LANGENSCHEIDTS
HANDWÖRTERBÜCHER

Muret-Sanders

Encyclopædic English-German
and German-English Dictionary

Enzyklopädisches englisch-deutsches
und deutsch-englisches Wörterbuch

* TOUSSAINT-LANGENSCHEIDT METHOD *

MURET-SANDERS

Encyclopædic English-German and German-English Dictionary

Giving the pronunciation according to the phonetic system employed in the
METHOD OF TOUSSAINT-LANGENSCHEIDT

Abridged Edition
(for School and Home)

PART II: GERMAN-ENGLISH

By
H. Baumann
Master of Arts of the University of London

Brought up to date by a supplement by
Professor E. Klatt

Published and Distributed in the
Public Interest by Authority of the
Alien Property Custodian under
License No. A-548, by

FREDERICK UNGAR PUBLISHING COMPANY
NEW YORK

★ METHODE TOUSSAINT-LANGENSCHEIDT ★

MURET-SANDERS

Enzyklopädisches englisch-deutsches und deutsch-englisches Wörterbuch

Mit Angabe der Aussprache nach dem phonetischen System der
METHODE TOUSSAINT-LANGENSCHEIDT

Hand- und Schulausgabe

TEIL II: DEUTSCH-ENGLISCH

Von
H. Baumann
Master of Arts of the University of London

Durch einen Nachtrag bis auf die heutige Zeit ergänzt von
Professor E. Klatt

Published and Distributed in the
Public Interest by Authority of the
Alien Property Custodian under
License No. A-548, by

FREDERICK UNGAR PUBLISHING COMPANY
NEW YORK

Copyright 1931 by
LANGENSCHEIDT'SCHE VERLAGSBUCHHANDLUNG, Berlin
*"Copyright vested in the Alien Property
Custodian, 1944, pursuant to law."*

PRINTED IN THE UNITED STATES OF AMERICA

Vorwort
zur vorliegenden Bearbeitung.

Der glänzende Erfolg der früheren Auflage dieses Wörterbuchs, das nicht nur dem Haus und der Schule, sondern auch in weiterem Sinne den zahlreichen praktischen Zwecken der Technik, der Wissenschaft und des Handels nach jeder Richtung hin dienen möchte, berechtigt mich zu der Hoffnung, daß das Werk auch in dieser neuen, vollendeteren Gestalt zahlreiche Freunde finden möge. Seit drei Jahren sind seitens der Berliner Verlagsbuchhandlung sowohl, wie auch meinerseits große Anstrengungen gemacht worden, um ein Buch, das schon so gute Dienste geleistet hat, ganz auf die Höhe unserer rasch fortschreitenden Zeit emporzubringen. Schon die Veränderungen in der deutschen Rechtschreibung und das stürmische Eindringen von neu gemünzten deutschen Wörtern machten eine Umarbeitung sehr wünschenswert. Aber auch auf englischem Gebiete haben die verflossenen Jahre wieder eine reiche Ernte von technischen, wissenschaftlichen und auch volkstümlichen Ausdrücken jeder Art gezeitigt, die eingeheimst werden mußten. Zugleich bot sich eine günstige Gelegenheit dar, den deutschen Wortschatz streng alphabetisch anzuordnen. Der Benutzer des Wörterbuchs wird jetzt jedes deutsche Wort, ob einfacher oder zusammengesetzter Art, genau an der abecelichen Stelle finden, an die es hingehört, ohne daß er nach Stamm oder Wurzel zu forschen braucht. Auch der Druck und die äußere Gewandung der Neubearbeitung zeigen einen merklichen Fortschritt. Kurz, es ist alles geschehen, um das Neueste und Beste zu liefern, das die Lexikographie unserer Zeit nur zu ersinnen vermag. Aber nichts auf der Welt, selbst nicht das feinste Wörterbuch, kann je Vollkommenheit erzielen. Es werden darum auch künftig Berichtigungen und Ergänzungen sowohl von der Verlagsbuchhandlung wie auch vom Verfasser stets mit Freuden entgegengenommen werden.

Da das Werk jetzt seinem Abschluß entgegengeht, so verbleibt es mir nur noch, denen zu danken, die mich bei der Arbeit so treu und wacker unterstützt haben. Die Beiträge flossen von vielen Seiten her. Doch möchte ich besonders die Herren

Preface
to the present Edition.

In view of the brilliant success of the former Edition of this Dictionary which, while serving for Home and School, also appeals to the wider circle of practical workers in the technical branches, and of professional and commercial men of all sorts, I have been emboldened to hope that, in this new and more perfect form, the work again may attract many friends. During the last three years, my Berlin Publishers have most strenuously seconded me in my efforts to raise a book, which has done such good services already, to the level of a highly progressive age. The changes in German Spelling, and the rapid influx of newly coined German words were in themselves sufficient to make a revision highly desirable. But also in English, the past few years have again matured a rich crop of technical and scientific, as well as popular expressions of every kind which had to be garnered. A favourable opportunity, moreover, presented itself for arranging the German vocabulary in more strictly alphabetical order. Those who consult the Dictionary will now find each German word, whether simple or compound, in exactly the alphabetical place to which it is entitled, so that he will have no further trouble about stems or roots. Also the print and the general 'get-up' of the Revised Edition show a marked improvement. In short, everything has been done to offer the latest and the best that modern lexicography can devise. But nothing in this world, not even a high-class dictionary, can ever attain perfection. Hence corrections and contributions will, also in the future, be gratefully received, both by the Publisher and the Author.

As the work is approaching its completion, I now feel it my pleasant duty to thank those who have so faithfully and ably assisted me in my task. Contributions came in from many sides. But I should make special mention of

Dr. E. A. Bayer und Kalau vom Hofe nennen, die mir bei der Umgestaltung des deutschen und englischen Textes, sowie auch bei der Lesung der Korrekturen viele nützliche Winke erteilt haben. Vorzüglichen Dank schulde ich auch Herrn Hauptmann a. D. Kannenberg, der mir bei der Drucklegung immerfort beratend zur Seite gestanden hat. Namentlich für die deutsche Rechtschreibung, Sprachlehre und Wortableitung, sowie auch für die Sichtung und Bereicherung des deutschen Wortschatzes waren seine Vorschläge mir stets vom höchsten Wert.

Zum Schluß noch dieser eine aufrichtige Wunsch: Möge auch diese verbesserte Auflage in den bewährten Händen des Hauses Langenscheidt sich bald die so reichlich verdiente Anerkennung verschaffen.

Brighton, Guildford Road 38

H. Baumann

Dr. E. A. Bayer and Mr. Kalau vom Hofe who, in the revision of the German and English articles and, besides, in the reading of the proofs, made many useful suggestions. My grateful acknowledgments are also due to Captain Kannenberg who, during the printing operations, was, at all times, ready to aid me with his kind advice. It was particularly in the German Spelling, Grammar, and Etymology, no less than in the arrangement and enlargement of the German vocabulary, that his proposals proved of the utmost value.

In conclusion, I would in all sincerity express this one wish: May also this Revised Edition, in the experienced hands of the Firm Langenscheidt, meet with the appreciation which it so richly deserves.

Brighton, 38 Guildford Road.

H. Baumann

Short Guide to German Pronunciation

[G. = German, E. = English, F. = French].

I. Introductory remarks.

1. The *standard pronunciation* of G., as here described, represents no particular province or part of the Empire. It is neither Hanoverian nor Saxon, neither Swabian nor Bavarian. Its home is all Germany, and not any particular centre, like Berlin, Dresden, Stuttgart, Munich, or, outside the Empire, Vienna. It is, generally speaking, the pronunciation of well educated Germans, of the stage, the pulpit, and the public platform, which tries to blend the dialectal peculiarities of North and South, of East and West.

2. The student who wishes to master the difficulties of G. phonetics should study the lessons on vowels and consonants, especially those on *ü, ä, ö, äu, eu, au*, the trilled *r*, the sharp hiss-sound *z*, and the characteristic G. ich-sound and ach-sound. He should also remember that the G. has nothing corresponding to the E. vowels in h*a*m, h*o*t, n*u*t; to E. *th* in *th*is, *th*orn; to *w* in *w*oe, *wh* in *wh*ich, *qu* in *qu*ite, or *j* in *j*aw; that the *er* in h*er*d is very different from the *er* in Herd; that the *aw* in l*aw* is only to be met with in G. dialects; and that the *g* in *g*nome, the *k* in *k*nee, the *l* in pa*l*m, the *p* in *p*sychology or recei*p*t, the *n* in hym*n*, which have become inaudible in E., retain their original sounds in the corrosponding G. words: Gnom, Knie, Palme, Psychologie, Rezept, Hymne.

The *diphthongal action* which characterizes some E. vowels [*a* in paper, *o* in code, &c.], and *voiced final consonants* [*b* in nob, *d* in lad, *g* in hug, *z* in coz, *v* in brave] are quite unknown in G. Terminal vowels, with few exceptions, such as **e** in Rose, are long in G.

The *articulation* of Germans is more vigorous, requiring much fuller play of the lips and the tongue, and stronger breathing action than that of people in the South of England.

3. The difference in *syllabication*, i. e. in the mode of splitting up words, should also be noticed: An *open syllable* is one which ends in a vowel. But a simple consonant between vowels in G. always goes to the next syllable [e=li=mi=nie=ren]. Digraphs and trigraphs, representing only one sound, such as ph, th, ch, sch, ß, st, x, z, in this rule, are counted as simple consonants: So=phist, A=thos, Lei=che, Fi=sche, Grü=ße, be=ste, He=xe, rei=zen. A *closed syllable* may end either in a single or a double consonant [mit, matt, dick = dikk], or in several consonants [hart, schlecht, krank, Kampf]. In syllabication the *last* of several such consonants goes to the next syllable: An=ker, Fin=ger, War=te, Rit=ter, Was=ser, Knos=pe, tap=fer, Ach=sel, krat=zen, Städ=te, Hak=ke [= Hacke].

Compounds are split up into their constituents, these again being subject to the general rules: Diens=tag, Tür=an=gel, Emp=fangs=an=zei=ge, Vor=aus=set=zung; hier=auf, her=ein, hin=aus, dar=über, war=um, wor=an, be=ob=ach=ten, voll=enden; Atmo=sphäre, Mikro=skop, Inter=esse; Brenn=nessel [Brennessel], Schiff=fahrt [Schiffahrt]; but: den(=)noch, Mit(=)tag, Ro=heit [not Roh=heit].

4. A G. vowel in the last syllable, if followed by a single consonant, is generally long. But there are many exceptions, especially with ch and sch: ab, äch, damit, frech, Gebüsch, Gekrach, Geruch, hat, hinab, hinweg, husch, in, Loch, mich, mit, noch, nötig, ob, &c.

II. Vowels.

These are originally sounds produced by the vocal chords and the cavities of the larynx. But the quality of the tone produced by them is differentiated in its passage through the throat, nose, and mouth. Vowels which are formed near the hard palate, such as G. i, e, ä, ö, ü, &c., are often called *front vowels*, those formed near the centre of the soft palate, as G. a, o, u, are described as *back vowels*.

Close i.

Resembling vowels in E. sl*ee*p, n*ea*t.

1. The front part of the tongue is raised very near to the hard palate, its point being kept close to the lower gums without actually touching. Opening of lips narrow. Avoid diphthongization by preventing the lower jaw and nether lip from making the slightest forward movement. G. flieh [flee thou] must be spoken with a pure undiphthongized vowel, and not like E. flea, and in dir [to thee] the voice must not be lowered before r, as in E. dear.

2. When *long*, this vowel is graphically expressed:
 a) by **ie**, as in lieben [to love], vier [four], nie [never], Rapie'r [rapier], Phantasie' [fancy].
 b) by **ieh**, as in Vieh [cattle], sieh [look], befiehl [order].
 c) by **ih**, as in ihre [her, their], ihm [to him].
 d) by **i**, as in mir [to me], dir [to thee], anti'k [antique].
 e) by **ee** in a few E. words, such as Spleen [spleen].

3. This **i** occurs as a *short* vowel in open unaccented syllables, as in Offizi'er [officer], an die Wa"nd [to the wall], Zitro'ne [lemon] which, in emphatic slow speech, however, would be pronounced long. It appears as y in Zylinder. See *close ü* 3.

Open i.

Like *i* in E. *i*ll, s*i*ck, l*i*p, dr*i*nk.

1. In passing from the previous *i* to this sound, we must still keep the point of the tongue near the lower gums. But the arch of the tongue is slightly flattened and lowered, and the opening of the lips increased. Carefully avoid the final vowel-sound in E. dut*y*. In G., this *i* is found only *short*.

2. It is met with mostly in closed syllables, especially before sibilants and double consonants, as in Liste [list], ißt [eats], wissen [to know], Ritz [chink], Schiffe [ships], Ritter [knight]; also before simple consonants, as in bin [am], im [in the], dari'n [therein], täglich [daily].

3. Only in a few exceptional cases, this vowel-sound appears as **ie**: Viertel [fourth part], vierzehn [fourteen].

4. Sometimes as y, see *open ü* 2b.

5. It should be noticed that the vowel *i* before *r* in G. retains its ordinary phonetic value [like *i* in sti*r*rup], and must not be allowed to approach the *i* in E. b*i*rd, g*i*rl, m*i*rth.

The student should practise side by side:
E. girt   G. girrte [cooed],
" flirt   " flirrte [glistened],
" stir   " Stirn [forehead].

Also in unaccented syllables, it keeps its full sound: Heldin [heroine] must be carefully differentiated from Helden [heroes].

Close ü.

Like the vowel u in French cru.

1. The tongue remains in the same position as for the close *i*-sound; but the lips must be well rounded. Thus we proceed from a high-front to a high-front-round vowel. It is essential that the tongue should not be retracted; else the sound produced will resemble the [pure or first] vowels in E. coo, do, shoe. In some dialects of the West and South of Germany, this *ü* is sounded like close *i*, which usage should not be imitated.

2. When *long*, this *ü*-sound appears in spelling:
 a) as *umlaut* or *mutation* or *modified u*: über [over], grün [green], für [for], müde [tired], Blüte [blossom].
 b) as **üh**: kühn [bold], führe [am leading], Stühle [chairs], Mühle [mill], Kühe [cows].
 c) as y in words derived from the Greek: lyrisch [lyrical], Analyse [analysis], Asyl [asylum, home].
 d) as **ue** in words from the F.: Revue' [review], Revenue' [income].

Other loan-words from the F. are spelt with ü: Lektüre [reading], Kostüm [costume], Tribüne [platform], Broschüre [pamphlet].

3. In a few foreign words, such as Bureau' [office], Hyazi'nthe [hyacinth], Physi'k [physics], Tyra'nn [tyrant], the close *ü* in open unaccented syllables is found *short*.

The y is sometimes pronounced like close i, e. g. in Zyli'nder [cylinder].

Open ü.

Like the vowel u in F. lutte.

1. Keep the tongue in the same position as for open *i*, lips well apart and rounded. Like the open *i*, it is found in closed syllables. In G. it is always short.

2. Graphically it is expressed:
 a) by **ü**: Bündel [bundle], Würde [dignity], Stürme [storms], kürzer [shorter], Nüsse [nuts], küsse [kiss].
 b) by y in certain words from the Greek: Myrte [myrtle], Gymna'sium [grammar-school], Nymphe [nymph].

This y is sometimes, but less correctly, pronounced like an open *i*. In Gips, Silbe, Kristall, Klistier — which are also of Greek origin — the G. has adopted both in spelling and pronunciation *i* for Greek ν; Ba'riton and Sinfoni'e, which have adopted the Italian *i*, rank side by side with Ba'ryton and Symphoni'e with the Greek y.
 c) by **u** in very few words from the F.: Budget [budget]. Other words from the F. are spelt with ü: Büste [bust], Perücke [wig].

3. The student must carefully distinguish:
Wüste [desert]   and wüßte [might know],
fühlen [to feel]   " füllen [to fill],
Hüte [hats]   " Hütte [hut],
büßte [expiated] " Büste [bust].

e.

Like the first part of the vowel-sound in game, pain.

1. In passing from close *i* to open *i*, we observed that the tongue had to recede a short distance from the hard palate. Retracting it once more about the same distance, or passing from the high-front to the mid-front vowel, we produce a new vowel-sound, that of a[i] in game, pain; but the usual E. diphthongizing of this vowel [gē-ⁱm, pē-ⁱn] must be carefully avoided. The opening of the lips is narrow, as in the case of close *i*.

2. It is met with *long*:
 a) as **e**: leben [to live], wem [to whom], den [*acc. sg.* of der], her [hither], lesen [to read].
 b) as **eh**: Lehm [clay], mehr [more], sehr [very], Weh [woe], Ehe [marriage].
 c) as **ee**: Meer [sea], Tee [tea], Teer [tar], scheel [squint-eyed], Schnee [snow], Seele [soul].
 d) as final é in words from the F.: Negligé [undress], Café [café], Abbé [abbé], Associé [partner].

It retains its full sound, even though it may not have the principal accent, e. g. in compounds such as a"nbe'ten [to adore], Wei"nle'se [vintage].

3. It is found *short* in unaccented open syllables, mostly in words of foreign origin:
Metho'de [method], Leva'nte [Levant], Melancholi'e [melancholy], Perücke [wig], Redakteu'r [editor], Sekretä'r [secretary], Thea'ter [theatre].

ä.

Resembling è in French père.

1. After assuming the *e*-position, as previously described, we must drop the lower jaw, and effect a wider opening of the lips. The sound produced is similar to that of the [undiphthongized or pure] vowel in hair, bear, care.

2. It is found *long*:
 a) as *umlaut* or *mutation* or *modified a* in: Käfig [cage], sägen [to saw], spät [late], täte [might do], Atmosphäre [atmosphere], Äther [ether].
 b) as **äh** in: Mähne [mane], Zähne [teeth], Zähre [tear], wählen [to choose], krähen [to crow].
 c) as **ai** in some words from the F.: Chaise [chaise].

Other F. words, like Militä'r [soldiery], Sekretä'r [secretary], have adopted the G. mutation.
 d) as **e** in some other F. loan-words: Karriere [career], Barriere [barrier], Dessert (*the t not to be pronounced!*) [dessert].
 e) Distinguish:
Ehre [honour]   from Ähre [ear of corn],
Meere [seas]   "   Mär(e) [tale],
wehre [defend] "   wäre [might be].

3. It is found *short* in closed syllables:
 a) as **ä** in: Bänder [ribbons], närrisch [foolish], Schätze [treasures], schärfer [sharper].
 b) as **e** in: fest [fast], Kette [chain], Scherflein [farthing, mite], Messe [mass], Ernte [harvest], Nerv [nerve], herrschen [to rule], wetzen [to whet].
 c) In such foreign words as Präla't [prelate], Zäsu'r [cæsura], Dämo'n [demon], the unaccented ä, in fluent familiar speech, becomes short.

4. The vowel-sound in E. hat, catch is not to be met with in G.

5. In comparing:
E. bet   with G. Bett [bed],
" nest   "   " Nest,
" sets   "   " setzt,
" send   "   " sende,
" hemming "   " hemmen [to check].
" kettle   "   " Kette [chain],

we should bear in mind that the G. *e*-sound requires a slightly wider lip-opening than the E. vowel. Some phoneticians consider the E. and the G. vowel identical.

6. The **er** in G. fern [far] is not pronounced like *er* in E. fern, but retains the original vowel-sound which we also find in E. merry and F. ternir.

Thus we must distinguish:
E. stern   from G. Stern [star],
" Ferdinand   "   " Ferdinand,
" perfect   "   " perfe'kt.
" perspective "   " Perspekti'v [telescope].

7. Some pairs of G. words exhibit identity in sound, together with differences both in meaning and spelling:
Welle [wave]   and Wälle [ramparts],
Felle [skins]   " Fälle [cases],
Lerche [lark]   " Lärche [larch-tree],
wende [turn]   " Wände [walls].

XI

Close ö.
Like the vowel in French *jeu*, *nœud*.

1. The tongue assumes the position for *ä* [in h*ai*r], while the lips are well rounded to form a mid-front-round vowel. This is an essential condition; otherwise a vowel, like that of E. h*er*d, b*ir*d would be produced which, as the student will readily observe, requires no rounding of the lips.

2. This vowel when *long* is found:
   a) as *umlaut* or *mutation* or *modified o* in: Töne [sounds], töte [kill], löfe [solve], Höfe [courts], höre [hear], Diarrhöe [diarrhœa], Euböa [Eubœa].
   b) as öh in: Söhne [sons], Löhnung [soldier's pay], Möhre [carrot], Köhler [collier], Öhr [eye of a needle].
   c) as eu in words from the F.: Regiſſeu'r [stage manager], Ingenieu'r [engineer], adieu' [adieu, good bye]. In other words from the F., the original eu has been changed into ö: Lifö'r [liqueur], Markö'r [marker], Möbel [furniture], Pöbel [mob], Manöver [manœuvre], pompö's [magnificent], porö's [porous], religiö's [religious].
   d) In some dialects of Central and South Germany, this rounded ö is pronounced like the unrounded e, so that löſe would sound like leſe [read], and Höfe like Hefe [yeast]. This dialectal usage must not be imitated, though in G. rhyming the ö and e are often, though mistakenly, treated as equivalents.

3. *Short ö*, like short *ä*, is met with in open, unaccented syllables, especially in foreign words: Öfono'm [farmer], Zöliba't [celibacy], Diöze'ſe [diocese], Phöni'zien [Phenicia].

Open ö.
Like the vowel-sound in F. *neuf*.

1. While the tongue assumes the position of *ä* [in Städte], the lips must be rounded. Phoneticians describe it as a mid-front-wide-round vowel. This vowel is always short in G. It is not found in E. The *u* in b*u*tter and in h*ur*t are not exact equivalents, approaching, as they do, the vowel-sound of *a* in f*a*t.

2. It occurs only as ö in: können [to be able], Förſter [forester], Mörder [murderer], Töchter [daughters].

3. The student must carefully study the difference between: E. g*u*tter and G. Götter [gods],
   „ g*u*nner „ „ Gönner [patron],
   „ l*u*st „ „ löſt [solves].
E. h*ur*t is totally unlike G. hört [hears] with its rounded long ö and its trilled r.

4. Distinguish also:
   G. Höfer [pedlar] from G. Höcker [hump],
   „ Röslein [little rose] „ „ Rößlein [little horse].

Terminal and unaccented e.
Resembling the short vowel of the final syllables in b*u*tter, *or*der, g*o*spel, lock*e*t, catch*u*p, gall*o*p.

1. This is a weaker form of the open ö previously described, and is generally met with as e: Schande [shame], Wandel [conduct], Leber [liver], Samen [seed], findet [finds], Gewehr [gun], Gedanke [thought].

2. In pronouncing „dieſe iſt", „konnte er", „lebte ich", the student must leave a clear cut between the final e and the initial vowel of the next word. The two vowels must on no account be slurred by means of what Alexander Ellis called the 'vanish-r'.

See paragraph on "Glottid before vowels", at the conclusion of V.

a.
Resembling *a* in E. b*a*r.

1. If the student, while successively articulating the vowels [only the vowels] in E. h*u*t, fl*a*t, and b*a*r, carefully follows up with his finger the movements of his tongue, he soon convince himself that the tongue, in framing the *a* of b*a*r, seems almost to slip away under his touch. The G. *a* is, in fact, a 'low-back vowel', and must be pronounced with the throat wide open, the tongue low down [but not so low down, as for the vowel-sound in l*a*w — which, only in some dialects of Germany, forms a substitute for *a*], and the lips a little wider apart than for the *a* in b*a*r.

Under no circumstances, should the G. *a*, whether long or short, whether in the centre or at the end of a word, be pronounced like the *a* in E. m*a*n, b*a*t, *a*ct, or in m*a*rauder, c*a*tastrophe, f*a*natical.

There is a long G. *a*, and a short G. *a*.

2. *Long a* is found:
   a) as **a** in: Vater [father], Samen [seed], Rabe [raven], Scham [bashfulness], Bart [beard], las [was reading], Waren [goods], da [there], Porzella'n [china].
   b) as **ah** in: Rahm [cream], fahren [to drive], kahl [bare], Draht [wire], ſah [saw].
   c) as **aa** in: Saal [hall], Haar [hair], Staat [state].
   d) as **i** in words from the F. with the diphthong *oi*: Reſervoir, Repertoire [repertory], Boudoir.

Notice that the plural of Saal is Säle, and the diminutive of Haar = Härchen, [with *one* ä].

3. Mark the phonetic differences in:
   E. theatre and G. Theater,
   „ sham „ „ Scham,
   „ rat „ „ Rat [counsel],
   „ cap „ „ Kap [headland].

4. The following pairs, though phonetically alike, exhibit different spelling and meaning:
   G. malen [to paint] and mahlen [to grind],
   „ Mal [mark] „ Mahl [repast],
   „ Aale [eels] „ Ahle [awl],
   „ Namen [names] „ nahmen [were taking].

5. The *short a* occurs as a:
   a) in closed syllables: kann [can], macht [makes], Stadt [town], Katze [cat], Karren [cart], lache [laugh], fange [catch], hart [hard].
   b) in open unaccented syllables [mostly in words of foreign origin]: Plati'n [platinum], Plaka't [placard], Phariſä'er [Pharisee], Mani'e [mania], Bagate'lle [trifle].

Close o.
Like the French *o* in m*o*t.

1. The tongue recedes still further than for G. *a* and E. *aw*. The lips show a narrow opening, and are rounded. The vowel produced is that of E. g*oa*t, b*o*ne, n*o*se, or rather of the first part of that vowel, because, as a rule, the E. ö is strongly diphthongized, especially in London. G. o, like French o, admits no second position of the lips such as would lead to the E. diphthong.

When accented, this vowel is invariably *long*.

2. In spelling, it is expressed:
   a) as **o**: Krone [crown], ſchon [already], hoch [high], rot [red], ſo [so], verlo'ren [lost], gebo'ren [born].
   b) as **oh**: Sohn [son], roh [raw], Bohne [bean], bohren [to bore], befo'hlen [ordered, bidden].
   c) as **oo**: Boot [boat], Moor [bog], Moos [moss].
   d) as **au** and **eau** in words from the F.: Sauce; Plateau', Niveau' [level].
   a) as **ow** in: Bowle [bowl].

3. Observe the difference in the vowel-sounds of:
   E. n*o*t, n*o*te and G. Not [need],
   „ r*o*t, wr*o*te „ „ rot [red],
   „ c*o*t, c*oa*t „ „ Kot [mud],
   „ l*o*st „ „ loſt [draws lots],
   „ *a*xiom „ „ Axio'm.

4. Notice the difference in meaning and spelling [together with identity in sound] of the following pairs:
   G. Sole [brine] and Sohle [sole of the foot],
   „ hole [fetch] „ hohle [hollow ones],
   „ [das] Moor [bog] „ [der] Mohr [black man].

5. This *o* occurs *short* in unaccented open syllables of a few foreign words: Komēt [comet], Pokāl [goblet], Morāl [morality], Topographīe [topography].

Open o.

Like the open vowel-sound in F. botte, somme.

1. In proceeding from a close *o* to an open *o*, we must, as the names suggest, increase the opening of the lips by a slight drop of the lower jaw, and at the same time allow the tongue to recede. The close and the open *o* are often called 'mid-back vowels'.

The G. open *o* cannot be counted as an equivalent of the E. vowel in *hot*, *cross* which is much more open, and closely approaches the sound of *a* in G. Laffe. Indeed, to a G. ear, E. mossy and G. Masse, E. donkey and G. danke would appear almost identical.

The G. *o* in Sorte has an open sound, and is very different from E. *o* in sort. The E. lord, when pronounced in a G. way, becomes Lord with an open *o*, a trilled *r*, and a voiceless or sharp *t*.

2. Open *o* occurs in G. only as a short vowel, and generally in closed syllables: koste [taste], Donner [thunder], Rosse [horses], borge [borrow], Knopf [button], voll [full], Wolf [wolf], ob [whether], von [from].

Some participles have the same short o-sound: gebrochen [broken], gesprochen [spoken], gefochten [fought], gescholten [scolded], geworfen [thrown], &c.

3. The same *o* occurs in a few words borrowed from the F.: Brosche [brooch], Lorgnette [eye-glass].

4. Notice the difference in meaning [owing to the phonetic distinction between the o-sounds] in the following pairs of G. homographs:

G. Rost [gridiron] and Rost [rust],
„ Schoß [lap] „ Schoß [sprout],
„ Floß [raft] „ floß [flowed].

Close u.

Like the French *ou* in *mou*.

1. The tongue, with its point downwards, rolls itself still further back, its top reaching to the arches of the palate, while the whole of it is right away from the front teeth. Lips with narrow opening and well rounded. The sound uttered would be the equivalent of *oo* in food, if the E. vowel were of a uniform quality throughout. The second position of the lips must again be carefully guarded against by the E. student. Also before *r*, as in nur, fuhr, it must not deviate into the vowel-sound of E. *your*, *sure*, *poor*. G. Tour considerably differs from E. tour [= tu^r-ᵊr or tu^r ᵊ] with its vocal murmur instead of the trilled G. *r*.

In accented syllables it is always long.

2. It is found *long*:

a) as **u** in: Flut [flood], Pflug [plough], Urkunde [deed], Ruß [soot], zu [to], zu'machen [to fasten up], nun [now], du [thou], Buch [book], Natu'r [nature].

b) as **uh** in: Ruhm [glory], Stuhl [chair], Schuh [shoe], Ruhe [rest].

c) as **ou** in words from the F.: Cour [courtship], Tour [excursion], Atout (the *t* at the end is not sounded!) [trump-card].

In Bluse &c., the F. *ou* has been changed into *u*.

3. The pronunciation of the following pairs is identical: [der] Ur [ure-ox] and [die] Uhr [watch].
Cour [courtship] „ Kur [cure].

4. The same **u** occurs *short* in open, unaccented syllables, especially of foreign words: Musi'k [music], Kuri'er [courier], Juwe'l [jewel], Husa'r [hussar], Gouverna'nte [governess].

Open u.

Like F. *ou* in *bouffe*, *course*.

1. In proceeding from the previous *u*-sound to this vowel, we must again depress the lower jaw, and thus effect a wider opening of the lips which are still kept rounded, and a corresponding lowering and flattening of the tongue. The nearest equivalent in E. is the vowel in foot, could, put; but the G. vowel is somewhat less open, and we most also beware of the diphthongal quality of the E. vowel.

This vowel-sound occurs only short, and generally in closed syllables. The two *u*-sounds are described in phonology as 'high-back-round vowels'.

2. It occurs in the orthographic forms:

a) of **u** in: Brust [breast], kurz [short], um [around], zum [to the], munter [cheerful], Genuß [enjoyment]. Mu'skel [muscle].

b) of **ou** in words from the F.: Tournü're [genteel manner]. Some F. loan-words have adopted **u**: Gruppe [group], Truppe [troop].

3. Distinguish the two *u*-sounds in:

G. Mus [stewed fruit] and muß [must],
„ flucht [curses] „ Flucht [flight],
„ sucht [seeks] „ Sucht [desire],

also in:

Fuß [foot] and Fluß [river],
Gruß [greeting] „ Guß [shower],
Ruß [soot] „ Kuß [kiss],

4. Compare the following:

E. club and G. Klub.
„ subject „ Subje'kt,
„ muse „ Muse.

III. Diphthongs.

ai, ei.

Resembling the E. vowel in *light*, *mine*.

1. In the G. diphthong, the weight rests more upon the first, in the E. more upon the second part of the vowel. The G. starts from a pure *a*, the E. from a sound akin to that of *u* in but or *o* in not.

In some G. dialects, especially of the South, the sound is almost identical with that of the diphthongized *a* in late, fame of the South of England.

2. In G. orthography, it appears:

a) as **ei** in: mein [my], Zeit [time], Ei [egg], drei [three], Geier [vulture].

b) as **ai** in: Hain [grove], Kaiser [emperor], Bai [bay], Laie [layman].

In naiv [ingenuous], the full vowel-sound is given to the *i*, not the *a*.

c) as **ay, ey** in names: Bayern [Bavaria], Cey'lon.

d) as **eih** in: leiht [lends], weiht [dedicates], Reiher [heron].

3. The following, though phonetically alike, differ both in spelling and meaning:

Laib [loaf] and Leib [body],
Saite [chord] „ Seite [side],
Main [name of G. river] „ mein [my],
Waise [orphan] „ Weise [tune],
Rain [slope, bank], Rhein [Rhine], and rein [pure].

äu, eu.

1. This diphthong is generally described as identical with E. *oy*, *oi* in boy, coy, loiter. But the G. diphthong requires rounding of the lips, and would appear to have for its first element, in the best pronunciation, the ö of könnte, and for its second a short ü. There are several dialectal varieties.

2. It is expressed in spelling by:

a) **äu** as *umlaut* or *mutation* or *modified au* in: Häute [hides], Kräuter [herbs], Säue [swine], Bäumlein [little tree].

b) **eu** in: heute [to-day], Reue [repentance], Euter [udder], Heu [hay], Leutnant [lieutenant].

3. In loan-words in ...**äum** and ...**eum**, as Jubilä'um [jubilee], Muse'um [museum], the two vowels [ä and u, e and u] have to be pronounced separately.

4. Notice the difference in meaning and spelling [together with identity in sound] of:

bläuen [to blue] and bleuen [to beat],
gräulich [greyish] „ greulich [awful],
Häute [hides] „ heute [to-day],
läute [ring the bell] „ Leute [people].

au.
Resembling E. *ou* in *house*.

1. In comparing G. **au** with E. *ou* in *house*, sound, we find that the opening of the lips and the throat in G. is much larger, and that the tongue is lower and flatter than in E. The initial element should be decidedly a pure G. a, and not the E. vowel in *not* or *but* or *hat*. In comparing G. baut [builds] with E. bout, we find that the E. diphthong in bout is shortened by the voiceless consonant t which follows it; such is not the case in G. baut.

2. Its spelling is generally **au**, rarely **auh**, as in: Frau [woman], bauen [build], Audie'nz [audience], Kra'kau [Cracow], rauh [rough].

oi, eo, ea, ua, ia &c.

Several other diphthongs may be found in imported words, names, &c.:

a) [French] **oi**: The first diphthongal element in G. is **o** [in the best F. it is the *u*-sound of *fou*], the second **a**, as in: Toilette [toilet]; Comptoir [office] is often spelt Konto'r.

b) **eo**, as in: The'odor, Theori'e [theory].

c) **ea**, as in: O'zean [ocean], Olea'nder [oleander].

d) **ua**, as in: Ja'nuar [January], Ka'suar [cassowary].

e) Several i-diphthongs, such as **ia, ie, io, iö, iu**, often lose their diphthongal character in fluent speech, the *i* approaching the E. consonant *y* in *yard*, yet.

Examples: Allia'nz [alliance], Gra'zie [grace], Traditio'n, offiziö'ö [semi-official], Gymna'sium [grammar-school].

IV. Nasal vowels.

These are to be met with only in words imported from the F., such as:

Chance, Amendeme'nt, Point, Pensée, Ballon, Cousin, Bassin, Pardon, Chambre, and are pronounced by good speakers as in F., but always long. The pure nasality of the vowel is not attainable, however, without considerable practice. The uvula has to be dropped so as to allow the nose to serve as a second resonance-chamber. Careless speakers neglect this, and substitute the nasal consonant *ng* which is met with in lo*ng*, so that Pardon becomes pardo'ng. This fault is very common in North Germany, and should be avoided. In such loan-words, as Bataillo'n, Postillo'n, the n is now generally pronounced as in the corresponding E. words battalion, postilion. In Pension, only the first n, and this not always, remains nasal.

V. Consonants.

1. According to their *origin*, they may be: lip-consonants: p, b, m, f, v [G. w]; point-and-teeth consonants: t, d, n, s, sh [G. sch], r, l; front-and-back consonants: k, several g's, ng, G. ich- and ach-sounds, &c.

2. According to their *mode of formation*, they may be divided into: stops or explodents or shut consonants which close the oral passage to the breath or voice: p, b, m, t, d, n, k, g, ng, &c., and continuants or central consonants which squeeze the breath or voice, leaving only a narrow central groove between the tongue and the palate: f, v, s, sh, r, l, G. ich- and ach-sounds, &c.

3. The names which phoneticians use refer both to the origin and formation of the sound. Thus **p** is described as lip-stop breath, **b** as lip-stop voice, **m** as lip-stop-voice nasal; **t** as point-stop breath, **d** as point-stop voice, **n** as point-stop-voice nasal; **k** as back-stop breath, **g** as back-stop voice, **ng** as back-stop-voice nasal; **f** as lip-teeth-continuant breath, **v** as lip-teeth-continuant voice; **s** as point-teeth-continuant voice; **r** as point-continuant voice; sharp **s** as teeth-continuant breath, flat **s** [E. z.] as teeth-continuant voice.

4. *Sharp or voiceless consonants* [p, f, t, k, &c.] are pronounced with more vigour than *flat or voiced consonants* [b, v, d, g, &c.]. A voiced consonant at the end of a G. word becomes voiceless. See *p, b* 1; *t, d* 1.

l.
More dental than E. *l*.

1. In pronouncing G. l, we must bring the tip of the tongue nearer the upper gums than in E., and not arch or raise the back of the tongue as in E.

2. In spelling, it is found as **l** and **ll**: Lohn [reward], viel [much], kalt [cold], all [all], Halle [hall].

3. In words, like Fabel [fable], Möbel [furniture], we may either, by skipping the e, make the **l** a separate syllable [fāb.l, möb.l], or, in slower speech, sound both the vowel and the consonant [fā'-bᵉl, mō'-bᵉl].

4. The **ll** [the 'l mouillé'] in words from the F., such as Billard, Postillon, Bataillon, is ordinarily pronounced like *ly* in E. ha*ly*ard.

m.

The same humming sound as in E. *mum*; but after a short vowel [as in Lamm], the G. *m* is shorter and sharper than an E. *m* [as in come].

1. Examples: Mond [moon], ihm [to him], Himmel [heaven], Lamm [lamb].

2. The *m* in the F. loan-words Champagner [champagne], Champignon, and others, has lost its nasal character; it retains it in Chambre garnie [furnished room].

n.
Like E. *n* in *new*.

1. Examples: nahm [took], ohne [without], Kanne [jug], Kind [child].

2. In pronouncing haben, raten, we may either skip the **e**, and voice **n** as a separate syllable [hāb.n, rāt.n], or we may, in slow speech, sound both the vowel and consonant [hā'-bᵉn, rā'-tᵉn].

3. See "IV. Nasal vowels".

4. In G. **gn** and **kn**, the **g** and **k** are always heard: Gnom [gnome], Knie [knee]. The F. *gn* in borrowed words, such as Kognak [F. brandy], Lorgnette [eye-glass], is pronounced as in F., or like E. *ny* in la*ny*ard. See also the next paragraph.

ng, nk.

1. The final consonants in E. lo*ng*, tha*nk* are the same as those in G. lang, Dank. But in North Germany the final *ng* of lang is very extensively pronounced like *nk*. This should not be imitated by the E. student. Also the consonant [ngg] in E. finger, longer is not allowed in G. Only in Latin words, like longus, longa, Germans employ the *ngg*.

On the other hand, in words of foreign origin, like Signa'l, A'gnes, Agno'stiker, Jgnora'nt, ma'gnum, the *gn* is sounded like *ngn* [sing-nā'l, &c.].

2. Examples: Finger [finger], Sänger [singer], länger [longer], springe [leap], Angst [anxiety], danke [thank], krank [ill], trinkst [drinkest].

r.

1. The G. **r** is a glottal trill. The tongue is arched and loosely supported against the lower gums, while its tip is made to vibrate by means of a well sustained breathing action.

There are in Germany, as in England, a great many local and individual r's. The E. vocal *r* [in far, further] is rare, and certainly not to be recommended. Good G. speakers trill all r's, whether initial, medial, or terminal, and the G. [like the F.] stage clings to the better tradition. A weaker guttural *r* is, however,

spreading in many G. towns, and the teachers are carrying on an unceasing warfare with this new comer.

The E. student should endeavour to trill all G. r's, also the final ones, and practise compound letters, like br, gr [in Bruder, groß], trying to arch his tongue, and to 'roll' the r, as most Irish and Scotch speakers do.

2. Examples: Karte [card], froh [glad], Schar [multitude], Bart [beard], knurre [growl], Rohr [reed], sehr [very], rheumatisch [rheumatical].

3. Compare the following:

G. arm [arm, poor] and E. arm,
„ hart [hard] „ „ hart, heart,
„ Firma „ „ firm,
„ Gürtel „ „ girdle,
„ Myrte „ „ myrtle,
„ Herde „ „ herd,

paying due heed to the differences, not only in the r, but also in the vowel-sounds.

It should be particularly noticed that G. vowels preceding an r are not affected by the r in the same way as E. vowels in the same position, but always retain their original sounds. Neither does the G. permit a transitional vowel [ᵊ] or murmur before the r such as is usually met with before the E. vocal r. Thus, while in *four* a second subsidiary vowel may be heard after the ō [fō-ᵊr or fō-ᵊ], no such deviation takes place in the vowel of vor [before]. See also *close i* 1, *open i* 4, *ü* 6, *open o* 1 and *close u* 1.

s.

In G., as in E., we find a sharp hissing s, and a flat buzzing s.

1. The sharp s is the same as in *sun*, *sing*, and in *ass*, *moss*. In G. it is met with chiefly before other consonants, and at the end of words.

In spelling, it appears:

a) as s or f in: Maske [mask], Knospe [bud], Husten [cough], als [when], uns [us], abends [in the evening], aus [out of], was [what].

b) as ss in: lasse [let], Masse [mass], Schüsse [shots].

c) as ß [in the Latin alphabet often denoted by ß]: Kuß [kiss], Gruß [greeting], groß [great].

d) as ç in words from the F.: avancieren [to advance], Garçon [waiter].

2. A G. spelling rule requires that, between vowels, ß can be used only when the preceding vowel is long.

Thus we distinguish:

Maße [measures] from Masse [mass],
Schöße [coat-tails] „ schösse [might shoot].
rußig [sooty] „ russisch [Russian].

Thus Kuß becomes in the plural Küsse,
„ Gruß „ „ „ „ Grüße.

Notice also the following distinctions:

As (♪) [ace] and aß (♩) [ate],
das [the, *neuter article*] and daß [that, *conjunction*]
[das and daß are phonetically the same].

As (♪) becomes in the plural Asse [aces],
aß (♩) „ „ „ „ .. aßen [were eating].

3. The flat s resembles the 'buzzes' in E. *zone*, *bees*, *rose*. It is found chiefly before and between vowels. Its only orthographic form [except in a few loan-words] is s: Sonne [sun], Reise [journey], Gemse [chamois], Linse [lentil].

4. It should be noticed that G. z [which will be specially referred to in another paragraph] is not a flat buzzing sound, like the E. z in *zone*, but a sharp 'hiss' [= E. ts]. Thus G. Zone [tsō-ne] materially differs from its E. homograph *zone*. Ziel [aim] [which in E. would be spelt: *tseel!*] also differs from *zeal*.

sch.

Like the *ch* in F. *chat*.

1. G. sch is not an exact equivalent of E. sh. The true G. sch requires a rounding and protruding, the E. *sh* only a narrow opening of the lips. G. sch is uttered with the tongue in an easy central position, E. sh with the blade of the tongue retracted, and closely approaching the hard palate.

2. It occurs in the graphic forms:

a) of sch in: scharf [sharp], Asche [ashes], Fleisch [flesh], zischt [hisses].

b) of inital s in the compound letters sp, st: Speise [food], sprechen [to speak], Stein [stone]. [In Hanover, Holstein, &c., initial sp, st retain the s-sound].

In a great portion of South Germany, also central and final *sp* and *st* are pronounced in this manner. At Stuttgart, Haspel [reel] is sounded like Haschpel, Last [burden] like Lascht, and ist [is] like ischt. Neither this custom nor the opposite one of pronouncing initial *sp* and *st* in the E. [that is, the original Low G.] way is to be recommended.

c) ch in words from the F.: Affoucheur, or E.: chartern [to charter]. In a few naturalized words, F. ch appears as sch: Schikane = F. chicane.

d) c in words from the Italian: Cello, Violincello.

3. There is a flatter sibilant to be met with in words borrowed from the F., as Journal, Courage. Many Germans, however, use their own sharp sibilant sch instead of the French j.

4. A few words from the E., such as Gentleman, Jockey, are pronounced with the F. j of *jour*, because the E. *j*-sound is unknown in G.

5. The sharper *tsh*, or rather *tsch* is common in G.: deutsch [German], rutsche [slither], Kutsche [coach]. In a few words from the Italian, like Cicero'ne [guide], the *c* is pronounced the same way.

w.

Like French *v* in *vu*, *avoir*.

1. G. w must, on no account, be pronounced like E. *w*. It is related to E. *v* in *violet*, *lavatory*.

North G. w, like E. *v*, is a lip-and-teeth sound, but Middle and South G. w is a pure lip-sound, or a lip-against-lip continuant, uttered with gently closed lips, and without the lower lip touching the upper teeth.

2. In spelling, it occurs:

a) as w in: Wasser [water], Löwe [lion].

b) as v in foreign words: Vaseli'n, Vademe'cum [pocket-book], Velozipe'd [cycle], trivia'l [commonplace]. In the two Latin loan-words Vogt [governor], and Veilchen [violet], the v retains its ordinary f-sound. Final v is always pronounced like f: brav [honest], relati'v [relative].

c) as u in the compound letter qu [which must not be pronounced, like E. *qu* in *quite*, with bagging of lips]: Quittung [receipt], quäle [torment].

The noun Queue [cue] which is borrowed from the F. is pronounced in the F. way [kö]. Also in Clique, Marquis the qu, as in F., is sounded as a k. In Bukett [† Bouquet], Kloake [drain-pipe] from cloaque, and Lakai [lackey] from laquais, the F. qu, also graphically, has become k.

p, b.

1. There is some difference in sound between an E. p and a G. p, an E. b and a G. b. The attack on the vowel following these lip-sounds is less clear in G. than in E., so that an E. ear seems to hear p-hein and b-hein instead of G. Pein [pain] and Bein [leg]. The final b in words like ab [off], Dieb [thief], lieb [dear], is equivalent to the *p* in E. *lap*, *keep*. Also b before t, as in liebt [loves], Abt [abbot], raubt [robs], should

sound like p in tipt. b before s, as in gāb's [gave its] liebſt [lovest], makes the s a sharp 'hiss', and sounds like p in caps, lips.

2. Examples for p: Pappel [poplar], ſchiebt [shoves], ob [whether], hab's [have it]; for b: bebe [quake], Bibel [bible], Amboß [anvil].

f, pf.

1. The G. f may be pronounced like the E. lip-teeth sound f in for, shift, although there is another G. f which, like G. w, does not require the lower lip to touch the upper teeth. The labiodental f is very generally made use of in uttering pf, a compound letter of frequent occurrence in G. In passing from the p- to the f-position in Pferd [horse], Kopf [head], we should slip the lower lip beneath the upper teeth.

2. The f is graphically expressed:
a) as f or ff in: fünf [five], Affe [ape], Schiff [ship].
b) as v in [the G. words]: viel [much], Vater [father], Vetter [cousin], von [of], vor [before]. Also in [the Latin words]: Subſtantiv [substantive], Dativ [dative]. See previous paragraph on w 2 b.
c) as ph and pph in words from the Greek: Photograph [photographer], Phosphor [phosphorus], Prophet [prophet]; Sappho [Sappho].
Words which are either of G. origin, as Efeu [ivy], or which have become thoroughly naturalized, like Elefant [elephant], Sofa [sopha], are now always spelt with f, though they had formerly ph. Trumpf [trump card] from F. triomphe, and Triumph [triumph] from Latin triumphus are different stages of the same Greek word thriambos.

t, d.

1. E. t and d are produced by pressing the point of the tongue *against the hard palate* just behind the gums; the G. t and d, which are true dentals, by pressing the upper surface of the tongue *against the gums* while the under part rests against the front teeth. The compound letters tr, dr, str can be more easily made to trill with the dental t and d.

The G. final d is voiceless, and the last letters of the G. Land have the same effect on an E. ear as those of E. lent. A G. beginner would probably pronounce E. cad, fad, nod like cat, fat, not.

2. In spelling, t occurs:
a) as t, dt or tt in: tat [did], Tür [door], Träne [tear]; Stadt [town], lädt [invites]; rette [save].
b) as th in words of foreign origin: Theater [theatre], Theologie [divinity], Thron [throne]; and in a few G. names beginning with Theo-: Theobald. **The sound of E. th is unknown in G.**
c) as terminal d in: geſund [sound], mied [shunned].
3. d occurs as initial or central d or Low G. dd in: da [there], meide [shun], edler [nobler], drei [three]; klabberadatſch [bang].

z.

Like ts in E. rats.

1. The G. z has a very different phonetic value from E. z. We must rapidly pass the point of the tongue from the upper gums to the lower front-teeth, so that a very sharp hiss [= ts] may be produced. This sound is of frequent occurrence.

We get the same sound when final s is preceded by either t or d: hat's [has it], fand's [found it].

2. Its spellings are:
a) z, tz, zz in: Ziel [aim], Kanzel [pulpit], Hitze [heat], Skizze [sketch].
b) ts, ds, tts in: Ratsherr [councillor], lud's [invited it], des Liebs [of the song], litt's [suffered it].
c) c in a few Latin and F. words before any front vowel: Cäſar, Ceres, Cicero, Cöleſtin [npr.]. Other words from the same foreign sources, which have become thoroughly naturalized in G., are now spelt with z: Zäſur, Zeder, Zitrone, Zöleſtin [min.], offiziös, Partizip.

d) t in the ti of Latin and F. terminations: Proportion [proportion], Station [station], Patient [patient]. Before unaccented e, G. zi may be substituted for Latin ti: Reagenzien [chemical tests]. But after f the ti prevails: Aktien, not Akzien [shares]. See x, 2 c.

k, g.

Like E. k, g in kernel, gap.

1. These palatal 'stops' are almost identical with the corresponding E. sounds; but in E. they appear 'thicker' because, with most E. speakers, the tongue covers a larger portion of the palate.

2. Orthographically k occurs:
a) as k, ck in: Kette [chain], Decke [cover].
b) as c [cc] in a few foreign words before a, o, and before consonants: Carmen, Cauſerie, Code, Claque, Courtoiſie [courtesy], Couſin[e], Creme. In the new G. spelling, k has taken the place of c in all naturalized foreign words. See also the next paragraph on x 2 c.
c) as ch in a few foreign words, mostly from the Greek: Charakter [character], Chloroform [chloroform], Cholera [cholera], Chor [choir], Chriſt [christian]. See the special paragraph on x.

3. The initial g in Gabe, Geld resembles the g in E. gale, gird; but in some parts of North Germany, the consonantal y-sound in yet is substituted for it, so that in the popular speech of Berlin, for instance, Gott [God] sounds like yŏt, and gūt [good] like yōot.

In spelling, it is represented:
a) by g or [Low G.] gg: Galle [gall], groß [great]; baggern [to dredge], Dogger [Dutch fishing smack], flügge [fledged].
b) by a central g, mostly in foreign words: Lagune [lagoon], Bagatelle [trifle], Kongreß [congress].
c) by gu in a few foreign words: Guillotine. In others the original gu has been changed into g: Droge [drug], Intrige [intrigue].

x.

Like x in E. tax.

1. In G. only the sharper x-sound [= ks] is known.
2. Its graphic forms are:
a) x in foreign words like: Xylographie [xylography], Examen [examination], lax [lax].
b) chſ, chs in words of G. origin: Achſel [shoulder], Eidechſe [lizard], Flechſe [sinew], Ochſe [ox], Lachs [salmon], Drechſler [turner]. Notice the x in the purely G. words Axt [axe], kraxeln [to climb].
gs in: flugs [instantly].
c) kt before i in foreign words: Aktion [action], Sektion [section], Lektion [lecture], Sanktion [sanction], Funktion [function], Konjunktion [conjunction].

The ich-sound and G. j (yot).

1. To pronounce ich correctly, shape the mouth for the consonant y in year, hue — which is the nearest equivalent to G. j — and then sharpen the feeble buzz by pressing the point of the tongue against the lower front-teeth. The ich-sound is called in phonology front-continuant breath, the j [or consonantal ŋ] front-continuant voice. Beginners should guard against the faulty sounds of ik, ish for ich.

2. The ich-sound is met with:
a) as initial ch in words of foreign origin: Chemie [chemistry], China, Charon, Cherubim.
b) as central or terminal ch in words of G. origin after consonants and front vowels [i, e, ä, ü, ö, &c.]: ich [I], recht [right], ſicher [sure], mächtig [mighty], Flüche [curses], Dolch [dagger], reich [rich], Töchter [daughters].
c) as terminal g after consonants and front vowels: Talg [tallow], Berg [mountain], Krieg [war], Weg [way], läg' [might lie], trüg' [might bear], Zeug [stuff].

3. The *j*-sound [yot-sound] occurs:

a) as **j** in: ja [yes], jene Jungfer [that spinster], jedes Jahr [each year], Jordan [Jordan], jubeln [to exult], Bajonett [bayonet].

b) as **y** in some foreign words: Yankee, loyal, Mayonnaise, Royalist.

c) in F. words with the 'l mouillé', also in F. and Italian words with *gn*: Taille [tā′l-jⁱ]; Lorgnon [eye-glass], Signora.

The ach-sound and central g.

1. The ach-sound [which is much heard in Scotland] originates between the back of the tongue and the soft palate. In passing from the 'front continuant' in 'ich' to the 'back continuant' in 'ach', the tongue retires from the hard palate, assuming a loose and flattened position, its point keeping in touch with the lower gums. If *u* precedes, the tongue, in adapting itself to the vowel, recedes still further, and the sound is formed at a somewhat lower point of the soft palate than after *a* or *o*.

Central *g* after back-vowels [a, o, u] is the flat ach-sound or, in the language of phonology, the back-continuant voice. We may start with the *g*-position in egg, and then loosen the tongue from the palate, allowing a thin stream of air to pass between.

2. The ach-sound appears:

a) as **ch** after back vowels: macht [makes], noch [yet], suche [seek], Bauch [belly]; as **cch** in [the Greek name]: Bacchus. See *k, g* 2c above.

b) as terminal **g** after back vowels: Tag [day], bog [bent], trug [carried], saug [suck thou].

In some G. dialects, after both front and back vowels, terminal **g** sounds like **f**.

3. The flat central *g*-sound *after back vowels* is found in: Tage [days], Bogen [arc], trugen [were carrying], Augen [eyes].

4. Central *g after consonants and front vowels* may be either the consonant *y* in *y*ell, distinctly buzzed, or the ich-sound, the latter esspecially in the South-West of Germany. The best pronunciation lies somewhere between the two.

Examples: bargen [were sheltering], Belgien [Belgium], Berge [mountains], Säge [saw], lege [lay], biege [bend], zöge [might pull], Züge [trains], säuge [suckle], eigen [own].

h.

1. Like *h* in E. *h*ome, *h*ill, strongly breathed. This is the pure aspirate, or breath without voice. The G. **h** requires more vigorous breathing than an E. *h*. The "dropping" of the *h* is seldom met with in Germany. But neither a central *h* between two vowels, as in ruhen [to rest], leihen [to lend], nor a terminal **h**, as in rauh, should be heard.

The G. **h** is largely employed in spelling to indicate length of vowel: ihn [him], Bühne [stage], ohne [without], Ruhm [glory].

2. The terminal inaudible **h** of stems, like droh-en [to threaten], froh [glad], is retained before inflectional and other syllables: drohte [threatened], fröhlich [merry]; but not before **heit**: Hoheit [highness] from stem hoh-; Rauheit [roughness], from rauh; Roheit [rudeness] from roh.

Glottid before vowels.

By tightly compressing the vocal chords, and then with a sudden effort reopening the glottis, we shall produce a kind of 'puff' which is called a *check glottid* or *glottal stop*. It is heard in: wie „ahnte" er es? [how did he surmise it?] In G. it is much used to prevent a consonant from gliding on to a following vowel. Thus un=ab=änderlich [unchangeable] is spoken in three distinct sections, with a check after „un" and „ab". In Vor=abend [eve], there is a distinct stop between the **r** and the **a**. Only short words, such as an in greif‿an, daran, aus in voraus, er in hat‿er, es ist‿es, ich in denk‿ich, &c. often allow the glide, and dispense with the glottid.

The E. student should pay great attention to this G. habit of putting a check or a 'clear cut' between words which must not, as is frequently done in E. [or French], be 'bound' or drawn together. Practise the following sentence in which the checks are denoted by ‖ :

Ich wandelte ‖ im Garten, da ‖ atmete ‖ ich frei ‖
I was walking in the garden, there I breathed freely,
und empfand ‖ in tiefer Seele ‖ eine ‖ innige
and felt deep within my soul an intense
Freude ‖ über alles Schöne ‖ und Herrliche ‖ in
joy at everything fair and glorious in
der Natur.
nature.

VI. Rules of G. Spelling.

A few rules have already been given in the description of vowels and consonants, see 13; *open ü* 2b & c; *ä* 2c; *close ö* 2c; *close u* 2c; *open u* 2b; *sch* 2c; *w* 2c; *z* 2c & d; *k, g* 2c, 3c.

1. All nouns, also adjectives used as nouns, have *capital initials*: Brot [bread], Asien [Asia], Gutes und Böses [good and bad things], der Reiche [the rich man]; also infinitives, ordinal numbers, &c. which play the part of nouns: Lesen und Schreiben [reading and writing], Wilhelm der Erste [William the First].

2. All adjectives derived from names of persons [Grimmsche Märchen Grimm's Tales], also adjectives in **er** derived from names of localities [Berliner Blätter Berlin papers], or forming part of geographical or historical designations [das Schwarze Meer the Black Sea; die Vereinigten Staaten the United States; der Siebenjährige Krieg the Seven Years' War], require *capitals*.

3. Adjectives in **isch** denoting a species, though derived from a noun proper [die lutherische Kirche the Lutheran Church; eine galvanische Batterie a galvanic battery], also adjectives in **sch** and **isch** derived from names of localities or nations [deutsche Waren German goods; die römischen Kaiser the Roman Emperors; das englische Volk the English people] have *small initials*. But also these adjectives take *capitals* if they form part of some proper name or title: das Deutsche Reich the German Empire; der Peloponnesische Krieg the Peloponnesian War; die Französische [or französische] Revolution the French Revolution.

4. All nouns and noun-adjectives, when forming part of some standing phrase or compound verb, also pronouns, though used like nouns, require *small initials*: heute morgen [this morning], mir ist angst [I am afraid], alt und jung [old and young], er nimmt teil [he takes part], wir halten haus [we keep house]; ein jeder, jedermann [each one], nichts anderes [nothing else], keiner von ihnen [none of them]; bei weitem [by far], ohne weiteres [without further ado], im großen (und ganzen) [on the whole], durch dick und dünn [through thick and thin], über ein kleines [after a little while]; etwas schwarz auf weiß haben [to have something in black and white]; mit wenigem auskommen [to subsist on small means].

D. Erklärung der bildlichen Zeichen ꝛc.

☞ Unmittelbar hinter dem **fettgedruckten** Titelworte stehend, beziehen sich diese Zeichen auf alle Bedeutungen des Titelkopfes. Steht das Zeichen nur hinter einer einzelnen Nummer, so hat es nur für den betr. Abschnitt des Artikels Geltung. Bei einem einzelnen Satze oder Worte stehend, gilt das Zeichen nur für diesen oder dieses.

	(Kein Zeichen)	Umgangs- und Schrift-sprache.
F	(familiär)	vertrauliche, nachlässige Sprechweise.
P	(populär)	Sprache des ungebildeten Volkes.
[P]	„	P in [...] = volksetymologisch.
☇	(Galgen)	Gauner- u. Diebes-sprache, Rotwelsch.
↘	(Komet)	selten, wenig gebräuchlich.
†	(Kreuz)	veraltet (bei Prsn. = gestorben). [boren).⎫
*	(Stern)	Neologi'smus, neues Wort (bei Prsn. = ge-⎬
*, **, ⁂	„	s. zs.-gesetzte Zeitwörter S. XXXVIII.
[*]	„	zB. [lt., * grch.] = Lehn- oder Fremdwort, zunächst ⎫
⌑	(Buch)	wissenschaftlich. [lt., letzthin grch. Ursprungs.⎬
⚘	(Blume)	Pflanze(nkunde).
⊕	(Zahnrad)	technisch, Handwerksausdruck.
⚒	(Hämmer)	den Bergbau betreffend.
⚔	(Schwerter)	militärisch.
⚓	(Anker)	Mari'ne, Schiffahrt, Schiffersprache.
♁	(Globus)	geographischer Name.
⚇	(Geldstück)	Handel, kaufmännisch.
⚴	(Posthorn)	Post, Telegraphie.
⛟	(Lokomotive)	Eisenbahn.
♪	(Note)	Musi'k.
⁺⁺⁺	(drei Kreuze)	unrichtig, mißverstanden.
=	(Gleichheitszeichen)	gleich, ebenso.

① bis ㊿ (Ziffern in e-m Kreise) verweisen auf die „Abgesonderten Bemerkungen" S. XXIII ff.; vgl. a. S. XXII, Nr. 6.

⚐ (Grenzpfahl) a) hinter dem deutschen Titelkopf: aus dem Englischen ins Deutsche übergegangen, b) vor e-m engl. Wort im Text: aus dem Dtsch. ins Engl. übergegangen.

(⚐) (dgl.) Übersetzung, zB. Gemeinplatz (⚐) [(commonplace)] oder Neubelebung, zB. Halle (⚐), vgl. unten [(...)].

[:], [P:], [?] (eckige Klammern) schließen die Angaben über den Wortursprung ein. — Vgl. a. S. XXII, Nr. 5. Der Doppelpunkt darin = (ur)verwandt mit //; [P:] = volksetymologisch zu // gezogen; [?] = Ursprung unsicher.

[(...)] Übersetzung des Fremdwortes, zB. Gevatter [(compater)], Gemeinplatz [(commonplace)].

( ) (runde Klammern): 1. Buchstaben in ( ) = doppelte Schreibweise mit oder ohne die Einklammerung, zB.: Arz(e)nei = Arzenei od. Arznei; labo(u)r = labour (engl. Schreibweise) od. labor (amerikan. Schreibweise). — 2. Worte in ( ) = die Einklammerung kann mitgelesen oder ausgelassen werden, zB.: to (strew with) sand = to strew with sand oder to sand. — 3. Worte mit or davor in ( ) = verschiedenerlei mögliche Übersetzungen, zB.: loose (or degenerate, depraved) morals pl. = loose morals od. degenerate morals od. depraved morals.

- (Divis): Die Wiederholung durch Divis in der englischen Übersetzung erläutert das folgende Beispiel: Her-reise f home- (or return-) journey or voyage = home-journey or return-journey or home-voyage or return-voyage.

=, ⁼ (Bindestriche) wiederholen mit großem (=) oder kleinem (⁼) Anfangsbuchstaben das vor ihnen stehende erste Glied der Zs.-setzung, zB.: Eid-genoß, =genossenschaft, ⁼genössisch (= Eidgenossenschaft, eidgenössisch).

D. Explanation of Signs, &c.

☞ Placed immediately after the **heavy-type** titleword or heading, these signs refer to all the meanings of the title-word. If the sign follow after a particular number, it applies only to that particular section of the article. If attached to a particular phrase or word, the sign applies only to such phrase or word.

	[No sign]	colloquial and literary style.
F	[familiar]	unrefined every-day language.
P	[popular]	vulgar language.
[P]	„	P in [...] = popular etymology.
☇	[Gallows]	flash language; [thieves'] cant.
↘	[Comet]	rare; little used.
†	[Cross]	obsolete [with names of persons = died].
*	[Star]	neologism, new word [of persons = born].
*, **, ⁂	„	see compound verbs, p. XXXVIII.
[*]	„	foreign loan-word; thus: [lt., * grch.] = taken ⎫
⌑	[Book]	scientific. [from Latin, but originally Greek.⎬
⚘	[Flower]	botanical; plant.
⊕	[Cog-wheel]	machinery; engineering.
⚒	[Crossed hammers]	mining term.
⚔	[Crossed swords]	military term.
⚓	[Anchor]	nautical [or boatmen's, watermen's, &c.] term.
♁	[Globe]	geographical term.
⚇	[Coin]	commercial language, business term.
⚴	[Post-horn]	postal, telegraphic term.
⛟	[Locomotive]	railway term.
♪	[Quaver]	musical term.
⁺⁺⁺	[Three crosses]	incorrect; misunderstood.
=	(Sign of equality)	equal(s), equal to.

① to ㊿ [Numbers within a circle] refer to the "Detached Observations" given on page XXIII, &c.; see also p. XXII,6.

⚐ [Boundary post] a) after a German heading: has passed from English into G. b) before an E. word in the context: has passed from G. into E.

(⚐) Translation, as Gemeinplatz (⚐) [(commonplace)], or revival, as Halle (⚐), see below [(...)].

[:], [P:], [?] [Square brackets or crotch(ets)] enclose the etymological explanations. See also p. XXII,5. The colon in the same = [originally] related to //; [P:] = by popular etymology assimilated to //; [?] = of uncertain origin.

[(...)] Translation of the foreign word, as: Gevatter [(compater)], Gemeinplatz [(commonplace)].

( ) [Round brackets or parentheses]: 1. Letters enclosed in ( ) denote a double mode of spelling as: Arz(e)nei = Arzenei or Arznei; labo(u)r = labour [English spelling] or labor [American spelling]. — 2. Words in ( ) denote, that what is enclosed in the bracket may either stand or be omitted, as: to (strew with) sand = to strew with sand or to sand. — 3. Bracketed words preceded by 'or' = alternative forms. Thus: loose (or degenerate, depraved) morals pl. = loose morals or degenerate morals or depraved morals.

- [Hyphen]: The following example is illustrative of the use of the hyphen in the E. translations: Her-reise f home- (or return-) journey or voyage = home-journey or return-journey or home-voyage or return-voyage.

=, ⁼ [Hyphens] repeat with either a capital [=] or small [⁼] initial the first part of the compound preceding either of these signs, as: Eid-genoß, =genossenschaft, ⁼genössisch [= Eidgenossenschaft, eidgenössisch.]

(Wiederholungszeichen) wiederholen mit großem (~) oder kleinem (²) Anfangsbuchstaben das zu Anfang eines Artikels stehende fettgedruckte Wort, den **Titelkopf**, z. B.:
Bann ban: in den ~ (= Bann) tun.
Abend-brot n supper; ohne ~ (= ohne Abendbrot) supperless; ²ländisch a. occidental, die 2e (= abendländische) Kirche the Roman (Catholic) Church.
(Teilstrich) wiederholt den abgetrennten Wortteil, z. B.:
befestig en: ... B/ung f (= Befestigung)
denaturier en: d/ter Spiritus (= denaturierter Sp.)
(Doppelstrich) bezeichnet Unvollendetlassung des Satzes, z. B.: gestern schrieb er uns, daß //
(‾‿ˇ͝) Das Zeichen ‾ über einem Selbst- od. Doppellaut bezeichnet, daß der betreffende Laut gedehnt zu sprechen ist; das Zeichen ‿ bezeichnet die geschärfte (kurze) Aussprache; das Zeichen ͝ bezeichnet die schwankende (lange oder kurze) Aussprache. Finden sich in mehrsilbigen Wörtern über diesen Zeichen zwei kleine Striche (″ oder ˝), so wird dadurch angegeben, daß auf der (je nachdem gedehnten oder geschärften Laute zu sprechenden) Silbe der Hauptton liegt, während die Silbe, in welcher über dem betreffenden Zeichen der Dehnung oder Schärfung bloß ein kleiner Strich steht (′, ˊ), nur einen schwächeren Nebenton hat und jede Silbe ohne darüber stehenden kleinen Strich (‿, -) tonlos ist. In **ab-beten** (‿‾‿) und **ab-betteln** (‿‿‿) z. B. hat die erste Silbe mit geschärftem Selbstlaut den Hauptton; in dem ersten Worte hat die zweite Silbe mit gedehntem Selbstlaut einen Nebenton und die dritte ist tonlos; in dem zweiten Worte hat die zweite Silbe mit geschärftem Selbstlaut einen Nebenton und die dritte ist tonlos. In **Berberis** (‿‿‿) dagegen ruht der Ton auf der ersten Silbe mit geschärftem Selbstlaut, während die beiden folgenden tonlos sind, und in dem zusammengesetzten fünfsilbigen **Berberis-beere** (‿‿‿‾‿) hat die erste Silbe mit geschärftem Selbstlaut den Hauptton, die vierte mit gedehntem Selbstlaut einen Nebenton, während die übrigen drei Silben (sämtlich mit geschärftem Selbstlaut) tonlos (oder unbetont) sind. — Der flüchtige Laut wird durch Einklammerung bezeichnet, z. B. **Bastion** ‿(‿)‾.

~, ² [Mark of repetition] repeats with a capital [~] or small [²] initial the heavy-type word or heading at the beginning of an article; thus:
Bann ban: in den ~ (= Bann) tun.
Abend-brot n supper; ohne ~ [= ohne Abendbrot] supperless; ²ländisch a. occidental, die 2e [= abendländische] Kirche the Roman [Catholic] Church.
/ [stroke] stands for the omitted part of a word, as:
befestig en: ...B/ung f [= Befestigung]
denaturier en: d/ter Spiritus [= denaturierter Sp.]
// [double stroke] denotes abridgment of the sentence, as in: yesterday he wrote to us that //
(-‾ ″ ‿, ˊ ͝) The sign ‾ over a vowel or diphthong signifies that it is sounded as *long*, the sign ‿ that it is sounded as *short*; the sign ͝ denotes a *variable* [either long or short] pronunciation. In words of two or more syllables, two accents [″ or ˝] over these signs indicate that the *principal accent or stress* rests on that same syllable [be its sound long or short], any syllable, with only *one* little dash over the sign of long or short [′, ˊ], having a weaker or *secondary accent*, and all other syllables without the little dash [-, ‿] remaining *unaccented*. Thus, for instance, in both **ab-beten** (‿‾‿) and **abbetteln** (‿‿‿), the first syllable with a short vowel has the principal accent; in the former word, the second syllable with a long vowel has a secondary accent, and the third remains without an accent; in the latter word, the second syllable with a short vowel has a secondary stress, and the third is without any accent. In **Berberis** (‿‿‿), on the contrary, the accent rests on the first syllable with a short vowel, the two following syllables remaining unaccented, and in the compound **Berberis-beere** (‿‿‿‾‿) of five syllables, the first syllable with a short vowel has the principal accent, the fourth, with a long vowel, a secondary accent, whereas the other three syllables [all with short vowels] are without any accents [or are unaccented]. — A *vanishing* or *fugitive* sound is enclosed in brackets, for instance **Bastion**: ‿(‿)‾.

E. Abkürzungen.   Abbreviations.

Vorbemerkung: Allgemein bekannte oder sich aus dem Zusammenhange von selbst ergebende Abkürzungen sind hier nicht aufgeführt. — Vgl. auch S. XXII,8.

Preliminary Observation: Abbreviations universally known, and such as are sufficiently explained by the context, are not given here. — See also p. XXII,8.

A

a. . . . auch, also (ā′l-hō)).
a. . . . adjective (ă′b-Ğᵉt-tĭw) Adjektiv(um), Eigenschaftswort.
abbr. . abbreviation (ă-brĭ-wĭēˊ-ʃᶜhᵉn) Abkürzung.
abh. . abhängig, dependent(ly) (dᵉ-pŏ′n-dᵉnt(-lᵉ).
abs. . . absolute (ă′b-ɮᵒ-l̅ŭt) absolu′t.
abstr. . abstra′kt, begrifflich abstract(ly) (ă′b-ɮtnăkkt(-lᵉ).
acc. . . accusative case (ă-kjŭˊ-ɮᵉ-tĭw kēs) Akkusativ, Wenfall.
act. . . active (ă′t-tĭw) Aktiv(um), Tätigkeitsform.
adv. . . adverb (ă′d-wᵉ̄b) Adverb(ium), Umstandswort.
agr. . . agriculture (ă′g-nᵉ̆-tŏl̆t-tʃᵉhᵉr) Ackerbau.
ahd. . . althochdeutsch, Old High German (ōld hăĭ dᵍŏˊᵉ-mᵉn).
alem. . alemannisch, Alemannic (ăt̆-ᵉ-mă′n-ĭt). [(7.-11. sæ.)]
allg. . . allgemein commonly (tᵒ′m̆-n-lᵉ).
Alt. . . Altertum, antiquity (ăn-tĭˊ-t-wᵉ̄-tᵉ). [Amerika.
Am. . Americanism (ă-mᵉ′R-ɮ̆-tᵉ-nĭʒm) engl. Ausdruck aus
anat. . anatomy (ă-nă′t-ᵉ-mᵉ) Anatomie, Körperbaulehre.
ant. . . antonym (ă′n-tᵒ-nĭm) Antony′m (Gegensatz z B. groß-klein).
Ap.G. . Apostelgeschichte, the Acts of the Apostles (ᵃhl ăkkt̥ ᵒᵛ).
ar. . . ara′bisch, Arabic (ă′R-ă-bĭt). [ᵃhl ă-pŏˊ ɮl].
arch. . architecture (ăˊR-t̆ᶜ-tᵉt-tʃhʳ) Architektur, Baukunst.
arith. . arithmetic (ă-nĭˊᵗh-mᵉᶜ-tĭt) Arithmetik, Rechenkunst.
art. . . article (ăˊR-tĭkl), Artikel, Geschlechtswort.

artill. . artillery (ăᵣ-tĭˊl̆-ɮ-ᵉR⁹) Artillerie, Geschützkunst.
ast. . . astronomy (ă-ɮtRŏˊn-ᵉ-mᵉ) Astronomie, Sternkunde.
astrol. . astrology (ă-ɮtRŏˊl̆-ᵉ-bĞᵉ) Astrologie, Sterndeuterei.
attr. . . attributiv attributive (ă-tR̆ĭˊb-ɮ̆-tĭw).
Ausſp. . Aussprache, pronunciation (pRᵒ-nᵒn-ɮĭᵉ-ēˊ-ʃᶜhᵉn).
aux. . auxiliary (ăˊ-gʒĭˊl̆-ĭᵒ-Rᵉ) Hilfs..., vgl. v/aux.

B

B. . . Bürger (Dichter, 1747-1794).
b. . . . bei(m) at (the), with (the) (ăt, wĭdh [dhᵒ]).
Bed. . . Bedeutung(en), signification(s) (ɮĭg-nᵉ-ɮ̆-tᵉˊ-ʃᶜhᵉn(ʒ).
Bem. . Bemerkung, remark (nᵉ-māˊʳt).
best. . . bestimmt, definite(ly) (dᵉˊf-ɮ-nĭt(-lᵉ).
betr. . . betreffend, relating to (nᵉ-lēˊ-tĭnɮ tᵒ).
bibl. . biblical (bĭˊb-l̆-t̆l) biblisch.
bisw. . . bisweilen, sometimes (ɮᵒˊm-tălmʒ).
Bn. . . Beiname, surname (ɮᵒˊᵉ-nēm).
b.s. . . bad sense (bĭd ɮᵉnɮ) im schlechten Sinne.
bjd. . . besonder(s), particular(ly) (pă̆ʳ-tĭˊ-t̆-ᵒ-l̆ᵉ(-lᵉ).
bſſ. . . . besser, better (bᵉˊt-ɮʳ).
bursch. . burschikos, student-like (ɮtᵊŭˊ-dᵉnt-lălt). [(dᵉ-nŏˊtĭnɮ).
bz. . . . bezeichnet, denotes (bᵉ-nŏˊtʒ), bezeichnend, denoting

C

card.numb. cardinal number (tā́r-dĭ-nʾl nŭm-bər) Grundzahl.
carp. . carpentry (kā́r-pʾn-trĕ) Zimmerhandwerk.
Cath. . Catholic (kăth-ŏ-lĭk) katho'lisch.
chin. . chine'sisch, Chinese (tchăī-nīʹs). [kunst.]
chm. . . chemistry (kĕ́m-ĭs-ktrĕ) Chemie, Stoffkunde, Scheide=
chron. . chronology (krŏ-nŏ́l-ŏ-dGĕ), Chronologie, Zeitrechnung.
cj. . . conjunction(kŏn-dGŭ́nkt-schʾn)Konjunktion,Bindewort.
co. . . . comic(al) (kŏ́m-ĭk, kŏ́m-ĭ-kʾl) komisch, scherzhaft.
coll. . collectively (kŏ-lĕ́k-tĭv-lĕ) kollekti'v, Sammelname.
comp. . comparative(kŏm-pā́r-ă-tĭv)Ko'mparativ,höhererGrad.
cond. . conditional(kŏn-dĭ́sch-ŏ-nʾl) Konditiona'lis, Bedingung.
contp. . contemptuously (kŏn-tĕ́m-tschŭ̆-ŏs-lĕ) verächtlich.
corr. . corrupt (kĭ-rŏ̆pt) verderbt.
cryst. . crystallography (kriss-tă-lŏ́g-ră-fĕ) Kristallkunde.
cycl. . . cycling (sai-klĭng) Radfahrwesen.

D

D. . . . Dichter, poet (pōʹ-ĕt). [dhĕ, ŏw, ʾw, tu dhĕ]
d. . . . . der, die, das, des, dem, den, the, of the, to the, the.
Dampfm. Dampfmaschine, steam-engine (stĭm éʹn-dGĭn).
dat. . . dative case (dēʹ-tĭv kēs) Dativ, Wemfall.
def. . . definite (dĕ́f-ĭ-nĭt) bestimmt. [schʾn].
Defl. Deflination, Fallabwandlung, declension (dĕ-klĕ́n-
dem.a.,pron. {demonstrative (dĕ-mŏ́n-strā-tĭv) adjective, pronoun hinweisendes Beiwort, Fürwort.
Df. . . . Dorf, village (wĭ́l-ĕdG).
dft. . . defective (dĕ-fĕ́k-tĭv) unvollständig.
d.h. . . das heißt, that is (to say) (thăt ĭs [tŭ sē]).
dim. . . diminutive (dĕ-mĭ́n-ĭu-tĭv) Diminuti'v, Verkleinerung.
distr.numb. distributive number (dĕ-sktrĭ́b-ĭu-tĭv nŭm-bər)
ds. . . . dies, this (miß). [Verteilungszahl.]
dse., dsr., dss. diese(r, s), this (miß), these (ahīß) rc.
dtsch. . deutsch, German (dGĕ́r-mʾn).

E

e. . . . . ein, a, an (ē oder ă, ʾn, ŏn). [ĭtsch éd dh-ĕr]
ea. . . . einander, one another (wŏn ă-nŭdh-ĕr), each other.
ebb. . . ebenda(selbst), at the same place (ăt dhĕ sēm plēʹs)
eccl. . . ecclesiastical (ĕ́k-lĭ-ĭsʹ-ă-ŝt-ĭ-kʾl) kirchlich, geistlich.
eccl.hist. ecclesiastical history (...hĭ́s-tŏ-rĕ) Kirchengeschichte.
e-e . . . eine, a, an (ē oder ă, ʾn, ŏn).
ehm. . . ehemals, formerly (fōʹr-mĕr-lĕ).
eigtl. . eigentlich, properly speaking (prŏ́p-ər-lĕ spī-kĭng).
elect. . . electricity (ĕl-ĕ́k-trĭs-ĭ-tĕ) Elektrizität.
ell. . . elliptical(ly) (ĕ-lĭ́p-tĕ-kʾl, ĕ-lĭ́p-tĕ-kʾl-lĕ) elli'ptisch, wort=
e-m . . einem, to a(n) (tū ă, ʾn, ŏn). [sparend.
e-n . . einen, a, an (ă, ʾn, ŏn) (acc.).
engl. . . englisch, English (ĭ́ng-glĭsch). [sĕnß.]
engS. . im enger(e)n Sinne, in a narrower sense (ĭn ă năʹr-ŏ-ĕr
ent. . . . entomology (ĕn-tŏ-mŏ́l-ŏ-dGĕ) Entomologie, Kerb=
e-r . . . einer, of a(n), to a(n) (ŏw-ă, tū ă, ʾn, ŏn). [tierlehre.
e-s . . . eines, of a(n) (ŏw-ă, ŏw ă'n, ŏn).
et. . . . etwas, something (ŝŏ́m-thĭng).
euph. {euphemistically (iū-fĕ-mĭ́s-tĕ-kă-lĕ) euphemistisch, be=
  schönigend, verhüllend.

F

F . . . . siehe Seite XVII see on p. XVII.
f. . . . . für, for (fʾr).
f. . . . feminine (fĕ́m-ĭ-nĭn), Femininum, weiblich.
fenc. . . fencing (fĕ́n-sĭng) Fechtkunst.
Fernspr. Fernsprechwesen, telephony (tĕ-lĕ́f-ŏ-nĕ).
fig. . . . figuratively (fĭ́g-ĭu-rā-tĭv-lĕ) bildlich.
Fl. . . . Fluß, river (rĭ́w-ĕr).
for. . . forestry (fŏ́r-ĕs-strĕ) Forstwirtschaft.
FR. . . . Freiligrath (Dichter, 1810—1876).
fr. . . . französisch, French (frĕnsch).
(++)fr. = {mit anderer Bedeutung (z. B. blamieren) oder
  anderer Form (z. B. Refrut, fr. recrue) with a
  different meaning [as blamieren] or form [as
  Refrut, recrue](wĭdh ă dĭ́f-ĕ-rʾnt mĭ-nĭng ŏr fŏʹrm).

++fr. = {ganz unfranzösisch, fr. fehlend, zB. Blamage, not
  to be found in French (nŏt tŭ bī sau̇nd ĭn frĕnsch).
frt. . . . fortification (fŏr-tĕ-fĭ-kē-schʾn) Befestigungswesen.
fut. . . . future (fiū-tschər) Futurum, Zukunft.

G

G . . . . Goethe (Dichter, 1749—1832).
gbr. . . . gebräuchlich, common(ly) (kŏ́m-ʾn(-lĕ).
geb. . . geboren, born (bŏ́rn) (* vgl. S. XVII).
geh. Spr. gehobene Sprache, elevated style (ĕ́l-ĕ-wē-tĕd stīl).
gen. . . genitive (dGĕ́n-ĕ-tĭv) Ge'nitiv, Wesfall.
geogn. . geognosy (dGē-ŏ́g-nŏ-sĕ) Geognosie, Gesteinkunde.
geol. . . geology (dGē-ŏ́l-ŏ-dGĕ) Geologie, Erdgeschichte.
geom. . geometry (dGē-ŏ́m-ĕ-trĕ)Geometrie, Raumgrößenlehre.
ger. . . . (gemein=germanisch, [common] Teutonic (tŏ́m-ĕn)
gest. . . gestorben, died (dāĭd) († vgl. S.XVII). [tiū-tŏ́-nĭk),
got. . . . gotisch, Gothic (gŏ́th-ĭk)
GR. . . . {Die Brüder Grimm (Jakob Ludwig, 1785—1863,
  und Wilhelm Karl, 1786—1859), Sprachforscher.
gr. . . . groß(e, er, es) great (grēt), large (lāʹrdG).
gr(am). grammar (grắm-ĕr) Grammatif, Sprachlehre.
grch. . . griechisch, Greek, Grecian (grĭk, grĭʹ-schʾn).
g.s. . . good sense (gŭd sĕnß) im guten Sinne.
gschr. . . geschrieben, written (rĭtn).

H

H . . . . Herder (Dichter u. Schr., 1744—1803).
h. . . . . haben to have (tŭ hăw), vgl. v/n.
hd. . . . hochdeutsch, High German (hāĭ dGĕ́r-mʾn).
hebr. . . hebräisch, Hebrew (hĭ́-brū).
her. . . heraldry (hĕ́r-ăl-drĕ) Heraldif, Wappenkunde.
hist. . . history (hĭ́s-tŏ-rĕ) Geschichte.
Hom. {homonym (hŏ́m-ŏ-nĭm, a. hŏ́-mʾs-) Homony'm (gleich=
  lautendes Wort mit anderer Bedeutung).
hort. . . horticulture (hŏ́r-tĕ-kăl-tschĕs) Gartenbau.
H.St. . . Hauptstadt, capital (kăʹp-ĭ-tʾl).
hunt. . hunting (hŏ́n-tĭng) Jagd(wesen). [lehre.
hydr. . hydraulics (hai-drăʹ-lĭks) Hydraulik, Wasserkraft=

I

ichth. . . ichthyology (ĭt-th-ŏʹl-ŏ-dGĕ) Fischkunde.
id. . . . idem, ebender(die, das)selbe, the same (dhĕ sēm).
idg. . . . indogermanisch, Indo-Germanic (ĭʹn-dŏ-dGĕ́r-mắn-ĭk).
imper. . imperative (im-pĕ́r-ă-tĭv) Imperativ, Befehl(sform).
imp(ers). impersonal (im-pĕ́r-ŝŏ-nʾl) unpersönlich.
impf. . . imperfect (im-pĕ́r-fĕt) Imperfekt(um), Vergangenheit.
ind. . . indicative (in-dĭ́-kă-tĭv) Indikativ, Wirklichkeit.
indef. . . indefinite (in-dĕ́f-ĭ-nĭt) unbestimmt. [form.]
inf. . . . infinitive mood (in-fĭ́n-ĕ-tĭv mūd) Infinitiv, Nenn=
int. . . . interjection (in-tĕr-dGĕ́kt-schʾn), Interjektion, Ausruf.
interr. . interrogative (in-tĕ-rŏ́-gă-tĭv) Frage(für)wort.
intr(ans). intransitive (in-trắn-ŝĭ-tĭv)intransiti'v, ziellos, s.v/n.
inv. . . invariable (in-wăʹ-rĭ-ă-bʾl) ohne Abwandlung.
iro. . . . ironically (ai-rŏ́n-ĭ-kă-lĕ) ironisch, spöttisch.
irr. . . . irregular (ĭ-rĕ́g-ĭu-lʾr) unregelmäßig.
it. . . . italienisch, Italian (ĭ-tăʹl-ĭʾn).

J

j., j-s, j-m, j-n {jemand, jemand(e)s, jemand(em), jemand(en),
  somebody, of, to somebody (sŏw, tŭ ŝŏ́m-bŏ-dĕ).
join. . . joinery (dGŏ́i-nĕ-rĕ) Tischlerhandwerk.
jur. . . juri'stisch, Rechtsausdruck, law term (lăʹ tĕʹrm).

K

Kg. . . König, king (kĭng).
KL. . . . Klopstock (Dichter, 1724—1803).
kl. . . . klein(e, er, es), little (lĭtl).
klt. . . keltisch, Celtic (ĕ́s-ʾl-tĭt).
Kochk. . Kochkunst, culinary art (tjū-lĕ-nʾ-rĕ āʹrt).
konkr. . konkret, körperlich concrete(ly) (kĭn-krĭt(-lĕ).
Ks. . . . Kaiser, emperor (ĕ́m-pĕ-rʾr).

L

L. . . . . Lessing (Dichter, 1729—1781).
l. . . . . lassen, to let (tᵉ lĕt).
lautm. . lautmalend, onomatopoetic (ŏn-ᵉ-măt-ᵒ-pᵒ-ĕᵗ-ĭt).
lit.s. . . literal sense (lĭᵗ-ᵗ-ᵃ-ʳˡ sĕnß) eigentlicher Sinn.
Lo. . . . London (lăⁿ-n-bᵉn), Londoner (of) London.
log. . . . logic (lŏ-bG-it) Lo'gik, Denklehre.
lt. . . . . lateinisch, Latin (lăᵗ-t-ⁿ).
LU. . . Luther (Reformator und Bibelübersetzer, 1483—1546).

M

m. . . . . machen, to make (tᵉ mēt).
m. . . . . masculine (măᵉ-ß-tĭᵘ-lĭn) Maskulinum, männlich.
mach. . machinery (mᵃ-schī'-nᵉ-rᵉ) Maschinenwesen.
madj. . madjarisch, Magyar (măᵍ-g-jär) (+ ungarisch).
man. . . manege (mᵃ-nēᵒ'G) Reitkunst. [lehre)
math. . mathematics (măth-ᵉ-măᵗ-t-ĭtß) Mathematik, Größen-
md. . . . mitteldeutsch, Middle German (mĭdl dGöʳ-mᵉn).
m-e. . . meine, my (maᵉ).
mech. . mechanics (mᵉ-tă'n-ĭtß) Mechanik, Triebwerklehre.
med. . . medicine (mĕᵈ-ᵒ-|ᵉ-ßĭn) Medizin, Heilkunde.
metall. . metallurgy (mĕᵗ-ᵗ-ᵃ-löʳ-bGᵉ) Hüttenkunde.
meton. { metonymisch, namenvertauschend, metonymic(al)
         { (mĕt-ᵒ-nĭʸm-ĭt, -ᵉ-fĭl).
mhd. . { mittelhochdeutsch, (11. bis 15. sœ.) Middle High
         { German (mĭdl haĭ bGöʳ-mᵉn).
min. . . mineralogy (mĭn-ᵉ-năˡ-ᵒ-bGᵉ) Steinkunde, Mineralogie.
mint. . . minting (mĭᵗⁿ-tĭnᵍ) Münzprägung. [iʳ-nᵃᵗ lăᵗ-tⁿ).
mlt. . . . mittellateinisch, mediæval Latin (mĕᵈ-ᵉ- oder mĭ-ᵈ-ᵉ-
m-m, m-n meinem to my (tᵉ maᵉ), meinen my (maᵉ) (acc.).
m-r, m-s meiner of ob. to my (ᵒw, tᵉ maᵉ), meines of my.
mst. . . . meist(ens), generally (bGᵉⁿ-ᵃ-rᵃ-lᵉ). [Sagenkunde.)
myth. . mythology (mᵉ-thŏl-ᵒ-bGᵉ) Mythologie, Götterlehre,

N

n. . . . . nach after (aᵃᶠ-ᵗ-ᵉʳ).
n. . . . . neuter (njuᵗ-tᵒʳ) Neutrum, sächlich.
ndd., ndtsch niederdeutsch, Low German (lō bGöʳ-mᵉn).
ndl. . . . niederländisch, holländisch Dutch (dătsch).
neg. . . { negation (nᵉ-gē-ᵉ-schᵉn) Verneinung.
         { negative(ly) (nĕᵍ-g-tĭw[-lᵉ]) verneinend.
nhd. . { neuhochdeutsch (seit 15. sœ.), New High German
         { (njuᵗ haĭ bGöʳ-mᵉn). fall.)
nom. . . nominative case (nŏᵐ-ᵉ-nᵃ-tĭw tēß) No'minativ, Wer-
nordd. . norddeutsch North German (nŏʳth bGöʳ-mᵉn).
npr. . . proper name (prŏᵒ'pᵒʳ nēm) Eigenname.
num. . . numismatics (njuᵗ-mĭß-măᵗ-t-ĭtß) Numisma'tik, Münz=
numer. numeral (njuᵗ-mᵉ-rᵃᵗ) Zahlwort. [kunde.)

O

o. . . . . ohne, without (wĭdh-aū'ᵗ).
obb. . . oberdeutsch, Upper German (ŏ'pᵒʳ bGöʳ-mᵉn).
obj. . . . object (ŏᵇ-bGᵉtt) Objekt, Ziel, Ergänzung.
od. . . . oder, or (ōʳ).
opt. . . . optics (ŏ'p-tĭtß) Optik, Lichtlehre.
ord.numb. ordinal number (ōʳ-ᵈ-ᵉ-nᵃᵗ năᵐ-bᵉʳ) Ordnungszahl.
orn. . . ornithology (ōʳ-ⁿ-thŏl-ᵒ-bGᵉ) Vogelkunde.
o.s. . . . oneself (wăn-ßĕ'lf) sich (selbst).
öst. . . . österreichisch, Austrian (ă'-ßtrᵉ-ᵃⁿ).
Ost=J. . Ostindien, East Indies (īßt_ĭ'n-bᵉf).

P

P, [P]. s. S. XVII see on p. XVII; p. = person.
paint. . painting (pē'n-tĭnᵍ) Malerei.
parl. . . parliamentary (pāʳ-l-ᵉ-mĕ'n-t-ᵃ-rᵉ) parlamentarisch.
part. . . participle (pāʳ-tᵉ-ßĭpl) Partizip(ium), Mittelform.
pass. . . passive (păᵉ-ß-ĭw) Passivum, Leideform.
path. . pathology (pᵃ-thŏl-ᵒ-bGᵉ) Pathologi'e, Krankheitslehre.
perf. . . perfect (pöʳ-fĕtt) Perfekt(um), Vorgegenwart.
pharm. pharmacy (fāʳ-mᵃ-ßᵉ) Arzneikunst.
phls. . . philosophy (fᵉ-lŏ'ß-ᵒ-fᵉ) Philosophie, Erkenntnislehre.
phot. . photography (fᵉ-tŏ'g-rᵃ-fᵉ) Photographie, Lichtbildkunst.
phys. . . physics (fĭ'ʓ-ĭtß) Physik, Naturlehre.

physiol. physiology (fĭß-ᵉ-ŏ'l-ᵒ-bGᵉ) Physiologie, Lebenslehre.
pl. . . . plural (pluᵗ-rᵃˡ) Plural(is), Mehrzahl.
poet. . . poetry (pŏᵉ-ᵉ-trᵉ) Poesie, Dichtkunst.
pol. . . . politics (pŏ'l-ᵉ-tĭtß) Politik, Staatskunst.
port. . . portugiesisch, Portuguese (pōʳ-tĭᵘ-gĭß). [gangenheit.)
p.p. . . past participle (păßt pāʳ-tᵉ-ßĭpl) Mittelform der Ver-
p.pr. . . present participle (prĕᶻ-ᵉnt pāʳ-tᵉ-ßĭpl) Mittelform)
pr. . . . preußisch, Prussian (prăᵒ'sch-ᵉn). [der Gegenwart.)
präd. . prädikati'v, aussagend, predicative (prĕ-dĭ'tt-ᵃ-tĭw.
pres. . . present [tense] (prĕᶻ-ᵉnt [tĕnß]) Präsens, Gegenwart.
pron. . . pronoun (prŏᵒ'-naun) Pronomen, Fürwort.
pros. . . prosody (prŏ'ß-ᵉ-bᵉ) Prosodie, Silbenmessung. [druck)
provc. . provincialism (prᵉ-wĭ'n-sch-ᵃ-lĭsm) mundartlicher Aus-
prp. . . preposition (prĕp-ᵉ-fĭ'sch-ᵉn) Präpositio'n, Verhältnis=
Prsn. . . Person, person (pöʳ-ßⁿ). [wort.)
prvz. . . provenza'lisch, Provençal (prō-wa-ßä'l).

R

R. . . . Rückert (Dichter 1788—1866).
refl. . . reflexive (rᵉ-flĕ'tt-ßĭw) reflexiv, (zu)rückbezüglich, s.)
regelm. regelmäßig, regular (rĕᵍ-g-jᵘ-lᵃʳ). [v/refl.)
rel. . . . religion (rᵉ-lĭ'bGᵉn) Religion.
rel. pron. relative (rĕ'l-ᵃ-tĭw) bezügliches Fürwort.
rhet. . . rhetoric (rĕᵗ-t-ᵒ-rĭt) Rhetorik, Redekunst.
rom. . . romanisch, Romanic (rᵒ-mă'n-ĭt).
röm. . . römisch, Roman (rŏᵒ'-mᵃn).
r-r. . . richtiger, more correctly (mŏʳ tᵒ-rĕ'tt-lᵒ).
russ. . . russisch, Russian (răᵒ'sch-ᵉn)

S

S. . . . Seite, page (pēbG).
s. . . . sieh(e), man sehe, see (ßĭ), refer to (rᵉ-föʳ' tĭĭ).
s. . . . substantive (ßŏ'b-ßtᵃn-tĭw) Hauptwort.
sae. . . sae'culum, century (ßĕ'n-tĭᵘ-rᵉ) Jahrhundert.
SCH. . Schiller (Dichter, 1759—1805).
schott. { schottisch, in Schottland üblich(er Ausdruck),
        { Scotch (ßtŏtsch). Scotticism (ßtŏ'ᵗ-t-ßĭßm).
Schr. . Schriftsteller, writer, author (rāᵉ'-tᵒʳ, ä'-thᵉʳ).
schwd. . schwedisch, Swedish (ßwĭ'-dĭsch).
schwz. . schweizerisch, Swiss (ßwĭß).
sculp. . sculpture (ßtŏ'lp-tĭsch-ᵉʳ) Bildhauerkunst.
s. d. . . sieh(e) dies, see this (ßĭ dhĭß).
s-e. . . seine, his, one's (hĭß, wănß).
sg. . . . singular (ßĭ'nᵍ-gĭᵘ-lᵃʳ) Singular(is), Einzahl.
SH. . . Shakespeare (schĕᵉ'-ßpĭʳ; Drama'tiker, 1564—1616).
skand. . skandina'visch, Scandinavian (ßtăn-bᵉ-nēᵒ'-wĭᵉⁿ).
sr., srt. Sanskrit, Sanskrit (ßăᵉⁿ-ßtrĭt).
sl. . . . slang (ßlănᵍ) Zunftausdruck.
s-m. . . seinem, to his, one's (tĭᵘ hĭß, wănß).
s-n. . . seinen, his, one's (hĭß, wănß) (acc.).
sn. . . sein (Verb), to be (tᵉ bĭ), vgl. v/n.
sog. . . sogenannte(r, s), so-called (ßᵒ tåld).
span. . spanisch, Spanish (ßpă'n-ĭsch).
spr. . . sprich, pronounce (prᵒ-naū'nß).
Sprichw. Sprichwort, proverb (prŏᵒ'w-ᵃʳᵇ).
s-r, s-s seiner, seines, of his, one's (ᵒw hĭß, wănß).
st. . . . statt, instead of (ĭn-ßtĕ'b ŏw).
St. . . . Stadt, town (taᵘn); vor Namen: Sankt, Saint [ßĕnt,)
s.th. . . something (ßŏ'm-thĭnᵍ) etwas. [ßᵃnt.)
subj. . . subjektiv(isch), subjective(ly) (ßŏb-bGĕ'ᵗ-tĭw(-lᵒ)).
subj. . . subjunctive (ßŏb-bGăⁿ'tt-tĭw) Konjunktiv, Vorstellung.
subst. . substantivisch, substantive(ly) (ßŏ'b-ßtᵃn-tĭw(-lᵉ); vgl. s.
südd. . süddeutsch, South German (ßauth bGöʳ-mᵉn).
sup. . . superlative (ßĭᵘ-pöʳ'-lᵃ-tĭw) Superlativ, höchster Grad.
surg. . surgery (ßöʳ-bGᵉ-rᵉ) Wundheilkunde.
surv. . surveying (ßᵉʳ-wēᵒ'-ĭnᵍ) Landvermessung.
Syn. . . synonym (ßĭ'n-ᵒ-nĭm) Synonym (sinnverwandt. Ausdruck).
synt. . . syntax (ßĭ'n-tătß) Syntax, Satzlehre.

T

T . . . Tieck (Dichter, 1773—1853).
tel. . . . telegraphy (tᵉ-lĕ'g-rᵃ-fᵉ) Telegraphie, Drahtpost.
th. . . . thing (thĭnᵍ) Ding; vgl. s. th.

thea. . . theatre (thī'-ä-tʳ) Thea'ter, Bühne.
theol. . theology (thē-ŏl'-ŏ-dʒĭ) Theologie, Gottesgelehrtheit.
trans. . transitive (träň-ßĭ-tiw) transitiv, zielend, f. *v/a.*
tschech. tschechisch, Czechic (tschĕ'-ĭt) (+ böhmisch).
türk. . . türkisch, Turkish (tör'-tisch). [druckerkunst.
typ. . . typography (tai-pŏ'g-rä-fĭ) Typographie, Buch-

U

U. . . . Uhland (Dichter, 1787—1862).
u. . . . und, and (änd, änd, ənd).
Übf. . . Übersetzung, translation (tränß-lē'-schən).
unanst. unanständig, indecent (in-dī'-ßənt).
univ. . {auf Universitäten bezüglich relating to universities (ju-nĭ-wör'-ßĭ-tĭs).
urspr. . ursprünglich, original(ly) (ŏ-rĭ'dʒ-ĭ-nəl, -nə-lĭ).
U.S. . . {United States of America (ju-nai'-tĕd ßtēts ŏw ä-mĕ'r-ĭ-fä) Vereinigte Staaten von Amerika.
usw. . . und so weiter, etc &c., and so on (änd ßo ŏn).

V

v. . . . . von, vom, of, by, from (ŏw, bai, from).
v. . . . . verb (wörb) Verb(um), Zeitwort. [Zeitwort.
v/a. . . verb active (wörb äk'-tiw), transitive verb zielendes
v/aux. auxiliary verb (ä-gfi'l-jə-rĭ wörb) Hilfszeitwort.
verk. . . verkürzt, abbreviated (ä-brī'-wiē-tĕd).
versch. . verschieden(e, r, s), various (wē'-rĭ-əß).
verw. . verwandt, related (rĭ-lē'-tĕd) (mst. durch : bz.).
vet. . . . veterinary art (wĕ't-ĭ-rĭ-nə-rĭ ārt) Tierheilkunde.

vgl. . . vergleiche, compare (fəm-pār'). [Zeitwort.
v/imp. . verb impersonal (wörb im-pör'-ßə-nəl) unpersönliches
Vn. . . Vorname, Christian name (krī'ß-tĭən nēm). [Zeitwort.
v/n. . . verb neuter (wörb njū'-tər), intransitive verb zielloses
v/n.(h.) {mit „haben" abgewandeltes zielloses Zeitwort intransitive verb conjugated with "haben" (in-trä'n-ßĭ-tiw wörb kŏ'n-dʒŭ-gē-tĕd widh "haben").
v/n.(sn) {mit „sein" abgewandeltes zielloses Zeitwort, intransitive (or neuter) verb conjugated with "sein".
v/n.(h.od.sn) {mit „haben" od. „sein" abgewandeltes zielloses Zeitwort, intransitive (or neuter) verb conjugated with either "haben" or "sein".
v/recip. {reciprocal verb (rĭ-ßĭ'p-rŏ-fəl wörb) rezipro'kes, wechselbezügliches Zeitwort. [Zeitwort.
v/refl. . reflexive verb (rĭ-flĕ'k-ßiw wörb) (zu)rückbezügliches

W

W . . . Wieland (Dichter, 1733—1813).
w. . . . werden, to become (tŭ bĭ-kŏ'm), to be (tŭ bī). [ßənß).
weit S. im weiteren Sinne, in a wider sense (in ə wai'-dər

Z

z. B. . . zum Beispiel, for instance (fŏr i'n-ßtənß).
zo. . . . zoology (fō-ŏ'l-ŏ-dʒĭ) Zoologie, Tierkunde.
zs. . . . zusammen together (tŭ-gĕ'dhər).
zsgz. . . zusammengezogen, contracted (kən-trä'k-tĕd).
Zssg(n) Zusammensetzung(en), compound word(s) (kŏ'm-paund wörd(s)).
zw. . . . zwischen, between (bĭ-twī'n).

F. Allgemeine Bemerkungen
über die innere Einrichtung des Werkes.

1. Rechtschreibung: Als Grundlage hat bei der Neubearbeitung die **amtliche Rechtschreibung von 1903** gedient, welche durch ihre grundsätzliche Annahme des **K** und **Z** statt des alten, nur für wenige Fremdwörter beibehaltenen **C** und Beschränkung des **th** auf griechische und wenige andere Wörter Hinweise auf die ältere Schreibung meistens unnötig macht. — Den Mitlaut **J** geben **wir** immer mit **J** (Jubel, Jahr), zur Unterscheidung von dem Selbstlaut **I** (Imme, Inland); — den **Ach**-Laut bezeichnen **wir** in der Aussprache durch ein gestrichenes **ch** (brach, Loch, Buch) zur Unterscheidung vom **Ich**-Laut, wie man ihn hinter **e** und **i** hört (Blech, Stich).

2. Wortschatz: Dieser hat eine wesentliche Bereicherung erfahren durch Aufnahme vieler, namentlich den neuen Gesetzbüchern und der Militärsprache entstammender Neubildungen und **Verdeutschungen**, neuer wissenschaftlicher oder technischer Wörter sowie österreichischer Sonderausdrücke u. Andersschreibungen. Auch ist eine große Zahl alltäglicher Redensarten zugefügt worden.

Fremdwörter, welche der Schreibung und dem Sinne nach genau in beiden Sprachen übereinstimmen, sind in der Regel weggelassen worden. Es fehlen z. B. Appendix (engl. appendix), Hysteron-Proteron 2c.; dagegen sind Aquarium, Chlamys, Meteor und vieles andere, namentlich Wissenschaftliches, bei dem eine Erläuterung angebracht schien, trotz der Übereinstimmung mit dem Englischen doch aufgenommen worden. Mit Namen, deutschen wie fremdländischen, ist ähnlich verfahren worden.

Eigennamen sind im allg. nicht besonders aufgeführt, wenn sie im Deutschen und im Englischen ganz gleich geschrieben werden. Aufgenommen sind die üblichen deutschen Vornamen, sowie an abecelicher Stelle die gebräuchlichsten Verkleinerungs- u. Koseformen; ferner geographische Namen, die in beiden Sprachen von ea. abweichen; z. B.:

F. General remarks
on the interior arrangement of the work.

1. Spelling: This new edition has been based on the *officially recognized spelling of 1903* which, by substituting **K** and **Z** for the former **C**, now retained only in a few foreign words, and by confining **th** to Greek and a few other words, has, in most cases, rendered references to the older orthography superfluous. — The consonantal German initial **J** we have always denoted by **J** [Jubel, Jahr], to distinguish it from **the** vowel-sound **I** (Imme, Inland); — the deep guttural **Ach**-sound has been rendered by a crossed **ch** [brach, Loch, Buch], to distinguish it from the palatal **Ich**-sound as heard after **e** and **i** [Blech, Stich].

2. The **vocabulary** has been largely increased by a number of German neologisms and **translations**, taken chiefly from the new G. Law Codes and military works, also by new scientific and technical terms, and special Austrian expressions or spellings. Our stock of colloquialisms has likewise been considerably added to.

Foreign words which, as regards both spelling and meaning, are identical in the two languages have generally been omitted. Thus Appendix (appendix), Hysteron-Proteron, &c. have been excluded; but Aquarium, Chlamys, Meteor, and other similar expressions, especially those of a scientific or technical nature which required elucidation, have found admittance despite their identity with the English. Names, both German and foreign, have been dealt with in the same manner.

Proper nouns or names, of identical spelling in German and English, have generally been left out. The ordinary German *Christian names* and — in alphabetical order — the corresponding familiar *diminutives* and *terms of endearment* have been admitted; also *geographical names* which differ in the two languages, for instance:

Oſtindien East Indies *pl.*; Genua Genoa.
Many of the *German* geographical names, used in England, have been transmitted through the medium of the French, e. g.: Cologne; but Englishmen, nowadays, are inclined to give foreign names with their original spelling and pronunciation; e. g.:

Leipzig ($´˘$) *npr. n.* Leipzig, not Leipsic.
Mainz ($´$) *npr. n.* Mainz or [*French*] Mayence.
Danzig ($´˘$) *npr. n.* Danzig, not Dantzig, Dantsic.

3. **Alphabetical Order** has been observed throughout also within each separate article, except where special reasons demanded a departure from it.

Special Lists are not given, not even of proper names. These and all other words must be looked for in their proper places within the one general alphabet. — Compare also No. 2 (Proper nouns).

In the arrangement of compounds a saving of space has frequently been effected by the device of putting an English attribute, which belongs to several nouns, only once, e. g.:

Kreide-formation, -gruppe *f. geol.* cretaceous formation, group = Kreide-formation *f geol.* cretaceous formation; Kreide-gruppe *f. geol.* cretaceous group.

4. **Pronunciation:** Special instruction for Englishmen in the pronunciation of German is given in the Author's revised 'Short Guide' on p. IX, &c. Also the paragraph on p. XVIII ($-^{I\,II}$, $˘\,´\,˘\,´$) deserves notice. Where necessary, fuller details have been furnished, in addition to these signs, see e. g. abdrechſeln, Agio, Aide etc.; and also above No. 1 [ch].

Compound foreign words, especially such as differ in their accentuation from the corresponding English words, have been provided with accents, e. g.: Gold-oxy'd *n chm.* auric o'xide.

5. **The Etymology,** contained in square brackets [ ], for the most part has been indicated by the simple designations "fr.", "lt.", "grch.", "ſkr", etc. A fuller account of the origin of a word has been added in those cases only which seemed specially to call for it. We may particularly mention the addition of English words of the same origin, as Vogel [ahd.: fowl]. See also [P], T̄, (T̄), [(…)], [:], [*] on p. XVII.

6. The **Detached Observations,** pp. XXIII, &c., contain, under ① to ㉒ instructions on matters of conjugation and declension. Thus every encircled figure in the text forms a reference, expressed in the smallest possible space, to a paragraph with the corresponding number on p. XXIII to XXXVIII.

7. **Roman figures** denote *classes of words* [e.g. **I** *a.*; **II** *s.* etc.], and, in compound articles, *separate cases*; the **Arabic figures**, on the contrary, denote the several *meanings of words*.

8. **Abbreviations.** These are explained on p. XVIII, &c.

Any abbreviation employed in the English rendering of a German compound may be easily explained by reference to the beginning of the article. Thus, if we find the word Saffian-einband *m* translated by: m.-binding, we can easily interpret it as: morocco-binding.

Abgesonderte Bemerkungen {referring to the signs ① to ㉾ in the Dictionary} Detached Observations

G. Abgesonderte Bemerkungen.
G.¹ Fallabwandlung.
I. Allgemein gültige Regeln.

1. Männliche (m) und Sächliche (n) haben eine übereinstimmende, Weibliche (f) eine davon abweichende eigne (Fall=)Abwandlung (, Biegung oder Beugung).
2. Alle Sächlichen (mit Ausnahme der Hauptwörter aus Eigenschaftswörtern ㉗) werden in der Einzahl stark abgewandelt (, gebogen oder gebeugt).
3. Alle Weiblichen (ausgenommen Hauptwörter aus Eigenschaftswörtern ㉗ und Vornamen ohne Geschlechtswort ㊴, ㊶) sind in der Einzahl unveränderlich (inv.).
4. In der Mehrzahl sind durchgängig Wer=, Wes= und Wen=fall gleichlautend u. der Wemfall der deutschen Abwandlungen (I bis III) auf ...n auslautend.
5. Zusammengesetzte Hauptwörter richten sich nach dem letzten Glied der Zusammensetzung (vgl. unten d u. ㉒).
6. Reine Zahl=, Maß= und Gewichtsbestimmungen lassen als solche (nicht als Gattungsnamen) die Mehrzahl unverändert gleich der Einzahl, z. B. 2 Paar Stiefel (aber: 2 Ehepaare), 3 Buch Papier (aber: 3 Bücher) [NB. „40 Köpfe" ist nicht Maßbestimmung, sondern bildlicher Ausdruck: Köpfe = Menschen]; ausgenommen sind: Weibliche auf e (z. B. 2 Ellen Band), Münznamen, außer Mark (z. B. 5 Pfennige, P und mint. ✠ 5 Pfennig; aber: 10 Mark), Zeit=teile u. =abschnitte (z. B. alle acht Tage), nur Jahr und Monat F auch inv.

II. Mehrfache Abwandlung.

Viele Hauptwörter folgen, oft mit veränderter Bedeutung, einer doppelten oder mehrfachen Abwandlung. Diese haben, ausgenommen die gemischte Abwandlung ㉝ bis ㉟, in den Mustern keine besondere Nr. ○ erhalten, sondern nur im Wörterbuch selber die ihnen zukommenden mehreren Nrn. ○. Die wichtigsten solcher Abwandlungspaare sind z. B.:
Wörter u. Worte ② u. ⑪, Lichter u. Lichte ④ u. ⑪, Drücke u. Drucke ⑦ u. ⑪, Böden u. Boden ⑳ u. ㉓, Monolithe u. Monolithen ⑪ u. ㊷, Claqueure u. Claqueurs ⑪ u. ㉛, Lyren u. Lyras ㊾ u. ㊻; von lt. ...um: Daten u. Data ㉘ u. ㊾, Adjektiva u. Adjektive ⑪ u. ㊾, Forums u. Fora u. ㊿; von lt. ...us: Musiker u. Jchthyosaurier ⑥, Kulte ⑬ u. Diafo'ne ㊾, Famulusse u. Globusse ⑯ u. ㊲, Bazillen u. Daktylen ㉗ u. ㉜, Modi u. Musici ㉘ od. inv.

III. Regeln für Wes= und Wem=fall der Einzahl.

Als Wesfallendung haben:	Wemfall=e steht
a) immer ...es: alle Wörter auf ...ß, ...sch, ...z, ...tz und solche mit Mitlauthäufung, z. B.: Arztes (nicht Arzts); die auf ...s und ß verwandeln dabei das s in ss und das ß nach kurzem Stammselbstlaut in ss, während ß nach langem Selbstlaut bleibt, z. B.: Glas: Glases (⏑ː⏑ː); Faß: Fasses (⏑ː⏑ː); aber Stoß: Stoßes (⏑ː⏑ː) (vgl. ㊋ D¹⁰).	entsprechend Wesfall ...es, Wemfall ohne e entsprechend Wesfall=s; ebenso wird e bei unmittelbar (ohne Geschlechtswort) nach Verhältniswörtern folgenden Hauptwörtern abgeworfen, z. B.: ein Mann von Geist (nicht Geiste) sowie vor Selbstlauten, z. B.: im Wald und auf der Heide..., aber: ich ging im Walde so für mich hin.
b) in der Regel ...s, weniger gut ...es: alle auf ...st, sowie allgemein die auf zwei und mehr Mitlaute auslautenden Einsilbigen, z. B.: des Mastes, Felles, Fettes, Gurtes ꝛc. (⌒ Masts, Fells, Fetts, Gurts).	
c) ...es und ...s gleichberechtigt: die übrigen Einsilbigen und die nicht unter d und e ausgenommenen Mehrsilbigen, z. B.: Reiches und Reichs, Generales und Generals.	
d) in der Regel ...s, weniger gut ...es: die Mehrsilbigen mit unbetonter Endsilbe, besonders auf ...ig, ...(l)ing, ...sal, ...sel, ...tum, sowie die zusammengesetzten Hauptwörter da, wo für das Grundwort Fall c gilt. (Vgl. ㊷.)	
e) immer ...s: Mehrsilbige auf (unbetontes) ...e, ...el, ...em, ...en, ...lein, ...er.	

G. Detached Observations.
G.¹ Table of Declensions.
I. General rules.

1. Masculine [m] and neuter [n] nouns are declined on a similar plan, but feminines [f] have a special declension of their own.
2. In the singular all neuters [with the exception of adjectival substantives ㉗] follow the strong declension.
3. In the sing. all feminines [except adjectives, when used as nouns ㉗, and f Christian names, when used without article ㊴, ㊶] are invariable [inv.].
4. In the plural the nominative, genitive and accusative are identical, the dative in the German declensions [I to III] terminates in ...n.
5. Compound substantives follow the declension of their last constituent [see d below and ㉒].
6. Names of numbers, measures, and weights as such [not as generic names] admit in the plural the unchanged singular, as 2 Paar Stiefel [but: 2 Ehepaare], 3 Buch Papier [but: 3 Bücher]. [Notice that 40 Köpfe is not denoting a measure, but stands in a figurative sense: Köpfe = Menschen]; exceptions are: feminines ending in e [e. g. 2 Ellen Band], names of coins, except Mark [e. g. 5 Pfennige, P & mint. ✠ 5 Pfennig; but: 10 Mark], divisions and periods of time [e. g. alle acht Tage], only Jahr and Monat F also inv.

II. Heteroclite Nouns.

Many substantives follow two or more declensions, often with modified meanings. In our Table, with the exception of the mixed declension ㉝ to ㉟, they have no special number ○ assigned to them. In the dictionary itself they appear with their several numbers ○ attached to them. Thus we frequently find such couples as:

III. How to form the Genitive and Dative Sing.

The genitive suffix may be:	The dative with ..e corresponds to the genitive with ..es; the dative without ..e to the genitive with ..s. The e is also omitted in nouns [without an article], when immediately preceded by a preposition, as: ein Mann von Geist [not Geiste]; also before vowels, as: im Wald und auf der Heide..., but: ich ging im Walde so für mich hin.
a) invariably ...es, in all substantives ending in ...s, ...ß, ...sch, ...z, ...tz, and in several consonants, such as Arztes [not Arzts]. Those ending in ..s change s into ss, those in ß with short root-vowels change ß into ss, while those in ß with long root-vowels retain the ß: Glas: Glases [⏑ː⏑ː]; Faß: Fasses [⏑ː⏑ː]; but Stoß: Stoßes [⏑ː⏑ː] [see ㊋ D¹⁰].	
b) usually ...s, less correctly ...es, in all monosyllabic nouns terminating in ...st, or, generally speaking, in two or more consonants, such as des Mastes, Felles, Fettes, Gurtes ꝛc. [⌒ Masts, Fells, Fetts, Gurts ꝛc.].	
c) indifferently either ...es or ...s, in all other monosyllabic nouns, and those polysyllabics which are not mentioned in d or e, such as: Reiches or Reichs; Generales or Generals.	
d) usually ...s, less correctly ...es, in all polysyllabic nouns of which the last syllable is unaccented, especially those in ...ig, ..(l)ing, ..sal, ..tum, and in all compounds of which the chief constituent falls under c. [see ㊷]	
e) invariably ...s, in polysyllabics of which the last [unaccented] syllable is ..e, ..el, ..em, ..en, ..lein, ..er.	

Abgesonderte Bemerkungen (beziehen sich auf die im Wörterbuche vorkommenden Zeichen ① bis ㊴) | Detached Observations

IV. Eigennamen. | IV. Proper nouns.

Wesfall der Einzahl. | **Genitive Singular.**

ohne Geschlechtswort — *mit Geschlechtsw.* | *without article* — *with article*

Wem- u. Mehrzahl. Wenfall | **dat. and acc. — Plural.**

α) immer ...s im Wesfall haben alle nicht unter β u. γ fallenden Eigennamen, z.B.: Paulas, Wilhelms, Homers Ilias (engl. Homer's Iliad), Berlins, Preußens, Otto von Bismarcks, Maria Stuarts, (Kaiser) Karls des Großen, Herrn (Professor) Müllers, Doktor Fausts (vgl. ㊕).

β) Wesfall auf ...s od. (bei Familiennamen weniger üblich) auf ...ns haben die auf unbetontes ...e, z.B.: Amalie(n)s ㊴, aber Goethes, ⸜ Goethens.

γ) Wesfall auf ...ens haben die auf ...s, ...ß, ...x, ...z, ...sch endenden deutschen Vornamen z.B.: Franzens, Fritzens, Maxens u., falls der Endmitlaut dabei unverändert bleibt, auch die andern Namen, z. B.: Horazens, dagegen nicht Vossens (Voß), Claudiussens (Claudius), Demosthenessens (Demosthenes), sondern in solchen Fällen besser ein Häkchen, also: Voß' Werke, Sokrates' Tod, Burns' Gedichte, engl. ☞ Burns's (or Burns') poems ꝛc. Bei geographischen Namen wählt man eine Umschreibung, z.B.: die Umgebung der Stadt Mainz oder von Mainz, aber nie: Mainz' Umgebung.

bleiben Personennamen unveränderlich, z. B.: des Cäsar, eines Cicero, des Alten Fritz, des Kaisers Karl, des Herrn Müller, des Doktors Faust, des jungen Goethe, des Philosophen Fichte, der Maria Stuart, der Tante Klara, der Julie (vgl. hierzu ㊴). Geographische Namen, bes. solche mit fremden Endungen unveränderlich zu lassen, z. B.: des Po, des Ural, liegt kein Grund vor; sie werden besser ebenso abgewandelt: des Po, des Urals, wie die deutschen: des Rhein(e)s, Main(e)s, Harzes.

α) ...s haben auf volle Selbstlaute endende Namen z. B.: zwei Paulas, die Tassos; auch: zwei Karls; ohne Endung: zwei Alexander; latinisiert: Scipio'nen, Otto'nen; sonst haben männliche, auf einen Mitlaut ausgehende Personennamen für gew. ...e: zwei Wilhelme, Heinriche.

β) Weibliche Namen auf unbetontes e hängen im pl. ein n an: zwei Julien, Marien, Brunhilden.

γ) zwei Felixe, Franze, Fritze, Maxe (vgl. α). Personennamen auf ...s, ...ß bilden keine Mehrzahl, wie etwa Augustusse, Sokratesse, sondern man behilft sich bei ihnen mit einer Umschreibung, nämlich: Männer wie Augustus, wie Sokrates.

α) The genitive invariably takes ...s in all proper nouns, not belonging to either β or γ, as Paulas, Wilhelms, Homers Ilias [Eng.: Homer's Iliad], Berlins, Preußens, Otto von Bismarcks, Maria Stuarts, [Kaiser] Karls des Großen, Herrn [Professor] Müllers, Doktor Fausts [see ㊕].

β) The genitive in ...s or ...ns [the latter is rare with surnames] is usually that of a name ending in unaccented e..., as Amalie[n]s ㊴, but Goethes, ⸜ Goethens.

γ) The genitive in ...ens is formed by all German Christian names ending in ...s, ...ß, ...x, ...z, ...sch, as Franzens, Fritzens, Maxens ㉟, and also by other names of which the final consonant requires no change, as Horazens, but not Vossens [Voß], Claudiussens [Claudius], Demosthenessens [Demosthenes]. In these cases, it is better to use the apostrophe, as: Voß' Werke, Sokrates' Tod, Burns' Gedichte, Eng. ☞ Burns's (or Burns') poems, &c. With geographical names a description is desirable, as: die Umgebung der Stadt Mainz, or von Mainz, but never: Mainz' Umgebung.

Names of persons remain uninflected, as des Cäsar, eines Cicero, des Alten Fritz, des Kaisers Karl, des Herrn Müller, des Doktors Faust, des jungen Goethe, des Philosophen Fichte, der Maria Stuart, der Tante Klara, der Julie [see ㊴]. Geographical names, especially with foreign endings should not remain uninflected, as des Po, des Urals, like the German names: des Rhein(e)s, Main(e)s, Harzes.

α) ...s is added to names with fully sounded final vowels, as zwei Paulas, die Tassos; also: zwei Karls. No plural suffix: zwei Alexander. Latinized forms: Scipio'nen, Otto'nen. In other cases names of males ending in consonants generally take ...e: zwei Wilhelme, Heinriche.

β) Feminine names ending in unaccented e add n in the pl.: zwei Julien, Marien, Brunhilden.

γ) zwei Felixe, Franze, Fritze, Maxe [see α]. Names of persons ending in ...s, ...ß form no plurals, such as Augustusse, Sokratesse, but are replaced by fuller expressions: Männer wie Augustus, wie Sokrates.

---

① G.!¹ Geschlechtswort (¹ bestimmtes, ² unbestimmtes)

	Nom.		Gen. *sg*		Dat.		Akk.	
m	¹der	²ein	¹des	²eines	¹dem	²einem	¹den	²einen
f	die	eine	der	einer	der	einer	die	eine
n	das	ein	des	eines	dem	einem	das	ein

① G.!¹ Article [¹definite, ²indefinite]

	Nom.	Gen. *pl*	Dat.	Akk.
	¹die	¹der	¹den	¹die

G.!² Hauptwörter
I. Starke Abwandlung
A. Mehrzahl auf ...er (nur *m* und *n*)
 a) mit Umlaut**) in der Mehrzahl.
Die Tilde (~) im *sg.* wiederholt den Nom. *sg.*

G.!² Substantives
I. Strong Declension
A. Plural in ...er [only *m* and *n* nouns]
a) with modified vowel [umlaut**)] in the *pl*.
The sign ~ in the *pl.* repeats the *nom. pl.*

② a, α ꝛc.*)					*m, n*			
Mann *m*	~(e)s	~(e)	~	Männer	~	~n	
Irrtum *m*	~(e)s	~(e)	~	Irrtümer	~	~n	
Gewand *n*	~(e)s	~(e)	~	Gewänder	~	~†	

*) 1, 2, a, α ꝛc. s. S. XXIII u. XXIV. — **) durch den Umlaut wird a und aa in ä, o und oo in ö, u in ü, au in äu verwandelt.

*) 1, 2, a, α, &c. see p. XXIII & XXIV. — **) Umlaut changes a and aa to ä, o and oo to ö, u to ü, au to äu.

Abgesonderte Bemerkungen { referring to the signs ① to ㊾ in the Dictionary. }				Detached Observations			
Die Tilde (~) im *sg.* wiederholt den Nom. *sg.*				The sign ~ in the *pl.* repeats the *nom. pl.*			
Nom.	Gen.	Dat.	Akk.	Nom.	Gen.	Dat.	Akk.
③ a*)			*m, n*				
Glas n (⌣)	Glases (⌣⌣)	Glase od. ~	~	Gläser (⌣⌣)	~	~n	~
Haus n	Hauses	Hause od. ~	~	Häuser	~	~n	~
Faß n (⌣)	Fasses	Fasse od. ~	~	Fässer (⌣⌣)	~	~n	~
b) ohne Umlaut**) in der Mehrzahl				b) without umlaut**) in the *pl.*			
④ a, α 2c.*)							
Bild n	~(e)s	~(e)	~	Bilder	~	~n	~
Reis n	Reises	Reise od. ~	~	Reiser	~	~n	~
⑤ Musikus m	~	~	~	Musiker	~	~n	~
⑥ Ichthyo=saurus m	~	~	~	Ichthyosaurier	~	~n	~
B. Mehrzahl auf ...e (*m,* ⌣ *n; f*)				B. Plural in ...e [*m,* ⌣ *n; f*]			
a) mit Umlaut**) i. d. Mehrzahl			*m, n*	a) with umlaut**) in the *pl.*			
⑦ a, α 2c.*)							
Ast m	~(e)s	~(e)	~	Äste	~	~n	~
Baum m	~(e)s	~(e)	~	Bäume	~	~n	~
Bischof m	~(e)s	~(e)	~	Bischöfe	~	~n	~
Choral m	~(e)s	~(e)	~	Choräle	~	~n	~
Saal m	~(e)s	~(e)	~	Säle	~	~n	~
Stoß m (⌣)	~es	~(e)	~	Stöße (⌣⌣)	~	~n	~
⑧ a*)							
Baß m (⌣)	Basses	Basse od. ~	~	Bässe (⌣⌣)	~	~n	~
Hals m	Halses	Halse od. ~	~	Hälse	~	~n	~
⑨ a, α 2c.*)	desgl. mit Tonwechsel			the same with change of accent			
A′ltar (⌣⌣)	~s	~	~	Altä′re (⌣⌣⌣)	~	~n	~
⑩ 3*)			*f*				
Hand f	~	~	~	Hände	~	~n	~
Auskunft f	~	~	~	Auskünfte	~	~n	~
Gans f	~	~	~	Gänse	~	~n	~
Nuß f (⌣)	~	~	~	Nüsse (⌣⌣)	~	~n	~
b) ohne Umlaut**) im *pl.*				b) without umlaut**) in the *pl.*			
⑪ a, α 2c.*)			*m, n*				
Hund m	~(e)s	~(e)	~	Hunde	~	~n	~
Maß n (⌣)	Maßes (⌣⌣)	Maß(e) (⌣⌣)	~	Maße (⌣⌣)	~	~n	~
Roß n (⌣)	Rosses (⌣⌣)	Rosse u. ~	~	Rosse (⌣⌣)	~	~n	~
Greis m	Greises	Greise u. ~	~	Greise	~	~n	~
Alta′r m (⌣⌣)	~(e)s (⌣⌣(⌣))	~(e) (⌣⌣(⌣))	~	Alta′re (⌣⌣⌣)	~	~n	~
⑫ a, α 2c.*)	desgl. mit Tonwechsel			the same with change of accent			
A′ltar m	~s (⌣⌣)	~	~	Altä′re (⌣⌣⌣)	~	~n	~
⑬ lateinische Wörter ohne Biegung im *sg.*, mit solcher im *pl.*				Latin nouns invariable in the *sg.*, inflected in the *pl.*			
Kultus m	~	~	~	Kulte	~	~n	~
Dualis m	~	~	~	Duale	~	~n	~
⑭ Dia′konus m	desgl. mit Tonwechsel			the same with change of accent			
	~	~	~	Diako′ne	~	~n	~
⑮ α*) {*art.*}							
Friedrich(ohne)	~s	(† od. F ~en)	(† od. F ~en)	Friedriche	~	~n	~
⑯ [mit *art.*]	Vgl. die Abwandlung der Eigennamen auf S. XXIVγ.						
der Friedrich	des ~	dem ~	den ~	die Friedriche	der ~	den ~n	die ~
Januar m	~, bff. ~s	~	~	Januare	~	~n	~
Habenichts m	~	~	~	Habenichtse	~	~n	~
Famulus m	~	~	~	Famulusse	~	~n	~
⑰ a*)							
Globus m	...sses	...sse u. ~	~	Globusse	~	~n	~
Erkenntnis n	...sses	...sse u. ~	~	Erkenntnisse	~	~n	~
⑱ 3*)			*f*				
Bilch f	~	~	~	Bilche	~	~n	~
Erkenntnis f	~	~	~	Erkenntnisse	~	~n	~

*) a, α 2c. f. S. XXIII f. **) Umlaut f. S. XXIV.   *) a, α. &c. see p. XXIII. &c. **) Umlaut see p. XXIV.

| Abgesonderte Bemerkungen | beziehen sich auf die im Wörterbuche vorkommenden Zeichen ① bis ㉜ | Detached Observations |

Die Tilde (~) im *sg.* wiederholt den Nom. *sg.*   The sign ~ in the *pl.* repeats the *nom. pl.*

	Nom.	Gen.	Dat.	Akk.		Nom.	Gen.	Dat.	Akk.
C.	ohne besondere Mehrzahlendung (s. auf ...er, ...el, ...en, ...e)				**C.**	Without a special plural suffix [...er, ...el, ...en, e...].			
⑲ e*)	a) mit Umlaut**) im *pl.* (m, n ~; f ~)			m, n		a) with umlaut**) in the *pl.* [m, n ~; f ~]			
	Vater m	~s	~	~		Väter	~	~n	~
	Kloster n	~s	~	~		Klöster	~	~n	~
⑳ e*)	Graben m	~s	~	~		Gräben	~	~	~
㉑ 3*)	Mutter f	~	~	~	f	Mütter	~	~n	~
	Tochter f	~	~	~		Töchter	~	~n	~
㉒ e*)	b) ohne Umlaut**) im *pl.* (nur m u. n)				m, n	b) without umlaut**) in the *pl.* [only m and n]			
	Maler m	~s	~	~		~	~	~n	~
	Esel m, Pudel m	~s	~	~		~	~	~n	~
	Gebirge n	~s	~	~		~	~	~n	~
㉓ e*)	Leben n†)	~s	~	~		~	~	~	~
	Kuchen m	~s	~	~		~	~	~	~
	Mädchen n	~s	~	~		~	~	~	~
	Kindlein n	~s	~	~		~	~	~	~
㉔ e*) ††)	Kindchen n	~s	~	~		{Kindchen od. Kinderchen}	~	~	~

II. Gemischte Abwandlung (m, n; f ~, s. ㊴)   **II.** Mixed Declension [m, n; f ~, see ㊴].

	Nom.	Gen.	Dat.	Akk.		Nom.	Gen.	Dat.	Akk.
㉕ a, α ꝛc.*)	sg. stark, pl. schwach				m, n	strong singular, weak plural			
	Hemd n	~(e)s	~(e)	~		Hemden	~	~	~
㉖ e*)	Auge n	~s	~	~		Augen	~	~	~
	Stachel m	~s	~	~		Stacheln	~	~	~
㉗	lateinische u. griechische Wörter, sg. unveränderlich					Latin and Greek nouns, invariable in the *sing.*			
	Epos n	~	~	~		Epen	~	~	~
	Bazillus m	~	~	~		Bazillen	~	~	~
	Genius m	~	~	~		Genien	~	~	~
	Trochäus m	~	~	~		Trochäen	~	~	~
	Pleonasmus m	~	~	~		Pleonasmen	~	~	~
	Anglizismus m	~	~	~		Anglizismen	~	~	~
㉘ e*)	lateinische, griechische u. italienische Wörter, im *sg.* stark, nicht zu empfehlen: *inv.*					Latin, Greek, and Italian nouns, strong in the *sing.*, not to be treated as *inv.*			
	Stu'dium n	~s, ~ ~	~	~		Stu'dien	~	~	~
	Lyze'um n	~s, ~ ~	~	~		Lyze'en	~	~	~
	Ga'nglion n	~s	~	~		Ga'nglien	~	~	~
	Konto n	~s	~	~		Konten	~	~	~
	Drama n	~s, ~ ~	~	~		Dramen	~	~	~
㉙ e*)	Kolleg n	~s	~	~		Kollegien	~	~	~
	Gratiale n	~s, ~ ~	~	~		Gratialien	~	~	~
㉚	desgl. mit Tonwechsel im *pl.*					the same with changed accent in the *pl.*			
	A'gens n	~	~	~		Age'nzien	~	~	~
㉛ e*)	Au'tor m	~s	~	~		Auto'ren	~	~	~
	Dä'mon m	~s	~	~		Dämo'nen	~	~	~
㉜	Da'ktylus [m]	~	~	~		Dakty'len	~	~	~

Größere Abweichungen sind an Ort u. Stelle angegeben, zB. } He'ros, Hero'en; Ka'ktus, Kakte'en; Ku'stos, Kusto'den.
More irregular forms are given in the dictionary, as

*) a, α ꝛc. s. S. XXIIIf. — **) Umlaut s. S. XXIV.
†) Ein *pl.* der Hauptwörter aus Nennformen fehlt meist, immer bei Begriffswörtern, zB. das Denken.
††) Solche doppelte Mehrzahl (Kindchen u. Kinderchen) haben alle Verkleinerungsformen der die Mehrzahl auf ...er bildenden Hauptwörter. (Nr. ②, ③ u. ④.)

*) a, α, &c., see p. XXIIIf. — **) umlaut see p. XXIV.
†) Infinitives, when used as substantives, are frequently and, when serving as abstract nouns, invariably without a *pl*.
††) These double plurals [Kindchen and Kinderchen] are found with all diminutives of such substantives as add ...er in the *pl.* [see ②, ③ and ④].

XXVII

| Abgesonderte Bemerkungen | referring to the signs ① to ㊾ in the Dictionary. | Detached Observations |

Die Tilde (~) im **sg.** wiederholt den Nom. sg.   The sign ~ in the **pl.** repeats the *nom. pl.*

	Nom.	Gen.	Dat.	Akk.	Nom.	Gen.	Dat.	Akk.
㉝ a, α ꝛc.*)	*sg.* **stark,** *pl.* **stark und schwach** ⑪ u. ㉕ m,				n strong singular, strong or weak plural ⑪ and ㉕			
Mast m	~(e)s	~(e)	~		Maste(n)	~	Masten	~
㉞ a, α ꝛc.*)	*sg.* **stark und schwach,** *pl.* **stark** ⑪ u. ㊶				strong or weak singular, but strong plural ⑪ and ㊶			
Magnet m	~(e)s u. ~en	~(e) u. ~en	~ u. ~en		Magnete	~	~n	~
㉟ γ Fritz†)	~ens u. ~'	(~en † od. F)	(~en † od. F)		Fritze	~	~n	~
㊱ a, α ꝛc.*)	*sg.* **stark und schwach,** *pl.* **schwach** ㉖ u. ㊸				strong or weak singular, but weak plural ㉖ and ㊸			
Ahn m	~(e)s u. ~en	~ u. ~en	~ u. ~en		Ahnen	~	~	~
Bauer m	~s u. ~n	~ u. ~n	~ u. ~n		Bauern	~	~	~
㊲ Herz n	~ens	~en	~		Herzen	~	~	~
Name**)	~ns	~n	~n		Namen	~	~	~
㊳ [m**)] Schade f	~ns	~n	~n		Schäden	•	~	~
㊴ 3, β*)				f				
Ama'lie f	~(n)s	~(† od. F ~n)	~(† od. F ~n)		Ama'lien	~	~	~
Mari'e f	~(n)s	~(† od. F ~n)	~(† od. F ~n)		Mari'en	~	~	~
Adelheid f††)	~(en)s	~(† od. F ~en)	~(† od. F ~en)		Adelheiden	~	~	~
㊵	*sg.* **schwach,** *pl.* **stark**			m	weak singular, strong plural			
Prahlhans m	~en	~ u. ~sen	~ u. ~sen		Prahlhänse	~	~n	~
㊶ Knes m	Knesen	~ u. sen	~ u. sen		Knese	~	~n	~

III. Schwache Abwandlung (nur *m* u. *f*, keine *n*)   **III. Weak Declension** [only *m* and *f*, no *n* nouns].
Mehrzahl auf …(e)n; stets ohne Umlaut.   *m* Plural in …(e)n; always without umlaut.

	Nom.	Gen.	Dat.	Akk.	Nom.	Gen.	Dat.	Akk.
㊷ Mensch m	~en	~en	~en		Menschen	~	~	~
Ochs m	Ochsen	Ochsen	Ochsen		Ochsen	~	~	~
Saß m	Sassen	Sassen	Sassen		Sassen	~	~	~
㊸ Herr m	~n	~n	~n		Herren	~	~	~
㊹ Bote m	~n	~n	~n		Boten	~	~	~
Ochse, Sasse m	~n	~n	~n		Ochsen, Sassen	~	~	~
㊺	desgl. mit Tonwechsel				the same with change of accent			
Au'gur m	Augu'ren	Augu'ren	Augu'ren		Augu'ren	~	~	~
Hi'strio m	Histrio'nen	Histrio'nen	Histrio'nen		Histrio'nen	~	~	~
㊻ Frau f	~	~	~	f	Frauen	~	~	~
Eins f	~	~	~		Einsen	~	~	~
Meß f	~	~	~		Messen	~	~	~
㊼ Kirmes f	~	~	~		Kirmessen	~	~	~
Königin f	~	~	~		Königinnen	~	~	~
㊽ Rede f	~	~	~		Reden,	~	~	~
Idee f	~	~	~		Idee'n	~	~	~
Mani'e (⌣́) f	~	~	~		Mani'en (⌣́⌣)	~	~	~
Fu'rie (⌣́⌣⌣) f	~	~	~		Fu'rien (⌣́⌣⌣)	~	~	~
die Ama'lie†††)	der ~	der ~	die ~		die Ama'lien	der ~	den ~	die ~
Leiter f, Kugel f	~	~	~		Leitern, Kugeln	~	~	~
㊾	mit fremder Endung im *sg.*, deutscher im *pl.*				*sg.* with a foreign, *pl.* with a German termination			
Firma f	~	~	~		Firmen	~	~	~
Krisis f	~	~	~		Krisen	~	~	~
	desgl. mit Tonwechsel				the same with change of accent			
㊿ Go'rgo f	~	~	~		Gorgo'nen	~	~	~
Diä'resis f	~	~	~		Diäre'sen	~	~	~

*) a, α ꝛc. s. Seite XXIII f.   *) a, α, &c., see p. XXIII &c.
**) Namen geht nach ㉓, Schaden nach ㉙.   **) Namen follows ㉓, Schaden ㉙.
†) **ohne** *art.*; **mit** *art.* nach ⑯.   †) **without** *art.*; **with** *art.* according to ⑲.
††) **ohne** *art.*; **mit** *art.* nach ㊻ u. ㊽.   ††) **without** *art.*; **with** *art.* according to ㊻ & ㊽.
†††) **mit** *art.*; **ohne** *art.* nach Nr. ㊴.   †††) **with** *art.*; **without** *art.* according to ㊴.

| Abgesonderte Bemerkungen {beziehen sich auf die im Wörterbuche vorkommenden Zeichen ① bis ㊿.} | Detached Observations |

IV. Niederdeutsche [französische] s-Abwandlung, Mehrzahl auf ...s (m, n und f)
Die Tilde (~) im **sg.** wiederholt den Nom. sg.

IV. Low German [French] Declension with plural in ...s [m, n and f nouns]
The sign ~ in the **pl.** repeats the nom. pl.

	Nom.	Gen.	Dat.	Akk.	Nom.	Gen.	Dat.	Akk.
(51) e*)				m, n				
	Salon m (⌣lǫ')	~s (⌣lǫ'ß)	~	~	Salons (⌣lǫ'ß)	~	~	~
	Portier (⌣tiē') m	~s (⌣tiē'ß)	~	~	Portiers (⌣tiē'ß)	~	~	~
	Genie n (Ge-ni')	~s (Ge-ni'ß)	~	~	Genies (-ni'ß)	~	~	~
(52) a*) [n								
	Sandwich	~es	~(e)	~	Sandwiches	~	~	~
(53) e*)								
	Atout n	~s, ⌢ ~ (⌣tū'ß, ⌢ ⌣tū')	~	~	Atouts (⌣tū'ß)	~	~	~
	Forum n	~s, ⌢ ~	~	~	Forums	~	~	~
(54) α*)								
	der Karl†	des ~	dem ~	den ~	die Karls	der ~	den ~	die ~
(55)	Korps n							
	(sprich: kōr)	(sprich: kōr)	(sprich: kōr)	(sprich: kōr)	(sprich: kōrß)	(sprich: kōrß)	(sprich: kōrß)	(sprich: kōrß)
(56) 3, α*)				f				
	Donna f	~	~	~	Donnas	~	~	~
	die Paula†	der ~	der ~	die ~	die Paulas	der ~	den ~	die ~
(57) 3, α*)								
	Paula††	~s			Paulas	~	~	~

V. Fremde (lateinische, italienische, griechische) Abwandlungen
V. Nouns of Foreign [Latin, Italian, Greek] Declension

	Nom.	Gen.	Dat.	Akk.	Nom.	Gen.	Dat.	Akk.
(58) z.T. e*)				m, n				
	Modus m	~	~	~	Modi	~	~	~
	Mu'sikus m	~	~	~	Mu'sizi (...tsi)	~	~	~
	Cicerone m	~	~	~	Ciceroni	~	~	~
	Kollo n	~s	~	~	Kolli	~	~	~
(59) e*)					(sprich: ~ītsīa)			
	Depo'nens n	~	~	~	Depone'ntia	~	~	~
	Faktum n	~s, ⌢ ~	~	~	Fakta	~	~	~
	Distichon n	~s, ⌢ ~	~	~	Disticha	~	~	~
㊿60 e*)								
	Dogma n	~s, ⌢ ~	~	~	Do'gmata	~	~	~
	Prono'men n	~s	~	~	Prono'mina	~	~	~
㊶61	Kodex m	~	~	~	Ko'dizes	~	~	~

VI. Zs.-gesetzte und lose verbundene Hauptwörter
VI. Compound Nouns and Double Forms

Zusammensetzungen, deren Glieder Hauptwörter sind (vgl. ㊾: adj. + adj. und ㊽: adj. + s.), biegen nur den letzten Wortteil nach der diesem zukommenden Abwandlung, falls nicht anders angegeben (s. Vollmacht), doch mit Bevorzugung der gekürzten starken Formen, vgl. S. XXIII d.

Compounds of which the constituent parts are substantives [see ㊾: adj. + adj. and ㊽: adj. + s.] inflect, unless otherwise prescribed [see Vollmacht], only the last constituent, according to its proper declension, but usually with the abbreviated strong forms, see p. XXIII d.

	Nom.	Gen.	Dat.	Akk.	Nom.	Gen.	Dat.	Akk.
㊷62 5, d*)								
	Bahnhof m	~s (⌢ ~es)	~ (⌢ ~e)	~	Bahnhöfe	~	~n	~
	Ave-Maria n	~ ~s	~ ~	~ ~	Ave-Marias	~ ~	~ ~	~ ~
㊸63	Jesus Christus	Jesu Christi	Jesu Christo	Jesum Christum				

*) a, α &c. s. S. XXIII f.
†) mit art. ††) ohne art.

*) a, α &c. see p. XXIII &c.
†) with art. ††) without art.

XXIX

| Abgesonderte Bemerkungen | {referring to the signs ① to ㊽ in the Dictionary.} | Detached Observations |

VII. Eigennamen mit Titeln wandeln **mit** art. (㉞) nur den Titel, **ohne** art. (㉟) nur den Namen ab

VII. Proper names attached to titles inflect, if **with** the art. ㉞, only the title; if **without** art. ㉟, only the name.

㉞ α *)
mit art. [with art.]
	Gen.	Dat.	Akk.
der Kaiser Karl (der Große)	des ~s ~ (des ~n)	dem ~ ~ (dem ~n)	den ~ ~ (den ~n)
der Papst Pius X.†)	des ~es ~ ~†)	dem ~(e) ~ ~†)	den ~ ~ ~†)
der (Herr) Professor Müller	des (~n) ~s ~	dem (~n) ~ ~	den (~n) ~ ~

㉟ α *)
ohne art. [without art.]
	Gen.	Dat.	Akk.
Kaiser Karl (der Große)	~s (des ~n)	~ (dem ~n)	~ (den ~n)
Papst Pius X.†)	~' ~†)	~ ~†)	~ ~†)
(Herr) Professor Müller	(~n) ~s	(~n) ~	(~n) ~

*) a, α ꝛc. s. S. XXIIIf.
†) Geschrieben immer nur X., gesprochen aber: der Zehnte, des ~n, dem ~n, den ~n.

*) a, α see p. XXIIIf.
†) Invariably written as X., but spoken of as: der Zehnte, des ~n, dem ~n, den ~n.

㊻ Eigenschafts= und Für=wörter.
Die starken Formen sind fett, die schwachen mager gedruckt.

Adjectives and Pronouns
With strong forms in fat-face type, weak ones in lean-face.

A. Starke Abwandlung.
1. Persönliches Fürwort.

A. Strong declension.
1. Personal Pronoun.

sg.	1.Prsn (m, f,n)	2.Prsn (m, f,n)	3.Prsn. m	f	n	pl.	1.Prsn (m, f,n)	2.Prsn (m, f,n)	3. Prsn (m, f, n)
Nom.	ich	du	er	sie	es	Nom.	wir	ihr	sie (Sie)
Gen.	*mein(er)¹)	*dein(er)¹)	*sein(er)¹)	*ihrer¹)	*sein(er)¹,²)	Gen.	*unser	*euer	*ihrer (Ihrer)
Dat.	*mir	*dir	ihm(*†)	ihr(*†)	ihm(*†)	Dat.	*uns	*euch	ihnen (Ihnen) } *sich
Akk.	*mich	*dich	ihn	sie	es	*sich	Akk.	*uns	*euch	sie (Sie)

* zugleich zurückbezüglich; zur Deutlichkeit wird oft selbst zugefügt.
1) für die veralteten oder poet. mein ꝛc. sind jetzt die volleren Formen [meiner ꝛc. üblicher.]
2) in einzelnen Wendungen noch: es.

* Also reflexive; for the sake of distinctness selbst is often added.
1) the obsolete or poetical forms mein etc. are now replaced by [the fuller forms meiner, &c.]
2) in a few expressions also: es.

2. Hinweisendes Fürwort ꝛc.
a

2. Demonstrative Pronoun, &c.
b

sg.	m	f	n	pl.	m f n
Nom.	dieser	diese	die(se)s	Nom.	diese
Gen.	dieses	dieser	dieses	Gen.	dieser
Dat.	diesem	dieser	diesem	Dat.	diesen
Akk.	diesen	diese	dieses	Akk.	diese

der, die, das: Gen. sg. dessen (m, n), deren (f), † nach ①, Gen. pl. deren (unbetont) ob. derer (betont), †nach①, Dat.pl. denen, sonst wie①

†) Die übrigen Eigenschafts= u. Fürwörter werden ebenso oder nach C 1 u. 2 abgewandelt.

†) The declension of other pronouns and adjectives is similar, or corresponding to C 1 and 2.

3. Eigenschaftswörter vor Hauptwörtern ohne Geschlechtswort ꝛc. †)

3. Adjectives before Substantives without article, &c. †)

sg.	m	f	n	pl.	m	f	n
Nom.	guter Mut	gute Hoffnung	sächliches Geschlecht	edle Männer	schöne Frauen	artige Kinder
Gen.	guten(†gutes*) ~es	guter ~	sächlichen († ...es*) ~(e)s	edler ~	schöner ~	artiger ~
Dat.	gutem ~e	guter ~	sächlichem ~(e)	edlen ~n	schönen ~	artigen ~n
Akk.	guten ~	gute ~	sächliches ~	eble ~	schöne ~	artige ~

†) So auch bsd. nach prp.: von ganzem Herzen, aus tiefster Seele; ferner: ich alter Mann, (Gen. fehlt), dir guter Frau, dich liebes Kind; aber im Plur. neigt der neuere Sprachgebrauch wieder der schwachen Form zu, sodaß man wohl häufiger: „wir armen Leute" als „wir arme Leute" hört vgl. ㊱C). Ebenso: solch, welch gutes Herz (wenn solch und welch inv.) (vgl. B*); and(e)re (, einige, einzelne, etliche, gewisse, manche, mehrere, verschiedene, viele, wenige, zwei, drei ꝛc.) reiche (++ reichen) Leute, Gen.: einiger ꝛc., zweier, dreier reicher (++, aber nicht selten: reichen) Leute ꝛc. vier ꝛc. reicher (nur so) Leute, Dat.: vielen, zwei ꝛc. reichen Leuten, Akk.: wenige, zwei ꝛc. reiche (++ reichen) Leute.

†) The same especially with prp.: von ganzem Herzen, aus tiefster Seele; also: ich alter Mann, [gen. not used], dir guter Frau, dich liebes Kind; but in the plural the modern usage again leans towards the weak forms, and wir armen Leute is now more popular than: wir arme Leute [see ㊱ C]. Also: solch, welch gutes Herz [when solch and welch are inv.; see B*]; and(e)re [, einige, einzelne, etliche, gewisse, manche, mehrere, verschiedene, viele, wenige, zwei, drei, &c.] reiche [not: reichen] Leute; gen.: einiger, &c., zweier, dreier reicher [F also: reichen] vier, &c. reicher [never: reichen] Leute; dat.: vielen, zwei, &c. reichen Leuten; acs.: wenige, &c. reiche [not reichen] Leute.

††) Anmerkung: Mehrere Eigenschaftswörter vor einem Hauptwort ohne Geschlechtswort sind stark, falls sie in gleich naher Beziehung zu ihm stehen (vgl. Anm.* zu C) z.B. nach langem, schwerem Leiden verstarb ...

††) Note: Several qualifying adj., if placed before a noun without article, follow the strong declension, provided they are in equally close relationship to the same, as nach langem, schwerem Leiden verstarb ... [see Note * to C].

*) Hier hat die schwache Endung auf ...n seit 17.—18. sae. die starke auf ...s bis auf wenige Ausnahmen (z. B. keineswegs) verdrängt, zum Teil schwankt der Brauch noch (z. B. keines= u. keinenfalls), nur bei adj. poss. ist die starke Endung geblieben (z.B. meines Wissens).

*) Since the 17. sae. the weak forms with ...n have, with few exceptions [as keineswegs], replaced the strong forms with ...s. In some cases, both forms are used [keines=, or keinenfalls]; only with poss. adj. the strong suffix ...s is firmly established [as meines Wissens].

| Abgesonderte Bemerkungen | beziehen sich auf die im Wörterbuche vorkommenden Zeichen ① bis ㊌ | Detached Observations |

B. Schwache Abwandlung
des Eigenschaftsworts nach bestimmtem Geschlechtswort, hinweisendem oder zurückbezüglichem Fürwort ꝛc.*)

B. Weak Declension
of qualifying adjectives after the definite article or a demonstrative or relative adjective, &c.*)

Einzahl — Singular | Mehrzahl — Plural

Nom.	der gute Mann *m*	die gute Frau *f*	das gute Kind *n*	die guten Männer *m*	die guten Frauen *f*	die guten Kinder *n*
Gen.	des guten ~(e)s	der guten ~	des guten ~(e)s	der ○ ~	der ○ ~	der ○ ~
Dat.	dem guten ~(e)	der guten ~	dem guten ~(e)	den ○ ~n	den ○ ~	den ○ ~n
Akk.	den guten ~	die gute ~	das gute ~	die ○ ~	die ○ ~	die ○ ~

*) Ebenso wenn an Stelle des Geschlechtsworts treten (Also if any of the following take the place of the article): dieser, jener, jeder, solcher, welcher (aber solch, welch vgl. A 3†), derselbe, selbiger, derjenige: derartige schwierigen (nicht: ...ge) Fragen, (bei)folgendes kleine (nicht: ...nes) Buch.

†) Stehen im Falle B mehrere Eigenschaftswörter vor dem Hauptwort, so sind sie sämtlich schwach (If in B several qualifying adj. precede the noun they all follow the weak declension), zB.: der gute, brave Mann; des guten braven Mannes ꝛc.

C. Gemischte Abwandlung
1. mit dem unbestimmten Geschlechtswort (nur *sg.*) oder einem wie dieses abgewandelten besitzanzeigenden Eigenschaftswort, sowie nach: kein, beide, alle, sämtliche.

C. Mixed Declension
1. with the indefinite article [singular only], or a possessive adjective declined like the same, also after kein, beide, alle, sämtliche.

sg.

Nom.	*m* (m)ein guter (edler) Mann	*f* (d)eine gute (edle) Frau	*n* (s)ein gutes (edles) Kind
Gen.	(m)eines guten (edlen) ~(e)s	(d)einer guten (edlen) ~	(s)eines guten (edlen) ~es
Dat.	(m)einem guten (edlen) ~(e)	(d)einer guten (edlen) ~	(s)einem guten (edlen) ~e
Akk.	(m)einen guten (edlen) Mann	(d)eine gute (edle) ~	(s)ein gutes (edles) ~

pl.

Nom.	*m* uns(e)re guten (edlen) Männer	*f* eu(e)re guten (edlen) Frauen	*n* ihre guten (edlen) Kinder
Gen.	uns(e)rer ○ (○) ~	eurer ○ (○) ~	ihrer ○ (○) ~
Dat.	unsern od. uns(e)ren ○ (○) ~n	euern od. eu(e)ren ○ (○) ~	ihren ○ (○) ~n
Akk.	uns(e)re ○ (○) ~	eure ○ (○) ~	ihre ○ (○) ~

*) Anm.: Von mehreren vor einem Hauptwort stehenden Eigenschaftswörtern steht (im Dat. sg. und Gen. pl.) das dem Hauptwort zunächststehende schwach, wenn es mit ihm einen einheitlichen Begriff bildet, zB. die Verleihung vieler Eisernen Kreuze, mit echtem Kölnischen Wasser (vgl. A 3††).

*) Note: If several adj. precede a *s.* [in the *dat. sg.* or *gen. pl.*] the one adjoining it follows the weak declension, provided it forms an inseparable adjunct of the *s.*, as die Verleihung vieler Eisernen Kreuze, mit echtem Kölnischen Wasser [see also Note †† to A 3.].

sg. 2. Zusammengesetzte Fürwörter. — *pl.* 2. Compound Pronouns.

Nom.	derselbe *m*	dieselbe *f*	dasselbe *n*	dieselben *m, f, n*	†) ebenso: derjenige, desjenigen ꝛc., aber bei derartig bleibt der... *inv.*	†) also: derjenige, desjenigen, etc., but in derartig the der... remains *inv.*
Gen.	desselben	derselben	desselben	derselben		
Dat.	demselben	derselben	demselben	denselben		
Akk.	denselben	dieselbe	dasselbe	dieselben		

D. Verlängerungsformen und Steigerung nach folgenden Musterbeispielen:

D. Formation of suffixes in comparison and declension after the following models:

	1. Stufe	2. Stufe	3. Stufe
¹ ohne Umlaut*)	voll,	voller,	vollst
² mit Umlaut*)	alt,	älter,	ältest
³ mit oder ohne Umlaut*)	glatt	glatter, / glätter,	glattest / glättest
⁴ mit (↘ ohne) Umlaut*)	naß	näßer, / ↘ nasser,	näßest / ↘ nassest
⁵ ohne (↘ mit) Umlaut*)	karg	karger, / ↘ kärger,	kargst / ↘ kärgst

	positive	comparative	superlative
¹ without umlaut*)	voll,	voller,	vollst
² with umlaut*)	alt,	älter,	ältest
³ with or without umlaut*)	glatt	glatter, / glätter,	glattest / glättest
⁴ with [↘ without] umlaut*)	naß	näßer, / ↘ nasser,	näßest / ↘ nassest
⁵ without (↘ with) umlaut*)	karg	karger, / ↘ kärger,	kargst / ↘ kärgst

6 Die Ausstoßung oder Nichtausstoßung des e in der Steigerung veranschaulichen die nebenst. Beispiele. { hold, holder, holdest / reich, reicher, reichst / edel, edler, ↘ edeler, edelst }

6 The examples here given illustrate the treatment of the e in comparison. { hold, holder, holdest / reich, reicher, reichst / edel, edler, ↘ edeler, edelst }

9 Auf ...er, ...el, ...en auslautende werfen gern das e vor Silben ab, wenn Steigerungs- oder Abwandlungsendungen hinzutreten, zB.: unser: uns(e)re; edel: ein edler Mann; edler als ...; vollkomm(e)ne Wesen. Dabei wird ss zu ß: angemessner [oder angemessener].

9 Adjectives ending in ...er, ...el, ...en often elide the e of these syllables, when suffixes of comparison or declension are added, as unser: uns(e)re; edel: ein edler Mann; edler als ...; vollkomm[e]ne Wesen. The ss changes into ß: angemessner [or angemessener].

10 Bei den Verlängerungsformen, sowohl in der Abwandlung wie in der Steigerung, gehen vor einem am Schlusse nachfolgenden e auslautendes ß und (nach kurzem Selbstlaut) ß bezüglich über in s und ss; zB. kraus, krause, krausem, krauser (a. comp.), krauses, krausest (sup.); blaß (♭), blasse ꝛc., blasser, a. comp.: blasser in blässer, sup. am blassesten u. blässesten; dagegen: heiß (♮), heiße ꝛc., heißer (a. comp.), am heißesten (sup.), groß (♮), große ꝛc., großer, größer (comp.), größte (sup.) (größte und beste sind die einzigen ohne e, alle übrigen an s und ß haben este).

Die Steigerungsformen werden ebenso abgewandelt wie die Grundform, zB. ein größerer nach ㊌ C ꝛc.

10 In the forms of declension or comparison the final ß is changed [before e] into s, and [after a shortened vowel] ß into ss: kraus, krause, krausem, krausen, krauser [also comp.], krauses, krausest [sup.]; blaß [♭], blasse, blassem, blassen, blasser, also comp. blasser or blässer, sup. am blassesten or blässesten; but: heiß [♮], heiße ꝛc., heißer [also comp.], am heißesten [sup.]; groß [♮], große ꝛc., großer, größer [comp.], größte [sup.]. [The only sup. without e are größte and beste, all other adj. in s or ß having este].

Comparatives and superlatives are declined throughout like the positive, as ein größerer according to ㊌ C, &c.

*) d. h. Verwandlung von a in ä, o in ö, u in ü.

*) i. e. change of a into ä, of o into ö, of u into ü.

| Abgesonderte Bemerkungen | referring to the signs ① to ㊾ in the Dictionary. | Detached Observations |

㊸ ²,³*) Hauptwörter aus Eigenschaftswörtern und Mittelformen (auch ihr *comp.* u. *sup.*)

G!⁴ Adjectives and Participles as substantives [also their *comp.* & *sup.*]

Einzelne ältere haben vollständig das Wesen von Hauptwörtern angenommen, z. B. Junge *m* [*adj.*] — aber nicht Junge(s) *n* — Feste *f* u. Untertan *m* [*p. p.*] und gehen dann nach ㊹, ㊺, ㊻. Auch Farbnamen (das Blau, das Immergrün) und Eigenschaftsbegriffe (das Recht, das Übel) wandeln mit Abstoßung des *adj.* **e** wie reine Hauptwörter ab: von Rechtswegen, in Blau, ein reines Deutsch; dagegen nach ㊿: im Grünen lagern, das ist etwas Rechtes. — Die starken Endungen sind fett, die schwachen mager gedruckt.

Some of the older ones have entirely assumed the character of nouns, as Junge *m* [*adj.*] — but not Junge(s) *n*, — Feste *f*, and Untertan *m* [*p. p.*], and may be declined according to ㊹, ㊺, ㊻. Also names of colours [das Blau, das Immergrün] and adjectival abstracts while casting off the *adj.* **e** [das Recht, das Übel] are declined like pure substantives: von Rechtswegen, in Blau, ein reines Deutsch; but ㊿: im Grünen lagern, das ist etwas Rechtes. — Fat-face type shows strong suffixes, lean-face the weak ones.

A. Mit dem bestimmten Geschlechtswort ꝛc. †) With the definite article, &c.

B. Mit dem unbestimmten Geschlechtswort ꝛc. ††) With the indefinite article, &c.

m	Einzahl Singular		Mehrzahl Plural	Einzahl Singular		Mehrzahl Plural	
Nom.	der ꝛc. †)	(²e) ~**e**	die (²en) ~**en**	ein ꝛc. ††)	(²er) ~**er**	uns(e)re ꝛc. ††)	(²en) ~**en**
Gen.	des (²en) ~**en**		der (²en) ~**en**	eines (²en) ~**en**		uns(e)rer (²en) ~**en**	
Dat.	dem (²en) ~**en**		den (²en) ~**en**	einem (²en) ~**en**		uns(e)ren (²en) ~**en**	
Akk.	den (²en) ~**en**		die (²en) ~**en**	einen (²en) ~**en**		uns(e)re (²en) ~**en**	

☞ Setze ein z. B. (Put as examples): groß (²) Gelehrt (~), gut (²) Deutsch (~), trauernd (²) Hinterblieben (~).

f							
Nom.	die ꝛc. †)	(²e) ~**e**	die (²en) ~**en**	eine ꝛc. ††)	(²e) ~**e**	eu(e)re ꝛc. ††)	(²en) ~**en**
Gen.	der (²en) ~**en**		der (²en) ~**en**	einer (²en) ~**en**		eu(e)rer (²en) ~**en**	
Dat.	der (²en) ~**en**		den (²en) ~**en**	einer (²en) ~**en**		eu(e)ren (²en) ~**en**	
Akk.	die (²e) ~**e**		die (²en) ~**en**	eine (²e) ~**e**		eu(e)re (²en) ~**en**	

☞ Setze ein z. B. (Put as examples): früher (²) Geliebt (~), alt (²) Bekannt (~), schön (²) Unbekannt (~).

n							
Nom.	das ꝛc. †)	(²e) ~**e**	die (²en) ~**en**	ein ꝛc. †) ~**es**	ein ²es ~**e**(s)	ihre ꝛc. †)	(²en) ~**en**
Gen.	des (²en) ~**en**		der (²en) ~**en**	eines ~**en**,	eines ²en ~**en**	ihrer (²en) ~**en**	
Dat.	dem (²en) ~**en**		den (²en) ~**en**	~**em**, ²em ~**en** (od. ~**em**)	ein ²es ~**e**(s)	ihren (²en) ~**en**	
Akk.	das (²e) ~**e**		die (²en) ~**en**	ein ~**es**,	ein ²es ~**e**(s)	ihre (²en) ~**en**	

☞ Setze ein z. B. (Put as examples): lieb (²) Klein (~), schön (²) Ganz (~), also: ein schönes Ganze (od. Ganzes).

C. Ohne Geschlechtswort ꝛc. †††) Without article, &c. †††)

sg.	*m*	*f*	*n*	*pl. m f n*	*m f n*	*m f n*	
Nom.	(²er) ~**er**	(²e) ~**e**	(²es) ~**es**	~**e**	²e ~**e**	wir (²en) ~**en**,	
Gen.	(²en, ✝²es) ~**en**	(²er) ~**en**	(²en, ✝ ²es) ~**en**	~**er**	²er ~**en** (od. ~**er**)	—	⸢\ (²e) ~**e**⸣
Dat.	~**em**, ²em ~**en** (od. ~**em**)	~**er**,²er ~**en**(od.~**er**)	~**em**,²em ~**en**(od.~**em**)	~**en**	²er ~**en**	uns (²en) ~**en**	
Akk.	(²en) ~**en**	(²e) ~**e**	(²es) ~**es**	~**e**	²e ~**e**	uns (²e) ~**e**	

☞ Setze die entsprechenden *m, f, n* Beispiele wie oben ein, z. B.: Put corresponding *m f, n* examples as above, e. g.: solch guter Bekannter, dir ungetreuem Beamten, von schönem Äußeren (od. Äußerem), liebe Bekannte, wir Wilden (SEUME) oder wir Wilde, wir Deutsche (BISMARCK) oder P wir Deutschen (vgl. ㊻ A 3†); Gen. *pl.* großer Gelehrten, besser als: großer Gelehrter (zumal dies auch Nom. *sg.* ist: especially as the latter is also *nom. sg.*).

㊹ Hauptwörter aus Eigenschafts-Hauptwortpaaren

Substantives compounded of adjective and substantive

wandeln ohne Worttrennung beide Wortteile ab

are declined in both parts which remain inseparable

A) Einzahl Singular (wie ㊿ B) Mehrzahl Plural   B) (wie ㊿ B)   C) (wie ㊿)

Nom.	der (dieser ꝛc.) Hohepriester	die Hohenpriester	die Langeweile	aber auch: die Lang(e)weile	
Gen.	des Hohenpriesters	der ~	der Langenweile	der ~	
Dat.	dem Hohenpriester	den ~ n	der Langenweile	der ~	
Akk.	den Hohenpriester	die ~	die Langeweile	die ~	

ein, kein ꝛc. Hoherpriester (wie ㊿ C); (zwei, viele ꝛc.) Hohepriester (wie ㊿ A 3†)   aus Langerweile (wie ㊿ A 3†) oder aus Lang(e)weile (㊹).

㊺ ⁵*) Hauptwörter aus Eigenschaftswortpaaren

Two adjectives forming one substantive

wandeln nur das zweite Wort ab, z. B.:   are declined only in the second part.

der ꝛc. †) Einjährig-Freiwillige, des (dem, den, *pl.* die, der, den, die) Einjährig-Freiwilligen, ein ꝛc. ††) Einjährig-Freiwilliger, zwei ꝛc. †††) Einjährig-Freiwillige.

*) f. Seite XXIII †) dieser, jener ꝛc. wie ㊿ B. ††) ein, kein ꝛc. wie ㊿ C. †††) ich, solch, viele, wenige ꝛc. wie ㊿ A. 3.

| Abgesonderte Bemerkungen {beziehen sich auf die im Wörterbuche vorkommenden Zeichen ① bis ㉙} | Detached Observations |

Gͫ͞. Zeitabwandlung.   Gͫ͞. Table of Conjugations.

I.

㊆ **)   **Hilfszeitwörter.**   **Auxiliary Verbs.**

a) sein (to be): Zur Bildung der zs.-gesetzten Zeiten der Vergangenheit solcher ziellosen Zeitwörter (v/n.), die einen Übergang, eine Ortsbewegung, ein Sein oder Werden ausdrücken; auch unabhängiges begriffliches Zeitwort.

a) sein (to be): used to form compound tenses of the past of such neuter verbs [v/n.] as denote a transition, a change of place, a being or a growing; also as an independent notional verb.

Einfache Zeiten.   Simple Tenses.

Wirklichkeit. *Indicative.*		Vorstellung. *Subjunctive.*	
Gegenwart. *Present.*	Vergangenheit. *Imperfect.*	Gegenwart. *Present.*	Vergangenheit. *Imperfect.*
sg. ich bin	*sg.* ich war	*sg.* ich sei	*sg.* ich wäre
du bist	du warst (warest)	du seiest od. seist	du wärest (wärst)
er (sie, es, man) ist	er (2c.) war	er (2c.) sei	er (2c.) wäre
pl. wir sind	*pl.* wir waren	*pl.* wir seien (sein)	*pl.* wir wären
ihr seid	ihr wart (waret)	ihr seiet	ihr wäret (wärt)
sie (Sie) sind.	sie (Sie) waren.	sie (Sie) seien (sein).	sie (Sie) wären.
Befehl(sform). *Imperative.*	Nennform der Gegenwart. *Infinitive Present.*	Mittelform der Gegenwart. *Present Participle.*	Mittelform der Vergangenheit. *Past Participle.*
sg. sei! (provc. od. † bis!, wiß!)	sein (poet. od. † wesen).	seiend (↘ † wesend).	gewesen (provc. P gewest).
pl. seid!			

Zusammengesetzte Zeiten.   Compound Tenses.

Wirklichkeit. *Indicative.*		Vorstellung. *Subjunctive.*	
Vorgegenwart. *Perfect.*	Vorvergangenheit. *Past Perfect.*	Vorgegenwart. *Perfect.*	Vorvergangenheit. *Past Perfect.*
ich bin gewesen.	ich war gewesen.	ich sei gewesen.	ich wäre gewesen.
1. Zukunft. *First Future.*	2. Zukunft. *Second Future.*	1. Bedingung. *1ˢᵗ Conditional.*	2. Bedingung. *2ⁿᵈ Conditional.*
ich werde sein.	ich werde gewesen sein.	ich würde sein.	ich würde gewesen sein.
Nennform der Vergangenheit. *Past Infinitive.*	Nennform der Zukunft. *Future Infinitive.*	Mittelform der Vergangenheit. *Past Participle.*	Mittelform der Zukunft. *Future Participle.*
gewesen sein.	sein werden.	↘ gewesen seiend.	↘ sein werdend.

b) haben (to have): Zur Bildung der zs.-gesetzten Zeiten der Vergangenheit der zielenden Zeitwörter (v/a.) und solcher ziellosen (v/n.), die eine Dauer oder einen Zustand ausdrücken; auch unabhängiges zielendes Zeitwort.

b) haben (to have): used to form compound tenses of the past of the active verbs [v/a.], and of such neuter verbs [v/n.] as denote a duration or a condition; also as an independent transitive verb.

Einfache Zeiten.   Simple Tenses.

Wirklichkeit. *Indicative.*		Vorstellung. *Subjunctive.*	
Gegenwart. *Present.*	Vergangenheit. *Imperfect.*	Gegenwart. *Present.*	Vergangenheit. *Imperfect.*
sg. ich habe	*sg.* ich hatte	*sg.* ich habe	*sg.* ich hätte
du hast	du hattest	du habest	du hättest
er (sie, es, man) hat	er (2c.) hatte	er (2c.) habe	er (2c.) hätte
pl. wir haben	*pl.* wir hatten	*pl.* wir haben	*pl.* wir hätten
ihr habt (habet)	ihr hattet	ihr habet	ihr hättet
sie (Sie) haben.	sie (Sie) hatten.	sie (Sie) haben	sie (Sie) hätten.
Befehl(sform). *Imperative.*	Nennform der Gegenwart. *Infinitive Present.*	Mittelform der Gegenwart. *Present Participle.*	Mittelform der Vergangenheit. *Past Participle.*
sg. habe!, hab'!; *pl.* habt (habet!)	haben.	habend.	gehabt.

Zusammengesetzte Zeiten.   Compound Tenses.

Wirklichkeit. *Indicative.*		Vorstellung. *Subjunctive.*	
Vorgegenwart. *Perfect.*	Vorvergangenheit. *Past Perfect.*	Vorgegenwart. *Perfect.*	Vorvergangenheit. *Past Perfect.*
ich habe gehabt.	ich hatte gehabt.	ich habe gehabt.	ich hätte gehabt.
1. Zukunft. *First Future.*	2. Zukunft. *Second Future.*	1. Bedingung. *1ˢᵗ Conditional.*	2. Bedingung. *2ⁿᵈ Conditional.*
ich werde haben.	ich werde gehabt haben.	ich würde haben.	ich würde gehabt haben.
Nennform der Vergangenheit. *Past Infinitive.*		Mittelform der Vergangenheit. *Past Participle.*	
gehabt haben.		↘ gehabt habend.	

c) werden: dient zur Bildung der Zukunft, Bedingung und Leideform; auch als unabhängiges begriffliches Zeitwort.

c) werden: serving either as auxiliary to form the future [shall, will], conditional [should, would], and passive [be], or as an independent notional verb [become].

Einfache Zeiten.   Simple Tenses.

Wirklichkeit. *Indicative.*		Vorstellung. *Subjunctive.*	
Gegenwart. *Present.*	Vergangenheit. *Imperfect.*	Gegenwart. *Present.*	Vergangenheit. *Imperfect.*
sg. ich werde	*sg.* ich wurde od. *poet.* ward	*sg.* ich werde	*sg.* ich würde
du wirst	du wurdest od. " wardst	du werdest	du würdest
er (sie, es, man) wird	er (2c.) wurde od. " ward	er (2c.) werde	er (2c.) würde

**) Abwandlung der zs.-gesetzten Zeitwörter s. S. XXXVIII.   **) See Conjugation of compound verbs on p. XXXVIII.

Abgesonderte Bemerkungen {referring to the signs ① to ㊆ in the Dictionary.}			Detached Observations
pl. wir werden ihr werdet sie (Sie) werden.	*pl.* wir wurden ihr wurdet sie (Sie) wurden.	*pl.* wir werden ihr werdet sie (Sie) werden.	*pl.* wir würden ihr würdet sie (Sie) würden.
Befehl(sform). *Imperative.* *sg.* werde! *pl.* werdet!	Nennform der Gegenwart. *Infinitive Present.* werden.	Mittelform der Gegenwart. *Present Participle.* werdend.	Mittelform der Vergangenheit. *Past Participle.* geworden (worden s. ㊆).
	Zusammengesetzte Zeiten.	**Compound Tenses.**	
Wirklichkeit. *Indicative.*		Vorstellung. *Subjunctive.*	
Vorgegenwart. *Perfect.* ich bin geworden.	Vorvergangenheit. *Past Perfect.* ich war geworden.	Vorgegenwart. *Perfect.* ich sei geworden.	Vorvergangenheit. *Past Perfect.* ich wäre geworden.
1. Zukunft. *First Future.* ich werde werden.	2. Zukunft. *Second Future.* ich werde geworden sein.	1. Bedingung. *1ˢᵗ Conditional.* ich würde werden.	2. Bedingung. *2ⁿᵈ Conditional.* ich würde geworden sein.
Nennform der Vergangenheit. *Past Infinitive.* geworden sein.	Nennform der Zukunft. *Future Infinitive.* ↘ werden werden.	Mittelform der Vergangenheit. *Past Participle.* ↘ geworden seiend.	Mittelform der Zukunft. *Future Participle.* ↘ werden werdend.

II. Starke Abwandlung. — Strong Conjugation.

Die (alten) **starkformigen** Zeitwörter lauten ab, d. h. sie verwandeln den Stamm= oder Wurzelselbstlaut sowohl im *impf.*, das in der 1. u. 3. Prsn. *sg.* keine besondere Endung hat und in der Vorstellungsform den **Umlaut** annimmt (z.B. bände), wie in dem auf ...en ausgehenden *p. p.* (z.B. binden — band — gebunden). Außer dem Ab= und Umlaut zeigen gewisse starke Zeitwörter mit dem Stammlaut e (ä) auch **Brechung**, d. h. Übergang in i (ie) in der 2. und 3. Prsn *sg.* der Gegenwart, sowie auch in der Befehlsform (z.B. gebe, gibst, gibt, gib; sehe, siehst, sieht, sieh; gebäre, gebierst, gebiert, gebier; s. ㊂, ㊃, ㊄, ㊅).

The [ancient or] **strong** verbs have **vowel change** [ablaut], i. e. they change their root-vowel, both in the *impf.*, which is without any particular termination in its 1ˢᵗ and 3ᵈ *p. sg.*, but with the **umlaut** [e. g. bände] in its subj. mode, and in the *p. p.* ending in ...en [as in: binden; *impf.* band, *p. p.* gebunden]. Certain strong verbs with the root-vowel e [ä] show not only change of the root-vowel and umlaut, but also **brechung**, i. e. change into i [ie] in the 2. and 3. *p. sg.* of the Present, and in the Imperative [as gebe, gibst, gibt, gib; sehe, siehst, sieht, sieh; gebäre, gebierst, gebiert, gebier; see ㊂, ㊃, ㊄, ㊅].

A. Dreilautige Ablautreihen: i, a, u ꝛc. — A. Verbs with three distinct root-vowels: i, a, u, etc.

㊆ ****§) binden.**
(Ablaute: i, a, u).

	Tätigkeitsform.	**Active Voice.**	
	Einfache Zeiten.	**Simple Tenses.**	
Wirklichkeit. *Indicative.*		Vorstellung. *Subjunctive.*	
Gegenwart. *Present.*	Vergangenheit. *Imperfect.*	Gegenwart. *Present.*	Vergangenheit. *Imperfect.*
sg. ich binde du bindest ob. bindst er (sie, es, man) bindet	*sg.* ich band du bandst (bandest) er (ꝛc.) band	*sg.* ich binde du bindest er (ꝛc.) binde	*sg.* ich bände du bändest er (ꝛc.) bände
pl. wir binden ihr bindet sie (Sie) binden.	*pl.* wir banden ihr bandet sie (Sie) banden.	*pl.* wir binden ihr bindet sie (Sie) binden.	*pl.* wir bänden ihr bändet sie (Sie) bänden.
Befehl(sform). *Imperative.* *sg.* bind(e)! *pl.* bindet!	Nennform der Gegenwart. *Infinitive Present.* binden.	Mittelform der Gegenwart. *Present Participle.* bindend.	Mittelform der Vergangenheit. *Past Participle.* gebunden.
	Zusammengesetzte Zeiten.	**Compound Tenses.**	
Wirklichkeit. *Indicative.*		Vorstellung. *Subjunctive.*	
Vorgegenwart. *Perfect.* ich habe gebunden du hast gebunden ꝛc.	Vorvergangenheit. *Past Perfect.* ich hatte gebunden du hattest gebunden ꝛc.	Vorgegenwart. *Perfect.* ich habe gebunden du habest gebunden ꝛc.	Vorvergangenheit. *Past Perfect.* ich hätte gebunden du hättest gebunden ꝛc.
1. Zukunft. *First Future.* ich werde binden.	2. Zukunft. *Second Future.* ich werde gebunden haben.	1. Bedingung. *1ˢᵗ Conditional.* ich würde binden.	2. Bedingung. *2ⁿᵈ Conditional.* ich würde gebunden haben.
	Leideform.	**Passive Voice.**	
Wirklichkeit. *Indicative.*		Vorstellung. *Subjunctive.*	
Gegenwart. *Present.* ich werde gebunden.	Vorvergangenheit. *Past Perfect.* ich war gebunden (worden).	Gegenwart. *Present.* ich werde gebunden.	Vorvergangenheit. *Past Perfect.* ich wäre gebunden (worden).
Vergangenheit. *Imperfect.* ich wurde (*poet.* ward) gebunden.	1. Zukunft. *First Future.* ich werde gebunden werden.	Vergangenheit. *Imperfect.* ich würde gebunden.	1. Bedingung. *1ˢᵗ Conditional.* ich würde gebunden werden.
Vorgegenwart. *Perfect.* ich bin gebunden worden.	2. Zukunft. *Second Future.* ich werde gebunden worden sein.	Vorgegenwart. *Perfect.* ich sei gebunden worden.	2. Bedingung. *2ⁿᵈ Conditional.* ich würde gebunden worden sein.
Befehl(sform). *Imperative.* *sg.* werde gebunden! *pl.* werdet gebunden!	Infinit. { *Present Inf.* gebunden werden. *Past Inf.* gebunden (worden) sein. *Future Inf.* ↘ werden gebunden werden.	Partic. { *Present Part.* ↘ gebunden werdend. *Past Part.* gebunden worden. *Future Part.* zu binden(d attributively)*).	

*) z.B. der Kranz ist erst zu binden; der zu bindende Kranz.
**§) Die Abwandlung der zs.-gesetzten Zeitwörter und (§) die verkürzten (est=)Endungen der S=Stämme s. S. XXXVII f.

*) e. g. der Kranz ist erst zu binden; der zu bindende Kranz.
**§) See Conjugation of compound verbs and [§] the contracted [est=]suffixes of the S=stems on p. XXXVII, &c.

Abgesonderte Bemerkungen (beziehen sich auf die im Wörterbuche vorkommenden Zeichen ① bis ㊹.) — Detached Observations

Nummer u. Ablaute	Nennform *Infinitive*	Gegenwart *Present* Wirklichkeit / Indicative	Vergangenheit *Imperfect* Indicative	Subjunctive	Befehlsform *Imperative* sg. u. pl.	Mittelform der Gegenwart und Vergangenheit
⑦② ** § (i, a, o)	sinnen a u. b f. *impf. subj.*	sg. ich sinne, du sinnst, er sinnt pl. wir sinnen, ihr sinnt*), sie sinnen	ich sann (⌣) du sann(e)st*) er sann ꝛc.	a) ich sönne ob. b) ich sänne sönnest, sännest	sinn(e)! (⌣*) sinnt! (⌣*)	sinnend (⌣⌣) gesonnen (⌣⌣⌣)
a	brechen	sg. ich breche, du brichst, er bricht pl. wir brechen, ihr brecht*), sie brechen	ich brach (⌣) du brach(e)st*) er brach ꝛc.	ich bräche (⌣⌣) du brächest (⌣⌣)	brich! (⌣) brecht! (⌣*)	brechend (⌣⌣) gebrochen (⌣⌣⌣)
	nehmen (kommen siehe ㊴)	sg. ich nehme, du nimmst (⌣) er nimmt (⌣) pl. wir nehmen, ihr nehmt*), sie nehmen	ich nahm (⌣) du nahm(e)st*) er nahm ꝛc.	ich nähme (⌣⌣) du nähmest er nähme ꝛc.	nimm! (⌣) nehmt! (⌣*)	nehmend (⌣⌣) genommen (⌣⌣⌣)
b	werfen	sg. ich werfe, du wirfst, er wirft pl. wir werfen, ihr werft*), sie werfen	ich warf (⌣) du warf(e)st*)	ich würfe (⌣⌣) du würfest (⌣⌣)	wirf! (⌣) werft! (⌣*)	werfend (⌣⌣) geworfen (⌣⌣⌣)
c ⑦③ ** § (e, a, o)	befehlen	sg. ich befehle, du befiehlst, er befiehlt pl. wir befehlen, ihr befehlt*), sie befehlen	ich befahl (⌣⌣) du befahl(e)st*) er befahl ꝛc.	ich beföhle (⌣⌣⌣) du beföhlest er beföhle ꝛc.	befiehl! (⌣⌣) befehlt! (⌣⌣*)	befehlend (⌣⌣⌣) befohlen (⌣⌣⌣)
d	stehlen	wie c; doch subj. impf. a. ⌐ stähle	☞ stehlen like befehlen, but subj. impf. also ⌐ stähle			
e	schelten	sg. ich schelte, du schiltst, er schilt pl. wir schelten, ihr scheltet, sie schelten	ich schalt (⌣) du schalt(e)st*) er schalt ꝛc.	ich schölte (⌣⌣) du schöltest er schölte ꝛc.	schilt! (⌣) scheltet! (⌣*)	scheltend (⌣⌣) gescholten (⌣⌣⌣)
f (ä, a, o)	gebären	sg. ich gebäre, du gebierst, sie gebiert pl. wir gebären, ihr gebärt*), sie gebären	ich gebar (⌣⌣) du gebar(e)st*) sie gebar ꝛc.	ich gebäre (⌣⌣), deutlicher: würde gebären	gebier! (⌣⌣) gebärt! (⌣⌣*)	gebärend (⌣⌣⌣) geboren (⌣⌣⌣)
⑦④ ** § (i, a, e)	bitten	sg. ich bitte, du bitt(e)st, er bittet pl. wir bitten, ihr bittet, sie bitten	ich bat (⌣) du bat(e)st*)	ich bäte (⌣⌣) du bätest (⌣⌣)	bitte! bitt'! (⌣*) bittet! (⌣*)	bittend (⌣⌣) gebeten (⌣⌣⌣)
	sitzen	sg. ich sitze, du sitzest u. sitzt, er sitzt pl. wir sitzen, ihr sitzt*), sie sitzen	ich saß (⌣) du saßest (⌣⌣)	ich säße (⌣⌣) du säßest (⌣⌣)	sitze! sitz'! (⌣*) sitzt! (⌣*)	sitzend (⌣⌣) gesessen (⌣⌣⌣)
(ie, a, e)	liegen	sg. ich liege, du liegst, er liegt pl. wir liegen, ihr liegt*), sie liegen	ich lag (⌣) du lag(e)st*)	ich läge (⌣⌣) du lägest (⌣⌣)	liege! lieg'! (⌣*) liegt! (⌣*)	liegend (⌣⌣) gelegen (⌣⌣⌣)
		☞ Vgl. schwören ⑦⑦ u. gehen ㊵.	☞ See also schwören ⑦⑦ and gehen ㊵.			

(Vorstellung: 1. Prsn. gleichlautend mit der 1. Prsn. des Indikativs, durchweg ohne Umlaut ob. Brechung und mit durchgehendem Biegungs-e, z. B. ich nehme, du nehmest, ihr nehmet ꝛc. — Subjunctive: 1. person the same as the 1. person of the ind., but without umlaut or breching, and with inflectional e throughout: er nehme, ihr nehmet ꝛc.)

B. Zweilautige Ablautreihen: ie, o, o ꝛc. mit Gleichlaut im *impf.* und *p. p.* (f. a. ㊶, ㊷.).
B. Verbs with two distinct root-vowels: ie, o, o, &c., same vowel in the *impf.* and *p. p.* [see also ㊶, ㊷].

a (i, ŏ, ŏ)	klimmen (auch ㊳)	sg. ich klimme, du klimmst, er klimmt pl. wir klimmen, ihr klimmt*), sie klimmen	ich klomm (⌣) du klomm(e)st*) er klomm ꝛc.	ich klömme (⌣⌣) du klömmest er klömme ꝛc.	klimm(e)! (⌣*) klimmt! (⌣*)	klimmend (⌣⌣) geklommen (⌣⌣⌣)
b (e, ŏ, ŏ)	fechten	sg. ich fechte, du fichtst, er ficht pl. wir fechten, ihr fechtet, sie fechten	ich focht (⌣) du focht(e)st*)	ich föchte (⌣⌣) du föchtest (⌣⌣)	ficht! (⌣) fechtet! (⌣)	fechtend (⌣⌣) gefochten (⌣⌣⌣)
⑦⑤ ** § c (ie, ŏ, ŏ)	riechen	sg. ich rieche, du riechst, er riecht pl. wir riechen, ihr riecht*), sie riechen	ich roch (⌣) du roch(e)st*)	ich röche (⌣⌣) du röchest (⌣⌣)	riech(e)! (⌣⌣) riecht! (⌣*)	riechend (⌣⌣) gerochen (⌣⌣⌣)
d	gießen	sg. ich gieße, du gieß(e)st, (†geußt) er gießt (†geußt) pl. wir gießen, ihr gießt*), sie gießen	ich goß (⌣) du goss(e)st*) er goß ꝛc.	ich gösse (⌣⌣) du gössest (⌣⌣) er gösse ꝛc.	gieß(e)! (⌣⌣) (†geuß! (⌣)) gießt! (⌣*)	gießend (⌣⌣) gegossen (⌣⌣⌣)
e	sieden (auch ㊴)	sg. ich siede, du siedest, er siedet pl. wir sieden, ihr siedet, sie sieden	ich sott (⌣) du sottest (⌣⌣)	ich sötte (⌣⌣) du söttest (⌣⌣)	sied(e)! (⌣⌣) siedet! (⌣⌣)	siedend (⌣⌣) gesotten (⌣⌣⌣)
f (au, ŏ, ŏ)	saufen	sg. ich saufe, du säufst, er säuft pl. wir saufen, ihr sauft*), sie saufen	ich soff (⌣) du soff(e)st*)	ich söffe (⌣⌣) du söffest (⌣⌣)	sauf(e)! (⌣⌣) sauft! (⌣*)	saufend (⌣⌣) gesoffen (⌣⌣⌣)
a	bieten	sg. ich biete, du biet(e)st (†beutst, ++beust), er bietet (†beut) pl. wir bieten, ihr bietet, sie bieten	ich bot (⌣) du bot(e)st*) er bot ꝛc.	ich böte (⌣⌣) du bötest (⌣⌣) er böte ꝛc.	biet(e)! (⌣⌣) ob. † beut! (⌣) bietet! (⌣⌣)	bietend (⌣⌣) geboten (⌣⌣⌣)
⑦⑥ ** § b (ie, ō, ō)	ziehen	sg. ich ziehe, du ziehst (†zeuchst), er zieht (†zeucht) pl. wir ziehen, ihr zieht*), sie ziehen	ich zog (⌣) du zog(e)st*) er zog ꝛc.	ich zöge (⌣⌣) du zögest (⌣⌣) er zöge ꝛc.	zieh(e)! (⌣⌣) ob. † zeuch (⌣) zieht! (⌣*)	ziehend (⌣⌣) gezogen (⌣⌣⌣)
c	wiegen	sg. ich wiege, du wiegst, er wiegt pl. wir wiegen, ihr wiegt*), sie wiegen	ich wog (⌣) du wog(e)st*)	ich wöge (⌣⌣) du wögest (⌣⌣)	wieg(e)! (⌣⌣) wiegt! (⌣*)	wiegend (⌣⌣) gewogen (⌣⌣⌣)
d (ü, ō, ō)	lügen	sg. ich lüge, du lügst, er lügt pl. wir lügen, ihr lügt*), sie lügen	ich log (⌣) du log(e)st*)	ich löge (⌣⌣) du lögest (⌣⌣)	lüg(e)! (⌣⌣) lügt! (⌣*)	lügend (⌣⌣) gelogen (⌣⌣⌣)

*) Die schleppenden Formen mit e (sinnet, brachest ꝛc.) sind nicht zu empfehlen. ** § wie S. XXXIII.

*) The full forms with e (sinnet, brachest, &c.) are not to be commended. ** § as on p. XXXIII.

Abgesonderte Bemerkungen / Detached observations

(referring to the signs ① to ⓸ in the Dictionary.)

Number & root-vowels	Nennform / Infinitive	Gegenwart / Present — Wirklichkeit / Indicative		Vergangenheit / Imperfect — Indicative	Subjunctive	Befehlsform / Imperative sg. u. pl.	Present Part. / Past Participle
㊆ a (ä, ō, ō)	gären (auch ㊵)	sg. ich gäre, du gärst, er gärt pl. wir gären, ihr gärt*, sie gären	*Vorstellung:* 1. Pers. gleichlautend mit der 1. Pers. des Indikativs, durchweg ohne Umlaut ob. Brechung und mit durchgehender Biegungs-e, z. B.: ich lese, du lesest 2c. throughout: 1. person of the indicative, but without umlaut or brechung and with inflectional e throughout, e.g.: ich lese, du lesest, er lese, ihr leset 2c.	ich gor (ˉ) du gorst (ˉ)*	ich göre (ˉ˘) du görest (ˉ˘)	gär(e)! (ˉ) gärt! (ˉ)*	gärend (ˉ˘) gegoren (˘ˉ˘)
㊆㊆ b (ö, ō, ō)	schwören (auch ㊵)	sg. ich schwöre, du schwörst, er schwört pl. wir schwören, ihr schwört*, sie schwören		ich schwor (ˉ) ob. schwur du schworst, schwurst	ich schwüre (ˉ˘) du schwürest (ˉ˘) 2c. †	schwör(e)! (ˉ)(˘) schwört! (ˉ)*	schwörend (ˉ˘) geschworen (˘ˉ˘)
ū, c (au, ō, ō)	schrauben (auch ㊵)	sg. ich schraube, du schraubst, er schraubt [schrauben pl. wir schrauben, ihr schraubt*, sie		ich schrob (ˉ) du schrob(e)st er schrob 2c.	ich schröbe (ˉ˘) du schröbest (ˉ˘) er schröbe 2c.	schraub(e)! (ˉ)(˘) schraubt! (ˉ)*	schraubend (ˉ˘) geschroben (˘ˉ˘)
㊆㊆ a (e, ō, ō)	scheren (auch ㊵)	sg. ich schere, du schierst (scherst), er schiert (schert) pl. wir scheren, ihr schert*, sie scheren		ich schor (ˉ) du schor(e)st* er schor 2c.	ich schöre (ˉ˘) du schörest (ˉ˘) er schöre 2c.	schier! (ˉ) schert! (ˉ)*	scherend (ˉ˘) geschoren (˘ˉ˘)
b	weben (auch ㊵)	sg. ich webe, du webst, er webt pl. wir weben, ihr webt*, sie weben		ich wob (ˉ) du wob(e)st*	ich wöbe (ˉ˘) du wöbest (ˉ˘)	web(e)! (ˉ) webt! (ˉ)*	webend (ˉ˘) gewoben (˘ˉ˘)
㊆㊆ (i, u, u)	schinden	sg. ich schinde, du schind(e)st, er schindet [schinden pl. wir schinden, ihr schindet, sie		ich schund (ˉ) du schund(e)st er schund 2c.	ich schünde (˘˘) du schündest (˘˘) er schünde 2c.	schind(e)! (˘)(˘) schindet! (˘˘)	schindend (˘˘) geschunden (˘˘˘)
㊆㊆ a	beißen	sg. ich beiße, du beiß(es)t, er beißt pl. wir beißen, ihr beißt*, sie beißen		ich biß (ˉ) du bissest (˘˘)	ich bisse (˘˘) du bissest (˘˘)	beiß(e)! (ˉ)(˘) beißt! (ˉ)*	beißend (ˉ˘) gebissen (˘˘˘)
b (ei, i, i)	reiten	sg. ich reite, du reit(e)st, er reitet pl. wir reiten, ihr reitet, sie reiten		ich ritt (˘) du ritt(e)st	ich ritte (˘˘) du rittest (˘˘)	reit(e)! (ˉ)(˘) reitet! (ˉ˘)	reitend (ˉ˘) geritten (˘˘˘)
c	leiden	sg. ich leide, du leid(e)st, er leidet pl. wir leiden, ihr leidet, sie leiden		ich litt (˘) du litt(e)st	ich litte (˘˘) du littest (˘˘)	leid(e)! (ˉ)(˘) leidet! (ˉ˘)	leidend (ˉ˘) gelitten (˘˘˘)
㊆㊆ (ei, ie, ie)	bleiben	sg. ich bleibe, du bleibst, er bleibt pl. wir bleiben, ihr bleibt*, sie bleiben		ich blieb (ˉ) du bliebst	ich bliebe (ˉ˘) du bliebest (ˉ˘)	bleib(e)! (ˉ)(˘) bleibt! (ˉ)*	bleibend (ˉ˘) geblieben (˘ˉ˘)
	preisen	sg. ich preise, du preis(es)t, er preist pl. wir preisen, ihr preist*, sie preisen		ich pries (ˉ) du priesest (ˉ˘)	ich priese (ˉ˘) du priesest (ˉ˘)	preise! u. preis! preist! (ˉ)*	preisend (ˉ˘) gepriesen (˘ˉ˘)

C. Zweilautige Ablautreihen: e, a, e 2c. / C. Verbs with two distinct root-vowels: e, a, e, &c.
mit Gleichlaut im pres. und p. p. / same vowel in the pres. and p. p.

a {	sehen	sg. ich sehe, du siehst, er sieht pl. wir sehen, ihr seht*, sie sehen		ich sah (ˉ) du sahst (ˉ)	ich sähe (ˉ˘) du sähest (ˉ˘)	sieh(e)! (ˉ)(˘)* seht! (ˉ)*	sehend (ˉ˘) gesehen (˘ˉ˘)
	lesen	sg. ich lese, du lies(es)t, er liest pl. wir lesen, ihr lest*, sie lesen		ich las (ˉ) du lasest (ˉ˘)	ich läse (ˉ˘) du läsest (ˉ˘)	lies! (ˉ) lest! (ˉ)*	lesend (ˉ˘) gelesen (˘ˉ˘)
㊆㊆ b (e, ā, e)	genesen	sg. ich genese, du genes(es)t, er genest [genesen pl. wir genesen, ihr genes(e)t*, sie		ich genas (˘ˉ) du genasest er genas 2c.	ich genäse (˘ˉ˘) du genäsest er genäse	genese! (˘ˉ˘) genest! (˘ˉ)*	genesend (˘ˉ˘) genesen (˘ˉ˘)
c	geben	sg. ich gebe, du gibst (˘), er gibt (˘) pl. wir geben, ihr gebt*, sie geben		ich gab (ˉ) du gabst (ˉ)	ich gäbe (ˉ˘) du gäbest (ˉ˘)	gib! (˘) gebt! (ˉ)*	gebend (ˉ˘) gegeben (˘ˉ˘)
d	treten	sg. ich trete, du trittst (˘), er tritt (˘) pl. wir treten, ihr tretet, sie treten		ich trat (ˉ) du trat(e)st	ich träte (ˉ˘) du trätest (ˉ˘)	tritt! (˘) tretet! (ˉ˘)	tretend (ˉ˘) getreten (˘ˉ˘)
㊆㊆ (ĕ, ā, ĕ)	essen	sg. ich esse, du issest ob. ißt, er ißt pl. wir essen, ihr eßt (esset*), sie essen		ich aß (ˉ) du aßest (ˉ˘)	ich äße (ˉ˘) du äßest (ˉ˘)	iß! (˘); eßt! (˘)* ob. esset! (˘˘)*	essend (˘˘) gegessen (˘˘˘)
㊆㊆ (ŏ, ā, ŏ)	kommen [ahd. qué-man: ㊸a]	sg. ich komme, du kommst (kömmst), er kommt (kömmt) [kommen pl. wir kommen, ihr kommt*, sie		ich kam (ˉ) du kamst er kam 2c.	ich käme (ˉ˘) du kämest (ˉ˘) er käme 2c.	komm! (˘) kommt! (˘)*	kommend (˘˘) gekommen (˘˘˘)
㊆㊆ a (a, u, a)	schaffen	sg. ich schaffe, du schaffst, er schafft pl. wir schaffen, ihr schafft*, sie schaffen		ich schuf (ˉ) du schuf(e)st*	ich schüfe (ˉ˘) du schüfest (ˉ˘)	schaff(e)! (˘)(˘) schafft! (˘)*	schaffend (˘˘) geschaffen (˘˘˘)
	waschen	sg. ich wasche, du wäsch(e)st, er wäscht pl. wir waschen, ihr wascht*, sie waschen		ich wusch (ˉ) du wusch(e)st*	ich wüsche (ˉ˘) du wüschest (ˉ˘)	wasch(e)! (˘)(˘) wascht! (˘)*	waschend (˘˘) gewaschen (˘˘˘)
b	backen	sg. ich backe, du bäckst, er bäckt pl. wir backen, ihr backt*, sie backen		ich buk (ˉ) du buk(e)st*	ich büke (ˉ˘) du bükest (ˉ˘)	back(e)! (˘)(˘) backt! (˘)*	backend (˘˘) gebacken (˘˘˘)
	fragen ₊₊	(bes. nordd. P.) ₊₊du frägst, er frägt r-r. nach ㊸ abzuwandeln		₊₊ ich frug (ˉ)	₊₊ ich früge (ˉ˘)		to be conjugated according to ㊸.

*) und **§) wie S. XXXIV; statt sieh! bei Hinweisungen 2c. auch siehe!

*) and **§) as on p. XXXIV; instead of sieh! the form siehe! is often used for references, &c.

Nummer	Nennform / Infinitive	Gegenwart / Present — Wirklichkeit / Indicative	Vergangenheit / Imperfect — Indicative	Subjunctive	Befehlsform Imperative. sg. u. pl.	Present Part. / Past Participle

Abgesonderte Bemerkungen {beziehen sich auf die im Wörterbuche vorkommenden Zeichen ① bis ⑨⑨} / Detached Observations

☞ ⑧⑥ u. ⑧⑦: Ehemals **verdoppelnde Zeitwörter**, z. B. got. haihald (hielt). ☞ ⑧⑥ and ⑧⑦: Ancient **reduplicating verbs**, thus: Gothic haihald [hielt].

	fallen	sg. ich falle, du fällst, er fällt pl. wir fallen, ihr fallt*), sie fallen	ich fiel (́) du fielst (́)*)	ich fiele (́ᴗ) du fielest (́ᴗ)	fall(e)! (́(ᴗ)) fallt! (́)*)	fallend (́ᴗ) gefallen (ᴗ́ᴗ)
a (a, ie, a)	blasen	sg. ich blase, du bläs(es)t, er bläst pl. wir blasen, ihr blast*), sie blasen	ich blies (́) du bliesest (́ᴗ)	ich bliese (́ᴗ) du bliesest (́ᴗ)	blase! od. blas! blast! (́)*)	blasend (́ᴗ) geblasen (ᴗ́ᴗ)
⑧⑥ **§	lassen	sg. ich lasse, du läßt(lässest), er läßt pl. wir lassen, ihr laßt*), sie lassen	ich ließ (́) du ließest (́ᴗ)	ich ließe (́ᴗ) du ließest (́ᴗ)	laß! (́) laßt!(lasset!)*)	lassend (́ᴗ) gelassen (ᴗ́ᴗ)
b (a, i, a)	fangen	sg. ich fange, du fängst, er fängt pl. wir fangen, ihr fangt*), sie fangen	ich fing (́) du fingst (́)*)	ich finge (́ᴗ) du fingest (́ᴗ)	fang(e)! (́(ᴗ)) fangt! (́)*)	fangend (́ᴗ) gefangen (ᴗ́ᴗ)
a (o, ie, o)	stoßen	sg. ich stoße, du stöß(es)t, er stößt pl. wir stoßen, ihr stoßt*), sie stoßen	ich stieß (́) du stießest (́ᴗ)	ich stieße (́ᴗ) du stießest (́ᴗ)	stoß(e)! (́(ᴗ)) stoßt! (́)*)	stoßend (́ᴗ) gestoßen (ᴗ́ᴗ)
b (u, ie, u)	rufen	sg. ich rufe, du rufst (rüfst), er ruft pl. wir rufen, ihr ruft*), sie rufen	ich rief (́) du riefst (́)*)	ich riefe (́ᴗ) du riefest (́ᴗ)	ruf(e)! (́(ᴗ)) ruft! (́)*)	rufend (́ᴗ) gerufen (ᴗ́ᴗ)
⑧⑦ **§ c au, ie, au	hauen	sg. ich haue, du haust, er haut pl. wir hauen, ihr haut*), sie hauen	ich hieb (́) du hiebst (́)*)	ich hiebe (́ᴗ) du hiebest (́ᴗ)	hau(e)! (́(ᴗ)) haut! (́)*)	hauend (́ᴗ) gehauen (ᴗ́ᴗ)
d (ei, ie, ei)	heißen	sg. ich heiße, du heiß(es)t, er heißt pl. wir heißen, ihr heißt*), sie heißen	ich hieß (́) du hießest (́ᴗ)	ich hieße (́ᴗ) du hießest (́ᴗ)	heiß(e)! (́(ᴗ)) heißt! (́)*)	heißend (́ᴗ) geheißen (ᴗ́ᴗ)

(Vorstellung wie vorhergehende Seite. / Subjunctive: as on the previous page.)

III.
Schwache Abwandlung. / Weak Conjugation.

Die (neuen) **schwachformigen** Zeitwörter nehmen im *impf.* und *p.p.* ohne Veränderung des Stammselbstlauts die Endungen ...(e)te und ...(e)t an.

The verbs of the [new or] **weak conjugation** leave their root-vowel unchanged, but add to the stem the suffixes ...[e]te and ...[e]t.

⑧⑧ **§	bauen	sg. ich baue, du baust, er baut pl. wir bauen, ihr baut*), sie bauen	ich baute (́ᴗ) du bautest	ich bau(e)te du bau(e)test	baue! (́ᴗ)† baut! (́)	bauend (́ᴗ) gebaut (ᴗ́)
	leben	sg. ich lebe, du lebst, er lebt pl. wir leben, ihr lebt*), sie leben	ich lebte (́ᴗ) du lebtest	ich leb(e)te du leb(e)test	lebe! (́ᴗ)† lebt! (́)	lebend (́ᴗ) gelebt (ᴗ́)
⑧⑨ **§	beten	sg. ich bete, du betest, er betet pl. wir beten, ihr betet, sie beten	ich betete (́ᴗᴗ) du betetest	ich betete du betetest	bete! (́ᴗ)† betet! (́ᴗ)	betend (́ᴗ) gebetet (ᴗ́ᴗ)
	reisen	sg. ich reise, du reis(es)t, er reist pl. wir reisen, ihr reist*), sie reisen	ich reiste (́ᴗ) du reistest	ich reis(e)te du reis(e)test	reise! (́ᴗ), reis! reist! (́)	reisend (́ᴗ) gereist (ᴗ́)
⑨⓪ **§	reizen	sg. ich reize, du reiz(es)t, er reizt pl. wir reizen, ihr reizt*), sie reizen	ich reizte (́ᴗ) du reiztest	ich reiz(e)te du reiz(e)test	reize! (́ᴗ)† reizt! (́)	reizend (́ᴗ) gereizt (ᴗ́)
	passen	sg. ich passe, du paßt (passest), er paßt pl. wir passen, ihr paßt(passet)*), sie passen	ich paßte (́ᴗ) du paßtest er paßte 2c.	ich paßte (́ᴗ) du paßtest er paßte 2c.	passe! (́ᴗ) oder paß! (́) paßt! (passet!)	passend (́ᴗ) gepaßt (ᴗ́)
⑨① **§	wünschen	sg. ich wünsche, du wünsch(e)st, er wünscht pl. wir wünschen, ihr wünscht*), sie [wünschen	ich wünschte (́ᴗ) du wünschtest	ich wünsch(e)te (́(ᴗ)ᴗ) du wünsch(e)test	wünsche! (́ᴗ)† wünscht! (́)*)	wünschend (́ᴗ) gewünscht (ᴗ́)
a ⑨② **§	wandeln	sg. ich wand(e)le, du wandelst, er wandelt pl. wir wandeln, ihr wandelt, sie [wandeln	ich wandelte (́ᴗᴗ) du wandeltest	ich wandelte (́ᴗᴗ) du wandeltest	wandle! (́ᴗ)† wandelt! (́ᴗ)*)	wandelnd (́ᴗ) gewandelt (ᴗ́ᴗ)
b	atmen	sg. ich atme, du atmest, er atmet pl. wir atmen, ihr atmet, sie atmen	ich atmete (́ᴗᴗ) du atmetest	ich atmete (́ᴗᴗ) du atmetest	atme! (́ᴗ)† atmet! (́ᴗ)	atmend (́ᴗ) geatmet (ᴗ́ᴗ)
	segnen	sg. ich segne, du segnest, er segnet pl. wir segnen, ihr segnet, sie segnen	ich segnete (́ᴗᴗ) du segnetest	ich segnete (́ᴗᴗ) du segnetest	segne! (́ᴗ)† segnet! (́ᴗ)	segnend (́ᴗ) gesegnet (ᴗ́ᴗ)
⑨③ **§	studieren	sg. ich studiere, du studierst, er studiert pl. wir studieren, ihr studiert*), sie [studieren 2c.	ich studierte (-́ᴗ) du studiertest	ich studierte (-́ᴗ) du studiertest	studiere! †) (-́ᴗ) studiert! (-́)*)	studierend (-́ᴗ) studiert (-́)

(Vorsilbe: 1. Präs gleichlaut. m. d. 1. Prä... des Ind., durchweg mit Biegungs-e; ich baue, du bauest, ihr bauet 2c. / Subj.: 1.p. the same as the 1.p. of the ind., with inflectional e throughout)

☞ Die Zeitwörter auf ...ieren [fr. ...er + dtsch. ...en] — nicht: einsilbige deutsche Stämme, wie zieren, schmieren — bleiben im *p. p.* ohne die Vorsilbe ge...

☞ The verbs ending in ...ieren [fr. ...er + dtsch. ...en] — but not the monosyllabic German stems, like zieren, schmieren — are formed without the prefix **ge**... in the *p. p.*

*) und **) wie S. XXXIV.

†) Der F Ausfall des e in der Befehlsendung der schwachen Zeitwörter wird durch ein Häkchen bezeichnet, zB.: leb' wohl!

*) and **) as on p. XXXIV.

†) The terminal F **e** cast off in the imperative of weak verbs is denoted by the apostrophe, as in: leb' wohl!

Abgesonderte Bemerkungen. {referring to the signs ① to ⑨⑨ in the Dictionary.} Detached Observations

Unregelmäßige Abwandlung. IV. Irregular Conjugation.

☞ ⑨④ u. ⑨⑤ sind starke, ⑨⑥ bis ⑨⑨ schwache unregelm. Zeitw. ☞ ⑨④ and ⑨⑤ are **strong**, ⑨⑥ to ⑨⑨ **weak** irregular verbs.

Number & root-vowels	Nennform / Infinitive	Gegenwart / Present Wirklichkeit / Indicative		Vergangenheit / Imperfect Indicative	Subjunctive	Befehlsform / Imperative sg. u. pl.	Present Part. / Past Participle
⑨④ ✱✱§ f. ⑦④ dreilautig	geh(e)n	sg. ich gehe, du gehst, er geht pl. wir geh(e)n, ihr geht*), sie geh(e)n		ich ging (ˊ) du gingst (ˊ)	ich ginge (ˊ˘) du gingest (ˊ˘)	geh(e)! (ˊ˘) geht! (ˊ)*)	gehend (ˊ˘) gegangen (˘ˊ˘)
f. ⑦⑤ f. zweilautig	steh(e)n	sg. ich stehe, du stehst, er steht pl. wir steh(e)n, ihr steht*), sie steh(e)n	Vorstellung: gleichlautend m. d. pl. des Ind. u. m. durchgehendem Biegungs=e, zB.: ich tue, du tuest ꝛc.; ich dürfe, könne, möge, müsse, wisse, wolle. Subjunctive: like the pl. of the indicative, and with inflectional e throughout.	ich stand (ˊ), südd.u.poet.stund	ich stünde (ˊ˘) bff. als: stände	steh(e)! (ˊ˘) steht! (ˊ)*)	stehend (ˊ˘) gestanden (˘ˊ˘)
⑨⑤ ✱✱§ zweilautig	tun [⑦⑨ f.]	sg. ich tue, du tust, er tut pl. wir tun, ihr tut, sie tun		ich tat, P tät du tat(e)st*)	ich täte (ˊ˘) du tätest (ˊ˘)	tu(e)! (ˊ˘) tut! (ˊ)*)	tuend (ˊ˘) getan (˘ˊ)
⑨⑥ ✱✱§ a	senden	sg. ich sende, du sendest, er sendet pl. wir senden, ihr sendet, sie senden		ich sandte (˘˘) ob. sendete (˘˘)	ich sendete (˘˘˘) du sendetest	sende! (˘˘)*) sendet! (˘˘)	gesandt (˘ˊ) ob. gesendet (˘ˊ˘)
b	nennen	sg. ich nenne, du nennst, er nennt pl. wir nennen, ihr nennt*), sie nennen		ich nannte (˘˘) du nanntest	ich nenn(e)te du nenn(e)test	nenne! (˘˘)*) nennt! (˘)*)	nennend (˘˘) genannt (˘ˊ)
	☞ ⑨⑥: Zeitwörter mit sog. Rückumlaut (a)				: Verbs with rückumlaut or restitution of **a**.		
⑨⑦ ✱✱§	bringen	sg. ich bringe, du bringst, er bringt pl. wir bringen, ihr bringt*), sie bringen		ich brachte (˘˘) du brachtest er brachte ꝛc.	ich brächte (˘˘) du brächtest er brächte ꝛc.	bring(e)! (ˊ˘)*) bringt! (ˊ)*)	bringend (˘˘) gebracht (˘ˊ)
	denken	sg. ich denke, du denkst, er denkt pl. wir denken, ihr denkt*), sie denken		ich dachte (˘˘) du dachtest	ich dächte (˘˘) du dächtest	denke! (˘˘)*) denkt! (˘)*)	denkend (˘˘) gedacht (˘ˊ)
	dünken	sg. mich (a. mir) ꝛc. (f. ⑥⑥ A₁) deucht pl. uns(acc.,a.dat.) ꝛc. (f. ⑥⑥ A₁) ob. dünkt		mich (mir) ꝛc. deuchte, dünkte	mich (mir) ꝛc. deuchte, dünkte	dünke! (˘˘)*) dünkt! (˘)*)	dünkend; gedeucht, gedünkt
	dürfen	sg. ich darf, du darfst, er darf pl. wir dürfen, ihr dürft*), sie dürfen		ich durfte (˘˘) du durftest	ich dürfte (˘˘) du dürftest	dürfe! (˘˘)*) dürft! (˘)*)	dürfend (˘˘) gedurft (˘ˊ)†
	können	sg. ich kann, du kannst, er kann pl. wir können, ihr könnt*), sie können		ich konnte (˘˘) du konntest	ich könnte (˘˘) du könntest	könne! (˘˘)*) könnt! (˘)*)	könnend (˘˘) gekonnt (˘ˊ)†
⑨⑧ ✱✱§	mögen	sg. ich mag, du magst, er mag pl. wir mögen, ihr mögt*), sie mögen		ich mochte (˘˘) du mochtest	ich möchte (˘˘) du möchtest	möge! (ˊ˘)*) mögt! (ˊ)*)	mögend (ˊ˘) gemocht (˘ˊ)†
	müssen	sg. ich muß, du mußt, er muß pl. wir müssen, ihr müßt*), sie müssen		ich mußte (˘˘) du mußtest	ich müßte (˘˘) du müßtest	müsse (˘˘)*) müßt (müsset)*)	müssend (˘˘) gemußt (˘ˊ)†
	wissen	sg. ich weiß (ˊ), du weißt, er weiß pl. wir wissen, ihr wißt*), sie wissen		ich wußte (˘˘) du wußtest	ich wüßte (˘˘) du wüßtest (˘˘)	wisse (˘˘) ob. wiß wißt (wisset)*)	wissend (˘˘) gewußt (˘ˊ)
	sollen	sg. ich soll, du sollst, er soll pl. wir sollen, ihr sollt*), sie sollen		ich sollte (˘˘) du solltest	ich sollte (˘˘) du solltest	solle! (˘˘)*) sollt! (˘)*)	sollend (˘˘) gesollt (˘ˊ)†
⑨⑨ ✱✱§	wollen	sg. ich will, du willst, er will pl. wir wollen, ihr wollt*), sie wollen		ich wollte (˘˘) du wolltest	ich wollte (˘˘) du wolltest	wolle (˘˘)*) wollt (˘)*)	wollend (˘˘) gewollt (˘ˊ)†

☞ Die unregelmäßigen Hilfszeitwörter **sein, haben, werden** f. unter ⑦⓪. ✱✱§ f. S. XXXIII. *) f. S. XXXIV u. XXXVI †.

☞ See in ⑦⓪ the irregular auxiliary verbs **sein, haben, werden**. ✱ §) see on p. XXXIII *) see on p. XXXIV *& XXXVI †.

---

†) An Stelle des *p.p.* der Hilfszeitwörter in ⑨⑧ u. ⑨⑨, mit Ausnahme von wissen, sowie der Zeitwörter: brauchen, lassen, machen, hören, sehen, helfen, heißen, lehren, lernen ist nach abhängigen Nennformen irrtümlich, aber durch den Sprachgebrauch eingebürgert, meist die Nennform getreten, zB.: er hätte es tun können (aber: er hat es gekonnt); ich habe sie singen hören (aber: hast du sie gehört?); sogar mit zweien solcher Nennformen: du hättest ihn nicht laufen lassen sollen, oder: sollen laufen lassen.

†) The auxiliary verbs in ⑨⑧ and ⑨⑨ except wissen, also the verbs: brauchen, lassen, machen, hören, sehen, helfen, heißen, lehren, lernen, though erroneously, yet by an established usage, require after dependent infinitives, instead of the *p. p.*, the infinitive. Thus: er hätte es tun können [but: er hat es gekonnt]; ich habe sie singen hören [but: hast du sie gehört?]; even with two such infinitives, as: du hättest ihn nicht laufen lassen sollen, or: sollen laufen lassen.

§) (e)t: Zeitwörter, deren Stamm auf einen S-Laut (f, ß, ff, z, tz, x) ausgeht, stoßen bei Verkürzung der 2. Prsn. sg. pres. (die impf.-Endung bleibt bei ihnen unverkürzt, zB. du aßest, nicht aßt) mit dem e zugleich s aus, zB. du lies(e)st d. i. liesest oder liest, du wäch(e)st, du reis(e)st, du reiß(e)st, du iss(e)st oder ißt, du läss(e)st oder läßt, du sitz(e)st.

(e)st: Die auf **sch** ausgehenden Stämme dagegen stoßen, wie alle übrigen, nur das e aus, z. B. du nasch(e)st, du wäsch(e)st, wie: du biet(e)st ꝛc. [ßt hat, zB. du brichst ꝛc.] **ßt** bedeutet, daß das betr. Zeitwort nur die verkürzte Form **est** desgl. nur die unverkürzte Form, zB. du siedest, er siedet.

§) [e]st **Verbs the stem of which terminates i.1 a hiss or an s-sound [f, ß, ff, z, tz, x]**, in contracting the 2. p. sg. pres. — the *impf.* does **not** contract its termination, as du aßest, not aßt — cast off the s together with the e, as in: du lies[e]st, i. e. liesest or liest, du wäch[es]t, du reis[e]st, du reiß[e]st, du iss[e]st or ißt, du läss[e]st or läßt, du sitz[e]st.

[e]st: The stems terminating in **sch**, like all other verbs, only elide the e, as du nasch[e]st, du wäsch[e]st, like: du biet[e]st, &c. [ßt, as du brichst, &c.] **ßt** signifies that the verb always uses the shorter form **est** signifies that it is never contracted, as du siedest.

| Abgesonderte Bemerkungen {beziehen sich auf die im Wörterbuche vorkommenden Zeichen ① bis ⑲} | Detached observations |

V.

**) Abwandlung der zusammengesetzten Zeitwörter.

Die echten zusammengesetzten Zeitwörter, in denen der Haupt= oder Hochton auf dem Zeitwort liegt, z. B. zerschlagen (⌣⌢⌣), sind untrennbar (*), die unechten, in denen er auf der Vorsilbe liegt, z. B. abschlagen (⌢⌣⌣), sind trennbar (**).

Die zs.=gesetzten Zeitwörter mit den Vorsilben be-, emp-, ent-, er-, ge-, ver-, zer- sind immer untrennbar; die mit den Vorsilben ab-, an-, auf-, aus-, bei-, dar-, ein-, fort-, gegen-, her(ab 2c.)-, hin(ab 2c.)-, mit-, nach-, nieder-, ob-, vor-, weg-, zu-, zurück-, zusammen- sind immer trennbar; die mit den Vorsilben durch-, hinter-, über-, um-, unter-, wieder- sind trennbar, wenn der Hauptton auf der Vorsilbe, dieselben nebst wider-, miß- und voll- untrennbar, wenn er auf dem Zeitwort liegt. Mit Haupt= oder Eigenschaftswörtern zs.=gesetzte oder von zs.=gesetzten Hauptwörtern abgeleitete Zeit=wörter nehmen, da sie den Ton auf dem voranstehenden Bestimmungswort haben, ein ge- im *p.p.* an, sind aber untrennbar und stets schwach (**), trennbar nur die mit Eigenschafts= oder Umstandswörtern zs.=gesetzten, welche nicht in einen einfachen Begriff verschmelzen, z. B. fehlschlagen (**).

Bei den untrennbaren Zeitwörtern behält die Vorsilbe ihre Stelle durch alle Formen, das *p.p.* wird ohne die Vorsilbe ge- gebildet und die *cj.* zu steht vor der Nennform, z. B. er umfängt (⌣⌢⌣), umfing (⌣⌢⌣) die Geliebte, hat sie umfangen (⌣⌣⌢⌣), hofft sie **zu** umfangen (⌣⌣⌢⌣).

In der Gegenwart, Vergangenheit und Befehlsform der trennbaren Zeitwörter folgt in Hauptsätzen die vom Zeitwort abgetrennte Vorsilbe nach; in Nebensätzen bleibt sie ungetrennt vor dem Zeitwort, z. B. ich fange **an**, ich fing **an**; fang(e) **an**!; daß ich zu weinen anfange, anfing (P und bisw. *poet. auch:* daß ich **an** zu weinen fange, fing). Die Vorsilbe ge- des *p.p.* u. die *cj.* zu beim *inf.* werden zwischengeschoben, z. B. er hat angefangen; er wünscht anzufangen.

**) Conjugation of compound verbs.

True compound verbs in which the primary accent rests on the verb, e.g. zerschlagen [⌣⌢⌣], are *inseparable* [*]; loose compounds in which the primary accent rests on the prefix, as abschlagen [⌢⌣⌣], are *separable* [**].

The compound verbs with the prefixes be-, emp-, ent-, er-, ge-, ver-, zer- are always *inseparable*; those with the prefixes ab-, an-, auf-, aus-, bei-, dar-, ein-, fort-, gegen-, her[ab 2c.]-, hin[ab 2c.]-, mit-, nach-, nieder-, ob-, vor-, weg-, zu-, zurück-, zusammen- are always *separable*; those with the prefixes durch-, hinter-, über-, um-, unter-, wieder- are *separable*, when the primary accent is on the prefix, the same, together with wider-, miß- and voll, *inseparable*, when it is on the verb.

Verbs either compounded with *substantives* and *adjectives*, or derived from compound nouns, being accented on the prefixed word, have ge- in the *p. p.*, but are *inseparable* and always weak [**]; only those compounded with adjectives or adverbs of quality are *separable* unless they are merged into one simple notion, as in fehlschlagen [**].

In all *inseparable* verbs, the prefix keeps its place throughout; the *p.p.* being formed without the prefix ge-, and the *cj.* zu preceding the *inf.*, as: er umfängt [⌣⌢⌣], umfing [⌣⌢⌣] die Geliebte, hat sie umfangen [⌣⌣⌢⌣], hofft sie **zu** umfangen [⌣⌣⌢⌣].

In the *pres.*, *impf.*, and *imper.* of *separable* verbs, the prefix, in a principal sentence, is detached from the verb and follows it; in a subordinate clause it retains its place before the verb, as in: ich fange **an**, ich fing **an**; fang(e) **an**!; daß ich zu weinen anfange, anfing [P and ⸺ *poet.* also: daß ich **an** zu weinen fange, fing]. The prefix ge- of the *p.p.* and the *cj.* zu with the *inf.* are inserted between the prefix and the root, as: er hat angefangen; er wünscht anzufangen.

*) zer-schla′gen (⌣⌢⌣) zu zerschla′gen	*sg.* ich zerschla′ge, du zerschlägst, er zerschlägt *pl.* wir zerschlagen, ihr zerschlagt, sie zerschlagen ☞ ⑤b*	ich zerschlu′g (⌣⌢)	zerschla′gen (ohne ge-)
**) a′b-schlagen (⌢⌣⌣) a′bzuschlagen (⌢⌣⌣⌣)	*sg.* ich schlage ab, du schlägst ab, er schlägt ab *pl.* wir schlagen ab, ihr schlagt ab, sie schlagen ab ☞ ⑤b**	ich schlug a′b (⌢⌣⌢)	a′bgeschlagen (⌢⌣⌣⌣)
/) a′n-erkennen a′nzuerkennen	ich erkenne an, du erkennst an, er erkennt an 2c. ⁒ ich anerkenne, du anerkennst, er anerkennt 2c.	ich erkannte an ⁒ich anerkannte	a′nerkannt (ohne -ge-)
***) ra′tschlagen (⌢⌣⌣) zu ra′tschlagen	*sg.* ich ra′tschlage, du ratschlagst, er ratschlagt *pl.* wir ratschlagen, ihr ratschlagt, sie ratschlagen ☞ ⑧***	ich ra′tschlagte (⌢⌣⌣)	gera′tschlagt (⌣⌢⌣⌣)

H. Maße, Gewichte, Münzen.

(Maß= und Gewichtsordnung vom 17. 8. 1868 mit den Abänderungsgesetzen vom 11. 7. 1884 und 26. 4. 1893.)

Die Abkürzungen sind reichsdeutsch in Antiqua, österreichisch in *Kursiv* und, im Gegensatz zum Englischen, sämtlich ohne Punkt.

Die Zehnerbrüche sind nach englischer Weise geschrieben: hoher Punkt statt Komma und keine Null davor.

*** im Deutschen Reich, in Deutsch=Österreich und in der Schweiz gültig; ** nur in Deutsch=Österreich gültig; * nur in der Schweiz gültig.

H. Measures, Weights, Coins.

[Regulations concerning measures and weights of Aug. 17th 1868, amended by the Acts of July 11th 1884 and April 26th 1893]

The abbreviations used in the G. Empire are printed in roman, those of Austria in italics, and unlike the English all without dots.

The decimals are written in the E. fashion with a dot, instead of the comma, and no zero before it.

*** used in the G. Empire, in German Austria, and Switzerland; ** used only in German Austria; * used only in Switzerland.

I. Maße. Measures.

A. Längenmaße. Linear Measures.

☞ Deutsch: m, m = **Meter** ($^1/_{10\,000\,000}$ des Erdmeridianquadranten); dcm, dm = **Dezimeter**; cm, cm = **Zentimeter**; mm, mm = **Millimeter**; μ = **Mikron**; dkm, dkm = **Dekameter**; hm, hm = **Hektometer**; km, km = **Kilometer**; μm = **Myriameter**.

(Engl.: 1 statutory [stat.] mile [m.] zu 8 furlongs [fur.] zu 10 chains zu 4 poles, perches od. rods [= $5^1/_2$ yards] zu 25 links; 1 yd. zu 3 feet [ft.] zu 12 inches [in.] zu 12 lines [l.].

1 m, m ***	. . . . . .	1 yd.	0 ft.	3 in.	4·4495 l.
1 dcm, dm ** = $^1/_{10}$ m	. . . .			3″	11·2449 l.
1 cm, cm *** = $^1/_{100}$ m	. . .				4·7245 l.
1 mm, mm *** = $^1/_{1000}$ m	. .				·4724 l.
1 μ ꓞ = $^1/_{1000}$ mm	. . . .				·0005 l.
1 dkm, dkm ** = 10 m	. . . .	10	″	2′ 9″	8·4948 l.
1 hm, hm ** † = 100 m	. . .	109	″	1′ 1″	8·9485 l.
1 km, km *** = 1000 m . . 1093	″	1′ 10″			9·4802 l.

(1 km ist nahezu $^5/_8$ „Englische" Meilen: is nearly $^5/_8$ of a mile: ·6214 m.); 1 μm . . . = 10 km: 6,2138 m. = 6 m. 376 yd. 1′ 0″ ·9446 l. — † Zoll, Fuß, Elle, Klafter, Rute, Meile ꝛc.

B. Flächenmaße. Superficial Measures.

☞ Deutsch: qm, m^2 = **Quadratmeter**; qdcm, dm^2 = **Quadratdezimeter** = $^1/_{100}$ qm; qcm, cm^2 = **Quadratzentimeter** = $^1/_{10\,000}$ qm; qmm, mm^2 = **Quadratmillimeter** = $^1/_{1\,000\,000}$ qm; a, a = **Ar**; ha, ha = **Hektar** = 100 a; qkm, km^2 = **Quadratkilometer**; μm^2 = **Quadratmyriameter** = 100 km^2.

↘ 1 Dekar = 10 a, 1 Deziar = $^1/_{10}$ a, 1 Zentiar = $^1/_{100}$ a.

(Engl.: 1 square mile [sq. m.] zu 640 acres [a.] zu 4 roods [ro.] zu 40 sq. rods zu 30·25 sq. yd. zu 9 sq. ft. zu 144 sq. in. zu 144 sq. l.)

1 qm, m^2 *** . .	1 sq. yd.	1 sq. ft.	110 sq. in.	8·5111 sq. l.
1 qd(c)m, dm^2 **	. . . .		15	„	72·0806 „
1 qcm, cm^2 ***	. . . .				22·3209 „
1 qmm, mm^2 ***	. . . .				·2232 „
1 a, a *** . . .	119 sq. yd.	5 sq. ft.	61 sq. in.	131·1114 „
1 ha, ha *** . .		2 a.	1 ro.	35 sq. rods	21·5826 sq. yd.
1 qkm, km^2 ***	. . .	·247 „	1 „	18 „	33·7612 „
1 μm^2 ***	38 sq. m.	416 „	3 „	37 „	16·8676 „

† Quadrat-rute, -fuß, -zoll, Morgen ꝛc.

C. Körper-, Raum- oder Kubikmaße. Cubic [or Solid] Measures.

☞ Deutsch: cbm, m^3 = **Kubikmeter**, auch Raummeter (rm), Festmeter (fm) oder Ster genannt.(↘ 1 **Hektoster** = 100 cbm, 1 **Dekaster** * = 10 cbm, 1 **Dezister** = $^1/_{10}$ cbm); cd(c)m, dm^3 = **Kubikdezimeter** = $^1/_{1000}$ m^3; ccm, cm^3 = **Kubikzentimeter** = $^1/_{1\,000\,000}$ cbm; cmm, mm^3 = **Kubikmillimeter** = $^1/_{1\,000\,000\,000}$ cbm; cbkm, km^3 = **Kubikkilometer**.

(Engl.: 1 cubic yard [c(ub). yd.] zu 27 cubic feet [c(ub). ft.] zu 1728 cubic inches [c(ub). in.]; 1 ton [t.] ⚓ = 100 c(ub). ft.; Am. 1 foot of board measure [ft. B. M.] = $^1/_{12}$ c(ub). ft.)

1 cbm, m^3 ***	{ 1 c(ub). yd. 8 c(ub). ft.	547·0516 c(ub). in.
	(Holz) Am.	423·7990 ft. B. M.
1 cdm, dm^3 **		61·0271 c(ub). in.
1 ccm, cm^3 **		105·4547 c(ub). l.
1 cmm, mm^3 ***		·1055 c(ub). l.
1 cbkm, km^3 ***	1 308 021 443 c(ub). yd. 14 c(ub). ft. 49·6155 c(ub). in.

† Kubikzoll, -fuß ꝛc.

D. Hohlmaße. Measures of Capacity.

☞ Deutsch: l, l = **Liter**; dcl, dl = **Deziliter**; cl, cl = **Zentiliter**; dkl, dkl = **Dekaliter**; hl, hl = **Hektoliter**; kl, kl = **Kiloliter**.

(Engl.: 1 quarter [qr.] zu 8 bushels [bu(s).] zu 4 pecks [pk.] zu 2 gallons [gal.] zu 4 quarts [qt.] zu 2 pints [pt.] zu 4 gills.)

1 l, l *** (= 1 cdcm)	. . . .	·2201 gal.	= 1 pt.	3·0431 gills.
1 dcl, dl ** = $^1/_{10}$ l	. .				·7043
1 cl, cl ** = $^1/_{100}$ l	. .				·0704
1 dkl, dkl * = 10 l	. .		2 gal.	1 pt.	2·4309
1 hl, hl *** = 100 l	. . .		22 „	0 „	·3090
1 kl, kl *** = 1000 l	. .		220 „	0 „	3·0905

† Becher, Flasche, Immi *, Kanne, Maß, Metze, Nößel, Ort, Pott, Quart, Quartier, Scheffel, Schoppen, Seidel, Seitel, Vierling, Wispel ꝛc.

☞ Getreide wird im Handel gewogen, gemessen nur zur Bestimmung der Qualität. | Grain, in commercial dealings, is generally weighed; it is measured only for the purpose of testing its quality.

II. Gewichte. Weights.

☞ Deutsch: kg, kg = **Kilogramm** (P Kilo) = 1000 g; g, g = **Gramm** = 1 ccm Wasser bei 4°C; dcg, dg = **Dezigramm** = $^1/_{10}$ g; cg, cg = **Zentigramm** = $^1/_{100}$ g; mg, mg = **Milligramm** = $^1/_{1000}$ g; dkg, dkg = **Dekagramm** oder Neulot = 10 g; hg, hg = **Hektogramm** = 100 g; μg = **Myriagramm** = 10 kg; dz od. q [Quintal] = **Doppel-** (od. metrischer) **Zentner** = 100 kg; t, t = **Tonne** = 1000 kg. 1 ton [t.] zu 20 hundredweights [cwt.] zu 8 stone [st.] zu 14 pounds [lb.] — oder zu 4 quarters [qr.] zu 28 lb.; 1 pound avoirdupois [lb. avdp.] = 7000 grains [gr.] troy; zu 16 ounces [oz.] zu 16 drams [dr.] zu $27^{11}/_{32}$ grains troy; 1 lb. troy (= 5760 gr.) zu 12 oz. zu 20 penny-weights [dwt.] zu 24 gr.

☯ 1 Last (Salz, Kalk) = 12 Tonnen.

1 kg, kg ***	. . . 2·204621028 lb. avdp. or	15432·349 gr. troy
1 g, g ***	. . . .	15·4323 gr.
1 dcg, dg ***	. . . .	1·5432 „
1 cg, cg ***	. . . .	·1543 „ } troy
1 mg, mg ***	. . . .	·0154 „
1 dkg, dkg **	. . . .	154·3235 „
1 hg, hg *	. . . .	1543·2349 „
1 μg	. . 22·0462 lb. avdp. or	154323·49 „
1 dz., q	{ od. 1 cwt. (= 112 lb.) 12 lb. 7 oz., &c.
	220·4621 lb. avdp. or 154323·49 „
	od. 1 ton (of shipping) 2 centals [ctl.] 4·6210 lb.
1 t, t	{ ·98 420 513 t. od. 19 cwt. 2 qr. 1 st. 6·6195 lb. } avdp.

🞰 1 Lori Steinkohle = 100 Ztr., böhmische Braunkohle = 200 Ztr.

† Zentner (Ztr.) = 100 Pfund (Pfd.), Quentchen, Lot, ꝛc.

III. Stückgüter, Zähl- und Zeitmaße. Piece Goods, Measures of Number and Time.

Abkürzungen: G. [Garn, yarn], H. [(Stab- und Faß-)Holz, (staves- and cask-)wood], K. [Kohlen, coals], Kw. [Kurzwaren, hardware], L. [Leder, leather], Lw. [Leinwand, linen], P. [Papier, paper], Pr. [Produktenhandel, trade in inland produce], R. L. [Rauchwaren und Leder, furs and leather], T. Lw. [Tuche und Leinwand, cloth and linen].

1 **Ballen** (P.) † (bis 1877) =	Schreibpapier 4800 sheets	1 (Neu-)**Buch** (P.) = 10 Hefte (zu 10 Bogen)	100 sheets
$^1/_{15}$ Pack = 10 Ries	Druckpapier . 5000 „	1 † **Buch** (P.) = 24 Schreib-	} papierbogen { 24 „
1 „ (T.) † = 12 Tücher (zu 32 Ellen)	12 cloths	(bis 1877) od. 25 Druck-	25 „
1 „ (L.) ‡ Zufteleder = 20 Rollen	120 pieces	1 **Bund** (G.) † = 20 Lopp od. Stück	18000 threads
1 **Band** (Pr.) Fische = $^1/_6$ Rolle	30 fishes	1 **Buschen** (L.) öft. = 10 Felle	10 hides
1 **Barchet** (T.) † südd. = $^1/_{45}$ Fardel 24 (auch 22) ells		1 **Decher** (R. L.) = $^1/_4$ Zimmer	10 pieces

1 Dutzend (Kw., Pr.)	12 pieces		1 Rolle (R. L.) Pergament (in London)	60 hides
englisches großes D.	13 "		1 Saum † (T.) = 22 Tücher (zu 32 Brabanter Ellen)	22 cloths
1 Fardel (T.) † = 45 Barchet	45 "		1 Schneller (G.) Baumwollgarn = 7 Gebinde	560 threads
1 Gebind(e) (G.) a) Baumwollgarn = 80 Fäden von 1½ Yards	80 threads		1 Schock (H. †, Lw.) = 3 Steigen (s. d.) (Pr.) = 4 Mandeln od. 6 Zehner	60 pieces
b) Leinengarn = 120 Fäden von 2½ Yards	120 "		1 Spindel (G.) a) Baumwollgarn = 18 Schneller b) Leinengarn = 2 Stück	10080 threads 5760 "
c) † = 9, 10, 18, 20, 40, 90 Fäden von 2—3 m	9—90 "		1 Steige, Stiege (H.; Pr. getrocknete Fische ꝛc.; Lw. †) = 20 Stück (Lw.: Ellen)	20 pieces
1 Gros (Kw.), kleines = 12 Dtz.	144 pieces		1 Strähne (G.) a) Leinengarn = 12 Gebinde b) Baumwollgarn = Schneller (s. d.)	1440 threads 560 "
großes = 12 kleine Gros	1728 "		c) † = 2 od. 3 Zaspel	180—2400 "
1 Großhundert (Kw.)	120 "		1 Stroh (Pr.) Heringe = 6 Wall	480 herrings
1 Großtausend (Kw., H.)	1200 "		1 Stück (G.) Leinengarn = 2 Strähnen	2880 threads
1 Heft (P.) = 10 Bogen	10 sheets		† = Lopf, Lopp, † (T. Lw.) =	900 "
1 Hundert (Kw.) od. Neugros = 10 Zehner	100 pieces		22 Tücher zu 32 Ellen	22 cloths
(R. L.)	104 "		1 Tausend (Kw.) = 10 Hundert	1000 pieces
1 Kiepe (Pr.) getrocknete Fische = 4 Steigen	80 fishes		1 Tonne (Pr.) Heringe	etwa 800 herrings
1 Lage (P.) = ½ Heft	5 sheets		1 Tuch (T.) s. Stück, Ballen, Saum; (Lw.) † = 50 Ellen	
1 Last (Pr.) Heringe = 12 Tonnen (s. d.)	9600 herrings		1 Wall (Pr.) Heringe	80 "
1 Lopf, Lopp od. Stück (G.) = 10 Gebind	900 threads		1 Zaspel †, Haspel (G.) = 10 od. 20 Gebind	90—800 threads
1 Mandel (Pr.) = 15 Stück, Lw. † = 15 Ellen	15 pieces		1 Zehner (Kw., Pr.) (s. Schock, Hundert)	10 pieces
1 Bauern-Mandel (Pr.)	16 "		1 Zimmer (R. L.) = 4 Decher (zu 10 Stück)	40 "
1 Pack † (P.) = 15 Ballen { Schreibpapier Druckpapier	72000 sheets 75000 "		1 Sonnenjahr (solar year) zu 365 24219879 mittleren Sonnentagen (mean solar days) zu 24 Stunden (hours) zu 60 Minuten (minutes) zu 60 Sekunden (seconds). Auch 1 Jahr = 12 Monate (months) = 52 Wochen (weeks) zu 7 Tagen (days). 1 Schaltjahr (leap year) = 366 Tage.	
† (T. Lw.) = 10 Stück (s. d.)	220 cloths			
1 Riem (P.) Packpapier = 2 † Ries 960 od. 1000 sheets				
1 (Neu=)Ries (P.) = 10 (Neu=)Buch	1000 "			
1 † Ries (P.) = 20 (†) Buch = 480 od. 500 "				
1 Ring (H.) = 4 Schock	240 pieces			
1 Rolle (Pr.) Stockfische	180 fishes			
(R. L.) Zuchten = 6 Felle	6 hides			

IV. Münzen. Coins.

A. Deutsche Reichswährung.

1. Banknoten:

5=, 10=, 50=, 100=, 500=, 1000=Rentenmark
10=, 20=, 50=, 100=, 1000=Reichsmark

2. Münzen:

Gold: 20=, 10=Mark
Silber: 5=, 2=Reichsmark
Nickel: 1=Reichsmark
      50=Reichspfennig
Aluminium=
  bronze: 10=, 5=Rentenpfennig
      10=, 5=Reichspfennig
Kupfer: 2=, 1=Pfennig
      2=, 1=Rentenpfennig
      2=, 1=Reichspfennig

B. Österreichische Währung.

1. Noten im Umlauf:

10=, 20=, 50=, 100=, 1000=Schilling

2. Münzen:

Gold: 25=, 100=Schilling
Silber: 2=, 5=Schilling
Kupfernickel: 1=Schilling
      50=Groschen
      1000=Kronen
      10=Groschen
      5=Groschen
Bronze: 100=, 200=Kronen
      1=, 2=Groschen

C. Schweizer Währung.

1. Noten im Umlauf:

5=, 20=, 50=, 100=, 500=, 1000=Franken

2. Münzen im Umlauf:

Gold: 10=, 20=, 100=Franken
Silber: ½=, 1=, 2=, 5=Franken
Nickel: 5=, 10=, 20=Rappen
Kupfernickel: 5=, 10=Rappen
Bronze: 1=, 2=Rappen

A

A, a (¹, f. S. XI) *n, inv.* (a. ⓢ) **1.** (Buchstabe) A, a. — **2.** *fig.* (Anfang; *ant.* 3, grch. Ω) (first) beginning; von A bis 3 from beginning to end, from first to last; Sprichw. wer A sagt, muß auch B sagen you can't say A without saying (F without you say) B, F in for a penny, in for a pound; *bibl.* das A und das Ω (Gott, f. Offenb. 1, 8 2c.; a. *fig.*) Alpha and Omega, the beginning and the ending.

A, a ♩ *n, inv.* 1a; A-Dur A major; A-Moll A minor; dieses Stück geht aus A-Dur ... is in A major. [Wien.

A mint. (auf dtsch., öst. Münzen) = Berlin,

a, a ⓢ (¹) [fr. *à*, it. *a*] *prp.* at (the rate of) //; a 2 Mark at (ⓢ a. @) two shillings each or a piece or a head; a 3 Prozent at three per cent.; a Konto (mit *gen.*) for the (or on) account of //; a vista [it.] at sight.

a (öft. *a*) *abbr.* = Ar.

a. *abbr.* = **1.** ♀ am, an der on (the), z.B. Frankfurt a. M. (bff. als a/M.) = F. am Main. — **2.** alt old. [the year.

A. *abbr.* = a'nno [lt. „im Jahre "] in

A. ob. a. ⓢ *abbr.* = akzeptiert (auf Wechseln) accepted. [*n, inv.* (a. ⓢ) modified a.]

Ä, ä (¹, f. S. X, XXIV**, XXX* u. XXXIII)]

ä! *int.* **1.** (¹) (Weinen) ah! (*SH.* heigh-ho). — **2.** (♪) (Ekel) fie!

aa (¹, f. S. XI) double a.

A-a F (♪¹) *n* ⓢ (o. pl.) *v.* Kindern: Aa machen to do a motion.

Aachen ♀ (¹♪♪) [„zu den) ~" ob. (Mineral-) Wäffern: lt. *A'quis(gra'ni)*] *npr/n.* Ⓓa. Aix-la-Chapelle, a. Aachen. — **Aachener** (¹♪♪♪) I *m* ⓢ, ~*in f* ⓢ inhabitant of A.... — II *a., inv.* of A... [machen.]

a-a-en F (♪¹♪) *v/n.* (h.) ⓢ = Aa (f. ds)

Aal (¹; *pl.* ~e: *Hom.* Ahle) [ahd.] *m* ⓤ (♪①) c. **1.** *ichth.* eel; kleiner ~ grig; *fig.* glatt (a. schlüpfrig) wie ein ~: a) (sehr listig) = ⓠglatt, b) (schwer zu fangen) elusive; er windet sich wie ein ~ he wriggles like an eel, weit S. F he's a slippery customer. — **2.** ⓢ (im Tuch) crease in the cloth.

aal-ähnlich (¹♪...; *Hom.* A(h)l=...; ⓠartig *a.* eel-like, eel-shaped; =**beere** ♀ *f* ⓢ f. Albeere; =**brut** *f* eel-fry, =fare; =**butt(e** *f*) *m, ichth.* = Hundszunge c.

aalen (¹♪) *v/n.* (h.) ⓢ to catch eels, to fish for eels.

Aal-fang (¹♪...) *m* ⓢ: a) eel-fishing; season for catching eels; b) ⓢ (Kasten) eelery; =**fänger** *m* eeler, eelman; ⓠförmig *a.* ⓢ anguilliform; =**flöße** ⓢ *f* = puppe; =**gabel** ⓢ *f* eel-spear, -prong; ⓠglatt *a.* (as) slippery as an eel; =**harpune** ⓢ *f* = Elger; =**haut** *f* eel-skin; =**molch** *m, zo. Am.* Neger-sl. Congo snake (*Amphiu'ma means*); =**mutter** *f, ichth.* eel-mother, ⚥ viviparous blenny (*Zo'arces vivi'parus*); =**puppe** ⓢ *f* eel-bob; =**quappe** *f, ichth.* a) = mutter; b) = raupe; =**quast(e** *f*) *m* ⓢ = puppe; =**raupe** *f, ichth.* burbot (*Lota vulga'ris*); =**reuse** ⓢ *f* eel-basket; =**stecher** *m* = gabel; =**stein** *m, min.* eelstone; =**strich** *m* dark (or light) stripe (along the back of a horse or cow); =**tierchen** *n, zo.* vinegar-eel (*Angui'llula ace'ti*); =**wehr** ⓢ *n* eel-weir.

a. a. O. *abbr.* = am angeführten Orte at the place quoted, *abbr.* l(oc). c(it). (f. l. c.). [sail.]

Aap ⚓ (¹) [ndb.: Affe] *m* ⓢ mizzen stay-

Aar (¹; *Hom.* Ar) [ahd.: erne: grch. *o'rnith*-] *m* ⓢc. u. ⓢ *poet.* (Adler) eagle.

Aar-gau ⓢ (¹♪...) [Mare, schwz. Fl.] *npr/m.* (♪ *n*) ⓓd. u. α. A(a)rgau; ~*er(in f* ⓢ) *m* ⓢ (¹♪♪♪) u. Ⓠisch (¹♪♪) *a.* ⓢ Argovian.

Aar-kirsche ♀ (¹...) *f* ⓢ = Elsbeere.

Aaron (¹♪♪; *Hom.* Aron) [hebr.] *npr/m.* Ⓓα. Aaron; ~**s-stab** (¹♪♪♪♪) *m* ⓢ = Aron.

Aar-weih(e *f*) *m* ⓢ *orn.* hen-harrier, kite.

Aas (¹; *Hom.* aß) [ahd.: effen] *n* ⓓa., a. ⓓa., †*pl.* ~ **1.** (Tierleiche) carcass, Abdeckerei: carrion; (Abfall beim Schlachten 2c.) offal; Sprichw. (bibl.) wo ein ~ ift, da sammeln sich die Adler (Matth. 24, 28) wheresoever the carcass is, there will the eagles be gathered together. — **2.** (Köder) *hunt.* u. Fischerei: bait, lure. — ⓢ Gerberei: (v. der Haut abgeschabtes Fleisch) fleshings *pl.* — **4.** P (Schimpfwort) beast.

Aas-anger (¹♪...) *m* ⓢ knacker's yard; =**blume** ♀ *f* carrion-flower (*Stape'lia, &c.*); ⓠfreffend *a.* ⓢ feeding on carrion, v. Käfern: ⚥ necrophagous; =**geier** *m, orn.* carrion-kite, carrion-vulture (*Catha'rtes percno'pterus*); =**geruch** *m* cadaverous smell or odour; =**grube** *f* carrion-pit.

aashaft (¹♪), **aasig** (¹♪) *a.* ⓢ **1.** carrion-like. — **2.** F *fig.* villainous, beastly.

Aas-jäger (¹♪...) *m* ⓢ *hunt.* pot-hunter; =**käfer** *m. ent.* carrion-beetle; =**krähe** *f, orn.* carrion-, gor-crow (*Co'rvus coro'ne*); =**seite** *f* fleshside.

aaßen (¹♪) *v/n.* (h.) ⓢ *hunt.* (fressen) to browse = aasen 2.

Aas-tier (¹♪) *n* ⓢ (Hyäne, Geier 2c.) beast of prey (which feeds on carrion).

A. B. öst. *abbr.* = Augsburger (f. ds) Bekenntnis.

ab (♪) [ahd.: of(f)] I *adv.* **1.** (Raum: a) Hut ab! hat(s) off!, off with your hat(s)!; der Knopf ift ab(=gegangen) the button is (or has come) off; ⚔ Gewehr ab! order arms!; b) (Entfernung) weit **vom** Wege **ab** a long way off the road; von da ab thence; c) (fort, verloren) ab fein to be done for, to be over. — **2.** (Zeit) **von jetzt ab** from now, from this day forward, henceforth; von da ab from that time (forward), thenceforth. — **3.** (abziehend) von fünf drei ab from five take three; ⓢ ab Diskonto less discount; ab an Unkosten less (or deducting) expenses or charges. — **4. auf und ab** f. auf II. — **5. ab und an** off and on; **ab und zu** now and then; ab und zu geh(e)n to go backwards and forwards. — **6.** *abbr.* (Bühnenweisung) = geht ab *exit*, geh(e)n ab *exeunt*; nach verschiedenen Seiten ab *exeunt severally,* f. auch II b 1. — **7.** in Zffgn f. her ⓠ, hin ⓠ; berg ⓠ, trepp ⓠ. — **II** *prp.* mit *dat.* 8. a) †(vgl. abhanden) ob. fübb. = von; b) [lt.?] ⓢ ab Berlin (to be) delivered yours; ab dort (to be) delivered at yours; ab Speicher ex(-)warehouse; ⚐ ab dep. [= departs, departure]; ab Brüssel from Brussels.

☞ ab-... (ⓢ...) Vorsilbe in Zffgn: I mit *v.* immer trennbar (**), f. S. XXXVIII (*ant.* an=..., auf=...) bz. ~: **1.** ⬋ Richtung von oben nach unten, z.B. abstürzen to tumble (or fall) down. — **2.** mst: Entfernen, Trennen, z.B. abgehen to walk off. — **3.** Verminderung, z.B. von et. abrechnen to deduct from a thing. — **4.** Verschlechterung *v.* Sachen, Erschöpfung von lebenden Wesen, z.B. sich die Schuhe ablaufen to wear out or down. — **5.** Verneinung, z.B. abbefehlen to countermand. — **6.** Töten, Vernichten, z.B. *hunt.* abfangen

---

♩ Musik; ⚥ Wissenschaft; ♀ Pflanze; ♁ Geographie; ⓢ Technik; ⚒ Bergbau; ⚔ Militär; ⚓ Marine; ⓢ Handel; ✉ Post; ⚐ Eisenbahn.

[abaasen] — 2 — [abbeten]

to despatch (with the hunting-knife). — 7. Nachbildung, ¿B. abschreiben to copy (by writing). — 8. Aneignung, ¿B. e-m et. abschmeicheln to coax a th. out of a p., to coax a p. out of a th. — 9. Vollenden, ¿B. abrechnen to settle (an account). — II mit a. u. s. 10. Verneinung, ¿B. abgeschmackt without taste, insipid; Abgeschmacktheit insipidity.

ab-aasen ⊕ (ᵟᵛᵛ) v/a. ⊛** = aasen 3.

ab-ackern (ᵟᵛᵛ) I v/a. ⊛a** 1. to separate by ploughing; e-m et. v. ſ-m Felde ⁎ to encroach on a p.'s... in ploughing. — 2. to plough completely. — II. ∼ n ⊛ u. **Ab-ackerung** f ⊛ encroachment.

Abaka ♀ (ᵛᵛ) f ⊛, m ⊛ = Manilahanf.

Abakus ⊕ (ᵛᵛ) [grch.] m, inv. (Alt.: Rechenbrett; arch. Kapitellplatte e-r Säule) abacus.

Abälard ⊕ npr/m. ⊛a. (fr. Scholastiker, 1079–1142) Abelard, (fr.) Abélard.

Ab-alienation ⚆ (ᵟ–(ᵛ)–⁺ᶠ⁽ᵛ⁾¹) [lt. äliën-] f ⊛ (Veräußerung) alienation.

ab-änderlich (ᵟᵛᵛ) a. ⊛ capable of alteration, alterable. [ility.]

Ab-änderlichkeit (ᵟᵛᵛᵛ) f ⊛ alterab-∫

ab-ändern (ᵟᵛᵛ) ⊛a** I v/a. 1. (et. an et. ändern) to alter (or modify) a th. in a th. — 2. (bessernd ändern) to correct, mend, rectify; e-n Gesetz-entwurf ⁎ to amend a bill. — 3. (umwandeln) to renovate, to recast. — II v/n. (ſn) 4. ♩ ♩ u. zo. to vary, to form a (new) variety.

Ab-änderung (ᵟᵛᵛ) f ⊛ (das Abändern) alteration; ∼en treffen to make changes; beſchränkte ∼ modification; beſſernde ∼ improvement, ſtärker: reform; (Ab-artung) variety, variation; parl. e-e ∼ beantragen to move an amendment to.

Ab-änderungs-antrag (⁵...) m ⊛ parl. amendment (to a bill or motion); e-n ∼ ſtellen to put (or move) an amendment; ⁼plan m scheme of improvement; ⁼vorſchlag m = ⁼antrag.

Abandon ⊛ (ä-ba-dą') [ſ... dtſch Bann] m ⊛ abandonment, d..... tion.

abandonnieren ⊛ (ᵛᵇᵈᵛᵛ) [fr.] v/a. ⊛ (verlaſſen) to abandon, to relinquish (premises, &c.), to quit.

ab-ängſten ⇗ (ᵟᵛᵛ) ⊛**, mſt **ab-ängſtigen** (ᵟᵛᵛ) ⊛** I v/a. to cause anxiety to a p.; e-m et. ⁎ to worry a th. out of a p. (or a p. into a th.). — II ſich ⁎ v/refl. to be (or live) in great anxiety (or mortal dread) about a th. — III ∼ n ⊛ u. **Ab-ängſt(ig)ung** f ⊛ anxiety (about a th.), ſtärker: (intense) anguish, agony. [to unmoor.]

ab-ankern ⇗ (ᵟᵛᵛ) v/a. u. v/n. (ſn) ⊛a**∫

ab-arbeiten (ᵟᵛᵛ) ⊛** I v/a. 1. (wegſchaffen) to work off; das Gröbſte von et. ⁎ to rough-work, mit der Art, dem Meißel: to chip, to rough-hew. — 2. (beenden) to complete or work out (one's task). — 3. (ermüden) to overtask, to overwork, F to work (or drive) one's men like slaves; Schul⁼sl: to fag; ab⁼gearbeitet worn out, jaded, fagged; abgearbeitetes Pferd jade, F crock. — 4. e-e Schuld ⁎ to pay (or clear) off ... by work or labour; ♩ ſ-e Überfahrt ⁎ to work one's passage out. — 5. ♩ ein Schiff vom Strande ⁎ to get a ship off or afloat, to float (or push) a vessel off the beach, to claw off the shore.

— II ſich ⁎ v/refl. 6. to overwork o.s., to toil hard, to drudge (one's life out), to sweat; vom Pferde ꝛc. auch: to strain; ſich (dat.) die Finger ⁎ to work the flesh off one's bones. — 7. ♩ to get clear of (a ship, &c.), to clear (a reef, &c.). — III ∼ n ⊛ u. **Ab-arbeitung** f ⊛ (vgl. I) 8. (ſ. 1) working off, rough-work(ing). — 9. (ſ. 2) completion of. — 10. (ſ. 4) clearing off by work. — 11. ♩ (ſ. 5) floating of.

ab-ärgern (ᵟᵛᵛ) v/a. u. v/refl. ⊛a** to vex, to mortify; ſtärker: to worry the life out of; ſich ⁎ to be or feel (greatly) vexed.

Ab-art (ᵟᶠ) f ⊛ 1. (Spielart) variety. — 2. † (Entartetes) degenerate species.

ab-arten (ᵟᶠᵛ) I v/n. (ſn) ⊛** (von der Art abweichen) to vary, to form a (new) variety. — II ∼ n ⊛ = Abartung.

Ab-artikulation ⚆ (ᵟᵛᵛᵛ⁻ᵗᶠ⁽ᵛ⁾¹) [neu=lt.] f ⊛ anat. (Gelenk) ≀ abarticulation.

Ab-artung (ᵟᶠᵛ) f ⊛ variety, variation.

ab-äſchern (ᵟᵛᵛ) ⊛a** I v/a. (mit Aſche reiben) to rub with ashes; Fiſche ⁎ (abſchleimen) to clean ... — II F ſich ⁎ v/refl. fig. (ermüden) to drudge, F to slave.

ab-äſen (ᵟᵛᵛ) v/a. ⊛** hunt. v. Rotwild: (weiden) to browse (on young trees).

ab-äſten (ᵟᵛᵛ) v/a. ⊛** agr. Bäume ⁎ to lop (or prune) ...; hort. to disbranch.

ab-ätmen ⊕ (ᵟᵛᵛ) v/a. ⊛b** to glow (and dry) in the muffle, (austrocknen) to desiccate; die Kapelle ⁎ (ausglühen) to glow the cupel.

ab-ätzen ⊕ (ᵟᵛᵛ) v/a. ⊛** to remove (or burn off) with caustics.

ab-äugeln (ᵟᵛᵛ) v/a. ⊛a** 1. e-m et. ⁎ (abloden) to get (or draw) a th. from a p. by ogling or by (casting) loving glances. — 2. hunt. den Jagdbezirk ⁎ ab. **ab-äugen** ⊛** (nach Wild abſuchen) to scour the country for game.

Abba (ᵛᵛ) [ſyr. „Vater"] m ⊛ u. ⊛⊛ abba.

ab-backen (ᵟᵛᵛ) ⊛b* I v/a. 1. Brot: to finish baking, Obſt: to dry. — II v/n. 2. (ſn) (auseinandergehen) to come asunder in baking; abgebacken (zu ſtark gebacken) ſein to be too much baked; das Brot iſt abgebacken the crust comes (or breaks) off the bread. — 3. (h.) (fertig backen) to finish baking.

ab-baden (ᵟᵛᵛ) v/a. ⊛** 1. to wash off (or remove) by bathing. — 2. ſ-e Marken ⁎ to use up one's bathing-tickets.

ab-baken ♩ (ᵟᵛᵛ) v/a. ⊛** 1. ⊕ Deichbau: to mark off with stakes. — 2. ♩ das Fahrwaſſer ⁎ to buoy (off) the fairway.

ab-balgen (ᵟᵛᵛ) ⊛** I v/a. ein Tier ⁎ to skin ...; (ſchinden) to flay; Erbſen ⁎ to shell ... — II F ſich ⁎ v/refl. fig. derb: to have a (good) wrestle or romp or tussle (mit e-m with a p.).

ab-bangen (ᵟᵛᵛ) v/a. u. ſich ⁎ v/refl. ⊛** = abängſtigen.

ab-barbieren (ᵟᵛᵛ) v/a. ⊛*/* to shave off (a p.'s beard or whiskers).

ab-baſten ⊕ (ᵟᵛᵛ) v/a. ⊛** to strip (trees) of the bast or inner bark.

Ab-bau (ᵟᶠ) m ⊛c. 1. agr. in ∼ bringen to put out of cultivation. — 2. outfarm(ing) (away from the chief estate). — 3. ⚒ a) working (of a mine), exhaustion (of ore); b) worked outmine; in ∼ bringen to exhaust.

ab-bau-en (ᵟᶠᵛ) ⊛** I v/n. (h.) 1. ⚔ (zurückziehen) to withdraw troops from the rear while engaging the enemy in the front. — II ſich ⁎ v/refl. 2. to build away from other farms, to settle down in an out-of-the-way place. — III v/a. 3. den Markt bauen u. ⁎ to put up and take down the booths. — 4. agr. to allot (plots of land). — 5. ⚒ : a) to work; b) eine Zeche ⁎ (aufgeben) to abandon a mine; c) das Grundwaſſer ⁎ (fortſchaffen) to drain (the water from ...). — 6. chm. eine organiſche Verbindung ⁎ (ſyſtematiſch zerlegen) systematically to split up an organic compound (so as to ascertain its structure).

Ab-baumen (ᵟᵛᵛ) v/n. (h.) ⊛** hunt. to come down from a tree, to fly off ...

ab-bäumen ⊕ (ᵟᵛᵛ) v/a. ⊛** Weberei: to take from the loom, to unroll.

Ab-bau-ſohle ⚒ (ᵟᵛᵛ...) f ⊛ level; ⁼ſtoß m face (of workings), wall; ⁼ſtrecke f board, headway.

ab-beeren (ᵟᵛᵛ) v/a. ⊛** to strip (a shrub, &c.) of berries; Trauben: to pick from the bunch, to strip a bunch of grapes.

ab-befehlen (ᵟᵛᵛ) v/a. ⊛c*/* to countermand; vgl. auch ab⁼... 5.

ab-behalten (ᵟᵛᵛ) v/a. ⊛a*/* den Hut ⁎ to keep one's hat off, to remain uncovered or bare-headed.

ab-beißen (ᵟᵛᵛ) ⊛a** I v/a. (h.) 1. to bite (off); ſich e-n Zahn ⁎ to break a tooth (in biting). — 2. fig. aller Scham den Kopf abgebiſſen h. to be dead to all sense of shame; ſich vor Lachen die Zunge ⁎ to split one's sides with laughing. — II ſich ⁎ v/refl. u. v/rpr. 3. to tire o. s. with biting. — 4. F (ſich) ea. ⁎ to be bickering and biting.

ab-beizen (ᵟᵛᵛ) I v/a. ⊛** 1. med. to cauterize. — 2. ⊕ mit e-r Feile ⁎ to take off with a file; mit Scheidewaſſer ⁎ to remove with aquafortis; Gerberei: to taw (skins); Metall-erze ⁎ (abbrennen) to pickle. ... — II ∼ n ⊛ u. **Ab-beizung** f ⊛ 3. med. cauterization.

ab-bekommen (ᵟᵛᵛ) v/a. ⊛*/* 1. F (losfriegen) to get off, to succeed in removing. — 2. (ſeinen Teil erhalten) to come in for (one's share of), to participate in; F e-e Tracht Prügel ⁎ to get a good beating; F er hat etwas (mit) ⁎ he got his share or P his whack.

ab-berſten (ᵟᵛᵛ) v/n. (ſn) ⊛** (ſ. berſten) to burst (or fly) off.

ab-berufen (ᵟᵛᵛ) v/a. ⊛b*/* to call away or back or home; Gott hat ihn ⁎ God has summoned him (to His eternal home); e-n Geſandten ⁎ to recall ...

Ab-berufung (ᵟᵛᵛ) f ⊛ call(ing) home, recall; ⚔ ∼ Militärpflichtiger i. b. Heimat bei Krieg summons (or order) to rejoin the ranks in time of war; ∼s⁼ſchreiben (⁵...) n ⊛ e-s Geſandten: letter(s) of recall.

ab-beſtell|en (ᵟᵛᵛ) v/a. ⊛*/* to countermand, counter-order; e-e Zeitung ⁎ to discontinue (taking in) a paper. — II ∼ n, **A|ung** f ⊛ counter-order.

ab-beten (ᵟᵛᵛ) v/a. ⊛** 1. (herbeten) ein Gebet ⁎ to say (off) ... mechanically, to reel off ..., to gabble ...; e-n Roſenkranz ⁎ to count (or tell)

Signs (see page XVII): F familiar; P vulgar; ʃ flash; ⇗ rare; † obsolete (died); * new word (born); ⁎ incorrect; ♪ music;

[abbetteln] — 3 — [abbrennen]

one's beads. — 2. (betend sühnen) to expiate by one's prayers. — 3. (betend abwenden) to avert by praying. — II ~ n ⊕ 4. (Sühne) expiation.
ab-betteln (⸗⸗) v/a. ⊕a** e-m et. ⸗ to get (or obtain) a th. from a p. by begging or soliciting.
ab-betten (⸗⸗) v/a. ⊕** I v/a. e-n Fluß ⸗ to turn (or divert) … into a new bed. — II sich ⸗ v/refl. sich von e-m ⸗ to give up sleeping (in the same bed) with a p.; sich von der Wand ⸗ to remove one's bed from the wall.
ab-beugen (⸗⸗) v/a. ⊕** = abbiegen, bsd. 4. [zählen.]
ab-bezahlen (⸗⸗⸗) v/a. ⊕** = abzahlen.⸣
ab-biegen (⸗⸗) ⊕ast** I v/a. 1. (ant. anbiegen) to bend off. — 2. (trennen) to detach. — 3. hort. (ablegen) to take layers (or slips) of. — 4. gram. = abwandeln. — II v/n. (sn) 5. in e-e andere Straße ⸗ to take a(nother) turning; vom Wege ⸗ to turn aside from …; wo die Straße abbog where the road branched off. — III ~ n ⊕ u. **Abbiegung** f ⊕ 6. turning; gram. f. 4.
Ab-bild (⸗⸗) [nhd.] ⊕b. 1. image, (faithful) copy; e-r Person: likeness, portrait; ein ~ von et. m. lassen to have a th. (faithfully) copied. — 2. fig. diese Worte sind das ~ seiner Gesinnung … the true reflection of his mind.
ab-bilden (⸗⸗) ⊕** I v/a. to copy, to portray, fig. to depict; in Gips, Wachs ⸗ to model (or mould) in …, in Metall: to emboss. — II sich ⸗ v/refl. to be reflected (or delineated) in. — III ~ n ⊕ = Abbildung 1.
Ab-bildung (⸗) f ⊕ 1. (s. abbilden I) copying; modelling. — 2. a) sketch; cut, picture, illustration; b) = Abbild 1.
ab-bimsen (⸗⸗) v/a. ⊕** to rub with pumice(-stone), to pumice.
ab-binden (⸗⸗) I v/a. ⊕** 1. (ant. anbinden) to unbind, to untie, to uncord. — 2. ein Kalb ⸗ to wean a calf. — 3. surg. to underbind, to tie (off), e-e Warze: to string. — 4. (fertig binden) ⊕ Böttcherei: to (new-)hoop (a cask); carp. to frame. — 5. fig. F e-n Bären ⸗ to pay off (or to discharge) a debt or an old score. — II ~ n ⊕ und **Abbindung** f ⊕ 6. (act of) unbinding, &c.; zu 3: ligature.
Ab-biß (⸗⸗) m ⊕a. 1. bite, biting off; for. u. hunt. nibbling (the buds). — 2. ♀ = Teufels-⸗.
Ab-bitte (⸗⸗) f ⊕ apology; e-m (auch: bei e-m) ~ tun to ask (or to beg, stärker: to implore or to crave) a p.'s pardon; öffentliche ~ (fr.) amende honorable.
ab-bitten (⸗⸗) I v/a. ⊕** 1. e-m et. ⸗ to beg a p.'s pardon for a th., stärker: to tender e. p. one's (humble) apologies for a th.; öffentlich ⸗ to make an amende honorable for. — 2. (erflehen) to obtain by begging (or imploring) a p.; (abwenden) to deprecate. — II **abbittend** p. pr. u. a. ⊕ 3. deprecatory.
ab-blasen (⸗⸗) ⊕a** I v/a. 1. (wegblasen) to blow off or away; die Möbel ⸗ to blow the dust off … — 2. ♪ e-e Melodie ⸗ to blow … (on a wind-instrument). — 3. (ankündigen) to sound (the hours, &c.). — 4. hunt. die Hunde ⸗ to call … off (or home) (with the bugle); die Jagd ⸗ to sound 'the death'. — 5. ⊕ den Dampf ⸗ to blow off the steam. — II v/n. (h.) 6. ⚔ (zum Rückzug blasen) to sound the retreat.
ab-blassen (⸗⸗) v/n. (sn) ⊕** to fade, to (grow) pale (= verschießen).
ab-blatten (⸗⸗) v/a. ⊕** 1. agr. to strip (or deprive) of leaves. — 2. den Weinstock ⸗ to trim. — 3. vom Wild: to browse.
ab-blattern (⸗⸗) v/n. (h.) ⊕a** path. v. der Haut: to peel after the small-pox.
ab-blättern (⸗⸗) ⊕a** I v/a. to strip of leaves, to deprive of foliage, to defoliate. — II v/n. (sn) u. sich ⸗ to shed the leaves or the foliage; (sich ablösen) to scale off; min., &c.: ⚙ to exfoliate, path.: ⚙ to desquamate (f. a. abblattern). — III ~ n u. **Abblätterung** f ⊕ min., &c. ⚙ exfoliation; path. ⚙ desquamation.
ab-bläuen (⸗⸗) ⊕** (blau machen) to give a bluish tint to, to dye blue; die Wäsche ⸗ to blue …
ab-bleiben (⸗⸗) v/n. (sn) ⊕** to keep (or remain) off or at a distance.
ab-bleichen (⸗⸗) I v/a. ⊕** to bleach (off), to finish bleaching. — II ⚑ v/n. (sn) ⊕ast** (p.p. a. ⊕**) = verbleichen.
ab-blitzen (⸗⸗) I v/n. (sn) ⊕** 1. v/imp. es hat (sich) abgeblitzt the lightning has ceased. — 2. ehm. von Flinten: to miss fire; fig. F (to suffer) fail(ure): to get a snub; e-n ⸗ lassen to give a p. a rebuff, to snub a p. — II v/a. ⊕** 3. = Gewehr abschießen. — III ~ n ⊕ 4. ⚔ flash in the pan.
ab-blühen (⸗⸗) I v/n. (h. u. sn) ⊕** 1. ♀ (ant. in Blüte stehen) to cease blossoming or blooming or flowering, to shed the bloom, F to go off. — 2. abgeblüht: a) fig. faded; sie ist abgeblüht she is passée; b) ♀ deflorate. — II ~ n ⊕ 3. fall of the blossom, deflorescence. [right through.]
ab-bohren ⚒ (⸗⸗) v/a. ⊕** to bore⸣
Ab-bohrer ⚒ (⸗⸗) m ⊕ long borer, terrier, ground-auger.
ab-borgen (⸗⸗) v/a. ⊕** e-m et. ⸗ to borrow a th. from (or of) a p.
ab-böschen (⸗⸗) v/a. u. v/n. (h.) ⊕** to slope, bsd. ⚔ frt. to scarp.
Ab-böschung (⸗⸗) f ⊕ slope, slant, ⚔ frt. escarp. [(in wax), to model.]
ab-bosseln (⸗⸗) v/a. ⊕** to emboss⸣
Ab-brand ⊕ (⸗⸗) m ⊙d. metall. loss in weight (or waste) of silver, &c. in the process of cleaning or testing.
ab-brassen ⚓ (⸗⸗) v/a. ⊕** die Segel ⸗ to brace aback and fill …
ab-braten (⸗⸗) v/a. ⊕a** to roast thoroughly; gut abgebraten well done.
ab-brauchen (⸗⸗) v/a. ⊕** to use up, to wear out. — II **ab-gebraucht** p. p. u. a. ⊕ used up, worn (out), von Redensarten: hackneyed, stale, trite.
ab-brauen (⸗⸗) v/a. ⊕** 1. to brew well. — 2. to finish brewing.
ab-bräunen (⸗⸗) v/a. ⊕** bsd. Kochkunst: to brown thoroughly, to roast brown.
ab-brausen (⸗⸗) I v/n. ⊕** 1. (h. u. sn) to cease fermenting or roaring. — 2. (sn) to rush off; 🚂 vom Dampfwagen: to steam out of the station, to steam off. — II v/a. 3. beim Bade: to douche.
ab-brechen (⸗⸗) ⊕a** I v/a. 1. (ant. anmachen) to break off, Blumen ꝛc.: to pluck (off), to pick; eine Brücke ⸗ to break (or pull) down a bridge; fig. alle Brücken hinter sich ⸗ to burn one's ships (or boats) behind one; die Eisen ⸗ f. u. Hufeisen, ⚔ Festungswerke ⸗ to dismantle …; ein Gebäude, eine Mauer ⸗ to pull down …, to demolish; das Gerüst ⸗ to take down the scaffolding; ⚔ die Glieder ⸗ to break off the files; Schmiede: die (Huf-)Eisen ⸗ to unshoe a horse; kurz ⸗ to snap (off); ⚔ das Lager ⸗ to break up (or move) the camp; der Sturm brach den Mast ab … carried away (or off) the mast; eine Mauer ⸗ to pull down …; Obst ⸗ to pick (or gather) fruit; ⚓ ein (altes) Schiff ⸗ to break (or rip) up a (condemned) vessel; ⊕ Schlosserei: e. Schloß ⸗ to pick (or to take off) a lock; die Spitze von et. ⸗ to break the point of a th.; gram. e. Wort ⸗ to divide …; e-n Zahn ⸗ to break (a piece of) a tooth, ein Zelt to strike … — 2. fig. (aufhören mit) to stop, to interrupt, plötzlich: to cut short, vorausgehend: to discontinue; die Arbeit ⸗ to knock off work; ⚔ e-e Belagerung ⸗ to raise a siege; alle Beziehungen ⸗ to sever (or cut off) all connexion (with); ⚔ ein Gefecht ⸗ to stop (or leave off) fighting; den Umgang mit e-m ⸗ to break off all intercourse with a p., to break with a p., F to cut (or drop) a p.; Unterhandlungen ⸗ to break off (or stop) one's negotiations. — 3. (ant. zulegen) = abziehen 5. — II v/n. 4. (sn) to break (or snap) off; 5. (h.) auf dem Jahrmarkte: to pack up. — 6. fig. (ant. fortfahren) to cease; kurz ⸗ to stop short; in der Rede ⸗ to come to a (dead) stop, to break down; von e-r Erzählung: to break off (abruptly); wir wollen hiervon ⸗! let us drop (or change) the subject! — 7. ⚔ zu zweien ⸗ to form (in) two deep. — III v/refl. 8. sich (dat.) etwas ⸗ (sich etwas versagen) to deny o.s. a thing; sich etwas am Munde ⸗ to go short of (food); sich an der Nahrung ⸗ to go without food, to pinch o.s.; sich nichts ⸗ not to deny (or stint) o.s. anything (or the least th.). — IV ~ n ⊕ u. **Ab-brechung** f ⊕ 9. breaking off, interruption; discontinuance; cessation; Maurerei: demolition; eines Wortes: division; fig. in der Rede ꝛc.: dead (or sudden) stop. — V **ab-gebrochen** p.p. u. a. ⊕ (D9) 10. broken off, &c. — 11. rhet. abrupt, jerky, disconnected; aphoristic; in kurzen Sätzen sprechen ⸗ to speak in broken sentences.
ab-brenn/en (⸗⸗) ⊕b** I v/a. 1. to burn down; eine Stadt ⸗ to destroy … by fire. — 2. (fortschaffen) to remove by fire or by burning or with corrosives. — 3. ein Feuerwerk ⸗ to let off (or display) fireworks. — 4. (fertig brennen) to finish burning, &c.; fast abgebrannt almost burnt (down). — 5. ⊕ Metalle ⸗ to refine (by fire), to treat

⚙ scientific; ♀ botanical; ⚱ geography; ⊕ machinery; ⚒ mining; ⚔ military; ⚓ marine; ⊛ commercial; ✉ postal; 🚂 railway.

in the refining furnace; Meſſing ꝛc. 2 (abbeizen) to pickle … (in nitric acid); Stahl 2 to temper …; ↓ ein Schiff 2 (zum Kalfatern reinbrennen) to bream; *chm.* ſchnell 2 laſſen to deflagrate. — **II** *v/n.* (ſn) 6. to be consumed (or devastated) by fire; von Perſonen: to suffer by (or to lose one's property through) a fire. — 7. vom Zündpulver: to flash (in the pan); *chm* ſchnell 2 to deflagrate. — 8. (zu Ende brennen) to cease burning; das Feuer 2 laſſen to let … drop or burn down. — **III** ~ *n* ⓔ 9. = A/ung. — **IV ab-gebrannt** *p.p.* u. *a* ⓕ 10. burnt (up), v. Gebäuden: ganz 2 burnt (down) to the ground, gutted; v. Perſonen: (made) homeless (by fire); *fig* F hard up (for cash); das 2e Haus the burnt-down house, the house (which was) consumed by the flames; (des Streichholz ꝛc.: used …; ~e(r) *m*, ~e *f* ⓕ sufferer (through fire). [flagrator.]
Ab-brenner (ᵍᵈ~) *m* ⓑ *phys., chm.* de-ꝛ
Ab-brennung (ᵍᵈ~) *f* ⓕ burning (down or up); e-r Stadt: conflagration; *chm.* deflagration; des Zündpulvers: flash in the pan. [(Abkürzung) abbreviation.]
Ab-breviatur (ᶨ⁻ʷ⁽ᵛ⁾⁻ᴵᴵ) [lt. *brev-*] *f* ⓕ
ab-brev(i)ieren (ᶨ⁻ʷ⁽ᵛ⁾⁻ᴵᴵ) [lt.] **I** *v/a.* ⓑ (abkürzen) to abridge, to abbreviate. — **II** ~ *n* ⓔ abridgment.
ab-bringen (ᵍᵈ~) **I** *v/a.* ⓜ** 1. (fortſchaffen) to take away or off, to remove; den Schmutz 2 to get off …; ↓ vom Ankergrunde 2 to unmoor. — 2. *fig.* e-n von et. 2 to turn (or divert) a p.'s thoughts from a th.; davon läßt er ſich nicht 2: F he will have it (so); ich will ihn ſchon davon 2 F I'll talk him out of it; das bringt uns weit von unſerm Gegenſtande ab this leads (or carries) us too far from our subject; e-n von e-r Gewohnheit 2 to break a p. of a habit;. e-n von ſeiner Meinung 2 to talk a p. over; eine Mode 2 to do away with …; Hunde ꝛc. von der Spur 2 to take … off the scent; e-n vom Trinken 2 to wean a p. from his drunken habits, to cure (or convert) a drunkard; wir brachten ihn von dieſem Vorhaben ab we put this scheme out of his head; er ließ ſich von ſ-m Vorſatze nicht 2 he could not be dissuaded from his design; ⓖ Waren 2 (an den Mann bringen) to dispose of goods, to clear off one's stock; e-n vom rechten Wege 2 to turn a p. from the right path, to misguide a p., to lead one astray. — **II** ~ *n* ⓔ u. **Ab-bringung** *f* ⓕ 3. removal; *fig.* diversion; dissuasion.
ab-bröckeln (ᵍᵈ~) ⓜa** **I** *v/a.* to take (or break) off in small pieces. — **II** *v/n* (ſn) u. *v/refl.* ſich 2 to crumble off; ⓞ vom Mauerputz ꝛc.: to scale (or peel) off; ⓓ Börſe: die Kurſe bröckelten ab (gingen zurück) prices crumbled away or weakened or gave way or declined.
Ab-bruch (ᵍᵈᶜʰ) *m* ⓓⓓ. 1. = abbrechen **IV**; ein Haus auf ~ verkaufen to sell a house (to be pulled down) for the materials or as old materials; *fig.* ~ freundſchaftlicher Beziehungen rupture. — 2. (Loslöſen) giving way, crumbling away. — 3. (Trümmerhaufen) fragments

pl., materials of a demolished building, wreckage; (weggeſchwemmtes Land) alluvial land. — 4. *fig.* (Benachteiligung) damage, injury, detriment; ~ leiden to suffer damage, &c.; e-m ~ tun to injure (or prejudice) a p.; dies tut ihm keinen ~ F that won't hurt him; e-r Sache 2 tun to do harm to a cause, &c.; dem Handel ~ tun to interfere with commerce, to undermine (or slacken, ſtärker: stop) trade; dies hat ſ-m Rufe ~ getan … detracted from or impaired, spoiled his reputation; ~ tuend derogatory, injurious.
ab-brüchig (ᵍᵈ~) *a.* ⓕ 1. brittle. — 2. *fig.* detrimental (to).
Ab-bruchs-arbeit (ᵍᵈᶜʰ~) *f* ⓑ eines Gebäudes demolition.
ab-brücken ⓞ (ᵍᵈ~) *v/n.* (h.) ⓜ** Pontonweſen: to break (or pull) down bridges, to take away a bridge.
ab-brühen (ᵍᵈ~) *v/a.* ⓜ** 1. Gemüſe: to (par)boil; ein Huhn ꝛc.: to boil, ein Schwein: to scald. — 2. *fig.* gegen alles abgebrüht (utterly) devoid of all shame, indifferent (ſtärker: callous) about one's honour, case-hardened.
ab-brüllen (ᵍᵈ~) ⓜ** **I** *v/a.* ein Lied 2 to bawl out …— **II** ſich 2 *v/refl.* to tire o.s. by roaring or bawling.
ab-brummen (ᵍᵈ~) *v/a.* ⓜ** 1. eine Rede 2 to mutter … — 2. F eine Strafe 2 to do time; ein Jahr 2 to serve a twelvemonth in jail, F to do a stretcher.
ab-bügeln (ᵍᵈ~) *v/a.* ⓜa** Wäſche: to iron; Schneiderei: to press down (the seams). [— **II** ~ *n* ⓔ discharge.]
ab-bürden (ᵍᵈ~) *v/a.* ⓜ** to unload.ꝛ
ab-bürſten (ᵍᵈ~) *v/a.* ⓜ** e-n Rock 2 to brush …; den Staub 2 to brush off …; der Schmutz läßt ſich 2, nicht 2 F … brushes off, the brush won't move (or take out) …
ab-büßen (ᵍᵈ~) **I** *v/a.* ⓜ** to expiate, to atone for; er hat es 2 müſſen he had to suffer for it; et. mit Geld 2 to pay a fine for; et. im Gefängnis 2 to sit in jail for. — **II** ~ *n* ⓔ u. **Ab-büßung** *f* ⓕ expiation, atonement.
Abc (--tſᴸ) *n, inv.* 1. ABC, alphabet; *fig.* noch beim ~ ſteh(e)n to be an abecedarian or a mere beginner, to be learning the rudiments. — 2. *fig.* (the first) rudiments *pl.*
Abc-bank (--tſᴵᴵ) *f* ⓑ lowest form; =**buch** *n* (first) spelling-book or primer; =**klaſſe** *f* lowest class; =**ſchule** *f* elementary school, früher: dame-school; =**ſchüler** *m*, =**ſchütz(e)** *m* abecedarian, (first) beginner; =**tafel** *f* abecedary.
Ab-dach (ᵍᵈ~) *n* ⓓ. 1. ⓞ *arch.* penthouse. — 2. (Schuppen) shed, outhouse.
ab-dachen (ᵍᵈᶜʰ) ⓜ** **I** *v/a.* 1. ↘ (*ant.* bedachen) to unroof, dem Sturme: to blow (or carry) off the roof. — 2. *arch.* u. *fig.* (böſchen) to build with a) slope, to incline, ↓ *frt.* to scarp. — **II** ſich 2 *v/refl.* to (form a) slope, to incline, to dip.
ab-dachig (ᵍᵈ~), **ab-dächig** *a.* ⓕ sloping, slanting; *adv.* on the slant, aslant.
Ab-dachung (ᵍᵈᶜʰ~) *f* ⓕ slope, declivity, gradient; (Böſchung) glacis, talus; eine ſanfte ~ a gentle incline or dip or rise; ↓ *frt.* (ſteile) ~ escarpment.

Ab-dachungs-grundlinie (ᵍᵈ~…) *f* ⓕ base of the glacis; =**koſten** *pl.* e-s Gebäudes cost (or expense) of unroofing …; =**verhältnis** *n*, =**winkel** *m* inclination, angle (of a slope), gradient; einer Böſchung: angle of a glacis.
ab-dämm|en (ᵍᵈ~) **I** *v/a.* ⓜ** 1. to dam up or in; Waſſer 2 to dike … — **II** ~ *n* ⓔ u. A/ung *f* ⓕ 2. damming up, e-s Sees ꝛc.: embankment. — 3. (nur A/ung) weir, (coffer-)dam.
Ab-dampf ⓞ (ᵍᵈ~) *m* ⓓⓒ. Dampfmaſchine: exhaust-, dead-steam. [=vorrichtung.]
Ab-dampf-apparat (ᵍᵈ~…) *m* ⓑ =ꝛ
ab-dampfen (ᵍᵈ~) **I** *v/n.* ⓜ** (h. u. ſn) 1. Flüſſigkeiten: to evaporate; 2 laſſen to evaporate, F to steam off, feſte Stoffe: ⚗ to volatilize. — 2. (ſn) F 🚂 u. ↓ der Zug, das Schiff iſt abgedampft … has steamed off or out of the station, out of the harbour. — **II** ⓞ *v/a.* ⓜ** 3. = 2 laſſen (ſ. 1). — **III** ~ *n* ⓔ 4. evaporation.
ab-dämpfen (ᵍᵈ~) *v/a.* ⓜ** 1. Flüſſigkeit: to evaporate, F to boil down. — 2. Kochkunſt: to stew (well). — 3 *fig.,* bſp. ♪ to deaden, to damp.
Ab-dampf-keſſel (ᵍᵈ~…) *m* ⓑ *phys. u. chm.* evaporating-kettle; =**pfanne** *f* evaporating-pan; =**ſchale** *f* evaporating-basin, -capsule, -dish.
Ab-dampfung (ᵍᵈ~) *f* ⓕ evaporation; ~**s**=… (~…) ⓑ = Abdampf=…
Ab-dampf-vorrichtung ⓞ (ᵍᵈ~…) *f* ⓕ evaporating-apparatus, evaporator.
ab-dank|en (ᵍᵈ~) ⓜ** **I** *v/a.* 1. (entlaſſen) einen Diener: to discharge, to dismiss, ſtärker: to send off, F to sack; Beamte (mit Penſion) to pension off; ⚔ e-n Offizier 2 to cashier …, (zur Diſpoſition ſtellen) to put … on half-pay; abgedankt dismissed, weitS. out of employment; abgedankter Sergeant ꝛc. (mit Gnadengehalt) pensioner; ein abgedankter Hauptmann a retired captain, a captain on half-pay; ⚔ ehm. Truppen 2 to disband …; ↓ ſ. abmuſtern 2. — 2. *fig.* ↓ ein Schiff 2 to lay up …, (als untauglich) to condemn …; F co. Kleider 2 to cast off … — **II** *v/n.* (h.) 3. to resign (one's post), to retire or withdraw (from a command, &c.); als Beamter: to leave the service; als Fürſt: to abdicate. — **III** ~ *n* ⓔ 4. = A/ung.
Ab-dankung (ᵍᵈ~) *f* ⓕ 1. genommene: resignation, retirement; eines Fürſten: abdication. — 2. gegebene: discharge; v. Beamten ꝛc.: dismissal, pensioning off.
Ab-dankungs-urkunde (ᵍᵈ~…) *f* ⓕ deed (or instrument) of abdication.
ab-darben (ᵍᵈ~) *v/a.* ⓜ** ſich (*dat.*) et. … Munde) 2 to deny o.s. a th., to pinch o.s.
ab-decken (ᵍᵈ~) *v/a.* ⓜ** 1. to uncover; ein Dach 2 to untile …; ein Bett 2 (a. *hort.* ein Beet 2) to strip …; den Tiſch 2 to clear the table, to remove the cloth, weitS. F to take away. — 2. (die Haut abziehen) Vieh 2 to skin (or flay) cattle.
Ab-decker (ᵍᵈ~) *m* ⓑ flayer, knacker.
Ab-deckerei (ᵍᵈ~ᴵᴵ) *f* ⓕ 1. flaying-house, (Schind-anger) knackery, flayer's pit. — 2. flayer's (or knacker's) trade.
Ab-decker-karren (ᵍᵈ~…) *m* ⓑ knacker's cart; =**leder** *n* † morkins' hides.
ab-deichen (ᵍᵈ~) *v/a.* ⓜ** = abdämmen.

[**Abderit**] — 5 — [**Abendmahl**]

Abderit (⌣‑́)[Abde'ra, grch. St.] m ⓶, ~in f ⓬ Abderite; *fig.* ~en *pl.* (Krähwinkler) wise men of Gotham, Gothamites *pl.*
abderitisch (⌣‑́) *a.* ⓺⓺ Abderian, mst *fig.* stupid, foolish, crazy, F cranky.
ab-dichten ↓ (⌣́⌣) *v/a.* ⓷⓽** (dicht machen) mit Werg 2 to caulk.
ab-dicken (⌣́⌣) *v/a.* ⓷⓽** Saft 2 to thicken ... (by boiling down).
ab-dielen ⓞ (⌣́⌣) *v/a.* ⓷⓽** 1. den Boden 2 to plank — 2. (durch Dielen trennen) to board off, to partition (with boards).
ab-dienen (⌣́⌣) *v/a.* ⓷⓽** 1. f‑e Zeit 2 to serve one's (full) time; F ⚔ fein Jahr 2 to serve one's year in the army. — 2. (dienend erstatten) to pay off (a debt) by one's services, to work off (a debt).
ab-dingen (⌣́⌣) *v/a.* ⓶ft** ob. ⓷⓽** 1. = abhandeln 4. — 2. e‑m et. 2: a) to hire a th. from (or of) a p.; b) to get (or obtain) a th. from a p. by bartering.
ab-disputieren (⌣́⌣⌣⌣) *v/a.* ⓷***/* e‑m et. 2 to dispute a p. a th.; *vgl.* abstreiten.
ab-dizieren (⌣⌣‑́⌣) [lt.] *v/n.* (h.) ⓷* to abdicate; *vgl.* abdanken II.
ab-docken (⌣́⌣) *v/a.* ⓷⓽** eine Schnur 2 to unwind ...   [domen.]
Abdomen (⌣⌣‑́) [lt.] *n* ⓷⓺ⓞ (Unterleib) ab-
abdominal (⌣⌣‑́) *a.* ⓺⓺ abdominal.
Abdominal-schuß (‑́...) *m path.* abdominal shot, shot in the abdomen.
ab-donnern (⌣́⌣) ⓶a** *v/imp.* es hat sich abgedonnert it has ceased (or left off, stopped) thundering.
ab-dorren (⌣́⌣) *v/n.* (fn) ⓷⓽** to dry and fall off, to be(come) parched up.
ab-dörren (⌣́⌣) *v/a.* ⓷⓽** to dry (or parch) thoroughly; ⓞ *metall.* to refine.
Ab-dörr-gerätschaften (⌣́⌣...) *f/pl.* ⓺⓺ drying-utensils; **=ofen** *m* refining furnace; **=prozeß** *m* drying-process.
Ab-dörrung (⌣́⌣) *f* ⓺⓺ drying.
ab-drängen (⌣́⌣) *v/a.* ⓷⓽** 1. e‑n 2 to push a p. off or away. — 2. e‑m den Platz 2 to push (or elbow) a p. aside; *fig.* e‑m et. ~ to squeeze a th. out of a p.
ab-drechseln (⌣́⌣) *v/a.* ⓶a** 1. (durch Drechseln fortschaffen) to remove in turning. — 2. (fertig drechseln) to round off (on the lathe), to finish turning. — 3. *fig.* abgedrechselte Verbeugung, Worte *pl.* formal bow, set phrases *pl.*
Ab-dreh-bank ⓞ (⌣́⌣...) *f* ⓺⓶ turner's lathe; **=eisen** *n* turner's chisel.
ab-drehen (⌣́⌣) *v/a.* ⓷⓽** 1. to twist off; einem Hühnchen den Hals 2 to wring a chicken's neck; einem Schlüssel den Bart 2 to wrench off the bit of a key; das Gas, das Wasser, den Hahn 2 (abstellen) to turn off the gas, the water(-supply), the tap; das elektrische Licht 2 to switch off the electric light. — 2. ⓞ (drechseln) to round off (on the lathe).
Ab-dreh-stahl (⌣́...) *m* ⓺⓶ = **=eisen**; **=späne** *m/pl.* shavings from the lathe; **=zeug** *n* turner's tools *pl.*
ab-dreschen (⌣́⌣) *v/a.* ⓓe. (ⓣb.) (e)ft** 1. *agr.* Getreide 2 to finish threshing. — 2. *fig.* abgedroschen commonplace, trite; abgedrosch(e)ne Redensart, Entschuldigung well-worn phrase, stale excuse; e‑n abgedrosch(e)nen Gegenstand behandeln to flog a dead horse. — 3. F (prügeln) to thrash soundly.

Ab-drift ↓ (⌣́⌣) *f* ⓺⓺ drift.
ab-dringen (⌣́⌣) I *v/a.* ⓶ft** e‑m et. 2 to extort (or wring) a th. from a p. — II ~ *n* ⓶⓷ u. **Ab-dringung** *f* ⓺⓺ extortion.
ab-drohen (⌣́⌣) *v/a.* ⓷⓽** e‑m et. 2 to obtain a th. from a p. by threats, to bully a p. out of a th.
Ab-druck[1] ⓞ (⌣́⌣) [abdrucken] *m* ⓺d. 1. (das Abdrucken) print(ing); ~ von 1000 Exemplaren edition of ...; e‑s Artikels reproduction of ... — 2. (Abgedrucktes) copy, impression; neuer ~ e‑s Buches reprint; Kupferstecherei: proof; *typ.* ~ vor der Schrift proof before letters; *phot.*proof of a photo(graph); (Lichtdruck)phototype.
Ab-druck[2] ⓞ (⌣́⌣) [abdrucken] *m* ⓺d. 1. (Gepräge) impression, print, mark; *geogn.* v. Fischen: ⚶ ichthyolite, v. Pflanzen: ⚶ dendrolite; ⓞ ~ in Gips plaster cast. — 2. fast † *fig.* (exact) likeness, counterpart. — 3. ⓞ (Drücker der Flinte) trigger.
ab-drucken ⓞ (⌣́⌣) *v/a.* ⓷⓽** to print; tausend Exemplare 2 to print (or strike) off ...; wieder 2 to reprint.
ab-drücken (⌣́⌣) *v/a.* ⓷⓽** 1. (drückend abformen) to mould. — 2. (drückend lösen) to squeeze off; ein Gewehr 2 to pull the trigger of ..., to discharge ..., to fire ...; e‑n Pfeil 2 to let fly ...; ein Türschloß 2 to snap (the spring of) a lock. — 3. *fig.* es drückt ihm das Herz ab it grieves him to the heart; die Angst u. Not will uns das Herz 2 ... are weighing us down. — 4. e‑n herzlich 2 F to give a p. a hearty squeeze.
Ab-druck-papier (⌣́⌣...) *n* ⓺⓶ copying-paper; **=stange** ⚔ *f* im Gewehrschlosse: stopper.
ab-dudeln F (⌣́⌣) *v/a.* ⓶a** ein Lied 2 to sing (or play) ... in a humdrum style or monotonously.
ab-duften (⌣́⌣) *v/n.* (fn) ⓷⓽** von e‑r Landschaft (*G.*): to grow hazy or misty.
Abduktion ⚶ (⌣⌣‑́⌣) [lt.] *f* ⓺⓺ *med. ꝛc.* (Abführung) abduction.
ab-dunst/en (⌣́⌣) I *v/n.* (fn) u. **ab-dünst/en** II *v/a.* ⓷⓽** to evaporate; F to steam off; ⓞ Salzsole: to graduate. — III ~ *n* ⓶⓷ = **/ung**.
Ab-dunstung, **Ab-dünstung** (⌣́⌣) *f* ⓺⓺ *phys., chm.* (f. abdunsten) evaporation, vaporization; ⓞ graduation.
Ab-dünstungs-... (⌣́⌣...) ⓺⓶ (meist Abdampf-...): **=bad** *n* vapour-bath; **~haus** *n* ⓞ Saline: drying-house, graduation-house.
ab-ebben (⌣́⌣) *v/n.* (h.) ⓷⓽** to ebb away.
ab-eb(e)nen (⌣́(⌣)⌣) *v/a.* ⓶b** to (make) level.   [= Abcschüler.]
Abecedari/er ⓶⓶, **A/us** ⓶⓺ (‑⌣‑́(⌣)⌣) *m*]
abecelich (‑‑tf‑́⌣) *a.* ⓺⓺ alphabetical.
ab-ecken (⌣́⌣) *v/a.* ⓷⓽** to round off at the corners or edges.   [off.]
ab-eggen (⌣́⌣) *v/a.* ⓷⓽** *agr.* to harrow]
ab-eichen (⌣́⌣) *v/a.* ⓷⓽** to gauge.
ab-eifern (⌣́⌣) sich 2 *v/refl.* ⓶a** to wear o.s. out with zeal or enthusiasm.
ab-eilen (⌣́⌣) ⓷⓽** I ⚲ *v/n.* (fn) to hurry (or bustle) away. — II sich 2 *v/refl.*: du brauchst dich nicht so abzueilen you need not be in such a hurry or bustle, you need not rush so.
ab-eisen (⌣́⌣) (Eis) *v/a.* ⓷⓽** to free (or clear) from ice. [⓺ = Silberpappel.]
Abele ⚘ ⚶ (‑⌣‑́) [ndd.; *fr. aube*(*l*)] *f*]

Abelmosch ⚘ (‑⌣‑́⌣) [ar. „Vater des Moschus"] *m* ⓶a. abelmosk (*Hibi'scus abelmo'schus*).
Abelmoschus-körner ⚘ (‑⌣‑́⌣...) *n/pl.* ⓺⓺ musk-, amber-seed(s *pl.*).
Abend (‑́⌣) [ahd.: eve(n[ing])] *m* ⓺d. 1. (*ant.* Morgen) evening; am ~, des ~s, abends (f. ds.) in the evening; des schönen ~s one fine evening; gestern 2 last night; diesen ~, heute 2 this evening, to-night; morgen 2 tomorrow evening or night; es wird ~, es geht auf (ob. gegen) den ~ (the) evening is drawing near; e‑m e‑n guten ~ sagen oder wünschen to wish a p. good evening; Sprichw. es ist noch nicht aller Tage ~ we have not seen the end of it yet; *vgl. auch* loben. — 2. (etwas) zu ~ essen to sup (off a th.), to have (some) supper; nichts zu ~ essen to go without supper. — 3. (=gesellschaft; f. ds) evening-party. — 4. (Tag vorher) am ~ vor der Schlacht on the eve of the battle; der heilige ~ (Weihnachtsabend) Christmas Eve. — 5. *bfd. bibl.* (Himmelsgegend) west, setting sun; gegen ~ (gelegen) to the west, western, occidental. — 6. *fig.* (Ende) conclusion, end; der ~ seines Lebens the declining years (or the autumn) of his life.
Abend-andacht (‑́⌣...) *f* ⓶ evening-prayers *pl.*; **=beleuchtung** *f* e‑r Landschaft evening-lights *pl.*; **=besuch** *m* evening- (or late) visit(or); **=blatt** *n* evening-paper; **=börse** ⚜ *f* (Versammlung von Börsenmännern nach der gewöhnlichen Börsenzeit) (stock-exchange) business transacted after the regular hours; **=brot** *n* supper; ohne ~ supperless; **=dämmerung** *f* (evening-)twilight; während der ~ F between the lights; **=dunkel** *n* dusk (of the evening); **=essen** *n* = **=brot**; **=essenszeit** *f* supper-time; **=falter** *m, ent.* hawk-moth; **=frist** *f* appointed hour of the evening; **=gang** *m* = **=spaziergang**; **=gebet** *n* = **=andacht**; **=geläut(e)** *n* evening-bells *pl.*; **=gesang** *m* Kirche: evening-hymn, *poet.* even-song; **=gesellschaft** *f* evening(-) party, soirée; große, feine ~ crush, ehm. rout; **=glanz** *m*, **=glut** *f* brightness, glow of the setting sun; **=glocke** *f* evening(-) bell, ehm. curfew (bell); **=glut** *f* f. **=glanz**; **=gottesdienst** *m* evening-service; *Cath. a.*: vespers *pl.*; **=grauen** *n* = **=dunkel**; **=himmel** *m* evening-sky; **=imbiß** *m*, **=kost** *f* = **=brot**; **=kreis** *m* = **=unterhaltung**; **=kühle/cool**(ness) of the evening; **=land** *n* Occident, West, *pl.* **=lande** (zf. fassend), **=länder** *n/pl.* (zf. fassend) western countries *pl.*; **=länder**(in *f* ⓶) *m* ⓶ inhabitant of a western country; **=ländisch** *a.* ⓺⓺ western, occidental; die ⓶e Kirche the Roman (Catholic) Church; **=landschaft** *f* evening-landscape.
abendlich (‑́⌣⌣) *a.* ⓺⓺ 1. referring to the evening; *adv.* in the evening. — 2. in ⓶er Stille in the calm of the evening. — 3. (westlich) westerly, occidental.
Abend-lied (‑́⌣...) *n* ⓺⓶ evening-song, *vgl.* **=gesang**; **=luft** *f* evening-air.
Abend-mahl (‑́⌣‑́...) *n* ⓺⓶ 1. = **Abendmahlzeit**. — 2. *rel.* the (holy) communion; das ~ halten (empfangen) to celebrate (to partake of) the Lord's supper.

♪ Musik; ⚶ Wissenschaft; ⚘ Pflanze; ☿ Geographie; ⓞ Technik; ⚒ Bergbau; ⚔ Militär; ↓ Marine; ⚜ Handel; ✉ Post; 🚂 Eisenbahn.

[Abendmahlsbrot] — 6 — [abfallen]

Abendmahls=brot (⌣−⌣…) n ⓘ consecrated bread (*Cath.* wafer); **=feier** f communion-service; **=gänger(in** f) m communicant; **=kelch** m chalice, *protestantisch*: communion-cup; **=streit** m dispute (or controversy) about the (holy) communion; **=tisch** m communion-table; **=wein** m sacramental wine.

Abend=mahlzeit (⌣−⌣…) f ⓘ supper; **=messe** f, **=mette** f, *Cath.* vespers *pl.*; **=musik** f serenade; **=punkt** m, *ast.* true West; **=rot** n (a. *fig.*=Abend 6) u. **=röte** f sunset glow, red evening-sky.

abends (⌣⌣) *adv.* in the evening; neulich ⚬ the other evening; spät ⚬, ⚬ spät late in the evening, late at night.

Abend=schein (⌣−⌣…) m ⓘ, **=schimmer** m = **=rot**; **=schicht**✕f night-shift; **=schule** f evening-classes *pl.*, night-school; **=segen** m = andacht; **=seite** f western aspect; **=spaziergang** m evening-walk; **=ständchen** n serenade; **=stern** m evening-star, (the planet) Venus; **⚬still** a. ⓘ calm as in the evening-hours; **=stimmung** f evening-mood; **=tau** m night-dew; **=tisch** m supper(-table); **=trunk** m evening-draught; **=unterhaltung** f evening(-)entertainment, evening(-) gathering; **⚬wärts** *adv.* westward, to the west; **=wind** m: a) night-breeze; b) = Westwind; **=zeit** f night-time, *poet.* eventide; **=zeitung** f = **=blatt**; **=zirkel** m = gesellschaft.

Abenteuer (⌣−⌣⌣) [mhd.; *fr. aventure* f] n ⓘ 1. *ehm.* Rittertum: (knight's) exploit or adventurous journey. — 2. *allg.*: adventure; (gewagtes Unternehmen) venture, risky undertaking; auf ⚬ ausgeh(e)n to go in search (or quest) of adventures; ein ⚬ besteh(e)n to meet with (F to have) an adventure; ein galantes ⚬ a love adventure.

Abenteuerin (⌣−⌣⌣) f ⓕ = Abenteurerin.

abenteuerlich (⌣−⌣⌣) a. ⓘ 1. adventurous, venturesome; *pol.* quixotic. — 2. *fig.* odd; eine ⚬e Geschichte a strange (or curious, romantic) affair.

Abenteuerlichkeit (⌣−⌣⌣) f ⓘ 1. adventurousness; strangeness; *pol.* quixotism. — 2. *fig.* strange (or curious) occurrence or adventure.

abenteuern (⌣−⌣⌣) v/n. (h.) ⓐa. to lead an adventurous (or a roving) life; ⚬der Ritter knight-errant.

Abenteurer (⌣−⌣⌣) m ⓘ, **~in** f ⓕ adventurer m, adventuress f; (Schwindler) auch: sharper, F high-flier; (fahrender Ritter) knight-errant, Don Quixote.

Abenteurer=geist (⌣−⌣…) m ⓘ adventurous spirit; **=leben** n adventurous life.

aber (⌣⌣) [ahd., *comp. von* ab] I *cj.* meist: but (stets an erster Stelle), schwächer: however; yet; er ist reich, lebt ⚬ auch sehr flott … at the same time, he spends his money freely; das ist ⚬ sehr drollig that's very droll, indeed; er sagt nein, hat es ⚬ doch getan … yet (or still) he has done it; nun ⚬ but now; oder ⚬, sonst ⚬ otherwise; ⚬, ⚬! *int.* there now!; what have you been about!; Weiß er es nicht? ⚬ doch! … F of course, he does! — II *adv.* again; ⚬ und ⚬mals over and over again; tausend und ⚬ tausend… thousands upon thousands

of … — III ~ n, *inv.* ob. ⓐ; er hat immer ein Wenn und ein ~ he is full of 'buts' or has always some objection; Sprichw. wer das Wenn und das ~ erdacht, hat sicher aus Häckerling Gold gemacht, he who argues best will win the day; ohne Wenn und ~ unreservedly. [peated (or double) ban.]

Aber=acht (⌣−⌣…) [mhd.] f ⓘ *ehm.* re-

ab=erben (⌣⌣⌣) v/a. ⓐ** e-m et. ⚬ to snatch s. th. from a p. by (the right of) inheritance.

Aber=glaube (⌣−⌣…) [mhd.] m ⓘ superstition; **⚬gläubig**✧, mst **⚬gläubisch** a. ⓕ superstitious.

ab=erkennen (⌣⌣⌣) I v/a. ⓐb*/* e-m et. ⚬ to dispossess a p. of a th. (by judgment); *jur.* Schadenersatz ⚬ to disallow compensation; etwas ⚬ to abjudicate, to deny. — II ~ n ⓘ u. **Ab=erkennung** f ⓕ dispossession by judicial decree; ~ bürgerlicher Rechte deprivation (*weitS.* loss) of civic rights.

Aber=klaue (⌣−⌣…) f ⓘ = Afterklaue.

aber=mal (⌣−⌣…) *adv.* f. abermals.

aber=malig (⌣−⌣⌣) a. ⓕ repeated; ⚬er Abdruck reimpression; nach ⚬er Erwägung, after repeated consideration, after reconsideration; *typ.* ⚬e Durchsicht (second) revisal (of proofs). [aber II.]

aber=mal(s) (⌣−⌣…) *adv.* once more (f. a.)

abern F (⌣⌣) v/n. (h.) ⓐa. to be (always) ready with a 'but' or an objection.

ab=ernten (⌣⌣⌣) I v/a., *agr.* den Acker ⚬ to get in the crop(s); das Getreide ⚬ to reap (or harvest) … — II v/n. (h.) to complete (or finish) the harvest.

Ab=erration ⚬ (⌣−⌣⌣-tß(⌣)") [lt.] f ⓕ (Abirrung des Lichtes 2c.) aberration.

Aber=raute ✧ (⌣−⌣…) [P aus lt. *abrótonum* n; *grch.*] f ⓕ = Eberreis; **=witz** [mhd.] m craziness, frenzy, mania; **⚬witzig** a. ⓕ crazy, frantic.

ab=essen (⌣⌣⌣) ⓐ** I v/a. die Kirschen vom Baum ⚬, den Baum ⚬ to eat (the cherries) off the tree; e-n Knochen ⚬ to pick … — II v/n. (h.) to finish dining; abgegessen h. to have done eating.

Abessini=en (⌣⌣−⌣(⌣)…) *npr.* ⓑ α. Abyssinia; Abessini=er(in f ⓕ) m ⓘ u.

abessinisch (⌣⌣−⌣) a. ⓕ Abyssinian.

Abf. *abbr.* = Abfahrt. [abschrägen.]

ab=facen ⊙ (⌣−ᵏ⌣) v/a. ⓑ** = abfauten,)

ab=fachen (⌣⌣⌣) v/a. ⓐ** to divide into partitions or compartments; e-n Schrank ⚬ to partition (off) …; Kunstschätze 2c. ⚬ u. *fig.* to classify …; to arrange …

ab=fädeln (⌣⌣⌣) v/a. ⓐa** Bohnen ⚬ to string; Perlen: to unstring.

ab=fadmen ↓ (⌣⌣⌣) v/a. ⓐb** to fathom.

ab=fahren (⌣⌣⌣) ⓐb** I v/n. (fn) 1. meist: to start (away), to set out; der Zug fuhr um 4 (Uhr) ab … left at four (o'clock); nach Köln ⚬ to leave for Cologne; sie fuhren ab a) im Wagen: they drove away; b) auf dem Fahrrad: they cycled off; mit dem Zug ⚬ to go by train; 🚂 Auf des Stationsvorstehers: ⚬! ready!, fire away! — 2. ⚓ *oft:* to set sail, von Dampfern: to steam off; vom Lande ⚬ to put (or sheer) off. — 3. F *fig.* (hastig weggehen) to make off; fahr ab! F be off!, (you may) hook it!; *derb:* (sterben) to depart (this life), F

co. to hop the twig. — 4. *fig.* e-n ⚬ lassen = abblitzen 2. — 5. = hinabfahren. — 6. (abgleiten) das Messer fuhr ihm ab his knife slipped. — II v/a. 7. to cart off or home. — 8. e-n Weg ⚬ to open up a road. — 9. (durch Fahren abnutzen) to wear out (by driving or riding); v/refl. die Räder fahren sich ab … are wearing out. — 10. (abtrennen) ihm wurde ein Fuß abgefahren he lost a foot by (or his foot was crushed in) a carriage accident. — 11. eine Schuld ⚬ to pay off … by driving or carting.

Ab=fahrt (⌣⌣) f ⓕ 1. (*abbr.* Abf.) departure; 🚂 es pfeift zur ~ the last whistle is blowing. — 2. ⚓ *oft:* sailing out of (or clearing the) port. — 3. ✧ F *derb fig.* (Tod) decease, death.

Ab=fahrts=flagge ⚓ (⌣⌣−⌣…) f ⓕ flag of departure; **=hafen** m port of departure; **=halle** f departure (or starting-) platform; **=ort** m, **=platz** m place of departure, starting-place; **=punkt** ↓ m starting-point; **=schuß** m, **=signal** n, **=zeichen** n signal of departure, starting-signal; **=zeit** f time of departure; **=zug** 🚂 m train ready to start.

Ab=fall (⌣⌣) [: offal, f. ~ 8] m ⓕ c. 1. (das Abfallen) der Blätter 2c.: fall of … — 2. (Böschung) declivity, slope. — 3. *fig.* (Lossagung) ~ von e-r Partei 2c. defection or secession from, zum Feinde: desertion, going over to; *hist.* ~ der Niederlande Revolt of the Netherlands (from). — 4. ↓ = Abtrift 2. — 5. *fig.* ✧ (Unterschied) contrast. — 6. *fig.* ✧ (*ant.* Beifall) disfavour. — 7. ⊙ (Abnahme an Gehalt, *bsd.* ✕) falling(-)off, diminution; ~ an Gewicht deficiency (F shortness) of weight, underweight; in ~ kommen to decline. — 8. (Unbrauchbares, meist Abfälle *pl.*) von Wolle 2c.: waste, rubbish; von Obst 2c.: refuse, garbage, beim Schlachten 2c.: offal, Küche: slops, leavings; ✕ tailings; Werkstatt: chips, clippings, shavings *pl.* — 9. ⓕ Uhrmacherei: (ruhende Hemmung) dead-beat.

Ab=fall=eimer (⌣⌣…) m ⓘ dust-pail; **=eisen** n scrap-iron.

ab=fallen (⌣⌣⌣) ⓐa** I v/n. (fn) 1. meist: to fall (off), to drop. — 2. ⚬ (leicht) ⚬d (von Früchten, Blättern 2c.) deciduous. — 3. *fig.* von e-m ⚬ to desert, to forsake a p.; *pol.* von einer Partei ⚬ to break away (or secede) from …, *rel.* auch: to renounce (one's faith). — 4. (wie Abfall 6) F to fail; F e-n ⚬ lassen to snub a p. — 5. (abmagern) to fall away; stark abgefallen emaciated; *weitS.* (sich verschlechtern) to degenerate, to deteriorate. — 6. (wie Abfall 8) to (be left as) waste. — 7. *fig.* es fällt (dabei) nicht viel für ihn ab F he won't gain much (by it) or be much the richer (for it). — 8. (wie Abfall 2) to slope (down), slant, shelve; steil ⚬d precipitous. — 9. (verschieden sein) to contrast, es fällt gegen Früheres sehr ab it is far inferior to …, F it makes a poor show after … — 10. ↓: a) to bear away; b) (abtreiben) to drift to leeward; c) ⊙ *typ.* (krumm stehen) to stand awry. — 11. ✕ *oft.* = abbrechen 7. — II v/a. 12. sich (*dat.*) den Hals ⚬ to

---

Signs (see page XVII): F familiar; P vulgar; F flash; ✧ rare; † obsolete (died); * new word (born); ⁺⁺ incorrect; ♪ music;

[abfällig] — 7 — [Abforderungsbrief]

break one's neck by a fall. — III ~ n ⊕ 13. = Abfall 1—3, 5—7. — IV **Abgefall(e)ne**[r] *m*) *f* ⊕ 14. deserter, renegade, turncoat; *rel.* apostate.
ab-fällig (⁸ᴶ~) *a.* ⊕1. inclined to fall off. — 2. ↘ (abschüssig) sloping, shelving. — 3. (*ant.* beifällig) depreciative, unfavourable; e-e ⸗e Kritik an adverse criticism; e-n ⸗ (abschlägig) bescheiden to give a p. a refusal or a rebuff or a snub. — 4. ⊕ (minderwertig) inferior. — 5. ⚘ (leicht abfallend) deciduous. — 6. = abtrünnig. — 7. ↘ (ungültig) void.
Ab-fall(s)=produkt ⊕ (⁸ᴶ...) *n* ⊕ waste-product; **⸗röhre** *f* waste-pipe; **⸗stoffe** ⊕ *m/pl.* waste-materials, ⸗substances.
ab-fangen (⁸ᴶ~) I *v/a.* ⊕b** 1. e-m die Tauben ⸗ to catch a p.'s ...; e-m das Wasser ⁊c. ⸗ to cut off a p.'s ...; e-m die Kunden ⸗ to take a p.'s customers away. — 2. (lauernd fangen) to seize; Briefe ⁊c. ⸗ to intercept — 3. (s. ab= ...6) *hunt.* Hirsche, Sauen ⸗ to kill ... with the hunting-knife. — 4. ⊕, ✕ (stützen) to prop,support.—II~n⊕ interception.
ab-färben (⁸ᴶ~) ⊕b** I *v/a.* to give the last dip (or dye) to a th. — II *v/n.* (h.) to lose (one's) colour, to fade.
ab-fasern (⁸ᴶ~) ⊕a** vom Tuch ⁊c.: (h.) ↘ sich ⸗ *v/refl.* to come off in threads or fibres, to ravel out, to fray.
ab-fassen (⁸ᴶ~) I *v/a.* ⊕** 1. (verfassen) to compose, to pen; *jur.* to draw up, to indite; höflich ⸗ to couch in polite terms; kurz abgefaßt concise(ly worded); in Prosa abgefaßt (written) in prose, in prosaic form. — 2. (ertappen) e-n bei et., auf der Tat ⸗ to catch a p. in the very act, stärker: to catch a p. red-handed). — 3. ⊕ (Waren in Pakete abwiegen) to measure (or weigh) off. — 4. *hunt.* eine Leine ⸗ to wind off a leash. — 5. ⊕ Schmiede: to bend. — II ~ n ⊕ 6. = Abfassung.
Ab-fasser (⁸ᴶ~) *m* ⊕, **~in** *f* ⊕ writer, inditer; *vgl. a.* Verfasser.
Ab-fassung (⁸ᴶ~) *f* ⊕ zu abfassen 1: composition; draft(ing); inditement.
ab-fasten (⁸ᴶ~) ⊕** I *v/a.* ⊕ to atone for ... by fasting. — II sich ⸗ *v/refl.* to fast for a long time, to starve o.s.
ab-faulen (⁸ᴶ~) *v/n.* (sn) ⊕** to rot off, to decay and drop off.
ab-fechten (⁸ᴶ~) ⊕b** I *v/a.* 1. e-m et. ⸗ to wrest a th. from a p. by fighting. — 2. von bettelnden Handwerksburschen: e-e Straße ⸗ to beg at every door, P to work a street. — II sich ⸗ *v/refl.* 3. to weary o.s. with fighting.
ab-federn (⁸ᴶ~) ⊕a** I *v/a* 1. e-n Rock ⁊c. ⸗ to pick the feathers off ...; ⊕ (mit Federn versehen) to provide with springs; *hunt.* Vögel ⸗ (durch e-n Stich mit einer ausgerissenen Schwungfeder in den Hinterkopf töten) to kill birds by pricking the back of the head with a pinion. — 2. (Vögel rupfen) to pluck. — II *v/n.* (h.) 3. (mausern) to moult.
ab-fegen (⁸ᴶ~) *v/a.* ⊕** 1. to sweep (off), to cleanse; den Staub ⸗ to dust. — 2. *hunt.* das Gehörn ⸗ to fray ...
Ab-feger (⁸ᴶ~) *m* ⊕ sweep(er), cleaner.
ab-feilen (⁸ᴶ~) *v/a.* ⊕** to file off, to cut off with a file, Münzen: to clip.

Ab-feil-raspel ⊕ (⁸ᴶ...) *f* ⊕ great rasp, rasp used for filing.
ab-feilschen (⁸ᴶ~) *v/a.* ⊕** = abhandeln 4.
ab-feimen (⁸ᴶ~) I *v/a.* ⊕** Milch ⁊c. ⸗ to skim (or scum) ... — II **ab-gefeimt** *p.p.* u. *a.* ⊕ *fig.* crafty, cunning; Ler Schurke arrant (or arch⸗)rogue or knave, deep scoundrel, F artful dodger.
ab-fertig/en (⁸ᴶ~) I *v/a.* ⊕** 1. (erledigen) to despatch, forward; eilig ⸗ to hurry forward; Geschäfte ⸗ to expedite. — 2. *fig.* (abweisen) e-n ⸗ F to send a p. about his business, to give a p. a set-down; e-n derb, grob ⸗ to send a p. off with a flea in his ear; e-n kurz ⸗ to be short (or brusque, offhandish) with a p., to snub a p.; sich mit Geld ⸗ l. to accept compensation; sie wollte sich nicht ⸗ l. etwa: she would not be put off. — II ~ n ⊕ 3. s. Ajung.
Ab-fertigung (⁸ᴶ~) *f* ⊕ 1. despatch. — 2. *fig.* (Abweisung) snub(bing).
Ab-fertigungs=amt (⁸ᴶ~...) *n* ⊕ despatching-office; ⊕ **⸗schein** *m*, **⸗schreiben** *n* declaration, Zollamt: permit; **⸗stelle** ⊟ *f* goods-platform.
ab-fetten (⁸ᴶ~) ⊕** I *v/a.* 1. Koch.: (schmalzen) to do up with lard. — 2. Suppe ⁊c. ⸗ to skim the fat off ... — II *v/n.* (h.) 3. (to give off) grease. [of moisture]
ab-feuchten (⁸ᴶ~) *v/a.* ⊕** to deprive)
ab-feuern (⁸ᴶ~) ⊕a** *v/a.* 1. ein Gewehr: to fire (off), to discharge; e-n Schuß ⸗ auf to shoot at. — II *v/n.* (h.) 2. ✕ (give) fire. — 3. (das Feuer erlöschen l.) to stop heating or firing, to let the fire drop. — III ~ n ⊕ u. **Ab-feu(e)rung** *f* ⊕ 4. firing, discharge (of fire-arms), ↓ broadside.
ab-fiedeln (⁸ᴶ~) *v/a.* ⊕** 1. *contp.* e. Lied ⸗ to scrape (or fiddle) ... — 2. ⊕ *metall.* (den Abstrich abziehen) to rake out the dross.
ab-fiedern ⊕ (⁸ᴶ~) *v/a.* ⊕a** Glas ⸗ to trim off ... (with the grossing-iron).
ab-fieren ↓ (⁸ᴶ~) *v/a.*; *Hom.* abvieren) *v/a.* ⊕** e. Tau ⸗ to veer (out) ...; to pay out ...
ab-filtrieren ⊕ (⁸ᴶ~) *v/a.* ⊕*/* to filter off, to pass through a filter.
ab-filzen (⁸ᴶ~) *v/a.* ⊕** 1. ⊕ to free from felt. — 2. (schelten) to scold, reprimand.
ab-finden (⁸ᴶ~) ⊕** I *v/a.* *jur.* e-n ⸗ to pay off; Gläubiger ⸗ to compound with ...; Prinzen ⸗ to make a grant to ...; seine Töchter ⸗ to settle money on ...; für Verluste: to indemnify or compensate for; man hat ihn mit einer Kleinigkeit abgefunden he was silenced (F squared) with a trifle. — II *v/refl.* sich mit e-m ⸗ to come to an arrangement (or understanding) with a p., gerichtlich: to (make a) compromise (or settlement) with a p.; sie haben sich dahin mit=ea. abgefunden, daß // they agreed that //; sich mit s-m Gewissen ⸗ to quiet one's conscience.
Ab-findung (⁸ᴶ~) *f* ⊕ *jur.* (legal) settlement, arrangement, mit Gläubigern: composition, *v.* Prinzen: grant to ...; (Schadloshaltung) indemnification.
Ab-findungs=geld (⁸ᴶ~...) *n* ⊕, **⸗quantum** *n*, **⸗summe** *f* (sum of) indemnity, (Schweigegeld) hush-money; **⸗vertrag** *m* agreement, compromise.
ab-fingern (⁸ᴶ~) *v/a.* ⊕a** = abzählen 1.

ab-fischen (⁸ᴶ~) ⊕** I *v/a.* 1. e-n Teich ⸗ to clear ... by fishing. — 2. *fig.* das Beste ⸗ to take the cream off; e-m et. ⸗ F to trick (or do) a p. out of a th. — II *v/n.* (h.) 3. to cease fishing.
ab-sitzen ⊕ (⁸ᴶ~) *v/a.* ⊕** Garn ⸗ (in Strähnen wickeln) to divide (or make) ... into skeins, to hank ...
ab-flachen (⁸ᴶ~) ⊕** I *v/a.* to level (or flatten) down; abgeflacht oblate. — II sich ⸗ *v/refl.* to flatten, to subside, to settle down, ↓ vom Meeresgrunde: to shoal. — III ~ n ⊕ u. **Ab-flachung** *f* ⊕ *cryst.* ~ der Kanten: bevelment.
ab-flammen ⊕ (⁸ᴶ~) *v/a.* ⊕** Gerberei: Leder ⸗ to tallow ...
ab-flauen (⁸ᴶ~) ⊕** I *v/a.* 1. ⊕ *metall.* Erze ⸗ to wash (or buddle) ... — 2. Tuchmacherei: to rinse. — II *v/n.* (h.) 3. ↓ (*ant.* auffrischen) der Wind flaut ab ..., is calming down; ⊕ Börse: die Kurse flauen ab prices are drooping or sagging or giving way.
Ab-flau-faß (⁸ᴶ...) *n* ⊕ washing(-)tub, (rinsing) buddle; **⸗herd** *m* (Waschbühne) washing(-)hearth, buddling-dish.
ab-flechten (⁸ᴶ~) *v/a.* ⊕b** to unplait.
ab-flecken (⁸ᴶ~) *v/n.* (h.) ⊕** to stain, *v.* Farben: to come off (in stains).
ab-flehen (⁸ᴶ~) *v/a.* ⊕** e-m et. ⸗ to obtain a th. by imploring a p.
Ab-fleisch=... (⁸ᴶ...) *s.* Ausfleisch=...
ab-fliegen (⁸ᴶ~) *v/n.* (sn) Waft** to fly off; von Mützen auch: to be blown off; *for.* von Holz: (dürr w.) to dry (and drop) off.
ab-fließen (⁸ᴶ~) *v/n.* (sn) ⊕d** to flow off or away; in e-n See ⸗ to drain into ...; ↓ das Hochwasser fließt ab the tide is receding; ⸗ l. to let run, to run off.
ab-flöhen (⁸ᴶ~) I *v/a.* ⊕** e-n Hund ⸗ to clear ... of fleas, to pick the fleas off ... — II sich ⸗ *v/refl.* to catch (or look for) one's fleas.
ab-flößen (⁸ᴶ~) *v/a.* ⊕** Holz ⸗ to float (or to raft) timber (down-stream).
Ab-flug (⁸ᴶ) *m* ⊕d.1. ~ der Störche ⁊c. flight ..., departure ... — 2. *for.* ~ des Holzes (winged) seed(s) borne off by the wind.
Ab-fluß (⁸ᴶ~) *m* ⊕a. 1. (Abfließen) flowing (or draining) off; discharge (aus from); *fig.* ⊕ ~ des Geldes withdrawal, in andere Länder: drain, efflux; *s. a.* Anfluß 1. — 2. (Stelle zum ~) gutter, gully, waste-pipe; sink; ⊕ *mach.* escape (-pipe). — 3. ~ e-s Teiches ⊕ outlet, waste.
Ab-fluß=graben (⁸ᴶ...) *m* ⊕ drain(ing-ditch); **⸗rinne** *f* trench; ⊕ Gießerei: cast; **⸗rohr** *n*, **⸗röhre** *f* escape- (or waste-)pipe; **⸗schleuse** *f* water-gate; **⸗venti'l** *n* escape-valve; **⸗wasser** *n* sewerage. [or away, to float away.]
ab-fluten (⁸ᴶ~) *v/n.* (sn) ⊕** to flow off)
ab-folgen ↘ (⁸ᴶ~) *v/a.* u. *v/n.* (sn) ⊕** = verabfolgen.
ab-fordern (⁸ᴶ~) I *v/a.* ⊕a** 1. e-m et. ⸗ to demand a th. of (or from) a p.; ✕ die Parole ⸗ to ask for the watchword; e-m Rechnung ⸗ to call a p. to account (for). — 2. ↘ Gott hat ihn abgefordert ... called him to Himself. — II ~ n ⊕ u. **Ab-forderung** *f* ⊕ 3. demand. — 4. (Abberufung) recall.
Ab-forderungs=brief (⁸ᴶ~...) *m* ⊕, **⸗schreiben** *n* letter(s) of recall.

⊕ scientific; ⚘ botanical; ⚲ geography; ⊕ machinery; ✕ mining; ⚔ military; ↓ marine; ⊕ commercial; ✉ postal; 🚂 railway.

[Abform] — 8 — [abgehen]

Ab-form ⊕ (ˊˋ) *f* ⊛ cast, mould, form.
ab-formen ⊕ (ˊˋ) *v/a.* ⊛** 1. to mould, to shape; in Gips ꝛc.: to (take a) cast (of). — 2. Schuhmacherei: (vom Leisten schlagen) to take off the last. [elicits.th. from a p.]
ab-forschen (ˊˋ) *v/a.* ⊕** e-m et. ⚲ to
ab-forsten (ˊˋ) *v/a.* ⊛**=abholzen 1.
ab-fragen (ˊˋ) *v/a.* ⊛** (⁺⁺ ⊛b**) 1. e-m et. ⚲ to question (stärker: to examine) a p. about a th.; e-m Geheimnisse, die Künste ⚲: F to pump a p. (dry). — 2. e-m Schüler die Aufgabe ⚲ to hear a pupil['s (home-)lesson(s)].
ab-fressen (ˊˋ) *v/a.* ⊛** 1. to eat off; Laub ꝛc.: to browse. — 2. *fig.* † der Kummer will ihm das Herz ⚲ (G.) grief is eating out his heart or is killing him.
ab-frieren (ˊˋ) *v/n.* (ſn) u. *v/a.* ⊛c** to freeze off, to be nipped by the frost; von Gliedern a. to get (or be) frost-bitten; es ſind ihm zwei Zehen abgefroren two of his toes were (genauer: came off by being) frost-bitten.
ab-fühlen (ˊˋ) *v/a.* ⊛** *fig.* e-m et. ⚲ to read (or guess) a p.'s thoughts.
Ab-fuhr (ˊˋ) *f* ⊕ 1. a. ~e ⊕ ⊛ (Wegfahren) von Holz, Ware ꝛc.: carrying (or carting) away (of) ..., carriage, cartage; ~ der Auswurfstoffe taking away (or removal of) refuse or rubbish or garbage, clearing the dust-bin, scavengers' work. — 2. burſch. *fenc.* (Kampfunfähigmachung) putting (an opponent) hors de combat; disablement.
Ab-führ-arbeit (ˊˋ...) *f* ⊛ Drahtzieherei: wire-drawing; =eisen *n* wire-drawing iron (vgl. abführen 9).
ab-führen (ˊˋ) I *v/a.* ⊛** 1. e-n ⚲ to take a p. off; in das Gefängnis ⚲ to march off to gaol; von Sachen: to carry off; e-n Fluß ⚲ to divert ... from its course. — 2. ⚔ Gefang(e)ne ⚲ to escort (or convey, remove) prisoners, Truppen ⚲ to march off troops; die Wache ⚲ to relieve guard. — 3. *hunt.* e-n Hund ⚲ (auf die Spur bringen) to put a dog on the scent, to train a hound for hunting. — 4. *fig.* e-n (unabsichtlich) vom Wege ⚲ to take a p. out of his way; das führt mich zu weit von meinem Gegenstande ab this carries me too far from ... — 5. *med.* von Mitteln: to purge, gewöhnl. to relieve the bowels of; als *v/n.* (h.) von Personen: to relieve one's bowels, to clear one's system, to take aperients or purgatives; ⚲d aperient, laxative, ⚲ cathartic; ⚲de Mittel ſ. Abführmittel. — 6. *bſd.* ⊛ eine Schuld ⚲ to discharge (or clear off) ..., eine Summe ⚲ to pay off ... — 7. *fenc.* e-n ⚲ to disable a p. — 8. e-n (schön) ⚲ to give a person a (nasty) rebuff. — 9. ⊕ (Goldſtangen) to draw (gold-wire). — II ~ *n* ⚂ 10. = Abführung. [wire-drawer.]
Ab-führer ⊕ (ˊˋ) *m* ⊛ Drahtzieherei:
Abfuhr-gesellschaft (ˊˋ...) *f* ⊛ company for the clearing of cesspools or dustbins; =karren *m* (parish) dust-cart, night-cart; =kosten *pl.* carriage.
Ab-führ-mittel (ˊˋ...) *n* ⊛ *med.* aperient (medicine), purgative, laxative; =mus *n* electuary (made) of senna-leaves.
Ab-fuhr-system (ˊˋ...) *n* ⊛ scavengering; cesspool-system.

Ab-führung (ˊˋ) *f* carriage, conveyance; e-r Summe: payment; *med.* purging; ⊛ wire-drawing.
Ab-führungs-gang (ˊˋ...) *m* ⊛, =kanal *m*, *anat.* secretory duct or canal; =mittel *n* = Abführmittel; =weg *m* = gang.
ab-füllen (ˊˋ) *v/a.* ⊛** 1. to take (or skim) off; das Fett von der Sauce ⚲ to skim the gravy. — 2. Bier ꝛc. ⚲ to draw off ..., to decant; in Flaschen: to bottle ...; ein Faß: to empty.
ab-furchen (ˊˋ) *v/a.* ⊛** to separate (or divide) by furrows.
ab-füttern, P **=futtern** (ˊˋ) I *v/a.* ⊛a** 1. Vieh ⚲ to feed ...; des Abends: to give the last feed (or provender) to ... (at night-time). — 2. F Freunde ⚲ to give a dinner-party (F a big feed) to ...— II ~ *n* ⚃ u. **Ab-fütterung** *f* ⊛ 3. (ſ.1) feeding; ~ der Pferde last feed of (or provender for) ...; (ſ.2) dinner-party, F big feed.
Ab-gabe (ˊˋ) *f* ⊛ 1. (Ablieferung) delivery; Politik ꝛc.: ~ der Stimme voting, polling. — 2. (Steuer) impost, duty, (Akziſe) excise; ⚔ ~ an den Staat royalty; ~n (bezahlen) to pay taxes; hohe ~n zahlen to be heavily taxed; drückende ~ (heavy) burden. — 3. ⊛ (Wechsel) draft.
Ab-gaben-bureau (ˊˋ...) *n* ⊛ excise-office; =frei *a.* exempt from taxes, duty-free; ⚲e Ware goods free of duty; =freiheit *f* immunity (from taxes); =pächter *m* farmer of taxes, *bibl.* publican; ⚲pflichtig *a.* dutiable; =verteilung *f* assessment of taxes; =wesen *n* taxation. [gallop off.]
ab-galoppieren (ˊˋˋ) *v/n.* (ſn) ⊛*/*⁺ to
Ab-gang (ˊˋ) *m* ⊕c. 1. setting out, start(-ing), departure; vor (nach) dem ~(e) des Zuges before (after) the train started. — 2. aus einer Stelle: retirement from; e-s Ministers: resignation; e-s Schauspielers: *exit*, (die Schlußworte des abtretenden Schauspielers) the actor's last words before his *exit*; ⚓ ~ e-s Schiffes: sailing ..., putting off to sea; beim ~e vom Gymnasium, vom Militär: on leaving school, the army. — 3. e-r Ware: sale; guten ~ h. to find (or to meet with) a ready sale, to go off well; schlechten ~ h. to sell badly; keinen ~ h. to remain (F to hang) on hand. — 4. (Verlust) waste, loss; beim Wiegen: deficiency; bei Flüssigkeiten: leakage; an Unkosten: charges to be deducted. — 5. *path. v.* Blut, Galle ꝛc.: flux (or loss) of ... — 6. = Abfall 8; in ~ kommen to fall into disuse, to go out of fashion.
ab-gängig (ˊˋ) *a.* ⊛ 1. (fehlend) deficient, missing. — 2. ⊛ (vgl. gängig) saleable, marketable. — 3. (abgenutzt) worn out; ⚲ werden to go out of fashion.
Ab-gängling (ˊˋ) *m* ⊕d. *path.* (unzeitig geborene Leibesfrucht) abortion.
Abgangs-bureau (ˊˋ...) *n* ⊛ outward (goods-)office; =dampf *m* dead steam.
Ab-gängsel (ˊˋ) *n* ⊛e. refuse.
Ab-gangs-prüfung (ˊˋ...) *f* ⊛ leaving-examination; =station *f* Fernſpr.: sending station; =winkel ⚔ *m* der Flugbahn angle of departure; =zeit *f* time of d.; =zeugnis *n* leaving-certificate.
ab-gären (ˊˋ) *v/n.*(h.) ⊛a**1. to ferment thoroughly. — 2. to cease fermenting.

Ab-gase ⊕ (ˊˋ) *n/pl.* ⚀a. = Abhitze.
ab-gattern ⚲ (ˊˋ) *v/a.* ⊛a** e-m et. ⚲ to coax (or worry) a p. out of a th.
ab-gaunern (ˊˋ) *v/a.* ⊛a** einem etwas ⚲ to swindle (or trick, F diddle) a p. out of a th.
▶ **ab-gearbeitet, -gebacken** ꝛc. (ˊˋ...) *p.p.* (u. *a.*) ſ. ab-arbeiten, -backen ꝛc.
ab-geben (ˊˋ) ⊛c** I *v/a.* 1. meiſt: to deliver (up), to hand over; Gepäck ⚲ to book (or deposit) one's luggage; e-n Brief bei e-m ⚲ to leave ... with a p.; e-m eigenhändig ⚲ to put into a p.'s hands; auf der Post ⚲ to (take to the) post. — 2. ein Urteil ⚲ to pass one's judgment; ſ-e Meinung ⚲ to offer one's opinion; eine Erklärung ⚲ to declare; ſ-e Stimme ⚲ to (give one's) vote, to poll. — 3. F e-m eins, et. ⚲ to give a p. a knock or a rap on his knuckles. — 4. ⊛ e-n Wechsel auf e-n ⚲ to draw (a bill) on a p. — 5. viel an Steuern ⚲ to be heavily taxed. — 6. (überlassen) to give up, to supply; ⊛ to sell; F um diesen Preis gibt man nichts davon ab it cannot be had (or made) at this price; er gibt niemand(em) was ab he keeps all to himself. — 7. (aufgeben) to get rid of, to give up. — 8. (vorstellen) to serve as; e-n Augenzeugen von et. ⚲ to be an eye-witness to a th.; die Mittelsperson ⚲ to play the intermediary, ⊛ to act as middleman; ⚔ e-n guten Soldaten ⚲ to make a good soldier. — II *v/imp.* 9. F es wird etwas ⚲ (Regen, Verdruß ꝛc.) we shall have (rain, trouble, &c.); es wird Schläge, Streit ⚲ it will come to blows, there will be a quarrel or a row. — III *v/n.* (h.) 10. Spiel: (*ant.* angeben) to deal for the last time. — IV *ſich* ⚲ *v/refl.* 11. ſich mit et. ⚲ to concern o.s. about a th.; ſich mit e-m ⚲ to have intercourse with a p.; ich kann mich nicht mit ihm ⚲ I won't have anything to do with him; geben Sie ſich damit nicht ab! don't meddle with it!; ſich mit schlechter Gesellschaft ⚲ to keep bad company; er gibt ſich zu viel mit diesem Menschen ab F he is too thick with ...; ⊛ ſich mit Aktien viel ⚲ to dabble a good deal in shares.
▶ **ab-gebildet, -gebrannt** ꝛc. (ˊˋ...) *p.p.* (u. *a.*) ſ. ab-bilden, -brennen ꝛc.
ab-gebrochen (ˊˋˋ) ſ. abbrechen IV; **~heit** (ˊˋˋ-) *f* ⊛ (o. *pl.*) abruptness; disconnected state.
ab-gedroschen F (ˊˋˋ) ſ. abdreschen 2; **~heit** F (ˊˋˋ-) *f* ⊛ triviality.
ab-gefeimt (ˊˋ) ſ. abfeimen II; **~heit** *f* (~-) *f* ⊛ artfulness, cunning, F depth.
ab-gefunden, -gegangen, -gegleitet, -gegossen, -gegriffen ꝛc. *p.p.* ſ. ab-finden, -gehen, -gleiten, -gießen, -greifen u.s.w.
ab-geh(e)n (ˊˋ)(ˇ) ⊛** I *v/n.* (ſn) 1. (*ant.* ankommen) to go off, to depart, to leave; ⚓ auch: to put to sea; das Schiff geht heute ab ... will sail to-day; der Dampfer geht ab ... is leaving port; Bühnenweisung: geht ab *exit*, geh(e)n ab *exeunt*; ⚲ laſſen: r) ⊛ Waren: to forward, to despatch; b) ⚓ Schiffe: to send out; c) ⚒ e-n Zug: to start; ⚲de Ladung outward cargo or goods; ⚲

Zeichen (ſ. S. XVII): F familiär; P Volkssprache; Γ Gaunersprache; ⚲ selten; † alt (auch gestorben); * neu (auch geboren); ⁺⁺ unrichtig;

[abgeizen] — 9 — [abgöttisch]

des Ministerium outgoing (or retiring) ministry. — 2. **ab** und **zu** geh(e)n to go to and fro; **auf** und **ab** geh(e)n f. auf II. — 3. (mit Tode) ⤶, F zur großen Armee ⤶ to depart this life, F to join the majority. — 4. *med. v.* Würmern 2c.: to pass (from the system). — 5. (sich loslösen) to come undone. — 6. (sich entfernen) to go away; von der Schule ⤶ to leave school; abgegang(e)ner Beamter official who has resigned, bisw. ex-official; von seiner Meinung ⤶ to change (or alter) one's opinion; geh(e)n Sie nicht von der Sache ab keep to the subject; er will von f-m Vorhaben nicht ⤶ he persists in his plan; hier geht der Weg ab here the road branches off. — 7. (Abzug leiden) to be reducible by; davon geht nichts ab nothing can be taken off; was ihm an Gabe abgeht, ersetzt er durch // what he lacks in ability he makes up by //; der rechte Takt geht ihm ab he is wanting in tact; sich nichts ⤶ lassen not to stint o.s. in any way; ⚙ hundert Mark geh(e)n für Spesen ab the charges (or expenses) come to five pounds. — 8 ⚙ (Absatz finden) to sell; reißend ⤶ to be in great demand, to find a ready (or rapid) sale, F to go off like steam. — 9. (enden) to end; alles ist gut abgegangen all passed off well; es ging nicht ganz glatt ab there was a hitch (somewhere). — II *v/a.* 10. (abnutzen) to wear down or use up (by walking); ↘ sich (*dat.*) die Beine nach et. ⤶ to run one's legs off for a th.; F *co.* abgegangen werden to be sent (or turned) off or adrift, to get the kickout or the sack. — 11. (abmessen) to pace off, to measure by steps. — III ~ *n* ㉓ 12. = Abgang 1 u. 2; ihr Abund Zu-gehen their coming and going, geh. Spr.: their *exits* and their entrances.

ab-geizen(ᵍ ᴸ ᵛ) ⓫*** I *v/a.* f-m Munde et. ⤶ to grudge o.s. a th., to stint o.s. of a th. — II **sich** ⤶ *v/refl.* to starve (o.s.) by one's avarice.— f. a. abkargen.

Ab-geklärtheit (ᵍ ᴸ -) *f* ⑯ *fig.* clearness.

Ab-gekratzte(§) (ᵍ ᴸ ᵛ) f. abkratzen III.

ab-gelagert (ᵍ ᴸ ᵛ) f. ablagern IV.

ab-gelebt(ᵍ ᴸ ᵛ) f. ableben IV; ~**heit** (~-) *f* ⑯ (*o. pl.*) decrepitude, senility, senile decay. I(~-) *f* ⑯ (*o. pl.*) remoteness.

ab-gelegen (ᵍ ᴸ ᵛ) f. abliegen III; ~**heit**/

ab-geloben (ᵍ ᴸ ᵛ) *v/a.* ⓫*/* to abjure.

ab-gemessen (ᵍ ᴸ ᵛ) *p.p. u. a.* ⑯ f. abmessen III; ~**heit** (~-) *f* ⑯ (*o. pl.*) 1. *v.* Personen: stiffness, reserved manner.—2. *v.* Sachen: exactness, precision.

ab-geneigt (ᵍ ᴸ ᵎ) f. abneigen II; ~**heit** (~-ᵎ) *f* ⑯ (*o. pl.*) disinclination; (Widerwillen) aversion (to or for).

ab-genutzt (ᵍ ᴸ ᵛ) f. abnutzen III.

ab-geordnet (ᵍ ᴸ ᵛ) *p.p. v.* abordnen; ~**e**[**r**] *m*) *f* (ᵍ ᴸ ᵛ) ⑰, Titel ⑭⑮ deputy, delegate. representative; (engl. Volksvertreter) Member of Parliament (M.P.); *parl.* der ~e für B. the Honourable Member for B.

Ab-geordneten-haus(ᵇ...) *n* ⑫ chamber of deputies, Engl.: House of Commons; **=wahl** *f* parliamentary election.

ab-geplattet (ᵍ ᴸ ᵛ) f. abplatten II.

ab-gerben (ᵍ ᴸ ᵛ) *v/a.* ⓫** 1. ⊕ Gerberei: to tan thoroughly. — 2. *fig.* F (durchprügeln) einen ⤶ to give a p. a good tanning or leathering or hiding.

ab-gerechnet (ᵍ ᴸ ᵛ) f. abrechnen I.

ab-gerieben (ᵍ ᴸ ᵛ) f. abreiben IV.

ab-gerissen (ᵍ ᴸ ᵛ) f. abreißen V; ~**heit** (ᵍ ᴸ ᵛ -) *f* ⑯ (*o. pl.*) 1. der Kleidung: raggedness. — 2. im Stil: abruptness, roughness, desultoriness.

ab-gerundet (ᵍ ᴸ ᵛ) f. abrunden III; ~**sein** (ᵍ ᴸ ᵛ ᴸ) *n* ㉓ roundness.

Ab-gesandte([**r**] *m*) *f* (ᵍ ᴸ ᵛ) [*p.p. v.* absenden]⑰, Titel ⑭⑮ 1. delegate, envoy, geheime(r) ~ emissary, päpstliche(r) ~ nuncio. — 2. (Gesandter) ambassador; (Bevollmächtigter) plenipotentiary.

Ab-gesang (ᵍ ᴸ ᵛ) *m* ①c. (*ant.* Aufgesang) last portion of a song; ehm., noch in Kirchenliedern: burden to a hymn.

ab-geschieden (ᵍ ᴸ ᵛ ᴸ) f. abscheiden I u. II; ~**heit**(ᵍ ᴸ ᵛ -) *f* ⑯ (*o. pl.*) retirement, stärker: seclusion.

ab-geschlagen (ᵍ ᴸ ᵛ ᵛ) f. abschlagen V; ~**heit**(~-) *f* ⑯ exhaustion, prostration.

ab-geschliffen (ᵍ ᴸ ᵛ ᵛ) f. abschleifen² 3; ~**heit** (ᵍ ᴸ ᵛ -) *f* ⑯ (*o. pl.*) polished manners, polish, refinement.

ab-geschlossen (ᵍ ᴸ ᵛ ᵛ) f. abschließen VI; ~**heit** (ᵍ ᴸ ᵛ ᴸ -) *f* ⑯ (*o. pl.*) seclusion; ~**heit** in sich compactness.

ab-geschmackt (ᵍ ᴸ ᵛ ᵛ) *fig.* I *a.* ⑯ insipid, absurd, silly; ⤶e Reden senseless talk. — II ~**e**(**s**) *n* ⑰ (*o. pl.*) absurdity. — ~**heit** (~-) *f* ⑯ insipidity, absurdity, preposterousness. — Vgl. ab=... 10.

ab-geschnitten (ᵍ ᴸ ᵛ ᵛ) *p.p. v.* abschneiden; ~**heit** (ᵍ ᴸ ᵛ ᵛ -) *f* ⑯ (*o. pl.*) (state of) being separated; isolation.

ab-geschossen(ᵍ ᴸ ᵛ ᵛ) *a.* ⑯(D 9) f. abschießen.

ab-geschworen (ᵍ ᴸ ᵛ ᴸ ᵛ) f. abschwören IV.

ab-gesehen (~) *p.p. v.* absehen (f. b.s, bsd. 7).

Ab-gesondertheit (ᵍ ᴸ ᵛ ᵛ -) *f* ⑯ (*o. pl.*) separateness, loneliness.

ab-gespannt(ᵍ ᴸ ᵛ ᵛ) f. abspannen III; ~**heit** (ᵍ ᴸ ᵛ -) *f* ⑯ (*o. pl.*) (Mattigkeit) enervation, exhaustion, languid state, languor; (Niedergeschlagenheit) depressed state, depression.

ab-gestanden (ᵍ ᴸ ᵛ ᵛ) f. abstehen V.

ab-gestorben (ᵍ ᴸ ᵛ ᵛ) f. absterben 2; ~**heit** (ᵍ ᴸ ᵛ ᵛ -) *f* ⑯ (*o. pl.*) (Gleichgültigkeit) indifference (for or to), apathy; eines Gliedes: deadness, torpor.

ab-gestoßen (ᵍ ᴸ ᵛ ᵛ) f. abstoßen, bsd. 3.

ab-gestumpft (ᵍ ᴸ ᵛ ᵛ) f. abstumpfen (bsd. 3); ~**heit** (ᵍ ᴸ ᵛ ᵛ -) *f* ⑯ (*o. pl.*), ~**sein** (ᵍ ᴸ ᵛ ᴸ) *n* ㉓ 1. ⊕ bluntness. — 2. *fig.* obtuseness, callousness.

ab-getan (ᵍ ᴸ ᵛ) *p.p.* f. abtun III.

ab-getragen (ᵍ ᴸ ᵛ ᵛ) *p.p.* f. abtragen 4; ~**sein** (ᵍ ᴸ ᵛ ᴸ ᴸ) *n* ㉓ der Kleider: threadbareness, shabbiness, F seediness.

ab-getreten (ᵍ ᴸ ᵛ ᵛ) *p.p. v.* abtreten.

ab-getrieben (ᵍ ᴸ ᵛ ᵛ) *p.p.* f. abtreiben 6.

ab-gewinnen (ᵍ ᴸ ᵛ ᵛ) *v/a.* ⓪a (b)*/* to win a th. of (or from) a p.; er hat mir (all) mein Geld abgewonnen he won all my money, *b.s.* F he fleeced me; ich kann der Sache keinen Geschmack ⤶ I have no taste for it, I don't see anything (attractive) in it, (es macht mir kein Vergnügen) it gives me no pleasure; e-m den Vorsprung ⤶ to get the start of a p., to steal a march upon a p.; ⚓ e-m Schiffe den Wind ⤶ to gain the weather-gage of a ship.

Ab-gewinnung (ᵍ ᴸ ᵛ ᵛ) *f* ⑯ winning, gain.

ab-gewogen (ᵍ ᴸ ᵛ) *p.p. von* ab-wägen und ab-wiegen (f. b.s).

ab-gewöhn/en (ᵍ ᴸ ᵛ) I *v/a.* ⓫*/* 1. e-m et. ⤶ to break a p. of a habit; sich (*dat.*) das Rauchen 2c. ⤶ to give up (or to leave off) smoking, &c. — II ~ *n* ㉓ u. A/ung *f* ⑯ 2. leaving off a habit. — 3. breaking a p. of a habit.

ab-gewonnen (ᵍ ᴸ ᵛ ᵛ) *p.p. v.* abgewinnen.

ab-gezehrt (ᵍ ᴸ ᵛ) *p.p.* f. abzehren III.

ab-gezogen (ᵍ ᴸ ᵛ ᵛ) *p.p.* f. abziehen V.

ab-gieren ⚓ (ᵍ ᴸ ᵛ) *v/a.* ⓫** to sheer off.

ab-gieß/en (ᵍ ᴸ ᵛ) I *v/a.* ⓪d** 1. to pour off. — 2. *chm.* (abklären) to decant. — 3. ⊕ (in e-r Form) to cast, to (shape in a) mould. — II ~ *n* ㉓ 4. = A/ung.

Ab-gießer ⊕ (~) *m* ㉒ moulder, former.

Ab-gießung (ᵍ ᴸ ᵛ) *f* ⑯ *chm.* (vorsichtige) ~ decantation; f. a. Abguß 1 u. 3.

ab-gipfeln (ᵍ ᴸ ᵛ) *v/a.* ⓪a** *hort.* Bäume ⤶ to top (or head, poll) …

ab-gittern (ᵍ ᴸ ᵛ) *v/a.* ⓪a** to rail (or fence) off, to separate by a railing.

Ab-glanz (ᵍ ᴸ) *m* ①a. (*o. pl.*) 1. reflected light or splendour, reflection. — 2. *fig.* ein schwacher ~ von a feeble copy of.

ab-glätten ⊕ (ᵍ ᴸ ᵛ) *v/a.* ⓫** (a. *fig.*) to (make) smooth, to polish, to give the last polish (or finish) to; ⊕ mit Bimsstein ⤶ to pumice(-stone).

ab-gleich/en (ᵍ ᴸ ᵛ) I *v/a.* ⓪aff** 1. to make even or smooth, to equalize. — 2. ⚙ Schuld und Forderung ⤶ to balance an account. — 3. ⊕ *arch.* eine Mauer ⤶ to (make) level; abgeglichen (von Flächen) flush; *mint. u. typ.* to adjust. — II ~ *n* ㉓ = A/ung.

Ab-gleich-feile ⊕ (ᵍ ᴸ -) *f* ⑯ equalling- (or smoothing-)file; **=stange** *f* Uhrmacherei: adjusting-tool, lever.

Ab-gleichung (ᵍ ᴸ ᵛ) *f* ⑯ des Bodens: levelling; ⚙ *mint.*, &c. adjustment; ~**s=**… (ᴸ…) ㉒ = Abgleich=…

Ab-gleich-wage *f* ⑯ *mint.* adjusting-scale or -balance; **=zirkel** *m* divider.

ab-gleiten (ᵍ ᴸ ᵛ) *v/n.* (ſn.) ⓪b** to glide (or slide, slip) off; ⊕ *v.* Fahrrad u. Automobil: to skid; *fig.* alle Ermahnungen gleiten an ihm ab he pays no heed (or he is deaf) to …; vom Pfade der Tugend ⤶ to drift (or stray) from the path of virtue.

ab-glimmen (ᵍ ᴸ ᵛ) *v/n.* (ſn) ⓪a** to cease glowing or glimmering; die ⤶de Kohle the dying embers *pl.*

ab-glitschen F (~) *v/n.* (ſn) ⓪** = abgleiten.

ab-glühen (ᵍ ᴸ ᵛ) I *v/a.* ⓪⊕ Eisen 2c. ⤶ to make … red-hot; *metall.* (ausbrennen) to anneal. — 2. Wein ⤶ to mull … — II *v/n.* (ſn) 3. to cease glowing, to cool down.

Ab-gott (ᵍ ᴸ) *m* (ⴕn) ②c. *abb. fig.* e-n (et.) zu f-m ~(e) machen to worship …, to idolize …; er machte das Gold zu f-m ~(e) he made money his god.

Ab-gott-anbeter(in *f*) *m* (ᵍⁿ…) ② ↘ = Götzendiener(in); **=dienst** *m* idol worship. [ben to worship idols.)

Ab-götterei (ᵍ ᴸ ᵛ ᵛ) *f* ⑯ idolatry; ~ treiben

Ab-göttin (ᵍ ᴸ ᵛ) *f* ⑰ (female) idol.

ab-göttisch (ᵍ ᴸ ᵛ) *a.* ⑯ idolatrous; *adv.* ⤶ verehren to worship (like an idol.)

♪ Musik; ♆ Wissenschaft; ✿ Pflanze; ⚯ Geographie; ⊕ Technik; ✕ Bergbau; ⚔ Militär; ⚓ Marine; ⚙ Handel; ✉ Post; 🚂 Eisenbahn.

Ab-gott(s)=schlange (ˢᴸ⌣...) f ㊷ zo. boa constrictor (*Boa constrictor*).
ab-graben (ˢᴸ⌣) v/a. ㊽b** 1. to level (or remove) by digging. — 2. e-m et. ⌢ to encroach upon a p.'s field by digging; *fig.* e-m den Boden unter den Füßen ⌢ to cut the ground from under a p.'s feet; e-m das Verdienst ⌢ to deprive a p. of his due, to do a p. out of his desert; e-m das Wasser ⌢ to cut off a p.'s water. — 3. ein Feld ⌢ to mark off ... by ditches.
ab-grämen (ˢᴸ⌣): sich ⌢ v/refl. ㊽** to pine away with grief; ein abgegrämtes Aussehen a haggard appearance.
ab-grasen (ˢᴸ⌣) v/a. ㊿** von Tieren: to graze; v. Menschen: to cut the grass; *fig.* to exploit, *co.* (oft aufsuchen) to frequent.
ab-greifen (ˢᴸ⌣) v/a. ㊽b** to wear (out) by much handling; von Büchern: abgegriffen well-thumbed; abgegriff(e)nes Geld light (or well-worn) coin.
ab-grenzen (⌣⌣) I v/a. ㊿** to mark (or define) the frontier (the boundary-lines or limits) of; *fig.* to keep (with)in bounds. — II ~ n ㉓ u. **Ab-grenzung** f ㊻ demarcation, delimitation.
Ab-grund (⌣) [ahd. = ohne Grund] m ①c. abyss, (Schlund ꝛc.) chasm, gulf; (sehr steil) precipice; (höllisch) *bibl.* bottomless pit; am Rande e-s ~es vorbei=geh(e)n to walk on the edge (or brink) of a precipice; *fig.* ~ der Liebe, Verzweiflung abysmal (or engulfing) depth of love, despair; ⌢tief (⌣ᴸ) *a.* ㊻ abysmal; ⌢wärts (⌣ᴸ) *adv.* down the precipice, downward, headlong.
ab-gucken F (⌣⌣) v/a. ㊽** 1. e-m et. ⌢ = absehen 3; das haben sie ihm abgeguckt (*SCH.*) they have copied it from him. — 2. sich (*dat.*) die Augen ⌢ to strain (or to wear out) one's eyes (or sight) by looking for.
Ab-gunst ⬊ (⌣⌣) f ⑩ (*o. pl.*), ⬊ **ab-günstig** *a.* ㊻ = Mißgunst, mißgünstig (s. d·s)
ab-gurgeln (⌣⌣) v/a. ㊽a** e-n ⌢ to throttle a p., to cut a p.'s throat.
ab-gürten (⌣⌣) v/a. ㊽** to ungird; den Degen ⌢ to unbuckle one's sword; ein Pferd ⌢ to unharness ...
Ab-guß (⌣⌣) m ⑧a. 1. (das Abgießen) pouring off or forth; *chm.* decantation. — 2. (das Abgegossene) poured-out liquid. — 3. (Abgießen in eine Form) casting, von Glocken ꝛc.: founding. — 4. (Bild) cast, copy; *typ.* plate; e-n ~ machen to take a cast. [casting.]
ab-guß-fertig (⌣⌣...) *a.* ㊻ ready for
Ab-guß-gerät (⌣⌣) n ㉒ implements (or tools) *pl.* for casting.
Abh. *abbr.* = Abhandlung.
ab-haaren (ˢᴸ⌣) ㊽** I v/a. to take off the hair, to scrape the hair off; ⊕ Gerberei: to unhair. — II v/n. (h.) v. Haustieren im Frühjahr ꝛc.: to lose one's hair; der Pelz haart ab the hair comes off the fur.
ab-haben F (ˢᴸ⌣) v/a. ㊼b** 1. den Hut ⌢ to have one's hat off. — 2. er will etwas ⌢ he demands his share or due.
ab-hacken (⌣⌣) v/a. ㊽** to chop (or cut) off; vgl. auch abhauen.
ab-hageln (⌣⌣) v/n. *imp.* (h.) und ㊽a** es hat (sich) abgehagelt it has ceased hailing; das Wetter hat (ob. es

sind) alle Blüten abgehagelt the hail has (or the hailstones have) knocked off (or beaten down) all the blossom(s).
ab-hägen (ˢᴸ⌣) v/a. ㊽** to hedge in.
ab-hagern (ˢᴸ⌣) v/n. ㉒a** = abmagern.
ab-häkeln (ˢᴸ⌣) v/a. ㊽** ein Muster: to copy (or do) in crochet-work.
ab-haken (ˢᴸ⌣) v/a. ㊽** 1. (loshaken) to unhook. — 2. *hort.* (Ableger am Boden festhaken) to fasten layers in the ground.
ab-halftern (⌣⌣) v/a. ㊽** to undo the halter of, to take the h. off (a horse); F auch *fig.* (sich) e-n ⌢ to get rid of a p.
ab-halsen (⌣⌣) v/a. ㊿** 1. (a. *fig.*) sich (*dat.*) et. ⌢ to get rid (or clear) of a th., to rid o. s. of a th. — 2. *hunt.* (einem Jagdhund das Halsband abnehmen) to take the collar off a hound.
ab-halt·en (ˢᴸ⌣) ㊽a** I v/a. 1. (fern halten) e-n von et. ⌢ to keep a p. off (or away from) a th.; *fig.* (hindern) to restrain, to prevent; e-n vom Studieren ⌢ to keep a p. from his books; wenn ich Sie im geringsten abhalte if I in the least detain you; lassen Sie sich von mir nicht ⌢ don't let me disturb you, don't mind me; ein bißchen Regen soll mich nicht ⌢ a few drops of rain shall not deter me. — 2. ꞉ die Wasser ⌢ to shut out ... — 3. = abwehren. — 4. (ausführen) to go through, (feiern) to celebrate; Gerichtstag ⌢ to sit in court, to hold a sitting; Gottesdienst wird um 11 Uhr abgehalten divine service will be held at 11 o'clock; eine Sitzung ⌢ to hold a meeting; *parl.* das Haus hat heute keine Sitzung abgehalten ... did not sit to-day; ꞉ Truppenschau ⌢ to hold a review, to review (a body of) troops; eine Vorlesung ⌢ to deliver (or give) a lecture. — II v/n. (h.) 5. ⚓ (den Kurs so ändern, daß das Schiff mehr vor dem Winde segelt) to turn the ship's head closer to the wind; auf et. ⌢ (zusteuern) to make (or head) for a th.; vom Lande ⌢ to bear off the land — III ~ n ㉓ 6. = A/ung.
Ab-halter ⚓ (⌣) m ㉒ (Tau z. Freihalten) guy.
Ab-haltung (⌣) f ㊻ 1. (Hinderung) hindrance; im Geschäfte: detention; ~ h. to be detained or engaged. — 2. (Ausführung) ~ e-s Festes celebration of ...; ~ e-r Schulinspektion inspection; ~ e-r Sitzung (holding a) meeting; ~ von Vorlesungen delivery (or course) of lectures.
Ab-haltungs=grund (⌣...) m ㉒ previous engagement, prevention.
ab-hämmern (⌣⌣) v/a. ㉒a** to knock (or strike) off with a hammer.
ab-handeln (⌣⌣) v/a. ㉒a** 1. ⬊ (verabreden) to negotiate. — 2. (erörtern) to treat (of), to discuss. — 3. (taufen) e-m et. ⌢ to purchase a th. of a p. — 4. (Preis mindern) etwas ⌢ to knock something off the price or the sum demanded; er läßt sich nichts ⌢ he won't be bartered down (or he won't take off) a farthing.
ab-handen (⌣⌣⌣) *adv.* ⌢ kommen to get lost; mir ist ein Buch ⌢ gekommen I missed (or had lost) one of my books; ~kommen (⌣...) n ㉓ loss of a th.
Ab-handler (⌣⌣) m ㉒ one who writes upon (or who discusses) a subject.
Ab-handlung (⌣) [nhd.] f ㊻ (abbr. **Abh.**)

schriftliche: treatise, essay, paper (über et. on a thing); mündliche: discourse or discussion (about or on a th.); religiöse: tract; gesammelte ~en e-r gelehrten Gesellschaft transactions *pl.*
Ab-hang (⌣) m ①c. 1. slope, declivity; jäher ~ steep descent or incline. — 2. e-s Hügels side; ꞉ (sloping) bank, gradient; ⚒ *frt.* glacis.
ab-hangen (⌣⌣) v/n. (h.) ㊽b**1. to hang down, to be suspended; von et. ⌢ to depend on a th. — 2. to hang at a (certain) distance from or off. — 3. *fig.* (abhängig sn) von e-m, von et. ⌢ to depend on ...; (an et. liegen) to turn or rest upon, to be dependent on; das hängt von Ihnen ab it rests with (or I leave it to) you; es von Umständen ⌢ lassen to act according to circumstances. — Vgl. a. abhängen II.
ab-hängen (⌣⌣) I v/a. ㊽** to take down, to detach; ⊕ to disconnect; ꞉ to uncouple. — II P oft ꞉⁺ als v/n. ㊽** im *pres.* u. *inf.* = abhangen. — III ~ n ㉓ ⊕ disconnexion.
ab-hängig (⌣) *a.* ㊻ 1. (abschüssig) sloping, inclined; *hort.* ⌢es Beet shelving bank; ⌢ m. to slope. — 2. *fig.* (unselbständig) dependent (von on); (bedingt) ⌢ von conditional upon; *gram.* ⌢e Rede oblique oration, ⌢er Satz subordinate clause.
Ab-hängigkeit (⌣⌣⌣) f ㊻ 1. (Abschüssigkeit) declivity. — 2. *fig.* (Unselbständigkeit) dependency (on others); *gram.* (Unterordnung) subordination.
Ab-hängigkeits=gefühl (⌣...) n ㉒ feeling of dependency or dependence; **=verhältnis** n dependent condition; in e-m ~ zu dependent upon, subordinate to.
Ab-hängling ⊕ (⌣⌣) m⊕d. *arch.* (hangender Schlußstein) hanging keystone, pendant.
ab-harken (⌣⌣) v/a. ㊽** to rake off.
ab-härmen (⌣⌣): sich ⌢ v/refl. ㊽** to pine away; abgehärmt care-worn.
ab-härt·en (⌣⌣) I v/a. u. v/refl. ㊽** (sich) gegen et. ⌢ to harden (o.s.) against ... — II ~ n ㉓ = A/ung. — III abgehärtet *p.p.* u. *a.* ㊻ hard, hardened, hardy; von Metallen: tempered; *fig.* gegen Strapazen ⌢ inured to fatigues
Ab-härtung (⌣⌣) f ㊻ (act of) hardening or tempering; inurement (gegen to).
ab-harzen (ˢᴸ⌣) v/a. ㊿** e-n Baum ⌢ to gather (or collect) the resin (or gum) of a tree.
ab-haschen (⌣⌣) v/a. ㊽** e-m et. ⌢ to snatch a th. from a p.('s grasp).
ab-haspeln (⌣⌣) v/a. ㉒a** 1. ⊕ Spinnerei: to reel off. — 2. *fig.* F to rattle off. [f ㊷ reeling-machine.]
Ab-haspel(ungs)=maschine ⊕ (⌣⌣(⌣)...)
ab-hasten (⌣⌣) ㊽** I v/a. to do hurriedly, to patch up hastily. — II v/refl. sich ⌢ to hurry too much, to bustle (along), *Am.* to hustle.
ab-hauen (ˢᴸ⌣) v/a. ㊽c** 1. to cut (or chop) off; einen Baum ⌢ to hew (or cut) down ..., to fell ...; e-m den Kopf ⌢ to behead (or decapitate) a p. — 2. P (schlagen) to thrash (soundly).
ab-häuten (⌣) ㊽** I v/a. to skin, flay, excoriate. — II v/n. (h.) to cast one's skin or slough, to peel (off). — III ~ n ㉓ skinning, excoriation.

[abheben] — 11 — [abteilen]

ab-heben (ᵇᴸᵘ) ⓥ (ⓥ)b** I v/a. 1. to lift off, to take off; die Speisen ⁓ to clear (away) the dishes, F to take away. — 2. abs. Kartenspiel: Sie müssen ⁓ you (have to) cut; wer hebt ab? who cuts?; zum Geben ⁓ to cut for (the) deal. — 3. ⊛ Geld ⁓ to draw ... from the bank. — II sich ⁓ v/refl. 4. to contrast (von with); Malerei ꝛc.: to stand out (in bold relief) against. — III ⁓ n ㉓ u. **Ab-hebung** f ㊻ 5. lifting, &c. wie I u. II. [hatchel, hackle, comb ...]
ab-hecheln (ᵇᴸᵘ) v/a. ⓐa** Flachs ꝛc. ⁓ to]
ab-heften (ᵇᴸᵘ) v/a. ⓑ** (losmachen) to unfasten, unhook, unpin, unclasp.
ab-hegen (ᵇᴸᵘ) v/a. ⓑ** = abhägen.
ab-heilen (ᵇᴸᵘ) v/n. (h. u. fn) ⓑ** to come off in healing, v. Wunden: to be (or to close in) healing.
ab-heischen (ᵇᴸᵘ) v/a. ⓠ** e-m et. ⁓ to demand a th. of a p.
ab-helfen (ᵇᴸᵘ) ⓥb** I v/a. 1. e-m den Rock ⁓ to help a p. off with his coat. — II v/n.(h.) 2. ⁓ e-m von et. ⁓ to help a p. out of (a scrape). — 3. e-r Sache ⁓ to remedy ...; e-m Fehler ⁓ to correct ...; e-m Übel(stande) ⁓ to redress a grievance; dem ist nicht mehr abzuhelfen that is beyond redress or past all remedy; ⁓d remedial. — III ⁓ ㉓ 4. = **Abhilfe**. [fondle (or hug, F cuddle) ...]
ab-herzen (ᵇᴸᵘ) v/a. ⓑ** ein Kind ⁓ to]
ab-hetzen (ᵇᴸᵘ) ⓑ** I v/a. 1. hunt. to run (or hunt) down. — 2. fig. to harass, to work to death, F to drive (like a nigger or like niggers). — II v/refl. sich ⁓ 3. to run and rush about; to overtire oneself, to (work like a) slave. — III ⁓ n ㉓, **Ab-hetzerei** (ᵇᴸᵘ) u. **Ab-hetzung** (ᵇᴸᵘ) f ㊻ 4. zu 1: running down. — 5. zu 2: harassing work.
ab-heulen (ᵇᴸᵘ) ⓑ** I v/a. to howl; ein Lied: to bawl out ... — II sich ⁓ v/refl. to cry (or sob) most bitterly.
ab(-)hier ⊛ (ᴸᴵᴵ) adv. from this place.
Ab-hilfe (ᵇᴸᵘ) f ㊸ remedy, redress; für et. ⁓ schaffen to remedy (or redress) a th.; dafür gibt es keine ⁓ there is no help for it; Mittel zur ⁓ remedial measures pl.; ohne ⁓ past redress.
Ab-hitze (ᵇᴸᵘ) f ㊸ (Gase, die aus Feuerungen, Öfen ꝛc. entweichen) gases escaping from hearths, furnaces, ovens, &c.
ab-hobeln (ᵇᴸᵘ) ⓐa** I v/a. 1. ⊛ to plane off; fein ⁓ to smooth (down); ein Brett ⁓ to rough-plane. — 2. fig. F e-n ⁓ to polish a p. — II sich ⁓ v/refl. 3. fig. to become refined.
ab-hold (ᵇᴸᵘ) [nhd.] a. ⓖⓖ e-m, e-r Sache ⁓ sein, to be ill-disposed towards (or to be averse to) ...; sie ist ihm ⁓ she is not well inclined towards him, F he is not in her good books.
ab-holen (ᵇᴸᵘ) v/a. ⓑ** 1. to fetch; er holte es hier ab he came to fetch it; ich holte es dort ab I went to fetch it; e-n am Bahnhofe ꝛc.: ⁓ to go to meet a p.; ich ging ihn ⁓ I called for him (at his house); ✉ Briefe ⁓ to call for ...; vom Briefträger: to collect ...; ⁓ lassen to send for. — 2. ⚓ ein Schiff vom Strande ⁓ to haul (or get) off ... — II ⁓ n ㉓ 3. fetching, &c. wie 1; ✉ der Briefe collection ... 4. ⚓ hauling off.

Ab-holer ✉ (ᵇᴸᵘ) m ㉒ (der seine Briefe von der Post selbst abholt) one who fetches (or calls for) his letters himself.
Ab-holung (ᵇᴸᵘ) f ㊻ = abholen II; ⁓s-fächer ✉ (ᵇ...) n/pl. ㉒ (sg. ⁓s-fach n) shelves pl. for letters to be called for.
Ab-hol-zeit ✉ (ᵇᴸᴸ) f ㊸ für Briefe: time (or hours) of collection or for clearance.
ab-holzen (ᵇᴸᵘ) v/a. ⓥ** 1. for. e-n Berg ꝛc. ⁓ to clear ...; e-n Wald: to cut down. — 2. e-n Baum ⁓ to prune (or thin) ... — 3. fig. (prügeln) e-n ⁓ to give a p. a sound beating or cudgelling.
ab-holzig (ᵇᴸᵘ) a. ㊿ for. v. Stämmen: (im Durchmesser von unten nach oben rasch abnehmend) tapering.
ab-horchen (ᵇᴸᵘ) v/a. ⓑ** e-m ein Geheimnis ⁓ to catch up ... by listening.
ab-hören (ᵇᴸᵘ) I v/a. ⓑ** e-m et. ⁓ to learn a th. from a p. by listening. — 2. (abfragen) e-n Schüler ⁓ od. e-m Schüler die Lektion ⁓ to hear a pupil's lesson; jur. Zeugen ⁓ to examine witnesses, to hear the evidence. — II ⁓ n ㉓ u. **Ab-hörung** f ㊻ 3. hearing; jur. examination.
Ab-hub (ᵇᴸ) m ⓓ. (o. pl.) 1. remains remnants, fragments pl. — 2. der Tafel: leavings pl. — 3. (Abfälle) refuse, waste, rubbish, garbage; ⚒ dross.
☞ **Ab-hülfe** f. **Abhilfe**.
ab-hülsen (ᵇᴸᵘ) ⓑ** I v/a. to peel; Erbsen ꝛc. ⁓ to shell ...; Gerste: to hull. — II sich ⁓ v/refl. to peel (or come) off.
ab-hungern (ᵇᴸᵘ): sich ⁓ v/refl. ⓐa** to starve o.s.; abgehungert aussehen to look (half) famished or starved.
ab-hüpfen (ᵇᴸᵘ) v/n. (fn) ⓑ** to hop (or skip) away. [(or glide) away.]
ab-huschen (ᵇᴸᵘ) v/n. (fn) ⓠ** to slip]
ab-husten (ᵇᴸᵘ) ⓑ** I v/a. Schleim ꝛc. ⁓ to cough up phlegm. — II sich ⁓ v/refl. to exhaust o.s. with coughing.
ab-hüten (ᵇᴸᵘ) v/a. ⓑ** e-e Wiese ⁓ to turn cattle into a meadow for grazing.
ab-hütten ⚒ (ᵇᴸᵘ) v/a. ⓑ** e-e Zeche ⁓ to shut down (or to abandon) a mine.
äbich(t) ⊛ (ᴸᵘ) [ahd.] a. ㊿ von Tuch: Le (linke) Seite wrong side of ...
Abi-etin ⚗ (ᵘ〻ᴸ) [lt.] n ⓓc. chm. (Tannenharz) abietin(e).
Abi-etin-säure (ᵘ...) f ㊸ abietic acid.
ab-irren (ᵇᴸᵘ) I v/n. (fn) ⓑ** to lose one's way, to stray; (abweichen) to deviate, fig. to err. — II ⁓ n ㉓ u. **Ab-irrung** f (ᵘ) deviation; des Verstandes: error (of judgment); des Lichtes: aberration.
Abiturient (ᵘ〻(ᵘ)ᴸ) [lt.] m ㊷ candidate for the leaving examination of a (German) college; ⁓en-exa'men (ᵘ〻(ᵘ)ᴸ...) n ㉒, ⁓prüfung f leaving-examination of (German) college students.
ab-jagen (ᵇᴸᵘ) ⓑ** I v/a. 1. ein Pferd ⁓ to override, to overdrive a horse. — 2. hunt. ein Revier ⁓ to shoot over an estate. — 3. fig. ♪ ein Stück ⁓ to rattle (or rush) through a piece. — 4. (entreißen) e-m et. ⁓ to recover a thing from a p. (by pursuit). — II v/n. (h.) 5. hunt. to finish hunting. — III sich ⁓ v/refl. 6. to rush (madly), to over-exert (or overwork) o.s.
ab-jammern (ᵇᴸᵘ): sich ⁓ v/refl. ⓐa** to moan (or wail) without cessation.

ab-jäten (ᵇᴸᵘ) v/a. ⓑ** e-n Garten: to weed (thoroughly). [unharness,]
ab-jochen (ᵇᴸᵘ) v/a. ⓑ** to unyoke, to]
Abjudikation (ᵘ〻ᴸ⁻ᵗᵇ(ᵘ)ᴸ) [lt.] f ㊻ (Aburteilung) abjudication.
ab-kälten (ᵇᴸᵘ) v/a. ⓑ** = abkühlen 1.
ab-kämmen (ᵇᴸᵘ) v/a. ⓑ** 1. to comb off; e-n ⁓ to comb ... — 2. ⊛ Wolle ⁓ to comb (or card) ... — 3. ⚔ die Brustwehr ⁓ to uncrown (or untop) ... by a (well-aimed) shot.
ab-kämpfen (ᵇᴸᵘ) v/a. ⓑ** e-m et. ⁓ to wrest (or take) a th. from a p. by conquest; ⚓ e-m Schiffe den Wind ⁓ to snatch the wind from ...
ab-kanten ⊛ (ᵇᴸᵘ) v/a. ⓑ** to round off; Steinschneiderei: to square; (schräg schneiden) to bevel; Tuchmacherei: das Tuch ⁓ to cut the list of ...
ab-kanzeln (ᵇᴸᵘ) v/a. ⓐa** 1. † (verkünden) to announce from the pulpit. — 2. fig. (ausschelten) to sermonize, reprimand, lecture, rebuke. [zeln 2.]
ab-kapiteln F (ᵇᴸᵘ) v/a. ⓐa** = abkan]
ab-kappen (ᵇᴸᵘ) v/a. ⓑ** 1. hort. e-n Baum ⁓ to top. — 2. norbd., bsd. ⚓ (abschneiden) to cut (or chop) off. — 3. P obb., md. fig. (schelten) to scold, F to blow up.
ab-kargen (ᵇᴸᵘ) v/a. ⓑ** e-m et. ⁓ to keep a p. short of a th.; sich (dat.) et. vom Munde ⁓ to deny o.s. a thing.
ab-karren (ᵇᴸᵘ) v/a. ⓑ** to cart off or away, to remove with a cart.
ab-karten (ᵇᴸᵘ) I v/a. ⓑ** to (pre)arrange; abgekartetes Handel, abgekartete Sache got-up (or deep-laid) scheme or plot, preconcerted plan, jur. collusion; F plant, put-up job, vorher abgekartet preconcerted, jur. collusive. — II ⁓ n ㉓ = **Abkartung** 1.
Ab-kartung (ᵇᴸᵘ) f ㊻ 1. (Handlung des Abkartens) previous arrangement. — 2. = abgekartete Sache (s. abkarten).
ab-kastei-en (ᵇᴸᵘ): sich ⁓ v/refl. ⓑ*/* to mortify one's flesh.
ab-kauen (ᵇᴸᵘ) v/a. ⓑ** to gnaw off; Pferd: das Gebiß ⁓ to champ (off) the bit; sich die Nägel ⁓ to bite one's nails.
Ab-kauf (ᵇᴸ) m ⓓ. purchase.
ab-kaufen (ᵇᴸᵘ) v/a. ⓑ** e-m et. ⁓ to buy (or purchase) a th. of a p.; e-m den ganzen Vorrat ⁓ to buy up (er to clear) a p.'s stock. [purchaser.]
Ab-käufer (ᵇᴸᵘ) m ㉒, ⁓in f ㊷ buyer,]
ab-kehlen (ᵇᴸᵘ) v/a. ⓑ** 1. ein Tier: to cut the throat of; ein Schwein: to stick. — 2. ⊛ join., &c. (mit Hohlkehlen versehen, auskehlen) to groove; abgefehlte Beine e-s Tisches fluted legs ...
Ab-kehr (ᵇᴸᵘ) f ㊸ (o. pl.) turning away from sin, &c., estrangement from friends, &c.; (Abscheu) aversion.
ab-kehren¹ (ᵇᴸᵘ) v/a. ⓑ** = abfegen 1.
ab-kehren² (ᵇᴸᵘ) ⓑ** I v/refl. (abwenden) sich ⁓ von to turn away (or aside) from, fig. to withdraw (one's support) from. — II v/n. (fn). v/refl. ⚒ (sich) ⁓ to leave the pit or the mine, to leave off work.
Ab-kehr (ᵇᴸᵘ) f ㊸ (o. pl.) m ㉒, ⁓in f ㊸ one who sweeps or dusts.
Ab-kehricht (ᵇᴸᵘ) n ⓓ. sweepings pl.
ab-keilen (ᵇᴸᵘ) v/a. ⓑ** 1. ⊛ to split (or cleave) with a wedge. — 2. F e-n et. ⁓ = abkaufen. — 3. P (hauen) to thrash.

㊼ scientific; ♀ botanical; ⚲ geography; ⊕ machinery; ⚒ mining; ⚔ military; ⚓ marine; ⊛ commercial; ✉ postal; 🚂 railway.

[abkeltern] — 12 — [abkühlen]

ab-keltern(⌣⌣) v a** I v/a. Wein: to press. — II v n. (h.) to finish pressing.
ab-ketten(⌣⌣) v a. ⑲** to unchain.
ab-kippen(⌣⌣) ⑲** I v/a. Nadlerei: to nip off; Münzen: to clip. — II v/n. (in) (umführen) to tilt (or topple) over.
ab-klagen(⌣⌣) v a. ⑲** e-m et. ⚤ to wring a th. from a p. by (harrassing) lawsuits.
ab-klammern(⌣⌣) v a. ⑲a** Wäsche ꝛc. ⚤ to take ... off the pegs, to unpeg …
ab-klappen(⌣⌣) v n.(in)⑲** to fail. [⚤.]
ab-klappern F(⌣⌣) v/a.⑲a** = ablaufen)
Ab-klär-...(⌣⌣...) ㊷ = Abklärungs-...
ab-klär/en(⌣⌣) ⑲** I v/a. 1. to clarify; chm. to decant; Sirup ⚤ to decolour…; Wein ꝛc.: to fine; Hefe ꝛc. to defecate. — II sich ⚤ v/refl. 2. to clear off. — 3. fig. to become clear; vom Wetter: to brighten up. — III ~ n ㉓ 4. = A/ung.
Ab-klärung (⌣) f ㊻ clarification; chm. decantation; des Zuckers: decoloration; des Weines: fining; der Hefe: defecation.
Ab-klärungs-methode (⌣⌣...) f ㊷ method of clarifying or fining; **mittel** n ingredient (or chemical drug) for clarifying or fining (i. a. Klär-…).
Ab-klatsch(⌣⌣) m ⑫a. 1. typ. impression; (Stereotypplatte) stereo(type plate). (Abdruck) proof-(sheet). vom Inschriften: squeeze. — 2. fig. (Abbild) copy, feeble imitation; thea. understudy.
ab-klatschen (⌣⌣) ⑪** I v/a. ⊙ (stereotypieren) to stereotype, to dab; typ. (abdrucken) einen Korrekturbogen ⚤ to strike (or pull) off a proof. — II v/n. (in) to fall with a crash. — III F sich ⚤ v/refl. to have a long gossip.
Ab-klatscher (⌣⌣) m ㉒, ~in f ㊷ 1. ⊙ dabber; typ. proof-printer. — 2. fig. F (Nachahmer) feeble imitator, plagiarist. [flushing with water.]
Ab-klatschung (⌣⌣) f ㊻ bei Wasserkuren:)
ab-klauben (⌣⌣) v/a. ⑲** e-n Knochen ⚤. das Fleisch von e-m Knochen ⚤ to pick (the meat off) a bone.
ab-klavieren (⌣w⌣) v/a. ⑲*/* to strum (or play) off in a mechanical way.
ab-klecksen (⌣⌣) v/a. ⑲*** to blot; to copy badly; to daub.
ab-kleiden (⌣⌣) v/a. ⑲** 1. ⊙ arch. (verstecken) to conceal by an imitation wall; carp. e-n Raum: to partition off; Maurerei: die Wände ⚤ to plaster … — 2. ⚓ das Tau ⚤ to take off the serving.
ab-klemmen (⌣⌣) v/a. ⑲** (sich) die Finger ⚤ to pinch (or squeeze) off one's fingers.
ab-klimpern (⌣⌣) v a. ⑲a** abfiedeln 1 und klimpern 2. [ring off.]
ab-klingeln (⌣⌣) v/a. ⑲a** Fernspr. to)
ab-klingen (⌣⌣) v n. ⑩t** 1. ♪ (verklingen) to die away. — 2. fig. v. Farben, Empfindungen (G.): to fade away. [brush.]
Ab-klopf-bürste (⌣⌣...) f ㊷ typ. letter-)
ab-klopfen (⌣⌣) v/a. ⑲** 1. to knock off; (abstäuben) to dust (off); Matten ꝛc. ⚤ to beat … — 2. ⊙ Saline: den Hungerstein ⚤ to scrape the pan; typ. einen Probebogen ⚤ to strike (or pull) off a proof; die Druckform ⚤ to plane down the form. — 3. ♪ v. Kapellmeister: (das Zeichen zum Aufhören geben) to give the signal to stop (playing). — 4. fig. e-n ⚤ (prügeln) to give a p. a good beating or hiding.

ab-klöppeln ⊕ (⌣⌣) v/a. ⑫a** 1. eine Spitze ⚤ to make bobbin-lace. — 2. ein Muster ⚤ to copy … with the bobbin.
ab-knabbern P(⌣)v/a.⑲a** to nibble off.
ab-knacken (⌣⌣) ⑲** I v/a. to snap (or break) off. — II v/n. (in) to crack off.
ab-knallen (⌣⌣) ⑲** I v/a. to blow off; e-e Flinte: to fire (off); chm. to detonate. — II v/n. (in) to explode, to go off; chm. to fulminate. — III ~ n ㉓ einer Flinte: discharge; chm. detonation, fulmination. [v/a. = abzwacken.)
ab-knappen ⑲**, **-knapfen** ⑨** F (⌣⌣))
ab-knappern (⌣⌣) v/a. ⑲a** = abknabbern. [fargen.]
ab-knausern F (⌣⌣) v/a. ⑲a** = ab=)
ab-kneifen (⌣⌣) v/a. ⑩b** to pinch off, to nip off; ⚓ den Wind ⚤ to ply to windward; im Schiffe den Wind ⚤ to gain the weather-side (or wind) of …
ab-knicken (⌣⌣) v/a. ⑲** 1. (a. v/n. [in]) to snap off. — 2. hunt. = abnicken.
ab-knickern (⌣⌣) v/a. ⑲a** = abfargen.
ab-knipsen (⌣⌣) v/a. ⑲** 1. to snip off …; das elektrische Licht ⚤ to switch off … — 2. (wegschnellen) to flip.
ab-knistern (⌣⌣) v/a. ⑲a** chm. Salze ⚤ (vom Kristallwasser befreien) to decrepitate.
ab-knöpfen (⌣⌣) v/a. ⑲** 1. to unbutton. — 2. F e-m et. ⚤ F to do (or cheat, swindle, diddle) a p. out of a th.
ab-knuppern F (⌣⌣) v/a. ⑲a** = abknabbern. [undo, to take off.)
ab-knüpfen (⌣⌣) v/a. ⑲** to untie, to)
ab-knutschen F (⌣⌣) v/a. ⑪** (caressingly) to hug and squeeze.
ab-kochen (⌣⌣) I v/a. ⑲** to boil (thoroughly); pharm. to decoct; ⚤ a. abs. (das Kochen beenden) to finish cooking; Gemüse ⚤ to parboil … — II ~ n ㉓ u. **A ung** f ㊻ (par)boiling; chm. decoction. [mark off with) charcoal.)
ab-kohlen (⌣⌣) a/v. ⑲*** carp. to)
ab-kommandier/en (⌣⌣⌣⌣) I v/a. ⑲*/* 1. (abbefehlen) et. ⚤ to countermand. — 2. (absenden) ⚔ e-n ⚤ to draft off to, to detail (on special service). to detail; zur Arbeit a/te Abteilung fatigue party. — II ~ n ㉓ u. **Ab-kommandierung** f ㊻ counterorder; ⚔ detachment.
Ab-komme (⌣⌣) m ㊹ = Abkömmling.
ab-kommen (⌣⌣) v/n. (in) ⑭** 1. to get off or away; fig. davon bin ich ab= gekommen I have given up (or dropped) the idea; ⚓ von der rechten Fahrt ⚤ to get off (or away) one's course; fig. von seiner Rede ⚤ to wander (or stray) from one's subject. to digress; vom Wege ⚤ to lose one's way; vom Winde ⚤ to fall to leeward; ⚤. (sich losmachen) to disengage o.s.; ich kann heute nicht ⚤ I cannot be spared today; könnten Sie morgen ⚤? could you get away to-morrow?; ich werde keine Minute ⚤ können I shall not have a minute to myself; fig. F er kann ⚤ he can (easily) be spared. we can dispense with him. — 3. billig davon ⚤ to get off cheaply; mit Gewinn ⚤ to come off well. — 4. (aus der Mode kommen) to go out of fashion; (außer Gebrauch kommen) to fall into disuse; die Sitte ist ganz abgekommen … is quite obsolete or antiquated; wir sind

davon abgekommen we have discontinued (or dropped) it. — 5. mit e-m über et. ⚤ (übereinkommen) to agree with a p. about a th. — 6. ⚔, hunt. gut ⚤ to aim (and fire) correctly. — 7. ⚓ (wieder flott w.) to get off, to be set afloat. — II ~ n ㉓ 8. ~ e-s Gesetzes ꝛc.: obsoleteness. — 9. (übereinkunft) agreement; ein ~ mit e-m treffen to arrange (or to come to terms) with a p.
Ab-kommenschaft (⌣⌣) f ㊻ (o. pl.) offspring, issue; descendants pl.
Ab-komm-kanone ⚔ (⌣⌣) f ㊷ (für Nichtübungen) cannon used for gun-laying drill. [dispensed with.]
ab-kömmlich (⌣⌣) a. ⑯ that can be)
Ab-kömmling (⌣⌣) m ⑩d. 1. (≁ ~in f ㊷) descendant. — 2. chm. derivative (body or compound). [malen) to portray.)
ab-konterfeien F (⌣⌣) v/a. ⑲* (abs.)
Ab-köpf-bank (⌣⌣...) f ㊷ Fischerei: bench for cutting off the heads of fish.
ab-köpfen (⌣⌣) v/a. ⑲** 1. to behead, to decapitate; Fische: to head. — 2. Gärtnerei: Bäume ⚤ to top (or poll) …
Ab-köpf-maschine (⌣⌣...) f ㊷ guillotine.
ab-kopieren (⌣⌣) v/a. ⑲*/* = kopieren.
ab-koppeln (⌣⌣) v/a. ⑲a** hunt. Hunde ⚤ to unleash …
ab-körnen (⌣⌣) v/a. ⑲** to pick the grains from; Rosinen ⚤ to stone …
ab-kosen (⌣⌣) v/a. ⑨** e-m et. ⚤ to coax (or wheedle) a p. out of a th.
ab-framen (⌣⌣) v/a. ⑲** = abräumen.
Ab-fratz-bürste (⌣⌣...) f ㊷ rough brush (for scraping), **=eisen** n scraper.
ab-kratzen (⌣⌣) v/a. ⑲** 1. to scrape (or scratch) off; sich den Schmutz von den Schuhen ⚤ to scrape one's ... 2. die Brotrinde ⚤ to grate (the) bread; ⊕ arch. e. Gebäude: to scrape. — II P v/n. (in) 3. (durchbrennen) to decamp; derb: (sterben) to hop the twig. — III **Abgekratzte**(s) n ㊿ (o. pl.) 4. scrapings pl.
Ab-kratzer (⌣⌣) m ㉒ scraper.
ab-krauten (⌣⌣) v/a. ⑲** to weed; (behacken) to hoe. [with circles.]
ab-kreisen (⌣⌣) v/a. ⑨** to mark off)
ab-krempen (⌣⌣) v a. ⑲** e-n Hut ⚤ to turn (or take) down the brim of …
ab-kreuzen (⌣⌣) v/a. ⑲** ein Meer ⚤ to cruise in or about …, to traverse … in cruising.
ab-kriegen F(⌣⌣)v/a.⑲**1.(abbekommen ⚤) to get one's share (P whack) of; weits. to come in for. — 2. (losbringen) ich kann es nicht ⚤ I cannot get it off.
ab-kritzeln (⌣⌣) v/a. ⑫a. to copy badly, to scribble. to scrawl.
ab-fröschen (⌣⌣) v/a. ⑨** to fry (lightly) in melted butter, &c.
ab-krümeln (⌣⌣) ⑲a** v/a., v/n. (in) sich ⚤ to crumble off or away.
ab-krümmen (⌣⌣) v/a., v/n. (in) u. sich ⚤ to bend down. to curve off.
ab-krusten (⌣⌣) v a. ⑲** Brot ⚤ to cut the crust off…; ⊕ Eisen ꝛc. ⚤ to scale …
ab-kugeln (⌣⌣) v/a. ⑲a** to (vote by) ballot; weits. to vote for or against.
Ab-kühl-apparat (⌣⌣...) m ㉖ refrigerator.
ab-kühl/en (⌣⌣) ⑲** I v/a. 1. to cool down (a. fig.); ⊙ to refrigerate; Getränke in Eis ⚤ to ice … — 2. fig. sein Zorn ⚤ to cool, to calm one's …; sein

---
Zeichen (s. S. XVII): F familiär; P Volkssprache; ⌐ Gaunersprache; ≁ selten; † alt (auch gestorben); * neu (auch geboren); ⁒ unrichtig;

[Abkühler] — 13 — [ablaufen]

Mütchen an e-m ≈ to vent (or let out) one's anger upon a p. — 3. ⊕ (im Abkühl-ofen) to anneal. — II sich ≈ v/refl. 4. to cool down, v. Personen a.: to calm down ... — III ~ n ⓶ 5. = A/ung. — IV ⚷ p.pr. u. a. ⊕⊕ 6. cooling, ⚹ refrigerant; fig. ⚷de Wirkung calming effect.
Ab-kühler (⁸ᴸ⌣) m ⓶ phys. refrigerator.
Abkühl-faß (⁸ᴸ…) n ⓶ cooling(-)vat, cooler; **gefäß** n = -apparat; **-ofen** m für Glas annealing-arch (or -oven).
Ab-kühlung (⁸ᴸ⌣) f ⓵ cooling (down); v. Personen: calmness; phys. refrigeration.
Ab-kühlungs-fläche (⁸…) f ⓶ cooling surface; **-mittel** n refrigerant; med. cooling draught or medicine; **-raum** m, **-zimmer** n ⊕ annealing chamber, refrigerator; refrigerating chamber, mit Eis: ice-room.
ab-kümmern (⁸ᴸ⌣) v/a. u. sich ≈ v/refl. ⓶a** to pine away with grief, to worry o. s. to death.
ab-künden (⁸ᴸ⌣)⊕⊕**, **ab-kündigen** (⁸ᴸ⌣) ⊕** v/a. to notify to; ein Brautpaar ≈ to publish the banns of ...
Ab-kunft (⁸ᴸ) f ⓵⓪ 1. origin, extraction, von gemeiner (edler) ~ of low (noble) descent or birth; von fürstlicher ~ of princely blood or lineage; von niedriger ~ of humble parentage or stock. — 2. ⚹ = abkommen 9.
ab-kuppeln (⁸ᴸ⌣) v/a. ⓶a** to uncouple.
ab-kuranzen (⁸ᴸ⌣) v/a. ⓪*/* = kuranzen.
ab-kürz/en (⁸ᴸ⌣) I v/a. ⓪** 1. to shorten, condense, abbreviate. — 2. Wörter ≈ to abridge ...; e-e Rede ≈ to cut short ... — 3. math. Brüche ≈ to reduce ...; Regel ꝛc.: to truncate. — 4. e-m den Lohn ≈, et. am Lohn ≈ to reduce (or curtail, F dock) a p.'s wages. — II ~ n ⓶ 5. = A/ung. — III ⚷d p.pr. u. a. ⓪⓪ 6. abbreviative. — IV **ab-gekürzt** p.p. u. a. ⓪⓪ 7. condensed; short; concise. — 8. math. = abgestumpft (s. abstumpfen).
Ab-kürzer (⁸ᴸ⌣) m ⓶ abbreviator.
Ab-kürzung (⁸ᴸ⌣) f ⓪⓪ abbreviation; abridgment; reduction; **~s-zeichen** (⁸…) n ⓶ abbreviature (-dash).
ab-küssen (⁸ᴸ⌣) v/a. ⓪** (auch sich ≈ v/rpr.) to kiss to one's heart's content; die Tränen ≈ to kiss off ..., to kiss away ...
ab-kutschieren (⁸ᴸ⌣) v/n (sn) ⓪*/* to drive away (in a coach).
Ab-lade-lohn (⁸ᴸ⌣ …) m ⓶ fee (or charge) for unloading.
ab-laden (⁸ᴸ⌣) I v/a. u. v/n. (h.) ⓪b** to unload; Erde ꝛc. ≈ a.: to shoot ...; ↓ Schiffsfracht ≈ to discharge a cargo; a. = ablagern 1. — II ~ n ⓶ = Abladung.
Ab-lade-ort (⁸ᴸ⌣ …) m ⓶, **-platz** m goodsyard, ↓ port of discharge, für Schutt: place where rubbish may be shot, ⚔ ꝛc.: dump, dumping-ground.
Ab-lader, **~-läder** (⁸ᴸ⌣) m ⓶ 1. allg.: unlader. — 2. auf Märkten ꝛc.: porter; (Verlader) shipper; ↓ heaver, lighterman. **~-lohn** (⁸…) m ⓶ = Ablade-l.
Ab-lade-stelle ⊕ (⁸ᴸ⌣ …) f ⓪ dumpingground (for inferior goods).
Ab-ladung (⁸ᴸ⌣) f ⓪ discharge; **~s-boot** ↓ (⁸…) n ⓶ lighter; **~s-schein** m certificate of discharge.
Ab-lage (⁸ᴸ⌣) f ⓪ (Ort) depot, dépôt, repository, von Holz: wood-yard.

ab-lager/n(⁸ᴸ⌣)⓶a** I v/a. u. v/refl. 1. (absetzen) a. geol. to deposit, (ablagen) bsd. Am. to dump (down). — 2. (trennen) to put in separate camps or depots. — 3. (lagern) to store (up). — 4. sich ≈ to lie in separate camps. — II v/n. (sn) 5. ⚹ to grow mellow (or to mature) by age; ≈ l. to store, to lay by, to season well. — III ~ n ⓶ 6. = A/ung 1. — IV **abgelagert** p.p. u. a. ⓪⓪ 7. gut ≈e Zigarre well-seasoned (or -matured) cigar; ≈er Madeira dry Madeira.
Ab-lagerung (⁸ᴸ⌣) f ⓪ 1. zu ablagern 3: storage. — 2. path. sediment, concretion; geol. deposit, bed.
Ab-lagerungs-ort (⁸…) m ⓶, **-platz** m (für Schutt) shoot, rubbish-yard.
Ab-laktation (⌣ᴸ⌣-(tß)⌣ᴸ) [lt.] f ⓪ hort. (Art Veredlung der Pflanzen) ablactation.
ab-lammen v/n. (h.) ⓪** to stop lambing. [Der Wind land-breeze.)
ab-landig ↓ (⁸ᴸ⌣) a. ⓪ (ant. auflandig)
ablang P (⌣ᴸ) [P aus It.] a. ⓪ oblong.
ab-langen (⁸ᴸ⌣) v/a. ⓪** to fetch down; ich kann's nicht ≈ I cannot reach it.
ab-laschen (~) v/a. ⓪** hort., for. Bäume ≈ to blaze ..., to mark ... for felling.
Ab-laß (⁸ᴸ) [ahd.] m ⓪ a. 1. (Abfluß) a) letting off, drain(age; b) (Ort) outlet, drain-pipe; sink; (Schleuse) flood-gate, outlet-sluice. — 2. (Aufhören) ohne ≈ without ceasing or cessation, incessantly, continuously. — 3. ⊕ (Abzug) deduction, abatement. 4. Cath. indulgence; e-m e-n (vollkommenen) ≈ erteilen to grant a p. a (plenary) remission of sins. [dulgence.)
Ab-laß-brief (⁸ᴸ…) m ⓶ letter of in-J
ab-lassen (⁸ᴸ⌣) [ahd.] ⓪a** I v/a. 1. to leave off or unfastened; s-e Hand von et. ≈ to keep one's hand(s) off a th. — 2. (abgehen l.) to let off; e-m Blut ≈ to bleed a p.; e-n Brief an e-n ≈ to write off ... to a p., to forward ... to a p.; (den) Dampf ≈ to blow off (the) steam; e-n Graben ꝛc. ≈ to drain (off) ...; ↓ ein Schiff vom Stapel ≈ to launch ...; ein Telegramm ≈ to send off a telegram, to (send a) wire; Wein vom Fasse ≈ to draw off ...; 🚂 e-n Zug ≈ to run ..., to start ..., to despatch ... — 3. ⊕ Glashütte: den Ofen ≈ to let (or cool) down ... — 4. ⊛ (erlassen) vom Preise ≈ to take off, to deduct; ich kann nicht einen Heller ≈ I cannot take off (or deduct) a farthing or make any reduction, I cannot bate a penny. — 5. (überlassen) to give up, käuflich: to sell, to dispose of; ⊛ unter dem Preise ≈, zum Selbstkostenpreise ≈ to sell below costprice; ich will es Ihnen billig ≈ I will let you have it cheap(ly). — II v/n. (h.) 6. (aufhören) to cease. — 7. (aufgeben) abstehen) von einer Gewohnheit ≈ to leave off a ...; er will davon nicht ≈ he won't desist from it or give it up. — III ~ n ⓶ = 8. Ablassung.
Ab-laß-geld (⁸ᴸ⌣) n ⓪ fee for an indulgence; **-graben** m ditch, drain; **-hahn** ⊕ m Dampfm.: delivery-cock; **-handel** m sale (or selling) of indulgences; **-händler** m seller of indulgences; **-jahr** n jubilee (-year); **-kram**, **-krämer** m = -handel, -händler; **-punkt**

m Sport: starting-point; **-rohr** ⊕ n waste-pipe; **-tag** m day of grace.
Ab-laßung (⁸ᴸ⌣) f ⓪ 1. letting off; drainage. — 2. (Aufhören) discontinuance.
Ab-laß-ventil ⊕ (⁸ᴸ…) n ⓶ delivery- (or outlet-)valve; **-woche** f (Fronleichnamswoche) Corpus Christi week; **-zettel** m (letter of indulgence).
Ab-laste-bogen ⊕ (⁸ᴸ⌣-ᴸ⌣) m ⓶ arch. discharging (or relieving) arch.
Ab-lativ (⁸-ᴸ⁻) [spät-lt.] m ⓪c., **~us** (⌣-ᴸ⌣) m ⓪ gram. ablative (case); ~us absolutus ablative absolute.
ab-latten ⊕ (⁸ᴸ⌣) v/a. ⓪** to unlath.
ab-lauben (⁸ᴸ⌣) v/a. ⓪** Bäume: to pluck the leaves off; Reben: to trim, prune.
ab-lauern (⁸ᴸ⌣) v/a. ⓶a** to watch for.
Ab-lauf (⁸ᴸ) m ⓪d. 1. = Abfluß 1, Ablaß 1. — 2. (Ort) sewer. — 3. man. start. — 4. (Zeit) expiration; ⊛ bei ~ des Wechsels on (or at) maturity, when the bill falls due; nach ~ dieser Frist, des Termins at the end of this time, of the period; nach ~ des Pachtvertrages when the lease ran (or runs) out or will expire; vor ~ des Jahres before the close of the year.—5. fig. (Ausgang) issue, termination. — 6. arch. ~ e-r Säule (oberster Teil des Säulenschaftes) escape, ~ apophyge. — 7. ↓ = Stapellauf.
Ab-lauf-balken ↓ (⁸ᴸ…) m ⓶ cradle.
ab-laufen (⁸ᴸ⌣) ⓪aft** I v/n. (sn) 1. bei Wettrennen: to start. — 2. fig. F er ist (gut) abgelaufen (abgeblitzt) F he had (or got) a (smart) rebuff; einen ≈ lassen to send a p. about his business, to snub a p.; fenc. s-n Gegner ≈ lassen to parry an assault of ... — 3. ↓ to put off or to sea; (vom Stapel ≈ lassen to launch. — 4. (abfließen) to run (or flow) off, to subside. — 5. (sich senken) to slope. — 6. (laufend vergehen) to come to an end; seine Uhr ist abgelaufen his watch has run down, fig. his sand (or race) is run; die Zeit (Frist) ist abgelaufen the time has expired or is up; ⊛ (fällig w.) to fall (or become) due, to lapse. — 7. (Ausgang nehmen) to terminate, end; das wird nicht gut ≈ it will lead to (or end in) trouble; wie ist Ihr Geschäft abgelaufen? how did you get on (with your business)?; es ist ziemlich gut abgelaufen it passed (or we came) off tolerably well. — 8. (sich abzweigen) to branch off. — II v/a. 9. a. v/refl. sich (dat.) et. ≈ to wear out in running; fig. sich die Beine nach et. ≈ to run one's legs off for a th.; sich die Hörner ≈ to sow one's wild oats; ich habe mir das an den Schuh(sohl)en abgelaufen I knew that long ago, I have it at my fingers' ends; vgl. ab- ... 4. — 10. im Turnier: e-n ≈ to unhorse a p. — 11. (laufend abgewinnen) to outrun; e-m den Rang ≈ to outstrip (or cut out) a p., to beat a p. (hollow), to take the wind out of a p.'s sails. — 12. die Läden ≈ to run from shop to shop, to go to every shop; die ganze Gegend ≈ to scour the whole neighbourhood. — III sich ≈ v/refl. 13. to tire o.s. with running. — IV ~ n ⓶ 14. running (or flowing) off; Zeit: termination. ↓ ~ e-s Taues slackening; ~ des Wassers receding (or outgoing)

♪ Musik; ⚛ Wissenschaft; ⚘ Pflanze; ⚘ Geographie; ⊕ Technik; ⚒ Bergbau; ⚔ Militär; ↓ Marine; ⊛ Handel; ✉ Post; 🚂 Eisenbahn.

[Abläufer] — 14 — [abliegen]

tide; ~(=laſſen) ↓ (~...) n ㉓ e-s Fahrzeuges: launching.
Ab-läufer ⊕ (ᵇᴸ·) m ㉒ Weberei: spool.
Ab-lauf-gerüſt (ᵇᴸ...) n ㉒ =balken.
Ab-lauf(s)-friſt (ᵇᴸ...) f ⊕ eines Wechſels maturity of ...; =röhre ⊕ f delivery- (or waſte-) pipe, gutter; =ſchleuſe ⊕ f discharging-sluice; =zeit ⊕ f = =friſt.
ab-laugen (ᵇᴸ·) I v/a. ⊛** to waſh (or rinse off) the lye, ⌘ to lixiviate; ⊕ Garn: ⚲ to waſh with lye. — II ~ n ㉓ des Garns: waſhing the yarn (in lye); ⌘ chm. lixiviation.
ab-lauſchen (ᵇᴸ·) v/a. ⊕** e-m ein Geheimnis ⚲ to learn a p.'s secret by listening or eavesdropping; er hat dies der Natur abgelauſcht, etwa: he is true to (or a close observer of) nature.
ab-lauſen F (ᵇᴸ·) v/a. u. v/refl. ſich ⚲ ⊛** to clean from lice.
Ab-laut (ᵇᴸ) m ⓒ c. gram. change of the radical vowel, ⸙ ablaut (ſ.S.XXXIII).
ab-lauten (ᵇᴸ·) v/n. ⊛** gram. to change the radical vowel. [by ringing.]
ab-läuten (~) v/a. v/n. ⊛** to announce
Ab-läuter-arbeit (ᵇᴸ·...) f ⊕ refining (work), ⚒ buddling; =faß n, =kiſte f buddle, waſhing-tub.
ab-läutern ⊕ (ᵇᴸ·) v/a. ⊛a** Flüſſigkeiten: to clarify, Zucker: to refine, gepochtes Erz: to waſh, to buddle.
Ab-laut-verb n ㉒ verb which changes its vowel for the purpose of inflexion.
ab-leben (ᵇᴸ·) ⊛** I ſich ⚲ v/refl. 1. von Zeit: to slip by. — 2. von Perſonen: to waſte (away), to wear o.s. out. — II v/n. (h., nur inf. u. p.p.) 3. to depart this life. — III ~ n ㉓ 4. (Tod) decease, death, jur. demise. — IV abgelebt p.p. u. a. ⊕ 5. worn (out), used up, decayed, von Greiſen: decrepit.
ab-lecken (ᵇᴸ·) v/a. ⊛** to lick off.
ab-ledern (ᵇᴸ·) v/a. ⊛a** 1. to take (or strip) the leather off; ♪ die Hämmer ⚲ to remove the leather (or felt) from ... — 2. F fig. e-n ⚲ (durchprügeln) to give a p. a (good) leathering or tanning.
ab-leeren (ᵇᴸ·) v/a. ⊛** eine Schüſſel ⚲ to empty ...; einen Baum ⚲ to strip ...
Ab-lege-maſchine ⊕ (ᵇᴸ·...) f ⊕ typ. automatic distributing machine.
ab-legen (ᵇᴸ·) ⊛** I v/a. 1. (ant. anlegen) to lay aside; Kleider ⚲ to take off; legen Sie ab! take off your things! — 2. (für immer) to leave (or caſt) off; er legte ſeine rauhe Art ab he grew gentler; von Schlangen: die alte Haut ⚲ to caſt the skin; fig. er hat die Kinderſchuhe (längſt) abgelegt he is no longer a child; abgelegte Kleider caſt-off clothes; fig. die Maske ⚲ to take off; Bogerei ⚲: Rock und Weſte ⚲ to strip (the upper part of the body); den Studenten ⚲ to drop ...; ⚔ den Torniſter ⚲ to lay down (or to relieve oneself of) one's knapsack; Trauer ⚲ to leave off (or to go out of) mourning. — 3. fig. (loswerden) to get rid of; ſ-e Fehler ⚲ to mend one's ways; eine Gewohnheit ⚲ to renounce ...; ſeine ſterbliche Hülle ⚲ to shuffle off this mortal coil. — 4. Spiel: eine Karte ⚲ to throw away ... — 5. (verrichten) to do; ein Bekenntnis ⚲ to confess; einen Eid ⚲ to

take ... (auf upon); ein Gelübde ⚲ to (make a) vow; eine Probe ⚲ von et. to give proof of ...; e-e Prüfung ⚲ to paſs ...; Rechenſchaft ⚲ to render an account of; Zeugnis ⚲: a) für, gegen e-n to give evidence for, againſt a p.; b) für et. to bear witneſs to ... — 6. ⊕: a) = abſenken 1; b) typ. to distribute (type); c) Bienenzucht: (e-n volkreichen Bienenſtock in 2 Teile teilen) to divide an overcrowded hive (in two). — 7. ⚓ ein Schiff ⚲ to put ... in dock. — II v/n. (h.) 8. ⚓ mit dem Schiffe ⚲ to put out (or off) to sea. — III ~ n ㉓ 9. = Ablegung.
Ab-leger ⊕ (ᵇᴸ·) m ㉒ 1. hort. layer, slip, shoot. — 2. Bienen: new swarm (of bees).
Ab-lege-ſatz ⊕ (ᵇᴸ...) m ⊕ typ. type (or matter) to be distributed; =ſpan m distributing rule; =zimmer n (Garderobe) (ladies') cloakroom.
Ab-legung (ᵇᴸ·) f ⊕ 1. eines Glaubensbekenntniſſes: profession (of a creed); jur. ~ einer Rechnung audit. — 2. ⊕ typ. distribution (of matter).
ab-lehnbar (ᵇᴸ·) a. ⊕ refusable.
ab-lehn/en (ᵇᴸ·) I v/a. ⊛** 1. to turn aside. — 2. fig. (zurückweisen) to decline, refuse; er lehnte es höflich ab he begged to be excused; parl. e-n Antrag ⚲ to reject (or throw out, negative) a motion; der Antrag wurde abgelehnt a.: the noes had it; jur. Geſchworene ⚲ to challenge jurymen. — II ~ n ㉓ 3. = A/ung.
Ab-lehnung (ᵇᴸ·) f ⊕ refusal, rejection, excuse; jur. ~ v. Geſchworenen: challenge.
Ab-lehnungs-fall (ᵇᴸ...) m ⊕ im ~e in case of refusal.
ab-leiern (ᵇᴸ·) v/a. ⊛a** 1. et. ⚲ to play s. th. on a barrel-organ. — 2. fig. to sing (or recite) monotonously, to drawl (out), to rattle off.
ab-leihen (ᵇᴸ·) v/a. ⊕** e-m etwas ⚲ to borrow a th. from a p.
ab-leiſten (ᵇᴸ·) I v/a. ⊛** 1. jur. einen Eid ⚲ to take an oath. — 2. ⚔ = abdienen 1. — II ~ n ㉓ u. **Ab-leiſtung** f ⊕ 1. ~ der Militärpflicht (rendering) military service, serving (one's time) in the army.
ab-leitbar (ᵇᴸ·) a. ⊕ derivable from.
ab-leit/en (ᵇᴸ·) I v/a. u. v/refl. ⊛** 1. vom Ziele: to turn off or aside; Störendes: to remove. — 2. einen von der rechten Bahn ⚲ to lead a p. astray; einen Fluſs lauf ⚲ to divert (or turn) the course of ...; Gaſe ⚲ to conduct away ...; med. Säfte ꝛc.: to draw off ...; elect. einen Strom ⚲ to ſhunt a current; Waſſer ꝛc. ⚲ to drain (off) .... — 3. (zurückführen) to retrace; j-s Herkunft ⚲ von to trace a p.'s descent back to; bib. gram. to derive from ... — 4. ſich ⚲ aus: dieses Wort läßt ſich aus dem Franzöſiſchen ⚲ ... is derived from ... — II ~ n ㉓ 5. = A/ung. — III ab-geleitet p.p. u. a. ⊕ 6. gram. ein ⚲es Dingwort a derivative noun. [conductor of electricity.]
Ab-leiter (~) m ⊕ phys. ~ der Elektrizität
Ab-leitung (~) f ⊕ 1. agr. turning off Gräben: drainage. — 2. diversion; gram. ~ e-s Wortes derivation, etymology; phls. (Folgerung) deduction.
Ab-leitungs-angriff ⚔ (~...) m ⊕ diversion; =draht m, elect. shunt-wire;

=graben, =kanal m drain, outfall; =mittel n, med.: ⚕ antispastic; =rechnung f = Differential-r.; =rinne f drain-pipe; =röhre ⊕ f waste, conduit-pipe, v. Gaſen: delivery-pipe or tube; =ſilbe f, gram. derivative syllable, derivational affix; =ſtange f des Blitzableiters rod of the lightning-conductor; =tabelle f, gr. etymological table; =wort n, gr. derivative. [turned off or diverted.]
ab-lenkbar (ᵇᴸ·) a. ⊕ capable of being
ab-lenk/en (ᵇᴸ·) ⊛** I v/a. 1. to turn aside or off, to draw off, to divert, to avert; j-s Aufmerkſamkeit ⚲ to divert a p.'s ...; Gefahren ⚲ to ward off ...; Verdacht ⚲ von to remove suspicion from ... — 2. phys. Lichtſtrahlen ꝛc. ⚲ to deflect ...; die Magnetnadel ⚲ to cause a deviation of ... — II v/n. (h.) 3. von et. ⚲ to turn aside, to deviate; von der Sache ⚲ to digress. — III ~ n ㉓ 4. = A/ung.
Ab-lenkung (ᵇᴸ·) f ⊕ 1. diversion. — 2. phys. deflexion, deviation.
Ab-lenkungs-angriff ⚔ (~...) m ⊕ (attack for the purpose of) diversion; =winkel m, phys. angle of deflexion.
ab-lernen (ᵇᴸ·) v/a. ⊛** e-m et. ⚲ to learn a th. by watching (or observing) a p.
Ab-leſe-fernrohr ⊕ (ᵇᴸ·...) n ⊕ telescope for reading in the distance.
ab-leſ/en (ᵇᴸ·) I v/a. ⊛a** 1. von einem Blatte, Inſtrument ꝛc: to read off; ein Gedicht ⚲ to read ...; e-m ins Geſichte ⚲ to read a th. in a p.'s face; Namen ⚲ to call over ... — 2. (durch Leſen abnutzen) to thumb (a book); ſich (dat.) die Augen ⚲ to ruin (or strain) one's sight by reading. — 3. Schule: betrügeriſch ⚲ von ... F to crib from ... 4. (ſammeln) Früchte ꝛc.: to pick (off), to gather; die Steine vom Felde ⚲ to pick up ... on the field; Raupen vom Baume ⚲ to pick ... off the tree, to clear the tree of ... — II ~ n ㉓ 5. = A/ung.
Ab-leſer (ᵇᴸ·) m ⊕a. 1. von Schriften ꝛc.: reader. — 2. v. Hopfen: picker.
Ab-leſung (ᵇᴸ·) f ⊕ 1. reading. — 2. (Einſammeln) gathering; ~ der Trauben vintage.
ab-leugn/en (ᵇᴸ·) I v/a. ⊛b** to deny, disavow, disown; eidlich ⚲ to forswear; ſ-n Glauben ⚲ to renounce ..., to abjure ... — II ~ n ㉓ = A/ung.
Ab-leugnung (~) f ⊕ denial, disavowal; renunciation; jur. disclaimer.
Ab-leugnungs-eid (ᵇᴸ·...) m ⊕ oath of abnegation, denial by oath.
Ab-liefer-... (ᵇᴸ·...) ⊕ = Ablieferungs-...
Ab-lieferer ⚔ (ᵇᴸ··) m ㉒ deliverer; (Überbringer) bearer, carrier.
ab-liefer/n (ᵇᴸ·) I v/a. ⊛a** to deliver (up), to hand over, ⚔ Waren ⚲ auch to consign. — II ~ n ㉓ = A/ung.
Ab-lieferung (ᵇᴸ··) f ⊕ delivery, ⚔ a. consignment; nach erfolgter ~ on delivery; verſpätete ~ late delivery.
Ab-lieferungs-prämie ⚔ (~...) f ⊕ premium; =ſchein m: a) vor der Lieferung: bill of delivery; b) nach der Lieferung: receipt; =termin m, =zeit f time (or day, date) of delivery, Börſe: (von Wertpapieren) settling-day.
ab-liegen (ᵇᴸ·) ⓓ** I v/n. (h.) 1. (a. fn) (entfernt ſein) to lie at a distance (from), to be far away (from). — 2. a. v/refl.

Signs (see page XVII): F familiar; P vulgar; ⸙ flash; ⚹ rare; † obsolete (died); * new word (born); ⁺⁺ incorrect; ♪ music;

[ablisten] — 15 — [abmucken]

sich 2 to get seasoned, von Obst: to ripen through lying, von Wein ꝛc.: to mature; mehr gbr. ablagern 5. — **II sich 2** v/refl. 3.f. 2. — 4. (schadhaft w.) to wear (o.s.) out (by lying); von Kranken: to get bedsores; sich die Haare 2 to lose one's hair through lying. — **III ab-gelegen** p.p. u. a. ⊛ (D9) 5. (entfernt) remote; ein 2es Dorf an out-of-the-way ...
ab-listen (ˢᴸ˅) v/a. ⊛** e-m et. 2 to trick (or cajole) a p. out of a th.; e-m ein Geheimnis 2 to draw ... out of a p.
ab-locken (ˢᴸ˅) v/a. ⊛** e-n von etwas 2 to entice a p. from a th.; fig. e-m et. 2 to coax (or talk) a p. out of a th., to wheedle a th. out of a p.; e-m Tränen 2 to draw tears from a p.'s eyes.)
ab-lohn/en, P ab-löhn/en (ˢᴸ˅) **I** v/a. ⊛** 1. einen 2 to pay (wages to) a p. — 2. mit Entlassung 2 to pay off, dismiss, discharge. — **II ~ n** ㉓ u. **A/ung** f 3. payment of (wages to) ...; discharge.
ab-lösbar (ˢᴸ-) a. ⊛ = ablöslich.
ab-löschen (ˢᴸ˅) **I** v/a. ⊛**1. (auslöschen) to extinguish. — 2. ⊕ (in kaltem Wasser abkühlen) to chill (by dipping into cold water), heißen Stahl a.: to temper; Kalt 2 (in Atzkalk verwandeln) to slake ... — 3. (abwischen) to wipe off, eine Tafel: to clean. — **II ~ n** ㉓ u. **Ab-löschung** f ⊛ 4. extinction; von Kalk: slaking.
ab-lösen (ˢᴸ˅) ⊛** **I** v/a. 1. to loosen. — 2. surg. ein Glied 2 to amputate, to cut off ...; die Haut 2 to strip off the skin. — 3. ein Kapital 2 to withdraw one's capital (from); Renten ꝛc.: to redeem; eine Verpflichtung: to discharge. — 4. (vertreten) to replace; ⚔ u. Posten, e-e Schildwache 2 to relieve guard, to go on sentry; abgelöst! relieve!, ⚓ to spell; e-n von seinem Posten 2 to step into a p.'s place, to undertake a p.'s duties. — **II sich 2** v/refl. 5. to come (or peel) off, in Schuppen: to scale off. — 6. (auch ea.) 2 to change places (with a p.); von Dingen: to come (or appear) by turns. — **III ~ n** ㉓ 7. = Ablösung. — 8. Malerei: ~ (Hervorheben) der Züge throwing into relief.
ab-löslich (ˢᴸ˅) a. ⊛ 1. (trennbar) separable. — 2. jur. redeemable.
Ab-löslichkeit (ˢᴸ-.) f ⊛ 1. separableness. — 2. jur. redeemableness.
Ab-lösung (ˢᴸ˅) f ⊛ 1. (vgl. ablösen) loosening; surg. amputation. — 2. jur. (e-r Strafe): commutation; ⊛ e-r Schuld redemption, liquidation, discharge of ... — 3. ⚔: a) (~ e-s Postens) relieving (guard), relief; ~vor! relieve!, sentry, on!, ⚓ spell!; b) (die ablösende Mannschaft) soldiers pl. going on guard, relief; c) v. Arbeitern: (fresh) relay or shift. — 4. ⚒ (Kluft) fissure; in Kohlen: parting.
Ab-lösungs-fonds (ˢᴸ-...) m ⊛, =summe f ⊛ redemption fund; =mannschaft f = Ablösung 3b u. c.
ab-loten ⊕ (ˢᴸ˅) v/a. ⊛** arch. to plumb.
ab-löten ⊕ (ˢᴸ˅) v/a. ⊛** to unsolder.
ab-luchsen (ˢᴸ˅ℱ˅) v/a. ⊛** e-m et. 2 to trick (or swindle, do) a p. out of a th.
Ab-luft* (ˢᴸ-) f ⊛ (schlechte Luft) foul air, vitiated atmosphere.
ab-lügen (ˢᴸ˅) v/a. ⊛d** e-m et. 2 to deny a th. to a p.'s face.

ab-mach/en (ˢᴸ˅) **I** v/a. ⊛** 1. (losmachen) meist: to detach; (fortnehmen) to take off. — 2. den Besatz e-s Kleides 2 to untrim (or to take the flounces off) a dress; vom Stiel 2 to take off the handle. — 3. (abschließen) to conclude; (ordnen) to arrange; bedingungsweise: to stipulate; schnell: to despatch; kurz: to cut short; mit einem ein Geschäft 2 to transact business with a p.; gütlich 2 to come to a friendly understanding with; e-n Handel: to close a bargain with a p.; eine Rechnung 2 to discharge (or settle) ...; e-n Streit 2 to settle (or adjust) a dispute; s-e Zeit 2 to serve one's time; abgemachter Preis (the) price agreed upon, fixed price; das ist abgemacht this is understood or settled; so gut wie abgemacht as good as settled; abgemacht! agreed!, all right!; abgemacht, sela! done, at last!; et. bei sich (dat.) 2 to determine (or resolve) a th. in one's own mind. — **II ~ n** ㉓ 4. fig. das ist ein ~ it's one (and the same) job. — 5. A/ung.
Ab-machung (ˢᴸ˅) f ⊛ arrangement, settlement, agreement; vertragsmäßige ~ stipulation; ⊛ liquidation; ⚓ jur. (Bestimmung des Verlustes, den der Versicherte erlitten hat) assessment of the loss sustained by the insured.
ab-magern (ˢᴸ˅) ⊛** **I** v/n. (sn) to grow thin or lean, to fall (or waste) away, to lose flesh. — **II** v/a. to waste; abgemagert emaciated. — **III ~ n** ㉓ u. **Ab-magerung** (ˢᴸ˅˅) f ⊛ wasting (of the body); emaciation.
ab-mähen (ˢᴸ˅) v/a. ⊛** to mow off (auch fig.); Korn: to cut (with a scythe).
ab-mahlen (ˢᴸ˅) v/n. (h.) ⊛** (p.p. abgemahlen) to finish (or cease) grinding.
ab-mahnen (ˢᴸ˅) **I** v/a. ⊛** e-n 2 von ... to dissuade a p. from ... — **II ~ n** ㉓ u. **Ab-mahnung** f ⊛ warning (or caution) against. [to mash thoroughly.]
ab-maischen ⊕ (ˢᴸ˅) v/a. ⊛** Brauerei:)
ab-malen (ˢᴸ˅) v/a. ⊛** 1. to paint; e-n 2 to portray ..., to paint a portrait of ...; nach dem Leben, nach der Natur 2 to paint (draw, sketch, take) from life. — 2. (kopieren) to copy. — 3. fig. to depict.
Ab-mangel* ⊛ (ˢᴸ˅) m ⊛ (Fehlbetrag) [deficit.]
ab-marken (...) v/a. ⊛** to mark.
ab-markten (ˢᴸ˅) v/a. ⊛** = abhandeln 4.
Ab-markung (ˢᴸ˅) f ⊛ agr. (Errichtung fester Grenzzeichen zw. Grundstücken) marking the boundaries between plots of land.
Ab-marsch (ˢᴸ˅) m ⊛ a. marching off; (Flankenbewegung e-s Heeres) flank movement (of troops); ~ aus dem Lager decampment; zum ~ trommeln to strike up the march; Befehl zum ~ marching-order.
ab-marschieren (ˢᴸ˅ᴸ˅) **I** v/n. (sn) ⊛** bsd. ⚔: to march off; links (rechts) abmarschiert! file left (right)!; einzeln 2 to file off. — **II ~ n** ㉓ = Abmarsch.
Ab-marsch-zeit (ˢᴸ˅) f ⊛ time of departure, marching-time.
ab-martern (ˢᴸ˅) ⊛a** **I** v/a. to torment, to torture. — **II sich 2** v/refl. körperlich: to fag o.s. (to death); geistig: to worry (o.s.), to fret. — **III ~ n** ㉓ u. **Ab-marterung** f ⊛ torment, torture; worry(ing), fretting.

ab-matten (ˢᴸ˅) v/a. u. v/refl. ⊛** 1. to fatigue (o.s.), stärker: to wear (o.s.) out; abgemattet wearied, exhausted, worn out, jaded, spent, F done up; vor Müdigkeit ganz abgemattet quite knocked up (F dead beat) with fatigue. — 2. ⊕ Goldarbeiterei: to dim, to deaden.
Ab-mattung (ˢᴸ˅) f ⊛ fatigue, weariness, stärker: exhaustion.
ab-meier/n (ˢᴸ˅) **I** v/a ⊛a** 1. einen Pächter 2 to turn a tenant out of his farm, to evict a tenant. — 2. F fig. = abfanzeln 2. — **II ~ n** ㉓ u. **A/ung** (ˢᴸ˅) f ⊛ 4. eviction (of a tenant).
ab-meißeln ⊕ (ˢᴸ˅) v/a. ⊛a** 1. (mit dem Meißel entfernen) to chisel off, Gravierkunst ꝛc.: to scoop. — 2. (zurichten) to chisel out, to shape with a chisel.
ab-meld/en (ˢᴸ˅) **I** v/a. ⊛** et. 2 to countermand a thing; e-n Fremden (auf der Polizei) 2 to give notice (to the police) of a stranger's departure; e-n Schüler (beim Direktor) 2 to give notice (to the headmaster) of a pupil's removal. — **II** = A/ung.
Ab-melde=schein (...) m ⊛, =zettel m written notice (to the police) of a removal or the departure of strangers, &c. [~ notice of a p.'s departure.]
Ab-meldung (ˢᴸ˅) f ⊛ counter-order; j-ds)
ab-mergel/n (ˢᴸ˅) [Mark n] **I** v/a. ⊛a** to emaciate, exhaust; F abgemergelter Mensch worn-out individual. — **II ~ n** ㉓, **A/ung** f ⊛ emaciation, exhaustion.
ab-merken (ˢᴸ˅) v/a. ⊛** e-m et. 2 to learn by watching (or observing) a p.; e-m et. an den Augen 2 to read a th. in a p.'s eyes.
ab-meßbar (ˢᴸ˅) a. ⊛ measurable; math. auch: mensurable; in 2er (kurzer) Frist within measurable distance.
Ab-meßbarkeit (ˢᴸ--) f ⊛ math. ⚛ mensurability, commensurability.
ab-mess/en (ˢᴸ˅) **I** v/a. ⊛**1. to measure off; (eichen) to gauge; mit der Wasserwage: to level; surv. to survey; nach der Schnur: to aline; Tuch 2 to cut off ... (by the yard-measure). — 2. (nach et. einrichten) to adjust to. — 3. fig. s-e Worte 2 to weigh one's words; s-e Worte nicht 2 to talk at random; mit abgemessenem Schritte with measured steps. — 4. (urteilen) to judge by a th.; andere nach sich 2 to judge (of) others by o.s. — **II ~ n** ㉓ 5. = A/ung. — **III ab-gemessen** p.p. u. a. ⊛ (D 9) 6. f. a. 3; (genau) precise; (umständlich) formal, stiff, ceremonious; (würdevoll) dignified.
Ab-messer (ˢᴸ˅) m ⊛ surveyor.
Ab-messung (...) f ⊛ (f. abmessen **I**) measurement; levelling; surveying; alinement; adjustment; math. mensuration.
ab-mieten (ˢᴸ˅) v/a. ⊛** to hire; e-m ein Haus 2 to rent ... from a p.
Ab-mieter (ˢᴸ˅) m ⊛, **~in** f ⊛ tenant.
Ab-mietung (...) f ⊛ hiring, renting, hire.
ab-mindern (ˢᴸ˅) **I** v/a. ⊛a** to lessen, to diminish. — **II ~ n** ㉓ u. **Ab-minderung** f ⊛ diminution.
ab-modeln (ˢᴸ˅) v/a. ⊛a** to model, * to copy (in forming or casting). [nect.]
ab-montieren (ˢᴸ˅ᴸ˅) v/a. ⊛*/* to discon-)
ab-mucken F (ˢᴸ˅) v/a. ⊛a** 1. to kill (off) secretly, P to do for, to remove,

⚛ scientific; ⚘ botanical; ⚲ geography; ⊕ machinery; ⚒ mining; ⚔ military; ⚓ marine; ⊛ commercial; ✉ postal; 🚂 railway

[abmüden] — 16 — [Abort]

to despatch, to make cold meat of, to connoble. — 2. *fig.* to snub.
ab-müden (ˢᴸᵛ) ⑨⁰**, **-mühen** (ˢᴸᵛ) ⑧** *v/a. u. v/refl.* = abmatten 1. [mucken 1.)
ab-murksen F (ˢᴸᵛ) *v/a.* ⑨⁰** = ab-)
ab-müßigen (ˢᴸᵛ) ⑧** I *v/a.* auch: sich (*dat.*) eine Stunde 2c. 2 to get an hour off (one's work). — II sich 2 *v/refl.* (von et.) to get away from (or to get rid of) a th.
ab-mustern (ˢᴸᵛ) I *v/a.* ⑨a** ①. ⊕ Weberei: (geblümt weben) to diaper. — 2. ⚓ (entlassen) die Mannschaft 2 to pay off the crew. — II ~ *n* ㉓ u. **Ab-musterung** *f* ㊻. ⚓ paying off the crew.
ab-nabeln (ˢᴸᵛ) *v/a.* ⑨a** ein Kind 2 to cut an infant's umbilical cord (and dress its navel).
ab-nagen (ˢᴸᵛ) *v/a.* ⑧** to gnaw (or to nibble) off, v. Personen: e-n Knochen 2 to pick a bone; *fig.* der Kummer nagt ihm das Herz ab ... is preying on his mind, stärker: is eating his (very) heart out.
ab-nähen (ˢᴸᵛ) ⑧** I *v/a.* 1. to quilt. — 2. (nähend abarbeiten) to pay off by sewing. — II sich 2 *v/refl.* 3. to sew continually or day and night.
Ab-nahme (ˢᴸᵛ) *f* ㊻ 1. (Fortnehmen) taking away or off; ~ Christi vom Kreuze descent from the cross; *surg.* ~ eines Beines amputation of ..., cutting off ...; ~ des Verbandes removal of the bandage. — 2. (Entgegennehmen) ~ e-s Eides von e-m taking an oath from a p.; swearing in (of) a p.; ~ einer Post checking (of) an incoming mail; ~ einer Rechnung audit(ing) ... — 3. ⚛ (Absatz) sale; ~ finden bei to find a ready sale with; bei ~ von ... on purchasing ... — 4. (Verringerung) decrease, diminution; in der ~ begriffen on the wane, abating, diminishing; in ~ kommen to fall off, to decline; ~ der Gesundheit failure of health, failing health, decline; *path.* ~ der Kräfte loss of strength, enfeeblement, depression; des Mondes: waning (of); der Tage: drawing in (of); des Wassers: subsiding (of). [contractor's trial.)
Ab-nahme=probefahrt (ˢᴸᵛ...) *f* ㉒
ab-narben ⊕ (ˢᴸᵛ) *v/a.* ⑧** Gerberei: to grain. [take) dainties stealthily.)
ab-naschen (ˢᴸᵛ) *v/a.* ⑨** to taste (or)
Ab-negation (ᵛ⁻ᵗᶠ(ᵛ)¹) [It.] *f* ㊻ denial.
ab-negieren (ᵛ⁻ᴸᵛ) [It. *abnega're*] *v/a.* ⑧* (ableugnen) to deny.
ab-nehmen (ˢᴸᵛ) ⑦a** I *v/a.* 1. (herabnehmen, entfernen) to take off; e-m den Bart 2 to shave a p.'s whiskers off; sich den Bart 2 lassen to have one's whiskers taken (or shaved) off; den Besatz von e-m Kleide 2 to untrim ...; *surg.* ein Glied 2 to cut off ...; das Heft von et. 2 to take the handle off a th.; Pferden die Hufeisen 2 to unshoe horses; den Hut vor e-m 2 to doff (or to take off) one's hat before a p.; Stieren das Joch 2 to unyoke bulls; Spiel: (die Karten) 2 to cut; e-m die Larve 2 to unmask a p.; (die Maschen) 2 to diminish the meshes; die Sahne von der) Milch 2 to cream the milk; die Mütze 2 s. o. Hut; das Obst vom Baume 2 to pluck (or gather) the fruit

off ...; sich (*dat.*) et. von e-r Sache 2 to take a portion (or slice) off a th.; die Siegel 2 von to unseal ...; die Speisen 2 to take away ...; das Tischtuch 2 to remove the cloth; den Verband 2 to take off the bandage. e-m die Waffen 2 to disarm a p. — 2. (weg-, an sich nehmen) e-m et. 2 to take a th. from a p., to deprive (or rob) a p. of a th.; e-m sein Geld 2 to rob a p. of his money, to fleece a p.; e-m e-e Last (Mühe) 2 to take a burden (a trouble) off a p. ('s shoulders); e-m Waren 2 to buy ... of a p.; ⚔ dem Feinde wieder 2 to recapture from ...; ⚛ e-m zuviel für et. 2 to overcharge a p. for a th. — 3. (entgegennehmen) to receive; *tel.* e-n Draht 2 to test ...; e-m e-n Eid 2 to put a p. on his oath; e-e Rechnung 2 to audit ...; e-m ein Versprechen 2 to obtain (or extract) a promise from a p., to make a p. promise (a th.). — 4. (Abbild nehmen) e-n 2 to paint a p. ('s portrait); sich photographisch 2 (aufnehmen) lassen to have one's photo(-graph) taken; eine Gipsmaske 2 to take a plaster-cast of a p.'s face. — 5. (entnehmen) aus et. 2 to infer (or judge) from a th., mit Sicherheit 2 to conclude; es läßt sich leicht 2 it can easily be seen. — II *v/n.* (h.) 6. (*ant.* zunehmen) to diminish, decrease, immer mehr: to grow less and less; (kürzer werden) to grow shorter; (schwinden) to decline, dwindle, fall away; ⚛ die Aufwärtsbewegung nimmt ab the boom is subsiding; die Flut nimmt ab the tide is receding; Gedächtnis: to be failing, to grow weak; Geschwindigkeit: to slacken; Geschwülste: to go down; Körper: to grow thin; Kräfte: to decrease; seine Kräfte nehmen ab his strength is failing him or waning; ⚛ der Kurssturz nimmt ab the panic is subsiding; Leistungen: to fall off; der Mond nimmt ab ... is on the wane; ⚛ die Nachfrage nimmt ab the demand is falling off; die Tage nehmen ab ... are drawing in; Wind 2c.: to abate, drop, calm (or go) down. — III ~ *n* ㉓ 7. = Abnahme 1 u. 2. — 8. = Abnahme 4. — 9. in ~ sein to be on the decrease; ⚛ die Preise sind im ~ ... on the downgrade or receding or going down; *phys.* ~ der Geschwindigkeit decrease (or retardation, slackening) of speed. — 10. Kinderspiel: (~ v. Maschen) cat's-cradle. — IV ㏂ *p.p.* u. *a.* ⑥⑥ 11. ㏂ de Gesundheit failing health; ♪ *diminuendo, decrescendo; math.* ㏂ de Reihe descending series; ㏂ de Geschwindigkeit decreasing (or retarded) speed.
Ab-nehmer (ˢᴸᵛ) *m* ㉒, **~in** *f* ㊻ 1. Obst-(2c.)pflücker: gatherer, picker. — 2. ⚛ buyer, purchaser, weitS. consumer, customer; der Artikel findet gute, keine ~ ... sells (or goes off) well, is unsaleable; das Blatt hat wenig(e) ~ ... has few readers or (Abonnenten) subscribers. — 3. (Hehler) receiver.
ab-neigen (ˢᴸᵛ) I *v/a. u. v/refl.* ⑧** to turn away (or aside) from; sich 2 auch: to be disinclined. — II **ab-geneigt** *p.p. u. a.* ⑥⑥ disinclined, disaffected;

(von) e-m 2 ill-disposed towards a p.; einem 2 sein to bear an ill feeling towards a p.; den Deutschen 2 anti-German; ich bin der Sache nicht 2 I am not averse to it; nicht 2 es zu tun not unwilling to do it; sich (*dat.*) e-n 2 m. to estrange a p.'s sympathies.
Ab-neigung (ˢᴸᵛ) *f* ㊻ 1. ⚛ *phys.* declination, deviation from. — 2. aversion (or disinclination) to, stärker: repugnance against; e-m ~ einflößen (von Sachen) to be repugnant to a p., (von Personen) to be repulsive to a p.; eine ~ fassen gegen to take a dislike to.
ab-nicken (ˢᴸᵛ) *v/a.* ⑧** *hunt.* ein Reh 2 to stab ... with the hunting-knife in the nape of the neck.
abnorm (ᵛ⁻) [It.] *a.* ⑥⑥ (regelwidrig) abnormal, exceptional.
Abnormität (ᵛᵛᵛ¹) *f* ㊻ abnormity.
ab-nötigen (ˢᴸᵛ) I *v/a.* ⑧** e-m et. 2 to extort a th. from a p.; e-m Bewunderung 2 to wring ... from a p.; e-m e-e Entschuldigung 2 to force a p. to apologize. — II ~ *n* ㉓ = Abnötigung.
Ab-nötigung (ˢᴸᵛ) *f* ㊻ extortion.
ab-nutschen ⊕ (ˢᴸᵛ) *v/a.* ⑨** (absaugen) Kristallmassen, Brotzucker 2c. 2 to absorb the moisture of crystals, loaf-sugar, &c. by means of an air-pump.
ab-nutzen bsd. nordd., **ab-nützen** bsd. südd. (ˢᴸᵛ) I *v/a. u.* sich 2 *v/refl.* ⑨⁰** 1. to wear (out). — 2. seine Kräfte 2 to use up ... — II ~ *n* ㉓ 3. = A/ung. — III **ab-genutzt** *p.p. u. a.* ⑥⑥ 4. worn (out), used up; sehr 2 well-worn, threadbare.
Ab-nutzung (ˢᴸᵛ) *f* ㊻ wear and tear, ⚛ attrition, detrition.
Ab-nutzungs=satz (ˢᴸᵛ...) *m* ㉒ *for.* (Hiebsatz, Maß für die jährliche Hiebsgröße) annual amount of timber to be felled.
ab-öden (ˢᴸᵛ) *v/a.* ⑧** to lay waste.
ab-ohrfeigen (ˢᴸᵛ) *v/a.* ⑧** e-n 2 to box a p.'s ears (well).
Abolitionist † (ᵛᵛᵛᵗᶠ(ᵛ)⁻ˢ) *m* ㉒ *Am.* Gegner der Sklaverei (1775—1863) abolitionist.
Abonnement (fr. ä-bö-n'ma') (ˢᴸᵛ) *n* ⑩ (Vorausbestellung) Buchhandel, Theater 2c.: subscription (auf to or for); im ~ by subscription; mit aufgehobenem ~ subscription-tickets (or passes) not available; aus dem ~ treten to discontinue (or drop) one's subscription; **~(s)=billett** (ˢᵗᶠ)...) *n* ⑫, **=karte** *f* = Zeitkarte; **=liste** *f* list of subscribers; **=preis** *m* subscription (-fee or -rate).
Abonnent (ᵛᵛˢᵗ) [⁺⁺ fr. (fr. *abonné*)] *m* ⑫, **~in** *f* ㊻ subscriber to.
abonnieren (ᵛᵛᴸᵛᵛ) [fr.] *v/a., v/n.* (h.) *v/refl.* ⑧ (vorausbestellen) (auf 2) to subscribe (auf to); im Opernhause abonniert sein to have a stall at the opera; auf e-e Zeitung abonniert sein to take in a (news)paper; Fernspr.: sich auf einen Draht 2 to rent a wire.
ab-ordnen (ˢᴸᵛ) I *v/a.* ⑨a** 1. to delegate; als Vertreter: to depute. — 2. (abbestellen) to countermand. — II *p.p.* als s. 3. *s.* Abgeordnete(r).
Ab-ordner (~) *m* ㉒ bsd. *pol.* (Wähler) constituent.
Ab-ordnung (ˢᴸᵛ) *f* ㊻ (vgl. abordnen) 1. delegation, deputation. — 2. (Abbestellung) countermand, counter-order.
Ab-ort (ˢᴸᵛ) *m* ⓒ. = Abtritt 2.

Zeichen (s. S. XVII): F familiär; P Volkssprache; ⌐ Gaunersprache; ⚲ selten; † alt (auch gestorben); * neu (auch geboren); ⁺⁺ unrichtig;

ab-ortiv ⚇ (⌣⌣́f) [lt.] *a.* ⓺ (zu früh geboren), bsd. *med.* abortive. [carriage.
Ab-ortus ⚇ (⌣⌣) [lt.] *m, inv. med.* mis-
ab-paaren (⌣⌣⌣) *v/a.* und *v/refl.* ⓼**
1. to (ar)range in couples. — 2. †*parl. v. politischen Gegnern:* sich 2 (sich paarweise der Abstimmung enthalten) to pair (off).
ab-pachten (⌣⌣chtv) I *v/a.* ⓼** e-m et. 2 to rent (a farm, &c.) from (or of) a p. — II ~ *n* ㉓ = Abpachtung.
Ab-pachter (⌣) *m* ㉒ tenant..
Ab-pachtung (⌣) *f* ㊻ lease.
ab-packen (⌣⌣⌣) *v/a.* ⓼** to unpack; Wagen: to unload.
Ab-packer (⌣⌣⌣) *m* ㉒ unpacker.
ab-palen F (⌣́⌣) *v/a.* ⓼** Erbsen, Bohnen: to shell ... [hieb 2 to parry ...
ab-parieren (⌣⌣⌣́) *v/a.* ⓼*/* *fenc.* e-n
ab-passen (⌣⌣⌣) *v/a.* ⓿** 1. to fit (or adapt) to; abgepaßte Serviette napkin with border. — 2. *fig.* to look out (or to lie in wait) for; die Gelegenheit 2 to watch for one's opportunity; die Zeit 2 to bide one's time; gut abgepaßt well timed, done in the nick of time. [die Gegend, Stadt 2 to patrol ...
ab-patrouillieren ⚔(⌣⌣trūl-j⌣́⌣) *v/a.* ⓼*/*
ab-pauken (⌣́⌣) ⓼** I *v/n* (h.) to cease beating the kettle-drum. — II P *v/a* (prügeln) to thrash soundly.
ab-peinigen (⌣́⌣⌣) *v/a.* ⓼** to torment.
ab-peitschen (⌣́⌣) *v/a.* ⓵** 1. et. 2 to whip a th. off (from), to bring a th. down with a whip. — 2. e-n 2 to horsewhip (or lash, scourge) a p.
ab-pellen P (⌣⌣⌣) *v/a.* ⓼** to skin, Kartoffeln: to peel (= abschälen 1).
ab-pelzen (⌣⌣⌣) ⓼** 1. ein Tier: to skin. — 2. P e-n 2 (prügeln) to thrash a p.
ab-perlen (⌣⌣⌣) *v/a.* ⓼** to unstring (*fig.* like) pearls.
ab-pfählen (⌣́⌣⌣) I *v/a.* ⓼** 1. to palisade, to fence in with palings. — 2. *surv.* to mark with stakes or poles; e-e Telegraphenlinie 2 to peg out a line. — II ~ *n* ㉓ u. **Ab-pfählung** *f* ㊻ 3. palisading. [distrainable.
ab-pfändbar (⌣⌣-) *a.* ⓺ *jur. v. Möbeln 2c.*]
ab-pfänden (⌣⌣⌣) *jur.* I *v/a.* ⓼** e-m f-e Sachen 2 to distrain (or seize) a p.'s goods and chattels. — II ~ *n* ㉓ u. **Ab-pfändung** *f* ㊻ distraint, seizure (by process of law).
ab-pfarren (⌣⌣⌣) *v/a.* ⓼** e-n Bezirk 2 to constitute ... as a separate parish.
ab-pfeifen (⌣́⌣⌣) ⓼** I *v/a.* ein Lied 2 to whistle (off) ...; ⚓ die Mannschaft 2 to pipe off ... — II *v/n.* (sn) (pfeifend davongehen) to go off whistling.
ab-pferchen (⌣⌣⌣) *v/a.* ⓼** Schafe 2 to pen off ..., to put ... in a separate fold.
ab-pflöcken (⌣⌣⌣) *v/a.* ⓼** 1. Wegebau: to peg off, to mark off with stakes. — 2. Wäsche 2 to take ... off the pegs.
ab-pflücken (⌣⌣⌣) *v/a.* ⓼** to pluck off, to pick; ein Hühnchen 2 to pluck ...
ab-pflügen (⌣́⌣⌣) *v/a.* ⓼** to plough off.
ab-picken (⌣⌣⌣) *v/a.* ⓼** to pick off.
ab-placken (⌣⌣⌣) ⓼** *v/a.* u. sich 2 *v/refl.* = abplagen.
ab-plagen (⌣́⌣⌣) ⓼** I *v/a.* to plague, to torment. — II sich 2 *v/refl.* to slave (or drudge) one's life out (mit etwas) over a th.).

ab-plaggen (⌣⌣⌣) *v/a.* ⓼** *agr.* Rasen 2 to cut sods (of grass); *vgl.* abrasen¹.
ab-plärren F (⌣⌣⌣) ⓼** I *v/a.* to bawl out. — II sich 2 *v/refl.* to tire o.s with bawling or crying or whining.
ab-platten (⌣⌣⌣) I *v/a* ⓼** to flatten. — II **ab-geplattet** *p.p.* u. *a.* ⓺ flattened; *geom.* (an den Polen) oblate.
ab-plätten (⌣⌣⌣) I *v/a.* ⓼** 1. Wäsche 2 to iron ... — 2. ⊕ Metall 2 to laminate... — II ~ *n* ㉓ 3. (*vgl.* 1) ironing; (*vgl.* 2) lamination.
Ab-platt-maschine ⊕ (⌣⌣...) *f* ㉒ (zur Abhobelung abgeschrägter Kanten) planing-machine for bevelling (the) edges.
Ab-plattung (⌣⌣⌣) *f* ㊻ *geom.* des Sphäroids: oblateness; *ast.* (Betrag, um den die Rotationsachse e-s Planeten kürzer ist als der Durchmesser des Äquators) amount by which a planet's axis of rotation is shorter than the diameter of its equator.
ab-platzen (⌣⌣⌣) *v/n.* (sn) ⓿** 1. to burst (or crack) off. — 2. *for.* to cut a path.
ab-plündern (⌣⌣⌣) *v/a.* ⓼** e-m et. 2 to rob a p. of a th.; e-n Baum 2 to strip ...
ab-pochen (⌣⌣⌣) *v/a.* ⓼** 1. to knock (or hammer) off; ⚒ to pound, stamp. — 2. e-m et. 2 to bully a p. out of a th.
ab-polieren (⌣⌣⌣́) *v/a.* ⓼*/* to polish (off), to remove by polishing.
ab-prägen (⌣́⌣⌣) ⓼** I *v/a.* 1. to impress, to stamp (with a die) on a th. — 2. ⊕ Geld 2 to coin or stamp (money), to mint. — II *v/n.* (h.) 3. to finish coining. — III sich 2 *v/refl.* 4. to impress o.s.
Ab-prägung (⌣́⌣⌣) *f* ㊻ impression.
Ab-prall (⌣́⌣) *m* ⓶*c.* = abprallen II.
ab-prallen (⌣́⌣⌣) I *v/n.* (sn.) ⓼** to rebound, recoil, fly back, auch *fig.* to glance off; aufschlagend 2 (bsd. v. Kanonenkugeln) to ricochet. — II ~ *n* ㉓ u. **Ab-prallung** *f* ㊻ rebound(ing), recoil (-ing); ⚔ ricochet; *phys. v. Licht, Schall 2c.:* reflection, reverberation.
Ab-prall(ungs)-winkel ⚇ (⌣⌣(⌣)...) *m* ㉒ *phys.* angle of reflection.
ab-prellen (⌣⌣⌣) *v/a.* ⓼** to cause to rebound or to recoil; *fig.* to repel.
ab-preschen (⌣⌣⌣) *v/a.* ⓵** ein Pferd 2 to overwork (or overdrive) a horse.
ab-pressen (⌣⌣⌣) *v/a.* ⓿** 1. to squeeze out of. — 2. *fig.* e-m et. 2 to obtain from a p. by (strong) pressure. — II ~ *n* ㉓ 3. = Abpressung.
Ab-preß-maschine ⊕ (⌣⌣...) *f* ㉒ Buchbinderei: backing-board.
Ab-pressung (⌣⌣⌣) *f* ㊻ extortion.
ab-pricken (⌣⌣⌣) *v/a.* ⓼** *surv.* u. ⚓ Seezeichen auf der Karte 2 to prick off ... on the chart (with pins).
ab-protzen ⚔ (⌣⌣⌣) [Protze] *v/a.* ⓿** ein Geschütz 2 to dismount (or unlimber) a piece of ordnance. [soundly.]
ab-prügeln F (⌣́⌣⌣) *v/a.* ⓶a** to thrash)
ab-puffen (⌣⌣⌣) ⓼** I *v/a.* (prügeln) to hit (hard), to whack. — II *v/n.* (sn) (abblitzen) to detonate, to decrepitate.
ab-pumpen (⌣⌣⌣) *v/a.* ⓼** 1. to put under the pump. — 2. e-n Brunnen 2 to pump a well dry, to exhaust a well. — 3. F = ableihen.
ab-punktieren (⌣⌣⌣́) *v/a.* ⓼*/* to mark off with dots or points, to dot.
ab-pusten F (⌣́⌣⌣) *v/a.* ⓼** = abblasen 1.

Ab-putz ⊕ (⌣⌣) *m* ⓶a. Maurerei: roughcast; zweischichtiger ~ e-r Wand two-coat plastering.
ab-putzen (⌣⌣⌣) I *v/a.* ⓿** 1. to wipe off; (stäuben) to dust off; (reinigen) to clean off, to cleanse, to scour. — 2. *carp.* to smooth ...; *typ.* die Ballen 2 to scrape ...; ⊕ Maurerei: ein Haus 2c. 2 to (give a coat of) plaster (to) ...; ein Licht 2 to snuff ...; die Nase 2 to blow ...; ein Pferd 2 to rub down ...; die Schuhe 2 to brush (the mud off) ...; ⚓ Taue 2 to scrape ... — 3. F e-n 2 (ausschelten) to give a p. a good scolding or talking-to. — II ~ *n* ㉓ u. **Ab-putzung** *f* ㊻ 4. cleaning (off). — 5. ⊕ Maurerei: coat of plaster; *s. a.* Abputz.
ab-quälen (⌣⌣⌣) *v/a.* u. sich 2 *v/refl.* ⓼** to worry (too much), *vgl.* abplagen.
ab-quetschen (⌣⌣⌣) *v/a.* ⓿** to squeeze (or pinch) off, to crush.
ab-quicken ⊕ (⌣⌣⌣) I *v/a.* ⓼** 1. Gold 2 to extract ... by means of quicksilver, to separate ... from amalgam. — 2. abgetriebenes Silber (mit Wasser) 2 to cool down fine silver. — II ~ *n* ㉓ u. **Ab-quickung** *f* ㊻ 3. extraction of gold, separation (from the amalgam).
ab-quirlen (⌣⌣⌣) *v/a.* ⓼** to beat up (with a twirling-stick), to twirl.
ab-rackern P (⌣⌣⌣) ⓶a** I *v/a* to work (too) hard, to drive (like a slave). — II sich 2 *v/refl.* to drudge, to slave.
ab-rädeln ⊕ (⌣⌣⌣) ⓶a.** Bäckerei: Teig 2 to round off ... with a paste-wheel.
ab-radieren (⌣⌣⌣́) *v/a.* ⓼*/* to erase.
ab-raffen (⌣⌣⌣) *v/a.* ⓼** 1. to snatch off the surface. — 2. *agr.* das geschnittene Getreide 2 to gather ... into sheaves. [who makes up sheaves.]
Ab-raffer(in *f*) (⌣⌣⌣) *m* ㉒ *agr.* reaper)
Abraham (⌣́⌣⌣) [hebr.] *npr/m* ㉒*a.* Abraham; *fig. (bibl.)* in ~s Schoß sitzen to be in A.'s bosom, *weitS.* F to be in clover, to be rolling in wealth; ~it (⌣⌣⌣́) *m* ㉒ Abrahamite; -itisch (⌣⌣⌣́) *a.* ⓺ Abrahamitic. [Keuschlamm.]
Abrahams-baum ♀ (⌣⌣...) *m* ㉒ =]
ab-rahmen¹ (⌣́⌣⌣) [Rahm = Sahne] *v/a.* ⓼** Milch 2 to cream off (or skim) ..., abgerahmte Milch *auch* skim-milk.
ab-rahmen² (⌣́⌣⌣) [Rahmen] *v/a.* ⓼** Bilder 2 to frame ... (well).
ab-rahmen³ *prov.* (⌣́⌣⌣) [Rahm = Ruß] *v/a.* ⓼** to cover with soot.
ab-rainen (⌣́⌣⌣) *v/a.* ⓼** Felder 2 to separate ... by banks; to balk off ...
Abrakadabra (⌣⌣⌣́⌣) *n* ㉓ (Zauberformel, Art Amulett) abracadabra.
ab-rändeln (⌣⌣⌣) ⓶a**, **ab-randen** (⌣⌣⌣) ⓼** *v/a.* to edge (off); ⊕ Münzen: a) to gnarl, to mill; b) (abfeilen) to clip.
Abrand-kraut ♀ (⌣⌣...) *n* ㉓ = Überreis.
ab-ranken (⌣⌣⌣) *v/a.* ⓼** den Wein 2 to trim (the tendrils of) a vine.
ab-rasen¹ (⌣́⌣⌣) [Rasen = Grasfläche] *v/a.* ⓿** einen Platz 2 to remove the turf (or lawn) from ...; *vgl.* abplaggen.
ab-rasen² (⌣́⌣⌣) [rasen = wüten] ⓿** sich 2 *v/refl.* to rave; to rush about.
ab-rasieren (⌣́⌣⌣́) I *v/a.* to shave off. — II sich 2 *v/refl.* to shave o. s. thoroughly, F to have a clean shave.

[abraspeln] — 18 — [abriegeln]

ab-raspeln ☉ (ˈˌˌ) v.a. ⓐ** to rasp off. to take off with a rasp.
ab-rasseln (ˈˌˌ) v.n. (ſn) ⓐ** to rattle off: to start with a rattling noise.
ab-raten (ˈˌˌ) I v/a. ⓐaſt** 1. (ant. anraten) e-m (v/n. [h.] von) et. ⓛ to dissuade a p. from a th., to warn (or caution) a p. against a th. — 2. (abmerken) e-m ein Geheimnis ⓛ to guess (or divine) a p.'s secret. — II ~ n 23. = Abratung.
Ab-rater ✕ (ˈˌˌ) m ⓶ dissuader.
Ab-ratung (ˌˌ) f ⓸⑥ dissuasion, warning.
ab-rauben † (ˈˌˌ) v/a. ⓐ** = rauben.
ab-rauchen (ˈˌˌ) I v/n. (ſn) ⓐ** to convert (or turn) into vapour; chm. to evaporate. — II ~ n 23 evaporation.
ab-räuchern (ˈˌˌ) v/a. ⓐa** to smoke (thoroughly or well). to fumigate.
Ab-rauch=raum (ˈˌˌ...) m ⓶ chm. evaporation-chamber; =ſchale ⓕ f, chm. evaporating-dish.
ab-raufen (ˈˌˌ) ⓐ** I v/a. to pull off. — II ſich (ea.) ⓛ v/rpr. to scuffle.
ab-rauhen ☉ (ˈˌˌ) v/a. ⓐ** Gußwaren ⓛ to polish, dress, trim ...
Ab-raum (ˈˌ) m ⓛd. (o. pl.) 1. bei einem Bau: rubbish; carp. chips pl.; for. loppings pl., dead wood; ⚒ (die in der Lagerſtätte nutzbare Mineralien bedeckenden unhaltigen Erd= und Gebirgsarten) barren country (or rock) superposed on mineraliferous strata. — 2. [mhd.] = Abräumung; ~ von Eis und Schnee clearing away (of) ice and snow.
ab-räum=en (for. u. ⚒ **ab-raumen**) (ˈˌˌ) I v/a. ⓐ** to clear off or away, to remove; Speiſen: to take away; ich ließ ⓛ I had the table cleared; Schutt: to cart away. — II ~ n 23 = Aˌ/ung.
Ab-räumer (ˈˌˌ) m ⓶ 1. one who clears (or carts) away. — 2. 🚂 Steinpflug der Locomotive: life-guard, cow-catcher.
Ab-raum=salze (ˈˌ...) n/pl. ⓶ mineral (or saline) deposit, ⌐ abraum-salts pl.: =ſtoffe m/pl. waste (substances).
Ab-räumung (ˈˌˌ) f ⓸⑥ removal; cartage.
ab-raupen (ˈˌˌ) v/a. ⓐ** agr. to clear ... of caterpillars.
ab-rechen (ˈˌˌ) v/a. ⓐ** agr. to rake (off).
Ab-rechling (ˈˌˌ) m(n) ⓛd. corn raked together after the thrashing operations.
ab-rechn=en (ˈˌˌ) I v/a. 1. (abziehen) to subtract; von et. ⓛ to deduct from a thing; das abgerechnet apart from this; Verluſte abgerechnet making allowance for..., setting aside ...; ⓓ die Tara ⓛ to allow for tare; fig. es läßt ſich an den Fingern ⓛ it may be easily ca.culated. it is quite evident. — 2. meiſt ⓞ (ausgleichen) to balance (F to square) accounts with; ich habe mit ihm abgerechnet we have settled accounts; fig. I am even with him. we are quits. — 3. to cease calculating. — II v/n. (h.) 4. to settle (accounts). — III ~ n 23 5. = Abrechnung. (Vgl.ab=...3.)
Ab-rechner (ˈˌˌ) m ⓶ liquidator.
Ab-rechnung, mit ⓞ f ⓸⑥ 1. (Abzug) deduction; nach ~ der Unkoſten deducting expenses; e-n Rabatt von 5%/₀ in ~ bringen to take off (or deduct) five per cent. discount. — 2. gegenſeitige ~ settling (of) accounts; mit e-m ~ halten to make up (or to settle) accounts with a p., fig. to pay a p. out for a thing. — 3. (Rechnungsabſchluß) balancing (of) accounts. (final) settlement.
Abrechnungs=kontor ⓐ (ˈˌˌ...) n ⓶, =ſtelle f clearing-house; =tag m settling-day, liquidation.
Ab-rechte (ˈˌˌ) [P aus ˈabich(t)] f ⓸⑧ Tuchmacherei: wrong (or left) side.
abrechten (ˈˌˌ) v/a. ⓐ⑨ ++ to dress the wrong side of (cloth).
Ab-rede (ˈˌˌ) f ⓸⑧ 1. (Verabredung) (mutual) understanding; F das iſt gegen (ob. wider) die ~ ... contrary to (our) agreement; mit e-m ~ nehmen (ob. treffen) über et. to agree (or stipulate) with a p. concerning a th. — 2. (Leugnung) denial; et. in ⓛ ſtellen ob. ziehen to deny (or contest) a th., to disavow a th.
ab-reden (ˈˌˌ) ⓐ** I v/a. u. v/n. (h.) 1. et. mit e-m ⓛ (verabreden) to arrange a th. with a p. — 2. (abraten) ich kann Ihnen weder zu= noch ⓛ I cannot advise you either way. — II ✕ ſich ⓛ v/refl. 3. to tire o.s. with (much) talking.
ab-regeln (ˈˌˌ) v/a. ⓐa** to regulate.
ab-regnen (ˈˌˌ) ⓑ** I v/n. (h., ✕ ſn) auch v/refl. die Wolke (oder es) hat (ſich) abgeregnet it has done raining; es laſſen to wait till the rain is over or holds up or abates. — II v/a. die Blüten ſind abgeregnet (worden) ... have been beaten down by the rain.
Ab-reib=bürſte ☉ (ˈˌˌ...) f ⓸⑥ bath-brush.
Ab-reibe=haut (ˈˌˌ) f ⓶, =leder, n Vergoldung: gilder's leather.
ab-reiben (ˈˌˌ) ⓐ** I v/a. 1. to rub off; reinigend: to clean off, to scour; abnutzend: to wear by rubbing, Tuch: to fray out; ſich (dat.) den Körper ⓛ to rub o.s. down; (wundreiben) to chafe; ⚓ ein Schiff ⓛ to hog ... — 2. ⓕ mit Bimsſtein ⓛ to pumice(-stone); den Putz ⓛ, eine Wand ⓛ to float a wall. — 3. (zerreiben) Farben ⓛ to grind (down) ... — II ſich ⓛ v/refl. 4. to get used up by friction. — III ~ n 23 5. = Abreibung. — IV. **ab-gerieben** p.p. u. a. ⓺⓺ (D9) 6. in den Bed. des inf. — 7. ⓛe Brotrinde bread raspings pl. — 8. von Münzen: defaced; light.
Ab-reiber ☉ (ˈˌˌ) m ⓶ v. Farben ꝛc.: grinder, rubber.
Ab-reibe=ſtroh (ˈˌˌ...) n ⓶ für Pferde: wisp of straw for rubbing down horses.
Ab-reibung (ˈˌˌ) f ⓸⑥ rubbing (off), friction, falte ~ (bei Waſſerfur) cold rub-down; der Haut ꝛc.: abrasion; (Abnutzung) detrition.
ab-reichen (ˈˌˌ) v/a. ⓐ** 1. et. ⓛ to (be able to) reach or touch. — 2. e-m et. (ver=)ⓛ to hand down a thing to a p.
ab-reifen¹ (ˈˌˌ) ⓐ** [reif] v/n. (ſn) to ripen. to become (F get) ripe.
ab-reifen² (˜) v/a. [Reif = Ring, Band] v/a. ⓐ** ⓕ Böttcherei: Fäſſer ⓛ to unhoop ... ⌐ Faden ⓛ to unstring (off).
ab-reihen (ˈˌˌ) v/a. ⓐ** Perlen ꝛc. vom
Ab-reiſe (ˈˌˌ) f ⓸⑧ ~ (nach //) departure (for //); vor meiner ~ nach // before setting out on my journey to //, previous to (my) leaving (or starting) for //.
ab-reiſen (ˈˌˌ) v/n. (ſn) ⓐ** to start or leave (nach P. for P.); to set out (on one's journey or travels); to depart; er reiſte (ſich) mit dem Schiff) nach dem Kap ab he sailed for the Cape; wir reiſen jetzt ab! F now we 're off or going!
Ab-reiß=block (ˈˌˌ...) m ⓶ date-block.
ab-reiß=en (ˈˌˌ) ⓐa** I v/a. 1. to pull (or tear, wrench) off; Bretter ⓛ to rip off ...; ein Schloß ⓛ to take off ... — 2. (niederreißen) to pull down; e-e Brücke ⓛ to break down ...; ⚒ e-e Ringmauer ⓛ to dismantle ... — 3. (zerreißen) to tear (up); abgeriſſene Kleider ragged ...; er war ganz abgeriſſen ... in rags and tatters. — 4. (aufzeichnen) to trace. — II v/n. (ſn) 5. to break (or snap) off or asunder; fig. meine Geduld reißt ab my patience is at an end, I am losing patience; es reißt gar nicht ab F it's a never ending job, there's no end to it. — III ſich ⓛ v/refl. 6. to come off or undone. — IV ~ n 23 7. = Aˌ/ung. — V **ab-gerissen** p.p. u. a. ⓺⓺ (D9) 8. ⓛer Faden broken thread; ⓛes Stück fragment; ſ. a. 3. — 9. fig. incoherent, abrupt; von Bemerkungen: desultory.
Ab-reißer (ˈˌˌ) m ⓶ 1. demolisher; arch. designer. — 2. (Reißſtift) tracer.
Ab-reiß=feder (ˈˌˌ...) f ⓶ tel. antagonistic spring; =kalender m tear-off calendar; block-almanac, date-block.
Ab-reißung (ˈˌˌ) f ⓸⑥ pulling off; demolition; ⚕ divulsion. [block.)
Ab-reiß=zettel (ˈˌˌ...) m/pl. ⓶ (Notizblock)
ab-reiten (ˈˌˌ) ⓐb** I v/a. 1. ein Pferd ⓛ to over-ride ...; abgeritt(e)nes Pferd broken(-down) ...; e-n Ort ⓛ to survey ... on horseback; ⚔ die Front ⓛ to ride down the front; ⚓ e-n Sturm ⓛ to weather a gale. — 3. (beim Reiten abſchlagen) to knock off in riding; ein Huf=eiſen ⓛ (verlieren) to cast a (horse's) shoe. — II v/n. (ſn) 4. (wegreiten) to start on horse-back. — 5. vom Wege ⓛ to ride off ..., to turn off ... in riding. — III ſich ⓛ v/refl. 6. to tire o.s. by (or with) riding, to ride very fast.
ab-rennen (ˈˌˌ) ⓐb** I v/a. et. ⓛ to knock off a thing in running; e-m den Weg ⓛ to outrun (or catch up) a p. — II v/n. (ſn) to run off or away, to start. — III ſich ⓛ v/refl. to rush and run; F er rennt ſich (faſt) die Beine, die Schuhſohlen ab he's (running and) rushing about like mad. — IV ~ n 23 start, starting.
ab-richten (ˈˌˌ) I v/a. ⓐ** 1. (dreſſieren) Tiere ⓛ to train ...; e-n Hund aufs Apportieren ⓛ to teach ... to fetch and carry; Jagdhunde ⓛ to enter ...; ein Pferd zum Ziehen ⓛ to break in ... to harness; fig. meiſt b.s. e-n zu et. ~ to drill (or coach) a p. into a th. — 2. (einrichten) to fit; ein Stück Arbeit: to adjust; (planieren) to level; glatt ⓛ to smooth; ⚓ ein Schiff ⓛ to rig out or up ... — II ~ n 23 3. Abrichtung.
Ab-richter (˜) m ⓶ 1. trainer. — 2. adjuster. [v. Pferden: brake, break.)
Ab-richte=wagen (ˈˌˌ...) m ⓷. Einfahren
Ab-richt=feile ☉ (ˈˌˌ...) f ⓶ mint. adjusting-file; =hammer m dressing-hammer; =ſtock m straightening-anvil.
Ab-richtung (ˈˌˌ) f ⓸⑥ 1. training; mehr geiſtig: coaching. — 2. ⓕ fitting, adjustment. [with a bolt, to bolt.)
ab-riegeln (ˈˌˌ) v/a. ⓐa** to fasten

Signs (see page XVII): F familiar: P vulgar; Ƒ flash; ✕ rare; † obsolete (died); * new word (born); ˌ+ incorrect; ♪ music;

[abrieseln] — 19 — [abschaffen]

ab-rieseln (ˢᴸ˘) v/n. (ſn, ˎh.) ⓐa** **1.** to trickle down. — **2.** to crumble off.
ab-riffeln ⊕ (ˢᴸ˘) v/a. ⓐa** to pull off with the flax-comb.
ab-rinden (ˢᴸ˘) **I** v/a. ⓖ** e-n Baum to bark (or peel off) ...; ◌ to decorticate; Brot ⁓ to cut the crust off ... — **II** ⁓ n ㉓ barking; ◌ decortication.
ab-ringeln (ˢᴸ˘) v/a. und ſich ⁓ v/refl. ⓐa** to detach rings or ringlets; to come off in ringlets.
ab-ringen (ˢᴸ˘) ⓜt*** **I** v/a. e-m ein Geſtändnis ⁓ to wrest a confession from a p.; ſich (dat.) die Hände ⁓ to wring one's ... — **II** ſich ⁓ v/refl. to tire (or weary, fatigue) o.s. with wrestling.
ab-rinnen (ˢᴸ˘) v/n. (ſn) ⓑ(a)** to run off, to flow (or trickle) down.
Ab-riß (ˢᴸ) m ⓐa. draft, design; (Skizze) sketch; kurzer ⁓ (Auszug) epitome, synopsis, abstract, (short) summary.
Ab-ritt (ˢᴸ) m ⓐc. (Wegritt) riding off (or setting out) on horseback.
ab-rogieren (˘˘ᴸ˘) [lt.] v/a ⓖ** (abſchaffen) to abrogate, to abolish. [... of reeds.]
ab-rohren (ˢᴸ˘) v/a. ⓖ** e-n Teich ⁓ to clear
ab-rollen (ˢᴸ˘) ⓐa** **I** v/a. (und ſich ⁓ v/refl.) to roll off or down; ↓ das Ankertau (ſchnell) ⁓ laſſen·to slip (or pay out) the cable; Draht ⁓ to uncoil ... — **II** v/n. (ſn) (rollend davoneilen) to roll away or down; fig. von der Zeit: to roll on.
ab-roſten (ˢᴸ˘) v/n. (ſn) ⓖ** to rust off.
ab-röſten (ˢᴸ˘) v/a. ⓖ** to roast (well or thoroughly).
ab-röten (ˢᴸ˘) ⓖ** **I** v/a. to dye red. — **II** v/n. (h.) to lose the red colour.
ab-rubbeln F (ˢᴸ˘) v/a. ⓐa** to rub (one's face) clean, to rub (off), to scour; ſich das Geſicht ⁓ to clean one's face.
ab-rücken (ˢᴸ˘) ⓖ** **I** v/a. to push off; typ. die Zeilen ⁓ to paragraph. — **II** v/n. (ſn) (wegrücken) to move off; ⚔ die Truppen ſind abgerückt ... have marched off. — **III** ⁓ n ㉓ ⚔ signal for returning to barracks at the conclusion of manœuvres.
ab-rudern (ˢᴸ˘) ⓐa** **I** v/n. (ſn) to row off. — **II** v/a. in Boot vom Lande ⁓ to push off (the land). [call.]
Ab-ruf (ˢᴸ) m ⓐd. recall; ⊕ auf ⁓ on
ab-ruf/en (ˢᴸ˘) ⓖb** **I** v/a. **1.** e-n ⁓ to recall a p.; e-n von ſeiner Pflicht ⁓ to call a p. off his duty; der Tod hat ihn abgerufen ... carried (or took) him off; abgerufen w. = ſterben; 🚂 den Zug ⁓ (im Warteſaal die Abfahrt verkünden) to call out the next train (on the platform). — **2.** die Stunden ⁓ to cry ... — **3.** e-n zum Theater ⁓ to call for a p. to go to ... — **4.** (ausrufen) to proclaim. — **5.** e-n (ein Schiff) ⁓ (mit der Stimme erreichen) können to be within call of a p. (within hail of a ship). — **II** ſich ⁓ v/refl. **6.** to shout o.s. hoarse. — **III** ⁓ n ㉓ **7.** = A/ung.
ab-rüffeln F (ˢᴸ˘) v/a. ⓐa** (severely) to reprimand, to talk sharply (or give a good scolding) to, F to blow up.
Ab-rufung (ˢᴸ˘) f ⓐ recall; proclamation; ⁓s... (ᴸ...) ⓐ = Abberufungs-...
ab-rühren (ˢᴸ˘) v/a. ⓖ** Kochk.: to stir (or beat) up with; Suppe mit e-m Ei ⁓ to beat up the soup (or broth) with ...
Ab-runde-Feile ⊕ f ⓐ round-off file.

ab-rund/en, ⁎ -ründen (ˢᴸ˘) **I** v/a. ⓖ** **1.** to round off, to make round — **2.** ⊕ ein Muſikſtück ⁓ to pearl ... — **II** ⁓ n ㉓ **3.** = A/ung **1.** — **III** abgerundet p.p. u. a. ⓖ **4.** round(ed off); ein ⁓er Satzbau a well-rounded (or -finished) period; ♪ des Spiel faultless execution.
Ab-rundung (ˢᴸ˘) f ⓐ **1.** rounding off; fig. finish. — **2.** (Rundſein) roundness.
ab-rupfen (ˢᴸ˘) v/a. ⓖ** to pluck (or pick) off; ein Huhn ꝛc. ⁓ to pluck ...
ab-rüſt/en (ˢᴸ˘) v/a. ⓖ** **1.** ⊕ ein Haus ⁓ (vom Baugerüſt entblößen) to take down the scaffolding from a house; arch. die (Lehr=)Bogen ⁓ to strike the centres. — **2.** ⚔ das Heer ⁓ (a. v/n. [h.]) to disarm, demobilize ..., to put ... on a peace-footing; ↓ ein Schiff ⁓ to unrig and lay up ... — **II** ⁓ n ㉓ **3.** = A/ung.
Ab-rüſtung ⚔ (ᴸ˘) demobilization, suspension of armaments; die ⁓ Europas the disarmament of Europe; ⁓s-Konferenz f ⓐ demobilization congress.
ab-rutſchen (ˢᴸ˘) v/n. (ſn) ⓖ** **1.** to glide off or down. — **2.** F (fortgehen) to slip (or make) off, to slope (off), to bolt, to hook it; (abfahren) to drive off, to leave (in a carriage, &c.); (ſterben) to die, F co. to hop the twig, to drop off the hook.
ab-rütteln (ˢᴸ˘) v/a. ⓐa** to shake off.
Abruzzen ♁ (˘˘˘) [it.; ⁎lt. Bru′ttium] pl. (Gebirge) the Abruzzi pl. (Mountains).
Abſ. abbr. = Abſatz; Abſender.
ab-ſäbeln (ˢᴸ˘) v/a. ⓐa** to sabre off.
ab-ſacken¹ (ˢᴸ˘) [Sack] v/a. ⓖ** ein Laſttier ꝛc. ⁓ to load ...
ab-ſacken² ↓ (⁓) [ſacken²] v/n. (ſn) ⓖ** mit dem Strome ⁓ to sag (or float, drift) down or with the stream.
ab-ſäen (ˢᴸ˘) v/a. u. abſ. ⓖ** ein Feld ⁓ (ganz beſäen) to sow (or seed) thoroughly.
Ab-ſage (⁓) f ⓐ **1.** ⚔ (Abbeſtellung) countermand(ing), counter-order; renunciation. — **2.** refusal (of an invitation).
Ab-ſage-Brief m ⓐ letter of refusal; ehm. (Fehdebrief) letter of defiance; challenge.
ab-ſagen (ˢᴸ˘) ⓖ** **I** v/a. **1.** e-m ⁓ to notify a p. of the discontinuance of a th.; e-m die Freundſchaft ⁓ to break with a p.; bſd. ehm.: e-m (den Frieden) ⁓ to (send a) challenge (to) a p.; ein abgeſagter Feind a professed (or sworn) enemy. — **2.** (abbeſtellen) et. ⁓ to countermand (ſtärker: to revoke) a th.; eine Einladung ⁓ to cancel an invitation; ein Eſſen ⁓ (verſchieben) to put off a dinner; eine Jagd ꝛc. ⁓ to declare ... off; et. ⁓ laſſen to excuse o.s. from a thing. — **II** v/n. (h.) **3.** (entſagen) einer Sache (dat.) ⁓ to renounce a th.
ab-ſägen (ˢᴸ˘) v/a. ⓖ** to saw off.
Ab-ſage-Schein (ˢᴸ˘...) m ⓐ ſüdd. = Wechſelproteſt; ⁼ſchreiben n = -Brief.
ab-ſahnen (ˢᴸ˘) v/a. ⓐa** = abrahmen¹.
Abſalom [hebr.] (˘⁻ᴸ, mſt ˢᴸ˘) npr/m ⓖα. (Sohn Davids, 1. Chron. 3,2) Absalom.
ab-ſalzen (ˢᴸ˘) v/a. ⓖ** to salt well.
ab-ſatteln (ˢᴸ˘) v/a. ⓐa** ein Pferd ⁓ to unsaddle ...; ein Packtier ⁓ to unload ...
Ab-ſatz (ˢᴸ) [:offset] m ⓐa. **1.** (Bodenſatz) sediment. — **2.** (Unterbrechung) interruption; in Abſätzen at intervals, by fits and starts; intermittently; ohne ⁓

without a break or a stop, uninterruptedly; ohne ⁓ austrinken ... at one draught; ohne ⁓ ſchreien ... without taking a breath; beim Diktat: new line; ♪ pause; im Gelände: terrace; ⚹ (Knoten im Halm) knot; ⊕ arch. e-r Mauer: offset; ⊕ Schuhmacherei: heel; mit hohen Abſätzen high-heeled; ſich auf den Abſätzen herumdrehen to turn on one's heels; e-r Treppe: landing; im Verſe: cæsura; ⚔ frt. am Wall: berm(e), relais; typ. in den Zeilen: paragraph (abbr. Abſ.). — **3.** ⓐ (Abgang) sale; reißenden ⁓ finden to meet with a ready (or rapid) sale or demand, to go off quickly or briskly; ſchlechten ⁓ h. to sell badly; es iſt kein ⁓ für ... da, der ⁓ iſt gleich Null there is no demand (or market, sale) for ...
Ab-ſatz-Ahle ⊕ (ˢᴸ˘...) f ⓐ pegging awl; ⁼draht ⊕ m wire for heels; ⁼fähig ⓖ a. ⓐ marketable, saleable; ⁼fleck ⊕ m heel-piece, heel-tap; ⁼gebiet ⓐ n outlet for export-goods; ⁼genoſſenſchaft f ⓐ co-operative association; ⁼koſten ⓐ pl. expenses connected with the sale (of goods); ⁼leder ⊕ n = -fleck; ⁼markt ⓐ m = ⁼gebiet; ⁼meſſer ⊕ n heel-shaver; ⁼pflock ⊕ m heel-peg, hob-nail; ⁼quelle ⓐ f (= ⁼gebiet); dem Handel neue ⁼n eröffnen to open up new markets for trade; ⁼ſtift ⊕ m = -pflock; ⁼ſtockung f stagnation of trade, stagnant market; ⁼weg ⓐ m = ⁼gebiet; ⁼weiſe adv. = in Abſätzen (ſ. Abſatz 2); ⁼zeichen n, typ. paragraph mark; ⁼zwecke ⊕ f = -pflock.
ab-ſäubern (ˢᴸ˘) v/a. ⓐa** to clean(se).
ab-ſäugel/n ⚘ hort. **I** v/a. ⓐa** u. **II** ⁓ n ㉓, A/ung f ⓐ f. abſäugen 2, 3.
ab-ſaugen (ˢᴸ˘) ⓜc(a. ⓖ)** **I** v/a. to suck (off). — **II** v/n. (h.) to cease sucking.
ab-ſäugen (ˢᴸ˘) **I** v/a. ⓖ** **1.** (entwöhnen) to wean. — **2.** hort. to inarch, graft, ablactate. — **II** ⁓ n ㉓ u. Ab-ſäugung f ⓐ **3.** zu **2:** ablactation.
☛ Abſce..., abſci... ſ. Abſze..., abſze...
Ab-ſchab(e)-Eiſen ⊕ (ˢᴸ(˘)...) n ⓖ grater, scraper, scraping-iron or -tool.
ab-ſchaben (ˢᴸ˘) **I** v/a. ⓖ** to grate, to scrape (off); (ſchälen) to pare; ⊕ Gerberei: to flesh out. — **II** ſich ⁓ v/refl. to wear out; abgeſchabt shabby, von Kleidern auch: shiny, threadbare, worn.
Ab-ſchabſel ⊕ (ˢᴸ˘) n ⓖ shavings, scrapings pl.; Gerberei: fleshings pl.
ab-ſchachern (ˢᴸ˘) v/a. ⓐa** e-m et. ⁓ to buy et. h. of a p. at a very low price.
ab-ſchachteln (ˢᴸ˘) v/a. ⓐa** (mit Schachtelhalm abſcheuern ꝛc.) to rub (or polish) with shave-grass or horse-tail.
ab-ſchachten ⚒ (ˢᴸ˘) v/a. ⓖ** (auszimmern) to line with framework of timber.
ab-ſchaffen (ˢᴸ˘) **I** v/a. ⓖ** **1.** (aufheben) to abolish; ein Amt, ein Feſt ꝛc. ⁓ to do away with ...; ein Geſetz ⁓ to repeal (or abrogate) ...; e-n Mißbrauch ⁓ to suppress ..., to put down ...; eine Verordnung ⁓ to set aside ..., to do away with ... — **2.** (loswerden) to get rid of, to part with; Diener ⁓ to dismiss (or send off) ...; ſeinen Wagen ⁓ to drop one's carriage. — **II** ⁓ n ㉓ u. Ab-ſchaffung f ⓐ **3.** abolition (of slavery); repeal (of statutes); suppression (of

---

◌ scientific; ⚘ botanical; ♁ geography; ⊕ machinery; ⚒ mining; ⚔ military; ↓ marine; ⓐ commercial; ⚲ postal; 🚂 railway.

[abschälen] — 20 — [abschlagen]

ab-schälen (ˈ⁻ᵛ) ⓈⒶ** I v/a. 1. to peel (off); Nüsse 2 to shell ... — 2. = abrinden I. — II sich 2. v/refl. allg.: to peel (or come) off; in Schuppen: to scale off.

ab-schalmen(ˈ⁻ᵛ)v/a.ⓈⒶ**for.=ablaschen.

Ab-schäl-schaufel (ˈ⁻...) f ⓺ agr. turf-cutter or -spade. [abschälen).

Ab-schälung (ˈ⁻ᵛ) f ⓺ peeling, &c. (f.

ab-schärfen (ˈ⁻ᵛ) v/a. ⓈⒶ** 1. (wetzen) to whet, ein Messer: to sharpen, to give an edge to ... — 2. ⊙ to edge off; carp. (abkanten) to chamfer.

Ab-schärfer ⊙ (ˈ⁻ᵛ) m ⓶ Schriftgießerei: ~ der Lettern kerned-letter maker.

ab-scharren (ˈ⁻ᵛ) v/a. ⓈⒶ** to scrape off.

Ab-scharricht (ˈ⁻ᵛ) m.u.n⓵d, **Ab-scharrsel** (ˈ⁻ᵛ) n ⓶ scrapings pl., shavings pl.

ab-schatten (ˈ⁻ᵛ) ⓈⒶ** I v/a. 1. to adumbrate, profile; a. fig. to sketch, outline. — 2. (schattieren) to shade off. II sich 2. v/refl. 3. fig. to stand out in dark tints (on a light ground). [(off).

ab-schattieren (ˈ⁻ᵛ)v/a.ⓈⒶ**/* to shade

Ab-schatt(ier)ung (ˈ⁻ᵛ, ˈ⁻ᵛ) f ⓺ adumbration, shading; soft gradation of tints, shade, hue; (Entwurf) sketch.

ab-schätzbar (ˈ⁻ᵛ) a. ⓺ appreciable, rateable; **~keit** (⁻⁻) f ⓺ rateability.

ab-schätz/en (ˈ⁻ᵛ) I v/a. ⓈⒶ** to estimate, berechnend, würdigend: to value; (taxieren) to appraise, tax; den Schaden auf 100 Mark 2 to value (or lay) the damage (done) at five pounds; abgeschätzte Grundstücke ꝛc. assessed ...; nicht abgeschätzt unassessed. — II ~ n⓶ = A/ung.

Ab-schätzer (ˈ⁻ᵛ) m ⓶ valuer, appraiser; e-r Steuer: commissioner of assessment.

ab-schätzig ⚭ (ˈ⁻ᵛ) a. ⓺ (verächtlich, W.) depreciative, contemptuous.

Ab-schätzung (ˈ⁻ᵛ) f ⓺ estimate, valuation; appraisement; assessment.

Ab-schätzungs-beamte(r) (ˈ⁻ᵛ...) m ⓶, **=kommissar** m = Abschätzer; **=kommission** f Commissioners pl. of (or for) Assessment, Assessment Committee.

ab-schaufeln (ˈ⁻ᵛ) v/a. ⓈⒶ** to shovel off, to remove with a shovel.

Ab-schaum (ˈ⁻ᵛ) [: offscum] ⓵d. 1. ⊙ (off)scum; (Schlacken) dross. — 2. fig. ~ der Gesellschaft scum of society; ~ der Menschheit dregs pl. of humanity.

ab-schäumen (ˈ⁻ᵛ) I v/a. ⓈⒶ**1. to skim (off), to scum. — 2. chm. ⚛ to despumate. — II ~ n ⓶ u. **Ab-schäumung** f ⓺ 3. skimming (off); ⚛ despumation.

ab-scheidbar (ˈ⁻ᵛ) a. ⓺ separable.

ab-scheid/en (ˈ⁻ᵛ) ⓈⒹ(e)st** I v/a. und v/refl. 1. to separate, physiol. to secrete, chm. to disengage, metall. to refine; es schied sich Sauerstoff ab oxygen was set free or liberated; fig. abgeschieden leben to live in retirement or seclusion, to lead a retired (or secluded) life. — II v/n. (ʃn) 2. to depart. — 3. (sterben) to depart this life; abgeschied(e)ne Seelen departed spirits, the departed. — III ~ n ⓶ 4. =A/ung. — 5. decease.

Ab-scheider (ˈ⁻ᵛ) m ⓶ one who separates; ⊙ metall. (Abtreiber) refiner.

Ab-scheidung (⁻⁻) f ⓺ separation; ⚛ chm. liberation; departure; **~s-mittel** n ⓶

chm. means of separating (or liberating) a substance, an element.

ab-scheiteln (ˈ⁻ᵛ) v/a. ⓆⒶ** das Haar 2 to part one's hair, to wear a parting.

ab-schelfe(r)n (ˈ⁻ᵛ) ⓈⒶ (Ⓠa)** v/a., v/n (h.) u. sich 2. v/refl. to scale (or peel) off; med. ⚛ to desquamate, to exfoliate.

ab-scheren (ˈ⁻ᵛ) I v/a. Ⓣa(a.ⓈⒶ)** den Bart: to shave (off); die Haare: to crop; Schafe: to shear; abgeschor(e)ne Wolle shearings pl. — II v/n. ⓈⒶ** ↓ (aus der Schleppvorrichtung abweichen) to sheer, to fall off. — III ~ n ⓶ hair-cutting.

Ab-scheu (ˈ⁻ᵛ) m ⓵d. († f ⓺) 1. (o. pl.) ~ vor (strong) aversion to, abhorrence (or detestation of; or for; großen ~ vor et. h. to loathe (or detest, abominate) ...; sein ~ vor dem Wasser his dislike of ...; e-m ~ einflößen to fill a p. with loathing; das Stück flößt mir ~ ein a ... gives me the horrors. — 2. (pl. ⚛) (Gegenstand des ~s) abomination, detestable object; er ist mir (od. für mich) ein ~ he is my (pet) aversion.

ab-scheuern (ˈ⁻ᵛ) v/a. ⓈⒶ** 1. to scour off, to use up by (or in) scouring; weits. to cleanse. — 2. (abnutzen) a.: sich 2. v/refl. to wear out by (or in) scouring.

ab-scheulich (ˈ⁻ᵛ) I a. ⓺ abominable, ein ~es Verbrechen a heinous (or an atrocious)crime; F (unangenehm) horrid, awful, dreadful; das 2e Ding the nasty (P beastly) thing; e-e 2e Geschichte an execrable (or a detestable) affair; das war 2 von ihm it was nasty of him. — II F adv. (derb, ungemein) es tut 2 weh it hurts awfully.

Ab-scheulichkeit (⁻⁻⁻) f ⓺ 1. detestableness, e-s Verbrechens: heinousness, atrociousness. — 2. (gräßliche Tat) outrageous (or atrocious) crime.

ab-schichten (ˈ⁻ᵛ) I v/a. ⓈⒶ** jur. to arrange (or divide) in(to) layers; geol. to stratify. — II ~ n ⓶ u. **Ab-schichtung** f ⓺ geol. stratification.

ab-schicken (ˈ⁻ᵛ) I v/a. ⓈⒶ** jur. to send off = absenden I. — II ~ n ⓶ u. **Ab-schickung** f ⓺ = Absendung.

ab-schieben (ˈ⁻ᵛ) Ⓣc** I v/a. 1. to push (F shove) off. — 2. fig. = abwälzen. — II v/n. (ʃn) 3. F (fortlaufen) to decamp, to slope, to hook it; F er ist abgeschoben he has sloped or made off.

Ab-schied (ˈ⁻ᵛ) m ⓵d. 1. departure; ~ vom Leben decease. — 2. (Lebewohl) leave-taking; beim ~ on leaving, on parting; von e-m ~ nehmen to take leave of a p., to bid a p. farewell, to say good-bye to a p.; ohne ~ weggeh(e)n to take French leave; der ~ fiel ihnen schwer they parted with heavy hearts. — 3. (Entlassung) dismissal; seinen ~ erhalten to be dismissed, F to get the sack; e-m den ~ geben to give notice to a p., to discharge a p.; seinen ~ nehmen to send in one's resignation or papers, ⚔ to quit (or leave) the service.

Ab-schieds-besuch (ˈ⁻ᵛ...) m ⓶ farewell(=) call or visit; **=essen** n. **=feier** f, **=geleit** n send-off; **=gesuch** n (tender of) resignation; sein ~ einreichen to tender one's resignation; **=kuß** m parting-kiss; **=rede** f farewell(-) (or valedictory)

address or speech; **=schmaus** m farewell dinner; **=trunk** m parting-cup, e-s Reiters: stirrup-cup; **=worte** m/pl. parting words pl.

ab-schiefern (ˈ⁻ᵛ) Ⓠa** I v/a. to take off in scales or flakes. — II sich 2. v/refl. to scale (or peel) off; ⚛ to exfoliate. — III ~ n ⓶ und **Ab-schieferung** f ⓺ scaling off, ⚛ exfoliation.

ab-schießen(ˈ⁻ᵛ)Ⓣc(e)ʃt** I v/a.1.Bomben auf den Feind 2 to ply ... with shells, to shell ...; ein Gewehr 2 to discharge a gun, to fire (off) a gun; e-e (Flinten=)Kugel 2 to shoot with a bullet; e-n Pfeil 2 to let fly ... — 2. (abreißen) to shoot off; ihm wurde der Kopf abgeschossen a cannon-ball took (or knocked) off his head. — 3. (herunterholen) to bring down by a shot. — 4. e-n 2 (übertreffen) to excel a p. in shooting; den Vogel 2 to carry the prize, to gain the day. — 5. hunt. ein Revier 2 to shoot over an estate. — II v/n. (ʃn) 6. ⚔ to fire a volley. — 7. to shoot (or rush) forth; von e-m Boote ꝛc.: to dart off swiftly; von Farben: to fade (away), v. Zeug, Tuch ꝛc.: to fly. — III ~ n ⓶ u. **Ab-schießung** f ⓺ 8. zu 1: discharge; zu 2: shooting off; zu 6: firing a volley.

ab-schiffen (ˈ⁻ᵛ) ⓈⒶ** I v/a. Waren 2 to ship (off) ..., ↓ to carry ... by (ship's) bottom. — II v/n. (ʃn) to sail, to steam off. — III ~ n ⓶ und **Ab-schiffung** f ⓺ shipping.

ab-schildern (ˈ⁻ᵛ) v/a. ⓆⒶ** to depict.

ab-schilfe(r)n (ˈ⁻ᵛ) v/a. u. v/n. (h.) ⓈⒶ (Ⓠa)** to scale off = abschelfe(r)n.

ab-schinden (ˈ⁻ᵛ) Ⓣa** I v/a. 1. to flay; (wund reiben) to chafe; abgeschund(e)ne Stelle gall. — 2. fig. e-n 2 to grind a p. (down), F to sweat a p. — II F sich 2. v/refl. 3. to toil and drudge, F to slave away, to work like a nigger.

ab-schirren (ˈ⁻ᵛ) v/a. ⓈⒶ** to unharness.

ab-schlachten (ˈ⁻ᵛ) v/a. ⓈⒶ** to slaughter; Menschen 2 auch: to butcher.

Ab-schlag (ˈ⁻ᵛ) m ⓵d. 1. for. = Abraum 1. — 2. (Abprallen) rebound(ing); Billard: die Banden haben einen guten 2 these are good (F lively) cushions. — 3. ⊙ (Prägen) striking off; (Abdruck) matrix. — 4. (Verschlag) partition. — 5. ⊙ Mühle: (Abzug) outlet. drain(-pipe); ⚒ (abgeleitetes Wasser) superfluous (or drained-off) water, overflow. — 6. † (Weigerung) refusal; ~ bekommen to meet with a rebuff. — 7. (Verminderung) ant. Aufschlag) abatement, fall (of prices); ohne ~ at the old price; in ~ geraten to (have a) fall, to go down. — 8. (Anrechnung) auf ~ on account; auf ~ von einer Summe in part-payment of ...; auf ~ bezahlen to pay by instalments.

Ab-schlag... (ˈ⁻ᵛ...) ƒ. Abschlags=...

ab-schlagen (ˈ⁻ᵛ) ⓈⒷ** I v/a. 1. to knock (or cut, hew, strike) off; e-m den Kopf 2 to cut a p.'s head off; Obst 2 to knock down ... — 2. (abformen) to strike off. — 3. (abbrechen; f. bs. 1) to pull (or break) down; ⊙ typ. das Format 2 to strip (or untie) the form(e); Maurerei: ein Gerüst 2 to take down a scaffolding; ↓ Segel 2 to unreef

Zeichen (ʃ. S. XVII): F familiär; P Volkssprache; Γ Gaunersprache; ⚛ selten; † alt (auch gestorben); * neu (auch geboren); ⁑ unrichtig;

[abschlägig] — 21 — [Abschneidung]

sails; ein Zelt ⁓ to strike ... — 4. (ableiten) das Wasser ⁓ to let (or drain) off ...; F sein Wasser ⁓ to make water. — 5. e-n ⁓ to thrash (or beat) a p. soundly. — 6. (zurückschlagen) to beat back; e-n Stoß, Hieb ⁓ to parry a thrust, a cut; ⚔ e-n Sturm, e-n Angriff ⁓ to repel (or repulse) an assault, an attack. — 7. (verweigern) to refuse; er hat es rund abgeschlagen he flatly declined (to do it); ich lasse es mir nicht ⁓, Sie dürfen es mir nicht ⁓ I won't be refused or denied. — 8. typ. = abklatschen I. — 9. ⚒ das Brot ꝛc. ⁓ to lower the price of ...; eine Münze ⁓ (abwürdigen) to depreciate ... — II sich ⁓ v/refl. 10. sich von f-m Wege ⁓ to stray from ... III v/n. (fn) 11. ⚒ aus der Art ⁓ to degenerate. — 12. † (mißraten) to fail. — 13. (a. h.) (abnehmen; ant. aufschlagen) to fall (in price); der Wein schlägt ab ... is losing (in) strength; die Hitze schlägt ab ... is abating; das kalte Wasser ⁓ lassen to take the chill off (abs.). — 14. Billard: (zurückprallen) to rebound. — 15. ⚔ to give the signal for 'march at ease'! — IV ⁓ n ㉓ 16. = A/ung. — V ab=geschlagen p.p. u. a.㉖(D9) (f. a. 7) 17. die Glieder sind mir, ich bin (an allen Gliedern) wie ⁓ F I am quite knocked (or done) up or dead-beat.

ab-schlägig (ᵍᴸ‿) I a. ㊻ negative; ⁓e Antwort refusal; ⁓er Bescheid rebuff. — II adv. e-n ⁓ bescheiden to refuse a p.; ⁓ beschieden w. to meet with a refusal.

ab-schläglich (ᵍᴸ‿) a. ㊻ u. adv. 1. = auf Abschlag (f. Abschlag 8) ⁓e Zahlung = Abschlag(s)zahlung. — 2. = abschlägig.

Abschlag(s)-dividende (ᵍᴸ‿...) f ㊻ interim dividend; =verteilung f (bei Konkurs) payment of a dividend (out of a bankrupt estate); =zahlung f payment on account, instalment.

Ab-schlagung (ᵍᴸ‿) f ㊻ 1. von Eicheln ꝛc.: knocking down. — 2. (Weigerung) refusal. — 3. ✤ fall (in price).

ab-schlämmen (ᵍᴸ‿) v/a. ㊽** 1. to clear of mud. — 2. Erze: to wash.

ab-schlecken obb. (ᵍᴸ‿) v/a. ㊽** = ablecken.

ab-schleichen (ᵍᴸ‿) ㊺ᵃfᵗ** I v/n u. sich ⁓ v/refl. to sneak away or off. — II v/a. e-m et. ⁓ to get a th. from a p. by sly means or in a sneaking way.

ab-schleifen¹ (ᵍᴸ‿) [Schleife] v/a. ㊽** 1. (fortschleifen) to drag off or away; to carry (away) on a sledge. — 2. ♪ Noten ⁓ (ineinander verschleifen) to slur ...

ab-schleif/en² (ᵍᴸ‿) [schleifen] I v/a. ㊺b** 1. to grind off, to take off by grinding or polishing. — 2. das Gröbste ⁓ to smooth or rub (off); ein Messer ⁓ to sharpen ... — 3. a. v/refl. fig. sich ⁓ to grow smooth, fig. to become polished or refined. — II ⁓en n ㉓ 4. = A/ung. — ⁓er (grinder, polisher.

Ab-schleifer ⊕ (ᵍᴸ‿) m ㉒, ⁓in f ㊵
Ab-schleifsel ⊕ (ᵍᴸ‿) n ㉒ (o. pl.) slip; grindings pl., shavings pl.
Ab-schleifung (ᵍᴸ‿) f ㊻ grinding (off); fig. polish(ing), refinement.
ab-schleimen (ᵍᴸ‿) v/a. ㊽** to free from slime; Zucker: to clarify.
Ab-schleißel (ᵍᴸ‿) n ㉒ particles pl. that have worn off.

ab-schleißen (ᵍᴸ‿) ㊺a(㊹)** = schleißen.
ab-schlendern F (ᵍᴸ‿) v/n. (fn) ㊺a** to saunter off or away. [away or off.)
ab-schlenkern F (ᵍᴸ‿) v/a. ㊺a** to fling)
ab-schleppen (ᵍᴸ‿) ㊽** I v/a. to drag (or carry) off. — II sich ⁓ v/refl. to tire o.s. with dragging heavy loads.
ab-schleudern (ᵍᴸ‿) v/a. ㊺a* to throw (or fling) off; den Reiter ⁓ to throw ...
Ab-schlicht-... (ᵍᴸ‿...) ㊻ = Schlicht=...
ab-schlichten (ᵍᴸ‿) v/a. ㊺a** to plane (off); carp. Holz ⁓ (zurichten) to dub ...
ab-schließ/en (ᵍᴸ‿) ㊵d** I v/a. 1. eine Tür ⁓ to lock (up) ..., to turn the key of ... — 2. a. v/refl. sich ⁓ (absperren) to shut off; ⊕ Dampfmaschine: den Dampf ⁓ to turn off ... — 3. a. v/refl. (beendigen) to terminate, to close. — 4. (zustande bringen) to accomplish, to achieve; eine Anleihe ⁓ to contract a loan; die von ihm abgeschlossenen Geschäfte pl. the business sg. done (or transacted) by him; einen Handel ⁓ to strike a bargain; ✤ die Handlungsbücher ⁓ to balance ...; eine Rechnung ⁓ to adjust (or close, settle) ...; einen Vertrag ⁓ to sign an agreement, pol. to conclude a treaty. — II v/n. (h.) 5. mit e-m ⁓ to come to an arrangement with a p. — 6. das Jahr schließt ab mit // ends in //; die Geschichte schließt ab mit // the story breaks off at //. — III sich ⁓ v/refl. 7. to shut (or lock) o.s. up; sich von der Welt ⁓ to seclude o.s. — IV ⁓en n ㉓ 8. = A/ung. — V ⁓d p.pr. u. a. ㊻ 9. conclusive. — VI ab=geschlossen p.p. u. a. ㊻(D9) 10. Red. des inf. — 11. (vollendet) complete; in sich ⁓ perfect; (vereinsamt) isolated, secluded; (sich absondernd) exclusive.

Ab-schließung f (ᵍᴸ‿) ㊻ locking (up), shutting off; vgl. Abschluß.
ab-schlingern (ᵍᴸ‿) v/a. ㊺a** die Masten ⁓ to roll away ... [away or off.)
ab-schlüpfen (ᵍᴸ‿) v/n. (fn) ㊺** to slip)
ab-schlürfen (ᵍᴸ‿) v/a. ㊺** to sip off.
Ab-schluß (ᵍᴸ) m ㊇a. 1. parl. e-r Debatte: closure; eines Handels, Vertrages: conclusion; e-r langwierigen Sache: winding-up; eine Sache zum ~ bringen to bring ... to an issue; zum ~ kommen (mit ...) to come to an arrangement (about ...), to bring ... to a conclusion; die Sache kam endlich zum ~ ... was at last settled or terminated; vgl. auch Austrag. — 2. ✤ ~ einer Rechnung closing (or balancing) of ...; (Verkauf) sale; es fanden nur wenige Abschlüsse statt but few sales were effected.

Ab-schluß-rechnung (‿...) f ㊻ final account; =tag m settling day; =wechsel m remittance for balancing accounts.
ab-schmarotzen (ᵍᴸ‿) v/a. ㊺**/* e-m et. ~ to coax (or wheedle) a th. out of a p.
ab-schmatzen F (ᵍᴸ‿) v/a. ㊺a** e-n ⁓ to cover a p. with kisses; f. a. abschnäbeln.
ab-schmecken (ᵍᴸ‿) I v/a. ㊺** dem Wein das Alter ⁓ to judge the age of wine by its flavour. — II ⁓d p.pr. u. a. = abschmeckig. [insipid; f. a. abständig.)
ab-schmeckig (ᵍᴸ‿) a. ㊻ unsavoury,)
ab-schmeicheln (ᵍᴸ‿) v/a. ㊺a** e-m et. ⁓ to coax (or flatter, wheedle) a p. out of a th. (vgl. ab=... 8). [werfen.)
ab-schmeißen P (ᵍᴸ‿) v/a. ㊺a** = ab=)

Ab-schmeißer F (ᵍᴸ‿) m ㉒ (Pferd, das gern abwirft) bucker, buckjumper.
Ab-schmelz-draht ⊕ (ᵍᴸ‿...) m ㊶ elect. fusible wire.
ab-schmelz/en (ᵍᴸ‿) I v/a. ㊺**, a. ㊺b(ef)t** 1. to melt (⚒ smelt) off. — 2. ⊕ metall. to separate by (s)melting. — 3. (schmelzen) to (s)melt thoroughly. — II v/n. ㊺b(ef)t** (fn) to (s)melt, to drop off in (s)melting. — III ~ n ㉓ u. Ab=schmelzung f ㊻ (s)melting off; fusion; eines Gletschers: ⚙ ablation.
ab-schmieden ⊕ (ᵍᴸ‿) v/a. ㊺** to finish by forging. [abschrägen (f. d.8 1).)
ab-schmiegen (ᵍᴸ‿) v/a. ㊺**=die Kanten)
ab-schmieren (ᵍᴸ‿) ㊽** I v/a. 1. F to copy badly. — 2. oft = abschreiben 2. — II v/n. (h.) (abschmutzen) to give off grease, typ. to blot, to maculate.
Ab-schmierer F (ᵍᴸ‿) m ㉒ 1. slovenly copyist. — 2. oft = Abschreiber 2.
ab-schmunzeln (ᵍᴸ‿) v/a. ㊺a** e-m et. ⁓ to obtain a th. from a p. by (smirking and) smiling. [off sheet.)
Ab-schmutz-bogen (ᵍᴸ‿...) m ㊶ typ. set-)
ab-schmutzen (ᵍᴸ‿) v/n. (h. u. fn) ㊺** to give off dirt or blots, to soil, to blot. Abschn. abbr. = Abschnitt.
ab-schnäbeln F (ᵍᴸ‿) sich (ea.) ⁓ v/rpr. ㊺a** to be billing and cooing.
ab-schnallen (ᵍᴸ‿) v/a. ㊺** to unbuckle; fig., bursch. e-m et. ⁓ to worry a th. out of a p. by constant begging.
ab-schnappen (ᵍᴸ‿) ㊽** I v/a. 1. ein Schloß ⁓ to slip a lock. — II v/n. (fn) 2. von einer Feder: to slip. — 3. (plötzlich aufhören) to break off suddenly (in the midst of a speech, &c.), to stop short.
Ab-schneide-maschine ⊕ (ᵍᴸ‿...) f ㊶ cutting-machine, für Flachs: flax-breaker.
ab-schneid/en (ᵍᴸ‿) ㊺c** I v/a. 1. meist: to cut (off), ⚒ auch: to head off; (durchschneiden) to sever; ⚔ dem Feinde den Rückzug, die Zufuhr ⁓ to cut off the enemy's retreat, supply; e-m die Kehle ⁓ to cut a p.'s throat (a. fig.); ich schnitt mir ein Stück Brot ab I cut myself a slice of bread. — 2. a) hort. Zweige ⁓ to lop off ...; surg. ein Glied ⁓ to amputate (or take off) ...; b) (sich) sich (dat.) die Nägel ⁓ to pare (or cut) one's nails; einem Vogel die Flügel ⁓ to clip a bird's wings; ⊕ schräg ⁓ to bevel. — 3. fig. e-m die Ehre ⁓ to backbite a p.; e-m alle Hoffnung ⁓ to blast a p.'s hopes; den Lebensfaden ⁓ to cut the thread of life; e-m den guten Namen ⁓ to blacken (or injure) a p.'s reputation, to take away a p.'s (good) name; e-m das Wort ⁓ to cut a p. short. — 4. Muster ⁓ (ausschneiden) to cut out (paper-)patterns. — 5. (abgrenzen) to delimitate. — II v/n. (h.) 6. a. sich ⁓ v/refl. (sich abheben) to form a strong contrast with. — 7. F gut (schlecht) ⁓ to turn out (or to get through) well (badly); er hat nicht gut abgeschnitten he did not do (or come off) well. — III ⁓ n ㉓ 8. = B/schneidung.
Ab-schneider (ᵍᴸ‿) m ㉒, ~in f ㊵ cutter
Ab-schneide-schere (ᵍᴸ‿) f ㊶ shears pl.
Ab-schneidung (ᵍᴸ‿) f ㊻ 1. cutting (off). — 2. surg.: amputation, abscission. — 3. fig.: (der Ehre) backbiting, slander.

♪ Musik; ⚙ Wissenschaft; ⚘ Pflanze; ⚲ Geographie; ⊕ Technik; ⚒ Bergbau; ⚔ Militär; ⚓ Marine; ✤ Handel; ✉ Post; 🚂 Eisenbahn.

ab-schnellen (ᵍᵍ⌣) ⑧** I v/a. to jerk (or flip) off; eine Feder: to snap. — II v/n. (ſn) to fly off (with a jerk).

ab-ſchnippe(l)n ⑧(⓶a)**, **ab-ſchnippern** ⓶a**, **ab-ſchnippſeln** ⓶a** ⋅ (ᵍᵍ⌣) v/a. to chip (or snip) off. [ſchnippſel.⎫

Ab-ſchnipperling ⊕(ᵍᵍ⌣) m ⓪d. = Ab-⎬

Ab-ſchnippſel (ᵍᵍ⌣) n ② chip(ping)s pl., clippings pl., snip.

Ab-ſchnitt (ᵍᵍ⌣) m ⓪c. **1.** cutting, cut, shred; (Zinsſchein) coupon. — **2.** ⓶: a) (Wechſel) bill; b) (Nachſchußſumme) appoint; math. e-s Kreiſes: segment; mint. einer Münze: exergue. — **3.** (abgegrenzter Teil) section, part, portion; eines Buches: chapter, paragraph, division; der Geſchichte: period, epoch. — **4.** pros. stop, pause; cæsura; thea. scene. — **5.** ⚔ frt. (Verſchanzung) (en)trenchment, trench; ⁓ im Gelände topographical section or unit; von ⁓ zu ⁓ vorgeh(e)n to advance from point to point.

Ab-ſchnitt(s)-linie ("...) ⊕ ⓯ cutting-line; **=ſchein** ⓶ m coupon; **=weiſe** adv. in sections; **=zeichen** n, typ. section (§).

Ab-ſchnitzel (ᵍᵍ⌣) n ② chip(ping)s pl., shred, cutting; geom. segment.

ab-ſchnitze(l)n (ᵍᵍ⌣) v/a. ⑨(⓶a)** to chip (or snip) off.

ab-ſchnorren P (ᵍᵍ⌣) v/a. ⑧** = ab-⌉

ab-ſchnüren (ᵍᴸ⌣) I v/a. ⑧**1.(losſchnüren) to unlace. — **2.** surg. eine Warze ② (abbinden) to tie off a wart. — **3.** (mit e-r geſpannten Schnur abmeſſen) to measure (or mark) off with a string or line. — II ⁓ n ② **4.** = Abſchnürung.

ab-ſchnurren (ᵍᵍ⌣) I v/a. **1.** P e-m et. ② to get a th. from a p. by begging. — **2.** (ableiern) ein Gebet: to rattle off. — II v/n (ſn). **3.** F to fly off with a whiz.

Ab-ſchnürung (ᵍᴸ⌣) f ⓯ alinement.

ab-ſchöpfen (ᵍᵍ⌣) v/a. ⑧**1. to skim off (a liquid); die Sahne von (der) Milch ② to cream the milk; abgeſchöpfte Milch skim-milk; den Schaum ② to scum. — **2.** fig. das (beſte) Fett von et. ② to take the cream off a. th., F to take the gild off the gingerbread.

Ab-ſchoß (ᵍᵍ) ⑧a. jur. tax paid on leaving a place, emigration tax.

ab-ſchoß-pflichtig ("...) a. ⓯ liable to pay the emigration tax.

ab-ſchrägen (ᵍᴸ⌣) I v/a. und v/refl. ⑧** **1.** to bevel, to slant off, to chamfer; abgeſchrägte Kante bevelled edge — **2.** Land. (böſchen) to slope; a. ſich ② v/refl. to slope. — II ⁓ n ② u. **Ab-ſchrägung** f ⓯ **3.** bevelling, slanting; (Böſchung) slope.

ab-ſchrammen (ᵍᵍ⌣) I v/a. ⑧** **1.** to scratch off. — II P v/n. (ſn) **2.** (fortlaufen) to slip (or make, move) off. — **3.** F verb: (ſterben) to die, F co. to kick the bucket, to pop (or hop) off.

ab-ſchränken (ᵍᵍ⌣) v/a. ⑧** **1.** (durch Schranken abgrenzen) to enclose, to mark with boundaries. — **2.** ⓯ in Glashütten: die glühende Glasmaſſe ② (zur Reinigung in kaltes Waſſer befördern) to chill and cleanse the liquid glass in cold water.

ab-ſchrapen (ᵍᴸ⌣), mſt **ab-ſchrappen** (ᵍᵍ⌣) v/a. ⑧** to scrape off.

Ab-ſchrapſel (ᵍᵍ⌣) n ㉒ scrapings pl.

ab-ſchrauben (ᵍᵍ⌣), ⑧** to screw ff, to unscrew; ſich ② f. to unscrew.

ab-ſchrecke/n (ᵍᵍ⌣) I v/a. ⑧** **1.** fig. to intimidate, dishearten, discourage; e-n von et. ② to deter a p. from a th., F to frighten a p. off a th.; er läßt ſich nicht leicht ② he is not easily discouraged or baffled. — **2.** e-m et. ② to frighten a p. out of a th. — **3.** ⊕ (abkühlen) Roh-eiſen: to chill; Kochk.: mit kaltem Waſſer ② to cool. — II ⁓ n ㉓ **4.** = A/ung. — III ②d a. ⑧ **5.** deterrent; ②des Beiſpiel warning (example); zum ②den Beiſpiel dienend exemplary; e-m als ②des Beiſpiel dienen to serve as a warning to a p.; fig. repulsive; ②d häßlich frightfully ugly; von ②dem Äußeren of forbidding appearance.

Ab-ſchreckung (ᵍᵍ⌣) f ⓯ intimidation; zur ⁓ dienend exemplary.

Ab-ſchreckungs-mittel ("...) n ㉖ deterrent; **=ſyſte'm** n system of intimidation; **=theorie'** f theory on the deterrent influence of punishment.

Ab-ſchreibe-gebühr (ᵍᴸ⌣...) f ⓯, **=geld** n copying-fee; **=maſchine** f copying press.

ab-ſchreib/en (ᵍᴸ⌣) I v/a. ⑨** **1.** to copy; (ins reine ſchreiben) to make a clean (or fair) copy of; jur. to engross. — **2.** von e-m ② (entlehnen) to plagiarize; von Mitſchülern ② F to crib from ...; (übertragen) ☞ to transcribe. — **3.** ⓶ (abrechnen) to write off, to deduct; e-m et. ② to credit a p. for a sum. — **4.** (abbeſtellen) to countermand (in writing); (abſagen) to revoke (in writing); ich werde ihm ② I shall write to him a) not to expect me (daß ich nicht komme), b) not to come (daß er nicht kommen ſoll); er hat mir abgeſchrieben he sent me a refusal or an excuse. — **5.** eine Feder, e-n Bleiſtift ② to use up a pen(cil) with writing; fig. ſich (dat.) faſt die Finger ② etwa: to be for ever scribbling. — II ⁓ n ㉓ **6.** = A/ung.

Ab-ſchreiber (ᵍᴸ⌣) m ㉒, **⁓in** (ᵍᴸ⌣) f ⓳ **1.** copyist. — **2.** (entlehnender Schriftſteller) plagiarist; Schule: cribber.

Ab-ſchreiberei (ᵍᴸ⌣||) f ⓯ **1.** (Geſchäft) copying. — **2.** b.s. von Schriftſtellern: plagiarism; ſtärker: literary theft.

Ab-ſchreibung (ᵍᴸ⌣) f ⓯ **1.** (Abſchrift) copy, ☞ transcript(ion). — **2.** (Entlehnen) plagiarism. — **3.** ⓶ transferring, crediting; **=en** (für Verſchliſſenes, Verluſte, Entwertetes) deductions (made for wear and tear, losses, depreciation).

ab-ſchreien (ᵍᴸ⌣) v/a. u. v/refl. ⑧** **1.** to cry (or bawl) out. — **2.** F ſich (dat.) die Kehle ②, ſich ② to shout o.s. hoarse.

ab-ſchreiten (ᵍᴸ⌣) ⑧b** I v/a. to measure by (one's) steps, to pace (off); ⚔ die Front ② to walk down the lines (to review on foot); der Kaiſer ſchritt die Front ſ-s Regiments ab the Emperor reviewed his regiment. — II v/n. (ſn) to step aside, (weggehen) to go away.

ab-ſchricken ⚓ (ᵍᵍ⌣) v/a. ⑧** ein Tau ② (abfieren) to pay out a cable; die Bolei-nen ② to check the bowlines.

Ab-ſchrift (ᵍᵍ⌣) f ⓯ copy, ☞ transcript, apograph; einer Urkunde: duplicate; jur. gerichtlich beglaubigte ⁓ legally attested copy; gleichlautende ⁓ true copy; für gleichlautende ⁓ for copy conform; ⁓ nehmen von // to take a copy of //; durch eine beglaubigte ⁓ beweiſen to exemplify.

ab-ſchriftlich (ᵍᵍ⌣) I a. ⓯ copied, ☞ transcriptive. — II adv. in duplicate.

ab-ſchröpfen (ᵍᵍ⌣) v/a. ⑧** e-m Blut ② to cup (or bleed) a person.

Ab-ſchrote (ᵍᴸ⌣) f sculp. large chisel.

ab-ſchroten ⊕ (ᵍᴸ⌣) v/a. ⑨** **1.** sculp. to chisel off; to rough-hew. — **2.** Malz ② to rough-grind ..., to bruise ...; Müllerei: Getreide ② (grob mahlen) to rough-grind corn. — **3.** Fäſſer ꝛc. ② lower ..., to shoot ... into the cellar.

Ab-ſchrot-mühle ⊕ (ᵍᴸ...) f ⓬ mill for rough-grinding corn.

ab-ſchrubbe(r)n (ᵍᵍ⌣) v/a. ⑧(⓶a)** **1.** to scrub, ⚓ to hog (the floor of a vessel). — **2.** ⊕ join. to rough-plane.

ab-ſchultern ⚔ (ᵍᵍ⌣) v/a. ⓶a** das Gewehr ② to take ... from the shoulder.

ab-ſchupp/en (ᵍᵍ⌣) ⑧** I v/a. Fiſche ꝛc.: to scale. — II v/n. (h.) u. ſich ② v/refl. to peel off. — III ⁓ n ㉓ u. **A/ung** f ⓯ scaling, ☞ desquamation.

ab-ſchürf/en (ᵍᵍ⌣) I v/a. ⑧**1. to take the scurf off; ſich (dat.) die Haut ② to rub off one's skin. — **2.** ⚒ Kohlen ꝛc. ② to dig (out). — II ⁓ n ㉓, **A/ung** f ⓯ **3.** scurf.

Ab-ſchuß (ᵍᵍ⌣) m ⑧a. **1.** rush(ing down), fall; (Abhang) declivity, slope. — **2.** Gewehr ꝛc.: discharge, firing, shooting; ⁓ des Wildes killing off the game.

ab-ſchüſſig (ᵍᴸ⌣) I a. ⓯ sloping; ſtärker: steep, precipitous; ② ſein to slope (down); Abſchüſſige pl. ⓯ zo. giraffes pl. (Deve'xa). — II adv. slopingly, precipitously; slopewise.

Ab-ſchüſſigkeit (ᵍᴸ⌣) f ⓯ steepness, precipitousness, declivity.

ab-ſchütteln (ᵍᵍ⌣) v/a. ⓶a** to shake off; ein Joch ② (a. fig.) to cast (or throw) off a yoke; Obſt: to shake down; fig. er ſchüttelt ſich (dat.) Vorwürfe ꝛc. leicht ab he soon gets over a scolding, &c.; von ſich ② to fling off, to rid o.s. of.

ab-ſchütten (ᵍᵍ⌣) v/a. ⑧** to pour (or throw) out of (a sack, &c.).

ab-ſchützen ⊕ (ᵍᵍ⌣) v/a. ⓯** **1.** Waſſer ② to shut off ... by means of a floodgate; ⊕ e-e Maſchine ꝛc.: to stop; einen Teich: to drain. — **2.** das Schutzbrett niederlaſſen to lower the flood-gate.

Ab-ſchützer (ᵍᵍ⌣) m ㉒ Maſchine: stopper.

ab-ſchwächen (ᵍᵍ⌣) I v/a. ⑧** to weaken, to enfeeble; e-n Ausdruck ② to gloss over, to qualify; e-n Fall, Sturz: to deaden; Farben: to tone (or soften) down; Börſe: abgeſchwächte Kurſe lower prices or quotations, weak(er) market. — II ſich ② v/refl. to grow weak(er), to lose (in) strength. — III ⁓ n ㉓ u. **Ab-ſchwächung** f ⓯ enfeeblement; qualification; attenuation.

ab-ſchwären (ᵍᵍ⌣) v/n. ⓰ (⑦)a** **1.** (ſn) to come off by ulceration, to fester away. — **2.** (h.) to cease festering.

ab-ſchwärmen (ᵍᵍ⌣) v/n. ⑧** Bienenzucht: **1.** (ſn) to leave (or fly off) in swarms. — **2.** (h.) to cease swarming.

ab-ſchwarten (ᵍᴸ⌣) v/a. ⑧** Speck ② to peel off (the skin of) bacon; ⊕ Zimmerei: to cut off the slabs.

ab-ſchwatzen F (ᵍᵍ⌣) v/a. ⑨** e-m et. ② to talk (or cajole) a p. out of a th.

Signs (see page XVII): F familiar; P vulgar; ⌐ flash; ⚲ rare; † obsolete (died); * new word (born); ⁺⁺ incorrect; ♪ music;

[abschweben] — 23 — [absetzen]

ab-schweben (ˢᴸ~) v/n. (ſn) ⊛** to move off, away or down(wards).

ab-schwefeln ⊕ (ˢᴸ~) I v/a. ⓐa** 1. (entſchwefeln) to desulphurate; Steinkohle ⚲ to coke coal. — 2. (ſchwefeln) to impregnate with (fumes of) sulphur. — II ~ n ㉓ und **Ab-schwef(e)lung** f ㊻ 3. desulphuration.

ab-schweif/en (ˢᴸ~) ⊛** I v/a. 1. ausſpülen (Wäſche): to rinse; Garn: to wash. II v/n. (ſn) 2. to deviate from; fig. to digress; ſchweifen Sie nicht ab! keep to the subject!, F don't ramble! — III ~ n ㉓ 3. = A/ung. — IV ⚶ p.pr. u. a. ㊻ 4. in allen Bed. des inf. — 5. fig. digressive, F rambling.

Ab-schweifung (ˢᴸ~) f ㊻ 1. deviation, excursion. — 2. fig. digression.

ab-schweißen (ˢᴸ~) v/a. ⓐ** Eiſen ⚲ to weld ... [kohle (glühen) to calcine ...]

ab-schwelen (ˢᴸ~) v/a. ⓑ** chm. Steinſ

ab-schwemmen (ˢᴸ~) v/a. ⓑ** 1. vom Waſſer: to carry off; Holz: to float. — 2. ⊕ Erze ꝛc.: to wash, ʑ to elutriate; Färberei: to rinse, cleanse. — 3. Pferde ⚲ to ride ... into the horse-pond.

ab-schwenden (ˢᴸ~) v/a. ⓑ** ein Grundſtück ⚲ (durch Verbrennen des Holzes oder Grases zum Pflügen vorbereiten) to make a plot of land arable (by burning off the timber or grass), to denshire.

ab-schwenk/en (ˢᴸ~) ⓑ** I v/a. 1. (abwaſchen) to rinse (off). — 2. das Waſſer vom Hute ⚲, den Hut ⚲ to shake (the water) off one's hat. — II v/n. (ſn) u. ſich ⚲ v/refl. 3. bſd. ⚔ to wheel off (aus der Linie) in Kolonnen ⚲ to file off in columns; nach der Seite ⚲ to wheel (or turn) aside; rechts abgeſchwenkt! right wheel! — III ~ n ㉓ u. A/ung f ㊻ 4. wheeling off, filing off.

ab-schwimmen (ˢᴸ~) ⓐ(b)** I v/a. j-e halbe Stunde ⚲ to swim one's half hour. — II v/n. (ſn) von Perſonen: vom Lande ⚲ to swim off (or away from) the land or shore; von Sachen: to drift (or float) away. — III ſich ⚲ v/refl. to tire (or exhaust) o.s. with swimming.

ab-schwindeln (~) v/a. ⓐa** e-m. et. ⚲ to swindle (or humbug) a p. out of a th.

ab-schwingen (ˢᴸ~) ⓑⁱ** I v/a. to shake off; Getreide: to winnow. — II ſich ⚲ v/refl. ſich vom Pferde ⚲ to jump (or leap) off (or from) one's horse. [off.]

ab-schwirren (ˢᴸ~) v/n. (ſn) ⊛** to buzzſ

ab-schwitzen (ˢᴸ~) ⓑ** I v/a. 1. ⊕ Gerberei: Felle: to heat. — 2. (durch Schwitzen entfernen) to sweat off. — II ſich ⚲ v/refl. 3. to perspire profusely or freely.

ab-schwör/en (ˢᴸ~) ⓑ b** I v/a. 1. e-n Eid ⚲ to take an oath; dem Teufel ein Bein ⚲ to forswear o.s. with a light heart. — 2. ſeinen Glauben ⚲ to abjure (or renounce) ... — 3. (ſchwörend ableugnen) to deny upon oath; ein Verbrechen ⚲, auch: to plead not guilty (to a charge); die Lehenspflicht e-m Herrſcher ⚲ to forswear one's allegiance to ... — II ſich ⚲ v/refl. 4. ſich von et. ⚲ to clear o.s. of ... by an oath. — III ~ n ㉓ 5. = A/ung. IV **ab-geſchworen** p.p. u. a. ㊻ (D 9) 6. ⚲er Feind sworn foe, bitter enemy.

Ab-schwörung (~) f ㊻ eines Eides: swearing; des Glaubens: abjuration, renunciation; jur. (Ableugnung) denial (upon oath). [Turnerei: swinging down.]

Ab-schwung (ᵇˢ) m ⓒ c. leap(ing) down;ſ

ab-segeln (ˢᴸ~) ⓐa** I v/n. (ſn) 1. ⚓ to sail away, to set sail; das Schiff ſegelt in drei Tagen ab ... will sail (or put to sea) in ... — 2. fig. F to pack up one's traps, derb co. (ſterben) to go on one's last journey, F to hop the twig, to kick the bucket. — II v/a. 1. ⚓ e-n Maſt ⚲ (abbrechen) to spring (or to carry away) ... — III ~ n ㉓ 4. Segelſport: (letzte gemeinſchaftliche Seglerfahrt des Jahres) last sailing trip of the year.

ab-ſehbar (ˢᴸ~) a. ㊻ within sight; nicht ⚲ lost to view; das Werk wird in ⚲er Zeit fertig w. ... be finished before long.

ab-ſeh/en (ˢᴸ~) ⓐa** I v/a. 1. (überblicken) to reach with the eye; ſoviel ich ⚲ kann as far as I can see; das Ende von et. ⚲ to foresee the end of a th.; der Ausgang iſt ſchwer abzuſehen it is difficult to foretell the upshot (or outcome) of it. — 2. fig. (begreifen) to conceive; es iſt noch gar nicht abzuſehen, wie das enden wird no one knows how ... — 3. (ſehend ablernen) e-m etwas ⚲ to learn a th. by watching (or observing) a p., vgl. Auge 5; einem et. an den Augen ⚲ to read a th. in a p.'s eyes. — 4. surv. (viſieren) to sight. — 5. ſein Ziel ⚲ to aim at a th.; es war auf mich abgeſehen it was meant (or intended) for me; es iſt auf Sie abgeſehen they have a design upon you, there's a plot against you; das Schickſal hatte es auf ihn (auf ſ-n Untergang) abgeſehen ... had marked him out as its victim; die Gelegenheit ⚲ to pick (or bide) one's opportunity. — II v/n. (h.) 6. von einem. et. ⚲ to turn one's eyes from ... — 7. (nicht in Betracht ziehen) fig. von et. ⚲ to take no account of a th.; abgeſehen von // oft: leaving // out of the question, setting aside; abgeſehen davon, daß // without counting that //, let alone that //, without mentioning that //. — 8. Schule: von e-m ⚲ to crib from ... — III ~ n ㉓ 9. über ~ beyond calculation. — 10. (Viſier) sight; surv. hinteres ~ back-sight. — 11. (Zielen) aim; ⚓ ob. † fig. (Abſicht) intention; ſein ~ auf et. haben to have a th. in view.

ab-ſehlich (ˢᴸ~) a. ㊻ = abſehbar.

Ab-ſeide ⚶ (ˢᴸ~) f ㊽ floss-silk.

ab-ſeifen (ˢᴸ~) v/a. ⓐ** 1. (waſchen) to (clean with) soap. — 2. ⊕ (entſeifen) to wash out the soap from.

ab-ſeigern ⊕ (ˢᴸ~) I v/a. und v/n. (h.) ⓐa** 1. e-n Schacht ⚲ to sink ...; (loten) to plumb. — 2. metall. to finish the (e)liquation of (metals). — II ~ n ㉓ u. **Ab-ſeigerung** f ㊻ 3. (e)liquation (of metals). [ing-bag.]

Ab-ſeihe-beutel (ˢᴸ~...) m ⓒ filter-ſ

ab-ſeihen (ˢᴸ~) I v/a. ⓐ** 1. hort. to strain (off). — II ~ n ㉓ u. **Ab-ſeihung** f ㊻ filtration, straining.

ab-ſein (ˢᴸ~) v/n. ⓐa** to be off or apart; nicht weit vom Wege ⚲ to be near one's ...; die Sache iſt ab ... is broken off.

Ab-ſeite (ˢᴸ~) f ㊻ 1. (Hinterſeite) reverse side (of a coin, &c.). — 2. ⊕ (geneigte Fläche) pane (of a roof). — 3. [ahd. P aus grch. Apſide] arch. (Seitenſchiff) apse-aisle, side-aisle. [part of ...]

ab ſeiten (ʲ¹/~) prp. (mit gen.) on theſ

ab-ſeits (ˢᴸ) I adv. aside, apart; ſich ⚲ halten to keep aloof. — II prp. (mit gen.) within a short distance from.

ab-ſend/en (ᵇˢ~) I v/a. ⊛** 1. Sachen: to forward, send off; ⊛ Güter auch: to consign; eilig: to despatch; Geld: to remit; Briefe: to post; zu Schiffe: to ship. — 2. Perſonen: to send out, ⚔ to detach; Abgeordnete: to depute; mit Aufträgen: to commission. — II p.p. als s. 3. ſ. Abgeſandte(r). — III ~ n ㉓ 4. = A/ung.

Ab-ſender (ᵇˢ~) m ⓑ, **~in** f ㊼ (abbr. Abſ.) sender, ⊛ consignor, shipper (of goods); auch Briefen: ~ N. forwarded by N.; ~ dieſes the writer of these lines.

Ab-ſendung (ᵇˢ~) f ㊻ ⊛ consignment; despatch; shipment; deputation; commission; ~s-**ort** (ˢᴸ~...) m ⓑ, -**ſtation** f station for the despatch of goods, forwarding office or station.

ab-ſengen (ᵇˢ~) v/a. ⓐ** to singe off, to scorch, to sear.

ab-ſenk/en (ᵇˢ~) ⓑ** I v/a. 1. ⊕ agr. Wein: to provine; hort. Ableger ⚲ to set (or plant) layers. — 2. ⚒ einen Schacht ⚲ to sink ... — II ſich ⚲ v/refl. 3. to slope, to incline. — III ~ n ㉓ = A/ung 1. [ſlip, ſhoot.]

Ab-ſenker ⊕ (ᵇˢ~) m ⓑ hort. layer,ſ

Ab-ſenkung (ᵇˢ~) f ㊻ 1. hort. layering. — 2. slope, incline. [ſentees.]

Abſenten-liſte (~...) f ⓑ list of ab-ſ

abſentieren (ˢᴸ~) [t.] ſich ⚲ v/refl. to absent o.s. (vgl. ſich entfernen).

Abſentismus † (~~~) m ⓓ (Fern vom Gute Wohnen der Großgrundbeſitzer) absenteeism.

Abſenz (~ˢ) [t.] f ㊻ (Abweſenheit) absence.

ab-ſetzbar (ˢᴸ-) a. ㊻ removable; ⊛ saleable, marketable; **~feit** (~-) f ㊻ removability; ⊛ saleability.

ab-ſetz/en (ᵇˢ~) ⓑ** I v/a. 1. (hinwegſetzen) to push off; v/refl. ſich von e-m ⚲ to sit away from a p.; ⚓ ein Boot vom Lande ⚲ to push off ...; von e-m andern Fahrzeuge ⚲ to put off (or to detach) ... — 2. (herabnehmen) die Mütze ⚲ to raise ...; den Reiter ⚲ (abwerfen) to throw the rider. — 3. (ab-, ausſteigen laſſen) e-n wo ⚲ to set a p. down; ſetzen Sie mich im Gaſthofe ⚲ put me down (or drop me) near the hotel. — 4. (innehalten) den Becher ⚲ to take ... off one's lips or mouth; ⚔ jetzt ab! ground arms! — 5. (et. unterbrechen) to break off a th.; die Zeile ⚲ to begin a new line. — 6. ♪ (stacca'to ſpielen) to play sharply. — 7. Tiere ⚲ (entwöhnen) to wean ... 8. (entfernen) e-n vom Amte ⚲ to remove a p. (from his post), to dismiss a p.; e-n König ⚲ to dethrone ..., to depose ... — 9. weitS.: Münzen ⚲ to withdraw ... (from circulation), to call in ... 10. (abſchneiden) to retrench; eine Summe vom Budget ⚲ to strike (or take) ... off the budget. — 11. ⊛ Waren ⚲ (verkaufen) to clear off (or to sell, to dispose of) one's stock; leicht abzuſetzen(b) marketable, saleable, meeting with a ready sale; Feigen laſſen ſich nicht ⚲ there is no sale for ... — 12. (abſondern)

⚶ scientific; ⚹ botanical; ☿ geography; ⊕ machinery; ⚒ mining; ⚔ military; ⚓ marine; ⊛ commercial; ✉ postal; ⛓ railway.

to deposit; auch: sich 2 to settle; beim Braten Fett 2 to give off dripping. — 13. (abheben) Farben 2 to set off ...; sich 2 u. v/n. (h.) (hervortreten) to show off well against ... — 14. typ. Manuskript 2 to set up ... (in type). — II v/n. (h.) 15. (vgl. 3) to break off, to stop, to pause; ohne abzusetzen without a break or a halt, beim Schreiben: with a running pen, beim Trinken: at a draught. — 16. (auch v/refl. sich 2) to be precipitated, to form a sediment or a deposit; ⚔ ein Gang setzt (sich) ab a lode runs off (in another direction). — III v imp. 17. es wird et. Böses 2 there is mischief (or trouble) brewing; es wird Hiebe 2 they will come to blows. — IV ~ n 23 18. in Reden ⁊c.: pause, hesitation. v. Tieren: weaning (i. a. A/ung).

Ab-setzung (ˇˇˇ) f 🌐 1. removal (from an office), discharge (from a situation); von Fürsten: deposition, dethronement; einstweilige: suspension. — 2. e-r Münze: depreciation, withdrawal (from circulation). — 3. (Niederschlag) precipitate, sediment. — 4. typ. e-s Bogens setting up (or putting) in type.

Ab-sicht (ˇˇ) f 🌐 1. intention; (Vorsatz) purpose, plan, design, scheme, project; (Ziel) end (in view), object; seine ~ erreichen to gain one's point; ich habe die ~ ihn zu besuchen I intend calling on him; et. mit ~ tun to do a thing intentionally or deliberately; ohne ~ unintentionally, without set purpose; es lag nicht in meiner ~, war nicht meine ~, zu // it was not my intention to //, it never entered my head to //; ich hatte nicht die leiseste ~ zu kommen I did not dream of coming; (feindselige) ~en auf et. haben to have designs upon a th.; er hat ~en auf sie he has an eye to (bisw. auch on) her; er tat's mit guter ~ he did it with a good intention, he meant it well; schlimme ~en verfolgen to have evil intentions, to be bent on mischief; in welcher ~? for what purpose?; jur. mit böswilliger ~ with malice prepense or aforethought — 2. † (Hinsicht) in ~ auf et. (oder gen.) as regards a th.

ab-sichtlich (ˇˇˇ) I a. 🌐 intentional; 2e Beleidigung deliberate insult. — II adv. intentionally, on purpose, of set purpose, designedly; meist b.s. deliberately; er ist 2 dahin gegangen he made a point of going there.

Ab-sichtlichkeit (ˇˇˇ) f 🌐 deliberateness; ~ eines Täters premeditation.

ab-sicht(s)=los (ˇˇˇ) a. 🌐 unintentional; =losigkeit (ˇˇˇˇ) f 🌐 want of an intention in a th.; =satz |(ˇˇˇ...) m 🌐 gram. (damit, um zu) clause expressing a purpose (in view); ab-sicht(s)=voll (ˇˇˇ) a. 🌐 intentional, adv. auch: purposely, on (or for the) purpose, vgl. absichtlich. [down.]

ab-sickern (ˇˇˇ) v/n. (sn) 🌐** to trickle
ab-sieben (ˇˇˇ) v/a. 🌐** to sift off.
ab-sieden (ˇˇˇ) I v/a. 🌐e**, 🌐** 1. to boil (thoroughly), pharm. to decoct. — 2. ⊙ Stoffe: to extract (or purify, cleanse) by boiling. — II ~ n 23 3. pharm. decoction.

ab-singen (ˇˇˇ) 🌐ü** I v/a. ein Lied: to sing off; Kirche: to chant (off); die Vögel sangen ihre Lieder ab ... carolled forth ... — II sich 2 v/refl. to sing o.s. hoarse.
ab-sinken (ˇˇˇ) 🌐ü** I v/n. (sn) to sink down. — II v/a. ⚔ (abteufen) to sink.
ab-sintern (ˇˇˇ) v/n. (sn) 🌐a** to trickle down (= absickern).

Absinth (ˇˇ) [fr., *grch.] m 🌐b. 1. 💠 ~ Wermut. — 2. (fr. Art Likör) absinth(e).

ab-sitzen (ˇˇˇ) 🌐e** I v/n. (sn) 1. von e-m (weit) 2 to sit away from a p. — 2. to get off (a horse), to dismount, to alight. — II v/a. (abnutzen) to wear out by sitting. — 4. e-e Schuld 2 to sit in jail (or to undergo imprisonment) for debt; s-e Schulzeit 2 to pass through a school; seine (Straf-)Zeit 2 F to do one's time.

ab-solden (ˇˇˇ) 🌐** Truppen ⁊c. 2 to pay off ..., to disband, to discharge ...

absolut (ˇˇˇ) [lt.] I a. 🌐 (ant. relativ) 1. absolute; 2er Herrscher a. monarch, autocrat; 2 (adv.) richtig absolutely correct. — 2. 🔬 phys. 2e Leere perfect vacuum. — II ~e(s) n 23 3. the absolute.

Absolution (ˇˇˇ-tz(ˇ)ˇˇ) [lt.] f 🌐 (Sündenvergebung) absolution. [solutism.]
Absolutismus (ˇˇˇ-ˇˇ) [neu-lt.] m 🌐 ab-]
Absolutist (ˇˇˇˇ) [lt.] m 🌐 defender of despotism, absolutist. [tist(ic).]
absolutistisch (ˇˇˇˇˇ) [lt.] a. 🌐 absolu-]
Absolutorium (ˇˇˇ-ˇ(ˇ)ˇ) [lt.] n 23 jur. (Freisprechung) acquittal, release.
absolvieren (ˇˇw-ˇˇ) [lt.] v/a. 🌐 1. (lossprechen) to acquit. — 2. (beendigen) seine Studien 2 to complete ..., to finish ...

ab-sonderlich (ˇˇˇˇ) a. 🌐 1. (eigentümlich) peculiar. — 2. (sonderbar) singular, curious, uncommon, out of the common, stärker: odd, strange, von 2er Größe of extraordinary size. — 3. mst adv. (besonders) especially.

Absonderlichkeit (ˇˇˇˇˇ) f 🌐 (vgl. absonderlich 1 u. 2) peculiarity; singularity, curiosity, oddity.

ab-sonder/n (ˇˇˇ) 🌐a** I v/a. 1. to set apart; to separate, divide (von et. from a th.); to detach; (vereinzeln) to isolate; ⚔ abgesonderter Truppenteil detachment. — 2. physiol. Galle ⁊c. 2 to secrete ... — 3. phls. to abstract. — II sich 2 v/refl. 4. to separate o.s., to dissociate o.s. from; 🌐 to dissolve partnership with; sich von der Welt 2 to retire from ...; v. d. Welt abgesondert secluded, (living) in seclusion. — III ~ n 23 5. = A/ung.

Ab-sonderung (ˇˇˇˇ) f 🌐 1. separation; isolation; seclusion. — 2. 🜨 geol. (Zerklüftung ob. Trennung der Gesteinsmassen) separation (or detachment) of mountain-groups or rocks; physiol. secretion; phls. abstraction. — 3. ⊙ im Konkurs: separate treatment (of a creditor).

Ab-sonderungs=drüse (ˇˇˇ...(ˇ˙ˇ)) f🌐physiol. secretory gland; =gefäß n = =organ; =graben m separating ditch; =orga'n n excretory duct, organ; =stoff m secreted matter, secretion; =strich m mark of division; =vermögen n, phls. power of abstraction (physiol. of secretion).

absorbierbar (ˇˇˇ-ˇ) a. 🌐 absorbable.
absorbieren (ˇˇˇˇ).[lt.] v/a. 🌐 (in sich aufnehmen) to absorb; 2d absorbent.

ab-sorgen (ˇˇˇ): sich 2 v/refl. 🌐** to be overwhelmed (or greatly troubled) with cares, to fret (or worry) too much.

Absorption (ˇˇˇ-tz(ˇ)ˇ) [lt.] f 🌐 (Aufsaugung) absorption; elektrische ~ electrification.
Absorptions=fähigkeit (ˇˇˇ-ˇ(ˇ)ˇˇ) ...) f 🌐, =kraft f, =vermögen n power of absorption, absorptive faculty.

ab-spalten (ˇˇˇ) v/a., v/n. u. sich 2 v/refl. 🌐** to split off, to cleave. [setzen 7.)
ab-spänen (ˇˇˇ) v/a. 🌐** to wean (= ab-]
ab-spann/en (ˇˇˇ) 🌐** I v/a. 1. e-n Bogen 2 to unbend ...; 🎵 Saiten 2 to slacken ...; Gewehr: to put to halfcock, auch: to halfcock; med. to relax. — 2. die Pferde vom Wagen 2, den Wagen 2 to take the horses from the carriage or out of the shafts, Stiere 2 to unyoke ... — 3. [adj. spanan = locken] F ob. † = abspenstig (i.d.) machen. — II ~ n 23 4. = A/ung. — III abgespannt p.p. u. a. 🌐 5. wie I. — 6. fig. (matt) weary, fatigued, unstrung, languid, stärker: done up, exhausted, worn out, dead-beat.

Ab-spannung (ˇˇˇ) f 🌐 unbending (a. fig.); (Erholung) relaxation; fig. (Ermattung) fatigue, languor, exhaustion.

ab-sparen (ˇˇˇ) v/a. 🌐** sich (dat.) et. (am Munde) 2 to stint o.s. (or to go short) of a thing, to deny o.s. a th.
ab-speisen (ˇˇˇ) 🌐** I v a. 1. e-n mit et. 2 to feed a p. on a th. — 2. fig. (abfertigen) mit leeren Worten 2 to put off with fair words. — II v/n. (h.) 3. to finish dining; sie haben abgespeist they have done (or finished) dining, their dinner (or repast) is over.

ab-spenen (ˇˇˇ) v/a. 🌐** s. abspänen.
ab-spenstig (ˇˇˇ) [abspannen 3] a. 🌐 einen 2 machen to estrange a p. from; Dienstboten ⁊c. 2 machen to unsettle ...; Kunden 2 machen to entice (or draw) customers away; e-r Sache 2 werden to desert a cause, abs. a. F to rat.

ab-sperr/en (ˇˇˇ) 🌐** I v/a. 1. (sperren) e-e Straße: to block; (abschließen) to shut off; (absondern) to confine. — 2. (hemmen) to stop, to obstruct. — 3. ⊙ den Dampf 2 to cut (or turn) off ... — II v refl. 4. fig. sich von der Welt 2 to seclude o.s. from everybody. — III ~ n 23 = 5. A/ung.

Absperr=hahn (ˇˇˇ...) m 🌐 stop-cock; =klappe ⊙ f = =ventil; =system n block-system.

Ab-sperrung (ˇˇˇ) f 🌐 1. (vgl. absperren) (solitary) confinement; stoppage, obstruction; seclusion. — 2. 🌐 prohibition (of trade). (Vgl. a. Sperrung.)

Ab-sperrungs=apparat ⊙ (ˇˇˇ...) m 🌐 tel. closing-apparatus; =system n: a) system of solitary confinement; b) 🌐 prohibitive system. [valve.]
Ab-sperr=venti'l ⊙ (ˇˇˇ...) n 🌐 check-]
ab-spiegeln (ˇˇˇ) I v/a. u. v/refl. 🌐a** to mirror; to reflect (a. fig.); sich 2 to be reflected. — II ~ n 23 u. Ab-spiegelung (ˇˇˇ) f 🌐 reflection.

ab-spielen (ˇˇˇ) 🌐** I v/a. 1. (von e-r Vorlage 2) 🎵 ein Lied auf der Orgel 2 to play an air on ...; vom Blatte 2 to play at (first) sight. — 2. (zu Ende spielen) to play to the end. — 3. (durch Spielen abnutzen) to wear out by playing. — 4. Billard: e-n Ball von der Bande 2 to

[**abspinnen**] — 25 — [**absteigen**]

drive a ball from ... — **II** *v/n.* (h.) 5. to leave off playing. — **III** ſich 2 *v/refl.* 6. to be enacted; *v.* Dingen: ſich gut 2 to go off well; *thea.,* &c.: die Szene ſpielt ſich ab ii // the scene is laid in //.

ab-ſpinnen (ᵍᴸ͜) *v/a.* ⓐ** to spin off; die Wolle vom Rocken 2 to empty the distaff; *fig.* Märchen 2 to tell fairytales, to spin yarns.

ab-ſpitzen (ᵍᴸ͜) *v/a.* ⓐ**⚒ 1. to break the point of, to blunt. — 2. to point, to sharpen; e-e Schreibfeder 2 to nib ... — 3. F *fig.* es auf et. 2 (abſehen) to have a th. in view, to plan a th.

Ab-ſplitz (ᵍᴸ) *m* ⓐ *a. for.* = Abſprung 3.

ab-ſplittern (ᵍᴸ͜) ⓐ** **I** *v/a.* to splinter (or split) off. — **II** *v/n.* (ſn) to come (or split) off in splinters.

Ab-ſprache ⚒ (ᵍᴸ͜) *f* ⓴ (Verabredung) (verbal) agreement or arrangement.

ab-ſprechen (ᵍᴸ͜) ⓐ** **I** *v/a.* (aberkennen; *ant.* zuſprechen) e-m et. 2: a) to dispossess (or deprive) a p. of a th. (by judicial decree), b) (in Abrede ſtellen) to dispute a p. a th.; e-m das Leben 2 to pass a death-sentence upon a p., to sentence a p. to death, *v.* Ärzten: to give over (a patient), *jur.* to abjudicate; ſeine Gabe läßt ſich nicht 2 ... cannot be questioned, there's no denying ... **II** *v/n.* (h.) (urteilen) über et. 2 to pronounce upon a th.; *b.s.* (abfällig urteilen) to cavil at a th., to dogmatize about a th. — **III** 2d *p.pr. u. a.* ⓴ dogmatic, censorious, positive; (ungünſtig) adverse; (anmaßend) overbearing, vom Charakter ꝛc.: arrogant.

Ab-ſprecher (ᵍ͜͜) *m* ㉒, **~in** *f* ⓰ dogmatizer, harsh (or censorious, peremptory) critic. [dogmatic tone.]

Ab-ſprecherei (ᵍᴸ͜) *f* ⓰ hasty judgment;ƒ

ab-ſprecheriſch (ᵍᴸ͜) *a.* ⓴ = abſprechend.

ab-ſprengen (ᵍᴸ͜) ⓐ** **I** *v/a.* **1.** ⚒ to blast off, to blow off (by an explosion). — 2. ⚔ Truppen 2 to cut off ... (from the main body). — 3. Blumen 2 to sprinkle ... (with water). — **II** *v/n.* (ſn) 4. (davonſprengen) to gallop off.

ab-ſprießen (ᵍᴸ͜) *v/n.* (ſn) ⓐd** to descend from (= abſtammen 1).

ab-ſpringen (ᵍᴸ͜) ⓐſ** **I** *v/n.* (ſn) 1. (nieder- u. weg-ſpringen) vom Pferde ꝛc. 2 to jump (or leap) off (or from) ... — 2. (ſich ablöſen) to crack (or burst, snap) off; *v.* Farbe *a.* to peel (or come) off; *v.* Glas *a.* to fly. — 3. (abprallen) to glance off, to rebound. — 4. *fig.* von e-r Partei 2 to dissociate o.s. (or to secede) from ..., F u. P to rat from ...; von e-m Gegenſtande 2 to fly off from a subject, to digress; ſpringen Sie nicht ab! keep (or stick) to the point!; F vom Abonnement 2 to drop one's subscription. — **II** ſich 2 *v/refl.* 5. to tire o.s. with jumping. — **III** ~ *n* ㉓ 6. secession (ſ. 4); *fig.* plötzliches ~ von e-m Gegenſtande digression ...

ab-ſpritzen (ᵍᴸ͜) ⓐ** **I** *v/a.* (ſn) to spurt off or back. — **II** *v/a.* to clean(se) with a hose or syringe.

Ab-ſprung (ᵍᴸ) *m* ⓒ. 1. leaping off or down; glancing off; vom Haſen ꝛc.: Abſprünge (Querſprünge) m. to double. 2. = abſpringen **III**. — 3. *for.* (ſchwächlicher Seitenſproß von Eichen, Pappeln u. Weiden) weakly young shoot.

ab-ſpulen ⊕ (ᵍᴸ͜) *v/a.* ⓐ** Garn: to wind off, to unwind, to unspool.

ab-ſpülen (ᵍᴸ͜) *v/a.* ⓐ** 1. to wash off, Wäſche: to rinse, Schüſſeln: to wash up. — 2. ⊕ Seide ꝛc.: to wash. — 3. (wegreißen) to wash away. [spooler.ƒ

Ab-ſpuler(in ⊕ *f*㊵) *m* ㉒ (ᵍᴸ͜)(˘) winder,ƒ

Ab-ſpül-waſſer (ᵍᴸ...) *n* ㉒ dish-water.

ab-ſpüren (ᵍᴸ͜) *v/a.* ⓐ** *hunt.* die Fährten des Wildes 2 to search for tracks.

Ab-ſtamm (ᵍᴸ) *m* ⓒ. *hunt.* † *ob. poet.* (H.) = Nachkommenſchaft.

ab-ſtammen (ᵍᴸ) *v/n.* (ſn) ⓐ** 1. to descend (von from); 2d aus // native of // — 2. *gram.* to be derived from.

Ab-ſtammung (ᵍᴸ͜) *f* ⓰ 1. descent, extraction; von vornehmer ~ of noble origin or birth or ancestry. — 2. *gram.* derivation of words, etymology.

Ab-ſtammungs-achſe ⚒ (ᵍᴸ͜ ...) *f* ⓺ central (or main) axis of a plant; **-geſchichte** *f* des Menſchen history of man's descent or origin; **-lehre** *f* theory of evolution or descent.

Ab-ſtand (ᵍᴸ) [(lt. *distaʼntia*)] *m* ⓒ. **1.** distance from ⚒ von vorwärts nach rückwärts; *ant.* Zwiſchenraum, ſeitlich), interval between; *arch.* space between; größter (kleinſter) ~ eines Planeten von der Sonne, ⚹ aphelion (perihelion). — 2. *fig.* (Unterſchied) disparity of age, difference. — 3. (Verzicht) renunciation; ~ nehmen von etwas = abſtehen 3. — 4. (Abtretung) cession.

Ab-ſtänder (ᵍᴸ͜) *m* ㉒ *for.* dead tree.

ab-ſtändig (ᵍᴸ͜) [abſtehen 4] *a.* ⓰ decayed, deteriorated; ⚘ von Waren: 2 werden to spoil (through lying by).

Ab-ſtands-geld (ᵍᴸ ...) *n* ㉒: a) (Entſchädigung) compensation, indemnification, hush-money; b) (Reukauf) forfeit; **-linie** *f, ast.* line of the apsides; **-punkt** *m, ast.* e-s Planeten ⚹ apsis; **-ſumme** *f* = -geld; **-winkel** *m* angle of elongation.

ab-ſtapeln (ᵍᴸ͜) ⓐ** **I** *v/a.* (*ant.* aufſtapeln) to take (down) from a stack.— **II** ⚒ *v/n.* (ſn) ⚓ Schiff: to be launched.

ab-ſtatten (ᵍᴸ͜) **I** *v/a.* ⓐ** to render; e-n Bericht 2 über to (send in a) report on; e-m e-n Beſuch 2 to pay a p. a visit, to call on (or to look up) a p.; Dank 2 für to return thanks for; e-m ſ-n Glückwunſch 2 to offer one's congratulations to a p. — **II** ~ *n* ㉓ und **Abſtattung** *f* ㊻ e-s Beſuches visit, call.

ab-ſtäuben (ᵍᴸ͜) *v/a.* ⓐ** to dust off. — **II** *v/n.* to fly off as dust.

Ab-ſtäuber (,͜) *m* ㉒ dust-brush, duster.

Ab-ſtech-eiſen ⊕ *n* ㉓ *hort.* edging-tool.

ab-ſtechen (ᵍᴸ͜) ⓐ** **I** *v/a.* 1. (ſtechend entfernen) to prick off; Raſen 2 to edge off (the lawn), to cut (sods); (ableiten) e-n Kanal 2 to cut ...; e-n Teich 2 to drain ...; Wein 2 to draw off ..., to tap ... — 2. *ehm.* (ſtechend beſiegen) e-n im Turnier (vom Pferde) 2 to bring down a p.; *fig.* ⚓ = ausſtechen 5; ⚓ einem Schiffe den Wind 2 to gain the weather-side of ...; Spiel: to trump, to over-trump. 3. ⚔ (abgrenzen) ein Lager 2 to trace out a camp (with a spade). — 4. (nachbilden) ein Muſter 2 to prick (out) a (paper-)pattern. — 5. ein Schwein: to stick. — **II** *v/n.* 6. (h.) (ſich ſcharf abheben) gegen (mit, von) et. 2 to contrast with; *fig.* to show off against; ſie ſticht ſehr von ihrer Schweſter ab she is totally unlike (or different from) ... — 7. ⚓ (ſn) vom Lande 2 to push off, to sheer off.

Ab-ſtecher (ᵍᴸ͜) [⚓] *m* ㉒ excursion, outing; e-n ~ nach Paris m. to take a trip to ...; *a. fig.* = Abſchweifung 2.

Ab-ſtech-graben (ᵍᴸ ...) *m* ㉒ ⚔ zu e-m Lager: trench for marking out a camp; **-pflug** *m, agr.* paring-plough.

ab-ſtecken (ᵍᴸ͜) *v/a.* ⓐ** 1. to unpin; das Haar 2 to undo. — 2. *surv.* to mark out; e-e Bahnlinie ꝛc.: to plot (out); die Grenzen 2 to delimitate the boundary or frontier; ⚔ ein Lager 2 to trace (or lay) out a camp; mit Pfählen ꝛc.: to stake out.

Ab-ſteck-fähnchen (ᵍᴸ ...) *n* ㉒ surveyor's flag; **-kette** *f* surveyor's chain; **-leine** *f, surv.* tracing-cord, marking-line; **-linie** *f* zu einem Gebäude ꝛc.: traced line; **-pfahl, -pflock** *m, surv.* (tracing-)picket; **-ſchnur** *f* = -leine; **-ſtab** *m,* **-ſtange** *f* staff (or rod) used in surveying.

Ab-ſteckungs-... (ᵍᴸ ...) ⓺ = Abſteck-...

ab-ſteh(e)n (ᵍᴸ͜) ⓐ** **I** *v/n.* (ſn, nur 2 1: h.) 1. (weg von et. ſtehen) to stand off (or away, apart, aloof) from. — 2. *hunt.* = abbaumen. — 3. (entſagen) von et. 2 to desist from ..., to leave off doing ...; von ſ-n Forderungen 2 to forego one's claims. — 4. (abſterben) to perish; abgeſtand(e)ner Fiſch dead (or stale) fish. — 5. (ſchal werden) to get stale, to turn; der Wein iſt abgeſtanden ... is flat, abgeſtand(e)nes Waſſer water which has stood for some time, in Teichen: stagnant water. — **II** *v/a.* 6. eine Stunde 2 to stand for ...; *v/refl.* ſich (*acc.*) 2, ſich (*dat.*) die Beine 2 to get tired with standing. — 7. ⚒ (abtreten) to abandon, to yield (up). — **III** ~ *n* ㉓ 8. distance from; desistence from; staleness (ſ. a. Abſtand). — **IV ab-ſtehend** *p.pr. u. a.* ⓰ 9. distant; ⚒ spreading; (ſparrig) ⚹ squarrose, ...ous; gleich weit 2d equidistant; 2de Ohren projecting ears. — **V ab-geſtanden** *p.p. u. a.* ⓰ (D9) 10. (*ant.* friſch) (verdorben) stale; *fig.* worn; vgl. 4 u. 5 u. abſtändig. [ceder, assignor.ƒ

Ab-ſteher ⚒ (ᵍᴸ͜) [abſtehen 3] *m* ㉒ *jur.*ƒ

ab-ſtehlen (ᵍᴸ͜) *v/a.* ⓐd** e-m et. 2 to rob a p. of a th.; er hat mir's abgeſtohlen he has stolen it from me; F *fig.* dem lieben Herrgott die Zeit (auch: die Tage) 2 to idle away (or to kill, waste) one's time or days.

ab-ſteifen (ᵍᴸ͜) *v/a.* ⓐ** 1. (ſtärken) Wäſche 2 to starch ... — 2. (ſtützen) ⊕ Mauern 2 to shore up ...; ⚒ to timber, to prop a wall, to support.

ab-ſteigen (ᵍᴸ͜) *v/n.* (ſn) ⓐ** 1. (*ant.* aufſteigen) to come down from; vom Pferde 2 to jump off one's horse, to dismount; vom Wagen 2 to alight from ... — 2 2de Achſe descending axis; *ast.* 2der Knoten descending node; 2de Linie der Verwandtſchaft descending line. — 3. (einkehren) bei Freunden 2 to stay with friends; im Gaſthofe 2 to put up at a hotel.

♪ Muſik; ⚹ Wiſſenſchaft; ⚒ Pflanze; ⚘ Geographie; ⊕ Technik; ⚒ Bergbau; ⚔ Militär; ⚓ Marine; ⚒ Handel; ⚒ Poſt; 🚂 Eiſenbahn.

Ab-steige=quartier (⁸ᴸ⌣…) *n* ⓮ (place of) accommodation; *b.s.* = Vorbell; sein ~ bei e-m nehmen to take up one's quarters (or to put up) at a p.'s house.

ab-stellbar (⁸ᴸ⌣) *a.* ⓰ *fig.* remediable.

ab-stellen (⁸ᴸ⌣) **I** *v/a.* ⓰⁎⁎ **1.** to place at a distance from. — **2.** ⊕ e-e Maschine: to stop (or ungear); *typ.* die Walzen: to throw off; Fernsprecher: abgestellt disconnected; Gas ꝛc. f. abdrehen 1. — **3.** *fig.* = abschaffen 1; Mißstände ꝛ to redress (or remedy) grievances. — **II** ~ *n* ⓫ u. **Ab-stellung** *f* ⓰ **4.** = abschaffen II. [off.

ab-stemmen ⊕ (⁸ᴸ⌣) *v/a.* ⓰⁎⁎ to chisel

ab-stempeln (⁸ᴸ⌣) **I** *v/a.* ⓰ₐ⁎⁎ to stamp; Fahrkarten ꝛ to check (off) …, (lochen) to clip; ⚓ Marken ꝛ to deface stamps. — **II** ~ *n* ⓫ u. **Ab-stemp(e)lung** (⁸ᴸ⌣(⌣)) *f* ⓰ stamping; von Fahrkarten: clipping; ⚓ von Marken: defacement.

ab-steppen (⁸ᴸ⌣) *v/a.* ⓰⁎⁎ to quilt.

ab-sterben (⁸ᴸ⌣) **I** *v/n.* (ſn) ⓰b⁎⁎ **1.** (allmählich sterben u. scheiden) to die off, to expire; (Glied: einschlafen) to get numb or torpid, to mortify, to be(come) paralysed; (hinwelken) to wither, to decay. — **2.** *fig.* e-r Sache abgestorben sein to be indifferent (stärker: to be dead) to a th.; den eitlen Dingen der Welt ꝛ to retire (or withdraw) from the vanities of the world. — **II** ~ *n* ⓫ **3.** (f. I) death; numbness; mortification; decay.

Abstergentia ⚕ (⌣⌣ᴸtj(⌣)⌣) [It.] *n/pl.* ⓰ *med.pharm.* (Reinigungsmittel) abstergent medicines, abstergents *pl.*

ab-steuern ↕ (⁸ᴸ⌣) ⓰ₐ⁎⁎ **I** *v/a.* ein Boot vom Ufer ꝛ to steer … off the shore. — **II** *v/n.* (h.) to steer away from …

Ab-stich (⁸ᴸ) *m* ⓭d. **1.** cutting off. — **2.** (Abbildung) pricked (off) pattern or drawing. — **3.** (Abzapfen) tapping, drawing off; ⊕ *metall.* running off. — **4.** (Gegensatz) set-off against, contrast.

ab-sticken (⁸ᴸ⌣) *v/a.* ⓰⁎⁎ to copy (or work) in embroidery.

ab-stieben (⁸ᴸ⌣) *v/n.* (ſn) ⓰aſt⁎⁎ *fig.* = abstäuben 1; *hunt.* vom Federwild: to fly off or away. [schrammen 2.

ab-stiefeln F (⁸ᴸ⌣) *v/n.* (ſn) ⓰ₐ⁎⁎ = ab=

Ab-stieg (⁸ᴸ) *m* ⓭d. descent; f. Aufstieg.

ab-stimm/en (⁸ᴸ⌣) ⓰⁎⁎ **I** *v/a.* ♪ to lower the pitch of (an instrument); ♪ (stimmen) to tune. — **2.** *fig.* (in Einklang bringen) to harmonize; gut abgestimmt well (-) tuned (or (-) balanced. — **II** *v/n.* (h.) **3.** (f-e Stimme abgeben) *parl.*, &c. to (give one's) vote; über et. ꝛ lassen to put (a proposal) to the vote, durch Teilung des Hauses: to divide the house (on a motion). — **III** ~ *n* ⓫ **4.** = A/ung.

Ab-stimmung (⌣) *f* ⓰ vote; geheime ~ secret voting (by ballot papers), ballot(ing), poll(ing); bei der ~ in voting, at the poll; durch ~ beschließen to vote; *parl.* namentliche ~ division; zur ~ vote!, *parl.* divide! e-e Frage, e-n Beſchluß zur ~ bringen to put … to the vote.

Ab-stimmungs=apparat (⁸ᴸ⌣…) *m* ⓮ *parl.* apparatus for registering votes; =zettel *m* voting (or ballot) paper.

ab-stinent (⌣⌣ᴸ) [It.] *a.* ⓰ (enthaltsam) abstinent; ~ *m* ⓬ = Abstinenzler.

Abstinenz (⌣⌣ᴸ) [It.] *f* ⓰ abstinence, von geistigen Getränken ꝛc.: F teetotalism.

Abstinenzler (⌣⌣ᴸ⌣) *m* ⓬ abstainer, auch F teetotaller. [stinence.

Abstinenz=tag (⌣⌣ᴸ…) *m* ⓮ day of ab-

ab-stippen F (⁸ᴸ⌣) *v/a.* ⓰⁎⁎ den (ob. das Fett, die Sauce vom) Teller ꝛ to soak up the gravy on one's plate with bread.

ab-stöckeln, ab-stöckern ⚓ (⁸ᴸ⌣) *v/n.* ⓰ₐ⁎⁎ to knock down with a stick. [off.

ab-stolzieren (⁸ᴸ⌣ᴸ) *v/n.* (ſn) ⓰⁎⁎ to strut

ab-stopfen ⚓ (⁸ᴸ⌣) *v/a.* ⓰⁎⁎ (das Feuern einstellen l.) to stop the firing. [to glean.

ab-stoppeln (⌣) *v/a.* ⓰ₐ⁎⁎ *agr.* ein Feld ꝛ

Ab-stoß (⁸ᴸ) *m* ⓭a. Fußball, gemischtes Spiel: drop-out, einfaches: goal-kick.

ab-stoßen (⁸ᴸ⌣) ⓰ₐ⁎⁎ **I** *v/a.* **1.** (stoßend entfernen) to knock (or thrust) off; die Ecken von et. ꝛ to take (or plane) the edges off a th.; sich (*dat.*) die Haut ꝛ to graze one's skin; *fig.* e-m das Herz ꝛ to grieve a p. to the (or to break a p.'s) heart; *fig.* sich (*dat.*) die Hörner ꝛ to sow one's wild oats; Kleider ꝛ to wear (or fray) … out at the edges; die Milchzähne ꝛ to shed one's (first) teeth; e-n Nachen vom Lande ꝛ to push a boat off the shore; ⚓ Waren, Aktien ꝛc. ꝛ to dispose of (or sell) goods, shares, &c.; sie haben das Tuch zu billigen Preisen abgestoßen they cleared the cloth at reduced prices. — **2.** ♪ eine Note: to play sharply; kurz abgestoßen *staccato*. — **3.** ⊕ eine Brettkante ꝛ to chamfer …; Gerberei: ein Fell ꝛ to take the grain off …; Steinhauerei: to hew; *arch.* Wände ꝛ to scrape walls; *carp.* to rough-plane. — **4.** (wegstoßen) to push away; Billard: einen Ball ꝛ to get (or force) … away from the cushion. — **5.** ein Kalb, Lamm ꝛ to wean … — **6.** *phys.* u. *fig.* (ant. anziehen 6b) to repel, ſ. a. ꝛ 9 u. 14. — **II** *v/n.* (ſn) **7.** ↕ vom Lande ꝛ to push (or shove) off the shore. — **III** sich ꝛ *v/refl.* **8.** (abnutzen) to get worn out at the edges. — **9.** *fig.* (wie 6). — **IV** ~ *n* ⓫ **10.** allg. knocking off. — **11.** ♪ staccato. — **12.** ⚓ hewing, &c. — **V** ꝛd *p.pr.* u. *a.* ⓰. **13.** Bed. des *inf.* — **14.** *fig.* repulsive, forbidding, (mürrisch) morose, gruff; das ~be, ꝛdes Wesen repulsiveness, moroseness. [knife.

Ab-stoß=messer ⊕ (⁸ᴸ…) *n* ⓮ paring-

Ab-stoßung (⁸ᴸ⌣) *f* ⓰ **1.** = abstoßen IV. — **2.** *phys.* repulsion. — ~s=… (ᴸ…) ⊕ = Abstoß=… [=zeichen ♪ *n* staccato.

Ab-stoß=zange (⁸ᴸ…) *f* ⓰ ⊕ bur-cutter;

ab-strafen (⁸ᴸ⌣) **I** *v/a.* ⓰⁎⁎ to punish (or correct) in a proper manner; (züchtigen) to chastise. — **II** ~ *n* ⓫ und **Ab-strafung** *f* ⓰ punishment, correction; (Züchtigung) chastisement.

abstrahieren ⚕ (⌣⌣ᴸ⌣) [It.] *v/a.* ⓭ (getrennt betrachten; absondern; verallgemeinern; Begriffe bilden) to abstract.

Ab-strahl (⁸ᴸ) *m* ⓭d. reflected ray.

ab-strahlen (⁸ᴸ⌣) ⓰⁎⁎ (= widerstrahlen) **I** *v/a.* to reflect (brightly). — **II** *v/n.* (ſn) to be reflected. — **III** ~ *n* ⓫ und **Ab-strahlung** *f* ⓰ reflection, lustre.

Ab-strahlungs=winkel (⁸ᴸ⌣…) *m* ⓮ angle of reflection.

abstrakt ⚕ (⌣ᴸ) [It.] **I** *a.* ⓰ (ant. konkret) abstract; ꝛe Wissenschaften abstract sciences. — **II** *adv.* in the abstract.

— **III** ~e ♪ *f* ⓰ (mit *pl.* ~en) Orgelbau (*ant.* Stecher) tracker(s *pl.*).

Abstraktion ⚕ (⌣⌣ᴸ) [It.] *f* ⓰ (Begriff[s=bildung]) abstraction; ~s=vermögen (ᴸ…) *n* ⓮ abstractive faculty.

Abstraktum ⚕ (⌣⌣ᴸ) [It.] *n* ⓭ abstract idea; *gram.* abstract noun. [unharness …

ab-strängen (⁸ᴸ⌣) *v/a.* ⓰⁎⁎ Pferde ꝛ to

ab-strapazieren F (⁸ᴸ⌣ᴸ) ⓰⁎/⁎ **I** *v/a.* e-e Sache: to wear out. — **II** sich ꝛ *v/refl.* to tire o.s. out, to slave (away).

ab-streben (⁸ᴸ⌣) *v/n.* (h.) ⓰⁎⁎ von et. ꝛ to tend (or get, fly) away from a th.

Ab-streich ſübd. (⁸ᴸ) *m* ⓭d. (Mindergebot; *ant.* Aufstreich) award(ing) to the lowest bidder. [lead; =eisen *n* scraper.

Ab-streich=blei (⁸ᴸ…) *n* ⓮ skimmed

ab-streichen (⁸ᴸ⌣) ⓰aſt⁎⁎ **I** *v/a.* **1.** to wipe off; sich (*dat.*) die Schuhe ꝛ to scrape one's … — **2.** ⚓ Korn, den Scheffel ꝛ to strike …; vgl. Abstreichmaß; e-n Posten e-r Rechnung ꝛ to strike off (or deduct) an item. — **3.** ⊕ Gerberei: Felle ꝛ to scrape …; Gießerei: die Unreinigkeiten ꝛ to scum or skim (the molten metal); *typ.* die Walze ꝛ to scrape up … — **4.** *hunt.* das Feld ꝛ to beat … (for game). — **II** *v/n.* **5.** (ſn) von Vögeln: to fly away, to leave the nest. — **6.** (h.) von Fischen: to finish spawning. — **III** ~ *n* ⓫ **7.** ⊕ Bleigießerei: drossing.

Ab-streich=holz ⊕ (⁸ᴸ…) *n* ⓮ strickle, strike(r); =löffel ⊕ *m* skimming ladle; =maß *n* für Getreide strike-measure; =meißel *m*, =messer *n*: a) Kattundruckerei: lint ductor; b) *typ.* e-r Walzendruckmaschine: raspatory; =riemen *m* razor-strop.

ab-streifbar (⁸ᴸ…) *a.* ⓰ capable of being (or fit to be) stripped off.

ab-streifen (⁸ᴸ⌣) ⓰⁎⁎ **I** *v/a.* **1.** to strip off; e-n Aal, Hasen ꝛc.: to skin …; weitS.: ein Tier ꝛ to flay … **2.** Handschuhe ꝛc.: to take off; e-n Rock: to slip off; e-e Schlange streift die Haut ab … casts its slough. — **3.** *fig.* et. ꝛ to divest o.s. of a th.; eine Gewohnheit ꝛ to lay aside … — **II** *v/n.* (ſn) **4.** to deviate; von Geschossen: to glance off.

ab-streiten (⁸ᴸ⌣) ⓰b⁎⁎ **1.** e-m et. ꝛ to wrest a th. from a p. by litigation. — **2.** (ableugnen) to dispute a p. a th.; e-m ein Recht ꝛ to contest a p.'s right; e-e Schuld ꝛ to deny …; ich lasse es mir nicht ꝛ I am quite positive about it.

Ab-strich (⁸ᴸ⌣) *m* ⓭d. **1.** (Abzug) sum struck off, deduction (made). — **2.** ⊕ (Schlacke) dross, scum, ſ abstrich.

ab-stricken (⁸ᴸ⌣) ⓰⁎⁎ **I** *v/a.* e-e Nadel ꝛ to knit off … — **II** *v/n.* (h.) to finish knitting. [to rub down, to curry.

ab-striegeln (⁸ᴸ⌣) *v/a.* ⓰ₐ⁎⁎ ein Pferd ꝛ

ab-strömen (⁸ᴸ⌣) ⓰⁎⁎ **I** *v/n.* (ſn) to stream away, to flow off rapidly; ↕ to be carried off by the current; *fig.* von e-r Menge: to disperse, to be scattered, to scatter. — **II** *v/a.* Uferland ꝛ to carry off …, to wash away …

abstrus ⚕ (⌣ᴸ) [It.] *a.* ⓰ (D 10) (schwer verständlich) abstruse.

ab-stück(e)ln (⁸ᴸ⌣) *v/a.* ⓰ (⓫a)⁎⁎ u. sich ꝛ *v/refl.* to crumble (or break) off.

ab-studieren (⁸ᴸ⌣ᴸ) sich ꝛ *v/refl.* ⓭⁎/⁎ to tire o.s. with poring over books, to study assiduously, to be a hard reader.

Signs (see page XVII): F familiar; P vulgar; ſ⸝ flash; ⸜ rare; † obsolete (died); * new word (born); ⁺⁺ incorrect; ♪ music;

[abſtufen] — 27 — [abtrennen]

ab-ſtufen (⁸ᴸ˘) v/a. u. ſich ² v/refl. ⁶⁸** 1. to form steps or grades, to grade; arch. to build in terraces; Erz: to (break off with the) pick. — 2. fig. to graduate, von Farben: to shade off.

Ab-ſtufung (˘) f ⁴⁶ 1. in Farben: gradation, (Schattierung) shade. — 2. Malerei: ~ (Abſchwächung) des Lichtes toning down ...

ab-ſtumpfen (⁸ᴸ˘) I v/a. und v/refl. ⁶⁸** 1. to blunt off, to take the edge(s) off; geom. abgeſtumpfter Kegel truncated cone. — 2. fig. ² to grow blunt. — 3. fig. die Sinne ꝛc.: (a. oft v/n.) to dull, deaden; gegen alles abgeſtumpft ſein to be indifferent (or dead) to everything. — 4. chm. Säuren ² to neutralize ... — II ~ n ²³ u. **Ab-ſtumpfung** f ⁴⁶ 5. ⊕ blunting; math. truncation (of a pyramid); fig. dulness, deadness; chm. neutralization.

ab-ſtürmen (⁸ᴸ˘) v/n. (ſn) ⁶⁸** (davoneilen) to rush (or hurry) off.

Ab-ſturz (⁸ˢ) m ⓞa. 1. (Fallen) headlong fall, F cropper. — 2. (Abhang) steep incline or slope.

ab-ſtürzen (⁸ᴸ˘) ⁶⁰** I v/a. 1. to hurl down (headlong). — 2. ſich (dat.) den Hals ² to (fall and) break one's neck. — II v/n. (ſn) 3. to fall headlong, to be precipitated (from a great height); ſ. ab-... 1. — 4. to form a sharp incline.

ab-ſtutzen (⁸ᴸ˘) v/a. ⁹⁰** 1. to trim off; Flügel ² to clip ...; Haar ² to crop ...; e-m Pferde den Schweif ² to dock a horse('s tail). — 2. hort. Bäume ² to top ..., prune ... — 3. arch. abgeſtutzte Säule truncated column. [abſteifen 2.⟩

ab-ſtützen (⁸ᴸ˘) v/a. ⁹⁰** to support =⟩

ab-ſuchen (⁸ᴸ˘) I v/a. ⁶⁸** 1. to search for and take off; e-m Baume Raupen ² to pick caterpillars off a tree. — 2. (durchſtöbern) to search for ... in all directions; e-e Gegend nach e-m ² to scour the country in search of a p.; ⚓ das Gelände ² to search the country (in all directions); hunt. ein Feld ² to beat ... — II ~ n ²³ und **Ab-ſuchung** f ⁴⁶ 3. search. [decoction.⟩

Ab-ſud ⚗ (˘ᴸ) m ⓞc. pharm.⟩

abſurd (˘˘) [lt.] a. ⁶⁶ (unſinnig) absurd, preposterous; ad absurdum führen to show the absurdity of; **~ität** (˘˘˘ᴸ) [lt.] f ⁴⁶ absurdity, preposterousness.

ab-ſüßen (⁸ᴸ˘) v/a. ⁹⁰** to (put) sugar (into), to sweeten, ⚗ to edulcorate.

Abſzeß ⚗ (˘ᴸ) [lt.] m ⓞa. path. (Eitergeſchwür) abscess.

Abſziſſe ⚗ (˘ᴸ˘) [lt.] f ⁴⁸ math. (Weitenabſtand) abscissa. [abscissas.⟩

Abſziſſen-achſe (˘ᴸ˘...) f ⁶² axis of⟩

Abt (˘) [ahd.; lt.; grch. v. "Abba"] m ⓞb. abbot; ehm.: infulierter (mit Biſchofsmütze geſchmückter) ~ mitred abbot.

Abt. abbr. = Abteilung.

ab-tafeln (⁸ᴸ˘) v/a. (h.) ⓐa** to finish dining, to rise from dinner.

ab-takeln ⚓ (⁸ᴸ˘) v/a. ⓐa** to unrig, dismantle; Maſten: to strip, Schiffe: to lay up; fig. abgetakelt used up, exhausted, done for, worn out, F washed out.

ab-tanzen (⁸ᴸ˘) ⁹⁰** I v/a. 1. e-n Walzer ꝛc. ² to dance ...; ſich (dat.) die Sohlen ² to wear out one's soles with dancing. — II v/n. 2. (ſn) von der Bühne ² to

dance off ...; (ſchaſſieren) to chassé. — 3. (h.) to finish dancing. — III ſich ² v/refl. 4. to tire o.s. with dancing.

ab-tauen (⁸ᴸ˘) v/n. (ſn) u. v a. ⁶⁸** to thaw off. [stagger away.⟩

ab-taumeln F (⁸ᴸ˘) v/n. (ſn) ⓐa** to⟩

Ab-tauſch (⁸ᴸ˘) m ⓐa. exchange, F swap; (Tauſchhandel) truck.

ab-tauſchen (⁸ᴸ˘) I v/a. ⁹¹** to exchange, F to swap, ⚑ to truck, to barter (gegen et. for a th.); Schach: abs. to exchange pieces. — II ~ n ²³ u. **Ab-tauſchung** f ⁴⁶ = Abtauſch. [little abbot.⟩

Äbtchen (˘˘) n ²³ (co. dim. von Abt)⟩

Abtei (˘ᴸ) [ahd., *lt.] f ⁴⁶ abbey; (Amt) abbacy, abbotship.

Abtei-kirche (˘˘...) f ⁶² abbey-church.

Ab-teil ⚏ (⁸ᴸ˘) m ⓞd. (Coupé) (railway-)compartment; ~ (erſter, zweiter Klaſſe first-, second-class) compartment; ~ für Damen, für Raucher ladies' c., smoking c.; in den ~ ſteigen to get into the compartment or carriage; ſteigen Sie in den ~! take your seat(s)!

ab-teilbar (⁸ᴸ˘) a. ⁶⁶ capable of being partitioned off; divisible.

ab-teilen (⁸ᴸ˘) I v/a. ⁶⁸** 1. to divide, (abſondern) to set apart; durch Verſchläge: to partition off; ⚑ Waren ² to parcel goods. — 2. die Haare durch e-n Scheitel ² to part one's hair; in Grade ² to graduate; in Klaſſen ² to classify. — II ~ n ²³ 3. = Abteilung 1.

abteilich (˘˘ᴸ˘) [Abtei] a. ⁶⁶ abbatial.

Ab-teilung (⁸ᴸ˘) f ⁴⁶ 1. division; portioning off; ⚑ v. Waren: parcelling, lotting (out); in Klaſſen: classification. — 2. (oft ++ ⸺ᴸ˘) (abbr. **Abt.**) a) (Abſchnitt) section; geſellſchaftlich: class; (gedruckte Spalte) column; Schule: division; e-r Behörde: department; e-s Spitals, Krankenhauſes: ward; ⚔ u. ⚓ division, detachment, Artill.: brigade; b) im Wagen ꝛc.: compartment; (Fach) partition.

Ab-teilungs-chef (⸺...) m ⁶² einer Behörde superintendent (or head) of a division or a department; departmental chief; **=unterricht** m mutual instruction; **=vorſteher** m = **=chef**; **=zeichen** n, typ. hyphen (-).

ab-telegraphieren (⁸˘˘˘ᴸ˘) v/a. ⁹³*/* to countermand by wire or telegraph.

ab-teufen ⛏ (⁸ᴸ˘) v/a. ⁶⁸** to deepen, to bore; einen Schacht ² to sink.

ab-tiefen ⊕ (⁸ᴸ˘) v/a. ⁶⁸** to hollow out, to deepen, to sink.

ab-tilgen ⚑ (⁸ᴸ˘) v/a. ⁶⁸** eine Schuld: to clear (or pay) off.

Äbt(iſſ)in (˘˘ᴸ˘) [ahd.] f ⁴⁷ abbess.

Äbtlein (˘˘) n ²³ = Äbtchen.

äbtlich (˘˘) a. ⁶⁶ abbatial.

ab-tönen (⁸ᴸ˘) v/a. ⁶⁸** paint. to tone down, to shade off; abgetönte Farben soft shades, neutral colours or tints pl.; fig. Schrifttum: fein abgetönte Charaktere finely balanced (or subtly drawn) characters pl.

ab-töten (⁸ᴸ˘) I v/a. ⁶⁸** nur noch fig. to mortify (the flesh); das Gefühl ² to subdue (or bridle, curb) one's passion. — II ~ n ²³ und **Ab-tötung** f ⁴⁶ bſd. rel. mortification (of the flesh).

ab-traben (⁸ᴸ˘) v/n. (ſn) ⁶⁸** to trot off.

Ab-trag (⁸ᴸ˘ pl. ⁸ᴸ˘) m ⓞd. 1. carrying off, eines Terrains: levelling, cutting, excavation. — 2. ° von der Tafel: clearing (of the table); (Abbub) leavings pl., refuse. — 3. (Entſchädigung) compensation; e-m ~ tun a) † to indemnify a p., b) (Schaden tun) to injure a p.

ab-trag/en (⁸ᴸ˘) ⓑ** I v/a. 1. to carry off or away; e-n Bau ² to pull down ...; e-e Brücke ² to break down ...; e-e Feſtung ² to raze ... (to the ground); einen Hügel ² to level ...; hunt. e-n Jagdfalken ² to train ... for the chase; e-n Leithund ² to lift ... off the scent; e-e Mauer um zwei Fuß ² to lower ... by two feet; die (Schüſſeln von der) Tafel ² to clear the table, to take away. — 2. (abzeichnen) to transfer (lines or figures). — 3. (abzahlen) to clear (or pay) off: Hypotheken: to wipe off. — 4. (abnutzen) to wear out; abgetragen worn, threadbare, shabby, shiny. — II ſich ² v/refl. 5. von Bäumen: to get exhausted (by bearing). — 6. (abgenutzt w.) to become threadbare. — III ~ n ²³ 7. = A/ung. — **IV** ²b a. agr. die Frucht (die die letzte Stelle in der Fruchtfolge einnimmt, mſt Hafer) last of the periodical crops.

ab-träglich ſübd. (⁸ᴸ˘) [Abtrag 3] a. ⁶⁶ (ſchädlich; ant. zuträglich) injurious.

Ab-trags-böſchung (⁸ᴸ˘...) f ⁴⁶ sloping bank of a railway-cutting; **=koſten** pl. expense of pulling down a house, levelling a mount, &c., ſ. abtragen 1

Ab-tragung (⁸ᴸ˘) f ⁴⁶ 1. carrying off, pulling down. — 2. fig. (Abzahlung) (full) payment, liquidation.

ab-trampeln P (⁸ᴸ˘) v/a. ⓐa** to knock (or wear) out by (constant) tramp(l)ing.

ab-träufe(l)n, ab-traufen (⁸ᴸ˘) v/n. (h.) ⓐa** to drip (or trickle) down.

Ab-treibe-herd ⊕ (⁸ᴸ˘...) m ⊕ refining-hearth, cupelling-furnace; **=hütte** f (re)finery; **=meiſter** m (master) refiner.

ab-treib/en (⁸ᴸ˘) I v/a. 1. to drive off or away. — 2. ⚐ (aus j-m Beſitze treiben) to turn off, expel, evict. — 3. for. (abholzen) to thin or clear (the wood), to fell (the trees). — 4. path. to expel (from the body), to purge off (worms, &c.); med. ein Kind ² to cause abortion, to bring on a miscarriage. — 5. agr. ein Feld mit der Herde ², eine Weide ² to graze cattle on pasture-land. — 6. (treibend abmatten) to overwork, Arbeiter: F to drive, sweat; abgetrieben jaded, spent. — 7. ⊕ metall. to (re)fine (by cupellation). — 8. ⛏ Geſtein ² to knock off (or quarry, split) rocks; e-e Galerie ² to drive ... — II v/n. (ſn) 9. ⚓ to drift off (to leeward). — III ~ n ²³ 10. = A/ung. — **IV** ²b p.pr. u. a. ⁶⁸ 11. Bed. des inf. — 12. med. abortive.

Ab-treibung (⁸ᴸ˘) f ⁴⁶ ejection; med. expulsion, der Leibesfrucht: abortion; ⊕ refining, cupellation; ⚓ drifting.

ab-trennbar (⁸ᴸ˘) a. ⁶⁶ separable.

ab-trennen (⁸ᴸ˘) I v/a. ⁶⁸** 1. Angenähtes: to unstitch, (abtrennen) to rip off. — 2. a. v/refl. (ſich) ² to separate or sever (o.s.) from; durch ein Gitter ² to fence (or rail) off; durch e-e Holzwand ² to partition off; durch e-e

---

⁴⁷ scientific; ⚘ botanical; ⚲ geography; ⊕ machinery; ⛏ mining; ⚔ military; ⚓ marine; ⚑ commercial; ✉ postal; ⚏ railway.

[abtrennlich] — 28 — [abwarten]

Mauer ⟲ to wall off; vgl. absondern 1 u. 4. — II ~ n ㉓ 3. = Abtrennung.
ab-trennlich (ᵇᵛ) a. ⓺ = abtrennbar.
Ab-trennung (ᵇᵛ) f ㊻ f. abtrennen 1. unstitching, &c. — 2. severance from. — 3. secession from.
ab-tretbar (ᵇᴸ-) a. ⓺ transferable, that may be transferred or ceded.
Ab-tretbarkeit (ᵇᴸ--)/f⓺ transferability.
ab-tret/en (ᵇᴸ) ⓶d** I v/a. 1. e-m das Kleid ⟲ to tread on a p.'s dress. — 2. a. v/refl. (abnutzen): den Absatz ⟲ to run down …; die Schuhe ⟲ to wear down …; Stufen ⟲ to wear out steps by treading on them. — 3. (entfernen) den Schmutz von den Schuhen ⟲, (sich) die Schuhe ⟲ to wipe the mud off one's … — 4. (fertigtreten) ⊙ Gerberei: Häute ⟲ to trample (or work) hides. — 5. fig. (überlassen) e-m et. ⟲ to cede (or surrender, transfer) a th. to a p.; jur. to assign, to convey to a p. (one's rights); an die Konkursmasse ⟲ to assign in bankruptcy. — II v/n. (fn) 6. (wegtreten, ant. antreten) to step aside, to withdraw; Bühnen-anweisung: tritt ab exit, treten ab exeunt. — 7. ⚔ to break ranks; fig. v. e-m Amte ꝛc. ⟲ to retire from …; von der Bühne ⟲ to go off the stage; vom Schauplatze ⟲ to make (or take) one's exit. — 8. (vgl. 5) von et. ⟲ to abandon a th. — 9. ⚹ (einkehren) to alight at; bei e-m ⟲ to stop (or stay) with a p. — III ~ n ㉓ 10. = A/ung.
Ab-treter (ᵇᴸ/) m ⓶ 1. transferrer; jur. a. assignor, ceder. — 2. (Matte) door-mat.
Ab-tretung (ᵇᴸ) f ㊻ 1. cession, surrender, transfer, jur. (Zession) assignment, conveyance. — 2. (Abgehen) retirement, withdrawal, v. d. Bühne: exit.
Ab-tretungs-urkunde (Z…)/f ㊶ (deed of) conveyance or cession or assignment.
Ab-trieb (ᵇᴸ) m ⓶d. 1. for.: a) felling of trees; b) timber cut down. — 2. Alpen: descent of the cattle (ant. Auftrieb). — 3. jur. = Näherrecht.
ab-triefen (ᵇᴸ) v/n. (fn) ⓺** ob. Gest** to drip (or trickle, run) down.
Ab-trift (ᵇᴸ) f ㊻ 1. agr. (right of) pasture (on other people's land). — 2. ⚓ (Drift) drift, leeway.
ab-trinken (ᵇᵛ) v/a. Gst** die Blume vom Bier ⟲ to sip off (or from) the cup.
ab-trippeln (ᵇᵛ) v/a. (fn) ⓶a** to trip (nimbly) off or away.
Ab-tritt (ᵇᴸ) m ⓶c. 1.† = Abtretung 2. — 2. (geheimer Ort) privy; in England (meist mit Wasser-verschluß) water-closet (W.C.); 🚻 ~ für Damen ladies' cloak-room; ~ für Herren gewöhnl. Aufschrift: (For) Gentlemen, weitS. Gentlemen's lavatory; auf den ~ gehen to go to the W.C. or closet, verhüllend: to go somewhere, to go to do s. th. — 3. hunt. ~ des Hirsches (Gras, das er beim Auftreten mit f-n Schalen abschneidet) † abature. foil(ing).
ab-trocknen (ᵇᵛ) ⓶b** I v/a. u. v/refl. 1. durch Luft: (auch sich ⟲) to dry off, to air, durch Reiben: to wipe (or rub) dry; sich (dat.) die Tränen (den Schweiß) ⟲ im Gesichte ⟲ to wipe the tears (the perspiration) off one's face. — II v/n. (fn) 2. to dry up, to wither. — 3. (vertrocknet abfallen) to shrivel up and drop.

ab-trollen F (ᵇᵛ) v/n. (fn) ⓺** to jog (or trot) off, F to toddle (off).
ab-trommeln (ᵇᵛ) ⓶a** I v/a. 1. einen Marsch ⟲ to drum (off) …; fig. auf dem Klavier ꝛc. ⟲ to strum … — II v/n. (h.) 2. to finish drumming. — 3. ⚔ to sound the retreat.   [tation, Küche: drainer.]
Ab-tropf-bank ⊙ (ᵇᴸ…) f ㊷ Zuckerfabri-
ab-tröpfeln ⓶a**, **ab-tropfen** ⓺** (ᵇᵛ) v/n. (fn) to drip (or drop, trickle) down or off; ⟲ lassen to drain off, chm. to distil.
Ab-tropf-gefäß ⊙ (ᵇᵛ) n ㊷ chm., -pfanne f Papierfabrikation: drainer, Zinngießerei: list-pan.
ab-trotzen (ᵇᵛ) v/a. ⓺** (trotzend erlangen) e-m et. ⟲ to wrest (or wring) a th. from a p. by obstinate resistance or open defiance or bold opposition.
ab-trumpfen (ᵇᵛ) v/a. ⓺** 1. Spiel: e-n ⟲ to overtrump a p. — 2. fig. e-n ⟲ to give a p. a sharp repartee or set-down.
ab-trünnig (ᵇᵛ) [ahd.: trennen] I a. ⓺ unfaithful; (v.) f-m Fürsten ⟲ disloyal to …; vom (ob. f-m) Glauben ⟲ w. to forsake (or desert) one's faith; Zer Christ apostate. — II ~e(r) m, ~e f ⓺ deserter; des Glaubens u. fig. e-r Partei: renegade, backslider; rel. apostate.
Ab-trünnigkeit (ᵇᵛ-)/f⓺ disloyalty, defection stärker: desertion, rel. apostasy.
Abts-hut (ᵇ…) m ㊷ abbot's cap or mitre; **Abt(s)-stab** m = Krummstab.
Abts-würde f abbacy, abbotship.
ab-tummeln (ᵇᵛ) v/a. ⓶a** ein Pferd ꝛc. ⟲ to fatigue … with violent riding.
ab-tun (ᵇᴸ) ⓹** I v/a. 1. (abnehmen) to take off (a coat, &c.); die Hand von e-m ⟲ to cast a p. off. — 2. (töten) to kill, Vieh: to slaughter; e-n Missetäter: to execute, to put to death; fig. von Sachen: to knock to pieces. — 3. (abschaffen) to abolish, eine Gewohnheit: to leave off; — 4. (erledigen) to dispose of; (beenden) to finish; schnell und flüchtig: to scamp; gütlich: to arrange; e-e Frage, e-n Streit ⟲ to settle a question, a dispute; et. kurz ⟲ to make short work of a th. — II sich ⟲ v/refl. 5. hunt. (angeschossen ob. krank vom Rudel abgehen) to leave the herd. — III ab-getan (ᵇᴸ·¹) pp. u. a. ⓺ 6. settled, (vorbei) all over; damit ist's noch nicht ⟲ it won't rest there; es ist mit zwei Worten ⟲ the matter lies in a nutshell.
ab-tünchen (ᵇᵛ) v/a. ⓺** (fertig tünchen) to finish whitewashing.
ab-tupfen (ᵇᵛ) v/a. ⓺** Feuchtigkeit: to dab up; eine Wunde: to wipe … dry (with lint). [shade) with Indian ink.]
ab-tuschen (ᵇᵛ) v/a. ⓺** to copy (or
Abukir ♀ (⟂-ᴸ) [ar.] npr/n. ⓶a. (ägypt. Reede) Aboukir; Seeschlacht von ~ (1798) battle of the Nile.   [abundance.]
Abundanz ⚹ (⌣⌣) [lt.] f ㊻ (Überfluß)
ab-urteilen (ᵇᵛ) v/a. ⓺** jur. (ein Schlußurteil fällen): 1. e-m et. ⟲ to dispossess a p. of a th. by judicial decree. — 2. e-n, et. ⟲ to prejudge a p., a th. — 3. über et. ⟲ to pronounce unfavourably upon a p., a th.; to criticize (or judge) a p., a th. severely, to pronounce hastily (or harshly) upon a p., a th.

Ab-urteilung (ᵇᵛ-) f ㊻ adjudication, harsh judgment or criticism.
ab-verdienen (ᵇᵛᴸ) v/a. ⓺** Geld ⟲ to pay off (a debt) by working for a p.
ab-verlangen (ᵇᵛᴸ) v/a. ⓺** e-m et. ⟲ to demand a th. of a p.
ab-vieren (ᵇᵛᴸ-) v/a. [Hom. abfieren) [vier] I v/a. ⓺** 1. ⊙ carp. to square. — II ~ n ㉓ u. **Ab-vierung** f ㊻ ⊙ squaring.
ab-visieren ⊙ (ᵇw-ᴸ) v/a. ⓺** surv. to sight (out), to survey.
ab-wachen (ᵇᵛ) sich ⟲ v/refl. ⓺** to tire o.s. with sitting up or watching.
Ab-wäge-… (ᵇᴸ…) ⓶ = Abwägungs-…
ab-wäg/en (ᵇᴸ) I v/a. ⓶b** u. ⓺** 1. ⚹ (mst ⓶b**) = abwiegen 1. — 2. ⚹ (mst ⓶b**) ⊙ surv. mit der Wasserwage ⟲ to level. — 3. (mst ⓶b**) fig. to weigh, to ponder out, (erwägen) to consider (carefully), to think well over, to meditate on; er wägt s-e Worte (auf der Goldwage) ab he weighs his words. — 4. (mst ⓺**) fig. die Staatsgewalten ⟲ to balance … — II ~ n ㉓ 5. = A/ung.
Ab-wäger ⚹ (ᵇᴸ-) m ⓶ surv. leveller.
Ab-wägung (ᵇᴸ-) f ㊻ balancing, weighing; ⊙ surv. levelling; bei genauer ⟲ der Umstände on close examination.
Ab-wägungs-instrument ⚹ (ᵇᵛ…) n ㊷ surv. levelling instrument, (spirit-) level; -kunst f art of levelling.
ab-walken ⊙ (ᵇᵛ) v/a. ⓺** Tuchfabrikation: das Tuch ⟲ to finish (the) fulling (of) the cloth; to mill the cloth thoroughly (well).
ab-wallen (ᵇᵛ) v/n. (fn) ⓺** 1. von Locken: to hang down. — 2. f. auf 11.
ab-wällen (ᵇᵛ) v/a. ⓺** Kochkunst: to boil (up) gently, to heat water, &c. till it gently boils.
ab-walzen (ᵇᵛ) ⓺** I v/a. ⊙ to level with a roller; den Rasen ⟲ to roll the grass. — II v/n. (fn) to waltz off.
ab-wälzen (ᵇᵛ) ⓺** 1. to roll off (or down) from. — 2. fig. von sich ⟲ to slip (or get) out of; eine Schuld von sich ⟲ to clear o.s. of a charge, to exculpate (or exonerate) o.s. from all blame.
ab-wamsen F (ᵇᵛ) v/a. ⓶a** to beat, thrash, cudgel (soundly).
ab-wandelbar (ᵇᵛ-) a. ⓺ capable of inflection; v. Hauptwörtern: declinable.
ab-wandeln (ᵇᵛ) ⓶a** I v/a. 1. gram. (a. sich ⟲ v/refl.) to inflect, ein Hauptwort: to decline, ein Zeitwort: to conjugate; dieses Wort läßt sich nicht ⟲ … cannot be inflected, suffers no change. — 2. (ändern) to modify. — II ~ n ㉓ u. **Ab-wand(e)lung** (ᵇᵛ(⌣)/) f ㊻ 4. gr. inflexion; (Fall-⟲) declension, (Zeit-⟲) conjugation. — 5. (Änderung) modification.
Ab-wärme ⊙ (ᵇᵛ) f ㊺ residue of heat (stored up in steam, gases, stoves, &c.)
ab-wärmen (ᵇᵛ) v/a. ⓺** to warm by degrees; ⊙ metall. den Hochofen ⟲ to heat the furnace.
ab-wart/en (ᵇᵛ) I v/a. u. v/n. (h.) ⓺** 1. et. ⟲ to wait for (the accomplishment of a th.); das Ende von et. ⟲ to stay to the end of a th.; die Gelegenheit ⟲ to bide one's opportunity or time; wir müssen es ruhig ⟲ we must wait and see (what will come of it); Sie

Zeichen (f. S. XVII): F familiär; P Volkssprache; ⌈ Gaunersprache; ⚹ selten; † alt (auch gestorben); * neu (auch geboren); ⁺⁺ unrichtig;

[Abwartung] — 29 — [abwerfen]

müssen's 2! have patience!, F don't be in (too much of) a hurry! — 2. (a. v/refl.) (pflegen) to wait upon; Kranke 2 to attend patients, to nurse invalids; Kinder, Blumen ꝛc. 2 to look after …; ein Pferd 2 to groom …; sein Geschäft 2, a. to see to …; ╲ sich 2 to take care of o.s. — II ~ n 23 3. = A/ung. — III 2d p.pr. u. a. 66 4. Bed. des inf. — 5. expectant; eine 2e Haltung einnehmen to temporize, to assume an attitude of expectation, pol. to sit on the fence.

Ab-wartung (ᵇᴸ⌣) f 46 1. biding (one's time). — 2. nursing; attendance on (a patient); attentions bestowed on (flowers, &c.); tending (domestic animals).

ab-wärts (ᵇᴸ) adv. 1. down(ward); s. berg2, strom2; der Weg führt 2 … leads downhill or descends; mit ihm geht's 2: a) he is on the downward slope; b) v. Alter: he is getting on in years; c) v. Vermögen: he is going down (in the world). — 2. (seitwärts) aside, off.

ab-waschen (ᵇᴸ⌣) I v/a. ⓈBb** 1. (waschend reinigen) to wash off, durch Baden: to bathe; (reinigen) to cleanse; e-m Kinde den Schmutz vom Gesicht abwaschen 2 to wash the dirt off a child's face; mit dem Schwamm 2 to sponge off. — 2. Geschirr 2 to wash (up) dishes and plates; Flecken mit Seife, Benzin 2 to take out stains with soap, benzine. — 3. (beschädigen) to damage by washing; die Farbe 2 to take (or wash) out. — 4. (waschend abnützen) die Ufer 2 to carry (or wash) away the banks. — II ~ n 23 5. = Abwaschung. — 6. Sprichw. es ist ein ~ it's killing two birds with one stone; es wäre ein ~ gewesen we might have done it in one stroke.

Ab-wasch-faß (ᵇᴸ…) n 62 washing-tub; =lappen m, dish-cloth; =magd f scullery-maid; =seife f washing soap; =tuch n =lappen.

Ab-waschung (ᵇᴸ⌣) f 46 washing (off); surg. lotion; chm. bath; rel. ablution.

Ab-wasch-wasser n water for washing up, dish-water; F u. P hog-wash.

Ab-wasser (ᵇᴸ⌣) n 62 u. 19 waste-water.

ab-wässern (ᵇᴸ⌣) v/a. ⓐa** to drain a field, ꝛc.; to soak herrings, &c.

ab-wechseln (ᵇᴸ⌣fg⌣) ⓐa** I v/a. to vary, to take alternately or in turns. — II v/n. (h.) to take place (or to come) alternately; in (ob. mit) et. 2 (to ex-)change for a th.; mit e-m regelmäßig 2 to alternate with a p.; mit=ea. 2 to relieve one another; mit e-m Dienste 2 to take a duty in turn. — III ~ n 23 (ex)change for, alternation with; Kleider zum ~ haben to have a change of clothes; s. Abwechselung. — IV 2d a. 66 alternate, alternating, alternative; (mannigfaltig) varying, varied; in 2er Reihenfolge in (alternate) succession; math. periodic; med. intermittent; adv. 2d (wechselweise) alternately; (der Reihe nach) in turn(s), by turns.

Ab-wechs(e)lung (ᵇᴸ⌣fg⌣) f 46 ~ der Jahreszeiten ꝛc. succession (or rotation) of …; (Mannigfaltigkeit) variety; er hat ~ nötig he requires a change (of scene, of occupation); ohne ~ monotonous(ly); ~ in et. bringen to diver-

sify a th.; zur ~, der ~ wegen by way of (a) change, for a change; 2s-weise (ᵇᴸ⌣) adv. = abwechselnd adv.

ab-wedeln (ᵇᴸ⌣) v/a. ⓐa** Fliegen 2 to drive off … by fanning.

Ab-weg (ᵇᴸ) m ⓤc. by-way, side-path; wrong way or track, (Umweg) roundabout way, devious path; fig. auf ~e führen to lead astray; auf ~e geraten to get off the right way or track, to go astray or adrift or wrong.

ab-wehen (ᵇᴸ⌣) ⓐa** I v/a. to blow off; vom Lande, vom Meere oder Wind landbreeze, sea-breeze. — II v/n. (h.) to calm down, to drop, to subside.

Ab-wehr (ᵇᴸ) f 46 1. defence; (Schutz) (safe)guard; zur ~ des Feindes (in order) to keep the enemy in check; fenc. parrying (of blows). — 2. = ~mittel.

ab-wehr/en (ᵇᴸ⌣) I v/a. u. v/n. (h.) ⓐa** 1. en et. ob. et. von e-m 2 to keep a th. off a p.; sich (dat.) die Fliegen 2 to drive off …. durch eine Decke to protect o.s. against … by; e-n Stoß 2 to parry (or ward off) …; ein (v/n. einem) Unglück 2 to avert …. — II ~ n 23 2. = A/ung. — III 2d p.pr. u. a. 66 3. Bed. des inf. — 4. defensive, protective, preventive.

Ab-wehrung (ᵇᴸ⌣) f 46 prevention.

Ab-wehr(ungs)-mittel (ᵇᴸ⌣(⌣)…) n means of defence; prevent(at)ive, preservative; protection.

ab-weichen¹ (ᵇᴸ⌣) [weich] I v/a. ⓐa** (weich machen) to soften (and loosen), to detach (or get off) by soaking or steeping. — II v/n. ⓐa** (in) (weich werden) to get soaked off, to come off in soaking or steeping. — III ~ n 23 = Abweichung¹.

ab-weich/en² (ᵇᴸ⌣) [weichen] I v/n. (in) ⓐafe** 1. von et. 2 to deviate from a th.; von der Pflicht (von der Wahrheit) 2 to depart (or swerve) from one's duty (from the truth); fig. von=ea. in et. 2 to differ (from one another) in a th.; ihre Meinungen weichen sehr von=ea. ab … are widely divergent. — 2. ⚓ to deflect; bsd. v. der Magnetnadel: (horizontal) to decline, (vertikal) to dip. — II ~ n 23 3. = A/ung². — III 2d p.pr. u. a. 66 4. in allen Bedeutungen des inf. — 5. divergent, different, discordant, at variance; gr. irregular, anomalous, fig. von der üblichen Sitte (Lehre) 2d eccentric (heterodox); adv. 2d von … divergently from … [diarrhœa.}

Ab-weichung¹ (ᵇᴸ⌣) f 46 path. (Durchfall)}

Ab-weichung² (ᵇᴸ⌣) f 46 1. deviation; v. e-r Lehre, Meinung: departure, divergence, discrepancy; ⚓ ~ der Geschosse deviation, error. — 2. ⚓ e-s Schiffes (von f-m Kurs): deflection, leeway; fig. (Abschweifung) digression; gram., &c.: a) ~ von der Regel anomaly …; b) (Ausnahme) exception (to the rule); c) (Freiheit) licence (of poets, &c.). — 3. ⚓ phys. variation; der Lichtstrahlen: deflection, der Magnetnadel: declination, dip; ast. sphärische ~ (spherical) aberration.

Ab-weichungs-instrument (ᵇᴸ…) n phys. declinator; =kompaß m declination-compass, azimuth; =kreis m circle of declination; =nadel f, ast. declination-needle; =winkel m der Magnetnadel: magnetic azimuth.

ab-weiden (ᵇᴸ⌣) v/a. ⓐa** 1. v. Tieren: to graze (or feed) on pastures. — 2. v. Hirten: to turn cattle into a meadow.

ab-weifen (ᵇᴸ⌣) v/a. ⓐa** Garn ꝛc.: to wind (or reel) off.

ab-weinen (ᵇᴸ⌣) v/a. ⓐa** sich (dat.) die Augen 2 to cry one's eyes out.

ab-weisen (ᵇᴸ⌣) I v/a. ⓐa** e-n 2 to refuse (or decline) the reception (or request) of a p.; hart 2 F to send (or turn) off; e-n kurz 2 to be very short with a p.; seien Sie nicht so 2d mit ihm don't be so offhandish with him; er läßt sich nicht 2 he will not take a (or will take no) denial, he won't be refused; das Gericht wies seine Klage ab … dismissed his case, nonsuited him; seine Ansprüche wurden abgewiesen … were rejected or not acknowledged; ⚔ e-n Angriff des Feindes 2 to beat back (or repel, repulse) the enemy's attack; etwas von sich 2 to discountenance (a plan); to decline to have anything to do with a th.; to resist a th. — II ~ n 23 = Abweisung.

Ab-weiser (⌣) m ⓐ 1. one who refuses, &c. (s. abweisen). — 2. ⚙ Wasserbau: groin, breakwater. — 2. (Prellstein) cornerpost; Straßenkante: kerbstone, curbstone.

ab-weißen (ᵇᴸ⌣) v/a. ⓐa** 1. ob wohin, (tünchen) to whitewash. — 2. ♧ Pflanzen 2 (bleichen) to whiten, blanch, etiolate.

Ab-weisung (ᵇᴸ⌣) f 46 refusal; harte ~ rebuff; ⚔ repulse; ♥ protest(ation), non-acceptance; fig. ~ e-r Beschuldigung denial …; jur. ~ einer Klage, ~s-bescheid (⌣…) m 62 non-suit(ed action); ~s-schreiben n letter of refusal.

Ab-weitung ⚓ (ᵇᴸ⌣) f = Abweichung² 2.

ab-welken (ᵇᴸ⌣) v/n. (in) ⓐa** to wither (and fall off); abgewelkt withered.

ab-wendbar (ᵇᴸ⌣) a. 66 preventable, avertible; ~keit f 46 preventability.

ab-wend/en (ᵇᴸ⌣) ⓐa** I v/a. to turn off or away; et. durch Bitten 2 to deprecate a th.; eine Gefahr 2 to avert …; seine Hand von e-m 2 to withdraw one's support from a p., stärker: to cast a p. off; e-n Hieb von sich 2 to parry (off) a thrust; ♥ einem die Kunden 2 to draw away the customers from a p.; ein Unglück 2 to prevent a mishap. — II sich 2 v/refl. to turn aside; fig. sich von einem 2 to take a dislike to a p. — III ~ n 23 = A/ung.

ab-wendig (ᵇᴸ⌣) a. 66 alienated; einen 2 machen von to draw a p. away from, to alienate (or detach, estrange) a p. from.

Ab-wendung (ᵇᴸ⌣) f 46 der Herzen ꝛc.: estrangement, alienation … from; der Aufmerksamkeit: diversion.

ab-werfbar (ᵇᴸ⌣) a. 66 capable of being cast (or thrown) off.

ab-werfen (ᵇᴸ⌣) ⓑb** I v/a. 1. zo. das Gehörn 2 to cast one's antlers; die Haut 2 to cast one's skin; das Joch 2 to shake off one's yoke; Kleider: to throw off, rasch: to slip off; die Maske 2 to take off …; den Reiter 2 to throw … — 2. v. Bäume 2 to bring down by a throw. — 3. Spiel: Fehlblätter 2, sich 2 to throw away useless cards, F to clear one's hand. — 4. eine Sache wirft et. ab (rentiert sich, bringt Gewinn) …

♪ Musik; ⚓ Wissenschaft; ♧ Pflanze; ⚘ Geographie; ⚙ Technik; ⚒ Bergbau; ⚔ Militär; ⚓ Marine; ♥ Handel; ✉ Post; 🚂 Eisenbahn.

[Abwerfofen] — 30 — [abziehen]

brings in something; zehn Prozent, e-n schönen Nutzen 2 to yield ten per cent., a handsome profit; das Geschäft wird wenig (nichts) 2 there is little (no) profit (or gain) to be made in this; Gewinn 2d remunerative. paying, profitable; nichts 2d unremunerative, unprofitable. — 5. metall. Schlacken 2 to remove slags; (garbrennen) to refine. — II sich 2 v/refl. 6. to tire o.s. with throwing. — 7. s. 3. — III v/n. (h.) 8. Würfelspiel rc.: to have the last throw.
Ab-werf-ofen ☉ (ᵍˡ᎔…) m ⊚ (s. abwerfen 5) refining furnace; **-pfanne** f refining pan; Zinngießer: list-pan, list-pot; **-saum** m Zinngießer: list-mark.
ab-wesend (ᵍˡ᎔) a. ⊚ u. ~e(r) m, ~e f ⊚ (ant. gegenwärtig) absent, von Hause: away from home; (fehlend) missing; seine Gedanken sind stets 2 he is very distracted or absent-minded; 2e Gutsherren absentee landlords; Sprichw. der ~e muß Haare l., die ~n h. immer unrecht absent ones are always in the wrong.
Ab-wesenheit (ᵍˡ᎔-) f ⊚ absence; s. glänzen 1; jur. non-appearance, vorsätzliche ~ contumacy; in ~ verurteilen to sentence (or punish) for contempt of court; ~ während e-r Tat alibi; dauernde ~ (von Gutsherren rc.) absenteeism; ~ des Geistes absence of mind, (mental) distraction. [s. th. of a p. by betting.]
ab-wetten (ᵍˡ᎔) v/a. ⊚** e-m et. 2 to win]
ab-wettern (ᵍˡ᎔) ⊚a** v/imp. u. v/refl. es wettert sich ab the storm is abating.
ab-wetzen (ᵍˡ᎔) v/a. ⊚** 1. die Spitze e-s Messers to blunt (off)…; Rost 2 to remove … in grinding. — 2. (abnutzen) to grind off. — 3. (schärfen) to sharpen, to whet.
ab-wichsen (ᵍˡtᵇ) v/a. ⊚** 1. to polish (boots well. — 2. F fig. = durchwichsen.
ab-wickelbar (ᵍˡ᎔) a. ⊚ geom. evolvable.
Ab-wickel-maschine (ᵍˡ᎔…) f ⊚ (un-) winding-machine.
ab-wickel/n (ᵍˡ᎔) I v/a. u. v/refl. ⊚a** 1. to unroll, unwind (a. fig.). — 2. math. e-e Kurve 2 to develop a curve. — 3. fig. (beenden) ein Geschäft 2 to wind up …, to dispatch …; s-e Sachen 2 to settle one's affairs. — II sich 2 v/refl. 4. to develop; das Ganze hat sich rasch abgewickelt … has been speedily arranged or dispatched. — III ~ n ㉓ 5. = A/ung.
Ab-wick(e)lung (ᵍˡ(᎔)~) f ⊚ unrolling; fig. ~ von Geschäften dispatch of business; math. einer Kurve: evolution, development; ☂ jur.~ Schulden: liquidation.
Ab-wick(e)lungs-bureau ↓(ˡ…) n ⊚ (Verwaltungsbehörde e-r [dtsch] Marinestation für außer Dienst gestellte Schiffe) naval board for auditing the accounts, and winding up the remaining business of men-of-war when put out of commission; **-kurve** f, math. evolvent.
ab-wiegeln (ᵍˡ᎔) ⊚a** I v/a. (ant. aufwiegeln) eine empörte Menge 2 to appease (or pacify, calm) a riotous multitude. — II v/n. (h.) to assume a peaceful attitude or tone.
ab-wiegen (ᵍˡ᎔) I v/a. ⊚c** u. ⊚** 1. meist ⊚c** bsb. ⊛ to balance, to poise; mit der Wage: to weigh. — 2. = abwägen 3. — II ~ n ㉓ und **Ab-wiegung** f ⊚ 3. balancing, weighing.

ab-wimmeln F (ᵍˡ᎔) v/a. ⊚a** 1. Schüler: to expel, Studenten: to rusticate. — 2. ⚔ Unteroffiziere: to reduce to the ranks. = 3. = abwerfen 3. [the pennant.]
ab-wimpeln ↓ (ᵍˡ᎔) v/a. ⊚a** to lower]
Ab-winde ☉ (ᵍˡ᎔) f ⊚ (Haspel) reel.
ab-winden (ᵍˡ᎔) ⊙** I v/a. 1. (ant. aufwinden) ein Knäuel rc. 2 to unwind, to wind (or reel) off (a. fig.). — 2. (ant. hochwinden) to lower (by means of a windlass). — II sich 2 v/refl. 3. to unwind, to come unwound.
Ab-winder ☉ (ᵍˡ᎔) m ⊚ one who winds; contrivance for winding, winder.
ab-winken (ᵍˡ᎔) v/a. ⊚** e-n 2 to call a p. off (or back) by beckoning to him; ⚔ e-m Soldaten 2 to beckon a soldier not to salute. [poll, lop.]
ab-wipfeln (ᵍˡ᎔) v/a. ⊚a** for. to top,]
ab-wippen (ᵍˡ᎔) v/n. (h.) u. sich 2 v/refl. ⊚** Turnen: am Barren (sich) 2 to swing on the parallel bar.
ab-wirbeln (ᵍˡ᎔) v/a. ⊚a** 1. ♪ Saiten 2 to loosen … by turning the peg. — 2. (abtrommeln) to play on the drum; ein Lied 2 to carol forth …
ab-wirken (ᵍˡ᎔) v/a. ⊚** 1. e-m Tiere die Haut 2, ein Tier 2 to uncase or skin (game). — 2. ⊚ to finish working (or kneading, weaving, &c.).
ab-wirren (ᵍˡ᎔) v/a. ⊚** to wind off.
ab-wirtschaften (ᵍˡ᎔) v/a., v/refl. u. v/n. ⊚** e-n Hausstand 2, sich 2 to wreck one's household, to ruin o.s.; er hat abgewirtschaftet he is done for.
ab-wischen (ᵍˡ᎔) v/a. ⊚¹** to wipe off, ⊘ to absterge; (reinigen) to clean off; (abstäuben) to dust off; mit nassem Tuch: to mop (up); mit Schwamm: to sponge off; den Mund 2 to wipe one's mouth; sich (dat.) die Tränen 2 to dry one's tears.
Ab-wisch-lappen (ᵍˡ᎔…) m ⊚ **-lumpen** m, **-tuch** n duster. [Schafen) pelt-wool.]
Ab-wolle ⊛ (ᵍˡ᎔) f ⊚ (Wolle von toten]
ab-wollen¹ ☉ (ᵍˡ᎔) [Wolle] v/a. ⊚** ein Fell 2 to remove the wool from a skin.
ab-wollen² (ᵍˡ᎔) [wollen] v/n. (h.) ⊚** das Blatt will nicht ab … won't come off.
ab-wracken ↓ (ᵍˡ᎔) v/a. ⊚** ein Schiff 2 to break up …; ein gestrandetes Schiff 2 (losbekommen) to bring off (or to set free) a stranded vessel or a wreck.
ab-wuchern (ᵍˡᶜʰᵛ) v/a. ⊚a** e-m Geld 2 to extort … from a p. by usury.
Ab-wurf (ᵍˡ᎔) m ⊚c. 1. thing cast aside, refuse. — 2. ⊚ rough-cast.
ab-würgen (ᵍˡ᎔) v/a. ⊚** I v/a. to throttle, to strangle, weit S. to butcher. — II sich 2 v/refl. to choke (whilst eating, &c.). — III ~ n ㉓ und **Ab-würgung** f ⊚ strangulation; wholesale slaughter.
ab-würzen (ᵍˡ᎔) v/a. ⊚** to season.
ab-zahlen (ᵍˡ᎔) I v/a. ⊚** et. 2 to pay off a th.; et. auf eine Schuld 2 to pay something on account of a debt; nach und nach 2 to clear off by degrees or by instalments or F by driblets; wöchentlich 2 to pay in weekly instalments. — II ~ n ㉓ = Abzahlung.
ab-zählen (ᵍˡ᎔) I v/a. ⊚** 1. to count off or over or out, to enumerate; parl. to tell; das läßt sich an den Fingern 2 that's easy reckoning or guessing; ⚔ zu zweien 2 to pair off, to detach in

pairs. — 2. (abziehen) to deduct. — II ~ n ㉓ 3. = Abzählung.
Ab-zahlung (ᵍˡ᎔) f ⊚ teilweise ~ payment on account, instalment; gänzliche ~ clearing off (a debt).
Ab-zählung (ᵍˡ᎔) f ⊚ counting out, enumeration; parl. telling.
Ab-zahlungs-geschäft ⊛ (ᵍˡ᎔…) n ⊚ firm carrying on business on the instalment system, s. abzahlen I.
ab-zahnen (ᵍˡ᎔) ⊚a** I v/a. ⊚ to indent. — II v/n. (h.) to finish teething.
ab-zanken (ᵍˡ᎔) v/a. u. v/recip. ⊚** to scold (well). (Vgl. a. ausanken u. zanken.)
ab-zapf/en (ᵍˡ᎔) I v/a. ⊚** e-m Blut 2 to bleed or cup a p.; ein Faß 2 to broach …; fig. F e-m Geld 2 to fleece (or drain) a p.; e-n Wassersüchtigen 2 to tap …; Wein 2 to draw off … — II ~ n ㉓ u. A/ung f ⊚ surg. ⊘ paracentesis; v. Blut: bleeding.
ab-zappeln F (ᵍˡ᎔) sich 2 v/refl. ⊚** to tire o.s. with moving and tossing about, to sprawl (or fidget) about.
ab-zäumen (ᵍˡ᎔) v/a. ⊚** ein Pferd 2 to unbridle …, to take the bridle off …
ab-zäunen (ᵍˡ᎔) I v/a. ⊚** to fence off or in; to cut off (land) by a hedge. — II ~ n ㉓ = Abzäunung 1.
Ab-zäunung (ᵍˡ᎔) f ⊚ 1. (act of) fencing (off), &c. — 2. enclosure.
ab-zehren (ᵍˡ᎔) ⊚** I v/a. 1. to consume; weit S. to waste, to emaciate; 2de Krankheit consumptive disease (vgl. a. Abzehrung). — II v/n. (sn) u. sich 2 v/refl. 2. to waste away, to fall off, to lose flesh, to grow thin. — III **ab-gezehrt** p.p. u. a. ⊚: 3. Beb. des inf. — 4. 2es Gesicht worn countenance.
Ab-zehrung (ᵍˡ᎔) f ⊚ path. wasting (away), stärker: emaciation, ⊘ tabes, (Entkräftung) atrophy, marasmus; die ~ bekommen to go into a consumption.
Ab-zeichen (ᵍˡ᎔) n ⊚ 1. meist: mark of distinction. — 2. ⚔ am Arme badge; ~ des Ranges von engl. Unteroffizieren u. Polizisten: stripe; für Verdienst: good-conduct badge or stripe. — 3. zo. mark of different colour, ⊘ macula. — 4. militärische u. amtliche ~ marks of distinction or rank or station; politische ~ party-badges pl.
ab-zeichnen (ᵍˡ᎔) I v/a. ⊚b** 1. (abbilden) to copy (from a drawing), to draw (from the original). — 2. (abgrenzen) to mark (off), mit Kreide: to chalk (off). — II sich 2 v/refl. ⊚b** 3. to appear in (well-defined) outlines, to be(come) delineated; sich scharf 2 to stand out in bold relief. — III ~ n ㉓, **Ab-zeichnung** f ⊚ 4. copy (from an original), sketch. — 5. delineation, outline (s pl.).
ab-zerren (ᵍˡ᎔) v/a. ⊚** to pull off.
ab-zetteln ☉ (ᵍˡ᎔) v/a. ⊚a** Weberei: to unwarp, unweave, undo (a warp).
ab-zeugen ↓ (ᵍˡ᎔) v/a. ⊚** = abtafeln.
ab-ziehbar (ᵍˡ᎔-) a. ⊚ deductible.
Ab-zieh-bild ☉ (ᵐˡ…) n ⊚ metachromatype; **-bilder-druck** m transfer-printing; **-blase** f still; **-bogen** m, typ. beim Widerdruck: tympan-sheet; **-bürste** f, typ. letter-brush.
ab-ziehen (ᵍˡ᎔) ⊙b** I v/a. 1. (ziehend entfernen) to pull down or off; die Handschuhe 2 to pull off one's gloves; den Hut 2

Signs (see page XVII): F familiar; P vulgar; ᵖ flash; ⚊ rare; † obsolete (died); * new word (born); ⁺⁺ incorrect; ♪ music;

[Abzieher] — 31 — [Achillenkraut]

to take off one's hat; F seine Kleider 2 to strip off one's clothes. — 2. ein Bett 2 to strip a bed; Bohnen 2 to string beans; einem Stiere das Fell 2, e-n Stier 2 to skin (or flay) a bullock; e-m die Kopfhaut 2 to scalp a p.; e-m die Larve 2 to unmask a p. — 3. (entfernen) den Schlüssel 2 to take out the key; ✱ die Saiten einer Geige 2 to unstring a violin. — 4. *fig.* seine Blicke von et. 2 to take one's eyes off a th.; j-s Gedanken 2 to divert a p.'s attention; die Hand (seinen Schutz) von e-m 2, *meist:* to withdraw one's support (or patronage) from a p.; die Kunden von e-m 2 to entice away the customers from a p.; von einer Partei 2 to draw (or lure) a p. (away) from ...; e-n von seinem Vorhaben 2 to turn a p. from his purpose. — 5. *math.* (abrechnen) to subtract, deduct; zieh 5 von 9 ab, so bleibt 4 take five from nine and four remain, auch kurz: 5 from 9 leave(s) 4; e-m etwas vom Lohne 2 to take (F dock) something off a p.'s wages; ⚭ et. vom Preise 2 to take (F knock) something off the price. — 6. ⚭ eine Farbe 2 to renew ...; ein Messer 2 to grind (or polish) a knife; ein Rasiermesser 2 to strop (or sharpen) a razor; (abhobeln) to plane off. — 7. (Wein ꝛc.) 2 to draw off (wine, &c.). — 8. (destillieren) to distil; (abgießen) to decant; auf Flaschen 2 to bottle; einen Teich 2 to drain off ...; stark abgezo(e)ner Weingeist rectified spirit; eine Suppe mit einem Ei 2 to beat up ... with an egg. 9. ⚙ *typ.* (eine Fahne) 2 to strike off (a proof), to pull (a proof), to take off (an impression); (abklatschen) to dab; *typ.* Farbe von den Walzen 2 to sheet the roller; einen Kupferstich 2 to transfer an engraving on. — II *v/n.* (sn) 10. to go away, to depart, F to be off; aus der Wohnung 2 to (re-)move; der Rauch zieht durch den Schornstein ab ... passes through (or out of) the chimney; ⚔ der Feind ist von der Festung abgezogen ... has raised the siege; von der Wache 2 (*ant.* aufziehen) to come off guard; aus dem Dienste 2 to leave service or one's place; leer 2 to come away empty-handed; mit Schimpf und Schande 2 to leave in disgrace; unverrichteter Sache (F mit langer Nase) 2 to go away disappointed. — III sich 2 *v/refl.* 11. von Zugtieren: to get worn out with (cart-)work. — IV ~ *n* ⓡ 12. = Abziehung. — V ab-gezogen *p.p. u. a.* ⓡ (D 9) 13. Beb. bes *inf.* — 14. *fig.* = abstrakt.
Ab=zieher(~) *m* ⓡ 1. *anat.* (Muskel) abductor. — 2. *typ.* proof-printer, puller.
Ab=zieh=feile(ˢᴸ...) *f* ⓡ smoothing-file; =klinge *f* knife-sharpener; =kolben *m* (helm of a) still; =leder *m* = riemen; =maschine *f* (Reinigungsmaschine v. Chaussee u. Asphaltstraßen) street-cleanser, scavenging roller; =muskel *m, anat.* = Abzieher 1; =pflug *m* draining-plough; =presse *f, typ.* proof-press; =riemen *m* (razor-)strop; =stein *m* whetstone.
Ab=ziehung(ˢᴸ) *f* ⓡ (vgl. abziehen I u. II) des Felles skinning; *anat.* der Muskeln:

abduction; (Abrechnen) subtraction; des Weines: drawing off; des Branntweines ꝛc.: distilling, rectifying; ⚙ (Schleifen) grinding; aus der Wohnung: removal; ⚔ der Truppen departure; ~s=vermögen *n* power of abstraction.
Ab=zieh=zahl(ˢᴸ...) *f* ⓡ subtrahend, number (to be) subtracted; =zeug *n* distilling apparatus or utensils *pl.*
ab=zielen(ˢᴸ) I *v/a. u. v/n.* (h.) ⓡ** auf et. 2 to aim at a th., to have a th. in view; es ist auf ihn dabei abgezielt it is meant (or intended) for him. — II ~ *n* ⓡ aim, purpose (in view).
ab=zimmern(ˢᴸ) *v/a.* ⓡa** *carp.* to square (correctly or accurately).
ab=zirkeln(ˢᴸ) I *v/a.* ⓡa** 1. (mit b. Zirkel messen) to measure off with compasses. — 2. *fig.* alles genau 2 to do things very accurately or precisely; seine Worte 2 (genau erwägen) to be over-particular (or over-nice) in one's speech, to weigh every word. — II ~ *n* ⓡ und **Ab=zirk(e)lung**(ˢᴸ(⌣)) *f* ⓡ 3. accurate measurement.
Ab=zucht(ˢᴸ) *f* ⓡ 1. *arch.* (Abfluß) sewer. — 2. ⚙ Gießerei: discharge-outlet.
Ab=zug(ˢᴸ, *pl.* ˢᴸ) *m* ⓞd. 1. v. Personen: departure; aus der Wohnung: removal; ⚔ (Rückzug) retreat; freier ~ einer Besatzung free (and honourable) withdrawal of a garrison; zum ~ veranlassen to dislodge, to eject; b) = Abmarsch. — 2. des Wassers ꝛc.: drainage, outflow; der Rauch hat keinen ~ there is no outlet for the smoke; (Kanal) channel, sewer. — 3. von einer Summe: deduction; am Gehalt ꝛc.: amount stopped off, deduction; ⚭ ~ von Zinsen bei sofortiger Zahlung discount; ~ am Gewicht (für Verpackung): tare; in ~ bringen to deduct, to allow; nach ~ der Kosten, der Spesen (after) deducting (all) expenses; charges paid; tohne in full, in cash. — 4. *agr.* einer Rebe: layer. — 5. *typ.* (Korrektur-2) proof, pull; Gravierkunst: (Probe-2) proof(-sheet); ~ in Fahnen: slip; *allg.* auch: impression; Kupferstich: ~ vor der Schrift proof before letters. — 6. ⚔ ⚙ am Gewehrschloß: trigger.
ab=züglich(ˢᴸ) *adv.* ⚭ 2 der (ohne die) Kosten deducting (or allowing for) expenses or charges.
Ab=zugs=bogen ⚭ (ˢᴸ...) *m* ⓡ *typ.* proof(-sheet); =bügel ⚭ *m* (am Gewehr) trigger-guard; =bühne ⚔ *f* plat; =dampf ⚙ *m* dead steam; =feder *f* Büchsenmacherei: trigger-spring; =flagge ⚓ *f* Blue-Peter; =freiheit *f* right of (free) emigration; =geld *n* (Abschoß) tax (levied) on emigrants; =gerinne *n* tail-race; =graben ⚭ *m* drain, sewer, conduit (-pipe); =grube *f* cesspool; =kanal *m* = =graben; überwölbter ~ = culvert; =kupfer *n, metall.* copper obtained from the scoria; =quelle *f* ⚭ outlet (or market, opening) for export trade; =rechnung *f, arith.* (calculation of) discount; =rinne ⚙ *f* gutter; =rohr *n*, =röhre *f* drain-pipe, waste-pipe; ⚙ Dampf auch: eduction-pipe; =schleuse *f* outlet-sluice; =teich *m* absorbing tank; ~wasser *n* Müllerei: tail-water; =zahl

f subtrahend; =zeit *f* time for leaving (a dwelling or a service).
ab=zupfen(ˢᴸ) *v/a.* ⓡ** to pluck off, to pull apart, Seide: to unravel.
ab=zwacken(ˢᴸ) *v/a.* ⓡ** 1. to pinch off. — 2. *fig.* e-m etwas 2 to squeeze a th. out of a p.; e-m etwas am Lohne 2 to cut down or reduce (F to dock) a p.'s wages; sich etwas (am Munde) 2 to stint o.s. of a thing.
ab=zwecken ⚀ (ˢᴸ) ⓡ** = abzielen.
ab=zweigen(ˢᴸ) ⓡ** I *v/a.* 1. e-n Baum 2 to lop the branches of ... — 2. (absondern) to detach, to set apart. — II sich 2 *v/refl.*, 2 *v/n.* (h.) 3. 🜨 ꝛc. to branch off, to form a (side-)branch. — III ~ *n* ⓡ 4. = Abzweigung.
Ab=zweigung(ˢᴸ) *f* ⓡ 1. detaching, (side-)branch. — 2. (Zweig) branch, offshoot (bsb. *fig.*), einer Bahn: branch line.
ab=zwicken(ˢᴸ) *v/a.* ⓡ** to nip off.
ab=zwingen(ˢᴸ) *v/a.* ⓡ** e-m et. 2 to wring (or wrest) a th. (by force) from a p., to extort a th. from a p.
ab=zwirnen ⚭ (ˢᴸ) *v/a.* ⓡ** to wind off.
a. c. *abbr.* = a'nni curre'ntis [It. laufenden Jahres] of (or in) the present year.

☞ **Aca...** f. Aka...; **Acce..., Acci...** f. Atze..., Akzi...; **Accl..., Acco..., Accu...** f. Affl..., Affo..., Affu...; **Ace...** f. Aze...

ach! [*ahd.*] I *int.* ah, oh; (Wehklage) alas!; 2 Gott! oh dear (me)!, stärker: good heavens!; 2 ja why, yes! yes, indeed!; 2 so oh, I see!; 2 was da! of course not, on no account!; 2 wo! not a bit of it! the idea (of such a thing)!; 2 daß (a. 2 wenn) er nur //! would he but //!, I wish (to goodness) he would //! — II **Ach** *n* ⓡ lamentation; ein ewig Weh und Ach an everlasting lamentation, an endless wailing; ach und weh schreien to raise (or set up) a pitiful cry; mit Ach und Krach with the greatest trouble, F by the skin of one's teeth, only just.
Achä=er(ˢᴸ⌣) [*grch.*] *m* ⓡ, ~in *f* ⓩ, **achä=isch**(⌣ᴸ⌣) *a.* ⓡ Achæan, weitS. Greek. [agate.
Achat(⌣ᴸ) [*mhd.,* * *grch.*] *m* ⓓc. *min.*
achat=ähnlich(⌣ᴸ⌣⌣) *a.* ⓡ, =artig *a.* agate-like, agatine; =farben *a.* agate-coloured; =haltig *a.* agate-bearing, ⌣ agatiferous. [(wandeln) to agatize.)
achatisieren(⌣ᴸ⌣⌣⌣) *v/a.* ⓩ (in Achat ver-)
Achat=kiesel(⌣ᴸ...) *m* ⓡ Egyptian pebble; =schleifer *m* agate-grinder; =schleiferei *f* ⓩ agate-mill; =schrift *f, typ.* ruby, Am. agate; =tulpe ⚘ *f* agate.
Ache rhein. (ˢᴸ) *f* (Nachen) (small) boat.
Achel⚭(ˢᴸ⌣) [*ahd.*] ⓡ (Granne) awn, chaff.
acheln F (ˢᴸ⌣) [*jüd.*] *v/n.* (h.) ⓡa. to eat.
Achene(⌣ᴸ⌣) *f* ⓩ [It., * *grch. a-chai'nion* sich nicht öffnend] *f* ⓡ (Schließfrucht) achene.
acherontisch(⌣⌣⌣⌣) [*grch.* A'cheron] *a.* ⓡ *myth.* Acherontian, weitS. infernal.
à cheval (á schwá'l) [fr.] ⓩ einer Straße (Truppenstellung zu beiden Seiten der Straße) astride a road, across a thoroughfare.
Achill(⌣ᴸ) *npr/m.* ⓑⓓⓔⓐ. f. Achille(u)s.
Achilea=ide(⌣⌣ᴸ⌣)*f* ⓩ=(Schaf-)Garbe.
Achille-ide (...le'm) son of Achilles.
achille=isch(⌣⌣ᴸ⌣) *a.* ⓡ *myth.* Achillean.
Achillen=kraut(⌣ᴸ⌣⌣) *n* ⓡ = Achillea.

⚛ scientific; ⚘ botanical; ⚲ geography; ⚙ machinery; ⚒ mining; ⚔ military; ⚓ marine; ⚭ commercial; ✉ postal; 🚂 railway.

[Achillesferse] [achtgeben]

Achilles-ferse (⌐ᷣ⌐ᷣ...) f ⓔ fig. (verwundbare Stelle) heel of Achilles, auch weak spot, weak part or side (of a p.); =flechse f, =fehne f, anat. (Hauptsehne zwischen Wade u. Ferse) tendon of Achilles.
Achilleus (⌐ᷣ⌐ᷣ) [grch.] npr/m. ⓰ ⓳ γ. (homerischer Held) Achilles.
Achiver (⌐ᷣ⌐ᷣ) m ⓴ hist. = Achäer.
a. Chr. (n.) abbr. = ante Christum (natum) [lt. vor Christo, vor Christi Geburt] before Christ, gewöhnlich B. C.
Achromasie ⌐ᷣ (⌐ᷣ⌐ᷣ) [grch.] f ⓸ phys. (Farblosigkeit, bsd. v. Linsen) achromatism.
achromatisch ⌐ᷣ (⌐ᷣ⌐ᷣ) [grch.] a. ⓸ phys. (farblos, bsd. v. Linsen) achromatic; ⓛ machen ob. **achromatisieren** ⌐ᷣ (⌐ᷣ⌐ᷣ) v/a. ⓽ phys. to achromatize. [tism.]
Achromatismus (⌐ᷣ⌐ᷣ) m ⓴ achroma-
Achs-band ⓸ (⌐ᷣ...) n ⓸, =blech n axle-tree clip, clip-plate; =bruch m, bsd. ⛓ breaking of the axle, axle-fracture; =büchse ⛓ f axle (or grease-)box.
Achse (⌐ᷣ⌐ᷣ) [ahd.: ax(-tree) †] f ⓸ 1. (Querholz an Rädern) axle(-tree); ⓖ auf der ~, per ~, zu(r) ~ befördern to convey (or carry) by road, to forward by wagon. — 2. ⌐ (um das sich et. dreht) math. axis; ⓺ um e-e ~ gereiht axile, axillary; min. mit drei senkrecht aufea. stehenden ~n trimetric. — 3. ⓸ mach. (Welle) arbor, beam, shaft.
Achs-eisen ⓸ (⌐ᷣ...) n ⓸ axle-tree bar.
Achsel (⌐ᷣ⌐ᷣ; Hom. Axel) [ahd.: axle Achse] f ⓸ 1. (Körperteil) shoulder (= Schulter); die ~n (oder mit den ~n) zucken to shrug one's shoulders; er zuckte leise mit den ~n he gave a slight shrug. — 2. fig. e-n über die ~ ansehen to look down upon a p., stärker: to give a p. the cold shoulder; etwas auf die leichte ~ nehmen to make light of a th.; F to take it easy; auf beiden ~n tragen to waver (or halt) between two parties, pol. to sit on the fence. — 3. anat. u. ⓺ axilla. — 4. ⓸ carp. ~ des Zapfens peg-shoulder.
Achsel-ader (⌐ᷣ⌐ᷣ...) f ⓸ anat. axillary vein; =band n: a) ⚔ (SCH.) shoulder-knot; b) arch., carp. = Tragband; c) Schneiderei: shoulder-piece; =bein n, anat. shoulder-blade; =drüse f axillary gland; =gelenk n shoulder-joint; =hemd n sleeveless shirt or shift; =höhle f arm-pit, ⓺ axilla; =klappe ⚔ f shoulder-strap, der Trompeter: wings pl.
ächseln ⓸ (⌐ᷣ⌐ᷣ) v/a. ⓶ a. carp. to tenon.
Achsel-schnur ⚔ (⌐ᷣ⌐ᷣ...) f ⓸ shoulder-points pl., epaulet; =sproß ⓺ m axillary shoot; =ständig ⓺ a. ⓸ axillary; =streifen m, =stück n shoulder-piece or -strap; am Hemde 2c.: gusset; acht¹ ⌠ II. — 4. ⓸ = Oktave.
=träger m time-server, opportunist; =trägerei f duplicity, double-faced-ness, opportunism; ⓛträgerisch a. double-dealing; temporizing; =troddel ⚔ f epaulet, shoulder-knot; =tuch n, Cath. amict; =zucken n shrug(ging) of the shoulders. [tree or with axes.]
achsen (⌐ᷣ⌐ᷣ) v/a. ⓽ to fit with an axle-
Achsen-arm (⌐ᷣ⌐ᷣ...) m ⓸ arm of an axle (-tree); ⓛbildend ⓺ a. ⓸ axile; =blech n axle-guard; =drehung f rotation; =förmig a. axiform; =geld ⓸ n wheel-age; =lager ⓸ n axle-bearing; =messer

m, opt.: ⌐ axometer; =nagel m am Wagen axle- (or linch-) pin; =neigung f, ast. obliquity of the ecliptic; =riegel ⓸ m transom, cross-timber; =ring m axle-hoop; =schiene f splint of the axle-tree; =schmiere f axle cart-grease; =schnitt m axial section; =schraube f axle-nut; =strahl m der Linse axial ray.
Achs-probe (⌐ᷣ⌐ᷣ...) f ⓸ mach. testing (or trial) of iron-axles; =schwenkung ⚔ f turning (or wheeling) of troops.
acht¹ (⌐ᷣ⌐ᷣ) [ahd.] numer. I card. numb. eight; je ⓛ Mark eight shillings each or a piece on a head; binnen ⓛ Tagen within a week; (heute) vor ⓛ Tagen a week ago, F a week to-day; über ⓛ Tage this day week; ⓺ mit ⓛ Staub-fäden ⌐ octandrian; math. die Zahl ⓛ betr. ⌐ octonary; mit ⓛen fahren to drive a carriage and eight; es ist, schlägt ⓛ(e) it is eight (o' clock), it is striking eight. — II ~ f ⓸ the number eight; eine ~ auf dem Eise 2c. beschreiben to describe an eight; F fig. lange ~ F (a p. as long as) a lamp-post.
Acht² (⌐) [ahd.: ächten] f ⓸ (Achtung) outlawry, ban(ishment), bsd. Alt.: proscription, ostracism, jetzt: boycott; e-n in die ~ erklären oder tun, mit der ~ belegen to outlaw, kirchlich: to excommunicate a p., ⓖ u. pol. to boycott a p.
Acht³ (⌐) [ahd.: achten] f ⓸ (o. pl.) (Aufmerksamkeit) außer ⓛ lassen to disregard, to overlook; außer aller ~ lassen to take no notice of; habt 2! take care!, look out!, s-e Gesundheit (ob. sich) in ⓛ nehmen, nicht in ⓛ nehmen to look after (or to study) one's health, to neglect one's health or o.s.; sich vor e-m in ⓛ nehmen to be on one's guard against (or to beware of) a p.; wir müssen uns in ⓛ nehmen we must mind our P's and Q's, we ought to be careful.
acht¹-armig (⌐ᷣ⌐ᷣ...) ⓸ with eight arms, zo. ⌐ octobrachiate; ⓛäugig a. with eight eyes, ⌐ octonocular.
achtbar (⌐ᷣ⌐ᷣ) [achten] a. ⓸ estimable; respected; ⓛ ein höchst ⓛes Haus a most respectable (or highly respected, greatly esteemed) firm. [bility.]
Achtbarkeit (⌐ᷣ) f ⓸ (o. pl.) respecta-
acht¹-beinig (⌐ᷣ⌐ᷣ...) a. ⓸ eight-legged; ⓛblumig ⓺ a.: ⌐ octopetalous.
Acht²-brief (⌐ᷣ⌐ᷣ...) m ⓸ writ of outlawry.
achte (⌐ᷣ⌐ᷣ) [acht¹] I card. numb. 1. P (wenn nichts nachfolgt) = acht¹. — II a. ⓸ ord. numb. 2. eighth; zum ⓛn eighthly; ⓛs Kapitel eighth chapter, chapter the eighth; am (ob. den) ⓛn Mai (on) the eighth of May, (on) May the eighth, May 8th. — III ~ f ⓸ 3. =
Acht-eck (⌐ᷣ⌐ᷣ...) n ⓸ math.: ⌐ octagon; ⓛeckig a. ⓸: ⌐ octagonal. [a half.]
achte-halb (⌐ᷣ⌐ᷣ) (7¹/₂) inv. a seven and
Achtel (⌐ᷣ⌐ᷣ) [nhd. achte Teil] I n ⓸ 1. eighth (part); das (ein) ~ vom Zentner the (an) eighth of a hundredweight, a stone. — 2. ♪ = ~note. — II ⓛ a. inv. 3. ein ⓛ Zentner = ⅛ of a Zentner.
Achtel-cicero (⌐...) f ⓸ typ. (Durchschuß) eight pica; =form(a't n) f, =größe f octavo volume or size; =freis m: ⓛ octant; =liter n (m) eighth of a litre;

=note ♪ f quaver; =pause ♪ f quaver (or eighth) rest; =petit f (Durchschuß) twelve to pica, hair-lead; =taft ⚔ m time of a quaver; =ton ♪ m = ~note.
achten (⌐ᷣ⌐ᷣ) [ahd.: Acht³] ⓸ I v/a. 1. (dafür halten) to esteem; für gut ⓛ to judge (or deem) it right or proper; wir ⓛ es für eine Ehre we esteem (or think) it an honour; wir ⓛ es für e-e Schande we consider it a disgrace; e-n, et. für nichts ⓛ to hold a p., a th. in mean (or the lowest) estimation; sie ⓛ ihn für verloren they give him up (or look upon him) as lost. — 2. (schätzen) to esteem; s. hochachten; gering ⓛ ob. nicht ⓛ to think lightly (or nothing) of ..., to have no opinion of ...; kein Ansehen der Person ⓛ to be no respecter of persons; das Geld nicht ⓛ to squander one's ...; die Gesetze ⓛ to respect ...; sein Leben nicht ⓛ to hold one's life cheap. — II v/n. (h.) 3. auf et. ob. e-r Sache (gen.) ⓛ to pay attention (or regard) to a th.; er achtet auf alles he attends to (or looks after) everything; sie ⓛ auf meine Worte nicht they won't listen (or pay any heed) to me; achtet auf meine Worte! mark my words! ohne auf // zu ⓛ without heeding //, despite (of) //. — III ⌐ v/refl. 4. sich nach et. ⓛ (mehr gbr. richten) to be guided (or ruled) by ...
ächten (⌐ᷣ) [ahd.: Acht²] I v/a. ⓸ to outlaw, weitS. to put a p. outside the pale of the law; mst Alt.: to proscribe a p., jetzt: to boycott a p. — II ~ n ⓴ = Achtung. — III ⓛd p.pr. u. a. ⓸ auch proscriptive.
Acht¹-ender (⌐ᷣ⌐ᷣ...) m ⓸ hunt. stag of eight branches (to his antlers).
achtens (⌐ᷣ⌐ᷣ) [acht¹] adv. eighthly, in the eighth place.
achtens-wert (⌐...) a. ⓸, ⓛwürdig estimable, worthy of esteem or regard.
Achter¹ (⌐ᷣ⌐ᷣ) m ⓸ [acht¹] 1. die Ziffer 8: einen ~ (eine 8) schreiben to write (or make) an eight. — 2. Maß: ~ (=lichte) pl. eights pl. — 3. Münze: eight-pfennig (or eight-kreuzer) piece. — 4. ⚓ eight-oared boat (= Achtruderer). — 5. eighth part (of a whole pound, &c.). — 6. (achtzeilige Strophe) ottava-rima.
achter² mst ⚓ (⌐) [ndd. (hd. Achter): after] a. u. prp. = hinter; nach ⓛn zu aft, astern; recht von ⓛn dead astern.
Achter² (⌐ᷣ⌐ᷣ) m ⓸ proscriber.
achter²-aus ⚓ (⌐ᷣ⌐ᷣ) (hinter dem Heck e-s Schiffes) adv. aft; on quarter-deck.
Achter²-deck (⌐...) n ⓸ quarter-deck.
achter-lei (⌐ᷣ⌐ᷣ) [acht¹] numer., inv. of eight kinds or sorts.
Achter²-luke ⚓ (⌐...) f ⓸ after-hatch way; ⓛlastig a. ⓸ a too much by the stern; =steven m stern-post. [octuple.]
acht¹-fach (⌐ᷣ⌐ᷣ) a. ⓸ eightfold, ⌐
acht²-fällig (⌐ᷣ⌐ᷣ) a. ⓸ outlawed.
acht¹-fältig (⌐ᷣ⌐ᷣ...) a.: ⌐ ⓛfach; =flächig a. math.: ⌐ octahedral; =flach n ⓸, =flächner m, math.: ⌐ octahedron; =füß(l)er m, zo.: ⌐ octopod.
acht²-geben (⌐...) v/n. ⓽ ⓶b** ⓳ ⓳ c** ⓞb** ⓯ (et.) ⓛ to pay attention (or heed) to auf e-n (a th.); geben Sie acht, daß keiner entkommt mind (or take care) that no one escapes; gebt acht, es wird Was-

Zeichen (s. S. XVII): F familiär; P Volkssprache; ⌐ Gaunersprache; ⌐ selten; † alt (auch gestorben); * neu (auch geboren); ⫶ unrichtig;

ser ausgegossen mind the water; gib auf das Feuer acht look to *or* watch …

acht¹-hundert ("cht…") *card. numb. inv.* eight hundred; ≗**jährig** *a.* [66] of eight years, eight years old, eight-year-old (child, &c.), 📖 octennial; ≗**jährlich** *a.* happening once in eight years; ≗**kantig** *a.* eight-edged; -**kant-eisen** ⚙ *n* [62] octagonal rolled bar-iron.

acht³-los (ʹcht-) *a.* [66] inattentive to, negligent (*or* unmindful) of; -**losig-keit** (ʹcht-⏑-) *f* [46] want of attention to, disregard of, unmindfulness of.

acht¹-mal *adv.* eight(-)times; ≗**malig** *a.* [66] (done) for the eighth time; ≗**männig** ✿ *a.*: 📖 octandrian; ≗**monatig** *a.* eight months old; ≗es Kind eight months' child; -**pfünder** ⚔ *m* [62] eight-pounder; ≗**räd(e)rig** *a.* eight-wheeled; (-**ruderer** *m* u.) ≗**ruderig** ⚓ eight-oared (boat).

achtsam (ʹcht-) [Acht³] *a.* [66] ≗ auf attentive to, careful (*or* mindful) of, alert to.

Achtsamkeit (ʹcht--) *f* [46] ~ auf attention to, care(fulness) (*or* mindfulness) of.

acht¹-säulig ("cht…) 📖 *a.* [66] octostyle; ≗**seitig** *a.* = ≗eckig, ≗flächig.

Achts-erklärung ("chts…) [Acht²] *f* [62] sentence of outlawry *or* banishment.

acht¹-silbig ("cht…") *a.* [66]: 📖 octosyllabic; -**spänner** *m* [62] carriage and eight; ≗**spännig** *a.* with (*or* drawn by) eight horses; ≗**stemp(e)lig** ✿ *a.*: 📖 octogynous; -**stundentag** *m* der Arbeiter: eight hours' day, eight-hour day; ≗**stündig** *a.* lasting eight hours; ≗**stündlich** *adv.* (u. *a.* happening) every eight hours.

acht¹-tägig ("cht…) *a.* [66] lasting eight days *or* a week; ≗**täglich** *a.* weekly; *adv.* once in eight days; ≗**teilig** *a.* of eight parts; 📖 ✿ octofid.

acht¹-und-vierzig ("cht…") *a. inv.* forty-eight; ~**er** *m* [22] revolutionary of '48 *or* of the year 1848; ~**stel-forma't** ⚙ *n* [62] *typ.* in 48⁰, in forty-eights.

Achtung (ʹcht⏑) [achten] *f* [46] (*pl.* ↘) **1.** (Achtsamkeit) attention; Ausruf: gebt od. paßt ~! attention!, a. look out!, mind! ⚔ ~! attention! b. Spiel: play!; auf e-n, auf et. ~ geben od. haben to pay attention to …, to look after …, to see to … — **2.** (Hochachtung) esteem for; e-m (große od. viel) ~ erweisen to pay great respect to a p.; große ~ genießen to be greatly respected; (nur) aus ~ gegen ihn, für ihn od. vor ihm out of (pure) regard for him; mit aller ~ vor Ihnen with all due deference to you; sich (*dat.*) ~ erwerben, sich (*dat.*) ~ zu verschaffen wissen to make o.s. respected, to gain (universal) esteem; bei e-m in ~ stehen to stand high in a p.'s opinion *or* estimation; sich bei e-m in ~ setzen to gain a p.'s respect, to establish one's credit with a p.; die schuldige ~ vor den Gesetzen beobachten to show a proper respect for the laws; ~ einflößend commanding respect, awe-inspiring.

Ächtung (ʹ⏑) *f* [46] outlawry, proscription (= Achtserklärung).

achtung-gebietend ("cht⏑…) *a.* [66] commanding (respect), imposing.

Achtungs-bezeigung (≗…) *f* [62] mark of esteem, tribute of respect; -**erfolg** *m* moral success, a. (fr.) *succès d'estime.*

Ächtungs-gesetz *n* [62] proscriptive law.

achtungs-los ("cht⏑…) *a.* [66] without respect; ≗**voll** *a.* respectful(ly *adv.*); ≗**wert** *a.* estimable; ≗**widrig(keit** *f* [46]) *a.* disrespectful(ness), irreverent(ness).

acht¹-weibig ✿ ("cht…) *a.* [66]: 📖 octogynous; ≗**wink(e)lig** *a.*: 📖 octagonal.

acht¹-zehn ("cht-ʹ) *card. numb.* eighteen; ~**ender** (≗…) *m* [22] stag (*or* head) of 18 points; ≗**flächig** *a.* [66] *min.*: 📖 octodecimal; ≗**jährig** *a.* eighteen years old.

acht¹zehnte (~⏑) *ord. numb.* [66][67] eighteenth; (~**l** *n* [22] u.) ≗**l** *a. inv.* eighteenth (part); ≗**ns** *adv.* in the eighteenth place.

acht¹-zeilig ("cht…) *a.* [66] of eight lines; ≗e Strophe, auch (it.) ottava(-)rima.

achtzig (ʹcht⏑) **I** *card. numb.* eighty; ≗ Jahre alt of fourscore years. — **II** die (Zahl) ~ *f* [46] the number 80. — **III** ~**er(in** *f* [47]) *m* [22] u. ≗**er** *a. inv.* octogenarian; in den ≗er Jahren (oder in den ~ern) v. Personen: turned (*or* over, past) eighty, v. d. Zeit: in the eighties.

achtzig-jährig (≗…) *a.* [66] octogenary; der, die ~e [67] octogenarian.

achtzigste (~⏑) *ord. numb.* [66][67] eightieth; (~**l** *n* [22] u.) ≗**l** *a. inv.* eightieth (part); ≗**ns** *adv.* in the eightieth place.

ächzen (ʹ⏑) [nhd.: ach] *v/n.* (h.) [90] to groan (and moan), to be full of aches and pains.

☞ **Aci…** s. Azi…

Acker (ʹ⏑) [ahd.: acre: lt. *ă'gĕr*] *m* [19] (doch vgl. ~ 3) **1.** field; den ~ bauen to till (*or* cultivate) the land *or* ground. — **2.** = ~beet. — **3.** [22]6. († Flächenmaß) acre; 30 ~ Landes thirty acres of land.

Acker-arbeit ("⏑…) *f* [62] agricultural labour; -**baldrian** ✿ *m* = Feldsalat.

ackerbar (ʹ⏑-) *a.* [66] arable, cultivable.

Acker-bau ("⏑ʹ) *m* [62] agriculture, farming; ~ treiben to till the land, to be engaged in husbandry *or* agriculture; ≗**bauend** *a.* [66] agricultural; -**bauer** *m* [62] = Ackersmann.

Ackerbau-gedicht ("⏑ʹ…) *n* [62] pastoral (*or* rustic) poem; -**gerät(schaft** *f*) *n* = Ackergerät(schaft); -**gesellschaft** *f* agricultural society; -**kunde** *f* science of agriculture, agriculturism; -**kundige(r)** *m* agriculturist; -**minister** *m* minister (England: President of the Board) of agriculture; -**ministerium** *n* öst. ministry (England: Board) of agriculture; -**schule** *f* agricultural college; ≗**treibend** *a.* [66] agricultural.

Acker-beet ("⏑…) *n* [62] ridge between two furrows; -**bestellung** *f* tillage; -**boden** *m* arable soil; -**bürger** *m* farming townsman.

Äckerchen (ʹ⏑⏑) *n* [23] *dim.* little field, small plot.

Acker-distel ✿ ("⏑…) *f* [62] way-thistle (*Ci'rsium arve'nse*); -**doppe** *f* (Knopper) acorn-cup; -**drossel** *f*, *orn.* rose-coloured thrush (*Turdus ro'seus*).

Ackerei (⏑⏑ʹ) *f* [46] tillage of land.

Ackerer (ʹ⏑⏑) *m* [22] small farmer.

Acker-erde ("⏑…) *f* [62] surface soil; -**feld** *n* field under cultivation, tilled land; -**fuchsschwanz** ✿ *m* field foxtail-grass (*Alopecu'rus agre'stis*); -**furche** *f* furrow; -**gänsedistel** ✿ *f* sow-thistle (*Sonchus arve'nsis*); -**gaul** *m* farm-horse; -**gerät(-schaft** *f*) *n* implement of husbandry; -**hahnenfuß** ✿ *m* corn-crowfoot (*Ranu'nculus arve'nsis*); -**hof** *m* farm(-yard); -**holunder** ✿ *m* = Attich; -**kamille** ✿ = Hunds-k.; -**klee** ✿ *m* = Sichel-k.; -**knecht** *m* ploughboy, ploughman; -**krähe** *f*, *orn.* rook; -**krume** *f* = -erde; -**land** *n* arable land; -**leute** *pl.* von -mann; -**lohn** *m* labourer's hire *or* wage(s); -**mann** *m* = -smann; -**männchen** *n*, *orn.* = Bachstelze; -**mennig** ✿ *m* = Odermennig;

ackern (ʹ⏑) [mhd.] **I** *v/a.* u. *v/n.* (h.) [92]a. to till (the land), to plough (the field); *fig.* to perform (write, &c.) with a great effort. — **II** ~ *n* [23] = Ackerung.

Acker-nüßchen ✿ ("⏑…) *n* [62] = Finkensame; -**parzelle** *f* small plot of land, allotment; -**pflug** *m* plough; -**rain** *m* ridge (of a field).

äcker-reich (≗…) *a.* [66] rich in arable land; landed (proprietor).

Acker-röte ✿ ("⏑…) *f* [62] field madder (*Shera'rdia arve'nsis*); -**schleife**, -**schlichte** *f* plough-drag; -**scholle** *f* clod (of earth); -**senf** ✿ *m* charlock (*Sina'pis arve'nsis*).

Ackers-mann ("⏑ʹ) *m* [62] farmer('s labourer), husbandman.

Ackerung (ʹ⏑⏑) *f* [46] tillage, husbandry, farming.

Acker-vieh ("⏑…) *n* [62] farm-cattle; ≗**weise** *adv.* in plots; -**werk** *n* farming; -**werkzeug** *n* = -gerät(schaft); -**winde** ✿ *f* bear-, corn-bind (*Convo'lvulus arve'nsis*); -**wirt** *m* farmer; -**wirtschaft** *f* farming, agriculture; -**wurz** ✿ [P aus lt. *a'corus*] *f* = Kalmus.

☞ **Aco…** s. Ako…

Aconitin 📖 (⏑k⏑-ʹ) [Akonit] *n* [11]c. (*o. pl.*) *chm.* aconitine.

☞ **Acro…**, **Act…**, **Acu…** s. Ak…

Acquit (ă-ki') [fr.] *n* [51] **1.** $ (Quittung) pour acquit (pür ~ erhalten), (payment) received (recd.). — **2.** Billard: ~ geben (aussetzen) to lead (off).

a. D. *abbr.* = außer Dienst retired, ⚔ on half-pay; Hauptmann a. D. half-pay captain.

A. D. *abbr.* = a'nno Do'mini [lt. im Jahre des Herrn] in the year of our Lord.

a d. *abbr.* = a da'to [lt. vom Tage (der Ausstellung)] from (this) date.

ad absurdum (ʹ⏑"⏑) [lt.] *adv.* s. absurd.

ad acta (ʹ"⏑) [lt.]: et. ≗ legen = zu den Akten legen (s. Akte).

adagio ♪ (ă-dā'-dʒō) [it.] *adv.* u. **Adagio** *n* [53] adagio; als *adv.* auch: slowly.

Adalbert (ʹ⏑⏑) *npr/m.* [15][16]α. Ethelbert.

Adam (ʹ⏑) [hebr.] *npr/m.* [51]α. Adam; *bibl.* den alten ~ ausziehen to put off the old man, to mend (one's ways); nach ~ Riese (r-r Ryse, Rechenbuch 1523), etwa: according to Cocker('s arithmetic).

adamisch (-ʹ⏑) *a.* [66] Adamic(al).

adamitisch (--ʹ⏑) *a.* [66] Adamitic(al).

Adams-apfel ("⏑…) *m* [62]: a) ✿ Adam's apple, plantain-tree; b) P *anat.* (Kehlknorpel) Adam's apple (= larynx); -**nadel** ✿ *f* Adam's needle (*Yucca*).

adäquat (⏑-ʹ) [lt.] *a.* [66] *phls.* adequate.

a dato $ (ʹ"⏑) [lt.] s. dato u. a d.

Addend (⏑ʹ) [lt.] *m* [42] *math.* addendum.

Addenda (⏑ʹ⏑) [lt.] *n/pl. inv.* (Beizufügendes) things to be added, addenda.

addieren (⏑ʹ⏑) [lt.] *v/a.* [93] (hinzufügen, zs-zählen) to add (*or* sum) up; (alles) zusammen ≗ to total (*or* cast) up; addiert man alles zusammen taking (*or* if we take) the sum total; falsch ≗ to cast up wrongly *or* incorrectly.

♪ Musik; 📖 Wissenschaft; ✿ Pflanze; 🌐 Geographie; ⚙ Technik; ⚒ Bergbau; ⚔ Militär; ⚓ Marine; $ Handel; ✉ Post; 🚂 Eisenbahn.

[Addition] — 34 — [Adreßkontor]

Addition (⌣⌣tß(ᵛ)ᴸ) [lt.] f ㊻ (Zusammenzählen) addition.
Additional-vertrag (⌣⌣tß(ᵛ)-ᴵᴵ...) m ㊽ additional agreement.
Additions-exe'mpel (⌣⌣tß(ᵛ)ᴵᴵ...) n ㊽ addition sum; **=fehler** m mistake (or error) in adding (up).
ade (-ᴸ) [adieu] int. u. **Ade** n ⑩ adieu, farewell, good-bye. [u. ㊷ = Storch.]
Adebar, Adebär norbd.(ᴵᴵᴸ) [ahd.] m ⑭d.
Adel¹ (ᴸᵛ) [ahd.: udal] m ㊒ (o. pl.) 1. (Adelstand) nobility, (die Abligen) the nobility, (all) titled people, people of noble birth; engS. in England.: peerage, weitS. aristocracy; niederer ~ gentry; von ~ sein to be of noble birth, co. to have a handle to one's name. — 2. fig. (innerer) ~ nobleness (of mind), nobility (of the soul).
Adel² provc. (⌣) m ㊒ = Jauche, Dünger.
Adelborst ↓ (ᴵᴵ....) m ㊒ holl. = Fähnrich zur See. [㊽ß. (Vn.) = Adeline.]
Adele (-ᴸᵛ) [fr.; dtsch. A'dela] npr/f. ㊴
Adelheid (ᴸᵛ-)npr/f.㊴㊻α.(Vn.)Adelaide.
ad(e)lig, äd(e)rig (ᴸ(ᵛ)ᵛ) a. ㊻ noble, F co. of blue blood; e-e Le Dame a titled lady, a lady of noble birth; sie ist 2 F co. she has a handle to her name. — II **~e(r)** m u. **~e** f ㊖ nobleman, lady of title; member of the nobility or aristocracy; engS. peer(ess).
Adeline (-ᵛᴸᵛ) npr/f. ㊴ u. ㊽ß. (Vn.) Adelina, dim. Addy.
adeln (ᴸᵛ) I v/a. ㊽a* 1. to ennoble, in Engl.: to raise to the peerage; er ist geadelt he has been made a peer (a baronet, (in den Ritterstand erhoben) nur persönlich: he has been knighted or been made a knight, he has had a knighthood conferred on him. — 2. fig. to dignify, exalt. — II **~** n ㉓ 3. = Adelung.
Adels-brief (ᴵᴵᵛ) m ㊽ patent of nobility; **=buch** n in England: peerage, Debrett's; **=diplom** (=brief; **=herrschaft** f aristocratic rule; **=hof** m = Edelhof.
Adel=sinn (ᴵᴵ...)m㊽noble sentiments pl.
Adels=kammer (ᴵᴵ...) f ㊻ Upper House, House of Lords; **=krone** f coronet; **=lexikon** n, **=register** n = =buch.
Adel=stand (ᴵᴵ...) m ㊽ nobility (vgl. Adel 1); in den (englischen) ~ erheben to raise to the peerage, weitS. to ennoble; Erhebung in den ~ being made a member of the nobility, in Engl.: being made a peer (of the realm), being raised to the Upper House; **=stolz** m aristocratic pride; **?stolz** a. ㊻ proud of one's noble descent.
Adelung (ᴸᵛᵛ) f ㊻ ennoblement.
Adept (ᵛᴸ) [lt.] m ㊽ (Eingeweihter) adept.
Ader (ᴸᵛ) [ahd.] f ㊻ 1. anat. bloodvessel; (Blut=)~ vein; (Schlag=)~ artery; path.†gold(e)ne ~ hemorrhoidal vein, piles pl.; e-m eine ~ öffnen oder schlagen, zur ~ lassen to bleed (F fig. to drain) a p.; man hat ihn stark zur ~ gelassen he has bled (or let blood) freely (auch fig.); (Blatt=)? nerve, nervure, vein (of a leaf); fig. er hat keine falsche ~ (an sich) he has not a grain of deceit in him, he is honest to the backbone. — 2. fig. seine (dichterische) ~ fließt he is in the vein; keine ~ (Anlage) zu et. haben to have no taste

(or talent) for a th. — 3. geol. vein; ⚔ lode, seam; ~ im Glase, in Edelsteinen ꝛc., auch: cloud, flaw; ☉ elect. ~ eines Kabels core (of a cable).
Äderchen (ᴸᵛᵛ) n ㉓ small vein, veinlet.
ader=förmig (ᴵᴵᵛ...) a. ㊻ having the form of veins; **=haut** f ㉗ choroid membrane (of the eye); **=haut=entzündung** f inflammation of the choroid, ꝛ choroiditis; **=holz** n (ant. Hirnholz) (beim Laufe der Fasern parallel geschnitten) wood cut along (or with) the grain.
ad(e)rig, äd(e)rig (ᴸ(ᵛ)ᵛ) a. ㊻ veined, full of veins; von Edelsteinen: clouded, flawy.
Ader=knoten (ᴵᵛ...) m ㊽ (bei Krampfadern) knotted vein, ꝛ varix; **=laß** m (SCH. =lässe f) surg. bleeding; **=laß=becken** n bleeding-basin; **=laß=eisen** n, surg. lancet, vet. fleam; **=lassen** n bleeding; **=lasser** m ㊽ bloodletter, ꝛ phlebotomist; **=laßkunst** f ꝛ phlebotomy.
adern, bff. **ädern** (ᴸᵛ) v/a. ㊽a. to mark with veins. [router-gauge.]
Abern=kratzer ⊙ (ᴵᴵ...) m ㊽ der Tischler
Ader=presse (ᴵᴵ...) f ㊽ surg. tourniquet; **?reich** a. ㊻ veined; **=schlag** m pulsation, pulse; a. = =laß; **=unterbindung** f tying up a vein; **=wasser** n lymph, bloodserum. [kleben, anhangen) to adhere.]
adhärieren (ᵛ-ᴸᵛ) [lt.] v/n. (h.) ㊼ (an-
Adhäsion ꝛ (ᵛ-(ᵛ)ᴸ) [lt.] f ㊻, **~s=kraft** f adhesion; **=wagen** ⚊ m adhesion-car.
adhäsiv ꝛ (ᵛ-ᴸf) [lt.] a. ㊻ adhesive.
adieu, Adieu (ä-biö') [fr.] int. u. n ⑨ farewell, good-bye, adieu; e-m ~ sagen to bid a p. farewell, to say good-bye to a p.
Ädil (-ᴸ) [lt.] m ㊽ röm Alt.: (öffentlicher Aufseher, höher Staatsbeamter) ædile; **=amt** (-ᴵᴵᵛᵛ) n ㊽, **~ität** (-ᵛᴸf) f ㊻ ædileship; **ädilisch** (-ᴸᵛ) a. ㊻ ædilian.
adj. abbr. = Adjektiv(um).
Adjektiv (ᴸᵛf) [lt.] n ⑪c. gram. (Eigenschaftswort) adjective; **?isch** (ᴸᵛᴸᵛ) a. ㊻ adjectival; adv. adjectively; **~=satz** m ㊽ adjective clause or sentence; **~um** (ᴸᵛᴵᵛᵛ) n ㊾ = Adjektiv.
adjes P (-ᴸ) int. = adieu.
Adjudikation (ᵛ-ᵛ-ᵛtß(ᵛ)ᴸ) [lt.] f ㊻ (Zuerkennung) adjudication.
adjudizieren (ᵛ-ᵛᴸᵛ) [lt.] v/a. ㊼ (zuerkennen) to adjudicate, to award to.
Adjunkt (ᵛᴸ) [lt.] m ㊽, ⑪b. adjunct; eines Professors: assistant; (Vertreter) substitute. [office.]
Adjustier=amt (ᵛᵛᴵᴵ...) n ㊽ gauging-
adjustier/en (ᵛᵛᴸᵛ) [lt.] I v/a. ㊼ Gewichte ꝛc.: to adjust; to test; to gauge (Münzen: to size. — II **~** n ㉓ = A/ung.
Adjustier=schraube f adjusting-screw.
Adjustierung (ᵛᵛᴸᵛ) f ㊻ adjustment, von Münzen: sizing. [bench.]
Adjustier=werk (ᵛᴵᴵ...) n ㊽ drawing-
Adjutant ⚔ (ᵛ-ᴸ) [fr., *span.] m ㊽ adjutant; eines Generals: aide-de-camp.
Adjutantur (ᵛ-ᵛᴸ) f ㊻ adjutancy; staff of the commander-in-chief.
Adler (ᴸᵛ) [mhd. Adel-Aar] m ㊽ eagle; junger ~ eaglet.
Adler=auge (ᴵᴵ...)n=blick;?äugig a. ㊻ eagle- (or keen-) eyed; **=blick** m eagle-eye; **=farn** ♀ m brake (Pte'ris aquili'na); **=flug** m eagle-flight; **=holz** ♀ n v. Himalaja: eagle- (or aloes-) wood, calambac (Aquilla'ria aga'llocha); **=horst** m aerie,

eyry; **=junges** n eaglet; **=nase** f aquiline nose; **=orden** m (der Rote [1705, 92], Schwarze ~ [1701]) order of the (red, black) eagle; **=stein** m, min. eagle-stone; ꝛ aetites; **=träger** ⚔ Alt. eagle-bearer; **=vitriol** m (tupferhaltiger Eisenvitriol) eagle (or Bayreuth, Salzburg) vitriol.
ad libitum (ᴸᴵᴵᵛ) [lt.] adv. (nach Belieben) at will, ad libitum (abbr. ad lib.).
adlig (ᴸᵛ, **Adlige(r)** f. adelig ꝛc.
Administration (ᵛᵛᵛ-tß(ᵛ)ᴵᴵ) [lt.] f ㊻ (Verwaltung) administration. [tive.]
administrativ (ᵛᵛᵛ-ᴸf) a. ㊻ administra-
administrieren (ᵛᵛᵛ-ᴸᵛ) v/n. ㊼ to administer. [strator, jur. a.: trustee.]
Administrator (ᵛᵛᵛ-ᴸᵛ) m ㉑ admini-
Admiral (ᵛ-ᴸ) [ar.] m ⑪ (⑦c. ↓ u. zo. admiral; (Schmetterling) red admiral.
Admiralität (ᵛ-ᵛ-ᴸ) f ㊻ admiralty (man beachte, daß in England: the Admiralty = Marineministerium).
Admiralitäts=amt (ᴵᴵ...) n ㊽, **=gericht** n Board (or Court) of Admiralty; **=inseln** ♀ npr/f/pl. Admiralty Islands.
Admirals=flagge (ᵛ-ᴸᵛ...) f ㊽ admiral's flag; **=schiff** n flag-ship; **=stab** m naval staff. [nung) admonition.]
Admonition (ᵛᵛᵛtß(ᵛ)ᴵᴵ) [lt.] f ㊻ (Ermah-
ad notam (ᴸᴵᴵ) [lt.]: 2 nehmen to take note of, to note down.
Adolf (ᴸᵛ) [ahd.] npr/m ⑮㊅α. (Vn.) Adolph(us), dim. Dolph(us).
Adonis (ᵛᴸᵛ) [grch., * phön.] m ⑯γ. I npr. myth. (schöner Jüngling) Adonis. II s. ♀ = **~röschen**. [(verse) (ᵛᵛ-ᴸf) Adonic.]
adonisch (ᵛᴸᵛ)a.㊻pros. 2 (erVers) Adonic
adonisieren (ᵛ-ᵛ-ᴸᵛ) v/a. ㊼ (putzen) to adonize, to deck out, to smarten up. [eye.]
Adonis=röschen (ᵛᴸᵛ...) n ㉓ pheasant's-
adoptieren (ᵛᵛᴸᵛ) [lt.] v/a. ㊼ (an Kindes Statt annehmen) to adopt, affiliate.
Adoption (ᵛᵛtß(ᵛ)ᴸ) [lt.] f ㊻ (Annahme an Kindes Statt) adoption, affiliation.
adoptiv (ᵛᵛᴸf) [lt.] a. ㊻ adoptive.
Adoptiv=kind (ᵛᵛᴵᴵ...) n ㊽ adoptive (or adopted) child; **=mutter** f, **=vater** m adoptive (or adopting) mother, father.
adoucieren (ᵛdu-ß-ᴸᵛ) [fr.] ㊼ ↓ u. metall. (härten, anlassen) to anneal, to [temper.]
Adr. abbr. = Adresse.
Adressant(in f ㊼) m ㊽ (ᵛᵛᵛ(ᵛ)) [fr.] (Absender[in] e-s Briefes ꝛc.) writer (or sender[in] v. Waren) consignor.
Adressat(in f ㊼) m ㊽ (ᵛᵛᵛ(ᵛ)) [fr.] (Empfänger[in] e-s Briefes ꝛc.) addressee; (Warenempfänger[in]) consignee; e-s Wechsels: drawee.
Adreß=buch (ᵛᴸ...)n㊽ directory, guide; **=bureau** n inquiry- (or registry-)office; **=debatte** f, parl. debate on the address.
Adresse (ᵛᴸᵛ) [fr.] f ㊻ address (auch an Fürsten; auf Briefen auch: direction; per ~, unter der ~ care of (c/o); ✱ ich habe die Waren an Ihre ~ befördert I have forwarded ... to you or to your address; sie sind nicht an die richtige ~ gelangt they failed to reach their destination; sich an die unrichtige ~ wenden to apply in the wrong quarters or to the wrong person, F to go to the wrong shop.
adressieren (ᵛᵛᴸᵛ) v/a. ㊼ to address, ✱ Güter: to consign; falsch 2 to misdirect.
Adreß=kalender (ᵛᴸ...) m ㊽ = =buch; **=karte** f (business-)card; **=kontor** n =

Signs (see page XVII): F familiar; P vulgar; ꟼ flash; ↘ rare; † obsolete (died); * new word (born); ⁺⁺ incorrect; ♪ music;

[adrett] — 35 — [Aftervollmacht]

=bureau; =zettel m auf Waren: label, ticket, docket. [schict) handy, skilled.
adrett (ᵕ◡) [fr. adroit] a. ⓖ smart, (ge=
Adria ♀ (⌣ᵕᵕ) npr/f ⑮ ⓖ α. (Meer) f.
Adrian ♀ = Hadrian. [adriatisch.]
adriatisch ♀ (-ᵕ◡ᵕ) a. ⓖ Adriatic; ~es Meer (a. Adria) the Adriatic (Sea).
adrig, ädrig (ᴵᵕ) a. ⓖ f. aderig.
adstringierend ⚔ (ᵕᵕᴸᵕ) [lt.] a. ⓖ med. (zusammenziehend) astringent.
Adular (ᵕ-ᴵ) [Adu'la ♀, Ostalpen] m ⑪c. min. adular, moon-stone.
A-Dur ♪ (ᴵᴵ) n, inv. ♪ A ♪.
adv. abbr. = Adverb(ium).
Advalorem-zoll (ᵕw-ᴵᴵᵕ)[lt. ad valo'rem dem Werte nach] m ⑫ advalorem duty.
Advent (ᴶᵕᵕ) [lt.] m ⑪b. rel. advent.
Adventiv-knospe ♀ (ᴶᵕᵕᴵᴵ...) f ⑫ adventitious bud. [season.]
Advents-zeit (ᴶᵕᵕ...) f ⑫ Advent-
Adverb (ᴶᵕᵕ) [lt.] n ⑳ gram. (Umstandswort) adverb; als ~ adverbial(ly); ᴸial(isch) (ᴶᵕᵕ(ᵕ)ᴵᴵ(ᵕ)) a. ⓖ adverbial; ~ium (ᴶᵕᵕ(ᵕ)) n ⑳ = Adverb.
Adversari-en ⓖ (ᵕwᵕᴵᴵ(ᵕ)ᵕ) [lt.] n/pl. inv. waste-book, journal, day-book.
Advokat (ᵕwᴵᴵ) [lt.] m ⓖ advocate; (Rechtsanwalt) solicitor, bei höheren Gerichtshöfen: barrister; erster ~ leading (or senior) counsel; e-n ~en (an)nehmen to engage counsel; die Sache e-m ~en anvertrauen to put the matter in a solicitor's (or lawyer's) hands; sich mit e-m ~en beraten to take counsel's advice; j-s Sache als ~ führen to defend (weitS. to conduct) a p.'s case; als ~ praktizieren to practise (or follow) the law.
Advokaten-gebühr (ᵕwᵕᴵᴵ...) f ⑫ lawyer's (or barrister's, counsel's, solicitor's) fee; =kniff F m lawyer's trick; =schreiber m solicitor's (or lawyer's) clerk; =stand m, =zunft f the Bar; weitS. the legal profession.
Advokatur (ᵕwᵕ-ᴵ) [lt.] f ⓖ meist: legal profession; zur ~ zugelassen werden to be called to the bar; (Praxis) solicitor's connexion.
advozieren (ᵕwᵕ-ᴵᵕ) [lt.] v/n. (h.) ⓖ to practise (or follow) the (profession of the) law, to practise at the bar; to plead (before a court).
adynamisch ⚔ (ᴵᴵᵕᴵᴵ) [grch.] a. ⓖ (kraftlos) weak, ⚔ adynamic.
A-ero..., ᴸ... meist ⚔ (ᴵᵕᵕ...) [grch. Luft=] ⓖ: ~dynamik f, phys. aerodynamics; ~lith (~ᴵᴵ) m ⑪c., ⑫ (Meteorstein) aerolite; ~meter (~ᴵᴵ) n (m) aerometer; ~naut (~ᴵᴵ) m ⑫ aeronaut; ~nautik f aeronautics; ᴸnautisch a. aeronautical; ~stat (~ᴵᴵ) m ⑪c. aerostat; ~statik f aerostatics; ᴸstatisch a. ⓖ phys. aerostatic(al).
a. f. abbr. = a'nni futu'ri [lt. nächsten Jahres] of next year, next year's.
äfern prov. (ᴵᵕ)[ahd.] v/a. ⑫a. (wiederholt vorbringen) to reiterate. [affability.]
Affabilität (ᵕᴵᵕᴵᴵ) [lt.] f ⓖ (Leutseligkeit)
Affäre (ᵕᴵᵕ) [fr. affaire] f ⓖ (Geschäft, Angelegenheit)affair, concern, business.
Äffchen (ᴶᵕᵕ) n ⓘ (dim. v. Affe) zo. little monkey; marmoset.
Affe (ᴵᵕ) [ahd.] m ⓖ 1. zo. allg. = (menschenähnlicher, ungeschwänzter) ape (simia), (langgeschwänzter) monkey. — 2. fig. von Personen: Hans ~ Jackanapes; co.

(v. Kindern) the little monkey or puppy; F s-m ~n Zucker geben to be brimming over with merriment; F e-n ~n an e-m gefressen haben to be infatuated with a p., to be foolishly fond of a p., to dote on a p. — 3. ✕ P (Tornister) knapsack. — 4. F (Rausch) e-n kleinen ~n haben F to be half-seas over or a little on, to have had enough or a drop too much.
Affekt (ᵕᴵ) [lt.] m ⑪b. emotion; (Leidenschaft) passion, impulse; (Innigkeit) ardour, warmth. [heit) affectation.]
Affektation (ᵕᵕᴶ-tʒ(ᵕ)ᴵᴵ) [lt.] f ⓖ (Geziert=
affektieren (ᵕᵕᴵᵕ) [fr.] I v/a. ⓖ to affect, to sham, F to put on side. — II affektiert a. ⓖ affected, studied; das ~e affectation, mannerism, (outward) show.
affektioniert † (ᵕᵕtʒ(ᵕ)ᴵ...) [fr.] a. ⓖ (liebevoll zugetan) affectionate, devoted.
Affekt-los (ᵕᵕᴶ-) a. ⓖ unimpassioned, cool and collected; =losigkeit (ᵕᵕ-ᵕ) f ⓖ freedom from passion.
äffen (ᴶᵕ) [mhd.] I v/a. ⑳ 1. to ape, to mimic. — 2. (foppen) to (be)fool, to mock, F to quiz. — II ~ n ⓘ = Äfferei.
Affen-abstammung (ᴶᵕᵕ...) f ⑫ des Menschen man's descent from the monkey; =art f species of apes; nach ~ monkey-like, monkey-fashion; ᴸartig a. ⓖ apish, monkey-like, ⚔ simious; ᴸe Geschwindigkeit lightning speed; =blume ♀ f monkey-flower (Mi'mulus); =brotbaum ♀ m baobab(-tree) (Adanso'nia digita'ta); =figur, =fratze f = =gesicht; =geschlecht n monkey-tribe, ⚔ quadrumana; =gesicht n monkey-face, ugly grimace.
affenhaft (ᴶᵕᵕ) a. ⓖ = affenartig.
Affen-haus (ᴶᵕᵕ...) n ⑳ monkey-house; =komödie f buffoonery, foolery; =könig m, zo. coaita (A'teles pani'scus); =liebe f foolish fondness (of parents); ᴸmäßig a. ⓖ = =artig; =mensch m monkey-like (or microcephalous) person; =pinscher m pug(-dog); =schande f great or scandalous (F beastly) shame; =schwanz m: a) monkey's tail; b) F fig. b.s. silly fool; =streich m tomfoolery, F skylarking; =weibchen ♀ n she-ape, she-monkey.
Äffer (ᴶᵕ) [ᴵ] m ⓖ 1. mocker, F quiz. — 2. zo. = Halbaffe, Lemuride.
Äfferei (ᴵᵕᴵ) f ⓖ 1. (Nachahmen) aping, mimicry. — 2. (Foppen) mockery. [bill.]
Affiche (ᵕᴵsch) [fr.] f ⓖ (Anschlag) poster,
affichieren (ᵕsch(ᴵᵕ) v/n. v/a. ⓖ to advertise (on posters), to post up bills.
affig P (ᴶᵕ) a. ⓖ 1. = affenartig. — 2. fig. foolish, silly. [filiation.]
Affiliation (ᵕ(ᵕ)-tʒ(ᵕ)ᴵᴵ) [lt.] f ⓖ affiliieren (ᵕ-(ᵕ)ᴵᵕ) [lt.] v/a. ⓖ (zugesellen) to affiliate; affiliiert affiliate(d).
Äffin (ᴶᵕ) [Affe] ⓖ 1. = Affenweibchen. — 2. fig. monkey-faced woman.
affinieren (ᵕᵕᴵᵕ) [fr.] v/a. ⓖ to refine.
Affinierung (ᵕ-ᴵᵕ) f ⓖ refining.
Affinität (ᵕ-ᴵᴵ) [lt.] f ⓖ (Verwandtschaft) bsd. chm. affinity.
Affirmation (ᵕᵕ-tʒ(ᵕ)ᴵᴵ) [lt.] f ⓖ (Bejahung, Bekräftigung) affirmation.
affirmativ (ᵕᵕ-ᴵf) [lt.] a. ⓖ (bejahend) affirmative. [bekräftigen) to affirm.]
affirmieren (ᵕᵕ-ᴵᵕ) [lt.] v/a. ⓖ (bejahen,
äffisch (ᴶᵕ) a. ⓖ = affenartig.
Affix(um) (ᵕᴵ(ᵕ)) [lt.] n ⑪a. (⑳) gram. (angehängte Silbe) affix.

affizierbar (ᵕᵕᴵ-) [lt.] a. ⓖ susceptible, impressionable; ~keit (~) [lt.] f ⓖ susceptibility, impressionability.
affizieren (ᵕᵕᴵᵕ) [lt.] v/a. ⓖ (einwirken auf) to affect; (ergreifen) to touch.
Affner ⓖ (ᴶᵕ) m ⑫ = Weberkamm.
Affodill ♀ (ᵕᵕᴵ) [Asphodill] m, n ⑪b. asphodel; ᴸartig (ᴵ...) a. ⓖ asphodelian; ~lilie f ⓖ = Taglilie.
Affresko (ᵕᴵ-) [lt.] n ⑳ (Wandgemälde) al-fresco (= Alfresko).
affrös (ᵕᴵ) [fr.] a. ⓖ (D 10) (gräßlich, abscheulich) horrible, awful, abominable.
Afghane (ᵕᴵᵕ) m ⓖ u. afghanisch a. ⓖ Afghan. [Mittelasiens: Afghanistan.]
Afghanistan ♀ (ᵕᴵᵕᴵᴵ) npr/n. ⑪α. Land
Afrika ♀ (ᴵᵕᵕ) [lt.] npr/n. ⑪α. Africa.
Afrika-forscher (ᴵ...) m ⓖ = =reisender.
Afrikander (ᵕᴵᵕ) m ⓖ Südafrika: (Abkömmling europäischer Ansiedler) Afrikander.
Afrikaner (-ᴵᵕ) m ⓖ, ~in f ⓖ, afrikanisch a. ⓖ African.
Afrika-reisende(r) (ᴵᴵᴵ...) m ⓖ African explorer or traveller.
aft ⚓ (ᴵ) adv. = hinten.
After¹ (ᴵᵕ) [ahd. (* ab): after] m ⓖ 1. anat.: anus. — 2. hind quarters pl., rump, posterior, backside, F behind.
After² (ᴵᵕ) n (m) ⓖ 1. (Abfälle) shreds pl., waste (matter). — 2. (Bienendreck) bees' excrements pl. — 3. ⚒ (Rückstand vom Erz) tailings pl.
After³... ⓖ, after³... ⓖ [ᴸ † adv. u prp. = nach(gemacht), unecht] f. Zssgn.
After³-aufklärung (ᴵ...) f ⓖ false enlightenment; =beredsamkeit f false (or spurious) eloquence; =biene f, ent. andrena (Anthre'na); =bildung f: a) path. malformation; (Neubildung) new formation; b) semi-education, spurious culture; =blatt ♀ n stipule; =bürge m second (or counter-)bail; =dichter m would-be poet; =dolde ♀ f = Trugdolde.
After³-drüse (ᴶᵕ...) f ⓖ anat. anal gland; =fratt (Wund=, Frattsein, Wolf) m chafed state (of a horse-rider), ⚔ intertrigo.
After³-frühlingsfliegen (ᴵᴵ...) f/pl. ⓖ perlids (Perlidae); =gebilde n, path.: ⚔ heteroplasm; =gelehrsamkeit f sham erudition, F smattering; =gelehrte(r) m pseudo-scholar, F smatterer; =heu n, agr. aftermath; =kegel m, math.: ⚔ conoid; =kind n: a) posthumous child; b) bastard; =klaue f, zo. dew-claw; =kohle f waste (of) coal; =könig m mocking-king, pretender; =korn n grain left after winnowing; =leder n Schuhm.: heel-piece (inside a boot); =leh(e)n n mesne (or arrière) fief; =mehl n coarse flour, pollard; =miete [nhd.] f subtenancy; =mieter, =mietsmann m sub(or under-)tenant; =moos ♀ n alga; =mutter f = Stiefmutter; =pacht f underlease; =pächter m sublessee; =pfand n jur. collateral security; =philosophie f pseudo-philosophy; ᴸreden [nhd.] v/n. ⓖ⁕* bibl. von e-m ᴸ to backbite a p.; =unternehmung f (Unterarbeit für den eigentlichen Unternehmer) work sublet by a contractor; ᴸvermieten v/a. ⓖ⁕ to underlet, sublet; =vermieter(in f) m one who underlets; =vermietung f underletting, subletting; =vollmacht f entail(ment).

⚔ scientific; ♀ botanical; ♀ geography; ⊙ machinery; ✕ mining; ⚔ military; ⚓ marine; ⓖ commercial; ⓥ postal; 🚂 railway.

[After¹-vorfall] — 36 — [Ahnung]

After¹-vorfall m falling (or dropping or bearing down) of the rectum or anus.
After³-weisheit (ˊᵕ...) f ⓺² spurious (or sham) wisdom; **=wesen** n inferior being; **=wissenschaft** f sham science; **=witz** m **=** =weisheit. [teln. ⚔ tenesmus.]
After¹-zwang (ˊ...) m der Afterschließmus=
ägä-isch ♀ (-ᴸᵛ) [grch.] a. ⓺ Ägäisches Meer (grch. Inselmeer) Ægean Sea.
Agar=Agar ♀ (ᴸᵛᴸᵛ) [malai.] n ⓽ⓓ agar-agar, Ceylon moss (Gracila'ria licheno'ides).
Agatha, Agathe (ᵛᴸᵛ) [grch. die Gute] npr/f. ⓹⓺ ⓺γ. ⓽⓷β. (Bn./Ags.) Agatha.
ägatisch ♀ (-ᴸᵛ) a. ⓺: ~e Inseln (westlich v. Sizilien, röm. Seesieg 241 v. Chr.) Ægates.
Agave ♀ (ᵛᴸᵛᵛ) [grch.] f ⓵⓼ agave (Aga've); amerikanische ~ = hundertjährige Aloe.
Agave=faser (ˊ...) f ⓵⓶ pita(-fibre), Mexican fibre or grass, (von Aga've ri'gida).
...age (...ᴸᵍᵛ) [fr. m] meist f.: a) in Wörtern fr. Ursprungs, z B. Etage f; b) an deutsche Wörter angehängt, z B. Stellage f [des]agenda.]
Agenda (ᵛᴸᵛ) [lt.] n/pl. inv. (zu Berhandeln=
Agende (ᵛᴸᵛ) [lt.] f ⓵⓼ 1. rel. (Gottes= dienstordnung) ritual; liturgy. — 2. ⚉ (Merkbuch) memorandum-(or note-)book.
Agens ⚔ (ᴸᵛ) [lt.] n ⓷⓪ chem. agent.
Agent (ᵛᴸ) [lt.] m ⓶⓶ (Geschäftsvermittler) agent, politischer: chargé d'affaires; ⚉ commission-agent, für Sendungen: forwarding agent; zum Werben und für Inserate: canvasser; geheimer: emissary.
Agenten=gebühr (ᵛᵛᵛ...) f ⓶⓶, **=provi= sion** f commission; **=stelle** f agency.
Agentschaft (ᵛᵛᵛ) f ⓵⓼, **Agentur** (ˊᵛᵛᴵᴵ) f ⓵⓼ agency(-business).
Agenzien (ᵛᴸ(ᵛ)ᵛ) pl. v. Agens (s. ds).
Agglomerat ⚔ (ᵛᴸᵛᴸ) [lt.] n ⓪c., **~ion** f (ˊᵛᵛᵛ-tₕ(ᵛ)ᴵᴵ) f ⓵⓼ agglomeration.
agglomerieren ⚔ (ᵛᴸᵛᴸᵛ) [lt.] v/a. ⓺⓷ (aufhäufen) to agglomerate.
Agglutination ⚔ (ᵛᵛᵛ-tₕ(ᵛ)ᴸ) [lt.] f ⓵⓼ (Zusammenkleben) agglutination.
agglutinierend ⚔ (ᵛᵛᴸᵛ) p.pr. u. a. ⓺⓺ ⓶e Sprachen agglutinant languages pl.
Aggregat ⚔ (ᵛᵛᴸ) [lt.] n ⓪c. aggregate.
Aggregation ⚔ (ᵛᵛᵛ-tₕ(ᵛ)ᴸ) [lt.] f ⓵⓼ (An= sammlung) aggregation.
Aggregat=zustand (ˊᴵᴵ...) m ⓺² (fest, flüssig ob. luftförmig) physical condition.
aggregieren (ᵛᵛᴸᵛ) [lt.] v/a. ⓺⓷ to aggregate, (einverleiben) to incorporate; ⚔ Offiziere ⓶ to attach ... to (a regiment).
aggressiv (ˊᵛᴵᴵ) [lt.] a. ⓺ aggressive.
Ägide (-ᴸᵛ) [grch.] f ⓵⓼ myth. (Götterschild) ægis, weitS. shield; unter j-s ~ under a p.'s protection. [(Bn.) auch: F Giles.]
Ägidius (-ᴸ(ᵛ)ᵛ) npr/m. ⓽⓶γ. Ægidius;]
agieren (ᵛᴸᵛ) [lt.] v/n. (h.) a⁰ to act; (eine Rolle spielen) a. to play one's part.
Ägina ♀ (-ᴸᵛ) npr/n. ⓽⓹α. (grch. Insel u. Stadt) Ægina. [a. ⓺ Ägineten.]
Äginet (---ᴵᴵ) m ⓺⓽, **~in** f ⓼⓼, **⚔isch** (---ᴵᴵ) m ⓺⓽, **~in** f ⓼⓼,
Agio ⚉ (ā'-dᵍō; meist fr. ā'-ǧī-ō) [lt.] n ⓵⓶ (Aufgeld) premium.
Agiotage ⚉ (ᵛ-ᴵᴵgᵛ) f ⓵⓼ (Börsenspiel) stock-jobbing, stock-exchange operation.
Agioteur ⚉ (~tₕ'ᵣᵗ) [fr.] m ⓪d. stock-jobber, stock-exchange operator.
agiotieren ⚉ (~ᴵᴵᵛ) [fr.] v/n. (h.) ⓺⓷ (an der Börse spielen) to operate (or gamble) in stocks or on the stock-exchange.
Agir (ᴸᵛ) [isländ.] npr/m. ⓽⓪α. myth. (Wasser= gott) Ægir; Sang an ~ Song to Ægir.

Ägis=(er)schütterer (ᴵᴵᵛ=(ᵛ)ᴸᵛᵛ) [grch.] m ⓶⓶ brandisher of the ægis (= Jupiter).
Agitation (ᵛᵛᵛ-tₕ(ᵛ)ᴸ) [lt.] f ⓵⓼ (Aufregung, Aufwiegelung) agitation.
Agitator (ᵛᵛᵛᴸ) [lt.] m ⓶⓵ (Wühler) agitator
agitatorisch (ᵛᵛᵛᴸᵛ) a. ⓺⓺ (wühlerisch) agitating; ⓶e Tätigkeit demagogic(al) activity, weitS. propagandism.
agitieren (ᵛᵛᴸᵛ) [lt.] v/a. u. v/n. (h.) ⓺⓷ to agitate, to stir (up), pol. to go on the stump, to stump the country.
Aglei ♀ (-ᴸ) [ahd.] *mlt. aquile'gia] f ⓵⓼ columbine (Aquile'gia).
Agnat (ᵛᴸ) [lt.] m ⓶⓶ jur. (Verwandter von väterlicher Seite; ant. Kognat) agnate.
agnatisch (ᵛᴸᵛ) [lt.] a. ⓺ agnatic.
Agnes (ᴸᵛ, s. S. XXIng) [grch. die Keusche] npr/f. ⓹⓺γ. (pl. Agne'jen) (Bn.) Agnes.
Agnostiker (ᵛᴸᵛᵛ) [grch.] m ⓶⓶ u. **agno= stisch** a. ⓺⓺ agnostic; **Agnostizismus** (ᵛᴸᵛᴸᵛ) m ⓶⓻ agnosticism.
Agonie (ᵛ-ᴸ) [grch.] f ⓵⓼ (Todeskampf) agony, death-struggle. [clasp.]
Agraffe (ᵛᵛᴸ) [fr.; *dtsch Krapfen] f ⓵⓼
Agrar=frage (ᵛᴸᴵᴵ...) f ⓺² agrarian question; **=gesetzgebung** f land legislation.
Agrari-er (ᵛᴸᵛᵛ) [lt.] m ⓶⓶, **agrarisch** (ᵛᴸᵛ) a. ⓺⓺ agrarian.
Agrar=politik (ᵛᴸᴵᴵ...) f ⓺² agrarian policy; **=verbrechen** n agrarian crime.
Agrikultur (ᴸᵛᵛᴵᴵ) [lt.] f ⓵⓼ (Ackerbau) agriculture; **~=chemie** f ⓵⓼ agricultural chemistry; **~=staat** m agricultural state.
Agronom ⚔ (ᵛᵛᴸ) [grch.] m ⓵⓶ agriculturist; **~ie** (ᵛᵛᵛᴸ) f ⓵⓼ (o. pl.) agricultural; **~isch** (ᵛᵛᴸᵛ) a. ⓺⓺ agricultural.
Ag(t)=stein † (ᵍᴸ) [Achat...] m ⓺² 1. Bernstein. — 2. (schwarzer) ~ = Gagat.
Aguti ⚔ (ᵛᴸ) [indian.] m(n) ⓶⓪ zo. (Gold= hase, Steißtier) agouti (Dasypro'cta Agu'ti).
Ägypten ♀ (-ᴸᵛ) npr/n. ⓽⓷α. Egypt.
Ägypter (~ᴸ) m ⓶⓶, **~in** f ⓼⓻, **ägyptisch** (~ᴸ) a. ⓺⓺ Egyptian. [Egyptologist.]
Ägyptolog(e) ⚔ (-ᵛᴸ(ᵛ)) [grch.] m ⓶⓶ (⓼⓼)
ah (ᴸ) int. ah!, oh!, pooh!; ⓶ was! oh no!, not at all!, not in the least!
a-ha (ᵛᴸ) int. ah!; auch ironisch: oh so!, oh ho!, ha ha!, now then!, F what oh!
A-hasver(us) (-ᵛᵛᴸ(ᵛ)) npr/m. ⓽⓹α. (⓵⓺γ.) 1. Ahasuerus (Esther 1,1 = Xerxes). — 2. (ewiger Jude) wandering Jew.
ahd. abbr. = althochdeutsch.
Ahl=beere ♀ (ᴵᴵ...; Hom. A(a)l=) f ⓺² s. Albeere; vgl. a. Ahl(en)=...
Ahle ⓿ (ᴸᵛ; Hom.s. Aal [ahd.= awl] f ⓵⓼ Schuhm.: awl; typ. bodkin, point.
ahl(en)=förmig ⓿ (ᴵᴵ(ᵛ)...) a. ⓺⓺ awl-shaped; **=macher** m ⓶⓶, **=schmied** m awl-maker, -smith. [⓶ to gauge ...]
ahmen ⚔ (ᴸᵛ) [mhd.: Ohm²] v/a. ⓺⓸ Fässer
Ahming ⚓ (ᴸᵛ) f ⓵⓼ (Skala am Schiff, welche dessen Tiefgang angiebt) scale indicating the draught of a ship.
Ahn (ᴸ) [ahd.] m ⓺⓺ ancestor; fast † = Großvater; **~en** pl. [uhd.] (Vorfahren) ancestors, forefathers, coll. ancestry; Adelige pl. von sechzehn ~en, auch: noblemen with sixteen quarterings.
ahnden (ᴸᵛ) [ahd.] v/a. ⓺⓷ 1. (rächen) to avenge; (tadeln) to censure, blame, (be= strafen) to punish; (züchtigen) to chasten, chastise; das Verbrechen wurde an ihm geahndet he suffered (punishment) for ..., he atoned for ... — 2. † = ahnen.

Ahndung (ᴸᵛ) f ⓸⓺ revenge; reproof; (Strafe) punishment, chastisement.
Ahne¹ (ᴸᵛ) [ahd.: Ahn] f ⓸⓼ ancestress; † od. obb. = Großmutter. [awn, beard.]
Ahne² ♀ (ᴸᵛ) [ahd.: awn] f ⓸⓼ (Granne)
ähneln (ᴸᵛ) [nhd. 18. sæ. aus † ähnlichen] v/n. (h.) u. v/rpr. ⓽⓶a. einem ⓶ to have (or bear) a slight resemblance to a p.; sich (ea.) ⓶ to resemble one another.
Ahnen¹ (ᴸᵛ) pl. von Ahn u. Ahne (s. ds).
ahnen² (ᴸᵛ) [mhd. aus mich ahn(de)t von † ahnden ⓶] v/a. u. v/n. (h.) ⓺⓷ (vermuten) to divine; (vorhersehen) to foresee, foreknow; es ahnt mir nichts Gutes I have strange forebodings; et. ⓶ lassen to foreshadow a th.; die Vorzeichen lassen das Kommende ⓶ coming events cast their shadows before.
Ahnen=bild (ᴵᴵᵛ...) n ⓺² ancestral portrait; **=gut** n = Fideikommiß; **=kultus** m in China ⓶c: worship of (one's) ancestors; **=probe** f proof of noble descent or of nobility; **=reihe** f (noble) line of ancestors; **=saal** m ancestral hall; **=stolz** m u. ⓼**stolz** a. pride, proud of one's (noble) ancestry or pedigree; **=tafel** f genealogical table or tree, pedigree. [m ancestor.]
Ahn-frau (ᴵᴵ...) f ⓺² ancestress; **=herr**
ähnlich (ᴸᵛ) [ahd. aus an- u. (g)leich: like] a. ⓺ bsb. v. Personen: resembling; e-m ⓶ sein ob. sehen to have (or show) a likeness to a p.; to be (or look) like a p.; er sieht f-m Vater sprechend ⓶ he is the image (F the very spit) of his father; ein zum Sprechen ⓶es Porträt a speaking likeness; er sieht sich nicht mehr ⓶ he does not look like the same person, he would not recognize him; das sieht Ihnen ganz ⓶ that's just like you, F that's you all over. — 2. bsb. v. Dingen: similar (or alike) to; ich habe nie et. ~es gesehen I never saw anything like it, I have never seen the like (of it); u. ⓶c(ē) (abbr. u. ä.) and the like; ⓶e Begriffe analogous ideas; ⓶e Stücke corresponding (math. homologous) parts pl.; ⓶ m. to assimilate.
ähnlichen † (ᴸᵛᵛ) v/n. (h.), v/a. u. v/refl. ⓺⓷ sich (dat.) ⓶ = ähneln.
Ähnlichkeit (ᴸᵛ-) f ⓸⓺ 1. resemblance (to or with a p.); frappante ~ striking likeness; e-e starke ~ haben mit j/i to bear a strong resemblance to ∥. — 2. fig. (Gleichförmigkeit) analogy, math., &c. similarity, (Verwandtschaft) affinity; diese Sprache hat viel ~ mit dem Russischen ... is very much like Russian.
Ähnlichkeits=kennzeichen (ᴵᴵᵛ-...) n ⓺² (v. Personen) mark of resemblance; **=punkt** m, math., phil. point of resemblance or similarity; **=schluß** m argument (or inference) by analogy, **=verhältnis** n analogy, **=zeichen** n, math. sign of similarity.
Ahnung (ᴸᵛ) [ahnen²] f ⓸⓺ 1. (Vorgefühl) presentiment, foreboding, schlimme: misgiving. — 2. (Vorstellung) idea, (Argwohn) suspicion; ich hatte keine ⓶ davon I had no idea (or I was unaware) of it; F er hatte keine blasse ⓶ davon he had not the slightest inkling (or the faintest notion) of it.

Zeichen (s. S. XVII): F familiär; P Volkssprache; Γ Gaunersprache; ⚔ selten; † alt (auch gestorben); * neu (auch geboren); ⁺⁺ unrichtig;

[ahnungsbang] — 37 — [Aktienhändler]

ahnungs-bang (⌣–...) a. ⓖ = Qvoll a. Qlos a. free from misgivings, unsuspecting; =**vermögen** n ⓖ faculty of foreseeing, prophetic gift; Qvoll a.: a) full of anxious presentiments or forebodings; b) von Sachen: ominous.

a-hoi ↓ (–⌣) int. (Zuruf) ahoy!

A-horn (⌣⌣) [ahd.: lt. a'cer] m ⓜ e. maple(-tree), f. Berg=2; vgl. Flader, Lehne³, Maßholder.³

a-hornen (⌣⌣⌣) a. ⓖ (made of) maple.

A-horn-gewächse ⟟ (⌣⌣...) f/pl. ⓖ ⟟ aceraceæ pl.; =**honig** m maple-honey; =**maser** ⟟ f bird's-eye maple; =**säure** f, chm. aceric acid.

Ährchen ⟟ (–⌣) n ⓖ spikelet, ⌣ spicula.

Ähre ⟟ (–⌣; Hom. Ehre, f. E. X) [ahd.: ear] f ⓖ spike-(of grass, &c.), ear (of corn); in ~n schießen to form (or to shoot into) ears, to ear; ~n lesen to glean.

ähren-bekränzt (⌣⌣...) a. ⓖ crowned with ears (of corn); =**bund** n ⓖ sheaf; =**feld** n cornfield in ear; Qförmig ⟟ a. ⌣ spicate(d); =**früchte** f/pl. (ant. Hülsenfrüchte), =**gräser** n/pl. cereals pl.; =**lese**(n n) f gleaning; =**leser**(in f) m gleaner; =**monat** m = August; Qreich a. rich in corn(fields); Qständig ⟟ a. ⌣ spicate(d); Qtragend ⟟ a. ⌣ spiked, ⌣ spicose.

ährig ⟟ (–⌣) a. ⓖ spiked, ⌣ spiciferous; bes. ... ährig in Zssgn, f. lang2 ⌣c.

Ahriman (––⌣) [perf. böser Geist] npr/m. ⓖa. rel. Ahriman (ant. Ormuzd).

ai (⌣) int. = ei. [toed sloth.

A-i, A-ï (⌣–) [brasil.] n ⓖ zo. three-

⬛ **Aich...** f. Eich...

Aide (ä'-b⌣) [fr.] m ⓖ Karten=, Kegel= ⌣c. spiel. partner. [busch) aigrette.

Aigrette ⤫ (ä-gr⌣⌣) [fr.] f ⓖ (Reiherfeder=

Ailantus ⟟ (–⌣⌣) [moluff. Götterbaum] m, inv. ailanthus (Aila'nthus).

A-is ♩(–⌣) n, inv. A sharp.

à jour (ä Gū'r) [fr. zu Tage] ⌣ gefaßt set hollow, in an à jour setting.

ajustieren (⌣Gü–⌣) [fr.] v/a. ⓖ to adjust.

Akademie (⌣⌣⌣–) [grch.] f ⓖ academy; Mitglied der engl. ~ (der Künste), a. oft: (Royal) Academician (R. A.); ~**stück** (⌣...) n ⓖ academical study or figure.

Akademiker (⌣⌣–⌣⌣) m ⓖ academician.

akademisch (⌣⌣–⌣) a. ⓖ 1. academic(al); Ler Bürger resident member of a university, weitS. (under)graduate; Le Tracht academicals pl., in England a. cap and gown; Les Viertel (¼ Stunde Verspätung) a quarter of an hour's grace; e-m e-e Le Würde erteilen to confer a(n academical) degree upon a p. — 2. fig. (schulmäßig; b.s. steif, pedantisch) scholastic, stiff, pedantic.

Akadi-en † ⟟ (⌣–(⌣)⌣) [indian.] npr/n. ⓖ a. Acadia, jetzt: Nova Scotia.

Akadi-er (⌣–(⌣)⌣) m ⓖ, **akadisch** (⌣–⌣; Hom. akkadisch) a. ⓖ Acadian.

Akajou¹ ⟟ (⌣–Gü) [fr., port., * südamer.] m ⓖ: ~(=**holz** n) (Art Mahagoni) mahogany (wood) (Cedre'la fi'ssilis).

Akajou² ⟟ (⌣–) [fr.; * inb. kä'dschu] m ⓖ phärm. (eßbarer Fruchtstiel v. Anaca'rdium occidenta'le, vgl. Cachou²) ~(=**baum** m) acajou(-tree), auch: cashewnut (-tree); ~**nuß** f = Cachounuß.

Akalephe ⌣ (⌣⌣–⌣) [grch.] f ⓖ zo. acaleph.

Akanthus ⟟ (⌣⌣⌣) [lt., * grch.] m, inv. ~**blätter** arch. acanthus leaves pl.

akataleptisch (⌣⌣⌣–⌣) [grch.] a. ⓖ pros. (ohne Fehlsilbe am Schlusse) acatalectic.

A-katholik südb. (⌣⌣–⌣) [grch.] m ⓖ (nicht katholischer Christ, bsd. Protestant) non-Catholic (Christian).

Akazi-e ⟟ (⌣–(⌣)⌣) [lt., * grch.] f ⓖ 1. (echte) ~ acacia (Aca'cia [ara'bica]). — 2. rote ~ hispid Robinia, Rose Acacia (Robi'nia hi'spida); weiße (ob. unechte) ~ common Robinia, a. locust-tree (R.pseudaca'cia).

Akelei ⟟ (–⌣–) f ⓖ = Aglei. [Acre.

Akka ⟟ (⌣–) npr/n. ⓖ a. (Hafenst. Palästinas)

akkadisch(⌣⌣–; Hom. akad...) a. ⓖ Accadian.

akkaparieren (⌣⌣⌣–⌣) [fr.] v/n. ⓖ (Waren wucherhaft aufkaufen) to produce (or make, create) a corner in a commodity, to corner the market.

Akklamation (⌣⌣–tß(⌣)–) [lt.] f ⓖ (Zuruf): durch ~ wählen to elect by acclamation.

akklamieren (⌣⌣–⌣) [lt.] v/a. ⓖ to acclaim.

Akklimatisation (⌣–––tß(⌣)–) [lt] f ⓖ (Einbürgerung) acclimatization.

akklimatisier/en (⌣–––⌣) [lt.] I v/a. ⓖ (einbürgern) to acclimatize; sich ⌣ to become acclimatized. — II ~ n ⓖ u. A/**ung** f ⓖ acclimatization.

Akkolade (⌣⌣–⌣) [fr.] f ⓖ (Klammer) typ. brace; ehm. (Ritterschlag) u. ⌣ accolade.

Akkommodation (⌣⌣⌣–tß(⌣)–) [lt.] f ⓖ (Anpassung) accommodation.

akkommodieren (⌣⌣⌣–⌣) ⓖ I v/a. (an bequemen, anpassen) to accommodate. — II sich ⌣ v/refl. to adapt o.s. to.

Akkompagnement ♩ (ä-tg-pä-nj'mg') [fr.] n ⓖ (Begleitung) accompaniment.

akkompagnieren ♩ (ä-tg-pän-ji'⌣) [fr.] v/a. ⓖ (begleiten) to accompany, ♩ auch to play the accompaniment to.

Akkord (⌣–) [fr.] m ⓖ ⓑ. 1. ♩ chord; harmony (a. fig.). — 2. (Stücklohn) price agreed upon; bei Lieferungen: contract; in ~ arbeiten (übernehmen) to do (to undertake) piece- (or job-)work; auf ~ by contract; im ~ by the job; j. der eine Arbeit in ~ nimmt contractor. — 3. ⓖ (Vergleich) settlement, mit den Gläubigern: arrangement, composition; den ~ zustande bringen to come to terms (with one's creditors).

Akkord-arbeit (⌣⌣...) f ⓖ piece- (or job-, task-)work, work done by contract; =**arbeiter**(in f) m piece-worker, jobber; =**bedingungen** f/pl. terms.

akkordieren (⌣⌣–⌣) [fr.] v/a. u. v/n. (h.) ⓖ bsd. ⓖ to arrange, compromise; to compound with one's creditors.

Akkordion ♩ (⌣–⌣⌣) n ⓖ(ⓖ) accordion.

Akkord-satz (⌣–⌣...) m ⓖ job-rate; =**vor-schläge** m/pl. terms offered by a contractor or for piece-work.

Akkouchement (⌣füsch-mg') [fr.] n ⓖ (Wochenbett) accouchement, confinement.

Akkoucheur (⌣tū-schö'r) m ⓖ d. accoucheur.

Akkoucheuse (⌣tū-schö'-f⌣) f ⓖ midwife.

akkouchieren (⌣tū-schi'⌣) ⓖ v/a. to deliver, als v/n. to attend a confinement.

akkreditieren (⌣––⌣–) [fr.] v/a. ⓖ to agree, ⌣ (beglaubigen) bei to accredit with.

Akkreditiv (⌣––⌣–f) [fr.] n ⓖ c. credentials pl.; ⓖ letter(s pl.) of credit.

Akkumulation (⌣⌣⌣–tß(⌣)–) [lt.] f ⓖ (An häufung) accumulation.

Akkumulator ⓧ (⌣⌣–⌣⌣) [lt.] m ⓖ (zum Aufspeichern e-r Kraft) accumulator.

akkumulieren (⌣⌣⌣–⌣) [lt.] v/a. ⓖ (an häufen) to accumulate, to pile up.

akkurat (⌣–⌣) [lt.] a. ⓖ = sorgfältig.

Akkuratesse (⌣⌣⌣–⌣) [lt.=fr.] f ⓖ (o. pl.) accuracy (= Sorgfalt).

Akkusativ (⌣–⌣–f) [lt.] m ⓖ c., ~**us**(⌣⌣–⌣w) m ⓖ (Wenfall) accusative, objective case; den ~ regierendes Zeitwort active (or transitive) verb. [acolyte.

Akoluth (⌣–⌣) [grch.] m ⓖ c. (Altardiener)

Akonit ⟟ (⌣⌣–) [grch.] n ⓖ c. aconite (= Sturmhut, Eisenhut).

Akonto-zahlung (⌣–⌣⌣⌣) [it. a conto, f. a ⓖ] f ⓖ payment on account.

Akotyledone(n pl.) ⌣ ⟟ (–⌣⌣⌣–) [grch. Keimblattlose] f ⓖ (Sporenpflanzen) acotyledon(s pl.) (= Kryptogame(n).

akquirieren (⌣⌣–⌣) [lt.] v/a. ⓖ (erwerben) to acquire. [bung) acquisition.

Akquisition (⌣⌣–tß(⌣)–) [lt.] f ⓖ (Erwer=

Akrobat (⌣⌣–) [grch.] m ⓖ (Seiltänzer) acrobat, (clever) gymnast, rope-dancer.

akrobatisch (⌣⌣–⌣) [grch.] a. ⓖ acrobatic.

Akropolis ⟟ (–⌣⌣⌣) [grch.] f, inv. (Stadtburg, bsd. die von Athen) acropolis.

Akrostichon (–⌣⌣⌣) [grch.] n ⓖ, a. ⓖ pros. (Namengedicht) acrostic.

Akt (⌣) [lt.] m ⓖ ⓑ. 1. (Handlung) act(ion); ~ der Verzweiflung desperate deed; von et. ~ nehmen to take (official) notice of a th. — 2. thea. (Aufzug) act.

Akte (⌣⌣) [lt.] f ⓖ, bsd. ~**n** pl. deeds, (legal) documents pl.; in die ~n eintragen to register; nach Durchsicht der ~n after searching (or examining) the deeds; zu den ~n (ad acta) legen to put (or lay) on the shelf, to shelve (mst fig.).

Akten-bündel (⌣⌣...) n ⓖ bundle of documents; =**deckel** m cover for legal documents; =**einsicht** f jur. inspection of deeds; searching (legal) documents; =**heft** n file (or roll) of legal documents, register; =**kammer** f office of the rolls; =**mappe** f portfolio; Qmäßig a. ⓖ documentary; =**mensch** m red-tapist; =**schnur** f red tape; =**schrank** m lawyer's (office-) shelves pl.; =**schreiber** m lawyer's (copying-)clerk; =**ständer** m shelf for deeds; =**staub** m dust of documents, fig. close air in a lawyer's office; =**stoß** m pile of (legal) documents or deeds; =**stück** n official document or deed; Qwidrig a. ⓖ contrary to authentic records; =**zimmer** n e-s Advokaten room to keep deeds in, vgl. =kammer.

...akter (..."⌣⌣) m ⓖ in Zssgn, zB. Ein2 play of one act.

Akti-e ⓖ (⌣tß(⌣)⌣) [nhd. 18. sæ.; * holl., fr.] f ⓖ share (in a joint-stock company); ~**n** ausgeben, besitzen to issue, to hold shares; wie stehen die ~**n**? how are the shares?, fig. how are things getting on? mit ~**n** wuchern, in ~**n** spekulieren to gamble (or speculate, F dabble) in stocks or shares.

Akti-en-abschnitt (⌣tß(⌣)...) m ⓖ coupon, (dividend-)warrant; =**ausgabe** f issue of shares or stock; =**bank** f joint-stock bank; =(**bier**)**brauerei** f joint-stock brewery; =**gesellschaft** f (abbr. A. G.) joint-stock company; =**handel** m stock-jobbing; =**händler** m stock-

[...aftig] — 38 — [Albion]

jobber, dealer in stocks; =**inhaber** m shareholder, proprietor (of shares); =**kapital** n (company's) share-capital; =**makler** m stockbroker, stockjobber; =**markt** m market for shares or securities; =**promesse** f share-certificate; =**schwindel** m market-rigging; =**spekulant** m, =**spieler** m market-manipulator; speculator in shares; =**verein** m = =**gesellschaft**; =**wesen** n stock-exchange transactions pl.; =**zeichnung** f subscription (for a joint-stock venture). ...**aktig** (..."ᴗ-) a. ⑥; in Zssgn, z.B. ein**2** of one act; ein**2e Posse** farce in one act.
Aktinometer ⟨ (ᴗ-ᴗ-ᴗ-) [grch.] n ② Strahlenmesser) actinometer.
Aktion[1] ♀ (ᴗᴗ-) npr/n. ⑩α. (grch. Vorgebirge, Schlacht 31 v. Chr.) Actium.
Aktion[2] (ᴗ-tz(ᴗ)-) [It.] f ⑯ ★ (†), man., &c. action. [v. Anteilscheinen) shareholder.]
Aktionär ⟨ (ᴗtz(ᴗ)-) [fr.] m ⑩C. (Inhaber
Aktions=**radius** ↓ (ᴗtz(ᴗ)-...) m (Dampfstrecke) radius of action; =**zentren** n/pl. der Atmosphäre centres of action or disturbance.
aktiv (-ᴗ-f) [It.] I a. ⑯ (tätig) active; ⚔ **2** Dienstzeit (bei der Fahne; ant. Reserve 2c.) (time of) active service (with the colours); Des Heer standing army. — II ~ n ⑩d. **1.** gr. active form or voice; **2.** ⑱ bsd. ~**a**, ~**en** pl. assets pl., estate; ~a u. Passiva assets and liabilities pl.
Aktiv=(**be**)**stand** (ᴗ-f...) m ⑫: a) ⚔ des Heeres effective (or actual) strength of ...; b) ⑱ =**kapital**; =**handel** m country's own (export- and import-) trade.
aktivieren öft. (ᴗ-w-ᴗ-) v/a. ⑬ to put into action; to make serviceable; to realize.
Aktivität (ᴗ-w-f) [It.] f ⑯ activity.
Aktiv=**kapital** ⑱ (ᴗ-f...) n ⑫, =**masse** f assets pl. of a bankrupt's estate; =**schulden** f/pl. outstanding debts, book-debts pl.; =**stand** m = =**bestand**.
Aktivum (-ᴗ-w-) [It.] n ㉘ = aktiv II.
Aktiv=**vermögen** (ᴗ-f...) n ⑫ = =**kapital**.
Akt=**modell** (-ᴗ-...) n ⑫ life model; =**saal** m room for (living) models; =**schluss** m, thea. end of an act. [actuality.]
Aktualität ⟨ (ᴗᴗ-ᴗ-) [It.] f ⑯ (Wirklichkeit)
Aktuar (ᴗᴗ-) [It.] m ⑩c., ~**ius** (ᴗᴗ(ᴗ)-) m ㉗ (Gerichtschreiber) actuary, registrar.
aktuell (ᴗᴗ-) [fr.] a. ⑯ actual; de Energie (lebendige Kraft) effective (or active) force.
Aktus (ᴗᴗ) [It.] m, inv. public act; (Schulfeier) speech-day.
Akupunktur ⟨ (ᴗᴗᴗ-) [It. Nadelstich] f ⑯ (orientalisches Heilverfahren) acupuncture.
Akustik ⟨ (ᴗᴗ-) [grch.] f ⑯ acoustics.
Akustiker ⟨ (ᴗᴗᴗ-) [grch.] m ㉒ acoustician.
akustisch ⟨ (ᴗᴗ-) [grch.] a. ⑯ acoustic(al).
akut ⟨ (ᴗ-) [It.] I a. ⑯ path. (heftig) acute. — II ~ m ⑩c. gram acute accent.
Akzeleration ⟨ (ᴗᴗᴗ-tz(ᴗ)-) [It.] f ⑯ (Beschleunigung) acceleration. [accelerate.]
akzelerieren ⟨ (ᴗᴗᴗ-) [It.] v/a. ⑬ to
Akzent (ᴗ-) [It.] m ⑩b. (Tonzeichen; Aussprache) stress, accent; e-n guten (reinen) ~ **haben** to speak with (or to have) a good (or pure) accent; vom Englischen auch: to speak without any foreign accent; irischer ~ Irish brogue.
Akzent=**lehre** (-ᴗ-...) f ⑫: a) theory of accentuation; b) (als Buch) treatise on accent(s); **2los** a. ⑯ without accent, unaccented; =**regel** f rule on accent(s).

akzentu=**ieren** (ᴗᴗᴗ-ᴗ-) I v/a. ⑬ to accent(uate), to put stress upon, to stress. — II ~ n ㉓ u. **Akzentu**-**ierung** f ⑯ accentuation, stress.
Akzent=**zeichen** (-ᴗ-...) n ⑫ (tonic) accent.
Akzepisse (ᴗ-ᴗ-ᴗ) [It. empfangen (zu) haben] n, inv. ob. ㉖ (Empfangschein) receipt.
Akzept ⑱ (ᴗ-) [It.] n ⑩b. (Annahme) acceptance; einen Wechsel zum ~ vorlegen to present a bill for acceptance; seine ~e einlösen to meet one's drafts; mangels ~(e)s in default of acceptance.
akzeptabel (ᴗᴗᴗ-) [It.] a. ⑯ (annehmbar) acceptable. [Wechsels) acceptor.]
Akzeptant ⑱ (ᴗᴗ-) m ㊷ (Annehmer eines
Akzeptation ⑱ (ᴗᴗ-tz(ᴗ)-) [It.] f ⑯ u. ~**s**=... (ᴗ-...) ⑫ = **Akzept**(=...).
Akzept=**blanko** (ᴗ-...) n ⑫ = =**kredit**; =**buch** n (book for) bills payable; =**geschäfte** n/pl. bill-brokerage.
akzeptieren ⑱ (ᴗᴗ-) v/a. ⑬ (annehmen) e-n Wechsel **2** to accept (or honour) ...; nicht **2** to refuse acceptance of, to dishonour; der Wechsel wurde akzeptiert, a. the bill met with due honour.
Akzept=**kredit** (ᴗ-...) m ⑫ blank credit; =**provision** f provision (or remittance) made for (honouring) a draft.
Akzessist (ᴗᴗ-) [It.] m ㊷ Beamtentum: unsalaried assistant or candidate.
akzessorisch (ᴗᴗᴗ-) [It.] a. ⑯ accessory.
Akzessorium (ᴗᴗ-(ᴗ)-ᴗ-) [It.] n ㉘ (Zubehör) accessory, appendage.
Akzidens (ᴗᴗ-) [It.] n ㉚ **1.** phls. (zufällige Eigenschaft; ant. Substanz) accidental property; (Zufall) accident. — **2.** meist pl. (Neben-Einkünfte) perquisites, F pickings pl. [sual, phls. auch: contingent.]
akzidentell (ᴗᴗᴗ-) a. ⑯ accidental, ca-
Akzidenz ⑱ (ᴗᴗ-) f ⑯ typ. (mst im pl.) (Rechnungsformulare u. dgl. kleine Sachen) display- (or job-)work.
Akzidenz=**arbeit** (ᴗ-...) f ⑫ job-work; =**drucker** m jobbing printer; =**druckerei** f jobbing-office, job-house, jobbing-firm; =**hobel** m shootboard. [(bsd. **2.**).]
Akzidenzien (ᴗᴗᴗ-ᴗ-) pl. v. Akzidens.
Akzidenz=**kasten** (ᴗᴗ-...) m ⑫ jobbing case; =**presse** f jobbing machine; =**schrift** f job-type; =**setzer** m jobbing compositor. [to excise.]
akzisbar † (ᴗᴗ-) a. ⑯ excisable, subject
Akzise † (ᴗᴗ-) [mlt.] f ⑱ **1.** (Verbrauchssteuer) excise; (Torsteuer) city-toll, town-dues pl.; ~ **auf etwas legen** to levy excise (weit**S.** to levy duty) upon a th. — **2.** (Ort) excise-office.
à la ... (ᴗᴗ ...) [fr.] adv. after (the manner of); in the style of; **2 like** (or à la) Heine; **2 chinoise** (...**schi**-nä**'s**) in the Chinese fashion.
Alaaf! (-ᴗ-) int. in Köln = hoch!
Alabaster (ᴗᴗᴗ-) [grch.] m ㉒ alabaster.
alabaster=**artig** (ᴗ-...) a. ⑯ alabastrian; =**bruch** n ⑫ alabaster-quarry.
alabastern (ᴗᴗᴗ-) a. ⑯ (of) alabaster.
Aland, **Alant**[1] (ᴗ-) [ahd.] m ⑩c. ichth. aland, chub (Leuci'scus); ide (Cypri'nus).
Alands=**inseln** (ᴗ-...) npr/f/pl. (finn. Inselgruppe) Aland Islands pl.
Alant[2] ♀ (ᴗ-, ᴗ-) [ahd., *?] m ⑩b.: echter ~ elecampane (I'nula Hele'nium); ~**beere** ♀ f s. Albeere. ⑯⑱α. Alaric.
Alarich ♀ (ᴗᴗ-) [ahd. Allherrscher] npr/m.

Alarm (ᴗ-) [fr., *It. zu den Waffen!] m ⑩b. alarm; ~ **blasen** ob. **schlagen** to sound an alarm, to call to arms; blinder ~ false alarm.
Alarm=**bereitschaft** (ᴗ-...) f ⑫ readiness for an alarm; =**glocke** f tocsin.
alarmieren (ᴗᴗᴗ-) [fr.] v/a. ⑬ to alarm.
Alarm=(**sammel**)**platz** (ᴗ-...) m ⑫ alarm-post or -meet; =**schuss** ⚔ m alarm-shot.
Alaun (ᴗ-) [mhd.; *It. alu'men] m ⑩c.chm. (Doppelverbindg. b. Aluminiumsulfats) alum.
alaun=**artig** (ᴗ-...) a. ⑯ aluminous; =**bad** n ⑫, =**beize** f, =**brühe** f alum-bath.
alaunen ⟨ (ᴗ-ᴗ-) I v/a. ⑱ to (steep in) alum. — II ~ n ㉓ aluming.
Alaun=**erde** (ᴗ-...) f ⑫ alumina (s. Tonerde); =**erde**=**metall** n, chm. aluminium; =**fabrik** f alum-works pl.; **2gar** ⊕ a. ⑯ (weißgar) dressed with alum, alumed; =**gerber** ⊕ m (Weißgerber) tawer; **2haltig** a. alumin(ifer)ous; =**hütte** ⊕ f = =**fabrik**.
alaunig (ᴗ-ᴗ-) a. ⑯ aluminous.
Alaun=**kristall** (ᴗ-...) n ⑫ alum crystal; =**kuchen** m alum-cake; **leder** n alumed (or white) leather; =**mehl** n, =**pulver** n powdered alum; **2saures Leder** alum-leather, white leather, **2saures Salz** aluminate; =**schiefer** m alum-slate; =**sieder** m alum-boiler; =**siederei** f =**fabrik**; =**ton** m = =**erde**; =**wasser** n aluminous water; =**werk** n = **fabrik**; =**zucker** m, pharm. alum-sugar, saccharine alum.
Albanese (ᴗ-ᴗ-) m ㊹, **Albanesin** (ᴗ-ᴗ-) f ㊺, **albanesisch** (ᴗ-ᴗ-) a. ⑯ = **Albanier(in)**, **albanisch**.
Albanien ♀ (ᴗ-(ᴗ)-ᴗ-) npr/n. ⑬α. Albania.
Albanier (ᴗ-(ᴗ)-) m ㉒, ~**in** f ㊶ u. **albanisch** (ᴗ-ᴗ-) a. ⑯ Albanian.
Albatros ꝉ (ᴗᴗ-) [span.; *ar. al batros = St. Peter] m, inv. ob. ⑬a. orn. albatross (Diome'dea). [hemb) alb.]
Albe[1] (ᴗ-) [ahd.; *It. a'lba] f ⑱ (Chor-
Albe[2] (ᴗ-) [mhd.; *It. a'lbula] f ⑱ ichth. ablet, bleak. [pappel.]
Alber ♀ (ᴗ-) [ahd., *It.] f ⑱ = Silber-
Al-beere ♀ (ᴗ-(ᴗ)-) [ndd.] = **Alant**[2]?] f ⑫ = Johannisbeere (schwarze).
albern (ᴗ-ᴗ-) [mhd. b.s. P: Alf (ahd. g.s. = all (ganz) wahr)] I a. ⑯ silly, F soft; Des Benehmen absurd conduct or ways pl.; Des Frauenzimmer, De Gans silly goose; Der Mensch simpleton; Des Geschwätz, Des Zeug foolish talk, nonsense, F twaddle. — II ~ v/n. (h.) ㉒a. to talk nonsense or F to talk twaddle, to play the fool. [ery.]
Albernheit (ᴗ-ᴗ-) f ⑯ silliness; tomfool-
Albert (ᴗ-ᴗ-) npr/m. ⑮ u. ⑯α. (Vn.) Albert.
Albertine (ᴗ-ᴗ-) npr/f. ㊴ u. ㊽β. Albertina. ꝉ (1485) Albertine line.]
albertinisch (ᴗ-ᴗ-) a. ⑯ ~**e Linie** hist.
Alb=**fuss** (ᴗ-...) m ⑫ = Drudenfuss; =**geschoss** n = Hexenschuss.
Albigenser (ᴗ-ᴗ-) [fr. v. ♀ Albi(geois)] m/pl. ㉒ hist. 1208 f. (religiöse Sekte Südfrankreichs) Albigenses pl.
albigensisch (ᴗ-ᴗ-) a. ⑯ Albigensian.
Albinismus ⟨ (ᴗ-ᴗ-) [neu-It.] m ㉗ (o. pl.) zo., ⚕ (Farbstoffmangel) albin(o)ism.
Albino (ᴗ-ᴗ-) [span.] m ⑮ albino; ~**neger** (ᴗ-...) m ⑫ leucoëthiops.
Albion ♀ (ᴗ-ᴗ-) [flt.] npr/n. ⑬α. poet. (Großbritannien) Albion; ein Sohn ~**s** (Brite) a son of Albion.

Signs (see page XVII): F familiar; P vulgar; Γ flash; ⟨ rare; ꝉ obsolete (died); * new word (born); ++ incorrect; ♪ music;

Albion=metall ⊕ (⌣⌣⌣...) *n* (zinnplattiertes Blei) albion-metal; **=presse** *f* (Handdruckpresse v. Cope) Albion press.

Albrecht (⌣́⌣) [ahd. der Adelglänzende] *npr/m.* ⑮ u. ⑯α. (Bn.) Albert.

Album (⌣́⌣) [lt.] *n* ㊵ u. ㉘ album.

Albumen ⚗ (⌣́⌣) [lt.] *n* ㉓ od. ㊱ (Eiweiß) albumen. [(Eiweißstoff) albumin.

Albumin ⚗ (⌣⌣́) [neu=lt.] *n* ⓑc. chm.⌢

Albumin=papier ⊕ *n* ㊵ phot. albumin-⌣
➤ Alc ... f. Alk ...   [paper.⌢

Alchemille ♀ ♃ (⌣⌣́⌣) *f* ㊽ = Sinnau.

Alchen (⌣́⌣) [Aal dim.] *n* ㉓ small (or young) eel, grig.

Alchimie (⌣⌣́) [mhd., *ar.=grch.] *f* ㊽ (Scheidekunst, Goldmacherei) alchemy.

Alchimist (⌣⌣⌣́) *m* ㊷ alchemist.

Alchimisterei (⌣⌣⌣⌣́) *f* ㊻ alchemistry, black (or hermetic) art.

alchimistisch (⌣⌣⌣́⌣) *a.* ⓖⓖ alchemistic(al).

Aldehyd ⚗ (⌣⌣́) [neu=lt. a'l(cohol) dehyd(-rogena'tus)] *m* (*n*) ⓑc. chm. aldehyde.

Aldina (⌣⌣́⌣) *f* ㊾ typ. (von Aldus Manu'tius, † 1587 i. Venedig) Aldine (edition).

Aldine (⌣⌣́⌣) *f* ㊾ typ. Aldine type. [*pl.*⌢

Aldinen (⌣⌣⌣) *pl.* Aldine editions or prints⌢

aldinisch (⌣⌣́⌣) *a.* ⓖⓖ Aldine.

Ale ♃ (⌣́⌣) *n* pl. von Aal (f. d.) (= Aale).

Alemanne (⌣⌣́⌣) *m* ㊵ Aleman(n)i.

alemannisch (⌣⌣⌣́⌣) *a.* ⓖⓖ Aleman(n)ic.

Aleppo=beule (⌣́⌣⌣⌣...) *f* ㊷ path. Aleppo boil; **=zitz** ⚙ *m* Aleppo calico.

alert [fr., *it.] *a.* ⓖⓖ (munter) alert.

Aleuron (⌣⌣́) [grch.] *n* ㊱ (Pflanzeneiweiß) aleuron.   [Aleutian Isles *pl.*⌢

ale=utisch (⌣⌣⌣́⌣) *a.* ⓖⓖ: ~e Inseln, **Ale=uten**⌢

Alexander [grch.] *npr/m.* ㉒α. (Bn.) Alexander, *dim.* Aleck, *co.* Sandy; *hist.* ~ der Große Alexander the Great.

Alexandri=en ♀ (⌣⌣⌣⌣) [grch.] *npr/n.* ㉓α. (bfd. Stadt in Ägypten) Alexandria.

Alexandriner (⌣⌣⌣⌣́⌣) **I** *npr/m.* ㉒, **~in** *f* ㊼ Alexandrian. — **II** *m* ㉒ *pros.* (jechsfüßiger jambifcher Bers) Alexandrine (metre).

alexandrinisch (⌣⌣⌣⌣́⌣) *a.* ⓖⓖ Alexandrian, Alexandrine. [Alice, Alicia.⌢

Alexi=a ♀ (⌣⌣⌣⌣) *npr/f.* ㊻ u. ㉓α. (Bn.)⌢

Alf (⌣́) *m* ㉓ b. f. Elf(e).

Alfanz † (⌣́⌣) [mhd.= Faut] ⓐa. **1.** (Hans Narr) buffoon. — **2.** = ~erei.

alfanzen †(⌣́⌣⌣) *v/n.*(h.)㉚ to fool about.

Alfanzerei faft † (⌣⌣⌣́⌣) *f* ㊻ tomfoolery.

alfanzig †(⌣́⌣⌣) *a.* ⓖⓖ silly, nonsensical.

Alfenid (⌣⌣́⌣)[fr.,*span.] *n*ⓑc. alfenid(e), white metal.   [⑯γ. (Bn.) Alphonso.⌢

Alfons (⌣́⌣) [span., *w/got.] *npr/m.* ⑮ u.⌢

alfonsinisch (⌣⌣́⌣⌣) *a.* ⓖⓖ a.*tr.* ~e Tafeln *f/pl.* Alphonsine tables.

Alfred ⚓ (⌣́⌣) *npr/m.* ⑮ ⑯α. od. ㉑α. (Bn.) Alfred, *dim.* Alf.   [Affresko.⌢

Alfresko [it. auf dem frischen (Kalt)] *f.*⌢

Algarot [it. Arzt, † 1604] **=pulver** (⌣⌣⌣...) *n* ㉒ † *med.* algaroth-powder.

Algarve ♀ (⌣⌣́) [ar.] *npr/n.* ㉓α. Algarbia, Algarve. [~**n** *pl.* algæ *pl.*⌢

Alge ♀ (⌣́⌣) [lt.] *f* ㊽ alga, sea-weed⌢

Algebra ⚗ (⌣́⌣⌣) [ar.] *f* ㊾ algebra.

algebra=isch ⚗ (⌣⌣́⌣) *a.* ⓖⓖ algebraic(al); ♃ lösen to solve algebraically.

Algebra=ist ⚗ (⌣⌣⌣́) *m* ㊷ algebraist.

algen=ähnlich, **=artig** ♀ (⌣́⌣...) *a.* ⚗ algoid, alg(ace)ous, fucoid(al); **=kunde** *f* ㊽ ♃ algology.   [Algeria.⌢

Algeri=en ♀ (⌣⌣⌣⌣) [Algier] *npr/n.* ㉓α.⌢

algerisch (⌣⌣́⌣) *a.* ⓖⓖ Algerian.

Algier (⌣́G=) [ar. die Inseln (= J=fo'sium das Paar)] *npr/n.* ㉓α. Algiers; ~**er(in** *f* ㊼) *m* ㉒ u. Lisch (⌣(G)⌣⌣⌣) *a.* ⓖⓖ Algerine, ...an.   [Algonquin(s *pl.*)⌢

Algonkin(s) ♀ (⌣⌣⌣) *m(pl.)* ㉕ (Indianer)⌢

Al=hambra ♀ (⌣⌣́⌣) [ar. die Rote] *f* ㊺ u. ㉕α. Alhambra.   [lineal) alidad(e).⌢

Al=hidade ⚗ (⌣⌣⌣́⌣)[ar.] *f* ㊽ *ast.* (Diopter=⌢

Alibi (mft ⌣́⌣⌣) [lt. ⌣́⌣ anderswo] *n* ⓑ od. *inv.* jur. alibi; fein ~ nachweisen to establish an (or to prove one's) alibi.

Alice (⌣́⌣⌣) [fr.] *f* ㊾ u. ㉓β. (Bn.) Alice.

Alignement ⚔ (á=li=nj'ma') [fr.] *n* ㊿ (vorbezeichnete Truppenfront) alinement.

Aliment (⌣⌣́) [lt.] *n* ⓑ b. jur., bsd. *pl.* ~**e** (Unterhaltungsbeiträge) alimony.

alimentations=berechtigt (⌣⌣⌣=tsch⌣)*II*...) *a.*ⓖⓖ entitled to alimony; **=gelder** *pl.* ㉒, **=kosten** *pl.* allowance (granted) for (or towards) a p.'s maintenance; **⚠pflichtig** having (or obliged) to pay alimony.

alimentieren (⌣⌣⌣⌣́⌣) [lt.] *v/a.* ㉓ (unterhalten) to maintain.

Alinea (⌣⌣́⌣) [lt.] *n* ㊻ typ. ([neuer] Abschnitt, Absatz) break, (fresh) paragraph.

aliquant ⚗ (⌣⌣́⌣) [lt.] *a.* ⓖⓖ math. (nicht ohne Rest aufgehend) aliquant.

aliquot ⚗ (⌣⌣⌣) [lt.] *a.* ⓖⓖ math. (ohne Rest aufgehend) aliquot.

Aliquot=töne ♪ (⌣́⌣...) *m* ㊷ harmonics *pl.*

Alizarin ⚗ (⌣⌣⌣́) [neu=lt., *ar. Al=iza'ri ☙ m Krapp] *n* ⓑc. chm. (Krapprot) alizari(n), purpurite; **~=tinte** *f* alizarin ink.

Alk (⌣́) [a/n.] *m* ⓑ b. u. ㊷ *orn.* auk.

alkäisch (⌣⌣́⌣) [Alkäos, grch. Lyriker, 600 v. Chr.] *a.* ⓖⓖ *pros.* Alcaic; ~e **Verse** *m/pl.* Alcaics *pl.* [*richter*) alcalde, alcayde.⌢

Alkalde (⌣⌣́⌣) [ar. der Kadi] *m* ㊵ (span. Dorf=⌢

Alkali ⚗ (⌣́⌣⌣, oft ⌣⌣́⌣) [ar. die Pottasche] *n* ㉗ (*pl.* Alka'lien) *chm.* alkali; ~ **bildend** alkaligenous; **mit ~ versetzen** to alkal(in)ize, to treat with an alkali.

alkali=artig ⚗ (⌣́...) *a.* ⓖⓖ alkaloid(al); **=gehalt** *m* ㊷ alkaline strength or percentage; **=metall(e** *pl.) n* ㉒ alkaline metal(s *pl.*).   [alkalimetry.⌢

Alkalimetrie ⚗ (⌣⌣⌣⌣́) [ar.=grch.] *f* ㊽⌢

Alkali=salze *n/pl.* ㊷ alkaline salts.

alkalisch (⌣́⌣⌣) *a.* ⓖⓖ *chm.* alkaline, alkalinous, lixivial.   [zation.⌢

Alkalisation ⚗ (⌣⌣⌣=tsch⌣́) *f* ㊻ alkali-⌢

alkalisier=en ⚗ (⌣⌣⌣⌣́⌣) **I** *v/a.* ㉓ *chm.* to alkalize; (in Alkali verwandeln) to alkalify. — **II ~n** ㉓, **A/ung** *f* ㊻ *chm.* alkalization.

Alkalo=id ⚗ (⌣⌣⌣́) *n* ⓑc. *chm.* alkaloid.

Alkanna ♀ (⌣⌣́⌣) [ar.] *f* ㊻ = Henna.

Alkibiades (⌣⌣́⌣⌣) *npr/m.* ⑯γ. (athenischer Feldherr, 450 bis 404 v. Chr.) Alcibiades.

Alkide (⌣⌣́⌣) *npr/m.* ⑯γ. (He'rkules) Alcides.

alkmanisch (⌣⌣́⌣) [Alkman, spart. Lyriker, 650 v. Chr.] *a.* ⓖⓖ *pros.* Alcmanian; ~**er Vers** Alcmanian verse or metre.

Alkohol (⌣́⌣⌣) [ar. das Feinste] *m* ⓑd. (⚗) *chm.* (Weingeist) alcohol; **⚠=artig** (⌣́...) *a.* ⓖⓖ alcoholic; **=äther** *m* ㊷ alcoholic ether; **⚠haltig** *a.* = **⚠artig**.

Alkoholiker (⌣⌣⌣́⌣) *m* ㉒ p. addicted to alcohol, p. suffering from alcoholism; drunkard.   [coholization.⌢

Alkoholisation ⚗ (⌣⌣⌣⌣=tsch⌣́) *f* ㊻ al-⌢

alkoholisch ⚗ (⌣⌣⌣́⌣) *a.* ⓖⓖ alcoholic; **⚠e Getränke** *n/pl.* alc. liquors, spirits *pl.*; **⚠ aufgeregt** alcoholically excited.

alkoholisieren ⚗ (⌣⌣⌣⌣⌣́⌣) *v/a.* ㉓ (mit Weingeist behandeln) to alcoholize.

Alkoholometer ⚗ (⌣⌣⌣⌣́⌣) *n* ㉒ *chm.* alcoholometer.   [Koran.⌢

Alkoran (⌣⌣́, oft ⌣́⌣ ⌣⌣) [ar.] *m* ⓑc. =⌢

Alkoven (⌣⌣́⌣) [fr. *alcôve f*; *ar.] *m* ㉓ (kleines Schlafzimmer) alcove; recess.

Alkuin (⌣⌣́⌣) *npr/m.* ㉕α. u. ㉖α. (engl. Gelehrter am Hofe Karls d. Gr.) Alcuin († 804).

all (⌣́) [ahd.] **I** *a.* u. *s.* ⓖⓖ (C1 u. ⓖⓖB), z. T. *inv.* all; **a)** *inv.* **1.** vor *dem.* u. *poss. pron.* ⚠(es) das (od. das ~es) all that; ⚠ **dies** (mein) **Gold** all this (my) gold; **mit ⚠(er) seiner Habe** with all his belongings; ⚠ **und jeder** (alle zusammen und jeder einzelne) each and every (one), *pl.* f. ⚠e; **bei ⚠ und jeder Gelegenheit** on every possible occasion; **sich mit ⚠ und jedem vertragen** to get on with everybody; **2.** *prädikativ* = ⚠e I b **3**; **3.** mst P *adv.* = **schon**; **b)** ~**e 1.** *nom. u. acc. sg. f. u. pl.* **sie kamen ⚠e** they all came; Bühnen=anweisung: ⚠**e ab** *omnes exeunt*; ⚠**e acht Tage once a week**; **ich sah fie ⚠e beide** I saw both of them, I saw them both (vgl. ⚠**en**); **alle drei Tage** every third day; **auf ⚠e Fälle** in any case, at all events; ⚠**e für einen und einer für ⚠e** all for each and each for all, individually and collectively; ⚠**e und jede one and all**; ⚠**e guten Geister** all good spirits *pl.*; ⚠**e Leute**, ⚠**e Menschen**, ⚠**e Welt** all (men), all the world, everybody; ⚠**e=n** (f. ds) ⚠**e Tage** (täglich) every day, daily; ⚠**e vierzehn Tage** once a fortnight; ⚠**e zwei Minuten** every two minutes, every other (or second) minute; ⚠**e zwei Tage** every other day; ⚓ ⚠**e Mann auf!** all hands on deck!; **er kennt sie ⚠e nicht** he does not know any of them; **er kennt sie nicht ⚠e** he does not know them all or all of them; **wir ⚠e** we all, all of us; **2.** *inv.* **mit** (trotz, zu) ⚠**edem** (oder ⚠**em**) with (despite, in addition to) all that; **trotz** (a. bei) ⚠**edem** for all that, nevertheless; **mit** (bei) ⚠**e diesem** with all this; **3.** ⚠(**e**) *adv.* F (zu Ende) at an end, all gone; **mein Geld ist ⚠e ...** is spent or has vanished; ⚠(**e) machen** to do away with, to finish, Geld: to spend; **P du kannst ⚠e werden!** be gone!, **F** (you can) take your hook!; **er ist einer von denen, die nicht ⚠e werden** there are (always) plenty of fools, and he is one of them; **c)** ⚠**em** *dat. sg.* **vor ⚠em above all**, **first and foremost**; **er ist zu ⚠em fähig** he is capable of anything; *vgl.* a. ⚠ b **2**; **d)** ⚠**en 1.** *gen. sg. m* u. *n* ⚠**en** (ob. ⚠**es Ernstes** (ⓖⓖ A 3*) in all seriousness, quite in earnest; *vgl.* ⚠**enfalls**; **2.** *acc. sg. m* u. *n* **ohne ⚠en Zweifel** without any (or the slightest) doubt; **3.** *dat. pl.* **ich nehme es mit ⚠en beiden auf F I defy the pair of them**; **vor ⚠en Dingen** first of all, above all (things); **unter ⚠en Umständen** under any circumstances; *vgl.* ⚠**enthalben**; **e)** ⚠**er 1.** *sg. nom. m* f. Anfang; **2.** *sg. gen. u. dat. f* **in ⚠er Eile** in a great hurry; **F post=haste; in ⚠er Frühe** quite (or very) early, in the early (hours of the) morning; **mit ⚠er Gewalt** (auch Macht)

[allabendlich] — 40 — [Allerweltsbürger]

with might and main; wer in Ler Welt könnte das sein? who on earth ...?, whoever ...?, F who the dickens ...?; vgl. ̃ a 1; 3. pl. gen. f. Ler-..., vgl. Ding 4; f) ̃es 1. nom.n ̃(e)s das (ob. das ̃es) all that; was ̃es whatever; wer ̃es whoever; ̃es Gute everything good; ̃es mögliche all kinds of things; everything; das ist ̃es that's all; ̃es eingerechnet, ̃es erwogen when all is said, considering all things; ̃es fließt (heraklitischer Satz:) all things are in a flux; er hat das ̃es (a. ̃es das) nur für sie getan he did all that only for her sake; er ist sein ̃es, er gilt ̃es he is his right hand; sie ist sein ̃es she is all in all to him; mein ein und mein ̃es my all, the only thing I possess; er wird ̃es aufbieten he will strain every nerve; ̃es zu seiner Zeit there's a time for everything; ich bin ̃en ̃es geworden (vgl. 1. Kor. 9, 22) I am made all things to all men; sie hat Wagen und Diener und wer weiß was ̃es ... and nobody (or Heaven) knows what (else); Gott weiß wer (oder was) ̃es da war Goodness knows who (or what) ...; was für Leute sind das nur ̃es? whoever are all these people? Sprichw. Ende gut, ̃es gut all's well that ends well; m.prp. Mädchen für ̃es maid of all work; sich in ̃es fügen to submit to everything; ̃es in ̃em all in all, (up)on the whole; hundert in ̃em a hundred all told; um ̃es in der Welt nicht not for all the world, F not for a pension. 2. gen. ̃es Ernstes f. Id. — II All n ⑱ (Welt-all) universe.
all-abendlich (͜...)a.⑯u.adv.; ̃abends adv. every evening or night.
Allah (̃-)[ar. der Gott]m⑱(o.pl.) Allah.
all-barmherzig (̃..."..) a.⑯ all-merciful; ̃bekannt a. notorious, universally known; ̃beliebt a. universally liked; ̃beneidet a. universally envied; ̃bereits adv. already; ̃besetzigend a. most blissful; ̃beweint a. mourned by all; ̃da" adv. there; ̃deutsch (̃...) a. pol. pan-German(ic); ̃deutschland n united (or all) Germany; ̃dieweil † ob. co. cj. since, because; ̃do"rt ͜ adv. = ̃da.
Alle¹ (̃͜) n, inv. Brettspiel: doublet.
alle² (̃͜) pl. u. adv. f. all Ib.
alledem (̃͜-) f. all Ib 2.
Allee (͜!) [fr. Gang] f ⑱ (doppelte Baumreihe) avenue (of trees), walk (between trees); schmale, enge: lovers' walk.
Allegat (͜-!)[it.]n⑱c., ~ion(͜--th(͜)!)f ⑯ allegation, quotation (of a passage).
Allegat-strich (̃...) m ⑱ = Anlagestrich.
allegieren (͜-!͜) [it.] v/a. ⑱ bsd. jur.: (anführen) to allege, quote, cite.
Allegorie ⚤ (͜-!) [grch.] f ⑱ allegory.
allegorisch ⚤ (͜-!͜) a. ⑯ allegoric(al).
allegorisieren (͜-!͜) v/n. (h.) ⑱ (in Gleichnissen, Bildern darstellen) to allegorize, to speak in allegories.
Allegorist ⚤ (͜-͜) m ⑫ allegorist.
allegretto (̃-) [it. munter] adv. u.
Allegretto n ⑱ allegretto; **allegro** ♪ (͜-!) [it.] adv. u. **Allegro** n ⑱ allegro.
allein (͜!) [mhd. all(ganz)=ein: alone] I a. inv. u. adv. alone, single, (o. Beistand) unaided, unassisted; er ̃ rauchte he alone smoked; ganz ̃ all alone, lonely; laß(t) mich ̃ leave me alone; sie lebt ganz ̃ she lives all alone or quite by herself, she leads a lonely life; sie steht ̃ da she stands alone in the world; er war ̃ da he was the only person present; ich möchte Sie ̃ sprechen I should like a private talk with you; sie muß alles ̃ tun she has to do everything herself, she has no assistance; schon ̃ der Gedanke the bare (or mere, very) thought (of it); nicht ̃ //, sondern auch not only //, but also; einzig und ̃ solely; Bühnenanweisung: solus (m), sola (f). — II cj. am Anfang des Satzes: but, however.
Allein-berechtigung (̃͜...) f ⑫ exclusive right; ̃besitz m, ̃betrieb m monopoly; ̃gesang ♪ m solo; ̃gespräch n soliloquy, monologue; ̃haft f solitary confinement; ̃handel ⚭ m monopoly; ~ treiben mit to monopolize; ̃händler ⚭ m monopolist.
Alleinheit (͜-!) f ⑫ (o. pl.) isolation, privacy; being (all in) one.
Allein-herr(in f) m (̃...) ⑫ (absolute) monarch, autocrat; ̃herrschaft f (absolute or unlimited) monarchy or authority, autocratic rule, autocracy; ̃herrscher(in) = ̃herr(in).
alleinig (͜-!)a. ⑯ exclusive; (ohnegleichen) unique; mit Ler Ausnahme von // with the sole exception of //, except only //; der ̃e Gott the (only) one God; für seinen ̃en Gebrauch for his separate (or sole, special) use; ⚭ für meine ̃e Rechnung for my sole account.
Alleinigkeit (͜-!) f ⑫ (o. pl.) exclusiveness; ~s-lehre (̃...) f ⑫ theol. doctrine of one God, monotheism.
Allein-sein (̃...) n ⑫ loneliness; ̃seligmachend a. ⑯ claiming the monopoly of all means of grace; ̃spiel ♪ n solo; ̃stehend a. isolated, von Gebäuden: detached, von Personen: alone in (or cast upon) the world, (ledig) single, unmarried; ̃verkauf m, ̃vertrieb m ⚭ monopoly.
alle-mal (̃͜!) adv. each time, always; invariably; ein für ̃ once for all; ̃ wenn whenever; ̃ig (̃͜) a. ⑯ happening each time or at all times; for the time being. [mande.]
Allemande (͜͜) [fr.] f ⑱ (Tanz) alle-∫
⚭ **Allemannen 2c.** f. Alemannen 2c.
allen-falls (̃͜) adv. 1. (zur Not) if need be, in the worst case, if the worst comes (or came) to the worst. — 2. (höchstens) at the most; zwei könnten noch ̃ untergebracht werden two might possibly (or at a pinch) be accommodated; ̃fallsig (̃͜) a. ⑯ (u. adv.) eventual(ly).
allent-halben (̃͜) adv. everywhere, on every side, on all sides; everyway.
aller-... (̃͜... u. ̃͜...) a. ⑯: ̃ärgst a. inv. = ̃hand; ̃art a. inv. = ̃hand; ̃äußerst a. ut(ter)most, very last; adv. in the highest degree.
All-erbarmer (̃͜) m ⑫ God of mercy.
aller-best (̃͜...) a. ⑯ best of all, very best; aufs ̃e in the best possible manner; ̃christlichst a. most Christian; ̃dings (̃͜) adv. certainly, surely, to be sure; das hat er doch nicht getan? ̃! ... indeed, he did (or has)!; Das wird (würde, könnte) er doch nicht tun? — ̃! ... indeed, he will (would, could)!, F rather!; ̃durchlauchtigst a. most Serene (Highness); ̃erst a. first an foremost; (zu) ̃ above all; ̃geringst a. very lowest, most humble; nicht im ̃en not in the least; ̃gnädigst a. (u. adv.) most gracious(ly); adv. ̃ einwilligen to consent most graciously; ̃größt a. greatest of all. [things.]
All-erha"lter ⚭ ⑫ Preserver of all (good)∫
aller-hand (̃͜... u. ̃͜...") a. inv. divers, sundry; ̃ (oder ̃lei, ̃art) Bücher books of all kinds; auf ̃ Art(en) in one way or other; ̃h"ei-ligen(=fest n, =tag m) n ⑫ (1. Nov.) eccl. All Saints' Day; ̃heiligst a) a. ⑯: most holy; Ler Vater (Papst) Holy Father; b) ~e(s) n ⑫: α) in einem Tempel: sanctuary; im jüdischen Tempel: Holy of holies; β) (Monstranz) the holy wafer; c) ~e f ⑱ (Jungfrau) Blessed Virgin; ̃höchst a. highest of all; der ~e (Gott) the Most High; ̃derselbe (~dieselbe) His (Her) Majesty; mit ~er Entschließung des Monarchen (öfter.) at His Majesty's gracious desire; ~e Bestimmungen regulations made by command of His Majesty; aufs ̃e, im ̃en Grade to the last degree, in the highest degree; ̃lei (̃͜͜) a) a., inv. = ̃hand; ̃ Leute all sorts and conditions of men; b) das ̃lei n ⑱ medley, hodge-podge; ♪ selections pl.; Literatur: miscellany; ̃lei-gewürz n mixed spice; ̃letzt a. very last; ⊙ die ̃en Neuheiten the latest novelties, up-to-date goods pl.; adv. last of all, in the end, ultimately; ̃liebst a. most charming or delightful; sie sah ̃ aus she looked lovely or most enchanting; adv. am ̃en bliebe ich hier I should like best (of all) to stay here; ̃mannsharnisch ⚥ m victor's garlic (A'llium victoria'le); ̃meist a.: die ̃en Menschen most people; adv. am ̃en mostly, generally, chiefly, principally; ̃mindestens adv. at the very least; ̃nächst a. next (or nearest) of all; adv. räumlich: close (F hard) by; zeitlich: ̃ens very soon; ̃neu(e)st a. quite new, F up to date, just in; die ̃e Mode the very latest fashion or novelty; (Straßenruf) das ~e! latest (or last) edition!; ̃ens adv. quite recently, just lately; ̃nötigst, ̃notwendigst a. most needful or indispensable; ̃orten, ̃orts adv. everywhere. [all things.]
All-erschaffer (̃͜͜) m ⑫ Creator of∫
aller-schlimmst (̃͜... u. ̃͜...) a. ⑯ worst of all; aufs ̃e in the worst manner possible; ̃schönst a. finest of all; ̃seelen(=fest n, =tag m) n ⑫ (2. Nov.) eccl. All Souls' Day; ̃seits (̃͜) adv. on all sides; ich empfehle mich ̃ I wish to be remembered to all, remember me (kindly) to the (or your, our) family-circle; ̃untertänigst a most humble, adv. very obediently; ̃wärts, ̃weg(en[s]), ̃wegs adv. everywhere.
Allerwelts=bürger (̃͜͜...) m ⑫ citizen of the world, cosmopolitan, cosmopolite;

Zeichen (s. S. XVII): F familiär; P Volkssprache; Γ Gaunersprache; ↘ selten; † alt (auch gestorben); * neu (auch geboren); ⫶ unrichtig;

[allerwenigſt] — 41 — [Alpe]

=freund *m* everybody's friend, auch⸗ hail-fellow well met (with everybody); =freundſchaft *f* good fellowship with all; =ferl F *m* smart fellow; =onkel *m* everybody's uncle.
aller⸗wenigſt (⸍⸣... u. ⸍⸣...") *a.* ⓺ least of all; *adv.* ⚲ens at the very least; ⚲werteſt *a.* most charming; der ~e ⓻ the posterior or backside.
alle⸗ſamt (⸍⸣) *adv.* all together, without (any) exception. [fellow]
Alles⸗freſſer (⸍⸣...) *m* ⓺ omnivorous/
alle⸗wege (⸍⸣⸍⸣) *adv.* 1. = allerwegen. — 2. at all times.
alle⸗weil(e) F (⸍⸣) *adv.* just now, presently; (immer) always. [occasion.]
all(e)⸗zeit (⸍⸣()⸍⸣) *adv.* always, on every/
All⸗gegenwart (⸍...) *f* ⓺ omnipresence, ubiquity; ⚲ge"genwä"rtig *a.* ⓺ omnipresent, ubiquitous; ⚲gema"ch *adv.* gradually, little by little.
all⸗gemein (⸍⸍⸍) **I** *a.* ⓺ general, ſtärker: universal; im ⚲en in general; im ⚲en genommen ob. geſagt generally speaking; ⚲ machen to generalize, to spread; das ⚲e Beſte the good of all, the common weal; zur ⚲en Kenntnis bringen to publish; ⚲e Kirchenverſammlung œcumenical council; ⚲e Maßregeln sweeping measures; ⚲es Stimmrecht manhood (or adult, universal) suffrage. — **II** *adv.* generally; ⚲ anerkannt, angenommen universally acknowledged, commonly accepted; es wird ⚲ behauptet it is commonly asserted; ⚲ verbreitet widely spread. — **III** ~e(s) *n* ⓺: das ~e und das Beſondere generalities and particularities *pl.*; er bewegt ſich ſtets im ~en he is always generalizing or talking in a general way; vom Einzelnen auf das ~e ſchließen to infer from particulars to generals, to draw an inductive conclusion. [health.)
Allgemein⸗befinden ("...) *n* ⓺ general/
Allgemeinheit (⸍⸍⸍) *f* ⓺ universality; commonness; generality
Allgemein⸗machung (⸍⸍⸍...) *f* ⓺ generalization, spread; popularization.
allgemein(⸗)verſtändlich (⸍⸍⸍...) *a.* ⓺ intelligible to the multitude.
Allgemein⸗werden ("...) *n* ⓻ = ⸗machung.
All⸗gewalt (⸍...) *f* ⓺ omnipotence, supreme power; ⚲gewa"ltig *a.* ⓺ omnipotent, all-powerful; ⚲gü"ltig *a.* universally valid; ⚲gü"tig *a.* infinitely good; der ⚲e Gott God in his supreme kindness or infinite goodness.
Allheit (⸍⸣) *f* ⓺ (o. *pl.*) (Geſamtheit) totality, (Allgemeinheit) universality.
all⸗hier (⸍") *adv.* here; in our town.
Allianz (⸍()⸍⸣) [fr.] *f* ⓻ (Bündnis) alliance.
Alliebe (⸍⸍⸣) [All⸗liebe] *f* ⓺ infinite love.
alliebend (⸍⸣) [all⸗l...] *a.* ⓺ all-loving.
Alligation (⸍⸍⸣⸍) [lt.] *f* ⓺ arith. (Miſchungsregel) alligation; ~s⸗rechnung *f* ("...) ⓺, *math., metall.* problem respecting alligation or alloys.
Alligator (⸍⸍⸍) [ſpan. *el lagarto* (*lt. lacerta*) bie Eidechſe] *m* ⓾ *zo.* alligator.
alligieren ⊕ (⸍⸍⸣⸍) [lt.] *v/a.* ⓽ (richtig miſchen) to alligate; to blend.
alliieren (⸍()⸍⸣) [fr.] *v/a.* u. ſich ⚲ *v/refl.* ⓽ to ally (o.s.); Alliierte(r) ⓻ ally.

Alliteration ⚁ (⸍⸍⸣⸍tß(⸍⸣)⸍) [lt.] *f* ⓽ *pros.* (Stab⸗reim) alliteration.
alliterieren ⚁ (⸍⸍⸍⸍⸍) *v/a.* u. *v/n.* ⓽ *pros.* to alliterate, to exhibit alliteration.
all⸗jä"hrig *a.* ⓺ happening once a year; ⚲jä"hrlich *a.* (u.*adv.*) annual(ly); =macht (⸍⸣) [nhd.] *f* ⓺ omnipotence; ⚲mä"chtig (ahd.) *a.* almighty (ſ. a. ⚲gewaltig); der ⚲e Gott, der ~e God Almighty; ⚲mä"h⸗lich (nhd. = all(ge)mä"chlich, P: Mal] *a.* (u.*adv.*) gradual(ly); *adv.* a. by degrees, little by little, step by step.
Allmande, Allmende (+od.ſübb. (⸍⸍⸣) [mhb.] *f* ⓸ (Gemeinde⸗gut, -alpe) common (land).
all⸗mo"natlich *a.* ⓺ monthly; *adv.* once a (or every) month; ⚲mo"rgens *adv.* every morning; =mu"tter *f* ⓺ mother of all (zB. nature); ⚲nä"chtlich *a.*, *adv.* nightly, (happening) every night.
Allobroger ☿ (⸍⸍⸣⸣) *npr/m.* ⓶ *hist.* (lt. Volk am Genfer See) Allobroges *pl.*
Allod (⸍⸣) [Ganzbeſitz] *n* ⓾ *c.*ehm. = Allodium.
Allodial⸗gut (⸍⸍⸣⸍...) *n* ⓼ allodial land, freehold estate. [freehold (estate).)
Allodium (⸍⸣(⸍)⸍) *n* ⓼ (Freigut) allodium,/
Allonge⸗perücke (ă⸗lā̃"⸍⸍G³...) [⸍+ fr.] *f* ⓺ full-bottomed wig (with long curls).
Allokution (⸍⸍⸣⸍tß(⸍⸣)⸍) [lt.] *f* ⓸ (feierliche Anſprache) allocution.
Allopath (⸍⸣⸍) [grch.] *m* ⓺ *(ant.* Homöo⸗ path) allopathist; ~ie (⸍⸍⸣⸍) *f* ⓸ allopathy; ⚲iſch (⸍⸍⸣⸍) *a.* ⓺ (durch entgegengeſetzte Mittel heilend) allopathic.
Allotria (⸍⸍⸣⸍⸣) [grch.] *n/pl. inv.*: ~ (Unſinn, Narrheiten) treiben to waste time on trivialities; to be up to one's tricks.
all⸗ſehend (⸍⸣⸍) *a.* ⓺ all-seeing.
a"ll⸗ſeitig *a.* ⓺ u.*adv.* universal(ly); ⚲ betrachten, erwägen to consider (or weigh) from every point of view; ~keit *f* universality, versatility (of a p.'s mind).
all⸗ſeits (⸍⸣) *adv.* = allerſeits; ⚲ſoglei"ch *adv.* immediately; ⚲ſtü"ndlich *a.* ⓺ u. *adv.* hourly, (happening) every hour; =tag (⸍⸣) *m* ⓺, des ~s, ⚲s *adv.* every day. ⚲tä"gig, mſt ⚲tä"glich *a.* daily, of daily occurrence; *fig.* common(place), usual, ordinary, trivial; =tä"glichkeit *f* commonness, commonplace character; triviality; ⚲tags (⸍⸣) *adv.* every day.
Alltags⸗anzug (⸍⸍⸣...) *m* ⓺ every-day suit (of clothes); =beſchäftigung *f* daily (or every day's) task; =geſchwätz *n*, =gewäſch *n* idle (or commonplace) talk; =kleid *n* every-day dress or garment; =koſt *f* ordinary fare; =leben *n* every-day (or work-a-day) life; =menſch *m* ordinary person, commonplace individual.
all⸗überall (⸍⸍⸍) *adv.* everywhere, in all places; ⚲umfaſſend (⸍⸣...) *a.* ⓺ all-embracing; ein ⚲es Wiſſen encyclopædic (or comprehensive) knowledge.
Allüren (⸍⸍⸣) [fr.] *f/pl.* ⓸ ways, manners, airs *pl.*; (Benehmen) conduct.
alluvial (⸍⸍⸣w(⸍)⸍) [neu⸗lt.] *a.* ⓺ (angeſchwemmt) alluvial. [um, alluvial soil.)
Alluvium ⚁ (⸍⸍⸣w(⸍)⸍) [neu⸗lt.] *n* ⓼ alluvi-/
All⸗vater (⸍⸣...") *m* ⓺ father of all, God; ⚲verſtändlich *a.* ⓺ intelligible to all; ⚲waltend *a.* supreme; ⚲weiſe *a.* all-wise, supremely wise; ⚲wiſſend *a.* omniscient, all-knowing; =wiſſenheit *f* omniscience; =wiſſer *m* p. pretending to know everything; =wiſſerei" *f*

superficial knowledge; ⚲wo *cj.* where; ⚲wöchentlich *a.* (happening) every week, ⚲hebdomadary; ⚲zeit (⸍¹) ſ. all(e)zeit; ⚲zu (⸍¹) *adv.* in Zſgn. mit *a.* getrennt: ⚲ groß (*a.*) much too great, too big by far; in Zſgn mit *adv.* zſ.⸗ geſchrieben: ⚲zubald (⸍¹...) *adv.* much too soon; ⚲zugenau *adv.* over-particular; ⚲zugut *adv.* far (or much) too kind; ⚲zuhauf *adv.* all of a heap; ⚲zulange *adv.* much too long (a time); ⚲zuſammen *adv.* all (taken) together, altogether; ⚲zuſehr *adv.* too much, overmuch; ⚲zuviel *adv.* too much, overmuch; ⚲ iſt ungeſund too much of a good thing (is good for nothing).
Alm [Alben *pl.*] *f* ⓸ alpine pasture.
Alma mater (⸍⸣⸍⸍) [lt. nährende Mutter] *f* (Hochſchule) Alma Mater, university.
Almanach ☿ (⸍⸣) [ar.⸗äg.] *m* ⓾ d. (Jahrbuch) almanac, calendar, als Titel *a.*: almanack.
Almandin ⚁ (⸍⸍⸣) [lt. v. *Alabanda*, St. i. Karien] *m* ⓾ c. *min.* (Granat) almandin(e).
Alm⸗anger (⸍⸍⸣) *m* ⓶ (Wieſenſtück neben der Almhütte) meadow adjoining a (Swiss) cowherd's alpine hut.
Almei ⊕ (⸍⸣) *n* ⓾ (weißes Nichts, unreines Zinkoxyd) tutty. [roſe; b) Edelraute.)
Almen⸗rauſch ♀ (⸍⸍⸣) *m* ⓶ = a) Alpen-/
Almerobb. (⸍⸣) [mhd.: ambry; *lt. armarium n*] *f* ⓸ (Schrank) cupboard, press.
Almoſen (⸍⸣) [ahd. P: Allmus; fr.; *grch. ἐλεημοσύνη f* Barmherzigkeit] *n* ⓼ alms (*sg.* u. *pl.*), charity; e-m ~ geben to bestow (an) alms on a p.; e-n um ein ~ bitten ob. anſprechen to beg (or ask) alms (or a charity) of a p.; von ~ leben to live on (people's) charity.
Almoſen⸗amt (⸍⸣⸍...) *n* ⓼ a) almonership; b) alms-house; =anſtalt *f* charitable institution; =büchſe *f* alms- (or poor-) box; =empfänger(in *f*) *m* one who lives on alms or charity, beggar (woman *f*); =geber(in *f*) *m* alms-giver; =geld *n* alms. [⚉ (Almoſenpfleger) almoner.)
Almoſenier (⸍⸍⸣, ⸍⸍⸣nie) [fr.] *m* ⓾ c., fr./
Almoſen⸗kaſſe (⸍⸣...) *f* ⓸ = ⸗büchſe; =pfleger(in *f*) *m* guardian (or overseer) of the poor; =ſammeln *n*, =ſammlung *f* collection for the poor.
Alo⸗e ♀ u. ⚉ (⸍⸍⸣) [mhd., grch., *hebr.*] *f* ⓸ (⚉) aloe(s); hundertjährige ~ agave.
alo⸗e⸗artig ♀ (⸍⸍⸣...) *a.* ⓺ aloid; =bitter *n* ⓼ alo(e)tine, *pharm.* aloes; =hanf *m* aloe-fibre, ⚉ mſt = Agaveſaſer; =holz *n* ⸣+⸣ = Adler⸗h. [*acid* ($C_{14}H_4(NO_2)_4O_2$).]
Alo⸗etin⸗ſäure (⸍⸍⸍⸍...) *f* ⓻ *chm.* aloetic/
Alo⸗in ☿ (⸍⸣) [Aloe] *n* ⓾ c. *chm.* alo-in(e), aloetine. [Aloysius.)
Alo⸗iſius (⸍⸍⸣) *npr/m.* ⓮ γ. (Vorname)/
Aloſe (⸍⸣) [lt., *flt.*] *f* ⓸ = Alſe.
Alp¹ (⸍) [ahd.: *elf*] *m* ⓐ b. 1. (Kobold) (hob)goblin, demon. — 2. (Alpbrücken) nightmare, incubus; *fig.* e-m ein ~ auf dem Herzen ſein to be (like) a great weight (or burden) on a p.'s mind.
Alp² (⸍) [flt.] *f* ⓸ = Alpe.
Alpaka ⚉ (⸍⸣) [ſpan., * peru.] *m*, *n* ⓶ (Baum⸗) Wollſtoff: alpaca. [at par.)
al pari ⚉ (⸍¹⸣) [it.] (dem Nennwerte gleich)/
Alp⸗drücken (⸍⸣...) *n* ⓻ = Alp¹ 2.
Alpe (⸍⸣) [mhd., *flt.*] *f* ⓸ 1. ⚉ meiſt: die ~n *pl.* the Alps *pl.*; die Schweizer ~n the Swiss Mountains; dieſſeit(s)

♪ Muſik; ⚁ Wiſſenſchaft; ♀ Pflanze; ⚉ Geographie; ⊕ Technik; ⚒ Bergbau; ⚔ Militär; ⚓ Marine; ⚈ Handel; ⚋ Poſt; 🚆 Eiſenbahn.

[älpeln] — 42 — [alt]

(jenseit(s) der ~n cisalpine (transalpine); Napoleon zog über die ~n Napoleon crossed the Alps. — 2. (Bergweideplatz) alpine meadow-land.

älpeln (⌣⌣) ⓥa., **alpen** (⌣⌣) ⓥ v/n. (h.) to live on an alpine dairy-farm.

alpen=artig (⌣⌣...) a. ⓐ alpine; =**bahn** ⛓ f ⓐ alpine (or mountain-) railway; =**bewohner(in** f) m inhabitant of the Alps; =**dohle** f, orn. alpine chough (Pyrrho'corax alpi'nus); =**fex** m = Bergfex; =**führer** m a) (Person) alpine guide; b) (Buch) guide(-book) to the Alps; =**gegend** f alpine region; =**glöckchen** n alpine soldanel (Soldanella alpi'na); =**glühen** n alp(en)-glow; =**horn** n: a) ♪ = Alphorn; b) (Bergspitze) (mountain-)peak; =**klub** m = verein; =**land** n alpine region or country; =**panora'ma** n alpine panorama; =**paß** m pass in the Alps; =**rebe** ⚘ f alpine clematis (Cle'matis alpi'na); =**reise** f tour in the Alps, alpine tour; =**rose** ⚘ f mountain-rose, alpine rose, rhododendron (Rhodode'ndron); =**steiger** m alpine climber; =**stock** m: a) (Gebirgsstette) alpine range; b) alpine pole, ⟙ alpenstock; =**straße** f road across the Alps, alpine road; =**trift** f alpine (or mountain-) pasture; =**veilchen** ⚘ n sow-bread, cyclamen (Cycla'men europae'um); =**verein** m Alpine Club; =**wirtschaft** f. a) alpine farm or farming; b) mountain-inn.

Alp¹=fuß (⌣⌣) m ⓐ = Drudenfuß.

Alpha (⌣⌣) [grch., *phön.] n ⓕ od. inv. das ~ u. das Omega = A und O (f. A 2).

Alphabet (⌣⌣⌣́) [grch.] n ⓐc. alphabet.

alphabetisch (⌣⌣⌣́⌣) I a. ⓐ alphabetic(al). — II adv. alphabetically, in alphabetical order or succession.

alphabetisieren (⌣⌣⌣⌣⌣́⌣) v/a. ⓐ (nach dem Abc ordnen) to arrange alphabetically.

Alphabet=schloß (⌣⌣⌣́...) n ⓐ letter-keyed (or puzzle-) lock; =**system** n alphabetical system.

Alphard (⌣⌣) npr/m. ⓐc. ast. (Stern) Alpha of the Hydra.

Alp²=hof (⌣...) m ⓐ alpine farm; =**horn** ⟙ ♪ alp-horn. [Alpen gehörig) Alpine.

alpin(isch) (⌣⌣(⌣)) [dtfch.-lt.] a. ⓐ (zu den)

Alpler m ⓐ. ~**in** f ⓐ (⌣⌣(⌣)) native (or cowherd) of the Alps, alpine dweller.

Alp¹=zopf (⌣⌣) m ⓐ = Weichselzopf.

Alquifoux (⌣⌣-fü) [fr., *ar.] n, inv. min. (Glasurerz) alquifou, potter's ore.

Alraun (⌣⌣) [ahd. aus all (ganz) u. Rune] m ⓐ. 1. a. **Alr(a)une** (⌣⌣(⌣)) f ⓐ myth. alruna. — 2. ⚘ **Alraun(wurzel** f) m mandrake (A'tropa Mandra'gora).

alraunenhaft ⚘ (⌣⌣⌣) a. ⓐ u. adv. like (or resembling) a mandrake.

als (⌣) [mhd.: as = also ganz so] cj. 1. (ganz so wie) a) as, like, for; in the capacity (or character) of; by way of; when, while, being; et. ⌂ bare Münze nehmen to take a th. for true; seine Bedeutung ⌂ Dichter his rank as a poet; ⌂ Ehrenmann handeln to act like a gentleman; er zahlte mir ⌂ Entschädigung ... by way of compensation; zu e-m ⌂ Freund sprechen to speak to a p. as a friend; ich betrachte ihn ⌂ einen Gegner I look upon him in the light

of an opponent; schon ⌂ Knabe war er when (or while) only a boy ...; ⌂ Mädchen benahm sie sich recht tapfer for a girl she behaved very bravely; ⌂ Mann sollte er // being (or as) a man he should //; thea. Irving trat ⌂ Hamlet auf I. appeared in the character of (or as) H.; er schrieb mir ⌂ ihr Vormund he wrote to me in the capacity of (or as) her guardian; ⌂ Vorwand dienen to serve as a pretext; etwas ⌂ (auch für) wahr annehmen to take a th. for true or granted; **b)** mst unübersetzt: er starb ⌂ Bettler he died (as) a beggar; das soll ihm ⌂ Warnung dienen this shall be a warning to him; sich vor Gericht ⌂ schuldig bekennen to plead guilty. — 2. (= nämlich, das ist 2c.) verschiedene Ursachen ⌂ (da sind) // divers causes, such as (or to wit) // — 3. Zeit: when; zur Zeit, damals ⌂ at the time when; sobald ⌂ as soon as; ⌂ ich betete when (or while) praying; ⌂ er nach B. abreiste on leaving for B. — 4. (= wie) so schön ⌂ ein Engel as beautiful as ...; so klug ⌂ (wie) zuvor no wiser than before; so viel ⌂ (abbr. f.v.a.) as much as; soviel (⌂) an mir ist, in m-n Kräften steht as far as lies in my power; ebenso viele ⌂ as many as; er ist zu dumm ⌂ daß er es verstehen könnte he is too stupid to understand it; er bot zu wenig, ⌂ daß ich es hätte annehmen können he offered too little for me to accept it; sowohl die Reichen ⌂ (auch) die Armen the rich as well as the poor, both rich and poor. — 5. nach comp.: **a)** than: er ist ärmer ⌂ ich he is poorer than I (am); er ist älter ⌂ ich, a. he is my senior; ich möchte lieber verhungern ⌂ stehlen I would rather starve than steal; **b)** nach Verneinungen: but: niemand sah es ⌂ (nur) mein Vater none but my father saw it; ich tat nichts weiter ⌂ was ich tun mußte (⌂ meine Pflicht) ... nothing but what I had to do (but my duty); kein and(e)rer ⌂ er nobody but he, no other than he; wer anders ⌂ sie? who else but she? **c)** ⌂ **ob**, ⌂ **wenn** as if, as though; es sieht aus ⌂ ob (⌂ wenn) es regnen wollte it looks as if it were (weniger richtig: was) going to rain; ⌂ ob einer behaupten wollte as who should say; ⌂ wäre es wirklich wahr as if (or though) it were really true.

als=bald (⌣⌣) adv. forthwith, directly; ⌂ rief er then he called at once (or immediately); ⌂**ig** (⌣⌣) a. ⓐ = baldig.

als=dann (⌣⌣) adv. then, after that, afterwards, upon that, thereupon.

Alse (⌣⌣) [It., *Kt.] f ⓐ ichth. shad (Clu'pea alo'sa).

Alsem ⚘ prov. W. (⌣⌣) [ahd., *?] m ⓐc. wormwood (= Wermut).

also (⌣⌣) [ahd. aus all=(ganz)so: also auch] I (a. ⌣⌣) adv. (Vergleich) thus, so, in this way or manner; nicht ⌂ don't say that; bibl. ⌂ sei es! be it so!; ⌂ bis gleich! au revoir!, I shall soon see you again! — II cj. (Schluß) therefore, consequently; er ist hier, ⌂ kann er nicht dort sein he is here, hence

...; soll er ⌂ wirklich //? is he then really to //?; nun ⌂! well then!, now then!

also=bald (⌣⌣⌣), ⌂**fort** (⌣⌣), ⌂**gleich** (⌣⌣⌣) adv. = alsbald.

alt¹ (⌣) [ahd.: old] I a. ⓐ(D²) mst: **old**. 1. (Lebensalter) er ist zwanzig (Jahre) ⌂ he is twenty (years old); wie ⌂ ist er? how old is he?, what is his age?; für wie ⌂ halten Sie ihn? how old do you think he is?, F what age do you take him for (or to be)?; er ist (doppelt) so ⌂ wie ich he is (twice) my age; ich bin älter als er I am his senior or older than he; er ist zehn Jahre älter als ich he is ten years my senior; die älteren Schüler(innen) the senior boys (girls) pl.; er sieht nicht so ⌂ aus wie er ist he does not look his age; über vierzig (Jahre ⌂) sein to be over (F on the wrong side of) forty; der ältere Bruder the elder brother; univ. ~er Herr (abbr. A. H.) (ehemaliges Mitglied [Ehrenmitglied] e-r studentischen Verbindung) former member of a students' club. — 2. (ant. jung, frisch) old; (bejahrt) aged, advanced (F well on) in years; so ⌂ wie Methu'salem as old as Methuselah or as the hills; ein ziemlich ⌂er Herr an elderly gentleman; sie ist sehr ⌂ geworden she has aged very much; er wird nicht ⌂ werden he won't make old bones; ⌂es Brot stale bread; ⌂er Käse ripe (or rotten, decayed) cheese; die ⌂e Leier, e-e ⌂e Geschichte the old story; ein ⌂er Sünder a hardened (or wicked old) sinner; Sprichw.: jung gewohnt, ⌂ getan as the twigs are bent, the tree's inclined; ⌂e Liebe rostet nicht old love never dies. — 3. (ant. neu) ancient; die ⌂en (ältesten) Anfänge der Kultur the early (earliest or first) beginnings ...; die ⌂en Briten the ancient (or old) Britons; ~er Bund = ~es Testament (s. u.); um ⌂er Freundschaft willen for old acquaintance' sake; ⌂e Geschichte ancient history; old story; ✕ ~er Mann (jeder verlassene Bergbau, auch jeder abgebaute Teil einer Lagerstätte) old workings pl., dead man; min. ~er roter Sandstein Old Red Sandstone; ⌂en Stiles (a. St., julian. Kalender) (of) old style (O. S.); ein ⌂er Streit a long-standing dispute; das ~e Testament (A. T.) the Old Testament; ⚥ die ~e Welt the Old World; in ⌂en Tagen, Zeiten in former days, in olden times, (in the days of yore; die gute ⌂e Zeit the good old times pl. — 4. (uralt, altmodisch) antique, old-fashioned, obsolete, of long (or old) standing. — 5. ⓐ (gebraucht) ⌂e Bücher, Möbel second-hand books, furniture; (erprobt) experienced; ein ⌂er (ausgedienter) Soldat an old veteran; Münze von ⌂em Schrot und Korn sterling money. — 6. (abgetragen) worn; (verfallen) decayed, in ruins; (baufällig) dilapidated; das Kleid ist schon ⌂ ... has seen its best days; ⌂es Zeug old lumber. — 7. F: a) = lieb: ein ⌂es fideles Haus! a jolly old boy! b) = unangenehm: ein ⌂er Querkopf an old fellow! — **II alt und jung** n, inv. (both) old and young (s. Alte 1).

Signs (see page XVII): F familiar; P vulgar; ⌐ flash; ⟍ rare; † obsolete (died); * new word (born); ÷ incorrect; ♪ music.

Alt² ♪ (ˊ) [it.] m ①b. alto, counter (or second) tenor. [cient) nobility.\
alt¹=ad(e)lig (ˊ"(ˇ)ˇ) a. ⑥ of old (or an=\
Alta-i (ˇ⸗ˊ⸗) [mongol. Goldgebirge]
npr/m. ⑬ a., ~gebirge n ⓺ in Zentral=
asien: Altai (Mountains pl.).
alta-isch (ˇ⸗ˇ) a. ⑥ Altaian, Altaic.
Altan (ˊˊ) [it. † alta'na f hohe] m ⓪c.,
\~e (ˇˊˇ) f arch. platform, gallery,
flat roof; (Balton) balcony.
Altar (ˊˊ) [ahd.; *spät=lt. altā'rĕ n] m ⑦
⑨⑪②c,d. altar; (Abendmahlstisch) com=
munion-table; zum ~ führen, gehen, oft =
to marry, to get married (at church).
Altar=aufsatz (ˊ...) m ⓺ altar-furniture;
=bild n altar-piece; =bildschirm m,
=blatt n altar-screen, reredos; =decke f
altar-cloth; =diener m sexton; =gerät
n = =aufsatz; =geschirr n communion-
plate; =himmel m canopy over an
altar. [2. protestantisch: sexton.
Altarist (ˇ⸗ˊ) m ⓷ katholisch: chaplain.—
Altar-kelch (ˊ"...) m ⓺ chalice; =kerze
f candle on the altar; =stück n = =bild;
=tuch n altar-cloth.
alt¹-backen (ˊ...) a. ⑥ stale; ♀begründet
a. old-established; ♀e Rechte vested
rights; ♀bekannt a. long-known; ♀be=
rühmt a. of ancient fame or renown;
♀bewährt a. approved, of long stand=
ing, of old repute, well-tested; ♀christ=
lich a. early Christian; ♀deutsch a.
Old German; Teutonic, Germanic.
Alte (ˇˊ) ⓺ **I** ~(r) m 1. F old man, greybeard, F old chap; die ~n the old ones,
the old folk or people; ~ und Junge
young and old; F der ~, unser ~r (Va=
ter) the old man, the governor, our
dad (vgl. ~ 4. F); Rat der ~n (Gerusia,
Senat) council (or assembly of (the)
Elders, senate; Sprichw. wie die ~n
sungen, so zwitschern die Jungen like
father, like son; the young pigs
grunt like the old sow. — 2. der ~
vom Berge [ar. Sche(i)ch el Dschiba'l] the
old man of the mountain. — 3. meist
klein geschrieben: (der gleiche) er ist immer
noch der ♀ he is the same as ever; er
ist nicht mehr der ♀ he is not what he
used to be; er ist wieder ganz der ♀ he
is quite himself again. — 4. F Stu=
denten= ꝛc.) sprache: father; meine ~n my
parents; mein ~r (Gatte) F my old
man, co. my hubbie (= husband);
(Meister) governor. — 5. (altgedienter
Soldat) veteran. — 6. die ~n (Völker)
the ancients pl.; unsere ~n our forefathers pl. — **II** ~ f 7. old woman, auch
F meine (gute) ~e my (dear) old
woman; die ~ F the old lady. —
8. von Tieren: (the) old one, mother.
— **III** ~(s) n (o. pl.) (oft klein geschrieben)
an old thing; ~s und Neues things
both old and new; das ist et. ~s that's
an old story, that's nothing new; es
bleibt (wir lassen) alles beim ♀n things
remain (we leave things) as they
were (before). [time-honoured.\
alt¹-ehrwürdig (ˊ...) a. ⑥ venerable; \
Alteklare (ˇˇˊˇ)[roman.] npr/f.⓸(Oliviers
Schwert im Rolandslied) Halteclere.
älteln (ˊˊ) v/n.(h.) ⓶ a. (als Älterer erscheinen
od. sich gebahren) to look old(-fashioned),
to have old-fashioned ways, to

appear (or behave) like an old (or aged)
man or woman. [= altern.\
alten (ˇˊ) (ahd.) v/n. (h. u. sn) ⑧⑨ poet.\
Alt¹-england (ˊ...") npr/n. ⑫ Old
England; ♀englisch a. ⑥ Old English.
Alten-teil (ˊˇ) m⑫ jur. reservation made
(or land set aside) for the parent(s)
on handing over the estate to the
heir(s), vgl. Altsitzer. [servation-deed.\
Alten-teil(s)-vertrag (ˊˇˊ...) m ⑫ re=
Alte(r)¹ (ˇˊ) m ⓺ f. Alte I.
Alter² (ˇˊ) [ahd.] n ⓶ **1.** (Dauer) age; er
ist von m=m ~ ... (of) my age, as old as
I (am); in m=m, s=m ~ at my, his age;
at my, his time of life; im ~ von 20
(Jahren) at the age of twenty; im
besten, blühendsten ~ in the vigour (or
prime) of life; ein hohes ~ erreichen to
attain a great age, to live to a green
old age; mittleren ~s middle-aged;
im mannbaren ~ stehen to have
reached man's estate; ⚒ jur. ~ im
Feld priority (of a discoverer or prospector). — 2. (hohes ~) old (or great)
age; decline (or autumn) of life;
man sieht ihm sein ~ nicht an he does
not look his age; Sprichw. ~ schützt vor
Torheit nicht age is not proof against
folly; F there is no fool like an old
fool. — 3. (Altertum) antiquity; von
~s her, seit ~s, vor ~s from ancient
times; in olden times, of old, of yore.
— 4. (Amts=♀) seniority. — 5. coll.
aged (or elderly) people; das ~ muß
man ehren we must honour old age.
älter (ˇˊ; pl. ~n, Hom. Eltern) ⑥ comp.
von alt²: older, elder; der ~e (abbr. d.
Ä.) the elder, nach Namen auch: sen(ior).
Alteration (ˇˇˇ=tsi(oˇ)ˊ) [it.] f ⓸ **1.** (Ver=
änderung) alteration. — 2. fig. (Er=
regung) (violent) emotion, excitement;
(Kummer) grief. [inv. my double.\
Alter ego (ˊˊˊˊ) [lt. (mein) zweites Ich] m,\
alterieren (ˇˇˊˇ) [it.] v/a. ⑬ **1.** (verän=
dern) to alter. — 2. fig. (erregen) to
excite; sich ♀ über to grieve over, to
feel vexed at. [the same age.\
...**alt(e)rig** (..."ˇ(ˇ)ˇ) a. ⑥, z.B. gleich♀ of\
Alter-mutter (ˊˊ...) f ⓺ ancestress.
altern (ˊˊ) ⓶ a. **I** v/n. (h. u. sn) to grow
(F to get) old or obsolete. — **II** v/a.
to make a. p. (look) old, F to age a. p.
alternativ (ˇˇˇˊf) [lt.] a. ⑥ alternative.
Alternative (ˇˇˇˊˊˇ) [it.] f ⓸ (Wahl zw.
zwei Dingen) alternative; keine ~ haben
to have no (F to have Hobson's) choice.
alternieren (ˇˇˇˊˇ) [it.] v/a. ⑬ (abwechseln)
to alternate; ♀d alternate.
alter=schwach a., =schwäche f s. Alters=...
Alters-folge (ˇˊ...) f ⓺ (order of) se=
niority; =genoß m, =genossin f one of
the same age, contemporary; =grau
a. ⑥ hoary, grey with age; =grenze f
limit of age; =klasse f people (or ani=
mals) of the same age or year; =prä=
sident m chairman by seniority; =rente
f old-age annuity; =ring m, path. der
Hornhaut white ring round the pupil
(caused by senile decay), ⚕ albugo,
leucoma; ♀schwach a. broken down (or
enfeebled by) age, decrepit, senile;
=schwäche f infirmity due to age, de=
crepitude, senility; =stufe f stage of
life; =unterschied m difference of age;

=versicherung f insurance for the aged;
=versorgung f old-age pension; =ver=
sorgungs-anstalt f, =haus n asylum
for the aged poor; =versorgungs-kasse
f provident (or old-age) fund; =zu=
lage f long-service increase of pay.
Altertum (ˇˊˇ) n ⓶ d. antiquity; das
graue ~ hoary antiquity, the dawn of
history; im grauen ~ at a remote period;
Altertümer pl. antiquities pl.
Altertümelei (ˇˊˇˇˊ) f ⓸ mania for
antiquities, antiquarianism.
altertümeln (ˇˊˇˇˊ) v/n. (h.) ⓶ a. to dabble
in antiquities, to have a liking (or
mania) for antiquarian research.
Altertümler (ˇˊˇˇ) m ⓺ antiquarian.
altertümlich (ˇˊˇˇˊ) a. ⑥ antique, ar=
chaic; ♀e Sitten old-world manners
pl.; ~keit (ˇˊˇˇˊˇ) f ⓸ antiqueness,
archaism, (apparent) antiquity.
Altertums=forscher (ˇˊˇˇ...) m ⓺ anti=
quary; archæologist; =forschung f
archæology; =gesellschaft f archæo=
logical society; =händler m dealer in
antiquities; =kenner m = =forscher;
=kunde f antiquarianism, archæology;
♀kundig a. ⑥ learned in antiquarian
matters; =kundige(r) archæologist;
=wissenschaft f = =kunde.
Älter-vater (ˊˇˇˊ) m ⓺ ancestor.
älteste (ˇˊˇ) **I** a. ⑥ sup. v. alt¹: oldest,
eldest. — **II** ~(r) u. ~ f ⑦ **1.** bsd. von
Geschwistern: the eldest, eldest; mein ~r
my eldest son. — 2. senior, superior,
die ~n pl.: a) der Kirchengemeinde: the el=
ders; b) der Kaufmannschaft: the syndics.
Ältesten-kollegium ⓸ (ˇ"...) n/pl. ⓶ body
of syndics, governing board; =recht n,
=würde f seniority, eldership.
Alt¹-flicker (ˊˊ...) m ⓺ mender of old
things, patcher, cobbler; ♀fränkisch
a. ⑥ old-fashioned, quaint, out of date;
F co. antediluvian; ♀gedient a. veteran.
Alt²-geige ♪ (ˊˊ...) f ⓺ = Bratsche.
Alt¹-gesell(e) (ˊˊ...) m ⓺ foreman, head-
workman; ganger; ♀gewohnt a. ⑥ long-
accustomed; ♀gläubig a. orthodox;
=gläubigkeit f orthodoxy; ♀gotisch a.
ancient (or old) Gothic; =grieche m old
(or ancient) Greek; =griechenland ⚥
n old (or ancient) Greece; ♀griechisch
a. old (or ancient) Greek, Hellenic;
=händler m (Trödler) second-hand dealer.
Althee ♀ (ˇˊ) [grch. Heiltraut] f ⓸ = Eibisch.
alt¹-hergebracht (ˊ...) a. ⑥, ♀herköm=
lich a. customary, traditional, ancient;
♀hochdeutsch a. (abb. ahd.) Old High
German (abbr. OHG.)
Altist ♪ (ˇˊ) m ⓸, ~in f ⑦ alto(-singer).
alt¹-jungfernlich (ˊ...) a. ⑥ old maidish;
=jungfernstand m ⓶ etwa: life of an old
maid; =kastilien ⚥ n Old Castile; ♀ka=
tholisch a. old-Catholic; ♀klassisch a.
classical, of the (ancient) classics;
♀klug a. precocious, grave beyond one's
years; =klugheit f precociousness,
precocity; =knecht m head-servant.
ältlich (ˇˊ) a. ⑥ elderly; oldish.
Alt-mannskraut (ˊˊˊ) ♀ n ⓶ = Beruf=
kraut; =meister m past-master, master
(of a company, &c.); der ~ (älteste
lebende Meister) der Musik the greatest
living representative of the musical
world, the highest living authority

⚛ scientific; ♀ botanical; ⚥ geography; ⊕ machinery; ⚒ mining; ⚔ military; ⚓ marine; ⚚ commercial; ✉ postal; 🚂 railway.

[altrömisch] — 44 — [Ammer]

in music(al matters); ˋmodiſch a. ⑥⑥ old-fashioned, antiquated, vgl. ˋfränkiſch; =mutter f great-grandmother, vgl. ˋnordiſch a. (Old)Norse; =philolog(e) m classical philologist; =preuße m native of one of the older provinces of Prussia; =preußen ⊕ n (die ſchon vor 1815 zu Preußen gehörenden Provinzen) Old Prussia; =reis [mhd.] m (Schuhflicker) ...altrig f. alt(e)rig. [cobbler.] alt¹=römiſch (⁸...) a. ⑥⑥ ancient Roman. Altruismus ⌐ (∪−⌐) [neu-lt.] m ② phls. (Comte, † 1857) (Nächstenliebe) altruism. Alt¹=ſachſe m, ˋſächſiſch a. Old Saxon. Alt²=ſänger ♪ (⁸...) m ⓶, ˋſängerin f alto (singer); =ſchlüſſel ♪ m alto-key, cleff on the third line. Alt¹=ſitzer (⁸...) m ⓶ one who has retained only a portion of his estate for his own use, vgl. Altenteil; =ſtadt f old(er part of a) town; die Londoner ~ the City (of London). [contralto.] Alt²=ſtimme ♪ f counter(-tenor); tiefe ~ ∫ alt¹=teſtamentlich (⁸...) a. ⑥⑥ relating to the Old Testament; =vater m ⓒ: a) patriarch; b) (Stammvater) progenitor; ˋväteriſch a. = ˋfränkiſch; ˋväterlich a. patriarchal; =vordern [ahd.] pl. ancestors pl.; =waſſer n (ehemaliger Flußarm) old branch of a river. Altweiber=fabel (⁸ᵛ...) f⑫, =geſchichte f, =geſchwätz, =gewäſch, =märchen n old woman's talk, idle gossip, tittle-tattle; ˋmäßig a. ⑥⑥ like an old woman, ⌐ anile; =ſommer m: a) (Spätherbſt) fine days in autumn, ‧ St. Martin's (or Indian) summer; b) (Spinnfäden) gossamer, floating cobwebs pl. alt¹=weibiſch (⁸...) a. ⑥⑥ old-womanish, weitS. fond of tittle-tattle or gossip. Aluminat ⌐ (∪−∪⌐) [lt.] n ②c. chm. (Tonerde=verbindung) aluminate. [minite.] Aluminit ⌐ (∪−∪⌐) [lt.] m ㉝c. min. aluAluminium ⌐ (∪−⁽∪⁾⌐) [lt.] n ② (o. pl.) chm. aluminium (Al); ~oxy'd n ② aluminium oxide, alumina (= Ton=erde). Alumnat (∪−⌐) [lt.] n ②c. boarding-school. [boarder, resident pupil.] Alumne ⓸, Alumnus ② (∪⁸∪) [lt.] m∫ alveolar ⌐ (∪ᵛ−⌐) [lt.] a. ⑥⑥ anat. (die Zahnhöhle betreffend) alveolar. Alveole ⌐ (∪ᵛ−⌐) [lt.] f⑫ (Zahnhöhle, Zahnfach) alveolus. [Alwin, Alvin.] Alwin (⁸⌣) npr/m. ⓯ ⓷ ob. ⓹ ⓶α. (Bn.) am (⁸) [an dem] prp. 1. ˋ Ende in the end, örtlich: at the end; Geſandter ˋ engliſchen Hofe ... to the Court of St. James('s); e-m ˋ Herzen liegen to be near to a p.'s heart; ˋ 1. März (on) the first of March, on March the first; ˋ Tage vor (nach) // on the eve (morrow) of //; ˋ Morgen in the morning; ˋ Tage vorher on the previous (or preceding) day; wer iſt ˋ Spiele? whose turn is it?, who plays?; Frankfurt a. M. (abbr. = ˋ Main) Frankfort-on-(the-) Main; vgl. a. a. D. — 2. ˋ mit inf., zB.: ˋ Sterben dying, noch ˋ Leben still alive; ˋ Einpacken ſein to be (busy) packing. — 3. ˋ vor sup.: a) unüberſetzt, zB.: ˋ beſten beſt: wer kämpfte ˋ tapferſten?, who fought most bravely?; er hielt ˋ längſten aus he held out (the) longest; ſie ſang ˋ ſchönſten she

sang the best, her singing was the most beautiful of all; ˋ ſchwierigſten with the greatest difficulty. Amalgam (∪∪⌐) [ar., *grch.] n ②c. (Queckſilberverbindung) amalgam. [gamation.] Amalgamation ⊕ (∪∪−tß(∪)⌐) f⓸ amalamalgamieren ⊕ (∪∪−⌐) v/a. ⑬ to amalgamate; fig. a.: to fuse, to blend. Amalgamier=werk ⊕ (∪∪−ᴵᴵ...) n ② amalgamating-works pl. Amali-a ⓹⓹ ⓶α., Amali-e ⓹⓽ ⓶β. (∪⁻⌐(∪)⌐) npr/f (Vn.) Amelia. Amalin=ſäure ⌐ (∪−ᴵᴵ...) f ⓶ chm. amalic acid ($C_{12}H_{14}N_4O_8$) Amanuensis (∪∪−∪⁸) [lt.] m (sg. inv., pl. ...jes) amanuensis, confidential clerk. Amarant ⓡ (∪−⁸) [grch. unverwelklich] m ㉝b.; ~blume (⁸...) f ⓶ amarant(h). amarant(en) (∪∪−⁸(∪)) a. ⑥⑥ amarant(h)ine. Amarant=farbe (∪∪−⁸...) f⓶, ˋfarben a., ˋfarbig a. amarant(h), amarant(h)-coloured, amarant(h)ine; =holz n palisander wood; =rot n, ˋrot a. = ˋfarbe ꝛc. Amarelle ⓡ (∪−⌐) [mhd., *it.] f⓶ morello, morel, Armenian cherry. Amaryllis ⓡ (∪−⌐) [grch.] f⓸ amaryllis. Amateur (∪∪tß'r) [fr.] m ②d. (⑸) (Kunſtfreund, Dilettant) amateur. Amazone (∪∪−∪) f⓶ [grch. P.⁺⁺ = bruſtlos; *ſemit. amaz ſtark] (triegeriſches Weib; Mannweib) Amazon; fig. virago (kühne Reiterin) bold horsewoman. amazonenhaft (∪∪⁻∪∪) a. ⑥⑥ Amazonlike. Amazonen-hut (⁸...) m ② archery-hat; =kleid n lady's riding-habit; =ſtrom ⓠ [(⁺⁺ P) braſil. Bootzerſtörer] m Amazon (River), auch Maranon. amazoniſch (∪∪−⌐) a. ⑥⑥ = amazonenhaft. Ambaſſade (ɑ∪ᵛ⁻) [fr.] f⓶ embassy. Ambe (⁸∪) [it.] f⓸ math. combination of two things; Lottoſpiel: double prize. Amber (⁸∪) [mhd., *ar.] m ⓶ 1. = Bernſtein. — 2. = Ambra. Amber=fett (⁸∪...) n ⓶ chm., =harz n ambrein(e); =ſalz n ambergris salt. Ambition (∪∪tß(∪)⌐) [lt.=fr.] f⓺ (Ehrgeiz) ambition. ambitiös (∪∪tß(∪)⁸) a. ⑥⑥ (D10) (ehrgeizig) Ambo-ina ⓠ (∪∪⌐) npr/n ⓹α. Moluttenjuſel: Amboyna. Amboß ⓸ (⁸⁸) [ahd. aus an= u. boßen: beat] m ⓷α. anvil, anat. (Gehörknöchelchen) ⌐ incus; zweihörniger ~ beak-iron, bickern; Hammer oder ~ (we must) either do or suffer, strike or be struck. Amboß=einſatz (⁸...) m ⓶ anvil-peg; =futter n = ˋſtock; =ſchenkel m anvil-side; =ſtempel m anvil-punch; =ſtock m bed, stock or block of an anvil. Ambra (⁸∪) [mhd., lt., *ar.] f⓹⓹, a. m, n ⓷⓷ ambergris; ˋfarben (⁸...) a. ⑥⑥, ˋfarbig a. amber(-coloured); ~holz n ⓶ yellow sandal-wood; ~kraut ⓡ n = Katzengamander. Am=broſia (∪⁻(∪)⌣) [grch. unſterbl. machend] f, inv. myth. (Götterſpeiſe) ambrosia. Ambroſiana (∪∪⁻∪⌐) f ⓸⓽ (Mailänder Bibliothek) Ambrosian library. ambroſianiſch (∼) a. ⑥⑥ of St. Ambrose; Der Lobgeſang (Tedeᵘᵘᵐ) Ambrosian chant. [delicious, luscious.] ambroſiſch (∪−⌐) a. ⑥⑥ ambrosial; weitS.∫ Ambroſius (∪⁻(∪)⁸) [lt., *grch.] npr/m. ⓺γ. (a. Vn.) Ambrosius, Ambrose.

ambulant (∪−⁸) [lt. wandelnd] a. ⑥⑥ itinerant; ⚔ ˋes Korps flying column. Ambulanz ⚔ (∪−⌐) [lt.] f ⓺⓺ (Feldlazarett) ambulance; ~wagen (⁸...) m ⓺⓶ ambulance(-cart or -wagon). Ameischen (⁻∪) n ㉓, dim. v. Ameise. Ameise (⁻∪) [ahd.: emmet, ant] f⓺⓺ ent. ant (Formi'ca), beſ. poet. emmet; weiße ~ (Termite) white ant. ameiſen=artig (⁸...) a. ⑥⑥ ant-like, ⌐ formicate; =äther m ⓶ formic ether; =bär, =freſſer m, zo. ant-eater or -bear (Myrmeco'phaga); =ei(er pl.) n ants' egg(s); =gäſte m/pl. (in Ameiſenneſtern beherbergte Blattläuſe ꝛc.) ant-cows pl.; =geiſt m ⓶ = ˋſpiritus; =haufen m ant-hill, ⌐ formicary; =igel m ant-eater (Echi'dna); =kriechen, =laufen n, med. ⌐ formication; =löwe m, ent. ant-lion, lion-ant; =pflanze(n pl.) f ⓡ (von ~ bewohnt) plant(s pl.) harbouring ants; ˋſauer a. chm. ˋſaures Salz ⌐ formiate; =ſäure f, chm.: ⌐ formic acid (CH_2O_2); =ſpiritus m formic spirit; =vögel m/pl. ant-birds (Formicariidae). Ameislein (⁻⁻) n ㉓, dim. v. Ameise. Amelioration (∪⁻(∪)−tß(∪)⌐) [lt.] f ⓺⓺ (Beſſerung) amelioration. Amel=korn ⓡ (∪⁻ᴵᴵ...) [grch. ?] n ⓶ spelt (= Dinkel); =mehl n starch. Amen (⁻⌐) [hebr.] adv. u. n ㉓ amen, so be it!; fig. (ja und) ~ zu et. ſagen, ſein ~ zu et. geben to agree (or consent) to a th.; das iſt (ſo gewiß) wie (das) ~ in der Kirche that's as sure as fate, it's a solid fact or truth. Amendement (ă-mg-bmg') [fr.] n ② (Zuſatz) amendment; ein ~ ſtellen (durchbringen) to move (to carry) an amendment. amendieren (∪∪−⌐) v/a. ⑬ parl. (abändern) to amend (a bill). Amerika ⓠ (∪−∪∪) [1507 *Ameri'go (*dtſch. Emmerich) Veſpucci] npr/n ⓹α. America. Amerikaner (∪∪−∪⁻) m ⓶, ~in f ⓺⓻, ame-rikaniſch (∪∪−∪⌐) a. ⑥⑥ American; ameri-kaniſches Duell American duel. amerikaniſier/en (∪∪∪∪⁻⌐) I v/a. ⑬ to Americanize. — II ~ n ㉓ u. A/ung f ⓺⓺ Americanization. [canism.] Amerikanismus (∪∪∪∪−⁸∪) m ⓶⓻ Ameri-Amethyſt ⌐ (∪∪⁸) [mhd., *grch.] m ①b. min. amethyst; ˋartig (⁸...) a. ⑥⑥, ˋfarben, ˋfarbig a. amethystine; =fluß m ⓶ min. fluor of amethyst. Ameublement (ă-mö-bl'⁻-mg') [fr.] n ⓶ (Hauseinrichtung) (complete set of) furniture. Amiant (∪∪⁸) [grch. unbefleckt] m ①b. min. amiant(h), amiant(h)us; ˋartig (⁸...) a. ⑥⑥, ˋförmig a. amiant(h)ine, amiant(h)iform, amiant(h)oid. Amiranten ⓠ (∪∪−⌐) npr/f/pl. ⓶ Stiller Ozean: Admiralty Islands. Ammann ſchwz. (⁸∪) [mhd. aus Amtmann] m ②c. high bailiff. Amme (⁸∪) [ahd.] f ⓺⓺ nurse (auch fig.), beſ. wet-nurse; (Hebamme) midwife. Amm(e)i ⓡ (⁸⁻) n ⓹⓸ ammi. Ammen=lied (er pl.) (⁸∪...) n ⓶ nursery-song(s), -rhyme(s pl.); =märchen n nursery-tale, fairy-tale, cock-and-bull story; =ſtube f nursery. Ammer¹ (⁸∪) [ahd.: (yellow-)hammer] f ⓺⓺ (m ⓶) orn. bunting (Emberi'za), beſ. yellow-hammer (= Goldammer).

Zeichen (ſ. S. XVII): F familiär; P Volksſprache; ſ Gaunerſprache; ‧ ſelten; † alt (auch geſtorben); * neu (auch geboren); ⁺⁺ unrichtig;

[Ammer] — 45 — [Amtsalter]

Ammer² ♀ (♫) [it.] f ⊕ (Kirsche) morello (= Morelle). [= Goldammer.]
Ammerling (♫) [Ammer¹] m ⊕d. orn.
Ammi ♀ f. Ammi(e)it.
Ammoniak ⚗ (ᴗ-(ᴗ)ᴗ) [neul-lt., v. b. *Ammons-oase (Siwah)] n ⊕e. (o. pl.) chm. ammonia (NH₃); kohlensaures ~ carbonate of ammonia (NH₄)₂ (CO₃); =alisch (ᴗ-(ᴗ)) a. ⊕ ammoniac(al).
ammoniak-artig (ᴗ-(ᴗ)ᴗ...) a. ⊕ ammoniac(al); =flüssigkeit f ⊕ liquid ammonia; =gas n ammonia gas, gaseous ammonia; =gummi ⊛ n (m) gum ammoniac; =salz n ammonia(cal) salt.
Ammonit ⚗ (ᴗ-ᴸ) [grch.] m ⊕ min. ammonite, auch: serpent- (or snake-)stone.
Ammoniter ♀ (ᴗᴸᴗ) npr/m ⊕, ~in f ⊕ bibl. (1. Mos. 19,38) Ammonite.
Ammonium ⚗ (ᴗᴸ(ᴗ)ᴗ) n ⊕ (o. pl.) chm. ammonium; ~-karbonat n kohlensaures Ammonium carbonate = kohlensaures Ammonium; ~-zinnchlorid n double chloride of tin and ammonium, pink salt.
Ammons-horn (♫ᴗ...) n ⊕ min. = Ammonit. [allgemeine) general pardon.]
Amnestie (ᴗᴸᴸ) [grch.] f ⊕ amnesty;
amnestieren (ᴗᴸᴸ) v/a. ⊛ (begnadigen) to amnesty, to pardon, to grant a pardon to (political offenders). [amoeba.]
Amöbe ♀ (ᴗᴸ) [grch. Wechselnde] f ⊕
A-Moll ♪ (ᴸ) n ⊕ f. A ♪.
Amom ♀ (ᴗᴸ) [grch.] n ⊕c. amomum.
Amor (ᴸᴗ) [lt.] m ⊕, a. ⊕ ⊚ myth. (Liebesgott) Cupid; (God of Love.)
Amorce (ᴗᴗᴗ) [fr. Köder] f ⊕(⊕)(Zündhütchen) detonating or percussion cap.
Amorette (ᴗᴗᴗ) [it.] f ⊕ little Cupid.
Amoriter ♀ (ᴗᴸᴸ) npr/m. ⊕, ~in f ⊕ bibl. Amorite. [los) amorphous.]
amorph(isch) ⚗ (ᴗ(ᴗ)f) [grch.] a. ⊕ (form-
Amortisation (ᴗᴗᴗ-tj(ᴗ)ᴸ) [fr.] f ⊕ (Tilgung): ~ einer Anleihe redemption of a loan; ~ e-s Wechsels (legal) extinction of a bill. [f sinking-fund.]
Amortisations-fonds (""...) m ⊕, =kasse
amortisierbar (ᴗᴗ-ᴸ-) a. ⊕ redeemable.
amortisier/en (ᴗᴗ-ᴸᴗ) [fr.] I v/a. ⊛ (abzahlen) to redeem; Schulden ⊊ to sink. — II ~ n ⊕ u. A/ung f ⊕ = Amortisation.
Ampel (♫ᴗ) [it.] f ⊕ (Lampe) (hanging or swinging) lamp; (hangende Blumenvase) suspended flower-pot. [(for).]
ampeln F (♫ᴗ) v/n. (h.) ⊕a. to try hard
Ampere (a'-pä'r) [fr. 1898, *Ampère, fr. Physiker, 1775—1836] n ⊕ ⊕. elect. (Maßeinheit der elektr. Stromstärke) ampere; ~-meter ⊕ (ᴗ'ᴗ) n ⊕ (Strommesser) amperemeter, ammeter; =stunde ("...) f (in e-r Stunde durch einen elektr. Strom entwickelte Kraft) ampere-hour; =volt (⌒ᴡ⁵) n (= 1 Watt ob. ¹⁄₇₄₆ Pferdekraft) ampere-volt.
Ampfer ♀ (♫ᴗ) [ahd.] m ⊕ dock (Rumex); kleiner ~ sheep's sorrel (R. Acetosella); krauser ~ curled dock (R. crispus); vgl. Sauerampfer; ~-klee ♀ (...) m ⊕ common wood sorrel (O'xalis).
Amphibi-e ⚗ (ᴗfᴸ(ᴗ)ᴗ) [grch. beiblebig] f ⊕ zo. amphibium, amphibious animal.
amphibien-artig ("...) a. ⊕, **amphibisch** (ᴗfᴸᴗ) a. amphibious.
Amphibi-en-kunde ("...) f ⊕ amphibiology; =leben n amphibious life; =lehre f = =kunde; =natur f amphibiousness.
Amphibium (ᴗfᴸ(ᴗ)ᴗ) n ⊕ = Amphibie.

Amphibrach ⚗ (ᴗf-⌣ᴸ) [grch.] m ⊕c., ~ys (ᴗfᴸ⌣ᴗ)m,inv.amphibrach(Versfuß⌣ᴸ⌣).
Amphiktyonen (ᴗfᴸᴗᴗ) [grch.] m/pl. inv., grch. Alt. amphictyons pl.; ~-bund ("...) m ⊕ (grch. Staatenbund zum Schutze der Heiligtümer ꝛc.): amphictyony, =gericht n Amphictyonic Council or Tribunal.
Amphiktyonie (ᴗfᴸᴗᴗᴸ) f ⊕ amphictyony.
Amphimacer ⚗ (ᴗfᴸ⌣tᵻ) [grch.] m ⊕ pros. amphimacer, cretic (Versfuß: -⌣-).
Amphi-theater (ᴗfᴸ...) [grch.] n ⊕ 1. amphitheatre. — 2. (Rampfplatz)arena. — 3. (Platz im Theater) amphitheatre; das ~ besuchen co. to be among (or up in) the gods. [amphitheatrical(ly).]
amphi-theatralisch (ᴗfᴸᴗᴗᴸᴗ) a. ⊕ u. adv.
Amphora ⚗ (ᴸfᴗ) [grch.] f ⊕, **Amphore** (ᴗfᴸᴗ) ⊕ (antikes irdenes Gefäß) amphora.
Amputation (ᴗᴗ-tj(ᴗ)ᴸ) [lt.] f ⊕(Abnahme e-s Gliedes) amputation; ~s-besteck ("...) n ⊕, =etui n surgical instrument case.
amputier/en (ᴗᴗᴸ) [lt.] surg. I v/a. ⊛ to amputate, to cut (or take) off (a limb). — II ~ n ⊕ u. A/ung f ⊕ amputation.
Amsel f/[ahd.: ouzel] f ⊕ orn. blackbird, ouzel (Turdus me'rula).
Amsel-feld ♀ (ᴸ♫ᴗ) n ⊕ (⚔ Schlacht bei Kossowo, 1389) plain of the blackbirds; =netz n, hunt. net (or toils pl.) for (catching) blackbirds.
Amstel-kraut ♀ (♫ᴗ...) n ⊕ meadow-rue (Thali'ctrum aquilegifo'lium).
Amsterdammer (ᴗᴗᴗᴗ) [Amsterdam] m ⊕, ~in f ⊕ inhabitant of Amsterdam.
Amt (ᴸ) [ahd., *flt.] n ⊕b. 1. appointment; (Behörde) board, politisch auch: department; (Pflicht) official duty, public function; (Pfründe) sinecure, es ist kein leichtes ~, ein schweres ~ it is no sinecure, a thorny task; ein ~ antreten to enter upon one's (official) duties; ein ~ bekleiden, versehen, e-m ~ vorstehen, e-s ~es walten to hold a situation, to fill a post, weitS. to officiate as, von Ministern a. to be in (or to hold) office, to be at the head of a (government-) department; sich um ein ~ bewerben to apply (or compete) for a post; e-n in ein ~ einführen to admit a p. into office, to install a p.; e-n in ein ~ (ein)setzen, ihm ein ~ übertragen to give a p. an appointment or a post, F to put a p. into a (nice) berth or screw; ein ~ niederlegen, aus dem ~e scheiden to resign one's office or charge, to throw up one's appointment, to leave one's post; im Genitiv: s. entsetzen 1; das ist nicht m-s ~es that is (F that's) no business of mine, that is beyond my province; was deines ~es nicht ist, da lasse deinen Vorwitz do not meddle (or don't interfere) with other people's business. — 2. obrigkeitliches ~ magistracy; kraft s-s ~es by virtue of one's office; von ~s wegen in one's official capacity, (lt.) ex officio. — 3. Amtsbezirk e-s Amtmannes: bailiwick, weitS. administrative sphere or district; Auswärtiges ~ Foreign Office. — 4. (Gerichts-)~ jurisdiction; vor das ~ müssen to be summoned (or to have to appear, stärker: to be hauled) before the Court. — 5. (Lokal) office (of a magistrate or public functionary);

(Gericht) court-house. — 6. (Innung) corporation. — 7. theol. ~ der Schlüssel power of the keys; eccl.: allg.: (divine) service; protestantisch: communion-service; Cath. mass; das ~ halten to officiate; to hold (or perform) the service. — 8. abs. = Fernsprechamt.
Amtchen (ᴸᴗ) n ⊕ dim. von Amt.
Amtei (ᴗᴸ) f ⊕ = Amtslokal. [tieren.]
amten (ᴸᴗ) [nhd. 19. sæ.] v/n. ⊕ = am-
Ämter-handel (ᴸᴗ...) m ⊕ barter of offices; =jagd =sucht; =schacher m =handel; =sucht f place-hunting; ♀süchtig a. ⊕ seeking office, covetous of a (good) berth.
amt-frei f. amtsfrei. [court-house.]
Amt-haus (ᴸ...) n ⊕ bailiff's residence,
amtieren (ᴗᴸᴗ) [dtsch-lt.] I v/n. (h.) ⊛ to officiate. — II ~ n ⊕ und **Amtierung** f ⊕ = Amtsverrichtung.
Amt-leute (ᴸᴸᴗ) m/pl. v. Amt-mann.
amtlich (ᴸᴗ) a. ⊕ official; nicht ⊊ unofficial, inofficial; vgl. halb⊊.
amt-los (ᴸᴸ) a. ⊕ out of office, retired.
Amt-mann (ᴸᴗ) m ⊕: a) preuß. farmer of a crown-domain; b) südd. bailiff; =justiciary; =mannschaft f bailiwick; ♀mäßig a. ⊕ = amtlich.
Amts-alter (ᴸ...) n ⊕ seniority (in office); =anmaßung f (unbefugte Ausübung e-s ~es) assumption of (official) authority; =antritt m entering on one's official duties, pol. accession to office; =befugnis f competence, authority; =beleidigung f insult (offered) to an official; =bewerber m applicant (or candidate) for an office; =bewerbung f canvassing (or competing) for a post; =bezirk m jurisdiction, eines Richters: venue; =blatt n official gazette; =bote m f. Bote 2; =bruder m colleague; ♀brüderlich a. ⊕ like a colleague; =charakter m: a) (amtliche Eigenschaft) official character; b) (Amtsbezeichnung) official title; =dauer f term (or tenure) of office; =diener m messenger of a court, beadle; =eid m official oath, oath of office; den ~ ablegen to be sworn in; et. auf f-n ~ nehmen to assert a th. on one's official oath; =entsetzung f discharge from office, dismissal; =erschleichung f surreptitious manner of securing a post or obtaining a situation; ♀fähig a. qualified for an appointment; =folge f: a) rotation in office; b) compliance with a summons (from the court); ♀frei a. off duty; ⊊e Zeit freetime, leisure-hours pl.; =führung f administration; =gebühren pl. official fees pl.; =gefälle n/pl. revenues pl. of a domain; =geheimnis n official secret; =gehilfe m (Adjunkt) assessor (of a court); assistant; =genoß, genosse m colleague; =genossenschaft f colleagueship; =gericht n lower court; =geschäft n professional (or official) duty; =gewalt f official authority; ♀halber adv. officially, for official reasons; =handlung f official act, eccl. ministration; =hauptmann m in Sachsen: head-magistrate, chief official; =hauptmannschaft f chief magistracy of a district; =hoheit f official dignity; =inhaber m functionary; eccl. incumbent; =kleid

[Amu=Darja] — 46 — [Ananas]

(=**ung** f) n official gown or robe; =**lokal** n magistrate's office; =**miene** f solemn air; F c-e ~ aufſetzen to look as serious as a judge; =**perſon** f official, functionary; =**pflege** f administration of public business; =**pflicht** f official duty; ♀**pflichtig** a. subject to the jurisdiction of a magistrate; =**reiſe** f official tour, eines Richters: circuit; =**richter** m judge in a lower court; =**ſache** f official business; ♀**ſäſſig** a. within a bailiff's jurisdiction; =**ſchreiber** m clerk of a (county-)court; =**ſiegel** n official seal; =**ſtube** f magistrate's office; =**ſtunden** f/pl. official hours pl.; =**tätigkeit** f performance of public business; außer ~ ſetzen to discharge from an official position; =**titel** m official title; =**tracht** f = =kleid; =**überſchreitung** f official excess; =**verbrechen** n malversation, offence committed in an (or abuse of one's) official capacity; =**verrichtung** f official function; =**vertreter** m deputy, eccl. (lt.) locum tenens; =**verwaltung** f administration; =**verweſer** m administrator; =**vogt** m bailiff; =**vogtei** f bailiwick; =**vorgänger** m predecessor; =**vorſtand** m head official; =**vorſteher** m (der über einen Amtsbezirk geſetzte Polizeibeamte) etwa: police superintendent; =**wechſel** m rotation in office; ♀**widrig** a. contrary to one's official duties; =**widrigkeit** f breach of official duty; =**willkür** f (Bureaukratismus) arbitrary rule (or conduct) of an official; =**wohnung** f official residence; =**zeichen** n (äußeres, die amtliche Eigenſchaft andeutendes Merkmal) official mark or stamp; =**zeit** f term of office; ♀**zuſtändig** a. competent.

Amu=Darja ♀ (⌣–⌣⌣) npr/m. Amu-Daria.

Amulett (⌣–⌣) [fr.; lt. P: amoli'ri; *ar. Anhängſel] ⓑb. charm, talisman.

Amur ♀ (⌣–́) [mongol. ſchwarzer Fl.] m ⓖa. (Fl. u. Land) Amur.

amüſant (⌣–⌣) [fr.] a. ⓖ (beluſtigend) amusing. [ment, entertainment.)

Amüſement (ä-mü-ſ'mã') [fr.] n ⓖ amuse-)

amüſieren (⌣–⌣–⌣) [fr.] v/a. und ſich ♀ v/refl. ⓖ to amuse (o.s.); wir haben uns ganz köſtlich amüſiert we had great fun, we enjoyed ourselves immensely.

Amygdalin ♀ (⌣⌣⌣–́) [grch.] n ⓑc. chm. amygdalin ($C_{20} H_{27} NO_{11}$).

Amyl ♀ (⌣–́) [grch.] n ⓖ chm. amyl; ~**alkohol** (–́⌣⌣) m ⓖ (Fuſelöl) amyl(ic) alcohol ($C_5 H_{12} O$); ~**azetat(lampe)** f n amyl-acetate (lamp).

an (–́) [ahd.: on] I prp. mit dat. u. acc. (vgl. auch am, ans): a) nach **verbs**: ſich an die Wand anlehnen to lean against the wall; (ſich) an et. (an)ſtoßen to knock against a th.; binden an to tie to; an et. denken, erinnern to think, remind of a th.; e-n an der Sprache erkennen to know a p. by his speech; an et. (nicht) glauben to (dis)believe in a th.; er hat nichts vom Geiſtlichen an ſich he has nothing clerical about him; es iſt ſchmählich an ihm gehandelt (auch geſündigt) worden he was shamefully done by; et. an die große Glocke hängen to spread a th. abroad, to blaze a th. about; ich hängte es an die Wand I hung (or suspended) it to the wall; es iſt nicht an dem that's not the case, it is not true; ich weiß, was an ihm iſt I know what (stuff) he is made of; es iſt nichts an ihm he is not worth (F not up to) much; ſoviel an mir iſt as far as I am able, as far as lies in my power; es iſt nicht an mir zu ſagen it is not for me to say; es iſt nichts an der Sache there is nothing in it; an et. ketten to chain to; an die Tür klopfen to knock at the door; an Kopfweh leiden to suffer from a headache; ſoviel an mir liegt for my part; die Schuld liegt an ihm the fault lies with me; das nagt an ſeinem Herzen it preys upon him; e-e Frage richten an to address a question to; ich ſchrieb an ihn I wrote to him; an den Aufgaben ſitzen to sit (F to pore) over one's lessons; ſündigen an.. ſ. o handeln; es läßt ſich vieles an ihm tadeln he has many faults; an et. teilnehmen to partake of a th.; an den Tiſch treten to step up to the table; an et. verhindern to prevent from (doing) a th., verkaufen an to sell to; ſich an e-m verſündigen to sin against a p.; an et. verzweifeln to despair of a th.; er eilte an uns vorbei he hurried past us; ich ging an ihm vorbei I passed by him; an dem (ob. am) Ufer wandeln to walk along the shore; ich wandte mich an ihn I applied to him; e-m et. an den Kopf werfen to throw a th. at a p.'s head; an et. zweifeln to doubt of a. th. b) **vor** s: ♀ an der Themſe on the Thames; ♂ an Bord geh(e)n to go on board; es ging ihm an den Hals (ans Leben) his life was at stake or in jeopardy; an der Hand der Statiſtik with the aid (or in the light) of statistics; dies liegt mir ſehr am Herzen I am greatly interested in ...; ich legte es ihm ans Herz I enjoined (or urged) it on him; an Land geh(e)n to go on land; ans Leben gehen ſ. o Hals; an die hundert Mark about (or nearly) five pounds; an demſelben Orte in the same place; an Ort und Stelle on the (very) spot; in bin an der Reihe, die Reihe iſt an mir it is my turn; Lehrer an e-r Schule master in a school; er ritt an meiner Seite he rode alongside of me or by my side; er ſtand an meiner Seite he stood by my side or beside me; an der Spitze der Truppen at the head of the troops; an ſ-r Stelle in his place; an demſelben Tage on the same day; an den Tag kommen to come to light; am Tiſch ſitzen to sit at (or by) the table; fünf an (der) Zahl five in number; c) **nach** s: es iſt ein Bote (ein Brief) an ihn da a messenger (a letter) for him has arrived; es iſt kein gutes Haar an ihm F he is a good-for-nothing; ſie ließen kein gutes Haar an ihm F they hadn't a (single) good word to say for him; aus Mangel an for want of; Rache an e-m üben to have (or take) one's revenge on; die Sache an ſich the thing in itself; an etwas Vergnügen finden to find pleasure in a th.; Vorrat an store of; Zweifel an doubt of; d) nach **a**: arm an poor in; gleich an Wert equal in value; krank an Herzen sick at heart; reich an // rich in //; (un)ſchuldig an guilty (innocent) of. — II adv. **von** dieſem Tage **an** from this day forth, henceforth; von jetzt an from now, from this (very) moment; von der Zeit (oder von da) an from that time (forth), ever since (then), after that.

...**an** (...–́) (hinan), z.B. berg=an uphill.

☛**an-...**(–́...) Vorſilbe I in Zſſgn mit verbs ſtets trennbar (**) ſ. S. XXXVIII (ant. ab=...) bz.: 1. Anfang der Handlung oder des Zuſtandes, z.B. anfaulen to begin to rot. — 2. Annäherung, z.B. anfliegen to fly near. — 3. Befeſtigung an et. anderes, z.B. annähen to sew on. — 4. Berührung mit dem Körper, z.B. anziehen to attract. — 5. Richtung auf et. hin, z.B. anrufen to call out to. — 6. Stoß gegen etwas, z.B. gegen etwas anlaufen to run against. — 7. Zuwachs, z.B. anſchwellen to swell up. — II in Zſſgn mit adv. ſ. aus, aneinander, anher.

Ana ♀ (–́) [ind.] m ⓖ num. (in Dtſch. Oſtafrika u. Oſt=indien) $^1/_{16}$ Rupie) anna.

Anabaptismus (⌣⌣⌣–́⌣) [grch.] m ② (o. pl.) rel. Anabaptism. [(= Wiedertäufer.)

Anabaptiſt (⌣⌣⌣–́) m ㊵ rel. Anabaptist.)

Anachoret (⌣⌣⌣–́) [grch.] m ⓖ (Klausner) anchorite, anchoret, recluse, **anachoretiſch** a. ⓖ anchoretic. [anachronism.)

Anachronismus (⌣⌣⌣–́⌣) [grch.] m ㉗)

anachroniſtiſch a (⌣⌣⌣–⌣–́) a. ⓖ (gegen die Zeitrechnung verſtoßend) anachronistic(al).

Anagramm a (⌣⌣–́) [grch.] n ⓑb. (durch Verſetzung der Buchſtaben umgebildetes Wort) anagram. [(⌣́⌣⌣)⊛** v/a. to assimilate.)

an-ähneln (–́⌣⌣) ⓐ**, **an-ähnlichen**)

Anakoluth a (⌣⌣⌣–́) [grch.] n ⓒc., ~**ie** (⌣⌣⌣–́) f ⓖ gram. (Unterbrechung im Satzbau) anacoluthon. [(ſchlange) anaconda.)

Anakonda (⌣⌣–́⌣) [braſil.] f ⓖ zo. (Rieſen-)

anakreontiſch a (⌣⌣⌣–⌣–́) a. ⓖ (nach Art des grch. Lyrikers Ana'kreon) Anacreontic.

Analekten a (⌣⌣–́⌣) [grch.] n/pl., inv. analecta, select pieces pl.; anthology.

analog a (⌣⌣–́) [grch.] a. ⓖ (ähnlich) analogous to or with.

Analogie a (⌣⌣⌣–́) [grch.] f ⓖ analogy (between, with); ~ h. with to bear analogy to, F to be on all fours with.

analogiſch a. (⌣⌣–́⌣) a. ⓖ (= analog), ♀ erklären to analogize.

Analogon a (⌣–́⌣⌣) [grch.] n ⓖ (Ähnliches, Entſprechendes) analogon, analogue.

Analphabet (⌣⌣⌣–́) [grch.] m ㊷ (der nicht leſen u. ſchreiben kann) analphabet(e), illiterate person. [analysis.)

Analyſe a (⌣–́⌣) [grch.] f ⓖ log., chm.)

analyſierbar a (⌣⌣⌣–́)–a. analysable; ~**keit** f ㊻ analysableness.

analyſieren a (⌣⌣⌣–́⌣) [grch.] v/a. ⓖ (in ſeine Beſtandteile auflöſen) to analyse.

Analyſis a (⌣–́⌣⌣) f ⓖ math. analysis.

Analytik a (⌣–́⌣⌣) [grch.] f ⓖ math. analytics pl.; ~**er** m ㉒ analyst.

analytiſch a (⌣(–́)⌣) a. ⓖ u. adv. analytic(ally).

Anämie a (⌣–́) [grch.] f ⓖ anæmia (= Blutarmut).

anamitiſch ♀ (⌣⌣–́⌣) [Anam, Land in Hinter-indien] a. ⓖ Anamese, Anamite.

Ananas ♀ (–́⌣⌣) [braſil.] f, inv. ob. ⓘ pine apple (Brome'lia).

Signs (see page XVII): F familiar; P vulgar; ⌐ flash; ⌏ rare; † obsolete (died); * new word (born); ⁺⁺ incorrect; ♪ music

[Ananasäther] — 47 — [anbolzen]

Ananas-äther (⌣⌣…) m ⊕ chm. pine-apple ether; **=beet** n pinery; **=eis** n, Kochk.: pine-apple ice; **=erdbeere** ⚘ f pine strawberry; **=gewächse** n/pl. ⚚ bromeliaceæ, zu den ~n gehörig ⚚ bromeliaceous; **=vogel** m, orn. humming-bird.

an-ankern (ᵍᴸ⌣) v/a. ⓒa** 1. ⚓ e. Schiff ≥ to moor a ship to. — 2. ⊕ arch. to fasten with iron braces or cramps.

Anapäst ⚚ (⌣⌣́) [grch.] m ⑬b. anapæst (Versfuß: ⌣⌣́).

anapästisch ⚚ (⌣⌣́⌣) a. ⑥⑥ anapæstic(al).

an-arbeiten (ᵍᴸ⌣) ⑥⑥** I v/n. (h.) gegen et. ≥ to work strenuously (or to bear up) against … — II v/a. an et. ≥ to join (or add) to … [anarchy.

Anarchie (⌣⌣́) [grch.] f ⑱ (Gesetzlosigkeit)*J*

anarchisch (⌣⌣⌣) [grch.] a. ⑥⑥ anarchic(al).

Anarchismus (⌣⌣⌣⌣) [grch.] m ㉗ anarchism. [=ſtiſch a. ⑥⑥ anarchistic).

Anarchist (⌣⌣⌣) [grch.] m ㊷ anarchist.

an-ärgern (ᵍᴸ⌣) v/a. ⓒa** ſich (dat.) ob. e-m die Schwindſucht ≥ to worry o.s. or a p. into a consumption.

an-arten ↘ (ᵍᴸ⌣) ⑥⑥** I v/a. to assimilate. — II v/n. (in) u. ſich ≥ v/refl. to be(come) assimilated to. — III ℒb p.pr., **an-geartet** p.p. ⑥⑥ innate, inborn.

anastaltiſch ⚚ (⌣⌣⌣⌣) [grch. hemmend] a. ⑥⑥ anastaltic, vgl. blutſtillend.

anastatiſch ⚚ (⌣⌣⌣) [grch.] a. ⑥⑥: typ. ℒer Druck (zur Vervielfältigung alter Drucke) anastatic printing.

Anästhesie ⚚ (⌣⌣⌣́) [grch.] f ⑱ path. (Empfindungsloſigkeit) anæsthesia.

anäſthetiſch ⚚ (⌣⌣⌣⌣) a. ⑥⑥ anæsthetic.

Anathem (⌣⌣́) [grch.] n ⑩c., **~a** (⌣⌣⌣), im Bannſluch: (⌣⌣⌣́⌣) n ⑩ u. ⑥⑥ (Bannſluch) anathema, (papal) excommunication.

an-atmen (ᵍᴸ⌣) v/a. ⓒb** = anhauchen 1.

Anatoli-en ⚢ (⌣⌣́(⌣)⌣) [grch.] npr/n. ⑬α. (Kleinaſien) Anatolia.

anatoliſch (⌣⌣⌣⌣) a. ⑥⑥ Anatolian.

Anatom ⚚ (⌣⌣́) [grch.] m ㊷ anatomist; **~ie** f ⑱: a) anatomy; b) dissecting room; ℒieren v/a. ≥ (zergliedern) to anatomize, dissect; **~iker** (⌣⌣́⌣) m ㉒ anatomist; ℒiſch a. ⑥⑥ anatomical.

Anatozismus (⌣⌣⌣⌣) [grch.] m ㉗ (Zinſeszins) compound interest.

an-ätzen (ᵍᴸ⌣) v/a. ⑥⑥** 1. ⊕ Kupferplatten: to etch. — 2. chm. to begin to erode.

an-äugeln (ᵍᴸ⌣) v/a. ⓒa** e-n ≥ to cast side-long glances at a p., to ogle a. p.

an-backen (ᵍᴸ⌣) v/a. u. v/n. (h.u.jn) ⓒb** 1. to bake gently. — 2. an et. ≥ (feſtbacken) to stick (or to bake) to a th.

an-bahnen (ᵍᴸ⌣) v/a. ⑥⑥** to prepare (or clear) the way for; neue Handelsbeziehungen ≥ to open up new channels (or markets) for trade.

an-ballen (ᵍᴸ⌣), ſich ≥ v/refl. ⑥⑥** to clot, ⚚ to conglobate.

an-bändeln, -bandeln (ᵍᴸ⌣) v/n.(h.) ⓒa** ≥ mit flirt with, to make up to.

an-bannen (ᵍᴸ⌣) v/a. ⑥⑥** e-n an et. ≥ to rivet a p. (as if by magic) to a th.; er war wie angebannt … spell-bound.

An-bau (ᵍᴸ) m ⑩d. 1. agr. cultivation (of a field). — 2. arch. (Neubau) additional building, (Baulichkeit) outhouse, wing (of a building); annex (Neuſtadt) new (part of a) town. — 3. (Anſiedelung) colony, settlement.

an-baubar (ᵍᴸ⌣) a. ⑥⑥ cultivable.

an-bauen (ᵍᴸ⌣) ⑥⑥** I v/a. 1. agr. to bring under cultivation, to till; fig. to cultivate (arts or sciences). — 2. arch. e-n Flügel ≥ to add a wing to (a building); to build an annex. — 3. e-n Ort ≥ to colonize a country. — II ſich wo ≥ v/refl. to settle down in …

An-bauer (ᵍᴸ⌣) m ㉒ 1. (Urbarmacher) pioneer, planter, squatter, cultivator. — 2. (Anſiedler) colonist, settler.

an-befehlen (ᵍᴸ⌣⌣) I v/a. ⑥⑥c*/* e-m et. ≥ to order (or command, enjoin) a p. to do a th., to bid a p. do a th. — II A/ung f ⑯ order, command, injunction.

An-beginn † ob. bibl. (ᵍᴸ⌣) m ⑩c. (o. pl.) first beginning, commencement; von ~ an from the (very) first.

an-behalten (ᵍᴸ⌣⌣) v/a. ⓒa*/* f-n Rock ≥ to keep on…, not to take off …

an-bei (ᵍᴸᴸ) adv. herewith (enclosed, annexed); ≥ folgt e. Muſter you herewith receive a sample, sample enclosed.

an-beißen (ᵍᴸ⌣) ⓒa** I v/a. to bite at (or a piece off) a th. — II ſich ≥ v/refl. to fasten one's teeth in. — III v/n. (h.): a) Fiſcherei: to bite (a. fig. F abs.); der Fiſch beißt an … rises (to the bait); b) fig. to swallow the bait, to be caught, to be taken in. — IV ~ n ㉓ fig. zum ~ most appetizing; zum ~ ſchön most enchanting or alluring.

an-belangen (ᵍᴸ⌣⌣) v/a., impers. ⓒ** to concern; was mich (dies) anbelangt as far as I am (this is) concerned.

an-belfern (ᵍᴸ⌣) ⓒa**, **-bellen** (ᵍᴸ⌣) ⑥⑥** I v/n. (h.) 1. to begin to bark. — 2. der Hund kommt angebellt … comes along barking. — II v/a. e-n (ſich, ea.) ≥ to snarl at a p. (at one another).

an-bequemen (ᵍᴸ⌣⌣) v/a. u. ſich ≥ v/refl. ⓒ*/* to accommodate a th. or o.s., to adapt (o.s.) to; ſich den Umſtänden ≥ to yield to circumstances.

an-beraum-en (ᵍᴸ⌣⌣) [nhd. (P ⁂: Raum)] I v/a. ⑥⑥*/* to appoint, assign, fix (a time, date). — II ~ n ㉓ u. A/ung f ⑯ appointment (of the day, the date).

an-beregt (ᵍᴸ⌣) a. ⑥⑥ jur. aforesaid.

an-bet-en (ᵍᴸ⌣) I v/a. u. v/n. (h.) ⑥⑥** e-n, vor e-m ≥ to adore, to worship a p.; er betet ſie an he idolizes her; vgl. Angebetete(r). — II ~ n ㉓ = A/ung.

an-betens=wert (ᴸ́⌣) a. ⑥⑥ = anbetungs=w.

An-beter (ᵍᴸ⌣) m ㉒, **~in** f ⑯ worshipper; (Liebhaber) admirer, ſtärker: adorer.

An-betracht (ᵍᴸ⌣) m, **An-betreff** (ᵍᴸ⌣) m: in ≥, ≥s f-r Lage considering (or respecting) his position; in ~, daß // taking into account (or consideration) that //. [= betreffen, anbelangen.*J*

an-betreffen (ᵍᴸ⌣⌣) v/a., impers. ⓒa*/*

an-betteln (ᵍᴸ⌣) v/a. ⓒa** to solicit alms of a p.; to importune a p. by begging.

An-betung (ᵍᴸ⌣) f ⑯ adoration, worship, von Götzen: idolatry; ≥s=wert (ᵍᴸ⌣…) a. ⑥⑥, ≥würdig a. adorable.

an-biedern F (⌣⌣́⌣) v/n. (h.) u. ſich ≥ v/refl. ⓒa** (ſich) mit (ob. bei) e-m ≥ to sidle (F to chum, F to pal) up to a p., to wheedle round a p., to hobnob with a p.

an-biegen (ᵍᴸ⌣) v/a. ⓒaſt** 1. (ant. abbiegen) to bend to(wards). — 2. Kanzlei u. ⚖ to annex; angebogen enclosed.

an-biet-en (ᵍᴸ⌣) ⓒa** I v/n. (h.) bei einer Auction: to start bidding, to bid first. — II v/a. (u. ſich ≥ v/refl.) to offer (o.s.); e-m ſeine Dienſte als // ≥ to tender one's services to a p. as //; f-e Hand ≥ to propose or to make an offer (to a lady). — III ~ n ㉓ = A/ung. — IV **an-geboten** ⦿ p.p. u. a. ⑥⑥ (D9) offered.

Anbieter (ᵍᴸ⌣) m ㉒, **~in** f ⑯: a) one who offers, ⦿ seller; b) first bidder.

An-bietung (ᵍᴸ⌣) f ⑯ offer(ing); (Vorſchlag) proposal.

an-bilden ↘ (ᵍᴸ⌣) v/a. ⑥⑥** e-m et. ≥ to inculcate a th. in(to) a p.

an-binden (ᵍᴸ⌣) ⓒ** I v/a. 1. (ant. abbinden) et. an et. ≥ (⌣⌣⌣) ≥ to tie a th. (fast) to a th.; ⚓ ein Boot ≥ to moor …; e-n Kettenhund ≥ to chain up a dog; fig. e-n kurz ≥ (ſtreng halten) to keep a strict hand over a p., to be strict with a p.; ein Tau ≥ to belay (or lash)…; weidende Tiere ≥ to tether … — 2. fig. e-m et. ≥ (aufbinden) to tell a p. a fib (or story) about a th.; F e-n Bären ≥ to run up a debt with a p. — 3. ⊕ ein Buch e-m andern ≥ to bind one book with another. — II v/n. (h.) mit e-m ≥ to enter into relationship with a p., mſt b.s. to pick a quarrel with a p. — III **an-gebunden** p.p. u. a. ⑥⑥ attached, fixed; fig. kurz ≥ gegen abrupt, short, offhandish with.

An-biß (ᵍᴸ) m ⑩a. (first) bite (at a th.).

an-blaken (ᵍᴸ⌣) v/a. ⑥⑥** to blacken.

an-blasen (ᵍᴸ⌣) v/a. ⓒa** 1. e-n, et. ≥ to blow at (or against) a p. or th.; das Feuer ≥ to blow up the fire. — 2. ♪ ein Horn ≥ to blow …; e-n Ton ≥ to sound a note; e-n ≥ to receive a p. with sound of trumpets; hunt. die Jagd ≥ to open the chase with bugle-sound; angeblaſen kommen to come (along) with flourish of trumpets. — 3. paint. die Farben ≥ to tone down …

an-blatten ⊕ (ᵍᴸ⌣) v/a. ⑥⑥** carp. to halve (together). [(linen, &c.).*J*

an-bläuen ↘ (ᵍᴸ⌣) v/a. ⑥⑥** to blue*J*

an-blecken F (ᵍᴸ⌣) v/a. ⑥⑥** to show one's teeth to. [attached or on.*J*

an-bleiben (ᵍᴸ⌣) v/n. (jn) ⑥⑥** to remain*J*

An-blick (ᵍᴸ) [nhd.] m ⑩c.sight; aspect; (Schauſtück) spectacle; beim (ober auf) den erſten ~ at the first glance; ſein (bloßer) ~ iſt mir zuwider I loathe the (very) sight of him.

an-blicken (ᵍᴸ⌣) v/a. ⑥⑥** to look (or glance) at, ſtarr: to stare (or glare) at, von der Seite: to leer at; zornig: to frown at, ſtärker: to look daggers at, zuwinkend: to wink at; vgl. a. anſehen.

an-blinken (ᵍᴸ⌣) v/a ⑥⑥** to twinkle at.

an-blinze(l)n (ᵍᴸ⌣) v/a. ⑩(ⓒa)** et. ≥ to gaze at a th. with twinkling eyes.

an-blöken (ᵍᴸ⌣) v/a. ⑥⑥** e-n ≥ to bleat (or low) at a p.

an-bohren (ᵍᴸ⌣) I v/a. ⑥⑥** 1. ⊕ to begin to bore or perforate; Harzbäume: to terebrate. — 2. ein Faß, den Wein ≥ to broach (or tap) a cask or barrel; ⚓ ein Schiff ≥ to scuttle … — II ~ n ㉓ und **An-bohrung** f ⑯ der Harzbäume terebration; ⚓ e-s Schiffes scuttling.

an-bolzen ⊕ (ᵍᴸ⌣) v/a. ⑥⑥** to (fasten with a) bolt to.

⚚ scientific; ⚘ botanical; ⚢ geography; ⦿ machinery; ⚒ mining; ⚔ military; ⚓ marine; ⦿ commercial; ⚐ postal; 🚂 railway.

[anborden] — 48 — [anderenfalls]

an-borden ⚓ (⌣⌣) v/a. ⑩** = entern.
an-borgen (⌣⌣) v/a. ⑧** c-n um Geld ⚑ to borrow money of a p.
An-bot (⁸ᴸ) n ①d. offer (= Angebot).
an-brassen ⚓ (⌣⌣) v/a. ⑩** to brace (the sails) in or up.
an-braten (⁸ᴸ⌣) ⑯a** I v/a. to (begin to) roast. — II v/n. (fr.) to burn (or stick) to the pan.
an-brausen (⁸ᴸ⌣) v/n. (fn) ⑩** meist: angebraust kommen to come rushing (or roaring) along, vom Zuge auch: to approach (or arrive) at full speed.
an-brechen (⌣⌣) ⑯a** I v/a. 1. ein Brot ⚑ to cut into a loaf; ⚔ ein Erzlager ⚑ to open (up) a lode; noch nicht angebrochen not broken into, (still) untouched; ein Faß ⚑ to broach a cask; f-e Vorräte ⚑ to break into one's provisions. — II v/n. (fn) 2. der Tag bricht an the day is dawning or breaking, it dawns; bei ⚑dem Tage at daybreak, at dawn; die Nacht bricht an night is setting in or coming on; mit ⚑der Nacht at nightfall. — 3. †(anfaulen) to (begin to) decay; angebrochen = anbrüchig. — III ~ n ㉓ = Anbruch 2.
an-brennen (⌣⌣) ⑯b** I v/n. (fn) 1. to catch fire, to begin to burn. — 2. Kochkunst: to burn (to the pan); angebrannt schmecken (riechen) to taste (to smell) of burning; fig. nichts ⚑ lassen to keep a sharp look-out. — II v/a. meist: to set alight, to set fire to, to kindle; ein Licht, e-e Zigarre ⚑ to light … — III angebrannt p.p. u. a. ⑯ die Kerze ist schon ⚑ (nicht mehr ganz) … partly gone or burnt.
an-bringen (⌣⌣) I v/a. ⑰** 1. to put (or fit) up, to fix (up); (unterbringen) to find room (or a place) for; (verwenden) to employ; (einrichten) to establish; (in e-e Stellung bringen) to procure (F to get) an appointment for; f-e Tochter ⚑ to settle … in marriage, F to get … off; gut angebracht appropriate, seasonable, well-timed; übel (a. schlecht) angebracht inappropriate, out of place; das ist bei ihm schlecht angebracht F that won't do with him. — 2. ⚑ f-e Waren ⚑ to dispose of …, to sell …; leicht (schwer) anzubringen(d) (un)saleable. — 3. ⊕ ein Schild an c-m Hause ⚑ to put (or affix) a signboard to a house; eine Treppe ⚑ to construct …; e-e Verbesserung ⚑ to make (or introduce) …; e-e Vorrichtung ⚑ to contrive …; — 4. (berichten) to report; jur eine Klage gegen e-n ⚑ to lodge a complaint against a p., als Polizeispion: to inform against a p. — 5. Gründe ⚑ to bring (or put) forward arguments; ein Wort für einen Freund ⚑ to put in a (good or kind) word for … — II ~ n ㉓ = Anbringung.
An-bringer (⌣⌣) m ㉒, ~in f ㊵ informer, denunciator; e-r Klage: plaintiff; ~ei f ㊻ informer-system; Schule: sneaking.
An-bringung (⌣⌣) f ㊻ 1. establishment, settlement. — 2. fig. report; information, denunciation.
An-bruch (⌣⌣) m ①d. 1. ⚔ (opening up of a) lode or body of ore; first output of a mine. — 2. ~ des Tages break (or dawn) of day, daybreak; beim ~ der Nacht at nightfall, at dusk. — 3. bsd.

for. ⚑ (Faulfleck e-s Baumes) decayed part or spot, rot (in a tree). — 4. ⚑ (angebrochne Ware) broken parcel or lot.
an-brüchig (⌣⌣) a. ⑯ slightly tainted or decayed or putrid; for. ⚑es Holz decayed (or rotten) wood; ⚑es Obst unsound (or damaged) fruit; der Zahn carious (or decaying) tooth; ~keit (⌣⌣–) f ㊻ putrescence, (incipient) decay, v. Obst: unsoundness.
an-brühen (⁸ᴸ⌣) v/a. ⑧** to scald, to soak in (or infuse with) boiling water.
an-brüllen (⌣⌣) v/a. ⑧** to bellow (or bawl, roar) at (f. anschreien).
an-brummen (⌣⌣) v/a. ⑧** to growl (or grumble) at, to talk gruffly to.
an-brüten (⁸ᴸ⌣) v/a. ⑩** to begin to hatch; angebrütetes Ei addle(d) egg.
Anchovis f. Anschowe.
Ancienniät ⚑ † (a-s̈(⌣)⌣⌣ᴸ) [fr. ancienneté] f ㊻ seniority (= Dienstalter).
An-dacht (ahd.) f ㊻ (religious) devotion or devoutness; (Gebet) devotional exercise; f-e ~ halten to attend to one's devotions; to be at (or to say one's) prayers; Mangel an ~ distraction; mit ~ devoutly, fervently; in ~ versunken wrapt in devotion.
An-dächtelei (⌣⌣ᴸᴸ) f ㊻ outward devotion, bigotry, cant. [devotion.]
an-dächteln (⌣⌣) v/n.(h.) ⑫a*:* to sham)
an-dächtig (⌣⌣) a. ⑯ 1. devout, pious, b.s. bigoted, saintly; (Andacht übend) devotional. — 2. fig. attentive; m-e ⚑en Zuhörer! beloved brethren!; adv. er hörte ⚑ zu he listened attentively.
An-dächtler (⌣⌣) m ㉒, ~in f ㊵ b.s. (false) devotee, hypocrite, F saint.
Andacht-…(⌣⌣…): ~s-buch n manual of devotion, spiritual guide; ⚑(s)-los a. lacking devotion, irreverent; ~(s)=losigkeit f want of devotion; ~(s)=stunden f/pl. devotional hours or exercises pl.; ~s-übungen f/pl. devotions pl.; ⚑(s)-voll a. devout, vgl. andächtig.
Andalusi-en (⌣⌣ᴸ(⌣)⌣) [Vandalen, s. sæ.] npr/n ㉓a. i. Süd-spanien: Andalusia.
Andalusi-er (⌣⌣ᴸ⌣) m ㉒, ~in f ㊵, an-dalusisch (⌣⌣ᴸ) a. ⑯ Andalusian.
Andamanen ⚑ (⌣⌣ᴸ⌣) npr/f/pl. ㊸ im Bengalischen Meerbusen: Andamans pl.
an-dämmen (⌣⌣) v/a. ⑧** to bar; Wasser ⚑ to dam up …
an-dampfen (⌣⌣) ⑧** I v/n. (fn) 1. to rise as steam. — 2. angedampft kommen to come steaming along or at full speed; mit der Zigarre: to puff the smoke of one's cigar at or in the face of. — II v/a. F e-n ⚑ (von Speisen) to invite a p. by a savoury (or an appetizing) odour or smell.
andante ♪ (⌣⌣) [it. gehend] adv. u.
Andante n ⑬ (langsam, mäßig) andante.
andantino ♪ (⌣⌣ᴸ) [it.] adv. u. Andantino n ⑬ andantino.
an-dauern (⁸ᴸ⌣) I v/n. (h.) ⑫a** to last; to continue; der Regen dauert an it keeps on raining. — II ~ n ㉓ continuousness. — III ⚑d p.pr. u. a. ⑯ lasting, continuous, uninterrupted; von Bemühungen xc.: sustained, steady.
Anden ⚑ (⌣⌣) [peru. Often] npr/f/pl. ㊸ die ~ (süd-amer. Gebirgskette) the Andes pl.; ~tanne ⚑ f araucaria (Arauca'ria).

an-denken (⌣⌣) I⚐ v/n. (h.) ⑰** 1. denk' (mal) an! only think!, F just fancy! — 2. to remember. — II ~ n ㉓: a) (o. pl.) memory; remembrance; zum ~ an in memory of, bsd. rel. in remembrance of; im ~ behalten to bear in mind; behalt mich in freundlichem ~ keep me in kind remembrance; das ~ an et. feiern to commemorate a th.; in gutem ~ bei e-m steh(e)n to be in good odour with a p.; b) (mit pl.) (Geschenke zum) ~ souvenir, keepsake.
and(e)re (⌣(⌣)⌣) (ahd.: other) I a. ⑯ (A₃†) (nur als Attribut) 1. other; Bücher other books; e-e ⚑ Brille another pair of spectacles; ⚑ Leute other people, others; das ⚑ Mal vgl. andermal; ein um das ⚑ Mal, ein Mal über das ⚑ time and again, repeatedly; sein Bruder ist ein ganz ⚑r Mensch … is quite another (or a different) sort of person; er kam am ander(e)n (nächsten) Morgen … on the next (or following) morning; ganz ⚑r Meinung sein to be of a totally different opinion. — 2. e-r oder der ⚑ some one or other; either (of the two); einmal über das ⚑ again and (or over and over) again; e-n Tag um den andern every other (or alternate) day; e-n Tag nach dem ander(e)n day after day; ein Jahr ins ⚑ gerechnet taking one year with another; ein ⚑es Hemd anziehen to change one's shirt or linen; ⚑r Ansicht (od. ander(e)n Sinnes) werden to change one's mind; ⚑ Saiten aufspannen to change one's tone; die ⚑ (verkehrte) Seite des Tuchs xc. the wrong (or reverse) side; — II ⚑(r) m, ⚑(e) f ㊼ (an)other; die (alle) ander(e)n (all) others; ein ⚑r another; der eine kannte den andern nicht neither (of them) knew the other; kein ⚑r als none other than, no other but; es ist keines ander(e)n Sache als seine it is nobody's business but his; F das machen Sie (e-m) ander(e)n weis tell that to your granny or to the marines; e-r um den ander(e)n alternately, by (or in) turns; unter e-m ander(e)n befehligen to be second in command, unter ander(e)n among the rest — III ⚑(s) n ㊼ (an)other; alles ⚑ everything else; eins brachte das ⚑ one thing led to another; etwas ⚑s something else; das ist et. ⚑s that's another thing, F that's another pair of breeches; von et. ander(e)m reden ob. sprechen to speak of s.th. else; eins ins ⚑ gerechnet one with the other; eins nach dem ander(e)n one thing after another; und noch vieles ⚑ and many other things (besides); nichts ⚑s als nothing (else) but; unter ander(e)m among other things; zum ander(e)n secondly; Sprichw. ein ⚑s ist versprechen, ein ⚑s halten it is one thing to promise, and another to perform; f. auch billig 1. [different, ⚑ heterogeneous.
ander-artig (⌣⌣⌣) a. ⑯ of another kind,
änderbar (⌣⌣–) a. ⑯ changeable. [ing.]
Änderei (⌣⌣ᴸ) f ㊻ chopping and chang-
ander(e)n-falls (⚑(⌣)⌣…) adv.: else, otherwise; in the contrary case.

Zeichen (f. S. XVII): F familiär; P Volkssprache; ⌐ Gaunersprache; ⚑ selten; † alt (auch gestorben); * neu (auch geboren); ⁺⁺ unrichtig,

[anderenteils] — 49 — [aneinanderbinden]

ander(e)n-teils (⸚⸚⸜⸌) adv.=anderſeits.
and(e)rer-ſeits (⸚⸚⸜⸌) adv.=anderſeits.
Ander-geſchwiſterkind (⸚⸚...) n ㉖ second cousin; ⸰mal adv. ein ⸰ another time; ⸰malig a. ⓺ happening another time.
ändern (⸚⸚) ⓐa. I v/a. 1. to change, to alter; teilweiſe ⸰ to modify; das ändert die Sache that alters the case; ſeinen Standpunkt ⸰ to shift one's ground; ſeinen Ton ⸰ to change one's tone, to talk in a different strain; zum Vorteil, Nachteil ⸰ to change for the better, for the worse; ſeine Wohnung ⸰ to change one's residence, to remove (to other quarters). — 2. (verhindern) to prevent; ich kann's nicht ⸰ I cannot help it; das iſt nicht zu ⸰ that cannot be helped or remedied; Sprichw. geſchehene Dinge ſind nicht mehr zu ⸰ what's done cannot be undone, it's (of) no use crying over spilt milk; was man nicht kann ⸰, muß man laſſen ſchlendern what cannot be cured must be endured. — II v/n. (h.) u. ſich ⸰ v/refl. 3. to change, alter; er hat ſich ſehr zu ſ-m Vorteil geändert he is (or has) greatly improved; die Sache (od. es) läßt ſich nicht ⸰ it can't be helped; das Wetter ändert ſich .. is changing; der Wind ändert ſich ... is shifting; ● von den Preiſen: to vary, to fluctuate — III ~ n ㉓ 4. = Änderung.
andern=... (⸚⸚...) adv. ſ. ander(e)n=...
anders (⸚⸚) adv. 1. otherwise; (verſchieden) differently; er iſt ganz ⸰ geworden he is quite different from what he was; es wird bald ⸰ kommen, werden things will take a new turn soon; ⸰ als differently from, other but; er ſpricht ⸰ als er denkt he says one thing and means another; das iſt nun (ein=)mal nicht ⸰ there it is, and it cannot be altered; ich kann nicht ⸰ I have no choice (in the matter); ich kann nicht ⸰, ich muß weinen I cannot help (or refrain from) crying, I cannot but weep; ſich ⸰ beſinnen to change one's mind; et ⸰ deuten to put a different construction on a th. — 2. (irgend) jemand ⸰ somebody (any one) else; irgendwo ⸰ somewhere (anywhere) else; niemand ⸰ als er nobody (else) but he; nirgend (=wo) ⸰ nowhere else; wer (was) ⸰ als er (dies)? who (what) else but he (this)?; wer könnte das ⸰ ſein als //? who could it be but //?; wo ⸰? where else? — 3. in Bedingungsſätzen: wenn ⸰, wofern ⸰ if indeed, provided that; wenn ⸰ nicht unless.
anders-denkend (⸚⸚...) a. ⓺ thinking otherwise, dissenting; ~e([r] m) f ㊲ one of a different opinion, dissentient.
anders-ſeits (⸚⸚⸌) adv. on the other hand.
anders-farbig (⸚⸚...) a. ⓺ of a different colour; ⸰geſinnt a. differently minded; ⸰geſtaltet a. heteromorphous; ⸰gläubig a., theol. ⚔ hederodox; =gläubige([r] m) f ㊲ one of a different faith or denomination, (Ketzer) heretic, (Seltierer, Diffident) dissenter; =meinende([r] m) f ㊲ =denkende(r); ⸰redend a. with a different speech; ⸰wie adv. (in) some other way, in some other manner; ⸰wo adv. elsewhere; =wo n jur. alibi; ⸰woher adv. from elsewhere; ⸰wohin adv. to some other place.
andert-halb F (⸚⸚) a. inv. (1½) one and a half; ⸰ Pfund a pound and a half; ⸰ Jahre eighteen months; ⸰ Fuß lang a.: ⚔ sesquipedal(ian); ⸰fach (⸚⸚) a. ⓺ chm.: Des Oxyd sesquioxide; ⸰ig (⸚⸚) a. ⓺ one-and-a-half times; math.: ⚔ sesquialter; ⸰jährig a. eighteen months old; ⸰kohlenſaures Salz: ⚔ sesquicarbonate.
Änderung (⸚⸚) f ㊻ change, alteration; beſſernde: improvement, beſchränkte: modification; ~ des Wetters change (or break) in the weather; ● der Preiſe: variation; ~ erfahren, erleiden to undergo (or suffer) a change; vgl. Abſ ⸰.
Änderungs-manie (⸌...) f ㊷, =ſucht f mania for changing; =vorſchlag m, parl. amendment; =wut f = =ſucht.
ander-wärtig (⸚⸚...) a. ⓺ other, further; ⸰wärts, ⸰weit [nhd. (P +⸌. weit): Weide Fahrt] adv elsewhere, in another place; ⸰weitig a.: a) = wärtig; adv. = wärts; b) (wiederholt) repeated; c) ⸰ über et. verfügen to dispose of a th. in a different way.
an-deuten (⸌⸚) ⓼⸌ I v/a. 1. to indicate, to intimate; er deutete mir an, daß // he gave me to understand that //; flüchtig, leicht ⸰ to make (a slight) allusion to, to hint, to suggest; paint., &c. to outline, to suggest. — 2. (vorherbedeuten) to announce, to foreshadow; Schlimmes ⸰ to forebode … — II ſich ⸰ v/refl. 3. to show o.s.; ſich gut ⸰ to promise well. — III ~ n ㉓ 4. = Andeutung. — IV ⸰d p pr u. a. ⓺ 5. indicative (or suggestive) of.
An-deutung (⸌⸚) f ㊻ 1. indication, intimation of, leiſe ~ (an, auf) allusion (to), suggestion (of); beleidigende: innuendo; eine ~ machen to (drop a) hint, to suggest. — 2. bildende Künſte: outline, sketch.—3. (Vorbedeutung) foreboding.
an-deutungs=weise (⸌⸌⸚) adv. by way of a suggestion or an allusion or a hint.
an-dichten (⸌⸚) I v/a. ⓼⸌ e-m et. ⸰ to ascribe (or impute) a th. falsely (or fantastically) to a p. — II ~ n ㉓ u. **An-dichtung** f ㊻ (false) imputation.
an-donnern ⚔ (⸌⸚) v/a. ⓶a⸌ to thunder at; e-n ⸰ to shout (or roar) at a p. with a voice of thunder; wie angedonnert daſteh(e)n to stand (as if) thunder-struck. [(Marru'bium).
An-dorn ⚘ (⸌⸚) [ahd.] m ⓶c. horehound)
Andorra ⚘ (⸚⸚) npr/n. ⓺a. (Republik in den Pyrenäen) Andorra; ~ betreffend, Bewohner(in) von ~ Andorran.
an-dorren (⸌⸚) v/n. (ſn) ⓼⸌ to adhere (or stick) to a th. in drying.
An-drang (⸌⸚) m ⓶c. 1. ~ von Menſchen throng, concourse, press, rush; thea. der ~ zu dieſem Stück iſt groß this piece draws large crowds or audiences; ● ~ zu e-r Bank run on a bank. — 2. path. ~ des Bluts ⸰c. congestion.
an-drängen (⸌⸚) ⓼⸌ v/a. e-n an die Wand ⸰c. ⸰ to press (or push) a p. against … — II ſich ⸰ v/refl. an e-n to press close to a p.; F to thrust o.s. on a p., to obtrude (o.s.) upon a p.

andre (⸚⸚) a. ſ. and(e)re.
Andreas (⸚⸌⸚) [grch. der Männliche] m, ㉟γ. (Bn.) Andrew, Andy.
Andreas=feſt (⸌...) n ㉖ =tag; =kraut n St. Andrew's cross or thistle (A'-cyrum crux André'ae); =kreuz n (×) cross of St. Andrew or St. Patrick, saltier; =orden m i. Schottland: Order of St. Andrew; =tag m St. Andrew's Day (30. Nov.)
an-drechſeln (⸌⸚ty) v/a. ⓶a⸌⸌ 1. einen Knopf oben an den Kegel ⸰ to turn (on the lathe) a knob to the ninepin. — 2. fig.: F-m et. ⸰ to palm a th. upon a p.; der Rock ſitzt ihm wie angedrechſelt ... fits him to perfection, F fits him (or sits) like a glove.
an-drehen (⸌⸚) v/a. ⓼⸌ 1. to begin to turn; fig. to set going; das Gas, Waſſer ⸰ to turn on ...; das elektriſche Licht ⸰ to switch on ... — 2. = andrechſeln. — 3. to fasten by twisting; fig. einem et. ob. eine Naſe ⸰ to fool (F to do or to gammon) a p. [andere.
andrer(=...), **andres** (⸚⸚) ſ. and(e)rer(=...),)
an-dreſchen (⸌⸚) v/n. ⓼⸌ ⓐe (auch ⓺b)(e)ſt⸌⸌ to begin to thrash.
an-dringen (⸌⸚) v/n. (ſn) ⓸i⸌⸌ 1. auf e-n ⸰ to press (or push) on towards a p.; ⚔ auf den Feind ⸰ to rush on ... — 2. das Blut bringt gegen den Kopf an ... rushes to the head. [drogynous.)
androgyniſch ⚔ (⸚⸚⸜⸚) [grch.] a. ⓺ an-)
an-drohen (⸌⸚) I v/a. ⓼⸌⸌ e-m et. ⸰ to threaten (or menace) a p. with a th. — II ~ n ㉓ u. **An-drohung** f ㊻ threat(ening), menace; jur. bei, unter ~ e-r Geldſtrafe under penalty of a fine.
Andromeda (⸚⸌⸚⸚) [grch.] npr/f ⓺ ㉟α. myth., ast. Andromeda.
An-druck (⸌⸚) m 1. ⓓd. pressing. — 2. ⓓd. ⚔ typ. going to press.
an-drucken ⚔ (⸌⸚) v/a. ⓼⸌⸌ typ. 1. (beidrucken) to add in printing. — 2. to set the printing-press going.
an-drücken (⸌⸚) I v/a. ⓼⸌⸌ to press (or squeeze) against or on to; die Tür ⸰ to close ... — II an-gedrückt p. p. u. a. ⓺ pressed (on to); ⸰ appressed.
an-duften (⸌⸚) v/a. ⓼⸌⸌ e-n ⸰ to exhale (or waft) fragrance towards a p
Äneas (-⸌⸚) [grch.] npr/m. ㉟ ⓲γ. Æneas.
an-ecken (⸌⸚) I v/a. ⓺⸌⸌ 1. (in Ecken anſtoßen) to push (or jam, squeeze) in(to) a corner. — 2. fig. (derb anrempeln) e-n ⸰ to push (or knock) against a p. — II v/n (h.) 3. Kegelſpiel: to graze the board with the bowl. [Vergil) Æneid.
Äne-ide (---⸌⸚) f ㊻ (Heldengedicht des röm.D.)
an-eifern (⸌⸚) I v/a. ⓶a⸌⸌ to stimulate, to rouse (to action). — II ~ n ㉓ und **An-eiferung** (⸌⸚⸚) f ㊻ stimulation.
an-eignen (⸌⸚) I v/a. und v/refl. ⓶b⸌⸌ ſich (dat.) et. ⸰ to appropriate a th. (to o.s.), to make it one's own; ſich eine Gewohnheit ⸰ to contract a habit; ſich eine Kunſt ⸰ to acquire (or master) ...; ſich e-n Namen ⸰c. ⸰ to adopt ...; physiol. (in ſich aufnehmen) to assimilate; (ſich et. anmaßen) to usurp a th. — II ~ n ㉓ u. **An-eignung** (⸌⸚⸚) f ㊻ appropriation, adoption; physiol. assimilation, gewaltſame ~ usurpation.
an-ein-ander (⸜⸌⸌) adv. together; ⸰binden (⸌⸌...) v/a. ⓶⸌⸌ to tie together;

♪ Muſik; ⚔ Wiſſenſchaft; ⚘ Pflanze; ⚲ Geographie; ⚙ Technik; ⚒ Bergbau; ⚔ Militär; ⚓ Marine; ● Handel; ✉ Poſt; 🜨 Eiſenbahn.

[aneinanderflechten] — 50 — [Anfang]

Taue ₂flechten v/a. ⓑ** to splice ...; ₂fügen v/a. ⓢ** to join together; =fügung f ㊻ juncture; ⊕ carp. assembling; ₂geraten v/n. ⓐa*/* kämpfend, streitend: to come to close quarters or to blows; ₂grenzen v/n. ⓠ** to be neighbours; bsd. ♀ to border on, to bound; ~ n ㉓ contiguity; ₂d a. ⓖⓖ contiguous; adjacent; ₂hängen v/n. ⓖb** und ₂hängen v/a. ⓢ** = ₂fleben; ₂hangend a. ⓖⓖ continuous, coherent; ₂fleben v/n. und v/a. ⓢ** to stick together. ↯ to conglutinate; ~ n: ↯ conglutination; ₂kommen=₂geraten; ₂prallen v/n. ⓢ** to collide; ~ n collision; =reiben n ㉓ mutual friction; ₂reihen v/a. ⓢ** to string together, to arrange side by side; =reihung f ㊻ arranging side by side; apposition; ₂rücken v/a. u. v/n. ⓢ** to move close together; =schlagen v/a. ㉓ concussion; ₂setzen v/a. ⓠ** to put close to each other, to join; ₂stoßen v/a. u. v/n. ⓖa** und ~ n ㉓: a) = ₂grenzen; b) = ₂prallen; ₂wachsen v/n. (ſu) ⓢb** to grow together, ↯ to coalesce; ~ n growing together, ↯ coalescence
Ane-is (-ᴗ́ᴗ) [grch.] f, inv. = Aneide.
Anekdote (ᴗᴗ́ᴗ) [grch.] f ㊽ (dim. Anekdötchen n ㉓) anecdote; alte ~ Joe Miller; ₂n-artig (ˮ...) a. ⓖⓖ, **anekdotenhaft** (ᴗᴗ́ᴗᴗ) a. ⓖⓖ anecdot(ic)al.
Anekdoten=jäger (ᴗᴗ́ˮ...) m ㊺, =liebhaber m anecdote-hunter; =sammlung f collection of anecdotes.
anekdotisch (ᴗᴗ́ᴗ) a. ⓖⓖ = anekdotenartig.
an-efeln (ᴗ́ᴗᴗ) v/a. ⓠa** et. efelt mich an, es efelt mich (mir) vor et., ich werde (od. fühle mich) von et. angefelt I feel a loathing for (or an aversion to) a th., it sickens me; das Fett efelt mich an ... turns my stomach, ... makes me heave; das Buch efelt mich an ... disgusts me.
an-elektrisch (ᴗ́ᴗᴗ) [grch.] a. ⓖⓖ (den elektrischen Strom leitend) anelectric(al).
Anemo-graph ↯ (ᴗᴗᴗ́f) [grch.] m ㊷, =meter ↯ (ᴗᴗᴗ́ᴗ) n (m) ㉒ phys. (Windmesser) anemograph, anemometer, wind-gauge; =logie ↯ (ᴗᴗᴗf) f ㊽ phys. (Windkunde) anemology.
Anemone (ᴗᴗ́ᴗ) [grch.] f ㊽ 1. ♀ (Windrös-chen) wind-flower (Anemo'ne nemoro'sa). — 2. zo. (See=)~ (sea-)anemone, ↯ actinia.
anemonen-artig ♀ (ˮ...) a. ⓖⓖ: ₂e Pflanzen f/pl. anemoneæ pl.
an-empfehl/en (ᴗ́ᴗᴗ) I v/a. ⓠc*/* e-m et. ₂ to (re)commend a p. a th.; wir haben ihm anempfohlen zu warten we have advised (or urged) him to wait. — II ~ n ㉓ u. A/ung f ㊻ recommendation; advice; (Reklame) puff(ing), (Lob) praise.
an-empfind/en (ᴗ́ᴗᴗ) I v/refl. ⓓ*/* sich e-m ₂ to adapt one's sentiments (or opinions) to those of another p.; anempfunden reflected. — II A/ung f ㊻ reflected (or adopted) opinion.
An-erbe (ᴗ́ᴗ) m ㊹ principal heir.
an-erben (ᴗ́ᴗ) v/a. ⓢ** ⚹ e-m et. ₂ to transmit a th. to a p. by inheritance (to), mst p.p. (e-m) anererbt hereditary (to).
an-erbiet/en (ᴗ́ᴗᴗ) I v/a. ⓠa*/* = anbieten. — II ~ n ㉓ u. A/ung f ㊻ offer, proposal; ein ~ annehmen to accept (or close with) an offer, freudig: to jump at it.

an-erkannt (ᴗ́ᴗᴗ) p.p. v. anerkennen u. a. ⓖⓖ u. adv. acknowledged; er ist ein ₂er Meister, ₂ermaßen (adv.) ein Meister he is a master of acknowledged repute; er ist ₂(ermaßen) ein Schuft he is admitted to be a scoundrel, he is a notorious rogue; ₂e Tatsachen established facts pl.; bayr. ₂er (rechtsfähiger) Verein (abbr. A. V.) association recognized by (the) law. [fit to be acknowledged.]
an-erkennbar (ᴗ́ᴗᴗ) a. ⓖⓖ recognizable,
an-erkennen (ᴗ́ᴗᴗ) I v/a. ⓖb*/* * 1. bsd. jur. to acknowledge, to recognize; e-n Anspruch ₂ to allow a claim; ein Kind (nicht) als (od. für) das seinige ₂ to (dis)own a child; e-e Schuld nicht ₂ to repudiate a debt; j-s Verdienst ₂ to do (full) justice to a p.'s merit; et. als Wahrheit ₂, nicht ₂ to admit, to disallow a th.; ♀ einen Wechsel ₂ to honour a bill. — 2. (loben) to appreciate, to approve. — II ₂d p.pr. u. a. ⓖⓖ 3. appreciative; sich ₂d (adv.) aussprechen über to express one's approbation of.
an-erkennens-wert (ᴗ́ᴗᴗ) a. ⓖⓖ worthy of acknowledgment or appreciation.
An-erkenntnis (ᴗ́ᴗᴗ) n ⑰ od. f ⑱ jur. acknowledgment; vgl. Anerkennung.
An-erkennung (ᴗ́ᴗᴗ) f ㊻ 1. recognition. — 2. gesetzliche ~ eines Kindes legitimation ... — 3. (Würdigung) approbation, appreciation; auf Ausstellungen: honourable mention; ich drückte ihm meine ~ aus I expressed my acknowledgment to him.
an-erkennungs-los (ˮ...) a. ⓖⓖ unappreciative; =schreiben n ㊲ letter of approbation or acknowledgment; =urkunde f recognitory act or deed; ₂würdig a. = anerkennenswert.
Anero-id (=barometer) ↯ (ᴗᴗᴗ́ᴗᴗ) [grch.] n ①c. (⓴) aneroid(-barometer).
an-erschaffen (ᴗ́ᴗᴗ) I v/a. ⓠa*/* to impart (or implant) by birth or in (the act of) creation. — II p.p. u. a. ⓖⓖ (D9) innate, inborn; vgl. angeboren.
an-erziehen (ᴗ́ᴗᴗ) v/a. ⓖb*/* e-m et. ₂ to impart a th. to (or to inculcate a th. in) a p. (by education); e-m anerzogen acquired by a p., bred in a p.
an-essen F (ᴗ́ᴗ) v/a. ⓢ** sich (dat.) e-n Bauch ₂ to grow fat (F pot-bellied) with eating, to gorge o. s. (with food), to eat voraciously.
an-fächeln (ᴗ́ᴗᴗ) v/a. ⓠa** to fan.
an-fachen (ᴗ́ᴗ) v/a. ⓢ** urspr. ⊕ (mit dem Blasebalg schüren) to breathe (up)on, bsd. zur Flamme ₂ to blow (up) into a flame, to set aflame; fig. Leidenschaften ₂ to rouse (or stir up) the passions; Zwietracht ₂ to foment discord.
an-fädeln (ᴗ́ᴗ) v/a. ⓠa** to string, to thread; fig. ein Gespräch ₂ to start (or enter into) a conversation with.
an-fahrbar (ᴗ́ᴗ-) a. ⓖⓖ accessible; für Wagen: passable; für Schiffe: navigable.
an-fahren (ᴗ́ᴗᴗ) ⓖb*/* I v/a. 1. (fahrend herbeibringen) to carry (or convey) by wagon or boat; (wogegen stoßen) mit dem Fahrzeug: e-n ₂ to run into (or against) a p.; (anlaufen) ⚓ e-n Hafen ₂c. ₂ to call (or touch) at ... — 2. fig. e-n (mit Worten) ₂ to rebuke (F to blow up, to fire out at, to pitch into) a p. — II v/n. (ſu)

3. ₂, angefahren kommen to come up (or along) in a carriage or ship; bei e-m ₂ to drive up at a p.'s house. — 4. ⚒ zur Arbeit ₂ to descend (or go down) the shaft. — 5. (ſu n. u. h.) (anstoßen) to dash (or push) against, to run foul of; der Wagen ist auf e-n Stein angefahren ... has struck against a stone; der Fuhrmann hat angefahren ... has run into another vehicle; ⚓ ein Schiff ₂ to foul ... — 6. fig. übel ₂ = übel anlaufen 2b. — III ~ n ㉓ 7. carriage, cartage. — 8. fig. rebuke, harsh taiking-to. [ing (or working) shaft.]
An-fahr=schacht ⚒ (ᴗ́ᴗ...) m ㊵ descend-
An-fahrt (ᴗ́ᴗ) f ㊻ 1. (Ankunft) arrival. — 2. ⚒ ~ in ein Bergwerk descent (into a mine). — 3. (=stelle) für Wagen: drive, avenue; für Schiffe: landing-place, quay, jetty.
An-fahr=weg (ᴗ́ᴗ) m ㊷ = Anfahrt 3.
An-fall (ᴗ́ᴗ) [mhd.: onfall] m ①c. 1. ⚹ (Fall) fall (against a th.); hunt. (Stelle wo sich gern Vögel niederlassen) settling- (or resting-)place for birds. — 2. ⚔ ꝛc. (Angriff) attack, assault, (Ansturm) onslaught, bei der Reiterei: shock; mörderischer ~ murderous attack (by an assassin). — 3. path. attack, fit, touch, seizure; neuer ~ relapse; e-n ~ von Krampf haben to be seized with the cramp, to have spasms; ſ. auch Husten₂, Schlag₂. — 4. jur. (Erbschaft) (falling-in) succession, reversion (of an estate). — 5. ⚹ Anfälle pl. (Einkünfte) revenue. — 6. ⊕ e-s Gewölbes spring (-ing) of a vault; ⚒ stay, prop.
an-fallen (ᴗ́ᴗᴗ) ⓖa** I v/n. (ſu) 1. to accumulate in falling; hunt. Vögel fallen an (laſſen ſich nieder) ... settle down, ... (take) rest. — 2. † e-m ₂ (zufallen) to fall to a p.'s share or lot. — II v/a. 3. bsd. ⚔ (angreifen) to fall upon, to attack, to assail, ungeſtüm: to make a dead-set at; eine Krankheit fiel ihn an ... attacked him, ... laid him low. — 4. hunt. der Leithund fällt die Fährte an ... takes up (or tracks) the scent.
an-fällig † (ᴗ́ᴗᴗ) a. ⓖⓖ reversionary.
An-falls-geld (ᴗ́ᴗ...) n ㊷, =recht n (bsd. Lehnsweſen) reversion.
An-fang (ᴗ́ᴗ) [mhd.] m ①c. (ant. Ende) beginning, commencement; ~ Januar early in January; ~ nächsten Jahres early (or at the beginning of) next year; Theater ꝛc.: ~ halb acht commence at half-past seven; am (ob. im) ~ at (or in) the beginning, at the start; am ~ des Jahrhunderts, a. in the early part (or years) of the century; im ~(e), gleich) von ~ an from the very commencement or outset, from the start, from the first; von ~ bis zu Ende from beginning to end, from first to last, from start to finish; Sprichw. aller ~ ist schwer all beginnings are difficult; große Dinge haben kleine Anfänge great things have small beginnings; in Zeitungen ꝛc.: groß gedruckter ~ (conspicuous) head-line in large type; ⚔ ~ e-s Feldzuges opening of ...; ~ († Tete) e-r Kolonne ꝛc. head ...; ~ e-r Krankheit ꝛc. origin of ...; e-r Rede ꝛc. exordium, introduction of ...;

Signs (see page XVII): F familiar; P vulgar; ⌐ flash; ⚹ rare; † obsolete (died); * new word (born); ⁺⁺ incorrect; ♪ music;

[anfangen] — 51 — [anfluchen]

~ der Schule reopening (or reassembling) of ...; ~ der Wissenschaft (first) elements of ..., rudiments of ...; den ~ machen mit to make a beginning with, to start with; to take the lead in; den ~ mit et. m. to begin (or to make a start) with ...; e-n ~ nehmen to commence, to crop up, (erscheinen, zu Tage treten) to arise, to come on the scene, to make one's appearance; e-m übel von ~ an steuern, vorbeugen to nip ... in the bud; f. a. anfangs.
an-fangen(ᵍᵘ) I v/a., v/n.(h.), v/impers., v/refl. ⓑ** 1. (beginnen; ant. aufhören) mst: to begin, commence, start; wieder ⓛ to begin afresh, to recommence, to resume; von vorn ⓛ to begin at the beginning; wieder von vorn ⓛ to begin over again; ⓛ zu schreiben to begin to write, to commence writing; es fängt mich an zu hungern I begin to feel hungry or F peckish; er hat klein angefangen he began (or started) in a small way; et. beim unrechten Ende (ob. verkehrt) ⓛ to begin (or start) a th. at the wrong end; zu arbeiten ⓛ to start work, to set to, F to cut in; einen Briefwechsel mit e-m ⓛ to enter into (or to open a) correspondence with a p.; ⚔ e-n Feldzug ⓛ to open ...; ein neues Leben, eine neue Lebensweise ⓛ to turn over a new leaf; e-n Prozeß mit e-m ⓛ to bring an action (or to proceed) against (or to go to law with) a p.; die Schule fängt wieder an ... is reopening or reassembling; von et. zu sprechen ⓛ to start a subject or topic; eine Unterhaltung mit e-m ⓛ to engage a p. in conversation. — 2. (sich einlassen auf, tun) to set about (doing a th.), to engage (or embark) in; ein Geschäft ⓛ to establish (or open) a business, to set up in (or to go into) business; Hader (Händel, Streit) mit e-m ⓛ to pick a quarrel with a p.; ein eigenes Hauswesen ⓛ to begin house-keeping; ⚔ Krieg ⓛ to open hostilities; er muß es anders ⓛ he must set about it differently; er läßt alles mit sich ⓛ you may do with him as you please or like; es ist mit ihm nichts anzufangen one can do nothing with him; er muß von neuem ⓛ he must start (or begin life) afresh; er fängt zu viel(erlei) an he has too many irons in the fire; er weiß nicht, was er ⓛ soll he does not know which way to turn or where to begin, F he's in a fix or in a tight corner or on his beam-ends; ich weiß nichts damit anzufangen I don't know what to do with it; was ist da anzufangen? what's to be done (now)?; was sollen wir heute ⓛ? what shall we do with ourselves to-day? — II ⓛb p.pr. u. a. ⓖ 3. = anfänglich; ⓖ Preis: ⓛd mit M 25 from 25 s. (twenty-five shillings).
Anfänger(ᵍᵘ) m ⓶, ~in f ⓵ 1. beginner, (Neuling) novice, tyro, learner, thea. debutant (e f); F new hand, greenhorn; ~ in et. sein to be a (mere) novice at a th. — 2. (Urheber) originator, author of.
an-fänglich(ᵍᵘ) a. ⓖ incipient, initial, original; adv. = anfangs.
an-fangs adv. in (or at) the beginning or commencement; (zuallererst) from (or at) the (very) first, to start with; gleich ⓛ from the very outset; ⓛ Januar ⁑ = Anfang (f. d.) J.
An-fangs-buchstabe (ᵍᵘ...) m ⓶ initial (letter); großer ⓛ capital (letter), typ.: F cap); =geschwindigkeit f initial velocity; =gründe m/pl. e-r Wissenschaft (first) elements, rudiments pl, the ABC of ...; zu den ~n gehörig elementary, rudimentary; e-n in den ~n unterrichten to ground a p. in the elements; =kolumne f, typ head-page; Vorschlag der ~ dropped head; =punkt m starting-point; =zeile f, typ. head-line.
an-färben(ᵍᵘ) v/a. ⓖ** to colour, to paint; (tuschen) to touch up; fig. to tinge. [taken hold of, tangible.]
an-faßbar (ᵍᵘ...) a. ⓖ that may be)
an-fassen(ᵍᵘ) ⓖ** I v/a. u. v/refl. to seize, to take (or get, lay, catch) hold of; et. beim (un)rechten Ende (ob. Zipfel) ⓛ to go the right (wrong) way to work, to get hold of the right (wrong) end of the stick; der Junge muß schon tüchtig mit ⓛ (helfen) the boy must now put his shoulders to the wheel or make himself useful; et. verkehrt ⓛ, a. to put the cart before the horse; fig. mit Glacéhandschuhen (rücksichtsvoll) ⓛ to treat gently or considerately; rauh (a. scharf) ⓛ to handle roughly, to take well in hand; am Kragen ⓛ to collar; sich weich, rauh ⓛ to feel soft, rough. — II v/n. (h.): a) angefaßt! faßt mit an! bear (or lend, give) a hand!; b) ⚘ (Wurzel fassen) to take root. — III ~ n ⓶ (act of) seizing, apprehension.
an-fauchen(ᵍᵘ) v/a. ⓖ** Katze: to spit at.
an-faulen (ᵍᵘ) I v/n. (ſn) ⓖ** to begin to decay or to rot, F u. P to go bad. — II ~ n ⓶ incipient decay, ⚕ putrescence. — III an-gefault p. p. u. a. ⓖ putrid, tainted, ⚕ putrescent; Obſt (half) decayed fruit. [keit f ⓖ contestability.)
an-fechtbar (ᵍᵘ...) a. ⓖ contestable;)
an-fechten(ᵍᵘ) v/a. ⓖb** 1. persönlich: to combat, assail; die Glaubwürdigkeit: to impeach; eine Meinung: to impugn (or contest); e. Testament (eine Wahl) ⓛ to dispute (or oppose) a will (an election). — 2. (versuchen) to tempt; (beunruhigen) to disturb; et. Böses ficht mich an ... is troubling my mind; was ficht ihn an? what's the matter with him?; laß dich das nicht ⓛ! never mind that!
An-fechtung (ᵍᵘ...) f ⓖ 1. contest(ation), jur. impeachment, impugnment. — 2. rel. (Versuchung) temptation; schwere ~ sore trial or tribulation.
An-fechtungs-grund (⁓...) m ⓶ jur. cause for impeachment.
an-feilen (ᵍᵘ) v/a. ⓖ** to begin to file; e-e Spitze an et. ⓛ to file a point to ...; ⓖ Waffenfabr.: to mark with a file.
an-feind/en (ᵍᵘ) I v/a. ⓖ** einen ⓛ to show ill-will (or enmity) to a p., to persecute (or malign) a p. — II ~ n ⓶ u. A/ung f ⓖ persecution, hostility.
an-fertig/en(ᵍᵘ) I. v/a. ⓖ** to make; in e-r Fabrik: to manufacture; ich ließ eine Übersetzung davon ⓛ I had it translated; eine Reinschrift ⓛ to produce a clean copy. — II ~ n ⓶ = A/ung.

An-fertiger(ᵍᵘ) m ⓶, ~in f ⓵ maker, manufacturer. [facture; production.)
An-fertigung (⁓) f ⓖ making, manu-)
an-fesseln (ᵍᵘ) v/a. ⓖa** to attach, fetter to; fig. an j-n Schreibtisch angefesselt sein to be chained to one's desk.
an-fetten (ᵍᵘ) v/a. ⓖ** to grease.
an-feucht/en(ᵍᵘ) I v/a. ⓖ** to moisten, stärker: to damp, to wet; fig. sich die Gurgel, die Kehle ⓛ F to moisten one's throat or clay, to wet one's whistle. — II ~ n ⓶ = A/ung. [tener, wetter.)
An-feuchter ⓖ (ᵍᵘ...) m ⓶ bsd. typ. mois-)
An-feucht-grube ⓖ (ᵍᵘ...) f ⓶ Papierfabrikation: sizing-vat, sizing-trough; =pinsel m damping-brush.
An-feuchtung(ᵍᵘ...) f ⓖ moistening, &c. f. anfeuchten I, ⚕: humectation; agr. ~ der Felder irrigation.
an-feuern (ᵍᵘ) I v/a. ⓖa** 1. den Ofen 2c. ⓛ to light (or heat) ..., ⓖ ⚔ Raketen, Zünder: to prime. — 2. fig. to fire (with passion), to inflame, to incite. — II ~ n ⓶ u. An-feu(e)rung (ᵍ-(ᵛ)⌣) f ⓖ 3. lighting, heating; Feuerwerk: priming. — 4 fig. incitement.
An-feuerungs-rede (⁓...) f ⓶ powerful harangue, stirring address or speech.
an-filzen ⓖ (ᵍᵘ) v/a. ⓖ** Hutmacherei: to begin to felt or to plank.
an-finden (ᵍᵘ...): sich ⓛ v/refl. ⓐ** to be found (again). [anfeuern.]
an-flammen (ᵍᵘ) v/a. u. v/refl. ⓖ** =)
an-flattern (ᵍᵘ) v/n. (ſn) ⓖa** to flutter (or fly) against; angeflattert kommen to come fluttering along.
an-flechten (ᵍᵘ) v/a. ⓐ** an et. ⓛ to join by plaiting (or twisting) on to ...
an-flehen (ᵍᵘ) I v/a. ⓖ** to implore; e-n (inständigst) um Gnade ⓛ to cry (pitifully) for mercy to a p. — II ~ n ⓶ u. An-flehung f ⓖ imploration, supplication (addressed to).
an-fletschen (ᵍᵘ) v/a. ⓐ** = anblecken.
an-flicken (⁓) v/a. ⓖ et. an et. ⓛ to patch (or sew) ... on to a th.; et. an et. ⓛ to tack a th. on to ...; F fig. sie will ihm et. ⓛ she wants to play him a trick.
an-fliegen (ᵍᵘ) ⓦaft** I v/n. 1. ⓛ, angeflogen kommen to fly near, to come flying along, to be borne along on wings; an et. ⓛ to fly (or strike) against a th. (with full force). — 2. to attach o.s. in flying; paint. wie angeflogen delicately laid on. — 3. fig. et. fliegt mir (a. v/a. mich) an ... occurs to me; alles fliegt ihm an, he's fortune's minion or favourite; im Lernen: he learns everything with the greatest ease. — II v/a. 4. e-e sanfte Röte flog ihre Wangen an a rosy blush tinged (or a tinge of red overspread) her cheeks.
an-fließen (ᵍᵘ) v/n. (ſn) ⓦd** ⓛ, angeflossen kommen to come flowing along; an et. ⓛ to flow to (or against) s. th.
an-flößen (ᵍᵘ) I v/a. ⓦ** 1. Holz ⓛ to float wood (or carry it as a raft) to a place. — 2. (anschwemmen) to deposit. — II ~ n ⓶ u. An-flößung f ⓖ 3. des Holzes: floating, rafting. — 4. v. Land: alluvial soil or deposit, alluvion.
an-fluchen (ᵍᵘ) v/a. ⓖ** e-m Böses 2c. ⓛ to curse and call down evil upon a p., to shower curses upon a p.'s head.

⚕ scientific; ⚘ botanical; ⓖ geography; ⓖ machinery; ⚒ mining; ⚔ military; ⚓ marine; ⓖ commercial; ⓖ postal; ⓖ railway.

[Anflug] — 52 — [Angeber]

An-flug (ˢᴸ) m ⓓd. 1. approach (or flight) of birds, &c.; (Aufliegen) soaring. — 2. ~ der Früchte: bloom, gloss; metall. (sehr dünner mineralischer Überzug) efflorescence; (angeschossener Salpeter) saltpetre crystals (or crust) forming; for. seeds pl. sown by the wind; (junges Holz) copse(-wood). — 3. fig. (Spur von et.) trace, touch, dash, very small quantity, sprinkling of; ~ von Bart down; ~ von Eifersucht, Neid slight attack (or fit) of jealousy, envy; ~ v. Röte red tinge or flush; ~ v. Säure suspicion of acid; leichter ~ v. Schnurrbart first signs pl. of a moustache; ein ~ v. Wissen a mere smattering.

An-fluß (ˢˢ) m ⓐa. 1. ~ des Wassers approach (or rise) of water; An- und Abfluß des Meeres high and low tide. — 2. (Anschwemmung) alluvium.

an-fluten (ˢᴸᵛ) v/n. (fn) ⓖ⁹** to flow (or float, rush) towards or against.

an-fordern (ˢᴸᵛ) v/a. ⓐa* 1.† to exact. — 2. ⅹ Lebensmittel ⁰ to requisition.

An-forderung (ˢᴸᵛ) f ⓐ⁶ demand, claim; ⅹ requisition; große (oder hohe) ~en an e-n stellen to require (or expect) a great deal of a p.; allen ~en genügen to meet all requirements, F to be quite up to the mark.

An-frage (ˢᴸᵛ) f ⓐ 1. demand; eine ~ richten an to put (or address) a question to; bei e-m wegen (ob. über) et. ⁰ tun to make inquiries of a p. about a th. — 2. parl. an die Minister: interpellation; für ~n an die Minister bestimmte Zeit question-time.

an-fragen (~) v/n. (h.), v/a. ⓖ⁸ (⁺* ⓖ⁵b.)** bei e-m (ob. v/n. e-n) ⁰ nach (um) et. to inquire of a p. about a th.; bitte, fragen Sie bei ihm an please apply to him.

an-freſſ/en (ˢᴸᵛ) v/a. ⓖ⁸** 1. to gnaw (or nibble) at. — 2. chm. to attack, beizend: to corrode, to eat into. — II P ſich ⁰ v/refl. 3. derb = aneſſen. — III ~ n ⓖ³ 4. = Ä/ung. — IV ⁰d p.pr. u. a. ⓖ⁶ 5.chm., path. corrosive, (äßend) caustic. — V an-gefreſſen p.p. ⓖ⁶ (D9) 6.v. Motten, Würmern ⁰ moth-, worm-eaten. — 7. path. vom Krebs ⁰ cancerous, gangrenous, Knochen: carious; der Zustand caries. — 8. Früchte ⁰: cankered, Zähne: carious, decayed. — 9. fig. vom Gifte ſchlechter Gesinnung ⁰ impregnated with the poison of rancorous feeling.

An-freſſung f ⓐ⁶ corrosion; path. caries.

an-freunden (ˢᴸᵛ) v/a. u. ſich ⁰ mit v/refl. ⓖ⁹** to make friends with; wir hatten uns lebhaft (mit=ea.) angefreundet we had formed a warm friendship.

an-frieren (ˢᴸᵛ) v/n. (fn) ⓘc** an et. ⁰ to freeze on (or fast) to a thing.

an-friſch/en (ˢᴸᵛ) I v/a. ⓐ¹** 1. to refresh, freshen up, renew; metall. Bleiglätte ꝛc.: to revive (or reduce) ...; der Lampe ⁰ to fill (or trim) ... — 2. fig. (anfeuern) to stir (up), to rouse, to fire; die Nerven ⁰ to brace the nerves. — II ~ n 3. = Ä/ung.

An-friſcher ⓞ (ˢᴸᵛ) m ⓐ² metall. workman who reduces litharge, &c.

An-friſch-gefäß ⓞ (ˢᴸˢ ...) n ⓐ⁶ (re)fining-vessel or -trough; =herd m, =ofen m (re)fining-furnace; =trog m = =gefäß.

An-friſchung (ˢᴸᵛ) f ⓐ⁶ freshening, refreshing (process); metall. reduction.

an-fugen ⓞ (ˢᴸᵛ) v/a. ⓖ*** = fugen 1.

an-fügen (ˢᴸᵛ) I v/a. und ſich ⁰ v/refl. ⓖ*** to adjoin, annex, add, attach, append; ein Siegel ⁰ to affix ...; das einem Briefe ꝛc. Angefügte the enclosure; ſich e-m ob. einer Sache ⁰ (anpaſſen) to attach o.s. to ... — II ~ n ⓖ³ und **An-fügung** f ⓐ⁶ annexing; addition.

an-fühlen (ˢᴸᵛ) ⓖ*** I v/a. 1. to feel, to touch. — 2. man fühlt es ihm an, daß // one feels that //. — II ſich ⁰ v/refl. 3. ſich hart, weich ⁰ to feel hard, soft.

An-fuhr (ˢᴸᵛ) f ⓐ⁶ 1. carriage, cartage. — 2. (Zufuhr) imports, imported goods pl.

an-führen (ˢᴸᵛ) v/a. ⓖ*** 1. (leiten) to be (or march) at the head of ...; ⅹ ein Heer ⁰ to command (or lead) an army; den Nachtrab ⁰ to bring up the rear; den Reigen, Tanz ⁰ to lead ... — 2. (anleiten) e-n zu etwas ⁰ to initiate (or tutor) a p. in ... — 3. (beibringen) als Beiſpiel: to instance; Beweiſe: to adduce; Gründe: to assign; Stellen: to quote, to cite; falſch ⁰ to misquote; vorher angeführt above-mentioned, aforesaid (vgl. a. a. D.); Tatſachen: to allege; zur Entſchuldigung ⁰ to plead in excuse; weiter hat er nichts (zu ſ-r Rechtfertigung) anzuführen he has nothing further to say (for himself). — 4. (hintergehen) to deceive, dupe, gull, cheat, F to take in, to diddle; ſich (von e-m) leicht ⁰ laſſen to be easily taken in by a p., to fall an easy prey to a p.; leicht anzuführen easily duped or imposed upon; gullible; nicht leicht anzuführen F up to snuff; wieder angeführt! F sold again! der Angeführte the p. victimized or imposed upon, the victim, the dupe, F the jay.

An-führer (ˢᴸᵛ) m ⓐ² 1. leader, chief, chieftain, captain; manager, controlling spirit; (oberſter) ~ commander (-in-chief); ~ e-s Komplotts ringleader. — 2. =in f ⓐ⁷ manageress, conductress, leader of (a choir). [captaincy.]

Anführer-schaft (ˢᴸᵛ) f ⓐ⁶ leadership,

An-führung (ˢᴸᵛ) f ⓐ 1. leadership, lead; guidance; ⅹ e-s Heeres ⁰: (chief or supreme) command. — 2. e-r Stelle: quotation; von Gründen: allegation.

An-führungs-fehler (ˢᴸᵛ ...) m ⓐ² misquotation; =zeichen n inverted commas pl. (for marking quotations), quotation mark („...", engl. "...").

an-füllen (ˢᴸᵛ) ⓖ*** I v/a. to fill up (mit et. with a th.); bis zum Übermaß ⁰ to cram, stuff; wieder ⁰ to replenish; angefüllt mit full of, replete with; die Straße iſt mit Wagen, Menſchen angefüllt ... is (over)crowded with ...; ⓖ den Speicher mit Waren ⁰ to stock ... — II ſich ⁰ v/refl. to be (F to get) filled with; mit Speiſe: to cram o.s. (with food), to gorge o.s. — III ~ n ⓖ³ u. **An-füllung** f ⓐ⁶ cramming, repletion; (over)crowding.

an-furchen (ˢᴸᵛ) v/a. ⓖ*** agr. (die erſte Furche ziehen) to plough the first furrow.

An-furt ⓙ ⁎ (ˢᴸᵛ) f ⓐ⁶ landing-place.

An-gabe (ˢᴸᵛ) [mhd.] f ⓐ 1. (Ausſage) declaration, assertion, beim Zollamte auch: entry; von Tatſachen: statement, ſtatiſtiſche: return, falſche: misstatement; als Zeuge: evidence; ~ des Tages date; nähere ~ (Auskunft) information; nähere ~n pl., oft: particulars pl.; ohne ~ von Gründen without assigning reasons, ſ-r ~ nach, zufolge from (or according to) what he says or asserts. — 2. ~ von Druckfehlern errata pl.; ~ des Haupt-Inhaltes summary. — 3. ~ (Anzeige) vor Gericht information, b.s. denunciation. — 4. (Anweiſung) instruction(s pl.) genaue: specification, detailed scheme.

An-gabe-liſte ⓛ (ˢᴸᵛ ...) f ⓐ⁶, **=zettel** m declaration of goods shipped.

an-gaffen F (ˢᴸᵛ) v/a. ⓖ*** to gape (ſtärker: to stare) at, höhniſch: to leer at.

an-gähnen (ˢᴸᵛ) v/a. ⓖ*** 1. to yawn at. — 2. e. Abgrund gähnt ihn an an abyss yawns (open-mouthed) before him.

An-gang (ˢᴸᵛ) m ⓓc. myth. good or evil omen attributed to the first person(s) or animal(s) that we meet when we first go out. missible;(tunlich)feasible.

an-gängig, an-gänglich (ˢᴸᵛ) a. ⓖ⁵ ad-

an-geb-bar (ˢᴸ-) a. ⓖ⁶ assignable.

an-geben (ˢᴸᵛ) ⓖc** I v/a. 1. (erklären) to state; ausführlich ⁰ to particularize, einzeln ⁰ to specify; den Grund für ⁰ to account for; Gründe ⁰ to assign reasons, to show cause (why); aus den angegeb(e)nen Gründen from (the) reasons mentioned; ⓖ Kurſe ⁰ to quote ...; in der Kürze ⁰ to sum up; e-n falſchen Namen ⁰ to give a false name; ♪ e-e Note ⁰ to sound ...; ⓖ Preiſe ⁰ to quote ...; eine Stunde ⁰ to appoint ...; ⓖ den Takt ⁰ to mark (or beat) time; den Ton ⁰: a) to give the key-note; b) fig. to set the fashion, to (take the) lead; ⓖ Waren zur Verzollung ⁰ to declare, to enter ...; den Wert von et. ⁰ to value a th.; auf Pateten: to declare the value of; zu wenig ⁰ to understate, ⁰ to enter short; ſtatiſtiſch: e-n als tot ꝛc. ⁰ to return a p. as dead, &c. — 2. (denunzieren) to denounce (a criminal, a crime), Mitſchuldige: F to split (or peach) on. — 3. (entwerfen, anordnen) to design, to deviſe; to suggest; ⓙ den Kurs ⁰ to shape one's course. — 4. ⓖ (als vom Preiſe abgehend in Anzahlung geben) ⁰ to give ... in part-payment; er zahlte 30 Mark bar und gab eine Uhr an ... and gave a watch into the bargain. — 5. (anzahlen) to pay on account, to pay a (first) deposit or an instalment. — 6. (treiben) Poſſen, Unſinn ⁰ to play (foolish) tricks or pranks; was werden ſie jeßt noch ⁰? F what will they be up to next? — II v/n. (h.) 7. Kartenſpiel: (ant. abgeben) to deal first, to have the first deal. — 8. die Feder will nicht ⁰ ... won't mark; ⓖ ein Hammer im Klavier will nicht ⁰ ... won't sound. — III ſich ⁰ v/refl. 9. to give o.s. up (to the police); ſich für (ober als) den Erben ⁰ to come forward as heir to ...; ⓖ ſich als fallit ⁰ to declare o.s. insolvent. — IV ~ n ⓖ³ 10. = Angabe. — 11.(ſ. 2) denunciation.

An-geber (ˢᴸᵛ) m ⓐ², **~in** f ⓐ⁷ 1. ~ e-s Planes author of ... — 2. ~ des Tones, Ton- ⁰

Zeichen (ſ. S. XVII): F familiär; P Volksſprache; ſ Gaunerſprache; ⁎ ſelten; † alt (auch geſtorben); * neu (auch geboren); ⁎⁺ unrichtig;

[Angeberei] — 53 — [angemessen]

leader (of fashion). — **3.** (Denunziant) informer, spy, in Schul=sl.: F sneak; jur.: ~ f=r Mitschuldigen approver; zum ~ werden to turn king's evidence.

An-geberei (⌣⌣–⌣) f ⓯ b.s. espionage, (system of) denunciation; Schul=sl.: tale-telling, F sneaking.

an-geberisch (⌣⌣–⌣) a. ⓰ **1.** ⟨ (erfinderisch) ingenious; der Kopf inventive genius. — **2.** (denunzierend) playing the informer, &c. (vgl. Angeber 3).

An-gebetete ([r] m) f⓰ (⌣⌣–⌣⌣) [anbeten]: der, die ⟨ (ihres, seines Herzens) the adored one, the idol (of one's heart).

An-gebinde (⌣⌣–⌣) n ⓶ ehm. bow (or lover's knot) presented to a knight by his lady-love; jetzt (Zueignung) (birthday, &c.) present or gift.

an-geblich (⌣–⌣) a. ⓰ u. adv. (der Angabe nach) as stated or alleged; ostensibly; dieser ⟨e Künstler this so-called (or self-styled) artist(e); eine Summe von ⟨ 500 Mark ... said (or supposed) to be (equal to) £ 25; ⊛ der ⟨e Wert the nominal value. [biegen.

an-gebogen (⌣⌣–⌣) p.p. u. a. ⓰ (D 9) f. an-

an-geboren (⌣⌣–⌣) p.p. u. a. ⓰ (D 9) inborn, innate, bred in, bisw. inbred; (erblich) hereditary; ⟨e Schwäche constitutional weakness.

An-gebot (⌣⌣–⌣) n ⓭d. **1.** bei Versteigerung: first bid. — **2.** ⊛ offer, tender; e. ~ m. to tender for; ~ u. Nachfrage supply and demand; Börse: es war einiges ~ there were a few buyers or inquiries; das ~ war stärker als die Nachfrage there were more sellers than buyers.

an-geboten (⌣⌣–⌣) p.p. f. anbieten.

an-gebracht (⌣⌣–⌣t) p.p. f. anbringen 1; ⟨ermaßen adv. (be)fittingly, at a suitable time, conveniently, seasonably.

an-gebrannt (⌣⌣–⌣) p.p. f. anbrennen.

an-gebunden (⌣⌣–⌣) p.p. f. anbinden.

an-gedeihen (⌣⌣–⌣) v/n. ⓭*/* nur im inf.: e-m et. ⟨ lassen to grant (or vouchsafe) a th. to (or to bestow it on) a p.; e-m eine gute Erziehung ⟨ lassen to give a p. a good education. [= andenken II.

An-gedenken (⌣⌣–⌣) n ⓴ geh. Spr. ob. poet.

an-geerbt (⌣⌣–⌣), **-geflogen** (⌣⌣–⌣), **-geflossen** (⌣⌣–⌣), **-gegangen** (⌣⌣–⌣), **-gegossen** (⌣⌣–⌣) p.p. f. an-erben, -fliegen, -fließen, -gehen IV, -gießen 4.

an-gegriffen (⌣⌣–⌣) p.p. f. angreifen; ~heit f ⓰ nervous or delicate state (of health), (physical) exhaustion.

An-gehänge (⌣⌣–⌣) n ⓰ appendage; zum Schmuck: pendant, drop, bob.

an-geh(e)n (⌣–⌣) ⓭** I v/n. (fn) **1.** (berg=a'n gehen) to mount. — **2.** (anfangen) to commence; wir wollen es damit sachte ⟨ lassen we won't be in a hurry about it; die Schule wird bald ⟨ school will soon reopen or be reopened; das Stück geht um 7 Uhr an the play will begin at 7 o'clock; ⊛ die Zinsen gehen von heute an the interest will run from this day; ⚓ ⊕ mit der Maschine ⟨ (fie in Betrieb setzen) to set the machine going or in motion, to start the machine or engine. — **3.** (in Brand geraten) to catch (or take) fire; das Holz will nicht ⟨ ... won't burn. — **4.** (verderben) to grow stale or putrid;

stark angegang(e)nes Wildbret high game (vgl. 12). — **5.** Kleid (sich anziehen l.): to go (or slip) on easily. — **6.** (leidlich sein) to be passable, tolerable; (tunlich sein) to be feasible, practicable; das geht nicht an that won't do; das ginge allenfalls noch an that might do on a pinch; sofern es ⟨ mag as far as it is possible, provided it can be done; es sacht ⟨ lassen not to trouble much, F to take it easy. — **II** v/a. (bff.: h., oft a.: fn) **7.** ⟨ den Berg ⟨ to climb (up) ... — **8.** e-n ⟨ to approach (or accost) a p.; der angeschossene Keiler geht den Jäger an the wounded boar rushes at the huntsman; fig. to apply to a p. (um et. for a th.). — **9.** (mst mit h.) das geht mich (⟨ mir) nichts an that does not concern (or interest, touch) me, that is no concern (or business) of mine; er geht uns nichts an he is nobody (or nothing) to us; was diese Sache angeht as regards this matter; was geht ihn das an? what has that to do with him?, what's that to him? — **III an-gehend** p.pr. u. a. ⓰ **10.** commencing; incipient; (unerfahren, ungeübt) inexperienced (workman, hand), raw (recruit), untried (author, &c.); der Advokat young (or budding) lawyer; der Student freshman; der Vierziger one (who is) just turned forty or not much over forty; bei der Nacht as the approach (or fall) of night, at nightfall or dusk. — **IV an-gegangen** p.p. u. a. ⓰ **11.** ⟨ kommen to come walking along. — **12.** (f. 4) = anbrüchig.

an-gehören (⌣⌣–⌣) v/n. (h.) ⓰ b.s. e-m ⟨ to belong (or appertain) to a p.; (verwandt fn) to be (a)kin (or related) to; e-r Gesellschaft ⟨ to be a member of ...

an-gehörig (⌣⌣–⌣) I a. ⓰ **1.** einem ⟨ belonging (or appertaining, related) to a p.; mir (dir, ihm, ihr) ⟨, als Prädikat: mine (yours, his, hers). — **II** ~e(r) m, ~e f ⓰ **2.** relation, relative; kinsman m, kinswoman f; meine ~en my kinsfolk or family or people; ~e pl. desselben Staates fellow-citizens pl. — **3.** alles mir ~e all my belongings or goods and chattels or (lt.) impedimenta pl.

An-gehörigkeit (~-) f ⓰ appurtenance; (Verwandtschaft) relationship, kinship.

an-geifern (⌣–⌣) v/a. ⓶a** to slaver over; bsd. fig. to slander, backbite.

an-gejahrt (⌣⌣–⌣) a. ⓰ (advanced) in years; ⟨e Herren elderly gentlemen.

An-geklagte ([r] m) f ⓰ (⌣⌣–⌣⌣) [p.p. v. anklagen] the accused, delinquent; Kriminal=prozeß: prisoner; Zivil=prozeß: defendant; Ehescheidungs=prozeß: respondent; f. a. Beschuldigter u. freisprechen.

Angel[1] (⌣⌣) [ahd.: angle] f ⓭, † ob. provc. m ⓶ **1.** der Tür. hinge; aus den ~n heben to unhinge; fig. zwischen Tür und ~ between two fires, between hammer and anvil; die Welt aus den ~n heben to shake the world (to its foundations). — **2.** (das, worum sich et. dreht) pivot (⟨=punkt), a. ⓰; sich um die ~ drehen to pivot. — **3.** zum Fischfange: a) (Haken) fishing-hook; b) (das ganze Werkzeug) angling-rod or -line; f-e ~ nach et., e-m auswerfen to

fish (or angle, hook) for ... — **4.** ~ e-r Klinge: spike (of a knife or sword).

Angel[2] ♀ (⌣⌣) [ahd. Speermann] npr/m. ⓰ hist. (Bewohner v. Angeln) Angle. [arrive.

an-gelangen (⌣⌣–⌣) v/n. (fn) ⓰*/* to

Angel[1]**-band** ⊕ (⌣⌣...) n ⓶ Schloff.: butthinge; **-blei** ⊕ n plummet sinkers pl.

An-geld (⌣⌣) n ⓭c. earnest (money).

an-gelegen (⌣⌣–⌣) [p.p. v. anliegen] a. ⓰ (D 9) near to one's heart, important; er hatte nichts ~eres zu tun, als zu // he did his utmost (so as) to //; sich (dat.) eine Sache ⟨ sein lassen to bestow great care upon (or to make a point of attending to) a thing; ich werde mir's ⟨ sein lassen, zu // I shall make it my business to //.

Angelegenheit (~-) f ⓰ affair, concern; jur. cause; Minister der auswärtigen ~en Foreign Secretary; sich in fremde ~en mischen, mengen to meddle (or interfere) with other people's business.

an-gelegentlich (⌣⌣–⌣), ⟨st (⌣⌣–⌣) a. ⓰ instant, pressing, urgent; mein ⟨ster Wunsch my (most) earnest desire; adv. urgently; sich ⟨(st) bemühen to try hard, to make a great effort, to exert o.s. to the uttermost; aufs ⟨ste empfehlen to recommend most warmly.

Ang(e)ler (⌣(⌣)⌣) m ⓶, ~**in** f ⓱ angler.

Angel[1]**-fisch** (⌣⌣...) m ⓰ ichth. thornback (Raia clavata); **-fischer** m angler; **-fischerei** f angling (-sport), fishing with the line; **-förmig** a. ⓰ ⍟ und zo. hooked, ⍚ hamate(d); **-gerät** n fishing-tackle; **-haken** m fishing-hook; **-haar** n (Seidendarm) silkworm gut.

Angelika (⌣–⌣⌣) [grch.] f Inpr. ⓰ ⍺. (Vorname) Angelica. — **II** ⍺ ob. ⓰ ♀ (Brustwurz) u. ♪ (Orgelregister) angelica, angelot.

Angel[1]**-leine** (⌣⌣...) f ⓶ = -schnur.

Angeln[1] (⌣⌣) [Angel[2]] npr. I n ⓷a. (Land) Anglia. — **II** m/pl. v. Angel[2].

angeln[2] (⌣⌣) I v/a. u. v/n. (h.) ⓶a. **1.** to angle (nach for), to fish with the line. — **2.** fig. (fangen) to catch, to ensnare; nach et. ⟨ to fish for a th.; (streben) to aspire to a th.; sie angelt nach ihm she is trying to capture (or F hook) him, she is setting up her cap at him. — **II** ~ n ⓷ **3.** ~ mit künstlichen Fliegen fly-fishing; ein guter Tag zum ~ a good day for fly-fishing or F a nibble.

an-geloben (⌣⌣–⌣) v/a. ⓰*/* geh. Spr. to promise (solemnly), to vow.

An-gelöbnis (⌣⌣–⌣) n ⓴, **An-gelobung** f ⓰ geh. Spr. solemn promise, vow.

Angel[1]**-platz** (⌣⌣...) m ⓶ convenient spot for anglers; **-punkt** m pivot; ast. pole; fig. cardinal point; einer Frage that on which a question hinges; **-rute** f angling-rod, fishing-rod.

Angel[2]**-sachse** (⌣⌣...) m ⓶ ⓰, **-sächsin** f ⓰, **-sächsisch** a. ⓰ Anglo-Saxon.

Angel[1]**-schnur** (⌣⌣...) f ⓰ fishing-line.

Angelus (⌣⌣⌣) n, inv. Cath. angelus.

angel[1]**-weit** adv.: die Tür steht (sperr=)⟨ offen ... is wide open; **-zapfen** ⊕ m ⓶ axle of a hinge; **-zeug** n fishing-tackle.

an-gemessen (⌣⌣–⌣) [p.p. v. anmessen] a. ⓰ (D 9) mit dat.: (passend) appropriate, adequate, fit; well adapted, den Umständen: suitable to; (entsprechend) conformable or proportionate to, adv. in conformity

[Angemessenheit] — 54 — [Angreifung]

with; Ses Benehmen proper conduct; der Jahreszeit ≤ seasonable; Ser Preis reasonable (or fair) charge(s); Se Strafe condign punishment; für ≤ halten to think fit; seinen Verhältnissen ≤ in keeping with his circumstances; der Zeit nicht ≤ out of season, untimely. **An-gemessenheit** (ᵕᵕᵕ⸝) f⑯(o.pl.) fitness, suitableness; des Benehmens: propriety.

an-genehm (ᵕᵕ⸝) **I** a. ⑯ **1.** (den Sinnen wohlgefallend) acceptable; agreeable, pleasant; ≤ von Geschmack palatable, savoury, grateful to the palate; Ses Leben comfortable life; Ses Wesen engaging (or pleasing) manners pl.; was dir ≤ ist just as you please; Sie sind mir stets ≤ you are always welcome; es ist mir ≤ zu hören I am pleased (or glad) to hear it; sich bei e-m ≤ machen to ingratiate o.s. with a p., to win a p.'s favour; bei Gott und Menschen ≤ zu machen (L.) to raise in favour both with God and man. — **2.** ⓖ (begehrt) in demand; Ser w.(von Preisen) ≤ to be looking up, to be improving. — **II ~e([r] m** f u. ~e(s) n ⑰ **3.** the agreeable.

an-genommen (ᵕᵕᵕ) p.p., s. annehmen. **Anger** (ᵕᵕ) [ahd.: ing] m ㉒ grass-plot, green(sward), meadow, pasture-land, common; **~blümchen** ⚥ (ᵕᵕᵕ…) n ㉖, **=blume** ⚥ f = Gänseblümchen.

an-geregter=maßen (ᵕᵕᵕᵕᵕ⸝⸝) adv. as (or in the manner) suggested, according to s. th. proposed or mentioned.

An-geregtheit (ᵕᵕᵕ⸝⸝) f ⑯ animation, animated state, liveliness. ⟦(gem.).⟧

Anger=gras ⚥ (ᵕᵕ…) n ㉖ = Rispengras. **an-gerissen** (ᵕᵕᵕ) p.p., s. anreißen II. **an-gesäuselt** F (ᵕᵕᵕ⸝) p.p. u. a. ⑯ half-seas over, slightly elevated, half tipsy. **an-geschlossen** (ᵕᵕᵕ) p.p. s.anschließen VI. **an-geschuldigt** (ᵕᵕᵕ) p.p. v. anschuldigen (s. ds.); ~e(r) m, ~e f ⑰ jur. defendant. **an-gesehen** (ᵕᵕᵕ) [p.p. v. ansehen] a. ⑯ (D 9) considerable, distinguished, (highly) esteemed; ⓖ Ses Haus respected firm, house of good standing; ≤ sein bei // to be well thought of by //; **~heit** (~⸝) f⑯(o.pl.) good repute. **an-gesessen** (ᵕᵕᵕ) p.p. ⑯ (D 9) s. ansitzen 1. **An-gesicht** (ᵕᵕᵕ) [mhd.] n ⓒ. **1.** (Anblick) nur gen. und dat.: im ~ (oder ≤s) des Strandes in sight of the shore; ≤s der ganzen Welt, des Feindes in the face (or eyes) of …, before…; e-n von ~ kennen to know a p. by sight. — **2.** (Antlitz) face, countenance; e-n ins ~ loben to praise a p. to his face; im Schweiße deines ~s in the sweat of thy brow; von ~ zu ~ face to face; dem Tode ins ~ schauen to look death in the face. — **3.** (Person) du holdes ~ (G.) thy dear face, my darling. ⟦nen 2,-stammen II.⟧ **an-gespannt** (ᵕᵕᵕ) gesammt (ᵕᵕᵕ⸝) s. anspann-. **An-gesteckt-sein** (ᵕᵕᵕ⸝) n ㉓ infectedness. **an-gestellt** (ᵕᵕᵕ) p.p. s. anstellen 2 u. 4: ~e(r) m, ~e f ⑰ employee, (Beamter) official. **an-gestrengt** (ᵕᵕᵕ) p.p. s. anstrengen II. ~**heit** (~⸝) f ⑯ severe effort or strain. **an-getan** (ᵕᵕᵕ) p.p. u. a. ⑯ (vgl. antun) dies ist ganz so (dazu, danach) ≤, daß es geschehen wird there is every appearance (or likelihood) of its happening; es ist nicht danach ≤ it is not

very likely; et. nicht ≤ finden to deem a th. inopportune. **an-getrunken** (ᵕᵕᵕ⸝) p.p., s. antrinken III. ~**heit** (ᵕᵕᵕ⸝) f ⑯ tipsiness. **an-gewachsen** (ᵕᵕᵕᵕ⸝) p.p. s. anwachsen 2. **An-gewäge** ⊙ (ᵕᵕᵕ⸝) n ㉒ Mühlenbau: supporting plank of a mill-arbour, spindle-block.

an-gewandt (ᵕᵕᵕ) p.p. s. anwenden II. **An-gewende** (ᵕᵕᵕ⸝) n ㉒ (Ackerteil, wo beim Pflügen umgewendet wird) part of the field where the plough(man) turns (round). **an-gewiesen** (ᵕᵕᵕ⸝) p.p. s. anweisen 1 u. 2. **an-gewinnen** † od. bibl. (ᵕᵕᵕ) [mhd.] v/a. ⓐ(b)*/* (gewinnend in Besitz nehmen) hatte ihm all sein Land angewonnen (4. Mos. 21, 26) had taken all his land out of his hand; gewann ihm Städte an (2.Chron.13, 19) took cities from him. **an-gewöhnen** (ᵕᵕᵕ⸝) v/a. u. v/refl. ⑯*/* e-m (sich) et. ≤, ↘ e-n (sich) an et. ≤ to accustom, habituate a p. or o.s. to a th.; sich (dat.) et. ≤ to contract a habit of … **An-gewohnheit** (ᵕᵕᵕ⸝) f ⑯, **An-gewöhnung** (ᵕᵕᵕ⸝) f⑯(old) habit; aus ~ from habit. **an-gezogen** (ᵕᵕᵕ) p.p. s. anziehen VI. **an-gießen** (ᵕᵕ⸝) **I** v/a. ⓓd* **1.** to pour against. — **2.** (anfeuchten) to moisten. — **3.** den Wein ≤ to broach … — **4.** ⊙ (an et. befestigen) to join by casting to …; fig. der Rock sitzt dir wie angegossen your coat fits you splendidly or like a glove, it is a perfect fit; er sitzt auf dem Pferde wie angegossen F he sits the horse as if he were glued to it. — **II ~** n ㉓ **5.** pouring against, &c. (s. T).

Angiosperme (n pl.) ⚥ ⚥ (ᵕᵕᵕ⸝) [grch.] f (Hüllsamer) angiosperm(s pl.).

an-girren (ᵕᵕ⸝) v/a. ⑯** to coo at.

Anglaise (a-glä̈-z̄) [fr. englisch(er Tanz)] f ⑯ (Reihentanz) country-dance.

an-glänzen (ᵕᵕ⸝) v/a. ⑯** to shine on, fig. to smile at.

an-gleichen (ᵕᵕ⸝) **I** v/a. ⓐst (⑯)** to assimilate (to or with). — **II ~** n ㉓ und **An-gleichung** f ⑯ assimilation.

an-gleiten (ᵕᵕ⸝) v/n. (sn) ⓑ** gegen et. ≤ to slip (and strike) against a th. **Angler(in)** (ᵕᵕ) s. Angeler(in).

Anglikaner (ᵕᵕᵕ⸝) [it. v. *Angel²] m ㉒, ~**in** f ⑰, **anglikanisch** (ᵕᵕᵕ⸝) a. ⑯ Anglican; die anglikanische Kirche (englische Staatskirche), a: the Church of England, the Established Church.

an-glimmen (ᵕᵕ⸝) ⓐa. u. ⓐ** **I** v/n. (h. u. sn) to begin to glow; to glimmer faintly. — **II** v/a. e-e Zigarre: to light. **anglisieren** (ᵕᵕᵕ⸝) [it.] v/a. ⑯ **1.** (englisch machen) to anglicize. — **2.** ein Pferd ≤ to dock a horse('s tail) (= englisieren). **Anglist** * (ᵕᵕ⸝) m ㉒, ~**in** f ⑰ (Kenner[in] des Englischen) anglicist.

Anglizismus (ᵕᵕᵕᵕᵕ⸝) [it.] m ㉗ (engl. Sprach-eigentümlichkeit) Anglicism.

Anglo-…(ᵕᵕ…) [Angel²] ⑯:**=ind(i)er(in** f) m, **≤indisch** a. Anglo-Indian; **=manie** (ᵕᵕᵕ⸝) f ⑯ (Vorliebe für englische Dinge u. Sitten) anglomania; **=normanne** m, **≤normannisch** a. Anglo-Norman. **an-glotzen** F (ᵕᵕᵕ) v/a. ⑯** e-n ≤ to stare (or glare, glower, gape) at a p. **an-glühen** (ᵕᵕ⸝) ⑯** **I** v/n. (sn) to begin to glow. — **II** v/a. to fire, to flush; Wein ≤ to mull …; angeglüht red-hot.

an-glup(sch)en F (ᵕᵕ⸝) v/a. ⑯ (⑪)** e-n ≤ to look hard or fiercely (or to leer) at a p. **Angora-garn** (ᵕᵕᵕ…) [Angora (ᵕᵕ⸝), St. i. Kleinasien] n ㉖, **=haar** n mohair; **=kaninchen** n, zo. Angora rabbit; **=katze** f, zo. A. cat; **=ziege** f, zo. A. goat.

Angostura ⚥ † (ᵕᵕᵕ⸝) npr/n. ⓜa. (jetzt. Ciudad Bolívar in Guayana) Angostura; ~**bitter(e[r]** (ᵕᵕ…) m ⑯ Angostura bitters pl.; ~**rinde** f Angostura bark.

an-grauen (ᵕᵕ⸝) v/n. (sn) ⑯** (grau zu werden anfangen) to turn grey.

an-greifbar (ᵕᵕ⸝) a. ⑯ assailable; ~**keit** (ᵕᵕ--) f ⑯ (o. pl.) assailableness.

an-greifen (ᵕᵕ⸝) ⓐb** **I** v/a. **1.** to seize (hold of), (anfassen) to handle; e-n bei seiner schwachen Seite ≤ to get round (or over) a p., to get on the right (or blind) side of a p.; ein Übel bei der Wurzel ≤ to strike at the root of an evil; Sprichw. wer Pech angreift besudelt sich they that touch pitch will be defiled. — **2.** (unternehmen) ein Werk ≤ to undertake …, to take … in hand; et. (un)geschickt ≤ to set about a th. in the right (wrong) way; et. richtig (verkehrt) ≤ to begin a th. at the right (wrong) end, to go the right (wrong) way to work. — **3.** Vorräte ≤ (anrühren) to break into …; Kapital ≤ to touch …; die Kasse ≤ (berauben) to rob the till. — **4.** (schwächen) to weaken, stärker: to exhaust, F to fag; die Augen ≤ to try (stärker: to hurt); die Gesundheit ≤ to injure one's health; die Nerven ≤ to affect …; m-e Nerven sind sehr angegriffen … unstrung; sich angegriffen fühlen to feel weak (F done up, seedy), to be (or feel) out of sorts; angegriffen aussehen to look worn (F washed out, seedy); Säure greift Metalle an acid eats into, corrodes …; der Schnee greift die Schuhe an … is bad for (the leather of) the boots. — **5.** (anfallen) to attack, assail; sie griffen ihn heftig an they fell upon them, they made a dead set at him; mit dem Bajonett ≤ to charge with the bayonet; von vorn, die Front ≤ to make a frontal attack; in der Flanke ≤ to take in flank, to attack (or take) the enemy's flank; ein Land ≤ to invade … — **II sich ≤** v/refl. **6.** sich rauh ≤ to feel rough (s. anfühlen II). — **7.** (sich anstrengen) to strain (o.s.), to exert o.s., to spend one's strength; sich zu sehr ≤ to overfatigue o.s., F to knock o.s. up. — **III ~** n ㉓ **8.** = Angreifung. — **IV ≤d** p.p. u. a. ⑯ **9.** trying, irksome, troublesome (erschöpfend) exhausting, (ermüdend) fatiguing, tiring, F fagging. — **10.** (anfallend) offensive, aggressive; der ~de, der ≤e Teil the aggressor, stärker: assailant.

An-greifer (ᵕᵕ⸝) m ㉒, ~**in** f ⑰ aggressor, assailant, eines Landes: invader. **an-greif(i)sch** F (ᵕᵕ⸝) a. ⑯ ⚭ Sachen: tempting to a p.'s greed or covetousness). — **2.** v. Personen: (sich gern et. aneignend) thievishly inclined, F long-fingered. **An-greifung** (ᵕᵕᵕ⸝) f ⑯ (Berühren) a) attiv: touch; b) passiv: ~ der Nerven nervous debility.

Signs (see page XVII): F familiar; P vulgar; ꟻ flash; ↘ rare; † obsolete (died); * new word (born); ⁺⁺ incorrect; ♪ music;

an-grenzen (⌣‿) I v/n. (h.) ⓜ** an et. ⌢ (mehr gbr. grenzen) to border (or abut) on a th, to be adjoining to a th. — II 2b a. ⓜ contiguous, adjoining, adjacent. — III ~ n ㉓ und **Angrenzung** f ㊻ contiguity, adjacency.
an-grienen (⌣‿) v/a. ⓜ** — angrinsen.
An-griff (‿‿) m ⓒc. 1. (Hand-anlegen) taking in hand, F tackling; et. in ~ nehmen to set about (doing) a th. — 2. bsd. ⚔ (feindlicher Anfall) attack (auf upon); mit blanker Waffe: charge; (Sturm) assault; ⚔ fenc. unerwarteter ~ diversion, sudden charge; den ~ aushalten to stand the brunt (of the battle); e-n ~ zurückschlagen to repel a charge; zum ~ blasen to sound the charge; sich zum ~ entwickeln to deploy for the attack; zum ~ vorgeh(e)n to take the aggressive, to charge; to (deliver an) attack. — 3. ⊕ ~ am Riegel (bolt-)toe.
An-griffs-befehl ⚔(‿‿...)m ⓑ order to attack; =**bewegung** f offensive movement; =**bündnis** n offensive alliance; =**krieg** m offensive (or aggressive) war; =**linien** f/pl. approaches pl.; =**punkt** m: a) point of attack; b) mech. point of application; =**schritt** m double quick step; =**signal** n charge; =**weise** adv. by way of attack, offensively, aggressively. [a broad) grin at, to leer at.}
an-grinsen (⌣‿) v/a. ⓜ** to (look with}
an-grunzen (⌣‿) v/a. ⓜ** to grunt at.
Angst (‿) [ahd. (: eng): anger (anguish u. anxiety fr., *It.)] I f ⓘ anxiety, stärker: anguish, (Schreck) fright, apprehension; (Unruhe) distress, trouble; in allen (a. tausend) Ängsten in mortal fear, F in a blue funk; ~ haben, in ~ sein to feel alarmed or anxious; ~ haben vor to be afraid of, to fear; in großer ~ schweben (a. leben) to be filled with dismay, F to be shaking in one's shoes; in ~ geraten to take alarm at; e-m ~ machen, e-n in ~ setzen to alarm (or terrify) a p.; nur keine ~! don't be alarmed or afraid!; schwere ~: epilepsy, falling sickness, auch als Fluch: hang it (all)!, confounded! — II ⌢ a. prädikativ: anxious, frightened, nervous; e-m, e-n ⌢ (und bange) machen to alarm, to frighten; ihm ward ⌢ u. bange he became greatly alarmed, he grew very uneasy or nervous; mir ist ⌢ I feel anxious; mir ward ⌢ um ihn I began to be anxious about him.
angst-beklommen (‿...) a. ⓜ (D 9) oppressed with fear, in agony.
ängsten ⌕ (‿) v/a. ⓜ = ängstigen.
angst-erfüllt (‿...) a. ⓜ full of fear or anxiety; =**geburt** f ⓑ (premature) confinement brought on by fright; fig. co. s. th. produced in an anxious hour; =**geschrei** n cry of distress, shriek of}
ängstig † (⌣) a. ⓜ = ängstlich. [terror.]
ängstig(ig)en (⌣(‿)) I v/a. u. sich ⌢ v/refl. ⓜ (⑨) to distress or alarm (a. p. or o.s.); (sich) zu Tode ⌢ to frighten (o.s.) to death; sich um e-n ⌢ to feel anxious (or solicitous, uneasy) about a p. — II ~ n ㉓ u. **Ängstigung** f ㊻ torment, anguish; alarm; uneasiness.
Angst-kind (‿...) n ⓑ only (or sickly) child (that causes much anxiety).

ängstlich (⌣) [ahd.] a. ⓜ 1. (schüchtern) nervous, timid, afraid, frightened, F funky; (angst-erfüllt) anxious, uneasy; (ängstigend) disquieting; die Sache ist nicht ⌢ there is no need for alarm; es wird mir ⌢ zumute I begin to feel alarmed; er ist zu ⌢ (um f-e Gesundheit besorgt) he coddles himself (too much); nur nicht ⌢! don't be afraid! — 2. (peinlich genau) scrupulous, precise; nicht sehr ⌢ not over-particular.
Ängstlichkeit (⌣‿) f ㊻ 1. (beunruhigende ~) anxiousness, uneasiness. — 2. (Schüchternheit, Verlegenheit) timorousness, timidity, shyness; embarrassment. — 3. (Genauigkeit) scrupulousness, preciseness, exactness.
Angst-meier F (‿...) m ⓑ timid (or nervous) person, (Feigling) coward; =**meierei** f timidity, nervousness, (Feigheit) cowardice; =**röhre** F f (Zylinderhut) chimney-pot (hat); =**ruf** m = =geschrei; =**schweiß** m cold sweat; ⌢**voll** a. ⓜ =erfüllt; =**zitternd** a. trembling with fear or fright, quaking.
an-gucken F (⌣‿) v/a. ⓜ** to look (or to peep) at; verstohlen: to cast a (sly) glance at (vgl. anschielen I).
Angulli (⌣‿) m, n ⓑ 6. (bengal. Zoll) ungulee (= 1.905 cm). [or on).}
an-gürten (⌣‿) v/a. ⓜ** to gird (about}
An-guß (‿‿) m ⓒa. 1. = angießen II. — 2. ⊕ (Gußzapfen) feeding- (or dead) head; typ. break of a letter, jet.
An-guß-farbe (‿‿...) f ㊻ coloured clay
Anh. abbr. = Anhang. [for glazing.}
an-haben (⌣‿) v/a. ⓜb** 1. Kleidungsstücke. ⌢ to have ... on, to wear ... — 2. e-m et. ⌢ (ihm schaden) wollen to have a design upon a p.; man kann ihm nichts ⌢ F he's not to be got at.
an-hacken (⌣‿) v/a. ⓜ** I F v/n. (h.) = anhaften I. — II v/a. Vögel: ⓜ** to peck at.
an-haften (⌣‿) I v/n. (h.) ⓜ** to stick (or cling) to. — II ~ n ㉓ adhesion.
An-hägerung (‿‿‿) f ㊻ (Ablagerung längs der Ufer) alluvial deposit along the banks. [haken 1. — 2. to crochet on.}
an-häkeln (⌣‿) v/a. ⓜa** 1. = an}
an-hak/en (⌣‿) I v/a. u. v/refl. ⓜ** 1. (sich) to hook (or hitch) on. — 2. ⚓ (anholen) to (seize with a) hook, e. Schiff: to grapple. — II A/ung f ㊻ hooking on, &c. (f. I).
an-halftern (⌣‿) v/a. ⓜa** ein Pferd: to (attach with a) halter.
an-halsen (⌣‿) v/a. ⓜ** hunt. 1. (e-m Hunde das Halsband anlegen) to put a dog's collar on. — 2. die Hunde ⌢ (auf die Spur bringen) to put ... on the scent.
An-halt (‿‿) I m ⓒc. 1. (Stützpunkt) support, prop, für die Füße: foothold; fig. ohne ⌢ adrift, without any footing-loose; fig. e-n ⌢ gewähren to give (or afford) a clue to; ~ gewinnen to gain a footing. — 2. (Innehalten) stoppage, pause. — 3. ⌢ (Ort des ~ens, bsd. 🚂) station. — II ⚜ [Burg; *~ 3] npr/n. ⓜα. 4. (dtsch. Herzogtum) Anhalt.
an-halten (⌣‿) ⓜa** I v/a. 1. et. ⌢ an to draw (or bring) a th. near (or close) to a th. — 2. (festhalten) to stop, to arrest; den Atem ⌢ to hold one's breath; Kricket: den Ball ⌢ to block the ball; Fußballspiel: to touch down; Güter ⌢ to

seize (or attach) ...; die Pferde ⌢, auch: to pull up — 3. e-n zu et. ⌢ (antreiben) to exhort, stärker: to urge a p. to do a th.; e-n zur Arbeit (zur Pflicht) ⌢ to keep a p. to his work (his duty); e-n zum Zahlen ⌢ to demand payment of a p., to dun a p. — 4. ♪ e-n Ton ⌢ (andauernd halten) to hold a note. — II v/n. (h.) 5. (stillhalten) to stop, to come to a stop or a standstill; vom Reiter ⁊c.: to pull up; der Zug hält nicht an the train does not stop, auch: it's a through-train. — 6. (fortdauern) to keep on, to last, to continue. — 7. um et. ⌢ to petition (or sue) for a th.; bei e-m um et. ⌢ to apply to a p. for ...; um ein Mädchen ⌢ to propose to a lady, to ask her in marriage; um e-e Stelle ⌢ to put up for (or to solicit) an appointment. — III sich ⌢ v/refl. 8. sich an eine(r) Sache ⌢ to attach o.s. to a th. — 9. (sich bezwingen) to check o.s. — IV 2b p.pr. u. a. ⓜ (u. adv.) 10. continual(ly), continuous(ly), constant(ly); es scheint 2b it keeps on snowing; das 2b schöne Wetter the long spell of fine weather. — 11. (beharrlich) persevering, (eifrig) assiduous, (stetig) steady, (hartnäckig) stubborn, obstinate — 12. ♪ sostenuto. — 13. med. (stopfend) binding. — V ~ n ㉓ 14. drawing near to ... — 15. (Festnahme) arrest. — 16. (Stillhalten) stop, stoppage. — 17. (Gesuch) application, weits. candidature for; ~ um e-e Dame suit, offer of marriage to ..., proposal to ... — 18. (Ausdauer) continuation, von Pers.: perseverance.
An-halter[1] ⊕ (‿‿) m ㉒ stützend: support, hemmend: catch, check; mech. regulator, governor.
Anhalter[2] (‿) [Anhalt4] I m ㉒ inhabitant of Anhalt. — II a. inv. = anhaltisch.
An-halte-stelle 🚂 (‿‿...) f ㊻ station; halting-place; =**punkt** m: a) (Station) station; b) surv. fixed point; mech. (Stützpunkt) fulcrum; c) ♪ fermata (⌢); =**zeichen** n sign to stop or for stopping.
anhaltisch ⚜ (⌣‿) a. ⓜ of Anhalt.
An-halts-ort (‿‿...) m ㉒ halting-place; =**punkt** m, fig. essential fact, important point; s. th. to go upon, clue.
an-hämmern (⌣‿) v/a. ⓜa** to fasten by hammering, to hammer to.
An-hang (‿‿) [mhd.] m ⓒc. 1. appendage; e-s Werkes: appendix; zur Vervollständigung: supplement; (Unwesentliches) accessory; (Nachtrag) addition, addendum. — 2. ⚖ ~ an Wechseln slip, endorsement; e-s Testaments: codicil to ... — 3. mst b.s. (Anhängerschaft) adherents, followers, hangers-on, partisans pl.; (Partei) party, following, faction; b.s. clique, gang. — 4. (Gefolge) retinue.
an-hangen (⌣‿) ⓜb** I v/n. (h.) 1. an et. (dat.) ⌢ to hang on to a th. or against a th., to adhere to a th. — 2. (anhaften) et. hängt e-m, e-r Sache an a th. cleaves (stärker: belongs) to a th.; fig. e-m wie e-e Klette ⌢ F to stick like a leech to a p. — 3. e-r Partei a. ⌢ to be attached to ...; dem Laster ⌢ to indulge in vice. II ~ n ㉓ 4. adhesion, fig. adherence. III 2b p.pr. u. a. ⓜ 5. adherent, adhesive, appendent; innig: inherent.

⚗ scientific; ⚘ botanical; 🜨 geography; ⊕ machinery; ⚒ mining; ⚔ military; ⚓ marine; ⬤ commercial; ✉ postal; 🚂 railway.

[anhängen] — 56 — [anjetzt]

an-hängen (ᵇᵛ) ⑧** **I** v/a. 1. to hang up (an einem Haken by a hook), to suspend; ↓ die Hängematten ⁀ to sling the hammocks; Sprichw. der Katze die Schelle ⁀ to bell the cat. — 2. (zufügen) to append (or add, annex) to a th.; eine Null ⁀ to add a cipher (F nought); ein Siegel ⁀ to affix a seal. — 3. fig. e-m eins ⁀ to play a p. a trick; e-m e-e Krankheit ⁀ to infect a p. with (or to give a p.) a disease; e-m einen Prozeß ⁀ to involve a p. in a lawsuit; e-m e-n Schimpf ⁀ to put (or cast) a slur upon a p.; e-m e-e Ware ⁀ to palm (off) goods on a p. — **II** P v/n. 4. = anhängen. — **III** sich ⁀ v/refl. 5. to cling (or adhere) to, to attach o.s. to; sich an e-n ⁀ to force o.s. on a p. — **IV** ~ n ㉓ 6. = Anhängung.
An-hänger (ᵇᵛ) [anhangen 3] m ㉒, ~**in** f ㊻ meist g. s.: adherent, supporter, follower, partisan; b. s. hanger-on to (vgl. Anhang 3); (Jünger) disciple.
An-hängerschaft (ᵇᵛ) f ㊻ (ohne pl.) 1. partisanship. — 2. = Anhang 3.
An-hänge=schloß (ᵇᵛ...) n ㉓ padlock; =**silbe** f, gram. suffix; =**wort** n, =**wörtchen** n, gram.: ⁀ enclitic.
an-hängig (ᵇᵛ) a. ⑥ 1. fast +adhering to, (eng verbunden) annexed to, (abhängig) dependent on. — 2. jur. (schwebend) pending; e-n Prozeß gegen e-n machen to enter an action (or a suit) against, to take (legal) proceedings against a p.
an-hänglich (ᵇᵛ) a. ⑥ attached (stärker: devoted) to; abs. auch affectionate; ~**keit** f ㊻ (o. pl.) attachment (stärker: devotion) to; (Treue) loyalty to; ~**keit** an e-n zeigen to show affection for a p.
An-hängsel (ᵇᵛ) n ㉒ 1. appendage (= Anhang 1). — 2. F = Hängsel.
An-hangs=register (ᵇᵛ...) n ㉒ zu einem Werke (table of) contents; =**tiere** n/pl. zo. appendiculata pl.; ⁀**weise** adv. by way of appendix. [— 2. appendage.]
An-hängung (ᵇᵛ) f ㊻ 1. suspension.
An-hau (ᵇᵛ) m ⓓd. for. first felling (or cutting) of wood in a forest.
An-hauch (ᵇᵛ) m ⓓd. 1. breath(ing on), ⁀ afflation. — 2. = Anflug 3.
an-hauchen (ᵇᵛ) v/a. ⑧** 1. to breathe on or at; f-e Finger ⁀ to blow ...; fig. die Farben sind wie angehaucht ... delicately laid on. — 2. fig. F = rüffeln.
an-hauen (ᵇᵛ) v/a. ⑨c** to begin to cut (up) or to hew (down); for. (anschalmen) to blaze; ⚒ to open (a mine).
an-häufeln (ᵇᵛ) v/a. ⑨a** to gather in(to) small heaps, agr., hort. Erde um eine Pflanze ⁀ to earth (or mould) up a plant, Kartoffeln: to hill up.
an-häuf/en (ᵇᵛ) **I** v/a. u. v/refl. ⑧** 1. to heap up. — 2. massenhaft: (sich) ⁀ to accumulate, to aggregate; fig. (vermehren) to increase, (aufspeichern) to hoard up. — **II** ~ n ㉓ = Äung. — **III** ⁀d a. ⑥ 4. accumulative.
An-häufung (ᵇᵛ) f ㊻ accumulation; (Bodensatz) deposit; path. ~ von Blut 2c. congestion; ~ von Hemmnissen, Geschäften block.
an-heben (ᵇᵛ) ⓐ(⑦)b** **I** v/a., v/n. (h.), bisw. sich ⁀ v/refl. 1. †ob. poet. fig. to begin; ein Lied ⁀ zu singen to commence singing, F to strike up a tune; abs.

er hub (also) an he began to speak thus; bibl. he lifted up his voice and said. — **II** v/a. 2. et. an et. ⁀ to lift (or raise) a th. close up to ... — 3. die Pumpe ⁀ (ansaugen lassen) to fetch (or start) a pump, to make a pump suck.
an-heftein (ᵇᵛ) v/a. ⑨a** to fasten.
an-heften (ᵇᵛ) **I** v/a. u. v/refl. ⑧** (sich) an et. (acc., ⁀ dat.) ⁀ to attach (or fasten) a th. (or o.s.) to, to affix to a th.; mit Stecknadeln: to pin a th. to; e-e Bekanntmachung ⁀ to announce by a bill that //; ein Buch an ein anderes ⁀ to stitch two books together; ans Kreuz ⁀ to crucify; ❀ Preise den Waren ⁀ to ticket goods. — **II** ~ n ㉓ und **An-heftung** f ㊻ affixture; von Zetteln: bill-posting; ⁀ attachment.
an-heilen (ᵇᵛ) **I** v/n. (ſn) und v/a. ⑧** to heal on or together; to join (or attach) by healing, ⁀ to agglutinate. — **II** ~ n ㉓ u. **An-heilung** f ㊻ healing (process), ⁀ agglutination.
an-heim (ᵛᴸ) [an Heim] adv. † = heim.
an-heimelln (ᵇᵛ) [ſchwz.] v/a. ⑨a** to remind one of home; alles heimelt mich hier an I feel quite at home here.
an-heim=fallen (ᵛ⁻ᴸ...) v/n. (ſn) ⑨a** to fall to (one's share or lot); der Vergangenheit ⁀gefallen buried in oblivion; ⁀**geben** v/a. ⑨c**, ⁀**stellen** v/a. ⑧** to suggest; e-m (j-s Urteil) et. ⁀ to leave a th. to a p.('s discretion); wir stellen Ihnen die Sache ganz anheim we leave the matter entirely in your hands or to you; es ist dir ⁀gegeben it lies (or rests) with you.
an-heiraten (ᵇᴸ⁻) v/a. ⑨** to acquire (or obtain) in wedlock; angeheiratet related by marriage.
an-heischig (ᵇᴸ⁻) [mhd. (₊₊ P): (ver)= heißen] a.: sich (gegen e-n) ⁀ machen zu et. oder et. zu tun to bind (or pledge) o.s. to a th.; ich mache mich dazu ⁀, oft: I undertake to do it.
an-heitern (ᵇᴸ⁻) v/a. ⑨a** to make merry; v. geistigen Getränken angeheitert tipsy, F elevated, a little on.
an-heizen (ᵇᴸ⁻) v/a. ⑧** (to begin) to heat (ſ. a. anfeuern).
an-helfen (ᵇᵛ) v/n. (h.) u. v/a. ⓑb** 1. e-m (e-n) ⁀ to help a p. to get a th. — 2. ell. e-m den Rock ⁀ (anziehen helfen) to help a p. on with his coat.
an-henken † ob. obb. (ᵇᵛ) v/a. ⑧** = anhängen 1. [hitherto.)
an-her ⁀ (ᵛᴸ), ⁀o † (ᵛᴸ⁻) adv. bis ⁀)
an-herrschen (ᵇᵛ) v/a. ⑨** e-n ⁀ (herrisch anfahren) to talk to a p. in an overbearing tone or F like a Dutch uncle.
an-hetzen (ᵇᵛ) **I** v/a. ⑨** 1. hunt. e-n Hirsch ⁀ to start ... — 2. fig. e-n zu et. ⁀ to egg a p. on to ...; e-n gegen e-n ⁀ to set (or incite) a p. against a p. — **II** ~ n ㉓ 3. = Anhetzung.
An-hetzer (ᵇᵛ) m ㉒, ~**in** f ㊻ b.s. instigator, abetter, jur. abettor, inciter.
An-hetzerei (ᵇᵛ⁻ᵇ) f ㊻ continued instigation. [citement.)
An-hetzung (ᵇᵛ) f ㊻ instigation, in-)
an-heucheln ⁀ (ᵇᵛ) v/a. ⑨a** to sham.
an-heuern ↓ (ᵇᴸ⁻) ⑨a** **I** v/a. Matrosen ⁀ to engage ..., to enroll ... — **II** v/n (h.) (sich anwerben lassen) to sign on.

an-heulen (ᵇᴸ⁻) ⑨a** **I** v/a. to howl at. — **II** v/n. (h.) F angeheult kommen to come howling along.
an-hexen (ᵇᵛ) v/a. ⑨** e-m et. ⁀ to inflict a th. on a p. by witchcraft.
An-hieb (ᴸ⁻) m ⓓd. for. = Anhau.
An-höhe (ᴸ⁻) [nhd.,* ſchwz.] f ㊻ eminence, elevation; allmählich ansteigende ~ swelling (or gently rising) ground.
an-holen (ᴸ⁻) v/a. ⑧** 1. (herbeiholen) to bring up. — 2. ↓ ein Tau ⁀ to haul in ...; die Boleine ⁀ to haul taut the bowline; die Schoten ⁀ to haul aft the sheets. — 3. ⚒ die Kübel: to hoist.
An-hol=part ↓ (ᴸ⁻...) m, n ⑳ tow-line; =**tau** ↓ n hawser.
an-hören (ᴸ⁻) ⑧** **I** v/a. 1. e-n, et. ⁀ to listen (or hearken) to, aufmerksam: to lend an ear (or to give a hearing) to; das ist nicht anzuhören I cannot endure (or bear to hear) this. — 2. dieser Vorschlag läßt sich ⁀ that sounds plausible, this seems acceptable. — 3. (anmerken) man hört ihm den Russen an one can tell by his speech that he is a Russian. — **II** sich ⁀ v/refl. 4. das Stück hört sich gut an ... is worth listening to; es hört sich unmelodisch an it sounds unmelodious or harsh. — **III** ~ n ㉓ u. **An-hörung** f ㊻ 5. hearing; listening to; jur. ~ von Zeugen examination of ...
an-hüpfen (ᵇᵛ) v/n. (ſn) ⑧** ⁀, angehüpft kommen to come hopping along.
Anhydrid ⁀ (ᵛ⁻ᴸ) [grch.] n ⓓc. chm. (wasserfreie Säure ob. Base) anhydrid(e).
Anhydrit ⁀ (ᵛ⁻ᴸ) [grch.] m ⓓc., min. (wasserfreier Gips) anhydrite.
Anilin (ᵛ⁻ᴸ) [neu=lt. 1840; port. (*ar.) anil Indigo] n ⓓc. chm. (aus Steinkohlenteer gewonnener Farbstoff) aniline.
Anilin=fabrik (ᴸ...) f ⑫ aniline works pl.; =**farbe** f aniline colour; =**rot** n, auch: Magenta red; =**tinte** f aniline ink.
animalisch ⁀ (ᵛᵛᴸᵛ) [lt.] a. ⑥ animal (= tierisch). [animalism.)
Animalismus ⁀ (ᵛᵛᴸᵛ) [lt.] m ⓓ)
Anime (ᴸ⁻ᵛ) n ⑳ (Flußharz), auch ⁀**gummi** n (m), ~=**harz** n anime-resin, courbaril (von Hymenaea courbaril).
animieren (ᵛᵛᴸᵛ) [lt.] v/a. ⑬ to urge on (ermutigen) to encourage; animiert (lebhaft) animated, lively, (erregt) excited.
animos (ᵛ⁻ᴸ) [lt.] a. ⑥ (D 10) hostile.
Animosität (ᵛᵛ⁻ᴸ) [lt.] f ㊻ animosity.
Anion ⁀ (ᵛ⁻ᵛᵛ) [grch.] n ⑳ (pl. Anio'nen) elect. (was sich am positiven Pole ausscheidet) anion.
Anis (ᵛᴸ) [lt. āne'thum Dill; *grch.] ⓓa. 1. ⁀ anise. — 2. (Samen) aniseed; ⚘ überzuckerter ~ candied aniseed.
Anis=brot (ᵛᴸ⁻...) n ⑳ aniseed-bread.
Anisett (ᵛ⁻ᴸ) [fr.] m ⓓb. = Anislikör.
Anis=holz (ᵛᴸ⁻) n ⑳ aniseed-wood; =**kuchen** m a.-cake; =**likör** m anisette; =**öl** n aniseed-oil; =**samen** m = Anis 2.
An-jagd (ᵛᴸ⁻) f ㊻ beginning of the hunt.
an-jagen (ᵇᴸ⁻) ⑨a** **I** v/a. 1. hunt. Wild: to start. — 2. (antreiben) die Pferde ⁀ to urge on ... — **II** v/n. (ſn) 3. ⁀, angejagt kommen to come galloping (or rushing) up or along.
an-jammern (ᵇᵛ) v/a. ⑨a** e-n ⁀ to address a p. in a lamenting tone.
an-jetzt † ob. poet. (ᵇᴸ) adv. = jetzt.

Zeichen (ſ. S. XVII): F familiär; P Volkssprache; ⁀ Gaunersprache; ⁀ selten; † alt (auch gestorben); * neu (auch geboren); ₊₊ unrichtig;

an-jochen (⸗⸗ch⸗) v/a. ⊕** Ochsen ≈ to yoke…, to couple … under the yoke.
Ank. abbr. = Ankunft.
an-kämmen (⸗⸗⸗) v/a. ⊕** to smooth (or arrange) with a comb.
An-kampf m ⑦c. wider ein übel, eine Unsitte: contention (or struggle) with …
an-kämpfen (⸗⸗⸗) v/n. (h.) ⊕** ≈ gegen to contend (or fight, struggle) against or with; fig. to militate against; to compete with.
an-karren (⸗⸗⸗) v/a. ⊕** to cart up.
An-kauf (⸗⸗) ⑦d. 1. purchase, weitS. acquisition. — 2.(das Angekaufte) purchase.
an-kauf/en (⸗⸗⸗) v/a. ⊕** I v/a. to buy, to purchase. — II sich ≈ v/refl. · sich wo ≈ to buy up property (and settle down) at a place. — III ~ n ㉓ = A/ung.
An-käufer (⸗⸗⸗) m ㉒, **~in** f ㊼ purchaser.
An-kaufs-preis (⸗⸗…) m ㉒ cost-price; purchase-money.   [acquisition.
An-kaufung (⸗⸗⸗) f ㊻ purchase.}
Anke¹ (⸗⸗) m ㊹ ichth. = Lachsforelle.
Anke² (⸗⸗) [ahd.] f ㊶ 1. prove. W. = Nacken. — 2. ⊕ Goldarbeiter: thimble(-stamp).
Anke³, **~n** schwz. (⸗⸗) [ahd.: lt. ü'nguen] m ㊹, ㉓ = Butter, Fett.
an-kegeln (⸗⸗⸗) v/n. (h.) ㉒a** to throw first at skittles.
an-kellen (⸗⸗⸗) v/a. ⊕** hunt. Enten ≈ to surprise wild ducks by stealing up to them in a rowing-boat.
Anker (⸗⸗) [ahd., lt., *grch.] m ㉒ 1. ⚓ anchor; kleiner ~ grapnel; großer ~ sheet-anchor; (e-n Sturm) vor ~ aushalten to ride out (a gale); der ~ faßt the an. bites; e-n ~ fischen to drag for an an.; vor ~ geh(e)n, sich vor ~ legen, ~ werfen to (come to an) an., to moor; den ~ lichten to weigh an., to trip the an.; den ~ seefest sorren to secure the an.; von dem ~ losreißen to part anchors; vor ~ liegen to (ride at) an.; vor ~ (liegend) at an.; vor ~ reiten, stampfen to ride hard; vor dem ~ spielen to ride easy; vor ~ treiben to drag the anchor. — 2. ⊕ arch. (Klammer) anchor, brace; e-r Dampfm.: grappling-iron. — 3. ⚡ phys. ~ am Magnet armature, keeper. — 4. † (Flüssigkeitsmaß) anker.
Anker-arm ⚓ (⸗⸗…) m ㉒ anchor-arm; **=balken** m anchor-beam,cat-head(s pl.).
an-kerben (⸗⸗⸗) v/a. ⊕** to mark with notches or with a notch.
Anker-boje ⚓ (⸗⸗…) f ㊸ anchor-buoy, dead-head; **=draht** m, tel. stay-wire; **=eisen** n grappling-iron; **=fest** a. ㊻ well-moored; 2er Grund good anchorground or anchorage; **=fliege** f, **=flügel** m fluke; **=förmig** a. anchor-shaped; **=geld** n anchorage; **=grund** m anchor(-ing)-ground, anchorage, berth; **=haken** m cat-hook; **=helm** m shank of an anchor; **=kette** f chain-cable; **=kreuz** n cross (or crowning) of the anchor; **=loch** n (Klüse) hawse; **=los** a. a) adrift, unmoored; b) elect. without armature.
ankern (⸗⸗) ⊕a. I v/n. (h.) 1. ⚓ to (cast) anchor, to moor. — 2. fig. auf et. ≈ to rest one's hopes upon a th.; nach et. ≈ to hanker after … — II v/a. 3. ⚓ e. Schiff ≈: a) to moor …; b) to provide … with anchorage. — 4. arch. to brace. — III ~ n ㉓ 5. ⚓ mooring.

Anker-platz ⚓ (⸗⸗…) m ㉒: a) = grund; b) (Reede) roadstead; **=recht** n right of anchorage; **=ring** m anchor-ring; **=rührung** f puddening; **=rute** f, **=schaft** m = =helm; **=schäkel** m shackle, jew's-harp; **=seil** n cable; **=stelle** f anchorage, vgl. auch =grund, =platz; **=schaufel** f = =fliege; **=stich** m clench of a cable; **=stock** m anchor-stock; **=tau** † n cable; **=tonne** f = Boje; **=uhr** f lever-watch (with anchor-escapement); **=winde** f capstan, windlass.
an-ketten F (⸗⸗⸗) v/a. ㉒a** to fix with a small chain.   [with a) chain to.}
an-ketten (⸗⸗⸗) v/a. ⊕** ≈ to (fasten)
an-keuchen (⸗⸗⸗) v/n. (ſn) ⊕** ≈, angefeucht kommen to come up panting.
an-kirren (⸗⸗⸗) v/a. ⊕** hunt. das Wild ≈ (ködern) to bait, to decoy (a. fig.).
an-kitten (⸗⸗⸗) v/a. ⊕** to fasten with putty (or cement) to, to cement.
an-kläffen (⸗⸗⸗) v/a. ⊕** to bark at.
an-klagbar (⸗⸗⸗) a. ㊻ impeachable, indictable; **~keit** f ㊻ impeachability.
An-klage (⸗⸗⸗) f ㊶ 1. accusation; indictment; eine ~ gegen e-n erheben to make (or bring) a charge against a p. — 2. (Beschuldigung) imputation against. — 3. (öffent.) information (laid against a p..), denunciation. — 4. jur. peinliche ~ arraignment; bsd. parl. impeachment.
An-klage-akte (⸗…) f ㊶ act (or bill) of indictment; **=bank** f (prisoner's) dock; **=jury** f grand jury.
an-klagen (⸗⸗⸗) v/a. u. v/refl. ⊕** 1. e-s Verbrechens 2c. ≈ to accuse (sich o.s.) of, to charge with (an offence); bsd. parl. to impeach for; vor Gericht: to arraign for, to indict of; s. a. Angeklagte(r). — 2. jur. to bring (or lay) an action against.
An-klage-punkte (⸗⸗…) m/pl. ㉒ heads pl. of the charge or indictment.
An-kläger (⸗⸗⸗) m ㉒, **~in** f ㊼ accuser; jur. indicter; (Denunziant) informer; öffentliche(r) ~ public prosecutor.
an-klägerisch (⸗⸗⸗) a. ㊻ accusatory.
An-klage-rede (⸗⸗…) f ㊶ opening speech of counsel for the prosecution; **=schrift** f = =akte; **=(zu)stand** m: e-n in ~ versetzen to arraign (or indict) a p., to put a p. in the dock.
an-klammern (⸗⸗⸗) v/a. u. v/refl. ㉒a** (sich an e-n, et.) ≈ to cling (or hang on) to.
An-klang (⸗⸗) m ⑦c. 1. sound of clashing bodies. — 2 introductory sound. — 3. (Gleichklang) ♪ accord; pros. vokalisch: assonance, (Stab-reim) alliteration. — 4. ♪ (Ähnlichkeit) Anflänge aus älteren Opern reminiscences or suggestions) of … — 5. fig. ~ (Gefallen) finden to meet with approval; das Stück hat wenig ~ gefunden … met with little applause, F … did not draw; die Sache findet keinen ~ … does not take (with the public); 🜨 von Waren: ~ finden to go off well, to meet with patronage.
an-klatschen (⸗⸗⸗) ⊕** I v/a. Regen: to splash against. — II v/a. = verflatschen.
an-kleben (⸗⸗⸗) v/a. to stick on, mit Kleister: to paste on, mit Leim: to glue on, mit Gummi: to gum on; hier dürfen keine Zettel angeklebt werden stick no bills. — II v/n. (h.) to stick

(or adhere, cleave) to; fig. ein Makel klebt ihm an there's a stain upon him. — III ~ n ㉓ von Zetteln: bill-sticking, posting up (of) advertisements. —
IV 2b p.pr. u. a. ㊻ adhesive.
An-kleber (⸗⸗⸗) m ㉒, **~in** f ㊼ v. Zetteln: bill-poster, bill-sticker.
an-klecken, mst **=kleckſen** (⸗⸗⸗) v/a. ⊕, ⊕** 1. e-m et. ≈ to bespatter a p. (a. fig.). — 2. (schlecht anstreichen) to daub (over).
An-kleide-kabinett(⸗⸗…) n ㉒ = =zimmer.
an-kleid/en (⸗⸗⸗) I v/a. u. v/refl. ⊕** e-n (sich) ≈ to dress a p. (o.s.); e-n ≈ to attire (or clothe) a p.; prächtig: to array, to deck out; in langem Gewande: to robe; sie kleidet sich jeden Tag anders an she changes her dresses (or apparel) daily. — II ~ n ㉓ = A/ung.
An-kleider (⸗⸗⸗) m ㉒, **~in** f ㊼ dresser.
An-kleide-spiegel (Z…) m ㉒ toilet-glass; (Drehspiegel) cheval-glass; **=zimmer** n dressing-room, kleineres auch: (lady's) boudoir.   [attire; F adornment.}
An-kleidung (⸗⸗⸗) f ㊻ dress(ing), toilet,
an-kleistern (⸗⸗⸗) v/a. ㉒a** to paste on.
an-klemmen (⸗⸗⸗) v/a. ⊕** to squeeze (or jam, pinch) against.
an-klingeln (⸗⸗⸗) ㉒a** I v/n. (h.) to ring at a p.'s door, to ring the bell. — II v/a. to call a p. up by ringing; Fernspr.: e-n ≈ to ring a p. up.
an-klingen (⸗⸗⸗) ⊕f** I v/n. (h.), ⚓ ſn) 1. to begin to sound or tinkle. — 2. (stimmen) to accord (or chime in) with. — 3. ♪ diese Melodie klingt an die Marseillaise an … reminds one of (or is suggestive of) …; pros. ≈ assonant, alliterative. — II v/a. 4. e-e Saite ≈ to sound … — 5. die Gläser (a. v/n. mit den Gläsern) ≈ to clink glasses.
an-klopfen (⸗⸗⸗) ⊕** I v/n. (h.) 1. an die Tür ≈ to knock (or rap) at the door; zweimal mit dem Türhammer ≈ to give a double knock (at the door). — 2. fig. bei e-m ≈ (anfragen) to sound (or inquire of) a p. about a th.; überall ≈ to apply everywhere. — II v/a. 3. to fasten by hammering. — III ~ n ㉓ 4. bsd. med. percussion.
An-klopfer (⸗⸗⸗) m ㉒ (j. der oder Hammer womit man anklopft) knocker. [knocker.}
An-klopf-ring (⸗⸗⸗) m ㉒ ring-shaped}
an-knallen (⸗⸗⸗) ⊕** I v/a. die Pferde ≈ to whip up … — II v/n. angeknallt kommen to arrive cracking one's whip.
an-knebeln (⸗⸗⸗) v/a. ㉒a** to gag.
an-kneipen (⸗⸗⸗) ⊕** I v/a. etwas ≈ to pinch (or squeeze) a th. against. —
II v/n. (h.) to carouse; angekneipt F fuddled, boozed, slightly on.
an-knöpfen (⸗⸗⸗) v/a. ⊕** to (fasten with a) button to.
An-knüpfe-…(⸗⸗⸗) = Anknüpfungs-=…
an-knüpf/en (⸗⸗⸗) ⊕** I v/a. u. v/refl. 1. et. an et. (acc.) ≈, et. e-r Sache ≈ to fasten (or tie) to a th.; ⚓ (zurren) to lash to; fig. eine Bekanntschaft ≈ mit to make a p.'s acquaintance; einen Briefwechsel mit einem ≈ to enter into (or open) a correspondence with a p.; ein Gespräch mit e-m ≈ to engage a p. in conversation; Verbindungen (Geschäfte) ≈ mit … to become connected (in business) with … — II v/n. (h.)

♪ Musik; ⚗ Wissenschaft; ♃ Pflanze; ♁ Geographie; ⊕ Technik; ⚒ Bergbau; ⚔ Militär; ⚓ Marine; 🜨 Handel; 🖂 Post; 🚂 Eisenbahn.

[Anknüpfung] — 58 — [anlaschen]

2. an et. ≈ to start from a th.; wieder ≈ to resume the thread; an Ihre Worte 2d referring to ... — 3. mit e-m ≈ to form a connexion with a p. — III ~ n ㉓ 3. = A/ung. — IV 2d a. ⑥⑥ 4. gram. conjunctional.

An-knüpfung (ˢᴸᵛ) f ㊻ 1. fastening, &c. (s. anknüpfen). — 2. connexion.

An-knüpfungs-punkt (ˢᴸᵛ...) m ㊷ fig. point of contact, (Ausgangspunkt) point of departure, starting-point.

an-knurren (ˢᴸᵛ) v/a. ㊽** e-n ≈ to growl (or snarl) at a p. (auch fig.).

an-ködern (ˢᴸᵛ) v/a. ㉒** to bait.

an-kommen (ˢᴸᵛ) I v/n. (fn) ㊽*** 1. (ant. abgehen) to arrive; ↓ to (get to) land; P = geboren werden; der Zug ꝛc. ist eben angekommen ... has (just) come in; sie kam zuerst dort an she was first on the spot; er kam um 5 Uhr in L. an he reached L. at 5 o'clock; wir werden gegen Mitternacht in Dresden ≈ we shall be (or we are due) at Dresden about midnight; 2de Personen, Züge ꝛc. oft: arrivals pl. — 2. (sich nähern) to approach (or get near to) a place; vgl. a. anfahren 3, anreiten 1. — 3. fig. (Aufnahme finden) gut (übel) ≈ to be well (ill) received, weitS. to meet with good (ill) success; da kommen Sie gut an, oft: you're very lucky; iro. da ist er schön angekommen he came to the wrong person or address, F he caught a Tartar; bei mir kommst du nicht an F that won't go down with me; da kommst du unrecht an you will find yourself mistaken (F in the wrong box); ● bei etwas gut (schlecht) ≈ to come off well (badly). — 4. (erreichen) to attain; da kann ich nicht ≈ I cannot reach it; fig. man kann ihm nicht ≈ there is no getting at him; er kann mir damit nicht ≈ F he won't get over me like that. — 5. einem ≈ (e-n behandeln) to behave to a p., to deal with a p.; wenn er mir so ≈ will if he treats me like that. — 6. es kommt ihn (ihm) die Lust an ... he has taken it into his head to ...; was kommt dich (dir) an? F what's the matter with you?; et. kommt mir (mich) schwer (oder hart, sauer) an F it comes hard to me; es kam mir (mich) schwer an zu sprechen I spoke with great difficulty or reluctance; der Schlaf kam mir (mich) an I began to feel sleepy. — 7. auf et., e-n ≈ (von et., e-m abhangen) to depend on a th., a p.; es kommt nur auf Sie an it depends entirely on you, it rests entirely with you; es kommt darauf an, ob // the chief thing is (to know) whether //; hier kam's bloß auf (das) Geld an that was a mere question (or matter) of money; es kam uns auf ein paar Mark nicht an we did not mind a few shillings; es kommt mir viel darauf an it is of great consequence to me; darauf soll es nicht ≈ that shall not stand in the way, never mind that; wenn es darauf nur ankommt if that is (or be) all; wenn es wirklich darauf ankäme if it came to the point; es kommt darauf an (ist fraglich) F it all depends; es darauf ≈ lassen F to chance (or risk) it. — II ~ n ㉓ 8. = Ankunft. — 9. = Unterkommen.

An-kömmling (ˢᴸᵛ) m ⑪d., ⚘ ~in f ㊼ 1. new-comer, arrival; (Fremde(r) stranger. — 2. (Neugeborene(r) new-born infant, F co. little stranger, new arrival, addition to the family.

an-köpfen ⊖ (ˢᴸᵛ) v/a. ㉘** Stecknadeln, Nägel ≈ to head pins, nails.

an-koppeln (ˢᴸᵛ) v/a. ㉒a** ≈ to couple or yoke (to an); hunt. to leash (hounds).

an-körnen (ˢᴸᵛ) v/a. ㉘** 1. hunt. (m. Körnern ködern) to bait with seeds. — 2. ⊖ Schlosserei: to mark with a centre-punch.

an-krähen (ˢᴸᵛ) v/a. ㉘** e-n ≈ to greet (or welcome) a p. with crowing.

an-krallen (ˢᴸᵛ) ㉘** I v/a. to seize with the talons or claws; bursch. e-n um et. ≈ (bitten) to press (or implore) a p. for a th. — II v/refl. sich an et. ≈ to cling to a th. with claws, to claw on to a th.

an-kränkeln (ˢᴸᵛ) v/a. ㉒a** der angebornen Farbe der Entschließung wird des Gedankens Blässe angekränkelt the native hue of resolution is sicklied o'er with the pale cast of thought (SH.H.).

an-kratzen (ˢᴸᵛ) v/a. ⑨⓪** 1. et. an die Wand ≈ to scratch a th. at the wall. — 2. F fig. sich (dat.) et. ≈ to make a little pile, to scrape some money together.

an-kreiden (ˢᴸᵛ) v/a. ㊵** to chalk up, to note with chalk; F er steht tief angekreidet he is deeply in debt; ≈ lassen to buy on credit or F on tick.

an-kreischen (ˢᴸᵛ) v/a. ㉚a(e)st (⑪)** to scream (or screech) at.

an-kriechen (ˢᴸᵛ) ⑮ds** I v/n. (fn) ≈ angekrochen kommen to come creeping (or crawling) along, to creep along. — II v/a. e-n, et. ≈ to crawl on to ...

an-kriegen F (ˢᴸᵛ) v/a. ㉘** 1. (ankommen) die Stiefel ≈ to get one's boots on. — 2. (einholen) to catch up. — 3. e-n ≈ (bestimmen) et. zu tun to get a p. to do a th.

an-künd/en geh. Spr. (ˢᴸᵛ) ㊺**, meist **an-fündig/en** (ˢᴸᵛ) ㉘** I v/a. to announce; in Zeitungen ꝛc.: to publish; (inserieren) to advertise; einem et. ≈ to notify a th. to a p. or a p. of a th.; es ward mir angekündigt, daß // I was informed (or advised) that //; feierlich ≈ to proclaim; vorher ≈ to herald; pomphaft ≈ to blazon forth; vorbedeutend ≈ to forebode, to prognosticate. — II sich ≈ v/refl. der Sturm kündet sich durch Vorzeichen an the storm is announced (or ushered in) by premonitory signs. — III ~ n ㉓ = A/ung.

An-künd(ig)er (ˢᴸᵛ(ᵛ)ᵛ) m ② announcer; informant; in Zeitungen: advertiser.

An-künd(ig)ung (~) f ㊻ announcement, notification, (Inserat) advertisement; feierlich: proclamation; Buch: prospectus.

An-kündigungs-kommando (Z...) n ㉒ ⚔ first word (or part) of a command; =schreiben n letter of advice; =signal n, elect. sending-signal; =wecker m, elect. signalling-bell.

An-kunft (ˢᵛ) f ⑩ (pl. ⚘) 1. arrival, coming; ~ der Post coming-in of the mail; ~ zu Hause return home; bei unserer ~ on our arrival, when we arrive(d); nicht erfolgte ~ non-arrival. — 2. eccl. ~ des Messias advent of Christ.

An-kunfts-bahnsteig 🚂 (ˢᴸ...) m ㉒, =halle f arrival-platform, arrival-side; =ort m, =punkt m place, point of arrival; =zeit f time of arrival.

an-kuppeln (ˢᴸᵛ) v/a. ㉒a** = ankoppeln.

an-kutschieren (ˢᴸᵛ) v/n. (fn) ⑨⅜/* ≈ angekutschiert kommen to drive up in a coach or carriage. [smile at a p.

an-lächeln (ˢᴸᵛ) v/a. ㉒a** e-n ≈ to]

an-lachen (ˢᴸᵛ) ㉛) [mhd.] v/a. ㉘** e-n ≈ to greet a p. laughingly or with a laugh; auch 2d Obst, ein Ort lacht uns an ... has an inviting (or a charming) look or aspect.

An-lage (ˢᴸᵛ) f ㊽ 1. (Anlegen) (act of) putting on, &c. — 2. Kapital(s)= investment in; (angelegtes Geld) invested capital. — 3. (Grundlegen) foundation; (Bau) construction; e-s Gartens: laying out of ...; öffentliche, städtische ~n pl. ornamental (or pleasure) grounds pl.; ~ einer chemischen Fabrik erection of chemical works. — 4. (Entwurf) design; outline; e-s Romans ꝛc.: plot, frame-work; bildende Künste: sketch; erste ~ (rough) draft. — 5. (Keim) germ. — 6. (Befähigung) aptitude; ~ zum Geschäftsmann business capacity; er hat keine ~ für die Bühne F he is not cut out for the stage; er hat keine ~ dazu he is not gifted that way, his talent does not lie in that direction; abs. ~n haben to be gifted, talented; path. (pre)disposition; sie hat ~ zur Schwindsucht she is inclined (or predisposed) to consumption. — 7. (Beigefügtes) enclosure; Sie empfangen in der ~ enclosed you receive, you receive herewith. — 8. (Verteilung von Steuern) assessment of taxes. — 9. ⊖ (Kolben des Gewehres) butt; arch. (Fuß, Grundlinie) foot, base; frt. (Böschung) escarpment.

An-lage-blatt (ˢᴸᵛ...) n ㉒ zur Korrekturabzug typ. rider to a proof-sheet; =kapital ● n invested capital or funds; =kosten pl. cost of construction; =strich m line denoting an enclosure.

an-lallen (ˢᴸᵛ) v/a. ㉘** to lisp at.

an-landbar ⚓ (ˢᴸᵛ) a. ⑥⑥ fit for landing.

An-lände ⚓ (ˢᴸᵛ) f ㊽ landing-place, quay; an diesem Ufer ist keine gute ~ this shore is not suitable for landing.

An-lande-brücke ⚓ (ˢᴸᵛ...) f ㉒ landing-stage, pier, jetty.

an-land/en ⚓ (ˢᴸᵛ) I v/n. (fn) ㊺** to land, to come to (or to get on) shore, to disembark. — II ~ n ㉓ = A/ung.

An-lande-platz ⚓ (ˢᴸᵛ...) m ㊷, =stelle f = Anlände; =zeit f time of arrival.

An-landung ⚓ (ˢᴸᵛ) f ㊻ landing, disembarkation; arrival. [soil.

An-ländung (~) f ㊻ alluvial deposit or]

an-langen (ˢᴸᵛ) ㉘** I v/n. (fn) wo ≈ to arrive at, to reach, F to get to. — II v/a. impers. was (so. soviel) diese Sache an(be)langt ob. 2d diese Sache (auch: diese Sache 2d) as regards (or as for, concerning) this matter; vgl. anbelangen.

an-längen ⚘ (ˢᴸᵛ) v/a. ㉘** Kochkunst: e-e Brühe ≈ to (make) thin ...

an-lappen F (ˢᴸᵛ) v/a. ㉘** = anschnauzen.

an-laschen (ˢᴸᵛ) v/a. ⑨⑴** 1. for. einen Baum ≈ to blaze ... — 2. ⊖ Schütze ≈ to put latchets (or strings) to ...

Signs (see page XVII): F familiar; P vulgar; ꝯ flash; ⚘ rare; † obsolete (died); * new word (born); ⁺⁺ incorrect; ♪ music;

[Anlaß] — 59 — [Anlehnslos]

An-laß (⁵ᴸ) [mhd.] *m* ⑧a. (Veranlassung) occasion, cause for, zum Handeln: motive, inducement for; ~ zu et. geben to give rise to a th.; ~ nehmen zu e-r Bemerkung to seize the opportunity for making a remark; er ist der ~ zu he is the cause of; der erste ~ zum Streite the origin of the quarrel; wir haben allen ~ dazu we have every reason for doing so; ohne allen ~ without (any) provocation, unprovokedly; aus ~ ... (*gen.*) = anläßlich. [starter.]

An-laß-apparat (ℒ...) *m* ⓜ u. *mach.*

an-lassen (⁵ᴸ) ⓐ** I *v/a.* 1. (anbehalten) seinen Rock ℒ to keep ... on; *fig.* sie ließen ihm nicht einmal das Hemd an they fleeced him (unmercifully). — 2. (anlaufen lassen) a) Wasser (in einen Teich), den Teich ℒ, die Wasser, die Mühle ℒ to let in the water; to set the mill going; b) Hunde aus Wild ℒ to slip hounds; c) ⊙ Metalle ℒ (weich machen) to temper, to anneal ...; Stahl blau ℒ (anlaufen lassen) to blue steel. — 3. ⊙ *mach.* (in Gang bringen) die Maschine (a. den Dampf) ℒ to set the machine going, to start it; to put on (or get up) steam. — 4. [†⚔] (anfahren) e-n barsch (hart, kurz) ℒ to give a p. a sharp talking-to. — II *sich* ℒ *v/refl.* 5. to appear; es läßt sich ganz danach an, als ob // it really seems as though //; die Sache läßt sich gut (schlecht) an the matter looks (does not look very) promising; das Wetter läßt sich gut an the weather promises well, it bids fair to be a fine day. — III ~ ⊙ *n* ⓶ 6. e-s Ofens: blowing-in (of); e-r Maschine: starting (of); e-r Mühle: opening of the flood-gate of.

An-lasser ⊙ (⁵ᴸ) *m* ⓶ *elect.* (Stromregler) resistance(s) inserted to moderate the strength of a current.

An-laß-hebel (⁵ᴸ...) *m* ⓶ starting-lever.
an-läßlich (⁵ᴸ) *adv.* occasionally; als *prp.* mit *gen.* on the occasion of.

An-laß-ventil (⁵ᴸ...) *n* ⓶ starting-valve; **=widerstand** *m* = Anlasser.

an-latschen F (⁵ᴸ) *v/n.* (fn) ⓜ**: ℒ, angelatscht kommen to come shuffling along, to have a shuffling gait.

An-lauf (⁵ᴸ) *m* ⓓd. 1. ~ des Wassers rising (or swelling) of ...; ⚓ (Fahrt des Schiffes) headway; heavy sea (washing over deck). — 2. a) (Ausholen) run, start for; e-n ~ nehmen to take a run (zum Springen for jumping), *fig.* to prepare for the start; b) (Angriff) rush (or dash) at; charge; im ersten ~ at the first onset. — 3. ⊙ (schiefe Fläche) slope; *arch.* ⚓ apophyge (= Ablauf 6).

an-laufen (⁵ᴸ) ⓐst** I *v/n.* (fn) 1. to begin to run; angelaufen kommen to come running up; die Pferde ℒ lassen to urge on ...; e-e Maschine ℒ lassen to set ... working, to start ... — 2. a) gegen et. ℒ (s. an... 6) to run (or strike) against a th.; heftig: to run full tilt into; mit dem Kopfe gegen die Wand ℒ to run (or knock) one's head against the wall; b) *fig.* schlimm, übel, *iro.* schön ꝛc. ℒ to meet with a (nasty) rebuff (F *iro.* with a nice or warm reception), weitS. to fail; e-n ℒ lassen to make a p. go into a snare or trap; mit sachlichem Subjekt:

das läuft gegen das Gesetz an it runs counter (or is contrary) to the law; *hunt.* das Wild läuft an ... comes within gunshot; die Sau läuft an ... ruskes upon the spear. — 3. ⚓ in e-n Hafen ℒ to call at ...; vgl. 8. — 4. (anschwellen) to swell, to rise; von Kosten ꝛc.: to increase, to run up; die Kosten liefen auf 200 Mark an ... came (F figured up) to ten pounds. — 5. (ansteigen) to rise (or slope) gently. — 6. a) (trübe werden) von Spiegeln: to (grow) dim, von Metall: to tarnish; angelaufen dull, dim, hazy; ein Glas schwarz ℒ lassen to smoke ...; ⊙ Schlosserei: Stahl blau ℒ lassen to blue ..., von Klingen auch: to damascene; b) *v.* Speisen: to get mouldy or musty. — II *v/a.* 7. e-n ℒ (belästigen) to importune a p. — 8. ⚓ (unterwegs) e-n Hafen, Land ℒ to touch ..., to make ... — III ~ *n* u. ~lassen *n* ⓶ 9. (vgl. I u. II) start; ~lassen ⚔ v. Truppen assault, charge; ⊙ einer Maschine: putting into gear; des Wassers: rising; der Zinsen: accumulation; (Trübewerden) dulness.

An-lauf-farbe (⁵ᴸ...) *f* ⓶ des Stahls annealing(-)colour; **=hafen** ⚓ *m* port of call; **=kolben** ⊙ *m, metall.* bloom, ball; **=sprung** *m* Turnerei: short leap preparatory to jumping.

An-laut (⁵ᴸ) *m* ⓓd. *gram.* initial sound, ſ anlaut; im ~ at the beginning (of a word or a syllable).

an-lauten (⁵ᴸ) *v/n.* (h.) ⓜ** *gram.* mit e-m Vokal ℒ to begin with a vowel; der 2de Konsonant the initial consonant.

an-läuten (⁵ᴸ) *v/a.* u. *v/n.* (h.) ⓜ** to announce by ringing the bell; to ring in.

An-lege-apparat (⁵ᴸ...) *m* ⓶ *typ.* an Tiegeldruckpressen: sheet-supporter; automatischer ~ automatic feeding-apparatus or feeder; **=gebühren** ⚓ *f/pl.* anchorage *sg.*; **=gelder** *n/pl.* = kapital; **=hafen** ⚓ *m* port of call; **=kapital** *n* (money for) investment; **=marke** *f, typ.* gauge-pin, lay-mark; **=maschine** ⊙ *f* Spinnerei: spreader, spreading-frame.

an-legen (⁵ᴸ) ⓜ** I *v/a.* 1. (heranbringen) meist: to apply (or lay, put) to; die Axt an e-n Baum ℒ to lay the axe to a tree; Blutegel ℒ to apply leeches to; die letzte Feile (ob. Hand) an et. ℒ to put the finishing touch(es) to a th.; Feuer ℒ to set fire to (a house), *jur.* to commit arson; das Gewehr ℒ (an die Backe legen) to level (or point) a gun (at); auf e-n das Gewehr ℒ to take aim at a p.; ⚔ legt an! — Feuer! present! — fire!; Hand ℒ to put one's shoulder to the wheel; mit Hand ℒ to lend a (helping) hand; Hand an sich selbst legen to attempt one's (own) life; den Hemmschuh ℒ to put on the brake or drag; einen Hund ℒ to chain up a dog; e-m Ketten, Fesseln ℒ to put a p. in chains, to cast him in irons; eine Leiter ℒ to raise (or put up) a ladder; einen Maßstab an et. ℒ to measure a thing (by a given standard); (den Nachen) ℒ to lay (a boat) alongside of; e-m Faße die Reifen ℒ to hoop a barrel or cask; ein Schiff zum Bau ℒ to lay (down) ... on the stocks; ⚓ die Schoten ℒ to haul home ...; Siegel ℒ to affix seals; *math.* einen Winkel (an einem Punkte) ℒ to apply an angle (at a point); e-m Pferde ꝛc. e-n Zaum ℒ to put a bridle on ...; *fig. auch:* to curb or check (a p.) — 2. (anziehen; *ant.* ablegen) to put on, to don; (Halb=)Trauer ℒ to go into (half-)mourning, seinen Sonntagsstaat ℒ to attire o.s. (or to dress o.s. up) in one's Sunday clothes. — 3. a) (einrichten) to construct; einen Durchstich ℒ to make a cutting; eine Eisenbahn ℒ to build ...; e-e Fabrik, ein Geschäft, eine Schule ℒ to set up (or to establish) a factory, a (house of) business, a school; einen Garten ℒ to lay out ..., to plant ...; ein Gemälde ℒ to sketch ...; e-e Kolonie, Niederlassung ℒ to establish ..., to found ...; einen Laden ℒ (eröffnen) to open ...; ⚔ ein Lager ℒ to pitch a camp; eine Stadt ℒ to found ...; von Natur für et. angelegt sein to be intended by nature for a th., to be cut out for a th.; b) *b.s.* to plot, contrive; ein angelegter Handel a preconcerted plan, F a put-up job, a (regular) plant; c) es auf et. ℒ to aim at; es war auf euch angelegt it was intended (or meant) for you; es war alles darauf angelegt, ihn zu verblenden everything was so arranged (or calculated) as to dazzle him. — 4. meist ⓜ: Geld (zu 5 Prozent) ℒ to put out ... (at 5 per cent.); Geld in et. ℒ to invest money in a th.; fest angelegt (permanently) invested, safely placed; wieviel wollen Sie ℒ? how much do you wish to spend?; seine Zeit gut ℒ to make good use of one's time. — II *v/n.* (h.) 5. auf e-n ℒ f. 1. — 6. *hunt.* (eine Meute an die zu verfolgende Fährte bringen) to put a pack of (or to lay the) hounds on the scent. — 7. *arch.* (Maße austragen) to lay out the measurements; *typ.* to feed, to lay on. — 8. ⚓ to moor; bei einem Schiffe ℒ to lay (a boat) alongside of ...; zum Aus- u. Einladen: to put to shore for lading (purposes). — III *v/impers.* 9. es legt bei ihm an he is growing stout or putting on flesh. — IV sich ℒ *v/refl.* 10. sich ℒ an to lean against, an ein feindliches Schiff: to board (or grapple) a ship. — V ~ *n* ⓶ 11. = Anlegung.

An-lege-platz (⁵ᴸ...) *m* = =stelle. [layer-on.}
An-leger (⁵ᴸ...) *m* ⓶, **~in** *f* ⓶ *typ.* feeder,
An-lege-schloß (⁵ᴸ...) *n* ⓶ (Vorlegeschloß) padlock; **=span** ⊙ *m, typ.* scale-board, reglet; **=stege** *m/pl., typ.* head-sides *pl.*, furniture; **=stelle** ⚓ *f* landing-place; **=tisch** ⊙ *m, typ.* horse.

An-legung (⁵ᴸ) *f* ⓶ 1. = Anlage 1, 2, 3. — 2. ~ von Kanälen cutting of canals, canalization; *surg.* ~ eines Verbandes application of a bandage. [leihe.}

An-leh(e)n (⁵ᴸ⌣) [ahd.] *n* ⓶ (⊙d.) = An=}

an-lehn/en (⁵ᴸ) I *v/a.* u. *v/refl.* ⓜ** 1. (sich) an et. ℒ to lean against (or upon) a th. (a. *fig.*); sich ℒ an (stützen auf) to find support in; ⚔ sich (seine) Flügel ℒ an to rest (one's column) against. — 2. die Tür ℒ to leave the door ajar or on the jar or upon the latch; er lehnte die Tür nur an he only half closed the door. — II ~ *n* ⓶ 3. = A/ung.

An-lehns-los (⁵ᴸ...) *n* ⓶ lottery-bond.

⚛ scientific; ♃ botanical; ♀ geography; ⊙ machinery; ⚔ mining; ⚔ military; ⚓ marine; ⓜ commercial; ✉ postal; 🚂 railway.

An-lehnung (ˢᴸᵛ) f ㊻ support; meist ⊕ prop; fig. in ~ an ... in support of, in connexion with.

an-lehren (ˢᴸᵛ) v/a. ㊿** e-m et. ㄥ to instruct (or train) a p. in a. th.

An-leihe (ˢᴸᵛ) [nhd. 18 sæ.] f ㊻ loan; bei e-m e-e ㄥ machen to borrow money of (or to get accommodation from) a p.; e-e (größere) ~ machen to raise (or contract) a loan; öffentliche (ob. Staats=) ~ public (or government-) loan.

An-leihe-amt (ˡ...) n ㊷ loan-office; =los n lottery-bond.

an-leihen obb. (ˢᴸᵛ) v/a. ㊿** bei e-m Geld ㄥ to borrow money of a p.

An-leihe-papier (ˡ...) n ㊷ eines Staates government-stock or -bond.

an-leimen (ˢᴸᵛ) v/a. ㊿** to glue on.

an-leit/en (ˢᴸᵛ) I v/a. ㊿** 1. (führen) to conduct, to guide (or direct) to a place. — 2. fig. (lehren) to instruct (or train) in a th. — II ~ n ㉓ a. = A/ung.

An-leiter (ˢᴸᵛ) m ㉒, ~in f ㊼ guide; (Lehrer[in]) instructor m, instructress f.

An-leitung (ˢᴸᵛ) f ㊻ 1. conducting; (Führung) guidance; (Unterweisung) instruction; e-m ~ zu e-r Wissenschaft geben to instruct a p. in the rudiments of ...; unter seiner ~ under his superintendence. — 2. (Schrift) manual, guide.

an-lernen (ᵍᵍᵛ) I v/a. ㊿** 1. to learn (= erlernen). — 2. e-n (zu et.) ㄥ to teach a p. a th.; v. Handwerkern: to apprentice. — II **an-gelernt** p.p. u. a. ㊻ 3. acquired by routine, mechanical.

an-liebeln (ˢᴸᵛ) v/a. ㉒a** to attract by amorous glances, to look lovingly at.

an-liegen (ˢᴸᵛ) I v/n. (h.) ㊹** 1. an et. (dat.) ㄥ to lie close (or near) to a th., to be adjacent (or contiguous) to a th.; (angrenzen) to border (or abut) on. — 2. von Kleidungsstücken: glatt ㄥ to sit close, to fit well. — 3. ⸚ e-m (a. v/a. e-n) mit Bitten ㄥ to entreat (or implore, solicit) a p. — 4. ⚓ (steuern nach) Nord (auch nordwärts) ㄥ to bear (or stand) to the north; seewärts ㄥ to stand (or make) for the offing. — II ~ n ㉓ 5. contiguity. — 6. (Wunsch) request; desire; er hatte kein dringenderes ~ nothing was nearer to his heart; ein ~ vorbringen to lay one's suit (or petition) before a p., stärker: to prefer a demand. — III ㄥd p.pr. u. a. ㊻ 7. (anstoßend) adjacent (a. math.), adjoining (land); das ㄥde Dorf the neighbouring village; vom Trikot ꝛc.: tight(ly fitting); adv. (beigefügt) herewith enclosed. — 8. ⚔ accumbent; appressed. — IV **angelegen** p.p. u. a. ㊻ 9. s. bsd. Artikel.

An-lieger (ᵛᴸᵛ) m ㉒ jur. (anwohnender Hausbesitzer) p. owning house-property (or living) close by (a street, &c.).

an-lispeln (ˢᴸᵛ) v/a. ㉒a** e-n ㄥ to speak in lisps to a p.; vom Winde ꝛc.: to speak in soft whispers to, to whisper to.

an-lock/en (˷) I v/a. ㊿** (ködern) to bait, Vögel: to decoy; allg. to allure, entice. — II ~ n ㉓ = A/ung. — III ㄥd p.pr. u. a. ㊻ attractive, stärker: tempting.

An-locker (ᵍᵍᵛ) m ㉒, ~in f ㊼ allurer, b.s. tempter; (Lockvogel) decoy(-bird).

An-lockung (ᵍᵍᵛ) f ㊻ allurement, enticement; ~s-mittel (ˡ...) n ㊷ decoy, bait.

---

an-loten ⚓ (ˢᴸᵛ) v/a. ㊿** (mit dem Lote bestimmen) to take soundings of.

an-löten (ˢᴸᵛ) v/a. ㊿** to solder to.

an-ludern (ˢᴸᵛ) v/a. ㉒a** hunt. (mit Luder ködern) to bait with a carcass.

an-lügen (ˢᴸᵛ) [ahd.] v/a. ㊇d** 1. e-n ㄥ to tell a p. a falsehood (or lie) to his face. — 2. e-m et. ㄥ falsely to impute a th. to a p.

an-luven ⚓ (ˢᴸᵛʷ) v/n. (h.) ㊿** (den Bug dem Winde zudrehen) to luff, to go to windward or to the weather-side.

Anm. abbr. = Anmerkung.

an-machen (ᵍᵛᵛ) I v/a. ㊿** 1. (befestigen; ant. abbrechen) to attach, to fix. — 2. (mischen) Farben ㄥ to temper ...; ⊕ den Kalk, Mörtel mit Wasser ㄥ to slake lime, to mix mortar; den Salat ㄥ to dress the salad; Zucker an eine Speise ㄥ to put sugar into a dish. — 3. engS. (verfälschen) to adulterate, F to doctor (up). — 4. Feuer ㄥ to light (or kindle) the fire; es ist kein Feuer angemacht there is no fire in the stove. — II P sich ㄥ v/refl. 5. sich an e-n ㄥ to force one's company on a p. — III ~ n ㉓ 6. fixing. — 7. (Einrühren) mixing (or stirring up) with.

an-mahnen (ˢᴸᵛ) v/a. ㊿** e-n an et. ㄥ to exhort (or admonish) a p. to do a th.

An-mahnung (ˢᴸᵛ) f ㊻ exhortation; ~s=schreiben (ˡ...) n ㊷ = Mahnbrief.

an-malen (ˢᴸᵛ) v/a. ㊿** to paint (over), to colour, tadelnd: to daub over.

An-mann (ᵍᵍᵛ) m ㉒c. Turnerei: leader.

An-marsch (ᵍᵍᵛ) m ㉒ ㊆a. approach; im ~ sein auf // to be advancing on //, to march on //.

an-marschieren ✕ (ᵍᵛᴸᵛ) v/n. (in) ㊽*/* ㄥ gegen // to march against//; anmarschiert kommen to come marching along.

An-marsch-weg (ᵍᵍᵛ...) m ㊷ marching-route. [Netze ㄥ to fasten the nets.]

an-maschen (ᵍᵍᵛ) v/a. ㊿** hunt. wied.)

an-maßen (ˢᴸᵛ) I v/refl. ㊿** 1. sich (dat.) et. ㄥ, † ob. geh. Spr. sich (acc.) e-r Sache ㄥ, to arrogate a th. to (schwächer: to claim a th. for) o.s.; sich e-n Titel ꝛc. ㄥ to assume, to usurp ...; ich maße mir kein Urteil (darüber) an I cannot presume to give an opinion; er maßt sich an ein Künstler zu sein he pretends to be an artist. — 2. sich (dat.) ㄥ (unterfangen) et. zu tun to venture (or take upon o.s.) to ... — II ㄥd p.pr. u. a. ㊻ 3. arrogant, insolent; (herrisch) overbearing, highhanded; (eingebildet) presumptuous, pretentious; (hochfahrend) haughty, F uppish, bumptious, ㄥdes Wesen assurance, arrogance, presumption; stärker: insolence. — III **an-gemaßt** p.p. u. a. ㊻ 4. a) aktivisch: Der Richter person assuming the dignity of a judge; b) passivisch: Der Titel assumed (or usurped) title.

an-maßlich (ˢᴸᵛ) a. ㊻ 1. usurped. — 2. arrogant, vgl. a. anmaßen II.

An-maßung (ˢᴸᵛ) f ㊻ 1. e-s Titels, Rechtes ꝛc.: assumption (or usurpation) of, encroachment upon. — 2. arrogance; (Eigendünkel) presumption, pretentiousness; (Unverschämtheit) insolence.

an-maßungs-voll (ˢᴸᵛ˷) a. ㊻ arrogant; vgl. auch anmaßen II.

---

an-mästen (ᵍᵍᵛ) v/a. ㊿** to fatten; sich (dat.) ein Bäuchlein, Fleisch ㄥ to eat well and grow stout, to put on flesh.

an-mauern (ᵍᵍᵛ) v/a. ㉒a** to build against a wall; fig. er stand wie angemauert da he seemed riveted (or fixed, rooted to the spot.

an-maulen P (ᵍᴸᵛ) v/a. ㊿** e-n ㄥ to be sulky (or in the sulks) with a p. [fee.|

An-melde-gebühr (ᵍᵍᵛ...) f ㊷ registry-|

an-meld/en (ᵍᵍᵛ) I v/a. u. v/refl. ㊿** 1. (sich) ㄥ to announce (o.s.); et. auf dem Standesamte ㄥ to give notice of a th. to the registrar (for births and deaths); e-m et. ㄥ to advise a p. of a th. — 2. jur. Berufung ㄥ to give notice of appeal; Fremde bei der Polizei ㄥ to notify the police of the arrival of ...; Gäste ㄥ to usher in (or to announce) ...; ein Patent ㄥ to take out ...; Schüler ㄥ to send in the name of ...; sich ㄥ to present o.s., to send in one's name; sich als fallit ㄥ to declare o.s. insolvent or bankrupt; ⚜ eine Tratte ㄥ to advise a draft; Waren beim Zollamte ㄥ to declare goods at the custom-house. — II ~ n ㉓ 3. = A/ung.

An-melder (ᵍᵍᵛ) m ㉒, ~in f ㊼ 1. one who announces s. th., informant. — 2. von Schulkindern: tell-tale, sneak.

An-melde-pflicht (ᵍᵍᵛ...) f ㊻ duty of giving notice (of the arrival of strangers); =schein ㄥ m über Warensendungen: certificate of arrival; =stelle f office for registering (persons, goods, &c.).

An-meldung (ᵍᵍᵛ) f ㊻ announcement; bei Gericht: notice; ⚜ auch: declaration; die ~ von Schülern findet heute statt names of new pupils will be received (or may be entered) to-day.

an-mengen (ᵍᵍᵛ) v/a. ㊿** to mix.

An-merke-buch ⸚ (ᵍᵍᵛ...) n ㊷ memorandum-, note-book; vgl. Notizbuch.

an-merken (ᵍᵍᵛ) v/a. ㊿** 1. to remark, observe, notice; e-m et. ㄥ to perceive a th. in a p.; man kann ihm nichts ㄥ one does not notice anything in him; man merkt s-m Werke die Hast an his work bears traces of haste. — 2. (notieren) to note (or jot, write) down; protokollarisch: to take a minute of; auf dem Kerbholz: to score; sich et. ㄥ to take (or to make a) note of a th.

an-merkens-... (ᵍᵍᵛ...) s. anmerkungs-...

An-merker (˷) m ㉒ annotator; scorer.

An-merkung (ᵍᵍᵛ) [nhd. 15. sæ.] f ㊻ observation, remark, note; (Randglosse) marginal note, im Text typ.: cut-in note; (Zusatz) rider; (Fußnote) foot-note; ~en zu e-m Buche machen to annotate a book; ~en über et. machen to comment on a th; ㄥs=wert (ᵍᵍᵛ...) a. ㊻, ㄥwürdig remarkable, noticeable.

an-messen (ᵍᵍᵛ) I v/a. ㊿** 1. e-m e-n Rock ㄥ to take a person's measure for a coat; er ließ sich e-n Anzug ㄥ he was measured for a suit. — 2. fig. (anpassen) to adapt (or adjust) to ...; II **an-gemessen** p.p. u. a. ㊻ 3. s. bsd. Art.

an-mischen (ᵍᵍᵛ) v/a. ㊿** = anmengen.

an-munden (ᵍᵍᵛ) v/a. ㊿** e-n ㄥ to please (or suit) a p.'s taste.

an-murren ⸚ (ᵍᵍᵛ) v/a. u. v/n. (h.) ㊿** (gegen) e-n ㄥ to grumble at a p.

Zeichen (s. S. XVII): F familiär; P Volkssprache; Γ Gaunersprache; ⸚ selten; † alt (auch gestorben); * neu (auch geboren); ⁒ unrichtig;

[anmustern] — 61 — [anölen]

an-mustern ⚓ ↓ (ˢᴸ⌣) ⓐa** (ant. ab=mustern) **I** v/a. Matrosen, Schiffsvolk ꝛc. ⚓ to enrol … — **II** v/n. (h.) to be enrolled, to sign on. — **III** ~ n ㉓ u.
An-musterung (ˢᴸ⌣⌣) f ㊻ enrolment.
An-mut (ˢᴸ) [Mut m] f ㊻ (o. pl.) (Grazie) grace, gracefulness; (Liebreiz) charm, loveliness, sweetness; comeliness, (Artigkeit) agreeableness; mit (ohne) ~ (un)gracefully; ~ verleihen to add (or give) charm to.
an-muten (ˢᴸ) **I** v/a. ⓑ** **1.** fast †= zumuten. — **2.** et. mutet mich an a th. pleases (or charms, delights) me. — **II** ~ n ㉓ **3.** = Anmutung.
an-mutig (ˢᴸ⌣) a. ㊶ graceful, charming, delightful; comely, agreeable, sweet; **~keit** ⚓ (ˢᴸ⌣⌣) f.㊻ = Anmut.
an-mut(s)-los (ˢᴸ⌣...) a. ㊶ ungraceful, plain, uncouth, vom Stil: rough, harsh, bald; **=losigkeit** f ㉒ lack of grace; ⚥reich, ⚥voll a. = anmutig.
An-mutung ⚓ (ˢᴸ⌣) f ㊻ **1.** (Zumutung) unreasonable demand. — **2.** ~ (Neigung) zu, für et. bent (or taste, liking) for a th.
Anna (ᴵ⌣) [hebr. Gnade] npr/f. ㊺ ⓑα. (Mutter Mariä; Vn.) Anna, Ann(e).
an-nadeln ⚓ (ˢᴸ⌣) v/a. ⓐa** to pin on to; Schuhmacherei: to sew (the welts) to the upper leather.
an-nageln (ˢᴸ⌣) v/a. ⓐa** to nail to, to fasten with nails to; fig. wie angenagelt as if fixed (or nailed) to the spot.
an-nagen (ˢᴸ⌣) v/a. ⓑ** to gnaw (or nibble) at; angenagt showing marks of teeth; vgl. auch benagen.
an-nahen (ˢᴸ⌣) v/n. (jn) u. sich ⚓ v/refl. ⓑ** to approach, to draw near.
an-nähen (ˢᴸ⌣) v/a. ⓑ** **1.** to sew on; mit Grätenstich: to herring-bone; glatt ⚓ to stitch down. — **2.** ↓ e-n Block ⚓ to seize a block; Segeltuch ⚓ (zurren) to lash.
an-näher/n (ˢᴸ⌣) **I** v/a. u. v/refl. ⓐa** **1.** (sich) ⚓ to approach, to draw near (or close) to. — **II** ~ n ㉓ **2.** = A/ung. — **III** ⚥d a. ㊶ **3.** approaching; sich (ea.) ⚥d math.: ⚙ convergent. — **4.** (ungefähr) approximat(iv)e; adv. = about, very nearly, close on; roughly (speaking), on a rough calculation.
An-näherung ⚓ (ˢᴸ⌣) f ㊻ **1.** approach (a. ⚔); der Nacht: approach of night, nightfall; fig. (Entgegenkommen) advance; e-e ~ (Versöhnung) zustande bringen to bring about a reconciliation. — **2.** ⚙ math. approximation, von Linien: convergence.
An-näherungs=graben ⚓ (ˢᴸ⌣...) m/pl. ㊷ frt. approaches pl., lines pl. of approach; **=kraft** f, phys.: ⚙ centripetal force; **=linien** f/pl. = graben; **=versuch** m attempt at reconciliation, advances pl.; **=wege** m/pl., **=werke** n/pl. = graben; **⚥weise** adv. approximately.
An-nahme (ˢᴸ⌣) f ㊻ **1.** e-s Geschenkes ꝛc.: acceptance; e-s Wechsels, a.: protection; willige ~ erteilen (verweigern) to (dis)honour (a draft); nicht erfolgte ~ non-acceptance. — **2.** (Ort) receiving-house or -office (for letters or parcels). — **3. a)** ~ an Kindes Statt adoption; ~ e-r Magd: engagement; e-s Schülers: admission; jur. ~ zum Bürgen acceptance of bail; **h)** eines Theaterstückes ꝛc.: reception; eines Gesetzes: carrying or passing (of a bill). — **4.** (Voraussetzung) assumption, supposition, ⚙ hypothesis; (Einbildung) fiction, fancy; auf diese ~ hin in this belief; in der ~, daß on the supposition that, in the belief that; nach der mäßigsten ~ at the lowest estimate, ⓧ at the lowest figure; v. Wechseln: mangels ~ for want of acceptance.
An-nahme=beamte(r) (ˢᴸ⌣...) m ㉜ receiving clerk; **=berechtigung** f right of admission; **=buch** n receipt-book; **=(post=)stempel** m (receipt) post-mark; **=stelle** f = Annahme 2; **=verweigerung** f refusal of acceptance.
Annalen (⌣ᴸ⌣) [lt.] f/pl. ㊸ (o. sg.) (Jahrbücher) annals, rolls pl.; die ~ der Geschichte historical records pl.; the pages of history. [annalist.⌐
Annalist (⌣⌣ᴸ) [lt.] m ㊷ (Annalen-schreiber)⌐
Annalistik (⌣⌣ᴸ⌣) f compiling of records.
an-nässen (ˢᴸ⌣) v/a. ⓐ** to moisten (or wet) a little. [Anna) Annie.⌐
Ännchen (ᴸ⌣) npr/n. ㉓α. (Vn.; dim. von⌐
an-nehmbar (ˢᴸ⌣) a. ㊶ acceptable, (zulässig) admissible, passable, (gefallend) agreeable, pleasing, von Meinungen: plausible; ⓧ der Preis, ⚥e Bedingungen fair price sg., reasonable terms pl.; **~keit** (ˢᴸ⌣⌣) f ㊻ (o. pl.) acceptability, admissibility; fairness.
an-nehmen (ˢᴸ⌣) ⓐa** **I** v/a. **1.** mst to accept; ein Anerbieten ⚓ auch: to close with an offer; ein Geschenk ꝛc.: to accept; das Gesetz ward angenommen the bill (was) passed; ⚔ e-e Schlacht: to accept; med. sein Magen nimmt feste Speisen nicht an … refuses solid food; e-n Vorschlag ⚓ to accept …, parl. ⚓ to agree to …; e-n Wechsel nicht ⚓ to refuse the acceptance of a bill. — **2.** (unternehmen, gut aufnehmen) Aufträge ⚓ to undertake orders; Besuche ⚓ to receive company; ein Gesuch ⚓ to accede to a request; zu Gnaden ⚓ to take into favour. — **3.** billigend: Ansichten, das Christentum ꝛc. ⚓ to embrace …; e-e Entschuldigung ⚓ to take …; Gründe ⚓ to admit …; eine Lehre ⚓ to espouse a doctrine; j-s Rat ⚓ to take (or follow) a p.'s advice; Vernunft ⚓ to listen to reason. — **4.** (sich aneignen) e-e Gestalt ⚓ to assume a form; eine Gewohnheit ⚓ to acquire (or fall into) …; e-e Haltung ⚓ to take up a position; eine andere Miene ⚓ to change one's countenance; e-n Namen ⚓ to assume (or adopt) a name; einen falschen Schein ⚓ to put on (or to give o.s.) a false appearance; von Sachen: leicht Schmutz ⚓d easily soiled; ⓧ den Kalk, das Öl ⚓ to mix readily with …; Färberei: die Farbe gut ⚓ to take … on (well). — **5. a)** (wählen, anwerben) einen Advokaten ꝛc. ⚓ to engage …; Arbeiter, Dienstboten: to hire; ⚔ als Rekruten ⚓ to enlist; **h)** an Kindes Statt ⚓ to adopt. — **6. a)** (voraussetzen) to assume, suppose, presume; et. als ausgemacht ⚓ to take a th. for granted; **b)** abs. (als wahr ⚓) to accept as true; man nimmt allgemein an, daß // it is commonly believed that //; man muß billigerweise ⚓, daß // it stands to reason that //. — **7.** hunt. den Hund ⚓ (an die Leine nehmen) to attach … to the leash; der Hund nimmt die Fährte an … takes up the scent; v. Wild: den Jäger ⚓ (ihn angreifen) to stand at bay, to turn on the huntsman, to charge the h.; den Äsungsplatz ⚓ (ihn besuchen) to go to graze. — **II** v/refl. **8.** sich einer Sache ⚓ to take charge (or care) of a th.; sich j-s ⚓ to take a p.'s part, to have a p.'s interest at heart, to interest o.s. in a p., to befriend a p. — **III** ~ n ㉓ **9.** = Annahme 1, 3, 4. — **IV an-genommen** p.p. und a. ㊶ (D⁹) **10.** accepted; assumed; ⚥es Kind adopted child; ⚥er Name adopted name, (it.) alias, eines Schriftstellers auch pseudonym, (fr.) nom de plume; nach übereinkommen: agreed upon; ⚓, daß es so sei supposing (or granting) it to be so; ⚓ sie zahlen nicht in case they should not pay. [nehmbar.⌐
an-nehmens=wert (ˢᴸ⌣ᴸ) a. ㊶ = an=⌐
An-nehmer (ˢᴸ⌣) m ㉒, **~in** f ㊵ one who accepts, &c.; e-s Wechsels: acceptor.
an-nehmlich (ˢᴸ⌣) a. ㊶ = annehmbar.
An-nehmlichkeit (ˢᴸ⌣⌣) f ㊻ **1.** ⚓ (o. pl.) acceptableness. — **2.** (Angenehmes) agreeableness; charm; delight(fulness); ~en pl. conveniences pl.; ~en des Lebens comforts pl., sweets of life.
An-nehmung (ˢᴸ⌣) f ㊻ = Annahme 1, 3, 4.
an-neigen (ˢᴸ⌣) v/a. u. v/refl. ⓑ** (sich) ⚓ to incline (or lean) towards; math.: to converge; vgl. auch zuneigen.
annektier/en (⌣⌣ᴸ⌣) [lt.] **I** v/a. ⓑ (sich aneignen) to annex. — **II** ~ n ㉓ = A/ung.
Annektierer (⌣⌣ᴸ⌣) m ㉒, **~in** f ㊵ annexer.
An-nektierung (⌣⌣ᴸ⌣) f ㊻ annexation.
Annette (⌣ᴸ⌣) [dim. v. Anna] npr/f. ㊺β. Annie.
an-netzen (ˢᴸ⌣) v/a. ⓑ** = annässen.
Annex (⌣ᴸ) [lt.] m ⓑa. **1.** (Anhang, Beilage) annex. — **2.** (Nebengebäude) (=bau) annexe.
Annexion (⌣⌣(⌣)ᴸ) [lt.] f ㊻ annexation.
an-nicken (ˢᴸ⌣) v/a. ⓑ** to nod to.
an-nieten (ˢᴸ⌣) v/a. ⓑ** to rivet to.
an-nisten (ˢᴸ⌣): sich ⚓ v/refl. ⓑ** sich an dem Hause ⚓ to build a nest on …
Anno, öft. **anno** (ᴸ⌣) [lt. im Jahr] ~ 1870 in (the year) 1870; co. F von ~ Tobak her, etwa: since the time of Queen Dick; since Adam; ~ dazumal many, many years ago, in the olden days.
an-noch † (ˢᴸ⌣) adv. as yet. [vgl. A.D.⌐
Annonce ⓧ ꝛc. (ă-ng'-β̂ˢ) [fr.] f ㊸ advertisement, vgl. Anzeige.
Annoncen=bureau (ᴸ⌣...) n ㉒, **=expeditio'n** f advertising office, advertisement-office; **=sammler** m canvasser (for advertisements); **=wesen** n advertising.
annoncieren (ă-nɡ-βᴸ⌣) [fr.] v/a. u. v/n. (h.) ⓑ to advertise. [nuity.⌐
Annuität (⌣⌣ᴸ) [lt.] f ㊻ (Zeitrente) an=⌐
annullierbar (⌣⌣ᴸ⌣) [lt.] a. ㊶ jur. defeasible, voidable, annullable; **~keit** (⌣⌣ᴸ⌣⌣) f ㊻ (o. pl.) defeasibleness.
annullieren (⌣⌣ᴸ⌣) [lt.] v/a. ⓑ (ungültig machen) to annul; to make void, ⓧ to cancel, to quash.
Anode ⚙ (⌣ᴸ⌣) [grch.] f, elect. (positiver Pol, Stromzuflußende; ant. Kathode) anode.
an-öhren (ˢᴸ⌣) v/a. ⓑ** to furnish with an ear or with a handle.
an-ölen (ˢᴸ⌣) v/a. ⓑ** to oil; sich ⚓ F fig. (sich betrinken) to lush up, to booze.

♪ Musik; ⚙ Wissenschaft; ♀ Pflanze; ⚨ Geographie; ⊕ Technik; ⚒ Bergbau; ⚔ Militär; ↓ Marine; ⓧ Handel; ⋄ Post; 🚂 Eisenbahn.

[anomal] — 62 — [Anrede]

anomal (ˊ◡) [grch.] *a.* ⓖ (unregelmäßig) anomalous; **~ie** (◡◡ˊ) *f* ⑯ anomaly; Äisch (◡◡◡) *a.* ⓖ = anomal.

anonym (◡◡ˊ) [grch.] *a.* ⓖ (namenlos) anonymous; **~ität** (◡◡◡ˊ) *f* ⑯ (o. pl.) anonymousness; **~us** (◡ˊ◡◡) *m* ⑬ anonymous writer or author or person.

an-ordn/en (ˊ◡◡) **I** *v/a.* ⓑ** to arrange, to (put in) order; (festsetzen) to appoint, fix; (unterbringen) to place, distribute, contrive; (regeln) to regulate, direct; (leiten) to conduct. — **II ~** *n* ㉓ = **A/ung.** — **III Äd** *p.pr.* u. *a.* ⓖ arranging, ordering, conducting, directing; a. regulative.

An-ordner (ˊ◡◡) *m* ㉒, **~in** *f* ㊼ p. who arranges or orders; director, conductor, organizer, v. Zeitungen, Zeitschriften: editor; F the life and soul of a th.

An-ordnung (ˊ◡◡) *f* ⑯ 1. arrangement; appointment, institution; in einzelnen Teilen: disposition (of the parts). — 2. des Haares: head-dress; *paint.* geschickte ~ clever combination or grouping; ♪ von Instrumenta'lmusik: instrumentation, orchestration. — 3. (Bestimmung) direction, appointment; ~ treffen, daß // to give orders (or instructions) that //, to arrange that //; auf f-e ~ by his direction or command.

an-organisch ⚛ (ˊ◡◡◡) [grch.] *a.* ⓖ (unbelebt) bes. *chm.*: inorganic.

a-normal (◡◡ˊ) [grch.-lt.] *a.* ⓖ †+ Verquickung von anomal und abnorm.

An-paarung (ˊ◡◡) *f* ⑯ (Paarung des Bastards mit einem Tier einer der Urrassen) pairing (of) a bastard with an animal of (the original) pure breed or stock.

an-packen (ˊ◡◡) *v/a.* ⓑ** to seize, to lay (or catch) hold of, to clutch; fest ⚲ to grip tightly; beim Kragen: to collar.

An-packer F (ˊ◡◡) *m* ㉒ brawler, bully.

an-pappen (ˊ◡◡) *v/a.* ⓑ** to paste on.

an-pass/en (ˊ◡◡) ⓝ** **I** *v/n.* (h.) 1. e-m Dinge ⚲ to be adapted (or fitted) for a th. — **II sich** ⚲ *v/refl.* 2. to adapt o.s. (or to conform) to; sich e-r Sache ⚲ to fit o.s. (or for) a th. — **III** *v/a.* 3. (anprobieren) (e-m) e-n Rock ꝛc. ⚲ to try (or fit) on ... — 4. (geeignet m.) to accommodate (or adjust) to; f-e Worte der Fassungskraft f-s ⚲ to suit ... to a p.'s capacity. — **IV ~** *n* ㉓ 5. = **A/ung.** — **V Äd** *p.pr.* u. *a.* ⓖ 6. suitable (or fit) for.

An-passung (ˊ◡◡) *f* ⑯ accommodation, adjustment, adaptation to; **~s-fähigkeit** *f* ⑫, **-vermögen** *n* adaptability.

an-patschen¹ F (ˊ◡◡) [Patsche Hand] *v/a.* ①** to (touch with a) paw.

an-patschen² F (◡ˊ◡) [patschen] *v/n.* (fn) ①** im Kote ⚲ ob. angepatscht kommen to come splashing along.

an-peitschen (ˊ◡◡) *v/a.* ①** to whip on.

An-pfahl ⚓ (ˊ◡) *m* ⓞd. upper stay or prop.

an-pfählen (ˊ◡◡) *v/a.* ⓑ** to attach (or fasten) to stakes or posts; am Spalier: to pale up; Weinstöcke: to prop (up).

an-pfeifen (ˊ◡◡) ⓑs ** **I** *v/a. fig.* F = anhauchen (schelten). — **II** *v/n.* (h.) die Lokomotive, der Zug kommt angepfiffen ... comes whistling along.

an-pflanz/en (ˊ◡◡) ⓝ** **I** *v/a.* to plant; Gärten: to lay out; Land: (urbar machen) to clear, (anbauen) to cultivate. — **II sich** ⚲ *v/refl. fig.* sich wo ⚲ to settle (down) in a place. — **III ~** *n* ㉓ = **A/ung** 1.

An-pflanzer (ˊ◡◡) *m* ㉒ planter, cultivator; (Ansiedler) settler, colonist.

An-pflanzung (ˊ◡◡) *f* ⑯ 1. *agr.* planting, cultivation. — 2. (Ansiedelung) plantation, settlement, colony.

an-pflöcken (ˊ◡◡) *v/a.* ⓑ** to fasten with pegs to; to peg to.

an-pflügen (ˊ◡◡) ⓑ** **I** *v/a.* to join (or enlarge) by ploughing. — **II** *v/n.* = anfurchen.

an-pfropfen (ˊ◡◡) *v/a.* ⓑ** 1. *hort.* to inoculate (or graft) on. — 2. (vollpfropfen) to cram with; mit Speisen: to gorge.

an-pichen (ˊ◡◡) *v/a.* ⓑ** 1. (mit Pech überziehen) to pitch (vgl. pichen). — 2. (mit Pech ankleben) to attach with pitch.

an-picken (ˊ◡◡) *v/a.* ⓑ** to peck (fruit).

an-pinseln (ˊ◡◡) *v/a.* ⓑ** to paint (or touch up) with a brush; to daub (over).

an-plappern (ˊ◡◡) *v/a* ⓐ** e-n ⚲ to jabber (or chatter) to a p.; to din in(to) a p.'s ears.

an-plärren (ˊ◡◡) ⓑ** **I** *v/a.* e-n ⚲ to bawl out (or shout) to a p. — **II** *v/n.* (h.) ⚲, angeplärrt kommen to come along bawling or shouting.

an-plätschern (ˊ◡◡) *v/n.* (h.) ⓐ** vom Wasser: an etwas ⚲ to plash against ...

An-pöbelung F derb (ˊ◡◡) *f* ⑯ abuse.

an-pochen (ˊ◡◡) *v/n.* (h.) ⓑ** an die Tür ⚲ to knock (or rap, tap) at ...

an-poltern (ˊ◡◡) *v/n.* (h.) ⓐ** 1. an die Tür ⚲ to give a loud rap (or knock) at ... — 2. angepoltert kommen to approach boisterously or noisily.

an-posaunen (◡ˊ◡◡) *v/a.* ⓑ**/* to blazon forth with sound of trumpets; *fig.* (hoch anpreisen) to puff.

An-prall (ˊ◡) *m* ⓞc. collision, impact; ⚔ shock, brunt of the battle.

an-prallen (ˊ◡◡) *v/n.* (fn) ⓑ** an etwas ⚲ to bound (or strike) against ..., to cannon (or dash) against ...

an-preien ⚓ (ˊ◡◡) *v/a.* ⓑ** ein Schiff ⚲ (anrufen) to hail ..., to speak ...

an-preis/en (ˊ◡◡) **I** *v/a.* ⓑ** to commend, extol, eulogize; to speak in glowing terms up; durch Reklame: to puff (up), crack up. — **II ~** *n* ㉓ = **A/ung.**

An-preiser (ˊ◡◡) *m* ㉒, **~in** *f* ㊼ eulogist.

An-preisung (ˊ◡◡) *f* ⑯ commendation, eulogy, loud praise; glowing account of; marktschreierisch: puff(ing), clap-trap.

an-prellen (ˊ◡◡) *v/a.* e-n ꝛc. ⚲ to dash (or knock) against a th.

an-pressen (ˊ◡◡) *v/a.* ⓝ** to press (or jam, squeeze) against.

an-prob(ier)en (ˊ◡◡◡,ˊ◡ˊ◡◡) ⓑ**(ⓑ*/*) *v/a.* Kleider ⚲ to try (or fit) on (a. p.'s) ...

an-prosten F (ˊ◡◡) *v/a.* ⓝ** to raise one's glass to (in drinking).

an-pumpen F (ˊ◡◡) *v/a.* ⓑ** *fig.* e-n ⚲ (von ihm borgen) to borrow money of ...

An-pumper F (~) *m* ㉒, **~in** *f* ㊼ borrower.

an-pusten F (ˊ◡◡) *v/a.* ⓑ** = anblasen **I**.

An-putz (ˊ◡) *m* ⓞa. (o. pl.) 1. adornment; (Kleider) finery; F *co.* fine togs *pl.* or toggery, rig-out. — 2. ⊕ = Abputz.

an-putzen (ˊ◡◡) ⓝ** *v/a.* to adorn, to dress up (in finery), F to titivate, to smarten up; e-n Weihnachtsbaum: to decorate or dress. — **II sich** ⚲ *v/refl.* to dress (o.s.) up, F to smarten (or spruce) o.s. up, to get o.s. up (for the occasion).

an-qualmen (ˊ◡◡) *v/a.* ⓑ** e-n ⚲ to envelop a p. in smoke. [pressen.

an-quetschen (ˊ◡◡) *v/a.* ①** = an=

an-quicken ⊕ (ˊ◡◡) *metall.* **I** *v/a.* ⓑ** to amalgamate. — **II ~** *n* ㉓ u. **An-quickung** *f* ⑯ amalgamation.

an-racken ⚓ (ˊ◡◡) *v/a.* ⓑ** das Segel ⚲ to fasten the sail with a parrel.

an-ranken (ˊ◡◡): sich ⚲ *v/refl.* ⓑ** to twine round (a tree); to cling to (a railing); sich an e-e Wand ⚲ to creep up ...

an-ranzen P (ˊ◡◡) *v/a.* ⓖ** (anfahren) to talk roughly (or severely) to, to rebuke, F to blow up. [slightly.

an-raspeln ⊕ (ˊ◡◡) *v/a.* ⓐa** to rasp

an-rasseln (ˊ◡◡) *v/n.* (fn) ⓐa** ⚲, angerasselt kommen to come rattling along.

an-raten (ˊ◡◡) **I** *v/a.* ⓐa** (*ant.* abraten) e-m et. ⚲ to advise a p. to do a th.; (empfehlen) to recommend; ich riet es ihm dringend an I urged him to do so, I urged it upon him. — **II ~** *n* ㉓ und **An-ratung** *f* ⑯ advice; auf sein ~ at his suggestion; on his advice.

an-rauchen (ˊ◡ˊ◡) **I** *v/a.* ⓑ** 1. to (blacken with) smoke. — 2. eine Zigarre ꝛc. ⚲ to begin to smoke ...; e-n Pfeifenkopf ⚲ to colour or season a (meerschaum-)pipe; angeraucht (smoke-)coloured, well-coloured, seasoned. — **II ~** *n* ㉓ 3. smoking; e-r Pfeife: colouring, seasoning.

an-räuchern (ˊ◡◡) **I** *v/a.* ⓑ** 1. to smoke (a little). — 2. *chm.* to fumigate. — **II ~** *n* ㉓ u. **An-räucherung** *f* ⑯ 3. smoking. — 4. *chm.* fumigation.

An-raum schles. (ˊ◡) *m* ⓞd. = Rauhreif.

an-rauschen (ˊ◡◡) *v/n.* (fn) ⓝ** ⚲, angerauscht kommen to approach with a rustling sound or a rushing noise.

an-rechnen (ˊ◡◡) **I** *v/a.* ⓑ** 1. to put (or set) down to one's account; wieviel rechnen Sie dafür an? how much do you charge for it?; e-m zuviel ⚲ to overcharge a p. for. — 2. *fig.* ich rechne es mir zur Ehre an I consider it an honour; e-m e-n Dienst hoch ⚲ to think very highly of a service rendered by a p.; sich (*dat.*) et. zum Ruhme ⚲ to glory in (or to boast of) a th.; sie rechnet es mir als Verbrechen an she puts it down to me as a crime; e-m et. als Verdienst ⚲ to give a p. full credit for a th. — **II ~** *n* ㉓ 3. = **A/ung.**

An-rechnung (ˊ◡◡) *f* ⑯ charge; *jur.* ~ Untersuchungshaft making allowance for the time already served (during the trial); in ~ bringen = anrechnen 1.

An-recht (ˊ◡) [nhd. 18. sæ.] *n* ⓞc. title to, right to; claim on; ein ~ haben auf to be entitled to.

An-rede (ˊ◡◡) *f* ⑯ 1. address; *rhet.* feierliche ~ bes. des Papstes allocution; plötzliche ~ apostrophe; an das Volk ꝛc.: harangue, des Richters an die Geschworenen: charge; e-e ~ halten an to address, to harangue. — 2. (das Anreden) die an einen richten to accost (or address) a p.; der Vokativ dient zur ~ ... is used in addressing a p. — 3. (~form) appellation; „Majestät" ist die ~ an Könige kings are addressed as "Majesty"; die ~ mit „Du" the "thouing" of a p.

Signs (see page XVII): F familiar; P vulgar; ⌐ flash; ⚲ rare; † obsolete (died); * new word (born); †+ incorrect; ♪ music.

An-rede-fall (ᵍᴸ˘...) *m* ⑫ *gram.* vocative (case); =**form** *f* = =weife.
an-reden (ᵍᴸ˘) *v/a.* ⑭** **1.** to address, auf der Straße: to accost; die Volksmenge: to harangue; e-n freundlich, hart ⚬ to talk gently, sharply to a p.; e-n mit „Durchlaucht" ⚬ to give a p. the title of "Highness". — **2.** e-n um e-n Dienst ⚬ to ask a service of a p.
An-rede-weife (⚬...) *f* ⑭ manner of addressing a p.; =**wort** *n,gr.*compellative.
an-regen (ᵍᴸ˘) I *v/a.* ⑭** **1.** *l. s., hunt.* Wild ⚬ (aufscheuchen u. forttreiben) to start (or beat up) game; *fig.* e-n ⚬ to stir (stärker: to stimulate, rouse, incite) a p.; angeregte Unterhaltung animated (or brisk, buoyant) tone; angeregte Unterhaltung animated (or lively) conversation. — **2.** e-n zu neuen Ideen, frischer Tatkraft ⚬ to call forth new ideas, fresh energy in a p.; *abs.* dieses Werk regt an ... is interesting, inspiring. — **3.** *et.* ⚬ to set a th. going; eine Frage ⚬ to bring up (or to moot) a question; einen Gegenstand ⚬ to start a subject; ein Unternehmen ⚬ to propose a scheme or venture; *et.* zuerst ⚬ to take the initiative (or lead) in a th. — **4.** (erwähnen) to touch upon (or to mention, to suggest) a th.; der angeregte Gegenstand the subject referred to or mentioned; angeregter= maßen *f. s.* — II ~ *n* ㉓ **5.** = Anregung. — III ⚬b *p.pr. u. a.* ⑥ **6.** stimulating, stärker: exciting, provoking; e-e ⚬de Melodie a stirring air.
An-reger (ᵍᴸ˘) *m* ㉒, ~**in** *f* ㊼ proposer, instigator, prime mover.
An-regung (ᵍᴸ˘) *f* ㊼ stimulation, stärker: excitement, provocation, (Anstoß) impulse; auf ~ von // at the instigation of //; *et.* in ~ bringen = anregen 3.
an-reiben (ᵍᴸ˘) *v/a.* ⑭** **1.** to rub against; Farben ꝛc.: to (begin to) grind or rub (down), zubereitend: to prepare (by grinding); Farben mit Wasser ⚬ to dilute ... — **2.** ein Zündholz ⚬ to strike a match. — **3.** Kochkunst: angeriebener Zwieback grated biscuit.
an-reichern ⊕ (ᵍᴸ˘) *metall.* I *v/a.* ⑭a** to enrich, ⊕ to improve. — II ~ *n* ㉓ und **An-reicherung** *f* ㊼ enrichment.
an-reihen (ᵍᴸ˘) ⑭** I *v/a.* **1.** Perlen ꝛc.: to string; e-e Bemerkung: to add to; *gram.* to co-ordinate; ⚬b copulative. — **2.** ⊕ Schneiderei: (m. großen Stichen anheften) to baste, to tack together. — II fich ⚬ *v/refl.* **3.** to take one's place, to rank; fich an=ea. ⚬ to form (in) a row, to join ranks. [needle.]
An-reih-nadel (ᵍᴸ...) *f* ⑫ stringing-)
An-reim ⚬ (ᵍᴸ) *m* ⑭d. *pros.* alliteration.
an-reifen (ᵍᴸ˘) *v/n.* (fn) ⑭** to arrive; angereist newly arrived; eine angereifte Person a p. (who has) lately arrived, a new comer.
an-reiß/en (ᵍᴸ˘) I *v/a.* ⑭a** **1.** to begin to tear, Bäume: to cut into; ⚬ (entwerfen) to trace. — **2.** (anbrechen) et. Ganzes, Geld, e-e Summe: to break into. — **3.** ⊕ *carp.* ꝛc.: das Holz ꝛc. ⚬ to mark ... — II **angerifen** *p.p. u. a.* ⑥ (D 9) **4.** slightly torn. — **5.** F *fig.* (*et.*) ⚬ (angeheitert) tipsy or F elevated, a little on.

An-reißer (ᵍᴸ˘) *m* ㉒ **1.** ⊕ Gießerei: scraper, rake. — **2.** P *berlin.:* (Kundenwerber) butcher's) tout.
an-reiten (ᵍᴸ˘) ⑭b** I *v/n.* (fn) **1.** ⚬, angeritten kommen to come riding up, to approach on horseback; ⚔ zur Attacke ⚬ to charge on horseback. — **2.** an e-n Stein ⚬ (anstoßen) to ride against ... — **3.** (voranreiten) to ride on, to advance on horseback. — II *v/a.* **4.** ein Pferd ⚬ (zuzureiten anfangen) to break in. — **5.** e-n ⚬ to accost a p. on horseback.
An-reiz (ᵍᴸ) *m* ⑭a. innerer: impulse; von außen: instigation, stimulation, irritation; auf *et.* Bestimmtes: incitement, provocation, ⚬ *med. u. a. fig.* stimulus.
an-reizen (ᵍᴸ˘) I *v/a.* ⑭** to irritate; zu *et.* ⚬ to incite (or provoke) to a th., to prompt (or instigate, induce) to do a th., to stimulate to a th. — II ~ *n* ㉓ = A/ung. — III ⚬b *p.pr. u. a.* ⑥ = anreizen III.
An-reizer (ᵍᴸ˘) *m* ㉒, ~**in** *f* ㊼ instigator, prompter, abetter, *jur.* ... or; tempter.
An-reizung (ᵍᴸ˘) *f* ㊼ = Anreiz.
an-rempeln F *derb* (ᵍᴸ˘) *v/a.* ⑭a** e-n ⚬ to jostle against (or to run into) a p.
an-rennen (ᵍᴸ˘) ⑭b** I *v/n.* (fn) **1.** ⚬, angerannt kommen to come running (up or along). — **2.** = anlaufen 2 (auch *fig.*). — **3.** to begin to run. — II *v/a.* **4.** den Kopf gegen an e-n Baum ꝛc. ⚬ to run (or bump) one's head against ... — **5.** e-n ⚬ to attack (F to rush) a p.; Polizei: to run a p. in; ⚓ ein Schiff ⚬ to foul a ship. [dresser; f. ~tifch.]
An-richte (ᵍᴸ˘) [*mhd.*] ⊕ sideboard;)
An-richte-kunft (ᵍᴸ˘...) *f* ⑫ art of serving (or dishing) up (a dinner); =**löffel** *m* tureen- (or pot-)ladle.
an-richten (ᵍᴸ˘) I *v/a.* ⑭** **1.** bfd. ⊕ die Speifen ⚬ to serve up (dinner); es ist angerichtet! dinner is ready or on the table!; ⊕ Farben ⚬ to mix colours. — **2.** Schaden ⚬ (anstiften) to do (or cause) damage, to do harm; *iro.* da haben Sie was Schönes angerichtet you have made a fine muddle (or F mess) of it, F now you have put your foot in it nicely; Uneinigkeit ⚬ to sow discord. — **3.** ⊕ = einrichten, vorbereiten. — II ~ *n* ㉓ **4.** dressing, preparation.
An-richter (ᵍᴸ˘) *m* ㉒, ~**in** *f* ㊼ **1.** dresser (of dishes). — **2.** ⊕ Gießerei: assayer.
An-richte-tifch (ᵍᴸ˘...) *m* ⑫ dresser, i. Speise= zimmer: sideboard; =**zimmer** *n* pantry.
An-richtung (ᵍᴸ˘) *f* ㊼ **1.** = anrichten II. — **2.** ⊕ Uhrmacherei: dial-train.
an-riechen (ᵍᴸ˘) *v/a.* ⑭c** e-m, e-r Sache *et.* ⚬ to scent (or perceive by the smell) a th. in a p., a th.; man riecht ihm an, daß one can tell by the smell that he.
an-ringeln (ᵍᴸ˘) ⑭a** I *v/a.* to fix with rings. — II *v/n.* (fn) to wind along.
An-ritt (ᵍᴸ) *m* ⑭c. **1.** approach on horseback, ⚔ oft: attack; cavalry charge. — **2.** first ride or attempt (on horseback).
an-ritzen (ᵍᴸ˘) *v/a.* ⑭** to scratch.
an-roden (ᵍᴸ˘) *v/a.* ⑭** *agr.* (urbar machen) to clear (for cultivation), to bring under the plough.
an-rollen (ᵍᴸ˘) ⑭** I *v/n.* (fn) ⚬, angerollt kommen to come rolling along;

to drive (or come riding) up in a coach. — II *v/a.* Fässer ꝛc. ⚬ to roll ... along.
an-roften (ᵍᴸ˘) *v/n.* (fn) ⑭** **1.** (roftig w.) to grow rusty. — **2.** to rust on to.
an-rüchig (ᵍᴸ˘) [*nhd.* (P.++: riechen): ruchbar, Gerücht] *a.* ⑥ ill-famed, disreputable, of ill repute, notorious, shady, stärker: infamous; ~**feit** (ᵍᴸ˘...) *f* ㊼ ill-repute, notoriety, stärker: infamy.
an-rücken (ᵍᴸ˘) ⑭** I *v/a.* einen Stuhl ꝛc.: to push (or move) near; ⚔ ⚬ laffen to bring (or move, march) up. — II *v/n.* a) (h.) die Uhr hat angerückt zum Schlagen the clock has given warning; b) (fn) bfd. ⚔ to come up, to draw near, to approach. — III ~ *n* ㉓ u. **An-rückung** *f* ㊼ approach; advance (of troops).
an-rudern (ᵍᴸ˘) *v/n.* (h. u. fn) ⑭a** **1.** ⚓ to row against; ans Ufer ⚬ to row ashore. — **2.** gegen den Strom ⚬ to row against the stream. — **3.** (anstoßen) to strike (against a th.) in rowing, to bump. — **4.** angerudert kommen to come rowing alongside or up.
An-ruf (ᵍᴸ) *m* ⑭d. **1.** appeal; um Hilfe: call (for help). — **2.** ⚔ ~ der Schildwache challenge. — **3.** Fernfpr.: call-signal.
an-rufen (ᵍᴸ˘) ⑭b** I *v/a.* **1.** e-n ⚬ to call a p.; Fernfpr.: to call (or ring) up; ein Schiff ⚬ to hail (or speak) ...; ⚔ e-e Runde: to challenge. — **2.** (anflehen) to implore; e-n um Hilfe ⚬, j-s Hilfe ⚬ to appeal to (or call upon) a p. for help; Gott ꝛc. ⚬ to invoke ...; e-n zum Zeugen ⚬ to call a p. as (or to) witness; *jur.* ein höheres Gericht ⚬ to appeal (to a higher court). — II ~ *n* ㉓ **3.** = A/ung.
An-rufer (ᵍᴸ˘) *m* ㉒, ~**in** *f* ㊼ **1.** one who calls or invokes. — **2.** *jur.* appellant.
An-rufung (˘) *f* ㊼ (f. anrufen I) appeal to; invocation (of God); ⚓ Hail(ing), speaking; ⚔ b. Poftens: challenge; *f. a.* Anruf.
An-rufungs-formel (ᵍᴸ˘...) *f* ㊼ invocatory formula, form(ula) of invocation; =**gericht** *n*, =**richter** *m* court, judge of appeal; =**schrift** *f jur.* appellatory libel.
an-rühmen (ᵍᴸ˘) *v/a.* ⑭** = anpreisen.
an-rühren (ᵍᴸ˘) I *v/a.* ⑭** **1.** *et.* ⚬ to touch a th.; rühr' es nicht an! (keep your) hands off!, don't meddle with it!, leave it alone!, let it be! F nicht rühr' an! (beileibe nicht) on no account! — **2.** (mifchen) to mix (or stir) up together. — II ~ *n* ㉓ u. **An-rührung** *f* ㊼ **3.** touching; mixing.
an-rutfchen F (ᵍᴸ˘) *v/n.* (fn) ⑭** angerutscht kommen to come sliding along.
ans (⚬) = an das, P a. an des (f. an); bis ⚬ äußerfte to the uttermost.
an-fä/en (ᵍᴸ˘) I *v/a.* ⑭** eine Frucht, ein Feld: to sow. — II ~ *n* ㉓ = A/ung.
An-fage (ᵍᴸ˘) *f* ⑭ **1.** = Ankündigung, Hofe: invitation. — **2.** Spiel: first call.
An-fage-... (⚬...) ⑫ = Ankündigungs=.
an-fagen (ᵍᴸ˘) I *v/a. u. v/refl.* ⑭** **1.** (fich) = ankündigen und anmelden 1; fage an! speak up! — **2.** Schule: ein (Rechen=) Exempel ⚬ to call out the answer to a sum. — **3.** Kartenspiel: die Farbe ⚬ to declare trumps; Sie fagen an it's your call; kein Spiel ⚬ to pass. — **4.** die Uhr fagt die Stunde an (hebt aus) the clock is warning. — II ~ *n* ㉓ **5.** ⚬ Anfagung.

[ansägen] — 64 — [anschießen]

ansägen (ˢᴸᵛ) v/a. ⊛** to saw into.
Ansager (ˢᴸᵛ) ㉒, ~in f ㊵ person who announces; messenger, summoner.
Ansageverfahren ⊛ (ˢᴸᵛ...) n ㉒ bei der Anmeldung zollpflichtiger Waren: (procedure for) declaring dutiable goods.
Ansagung (ˢᴸᵛ) f ㊻ 1. = Ankündigung. — 2. (Entbietung) summons.
ansammeln (ˢᴸᵛ) I v/a. u. v/refl. ⊛a** (sich) to collect, gather, (a)mass; von Truppen ꝛc.: to assemble; Schätze ♀ to accumulate ..., to hoard (or pile) up ƒ — II ~ n ㉓ = Ansammlung 1.
Ansammler (ˢᴸᵛ) m ㉒ 1. ~, ~in f ㊵ collector. — 2. accumulator (a. elect.).
Ansammlung (~) f ㊻ 1. collection, accumulation. — 2. (Haufen) heap, pile; ~ von Leuten gathering, crowd; ~ von Schätzen hoard(ed treasures).
ansässig (ˢᴸᵛ) I a. ㊿ domiciled; im Auslande ♀ settled abroad; sich ♀ machen, ♀ werden in to take up one's residence at, to settle in. — II ~e(r) m, ~e f ㊻ (old) resident.
Ansässigkeit (ˢᴸᵛ~) f ㊻ residency.
Ansatz (ˢᴸᵛ) m ⑦a. 1. meist: piece added or adjoined. — 2. ⚭ anat. appendage, epiphysis. — 3. ♪ an Blasinstrumenten: lengthening-piece; (Mundstück) mouth-piece. — 4. ⊕ (Ferse, Nase) peg, catch; ♐ ~ es Schienenstuhls shoulder of a chair; ⚓ (oberster Teil des Vorderstevens) head-piece of the stem. — 5. a) e-r Rechnung: (preliminary) statement, arrangement (of a proportion or a rule of three sum); b) für Geliefertes ob. Geleistetes: charge, fee; die Ansätze e-r Rechnung the items of a bill; die Ansätze des Anwalts sind mäßig the solicitor's charges are moderate; einem in ~ bringen to put to one's account; c) (Abschätzung) valuation, appraisement. — 6. ~ von Land an e-m Flusse desposit(ion) of land, ⚭ alluvium; Kochkunst: scrapings pl. (of the pan), crust, (Bodensatz) sediment, deposit; ♀ germ or spore (of a plant). — 7. beim Spiel: start. — 8. fig. ~ (Anlage) zu et. disposition to s. th. — 9. (Ansetzen v. Blasinstrumenten) tonguing, blowing. — 10. = Anlauf 2; auf den ersten ~ at the first start or go.
Ansatzberichtigung (ˣ...) f ㊷ rectification of an account; eisen ⊛ n adjoint-piece; feile ⊕ f small (or hand-) file; größe f, math. differential value; preis ⊛ m (amount of) taxation; rechnung f rule of three; stück n piece (that can be) joined on, eking-piece; es Tisches: leaf; ♪ = Ansatz 3.
ansäuern (ˢᴸᵛ) v/a. ⊛a** 1. den Teig ♀ to leaven ... — 2. to (make) sour; bfd. chm. (säuerlich m.) to acidify, acidulate.
Ansaugegebiß (ˢᴸᵛ...) ⊛ n Zahntechnik: set of teeth attached (or acting) by suction; suction-plate.
ansaugen (ˢᴸᵛ) ⊛c(ˢˢ)** I v/a. 1. to begin to suck; das Kind will nicht ♀ ... refuses the breast. — 2. to suck up; ⚓ e-e Pumpe ♀ lassen to fetch (or light) ... — II sich ♀ v/refl. 3. to attach o.s. by suction; von Blutegeln: to take. — III ~ n ㉓ 4. sucking, suction.

Ansäung (ˢᴸᵛ) f ㊻ sowing; for. neue ~en m. to replant or restock (a forest).
ansäuseln (ˢᴸᵛ) v/a. ⊛a** vom Winde: to fan, to cool, to waft towards; F angesäuselt half seas-over, slightly on.
ansausen (ˢᴸᵛ) v/n. (in)⊛** 1.to rush on. — 2. ♀, angesaust kommen to sweep (or come) along with a rush or roar.
anschaben (ˢᴸᵛ) v/a. ⊛** to commence (or start) scraping.
anschaff/en (ˢᴸᵛ) I v/a. ⊛a** 1. = anerschaffen I. — II v/a. u. v/refl. ⊛** 2. (besorgen) e-m et. ♀ to procure (or provide) a th. for a p.; Lebensmittel: to cater for a p.; sich (dat.) et. ♀ to furnish (or supply) o.s. with a th.; sich Kleider ♀ to buy o.s. clothes, F to rig o.s. out; sich Möbel ♀ to furnish one's house; sich Pferd und Wagen ♀ to set up a carriage and pair; er muß das Geld ♀ he must find (or provide) the money; dafür ließe sich ein Haus ♀ it would be enough to buy a house with. — 3. ⚭ = A/ung (f. d. 2) m. — 4. prov. (Herbeizuschaffendes bestellen, bfd. beim Kellner) to order of a p.
Anschaffer ⚫ (ˢᴸᵛ) m ㉒ purveyor. — 2. (Verwaltungsbeamter) administrator.
Anschaffung (ˢᴸᵛ) f ㊻ 1. purveyance, acquisition, providing for; durch Kauf: purchase. — 2. ⊛ keine ~ m. to make no provision (for payment); wieder ~ machen (das Lager vervollständigen) to lay in a fresh stock or supply; (Deckung) provision (of funds); ~ von Rimessen remittances pl., reimbursement.
Anschaffungskosten (ˣ...) pl. ⊛ prime (or first) cost; preis m (wien.) cost-price (= Selbstkostenpreis).
anschäften ⊕ (ˢᴸᵛ) v/a. ⊛** Äxte, Hämmer ♀ to helve ..., to put (new) handles to ...; Gewehre ♀ to stock ...
anschälen (ˢᴸᵛ) v/a. ⊛** to begin to peel or to pare; for. Bäume: to blaze.
anschalmen (ˢᴸᵛ) v/a. ⊛** for. = anlafchen 1 und anschälen.
anscharren (ˢᴸᵛ) v/a. ⊛** to scratch at.
anschau/en (ˢᴸᵛ) I v/a. ⊛** 1. geh. Spr. ob. obb. = ansehen. — 2. rel., phls. to contemplate, (erkennen) to perceive intuitively. — II ~ n ㉓ 3. view, contemplation. — 4. rel. intuitive vision. — 5. = A/ung 1. — III ♀d p.pr. u. a. ㊿ 6. Bed. des inf. — 7. (betrachtend) contemplative; intuitive. — 8. = anschaulich.
anschauenswert (ˢᴸᵛ.ᴸ) a. ㊻ worthy of contemplation or inspection.
Anschauer (ˢᴸᵛ) m ㉒, ~in f ㊵ looker-on, onlooker, spectator (f ...ress).
anschaufeln (ˢᴸᵛ) v/a. ⊛a** to shovel up.
anschaulich (ˢᴸᵛ) a. ㊻ intuitive; (augenscheinlich) evident, obvious, manifest; (sichtbar) visible; ♀ machen to demonstrate, illustrate; to make clear; ♀ schildern to describe in a telling (or graphic) way; keit (ˢᴸᵛ~) f ㊻ (o. pl.) obviousness, clearness, plainness.
Anschauung (ˢᴸᵛ) f ㊻ 1. geh. Spr. contemplation; (Vorstellung) perception, notion. — 2. phls. intuition. — 3. (Ansicht) view, mode of viewing things, (Vorstellung) idea, notion; nach kaufmännischer ~ from a commercial point of view.

Anschauungsbegriff (ˢᴸᵛ...) m ㊷ intuitive notion; erkenntnis f intuitive science or faculty; kreis m sphere of observation or intuition; lehre f, unterricht m Pädagogik: intuitive method of instruction, object-teaching, object-lesson; vermögen n = erkenntnis; weise f = Anschauung 3.
Anschein (ˢᴸᵛ) m ①d. (o. pl.) 1. a) appearance; dem ~e nach, nach dem ~e zu urteilen apparently, to judge from (outward) appearances; es hat (ganz) den ~, als ob // it very much looks as if //; b) subjektiv: semblance; es hat den ~ it seems; dem ~e nach seemingly; c) (Wahrscheinlichkeit) likelihood; allem ~ nach to all appearances, in all probability. — 2. (Schein) look; sich den ~ (als ob ober als ob) geben to pretend (that or as if), to make (people) believe that; den ~ erwecken (als ob) to make an impression (as if).
anscheinen (ˢᴸᵛ) I v/a. ⊛** die Sonne scheint e-n, et. an ... shines upon a p., a th. — II ♀d p.pr. u. a. ㊿ (u. adv.) apparent(ly), seeming(ly), adv. auch: to all appearances.
anschellen (ˢᴸᵛ) v/n.(h.)⊛**to announce by ringing (or touching) the bell.
Anschere ⊕ (ˢᴸᵛ) f ㊻ Weberei: warp.
anscheren (ˢᴸᵛ) v/a. 1. ⊛a** to (begin to) shear or shave. — 2. ⊛** Weberei: die Kette und ⚓ ein Tau ♀ to warp ...
Anscherpfahl ⊕ (ˢᴸᵛ...) m warping-post.
anschichten (ˢᴸᵛ) v/a. ⊛** to pile up (in layers), to stack up; geol. to stratify.
anschick/en (ˢᴸᵛ) I sich ♀ v/refl. ⊛** sich ♀ zu et., et. zu tun to prepare (o.s.) for, to get ready for, to set about doing a th. — II v/a. to arrange, appoint. — III Anschickung f ㊻ vor der Handlung: preparation (or getting ready) for.
anschieben (ˢᴸᵛ) ⑦c** I v/a. 1. to push (or shove) against or on to. — II v/n. (h.) 2. angeschoben kommen to come shuffling (or slouching) along. — 3. Kegelspiel: to have the first throw, to bowl (or throw) first.
Anschieber (ˢᴸᵛ) m ㉒ 1. he that bowls first, first bowler. — 2. = Anschiebestül.
Anschiebering (ˢᴸᵛ...) m ㊷ es Regenschirms: runner; stück n es Tisches: leaf; tisch m telescope-table.
Anschiebsel (ˢᴸᵛ) n ㉒ appendage, piece added to; (Zusatz) supplement.
anschielen (ˢᴸᵛ) I v/a. ⊛** e-n ♀ to squint (or leer) at a p.; verstohlen: to cast a sidelong glance at a p. — II ♀ n ㉓ ogling, side-glance.
Anschieler F (ˢᴸᵛ) m ㉒, ~in f ㊵ ogler.
anschienen (ˢᴸᵛ) v/a. ⊛** surg. to splint; ⊕ to fix with iron bands.
anschießen (ˢᴸᵛ) ⑦c(es)** I v/n. (in) ⊛ 1. ♀, angeschossen kommen to rush (or shoot) along. — 2. ⚭ chm. in ober zu Kristallen ♀ to shoot into crystals, to crystallize. — 3. (zu schießen anfangen) to commence shooting, to have (the) first shot, to shoot first. — II v/a. 4. e-e neue Büchse ꝛc.: to test (or try) — 5. ein Fest ꝛc.: to announce (or salute) ... by shots. — 6. hunt. Wild ♀ to wound ... by firing or shooting; F fig. angeschossen (verliebt) sein to be

Zeichen (s S. XVII): F familiär; P Volkssprache; ↗ Gaunersprache; ⚓ selten; † alt (auch gestorben); * neu (auch geboren); ⁺⁺ unrichtig;

[Anschießfaß] — 65 — [anschmeicheln]

crazy or (madly) in love. — 7. ☉ typ. zwei Kolumnen ○ to add …; Schneiderei: die Ärmel ○ to put (or fit) in … — III ~ n ⑳ 8. ~ eines Festes ꝛc.: announcement of … by gun-shots; von Feuerwaffen: firing test; ⚗ chm. crystallization.

An-schieß-faß(⸚…) n ⑫, **-kessel** m, chm. crystallizing-pan or -vessel, crystallizer; **-messer** n, **-pinsel** m ☉ Vergolderei: gilding brush or pallet.

an-schiffen (⸚) ⓜ** I v/a. Waren ○ to take goods aboard, to ship goods. — II v/n. (in) angeschifft kommen to approach a ship; an e-e Insel ○ to touch at an island. — III ~ n ⑳ u.

An-schiffung f ㊻ v. Waren: shipment.

an-schiften(⸚)v/a.ⓜ**1.☉carp.to join (rafters) together. — 2. fig. = anstiften.

an-schilden (⸚) v/a. ⓜ** hort. to scutcheon-graft. [grow mouldy.⟩

an-schimmeln (⸚) v/n. (in) ⓜa** to⟨

an-schimmern (⸚) v/a. ⓜa** to gleam upon. [harness, weits. to put to.⟩

an-schirren (⸚) v/a. ⓜ** Pferde: to⟨

An-schlag (⸚) m ⓞd. 1. striking (or shock) against; Tennis: service; Ihr ~! your service! ~ der Glocke stroke (or ringing, peal) of … — 2. ~ der Wellen ans Ufer breaking of waves against the shore. — 3. ♪ a) das Klavier, der Klavierspieler hat e-n leichten ~ … a light (or delicate) touch; b) (ant. Nachschlag) strongly accented part of the bar. — 4. (Plakat) placard; poster, bill; ein Haus ist im ~ (zur Versteigerung) … is put up for sale; durch ~ öffentlich bekanntmachen to announce on posters or bills, to post up, to bill. — 5. ⚔ ~ des Gewehrs levelling of …; die Flinte ꝛc. im ~(e) halten auf // to take aim at // — 6. fig. (Entwurf) project; schlechter ~ ill-concocted scheme; heimlicher ~ plot; Anschläge m. gegen to conspire (or plot) against; Anschläge gegen j-s Leben machen to attempt a p.'s life. — 7. (Schätzung) valuation, estimate; gesetzlich: taxation; ~ der staatlichen Einnahmen und Ausgaben: budget; e-m oberflächlichen ~e nach at a rough estimate or calculation; in ~ bringen to take into account or consideration, to allow for; die Kosten in ~ bringen to calculate (or consider) the expense(s); dies kommt nicht in ~ that counts (or goes) for nothing, F that's no consideration. — 8. Kinderspiel: hide-and-seek. — 9. ☉ der Tür, e-s Fensters: rabbet; e-r Glocke: rim; e-r Taschenuhr: warning-piece. — 10. hunt. bark (or challenge) of hounds.

An-schlag(e)-brett (⸚(⸳)…) n ⑫ noticeboard; **-faden** m Schneiderei: basting-thread, -cotton; **-holz** ⊕ n mill-clapper.

an-schlagen(⸚)ⓑ** I v/a. 1. mst: to strike against, to knock at; (festmachen) to fix to, to affix to; mit Nägeln: to nail to; ein Haus ○ to put … up for auction, to post up the sale of …; Zettel ○ to stick (or post) up … — 2. Licht ○ to strike a light. — 3. ♪ die Glocke ○ to ring (or toll) the bell; die Uhr schlägt die Stunden an … strikes the hours; e-e Saite ○ to touch a chord; e-n andern Ton ○ to change one's tune or manner. — 4. ⚔ das Gewehr ○ to level one's gun (auf e-n at a p.). — 5. e-n Zuckerhut ○ (anbrechen) to start …; ⚒ e-e Erzader ○ to strike a lode or vein. — 6. e. Faß ꝛc. ○ = anstechen 2. — 7. Kinderspiel: e-n ○ (abs.) to play hide-and-seek. — 8. (abschätzen) to estimate, to value; et. hoch ○ to think much (or highly) of a th.; zu hoch ○ to overestimate, to overrate; zu niedrig ○ to underrate; wie hoch schlägt er es an? (wieviel verlangt er?) how much does he ask for it?; ⊕ die Kosten lassen sich auf 500 Mark ○ … may be put down at £ 25. — 9. Schneiderei: einen Ärmel ○ to baste (or run) together …; Strickerei: e-n Strumpf ○ to begin to knit … — 10. ↓ ein Segel ○ to bend … to its yard. — II abs. od. v/n. (h.) 11. to strike the first blow; Ballspiel: to serve (the ball); Sie schlagen an! your service! — 12. an et. ○ to strike (or dash) against a th.; von Wellen: to break against, ↓ (plätschern) to ripple. — 13. (schallen) (to begin to) sound; die Glocke schlägt an … is ringing, tolling; von Vögeln: to begin to sing; von Hunden: to (begin to) bark, to give tongue; auf der Trommel ○ to roll (a drum). — 14. (Wurzel schlagen) to take root. — 15. vom Essen ꝛc.: bei e-m ○ (e-m gut bekommen) to agree with a p.; von Arzneien: to act, to take effect on; die Kur schlägt bei ihm trefflich an … is working wonders with him; bei ihm will nichts (mehr) ○ he is beyond (or past) all remedy. — III ~ n ⑳ 16. striking at; affixing (or nailing) to; posting (up); an die Glocke: ringing, tolling; der Wellen: breaking; der Hunde: barking; vom Trommler: roll; von Speisen ꝛc.: salutary (or beneficial) effect.

An-schläger (⸚) m ⑫ 1. Person: a) ☉ auf Bauten: p. that fixes (doors, &c.); b) ⚒ im Förderschachte: hanger-on (of buckets), onsetter; c) Tennis: server. — 2. Gerät: a) ☉ Uhrmacherei: scapement; b) ♪ (Hämmerchen im Klavier) jack.

An-schlage-rad ☉ (⸚…) n ⑫ der Uhr: warning-, striking-wheel.

an-schlägig, ⚹ **an-schlägisch** (⸚) a. ⓗ ingenious, inventive, clever, full of resource; (anstellig) handy, smart.

An-schlag(s)-höhe (⸚…) f ⊕ ⚔ breast-height; **-säule** f advertising pillar, column with advertising spaces; **-winkel** ☉ (Winkelhaken) back-square; **-zettel** m = Anschlag 4.

an-schlämmen (⸚) v/a. u. v/refl. ⓜ** (sich) ○ to fill (or to get choked) with mud; Land ○ to deposit …

an-schleichen (⸚) v/n. (in) u. sich ○ v/refl. ⓜa** ○, angeschlichen kommen to approach stealthily, to creep near to, to come crawling (or sneaking) along.

an-schleifen¹ ☉ (⸚) [schleifen¹] v/a. ⓜd** ○ to begin to grind; to set an edge on; Facetten ○ to cut facets; e-e Spitze ○ to grind to a point.

an-schleifen² (⸚) [Schleife] v/a. ⓜ** 1. e-n, et. angeschleift bringen (heranbringen) to convey (or carry, drag) … on a sledge or a sleigh. — 2. Weberei: (anknüpfen) to slip-knot.

an-schlendern (⸚) v/n. (in) ⓜa** ○, angeschlendert kommen to come sauntering (or trailing) along, F to jog along.

an-schleppen (⸚) v/a. ⓜ** Steine ꝛc.: to drag along, to haul (along).

an-schleudern (⸚) v/a. ⓜ** to fling (or hurl, throw) against or at.

an-schlichten ☉ (⸚) v/a. ⓜ** Weberei: die Kette ○ to dress the warp.

an-schließen (⸚) ⓞd** I v/a. 1. to (fasten with a) padlock; Gefangene: to put in irons, to chain (up). — 2. (anfügen) to join, to add, to annex; e-m Briefe: to enclose. — 3. ⚔ Marsch: schließt euch an! close ranks! — II sich ○ v/refl. 4. sich an e-n oder sich e-m ○ to attach o.s. to (or to side with) a. p., to join (forces with) a p., to throw one's lot in with a p.; sich einer Gesellschaft ○ to join a society or party; darf ich mich Ihnen ○? may I make one of you or of your party?; ⛴ der Zug schließt sich (an den Dampfer ꝛc.) an … is timed to meet the steamer, &c.; abs. sich leicht (schwer) ○ to be (un)companionable, (un)sociable. — III v/n. (h.) 5. (passen) von e-r Tür: to be well jointed or hung; von Kleidungsstücken: eng ○ to fit tightly. — 6. man. die Schenkel ○ to sit close, to grip the horse well. — IV ~ n ⑳ 7. = Anschluß. — 8. v. Kleidungsstücken: tight (or close) fit. — V ⓑd p.pr. ⓞ 9. ⓑd an seine astronomischen Studien widmete er sich auch der Optik in conjunction with his astronomical studies he also applied himself to optics. — VI an-geschlossen p.p. u. a. ⓞ (D9) 10. Bed. des inf. — 11. Fernspr.: (nicht) ○ (dis)connected; put (off) on.

an-schlingen (⸚) v/a. ⓞi** to fasten (or tie) with a noose to.

an-schlitzen(⸚)v/a.ⓜ**to begin to slit.

An-schluß(⸚)m⑧1.addition,accession, gezwungen:annexation; im ~ an referring to; (das Angefügte) th. added or annexed; von e-m Briefe: enclosure. — 2. (genaues Passen) e-s Rockes ꝛc.: tight fit. — 3. (das Sich-anschließen) joining, stärker: union; der ~ an den Zollverband the entry into the customs-union. — 4. ⛴ ~ der Züge (direct) communication (or correspondence) between …; dieser Zug hat keinen ~ … meets no other train, has no communication; den ~ versäumen to miss the (corresponding) train, a. fig. to come too late. — 5. Fernspr.: um ~ ersuchen to ask to be put on to.

An-schluß-bahn ⛴ (⸚…) f ⛴ junction-railway, branch-line; **-dose** ☉ f, elect. connecting-box; **-fahrscheinheft** n book of transfer tickets; **-geleise** n junction; **-linie** f = -bahn; **-punkt** m, **-station** f = -geleise; **-wagen** m slip-carriage; **-zug** m corresponding (or connecting) train.

an-schmachten (⸚) v/a. ⓜ** e-n ○ to cast amorous glances at a p., to make sheep's eyes at a p. [rauchen I.⟩

an-schmauchen F (⸚) ⓜ** = an-⟨

an-schmecken (⸚) v/a. ⓜ** e-r Speise et. ○ to (notice by the) taste that a dish …, to taste s.th. in a dish.

an-schmeicheln (⸚) ⓜa** I v/a. e-m et. ○ to coax (or flatter) a p. into s. th. —

♪ Musik; ⚗ Wissenschaft; ♀ Pflanze; ⚲ Geographie; ☉ Technik; ⚒ Bergbau; ⚔ Militär; ↓ Marine; ⚏ Handel; ⚐ Post; ⛴ Eisenbahn.

[anschmeißen] — 66 — [Anschwellung]

II v/refl. sich (bei) e-m ≤ to ingratiate (or insinuate) o.s. with a p.
an-schmeißen F (ᵍˡ˘) v/a. ⊛a** 1. = anschütten. — 2. e-m et. ≤ to dash (or fling, throw) something at a person.
an-schmelzen (ᵍˡ˘) v/a. ⊛(Tb(ef)t)** to solder on; to fasten by smelting.
an-schmieden (ᵍˡ˘) v/a. ⊛** 1. to join by forging. — 2. Verbrecher ≤ to put ... in irons, to chain up ...; fig. an das Laster angeschmiedet enthralled by vice.
an-schmiegen (ᵍˡ˘) ⊛** I v/a. to apply, to press closely to; to adapt to. — II sich ≤ v/refl. sich an et., an e-n ≤ to hug, to cling to; to nestle (F to snuggle) up to a th., a p.; fig. sich e-m oder an e-n ≤ to fall in (or to comply) with a p.'s ideas; sich dem herrschenden Geschmack ≤ to conform with the prevailing taste.
an-schmiegend (ᵍˡ˘), **an-schmiegsam** (ᵍˡ˘) a. ⊛ supple, pliant (auch fig.).
an-schmieren (ᵍˡ˘) v/a. ⊛** 1. to (be)daub, besmear, grease (up). — 2. (fälschen) Wein: to doctor (up). — 3. F fig. e-n ≤ (betrügen) to cheat (F to let in, to diddle) a p.; e-n mit et. ≤ to take a p. in with a th., to palm a th. off on a p.
An-schmier-maschine ⊕ (ᵍˡ˘) f ⊛ der Buchbinder: sizing-machine.
an-schminken (ᵍˡ˘) v/a. ⊛** = schminken.
an-schmitzen † (ᵍˡ˘) v/a. ⊛** (besudeln) to soil. [to smirk (and smile) at a p.]
an-schmunzeln F (ᵍˡ˘) v/a. ⊛a** e-n ≤)
an-schnallen (ᵍˡ˘) v/a. ⊛** 1. to buckle on or up; den Degen: to gird on. — 2. fig. derb: sich e-e Braut, Liebste ≤ (anschaffen) to find (or get) a sweetheart.
An-schnaller (~) m ⊛ v. Schlittschuhen man who straps on (people's) skates.
An-schnall-sporen (ᵍˡ˘ ...) m/pl. ⊛ jack-boot spurs pl. [in a p.'s ears.]
an-schnarchen (ᵍˡ˘) v/a. ⊛** to snore)
an-schnauben (ᵍˡ˘) u. ⊛c** I v/a. 1. Pferd: to snort, feuchend · to roar. — 2. fig. = anschnauzen. — II v/n. 3. angeschnaubt kommen to come puffing along.
an-schnauzen F (ᵍˡ˘) v/a. ⊛** derb: to reprimand; F to bully, to blow up.
An-schneide-messer (ᵍˡ˘ ...) n ⊛ (Tranchiermesser) carving-knife.
an-schneiden (ᵍˡ˘) v/a. ⊛c** 1. to take a cut off, to begin to cut or to carve; das Brot ≤ to cut a (fresh) loaf; ein angeschnittener Braten a joint in cut. — 2. fig. e-e Frage ≤ to start (or broach) a subject. — 3. auf den Kerbhölze: to tally, to notch. — 4. hunt. v. Hunde: (anfressen) to begin to feed on the game.
an-schnellen (ᵍˡ˘) ⊛** I v/a. to jerk against. — II v/n (fn) = anprallen.
an-schniegeln F (ᵍˡ˘) v/a., (sich) v/refl. ⊛a** to smarten (o.s.) up, to trick (o.s.) out, to deck (o.s.) out, to adorn (o.s.).
An-schnitt (ᵍˡ) m ⊛c. 1. v. Schinken, Brot ꝛc.: first cut or slice. — 2. (Schnittfläche) cut(ting). — 3. ⚒ in das Kerbholz: notch, score.
an-schnitze(l)n (ᵍˡ˘) v/a. ⊛ (⊛a)** et. an e-n Stock ≤ to carve a th. or ...
an-schnüffeln F (ᵍˡ˘) v/a. ⊛a** to smell (out), to scent, to sniff at.
an-schnüren (ᵍˡ˘) v/a. ⊛** 1. to lace (or string) on; e-n an die Folter ≤ to

tie (or fasten) a p. to the rack. — 2. ⊕ Weberei: to tie up, to fasten on.
an-schobern (ᵍˡ˘) v/a. ⊛a** Heu: to stack up. [bepflanzen) to replant.)
an-schonen (ᵍˡ˘) v/a. ⊛** for. (wieder)
an-schoppen (ᵍˡ˘) I v/a. u. v/refl. ⊛** bsd. path. den Leib, sich ≤ to gorge (o.s.), to choke (o.s.); to obstruct, to become obstructed. — II **An-schoppung** (ᵍˡ˘) f ⊛ path. (Anfüllung mit Blut) engorgement, obstruction, congestion.
Anschove ⊛, **Anschovis** inv. (˘ˡ˘w) [engl., *span.] f, ichth. anchovy.
an-schrammen (ᵍˡ˘) v/a. ⊛** I v/a. to scratch. — II F v/n. (fn) angeschrammt kommen to come trotting along.
an-schrauben ⊕ (ᵍˡ˘) v/a. ⊛c** u. ⊛** sep. ≤ to screw on or up; e-m Daumenstöcke ≤ to apply thumb-screws to a p.
An-schraub-sporen (ᵍˡ˘ ...) m/pl. ⊛ screw- (or cavalry-) spurs pl.
an-schreiben (ᵍˡ˘) I v/a. ⊛** 1. to write (or put) down; in e-m Buche: to book, mit Kreide: to chalk up, Kricket, Billard: to score; im Rechnungsbuche: to debit (to a p.); ≤ lassen to take on credit (F on tick). — 2. fig. von Schülern ꝛc.: gut angeschrieben sein to have high marks; bei e-m gut (übel) angeschrieben sein oder stehen to be in a p.'s good (bad) books; schlecht angeschrieben sein to be in ill repute, to have a bad name. — II ~ n ⊛ 3. writing down; booking; marking; scoring. — 4. (Erlaß) rescript; (Ansuchen) application. — 5. (Rundschreiben) circular.
An-schreiber (ᵍˡ˘) m ⊛ Kricket ꝛc.: scorer.
An-schreibe-tafel (ᵍˡ˘ ...) f ⊛, =tisch m scoring-board or -table.
an-schreien (ᵍˡ˘) v/a. ⊛** e-n ≤ to hoot at a p.; et. ≤ (ankündigen) to shout (or call) out a th.; ein Schiff: to hail.
an-schreiten (ᵍˡ˘) v/n. (fn) ⊛b** ≤, angeschritten kommen to come striding along, to approach with long strides.
An-schrot ⊕ (ᵍˡ) n ⊛d., ~e (ᵍˡ˘) f ⊛ v.Tuch: selvedge; list; wale (=Salband).
an-schroten (ᵍˡ˘) v/a. ⊛** 1. ein Faß ≤ to roll up a cask. — 2. ⊕ Tuchmacherei: to put the selvedge on (cloth).
An-schub (ᵍˡ) m ⊛d. Kegelspiel: den ~ h. to have first bowl; to bowl first.
an-schuhen (ᵍˡ˘) v/a. ⊛** ⚒ (a. v/refl.) to shoe a p. or o.s. — 2. ⊕ Stiefel ≤ (vorschuhen) to new-front (or new-foot) ...; Pfähle ≤ to tip stakes (or posts) with iron, to shoe piles.
an-schuldigen (ᵍˡ˘) v/a. ⊛** e-n eines Verbrechens ≤ to accuse a p. of (or charge him with) ...; jur. to incriminate; der Angeschuldigte the accused, vor Gericht: the defendant, the prisoner.
An-schuldigung (~) f ⊛ indictment (oft = Anklage); jur. auch: inculpation.
an-schüren (ᵍˡ˘) v/a. ⊛** to poke (or stir) a fire; fig. to kindle (the passions).
An-schürer (ᵍˡ˘) m ⊛ fig. firebrand.
An-schuß (ᵍˡ) m ⊛ 1. ~ des Wassers shoot, rush. — 2. chm. crystallization, Zuckerfabrikation: crop. — 3. ⚒ (erster Schuß) first shot; den ~ h. to shoot first, to have the first shot. — 4. hunt. a) (~wunde) gunshot wound; b) (~ort) spot where the game received the first shot.

An-schutt, -schütt (ᵍˡ) m ⊛c. alluvium.
an-schütten (ᵍˡ˘) I v/a. ⊛** 1. to pour (or throw) against. — 2. ⊕ mit Erde ≤ to fill (or bank) up. — 3. Getreide ≤ (aufstapeln) to store up ... — II ~ n ⊛ u. **An-schüttung** f ⊛ 4. filling up; storage.
Anschütz-apparat ⊕ (ᵍˡ˘ ...) m ⊛ phot. Anschütz(-apparatus).
an-schütten (ᵍˡ˘) v/a. ⊛** 1. Müllerei: (Wasser anlassen) to turn on or let in (water). — 2. Wasserbaukunst: ein Wehr ≤ (eindämmen) to dam up a weir.
an-schwängern (ᵍˡ˘) I v/a. ⊛a** chm. to impregnate, to saturate with. — II ~ n ⊛ und **An-schwängerung** (ᵍˡ˘) f ⊛ chm. impregnation, saturation.
an-schwanken (ᵍˡ˘) v/n. (fn) ⊛** to totter against; ≤, angeschwankt kommen to stagger (or totter, reel) along.
an-schwänzeln (ᵍˡ˘) v/n. (fn) ⊛a** der Hund kam angeschwänzelt ... came (along) wagging its tail.
an-schwären (ᵍˡ˘) v/n. (h.) ⊛a** to begin to fester or to suppurate.
an-schwärmen (ᵍˡ˘) ⊛** I v/n.(h.) 1. von Bienen: to begin to swarm. — 2. angeschwärmt kommen to come (or approach) in swarms. — II v/a. 3. e-n huldigend: to address a p. in terms of admiration or homage, F to gush (up to) a p.; von Verliebten: to write effusive (or gushing) letters to a p.
an-schwärz/en (ᵍˡ˘) I v/a.⊛** to blacken, fig. to slander, backbite; to cast an aspersion upon; F to run down; bei e-m ≤ to speak badly of a. p. to a p. — II ~ n ⊛ blackening; fig. f. A/ung.
An-schwärzer (~) m ⊛, ~in f ⊛ fig. detractor, slanderer, backbiter, calumniator.
An-schwärzerei (ᵍˡ˘ ...), **An-schwärzung** (ᵍˡ˘) f ⊛ fig. disparagement, back-biting, calumniation, defamation.
an-schwatzen (ᵍˡ˘) v/a. ⊛** e-m et. ≤ to talk a p. into (buying) a th.
an-schwefeln (ᵍˡ˘) v/a. ⊛a** to (fumigate or treat with) sulphur.
An-schweif (ᵍˡ) m ⊛d. 1. ⊕ Weberei: warp. — 2. ⊕ (Ende des Tuches) selvedge, list.
an-schweifen (ᵍˡ˘) v/a. ⊛** Weberei: to warp (= anscheren 2).
An-schweif-haspel ⊕ (ᵍˡ˘ ...) f ⊕, =winde f warping-reel; =rahmen m warp(ing)-frame; =rolle f warping-bobbin.
an-schweißen (ᵍˡ˘) v/a. ⊛** 1. to weld together; vgl. anlöten, anschmieden. — 2. hunt. = anschießen 6.
an-schwellen (ᵍˡ˘) I v/a. ⊛b** 1. to swell (up or out), sackartig: to bag, to puff; von Flüssen: to rise; von Geldern, Schulden ꝛc.: to increase, to run up to; von Segeln: to belly, to bunt. — 2. ♪ to swell; einen Ton ≤ und wieder schwach werden lassen to hold a note. — II v/a. ⊛** 3. to distend, inflate, puff; der Bach ist durch den Regen angeschwellt the stream is swollen with rain. — III ~ n ⊛ 4. = Anschwellung. — 5. ♪ crescendo. — IV ≤ d p.p. u. a. ⊛ 6. swelling; path. intumescent.
An-schwellung (ᵍˡ˘) f ⊛ 1. swell(ing); e-s Flusses: rise; (Zunahme) increase. — 2. ⊛ ~ an der Oberfläche von Samen caruncle. — 3. ⚕ (Hervorragung) protuberance; path. tumour, intumescence.

Signs (see page XVII): F familiar; P vulgar; ⌐ flash; ⧹ rare; † obsolete (died); * new word (born); ⁒ incorrect; ♪ music;

[anschwemmen] — 67 — [Ansicht]

an-schwemmen (⌐⌐) I v/a. ⊛** u. II ~ n⌐ u. **An-schwemmung** f ⊛ = anflößen. — III **an-geschwemmt** p.p. ⊛ alluvial; ↓ ⌐es Wrackgut flotsam and jetsam; ⌐es Land alluvion, alluvial soil.

an-schwimmen (⌐⌐) v/n. (sn) ⊛a(b)** ⌐, angeschwommen kommen to come swimming (or floating) up; ans Ufer ⌐ to swim ashore or to shore; gegen den Strom ⌐ to swim against the stream or the current.

an-schwindeln (⌐⌐) v/a. ⊛a** e-n ⌐ to swindle (or humbug, bamboozle) a p.

an-schwöden ⊕ (⌐⌐) v/a. ⊛** Weißgerberei: Felle ⌐ to cleanse and treat ... with lime-water.

an-segeln ↓ (⌐⌐) ⊛a** I v/n. (sn) 1. ⌐, angesegelt kommen to approach sailing, to come booming (along). — II v/a. 2. ein Riff ⌐c. ⌐ to run foul of ... — 3. e-n (Not-)Hafen ⌐ to put (or run) into port; Land ⌐ to make for land.

an-sehen[1] (⌐⌐) ⊛a** I v/a. 1. to look at, to face, to eye, aufmerksam: to view; e-n über die Achsel ⌐ s. u. Schulter; et. von der falschen Seite ⌐ to look at a th. in the wrong light; genau (erwägend, prüfend) ⌐ to consider, to examine (closely), to look (or gaze) at, to behold, to scrutinize; er kann mich nicht gerade ⌐ he cannot look straight at me; e-n finster (wütend) ⌐ to give a p. a black (an angry) look; e-n giftig ⌐ to look daggers at a p.; e-n groß ⌐ to open one's eyes wide (or to look astonished) at a p.; e-n sauer ⌐ to make sour faces at a p.; e-n scharf (schief, scheel) ⌐ to look hard (askance) at a p.; e-n über die Schulter (auch Achsel) ⌐ to look down on a p.; verliebt ⌐ to make sheep's eyes at; e-n verstohlen ⌐ to cast a sly glance at a p.; von oben herab ⌐ to turn up one's nose at; sie sah mich von oben bis unten an she eyed me from head to foot; e-n wütend ⌐ s. o. finster. — 2. et. auf et. (hin) ⌐ to examine a th. as to its suitability for a th. — 3. fig. et. mit dem Rücken ⌐ (müssen) to (have to) turn one's back upon a th., (to be obliged to) forsake (or abandon) a th. — 4. et. mit ⌐ (ohne zu handeln) to look (passively) on at a th., to witness a th. (silently); et. stillschweigend (mit) ⌐ to be a silent witness to a th., weit⌐ to tolerate a th.; ich kann es nicht länger mit ⌐ I cannot stand it any longer. — 5. e-n für einen anderen (et. für et. anderes) ⌐ to (mis)take one person (one thing) for another; wofür sieht er mich an? what does he take me for?; ich sehe ihn für den Dieb an I look upon him as (or I believe him to be) the thief. — 6. (auffassen) als et. ⌐ to consider (or regard) as, to take for; fig. et. anders, durch e-e andere Brille ⌐ to see a th. with other eyes or in a different light; alles im günstigsten Lichte (von der schlimmsten Seite) ⌐ to see the bright (dark) side of everything; wie wir die Sache ⌐ to our way of thinking; wie man es auch ⌐ mag in whatever light one may look at it, in whatever way you may take

it. — 7. (berücksichtigen) to pay regard to; die Person nicht ⌐ (bibl.) to be no respecter of persons; ich sehe es auf 100 Mark nicht an I do not mind a fivepound note. — 8. e-m et. ⌐ = anmerken 1 (s. ds.); man sieht ihm sein Alter nicht an he does not look his age. — 9. ⌐ e-m et. ⌐ (durch den Blick mitteilen) to impart a th. to a p. by a glance or look. — II v/n. (h.) 10. F sieh mal an!, seh' mal einer an! F well, I never!, now, did you ever!, there, now! — III sich ⌐ v/refl. 11. (aussehen) das sieht sich gut an that looks well, it impresses one favourably. — IV **an-gesehen** p.p. u. a. ⊛ 12. s. ds. **An-sehen**[2] (⌐⌐) n ⌐ 1. (Sehen) looking at; view; bei flüchtigem ~ at the first glance; das ~ hat man umsonst seeing costs nothing; e-n von ~ kennen to know a p. by sight; fig. vom (bloßen) ~ wird man nicht satt one cannot live on the smell of a (good) thing. — 2. (Ansehen) appearance, look; (Äußeres) outside, exterior, (äußerer Eindruck) air, mien; auch complexion (of affairs, &c.); allem ~ nach to judge from appearances, on the face of it; die Sache hat jetzt ein anderes ~ (gewonnen) things have assumed a different aspect; abs., b.s. sich ein ~ geben to put on (or to give o.s.) airs; er weiß sich ein ~ zu geben he knows how to impress (or to impose upon) the world. — 3. (Rücksicht) regard; consideration; ohne ~ der Person without distinction (bsd. bibl. respect) of persons. — 4. (Achtung) credit, prestige; (Geltung) authority; in ~ bringen to bring into repute or vogue; e-n um sein ~ bringen to discredit a p.; ein Mann von (großem) ~ a man of (great) influence or consequence; sein ~ zur Geltung bringen to wield great power, to exert one's influence; großes ~ genießen, in hohem ~ stehen to enjoy great esteem, to be held in great respect; to be highly thought of; sich ~ verschaffen to make o.s. respected (by all).

an-sehnlich (⌐⌐) a. ⊛ 1. (anziehend) handsome, imposing; das ⌐ste Haus the best-looking house. — 2. (bedeutend) considerable, ample, (hervorragend) conspicuous, (bemerkenswert) remarkable; ⌐e Gelehrte m/pl. eminent scholars pl.; ⌐e Mittel n/pl. large means or funds pl.; ⌐e Mitgift handsome dowry. — 3. (angesehen) notable, (highly) respected.

An-sehnlichkeit (⌐⌐) f ⊛ (o. pl.) imposing appearance; considerableness; e-r Person: conspicuousness, eminence.

An-sehung (⌐⌐) f ⊛ nur adv.: in ~ (mit gen.) with regard to, in respect of; in ~ dessen as for (or as regards) that matter.

an-seilen (⌐⌐) v/a. ⊛** e. Schiff ⌐ to tie (or fasten) ... to a line or cable.

an-sengen (⌐⌐) v/a. u. v/n. (sn) ⊛** to singe (or burn) a little.

an-setzbar (⌐⌐-) a. ⊛ capable of being (or fit to be) put on or applied to, &c. (s. ansetzen I und II).

An-setz-blatt ⊕ (⌐⌐...) n ⊛, typ. flyleaf; -blech e-r Feile plain edge; =pappe ⊕ f Buchbinderei: strong pasteboard.

an-setzen (⌐⌐) ⊛** I v/a. 1. a) (haftend befestigen) to put (or set) on, to apply to; (anpassen) to adapt to; (anstücken) to add to; Ärmel, Knöpfe ⌐ to sew on ...; b) den (Violin-)Bogen, den Pinsel ⌐ to take up the bow, the brush; to begin to play (the violin), to paint; c) (straff spannen) to tauten, to haul taut. — 2. den Becher ⌐ to put the cup to one's lips; Blutegel ⌐ to apply leeches to; die Feder ⌐ to put pen to paper; die Flöte ⌐c. ⌐ to put ... to one's mouth; die Sporen ⌐ to set (F to clap) spurs to the horse; zum Verkauf ⌐ to put up for sale. — 3. Tinte, Essig, Litör ⌐ to mix the ingredients for..., to make or brew or prepare...; Feuerwerkerei: den Satz ⌐ to mix the composition. — 4. eine Zeit ⌐ (bestimmen) to fix, appoint ...; Tag und Stunde ⌐ to name the day and hour. — 5. (niederschreiben) to note down; (abschätzen) to tax, (anrechnen) to charge to, to put down to; Preise: to quote; e-m e-n zu hohen (zu niedrigen) Preis ⌐ to overcharge (undercharge) a p. for a th. — 6. arith. ein Exempel ⌐ to put down (or state) a sum; math. e-e Gleichung ⌐ to put up (or form) an equation. — 7. auch v/n. (h.) (entwickeln) to produce; Blätter, Sprößlinge ⌐c. ⌐ to put forth (or on) ...; Früchte ⌐ to form ...; die Frucht des Baumes setzt an the fruit ... begins to show; path. die Gicht setzt Knoten bei ihm an ... is settling in his joints; die Kartoffeln setzen gut an ... are doing (or promising) well; Fleisch ⌐ to put on flesh; Rost ⌐ to grow (or turn) rusty. — II v/n. (h.) 8. s. 7. — 9. (versuchen) to attempt, to try (= [es] auf et. ⌐); noch einmal ⌐ to begin again or anew; er setzte zweimal an he started twice; zu et. ⌐ to set to and do a th.; zum Laufen ⌐ to take a run before leaping; angesetzt kommen to come rushing (or racing) along. — 10. ⌐ die Erze setzen an the lode is continuous. — 11. Dominospiel: der Gewinner setzt an the winner begins the new game. — III sich ⌐ v/refl. 12. sich an et. ⌐ to attach o.s. to ...; chm. to (leave a) deposit, to be deposited, in Kristallen: to crystallize. — 13. to form (o.s.). — IV ~ n ⊛ 14. = Ansetzung.

An-setzer (⌐⌐) m ⊛ Spiel: one who plays first, beginner of the game.

An-setz-punkt (⌐⌐...) m ⊛ point of application; =stück ⊕ n = Ansatzstück.

An-setzung (⌐⌐) f ⊛ (s. ansetzen) putting on, application; e-r Zeit: appointment; eines Blas-instrumentes: tonguing; eines Preises: quotation; ⌐ der Frucht: formation. [=teil m, anat. attachment.]

An-setzungs-ort (⌐⌐...) m ⊛, =rand m,

An-seuchung (⌐⌐) f ⊛ infection.

An-sich-halten ⌐ (⌐⌐) n ⊛ self-restraint, self-command; reserve.

An-sicht (⌐⌐) [nbd.] f ⊛ 1. a) view; sight; (Besichtigung) inspection; ⊛ e-m Waren zur ~ schicken to send a p. goods on approval (F on appro'); zur gefälligen ~ for your kind inspection; v. Schriften: for your kind perusal; et. aus eigener ~ kennen to know a th. from personal

---

⌐ scientific; ⌐ botanical; ⌐ geography; ⊕ machinery; ⌐ mining; ⌐ military; ↓ marine; ⊛ commercial; ⌐ postal; ⌐ railway.

[ansichtig] — 68 — [Anspruch]

observation; ⊕ bei ~ des Gegenwärtigen on receipt of the present; **b)** (Anblick) aspect; v.b. Seite: side-view; *paint.* perspektivische ~ perspective view. — 2. (Meinung) opinion, view; (Überzeugung) conviction; ich bin ganz Ihrer ~, schließe mich Ihrer ~ an I quite agree with you(r opinion); and(e)rer ~ sein als to differ (in opinion) from; derselben ~ sein wie to share the view(s) of, to be of the same way of thinking as; seine ~ aussprechen to speak one's mind; es herrscht nur e i n e ~ darüber there is but one opinion (or voice) about it; er hat sehr schiefe ~en he is a queer-headed fellow; nach meiner ~ in my opinion or estimation, to my mind, (according) to my way of thinking; nach der ~ aller by general consent.
an-sichtig (⌐ℐ) [adj.] *a.* e-j-s (e-n) ~ werden to catch (or get a) sight of a p.
An-sichts=(post)karte (⌐ℐ...) *f* ⊕ picture postcard, pictorial postcard; **=sache** *f* matter of opinion or of taste; **=seite** *f* front(view), frontispiece; **=sendung** ⊕ *f* consignment (or parcel sent) for inspection or on approval. [ment.]
An-siedelei (⌐ℐ) *f* ⊕ colony, settle-
an-siedeln (⌐ℐ) *v/a.* u. (sich) *v/refl.* ⓐ a** to settle; to colonize; to establish (o.s.), locate (o.s.). [(planting of a) colony.]
An-sied(e)lung (⌐ℐ) *f* ⊕ settlement,
an-sieden (⌐ℐ) *v/a.* ⓒe** ⓒ** 1. to boil. — 2. ⊕ Färberei: to ungum.
An-siedler (⌐ℐ) *m* ⊕ settler, colonist; *Am.* u. Australien: squatter; die ersten ~ Amerikas the Pilgrim Fathers.
An-siedlung (⌐ℐ) *f* ⊕ s. Ansied(e)lung.
an-siegeln (⌐ℐ) *v/a.* ⓐa** to seal.
an-sillen (⌐ℐ) *v/a.* ⓒ** *hunt.* den Lockvogel ⊕ to fasten ... (to the string).
an-singen (⌐ℐ) ⓓf** I *v/a.* e-n, et. ⊕ to welcome ... with a song, to praise (or address) ... in song. — II *v/n.* (h.) to begin to sing, to pitch a note.
an-sinnen (⌐ℐ) I *v/a.* ⓒ** gew. *b. s.*: e-m et. ⊕ (zumuten) to expect (or demand) s. th. (unreasonable or unpleasant) of (or from) a p. — II ~ *n* (unfair or strange) demand; e-m ein ~ stellen to put a(n unreasonable) request to a p.
an-sintern (⌐ℐ) *v/n.* (sn.) ⓐa** *min.*, *geol.* to form stalactites.
An-sitz (⌐ℐ) *m* ⓐa. 1. ⚒ domicile. — 2. *hunt.* (Hinterhalt) hiding place for huntsmen; auf dem ~ sein = ansitzen 3.
an-sitzen (⌐ℐ) *v/n.* (sn.) ⓓ** 1. ⊕, angesessen sein to be domiciled or settled; angesessen resident. — 2. (festsitzen) to be attached to, v. Kleidern x.: to fit tightly. — 3. *hunt.* to sit up.
an-spalten (⌐ℐ) ⓒ** I *v/a.* to make a split in. — II *v/n.* (sn) ⊕, angespalten sein to (begin to) split.
An-spann (⌐ℐ) *m* ⓐc. team (of horses, &c.).
an-spannen (⌐ℐ) ⓐ** ⓒ**1. to stretch; den Bogen, die Sehne ⊕ to bend ...; ♪ eine Saite ⊕ to tighten ... — 2. *fig.* to brace (up); alle (seine) Kräfte ⊕ to put forth all one's strength, to strain every nerve, to exert o.s. to the uttermost; den Geist ⊕ to rack one's brain(s); e-n ⊕ to keep a p. to his work or F with his nose to the grindstone; durch an-

gespannte Arbeit by (dint of) great exertion. — 3. die Pferde, den Wagen ⊕, *a. abs.* to put the horses to; ⊕ lassen to order the carriage out. — II ~ *n* und **An-spannung** *f* ⊕ 4. tension, strain, exertion. — 5. befiehl das Anspannen! have the horses put to!
an-speien (⌐ℐ) *v/a.* ⓒ** to spit at or upon; e-n ⊕ oft: to spit in a p.'s face.
an-speilern ⊕ (⌐ℐ) *v/a.* ⓐa** to fasten (or fix) with skewers.
an-spicken (⌐ℐ) *v/a.* ⓒ** to lard; *fig.* (an)gespickter Beutel well-lined purse.
An-spiel (⌐ℐ) *n* ⓐd. Kricket: first innings; Fußball: first kick, kick-off; Karten: lead.
an-spielen (⌐ℐ) I *v/n.* (h.) u. *v/a.* ⓒ** 1. ♪ ein Tonstück x.: to begin to play. — 2. ein Instrument ⊕ (probieren) to try ... — 3. Spiel: *abs.* to play first, to have the first throw, &c.; Kartenspiel: ⊕ (have the) lead; Billard: einen Ball ⊕ to put on a ball, Lawntennis: to serve a ball; Whist: eine Farbe ⊕ to lead a suit; die angespielte Farbe nachspielen to return the lead. — 4. (berühren) to touch (lightly). — 5. *fig.* auf etwas ⊕ (hindeuten) to allude to a th., to hint (at) a th.; auf was will er ⊕? what is he driving at or referring to? — II ~ *n* 6. Karten: lead; *f.a.* Anspiel(ung).
An-spieler (⌐ℐ) *m* ⓐ he who leads or plays first, &c., first hand; Kricket: first bowler (*f.* anspielen).
An-spielung (⌐ℐ) *f* ⊕ *fig.* allusion, hint, feindselige: insinuation; leise ~ auf faint allusion to, gentle hint at; das ist e-e ~ auf Sie this is meant (or intended) for you; mit ~ auf in allusion to, alluding (or referring) to.
an-spießen (⌐ℐ) *v/a.* ⓒ** 1. to (run through with a) spear. — 2. Kochkunst: to (put on the) spit; † to broach.
an-spinnen (⌐ℐ) ⓐa** I *v/a.* 1. to begin to spin. — 2. (anknüpfen) e-n Faden ⊕ to join a thread; *fig.* to contrive; eine Unterhaltung ⊕ to start ...; Ränke x. ⊕ to hatch a plot, &c. — II sich ⊕ *v/refl.* 3. von einer Raupe: it encloses (or wraps) itself in a cocoon. — 4. *fig.* to arise; es spann sich e-e feste Freundschaft zwischen ihnen an a close friendship sprang up between them.
an-spitzen (⌐ℐ) *v/a.* ⓒ** to sharpen, to point; wieder ⊕ to put a new point to.
an-splissen, **=splitzen** ⚓ (⌐ℐ) *v/a.* ⓒ** ein Anfertau ⊕ to splice a cable.
An-sporn (⌐ℐ) *m* ⓒc *fig.* spur(ring); (Antrieb) inducement, stimulus, encouragement.
an-spornen (⌐ℐ) I *v/a.* ⓒ** to give the spurs to, to spur on to; (anstacheln) to goad (or egg) on, to stimulate, stärker: to rouse, to put on one's mettle; Schüler: to push; er muß angespornt werden he wants rousing (up) or spurring on. — II ~ *n* ⊕ u. **An-spornung** *f* ⊕ spurring (on); stimulation, incitement, vgl. Ansporn.
An-sprache (⌐ℐ) [mhd.] *f* ⊕ 1. (kleine, mst feierliche Rede) (short) address. — 2. ♪ e-s Instruments ⊕: intonation, tone.
an-sprechen (⌐ℐ) ⓐa** I *v/a.* 1. e-n ⊕ to speak to, to address, auf der Straße: to accost a p.; ⚓ ein Schiff ⊕ to speak ... — 2. e-n um et. ⊕ to beg (or request)

a th. of a p., to ask a p. for a th. — 3. *hunt.* u. allg.: ein Tier x. ⊕ (nach dem Anschauen ob. der Fährte richtig erraten ob. bezeichnen) to pronounce, to call; einen Hund für einen Wolf ⊕ to take a dog for ... — 4. (geltend machen) to (lay) claim (to). — 5. *fig.* e-n (⇌ e-m) ⊕ (e-m zusagen) to impress, stärker: to interest; (anmuten) to please; *abs.* das Stück spricht (die Menge) an ... takes, ... draws. — II ~ *n.* (h. u.) 6. ⚑ = vorsprechen. 7. ♪ v. Orgelpfeifen x. ⊕ to emit (or give forth) a sound or a note. — III ⓑ *p.pr.* u. *a.* ⊕ 8. oft: pleasing, prepossessing, attractive; sie hat etwas sehr ~des she has s. th. very engaging (or charming, taking) in her ways.
an-spreizen (⌐ℐ) ⓒ** I *v/a.* to prop, to stay. — II *v/refl.* sich an et. ⊕ to sprawl (or lean) against a th.
an-sprengen (⌐ℐ) ⓒ** I *v/n.* (h.) und *v/a.* 1. to (begin to) blow up a mine, &c. — 2. (auf) e-n ⊕ to gallop up to a p.; angesprengt kommen to come on at full gallop or at full tilt. — II *v/a.* 3. (anfeuchten) to (be)sprinkle with; (abbrausen) to douche. — 4. (sprenklicht machen) to speckle; v. Haar: angesprengt touched with grey. — III ~ *n* ⊕ u. **An-sprengung** *f* ⊕ 5. approach(ing) at full gallop. -- 6. (Besprengung) sprinkling.
an-springen (⌐ℐ) ⓓf** I *v/n.* 1. (sn): a) ⊕, angesprungen kommen to come jumping (or skipping, bouncing) along; Galopp ⊕ to (put to a) gallop; an et. ⊕ to leap against a thing; b) das Glas ist angesprungen ... is slightly cracked. — 2. (h.) to take the first leap, to jump first. — II *v/a.* 3. einen feindlich ⊕ to spring (or rush, fall, set) upon a p. — III ~ *n* ⊕ 4. *man.* (first) leap, rush, jump; ~ zum Galopp galloping (away).
an-sprit/en (⌐ℐ) ⓒ** I *v/a.* to (be-)sprinkle with; Pflanzen: to syringe; e-n Kot x. ⊕ to splash (or bespatter) a p. with ... — II *v/n.* (sn) an etwas ⊕ to splash (or be squirted) against a th. — III ~ *n* ⊕ u. **A/ung** *f* ⊕ sprinkling; *hort.* syringing; v. Kot: splash (of mud).
An-spruch (⌐ℐ) *m* ⓓd. ~ auf claim to; ältere Ansprüche prior claims *pl.*; (Forderung) demand (auf for); *jur.* title to; ~ haben auf (ob. an) to be entitled to; auf et. ~ machen ob. erheben to make pretensions (or lay claim) to a th.; schlecht begründete Ansprüche ill-founded pretensions *pl.*; er macht ~ auf hohe Fähigkeiten he pretends to be highly gifted; große (keinerlei) Ansprüche m. to have great (no) pretensions; er macht keine großen Ansprüche she does not assume (or aspire) to much, she is very unpretentious; j-s Aufmerksamkeit x. in ~ nehmen to engage, stärker: to engross ...; j-s Dienste, Güte in ~ nehmen to have recourse to ...; j-s Hilfe in ~ nehmen to call in a p.'s aid; j-s Zeit sehr in ~ nehmen to take up ...; to encroach (or trespass) on ...; Kräfte, Mittel aufs höchste in ~ nehmen to tax ... to the utmost; seine Rechte in ~ nehmen to vindicate ..., to assert ...; den neuesten Ansprüchen gemäß accord-

Zeichen (s. S. XVII): F familiär; P Volkssprache; Γ Gaunersprache; ⚑ selten; † alt (auch gestorben); * neu (auch geboren); ✚ unrichtig;

ing (or coming up) to the latest requirements, quite up to date, von Häusern ꝛc. auch: with all the modern improvements; er ist sehr in ~ genommen he is very much engaged or very busy.

an-spruchs-frei (˶ˏch...) *a.* [66], ~**los** *a.* free from pretensions, unpretending; (schlicht) unassuming; Kleider: plain; -**losigkeit** *f* [62] unpretendingness; plainness; -**verjährung** *f jur.* limitation of claims; ~**voll** *a.* pretentious; (wählerisch) fastidious, fussy; (mit hohen Anforderungen) exacting; (anmaßend) arrogant, assuming; ~es Wesen pretentiousness.

an-sprudeln (˶ʹ⏑) *v/a. u. v/n.* (sn) [92]a** to (make) bubble (or spout) against …

an-sprühen (˶ʹ⏑) *v/a. u v/n.* (sn) [88]** to (let) fly (or flash) against …

An-sprung (˶ˏ) *m* [7]c. **1.** leap at. — 2 (Milchschorf) milk-scab, 🎓 impetigo.

an-spucken F (˶ˏ⏑) *v/a.* [88]** = anspeien.

an-spulen ⚙ (˶ʹ⏑) *v/a.* [88]** to (begin to) reel, to fix (the thread) to the spool.

an-spül/en (˶ʹ⏑) **I** *v/n.* (h.) und *v/a.* [88]** (an) etwas ~ to wash (the shore); to ripple against s.th.; angespültes Land alluvial soil. — **II** ~ *n* [23] u. **A/ung** *f* [46] wash(ing ashore); 🎓 alluvion.

an-stacheln (˶ˏch⏑) *v/a.* [92]a** to stimulate, goad on, incite to (vgl. anspornen).

an-stählen ⚙ (˶ʹ⏑) *v/a.* [88]** to steel; to overlay (or edge) with steel.

An-stalt (˶ˏ) *f* [46] **1.** (Zurüstung) preparation (or arrangement) for; ~en m. zu et. to get ready (or to prepare) for a th.; (die nötigen) ~en treffen für to take one's measures (or to provide, arrange) for. — **2.** (Einrichtung) establishment, institution; typographische ~ printing office, printing works *pl.*; ~ für Irre lunatic asylum.

An-stalts-geistliche(r) (˶ˏ...) *m* [62] chaplain to some public institution.

an-stammen (˶ˏ⏑) **I** 🗡 *v/a.* [88]** to bequeath upon. — **II an-gestammt** *p.p. u. a.* [66] (ererbt) hereditary.

an-stampfen (~) *v/n.* (sn) [88]** sie kamen angestampft they came stamping along.

An-stand (˶ˏ) *m* [7]c. (1-3 o. *pl.*) **1.** ([gutes] Auftreten) (good) address; (Haltung) bearing, carriage; deportment; (Schicklichkeit) decorum, propriety; sein edler ~ his gentlemanly behaviour or manners *pl.*; keinen ~ haben to be well-mannered, to have good breeding; den ~ beiseite setzen to set aside the rules of decency; ~shalber for decency's sake, for the sake of respectability; mit ~ decently, decorously, properly. — **2.** (Aufschub) delay; das soll keinen ~ haben it shall be done without demur. — **3.** (Bedenken) hesitation; das leidet keinen ~ there is no difficulty about that; (keinen) ~ nehmen, et. zu tun (not) to think twice before doing a th., to be loath (ready) to do a th.; nimm es ohne ~ … without further ado, … without (much) ceremony; das hat (gar) keinen ~ there is nothing to be said against it, that is understood. — **4.** *hunt.* stand, stable, (appointed) place; auf den ~ gehn to go shooting (from a hiding-place); auf dem ~ stehn to lie in wait, to be in cover or on the look out.

An-stand-... (˶ˏ...) [62] = Anstands-..

an-ständig (˶ˏ⏑) *a.* [66] u. *adv.* **1.** becoming, decent, decorous, Fußballspiel: fair; fast † e-m ~ = anstehend 5 b; ~es Benehmen proper behaviour, von Herren a. gentlemanly conduct, von Damen: ladylike demeanour; ein ~es Mädchen a respectable girl; sich ~ benehmen to behave decently, or properly, auch: to behave o.s.; ~ gekleidet respectably (or nicely) dressed, presentable. — **2.** (genügend) er hat ein ~es Auskommen … a comfortable income; e-n ~en Lohn erhalten to receive fair (or decent) wages; *iro.* ~ (tüchtig) bezahlen (müssen) F to (have to) pay through the nose.

An-ständigkeit (˶ˏ⏑-) *f* [46] **1.** decency; decorum; propriety; respectability; reputableness. — **2.** einzeln: civility.

An-stands-besuch (˶ˏ...) *m* [62] formal call; -**brief** *m* letter of respite or grace; -**dame** *f* chaperon; in Gesellschaft: die ~ spielen to play propriety; -**gefühl** *n* tact; sense of propriety; ~**halber** *adv.* s. Anstand 1; -**lehrer** *m* (ladies') professor of deportment; ~**los** *a.* [66] u. *adv.* unhesitating(ly); -**person** *f* **a)** = -dame; die ~ spielen to play propriety; **b)** bei einem Pärchen: bisw. F gooseberry; -**regeln** *f/pl.* rules *pl.* of etiquette; -**rolle** *f*, *thea.* part of a worthy gentleman or matron; -**übungen** *f/pl.* lessons *pl.* in deportment; -**visite** *f* = -besuch; ~**widrig** *a.* improper; unbecoming; indecent.

an-stänge(l)n, -stangen (˶ˏ⏑) *v/a.* [88] ([92]a)** Bohnen ꝛc. to stick, to provide with sticks or poles.

an-stapeln (˶ʹ⏑) [92]a** **I** *v/a.* Holz ꝛc.: to pile (or store) up. — **II** F *v/n.* (sn) ~, angestapelt kommen to come stalking along.

an-starren (˶ˏ⏑) *v/a.* [88]** to stare (stärker: to glare) at.

an-statt (⏑ˏ) [nhd. 16. *sæ.*] **I** *prp.* (mit *gen.*) instead of, in lieu of, in the place of; ~ ihrer in her (or their) stead. — **II** *cj.* ~ daß er kam, ~ zu kommen instead of (his) coming.

an-stauben (˶ʹ⏑) *v/n.* (sn) [88]** **1.** to cling like dust. — **2.** to become covered with dust, to grow dusty.

an-stau/en (˶ʹ⏑) **I** *v/a. u. v/refl.* [88]** Wasser ~ to dam up …; das Wasser staut sich an … is rising. — **II** ~ *n* [23] = A/ung.

an-staunen (˶ʹ⏑) *v/a.* [88]** to gaze (or stare) at; to look wonderingly at.

an-staunens-wert (~...) *a.* [66], ~**würdig** *a.* astonishing, amazing, wonderful.

An-stauner (˶ʹ⏑) *m* [22], ~**in** *f* [47] staring person, p. looking amazed.

An-stauung (˶ʹ⏑) *f* [46] swell (of water).

an-stechen (˶ˏ⏑) **I** *v/a.* [73]a** **1.** to prick. — **2.** (anbrechen) ein Faß ~ to broach (or tap) …; das Faß ist angestochen … on tap; Käse ꝛc. ~ to cut into … — **II** ~ *n* [23] **3.** prick, puncture. — **4.** = Anstich.

An-steck-ärmel (˶ˏ...) *m* [62] shamsleeve; -**bohrer** ⚙ *m* first bit; tap-borer.

an-stecken (˶ˏ⏑) [mhd.] **I** *v/a.* [88]** **1.** to stick on; Bänder ꝛc.: to pin on, to fasten (with pins). — **2.** den Degen ~ to gird on …; einen Ring ~ to put on … — **3.** (anzünden) ein Licht ꝛc.: to light; das Haus ~ to set the house ablaze or on fire; e-n Wald ꝛc. ~ to fire … — **4.** e-n mit e-r Krankheit ~ to infect a p. with …; angesteckt werden to catch a disease, to take the infection; *fig.* durch schlechten Einfluß ~ to contaminate a p. by …; durch Gift: to poison, to taint. — **II** ~ *n* [23] **5.** (act of) pinning on, &c.; s. I u. Ansteckung. — **III** ~**d** *p.pr. u. a.* [66] **6.** infectious, contagious; poisonous; die Cholera ist ~d, auch: … catching.

An-stecker (˶ˏ⏑) *m* [22] **1.** ⚙ Spinnerei: pinner. — **2.** ~ von Laternen lamp-lighter. — **3.** ⚙ (Verlängerung) lengthening-piece.

An-steck-nadel (˶ˏ...) *f* [62] pin for fastening s. th.

An-steckung (˶ˏ⏑) *f* [46] *med.* infection, contagion; taint; der ~ wehrend anti-contagious, prophylactic; *fig.* der ~ zugänglich contaminable; frei von ~ uninfected, untainted, immune; clean.

An-steckungs-fähigkeit (˶ˏ⏑...) *f* [62] *med.* contagiousness; -**gift** *n*, -**stoff** *m* (a. *fig.*) contagious matter; virus; 🎓 effluvium, miasma; von ~en befreien to disinfect.

an-steh(e)n (˶ʹ(⏑) *v/n.* (h. und sn) [94]** **1.** meist: to be contiguous, to stand close to; ~d. a) (nächstkünftig) next; b) ⚘ contiguous. — **2.** *hunt.* to take up one's stand; s. Anstand 4. — **3.** ⚒ (zutage treten) to crop out; ~des Gestein primary rock. — **4.** (angeschrieben stehen) et. steht noch im Schuldbuche an a debt is still on the books or still due; von einem Termine: to be fixed for. — **5. a)** von Kleidern: der Rock steht dir gut an … fits you well, … is just your fit; **b)** *fig.* (sich schicken) e-m ~ to become a p., to be becoming or seemly for a p.; es würde dir übel ~ zu // it would be unbecoming of you to //; it would not do for you to //, F it would be bad form of you to //; es steht ihr alles gut an she has a nice (or graceful) way of doing things. — **6.** 🗡 (antreten) to enter (a service), to join (a party). — **7.** (genehm sein) e-m ~ to suit (or please) a p.('s taste); das steht mir schlecht an that's not what I want or should like; das Haus würde mir wohl ~ F … would be just the thing for me. — **8.** (sich verzögern) to be delayed, deferred; lange ~ to hang fire; es wird lange ~ bis // it will be a long time before //; ~ lassen to put off, to postpone. — **9.** (schwanken) to waver; (zögern) to hesitate; (Bedenken tragen) to scruple; ich stehe an es zu tun I am in two minds as to whether to do it or not.

an-steifen (˶ʹ⏑) [88]** **I** *v/a.* Wäsche ~ (absteifen) to starch. — **II sich** ~ *v/refl.* (anstemmen) to put one's feet against, bsd. *fig.* to fight (or struggle) against.

an-steigen (˶ʹ⏑) **I** *v/n.* (sn) [81]** **1.** von Menschen ꝛc.: to ascend, mount; angestiegen kommen to stalk along; F *fig.* mit et. angestiegen kommen to broach (or introduce) a subject. — **2.** vom Boden: to rise, slope; steil ~d steep; 500 Fuß (*acc.*) über den Meeresspiegel ~d rising five hundred feet above sea-level; ~des Kleid highneck dress. — **3.** (anwachsen) vom Wasser ꝛc.: to increase, to rise. — **II** ~ *n* [23] u. **Ansteigung** *f* [46] **4.** ascent; slope; rise (of the ground or the water).

[anstellbar] — 70 — [anstreichen]

an-stellbar (ʃʃ-) *a.* ⓖ qualified for a post, fit to be appointed.
an-stellen (ʃʃ~) ⓖ** **I** *v/a.* 1. e-n zu et. ⓛ to appoint (or employ) a p. to do a th.; *hunt.* die Treiber ⓛ to post (or place) the beaters. — 2. (mit e-m Amte bekleiden) e-n ⓛ to put a p. in a place, to give him an appointment; (einsetzen) to install; angestellt sein to be in a situation or F in a berth; von Ministern: to be in office; weitS. to hold (or have) a position; angestellt werden to find (or obtain, F get) employment; nicht angestellt out of employment, F out of a berth or job. — 3. (anwerben) to engage, to hire; (anspornen) to incite, urge on, induce; falsche Zeugen ⓛ to suborn false witnesses. — 4. (veranstalten) to contrive, eine Jagd ꝛc.: to arrange, to set on foot; Betrachtungen über et. ⓛ to reflect on a th.; ⓧ *mach.* das Getriebe ⓛ to start the machinery; eine Klage ⓛ = anstrengen 2; eine Untersuchung über et. ⓛ to inquire into a th.; einen Vergleich ⓛ to institute a comparison; wie hast du das angestellt? how did you manage it?; was hast du angestellt? F what have you been up to?; ich weiß nicht wie ich es ⓛ soll … how to set to work; wie soll ich es ⓛ, das Huhn zu braten? how shall I manage (or contrive) to roast the fowl? — 5. ⓧ Waren ⓛ to offer ... **II** sich ⓛ *v/refl.* 6. (vgl. 1) to post (or place) o.s. — 7. (vgl. 4) sich (un)geschickt ⓛ to go (or set) to work cleverly (clumsily). — 8. sich fromm ꝛc. ⓛ (gebärden) to affect an air of piety, &c.; sich jämmerlich ⓛ to cut a sorry figure; sich ⓛ als ob (oder als wenn) // — **III** ~ *n* ⓛ 9. = Anstellung 1.
An-steller ↘ (ʃʃ~) *m* ⓛ, ~**in** *f* ⓖ employer.
an-stellig (ʃʃ~) [schwz.] *a.* ⓖ handy, skilful; apt, clever; ~**keit** (ʃʃ~) *f* ⓖ skill, ability; aptitude, cleverness.
An-stellung (ʃʃ~) *f* ⓖ 1. placing; (Ernennung) appointment; (Einsetzung) installation. — 2. (Stelle) a) als Beamter: appointment, post; höhere: office; b) allgemein: situation; eine gute ~ haben to have a good appointment, F to be in a good berth; eine sichere ~ a fixed appointment, F a safe berth.
an-stellungs-berechtigt (ʃʃ~…) *a.* ⓖ als Beamter: entitled to an appointment; ⸗**fähig** *a.* qualified for a post or an appointment; ⸗**patent** *n* ⓖ e-s Offiziers commission; ⸗**prüfung** *f* ⓖ qualifying test; für Beamte: competitive examination; für Lehrer: certificate examination; ⸗**verhältnisse** *n/pl.* circumstances determining appointments.
an-stemmen (ʃʃ~) *v/a.* und *v/refl.* ⓖ** (sich) ⓛ gegen to press (with one's feet) against, *fig.* sich gegen et. ⓛ to offer strenuous opposition to a th., to set o.s. against a th. (vgl. ansteifen II.)
an-sterben † (ʃʃ~) *v/n.* (ʃn) ⓖb** jur. durch Todesfall anheimfallen.
an-steuern ↓ (ʃʃ~) ⓖa** **I** *v/a.* das Schiff ans Land ⓛ to steer the ship towards the shore. — **II** *v/n.* (ʃn) F ⓛ, angesteuert kommen to come ashore, to make for land.

An-steu(e)rung ↓ (ʃʃ(~)~) *f* ⓖ (Hinansteuern an die Küste) making land; ~**s-tonne** (⹀…) *f* ⓖ buoy marking an inlet of the sea or the mouth of a river.
An-stich (ʃʃ) *m* ⓖd. 1. e-s Fasses: broaching; ein frischer ~ a fresh tap or cask. — 2. des Obstes (durch Würmer): canker.
an-sticheln (ʃʃ~) *v/a.* u. *v/n.* (h.) ⓖa** 1. to (begin to) stitch. — 2. *fig.* to taunt (by sly allusions); to chaff, quiz, tease.
An-stich-faß (ʃʃ~…) *n* ⓖ cask on tap; ⸗**geld** ⓛ (Zapfgeld) beer-duty.
an-sticken (ʃʃ~) *v/a.* ⓖ** 1. to add (by way of) embroidery. — 2. to begin to embroider.
an-stiefeln F (ʃʃ~) ⓖa** **I** *v/a.* u. *v/refl.* (sich) ⓛ to put on boots. — **II** *v/n.* (ʃn) angestiefelt kommen to come striding up or stalking along.
An-stieg (ʃʃ) *m* ⓖd. ascent.
an-stieren P (ʃʃ~) *v/a.* ⓖ** e-n ⓛ to stare (or glare) at a p.
an-stift/en (ʃʃ~) **I** *v/a.* ⓖ** 1. (mst Schlimmes) ⓛ (verursachen) to cause, (hervorrufen) to provoke; (befördern) to aid, to abet; er wird Unheil ⓛ he will do (or is breeding) mischief. — 2. (anreizen) to induce, set on, instigate; e-n zu et. ⓛ to set (or egg) a p. on to a th., to incite a p. to do a th., to put a p. up to a th.; heimlich: to suborn (false witnesses). — 3. ⓧ (annageln) to peg, pin. — **II** ~ *n* ⓖ 4. = A/ung.
An-stifter (ʃʃ~) *m* ⓖ, ~**in** *f* ⓖ abetter, *jur.* abettor; instigator; prime mover or author; promoter; suborner; (Rädelsführer) ringleader.
An-stiftung (~) *f* ⓖ provocation; abetment; incitement; instigation; machination; subornation; auf ~ von et. the instigation of, on the suggestion of.
an-stimmen (ʃʃ~) **I** *v/a.* ⓖ** 1. ♪ ein Instrument: to tune. — 2. ♪ ein Lied: to intonate; *abs.*: a) to begin to sing; b) to strike up (a tune); in der Kirche auch: to lead (the choir). — 3. *fig.* (immer wieder) das alte Lied, die alte Leier ⓛ to be (for ever) harping on the same string; ein Klagelied ⓛ to break out in lamentations, einen anderen Ton ⓛ to change one's tune or tone. — **II** ~ *n* ⓖ u. **An-stimmung** *f* ⓖ 4. ♪ intonation.
an-stinken F (ʃʃ~) ⓖf** e-n ⓛ to waft an offensive smell towards a p., *fig.* u. *bibl.* to stink in a p.'s nostrils.
an-stöhnen (ʃʃ~) *v/a.* ⓖ** e-n ⓛ to groan at a p., to receive a p. with groans.
an-stolpern (ʃʃ~) *v/n.* (ʃn) ⓖa** an et. ⓛ to stumble against a th.; angestolpert kommen to come stumbling along.
an-stopfen (ʃʃ~) *v/a.* ⓖ** to cram, to stuff with; *typ.* to fill the balls.
An-stoß (ʃʃ) *m* ⓖa. 1. shock, collision; Fußballspiel: kick-off; meist *fig.* impulse, impetus; den ersten ~ zu et. geben to start a th., stärker: to take the initiative in a th. — 2. = Anfall 3 u. Anfechtung 2. — 3. (Hemmnis) obstacle, check, impediment; ohne ~: a) without a hitch; b) without hesitation or faltering or stuttering; beim Lesen auch: fluently. — 4. *fig.* (Ärgernis) e-n Stein des ~es sein to be a stumbling-block to a p.; ~ erregen, geben to give (or cause) offence; bei e-m ~ erregen to scandalize (or shock) a p.; ~ an et. nehmen to take umbrage (or offence) at a th. — 5. ⓧ Bäckerei: ~ am Brote kissing-crust; Schneiderei: eking, eking-piece; *carp.* butting-joint.
an-stoß/en (ʃʃ~) ⓖa** **I** *v/a.* 1. to push, strike, knock (against); die Gläser ⓛ to touch (or clink) glasses (together); auf j-s Wohl ⓛ to drink a p.'s health; ea. mit den Ellenbogen ⓛ to nudge one another. — 2. (anschieben) e-e Röhre an eine andere ⓛ to join pipes together; ein Stück Tuch an ein anderes ⓛ to renter. — **II** *v/n.* (o. ʃ: h.) 3. to strike (or knock) against; bfS. von Pferden: to stumble; an die Wand ⓛ to touch the wall. — 4. = Anstoß (s. ds 4) erregen. — 5. (stocken) beim Reden. to hesitate, to falter; (stottern) to stutter; mit der Zunge ⓛ to speak thick, to have an impediment (of speech), to lisp. — 6. gegen (ob. wider) et. ⓛ to offend against. — 7. (angrenzen) to border upon, to be next-door (or adjoining) to; to abut on. — 8. (ʃn) das Obst ist angestoßen (anbrüchig) ... damaged, … unsound. — **III** ~ *n* ⓖ 9. collision; mit den Gläsern: clinking; beim Reden: hesitation; mit der Zunge: impediment (or thickness) of speech, lisp. — 10. = angrenzen III. — 11. ⓧ Schneiderei: fine-drawing. — **IV** ⓛ*b* *p.pr.* u. *a.* (ʃ. I u. II). 12. (den Anstoß gebend) impulsive. — 13. = angrenzend (ʃ. angrenzen II).
An-stoß-erreger (ʃʃ…) *m* ⓖ, ~**in** *f* ⓖ p. causing a scandal or giving offence.
an-stößig (ʃʃ~) *a.* ⓖ (e-m) ⓛ obnoxious, objectionable (to a p.), stärker: shocking, scandalous; fürs Ohr: offensive; (schlüpfrig) slippery: er fand es ⓛ he was shocked or scandalized (by it).
An-stößigkeit (ʃʃ~) *f* ⓖ obnoxiousness, scandalousness; offensiveness.
An-stoß-naht (ʃʃ…) *f* ⓖ Schneiderei: rentering; ⸗**schiene** *f* ⓖ und ⓧ *artill.* headplate; ⸗**schnur** *f* (an Kleidern) chain-lace; ⸗**schwelle** 🜨 *f* joint-sleeper.
an-strahlen (ʃʃ~) *v/a.* ⓖ** to shed rays (or to shine) upon; *fig.* to beam on.
an-stranden ↓ (ʃʃ~) *v/n.* (ʃn) ⓖ** to run aground; to be cast ashore.
an-strängen (ʃʃ~) *Hom.* anstrengen) *v/a.* ⓖ** die Pferde ⓛ to put the horses to (the carriage). [centripetal force.]
An-strebe-kraft ⁊ (ʃʃ~…) *f* ⓖ *phys.*
an-streben (ʃʃ~) ⓖ** **I** *v/n.* (h.) 1. to tend upwards; hoch ⓛ to soar. — 2. gegen et. ⓛ to struggle (or strive) against a th. — **II** *v/a.* 3. et. ⓛ to strive for (or after) a th., to aspire to a th.; die Freiheit, die Krone kühn ⓛ to make a bold bid for liberty, for the crown.
an-streichen (ʃʃ~) *v/a.* ⓖaft** 1. et. an et. ⓛ to rub a th. against a th. — 2. ⓧ Bäckerei: mit Eiweiß ⓛ to glaze (over). — 3. (anmalen) to paint; mit Firnis ⓛ to varnish (over); liederlich ⓛ to daub, smear; mit Leimfarbe ⓛ to colour; mit Mauerfarbe ⓛ to limewash; mit Teer ⓛ to tar; weiß ⓛ a) to paint white; b) (tünchen) to white-

---

Signs (see page XVII): F familiar; P vulgar; ⸗ flash; ↘ rare; † obsolete (died); * new word (born); ⹋ incorrect; ♪ music;

[Anstreicher] — 71 — [anticken]

wash. — 4. (anmerken) to mark or underline (a passage); Drohung: das will ich dir ⇄ I'll chalk that up against you; F I'll pay you out for it.
An-streicher⊕(ˢᴸᵛ) m ㉒ (house-)painter, whitewasher; ~=...(⸺...)⊛f.Anstreich=...
An-streicherei (ˢᴸᵛ) f ㊻ daub.
An-streich=pinsel (ˢᴸ...) m ㉒ brush.
an-streifen (ˢᴸᵛ) v/n. (h.) ⊛** an et. ⇄ to touch a th. (s)lightly, to graze a th.
an-strengen (ˢᴸᵛ); Hom. anstrangen)⊛*
I v/a. 1. (a. v/refl.) (anspannen) ein Seil: to tighten, to stretch; fig.: seine Kräfte ⇄, sich ⇄ to put forth (or to exert) one's strength, to exert o.s.; seinen Geist, Witz ꝛc. ⇄ to rack one's brain; übermäßig ⇄ to overtax; alle Kräfte ⇄ to strain every nerve; ob für die Augen trying to the eyes or to one's sight. — 2. jur.: eine Klage (einen Prozeß) gegen e-n ⇄ to bring (or lay) an action(or to take proceedings) against a p. — II sich ⇄ v/refl. 3. to exert o.s.; sich mächtig ⇄ to make a mighty effort, to put one's shoulder to the wheel, sich über die Maßen, die Kräfte ⇄ to over-exert (or overstrain) o.s., F to overdo it; F fig. sich ⇄ (freigebig sein) to be liberal, F to come down handsomely. — III **an-gestrengt** p.p. u a. ㊻ 4. intense, strenuous, trying; durch ⇄e Arbeit through (sheer) hard work; ⇄e Aufmerksamkeit close attention; adv. ⇄ arbeiten to work hard, to labour strenuously, to plod on, (studieren) to study hard.
An-strengung (ˢᴸᵛ) f ㊻ application; exertion; große ~ strain; durch vereinte (eigene) ~ by united (by one's own) efforts; ohne ~ without any exertion or trouble, leisurely, easily; Sport, pol., &c. ohne ~ gewinnen to have a walk-over. [sprinkle salt on.]
an-streuen (ˢᴸᵛ) v/a. ⊛** Salz ⇄ to.⌋
An-strich (ˢᴸ) m ⓘd. 1. ⊕· a) (Anstreichen) (house-)painting; mit Leimfarbe: colouring; mit Mauerfarbe: whitewashing, limewashing; b) (das Aufgestrichene) der erste, letzte ~ the first, last coat of paint; (Firnis) (coat of) varnish. — 2. fig. appearance; leiser: tinge; dash; gloss; touch; breath; äußerer ~ outward appearance, veneer; von Gelehrsamkeit: smattering; sich e-n gelehrten ~ geben to assume a learned air; e-m Ding e-n guten ~ geben to give a fine look (or gloss) to a th., to show a th. off to advantage; e-n pedantischen ~ haben to smack of pedantry. — 3. ♪ (Bogenstrich) stroke of the bow.
an-stricken (ˢᴸᵛ) v/a. ⊛** to join (by) knitting; to knit on to; Strümpfe ⇄ to (new-)foot ...
an-striegeln (ˢᴸᵛ) v/a. ⊛a** e-m Pferde die Haare ⇄ to curry a horse.
an-strömen (ˢᴸᵛ) ⊛** v/n. (sn) ⇄, angeströmt kommen to flow (or stream) towards, to come rushing along. von Menschen: to flock (or crowd) near; gegen das Ufer ⇄ to wash (against) ...
an-stück(el)n (ˢᴸᵛ) v/a. ⊛a(⊛)** to piece on to, to patch; (verlängern) to eke out.
An-stücker (ˢᴸᵛ) m ㉒, ~in f ㊵ patcher.
An-stückfel (ˢᴸᵛ) n ㉒ patch.

An-sturm (ˢᴸ) m ⓘc. charge, assault; erster ~ (first) onset or shock; ⚔ brunt (of the battle); ~ auf die Schanzen storming (of) the trenches.
an-stürmen (ˢᴸᵛ) I v/n. (sn) ⊛** to charge, to (make an) assault, gegen, wider, auf et. ⇄ u. v/a. et. ⇄ to rush upon a th.; (auf) e-n ⇄, auch et. ⇄ to lay siege to a p.; ⚔ auf e-e Stellung ⇄ to storm (or rush) a position. — II ~ n ㉓ = Ansturm. [shock.⌋
An-sturz (ˢᴸᵛ) m ⓘc. der Feinde, Wogen:⌋
an-stürzen (ˢᴸᵛ) v/n. (sn) ⊛** ⇄ gegen to tumble against; angestürzt kommen to arrive in hot haste.
an-stutzen (ˢᴸᵛ) v/a. ⊛** 1. to look amazed at. — 2. (stürzen) to curtail.
an-stützen (ˢᴸᵛ) ⊛** I v/a. to prop. — II sich ⇄ v/refl. to lean against.
an-suchen (ˢᴸᶜʰᵛ) I v/n. (h.) ⊛** bei e-m um et. ⇄ to apply to (or to solicit) a p. for a th., bei der Obrigkeit: to petition for a th.; um Erlaubnis ⇄ to ask for permission or leave. — II ~ n㉓ application, solicitation, petition; auf (dringendes) ~ von // at the (urgent) request of //, at (or by) the (special) desire of //. [tioner, applicant.⌋
An-sucher ⸢(ˢᴸᵛ) m ㉒, ~in f ㊵ peti-⌋
An-suchung ⸢(ˢᴸᶜʰᵛ) f ㊻ = Ansuchen.
An-such(ungs)=schreiben (ˢᴸᶜʰ(ᵛ)...) n ㉓ petition, requisition. [gumming.⌋
An-sud ⊕ (ˢᴸ) m ⓘd. Färberei: un-⌋
an-summen¹ (ˢᴸᵛ) ⊛** v/n. e-n ⇄ to buzz in a p.'s ear. — II v/n. (sn) ⇄, angesummt kommen to come buzzing along.
an-summen² (ˢᴸᵛ) [Summe] ⊛** v/a. und sich ⇄ v/refl. to accumulate, to sum up; von Ausgaben ꝛc.: to run up.
an-süßen (ˢᴸᵛ) v/a. ⊛** to sweeten (auch fig.); chm.: ⸗ to edulcorate.
☛ **Ant**¹..., ⇄... (ˢ...) [: ent...,* idg.] ꝫB.: Antwort answer. [tisch.⌋
☛ **Ant**²..., ⇄... (ˢ...) [grch.] ꝫB. antarf-⌋
Ant-agonismus ⸗ (⸺⸍⸌) [grch.] m ㉗ (Gegnerschaft) antagonism. [gonist.⌋
Ant-agonist (⸺⸍) m ㉘ (Gegner) anta-⌋
ant-agonistisch (⸺⸌) a. ㊻ antagonistic.
an-tafeln ⸗ (ˢᴸᵛ) v/a. ⊛a** = auftafeln.
an-tanzen (ˢᴸᵛ) ⊛** I v/n. 1. (h.) to dance first; to open the ball. — 2. (sn) an et. ⇄ to knock against a th. in dancing. — 3. angetanzt kommen to come up dancing; to trip along; (auftreten, erscheinen) to appear on the scene, to arrive; e-n ⇄ lassen to command a p.'s attendance, F to make a p. dance attendance (on oneself). — II v/a. 4. sich (dat.) die Schwindsucht ⇄ to dance o.s. into a consumption.
an-tappen (ˢᴸᵛ) v/n. (h. u. sn) ⊛** 1. an et. ⇄ to touch a th. in groping about; leise. to tap at. — 2. ⇄, angetappt kommen to come on groping.
ant-arktisch ♀ (⸌) [grch.] a. ㊻ (im südlichen Polarkreise gelegen) antarctic.
an-tasten (ˢᴸᵛ) I v/a. ⊛** 1. to touch; das Kapital ⇄ to touch (or draw on) one's capital. — 2. fig., b.s. to attack, invade; to infringe (or encroach) upon a. p.'s right; et. ~de(r), **An-taster**(in f ㊵ m ㉒ invader, &c. — II ~ n ㉓ und **An-tastung** f ㊻ 3. touch(ing), von Rechten: infringement of, encroachment upon.

an-taumeln (ˢᴸᵛ) v/n. (sn) ⊛a** 1. ⇄, angetaumelt kommen to reel along. — 2. gegen et. ⇄ to stagger against a th.
ante-datieren ⸗ (⸍⸌⸍⸌) [lt.] v/a. ⊛ to antedate (mehr gebr. zurückdatieren)
ante-diluvianisch ⸗ (⸍⸌⸌⸍w(⸌)⸍) [lt.] a. ㊻ (vorsintflutlich) antediluvian.
an-teeren ⊕ u. ⚓ (ˢᴸᵛ) v/a. ⊛** to tar.
An-teil (ˢᴸ) m (⚓ n) ⓘd. 1. portion, share; j-n ~ erhalten to come in for one's share; e-n gleichen ~ fordern to ask (for) one's half-share; ~ an e-r Beute ꝛc. F whack, lot; ~ haben an to partake of, to share in; ~ an e-r Firma haben to be partner (in a firm); ~ am Geschäftsgewinn percentage (or royalty) on the profits. — 2. (Teilnahme) interest, sympathy; ~ nehmen an to interest o.s. in, to concern o.s. about; wir nehmen herzlichen ~ an Ihrem Mißgeschick we heartily sympathize with your misfortune; tätigen ~ nehmen an // to take an active part in //.
Anteil=haber (ˢᴸ...) m ㊻ participant, partner. [one's share.⌋
an-teilig (ˢᴸᵛ) a. ㊻ proportionate to⌋
an-teil=los (ˢᴸ...) a. ㊻ indifferent; =losigkeit f ㊵ indifference; =nahme f ㊻ sympathy, concern(ment).
An-teils=..., ⇄... (ˢᴸ...) f. Anteil=..
An-teil=schein (ˢᴸ...) m ㊻ share certificate; ⇄voll a. ㊻ sympathetic; =wirtschaft f, agr. payment of rent (for a farm) partly in cash, partly in kind.
Antenne (⸍⸌ᵛ) [lt.] f ⊛ 1. ⚓ (Rahe) lateen-yard. — 2. zo. (Fühler) feeler, ⸗ antenna.
Ante-pänultima (⸍⸌⸍⸌⸍) [lt.] f ㊼ gr. (vorletzte Silbe) antepenultimate (syllable).
Ante-zedenzien (⸍⸌⸍(ᵛ)⸍) [lt.] f/pl. ㉚ (Vergangenheit, Vorleben) antecedents pl.
Anthere ⸗ ♀ (⸌⸍) [grch.] f ⊛ (Staubbeutel) anther, ~n=schlauch m ㊻ utricle.
Anthologie ⸗ (⸍⸌⸍⸌) [grch.] f ⊛ (Blütenlese) anthology, selection. [logical.⌋
anthologisch (⸍⸌⸍⸌) [grch.] a. ㊻ antho-⌋
Anthrachinon ⸗ (⸌⸍⸌⸍) [grch.] n ⓘc. chm. anthraquinone ($C_{14}H_8O_2$).
Anthrazen ⸗ (⸍⸌⸍) [grch. anthrax Kohle] n ⓘc. (o. pl.) chm. (fester Kohlenwasserstoff) anthracene.
Anthrazit ⸗ (⸌⸍⸍tȥ⸍) [grch.] m ⓘc. min. (Kohlenblende, Glanzkohle) anthracite; ⇄=haltig (⸍...) a. ㊻ anthracitic.
Anthropolog ⸗ (⸍⸍⸌ᵛ⸍) [grch.] m ㉘, ~e ㊹ anthropologist; ~ie ⸗ (⸍⸍ᵛᵛ⸍) ㊼ (Lehre vom Menschen) anthropology; ⇄isch (⸌⸌⸍ᵛ) a. ㊻ anthropological.
anthropomorph(isch) ⸗ (⸌⸌⸌f(ᵛ))[grch.] a. ㊻ (v. Menschengestalt) anthropomorphous.
Anthropophag ⸗ (⸌⸌⸍f⸍) [grch.] m ⓷, ~e (⸌⸌⸌f⸍) (Menschenfresser) cannibal; ~en pl. auch: anthropophagi; ⇄isch (⸌⸌ᵛ⸍f⸌ᵛ) a. ㊻ anthropophagous.
☛ **Anti**..., ⇄... (⸍ᵛ...) [grch. gegen; lt. vor] in Zssgn mst: anti(-)...
Anti-bacchius ⸗ (⸍⸍⸌⸌) [lt.,* grch.] m ㊳ pros. antibacchius (⸌⸌⸌⸍).
anti-chambrieren (⸍⸌⸍ᶜʰ⸍⸌ᵛ) [fr.] v/n. (h.) ⊛ (im Vorzimmer warten) to wait in the antechamber; F to dance attendance upon.
Anti-christ (⸍ᵛ⸌) m ㉘, ⓘc. rel. Antichrist; ⇄lich (⸍⸌⸍ᵛ) a. ㊻ antichristian.
an-ticken (ˢᴸᵛ) v/a. ⊛** to touch lightly; den Pendel, die Uhr ⇄ to set ... going.

⸗ scientific; ♀ botanical; ♁ geography; ⊕ machinery; ⚒ mining; ⚔ military; ⚓ marine; ⊛ commercial; ✉ postal; 🚂 railway.

anti-deutſch (ˈˌ‿ˌ) *a.* Ⓖ (deutſch-feindlich) anti-German. [(Gegengift) antidote.]
Anti-dot (ˈˌ‿ˌ) Ⓓc., **~on** (‿ˈ‿ˌ) [grch.] *n* Ⓓ
an-tiefen ↓ *v/n.* (h.) ⊛** to sound (on approaching the shore).
Anti-friktions-metall ⊕ (‿‿‿tȥ(‿)ˌˌ...) *n* Ⓑ (ſchwer abnutzbares [Lager-] Metall zu Zapfenlagern ꝛc.) antifriction metal.
antik (‿ˌ) [fr.] *a.* Ⓖ antique; *adv.* in an antique style; **~e** (‿ˌ‿) *f* Ⓘ **a)** Kunſt: antique art, (the) antique; **b)** Kunſtwert: antique work, antiquity.
Antiken-händler (‿ˌˌ‿...) *m* Ⓑ dealer in antiquities (F in curios); **=handlung** *f*, **=laden** *m* oft: old curiosity-shop; **=ſammlung** *f* collection of antiquities.
antikiſieren (‿‿ˌˌ‿) *v/n.* (h.) u. *v/a.* Ⓖ to work after an antique pattern.
Anti-klimax ↗ (ˈ‿‿ˌ) [grch.] *f* Ⓘ (Gegenſteigerung) anticlimax.
anti-klinal ↗ (‿‿ˌ) [grch.] *a.* Ⓖ geol. ♀, *anat.* (dach-artig geneigt: ∧) anticlinal.
Anti-libanon ↗ (ˈ‿‿‿) npr/m. Ⓑ α. (Gebirge in Syrien) Anti-Lebanon.
Antillen ♀ (‿ˈˌ) npr/f/pl. Ⓘ (Weſt-indien) Antilles; Kleine ~ Lesser Antilles; **~meer** (‿ˈˌˌ) *n* Ⓑ Caribbean Sea.
Antilope ↑ (‿‿ˈ‿) [engl., *?] *f* Ⓘ zo. antelope (Anti'tope); zu den ~n gehörig antelopian, antilopine.
Antimon ↗ (‿‿ˈ) [16. sæ. ar., grch.?] *n*, *a. m* Ⓓc., *chm., min.* antimony (Sb = stibium); mit ~ verbunden antimoniated; zum ~ gehörig antimonial.
antimon-artig ↗ (ˌˌ...) *a.* Ⓖ antimonial; **=blei** *n* Ⓑ slag-lead; **=blende** *f* red antimony (ore); **=blüte** *f* antimony-bloom, antimonious acid; **=chlori'd** *n* antimony trichloride (Sb Cl₃); **=glanz** *m* antimony trisulphide (Sb₂S₃); **ℨhaltig** *a* antimonial, antimoniferous.
antimonig, antimoniſch ↗ (‿‿ˈ‿) *a.* Ⓖ *chm., min.* antimonious, antimonial; ℨe Säure antimonious acid (HSbO₂); ℨ-ſaures Salz antimonite.
Antimon-oxy'd ↗ (‿‿ˈˌ...) *n* Ⓑ oxide of antimony (Sb₄O₆); **ℨſauer** *a.* Ⓖ antimonic; ℨſaures Salz antimoniate; **=ſäure** *f* antimonic acid (HSbO₃, 2H₂O).
Antimonyl-kalium-tartrat ↗ (ˌˌ(‿)‿‿ˌˌ) *n* Ⓓc. *chm.* = Brechweinſtein.
Anti-nomie ↗ (‿‿‿ˈ) [grch.] *f* Ⓘ (innerer Widerſpruch) antinomy.
Antiochia ♀ (‿‿ˈ‿‿) Ⓑα., **Antiochien** (‿‿‿ˈ‿‿) Ⓑα. *npr/n.* (alte ſyr. St., jetzt Antakia) Antioch.
Anti-parallelogramm (‿‿‿‿‿ˈ) [grch.] *n* Ⓓc. ↗ *math.* quadrangle of which two sides are parallel, and the other two equal, but not parallel.
Anti-pathie (‿‿‿ˈ) [grch.] *f* Ⓘ (Abneigung) antipathy, dislike, aversion.
anti-periſtaltiſch ↗ (‿‿‿‿ˈ‿) [grch.] *a.* Ⓖ *physiol. v.* Darmbewegungen: (rückgängig) antiperistaltic; ℨe Mittel = Brech-m.
Anti-pode (‿‿ˈ‿) [grch.] *m* Ⓘ (Gegenfüßler), meiſt im *pl.* ~n antipodes (a. *fig.*).
anti-podiſch (‿‿ˈ‿) *a.* Ⓖ antipodal, antipodean; *fig.* diametrically opposed.
an-tippen F (ˈ‿‿) *v/a.* ⊛** to tap.
Anti-pyrin ↗ (‿‿‿ˈ) [grch.] *n* Ⓓc. *chm.* antipyrin(e).
Antiqua ⊕ (‿ˈ‿) [It.] *f* Ⓘ *typ.* Roman (type); **~kaſten** (ˌ...) *m* Ⓑ Roman case.

Antiquar (‿‿ˈ) [It.] *m* Ⓓc., *a.* Ⓘ **1.** (Altertumskenner) antiquary, antiquarian. — **2.** (Händler) second-hand bookseller.
Antiquariat (‿‿‿ˈ) [It.] *n* Ⓓc. second-hand book-stall or bookseller's shop; **~s-buchhändler** *m* Ⓑ = Antiqua'r 2; **~s-buchhandlung** *f* = Antiquaria't.
antiquariſch (‿‿ˈ‿) [It.] *a.* Ⓖ *adv.* **1.** ↘ archæological. — **2.** buchhändleriſch: Les Lager stock of second-hand books; ein Buch ℨ kaufen to buy ... second-hand.
Antiqua-ſchrift (‿ˈˌ...) *f* Ⓑ Roman (letters pl. or character), roman.
antiquieren (‿‿ˈ‿) [It.] Ⓘ **I** *v/a.* (ſn) veralten. — **II** *v/a.* (abſchaffen) to abolish.
Antiquität (‿‿‿ˈ) [It.] *f* Ⓘ antiquity; ~en *pl.* (alte Überreſte, altertümliche Artikel) antiquities, old curios(ities) *pl.*
Antiquitäten-händler (‿‿‿‿ˌˌ...) *m* Ⓑ dealer in antiques or in articles of virtu; **=laden** *m* old curiosity-shop; **=ſammler** *m* collector of curios(ities).
Anti-ſemit (‿‿ˈ) *m* Ⓘ (Judenfeind) Anti-Semite, Jew-baiter; Liſch *a.* Ⓖ anti-Semitic; **~i"smus** *m* Ⓑ anti-Semitism.
anti-ſeptiſch ↗ (‿‿ˈ‿) *a.* Ⓖ antiseptic.
Anti-ſtrophe ↗ (‿‿ˈ‿) [grch.] *f* Ⓘ (Gegengeſang in der grch. Lyrik) antistrophe.
Anti-theſe ↗ (‿‿ˈ‿) [grch.] *f* Ⓘ *rhet.* (Gegenſatz) antithesis; weitℨ. the very opposite.
anti-zipando (‿‿‿ˈˌ‿) [It.] *adv.* in anticipation.
Anti-zipation (‿‿‿ˈ‿) *f* Ⓘ anticipation.
anti-zipieren (‿‿‿ˈ‿) *a.* Ⓖ (im voraus tun, genießen ꝛc.) to anticipate.
Ant-litz (ˈ‿) [ahd.] *n* Ⓓc. *a. bſb. bibl. u. poet.* face, countenance; e-m ins ~ ſagen ꝛc. ... to a p.'s face, ſtärker: in a p.'s teeth.
an-toben (ˈ‿‿) *v/n.* (ſn) ⊛** ℨ, angetobt kommen to come roaring along.
Anton (ˈ‿) [It.] *npr/m.* Ⓑα. (Bn) Ant(h)ony. [to begin to sound.]
an-tönen (ˈ‿‿) *v/n.* (h. u. ſn) u. *v/a.* ⊛**]
Antoni-a, -e (‿ˈ‿(‿)‿) *npr/f.* Ⓑ Ⓘβ. (Bn) Antonia, Antoinette, *dim.* Netty.
Antoninus-wall ♀ (‿‿ˈ‿‿) *m* Ⓑ (ſchott.Grenzwall zw. Forth u. Clyde) Antonine's wall.
Antonius-feuer (‿ˈ‿(‿)‿...) *n* Ⓑ *path.* (Rotlauf, Geſichtsroſe) St. Anthony's fire; **=kreuz** *n* (T) Saint Anthony's cross, tace.
Ant-onomaſie ↗ (‿‿‿‿ˈ) [grch.] *f* Ⓘ *rhet.* (Umſchreiben v. Eigennamen) antonomasia.
Ant-onym ↗ (‿‿ˈ) [grch.] *n* Ⓓc. (entgegengeſetzter Begriff) antonym.
an-traben (ˈ‿‿) *v/n.* (ſn) ⊛** to trot; angetrabt kommen to come at a trot.
An-trag (ˈ‿) *m* Ⓓd. **1.** proposition, proposal; *parl.* motion; einen ~ ſtellen, einbringen to put (or bring forward) a motion, to move; einen ~unterſtützen to second a motion; der ~ ging (fiel) durch the motion was carried (lost); der ~ ward (mit e-r Stimmenmehrheit von //) abgelehnt the motion was rejected (by a majority of //). — **2.** (Heirats-ℨ) offer; e-r Dame e-n ~ m. to propose or make an offer to a lady.
an-tragen (ˈ‿‿) Ⓑb** **I** *v/a.* **1.** (herbeitragen) to carry up to; ⊕ *arch.* Putz an e-e Wand ℨ to plaster ...; Vergolderei: Blattgold ℨ to lay on gold-leaf. — **2.** auch *v/refl.* (anbieten) (ſich) ℨ to offer (o.s.); mir iſt eine Stelle angetragen

worden I have been offered a post; einer Jungfer Herz und Hand ℨ to make an offer (or to propose) to a spinster. — **II** *v/n.* (h.) **3.** auf et. ℨ to make a proposal; *parl. u. jur.* to put a motion, to move; auf die Tagesordnung ℨ to move the previous question.
Antrag(s)-formula'r (ˈ‿‿...) *n* Ⓑ form of application; **=ſteller** *m* proposer; *parl.* mover (of a resolution); **=vergehen** *n* *jur.* offence dealt with at the request of the injured party.
an-trauen (ˈ‿‿) *v/a.* ⊛** to marry to; ſich (*dat.*) ein Mädchen ℨ laſſen to wed (or espouse) ...; angetraut wedded to.
an-träufen (‿) *v/a.* ⊛** to drip on to.
an-treffen (ˈ‿‿) **I** *v/a.* Ⓑa** (*impf.* traf an) to meet (or to fall in) with; gelegentlich: to come across; zufällig: to chance (or hit) upon; nicht anzutreffen(d) not to be found. — **II** ~ *n* Ⓑ meeting.
An-treibe-holz ⊕ (ˈ‿‿...) *n* Ⓑ wood used for the refining furnace.
an-treiben (ˈ‿‿) Ⓑ** **I** *v/a.* **1.** et. an et. ℨ to drive (or push, float) a th. against ... — **2.** (feſtſchlagen) den Hut ℨ f. auf, ein-treiben; e-n Nagel ℨ to drive in; ⊕ Böttcherei: Reifen ℨ to drive the hoops. — **3.** *fig.* (anregen) to incite, prompt, stimulate, egg on, goad on, spur on, urge on; *hort.* Pflanzen ℨ to force ... — **II** *v/n.* **4.** (ſn) to come floating, ans Land: to drift ashore. — **5.** (h.) ℨ to begin to shoot. — **III** ~ *n* Ⓑ **6.** = Antreibung. — **IV** ℨd *p.pr. u. a.* Ⓑ **7.** impulsive; Ⓛde Kraft moving force.
An-treiber (ˈ‿‿) *m* Ⓑ one who drives, &c.; *fig.* instigator, prompter; Werkſtatt: foreman; ⊕ Böttcherei: hoop-driver.
An-treibung (ˈ‿‿) *f* Ⓑ driving, pushing; incitation, stimulation; ſ. *a.* Antrieb.
an-treten (ˈ‿‿) Ⓑd** **I** *v/n.* (ſn) **1.** F bei e-m ℨ to call on a p. — **2.** (ſich aufſtellen; *ant.* abtreten) to take one's place; ⚔ to fall in(to line or position); to form (in ranks); zum Tanze ℨ, auch: to stand up. — **3.** (zuerſt gehen) mit dem linken Fuße ℨ to set out with the left foot. **II** *v/a.* **4.** (feſttreten) to stamp (or tread) down. — **5.** ℨ to step up to; e-n (anreden) to accoſt a p.; raſch tritt der Tod den Menſchen an (SCH.) death comes upon us unforeseen. — **6.** *fig.* (übernehmen) ein Amt, eine Stelle ℨ to enter on one's duties, to undertake a place; den Beweis (der Wahrheit) ℨ to produce evidence for; eine Erbſchaft ℨ to enter on (or to take possession of) an inheritance; ſie hat ihr achtes Jahr angetreten she is just turned seven; die Regierung ℨ to take the reins of government; eine Reiſe ℨ to set out on a journey. — **III** ~ *n* Ⓑ und **Antretung** *f* Ⓘ **7.** = Antritt.
An-trieb (ˈ‿) *m* Ⓓd. **1.** impulse; (Beweggrund) motive, incentive, inducement; *phys.* impetus; *mech.* accelerating (or propelling) force; aus eignem ~ one's own accord, spontaneously; aus freiem ~ of one's own free will; aus innerem ~ from inclination, by impulse; aus natürlichem ~ by instinct; nach plötzlichem ~ handeln to act on the spur of the moment. — **2.** ⊕ *elect.* elektriſcher

---

Zeichen (ſ. S. XVII): F familiär; P Volksſprache; Γ Gaunerſprache; ↘ ſelten; † alt (auch geſtorben); * neu (auch geboren); ⁺⁺ unrichtig;

~ electric propulsion or power; mit elektrischem ~ versehene Wagen electrically propelled (or driven) cars.

an-trinken (⸗⸗) ⊕ſt** I v/refl. 1. ſich (dat.) einen Rauſch 2 to get tipsy (F fuddled); ſich Courage 2 to stimulate (or fire) one's courage by (having a) drink. — 2. ſich (acc.) 2 to drink hard, F to liquor (or lush) up. — II v/n. (ſn) 3. to drink first. — III **an-getrunken** p.p. u. a. ⊕(D9) 4. (betrunken) tipsy, F slightly on, half-seas over, fuddled. — 5. Les Glas ... partly emptied.

An-tritt (⸗⸗) m ⊕c.1. (ſ. antreten 2) taking one's place or stand. — 2. ~ e-s Amtes entering on one's duties, installation; Anzeige: Geſucht zu ſofortigem ~ Wanted immediately or at once; ~ einer Erbſchaft entering upon an inheritance; ~ der Regierung accession to the throne; ~ e-r Reiſe starting (or setting out) on a journey. — 3. (erſtes Auftreten) thea., &c. first appearance, (fr.) debut; (Anfang) commencement. — 4. ⊕ (Stufe) first step (of a staircase); (Schemeltritt) foot-step.

An-tritts=audienz (⸗⸗...) f ⊕ eines Gesandten: first audience; **=beſuch** m first visit; **=geld** n bezahlen to pay one's footing; **=predigt** f first sermon; anglikaniſch: ſeine~halten to preach one's first sermon; **=rede** f inaugural speech or address; parl. maiden - speech; **=rolle** f debut; **=ſchmaus** m installation-dinner, inaugural banquet.

an-trocknen (⸗⸗) v/n. (ſn) ⊕b** 1. to begin to dry. — 2. an et. 2 to dry on to a th., to adhere to a th. in drying.

an-trommeln (⸗⸗) v/n. (h.) ⊕a** 1. an et. 2 to drum on a th. — 2. (anfangen zu trommeln) to commence drumming.

An-trunk (⸗⸗) m ⊕c. (erſter Trunk) first drink; den ~ tun, haben to drink first.

an-tun (⸗ʹ) I v/a. und v/refl. ⊕** 1. faſt † ein Kleid 2c. 2 to put on ...; — 2. (zufügen) F tun Sie mir das nicht an! do not inflict this (disgrace) upon me!, spare me this humiliation!; e-m Ehre 2 to do honour to a p.; wollen Sie mir die Ehre 2? will you do me the honour? ſich (dat.) Gewalt 2 to put a restraint (or check) on o.s., to overcome one's disinclination or reluctance; dem Sinne e-s Wortes Gewalt 2 to twist (or strain) the meaning of a word; einem Weibe Gewalt 2 to ravish a woman; ſich ein Leid(s) 2 to lay hands upon o.s., to do away with o.s.; e-m e-n Schimpf 2 to offer a p. an affront; ſich Zwang 2 to restrain o.s., to keep o.s. in check. — 3. es e-m 2 to bewitch (or fascinate) a p. — 4. ⊥ einen Hafen, das Land 2 (zu erreichen ſuchen) to stand in (or to make) for a port, for (the) land. — II **an-getan** p.p. 5. ſ. bs.

an-tupfen (⸗⸗) v/a. ⊕** to touch lightly (with a finger, sponge, &c.).

an-tuſchen (⸗⸗) v/a. ⊕** to paint in (or to touch up with) Indian ink.

Antw. abbr. = Antwort.

Antwerpen ♀ (⸗⸗) npr/n. ⊕α. (belgiſche Provinz u. Stadt) Antwerp, (fr.) Anvers.

Ant-wort (⸗⸗) [ahd. aus Ant-¹ u. Wort n] f ⊕ 1. (ant. Frage) answer, reply, jur. rejoinder; tel. ~ bezahlt reply paid (abbr. R.P.); bitte um ~ an answer will oblige; um ~ wird gebeten (abbr. U. A. w. g.) an answer is requested (a. a. i. r.), (fr.) répondez s'il vous plaît (R. S. V. P.); gleich mit einer ~ bei der Hand ſein to be quick at repartee; auf ~ dringen to insist on an answer; eine ~ geben to make reply, to give an answer; er gab keine ~ he made no response; iſt eine ~ mitzunehmen? is there an(y) answer?; ~ ſchicken to send back word; keine~ſchuldig bleiben: a) beim Examen: to answer every question, F to floor the paper; b) to be never at a loss for an answer; ⊕ in ~ auf Ihr Geehrtes replying (or in reply) to your favour; Sprichw. keine ~ iſt auch eine ~, etwa: silence gives consent. — 2. eine abſchlägige ~ bekommen to meet with a refusal or rebuff; keine abſchlägige ~ annehmen to take no denial; eine bejahende (verneinende) ~ geben to give an affirmative (a negative) reply, vgl. antworten am Schluß; endgültige ~ final answer or decision; ſchlagfertige ~ repartee; e-m eine ſchlagfertige ~ geben to give a p. a smart reply or answer. — 3. ~ auf die Thronrede address in answer to the King's speech. — 4. Rede und ~ über et. ſteh(e)n to give an account of s. th.; to (have to) answer for s. th.

ant-worten (⸗⸗) [ahd.] v/a. und v/n. (h.) ⊕ *,* e-m 2 to answer a p., to give a p. an answer, to (make) reply to a p.; grollend 2 to retort upon; umgehend 2 to reply by return (of post); auf e-e Frage, e-n Brief 2 to answer a question, a letter; darauf läßt ſich nichts 2 that is unanswerable; er weiß ſtets etwas zu 2 he is never at a loss for an answer; mit ja (nein) 2 to say yes (no), to answer in the affirmative (negative).

ant-wortlich* ⊕ (⸗⸗) adv. m. gen. in reply to, in answer to (bff. in Beantwortung).

Ant-wort(s)=ſchreiben (⸗⸗...) n ⊕ reply, letter sent in response to; **=ſchrift** f jur. 2c. reply; rejoinder.

An= und Abfuhr ⊕ (⸗⸗⸗⸗) f ⊕ (o. pl.) v. Gütern: carriage, conveyance, cartage.

An-und-für-ſich-ſein (⸗⸗⸗⸗) n ⊕ phls. etwa: abstract existence.

an-vermählen (⸗⸗⸗) v/a. ⊕*/* to wed to.

an-verſuchen F (⸗⸗⸗) v/a. ⊕*/* einen Rock 2c.: to try on, to fit on.

an-vertrauen (⸗⸗⸗) I v/n. und v/refl. ⊕*/* 1. e-m et. 2 (übergeben) to entrust (or commit) a th. to a p.('s care); e-m Geld 2 to deposit ... with a p.; anvertrautes Gut deposit, (property in) trust; ich will das Kind ſeiner Obhut 2 ... give the child in his charge or custody. — 2. e-m et. 2 (mitteilen) to confide a th. to a p.; ſich e-m 2 to make a confidant of a p., to open one's heart to a p. — II ~ n ⊕ und **An-vertrauung** f ⊕ 3. entrusting, commitment; depositing; trust.

an-verwandt (⸗⸗⸗) I a. ⊕ = verwandt (ſ. bs); er iſt mir 2 he is a relative (or kinsman) of mine. — II ~e(-n) m, ~e(r) f ⊕, a. **~in** ⊕ ⊕ kinsman (kinswoman f); durch Heirat: relation by marriage.

An-verwandtſchaft (⸗⸗⸗) f ⊕ kinship, durch Heirat: relationship by marriage.

an-vetter(michel)n F (⸗⸗(⸗⸗)⸗) ⊕a** ſich 2 v/refl. to thrust (or force) one's company on; to curry favour with.

Anw. abbr. = Anweiſung.

An-wachs (⸗⸗) m ⊕a. 1. growth; increase; med., &c ⊕: accretion; des Waſſers: rising; von Angeſchwemmten: alluvion, alluvial deposit or soil. — 2. (das Anwachſende) that which grows; hort. young shoots or trees pl.; (Unterholz) coppice, copse; (die Jugend) the rising generation. — Vgl. a. Anwuchs.

an-wachſ/en (⸗⸗) I v/n. (ſn) ⊕b(e)ſt** 1. (Wurzel ſchlagen) to take root. — 2. (feſtwachſen) to grow to or together; to adhere to; angewachſen zo. hidebound; ⨁ adnate; F fig. die Zunge iſt ihr nicht angewachſen she has a voluble (b.s. loose) tongue. — 3. (zunehmen) to grow, increase, augment; ♪ Töne 2 laſſen to swell ... — 4. (aufwachſen) to grow up. — II ~ n ⊕ 5. = Anwachs 1; (Wurzelſchlagen) taking root; (Feſtgewachſenſein) adhesion. — 6. **A/ung** f ⊕ jur. ~ des Beſitzes increase, accrescence.

an-wackeln (⸗⸗) v/n. (ſn) ⊕a** 2, ſie kamen angewackelt ... waddling along.

An-walt (⸗⸗) [mhd.] m ⊕⊕c. ſ. Advokat; e-n ~ annehmen to retain counsel; als ~ auftreten for to appear as counsel for; e-n ~ um Rat fragen to take counsel's opinion; fig. ſich zum ~ e-r verlorenen Sache m. to make o.s. the advocate (or champion) of a forlorn cause.

an-waltlich (⸗⸗) a. ⊕ concerning (or relating to) members of the Bar.

An-waltſchaft (⸗⸗) f ⊕ attorneyship; solicitor's profession; (Genoſſenſchaft) the Bar; **A/lich** a. ⊕ = anwaltlich.

An-walts=gebühren (⸗⸗...) f/pl. ⊕ counsel's (or solicitor's) fee; **=kammer** f etwa: the Bar; the Inns pl. of Court; the Law Society.

an-walzen (⸗⸗) ⊕** I v/a. 1. die Erde 2 to roll down the earth (with a roller). — II v/n. (h.) 2. Tanz: to begin to waltz. — 3. 2, angewalzt kommen to come rolling (waltzing) along.

an-wälzen (⸗⸗) v/a. ⊕** to roll against or on to. [two fields.)

An-wand (⸗⸗) f ⊕ agr. ridge between)

an-wandeln (⸗⸗) ⊕a** I v/n. (ſn) 2, angewandelt kommen to come sauntering (or walking) along. — II v/n. (ſn) u. v/a. e-n (⸗ e-m) 2 to come over a p.; es wandelt mich eine Laune an I feel in a humour to; es wandelte mich eigentümlich an I was seized (or I felt prompted) with peculiar sensations; was wandelt ihn an? what is the matter with him? (ſ. a. ankommen 6).

An-wand(e)lung (⸗⸗(⸗)⸗) f ⊕ access; med. &c. attack, fit; e-e ~ von Ohnmacht a fainting fit; in einer ~ von Schwäche (Großmut) in a weak (generous) moment; plötzliche ~ sudden impulse.

an-wandern (⸗⸗) v/n. (ſn) ⊕a** wo 2 oder angewandert kommen to come tramping (or marching, journeying) along; F to come on shanks' pony.

an-wanken (⸗⸗) v/n. (ſn) ⊕** 2, angewankt komm... ..o come tottering up.

[anwärmen] — 74 — [Anzahlung]

an-wärmen (⌂⌂⌣) v/a. ⊛** to begin to heat (the furnace); Getränke ⌂ to take the chill off …, to mull …
An-wärter (⌂⌂⌣) m ㉒, ⟋ ~in f ㊵ 1. (Person, die Anspruch auf eine Erbschaft hat) reversioner, one who has expectations of a reversion; heir apparent. — 2. ~ zum Staatsdienste candidate for …
An-wartschaft (⌂⌂⌣) f (Anheimfall) reversion of; (Aussicht auf) prospect of; (Anrecht auf) claim to, bei e-r Pfründe: next presentation to; 2lich (⌂⌂⌣⌣) a. ⊛ reversionary. [ore).}
An-wäsche ⚒ (⌂⌂⌣) f ㊽ washing (of
an-waschen (⌂⌂⌣) v/a. ⊛b**. 1. Wäsche ⌂ to soak or steep … — 2. ein Bild ⌂ (tuschen) to paint (or wash) … in Indian ink.
an-wässern ⟋ (⌂⌂⌣) v/a. ⊛a** to moisten (a little), to sprinkle (with water).
an-watscheln (⌂L⌣) (v/n. (fn) ⊛a** angewatschelt kommen to come waddling along.
an-weben ⊙ (⌂L⌣) ⊛b** od. ⊛** to join (or attach, fasten) by weaving.
an-wedeln (⌂L⌣) v/a. ⊛a** 1. vom Hunde: e-n ⌂ to wag its tail at a p. — 2. (fächeln) to cool with a fan.
an-wehen (⌂L⌣) ⊛** I v/a. e-n, et. ⌂ to blow (or breathe) upon …; wenn ihn nur ein Lüftchen anweht, liegt er schon da the least breath of wind knocks him down, fig. mit dem Hauche der Begeisterung ⌂ to inspire with enthusiasm; es weht mich hier heimatlich an this (place) reminds me of home. — 2. das glimmende Feuer zu heller Flamme ⌂ to fan (up) the embers into a bright flame. — 3. Schneehaufen ⌂ (anhäufen) to drift snow. — 4. fig. eure Luft hat mir's angeweht your air (here) has infected me with it. — II v/n. 5. Schnee weht an snow is drifting this way. — III ~ n ㉓ 6. breath, fig. afflatus; von Schnee: drifting.
an-weichen (⌂L⌣) v/a. ⊛b**to soak(a little).
an-weisbar (⌂L⌣) a. ⊛ assignable. [bank.)
An-weise-bank ⊕ (⌂L⌣…) f ㉒ (deposit-}
an-weisen (⌂L⌣) v/a. ⊛** 1. (anleiten) to direct, to instruct; angewiesen fn, zu to have orders (or instructions) to; e-n zu et. ⌂ to put one in the way of a th. — 2. e-n mit e-r Forderung ⌘. an e-n ⌂ to refer a p. to a p.; auf Gemeinde-unterstützung angewiesen depending (or thrown) on the parish; fig. er ist auf sich angewiesen he is dependent on himself; ich bin auf meinen Lohn angewiesen I have nothing but my wages (to depend upon). — 3. e-m et. ⌂ to assign a th. to a p.; ⊕ Geld ⌂: a) für eine Sache: to appropriate, to set apart; b) einer Person: to assign ⌘; e-n auf e-e Bank ⌂ to pay a p. through a bank; e-m e-n Platz im Theater ⌘. ⌂ to show a p. to his seat.
An-weiser (⌂L⌣) m ㉒, ~in f ㊵ 1. instructor, adviser; assigner. — 2. ~ der Plätze bei einer Feier: steward.
an-weißen (⌂L⌣) v/a. ⊛** e-e Wand ⌂ to whitewash a wall.
An-weisung (⌂L⌣) f ㊽ 1. (Anordnung) direction, instruction; precept; jur. (schriftliche Aufforderung) order (in writing); (Befehl) injunction; (Rat) advice; e-m ~ geben, daß er et. tun soll

to order (or to enjoin upon) a p. to do a th.; ich erhielt ~ zu I was instructed to; kurze ~ (Anleitung) zum Schachspiel short guide to chess. — 2. ~ e-s Platzes: allocation, einer Zahlung: assignment, draft, cheque; ⟋ money-order (f. Geld-, Post-⌂); ~ (Übertragung) einer Schuld transfer of a debt to; ⊛ ~ auf Order (auf den Inhaber lautend) bill (or cheque) to order (to bearer). — 3. ⚒ das Erz hat gute ~ the ore is opening out well or promising well.
An-weisungs-buch ⊛ (⌂…) n ㉒ chequebook; =schein, =zettel m draft, cheque.
An-welle (⌂L⌣) f ㊽ agr. ridge.
an-wendbar (⌂⌂-) a. ㊻ appli(c)able to, available for; (ausführbar) feasible, practicable; allgemein ⌂, in allen Fällen ⌂ of general (stärker: of universal) application; das ist auch hier ⌂ it applies (or holds good) also in this case; zu diesem Zwecke ⌂ answering (or adapted for) this purpose; ~keit (⌂⌂⌣) f ㊽ applicableness; feasibility, practicableness, adaptability.
an-wenden (⌂⌂⌣) I v/a. ⊛a** 1. et. zu et. ⌂ to employ (or use) a th. for a th.; seine Kräfte ⌂ to exert o.s.; Mühe bei et. ⌂ to take pains with a th., to bestow pains upon a th.; seine Zeit ⌘. gut ⌂ to make good use of …; etwas nützlich ⌂ to turn a th. to good account; unnütz ⌂ to waste; übel (auch falsch, ungehörig) ⌂ to misapply; sein Geld schlecht ⌂ to misspend (stärker: to throw away) one's money; das ist bei uns schlecht angewandt F it won't do with us; F mehr (Geld) kann ich nicht ⌂ I cannot afford more. — 2. e-e Regel ⌂ to apply … to; sich ⌂ l. to be applicable to. — II **an-gewandt** (⌂⌂⌣) p.p. u. a. ㊻ 3. ⌂e Chemie experimental chemistry; ⌂e Geometrie ⌘. applied geometry, &c.; phls. ⌂er Begriff concrete notion.
An-wendung (⌂⌂⌣) f ㊽ 1. employment, use; zur (od. in) ~ bringen to put into practice, to apply. — 2. (Beziehung auf) application; ~ finden, zur ~ kommen to bear upon; to apply to; verkehrte ⌂ misapplication. [application.}
An-wendungs-weise (⌂…) f ㊷ mode of}
an-werben (⌂⌂⌣) ⊛b** I v/n. (h.) um et. ⌂ to canvass for et. — II v/a. (bfd. ⚒) to enlist, enrol, ehm. auch to press; Truppen ⌂ to levy (or raise) …; sich ⌂ lassen to take service with, to enlist (as a soldier). — III ~ n ㉓ und **An-werbung** f ㊽ zum Kriegsdienste: enlistment, levy; von Arbeitern: engagement, F taking on. — IV **An-geworb(e)ne(r)** m ㉒; ⚒ recruit; rel. proselyte.
an-werfen (⌂⌂⌣) ⊛b** I v/n. (h.) to have (the) first throw, to throw (or play) first. — II v/a. an et. ⌂ to fling against a th.; ⊕ arch. Mörtel an eine Wand ⌂, eine Wand mit Mörtel ⌂ to plaster a wall; F einen Rock ⌂ to whip on a coat. — III ~ n ㉓ = Anwurf 1.
An-wesen bsd. südd. (⌂L⌣) n ㉓ (Besitztum) estate, property, jur. auch messuage.
an-wesend (⌂L⌣) (ant. abwesend) I a. ㊻ present; er war bei ihrer Beratung ⌂ he was present at (or he attended) their conference. — II ~e(r) m, ~e f ㊵ person

present; die ~en those present, weitS. the spectators pl., the audience; die ~en sind stets ausgenommen present company (is or are) always excepted.
An-wesenheit (⌂L⌣-) [nhd. 17. sac.] f ㊽ (o. pl.) presence; attendance; ~s-verzeichnis (⌂…) n ㉓ muster-roll.
an-wettern (⌂⌂⌣) ⊛a** I v/a. e-n ⌂ to thunder (or to bawl out) at a p. — II v/n. (fn) auf e-n ⌂ to rush upon a p.
an-wetzen (⌂⌂⌣) v/a. ⊛** e-e Spitze an et. ⌂ to grind a th. to a point.
an-widern (⌂⌂⌣) v/a., ⟋ v/n. (h.) ⊛a** e-n, bisw. e-m ⌂ = anekeln.
an-wiehern (⌂⌂⌣) v/a. ⊛a** von Pferden: to neigh (or whinny) at.
an-wimmern (⌂⌂⌣) v/a. ⊛a** e-n ⌂ to address a p. in a whining tone.
an-winken (⌂⌂⌣) v/a. ⊛** 1. e-n ⌂ to beckon to a p. — 2. ⚓ ein Schiff ⌂ to ease off the sheets of the forestay-sails and jib (so as to go to windward).
an-winseln (⌂⌂⌣) v/a. ⊛a** = anwimmern.
an-wirken (⌂⌂⌣) ⊛** I ⟋ v/n. (h.) gegen et. ⌂ to strive (or work) against a th. — II ⊙ v/a. = anweben. [or against.}
an-wischen (⌂⌂⌣) v/a. ⊛** to wipe on.
an-wohnen (⌂L⌣) v/n. (h.) ⊛** 1. e-m, e-m Flusse ⌘. ⌂ to live next to (or close by) …; ⌂d neighbouring; e-m Flusse ⌂d riverain. — 2. = beiwohnen 1.
An-wohner (⌂L⌣) m ㉒, ~in f ㊵ neighbour; die ⌂ des Meeres people living by the sea, seaside folks pl.; ~schaft (⌂L⌣) f ㊽ (o. pl.) neighbourhood; ~schaft e-s Flusses, riverside dwellers pl.
An-wuchs (⌂L⌣) m ⊛ 1. (Anwachsen der Pflanzen ⌘.) growth, fig. der Bevölkerung ⌘.: increase. — 2. for. junger ~ (Bäume v. 30—40 Jahren) stock of young, full-grown trees; vgl. Anwachs, Anwachsung.
an-wünschen (⌂⌂⌣) I v/a. ⊛** e-m et. ⌂ to wish a person something (bad). — II ~ n ㉓ und **An-wünschung** f ㊽ wish(ing); von et. Bösem: imprecation.
An-wurf (⌂L⌣) m ⊙c. 1. (erster Wurf) first throw; Fritz hat den ~ Fred throws first; ⊛ = Anzahlung. — 2. (Angeworfenes) ⊕ Maurerei: plaster(ing), roughcast; auch = Anländung (f. bsd.); Tuchmacherei: selvedge. — 3. † mint. (minting-)mill for larger coins.
an-würfeln (⌂⌂⌣) v/n. (h.) ⊛a** = anwerfen I. [balancing-pole.}
An-wurf-schlüssel (⌂L⌣…) m ㉒ mint.}
an-wurzeln (⌂⌂⌣) v/n. (fn) und v/refl. ⊛a** sich ⌂ to take (or strike) root; er stand wie angewurzelt da he stood (as if) rooted (or fixed) to the spot.
An-zahl (⌂L) f ㊽ (ohne pl.) number, quantity; große ~ von Leuten crowd, host, throng, mob, multitude; gang (of convicts, &c.), party (of soldiers, &c.); mit Prädikat im pl.: eine große ~ der Kühe ist (ob. sind) umgekommen a great many (or a great part, number) of the cows **have** perished.
an-zahlen (⌂L⌣) I v/a. ⊛** to pay on account. — II ~ n ㉓ = Anzahlung.
an-zählen (⌂L⌣) v/n. (h.) ⊛** to begin to count or to enumerate.
An-zahlung (⌂L⌣) f ㊽ payment on account; first payment, (first) instalment, part-payment.

Signs (see page IX): F familiar; P vulgar; ⌐ flash; ⟋ rare; † obsolete (died); * new word (born); ⁒ incorrect; ♪ music;

[anzapfen] — 75 — [anzüglich]

an-zapfen (ˢᴸ~) v/a. ⊕** 1. ein Faß ♀ to broach (or tap) ... — 2. ⊕ Bäume ♀ to tap (or box) ... — 3. F fig. e-n ♀ (aussaugen) a. e-n um Geld ♀ to get (stärker: to extort) money from a p., (ausholen) to pump a p. dry; parl. e-n Minister ♀ to put a question to..., (zum Reden veranlassen) to draw...; (reizen) to irritate (or provoke) a p.; (necken) to chaff a p.

an-zaubern (ˢᴸ~) v/a. ⊕a** e-m ♀, to fascinate a p.; e-m et. ♀ to bewitch a p. with a th.; angezaubert spell-bound.

an-zäumen (ˢᴸ~) v/a. ⊕** ein Pferd ♀ to bridle ..., to put the bridle on ...

an-zechen (ˢᴸ~) sich ♀ v./refl. ⊕** to take a drop too much, to drink too freely, to get tipsy.

An-zeichen (ˢᴸ~) n ⊕ allg.: mark, sign, token; (Andeutung) indication; path., &c. symptom; (Vorbedeutung) foreboding, omen, presage; sicheres ~ sure sign; wenn nicht alle ~ trügen unless we are greatly mistaken or deceived.

an-zeichnen (ˢᴸ~) v/a. ⊕b** to mark, mit Bleistift: to (mark with) pencil.

An-zeige (ˢᴸ~) f ⊕ 1. intimation, notice; (Kunde) intelligence; ~ des Wertes declaration of value; amtliche ~ notification; briefliche ~ advice; gerichtliche ~ legal notice; ~ (Anklage) bei Gericht information, denunciation; öffentliche ~ (Annonce) bsd. in Zeitungen: advertisement; telegraphische ~ telegram, wire (message); von et. ~ machen to give notice of (or information about) a th., to report a th. — 2. (Ankündigung) (public) announcement; advertisement; (Reklame) puff; (Besprechung e-s neuen Buches ob. Kunstwerks) review.

Anzeige = amt (ˢᴸ~...) n ⊕ intelligence-office; **=beweis** m circumstantial evidence; **=blatt** n advertisement-sheet; **=brief** m circular (letter).

an-zeigen (ˢᴸ~) ⊕** I v/a. (andeuten) to indicate, to show; (bedeuten) to signify; (ankündigen) to announce; (kundgeben) to notify, to give notice of; in Zeitungen: to advertise, to publish; den Wert ♀ to declare the value of; den Empfang ♀ to acknowledge (receipt of); das zeigt nichts Gutes an this augurs evil, it is a bad sign or omen; e-m et. ♀ to advise (or apprise, inform, acquaint) a p. of a th., amtlich: to notify a p. of a th.; man wird es mir ♀ I shall be told of it; e-n bei Gericht ♀ to inform (or lay information) against a p., stärker: to denounce a p.; e-m etwas ♀ lassen to send word to a p. (of what has happened); ⊖ Preise: to quote. — II sich ♀ v./refl. to make o.s. known. — III ~ n ⊕ = Anzeigung. — IV ♀ᵇ p.pr. und a. ⊕ indicative of; ♀ᵈᵉˢ Fürwort demonstrative pronoun. — V an-gezeigt p.p. u. a. ⊕ manifested, indicated; es ist ♀ (ratsam) so zu handeln it is expedient (or advisable, proper) to act that way.

An-zeige-pflicht (ˢᴸ~...) f ⊕ obligation to give notice to the police.

An-zeiger (ˢᴸ~) m ⊕ 1. (a. ~in f ⊕) indicator; e-s Verbrechens: informer; ⚔ ~ an der Schießscheibe marker. — 2. (Zeitung) Intelligencer, Advertiser, Gazette, &c. — 3. ⊕ mech. indicator; pointer. — 4. math. index, exponent.

An-zeigung (ˢᴸ~) f ⊕ (s. anzeigen I): ~ e-s Mordes information about a murder; ⊛ der Preise: quotation; vgl. a. Anzeige.

an-zetteln (ˢᴸ~) I v/a. ⊕a** 1. ⊕ Weberei: to warp. — 2. fig. e-e Verschwörung ꝛc.: to frame, hatch, contrive, devise; er hat das Ganze angezettelt he has set the whole thing going, he is at the bottom of it all. — II ~ n ⊕ u. **An-zett(e)lung** f ⊕ 3. (zu 1) warping. — 4. (zu 2) fig. intrigue, hatching (or brewing) of plots.

An-zettler (ˢᴸ~) m ⊕, ~in f ⊕ 1. ⊕ Weberei: warper. — 2. fig. plotter, schemer, intriguer, author of a plot.

an-ziehbar (ˢᴸ~) a. ⊕ magnetisch ꝛc.: attractable; **~keit** f ⊕ attractableness.

an-ziehen (ˢᴸ~) ⊕b** I v/a. 1. a. v/refl. Kleider: to put on, F to don; Stiefel ♀ to pull on ...; hastig ♀ to slip (or throw, whip) on; sich ♀ to dress (o.s.); sich fein, schmuck, auch: F to smarten (or spruce, tog, trick) o.s. up; e-m seinen Rock ♀ (helfen) to help a p. on with his coat; andere Kleider ♀ to change one's clothes; dieser Rock ist noch anzuziehen ... can still be worn; F den bunten Rock ♀ (Soldat werden), to don the red coat, to enlist; fig. bibl. einen neuen Menschen ♀ to put on the new man; warm angezogen warmly clad or clothed; gut angezogen well dressed. — 2. (in Bewegung setzen) die Glocke ♀ to pull (stärker: to tug at) the bell; von Pferden: den Wagen ♀ (to begin) to draw (or to pull) ... — 3. (anspannen) to strain; ein Seil: to stretch; eine Schraube: to tighten, to drive home; die Zügel ♀ to draw in (or to pull hard at) the reins. — 4. (zs.-ziehen) die Lippen: to draw together. — 5. die Tür ♀ (zuziehen) to close ..., to draw ... to. — 6. (auch v/n.): a) sich ♀ ziehen (or suck) in, to absorb; den Geruch von et. ♀ to become impregnated with the smell of a th.; b) (an sich ziehen; ant. abstoßen) magnetisch ꝛc.: to attract; (interessieren) to engage, interest; von Schaustücken: to draw; c) den Atem ♀ to hold one's breath; d) von der Pumpe: to suck (or draw up) the water. — 7. (großziehen) to raise; Vieh: to rear, breed; Bäume: to plant, cultivate, grow; Arbeiter ♀ (ausbilden) to train (or instruct) ... — 8. fig. eine Schriftstelle ♀ to quote, cite; die angezog(e)nen Fälle the examples or cases mentioned or referred to; angezog(e)ne Stellen references pl., cases quoted, cases in point. — 9. hunt. v. Vorstehhund: (die frische Spur verfolgen) to follow (up) a fresh scent. — II v/refl. 10. f. 1. — III v/n. (11-14: h.), 15 u. 16: fn) 11. f. 6; das Salz zieht an (wird feucht) ... is becoming (or getting) damp. — 12. Schach: to move first, to have the first move. — 13. (anfangen zu wirken, auch impers.) to take effect, to begin to act; vom Mörtel: to bind; von Nägeln: to clinch; v. Gewinden ꝛc.: scharf ♀ to have a great pull, to act with great force or power; vom Leim: to stick; F es zieht nichts bei ihm an it's all lost upon him; ⊛ die Preise ziehen an (steigen) prices are rising, hardening, looking up, improving, stiffening; bei ♀ᵈᵉⁿ Kursen in a rising market, with quotations tending upwards. — 14. die Kälte (das Wetter ob. es) zieht an it is getting colder or sharper, the cold is increasing. — 15. ♀, angezogen kommen to arrive; von Truppen: to come marching; F fig. mit et. angezogen kommen to bring a matter forward, to broach a subject, to talk about it. — 16. (den Dienst antreten) to enter service or a place. — IV ~ n ⊕ 17. z.B. der Kleidung: putting (or pulling) on; sie ist noch nicht fertig mit (dem) ~ she has not finished (or done) dressing; ⊛ der Preise: rise, hardening, improvement; ~ in e-e Wohnung installation; ~ von Dienstboten going into service; vgl. a. Anziehung u. Anzug 3, 4, 5. — V ♀ᵇ p.pr. u. a. ⊕ 18. in den Bed. des inf. — 19. fig. (w.) attractive, weitS. interesting; nicht ♀ᵇ unattractive, uninteresting, uninviting; das ~ᵇᵉ e-r Sache the charm of ... — 20. med. (zs.-ziehend) astringent. — VI **an-gezogen** (ˢᴸ~) p.p. u. a. ⊕ (D 9) 21. s. 1, 8, 15.

An-zieher (ˢᴸ~) m ⊕ 1. (bisw. a. ~in f ⊕) (Ankleider) dresser. — 2. ⚛ anat. = Anziehmuskel. — 3. (Gerät) für Schuhe ꝛc.: shoehorn, boot-hook; für Knöpfe: button-hook.

An-zieh-muskel (ˢᴸ...) m ⊕ anat.: ⚛ adductor, adducent muscle.

An-ziehung (ˢᴸ~) f ⊕ phys. attraction; der Erde: gravitation; e-r Schriftstelle: quotation; molekulare ~ molecular attraction, adhesion and cohesion.

An-ziehungs-kraft (ˢᴸ~...) f ⊕ power of attraction, attractive force; **=kreis** m, phys. sphere of attraction; **=muskel** m = Anzieh-; **=punkt** m point (or centre) of attraction; **=vermögen** n = =kraft.

an-zisch(e)n (ˢᴸ~) ⊕ ⊕a** e-n ♀ to hiss at a p.; to whisper to a p.

an-zotteln F (ˢᴸ~) v/n. (fn) ⊕a** sie kamen angezottelt: F ... toddling along.

An-zucht (ˢᴸ~) f ⊕ [anziehen 7] raising, agr. breeding; hort. cultivation, growing. [with sugar, to sugar over.]

an-zuckern (ˢᴸ~) v/a. ⊕a** to (sprinkle)

An-zug (ˢᴸ~ ob. ~) m ⊕d. 1. [18. sæ.,** md.] (Bekleidung) attire, clothing, garb; ein neuer ~ new clothes pl.; vollständiger ~ (complete) suit (of clothes); für Frauen: costume; ein zweiter ~ zum Wechseln a change of clothes; in vollem ~e in full dress. — 2. (Garnitur) ein ~ Spitzen a set of lace. — 3. (Anrücken) approach; im ~e sein to draw near, to approach, v. Sachen: to be in preparation or on the carpet, v. Gewitter: to be brewing or gathering; F es ist et. im ~e there's s. th. in the wind or on the card. — 4. (Eintritt) going into service. — 5. Schachspiel: (erster Zug) opening (or first) move.

an-züglich (ˢᴸ~) a. ⊕ (auf et. (b.s.) anspielend) suggestive, pointed, poignant, offensive, sarcastic, cutting; ♀ w. to become personal; ♀ᵉ Redensart insinuation, personal (or pointed) remark; ♀ᵉʳ Scherz cutting joke.

⚛ scientific; ✿ botanical; ♀ geography; ⊕ machinery; ⚒ mining; ⚔ military; ⚓ marine; ⊛ commercial; ✉ postal; 🚂 railway.

[Anzüglichkeit] — 76 — [apothekern]

An-züglichkeit(⸗⸗⸗) f ⓺ suggestiveness, offensiveness; personality; pointedness; auch = anzügliche (f. b.) Redensart.
An-zugs-kosten (⸗⸗ ...) pl. ⓺ expenses: a) for dress, b) for removal; =stoff m material for (whole) suits, ⓺ suiting; =tag m day of entering service.
an-zünden (⸗⸗) [nhd.] I v/a. ⓺** ein Licht 2c.: to light; ist das Gas angezündet? is the gas alight?; (anstecken) to kindle, to set alight or ablaze, mit e-m Streichholz: to apply a match to; (in Brand stecken) to set on fire, to ignite; wieder ⸗ to rekindle; sich (dat.) eine Zigarette ⸗ to light (up) one's cigarette. — II ~ n ⓶ = Anzündung.
An-zünder (⸗⸗) m ⓶ 1. (auch ~in f ⓺) lamplighter. — 2. (Stange mit Spiritusflamme zum Gasanzünden) lamplighter's rod; f. a. Feuer⸗. [alight; ignition.]
An-zündung (⸗⸗) f ⓺ lighting; setting]
an-zupfen ~ (⸗⸗) v/a. ⓺** einen ⸗ to pluck (or pull) a p. (by the sleeve).
an-zwängen (⸗⸗) v/a. ⓺** to force on, to squeeze (or press) on tightly.
an-zwecken ⓺ (⸗⸗) v/a. ⓺** to fasten with hobnails; to nail (or tack) on.
an-zweifeln (⸗⸗) v/a. ⓶a** et. ⸗ to doubt a th., to have (one's) doubts about a th., (bestreiten) to contest a th. — II ~ n ⓶ u. **An-zweif(e)lung** f ⓺ doubting a th.; contesting a th.
an-zwinkern (⸗⸗) v/a. ⓶a** (zwinkernd anblicken) to blink (or wink) at. [to or on.]
an-zwirnen ⓺ (⸗⸗) v/a. ⓺** to twist]
a. o. abbr. = außerordentlicher (Prof. 2c.).
Aol (⸗) npr/m. ⓺α. poet. = Aolus.
Aoli-a ⓺ (⸗(⸗)⸗) [grch.] npr/n. ⓺α. Æolia, Æolis.
Aoli-er (⸗⸗(⸗)⸗) m ⓶, ~in f ⓺ Æolian.
Aolipile ⓺ (⸗⸗⸗⸗) [grch.-lt.] f ⓺ phys. (Lötrohrlampe) æolipile, æolipyle.
äolisch (⸗⸗)[grch.] a. ⓺ Æolian, Æolic; der (altgriechischer) Dialekt, ~(e) n ⓺ Æolic.
Aols-harfe ♪ (⸗⸗ ...) f ⓶ (Windharfe) Æolian harp or lyre.
Aolus (⸗⸗) [lt., *grch.] npr/m. ⓺γ., myth. (Gott der Winde) Æolus.
Aon (⸗⸗) [grch.] m ⓶ (Weltalter), bsd. pl. ~en (⸗⸗) æon; Aen-lang a. ⓺ lasting for ages, never ending, eternal.
Aorist ⓺ (⸗⸗) [grch.] m ⓶b. gram. aorist.
Aorta ⓺ (⸗⸗) [grch.] f ⓺ anat. (große Pulsader) aorta; dazu gehörig: aortic.
Aorten-entzündung (⸗⸗⸗ ...) f ⓶ path. ⓺ aortitis; =kammer f, anat. (untere Herzkammer) ventricle of the heart.
a. p. abbr. = a'nni praete'riti [lt. vergangenen Jahres] (of or in) the past (or preceding, previous) year.
apagogisch ⓺ (⸗⸗⸗⸗) [grch.] a. ⓺ apagogical; Aer Beweis (redu'ctio ad absu'rdum) apagogical (or indirect) proof.
Apanage (⸗⸗⸗) [fr.] f ⓺ (fürstliches Einkommen) civil list; royal grant.
apanagieren (⸗⸗⸗⸗) v/a. ⓺ e-e fürstliche Person ⸗ to make a (royal) grant to ..., to settle a civil list upon ...
apart (⸗⸗) [nhd. 17. sæ., *fr.] I a. ⓺ singular, odd; sie hat ein Aes Gesicht her face is out of the common, she has interesting (or uncommon) features; sie hat et. ~es (an sich) she has something out of the common — II adv. apart.

Aparte (⸗⸗⸗) [lt. a parte beiseite] n ⓺ thea. (et. beiseite Gesprochenes) an aside.
Apathie (⸗⸗⸗) [grch.] f ⓺ (Stumpfsinn) apathy; **apathisch** (⸗⸗) a. ⓺ apathetic.
Apatit ⓺ (⸗⸗⸗) [grch.] m ⓶c. min. (phosphorsaurer Kalt) apatite, phosphorite.
Apatsche(n pl.) (⸗⸗⸗) npr/m. ⓺ (Indianerstamm) Apache(s).
Apennin(en pl.) ⓺ (⸗⸗⸗)[flt. pen Fels] npr. m ⓶d. (ital. Gebirgskette) Apennines pl.
Apetale(n pl.) ⓺ (⸗⸗⸗) [grch. blumenblattlose] f ⓺ (Kronenlose) apetalous plant(s).
Apfel (⸗⸗) [ahd.] m ⓶ apple; Kochkunst: in Teig gebackener ~ apple turnover; fig. in den sauren ~ beißen (müssen) to (have to) swallow a bitter pill, to make the best of a bad bargain, to make a virtue of necessity; es konnte kein ~ zur Erde fallen (so groß war das Gedränge) one might have walked over their heads; Sprichw. der ~ fällt nicht weit vom Stamm like father, like son; he's a chip of the old block; ~ der Zwietracht apple of discord.
apfel-artig ⓺ (⸗⸗ ...) a. ⓺ ⓺ pomaceous; =äther ⓺ m ⓶ chm. malic ether; =auflauf m apple-puff; =baum ⓺ m apple-tree (Pirus malus); =biß m Adams ~ Adam's bite of the apple; =blech n apple-roaster; =blüte f apple-blossom; ⓺ braun a. dapple-bay.
Apfel-brater (⸗⸗ ...) m ⓺ fig. (Weichling) effeminate man, coddle, molly(coddle).
Apfel=brecher ⓺ (⸗⸗ ...) m ⓶ (Werkzeug) apple-crook; =brei m apple-sauce.
Apfelchen (⸗⸗⸗) n ⓶ dim. v. Apfel.
Apfel=dorn ⓺ (⸗⸗ ...) m ⓶ crab-tree; =ernte f apple(-)harvest; =falbe(r) m dapple light-bay horse; ⓺ förmig a. ⓺ apple-shaped; =frau f apple-woman; =gehäuse n apple-core; ⓺ grau a. dapple-grey; =grieß m = gehäuse; ⓺ grün a. ⓺ apple-green; =kammer f apple-loft; =kloß m apple(-)dumpling or (-)pudding; =krapfen m apple(-)fritter; =kuchen m apple(-)tart; =most m new cider; =mus n apple(-)sauce; =pastete f apple(-)pie; =quitte ⓺ f apple- (or English) quince (Cydo'nia vulga'ris, var. malifo'rmis); =röster m = pfanne; ⓺ sauer a.: =säure f, chm. malic, sorbic; ⓺ saures Salz malate, sorbate; =säure f, chm. malic (or sorbic) acid; =schimmel m dapple-grey horse; =schnitte f, =schnitz m apple(-)ring, dried apple(-)chip (meist im pl.).
Apfelsine ⓺ norddt. (⸗⸗⸗)[ndl. Apfel aus Sina † = China] f ⓺ (China- or sweet) orange.
Apfelsinen=baum ⓺ (⸗⸗⸗ ...) m ⓶ orange-tree (Citrus Aura'ntium, var. sine'nsis); =kern m orange-pip; =schale f orange-peel.
Apfel=stecher (⸗⸗ ...) m ⓶ apple-corer; =stiel m stalk of an apple; =torte f = =kuchen; ⓺ tragend a. ⓺ ⓺ pomiferous; **Apfel=trank** (ahd.), **Apfelei**, **Apfel=wein** m cider; **Apfel=presse** f cider-press.
Aphärese ⓺ (⸗i⸗⸗) ⓺, **Aphäresis** (⸗f⸗⸗) ⓺ [grch.] f. surg. (Abnahme eines Gliedes und gram. Abfall des Anlautes) aphæresis.
Aphelium ⓺ (⸗f(⸗)⸗) [lt., *grch.] n ⓶ ⓺ ast. (Sonnenferne e-s Planeten) aphelion.
Aphorismus ⓺ (⸗f⸗⸗⸗) [grch.] m ⓶ (Gedankensplitter, Denkspruch) aphorism.
aphoristisch (⸗⸗⸗⸗) a. ⓺ (u. adv.) (abgerissen, hingeworfen) aphoristic(ally).

Aphrit ⓺ (⸗f⸗) [grch.] m ⓶c. min. (Schaumkalt) aphrite.
Aphrodite (⸗f⸗⸗⸗) [grch.; *Astarte] npr f. ⓺ ⓺β. myth. (Göttin der sinnlichen Liebe) Aphrodite. [(schwamm) aphthæ.]
Aphthen ⓺ (⸗ft⸗) [grch.] pl. path. (Mund-)
aplanatisch ⓺ (⸗⸗⸗⸗) [grch.] a. ⓺ opt. (ohne sphärische Abweichung) aplanatic.
Aplom ⓺ (⸗⸗) [grch.] m ⓶c. min. aplome.
apodiktisch (⸗⸗⸗⸗) [grch.] a. ⓺ (u. adv.) (unumstößlich) apodictic(ally).
Apodosis ⓺ (⸗⸗⸗⸗) [grch.] f, inv. (das aus e-m Bedingungssatz Folgende) apodosis.
Apogäum ⓺ (⸗⸗⸗⸗) [lt., *grch.] n ⓶ (größte Erdferne des Mondes) apogee.
Apokalypse ⓺ (⸗⸗⸗⸗⸗) [grch.] f ⓺ bibl. (Offenbarung des Johannes) Apocalypse.
apokalyptisch (~) a. ⓺ apocalyptic(al).
Apokope ⓺ (⸗⸗⸗⸗) [grch.] f ⓺ (Wortkürzung am Ende) apocope.
Apokryph ⓺ (⸗⸗⸗f) [grch.] n ⓶, mst pl. ~en bibl. (Geheimschriften) (the) Apocrypha pl.
apokryph(isch) ⸗⸗⸗f(⸗) a. ⓺ apocryphal.
Apoll (⸗⸗), ~o(n) (⸗⸗) npr/m. ⓺α. myth. (Gott der Künste 2c.) Apollo.
apollinisch (⸗⸗⸗⸗) a. ⓺ Apolline, Apollinic. [apologue.]
Apolog ⓺ (⸗⸗⸗) [grch.] m ⓶ (Lehrfabel)
Apologet ⓺ (⸗⸗⸗⸗) m ⓶ (Verteidiger) apologist; ~ik (⸗⸗⸗⸗) f ⓺ apologetics; =isch a. ⓺ apologetic(al). [apology.]
Apologie (⸗⸗⸗⸗) f ⓺ (Verteidigungsschrift)
apoplektisch (⸗⸗⸗⸗) [grch.] a. ⓺ path. apoplectic. [fluß) apoplexy.]
Apoplexie ⓺ (⸗⸗⸗⸗) [grch.] f ⓺ (Schlag-)
Aposepedin ⓺ (⸗⸗⸗⸗⸗) [grch.] n ⓶c. (ohne pl.) chm. aposepedin (= Leuci'n).
Apostasie (⸗⸗⸗⸗) [grch.] f ⓺ rel. Abfall (vom Glauben) apostasy. [apostate.]
Apostat(a) (⸗⸗⸗, ⸗⸗⸗⸗) [grch.] m ⓶ (⓺)
Apostel (⸗⸗⸗) [ahd.; * grch. Bote] m ⓶ 1. apostle, weitS. emissary. — 2. (Schweif des Papierdrachens) tail of a kite.
Apostel=amt (⸗⸗ ...) n ⓶ apostleship, apostolate; =geschichte f Acts of the Apostles; =häuschen n niche for a statue = Bilder-nische; =pferd n: auf dem ~e reiten (zu Fuß gehen) to ride on shanks' pony, to tramp it.
Apostel=schaft (⸗⸗⸗⸗) f ⓺, =tum (⸗⸗⸗) n ⓶, **Apostolat** (⸗⸗⸗⸗) n ⓶c. = Apostelamt.
apostolisch (⸗⸗⸗⸗) a. ⓺ apostolic(al); ~es Glaubensbekenntnis the Apostles' Creed. [apostrophe (').]
Apostroph (⸗⸗⸗f) ⓺ m ⓶c., gram.
apostrophieren (⸗⸗⸗⸗f⸗) v/a. ⓺ to apostrophize, to mark with an apostrophe.
Apotheke (⸗⸗⸗⸗) [mhd.; *grch. Niederlage] f ⓺ (Arzneiladen) chemist's (~ apothecary's) shop, im Hospital, für Arme: dispensary; in der ~ gebräuchlich officinal; in die ~ geh(e)n to go to the chemist's.
Apotheker (⸗⸗⸗) [mlt.] m ⓶, ⓺⓺ chemist (and druggist), geprüfter: pharmaceutical chemist, Am. u. schott.: apothecary.
Apotheker=buch ("...) n ⓶ pharmacopœia, dispensary; =gehilfe m chemist's assistant; =gewicht n apothecaries' weight; =kunst f pharmacy, pharmaceutics; =lehrling m chemist's apprentice.
apothekern F (⸗⸗⸗⸗) [grch.] v/n. (h.) ⓶a. 1. (Medizin nehmen) to take physic. — 2. (das Gewerbe als Apotheker ausüben) to be a chemist, to dispense medicines.

Zeichen (s. S. XVII): F familiär; P Volkssprache; ⸀ Gaunersprache; ~ selten; † alt (auch gestorben); * neu (auch geboren); ⁓ unrichtig;

[**Apothekerordnung**] — 77 — [**Ärarialvermögen**]

Apotheker=ordnung (⌣⌣ᴸ⌣...) f ㊷ dispensatory; **=rechnung** f chemist's account; fig. (hohe Rechnung) heavy (or doctor's) bill; **=waren** f/pl. oft: (pharmaceutical) drugs pl.; **=wissenschaft** f pharmacology, (lt.) materia medica.
Apotheose ⚗ (⌣⌣ᴸ⌣) [grch.] f ㊻ (Vergötterung) apotheosis, deification.
Appala(tsch)en ♀ (⌣⌣ᴸtisch) npr/m/pl. ㊸ a) (Gebirge) Appalachian Mountains, Alleghanies; b) (Indianer) Appalaches.
Apparat ⊕ (⌣ᴗᴸ) [lt.] m ㊷c. (Vorrichtung) apparatus, weitS. contrivance, appliance; (Fernsprecher) telephone; bleiben Sie am ~ stay at the instrument; gelehrter ~ (Stoff) material(s pl.) for a learned disquisition or treatise.
Apparat=tagebuch (ᴸ...) n ㊷ tel. tablet-check; **=tisch** m work-table.
Appartement (⌣⌣⌣mąˊ) [fr. Gemach] n ㊵ 1. chamber, room. — 2. [⌣̇⊥ fr.] (a. m) water-closet (W. C.).
Appell (⌣ᴸ) [fr.] m ㊶b. 1. ⚔ (roll-)call; hunt. der Hund hat ~ ... is well trained; ~ (Ruckruf) blasen to sound the recall. — 2. jur. = Appellation.
Appellant (⌣⌣ᴸ) [lt.] m ㊷. **~in** f ㊵ (Berufungskläger[in]) appellant; plaintiff in error.
Appellat ⚗ (⌣⌣ᴸ) [lt.] m ㊷, **~in** f ㊵ jur. (Berufungsbeklagte(r)) appellee; defendant in error. [(Berufung) appeal.]
Appellation ⚗ (⌣⌣=tsch(⌣)ᴸ) [lt.] f ㊻ jur.
appellativ ⚗ (⌣⌣⌣ᴸf) [lt.] a. ㊽, **~n** ㊷c., **~um** (⌣⌣ᴸmv) n ㊾ gram. appellative (noun). [pealable.]
appellierbar (⌣⌣ᴸ-) [lt.] a. ㊽ jur. ap-
appellieren (⌣⌣ᴸv) [lt.] v/n. (h.) ㊽ jur. (Berufung einlegen) to appeal (to a higher court), to take the matter to a higher court or tribunal; to move for a new trial; fig. an die Nachwelt ♀ to make an appeal to ... [ground.]
Appell=platz ⚔ (⌣ᴸ⌣) m ㊷ mustering
Appertinenz (⌣⌣⌣ᴸ) [lt.] f ㊻ (Zubehör) bsd. pl. ~en ob. ~ien㉚ appurtenances pl.
Appetit (⌣⌣ᴸ, a. ⊃⌣ᴸ) [fr.] m ㊷c. (Eßlust) appetite (auf ob. nach et. for s.th); fig. (Neigung) auch: longing for; ich bekam ~ I began to get hungry (F to feel peckish); e-m den ~ benehmen to take away (or to blunt the edge of) a p.'s appetite; ich habe keinen ~ I have no appetite, my appetite is failing me or gone; starken ~ haben, (ver)spüren to have a good (or a sound) appetite; das wird Ihnen ~ machen it will give you an (or sharpen your) appetite; den ~ reizend appetizing; Sprichw. der ~ kommt beim Essen, etwa: the more one has the more one wants.
Appetit=bissen (⌣⌣ᴸ...) m ㊷ appetizing morsel; **=brötchen** n piquant sandwich.
appetitlich (⌣⌣ᴸ⌣) a. ㊽ appetizing.
appetit=los (⌣⌣ᴸ...) a. ㊽ without an(y) appetite; **=losigkeit** f ㊷ want of appetite; **~machendes Mittel**, **=mittel** n appetizer, s. th. piquant.
Appisch (ᴸ⌣) [lt. (Via) A'ppia] a. ㊽: **~e Straße** Appian road.
applanieren (⌣⌣ᴸ⌣) [fr.] v/a. ㊹ (ebnen) to level (down).
applaudieren (⌣⌣ᴸ⌣) [lt.] v/n. (h.) u. v/a. ㊹ (beklatschen) to applaud; to cheer.

Applaus (⌣ᴸ) [lt.] m ㊷a. (Beifall) applause; das Publikum zum ~ hinreißen to bring down the house, to carry away the audience.
Applikatur ♪ (⌣⌣ᴸ) [lt.] f ㊻ fingering.
applizieren (⌣⌣ᴸ⌣) [lt.] v/a. ㊹ to apply; F e-m Ohrfeigen ♀ to box a p.'s ears.
Appoint ⊕ (a-peˊa) [fr.] m ㊶. 1. (Wechsel) per ~ trassieren to settle (the balance) by way of a draft. — 2. (Aktienteil) share certificate.
apport! (⌣ᴸ) [fr. bring] int. fetch!, go!
apportieren (⌣⌣ᴸv) [fr.] v/a. ㊹ bsd. hunt. to fetch and carry.
Apportier=hund (⌣⌣ᴸ⌣) m ㊷ hunt. retriever. [(Beifügung) apposition.]
Apposition ⚗ (⌣ᴸ-tsch(⌣)ᴸ) [lt.] f ㊻ gram.
appositionell a. (⌣ᴸ-tsch(⌣)ᴸ) a. ㊽ u. adv. as (or by way of) apposition.
Appreteur ⊕ (⌣-t∂ˊr) [fr.] m ㊷d. (Zurichter v. Tuch ꝛc.) dresser, finisher (of cloth).
appretieren (⌣⌣ᴸ⌣) [fr.] v/a. ㊹ (zurichten) to dress or finish (cloth, &c.).
Appretur ⊕ (⌣⌣ᴸ) [fr.] f ㊻ (Zurichtung v. Tuch ꝛc.) dressing, finish; (Satinieren) glazing; **~papier** n ㊷ pressed paper.
Approbation ⚗ (⌣⌣=tsch(⌣)ᴸ) [lt.] f ㊻ (Billigung) approbation.
approbieren (⌣⌣ᴸ⌣) [lt.] v/a. ㊹ to approve; approbierte Klinge proof-blade.
Approche ⚔ (⌣ᴸsch) [fr.] ㊹ frt., meist pl. **~n** approaches pl., parallels pl.
approximativ ⚗ (⌣⌣⌣ᴸf) [lt.] a. ㊽ (annähernd) approximative.
Aprikose ♀ (⌣⌣ᴸ⌣) [ndl., fr., * ar.=lt.] f ㊻ 1. apricot. — 2. **~n=baum** ♀ (ᴸ...) m ㊷ apricot-tree (Prunus Armeni'aca); **~n=marmelade** f apricot-jam.
April (⌣ᴸ) [mhd., *lt.] m ㊷c. April; der erste ~ the first of April, auch: All Fools' Day; einen in den ~ schicken to make an April-fool of a p.; to send a p. on a fool's errand.
April=glück (⌣ᴸ...) n ㊷ short spell of good luck, F lucky chance; **=(s)narr** m April-fool; **=regen** m A.-shower; Sprichw. ~, Maisegen April - showers bring May-flowers; **=wetter** n April-weather.
apriorisch ⚗ (⌣-ᴸ⌣) [lt.] a. ㊽ phls. (voraussetzungslos) a priori. [merkt] by the by.]
apropos (⌣⌣poˊ) [fr.] adv. (nebenbei be-
Apside ♀ (⌣ᴸ⌣) f ㊸, **Apsis** (ᴸ⌣) f (sg. inv., pl. 'Apsi'den) [grch.] 1. ⊕ arch. (halbkreisförmige Nische) apse. — 2. ⚗ ast. (Kehrpunkt eines Planeten) apsis.
Apteren ♀ (ᴸ⌣⌣) [grch.] pl., zo. (flügellose Insekten) aptera, apterans pl.
aptieren (⌣ᴸ⌣) [lt.] v/a. ㊹ to adapt.
Apuli=en ♀ (⊃ᴸ(⌣)⌣) npr/n. ㉓α. (ital. Landschaft) Alt.: Apulia, jetzt: Puglia.
Apuli=er (⊃ᴸ(⌣)⌣) m ㊷, **~in** f ㊵, **apulisch** (⊃ᴸ⌣) a. ㊽ Apulian.
Apyrit ⚗ (⌣⌣ᴸ) [lt.] m ㊷c. 1. min. (roter Turmalin) rubellite. — 2. ⚔ smokeless powder (used in Sweden). [aqueduct.]
Aquädukt (⊃ᴸ⌣) [lt.] m ㊶b. (Wasserleitung)
Aquafort (⌣⌣ᴸ) [lt.] n ㊶ (o. pl.) (Kupferstich) aquafortis (engraving); etching; **~ist** m ㊷ (Radierer) aquafortist, etcher.
Aquamarin ⚗ (⌣⌣⌣ᴸ) [lt.] m ㊷c. min. (Art Beryll) aquamarine.
Aquarell (⌣⌣ᴸ) n ㊶b., auch: **~e** (⌣⌣ᴸ⌣) f ㊵ [it.] painting in water-colours.
Aquarell=farbe (ᴸ...) f ㊵ water-colour.

aquarellieren (⌣⌣⌣ᴸ⌣) [it.] v/a. u. v/n. (h.) ㊹ to paint in water-colours.
Aquarell=maler (⌣⌣ᴸ...) m ㊷ water-colour painter; **=malerei** f painting in water-colours; **=skizze** f water-colour sketch.
Aquarium ⚗ (⌣ᴸ(⌣)⌣) [lt.] n ㉓ (Behälter für Wassertiere) aquarium.
Aquatinta (⌣⌣ᴸ⌣) [it.] f ㊻ paint. (Art Kupferstich) aquatint(a).
Äquator ⚗ (⌣ᴸ⌣) [lt.] m ㊷ ast., ♀ (Mittellinie der Erdkugel ꝛc.) Equator; magnetischer ~, a. aclinic line; **Lial** (---(⌣)ᴸ) a. u. **~ial** n ㊷c. equatorial (telescope); sich Lial einstellen to set equatorially.
Aquavit (⌣⌣ᴸw⌣) [lt.] m ㊷c. (Likör) aquavitæ, spirits pl., alcohol(ic liquor).
Äquilibrist (⌣⌣⌣ᴸ) [lt.] m ㊷, **~in** f ㊵ equilibrist; (Seiltänzer) rope-dancer.
äquilibristisch (⌣⌣⌣ᴸ⌣) a. ㊽ equilibristic.
äquinoktial ⚗ (⌣⌣⌣=tsch(⌣)ᴸ) a. ㊽ (Tag- u. Nachtgleiche betreffend) equinoctial.
Äquinoktial=kreis (ᴸ...) m ㊷ equinoctial (line), equator; **=sturm** m equinoctial gale. [(Tag- u. Nachtgleiche) equinox.]
Äquinoktium ⚗ (⌣⌣ᴸ=tsch(⌣)⌣) [lt.] n ㉓ ast.
Aquitani=en ♀ (⌣⌣ᴸ(⌣)⌣) npr/n. ㉓α. (Südwesten Galliens) Aquitania, Aquitain(e).
äquivalent ⚗ (⌣-vw⌣ᴸ) [lt.] a. ㊽ u. **~n** ㊶b. equivalent; **~** a. ⚙ consideration.
Äquivalenz ⚗ (⌣-vw⌣ᴸ) [lt.] f ㊻ chm. (Gleichwertigkeit der Atome) equivalence.
Ar (ᴸ; Hom. Aar) [fr. are m; *lt. a'rea f] n (m) ㊷c.6. (abbr. a, Flächenmaß) are, fig. er hat weder ~ noch Halm he does not own an acre of land.
Ara ⚗ (ᴸ⌣) m ㊶ f. Ara'ra. [raum) era.]
Ära (ᴸ⌣); pl. Hom. Ähren) [lt.] f ㊹ (Zeit-
Araber (ᴸ⌣⌣) [Nomade] m ㊷ 1. ~, **~in** (⌣ᴸ⌣) f ㊵ Arab(ian). — 2. (Pferd) Arab (steed); (thoroughbred) Arabian horse.
Arabeske (⌣⌣ᴸ⌣) [fr.] f ㊸ (bsd. pl. ~n) arabesque (ornament), moresque (work).
Arabi=en ♀ (⌣ᴸ(⌣)⌣) npr/n. ㉓α. Südwesten Asiens: Arabia; das Glückliche ~ Arabia Felix, † ob. poet. Araby the Blest.
arabisch (⌣ᴸ⌣) a. ㊽ Arabian; die Le Sprache, das **~(e)** n ㊶ Arabic; Les Gummi gum arabic; **~er Meerbusen** m Arabian Gulf; Le Redeweise Arabism; Le Zahl, Ziffer arabic figure.
Arachniden ⚗ (⌣⌣ᴸ⌣) [grch.] pl., zo. (Spinnentiere) arachnids, arachnid(e)ans pl.
Aragoni=en ♀ (⌣⌣ᴸ(⌣)⌣) [Aragon, Fluß] npr/n. ㉓α. (span. Landschaft, ehm. Königreich) Aragon. [(⌣⌣ᴸ) a. ㊽ Aragonese.]
Aragoni=er (⌣.) m ㊷, **~in** f ㊵, **aragonisch**
Aragonit ⚗ (⌣⌣⌣ᴸ) [lt.] m ㊷c. (kohlensaurer Kalk) aragonite.
Aralia ♀ (-ᴸ(⌣)⌣) f ㊵ aralia; schaftblütige ~ sarsaparilla (Ara'lia nudicau'lis).
Aral=see ♀ (ᴸ⌣⌣) [kirgis. Inselsee] npr/m. ㉓ i. Westasien Sea of Aral, Aral Sea.
Aramäer (⌣⌣ᴸ⌣) m ㊷, **~in** f ㊵ **aramäisch** a. ㊽ (syro=chaldä'isch) Aramean, Aramaic.
Aräometer ⚗ (⌣⌣⌣ᴸ⌣) [grch.] n ㊷ phys. (hydrosta'tische Senkwage) aræometer; **Aräometrie** (⌣⌣⌣ᴸ) f ㊻ aræometry; **aräometrisch** (⌣⌣⌣ᴸ⌣) a. ㊽ aræometric(al).
Arar (⌣ᴸ) [lt.] n ㊷c. (Staatsschatz) (public) treasury, exchequer.
Ara(ra) ⚗ (⌣⌣, vᴸ⌣⌣) m ㊶ orn. ara.
Ärarial=schuld (--(⌣)ᴸ⌣...) f ㊷ national debt; **=vermögen** n public funds pl., state (or national) property.

[ärarisch] — 78 — [Arbeitsmarkt]

ärarisch (-⌣) *a.* ⊛ relating to the public treasury, ærarian, fiscal.
Ärarium (-⌣) [lt.] *n* ⊛ = Ärar.
Araukani-en ♀ (⌣-⌣(⌣)) [indian. Rebellen] *npr/n.* ⊛a. im Süden von Chile, Süd-am.: Araucania. [araucaria.]
Araukaria ♀ (⌣-⌣(⌣)) *f* ⊛,⊛ (Andentanne))
Arbeit (⌣-) [ahd.: slaw. *rabo'ta* Frondienst] *f* ⊛ **1.** (das Schaffen) work; ~ im (außern) Hause indoor (outdoor) work; ~ aufs Stück piecework, job(bing work); kopfbrechende: headwork; auferlegte: task, imposition; mühevolle: labour, toil; ~ bekommen to get (or find) employment; die ~ einstellen to stop (or throw up) work, auch: to (go on) strike; e-m ~ geben to give a p. employment, to engage a p.; gemeine, erniedrigende ~ verrichten to do drudging work, to drudge, to slave; **an die ~** geh(e)n, sich an die ~ machen to go (or set) to work; e-n an die ~ geh(e)n heißen to set a p. to work; **auf (die) ~** geh(e)n to go to one's daily labour; **bei der ~** sein to be at work; et. **in ~** nehmen to take a task (or job) in hand; et. **in ~** geben to give a th. out to be made; **in ~** sein oder steh(e)n: a) vom Arbeiter: to have work or employment, von Bedienten: to be in a place; b) von einer Sache: to be taken in hand; Ihr Rock ist in ~ ... is in hand; der Stuhl ist in ~ ... is being made, repaired; c) von e-r Maschine: to be going or working; **ohne ~** out of work, out of employment, without a job; **von s-r Hände ~** leben to live by manual labour or by the sweat of one's brow; Schüler **zur ~** anhalten, bei der ~ beaufsichtigen to keep ... to their work, to superintend ... in their studies. — **2.** (Erzeugnis der ~) performance; seine ~en in diesem Fache his efforts in this department; künstlerische ~ work of art; schriftliche ~ composition; häusliche, schriftliche ~en der Schüler: home tasks or home lessons *pl.*, zur Strafe: imposition; f. a. 6. — **3** (Anstrengung) fatigue, vgl. 1; *fig.* er hat seine ~ he has all his work cut out for him, he has his hands full; es hat uns viel ~ gemacht it has caused (or given) us a great deal of trouble. — **4.** (Art der Ausführung) workmanship; (Gestaltung) shape, make; deutsche ~ German make, goods (or things) *pl.* made in Germany, German-made goods *pl.* — **5.** (Gärung) fermentation; der Wein ist in ~ ... is fermenting or working. — **6** ⊛ bossierte, erhab(e)ne ~ embossed (or raised) work; eingelegte ~ inlaid work; getrieb(e)ne ~ chased work; mechanische ~ (Leistung) einer Kraft mechanical effect; gestickte ~ embroidery; ~ in Stein stonework. — **7.** Sprichw. ~ macht das Leben süß no sweet without sweat; nach getaner ~ ist gut ruhen after the work is done, repose is sweet; wie die ~, so der Lohn as the work, so the pay.
arbeiten (⌣-⌣) [ahd.] ⊛ **I** *v/n.* (h.) **1.** to (do) work; schwer ~ to labour (hard), to toil (and drudge); tüchtig ~ to do good work, to put one's shoulder to the wheel; **an et. ~** to work at a th.,

to be at work on a th., to be engaged in a th.; **aufs Stück ~** to do piecework or jobbing-work; **bei e-m** (a.: für e-n) ~ to work for a p., to be employed by a p. or in a p.'s employ; **bei e-m** lassen to employ (a tradesman, &c.) regularly; bei welchem Schneider lassen Sie ?? who is your tailor?; **fürs Brot, im Tagelohn ~** to work for daily wages; **gegen den Strom ~** to toil against the stream; e-m **in die Hand ~** to aid (or assist) a p.; ♠ ~ (Geschäfte machen) in ... to deal (F to do) in ...; vom Fürsten: **mit** dem Minister ~ to be closeted with ...; **wie ein Pferd ~** to work like a slave or, like a nigger; e-n schwer ~ lassen to work a p. hard, für geringen Lohn: to grind a p. down, to sweat a p.; Sprichw. wer nicht arbeitet, soll auch nicht essen no mill no meal. — **2.** von Sachen: ⊛ sein Geld ~ lassen to employ (or invest) ...; vom Holz: (sich ausdehnen und zf.-ziehen, sich werfen) to warp; von Maschinen: to work, go; die Lokomotive arbeitet mit vollem Dampfe has all its steam up; vom Wein, Bier: (gären) to ferment; vom Teige: (aufgehen) to rise; ⚓ das Schiff arbeitet ... is labouring; die See arbeitet ... is heavy or rough. — **II** *v/a.* **3.** to work, make; (formen) to shape, fashion; den Acker: to till; einen Aufsatz, ein Buch: to compose; aus dem groben ~ to do in the rough; to rough-hew. — **4.** auch *v/refl.* ein Pferd (a. sich) zuschanden, zu Tode ~ to tire (or fatigue, wear out, weary) a horse (o.s.); sich krank ~ to work o.s. ill. — **III sich ~** *v/refl.* **5.** f. 4. — **6.** (ans Ziel kommen) sich durch den Schnee ~ to work one's way through ...; sich aus e-r Lage (heraus-)~ to extricate o.s. from a position. — **7.** *v/impers.* es arbeitet sich schlecht, wenn // one works badly (or it is difficult to work, work comes hard) when //. — **IV** ~ *n* ⊛ **8.** work(ing), labour(ing); des Ackers: tillage. — **V** ⊛b *p.pr. u. a.* ⊛ **9.** working; die Oben Klassen the working classes; labouring men *pl.*
Arbeiter (⌣-⌣) [ahd.] *m* ⊛, **~in** ⊛ *f* **1.** worker, workman *m*, workwoman *f* (vgl. Arbeits-mann, -frau); geistiger: brainworker; eine gute ~in a hard-working woman, a good worker or workingwoman; Sprichw. jeder ~ ist seines Lohnes wert the labourer is worthy of his hire. — **2.** (Tagelöhner) (day-)labourer, *agr.* field-hand. — **3.** (Handarbeiter) operative, mechanic; (Handwerker) artisan; (Fabrik-arbeiter) factory-hand; (Hafen-arbeiter) docker; (Erdarbeiter) navvy; schwarze, gelbe ~ black, yellow labourers *pl.* or labour; in Geschäften, Fabriken 2c.: es fehlt uns an ~n we are short of hands, we are short-handed.
Arbeiter-abteilung ⚔ (⌣-⌣...) *f* ⊛ fatigue-party; **=ausstand** *m* (workmen's) strike; **=(bahn)zug** *m* workmen's train; **=bildungschule** *f* school for instruction of workmen; **=buch** *n* workman's book; **=bund** *m* working men's union, trade(-)union; **=frage** *f* labour question; **=führer** *m* labour leader; **=genossenschaft, =gesellschaft** *f*

working men's club or society; **=karte** *f* ticket for workmen; **=mangel** *m* lack of workmen, shortness of labour(ers) or hands; **=partei** *f* labour party; **=personal** *n* staff of workmen, hands *pl.*
Arbeiterschaft (⌣-⌣⌣) *f* ⊛ (o. *pl.*) workmen *pl.*, the working class(es *pl.*).
Arbeiter-schutz(gesetzgebung) *f* (*m* (⌣-⌣...) ⊛ (legislation for the) protection of the working classes; **=sperre** *f* lock-out (of workmen); **=stand** *m* (the) working class(es *pl.*); **=unruhen** *f/pl.* labour riots or troubles *pl.*; **=verband** *m*, **=verein** *m* = **=bund**; **=versicherung(sgesetz** *n*) *f* working men's insurance (law); **=vertreter** *m* representative (or delegate) of the working class(es), im engl. Unterhause: labour member; **=wohnungen** *f/pl.* artisans' dwellings *pl.*, lodgings for working men or workmen; **=zug** *m* = **=bahnzug**.
Arbeit-geber (⌣-...) *m* ⊛ employer (of labour), master; **los** *a.* ⊛ f. arbeits-...; **=müde** *a.* weary of work; **=nehmer** *m* employee, workman.
arbeitsam (⌣-⌣) [ahd.] *a.* ⊛ laborious, industrious, diligent, von Schülern: studious, F plodding. [(working) ant.]
Arbeits-ameise (⌣-...) *f* ⊛ neuter (or)
Arbeitsamkeit (⌣-⌣⌣) *f* ⊛ laboriousness, industry, diligence; studiousness, F plodding (f. arbeitsam).
Arbeits-amt (⌣-...) *n* ⊛ labour bureau; **=anstalt** *f* zur Zwangsarbeit house of correction; **=aufseher** *m* foreman; **=bank** *f* work(ing)-bench; **=beutel** *m* work(-ing)-bag, für Damen auch: reticule; **=biene** *f* working bee; **=buch** *n* (Wanderbuch) workman's pass(port); **=dienst** ⚔ *m* fatigue-duty; **=draht** *m*, *elect.* bei Straßenbahnen *m.* Oberleitung: overhead wire (for working electric [tram-]cars); **=einheit** *f* unit of work; **=einstellung** *f* turn-out (of workmen), strike; **=fähig** *a.* ⊛ able to work, able-bodied; **=feld** *n* field of activity, sphere of action; **=frau** *f* working woman; **=genoß** *m* fellow-workman; **=gerüst** *n* scaffolding; **=gewölbe** ⊕ *n* des Hochofens: working- (or temp-)arch; **=haus** *n* für Bettler: workhouse; (Strafanstalt) house of correction; **=kammer** *f*, *chm.* laboratory; **=kasten** *m*, **=kästchen** *n* tool-box, für Damen: work-box; **=kittel** *m* (workman's) blouse or frock; **=kleider** *n/pl.* working-clothes; **=kontakt** *m*, *tel.* transmission contact; **=korb** *m*, **=körbchen** *n* work-basket; **=kraft** *f*: a) working-power; b) ~kräfte *pl.* (Arbeiter) (body of) workmen, hands *pl.*; **=leistung** ⊕ *f* work performed or done; **=leute** (*pl.* zu mann; f. ds) workmen, working men or people *pl.*; **=loch** ⊕ *n* working-hole; am Dampfkessel *m.* man-hole; **=lohn** *m* wages *pl.*; **=los** *a.* out of work, without employment, F u. ⊛ out of a job; die ~losen the unemployed *pl.*; die Frage der ~losen oft: the unemployed question; **=losigkeit** *f* want of employment, unemployment; **=mann** *m* (*pl.* =leute; f. ds) workman, working man, labouring man, (unskilled) labourer; **=markt** *m* labour market;

Signs (see page XVII): F familiar; P vulgar; F flash; ⚡ rare; † obsolete (died); * new word (born); ++ incorrect; ♪ music;

[Arbeitsmaschine] — 79 — [ärgern]

=maschine ⚙ f operator; =ministerium n England: Labour Department of the Board of Trade; =nachweis m information respecting the labour market, labour intelligence, guide to employment; =nachweisanstalt f employment agency or bureau, labour bureau; =personal n men (or hands) pl. employed; =pferd n working horse; fig. hard-working fellow; =preis m price of labour; =raum, =saal m workroom; chm. laboratory (Schulzimmer) study, schoolroom; =scheu a. loth to work; =scheu f laziness; =schicht f shift (of hands); =schule f industrial school; =sperre f lock-out; =stätte f place where the work is done, für rauhere Arbeit: labour-yard, vgl. =raum; =strom m, tel. transmission (or working) current; =stube f e-s Gelehrten: study, F sanctum; e-s Geschäftsmannes ꝛc.: office; e-s Künstlers: studio; vgl. =raum; =stunde f working-hour, in Schulen: preparation; =stunden-buch n time-book; =tag m working-day; =tasche f = =beutel; =teilung f division of labour; =tisch m work-table; (Schreibtisch) (writing-)desk; =tür f, metall. working-door.
arbeit-suchend(ˆ-...) a. ⚙ seeking work.
arbeits-unfähig (⁵ˡ...) a. ⚙ unfit for work; disabled; =**unfähigkeit** f ⚙ incapacity for work(ing); =**vertrag** m jur. working (or labour) contract, agreement about (the) work to be performed; =**voll** a. toilsome, laborious; =**zeit** f working-time, der Schüler: hours pl. of study; =**zelle** f im Gefängnis: labour-cell; =**zeug** n: a) working costume; b) (Werkzeug) tools pl.; =**zimmer** n = =stube.
arbeit-voll, =**zeit** (ˆ-...) s. Arbeits...
Arbitrage ⚙ (ˆˡQˇ) [fr.] f ⚙: ~, ~**rechnung** f ⚙ arbitration of exchange.
arbiträr (ˆˆˡ) [fr.] a. ⚙ (nach Gutdünken) arbitrary.   [arbitration.]
arbitrieren (ˆˆˡˇ) v/a. ⚙ to settle by
Arbuse ⚘ (ˆˡˇ) [fr., *It.] f ⚙ = Wassermelone u. Erdbeer-baum.
Archa-ismus ⚙ (ˇ-ˇˡˇ) [grch.] m ²⁷ (Altertümlichkeit) archaism.   [antiquated.]
archa-(ist)isch ⚙ (ˇˡˇ, ˇ-ˇˡˇ) a. ⚙ archaic,
Archäolog ⚙ (ˇˇˡ) [grch.] m ⚙, ~**e** ⚙ (Altertumsforscher) archæologist; =**ie** f ⚙ archæology; 2**isch** ⚙ archæological(al).
Arche (ˡˇ) [ahd., *It. ä´rcā] f ⚙ 1. ark; bibl. (Bundes-Lade) Ark of the Covenant; ~Noah(s) (Noä) Noah's ark (a. Spielzeug). — 2. (Kasten zum Fischfange) (eel-)trunk. — 3. ⚙ Brückenbau: coffer-dam; (Windkasten an Orgeln) windchest. [schnecke.]
Archen-muschel (ˣˇ...) f ⚙ zo. = Kahn-]
Archibald † (ˡˇˇ) [engl.] npr/m. ⚙ α. (Vn.) Archibald, dim. Archie, Archy.
Archidiakonat (ˇˇˇˡ) n ⚙ c. eccl. archdeaconry.   [archdeacon.]
Archidiakonus (ˇˇˡˇˇ) [grch.] m ⚙ eccl.]
archilochisch ⚙ (ˇˇˡˇ) [grch.] a. ⚙ pros. Der Vers Archilochian (metre).
Archimandrit (ˇˇˡˡ) [grch.] m ⚙ eccl. (Oberabt) archimandrite.
Archi(m)bald (ˡˇˇ) = Archibald.
archimedisch (ˇˇˡˇ) [Archime'des, grch. Mathematiker, 287-212 v. Chr.] a. ⚙ Archimedean; ⚙ mech. Die Schraube Archimedean screw, ↓ screw-propeller.

Archipel (ˇˇˡ) [grch.] m ⚙ e. (Inselmeer) archipelago.
Architekt (ˇˇˡ) [grch.] m ⚙ (Baumeister) architect; ~**onik** (ˇˇˇˡˇ) f ⚙ (Bauwissenschaft) architectonics; 2(**on**)**isch** (ˇˇˇ(ˡ)ˇ) a. ⚙ architectonic, architectural; ~**ur** (ˇˇˇˡ) [It.] f ⚙ architecture.
Architrav (ˇˇˡf) [it., *grch.=It.] m ⚙ c., ⚙ arch. (Balken über den Säulen) architrave.
Archiv (ˇˡf) [It., *grch.] n ⚙ c. (Urkundensammlung) archives pl., record-office, roll-chamber, public records pl.; 2**alisch** (ˇˇmˡˇ) [It.] a. ⚙ archival (= urkundlich); ~**ar** (ˇˇmˡ) [It.] m ⚙ c. recorder; auch = Archivdirektor.
Archiv-beamte(r) (ˇˇˡˇ...f...) m ⚙ Recorder; =**direktor** m Master of the Rolls; =**gebäude** n, =**saal** m record-office, muniment-room; =**stück** n authentic document or deed.
Archont (ˇˇˡ) [grch.] m ⚙ archon; ~**at** (ˇˇˇˡ) [grch.] n ⚙ c. archonship.
Ardennen ⚘ (ˇˇˡˇ) [flt. großer Wald] npr/f/pl., inv., **Ardenner-wald** (ˇˇˇˇˡ) npr/m. ⚙ (Forest of) Ardennes pl.
Areal (ˇˇˡ) [It.] n ⚙ c. (Flächeninhalt) area.
Areka-nuß⚘ (ˇˡˇˇ...) [malabar.] f ⚙ Indian (or betel-) nut; =**palme** f areca.
Aremorica ⚘ (ˇ-ˇˡˇ) f. Armorika.
Arena (ˇˡˇ) [It. Sand(platz)] f ⚙ im Amphitheater: arena; für Stiergefechte: bull-ring; im Zirkus: circle, ring, F the tan.
Arendator ꝛc. f. Arrendator ꝛc.
Areopag (ˇ-ˇˇˡ) m ⚙ c. [grch.] grch. Gesch.: (hoher Gerichtshof in Athen) Areopagus; ~**itikus** (ˇ-ˇˇˇˡˇˇ) m ⚙ (o. pl.) (Rede des Iso'krates) Areopagitic (oration).
Ares (ˡˇ) [grch.] npr/m. ⚙ γ. myth. (Kriegsgott) Ares, mehr gbr. lt. Mars.
arg (ˡ) [ahd.] **I** a. ⚙ 1. bad, evil (comp. ärger worse, sup. ärgst worst): ein 2er, der ärgste Schelm, Fuchs an arrant knave, the veriest rogue; jur. ärgere Hand (unebenbürtiger Ehegatte) husband of inferior birth or rank. — 2. (übermäßig stark) very great, tremendous, awful; 2es Versehen gross mistake, 2e Krankheit severe (or serious) illness; 2e Verwüstung sad havoc; das ist denn doch (gar) zu 2! that's too bad or worse than ever! that beats everything! — 3. = ärgerlich. — 4. (höchst leichtfertig) frivolous. — **II** adv. 5. badly, ill; mach's nicht (auch: treib's nicht) zu 2! be as gentle as you can!, F draw it mild!; Sie machen es zu 2! you are going too far, F you come it too strong!; er macht (auch: treibt) es doch gar zu 2! his goings-on are outrageous or beyond endurance!; ärger als je worse than ever; immer ärger worse and worse; es wird immer ärger things are going from bad to worse; sie schrie noch ärger, am ärgsten she screamed even louder, louder than any; sie quälen ihn gar zu 2 they are tormenting him most cruelly; es wird nicht so 2 sein it won't be as bad as we (they, &c.) think, it will come all right in the end; so 2 ist es mit seinem Wissen auch nicht his knowledge is not so (very) wonderful or extraordinary; 2 nach (ob. hinter) et. her sein to be mad after (F keen upon) a th.;

was zu 2 ist, ist zu 2 that's too much of a joke or a good thing; ärger konnte es nicht kommen it (or things) couldn't have been (or turned out) worse. — **III** ~ n ⚙, ⚙b. (o. pl.) 6. das ~**e** meiden to shun evil; an nichts ~**es** denken to mean no harm, to suspect nothing (bad); ich sehe nichts ~**es** dabei I don't see anything bad (or much harm) in it; die Welt liegt im ~**en** the whole world lieth in wickedness; wenn es zum Ärgsten kommt if the worst comes to the worst; die Sache liegt noch im ~**en** the matter is still in a bad way or in (great) jeopardy; (o. pl.) evil, wickedness; ohne Arg without malice, guileless, harmless; ohne Arg sein to bear no malice; kein Arg haben to act with good faith. — **IV** m 7. der ~**e** (bibl. der 2e, böse Feind) the Evil one (= devil).
Argand (är-ga´) (Physiker aus Genf): ~(**gas**)**brenner** m ⚙ Argand's (gas-)burner; 2(**i**)**sch** (ˇˇ, ˇˇˡ) a. ⚙: ⚙ 2(**i**)**sche Lampe** (mit zyli'ndrischem Docht) Argand lamp.
Argei-er (ˇˇˡˇ) [grch.] npr/m. ⚙, **argei-isch** a. ⚙ grch. Alt.: Argive, Greek.
Argentan ⚙ (ˇˇˡ) [It.] n ⚙ c. metall. (Neusilber) German silver, white copper.
Argentin⚘ (ˇˇˡ) n ⚙ c. (o. pl.) metall. (versilbertes Weißmetall) argentine [gentina.
Argentini-en ⚘ (ˇˇˡ(ˇ)ˇ) npr/n. ⚙. Ar-]
argentinisch (ˇˇˡˇ) a. ⚙ Südamerika: ~**e** Republik Argentine Republic; die ~**en** Staaten the Argentines pl.
ärger¹ (ˡˇ) comp. v. arg (s. ds., bsb. 1 u. 5).
Ärger² (ˡˇ) [nhd. (ubb.): arg] m ⚙ (Verdruß) annoyance, vexation; (Zorn) anger, wrath; (Groll) spite; aus ~ out of spite; ihm zum ~ to vex (or spite) him; zu seinem großen ~ to his great mortification; seinen ~ an e-m auslassen to vent one's ill-humour on a p.; ich habe schon viel ~ gehabt I have had many annoyances or much to put up with; er macht mir viel ~ he gives me a good deal of trouble.
ärgerlich (ˡˇˇ) a. ⚙ 1. (zum Ärger geneigt) easily provoked, irritable, irascible. — 2. (Ärger empfindend) angry (with a p., about a th.), vexed at, nettled at; e-n 2 machen to vex a p.; 2 sein to be cross (or displeased) with; 2 werden to grow angry, to lose one's temper. — 3. (Ärger erregend) e-m 2 vexatious, aggravating, annoying, provoking; 2e Sache nuisance, troublesome (or tiresome) business; das ist sehr 2 it's most provoking. — 4. (Ärgernis erregend) scandalous, giving offence, shocking.
Ärgerlichkeit (ˡˇˇˇ) f ⚙ (vgl. ärgerlich) 1. irritability, irascibility, &c. — 2. = Ärger. — 3. ~**en** pl. vexatious affairs, annoyances, troubles pl.
ärgern (ˡˇ) [ahd.] ⚙ **I** v/a. 1. e-n 2 to make a p. angry or vexed; to annoy, vex, mortify, aggravate, provoke, nettle a p.; to upset a p.'s temper, to put a p. out; e-n (halb)tot 2, e-m die Schwindsucht an den Hals 2 to vex a p. to death; es kann e-n furchtbar (F schändlich) 2, wenn man sieht // it's most galling (or aggravating) to see //. — 2. (bsb. bibl.) to scandalize; ärgert dich

⚙ scientific; ⚘ botanical; ⚘ geography; ⚙ machinery; ⚒ mining; ⚔ military; ↓ marine; ⚙ commercial; ✉ postal; 🚂 railway.

[Ärgernis] — 80 — [Armengeld]

dein rechtes Auge if thy right eye offend thee. — II v/refl. 3. sich 2 (über) to feel angry or vexed (at a th., with a p.); ärgere dich nicht zu sehr! don't fret (or worry) too much!; sich über et. tot 2 to worry o.s. to death about a th.

Ärgernis (ˊˇˇ) [nhd.] n ⑰ (\ f ⑱) 1. (= Anstoß 4, f. ds) scandal, offence; ein öffentliches ~ geben to raise a great scandal. — 2. (f. Ärger) annoyance, vexation, spite, &c.

arg=gesinnt (ˊ...) a. ⑥⑥ malicious.

Argheit (ˊˇ) f ⑥⑥ wickedness, malice.

arg=herzig (ˊˇ) a. ⑥⑥ = 2gesinnt.

Argiver (ˇˊˇˇ) [lt.] m ㉒, **argivisch** (ˇˊˇˇ) a. ⑥⑥ = Argeier, argeiisch.

Arg=list (ˊˇ) [ahd.] f ⑥⑥ craft(iness), artfulness, cunning(ness).

arg=listig (ˊˇˇ) [mhd.] a. ⑥⑥ crafty, cunning; jur. 2e († doloſe) Täuschung malicious fraud; fraudulent device or practice; false pretence; **~feit** f ⑥⑥ =Arglist.

arg=los (ˊˇ) [nhd.] a. ⑥⑥ (ohne Falsch) guileless; (unschuldig) innocent, simple; (harmlos) harmless, inoffensive, unsophisticated; (nichts ahnend) unsuspecting.

Arg=losigkeit (ˊˇˇ~) f ⑥⑥ guilelessness, harmlessness, inoffensiveness.

argolisch (ˇˊˇ) a. ⑥⑥ grch. Alt.: Argolic.

Argon (ˊˇ) [grch.] n ㊿ (o. pl.) chm. (1895 in der Luft entdecktes seltenes Gas) argon.

Argonaut (ˇˇˊ) [grch. Argoschiffer] m ㉒ 1. myth. Argonaut. — 2. ↗ zo. paper-nautilus. [ition of the Argonauts.]

Argonauten=zug (ˇˇˇˇ...) m ㉒ exped-

Argonnen ♀ (ˇˊˇ) npr/f/pl. inv., **Argonner=wald** (ˇˊˇ) npr/m. ㉒ (o. pl.) am linken Maas=ufer: Argonne Forest.

Argot ♀ (ˊgo) [fr. (corr. aus Arabie)] n ⑬ (Gaunersprache) cant, flash (speech), thieves' slang or jargon.

Ärgste (ˊˇ) n ⑰ f. arg III.

Argument (ˇˇˊ) [lt.] n ⑩b. (Beweisgrund) argument; **~ation** (ˇˇˇˇ~tsˇˊ) f ㊻ argumentation; 2ieren (ˇˇˊˇ) v/n. (h.) ⑬ to argue. [m, zo. Argus.]

Argus (ˊˇ) [grch.] npr/m. ⑬ γ. myth. u.]

Argus=auge (ˊ...) n ㉒: ~n haben to be argus-eyed; **2äugig** a. ⑥⑥ (wachsam) argus-eyed, vigilant; **=fasan** m argus-pheasant (Argus giganteˊus).

Arg=wille (ˊ...) m ㉒ ill-will, malevolence; **2willig** a. ⑥⑥ malevolent; evil-minded; **=willigkeit** f = =wille.

Arg=wohn (ˊˇ) [nhd. aus arg u. Wahn] m ⑩d. suspicion, mistrust; ~ hegen gegen e-n to harbour (or have) a suspicion against a p., to be suspicious of a p., to suspect a p.; j=s erregen to raise a p.'s suspicion; ~ fassen, schöpfen to grow suspicious of; frei von ~, 2=los free from suspicion, unsuspecting; voll ~, 2=voll = argwöhnisch.

arg=wöhnen (ˊˇ~)[ahd.]v/n.(h.)u.v/a.⑬*ˣ*ˣ to suspect, to have one's suspicions; et. 2 to have an inkling of a th.

arg=wöhnisch (ˊ~)a.⑥⑥ suspicious or apprehensive of; 2es Wesen suspiciousness.

a. Rh. abbr. = am Rhein on (the) Rhine.

Ariadne (ˇˇˊˇ) npr/f. ㉒β. myth. (Geliebte des Theseus) Ariadne; **~=faden** m ㊷ (der zur Rettung führt) Ariadne's clue.

Arianer (ˇˊˇˇ) [Ariˊus, Sektierer um 325] m㉒, **~in** f㊺, **arianisch** a. ⑥⑥ eccl. Arian.

Arianismus (ˇˇˊˇ) m ㉗ Arianism.

Ari=e ♀ (ˊˇˇ) [it.] f ㊺ air, bisw. a. (it.) aria; (Melodie) tune; (Lied) song, ditty; kleine ~, **Ari=ette** (-ˇˇˇ) f ㊺ ariette.

Ari=er (ˊˇˇ) m ㉒ (Indo=germane) Aryan.

Arimathia ♀ (ˇˇˊˇ) npr/n. ㉚α. (bibl. Ort auf dem Berg Ephraim) Arimathæa.

arisch (ˊˇ) a. ⑥⑥ (indo=germanisch) Aryan.

Aristarch (ˇˇˊ) npr. u. s/m. ⑩b. u. ㉒ (strenger grch. Kriˊtiker) Aristarch(us).

Aristokrat (ˇˇˇˊ) [grch.] m ㊷ aristocrat; die ~en the aristocracy, F the upper ten; ~**ie** (ˇˇˇˇˊ) f ㊸ aristocracy, F the (upper) classes; **2isch**(ˇˇˊˇ)a.⑥⑥ aristocratic; die 2ische Welt high life, the upper ten, society (people), F the fine folk(s). [f/pl. ㊺ aristolochiaceæ.]

Aristolochiazeen ♀(ˇˇˇˇˇˇ)[grch.]

aristophanisch (ˇˇˇˊˇ)[grch.D.Aristophanes 5.sæ.v.Chr.] a. ⑥⑥ of (or like) Aristophanes, Aristophanic; ~**e Komödie**, Satire Aristophanic comedy, satire.

Aristoteles (ˇˇˊˇˇ) npr/m. ⑯γ. (grch. Philosoph,384-322 v.Chr.)Aristotle, ...eles; Jünger m des ~, **Aristoteliker** (ˇˇˇˊˇˇ) m ㉒ Aristotelian; **aristoteˊlische Schule** Aristotelian School.

Arithmetik (ˇˇˊˇ. u. ˇˇˊˇ) [grch.] f ㊺ (Rechenkunst) arithmetic.

arithmetisch (ˇˇˊˇˇ) [grch.] a. ⑥⑥ arithmetical; 2e Reihe ar. progression; 2e Zeichen typ. ar. signs pl.

Arkade (ˇˊˇ) [fr.] f ㊺ 1. arch. (Bogengang) arcade; mit e-r ~ versehen arcadian. — 2. ⊕ Weberei: neck-twine.

Arkadi=en ♀ (ˇˊˇ(ˇ)ˇ) npr/n. ㉓α. grch. Geogr.: (peloponnesisches Hochland) Arcadia.

Arkadi=er (ˇˊˇ(ˇ)ˇ) m ㉒, **~in** f ㊺, **arkadisch** (ˇˊˇˇ) a. ⑥⑥ (a. poet. ländlich einfach) Arcadian. [Arkansas.]

Arkansas ♀ (ˊˇˇˇ) [indian.] n, inv.]

Arkanum ☿ (ˇˊˇˇ) [lt.] n ㊾: a) (Geheim-mittel) nostrum; b) weitS. (Geheimnis) secret. [büchse] f ㊺ arquebuse.]

Arkebuse ☿ (ˇˇˊˇ) [fr., it., *holl. Hakenbüchse]

arktisch ♀ (ˊˇ) [grch.] a. ⑥⑥ (im nördlichen Polarkreise) arctic. [[ahd.] = Elsbeere.]

Arles=baum ♀ (ˊˇ...) m ㉒, **=beere** f]

Arm¹ (ˊ) [ahd.] m ⑩b. 1. meist: arm (a. fig. u. ⊕); der rechte ~ the right arm, ⚔ the sword-arm; ⚔ Gewehr in ~! support arms!; ~ in ~ gehen to go arm in arm; mit gekreuzten ~en with folded arms; in die ~e schließen to clasp in one's arms, to hug, to embrace. — 2. fig. die ~e (Ellbogen) frei haben to have elbow-room; e-m unter die ~e greifen (beistehen) to give a p. a lift; sich aus j=s ~en reißen to tear o. s. away from a p.; sich e-m in die ~e werfen to cast o.s. upon the mercy of a p.; der weltliche ~ the secular arm, temporal power. — 3. ~ eines Flusses tributary, branch; e=s Leuchters: branch; e-r Gabeldeichsel: shaft; e=s Schiebkarrens: handle; der Segelstange: yard-arm; e-r Wage: cross-bar; einer Schnellwage: tail; des Weiners: limb, finger; des Zifferblattes e=s Telegraphen: hand.

arm² [ahd.: yearn] I a. ⑥⑥ (comp. ärmer, sup. ärmst) 1. poor, needy; indigent, necessitous, (ohne Geld) penniless, impecunious, F hard up; so 2 wie Hiob, wie eine Kirchenmaus as poor as Job, as a church-mouse; 2 an Geist, bibl. geistlich arm poor in spirit; 2 an Vernunft lacking intelligence; um zwei Mark ärmer poorer by ...; sich 2 bauen (trinken) to ruin o.s. by building (drinking). — 2. bemitleidend: mein 2es Kind! poor child!; 2er Schlucker, Teufel! poor fellow!, P poor devil!; verächtlich: = armselig. — 3. Sprichw. besser 2 mit Ehren, als reich mit Schande better honest poverty than shameful wealth. — 4. 2er Sünder poor wretch; (zum Tode Verurteilter) culprit under sentence of death. — II ~e(r) m, ~e f ㊺ 5. poor person; die ~en pl. the poor, the destitute; reich und 2 (the) rich and (the) poor; (öffentlich) unterstützter ~er pauper; ich ~er! F poor me!

Armada (ˇˊˇ) [span. Rüstung] f ㊺ span. Flotte 1588: (the Invincible) Armada.

Armadill (ˇˇˊ) [span.] n (m) ⑩b. zo. (broad-banded) armadillo (Daˊsypus).

arm¹=**ähnlich** (ˊˇˇ) a. ⑥⑥ brachial.

Armatur (ˇˇˊ) [lt.] f ㊺ 1. ⚔ u. ⚓ e=s Soldaten, Schiffes ꝛc. = Ausrüstung. — 2. ~ e=s Magneten ꝛc.: armature; keeper; ⊕ eines Dampfkessels armature of a boiler; boiler-fittings pl.

Arm¹=**band** (ˊ...) n ㉒ bracelet; ⊕ Wagner: =bänder arm-loops pl.; **=bewegung** f beim Schwimmen: stroke; **=binde** f: a) (Erkennungszeichen) badge; b) (Bandage) bandage, sling; **=bolzen** ⚔ m Mörser=Lafetten: running-up bolt; **=bruch** m fracture of an arm.

Armbrust (ˊˇ) [mhd. (P); *milt. arcubaliˊsta] f ㊺ ㉒ ⊕ crossbow; **~=bolzen** ㉒ bolt; **~=macher** m (cross)bow-maker; **~=schütze** m archer, crossbow man.

Ärmchen (ˊˇ)n ㉓ dim. v. Arm¹: armlet, little arm. [one's arm.]

arm¹=**dick** (ˊˇ) a. ⑥⑥ as big as an (or]

Armee ⚔ (ˇˊ)[fr.] f ㊺ (part of an) army (vgl. Heer); fig. zur großen ~ abgeh(e)n (sterben) to go where the good niggers go, to join the majority.

Armee=befehl (ˇˊ...) m ㊷ order of the day; general order; **=bericht** m military report; **=korps** n army-corps; **=lieferant** m army-contractor; **=ober-kommando** n supreme (or chief) command of an a.; **=train** m wagon-train.

Ärmel (ˊˇ) [ahd.: Arm] m ㉒ 1. sleeve; die ~ zurückschlagen to tuck up one's sleeves; ohne ~ sleeveless; fig. e-n beim ~ zupfen to pull a p. by the sleeve, (mahnen) to remind a p. of a th.; et. aus dem ~ schütteln to do a th. offhand,to extemporize(a speech,&c.). — 2. ⊕ ~ der Buchbinder arm-leather.

Ärmel=aufschlag (ˊˇ...) m ㊷ cuff, ⚔ facings pl.; **=loch** n arm-(or sleeve-)hole; **2los** a. ⑥⑥ sleeveless; **=meer** ♀ n the (British) Channel; **=patte** ⚔ f = =auf-schlag; **=schoner** m butcher's sleeve.

Armen=anstalt (ˊˇ...) [arm²] f ㊷ alms-house(s pl.), home (or refuge) for the poor, der engl. Gemeinden: workhouse, union; **=apotheke** f dispensary; **=arzt** m medical officer of health; **=aufseher** m (bezahlter) relieving officer; **=behörde** f overseers (or guardians) pl. of the poor; **=becken** n, **=büchse** f, poor-box; **=geld** n: a) poor-rate(s pl.);

Zeichen (f. S. XVII): F familiär; P Volkssprache; ♀ Gaunersprache; ⟨ selten; † alt (auch gestorben); * neu (auch geboren); ++ unrichtig;

b) alms; =gesetz n poor-law; =haus n a) = =anstalt; b) (Arbeitshaus) workhouse, a. union; außerhalb des Hauses unterstützt werden to be in receipt of (or to receive) outdoor relief.
Armeni=en ♀ (⌣⌣́⌣⌣) [med.] npr/n. ℬα. (vorder=asiatisches Gebirgsland) Armenia.
Armeni=er (⌣⌣́⌣⌣) m ㉒, ~in f ㊼, armenisch (⌣⌣́⌣⌣) a. ⑯ Armenian.
Armen=kasse (⌣́⌣⌣⌣) [arm²] f ㉒ fund for the (relief of the) poor; =kasten m = =büchse; =kommissär m = =aufseher; =liste f list of paupers; =pflege f: a) relief of the poor; b) poor-law system; =pfleger m guardian of the poor, =rat m poor-law commissioners pl.; vgl. =behörde; =recht n poor-law; =schule f charity-school; =schüler m charity-boy; =steuer f poor-rate; =stock m = =büchse; =sünder=... = Armesünder=...; =unterstützung f = =pflege a; =verband m union; =verpflegung, =verwaltung f poor-law administration; =viertel n poor quarter (of a town), slum-district; =vogt m beadle; =vorsteher m = =pfleger; =wesen n: a) charity organization, a. = =pflege b; b) (Elend) pauperism, destitution.
Arme=ritter (⌣⌣́⌣⌣) [corr. aus fr. amourettes] m/pl. ⑱ Kochkunst: fritters pl.
Armes=... (⌣⌣...) f. Arms=... u. Armlänge.
Armesin (⌣⌣́⌣) n ⑩c. (Art Taft) armozine.
Armesünder (⌣⌣́⌣⌣) m ⑱ vgl. arm² 4.
Armesünder=gesicht (⌣́...) n ㉒ woeful countenance; =glöckchen n funeral bell tolled at executions; =stuhl m im Gotteshause: stool of repentance; =zelle f im Zuchthause: condemned cell.
Arm¹=feile ⊙ (⌣́...) f ㉒ arm-file, rubber; =flor m mourning-band (or black band) round the arm; ⒒förmig a. ⑯ arm-shaped; ⚕ brachial, ⚘ (ästig) brachiate; =füßer m, zo. ⚘ brachiopod, =geige ♪ = Bratsche; =gelenk n, anat. ⚘ brachial joint; =grube f, =höhle f arm-pit, -hole.
armieren (⌣⌣́⌣) [fr.] I v/a. ⑬ 1. ⚔ ein Heer: to arm; ⚓ ein Schiff: to equip. — 2. ⊙ Balken: to truss, arm. — 3. e=n Magnet: to arm, cap. — II ~ n ⑳ u. Armierung f ㊻ 4. e=s Magneten: armature; ⚓ armature, guns and torpedoes pl. ...armig (...⌣́) ⑯, z.B. lang=long-armed.
Armillar=sphäre ⚘ (⌣⌣⌣́⌣) f ㉒ † ast. ⚘ Messen b. Stundenwinkels: armillary sphere.
Arminianer (⌣⌣(⌣)⌣́⌣) [Armi'nius, Sektierer, †1609] m ㉒ eccl. Arminian. [ianism.]
Arminianismus (⌣⌣(⌣)⌣⌣́⌣) m ㊲ Armin=]
Arm¹=kissen (⌣́...) n ㉒ = =polster; =korb m, =körbchen n (little) hand-basket; =lampe f bracket-lamp; =länge f arm's length; =lehne f arm= (or elbow-) rest of a chair; =leuchter m a) chandelier; b) ♀ (Art Alge) fetid chara or stonewort (Chara fe'tida).
ärmlich (⌣́⌣) [abd.] a. ⑯ poor, miserable, needy; fig. thin, lean; ein Les Ansehen h. to look poverty-stricken; adv. ⒉ gekleidet shabbily dressed; ~keit f ㊻ poorness; misery, poverty, shabbiness.
Ärmling (⌣́⌣) m⑩d. false sleeve.
Arm¹=loch (⌣́...) n ㉒ sleeve-hole; =molch m, zo. siren (Siren lacerti'na).
Armorika ♀ (⌣⌣́⌣⌣) [flt. am Meere] npr/n. ⑩α. (Bretagne und Normandie) Armorica.

Arm¹=polster (⌣́...) n ㉒ elbow-cushion; =ring m = =band; =säule f finger-post; =schiene f: a) ⚔ am Harnisch: armlet; b) surg. splint; =schild: a) m buckler; b) n badge; =schleife f sleeve(-knot).
arms=dick (⌣́...) [Arm¹] a. ⑯ as thick (or big) as an arm; =dicke f ㉒ thickness (or width) of an arm.
armselig (⌣́⌣⌣) [aus mhd. † Armsal f (*arm²) u. =ig] a. ⑯ (elend) miserable, wretched, beggarly, poor; (erbärmlich) paltry, mean; (kläglich) piteous; ein Ler Kram a trumpery affair.
Armseligkeit (⌣́⌣⌣=) f ㊻ 1. misery, wretchedness, paltriness, beggarliness. — 2. =en pl. (erbärmliche Dinge) paltry matters pl., beggarly concerns pl.
Arm¹=sessel (⌣́...) m ㉒ arm= (or easy-) chair; =spange f bangle, bracelet.
Armstrong (⌣⌣) npr/m. ⑩α. (engl. Fabrikant): ~=kanone ⚔ f ㉒ Armstrong gun.
Arm¹=stuhl (⌣́...) m ㉒ arm-chair.
Armsünder=... (⌣⌣́⌣...) f. Armesünder...
Armut (⌣́=) [arm²] f ㊻ (o. pl.) 1. poverty, stärker: indigence; penury, need(iness); äußerste: abject need, utter destitution, distress, pauperism; ~ an Blut poorness of blood; ~ an Geist lack of wit; Sprichw.: ~ schändet nicht poverty is no vice; ~ tut weh poverty is a sharp weapon or is hard to bear. — 2. (geringe Habe) mein bißchen ~ the little (or the few things) that I have. — 3. coll. the poor, the destitute, the indigent.
Armuts=schein (⌣́...) m ㉒, =zeugnis n certificate of poverty; fig. sich selbst ein Armutszeugnis ausstellen to prove (or show) one's incapacity or unfitness.
Arm¹=voll (⌣́...) m ㉒ armful; =welle f Turnerei: muscle-grinder; ⒉weise adv. by armfuls.   [Arnaut.]
Arnaute ♀ (⌣⌣́⌣) [türk.] m ㊹ Arnaut,]
Arnheimer (⌣́⌣⌣) [Arnheim, St.] m ㉒ (Geldschrank) money-safe.
Arnika ♀ (⌣́⌣⌣) [mlt. *grch.] f ㊾ 1. ♀ arnica (A'rnica monta'na). — 2. pharm., a. ~=tinktur (⌣́...) f ㉒ arnica (tincture).
Arom (⌣́) [grch.] n ⑩c., ~a (⌣́⌣) n ⑳ aroma, fragrance, weit S. (sweet) scent, perfume (= Duft¹ 2).
aromatisch (⌣⌣́⌣) a. ⑯ aromatic, fragrant; scented, perfumed, spicy.
Aron ♀ (⌣́⌣) [grch.] m ⑩ arum.
Arpeggiatur ♪ (⌣⌣Gä́⌣) [it.] f ㊻ (harfenähnlicher Anschlag, Tonbrechung) arpeggio.
Arrak (⌣́⌣) [ar.] m ⑩d., ⚘ arrack, F rack.
Arrangement (ă=rɑ̃=G̃⌣́=mɑ̃) [fr.] n ⑳ (Anordnung) arrangement.
arrangieren (ă=rɑ̃=G⌣́⌣) [fr.] v/a. (ordnen) to arrange; ⊙ v/refl. sich mit j=n Gläubigern ⒉ to compound (or arrange, settle) with one's creditors.
Arras ⚕ (⌣́⌣) [fr. St.] m, inv. (Rasch) serge.
Arrendator (⌣⌣⌣́⌣) [lt.] m ㉑ = Pächter.
arrendieren (⌣⌣⌣́⌣) [lt.] v/a. ⑬ = pachten.
Arrest (⌣⌣́) [mlt.] m ⑩b. 1. von Sachen: seizure, attachment; ~ (Beschlag) auf et. legen, et. mit ~ belegen to seize, attach, detain a th.; ⚓ auf ein Schiff: embargo. — 2. bsd. ⚔ von Personen: (Haft) arrest, strenger: close arrest; von Schülern: detention; ⚔ e=n Soldaten mit ~ bestrafen to put ... under arrest; Schüler: to keep in, to detain (after school).

Arrestant (⌣⌣⌣́) [mlt.] m ㊽, ~in f ㊻ 1. (Gefangene(r) prisoner. — 2. jur. distrainer.
Arrestat (⌣⌣⌣́) [mlt.] m ㊽ 1. = Arrestant 1. — 2. jur. person distrained.
Arrestation (⌣⌣⌣=tsj(⌣)⌣́) [mlt.] f ㊻ arrestation, &c. (= Verhaftung).
Arrest=legung (⌣⌣́...) f ㊻ seizure; =lokal n lock-up; ⚔ guard-room; F blackhole; =schlag m = Beschlagnahme; =strafe f = Arrest 2; =stube f, =zimmer n = =lokal.
arretieren (⌣⌣⌣́⌣) [fr.] v/a. ⑬ to arrest, apprehend, seize; F to collar; ich ließ ihn ⒉ I gave him into custody; Güter ⒉ to distrain..., to attach... [hension.]
Arretierung (⌣⌣⌣́⌣) f ㊻ arrest, appre-]
Arri=ere=garde=(=stellung) ⚔ (ă=riẵ́r...) [fr.] f ㉒ rear-guard (position).
arrogant (⌣⌣⌣́) a. ⑯ arrogant; Arroganz f ㊻ (Anmerkung) arrogance
arrondieren (⌣⌣⌣́⌣) [fr.] v/a. u. v/refl. ⑬ (sich ⒉) (abrunden) to round off (one's lands). [Uhrenfabr.: finishing engine.]
Arrondier=maschine ⊙ (⌣⌣⌣́⌣...) f ㉒]
Arrondierungs=politik (⌣⌣⌣́⌣...) f ㉒ policy of rounding off one's lands or estates.
Arrowroot ♀ (ă'r=⌣=Rūt) [engl.] n ⑪ (Stärkemehl v. Mara'nta arundina'cea rc.). arrowroot.
Arsch P (⌣) [ahd.: arse] m ⑩a. arse, backside, weniger anstößig: behind, posterior.
Arsch=leder ⚒ (⌣́...) n ㉒ breech-leather.
ärschlings (⌣́⌣) adv. backwards.
Arsen¹ ⚘ (⌣́) [grch.] n ⑩c. (o. pl.) chm. (im Arsenik enthaltenes Element) arsenic (As).
Arsen² (⌣́) f/pl. v. Arsis (f. ds).
Arsenal (⌣⌣⌣́) [it. *ar.] n ⑩ = Zeughaus.
Arsen=blei (⌣́...) n ⑩ arseniate of lead; =chlorid n chloride of arsenic (As Cl₃); =hexoxyd n (reines Arsenik) arsenious oxide or anhydride (As₄O₆, † As₂O₃).
arsenig ⚘ (⌣́⌣) a. ⑯ chm. arsenious; Le Säure arsenious acid (H₃As O₃); ⒉saures Kali potassium arsenite; basisch ⒉saures Kupferoxyd (Scheeles Grün) basic arsenite of copper.
Arsenik ⚘ (⌣́⌣) n ⑩e., min., chm. (durch Rösten arsenhaltiger Erze gewonnenes giftiges Pulver; Arsen=hexoxyd) (white) arsenic, arsenic powder, als Rattengift: F ratsbane; mit ~ verbinden to arsenicate. [arsenical.]
arsenikalisch ⚘ (⌣⌣⌣́⌣) [grch.] a. ⑯]
Arsenik=blume (⌣⌣́...) f ㉒, =blüte f = Arsenhexoxyd, a. flowers pl. of arsenic, smelting-house smoke (As₂O₃); =butter f chloride (or butter) of arsenic; =essen n, med. arsenic habit, ⚘ arsenicophagy; ⒉haltig a. ⑯ containing arsenic, arsenical, arseniferous; =kies m arsenical pyrites = Arsenkies; =metall n: ⚘ arseniuret; =spiegel m arsenic-mirror; =vergiftung f poisoning by arsenic, arsenic poisoning.
Arsen=kies (⌣́...) m ⑩ min., chm. arsenical pyrites; =nickel n, m arsenical nickel; ⒉sauer a.: ⒉saures Salz arseniate (of lead, &c.); =säure f arsenic acid (H₃As O₄); =wasserstoff m arseniuret(t)ed hydrogen (As H₃).
Arsis ⚘ (⌣́⌣) [grch.] f ㊾ pros., &c. arsis, emphasis, accented syllable.
Art. abbr. = Artikel.

Art¹ (ʟ) [mhd.: flaw. *rot* Art] **1.** ~ (und Weise) manner, mode; auf diese ~ in this way, at that rate; auf die eine oder die andere ~ some way or other; auf irgend eine ~ anyhow; auf keinerlei ~ nowise; auf welche ~? in what way?, how?; in seiner ~ in his (or its) way; einzig in seiner ~ unique; nach ~ von after the manner (or style) of; nach ~ einer gebildeten Dame in a ladylike fashion; diese Dinge sind von der ~, daß // these things are of such a nature as to // mit *inf.*; nichts der ~ nothing of the kind, no such thing; Leute von dieser ~ people of this description, that sort of people; von allerlei ~ of many (or all) kinds, multifarious; es lag nicht in seiner ~ that was not his way (of doing things), it was not in his nature or composition; ganz in deiner ~ just like you. — **2.** (die rechte Art) the right way, F good form; er hat keine ~ he has no manners; das hat keine ~ F that's not the thing, that's bad form; das ist keine ~ that's not the way to do things; daß es (nur so) eine ~ hat admirably, thoroughly (well); F with a vengeance. — **3.** (Gattung) kind, sort, description; ein Mann s-r ~ a man of his stamp; nicht von sehr feiner, besonderer ~ not very high-class, F nothing particular, v. Leuten a.: F not very classy; Leute von gewöhnlicher ~ the common run of people; von guter ~ good-natured; sie sind alle von der nämlichen ~ they are all tarred with the same brush; zwei (alle) von derselben ~ F two (all) of a kidney; so ziemlich von derselben ~ much of a muchness, F six of one and half-a-dozen of the other; eine ~ Gelehrter F a bit of a scholar; was für eine ~ von Menschen? what class of people? aus der ~ schlagen to degenerate. Sprichw. ~ läßt nicht von ~ like will stick to like, blood is thicker than water, &c. — **4.** Naturgeschichte: species, order, tribe, race, class; e-e besondere ~ Schafe a particular breed of sheep.
Art² † (ʟ) [ahd.: lt. *ara're*] *f* ⑯ a) (Pflügung) ploughing, tillage; b) = ~acker.
Art²-acker (″...) *m* ⑫ arable land or field.
artbar (ʟ-) [Art²] *a.* ⑯ agr. (urbar, tragbar) arable, cultivable, bearing fruit.
Art¹-begriff (″...) *m* ⑫, =charakter *m* specific (or typical) character.
Artemis (ʟ~) [grch.] *npr/f.*, *inv. myth.* Artemis, (lt.) Diana.
arten (ʟ~) ⑯ **I** (fast †) *v/n.* (sn) **1.** (auch sich ⌒ *v/refl.*) to be of a certain quality or kind; nach e-m (sich) ⌒ to take after a p. — **2.** (gedeihen) (gut) ⌒ to thrive, prosper, succeed. — **II** ⌣ *v/a.* **3.** to form. — **III** ge-artet *p.p. u. a.* ⑯ **4.** of a certain quality or nature; disposed; gut (schlecht) ⌒es Kind well-bred (ill-behaved) child; so ⌒ of such a kind or disposition; such. [species.
arten-reich (″~ʟ) *a.* ⑯ ⚥, *zo.* rich in]
Arteri-e ⌣ (ʟ(~)~) [grch.] *f* ⑯ *anat.* (Pulsader) artery; Öffnung der ~n ⌣ arteriotomy; zu den ~n gehörig, **arteri-ell** (~~ʟ) *a.* ⑯ arterial.

Arteri-en-erweiterung (~ʟ(~)~...) *f* ⑯ aneurism; =öffnung *f* arteriotomy; =presse ⌣ *f* compressor; =zange *f* artery-forceps. [arterial.]
arteriös ⌣ (~(~)ʟ) [lt.] *a.* ⑯ *anat.*]
artesisch (~ʟ~) [Artois⌣] *a.* ⑯ Artesian; der Brunnen Artesian well, bore-well.
Art²-feld (ʟʟ) *n* ⑫ = Artacker.
Arthralgie ⌣ (~~ʟ) [grch.] *f* ⑯ *path.* (Gelenkschmerz) arthralgia.
...artig (ʟ~) [Art¹] *a.* ⑯ in Zssgn. (geartet) resembling, like, &c., z.B. gleich⌒ of the same kind; silber⌒ silver-like.
artig (ʟ~) [Art¹] *a.* ⑯ **1.** (brav) v. Kindern: good, well-behaved; sei ⌒! be good!, there's a dear (child); seid ⌒! be good boys (girls)!, behave yourselves!; (höflich) polite, courteous; (liebenswürdig) amiable, gegen Damen: gallant; sich ⌒ benehmen to behave nicely, to be on one's best behaviour; er sagt ihr viel ⌒es he pays her many compliments; *iro.* ich finde es ⌒, daß Sie mir sagen // you're a fine fellow to tell me //. — **2.** (niedlich) nice, pretty, graceful; F ein ⌒es (tüchtiges) Stück a fine (F jolly) piece.
Artigkeit (ʟ~-) *f* ⑯ **1.** im Benehmen: good behaviour; bsd. der Schulkinder: good conduct; (feines Benehmen) good manners *pl.*, courteousness, courtesy, gegen Damen: gallantry. — **2.** in der Rede: compliment; ~en civilities, courteous (or polite) words *pl.*; e-m ~en über et. sagen to compliment a p. on a th. — **3.** (Anmut) prettiness, gracefulness.
Artikel (~ʟ~) [lt.] *m* ⑫ ⓐ, *gr.*, &c.: article; (Ware) auch: commodity; die neuesten ~ the latest novelties or fashions *pl.*; (Leit⌒) leading article.
Artikel-brief (~ʟʟ...) *m* ⑫ articles (or statutes) *pl.* of the navy; ⌒los *a.* ⑯ without article; =schreiber *m* für Zeitungen: leader-writer, par(agraph)-writer; ⌒weise *adv.* by the article.
Artikulation (~~~tʟ(~)ʟ) [lt.] *f* ⑯ (Lautbildung, deutliche Aussprache) articulation.
artikulieren (~~ʟ~) [lt.] *v/a.* ⑬ (deutlich aussprechen) to articulate.
Artillerie ⚔ (ʟ⌣~ʟ) [fr.] *f* ⑯ artillery, gunnery; (Geschütze) ordnance; reitende ~ horse-artillery; schwere ~ des Feldheeres heavy artillery.
Artillerie-brigade (″...) *f* ⑫ artillery-brigade; =chef, =direktor *m* in England seit 1904: Master General of the Ordnance; =feuer *n* cannonade; =offizier *m* artillery-officer; =regiment *n* artillery-regiment; =schießplatz *m* gunnery practising-ground; =schule *f* school of gunnery; =train *m* ar.-train; =wagen *m* tumbrel; =werkstätte *f* arsenal; artillery workshops *pl.*; =wesen *n* gunnery, gunning (of an army); artillery matters *pl.*; =zug *m* train of artillery.
Artillerist ⚔ (~~ʟ~) [fr. *artilleur* mit lt. Endg.] *m* ⑫ artilleryman, gunner, (der das Geschütz richtet) gun-layer; (der das Geschütz bedient) gun-server; ⌒isch *a.* ⑯ belonging (or referring) to the artillery.
Artischocke ⚥ (~~ʟ~) [it.; *ar.* Erddistel] *f* ⑯ artichoke; ~n-boden (″...) *m* ⑫, =käse *m* crown of an artichoke.
Artist (~ʟ) [fr.] *m* ⑫ (Künstler) (circus or music-hall) artist(e); acrobat, clown.

artistisch (~ʟ~) [fr.] *a.* ⑯ artistic.
Artistschaft (~ʟ~) *f* ⑯ world of artist(e)s; music-hall performers *pl.*
Art²-land (″...) *n* ⑫ = Artacker.
Art¹-name (″...) *m* ⑫ specific (or class-) name.
Artur (ʟ~) ⓐ *a.*, **Artus** (ʟ~) ⑯ γ. [flt.] *npr/m.* Arthur; König Arturs (Artus') Tafelrunde King Arthur's Round Table; ~sage (″...) *f* ⑫ Arthurian legend.
Arum ⚥ (ʟ~) [lt.] *n* ⑫ = Aron.
Arve ⚥ (ʟ~) *f* ⑯ = Zirbelkiefer.
Arz(e)nei (⚥(~)ʟ) [mhd.: Arzt] *f* ⑯ medicine, physic; (~ware) drug; flüssige: draught, potion; nervenstärkende: tonic; für bestimmte Leiden: specific; e-m ~ geben to physic a p.; ~ einnehmen to take medicine or physic.
Arz(e)nei-bereitung (⚥(~)″...) *f* ⑫ making up (of) prescriptions; =bereitungskunst *f*: ⌣ pharmacy, pharmaceutics; =buch *n* dispensatory, ⌣ pharmacopœia; =formel *f* (medical) prescription; =geschäft *n* drug-stores *pl.*; =geschmack *m* medicinal taste; =glas *n* phial; =händler *m* druggist; =kasten *m* medicine-chest; =kräuter *n/pl.* medicinal (or officinal) herbs, simples *pl.*; =kunde, =kunst, =lehre *f* pharmacy, pharmacology, medicine.
arz(e)neilich (⚥(~)ʟ~) *a.* ⑯ medicinal, medical; *pharm.* officinal.
Arz(e)nei-mittel (⚥(~)″...) *n* remedy, medicine; =mittel-lehre *f*: ⌣ materia medica; =pflanze ⚥ *f* medicinal (or officinal) plant; =schrank *m* = =kasten; =taxe *f* official price (or rate) of drugs; =trank *m* potion; herb-tea; =verschreibung, =vorschrift *f* = =formel; =ware *f* drug; =wesen *n* (things *pl.* relating to) pharmacy; =wissenschaft *f* medical science; =wissenschaftlich *a.* ⑯ medical; =zettel *m* label for drugs and medicines.
Arzt (⚥) [ahd.; *grch. arch-iatro's*] *m* ⑦ a. physician (der konsultiert wird); sonst: medical man or practitioner; F hoher ~ (s. Hausarzt); praktischer ~ und Wundarzt general practitioner, auch oft: surgeon; mein ~ my medical adviser or man; weiblicher ~, **Ärztin** *f* ⑯ lady (or female) doctor; den ~ holen lassen to send for the doctor; er zog einen ~ zu Rate he took medical advice.
Arzt-gebühr (⚥...) *f* ⑫ doctor's fee.
ärztlich (⚥~) *a.* ⑯ medical; ⌒e Hilfe in Anspruch nehmen to call in medical assistance, to have (or take) medical advice; ⌒ behandeln to attend (a patient); ⌒ untersucht werden to pass a medical examination, F to pass the doctor; ⌒es Personal medical staff; ⌒e Verordnung medical prescription.
As¹ (⚥) [fr.] *n* ⓐ Spiel: ace; Herz-As ace of hearts. [(Apothekerpfund) as.]
As² (⚥) [lt. *ās m*] *n* ⓐ (römische Münze;]
As³ (ʟ) *gen. u. pl. v.* A.
As⁴ ♪ (ʟ) *n*, *inv.* A flat; As-Dur (As-Moll) A flat major (minor).
Asa foetida (ʟ-⌣~) [perf. *a'sa* Harz u. lt. *f(o)e'tida*] *f* = stinkender Asant.
A-Saite ♪ (″ʟ~) *f* ⑯ la, A-string.
Asant ⚥ (~ʟ) [Asa] *m* ⑫ b. *pharm.* stinkender ~ asafœtida; wohlriechender ~ benzoin(e).

Asbestᚱ (⌣⌢) [grch. unverbrennlich] m ①a. min. asbestos; biegsamer amiant(h)us.
asbest-ähnlich (⌣⌢...) a. ⓺, ⚯artig, ⚯förmig a. asbestic, asbestine; amianthoid; **⚯gasofen** m ⓶ asbestos stove; **⚯gewand** n asbestos garment; **⚯packung** f asbestos packing.

Ascenseur ⊕ (ä-ßa-ßö'r) [fr.] m ①d. (a. ⓾) (hydraulische Hebemaschine) hydraulic lift or elevator.

Asch¹ ⊕ u. *prov.* (⌣) [ahd.] m ①a. (flower-)pot; (Napf, Satte 2c.) bowl.

Asch² ⊕ m ①a. *ichth.* = Äsche.

Aschanti ♀ (⌣⌣) *npr/n.* (Land) u. m, *inv.* (Volk in West-afrika) Ashanti, Ashantee.

asch-artig (⌣...) a. ⓺ ashy, ⚯ ciner(ac)eous; **⚯becher** m ⓶ = Äschen-b.; **⚯behälter** m = ⚯eimer; ⚯**bleich** a. = ⚯fahl; ⚯**blond** a. ashy-fair.

Asche (⌣⌣) [ahd.: ash(es)] f ⓺ 1. ashes *pl.*; aus der ~ erstehen (wieder aufblühen) to rise from one's ashes or from the ruins; in ~ verwandeln, zu ~ (ver)brennen to reduce to ashes, *chm.* ᚱ: to incinerate; in ~ legen to lay in ashes, to burn down. — 2. *poet.* (sterbl. Reste) ashes *pl.*, dust; *rel.* mortal (or earthly) remains *pl.*; Friede seiner ~! may he rest in peace! — 3. *bibl.* in Sack und ~ büßen to do penance in sack-cloth and ashes. — 4. ⊕ ausgelaugte ~ buck-ashes *pl.*

Äsche (⌣⌣) [ahd.] f ⓺ *ichth.*: grayling, umber(*Thyma'llus* [*vulga'ris*]). [-bucket.⎫

Asch-eimer (⌣...) m ⓶ ash-pan, -bin,⎭

aschen (⌣⌣) *v/a.* ⓸ Gießerei: die Formen ⚯ to ash (or wash) the moulds.

aschen-ähnlich (⌣⌣...) [Asche] a. ⓺ = aschartig, **⚯becher** m ⓶ ash-tray; **⚯brenner** ⊕ m ash-consumer; **⚯brödel** (⌣⌢...) [uhd.] n (m) Ashputtle, Cinderella, weitS. (domestic) drudge, scullion; **⚯eimer** m = Ascheimer; **⚯fall** m: a) shower of ashes; b) ⊕ (Kasten unter dem Rost) ash-pan; **⚯fall-tür** f ash-pit door; **⚯grube** f ash-pit; **⚯kasten** m = Ascheimer; **⚯kegel** m der Vulkane cone of cinders; **⚯klappe** f ash-pit; **⚯krug** m cinerary (or funeral) urn; **⚯lauge** f lye (of wood-ashes); **⚯ofen** ⊕ m Glashütte: ash-furnace; **⚯pflanze** ♀ f cineraria; **⚯puttel** n = **⚯brödel**; **⚯raum** m ash-pit; **⚯regen** m rain of ashes; **⚯salz** n = Pottasche; **⚯sieb** m cinder-sifter; **⚯urne** f = **⚯krug**; **⚯tuch** n bucking-cloth; **⚯zieher** m, *min.* tourmaline. — Vgl. auch Asch⚯...

Ascher (⌣⌣) m ⓶ 1. ⊕: a) ash-barrel Gerberei: (Kalkgrube) lime-pit; (gelöschter Kalt) slaked lime; b) (ausgelaugte Asche) lixiviated (or buck-) ashes *pl.*; c) *metall.* soap-boiler's ashes *pl.* — 2. = Äsche.

Ascher-faß ⊕ (⌣⌣...) n ⓾ liming-tub; **⚯grube** f lime- (or tanner's) pit. [lb.⎫

Ascherig ⊕ schwz. (⌣⌣) m ①d. = Äscher.⎭

Ascher-kalk (⌣⌣⌣) m ⓶ lime.

Ascher-mittwoch (⌣⌣⌣) m ⓶ Ash-Wednesday; ⚯**lich** (⌣⌢) a. ⓺ penitential.

äschern (⌣⌣) *v/a.* ⓶a. 1. (einäschern) to reduce to ashes. — 2. to burn ashes am Aschermittwoch: to strew with ashes. — 3. ⊕ Gerberei: to steep in lime; Wäsche ⚯ (laugen) to buck, to boil ... in soda-water. [flux.⎫

Ascher-salz ⊕ (⌣⌣...) n ⓶ Gießerei: lime-⎭

asch-fahl (⌣...) [Asche] a. ⓺, ⚯**farben**, ⚯**farbig**, ⚯**grau** a. ash-coloured; ash-grey, ashy grey, ⚯ ciner(ac)eous; F das geht ins Aschgraue this beats all, that's too much of a good thing).

ascht ⚯, **aschig** (⌣⌣) a. ⓺ = aschartig.

Äsch-kasten (⌣...) [Asche] m ⓶ = ⚯eimer; **⚯kraut** ♀ n cineraria; **⚯kuchen** m: a)[Asch'⎫ bun, scone; b) [Äsche] cake baked in hot ashes; **⚯lauch** ♀ [ahd. *corr.* P] = Schalotte; **⚯loch** n ash-hole; **⚯meise** f, *orn.* marsh-titmouse; **⚯sieb** m f. Aschen-: **⚯wurzel** ♀ dittany (*Dicta'mnus*).

äschyle-isch (⌣⌣⌢) [Aschylos, Aschylus, grch. Tragiker, 525 bis 456 v. Chr.] a. ⓺ of Æschylus, Æschylean.

Ase (⌣⌣) [isländ.] m ⓸ *nord. myth.* As, ~n *pl.* Æsir (nordisches Göttergeschlecht).

äsen (⌣⌣) *v/a.* ⓽ *hunt.* (weiden) to browse, to graze. [Fäulnis) aseptic.⎫

aseptisch ᚱ (⌣⌣⌣) [grch.] a. ⓺ (frei von⎭

Aser¹ (⌣⌣), *pl. von* Aas.

Äser² *prov.* (⌣) [mhd.] m ⓶ *hunt.* (Speisesack, Ranzen) wallet.

Asiat (⌣⌣⌢) m ⓶, ~**in** f ⓷, **asiatisch** (⌣⌣⌣) a. ⓺ Asiatic; bisw. n. Asian; asiatische Cholera Asiatic cholera.

Asi-en ♀ (⌣(⌣)⌣) *npr/n.* ⓶a. Asia.

Askariden ᚱ (⌣⌣⌢⌣) [grch.] f/pl. ⓺ (Faden-Spul-würmer) ascaridæ, ascarides *pl.*

Askese (⌣⌢) [grch.] f ⓺ (strenge Bußübung ob. Enthaltung) asceticism.

Asket (⌣⌢) m ⓶ u. **asketisch** a. ⓺ ascetic.

Asklepiadazee(n *pl.*) ᚱ ♀ (⌣-(⌣)-⌣⌢⌣) [grch.] f ⓺ asclepiadaceæ.

Asklepiadeen ᚱ (⌣⌣⌣⌢⌣) [grch.] m/pl. ⓶ (Verse) *pl.* Asclepiadean verse or metre.

asklepiadisch ᚱ (⌣-(⌣)-⌣⌢) [grch.] a. ⓺ bsd. *pros.* 2er Vers Asclepiad(ean), Asclepiadic.

Asklepi-os, -us (⌣⌢(⌣)⌣) [grch.] *npr/m.* ⓺γ. = Äskulap.

Äskulap (⌣-⌣⌢) [lt.] *npr/m.* ①e., ⓺α. *myth.* (Gott der Heilkunde) Æsculapius; **⚯fisch** (⌣-⌣⌢) a. ⓺ Æsculacian, weitS. medical.

asomatisch ᚱ (⌣-⌣⌢) [grch.] a. ⓺ (unkörperlich) asomatous.

Äsop, ~**os** (⌣⌢(⌣)) *npr/m.* ①e. u. ⓺α, γ. (grch. Fabeldichter) Æsop(us);

äsopisch (⌣⌢⌣) a. ⓺ Æsopian; 2e Fabeln *f/pl.* Æsop's fables *pl.*

Asow ♀ (⌣⌢f) *npr/n.* ⓺α. Azov; Süd-rußland: ~sches Meer Sea of Azov.

Aspalath(a)-holz ♀ (⌣⌣ᴵᴵ(⌣)⌣⌢) n ⓶ (Rosenholz, falsches Ebenholz) aspalathus.

Asparagin (⌣⌣⌣⌢) n ⓺ *chm.* (Alkaloid des Spargels) asparagin(e) ($C_4H_8N_2O_3$).

☞ Aspe ♀ (⌣⌣) f ⓺ 2c. s. Espe 2c.

Aspekt ᚱ (⌣⌢) [lt.] m ⓶ bsd. *ast.* aspect.

Asper (⌣⌣) [neu-grch.] m ⓶ *num.* asper.

Asphalt (⌣f⌢, oft ⌣f⌣) [grch.] m ①b. *min.* (Erd-harz, -pech) asphalt.

asphalt-haltig (⌢...) a. ⓺ asphaltic.

asphaltier/en ⊕ (⌣f⌣⌣⌢) [grch.] I *v/a.* ⓺ to asphalt, bituminize. — II ~ **n** ⓶ u. **A/ung** f ⓺ bituminization; asphalt-paving, asphalt-roofing.

asphaltisch (⌣f⌣⌢) [grch.] a. ⓺ asphaltic.

Asphalt-lack (⌣f...) m ⓶ (black) japan; **⚯negativ** n, *phot.* asphaltotype; **⚯pappe** f tar-roofing; **⚯pflaster** n asphalt(ic) pavement, F asphalt. [Affodill 2c.⎫

Asphodill ♀ (⌣f⌣⌢) [grch.] m ①b. 2c. =⎭

Asphyxie ᚱ (⌣f⌣⌢) [grch.] f ⓺ *path.* (Erstickung) asphyxia.

Aspik (⌣⌢) [fr.] m ①c. (Speise mit gallertartigem Überzug) aspic (jelly).

Aspirant (⌣-⌣⌢) [lt.] m ⓶ (Bewerber) aspirant, candidate. [aspirate(d letter).⎫

Aspirata ᚱ (⌣-⌣⌢⌣) [lt.] f ⓺ gr. (Hauchlaut);⎭

Aspiration (⌣-⌢-tß(⌣)ᴸ) f ⓺ (Aussprache mit e-m Hauchlaute; *fig.* Streben) aspiration, (Atmen) breathing.

aspirieren (⌣-⌣⌢) [lt.] *v/a.* ⓺ *gram.* to aspirate; *fig.* to aspire to.

aß (⌣ᴸ) *impf.* von essen.

Assagai(e) (⌣⌣ᴸ(⌣)) [hottent.-ind.] m ⓶ (Wurfspieß b. Kaffern) assagai, (h)assegai.

Assam ♀ (⌣⌢) [ind.] *npr/n.* ⓺a. in Ost-J.: Assam; aus ~, ~**it** (⌣⌣⌢) m ⓶ Assamese.

assanier/en ⊕ (⌣-⌣⌢) [lt.] I *v/a.* ⓺ (gesundheitlich einrichten) to sanitate. — II ~ **n** ⓶ u. **A/ung** f ⓺ sanitation.

Assassine (⌣⌣⌢) [fr.] m ⓸ assassin.

Assaut ☒ (ä-ßo') [fr.] m ①d. (Angriff im Zweikampf, Fechtübung) assault, lunge.

äße (ᴸ⌣) *subj. impf. v.* essen.

Assekurador (⌣⌣⌣⌢) [span.] m ⓶, **Assekurant** [lt.] ⊕ (⌣⌣⌢) m ⓶ (Versicherer) insurer; ⚓ underwriter.

Assekuranz (⌣⌣⌢) ⊕ f ⓺ insurance; ⚓ underwriting; s. Versicherung(s-...).

Assekurat ⊕ (⌣⌣⌢) [mlt.] m ⓶ (Versicherter) person insured.

assekurierbar (⌣⌣⌢⌣) a. ⓺ insurable.

assekurieren (⌣⌣⌣⌢) *v/a.* ⓺ to insure.

Assel (⌣⌣) [lt.] f ⓺ (a. m ⓶) *zo.* wood-louse (*Oni'scus*); (Tausendfuß) scolopendra.

Assemblee (ä-ßa-blē') [fr.] f ⓺ (Versammlung) assembly.

assentieren öft. ☒ (⌣⌣⌢) [lt.] *v/a.* ⓺ (für den Militärdienst tauglich erklären) to accept for military service.

assen, äßen (ᴸ⌣) *v/a.* ⓽ *hunt.* = äsen.

Assessor (⌣⌣⌣) [lt.] m ⓶ (assessor, junior (or assistant) judge.

Assibilation ᚱ (⌣⌣⌣-tß(⌣)ᴸ) [lt.] f ⓺ *gram.* (zischende Aussprache) assibilation.

Assignant ⊕ (⌣⌣⌢) [lt.] m ⓶ (Aussteller) drawer. [drawee.⎫

Assignat ⊕ (⌣⌣⌢) [lt.] m ⓶ (der Bezogene)⎭

Assignatar (⌣⌣⌢) m ①c. (Bevollmächtigter) assignee. [(Geldschein) assignat.⎫

Assignate (⌣⌣⌢) [fr.] f ⓺ fr. Geschichte:⎭

assignieren (⌣⌣⌢) *v/a.* ⓺ = anweisen 3.

Assimilation ᚱ (⌣⌣⌣-tß(⌣)ᴸ) [lt.] f ⓺ *physiol.* (Ähnlichmachung, Einverleibung) assimilation; **⚯kraft** (...) ⓺ assimilative power.

assimilatorisch ᚱ (⌣⌣⌣⌣-⌢) [lt.] a. ⓺ (ähnlich machend, einverleibend) assimilatory.

assimilierbar (⌣⌣⌣⌢) [lt.] a. ⓺ assimilable, capable of assimilation; **~keit** (⌢) f ⓺ (o. *pl.*) assimilability.

assimilier/en ᚱ (⌣⌣⌣⌢) [lt.] I *v/a.* ⓺ (ähnlich machen) (sich *dat.*) et. ⚯ to assimilate ... — II ~ **n** ⓶ = Assimilation. — III 2d *p.pr.* u. a. ⓺ assimilative. — IV A/ung f ⓺ = Assimilation.

Assisen (⌣⌢⌣) [fr.] *f/pl.* ⓺ (Schwurgericht) assizes *pl.*; vor die ~ verweisen to commit for trial.

Assistent (⌣⌣⌢) [lt.] m ⓶ (Gehilfe) assistant, (under)clerk. [surgeon.⎫

Assistenz-arzt (⌣⌣⌣⌢...) m ⓶ assistant-⎭

assistieren (⌣⌣⌢) [lt.] *v/a.* ⓺ e-m ⚯ (Hilfe leisten) to assist a p.

Associé (⌣⌣ß(⌣)ᴸ) [fr.] m ①d. (Teilhaber) partner; stiller ~ sleeping partner.

[Associégesuch] — 84 — [Äthylen]

Associé-gesuch (⌣⌣ᵋ(⌣)ᴴ...) n 62, Associé gesucht partner wanted or required.
Assonanz (⌣⌣ᴸ) [lt.] f 46 (Anklang) assonanz-)
assonierend (⌣⌣⌣ᴸ) a. 66 assonant. [ance.]
assortieren (⌣⌣ᴸ⌣) [fr.] v/a. u. v/refl. 93 (nach Arten ordnen) to (as)sort; ❋ sich mit et. ℒ (versehen) to lay in a stock of a th., to get in a (fresh) supply of a th. [❋b. assortment.]
Assortiment (⌣⌣⌣ᴸ, fr. ä-ßōr-ti-mąg') [fr.] n}
Assoziation (⌣-(⌣)-tß(⌣)ᴸ) [lt. só'ciūs] f 46 (Vereinigung) association; ❋ (trading) company, partnership; ~s-firma ❋ ("...) f 62 firm. [ciate.]
assoziieren (⌣-(⌣)ᴸ⌣) [lt.] v/a. 93 to asso-}
Assyri-en (⌣ᴸ(⌣)⌣) npr/n. 93α. Assyria.
Assyri-er (⌣) m 22, ~in f 47 u. assyrisch (⌣ᴸ⌣) a. 66 Assyrian.
Assyriologie (⌣ᴸ(⌣)⌣⌣ᴴ) f 48 assyriology.
a. St. abbr. = alten Stils (julian. Kalender) of old style (s. alt¹ 3).
Ast (ᵋ) [ahd.] m ⓓb. 1. branch (a. fig.); sich in Äste teilen to branch out, to ramify. — 2. F (Auswuchs) hunch, hump; fig. sich (dat.) e-n ~ lachen to split with laughter. — 3. (Stelle im Holz) knot, knob. — [Erdmagnetismus) astatic.]
astatisch ☌ (⌣ᴸ⌣) a. 66 (frei vom)
Ästchen (ᵋ⌣) n 23, dim. v. Ast, branchlet, bough, twig, sprig. [(=Urbanität.)]
Aste-ismus (⌣⌣ᴸ⌣) [grch.] m 27 urbanity}
ästeln (ᵋ⌣): sich ℒ v/refl. 93a. to put forth (or shoot out) branches.
asten, ästen (ᵋ⌣) I v/n. (h.) u. sich ℒ v/refl. 89 to branch out, to form branches to ramify. — II ge-ästet p.p. und a. 66 branchy, ☌ ramose, vgl. auch ästig.
Aster ♀ (ᵋ⌣) [grch.] f 48 (China-)aster; ℒartige Pflanzen f/pl.: ☌ asteraceæ pl.
Asterisk-os, -us (⌣⌣ᴸ⌣) [grch.] m 22 typ. (Sternchen) asterisk (*).
Astero-id ☌ (⌣⌣ᴸ) [grch.] m 36c. ast. (kleiner Planet) asteroid.
Asthenie ☌ (⌣⌣ᴸ) [grch.] f 48 path. (Kraftlosigkeit) asthenia, debility.
Ästhetik ☌ (-ᴸ⌣) [grch.] f 46 phls. (Kunstwissenschaft) æsthetics; **Ästhe'tiker** m 22 æsthetic(ist); **ästhetisch** a. 66 æsthetic.
Asthma ☌ (ᵋ⌣) [grch.] n 50 path. asthma; **Asthmatiker** (⌣ᴸ⌣) m 22, **asthmatisch** (⌣ᴸ) a. 66 (engbrüstig) asthmatic. [pl.}
Ast-holz (ᵋᵋ) n 62 branch-wood, loppings}
ästig (ᵋ⌣) a. 66 (verzweigt) branchy, ramified; (knorrig) gnarled, knotted.
astigmatisch ☌ (⌣ᴸ⌣) [grch.] a. 66 path. astigmatic. [störung) astigmatism.]
Astigmatismus ☌ (⌣⌣-ᵋ⌣) m 27 (Seh-}
Äsling (ᵋ⌣) m ⓓd. Faltneiser: brancher.
Ast-loch (ᵋ...) n 62 knot-hole; ℒlos a. 66 branchless; =moos n: ☌ hypnum.
Astrachan ♀ (⌣⌣ᵋ) [ar.-pers. * Hāǵschi Tarchân] 50(α.) I npr/n. Astrakhan. — II m (Plüsch) astrakhan; mit ~ eingefaßt, verbrämt astrakhan-trimmed.
Astral-lampe (⌣ᴸ...) f 62 astral lamp; =leib m Spiritismus: astral body; =licht n, ast. der Milchstraße: astral light.
Astr(o)-it ☌ (⌣(⌣)ᴸ) [grch.] m 46 min. (versteinertes Strahltier) astr(o)ite.
Astrolabium ⚗ (⌣⌣ᴸ(⌣)⌣) [lt.,*grch.] n 28 (Sternhöhenmesser) astrolabe.
Astrolog, ~e ☌ (⌣⌣ᴸ) [grch.] m 42, ~ie (⌣⌣⌣ᴸ) f 48 (Sterndeuter) astrologer; ~ie (⌣⌣⌣ᴸ) f 48 astrology; ℒisch (⌣⌣ᴸ⌣) a. 66 astrologic.

Astronom ☌ (⌣⌣ᴸ) [grch.] m 42 astronomer; co. star-gazer; ~ie (⌣⌣⌣ᴸ) f 48 (Sternkunde) astronomy; ℒisch (⌣⌣ᴸ⌣) a. 66 astronomic(al).
Astrophotographie ☌ (⌣ᴸ-⌣⌣ᴸ) [grch.] f 48 (o. pl.) phot. astrophotography.
Astrophysik ☌ (⌣⌣ᴸ⌣) f 46 (Physik der Gestirne) astro-physics.
Astroskop (⌣⌣⌣ᴸ) [grch.] n ⓓc. ast. (Sternfernrohr) astroscope.
ast-ständig ♀ (ᵋ...) a. 66 ramous.
Astuar(ium) ☌ (-⌣ᴸ[(⌣)⌣]) [lt.] n ⓓc.(28)♀ (Flutmündung) estuary. [of(f) branches.]
Ästung (ᵋ⌣) f 64 for. (Ab-ästung) lopping}
Asturi-en ♀ (⌣ᴸ(⌣)⌣) npr/n. 93α. (ehm. span. Fürstentum, jetzt Ovi-e'do) Asturias.
Asturi-er (⌣ᴸ⌣) m 22, ~in f 47, asturisch (⌣ᴸ⌣) a. 66 Asturian.
Ast-verhau (ᵋ...) ⚔ m 62 defence constructed of branches (of trees); =werk n branches, boughs pl. (of a tree).
Äsung (ᴸ⌣) f 64 agr. (Weideland) pasture; hunt. grazing, browsing.
Äsungs-platz (ᴸ...) m 62 pasture-land; hunt. feeding-place.
Asyl (⌣ᴸ) [grch.] n ⓓc. (Zufluchtsort) (place of) refuge; für Irrsinnige ꝛc.: asylum, home; (Schutz) sanctuary; ~ für Obdachlose (Nachtherberge) night-shelter, e-r engl. Gemeinde: casual ward; ~=recht (⌣ᴸ...) n 62 right of sanctuary.
Asymptote ☌ (⌣⌣ᴸ⌣) f 48 math. (gerade Linie, der sich eine Kurve nähert, ohne sie zu schneiden) asymptote.
asyndetisch ☌ (⌣⌣ᴸ⌣) [grch.] a. 66 (verbindungslos) asyndetic.
Aszese, Aszet, aszetisch s. Askese ꝛc.
Aszidien ☌ (⌣ᴸ(⌣)) [grch.] pl., zo. (Seescheiden) ascidia pl. [(Old Testament) O. T.]
A. T. abbr. = Altes Testament = O. T.}
Atakamit ☌ (⌣⌣ᴸ) [Ataca'ma ♀ in Chile] m ⓓc. (o. pl.) min. (Kupfersmaragd) atacamite, oxychloride of copper.
Atavismus ☌ (⌣⌣ᵋ⌣) [lt.] m 27 (o. pl.) (den Ahnen entlehnte Eigentümlichkeit) atavism.
Ate (ᴸ) [grch.] npr/f., inv., myth. (Schuld) Ate.
Atelier (⌣⌣ᴸ) [fr. Werkstatt] n 50 studio; photographisches ~ photographic studio; ~=zigeuner (⌣...) m 22 Malerei: gipsy serving as artist's model.
Atellanen pl. (⌣⌣ᴸ⌣) [lt.] f 48 röm. Alt.: (Volksschauspiele) Atellan(s pl.)
Atem (ᴸ⌣) [ahd.] m 23e. (ohne pl.) breath; (Atmen) breathing, respiration; kurzer ~ short(ness of) breath, short-windedness; außer ~ out of breath, F puffed, von Pferden ꝛc.: blown; außer ~ kommen to get out of breath; in e-m ~ in (one and) the same breath; den ~ an-, zurückhalten to hold one's breath; den letzten ~ aushauchen to breathe one's last; guten ~ besitzen to be long-winded; to have good lungs; ❋ den Feind in ~ halten to keep the enemy on the move, to pursue (or harass) the enemy; ~ holen ob. schöpfen to take breath; tief ~ holen to draw (or heave) a deep breath; ~ schöpfen lassen (to allow to) breathe; wieder zu ~ kommen to recover one's breath, to breathe again; laß mich erst zu ~ kommen give me breathing-time; mit verhaltenem ~ with bated breath.
atembar (ᴸ⌣) a. 66 breathable, respirable. ~keit (~) f 46 respirability.

Atem=beklemmung (ᴸ⌣...) f, =beschwerde f, path. difficulty of breath(ing), ☌ dyspnœa; =holen n respiration; =loch n, ent. spiracle; ℒlos a. 66 breathless; ℒlose Stille dead silence; =losigkeit f breathlessness; =not f, path. heavy breathing, vgl. =beschwerde; (sehr) schwere ~ (great) shortness of breath, ☌ orthopnœa. — Vgl. auch: Atmungs=...
a tempo (ᴸᵋ⌣) [it.] adv. (rechtzeitig) in (the nick of) time; (gleichzeitig) at the same time, simultaneously.
A-tempo-hieb (ᴸᵋ⌣...) m 62, =stoß m fenc. simultaneous thrust.
Atem=zug (ᴸ...) m 62 respiration; bis zum letzten ~e to one's last breath or gasp; in einem ~e in the same breath.
Athal ☌ (-ᴸ) n ⓓc. chm. (Cetylalkohol) ethal ($C_{16}H_{34}O$). [ethane (C_2H_6).]
Äthan ☌ (-ᴸ) n ⓓc. chm. (Äthylwasserstoff)}
athanas(ian)isch (⌣⌣ᴸ(⌣ᴴ)) [Athana'sius, Bischof] a. 66 Athanasian; eccl. ~es Glaubensbekenntnis Athanasian Creed.
Athe-ismus ☌ (⌣⌣ᵋ⌣) [grch.] m 27 atheism; **Athe-ist** (⌣⌣ᵋ) m 42 (Gottesleugner) atheist; **athe-istisch** (⌣⌣ᵋ⌣) a. 66 atheist(ic), atheistical.
Athen (⌣ᴸ) [grch.] npr/n. 93α. Athens; Sprichw. Eulen nach ~ tragen to carry coals to Newcastle. [næum.]
Athenäum (⌣⌣ᴸ) [lt.,*grch.] n 28 Athe-}
Athene (⌣ᴸ) npr/f. 94ᵋβ. myth. (Göttin der Künste ꝛc.) Athene, (it.) Minerva.
Athen(i-ens)er (⌣-(⌣)ᵋ⌣, ⌣ᴸ⌣) m 22, ~in f 47, **athen(i-ens)isch** a. 66 Athenian.
Äther (ᴸ⌣) [grch.] m 22 poet. (Himmelsraum), phys., chm. ether; mit ~ erfüllt ethereal; chm. in ~ verwandeln to etherize; surg. mit ~ betäuben to narcotize with ether, to etherize.
Äther=bildung (ᴸ⌣...) f 62 aus Alkohol: etherification; =dämpfe m/pl. ether(eal) vapours pl.; =förmig a. 66 etheriform.
ätherhaft (ᴸ⌣⌣) a. 66 ethereous.
äther=haltig (ᴸ⌣...) a. 66 containing ether, ethereous.
ätherisch (-ᴸ⌣) [grch.] a. 66 1. poet. (himmlisch) ethereal, ...ous. — 2. chm. ℒe Öle essential (or volatile) oils pl.; phys. ℒe Stoffe imponderabilia pl.
ätherisierbar ☌ (---ᴸ) [grch.] a. 66 surg. etherizable.
ätherisieren ☌ (---ᴸ) [grch.] v/a. 93 surg. (mit Äther befeuchten, betäuben) to etherize.
äther=leicht (ᴸ⌣...) a. 66 (as) light as ether, very light, F (as) light as love.
atherman ☌ (⌣⌣ᴸ) [grch.] a. 66 phys. (Wärme nicht durchlassend) atherm(an)ous.
Äther=narkose (ᴸ⌣...) f 62 med. narcosis produced by ether, etherization; =öl n, chm. etherol; =säure f, chm. lampic acid; =schwefelsäure f = Äthyl=s.; =weinsäure f, chm. ethyltartaric acid, tartrovinic acid.
Äthiopi-en ♀ (-(⌣)ᴸ(⌣)) [grch.] npr/n. 93α. Ethiopia; **Äthiopi-er(in** f 47) m 22, **äthiopisch** a. 66 Ethiopian.
Athlet (⌣ᴸ) [grch.] m 42 athlete; ~ik f 46 athletics; ℒisch a. 66 athletic.
Äthyl (-ᴸ) [grch. aith(er)-hyle] n ⓓc. chm. ethyl (C_2H_5); =äther ("...) m 22 ethylic ether ($C_4H_{10}O$).
Äthylen ☌ (---ᴸ) [grch.] n ⓓc. chm. (ölbildendes Gas) ethylene, olefiant gas (C_2H_4).

Zeichen (s. S. XVII): F familiär; P Volkssprache; ⚡ Gaunersprache; ⸵ selten; † alt (auch gestorben); * neu (auch geboren); ⧾ unrichtig;

Äthyl-jodid (-ᴗ...) n ⓺ chm. ethyl iodide (C_2H_5J); =**schwefelsäure** f, chm. sulphovinic acid; =**wasserstoff** m, chm. ethyl hydride (= Ätha'n).

Ätiologie ⚘ (-(ᴗ)ᴗ⌣ᴗ) [grch.] f ⓴ path. (Lehre v. den Ursachen, bsd. der Krankheiten) ætiology.

Atlant (ᴗ⌣) [grch.] m ⓬ = Atlas¹ 3.

Atlanten=... (ᴗᴗ⌣...) f. Atlas¹...

Atlantis ⚘ (ᴗ⌣ᴗ) [grch.; *(Ma)atlan = Mexiko] f, inv. (sagenhafte Insel) Atlantis.

Atlantisch ⚥ (ᴗ⌣ᴗ) [grch.] a. ⓺ ~es Meer, ~er Ozean the Atlantic (Ocean); jenseit des ~en Meeres transatlantic.

Atlas¹ (⌣ᴗ) [grch.] m ⓲, Wa. (pl. a. Atlanten) I npr. 1. myth. u. ⚥ Atlas (a. arch. = Gebälkträger). — II s. 2. ⚘ anat. (erster Halswirbel) atlas. — 3. [nhd. 1595] (Kartenwerk) atlas. [stoff] satin.

Atlas²(⌣ᴗ) [mhd.,*ar.] m ⓬, Wa. (Seiden-)

atlas²=artig (⌣ᴗ...) a. ⓺ satined; =**band** n ⓬ satin-ribbon; =**barchent** m satin-top; =**beere** ⚵ f = Elsbeere; =**brokat** m satin-brocade; =**falter** m, ent. atlas(-moth); =**format** n, typ., &c. atlas (-folio), large square folio.

Atlas¹=gebirge ⚥ n Atlas (Mountains).

Atlas²=köper (⌣ᴗ...) m ⓬ satin-tweel.

atlassen (⌣ᴗᴗ) a. ⓺ (D 9) (made of) satin.

Atlas²=weber (⌣ᴗ...) m ⓬ satin-weaver; =**stein** m, min. satin-spar; =**zeug** n

Atm. abbr. = Atmosphäre. [satinet.]

atmen (⌣ᴗ) [mhd.: Atem] ⓶b. I v/n. (h.) 1. meist: to breathe; schwer ⚷ to gasp (for breath); tief ⚷ to fetch (or draw) a deep breath. — 2. fig. (hauchen): die Nelken ⚷ duftig ... exhale (or diffuse, waft, spread, emit) a sweet scent. — II v/a.u. v/refl. 3. e-e reine Luft ⚷ to breathe (or inhale) a pure air. — 4. (bekunden) to manifest; alles atmet Freude joy dwells in every eye; (verbreiten) to spread. — III ~ n 5. — Atmung. — IV ⓶d p.pr. und a. ⓺ 6. breathing; schwer ⚷ short- (für Tiere: broken-)winded.

ätmen (⌣ᴗ) v/a. ⓶b. — abätmen.

atmig (⌣ᴗ) a. ⓺ vet. broken-winded.

...atmig (⌣¹ᴗ), zB. kurz⚷ short of breath.

Atmosphäre ⚘ (ᴗᴗf ᴗ) [grch.] f ⓴ (Lufttreis) atmosphere; eine schwüle ~ a stifling air; =**druck** (⌣...) m ⓬ (Luftdruck) atmospheric pressure.

atmosphärisch ⚘ (ᴗᴗfᴗ) [grch.] a. ⓺ phys. atmospheric; ⚷e Maschi'ne atmospheric engine; hot-air (or caloric) engine.

Atmung (⌣ᴗ) f ⓴ breath(ing), respiration; ~**s=bewegung** (⌣ᴗ...) f ⓴ respiratory movement; =**beschwerde** f heavy breathing, vgl. Atem=...; =**geräusch** n respiratory sound or murmur; =**organe**, =**werkzeuge** n/pl. anat. respiratory organs pl. Bgl. a. Atem=...

Ätna ⚥ (⌣ᴗ) npr/m. ⓶α. Berg auf Sizilien: (Mount) Etna.

Ätoli-en ⚥ (-ᴸ(ᴗ)ᴗ) npr/n. ⓶α. Ætolia.

Ätoli-er m ⚥, **ätolisch** a. ⓺ Ætolian.

Atoll ⚥ (ᴗ⌣) [malai. Einschließung] n ⓶b. u. ~**e** f ⓴ (ringförmige Koralleninsel) atoll.

Atom ⚘ (ᴗ⌣) [grch.] n ⓶c. chm., phys. (kleinstes Teilchen) atom, weitS. minute particle; fig. nicht ein ~ not an atom, not a speck. [weight, equivalent.]

Atom-gewicht ⚘ (ᴗ⌣...) n ⓬ atomic

atomisch ⚘ (ᴗ⌣ᴗ) [grch.] a. ⓺ atomic.

Atomismus ⚘ (ᴗ-ᴸᴗ) [grch.] m ⓶ (naturwissenschaftliche Atomtheorie) atomism.

Atomist ⚘ (ᴗ-⌣) [grch.] m ⓬ atomist; ~**istik** (ᴗ-⌣ᴗ) f ⓴ atomic theory; Lisch a. ⓺ chm. atomic. [Wertigkeit.]

Atomität ⚘ (ᴗ---ᴸ) [grch.] f ⓴ = atomic theory; =**verhältnis** n, =**wesen** n atomicity.

Atonie ⚘ (ᴗ-ᴸ) [grch.] f ⓴ path. atony, (bodily) weakness, debility, lack of strength.

atonisch (ᴗ⌣ᴗ) [grch.] a. ⓺ med. (erschlafft) atonic, relaxed.

Atout (à-tu') [fr.] n ⓶ (Trumpf) trump card.

Atrament=stein ⚘ (--ᴸ=ᴸ) m ⓬ min. = Eisenvitriol.

Atride (ᴗ⌣ᴗ) [grch.] m ⓴ (Nachkomme des A'treus) Atrides, pl. Atridæ.

Atrophie ⚘ (ᴗᴗᴸ) [grch.] f ⓴ (Abzehrung, Abmagerung) atrophy.

Atropin (ᴗ-ᴸ) [grch.] n ⓶c. (Alkaloid der Belladonna) atropine ($C_{17}H_{23}NO_3$).

ätsch! F (⌣) int. (Schadenfreude 2c.) etwa: serves you right!, sold again!, wouldn't you like it!

Atschin ⚥ (⌣ᴸ) npr/n. ⓶α. (Staat auf Sumatra) Achin; ~**ese** (ᴗᴗ⌣) m ⓬, ~**esin** f ⓴, **Lesisch** a. ⓺ Achinese.

Attaché (ᴗᴗ⌣ᴸ) [fr.] m ⓬ attaché.

Attacke ⚔ (ᴗ⌣ᴗ) [fr.] f ⓴ (Angriff) attack; (zur) ~ reiten ta make a cavalry-charge.

attackieren ⚔ (ᴗᴗ⌣ᴗ) [fr.] v/a. ⓴ to (make an) attack, to charge.

Attentat (ᴗᴗ⌣) [lt.] n ⓶ (Mordanschlag) attempt on a p.'s life; murderous attack; ein ~ auf e-n machen to attempt a p.'s life. [assassin.]

Attentäter F (ᴗᴗ⌣ᴗ) m ⓬ (would-be)

Atter † (⌣ᴗ) [mhd.] f ⓴ = Natter.

Attest (ᴗ⌣), ~**at** (ᴗᴗ⌣) [lt.] n ⓶b. (Zeugnis, Bescheinigung) certificate, attestation; ein ~ ausstellen to grant a certificate.

attestieren (ᴗᴗ⌣ᴗ) v/a. ⓴ to certify, attest.

Attich ⚵ (⌣ᴗ) [ahd.;* grch. akte´] m ⓶d. dwarf-elder (Sambu'cus e'bulus, E'bulum hu'mile). [II arch. f ⓴ (Muffat) attic.]

Attika ⚥ (⌣ᴗᴗ) I npr/n. ⓶α. Attica.

Attila¹ (⌣ᴗᴗ) [got. Väterchen] npr/m. ⓶α. (Hunnenkönig, 451) Attila. [hussar tunic.]

Attila² ⚔ (⌣ᴗᴗ) [madj.] ⓶ (Husarenrock)

attisch (⌣ᴗ) a. ⓺ Attic; ⚷es Salz Attic salt; ⚷e Redeweise atticism. [attitude.]

Attitüde (ᴗᴗ⌣ᴗ) [fr.] f ⓴ Kunst: (Haltung)

Attizismus (ᴗᴗ⌣ᴗ) [lt.] m ⓶ atticism.

Attizist (ᴗᴗ⌣) [lt.] m ⓬ atticist.

Attraktion ⚘ (ᴗᴗtß(ᴗ)ᴸ) [lt.] f ⓴ (Anziehung) attraction. [artikel] take-in, catch.

Attrappe ⓫ (ᴗ⌣ᴗ) [fr.,*dtsch.] f ⓴ (Scherz-)

Attribut (ᴗᴗ⌣) [lt.] n ⓶c. (Sinnbild) emblem, symbol; (äußeres Zeichen) attribute; log. predicate; gr. adjunct.

attributiv(isch) (ᴗᴗ⌣f, ᴗᴗ⌣ᴗᴗ) a. ⓺ bsd. gram. attributive. [monia.]

Ätz=ammoniak (⌣...) n ⓬ (caustic) am-

ätzbar (⌣ᴗ) a. ⓺ corrodible, ...sible; ~**keit** f ⓴ (o. pl.) corrodibility, ...sibleness.

Ätz=beize (⌣...) f ⓬ Zeugdruck: discharge; =**bild** n etching; =**brett** n etching-board; =**druck** ⓶ a) Zeugdruck: chemical discharge-work; b) (Gedrucktes) discharge-style (print); c) (Kupferstich: etching engraved with caustic (water).

Atzel (⌣ᴗ) [mhd.] f ⓴ 1. orn. magpie (= Elster). — 2. F wig (= Stutzperücke).

ätzen (⌣ᴗ) [mhd.: eat] ⓴ I v/n. (h.) u. sich ⚷ v/refl. 1. to eat, feed, graze. — II v/a. 2. Tiere, auch (jur.) Gefangene: to feed, to give food to, stärker: to gorge. — 3. (ködern) to bait, to lure.

ätzen (⌣ᴗ) [ahd.: eat, etch] I v/a. ⓴ 1. v. Tieren (bsd. Vögeln): die Jungen ⚷, hunt.: Geflügel ⚷, auch Kinder ⚷ = atzen. — 2. ⓺ (sich einfressen) to corrode, to eat into; surg. to cauterize; Kupferstecherei: to etch. — II ~ n 3. — Ätzung. — III ⓶d p.pr. u. a. ⓺ 4. (f. I) auch :caustic (a. fig.), corrosive.

Ätz=grund (⌣...) m ⓬ etching-ground; =**kali**, n (Kaliumhydroxyd) caustic potash, potassium hydrate; =**kalk** m (Kalziumhydroxyd) caustic lime, quicklime; =**kraft** f causticity; =**kunst** f Kupferstecherei: etching; =**lauge** f caustic lye; =**mittel** n corrosive, caustic; =**nadel** f Gravierkunst: etching-needle; =**natron** n, chm. (Natriumhydroxyd) caustic soda, sodium hydrate; =**stein** m = =kali; =**stift** m stick of caustic, (Höllenstein) stick of nitrate of silver; =**stoff** m = =mittel; =**sublima't** n, pharm. (Quecksilberchlorid) corrosive sublimate (of mercury). [2. (Köder) bait.]

Atzung (⌣ᴗ) f ⓴ hunt. ob. † 1. food. —

Ätzung (⌣ᴗ) f ⓴ surg. cauterization, Gravierkunst: etching, aquatint(a).

Ätz=verfahren (⌣...) n ⓶ caustic process; =**wasser** n aquafortis; mordant; =**zeichnung** f etched copper-plate.

a u. ⓫ = a uso [it. dem Gebrauche gemäß] according to usage, as usual.

Au¹ (ᴸ) f ⓴ = Aue¹.

au² (ᴸ) int. (Schmerz) ⚷!, ⚷ weh! oh! — 2. P bei e-m faulen Witz, Kalauer: oh!, I never!, did you ever (hear the like)?

auch (ᴗ⌣) [ahd.: eke] cj. 1. (ebenfalls) also; too; likewise: a) ⚷ er sagte es he also ..., he too ..., also he ...; ich glaube es I believe it — ich ⚷! so do I!; sie hat ihn gesehen she has seen him — wir ⚷! so have we!; er war ein Dichter und ⚷ ein Held ... and a hero withal; sie gab mir Wein und ⚷ Geld ... and money as well (F to boot); Gewehre und dazu ⚷ Patronen ... and cartridges into the bargain; du bist ⚷ so einer! you're another!; nicht nur gut, sondern ⚷ klug not only kind, but also wise; sowohl gestern ⚷ heute both yesterday and to-day; b) aber ⚷, doch ⚷: das Kleid ist schön, aber ⚷ teuer ... beautiful and proportionately dear — das wußten Sie doch ⚷! you, surely, must have known it!; ich gebe dir das Buch, nun lies es (aber) ⚷! ... now mind (or be sure) and read it! — das will ich aber ⚷ tun certainly, I will (vgl. aber I); c) ⚷ nicht: ich kann's nicht I cannot do it — ich ⚷ nicht nor (or neither) can I; er hat keine Freude he has no pleasure — wir ⚷ nicht (or neither) have we, nor we either. — 2. steigernd: (selbst, sogar) even; ⚷ das kleinste Tröpfchen even the smallest drop; ohne ⚷ nur zu weinen without so much as a tear; ⚷ du hast nicht (einmal) gewartet nay, you did not even wait; ⚷ nicht einer not (a single) one; er mag gehen oder ⚷ bleiben ... or

[Aucklandsinseln] — 86 — [auf]

(even) stay. — **3.** zugeftehend: **wenn** ⁂, **ob** ⁂, **wenn** ⁂ **fchon**, **wenn** ⁂ **gleich** even if, even though; although; wenn ich ihn ⁂ nur fehen darf if I may only see him; ob er ⁂ noch fo groß ift, wie groß er ⁂ ift be he ever so big, however tall he may be; wenn fie ⁂ tanzen kann though (or granted) she can dance; fo fehr er ⁂ lief however fast he ran; fo fehr ich es ⁂ bedaure much as (or however much) I regret it; ob er ⁂ ftudiert hat, fo weiß er doch nichts though he has (or may have) studied, yet he knows nothing. — **4.** verallgemeinernd: **was** er ⁂ (**immer**) fagen mag whatever he may say; **wer** es ⁂ (**immer**) fei whoever it may be; **wie** dem ⁂ fei however this may be; auf welche Art ⁂ immer in whatever way, how(so)ever; wo ⁂ immer where(so)ever; fooft er ⁂ kommen mag however often (fchwächer: whenever) he may come. — **5.** verftärkend: indeed; das ift ⁂ wahr that's really true, that's true enough; fo ift's ⁂! why, so it is!; er ift aber ⁂ gar nicht blöde he is certainly not at all shy; es hat ⁂ nur wenig geregnet don't forget how little rain we have had; fo wird's ⁂ wohl fein! no doubt (or I believe) you are right! — **6.** in Wunfch- u. Fragefätzen: kann ich ⁂ (wirklich) **auf ihn bauen**? (how) can I rely upon him?; wozu (denn) ⁂? (now) what is the use of it? — **7.** zur Begründung: wie bift du geputzt? — ich will ⁂ auf den Ball quite so, I am going to the ball. — **8.** iro.: das hilft ihm ⁂ was Rechtes! I hope it will do him (much) good! du kommft ⁂ wirklich gelegen! a nice time for you to come, indeed!

Aucklands-infeln ♀ (⁂) npr/f/pl. ⁂ (Infeln füdl. von Neufeeland) Auckland Isles pl. [von Britifch-Indien] Oudh.]
Audh ♀ (⁂) npr/n. ⁂α. (nordöftl. Proving)
Audi-enz (-⁂) [fr.] f ⁂ (Gehör, Zutritt) audience (beim König of the king), bei e-m ~ erhalten to be admitted to (or to come into) the presence of a p.
Audi-enz-faal (⁂...) m ⁂, =zimmer n audience- (or presence-) chamber or room. [gerichtsrat.]
Auditeur (-⁂tö'r)[fr.] m ⁂d. ⁂ = Kriegs-]
Auditor (-⁂) [it.] m ⁂ (ehm. jur. Beifitzer) judge-advocate, assessor.
Auditorium (-⁂) [it.] n ⁂ **1.** (Hörfaal) lecture-room. - **2.** (Zuhörerfchaft) audience; das verfammelte zahlreiche ~ the assembled crowd of hearers or listeners.
Au(-e¹ (⁂) [ahd.: ait, eyot, island] f ⁂ (⁂) (Wiefengrund) (rich) pasture-land; (low-lying) meadow-land, fresh green fields pl.; fertile plain. [fchaf] ewe.]
Au-e² (⁂) [ahd.: ewe: lt. ovis] (Mutter-]
Au-er (⁂) [ahd.] m ⁂ zo. = ~ochs.
Au-er-balz (⁂...) f ⁂ pairing-time for mountain-cocks; **=geflügel** n woodgrouse, heath-fowl; **=hahn** [mhd.] m mountain-cock, cock of the wood; **=henne** f, **=huhn** [mhd.] n (Te'trao uroga'llus) mountain-hen; **=kalb** n calf of an aurochs, **=ochs** [ahd.] m aurochs, ureox, European bison (Bos primige'nius).
Auf¹ (⁂) [ahd.] m ⁂c. hunt. = Uhu.

auf² (⁂) [ahd.: up] **I** prp. räumlich: mit dat. auf die Frage **wo**?, mit acc. auf die Frage **wohin**? **1.** on, upon; das Buch liegt ⁂ dem Tifche the book is lying on the table; ich habe es ⁂ den Tifch gelegt I put it on the table; blind ⁂ beiden Augen blind in (or of) both eyes; ⁂ Ehre! upon my honour!; ⁂ Erden on this earth; ⁂ der Harfe fpielen to play on the harp; er lebt ⁂ Koften von he lives upon or at the expense of; ⁂ Kredit on credit; ⁂ diefer Seite on this side; ⁂ der Stelle on the spot; ⁂ dem Verdeck on deck; ⁂ einen Wechfel ⁂ e-n ziehen to draw upon a p. (for a certain sum). — **2.** durch andere prp. ⁂ dem Balle at the ball; alle bis ⁂ einen all except (or but) one; ⁂ e-e große Entfernung at a great distance; ⁂ e-n fchießen to fire (or shoot) at a p.; ⁂ der Schule, Univerfität at school, at the university; ⁂ der See at sea; ⁂ der Straße herumlaufen to run about the street; ⁂ geradem Wege by the straightest route; ⁂ welchem Wege kommt er? by which road is he coming?; ⁂ der Flotte dienen to serve in the navy; ⁂ dem Hofe in the yard; ⁂ dem Lande in the country; auf der Straße in (Am. on) the street; kein Menfch ⁂ der Welt nobody in the world; er ift ⁂ f-m Zimmer he is in his room; ⁂ dem Zuge in the train; ⁂ die Straße (den Hof) laufen to run into the street (the yard); ⁂s Land reifen to go into the country; es fiel ⁂ die Erde it fell to the ground; er ift ⁂ den Markt fchicken to send a p. to the market; ⁂ die Poft, die Polizei, fein Zimmer gehen to go to the post-office, to the police-station, to one's room; ⁂ einen Baum klettern to climb up a tree; fich ⁂ Piftolen fchlagen to fight with pistols. — **3.** zur Bezeichnung des Objekts: ⁂ e-e Frage (e-n Brief) antworten to answer a question (letter); ⁂ ⁂ den Inhaber lautende Obligationen bonds (payable) to bearer; Wechfel ⁂ hier bill (of exchange) on this place, on ours. — **4.** bei Zahlenangaben: foviel ⁂ den Mann so much each (person) or a head; die Koften belaufen fich mindeftens ⁂ (ob. ⁂ mindeftens) 1000 Mark the expenses amount to at least fifty pounds or come to 50 pounds at least; ⁂ ein Pfund gehen 20 Schilling... go to a pound; ein Druck von 10 Pfund ⁂ den Quadratzoll... ten pounds to the square inch. — **5.** bei Zeitbeftimmungen: ⁂ den Abend towards evening; ⁂ e-n Augenblick for a moment; ⁂ den erften Blick at the first glance, at a glance; ⁂s (ganze) Leben, ⁂ Lebenszeit for life, for a life-time; ⁂ die Minute to the minute; ⁂ f-r Reife during (or on) his journey; ⁂ frifcher Tat (ertappt caught) in the very act or red-handed; ⁂ Wiederfehen! till we meet again!, (fr.) au revoir!; es geht ⁂ neun it's going on for nine; es ift drei Viertel ⁂ fünf, ein Viertel ⁂ drei is a quarter to five, a quarter past two; ⁂ ⁂ Zeit (abbr. **a. Z.**).

on credit; ⁂ zwei Monate at two months' credit; **bis** ⁂ **den heutigen Tag** up to this (or the present) day; bis ⁂ weiteres until further notice. — **6.** (gemäß) ⁂ meinen Befehl by my order; ⁂ Ihre Bitte at your request; ⁂ Grund von by reason of; **auf das hin** on the strength of that. — **7.** (Art und Weife, Mittel ꝛc.) oft durch adv., zB.: ⁂ andere Art differently, otherwise; ⁂ indirektem Wege indirectly; ⁂ halbem Wege half-way; ⁂ folgende Art in the following manner; ⁂ alle Fälle (= jedenfalls) in any case; ⁂ einmal all at once; ⁂ deutfch in German; ⁂ franzöfifche Art in (or after) the French fashion; ⁂s Geratewohl at random; ⁂ Ihre Gefahr hin at your risk; ⁂ feine Koften kommen to cover one's expenses; ⁂ Sicht at sight; vor dem sup.: ⁂s äußerfte to the uttermost; er ift ⁂s Äußerfte gefaßt he is prepared for the worst; ⁂s befte in the best way (possible); ⁂s billigfte at the cheapest rate, most moderately; ⁂s deutlichfte most distinctly; ⁂s höchfte in the highest degree; ⁂s fchnellfte in the quickest way possible, as soon (or quickly) as possible. — **8.** (Reihenfolge) ⁂ e-n, ⁂ et. folgen to succeed (or follow) a p., a th.; es kamen Briefe ⁂ Briefe there came letter(s) upon letter(s) or one letter after another; ⁂s neue again, afresh, anew, once more. — **9.** Idiotismen: ⁂ Befuch fein bei // to be staying with //, ⁂ die Jagd (⁂ Reifen) gehen to go hunting (travelling); et., viel ⁂ fich haben to be of great consequence or import(ance); es hat nichts ⁂ fich it does not (much) matter; ⁂ j-s Gefundheit (auch: Wohl) trinken to drink (to) a p.'s health, to toast a p.; ⁂ ⁂ Wache ziehen to mount guard. — **II** adv. **10.** (nach oben hin) up(wards); aloft; on high. — **11.** ⁂ **und ab** (von oben nach unten) up and down; (hin und her) to and fro; eine Mark ⁂ oder ab ... more or less; das ~ und Ab the ups and downs (of life); bf. in Verbindung mit v. der Bewegung, zB.: ⁂ und ab geh(e)n, wallen, wandeln, ziehen to walk, float, saunter, travel up and down or to and fro; ⁂ und ab fteigen to ascend and descend, vom Pferde: to mount and dismount; ⁂ **und davon** gehen, ziehen, fich ⁂ und davon machen to run (or be) off, F to bolt, to hook it; er war fchon ⁂ und davon he was already gone or flown; ⁂ **und nieder** hüpfen to hop up and down; ⚓ der Anker ift ⁂ und nieder the anchor is apeak. — **12.** (offen) die Tür ift auf ... open; die Augen ⁂! open your eyes! — **13.** ell. noch ⁂ (nicht zu Bett) fein to be up or astir; er ift noch ⁂ he is not in bed yet; find fie fchon um fechs (Uhr) auf? are they up (or do they rise) as early as six (o'clock)?; ⚔ Gewehr ⁂! shoulder arms!; ⚓ Anker ⁂ fein to be aweigh. — **14. von ... ⁂** from, zB.: von klein, von Jugend ⁂ from childhood, from a child; von der Pike ⁂ dienen to serve from the ranks. — **III** int. ⁂! ⁂!, frifch

Signs (see page XVII): F familiar; P vulgar; ⌐ flash; ⸸ rare; † obsolete (died); * new word (born); ⁺⁺ incorrect; ♪ music:

[auf...] — 87 — [aufbleiben]

2! (let us be) up!, cheer up!, be alive!, go it! — **IV** ⌇ *cj.* ⌇ **daß** (= damit) in order that; ⌇ daß nicht lest, for fear that. [auf, straßab.]
...auf (...*¹*), ʒB. bergauf, bergab; straß-
☞ **auf-...** (*¹¹*...) Vorſilbe in Zſſgn. mit *verbs* immer trennbar (**) (*ant.* ab-...) bʒ. --
1. Richtung, Bewegung nach oben, ʒB. aufflie-gen to fly up. — 2. Öffnen, ʒB. aufſchneiden to cut open. — 3. Verbrauch, Vollendung, ʒB. aufbrennen to burn up. — 4. Be-ſtimmung, ʒB. Eis auftauen to thaw ... — 5. bei Tonwörtern: Wecken, ʒB. auf-geigen to rouse by fiddling. — 6. Aus-breiten, ʒB. auftiſchen to serve up. — 7. Auflegen, ʒB. aufbürden to lay on (a p.'s shoulders). — 8. Wiederholung, ʒB. aufwärmen to warm up. — 9. Zu-wachs, ʒB. aufſchwellen to swell up.
auf-ächzen (*¹¹⌣*) *v/n.* (h.) ⓦ** to groan heavily, to draw (or heave) a deep sigh.
auf-ackern (*¹¹⌣⌣*) *v/a.* ⓦa** to plough up or over again, to break (the ground).
auf-arbeiten (*¹¹⌣-⌣*) ⓦ**I *v/a.* 1. den Vorrat ⌇ to work (or use) up; Rückſtände ⌇ to work (or clear) off arrears. — 2. (öff-nen) to break open, e-e Tür ⌇ to force (open) ... — 3. (auffriſchen) Röcke ꝛc.: to renovate, to do up. — **II** *v/n.* (h.) 4. (vollenden) to finish (a task). — **III** ſich ⌇ *v/refl.* 5. to over-exert o.s. — 6. (emporſtreben) to work one's way up.
auf-atmen (*¹¹⌣*) *v/n.* (h.) ⓑb** to breathe again or freely; to utter a sigh of relief; auch: *fig.* (wieder frei) ⌇ to re-cover, to feel relief, to revive.
auf-ätzen (*¹¹⌣*) *v/a.* ⓦ** 1. *surg.* (durch Ätzmittel öffnen) to open by corrosives. — 2. ⊕ eine Kupferplatte ⌇ to etch ...
auf-backen (*¹¹⌣⌣*) ⓑb** I *v/a.* 1. (wieder) ⌇ to bake afresh. — 2. alles Mehl ⌇ to use up ... in baking. — 3. (aufkleben) to bake on to; Roſinen ⌇ to garnish with ... — **II** *v/n.* (ſn) 4. auf et. ⌇ to adhere (or stick) to a th. in baking.
auf-bähen (*¹¹⌣*) *v/a.* ⓦ** to open by (or with) poulticing.
auf-bahren (*¹¹⌣*) I *v/a.* ⓦ** den Sarg ⌇ to put the coffin on the bier; die Leiche (feierlich) ⌇ to lay out the body (in state). — **II Auf-bahrung** *f* ⓦ von Fürſten ꝛc.: lying-in-state.
auf-ballen (*¹¹⌣⌣*) *v/a.* ⓦ** to put (or heap, pile) up in bales.
auf-bänken ⊙ (*¹¹⌣*) *v/a.* ⓦ**: das Feuer eines Dampfkeſſels ⌇ (durch Öffnen der Feuer-keſſel u. Schließen der Aſchenfälle klein halten) to keep down ..., to moderate ...
auf-banſen (*¹¹⌣*) *v/a.* ⓦ** *agr.* Korn ⌇ to pile up (sheaves in a barn).
Auf-bau (*¹¹*) *m* ⓓd. 1. erection, e-s Kunſtwerkes: composition. — 2. super-structure; ~ (Oberteil) e-s Wagens body of a coach.
auf-bauen (*¹¹⌣*) *v/a. u. v/refl.* ⓦ** 1. to build (or raise) up, to erect; ſchnell ⌇ to run up; wieder ⌇ to rebuild, to reconstruct; ſich ſtufenweiſe ⌇ to rise gradually or step by step. — 2. zu Weihnachten ⌇, auch *abs.* ⌇ to set out the Christmas gifts, to arrange the Ch. presents (under the Christmas tree).
auf-baumen (*¹¹⌣*) *v/n.* (h.) ⓦ** 1. = auf-bäumen. — 2. *hunt. v. Raubtieren:* to climb

up (or to seek refuge on) a tree; *v. Vögeln:* to perch, to settle on a tree.
auf-bäumen (*¹¹⌣*) ⓦ** I *v/a.* ⊕ Weberei: die Kette ⌇ to beam, to wind up ...; das Gewebe ⌇ to take up ... — **II** ſich ⌇ *v/refl.* von Pferden: to rear, to prance, *fig.* ſich ⌇ gegen to struggle (or rebel, F kick) against.
auf-bauſchen (*¹¹⌣*) ⓓ** I *v/a.* to puff (up); F vom Frauenkleide: to puff (or swell) out; *fig.* to exaggerate. — **II** *v/n.* (h.) *u. v/refl.* to swell, to bag (out).
Auf-bauten ⌇ (*¹¹⌣*) *pl.* (die geſchloſſenen Räume auf dem Oberbau e-s Schiffes) upper works of a ship.
auf-befinden (*¹¹⌣⌣*), ſich ⌇ *v/refl.* ⓓ*/* to be (still) up (= noch auf ſein; ſ. auf 13).
auf-begehren (*¹¹⌣⌣*) *v/n.* (h.) ⓑ*/* to inveigh against, to be up in arms.
auf-behalten (*¹¹⌣⌣*) I *v/a.* ⓦa*/* 1. den Hut ⌇ to keep one's hat on. — 2. die Augen ⌇ to keep one's eyes open. — **II** *n* ⓦ 3. das ~ des Hutes iſt nicht erlaubt: hats to be taken off!, hats off!; please remove (your) hats!
auf-beißen (*¹¹⌣*) *v/a.* ⓦa*/* to bite open; Nüſſe ⌇ to crack nuts.
auf-beizen (*¹¹⌣*) *v/a.* ⓦ** = aufätzen 1.
auf-bekommen (*¹¹⌣⌣*) *v/a.* ⓦ*/* 1. eine Tür ꝛc.: to get open; einen Hut: to get on. — 2. (auf-eſſen) to eat up, F to polish off. — 3. Schule: wir haben etwas ⌇ we had a lesson set us, we have some lessons to do.
auf-bereiten ⚒ (*¹¹⌣⌣*) I *v/a.* ⓦ*/* 1. *metall.* Erz ⌇ to dress (or concentrate, prepare) ore(s); naß: to wash (or buddle) ores. — 2. Statiſtik: die Zählkarten ⌇ to prepare the census cards. — **II** ~ *n* ⓦ 3. = Aufbereitung.
Auf-bereitung ⚒ (*¹¹⌣⌣*) *f* ⓦ (mechaniſche Trennung der nutzbaren Mineralien vom Ge-ſtein) ore-dressing, mechanical preparation of ore(s); **~s-anſtalt** ⚒ *f* ⓦ dressing- (or concentration) works *pl.*; **~s-maſchine** ⚒ *f* ⓦ (Walz-, Poch-werk ꝛc.) dressing-machine or -mill.
auf-berſt/en (*¹¹⌣⌣*) I *v/n.* (ſn) ⓑe** ꝛc. (ſ. berſten) to burst (open); to split, to crack; *v.* der Haut, auch: to chap. — **II** ~ *n* ⓦ *u.* **A/ung** *f* ⓦ bursting, split(ting), crack(ing), chap(ping).
auf-beſſer/n (*¹¹⌣⌣*) I *v/a.* ⓦa*/* to better, improve, ameliorate; das Gehalt eines Beamten ⌇ to raise (or increase) the salary of ... — **II** ~ *n* ⓦ und **A/ung** *f* ⓦ improvement, amelioration, rise of salary, increase of pay.
auf-bewahr/en (*¹¹⌣⌣*) I *v/a.* ⓦ*/* to keep, save, preserve, lay up, put by, Lebensmittel ꝛc. auch: to store (up); *fig.* to treasure (or hoard) up; gut auf-bewahrt in safe keeping; das läßt ſich nicht ⌇ it does not keep; *fig.* zu großen Dingen aufbewahrt spared for great things. — **II** ~ *n* ⓦ = A/ung.
Auf-bewahrer (*¹¹⌣⌣*) *m* ⓦ custodian.
Auf-bewahrung (*¹¹⌣⌣*) *f* ⓦ keeping, preservation, *v.* Lebensmitteln ꝛc. auch: storage, storing; e-m et. zur ~ geben to give a th. in charge of a p.; e-m et. entruſt a th. to a p.'s custody.
Auf-bewahrungs-ort (*¹...*) *m* ⓦ, **-platz** *m*, **-raum** *m* depository, receptacle,

storehouse; für Möbel auch: warehouse; für Koſtbarkeiten: safe-room; **-zimmer** *n* cloak-room, luggage-office.
auf-biegen (*¹¹⌣*) *v/a.* ⓦaſt** (in die Höhe biegen) to bend upwards; (aufmachen, öffnen) to unfold, bend open.
auf-bieten (*¹¹⌣*) I *v/a.* ⓦa*/* 1. (verkünden) to proclaim, ein Brautpaar ⌇ to publish the banns of ...; F *fig.* e-n ⌇ (ſchmähen) to abuse a person. — 2. (aufrufen) to call up, to summon; ⚔ Soldaten: to raise, to levy; die Landwehr: to call out; das Volk in Maſſe ⌇ to call the people to arms; to raise the country. — 3. *fig.* (anſtrengen) alle ſ-e Kräfte, alle (ſ-e) Mittel, alles (Mögliche) ⌇ to make every possible effort, to do one's (very) utmost, to work with might and main; to strain every nerve; ſ-n ganzen Einfluß ⌇ to use one's interest (or influence) to the fullest extent, ſtärker: to move heaven and earth. — **II** ~ *n* ⓦ *u.* **Auf-bietung** *f* ⓦ 4. proclamation; publishing (of banns; ⚔ levy, call(ing) to arms; mit ~ aller Kräfte with the utmost exertion, by a mighty effort.
auf-binden (*¹¹⌣*) *v/a.* ⓓ*/* 1. (aufknüpfen) to untie, unbind, undo; weitS. to loosen. — 2. (befeſtigen) to tie up; ⚓ ein Segel ⌇ to furl ...; ſich ſelbſt eine Rute ⌇ to make a rod for one's own back. — 3. F *fig.* e-m et. (auch: e-n Bären) ⌇ (e-n anführen) to palm s th. off on a p., to impose on a p., F to gammon (or hoax) a p.; er läßt ſich alles ⌇ F anything will go down with him, he swallows anything. — 4. Getreide ⌇ to bind ... into sheaves. — 5. Kleid ꝛc.: to tuck up; Haar: to do (or tie) up.
auf-blähen (*¹¹⌣*) ⓦ** I *v/a.* to (cause to) swell, to puff up or out, blow out, inflate; der Wind bläht die Segel auf the wind fills ... — **II** ſich ⌇ *v/refl.* to be puffed (and *fig.* vor Stolz) with pride. — **III** ~ *n* ⓦ *u.* **Auf-blähung** *f* ⓦ swelling, inflation, bloatedness; *med., vet.* flatulence. — **IV auf-gebläht** *p.p. u. a.* ⓦ swollen, swoln, (aufgebunſen) bloated; *med.* flatulent.
auf-blaſen (*¹¹⌣*) ⓦa** I *v/a. u. v/refl.* 1. = aufblähen I u. II. — **II** *v/a.* 2. to fill with wind; eine Blaſe ꝛc.: to distend, to blow out. — 3. (öffnen) der Wind blies die Tür auf the wind blew the door open. — 4. (in die Höhe blaſen) to blow up. — 5. ⚔ e-n Tuſch, e-e Fanfare ⌇ to sound a flourish (of trumpets); zum Rückzuge ⌇ to sound the retreat; e-n Tanz ⌇ to strike up for a dance. — **III auf-geblaſen** *p.p. u. a.* ⓦ 6. puffed up, ſ. I u. II. — 7. bloated; *med.* flatulent. — 8. *fig.* haughty, pompous, F bumptious.
auf-blättern (*¹¹⌣⌣*) ⓦa*/* I *v/a.* 1. ein Buch ⌇ to turn over the leaves of a book. — 2. eine Roſe ⌇ to open (or unfold) the leaves (or ⚘ petals) of a rose. — **II** ſich ⌇ *v/refl.* 3. (ſ. 2) to open.
auf-bleiben (*¹¹⌣*) *v/n.* (ſn) ⓦ** 1. (offen bleiben) to remain open. — 2. (nicht zu Bett gehen) to stay (or sit, stop) up, to keep late hours.

[**Aufblick**] — 88 — [**aufdrehen**]

Auf-blick (⏜⏝①) m ⑦c. upward glance; im ~ zu // (reverently) looking up to //, raising one's eyes to //.
auf-blicken (⏜⏝) v/n. (h.) ⑱** 1. to raise (or lift up) one's eyes to; fig. zu e-m mit Achtung ≈ to look up to a p., to respect a p. — 2. (aufblitzen) ⊕ metall. to gleam, to shed lustre, to brighten.
auf-blitzen (⏜⏝) I v/n. (n u. h.) ⑱** = aufblicken 2; fig. von Gedanken: to flash (through one's mind). — II ~ n ㉓ lightning(-glance); flash (of light), sudden gleam.
auf-blöcken (⏜⏝) v/a. ⑱** zu enge Stiefel ≈ (auf den Block schlagen) to block ..., to put ... on the tree.
auf-blühen (⏜⏝) I v/n. (n) ⑱** 1. to (begin to) blossom or bloom or flower; voll aufgeblüht full-blown. — 2. fig. ≈de Schönheit budding beauty; ≈de Stadt rising (or flourishing, prospering) town. — II ~ n ㉓ 3. blossoming. — 4. fig. rise, growth, prosperity.
auf-bohne(r)n ⊕ (⏜⏝) v/a. ⑱ ⓖa)** den Fußboden ≈ to wax (or polish) the floor.
auf-bohren ⊕ (⏜⏝) v/a. ⑱** to bore open, to open by boring.
auf-bojen ⌇ (⏜⏝) v/a. ⑱** (auf dem Wasser flott erhalten) to buoy (up).
auf-borgen (⏜⏝) v/a. ⑱** to borrow, to take up loans.
Auf-borger (~) m ㉒, ~in f ㊶ borrower.
auf-brassen ⌇ (⏜⏝) v/a. ⑲** (auf den Wind brassen) to bring (or heave) to; (die Luvbrassen anholen) to brace in.
auf-braten (⏜⏝) v/a. ⓖa** to roast afresh, to fry again.
auf-brauchen (⏜⏝⏜) v/a. ⑱** to use up, to wear out; (verzehren) to consume.
auf-brauen v/a. ⑱** 1. = brauen. — 2. to use up in brewing.
auf-brausen (⏜⏝) I v/n. (h. u. n) ⑨** 1. to bubble up, to effervesce; vom Wein: to ferment; von der See: to surge. — 2. fig. to fly into a passion; er braust leicht auf he quickly fires up. — II ~ n ㉓ 3. effervescence; fermentation; chm. ebullition; fig. (burst of) passion, fit of temper. — III ≈d p.pr. u. a. ㊿ 4. effervescent; fig. hot-tempered, irascible.
auf-brechen (⏜⏝) ⓖa** I v/a. 1. e-n Brief ≈ to open a letter; mit dem Hebel ≈ to prize up; ein Schloß ≈ to pick a lock; eine Tür ≈ to break (or force) open ... — 2. hunt. ein Hochwild: to disembowel, to eviscerate. — 3. agr. (umpflügen) to plough. — 4. ⊕ das Pflaster ≈ to tear (or take) up the pavement. — II v/n. (n) 5. (sich öffnen) to (burst) open; von Geschwüren: to break (open); von der Haut: to crack, to chap. — 6. (rasch fortziehen) to start, to move off, to set out (on a journey), F to decamp; ⚔ to break up the camp. — III ~ n ㉓ 7. breaking open; von Schlössern: lock-picking; hunt. evisceration.
Auf-brech-loch ⊕ (⏜⏝...) n ㊷ des Glasofens: tunnel (for the melting-pot).
auf-breiten (⏜⏝) v/a. ⑱** to spread (out), to display; das Tischtuch ≈ to lay (or spread) the cloth.
Auf-breit-maschine ⊕(⏜⏝...) f ㊻ Spinnerei: blower and spreader.

auf-brennen (⏜⏝) ⓑ** I v/n. (n) 1. to catch fire, to flare up; fig. to fly into a passion. — II v/a. 2. (aufbrauchen, f. auf-... 3) to burn up; to consume by burning. — 3. (durch Feuer auffrischen) to renovate (or to freshen up) by fire. — 4. e-m eine Kugel (oder F eins) ≈ to fire at (or on) a p., to put a bullet into a p. — 5. e-m (ob. auf et.) ein Zeichen ≈ to mark (or brand) a p., a th. with a red-hot iron.
auf-bring/en (⏜⏝) I v/a. ⑰** 1. (öffnen) to (get) open. — 2. (aufrichten) to raise (up); (aufziehen) auch: to rear, to bring up. — 3. ein Geschäft ≈ (emporbringen) to push (or nurse) a business. — 4. (emporschaffen) to move up, to lift; Getreide (auf den Boden) ≈ to garner grain; to take (or hoist) up grain into the loft; ⚓ Stängen u. Rahen ≈ (an der Bemastung befestigen) to put (or fix) up the yards. — 5. e-e Mode ≈ (einführen) to introduce (or set, start) a (new) fashion. — 6. (herbeischaffen) Geld ꝛc.: to raise, gemeinschaftlich: to club together; die Kosten ≈ to bear (or defray) the expenses; ⚔ Truppen: to levy, muster; Zeugen, Beweise: to produce; ⚓ ein Schiff ≈ (im Krieg als Prise fortnehmen) to capture (or bring in) a (vessel as a) prize, to make a prize. — 7. fig. (aufreizen) to provoke, irritate; das wird ihn sehr ≈ it will put him out terribly; (aufhetzen) to set (or egg on) against a p. — II ≈ 8. = ≈ung. — III aufgebracht p.p. u. a. ㊿ 9. f. 1 bis 6. — 10. fig. (f. 7) (gegen e-n, über et.) angry (with a p., at or about a th.); er ist sehr ≈ he is very indignant, in a towering rage, in high dudgeon; leicht ≈ easily put out, irascible, hot-tempered, F short-tempered. [prize or of prizes).
Auf-bringer ⌇ (⏜⏝) m ㉒ captor (of a)
Auf-bringung (⏜⏝) f ㊻ raising (up); einer Mode: introduction; ⚔ levy; ⚓ capture (of a prize); fig. provocation.
auf-brocken (⏜⏝) v/a. ⑱** to break into (small) pieces, (krümeln) to crumb.
auf-brodeln (⏜⏝) v/n. (n) ⓖa** to bubble up; to boil up; to effervesce.
Auf-bruch (⏜⏝ch) m ⑦d. 1. agr. (Pflügen) ploughing. — 2. (Verlassen) start(ing). move, departure, ⚔ camp.: decampment; e-r Gesellschaft: break-up; v.d. Tafel: rising from dinner. — 3. hunt. bowels, entrails, guts pl. — Vgl. aufbrechen III.
auf-brühen (⏜⏝) v/a. ⑱** = aufkochen.
auf-brüllen (⏜⏝) v/n. (h.) ⑱ ** to roar (aloud); von Rindern: to low, to bellow.
auf-brummen (⏜⏝) v/a. ⑱** I v/n. (h.) 1. to growl. — 2. ⚓ = auffahren 6. — II v/a. 3. burich.: e-m einen dummen Jungen ≈ to provoke a p. to a duel.
auf-buchten ⌇ (⏜⏝chtv) v/n. (n) ⑱** von Schiffen: (kielbrüchig w.) to become broken-backed or hogged. [put up) booths.]
auf-buden (⏜⏝) v/n. (h.) ⑱** to erect (or)
auf-bügeln (⏜⏝) v/a. ⓖa** to (press down with a hot) iron; einen Hut ≈, oft: to do up a hat. [sides of) a ship.]
auf-bujen ⌇ (⏜⏝) v/a. ⑱** to plank (the)
auf-bullern P (⏜⏝) v/n. (h.) ⑱** 1. to bubble up. — 2. fig. (aufbrausen) to boil over (with anger).

Auf-bund (⏜⏝) m ⑦c. tying-up of the hair, hair tied up.
auf-bürden (⏜⏝) I v/a. ⑲** 1. e-m et. ≈ (auch fig.) to burden (F to saddle) a p. with a th., to impose (or lay) s. th. on him. — 2. fig. (zur Last legen) to impute (a th.) to, to throw (or put) the blame (for a th.) on a p. (Vgl. auf-... 7). — II n ㉓ u. **Auf-bürdung** (⏜⏝) f ㊻ 3. burdening; imposition. — 4. fig. imputation.
auf-bürsten (⏜⏝) v/a. ⑱** 1. to brush up; e-n Hut ≈, a.: to trim (or do) up .... — 2. (hoch bürsten) die Haare: to brush up or back. [crown a king (at draughts).]
auf-damen (⏜⏝) v/a. ⑱** Brettspiel: to)
auf-dämmen (⏜⏝) v/a. ⑱** to dam up.
auf-dämmern (⏜⏝) [nhd. 18. sæ.] v/n. (n u. h.) ⓖa** Tag: to dawn, to break; fig. eine schwach ≈de Hoffnung a faint gleam (or dim ray) of hope.
auf-dampfen (⏜⏝) v/n. (n) ⑱** to steam up, to rise as steam or smoke.
auf-dauern (⏜⏝) v/n. (h.) ⓖa** v. Kranken, Bettlägerigen: (aufbleiben) to stay up, to remain out of bed.
auf-decken (⏜⏝) I v/a. ⑱** 1. (auflegen) to cover over; das Tischtuch ≈, abs. ≈ to lay the cloth. — 2. (bloßlegen) to uncover, to (lay) bare; fig. to disclose, to reveal; sein Spiel ≈ to show one's hand or cards, F to give the game away; einen Mißbrauch ≈ to expose an abuse. — II ~ n ㉓ u. **Auf-deckung** f ㊻ 3. laying the cloth. — 4. fig. disclosure, revelation; exposure.
auf-deichen (⏜⏝) v/a. ⑱** to dike.
auf-dingen ⌇ (⏜⏝) v/a. ⒟ft** als Lehrling ≈ to bind as an apprentice to.
auf-docken (⏜⏝) v/a. ⑱** 1. hunt. to wind (or roll) up the leash. — 2. agr. Getreide ꝛc.: to put in shocks, to shock.
auf-donnern (⏜⏝) ⓖa** I v/n. (n) to open with a thundering noise. — II ⌇ v/a. to rouse (or waken) with peals of thunder. — III v/refl. sich ≈ to dress o.s. up = aufputzen II. — IV aufgedonnert p.p. u. a. ㊿ dressed up (to the nines), decked out, looking smart. F got up (for the occasion).
auf-doppeln ⊕ (⏜⏝) v/a. ⓖa** 1. Schuhmacherei: (st-nähen) to close, to sew together. — 2. ⚔ die Reihen ≈ to join two ranks (together).
auf-dörren (⏜⏝) v/a. ⑱** Obst: to dry; Malz ≈ (darren) to kiln-dry ...
auf-drängen (⏜⏝) v/a. und v/refl. ⑱** 1. (drängend öffnen) to push open; eine Tür: to break open. — 2. (heben) to rise (with great force). — 3. fig. (sich) ≈ (aufnötigen) e-m et. ≈ to force (or press) a th. on a p.; sich e-m ≈ to obtrude (or thrust) o.s. upon a p.; die Zweifel, die sich mir ≈ the doubts which crowd into my mind.
auf-drehen (⏜⏝) ⑱** I v/a. 1. auch sich ≈ v/refl. to untwine, untwirl, untwist; (ausspinnen) to ravel out; ⚓ ein Tau: to unstrand, v. Tauenden: sich ≈ to fag; aufgedrehtes Tauende fag(-end). — 2. (öffnen) den Hahn: to turn on; eine Schraube: to unscrew. — 3. (nach oben drehen) to turn up(wards). — 4. einen Stocke-n Knopf ≈ to screw a knob on a stick. — II ~ n ㉓ 5. untwining; un-

---

Zeichen (f. S. XVII): F familiär; P Volkssprache; ⌜ Gaunersprache; ⌇ selten; † alt (auch gestorben); * neu (auch geboren); ⁺⁺ unrichtig;

[**Aufdrehſcheibe**] — 89 — [**auffangen**]

ravelling; unscrewing; screwing on. [throwing-wheel.]
Auf-dreh-ſcheibe ⊕ (ᴵᴵᴸ...) f ⓬ Töpferei;
auf-dreſchen (ᴵᴵᴸ◡) v/a. ⓾e (a. ⓾b)(e)ſt** to thrash out all the sheaves.
auf-drieſeln (ᴵᴵᴸ) ⓾a** = aufdrehen 1.
auf-dringen (ᴵᴸ◡) [mhd.] ⓾ſt** I v/n. (ſn) zu et. ⓵ (ſich emporheben)to rise (or strive up, press up) to …. — II v/a. u. v/refl. ⁗ = aufdrängen 3.
auf-dringlich (ᴵᴸ◡) a. ⓺⓺ obtrusive, importunate; officious; ℓe Reklame flaring advertisement; **~keit** (ᴵᴸ◡-) f ⓺⓺ obtrusiveness; officiousness.
Auf-dringling (ᴵᴸ◡) m ⑪d. intruder.
auf-dröſeln (ᴵᴸ◡) v/a. ⓾a** to untwine, untwist (= aufdrehen 1).
Auf-druck (ᴵᴸ) m ⓬c. 1. (das Aufdrucken) printing (on). — 2. (Aufgedrucktes) s. th. (im)printed (on), print.
auf-drucken (ᴵᴸ◡) v/a. ⓾⓾** to imprint, to print on; Stempel ⓵ to stamp on.
auf-drücken (ᴵᴸ◡) v/a. ⓾⓾** 1. (aufprägen) to impress (or print, stamp) on; ein Siegel ⓵ to set a seal to; den Lippen Küſſe ⓵ to imprint kisses on the lips. — 2. (öffnen) to press (or break) open.
auf-dunſen (ᴵᴸ◡) I v/a., v/n. (ſn) u. ſich ⓵ v/refl. ⓾⓾** to swell up or out. — II **auf-gedunſen** p.p. u. a. ⓺⓺ (D 9) puffed up or out, v. Körperteilen a.: swoln (out), flabby; ℓes Geſicht bloated face.
auf-dunſten (ᴵᴸ◡) I v/n. (ſn) ⓾⓾** to evaporate, to steam away. — II **~n** ⓶⓷ u. **Auf-dunſtung** f ⓺⓺ evaporation.
auf-duven ⬇ (ᴵᴸmv) v/n. (h.) ⓾⓾** (abfallen) to bear (the ship) up or round.
auf-eggen (ᴵᴸ◡) v/a. ⓾⓾** to lay open (or break) by harrowing, to harrow.
auf-ein-ander (ᴸ–ᴸ◡) adv. one upon (or after) another; atop of one another; **~folge** (ᴸ…) f ⓬ succession; **ℓfolgen** v/n. ⓾⓾** to succeed (each other or one another); **ℓfolgend** a. ⓺⓺ successive; **ℓhäufen** v/a. ⓾⓾** to heap (or pile) up; **=häufen** n accumulation; **=legen** n, geom. superposition; **=liegen** n ⚇ incumbency; ⚇ unregelmäßiges: overlapping; **ℓliegend** a. lying atop (of) one another,⚇ incumbent; **ℓplatzen** v/n. ⓾⓾** to clash (together), to knock against each other, to collide; **=platzen** n der Geiſter clashing (together), conflict; **=ſtoß** m collision; **ℓſtoßen** v/n. ⓾a** = **ℓplatzen**; **ℓtreiben** ⬇ v/n. ⓾⓾** von Schiffen: to run foul of one another; **=treiben** ⚇ n fouling.
auf-eiſen (ᴵᴸ◡) v/a. ⓾⓾** e-n Teich, Fluß, Straße ⓵ to break (open) the ice on …, to clear … of ice.
aufen†(ᴵ◡) [ahd.: auf] v/n. (h.) u. v/a. ⓾⓾ (aufbringen, mehren) to grow, to increase.
Auf-ent-halt (ᴵᴵ◡ᴸ) m ⓬c.1.(Ort)dwelling (-place), ſtändiger: (permanent) residence, domicile, beliebter: haunt; ſein jetziger ~ iſt unbekannt his present whereabouts are unknown; ohne feſten ~ without settled abode, vagrant; von Völkern: nomadic. — 2. (Verweilen) stay, kurzer: sojourn; ſ-n ~ nehmen bei to stay(or remain) with.—3. hindrance, stoppage, (Verſpätung) delay; ohne ~ without stopping; 🚂 wie lange iſt der in N.? how long shall we stop at N.?; wir hatten 10 Minuten ~ we had a ten minutes' stoppage or halt, we stopped ten minutes (for refreshment).
Auf-ent-halts-beſchränkung (ᴵᴵ◡ᴸ…) f ⓬ jur. pol. restriction imposed on the right (of aliens) to stay in a country; **=dauer** f time of stay; 🚂 stoppage, time for refreshment; **=karte** f foreign resident's card or permit or licence; **=ort** m = Aufenthalt 1; **=zeit** f = =dauer.
auf-erbauen (ᴵᴸ◡ᴸ◡) v/a. ⓾⓾*/* to build (up) = aufbauen; fig. = erbauen.
auf-erlegen (ᴵᴸ◡ᴸ◡) I v/a. ⓾⓾*/* (auflegen) e-m et. ⓵ to impose (or enjoin) a th. on a p., ſtärker: to dictate a th. to a p.; e-m e-n Eid ⓵ to put a p. to his oath; e-m e-e Pflicht ⓵ to lay (or impose) a duty on a p.; Strafen: to inflict; ſich (dat.) Zwang ⓵ to force (or check, restrain) o.s.; ſich keinen Zwang ⓵ to put no restraint on o.s., to be free and easy (in one's manners); et. Auferlegtes = imposition, task (imposed upon a p.); check; burden. — II **~n** ⓶⓷ u. **Auferlegung** f ⓺⓺ imposition; infliction.
auf-erſteh(e)n (ᴵᴸ◡ᴸ◡) I v/n. (ſn) ⓾⓸*/* (aufſtehen, bſd. v. Tode) to rise up (from the dead); Auferſtand(e)ne(r) ⓺⓺ a p. risen from the dead or the grave; wie ein vom Grabe Auferſtandener ausſehen to look like a corpse.— II **~n** ⓶⓷ = A/ung.
Auf-erſtehung (ᴵᴸ◡ᴵᴸ◡) f ⓺⓺ rel. rising (from the dead or grave), resurrection.
Auf-erſtehungs-feſt (ᴸ…) n ⓬ Easter-festival; **=mann** m (Leichenausgräber) resurrection-man,body-snatcher; **=tag** m day of resurrection; resurrection-day.
auf-erwachen (ᴵᴸ◡◡◡) v/n. (ſn) ⓾⓾*/* (aufwachen) to awake; fig. vom Tode ⓵ to rise from the dead (= auferſtehen).
auf-erweck/en (ᴵᴸ◡ᴸ◡) I v/a. ⓾⓾*/* geh. Spr. (aufwecken) to raise (from the dead), to resuscitate. — II **~n** ⓶⓷ = A/ung.
Auf-erwecker (ᴵᴸ◡ᴸ◡) m ⓺⓺ one who raises the dead; Chriſtus wird unſer ~ ſein will call us to life (again).
Auf-erweckung (ᴵᴸ◡ᴸ◡) f ⓺⓺ raising (zB. of Lazarus); resuscitation.
auf-erziehen (ᴵᴸ◡ᴸ◡) I v/a. ⓾b*/* (aufziehen) to bring (or rear) up, to nurse, to educate. — II **Auf-erziehung** f ⓺⓺ bringing-up of, education.
auf-eſſen (ᴵᴸ◡) v/a. ⓾⓷** to eat up, to consume, to devour; F to gobble up.
auf-fädeln, nbb. **auf-fädmen**(ᴵᴸ◡) ⓾a,b** I v/a. (auf den Faden:: fädeln) to thread, to string. — II v/refl. ſich ⓵ to ravel out.
auf-fahren (ᴵᴸ◡) ⓾b** I v/n. (ſn) 1. von einer Tür ⓶c.: to fly open. — 2. (aufſteigen) to mount, to go (or rise) up; gen Himmel ⓵ to ascend to heaven. — 3. a) von Perſonen: (auffpringen) to rise suddenly, to spring up; aus dem Schlaf, vor Schreck: to start (or jump) up; b) von Sachen: (emporfliegen) der Staub fährt auf die duſt rises (or flies) up. — 4. fig. (in Zorn geraten) to fire up, to fly into a passion or a temper. — 5. (feierlich einziehen) to enter in state; (vorfahren) to drive up (in a carriage). — 6. (h. u. ſn) ⬇ (auf den Grund geraten) to run aground or on the sands, to strike (on) the rocks, to ground, &c.; 🚂 (zuſtoßen) to collide, to run into (another carriage). — II v/a. 7. (hinfahren u. aufpflanzen) to place, to range; die Kutſchen ⓵ laſſen to draw up … (in a line); ⚔: to park (the artillery), to plant (the cannon); ſchweres Geſchütz ⓵ to bring up the heavy guns (auch fig.); eine Batterie ⓵ l. to bring a battery into action or to the front; co. eine Batterie Flaſchen ⓵ l. to put up a long row of bottles. — 8. (erhöhen) Erde auf Wieſen ⓶c. ⓵ to raise the soil on …; auf eine Landſtraße Kies ⓵ to gravel (or macadamize) a road. — 9. (beſchädigen) den Torweg: to damage, to break open; (öffnen) e-n Weg: to cut up; ⚒ to drive or run (galleries, tunnels). — III **~n** ⓶⓷(f. I u: II) 10. zB.: start(ing), fig.(Heftigkeit) (fit of) passion; ⬇ stranding, running aground; 🚂 collision. — Vgl. auch Auffahrt. — IV ⓶b p.pr. u. a. ⓺⓺ 11. fig. (heftig) hasty, passionate; (jähzornig) irascible, hot-tempered.
Auf-fahrt (ᴵᴸ) f ⓺⓺ 1. rising; ſüdd. Chriſti ~ ascension of Christ (into heaven); ~ in e-m Luftballon balloon-ascent; ⚒ aus dem Schacht: ascent; in e-m Wagen: driving up; (Zugang) approach, vor e-m Hauſe: drive, auch avenue; 🚂 rising ground; arch., frt. (Rampe) ramp, ascent. — 2. (feierlicher Aufzug) entry in state, procession. — 3. (Einzug auf e-m Gute) entering into possession.
auf-fallen (ᴵᴸ◡) ⓾a** I v/n. (ſn) 1. (auf et. fallen) to fall (or strike) upon. — 2. hunt. v. Vögeln: (ſich niederlaſſen, plötzlich niederſchwirren) to make a sudden descent, to swoop down; v. Vorſtehhund: auf e-e Fährte ⓵ to find the scent. — 3. (durch Fallen ſich öffnen) to open by falling. — 4. fig. e-m ⓵ (Befremden einflößen) to strike, to surprise, ſtärker: to shock a p.; auch abs. ⓵ to attract attention or notice; es wird allgemein ⓵, daß // everybody will notice that //. — II v/a. 5. ſich (dat.) den Kopf ⓵ to break one's head in falling. — III **~n** ⓶⓷ 6. phys. v. (Licht=)Strahlen ⓶c.: incidence; einer Kugel: impact. — IV ⓶b p.pr.u.a. ⓺⓺ 7. Bed. ⓵.inf. — 8. = auffällig.
auf-fällig (ᴵᴸ◡) a. ⓺⓺ striking (resemblance, &c.), surprising, remarkable, conspicuous; (ſchnurrig) curious, odd; ℓer Anzug showy(Floud) attire; ⓵ (adv.) gekleidet gaudily dressed; es war mir ⓵, daß // I thought it curious (or extraordinary) that //, it surprised me that //; die Sache hat et. ~es there is something strange about it.
Auf-fälligkeit (ᴵᴸ◡-) f ⓺⓺ striking character, remarkableness; strangeness; der Sitten: eccentricity; Kleider: showiness.
auf-falten (ᴵᴸ◡) v/a. ⓾⓾** 1. die Hände ⓵ to lift up one's folded hands. — 2. (aus=ea=falten) to unfold, unplait; (Falten ausmachen) to take out creases. — 3. (in Falten legen) to fold (up); to lay (or put) in folds.
auf-fangbar (ᴵᴸ◡-) a. ⓺⓺ seizable.
Auf-fang(e)-apparat(ᴵᴸ(◡)…) m ⓬ chm. vessel for collecting gases; **=gabel** f, typ. des Zylinders: cylinder catch; **=glas** n, opt. object-glass, objective.
auf-fang/en (ᴵᴸ◡) I v/a. ⓾b** 1. catch (up), haſtig: to snatch (up);

[**Auffangespitze**] — 90 — [**auffüttern**]

einen Ball ~ to catch a ball. — 2. (einsammeln) to collect, gather (rainwater, &c.); Briefe, Strahlen: to intercept; einen Hieb: to parry; Neuigkeiten: to pick up; Telegramme: to tap the wire; ich konnte nur ein paar Worte ~ catch only a word or two. — 3. ⚓ den Wind ~ to take the wind out of a ship's sails; den Anker ~ to get (or haul) up ... — II ~ n ⚥ 4. = A/ung.

Auf-fang(e)-spitze (⸺‿...) f ⚥, **-stange** f des Blitzableiters: metallic point of the lightning-rod.

Auf-fangung (⸺‿)/⚥(s.auffangen) catching; capture; collection; interception.

auf-färben (⸺‿) v/a. ⚥** Malerei: to colour again; ⚥ to dye (or dip) afresh. (auf-frischen) to touch (or freshen) up;

auf-fase(r)n (⸺‿) v/a.(u.v/refl. ⚥ (⚥a)** to unravel, ravel out, fray (out).

auf-fassen (⸺‿) v/a. ⚥** 1. körperlich: to catch (or pick) up; eine Masche ~ to take up a stitch; Perlen: to thread. — 2. sinnlich: to perceive, conceive; geistig: to apprehend; von Grund aus: to comprehend, understand, F to take in; eine Rolle, Stelle richtig ~ to interpret (or read) ... correctly; ich fasse es anders auf I look at it in a different light, I take it in another sense; et. falsch ~ to take a wrong view of a th., to misunderstand (or misconstrue, misinterpret) it; abs. schwer (rasch) ~ to be slow (quick) of apprehension or comprehension or understanding.

Auf-fassung (⸺‿) f ⚥ 1. conception; apprehension, comprehension, grasp; nach meiner ~ as I take (or understand, conceive) it, from my point of view. — 2. (Deutung) interpretation, reading, version; falsche ~ misconstruction, misinterpretation.

Auf-fassungs-art (⸺‿...) f ⚥ apprehension, point of view; **-fähigkeit**, **-gabe**, **-kraft** f, **-vermögen** n perceptive faculty, power of conception or apprehension, intellectual grasp; phls.: ⚥ perceptivity; **-weise** f = -art.

auf-feilen (⸺‿) v/a. ⚥** 1. to file (again). — 2. (aufputzen) to polish by filing. — 3. (öffnen) to open by filing.

auf-feuchten (⸺‿) v/a. ⚥** to moisten (or wet) again; to damp afresh.

auf-fiedeln F (⸺‿) v/a. u. v/n. (h.) ⚥a** eins ~, (zum Tanze) ~ to strike up a dance on the fiddle; to play (dance-music) on the violin.

auf-fieren ⚓ (⸺‿) v/a. ⚥** (schlaff m.) die Schoten ~ to slacken the sheets.

auf-findbar (⸺‿) a. ⚥ discoverable.

auf-find/en (⸺‿) [nhd. 18. sæ.] I v/a. ⚥** to find (out), to trace; Geheimes: to discover. — II ~ n ⚥ = A/ung.

Auf-finder (⸺‿) m ⚥, ~**in** f ⚥ finder.

Auf-findung (⸺‿) f ⚥ discovery.

Auf-findungs-gabe (⸺‿), **-kunst** f talent for discovery.

auf-firnissen (⸺‿) v/a. ⚥** to new-varnish, to varnish afresh.

auf-fischen (⸺‿) v/a. ⚥** to fish up or out; auch fig. to pick up, to find.

auf-flackern (⸺‿) I v/n. (ſn) ⚥a** to flare (or flicker) up, chm. to deflagrate. — II ~ n ⚥ chm. deflagration;

fig. das letzte ~ der Lebensflamme the last spark (or remnant) of life; poet.: the last flicker of the vital flame, auch: life's dying embers.

auf-flammen (⸺‿) I v/n. (ſn) ⚥** to blaze up, to burst into flame(s); fig. to break out (or fly) into a passion. — II ~ n ⚥ fig. ~ der Leidenschaft burst (or hot fit) of passion.

Auf-flammung (‿) f ⚥ 1. blazing-up, blaze. — 2. * (Explosion) explosion.

auf-flattern (⸺‿) v/n. (ſn) ⚥a** to flutter up(wards).

auf-flechten (⸺‿) v/a. ⚥b** 1. einem Mädchen die Haare ~ to plait a girl's hair. — 2. (Geflochtenes auflösen) to unplait, to unbraid; sich (dat.) die Haare ~, auch: to undo (or to let down) one's hair; ein Tau: to untwine.

auf-flicken (⸺‿) v/a. ⚥** to patch (or vamp) up; to mend, repair; F to botch.

auf-fliegen (⸺‿) I v/n. (ſn) ⚥ast** 1. mst: to fly (or soar) up, v. Vögeln a. to burst upon the wing; vom Luftballon: to rise, to ascend. — 2. in die Luft ~ to explode; ~ lassen: to blow up; eine Mine: to spring; e-n Luftballon: to let off; fig. (in Rauch) ~ (enden) to collapse; to end in smoke; e. Unternehmen ~ lassen to drop ... — 3. (auffspringen) to rise suddenly; von Schlössern zc.: to fly open. — II ~ n ⚥ 4. (f. I) zB. eines Schiffes: explosion.

auf-flimmern (⸺‿) v/n. (h.) ⚥a** to glimmer, gleam, glitter, sparkle.

Auf-flug (⸺) m ⚥d. 1. soaring (up); (heavenward) flight; eines Luftballons: ascent. — 2. hunt. (flügge Brut) brood of fledged partridges, &c.

Auf-forderer (⸺‿) m ⚥, **-forder(r)erin** f ⚥ summoner, challenger.

auf-fordern (⸺‿) I v/a. ⚥a** 1. bittend: to beg, entreat; befehlend: to bid, order; bringend: to urge; ermunternd: to exhort; freundlich: to invite; gerichtlich: to summon; e-e Dame zum Tanz ~ to ask a lady to dance with one; to take a partner; darf ich Sie zum nächsten Tanze ~? may I have the pleasure of the next dance?; ~de Reden f/pl. provoking (or inciting) speeches pl. — 2. ⚔ eine Festung zur Übergabe ~ to summon ... (to surrender). — II ~ n ⚥ 3. = Aufforderung.

auf-fördern ⚒ (⸺‿) v/a. ⚥a** Saline: die Sole ~ to raise the brine; ⚒ to draw up.

Auf-forderung (⸺‿) f ⚥ request, demand, requisition; gesellschaftlich: invitation; gerichtlich: summons; parl. ~ zur Beobachtung der Geschäftsordnung call to order; zum Kampfe: challenge; ⚒ ~ zur Nachzahlung (auf Aktien) call (on the shareholders); jur. e-e ~ ergehen lassen to issue an appeal.

Auf-forderungs-schreiben (⸺‿...) n ⚥ letter of invitation; summons.

auf-formen ⚒ (⸺‿) v/a. ⚥** e-n Hut ~ to put ... upon the block, to block ...

auf-forsten (⸺‿) v/a. ⚥** for. to plant afresh, to afforest, to reafforest.

auf-fressen (⸺‿) v/a. ⚥** to eat up (greedily), to devour; fig.: der Gram frißt ihn auf grief is preying upon him or his mind; F er könnte sie (vor Liebe) ~ he is madly in love with her,

he is so fond of her that he could eat her. [burst with the frost.]

auf-frieren ⚓ (⸺‿) v/n. (ſn) ⚥c** to

auf-frisch/en (⸺‿) I v/a. u. v/refl. ⚥** (sich ~) to freshen up, to revive; to put new life (or vigour) into; Gemälde: to touch up; das Andenken an et. ~ to refresh (or renew) the memory of ...; sein Latein (wieder) ~ to rub (or brush) up one's Latin. — II v/n (ſn) vom Wind: ⚓ (frisch aufsteigen; ant. abflauen) to freshen. — III ~ n ⚥ u. A/ung f ⚥ freshening up, revival, &c. (f. 1).

auf-fugen, auf-fügen ⚒ (⸺‿) v/a. ⚥** Wagnerei: die Felgen auf die Speichen ~ to join the fellies to the spokes.

auf-führbar (⸺-) a. ⚥ capable of being (or fit to be) erected (or played, performed); practicable; von Schauspielen: performable, fit for the stage; ~es Stück: acting play or drama.

auf-führ/en (⸺‿) ⚥** I v/a. 1. ein Gebäude: to build, erect; eine Mauer (höher) ~ to raise a wall; ⚔ Schanzen ~ to throw up trenches. — 2. (aufschichten) Erde um um Baum ~ to heap up ... round a tree. — 3. ⚔ die Wache ~ to mount (or relieve) guard; eine Schildwache ~ to post (or set) a sentry; Geschütze ~ to post (or plant) cannon. — 4. (vor die Augen führen) to bring up; Zeugen ~ to produce witnesses; Besiegte im Triumphe ~ to lead captives in triumph; eine Stelle aus e-m Buche ~ to quote a passage from ...; ⚒ e-n Posten in der Rechnung ~ to enter (or specify) an item in the account. — 5. (öffentlich darstellen) bsb. thea. ein Stück, eine Rolle: ~ to act, perform, play. — II sich ~ v/refl. 6. to behave (or conduct) o.s.; sich schlecht ~ to misbehave (or misconduct) o.s.; führen Sie sich nicht wie (ob. als) ein Kind auf! don't behave (or go on) like a child! — III ~ n ⚥ u. Auf-führung f ⚥ 7. (zu 1) building, erection. — 8. (zu 4) production (of witnesses); quotation; ⚒ specification. — 9. (zu 5) thea. acting, performance; zur ~ bringen to mount, to (put on) the stage. — 10. (zu 6) behaviour, conduct, (Lebensart) breeding, manners pl.; schlechte ~ bad conduct, ill behaviour, misconduct; iro. (das nenne ich mir eine) schöne ~ (these are) fine doings or goings-on!

Auf-führungs-recht (⸺‿...) n⚥thea. acting right; **-zeugnis** ncertificate of conduct.

auf-füllen (⸺‿) v/a. ⚥** 1. e-e Lücke ~ to fill up (or stop) a gap; Wein ~ to cask (or bottle) wine; arch. (anschütten) to heap (or bank) up (earth). — 2. Suppe ~ to serve up soup. — II ~ n ⚥ und Auf-füllung f ⚥ 3. filling up; ~ auf Flaschen bottling.

auf-funkeln (⸺‿) v/n. (h.) ⚥a** to sparkle, to shine forth (vividly).

auf-furchen (⸺‿) v/a. ⚥** to furrow.

auf-fußen (⸺‿) v/n. ⚥** to alight, to set one's foot on the ground.

auf-futtern F (⸺‿) = auffüttern 1 u. 2.

auf-füttern (⸺‿) I v/a. ⚥a** 1. Kälber zc.: to breed, to rear. — 2. Heu zc.: to feed on, to consume as fodder. — 3. ⚒ to line; mit Holz ~ to case.

Signs (see page XVII): F familiar; P vulgar; ⚡ flash; ⟍ rare; † obsolete (died); * new word (born); ₊₊ incorrect; ♪ music:

[Aufgabe] — 91 — [aufglätten]

II ~ n ㉓ u. **Auf-fütterung** (ᴗᴗ) f ㊻ 4. rearing (or feeding) up; ⊕ lining.
Auf-gabe (ᴗᴗ) [mhd.] f ㊻ 1. delivery; e-s Briefes: posting; e-s Telegramms: handing in (of a telegram); wiring (a message); des Gepäcks: booking; ⌬ ~ zur Post posting (a letter, &c.) — 2. Schule ꝛc.: task; e-r ~ gewachsen equal to a task; f-r ~ nicht gewachsen unequal to one's task, F not up to the mark; häusliche ~ home lesson; schriftliche ~ (written) exercise; mathematische ~ (mathematical) problem; sum; ~ e-s Rätsels proposition of (or setting, proposing) a riddle; e-m e-e ~ abhören to hear a p.'s lesson; eine ~ geben to set (a p.) a task; sich an eine ~ machen to set about a thing, to undertake a task; seine ~n machen to do one's lessons or sums; sich et. zur ~ m. to make s. th. one's business; es war die ~ seines (ganzen) Lebens he made it his life-task; ⌬ Ihrer ~ gemäß, laut ~ as per advice, by your order or instructions. — 3. (Fahrenlassen) giving up; abandonment; eines Amtes: resignation; eines Rechtes ꝛc.: surrender; ⌬ wegen ~ des Geschäfts (on) retiring from business.
Auf-gabe-amt ⌬ (ᴗ...) n ㉒ issuing office.
auf-gabeln (ᴗᴗ) v/a. ㉒a** 1. to take up (or seize) with a fork. — 2. F fig. to pick up (with a p.).
Auf-gaben-buch (ᴗ...) n ㉒, **-heft** n exercise-book; **-sammlung** f collection of (mathematical,&c.) problems or exercises.
Auf-gabe-ort ⌬ (ᴗᴗ...) m ㉒ place where a letter (or a telegram) was (or is) despatched; **-schein** ⌬ m receipt (of delivery); **-station**, **-stelle** f sending station; **-zeit** ⌬ f time of issue or despatch.
Auf-gang (ᴗᴗ) m ㉒c. 1. going up, rising, rise, ascent; phys. e-s Kolbens: up-stroke; fig. (Wachsen) growth; zum ~ bringen to make grow. — 2. ✶ der Gestirne rising; † = Osten. — 3. (Aufstieg) rising ground; (Treppe) staircase, stairs pl. — 4. (Sichöffnen) opening; von Eis: break-up.
Auf-gangs-punkt (ᴗᴗ...) m ㉒ ~ der Sonne point where the sun rises.
auf-gären (ᴗᴗ) v/n. (in, h.) ㉒a** und ㊽** to rise in fermenting.
auf-gattern F (ᴗᴗ) v/a. ㉒a** fig. to pick (or fish) up, to meet by chance.
auf-geben (ᴗᴗ) I v/a. ㉒c** 1. to deliver; e-n Brief: to post, to put in the letter-box; Gepäck: to book; ein Telegramm: to hand in, to send; ⌬ eine Bestellung ~ to give an order. — 2. ⊕ im Hoch-ofen: die Gicht ~ to charge (or feed) the furnace. — 3. Speisen ~ (auftragen) to serve (up) ... — 4. Ballspiel: den Ball ~ to serve (the ball). — 5. e-m et. ~ (anbefehlen) to commission (or order) a p. to do a th.; (zur Lösung vorlegen) to set (or impose) a task on a p.; ein Rätsel, et. zu raten ~ to propose (or propound, set) a riddle; eine Schulaufgabe: to set (as home task); die uns aufgegeb(e)nen Arbeiten (Rechnungen) our home lessons (home sums). — 6. (fahren lassen) to give up or over; eine Bekanntschaft ~ to drop an acquaintance, to cut a p.; den Geist ~ to give up the ghost, to breathe one's last, to expire; sein Geschäft ~ to retire from business; eine Gewohnheit: to leave off; alle Hoffnung: to abandon, to give up, to lose; einen Kranken ~ to give over (or up) a patient; den Militärdienst ~ to leave the army; Schachspiel: eine Partie als verloren ~ to throw up a game; ein Recht ~ to yield up a right; e-e Sache ~ to relinquish (F to clear out of) a th.; ⚔ e-e Stellung ~ to abandon (or surrender) a position. — II ~ n ㉓ 7. = Aufgabe.

Auf-geber (ᴗᴗ) m ㉒, **~in** f ㊸ von Waren: consignor, e-s Briefes: sender; e-s Rätsels: proposer; ⊕ der Gicht: p. who charges the furnace.
Auf-gebe-trichter ⊕ (ᴗᴗ...) m ㉒ metall. charging-cone, ore-funnel.
auf-gebläht (ᴗᴗ) p.p. u. a. ㉖ f. aufblähen.
auf-geblasen (ᴗᴗ) p.p. f. aufblasen III; **~heit** (ᴗᴗ-) f ㊻ haughtiness, conceit, F bumptiousness.
Auf-gebot (ᴗᴗ) n ㉔d. (vgl. aufbieten) 1. publication; jur. (behördliche Aufforderung zur Anmeldung von Rechten u. Ansprüchen) public notice to heirs, creditors, &c. to send in their claims; eccl.: e-s Brautpaares: publishing the banns (of matrimony); dies ist das dritte ~ this is the third time of asking; Einspruch gegen die ~e erheben to forbid the banns; eine Dispensation vom ~ erkaufen to obtain a marriage-license.—2. (Aufruf) summons, call; ⚔ von Truppen: raising, calling out; (aufgebotene Truppen) troops (or men) called out; allgemeines ~ levy en masse; Landwehr zweiten ~s, etwa: second reserve. — 3. (Anstrengung) fig. mit ~ aller Kraft with the utmost exertion; with might and main.
auf-gebracht (ᴗᴗ) f. aufbringen; **~sein** n ㉓ (o. pl.) anger, indignation, stärker: rage.
Auf-gebung (ᴗᴗ) f ㊻ = Aufgabe 1 u. 3.
auf-gedonnert (ᴗᴗ) p.p. f. aufdonnern II.
auf-gedunsen (ᴗᴗ) f. aufdunsen II; **~heit** f ㊻ puffiness, bloatedness; des Stils: bombast, turgidity, exuberance; F gas.
auf-gegangen (ᴗᴗ) p.p. v. aufgehen.
auf-geh(e)n (ᴗᴗ) [mhd.] v/n. (fn) ㊽ 1. ⤴ = aufsteigen; der Vorhang ging auf the curtain rose; auf und ab (ob. davon) geh(e)n f. auf 11; vgl. 3. — 2. (anschwellen) vom Teige: to rise, to swell. — 3. v. Staub, Rauch ꝛc.: to rise, to ascend. — 4. (sichtbar werden) von Pflanzen, von der Saat: to come (or spring) up; to shoot up or forth; von Gestirnen: to rise; ♂der Stern (a. fig.) rising star; die Sonne ist auf (=gegangen) the sun is up; F es geht mir ein Licht auf, die Augen geh(e)n mir auf I begin to see (it in its true light) or to understand (the drift of it), it dawns upon me that //, vgl. 5 am Schluß. — 5. (sich öffnen) to open, F to come undone; von Briefen: to come open or unsealed; vom Eise: to break up; von Geschwüren: to break, to burst; von geflochtenem Haar: to come unplaited or unbraided; von Kleidungsstücken: to come unbuttoned or unhooked; von Knoten: to come untied; von einer Naht: to come unstitched, to give way; v. Schnallen: to come unbuckled; von Schnüren: to come unlaced; es ging ihm plötzlich der Gedanke auf, daß // it flashed through his mind that //, it suddenly occurred to him that //, vgl. 4. am Schluß. — 6. (fig. entfalten) von Blumen: to unfold; ganz aufgegangen, auch: full-blown; fig. es geht ihm das Herz dabei auf it gladdens his heart, it lifts his heart good. — 7. arith. (keinen Rest geben) 7 geht in 14 auf 7 divides (or F goes) into 14 without a remainder; 5 geht nicht in 9 auf 9 is not divisible by 5 without a remainder; 6 von 6 geht auf 6 from 6 leaves nought; es geht (gerade oder Null für Null) auf there is no remainder; Rechnungen ꝛc. gegen=ea. ~ lassen to balance (or set off) ... one against the other. — 8. (verschwinden) to vanish, schmelzend: to melt (away), vom Schnee: to thaw; in Asche ~ to be turned (or reduced) to ashes; in Dunst, Rauch ~ to end in smoke; in et. ~ to be(come) merged (or absorbed) in a th.; fig. in f-r Arbeit ganz ~ to be heart and soul (or to be deeply engrossed) in one's work. — 9. (verbraucht w.) to be used up, to be consumed or spent; es geht viel Holz auf the wood is going fast; (viel) Geld ~ lassen bei to spend money (lavishly) over, ⌬ to sink (or drop) large sums (or a good bit of money) in; F er läßt gern viel ~, auch: he is open-handed. — II v/a. 10. sich (dat.) die Füße ~ to walk one's feet sore. — III ~ n ㉓ 11. = Aufgang; beim ~ des Vorhangs on the rising of the curtain, on the curtain rising.
auf-geien ⚓ (ᴗᴗ) v/a. ㊽** Segel ~ (festmachen) to brail (or clew) up ... [(sails).]
Auf-geier (ᴗᴗ) m ㉒ one who brails up
auf-geigen (ᴗᴗ) ⌬**(f.auf-...5)=** aufsiedeln.
auf-geklärt (ᴗᴗ) f. aufklären III; **~heit** (ᴗᴗ-) f ㊻ (o. pl.) = Aufklärung 2.
auf-gekratzt (ᴗᴗ) p.p. f. aufkratzen II.
Auf-geld (ᴗᴗ) n ㉔d. 1. extra charge; premium; ⌬ Börse: (für Stundung) contango. — 2. (Angeld) earnest (money).
auf-gelegt (ᴗᴗ) p.p. f. auflegen IV.
auf-geräumt (ᴗᴗ) p.p. f. aufräumen III; **~heit** f ㊻ merriment, mirth, good (or merry) humour. [IV u. Aufregung 2.]
auf-geregt (ᴗᴗ), **~heit** f ㊻ f. aufregen
Auf-gesang (ᴗᴗ) m ㉒c. (ant. Abgesang) ehm. u. noch in Kirchenliedern: introductory part of a song or hymn.
auf-gesprungen (ᴗᴗ) f. aufspringen 3.
auf-getrieben (ᴗᴗ) f. auftreiben IV; **~heit** (ᴗᴗ-) f ㊻ med. intumescence.
auf-gewältigen ⚒ (ᴗᴗ) v/a. ㊽*/* einen Schacht ~ to clear (or drain) ...
auf-gewärmt (ᴗᴗ) p.p. f. aufwärmen.
auf-geweckt (ᴗᴗ) p.p. f. aufwecken III. **~heit** f ㊻ liveliness, sprightliness; des Verstandes: brightness, sharpness.
auf-geworfen (ᴗᴗ) p.p. f. aufwerfen 6.
auf-gießen (ᴗᴗ) I v/a. ㊽d** to pour upon; to infuse; Tee ~ to pour (fresh) water on the tea; (mit kochendem Wasser bereiten) to make (fresh) tea. — II ~ n ㉓ f. I; Tee ꝛc.: infusion.
Auf-gießer (ᴗᴗ) m ㉒ metall. feeder.
Auf-gieß-löffel ⊕ (ᴗᴗ...) m ㉒ metall. feeding-ladle.
auf-glätten (ᴗᴗ) v/a. ㊽** to polish.

⚛ scientific; ♣ botanical; ⚲ geography; ⊕ machinery; ⚒ mining; ⚔ military; ⚓ marine; ⌬ commercial; ⌬ postal; 🚂 railway.

auf-glimmen (‿́‿) *v/n.* (ſn) [30a] (a. [30])** to gleam, glitter, glow, twinkle.
auf-glühen (‿́‿) *v/n.* (ſn) [30]** v. d. Sonne: to rise with a (red) glow.
auf-grab/en (‿́‿) I *v/a.* [30b]** 1. die Erde ≈ to dig up ...; rings um einen Baum: to bare the roots (of a tree). — 2. = ausgraben. — 3. (eingravieren) einen Namenszug ꝛc.: to engrave ... on. — II ~ *n* [23] u. **A/ung** *f* [46] 4. excavation.
auf-greifen (‿́‿) [30b]** *v/a.* I to take (or snatch) up; einen Dieb: to apprehend, catch; *fig.* einen Gedanken ≈ to catch at an idea. — II *v/n. hunt.* v. Leithund: to be on (or to follow) the scent.
auf-grünen (‿́‿) *v/n.* (ſn) [30]** to become green (again), to be clothed in (new) verdure; weitS. to revive. [ſehen 1.
auf-gucken F (‿́‿) *v/n.* (h.) [30]** = auf-
auf-gürten (‿́‿) *v/a.* [30]** 1. e-m Pferde den Sattel ≈ to saddle a horse. — 2. (aufschürzen) ein Kleid ≈ (a. *v/refl.* **ſich** ≈) to tuck up one's dress. — 3. (den Gurt löſen) to ungird; to loosen the belt.
Auf-guß (‿́) *m* [5] (Aufgießen; Aufgegossenes) infusion; v. Tee, ꝛc.: es ist nur ~ the tea, coffee is very weak, F it's only wash; **~-tierchen** *n* [62] *zo. pl.*: ⚭ infusoria.
auf-haben (‿́‿) *v/a.* [70b]** 1. den Hut ≈ to have one's hat on; ⚓ alle Segel ≈ to crowd all sails, to carry (or to be under) a full press(ure) of canvas. — 2. (offen haben) den Mund ≈ to have one's mouth open. — 3. Schule: wir haben viel (zu viel) auf we have plenty of (too much) homework.
auf-hacken (‿́‿) I *v/a.* [30]** 1. to cut up or open (with a hoe, &c.); to grub up; eine Straße ≈ to pick up a road. — 2. (fertig hacken) das Holz ≈ to finish chopping or cutting ... — II ~ *n* [23] 3. (ſ. 1) hoeing; picking (up); der Erde um einen Baum: baring the roots.
auf-häkeln (‿́‿) *v/a.* [32a]** 1. = aufhaken. — 2. to use up in crochet-work.
auf-haken (‿́‿) *v/a.* u. *v/refl.* [30]** (**ſich**) ≈ to unhook, unclasp, unbuckle.
auf-halsen F (‿́‿) *v/a.* [30]** = aufbürden I. [(Fenſterwirbel) sash-fastener.
Auf-halt(e)-haken ⚙ (‿́(‿)...) *m* [62]
auf-halten (‿́‿) [30a]** I *v/a.* 1. (offen halten) to hold open; e-m eine Stelle: to keep open; *fig.* die Hand ≈ to hold out the open hand. — 2. (a. *v/refl.*) (hemmen) to check, to give a check to, to stop, im Fallen: to support; (hinhalten) to put off, to delay; einen Fall ≈ to break a fall; den Strom ≈ to stem the tide; ♪ e-n Akkord: to suspend; ich will Sie nicht lange ≈ I will not detain (or keep) you long; ſich unnütz mit (od. bei) et. ≈ to waste one's time over a th.; ſich bei Kleinigkeiten ≈ to stick at trifles. — II **ſich** ≈ *v/refl.* 3. ſ. 2. — 4. ſich wo ≈ (verweilen) to stay (or abide) at a place; ſich bei e-m ≈ to stay (or live) with a p.; ſich im Freien ≈ to keep in the open air; *fig.* ſich bei einer Sache ≈ to enlarge (or dwell) on a matter. — 5. ſich über e-n, et. (tadelnd) ≈ to find fault with (or to criticize) a p., a th. — III ~ *n* [23] 6. = Aufenthalt 2 u. 3. — 7. *mech.* check. — IV **Lb** *p.pr.* u. *a.* [66] 8. Vcb. des *inf.* — 9. *phys.* retarding.

Auf-halter (‿́‿) *m* [22] 1. ⚙ = Aufhalteriemen; *tel.* stop-work; interruptor. — 2. ⚓ ~ der Kabelkette relieving rope, relieving tackle.
Auf-halt(e)-riemen (‿́(‿)...) *m* [62] Sattlerei: breech(ing); **-ring** *m* am Pferdegeschirr: stopping-ring. [— 2. ♪ suspension.
Auf-haltung (‿́‿) *f* [46] 1. = aufhalten III.
auf-hämmern (‿́‿) *v/a.* [32a]** 1. (loshämmern) to open by hammering. — 2. (festhämmern) to fix by hammering. — 3. (aufwecken) to rouse by hammering.
Auf-hänge-band (‿́‿...) *n* [62] truss, suspensor; **-boden** ⚙ *m* Bleiche und *typ.* hanging-room, drying-loft; **-kreuz** ⚙ *n*, *typ.* printer's peel; **-leine** *f* line for (hanging up and) drying (clothes, &c.).
auf-hängen (✝ **auf-hangen**) (‿́‿) [30] (✝ [30b])** I *v/a.* u. *v/refl.* 1. (hoch hängen) to hang (up); Gemälde ≈, a. to put up pictures; Wäsche ≈ to hang out linen; an der Decke ≈ to suspend from the ceiling; e-n ≈ (aufhenken) to hang a p. (by the neck); **ſich** ≈ to hang o.s. — 2. einem et. ≈ to palm a th. off on a p. — II ~ *n* [23] 3. = Aufhängung.
Auf-hänge-punkt (‿́‿...) *m* [62] e-r Wagſchale: point of suspension; **-ſeil** *n* = -leine.
Auf-hänger *m* u. **Auf-hängſel** *n* (‿́‿) [22] something to hang a th. (up) by; am Kragen: tab. [suspension.
Auf-hängung (‿́‿) *f* [46] hanging (up),
auf-harken (‿́‿) *v/a.* [30]** to rake.
auf-härten (‿) *v/a.* [30]** 1. to make (again) hard. — 2. ⚓ e. Tau ≈ to twist the strands of a rope, to twist a rope hard.
auf-haſchen (‿) *v/a.* [31]** to snatch up.
auf-haſpeln (‿́‿) [32a]** I *v/a.* 1. Garn: to wind (off). — 2. (emporwinden) to wind (or hoist) up. — II *fig.* **ſich** ≈ *v/refl.* 3. to rise (or recover) slowly.
auf-hauen (‿́‿) [30c]** I *v/a.* 1. to hew (or break, cut) open; Geſchlachtetes: to cut up. — 2. (fertig hauen) Holz: to finish chopping. — 3. ⚙ eine Feile: (auffriſchen) to cut anew. — II *v/n.* (h.) 4. auf den Tiſch ≈ to strike ... (with one's fist). [chisel.
Auf-hauer ⚙ (‿́‿) *m* [22] Schloſſerei: bolt-
auf-häufeln (‿́‿) *v/a.* [32a]** to form into small heaps; *agr.* to earth, hill.
auf-häufen (‿́‿) I *v/a.* u. *v/refl.* [30]** to heap (or store) up; Geld, Schätze: to pile (or hoard) up; to amass; **ſich** ≈ to accumulate; vom Schnee: to drift; ein aufgehäuftes Maß a good and full measure; et. Aufgehäuftes heap, pile. — II ~ *n* [23] = Aufhäufung.
Auf-häufer (‿́‿) *m* [22], **~in** *f* [47] accumulator; v. Schätzen: amasser, hoarder.
Auf-häufung (‿́‿) *f* [46] piling up; amassment, accumulation, ⚭ acervation.
Auf-hebe-binde (‿́...) *f* [62] truss, suspensor; **-muskel** *m*, *anat.* ⚭ attollent muscle.
auf-heben (‿́‿) [78] ([77]b)** I *v/a.* 1. to pick up. — 2. (emporheben) die Augen: to lift (or raise) up; e-n vom Boden ≈ to help a p. up; die Hand gegen e-n ≈ to lift one's hand against a p.; ein Kleid: to hold (or pull) up; *fig.* den Handſchuh ≈ to take up the gauntlet; *mech.* mit e-m Hebel: to purchase, to prise up. — 3. (aufbewahren) to put away, Wertſachen: to lay (or treasure) up; gut, ſicher aufgehoben in good hands, in safe keeping; *fig.* bei ihm bin ich gut aufgehoben he makes me very comfortable (at his house); dort war ich gut aufgehoben I was well looked after there; *iro.* der iſt beſorgt und aufgehoben (*SCH.*) etwa: he is dispatched once and for all; et. vor e-m ≈ to keep a th. from, to guard it against a p. — 4. (überrumpeln) to seize (suddenly); to capture; e-e Spielhölle ≈ to raid a gambling-house; ⚔ einen Poſten: to surprise (and capture). — 5. (aufhören machen) to do away with, to put an end to; to stop, to arrest; ⚔ eine Belagerung ≈ to raise a siege; ⚓ den Beſchlag ≈ to take off the embargo; Einrichtungen, Bräuche: to abolish; ⚖ e-e Genoſſenſchaft ≈ to dissolve partnership; ein Geſetz ꝛc.: to repeal; ⚔ das Lager: to move, to break up; e-e Sitzung: to dissolve; *parl.* to adjourn the House; einen Streit: to end; die Tafel ≈ to rise from the table; ein Urteil: to quash, to reverse; eine Verordnung: to abrogate; eine Verlobung ≈ to break off (or cancel) an engagement; e-n Vertrag ≈ to cancel an agreement; to annul a treaty; Sprichw. aufgeſchoben iſt nicht aufgehoben forbearance is no(t) acquittance. — 6. (ausgleichen) eins gegen das andere ≈ to balance one with the other; *v/rpr.* ſie heben **ſich** (ea. od. gegenſeitig) auf they neutralize (or cancel, balance, compensate) each other. — 7. *math.* e-n Bruch ≈ to reduce a fraction (to its lowest terms); ſich ≈ (laſſen) to cancel. — II **ſich** ≈ *v/refl.* 8. ſ. 6 u. 7. — 9. ſich vom Erdboden ≈ to get up, to raise o.s., F to pick o.s. up. — III ~ *n* [23] 10. picking (or raising) up; beim ~ der Tafel when the dinner-party was (all) over, when the company rose from the table; ~ der Hände (bei Abſtimmungen) show of hands; *math.* reduction (of fractions). — 11. *fig.* viel ~s von et. machen (mit et. großtun) to make a great fuss about a th.; viel ~s um nichts much ado about nothing (auch Titel e-s Luſtſpiels von *SH.*). — IV **Lb** *p.pr.* u. *a.* [66] 12. in den Bed. des *inf.* — 13. bisw.: (abſchaffend) abrogative; (entkräftend) derogatory; (ausgleichend) compensative.
Auf-hebe-tau ⚓ (‿́‿) *n* [62] spanker-brail.
Auf-hebung (‿́‿) *f* [46] 1. = aufheben 10. — 2. (Wegnahme) seizure; ⚔ ~ eines Poſtens surprising (and capturing) a post. — 3. (Hemmung im Fortgange): **a)** zeitweilige: suspension; dauernde: suppression; annulment; **b)** fr. *hist.* ~ des Edikts von Nantes Revocation of the Edict of N. (1685); *jur.* ~ eines Erkenntniſſes rescission of a verdict; e-s Geſetzes: repeal; e-r Klage: nonsuit; e-r Sitzung, Verſammlung: breaking up, dissolution; ~ der Tafel (general) rising from the table; ⚖ ~ des Verkehrs suspension of intercourse.
Auf-hebungs-befehl (‿́...) *m* [62] order of annulment; **-gericht** *n* court of cassation; **-zeichen** ♪ *n* natural (note) ♮.
auf-hefteln (‿́‿) *v/a.* [32a]** to unhook.
auf-heften (‿́‿) *v/a.* [30a]** 1. (in die Höhe heften) to fix (or pin) up. — 2. (befeſtigen)

[**aufheißen**] — [**aufknabbern**]

to tack (or stitch) on. — 3. *fig.* = auf=
binden 3. — 4. (losmachen) to undo.
auf-heißen ⚓ (ᴵᴸ˘) v/a. ⑨** die Flagge:
to hoist (up); zur Trauer: to fly the
flag at half-mast (high); die Anker
sind aufgehißt the anchors are a-weigh.
auf-heitern (ᴵᴸ˘) I v/a. u. v/refl. ⓐa**
to brighten (or clear) up; das Gemüt
≈ to cheer a p.('s thoughts); dies
heiterte ihn sehr auf this quite livened
him up; vom Wetter: es heitert sich auf
it is clearing up, it's getting brighter;
mit aufgeheiterten Zügen with a (more)
cheerful (or with a brighter) countenance. — II ~ n ㉓ = Aufheiterung.
— III ≈b *p.pr. u. a.* ⑯ in den Beb. des *inf.*;
auch: cheerful, cheery, exhilarating.
Auf-heiterung (ᴵᴸ˘˘) f ⑯ brightening
(or cheering) up; serenity, exhilara-
tion. [*sg. ob. pl.* of) diversion.]
Auf-heiterungs=mittel (≈...)n ⑫(means)
auf-helfen (ᴵᴸ˘˘) v/n. (h.) u. v/refl. ⓑb**
einem ≈ to help a p. up; (beistehen) to
assist (or support) a p.; e-m Kranken
≈ to set a patient on his legs (again);
dem ist nicht mehr aufzuhelfen he is past
help or cure; sich (*dat.*) ≈ to raise o.s.
Auf-helfer (ᴵᴸ˘˘) m ㉒ 1. one who helps.
— 2. (Bettvorrichtung) cord which assists an invalid in raising himself.
auf-hellen (ᴵᴸ˘˘) I v/a. u. v/refl. ⑧** to
clear; eine Flüssigkeit: to clarify; *fig.* eine
Frage: to elucidate; das Wetter hellt
sich auf the weather is clearing up.—
II ~ n ㉓ u. **Auf-hellung** f ⑯ clarification; *fig.* elucidation, enlightenment.
auf-henken *obb.* (ᴵᴸ˘˘) ⑧** = aufhängen 1.
auf-hetzen (ᴵᴸ˘˘) I v/a. ⑨** 1. to rouse,
start. — 2.*fig.*(aufreizen) to incite, to egg
on; er hetzt sie gegen-ea. auf he stirs
up strife between them, he sets them
by the ears. — II ~ n ㉓ ≈. = A/ung.
Auf-hetzer (ᴵᴸ˘˘) m ㉒, ~in f ㊵ instigator, inciter; ~ei (ᴵᴸ˘˘ᴸ˘) f ⑯ instigation,
incitement, stirring-up (of) strife;
≈isch (ᴵᴸ˘˘) a. ⑯ inciting; Rede: inflammatory, revolutionary.
Auf-hetzung (ᴵᴸ˘˘) f ⑯ incitement.
Auf-hilfe (ᴵᴸ˘) f ⑯ succour; assistance.
auf-hissen ⚓ (ᴵᴸ˘˘) v/a. ⑨** = aufheißen.
auf-hocken F (ᴵᴸ˘˘) ⑧** I v/n. (in) to get
on some one's back. — II v/a. ⓒ-n ≈
to take a p. on one's back. — III ~
n ㉓, auch **Auf-hock=spiel** n ㉒ Turnerei:
(game of) high cockalorum.
auf-höhen (ᴵᴸ˘) v/a. ⑧** 1. to make
higher, to raise. — 2.*paint.* to set off.
auf-holen (ᴵᴸ˘) v/a.⑧** 1. Fallengelassenes:
to fetch (or draw) up. — 2. ⚓ a) (in
die Höhe winden) to haul up; ein Boot: to
hoist up; ein Schiff ≈ (ans Ufer winden) to
draw up ... (for repairs); to ground
...; b) (luvwärts bewegen) die Brassen ≈
to brace the sails in; das Schiff wieder
≈ to bring ... to the wind.
Auf-holer (ᴵᴸ˘) m ㉒ 1. zum Heraus=
ziehen von Erdbohrern: lifting tackle. —
2. ⚓ ~ (Tau) e-s Stagsegels halyard.
auf-horchen (ᴵᴸ˘˘) v/n. (h.) ⑧** to listen,
to hearken; hoch ≈ to listen very attentively, to prick up one's ears.
auf-hören (ᴵᴸ˘˘) [mhd.] I v/n. (h.) ⑧**
1. = aufhorchen. — 2. (ablassen; *ant.* anfangen) to cease, stop, end, finish; (ab-

brechen) to discontinue; ≈ zu arbeiten:
a) to knock off work; b) to strike; ≈ zu
weinen to leave off crying; ≈ zu zahlen
to stop payment; der Regen hört auf ...
is holding up; der Sturm hat aufgehört
... has calmed (or gone) down, is blown
over; die Unterhaltung hört auf ... is
flagging; F da hört alles auf! that's too
much of a good thing!; in Geldsachen
hört die Gemütlichkeit auf business is
business; hör' auf! (schweig) hold your
tongue!— II ~ n ㉓ 3. cessation, stop,
end, finish; discontinuation; ohne ~
without intermission (= unaufhörlich).
auf-hüpfen (ᴵᴸ˘) v/n. (in) ⑧** to bound
(or leap) up; vom Balle: to rebound.
auf-husten (ᴵᴸ˘) ⑨** v/n. (h.) bsd. laut
≈ to cough violently.
auf-jagen (ᴵᴸ˘) v/a. ⑧** 1. *hunt.* Wild ≈
(aufscheuchen) to scare, frighten, rouse
(a hare or a rabbit); to start (a deer);
to flush (a bird); to unearth or draw
(a fox). — 2. ⚓ ein Schiff ≈ (einholen)
to overtake a ship at sea.
auf-jammern (ᴵᴸ˘˘) v/n. (h.) ⓐa** to
wail (or lament, moan) aloud.
auf-jauchzen (ᴵᴸ˘˘) v/n. (h.) ⑨** to utter
a shout of joy, to exult at.
auf-jubeln (ᴵᴸ˘˘) ⓐa**, F **auf-juchen**
(ᴵᴸ˘ch) ⑧** v/n. (h.) u. v/a. = aufjauchzen.
auf-kämmen (ᴵᴸ˘˘) v/a. ⑧** 1. Haare ≈. ≈ to
comb ... up or afresh; Perücke: to dress.
— 2. ⨁ *mech.* to furnish (a cogwheel)
with new cogs. [set up) edgeways.}
auf-kanten ⊕ (ᴵᴸ˘˘) v/a. ⑧** to put (or)
auf-kantern (ᴵᴸ˘˘) v/n. (in) ⓐa** Renn=
sport: to canter to the starting-post.
auf-kappen (ᴵᴸ˘˘) v/a. ⑧** to (cover
with a) cap; *hunt.* den Falken ≈ to hood —
auf-karren (ᴵᴸ˘˘) v/a. ⑧** = auffahren II,
bsd. 8. [⚓ den Anker: to cat, to fish (up).}
auf-katten ⑧**, -katzen ⑨** (ᴵᴸ˘˘) v/a.}
Auf-kauf (ᴵᴸ˘) m ⓓd. buying up, (speculative) purchase; forestalling.
auf-kaufen (ᴵᴸ˘˘) I v/a. ⑧** to buy (or
take) up; to forestall (the market);
ehm. to engross; Wechsel ≈, auch: to discount bills. — II ~ n ㉓ = Aufkauf.
Auf-käufer (ᴵᴸ˘˘) m ㉒, ~in f ㊵ (speculative) buyer; forestaller; ehm. engrosser; (der den Alleinhandel an sich bringt)
monopolist. [aufstellen) to pile (up).}
auf-kegeln (ᴵᴸ˘˘) v/a. ⓐa** (in Kegelform)
auf-kehren (ᴵᴸ˘˘) v/a. ⑧** 1. to sweep
up; to turn up. — 2. ⨁ Goldschmied:
to stamp. [*pl.*) scrapings *pl.*}
Auf-kehricht (ᴵᴸ˘˘) m u. n ⓓd. sweepings
auf-keimen (ᴵᴸ˘˘) I v/n. (in) ⑧** to bud,
germinate, shoot up; *fig.* to rise,
begin; ≈b budding, ⨯ nascent; ≈de
Liebe dawning love. — II ~ n ㉓ und
Auf-keimung f ⑯ germination; *fig.*
rise, beginning. [pressing (grapes).}
auf-keltern (ᴵᴸ˘˘) v/a. ⓐa** to finish}
auf-kippen (ᴵᴸ˘˘) v/n. (h.) ⑧** to tilt
(or tip) up. [(or putty) on.}
auf-kitten (ᴵᴸ˘˘) v/a. ⑧** to cement}
auf-klaffen (ᴵᴸ˘˘) v/n. (h.) ⑧** von Spal=
ten 2c. to gape (open), to yawn.
auf-klaftern (ᴵᴸ˘˘) v/a. ⓐa** Holz: to put
(or pile) up in fathoms, to cord (up).
auf-klappen (ᴵᴸ˘˘) v/a. ⑧** 1. einen
Hut ≈ to turn up (the brim of) ...;
einen Tisch ≈ to open or put up (the

leaves of) ... — 2. (öffnen) ein Messer:
to unclasp. — II v/n. (in) ⑧** 3. (sich öffnen)
von Türen 2c.: to (fly) open (with a
bang). — 4. auf et. ≈ (aufschlagen) to
fall on a th. with a bang.
auf-klaren ⚓ (ᴵᴸ˘) ⑧** I v/a. e. Tau: to
coil up. — II v/n. v. Wetter = aufklären 1.
auf-klär/en (ᴵᴸ˘) v/a. u. v/refl. ⑧**
1. e-e Flüssigkeit: to clarify; das Wetter
(oder es) klärt sich auf the weather is
clearing up, the clouds are dispersing, it is setting in fair; ⨯ das Gelände
≈ to reconnoitre the country.—2.*fig.*
den Geist: to clear up, to enlighten;
eine Frage ≈ to elucidate (or clear up,
throw light upon) a question; ein
Geheimnis ≈ to solve a mystery; e-n
über einen Irrtum ≈ to correct a p.'s
mistake, to set a p. right concerning
a th.; es hat sich alles aufgeklärt everything has been (fully) explained or
cleared up. — II ~ n ㉓. = A/ung.
— III **auf-geklärt** *p.p. u. a.* ⑯ 4. Beb.
des *inf.* — 5. *fig.* (j. 2) enlightened,
civilized, (vorurteilsfrei) unprejudiced,
open-minded, liberal-minded.
Auf-klärer (ᴵᴸ˘) m ㉒ one who enlightens;
pioneer of progress; ⨯ scout; ~ei
(ᴵᴸ˘ᴸ˘) f ⑯ pseudo-culture, sham civilization; ≈isch (ᴵᴸ˘) a. ⑯ bent on
enlightening people.
Auf-klärigt (ᴵᴸ˘) n (m) ⓓd.(*o.pl.*) sham
enlightenment, sham culture.
Auf-klärung (ᴵᴸ˘˘) f ⑯ 1. ⨯ reconnoitring,
reconnaissance, scouting; *fig.* (Aus=
kunft) intelligence, (Erklärung) explanation; e-m ~ über et. geben to enlighten
a p. on a th.; sich ~ über et. verschaffen
to get a matter fully explained. —
2. (Bildung) enlightenment, liberal-
mindedness; (progress of) civilization; der Fortschritt der ~ the march
of (human) progress.
Auf-klärungs=dienst ⨯ (ᴵᴸ˘...) m ㉒
reconnoitring (or scouting) duties *pl.*;
=eskadron f squad of scouts; =sucht
f mania for enlightening people;
≈süchtig a. ⑯ (madly) bent on reforms;
=wesen ⨯ n intelligence-department.
auf-klauben (ᴵᴸ˘˘) v/a. ⑧** to glean, to
pick up; einen Knoten: to undo.
auf-kleben (ᴵᴸ˘˘) I v/a. ⑧** to paste (up
or on); to gum on; Freimarken: to
affix; ⨁ Etiketten ≈ to label; ⊕ Karten
auf Leinwand ≈ to mount maps on
cloth. — II v/n. (h.) ⑧** to stick on. [on.}
auf-fleck(s)en (ᴵᴸ˘˘) v/a. ⑧ (⑨)** to daub}
auf-kleistern (ᴵᴸ˘˘) v/a. ⓐa** to paste on.
auf-klettern (ᴵᴸ˘˘) ⓐa**, **auf-klimmen**
(ᴵᴸ˘ ⑧ (⑨)**) v/n. (in) to climb up.
auf-klinken (ᴵᴸ˘˘) v/a. ⑧** eine Tür ≈
unlatch, to put back the latch of.
auf-klopfen (ᴵᴸ˘˘) ⑧** I v/n. (h.) 1. to
knock on; ♪ v. Kapellmeister: (b. Zeichen
zum Anfangen geben) to give the signal
for beginning, to start the orchestra
or band. — II v/a. 2. to knock open;
eine Nuß: to crack. — 3. (befestigen) to
fix by knocking. — 4. (aufflreißen) eine
Matraze: to beat up. — 5. (aufwecken) to
rouse (or awaken, call) by knocking.
Auf-klopf=hammer ⨁ (ᴵᴸ˘...) m ㉒ des
Nabelmachers: heading-hammer. [(up).}
auf-knabbern (ᴵᴸ˘˘) v/a. ⓐa** to crunch}

♪ Musik; ⚶ Wissenschaft; ❦ Pflanze; ⚘ Geographie; ⊕ Technik; ⚒ Bergbau; ⨯ Militär; ⚓ Marine; ⊛ Handel; ⚭ Post; 🜊 Eisenbahn.

auf-knacken (⏑⏑) v/a. ⊛** eine Nuß ꝛ to crack (open) a nut; *fig.* e-m et. (ob. e-e harte Nuß) aufzuknacken geben to give a p. a nut to crack *or* a riddle to solve.
auf-knallen (⏑⏑) ⊛** I v/a. e-m et. ꝛ to fire (F to pot) at a p. — II v/n. (ſn) (knallend aufſliegen) to burst, explode.
auf-knebeln (⏑⏑) v/a. ⊛a** 1. to (fasten with a) gag. — 2. (entknebeln) to ungag. [with pincers.|
auf-kneipen (⏑⏑) v/a. ⊛** to open
auf-knöpfen (⏑⏑) I v/a. u. v/refl. ⊛** to unbutton, F *fig.* ſich ꝛ to unbosom o.s., to become communicative; derb: die Ohren ꝛ (aufpaſſen) to listen with both ears, to keep one's ears open. — II auf-geknöpft p.p. ⊛ outspoken, open.
auf-knoſpen (⏑⏑) v/n. (ſn) ⊛** to (begin to) blossom, &c. (= aufblühen 1).
auf-knüpfen (⏑⏑) I v/a. ⊛** 1. (in die Höhe binden) to tie up; (aufhängen) to hang (F to string) up, to suspend. — 2. (löſen) to untie, undo, unknot. — II v/ꝛ, **Auf-knüpfung** f ⊛ 3. tying up; (Aufhängen) hanging; (Auflöſen) untying.
auf-kochen (⏑⏑) ⊛** I v/n. (ſn, h.) 1. to boil; *fig.* er kocht raſch auf his blood (F his monkey) is soon up, he is easily roused; Gemüſe ꝛ l. to parboil. — II v/a. 2. to boil up. — 3. (auffriſchen) to warm up, to do up again. — 4. (aufbrauchen) to use up in cooking.
auf-kommen (⏑⏑) I v/n. (ſn) ⊛** 1. vom Boden: ꝛ to get (or rise) up; *fig.* von einer Krankheit wieder ꝛ to regain (*or* recover) one's health *or* strength; er kommt nicht wieder auf he is past recovery, he's done for. — 2. *fig.* (Glück haben) to prosper, thrive, to make one's way. — 3. (heranwachſen) to come up, grow, increase. — 4. (entſtehen) to come into use; (ſich behaupten) to gain ground, to make headway; von Gebräuchen, Moden: to find favour, to get into vogue; F to take, to catch on; (gedeihen) to thrive, prosper; Gedanken, Zweifel kamen in mir auf ... arose (*or* sprang up) in my mind; einen Zweifel nicht in ſich ꝛ laſſen to suppress a doubt; niemand neben ſich ꝛ laſſen to admit (*or* suffer) no rival; er kann nicht gegen dich ꝛ he cannot prevail against (*or* cope with) you, he is no match for you. — 5. (e-m) für et. ꝛ (einſtehen) to make o.s. answerable (*or* responsible) (to a p.) for a th.; er ſoll mir dafür ꝛ I shall look to him (for it). — 6. (gelöſt werden) von Geld: to come in. — 7. (offen werden) to (come) open; von e-m Geſchwür: to break (open); *fig.* von einer Stelle: to become (*or* fall) vacant. — 8. ⚓ e-m andern Schiff ꝛ (es einholen) to overtake (*or* gain on) another ship; eine Bö kommt auf (nähert ſich ſchnell) a squall is approaching *or* at hand. — II ~ n ㉓ 9. getting up, rise, recovery; man zweifelt an ſeinem ~ his life is despaired of; (Emporkommen) prosperity, growth, advance; (Gelingen) success;(Entſtehen) rise, origin;(Einſetzung) establishment; (Verbreitung) spread.
Auf-kömmling ↘ (⏑⏑) m ⓓ upstart.
auf-können (⏑⏑) v/n. (h.) ⊛** to be able to get up *or* rise.

auf-köpfen ⊕ (⏑⏑) v/a. ⊛** Stecknadeln ꝛ to head pins (= anköpfen).
auf-koppeln (⏑⏑) ⊛a** = abkoppeln.
auf-korken (⏑⏑) v/a. ⊛** to uncork.
auf-kramen (⏑⏑) v/a. ⊛** (in Ordnung bringen) to arrange, to put in order.
auf-kratzen (⏑⏑) I v/a. ⊛** 1. e-n Namen: to engrave; ♪ ein Lied: to scrape (on a violin, &c.); die Erde: to turn up. — 2. (wund kratzen) auch v/refl. ſich ꝛ to scratch (o.s.) sore. — 3. v. Hühnern: die Körner ꝛ to scratch up the seeds. — 4. ⊕ Hutmacherei: to raise; eine Mauer: to scrape; Tuchmacherei: (mit einer Karde) ꝛ to raise (*or* dress) the nap (of cloth); Wolle: to card. — II auf-gekratzt p.p. u. a. ⊛ 5. in den Bed. des *inf.* — 6. F *fig.* in excellent spirits, in a merry mood; jolly.
Auf-kratzer ⊕ (⏑⏑) m ㉒, ~in f ㊵ von Seide: dresser; von Tuch: carder.
Auf-kratz-holz ⊕ (⏑⏑...) n ㉒ bſd. Tuchm.: napping-frame; =kamm m n.-comb; =maſchine f friezing-machine, raising- (*or* napping-)machine, gig.
auf-kräuſeln (⏑⏑) v/a.u.v/refl. ⊛a** (ſich) die Haare ꝛ to curl up (*or* frizzle) ...
auf-kreiſchen (⏑⏑) v/n. (h.) ⊛a⊛** to shriek, to set up a scream.
auf-krempeln (⏑⏑) v/a. ⊛a** 1. ⊕ Wolle: to card (again). — 2. = aufkrempen.
auf-krempen (⏑⏑) v/a. ⊛** to tuck up; einen Hut: to turn up (the brim of); die Hoſen ꝛ to turn up one's trousers.
auf-kriechen (⏑⏑) v/n. ⊛dſt ⊛** to creep (*or* crawl, sneak up) to. [bekommen.]
auf-kriegen F (⏑⏑) v/a. ⊛** = auf-⎯|
auf-krimpen ↘ (⏑⏑) v/n. (h.) ⊛** Wind: to keep (even) pace with the sun.
auf-krümmen (⏑⏑) v/a. u. v/refl. ⊛**: (ſich) ꝛ to bend upwards. [kündigen.]
auf-künden obb. (⏑⏑) v/a. ⊛** = auf-⎯|
auf-kündigen (⏑⏑) ⊛** I v/a. ꝛ to give a p. warning *or* notice; v. Hauswirt ob. Gutsherrn: to give a tenant notice to quit; v. Hausherren u. Bedienten: to give a month's notice to, pay a month's wages in lieu of notice; es iſt ihm aufgekündigt worden he received warning *or* notice; ohne aufzukündigen without (giving) previous notice; eine Hypothek ꝛ to call in a mortgage; e-m die Freundſchaft ꝛ to break (*or* to sever one's friendship) with a p.; den Gehorſam ꝛ to refuse obedience to. — II ~ n ㉓ = Aufkündigung.
Auf-künd(ig)ung (⏑⏑⏑) f ㊵ warning, notice; ~ des Gehorſams refusal to obey; e-s Kapitals: recall; e-s Kontrakts: revocation; ⚔ e-s Waffenſtillſt.: termination.
Auf-künd(ig)ungs-brief (⏑⏑⏑...) m㉒ written notice; =friſt f, =termin m; =zeit f time allowed for giving notice.
Auf-kunft † (⏑) f ⑩ recovery.
auf-küſſen (⏑⏑) v/a. ⊛** to open (*or* to rouse from sleep) by kisses.
Aufl. *abbr.* = Auflage 3.
auf-lachen (⏑⏑ch) v/n. (h.) ⊛** laut ꝛ to burst out laughing, to indulge in a hearty laugh.
Auf-lade-gebühr (⏑⏑⏑...) f ㉒, =lohn m loading(-charges pl.),(cost of) packing.
auf-lad/en (⏑⏑) I v/a. ⓢb** 1. to lay a load (*or* burden) on; Frachtgüter ꝛ to load goods. — 2. e-m (ſich) et. ꝛ to

charge a p. (o.s.) with s. th.; ſich eine große Verantwortlichkeit ꝛ to take a great responsibility on o.s. *or* on one's shoulders. — II ~ n ㉓ = A/ung.
Auf-lader, Auf-läder (⏑⏑⏑) m ㉒ loader; packer, porter; ~ von Steinkohlen coal-heaver; ~lohn m f. Auflade=...
Auf-ladung (⏑⏑) f ㊻ loading; *fig.* imposition; ~s=... (...) ㉒ = Auflade=...
Auf-lage (⏑⏑) f ㊻ 1. (Auflegen, Auferlegung) laying-on, imposition; (aufgelegte Steuer) impost, tax. — 2. (Zſ.kunft, bſd. einer Zunft) meeting (of a corporation); (Zunftgeld) subscription. — 3. Buchhandel: edition; neue (unveränderte) ~ reprint, reimpression, vermehrte und verbeſſerte ~ revised and enlarged edition; wie ſtark iſt die ~? how many copies have been printed?; fünf ~n erleben to run through five editions.
auf-lager/n (⏑⏑) I v/a. ⊛a** 1. ⊛ Waren: to store up, to warehouse. — 2. (über ea. lagern) to lay over each other, *geol.* ⚯: to superpose. — II ~ n ㉓ = A/ung.
Auf-lager-ſyſtem n ㉒ Brücke: cantilever.
Auf-lagerung (⏑⏑⏑) f ㊻ 1. storage, warehousing. — 2. *geol.* ⚯: superposition, stratification.
auf-landig ↘ (⏑⏑) a ㊻ (ant. ablandig): ⸗er Wind sea-breeze.
auf-langen F (⏑⏑) v/a. ⊛** von der Erde ꝛ to take (*or* pick) up.
Auf-langer ↘ (⏑⏑) m ㉒ Schiffbau: (oberes Ende der Spanten) futtock.
auf-laſſ/en (⏑⏑)[mhd.] I v/a. ⊛a** 1. e-n ꝛ: a) der auf iſt: to let a p. sit up; b) der liegt: to let a p. get up. — 2. die Tür ꝛ to leave open; den Rock ꝛ to leave unbuttoned. — 3. eine Stelle: to leave vacant; ⚒ ein Bergwerk: to abandon; aufgelaſſene Grube disused pit; *jur.* ein Gut ꝛ (abtreten) to cede (*or* convey) real estate to. — II ~ n ㉓ 4. = A/ung.
auf-läſſig ⚒ (⏑⏑) a. ㊻ von e-r Grube: abandoned, disused.
Auf-laſſung (⏑⏑) f ㊻ leaving open; *jur.* (Übertragung v. Grundeigentum) cession (*or* conveyance) of real estate; ⚔ ~ einer Feſtung (Entfeſtigung) dismantling a fortress; ⚒ einer Grube: abandonment.
Auf-lau(e)rer (⏑⏑⏑) m ㉒ one lying in wait *or* in ambush; waylayer; lurker.
auf-lauern (⏑⏑⏑) I v/n. (h.) ⊛a** e-m ꝛ to lay an (*or* to lie in) ambush for a p.; to waylay a p.; um ihn zu verraten: to spy a p. out, to watch a p.('s movements). — II ~ n ㉓ und **Auf-lau(e)rung** f ㊻ lying in wait *or* in ambush, ambuscade.
Auf-lauf (⏑⏑)[mhd.] m ⊕d. 1. concourse (of people); *vgl.* Aufruhr; es entſtand ein ~ a large crowd (of people) assembled, there was a great rush *or* commotion (among the people); e-n ~ erregen to raise (*or* cause) a tumult. — 2. (Backwerk) puff-paste, cream-cake, sponge-cake. — 3. ⊕ *arch.* (Fahrbrücke) bridge of boards, gangway.
auf-laufen (⏑⏑) ⊛aſt** I v/n. (ſn) 1. ⊛ = hin. ꝛ. — 2. (anſchwellen) to swell; Kochkunſt: der Teig läuft auf ... is rising *or* heaving; Fleiſch im Waſſer ꝛ laſſen to scald ...; ⊛ v. Geldſummen: to run (*or* swell) up, to increase; vom Kapital

Signs (see page XVII): F familiar; P vulgar; ⌐ flash; ↘ rare; † obsolete (died); * new word (born); ++ incorrect; ♪ music;

[Aufläufer] — 95 — [aufluven]

aufgelauf(e)ne Zinsen accumulated interest; ⚓ ≈des Wasser high water, rising tide. — 3. hunt. einen Keiler ≈ lassen to receive the wild boar's charge. — 4. ⚓ ein Schiff läuft auf (auf den Grund) ... runs aground or ashore; e-m andern Schiff ≈ (sich von hinten nähern) to steal up to a ship by the stern; das Volk ≈ lassen to man the yards. — II v/a. 5. sich (dat.) die Füße ≈ to run one's feet sore. — 6. e-e Tür ≈ (aufsprengen) to break a door open with a rush. — III ~ n ㉓ 7. swell, swelling, rising; (Aufblähung) inflation, med. und vet. flatulence; von Zinsen: accumulation; ⚓stranding (of boats). **Auf-läufer** (ᴵᴸ‿) m ㉒ 1. metall. stoker, charger, charging man. — 2. Kochkunst: = Auflauf 2. — 3. ⚓ auch **Auf-laufer** (halb befahrener Matrose) younker, ship's boy. [scupper-hole.| **Auf-lauf-rinne** ⚓ (ᴵᴸ‿...) f ㉖ scupper,| **Auf-laurer** (ᴵᴸ‿) m f. Auflauerer. **auf-lauschen** (ᴵᴸ‿) v/n. (h.) ㉛** to listen attentively, to prick up one's ears. **auf-lavieren** ⚓ (‿ᴸᴸ‿ᴸ‿) v/n. (h., fn) ㉛*/* to ply to windward; to tack. **auf-leben** (ᴵᴸ‿) I v/n. (fn) ㉛** (wieder) ≈ to revive, to come to life again; davon lebte er neu auf that gave him new life (and strength) or a new lease of life. — II ~ n ㉓ revival; der Künste ꝛc., auch: renascence, als Periode: (fr.) Renaissance. [Hunden ꝛc.: to lap up.| **auf-lecken** (ᴵᴸ‿) v/a. ㉛** to lick up; von| **Auf-lege-brettchen** ⊙ (ᴵᴸ‿...) n ㉓ Färberei: spreading-board; **maschine** f Spinnerei: spreading-machine. **auf-legen** (ᴵᴸ‿) ㉛** I v/a. 1. ein Pflaster ꝛc.: to apply; ⚔ das Gewehr ≈ to put the rifle on the rest. — 2. die Ellbogen ≈ to rest one's elbows on; e-m die Hände ≈ to lay (one's) hands on a p.; dem Pferde einen Sattel (eine Schabracke) ≈ to saddle (to caparison) a horse; Schminke ≈ to lay on rouge, to paint; das Tischtuch ≈ to spread (or lay) the cloth. — 3. fig. von Schweinen: viel Fett ≈ to put on fat. — 4. einen Strumpf ≈ (zu stricken anfangen) to begin to knit, to set up ... — 5. fig. = auferlegen; Sprichw. Gott legt uns nicht mehr auf, als wir tragen können Heaven suits the burden to the back. God tempers the wind to the shorn lamb. — 6. ein Buch ≈ to edit ..., to publish ...; (neu oder wieder) ≈ to reprint, to republish. — 7. (offen hinlegen) Bücher, Zeitschriften ꝛc. ≈ to lay out; Börse: eine Anleihe ≈ to invite subscriptions for a loan; Spiel: Bank, Pharao ≈ to keep (or hold) the bank; ein Achtel (Vier) ≈: a) vom Wirte: to broach a cask of beer; b) von einem Gaste: to treat the company to ...; die Karten ≈ to spread one's cards on the table. — 8. ⚓ ein (Handels-)Schiff ≈ (abtakeln) to (unrig and) lay up ...; aufgelegte Schiffe n/pl., auch: ships pl. in ordinary. — II sich ≈ v/refl. 9. to rest on one's elbow. — 10. man. ein Pferd legt sich auf ... pulls hard at the bit. — III ~ n ㉓ 11. = A/ung. — IV **auf-gelegt** p.p. u. a. ㉖ 12. in allen Bedeutungen des inf.; ⚔ ≈ schießen to

shoot with (or from) a rest or a support. — 13. fig. disposed to, inclined to, in a (fit) frame of mind for; zu et. ≈ sein to be (or feel) in the humour (or vein) for a th.; ich bin nicht zum Radfahren ≈ I am not in the (right) mood for cycling; gut (schlecht) ≈ in a good (bad) humour or temper. **Auf-leger** (ᴵᴸ‿) m ㉒, ~in f ㊵ one who applies, imposes, inflicts, &c. **Auf-lege-stück** (ᴵᴸ‿...) n ㉖ für Stickereien: appliqué (work). **Auf-legung** (ᴵᴸ‿) f ㊵ eines Pflasters: application; der Hände: laying-on, imposition; einer Strafe: infliction. **auf-lehnen** (ᴵᴸ‿) I v/a. u. sich ≈ v/refl. ㉛** 1. (sich) ≈ to lean (or rest) on (one's elbow, &c.). — 2. sich ≈ (emporrichten) to raise o.s.; von Pferden: (sich bäumen) to rear, to prance. — 3. fig. (sich empören) sich gegen et. oder e-n ≈ to resist, to rebel (or to rise in arms) against ...; mit Worten: to cry out against ...; (sich wehren) to resist, F to kick against ... — II ~ n ㉓ und **Auf-lehnung** f ㊵ 4. resistance, rebellion, insurrection. **auf-leimen** (ᴵᴸ‿) v/a. ㉛** 1. to glue upon or to. — 2. (wiederherstellen) bsd. ein Gemälde: to put new canvas to. **auf-lesen** (ᴵᴸ‿) v/a. ㉛a** 1. to gather, to pick up; Ähren: to glean. — 2. ⚕ eine Krankheit ꝛc.: to catch a disease, &c. **Auf-leser** (ᴵᴸ‿) m ㉒, ~in f ㊵ gatherer, collector; gleaner (= Ährenleser). **auf-leuchten** (ᴵᴸ‿) v/n. (h., fn) ㉛** to flash up, to beam (or shine) forth. **auf-lichten** (ᴵᴸ‿) v/a. ㉛** Malerei: to brighten up, to enliven; (Lichter aufsetzen) to set off the lights. **auf-liegen** (ᴵᴸ‿) ㉛** I v/n. (fn) 1. auf et. ≈ to lie (or rest) on a th.; fest ≈ to fit tightly. — 2. e-m ≈ (zur Last fallen) to weigh heavily on a p.; to be incumbent. — 3. (offen liegen) Spiel: was liegt auf (ist Trumpf)? what are trumps?; von Waren: to be exposed for sale; von Zeitschriften: to be kept. — 4. ⚓ v. Handelsschiffen: (aufgelegt sein) to be laid up. — II v/a. u. sich ≈ v/refl. 5. den Rücken ≈, sich ≈ (wund liegen) to become bedsore (= sich durchliegen). — III ~ n ㉓ 6. lying (or resting) on; incumbency; von Kranken: bedsoreness. [curl.| **auf-locken** (ᴵᴸ‿) v/a. ㉛** die Haare ≈ to| **auf-lockern** (ᴵᴸ‿) v/a. und sich ≈ v/refl. ㉛a** 1. Knoten: to loosen; fig. to relax, to slacken. — 2. ein Bett: to shake up; agr. den Boden ≈ to break (or loosen) the ground; to scarify the soil. **auf-lodern** (ᴵᴸ‿) I v/n. (fn) ㉛a** to blaze (or flare) up; fig. to fire up; leicht 2d irascible, quick-tempered. — II ~ n ㉓ blaze; leidenschaftliches ~ violent (fit) of passion or temper. **auf-löffeln** F (ᴵᴸ‿) v/a. ㉛a** to spoon up, to take up with a spoon. **auf-lösbar** (ᴵᴸ-) a. ㊻ (dis)soluble, dissolvable; math. solvable; nicht ≈ insoluble, insolvable; ~keit (ᴵᴸ-) f ㊵ (dis)solubility; math. solvability. **Auf-löse-...** (ᴵᴸ‿) ㉖ = Auflösungs-. **auf-lösen** (ᴵᴸ‿) I v/a. u. sich ≈ v/refl. ㉛** 1. (entwirren) to loosen, disentangle, unravel; Knoten: to undo; ⊙ typ. die

Kolumnen: to untie; Schuhriemen: to unlace; aufgelöstes Haar dishevelled hair. — 2. fig. ein Geheimnis ≈ to clear up a mystery; ein Rätsel ≈ to solve a riddle or puzzle. — 3. (zerlegen) to dissolve, resolve, decompose, (zersetzen) to disintegrate, to disorganize; Farben im Wasser ≈ to dilute (or temper) colours; Phosphor in Äther ≈ to solve phosphorus in ether; chm. in seine Bestandteile ≈ to resolve into its components, to split up, to analyse; math. Gleichungen, Klammern ≈ to solve (or reduce) equations, brackets; fig. sich in nichts, in allgemeines Wohlgefallen ≈ to fall to the ground, to come to nothing or to nought; sich ≈ (sterben) to pass away; to expire; in Tränen aufgelöst melted into tears; ♪: eine Dissonanz ≈ to resolve a discord; e-e Note ≈ (durch das Auflösungszeichen wiederherstellen) to restore a note. — 4. (aufhören m.) to dissolve, to break up; die Bande der Freundschaft ≈ to sever the ties (or bonds) of friendship; eine Ehe ≈ to dissolve a marriage, to untie the matrimonial knot; ✱ ein Geschäft ≈ to wind up ...; e-e Handelsgesellschaft ≈ to dissolve partnership; ⚔ ein Korps ≈ to disband troops; e-e Versammlung ≈ to dissolve (or break up) a meeting; die Versammlung löste sich auf the meeting dispersed or broke up. — II ~ n ㉓ 5. = A/ung 1—3. — III 2b p.pr. u. a. ㊻ 6. in den Bed. des inf. — 7. ⚗ (dis)solvent; (verdünnend) diluent; ≈des Mittel (dis)solvent. — IV **auf-gelöst** p.p. u. a. ㊻ 8. Bed. des inf. — 9. chm. ≈es Gold gold solution. **auf-löslich** (ᴵᴸ‿) a. ㊻ = auflösbar. **Auf-lösung** (ᴵᴸ‿) f ㊵ 1. (Entwirren) loosening, disentanglement. — 2. fig. eines Geheimnisses: elucidation; ~ des Knotens im Drama unravelling ~ des plot, (fr.) dénouement; parl. ~ in ein Komitee going into committee; (Zersetzung) decomposition, disintegration, disorganization; chm. analysis; med. von Sterbenden: break-up, final stage, approaching end; der Kranke geht s-r ~ entgegen the patient is sinking fast or dying; (Tod) death, decease; math. von Gleichungen: solution; von Brüchen: reduction; ♪ e-r Dissonanz: resolution. — 3. (Aufhebung des Bestandes, e-r Versammlung ꝛc.) dissolution, breaking up, break-up; e-r Ehe: divorce; ⚔ von Truppen: disbandment. — 4. (Ergebnis des Auflösens) chm. solution; ~ von Jod in Alkohol alcoholic iodine solution, solution of iodine in alcohol. **Auf-lösungs-dekret** (ᴵᴸ‿...) n ㉖ decree of dissolution; ≈fähig a. ㊻ soluble, solvable; ≈fähigkeit f solubility, solvability; ≈kraft f dissolving power, opt. dissolvent force; ≈mittel n (dis)solvent; ≈vermögen n = ≈kraft; ≈wissenschaft f: ⚗ analytics; ≈wort n e-s Rätsels answer; ≈zeichen n: a) gr. ⚗ diæresis (¨); b) ♪ natural (♮). **auf-löten** ⊙ (ᴵᴸ‿) v/a. ㉛** 1. to solder on. — 2. (loslöten) to unsolder. [luven.| **auf-luven** ⚓ (ᴵᴸʷ‿) v/n. (hn) ㉛** = an=|

⚗ scientific; ⚘ botanical; ⚱ geography; ⊕ machinery; ⚒ mining; ⚔ military; ⚓ marine; ✱ commercial; ✉ postal; 🚂 railway.

auf-machen (ᵘᵇᶜʰʲ) ⊛** I v/a. 1. e-e Tür w. to open, undo; (aufschließen) to unlock; wenn geschellt od. geklopft wird: to answer the bell or the door. — 2. die Augen 2 to open one's eyes; ein Bett: to make up, to turn down; eine zugekorkte Flasche: to uncork; Kartoffeln: to dig up, to lift; einen Knoten 2 to untie a knot; Nüsse: to crack (open); die Ohren 2 to prick up one's ears; ein Paket 2 to undo (or unpack) a parcel; e-n Schirm: to put up; ein Schnürleib 2 to unlace (or unfasten) stays; Verklebtes: to unfasten, to undo; Zugeknöpftes: to unbutton. — 3. ⊛ ein Konto 2 (eröffnen) to open an account; eine Faktura 2 to make out an invoice. — II sich 2 v/refl. 4 to (a)rise, get up, set out; sich 2 nach to start (or make) for; der Wind macht sich auf the wind is springing up; sich auf und davon machen f. auf 11. — 5. (sich zu et. anschicken) to set about a th. — III ~ n ⓖ 6. = A/ung.

Auf-machung (~) f ⓖ opening, &c.; ⊛ ~ einer Rechnung opening (or statement) of an account; (innere Verpackung e-r Ware) inside packing; ⚓ (Seeschädenberechnung) making up the average, estimate of sea-damage, calculating losses (suffered) at sea.

auf-mahlen (ᵘˡ˘) v/a. ⊛** (f. mahlen) to grind all, to finish grinding.

auf-malen (ᵘˡ˘) v/a. ⊛** 1. auf et. 2 to paint on a th. — 2. ein Gemälde (auffrischen) to freshen up; (instand setzen) to retouch; (neu) 2 to paint anew. — 3. (aufbrauchen) alle Farbe 2 to use up all the paint.

Auf-marsch, meist ⚔ (ᵘˢ) m ⓐ. marching up; drawing up; deploy(ment); ~ v. Truppen: tactical evolution of ...; ~ e-s Heeres strategical movement of ...

Auf-marsch-gelände (ᶻ...) n ⓖ ground on which to draw up troops or to make an evolution.

auf-marschieren, meist ⚔ (ᵘˡ˘) v/n. (in) ⊛*/* to form (into) line; zum Gefecht: to deploy; ⚔ in Linie 2 to form a line; in Schlachtordnung 2 lassen to draw up (in battle-array); weitS. 2 lassen to marshal, to muster; (aufzählen) to enumerate; ~lassen (ᵘˡ˘ˍᵘ˘) n ⓖ deployment, evolution (of troops); muster; (Aufzählung) enumeration.

Auf-marsch-linie (ᵘˢ...) f ⓖ line of march; ᐅzeit f time allowed (or fixed) for marching up.

Auf-maß (ᵘˡ) n ⓐ. heaped-up measure.

auf-mauern (ᵘˡ˘) v/a. ⓐ** to build up (with brick); ⚓ (höher mauern) to raise.

auf-meißeln ⊕ (ᵘˡ˘) v/a. ⓐ** to (force or break) open with a chisel.

auf-merken (ᵘˢ˘) ⊛** I v/a. to mark, to note (or put, write, jot) down. — II v/n. (h.) 2 auf to give (or pay) attention (or heed) to, to attend to, to give ear (or one's mind) to; du hast nicht aufgemerkt you did not listen.

Auf-merker (ᵘˢ˘) m ⓖ, ~in f ⓖ (attentive) listener, eavesdropper.

auf-merksam (ᵘˢ˘) a. ⓖ 1. attentive (auf et. to a th.), mindful of; e-n auf et. 2 machen to call (or draw) a p.'s attention to a th.; auf eine Gefahr 2 w. to become alive to or aware of ...; adv. 2 prüfen to examine carefully or closely. — 2. fig. attentive to; (höflich) obliging to, courteous to, polite to; er ist sehr 2 gegen sie he shows her every (possible) attention.

Auf-merksamkeit (ᵘˢ--) f ⓖ 1. attention; j-s ~ von et. ablenken to divert a p.'s att. from a th.; j-s ~ erregen (fesseln) to attract (or rivet) a p.'s att.; j-s ~ auf et. (hin)lenken to direct a p.'s att. to a th.; mit gespannter ~ lauschen to listen with eager att., to listen intently; e-m (seine) ~ schenken to pay attention to a p. — 2. fig. (Artigkeit) attention, attentiveness; (Höflichkeit) courtesy, civility; e-m große ~(en) erweisen to pay great respect to a p.; eine zarte ~ a delicate attention.

auf-messen (ᵘˡ˘) v/a. ⊛** e. Feld 2 (vermessen) to survey a field; Korn 2 to measure and put up corn (in a barn).

auf-mischen (ᵘˢ˘) v/a. ⓖ** Wein 2 to mix (or blend) different wines.

auf-montieren ⊕ (ᵘˡ˘) v/a. ⊛*/* to mount; e-n Motorwagen: to connect.

auf-mucken F (ᵘˢ˘) v/n. (h.) ⊛** to speak up boldly, to resist; to kick against the pricks; gegen et. 2 to rebel (F to kick) against a th.

auf-muntern (ᵘˢ˘) I v/a. ⓐ** to rouse; (aufheitern) to cheer (up); (anreizen) to encourage, inspire, incite, egg on. — II ~ n ⓖ u. **Auf-munterung** f ⓖ encouragement, incitement; er fand keine ~ he met with no encouragement.

auf-münzen (ᵘˢ˘) v/a. ⓖ** to imprint on.

auf-müssen (ᵘˢ˘) v/n. (h.) ⊛** ich muß auf (= aufstehen) I must get up; die Tür, das Fenster muß auf(gemacht w.) ... must be opened, ... is to be left open.

auf-mutzen F (ᵘˢ˘) [mhd.] v/a. ⓖ** e-m et. 2 (vorrücken) to cast s. th. in a p.'s teeth, to blame a p. for a th.

auf-nageln (ᵘˡ˘) v/a. ⓑ** to nail down.

auf-nagen (ᵘˡ˘) v/a. ⊛** 1. to gnaw open. — 2. to consume by gnawing.

Auf-näh-arbeit (ᵘˡ...) f ⓖ appliqué work.

auf-nähen (ᵘˡ˘) ⊛** I v/a. 1. to sew on. — 2. sich (dat.) die Finger 2 (wund nähen) to sew one's fingers sore. — 3. den Zwirn 2 to use up ... in sewing. — II sich 2 v/refl. 4. von einer Naht 2. to come unstitched.

Auf-nahme (ᵘᴸ˘) f ⓖ 1. (das Aufnehmen) taking up, reception; physiol. (in sich): assimilation, absorption. — 2. (Zulassung) admittance, admission; von Soldaten, Schülern ⁊c. auch: enrolment; als Bürger in den Staatsverband: naturalization, enfranchisement; fremder Sitten ob. Wörter: adoption. — 3. (Empfang) reception; e-m e-e freundliche ~ bereiten to give a p. a hearty welcome; er fand bei ihr eine kühle ~ he met with a cool reception at her hands; ⊛ einer Tratte gute ~ bereiten duly to honour (or to pay due honour to) a draft. — 4. ~ von Kapitalien taking up of capital; loan. — 5. (Aufzeichnung) surv. topographische ~ measurement, (topographical) survey; flüchtige ~ hasty sketch; geographische ~ eines Landes mapping-out a country; jur. ~ von Beweisen deposition(s pl.); ~ e-s Protokolls drawing up of the minutes; ⊛ ~ eines Inventariums making (up) of an inventory; ~ des Warenlagers taking stock; phot. sitting; taking a p.'s likeness; (das Bild) photograph(ic view); tel. ~ nach dem Gehör reading by sound. — 6. (Emporkommen) prosperity; (Erfolg) success; in ~ bringen to bring forward, push, promote; in ~ kommen to come into fashion or vogue, to meet with a good reception, F to catch on (well); in ~ sein to be in vogue, F to be all the rage; das Stück hat gute ~ gefunden the piece has taken (F caught on) well.

Auf-nahme-bedingungen (ᵘᴸ...) f/pl. ⓖ terms pl. of admission; ᐅfähig a. ⓖ qualified (or suitable) for admission; eligible; admissible; ⊛ (vom Markte) capable of absorbing; für Baumwolle ist der Markt noch 2 there is (still) a demand (or an opening) for cotton on the market; ᐅfähigkeit f admissibility; eligibility; ᐅprüfung f entrance-examination; ᐅschein m certificate of admission; ᐅschiff ⚓ n zur Küstenvermessung: survey-ship; ᐅstellung ⚔ f covering position, cover; 2würdig a. worthy of admittance.

auf-naschen (ᵘˢ˘) ⓖ** to eat up (dainties) on the sly; to spend or waste (money) on dainties.

auf-nehmbar (ᵘˡ˘) a. ⓖ admissible.

auf-nehmen (ᵘˡ˘) ⓐ** I v/a. 1. (aufheben) to raise, to lift up; vom Boden 2 to pick up; fig. den Fehdehandschuh 2 to take up the gauntlet or challenge. — 2. die Stube 2 to scrub out the room, to wash the floor. — 3. es mit e-m 2 to compete (or cope) with a p.; er kann es mit jedem 2 he is a match for any one; den Kampf mit e-m 2 to enter into a contest (or to try conclusions) with a p. — 4. den fallengelassenen Faden, eine Masche (wieder) 2 to take up a stitch; hunt. die Spur (ob. Fährte) 2 to catch (or find, recover) the scent; fig. den Faden der Erzählung wieder 2 to pick up the thread of the story; die Arbeit wieder 2 to resume work. — 5. et. (in sich) 2 to receive, absorb; (beherbergen) to harbour, shelter; das Wort ist in unsere Sprache aufgenommen ... passes current in our language; der Saal kann 80 Kinder 2 the hall holds or can seat ... — 6. (einverleiben) e-n 2 to admit a p. (in)to; er ließ sich in den Klub 2 he joined the club; Artikel in ein Blatt 2 to insert (or put) ... in a paper. — 7. als Gast 2 to receive (hospitably); (bewirten) to entertain; gut aufgenommen werden to meet with a good reception at a p.'s hands. — 8. (auffassen) et. gut (übel) 2 to take a th. in good (bad) part; et. als Beleidigung (Scherz) 2 to look upon a th. as an insult (a joke); sie wird es dir hoch 2 she will think it very kind of you. — 9. (borgen) to take up or raise or borrow (money); e-e Anleihe 2 to contract a loan. — 10. (zu Papier bringen) surv., &c.: e-n Grundriß 2 to survey; ⚓ a. to map out; ⊛ den Lager-

---

Zeichen (f. S. XVII): F familiär; P Volkssprache; Γ Gaunersprache; ᐳ selten; † alt (auch gestorben); * neu (auch geboren); ⁑ unrichtig;

[aufnehmenswert] — 97 — [aufrechnen]

bestand ≈ to take stock; ein Protokoll ≈ to draw up the minutes; ein Verzeichnis ≈ to make an inventory; *phot.* to photograph, F to take (a likeness of); ⊕ *tel.* nach dem Gehör ≈ to read by sound. — **II** sich ≈ v/refl. 11. to rise (again); bsd. fig. (gedeihen) to prosper, to thrive. — **III** ~ n ㉓ 12. = Aufnahme.

auf-nehmens-wert (ᴵᴸ⌣...) a.⊛, ≈würdig worthy of being (or deserving to be) admitted, received, inserted.

auf-nieten ⊕ (ᴵᴸ⌣) v/a. ⊛** to rivet on.

auf-notieren (ᴵᴸ⌣⌣) v/a. ⊛*/* to note (or put, write) down; ⊛ to book.

auf-nötigen v/a. ⊛** e-m et. ≈ to press (or urge, force) a th. upon a p.

auf-opfer/n (ᴵᴸ⌣) **I** v/a. u. v/refl. ⊛a** (sich) ≈ to sacrifice (o.s.) to; to offer (o.s.) up; sich einem, e-r Sache ≈ (sich hingeben) to devote o.s. (or to give o.s. up) to a p., a. th.; sich, sein Leben ≈ für to lay down one's life for. — **II** ~ n ㉓ = A/ung. — **III** ≈d *p.pr.* u. a. ⊛ devoted to; ≈de Liebe self-sacrificing love, (pure) devotion.

Auf-opferung f ㊻ (self-)sacrifice; (blind) devotion; ≈s-fähig a. ⊛ capable of self-denial, self-denying.

auf-pack/en (ᴵᴸ⌣) v/a. ⊛** 1. to pack up on, to load on; *fig.* da habe ich mir (et)was Schönes aufgepackt I have taken a nice burden on myself. — 2. *abs.* (aufbrechen) to start, F to pack and be off.

auf-palmen ⊥ (ᴵᴸ⌣): sich ≈ v/refl. ⊛** to climb hand over hand.

auf-päppeln (ᴵᴸ⌣) v/a. ⊛a** ein Kind ≈ to bring up ... by hand or with the bottle.

auf-pappen (ᴵᴸ⌣) v/a. ⊛** 1. to paste on. — 2. F to eat (or gobble) up.

auf-passen (ᴵᴸ⌣) ⊛** **I** v/n. (h.) 1. to attend; to listen (attentively); to be on one's guard; to (be on the) watch for; aufgepaßt! attention!, mind!, look out!, look alive!; paß' (nur) auf! mark my word! — 2. e-m ≈ to waylay a p.; e-m ≈ lassen to have a p. watched. — **II** v/a. 3. e-n Deckel auf eine Schachtel ≈ to fit a cover on a box. — 4. einen Hut ≈ to try on.

Auf-passer (ᴵᴸ⌣) m ㉒, ~in f ㊼ p. who watches, (police-)spy; (Horcher) listener; den ~ für Mitschüler spielen F to be (or stand) cave. [espionage.)

Auf-passerei (ᴵᴸ⌣ᴵᴵ) f ㊻ spying, b.s.)

auf-pauken (ᴵᴸ⌣) v/n. (h.) ⊛** auf die Trommel ≈ to beat the drum violently.

auf-pausen (ᴵᴸ⌣) Zeichnungen ≈ (durch Schwärzen ꝛc. der Rückseite übertragen) to trace ..., to pounce ....

auf-peitschen (ᴵᴸ⌣) v/a. ⊛** to whip up.

auf-pfählen (ᴵᴸ⌣) v/a. ⊛** to empale; to fix on (or to fasten with) stakes.

auf-pfeifen (ᴵᴸ⌣) v/a. u. v/n. (h.) ⊛b** to play upon a whistle or a fife.

auf-pflanzen (ᴵᴸ⌣) ⊛** **I** v/a. to set up; ⚔ : eine Fahne ≈ to mount (or plant) a flag, to raise a standard; das Seitengewehr ≈ to fix bayonet. — **II** sich ≈ v/refl. to take one's place or stand or position. [(or fix) with pegs.)

auf-pflöcken (ᴵᴸ⌣) v/a. ⊛** to fasten)

auf-pflügen (ᴵᴸ⌣) v/a. u. agr. to plough up. [upon.)

auf-pfropfen (ᴵᴸ⌣) v/a. ⊛** to (en)graft)

auf-pichen (ᴵᴸ⌣) v/a. ⊛** to (fasten on with) pitch. [— 2. to pick open.)

auf-picken (ᴵᴸ⌣) v/a. ⊛** 1. to pick up.)

auf-plätten (ᴵᴸ⌣) v/a. u. v/refl. ⊛** = aufbügeln.

auf-platzen (ᴵᴸ⌣) v/n. (ſn) ⊛** to burst open, to fly asunder, to explode.

auf-plump(ſ)en F (ᴵᴸ⌣) v/n. (ſn) ⊛(⊛)** to plump down, to fall heavily.

auf-plustern F (ᴵᴸ⌣) v/a. u. v/refl. ⊛a** ein Vogel plustert sein Gefieder od. sich auf a bird ruffles its feathers.

auf-pochen (ᴵᴸ⌣ⱷ) ⊛** **I** v/n. (h.) 1. vom Herzen: to beat fast, to throb, F to bump. — 2. mit der Faust ꝛc. auf den Tisch ≈ to knock on the table. — 3. *fig.* (trotzen) to show a refractory (or defiant) spirit. — **II** v/a. 4. (pochend öffnen) to knock open.

auf-polieren (ᴵᴸ⌣ᴸ⌣) v/a. ⊛*/* to polish (or furbish) up; to rub (or touch) up.

auf-polstern (ᴵᴸ⌣) v/a. ⊛a** to stuff, to upholster; to pad afresh.

auf-prägen (ᴵᴸ⌣) v/a. ⊛** ein Bild ꝛc.: to imprint, to impress (or stamp) on.

auf-prallen (ᴵᴸ⌣) **I** v/n. (ſn) ⊛** to rebound, to bounce; ⚔ to ricochet. — **II** ~ n ㉓ rebound(ing); ⚔ ricochet.

auf-prasseln (ᴵᴸ⌣) v/n. (ſn) ⊛** Flamme: to flare up with a crackling noise.

auf-pressen (ᴵᴸ⌣) v/a. ⊛** 1. to press again. — 2. eine Verzierung ꝛc.: to imprint, to (im)press on. — 3. to press open.

auf-probieren (ᴵᴸ⌣ᴸ⌣) v/a. ⊛*/* e-n Hut ꝛc. ≈ to try on ... (= aufpassen 4).

auf-protzen ⚔ (ᴵᴸ⌣) [Protze] **I** v/a. u. v/n. ⊛** Geschütze ≈ to limber (up) ordnance. — **II** ~ n ㉓ limbering (up).

auf-pudern (ᴵᴸ⌣) v/a. ⊛a** to repowder; to use up in powdering.

auf-puffen (ᴵᴸ⌣) ⊛** **I** v/a. Haar, Ärmel ≈ to puff up ... **II** v/n. das Pulver pufft auf ... decrepitates.

auf-pullen ⊥ (ᴵᴸ⌣) [engl.] v/a. ⊛** Sport: (verhalten) to pull up, to pull (a horse).

auf-pumpen (ᴵᴸ⌣) v/a. ⊛** 1. to pump up, to heave. — 2. F Geld: to borrow (on all sides); F to get things on tick.

auf-purren ⊥ (ᴵᴸ⌣) v/a. ⊛** die Schiffswache ≈ (wecken) to call the watch.

Auf-putz m ⊛ a. 1. = aufputzen **III**. — 2. (Anzug) dress, attire; adornment, finery; ein seltsamer ~ F a curious get-up. — 3. allgem. (Schmuck) ornament; ⊕ für Mauern: coat(ing) of plaster.

auf-putzen (ᴵᴸ⌣) ⊛** **I** v/a. Leuchter ꝛc. ≈ to clean(se), brighten, polish; ⊕ Hüte ꝛc.: to do (or trim) up; *fig.* (über-arbeiten) to retouch. — **II** v/a. (u. sich ≈ v/refl.) to adorn (o.s.), attire (o.s.), smarten (o.s.) up; sie war lächerlich aufgeputzt F she was got up in a ludicrous fashion; sich wie einen Pfingstochsen (☞ wie ein Pfingstochse) ≈ to attire o.s. most gorgeously, F to put on one's Sunday best; Zimmer: F to tidy up. — **III** ~ n ㉓ clean(s)ing; retouching.

Auf-putzer (ᴵᴸ⌣) m ⊛, ~in f ㊼ clean(s)er, polisher; trimmer.

auf-qualmen (ᴵᴸ⌣) v/n. ⊛** Rauch qualmt auf smoke is rising.

auf-quellen (ᴵᴸ⌣) **I** v/n. (ſn) ⊛b** 1. to gush forth, to spring (or well) up; (ſiedend) to bubble up. — 2. to open with a gush. — 3. (anſchwellen) to swell up; to rise. — **II** v/a. ⊛** 4. Erbſen ꝛc.: to soak, to steep. — **III** ~ n ㉓ 5. springing (or bubbling) up, &c.

auf-quetschen (ᴵᴸ⌣) v/a. ⊛** (quetſchend öffnen) to squeeze open.

auf-quirlen (⌣) v/a. ⊛** to twirl (again), to stir up, Eier: to whisk, to beat up.

auf-raff/en (ᴵᴸ⌣) ⊛** **I** v/a. to snatch (or rake) up; von Frauen: die Kleider ≈ tuck (or gather) up ...; aufgerafftes Gesindel riffraff. — **II** sich ≈ v/refl. to rise (or get up) quickly, to pull o.s. together; *fig.* auch: to recover from.

auf-ragen (ᴵᴸ⌣) v/n. (h.) ⊛** (hoch) ≈ to rise aloft, to tower (up).

auf-rahmen ⊕ (ᴵᴸ⌣) v/a. ⊛** Tuchfabr.: (auf Rahmen ſpannen) to stretch on tenters.

auf-ranken (ᴵᴸ⌣) v/n. u. sich ≈ v/refl. ⊛** to climb (or creep) up.

auf-rappeln F (ᴵᴸ⌣) v/n. u. v/refl. ⊛a** e-n ≈ to stir up a p.; sich zu et. ≈ to pull o.s. together for s.th.

auf-rasseln (ᴵᴸ⌣) v/n. (ſn) ⊛a** to open (or to rise) with a rattling noise.

auf-rauchen (ᴵᴸ⌣ⱷ) ⊛** **I** v/n. (ſn) to rise as smoke. — **II** v/a. eine Pfeife: to finish; den Tabak ≈ to smoke (up) ...

auf-räufeln (ᴵᴸ⌣) v/a. ⊛a** Gestricktes: to ravel out. [wirkerei: raising-iron)

Auf-rauh-eisen ⊕ (ᴵᴸ...) n ㉓ Borten-)

auf-rauhen ⊕ (ᴵᴸ⌣) v/a. ⊛** to roughen. Tuch: to nap, to dress; Wolle: to card.

Auf-rauher ⊕ (ᴵᴸ⌣) m ㉒, ~in f ㊼ Tuchmacherei: dresser, carder.

auf-räum/en (ᴵᴸ⌣) [mhd.] **I** v/a. u. v/n. (h.) ⊛** 1. (wegſchaffen) to carry off, remove; *typ.* to clear (or put) away. — 2. (freimachen) to clear, disencumber, ⚔ das Gefechtsfeld (nach dem Gefecht) ≈ to clear the battle-field; ⊛ ſein Lager ≈ to clear (out) one's stock; mit e-r Ware ≈ to sell off, to dispose of ...; ⚔ *artill.* das Zündloch ≈ to clear (or pick) the touch-hole. — 3. (ordnen) to set in order, to put to rights, to clear up; ein Zimmer: F to tidy up. — 4. *fig.* unter den Beamten ≈ to purge the (civil) service; unter ſ-r Dienerſchaft: to make a clean sweep (in one's household); mit seinen früheren Ansichten ≈ to throw up (or over) one's former opinions; der Krieg hat unter der Bevölkerung aufgeräumt the war has wrought (or made) havoc among ...; die Cholera räumt im Hospital auf ... is emptying the hospital. — **II** ~ n ㉓ 5. = A/ung; es fand sich beim ~ it was found when the room was cleared. — **III** auf-geräumt *p.p.* u. a. ⊛ 6. Bed. des *inf.* — 7. *fig.* merry, cheerful, blithe, jovial, F jolly.

Auf-räumer (ᴵᴸ⌣) m ㉒ 1. (a. ~in f ㊼) p. who clears up; *typ.* one who clears away or distributes (type). — 2. ⊕ Büchſenm.: boasting-chisel; Uhrm.: broach, puncher. — 3. ⚔ *artill.* = Aufreiber

Auf-räumung (ᴵᴸ⌣) f ㊻ carrying off; clearing up, clearance; F tidying up.

auf-rauschen (ᴵᴸ⌣) v/n. (ſn) ⊛** to open (or rise, fly up) with a rustling noise.

auf-räuspern (ᴵᴸ⌣) v/a. u. v/refl. ⊛a** den Schleim ≈ to expectorate; sich ≈ to clear one's throat.

auf-rechen (ᴵᴸ⌣) v/a. ⊛** to rake up.

auf-rechnen (ᴵᴸ⌣) v/a. u. v/n. (h.) ⊛b** 1. (anrechnen) to reckon (or count) up;

♪ Musik; ⚛ Wissenschaft; ⚘ Pflanze; ⚲ Geographie; ⊕ Technik; ⚒ Bergbau; ⚔ Militär; ⊥ Marine; ⊛ Handel; ✉ Post; 🚂 Eisenbahn.

[Aufrechnung] — 98 — [aufrühren]

to enumerate, specify; e-m et. ₂ to charge ... to a p.'s account. — 2. (ausgleichen) et. mit=ea. ₂ to balance (or square) accounts; jur. der 2de Teil the compensating party.

Auf-rechnung (ᴹᴸ∪) f ⓯ balancing; settlement; F squaring of accounts; jur. compensation.

auf-recht (ᴹᴸ) [ahd.: upright] a. ⑥⑥ (v. adv.) upright, erect; (gerade) straight; (senkrecht) vertical(ly), perpendicular (-ly); (sich) ₂ (er)halten to maintain (o.s.), to sustain (o.s.), to support (o.s.), to keep (o.s.) afloat; durch Hoffnung: to buoy (o.s.) up; ₂ geh(e)n to walk upright; den Kopf (a. sich) ₂ halten to hold up one's head; fig. to hold one's own; ₂ sitzen to sit up; ₂ sich(e)n to stand erect; ₂(=)stehend her. rampant; ₂ stellen to set on end. [maintain.]

auf-recht-(er)halten (ᴹᴸ...) v/a.⓯a⁂ to)

Auf-recht-(er)haltung (ᴹᴸ...) f⓯ maintenance, support; e-s Rechtes: vindication.

auf-recken (ᴹᴸ) v/a. ⓯⁂ to reach (or lift) up; den Hals: to stretch; to crane forward; die Ohren: to prick up one's ears.

auf-reden (ᴹᴸ) ⓯⁂ e-m ₂ = aufhetzen ₂; e-m et. ₂ = anschwatzen.

auf-reg/en (ᴹᴸ) I v/a. u. v/refl. ⓯⁂ 1. das Meer 2c.: to agitate, to set in motion; das ganze Haus: to rouse, to stir. — 2. fig. Bedenken 2c.: to give rise to, stärker: to excite, raise, stir up. — 3. fig. e-n: to agitate, exite; (beunruhigen) to alarm, disturb, unsettle, upset; sich über et. ₂ to get excited (or alarmed, upset) about a th. — II ~ n ㉓ 4. = A/ung. — III 2d p.pr. u. a. ⑥⑥ (f.I) 5. exciting, med. a. irritant; (bemrubigend) alarming; (aufrührerisch) seditious. — IV auf-geregt p.p. u. a. ⑥⑥ (f.I) 6. excited, flurried; von 2em Wesen of an excitable nature. of quick temper.

Auf-regung (∼) f ⓯ 1. (das Aufregen) agitating, &c. (f. aufregen I). — 2. (Aufgeregtsein) agitation; emotion; flurry; flutter (of excitement); stärker: turmoil; in ~ geraten (sein) to grow (to be) excited or alarmed or upset: in ~ bringen, versetzen = aufregen I; die Stadt ist in ~... alarmed or in a (state of) commotion or in an uproar.

Auf-regungs=mittel (ᴸ...) n ⓰ med. stimulant; irritant.

auf-reib/en (ᴹᴸ) ⓯¹⁂ I v/a. 1. to rub on; ein Zimmer: to scrub (down). — 2. (wund reiben) to rub sore; to gall. to chafe. — 3. (aufbrauchen) die Farbe ist aufgerieben = is all ground (up) or crushed. — 4. (auch sich ₂ v/refl.) fig. (vernichten) to destroy, to annihilate; ⚔ ein Heer ₂, auch: to cut (or wipe) up; die aufgeriebene Mannschaft the troops who perished; (untergraben) to undermine; (erschöpfen) to exhaust; e-e 2de Arbeit a wearing task; sich ₂ to wear o.s. out. — II v/n. 5. auf et. ₂ to rub on a th. — III ~ n ㉓ 6. = A/ung.

Auf-reiber ⊙ (ᴹᴸ) m ㉒ (Löffelbohrer) wimble; (Nagelbohrer) gimlet; (Zentrumbohrer) centre-bit.

Auf-reibung (ᴹᴸ) f ⓯ rubbing up; (Vernichtung) destruction, annihilation; (Erschöpfung) exhaustion.

auf-reihen (ᴹᴸ) v/a. ⓯⁂ Perlen 2c.: to (file on a) string, to thread.

auf-reiß/en (ᴹᴸ) ⓯a⁂ I v/a. 1. to tear open, to rend; die Tür 2c.: to fling (or burst) open. — 2. die Augen weit ₂ to open one's eyes wide; das Maul ₂ to open one's mouth wide (in speaking, &c.); (gähnen) to gape, to yawn; von die Dürre: den Boden ₂ to crack ...; to die Hand an e-m Nagel ₂ to tear one's hand (open) by a nail; eine Naht: to rip up; ⊕ Schienen, Straßenpflaster ₂ to take up rails, the pavement; fig. e-e alte Wunde wieder ₂ to reopen old sores; agr. ein Brachfeld ₂ to clear fallow ground. — 3. (emporreißen) to tear up. — 4. (aufzeichnen) to draw, sketch, design. — II v/n. (fn) 5. to burst, crack, split; to give way; in der Naht ₂ to come unstitched. — III sich ₂ v/refl. 6. to spring up suddenly. — IV ~ n ㉓ u. **Auf-reißung** f ⓯ 7. (f.I) der Haut: chap(ping), crack(ing); des Pflasters 2c. taking up.

auf-reiten (ᴹᴸ) ⓯b⁂ I v/n. (fn) in bestimmter Ordnung: to ride up in a line or in files; nahe: to ride up close to a p., a th. — II v/a. (wund reiten) to gall (or chafe, make sore) by riding; sich ₂ to chafe o.s. by (or in) riding.

auf-reiz/en (ᴹᴸ) I v/a. ⓯⁂ to incite, provoke, stir up; die Leidenschaften: to work up, fire, rouse; er reizte ihn dazu auf he egged him on to do it; e-n gegen andere ₂ to set a p. against others. — II ~ n ㉓ = A/ung. — III 2d p.pr. u. a. ⑥⑥ stirring, irritating, provocative; von Reden: inflammatory.

Auf-reizer (ᴹᴸ) m ㉒, ~in f ㊹ inciter, provoker, instigator, stimulator.

Auf-reizung (ᴹᴸ) f ⓯ incitation, provocation, instigation.

auf-renn/en (ᴹᴸ) ⓯b⁂ I v/n. (fn) = auflaufen 1 u. 4. — II v/a. = auflaufen 5 u. 6; er ist so dumm, man kann mit ihm Tür und Tor ₂ he is a blockhead. — III sich (ea.) ₂ v/rpr. (aufspießen) to run one another through the body. [Schiffes: metacentre.]

Auf-richte=mome'nt ⚓ (ᴹᴸ...) n ㉑ e-s)

auf-richt/en (ᴹᴸ) ⓯⁂ I v/a. 1. et. Liegendes: to raise, to set up; ⚓ ein gekieltes Schiff: to right; her. aufgerichtet salient. — 2. fig. e-n in seinem Kummer ₂ to comfort (or console) a p.; j-s Mut wieder ₂ to revive (or raise) a p.'s courage. — 3. Mauern, Altäre 2c.: to raise, to erect; fig. einen Bund: to contract; ein Reich: to found; Schulen: to establish. — II sich ₂ v/refl. 4. to raise o.s. (up), to arise from; to stand up; sich im Bett ₂ to sit up in bed; sich stolz ₂ to draw o.s. up (to one's full length); sich wieder ₂ (erholen) to recover from. — III ~ n ㉓ 5. = A/ung.

Auf-richter (ᴹᴸ) m ㉒ raiser, setter-up; anat. (Aufrichtmuskel) erector.

auf-richtig (∼) a. ⑥⑥ sincere, candid; (offen) open, frank; (ehrlich) honest, upright, straightforward; ₂ gesagt frankly speaking, to speak candidly or openly.

Auf-richtigkeit (ᴹᴸ∼) f ⓯ sincerity, candour; openness, frankness; uprightness, straightforwardness.

Auf-richtung (ᴹᴸ∼) f ⓯ raising, erection; (Tröstung) comfort, consolation; (Gründung) foundation, establishment.

auf-riegeln (ᴹᴸ) v/a. ⓯a⁂ to unbolt, to unbar, to unhasp.

auf-ringeln (ᴹᴸ) v/a. u. sich ₂ v/refl. ⓯a⁂ 1. to form into ringlets or coils; Schlange: to coil up; Rauch: to curl up. — 2. (aus=ea.) Locken 2c.: to uncurl.

Auf-riß (ᴹᴸ) m ⓐa. (Zeichnung) design, draught, sketch; arch. (äußere Ansicht) elevation; (Vorder=ansicht) front; perspektivischer: scenography; Zeichenkunst: construction. [ing compasses pl.]

Auf-riß=zirkel ⊙ (ᴸ...) m ㉒ construct-]

auf-ritzen (ᴹᴸ) v/a. ⓯⁂ to slit (or rip) open; die Haut: to scratch (open).

auf-roll/en (ᴹᴸ) ⓯⁂ I v/n. (fn) 1. to roll up; der Vorhang rollt (geht) auf the curtain rises. — II v/a. u. v/refl. 2. (aufwickeln) to roll (or coil) up. — 3. die Haare in Locken ₂ to curl ...; sich ₂ to curl, to form curls or ringlets. — 4. ⊙ Färberei: den Rand, Saum: to roll up; Tuchm.: auf die Zeugrolle ₂ to calender. — 5. ? sich 2d, aufgerollt ⚤: convolute, spiral. — 6. (3f.=gerolltes entfalten) (sich) ₂ to unroll, uncoil, unfurl; fig. e-e Frage ₂ to broach a question.

Auf-roller ⊙ (ᴹᴸ) m ㉒ Spinnerei: fleeceroller; Drahtwalzwerk: roller.

auf-rück/en (ᴹᴸ) [mhd.] ⓯⁂ I v/n. (fn) to move up(ward), to rise; Fußballspiel: to back up; in eine höhere Stelle: to be promoted, F to get a lift; ⚔ ist zum Hauptmann, Leutnant 2c. aufgerückt he has been promoted to captain, to lieutenant, &c.; e-n ₂ lassen to promote a p., to move him up, F to give a p. a lift. — II v/a. to move up(ward); fig. bibl. (vorwerfen) to reproach (or upbraid) with. — III ~ n ㉓ u. **Auf-rückung** f ⓯ promotion; advancement (in rank or position).

Auf-ruf (ᴹᴸ) m ⓐ d. 1. (lauter Ruf) (out-)cry. — 2. (Aufforderung) calling up, call; (Befehl) summons; eines Fürsten: proclamation; einen ~ erlassen to (make an) appeal to the public; ~ der Zeugen calling (the names of) witnesses.

auf-rufen (ᴹᴸ) I v/a. ⓯b⁂ to call up; in der Schule: to call upon (a pupil); einzeln mit Namen ₂ to call over; e-n zum Zeugen ₂ to call a p. to witness; e-n durch die Zeitungen ₂ to advertise for a p. in the papers. — II ~ n ㉓ u. **Auf-rufung** f ⓯ calling up, call.

Auf-ruhr (ᴹᴸ) [:uproar] m⓪⑦d. 1. (Empörung) rebellion; (Aufstand) rising, insurrection, sedition; (Meuterei) mutiny; (Umwälzung) revolution; in ~ geraten to grow rebellious or mutinous, to rebel, to rise in arms; in hellem (ob. offenem) ~ in open revolt, all up in arms; einen ~ stillen, unterdrücken to quell, to crush out a rebellion. — 2. (Unruhe) commotion, riot, disturbance; (Getümmel) tumult, turmoil; einen ~ anstiften to cause a riot to excite a tumult, to raise a disturbance.

Auf-ruhr-akte (ᴸ...) f ㉑ =gesetz.

auf-rühren (ᴹᴸ) v/a. ⓯⁂ to stir (up), to rouse (up); das Feuer: to stir, to poke; fig. alte Geschichten 2c. (wieder) ₂

Signs (see page XVII): F familiar; P vulgar; ſ flash; ∖ rare; † obsolete (died); * new word (born); ⁺⁺ incorrect; ♪ music.

to rake up old grievances, the past, &c.; die Leidenschaften: to stir, to inflame; das Volk: to rouse to revolt.
Auf-rührer (ᴗ́ᴗ) m ㉒, ~**in** f ㊵ rebel; rioter; insurgent; mutineer; ᴌiſch a. ㊺ rebellious; riotous; insurrectional (movement); mutinous (conduct); inflammatory (speeches); seditious (language).
Auf-ruhr-geſetz (ᴗ́...) n ㉒ riot (or mutiny) act; =**ſtifter(in** f) m plotter, agitator; fig. firebrand.
auf-rüſten (ᴗ́ᴗ) v/a. ㊽** 1. to raise a scaffolding. — 2. (einrichten) to arrange; (ſchmücken) to adorn, to decorate.
auf-rütteln (ᴗ́ᴗ) I v/a. ㉒a** to shake, to stir up; e-n aus dem Schlafe ♁ to rouse up (by shaking); auch v/refl. ſich ♁ to shake off one's lethargy; to make fresh exertions.
aufs (¹) = auf (ſ. das 7) das. [aufbürden 1.)
auf-ſacken (ᴗ́ᴗ) v/a. ㊽** = aufladen u.)
Auf-ſage (ᴗ́ᴗ) f ㊻ = Aufkündigung.
auf-ſag|en (ᴗ́ᴗ) I v/a. ㊽** 1. e-e Lektion: to say, repeat; e-e Gedicht ꝛc.: to recite. — 2. = aufkündigen I. — II ~ n ㉓ = A/ung.
auf-ſägen (ᴗ́ᴗ) v/a. ㊽** 1. to saw open. — 2. to saw up (all the wood).
Auf-ſagung (ᴗ́ᴗ) f ㊻ 1. recitation. — 2. = Aufkündigung.
auf-ſammeln (ᴗ́ᴗ) I v/a. ㉒a** to gather (up), to collect; einzeln: to pick up; in Haufen: to hoard up. — II ~ n ㉓ und
Auf-ſamm(e)lung f ㊻ gathering (up), collection; hoarding up, hoards pl.
auf-ſäſſig (ᴗ́ᴗ) a. ㊺ 1. hostile, opposed; e-m ♁ ſein to have a grudge against a p. — 2. (widerſpenſtig) rebellious; refractory; ♁ w. to become unruly, to rebel.
Auf-ſäſſigkeit (ᴗ́ᴗ-) f ㊻ 1. ill-will. — 2. (Widerſpenſtigkeit) insubordination.
auf-ſatteln (ᴗ́ᴗ) v/a. ㉒a** 1. ein Pferd: to saddle. — 2. ⊕ carp. aufgeſattelte Treppe saddled stairs or steps pl. — 3. ⚒ (Schachtzimmerung erhöhen) to raise the timbering of the shaft. — II ~ n ㉓ u. **Auf-ſatt(e)lung** (ᴗ́ᴗ(ᴗ)ᴗ) f ㊻ saddling.
Auf-ſatz (ᴗ́ᴗ) [mhd.] m ①a. 1. mſt of head-piece, top(-piece), crest; ~ (Anſatzröhre) für Springbrunnen: jet-pipe, adjutage; ♪ an Blasinſtrumenten: reed; ⚔ artill. tangent-scale. — 2. (Tafel=²) centre-piece, epergne; (Porzellangeſchirr) china service. — 3. arch. ornamental top or head-piece. — 4. (Kopfputz) head-dress; top-knot. — 5. (ſchriftliche Behandlung e-s Themas) Schule: composition, essay; lateiniſcher ~ Latin theme; in e-r Zeitſchrift: article, feuilletoniſtiſcher: essay; gelehrter: treatise, paper; vermiſchte Aufſätze miscellanies; (Denkſchrift) memoir.
Auf-ſatz-thema (ᴗ́ᴗ...) n ㉒ der Schüler: subject for an essay.
auf-ſäubern (ᴗ́ᴗ) v/a. ㉒a** to clean up.
auf-ſaufen P derb (ᴗ́ᴗ) v/a. ㊵f** to drink (or guzzle) up, to swill; F to drain off.
auf-ſaugbar (ᴗ́-) a. ㊺ absorbable.
auf-ſaug|en (ᴗ́ᴗ) I v/a. ⑦c(㊽)** 1. to suck up or in; to absorb; med. ♁d(es Mittel) absorbent. — 2. to suck open; (wund ſaugen) to make sore by sucking. — II ~ n ㉓ 3. = Aufſaugung.
auf-ſäugen (ᴗ́ᴗ) v/a. ㊽** to suckle up; ein Kind auch: to nurse; fig. im Haß des Papſttums aufgeſäugt (SCH.) reared ...

Auf-ſaugung (ᴗ́ᴗ) f ㊻ absorption.
auf-ſchaben (ᴗ́ᴗ) v/a. ㊽** to scrape (or scratch) off or up; to scrape open.
auf-ſchanzen (ᴗ́ᴗ) v/a. ⑨** to trench; to throw up; to heap (or pile) up.
auf-ſchärfen (ᴗ́ᴗ) v/a. ㊽** 1. to whet, to sharpen (up); ⊕ e-n Mühlſtein: to edge, to notch. — 2. hunt. (dem Wild die Haut aufſchneiden) to cut open. — 3. (ritzen) die Haut: to scratch (open).
auf-ſcharren (ᴗ́ᴗ) v/a. ㊽** (aufgraben) von Hühnern: to scratch up.
auf-ſchauen (ᴗ́ᴗ) v/n. (h.) ㊽** 1. to look (or glance) up to; to lift up one's eyes. — 2. = aufpaſſen 1.
auf-ſchaufeln (ᴗ́ᴗ) v/a. ㉒a** to shovel up; to throw up with a spade.
auf-ſchäumen (ᴗ́ᴗ) v/n. (ſn) ㊽** to foam up, froth, effervesce; ſiedend: to boil up.
auf-ſchellen (ᴗ́ᴗ) v/a. ㊽** to ring up, to waken by ringing.
auf-ſchenken (ᴗ́ᴗ) v/a. ㊽** den Ball: to throw (up), ſ. aufſchlagen 1.
auf-ſcheren (ᴗ́ᴗ) v/a. ⑦a (㊽)** ⊕ Weberei: to warp; ⚓ Takelwerk: to coil (up).
auf-ſcheuchen (ᴗ́ᴗ) v/a. ㊽** hunt., allg. u. fig. to scare, to start, ſ. aufjagen 1.
auf-ſcheuern (ᴗ́ᴗ) v/a. ㉒a** 1. to scour, cleanse; Geſchirr: to wash up (dishes). — 2. (wund reiben) to chafe, to make sore; ſich (dat.) die Haut ♁ to scour off one's skin, to rub o.s. sore.
auf-ſchicht|en (ᴗ́ᴗ) I v/a. ㊽** to stack (or pile) up, to range in layers; geol. ⚐: to stratify. — II ~ n ㉓ = A/ung.
Auf-ſchichter (ᴗ́ᴗ) m ㉒, ~**in** f ㊵ piler-up; Ziegelei: one who stacks bricks.
Auf-ſchichtung (...) f ㊻ stack(ing), piling-up; superposition, geol. auch ⚐ stratification. [zum Himmel ♁ to send up ...)
auf-ſchicken (ᴗ́ᴗ) v/a. ㊽** Blicke, Seufzer)
auf-ſchieb-bar (ᴗ́-) a. ㊺ postponable; nicht ♁ admitting (of) no delay.
auf-ſchieb|en (ᴗ́ᴗ) I v/a. ⑦c** 1. (in die Höhe ſchieben) to lift (or push) up; (öffnen) to push (F to shove) open; den Riegel ♁ to unbolt (the door, &c.). — 2. fig. to put (or stave) off; auf beſtimmte Zeit: to postpone, to defer; auf kurze Zeit: to adjourn (a meeting); zögernd: to delay; es läßt ſich ♁ it brooks no delay; Sprichw. aufgeſchoben iſt nicht aufgehoben omittance is no acquittance; beſſer aufgeſchoben als aufgehoben better late than never. — II ~ n ㉓ 3. = A/ung.
Auf-ſchiebling (ᴗ́ᴗ) m ㉒ an Dachſtuhl: caves-board, eaves-catch.
Auf-ſchiebung (ᴗ́ᴗ) f ㊻ postponement, delay; von Tag zu Tag: procrastination.
auf-ſchienen (ᴗ́ᴗ) v/a. ㊽** to fasten (down) with iron bands.
auf-ſchieß|en (ᴗ́ᴗ) ⑦c(ef)**, I v/a. 1. ein Tor ꝛc.: to burst open. — 2. ⚓ ein Tau: to (wind into a) coil. — II v/n. (ſn) 3. (emporſchießen) to shoot (or rise) up suddenly; vom Waſſer: to rush or leap, spirt) up. — 4. (aufwachſen) to grow up rapidly; wie Pilze ♁ to spring up like mushrooms; in Saat ♁ to run into seed; lang aufgeſchoſſener Menſch long lanky fellow, overgrown boy.
auf-ſchirren (ᴗ́ᴗ) v/a. ㊽** to harness.
auf-ſchlacken ⊕ (ᴗ́ᴗ) v/n. (h.) ㊽** Gießerei: to be reduced to scoria or dross.

Auf-ſchlag (ᴗ́ᴗ) m ①d. 1. (Niederfallen auf et.) striking down upon; ⚔ ~ e-s Geſchoſſes impact of a projectile, (Anſtreifen) graze. — 2. aufſchlagen III. — 3. am Rock, an der Uniform: facing, lapel; mit rotem ~ with red facings, faced with red; am Ärmel: cuff; an Stiefeln: (Stulpe) top; am Hut: (Krempe) brim. — 4. ♣ (Preiserhöhung; ant. Abſchlag 7) advance; rise (or improvement) of prices; (erhöhte Steuer, Ausgabe) additional duty, expense; extra cost; (Übergewicht) overweight. — 5. ♪ u. pros. arsis. — 6. Spiel: turning up (of) a card; Tennisſpiel: service; Ihr ~! your service. — 7. ⊕ Weberei: warp. — 8. for. (Holznachwuchs aus Eicheln, Bucheln) seedlings pl. from acorns, beech-nuts.
auf-ſchlag|en (ᴗ́ᴗ) ⑤b.** I v/a. 1. (emporſchlagen) die Augen ♁ to raise (or cast up) one's eyes; einen Ball ♁ to throw (or send) up a ball, Tennis: to serve; den Schleier: to put up. — 2. die Ärmel: to tuck up; e-e Hutkrempe: to turn up. — 3. (erhöhen) to enhance, to raise; ſeine Waren ♁ f. 12. — 4. fig. ein Gelächter ♁ to set up a laugh, to burst out laughing. — 5. (errichten) ein Bett ꝛc. ♁ to make (or put) up ...; ein Gerüſt: to erect; ⚔ ein Lager, ein Zelt ♁ to erect or pitch, put up) a camp, a tent; ſeine Wohnung an einem Orte ♁ to take up one's abode somewhere. — 6. (öffnen) to (break) open; Eier: to crack; ein Faß ♁ (auffpunden) to knock the bung out of ...; e-m den Kopf ♁ to split a p.'s ... (open). — 7. ein Buch: to open; eine Stelle in einem Buche ♁ to look (or hunt) up a passage; das Wörterbuch ♁ to consult; Spiel: eine Karte ♁ to turn up ... — 8. (feſtmachen) to fasten (or fix) by blows; ein Hufeiſen ♁ to put a shoe on a horse; e-n Schuh ♁ (den Leiſten) ſchlagen to put (or fix) ... upon the last. — 9. ⚓ ein Tau ♁ a) to coil a rope; b) (in ſ-e Duchten zerlegen) to untwist a rope, to undo the strand. — II v/n. (ſn) 10. (ſteigen) to move up (rapidly); (aufſchnellen) to rebound, to bounce (or spring up); in Flammen: to blaze up. — 11. ein Gelächter ſchlug auf (brach aus)... burst (or broke) forth. — 12. ♣ (ant. abſchlagen 13) to rise (in price), to advance, to improve; mit ſ-n Waren (v/a. ſeine Waren) ♁ to put up (or raise) the price(s), to ask for higher prices; die Wolle ſchlägt auf ... is looking (or going) up, ... is rising (in price). — 13. auf den Boden ꝛc. ♁ to strike hard upon the ground, &c.; to come down with vehemence; ⚔ v. Geſchoſſen: to ricochet. — III ~ n ㉓ 14. raising (up); bſd. fig. ~ der Augen casting (or turning up) (of) the eyes, upward glance; e-s Gerüſtes: erection; e-s Lagers: encampment; beim ~ eines Buches: on opening a book.
Auf-ſchläger (ᴗ́ᴗ) m ㉒ Tennis: server.
Auf-ſchlagung (ᴗ́ᴗ) f ㊻ = aufſchlagen III.
Auf-ſchlag-waſſer ⚒ (ᴗ́ᴗ-ᴗᴗ) n ㉒ für Waſſerräder, Turbinen ꝛc. water as motive power; =**zünder** ⚔ m, artill. (ant. Zeit-, Brenn-zünder) percussion-fuse.
auf-ſchleifen¹ (ᴗ́ᴗ) [ſchleifen] v/a. ⑤b** etwas auf Glas ꝛc. ♁ to grind ... on ...

[aufschleifen] — 100 — [aufschwänzen]

auf-schleifen² (⁻ᴸ◡) [Schleife] v/a. ⊕** 1. to drag along (on a sledge). — 2. zu e-r Schleife zu die. [ing-up slip.]
Auf-schlepp-helling ⚓ (⁻) f ⑫ haul-
auf-schließen (⁻ᴸ◡) I v/a. u. v/refl. ⑥d** 1. (sich) ≳ to unlock; fig. to unfold; einem sein Herz ≳ to open (or pour out) one's heart to a p.; chm. e-e schwer lösliche Substanz: to render soluble, disintegrate, break up, durch Flußmittel: to flux. — 2. ⚒ to open or explore or develop (a mine); der Gang schließt sich auf die Lode is widening (out). — 3. ⚔ die Rotten, Glieder ≳ to close the ranks; aufgeschlossen! close ranks! — II ~ n ㉓ 4. = Aufschließung.
Auf-schließer (⁻ᴸ◡) m ㉒, ~in f ㊵ opener; turnkey; thea. box-keeper.
Auf-schließung (⁻ᴸ◡) f ㊻ unlocking, &c. (f. aufschließen I); ⚒ exploration. — Vgl. Aufschluß. [development work(s).]
Auf-schließungs-arbeiten („...) f/pl. ㉒
auf-schlingen (⁻ᴸ◡) v/a. u. v/refl. ⑥f** 1. (in die Höhe schlingen) to tie up with a loop, ⚓ to sling up. — 2. (losbinden) to untie; Verwickeltes: to disentangle. — 3. (verschlucken) to swallow (or gulp) down.
auf-schlitzen (⁻ᴸ◡) v/a. ⊕** to rip up or open; die Haut: to gash; die Nase ꝛc.: to slit; ⚓ Segel: to s(p)lit.
Auf-schlitzer (⁻ᴸ◡) m ㉒ ripper. [aloud.]
auf-schluchzen (⁻ᴸ◡) v/n. (h.) ⊕** to sob
auf-schlürfen (⁻ᴸ◡) v/a. ⊕** to sip up.
Auf-schluß (⁻ᴸ) m ⑧a. 1. unlocking, opening; (Lösung) solution; fig. disclosure, explanation; ~ über et. geben to throw light on a th.; e-m ~ über et. gewähren to vouchsafe a p. information respecting a th.; sich ~ über et. verschaffen to acquaint o.s. with the facts of a case; um näheren ~ bitten to ask for full information or particulars. — 2. ⚒ open lode.
auf-schmauchen F (⁻ᴸ◡) ⊕**, **-schmausen** (⁻ᴸ◡) ⊕**, **-schmeißen** F (⁻ᴸ◡) ⊕a** v/a. = auf-rauchen, -essen, -werfen.
auf-schmelzen (⁻ᴸ◡) I v/a. ⊕** 1. to melt (⚒ smelt) on. — 2. (öffnen) to open by (s)melting. — 3. (auflösen) to (s)melt down; to dissolve by heat. — II v/n. (sn) ⑥b(ef)** to be(come) fixed by (s)melting; to open by (s)melting.
auf-schmieden (⁻ᴸ◡) v/a. ⊕** 1. to fix by forging. — 2. to use up in forging.
auf-schmieren F (⁻ᴸ◡) v/a. ⊕** 1. to smear on; Butter ≳ to spread butter on, to butter (the bread). — 2. (verbrauchen) to use up in smearing, F fig. in scribbling. — 3. F e-m et. ≳. f. anschmieren 3.
auf-schmoren (⁻ᴸ◡) v/a. ⊕** Kochkunst: 1. Gemüse ꝛc. in Butter ≳ to do up ... in butter. — 2. to use up in stewing.
auf-schmücken (⁻ᴸ◡) v/a. und v/refl. ⊕** et., e-n, sich ≳ to adorn (or dress) ...
auf-schnallen (⁻ᴸ◡) v/a. ⊕** 1. to buckle up. — 2. (öffnen) to unbuckle.
auf-schnappen (⁻ᴸ◡) ⊕** I v/a. 1. to snatch (or catch) up; F fig. eine Nachricht: to pick up. — II v/n. (h.) 2. nach Luft: to gasp for breath. — 3. F = aufatmen. — 4. (in die Höhe fahren) to fly up; (aus-ea.fahren) to fly (or burst, spring) open.
auf-schneid/en (⁻ᴸ◡) ⊕c** I v/a. 1. aufs Kerbholz: to score up. — 2. (öffnen) to

cut (or rip) open; (spalten) to split (open); (sezieren) to dissect; ein Buch ≳ to cut open a book; die Blätter e-s Buches ≳ to cut the leaves of a book. — 3. Braten, Wurst ꝛc.: to cut up in(to) slices; to carve. — 4. to cut up all (the meat, &c.) — II v/n. (h.) 5. fig. (prahlen) to boast, brag, swagger; (übertreiben) to exaggerate; to talk big; F to tell a cram, to stretch, to draw (or pull) the long bow; das heißt aufgeschnitten! F that's a good one!, what a story!, what yarns to spin! — III ~ n ㉓ 6. = A/ung.
Auf-schneider (⁻ᴸ◡) m ㉒, ~in f ㊵ cutter, carver; (Anatom) dissector; (Prahler) boaster, braggart, swaggerer, F gasbag; (Lügner) story-teller, liar; **~ei** (⁻ᴸ◡ᴸ) f ㊻ brag(ging), swagger, bounce, big talk or words pl., gasconade, F gas; (Unsinn) blarney; Lisch (⁻ᴸ◡) a. ⑥⑥ boastful; flaming (description), exaggerated (account).
Auf-schneidung (⁻ᴸ◡) f ㊻ 1. cutting (or ripping) open, &c.; surg. incision, dissection. — 2. fig. = Aufschneiderei.
auf-schnellen (⁻ᴸ◡) ⊕** I v/a. 1. to fling (or jerk) up. — II v/n. (sn) und sich ≳ v/refl. 2. (auffliegen) to spring (or fly) up (with a jerk). — 3. (sich öffnen) to open suddenly.
Auf-schnitt (⁻ᴸ) m ⓒc. 1. (Aufschneiden) cutting (up). — 2. (Aufgeschnittenes) cut; (Kerbe) notch; (Schlitz) slit; (Wunde) gash; surg. incision; kalter ~ cold slices of meat, articles sold in a ham-and-beef shop.
auf-schnitze(l)n (⁻ᴸ◡) ⑨ (⑨a)** 1. to carve on. — 2. to use up in carving.
auf-schnobern (⁻ᴸ◡), **auf-schnüffeln** (⁻ᴸ◡) v/a. ⊕** to trace by the scent.
auf-schnupfen (⁻ᴸ◡) v/a. ⊕** 1. durch die Nase: to sniff up. — 2. allen Tabak ≳ to use up all one's snuff.
auf-schnüren (⁻ᴸ◡) v/a. ⊕** 1. to lace (or tie) upon. — 2. auch v/refl. (lösen) to untie, uncord, unfasten; sich ≳ to unlace o.s.; to come unlaced. — 3. (auf eine Schnur reihen) to (put on a) string.
auf-schobern (⁻ᴸ◡) ⊕a**, **-schocken** (⁻ᴸ◡) ⊕** v/a., agr. Heu ꝛc.: to stack up.
auf-schöpfen (⁻ᴸ◡) v/a. ⊕** to scoop (or ladle) up, to empty with a) scoop.
Auf-schößling (⁻ᴸ◡) m ⓓ. von Pflanzen: shoot, sprig; von Menschen: stripling, overgrown lad or girl; a. fig. upstart.
auf-schrammen (⁻ᴸ◡) v/a. ⊕** die Haut: to scratch, graze, rub off, raise.
auf-schrauben (⁻ᴸ◡) v/a. ⊕ ⓒ** 1. to screw on. — 2. (emporschrauben) to screw up; fig. (rühmen) to puff up, to praise to the skies, ⊛ to boom. — 3. (öffnen) to unscrew; to screw off; sich ≳ lassen to unscrew, to come off by turning.
auf-schrecken (⁻ᴸ◡) I v/n. (sn) ⑥a** (impf. schrak auf) to start (up) with fright at; to be(come) startled by. — II v/a. ⊕** to startle, to alarm; einen aus dem Schlafe ≳ to rouse a p. from his slumber. — III ~ n ㉓ start(ing), frightening; affright. [fig. outcry.]
Auf-schrei (⁻ᴸ) m ⓓ. shriek, scream;]
auf-schreiben (⁻ᴸ◡) v/a. ⓘ** 1. to write (or note, book) down; im Konzept: to take down roughly; die Points bei Spielen: to score; ⊛ (eintragen) to enter, to book;

Schuldposten auch: to charge (to a p.'s account). — 2. schreibend verbrauchen: Federn, Tinte ≳ to use up ...
auf-schreien (⁻ᴸ◡) ⊕** I v/n. (h.) to cry out or aloud; to scream, to shriek; bsd. fig. to raise an outcry; gellend: to yell. — II ~ n ㉓ = Aufschrei.
Auf-schrift (⁻ᴸ) f ㊻ 1. e-s Briefes: address, direction; ohne ~ without address, undirected (letter); auf e-r Flasche: ticket, label; auf e-m Grabe: epitaph. — 2. (Inschrift) inscription; (Überschrift) superscription, e-s Kapitels ꝛc.: heading, title.
auf-schroten (⁻ᴸ◡) v/a. ⊕** 1. (grob gemahlen) Korn: to bruise. — 2. (öffnen) to open with a punch or chisel. — 3. (emporwalzen) ein Faß: to roll up from the cellar. [bit, (square-pointed) peg.]
Auf-schroter ⊕ (⁻ᴸ◡) m ㉒ rimer, riming-
Auf-schub (⁻ᴸ) m ⓓ. (ohne pl.) delay, beabsichtigter: adjournment; gewährter: respite; e-s Todesurteils: reprieve; der Zahlung: postponement, deferment; (Verschleppung) procrastination; ohne ≳ without delay, forthwith; die Sache duldet, leidet keinen ~ ... brooks (or admits of) no delay, is most urgent; ~ bringt Gefahr delays are dangerous.
Auf-schub(s)-befehl („...) m ㉒ reprieve; **=brief** m letter of respite.
auf-schultern (⁻ᴸ◡) v/a. ⓒa** to (take on one's) shoulder.
auf-schüren (⁻ᴸ◡) v/a. ⊕** = anschüren.
auf-schürfen (⁻ᴸ◡) v/a. ⊕** die Haut: to graze. [schürzer.]
Auf-schürz-band (⁻ᴸ ...) n ㊵ = Auf-
auf-schürzen (⁻ᴸ◡) [mhd.] I v/a. u. v/refl. ⊕** 1. ein Kleid (a.: sich) ≳ to tuck (or pin, loop) up one's dress; ⚓ ein Segel: to unfurl. — 2. (auflösen) to untie, to undo. — II ~ n ㉓ 3. = A/ung.
Auf-schürzer (⁻ᴸ◡) m ㉒ von Kleidern: dress-holder, ehm. page. [tucker.]
Auf-schürz-falte (⁻ᴸ ...) f ㊵, **=knoten** m]
Auf-schürzung (⁻ᴸ◡) f ㊻ tucking (or pinning, looping) up; untying, undoing. [(or serve) up.]
auf-schüsseln (⁻ᴸ◡) v/a. ⊕** to dish]
auf-schütteln (⁻ᴸ◡) ⓒa** 1. to shake up; ein Federbett: to beat up; e-n ≳ = aufrütteln. — 2. to raise (or lift, bring, send) up by shaking.
auf-schütt/en (⁻ᴸ◡) I v/a. ⊕** 1. to pour (or put) on; ehm. Pulver ≳ to prime a gun; Müllerei: Getreide ≳ to put grain into the mill-hopper. — 2. (aufspeichern) to store (or pile) up, to amass; Korn: to garner. — 3. (aufwerfen) e-n Damm: to throw (or raise) up; Straßenbau: Erde ≳ (lagern) to deposit ...; Schotter, Kies ≳ to metal, to gravel the roads. — II ~ n ㉓ 4. = A/ung 1.
Auf-schütter ⊕ (⁻ᴸ◡) m ㉒ workman who charges the furnace, &c.
Auf-schütt-faß (⁻ᴸ ...) ⊕ n ㊵ Färberei: settling-vat; **=junge** m vat-boy.
Auf-schüttung (⁻ᴸ◡) f ㊻ 1. pouring (or putting) on; storage. — 2. ⊕ (Erdarbeit) dike, mound, embankment.
auf-schützen (⁻ᴸ◡) v/a. ⊕** Müllerei: to open the flood-gates.
auf-schwänzen (⁻ᴸ◡) ⊕** I v/a. 1. Kochkunst: einen Fisch ≳ to serve up ... with the tail stuck in(to) its mouth. —

Zeichen (f. S. XVII): F familiär; P Volkssprache; Γ Gaunersprache; ⚒ selten; † alt (auch gestorben); * neu (auch geboren); ⁺⁺ unrichtig;

[aufschwärzen] — 101 — [aufsperren]

— 2. ein Pferd ≈ f. aufschweifen 1. — 3. ♥ Börse: die Baissiers ≈ (sie zwingen, die ihnen fehlenden Stücke zu hohen Kursen anzunehmen) to squeeze the bears (by forcing them to buy, when there is a shortage of stocks). — 4. fig. e-n ≈ = aufreizen. — II sich ≈ v/refl. 5. vom Pfau: to spread its tail. [afresh.}

auf-schwärzen (ᴴᴸ◡) v/a. ⓖ** to blacken

auf-schwatzen F (ᴴᴸ◡) v/a. ⓖ** e-m et. ≈ to talk a p. into a th., vgl. anschwatzen.

auf-schweben (ᴴᴸ◡) v/n. (fn) ⓖ** to soar up, to float upwards.

auf-schweifen (ᴴᴸ◡) v/a. ⓖ** 1. ein Pferd ≈ to truss (or tuck) up a horse's tail. — 2. ⊙ Seilerei: Garn ≈ to warp …; Weberei: aufgeschweiftes Muster (mit verschiedenfarbiger Kette) variegated pattern.

auf-schweißen ⊙ (ᴴᴸ◡) v/a. ⓖ** Schmiede: to weld to, to join by welding.

auf-schwellen (ᴴᴸ◡) I v/n. (fn) ⓖb** to swell up (f. auf= 9); Flüsse: to rise; (zunehmen) to increase. — II v/a. ⓖ** to inflate, to puff up. — vgl. anschwellen.

auf-schwemmen (ᴴᴸ◡) v/a. ⓖ** 1. to float (or wash) on to; (ablagern) to deposit; geol. aufgeschwemmtes Land alluvial (⊘ thalassic) land; aufgeschwemmter Schlick deposit of warp. — 2. (aufschwellen m. e. Tier: to bloat, inflate.

auf-schwingen (ᴴᴸ◡) ⓖj** I v/a. ⓖ** to swing (up); ein Schwert ≈ to brandish. — II sich ≈ v/refl. to swing o.s. up; to rise (in the air); von Vögeln: to soar up; fig. a. to make one's way (in the world); sich zu et. (Kühnem, Schwerem) ≈ to brace o.s. up to a th. — III ~ n ㉓ = Aufschwung.

Auf-schwung (ᴴᴸ) m ⓒc. 1. Turnkunst: swinging up. — 2. (Aufflug) soaring (up); fig. auch: high flight; plötzlicher ~ sudden growth; ♥ advance (of prices), boom (in the market); einen ~ nehmen to rise, to go up, to advance; einen neuen ~ nehmen to revive, to spring up afresh.

auf-segeln ⊥ (ᴴᴸ◡) v/n. (h. u. fn) ⓖa** 1. einen Fluß ≈ to sail up a river. — 2. (sich festlegen) to run aground.

auf-sehen (ᴴᴸ◡) [mhd.] I v/n. (h.) ⓖa** 1. to look up. — 2. (achthaben auf) to look (or see) after. — II ~ n ㉓ 3. (Verwunderung) surprise, shock; (öffentliches Gerede) noise; ärgerliches: scandal; ~ erregen oder machen to cause (or create) a sensation, to make a great stir, durch Auffälliges oder Neumodisches: F to cut a great dash; ~ erregend sensational; striking; F dashing; etwas ~ Erregendes s.th. which attracts notice, F a bang-up affair; wenig ~ machen to attract little attention; um ~ zu vermeiden to avoid notice.

Auf-seher (ᴴᴸ◡) m ㉒, ~in f ㊵ overseer; inspector; F boss; ~ über ein Gut bailiff of an estate; (Wertmeister) foreman; (Vorsteherin) forewoman; (Verwalter[in]) manager(ess), (Armenpfleger) guardian; (die Aufsicht führender Schüler) monitor; ⚒ (Schachtmeister) overlooker, banksman; ein englisches Hofe: ~ der königlichen Dienerschaft Controller of the (King's, Queen's) Household; von Museen: custodian, keeper; bei Wett-

rennen: steward; ~amt (ᴴᴸ…) n ㉒, =schaft f, =stelle f ㊻ overseership; inspectorship, custodianship.

auf(-)sein (ᴴᴸ) I v n. (ⓖa** f. auf 12, 13. — II ~ n ㉓ bei Nacht: sitting up.

auf-setzbar (ᴴᴸ◡) a. ⓖ fit to (be) put on.

auf-setz|en (ᴴᴸ◡) ⓖ** I v/a. 1. to put on; einem Hause das Dach ≈ to raise the roof of a house; Schuhmacher: einen Fleck ≈ to put (or sew) on a patch; den Fuß (leicht) ≈ to step (lightly) on the ground; den Hut, die Mütze ≈ to put on (or to don) one's hat, one's cap; setzen Sie Ihren Hut auf! be covered!; die Schüsseln, das Essen ≈ to dish up; ⊥ die Segel, Stengen ≈ to hoist (or sway) up …; Damspiel: einen Stein ≈ to crown a king; arch. noch ein Stockwerk ≈ to add another story; Wasser (zum Kochen) ≈ to put water on (to boil); ein Zündhütchen ≈ to put on a percussion-cap. — 2. fig. ein Gesicht, eine Miene ≈ to put on a face; F seinen Kopf ≈ to be obstinate; um allem die Krone aufzusetzen to crown all; dies setzt dem Ganzen die Krone auf that is the crowning deed; beats (or crowns, tops) all. — 3. (niederschreiben) to set (or put) down in writing; einen Vertrag ≈ to draw up an agreement; eine Rechnung ≈ to make up an account; jur. eine Urkunde ≈ to draft a deed; flüchtig ≈ to sketch (roughly); (sorgfältig abfassen) to compose. — 4. (aufreihen) Kegel ≈ to set up ninepins; Kugeln ꝛc.: to pile up; Garben: to stack up; typ. Buchstaben ≈ to set (up) type; Zwiebelfische ≈ to sort pie. — II v/n. (h.) 5. = aufsitzen. — III sich ≈ v/refl. 6. = aufsitzen 1 u. 3; von Hunden ꝛc: sich auf die Hinterfüße stellen ≈ to get (or sit) up on its hindlegs. — 7. fig. sich gegen e-n ≈ to rise (up) against a p. — IV ~ n ㉓ 8. = Aufung.

Auf-setzer (ᴴᴸ◡) m ㉒, ~in f ㊵ ⓖ 1. one who puts on, sets up, stacks up, &c. (f. aufsetzen). — 2. ⊙ Spinnerei: ~ an der Mulemaschine (der das Vorgespinst in den Rahmen bringt) creel-filler.

Auf-setzung (ᴴᴸ◡) f ㊻ putting on; e-s Briefes, einer Urkunde: draft(ing); einer Schrift: drawing up, composition; (Aufstapeln) piling up.

auf-seufzen (ᴴᴸ◡) v/n. (h.) ⓖ** (tief) ≈ to heave (or draw) a (deep) sigh.

Auf-sicht (ᴴᴸ) f ㊻ (o. pl.) inspection, supervision, superintendence; polizeilich: surveillance; die ~ h., führen über to have (or to be in) charge of; Klassenarbeit: unter ~ under supervision, unter ~ (stehend) under control, von Irren: under restraint; unter polizeilicher ~ stehen to be under police-supervision, auch: to be a ticket-of-leave man.

Auf-sicht(s)-behörde (ᴴᴸ…) f ㉒ board of control or of visitors; e-r Aktiengesellschaft: board of supervision, managerial board; =bezirk m inspector's district; =komitee n supervising committee; =maßnahme(n pl.) f Zoll: regulation(s pl.) for the control of imports; =rat m board of visitors; ♥ board of directors, für Prüf. v. Rechnungen: board of auditors; =personal n superintending staff.

auf-sieden (ᴴᴸ◡) v/a. u. v/n. (fn, h.) ⓖe** u. ⓖ** = aufkochen; ⊙ Silber ꝛc.: to blanch.

auf-siegeln (ᴴᴸ◡) v/a. ⓖa** 1. to seal on, to fasten down by sealing. — 2. (öffnen) to unseal; to unfasten the seal.

Auf-singer ⊥ (ᴴᴸ) m ㉒ singer-out.

Auf-sitz ⚔ (ᴴᴸ) m ⓖa. (o. pl.) mst: zum ~ bereit sein to be ready to mount.

auf-sitzen (ᴴᴸ◡) I v/n. (h., ⚔ fn) ⓖ** 1. im Bette: to sit up. — 2. = aufbleiben 2. — 3. (sich aufsetzen) to sit down on, to sit upon; vom Geflügel: to perch, to roost; (zu Pferde steigen) to mount (on horseback); ⚔ ≈!, aufgesessen ≈ to horse!; Pferd, das den Reiter schwer ≈ läßt … difficult to mount; e-n hinter sich ≈ lassen to take a p. up behind; F fig. ≈ lassen (im Stiche lassen) to leave in the lurch; (zum Narren halten) to fool, F to sell. — 4. (festsitzen) to stick fast (in the mud); fig. (in Verlegenheit sein) to be in a fix or a hole; to be dumbfounded; ⊥ ein Schiff sitzt auf … has run aground; ⚔ die Patrone sitzt auf the cartridge is home; ♀ ♂de Blüten f/pl. sessile flowers pl. — II ~ n ㉓ 5. sitting up; ⚔ Befehl zum ~ geben to give orders to mount.

Auf-sitzer m ㉒ (schwer zu beantwortende Frage) poser, teaser, hard nut to crack.

Auf-sitz-geld (ᴴᴸ…) n ㉒ fee for the riding master; =stange f für Vögel: perch, roost.

auf-sollen F (ᴴᴸ◡) v/n. (h.) ⓖ** ell. was soll ich schon so früh (noch so spät) auf? why should (F what's the use if) I get up so early (sit up so late)?

auf-sorren ⊥ (ᴴᴸ◡) v/a. ⓖ** die Hängematten ≈ to lash up the hammocks.

auf-spähen (ᴴᴸ◡) v/a. ⓖ** to espy.

auf-spalten (ᴴᴸ◡) ⓖ** I v/a. to split (open), to cleave. — II v/n. (fn) u. sich ≈ v/refl. to burst, crack, split.

auf-spannen (ᴴᴸ◡) v/a. ⓖ** 1. to stretch, to strain; e-n Bogen: to bend; Netze: to spread; einen Schirm: to put up; ein Zelt: to pitch; Saiten ≈ to string an instrument; fig. andere Saiten ≈ to change one's tone; gelindere Saiten ≈ to give way, F to come down a peg. — 2. ⊥ Segel ≈ to set sails; alle Segel ≈ to sail under full pressure of canvass, fig. to exert o.s. to the utmost; mehr Segel ≈ to clap on more sails. — 3. ⊙ Buchbinderei: Karten ≈ to mount maps.

auf-sparen (ᴴᴸ◡) v/a. ⓖ** 1. to (keep in) reserve for; e-n Notpfennig ≈ to save up (or to lay by) for a rainy day; Aufgespartes savings pl. — 2. = aufschieben 2.

Auf-speich(e)rer (ᴴᴸ)(◡) m ㉒, **Auf-speich(r)e-rin** f ㊵ p. who stores up.

auf-speichern (ᴴᴸ◡) v/a. ⓖa** to store, garner, lay in, hoard up; aufgespeicherte Waren f/pl. warehoused goods pl.; phys. Elektrizität ≈ to accumulate…, to store up … — II Auf-speicherung f ㊻ storing, storage, &c.

auf-speisen (ᴴᴸ◡) v/a. ⓖ** = aufessen.

auf-sperr|en (ᴴᴸ◡) I v/a. ⓖ** 1. to open (wide); das Maul ≈ to gape, to stand gaping; F Mund und Nase ≈ to be struck dumb with.. — 2. (südd.) (aufschließen) to unlock. — II ~ n ㉓ u. **Auf-sperrung** f ㊻

[aufspielen] — 102 — [aufstellen]

3. opening; ~ der Augen vor Verwunderung: amazement, des Mundes: gaping.
auf-spielen (ˡˡ‿) ⓖ⁎⁎ **I** v/a. u. v/n. (h.) ♪ einen Walzer ꝛc.: to strike up; spielt auf! play away! Sprichw. wem's Glück aufspielt, der hat gut tanzen he dances well to whom Fortune pipes. — **II** sich 2 v/refl. (sich ein Ansehen geben) to put on (or to give o.s.) airs; F to show off; sich als Heiligen (┼Heiliger) 2 to pose as a (or to play the) saint.
auf-spießen (ˡˡ‿) ⓖ⁎⁎ to spit; Fleisch, auch: to broach; mit dem Speer: to spear, run through, pierce; mit den Hörnern: to gore; als Todesstrafe: to impale. [put on a spindle.]
auf-spindeln (ˡˡ‿) ⓖa⁎⁎ v/a. Garn: to⌋
auf-spinnen (ˡˡ‿) v/a. ⓖa⁎⁎ 1. (auch abs.) to spin up; to work up in spinning. — 2. sich (dat.) die Finger 2 to spin one's fingers sore.
auf-spreizen (ˡˡ‿) ⓖ⁎⁎ **I** v/a. to spread (or stretch) out. — **II** sich 2 v/refl. to sprawl o.s. out; fig. sich 2 to assume an air of importance, to strut about like a lord; aufgespreizt: F bumptious.
auf-sprengen (ˡˡ‿) v/a. ⓖ⁎⁎ 1. to burst (or force) open; to blow up (with gunpowder). — 2. hunt. Rebhühner ꝛc. 2 to rouse ... — 3. Wasser auf et. 2 to sprinkle water on a th.
auf-sprießen (ˡˡ‿) v/n.(sn)ⓖd⁎⁎ to shoot (or spring, sprout) up; to germinate.
auf-springen (ˡˡ‿) **I** v/n. (sn) ⓓs⁎⁎ 1. (emporspringen) to spring (or bounce) up; to start to one's feet; vor Freude 2 to jump for joy. — 2. (sich öffnen) to fly open. — 3. (aufbersten) to burst open, to split asunder; die Hände (Lippen) springen mir in der Kälte auf the cold chaps my hands (cracks my lips); aufgesprung(e)ne Hände chapped hands; ♀ Kapseln: 2d: ⚘ dehiscent. — **II** ~ n ㉓ 4. springing up; des Balles: bouncing (up); der Tür: bursting open; der Hände: chapping, cracking, ⚘ rhagades pl.; ♀ der Samenhülsen: ⚘ dehiscence.
auf-spritzen (ˡˡ‿) ⓖ⁎⁎ **I** v/n. (sn) 1. to squirt (or splash, fly) up. — **II** v/a. 2. to squirt up; to sprinkle (or squirt) on. — 3. (öffnen) ein Geschwür 2 to open ... by injections. [sprießen.]
auf-sprossen (ˡˡ‿) v/n. (sn) ⓖ⁎⁎ = auf-⌋
auf-sprudeln (ˡˡ‿) v/n. (sn) ⓖa⁎⁎ 1. (aufwallen) to bubble (or boil) up (s. auch aufschäumen). — 2. fig. = auffahren 4.
auf-sprühen (ˡˡ‿) v/n. (sn) ⓖ⁎⁎ to sparkle up, to fly up in sparks.
Auf-sprung (ˡˡ‿) m ⓞc. Turnerei: leaping up; bound. [wind, spool, reel.]
auf-spulen (ˡˡ‿) v/a. ⓖ⁎⁎ Garn: to⌋
auf-spülen (ˡˡ‿) v/a. ⓖ⁎⁎ 1. Sand ꝛc.: to deposit ... on. — 2. Geschirr: to wash up.
auf-spunden, auf-spünden ⓞ (ˡˡ‿) v/a. ⓖ⁎⁎ ein Faß 2 to unbung a cask.
auf-spüren (ˡˡ‿) v/a. ⓖ⁎⁎ hunt. to hunt up or out (a. fig.); to trace, track, search out, smell out, scent, ferret (out).
auf-stacheln (ˡˡ‿) v/a. ⓖa⁎⁎ to goad (or spur) on; meist fig. to stimulate, to incite; Leidenschaften 2 to rouse (or work up) passions.
auf-staffieren (ˡˡ‿ˡ‿) v/a. ⓖ⁎/⁎ to trim (or dress) up (= ausstaffieren).

auf-stampfen (ˡˡ‿) ⓖ⁎⁎ **I** v n. (h.) 1. to stamp on the ground; to stamp one's feet. — **II** v/a. 2. to fasten by stamping or battering. — 3. (öffnen) to open by stamping or kicking.
Auf-stand (ˡˡ‿) m ⓞc. 1. ↘ rising; F (mit dem Stuhle rücken und) ~ machen to rise from the table. — 2. rising, rebellion, insurrection, s. Aufruhr 1. — 3. ⚒(Bericht) report on the condition of a mine. — 4.arch. (Säulenplatte) plinth.
auf-ständig, auf-ständisch (ˡˡ‿) a. ⓖⓖ rebellious, seditious, revolutionary; 2e Bewegung insurrectionary movement; ~e(r) ㊼ rebel, insurgent.
Auf-stands-versuch (ˡˡ‿...) m ⓖ⁑ attempt at insurrection, attempted rebellion.
auf-stapeln (ˡˡ‿) **I** v/a. ⓖa⁎⁎ (ant. abstapeln) to pile (or heap, stack) up; ⚜ to store (up). — **II** ~ n ㉓ = A/ung.
Auf-stapler(in f) m ⓖ⁎⁎ one who piles up, &c. [accumulation; ⚜ storage.]
Auf-stap(e)lung (ˡˡ‿(‿)) f ㊻ piling up,⌋
auf-starren (ˡˡ‿) v/n. (h.) ⓖ⁎⁎ 1. zum Himmel 2 to stare up to heaven. — 2. (starr emporstehen) to bristle up.
auf-stau/en (ˡˡ‿) **I** v/a. ⓖ⁎⁎ 1. (auf ea. packen) to pile up; ⚓ die Ladung 2 to stow away ... in the hold of the ship. — 2. das Wasser 2 to dam up ... — **II** A/ung f ㊻ 3. Wasserbau: dammed (up) water.
auf-stechen (ˡˡ‿) ⓖa⁎⁎ **I** v/a. 1. to (open by) puncture, to prick open; ein Geschwür: to lance. — 2. ⚒ Kupferstecherei: e-e Platte 2 to retouch a (copper) plate. — 3. (befestigen) to fasten by stitches. — 4. (umrühren) Korn ꝛc.: to turn up or over. — 5. ⚓ die Halsen u. Schoten 2 to give up (or raise, rise) the tacks and sheets; zwei Taue 2 to tie two ropes together. — **II** v/n. ⓖ⁑ 6. ⚓ bei dem Winde 2 to ply to windward.
auf-stecken (ˡˡ‿) **I** v/a. ⓖ⁎⁎ 1. (in die Höhe stecken) to put (or stick) up; ein Kleid: to catch up; mit Nadeln: to pin up; sich (dat.) das Haar 2 to do (or tuck) up one's hair. — 2. (aufrichten) Futter 2 to put fodder on the rack; ein Licht 2 to put a candle into the candle-stick; ⚓ die Flagge 2 to hoist the flag; ⚔ das Seitengewehr 2 to fix bayonets. — 3. fig. eine Amtsmiene 2 to put on an official air; einem ein Licht über et. 2 to enlighten a p. on a subject. — 4. [ndd.] F et. 2 (aufgeben) to give up; F to throw up (the game). — **II** ~ n ㉓ 5. catching up (of a dress); (Verzicht) renunciation.
Auf-stecker ⓞ (ˡˡ‿) m ㉒, ~in f ㊼ pinner; Spinnerei: reeler, winder.
Auf-steck-kamm (ˡˡ‿...) m ㉒ dressing-comb; =nadel f (patent) dressholder; safety-pin; patent hooks and eyes pl.
auf-steh(e)n (ˡˡ(‿)) **I** v/n. ⓖ⁎⁎ (1—3: h. u. fn, 4—6: sn) 1. (offen stehen) to stand open. — 2. (aufet. stehen) to stand upon; beim Baden 2 to (be able to) touch the ground. — 3. (aufrecht stehen) to stand upright. — 4. (sich erheben) to stand up, to get up; aus dem Bette auch: F to turn out (of bed); von Tisch 2 to rise from the table; er steht früh auf he is an early riser; sind sie noch nicht aufgestanden? are they not up yet?; fig.

er ist mit dem linken Fuß zuerst aufgestanden he got out on the wrong side of the bed; wer den anführen will, (der) muß früher 2 you must rise betimes to get the better of him; he is not easily taken in; ⚓ das Schiff steht auf ... is righting herself; von Fischen: to rise to the surface. — 5. fig. (erscheinen) von Propheten ꝛc.: to arise, to appear. — 6. (sich empören) to rise (up in arms), to rebel. — **II** ~ n ㉓c. 7. rising, &c. (s. I); spätes ~ getting up late, F fashionable hours pl.; ~ des Wildes aus s-m Lager breaking cover.
auf-steifen ⓞ (ˡˡ‿) v/a. ⓖ⁎⁎ mit Stärke 2 to (stiffen up with) starch.
auf-steig/en (ˡˡ‿) **I** v/n. (sn) ⓖ⁎⁎ 1. (ant. absteigen) to mount; to rise; von Vögeln: to soar (up); zu Pferd: to mount on horse-back, to mount (F to get on) one's horse; (auf) den Berg 2 to ascend the mountain; auf eine Leiter 2 to climb up a ladder; in einem Ballon 2 to go up (or ascend) in a balloon; e-n Drachen 2 lassen to fly a kite; der Wind steigt auf ... is springing up. — 2. (entstehen) to arise, F to pop up; ein Gewitter steigt auf there is a storm brewing. — 3. fig. mir stieg ein Gedanke auf a thought struck (or occurred to) me. — **II** ~ n ㉓ 4. = A/ung.; ~ der Flut rising of the tide; eines Gewitters gathering of a storm. — **III** 2d p.pr. u. a. ⓖⓖ 5. mounting, &c. (s. I); schroff 2d steep(ly ascending).
Auf-steigung (‿) f ㊻ ascent; ast. gerade, schiefe ~ right, oblique ascension.
auf-stellen (ˡˡ‿) ⓖ⁎⁎ **I** v/a. 1. to set (or put) up; in Ordnung: to arrange, to set in order; in Haufen: to pile (or stack) up; eine Falle (Schlinge) 2 to set a trap (a snare); eine Leiter 2 to raise a ladder; Maschinen: to fit up, mount, erect; Netze: to spread; eine Säule 2 to erect (or raise) a statue; Waren zum Verkauf 2 to expose goods for sale; aufbewahrend: to deposit, store, warehouse. — 2. arch. die Lehrbogen 2 to set the centres. — 3. ⚔ eine Batterie 2 to set up (or raise) ...; eine Schildwache 2 to post a sentry; Truppen zum Gefecht ꝛc. 2 to draw up troops (in battle-line). — 4. fig. Bedingungen 2 to make terms or conditions; e-e Behauptung 2 to advance (or make) an assertion; e-n Beweis 2 to furnish proof or evidence; einen Grundsatz 2 to lay down a principle; e-n als Kandidaten 2 to put a p. up (or to propose a p.) as candidate; bei Wahlen auch: to nominate a p.; ⚜ eine Rechnung 2 to draw (or make) up an account; e-m zum (ob. als) Vorbild 2 to put up as a pattern, to hold up as a model to a p.; Zeugen 2 to produce witnesses. — 5. (vornehmen) mit e-m, e-r Sache et. 2 to do with ...; es läßt sich nichts mit ihm ~ there's nothing to be done with him. — **II** sich 2 v/refl. 6. to form, to draw up; ⚔ den Soldaten auch to fall in (line); sich zur Schlacht 2 to form in battle-line; sich hinter ea. 2 (a. von Wagen) to stand in file or in a line. — **III** ~ n ㉓ 7. = Aufstellung.

Signs (see page XVII): F familiar; P vulgar; ꜰ flash; ↘ rare; † obsolete (died); * new word (born); ⁑ incorrect; ♪ music;

[Aufsteller] — 103 — [Auftrag]

Auf-steller (⁻⁻◡⁻) m person who sets up, &c.; ⊕ von Maschinen: litter.
Auf-stell-gleis (⁻⁻...) n des Bahnhofs: siding for arranging trains, &c.
Auf-stellung f 1. setting (or putting) up; von Maschinen 2c.: erection; von Waren zum Verkauf: display (for sale); im Magazin: warehousing. — 2. ⚔ ~ der Truppen in Schlachtordnung: disposition of troops; (drawing up in) battle-array; ~ nehmen to take up a position, to form up; ~ in Linie parade; zwei=(drei=)glied(e)rige ~ formation of two (three) deep; staffelförmige ~ echelon; ⚓ auf den Rahen ~ nehmen to man the yards; ~ der Geschütze mounting of guns. — 3. fig. (Darlegung) statement, assertion; ~ als Kandidat candidature, nomination; von Zeugen: production.
Auf-stellungs-kosten ("...) pl. cost(s pl.) of putting (or fitting) up, &c.
auf-stemmen (⁻⁻◡⁻) ⊛** I v/a. u. v/refl. 1. den Arm, sich ⚲ auf den Tisch 2c. to lean (one's arm) upon the table, &c. — 2. fig. sich ⚲ gegen to resist (or oppose). — II v/n. 3. ⊕ to force open with a crow-bar, F to prize up.
auf-stempeln (⁻⁻◡⁻) v/a. ⊛a** to stamp (up)on or anew.
auf-steppen (⁻⁻◡⁻) ⊛** to quilt on.
auf-sticken (⁻⁻◡⁻) v/a. ⊛** (et.) ⚲ auf to embroider (s.th.) upon.
auf-stieben (⁻⁻◡⁻) [mhd.] v/n. (ſn) Gaſt**, bſd. hunt. v. Rebhühnern: to rise (or fly) up.
Auf-stieg m ⓓd. 1. ascent. — 2. am Fahrrad: step (an den neuen safety bicycles fehlt dieser); Auf= und Abſtieg ascent and descent, going up and coming down.
auf-stöbern (⁻⁻◡⁻) v/a. ⊛** 1. to stir (or rouse) up; bſd. hunt. to start, discover, track. — 2. fig. to ferret (or rout) out, to hunt up, to unearth.
auf-stöhnen (⁻⁻◡⁻) v/n. (h.) ⊛** to fetch (or utter) a (deep) groan.
auf-stöpseln (⁻⁻◡⁻) v/a. ⊛a** to uncork.
auf-stören (⁻⁻◡⁻) v/a. ⊛** 1. Feuer: to stir (or rake) up. — 2. e-n ⚲ to rouse (or startle, disturb) a p.; ⚔: to start.
auf-stoßen (⁻⁻◡⁻) ⊛a** I v/a. 1. (öffnen) to push (or thrust, fling) open; ein Faß: to stave in; sich (dat.) das Knie ⚲ to bruise (or graze, chafe) one's knee. — 2. (in die Höhe stoßen) to push (or throw, kick) up. — 3. hunt. Haſen ⚲ = aufjagen 1. — II v/n. (h. [in 4,5] u. ſn) 4. (im Faſſe gären) to ferment, rise, work; (sauer werden) to turn acid. — 5. von genoſſenen Speiſen: Zwiebeln ſtoßen mir auf onions rise (or repeat) with me; es ſtößt mir fortwährend auf I am full of wind, I suffer from flatulency; er das soll ihm sauer ⚲ he shall pay dearly for that. — 6. (vorkommen) to occur to; to (come by) chance upon; to light upon; mir iſt nie ſo etwas aufgeſtoßen I never saw (or heard) the like; mir ſtieß ein Zweifel auf a doubt crossed my mind. — 7. (auf et. ſtoßen) to knock (or run) against, (zurückprallen) to rebound on. — 8. ⚓ auf den Grund ⚲ to run aground. — III ~ n 9. pushing open or up, &c. (ſ. 1 u. 2); von Genoſſenem: belching,

breaking the wind (upwards), ꝛ (e)ructation; ſaures: heartburning; (Zuſammentreffen) (casual) meeting.
auf-stößig (⁻⁻◡⁻) a. ⊛ 1. von Getränken: (heftig) dreggy; (ſchal) vapid, flat. — 2. (unwohl) von Kindern: unwell, sickly; F poorly.
auf-strahlen (⁻⁻◡⁻) v/n. (h.) ⊛** to rise radiantly; to shine (or beam) forth; ich ſehe neue Hoffnung ⚲ I see a gleam (or a new dawn) of hope.
auf-sträuben (⁻⁻◡⁻) v/a. u. v/refl. ⊛** to (make the hair &c.) stand on end.
auf-streben (⁻⁻◡⁻) I v/n. (h.) ⊛** to strive (or tend) upwards; fig. zu et. ⚲ to aspire to a th.; ⚲d ascending, ascendant, fig. aspiring. — II ~ n ascending (or upward) tendency; aspiration.
auf-strecken (⁻⁻◡⁻) v/a. ⊛** zum Himmel ⚲ to stretch out (or up) to heaven.
Auf-streich ſüdd. (⁻⁻) m ⓓd. (Verſteigerung) auction, public sale (ant. Abſtreich).
auf-streichen (⁻⁻◡⁻) ⊛aſt** I v/a. (ſn) 1. = aufſtreifen II. — II v/a. 2. Butter ⚲ to butter (bread); Pflaſter ⚲ to spread a plaster on; Farbe ⚲ to lay on paint. — 3. (in die Höhe ſtreichen) die Ärmel 2c. to turn (or tuck) up, den Schnurrbart ⚲ to twirl up. — 4. ♩ = aufſiedeln. — III ~ n 5. (act of) spreading, &c.; turning up (one's sleeves), &c.
auf-streifen (⁻⁻◡⁻) ⊛** I v/a. 1. die Ärmel od. Arme ⚲ to tuck (or turn) up one's sleeves. — 2. (öffnen) sich (dat.) die Hand ⚲ und v/refl. sich (acc.) ⚲ to graze or tear (the skin off) one's hand, &c. — II v/n. (ſn) 3. (auf den Boden ſtreifen) von Türflügeln 2c.: to scrape the floor; to sweep the ground.
auf-streuen v/a. ⊛** to strew (or sprinkle) upon; Zucker ⚲ to sugar.
Auf-strich (⁻⁻) m ⓓd. 1. = Aufſtreich. — 2. up-stroke of a pen; ♩ up-bow.
auf-stricken (⁻⁻◡⁻) v/a. ⊛** 1. to work up in knitting. — 2. eine Maſche ⚲ (aufnehmen) to take up a stitch.
auf-striegeln (⁻⁻◡⁻) ⊛a** I v/n.(h.)Pferd 2c.: to dress the hair with a curry-comb; to comb (or curry) up or upwards); — II F fig. sich ⚲ v/refl. to trick o.s. out, to smarten (or spruce, trim) o.s. up.
auf-stufen (⁻⁻◡⁻) ⊛** I v/a. to raise gradually. — II v/n. (ſn) u. sich ⚲ v/refl. to rise by degrees. — III **Auf-stufung** f gradual ascent; rhet. climax.
auf-stülpen (⁻⁻◡⁻) v/a. ⊛** 1. einen Hut ⚲ to turn up (the brim of) ...; aufgeſtülpte Naſe turned-up nose. F aufgeſtülpte Naſe turned-up nose. — 2. F e-m, sich (dat.) die Mütze 2c. ⚲ to clap (or put) on ... (hurriedly).
auf-stürmen (⁻⁻◡⁻) ⊛** I v/n. (ſn) 1. to rush up. — II v/a. 2. (aufregen) to excite, agitate. — 3. (aufbrechen) ein Tor 2c.: to (break) open by assault; to storm (and force open).
auf-stürzen (⁻⁻◡⁻) ⊛** I v/a. = aufſtülpen 2. — II v/n. (ſn) mit dem Kopfe auf e-n Stein ⚲ (a. abs.) to fall (heavily) and strike one's head against a stone.
auf-stutzen (⁻⁻◡⁻) ⊛** I v/n. (h.) 1. to look up with surprise; to start at. — II v/a. 2. = aufſtülpen 1. — 3. to trim (up); neu: to renovate; mit ſchönen Redensarten ⚲ to interlard with fine phrases. — III sich ⚲ v/refl. 4. ſ. aufputzen II.

auf-stützen (⁻⁻◡⁻) I v/a. u. v/refl. ⊛** to support by, to prop up with; arch. to stay, to shore; sich ⚲ to lean (or rest) on a table, one's elbows, &c. — II ~ n supporting, propping (up), &c.
Auf-stutzer (⁻⁻◡⁻) m trimmer.
auf-suchen (⁻⁻◡⁻) I v/a. ⊛** to seek (for, after); to (make) search for, to track to trace; to look for, in e-m Buche: to look up, to hunt after or for; e-n ⚲ to go to see a p., to look a p. up, to call on a p.; ⚔ den Feind ⚲ to be on the look-out for (or on th track of) the enemy; seine alte Gegend wieder ⚲ to revisit (or to resort to) one's old haunts; e-n ⚲ l. to have a p. searched for; die Lage e-s Ortes ⚲ to take the bearings of ... — II ~ n = Aufſung **Auf-sucher** (⁻⁻◡⁻) m, ~in f p. who seeks (or searches) for, investigator
Auf-suchung (⁻⁻◡⁻) f ⊛ search for, quest
auf-summen[1] (⁻⁻◡⁻) ⊛**/*: **auf-summieren** (⁻⁻◡⁻) ⊛**/*: sich ⚲ v/refl. to sum (or cast) up; sich ⚲ a.: to total (or run) up
auf-summen[2] ⊛**, **auf-summen** ⊛** (⁻⁻(◡)⁻) v/n. (ſn) (summend auffliegen) to buzz up
auf-tafeln (⁻⁻◡⁻) v/a. ⊛a** 1. to dish up. — 2. ⊕ Tuchm.: (falten) to fold up
auf-tafeln ⚓ (⁻⁻◡⁻) I v/a. u. v/refl. ⊛a** ein Schiff: to rig up; nicht gut aufgetafelt not (rigged) shipshape; sich ⚲ F fig. to rig o.s. out; aufgetafelt (fein gepußt) well rigged out, smartly dressed, F togged out, got up (for the occasion). — II **Auf-taf(e)lung** (⁻⁻(◡)⁻) f rigging (up); F (feiner Puß) smart clothes, F fine toggery or rigout.
Auf-takt ♩ u. pros. (⁻⁻) m ⓒc. arsis; (Vorſchlag[ſilbe]) anacrusis. [to bowse.)
auf-taljen ⚓ (⁻⁻◡⁻) ⊛** (aufwinden))
auf-tauchen (⁻⁻◡⁻) I v/n. (ſn) ⊛** to rise (up); to emerge (from the water); weitS. und fig. (erſcheinen) to appear (on the surface); to come in sight, to turn up; plötzlich ⚲ (suddenly) to spring up, F to pop up; es tauchte ein Gerücht auf a rumour was set afloat. — II ~ n (a)rising; emersion; appearance
auf-tauen (⁻⁻◡⁻) I v/n. (ſn) das Eis taut auf ... thaws, runs, melts; fig auch: to grow warm, to lay aside one's reserve, to unbend. — II v/a et. ⚲ to thaw; a. (cause to) melt; F fig e-n ⚲ to warm a p.'s heart. — III ~ n thaw; beim ~ des Schnees (at the time) when the snow thaws or melts
auf-teil-en v/a. ⊛** Land 2c.: to parcel out, to allot. — II ~ n ⚲ unt **A**ung f parcelling out, allotment
Auf-tief=amboß ⊕ (⁻⁻...) m chasing anvil. [to chase, to emboss, to raise.]
auf-tiefen ⊕ (⁻⁻◡⁻) v/a. ⊛** Kupferſchmiede:]
Auf-tief=hammer ⊕ (⁻⁻...) m chasing-hammer; =meiſel m drift.
auf-tippen (⁻⁻◡⁻) v/a. ⊛** = auftupfen 1.
auf-tiſchen F (⁻⁻◡⁻) v/a. ⊛** Speiſen: to dish (or serve) up; e-n et. ⚲ to regale a. p. with a th.; fig. alte Geſchichten ⚲ to tell (or to warm up) old tales.
Auf-trag (⁻⁻) m ⓓd. 1. (Aufgetragenes) commission; charge; (Weiſung) injunction, instruction; m. mandate; er kam in ihrem ~e he came by her orders, in her name; im ~e von by

---

⚛ scientific; ⚘ botanical; ⚲ geography; ⊕ machinery; ⚒ mining; ⚔ military; ⚓ marine; ⊛ commercial; ✉ postal; 🚂 railway.

[auftragen] — 104 — [aufwälzen]

order of, on behalf of; im ~e der Regierung by government order; im ~e meines Vaters teile ich Ihnen mit // my father directs me (or I am directed, instructed by my father) to tell you //; e-n ~ für e-n besorgen to do a commission for a p.; sich e-s ~es entledigen to carry out an order, to deliver a message; einen ~ zu etwas halten to be charged (or commissioned) with s.th.; ⊕ (Bestellung) order; Ihrem ~e gemäß in accordance with your instructions; wir haben Ihren ~ ausgeführt we have executed your order, your order has been attended to; e-n ~ zurücknehmen to countermand an order. — 2. von Farben: laying on of colours, coat of paint.

auf-tragen (ᴵᴵᴸᵛ) ⑤b⋆⋆ **I** v/a. 1. Speisen: to serve (or dish) up; auch abs. es wird aufgetragen dinner is being served (up); ♀ lassen to send in the dinner. — 2. (auf Papier zeichnen) to lay (or trace) out. — 3. (aufstreichen) to lay on; eine Farbe, auch: to apply, to touch; dick ♀ to impaste, to set thick; fig., auch abs. stark, dick ♀ to exaggerate, F to lay it on (thick); Schminke ♀ to paint, to rouge. — 4. ⊕ Erde ♀ aufschütten 3. — 5. e-m et. ♀ to commission (or charge) a p. with a th.; e-m ♀ et. zu tun to commission (or enjoin, order) a p. to do a th.; mir wurde ein heikles Geschäft aufgetragen I had a delicate task entrusted (to) me. — 6. Kleidungsstücke: to wear out, to use up. — **II** v/n. 7. s. I u. 3. — 8. (aufbauschen) to swell, puff, bulge; diese Stoffe tragen stark auf these materials are very stout or bulky. — **III** ~ n ㉓ 9. = Auftrag.

Auf-träger ↖ (ᴵᴵᴸᵛ) m ⑫ 1. Kellner: waiter. — 2. ⊕ = Auftraggeber.

Auf-trag-geber ⊕ (ᴵᴵᴸᵛ...) m ⑫: one who orders, buyer, customer; principal; =handel ⊕ m commission-business; =nehmer m p. (or party) commissioned.

Auf-trag(s)-ausführung (ᴵᴵᴸᵛ...) f ⑫ execution of an order; =besorger ⊕ m commission-agent; ♀weise adv. by way of commission.

Auf-tragung (ᴵᴵᴸᵛ) f ⑯ 1. = Auftrag 2. — 2. paint. application of colours; typ. ~ der Farbe: inking; fig. starke ~ exaggeration.

Auf-trag-walze ⊕ (ᴵᴵᴸᵛ...) f ⑫ typ. (distributing-, inking-, printing-)roller, inker; =zettel ⊕ m e-s Börsenagenten list of (buying and selling) orders.

auf-trampe(l)n, auf-trappe(l)n F (ᴵᴵᴸᵛ) v/n. (sn) ⑱ (⑫a)⋆⋆ to stamp or tramp or patter (on the ground).

auf-träufe(l)n, -traufen (ᴵᴵᴸᵛ) ⑱ (⑫a)⋆⋆ **I** v/n. (sn) to fall in drops, to drip on. — **II** v/a. to drop (a fluid) on.

auf-treffen (ᴵᴵᴸᵛ) ⑫a⋆⋆ **I** v/n. (sn) to strike upon; vgl. antreffen. — **II** v/a. e-n ♀ to find a p. up or out of bed.

auf-treib/en (ᴵᴵᴸᵛ) ⑥¹⋆⋆ **I** v/a. 1. to drive (up); vgl. eintreiben 1. — 2. (aufbrechen) eine Tür: to break open. — 3. (ausdehnen) to swell (out), to blow (or puff) up; ⊕ Metallarbeiten: to chase, to beat out. — 4. Staub, Wellen ♀ to raise ...; e-n aus dem Bette ♀ to drive a p. out of

bed; hunt. Wild: to rouse, to start. — 5. (ausfindig machen) to hunt out or up, to get hold of; Neuigkeiten: to pick up; Geld ♀ to raise money or F the wind; die Mittel ♀ to find the means (or F the money) for; Volk ♀ to levy troops, to press sailors. — **II** v/n. (sn) 6. ↓ to be driven (or to drift) ashore, to run aground. — 7. to swell up, to distend. — 8. (aufgehen) von Pflanzen: to shoot (or come, spring) up. — **III** ~ n ㉓ 9. = A/ung.; das ~ der Mittel the supply of funds. — **IV auf-getrieben** p.p. u. a. ⑥⑥ (D 9) 10. bes. path. blown out, bulged, bloated, puffed, inflated.

Auf-treibung (~) f ⑯ driving in (a hat), breaking open (a door, &c.; Bildhauerei: embossment; path. = Aufgetriebenheit.

auf-trennen (ᴵᴵᴸᵛ) v/a. ⑱⋆⋆ to undo, unstitch; to rip open.

auf-treten (ᴵᴵᴸᵛ) ⑫d⋆⋆ **I** v/n. (sn, ohne Fortbewegung: h.) 1. to step forth; leise ♀ to tread softly; fest ♀ to walk with a firm step, fig. to act firmly, to put down one's foot. — 2. fig. (verfahren) to proceed; leise, vorsichtig ♀ to proceed gently, warily; entschieden, herzhaft ♀ to act resolutely, determinedly. — 3. fig. (sich zeigen) to present o.s.; als Kandidat ♀ to offer o.s. (or to come forward, to put up) as a candidate; als Kanzelredner ♀ to mount the pulpit; als Mitbewerber ♀ to set up as a rival; thea. auf der Bühne, als Schauspieler ♀ to appear on the scene, to come on the stage; to tread the boards; zum erstenmal: to make one's début; zum letztenmal: to make one's farewell bow (to the audience); gegen e-n ♀ to rise up against a p., to accuse (or denounce, oppose) a p.; jur. als Kläger gegen e-n ♀ to bring an action against a. p. — 4. mit sachlichem Subjekt: es trat ein Gerücht auf a rumour arose; die Krankheit tritt verheerend auf ... is raging fiercely, ... is causing great ravages. — **II** v/a. 5. (festtreten) to press down by treading or stamping, to stamp down. — 6. (öffnen) eine Nuß ♀ to break open ..., by stamping on it; eine Tür ♀ to kick ... open. — **III** ~ n ㉓ 7. man. style of pacing. — 8. (Benehmen) bearing, demeanour; freches ~ impudence, F bounce. — 9. (Erscheinen) appearance; thea. erstes ~ début; med. e-r Krankheit: outbreak. — Vgl. a. Auftritt.

Auf-trieb (ᴵᴵᴵ) ⑪d. 1. ↓ (aufwärtstreibende Kraft) buoyancy. — 2. ~ des Alpenviehs departure of the cattle for the Alpine pastures; ⊕ cattle driven (or brought) to market, cattle-supply (ant. Abtrieb).

Auf-triebs-vermögen ⊕ (ᴵᴵᴵ...) n ⑫ e-s Luftschiffes ꝛc.: ascending force.

auf-trinken (ᴵᴵᴸᵛ) ⑱f*⋆⋆ to drink up, to imbibe, in e-m Schlucke ♀ to empty ...

Auf-tritt (ᴵᴵᴰ) m ⑪c. 1. (Gangart) gait, step. — 2. = auftreten 8 u. 9. — 3. bes. thea. scene; ein blutiger ~ a gory act; ein bedauerlicher ~ a painful incident; e-n ~ machen oder veranlassen to create (or make) a scene; e-n ~ mit e-m haben to have an altercation with a p. — 4. ⊕ ~ an e-m Wagen step; man. zum Aufsteigen: horse-block, -stone; ⚔ frt. banquette.

Auf-tritts-stichwort (ᴵᴵᴸ...) n ⑫ thea. cue; er überhörte das ~ he missed his cue.

auf-trocknen (ᴵᴵᴸᵛ) ⑫b⋆⋆ **I** v/n. (sn) to dry up. — **II** v/a. to dry up; Tränen ꝛc. to wipe off; ↓ (undicht m.) to make leaky.

auf-trommeln (ᴵᴵᴸᵛ) ⑫a⋆⋆ **I** v/n. (h.) to (beat the) drum. — **II** v/a. to rouse by (the sound of) the drum; (anwerben) to drum up. [⑫a⋆⋆, ⑱⋆⋆ = aufträufeln.]

auf-tröpfeln, auf-tropfen (ᴵᴵᴸᵛ) v/a. (h.)

auf-trumpfen (ᴵᴵᴸᵛ) v/n. (h.) ⑱⋆⋆ 1. to play trumps. — 2. e-m ♀ (grob werden) to give a p. a bit of one's mind.

auf-tuchen ↓ (ᴵᴵᴸᵛ) v/a. ⑱⋆⋆ Segel: to furl.

auf-tun (ᴵᴵᴵ) ⑭⋆⋆ **I** v/a. 1. (öffnen) to open; den Beutel ♀ to loosen one's purse-strings; das Essen ♀ (auftragen) to dish (or serve) up the dinner; er wagt den Mund nicht aufzutun he dare not open his mouth; die Ohren ♀ to hearken; die Tür ♀ to open (or unlatch, unlock) the door. — 2. den Hut ꝛc. ♀ to put on. — **II sich** ♀ v/refl. 3. to open; ⚔ to be widening (up), to extend in width; von Blumen: to expand; s-e Lippen taten sich auf ... parted; ein Abgrund tut sich auf ... yawns. — 4. (sich zeigen) to appear, to show o.s.; bes. fig. es tun sich uns gute Aussichten auf we have good prospects (opening up to us); ⚔ eine Gesellschaft tut sich auf ... is forming. — **III** ~ n ㉓ 5. opening.

auf-tupfen (ᴵᴵᴸᵛ) v/a. ⑱⋆⋆ 1. m. d. Finger: to touch lightly. — 2. Punkte ♀ to dot.

auf-türmen (ᴵᴵᴸᵛ) ⑱⋆⋆ **I** v/a. to heap (or pile, raise) up. — **II sich** ♀ v/refl. to rise aloft; to tower over (or above); (sich ansammeln) to accumulate, grow. — **III** ~ n ㉓ u. **Auf-türmung** f ⑯ heaping up, &c. (s. I u. II); accumulation.

auf-wachen (ᴵᴵᴸᶜʰᵛ) v/n. (sn) ⑱⋆⋆ to awake, to wake (up) (a. fig.); plötzlich ♀ to start up (from one's sleep). [to (a)wake aufwachen u. to (a)waken aufwecken werden in England sehr viel verwechselt!]

auf-wachsen (ᴵᴵᴸᵗʃᵛ) **I** v/n. (sn) ⑤b(et)t⋆⋆ to grow up; zum Manne ♀ to grow up to man's estate. — **II** ~ n ㉓ growth, growing in (wo)manhood.

auf-wagen (ᴵᴵᴸᵛ): sich ♀ v/refl. ⑱⋆⋆ to venture to rise after an illness, &c.

auf-wägen (ᴵᴵᴸᵛ) v/a. ⑫b⋆⋆ = aufwiegen.

auf-wall/en (ᴵᴵᴸᵛ) [mhd.] **I** v/n. (sn, ↖ h.) ⑱⋆⋆ 1. to bubble up; durch Hitze: to boil up, to wallop; brausend: to effervesce. — 2. fig. vom Rauch, Staub: to rise; von der See: to rage, to roll; von Menschen: to fret and fume, to boil over with passion. — **II** ~ n ㉓ 3. = A/ung.

auf-wällen (ᴵᴵᴸᵛ) v/a. ⑱⋆⋆ Kochkunst: to boil gently, to (put on the) simmer.

Auf-wallung (ᴵᴵᴸᵛ) f ⑯ bubbling (up); chm. ebullition; effervescence; fig. e-r Leidenschaft: (fit of) passion; des Augenblicks: (passing) emotion; der Freude: elation, flush (of joy); des Zorns: outburst.

auf-wältigen ⚒ (ᴵᴵᴸᵛ) v/a. ⑱⋆⋆ Schacht: to drain a shaft, to pump ... dry.

auf-walzen (ᴵᴵᴸᵛ) v/a. ⑯⋆⋆ to put (or wind) on a roller or cylinder; typ. Farbe ♀ to roll (or beat) the form.

auf-wälzen (ᴵᴵᴸᵛ) v/a. ⑯⋆⋆ 1. to roll up. — 2. to roll down upon; fig. = aufbürden I. — 3. (auftürmen) to heap up.

Zeichen (s. S. XVII): F familiär; P Volkssprache; ┌ Gaunersprache; ↖ selten; † alt (auch gestorben); ⋆ neu (auch geboren); ⋆⋆ unrichtig;

[Aufwand] — 105 — [aufwinden]

Auf-wand (ˣˣ) *m* ⊙c. (*pl.* ⁀) expense, expenditure; unnützer: waste; in der Lebensweise: sumptuousness, luxury; (Pracht) pomp, splendour; von Worten: display, profusion; mit großem ~ von Gelehrsamkeit with a great show of learning; großen ~ machen to spend one's money freely or lavishly, to live in (a costly) style or in great style, F to do the grand. [law.]

Auf-wands-gesetz (ˣ...) *n* ⓶ sumptuary)

auf-wärmen (ˣˣˣ) I *v/a*. ⓼** to warm up (again); *fig.* to repeat (over again), to rake up (old stories). — **II auf-gewärmt** *p.p.* ⓺ hackneyed, stale; Les Essen warmed up scraps *pl.*, hash, (fr.) réchauffé; Le Geschichte, Ler Kohl well-worn tale, F chestnut.

Auf-warte-bursche (ˣˣˣ...) *m* ⓶ occasional attendant or waiter; =frau *f* = Aufwärterin, =geld *n*, =lohn *m* pay (or fee) for attendance; F tip for the waiter or waiting-woman.

auf-wart|en (ˣˣˣ) I *v/n*. (h.) ⓼** 1. bei Tische ⓶ to wait at table; e-m ⓶ to attend on a p. — 2. e-m ⓶ (seine Ehrerbietung bezeigen) to wait on a p.; to pay one's respects (or a visit) to a p.; `-e-m fleißig ⓶ to dance attendance on a p. — 3. e-m mit et. ⓶ to wait on a p. with a th.; bsd. bei Tisch: kann ich Ihnen (noch) mit et. ⓶? may I help you to anything (else)? womit kann ich Ihnen ⓶? what is your pleasure?, what are your orders?, what can I show you or do for you?; ich will gleich damit ⓶ (y(r order) shall be attended to at once; höfliche Bejahung: aufzuwarten! at your service! — 4. v. Hunden: to beg. — II ~ *n* ⓶ 5. = A/ung.

Auf-wärter (ˣˣˣ) *m* ⓶, ~in *f* ⓸ attendant, *f* a. waiting-woman, (Kellner[in]) waiter, waitress; ~(in) auf Schiffen steward(ess); ~dienst (ˣ...) *m* ⓶ duties *pl.* of an attendant, &c.

auf-wärts (ˣˣ) *adv.* upward(s); uphill; fluß⓶ up the river; zu Wasser ⓶ fahren to go up-stream; ⓶ steigen to ascend; Haare ⓶ kämmen to comb ... up or back.

Auf-wärts-bewegung ⓸ (ˣˣˣ...) *f* ⓶ der Kurse: upward move(ment) or tendency, buoyant tone of the market; rise.

Auf-wartung (ˣˣˣ) *f* ⓸ 1. waiting; service: attendance on; sie hat ein Mädchen zur ~ she has a maid to wait on her; er hat die ~ bei mir he waits (or is in waiting) on me — 2. e-m seine ~ machen = aufwarten 2.

auf-waschen (ˣˣˣ) I *v/a*. ⓼b** 1. den Fußboden, bsd. das Küchengeschirr ⓶ to wash up ...; (scheuern) to scour. — 2. to use (up) in washing. — 3. sich (*dat.*) die Hände ⓶ (wund waschen) to wash one's hands sore. — II ~ *n* ⓶ 4. washing up (f. I). Sprichw. das ist ein ~ it's (all) one doing; F it's all one job.

Auf-wäscher (ˣˣˣ) *m* ⓶, ~in *f* ⓸ scullion, dish-washer, cleaner, *f* scullery-maid, woman that washes up (the dishes).

Auf-wasch-faß (ˣˣˣ...) *n* ⓶ washing-up pan (or tub); =frau scullery-maid; =küche *f* scullery; =wasser *n* water for washing-up; (Spülicht) dish-water, dish-wash; (Schmutzwasser) a. hog-wash.

auf-weben ⊙ (ˣˣˣ) *v/a*. ⓼b** 1. to weave on (to). — 2. to work up in weaving. — 3. (auftrennen) to unravel.

auf-weck|en (ˣˣˣ) I *v/a*. ⓼** 1. to call up, to rouse (from sleep); to awaken; vgl. aufwachen; durch Klopfen an die Tür: to knock up; vom Tode ⓶ to raise (from the dead); to (re)call to life; *fig.* to resuscitate; (aufmuntern) to enliven, to cheer up. — II ~ *n* ⓶ 2. = A/ung. — III auf-geweckt *p.p. u. a.* ⓺ 3. Bed. des *inf.* — 4. *fig.* wide-awake, bright, smart, lively; (heiter) cheerful.

Auf-wecker (ˣˣˣ) *m* ⓶ 1. rouser, awakener; *p.* who calls people up in the morning. — 2. (uhr) alarum(-clock).

Auf-weckung (ˣˣˣ) *f* ⓸ (a)wakening.

auf-wehen (ˣˣˣ) ⓼** I *v/n*. (ĭn) 1. der Wind weht auf the wind is rising. — 2. to be blown open (by the wind). — II *v/a*. 3. to raise by blowing, to blow up. — 4. to blow open. — 5. (wehend bloßlegen) to lay bare. — 6. (wehend aufschwellen) to swell (or puff) up with blowing; to inflate.

auf-weichen (ˣˣˣ) ⓼** I *v/a*. to soften, to mollify; durch Feuchtigkeit: to soak; *path.* Geschwüre *x.* ⓶ to open by fomentation; Les Mittel: ⁊ emollient. — II *v/n*. (ĭn) to become softened, soaked, sodden, &c. — III ~ *n* ⓶ u.

Auf-weichung *f* ⓸ softening; soaking; *path.* fomentation.

auf-weinen (⁀) ⓼** I *v/n*. (h.) laut ⓶ to break into tears. — II *v/a*. to awaken (or rouse) by weeping or crying.

auf-weisbar (ˣˣˣ) *a*. ⓺ producible.

auf-weis|en (ˣˣˣ) ⓼** I *v/a*. to exhibit, einen Befehl: to produce; guten Erfolg ⓶ to show good results; et. aufzuweisen h. to have s. th. to show, (besitzen) to have s. th. to boast of. — II sich ⓶ *v/refl*. sich ⓶ als to prove to be. — III ~ *n* ⓶ = A/ung.

auf-weißen (ˣˣˣ) *v/a*. ⓼** to whitewash (anew); to whiten. [duction; show.)

Auf-weisung (ˣˣˣ) *f* ⓸ exhibition, pro-)

auf-weiten (ˣˣˣ) *v/a*. ⓼** to widen (out), to expand, to extend in width.

auf-wend|en (ˣˣˣ) ⓼a** I *v/a*. 1. ⁀ sein Auge zum Vater ⓶ (*G.*) to look up to Heaven. — 2. *fig.* (aufbieten) to spend, lay out, employ, devote; viel Geld ⓶ to put o.s. to great expense; alles ⓶, alle s-e Kräfte ⓶ to strain every nerve; die aufgewendete (aufgewandte) Mühe the pains bestowed on a th.; unnütz ⓶ to waste, to squander. — II *v/n*. (h.) 3. ⚓ to put (or tack) about a ship. — III ~ *n* ⓶ u. A/ung *f* ⓸ 4. employment, *v.* Geld: expenditure, (Kosten) expense.

auf-werfen (ˣˣˣ) ⓶d. *sep.* I *v/a*. 1. eine Tür *x.* to throw (or fling) open; mit Würfen: to break open by (stone-)throwing. — 2. die Karten ⓶ to throw up; eine Fahne: to unfurl, to raise. — 3. *fig.* (= aufstellen 4) e-e Frage: to put; einen Zweifel ⓶ to raise. — 4. (auf et. throwen) to throw (down) upon. — 5. (emporwerfen) to throw up; den Ball: to toss up; Blasen, Schaum ⓶ to throw (or send) up bubbles, froth; *fig.* viel Staub ⓶ to make a great stir. — 6. die Hand, den Kopf: to hold (or raise) up; den Mund: to purse up; die Nase: to put up; natürlich aufgeworfene Lippen *f pl.* pouting lips *pl.*; aufgeworfene Nase turned-up nose. — 7. (aufschütten) to heap (or pile) up; Schanzen: to throw up; Deiche, Erdwälle ⓶ to construct; einen Graben ⓶ to (dig a) trench; ※ eine Schanze ⓶ to throw up earth-works, to entrench o.s. — II sich ⓶ *v/refl*. 8. (sich als oder zum Richter ⓶ (oft mit dem Nebensinne der Anmaßung) to set up as (or for) a judge, to assume judicial authority; *jur.* sich zum Kläger ⓶ to appear as plaintiff against; er warf sich vor der Welt zu ihrem Verteidiger auf he proclaimed himself before the world her champion. — 9. (sich erheben) sich gegen e-n ⓶ to rise (up), revolt, rebel against a p. — 10. ⊙ von Brettern: (sich krümmen) to warp, to cast. — III ~ *n* ⓶ 11. = A/ung.

Auf-werfer ⊙ (ˣˣˣ) *m* ⓶, **Auf-werf-hammer** *m* ⓶ der Schmiede lift-hammer.

Auf-werfung (ˣˣˣ) *f* ⓸ throwing (or flinging) open or up, &c. (f. aufwerfen I u. II).

auf-wichsen (ˣˣˣ*fgv*) *v/a*. ⓼** 1. to brush (or polish) up with blacking, &c. — 2. F (auch) *v/refl*. = aufputzen II. — 3. (emporwichsen) den Bart: to brush up, den Schnurrbart: to twirl up.

auf-wickeln (ˣˣˣ) I *v/a*. u. *v/refl*. ⓶a** 1. to wind (or roll) up; (auf et. wickeln) to wind upon; ⊙ Zwirn, Garn (zu e-m Knäuel) ⓶ to wind (up) ... into a ball, to ball ...; ⚓ Taue *x.*: to coil; ⁊ aufgewickelt ⁊: convolute; die Haare ⓶ to put one's hair in (curl-)papers. — 2. (aus-ea. wickeln) durch *verbs* mit un..., *z.B.*: to unwind, uncoil, unwarp; *fig.* einen Knoten, sich ⓶ to unravel, to unfold. — II ~ *n* ⓶ u. **Auf-wick(e)lung** *f* ⓸ 3. winding (or coiling) up, &c.; ⁊: convolution. — 4. unwinding &c.

Auf-wiegelei (ˣˣˣ*ʋ*) *f* ⓸ = aufwiegeln II.

auf-wiegeln (ˣˣˣ) [*schwz.*] I *v/a*. ⓶a** (*ant.* abwiegeln) (aufreizen) to stir up, to provoke; to incite (to mutiny or rebellion); das Volk ⓶d, oft demagogic(al), seditious (language). — II ~ *n* ⓶ u. **Auf-wieg(e)lung** *f* ⓸ stirring up, provocation; incitement.

auf-wiegen (ˣˣˣ) ⓶c** to (counter-)balance, to compensate for; et. mit Gold ⓶ to pay for a th. (its weight) in gold; dies wiegt alle Nachteile auf this makes up for all shortcomings or disadvantages.

Auf-wiegler (ˣˣˣ) *m* ⓶, ~in *f* ⓸ (Wühler) agitator, demagogue; (Hetzer) stirrer-up (of strife); (Anstifter) instigator; (Aufrührer) plotter; Lisch *a.* ⓺ seditious, mutinous; *v.* Reden *a.*: inflammatory.

Auf-wiegelung (ˣˣˣ) *f* ⓸ = aufwiegeln II.

auf-wiehern (ˣˣˣ) *v/n*. (h.) ⓶a** *v.* Pferden: to neigh aloud; to commence neighing; von Menschen: to burst out laughing. [nerei: copping-wire; rim.)

Auf-winde-draht ⊙ (ˣˣˣ) *m* ⓶ Spin-)

auf-winden (ˣˣˣ) ⓶** I *v/a*. u. *v/refl*. (*ant.* abwinden) 1. = aufwickeln 1. — 2. (sich) ⓶ = auflösen 1; Seide ⓶ to sleave silk. — 3. to wind up (with a windlass); mit einer Hebevorrichtung: to hoist; ⚓ den Anker aus dem Grunde ⓶

♪ Musik; ⁊ Wissenschaft; ⚘ Pflanze; ⊕ Geographie; ⊙ Technik; ※ Bergbau; ※ Militär; ⚓ Marine; ✻ Handel; ✉ Post; ⛴ Eisenbahn.

[Aufwinder] — 106 — [Auge]

(lichten) to weigh (or start) the anchor; ein Fahrzeug ≈ (aufholen) to haul up (or to ground) ... — **II** sich ≈ v/refl. 4. f. 1 u. 2. — 5. to take a winding upward course, to wind up a slope or hillside. [winds up, &c., winder.]

Auf-winder (ᴗ́ᴗᴗ) m ㉒, **~in** f ㊼ p. who **Auf-winde-rad** (ᴗ́ᴗᴗ...) n ㉒ = =draht.

auf-wirbeln (ᴗ́ᴗᴗ) ⓐa** **I** v/n. (ſu) 1. to whirl up. — 2. von Lerchen: to rise up warbling or carolling. — **II** v/a. 3. ≈, a. ≈l. to raise up; l.s. Staub ≈ F to kick up (a) dust; fig. (viel) Staub ≈ to make a (great) stir, to cause a (mighty) commotion. — 4. Fenster: to unbolt.

auf-wirken (ᴗ́ᴗᴗ) v/a. ⑧** 1. das Garn: to work up in weaving. — 2. (kneten) Brot ≈ to knead the dough; to make up the loaves. — 3. hunt. (aufschneiden) ein Wild ≈ to (skin and) cut up ...

auf-wischen (ᴗ́ᴗᴗ) v/a. ⑨** to wipe (or mop) up; ⚓ to swab.

Auf-wischer (ᴗ́ᴗᴗ) m ㉒, **Auf-wisch-lappen** (ᴗ́ᴗ...) m ㉒, **=tuch** n dish-cloth; flannel (or rug) for wiping up, mop; ⚓ swab(ber).

auf-wogen (ᴗ́ᴗᴗ) v/n. (ſu) ⑧** to rise in billows, to surge up; See: hoch ≈b rolling heavily, storm-tossed.

auf-wollen (ᴗ́ᴗᴗ) v/n. (h.) ⑨** to wish to rise; das Fenster, der Deckel will nicht auf ... won't open, won't come undone, won't come off.

auf-wühlen (ᴗ́ᴗᴗ) v/a. ⑧** die Erde: to turn up; von Kanonenkugeln ꝛc.: to rake up; das Meer: to toss (or lash) up; von Schweinen: mit dem Rüſſel ≈ to root (or rip) up (trees, &c.); e-e alte Wunde: to open, to rip up; fig. das Land, Volk ≈ to stir up the country, the people.

Auf-wurf (ᴗ́ᴗ) m ⓓc. 1. (das Aufwerfen) throwing up. — 2. (aufgeworfene Erde) embankment; bank; dam; mound.

auf-zähl/en (ᴗ́ᴗᴗ) **I** v/a. ⑧** allg. to count up; einzeln: to enumerate, to reckon up singly; ſtatiſtiſch: to return; Geld: to pay (F to plank) down; e-m zehn Hiebe ≈ to administer ten lashes to a p. — **II** ~ n ㉓ = A/ung.

Auf-zähler (ᴗ́ᴗᴗ) m ㉒ enumerator.

Auf-zählung (ᴗ́ᴗᴗ) f ㊻ counting; enumeration; ſtatiſtiſche: return.

auf-zaubern (ᴗ́ᴗᴗ) v/a. ⓐa** 1. to open by magic. — 2. (aufrufen) to call up by magic, to raise (spirits) by witchcraft.

auf-zäumen (ᴗ́ᴗᴗ) v/a. ⑧** to bridle, to bit; fig. den Esel beim Schwanz ≈ to put the cart before the horse.

auf-zehren (ᴗ́ᴗᴗ) ⑧** **I** v/a. (auf-essen) to consume, to eat up; (auffaugen) to absorb; (erschöpfen) to exhaust; fig. sein Vermögen: to spend, dissipate, waste, lavish. — **II** ~ n ㉓ u. **Auf-zehrung** f ㊻ consumption; absorption; exhaustion; fig. dissipation, waste.

auf-zeichn/en (ᴗ́ᴗᴗ) **I** v/a. ⑨b** 1. to design, sketch, draw; eine Bahnlinie: to trace. — 2. (aufſchreiben) to note (or take, write) down; geſchichtlich: to chronicle, to record; ♔ to book (down), enter, charge. — **II** ~ n ㉓ 3. = A/ung.

Auf-zeichner (ᴗ́ᴗᴗ) m ㉒, **~in** f ㊼ person who traces, notes down, books, &c.; chronicler. [sketch; note.]

Auf-zeichnung (ᴗ́ᴗᴗ) f ㊻ design;

Auf-zeichnungs-buch (ᴗ́ᴗᴗ...) n ㉒ notebook, memorandum-book.

auf-zeigen (ᴗ́ᴗᴗ) v/a. ⑧** to show up, vgl. aufweisen I. [tear) up or open.]

auf-zerren (ᴗ́ᴗᴗ) v/a. ⑧** to pull (or

Auf-zieh-brücke (ᴗ́ᴗ...) f ㉒ draw-bridge.

auf-zieh/en (ᴗ́ᴗᴗ) ⓑb** **I** v/a. 1. (emporziehen) to draw (or pull, wind) up; ⚓ den Anker ≈ (lichten) to weigh (the) anchor; die Brauen ≈ to knit one's brows; die Brücke: to draw; den Eimer: to wind up; Flaggen: to hoist (up); Hoſen: to hitch up; Kleid: to tuck up. — 2. (aufwiegen) to weigh, balance, poise. — 3. (ziehend öffnen) to draw (or pull) open; den Kork e-r Flaſche ≈ to uncork a bottle; einen Riegel: to draw; die Schleuſen: to open; den Vorhang: to draw up; ſich ≈ to get loose; to come undone, to unwind; auf= und zu=ziehen to open and shut. — 4. ☉ den Hahn eines Gewehrs ≈ to cock (or make ready) a gun; eine Uhr: to wind up; ſtark ≈ to overwind; et. das ſich ſchwer ≈ läßt a th. difficult to wind up. — 5. (auf et. ſpannen) Karten ꝛc. auf Leinwand ≈ to mount ... on canvas; ♪ Saiten auf eine Geige ≈ to string a violin; fig. gelindere Saiten ≈ to come down a peg, to climb down (a bit). — 6. (großziehen) ein Kind: to bring (or train) up; Vieh: to rear, raise, breed. — 7. (hinhalten) to keep in suspense, to put off. — 8. (foppen) to tease, quiz, rally, jeer; to make game of; e-n mit et. ≈ F to chaff a p. with a th. — 9. ☉ Färberei: die Küpe ≈ to prepare the vat. — 10. ⚒ einen Schacht: to work. — **II** v/n. (ſu) 11. auf und ab ꝛc. ziehen vgl. 11. — 12. (ſich zur Schau ſtellen) ≈, aufgezogen kommen to march up (in procession); ⚔ to mount guard (ant. abziehen 10). — 13. F fig. ≈, aufgezogen kommen to make one's appearance; prächtig ≈ to come (up) in splendid style. — 14. (mit et. ankommen) mit et. aufgezogen kommen to bring forward; to produce, to show. — 15. (ſichtbar werden) von Geſtirnen: to rise; ein Gewitter zieht am Himmel auf a storm is approaching or brewing. — **III** v/refl. ſich ≈ 16. f. 3 u. 4. — **IV** ~ n ㉓ 17. (ʒu 1) thea. ~ des Vorhangs rise of the curtain. — 18. (ʒu 6) breeding (cattle-) rearing. — 19. (ʒu 8) teasing, railery; er liebt das ~ he is fond of teasing, F he likes a bit of chaff. — 20. (ʒu 12) ⚔ ~ der Wache mounting guard.

Auf-zieher (ᴗ́ᴗᴗ) m ㉒, **~in** f ㊼ one who draws (or winds, mounts) up, &c.; (Fopper) teaser, quiz(zer); **~ei** (ᴗᴗᴗ́) f quizzing, jeering, F chaff, kidding.

Auf-zieh-fenſter (ᴗ́ᴗ...) n ㉒ sash-window; **=loch** n der Uhr: key-hole; **=muskel** m, anat. adducent muscle.

Auf-zucht (ᴗ́ᴗ) f ㊻ ohne pl.) breeding, rearing, raising, &c. (ſ. aufziehen 6).

auf-zucken (ᴗ́ᴗᴗ) v/n. (h.) ⑧** to rise (or start up) with a convulsive motion or a jerk; v. Flammen: to blaze up.

Auf-zug (ᴗ́ᴗ) m ⓓd. 1. train; bſd. eccl. procession; zu Pferde: cavalcade; ~ v. Dienern: train of attendants; glänzen-

der ~ brilliant pageant, splendid display or show. — 2. F (Tracht) array, attire; weitS. dress; in ſeltſamen ~e in strange attire, curiously attired. — 3. thea. (Akt) act. — 4. (Emporziehen) raising, lifting, hoisting; (Fahrſtuhl) lift, elevator; hydrauliſcher ~ hydraulic lift; (Kran) crane. — 5. Turnerei: pull-up. — 6. ☉ Weberei: (Kette) chain, warp; typ. ~ des Deckels, Zylinders packing; harter ~ hard packing.

Auf-zug(s)-feder (ᴗ́ᴗ...) ☉ f ㉒ Uhrm.: maintaining power (of a clock); going-wheel; **=klappe** f e-r Zugbrücke f half of a draw-bridge. — Vgl. a. Aufzieh=...

Auf-zunehmende([r] m) f (ᴗ́ᴗᴗᴗ) ㊲ one to be admitted or received, candidate for admission.

auf-zupfen (ᴗ́ᴗᴗ) v/a. ⑧** 1. Pflanzen: to pull up, to pluck out. — 2. (auflöſen) to pluck (or pick) to pieces. — 3. (aufziehen) e-e Schleife: to untie. [3.)

auf-zwängen (ᴗ̑ᴗ) v/a. ⑧** = aufzwingen

auf-zwecken (ᴗ́ᴗᴗ) v/a. ⑧** Schuhmacherei ꝛc.: to fasten on with pegs.

auf-zwicken (ᴗ́ᴗᴗ) v/a. ⑧** 1. ☉ = aufzwecken. — 2. to open with nippers.

auf-zwingen (ᴗ́ᴗᴗ) ⓓf** **I** v/a. 1. e-m et. ≈ to press (or force) a th. upon a p. — 2. e-m e-e Portion Essen ≈ to force ... down a p. — 3. (öffnen) to force (or break) open. — 4. (mit Gewalt aufſetzen) to force on. — **II** v/refl. 5. ſich (e-m) ≈ (aufdrängen) to obtrude (or thrust) o.s. on a p., to force one's company on a p.

Aug-apfel (ᴗ́ᴗᴗ) [ahd.] m ㉒ 1. ball (or apple) of the eye; eyeball. — 2. (Augenſtern) pupil; fig. er iſt ſein ~ (Liebling) he is the apple of his eye, he is his darling.

Auge (ᴗ́ᴗ) [ahd.: eye] n ㉖ 1. eye; blaue ~n pl. blue eyes pl.; ein blau-(geſchlagen)es ~ a black eye; fig. e-m in die ~n ſehen to look a p. full in the face; mit einem blauen ~ davonkommen to get off with a small loss, to have a narrow escape; mit bloßem, unbewaffnetem ~ with the naked eye; künſtliches ~ artificial eye; die ~n aufſchlagen (niederſchlagen) to lift up (to cast down) one's eyes; große ~n machen to open one's eyes wide, to be all eyes, vgl. 4; die ~n geh(e)n ihm über his eyes are swimming with tears; die ~n betr. ocular; path., &c.: ☉ ophthalmic; ⚔ ~n rechts (links)! eyes right (left)!; ich habe (die ganze Nacht) kein ~ zugetan I did not sleep a wink (all night). — 2. (Geſicht, Sehkraft) er hat gute (ſchlechte) ~n he has a good (bad) sight, his (eye-)sight is good, bad; ſcharfe (ſchwache) ~n haben to be keen-sighted (weak-sighted); von Brillen: für je-s ~ paſſend suitable for a p.'s sight; das ſchadet den ~n it injures the sight or hurts the eyes; es ſtrengt die ~n an it tries the eyes; fig. es fällt, ſpringt in die ~n it is obvious, manifest; in die ~n fallend, auch: striking, conſpicuous; e-n feſt ins ~ faſſen to fix one's glance upon a p.; ſoweit die ~n reichen as far as the eye (or the sight) can reach, within (one's) ken; vor aller ~n before the public gaze, openly, publicly; vor j-m geiſtigen (ob. inneren)

Signs (see page XVII): F familiar; P vulgar; F flash; ⚹ rare; † obsolete (died); * new word (born); ⁺⁺ incorrect; ♪ music.

[Äugelchen] — 107 — [Augment]

~ before (or in) his mind's eye; vor j-s ~n Gnade finden to find favour in a p.'s eyes. — 3. (sehende Person) vor Gottes ~n before (the sight of) God; unter f-n eigenen ~n under his very eyes or nose; unter vier ~n face to face; sich unter vier ~n besprechen to have a private talk or interview; Gespräch unter vier ~n (fr.) tête-à-tête; wenn zwei ~n weniger sind, etwa: should anything happen (in the family). — 4. (Acht, Absicht) ein ~ auf e-n haben to have (or keep) one's eye upon a p., to look (well) after a p.; er hat ein ~ (Heiratsabsichten) auf sie he is making up to her; e-n im ~ behalten, nicht aus den ~n verlieren to keep watch over a p.; to watch a p. (closely); er läßt ihn nicht aus den ~n, a. he does not trust him out of sight; et. Neues ins ~ fassen to concoct (or hatch) a new plan; die ~n offen halten to keep one's eyes open, to keep a sharp look-out; ganz ~ und Ohr sein to be all eyes and ears; die Ehrfurcht gegen e-n aus den ~n setzen to set aside the respect due to a p.; du mußt die ~n überall haben you must have your eyes about you; ihm werden die ~ übergehen he will open his eyes (wide), he will be surprised, vgl. 1; er wandte fein ~ von ihr he never took his eyes off her; aller ~n auf fich ziehen to attract general attention or notice; ein ~ bei et. zudrücken to overlook (or connive at) a th.; Sprichw. aus den ~n, dem Sinn out of sight, out of mind. — 5. fig. ich tue alles, was ich ihm an den ~n absehen kann I anticipate all his wishes, vgl. absehen 3; e-m den Daumen aufs ~ setzen to keep a firm hand over a p.; das paßt wie die Faust aufs ~ it's beside the purpose; geh mir aus den ~n get out of my sight; der Geiz sieht ihm aus den ~n he has an avaricious look (about him); er ist f-m Vater wie aus den ~n geschnitten he is the image (or F the spit) of his father; in meinen ~n in my opinion, as I look upon it; ich bin ihm ein Dorn im ~ he abhors (or detests) me; dem Tod (feck) ins ~ sehen to look death (boldly) in the face; wir sehen es mit ander(e)n ~n an we take a different view of it; e-m unter die ~n treten to present o.s. before (or to face) a person; die ~n sind bei ihm größer als der Magen his eyes are larger than his appetite. — 6. ⚘ (Knospe) germ, bud; ~n treibend germinating, budding. — 7. ~ (Loch) im Brot, Käse: hole; ⊕ arch. ~ (Öse) eines Bolzens eye of a bolt; ⊕ typ. ~ des Buchstaben am Schriftkegel face of a letter; ⚓ (Schlinge) im Tau ꝛc.: eye. — 8. ~n pl. auf Karten, Würfeln ꝛc.: points pl.

Äugelchen (͟ᴗ) n ㉓, dim. = Äuglein 1.
äugeln (͟ᴗ) ㉒a. I v/n. (h.) to ogle, to leer at. — II v/a. hort. = okulieren.
äugen (͟ᴗ) v/n. (h.) ⊛ bsd. hunt. = äugeln 1.
Augen=acht (͟ᴗ...) m ㉒ min. cat's eye; **=achse** f, anat. axis of the eye; **=arterie** f, anat.: ⚕ ophthalmic artery; **=arzt** m oculist, F eye-doctor; **=ausstechen** n putting (or punching) out (of) an eye; **=balsam** m ointment (fig. balm) for the eyes; **=beschreibung** f: ⚕ ophthalmography; **=besichtigung** f: ⚕ ophthalmoscopy; **=binde** f bandage (over the eye); **=bindehaut** f, anat.: ⚕ conjunctiva; **=blende** f = =leder.
Augen=blick (͟ᴗ͟ᴗ) m ㉒c. 1. (kurze Zeit) moment, instant; alle ~(e), jeden ~ every moment or instant, momentarily; er kann jeden ~ kommen he may come (at) any minute; auf einen ~ for a moment; bis zu diesem ~ up to this very moment or instant, till now; für den ~ for the time (being); im ~e in a trice, in a twinkling (of the eye); (soeben) just now; in dem ~, als (auch: wo) at the (very) instant when; von dsm ~e an henceforth. — 2. (Zeitpunkt) entscheidender ~ critical moment; die letzten ~e eines Sterbenden (last) dying moments; lichte ~e (eines Irren) lucid intervals; im letzten ~ at the last moment, just before the end, at the eleventh hour; im rechten, richtigen ~ (just) at the right moment, in the nick of time; einen günstigen ~ wahrnehmen to watch (or wait) for one's opportunity.
augen=blicklich (͟ᴗ͟ᴗ) I a. ㉖ instantaneous, immediate; (vorübergehend) momentary; m-e ꝛe Lage my present position. — II adv. auch: augen=blicks for the moment, for the present, just now; (sofort) in a moment, immediately, instantly, on the spot.
Augenblicks=bild (͟ᴗ͟ᴗ...) n ㉒ instantaneous photograph, F snap-shot; von e-m, von et. ein ~ aufnehmen, oft: to snapshot (or kodak) a p., a th.; **=photograph** m kodakist, F snap-shooter; **=photographie** f a) instantaneous photography; b) = =bild.
Augen=bogen (͟ᴗ...) m ㉒ anat. iris; **=braue** f (eye)brow; die ~n falten, zusammenziehen to knit one's brows; **=butter** f, med. secretion from (F gum of) the eyes; **=diener** m eye-servant, toady, adulator; **=dienerei** f toadyism; **=dienst** m: a) = =dienerei; b) ⚘ = =trost b; **=entzündung** f, path. inflammation of the eye(s), ⚕ ophthalmia; **=fällig**(**keit**) = =scheinlich(keit); **=fell** n, path. film of the eye, ⚕ pterygium; **=fleck**(**en**) m speck in the eye, ⚕ leucoma; **=flimmern** n twitching of the eye; ⚘**=förmig** a. ㉖ eyeshaped, ⚕ oculiform; **=funkeln** n sparkling of the eyes, path.: ⚕ photopsia; **=geschwulst** f. path.: ⚕ exophthalmy; **=glas** n: a) allg.: eyeglass; F quizzing-glass; (Opernglucker) operaglass; (Vergrößerungsglas) magnifying glass, lens; (Fernglas) telescope; b) opt. (Okularglas) eyepiece; **=heil=anstalt** f (or ophthalmic) hospital; **=heilkunde** f: ⚕ ophthalmology; **=höhle** f socket of the eye, ⚕ orbit; die ~ betr.: orbital; **=klappe** f = =leder; **=klinik** f = =heil=anstalt; **=kneifer** F m nippers pl.; ⚘**krank** a. suffering from the eyes; **=krankheit** f eye-disease, ⚕ =leiden; **=leder** n der Pferde: winkers pl., eye-flap; **=lehre** f: ⚕ ophthalmology; **=leiden** n. path. affection of the eye; **=licht** n (eye-)sight; er verlor sein ~ he lost his sight; **=lid** n eyelid; das ~ betr.: ⚕ palpebral; **=liderkrampf** m. path.: ⚕ nystagmus; ⚘los a. eyeless; **=lust** f = =weide; **=maß** n measure taken by the eye; ein gutes ~ haben to have a correct eye; **=merk** n object in view; sein ~ auf et. richten to have a th. in view or in one's mind, to aim at a th.; **=messer** m. med. (Instrument): ⚕ ophthalmometer; **=mittel** n ophthalmic (remedy), vgl. =salbe, =wasser; **=nerv** m. anat.: ⚕ optic nerve; **=nicht**(**s**) n. pharm. (Zinkoxyd) white tutty, zinc-flowers pl.; **=operation** f operation (to be) performed on the eye(s); **=paar** n pair of eyes; **=pflege** f nursing of (or care bestowed on) the eyes; **=pulver** n: a) pharm.: ⚕ xerocollyrium; b) fig. (kleine Schrift) small print or type; diamond-type; **=punkt** m, paint. point of sight or vision; **=salbe** f eye-salve, ointment for the eyes; **=schein** m appearance; nach dem ~ (zu urteilen) according to (all) appearances, to judge from appearances, evidently, obviously; (Besichtigung) inspection, examination; et. in ~ nehmen to inspect (or examine) a th.; ⚘**scheinlich** a. visible, (self-)evident, obvious; adv. apparently, visibly, evidently, obviously, to judge from appearances; ꝛer Beweis ocular demonstration; **=scheinlichkeit** f visibility, (self-)evidence, obviousness; **=schirm** m eye-shade; **=schleim** m, **=schmalz** n = =butter; **=schmaus** m = =weide; **=schwäche** f, path. weakness of the eye(s), weak sight; **=spiegel** m: a) = =weide; b) surg. ophthalmoscope; **=sprache** f language of the eyes; **=sprosse** f am Hirschgeweih brow-antler; **=stechen** n shooting pain in the eye; **=stein** m: a) = =achat; b) pharm. = Zinkvitriol; **=stern** m, anat. pupil, iris; **=täuschung** f optical delusion; **=triefen** n running of the eyes, blear-eyedness; **=trost** m: a) = =weide; b) ⚘ eyebright, euphrasy (Euphra'sia); **=verdreher** m. fig. hypocrite; **=wasser** n eye-lotion, ⚕ collyrium; **=wassersucht** f, path.: ⚕ hydrophthalmia; **=weh** n pain in the eye(s); **=weide** f s.th. to feast one's eyes upon, delightful sight; **=weite** f range of vision; **=wimper** f eyelash; **=winkel** m, anat. corner of the eye; ⚕ canthus; **=wurz** f woodanemone (Anemo'ne nemoro'sa); **=zahn** m eye- (or canine) tooth; **=zeuge** m eyewitness; weitS. looker-on; **=zeugnis** n ocular evidence; **=zittern**, **=zucken** n, path.: ⚕ nystagmus.
Augias (͟—͟ᴗ) [grch.] npr. m. ㉖γ. myth. Augeas, Augias; fig. den ~=stall ausmisten (wie Herkules) to cleanse the Augean stables. [honeycombed.]
augig ⚔ (͟—ᴗ) a. ㉖ (blasig) porous.
äugig (͟—ᴗ) a. ㉖ 1. eyed; bsd. in Zssgn.. zB.: blau=⚔ blue-eyed. — 2. with eye-like spots, ⚕ ocellated.
Augit ⚘ (-͟—) [grch.] m ㉔c. min. augite, pyroxene; grüner ~ malacolite; **~=porphyr** m ㉔ augite porphyry.
Äuglein (͟—͟—) n ㉓ (dim. von Auge) 1. little eye. — 2. hort. bud.
Augment ⚕ (-͟—) [lt.] n ㉔b. gr. augment.

⚕ scientific; ⚘ botanical; ♁ geography; ⊕ machinery; ⚒ mining; ⚔ military; ⚓ marine; ⚙ commercial; ✉ postal; 🚂 railway.

[Augmentation] — 108 — [ausbacken]

Augmentation ⚥ (-ˇ-tſ(ˇ)ᴸ), **Augmentierung** (-ˇᴸˇ) [lt.] f ⓶ (Vermehrung) augmentation.

Augsburg ♀ (ᴵᴵˇ) npr/n. ⓾α. Augsburg; ~er (in f ㊸) m ㉒ native of Au.; ~er a., inv. of Augsburg; ~er Bekenntnis f. augsburgiſch;~er Religionsfriede (1555) the Religious Peace of Augsburg.

augsburgiſch (ᴵᴵˇˇ) a. Augsburgian; ~es Bekenntnis (abbr. öſt. A. B.), ~e Konfeſſion (1530) Augsburg Confession.

Augur (-ᴸ) [lt.] m ㉛④㊺ röm. Alt.: augur.

Augurium (-ᴸ(ˇ)ˇ) [lt.] n ㉘ (Wahrſagen) augury. weitS. prognostication.

Auguſt¹ (-ˇ) [ahd., *lt.] m ⑥ b. (month of) August; am 1. ~ on the first of August.

Auguſt² (ᴸˇ) [lt.] m I npr. ⑮⑨α. (Vn.) Augustus; dim. Guss. — II ⓒc. Zirkus: clown. — III ~a ⓺⑲α., ~e ⓾⑭β. (-ˇˇ) npr/f. (Vn.) Augusta; dim. Gussy, Gussie.

auguſte-iſch (ˇᴵˇˇ) a. ⓺ of Augustus; das ~e Zeitalter the Augustan age.

Auguſtin (ᴵˇ-) ⑮⑥α, ⓺⑭α., ~us (ˇᴵᴸˇ) ⑥γ. [lt.] npr/m. Augustin(us), Austin.

Auguſtiner (-ˇᴸˇ) [lt.] m ㉒, ~in f ㊸ eccl. Augustine (or Austin) friar, nun; ~=barfüßer (ᴸ...) m ㉒ barefooted Austin friar; =mönch m =Auguſtiner; =nonne f =Auguſtinerin; =orden m (1244) order of the Augustinians.

auguſtiſch (-ˇᴸ) a. ⓺ = auguſteiſch; ſein ~es Alter blühte der deutſchen Kunſt (SCH.) no age of patrons fostered German art.

Auguſtus (-ˇᴸˇ) [lt.] npr/m. ⑥γ. (röm. Kaiſer, 31 v. Chr. bis 14 n. Chr.) Augustus.

Auktion (-tſ(ˇ)ᴸ) [lt.] f ㊻ (Verſteigerung) (sale by) auction; public sale; in die ~ geben, tun to put up for sale, to sell by auction. [ſteigerer] auctioneer.]

Auktionator (-tſ(ˇ)-ᴸˇ) [lt.] m ㉛ (Verſ-) **auktionieren** (ˇˇ) v/a. ⑲ (verſteigern) to sell by auction, to bring to the hammer.

Auktions=ausrufer (-tſ(ˇ)ᴸ...) m ㉒ crier (at auctions); =hammer m auctioneer's hammer; =katalog m, =liſte f catalogue (of goods for sale); =kommiſſa'r m = Auktiona'tor; =lokal n auction-room.

Aufuba ♀ (ᴵ-ˇ) [jap. aoki (grün) ba (Blatt)] f ㊿ aucuba.

Aula (ᴸˇ) [grch.] f ㊾ u. ⓺ hall in universities, colleges, &c.

Aurat ⚥ (-ᴸ) [lt.] n ⓒc. chm. (Goldſäureſalz) aurate.

Aurel (-ᴸ) [lt.] npr/m. ⓾④α. (Vn.) = ~ius, ~ia (-ᴸˇˇ) ⑤⓾., ~i-e (ˇ) npr/f. ⓾④β. (Vn.) Aurelia; ~ius (-ᴸ(ˇ)ˇ) npr/m. ⑥γ. (Vn.) Aurelius.

Auren-kraut ♀ (ᴵᴵᴸ) [lt.] n ㉒ = Tauſendgüldenkraut (echtes).

Aureole (-ˇᴸˇ) [fr.] f ㊽ (Strahlenkranz) aureola (auch ast.).

Aurikel ♀ (-ᴸ) [lt. Öhrchen] f ㊽ bear's ear; French cowslip (Pri'mula auri'cula).

Aurin (-ᴸ) [lt.] n ⓒc. 1. chm. (gelber Farbſtoff) aurin ($C_{19}H_{14}O_3$). — 2. ♀ roter ~ = Tauſendgüldenkraut (echtes).

Auripigment ⚥ (-ˇˇᴸ) [lt.] n ⓒb. min. orpiment; yellow sulphide of arsenic, arsenious sulphide (As_2S_3).

Aurora (-ᴸˇ) [lt.] f ⓺⓾α.,㊾β. (Morgenröte) dawn (of day); als npr/f., myth. Aurora. [= v. w. o.]

a. u. s. abbr. = lt. a'ctum ut su'pra]

---

aus(ᴸ) [ahd.: out] I (ant. in) prp. mit dat., meiſt durch out of, from, off, of, by, for, &c. gegeben. 1. Hervor-gehen, -kommen: oft ~ ... heraus: ~ der Kirche kommen to come out of church; Waſſer ſpringt ~ der Erde (heraus) water wells up from the earth; ~ dem Fenſter ſehen to look through (or out of) the window; ~ einem Glaſe trinken to drink out of a glass; e-n ~ dem Hauſe werfen to turn a p. out (of doors) e-n ~ dem Graben ziehen to pull a p. out of the ditch; das Schwert ~ der Scheide ziehen to draw one's sword from the scabbard; e-m ~ dem Wege gehen to go out of a p.'s way; geh mir ~ den Augen! out of my sight! — 2. Aufhören: ~ den Angeln off the hinges, ~ den Fugen, ~ dem Leim out of joint; er iſt ~ der Lehre (hat ausgelernt) he has served his apprenticeship; ~ der Mode out of fashion. — 3. Herſtammung, Quelle: er iſt ~ London he comes from London, is a native of Lo.; ich entnehme ~ Ihrem Briefe I observe (or understand) from your letter; ich will e-n Künſtler ~ ihm machen I want to make him an artist; man ſieht ~ ſeinem Briefe one can see (or judge) by his letter; ~ einer alten Familie ſtammen to descend (or come) from an ancient stock; er ſtammte ~ dem Volke he was of humble (or lowly) origin; ~ dem Franzöſiſchen überſetzt translated from the French; was iſt ~ ihm geworden? what has become of him?; es iſt nichts ~ der Sache geworden nothing has come of it, the scheme has failed or has fallen to the ground. — 4. Zuſammenſetzung: ~ Gold (gemacht) (made) of gold; ~ Holz bauen to build (out) of wood; das Waſſer beſteht ~ Waſſerſtoff und Sauerſtoff water consists of hydrogen and oxygen; einen ~ ihrer Mitte wählen to choose one from among their number; ~ unſerer Mitte from among ourselves. — 5. Beweggrund: ~ freier Wahl of one's own free choice; ~ Mitleid, Neugier from (or out of) pity, curiosity; ~ Furcht vor for fear of; ~ dieſem Grunde for this reason; ~ reiner Torheit, Unwiſſenheit through sheer folly, ignorance; ~ Vorſicht as a (matter of) precaution, to make sure; mit Zeitwörtern: ſie macht ſich nichts ~ ihm she does not care for him. — 6. Art und Weiſe: ~ vollem Halſe ſchreien to shout at the top of one's voice; ~ freier Hand zeichnen to draw freehand; ~ dem Kopfe, Gedächtnis by rote, from memory; ~ allen Kräften with might and main; ⚥ ~ erſter (zweiter) Hand kaufen to buy (at) first (second) hand. — II adv. 7. ... ~aus mit s. zu einem adv. verſchmelzend: jahr-~; jahr-ein from one year's end to another; year after year; land-~, land-ein in every part of the globe. — 8. von ... ~: von da (oder von dieſer Stelle) aus (from) hence, from this place; von Grund ~ thoroughly; von Hauſe ~ originally; von Hauſe ~ arm ſein to start with no property (of one's own); von dieſem Standpunkte

---

~ from this point of view. — 9. (zu Ende) ~ ſein to be out or over or finished or at an end; es iſt ~ mit ihm it is all over with him; he is done for; die Flaſche iſt ~ (geleert) the bottle is empty; die Kirche iſt ~ church is over. — 10. ell. mit zu ergänzendem v.: ~ (war) ſein Ringen! his struggles were over!; (trinke) ~ bis zur Neige! drink up (your glass)!; er iſt ~ (gegangen) he is out. — 11. ~ und ein (gehen) to go and come; er weiß nicht ~ und ein, weder ein noch ~ he does not know which way to turn, he is in a (tight) corner or at his wits' end.

aus-... (ᴵᴵ...) Vorſilbe in Zſſgn mit verbs immer trennbar (**): 1. Hervor-gehen, -kommen, z.B. Kriechen to crawl forth (ant. ein-...). — 2. Vollendung, Abſchluß, z.B. Leſen to finish (or cease) reading. — 3. Wahl, z.B. Suchen to select. — 4. Veröffentlichung: Läuten to announce by bell - ringing. — 5. Schauſtellung, z.B. Kramen to display, to exhibit.

aus-ackern (ᴵᴵˇ) v/a. ⓐ** to plough up or thoroughly. [überantworten.]

aus-antworten ⚊ (ᴵᴵˇᴸˇ) v/a. ⓐ** =]

aus-apern ſchwz. (ᴵᴵˇᴸ) v/a. ⓐ** (ſchneefrei machen) to clear of (the) snow.

aus-arbeiten (ᴵᴵˇᴸˇ) ⓐ** I v/n. (h.) 1. to cease working; von Wein ꝛc. auch: to cease fermenting. — II v/a. 2. to work out; (vollkommen m.) to elaborate, to perfect; ſchriftlich: to compose; einen Plan ~ to draw up a scheme; ſein ausgearbeitet highly finished, elaborate; (abrichten) to break in, to train. — 3. ⊕ to work; (geſtalten) to fashion; aus dem gröbſten: to rough-hew; (ausmeißeln) to carve, to engrave. — III ſich ~ v/refl. 4. ſich (körperlich) tüchtig ~ to exert o.s. to the utmost, to work with all one's might, to do hard (or solid) work. — IV ~ n ㉓ u. A/ung f ㊻ 5. elaboration; ſchriftliche A/ung composition; (Dreſſierung des Pferdes) breaking-in, training.

aus-arten (ᴵᴵˇˇ) I v/n. (ſn.) v/refl. ⓐ** (ſich) ~ in to degenerate into; ihr Jauchzen artete in Geheul aus their exultation was turned (or converted) into howling; ausgeartete Sitten f/pl. loose (or degenerate, depraved) morals pl. — II ~ n ㉓ u. Aus-artung f ㊻ degeneracy, deterioration; (Entſittlichung) depravity, decadence.

aus-äſte(l)n (ᴵᴵˇ) ⓐ (ⓐ)ᴸ** I v/a., hort. einen Baum: to disbranch, to cut the branches off (a tree), to prune. — II ſich ~ v/refl. (verzweigen) to ramify. — III ~ n ㉓ und Aus-äſt(el)ung f ㊻ pruning; (Verzweigung) ramification.

aus-atm/en (ᴵᴵˇ) ⓐ** I v/n. (h.) 1. (ant. einatmen) to breathe forth, to exhale. — 2. fig. (ſterben) to breathe one's last, to expire. — II v/a. 3. die Luft aus~ und ein-atmen to breathe; Düfte: to exhale. — III ſich ~ v/refl. 4. (verſchnaufen) to recover one's breath, to take breath or rest. — IV ~ n ㉓ u. A/ung f ㊻ 5. breathing, exhalation; Aus- und Ein-atmen respiration.

aus-ätſchen F (ᴵᴵˇ) v/a. ⓐ** to jeer (at), to chaff, quiz, tease, mock.

aus-backen (ᴵᴵˇ) v/a. u. v/n. (h. u. ſn) ⓺b**

Zeichen (i. S. XVII): F familiär; P Volksſprache; ⌐ Gaunerſprache; ⚊ ſelten; † alt (auch geſtorben); * neu (auch geboren); ⚌ unrichtig;

[ausbaden] — 109 — [ausbleichen]

1. to bake sufficiently or thoroughly; nicht ausgebacken slack-baked. — 2. ausgebacken haben to have done baking.
aus-baden (⁂) ⊛** I v/n. (h.) 1. to have done bathing. — II v/a. 2. (ausspülen) to rinse, to wash. — 3. fig. (für et. büßen) et. ⸺ to suffer for a p.'s fault.
aus-baggern ⊕ (⁂) v/a. ⊛a** e-n Hafen 2c.: to dredge, to deepen by dredging.
aus-baken ⸸ (⁂) ⊛** to mark (out) by means of beacons or buoys.
aus-baldowern P (⁂) [⁂] v/a. ⊛a*/* (austundischaften) to spy (or ferret) out; Diebesgelegenheiten: to put up a job.
aus-balgen, aus-bälgen (⁂) v/a. ⊛** 1. to skin, flay. — 2. (ausstopfen) to stuff.
Aus-balger, -bälger (⁂) m ㉒, ~in f ㊼ (bird-)stuffer, ⚔ taxidermist. [bale.\
aus-ballen (⁂) v/a. ⊛** to unpack, un-\
aus-ballottieren (⁂⁂) v/a. ⊛*/* (durch Abstimmung ausstoßen) to blackball.
Aus-bau (⁂) m ⓓd. 1. innerer: completion of (the interior of) a building; fig. final development, extension, consolidation. — 2. ⚒ e-s Ganges: working; ~(ung f) der Gruben timbering (and walling), casing; wasserdichter: tubbing. — 3. arch. (Erker) jetty; (Fensternische) bay(-window); einer Kirche: exedra.
aus-bauchen (⁂) ⊛** I v/a. to belly (or puff) out; to swell; (ausweiten) to widen out; erhaben od. vertieft ⸺ to emboss, to chase. — II v/n. (in) u. sich ⸺ v/refl. die Mauer baucht aus the wall bulges (out), (springt vor) juts out; arch. ausgebauchter Gang arched way. — III ~ n ㉓ u. Aus-bauchung f ㊼ belly(ing); e-r Säule: swelling, ⚔ entasis.
aus-bauen (⁂) ⊛** I v/a. 1. (fertig bauen) to finish (the interior of a building, a railway-line, &c.), to complete; fig. to develop, extend, consolidate. — 2. (ausbessern) to repair; arch. wieder ⸺ to restore. — 3. (vorspringend bauen) to build out. — 4. (erschöpfen) agr. und ⚒ to exhaust. — II v/n. (h.) 5. to cease building. — III ~ n ㉓ u. Ausbauung f ㊼ 6. completion; restoration; exhaustion; f. Ausbau 2. [bulge) out.\
aus-bauschen (⁂) v/a. ⊛** to puff (or/
aus-bedingen (⁂) ⊛t*/* 1. to stipulate. — 2. sich (dat.) et. ⸺ to reserve a th. to o.s.; dies ausbedungen (ausgenommen) with this exception or reservation. — II ~ n ㉓ und Aus-bedingung f ㊼ 3. stipulation, reservation.
aus-beeren (⁂) v/a. ⊛** to strip of berries; to pick the b. off springes.
aus-beichten (⁂) ⊛** I v/a. 1. et. ⸺ to make a full confession of s.th. — 2. e-n ⸺ to question a p. closely. — II v/n. (h.) 3. to finish confessing.
aus-beißen (⁂) ⊛a** I v/a. 1. to bite out; sich (dat.) einen Zahn ⸺ to break (off) a tooth (in biting). — 2. (vertreiben) to drive away by biting; fig. (verdrängen) to supplant (a rival). — II v/n. 3. ⚒ (vorragen) to crop out.
aus-beizen (⁂) v/a. ⊛** to remove with caustics or corrosives; to cauterize.
aus-bersten (⁂) v/n. ⊛e** ⊛t. (f. bersten) in Lachen ⸺ to burst out laughing.
Aus-besserer (⁂) m ㉒, Aus-besse(re)rin f ㊼ mender, repairer; (Flicker) botcher,

patcher; vamper; (Flickschneider) jobbing tailor; (Flickschuster) cobbler; ~ in v. Wäsche: needlewoman, v. Strümpfen: darner.
aus-besser/n (⁂) I v/a. ⊛a** 1. to mend, to repair; Kunstwerke: to restore. — 2. (flicken) to patch up (clothes), to cobble or vamp (boots); (stopfen) to darn (stockings); (nachbessern) to retouch or touch up (pictures); to correct (an essay); (aufputzen) to trim up (a bonnet); ⸸ to refit (ships); ich ließ meine Uhr ⸺ I had my watch mended or repaired or seen to. — II ~ n ㉓ u. Aus-besserung f ㊼ 3. mending, &c.; sich in ~ befinden to be under (or to undergo) repair.
Aus-besserungs-kosten (⁂...) pl. ㉖ expenses pl. of repair; repairs pl.
aus-beten (⁂) v/n. (h.) u. v/a. ⊛** to finish praying; to pray to the end.
aus-betten (⁂) v/a. ⊛** Gäste: to bed (or sleep) out (of the house).
Aus-beute (⁂) f ㊼ produce, gain, yield; ⚒ output; (Gewinn) reichliche ~ geben to give good results, to pay well; ⚒ e-e ~ liefernde Zeche, a. ~zeche (⁂...) f ㉝ productive (or paying) mine.
aus-beuteln (⁂) v/a. ⊛** 1. ⊕ Müllerei: to bolt. — 2. F fig. (ausgeben) to spend, to disburse. — 3. F (a. v/refl.) e-n ⸺ (von Geld entblößen) to drain a p.'s purse, to fleece (or bleed) a p.; sich ⸺ F to part with one's cash.
aus-beut/en (⁂) I v/a. ⊛** to put (or turn) to (good) account; agr. to cultivate, to farm; ⚒ eine Mine: to work; fig. et. für seine Zwecke ⸺ to make capital out of a th., to exploit a th.; Arbeiter ⸺ to grind down (or sweat, drive) workmen. — II ~ n ㉓ = A/ung.
Aus-beuter m ㉒, ~in f ㊼ exploiter; v. Arbeitern oft: sweater, slave-driver, v. Möbelarbeitern a.: slaughterer.
Aus-beutertum (⁂~)n㉓d.Arbeitersprache: sweating (system), slave-driving.
Aus-beutung (⁂) f ㊼ agr. cultivation, farming; ⚒ mining, fig. exploitation; v. Arbeitern: sweating.
Aus-beutungs-feld ⚒ (⁂...) n ㉒ mining-claim; -kosten pl. working expenses pl.; -system n sweating (or grinding) system, slave-driving.
aus-bezahl/en (⁂) I v/a. ⊛*/* to pay in full, to pay off; to make up the full amount; in e-r Bank 2c.: to pay over the counter; ⊛ sofort to pay cash down. — II ~ n ㉓ u. A/ung f ㊼ payment.
aus-biegen (⁂) ⊛a** I v/a. to bend (or turn) out(wards); (ausweiten) to widen, expand. — II v/n. (jn) e-m Wagen ⸺ (ausweichen) to make room for, to get out of the way of ...; ⚄ e-n Zug ⸺ lassen to shunt a train.
aus-bieten (⁂) ⊛a** I v/a. 1. zum Verkauf: ⸺ to exhibit for sale; billig ⸺ to offer at a cheap rate; laut u. öffentlich ⸺ to hawk about (one's wares). — 2. (überbieten) to outbid —. II sich ⸺ v/refl.3.to offer one's services publicly. — III ~ n ㉓ 4. = Ausbietung.
Aus-bieter (⁂) m ㉒ one who offers s.th. for sale; auctioneer. [hawking.\
Aus-bietung (⁂) f ㊼ display of goods;/
aus-bilden (⁂) ⊛** I v/a. und v/refl. (sich) ⸺ to form (o.s.); entwickelnd: to

develop (o.s.); vervollkommnend: to (grow) perfect; den Geist: to cultivate, to improve; lehrend: to instruct; verfeinernd: to polish; ⚔ to drill, to exercise; sich zum Advokaten ⸺ to study (or qualify) for the law; ein Geschwür bildet sich aus an ulcer is gathering or growing to a head. — II ~ n ㉓ = Ausbildung.
Aus-bildung (⁂) f ㊼ formation, development; cultivation; med. ~ e-s Geschwürs gathering of an ulcer; ⚔ ~ in Abteilungen drilling in sections, squad exercise; praktische ~ practical instruction; theoretische ~ (Dienstunterricht) theoretical instruction; von Personen: instruction, education, (professional) training, polish(ing).
aus-binden (⁂) v/a. ⊛** 1. et. ⸺ to untie and take out of a parcel. — 2. ⊕ arch. to assemble, to join; typ. die Kolumne ⸺ to tie up the column.
Aus-biß (⁂) m ⓓa. geol. = Ausstrich.
aus-bitten (⁂) v/a. ⊛** 1. sich (dat.) et. ⸺ to ask (or beg) for a th.; sich von e-m eine Gunst ⸺ to solicit a favour of a p.; darf ich mir die Ehre ⸺, Sie zu begleiten? may I have the honour of accompanying you?; das bitte ich mir aus, will ich mir ausgebeten h. I (must) insist on that; verbietend: du rührst es nicht an, das bitte ich mir aus! I won't allow you to (or have you) touch it!, don't you touch it (on any account)! — 2. ausgebeten (eingeladen) sein to be invited (or asked) out. [off tap.\
Aus-blase-hahn ⊕ (⁂...) m ㉒ blow-/
aus-blasen (⁂) [ahd.] v/a.⊛a** 1. ein Ei ⸺ to blow an egg. — 2. (ausdehnen) to extend (or puff out) by blowing. — 3. (auslöschen) to blow out (a candle); e-m das Lebenslicht ⸺ to kill a p., P to put out a p.'s light, to do for a p. — 4. (verkündigen) to proclaim by sound of trumpet. — 5. (zu Ende blasen) to cease blowing (a wind-instrument). — 6. ⊕ e-n Dampfkessel ⸺ to blow off a boiler; metall. den Hochofen ⸺ to blow (out) the furnace; typ. den Setzkasten m. d. Blasebalg ⸺ to clear (or cleanse) the letter-case by means of ...
aus-blättern (⁂) v/a. ⊛a** 1. to turn over (all) the leaves (of a book). — 2. to pluck off the leaves (of a plant).
aus-bleiben (⁂) I v/n. (in) ⊛** 1. to stay away, to fail to come, not to appear; er blieb lange aus he did not come till late; ich werde nicht lange ⸺ I shall not be long (in coming); die ganze Nacht ⸺ to stay (or stop) out all night; das kann nicht ⸺ it must come to this (in the end); die englische Post ist ausgeblieben the English mail has not come in or is overdue. — 2. ⊛ mit der Zahlung ⸺ to be in arrear (with one's payment); jur. (nicht erscheinen) to make default; med. das Fieber bleibt aus ... intermits, hit ganz ausgeblieben ... has left me. — II ~ n ㉓ 3. staying away; non-appearance; der Post 2c.: non-arrival; der Zahlung: non-payment; jur. (Richterscheinen vor Gericht) default; vorsätzliches: contempt of court, contumacy.
aus-bleichen (⁂) I v/n. (in) ⊛a** to fade. — II v/a. ⊛** to bleach out.

♪ Musik; ⚔ Wissenschaft; ⚘ Pflanze; ⚱ Geographie; ⊕ Technik; ⚒ Bergbau; ⚔ Militär; ⸸ Marine; ⊛ Handel; ⛨ Post; ⚄ Eisenbahn.

[ausbleien]

aus-bleien (ᵘᴸ˅) v/a. ⓢ** to (fill with) lead; Zähne ≗ (plombieren) to stop ...
Aus-blick (ᵘᴳ) m ⓓc. look-out, prospect.
aus-blitzen (ᵘᴸ˅) v/n.(h.)⓽⁰** es hat ausgeblitzt the lightning has ceased.
aus-blühen (ᵘᴸ˅) ⓢ** I v/n. (h., jn) 1. a) to cease blooming or blossoming; fig. to fade; b) to blossom forth. — 2. min. (auswittern) to effloresce. — II ~ n ㉓ u. **Aus-blühung** f ㊻ 3. last bloom; min. efflorescence.
aus-bluten (ᵘᴸ˅) ⓢ** I v/n. (h.) to cease bleeding. — II v/a. s-n Leben ≗ to shed one's life-blood, to bleed to death.
aus-bohren ⊙ (ᵘᴸ˅) ⓢ** I v/a. 1. to bore up or out; to drill; Schraubenmutter: to worm, tap; trichterförmig: to chamfer. — 2. (herausschaffen) den Spund (aus dem Fasse) ≗ to draw the bung (with a gimlet). — II v/n. (h.) 3. to finish boring.
aus-boyen ↓ (ᵘᴸ˅) v/a. ⓢ**e-e Sandbank 2c.: to indicate ... by means of buoys.
aus-borgen (ᵘᴸ˅) v/a. ⓢ** to lend out.
aus-bracken (ᵘᴸ˅) v/a. ⓢ** (Vieh 2c.: ausmerzen) to separate from the rest.
aus-braten (ᵘᴸ˅) ⓢa** I v/n. 1. (jn) to run out in roasting. — 2.(h.) to roast well. — II v/a.3.to roast thoroughly; Schmalz ≗ to let the dripping run off (the joint).
aus-brauchen(ᵘᴸ˅)v/a.ⓢ**1. = aufbrauchen. — 2. ausgebraucht h. (nicht mehr brauchen) to use no more; to put aside.
aus-brausen (ᵘᴸ˅) v/n. (h.) u. v/refl. ⓽⁰** vom Winde 2c.: (sich) ≗ to cease roaring; von Gärendem: to cease fermenting; fig. to calm (or settle, cool) down.
aus-brechen(ᵘᴸ˅)[mhd.]ⓐa** I v/a.1. to break (out) with an effort, to force out; hort. Äste, Bäume ≗ to prune (or lop) a tree; ⊙ das Bier ≗ to pour ... from the boiler into the trough; Erbsen: to shell; ⚒ e-n Gang ≗ to work a lode; Honig aus den Bienenstöcken ≗ to cut the honey-combs; überflüssige Knospen ≗ to nip off the buds; Steinbruch: Marmor 2c.: to quarry; ein Messer: to notch; ⚒ e-n Schacht: to sink; Wachs ≗ s. Honig ≗; e-n Zahn: to take (or pull) out; die Zähne aus e-m Kamm ≗ to break off the teeth of a comb. — 2. (erbrechen) to bring (or throw) up; das Ausgebrochene vomit. — 3. hunt. Wildschwein: den Boden nach Fraß ≗ (aufwühlen) to root up the soil. — II v/n. (jn) 4. (hervortreten) (aus dem Gefängnis) ≗ to break out of prison, to escape (from prison); von Gewässern: to overflow (the banks); ⚔ (einen Ausfall m.) to sally forth, to make a sortie; Rennsport: to leave the racecourse. — 5. fig. (plötzlich entstehen) von Feuer, Krieg, Aufruhr, Krankheit: to break out; to arise, originate; vom Gewitter: to break; ihm brach ein heftiger Schweiß aus he broke out in a violent perspiration, he was in a bath of perspiration; ● es sind zwei Fallimente ausgebrochen two houses have stopped payment or have been declared bankrupt, there have been two failures. — 6. in et. (acc.) ≗: in ein Gelächter ≗ to burst out laughing; in Klagen ≗ to utter lamentations; in Tränen ≗ to break out (or burst) into tears. —

III ~ n ㉓ 7. e-s Zahnes: extraction; v. Bruchsteinen: quarrying; Erbrechen: vomiting; ~ aus dem Gefängnisse: breaking-out of prison; ⚔ (Ausfall) sortie.
aus-breit/en(ᵘᴸ˅)I v/a.u.v/refl.ⓢ**1.(sich) ≗ über (acc..a.dat.) to spread, expand, extend; die Arme, Flügel: to stretch out; (aus-ea.-falten) to display, unfold; das Land breitet sich vor uns aus the landscape unfolds itself to our view; ⊙ typ. die Druckbogen ≗ (aushängen) to hang up the proofs; ↓ die Segel: to spread; sich weiter ≗ to gain ground, to make headway. — 2. (in Umlauf setzen) to circulate or promulgate (news), to spread abroad; Kenntnisse: to diffuse; (zerstreuen) to disseminate; (fortpflanzen) to propagate; die Kunde breitete sich rasch aus the news was soon in everybody's mouth. — II ~ n ㉓ 3. A/ung. — III aus-gebreitet p.p.u.a. ⓺⁶ 4. extended; ⚘ (abstehend) ⚯ patulous; ≗e Bekanntschaft, Verbindungen extensive circle of friends, large connexion.
Aus-breiter (ᵘᴸ˅) m ㉒, ~in f ㊻ (f. ausbreiten) spreader; disseminator.
Aus-breitung (ᵘᴸ˅) f ㊻ expansion, extension; circulation, promulgation; diffusion; dissemination; propagation; e-r Seuche: spread; ≗s-fähig (≗...) a. ⓺⁶ diffusible; ~s-sucht f ㊷ proselytism; propagandism.
aus-brennen (ᵘᴸ˅) ⓢb** I v/a. 1. to burn, Ziegel: to bake; e-m die Augen ≗ to burn out a p.'s eyes; fig. dem Tage die Augen ≗ (bei Tage Licht brennen) to burn daylight. — 2. surg. e-e Wunde: to cauterize; ⊙ Fässer: (ausschwefeln) to sulphur; ⚒ artill. das Zündloch 2c.: to enlarge. — 3. auch v/n. (h.) (fertig brennen) to finish burning (bricks) or baking (pottery). — II v/n. 4. (h.) s. 3. — 5. (in) to cease burning; das Feuer ≗ lassen to let the fire go (or drop) out; ausgebrannter Vulkan extinct volcano. — 6. (inwendig verbrennen) to be internally consumed by fire, von Häusern, a..: to be gutted. — III ~ n ㉓ 7. burning (out); surg. cauterization; ⚒ artill. ~ der Rohrseele 2c.: enlargement.
aus-bringen (ᵘᴸ˅) v/a. ⓢ**1.(fortschaffen) to bring out, to get off; ↓ ein Boot ≗ to hoist out a boat; den Anker mit dem Boote ≗ to boat an anchor. — 2. e-n Fleck(en) ≗ to get out a stain. — 3. e-e Gesundheit ≗ to give a toast; j-s Gesundheit ≗ to propose (or drink) a p.'s health, to toast a p. — 4. Junge ≗ (ausbrüten) to hatch ... — 5. ⊙ typ. e-e Zeile ≗ (durch weitläufigeres Setzen) ant. einbringen 3) to space out a line.
Aus-bringer (ᵘᴸ˅) m ㉒, ~in f ㊻ eines Trinkspruches proposer of a toast.
Aus-bruch (ᵘᴸch) m ⓓd. 1. = ausbrechen III. — 2. eines Vulkans: eruption; e-s Aufruhrs: outbreak; e-r Krankheit: breaking out, outbreak; einer Leidenschaft: (out)burst; ~ des Wahnsinns fit of madness; zum ~(e) kommen to break (or burst) out, to appear; nicht zum ~ kommen lassen to nip in the bud, to prevent (from breaking out). — 3. (hochfeiner Wein) wine from picked grapes; (Vorlauf) wine of the first press.

[ausdauern]

aus-brühen (ᵘᴸ˅) v/a. ⓢ** to scald.
aus-brüllen (ᵘᴸ˅) v/n. (h.) ⓢ** 1. to roar aloud. — 2. to cease roaring.
aus-brüten (ᵘᴸ˅) ⓢ** I v/a. 1. Eier: to sit on, künstlich: to incubate; Küchlein: to hatch; Krankheiten: to breed. — 2. fig. (ersinnen) to hatch out, to concoct, to plot. — II v/n. (h.) 3. to cease hatching. — III ~ n ㉓ u. **Aus-brütung** f ㊻ 4. hatch(ing); incubation.
aus-buchsen, aus-büchsen ⊙ (ᵘᴸtʃ˅) v/a. ⓽⁰** eine Nabe 2c.: to box.
aus-buchten (ᵘᴸ˅) v/a. ⓢ** to bend outwards; ↓ eine ausgebuchtete Küste a coast with many bays and inlets, an indented coast-line. — II **Aus-buchtung** f ㊻ der Küste 2c.: indentation.
aus-buddeln P (ᵘᴸ˅) v/a. ⓟa** to scratch out of the ground; vgl. auskratzen.
aus-bügeln (ᵘᴸ˅) ⓟa** I v/a. 1. Falten ≗ to press (or smooth) creases by ironing. — 2. to iron thoroughly. — II v/n. (h.) 3. to cease ironing.
aus-bühnen ⚒ (ᵘᴸ˅) ⓢ** e-n Schacht ≗ (austonnen) to brattice or line ...
Aus-bund (ᵘᴸ) m ⓓc. meist F fig. (Muster) pattern (of excellence); paragon (of beauty); prodigy (of wisdom, learning); er ist der ~ von ihnen allen he is the best (or worst) of them all; ein ~ von Narrheit, Tollheit an out-and-out fool; a madcap; ein ~ von Schurke(rei) an arrant knave. [quisite, select.)
aus-bündig F (ᵘᴸ˅) a. ⓺⁶ excellent, ex-⌐
Aus-bürger †(~) m ㉒ (nicht in der Stadt wohnend) non-resident citizen; suburban.
aus-bürsten (ᵘᴸ˅) v/a. ⓢ** einen Rock ≗ to brush a coat (thoroughly); ⊙ typ. die Form ≗ to brush the form.
aus-büßen (ᵘᴸ˅) ⓽⁰** I v/a. 1. to expiate, to atone (or make amends) for. — 2. (ausbessern) to repair, to do up. — II v/n. (h.) 3.to make full atonement, to complete one's time of penance; er hat ausgebüßt his sufferings are over.
aus-buttern (ᵘᴸ˅) ⓟa** I v/a. viel aus der Milch ≗ to get much butter by churning. — II v/n. (h.) to leave off churning.
aus-dämmen ⊙ (ᵘᴸ˅) v/a. ⓢ** 1. Gießerei: die Formen ≗ to repair the moulding. — 2. Wasserbaukunst: to dam out.
aus-dampfen (ᵘᴸ˅) ⓢ** I v/n. (jn) 1. to pass off as vapour; to steam away. — 2.to cease steaming. — II v/a. 3. to evaporate. — III ~ n ㉓ 4. = A/ung.
aus-dämpfen (ᵘᴸ˅) v/a. ⓢ** 1. (ausdampfen m.) to cause to evaporate. — 2. (auslöschen) Kohlen: to damp out, smother. — 3. (durch Dampf austreiben) to expel by steam(ing); to smoke out.
Aus-dampfung (ᵘᴸ˅) f ㊻ steaming off, evaporation. [&c. (= ausweichen 1).)
aus-därmen(ᵘᴸ˅)v/a.ⓢ**to eviscerate,⌐
Aus-dauer (ᵘᴸ˅) f ㊸ (ohne pl.) perseverance, persistence; (Fleiß) assiduity; (Ausharren) endurance, steadiness, tenacity of purpose; von Pferden 2c.: haben to have (great) staying power.
aus-dauern (ᵘᴸ˅) ⓢa** I v/n. (h.) 1. to persevere, (beharren) to persist, hold out, last; Sport: to stay. — 2. ⚘ von Pflanzen: to be perennial. — II v/a. 3. (ertragen) to endure. — III ≗d p.p. u. a. ⓺⁶ 4. persevering; persistent;

Signs (see page XVII): F familiar; P vulgar; ꜝ flash; ⚮ rare; † obsolete (died); * new word (born); ₊* incorrect; ♪ music;

[ausdehnbar] — 111 — [auseinandergehen]

(gebulbig) patient, enduring. — 5. ♃ (das ganze Jahr dauernd) perennial.
aus-dehnbar (ᴵᴵ◡-) *a.* ⁶⁶ dehnbar, *phys.* = verdünnbar; ~**keit** (ᴵᴵ--) *f* ⁴⁶ (o. *pl.*) = Dehnbarkeit; *phys.* = Verdünnbarkeit.
aus-dehn/en (ᴵᴵ◡) **I** *v/a.* u. *v/refl.* ⁶⁸** (ſich) ♃ 1. allg.: to stretch, extend, expand; (breiter m., w.) to enlarge, widen out, distend; ([ſich] verlängern) to lengthen, zeitlich: to prolong; ſich ♃ (wachſen) to increase; die Wärme dehnt Metalle aus heat expands metals; Gold dehnt ſich unter dem Hammer aus gold spreads … — 2. *fig.* ſein Geſchäft ♃ to enlarge one's business; eine Erzählung ♃ to spin out a (long) yarn. — **II** ~ *n* ²³ 3. = A/ung 1. — **III** (ſich) ♃b *p.pr.* u. *a.* ⁶⁶ 4. extending; ſich weit ♃b expansive; far-reaching. — **IV aus-gedehnt** *p.p.* u. *a.* ⁶⁶ 5. extensive; wide(-spread); vast; *v.* Erzählungen (long) drawn-out; ♃ Praxis large (or considerable) connexion; in ♃em Sinne in the widest sense (of the word).
Aus-dehnung (ᴵᴵ--) *f* ⁴⁶ 1. extension; enlargement; in die Breite: widening; in die Länge: lengthening; *phys.* dilatation; expansion. — 2. *geom.*, &c. dimension; ~ (Rauminhalt) feſter Körper (solid) contents *pl.*; ein Werk ꝛc. von großer ~ … of large range.
Aus-dehnungs-koeffizient (∠…) *m* ⁶² *phys.* coefficient of expansion; **=kraft** *f*, **=vermögen** *n* expansive force.
aus-denken (ᴵᴵ◡) ⁶⁷** **I** *v/a.* ſich (*dat.*) et. ♃ to imagine (or devise) s.th.; to contrive (or invent) a th.; Gedanken ♃ to ponder over …; das Unglück läßt ſich gar nicht ♃ … cannot be conceived, baffles our imagination. — **II** *v/n.* (h.) to cease thinking.
aus-deuten (ᴵᴵ◡) **I** *v/a.* ⁶⁹** Träume ꝛc.: to explain, interpret, expound, (entziffern) to decipher; et. falſch ♃ to misinterpret (or to put a wrong construction on) a th. — **II** ~ *n* ²³ u. **Aus-deutung** *f* ⁴⁶ explanation; interpretation.
aus-dichten¹ (ᴵᴵ◡) [dichten²] *v/n.* (h.) ⁶⁹** to cease writing poetry.
aus-dichten² ⚓ (ᴵᴵ◡) [dicht¹] *v/a.* ⁶⁹** (kalfatern) to caulk, to make tight.
aus-dielen ⊕ (ᴵᴵ◡) *v/a.* ⁶⁶ to board, to plank; den Fußboden: to floor.
aus-dienen (ᴵᴵ◡) **I** *v/n.* (h.) ⁶⁸** (ſeine Zeit) ♃ to serve (or complete) one's time; der Rock hat ausgedient … has seen its best days. — **II aus-gedient** *p.p.* u. *a.* ⁶⁶ no longer fit for service, superannuated; *v.* Beamten: pensioned off, retired; ♃er Profeſſor emeritus professor; ⚔ time-expired, veteran.
aus-dingen (ᴵᴵ◡) *v/a.* ⓘft*** = ausbedingen.
aus-docken ⚓ (ᴵᴵ◡) *v/a.* ⁶⁶ ein Schiff:⌋ [to undock.⌋
aus-donnern (ᴵᴵ◡) *v/n.* (h.) ⓶a** to cease thundering, *fig.* to cease scolding.
aus-dorren (ᴵᴵ◡) *v/n.* (ſn) ⁶⁸** to dry up, to wither; *fig.* to pine away.
aus-dörren (ᴵᴵ◡) **I** *v/a.* ⁶⁸** to dry up, parch, scorch; (austrocknen) to season (timber). — **II aus-gedörrt** *p.p.* dried up, parched; sapless (plant); arid (region).
aus-drechſeln (ᴵᴵ◡ᵗʸᵖ) *v/a.* ⓶a** 1. to hollow out (or finish) by turning on a lathe. — 2. *fig.* to finish with care; ausgedrechſelt well (or accurately) made. [(in)side-tool.⌋
Aus-dreh-ſtahl (ᴵᴵ…) *m* ⁶² ⊕ Drechſlerei:⌋
aus-drehen (ᴵᴵ◡) ⁶⁸** **I** *v/a.* 1. = ausdrechſeln. — 2. (auslöſchen) eine Lampe, das Gas: to turn off; to put out, das elektriſche Licht: to switch off. — **II** ſich ♃ *v/refl.* 3. die Schraube hat ſich (od. iſt) ausgedreht … has lost its grip; the thread of the screw is worn out.
aus-dreſchen (ᴵᴵ◡) ⓔ (a. ⁷⁵b)** **I** *v/a.* 1. Korn, Garben, a. *abs.*: to thrash (or beat) out; *fig.* ausgedroſch(e)nes Stroh hackneyed saying, trite remark. — 2. (durch Dreſchen erhalten) to obtain by thrashing. — 3. F *fig.* (prügeln) to thrash soundly. — **II** *v/n.* (h.) 4. ſ. 1; ausgedroſchen h. to have done thrashing.
Aus-druck (ᴵᴵ◡) *m* ⓒc. *fig.* 1. expression (auch *math.*); in allgemeinen Ausdrücken in general terms; beſchönigender ~ euphemism; bildlicher ~ figure of speech; gemeiner ~ vulgarism; veralteter ~ archaism; zum ~ bringen to give expression (or voice) to, to express, to put into words, to voice. — 2. (~sweiſe) diction, style; (Redewendung) phrase, (Ausſprache) articulation; redneriſch: elocution; ſchwülſtiger ~ high-flown language. — 3. ~ haben to be expressive; ihr Geſicht hat keinen ~ her face lacks expression, looks vacant; Kunſt: life, animation, action; passion.
aus-drückbar (ᴵᴵ◡-) *a.* ⁶⁶ expressible.
aus-drucken (ᴵᴵ◡) ⓬** meiſt *typ.* **I** *v/a.* 1. (fertig drucken) to finish printing; e-e Form ♃ to work off a form; das Werk wird bald ausgedruckt ſ-n the work will soon be worked off. — 2. ungekürzt: to print in full; gut ♃ to (im)print clearly. — **II** *v/n.* (h.) 3. to cease printing.
aus-drück/en (ᴵᴵ◡) **I** *v/a.* ⓬** 1. einen Stempel: to impress, to imprint. — 2. (auspreſſen) to press (or squeeze) out; to strain off, ein Auge: to gouge (out). — 3. (auslöſchen) to put out by pressing. — 4. (a. *v/refl.*) *fig.* to utter, to convey; ſich ob. ſeine Gefühle durch Worte ♃ to express o.s. or one's feelings in words; ſ-e Gedanken in Verſen ♃ to clothe one's thoughts in verse; ſeine Meinung, Anſicht ♃ to state one's opinion; ſich deutlich (gut) ♃ to speak plainly (well); ſich derb, grob ♃ to use strong words, to talk rudely; ſich fließend ♃ to have a good flow of language; wie man ſich gewöhnlich ausdrückt in common parlance; ſich gelinde über et. ♃ to put it mildly; ſich kurz ♃ to be brief; ſich verblümt ♃ to veil one's meaning; nicht auszudrücken(d) beyond expression, inexpressible. — **II** ~ *n* ²³ 5. = A/ung. — **III** ♃b *p.pr.* u. *a.* ⁶⁶ 6. expressive of.
aus-drücklich (ᴵᴵ◡ u. ᴵ◡◡) *a.* ⁶⁶ (u. *adv.*) express(ly), explicit(ly); positive(ly); *adv.* auch: in a formal manner, in due form; (abſichtlich) intentional(ly), on purpose, purposely; ♃er Befehl express command, strict order, special injunction; ~**keit** (~) *f* ⁴⁶ explicitness.
Aus-drucks-art (ᴵᴵ◡…) *f* ⁴⁶ = =weiſe; **=bewegung** *f* expressive movement or gesture; **=fülle** *f* expressiveness; copiousness (of style); ♃**leer** *a.* ⁶⁶, ♃**los** *a.* void of expression; inexpressive; blank or vacant (look); **=loſigkeit** *f* lack of expression, inexpressiveness; ♃**voll** *a.* expressive, suggestive; Worte: significant; Augen: eloquent; **=weiſe** *f* mode of expression or utterance; weitS. language, style, phraseology.
Aus-drückung (ᴵᴵ◡) *f* ⁴⁶ 1. impress(ion), stamp. — 2. *fig.* (form of) expression.
Aus-druſch (ᴵ◡) *m* ⓓd. *agr.* number of sheaves thrashed (at one time).
aus-duften (ᴵᴵ◡) ⓽** **I** *v/n.* e-n Geruch, a. *abs.*: to exhale. — **II** *v/n.* (h.) to cease spreading perfume; to lose one's scent.
aus-dulden (◡) ⁶⁹** **I** *v/a.* to endure to the end. — **II** *v/n.* (h.) to cease suffering; er hat ausgeduldet his sufferings are at an end, he will suffer no more.
aus-dunſtbar, -dünſtbar (ᴵᴵ◡-) *a.* ⁶⁶ evaporable; ⚷ *physiol.* perspirable; ~**keit** *f* (.~) ⁴⁶ evaporability; perspirability.
aus-dunſt/en, -dünſt/en (ᴵᴵ◡) ⓽** **I** *v/n.* (h.) 1. to evaporate, vaporize; (verduften) to exhale; durch die Haut: to perspire, F u. P to sweat. — **II** *v/a.* 2. to evaporate; to exhale; Krankheitsſtoffe ꝛc.: to sweat out. — **III** ~ *n* ²³ 3. = A/ung 1.
Aus-dunſtung, -dünſtung (ᴵᴵ◡) *f* ⁴⁶ 1. (das Ausdünſten) evaporation, exhalation; perspiration, F u. P sweating. — 2. (das Ausgebünſtete) exhalation; steam; ſchädliche ~ noxious vapours, foul gases, effluvia *pl.*; ⚒ choke-damp.
Aus-dünſtungs-meſſer (ᴵᴵ◡…) *m* ⁶² ⚷ atmometer; evaporimeter. [angles.⌋
aus-ecken (ᴵᴵ◡) *v/a.* ⓬** to cut out in⌋
aus-eggen (ᴵᴵ◡) *v/a.* ⁶⁶ *agr.* **I** *v/a.* to harrow out or up. — **II** *v/n.* (h.) to finish (or cease) harrowing.
aus-ein-an-der (--◡◡) *adv.* asunder; apart, separate(ly); weit ♃ far from each other; ſie ſind um zwei Jahre ♃ they were born within two years of each other; ♪ Sänger u. Begleitung ſind ♃ (geraten) … have not kept time.
aus-ein-an-der-… (--◡◡…), in Verbindung u. Zſſg mit *verbs* immer trennbar (**), bezeichnet: **A.** Trennung, zB. ♃**brechen**. — **B.** Entwirren, zB. ♃**wirren**. — ♃**brechen** *v/a.* u. *v/n.* (ſn) ⓬a** to break asunder or off or in two; ♃**breiten** ⓬** to unfold, spread out, lay open; ♃**bringen** *v/a.* ⓬** Streitende ꝛc.: to separate from each other; to part; Freunde: to set at variance; ♃**drehen** *v/a.* ⓬** to untwist; ♃**fahren** *v/n.* (ſn) ⓺b** to move (or go, fly) asunder; weitS. to disperse; ♃**fallen** *v/n.* (ſn) ⓺a** to fall asunder, to go to pieces; ♃**falten** *v/a.* ⓬** to unfold, to unfurl; ♃**fliegen** *v/n.* (ſn) ⓹f** to fly asunder or in different directions; ♃**geh(e)n** *v/n.* (ſn) ⓺** *v.* Perſonen: to part company; von e-r Verſammlung: to break up, to disperse; ⚔ to disband; ♃ laſſen to dismiss; von Strahlen: to diverge, von Wegen: to branch off; *fig.*: die Anſichten gehen weit auseinander … are very much divided or differ very much; ♃**gehende** Anſichten *f/pl.* divergent (or different) opinions *pl.*; *v.* Sachen: (entzweigehen) to fall to pieces,

---
⚷ scientific; ✿ botanical; ⊕ geography; ⊙ machinery; ⚒ mining; ⚔ military; ⚓ marine; ⬤ commercial; ✉ postal; 🚂 railway.

[Auseinandergehen] — 112 — [ausfaulen]

to come asunder; =geh(e)n n ㉓ separation, dispersal; einer Schule, des Parlaments: breaking-up; beim ~ on parting; der Strahlen, fig. der Meinungen: divergence; von Zusammengefügtem: dislocation; ⚔ zerstreutes ~ der Truppen disbandment; ≗halten v/a. ⑥a** to keep asunder or separate or distinct; to discriminate between; =halten n ㉓ separation, distinction; ≗jagen v/a. to disperse, scatter; mit e-m Keil: to cleave or drive asunder (with a wedge); ≗kommen v/n. (in) ⑥4** to become separated; im Gedränge ⟳ to lose one another in the crowd; ≗laufen v/n.(in)⑥asi** =≗gehen; ⊕ (zu flüssig w.) to melt away; ~ n ㉓ = =gehen; ≗legen v/a.⑥8** to take asunder; Maschinen: to take to pieces; Zeuge: to spread (or lay) out; ⚔ Truppen: to disperse (regiments); to quarter apart; fig. (erklären) to explain; ~ n ㉓ u. =legung f ㊻ von Maschinen: taking to pieces; von Stoffen: laying out (for show); fig. (Erklärung) explanation; ≗liegen v/n. (h.) ⑭** to lie at a distance from one another; ~ n ㉓ separateness; ≗machen v/a. ⑥8** to undo; mit Mühe: to force asunder; die Beine ⟳ to put one's legs apart, F to straddle (one's legs); fig. (entwirren) to disentangle; ~n㉓undoing, ↓ unfurling; fig. disentanglement; ≗nehmen v/a. ⑭a** eine Maschine, ⚔ ein Gewehr ꝛc.: to take to pieces; to dismount; eine elektrische Batterie: to break up; anat. ein Gerippe ꝛc.: ⚕ to disarticulate; ~ n ㉓ dismounting; anat. disarticulation; ≗reißen v/a. u. v/n. (in) ⑥a** to tear (or rend) asunder, to pull apart; ≗richten v/a. ⑥9** to cause to diverge; ≗rollen ⑥8**: a) v/a. to unroll; b) v/n. (in) to come unrolled; ≗rücken v/a. u. v/n. (in) ⑥8** to move apart; v/n. (sich ≗setzen) to move one's chairs apart; ≗setzen ⑩** v/a. to put (or set, place) apart or asunder; (scheiden) to decompose, to analyse; (darlegen) to set forth; (klar machen) to expound; (erörtern) to discuss; Personen (in betreff des Mein und Dein) ⟳ to arrange (money) matters between ...; sich ⟳ v/refl. to sit apart; fig. sich mit e-m wegen e-r Sache ⟳ to come to an understanding with a p. about a matter; ⚜ sich mit seinen Gläubigern ⟳ to come to terms (or to arrange, to compound) with one's creditors; ~ n ㉓ u. =setzung f ㊻ putting apart or asunder; analysis; exposition; discussion; arrangement (of money matters); ⚜ =setzung mit seinen Gläubigern: arrangement, composition; (Abwicklung von Rechnungen) liquidation, settlement; ≗spreizen v/a. ⑩** die Beine ⟳ = ≗machen; ≗sprengen v/a. ⑥8** to burst asunder, to blow up; den Feind: to scatter; ≗steh(e)n v/n. (h.) ⑩** = abstehen 1; ⸙ u. zo. ≗stehend: ⚗ dehiscent; ≗stellen v/a. und sich ⟳ v refl. ⑥8** to place (o.s.) at some distance (or apart, away) from each other; ≗stieben v/n. (h.) ⑭äst** to fly (or run) in different directions; ≗treiben v/a. ⑥1** = ≗jagen; ≗treten ⑧d. v/n. (in) = sich ≗stellen; v/a. to

flatten (or break) by stamping; ~ n ㉓ breaking by stamping; Abstimmung durch ~ e-r Versammlung (voting by) division; ≗tun v/a. und v/refl. ⑤** = ≗machen u. ≗legen; ≗wickeln ⑩a** v/a. to unwrap, to unroll; sich ⟳ v/refl. von Schlangen: to uncoil; ≗wirren v/a. ⑥8** to disentangle; ≗ziehen ⑭b** v/a. to draw (or pull) asunder; to stretch out or apart; ⚔ ein Bataillon zum Gefecht: to put (or draw up) in loose formation or in skirmishing order; v/n. (in) to move apart; to remove into separate localities; to take different routes.
aus-eisen (᷾‿‿) v/a. ⑩** et. ⟳ to dig a th. out of the ice, to clear a th. of (the) ice.
aus-eitern (᷾‿‿) v/n. ⑩** path. 1. (h.) v. Geschwüren: a) (aufhören zu eitern) to cease festering; b) (stark eitern) to discharge freely. — 2. (in) v. Krankheitsstoffen: to flow out (as pus) by suppuration.
aus-erkoren (᷾‿᷾‿) I p.p. von † auserküren u. a. ⑥(D9) chosen, select(ed), choice; von Truppen: picked; meist theol. predestin(at)ed, elect; weiß. (well-)beloved. — II ~e(r) m, ~e f ㊻ = Auserwählte(r) (f. auserwählt).
aus-erlesen (᷾‿‿‿) I v/a. ⑥a*/* = ausersehen. — II p.p. und a. ⑥(D9) (ausgewählt, vorzüglich) picked, (specially) selected, carefully chosen; v. Sachen: exquisite, choice; die ⟳ste Mannschaft the flower of the army, the pick of the men; etwas ~es a choice article.
Aus-erlesenheit (᷾‿‿‿) f ㊻ (ohne pl.) choiceness, selectness, exquisiteness.
aus-ersehen (᷾‿‿‿)Iv/a.⑥a*/* to choose, select, pick (out); to single out; für ein Amt ꝛc.: to designate; zu größeren Dingen destined for greater things; er war dazu ⟳, es zu tun it was allotted to him to ..., he was chosen to ... — II ~ n ㉓ u. A/ung f ㊻ choice, selection; designation.
aus-erwähl/en (᷾‿‿‿) I v/a. ⑥*/* to choose, to select. — II ~ n ㉓ = A/ung.
aus-erwählt (᷾‿‿‿) p.p. ⑥ elect, von der Vorsehung: predestin(at)ed; bibl. Les Rüstzeug chosen vessel (of the Lord); viele find berufen, aber wenige ⟳ many are called, but few chosen; ~e(r) m, ~e f ㊻ one chosen or selected; theol. die ~en pl. God's elect pl.; F s-e ~e, die ~e seines Herzens the lady of his choice, the beloved of his heart, F his lady love.
Aus-erwählung (᷾‿‿‿) f ㊻ choice, selection, für ein Amt ꝛc.: election.
aus-erzählen (᷾‿‿‿) v/n. (h.) ⑥*/* to finish a tale or story.
aus-essen (᷾‿‿) ⑥** to eat up, eine Schüssel: to finish or empty; F fig. man muß ⟳, was man eingebrockt hat we must put up with the consequences of our actions; Sprichw. as you brew, so you must drink; as you have made your bed, so you must lie on it.
aus-fachen ⊕ (᷾‿ch‿) v/a. einen Schrank: to provide with shelves.
aus-fädeln (᷾‿‿) v/a. u. v/refl. ⑥** 1. eine Nadel: to unthread; Perlen: to unstring; sich ⟳ to come unstrung. — 2. (ausbriefeln) to ravel out, to unravel.
aus-fahren (᷾‿‿) ⑥bst** I v/n. (in) 1. im Wagen ꝛc.: to drive out, to go for a (carriage-)drive, to take a drive or a

ride, to go out boating or cycling. — 2. von e-m Orte ⟳ to set out from (or to leave) a place; ⚒ (aus dem Schacht fahren) to ascend (the shaft), to leave the pit; ⚓ (aussegeln) to put to sea; aus Kanälen: to disembogue. — 3. (hinausstürzen) to rush (or hurry) off. — II v/a. 4. to take a p. for a drive or a ride. — 5. Wege: to wear out by carting; ein Geleise ⟳ (tiefer machen) to cut (or break) up a road; fig. ein ausgefahr(e)nes Geleise a beaten track, the same old groove; ausgefahr(e)ner Weg road with deep ruts. — III ~ n ㉓ 6. = Ausfahrt I. — 7. path. eruption, (breaking out in a) rash.
Aus-fahr-schacht ⚒ (᷾‿‿...) m ㊷ upcast(-shaft or -pit); ascending shaft.
Aus-fahrt (᷾‿‿) f ㊻ 1. (carriage-)drive, riding (or driving) out; von einem Orte weg: departure (auch ⚓); ⚒ ascent. — 2. (Torweg) gateway, carriage-gate; (Fahrweg durch den Park) drive; ⚓ aus Kanälen: disemboguement.
Aus-fall (᷾‿‿) m ⑩c. 1. = ausfallen III. — 2. (Wegfall) deficiency, falling off; (Verlust) shortage, shrinkage, loss; Finanzwesen: deficit; einen ~ decken to cover losses. — 3. (Angriff): a) ⚔ aus einer Festung: sortie, sally; b) fenc. pass, thrust, lunge; c) fig. attack; in Worten: invective; (Beleidigung) insult. — 4. (Ergebnis) result, issue, F upshot.
aus-fallen (᷾‿‿) ⑥a** I v/n. (in) 1. vom Haar ꝛc.: to fall (or come) off; die Zähne fallen ihm aus he is losing his teeth; chm. von Bodensätzen: to be deposited or precipitated, to settle down. — 2. (unterbleiben) to be omitted; die Vorstellung ꝛc. fällt aus ... does not take place; die Schule fällt heute aus there is no school to-day. — 3. a) ⚔ aus e-m Tore: to sally forth; b) fenc. to lunge (out); c) fig. (in Worten) gegen einen ⟳ to assail (or attack) a p., to inveigh against a p. — 4. gut, schlecht ⟳ to turn out well, ill; to prove good, bad; es fiel anders aus, als ich erwartet hatte things took a different turn from what I had expected; das Urteil fiel zu seinen Gunsten, Ungunsten aus the verdict went in his favour, against him. — II v/a. 5. sich (dat.) einen Zahn ⟳ to break ... by a fall; aus dem Gelenke: to dislocate (one's shoulder), to put (an arm) out of joint. — III ~ n ㉓ 6. ~ der Haare fall of the hair, ⚗ depilation. — IV ⟳d p.pr. u. a. ⑥ 7. Beb. des inf. — 8. fig. aggressive; (beleidigend) insulting.
Aus-fall(s)-gatter (᷾‿‿ ...) n ㊵, =pforte f † ⚔ frt. sally-port; postern(-gate).
aus-färben ⊕ (᷾‿‿) v/a. ⑥8** Stoffe ⟳ to give the last dye (or dip) to ...
aus-fasern (᷾‿‿) ⑭a** I v/a. Näherei: to unravel, Gewebes: to unweave. — II v/n. (in) u. sich ⟳ v/refl. to ravel (or fray) out, to (be)come unravelled.
Aus-faser-zylinder ⊕ (᷾‿‿ ...) m ㊷ Papierfabrikation: ravelling roller.
aus-faulen (᷾‿‿) ⑥8** v/n. (in) ⑥** 1. von Pflanzen: to become hollow by decay. — 2. (herausfaulen) to rot out. — 3. (tief) ⟳ v. Zähnen, Knochen: to become carious.

Zeichen (s. S. XVII): F familiär; P Volkssprache; ⸕ Gaunersprache; ⸍ selten; † alt (auch gestorben); * neu (auch geboren); ⁺⁺ unrichtig;

[ausfechten] — 113 — [Ausführer]

aus-fechten (⁽ᵘˡ˘⁾) v/a. ⓑ** to fight out (quarrels), to settle (differences) by having recourse to arms; et. mit e-m 2 to fight a th. (F to have it) out with a p.; eine Ehrensache 2 to fight a duel.

aus-fegen (⁽ᵘˡ˘⁾) v/a. ⓈⓈ** Schmutz: to sweep (out or clean); das Zimmer 2 to clean out ...; to give ... a sweep.

Aus-feger (⁽ᵘˡ˘⁾) m ㉒, ~in f ㊵ sweeper.

Aus-fegsel (⁽ᵘˡ˘⁾) n ㉒ sweepings pl.

aus-feilen (⁽ᵘˡ˘⁾) I v/a. ⓈⓈ** 1. to file out; ⓔ e-e Säge ꝛc.: to tooth (by filing), to indent. — 2. (ausarbeiten) to smooth (with a file); eine Arbeit 2 to give the last finish(ing touch) to a piece of work; fig. a.: to elaborate. — II ~ n ㉓ 3. filing (out); fig. finishing touch.

aus-fenstern F (⁽ᵘˡ˘⁾) v/a. ⓐ** (schelten) to rebuke, scold.

aus-fertig/en (⁽ᵘˡ˘˘⁾) I v/a. ⓈⓈ** 1. e-n Befehl ꝛc.: to dispatch, expedite; e-e Urkunde ꝛc.: to draw up. — 2. jur. e-n Akt 2 to execute a deed; doppelt ausgefertigt (done) in duplicate; ⓗ die Fakturen über et. 2 to invoice a th.; eine Rechnung 2: to make out. — II ~ n ㉓ 3. -A/ung.

Aus-fertiger (⁽ᵘˡ˘˘⁾) m ㉒, ~in f ㊵ person who dispatches; copying clerk.

Aus-fertigung (⁽ᵘˡ˘˘⁾) f ㊻ 1. despatch; jur. draft(ing). — 2. - (Schriftstück) jur. (engrossed) copy; ⓗ invoice; in doppelter ~ in duplicate copies.

Aus-fertigungs-gebühren (⁽¯˘˘˘⁾...) f/pl. fee for executing (or engrossing) a deed.

aus-fetten (⁽ᵘˡ˘⁾) v/a. ⓈⓈ** to free from grease or fat; Wolle: to scour, clean.

aus-feuern (⁽ᵘˡ˘⁾) ⓐ** I v/a. 1. ein Zimmer ꝛc.: to warm (thoroughly). — II v/n. (h.) 2. ⚔ to cease firing. — 3. F Pferd: (ausschlagen) to lash out, to kick.

aus-filzen (⁽ᵘˡ˘⁾) v/a. ⓐ** 1. Schuhe ꝛc.: to furnish with felt. — 2. ⊕ Sattlerei: (ausstopfen) to stuff with hair, &c.

aus-findbar (⁽ᵘˡ˘⁾) a. ⓑ discoverable.

aus-findig (⁽ᵘˡ˘⁾) a. ⓑ: 2 machen to find (or make) out; to discover; to trace out; 2 zu m. suchen to search (or look out) for; to hunt for news. I (within).

aus-firnissen (⁽ᵘˡ˘˘⁾) v/a. ⓐ** to varnish.

aus-fischen (⁽ᵘˡ˘⁾) ⓐ** I v/a. 1. to fish out. — 2. fig. (aufspüren) to ferret out. — 3. (leer fischen) einen Teich 2 to clear a pond (of fish), to drag a pond. — II v/n. (h.) 4. to cease fishing.

aus-flackern (⁽ᵘˡ˘⁾) v/n. ⓐ** 1. (h.) to cease flickering. — 2. (sn) to go out.

aus-flammen (⁽ᵘˡ˘⁾) ⓐ** I v/n. (h.) to cease blazing. — II v/a. ⚔ artill. ein Geschützrohr: to flash off, to scale.

aus-flattern (⁽ˡ˘⁾) v/n. (sn) ⓐ** to flutter forth; f. aus-fliegen.

aus-flechten (⁽ᵘˡ˘⁾) v/a. ⓑ** 1. to line with wickerwork. — 2. to unplait, to untwist (= aufflechten 2).

Aus-fleisch-eisen (⁽ᵘˡ˘˘⁾...) n ㉒ (currier's) fleshing-iron or -knife.

aus-fleischen ⊕ (⁽ᵘˡ˘⁾) v/a. ⓘ** Gerberei: to flesh; to scrape off (the skin).

Aus-fleisch-messer (⁽ᵘˡ˘⁾...) n ㉒ = -eisen.

aus-flicken (⁽ᵘˡ˘⁾) v/a. ⓐ** (ausbessern) to mend; gröber: to patch or botch (up) (Stücke aufsetzen) to piece, to vamp (up); Strümpfe: to darn; ein Haus: to repair, patch up; schlecht 2 F to blow together.

aus-fliegen (⁽ᵘˡ˘⁾) I v/n. (sn) ⓦaft** to fly out or away; aus dem Neste: to take wing, to leave the nest; die Vögel sind ausgeflogen the birds are flown (a. fig.); fig. v. Menschen: (entfliehen) to run away, to bolt; (reisen) to take (or to go on) a trip; (das Heim verlassen) to leave home. — II ~ n ㉓ f. Ausflug 1 u. 2.

aus-fließen (⁽ᵘˡ˘⁾) I v/n. (sn) ⓦd** 1. von Flüssigkeiten: to flow (or run) out or away; (ausströmen) to gush forth; aus Fässern: to leak; Wasser 2 l. to let off ...; Geschwür: to discharge, suppurate. — 2. fig. u. phys. to emanate (or issue) from. — II ~ n ㉓ 3. = Ausfluß 1.

Aus-flucht (⁽ᵘˡ⁾) f ㊿ 1. loophole (a. fig.). — 2. fig. (Ausrede) subterfuge, shift, excuse; (Vorwand) pretext, blind, plea; (Vorbehalt) mental reservation; eine elende ~ a paltry (or lame) excuse; eine leere ~ a shallow pretext; Ausflüchte m. to shuffle, to prevaricate.

Aus-flug (⁽ᵘˡ⁾) m ⓓ. 1. der Vögel: flying out (of the nest); flight; fig. von einem jungen Menschen: sein erster ~ his first journey or venture or experience (in life). — 2. fig. (kleine Reise) trip, excursion, outing, run, jaunt; einen ~ m. to make an excursion, to take a (short) trip to; j. der einen ~ macht = Ausflügler. — 3. (Flugloch) e-s Bienenstocks: entrance; eines Taubenschlags: opening (of a pigeon-house), pigeonhole.

Aus-flügler (⁽ᵘˡ˘⁾) m ㉒ excursionist, tourist, holiday-maker, F tripper.

Aus-fluß (⁽ᵘˡ⁾) m ⓓa. 1. (das Ausfließen) flowing (or running) out, outflow; von Blut, Eiter ꝛc.: discharge, secretion; phys. (Ausströmen) effluence, emanation. — 2. path. (das Ausgeflossene) pus, (discharged) matter. — 3. (Ort des Ausfließens) outlet, passage; (Mündung) orifice; e-s Flusses: mouth; er Dachrinne: (water-)spout; (conduit-)pipe; gutter.

Aus-fluß-geschwindigkeit (⁽ᵘˡ˘...⁾) f ㉒ phys. velocity of efflux or of a jet; =loch n gully-hole; =rohr n, =röhre f ⊕ e-r Pumpe: outlet- (or delivery-) discharge-, jet-)pipe.

Aus-flut (⁽ᵘˡ⁾) f ㊻ gutter; ⚒ adit.

aus-fluten (⁽ᵘˡ˘⁾) v/n. (sn) ⓈⓈ** to flow out, to stream forth; to disembogue.

aus-folgen (⁽ᵘˡ˘⁾) v/a. ⓈⓈ**: 2 (lassen) to hand over, to deliver (= ausliefern).

aus-fordern (⁽ᵘˡ˘⁾) v/a. ⓐ** u. Aus-forderung f ㊻ = herausfordern ꝛc.

aus-fördern ⚒ (⁽ᵘˡ˘⁾) v/a. ⓐ** to extract, to put out. — II ~ n ㉓ und Aus-förderung f ㊻ extraction, output.

aus-forsch/en (⁽ᵘˡ˘⁾) I v/a. ⓐ** 1. a) eine Sache: to (try to) find out; to search (or pry) into; to investigate; b) to sift, explore. — 2. e-n 2 to sound (F to pump) a p.; er läßt sich nicht 2 he won't be drawn. — II ~ n ㉓ 2. = A/ung.

Aus-forscher (⁽ᵘˡ˘⁾) m ㉒ investigator.

Aus-forschung (⁽ᵘˡ˘⁾) f ㊻ search(ing); sounding; investigation; meist jur. inquiry; (Aushorchen) F pumping.

Aus-fracht ⓗ (⁽ᵘˡ⁾) f ㊻ outward freight; ~ u. Rückfracht out(ward) and home f.

aus-fragen (⁽ᵘˡ˘⁾) ⓈⓈ (⁽⁾ᵘˡ**) I v/a. 1. (ausfindig m.) to find out by inquiry or by asking (questions). — 2. e-n 2 (ausforschen), von e-m et. 2 to question (or interrogate, sound) a p. about a th.; scharf: to cross-question, cross-examine, catechize; e-n zudringlich (F fig. bis aufs Hemde, Blut) 2 to torment a p. with queries; ⚓ ein Schiff: to hail. — II v/n. (h.) 2. to cease questioning. — III 2d p.pr. u. a. ⓐ 4. inquisitorial.

Aus-frager (⁽ᵘˡ˘⁾) m ㉒, ~in f ㊵ b.s. interrogator, questioner; ~ei (~¯¯) f ㊲ (inquisitive) questioning, F pumping.

aus-fransen (⁽ᵘˡ˘⁾) ⓐ** I v/a. to fringe. — II sich 2 v/refl. to ravel (or fray) out.

aus-fräsen ⊕ (⁽ᵘˡ˘⁾) v/a. ⓐ** e-n Rand 2 to bead (or curl, crisp) a border.

aus-fressen (⁽ᵘˡ˘⁾) ⓈⓈ** I v/a. 1. v. Tieren: den Trog, die Schüssel 2 to clear (or empty) ...; P derb v. Menschen: = ausessen (a. fig.); F fig. er hat wieder etwas ausgefressen he has been up to mischief (or up to his tricks) again. — 2. (aushöhlen) Käse: to hollow out; v. Säuren: to corrode. — II v/n. (h.) 3. to have done eating.

aus-frieren (⁽ᵘˡ˘⁾) v/n. ⓒ** 1. (sn): a) to freeze thoroughly or to the bottom; et. 2 l. to freeze a th., to let a th. congeal; b) (erfrieren) to perish with cold, to be(come) frost-bitten. — 2. (h.) es hat ausgefroren it has left off freezing.

aus-fugen ⊕ (⁽ᵘˡ˘⁾) v/a. ⓈⓈ** Maurerei: to fill up (or flush) the joints of a wall.

Aus-fuhr ⓗ (⁽ᵘˡ⁾) f ㊻ export(ation).

Aus-fuhr-abgabe (⁽ᵘˡ...⁾) f ⓑ = -zoll; -artikel m article of export, pl. auch: goods pl. for export(ation), export (or outward) goods, exports pl.

aus-führbar (⁽ᵘˡ⁻⁾) - a. ⓑ 1. achievable; (tunlich) practicable, feasible; leicht, schwer 2 easy, difficult to accomplish; nicht 2 impracticable. — 2. ⓗ exportable.

Aus-führbarkeit (~¯) f ㊻ (o. pl.) practicability, practicableness, feasibility.

Aus-fuhr-dock n dock for export goods.

aus-führ/en (⁽ᵘˡ˘⁾) I v/a. ⓈⓈ** 1. to lead (or take) out, Pferde ꝛc. auch: to exercise; Kinder 2 to take children for a walk. — 2. F (entwenden) to pilfer, to abstract, F to nick, pinch, prig. — 3. ⓗ Waren ꝛc. 2 to export (or ship) ... to, to sell ... abroad or in foreign parts. — 4. (fortschaffen) med. die Galle ꝛc. 2 = abführen 5. — 5. (bewerkstelligen) to put into execution; to carry into effect, to carry out (a plan, a resolution); to perform (a task); allg.: to accomplish) a th.; e-n Auftrag 2 to effect an order; e-n Bau: to erect; Kunstwerke: to execute; e-e Rechnung 2 to work out a problem or a sum (in arithmetic); Verbrechen: to perpetrate; eine Zeichnung mit der Feder, mit Tusche 2 to make a pen-and-ink sketch; etwas geschickt 2 to manage a th. well; er kann es nicht 2 he cannot carry it through; sich 2 lassen to be practicable; von e-m Redner: er führte (etwa) folgendes aus he argued (or remarked) as follows. — 6. (eine behandeln) to particularize, specify; et. weiter 2 to follow up a th. — II ~ n ㉓ 7. = A/ung.

Aus-führer (⁽ᵘˡ˘⁾) m ㉒, ~in f ㊵ 1. ⓗ von Waren ꝛc.: exporter. — 2. (Vollbringer) performer, accomplisher; ⓣ Tat auch: doer, e-r Missetat: perpetrator.

♪ Musik; ⚛ Wissenschaft; ⚘ Pflanze; ⚲ Geographie; ⊕ Technik; ⚒ Bergbau; ⚔ Militär; ⚓ Marine; ⓗ Handel; ✉ Post; 🚂 Eisenbahn.

[**Ausfuhrerlaubnis**] — 114 — [**ausgehen**]

Aus-fuhr-erlaubnis ❋ (ᴵᴵᴸ...) f ㉒ declaration (of outward goods), permit for exportation; =**geschäft** n export house; =**handel** m export (or outward) trade; =**haus** n =geschäft.

aus-führlich(ᴵᴵᴸ) a.㊋ (u. adv.) (ins einzelne gehend) detailed, (umständlich) circumstantial(ly); (weitläufig) copious(ly), (weit ausgedehnt) ample; adv. auch: in detail, at full length, minutely; ⚥er Bericht full particulars pl.; ⚥ beschreiben, erzählen to describe fully, to give full details of, to circumstantiate, to particularize; ~**keit** (~-) f ㊻ fulness, completeness, copiousness.

Aus-fuhr-prämie ❋ (ᴵᴵᴸ...) f ㉒ premium or bounty (on exports), drawback.

Aus-führung (ᴵᴵᴸ) f ㊻ leading out, &c.; ❋ = Ausfuhr; e-s Baues: erection; fig. (Verwirklichung) execution, performance, e-s Verbrechens: perpetration; (Anordnung) arrangement, disposition, eines Redners: argument; zur ~ bringen to carry into effect, to execute; zur ~ kommen to be put into execution, Gesetz: to come into force.

Aus-führungs-befehl (ᴵᴵᴸ...) m ㉒ instruction for the execution or performance of a th.; =**bestimmung** f order for putting a (new) law into effect or force; =**gang** m, anat. excretory duct, ⚧ emunctory; =**rohre** n, =**röhre** f discharge-pipe; =**weg** m = gang.

Aus-fuhr-verbot (ᴵᴵᴸ...) n ㉒ prohibition of exportation; =**vergütung** f = =prämie; =**waren** f/pl. = =artikel; =**zoll** m export-duty, duty on outward (or export) goods.   [up, &c.¬

aus-füllbar (ᴵᴵᴸ-) a. ㊋ fit to be filled⌐

aus-füll/en (ᴵᴵᴸ) I v/a. ㊋** 1. to fill up; ein Formular ⚥ to fill up (or out) a form. — 2. fig. eine Lücke ⚥ to stop (or fill) a gap; s-e Stellung würdig ⚥ to fill a post worthily, to do credit to one's position; dieser Gedanke füllte seine ganze Seele aus ... engrossed his whole mind or all his thoughts; seine Zeit (gut) ⚥ to employ one's time (profitably). — 3. ⊕ mit Blei ⚥ to fill up with lead; mit Watte ⚥ to stuff with wadding, to pad; Maurerei: die Fugen ⚥ to flush the joints; einen Weg mit Steinen ⚥ to metal a road; Zähne ⚥ (plombieren) to stop teeth. — 4. (ausleeren) das Faß ⚥ to empty the cask; Wein: to draw off. — II ~ n ㉓ 5. = A/ung 1. — III ⚥d p.pr. u. a. ㊋ 6. Bed. des inf. — 7. gr.: ⚧ expletive.

Aus-füllung (ᴵᴵᴸ) f ㊻ 1. filling up or out; der Zeit: employment; (Ausstopfen) padding. — 2. ⊕ arch. (Schutt und Steine) fillings pl.; ballast; rubble (-stones pl.); metal.

Aus-füllungs-masse (ᴸ...) f ㉒ material for filling up; =**wort** n gr.: ⚧ expletive; (Flickwort) padding.

aus-füttern¹, F **-futtern¹** (ᴵᴵᴸ⌣) [**Futter¹**] ㉒a** v/a. 1. Vieh, ⚥ Personen: to fatten. — 2. (leeren) ⚥ to empty ... by feeding.

aus-fütter/n², F **aus-futter/n²**, ⊕ (ᴵᴵᴸ⌣) [**Futter²**] I v/a. ㊋** 1. c-n Rock ⚥ to line a coat (throughout); mit Stroh ⚥ to pad (or stuff) with straw; typ. den Kasten ⚥ to paper the case. —

II ~ n ㉓ u. A/**ung** f ㊻ 2. lining, padding, stuffing. — 3. ⇩ ~ der Stückpforten half-port(s pl.).

Ausg. abbr. = Ausgabe 3.

Aus-gabe (ᴵᴵ⌣) f ㊻ 1. (Ausgegebenes) expense, expenditure, outgoings pl.; (Auslage) outlay, disbursement; kleine ~n pl. petty expenses pl.; außerordentliche ~n pl. extra(ordinary) expenses, extras pl.; die ~n beschränken to reduce one's expenses, F to draw in; ~n und Einnahmen ins Gleichgewicht bringen to live within one's income, bei schmalen Mitteln: to make both ends meet; seine ~n übersteigen die Einnahmen he outruns the constable. — 2. (Ausgeben) ✉ der Briefe: delivery; ❋ von Aktien, Anleihen, Banknoten ꝛc.: issue. — 3. Buchhandel, typ. eines Buches: edition, issue; neue (unveränderte) ~ reprint, in äußerlich veränderter Form: new issue (of a book in cheaper or costlier editions); ~ mit Noten verschiedener Erklärer variorum edition; rechtmäßige ~ copyright edition.

Aus-gabe-... (ᴸ...) ㉒: ~(n)-**buch** n cash-book of expenses; ~(n)-**budget** n budget; estimated expenditure; =**bureau** n, =**posten** m item of expenditure; =**schalter** m für Billette ꝛc.: booking- (or ticket-) office; =**stelle** f issuing office, für Gepäck: luggage (or parcel-) office.

Aus-gang (ᴵᴵ) m ⑦c. 1. going out (Abreise) departure; e-n ~ machen to go (or walk) out; der erste ~ nach e-r Krankheit the first airing; es ist sein erster ~ it is the first time he has been out of doors or outside the house; erster ~ einer Wöchnerin: (Kirchgang) churching; von Dienstboten ꝛc.: seinen, ihren ~ haben to have one's day (or afternoon, evening) out; ❋ ~ (Ausfuhr) v. Waren: export(ation); pol.mst pl. Ausgänge (ant. Eingänge) im Staatshaushalt: outgoings pl., expenditure sg. — 2. (Öffnung) outlet; way out; egress; geheimer: private door; eines Flusses, Hafens: mouth; eines Hohlweges, Kellers: head; eines Engpasses: (fr.) débouché; ⚔ ʲrt. (fr.) sortie; e-s Theaters ꝛc.: exit. — 3. (Ende) end, conclusion; mit ~ des Jahres at the close of the year; zum ~ bringen to conclude, to bring to a conclusion; der Prozeß geht dem ~ entgegen ... is drawing to a close. — 4. (Erfolg) issue, event, F upshot; (Lösung) im Roman ꝛc. (final) catastrophe; (fr.) dénouement; e-n guten, schlechten ~ nehmen to terminate well, badly.

Aus-gangs-deklaration ❋ (ᴵᴵᴸ...) f ❋ = =**zettel**; =**hafen** m a) ❋ shipping-port, b) für Personen: port of embarkation; =**handel** ❋ m export trade; =**kolumne** ❋ f, typ. end of a break; partly filled end-page; =**pforte** f outlet, gate; =**punkt** m starting-point, point of departure (auch fig.); =**rohr** n von Maschinen: waste- (or eduction-) pipe; =**tor** n, =**tür** f = =**pforte**; =**waren** ❋ f/pl. exports pl.; =**zeile** f, typ. last line of a break; =**zettel** ❋ m permit; ❋ =**zoll** m = Ausfuhrzoll.

aus-gären (ᴵᴵᴸ⌣) ㊆a (㊇)** I v/n. 1. (h.) to cease fermenting (= abgären 2). — 2. (in) (heraustreten) to overflow in

fermenting. — II v/a. 3. vom Wein ꝛc.: alle Unreinigkeit ~ to throw off all impurity in fermenting.

aus-geben (ᴵᴵᴸ⌣) ㊅c** I v/a. 1. (zu Ende geben) das Stück konnte nicht ausgegeben werden the piece could not be played (right) to the end. — 2. Geld ⚥ (verschieden: 3 u. 5) to spend money; (auslegen) to lay out; auf der Reise wird das Geld schnell ausgegeben (oder gibt sich das Geld schnell aus) money is quickly spent (or soon goes) in travelling; alles ⚥, was man verdient to live up to one's income or up to the hilt; fig. wer ausgibt (andere ansteht) muß auch einnehmen who gives must take. — 3. ❋ eine Anleihe, Aktien ꝛc. ⚥ (im Umlauf setzen) to issue, to emit; schlechtes Geld ⚥ to utter false coin; neu auszugebende Aktien new shares to be issued. — 4. (verteilen) to give out, Almosen, die Briefe auf der Post ꝛc.: to distribute; (aushändigen) to deliver; in einer Wirtschaft: das Nötige ⚥ to give out sufficient (for the day); ⚔ die Losung ⚥ to pass the watch-word; Buchhandel: ein Buch ⚥ (verbreiten) to publish (or circulate) a book. — 5. (von sich geben) Dämpfe: to give off; Geld ⚥ (ausleihen) to put out ... — 6. (abwerfen) a. v.n. (h.) to yield, produce, bear; der Roggen gibt das zehnte Korn aus ... yields tenfold. — 7. (a. v/refl. sich) für ⚥ to pass (or palm) o.s. off as s.th.; er gibt sich für einen Offizier aus he pretends to be ..., he calls himself ... — II v/n. (h.) 8. §. 6. — 9. (aufquellen) von gelöschtem Kalk ꝛc.: to rise, to swell. — 10. hunt. vom Hunde: to give tongue. — 11. ♪ das Horn gibt aus ... sounds. — III sich ⚥ v/refl. 12. §. 7, auch 2. — 13. sich (ganz) ⚥ (sein Geld ꝛc. ⚥) to spend one's last or all one has, F to run out of (or short of) cash. — IV ~ n ㉓ 14. = Ausgabe 1 u. 2.

Aus-geber (ᴵᴵᴸ⌣) m ㉒, ~**in** f ㊵ person who spends, issues, &c. (s. ausgeben); (Verwalter[in]) steward(ess), caterer; ~**in** auch: (lady) housekeeper.

Aus-gebot (ᴵᴵᴸ⌣) n ⑪d. 1. announcement of sale. — 2. = Angebot.

Aus-geburt (ᴵᴵᴸ⌣) f ㊻ meist b.s. etwa: offspring, product; creation, creature; ~ der Hölle hellish (or hell-born) monster, child of hell; (Hirngespinst) phantom, illusion; seltsame ~ (des Gehirns) strange hallucination (of the mind).

Aus-gedinge (ᴵᴵᴸ⌣) n ㉓ 1. = Altenteil.

aus-gefeimt (ᴵᴵᴸ⌣) a. ㊋ cunning, artful = abgefeimt (s. abfeimen II).

aus-gegangen (ᴵᴵ⌣⌣) p.p. v. ausgehen.

Ausgeh(e)-anzug (ᴵᴵᴸ(⌣)...) m ㉒, =**kleid** n walking-costume, walking-dress.

aus-geh(e)n (ᴵᴵᴸ(⌣)) ㊆** I v/n. = a) (zu) 1. (das Haus verlassen) to go out (of doors), to take a walk or a stroll, to walk abroad; sie geht viel aus she goes about a good deal; er darf nicht ⚥ he is not allowed to go (or be) out, he has to keep indoors. — 2. (aus etwas hervorgehen) (mit a.) frei, ledig, los ⚥ to go (or get off) scot-free; ohne Bezahlen: to pay nothing; leer ⚥ to go away empty(-handed), to get

Signs (see page XVII): F familiar; P vulgar; Ƿ flash; ⟋ rare; † obsolete (died); * new word (born); ₊₊ incorrect; ♪ music;

[Ausgehetag] — 115 — [ausgreifen]

nothing, to be left out (in the cold). — 3. (sich ausziehen lassen) von Kleidern: to come off (easily); die Stiefel geh(e)n leicht an und aus the boots easily slip on and off. — 4. (auf=, los=gehen) to come undone. — 5. (schwinden, erlöschen) to fail, to vanish; der Atem geht mir aus I am getting out of breath; die Geduld geht mir aus I am losing patience; die Farbe wird leicht 2 ... easily fade; das Geld war mir aus= gegangen I had spent all my cash, my money was gone; die Haare, Zähne geh(e)n ihm aus he is losing his hair, teeth; die Kräfte geh(e)n ihm aus his strength begins to fail; die Lebensmittel geh(e)n ihnen aus they are running short of provisions; das Licht, Feuer geht aus ... is going out; von Pflanzen: to wither, to die; ⊛ der Artikel ist uns ausgegangen we are (cleared) out of... — 6. (ein Ende nehmen) to end, close, terminate. — 7. ⊕ typ. so setzen, daß der Text mit der Seite aus= geht to make up a page. — 8. ✕ von einem Flöz (zutage) 2 to crop (out). — 9. (erscheinen) von Schriften: to appear, to come out; von einer Idee: to eman= ate; einen Befehl, ein Verbot 2 lassen to promulgate (or issue) — 10. mit abhängiger prp.: auf: a) auf einen Vokal 2 to end in ...; b) auf etwas 2 to aim at a th.; auf Abenteuer 2 to go in quest (or in search) of adventures; auf Bettel 2 to go (a-)begging; auf Betrug 2 to be bent on cheating; auf j-s Verderben 2 to plot a p.'s ruin; er ging darauf aus, uns zu verderben he meant to ruin us, he schemed our ruin; in: in eine Spitze 2 (auslaufen) to end in a point; über: über etwas 2 (sich verbreiten) to spread over; von: von e-m Orte, fig. von e-m Grundsatze 2c. 2 to proceed from ...; ich ging davon, von dem Glauben aus, daß // I started on the supposition that //, I was led to believe that //; der Vorschlag geht von ihm aus the proposal comes (or eman= ates) from him. — b) (h. u. sn) 11. (auf= hören zu gehen) v. Teige: to cease rising. — II v/a. 12. (ausweiten) Schuhe: to stretch in (or with) wearing. — 13. (ausmessen) einen Saal: to pace out. — III sich 2 v/refl. 14. sich recht 2 to take good (walking) exercise or long walks. — IV ~ n ㉓ 15. going out, outing; Aus= und Eingeh(e)n going in and out; going out and coming in; (Erlöschen) extinction; von Vorräten: exhaustion; shortness; (Endigen) end (-ing), termination, issue; (Erscheinen) publication; promulgation. — Bgl. a. Ausgang. — V aus-gehend p.pr. u. a. ⊛ 16. ⊛ ⒟e Fracht outward freight; ⒟e Post departing mail; ⚓ ⒟es Schiff outward-bound ...; ⊛ ⒟e Waren f/pl. export goods pl.; ~e(s) n ⊕ geogn. sur= face-edge, outcrop. [day out, day off.)
Aus-geh(e)=tag (ᴵᴵ(∨)...) m ㉒ (servant's)}
aus-geigen ♪ (ᴵᴵ∨) ⊛** I v/a. ein Stück 2 to finish a piece on the violin. — II v/n. (h.) to cease fiddling.
aus-geizen (ᴵᴵ∨) v/a. ⊛** agr. Reben, Tabak 2c.: to prune, thin out, trim.

aus-gelassen (ᴵᴵ∨∨) I p.p. in allen Bed. des inf. (s. auslassen). — II a. ⊛ (D.9) fig. 1. (ungebunden) unrestrained, un= bridled, unruly, riotous; (ausschweifend) dissolute, loose. — 2. (übermütig, lustig) frolicsome, wanton; very jolly or merry; (ungestüm) boisterous; rompish, skittish; 2e Lustigkeit exuberant (or high) spirits pl.; 2es Mädchen tomboy.
Aus-gelassenheit (ᴵᴵ∨∨-) f ⊛ unruliness; dissoluteness; wantonness; boister= ousness; rompishness, skittishness; exuberance (of spirit), high spirits pl.
aus-gemacht (ᴵᴵ∨∨) I p.p. in allen Bed. des inf. (s. ausmachen). — II a. ⊛ 1. (ge= wiß) certain, sure; eine 2e Sache an established fact, an understood thing; eine längst 2e Gewißheit a foregone conclusion. — 2. (vollendet) accom= plished, settled; ein 2er Gauner a notorious (or thorough) scoundrel.
aus-gemergelt (ᴵᴵ∨∨)p.p.s.ausmergeln II.
aus-genießen (ᴵᴵ∨ᴵ∨)v/a. ⊛d*/* sein Leben: to enjoy ... thoroughly or to the utmost.
aus-genommen (ᴵᴵ∨∨) I p.p. in allen Bed. des inf. (s. ausnehmen). — II prp. u. adv. except(ing), with the exception of, save; keinen 2 without (a single) ex= ception, F u. Sport: bar none; nur diese beiden 2 all but these two; Rennsport: ich wette auf sämtliche Pferde, eins 2 I back the field bar one. — III cj. 2 daß except (or save) that; (wenn nicht) unless.
aus-geschieden (ᴵᴵ∨∨)p.p.s.ausscheiden 3.
aus-gestalt/en (ᴵᴵ∨∨) I ⊛*/* to shape (s. gestalten); (entwickeln) to develop. — II A/ung f ⊛ putting into a (more perfect) shape or form; ~ des Ver= kehrs 2c. development of traffic, &c.
aus-gestorben (ᴵᴵ∨∨) p.p. s. aussterben 2.
aus-gesucht (ᴵᴵ∨ᴵ) I p.p. in allen Bed. des inf. (s. aussuchen). — II a. ⊛ exqui= site, choice; aufs Feste gekleidet most elegantly dressed, F dressed (up) to the knocker or to the nines.
aus-gezeichnet (ᴵᴵ∨ᴵ∨)Ip.p.in allen Bed. des inf. (s.auszeichnen). — II.a. ⊛ excellent, distinguished, eminent; ein Schütze capital (F crack) shot; adv. es geht ihm 2 he is getting on exceedingly well.
aus-giebig (ᴵᴵ∨∨) a. ⊛ u. adv. = ergiebig.
aus-gießen (ᴵᴵ∨) I v/a. ⊛d** 1. to pour out, (weggießen) to pour away, (ver= schütten) to spill; fig. die Schale des Zornes über e-n 2 to vent (or let out) one's anger (bibl. to pour out vials of wrath) on a p. — 2. (auslöschen) Feuer 2 to put out fire with water. — 3. (ausfüllen) to fill up (with lead); mit Blei ausgegossener Stock loaded (or leaded) cane. — II ~ n ㉓ und Aus-gießung f ⊛ 4. pouring out; effusion; rel. ~ des Heiligen Geistes descent of the Holy Ghost; (Aus= löschen) extinction.
aus-gipsen ⊕ (ᴵᴵ∨) v/a. ⊛** to fill or stop up with plaster (of Paris).
aus-glätten (ᴵᴵ∨) v/a. ⊛** Falten: to take out by smoothing, to smooth.
aus-gleich (ᴵᴵ) m ⒈d. arrangement, (final) settlement, (Vertrag) treaty, agreement, vgl. a. Ausgleichung.
aus-gleichbar (ᴵᴵ-) a. ⊛ reconcilable.

aus-gleich/en (ᴵᴵ∨) I v/a. ⊛a§** 1. to equalize, (ebnen) to make even, to level (down); fig. ein ausgeglich(e)ner Mensch a person who has steadied (or settled) down (in life). — 2. (a. v/refl.) fig. e-e Schwierigkeit: to smooth down; e-n Streit: to settle, arrange, adjust; sich 2 (vergleichen) to come to an agreement or to terms, to settle, to make a compromise with; das wird sich bald wieder 2 that will soon come right again. — 3. ⊛ eine Rechnung 2 to balance (or settle, square) an account; alle Rechnungen mit e-m ausgeglichen h. to be quits or square with a p — 4. (vergüten) to compensate; to make good (a loss). — II ~ n ㉓ 5. = A/ung.
Aus-gleicher (ᴵᴵ∨) m ㉒, ~in f ㊻ 1. (Er= setzer) compensator. — 2. ⊛ adjuster. — 3. fig. (Versöhner) peace-maker. — 4. Tennis: handicapper.
Aus-gleichs=verfahren ⊛ (ᴵᴵ...) n ⊛ arrangement with (the) creditors for the purpose of preventing bankruptcy (proceedings); s. a. Ausgleichungs=...
Aus-gleichung (ᴵᴵ∨) f ⊛ equalization; levelling; arrangement; adjustment (of differences); ⊛ (Abrechnung) balance, balancing, settlement, clearing (of drafts); zur ~ e-r Rechnung in full (dis= charge) of ...; zur ~ unserer Tratte as a cover for our draft; phls. Gesetz der ~ law of compensation; Finanz: ~ der Steuern (equable) adjustment of taxes.
Aus-gleichungs=batterie (ᴵᴵ...) f ⊛ elect. compensating-battery, =betrag ⊛ m (amount of) balance, =haus n für Schecks: clearing-house, =pendel ⊕ m, n compensation-pendulum; jur. =pflicht f e-s Miterben obligation to compensate (or pay off) other heirs; =versuch m attempt at a compromise; =zölle m/pl. countervailing duties pl.
aus-gleiten (ᴵᴵ∨) I v/n. (sn) ⊛b** to (make a) slip, to slide (down), to miss one's footing; fig. to take a false step. — II ~ n ㉓ slip(ping).
aus-glimmen (ᴵᴵ∨) v/n. (sn) ⊛a (a. ⊛**) to die away with a glimmer.
aus-glitschen F ⊛** (~) = ausgleiten.
aus-glüh/en (ᴵᴵ∨) ⊛** I v/n. 1. (h.) to cease glowing; to cool down. — 2. (sn) (verbrennen) to be consumed by fire. — II v/a. ⊕: to heat thoroughly; Metalle 2c.: to anneal; chm. unschmelzbare Körper: to calcine. — III ~ n ㉓ u. A/ung f ⊛ annealing; calcination.
aus-grab/en (ᴵᴵ∨) I v/a. ⊛b** 1. to dig out or up; hunt. Füchse 2c.: to unearth, to dig; Leichen: to exhume, to disinter. — 2. (aushöhlen) to excavate, to hollow (out), den Boden: to cut away; Brunnen: to sink; Gravierkunst: vertiefte Figuren 2 to engrave. — II ~ n ㉓ 3. = A/ung.
Aus-gräber (ᴵᴵ∨) m ㉒ excavator.
Aus-grabung (~) f ⊛ digging out or up; excavation; archäologische ~en archæo= logical excavations or explorations; e-r Leiche: exhumation; Gravierkunst: engrav= ing; die-sinking; ⛏(Abtragung) cutting.
aus-gräten (ᴵᴵ∨) v/a. ⊛**: einen Fisch 2 to take out the bones of a fish.
aus-greifen (ᴵᴵ∨) ⊛b** I v/n. (h.) 1. to stretch (out) one's arms or legs; bsb.

⚗ scientific; ♀ botanical; ♁ geography; ⊛ machinery; ✕ mining; ⚔ military; ⚓ marine; ⊛ commercial; ✉ postal; 🚂 railway.

[Ausgriff] — 116 — [aushecken]

man. to step out (well); to take long strides; mein Pferd greift tüchtig aus ... is a good stepper; ein Pferd ⁂ lassen to give ... its head; vom Ruderer: weit ⁂ to pull with a long stroke. — II v/a. 2. (wählen) to pick out, to select. — 3. (betasten) to handle. — 4. (aushöhlen) to wear by handling.
Aus-griff (ᴵᴵ⌣) m ⒞. der Pferde: stride.
ausgrübeln (ᴵᴵ⌣) I v/a. ⓶a** to think (or puzzle) out; Plan: to devise; (entdecken) to ascertain; to get to the bottom of. — II ~ n ㉓ u. **Ausgrüb(e)lung** f ⓮ rumination, device; discovery.
aus-gründ/en (ᴵᴵ⌣) I v/a. ⓮** 1. ⓺ (austehlen) to chamfer, to flute. — 2. fig. to (un)fathom (a mystery). — II ~ n ㉓ u. **A/ung** f ⓮ 3. hollow; groove; fluting; fig. (un)fathoming, elucidation.
aus-grünen (ᴵᴵ⌣) v/n. ⓮** 1. (h.) to lose one's verdure; to cease sprouting. — 2. ⚘ (in) (Knospen) to bud; to grow green.
Aus-guck (ᴵᴵ⌣) m ⒞. u. ⓰ 1. ⚓ (das ~en) watch; e-n ~ halten = ausgucken I. — 2. (Schönsicht) (fine) look-out or view.
aus-gucken (ᴵᴵ⌣) ⚓** I v/n. (h.) ⚓ to keep a (good or sharp) look-out. — II v/a. sich (dat.) die Augen ⁂ to stare one's eyes out or o.s. blind.
Aus-gucker ⚓ ᴵᴵ⌣ m ⓶ look-out man.
Aus-guß (ᴵᴵ⌣) m ⓼a. 1. pouring out. — 2. ⊕ ⚘ = Abguß 3; metall. (das Ausgegoffene) ingot. — 3. (Goffe in der Küche) sink(-hole); e-s Gefäßes, e-r Dachrinne: spout; e-r Röhre: mouth; Küche: am ~ stehen to stand at the sink. — 4. ⚘ fig. ~ von Gefühlen effusion, F gush (= Erguß).
Aus-guß-kelle (ᴵᴵ⌣ ...) f ⓰, **-löffel** m ⓰ casting-spoon or -ladle; **-rinne, -röhre** f einer Pumpe ꝛc. drain- (or conduit-, waste-)pipe; **-wasser** n waste-water; dish-wash or -water.
aus-haaren (ᴵᴵ⌣) v/n. (h.) ⓮** to lose one's hair (f. a. ausfallen 1).
aus-haben F (ᴵᴵ⌣) v/a. ⓫b** ell. für ausgelesen, -getrunken, -gezogen haben ꝛc., z. B. er hat das Buch, das Glas, den Rock schon aus he has already read the book (through), emptied the glass, taken off his coat.
aus-hacken (ᴵᴵ⌣) v/a. ⓮** 1. die Augen ꝛc.: to pick out; f. Krähe. — 2. aus dem Boden ꝛc.: to take (or get) out with a sharp-edged tool; to grub up; Kartoffeln: to hoe out. — 3. (auszacken) to cut out; to pink. — 4. Fleisch ⁂ to cut up an ox, &c. (vgl. aushauen 5).
aus-hageln (ᴵᴵ⌣) v/impers. (h.) ⓶a** es hat ausgehagelt it has done hailing.
aus-haken (ᴵᴵ⌣) v/a. ⓮** (a. sich ⁂ v/refl.) to unhook, unhitch, unclasp.
aus-halftern (ᴵᴵ⌣) v/a. ⓶a** (a. sich ⁂ v/refl.) to unhalter, to slip the halter.
aus-hallen (⌣) v/a. (h., in) ⓮** to sound at a distance; to cease sounding.
aus-halt/en (ᴵᴵ⌣) ⓮a** I v/a. 1. (ausbauern lassen) to sustain; eine Silbe ⁂ to dwell on a syllable; ♪: e-n Ton, e-e Note ⁂ to hold a note; ausgehalten (sos)tenuto. — 2. (ertragen) einen Angriff ⁂ to (with)stand (or to bear up against) an attack or a charge; die Probe ⁂ to stand the test; Schmerzen, Strapazen: to endure, undergo, bear;

er hat viel ⁂ müssen he has had a great deal to put up with; ⚓ einen Sturm ⁂ to weather a storm or a gale; einen Sturm vor Anker ⁂ to ride out a gale; ich kann es nicht mehr ⁂, es ist nicht mehr auszuhalten I cannot stand (or bear) it any longer (f. a. III); ich kann es vor Müdigkeit nicht mehr ⁂ I am done up with fatigue; F I am dead-beat. — 3. mit acc. der Zeit f. 4. — II v/n. (h.) 4. (ausbauern) to persevere, persist, continue; bei ihr halten die Dienstboten nicht lange aus servants do not stay (for) long with her; seine Lehrjahre, seine Zeit ⁂ to serve one's (full) time; der Rock wird noch einen Winter ⁂ ... will last another winter; ⚘ die Farbe hält nicht aus ... flies quickly, fades easily; fenc. auf dem Stoß ⁂ to remain on the lunge; es ist mit ihm nicht auszuhalten he is unbearable or intolerable. — 5. abs. (standhalten) to suffer; to hold out; gegen et. ⁂ to withstand (or resist) a th. — III ~ n ㉓ 6. = A/ung; das ist nicht zum ~ that is beyond (all) endurance or forbearance, it is more than I can stand or bear.
Aus-haltung (ᴵᴵ⌣) f ⓮ e-s Tones: sustaining, lengthening; (Beharren) perseverance. [pause, corona, hold (⌢).)
Aus-haltungs-zeichen ♪ (⌣...) n ⓶
aus-hämmern ⊕ (ᴵᴵ⌣) v/a. ⓶a** 1. die Beulen e-r Schüssel ⁂ to beat out dents in a dish. — 2. to hammer out; to flatten (or widen) out by hammering.
aus-händigen (ᴵᴵ⌣) I v/a. ⓮** e-m et. ⁂ to hand a th. over to a p.; ⚘ to deliver a th. to a p. — II ~ n ㉓ und **Aus-händigung** f ⓮ delivery, surrender; Börse: ~ der verkauften Fonds delivery of stock.
Aus-hang (ᴵᴵ⌣) m ⒞. 1. ⚘ von Waren: show, display; (Anschlag) placard. — 2. ⚘ goods pl. exhibited for sale.
Aushänge-bogen ⊕ (ᴵᴵ⌣...) m ⓶ typ. clean sheet, last proof, advance-sheet; **-exemplar** ⊕ ⚘ n, typ. author's slip.
aus-hängen (ᴵᴵ⌣) v/n. (h.) ⓫b** to hang out; von Waren: to be exposed for sale; von einem Zettel: to be put up.
aus-hängen (ᴵᴵ⌣) I v/a. ⓮** 1. auch v/refl. to unhook; sich ⁂, a. to come unhooked; eine Tür ⁂ to unhinge; den Radschuh ⁂ to take off the drag; Maschinenteile: to unhang, to ungear. — 2. (ausstellen) to display, to show; Waren: to expose (or exhibit) for sale; Schild: to post (or put) up; Flagge: to hang out. — II P oft ⚘⁺ v/n. 3. = aushangen. — III ~ n ㉓ 4. = A/ung; 'contp. nur zum ~ only for (outside) show; nothing but an advertisement.
Aus-hänge-schild (⌣...) n ⓶ sign-board; auf dem Dach: F sky-sign; (Reklame) advertisement, puff; **-zettel** m placard; ~ anheften to put (or stick) up bills.
Aus-hängung (ᴵᴵ⌣) f ⓮ unhooking, &c.; von Waren: display, exposure for sale.
aus-harren (ᴵᴵ⌣) I v/n. (h.) ⓮** to persevere (in one's efforts); to hold out; im Unglück ⁂ to bear up against (or under) misfortune. — II ~ n ㉓ perseverance; endurance; fortitude in suffering or misfortune.

aus-haspen (ᴵᴵ⌣) v/a. ⓮** e-e Tür: ot unhinge, to take off the hinges.
Aus-hau (ᴵᴵ⌣) m ⓭d. for. 1. (das ~en) thinning (or clearing) the wood. — 2. (Lichtung) glade. — 3. (Ausgehauenes) loppings pl.
Aus-hauch (ᴵᴵ⌣) m ⓭d. breathing out; breath; exhalation; Blumen: fragrance.
aus-hauchen (ᴵᴵ⌣) I v/a. ⓮** to exhale; to breathe out or forth; den Geist, das Leben ⁂ to breathe one's last, to expire. — II ~ n ㉓ u. **A/ung** f ⓮ exhalation; last breath, expiring.
Aus-hau(e)-eisen ⊕ (ᴵᴵ⌣(⌣)...) n ⓶ punch, punching tool; metall. tapping-rod.
aus-hauen (ᴵᴵ⌣) I v/a. ⓭c** 1. (aushöhlen) to hollow out, to excavate; ein Grab im Felsen ⁂ to cut a tomb out of the living rock. — 2. hort. Zweige und Äste aus einem Baume, den Baum ⁂ to lop a tree; for. den Wald ⁂ (lichten) to clear the wood. — 3. sculp. j-s Standbild ⁂ to make a statue of a p.; eine Figur in Marmor ⁂ to carve (or hew) out ... in marble; mit dem Meißel: to chisel out. — 4. ⚒ to work, to dig; ausgehauen worked out. — 5. Schlächter: einen Ochsen (zum Verkaufe) ⁂ to cut up an ox (for sale). — 6. F derb: (prügeln) to whip, to flog. — II ~ n ㉓ 7. hollowing (out); e-s Waldes: clearance; sculp. carving out; ⚒ e-s Feldes exhaustion of a mine.
aus-häuten (ᴵᴵ⌣) v/a. u. v/refl. ⓮** to skin, to flay; sich ⁂ to cast one's skin.
aus-heb/en (ᴵᴵ⌣) ⓭(⓻)b** I v/a. 1. Steine, Wurzeln: to pull (or lift) out. — 2. Bier, Wein ⁂ (mit dem Heber) to draw off; Blumen aus den Töpfen ⁂ to unpot, to pot out ...; Nest ꝛc. ⁂ to take ... from the nest; auch fig. die Polizei hob das Nest aus the police unearthed (or pounced on) the whole gang or raided the premises; e-e Tür: to unhinge; sich (dat.) die Schulter ⁂ to dislocate (or put out) one's shoulder. — 3. hunt. e-e Sau: to lift ... by the hind feet; ⊕ Gießerei: das Modell (aus der Form) ⁂, den Guß ⁂ to lift the casting; typ. die Form ⁂ to lift out the form; Zeilen aus dem Winfelhaken ⁂ to empty the stick. — 4. ⚔ frt. die Schützengräben ⁂ to open the trenches. — 5. (auswählen) to select, to pick out; ⚔: Truppen ⁂ to raise (or levy) troops; Rekruten ⁂ to enlist recruits; Ausgehob(e)ne(r) m ⓰ (fresh) recruit, conscript. — II v/n. (h.) 6. die Uhr hebt aus the clock is warning. — III ~ n ㉓ 7. = A/ung.
Aus-heber ⊕ (ᴵᴵ⌣) m ⓶ zum Ausheben von Maschinen: disengaging-apparatus; uhrm.: lifter, ratch.
Aus-hebe-span ⊕ (ᴵᴵ⌣...) m ⓶ typ. setting- (or composing-)rule; **-stab** m Glasmacherei: ferret.
Aus-hebung (ᴵᴵ⌣) f ⓮ pulling out; drawing off; hort. unpotting; ⚔ levy, recruiting; conscription; zu besonderem Dienst: draft(ing off), detachment.
aus-hecken (ᴵᴵ⌣) ⓮** I v/n. (h.) 1. to cease hatching. — II v/a. 2. to hatch (young ones). — 3. F fig. Pläne ꝛc.: to hatch or lay or get up (plots), to concoct or devise (schemes); Gerüchte: to invent.

Zeichen (f. S. XVII): F familiär; P Volkssprache; ⎡ Gaunersprache; ⚘ felten; † alt (auch gestorben); * neu (auch geboren); †† unrichtig;

[aus·heilen] — 117 — [Auskleidezimmer]

aus-heilen (ᵘᴸ˘) I v/a., v/n. (h.), v/refl. ⓖ** to cure (or heal) thoroughly. — II ~ n ㉓ u. A/ung f ㊻ complete (or radical) cure, restoration to health.
aus-heizen (ᵘᴸ˘) v/a. ⓐ** neuen Ofen, frisch geweihte Stube: to warm thoroughly.
aus-helfen (ᵘᴸ˘) ⓑd** I v/n. (h.) 1. † bsd. bibl. (aus der Not helfen) to aid, succour, assist. — 2. (aus der Verlegenheit helfen) e-m mit et. 2 to accommodate (or supply) a p. with a th.; sie hilft ihm oft aus she often gives him a lift or helps him out of a scrape; er hilft uns häufig mit Geld aus he frequently advances us (or supplies us with) money; v. Sachen: in Ermangelung e-s Klaviers wird e-e Gitarre 2 ... a guitar will do (just as well). — II v/a. 3. e-m den Rock 2 to help a p. off with his coat. — III ~ n ㉓ 4. = Aushilfe.
Aus-helfer (ᵘᴸ˘) m ㉒ occasional help (-er); (Ersatzmann) odd man.
aus-heulen (ᵘᴸ˘) v/n. (h.) ⓖ** to cease (or finish) howling.
Aus-hieb (ᵘᴸ) m ⓓd. 1. fenc. (Hieb des ausfallenden Fechters) lunge, thrust. — 2. for. = Aushau. — 3. ✕ cutting (through) the rock, tunnelling, driving.
Aus-hilfe (ᵘᴸ˘) f ㊻ succour, (temporary) assistance, (timely) help; mit Geld a. accommodation; zur ~ by way of a makeshift; in Ermangelung von et. Besserem zur ~ dienen to serve as (or to be) a last resource or a stop-gap; zur ~ dienend subsidiary, supplementary.
Aus-hilfe-gesuch (ᵘᴸ˘...) n ㉒ request for help; =fellner m occasional waiter; =mast ↓ m spare mast, jury-mast; =schauspieler m super(numerary).
aus-hilflich ↘ (ᵘᴸ˘) adv., **aus-hilfsweise** (ᵘᴸ˘) by way of a makeshift or stop-gap; weit≈. temporarily.
aus-hobeln ⊕ (ᵘᴸ˘) v/a. ⓐa** to plane (off or out). [up hoping.)
aus-hoffen (ᵘᴸ˘) v/n. (h.) ⓖ** to give
aus-höhlen (ᵘᴸ˘) I v/a. ⓖ** 1. to hollow out; durch Graben: to excavate; der Tropfen höhlt den Stein aus ... wears (away) the stone. — 2. ⊕ (austiefen) to gouge; (furchen) to groove; (ausweiten) to scoop out. — II ~ n ㉓ 3. = A/ung 1. — III aus-gehöhlt p.p. u. a. ⓖ 4. concave; ⚡ channelled, ⚘ canaliculate(d); (buchtig) sinuous.
Aus-höhlung (~) f ㊻ 1. hollowing (out); excavation. — 2. hollow, groove.
aus-höhnen ↘ (ᵘᴸ˘) ⓖ** = verhöhnen.
aus-holen (ᵘᴸ˘) ⓖ** I v/n. (h.) mit der Hand zum Schlage, Wurfe 2c. 2 to raise (or lift) one's arm for striking, throwing, &c.; zum Sprunge 2 to take a run before jumping; ↓ beim Rudern lang 2 to pull a long stroke; fig. im Erzählen weit 2 to go far back; to give a circumstantial account. — II v/a. e-n 2 (ausforschen) to sound, F to pump a p.
Aus-holer (ᵘᴸ˘) m ㉒ 1. (auch ~in f ㊼) = Ausfrager. — 2. ↓ (Tau) ↘ des blinden Segels sprit-sail halyard; ~ des Klüvers outhaul(er) of the jib.
aus-holzen (ᵘᴸ˘) v/a. ⓐ** 1. = abholzen 1. — 2. (a. **aus-hölzen**) ⊕ Schuhm.: die (hölzernen) Absätze 2 (ausschweifen) to pare (or to slope) the heels.

aus-horchen (ᵘᴸ˘) I v/a. ⓖ** 1. e-n 2 (ausforschen) to sound, to pump, F to pump a person; bisw. v/n. (h.) bei e-m 2 to listen, to play the eavesdropper. — 2. med. den Zustand der Brust 2: ⚕ to auscultate. — II ~ n ㉓ 3. sounding, &c. (f. I); med.: ⚕ auscultation.
Aus-horcher (ᵘᴸ˘) m ㉒, bisw. ~in f ㊼ one who draws out (people's secrets).
aus-hören (ᵘᴸ˘) v/a. ⓖ** to hear to the end, to hear out, to hear (it) all.
Aus-hub (ᵘᴸ) m ⓓd. 1. (Auswahl) choice, selection. — 2. (Auserlesenes) the pick (of the basket), the flower, F the cream. — 3. = Aushebung.
☞ **Aus-hülfe** 2c. f. Aushilfe 2c.
aus-hülsen (ᵘᴸ˘) v/a. ⓐ** to hull, to husk; Erbsen 2c.: to shell; Gerste: to peel.
aus-hungern (ᵘᴸ˘) v/a. ⓐa** to famish, to starve; ✕ eine Festung 2 (zur Übergabe zwingen) to reduce ... by famine, to starve ... into surrender; ausgehungert famished, ravenous, starved; ausgehungertes Geschöpf starveling.
aus-hunzen F (ᵘᴸ˘) v/a. ⓐ** e-n 2 to reprimand (or scold) a p.
aus-husten (ᵘᴸ˘) ⓖ** I v/a. (auswerfen) to cough up; Schleim, a.: to expectorate. — II v/n. (h.) to cease coughing.
aus-jagen (ᵘᴸ˘) v/a. ⓖ** e-n 2 to expel a p.; to hunt him off; fig. e-m den Angstschweiß 2 to make a p. sweat, to frighten a p. into fits; den ganzen Wald 2 to hunt all over the forest.
aus-jammern (ᵘᴸ˘) ⓐa** I v/n. (h.) to cease lamenting. — II sich 2 v/refl. to relieve o.s. by lamentations.
Aus-jät-eisen (ᵘᴸ...) n ㉒ agr. weed(ing)-hook; hoe. [out; to clear of weeds.)
aus-jäten (ᵘᴸ˘) v/a. ⓖ** to weed (or root))
aus-jauchzen (ᵘᴸ˘) ⓖ** sich 2 v/refl. sich (recht) 2 to indulge in loud jubilation.
aus-jochen (ᵘᴸ˘) v/a. ⓖ** to unyoke.
aus-kämmen (ᵘᴸ˘) v/a. ⓖ** 1. to comb (out); das Haar 2 to give the hair a good (or thorough) combing; ausgekämmte Haare n/pl.: a) well-combed hair; b) hair that has come out (or off) in combing, combings pl. — 2. ⊕ Spinnerei: Wolle 2 to comb (or card).
aus-kämpfen (ᵘᴸ˘) ⓖ** I v/n. (h.) to cease fighting; fig. er hat ausgekämpft he has done fighting, his struggles are over. — II v/a. einen Kampf 2 to do (stout) battle; to fight it out.
aus-kauen (ᵘᴸ˘) ⓖ** I v/n. (h.) to finish chewing. — II v/a. Tabak 2c.: to chew ...; ↓ fig. das Schiff kaut das Werg aus ... works out the oakum.
Aus-kauf (ᵘᴸ) m ⓓd. buying out or off.
aus-kaufen (ᵘᴸ˘) I v/a. ⓖ** 1. e-n 2 to buy a p. out; et. 2 (aufkaufen) to buy up a th.; e-n Laden 2 to purchase the whole stock; fig. e-e Gelegenheit, die Zeit 2 to make the most of ... — 2. e-n 2 (ausdrängen) to outbid a p., to forestall a p. in buying; Teilhaber 2 to buy out partners. — II ~ n ㉓ 3. = Auskauf.
aus-kegeln (ᵘᴸ˘) ⓐa** I v/a. ein Schwein 2 to play skittles (or ninepins) for ... — II v/n. (h.) to cease playing skittles.
aus-kehlen (ᵘᴸ˘) I v/a. ⓖ** to flute, to chamfer, channel. — II ~ n ㉓ u. **Aus-kehlung** f ㊼ flute, channel, groove.

Aus-kehr (ᵘᴸ) f ㊻ fig. die (gründliche) ~ von nutzlosen Beamten 2c. a (thorough) sweep among worthless officials, &c.
aus-kehren (ᵘᴸ˘) I v/a. ⓖ** to sweep (out); Schiff: to swab. — II ~ n ㉓ sweep (-ing); fig. das wird sich beim ~ finden it will be found when all is over.
aus-keilen (ᵘᴸ˘) ⓖ** I v/a. 1. ⊕ to fasten with wedges, to wedge. — 2. F fig. e-n 2 = durchprügeln. — II v/n. (jn) 3. v. Pferden: (treten) to kick, (ausschlagen) to lash out. — 4. auch sich 2 v/refl. ✕ ([sich] keilförmig zuspitzen) to pinch out, dwindle, run (out) to a point.
aus-keimen (ᵘᴸ˘) ⓖ** I v/n. 1. (in) to germinate, to shoot out. — 2. (h.) to cease germinating. — II v/a. 3. Kartoffeln 2 (entkeimen) to clear ... of shoots.
aus-keltern (ᵘᴸ˘) ⓐa** = abkeltern.
aus-kennen (ᵘᴸ˘) ⓖb** v/a. to know from. — II [obb.] sich 2 v/refl. (Bescheid wissen) to know (the locality), to be quite at home (in a th.); er kennt sich nicht mehr aus he has lost his bearings; he is at his wits' end.
aus-kerben (ᵘᴸ˘) I v/a. ⓖ** to notch, jag, indent; (auszacken) to scallop; ⚘ ausgekerbt crenated. — II ~ n ㉓ und **Aus-kerbung** f ㊻ notch, indentation.
aus-kernen (ᵘᴸ˘) I v/a. ⓖ** to take the pips out of fruit, to stone plums, to shell peas, &c.; ✕ das Erz 2 to separate the good ore from worthless admixtures. II ~ n ㉓ stoning, &c., pharm. ⚕ enucleation. [kettle-shape.)
aus-fesseln (ᵘᴸ˘) v/a. ⓐa** to form in)
Aus-fesselung ✕ (ᵘᴸ˘) f ㊻ sinking (or falling in) of the bottom.
aus-kitten (ᵘᴸ˘) v/a. ⓖ** to cement.
aus-klagbar (ᵘᴸ) a. ⓖ jur. actionable.
aus-klagen (ᵘᴸ˘) ⓖ** mst jur. I v/a. to sue; to take (or lay an) action against a p.; e-e Schuld, e-n Wechsel 2 to sue for ... — II v/n. (h.) to cease complaining; to stop proceedings against. — III ~ n ㉓ = A/ung. — IV ~de(r) m u. ~de f ㊻ plaintiff. [proceedings pl. against.)
Aus-klagung (~) f ㊻ (law)suit or legal)
aus-klatschen (ᵘᴸ˘) ⓐ** I v/a. 1. to blab (out), abs. (u. ⓖ 2) to enjoy a good gossip. — 2. F ein Kind: to slap. — II v/n. (h.) 3. to cease gossiping.
aus-klauben (ᵘᴸ˘) [mhd.] v/a. ⓖ** to pick out; ✕ Erze 2 to sort (or pick) with the hand; ausgeklaubt hand-picked; F fig. to ferret (or find) out; to work (or worry) out by hard thinking.
aus-kleben (ᵘᴸ˘) v/a. ⓖ** 1. e-n Kasten: to line with paper; eine Wand mit Papier 2 to paper a wall; et. 2 to paste a th. over. — 2. (mit Mörtel 2c. klebend ausfüllen) to fill up (with mortar, &c.), to stop up a hole or a gap.
aus-kleiden (ᵘᴸ˘) v/a. und v/refl. ⓖ** 1. (sich) 2 to undress, unrobe, disrobe; to take off a p.'s clothes (one's clothes); von Rennpferden, Faustkämpfern: 2, ausgekleidet werden: to strip, to peel. — 2. ⊕ (e-n hohlen Raum) mit et. 2 (ausfuttern) to line, coat, face; mit Holz: to board, plank, timber; mit Täfelwerk: to wainscot.
Aus-kleide-zimmer (ᵘᴸ˘...) n ㉒ (un-) dressing-room; lady's boudoir.

aus-kleistern (‴‿) v/a. ⊛a** to paste over, to line (on the) inside with paste.
aus-klengen (‴‿) v/a. ⊛** Samen ⚂ to pick (or take) ... from the (pine-)cones.
aus-klingeln (‴‿) ⊛a** I v/n. (h.) to cease ringing the bell. — II v/a. (kund-tun) to publish by bell-ringing.
aus-klingen (‴‿) v/n. öft** 1. (h.) von Tönen: to die away. — 2. (in, h.) (ausshallen) die Rede klang in ein Hoch ausshallen) die Rede klang in ein Hoch aus the speech ended in (or was greeted with) cheers or loud hurrahs.
aus-klopfen (‴‿) v/a. ⊛** to beat out; Teppiche ⚂ to beat carpets; den Staub aus den Kleidern, die Kleider ⚂ to beat the dust out of (the) clothes; die (Asche aus der) Tabakspfeife ⚂ to knock the ashes out of a pipe; eine verstopfte Pfeife ⚂ to clear a pipe; fig. einem den Rock, das Wams auf dem Leibe ⚂ to dust a p.'s jacket, to thrash a p.; ⊕ Beulen im Metall, aus e-m Kessel ⚂ to beat (or take) out dents.
Aus-klopfer (‴‿) m ⊠ 1. p. who beats carpets, &c. — 2. (Ausklopfstock) switch (or cane) for beating clothes, &c.
aus-klügeln (‴‿) v/a. ⊛a** to puzzle out; to discover by subtle reasoning.
Aus-klüg(e)lung (‴(‿)‿) f ⊛ puzzling out; solution (of a problem) by dint of hard thinking; s. aus-grübeln, -tüfteln.
aus-kneifen F (‴‿) v/n. (in) ⊛öft** (heim-lich entkommen) to slip off, bolt, decamp, slope; to hook it, to (do a) bunk.
aus-kneten (‴‿) v/a. ⊛** to knead thoroughly. [würfeln.]
aus-knobeln F (‴‿) v/a. ⊛a** = aus-
aus-knurren (‴‿) v/n. (h.) ⊛** ausgeknurrt haben to have done snarling.
aus-kochen (‴‿) ⊛** I v/n. 1. (h.): a) v. Dingen: to cease boiling fig. vom Zorn: to cool down; b) von Personen: to cease cooking; c) (recht od. gehörig) ⚂ to boil thoroughly — 2. (in) (übertochen) to boil over. — II v/a. 3. (gehörig) ⚂ to boil (thoroughly) out, to remove (or expel) by boiling; den Saft aus Fleisch ⚂ to extract ... by boiling; ausgekochtes (Suppen-)Fleisch juiceless meat. — 4. Gefäß, Garn ⚂c. ⚂ (reinigen) to cleanse in (or with) boiling water; to scald, to boil; Baumwolle, Seide, auch: to scour; pharm. to decoct (herbs). — 5. Dämpfe ⚂c. ⚂ (ausstoßen) to throw up (or give forth) in boiling. — 6. (gar machen) das Fleisch ist nicht ausgekocht the meat is not sufficiently boiled or not quite done. — III ~ n ⚂ u. **Aus-kochung** f ⊛ 7. boiling thoroughly, boiling out, &c.; pharm. decoction; (durch Abdampfen:) boiling down.
aus-kommen (‴‿) I v/n. (in) ⊛** 1. fast † — herauskommen. — 2. (aus dem Ei ausschlüpfen) to come out of (or to leave) the shell. — 3. fast † (aus-brechen) vom Feuer: to break out. — 4. bibl. (ruchbar w.) to spread (or get) abroad. — 5. (zu Ende kommen) das Faß kommt heute noch aus ... will be finished (or emptied) to-day. — 6. (aus-reichen) mit et. ⚂ to manage to live (or subsist) upon s. th.; mit diesem Gelde werde ich schon ⚂ (können) I shall be able to live on this sum, I shall make

it last or do; damit kann man nicht ⚂ that won't suffice (or be sufficient) to make two ends meet; that won't be enough to live upon; bequem, be-haglich ⚂ to be in easy circumstances; mit wenig Mitteln lange ⚂ to make a little money go a long way; mit dieser Entschuldigung werden Sie nicht ⚂ this excuse will not avail (or help) you; Sprichw. mit vielem hält man haus, mit wenigem kommt man aus enough is as good as a feast. — 7. (in Frieden leben) mit e-m, mit-ea. ⚂ to be on good (or friendly) terms with a p.; mit ihm ist nicht auszukommen nobody can get on with him; sie kommen schlecht mit-ea. aus they don't hit it off well, they cannot agree (well), they are always at logger-heads; es läßt sich schwer mit ihm ⚂ he is difficult to manage; F he's a trouble-some customer (to deal with); sie wird schon mit ihm ⚂ F she'll manage him all right. — II ~ n ⚂ 8. das Aus- und Ein-kommen coming in and out. — 9. (Unterhalt) livelihood, living, competency; sein anständiges, gutes ~ haben to have a decent (or comfortable) income; sein knappes ~ haben to have (just) enough to keep body and soul together. — 10. (friedliches Zs.-leben) living in peace together; es ist kein ~ mit ihm it is impossible to live with him, nobody can get on with him.
aus-kömmlich (‴‿) a. ⊛ (u. adv.) suffi-cient(ly); ein ⚂es Amt a post to which a competent salary is attached, a good appointment; der Lohn living wage; ⚂ besoldet well salaried.
aus-koppeln (‴‿) v/a. ⊛a** hunt. to uncouple (or slip) the hounds.
aus-körnen (‴‿) v/a. ⊛** agr. to shake (or pick) out the grains of; Getreide: to shell; ⊕ Baumwolle: to clean, to gin.
aus-kosten (‴‿) v/a. ⊛** 1. to taste (or enjoy) thoroughly. — 2. ⌇ (auswählen) to select (or pick out) by tasting.
aus-kragen ⊕ (‴‿) ⊛** arch. I v/a. (durch Kragsteine stützen) to corbel. — II v/n. (in) (vorragen) to jut out; (auf Kragsteinen ruhen) to be corbelled.
Aus-kragung (‴‿) f ⊛ arch. projection.
aus-krähen (‴‿) ⊛** I v/a. Hahn: to announce ... by crowing; F fig. et. ⚂ to proclaim a th. upon the housetops. — II v/n. (h.) to cease crowing.
aus-kramen (‴‿) I v/a. ⊛** 1. (zur Schau stellen) to display, exhibit (s. aus-... 5); ⊛ to expose for sale; fig. sein Wissen ⚂ to show off; Geheimnisse: to divulge, to let out. — 2. (ausräumen) to clear (or strip) of furniture. — II ~ n ⚂ u. **Aus-kramung** f ⊛ 3. display(ing); ⊛ ex-hibition; removal of furniture.
aus-kratzen (‴‿) ⊛** I v/a. 1. to scratch (or scrape) out or off; ea. die Augen ⚂ to scratch (or tear) one another's eyes out; Geschriebenes, auch: to erase; to take out (with a knife). — 2. ⊕ metall. den Hochofen ⚂ to draw out the fur-nace. — II F v/n. (in) 3. (weglaufen) to scamper (or run) off, to decamp, to take to one's heels. — III ~ n ⚂ u. **Aus-kratzung** f ⊛ 4. scratching out; erasure. — 5. F (ignominious) flight.

aus-krebsen (‴‿) v/a. ⊛** einen Bach ⚂c. ⚂ to clear ... of crayfish.
aus-krempeln ⊕ (‴‿) v/a. ⊛a** Wolle ⚂ (tragen) to card ... thoroughly.
aus-kriechen (‴‿) ⊛öft** I v/n. (in) aus dem Ei ⚂ to come (or creep) out of the shell (s. aus-1). — II v/a. an Ort: to search (or ferret) out; alle Winkel ⚂ to hunt (or spy about) in every nook and corner.
aus-kugeln (‴‿) I v/a. ⊛a** to ballot (out). — II ~ n ⚂ **Aus-kugelung** f ⊛ ballot(ing).
aus-kühlen (‴‿) v/a. v/refl. (sich ⚂) und v/n. (in) ⊛** to cool thoroughly.
Auskultant ⚂ (‿‿) [it.] m ⊠ hearer.
Auskultation ⚂ (‿‿‿(‿)‿) [it.] f ⊛ med. der Brust ⚂c.: auscultation, stethoscopy.
Auskultator (‿‿‿‿) [it. Zuhörer] m ⊠ jur. ehm., noch öft., etwa: young barrister attending the courts. [thoscopic.]
auskultatorisch ⚂ (‿‿‿‿) a. ⊛ med. ste-
auskultieren ⚂ (‿‿‿‿) [it.] v/a. ⊛ med. (behorchen) to practise auscultation, to diagnose diseases of the heart or lungs through the sounds in the chest.
aus-kundschaft/en (‴‿) I v/a. ⊛** 1. das Land: to explore; ⚔ to scour, reconnoitre. — 2. e-n ⚂ (auffinden) to discover (or spy out) a p. after a pro-longed search. — II ~ n ⚂ 3. = Aung.
Aus-kundschafter ⚂ (‴‿) m ⊠, ~in f ⊛ scout, informer; s. a. Kundschafter.
Aus-kundschaftung (‴‿) f ⊛ explora-tion; ⚔ reconnoitring; spying.
Aus-kunft (‴‿) f ⊛ 1. (Belehrung) infor-mation; intelligence; nähere ~ erteilen über to give full particulars of; nähere ~ hierselbst! Inquire within!, For par-ticulars apply within!; ~ wird erteilt von //! inquire of //!; über et. ~ ver-langen to make inquiry (or to ask for information) about a th. — 2. = Auskunftsmittel. [bureau.]
Aus-kunftei * (‿‿‿‿) f ⊛ = Auskunfts-
Aus-kunft(s)-bureau (‴‿...) n ⊠ in-quiry office; -erteiler m informant, ⊛ referee; -erteilung f information; -mittel n resource, expedient; ver-zweifelte ~ pl. desperate shifts pl.; zu verzweifelten ~n greifen müssen to be put to one's last shifts.
aus-künsteln (‴‿) v/a. ⊛a** to devise (or contrive) cunningly or cleverly.
aus-kuppeln ⊕ (‴‿) v/a. ⊛a** to dis-connect, disengage, ungear, un couple.
aus-kurieren (‴‿) ⊛*/** = ausheilen.
aus-lachen (‴‿) ⊛** I v/n. (h.) to cease laughing. — II v/a. (aushöhnen) e-n ~ über (wegen) etwas to laugh at (or to deride) a p. for a th.; Sie müssen mich nicht ⚂ don't (or you must not) laugh at (or make fun of) me; (lächerlich machen) to (turn into) ridicule; er läßt sich nicht gern von den Nachbarn ⚂ he does not like to be laughed at by (or to be made the laughing-stock of) the neighbours. — III sich ⚂ v/refl. (sich satt lachen) to laugh immoderately; to cease laughing. — IV ~ n ⚂ derision.
aus-lachens-wert (‴‿...) a. ⊛. ⚂wür-dig ridiculous, absurd, ludicrous.
aus-lad/en (‴‿) ⊛bs** I v/a. 1. Waren aus e-m Wagen, e-n Wagen ⚂ to un-load goods, a van; ⚓ ein Schiff ⚂ (löschen) auch: to discharge, clear, lighten ...;

Signs (see page XVII): F familiar; P vulgar; ꜰ flash; ⚂ rare; † obsolete (died); * new word (born); +† incorrect; ♪ music;

[Ausladeort] — 119 — [auslegen]

den Ballast aus einem Schiffe ⁓ to unballast a ship; ⚔ 🚂 **Truppen ⁓** to disembark troops. — **2.** ⚙ *phys.* (entladen) to discharge. — **3.** *paint.* Teile e-s Bildes ⁓ (hervortreten l.) to set off...
II *v/n.* (jn) **4.** *paint.* to stand (in relief); *arch.* Gesims 2c.: to project. — **III** ⁓ *n* ㉓ **5.** = A/ung; *phys.* ⁓ e-s Elektrophor's discharge of an electrophorus.

Aus-lade-ort (⁓⁓...) *m* ㊷, *f* place for unloading; ⚓ landing-place or -pier, wharf, quay.

Aus-lader (⁓⁓) *m* ㊷ **1.** ⚓ lighterman. — **2.** ⚙ Instrument: *elect.* discharging-rod.

Aus-lade-zeug (⁓...) *n* = Kugelzieher.

Aus-ladung (⁓⁓) *f* ㊻ unloading; discharge; *arch.* ⁓ e-s Gesimses projection; sally; *path.* eine kropfige ⁓ am Halse a goitrous growth of the neck.

Aus-ladungs-... (⁓⁓...) ㊷ = Auslade-...

Aus-lage (⁓⁓) *f* ㊸ **1.** (ausgelegtes Geld) outlay, disbursement, advance; e-m seine ⁓ wiedererstatten to reimburse a p.; zu seinen ⁓n kommen to (re)cover (one's) expenses. — **2.** (etwas offen Hingelegtes) die ganze ⁓ auf der Tenne the corn spread on the (barn-)floor; bsd. 🏪 (zur Schau gelegte Waren) display, show; (Schaufenster) show-window, shop-front. — **3.** *fenc.* first position, guard.

Aus-lage-nota 🏪 (⁓...) *f* ㊻, **=rechnung** *f* note of disbursement(s). [lagern II.]

aus-lagern (⁓⁓) *v/n.* (jn) ㊹** = ab-

Aus-land (⁓⁓) [nhd.] *n* ②c. (*pl.* ⁓) foreign country or parts *pl.*; im Ju= und ⁓ e at home and abroad; Reise ins ⁓ journey (or tour) abroad, foreign travels *pl.*; aus dem ⁓ e from abroad, ins ⁓ abroad; 🏪 fürs ⁓ bestimmt, ins ⁓ gehend outward bound; *coll.* dem ⁓ zum Gelächter (U.) the laughing-stock of foreigners or foreign lands.

Aus-länder (⁓⁓) *m* ㊷, **⁓in** *f* ㊵ foreigner, alien; **⁓ei** (⁓⁓⁓) *f* ㊻ mst *b.s.* predilection (or mania) for foreign things; affectation of foreign manners.

aus-ländisch (⁓⁓) *a.* ㊺ foreign, alien; (fremdartig) outlandish; ♃ u. *zo.* exotic.

Aus-lands-paß (⁓⁓...) *m* ㊷ passport for abroad; **=reise** *f* = Reise ins Ausland (s. d₈); **=sucht** *f* = Ausländerei.

aus-langen (⁓⁓) *v/n.* (h.) ㊹** **1.** *fig.* (ausreichen) das Geld wird ⁓ the money will suffice or last; ich kann damit ⁓ I can make it do or make shift with it. — **2.** (die Hand ausstrecken) to stretch out (or reach forth) one's hand.

Aus-laß (⁓⁓) *m* ⑧a. outlet.

aus-lass/en (⁓⁓) ⑥** **I** *v/a.* **1.** eine Stelle: to omit, to leave out, to pass over; (überspringen) to skip (over); ♪ to slur over; Billard: einen Ball: to miss; Unterkleider: to leave off. — **2.** (hervorkommen od. entweichen lassen) to let escape, to emit; ⊕ Dampf ⁓ to let (or blow) off the steam; *fig.* seinen Ärger, Verdruß an e-m ⁓ to let out one's anger, to vent one's ill humour upon a p.; seine Galle, Wut ⁓ to vent (or to give vent to) one's passion, rage on a p.; seine Rache an einem ⁓ to wreak one's vengeance upon a p. — **3.** *a. v/refl.* (kundgeben) to manifest; seine Ansichten, sich über et. ⁓ to express one's opinion,

o.s. upon a th.; to speak one's mind about a th.; sich des längeren und breiteren über et. ⁓ to expatiate (or enlarge) upon a th.; *abs.* sich gegen e-n ⁓ to unbosom o.s. (or to open one's heart) to a p. — **4.** Kochkunst: Fett ⁓ to melt; Honig: to strain. — **5.** Schneiderei: (weiter machen) to let out (the seams), (länger machen) to let down (a tuck). —
II sich ⁓ *v/refl.* **6.** **⁓ 3.** — **III** ⁓ *n* ㉓ **7.** = A/ung. —**IV aus-gelassen** *p.p.* u. *a.* **8.** s. b.

Aus-laß-rohr ⊕ (⁓⁓...) *n* ㊷, **=röhre** *f* outlet- (or discharge-)pipe; waste-pipe.

Aus-lassung (⁓⁓) *f* ㊻ letting out, &c. (s. auslassen); ⊕ **⁓ von Dampf** letting off steam; (Weglassung) omission; word(s *pl.*) omitted; *gr.* von Worten: ellipsis; des Endvokals vor einem folgenden Vokal: elision; (Äußerung) manifestation, utterance, der Freude 2c.: effusion.

Aus-lassungs-fehler (⁓⁓...) *m* ㊷ omission; **=zeichen** *n gr.* apostrophe, mark of elision; *typ.* auch: caret (∧).

Aus-laß-ventil ⊕ (⁓⁓...) *n* ㊷ Dampfm.: outlet- (or discharge-, escape-)valve.

Aus-lauf (⁓⁓) *m* ⓪d. **1. a)** (Auslaufen des Wassers 2c.) running (out), outflow; aus einem lecken Fasse: leakage; **b)** (Ausmündung) bei einem Flusse: mouth, outlet. — **2.** v. e-m Orte aus: start, departure; Tennis: margin; ⚓ setting sail. — **3.** ⚔ (Karrenvoll) barrow-load, barrowful. — **4.** *arch.* (Aus-tragung, -ladung) projection.

aus-lauf/en (⁓⁓) Gast** **I** *v/n.* (1: h., 2 f.: jn) **1.** (aufhören zu laufen) to cease running. — **2.** (sich in Bewegung setzen, abfahren) to set out; to depart, to leave; bsd. bei Wettrennen: to start; ⚓ to set sail; aus dem Hafen ⁓ to clear (or leave) a port; to put to sea; von einer Flotte auch: to go on a cruise, to take a trip; das Geschwader war ausgelaufen the squadron was (manœuvring) at sea or cruising about. — **3.** (ausgehen) to go out, F to have (or take) a run (out); Gänge abmachen to go on (or to do) errands. — **4.** (ausrinnen) von einer Sanduhr, von Wasser: to run out; von Gefäßen: to leak; durch Überfüllung: to run (or flow) over, to overflow. — **5.** (endigen) to taper; in eine Spitze ⁓ to end in (F to run to) a point; das Land läuft in ein Vorgebirge aus... runs out (or narrows) into a promontory; *fig.* auf etwas ⁓ to terminate (or result) in s.th. — **6.** ⊕ *arch.* (vorragen) to jut out, to project. — **7.** v. Strahlen: to radiate, to diverge; von Wurzeln: to spread; to run into suckers. — **8.** ⚓ das Ankertau 2c. ⁓ lassen to slip the cable, &c. — **II** *v/a.* **9.** eine Bahn ⁓ (zu Ende laufen) to run from one end of a course to the other. — **10.** sich (*dat.*) die Schuhe ⁓ to stretch one's boots by walking. — **III** sich ⁓ *v/refl.* **11.** (tüchtig laufen) to have a good (long) run or a stiff walk, to take good exercise. — **12.** (durch Laufen weiter werden) to grow wider by running. — **13.** ⁓ (sich ausschleifen) to wear off (or out) by friction. — **IV** ⁓ *n* ㉓ **14.** course; departure; Sport 2c.: start; ⚓ going to sea; cruising (excursion); Befehl zum ⁓ sailing-orders *pl.*; zum ⁓ bereit ready for sailing, v. Dampfern: with steam up; ⁓ v.

Strahlen: radiation; v. Wurzeln: spreading; in eine Spitze: tapering off; end.

Aus-laufer (⁓⁓) *m* ㉒ **1.** (a. **⁓in** *f* ㊵) (Lauf-bursche, -mädchen) errand-boy, -girl; runner; *typ.* printer's devil. — **2.** ⚔ (Hundsläufer) draw-boy.

Aus-läufer (⁓⁓) *m* ㉒ **1.** = Ausläufer. — **2.** (Abzweigung): **a)** ♃ ramification; **b)** ♀ ⁓ e-s Gebirges: spur; ⚔ ⁓ e-s Ganges branch of a lode; **c)** *fig.* (a. Eisenbahnwes.) branch. — **3.** ♃ (Ranke) offshoot, sucker, ⁊ stolon; ⁓ treibend ⁊ stoloniferous.

Auslauf-hafen ⚓ (⁓⁓...) *m* ㊷ port of departure; **=karren** ⚔ *m* wheel-barrow; **=platz** *m* Wettrennen: starting-post.

aus-laug/en (⁓⁓) **I** *v/a.* ㊹** *chm.* u. ⊕ to lixiviate; to steep in lye; Wäsche: to buck; Holzasche: to leach; Erze: to wash, to buddle; *pharm.* (ausziehen) to extract. — **II** ⁓ *n* ㉓ u. A/ung (⁓⁓) *f* ㊻ lixiviation; bucking, &c.; extraction.

Aus-laut (⁓⁓) *m* ⓪d. *gr.* final sound; Abfall des ⁓s ⁊ apocope; im ⁓, als ⁓ at the end of a word or syllable.

aus-lauten (⁓⁓) *v/n.* (h.) ㊹** *gram.* to terminate (or end) in; ⁓d *p.pr.* u. *a.* ㊺ forming a termination, terminal, final.

aus-läuten (⁓⁓) ㊹** **I** *v/n.* (h.) **1.** to cease ringing the bell(s); es hat ausgeläutet the bells have stopped. — **2.** e-m Verstorbenen ⁓ to ring the funeral bell for a p. — **II** *v/a.* **3.** (s. auch.) **4.** et. ⁓ to announce (the end of) s.th. by bell-ringing; das alte Jahr ⁓ to ring out the old year (and ring in the new one).

aus-leben (⁓⁓) ㊹** **I** *v/a.* eine Zeit: to live to (see) the end of. — **II** *v/n.* (h.) er hat ausgelebt his life is spent, he has ceased living. — **III** sich ⁓ *v/refl.* to wear o.s. out, to waste one's vital powers; *durch* Genüsse: to lead a life of pleasure; durch Wirksamkeit: to live a full life, to attain the ends of (one's) life.

aus-leck/en (⁓⁓) ㊹** **I** *v/n.* (jn) = auslaufen 4. — **II** *v/a.* Flüssiges mit d. Zunge: to lick up, von Tieren a.: to lap up. — **III** ⁓ *n* ㉓ leakage; licking.

aus-ledern (⁓⁓) *v/a.* ㊹a** **1.** to line with leather. — **2.** *fig.* = durchprügeln.

aus-leer/en (⁓⁓) *v/a.* ㊹a** **1.** to empty (out); das Glas, den Wein: to drink up; den Briefkasten ⁓ to clear the letter-box; e-n Teich ⁓ to drain a pond; ein Haus ⁓ to clear ..., (plündernd) to ransack ...; j-s Börse ⁓ to rifle a p.'s pocket; to fleece a p. — **2.** *fig.* sein Herz ⁓ to pour out one's heart to. — **II** sich ⁓ *v/refl.* to empty (o.s.). — **III** ⁓ *n* ㉓ **4.** = A/ung. — **IV** ⁓d *p.pr.* u. *a.* ㊺ **5.** emptying, &c.; *med.* ⁓d (es Mittel) aperient, laxative.

Aus-leerung (⁓⁓) *f* ㊻ emptying, &c. (s. ausleeren); *med.* evacuation, opening (or relief) of the bowels, motion.

Aus-leerungs-mittel (⁓⁓...) *n* ㊷ *med.* purgative; **=pumpe** *f* exhausting pump or syringe; **=rohr** *n*, **=röhre** *f* evacuation- (or waste-)pipe.

Aus-lege-bank ⊕ (⁓...) *f* ㊻ *typ.* **=tisch** *b*; **=holz** ⊕ *n*, *join.* veneer; inlaid piece.

aus-leg/en (⁓⁓) ㊹** **I** *v/a.* **1.** (ausbreiten) to spread (or lay) out; 🏪 Waren: to display, to expose for sale. — **2.** *fig.* (erklären) to explain, interpret, ex-

---
⚗ scientific; ♃ botanical; ♀ geography; ⊕ machinery; ⚔ mining; ⚔ military; ⚓ marine; 🏪 commercial; ✉ postal; 🚂 railway.

[Ausleger] — 120 — [ausmachen]

pound; et. als Beleidigung 2 to take s.th. as an insult; als Hochverrat 2 to construe into treason; e-m et. als Stolz 2 to set (or put) a th. down to a p.'s pride; et. gut (übel) 2 to put a good (bad) construction upon a th.; falsch 2 to misconstrue, to put a wrong construction upon; 2d explanatory, ⚔ exegetical. — 3. Geld für e-n 2 to lay on money for a p.; sein Geld auf Zinsen 2 to put (out) ... at interest. — 4. agr. Erbsen 2 (säen) to sow peas. — 5. ⊕ (als Verzierung einlegen) to inlay, to (in)crust; ausgelegte Arbeit inlaid work; veneering; Holz mit Furnieren 2 to veneer; Stahl mit Gold ob. Silber 2 to damascene...; den Fußboden 2: a) mit Holz: to board; b) mit Kieseln: to lay out with pebblework; c) mit Steinplatten: to tile; mit Steinwürfeln: to tesselate. — 6. ⊕ typ. (Bogen fangen) to pick up (the printed sheets). — 7. ⚔ ein Geschütz 2 to dismount a gun. — 8. ⚓ ein Schiff auf die Reede 2 to lay out ... — II F v/n. (h.) 9. (fett w.) to grow stout. — 10. ⚓ v. Matrosen: (auf die Rahen hinausgehen) to man the yards. — III sich 2 v/refl. 11. (sich vorbeugen) bsd. fenc. to take one's guard. — IV ~ n ⊕ 12. = A/ung.

Aus-leger (ᴵᴵ˘) m ⊕ 1. (a. ~in f ⊕) a) (Erklärer) interpreter; commentator; expounder (of the gospel); b) ⊕ typ. (Bogenfänger[in]) taker-off, sheet-collector. — 2. ⊕ typ. (mechanische Vorrichtung) flyers, flies pl.; sheet-deliverer. — 3. ⚓ a) bei Schiffen: (Stange ob. Spiere zur Anbringung v.Netzen, Segeln ob. Torpedos) boom; b) bei Sportbooten (Stahlgestell als Auflage für die Riemen) und bei polynesischen Booten (durch Querhölzer mit dem Boot verbundener Seitenbaum): outrigger.

Aus-leger-boot ⚓ (ᴵᴵ˘...) n ⊕ zu Wettrennen: outrigger; -brücke f cantilever bridge.

Aus-legerei (ᴵᴵ˘ᴵᴵ) f ⊕ meist b.s. misconstruction, strained interpretation.

Aus-lege-stäbchen ⊕ (ᴵᴵ˘...) n⊕ = -Holz; -tisch m: a) salesman's stall; b) ⊕ typ. table for spreading out printed sheets, fly-board, taking-off board.

Aus-legung (ᴵᴵ˘) f ⊕ 1. = Auslage 2. — 2. fig. (Erklärung) explanation, (jur. &c.) interpretation, exposition; der Heiligen Schrift, auch: exegesis; (Lesart) reading; falsche ~ misconstruction; e-e doppelte ~ zulassend admitting of two constructions, ambiguous, with a double-entente. — 3. ⊕ incrustation; damascening; inlaid flooring.

Aus-legungs-kunde (ᴵᴵ˘...) f ⊕, -kunst f, science of exposition; -weise f mode of interpretation; -weise adv. by way of exposition or interpretation; -wissenschaft f ⚔ exegesis; hermeneutics pl.

aus-leiden (ᴵᴵ˘) ⊕c** = ausdulden.

aus-leiern ⊕ (ᴵᴵ˘) v/a. ⊕a** to wear out by friction; ausgeleiert worn out, widened out (and loosened) by friction or constant wear.

aus-leih/en (ᴵᴵ˘) I v/a. ⊕** to let out (on hire), to lend out; v. Banken u. Geldleihern: to loan; sein Kapital auf Zinsen 2 to put out one's principal at interest. — II ~ n ⊕ = A/ung.

Aus-leiher (ᴵᴵ˘) m ⊕, ~in f ⊕ lender; v. Pferden: livery-stable man.

Aus-leihung (ᴵᴵ˘) f ⊕ letting out on hire, &c. (s. ausleihen I); loan.

aus-lenken (ᴵᴵ˘) v/n. ⊕** = ausbiegen II.

aus-lernen (ᴵᴵ˘) I v/a. u. v/n. (h.) ⊕** to learn (or study) thoroughly or completely; to make o.s. master of a subject, an art, &c.; ausgelernt h. to have learnt enough; v. Lehrlingen: to have served one's time; v. Schülern: to have done schooling or learning; Sprichw. man lernt nie aus we are never too old to learn, we live and learn. — II aus-gelernt p.pr. u. a. ⊕. s. I; a.: accomplished; (erfahren) experienced; der Schalk, Fuchs arrant knave, cunning rogue, F old (or practised) hand.

Aus-lese (ᴵᴵ˘) f ⊕ 1. (Auswahl) choice; zo., physiol. natürliche ~ natural selection. — 2. (auserlesener Wein) choice(st) wine; fig. (Auserlesenes) pick (of the basket), the cream, the very best.

aus-lesen (ᴵᴵ˘) ⊕a** I v/a. 1. to select, to choose; (einzeln aussuchen) to single (or pick) out; (sortieren) to sort, pick, cull; Ausgelesenes selection, pick. — 2. (zu Ende lesen, s. aus 2.) to finish reading, to peruse. — II v/n. (h.) 3. to cease reading; to read to the end. — III ~ n ⊕ 4. selection, choice; sorting; reading through, perusal of a letter, &c.

Aus-leser (ᴵᴵ˘) m ⊕, ~in f ⊕ person who selects or picks; sorter, culler.

aus-leuen ⚓ (ᴵᴵ˘) v/a. ⊕** Sturzgüter 2 to unload ... with the girt-line, to whip up ...

aus-lichten (ᴵᴵ˘) v/a. ⊕** 1. for. einen Wald 2 to thin (the trees of) a forest; hort. Bäume 2 to prune (or lop) trees. — 2. ⚓ (teilweise ausladen) to lighten.

Aus-lieferer (ᴵᴵ˘) m ⊕ deliverer; in Verlagsbuchhandlungen &c.: delivery-clerk.

aus-liefern (ᴵᴵ˘) I v/a. ⊕a** to deliver (up), to give up, to hand over; Gestohlenes: to restore; Buchhandel: to deliver a serial work; jur. to surrender; e-n Verbrecher, auch: to extradite; wir sind ihm ausgeliefert we are in his power or at his mercy. — II ~ n ⊕ = A/ung.

Aus-lieferung (ᴵᴵ˘) f ⊕ delivery; v. Entwendetem: restitution; jur. surrender; v. Verbrechern an e-n fremden Staat: extradition, handing over to a foreign state.

Aus-lieferungs-buch ⊕ (ᴵᴵ˘...) n ⊕ delivery-book; -provision ⊕ f (Entschädigung für den Kommissionär) agent's commission for delivery; -schein m bill of delivery, delivery-order; -tag m day of delivery; -vertrag m über Auslieferung von Verbrechern: extradition treaty; über Auswechselung von Kriegsgefangenen: cartel; -zettel m = -schein.

aus-liegen (ᴵᴵ˘) ⊕** I v/n. (h.) u. v/refl. 1. = abliegen 2. — II v/n. (h.) 2. to be on show; von Zeitungen: to be kept; hier liegt die Kölnische Zeitung aus the Cologne Gazette is taken in (here). — 3. fenc. to take one's guard. — 4. ⚓ Wachtschiff: to be posted (or stationed) at the mouth of the harbour.

Aus-lieger ⚓ (ᴵᴵ˘) m ⊕ 1. outrigger (= Ausleger 3). — 2. (Wachtschiff) guard-ship, revenue-cutter.

aus-loben (ᴵᴵ˘) v/a. ⊕** et 2 (öffentlich e-e Belohnung für ein Zustandebringen v. et. aussetzen) to make a public offer of a reward for s.th. (to be accomplished).

aus-lochen ⊕ (ᴵᴵ˘⊕˘) v/a. ⊕** carp. to mortise. [scoop out] with a spoon.)

aus-löffeln (ᴵᴵ˘) v/a. ⊕a** to empty (or

aus-lohnen (ᴵᴵ˘) v/a. ⊕** to pay off.

aus-lösbar (ᴵᴵ˘-) a. ⊕ redeemable.

aus-löschbar (ᴵᴵ˘-) a. ⊕ quenchable.

aus-löschen (ᴵᴵ˘) I v/a. ⊕** 1. Feuer &c. 2 to extinguish (or put out, quench)..., Gas: to turn off, elektrisches Licht: to switch off. — 2. Geschriebenes: to efface, to obliterate, (auswischen) to wipe (or blot) out, (auskratzen) to scratch out, to erase. — II v/n. (in.) ⊕b(e)ft** 3. to go (or drop) out, to be(come) extinguished; v. Geschriebenem: to be(come) effaced. — III ~ n ⊕ 4. = A/ung.

Aus-löscher (ᴵᴵ˘) m ⊕ 1. (a. ~in f ⊕) extinguisher; bsd. fig. (Vertilger) destroyer, exterminator. — 2. (Löschhorn, extinguisher. [vgl. auslöschbar.)

aus-löschlich (ᴵᴵ˘) a. ⊕ extinguishable.)

Aus-löschung (ᴵᴵ˘) f ⊕ extinction; effacement; obliteration; von Buchstaben: deletion.

aus-los/en (ᴵᴵ˘) I v/a. ⊕** to allot; to distribute (or draw) by lot(s); Tennis: to toss; (auswürfeln) to raffle for; ⚓ e-n geloste Staatsschuldscheine m/pl. drawn bonds pl. — II ~ n ⊕ = A/ung.

aus-lös/en (ᴵᴵ˘) I v/a. ⊕** 1. to loosen; ⊕ to uncouple, ungear, disengage; einen Wecker 2 to start an alarum; surg. aus den Gelenken 2 to disarticulate; fig. die durch solche Mannestat ausgelöste Begeisterung the enthusiasm aroused (or called forth) by such a noble deed. — 2. auch v/refl. sich 2 (frei machen) to redeem (o.s.), (loskaufen) to ransom; mech. e-e Kraft 2 to set free ..., to release ...; jur. Verpfändetes: to replevy, to recover; ⚓ e-n Wechsel 2 to cash. — II ~ n ⊕ 3. = A/ung.

Aus-losung (ᴵᴵ˘) f ⊕ allotment; ⚓ drawing of bonds; Tennis: draw, toss.

Aus-lösung (ᴵᴵ˘) f ⊕ loosening, &c.; mech. s.th. which releases (or sets free) the potential forces (stored up) in a body; ~ einer Uhr: detent, ratch(et); (Befreiung) redemption, ransom, deliverance. [Kriegsgefangene: cartel.)

Aus-lösungs-vertrag ⚔ ("...) m ⊕ betr.)

aus-lotsen ⚓ (ᴵᴵ˘) v/a. ⊕** to pilot out of port, to take out to sea.

aus-lüften (ᴵᴵ˘) I v/a. ⊕** to air (thoroughly); to ventilate. — II sich 2 v/refl. to take an airing. — III ~ n ⊕ u. **Aus-lüftung** f ⊕ airing.

aus-lugen (ᴵᴵ˘) v/n. (h.) ⊕** to be on the lookout, vgl. ausgucken.

aus-mach/en (ᴵᴵ˘) ⊕** v a. 1. (herausbringen): a) to get (or fetch) out; Flecke auch: to take out, to remove; Falten aus Kleidern 2 (ausplätten) to smooth out ... with a hot iron; Feuer: to put out, to extinguish; b) Austern, Krebse: to open, to take out of the shell; Hülsenfrüchte: to hull, husk, shell. — 2. (zu Ende bringen) to put an end to, to end, to finish. — 3. F (entleeren) den Wein im Glase, das Glas 2 to

Zeichen (s. S. XVII): F familiär; P Volkssprache; Γ Gaunersprache; ⟍ selten; † alt (auch gestorben); * neu (auch geboren); ++ unrichtig.

[Ausmachung] — 121 — [ausniesen]

drink off the wine. — 4. (einen Streit beilegen) mit e-m et. auszumachen haben to have a bone to pick with a p.; e-n Streit mit e-m 2 to settle a difference with a p.; das mögen die beiden miteinander 2 the two may settle (or arrange) that between them (-selves). — 5. (feststellen) to decide, to determine; (übereinkommen) to agree upon; (ausbedingen) to stipulate; dies darf als ausgemacht gelten this may be taken for granted; vgl. ausgemacht. — 6. ohne pass. (betragen) to come to, to total up to; wieviel macht das aus? what does it come (or amount) to?; (bilden) to form; zwei Zimmer machen meine (ganze) Wohnung aus ... constitute my (whole) dwelling; einen (notwendigen) Teil von et. 2 to form a(n essential) portion or a(n integral) part of a th. — 7. (das Wesen von etwas bilden) das macht nichts aus (hat nichts zu bedeuten) that does not matter, it's of no consequence, never mind that; würde es Ihnen et. 2, wenn //? would it make any difference to you if //? — II ~ n ㉓ 8. = A/ung. — III ausgemacht p.p. u. a. ㊻ 9. f. bsd. Art.
Aus-machung (ᴗ—ᴗᴗ) f ㊻ getting (or taking) out; e-r Streitigkeit: agreement, settlement, arrangement.
aus-mahlen (ᴗ—ᴗᴗ) ⓼** (p.p. ausgemahlen) I v/a. Getreide: to grind (all) up. — II v/n. (h.) to cease grinding.
aus-mal en (ᴗ—ᴗᴗ) ⓼** I v/a. 1. (anstreichen) ein Zimmer: to paint; (tuschend illuminieren) Kupferstiche 2c.: to illuminate, to colour; Wappen: to emblazon. — 2. ein Gemälde 2 (zu Ende bringen) to finish painting, to put the finishing touches to ... — 3. fig. to delineate, sketch, depict; (ausschmücken) to amplify; sich (dat.) et. im Geiste 2 to picture a th. to o.s., to fancy a th. — II v/n. (h.) 4. to cease painting. — III ~ n ㉓ 5. = A/ung.
Aus-maler (ᴗ—ᴗᴗ) m ㉒. ~in f ㊼ colourer, illuminator; fig. delineator; (übertreiber) exaggerator.
Aus-malung (~) f ㊻ painting, &c. (f. ausmalen I); (Beschreibung) delineation, sketch; (Vorstellung) fancy(-picture).
Aus-marsch bsd. ⚔ (ᴗ—ᴗ) m ⓞa. marching out; für längere Zeit, in den Krieg 2c.: departure, setting out on a (long) march.
aus-marschieren (ᴗ—ᴗ—ᴗ) v/n. ⓽** 1. (in) to march (out or off); to set out on a (long) march, to turn out. — 2. (h.) to cease marching. [or thoroughly.
aus-mästen (ᴗ—ᴗᴗ) v/a. ⓼**to fatten well]
aus-mauern ⊕ (ᴗ—ᴗᴗ) v/a. ⓽a** arch. to wall (up); to line (or fill) with bricks or stones or masonry; ausgemauertes Grab brick-grave; tomb; ⚒ ausgemauerter Gang arched level or tunnel.
aus-mause(r)n (ᴗ—ᴗᴗ) v/n. (h.) ⓽ (⓽a) ⓼** von Vögeln: to cease moulting or mewing.
aus-meißeln ⊕ (ᴗ—ᴗᴗ) ⓽a** I v/a. (aushöhlen, ausarbeiten) to work (out) with a chisel, to chisel out; sculp., &c. to carve (in stone, &c.), to engrave, (en-)chase; ausgemeißelte (zifelierte) Arbeit chased work; ein geistiges Werk sorgsam 2 to elaborate, to polish ... — II v/n. (h.) bsd. ausgemeißelt haben to have done

chiselling. — III ~ n ㉓ und **Ausmeißelung** (ᴗ—ᴗᴗ) f ㊻ chiselling; carving; sculpture; fig. elaboration.
aus-melken (ᴗ—ᴗᴗ) ⓼ (a. ⓽b)** I v/a. der Kuh die Milch 2, die Kuh oder das Euter 2 to milk ... out, to milk ... dry, to drain ... by milking. — II v/n. (h.) to cease milking.
aus-mergeln (ᴗ—ᴗᴗ) v/a. ⓽a** to impoverish; vgl. abmergeln.
aus-merzen (ᴗ—ᴗᴗ) I v/a. ⓽** (aussondern) to pick (or sort) out, to weed out; (verwerfen) to cast off, to reject; ein Gesetz: to abolish; Namen aus einer Liste: to expunge, strike out; Schriftstellen: to suppress; math. Größen aus einer Gleichung: to eliminate; einen Schandfleck: to efface, to blot out. — II ~ n ㉓ u. **Ausmerzung** f ㊻ rejection; abolition; expurgation; elimination; effacement.
aus-meßbar (ᴗ—ᴗᴗ) a. ㊻ measurable.
aus-meß|en (ᴗ—ᴗᴗ) ⓼** I v/a. 1. (vermessen) to measure (mit dem Meter by the metre, mit der Elle with a yard-measure); ein Zimmer: to take the dimensions of; Land: to survey; math. den Rauminhalt e-s Körpers 2 to find the cubic (or solid) contents of a body; Faß, Schiff: to gauge. — 2. (nach Maß austeilen, verkaufen) to distribute (or sell) by measure (by the metre, litre, pint, &c.); ⊕ to (sell by) retail. — II v/n. (h.) 3. to cease measuring. — III ~ n ㉓ 4. = A/ung 1.
Aus-messer (~) m ㉒ p. who gauges, &c.; (Feldmesser) (land-)surveyor.
Aus-messung (ᴗ—ᴗᴗ) f ㊻ 1. measure(ment); survey(ing); gauging; math. mensuration; von Körpern: solid geometry; ⊕ selling by retail; retail trade. — 2. *(Ausdehnung, Größe) dimension, size.
aus-mieten (ᴗ—ᴗᴗ) v/a. ⓽** 1. e-n 2, e-m die Wohnung 2 (ihn verdrängen) to oust (or push out) a p. by offering a higher rent). — 2. e-n 2 (wo einmieten) to find lodgings (or apartments) for a p.
Aus-mischung (ᴗ—ᴗᴗ) ⊕ f ㊻ 1. mixture. — 2. paint, ⊕, &c. ~ der Farbentöne blend(ing) of colours.
aus-misten (ᴗ—ᴗᴗ) v/a. ⓽** den Stall 2c.: to clear ... of manure or (horse-)dung; fig. den Augiasstall 2 to cleanse the Augean stables; F eine Schrift 2 to correct (or weed out) the grossest mistakes in ...
aus-mitteln (ᴗ—ᴗᴗ) I v/a. ⓽a** (ausfindig m.) to find out, ascertain, discover. — II **Aus-mitt(e)lung** (ᴗ—(ᴗ)—ᴗ) f ㊻ finding out discovery.
aus-möblieren (ᴗ—ᴗ—ᴗ) v/a. ⓽** to furnish or fit up (a house, a room) throughout.
aus-montieren ⚔ (ᴗ—ᴗ—ᴗ) I v/a. ⓽** to accoutre, to equip (thoroughly). — II ~ n ㉓ u. **Aus-montierung** f ㊻ accoutrement, equipment; weit S. outfit.
aus-münden (ᴗ—ᴗᴗ) I v/n. (h.) u. v/refl. ⓽**: in etwas 2 to discharge, to empty (or flow) into s.th.; to open (out) into s.th.; auf zwei Straßen 2 to lead into (or to connect) ... — II **Aus-mündung** f ㊻ (Mündung) mouth (of a river, &c.); outlet.
aus-münzen (ᴗ—ᴗᴗ) I v/a. ⓽** to coin; ⊕ geringer 2 to debase (the coinage). — II ~ n ㉓ u. **Aus-münzung** f ㊻ coinage; aus schlechter Legierung: debasement.

aus-müssen F (ᴗ—ᴗᴗ) v/n. (h.) ⓼** von Personen: to be obliged to go out; die Stiefel müssen aus ... must come off.
aus-mustern (ᴗ—ᴗᴗ) I v/a. ⓽a** (verwerfen) to discard, reject; (ausmerzen) to pick out, to eliminate; ⚔ Soldaten als dauernd untauglich 2 to discharge ...; das Betriebsmaterial 2 to overhaul the stores; ausgemusterte Pferde cast horses; ⊕ ausgemusterte Ware cast-off (or discarded) goods pl., refuse. — II ~ n ㉓ u. **Aus-musterung** (ᴗ—ᴗᴗ) f ㊻ rejection; discharge; overhauling.
aus-nähen (ᴗ—ᴗᴗ) I v/a. ⓼** 1. to finish sewing. — 2. (ausziehen) to embroider, to work; ausgenähte Arbeit fancy-work, embroidery. — 3. fig. sich (dat.) die Augen 2 to ruin o.'s eyes with sewing. — II ~ n ㉓ 4. embroidery, fancy-work, mit Blumen: diaper-work.
Aus-nahme (ᴗ—ᴗᴗ) f ㊸ exception; anomaly; mit ~ von with the exception of, except(ing), save; alle ohne ~ all to a man; feine Regel ohne ~ (there is) no rule without an exception; die ~ bestätigt die Regel the exception proves the rule; eine ~ von der allgemeinen Regel bilden to form an exception to the general rule; mit e-m, et. eine ~ machen to except a p., a th., (v. Steuern 2c. befreien) to exempt a p.
Aus-nahmefall (ᴢ...) m ㊷ exceptional case; =frachtsätze m pl. differential rates pl.; =gericht(shof m) n special tribunal; =gesetz n exceptional law.
aus-nahms-los (ᴗ—...) a. ㊻ admitting of no exception, universal; without exception; =losigkeit f ㊻ universality; 2weise adv. by way of exception, exceptionally; (nur einmal) for once in a way.
Aus-nähung (ᴗ—ᴗᴗ) f ㊻ = ausnähen II.
aus-naschen (ᴗ—ᴗᴗ) v/a. ⓽** to rob (of dainties), to pilfer (eatables).
aus-nehm|en (ᴗ—ᴗᴗ) ⓼a** I v.a. 1. to take out; (ausleeren) to empty; (plündern) to rifle; (ausweiden) to disembowel, to gut; Bienenstöcke 2 to cut the honeycombs; Vögel aus dem Neste, Nester 2 to take young birds from the nest(s); to go birdnesting; einen Zahn: to extract; Kochk.: Fisch, Wildbret 2 to dress fish, game; Geflügel 2 to draw (or truss) poultry. — 2. Waren auf Borg 2 (auswählen) to take (up) ... — 3. (ausschließen) to except, to exclude; dies eine ausgenommen except (or all but) this one; eins ausgenommen with one single exception, all but one. — II sich 2 v/refl. 4. to form an exception. — 5. (aussehen) sich gut (schlecht) 2 to show up well (ill); sich vorteilhaft 2 to show to advantage: von oben nimmt es sich hübscher aus it presents (or has) a prettier effect from above; er nahm sich stattlich darin aus he looked magnificent in it. — III ~ n ㉓ 6. = A/ung. — IV 2d p.pr., a. ㊻ u. adv. 7. (vorzüglich) exceeding(ly), uncommon(ly). — V aus-genommen f.b.
Aus-nehmung (ᴗ—ᴗᴗ) f ㊻ taking out, &c.; der Nester: birdnesting; e-s Zahnes: extraction; bisw. a. = Ausnahme.
aus-niesen (ᴗ—ᴗᴗ) v/n. (h.) u. sich 2 v/refl. ⓽**: to sneeze vehemently.

[ausnippen] — 122 — [ausrauben]

aus-nippen (ᴵᴸ˘) v/a. ⑱** to sip up.
aus-nutz/en, aus-nütz/en (ᴵᴸ˘) I v/a.⑨**
1. to utilize, to make (good, excellent) use of, to make the most (or the best) of; to turn to account; etwas zu seinem Vorteile ∠ to turn a th. to one's advantage, to exploit a th.; einen Vorteil ∠ to pursue (or follow up) an advantage; er nutzt jeden, alles aus he makes (good) use of everybody, everything; Arbeiter ꝛc. ∠ to work ... (unmercifully), F to drive, sweat ... — 2. = abnutzen I. — II ~ ㉓ n u. A/ung f ㊻ 3. utilization, exploitation.
aus-öden (ᴵᴸ˘) v/a. ⑨** to desolate.
aus-ösen ↓ (ᴵᴸ˘) v/a. ⑨** (ausschöpfen) to bail out. to free from (water).
aus-packen (ᴵᴸ˘) v/a. ⑱** 1. seine Sachen aus dem Koffer. den Koffer ∠ to unpack one's things, one's box; Waren, auch: to uncase, to unbale; to open (a parcel). — 2. (ausframen) to spread out; F fig. Neuigkeiten: to spread about.
Aus-packer (ᴵᴸ˘) m ㉒, **~in** f ㊵ p. who unpacks or unloads, (un)packer.
aus-parieren (ᴵᴸ˘ᴸ˘) v/a. ⑱** e-n Streich ꝛc. ∠ to parry (or ward off) ...
aus-pauken (ᴵᴸ˘) ⑱** I v/a. 1. to drum out. — 2. burich.: e-n Streit ∠ to fight out ...
II v/n. (h.) 3. burich. to cease duelling.
aus-peilen ↓ (ᴵᴸ˘) v/a. ⑱** den Grund ∠ to sound the bottom.
aus-peitschen (ᴵᴸ˘) v/a. ⑪** to (horse-)whip, to scourge (publicly), to flog; e-m et. ∠ to whip a p. out of a th.
aus-pfählen ⊕ (ᴵᴸ˘) I v/a. ⑱** to pale, to support with piles. — II ~ n ㉓ u. **Aus-pfählung** f ㊻ pile-work.
aus-pfänd/en (ᴵᴸ˘) I v/a. ⑱** einen Schuldner ∠ to distrain (or seize) a debtor's goods, to put an execution in(to) his house. — II ~ n ㉓ = A/ung.
Aus-pfänder (ᴵᴸ˘) m ㉒ person who levies (or puts in) a distress; (Gerichts-diener) bailiff seizing goods.
Aus-pfändung (˘)f㊻ distraint, distress, seizure (of goods), execution (put into a house); **~s-befehl** m ㉒ distress warrant, writ (for a distraint of goods).
aus-pfarren (ᴵᴸ˘) v/a. ⑱** to sever from a parish. — II **Aus-pfarrung** f ㊻ severing from a parish.
aus-pfeifen (ᴵᴸ˘) v/a. ⑱b** 1. bfd. thea. Schauspieler, ein Stück: to hiss (off the stage), sl. to goose; stärker: to howl (or hoot) at. — 2. (zu Ende pfeifen) to finish whistling.
aus-pferchen (ᴵᴸ˘) v/a. ⑱** Schafe: to unpen, unfold, let out into the fields.
aus-pflanzen (ᴵᴸ˘) v/a. ⑨** to transplant, ins freie Beet: to bed out; aus einem Topfe: to pot out.
aus-pflastern (ᴵᴸ˘) v/a. ⑨a** einen Hof, Keller: to pave (over).
aus-pflücken (ᴵᴸ˘) v/a. ⑱** 1. hort. Obst: to pick out; (ausrupfen) to pluck up. — 2. ↓ alte Taue: to untwist, to pick.
aus-pflügen (ᴵᴸ˘) v/a. ⑱** 1. to plough up. — 2. to unearth in ploughing.
aus-pfützen ⚒ (ᴵᴸ˘) v/a. ⑨** das Wasser, die Grube ∠ to pump a pit dry, to draw the ground-water.
aus-pichen (ᴵᴸ˘) I v/a. ⑱** ⊕ to pitch (out). — II fig. **aus-gepicht** p.p. u. a.

㊺ hardened, well seasoned; ∠e Gurgel capacious gullet, thirsty throat; ∠er Magen, etwa: india-rubber (or cast-iron) stomach, splendid digestion.
aus-picken (ᴵᴸ˘) v/a. ⑱** to pick out.
aus-pinseln (ᴵᴸ˘) v/a. ⑫a** to blot out with (a stroke of) the (paint-)brush.
Auspizium (-ᴸtʃ(˘)ᴸ) [It.] n ㉓ röm. Alt.: (Vogelschau) (bfd. **Auspizien** pl.) auspices pl.; unter günstigen Auspizien under favourable auspices, auspiciously.
aus-plappern F (ᴵᴸ˘) = ausplaudern.
aus-plätten (ᴵᴸ˘) v/a. ⑱** to iron out, to smooth (or take out) by ironing.
aus-platzen (ᴵᴸ˘) v/n. (fn) ⑨** 1. von einer Naht: to burst (asunder). — 2. fig. in ein Gelächter ∠ (ausbrechen) to burst out laughing or into a loud laughter.
Aus-plauderer (ᴵᴸ˘˘) m ㉒, **-plaud(r)erin** f ㊵ babbler, prattler, tell-tale.
aus-plaudern (ᴵᴸ˘) I v/a. to blab (or let) out, to divulge (a secret). —
II v/n. (h.) to cease prattling. —
III sich ∠ v/refl. to indulge in a good, long chat. — IV ~ n ㉓ u. **Aus-plauderung** (ᴵᴸ˘) f ㊻ blab(bing), prattling, taletelling, babbling.
aus-plündern (ᴵᴸ˘)v/a.⑫a**= plündern.
aus-pochen (ᴵᴸ˘)⚒) v/a. ⑱** 1. bfd. hunt. to dislodge. — 2. = auspfeifen 1.
aus-polier/en (ᴵᴸᴸ˘) v/a. ⑱*/* to polish well; Metalle: to burnish, to brighten, to furbish up.
aus-polstern (ᴵᴸ˘) v/a. ⑫a** Stühle: to stuff; Kleider: to pad (out); Bettdecken: to quilt; mit Watte: to wad; ausgepolsterte Schultern, Waden padded ...
aus-posaunen (ᴵᴸ˘ᴸ) v/a. ⑱*/* to trumpet (or blazon) forth; to announce with a flourish of trumpets; fig. sein eigenes Lob ∠ to sound one's own trumpet; ⚓ Waren: to puff, to praise up; durch Reklame: to advertise.
aus-präg/en (ᴵᴸ˘) I v/a. u. v/refl. ⑱**
1. Münze, Gold ꝛc.: to coin. — 2. das Bild auf einer Münze: (auch sich ∠) to mark (or stamp) distinctly. — ⊕ 3. = A/ung. — III **aus-geprägt** p.p. u. a. ㊺ 4. distinct, pronounced; scharf ∠er Charakter strongly marked character; scharf ∠e Züge m/pl. well-marked (or sharp) features pl. [stamp.]
Aus-prägung (˘) f ㊻ coinage; (distinct))
aus-prahlen (ᴵᴸ˘) v/n. (h.) u. v/a. ⑱** to utter (or speak) boastfully; to brag.
aus-pressen (ᴵᴸ˘) v/a. ⑨** 1. to press (or squeeze) out (juice); Öl aus etwas ∠ to press oil out of ...; ausgepreßte Zitrone squeezed lemon. — 2. fig. e-m Geld ∠ to extort (or draw) ... from a p., to squeeze ... out of a p.; e-m Klagen, Tränen ∠ to draw sighs, tears from a p. — II ~ n ㉓ u. **Aus-pressung** f ㊻ 3. pressing out; (von Geld) extortion.
aus-proben (ᴵᴸ˘) ⑱**, **aus-probieren** (ᴵᴸ˘ᴸ) ⑱*/*, **aus-prüfen** (ᴵᴸ˘) v/a., to try (or test, examine) thoroughly, to put to the test; Wein(e) ∠ (versuchen) to sample (or taste) wine(s).
aus-prügeln (ᴵᴸ˘) v/a. = durchprügeln.
Aus-puff ⊕ (ᴵᴸ˘) m ㉒c. exhaust, escape; **~dampf** m ㉒, **-luft** f exhaust-steam; **-klappe** f exhaust-valve; **-maschine** f steam-engine without a condenser.

aus-pumpen (ᴵᴸ˘) I v/a. ⑱** to pump out; das Wasser aus dem Keller ∠, den Keller ∠ to pump the cellar dry; phys. die Luft ∠ to exhaust (or rarefy) the air; to produce a vacuum; F fig. e-n ganz ∠ to empty a p.'s pockets, to fleece a p. — II ~ n ㉓ u. **Aus-pumpung** f ㊻ pumping(out); phys. der Luft: exhaustion, rarefaction.
aus-punktieren (ᴵᴸ˘ᴸ) v/a. ⑬*/* 1. to mark out with dots; ein Muster ∠ to prick out a pattern; ⊕ typ. e-e Zeile ∠ to run out ... with full points. —
2. (erforschen) to divine (by geomancy).
aus-pusten F (ᴵᴸ˘) v/a. ⑨** ein Licht ꝛc. to blow out ...
Aus-putz (ᴵᴸ˘) m ㉒a. (o. pl.) 1. ornament(ation), trimming(s pl.); F titivation; (weiblicher Putz) finery, adornment(s pl.); F (fine) toggery. —
2. Hoftunft: dressing.
aus-putzen (ᴵᴸ˘) ⑨** I v/a. 1. (ausloschen) to snuff out (a candle). —
2. hort. Bäume ∠ (beschneiden) to prune (or lop) ...; Reben: to trim; Knospen: to nip off; ⊕ (die Kanten von etwas abnehmen) to bevel (or round) off, to pare; die Spitzen von etwas ∠ to blunt off a th., to clip a th. — 3. (reinigen) to cleanse; einen Kanal: to dredge. —
4. (fertig m.) to put the finishing touches to. — 5. (ausschmücken) to decorate; a. v/refl. sich ∠ to deck (o.s.) out, to adorn (o.s.), to dress (o.s.) up, to smarten (o.s.) up, F to titivate (o.s.); Zimmer: to trim (up); to deck out; Kochkunst: to dress. — 6. (ausleeren) die Schüsseln: to clear, to empty. — 7. (schelten) to scold, to reprimand, F to blow up. — II ~ n ㉓ u. **Aus-putzung** (ᴵᴸ˘) f ㊻ 8. snuffing out, &c.
aus-quartier/en (ᴵᴸᴸ˘) ⑬*/* I v/a. to shift; ⚔ to quarter (or billet) out. —
II sich ∠ v/refl. to shift (or change) one's quarters or lodgings. — III ~ n ㉓ u. A/ung f ㊻ ⚔ billeting out; change of quarters or lodgings.
aus-quetschen (ᴵᴸ˘) v/a. ⑪** to squeeze (or press) out; er läßt sich ∠ wie eine Zitrone you can squeeze anything out of him, he is most yielding or obliging.
aus-radieren (ᴵᴸ˘ᴸ˘) v/a. ⑬*/* to erase.
Aus-radung (ᴵᴸ˘) f ㊻ = Abfindung.
aus-rahmen (ᴵᴸ˘) v/a. ⑱** to unframe.
aus-rändel/n ⑫a**, **-rand/en** u.**-ränd/en** ⑨**, **=rändern** ⑫ (alle: ᴵᴸ˘) I v/a.
1. to emarginate (a. ⚘); mint. to mill; ausgerandet ꝛc., ⚘ emarginate(d). —
2. (austerben) to jag — II ~ n ㉓ u. A/ung f ㊻ 3. emargination (a. ⚘).
aus-rangieren (ᴵᴸrgᴸ˘) ⚔ [fr.] v/a. ⑬*/* to discard, to cast off (= ausmustern).
aus-ranken (ᴵᴸ˘) v/n. (h.) ⑱** to put forth (or send out) tendrils.
aus-rasen (ᴵᴸ˘) v/n. (h.) u. sich ∠ v refl.
1. to calm down; vom Winde auch: subside, to blow over. — 2. (f-r Wut, Luft m.) to give full vent to one's fury.
aus-rasieren (ᴵᴸᴸ˘) v/a. ⑬*/* den Bart ∠ (stellenweise rasieren) partly to shave off ...
aus-rasten (ᴵᴸ˘) ⑨** = ausruhen III.
aus-raten (ᴵᴸ˘) v/a. ⑱a** Tennis: to toss.
aus-rauben (ᴵᴸ˘) v/a. u. v/n. (h.) ⑱** to rob, to pillage (= plündern).

Signs (see page XVII): F familiar; P vulgar; Γ flash; ⋄ rare; † obsolete (died); * new word (born); ++ incorrect; ♪ music;

aus-rauchen (⁻ˡ˘) ⊛** **I** v/a. seine Pfeife ⁀ to finish one's pipe. — **II** v/n. (h.) to cease smoking; to smoke one's last pipe.

aus-räuchern (⁻ˡ˘) **I** v/a. ⊕a** 1. Bienen ꝛc.: to (expel by) smoke, to smoke out. — 2. to fumigate; ⊕ mit Schwefeldämpfen: to sulphur; Fleisch, Fisch: to smoke-dry. — **II ~** n ⊚ u. **Aus=räucherung** (⁻ˡ˘) f ⊕ 3. smoking (out); fumigation; ⊕ sulphuring.

aus-raufen (⁻ˡ˘) ⊛** **I** v/a. Unkraut ꝛc.: to pull (or pluck) up or out; sich (dat.) die Haare ⁀ to tear one's hair out. — **II** v/n. (h.) to leave off squabbling and fighting. — **III** sich ⁀ v/refl. to indulge in a free fight; von Kindern: to have a good romp. [burl (=noppen).]

aus-rauhen ⊚ (⁻ˡ˘) v/a. ⊛** Tuch ⁀ to}

aus-räumen (⁻ˡ˘) **I** v/a. ⊛** 1. to clear away; (ausleeren) to empty (out); die Möbel aus dem Zimmer, das Zimmer ⁀ to clear the room (of furniture), beim Ausziehen: to remove the furniture; den Ofen ⁀ to clear the grate or stove; to rake out the fire or the ashes; ⊛ Waren: to clear off. — 2. (reinigen) ein Haus, Zimmer: to clean up; e-n Hof, Platz: to sweep up; Abflußröhren, Kloaken ꝛc.: to cleanse, to clear (out), to unstop. — **II ~** n ⊚ 3. = A/ung.

Aus-räumer (˘) m ⊚ 1. (a. **~in** f ⊕): a) one who clears; cleaner; b) h: Möbel: furniture-remover. — 2. Werkzeug ⚒ Schlosserei: (Senker) counter-sink; ⚒ (Räumnadel) wire-riddle; wad-hook.

Aus-räumung (⁻ˡ˘) f ⊕ clearance; removal (of furniture); clean(s)ing (up); sweep-up (vgl. ausräumen); **~=kosten** (⁻...) pl. ⊕ cost of (or charges pl. for) removal (of furniture).

aus-räuspern (⁻ˡ˘) ⊛a** **I** v/a. Schleim ꝛc.: to expectorate, to cough (or hawk) up. — **II** sich ⁀ v/refl. to clear one's throat. — **III ~** ⊚ expectoration.

aus-rechen (⁻ˡ˘) v/a. ⊛** hort. Wege: to (clear with the) rake.

aus-rechenbar (⁻ˡ˘ˋ) a. ⊕ math. calculable; schwer ⁀ difficult to calculate.

aus-rechn/en (⁻ˡ˘) **I** v/a. ⊛b** to calculate to compute; (sch=zählen) to cast (or reckon) up; falsch ⁀ to miscalculate; nicht auszurechnen(d) incalculable, impossible to compute. — **II~**n⊚=A/ung.

Aus-rechner (⁻ˡ˘) m ⊚, **~in** f ⊕ calculator, computer, reckoner.

Aus-rechnung (⁻ˡ˘) f ⊕ calculation, computation, reckoning.

aus-recken (⁻ˡ˘) v/a. u. v/refl. ⊛** 1. (ausstrecken) to extend, stretch out. — 2. (lang ziehen) (sich ⁀) to distend, to stretch (or draw) out; (aushämmern) to beat out.

Aus-rede (⁻ˡ˘) f ⊕ subterfuge; plea; pretext, pretence, shift; lahme, leere **~** pl. lame (or paltry) excuses pl., **~** machen to excuse o.s. from doing a th., to shuffle (F to back) out of a th.; gerichtliches ~ legal quibble.

aus-reden (⁻ˡ˘) ⊛** **I** v/n. (h.) 1. to finish (or cease) speaking; lassen Sie mich ⁀ let me have my say, let me finish my remark; e-n nicht ⁀ lassen to cut a p. short, to interrupt a p.('s speech). — 2. frei ⁀ to speak one's mind, to speak up or out, to express o.s. freely. — **II** v/a. 3. (s. 1) einen Satz ⁀ to finish a sentence. — 4. (äußern) to utter, to express. — 5. (besprechen) to talk (a matter) over, to discuss. — 6. e-m et. ⁀ to dissuade a p. from (doing) a th., to talk (or argue) a p. out of a th.; das lasse ich mir nicht ⁀ I won't be talked out of it. 7. (richtig sagen) to express correctly. — **III** sich ⁀ v/refl. 8. to speak at full length; sich mit e-m ⁀ (ausfprechen) to have a confidential talk with a p. 9. (sich erschöpfen) to exhaust one's stock of words or of conversation. — 10. (sich herauswinden) to extricate (or exculpate) o.s.; sich mit et. ⁀ to plead (a good excuse for) a th., F to wriggle out of a th.

aus-reeden ⚓ (⁻ˡ˘) **I** v/a. ⊛** ein Schiff ⁀ to rig, to fit out. — **II ~** n ⊚ u. **Aus=reedung** f ⊕ rig(ging), outfit.

aus-regnen (⁻ˡ˘) ⊛b** **I** v/n. (h.) u. v/refl. impers. = abregnen I. — **II** v/a. (aushöhlen) v. Regen: to wash out (a road).

Aus-reibe-holz ⊚ (⁻ˡ˘...) n ⊚, **=knochen** m Schuhmacherei: polisher, burnisher.

aus-reiben (⁻ˡ˘) **I** v/a. ⊕** 1. Flecke(n) ⁀ to rub out stains; Kleider ⁀ to clean clothes by rubbing (them); sich (dat.) die Augen ⁀ to rub one's eyes. — 2. e-e Schüssel ꝛc.: to wipe out. 3. ⊕ Schuhm.: (glätten) die Nähte ⁀ to polish (or burnish) the seams. — **II ~** n ⊚ 4. rubbing (out), &c. (s. I).

aus-reichen (⁻ˡ˘) ⊛** **I** v/n. (h.) 1. v. Sachen: ⁀ (genügen) für to suffice for; das reicht kaum aus that's barely enough; das Mehl wird ⁀ (bis dahin) the flour is not sufficient flour, the flour will not last (until then). — 2. v. Personen: mit et. ⁀ (auskommen) to make a th. do, to make shift with a th., (only just) to manage with a th. — **II** ⁀d p.pr. u. a. ⊚ 3. ⁀d (genügend) für sufficient for.

aus-reifen (⁻ˡ˘) v/a. u. v/n. (s. u. h.) ⊛** to ripen or mature (thoroughly or fully).

Aus-reise ⚓ (⁻ˡ˘) f ⊕ = Abreise.

aus-reisen (⁻ˡ˘) v/n. ⊛** 1. ⚒ (s) abreisen. — 2. (h.) ausgereist h. to have travelled enough.

aus-reißen (⁻ˡ˘) ⊛a** **I** v/a. 1. mst: to tear (or pluck) out; sich (dat.) die Haare ⁀ to tear one's hair; Bäume, Pflanzen: to pull up, mit der Wurzel: to uproot; Zähne ⁀ to pull out (or draw, extract) teeth; F fig. er reißt sich kein Bein dabei aus (wird sich nicht krank arbeiten) he does not hurt (or kill) himself over the job. — **II** v/n. (s/n) 2. (aus-ea.-gehen) to tear (asunder); von einem Damme ꝛc.: to break (down); von einer Naht: to come unstitched, to burst; vom Unterfutter auch: to split, to give way; fig. meine Geduld reißt aus ... is at an end. — 3. F (weglaufen) to escape, F to bolt, to scamper off, to cut one's stick, to hook it; fig. er riß aus wie Schafleder he was off like a shot; reiß aus! take to your heels!, be off!, F cut it!; ⚔ (fahnenflüchtig w.) to desert; von Pferden ꝛc.: to run away, to tear off. — **III ~** n ⊚ 4. plucking out; (mit der Wurzel) uprooting; (Flucht) escape; von Pferden ꝛc.: running away; ⚔ desertion.

Aus-reißer (⁻ˡ˘) m ⊚ 1. p. who plucks out or pulls up, &c. — 2. (Flüchtling) fugitive, runaway, &c. ⚔ (Fahnenflüchtiger) deserter; ⚔ (abgeirrtes Geschoß) wide (or wild) shot, stray bullet.

Aus-reißerei (⁻ˡ˘⁻) f ⊕ frequent desertion (i. a. ausreißen III).

aus-reiten (⁻ˡ˘)⊛b** **I** v/n.(s/n) 1. (spazierenreiten) to ride out (on horseback), to take a ride. — 2. von einem Orte ⁀ to depart (on horseback) from a place. — **II** v/a. 3. ein Pferd ⁀ to give ... an airing, to exercise ... — 4. (zureiten) to break in thoroughly. — 5. einen Raum ⁀ (ausmessen) to ride over (the grounds, a course). — **III ~** n ⊚ 6. riding out (on horseback). [ed messenger.)

Aus-reiter (⁻ˡ˘) m ⊚ outrider; mount-)

aus-renken (⁻ˡ˘) **I** v/a. ⊛** path. ein Glied ⁀ to put out of joint, to dislocate, to sprain; sich das Handgelenk ⁀ to put out (or to sprain) one's wrist. — **II ~** n ⊚ u. **Aus=renkung** f ⊕ dislocation, sprain, ᴧ luxation.

aus-rennen (⁻ˡ˘) ⊛b** **I** v/n. 1. (h.) to cease (or finish) running. — 2. (s/n) von e-m Orte ⁀ to start (one's run) from ... — **II** v/a. 3. e-n Raum ⁀ to run over a course. — 4. e-m mit der Lanze das Auge ⁀ (ausstoßen) to thrust out a p.'s eye with ...; sich (dat.) ein Auge ⁀ to knock out one's eye (by running into s. th.). — **III** sich ⁀ v/refl. 5. to enjoy a long run or walk. — **IV ~** n ⊚ 6. running out, &c. (s. I u. II). [roden.)

aus-reuten (⁻ˡ˘) [uhd.] v/a. ⊛** = aus-)

aus-richt/en (⁻ˡ˘) **I** v/a. u. sich ⁀ v/refl. ⊛** 1. to straighten (out); to adjust; ⚔ die Glieder ⁀ to dress the ranks; sich ⁀ to dress ranks. — 2. bsd. ⚒ (aufspüren) to explore, (aufschließen) to develop (a mine), to discover. — 3. (bestellen) einen Auftrag ⁀ to do a commission; e-e Bestellung, Botschaft ⁀ to deliver a message; richten Sie ihm meinen Gruß aus give him my compliments or kind regards; remember me (kindly) to him; ich werde es ⁀ I will attend (or see) to it. — 4. (ausführen) to do, accomplish, perform; er kann nur wenig ⁀ he can do but little good, his efforts are of little avail; mit guten Worten läßt sich viel ⁀ much can be effected by kind words; es läßt sich nichts damit ⁀ it has proved ineffectual, it did (or does) not succeed. — 5. (erlangen) to obtain, to succeed in; nichts ⁀ to fail; F to come away empty(-handed); ich kann nichts bei ihm ⁀ I cannot prevail upon him (to do it), I have no influence over him; damit ist nichts (wenig) ausgerichtet no (little) good will ensue from it or F will come of it; that's of no (little) use. — 6. ein Gastmahl, eine Hochzeit ⁀ (veranstalten) to give (or pay for) a banquet (or dinner), a wedding-party. — 7. ⊕ Maschinenteile ⁀ (aus-ea.-nehmen) to take ... to pieces, to disconnect. — **II ~** n ⊚ 8. = A/ung.

Aus-richter (⁻ˡ˘) m ⊚, **~in** f ⊕ one who adjusts, &c.; e-r Botschaft: bearer; e-s Testaments: executor (f executrix); ⚒ e-s Ganges: explorer.

⊕ scientific; ♃ botanical; ♀ geography; ⊕ machinery; ⚒ mining; ⚔ military; ⚓ marine; ⊕ commercial; ✉ postal; 🚂 railway.

[**Ausrichtung**] — 124 — [**ausschälen**]

Aus-richtung (⁻⁻⌣⌣) f ㊻ adjustment; ⚔ exploration; performance, execution.
aus-riefen ⊙ (⁻⁻⌣) v/a. ㊽** arch. to flute, to channel; Gewehrlauf: to rifle; to groove; ≀ ausgerieft ⚯ striated.
Aus-ring(e)-maschine ⊙ (⁻⁻⌣(⌣)...) f ㊷ wringing-machine, wringer.
aus-ringen (⁻⁻⌣⌣) ㊲n** I v/a. 1. das Wasser aus der Wäsche, die Wäsche ≀ to wring (out) linen. — 2. seine Glieder ≀ od. v/refl. sich ≀ to exercise one's limbs by wrestling. — 3. der Streit ist ausgerungen the strife is ended. — II v/n. (h.) 4. fig. er hat ausgerungen his struggles are over; he has gone to rest.
aus-rinnen (⁻⁻⌣⌣) ⊙fr** (fn) ㊲b(a)** aus Fässern ꝛc.: to run (or leak) out.
aus-rippen ⊙ (⁻⁻⌣⌣) v/a. ㊽** Tabaksblätter ≀ to unrib tobacco.
Aus-ritt (⁻⁻⌣) m ㊵c. ride (out), excursion on horseback (= ausreiten III).
aus-röcheln (⁻⁻⌣⌣) ㊶a** I v/a. das Leben ≀ to gasp one's last (breath). — II v/n. (h.) to expire (with death-rattles).
Aus-rode-maschine ⊙ (⁻⁻⌣⌣...) f ㊷ agr. zum Ausreißen v. Baumstümpfen: grubber.
aus-rod/en (⁻⁻⌣⌣) I v/a. ㊽** agr. u. for.: to root out; Wurzelstöcke: to grub up; (urbar machen) Land: to clear (for tillage); Wälder, a.: to hew down. — II ~ n ㉓ u. ≀ung f ㊻ rooting out; clearance.
aus-rollen (⁻⁻⌣⌣) ㊽** I v/n. (h.) 1. to cease rolling (v. Donner ꝛc.: rumbling). — II v/a. 2. Teig: to roll out; ⊙ a.: to flatten out. — 3. (auswickeln) to unroll. — III sich ≀ v/refl. 4. to come unrolled.
aus-rottbar (⁻⁻⌣-) a. ㊺ eradicable.
aus-rotten (⁻⁻⌣⌣) [mhd.] v/a. ㊽** Unkraut, fig. ein Laster ꝛc.: to root out, extirpate, eradicate; ein Übel: to stamp out, put down; Volksstämme: to exterminate, wipe out; fig. s. Stiel.
Aus-rotter (~) m ㉒, ~in f ㊷ extirpator, exterminator; destroyer.
Aus-rottung (⁻⁻⌣⌣) f ㊻ extirpation; eradication; extermination; ~s-krieg (...) m ㉒ war of extermination.
aus-rücken (⁻⁻⌣⌣) ㊽** I v/a. to disengage; bsd. ⊙ mach. (aus dem Getriebe bringen) auch: to ungear; aus- und einrücken to ship and unship the gear, to connect and disconnect; typ. eine Zeile ≀ (ant. einrücken) to begin a full line; to make no break or (fresh) paragraph. — II v/n. (fn) ⚔ to move out of camp, to turn (or march) out; F (fortlaufen) to decamp. [gaging-gear.]
Aus-rück-zeug ⊙ (⁻⁻⌣...) n ㉒ mach. disen-⌐
Aus-ruf (⁻⁻⌣) m ⑪(⌣⑦)d. 1. exclamation, shout, outery, der überraschung auch: ejaculation; gram. interjection. — 2. (Ankündigung) proclamation; durch öffentlichen ~ bekannt-m. to proclaim.
aus-rufen (⁻⁻⌣⌣) ㊲b** I v/n. (h.) 1. to exclaim, to cry (or call) out; verwundernd auch: to ejaculate. — II v/a. 2. Waren zum Verkaufe: to cry, to call out; vor Läden: F to tout. — 3. (ankündigen) to announce, to proclaim; et. ≀ to publish a th. by the town-crier; e-n als (a. zum) König ≀ to proclaim a p. king. — III ~ n ㉓ 4. = Ausruf.
Aus-rufer (⁻⁻⌣⌣) m ㉒ (public) crier; bellman; vor Läden: F tout (Hausierer)

hawker; ~ und Verkäufer von Zeitungen newspaper-boy or -man.
Aus-rufung (⁻⁻⌣) f ㊻ = Ausruf; ~s-wort ("...) n ㉖ interjection; =zeichen n note (or point, sign) of exclamation, exclamation-mark, typ. (!) auch: screamer.
aus-ruhen (⁻⁻⌣⌣) ㊽** I v/a. 1. den Geist, den Leib ꝛc.: to rest one's mind, one's body, &c. — II sich ≀ v/refl. 2. to (take) rest from; to repose, to take one's ease. — III v/n. (h.) 3. = 2; auf s-n Lorbeeren ≀ to rest on one's laurels. — 4. seine Pferde ꝛc. ≀ lassen to rest ..., to give ... a rest, to breathe ... 5. (zur Genüge ruhen) haben Sie ausgeruht? are you (or do you feel) rested? — IV ~ n ㉓ 6. rest, breathing(-time), repose; (Erholung) recreation.
aus-rühren (⁻⁻⌣) v/a. ㊽** to spill in (or while) stirring or twirling.
aus-runden, aus-ründen (⁻⁻⌣⌣) v/a. ㊽** 1. (aussöhlen) to hollow out. — 2. ⊙ (ausbauchen) to round off, to give a round shape to. — 3. auch v/refl. sich ≀ to be well rounded (or finished) off.
aus-rupfen (⁻⁻⌣⌣) v/a. ㊽** to pull (or pluck) out; einer Gans die Federn ≀ to pluck a goose (auch fig.).
aus-rüst/en (⁻⁻⌣⌣) I v/a. u. v/refl. ㊽** to furnish with; sich ≀ to get ready, to prepare; fig. der Himmel hat ihn mit glänzenden Gaben ausgerüstet Heaven has provided (or endowed) him with brilliant gifts; ⚔ Truppen: to equip, arm, accoutre; ⚓ ein Schiff: to rig (or fit) out, (bemannen) to man; Kriegsschiff: fertig für den Dienst ≀ to put into commission. — II ~ n ㉓ = ≀ung.
Aus-rüstung (~) f ㊻ bsd. ⚔ u. ⚓ equipment; armament; accoutrement; appointments pl.; outfit; für einzelne a.: kit; ~s-gegenstände ⚔, ⚓ (...") m/pl. ㉒ articles pl. (required) for the equipment of troops or a ship('s crew), for the outfit of an expedition, &c.
aus-rutschen F (⁻⁻⌣⌣) v/n. (fn) ⑪** to slip, to glide (= ausgleiten).
Aus-saat (⁻⁻⌣) f ㊷ agr. 1. (Aussäen) sowing. — 2. (Ausgesätes) seed(-corn).
aus-säckeln ㊶a**, **aus-sacken** ㊽** (⁻⁻⌣⌣) v/a. to take out of a bag or sack, to empty (out of) a pocket or bag or sack; fig. e-n ≀ = ausbeuteln 3.
aus-säen (⁻⁻⌣) ㊽** I v/a. agr. to sow (auch abs.); fig. auch: to disseminate or scatter (seeds of discord, &c). — II v/n. (h.) er hat ausgesät he has done sowing. — III ~ n ㉓ = Aussäung.
aus-sagbar (⁻⁻⌣-) a. ㊺ log. predicable.
Aus-sage (⁻⁻⌣) f ㊽ 1. assertion; bestimmte: declaration; seiner ~ nach according to his account or statement; auf seine ~ hin acting on the information given by him; ⚔ der Einwohner, der Gefangenen intelligence obtained from (or information given by) the inhabitants, the prisoners; jur. (gerichtliche) ~ deposition, evidence; (Zeugnis) testimony; eidliche ~ declaration on oath, sworn evidence, affidavit. — 2. gram. predicate, verb.
aus-sagen (⁻⁻⌣⌣) v/a. ㊽** 1. (zu Ende sagen) to finish saying. — 2. meist neg. (durch Worte erschöpfen): seine Wunder werden

nimmer ausgesagt ... can never be fully described or expressed or told. - 3. jur. (sich äußern, auch abs.) to depose; eidlich ≀ to attest (or declare, state) on oath; et. gegen einen ≀ to charge a p. with a th.; der Schutzmann sagt aus, er habe ihn um 10 Uhr dort festgenommen the constable deposes (or speaks) to having arrested him there at ten o'clock. — 4. (berichten) to (make a) report. — 5. meist gram. to enunciate, to predicate.
aus-sägen (⁻⁻⌣⌣) v/a. ㊽** I to saw out. — II v/n. (h.) to finish sawing.
Aus-sager (⁻⁻⌣) m ㉒, ~in f ㊷ witness.
Aus-sage-satz (⁻⁻⌣⌣) m ㉒ sentence of affirmation; =weise f mood; =wort n = Aussage 2.
aus-salzen ⊙ (⁻⁻⌣⌣) v/a. ㊾** chm. Seife ≀ to separate soap by means of salt.
Aus-satz (⁻⁻⌣) [mhd. 13. sae.] m ㉔a. 1. Billard: lead. — 2. (im Spiele) stake(s pl.), pool (= Einsatz). — 3. (Krankheit) leprosy (a. fig.); schuppiger: elephantiasis; von Schafen ꝛc.: rot, scab; ≀ v. Bäumen: scurf.
aus-sätzig (⁻⁻⌣) I a. ㊺ leprous. — II ~(r) m, ~e f ㊷ leper, lazar; Spital für ~e, a. =en-haus (...") n ㉒ leper(or lazar-)house, hospital for lepers.
aus-säuern ⊙ (⁻⁻⌣⌣) v/a. ㊶a** chm. to extract (or remove) the acid(ity) from.
aus-saufen (⁻⁻⌣⌣) ㊲f** I v/a. to drink up; den Eimer ≀ to empty the pail; von Menschen derb auch: F to swill. — II v/n. (h.) to cease drinking, F to stop swilling or guzzling or boozing.
aus-saugen (⁻⁻⌣⌣) ㊲c** I v/a. 1. das Mark aus einem Knochen, einen Knochen ≀ to suck (the marrow out of) a bone; (erschöpfen) to suck dry, to exhaust; fig. einen ≀ to live (or sponge) upon a p.; (beschwindeln) to bleed or drain or fleece a p. (to the last farthing); ein Land, Volk: to impoverish (F to eat up) with taxation; to grind; to draw the life-blood from. — II v/n. (h.) 2. ein Kind ≀ lassen to suckle (or nurse) ... the full time. — 3. to cease sucking. — III ~ n ㉓ 4. sucking; exhaustion; fig. sponging; fleecing; med. ⚯ exsuction.
aus-säugen (⁻⁻⌣⌣) v/a. ㊽** I. ein Kind ≀ to suckle ... well; s.a. aussaugen 1. — II v/n. (h.) to cease suckling or nursing.
Aus-sauger (⁻⁻⌣) m ㉒, ~in f ㊷ chm. von Wunden, Blut ꝛc.: sucker; ≀ parasitical plant; meist fig. sponger; stärker: blood-sucker, extortioner; ~ei f ㊷ extortion.
Aus-saugung (⁻⁻⌣) f ㊻ = aussaugen III.
Aus-sä-ung (⁻⁻⌣) f ㊻ sowing.
aus-schaben (⁻⁻⌣⌣) v/a. ㊽** 1. to scrape (or hollow) out. — 2. (ausradieren) to erase. — 3. ⊙ Gerberei: to flesh. — II ~ n ㉓ 4. scraping out; erasure.
aus-schachten ⚒ u. ⊙ (⁻⁻⌣) I v/a. ㊽** to sink, deepen, excavate. — II ~ n ㉓ a. **Aus-schachtung** f ㊻ excavation.
aus-schaffen ⚓ (⁻⁻⌣⌣) v/a. ㊽** = herausschaffen. [≀ to fit ... with gunports.⌐
aus-schäften ⚓ (⁻⁻⌣⌣) v/a. ㊽** ein Schiff⌐
aus-schalen (⁻⁻⌣⌣) v/a. ㊽**. 1. Austern ꝛc. ≀ to take ... out of the shell. — 2. ⊙ (mit Brettern bekleiden) to line with boards, to plank, to lath (a ceiling).
aus-schälen (⁻⁻⌣⌣) ㊽** I v/a. u. v/refl. 1. den Kern ≀ to take out ...; F kaum =

Zeichen (s. S. XVII): F familiär; P Volkssprache; ⌐ Gaunersprache; ⚮ selten; † alt (auch gestorben); * neu (auch geboren); ⁂ unrichtig;

[**ausschallen**] — **125** — [**ausschlagen**]

plündern. — 2. Bohnen ꝛc.: to shell, Äpfel, Eier ꝛc.: to peel, Bäume: to bark; sich 2 to peel. — II v/n. (h.) 3. ausgeschält h. to leave off shelling, peeling.

aus-schallen (ᴵᴸ◡) v n. (h. u. sn) ⑱ (impf. u. p.p. a. ⑲b)* = ausklingen.

aus-schalten (ᴵᴸ◡) I v/a. ⑱** to eliminate; aus dem Verkehrsleben 2 to remove (or shut out) from the flow of traffic; tel., elect., fig. to disconnect, to put out of circuit, to break the circuit of; elektrisches Licht: to switch off. — II ~ n ㉓ = Ausschaltung.[breaker, cut-out.]

Aus-schalter ⊙ (ᴵᴸ◡) m ㉒ elect. contact-

Aus-schaltung (ᴵᴸ◡) f ㊺ elimination; elect. disconnection, circuit-breaking.

aus-schämen (ᴵᴸ◡) v/refl. ⑱** sich die Augen 2 to be ashamed of looking any one in the face.

Aus-schank (ᴵᴸ) m ⑦c. 1. retail(ing) of liquor. — 2. Ort: public(-)house, bar, beer-shop, ale-house. — 3. Anzeige: ~ von Bier ale on tap, beer on draught.

aus-scharren (ᴵᴸ◡) ⑱** I v/a. Körner ꝛc.: to scratch (or rake) up; Leichen ꝛc.: to disinter, to dig up. — II v/n. (h.) mit dem Fuß beim Bücklung ꝛc. 2 to scrape (with) one's feet.

aus-scharten ⊙ (ᴵᴸ◡) v/a. ⑱** das Leder 2 to notch (or jag) ... [to shade.]

aus-schatt(ier)en (ᴵᴸ◡, ᴵᴸ◡) v/a. ⑱ (⑬)**

Aus-schau (ᴵᴸ) f ㊺ lookout; ~ halten nach to be on the lookout for, to watch for.

aus-schauen (ᴵᴸ◡) [obb.] v/n. (h.) ⑱** 1. = ausgucken. — 2. bsd. südd. = aussehen 4.

aus-schaufeln (ᴵᴸ◡) v/a. ⑫a** 1. to shovel out; to scoop (or throw) out with a shovel; ein Grab: to dig (with a shovel). — 2. ⚓ to bail out (a boat).

aus-schäumen (ᴵᴸ◡) ⑱** I v/n. 1. (h.) to cease foaming (fig. raging). — 2. (sn) a. sich 2 v/refl. to exhaust (o.s.) by foaming. — II v/a. fig. 3. Gift und Galle 2 to fret and fume.

aus-scheid/en (ᴵᴸ◡) ⑪** I v/a. 1. to separate from; chm., math., &c. to eliminate from; durch Fällung: to precipitate, durch Kristallisation: to crystallize out; physiol. aus dem Blute: (absondern) to secrete from; (ausstoßen) to expel; to eject, to excrete; fremde Stoffe 2 to clear off foreign matter. — II v/refl. sich 2 2. to separate from; physiol. to be(come) disengaged (or secreted) from. — III v/n. (sn) 3. aus e-r Gesellschaft 2 (austreten) to withdraw from ...; aus e-r Stellung 2 to retire from a post, to give up a position; ausgeschied(e)ner Beamter retired (or pensioned) ... — IV ~ n ㉓ 4. = A/ung. — V 2 b p.pr. u. a. ⑯ 5. Bed. des inf. — 6. physiol.: secretory, excretory (vessels). — 7. ❀ 2 de Direktoren outgoing (or retiring) directors.

Aus-scheidung (ᴵᴸ◡) f ㊺ separation; elimination; chm. precipitation; physiol. secretion, excretion; (Zurücktreten) withdrawal (or retirement) from.

aus-scheinen (ᴵᴸ◡) v/n. (h.) ⑪** to cease shining. [= ausklingeln.]

aus-schellen (ᴵᴸ◡) v/n. (h.) und ⑱**

aus-schelten (ᴵᴸ◡) ⑬e** I v/a. 1. e-n 2 to scold (or chide, F blow up) a p.; (schimpfen) to abuse. — II v/n. (h.) 2. to cease scolding. — III sich 2: 3. v/refl. to vent

one's anger in scolding. — 4. v/rpr. sich (ea.) 2 to abuse one another. — IV ~ n ㉓ 5. scolding, &c. (f.I.) abuse.

aus-schenken (ᴵᴸ◡) I v/a. ⑱** 1. to distribute as presents, to give away. — 2. to pour out (from a vessel). — 3. to sell (liquor) by retail, to retail. — II ~ n ㉓ 4. retail liquor-trade; vgl. Ausschank.

aus-scheren (ᴵᴸ◡) v/a. ⑨a (a. ⑱)** 1. ⊙ das Tuch 2 to give the cloth the last shearing. — 2. ⚓ ein Tau: to unreeve.

aus-scheuern (ᴵᴸ◡) ⑫a** I v/a. e-n Kessel 2 to scour (out); ein Zimmer: to scrub (out). — II v/n. (h.) ausgescheuert haben to have done scouring, &c. — III sich 2 (abnutzen) v/refl. to wear out by friction.

aus-schicken (ᴵᴸ◡) I v/a. ⑱** 1. to send out; Boten a.: to dispatch; Laufburschen: to send on errands; ✕ (abkommandieren) to detail or detach (on special service); abs. nach e-m, et. 2 to send for a p., for a th. — II ~ n ㉓ u. **Aus-schickung** f ㊺ dispatch; detachment; expedition; eines Rundschreibens: circulation.

aus-schieben (ᴵᴸ◡) v/a. ⑦c** 1. to push (F to shove) out or forth; ⊙ Bäckerei: das Brot 2 to draw bread (from the oven). — 2. einen Tisch ꝛc.: to draw out telescope-fashion. — 3. Kegelspiel: to play off.

Aus-schieber (ᴵᴸ◡) m ㉒ 1. (a. ~in f ㊺) p. who pushes (out), &c. — 2. ⊙ Tischlerei: ~ e-s Eßtisches leaf of a telescope-table.

Aus-schieß=brett ⊙ (ᴵᴸ ...) n ㉒ typ. imposing-board.

aus-schieß/en (ᴵᴸ◡) ⑦c(e)t** I v/a. 1. e-m ein Auge 2 to shoot out a p.'s eye; ein Gewehr 2: a) (abnützen) to wear out ... (by much shooting); b) = einschießen. — 2. e-n Preis 2 to shoot for a prize. — 3. Strahlen, Blicke: to dart forth. — 4. ♣ Blumen 2 (treiben) to sprout or shoot (forth); ⚕ das Gebirge schießt Nebenäste aus ... sends out spurs, ... branches out. — 5. ♣ (prüfend aussondern) to cast (or sort) out, to reject. — 6. ⊙ Bäckerei: Brot 2 to draw ...; typ. einen Bogen 2 to impose ...; 2 zum Ineinanderlegen to impose as inset; ⚓ den Ballast 2 (wieder ausladen) to discharge (or unship, shoot) ...; to unballast (a ship). — II v/n.: a) (sn) 7. von Blut: to gush out; von Funken: to fly forth. — 8. ♣ v. Knospen: to sprout forth, to shoot out or up. — 9. arch. (vorspringen) to project, to jut forth; b) (h.) 10. to cease shooting. — 11. ⚓ Wind: to veer. — III v/n ㉓ 12. = A/ung.

Aus-schießer (ᴵᴸ◡) m ㉒, ~in f ㊺ 1. person who shoots out, &c. — 2. ⊙ Papierfabrikation: gatherer, sorter.

Aus-schieß=platte ⊙ (ᴵᴸ ...) f ㊺, =stein m typ. imposing-stone.

Aus-schießung (ᴵᴸ◡) f ㊺ shooting out or forth; (Preisschießen) prize-shooting; ⊙ typ. imposition; ⚓ unballasting.

aus-schiffen (ᴵᴸ◡) ⑱** I v/a. (sn) ⚓ to put to sea, to set sail. — II v/a.: a) ✓ Personen u. ✕ Truppen: to land, disembark; b) ⚓ Güter 2 bff. = löschen ². — III sich 2 (das Schiff verlassen) to (go to) land, to disembark. — IV ~ n ㉓ u. **Aus-schiffung** (ᴵᴸ◡) f ㊺ discharge; landing; disembarkation.

aus-schimpfen (ᴵᴸ◡) ⑱** I v/a. u. v/refl. to revile, to abuse; (ausschelten) to scold,

to chide; sich einmal recht 2 to pour forth abuse to one's heart's content. — II v/n. (h.) to leave off abusing. — III ~ n ㉓, **Aus-schimpferei** (ᴵᴸ◡) f ㊺ revilement, abuse; abusive language.

aus-schinden (ᴵᴸ◡) v/a. ⑦*** Tiere 2 (abbalgen) to flay ..., to skin ...

aus-schirren (ᴵᴸ◡) v/a. ⑱** 1. to unharness, unyoke; to take out (of harness). — 2. ⊙ Maschinenteile: to ungear.

aus-schlachten ⊙ (ᴵᴸ◡) v/a. ⑱** Schlächterei: to cut up (a sheep, &c.) for sale; F fig. ein Gut 2 to parcel out an estate.

Aus-schlachter (ᴵᴸ◡) m ㉒ (retail) butcher; Schriftstellerei: (agent who acts as) intermediary between authors and publishers.

aus-schlacken ⊙ (ᴵᴸ◡) v/a. ⑱** metall. to free or separate (metal) from dross.

aus-schlaf/en (ᴵᴸ◡) ⑨a*** I v/n. (h.) und sich 2 v/refl. to have a long sleep, to enjoy a good night's rest; ich habe nicht ausgeschlafen I have not had my full amount of sleep. — II v/a. (vertreiben) to sleep upon, to forget in one's sleep; e-n Rausch 2 to sleep off the effects of drink, to sleep o.s. sober.

Aus-schlag (ᴵᴸ) m ⑦d. 1. Ballspiel: first ball, service; den ~ tun to throw the first ball; to serve the ball. — 2. (Pflanzentriebe) sprouts, shoots pl. — 3. path. ~ (der Haut) eruption, rash, breaking-out (of the skin); ⚕ exanthem(a); pimple, pustule, F heat-bump; e-n ~ bekommen to have a rash (coming out), to come out in pimples or pustules. — 4. (Neigung) der Wage ꝛc.: turn(ing) of the scale(s); der Wage den ~ geben to turn (or weigh down) the scale, to cast the balance; der Magnetnadel: deflection; des Pendels: amplitude; des Gewichts: casting weight. — 5. fig. (Erfolg) turn (of affairs), issue (of events); e-r Sache den ~ geben to decide a matter (zugunsten von in favour of); er gab dabei den ~ he clinched the matter, he brought it to a definite conclusion, als Vorsitzender: he settled it by his casting vote; 2=gebend f. bsd. Art.

aus-schlag-artig (ᴸ ...) a. ㊶ path.: ⚕ exanthematic; =eisen ⊙ n ㉒ punch(er).

aus-schlag/en (ᴵᴸ◡) ⑨b** I v/a. 1. einen wacker 2 to beat (or thrash) a p. soundly. — 2. (forttreiben) to drive away, to expel; Ballspiel: den Ball 2 to serve the ball; fenc. e-n Hieb 2 (parieren) to parry a thrust. — 3. (auslöschen) to extinguish by knocking, to stamp out. — 4. (ausstrecken) die Arme in die Luft 2 to stretch out one's arms. — 5. die ausgerungene Wäsche ꝛc.: to untwist, to unfold. — 6. ⊙ Gerberei: die Felle 2 (aus dem Äscher nehmen) to pull ... out of the lime-pit. — 7. (ausleeren, gewinnen) den Dotter, das Ei 2 to beat up an egg; ✕ das Erz aus dem tauben Gestein 2 to (hand-)pick a lode, to pound the ore. — 8. e-m ein Auge 2 to knock out a p.'s eye; e-m Fasse den Boden 2 to stave (in) a cask; fig. das schlägt dem Fasse den Boden aus (gibt ihm ꝛc. den Rest) that settles (or finishes) him, F that does for him; weit S. that spoils the whole thing; ⊙ Löcher in eine Metallplatte ꝛc.: to

♪ Musik; ✿ Wissenschaft; ❀ Pflanze; ⚕ Geographie; ⊙ Technik; ✕ Bergbau; ✕ Militär; ⚓ Marine; ❀ Handel; ✉ Post; 🚂 Eisenbahn.

stamp (or punch) out; *metall.* (aus-hämmern) to flatten (or hammer) out. — 9. (bekleiden) to trim (or dress) up with; mit Tuch, Brettern ⁂ to line with cloth, boards; mit Papier ⁂ to (line with) paper; e-n Saal mit Tapeten ⁂ to hang … with tapestry. — 10. *fig.* (abweisen) to refuse or decline (a p.'s offer); stärker: to reject. — 11. von Glocken: (die Stunden) ⁂ to strike (the hours); F e-c ausgeschlagene Stunde a full hour. — 12. (hervortreten lassen) vom Feuer: Flammen ⁂ to send forth …, to blaze forth …; von Pflanzen: ⚘ Blätter ⁂ to shoot forth …; von e-r Wand: Feuchtigkeit ⁂ to sweat. — II *v/n.* (13-16: h., 17-19: fn) 13. (den 1. Schlag tun) to strike first, to give the first blow; Ballspiel: to serve the ball; to bowl (first). — 14. (zu Ende schlagen) to cease striking; Singvögel: to leave off singing; F to go out of song; von Uhren: die Stunde hat ausgeschlagen the (full) hour has struck. — 15. (vgl. 4) mit der Hand ⁂ to strike out with one's hand; von Pferden: hinten ⁂ to lash out; nach e-m ⁂ to kick (out) at a p. — 16. von der Wage: nach e-r Seite ⁂ to incline, to turn, to be weighed down. — 17. (hervorbrechen) to break out; das Feuer schlägt zum Dache aus the flames are leaping up to the roof; *agr., hort.,* ⚘ Blätter, Knospen treiben) to sprout, shoot, bud; to burst into leaf; to come out (in shoots); *path.* von der Haut: to come out in a rash, to break out (in pimples). — 18. die Wände schlagen aus … show damp; der Frost schlägt an der Wand aus the wall is covered with hoar-frost or crystals; *chm.* vom Salpeter ⁊c.: to effloresce. — 19. *fig.* gut, nach Wunsch ⁂ (ablaufen) to turn out well, to succeed; es schlug zu s-m Nutzen aus it brought him in a profit, he (was) benefited by it. — III sich ⁂ *v/refl.* 20. to have a good fight or scuffle. — 21. to cease fighting or scuffling. — IV ⁓ *n* ⁂ u. A/ung *f* ⁂ 22. service (of a ball); refusal (of an offer); striking (the hours); first blow or throw (in a fight or a game); turn (of the scale); ⚘ sprouting, budding; *path.* rash, eruption; damp or sweat (of walls); *chm.* efflorescence.

Aus-schläger (ᴴᴸ⌣) *m* ⁂, ⁓**in** *f* ⁂ 1. one who serves a ball; ⚒ picks the ore, &c. — 2. Pferd: kicking horse, kicker.

Aus-schlag-fäustel ⊙ (ᴴᴸ…) *m* ⁂ pounding-hammer; ⁼**fieber** *n, path.* exanthematic fever; ⁂**gebend** *a.* ⁂ decisive; ⁂e Stimme casting vote; ⁼**schuppen** ⚘ *m* bes Blattes, bei Farnen ⁊c. ⟋ ramentum; ⁼**steiger** ⚒ *m* foreman of sorters; ⁼**wald** *m, for.* mit gleichaltrigem Holz: timber of uniform growth or age.

aus-schlämmen (ᴴᴸ⌣) *v/a.* ⁂** Teiche ⁊c.: to clear of mud, weit S. to dredge.

aus-schleifen¹ (ᴴᴸ⌣) [schleifen¹] ⁂b** I *v/a.* to grind (or whet) thoroughly; to remove by grinding; e-e Klinge ⁂ to grind hollow. — II sich ⁂ *v/refl.* to get worp (out) by grinding or friction. — III *v/n.* (h.) to cease grinding.

aus-schleifen² (ᴴᴸ⌣) [Schleife] *v/a.* ⁂** to drag out (on a sledge).

aus-schleimen (ᴴᴸ⌣) *v/a.* ⁂** to free from slime, e-n Fisch: to clean.

aus-schlenkern (ᴴᴸ⌣) *v/a.* ⁂a** to jerk out or off. [out or away.

aus-schleppen (ᴴᴸ⌣) *v/a.* ⁂** to drag]

aus-schleudern (ᴴᴸ⌣) *v/a.* ⁂a** 1. to hurl forth; ⊙ mit der Schwungmaschine: to centrifuge. — 2. e-m ein Auge ⁂ to knock out a p.'s eye with a sling.

aus-schlichten ⊙ (ᴴᴸ⌣) *v/a.* ⁂** *metall.* (glattschlagen) to stretch, smooth, flatten out; Gerberei: Leder ⁂ (verfeinern) to pare…; Weberei ⁊c.: to size, to dress the warp.

aus-schließ/en (ᴴᴸ⌣) I *v/a.* und *v/refl.* ⁂d** 1. e-n (aus dem Hause) ⁂ to shut (or lock) a p. out, Arbeiter: to lock out. — 2. e-n, sich ⁂ (ausfondern) to exclude a p., o.s.; ich schließe niemand davon aus I except nobody; das eine schließt das andere nicht aus the one does not preclude (or bar) the other; weitere Zugeständnisse ⁊c. sind ausgeschlossen … are out of the question, … are impossible; sich von et. ⁂ to separate (or sever) o.s. from a th., to secede from a party, &c.; von der Advokatur ⁂ to disbar; von der Kirchengemeinschaft ⁂ to excommunicate; aus e-r Gesellschaft: to expel. — 3. e-n Gefangenen ⁂ (aus den Ketten lösen) to unchain … — 4. ⊙ *typ.* eine Zeile ⁂ to justify. — II ⁓ *n* ⁂ 5. = A/ung. — III ⁂d *p.pr.* u. *a.* ⁂ 6. = ausschließlich. — IV **aus-geschlossen:** 7. *p.p.* u. *a.* ⁂ (D9) in den Bed. des *inf.,* f. bsd. 2. — 8. *adv.* und *prp.* except(ing), with the exclusion of.

aus-schließlich (ᴴᴸ⌣) I *a.* ⁂ exclusive; ⁂es Recht mit et. zu handeln ⁊c. monopoly; bis (zur) Seite 20 ⁂ up to page 20 exclusively. — II *prp.* mit *acc.* ob. *gen.* exclusive (or to the exclusion) of. [exclusiveness.]

Aus-schließlichkeit (ᴴᴸ⌣) *f* ⁂ (o. pl.)]

Aus-schließung (ᴴᴸ⌣) *f* ⁂ 1. = Ausschluß 1; *jur.* f. ⁓**frist**. — 2. ⊙ *typ.* justification; a. = Ausschluß 2.

Aus-schließungs-frist (ᴴᴸ…) *f* ⁂ *jur.* term of preclusion; ⁼**system** *n* prohibitive system; ⁂**weise** *adv.* by way of exclusion; exclusively.

aus-schluchzen (ᴴᴸ⌣) ⁂** I *v/a.* 1. Worte ⁂ to sob out … — II *v/n.* 2. (h.) to cease sobbing. — 3. (fn) in Tränen ⁂ to burst out in sobs and tears.

aus-schlummern (ᴴᴸ⌣) *v/n.* (h.), *v/refl.* u. *v/a.* ⁂a** 1. to slumber enough. — 2. to cease slumbering.

aus-schlüpfen (ᴴᴸ⌣) *v/n.* (fn) ⁂** 1. to creep out (of the egg). — 2. (entfahren) das Messer schlüpfte aus the knife slipped (out of his or her hands).

aus-schlürfen (ᴴᴸ⌣) *v/a.* ⁂** Flüssiges: to sip (up); ein Ei ⁂ to suck an egg.

Aus-schluß (ᴴᴸ) *m* ⁂a. 1. exclusion, seclusion; mit ⁓ von ob. *gen.* to the exclusion (or with the exception) of; *jur.* Verhandlung mit ⁓ der Öffentlichkeit proceedings *pl.* to which the public are not admitted, private proceedings. — 2. ⊙ *typ.* spaces, justifiers *pl.*; großer ⁓ quadrat.

aus-schmähen, ⚘ **aus-schmälen** (ᴴᴸ⌣) *v/a.* u. *v/n.* (h.) ⁂** to scold, to chide.

aus-schmausen (ᴴᴸ⌣) ⁂** = ausessen.

aus-schmelzen (ᴴᴸ⌣) I *v/a.* ⁂(Tb[ei]t)** 1. to melt; ⊙ Metalle: to smelt, fuse; Talg: to try (out). — 2. (h.) to cease melting. — III ⁓ *n* ⁂ und **Aus-schmelzung** *f* ⁂ 3. (s)melting; fusion.

aus-schmettern (ᴴᴸ⌣) ⁂a** I *v/a.* die Trompete schmettert ein Lied aus … is sounding (or blazoning forth) a tune. — II *v/n.* (h.) die Trompete hat ausgeschmettert … has ceased sounding.

aus-schmieden (ᴴᴸ⌣) ⁂** I *v/a.* 1. ⊙ Metalle: to forge (or hammer) well; (ausdehnen) to stretch under the hammer. — 2. Gefangene: to free from chains, to unfetter. — II *v/n.* (h.) 3. ausgeschmiedet haben to have done forging.

aus-schmieren (ᴴᴸ⌣) *v/a.* ⁂** 1. to smear (inside); ⊙ mit Fett, Pech, Teer ⁂ to (smear with) grease, pitch, tar; Maurerei: die Fugen ⁂ to point the joints of a wall. — 2. F *nur b.s.* = ausschreiben 3 b. — 3. F *fig.* e-n ⁂ (schlagen) to thrash a p. (soundly).

Aus-schmierer (ᴴᴸ⌣) *m* ⁂, ⁓**in** *f* ⁂ *fig.* compiler, *b.s.* plagiarist; ⁓**ei** (⁻ᴴᴸ) *f* ⁂ compilation, *b.s.* plagiarism.

aus-schmollen (ᴴᴸ⌣) *v/n.* (h.) u. *v/refl.* ⁂** to cease sulking or moping.

aus-schmoren (ᴴᴸ⌣) ⁂** I *v/a.* to stew, to extract by stewing. — II *v/n.* (h., fn) to stew, to run out in stewing.

aus-schmück/en (ᴴᴸ⌣) I *v/a.* ⁂** 1. (auch *v/refl.*) e-n Raum: to adorn, to ornament; to decorate; ein Kleid mit Bändern ⁊c. ⁂ to trim … with ribbons, sich ⁂ to attire o.s., to dress o.s. up, F to adorn o.s. — 2. e-e Erzählung ⁂ to embellish (F to trick up) a story. — II ⁓ *n* ⁂ = A/ung.

Aus-schmücker (ᴴᴸ⌣) *m* ⁂, ⁓**in** *f* ⁂ decorator; des Stils: ornate (or florid, flowery) writer.

Aus-schmückung (ᴴᴸ⌣) *f* ⁂ adornment, ornament, decoration; (Kleidung) attire, dress; der Rede: embellishment.

aus-schnallen (ᴴᴸ⌣) *v/a.* ⁂** to unbuckle.

aus-schnappen (ᴴᴸ⌣) *v/n.* (h.) ⁂** to snap off, to go off suddenly.

aus-schnarchen (ᴴᴸ⌣) *v/n.* (h.) ⁂** to cease (or to have done) snoring.

aus-schnauben (ᴴᴸ⌣) ⁂c** u. ⁂** I *v/n.* (h.) to recover one's breath. — II *v/a.* u. *v/refl.* die Nase, sich ⁂ to blow one's nose; Blut ⁊c. ⁂ to bring up … by blowing one's nose, v. Walfisch: to blow (or send, spirt) up … through the nostrils.

aus-schnaufen F ⚘ (ᴴᴸ⌣) *v/n.* (h.) ⁂** (sich verschnaufen) to get one's breath.

Aus-schneide-bilder ⊙ (ᴴᴸ…) *n/pl.* cut-paper work; ⁼**kunst** ⊙ *f* cutting silhouettes out of paper, ⟋ psaligraphy; Tischlerei: sawing in curves; ⁼**messer** *n* paring-knife.

aus-schneid/en (ᴴᴸ⌣) I *v/a.* ⁂c** 1. (herausschneiden) to cut out or away, Holzwert: to carve; *hort.* e-n Baum: to lop, to prune; *surg.* ein Gewächs: to cut out, ⟋ to extirpate; Waben aus den Bienenstöcken ⁂ to cut the honeycombs; ausgeschnittene Zeitungsartikel *m/pl.* newspaper clippings or cuttings *pl.* — 2. Schneiderei: Ärmel ⁂ to slope (out)…; ein Kleid ⁂ to cut… low; ausgeschnittenes Kleid low(-necked)

Signs (see page XVII): F familiar; P vulgar; ſ flash; ⚘ rare; † obsolete (died); * new word (born); ⁺⁺ incorrect; ♪ music;

[Ausschneider] — 127 — [ausschweifen]

dress; Rock mit ausgeschnittenen Vorderschößen cut-away coat. — 3. Papier ꝛc. ⌇ to cut paper into figures or patterns; ein Bild ꝛc. ⌇ to cut ... (out of paper, &c.); Zeug ⌇ (durchstechen ꝛc.) to pink, to prick out; ausgeschnittene Arbeit cut cloth- (or paper-)work; bogenförmig, wellenförmig ⌇ to slope, to scallop; zackenförmig ⌇ to jag (out). — 4. ⚓ für den Kleinverkauf: to sell by retail, Tuch: to sell by the yard. — II ~ n ㉓ 5. = A/ung.

Aus-schneider (ᴵᴵ‿) m ㉒. ~in f ㊼ one who cuts out, v. Mustern: pinker, v. Kleidern: cutter-out; von Bäumen: pruner; ⚓ retailer.

Aus-schneidung f ㊼ cutting (out); surg. excision, extirpation; ⚓ retail (trade).

aus-schneien (ᴵᴵ‿) v/impers. (h.) ⑧**: es hat ausgeschneit it has ceased snowing.

aus-schneite(l)n ⊕ (ᴵᴵ‿) v/a. ⑧ (㉒a)** hort. Bäume: to prune, to lop.

aus-schneuzen (ᴵᴵ‿) v/a. ⑨** 1. a. v/refl. sich ⌇ to blow one's nose. — 2. ein Licht ⌇ (auslöschen) to snuff out a candle.

Aus-schnitt (ᴵᴵ‿) m ⓜ c. 1. ⚓ retail (trade); im ~(e) verkaufen ⌇ (sell by) retail, to sell by the yard. — 2. (Herausschneiden) cutting (out). — 3. (Lücke) cut(ting); bogenförmiger sweep; gezackter: indenture; arch. bay; ~ des Ärmels sloping (out); Leibchen mit ~ low body; ⊕ Schlosserei: ~ im Schlüsselbarte ward; typ. ~ für die Zurichtung overlay. — 4. (Ausgeschnittenes) ~ aus e-r Zeitung newspaper cutting or clipping; math. e-s Kreises: sector.

Aus-schnitt-handel ⚓ (ᴵᴵ‿...) m ㉒, -handlung f retail (business, trade); -händler m retail dealer; linendraper; -laden m retail shop; -waren f/pl. retail goods; (Ellenwaren) dry goods pl.

aus-schnitze(l)n (ᴵᴵ‿) v/a. ⑨ (㉒a)** to carve (out), to sculpture.

aus-schnüffeln F (ᴵᴵ‿) v/a. ㉒a** to sniff (or scent, ferret) out, F to nose.

aus-schnupfen (ᴵᴵ‿) v/a. u. v/refl. ⑨** seine Dose ⌇ to empty ... by taking snuff; sich ⌇ to blow one's nose.

aus-schnüren (ᴵᴵ‿) v/a. ⑧** 1. to untie (a parcel). — 2. (a. v/refl.) e-n (sich) ⌇ to unlace a p. (o.s.) or a p.'s (one's) stays.

aus-schöpf/en (ᴵᴵ‿) v/a. ⑧** I v/a. 1. (ausleeren) to scoop out, empty, drain off (a. fig.); den Brunnen ⌇ to exhaust the well; ⚓ das Wasser aus e-m Kahne ⌇ e-n Kahn ⌇ to bail out a boat. — 2. bsd. metall. to ladle (out). — II v/n. (h.) 3. ausgeschöpft h. to have done drawing water. — III ~ n ㉓ 4. = A/ung.

Aus-schöpfer (ᴵᴵ‿) m ㉒ 1. a. ~in f ㊼ scooper. — 2. = Ausschöpfkelle.

Aus-schöpf-kelle ⊕ (ᴵᴵ‿...) f ㊼, -löffel m ladle, scoop(er).

aus-schoten (ᴵᴵ‿) v/a. ⑧** to shell.

aus-schrägen (ᴵᴵ‿) v/a. ⑧** arch. ein Fenster ꝛc. ⌇ to splay (or chamfer) ...

aus-schrapen (ᴵᴵ‿), mst. aus-schrappen (ᴵᴵ‿) v/a. ⑧** 1. (auskratzen) to scrape out. — 2. ⚓ die Kabelgarne ⌇ to untwist the ends of the strands.

aus-schrauben (ᴵᴵ‿) v/c** u. ⑧** I v/a. to unscrew. — II sich ⌇ v/refl. = ausdrehen II. — III v/n. (h.) to cease (or stop) screwing.

aus-schreiben (ᴵᴵ‿) ⑩** I v/a. 1. to finish writing (auch abs.). — 2. (ungefürzt schreiben) to write out, to write in full. — 3. (abschreiben): a) meist g.s. to copy, to transcribe; ausgeschriebene Rollen f/pl. written parts pl.; ⚓ die Posten e-r Rechnung, e-e Rechnung ⌇ to extract (or draw out, make up) an account; b) b.s. aus e-m Buche ⌇ to plagiarize (stärker: to pilfer) from ... 4. (aus der Liste streichen) e-n Lehrling ⌇ to enter ... as journeyman. — 5. seine Hand(schrift) ob. sich ⌇ to form (or improve) one's handwriting; ausgeschrieb(e)ne Hand flowing (or round) hand. — 6. (ankündigen) to publish, announce, proclaim; einen Bußtag ⌇ to appoint; e-n Konkurs ⌇ to issue a statute in bankruptcy; e-n Preis ⌇ to offer a prize; e-n Reichstag, Landtag ⌇ to convoke (or summon) parliament, the diet; (eine Konkurrenz über) eine Stelle ⌇ to advertise a vacancy; Steuern ⌇ to impose (or lay on) taxes; e-e Versammlung ⌇ to call a meeting; Wahlen ⌇ to issue writs for elections, von Ministern auch: to appeal to the country; e-n Wettbewerb ⌇ to invite (public) competition, für Kandidaten: to offer a post by (public) announcement, to advertise an appointment; ⚔ e-e Lieferung ⌇ to requisition supply. — II sich ⌇ v/refl. 7. (erschöpfen) to exhaust one's literary powers, to weaken one's intellectual powers by (too much) writing. — III v/n. (h.) 8. to cease writing. — IV ~ n ㉓ 9. = A/ung.

Aus-schreiber (ᴵᴵ‿) m ㉒ Abschreiber; -ei (ᴵᴵ‿ᴵ) f ㊻ = Abschreiberei.

Aus-schreibung (.‿.) f ㊻ copy, transcription; ⚓ e-r Rechnung: abstract (of an account); b.s. e-s Buches: plagiarism; e-s Reichstages: convocation; v. Steuern: imposition; ⚔ v. Lebensmitteln: requisition.

aus-schreien (ᴵᴵ‿) ⑩** I v/a. 1. to cry (or shout) out; F to bawl (one's lungs) out. — 2. e-n für (ob. als) et. ⌇ to report a p. to be ..., lobend: to extol (F to puff, to boom) a p. as (being)...; b.s. to cry down (or defame) a p. as ... — 3. s-e Stimme ⌇ to strain one's voice. — II v/n. (h.) 4. to cease crying out. — III sich ⌇ v/refl. 5. to scream lustily, sich den Hals ⌇ F to bawl at the top of one's voice, to scream one's lungs out.

aus-schreiten (ᴵᴵ‿) ⑩b** I v/n. (fn) 1. (wacker, tüchtig) to step out (well); to take long (and vigorous) strides. — 2. fig. to exceed the bounds; to overstep the mark. — II v/a. 3. = abschreiten I. — III ~ n ㉓ und Aus-schreitung f ㊻ 4. fig. (Übertretung) transgression, stärker: outrage, (Ungebühr) excess; (Tumult) riot, tumult, uproar.

aus-schroten (ᴵᴵ‿) v/a. ⑧** 1. Bier ⌇ (faßweise verkaufen) to sell beer by the barrel. — 2. Fässer ⌇ (emporwinden) to pull (or lift) ... out of a cellar.

aus-schulen (ᴵᴵ‿) v/a. ⑧** e-e Gemeinde ⌇ to detach ... from a school-district.

aus-schuren ⊕ (ᴵᴵ‿) v/a. ⑧** metall. = ausblasen 6.

aus-schüren ⊕ (ᴵᴵ‿) v/a. ⑧** metall. to draw the slags.

aus-schürfen ⚒ (ᴵᴵ‿) v/a. ⑧** to dig out, to uncover; e-n Gang ⌇ to open (or follow up) a lode.

Aus-schuß (ᴵᴵ‿) m ⓜ a. 1. = Ausschießung. — 2. (Untaugliches) refuse, rubbish, waste, trash; ⚓ auch: spoilt (or soiled, defective) goods pl.; (first, second) rejections pl. — 3. (Auserlesenes) choice article, select goods pl. — 4. (Kommission) committee, (managing) board; e-r Bank: board of directors; parl. enger(er) ~ select committee, allgemeiner ~ committee of the whole house; geschäftsführender ~ committee of management; ständiger ~ standing committee; ~ zu Wahlzwecken b.s. bsd. Am. caucus. — 5. path..⚔ spot where the bullet leaves the body.

Aus-schuß-bogen (ᴵᴵ‿...) m ㉒ f. -papier; -mitglied n member of a board, committee-man; -papier n (äußerste Lagen) outside paper or sheets pl., outsides pl.; typ. waste paper; -sitzung f committee-meeting; -ware ⚓ f damaged goods, rejections, remnants pl.; -wolle ⊕ f waste-wool.

aus-schütteln (ᴵᴵ‿) v/a. u. sich ⌇ v/refl. ⓶a** Kleider: to shake (out).

aus-schütt/en (ᴵᴵ‿) ⑧** I v/a. 1. (ausgießen) to pour out or forth; das Korn aus dem Sack ⌇ to shoot out the corn.... den Sack ⌇ to empty the sack; fig. sein Herz ⌇ to unbosom o.s., to pour out one's heart to a. p.; das Kind mit dem Bade ⌇ to cast away the good with the bad. — 2. (zufüllen) e-n Graben to fill up. — 3. ⚓ eine Konkursmasse ⌇ (verteilen) to divide a bankrupt's estate; Dividenden ⌇ to distribute (or declare) dividends. — II sich ⌇ v/refl. 4. fig. sein Herz ⌇ (f. 1). — 5. F sich vor Lachen ⌇ to split (one's sides) with laughing. — III ~, &c. ~ n ㉓ u. A/ung f ㊻ 6. pouring out, &c. — 7. ⚓ ~ der Masse division (or apportionment) of the bankrupt's estate; ~ v. Dividenden distribution (or declaration) of dividends; ~ v. Geldern (great) abundance of money.

aus-schwärmen (ᴵᴵ‿) ⑧** I v/n. 1. (fn) v. Bienen ꝛc.: to swarm (out); ⚔ to deploy, to skirmish; in Schützenlinien ⌇ to advance (or attack) in loose formation. — 2. (h.) to cease swarming or fig. rioting; hat er endlich ausgeschwärmt? has he steadied (or settled) down at last? — II ~ n ㉓ swarming, &c.; ⚔ deploy(ment).

aus-schwatzen, aus-schwätzen F (ᴵᴵ‿) v/a., v/n. u. v/refl. ⑨** = ausplaudern I, II, III und ausreden 6.

aus-schwefeln (ᴵᴵ‿) v/a. ⑨a** to (fumigate or strew with) sulphur; ein Faß ꝛc.: to match. — II ~ n u. Aus-schwef(e)lung f ㊻ sulphur(iz)ation.

aus-schweif/en (ᴵᴵ‿) v/a. ⑧** I v/a. 1. (wellen) to scallop, notch; (auszacken) to indent, jag; ⚓ Blätter: ausgeschweift imbricate(d), sinuated. — 2. (ausspülen) Wäsche: to rinse. — II v/n. (fn u. h.) 3. fig. meist b.s. to ramble, to stray; im Reden: to digress. — 4. sinnlich: to commit excesses, to lead a dissolute (or fast, debauched, dissipated) life. — III ~ n ㉓ 5. = A/ung. — IV ⚓ b p.pr. u. a. ㊻

⚛ scientific; ⚘ botanical; ⌇ geography; ⊕ machinery; ⚒ mining; ⚔ military; ⚓ marine; ⚓ commercial; ✉ postal; 🚆 railway.

[Ausschweifung] — 128 — [außer]

6. in den Beb. des inf. — 7. dissolute, disorderly, debauched, dissipated, licentious; (übertrieben) excessive; (überspannt) eccentric; ⸺de Reden führen to indulge in extravagant (or wild) talk; ein ⸺des Leben a life of dissipation or indulgence.

Aus-schweifung (ᴵᴸᵛ) f ⑯ sweep, curve; (Abschweifen) digression; (Übertreibung) excess; (Überspanntheit) eccentricity; (liederliches Leben) dissoluteness, debauchery, licentiousness, dissipation; zur ~ verleiten to debauch; ~s-kreis (ᶻ...) ⊕ m ⑫ circle of excursion.

aus-schweißen ⊕ (ᴵᴸᵛ) ⓐ** I v/a. Maurerei: die Fugen ⸺ to point the joints (roughly); Schmiede: Eisen ⸺ to weld out iron. — II v/n. (h.) hunt. to bleed.

aus-schwelgen (ᴵᴸᵛ) v/n. (h.) ⑱** to discontinue one's revelry or debauchery.

aus-schwemmen (ᴵᴸᵛ) v/a. ⑱** to wash (or flush) out; to rinse, to cleanse.

aus-schwenken (ᴵᴸᵛ) ⑱** I v/a. Glas, Wäsche ꝛc. ⸺ to rinse … — II v/n. ⊕ Uhrm.: die Spindel schwenkt aus … escapes.

aus-schwingen (ᴵᴸᵛ) ⊕ fr** I v/a. 1. (ausbreiten) to spread out by swinging; ↓ ein Boot ⸺ (aussetzen) to swing (out) a boat. — 2. (schütteln) to shake; (reinigen) to cleanse by shaking; den Flachs ⸺ to swing(le), to scutch; Getreide: to winnow, to fan. — II v/n. (h.) 3. to cease swinging or oscillating; hunt. Birkwild: to fly out of a tree. — III sich ⸺ v/refl. 4. Turner am Reck: to swing (round).

aus-schwitzen (ᴵᴸᵛ) ⑱** I v/n. 1. (h.) to cease perspiring. — 2. (in) (heraussickern) von Harzen: to exude. — II v/a. 3. to sweat (out), to exude. — 4. (durch Schwitzen loswerden) to sweat out (of one's system); eine Krankheit ⸺, auch: to go through a sweating cure. — 5. F co. (vergessen) to forget. — III ~ n ㉓ u. **Aus-schwitzung** f ⑯ 6. sweating (cure); path.: ✻ exudation.

aus-segeln ↓ (ᴵᴸᵛ) ⓐ** I v/n. (in) 1. aus e-r Meerenge: to disembogue. — 2. = absegeln I. — 3. (gegen den Strom segeln) to sail up-stream or against the tide. — II v/a. 4. ein Kap ꝛc. ⸺ (umsegeln) to steer clear of … — III ~ n ㉓ 5. disemboguement; aus dem Hafen: sailing.

aus-sehen (ᴵᴸᵛ) ⓐ** I v/a. 1. (zu Ende sehen) to see out or to the end. — 2. sich (dat.) (fast) die Augen ⸺ (blind sehen) to stare one's eyes out, to wear out one's eyesight; nach etwas ob. e-m ⸺ to look out for … — II v/n. (h.) 3. zum Fenster ⸺ to look out of the window. — 4. (äußerlich erscheinen): to appear; a) mit a.: appetitlich ⸺ to look appetizing, auch fig. von Personen: to look neat or nice; gut (gesund) ⸺ to look well; (hübsch) to have a good appearance, to be good-looking; iro. da sehe ich gut aus there I am in a fine pickle; prächtig ⸺ to look splendid, F to be in fine form or condition; rüstig (für sein Alter) ⸺ to look hale and hearty for one's age; iro. sie muß schön ⸺ F she must look a (fine) sight; er sah schrecklich aus he looked awful or a terrible object; b) er sieht aus, als könnte er nicht bis fünf zählen he looks as if he could not say boo to a goose; nach etwas (recht Großem, Vornehmem) ⸺ to make a great show; to look a fine gentleman; er sieht ganz danach aus he looks it; iro. ihr seht mir ganz danach aus you are the right man (F the right sort) to do it; er sieht wie 60 Jahr alt aus, wie wenn (als ob) er 60 Jahr alt wäre he looks sixty (years old); wie sieht sie aus? what is she like?, how does she look; c) als v/impers. es sieht mißlich, F faul mit ihm ob. um ihn aus he is in difficulties or in a bad way; wie sieht's bei dir aus? how are things with you?; wie sieht's in der Welt aus? co. how goes the world?; wie sieht's mit Ihrem Geschäft aus? how are you getting on in business?, what about your business?; es sieht nach Regen aus, als ob es regnen wollte there's every appearance of rain coming, it looks as if it were going to rain. — III ~ n ㉓ 5. aspect, look, appearance; nach dem äußeren ⸺ zu urteilen to judge from outward appearances; nach seinem ~ ist er ein gemeiner (feiner) Mensch F he has a low (superior) look about him; er hat ein verdächtiges ~ he looks or appears to be a suspicious character; das gibt den Dingen ein anderes ~ that puts a new face on things; einer Sache ein schönes ~ geben to whitewash …, to gloss … over; frisches, gesundes ~ fresh complexion, healthy look or appearance. — IV ⸺d p.pr. u. a. ⑯ 6. in den Beb. des inf., z. B.: gut ⸺d good-looking, of fine appearance; schlecht ⸺d illfavoured. — 7. weit ⸺d (sich in die Zukunft erstreckend) (being) far from realization; von Plänen: far-reaching, extensive. [geigern.]

aus-seigern ⊕ (ᴵᴸᵛ) v/a. ⓐ** = ab-

aus-seihen (ᴵᴸᵛ) v/a. ⑱** to filter = abseihen. [clarify honey.]

aus-seimen (ᴵᴸᵛ) v/a. ⑱** Honig ⸺ to

aus-sein (ᴵᴸᵛ) v/n. (in) ⓐ** 1. to be over; s. aus 9, 10. — 2. sie sind nach ihm aus they have gone to fetch him, they are after him; fig. auf (ob. nach) et. ⸺ to be in search (or quest) of a th., to be after a th.

außen (ᴸᵛ) [ahd.; * aus] adv. (ant. innen) out, without, (on the) outside. outwardly; (draußen) out of doors, abroad; nach ⸺ (zu, hin) outwards; von ⸺ her from without, from (the) outside; ⸺ befindlich outward, exterior; nach innen und ⸺ both inward(ly) and outward(ly), within and without; von ⸺ besehen, betrachtet seen (or judging) from the outside; ⸺ bleiben (ausbleiben) to stay out(side) or away.

Außen-abteilung ⚔ (ᶻ...) f ⑫ detached section, outpost; =bahnhof 🚂 m outer station; =beplankung ↓ f outside planking; =beplattung ↓ f outside plating; =bords ↓ adv. outboard, outside; =böschung ⚔ f, frt. counterscarp; =deck ↓ n outer deck.

aus-senden (ᴵᴸᵛ) I v/a. ⓐ** 1. Strahlen ⸺ to emit (or dart) rays. — 2. to send out or forth (= ausschicken I). — II ~ n ㉓ 3. = Aussendung.

Außen-dienst (ᴵᴸ...) m ⑫ outdoor service or duty; =ding n external object.

Aus-sendling (ᴵᴸᵛ) m ⑪d. emissary.

Außen-dock ↓ (ᴵᴸᵛ) n ⑫ wet dock.

Aus-sendung (ᴵᴸᵛ) f ⑯ 1. emission. — 2. = ausschicken II.

Außen-fahrgast (ᴵᴸ...) m outside passenger; =gebäude n outhouse.

aus-sengen (ᴵᴸᵛ) v/a. ⑱** to singe (on the) inside, to singe thoroughly.

Außen-graben ⚔ (ᴵᴸ...) m ⑫ frt. advanced ditch; =hafen ↓ m outer harbour or port; =handel m foreign trade; =haut f outer skin; ↓ = =beplattung; =kelch ♀ m ♀ calycle; =klüver ↓ m flying jib; =kreise m/pl. Börse ꝛc.: outsiders pl.; =liek ↓ n fore-leech; =linie f outline, contour; =mauer f outer (or exterior) wall; =passagier m outside passenger; =schlag m, agr. Fruchtfolge: outfield; =seite f outside, surface; outward appearance; exterior; =sitz m Straßenbahn: outside seat; =stände ⚙ m/pl. outstanding debts or claims pl.; =stehend p.pr. u. a. ⑯ standing out(side); =tür f outer door; =wache ⚔ f outer watch or guard; =wand f = =mauer; =wall ⚔ m, frt. exterior rampart; =welt [nhd. 18. sae.] f external (or outer, visible) world; =werk ⚔ n, frt. advanced (or detached) work or fort, outwork; =winkel m, math. exterior angle.

außer (ᴵᴸᵛ) [ahd.; * auß] I prp. mst mit dat. 1. räumlich: (außerhalb) beside(s), outside; ⸺ j-s Bereich beyond (or out of) a p.'s reach; ⸺ dem Hause out of doors; ⸺ dem Hause essen (schlafen) to dine (to sleep) out; ⸺ Landes (gehen to go) abroad; ⸺ der Stadt outside the town. — 2. ⸺ acht, ⸺ Betracht lassen to leave out of account; to neglect, overlook, slight; ⸺ aller Acht lassen to pay no heed (whatever) to, entirely to overlook; sich ⸺ Atem laufen to get out of breath by running; ⸺ Dienst (dienstfrei) off duty; (ohne Stelle) out of employment; vgl. a. D.; ⸺ Fassung kommen to lose one's presence of mind; ⸺ Frage, ⸺ Zweifel beyond all doubt; ⸺ Kurs setzen to withdraw from circulation; ⸺ Stand setzen to disable; ⸺stande s. ds.; ⸺ der Zeit out of season, at the wrong time. — 3. ⸺ sich sein to be beside o.s.; vor Freude ⸺ sich sein to be mad (or frantic) with joy; e-n vor Schreck ⸺ sich bringen to frighten a p. out of his wits. — 4. (nebst) in addition to; apart from; independently of; sein einziges Werk ⸺ den Gedichten his only work other than (or apart from) the poems. — 5. (ausgenommen) save, except, barring, besides; alle ⸺ ihm all but he (F him); ⸺ uns ließ sich niemand sehen besides us there was nobody to be seen; ⸺ den Möbeln hat er nichts he has nothing but (or save, except) the (bare) furniture; Rennsport: alle Renner ⸺ einem (all) the field bar one. — II cj. ⸺ daß but (or save, except) that; ⸺ daß er Geld hat besides having money; ⸺ wenn if not, unless; er lacht nie, ⸺ wenn er gewinnt he never laughs, except when he wins.

[außeramtlich] — 129 — [Aussicht]

außer=amtlich (⁻⌣…) *a.* ⊕ extra-official, unofficial; private; **⚘blattständig ？** *a.* extra-foliaceous.

außer=dem (⁻⌣⌣) **a)** *adv.* (überdies) besides; moreover; without mentioning that; **b)** ⚘ **daß** *cj.* except (or save) that he is … or in addition to his being …

außer=dienstlich ⚓ (⁻⌣…) *a.* ⊕ outside (or not belonging to) one's (regular) duty or duties; off duty; **=dienst-stellung** ⚓ *f* ⊕ e-s Kriegsschiffes putting a man-of-war out of commission.

äußere (⁻⌣⌣) **I** *a.* ⊕ **1.** im Positiv nur Attribut, nicht Prädikat (dafür äußerlich, s. ds); *comp.* fehlt, *sup.* äußerst (s. ds); outward; outer; exterior; external; ⚘ Ansehen, ⚘ Erscheinung (outside) appearance; ⚘r Schein (mere) semblance, outward show. — **II ⚘(s)** *n* ⊕ **2.** outside, exterior; sein ⁓s ist das Beste an ihm he is all outsideshow; nach seinem ⁓n muß er ein Mann von Stande sein to judge from his manners (or his bearing), his look) he must be a man of position. — **3.** *pol.* Minister des ⁓n minister of foreign affairs, England: Foreign Secretary; Ministerium des ⁓n Foreign Office.

außer=ehelich (⁻⌣…) *a.* ⊕ illegitimate, born out of wedlock, natural; **⚘etat-mäßig** *a.* (im Budget nicht vorgesehen) not budgeted, unprovided for in the budget; **⚘europäisch** *a.* extra- (or non-) European; **⚘gerichtlich** *a.* extra-judicial; **⚘gesetzlich** *a.* unlawful; **⚘gewöhnlich** *a.* extraordinary, unusual, uncommon; etwas ⁓es s.th. out of the ordinary, s.th. out of the common.

außer=halb (⁻⌣⌣) **I** *prp.* meist mit *gen.*, bisw. mit *dat.* = außer 1; ⚘ der Mauern liegend extramural. — **II** *adv.* outside, on the outside; externally; von ⚘ from outside, (aus e-m fremden Lande) from abroad.

außer=kirchlich (⁻⌣…) *a.* ⊕ non-ecclesiastic; **=kurs=setzung** ⊕ (⁻⌣⌣⌣) *f* ⊕ (Entwertung) demonetization.

äußerlich (⁻⌣⌣) **I** *a.* ⊕ (*ant.* innerlich) **1.** = äußere I; *adv.* = außerhalb II; *fig.* apparent(ly), seeming(ly); ⚘e Frömmigkeit outward (or sham) piety; ⚘es Heilmittel topical remedy; auf Medizinflaschen: for external application; ⚘ anzuwenden to be applied externally. — **2.** (oberflächlich) superficial(ly). — **3.** ⚘er Wert e-r Münze ꝛc.: extrinsic value. — **II ⚘e(s)** *n* ⊕ **4.** = äußere 2.

Äußerlichkeit (⁻⌣⌣⌣) *f* ⊕ **1.** (das Äußerlichsein) outwardness; superficiality. — **2.** (äußerliches Ding) externals *pl.*; bloße ⁓en *pl.* mere formalities *pl.*, F only a matter of form.

äußern (⁻⌣) ⊕ *a.* **I** *v/a.* **1.** Furcht, Freude ⚘ to manifest, show … — **2.** (aussprechen) to utter, express; eine Meinung, a.: to advance. — **II.** sich ⚘ *v/refl.* **3.** von Dingen: to manifest (or display, show) itself; von Blattern ꝛc.: to break out. — **4.** (sich aussprechen) to express (or declare) o.s., to give utterance to one's thoughts or opinions. — **III ⁓** *n* ⊕ **5.** = Äußerung 1.

außer=ordentlich (⁻⌣⌣⌣): **I.** *a.* ⊕: **a)** (⚘gewöhnlich) extraordinary, out of the common; ⚘er (*abbr.* **a. o.**) Professor assistant professor, university lecturer; ⚘er Gesandter ambassador extraordinary; ⚘e Ausgaben *f/pl.* extra expenses, extras *pl.* — **b)** (ungewöhnlich) astonishing, amazing, prodigious; (vorzüglich) remarkable; (ungeheuer) enormous; in ⚘en Fällen in cases of emergency; ⁓es leisten to do wonders. — **II.** *adv.* ⚘ reich of extraordinary wealth, immensely rich.

Außer=ordentlichkeit (⁻⌣⌣⌣⌣) *f* ⊕ extraordinariness; remarkableness.

Außer=sich=sein (⁻⌣⌣⌣) *n* ⊕ ecstasy; vor Zorn: exasperation, frenzy.

außer=sinnlich (⁻⌣…) *a.* ⊕ supersensual.

äußerst (⁻⌣) **I** *adv.* **1.** extremely, exceedingly; ⚘ geschmackvoll of exquisite taste; ein ⚘ angenehmer Gesellschafter a most pleasant companion; ⚘ gebildet highly accomplished; ⚘ glücklich supremely happy. — **II** ⚘**e** (⁻⌣⌣) *a.* ⊕ (*sup.* von äußere) **2.** outermost; most remote; ⚘e Grenze utmost limit. — **3.** *fig.* im ⚘en Elende in the greatest (or in utter) misery or distress; im ⚘en Falle in case of necessity or urgency, if the worst came (or comes) to the worst; die ⚘e Not extreme (or the last) necessity; der ⚘e Preis the lowest possible (F the bottom) price; von ⚘er Wichtigkeit of the utmost (or highest) importance. — **III ⁓e(s)** ⊕, oft klein geschrieben: **4.** extreme (case), extremity; sein ⁓es tun to do one's utmost or best, to make a supreme effort, to strain every nerve; das ⚘e wagen to risk (one's) all; die Dinge auf das ⚘e treiben to push matters to extremes; *adv.* aufs ⚘e extremely, to the utmost; es aufs ⚘e ankommen lassen, zum ⁓en kommen lassen to bring matters to a climax; sie ist aufs ⚘e um ihn besorgt she is extremely nervous about him; e-n aufs ⚘e bringen to tire out a p.'s patience; aufs ⚘e gebracht put to one's last shifts; wir sind aufs ⚘e gefaßt we are prepared for the worst; bis zum ⚘en right to the bitter end; wenn es zum ⁓en kommt in the worst case.

außer=stande (⁻⌣⌣⌣) sein zu to be unable (or not to be in a position) to.

Äußerung (⁻⌣⌣) *f* ⊕ **1.** manifestation, expression. — **2.** (Ausspruch) utterance, saying; (Bemerkung) remark, observation, stärker: declaration; ⁓en *pl.* der Freundschaft ꝛc.: demonstrations *pl.* of…

außer=weltlich (⁻⌣…) *a.* ⊕ extramundane; **⚘wesentlich** *a.* non-essential, contingent; **⚘zeitlich** *a.* unseasonable.

aus=setzen (⁻⌣⌣) ⊕** **I** *v/a.* **1.** mit etwas ⚘ (ausfüllen, besetzen) to line (or face) with s.th.; mit Pflastersteinen: to pave. — **2.** (hinaussetzen) to put out; *hort.* Bäume ꝛc.: to transplant; ⚓ eine Schildwache: to post, station, set; ⚓: Mannschaft aus dem Schiffe ans Land ⚘ to disembark (or land) troops; ein Boot aus dem Schiffe ins Wasser ⚘ to hoist out, to launch (or lower) a boat; die Segel ⚘ to set, to spread. — **3.** (zur Schau stellen) to expose (to view). — **4.** *a. v/refl.* (bloßstellen, preisgeben) meist mit *dat.*: e-n et. (sich) der freien Luft, dem Spotte ꝛc. ⚘ to expose (or lay open) a p., a th. (o.s.) to …; sich einer Gefahr, einem Risiko ⚘ to incur (stärker: to court) danger, to run a risk; sein Leben unnütz der Gefahr ⚘ to jeopardize …; dem setze ich mich nicht wieder aus F I shall keep out of this another time; e-n dem Gelächter der Leute ⚘ to hold a p. up to ridicule; der Verfolgung ausgesetzt liable to persecution; ein neugeborenes Kind: to expose; einen Matrosen an öder Küste: to maroon, to turn adrift; ⚘ dem feindlichen Feuer ausgesetzt exposed to (or within range of) the enemy's guns, under fire; *chm.* der Wirkung einer starken Säure ⚘ to treat with a strong acid. — **5.** auch *v/refl.* u. *v/n.* (h.) Spiel: to play first, to have the lead; Brettspiel auch: to move (first); Billard: seinen Ball ⚘, (sich) ⚘ to (take the) lead. — **6.** (festsetzen) to fix, to appoint; einen Preis, eine Belohnung ⚘ to offer a prize, a reward; e-m e-e Summe ⚘ to allow a p. a sum; to allowance a p., to settle an annuity or a (fixed) sum (up)on a p.; ausgesetzter Betrag, das Ausgesetzte allowance; letztwillig ⚘ to (leave by) will; to bequeath (up)on a p. — **7.** (nicht stattfinden lassen) seine Arbeit ⚘: **a)** (ganz) to discontinue, to stop; **b)** zeitweilig: to suspend; (aufschieben) to postpone, delay, put off, adjourn; *jur.* etwas ⚘, auch: to let a matter stand over; ⚘ einen Posten in einer Rechnung ⚘ to set out an entry. — **8.** (als tadelhaft hervorheben) an e-m, an einer Sache et. ⚘, auszusetzen haben to take exception to …, to find fault with …, to pick holes in …; was haben Sie an ihm (daran) auszusetzen? what is your objection to him (to it)? es ist nichts daran auszusetzen there is no fault to be found with it, it is unexceptionable. — **9.** ⊕ *typ.* (nicht abkürzen) to set up (or to print) at full length. — **10.** (zu Ende setzen) ⊕ *typ.* to finish setting up a sheet, to work off copy; ♪ to finish composing. — **II** *v/n.* (h.) **11.** f. **5.** — **12.** mit et. ⚘: **a)** von Personen: = **7**; ohne auszusetzen without stopping or break or intermission; **b)** von Sachen: to pause, stop, break off; vom Pulse, Fieber: ⚘d intermittent. — **13.** ⚘ der Gang setzt aus (geht zutage) … crops out. — **III** sich ⚘ *v/refl.* **14.** f. **4** und **5.** — **IV** ⁓ *n* ⊕ **15.** = Aussetzung.

Aus=setzling (⁻⌣⌣⌣) *m* ⊕d. exposed child; ⚓ an öder Küste zur Strafe: maroon.

Aus=setzung (⁻⌣⌣) *f* ⊕ (Besetzen) lining, facing; von Bäumen: transplantation; e-s Kindes ꝛc: exposure; (Vermächtnis) bequest; (Unterbrechung) discontinuation, interruption; ⊕ ~ (Einstellung) der Zahlung suspension of payment; (Vertagung) adjournment; (Befristung) criticism; (Aufhören) stoppage, des Pulses: intermittence; *jur.* ~ des Strafvollzuges postponement of the execution.

Aus=sicht (⁻⌣) *f* ⊕ **1.** (Blick ins Freie, Gegend) view, outlook, perspective; ein Fenster hat die ~ auf, in, über … looks into,

♪ Musik; ⚗ Wissenschaft; ⚘ Pflanze; ⚘ Geographie; ⊕ Technik; ⚒ Bergbau; ⚔ Militär; ⚓ Marine; ⚘ Handel; ⚘ Post; 🚆 Eisenbahn.

[**ausſichtslos**] [**ausſprechen**]

looks down on, commands a view of; mit ~ auf den See facing the lake; ~ nach Oſten eastern aspect. — 2. fig. (Zukunft) prospect; nicht die geringſte ~ F not the ghost of a chance; ſchöne (auch hübſche) ~en pl. (als Erbe) good prospects or expectations pl.; es bietet gute ~en it bids fair to; er hat keine ~en, gute ~en ... no prospects, s.th. good in view; es iſt keine ~ dazu vorhanden, daß // it is very unlikely that //; et. in ~ nehmen to contemplate (or plan, propose, purpose) a th.; es ſteht eine Kurserhöhung in ~ there is every prospect of a rise; et. in ~ ſtellen to hold out a prospect of a th., to promise a th.

aus-ſichts-los (ᴵᴵ⌣...) a. ⑯ fig. without prospects; hopeless; =loſigkeit f ㊻ fig. absence of prospects; hopelessness; =punkt m spot affording (or commanding) a good view; belvedere; ㊒reich a. fig. rich in prospects; =turm m lookout (tower) ⟍ (fr.) belle-vue; =wagen m Am. observation-car; =warte f = =turm.

aus-ſickern (ᴵᴵ⌣) v/n. ㉑a** 1. (in) to ooze (out), to trickle out. — 2. (h.) to stop (or cease, leave off) trickling.

aus-ſieben (ᴵᴵ⌣) v/a. ㉓** to sift.

Aus-ſiebſel (ᴵᴵ⌣) n ㉒ siftings pl.

aus-ſieden (ᴵᴵ⌣) ㊴e** u. ⑬** I v/n. (h. u. ſn) = ausſochen 1. — II v/a. = ausſochen II; ⊕ Silber ㊴ to blanch ...

aus-ſingen (ᴵᴵ⌣) ⑬i** I v/n. (h.) 1. to cease (or stop) singing. — II v/a. 2. ein Lied ㊴ to sing out or through. — 3. von der Lerche: den Lenz ㊴ to carol (or warble) forth the arrival of spring. — 4. ſeine Stimme ㊴ (ausbilden) to train (or form) ...; ausgeſu(e)ne Stimme: a) trained voice; b) (abgeſungen) voice impaired (or ruined) by (too much) singing. — III ſich ㊴ v/refl. 5. ſich einmal ordentlich ㊴ to have a good singing practice. — 6. ſie hat ſich ausgeſungen she lost (or ruined) her voice through (or by) too much singing.

aus-ſinnen (ᴵᴵ⌣) v/a. ㉒** to contrive, devise, plot, scheme; ſ. ausdenken I.

aus-ſitzen (ᴵᴵ⌣) ㉓** I v/n. (h.) 1. mit Waren: to keep a(n outdoor) stall. — 2. ſ. 3. — II v/a. 3. ſeine Zeit ㊴, auch v/n. (h.) von Gefangenen ꝛc.: to sit out (F to do) one's (full) time. — 4. F Eier, Junge ㊴ = ausbrüten 1.

aus-ſöhnbar (ᴵᴵ-) a. ⑯ reconcilable, conciliatory; v. Fehlern: (ſühnbar) expiable.

aus-ſöhn/en (ᴵᴵ⌣) v/a. u. v/refl. ㉓** e-n (ſich) mit e-m, mit etwas ㊴, auch mit dat. e-n e-m ㊴ to reconcile a p. (o.s.) to or with ...; ſich mit e-m ㊴ a.: F to make it up with a p.; ſich mit et. ㊴ a..: to become reconciled (or to take more kindly) to a th. — II ~ n ㉓ = A/ung. [ciler, peacemaker.)

Aus-ſöhner (ᴵᴵ⌣) m ㉒, ~in f ㊵ recon-

Aus-ſöhnung (ᴵᴵ⌣) f ㊻ reconciliation.

aus-ſonder/n (ᴵᴵ⌣) I v/a. ㉒a** = ausſcheiden 1; (auswählen) to sort, to pick (out), to single out; (ausmuſtern) to cast out, to reject. — II ~ n ㉓ = A/ung f ㊻ = Ausſcheidung. — Vgl. a. abſondern.

aus-ſorgen (ᴵᴵ⌣) v/n. (h.) ㉓** für e-n ausgeſorgt h. to have done looking after a p.; er hat ausgeſorgt his cares (or troubles) are over or ended.

aus-ſortieren (ᴵᴵ⌣ᴵ⌣) v/a. ⑬*/* (ordnen) to (as)sort; (beiſeite ſetzen) to lay aside.

aus-ſpähen (ᴵᴵ⌣) ⑬** I v/a. 1. (nach) et. ㊴ to look out for a th., to watch for a th. — II v/a. = auskundſchaften I. — III ~ n ㉓ = Ausſpähung.

Aus-ſpäher (ᴵᴵ⌣) m ㉒, ~in f ㊵ lookout man; (Spion) spy; ~ei (ᴵᴵ⌣ᴵᴵ) f ㊻ spying; Polizei: espionage.

Aus-ſpähung (⌣) f ㊻ spying, search.

Aus-ſpann (ᴵᴵ⌣) m ⓒc., ~(e) f ㊻(㊽) (Umſpann-ort) relay; stage; (Raſt-ort für Pferde) baiting-place or -stable.

aus-ſpann/en (ᴵᴵ⌣) I v/a. ㉓** 1. auch v/refl. (ausdehnen) die Arme (ſich) ㊴ to extend, to stretch (out), die Finger ㊴ to distend; Flügel ㊴ to spread out; Segel ㊴ to spread, to unfurl; ⊕ Weberei: die Ketten auf den Tummler ㊴ to stretch the warp ... — 2. e-e Stickerei (aus dem Rahmen) ㊴ to take ... down from the (tambour-)frame; Ochſen ㊴ to unyoke oxen; bſd. die Pferde, den Wagen ㊴ to take horses out of the shafts; to unharness horses; abs. in e-m Gaſthof ㊴ to put up (or to turn in) at a hotel; hier wird ausgeſpannt! good stabling (provided)!; abs. ㊴, ſich ㊴ (ſ-n Geiſt ausruhen laſſen) to unbend (or relax) one's mind, to (take) rest, to rest one's brain. — II ~ n ㉓ 3. = A/ung 1.

Aus-ſpannung (⌣) f ㊻ 1. extending, &c., der Pferde: unharnessing; des Geiſtes: relaxation. — 2. = Ausſpann.

aus-ſparen (ᴵᴵ⌣) ㉓** I v/a. 1. (ausnutzen) to make the best (use) of. — 2. ⊕ Zeichenkunſt, Schriftgießerei ꝛc.: (unausgefüllt laſſen) to leave free or open. — II v/n. (h.) 3. ausgeſpart haben to have saved enough. [off joking.)

aus-ſpaßen (ᴵᴵ⌣) v/n. (h.) ㊽** to leave)

aus-ſpazieren ⟍ (ᴵᴵ⌣ᴵ⌣) v/n. ⑬*/* 1. (ſn) to go (out) for a walk. — 2. (h.) ausſpaziert haben to have done walking.

aus-ſpeien (ᴵᴵ⌣) v/a. u. v/n. (h.) ⑬** to spit (out, forth), to expectorate; (ausbrechen) to vomit, to throw up; Gift und Galle ㊴ to fret and fume; to fly into a passion.

aus-ſpelzen (ᴵᴵ⌣) v/a. ㊽** agr. die Körner ㊴ to husk the corn.

aus-ſpend/en (ᴵᴵ⌣) I v/a. ㉓** to distribute, to dispense; to administer (the sacrament). — II ~ n ㉓ = A/ung.

Aus-ſpender (ᴵᴵ⌣) m ㉒, ~in f ㊵ distributor, dispenser; administrator.

Aus-ſpendung (ᴵᴵ⌣) f ㊻ distribution, dispensing; administration.

aus-ſperren (ᴵᴵ⌣) I v/a. ㉓** 1. (ausſpreizen) to distend, to spread out; typ. Zeilen ㊴ to space out ...; mit ausgeſperrten Beinen with straddled legs, astride. — 2. = ausſchließen 1; Arbeiter ㊴ to lock out workmen. — II ~ n ㉓ u. **Aus-ſperrung** f ㊻ 3. spreading, &c.; der Arbeiter durch die Arbeitgeber: lock-out; (ant. Ausſtand 3).

aus-ſpicken (ᴵᴵ⌣) v/a. ㉓** mit et. ㊴ to lard (or interlard) with s.th. (a. fig.).

aus-ſpielen (ᴵᴵ⌣) I v/a. 1. (zu Ende ſpielen) to play to the end; e-e Partie ㊴ to finish a game; Tennis: to play it out; ſ-e Rolle ㊴ to act (or go through) one's part; er hat ſ-e Rolle ausgeſpielt he has played his part, he is played out or done for. — 2. (a. v/n., h.) Spiel: e-e Karte ㊴ to play (or throw out) ...; eine Farbe wieder ㊴ to return the (or one's partner's) lead; wer ſpielt aus? who leads?; fig. den letzten Trumpf ㊴ to play one's last trumpcard; einen gegen den andern ㊴ to play off one (person) against the other. — 3. (als Preis ausſetzen) to play (or raffle) for. — 4. (a. v/refl.) ♪ eine Geige ㊴, d. h. durch längeres Spiel: a) verbeſſern: to improve ... by constant playing; b) verſchlechtern: to wear out (or to impair) ... by playing ⊕ der Zapfen hat ſich ausgeſpielt ... is (or works) too loose, is worn out. — II v/n. (h.) 5. ſ. 2. — 6. to finish playing. — III ſich ㊴ v/refl. 7. ſ. 4. — 8. ſich ausgeſpielt haben to have played all one's (best) cards. — IV ~ n ㉓ 9. e-s Gewinnes: raffle, lottery. — 10. Kartenſpiel: ſind Sie am ~? is it your lead?, do you lead?

Aus-ſpieler (ᴵᴵ⌣) m ㉒, ~in f ㊵ person who plays (out) or leads or raffles, &c.

Aus-ſpielung ⟍ (⌣) f ㊻ = ausſpielen IV.

aus-ſpinnen (ᴵᴵ⌣) ㉒a** I v/a. 1. to finish spinning; fig. ſein Lebensfaden iſt ausgeſponnen his thread is spun. — 2. (ausziehen) to draw out; auch fig. zu lang ㊴ to spin out too long. — 3. fig. (ausſinnen) to imagine, contrive, think out, devise, plot, scheme. — II v/n. (h.) 4. to have done spinning.

aus-ſpintiſieren F ⟍ (ᴵᴵ⌣ᴵ⌣) v/a. ⑬*/* = ausſpinnen 3. [(or ferret) out.)

aus-ſpionieren (ᴵᴵ⌣ᴵ⌣) v/a. ⑬*/* to spy)

aus-ſpitzen ⚔ (ᴵᴵ⌣) ㊽** = ausfeilen 4.

aus-ſpöttel/n ㉒a**, -ſpott/en ㊽** (ᴵᴵ⌣) I v/a. e-n ㊴ to mock (or ridicule, deride) a p. — II ~ n ㉓ u. A/ung ㊻ mockery, derision.

Aus-ſprache (ᴵᴵ⌣) f ㊸ 1. pronunciation; ⊘ elocution; fremdartige, reine, mundartliche ~ foreign, pure, provincial accent; iriſche ~ (Irish) brogue; (un)deutliche ~ (in)distinct articulation; Bezeichnung der ~ notation of sounds. — 2. = Erörterung.

Aus-ſprache-bezeichnung (ᴵᴵ⌣ᴵᴵch⌣...) f ㊻ phonetic notation; =lehrer m teacher of elocution; =wörterbuch n pronouncing dictionary.

aus-ſprechbar (ᴵᴵ⌣-) a. ⑯ utterable, pronounceable, speakable; nicht ㊴ unutterable.

aus-ſprechen (ᴵᴵ⌣) ⑬a** I v/a. 1. ein Wort ꝛc.: to pronounce; deutlich ㊴ to articulate; die letzten Worte, die er ausſprach ... which he uttered or spoke; ein ſchwer auszuſprechendes Wort a word difficult to pronounce, F a jawbreaker. — 2. (zu Ende ſprechen) to speak to the end, to ㊴ Satz: to finish; abs. laſſen Sie mich ㊴ let me have my say (out), hear me to the end. — 3. (ausdrücken) to express; ſeine Anſicht ㊴ to speak one's mind, to give one's opinion; ein Urteil ㊴ to give a verdict; to pass a sentence (of death) upon a p. — II v/n. (h.) 4. ſ. 2. —

Signs (see page XVII): F familiar; P vulgar; ℱ flash; ⟍ rare; † obsolete (died); * new word (born); ⁺⁺ incorrect; ♪ music.

[**ausſprechlich**] — 131 — [**ausſtecken**]

III ſich 2 v/refl. 5. ſich über etwas 2 to express o.s. (or one's opinion) about a th.; ſich umſtändlich, vollſtändig über et. 2 to make a clear breaſt of it; ſprechen Sie ſich (deutlich) aus! speak up!, ease (or unburden) your mind!; ſich gegen=ea. 2 to exchange (one's) ideas; ſich für (gegen) e-n 2 to declare for (against) a p.; ſich gegen et. 2 to oppose (or object to) a th.; ſich mit e-m 2 to have a (quiet) talk with a p. — 6. (ſich offenbaren) to be(come) manifest or apparent; in dem Werk ſpricht ſich Talent aus the work shows (or bears signs of) ...; ſein Charakter ſpricht ſich in ſ-n Zügen aus ... is visible in (or is stamped on) his features. — IV ~ n 23 7. = Ausſprache u. Ausſpruch. — V aus-geſprochen p.p. u. a. 66 (D9) 8. in den Bed. des inf. — 9. (entſchieden) decided; (offenherzig) outspoken, straightforward; ſeine 2e Abſicht his avowed (or professed) intention.

aus-ſprechlich ~ (ᴗᴗ) a. 66 utterable.

Aus-ſprechung (~) f 46 = ausſprechen IV.

aus-ſpreiten ~ 68**, mſt **aus-ſpreizen** 60** (ᴗᴗ) v/a. to spread out, to distend, die Beine: to straddle; im Zirkus ꝛc.: die Beine horizontal 2 to do the splits; mit ausgeſpreizten Beinen with straddled legs, astraddle, astride.

aus-ſprengen (ᴗᴗ) I v/a. 68** 1. ein Stück aus dem Felſen: to blast, to blow up (with gunpowder). — 2. Waſſer: to sprinkle. — 3. fig. eine Nachricht 2 (verbreiten) to spread ... about, to set ... afloat, to circulate ... — II ~ n 23 u. **Aus-ſprengung** f 46 4. blasting, &c.; fig. e-s Gerüchtes: circulation.

aus-ſpringen (ᴗᴗ) Oft** I v/n. (1: h., 2 u. 3: ſn) 1. to cease springing, leaping, von Springbrunnen: to cease playing. — 2. (herausſpringen) von Lebendem: to leap (or jump) out; aus dem Kerker: to (make one's) escape; F (den Beruf wechſeln) to change one's vocation; von Lebloſem: to break away, to burst forth; ↓ der Anker ſpringt aus the anchor starts. — 3. (vorſpringen) to jut out, to project; ✕ frt. 2der Winkel salient angle. — II v/a. 4. (ausrenken ꝛc.) ſich (dat.) die Hüfte 2 to dislocate one's hip. — III ſich 2 v/refl. 5. to jump (or skip, romp) to one's heart's content. — IV ~ n 23 6. leap(ing); escape; (Vorſprung) projection; (Ausrenken) dislocation.

aus-ſpritz/en (ᴗᴗ) 60** I v/a. 1. Flüſſigkeiten: to spout (or squirt) out; to sputter forth; die (Tinte aus der) Feder 2 to spirt (or sling) the ink out of the pen. — 2. Feuer 2 (löſchen) to put out a fire (with a hose). — 3. Straßen: to water, flush. — 4. med. Wunden, Gefäße: to inject, to syringe. — II v/n. 5. (ſn) (herausſpringen) to spirt (or gush) out. — 6. (h.) ausgeſpritzt haben to have done syringing, &c. — III ~ n 23 7. = A/ung. **Aus-ſpritzung** (~) f 46 spouting out, &c.; (ſ. ausſpritzen I); (Auslöſchen) extinction; med. (auch Flüſſigkeit zur) ~ injection.

Aus-ſpruch (ᴗᴗ) m Ⓓ d. saying, utterance; e-s Orakels: response; (Urteil) sentence, judgment, decision; der Geſchwornen: verdict; of the jury; der Schieds-richter: award; ſich ihrem ~ unterwerfen to abide by their award; (Lehrſpruch) sententious saying, ⚘ apophthegm, dictum; (Bemerkung) remark; einen ~ tun to pronounce one's opinion; vom Richter: to pronounce judgment upon.

aus-ſprudeln (ᴗᴗ) 68a** I v/a. 1. Waſſer: to sputter out or forth (auch fig.). — II v/n. 2. (ſn) to bubble forth, to gush out. — 3. (h.) ausgeſprudelt haben to have done sputtering or bubbling.

aus-ſprühen (ᴗᴗ) 68** I v/a. 1. Flammen 2 to throw (or cast) up ...; to eject, belch, vomit ... — II v/n. 2. (ſn) to be thrown (or cast) up; to leap up; v. Funken: to fly (or dart) up. — 3. (h.) to cease throwing (or leaping) up.

Aus-ſprung (ᴗᴗ) m Ⓒ f. ausſpringen IV.

aus-ſpucken F (ᴗᴗ) 68** = ausſpeien.

aus-ſpuken (ᴗᴗ) v/n. (h.) 68** v. Geſpenſtern: to cease haunting a place; v/impers. es hat hier ausgeſpukt the house is no longer haunted; fig. hat es bei ihm ausgeſpukt? is his mad fit over?

aus-ſpülen (ᴗᴗ) I v/a. 68** 1. von Gewäſſern: a) (auswerfen) to deposit on the bank; b) (aushöhlen) to carry (or wash) away; das Ufer: to eat (or wear) away; e-e Mauer: to undermine. — 2. mit perſönlichem Subjekt: Gefäße: to wash (out), to flush; Gläſer: to rinse (out); Küchengeſchirr: to wash up (auch abs.); ſich (dat.) den Mund 2 to rinse one's mouth; ⊕ Färberei ꝛc.: Tuche 2 to wash (off) ... — II ~ n 23 u. **Aus-ſpülung** f 46 3. ~ des Ufers: erosion; v. Gefäßen: rinsing, washing.

aus-ſpüren (ᴗᴗ) v/a. = aufſpüren.

Aus-ſpürer (~) m 22 spy, informant.

Aus-ſpürung (~) f 46 tracking, tracing.

aus-ſtaffier/en (ᴗᴗᴗ) [nhd. 17. sae.] 68** I v/a. to provide (or furnish) with; ſchmückend: to trim (or dress) up; ↓ ein Schiff (auftakeln) to rig ...; e-n mit etwas 2 (ausrüſten) to equip a p. with a. th. — II ſich 2 v/refl. to equip o.s.; to fit (or rig) o.s. out; mit Putz: F to smarten o.s. up. — III ~ n 23 ~ A/ung. **Aus-ſtaffierer** (ᴗᴗᴗ) m 22 outfitter.

Aus-ſtaffierung (~) f 46 trimming (or dressing, rigging) up; (Ausrüſtung) equipment, fit(ting-)out; accoutrement, outfit; F turn-out.

aus-ſtaken ⊕ (ᴗᴗ) v/a. 68** arch. (mit Pfählen ob. Lattenwerk ausrüſten) to insert stakes (or laths) in plaster-work; ein Fach 2 to stake a panel.

aus-ſtampfen (ᴗᴗ) v/a. 68** to stamp (or beat) out; weiſ. to pound.

Aus-ſtand (ᴗᴗ) m Ⓒ c. 1. ⚘ (Forderung) ein Poſten, der noch in ~ iſt an item still in arrear; nicht einzutreibende Ausſtände pl. bad debts pl.; Ausſtände u. Schulden pl. assets (or outstandings) and liabilities pl., arrears pl. — 2. (Friſt) delay. — 3. (Arbeitseinſtellung) strike; turn-out; im ~ ſein to be on strike; in den ~ treten to (go on) strike, to strike (or stop, leave) work, to turn out; (ant. Ausſperrung).

aus-ſtändig (ᴗᴗ) a. 66 1. outstanding (debt). — 2. (being) on strike, striking; ~e(r) m 67 (a. **Aus-ſtänder** m 22) (work)man (out) on strike; striker.

Aus-ſtands=ausſchuß (ᴗᴗᴗ...) m 62, =komitee n strike(-)committee; =bewegung f strike(-)movement; =führer m strike(-)leader; =kaſſe f strike(-)fund; =lohn m, =unterſtützung f strike(-)pay.

aus-ſtanzen ⊕ (ᴗᴗ) v/a. 60** to punch (or stamp) out.

aus-ſtatten (ᴗᴗ) I v/a. 60** 1. to equip, to fit out; einen Sohn: to establish, to set up (in business); eine Tochter, die heiratet: to furnish a trousseau (eine Mitgift: a dowry) for; die Kinder, aus: to portion off. — 2. auch v/refl. verallgemeinert: (ſich) mit et. 2 to provide (or supply) (o.s.) with a th.; to fit (o.s.) out with a th.; fig. die Natur hat ihn reich (ſtiefmütterlich) ausgeſtattet nature has richly endowed (has been niggardly in her gifts to) him; thea. ein Stück: to mount; Buchhandel: ſchön ausgeſtattet beautifully got up. — II ~ r 23 3. = Ausſtattung 1.

Aus-ſtattung (ᴗᴗ) f 46 1. equipment, establishment; endowment. — 2. e-r Tochter: (Ausſteuer) marriage(-)outfit, (wedding-)trousseau, (Mitgift) dowry, (marriage-)portion; ohne ~ dowerless. — 3. eines Buches: get(ting)-up; thea. scenery; eines Ladens: fittings pl.

Aus-ſtattungs=gegenſtände (ᴗᴗ...) m/pl. 62 stores pl.; thea. property; =koſten pl. cost of equipment; =ſtück n, thea. elaborately mounted piece; (Christmas) pantomime; 2weiſe adv. by way of dotation or of a dowry. [duſt.]

aus-ſtauben, -ſtäuben (ᴗᴗ) v/a. 68** to]

aus-ſtechen (ᴗᴗ) I v/a. 68a** 1. to dig (or prick) out; e-m die Augen 2 to put (or gouge) a p.'s eyes out; das Kernhaus aus Äpfeln 2 to core apples; Raſen, Torf 2 to cut turf, peat. — 2. das Faß, Wein aus einem Faſſe 2 (abziehen) to draw off wine (by means of a siphon); F: e-e Flaſche 2 (trinken) to crack a bottle of wine; ein Glas Wein 2 to drink (or toss) off ...; einen Graben 2 to dig a trench, to make a ditch. — 3. hohl, in Holz 2 (ausarbeiten) to engrave, to carve; eine Platte 2 (vollenden) to finish a copper engraving; ein Muſter ꝛc. mit Nadeln 2 to prick out ... — 4. (gewachſene) Kanten, Spitzen mit e-r Hummer-ſchere 2 to enlarge lace with the claw of a lobster. — 5. e-n 2 (beim Turnier aus dem Sattel heben) to unhorse (or dismount) a p.; fig. (ausdrängen) to oust; to supplant; to cut a p. out, F to put his nose out of joint; (überflügeln) to outdo, to surpass. — 6. ↓ dem Anker mehr Tau 2 to pay (or reel) out more cable. — II aus-geſtochen p.p. und a. 66 7. Beb. des inf. — 8. (extrafein) exquisite, choice. — 9. (grubig) pitted.

Aus-ſtecher ↓ (ᴗᴗ) m 22 ehm. (Art Bugſpriet ohne Klüverbaum) boom for the bowsprit in small vessels without a jib-boom, sliding bowsprit.

aus-ſtecken (ᴗᴗ) v/a. 68** 1. eine Fahne ꝛc.: to put (or stick) out; bſd. zur Schau: to expose, show, display. — 2. = abſtecken 2. — 3. Bohnen ꝛc.: to plant. — 4. ↓ das Ankertau auf den Tamp 2 to veer the cable to the clench.

⚘ scientific; ⚘ botanical; ⌖ geography; ⊕ machinery; ⚒ mining; ✕ military; ↓ marine; ⚘ commercial; ✉ postal; 🚂 railway.

aus-steh(e)n I v/n. (jn u. h.) 1. als Krämer: to keep a stall; von den Waren als Subjekt: to be exposed for sale. — 2. a) von Geld: to stand out, to be outstanding or owing; er hat viel (Geld) ⁓ he has a great deal of money owing to him (f. 5); ⦿ ⓇeGelder, Forderungen pl. outstanding debts, arrears pl.; b) weiß. (noch zu erwarten sein) to be in arrear(s); die ⓇDe (fällige) Post the overdue mail. — 3. mit acc. der Zeitdauer: to stand to the end of; die Predigt ⁓ to stand till the sermon is over. — 4. (streiten) to strike, to stand out for higher wages, shorter hours, &c. — II v/a. 5. (überstehen; vgl. A. 3) to endure; Hitze und Kälte gut ⁓ können to be inured to ...; Schmerzen: to suffer; e-e Strafe: to undergo; er hat viel auszusteh(e)n he has a great deal to put up with (f. 2). — 6. ich kann ihn, das nicht ⁓ (leiden) I cannot bear (F I can't stomach) him, it. — III ⁓ n 7. v. Waren: exposure for sale; von Schulden: arrear(s pl.) of payment. — IV **aus-stehend** p.pr. und a. 8. in den Bed. des inf. — 9. (streikend) on strike; ⁓de(r) workman who has struck (for higher wages, &c.).

aus-steifen v/a. 1. ein Kleid ⁓ (mit Steifleinen füttern) to line a dress with buckram. — 2. einen Schacht ⁊c. ⁓ (stützen) to prop, stay, shore; (mit Holz auskleiden) to timber.

aus-steigen I v/n. 1. (jn): aus dem Wagen ⁓ to get out of ...; to alight from ...; aus dem Schiffe ⁓ to disembark, to land; 🚂 to get out of (or to leave) the train, to alight on the platform. — (h.) to cease rising. — II ⁓ n 3. landing, &c.; beim ⁓ on alighting, &c.

aus-steinen v/a. Pflaumen ⁊c. ⁓ to stone (plums, &c.), to take the stones (or kernels) out of (plums, &c.).

aus-stell/en I v/a. 1. to put out or forth, to expose (to view); Netze: to spread; ✕ Posten: to station. — 2. (zur Schau stellen) to show or display (goods); Gemälde ⁊c.: to exhibit; eine Leiche: to lay out; ausgestellt on view; et. Ausgestelltes exhibit; show-goods pl. — 3. (tabeln) ⁓ auszusetzen 8. — 4. (ausfertigen) e-m e-n Paß ⁓ to make out a passport for a p., eine Urkunde: to draw up; e-m ein Zeugnis ⁓ to give a p. a reference or character; ⦿ e-e Quittung ⁓ (to give a) receipt; e-n Wechsel auf e-n ⁓ to draw upon a p. — II ⁓ n 5. = A/ung 1.

Aus-steller (⁓) m, **~in** f 1. p. who draws up a receipt, &c.; von Urkunden: draftsman; ⦿ ⁓ e-s Wechsels drawer (or giver) of a bill. — 2. (Beschicker e-r Ausstellung) exhibitor.

Aus-stellung f 1. (Kunst-, Industrie-, Welt-) ⁓ exhibition, show; von Waren: exposure, show, display; einer Leiche: lying-in-state; von Posten, Schildwachen: stationing. — 2. (Tadel) stricture, censure; an et., e-m ⁓en machen to find fault with (F to pick holes in) ...

Aus-stellungs-gebäude (⁓...) n exhibition(-building); **=gegenstand** m exhibit(ed article); **=ort** m e-s Schriftstückes: place of issue; **=raum, =saal** m show-room; **=tag** ⦿ m eines Wechsels date of a bill.

aus-stemmen ⦿ v/a. to (hollow with a mortise-)chisel. [quilt.]

aus-steppen ⦿ (⁓) v/a. Näherei: to

Aus-sterbe-etat (...) m ⦿ auf den ⁓ kommen oder gesetzt werden to be destined to die (out) or to go out of use; von Ämtern: to lapse.

aus-sterben I v/n. (jn) b** 1. (aufhören) to become extinct; to die out; sie werden bald ⁓ they will soon be extinct; their days are numbered; ausgestorben p.p. extinct. — 2. (veröden) to become desolate; ausgestorb(e)ne Straße deserted (F dead-alive) street. — II ⁓ n 3. extinction; desolation; (Entvölkerung) depopulation; im ⁓ dying out, on the decrease.

Aus-steuer f e-r Braut: (Möbel, Kleidung ⁊c.) trousseau; (Mitgift) dowry; (marriage-) portion.

aus-steuern ⦿ a** I v/a. = ausstatten 1 und 2. — II v/n. (jn) ⏚ to steer out of (or away from) a place.

Aus-stich m ⓐd. (der beste Wein eines Berges oder Jahres) choicest wine, vgl. Ausbruch 3; (Aus-erlesenes) auch: **~ware** (...) f prime quality, finest brand.

aus-sticken ⦿ v/a. 1. ein Kleid ⁓ to embroider, to fill (or adorn) with embroidery. — 2. = aussteppen.

aus-stöbern v/a. a** 1. hunt. to drive (or hunt) out. — 2. (spürend ausfindig machen) to search (or ferret) out.

aus-stochern v/a. a** to pick out; etwas aus den Zähnen, sich (dat.) die Zähne ⁓ to pick one's teeth.

aus-stocken ⦿ v/a. agr. einen Wald: to clear of stumps or stubs.

aus-stopf/en I v/a.** Sessel, Bälge ⁊c. zu stuff; mit Baumwolle, Watte: to pad, to wad. — II ⁓ n = A/ung.

Aus-stopfer (⁓) m bird-stuffer, ⁓ taxidermist, weitS. naturalist.

Aus-stopfung (⁓) f stuffing; padding, wadding; von Tieren: ⁓ taxidermy.

Aus-stoß m ⓐa. 1. fenc. thrust, lunge; Schwimmen: stroke. — 2. ⦿ bei Bierbrauern (Abzapfen des Biers): tapping the cask; Feuerwerk: burster.

aus-stoßen v/a. I v/n. (h.) 1. fenc. to thrust, to lunge; schwimmend: to strike out. — II v/a. 2. to push (or thrust) out; (auswerfen) to discharge; e-m ein Auge ⁓ to knock out a p.'s eye; dem Fasse den Boden ⁓ to stave in a cask; ⏚ die Marssegel ⁓ to set out the top-sails. — 3. aus einem Verein ⁊c. ⁓ to expel, exclude, turn out; to send to Coventry, (austreiben) to oust, eject; (verbannen) to banish, ostracize; aus der Kirche ⁓ to excommunicate; aus dem Regiment ⁓ to drum (or turn) out (of the regiment). — 4. gram.: Buchstaben ⁊c.: to drop; Vokale, auch: to elide; math. to eliminate; physiol. to excrete. — 5. (hervortreten lassen) to throw up, to give forth; mit persönl. Subjekt: to utter, to ejaculate; e-n Fluch ⁓ to swear (an oath); Schmähungen: to launch (or pour) forth; einen Schrei ⁓ to (set up a) scream; to yell; Seufzer: to heave, to draw; F to fetch. — 6. ⦿ Hutm.: to put the felt on the block; join. eine Nut ⁓ to shoot a joint. — III ⁓ n und **Aus-stoßung** f 7. aus einem Verbande: expulsion, exclusion, ejection; ✕ aus dem Heere: dismissal (or discharge) from the army; aus der Kirche: excommunication; aus dem Lande: banishment; der Lichtstrahlen: radiation; math. einer Unbekannten: elimination; von Tönen, Worten: utterance, ejaculation; eines Vokals: elision.

aus-strahlen ⦿ I v/n. (jn) to (ir)radiate; to beam (forth); ein Glanz ⁓ strahlt aus von einem Punkte ... issues (or shines forth) from a point. — II v/a. Licht ⁊c.: to radiate; to send (or give) forth; ⁓ to emit. — III ⁓ n und **Aus-strahlung** f 4 (ir)radiation; beam(ing); lustre; phosphorischen Lichtes: phosphorescence; ⁓ v. Wärme, Licht, chemischen Strahlen: emission.

aus-strecken ⦿ I v/a. to extend; die Hand nach et. ⁓ to stretch (or put, reach) out one's hand for a th.; den Arm ⁓ to throw (or shoot) out one's arm; die Zunge: to stretch out. — II sich ⁓ v/refl. to stretch o.s. (out); sich lang ⁓ to lie full length, to lie sprawling (on the ground).

Aus-strecker (⁓) m, **Aus-streck-muskel** (...) m bsd. anat. extensor muscle.

Aus-streckung f stretch(ing); extension.

aus-streich/en ⦿ a** I v/a. 1. to strike (or cross) out, to run one's pen through, bsd. math. beim Heben: to cancel; ein Rennpferd aus der Liste: to scratch. — 2. (glatt streichen) to smooth down, to level; die Falten ⁓ to take out plaits or creases. — 3. e-e Form zum Backen ⁓ (innenbig bestreichen) to butter (or grease) a shape. — 4. agr. die Furchen ⁓ (austiefen) to deepen the furrows. — 5. (ausfüllen) to stop (or fill) up; ⦿ Maurerei: die Fugen ⁓ to flush (up) the joints. — II v/n. (jn) 6. (umherschweifen) to roam (or rove) about; hunt. Vögel ⁓ lassen to let ... rise (before one shoots); Wild ⁓ lassen to give law to the game. — 7. beim Schwimmen: to strike out. — 8. ✕ der Gang streicht zutage aus the lode crops out. — III ⁓ n u. A/ung f 9. erasure; (Schwimmstoß) stroke; ✕ outcrop(ping).

aus-streifen (⁓) I v/n. (jn) to make an excursion; to rove (or roam) about; ✕ to beat up (or to scour) the country. — II (auch **aus-streifeln** a**) v/a. Erbsen ⁊c. to shell ...

aus-streiten v/a. b** einen Streit ⁓, auch abs. oder v/n. (h.) to fight out a quarrel; to finish disputing.

aus-streuen v/a. ⦿ to strew (about), to disseminate, to spread (about); hier und da ⁓ to scatter; Samen ⁓ to sow seed; fig. Gerüchte, Neuigkeiten: to circulate.

Aus-streuer m, **~in** f disseminator, person who spreads (or circulates) news.

Aus-streuung (⁓) f 1. dissemination; circulation. — 2. ⁓en false reports pl.

Aus-strich (⁻⁻) m ⓓd. **1.** geol. outcrop. — **2.** ⚒ granular (or stream-)tin.
aus-ström/en (⁻⁻⌣) ⓖ** **I** v/n. (ſn) **1.** to stream (or gush) forth, to flow out; v. Flüſſen: ins Meer ⌒ to flow (or empty, fall) into the ocean; von Gaſen, Dampf ꝛc.: to escape; phys. vom Lichte ꝛc.: to emanate, to radiate. — **2.** etwas ⌒ laſſen = **3.** — **II** v/a. **3.** to pour (or send) out or forth; to emit, give forth; Waſſer ⌒ (l.) to discharge, let off …; fig. Empfindungen: to pour (or gush) forth; Segen ⌒ (l.) auf to pour down blessings upon. — **III** ~ n ㉓ **4.** = A/ung.
Aus-strömung (⌣) f ㊻ outflow; von Gas: escape; phys. emanation, effluence; der Elektrizität: flow; von Waſſer: discharge; ♪ mit einer ~ der Stimme with one (or a single) breath; fig. ~en pl. des Herzens effusions pl. (of the heart), F gush sg.
Aus-strömungs=rohr ⊕ (⁻⁻…) n ㉒ mach. blast- or delivery-)pipe.
aus-stückeln ⊕ (⁻⁻⌣) v/a. ⓐa** carp. Holz ⌒ (zuschneiden) to saw out wood.
aus-studieren (⁻⁻⌣⁻) **I** v/a. **1.** e-n, etwas ⌒ to make a thorough study of … — **II** v/n. (h.) **2.** to complete one's studies; to cease studying. — **3.** Hochschule: ausstudiert haben to have gone through a full (academical) course, to obtain (or take) one's degree. — **4.** ein ausstudierter Gauner an expert (or arrant) knave.
aus-stürzen (⁻⁻⌣) v/a. ⓖ** **1.** ein Behältnis: to empty by tilting up; den Inhalt: to shoot out; ein Glas Wein: to toss off. — **2.** sich den Arm ⌒ = ausfallen II.
aus-such/en (⁻⁻⌣♦) ⓖ** **I** v/a. **1.** to choose, select, pick out (f. aus=…3); Sie dürfen sich et. Beliebiges ⌒ you may have your pick, you may pick and choose; ⚫ hier kann man ⌒ we offer a large selection or a great choice (of goods). — **2.** (durchsuchen) to search thoroughly. — **II** v/n. (h.) **3.** hunt. v. Hunde: weit ⌒ to run a length. — **4.** to stop searching. — **III** ~ n ㉓ **5.** = A/ung; das ~ haben (unter) to have the pick (of). — **IV** aus-gesucht p.p. u. a. ㊻ **6.** ſ. bſd. Art.
Aus-suchung (⁻⁻⌣♦) f ㊻ choosing, choice, selection; sorting.
aus-süßen (⁻⁻⌣) v/a. ⓖ** to edulcorate.
Aus-süßung (⌣) f ㊻ ⚗ edulcoration.
Auſt, nordd. (⁻) [Auguſt²] m ⓑb. **1.** = Ernte. — **2.** ent. (Eintagsfliege) ephemeral fly, ⚗ ephemera.
aus-täfeln (⁻⁻⌣) v/a. ⓐa** arch. to wainscot; Fußböden ⌒ = parkettieren.
aus-tändeln (⁻⁻⌣) v/n. (h.) ⓐa** to cease trifling or toying or flirting.
aus-tanzen (⁻⁻⌣) ⓖ** **I** v/n. **1.** (ſn) aus- und ein-tanzen to dance in and out. — **2.** (h.) to finish dancing. — **II** v/a. **3.** einen Tanz ⌒ to finish … — **III** sich ⌒ v/refl. **4.** to enjoy (or have) a good long dance.
aus-tapezieren (⁻⌣⌣⁻) v/a. ⓖ*/* to hang (or cover) with tapestry; mit Papiertapeten: to paper.
aus-taſten (⁻⁻⌣) v/a. ⓖ** to search (or find) out by the touch.
Aus-tauſch (⁻⁻) m ⓓa. durch Tauschhandel: barter, exchange; ~ von Anſichten ꝛc.

interchange of views or ideas; ~ von Gefühlen ꝛc.: reciprocity.
aus-tauſchbar (⁻⁻⌣) a. ㊻ exchangeable, interchangeable.
aus-tauſchen (⁻⁻⌣) **I** v/a. ⓖ** et. mit et. anderem ⌒ to exchange one th. for (or with) another; ⚫ to barter, to truck; F to swap; Gefühle ꝛc.: to reciprocate; Meinungen: to interchange; Worte, Blicke: to bandy; Gedanken ⌒ to compare notes; er iſt (rein ob.) wie ausgetauscht he is quite changed, like another person. — **II** ~ n ㉓ u. **Austauſchung** f ㊻ = Austauſch.
aus-teil/en (⁻⁻⌣) **I** v/a. to distribute (or dole out, mete out) to, among; ⌒ unter, auch: to divide between, among; Almoſen ꝛc. ⌒ to dispense alms, give to; Befehle ⌒ to give orders to; Gnaden ⌒ to bestow favours upon; Prügel ⌒ to deal (out) blows to; eccl. Sakramente: to administer; Titel ⌒ to confer titles upon. — **II** ~ n ㉓ = A/ung.
Aus-teiler (⁻⁻⌣) m ㉒, ~in f ㊼ distributor; von Arzneien im Hoſpital: dispenser. [administration.)
Aus-teilung (⁻⁻⌣) f ㊻ distribution;
Auſter (⁻⌣) [grch.] f ㊻ zo. oyster (O'strea); beſte engliſche ~n pl. natives pl.; ~n fangen to dredge for oysters.
Auſter(n)=bank (⁻…) f ㊷ oyster-bed or -ground or -park; layings pl.; vgl. =park; =brecher m oyster-knife; =brut f spat; =dieb m, orn. = =fiſcher b; =fang m oyster-dredging; =fiſcher m: a) dredger; b) orn. oyster-catcher (Haema'topus); =händler(in f) m oyster-man (-woman); =korb m oyster-basket; =kultur f = =zucht; =laden m oyster-shop; =lager n = bank; =meſſer n = =brecher; =park m oyster-preserve (for fattening oysters); ⌒reich a. ㊻ abounding in oysters; =ſchale f oyster-shell; =ſchleppnetz (oyster-)dredge; =ſtein m, =verſteinerung f: ⚲ ostracite; =zucht f oyster-culture or -farming; =züchter m oyster-culturist.
Aus-tief=… ⊕ (⁻⁻…) ㉒ = Auftief=….
aus-tiefen (⁻⁻⌣) v/a. ⓖ** **1.** to deepen, e-n Schacht: to sink; (ausbaggern) to dredge, (ausgraben) to excavate; ⊕ Kupferſchmiede: Keſſel ⌒ to beat out …; ausgetieft hollow, concave. — **2.** (ausmeſſen) to fathom.
Aus-tiefung (⁻⁻⌣) f ㊻ deepening, &c. (f. austiefen); (Höhlung) hollow, cavity.
aus-tilgen (⁻⁻⌣) **I** v/a. ⓖ** (auslöschen) to efface; Schrift, auch: to obliterate; (ausrotten) to exterminate, uproot, destroy, eradicate; fig. Laſter ꝛc.: to extirpate; Schulden: to discharge, pay off, wipe out. — **II** ~ n ㉓ u. **Austilgung** f ㊻ effacement; obliteration; extermination; extirpation; einer Schuld: discharge, liquidation.
aus-toben (⁻⁻⌣) ⓖ** **I** v/n. (h.) u. **ſich** ⌒ v/refl. to cease raving, to calm down; von der tollen Jugend: to sow one's wild oats, to lead a fast life; vgl. austollen II u. III; Sprichw. Jugend muß ⌒, young folks must have their fling; boys will be boys. — **II** v/a. to give full vent to (one's passion).
aus-tollen (⁻⁻⌣) ⓖ** **I** ⊕ v/a. Putzmacherei: (mit Tollen verſehen) to goffer, to crimp.

— **II** F v/n. (h.) to desist from one's riotous (or fast) living; vgl. austoben I.
— **III** F ſich ⌒ v/refl. to have a good romp; to have one's fling; ſtärker to give free course to one's folly.
aus-tönen (⁻⁻⌣) v/n. (h.) ⓖ** to die away.
aus-traben (⁻⁻⌣) v/n. ⓖ** **1.** (ſn) to trot (out). — **2.** (h.): a) ein Pferd ⌒ laſſen, auch v/a. ein Pferd ⌒ to put … at a (full) trot; b) ausgetrabt haben to have done trotting.
Aus-trag (⁻⁻) m ⓓd. **1.** (Entſcheidung, bſd. gerichtliche) decision; settlement; gütlicher: amicable arrangement; ſchiedsrichterlicher: arbitration; bis zum ~e der Sache till the matter is settled or arranged; vor ~ der Sache while the case is still pending. — **2.** (Ausgang) issue, decision; zum ~(e) bringen to determine, to decide; to bring to a head or a decision or a conclusion.
aus-trag/en (⁻⁻⌣) ⓖbſt** **I** v/a. **1.** to carry out; ein Kind ⌒ to take out a child in arms; (abliefern) zB. Brot ⌒ to carry round (or deliver) … to the customers; ⚫ Briefe: to deliver, to take round. — **2.** ⚫ Poſten aus einem Buche ⌒ to transfer entries. — **3.** (fortſchaffen, leeren) to empty out. — **4.** (in Umlauf setzen) meiſt b.s. to blab out; (verleumden) to defame, backbite, slander. — **5.** (zu Ende tragen) ein Kleid ⌒ to wear … its full time; vollends ⌒ to wear (right) out; ausgetrag(e)nes Kind nine months' child; fig. ausgetrag(e)ner Junge resolute (b.s. cunning or impudent) fellow. — **6.** (entſcheiden, ſchlichten) to bring to a decision or a close; to decide; als Schiedsrichter: to arbitrate. — **II** v/n. (h.) **7.** mit acc. des Preiſes: das Ganze trägt zehn Mark aus … amounts (or comes) to ten shillings; es wird die Koſten nicht ⌒ it won't cover the expense(s); es trägt nicht viel aus it does not much matter. — **III** (ſich) ⌒ v/refl. u. v/n. **8.** von Bäumen: (ſich erſchöpfen) to leave off bearing; ſich ausgetragen haben to be past bearing. — **IV** ~ n ㉓ **9.** = A/ung.
Aus-träger (⁻⁻⌣) m ㉒, ~in f ㊼ **1.** carrier, errand-boy; von Briefen: letter-carrier, postman; von Zeitungen: newspaper-boy. — **2.** b.s. (Ausplauderer) tell-tale, scandalmonger; (Verleumder) slanderer, backbiter. [scandal.)
Aus-trägerei (⁻⁻⌣⁻) f ㊻ tittle-tattle,)
Aus-trage=rohr (⁻⁻⌣…) n ㉒, =röhre f discharge-pipe; =zeit ⚫ f für Briefe ꝛc. (usual) time (or hour) of delivery.
Aus-trägler (⁻⁻⌣) m ㉒ = Altſitzer.
Aus-tragung (⁻⁻⌣) f ㊻ der Briefe: delivery; (Klatſch) idle gossip; (Verleumbung) defamation (of character), slander; (Entſcheidung) decision.
Auſtral=aſi=en ♀ (⁻⁻…) [lt. Süd-] npr/n. ㉓α. (oſtindiſcher Archipel) (East) Indian Archipelago (engl. Australasia = Auſtralkontinent mit Tasmanien u. Neuſeeland, auch mit Ozeanien); =gegenden f/pl. austral (or antarctic) regions pl.
Auſtrali=en ♀ (⁻⁻(⌣)⁻) [lt. Südland] npr/n. ㉓α. Australia.
Auſtrali=er (⁻⁻(⌣)⁻) [lt.] m ㉒, ~in f ㊼, **auſtraliſch** (⁻⁻⌣) a. ㊻ Australian.
Auſtralit ⚗ (⁻⁻⁻) m ⓓc., min. australite.

[Australlicht] — 134 — [auswählen]

Austral-licht(-ˈ...) n ⑫ aurora australis; =**neger** m ⑫ = Australier; =**ozean** ♀ m Pacific (Ocean); =**sand** m, min. Sydney-earth; =**schein** m = =licht.
aus-trampeln (ˈˈ‿) v/a. ⑫a** to stamp (or trample) out, verhöhnend: to receive with trampling of feet.
aus-trauern (ˈˈ‿) v/n (h.) ⑫a** 1. to mourn the full time. — 2. to leave off (or to go out of) mourning.
aus-träufeln (ˈˈ‿) ⑫a** = träufeln.
aus-träumen (ˈˈ‿) ⑥** I v/n. (h.) 1. to leave off dreaming. — II v/a. 2. e-n Traum ℒ to finish ...; fig. der schöne Traum war ausgeträumt the beautiful dream was at an end. — 3. sich (dat.) et. ℒ to dream of a th., to imagine a. th.
aus-treib/en (ˈˈ‿) ⓺** I v/a. 1. to expel, to drive out; jur. aus dem Besitze ℒ to evict; ⚔ den Feind, hunt. das Wild: to dislodge; fig. e-m den Hochmut, den Dünkel ℒ to take the conceit out of a p.; Teufel: to cast out, to exorcize. — 2. auch abs. (Vieh) ℒ to drive (or take) out cattle to pasture. — 3. ♃ Knospen, Keime: to shoot forth; e-m den Schweiß ℒ to put (F to send) a p. into a perspiration, F to make a p. sweat. — II v/n. (sn) 4. ♃ von Keimen: to shoot forth. — III~n ㉓ 5. = A/ung.
Aus-treibung (ˈˈ‿) f ㊻ expulsion, jur. eviction; der Geister: exorcism.
aus-trennen (ˈˈ‿) v/a. ⓺** to rip up; das Futter aus einem Kleide: to take out.
aus-treten (ˈˈ‿) ⓺d** I v/n.: a) (sn) 1. to step (or walk) out; ⚔ aus Reih' und Glied ℒ to quit (or leave) the ranks, to fall out. — 2. (ausscheiden) ℒ aus ℒ to go out; to withdraw (or retire) from; to sever one's connexion with; aus e-m Amte ℒ to resign one's post or situation; ☉ aus e-r Firma, e-m Geschäfte ℒ to retire from (a house of) business; aus e-r Gesellschaft ℒ to discontinue one's membership (in a society or an association). — 3. (aus den Schranken treten) bsd. vom Wasser: to overflow (its banks); med. vom Blut: (aus den Gefäßen) ℒ: ♃ to extravasate. — b) (h.) 4. ausgetreten haben to have done treading or kicking. — II v/a. 5. (herausbringen) to get out by treading or stamping; Weintrauben ℒ to tread ...; sich (dat.) den Fuß ℒ to put one's foot out of joint. — 6. (einschlagen) to break open by kicking, to kick open. — 7. (aushöhlen) Stufen ℒ to wear (or hollow) out ... by treading; Schuhe ℒ (ausweiten) to stretch, to widen ..., (abnutzen) to wear down ...; fig. sie hat die Kinderschuhe ausgetreten she is out of her teens, she's no longer a child; ausgetreten worn down, well worn; ausgetret(e)ner Weg beaten track. — 8. (fortschaffen) Feuer: to stamp (or trample) out. — III sich ℒ v/refl. 9. die Schuhe treten sich aus ... are wearing out. — IV ~ n ㉓ u.
Aus-tretung f ㊻ 10. stepping out; aus e-m Amte, Geschäfte 2c.: resignation; withdrawal, retirement; des Flusses: overflow, inundation; med. des Blutes: ♃ extravasation; surg. e-s Gliedes: sprain. — Vgl. Austritt.

Austria (ˈˈ(‿)) [dtsch=lt.] f ㊾a. = Österreich.
aus-trillern (ˈˈ‿) v/a. ⑫a** ein Lied ℒ to finish trilling (or quavering) ...
aus-trinken (ˈˈ‿) v/a. ⓓit** 1. to drink up or off (in einem Zuge: at a (or one) draught); bis auf den letzten Tropfen ℒ to drink to the last drop; F to drain off; e-e Flasche: to empty, to finish, F to tipple off; abs. trink aus! drink up!, finish your glass! — 2. to stop drinking; er hat ausgetrunken he has had enough (to) drink.
Aus-tritt (ˈˈ‿) m ⓓc. 1. = austreten IV. — 2. ~ aus einer Kirche leaving (or severance, secession from) a church, ~ aus dem Leben departure, demise, decease, aus der Welt: seclusion. — 3. ♃ ast. ~ aus einer Verfinsterung emersion, egress. — 4. (Ort) mst arch.: a) (oberes Treppen=ende) top of the staircase, landing; b) (Vorzimmer) antechamber, ante-room.
Aus-tritts=bogen (ˈˈ...) m ⑫ ast. arc of vision; =**erklärung** f notice of withdrawal; resignation; =**punkt** m, ast. point of emersion.
aus-trockn/en (ˈˈ‿) ⑫b** I v/a. to (make) dry, to dry up; (trocken legen) to drain, ♃ to desiccate; eine Schüssel (mit einem Tuche) ℒ to wipe ... dry (with a cloth); med., &c. ℒde Mittel desiccatives pl.; von der Hitze ausgetrocknet parched up; gut ausgetrocknetes Holz well-seasoned wood; ausgetrocknete Kehle parched throat. — II v/n. (sn) to dry (or become) dry; von Teichen 2c.: to dry up; to be drained off. — III ~ n ㉓ = A/ung.
Aus-trocknung (ˈˈ‿) f ㊻ drying, draining (of marshes); ♃ desiccation.
aus-trommeln (ˈˈ‿) v/a. ⑫a** to publish by (beat of) the drum; fig. to make (publicly) known.
aus-trompeten (ˈˈ‿) v/a. ⓺*/* to proclaim (or announce) by sound of trumpet; fig. to trumpet (or blazon) forth, to spread (or publish) abroad.
aus-tröpfeln (ˈˈ‿) v/n. ⑫a** 1. ℒ und **aus-tropfen** (‿) v/n. ⓺** (sn) to trickle out, to drip. — 2. (h.) to cease trickling or dripping; F es hat ausgetröpfelt it has quite stopped dripping or drizzling or raining.
aus-tüfteln F (ˈˈ‿) v/a. ⑫a** to contrive with elaborate care, to think out.
aus-tun (ˈˈ‿) ⓺** I v/a. 1. = ausziehen 1, ausnehmen 1. — 2. F (auslöschen) to put out, to extinguish. — 3. ↘ einen Knaben in die Lehre ℒ to apprentice..., zu andern Leuten: to put... out to board. — 4. obb. P = ausleihen. — II sich ℒ v/refl. 5. wie bei den verbs unter 1. — III ~ n ㉓ 6. (Ausziehen) undressing; (Auslöschen) extinction; (ausleihen) investment. [to empty by dipping.]
aus-tunken (ˈˈ‿) v/a. ⓺** to dip out,∫
aus-tuschen (ˈˈ‿) v/a. ⓺** to shade (or paint or touch up) with Indian ink.
aus-üb/en (ˈˈ‿) I v/a. ⓺** 1. to practise, exercise; ein Gewerbe ℒ to carry on (or ply) a trade.— 2. (fühlbar m.) Druck auf e-n ℒ to put pressure on a p.; Einfluß ℒ to exert l's influence; Rache an e-m ℒ to wreak vengeance on a p.; Verbrechen: to commit, perpetrate. — II ℒd p.pr. u. a. ㊿ 3. practising, practical; ℒder Arzt medical man or practitioner; ℒde Gewalt executive power. — III ~ n ㉓ 4. = A/ung 1.

Aus-übung (ˈˈ‿) f ㊻ 1. exercise; eines Verbrechens: commission, perpetration. — 2. in ~ bringen to put in(to) practice or execution; in der ~ m-s Berufes in the pursuance of (or in pursuing) my vocation, in the exercise of my calling; in der ~ seines Berufes sterben to die in (full) harness.
Aus-verkauf ☉ (ˈˈ‿) m ⓓd. selling off or out; (general) clearance- (or rummage-) sale, clearing sale; geretteter Waren: salvage-sale.
aus-verkaufen (ˈˈ‿) v/a. u. v/n. (h.) ⓺*/* 1. ☉ to sell off or out; to clear off one's stock; der Artikel ist ausverkauft ... all sold, ... exhausted. — 2. thea. das Haus ist ausverkauft every seat is booked or taken; the theatre is full; F the house is sold out.
aus-verschämt P (ˈˈ‿) [nbb.] p.p. u. a. ㊿ impudent (= unverschämt).
aus-wachsen (ˈˈtß‿) ⓺b(ef)r** I v/n. (sn) 1. (a. v/refl. sich) ℒ to attain one's full growth; ℒ zu to grow into; chm. zu Kristallen ℒ to vegetate, to ramify. — 2. a) vom Korn: (auskeimen) to sprout out (in the ears); b) von Menschen: to grow deformed, to become humpbacked. — 3. von Wunden: to heal (or close) up. — II v/a. 4. Kleider ℒ to outgrow one's clothes. — III sich ℒ v/refl. 5. s. 1. — IV~n ㉓ 6. (full) growth; development; des Kornes: sprouting; F das ist zum ~ (langweilig) nach 2 b) that tires (or bores) one to death. — V aus-gewachsen p.p. u. a. ㊿ (D 9) 7. full-grown, grown-up, (voll entwickelt) fully developed, (quite) mature(d); ein ℒer Mensch an adult.
aus-wagen (ˈˈ‿): sich ℒ v/refl. ⓺** to venture (to go) out or (to come) forth.
aus-wägen (ˈˈ‿) v/a. ⓓb** 1. = auswiegen 1. — 2. (wägend aussuchen) to select by weight; fig. von Geistigem: et. richtig ℒ to form a correct estimate (or a true conception) of a th.
Aus-wahl (ˈˈ‿) f ㊶ 1. (Auswähl=) choice; des Besten unter vielen Gegenständen: selection; Sie haben die ~ you have the choice, (you may) choose which you like; eine ~ treffen unter to take (or make) one's choice among; to have one's pick of. — 2. (Vorrat) e-e große (reiche) ~ von Sachen a large (rich) assortment of articles; (Ausgewähltes) choice articles pl.; the pick (of the bunch); the finest brand; (feinste Gesellschaft) the élite, the cream of society, the upper ten (thousand).
aus-wählen (ˈˈ‿) ⓺** I v/a. (aus oder unter vielen) et. ℒ to choose s.th. (from among many); aus vielen ℒ to pick out of many; sich (dat.) ob. s-m Sohne e-e Gattin ℒ to select a wife for o.s., one's son; ausgewählt choice, select, exquisite, excellent. — II v/n. (h.) ausgewählt h. to have made one's selection or given one's vote. — III ~ n ㉓ = Auswahl.

Signs (see page XVII): F familiar; P vulgar; Γ flash; ↘ rare; † obsolete (died); * new word (born); ⁺⁺ incorrect; ♪ music;

Aus-wahl-sendung (ˡˡ...) f ② goods pl. sent to select from.
Aus-wählung (ˡˡ◡) f ㊻ = Auswahl.
aus-walken ⊙ (ˡˡ◡) v/a. ⑧⁺⁺ Tuchfabrikation: to full thoroughly (= abwalken).
aus-walzen (ˡˡ◡) ⑧⁺⁺ **I** v/a. **1.** agr. Getreide ℒ to roll out the grains. — **2.** ⊙ metall. (ausstrecken) to roll, to mill, to pass between the rollers. — **II** v/refl. **3.** sich recht ℒ (tanzen) to waltz to one's heart's content, to enjoy a good waltz. — **III** v/n. (h.) **4.** to stop waltzing.
Aus-wand(e)rer (ˡˡ◡(◡)◡) m ②, **=wand(r)erin** f ㊼ emigrant; (Kolonist) settler; ~z... (ℒ...) ② f. Auswanderungs-...
aus-wander/n (ˡˡ◡) ⑨a⁺⁺ **I** v/n. (ſn) **1.** to emigrate; to quit (or leave) one's (native) country; to settle abroad; von Zugvögeln und Völkern: to migrate. — **2.** (h.) ausgewandert haben to rest from one's wanderings or travels. — **II** v/a. **3.** ein Land ℒ to explore a country (in all directions). — **III** ~ n ㉓ **4.** = A/ung. **IV** **ausgewandert** p.p. ⑥: ~e(r) m und ~e f ㊻ **5.** emigrant; ~sein n ㉓ = A/ung.
Aus-wand(e)rung (ˡˡ◡(◡)◡) f ㊻ emigration, expatriation, eines ganzen Volkes: exodus; von Zugvögeln und Völkern: migration; gegenseitige: intermigration.
Aus-wanderungs-fieber (ℒ...) n ② fig. mania for emigration; **=gesetz** n law respecting emigration; **=schiff** n emigrant-vessel; **=sucht** f = -fieber.
aus-wärmen (ˡˡ◡) v/a. ⑧⁺⁺ **1.** (a. v/refl. sich ℒ) to warm (o.s.) thoroughly. — **2.** ⊙ (ausglühen) to anneal.
aus-wärtig (ˡˡ◡) a. ㊻ foreign; meine ℒen Freunde my friends abroad; ℒes Mitglied im In-(Aus-)land country (foreign) member; in England: ~es Amt od. Ministerium, Ministerium des ~en Foreign Office; Minister des ~en, der ℒen Angelegenheiten Foreign Secretary.
aus-wärts (ˡˡ◡) adv. **1.** (ant. einwärts) outward(s); ℒ gehen, die Fußspitzen ℒ kehren to turn one's toes out; mit ℒ gebogenen Füßen (wie ein Kamel) splayfooted. — **2.** (außerhalb) out of doors; nach ℒ (on the) outside; von ℒ from without; es ist keine Nachricht von ℒ da there is no news from abroad; Briefe von ℒ foreign letters pl.; ℒ essen to dine out; ℒ schlafen to sleep away from home, to sleep out.
Aus-wärts-drehung (ℒ...) f ② der Hand: ♁ supination; **=setzen** n der Füße walking with turned-out feet or toes.
aus-wasch/en (ˡˡ◡) ⑧b⁺⁺ **I** v/a. u. v/refl. **1.** Flecke ic, Schmutz aus etwas ℒ meist: to wash out or off, weits. to cleanse, chm. auch: ♁ to edulcorate; die Farbe aus dem Kleide (oder das Kleid) ist ausgewaschen the dye (of the dress) has come off (or out) in washing; sich ℒ to come off (or out) in washing; es läßt sich leicht ℒ it is easily removed by washing. — **2.** ⊙ Wolle, Tuche ic.: to scour, wash, clean. — **3.** (ausspülen) Gläser ic.: to rinse; med. eine Wunde: to bathe. — **4.** den Sand aus dem Ufer, das Ufer ℒ (fortspülen) to wash away the sand from (under)... — **II** ~ n ㉓ **5.** = A/ung; pharm. Mittel zum ~ lotion.

Aus-waschung (ˡˡ◡) f ㊻ washing out, cleansing; ♁ ablution; abstersion; chm. edulcoration.
aus-wässern (ˡˡ◡) **I** v/a. ②a⁺⁺ to (soak in) water; zum Entsalzen to (put in) soak; pharm. ♁ to macerate. — **II** ~ n ㉓. **Aus-wässerung** f ㊻ soaking; pharm. ♁ maceration.
Aus-wässerungs-linie ⊥(ℒ...) f ② load-line.
aus-wattieren (ˡˡ◡◡) v/a. ⑧⁺/⁺ to pad = wattieren. [cancel.]
Aus-wechsel-blatt ⊙ (ˡˡ◡tʃ◡) n ② typ.
aus-wechsel/n (ˡˡ◡tʃ◡) ②a⁺⁺ **I** v/a. **1.** = austauschen **I.** — **2.** ⚒ einen Schacht ℒ to new-line (or repair) a shaft. — **II** v/n. (h.) **3.** hunt. vom Wilde: (ein Revier verlassen) to leave the (old) haunt or ground. — **III** ~ n ㉓ **4.** = A/ung.
Aus-wechs(e)lung (ˡˡ◡ˡˡ◡) f ㊻ exchange, change; **~s-kasse** (ℒ...) f ② für Banknoten: redemption-office; **~s-vertrag** m cartel (or treaty) for the exchange of prisoners.
Aus-weg (ˡˡ◡, ⤸ ˡˡ◡) m ⓪d. **1.** way out, egress, outlet. — **2.** fig. (Ausflucht) backdoor, loophole; (Auskunftsmittel) expedient, shift; sich e-n ~ offen lassen to leave o.s. a loophole; ich weiß mir keinen ~ mehr I am at my wits' end, F I am in a fix, in a (tight) corner, in a hole; es gab keinen andern ~ there was no other way left (out of it).
aus-wehen (ˡˡ◡) ⑧⁺⁺ **I** v/n. **1.** (h.) = abwehen **II**; ⊥ von Flaggen und Wimpeln: (im Winde flattern) to flutter in the breeze. — **2.** (ſn) ein Licht weht aus a candle is blown out. — **II** v/a. vom Winde: (auslöschen) to blow out (vgl. 2).
aus-weichbar (ˡˡ◡-) a. ㊻ avoidable.
Aus-weiche ▤ (ˡˡ◡) f ② shunt(ing), siding, (turn-out) switch.
Aus-weich(e)-geleise ▤ (ˡˡ(◡)...) n ② siding(-way); shunting-line; **=hebel** ⊙ m switch-lever.
aus-weich/en¹ (ˡˡ◡) [weichen] **I** v/n. (ſn) ⑥a⁺⁺ **1.** to avoid (or shun) a p. or a th.; to shirk a th.; abs. to step aside; durch Bücken: to duck; durch Seitensprung: to dodge; e-r Sache (geſchickt): to evade, to elude; et. Unliebsamem gut ℒ to give a wide berth to; ⚒ e-m Stoße ic. to parry; ▤ to shunt. — **2.** e-m Wagen ic.: to make way for, to go out of the way of; in weitem Bogen: to give a wide berth to. — **3.** mit sachlichem Subjekt: vom Sand ic.: unter dem Fuße ℒ to give way (or to yield) under one's feet; ♪ aus e-m Tone in den andern ℒ to pass from one key to another. — **II** ~ n ㉓ **4.** = A/ung; phys. ~ (größter Schwingungsbogen) e-s Pendels (auch ast. Winkelabstand e-s Planeten von der Sonne) elongation. — **III** ℒd p.pr. u. a. ⑥ **5.** Bed. des inf. — **6.** evasive, elusive; ℒd antworten to give an evasive reply, to shuffle.
aus-weichen² (ˡˡ◡) [weich] v/a. und v/n. (ſn) ⑧⁺⁺ to soften (or soak) thoroughly.
Aus-weich(e)-platz (ˡˡ(◡)...) m ② od. **=stelle** f shunting-place, siding-place, turn-out track; **=schiene** f siding- (or turn-out) rail; **=zunge** f switch(-tongue).
Aus-weichung (ˡˡ◡) f ㊻ avoiding; evasion; elusion; ♪ transition from one key to another; der Stimme: modula-

tion; path. (Lageveränderung) displacement of some part of the body.
aus-weiden (ˡˡ◡) [nhd.: (Einge)weide] **I** v/a. ⑨⁺⁺ **1.** Wild: to eviscerate; to disembowel; bsd. Fische: to gut; Geflügel: to draw. — **2.** to graze (off) the pasture. — **II** ~ n ㉓ u. **Aus-weidung** f ㊻ **3.** evisceration; disembowelment.
aus-weinen (ˡˡ◡) ⑧⁺⁺ **I** v/a. **1.** sich (dat.) die Augen ℒ to cry one's eyes out. — **2.** f-e Tränen ℒ (erschöpfen) to shed many tears, F to cry one's eyes out. — **3.** f-n Schmerz ℒ (erleichtern) to relieve (or alleviate, lighten) one's grief with weeping. — **II** sich (recht) ℒ v/refl. **4.** a) (sich erleichtern) to pour forth one's grief in tears, F to have a good cry; b) (sich erschöpfen) to be all tears, F to cry one's heart out.
Aus-weis (ˡˡ◡) m ⓪a. **1.** statement; monatlicher ~ der Bank monthly return of the Bank; nach ~ der Bücher as the books (will) prove or show. — **2.** (Beweis, Legitimationspapiere) proof (of identity), certificate, voucher; weits. legal evidence of one's identity; documentary proof.
aus-weis/en (ˡˡ◡) ⑨⁺⁺ **I** v/a. einen ℒ to turn a p. out (of doors); Pächter: to evict; aus dem Lande ic.: to expel, banish, exile. — **II** ~ n ㉓ u. sich ℒ v/refl. (zeigen) to show, to prove; (funtun) to manifest; auch abs. wie die Briefe ℒ according to (the tenor of) ...; as appears from (the purport of) ...; sich ℒ to give an account of o.s., to prove one's claims; (sich über) seine Identität ℒ to establish (or prove) one's identity; a. impers. es wird sich bald ℒ (zeigen) we shall soon see; time will show (whether it's true). — **III** ~ n ㉓ = A/ung. [Bücher = nach Ausweis (f. ds.).]
aus-weislich (ˡˡ◡) adv. mit gen.: ℒ der
aus-weißen ⊙ (ˡˡ◡) v/a. ⑨⁺⁺ ein Zimmer ℒ: to whitewash, to lime-wash.
Aus-weißung (ˡˡ◡) f ㊻ eines Zimmers: whitewashing a room.
Aus-weisung (ˡˡ◡) f ㊻ **1.** turning out; eviction; expulsion; banishment. — **2.** polizeiliche: (Legitimation) proof of identity. [of expulsion, &c.]
Aus-weisungs-befehl (ˡˡ◡(◡)...) m ② order
aus-weiten (ˡˡ◡) **I** v/a. u. v/refl. ⑨⁺⁺ et., sich ℒ to widen, to enlarge; sich ℒ a.: F to give; Handschuhe, Schuhe ic.: to stretch; ⊙ (ausböhlen) to scoop out. — **II** ~ n ㉓ = Ausweitung.
Aus-weit(e)-stock (ˡˡ◡(◡)...) m Handschuhm.: stretching-stick, (glove-)stretcher.
Aus-weitung (ˡˡ◡) f ㊻ widening (out), enlargement, durch Strecken: stretching.
aus-wendig (ˡˡ◡) ⑧ **I** a. u. adv. **1.** (ant. inwendig) without; outward(ly); external(ly); inwendig und ℒ within and without, inside and out. — **2.** adv. ℒ lernen to learn by heart or by rote, to commit (a passage) to memory, F to get (up) by heart; et. ℒ können, wissen to know a th. by heart, to have it at one's fingers' ends. — **II** ~e(s) n ㉓ **3.** outside, exterior.
aus-werden F (ˡˡ◡) v/n. (ſn) ⑦c⁺⁺ v. Spielen ic.: to (come to an) end; v. Spielenden: to go out.

⚗ scientific; ❦ botanical; ⊕ geography; ⊙ machinery; ⚒ mining; ⚔ military; ⊥ marine; ⓜ commercial; ✉ postal; ▤ railway.

[aus-werfen] — 136 — [auszeichnen]

aus-werfen (ᴴᴗ) ⓑ** I v/a. 1. einem ein Auge 🕮 to knock out a p.'s eye by a throw. — 2. (hinwerfen) to cast (or throw, fling) out or forth; die Angel nach et. (fig. nach e-m) 🕮 to angle (or fish) for ...; ⚓ den Anker: to cast, to drop; das Lot: to cast, to heave. — 3. (ausstoßen) v. Vulkanen: Asche, Feuer ꝛc. 🕮 to cast (or throw, belch) up or forth; Blut ꝛc.: to spit, to cough (or bring) up, 𝔐 to expectorate. — 4. = ausweiden 🕮. — 5. (ausgraben) Erde aus e-m Graben, e-n Graben 🕮 to throw up the earth, to cast (or dig) a trench. — 6. 🏛 Posten im Rechnungsbuche: to put to account; eine Rechnung: to draw out. — 7. e-m eine Summe für et. 🕮 (aussetzen) to allow (or grant) a p. a certain sum for s.th.; e-m eine Rente 🕮 to settle an annuity on a p. — 8. (auslöschen) to put out (fire) by throwing on earth, &c. — II v/n. (h.) 9. = anwerfen I. — 10. (das Spiel ausmachen) to end a game (of skittles, &c.) by a throw. — 11. to finish throwing. — III ~ n 🕮 12. = Auswerfung.
Aus-werfer ⚒ (ᴴᴗ) m 🕮 zur Entfernung der Patronenhülse nach dem Feuern: ejector.
Aus-werfung (~) f 🕮 throw(ing); ~ des Lotes, Netzes cast of the lead, net; v. Vulkanen: eruption; v. Blut ꝛc.: expectoration.
aus-wettern (ᴴᴗ) v/n. (h.) u. sich 🕮 v/refl. 🏛** es hat ausgewettert the fury of the storm has abated; fig. er hat ausgewettert he has ceased storming and raging, his passion has calmed down.
aus-wetzen (ᴴᴗ) v/a. 🏛** eine Scharte 🕮: to grind out a notch; b) fig. to wipe off a disgrace or an old score; e-n Schimpf 🕮 to avenge an insult.
aus-wichsen (ᴴᴗ⚓⚒) v/a. 🏛** 1. to (polish with) wax. — 2. F fig. to thrash.
aus-wickeln (ᴴᴗ) v/a. 🏛a** to unwind, unwrap, unfold, unroll, ein Kind: to unswathe; fig. to extricate, disentangle.
aus-wieg/en (ᴴᴗ) I v/a. 🏛c** Waren: to weigh out, 🏛 to (sell by) retail. — II ~ n 🕮 u. A/ung f 🕮 retail trade.
aus-winden (ᴴᴗ) v/a. 🏛** 1. = auswringen 1. — 2. (mit der Winde ausheben) to raise by means of a windlass.
aus-wintern (ᴴᴗ) 🏛a** I v/a. 1. to expose to the rigour of winter; to (bring through the) winter. — 2. Kinder, sich 🕮 (abhärten) to inure children, o.s. to the frost. — II v/n. 3. (h.) = überwintern. — 4. (sn.) v. Pflanzen: (im Winter absterben) to die during the winter. — III v/impers. 5. es hat ausgewintert (the) winter is over or has departed or is gone. [top.)
aus-wipfeln (ᴴᴗ) v/a. 🏛a** Bäume: to)
aus-wirken (ᴴᴗ) 🏛** I v/n. (h.) 1. to cease working or operating. — II v/a. 2. (erlangen) to obtain, to get; (ausrichten) to effect, bring about, accomplish, F to work; et. bei e-m 🕮 to obtain a th., a favour from a p., F to get a th. out of a p.; ich habe nichts bei ihm (für mich) 🕮 können I could not prevail upon him to do anything for me; I did not succeed with him; e-n Gerichtsbefehl gegen einen 🕮 lassen to obtain (or procure) a warrant against

a p.; ein Patent: to take out. — 3. 🜊 Bäckern: den Teig 🕮 to knead the dough; Hufschmiede: den Huf 🕮 to pare a horse's hoof. — 4. hunt. den Hirsch: to uncase.
aus-wirren (ᴴᴗ) v/a. 🏛** (aus-ea.-wirren) to unravel, untwist, disentangle.
aus-wischbar (ᴴᴗ) a. 🕮 effaceable.
aus-wischen (ᴴᴗ) v/a. 🏛** 1. den Staub aus dem Glase, das Glas: to wipe off; sich (dat.) den Schlaf aus den Augen, die Augen 🕮 to rub one's eyes; F fig. e-m die Augen 🕮 (ihn betrügen) to dupe a p.; ⚔ artill. ein Geschützrohr 🕮 to sponge out the barrel of a gun. — 2. (tilgen) to expunge, to efface; Geschriebenes: to blot out. — 3. F e-m eins (e-n Schlag ꝛc.) 🕮 to deal a p. a blow, to hit out at a p., fig. (e-m Vorwürfe machen) to reprimand (or rebuke) a p., F to blow him up.
aus-witter/n (ᴴᴗ) 🏛a** I v/a. 1. (ausspüren) hunt. u. fig. to (find the) scent, to get scent (or wind) of. — 2. (der Luft aussetzen) to expose to the air; Holz ꝛc.: to season. — II v/n. (sn) 3. (durch die Witterung leiden) to decompose (or to fall to dust) through exposure to the air; chm., min. to effloresce; von Holz: to get seasoned. — III ~ n 🕮 u. A/ung f 🕮 4. scenting; decomposition; chm., min. efflorescence, v. Holz: seasoning.
aus-wollen F (ᴴᴗ) v/n. (h.) 🕮 ** to wish (or want) to go out.
aus-wringen (ᴴᴗ) 🏛** = auswringen 1.
Aus-wuchs (ᴴᵗ) m 🏛a. 1. = auswachsen IV. — 2. (das Ausgewachsene) (out-)growth, excrescence, protuberance; (Buckel) hump(back), hunch; 🜊 tumour, 𝔐 apophysis; fleischiger ~ fleshy growth, orn., &c. 𝔐 caruncle; path. der Knochen: 𝔐 exostosis. — 3. fig. (Mißstand) abuse, drawback; meist pl. Auswüchse des Geistes eccentricities pl.; der Phantasie: aberrations, ravings pl.
aus-wühlen (ᴴᴗ) v/a. 🏛**to dig (or grub, root) up; (aushöhlen) to undermine.
Aus-wurf (ᴴᴗ) m 🜊c. 1. = Auswerfung; wer hat den ~ 🕮? who has the first throw?, who throws first? — 2. (das Ausgeworfene) anything cast (or thrown) up; des Meeres: sea-weed; (Strandgüter) wreckage, ⚓ jetsam and flotsam, aus dem Körper: excretion; aus dem Munde: expectoration, 𝔐 sputum; (Speichel) saliva; (Schleim) phlegm; er hat starken ~ he expectorates freely; eines Vulkans: lava. — 3. bfd. 🏛 (Abfälle) (off)scum, refuse, trash; typ. wastesheets pl.; (Schund) garbage, rubbish; ~ der Menschheit (the) dregs pl. (or scum) of humanity. [gamble) for (with dice).)
aus-würfeln (ᴴᴗ) v/a. 🏛a**to raffle (or)
Aus-würfling (ᴴᴗ) m 🜊d. outcast.
Aus-wurf(s)-stoffe (ᴴᴗ...) m/pl. 🕮 excrements pl.; ⚓ware f 🜊 s(p)oiled goods, rejections pl., F rubbish, refuse.
aus-wüten (ᴴᴗ) 🏛** = ausrasen 🕮.
aus-zack/en (ᴴᴗ) I v/a. 🏛** to indent, jag, tooth; wellenförmig: to scallop. — II ~ n = A/ung. — III aus-gezackt p.p. u. a. 🏛 indented, &c. (s. I); 🜊 denticulate(d), dentated; 🖉 der überge-schlagener Kragen Vandyke (collar).
Aus-zackung (ᴴᴗ) f 🕮 indentation; 🜊 denticulation.

aus-zahlbar (ᴴᴗ) a. 🕮 payable.
aus-zahl/en (ᴴᴗ) I v/a. 🏛*** to pay out or away or down, to disburse (money); Arbeiter(n den Lohn) 🕮 to pay off workmen, to pay (them) their wages; 🏛 s-e Gläubiger vollständig 🕮 to pay one's creditors in full, to pay twenty shillings in the pound; F fig. wart', ich will dich 🕮! wait, I'll pay you out (some day)! — II ~ n 🕮 = A/ung.
aus-zählen (~) v/a. 🏛*** 1. = zählen. — 2. (ausbreiten) to lay out; (nach dem Stück verkaufen) to sell by the piece. — 3. (fertig zählen) to count to the end; to cease counting. [payor; paymaster; cashier.)
Aus-zahler (ᴴᴗ) m 🕮, ~in f 🕮 payer,)
Aus-zahlung (ᴴᴗ) f 🕮 payment, disbursement; paying off.
aus-zähneln 🔘 (ᴴᴗ) 🏛a** = auszacken.
aus-zahnen (ᴴᴗ) 🏛** I v/n. (h.) to finish (or have done) teething; das Kind hat ausgezahnt a. the child has all its teeth. — II v/a. = auszacken I.
aus-zanken F (ᴴᴗ) v/a., v/n. (h.) u. sich 🕮 v/rpr. 🏛** to scold (f. ausschelten).
aus-zapfen (ᴴᴗ) v/a. 🏛** 1. den Wein aus dem Fasse, das Faß 🕮 to draw (or tap) off the wine (from the cask). — 2. (ausschenken) to sell by retail.
aus-zappeln (ᴴᴗ) v/n. (h.) 🏛a** to cease fidgeting or sprawling.
aus-zausen (ᴴᴗ) v/a. 🏛** e-m die Haare 🕮 to pull (or pluck) out a p.'s hair.
aus-zechen (ᴴᴗ) 🏛** I v/a. to drink (or quaff) off. — II v/n. (h.) ausgezecht h. to have done carousing, boozing.
aus-zehr/en (ᴴᴗ) 🏛** I v/a. u. v/refl. 1. (aufzehren) to consume; ein Land: to impoverish, drain, exhaust; sich 🕮 to pine (or waste) away. — 2. (abzehren) to waste. — II v/n. 3. (h.) to cease consuming. — 4. (sn) u. sich 🕮 v/refl. to fall off (in strength), to lose flesh. — III ~ n 🕮 5. = A/ung 1. — IV 🜊 p.pr. u. a. 🕮 b. 6. in den Bed. des inf.; path. 🜊 Fieber hectic fever.
Aus-zehrung (~) f 🕮 1. consumption, impoverishment, exhaustion. — 2. path.: 𝔐 tabes; (Schwindsucht) (pulmonary or spinal) consumption; 𝔐 phthisis; die ~ bekommen to go into a consumption or decline; die ~ h. to be consumptive or in a consumption; sie hat die ~ a. she is (rapidly) wasting away.
aus-zeichn/en (ᴴᴗ) ⓑ** I v/a. 1. eine Figur ꝛc.: to finish (drawing). — 2. (hervorheben) to mark (or point) out; to note, to notice; sich (dat.) einen Weg 🕮 (abstecken) to lay (or trace) out a road; 🏛 Waren: to ticket, label, mark; durch Zahlen: to number; typ. durch fette Schrift 🕮 to distinguish (or display) by means of fat (or bold, clarendon) type. — 3. e-n 🕮 (mit Hochachtung behandeln) to treat a p. with marked distinction or respect. — 4. (unterscheiden) to distinguish from. — II sich 🕮 v/refl. 5. to distinguish (or signalize) o.s. by; to make o.s. (or to become) conspicuous by; sich in et. 🕮 to excel in a th.; er zeichnete sich dadurch aus, daß er die Armen schonte he distinguished himself by his considerate treatment of the poor. — III ~ n 🕮 6. = A/ung 1. — IV aus-gezeichnet 7. s.d.

Zeichen (s. S. XVII): F familiär; P Volkssprache; ⌐ Gaunersprache; 🜊 selten; † alt (auch gestorben); * neu (auch geboren); ⁺⁺ unrichtig;

[Auszeichnung] — 137 — [A. V.]

Aus-zeichnung (⸗⸗‿) f ⓴ 1. marking. &c.; ⓦ der Waren: ticketing, &c. — 2. (Ehrung) distinction, eminence; eine Prüfung mit ~ bestehen to pass ... with (high) honours; dies ist eine große ~ für ihn F that is a great feather in his cap or s.th. (for him) to be proud of.

Aus-zeichnungs-schriften (⸗...) f/pl. typ. display-, fancy-type; ⸗wert, ⸗würdig a. ⓰ worthy of distinction, worthy of (or deserving) special notice.

aus-zerren (⸗⸗‿) v/a. ⓰** to pull out, to pluck off; gewaltsam: to drag off.

aus-ziehbar (⸗⸗‿) a. ⓰ fit to be taken off, &c. (s. ausziehen); phys. (dehnbar) ductile; **~keit** f ⓪. pl.) phys. ductility.

aus-ziehen (⸗⸗‿) ⓖb** I v/a. 1. a. v/refl. Kleidungsstücke: to take (or get, pull) off; e-n ⸺ to undress, disrobe, strip a p.; er ist ausgezogen, hat sich ausgezogen he is undressed; sich ⸺ to take off one's clothes or garments; to undress or strip (o.s.); Sport: to peel; Handschuhe, Stiefel ⸺ to pull off ...; e-n bis aufs Hemd ⸺ to strip a p. naked or bare, fig. to fleece a p.; F e-n rein ⸺ (berauben) to strip (or fleece) a p., to despoil him of everything; e-m (sich dat.) den Mantel ⸺ to uncloak a p. (o.s.); bibl. den alten Menschen (od. Adam) ⸺ to put off the old man; to mend (one's ways). — 2. (herausziehen) to take (or draw) out of; ⸺ die Kugel, den Schuß ⸺ to draw the charge; die Kugel aus der Wunde: to extract the bullet; das Schwert aus der Scheide ⸺ to draw (or unsheathe) one's sword; sich e-n Zahn ⸺ lassen to have a tooth (taken) out or drawn; hunt. Federwild ⸺ to truss poultry. — 3. aus Pflanzenstoffen 2c. e-n Extrakt ⸺ to extract from ...; Rhabarber durch heißen Aufguß ⸺ to infuse ...; Stellen aus einem Buche, ein Buch ⸺ to make extracts (or to abstract) from a book; kurz zs.-fassen) to abridge, to summarize; ausgezog(e)ner Stoff, ausgezog(e)ne Stelle extract; ⓦ Rechnungen ⸺ to make out ...; math. eine Quadratwurzel ⸺ to extract a square-root. — 4. (ausdehnen, recken) to stretch, extend, distend. — 5. (zu Ende ziehen) eine Linie, Furche: to draw, to make. — 6. ⓦ einen Büchsenlauf ⸺ (ausriefen) to rifle a gun. — II sich ⸺ v/refl. 7. f. 1. — III v/n. 8. (sn): a) (wegziehen) to change (or leave, quit, shift) one's lodging or apartments, to (re)move, to move into new quarters; mit Sack und Pack ⸺ to leave the country, F to clear out (with bag and baggage); in Scharen ⸺ to set out (or march off) in bands or in gangs or in a procession; auf die Jagd ⸺ to go (a-)hunting; ⚔ in den Krieg ⸺ to take the field; b) F (sich eilig fortmachen) to hasten (or to scamper) away. — 9. (h.) ausgezogen haben to have done pulling, &c. — IV ~n ⓴ 10. taking off, &c.; (Berauben) spoliation; der Zähne 2c.: extraction; aus der Wohnung: removal, (re)move; im ~ begriffen sein to be moving or on the move. — Vgl. Auszug.

Aus-zieher (⸗⸗‿) m ⓴ 1. undresser (vgl. ausziehen 1). — 2. ⓦ im Gewehr: extractor.

Aus-zieh-gleis (⸗⸗...) n ⓰ des Bahnhofs sliding rail; **=maschine** ⓞ f Wasserbau: (pile-)withdrawing engine; **=schacht** ⚒ m upcast-shaft or -pit; **=tisch** m sliding (or telescope-)table.

Aus-ziehung F (⸗⸗‿) f ⓰ = ausziehen IV.

aus-zieren ⓞ (⸗⸗‿) = ausschmücken.

aus-zimmern ⓞ (⸗⸗‿) v/a. ⓦa** ⚒. einen Schacht ⸺ : to (line with) timber.

aus-zirkeln (⸗⸗‿) ⓦa** = abzirkeln.

aus-zischen (⸗⸗‿) v/a. u. v/n. (h.) ⓰** Schauspieler: to hiss (off the stage)); to cease hissing; ausgezischt w. F to get the goose. [palpitating.]

aus-zucken (⸗⸗‿) v/n. (h.) ⓰** to cease)

Aus-zug (⸗‿) m ⓓ. 1. aus e-r Wohnung: removal, move; aus einem Lande: emigration; weit S. departure; bibl. exodus. — 2. (Schublade) drawer. — 3. (Auszugs-platte) leaf (of a telescope-table). — 4. Lotterie (Gezogenes) (result of) drawing; number (or lot) drawn. — 5. ~ aus einem Buche: extract, epitome, summary; aus einer Rechnung 2c.: abstract; Auszüge machen aus to take extracts from, to abstract (or cull) from; im ~(e) darstellen to summarize, to epitomize. — 6. (Wirtschaftes, Bestes) chm., pharm. extract, (quint)essence, decoction; wässeriger, weiniger ~ watery, vinous extract or tincture. — 7. jur. = Ausgedinge, Altenteil. — 8. ⚔ schwz. troops of the regulars pl. [Auszug 3.)

Aus-zug-blatt (⸗‿...) n ⓰, **=brett** n =)

Aus-züger (⸗‿) m ⓰ = Altsitzer.

aus-züglich (⸗‿) adv. by way of extract, in the form of a summary or an abstract; briefly (stated).

Aus-zug(s)-fest (⸗‿...) n ⓰ der Juden: Passover; **=hieb** m, for. cutting away the rank growth of underwood; **=macher** m abbreviator; epitomizer; **=mehl** n, Müllerei: superfine (or best quality of) flour; **=platte** f = Auszug 3; ⸺weise adv. = auszüglich.

aus-zupfen (⸗‿) ⓰** I v/a. 1. = ausrupfen. — 2. etwas ⸺ to pick (the threads of) s.th.; Seide 2c.: to unravel; ausgezupfte Leinwand lint. — II v/n. (h.) 3. ausgezupft haben to have done plucking or picking, pulling) out.

Aus-zupfer ⓞ (⸗‿) m ⓰, **~in** f ⓰ p. who picks out the threads of.

aus-zürnen (⸗‿) v/n. (h.) ⓰** to relent in one's anger; er hat ausgezürnt his fit of passion (or temper) is over.

Aut¹ * F (‿) n ⓒ. = Automobil.

auteln* F (‿) v/n. ⓰a. = mit dem Automobil (f. bs.) fahren.

authentisch (‿⸗‿) [grch.] a. ⓰ (echt) authentic; genuine; ⸺ machen, ⸺ **authentisieren** v/a. ⓰ to authenticate.

Authentizität (‿⸗‿⸗) f ⓰ (Echtheit) authenticity.

Autler* F (‿) m ⓰, **~in** (‿‿) f ⓰ = Automobilist(in).

Autler-falle* (⸗‿...) f ⓰ motor-trap.

Auto¹ F [span., port.] ⓰ = Autodafé.

Auto² * F (‿) n ⓰ = Automobil.

☞ **Auto...** (‿‿) [grch. selbst] f. Zssgn.

Autobiograph/ie (‿‿‿⸗‿) f ⓰ autobiography; **a/isch** (‿‿‿⸗‿) a. ⓰ autobiographical. [omnibus.)

Autobus* F (‿‿‿) m ⓲ = Automobil-)

autochthon. Lisch (‿⸗‿(‿) [grch. eingeboren] a. ⓰ autochthonous; aboriginal; **~e** ⚢ (‿‿‿)m ⓸ autochthon; aborigines pl.

Autodafé (‿‿‿⸗) [port.] n ⓠ Cath. ecol. (Ketzer-verbrennung) auto-da-fé, act of faith.

Autodidakt ⚢ (‿‿⸗) [grch.] m ⓰ (der ohne Lehrer gelernt hat) self-taught p.; auch bisw. autodidact; **~entum** n ⓓd. (o.pl.) self-instruction.

autodynamisch ⚢ (‿‿‿⸗‿) [grch.] a. ⓰ med. (selbstwirkend) autodynamic.

Autogramm (‿‿⸗) [grch.] n ⓑ. = Autograph b.

Autograph (‿‿⸗) ⓔ, ⓒc., ⓓ. ⓰ a) m (Kopierpresse) copying-press; b) n (m) (Handschrift) autograph; **~ie** (‿‿‿⸗) f ⓰ autography; copying-machine; **Lisch** (‿‿⸗‿) a. ⓰ autographic; **Lischer Abdruck** autograph(y).

Autoklav (‿‿⸗) [fr.,*grch.=lt. Selbstschließer] m ⓲c. (Schnellkochtopf) autoclave.

Autokrat (‿‿⸗) [grch.] m ⓰ (Selbstherrscher) autocrat; **~ie** (‿‿‿⸗) f autocracy; **Lisch** a. ⓰ autocratic.

Automat (‿‿⸗) [grch.] m ⓰ automaton; self-acting machine; (Verkaufs-) automatic machine, penny-in-the-slot (machine); **Lisch** ⚢ (‿‿‿⸗‿) a. ⓰ (selbsttätig) automatical(ly).

Automobil (‿‿‿⸗) [grch.=lt.] n ⓒc. motor (car), automobile; Kutscher, Lenker e-s ~s driver of a motor (car), (fr.) chauffeur; im, mit dem ~ fahren to go (or drive) in a motor (car), to motor, to go motoring; **~anzug** (‿...) m ⓰ motor costume or dress; **=brille** f motor goggles pl.; **=droschke** f motor cab; **=fahrrad** n motor cycle.

Automobilismus (‿‿‿‿⸗) m ⓲ automobilism, motoring.

Automobilist (‿‿‿⸗) m ⓰ motorist.

Automobil-omnibus (‿‿‿⸗‿) m ⓲ motor (omni)bus; **=radfahrer** m motor cyclist; **=schleier** m motor veil; **=schuppen** m motor shed, (fr.) garage; **=steuerrad** n steering-wheel of a motor.

autonom (‿‿⸗), **Lisch** (‿‿⸗‿) a. ⓰ (selbständig) autonomous; **~ie** (‿‿‿⸗) f ⓰ autonomy.

Autoplastik ⚢ (‿‿⸗‿) [grch.] f ⓰ (Neubildung v. abgestorbenen Teilen) autoplasty.

Autopsie ⚢ (‿‿⸗) [grch.] f ⓰ autopsy.

Autor (‿‿) [lt.] m ⓓ (Verfasser, Urheber) author, writer; **~exemplar** (⸗...) n ⓰ presentation-copy; **~isation** (‿‿‿‿⸗‿) f ⓰ authorization; **Lisieren** (‿‿‿⸗‿) ⓰ f. bevollmächtigen.

Autorität (‿‿‿⸗) [mhd.,*lt.] f ⓰ 1. (Ansehen, Macht; Zeugnis) authority; auf f-e ~ hin on his authority; ich habe es von guter ~ (Quelle) I have it on the best authority or from a good source. — 2. (Gewährsmann) authority; als erste ~ gelten to be looked up to as (or considered) the highest authority.

autoritativ (‿‿‿⸗f) a. ⓰ authoritative.

Autorschaft (‿‿‿) [lt.] f ⓰ authorship.

Autotypie ⓞ (‿‿⸗) [grch.] f ⓰ (Tonätzung) autotype.

auweh (‿⸗) int. oh!, alas! (= o weh!).

Auxiliar-truppen (‿‿(‿)⸗...) [lt.] f/pl. auxiliary troops (vgl. Hilfs-...).

Auxometer ⚢ (‿‿⸗‿) [grch.] n (m) ⓰ (Vergrößerungsmesser) auxometer.

A. V. abbr. = Anerkannter (f. b.) Verein.

♪ Musik; ⚢ Wissenschaft; ♣ Pflanze; ♀ Geographie; ⓞ Technik; ⚒ Bergbau; ⚔ Militär; ⚓ Marine; ⓦ Handel; ✉ Post; 🚂 Eisenbahn.

Aval ⚥ (⌣ˢ) [fr.] m ⓐc. u. ⑩ (Wechselbürgschaft) surety; **Lieren** (⌣⌣ˡ) v/a. ⑬ (e-n Aval ausstellen) to stand security.

Avance (ă-wg̀'-ß̆) [fr.] f ⑭ **1.** = Entgegenkommen; e-m ~n machen to make advances to a p. — **2.** ⚘ = Geldvorschuß.

Avancement (ă-wg-ßmg̀') [fr.] n ⓟ promotion; advancement(= Beförderung).

avancieren (ă-wg-ß̆-ʹ) [fr.] **I** v/n. (ſn) to be promoted, to rise (in the army, navy, service); er ist zum Oberſten avanciert he has been promoted to a colonelcy; auch: he was promoted to colonel or made a colonel; (vorrücken) to advance. — **II** v/a. e-e Uhr ⌚ (vorſtellen) to put on a watch. — **III Avancierte(r)** ⚔ m ⑰ (Unter-offizier) non-commissioned officer.

Avantageur ⚔ (ă-wg-tă-Ǧö'r) [+fr.] m ⓐd. (Offizier-aſpirant) † = (Fahnen-)Junker.

Avantgarde ⚔ (ă-wg̀''-⌣ˡ) [fr.] f ⑱ (Vortrab) vanguard.

Ave (ʹwˢ) [lt.] n, inv. ~=Mari'a ⑩ (a. inv.) Ave (Mary); ~=Maria=Läuten n Angelus(-bell).

Aventin ♀, ~us ⓐa,⑯γ. (⌣wˡ(⌣)) [lt.] npr/m.a.Liſcher Hügel(Mount)Aventine.

Aventüre (⌣wˡ⌣ʹ) [fr.] f ⑱ bold venture; (Abenteuer) adventure.

Aventurin (⌣wˢʹ⌣ʹ) [it.] m ⓐc., ~=stein (ʹ⌣ʹ) m ⓜ min. aventurin(e) (a. ⊙).

Avers (⌣wˢ) [fr.] m ⓐa. einer Münze: obverse, &c. (= Bildseite; ant. Revers.

Aversion (⌣w⌣(ˢ)ˡ) [lt.] f ㊻ (Abneigung) aversion, (utter) dislike.

Averſ(ion)al=ſumme (⌣wˢ(⌣)-ʹ⌣) [lt.] f ⑬ = quantum n, **Averſum** (⌣wˢʹ) n ⑨, ㉘ = Abfindungs-...

avertieren (⌣w⌣ˡʹ) [fr.] v/a. ⑬ e-n ⚘ (benachrichtigen) to advise, inform a p. of.

Avertiſſement (ă-wär-tı̆-ßmg') [fr.] n ⑩ (Benachrichtigung, Ankündigung) announcement, advice, notice.

Avis (ă-wı̆') [fr.] m ⓐa. advice, information; ~=brief (ʹ...) m ⑫ letter of advice; ~=dampfer m steam-tender.

aviſieren (⌣w-ʹ⌣) [fr.] **I** v/a. ⑬ e-m et. ⚘ (anzeigen) to advise (or inform, apprise) a p. of ... — **II** ~ n ㉓ und **Aviſierung** f ㊻ advice. [boat, aviso.]

Aviſo ehm. ⚓ (⌣ˡʹ) [it.] m ⑩ dispatch-
a vista ♀ (⌣wˢʹ) [it.] adv. at sight (vgl. a).

Awaren (⌣ˡʹ) npr/pl. ⑲ hist. (Volk) Avars pl.

axial ⚲ (⌣(ʹ)ˡ) [lt.] a. ⑥⑥ (eine Achse bildend) axial. [axillary.]

axillar ⚲ (⌣⌣ˡ) [lt.] a. ⑥⑥ (achselständig)

Axinit ⚲ (⌣ˡ) [grch.] m ⓐc. min. (Beilstein) axinite, thumite, thumerstone.

Axiom ⚲ (⌣ˡʹ) [grch.] (Grundſatz) axiom.

Axiometer ⚓ (ˡ(⌣)-ˡˡ) [grch.] n (m) ② (Ruderzeiger) tell-tale (of the tiller or rudder); axiometer.

Axolotl (⌣ˡ⌣, ⌣⌣ˡ) [mex.] m ⑩ zo. axolotl, siredon (Ambly'stoma tigri'num, mexica'num).

Axt (ˡ) [ahd.] ♀ axe, adz(e)] f ⑩ große ~ axe; kleine ~ (small) hatchet, adze; die ~ an den Baum (od. an die Wurzel) legen (das Werk beginnen) to lay the axe to the tree; to set to work; Sprichw. der ~ den Stiel nachwerfen to throw the helve after the hatchet.

Äxtchen (ˡ⌣) n ㉓ dim. v. Axt

Axt=helm (ˡ...) m ⑫, =stiel handle (or helve) of an axe.

a. 3. abbr. = auf Zeit (ſ. Zeit 5).

Az. ⚔ artill. = Aufſchlagzünder.

Azale-in (⌣⌣ˡʹ) n ⓐc. (o. pl.) (violettrote Anili'nſarbe) azalein.

Azali-e ♀ (⌣⌣ˡ(⌣)⌣) [grch. Fels-...] f ⑱ azalea (Aza'lea).

Azarole ♀ (⌣⌣ˡʹ⌣) [span., *ar.] f ⑱ azarole(-tree), Neapolitan medlar (Crataeʹgus Azaro'lus). [acid $(C_9H_{16}O_4)$.]

Azela-in-ſäure ⚲ (⌣⌣ˡ--...) f ㊻ acelaic

Azetat ⚲ (⌣⌣ˡʹ) [lt.] n ⓐc. chm. (eſſigſaures Salz) acetate. $(C_2H_6O.)$.

Azeton ⚲ (⌣⌣ˡʹ) [lt.] n ⓐc. chm. (Eſſiggeiſt)

Azetyl ⚲ (⌣⌣ˡʹ) [lt.-grch.] n ⓐc. chm. (organ. Radikal) acetyl(e) (C_2H_3O).

Azetylen ⚲ (⌣⌣ˡʹ) [lt.-grch.] n ⓐc. chm. (im großen aus Kalziumkarbid dargeſtellt) acetylene; ~=lampe ⊙ (ʹ...) f ⑫ acetylene lamp.

Azimut ⚲ (⌣⌣ˡʹ) [span.,* ar. die Wege pl.] m (n) ⓐc. ast. (Winkelbogen des Horizonts zw. dem Mittagspunkt u. dem Höhenkreiſe eines Sternes) azimuth; ~=al=kompaß ⚓ (⌣⌣ˡʹ--...) m ⑫ azimuth compass; ~=al=kreis m azimuth (circle).

Azincourt (ă-ʃg-ku'r) [fr.] npr/n. ⑩ α. hist. (fr. Dorf, Sieg Heinrichs V. von England über die Franzoſen 25. Okt. 1415) Agincourt.

Azo=benzol ⚲ (ʹtß-...) n ⑫ chm. $(C_{12}H_{10}N_2)$ azobenzene, azobenzol; =farbstoffe m/pl. azobenzene dyes pl.

azoiſch ⚲ (⌣tßˡʹ) [grch.] a. ⑥⑥ geol. (ohne organische Überreſte, archäiſch) azoic.

Azoren ♀ (⌣ˡʹ) [port. Habichts-...] npr/pl. ⑱ α. (portugieſiſche Inſelgruppe im Atlantiſchen Ozean) Azores pl.; **azoriſch** a. ⑥⑥ Azorian. [reste] azo(t)ic.]

azotiſch ⚲ (⌣tßˡʹ) a. ⑥⑥ (ohne organiſche Über-

Azteke (⌣tßˡʹ) [(Maz)aßt(lan) Mexiko] m ㊾, **Aztekin** f ㊼, **aztekiſch** a. ⑥⑥ hist. Aztec.

Azur (⌣tßˡʹ) [fr. l'azur, *+ aus *perſ. Laſur, j. b.] m ㉙ min. lapis lazuli; poet. azure, sky-blue; =blau a. ⑥⑥ =blau n ⑫ azure; ~=farbe f = Azur (n).

azurn (⌣tßʹ) a. ⑥⑥ azure. [azurite.]

Azurit ⚲ (⌣tßˡʹ) m ⓐc. (Kupferlaſur)

B

B, b (ˡ) n, inv. (Buchstabe) B, b; vgl. A 2.
B, b ♪ n, inv. ♪ (der halbe Ton zwiſchen A und H) B flat; **B=Dur** B flat major; **B=Moll** B flat minor; als Erniedrigungszeichen: flat (♭); **B=Quadrat** ♮ = H.
B, chm. Symbol für Bor.
B. ⚘ abbr. auf Kurszetteln = Brief.
ba (ˡ) int. höhnend, etwa: bah!, pooh!. P yah!; F er kann nicht ba ſagen he cannot say bo(h) to a goose; F he is a silly (fellow) or a dunce.
bä (ˡ) [lautm.] int. (Bezeichnung des Schafgeblöts) baa.
Baal (ˡ u. ˡʹ)[hebr. Herr] npr/m. ⑩ α. myth. (Gott der Babylonier und Phönizier) Baal.
Baal=anbeter (ˡ(⌣)...), =diener, =pfaffe, =priester m ⑯ worshipper of Baal, Baalite, weitS. idol-worshipper.
Baba (ˡʹ) f ⑳ Kinderſprache: (Bettchen) in die ~ gehen to go to bye-bye.
Babbelei F (⌣⌣ˡ) f ㊻ babble, twaddle.
babbeln F (ʹ⌣) [ndd. lautm.] v/n. (h.) ⓐa. to babble, prattle, jabber.
Babel (ˡʹ) [Babylon] npr/n. ⑩ α. hist. Babel (auch fig. babel = Verwirrung); bibl. Turm zu ~ Tower of Babel.
Babine ⚥ (⌣ˡʹ) [ruſſ.] f ⑱ Kürschnerei: Russian (brown) catskin.

Babirussa ⚲ (-⌣ˡ⌣) [malai.] m (n) ⑩ zo. (Hirſch-eber) babiroussa, Indian hog.
Babu-in (ˡʹ) [fr.] m ⓐc. zo. baboon.
Babusche (⌣ˡʹ) [perſ.] f ⑱ (Pantoffel) babooche, pointed (flat-heeled) slipper.
Babylon (ˡ⌣⌣) [bab-ilu Pforte Gottes] npr/n. ⓐα. hist. Babylon (= Babel); **~i-en** (⌣ˡ f ㊼) npr/n. ㉓α. Babylonia; **~i-er** (⌣ˡ f ㊼) m ㉓ (-⌣ˡ(⌣)⌣), **Liſch** a. ⑥⑥ Babylonian; bibl. Liſche Verwirrung confusion of tongues.
Bacchanal (⌣ʹ) [grch.] n ⓐc. u. ㉙ myth. mſt pl. ~ien (Bacchusfest) bacchanals, bacchanalia pl.; (Zechgelage) drinking-bout; ſtärker: (wild) orgies pl.
Bacchant (⌣ʹ) [grch.] m ㊷, ~in f ㊼ (Bacchusdiener[in]) bacchant, priest(ess) of Bacchus; Bacch(ant)in f auch: bacchante, raſende: maenad.
bacch(ant)iſch (⌣ˢʹ, ⌣ʹ) a. ⑥⑥ bacchantic; bacchanal(ian).
bacch(e)-iſch (⌣ˢʹ, ⌣ʹ) [grch.] a. ⑥⑥ **1.** pros. bacchiac. — **2.** ſ. bacchantiſch.
Bacche-us, Bacchius ⚲ (⌣ˢˡʹ) [grch.] m ㉗ pros. bacchius (Versfuß: ⌣ˡˡ).
Bacchus (ˢʹ) [lt.; grch.;* perſ. bagh Weinberg] npr/m. ⑩ γ. myth. (Gott des Weines) Bacchus; ~=bruder F (ʹ...) m ⑫ drunk-

ard; =fest n bacchanals pl.; =lied n bacchanalian song; =stab m thyrsus.
Bach (ˢʹ) [ahd.] m ⓐc. brook, rivulet, stream(let); weitS. water - course; Sprichw. kleine Bäche machen große Flüsse every little helps, small gains make large profits.
Bach=amſel (ˢʹ...) f ⑫ orn. water-ousel (Cinclus aqua'ticus); =binſe ♀ f water-bulrush (Iuncus conglomera'tus); =blume f = Dotterblume; =bunge [nhd. 16. sae.] ♀ f brooklime (Vero'nica Beccabu'nga).
Bache (ˢʹ) [ahd.: bacon] f ⑱ hunt. wild sow.
Bächelchen (⌣⌣ˡ) n ㉓ = Bächlein.
Bacher (ˢʹ) [Bache] m ⑫ (two-year-old) wild boar.
Bach=fahrt (ˢʹ...) f ⑫ (Schlucht) ravine, gully; =forelle f, ichth. brook-(or river-)trout (Salmo fa'rio); =hol(un)der ♀ m = Schneeball; =krebs m, zo. crayfish (A'stacus); =kresse ♀ f = Brunnenkresse.
Bächlein (ˢʹ) n ㉓ dim. v. Bach brooklet, rill, streamlet.
Bach=minze (ˢʹ...) f round-leaved mint (Mentha rotundifo'lia); =reich a. ⑥⑥ abounding in brooks; rilly; =stelze [nhd.] f, orn. wagtail (Motaci'lla); weiße ~

Signs (see page XVII): F familiar; P vulgar; ⌜ flash; ⌟ rare; † obsolete (died); * new word (born); ⁺⁺ incorrect; ♪ music;

[back] — 139 — [Badeordnung]

water-wagtail; gelbe ~ yellow wagtail: =weide ⚓ f osier (*Salix helix*).
back¹ ⚓ ⬇ (⸝) [engl.] *adv.* (rückwärts gewendet) aback; (hinten) abaft.
Back² (⸝) [ndd.] *f* ⊕, ⚓ *n* ⊕c. **1.** ⬇ a) (Schüssel für das Schiffsvolk) bowl, platter (for the mess); b) (ehm. Vorderkastell) forecastle; c) (beim Kalfatern gebrauchtes Fahrzeug) punt. — **2.** ⊙ (Kasten, Abteilung) locker; partition; berth.
Back³=apfel (⸝...) [backen] *m* ⊕ baked (or baking) apple; ⊙**berechtigt** *a.* ⊕ licensed to bake; =**birne** *f* baked (or baking) pear; =**blech** *n* baking(-)tin; plate (or board) used for baking.
Back¹=bord ⬇ (⸝⸝) *n* (*m*) ⊕c. (linke Schiffsseite vom Steuer aus) port, ehm. larboard; das Schiff frängt nach ~, legt sich nach ~ über, liegt auf der ~=seite ... heels (or lists) to port; Helm an ~! link a-port!; ~=**seite** (⸝...) *f* ⊕ = Backbord; ~(s)=**wache** *f* port-watch.
back¹=brassen ⬇ (⸝⸝⸝) *v/a.* ⊕: die Segel ⚓ to (brace) back ...
Back³=brett (⸝⸝) *n* ⊕ =blech.
Back²=deck ⬇ (⸝⸝) *n* ⊕ forecastle deck.
Bäckchen (⸝...) *n* ⊕ *dim. v.* Backe.
Backe (⸝...) [ahd.] *f* ⊕, ~**n¹** *m* ⊕ **1.** (Wange) cheek (auch ⊕); mit dicken, runden ~n chubby(-faced); mit roten ~n rosy-cheeked, mit eingefallenen ~n hollow-cheeked, F lantern-jawed; er hat eine dicke ~ he has a swoln cheek or face; *fig.* mit leeren ~n kauen to live on hope; die ~n voll nehmen to talk big. — **2.** (Kinnbacken) jaw(-bone). — **3.** ⊙ *arch.* ~n *pl.* eines Kami'ns: cheeks, sides *pl.*; Drechslerei: ~n *pl.* coving *sg.*, sides *pl.*; ~ am Gewehrkolben butt-end; Schlosserei: ~n *pl.* e-s Schraubstockes: jaws *pl.* — **4.** ⚔ artill. (Lauflatte) ribbon. — **5.** ⬇ ~n *f/pl.* od. *m/pl.* des Mastes cheeks, hounds, bibbs *pl.*
backen (⸝...) [ahd. bake, grch. pho'gō röste] **I** *v/a.* **1.** ⊕b. a) Brot *ic.*: to bake; frisch, alt(ge)backenes Brot new, stale bread; b) Kochkunst: in der Pfanne mit Butter *ic.* to fry; Austern *ic.* to scallop; Fleisch *ic.*: braun, scharf ⚓ to roast well, to brown; Eier in (brauner) Butter ⚓ to poach ... — **2.** ⊕ b. (dörren) meist: to dry, ⊕: Stahl ⚓ (aus Eisen herstellen) to puddle, to cement ...; Ziegelsteine ⚓ to burn (or bake) tiles or bricks. — **3.** F *fig.* (schaffen) neugeback(e)ner Adel new-fangled (or mushroom) nobility; *bsd. pol.* new batch of peers. — **II** *v/n.* **4.** ⊕ u. ⊕b. in Backofen: to be baking or cooking; in der Pfanne: to be frying; das Brot hat nicht genug gebacken the bread is not baked enough. — **5.** (zu u. h.) ⊕ (sich-kleben) to adhere, to stick (together), to cake (together), vom Leim *ic.*: to bind; durch Hitze oder Kälte: (fest werden) to clot, to conglomerate; (hart werden) to harden; (starr werden) to grow rigid; (gefrieren) to congeal; der Schnee backt (ballt) the snow cakes together. — **III** ~ *n* ⊕ **6.** baking; in der Pfanne: frying; ⊕ der Ziegel: burning. —
IV Ge=back(e)ne(s) ⊕ *n* ⊕ **7.** = Gebäck.
backen³ ⚓ (⸝⸝) [engl.] *v. n.* (h.) ⊕ Sport: (auf ein Pferd wetten) to back (a horse).

Backen=ansatz (⸝⸝...) *m* ⊕, =**ausschnitt** *m* ⊕ des Gewehrkolbens: cheek-piece; =**bart** *m* (pair of) whiskers *pl.*; mit einem ~, ⊙**bärtig** *a.* ⊕ whiskered; =**bein** *n. anat.* cheek- (or jaw-)bone; =**bohrer** ⊕ *m* Schlosserei: master-tap; =**drüse** *f, anat.* buccal gland; =**haube** *f* (lady's) dresscap; =**höhle** *f, anat.* buccal cavity; =**knochen** *m, anat.* = =bein; =**muskel** *m. anat.* trumpeter's (⸌ buccinator) muscle; =**riemen** *m*: a) ⚓ = =Schuppenfette; b) ⸌ Sattlerei: collar-head; =**streich** *m* slap in the face; (Ohrfeige) box on the ear; =**tasche** *f, zo.* cheek-pouch; =**zahn** *m, anat.* molar (tooth), double tooth, grinder.
Bäcker (⸝⸝) [backen] *m* ⊕, ~**in** *f* ⊕ baker, *f* baker's wife; Sprichw. das ist wie beim ~ die Semmel (ein fester Preis) there is a fixed charge; besser zum ~ als zum Apotheker (it's) better to pay a butcher's bill than a doctor's.
Bäcker=(be)scheider (⸝⸝...) ⊕ *m* ⊕ sifter; =**beine** *n/pl.* knock-kneed legs *pl.*; =**beinig** *a.* ⊕ knock-kneed; =**brot** *n* baker's (or shop-)bread; =**bursche** *m* baker's boy; =**dutzend** *n* (13 Stück) baker's dozen. [ware.
Bäckerei (⸝⸝) *f* ⊕ s. Backstube, Back=]
Bäcker=gesell(e) (⸝⸝...) *m* ⊕ baker's man, journeyman baker; =**gewerbe**, =**gewerk**, =**handwerk** *n* baker's trade or business; =**laden** *m* baker's shop; =**meister** *m* master baker; =**schabe** *f* black beetle; =**gast** ⬇ *m* (Marinebäcker) ship's baker; =**scheider** *m* = =bescheider.
Back³=fisch (⸝...) *m* ⊕: a) fish for frying; b) fried fish; c) F *fig.* (Mädchen) girl in her teens, school-girl (in short dresses), F bread-and-butter miss; =**form** *f* baking(-)mould; tin for baking; =**geld** *n* baker's fee (for baking); =**gerät** *n* baking utensils *pl.*; =**gerechtigkeit** *f* baker's license; =**hähnchen** *n*, =**hähn(d)el** F *n* roast chicken; =**haus** *n* = =stube; =**hitze** *f* heat of a baker's oven; intolerable heat.
...backig, =bäckig (...⸝) [Backe] *a.* ⊕, *zB.* rot⸝ red-cheeked.
Back³=kohle (⸝...) *f* ⊕ baking-coal.
back¹=legen ⬇ (⸝⸝⸝) = backbrassen.
Back³=mulde (⸝...) *f* ⊕ = =trog; =**obst** *n* dried fruit; =**ofen** *m* (baker's) oven; ein ~ voll a batch (of bread); =**pfanne** *f* frying-pan.
Back=pfeife F (⸝...) | = Backe] *f* ⊕ box on the ear (= Backenstreich); ⸌ baking powder.)
Back³=pflaume (⸝...) *f* ⊕ prune; =**pulver**
Back¹=quartier ⬇ (...⸝) ⊕ larboard quarter.
Back³=rädchen (⸝...) *n* ⊕ jagging iron; =**schaufel** *f* = =scheibe *f*, =**scheit** *n*, =**scheibe** *f* (baker's) peel.
Backschisch (⸝⸝) [türk., *pers.* Geschenk] *n, inv.* (Trinkgeld) baksheesh, bakshish.
Back³=schüssel (⸝⸝) *f* baking dish or pan.
backsen (⸝⸝) ⊕ ein Geschütz *ic.* eine schwere Last ⚓ (vom Flecke schieben) to shift, (mit der Talje aufwinden) to bouse.
Backs=gasten ⬇ (⸝...) [Back²] *m/pl.* ⊕ castle-crew.
Back=spiere ⬇ (⸝...) *f* ⊕ lower boom.
Back³=stag (⸝⸝) *n* ⊕ guy; shrouds *pl.*; ⸝=**weise** (⸝⸝...) *adv.* abaft the beam; on the quarter; ~**s=wind** *m* ⊕ quarter-wind, weits. favourable breeze.

Back³=stein (⸝...) *m* ⊕ brick; =**stein=bau** ⊕ *m* brick building; =**stein=mauerung** *f* brick masonry; =**stube** *f* bakehouse, bakery; =**tag** *m* baking day; =**teig** *m* dough; =**trog** *m* kneading-trough; =**ware** *f*, =**werk** *n*: a) baker's ware; b) (Kuchen *ic.*) pastry, confectionery; =**zahn** (⸝⸝) [Backe] *m* ⊕ = Backenzahn.
Bad (nordd. ⸝, südb. ⸝, *pl.* ⸝) (ahd.: bath; *bähen) *n* ⊕c. **1.** bath; im Freien: F bathe, dip (in the sea); durch Untertauchen: ducking; durch Naßwerden: soaking, F sousing; frühes kaltes ~ F morning tub; (Sturz)~ shower-bath; ein ~ nehmen to take (or have) a bath; (Badeanstalt) baths *pl.* — **2.** *fig.* e-m ein ~ rüsten, her- ob. zu=richten, e-m das ~ (ge)segnen (Schlimmes bereiten) to put a p. in a great predicament, F to make it hot for a p.; † ausschütten L — **3.** ⊙ (Färberei) bath, dip; *chm., &c.* bath, balneum. — **4.** (Ort mit Heilquellen) medicinal springs *pl.*, spa; in's ~ reisen to go to a watering-place or healthresort; in's Seebad: to go to the seaside or to a marine health-resort; warme Bäder bei den Alten: thermæ *pl.*
Bade=anstalt (⸝⸝...) *f* ⊕ bathing-establishment, baths *pl.*; =**anzug** *m* bathing-dress or -costume; =**arzt** *m* physician at a watering-place; =**diener** *m* (bathers') male attendant; =**einrichtung** *f* bathing-accommodation; =**frau** *f* (Aufwärterin) ladies' attendant; =**gast** *m* visitor at a spa or a health-resort or a watering-place; ⬇ (zum Schiffspersonal gehöriger Nicht=Seemann, wie Schiffsarzt *ic.*) etwa: outsider, loafer; =**gelegenheit** *f* opportunity for bathing; =**handschuhe** *m/pl.* Turkish gloves *pl.*; =**handtuch** *n* bath towel; =**haube** *f* = =**kappe**; =**haus** *n* = =anstalt; =**hose(n.** *pl.*) *f* bathing-drawers *pl.*; =**inhaber** *m* proprietor of baths; =**kappe** *f* (lady's) oilskin cap; =**karren** *m* im Seebad: bathing-machine; =**kur** *f* use of medicinal springs, weits. stay at a health-resort; eine ~ in T. gebrauchen to take the waters (or the cure) at T.; =**liste** *f* list of visitors or arrivals (at a watering-place); =**mantel** *m* bathing-gown; =**meister** *m*: a) manager of the baths; b) swimming-master.
baden¹ (⸝⸝) ⊕ **I** *v/a.* ein Kind *ic.*: to bathe; ein Pferd ⚓ (schwemmen) to ride into the) water. — **II** *v/n.* (h.) u. **sich** ⚓ *v/refl.* bsd. im Freien: to bathe; warm, kalt ⚓ to take a warm, a cold bath; in Schweiß gebadet perspiring profusely, F in a bath of perspiration; in Tränen, in Blut gebadet melting in tears. swimming in blood. — **III** ~ *n* ⊕ bathing; in der See: sea-bathing; F dip in the ocean. — **IV** ⸝**de(r)** *m*. ~**de** *f* ⊕ bather.
Baden² ⚥ (⸝⸝) *npr.n.* ⊕ **1.** (südb. Land) (grand-duchy of) Baden. — **2.** (Stadt) Baden. |Badenese, native of Baden.)
Baden(f)er(in *f*) *m* ⊕ (⸝⸝(⸝), ⸝⸝(⸝))
badensisch (⸝⸝⸝) *a.* ⊕ = badisch.
Bade=ordnung (⸝⸝...) *f* ⊕ regulations *pl.* for the use of baths at a spa; =**ort** *m* = Bad 4; deutsche =**örter** *pl.* German spas *pl.*; =**platz** *m* bathing-place.

⸌ scientific; ⚓ botanical; ⚥ geography; ⊙ machinery; ⛏ mining; ⚔ military; ⬇ marine; ⚭ commercial; ⚬ postal; 🚂 railway.

Bader faſt † (⸺) [mhd.] m ㉒ (Heil=gehilfe) barber(-surgeon).
Bade=raum (⸺...) m ㉒ = =plaꜩ.
Baderei (⸺⸻) f ㊻ 1. F (Badeanſtalt) baths pl. — 2. † barber's shop. [ing-place.
Bade=reiſe (⸺⸻...) f ㉖ trip to a water-
Bäder=geſell(e) (⸺⸻...) m ㉖ barber's assistant or man. [balneology.
Bäder=kunde (⸻...) f㉖: ⚥ balneography,
Bade=ſchiff (⸺⸻...) n ㉖ floating baths pl.; =ſchrank m shower-bath; =ſchwamm m bath-sponge (Euspo'ngia); =ſtelle f = =plaꜩ; =ſtrand m beach (suitable for bathers; =ſtube [ahd.] f: a) bath-room; b) (Schwiꜩraum) hot-room; im Orient: hummum; =tuch n bath-towel; =wagen m = =karren; =wanne f bath, F tub; ⚥warm a. ㊺ (lauwarm) tepid; =wärme f temperature for bathing; =waſſer n water for bathing; =zeit f bathing-hours pl.; =zelle f (bathing-)cabin or box; =zelt n tent for bathers; =zeug n bathing-linen; =zimmer n = =ſtube.
Badian ⚥ (-⸻) m ⓑc., ~e (-⸻) f ㊸ [perſ.] badian (Frucht) = Stern=anis).
badiſch (⸻) a. ㊻ of Baden, Badenese.
bäen (⸻) v/n. (h.) ㊽ v. Schafen: to bleat, to baa (ſ. bä).
Baſel ⚥ (⸻) [it. *bavella*] m ㉒ (Aus=ſchußware) damaged (or soiled) goods pl.
baff (⸻) int. bang!, pop!
bäffen (⸻) [mhd.] v/n. ㊽ (bellen) to bark.
Baffin(s)=bai ⚥ (⸻⸻) npr/f. ㉖ (Bai weſt=lich von Grönland) Baffin('s) Bay.
Bagage (⸻⸻) [ndl.; * fr.] f ㊺ 1. (Gepäck) 🞨 baggage; weitS. (traveller's) luggage. — 2. Schimpfwort: (Geſindel) rabble, riff-raff, mob.
Bagage=kammer (⸻...) ⚥ f ㉖ slop-room; =karren, =wagen m baggage-cart or -wagon; =pferd n bat-horse. — Vgl. auch Gepäck...
Bagaſſe (⸻⸻) [fr.] f ㊸ (Zuckerrohrſtroh als Feuerungsmaterial) bagasse, begasse.
Bagatelle (⸻⸻⸻) [fr.] f ㊺ bagatelle, trifle; für eine ~ kaufen to buy for a mere trifle or F song.
Bagatell=gericht (⸻⸻...) n ㊺ jur. lower court; =klage f petty cause; ⚥=mäßig adv. as a trifle; ⚥ behandeln to treat in an offhandish way; =prozeß m = =klage; =richter m (police) magistrate; =ſache f = =klage; =ſchulden f/pl. petty (or small) debts pl.
Bagdad ⚥ (mſt ⸺) [perſ. ⸺] npr/n. ⓑα. (türk. St. in Vorderaſien) Bagdad; ~=bahn (⸻...) f ㊺ Bagdad railway or line.
bägern ⚥ (⸻) [ahd.: bicker] v/a. ⓑa. (plagen, quälen) to worry, plague, vex, torment.
Bagger ⊙ (⸻) [ndl.] m ㉒ = ~maſchine.
Bagger=boot (⸻...) n ㉖ dredging boat, dredger; mud-boat or -lighter; =eimer m bucket of dredging engine; =haken m drag; =maſchine f dredge(r), dredging machine or engine. [baggern.
baggern ⊙ (⸻) [ndl.] v/a. ⓑa. = aus=
Bagger=netz (⸻...) n ㉖ dredge; drag-net; =ponton m, =prahm m, =ſchiff n = =boot; =torf m drag-peat; =trommel f = dredging tumbler.
Bagien=braſſe ⚓ (⸻⸻) f ㊺ cross-jack (brace); =rahe f square-sail yard; =ſegel n cross-jack sail, miz(z)en-sail.

Bagno (bä'n-jo) [it. Bad] n (m) ㉓, auch ㊽ (Gefängnis ꝛc.) bagnio.
bah int. 1. (⸻) verächtlich: pshaw!, pooh!; (Unſinn) bosh! — 2. (⸻) = ba.
👉 **bäh** (⸻) ꝛc. ſ. bü ꝛc.
Bäh(e)=lappen (⸻⸻...) m ㉖ stupe; =mittel n s.th. used for fomentation.
bähen[1] ⚥ (⸻) [ahd.] I v/a. ㊺ 1. Holz ⚥ to warm, to heat ...; Pflanzen ⚥ (treiben) to force ... — 2. med. kranke Glieder ⚥: a) durch warme Umſchläge: to foment; b) an=feuchtend: to bathe, to stupe. — II ⚥ v/n ㉓
bähen[2] = bäen. [3. = Bähung 1.
Bäh=lappen, =mittel ſ. Bäh(e)=...
Bahn (⸻) [mhd.] f ㊻ 1. (beaten) track, road, way; (ebener Weg) level track, smooth road or way; eine freie ~ a clear path, an open road, ſ. a. 3; die ~ brechen, ~ machen to pave (or prepare) the way, to (act as) pioneer, fig. to make a start; ſich ~ brechen to make (or push, work) one's way, to make headway, v. Anſichten ꝛc.: to be gaining ground, to spread; eine neue ~ einſchlagen to strike out a new path or track, fig. a. to take a new departure; auf die rechte ~ führen ob. bringen to put on the right track, to lead into the right path (auch fig.); ſeine ~ gemächlich verfolgen to pursue the even tenor of one's way. — 2. oft fig. e-m die ~ abgewinnen (ihm vorlaufen) to get the start of a p., to overtake a p.; auf der betretenen ~ bleiben to continue in (or to pursue) the old groove; die Unterhaltung in gemütlichere ~en einlenken to turn the conversation into a more congenial channel; ~ der Ehre, des Ruhmes honourable, glorious career. — 3. auf dem Eiſe: ~ fegen to sweep the snow (away); to clear the ice; ſ. Eisbahn. — 4. 🚂 (Eiſenbahn) railway (line), kurz: line, Am. railroad; mit der ~ fahren to travel (or go) by rail(way); mit der (ob. per) ~ ſenden to send by rail; die ~ iſt frei! line clear!, all right!; die ~ iſt geſperrt! line blocked!, caution!; ast. der Geſtirne: course; der Planeten: orbit; e-s Kometen: track, path; phys. ~ (durchlaufener Raum) path (of a projectile), space (traversed by a falling body), (Flug=~) trajectory (of a bullet). — 5. Kampfplaꜩ ꝛc.: arena; ring; die ~ betreten to enter the lists; ſ. Kegel=, Lauf=, Reit=, Rennbahn. — 6. ⊙ (glatte Fläche an Werkzeugen) meiſt: face. — 7. (Maß für Zeuge, Tapeten ꝛc.) breadth, width (in England gewöhnlich = 1 yard).
Bahn=arbeiter 🚂 (⸻) m ㉖ railway-man; =aufſeher 🚂 m overseer (or inspector) of the line; =bau 🚂 m (pl. =bauten) railway-construction; =be=amte(r) 🚂 m railway-official; =betrieb 🚂 m working of a railway; ⚥brechend a. ㊺ fig. opening the way; striking out new paths or in new directions; ⚥ wirken to (act as) pioneer, to do pioneer('s) work; ⚥es Genie original (or inventive) genius; =brecher m (bſſ. fig.) pioneer; original inventor; =brücke 🚂 f railway-bridge, viaduct; =dienſt 🚂 m railway-service; =einheit f property and stock of a railway.
bahnen (⸻) v/a. ㊽ einen Weg ⚥: a) to prepare (or pave) the way; to open up

a new path or track; b) (ebenen) to level (down); c) (leichter machen) bſſ. fig. to smooth the way for, to facilitate; e-m (dat.) e-n Weg durchs Gedränge ⚥ to force (or edge, elbow, push, squeeze) one's way through the crowd; ⚥ durch den Feind: to cut one's way through the foe; ſich (dat.) den Weg ⚥ to make one's way (in the world); to carve out a career for o.s.; e-m den Weg zu etw. (zu j-m Glücke) ⚥ to put a p. in the way of a th. (of a good th.).
Bahnen... (⸻⸻) ſ. Bahn=...; ⚥ v. Stoffen: ⚥weiſe adv. by widths.
bahn=frei ⚥ (⸻...) a. ㊺ delivered free at station; =geleiſe 🚂 n ㉖ line of rails; =häuschen 🚂 n = =wärterhäuschen.
Bahnhof 🚂 (⸺⸻) m ㉖ (railway-)station; großer: terminus; ~=direktor, ~=inſpek=tor m = =vorſteher; ~(s)=reſtauration f (Wirtſchaft) refreshment-room (of a station); ~(s)=reſtaurateur (Wirt) m refreshment contractor; ~s=vorſteher m station-master; ~s=wirtſchaft f = =reſtauration.
...bahnig (⸻) ㊺ in Zſſgn, zB.: breit=⚥ of great (or full) width; zwei=⚥ ꝛc. ⚥ of two, &c (full) widths.
Bahn=körper 🚂 (⸻...) m ㉖ permanent way; =kreuzung f railway-crossing; ⚥lagernd ⚥ a. ㊺ v. Gütern: to be kept till called for; =linie 🚂 f railway-line; ⚥los a. pathless, trackless; =meiſter 🚂 m inspector of (works on) the permanent way; =meiſterwagen m trolly; =netz n railway-net; =planum n formation level; =poſt 🕮 f travelling post-office (T. P. O.); =poſtamt 🕮 n railway post-office; =poſtzug 🕮 m mail-train; =profil 🚂 n railway-section; =räumer m sweeper, fender; cow-catcher; =ſchlitten m snow-plough; =ſchwelle f sleeper; =ſteig m (Perron) platform; =ſteig=karte f (railway-)platform ticket; =ſteig=ſperre f collection of tickets at the gate (of the platform); =ſtollen m tunnel; =ſtrecke f, =ſtück n section of a railway; =transport m goods-traffic, carriage (or transport) of goods by rail; =ver=kehr m railway-traffic; =wart ⚥ m, mſt =wärter m watchman, points-man, signalman, lineman; =wärter=häuschen n watchman's (or points-man's, lineman's) hut; signal-box; =zug n (railway-)train.
Bahre (⸻) [ahd.: barrow; *(ge)bären: lt. fé'rō trage] f ㊺ 1. (Trage) für Steine ꝛc.: (hand-)barrow; für Kranke: stretcher; für Tote: bier, hearse. — 2. (Sarg) coffin; von der Wiege bis zur ~ from the cradle to the grave.
Bahren... (⸻) ſ. Bahrrecht ꝛc.
Bahr=recht (⸻...) n ㉖ ehm. ordeal of the bier; =tuch n pall, (Sargtuch) hearse-cloth; =tuchhalter m pall-bearer.
Bähung (⸻) f ㊻ 1. warming, &c. (ſ. bähen); med. fomentation, bathing. — 2. = Bäh(e)mittel.
Bai (⸻; *Hom.* bei) [ndd., *it.] f ㊺ bay, kleine: creek, cove, bight; ⚓ v. Schiffen im Sturm: in eine ~ getrieben embayed.
Ba=ikal=ſee ⚥ (⸻⸻⸻) npr/m. ㊾e. (o. pl.) in Südſibirien: Lake Baikal.

Zeichen (ſ. S. XVII): F familiär; P Volksſprache; ⸺ Gaunerſprache; ⸺ ſelten; † alt (auch geſtorben); * neu (auch geboren); ⁺⁺ unrichtig;

Bai=salz ⊤ (ᵘ...) n ⓺ (Seesalz) sea-salt.
Baiser (bä-ſe') [fr. Kuß] n (m) ⓾ (Schaumgebäck) cream-puff or -bun; meringue.
Baisse (bä'-ß³) [fr.] f ⓸ (ant. Hausse) decline or depression (of the market), fall or drop (of prices, slump); auf die ~ spekulieren to speculate (or operate) for a fall, to bear the stocks.
Baisse=clique ⓸ (ᶻ...) f ⓸, operators pl. for the fall, bearish clique; **=moment** n (et. das die Kurse ungünstig beeinflußt) bear point; **=partei** f =clique; **=spekulation** f bearish speculation; **=strömung**, **=tendenz** f bearish tone, downward tendency; **=syndikat'n** ring for bearing (or depreciating) a stock.
Baissier (bä-ße') [fr.] m ⓾ bear; seller; person operating for a fall.
Bajadere (ᵘᵛᴸᵛ) [port.] f ⓸ (indische Tänzerin) bayadère, dancing girl.
Bajazzo (ᵛᵇᶻ) [it. *pagliaccio*] m ⓾ und ⓸ pantaloon, ſ. Hanswurst.
Bajonett ⚔ (ᵛᵛᴸ) [fr. v. Bayonne, St.] n ⓵b. bayonet; ~ ab! unfix bayonets!; ~ an ein Ort bringen to unfix bayonets; das ~ aufpflanzen, aufstecken to fix bayonets; fällt das ~! charge bayonets!; mit gefälltem ~ angreifen, einnehmen to charge with fixed bayonets or with (the) bayonet at the charge, to carry (or take) at the point of the bayonet; mit dem ~ verwunden to (wound with the) bayonet.
Bajonett=angriff ⚔(ᵛᵛᴸ...) m ⓸ bayonet-charge; **=exerzieren**, **=fechten** n b.-exercise, crossing (of) bayonets; **=hülse** f bayonet-socket. [with the) bayonet.]
bajonettieren ⚔(ᵛᵛᴸᵛ) v/a. ⓸ to (charge)
Bajonett=ring ⚔(ᵛᵛᴸ...) m ⓸ bayonet-clasp; locking-ring (a. ⚙); **=verschluß** m bayonet-catch; **=vorschrift** f rules pl. for bayonet-fighting.
☞ **Bakchos** f. Bacchus 2c.
Bake (ᴸᵛ) [ndb. beacon] f ⓸ 1. *surv.* u. ⚔ (Fluchtstab) directing staff. — 2. ⚓ (Seezeichen) seamark; (Landtennung) landmark; (Feuerzeichen) beacon(-fire); (Boje) buoy.
Bakel [lt.] m ⓸ (Stock, bsd. des Schulmeisters) (schoolmaster's) ferule, (birch) rod, birch, cane.
baken ↓ (ᴸᵛ) v/a. u. v/n. (h.) ⓼ (mit Baken bezeichnen) to buoy (off), to mark (off) dangerous points or courses with beacons.
Baken=boje ↓ (ᵘ...) f ⓸ buoy; **=feuer** n beacon-light; **=tonne** f = =boje.
Baker ↓ (ᴸᵛ) m ⓸ overseer of buoys.
Bakkalaureat (ᵛᵛᴸ) [lt.] n ⓵c. (full) bachelor's degree.
Bakkalaureats=examen (ᶻ...) n ⓸, **=prüfung** f (pass-)examination for a degree.
Bakkalaure-us (ᵛᵛᴸᵛ) [lt.] m ⓸: ~ der Theologie bachelor of divinity; *Baccalau'reus a'rtium libera'lium*, bachelor of arts (*abbr.* B. A.).
Bakteri-e ᚕ (ᵛᴸᵛ(ᵛ)ᵛ) [grch.] f ⓸ (Spaltpilz) bacterium, microbe, schizomycete.
bakteri-ell ᚕ (ᵛᵛ(ᵛ)ᵇ) *a.* ⓺ bacterial.
bakteri-en-artig ᚕ (ᵛᵘ(ᵛ)ᵛ...) *a.* ⓺ bacterioid; **=förmig** *a.* bacteriform; **=forscher** m ⓸ bacteriologist; **=kunde** f ⓸ **=teriology**. [⓸ ᚕ bacteriologist.]
Bakteriolog ᚕ, ~e (ᵛᵛ(ᵛ)ᴸ) m ⓸,]
Baktri-er (ᴸᵛᵛ) [Alt.: Baktra, Baktri-en ♀] m ⓸, **=in** f ⓸, **baktrisch** *a.* ⓺ Bactrian.

Bä=lamm (ᵘ...) n ⓸ Kinderspr.: baa-lamb.
Balance (bä-lɑ̃-ß³) [fr.] f ⓸ 1. balance = Gleichgewicht. — 2. ↓ (für Kauffahrteischiffe Angabe der Ladung) invoice of the cargo; **~=ruder** ↓ n balanced rudder.
Balancier ⚙ (bä-lɑ̃-ße') [fr.] m ⓾ beam; e-r Dampfmaschine: working (or engine-) beam. [beam-engine.]
Balancier=(dampf)maschine ⚙(ᶻ...) f ⓸]
balancieren (bä-lɑ̃-ß³ᴸᵛ) [fr.] v/a., v/refl. u. v/n. (h.) ⓼ (im Gleichgewicht halten) to poise; bsw. a. ⓸ to (strike a) balance.
Balancier=maschine (ᶻ...) f ⓸ ſ. Dampfmaschine; **=pflug** m balance-plough; **=presse** f z. Ausschneiden v. Papier, Leder 2c.: punching press; **=spanten** ↓ n/pl. balance-frames pl.; **=stange** f Uhrmacherei: balancing-rod; der Seiltänzer: (bä-lɑ̃-ß³ᵘ'ʳ...) (balancing) pole; **=zapfen** m beam-gudgeon. [*zo.*balanid, balanus.]
Balane ᚕ (ᵛᴸᵛ) [grch.] f ⓸ (Meer-eichel)]
bald (ahd.: bold] *adv.* ⓺ (D 2) 1. soon; in der Zukunft: presently, shortly, ere long; sehr ⓶ speedily, F in no time; er lernte es sehr ⓶ he learnt it in a very short time, he was not long learning it; er wird ⓶ kommen he will soon be here, F he won't be long; zu ⓶ too soon, too early, vgl. allzu⓶; so ⓶ als möglich, a. möglichst ⓶ as soon as possible or feasible, as soon as ever it can be, at the earliest date (or moment) possible; brieflich oft: at your earliest convenience; ⓶ darauf, ⓶ nachher a short time or a little while) after(wards); je bälder, je lieber the sooner the better. — 2. (leicht) easily; das ist ⓶ gesagt, aber schwer getan that is sooner said than done. — 3. (beinahe) almost, ich wäre ⓶ gestürzt I nearly tumbled, es ist ⓶ drei Uhr F it's getting on for three. — 4. (schnell) wie ⓶ die Zeit hingeht! how quickly time flies! — 5. **bald ... bald ...** (rasche Aufeinanderfolge) now ... now ...; now ... then ...; at one time ..., at another time ...; ⓶ dieses, ⓶ jenes first this thing, then that; ſo ⓶, ſo ⓶ sometimes this way, sometimes that now; one way, now the other; ⓶ hier, ⓶ dort here one day, there the next.
Baldachin (ᵛᵘᵇ-) [it. von * Baldach = Bagdad] m ⓵c. canopy; (Thron) dais; mit einem ~ bedeckt canopied; ohne ~, bisw. uncanopied. [bearer.]
Baldachin=träger (ᶻ...) m ⓸ canopy-]
Bälde (ᴸᵛ) f ⓸ (o. *pl.*) in ~ = bald ⓶.
baldig, ⓶st (ᴸᵛ) *a.* (D 2) ⓺ speedy; auf ⓶es Wiedersehen! may we soon meet again!, (fr.) au revoir!; ich bitte um ⓶(ſt)e, ⓶ſt um Antwort please write at your earliest convenience, ⓼ an early reply (or answer) will oblige.
bald=möglichst (ᵇ...) *adv.* as soon as (ever) possible = ſo bald (ſ. bs) als möglich.
Baldowerer (ᶻᵛᵘᵛᵛ) m ⓸ one who tracks down (F who splits on) criminals, tracker, F split.
Baldrian ♀ (ᴸᵛᵛ) [mhd.=*lt. valeria'na* heilkräftige] *m* ⓵c. valerian (*Valeria'na*); echter ~ (*V. officina'lis*) great wild v., cut-heal, all-heal; griechischer ~ = Himmelsleiter; kleiner ~ (*V. dio'ica*) marsh v.; **~=extrakt** (ᶻ...) m ⓸ extract of v.

=öl n valerole; **=säure** f, *chm.*: ⚗ valer-(ian)ic acid ($C_5H_{10}O_2$); **=wurzel** f v. root.
bald=tunlichst (ᵇ...) *adv.* = ⓶möglichst.
Balduin (ᵛᵛ-) *npr./m.* ⓵b⓸⓺α. Baldwin.
Balearen ♀ (ᵛᵛᴸᵛ) [grch.Schleuderer] *npr./pl.* ⓸ die ~, auch Balearische Inseln f/pl. östlich v. Spanien: Balearic Islands pl.
Balg (⁰) [ahd.: bellows] m ⓶b. 1. (weiche Hülle): a) v. Erbsen 2c.: husk, pod, shell; von Gräsern: glume; *path.* cyst; b) (Tierfell) skin, hide, e-s Hasen 2c., auch: case; v. Schlangen: slough; v. lebenden Tieren, bsd. zur Bezeichnung der Hautfarbe: coat; Sprichw. stirbt der Fuchs, so gilt der Balg when the fox is dead his skin is sold; als Spiel: Jack's alight or alive. — 2. *pl.* auch **~en** ⓶ (Blasebalg) (pair of) bellows; die Bälge (ob. Balgen) e-r Orgel treten to work (or blow) the bellows of an organ. — 3. (ausgestopftes Tier) stuffed animal; *hunt.* stuffed decoy-bird; ~ e-r Puppe body of a doll; dicker ~ (Bauch) paunch. — 4. Schimpf-, bisw. auch Kosename: F oft *n*, *pl. a.* ⓶, meist *contp.*: (unartiges Kind) brat, imp, chit; (Knabe) urchin; (Weibsbild) wench, F baggage.
Balge (ᴸᵛ) [fr. *baille*] f ⓸ ⚙ (flache Bütte) low tub, zum Waschen: wash-tub; ↓ (Hälfte e-r Tonne) half-tub (= Deckwasch⓶).
balgen (ᴸᵛ) [Balg] ⓺ **I** v/a. 1. = abbalgen I. — **II** sich ⓶ v/refl. 2. (sich häuten) to shed (or cast) the skin or slough. — 3. (sich raufen) to scuffle, wrestle, fight, zum Scherz: to romp. — **III** ~ n ⓶ 4. skinning. — 5. (Rauferei) scuffle, wrestle, fight, tussle, scrimmage, zum Scherz: romp.
Balgen=gebläse ⚙ (ᵇ...) [Balg 2] *n* ⓸ blowing-action; **=gerüst** n einer Feldschmiede: bellows-frame; **=klappe** f valve of the bellows; **=kopf** m bellows-head; **=register** n stop of the bellows; **=treter** m bellows- (or organ-)blower; **=werk** n organ-bellows.
Balger (ᴸᵛ) m ⓸ scuffler, wrestler.
Balgerei (ᵛᵛᴸ) f ⓺ = balgen 5.
Bälge=treter (ᵇ...) m ⓸ = Balgentreter.
Balg=frucht ♀ (ᵇ...) f ⓸ caryopsis; **=geschwulst** f, *path.* encysted (or cystic) tumour; (sebaceous) cyst; (Kropf) wen; **=kapsel** f air-bag, ⚚ follicle.
Bälglein (ᴸᵛ) n ⓶ *dim.* v. Balg (Grasteich) glume; inneres ~ glumelle, glumella.
Balje (ᴸᵛ) 1. ↓ (Durchfahrt zwischen Sandbänken 2c.) passage between shallows, narrow channel. — 2. = Balge.
Balk (ᵇ...) = Balken=.
Balkan ♀ (ᴸ¹) [türk. Gebirge] *npr./m.* ⓵α. der ~, auch **=gebirge** (ᶻ...) *n* ⓸ Balkans, Balkan Mountains pl.; **=halbinsel** f Balkan Peninsula; **=länder**, **~=staaten** pl. Balkan States pl.
Bälkchen (ᴸᵛ) *n* ⓶ (*dim.* von Balken) little beam or joist or girder.
Balken (ᴸᵛ) [ahd.: balk] *m* ⓶ 1. ⚙ meist *arch.* beam; (Decken=)~ joist; (Trägerschwelle) girder; *bibl.* du sollst den ~ aus deinem eig(e)nen Auge ziehen thou shalt cast the beam out of thine own eye; Sprichw. das Wasser hat keine ~ there's no bridge across the sea, the sea is not planked over. — 2. am Pfluge: (plough-)beam; an der Wage: beam (of the scales); der Brückenwage:

[Balkenanker] — 142 — [Bammel]

lever. — 3. *her.* fess(e), chevron. — 4. *anat.* ~ des Gehirns: ♋ (corpus) callosum. — 5. ♪: ~ der Violine bassbar. — 6. (Scheunenboden) loft (of a barn). **Balken-anker**⊙(ˇ⌣...) *m* ㉒ brace. ⊙ =**band** *n* beam-tie; strap; =**brücke** *f* girder-bridge; =**decke** *f* timbered ceiling; =**fach** *n* interstice, case-bay, =**gerüst** ⚔ *n* skeleton-frame; =**holz** *n* square(d) timber; ♀**kantig** *a.* squared; =**keller** *m* raftered cellar; =**kopf** *m* beam-head, end of a joist; ↓ beam-end; =**lage** *f* position of joists; ↓ tier of beams, für den Stapellauf: bilgeways *pl.*; =**querschnitt** *m* scantling; =**streif** *m*, *her.* = Balken 3; =**stütze** *f* stay, prop; =**träger** *m* (breast-)summer; transom; =**wage** *f* steelyard; =**weite** *f* interjoist; =**werk** *n* timber framework of a building, &c. **Balkon** (vlq' ob. ˇ⌣ @c.) [fr.; it.; *Bʳdjch⁀ Balken] *m* 1. *arch.* (Altan) balcony; mit ~en versehen balconied. — 2. *thea.* (Galerie vor der 1. Logenreihe) dress-circle. **Balkon-fenster** (ˇ...) *n* @ *arch.* balcony-window; =**gärtnerei** *f* floriculture on balconies, weitS. window-gardening; =**säule** *f*, =**träger** *m* balcony-support; =**zimmer** *n* = Erkerzimmer. **Balk-weger** ↓ ⊙ (ˇˇˇ) *m* ㉒ clamp of the deck-beams. **Ball**¹ (ˇ) [ahd.: ball] *m* ①b. 1. zum Spielen: ball; (Schlagball) tennis-ball; ~ spielen to play ball, tennis; Kricket: den ~ gegen den Dreistab werfen to bowl; den ~ (mit der Keule) zurückschlagen to bat; mit aller Macht: to drive (or swipe) the ball. — 2. (Billardkugel) billiard-ball; den ~ ins Loch machen to pocket a ball; den ~ verfehlen to miss a ball; den ~ an die Bande spielen, stoßen lassen to put the ball close against the cushion, to cushion (the ball); gefleckter (Spiel-)~ spot(-ball); Anstoßen zweier Bälle durch den SpielB cannon. — 3. (andere runde Körper) *poet.* (Himmelskörper) globe (vgl. Erd-, Sonnen-2 und Reichsapfel, Schnee-, Zeit-2); ⊙ metall. (Luppe) ball, loop.

Ball² (ˇ) [fr., it.] *m* ⓪b. (Tanzfest) ball; dance; großer: dress-ball; im Kostüm: fancy-ball; auf dem ~ at the ball; auf den ~, auf viele Bälle gehen to go to a ball, to many dances. **Ballade** (vˇv) [prvz. Tanzlied] *f* ㊽ (erzählende Dichtung) ballad; ~**n-dichter** (ˇ...) *m* @ ballad-writer or -maker; ~**n-dichtung** *f* @ ballad literature; ~**n-schreiber** *m* = ~n-dichter. 　　[ball-costume.] **Ball**²**-anzug** (ˇ...) *m* ㉒ full dress;⌉ **Ballas-rubin** (ˇˇˇ) [pers., aus *Balaschan, St.] *m* ㉒ (blaßroter Rubin) balass-ruby. **Ballast** ↓ (ˇˇ) [ndd., *dän.] *m* ⓪b. ballast(ing); ~ einschießen (einnehmen) to take (or shoot) in ballast; ~ ausschießen (ausladen) to shoot (or discharge) ballast; den ~ über Bord werfen to cast the ballast over board; mit ~ ballasted; *fig.* überflüssiger ~ in Büchern x. : padding. **Ballast-ausschießer** ↓ (ˇ...) *m* ㉒ ballast-heaver or -lighter. 　　[ballast.] **ballasten** ↓ (ˇˇˇ) *v/a.* ㉙ to (load with)⌉ **Ballast-ewer** (ˇˇ...) *m* ㉒ =**leichter**; =**fracht** *f*, =**ladung** *f* dead-freight; =**l(e)ichter** *m*, =**schiff** *n*, =**schute** *f* ballast-lighter, -boat.

Ball²**-besucher** (ˇ...) *m* ㉒ p. invited to a ball, frequenter of balls. **Bällchen** (ˇv) *n* ㉓ 1. dim. v. Ball¹ u. ². — 2. dim. v. Ballen: ⚙ small bale. **Bällchen-atlas**⚙ (ˇ...) *m* ㉒ inferior satin. **Ballei** (vˇ) [fr.] *f* ㊻ (Ordensbezirk, bsd. des Malteser-ordens) commandery. 　　[chisel.] **Ball-eisen**⊙ (ˇ...) *n* ㉒ carving, paring-⌉ **Ballen**¹ (ˇv) [ahd.: *Ball¹] *m* ㉓ 1. =Ball¹. — 2. *anat.* (fleischiger Teil) ball (of the hand, the foot); ♋ thenar eminence, v. Tieren: sole. —3. *fenc.* (schützende Lederkugel) button (of a rapier or foil). — 4. ⚙ (verpackte Waren) bale, pack(et), parcel, bundle; *auch* Maßbestimmung: ~ Papier paper-bag of ten reams. — 5. ⊙ (Rundung am Fausthobel) handle (of the plane); ehm. *typ.* (Tupf-)~ ball, dabber. **ballen**² (ˇv) [mhd.] ⌐ *v/a.* 1. to form (or make up) into a ball or bale, into balls or bales; ♋ to conglomerate, to conglobate; die Hand zur Faust 2 to clench (or double) one's fist. — 2. Schnee 2 (auch schnee-2) to make (or throw) snowballs. — II *v/n.* (h.) und sich 2 *v/refl.* 3. to gather into a ball; der Schnee ballt the snow clings (or cakes) together (f. backen 5). **Ballen-binder**⚙ (ˇv...) *m* ㉒ packer; =**binder-lohn** *m* package; =**blume** *f* *arch.* des engl.-got. Stils 14. sae. ball-flower; =**degen** *m*, *fenc.* foil; =**eisen**⊙ *n* = Balleisen; =**gicht** *f*, *path.* gout in the thenar muscle, =**gut** ⚙ *n* bale-goods *pl.*; =**meißel** *m* = =eisen; =**schnur** *f* packing-thread or cord; =**ware** ⚙ *f* = =gut; ♀**weise** *adv.* in bales; =**zink** ⚙ *n* zinc in balls; =**zinn** *n* rolled tin, tin in rolls. 　　[pop-gun.] **Baller-büchse** (ˇˇ...) *f* ㉒ (Spielzeug)⌉ **Ballerina**, ...ne (vvˇv) [it.] *f* ㊾, ⚙ *thea.* (Kunsttänzerin) ballet-dancer, ballerina. **ballern, bällern** F (ˇv) *v/n.* (h.) ㉙*a.* to make a noise; mit e-r Ballerbüchse: to shoot with a pop-gun. **Ballett** (vˇ) [fr.; *Ball²] *n* ⓪b. *thea.* (Kunsttänzer Tanz) ballet. **Balletteuse** (vvˇv) [++ fr.] *f* ㊽ *thea.* (Tanzkünstlerin) ballerina. **Ballett-kunst** (vˇ...) *f* ㉒ ballet-dancing, ♋ chore(o)graphy; =**meister** *m* ballet-master; =**schülerin** *f* ballet-girl, figurante; =**tänzer(in** *f*) *m* ballet- (or opera-)dancer, *f auch:* ballerina. **Ball**²**-fest** (ˇˇ) *n* ㉒ ball in connexion with a fête; ♀**förmig** *a.* ㊻ spherical, globular; =**gast** *m* = =besucher; =**haus** *n* ehm. tennis-court; =**holz** *n* Kricket: bat, vgl. =netz. **ballhornisieren** (ˇvvvˇ) [Johann Balhorn, Buchdrucker in Lübeck, 1530—1603] *v/a.* to spoil things by trying to mend them. **ballig** ⊙ (ˇv) [Ball¹] *a.* ㊻ (schwach gewölbt) slightly convex; 2 drehen to turn spherically or into (the shape of) a ball. **Balliste** ⚔ (vˇv) [grch.] *f* ㊽ Alt. : (Wurfmaschine) ballista. 　　[of projectiles.] **Ballistik** ⚔ (vˇv) *f* ㊻ ballistics, science⌉ **ballistisch** ⚔ (vˇv) *a.* ㊻ ballistic. **Ball**¹**-kelle** (ˇˇ...) *f* ㉒ =**holz**; ²**kleid** *n* ball-dress; =**königin** *f* belle of the ball; =**kugel** *f* ball; ¹**netz** *n* Tennis: racket; (Federball) battledore. 　　[room.] **Ballokal** [Ball²-lokal] *n* ball-, dancing-⌉

Ballon (vlq') [fr.; *Ball¹] *m* ㊿ 1. balloon (a. *chm.* = Rezipie'nt); (Fußball) football. — 2. ⚙ (große Flasche für Säuren) carboy. — 3. (Luftballon) balloon. **Ballon-fahrt** (ˇ...) *f* ㉒ = Luftschiffahrt; =**post** *f* balloon-post; =**train** *n* ㊿ b.-train. **Ballot** (bä-lo') [fr.] *n* ㊿ (kleiner Ballen von 30-60 kg) ballot; ~ **kugel** *f* (ballot-)ball. **Ballotage** (vvˇq) [fr.] *f* ㊽ (voting by) ballot, balloting (= Kugelung). **ballotieren** (vvˇv) [fr.] ⌐ I *v/n.* (h.) u. *v/a.* ㊽ to (vote by) ballot; e-n hinaus 2 to blackball a p.; 2de *pl.* ㊼ voters *pl.* (by ballot). — II ~ *n* ㉓ = Ballotage. **Ball**²**-saal** (ˇˇ...) *m* ㉒ = Ballsaal; =**schläger(in** *f)* *m* = ¹**spieler(in);** ¹**schlegel** *m:* a) = =**holz;** b) = =**netz;** ²**schuhe** *m/pl.* für Herren: pumps *pl.*, für Damen: dancing-shoes *pl.*; ¹**spiel** *n* playing ball; (playing) tennis; ¹**spieler(in** *f)* *m* p. playing ball; tennis-player; Kricket: bowler; batsman; ¹**stäbe** *m/pl.* Kricket: wickets *pl.*; ²**toilette** *f* = =anzug. **Balme** (ˇv) [prvz.: fr. baume] *f* ㊽ (überhängende Felswand) rocky ledge or shelf. **Balneologie** ♋ (vvvˇv) [grch.] *f* ㊽ (Bädertunde) ♋ balneology. **Balneotherapie** ♋ (vvvvˇv) *f* ㊽ (Badeheilkunst) ♋ balneotherapeutics. **Balsam** (ˇv) [ahd., *hebr.] *m* @c. balsam (a. ♀), balm (a. *fig.*); ~ erzeugend, hervorbringend, tragend: ♋ balsamiferous; *med.* (Salbe) salve, ointment. **Balsam-apfel** ♀ (ˇ...) *m* ㉒ balsam-apple (*Momo'rdica Balsami'na*); =**baum** ♀ *m* bal(sa)m-tree; =**büchse** *f* balm-box; =**duft** *m* balsam(ic) scent or fragrance; =**feige** *f* balsam-fig (*Clu'sia ro'sea*); =**fichte** ♀ *f* balsam-fir, balm of Gilead (*A'bies* u. *Pinus balsa'mea*); =**geruch, =hauch** *m* = =duft; =**holz** ♀ *n* xylobalsamum (*A'myris opoba'lsamum*). 　　[to perfume.] **balsamieren** (vvˇv) *v/a.* ㊽ to embalm;⌉ **balsamig** (ˇvv) *a.* ㊻ = balsamisch. **Balsamine** ♀ (vˇv) *f* ㊽ balsam(ine) (*Impa'tiens Balsami'na*); ~**n-samen** (ˇ...) *m* ㊺ seeds *pl.* of balsam. **balsamisch** (vˇv) *a.* ㊻ balsamic; balmy; (erquickend) soothing, refreshing. **Balsam-kraut** ♀ (ˇ...) *n* ㉒: a) balsam-herb (*Dianthe'ra re'pens*); = Bisamkraut; =**pappel** *f* tacamahac (*Po'pulus balsami'fera*); 2**schwitzend** *a.* ㊻ balsam-sweating; =**staude** ♀ *f* balsam-shrub; =**strauch** *m* bdellium (shrub) (*Commi'phora* ob. *Balsamode'ndron*); =**tanne** *f* = =fichte. **baltisch** ♀ (ˇv) *a.* ㊻ Baltic; ~es Meer (mehr gebräuchlich: Ostsee) Baltic (Sea). **Baluster** (vˇv) [fr.] *m* ㊺ *arch.* baluster. **Balustrade** (-vˇv) [fr., it.] *f* ㊽ *arch.* (Brustlehne, Geländer) balustrade; parapet. **Balz** (ˇ) [it.] *f* ㊽ ⓪a. *hunt.* (Paarung größerer Waldvögel) coupling, pairing. **balzen** (ˇv) *v/n.* (h.) ㊿ to pair, to mate. **Balz-zeit** (ˇˇ...) *f* ㉒ pairing season of birds. **Bambus** ♀ (ˇv) [malai.] *m*, *inv.*, ⓪ bamboo; ~**arten** (ˇ...) *f/pl.* ㉒: ♋ bambuseæ *pl.*; 2**artig** ♀ *a.* ㊻: ♋ bambusaceous; =**rohr** *n* bamboo (*Bambu'sa arundina'cea*); japanisches: wanghee; =**stock** *m* bamboo- (or Indian) cane; =**zucker** *m* tabasheer. **bam** (ˇ) *int.* (Glockengeläute nachahmend) bim, 2, bum dingdong (bell). 　　[Angst.] **Bammel**¹ berl. (ˇv) *m* ㉒ (o. *pl.*) =⌉

Signs (see page XVII): F familiar; P vulgar; ⟋ flash; ⟍ rare; † obsolete (died); * new word (born); ++ incorrect; ♪ music;

[**Bammel**] **Bammel**² F (⌣⌣) f ⑱, **~age** F (⌣⌣⌣) f ⑱, **~ei** F (⌣⌣) f ⑱ tassel; dangling fringe, &c.; (Dhr²) pendant, drop.
bammeln F (⌣⌣) v/n. (h.) ⑱a. to dangle.
Bams (⌣) m ⑱a. saddle-cushion.
bamsen (⌣⌣) [**Bams**] v/a. ⑳ Felle ꝛc.: to beat. [(Statthalter) ban.]
Ban (⌣) [slaw.; *perj. Herr] m ⑪c.
banal (⌣⌣) [fr.; *dtsch. Baun] a. ⑯ (alltäglich) hackneyed, trite, humdrum; (bedeutungslos) trivial, trifling.
Bananas-feige ♀ (⌣⌣⌣) f ⑱ banana.
Banane ♀ (⌣⌣) [brasil., afrik.?] f ⑱: a) Frucht: banana; b) Baum = **~n-baum**.
bananen-artig ♀ (⌣⌣⌣⌣)a. ⑯ banana-like, ⚙ scitamineous, musaceous; **=baum** ♀ m ⑫ banana(-tree) (*Musa sapie'ntum*); **⚟freffend** a. ⚙ bananivorous; **=fresser** m, orn. banana- (or plantain-)eater (*Muso'phaga*); **=pisang** ♀ m = **=baum**.
Banat (⌣⌣) [Ban] m ⑪c. (ungarische Mark oder Grenzprovinz) banate.
Banause (⌣⌣) [grch.] m ㊹ (gemeiner Mensch) p. of low breeding, F (low) cad; (Lohnarbeiter) (common) workman.
Banausie (⌣⌣⌣) f ⑱ shoppiness.
banausisch (⌣⌣⌣) [grch.] a. ⑯ (gemein) ignoble, low; (handwerksmäßig) shoppy.
band¹ (⌣) impf. von binden.
Band² (⌣) [ahd.: band] I m ⓪b. 1. (Einband) binding; cover. — 2. (eingebundenes Buch) volume; tome. — II n ⓪b. 3. (nordd. a. m): a) (Bindfaden, Schnur) thread; string, cord; zum Aktenschnüren ꝛc.: tape, bei der engl. Regierung: red tape; b) (Gewebe zum Binden, bsd. zum Putz) ribbon; (Binde-) Bändchen an Damenhüten: (bonnet-)string; übersponnenes **~** guipure lace, gimp; c) Trictrad: point of a backgammon board. — 4. phys. des Spektrums: band. — 5. (aus Stroh oder Weiden geflochtenes **~**) band, strap. — 6. anat. (fehniges) **~**: ligament, tendon; Lehre von den Bändern: ⚙ (syn)desmology. — 7. (Reifen) eisernes **~** iron band; als Schmuck: ring, circlet; bsd. am Arm: bracelet; F fig. außer Rand und **~** = out of (all) bounds, beyond control; aus Rand u. **~** geraten to get out of hand. — 8. ⊕ **~** um Fässer, Balken ꝛc.: hoop; (Radreifen) tire, tyre; arch. (Borte) moulding, fillet; Schlofferei ꝛc.: eine Krampe bildendes **~** cramp (-iron); mech. Bänder pl. des Wattschen Parallelogramms: links pl.; typ. **~** der Schnellpresse tape. — 9. surg. (Verband) bandage; ligature. — III n ⓪b. 10. (Bindendes, Hemmendes) bond, trammel; bsd. **~e** pl. (Fesseln) fetters, irons pl.; in Ketten und **~en** in chains; in **~e** schlagen ob. werfen to load with irons, to chain up. — 11. (geistig Verknüpfendes) bond, tie; **~** der Ehe nuptial (or matrimonial) knot. — **IV** **~** ⓪b. 12. (Maß: 30 Fische) thirty fishes.
Band-achat (⌣⌣⌣) m ⑫ min. ribbon-agate.
Bandage (⌣⌣⌣) [fr.; *dtsch. Baud] f ⑱ 1. bsd. surg. (Verbandzeug) bandage. — 2. auch ⊕ (Radreifen) tire, tyre.
Bandagen-glühofen ⊕ (⌣⌣⌣⌣) m ⊕ tire-heating furnace; **=macher** m, surg. bandage- (or truss-) maker; ⊕ tire-maker; **=walzwerk** ⊕ n tire-rolling mill.

bandagieren (⌣⌣⌣⌣) [fr.] v/a. ⑱ bsd. surg. to apply bandages; to bandage.
Bandagist (⌣⌣⌣) [fr.] m ⑫ 1. surg. = Bandagenmacher. — 2. person who (applies) bandages, bandager.
band-ähnlich (⌣⌣⌣) a. ⑯, **=artig** a.: a) ribbon-like or -shaped; b) zo., ich. streaked, ⚙ tænioid; anat. ligamentous; **=alge** ♀ f ⑫ tangle (*Lamina'ria*).
Bandanen-druck ⊕ (⌣⌣⌣⌣) m ⑫ Zeugweberei: bandanna.
Band-assel (⌣⌣⌣) f ⑫ zo. streaked centipede; **=aufnäher** m an der Nähmaschine: ribbon-sewer; **=balken** ⊕ m, carp. tie-piece; brace; **=beinfügung** f, anat.: ⚙ synneurosis, syndesmosis; **=bohrer** m, carp. barwimble; broad awl.
Bändchen (⌣⌣) n ⑭ dim. v. Band I u. II small ribbon or bow. [**~** loose cover.]
Band-deckel (⌣⌣⌣) m ⑫ book cover; loser]
Bande (⌣⌣) [fr.; *dtsch. Band] f ⑱ 1. (Rand) border; (Schranke) barrier; Billard: cushion; Ball dicht an der **~** close ball, **~** bekommen, an die **~** legen to cushion (a ball). — 2. a) (Truppe) troop, body, crew; von Arbeitern ꝛc.: gang; meist b.s. **~** von Dieben set (or pack) of thieves; **~** von Räubern band of highwaymen or brigands; b) (Musik²) [it.] **~** von Blechmusikanten ꝛc. (German)]
bände (⌣⌣) subj.impf.v.binden. [band.]
Band-einfasser ⊕ (⌣⌣⌣) m ⑫ Nähmaschine: ribbon-binder; **=einfassung** f lacing; **=eisen** ⊕ n band- (or strap-)iron; min. (nickelreiches Meteoreisen) ⚙ tænite.
Bandelier × (⌣⌣⌣) [fr.bandoulière; *dtsch. Band] n ⑪c. bandoleer, shoulder-belt.
Banden-chef (⌣⌣⌣) m ⑫, **=führer** m chief (or leader) of a band or gang.
Bänder-besatz (⌣⌣⌣) [Band²³] m ⑫ Kleid ꝛc.: trimming with ribbons or bows.
bände-reich (⌣⌣⌣) [Band² 2] a. ⑯ rich in volumes, in many volumes; voluminous. [⚙ (syn)desmology.]
Bänder-lehre (⌣⌣⌣) [Band²6] f ⑫ anat.:]
bändern (⌣⌣) ⊕ v/a. ⑱a. to form into ribbons or stripes; (streifig machen) to stripe, to streak.
bände-weise (⌣⌣⌣) [Band²2] adv. by volumes; **=zahl** f ⑫ number of volumes.
Band-fabrik (⌣⌣⌣) f ⑫ ribbon-factory; **=farn** ♂ m: ⚙ vittaria; **=fisch** m, ichth. ribbon-fish; auch: ⚙ cepola; **=flechte** ♀ f (*Eve'rnia furfura'cea*) evernia; **=förmig** a. ⑯: a) **=artig** b) ♀ ligulate, ligulated; auch ♀ ⚙ linear; **=gras** n, ♀ a. painted lady-grass (*Pha'laris picta*); **=hafen** ⊕ m a) (Reißzieher) hoop-cramp; b) (Haken, um eine Tür einzuhängen) hinge-hasp; **=handel** ⊕ m ribbon-trade; **=handlung** f; **=händler** ⊕ m haberdasher; **=holz** n für Fässer: hoop-wood.
bandieren ⊕ (⌣⌣⌣) v/a. ⑱ = bändern.
bandig P nordd. (⌣⌣) I a. ⑯ (mächtig, tüchtig) powerful, capable; ein **~er** Kerl, a smart chap. — II adv. (außerordentlich) extremely. [work in two volumes.]
…bändig (…⌣⌣) a. ⑯: zwei=bes Werk]
bändigen (⌣⌣⌣) v/a. ⑱ wilde Tiere, Leidenschaften ꝛc.: to tame, subdue, master; Pferde: to break in; bsd. fig. to bridle, restrain, check.
Bändiger (⌣⌣⌣) m ⑫, **~in** f ㊵ tamer, subduer, conqueror; breaker-in.

[**bangen**]
Bändigung (⌣⌣⌣) f ㊻ taming (a lion, &c.), breaking in (a horse).
Bandit [it.; *dtsch. Baun] m ⑫ (Straßenräuber) bandit (pl. bandits, banditti), brigand; bravo.
Banditen-führer (⌣⌣⌣⌣) m ⑫ chief (or captain, leader) of bandits; **=haft** (⌣⌣⌣) a. ⑯ bandit-like; **=mord** m (für Sold verübter Mord) murder by a hired assassin; **=wesen** n brigandage, brigandism; highway robbery.
Band-jaspis (⌣⌣⌣) m ⑫ ribbon-jasper; **=kram** ♣ m = **=handel, =laden; =krämer** ♣ m = **=händler; =laden** m ribbon-shop.
Bändlein (⌣⌣) n ㉓ = Bändchen.
Band-macher(in (⌣⌣⌣) m ⑫ ribbon-maker; **=marmor** m streaked marble; **=maschine** ⊕ f drawing-frame; **=maß** n tape-measure; **=messer** ⊕ n Böttcherei: hoop(ing)-knife; **=mühle** f ribbon-mill; **=nadel** f tape-needle; **=nagel** m, carp. clamp- (or clout-) nail; **=natter** f, zo. ribbon-snake.
band-, niet- und nagelfest (⌣⌣⌣⌣⌣) a. ⑯ riveted to the spot. [line (s. Teil I).]
Bandolin ⊕ (⌣⌣⌣) [fr.] n ⑪c. bando-]
Band-reif (⌣⌣⌣) m ⑫ Böttcherei: hoop; **=rolle** f, typ. tape-pulley, flying drum; **=rose(tte)** f rose-knot, rosette; **=säge** ⊕ f: a) endless (or band-, ribbon-, strap-) saw; b) (Drehbank) bench-saw; **=scheibe** f: ⚙ meniscus; **=schleife** f ribbon tied in a bow or a knot, (silk) bow; favour; **=stein** m, arch. eines Bogens springer, springing-stone; **=streif(en)** m, her. (Schrägbalken) cot(t)ise, bend; **=streifig** a. Naturgesch.: streaked, banded; **=stuhl** ⊕ m ribbon-loom; **=träger** m, tape-carrier; **=tresse** f livery-lace; **=vereinigungsmaschine** ⊕ f Spinnerei: lapping-machine; **=waren** ♣ f/pl. small wares, ribbons pl.; **=weber** ⊕ m ribbon-weaver; **=weberei** f ribbon-manufacture; **=weide** ♀ f = Korbweide; **=wirkerei** ⊕ f = **=weberei; =wurm** m, zo. tapeworm, ⚙ tænia, cestoid; **=zünder** × m, artill. tape-fuse.
bang (⌣) [nbd.: eng(e)] a. ⑯ (D3,7) attributives a. (ängstlich) anxious, alarmed, frightened; ein **~es** Mädchen a timid or nervous girl; (ängstigend) disquieting, alarming; in **~er** Erwartung in anxious suspense; in banger Sorge um solicitous about. [haus]bungalow.]
Bangalo (⌣⌣) [ind.bangla] n ⑬ (Sommer-]
bange¹ (⌣⌣) präditatives a. und adv. ich bin **~** oder mir ist (angst und) **~** um … I am most anxious about …; mir ist **~** davor I dread it; **~** machen gilt nicht!, you (or that) won't frighten me!, don't try to bully (or scare) us!; ihm ist sehr **~** für (oder um) sein Leben oder daß er stirbt he is in great apprehension (or fear) for his life; e-m (⇘ e-n) e-m, vor et. **~** m. to make a p. afraid of …; nur nicht **~!** never fear!
Bange² F (⌣⌣) f ⑱ (o. pl.) = Angst I.; feine **~** haben to be without fear.
bangen (⌣⌣) ⊕ I v/n. (h.), v/impers. und sich **~** v/refl. 1. ich bange (mich), es bangt mich für mein Leben I am afraid of death, I tremble for my life; bangen (G., Egmont) langen und **~** in schwebender Pein, to fret and sorrow

⚙ scientific; ♀ botanical; ♁ geography; ⊕ machinery; ⚒ mining; × military; ⚓ marine; ♣ commercial; ✉ postal; 🚂 railway;

[Bangert]

in anguishing grief. — 2. nach et. ⌇ (sich sehnen) to long (or yearn) for a th. — **II** v/a. 3. (bange m.) to make uneasy or afraid. — **III** ~ n ⊕ 4. fear; disquietude; anxiety; stärker: anguish.
Bangert⌇(⌣) [Baumgarten] m ⊕ d. orchard.
Bangigkeit (⌣) f ⊕ = bangen III; Angst und ⌇ dread and dismay.
bänglich (⌣) a. ⊕ rather anxious, somewhat uneasy or nervous.
Baniane ♀ (-(⌣)⌣) [sft.] f ⊕, ~n=feigen= baum ("…) m ⊕ banyan, banian-tree (Ficus benjami'na, F. i'ndica).
Banjane (⌣⌣) [ind.] m ⊕ (Hindukaste der Kaufleute in Ost-J.) banian. [deck.⌋
Banjer ↓ (⌣) m ⊕ (zwischendeck) half-
Bank[1] (⌣) [ahd.: bank] f ⊕ **1.** (Sitz) (wooden, stone, &c.) bench; in der Schule: form; Kirche: pew; im Garten, Boot 2c.: seat, bench; (Rasensitz) bank (of grass); thea. vor leeren Bänken spielen to play to empty benches; auf der ersten ~ in the front row. — 2. parl.: ~ der Minister Treasury Bench; ~ der Oppositionsführer Front Opposition Bench. — 3. fig. et. **auf die lange ~ schieben** (aufschieben) to put off (or to delay) a th.; F **durch die** ~ (ohne Ausnahme) without exception, one with another, indiscriminately; **hinter** (oder **über**) die ~ werfen (beiseite- legen) to throw aside. — 4. (Sand-)~ (sand-)bank; weits. shelf; shoal, shallow. — 5. ⊕ (Werktisch) work- (or joiner's) bench; (Drehbank) lathe. — 6. (Ladentisch) counter, stall. — 7. ⚔ artill. (Geschützbank) barbette.
Bank[2] (⌣) [it., = dtsch.] ⊕ **1.** ⚜ bank, banking establishment; Geld in e-r ~ niederlegen to put money into a bank; in welcher Bank hat er sein Geld stehen? where does he bank?, who is his banker?; in e-r ~ zahlbar bankable, payable at a bank. — 2. Kartensp.: bank, gaming-table; die ~ halten to keep bank; die ~ sprengen to break the bank.
Bank[2]=**abschluß** ⚜ (⌣…) m ⊕ balance- sheet of a bank; =**agio** n bank-agio; =**aktie** f, =**anteil** m bank-share; =**an-** teilseigner m shareholder in a (joint- stock) bank; =**anweisung** ⚜ f banker's note, cheque; =[1]**arbeit** ⚜ f sedentary work; =[2]**ausweis** ⚜ m = abschluß; =**beamte(r)** m bank-official, clerk of a bank; =[1]**bein** ⊕ n foot of a bench; =[2]**bericht** ⚜ m return of a bank; =[1]**bohrer** ⊕ m auger; =[2]**bruch** ⚜ m, ⌇**brüchig** a. ⊕ = bankerott II, I.
Bänkchen (⌣) n ⊕ dim. von Bank[1] small (or little) bench.
Bank[2]=**direktor** ⚜ (⌣…) m ⊕ director (or manager) of a bank; =**diskont(o)** m a) banker's discount; b) (Zinsfuß der Banken) bank-rate; =[1]**durchschlag** ⊕ m Schlosserei; =[1]**eisen** ⊕ n: a) (Hols- krampe) cramp-iron, zur Befestigung eines Gegenstandes in der Wand: clamp for fixing a shelf, &c. to the wall; b) (Bank-hafen, =zwinge, =schraube) bench- hook or -screw, bench-cheek.
Bänkel=sänger (⌣…) m ⊕ street-singer; negro-minstrel; wretched rhymester.
bank(e)rott (⌣(⌣)⌣) [it.] **I** a. ⊕ bank- rupt, insolvent, F broken, smashed

up, gone to smash; sich für ⌇ erklären to declare o.s. (a) bankrupt, gerichtlich: to file a petition in bankruptcy, Lo. Börse: (durch Hammerschlag) ⌇ erklärt werden to be hammered. — **II** ~ m ⊕b. bankruptcy, insolvency, failure, F crash, smash; ~ m. to become (a) bank- rupt, to fail (in business), F to shut up shop. [claration of bankruptcy.⌋
Bank(e)rott=erklärung (⌣…) f ⊕ de-
Bank(e)rotteur (⌣(⌣)⌣'r) m ⊕d. = Bank(e)rottierer.
bank(e)rottieren (⌣(⌣)⌣⌣) [it.] v/n. (h.) ⊕ to become insolvent; F to go to smash.
Bank(e)rottierer (⌣(⌣)⌣⌣) m ⊕ [it.] bankrupt, defaulter; insolvent firm; broken merchant, F lame duck.
Bankert (⌣) [mhd.; *Bank] m ⊕d. natural or illegitimate child; bastard.
Bankett (⌣) n ⊕b. [it.; *dtsch. Bank] (Festmahl) banquet, feast.
Bankette (⌣) ⊕ [fr.] f ⊕ (erhöhter Fuß- steig) (raised) footway, ⚔ banquette; (Böschung) bank, slope; ⚒ side-pace.
bankettieren (⌣⌣⌣) [Bankett] v/n. (h.) ⊕ (ein Festmahl halten) to (give a) banquet.
Bank[2]=**gebäude** ⚜ (⌣…) n ⊕ bank; =**geld** ⚜ n bank-money; =**geschäft** n banking business; =**geschäfte** n/pl. banking (transactions &c.); =**gebung** (=**gebung** f) n statute(s pl.) regulat- ing the business of a bank; =[1]**haken** ⊕ m = eisen b; =[2]**halter** m Kartenspiel: banker, keeper of the bank; (Spiel- gehilfe) croupier; =**haus** ⚜ n banking firm or house or establishment; =**herr** m = halter; =[1]**hobel** ⊕ m, carp., &c. (great) bench-plane; jointer; =**horn** ⊕ n Schlosserei: two-beaked anvil.
Bankier (⌣⌣'e') [fr.; *Bank[2]] m ⊕ **1.** ⚜ banker; (Geldwechsler) money-changer; (großer Finanzmann) financier. — 2. Karten- spiel: banker (= Bankhalter).
Bankier=geschäft (⌣…) n ⊕, =**haus** n ⊕ banking firm or house; =**provision** f banker's commission or profit.
...=bänkig (…"⌣) a. ⊕: schmal⌇, zehn⌇ with narrow, with ten benches.
Bankiva=huhn (⌣⌣⌣⌣⌣) n ⊕ orn. ban- tam fowl, bantain (Gallus banki'va).
Bank[2]=**konto** ⚜ (⌣…) n ⊕ bank(ing) account; =[1]**lehne** f back of a bench; =[2]**mark** f = Banko 2; ⌇**mäßig** ⚜ a. ⊕ cus- tomary in banks; Wertpapiere: bankable, negotiable; =[1]**meißel** ⊕ m Schlossf.: cold (or hewing) chisel; =**messer** n Schlächterei: chopper; cleaver; =**note** ⚜ f bank- note; =**noten=umlauf** m paper currency.
Banko ⚜ (⌣-) [it.] n ⊕ (o. pl.) **1.** = Bank- geld. — 2. (Hamburger Rechnungsmünze) mark banco, banco mark; ~=**a'gio** n bank-agio. [boy (of a form).⌋
Bank[1]=**primus** (⌣…) m ⊕ Schul=sl. first⌋
bankrott (⌣) 2c. s. bank(e)rott.
Bank[2]=**satz** ⚜ (⌣…) ⊕ m ⊕ bank-rate; =[1]**schlächter** m stall-butcher; =**schraube** ⊕ f = eisen b; =[2]**valuta** ⚜ f = geld; =[1]**wagen** ⊕ m break, (fr.) char à banc; =[2]**währung** ⚜ f = geld; =**wechsel** ⚜ m von e-r Bank auf die andre gezogen: bank- bill; =**wesen** ⚜ n banking; =**zettel=buch** n cheque-book; =[1]**zwinge** ⊕ f = eisen b.
Bann (⌣) [ahd.: ban] m ⊕b. **1.** (Zwang) constraint; (Zauber) spell; unter dem

[bar]

~ von et. oder einem stehen to be under the spell (or influence) of…, stärker: to be spell-bound (or fascinated) by… — 2. bsd. ehm.: **a)** Amtsbezirk; **b)** Amtsgewalt; **c)** die Untergebenen; **d)** Aufgebot, Verbot; **e)** Strafe der Acht, meist: ban; mit dem ~e belegen, in den ~ tun to put under the ban; to banish, to outlaw. — 3. (Kirchenbann) anathema; in Bezug auf abgesprochene Rechte: excommunication; in den ~ tun to anathematize; to ex- communicate; to (lay under an) in- terdict. — 4. gesellschaftlich oder geschäft- lich in den ~ tun to boycott, to taboo, to send to Coventry; weits. to snub.
Bann=brief (⌣…) m ⊕ = bulle; =**bruch** m breach (or infraction) of the ban; =**bulle** f bull of excommunication.
bannen (⌣) [Bann] v/a. ⊕ **1.** (fesseln) to captivate, (bezaubern) to enchant; to fas- cinate. — 2. **a)** (mit Gewalt festpflanzen) to transfix, Geister: to lay; e-n in e-n Kreis ⌇ to detain a p. in a magic circle; auf den Stuhl, ins Haus ge- bannt pinned down to one's chair, confined to the house; **b)** Geister ⌇ (heraufbeschwören) to conjure (or raise) … — 3. (austreiben) to cast out or to exorcize (evil spirits); to expel; eccl. to excommunicate.
Banner[1] (⌣) [bannen] m ⊕ conjurer.
Banner[2] (⌣) [mhd.; fr. bannière; *dtsch Band] n ⊕ (Heerfahne) ehm., jetzt fig. u. poet. banner; ⚔ 2c. jetzt: flag, standard, ~=**herr** (⌣…) m ⊕ (knight-)banneret; =**träger** m standard-bearer, ⚔ ensign.
Bann=fluch (⌣…) m ⊕ = Bann 3; =**friede** m ⊕ enclosure, fence; =**herr** m lord of the manor, justiciary; =**leute** pl. vassals pl.; =**meile** f boundary (or precincts pl.) of a town; =**strahl** m Cath. eccl. sentence of excommunication; den ~ schleudern to fulminate (an anathema). [agr. (bay of a) barn.⌋
Banse (⌣) [ndb.] f ⊕, ~**(n**[1]) m ⊕ (⌇)⌋
bansen[2] (⌣) v/a. ⊕ (Garben einschichten) to pile up the sheaves in the barn.
Bantam ♀ (⌣) npr/n. ⊕ α. (St. auf Java) Bantam; ~=**huhn** (⌣⌣…) n ⊕ orn. bantam (= Bankivahuhn).
Banting=kur ⚕ (⌣⌣⌣) [vom engl. Kaufmann Banting 1863 zuerst an sich angewandte Kur des engl. Arztes Harvey] f ⊕ eine ~ (gegen Beleibtheit) durchmachen to go through (or to undergo) a course of banting.
Banus (⌣) [slaw.] m, inv. = Ban; ~**würde** (⌣…) f ⊕ = Banat. [brotbaum.⌋
Baobab ♀ (-⌣⌣) [äthiopisch] m ⊕ = Affen-⌋
Baptismus (⌣⌣⌣) [lt., *grch.] m ⊕ (Taufe v. Erwachsenen) (adult) baptism.
Baptist (⌣⌣) [grch.] **I** npr/m. ⊕⊕⊕⊕⊕ (☧) Baptist. — **II** ~ m ⊕, ~**in** f ⊕ eccl. (Taufgenosse; in England: Art Dissenter) Baptist. [community or congregation.⌋
Baptisten=gemeinde (⌣…) f ⊕ Baptist⌋
Baptisterium (⌣⌣⌣⌣⌣) [lt., *grch.] n ⊕ eccl. chapel (or part of a church set aside) for baptism.
baptistisch (⌣…) a. ⊕ Baptist(ic).
bar[1] (⌣) [ahd.: bare] **1.** bare, destitute, (nackt) naked; mit ⌇em Haupte bare- headed. — 2. (offen baliegend) pure, unmixed, ⌇e Erdichtung mere fiction, ⌇er Unsinn sheer nonsense. — 3. (blank

aufgezählt) 2(es) Geld ready cash or money; 2 bezahlen to pay in cash, F to pay cash down; für, gegen 2(es Geld) for cash; tausend Mark in 2 ... in cash; 2e Auslage money out of pocket, disbursement; 2er Ertrag net proceeds pl.; 2e Zahlung cash (or ready-money) payment; Sprichw. 2 Geld lacht, etwa: money makes the mare go; fig. et. für 2(e Münze), für 2en Ernst nehmen to believe firmly in a th., F to take a th. for gospel-truth, to swallow a th. — 4. (ledig, los) mit gen. oder mit von, bisw. an: destitute (or devoid) of; alles menschlichen Gefühls 2 dead to all human sentiment.

Bar² ⚘ (⌣́) [amer.] f ⑤⑥ (Ausschank, Stehbierhalle) (American) bar.

...bar (...-́) [ahd.: lt. -fer; grch. -phŏros] a. ⑥⑥ i. Zssgn. fruchtbar 2c.

Bär¹ (⌣́) [ahd.: bear] m ㊷ 1. zo. (male) bear; weiblicher ~ f. ~in, a. female bear; brauner ~ brown bear (Ursus arctos); schwarzer ~ (U. america'nus); (australischer) grauer ~ grizzly bear (Phascola'rctos cine'reus); junger ~ bear-whelp, bear's cub; fig. ungeleckter 2 unlicked cub. — 2. ast. (Sternbild) der Große ~ the Great(er) Bear, Charles'(s) Wain; der Kleine ~ the Lesser Bear. — 3. fig. j. abbinden 5; anbinden 2; aufbinden 3; Fell 2. — 4. ent. = Bären-raupe, -spinner.

Bär² (⌣́) [ahd.: boar] m ㊷ = Eber.

Bär³ ⊙ (⌣́) (Rammklotz) m ㊷ ram(mer); ⚒ (Hammer-2) hammer-block.

Baracke (⌣⌣́) [fr., *span.] f ㊽ barrack, (bsd. ⚔) hut; fig. alte ~ (tumbled-down) hovel; ~n-lager ⚔ ('..) n ⑫ hut-camp; ~n-system n, med. barrack-system (for sanitary encampment).

Baranke (-⌣́) [poln.] f ㊽, ~n-fell (''...) n ⑫ Astrakhan fur or lambskin; ⚔ (Pelzverbrämung der Husarendolmans) fur trimming of a hussar dolman.

Bar-artikel ⊙ (''...) m ⑫ ready-money article. [barter.]

Baratt (⌣́) [it.] m ⓑ. (Warentausch)]

Baratterie ⚓ (⌣⌣⌣́) ⊙ (Schädigung des Reeders od. Frachteigentümers durch die Schiffsmannschaft) loss inflicted on the ship-owner (or shipper of goods) by the crew, called: barratry.

Baratt-handel (⌣⌣́) m ⑫ = Baratt. **barattieren** (⌣⌣⌣́) [it.] v/n. (h.) ⑬ (Waren austauschen) to barter.

Bar-auslage (''...) f ⑫ actual expense or outlay, money out of pocket.

Barbar (⌣́) [grch.] m ㊲e., ~in f ⓰ 1. grch. Alt. (Nichtgrieche) barbarian. — 2. fig. (roher, grausamer Mensch) barbarian, savage. [⚘ Barb, Babby.]

Barbara (⌣⌣⌣) npr/f. ⑤⑥ α. Barbara.

Barbarei¹ (⌣⌣⌣́) f ㊽ von Ungebildeten: barbarousness, barbarism; von Blutdürstigen: savageness; den Künsten ꝛc. gegenüber: vandalism. [† = Berberei.]

Barbarei² ⊙ (⌣⌣⌣́) npr/f. inv. Barbary,]

Barbaren-weise (⌣⌣⌣⌣́) f ⑫ (u. 2 adv.) (after the) manner of barbarians.

Barbaresken-staaten ⊙ (⌣⌣⌣⌣⌣́) m/pl. ⑫ die ~ the Barbary States pl.

barbarisch (⌣⌣́) a. ⑥⑥ meist: (ungebildet) barbarous (a. fig.); (blutdürstig) ferocious, truculent; F (ungeheuer) enormous.

Barbarismus (⌣⌣⌣́) [grch.] m ㉗ gram. (Sprachfehler) barbarism.

Barbarossa (⌣⌣⌣́) [it. Rotbart] npr/m. ⑤⑥ α. (Kaiser Friedrich I., 1152—90), Barbarossa.

Bärbchen (⌣́⌣) n ㉓ dim. von Barbara (f. ds.), bisw. auch Bab.

Barbe (⌣́) f ㊽ 1. [ahd., *lt. Bart] ichth. barbel (Barbus vulga'ris). — 2. (Spitzenstreifen an Frauenhauben) lace-lappet (of a woman's cap). — 3. Kupferstecht.: barb.

bär¹-beißig F ('̈...) a. ⑥⑥ morose; gruff; like a bear, F grumpy; **~keit** f ㊻ morosity; gruffness.

Bärbel (⌣́⌣) n ㉒, **~chen** (⌣⌣́) n ㉓ dim. von Barbara (f. ds. u. Bärbchen).

Barben-kraut ♀ (⌣́⌣) n ⑫ winter-cress, rocket-gentle (Barba'rea vulga'ris).

Bar-bestand mst ⊙ ('̈...) m ⑫ balance in cash; metallic reserve; **-betrag** m amount in cash.

Barbier (⌣⌣́) [fr.] m ⓑc. barber, contp. shaver; (Friseur) hair-dresser.

Barbier-becken ('̈...) n ⑫ shaving-basin; **-beutel** m barber's bag or pouch.

barbieren (⌣⌣⌣́) [Barbier] I v/a. u. sich 2 v/refl. ⑬ e-n 2 to shave a p., to give a p. a shave; sich 2 lassen to have (or get) a shave; F fig. (betrügen) e-n (über den Löffel) 2 to trick (F to take in or diddle) a p. — II ~ n ㉓ shaving.

Barbier-gehilfe (⌣⌣⌣́) m ⑫, **-gesell(e)** m barber's man or assistant; **-laden** m, **-stube** f barber's shop, (Frisierstube) hairdressing-saloon; **-messer** n razor; **-riemen** m razor-strop; **-zeug** n shaving case or things pl. or utensils pl.

Barch prov. (⌣́) [ahd.: barrow] m ⓑ. barrow, castrated male hog.

barchen (⌣́⌣) | **Barchent** a. ⑥⑥ (of) fustian.

Bärchen (⌣́⌣) n ㉓ (dim. von Bär) bear-whelp, cub (of a bear).

Barchent ⊙ (⌣́⌣) [mhd., *ar.] m ⓑ. fustian; geköperter ~ dimity; glatter ~ bed-tick. — II 2 a. ⑥⑥ = barchen.

Barches (⌣́⌣) [hebr. Segen] m, inv. (Ostertuchen) unleavened Passover cake.

bardauz F (⌣⌣́) int. bang!, crash!

Barde (⌣́) [flt.] m ㊷ (altkeltischer Sänger) bard; weitS. (Dichter) minstrel, poet; **~n-chor-gesang** (⌣''...) m ⑫ bardic lay.

Bardi(e)t (⌣⌣́) n ⓑc. bard's (war-)song.

bären-artig (''...) a. ⑥⑥ ursine, bear-like; **-beißer** m ㊷ zo. (Hund) bull-dog; **-decke** f = -haut; **-dill(e) f** m ♀ = Bärwurz; **-fell** n bear's skin; **-fenchel ♀** m = Bärwurz; **-führer** m bear-leader; F fig. tutor; **-grube** f bear-pit. [⚘ ursine.]

bärenhaft (⌣⌣⌣́) a. ⑥⑥ bearish, bearlike;]

Bären-haut (''...) f ⑫ bear's (or bear-) skin; fig. auf der ~ liegen to idle (away one's time); (fauler F m lazy or idle fellow, lazy-bones); **-häuterei** F f sloth; **-hetze** f = -jagd; **-hunger** m f. 2mäßig; **-jagd** f bear-baiting or -hunting; **-jäger** m one who hunts bears; **-klau** ♀ (f, m a.) hogweed (Heracle'um); b) = Akanthus; **-lauch** ♀ m wild garlic (A'llium ursi'num); **-maki** m, zo. arctocebus (Arctoce'bus calabare'nsis); **-marder** m zo. ♀ arcticus; 2mäßig a. (as clumsy or savage) as a bear; fig. 2er Hunger wolfish appetite or hunger; **-mütze** ⚔ f bearskin cap, der Garbegrenadiere: busby; **-raupe** f, ent. (Raupe des -spinners) bear(-caterpillar); **-schote ♀** f wild licorice (Astra'galus glycy-phy'llos); **-spinner** m, ent. tiger-moth; ⚘ arctia; **-traube ♀** f: immergrüne ~ red bear-berry, bear's bilberry (Arcto-sta'phylos Uva ursi); **-zwinger** m bear-garden, auch = -grube.

Barett (⌣⌣́) [fr., it.] n ⓑ. bsd. der kath. Geistlichen: barret; der engl. Studenten u. Graduierten: (student's or graduate's) cap.

Bar-frost ('̈...) m ⑫ frost without snow; blackfrost; **2fuß** a. ⑥⑥ u. adv. bare-legged, -footed; **2 geh(e)n** to go bare-footed; **-füßelen** n bare-footed child; **-füßer(in)** f m, Cath.eccl. bare-footed friar or monk (f nun); **2füßig** (⌣⌣́) a. ⑥⑥ = 2fuß.

barg¹ (⌣́) impf. v. bergen. [= Barch.]

Barg² prov. (⌣́) m ⓑc. = Barch.

Bar-geschäft ⊙ ('̈...) n ⑫ cash (or ready-money) purchase; **2haupt, 2häuptig** a. ⑥⑥ u. adv. bare-headed.

Baribal (⌣⌣́) [indian.] m ㊵ zo. (amerikanischer Bär) baribal (Ursus america'nus).

Barilla ⚗ (⌣⌣́ja) [span.] f ㊽ chm. (rohe Soda) barilla; **~asche** f ㊽ chm. pulverin(e), **~soda** f, aus der Asche von Strandpflanzen: barilla (soda).

Bärin (⌣́⌣) f ㊼ (weiblicher Bär) she-bear.

Bariton ♪ (⌣́⌣) [it., *grch.] m ⑫ (Mittelstimme) baritone; ~ singen to sing b.; **~ist ♪** (⌣⌣⌣́) m ㊷ baritone (singer).

Barium ⚗ (⌣́⌣) [grch. bar(y's) schwer + lt. -ium] n ㊵ (o. pl.) chm. barium (Ba).

Barium-oxyd (⌣''...) n ⑫ barium (or baric) oxide (BaO); **-sulfat** n barium sulphate; **-superoxyd** n peroxide of barium (BaO₂). [chant-vessel, barque.]

Bark¹ ⚓ (⌣́) [it.] f ㊽ three-masted mer-]

Bark² ⊙ (⌣́) m ⓑ. = Barch.

Barka ♀ (⌣́⌣) npr/f. ⑤⑥ α. Landschaft in Nordafrika: Barca. [Gondellied) barcarole.]

Barkarole ♪ (⌣⌣⌣́) [it.] f ㊽ (venezianisches)]

Barkasse ⚓ (⌣⌣́) [span.] f ㊽ (größtes Boot auf Kriegsschiffen) launch.

Bar-kauf ⊙ ('̈...) m ⑫ = -geschäft.

Barke ⚓ (⌣́) [mhd., *it.] f ㊽ 1. (Boot) barque. — 2. (plattes Flußfahrzeug) barge.

Barkerole ♪ (⌣⌣⌣́) [it.] f ㊽ = Barkarole.

Bark-halter ⚓ ('̈...) m ⑫ rib(-)band; **-holz** n wale, sheer-rail.

Bär¹-lapp ♀ (''...) m ⓑc. club-moss (Lycopo'dium); **~mehl** n ⊙, **~staub** m lycopodium powder, witch-meal.

Bar-lauf(en) n) m (⌣⌣́) [Barren 2] ⊙ Lauf- u. Fangspiel: (prisoner's) base.

Bärlein (⌣́⌣) n = Bärchen.

Bärm-brot (⌣́⌣) n ⑫ leavened bread.

Bärme (⌣́) [ndd.: barm] f ㊽ (o. pl.) leaven, vom Biere: yeast (= Hefe).

barmen ⚘ (⌣́) v/n. (h.) ⑬ to lament.

barmherzig (⌣⌣́) a. ⑥⑥ (auch) armherzig = lt. misericors] I a. ⑥⑥ merciful (gegen e-n to a p.), schwächer: charitable; seid 2 mit mir! have pity on me!; eccl. 2e Brüder (Schwestern) brethren (sisters) pl. of charity. — II **~e(r)** m, **~e** f ⑰ compassionate (or charitable) person.

Barmherzigkeit (⌣⌣⌣-) f ㊽ (o. pl.) mercifulness, (schwächer) pity (with a p., on a p.); aus ~ out of charity; an e-m ~ üben to show mercy to a p., to have compassion on a p. [(Krippe) crib.]

Barn prov. (⌣́) [mhd.: barn] m ⓑ.

[Barnabas] — 146 — [Basiliskenanblick]

Barnabas (⏑⏑⏑) [hebr.] npr/m. ⓖγ. (Vn.) Barnabas, Barnaby; **Barnabit**(en pl.) (⏑⏑¹⏑) m ② Cath.eccl. Barnabite(s pl.).
☞ **Baro...**(⏑⏑¹..)[grch.ſchwer] ſ.=meter 2c.
barock (⏑⏑) [port.] a. ⓖⓖ eccentric, quaint; ein ℒer Kerl F a rum chap; **~heit** (⏑⏑⏑) f ⓖⓖ eccentricity, quaintness; **~perlen** (⏑..) f/pl. ⓖ Scotch pearls pl.; **~ſtil** m, arch. grotesque (auch rococo) style.
Bär-ohr ♀ (⏑⏑) n ⓖ = Aurikel.
Barometer ⚯ (⏑⏑⏑⏑) [grch.] n(m) ⓖ phys. (Meßinſtrument für Luftſchwere, Wetterglas) barometer, (weather-)glass; das ~ ſteht auf veränderlich (a. fig.) the barometer (or glass) indicates a change (in the weather); das ~ ſteht hoch, niedrig the glass is high, low; **~ſtand** (⏑..) m ⓖ height of the b.
Barometrie ⚯ (⏑⏑⏑¹) [grch.] f ⓖ barometry. [barometric(al).]
barometriſch ⚯ (⏑⏑⏑⏑) [grch.] a. ⓖⓖ phys.
Baron (⏑¹) [fr.,*flt. ob.*ahd. Mann] m ⓖⓒ., Titel ⓖⓖ (Freiherr) baron; als ~ leben = baroniſieren II. [barony.]
Baronat (⏑⏑¹) [fr.-It.] n ⓖⓒ. baronage,
Baroneſſe (⏑⏑⏑⏑) [++ fr.] f ⓖ **1.** (Freifrau) baroness. — **2.** (Freifräulein) daughter of a baron; die ~ N.N. the (Right)Honourable Lady (or Miss)***.
Baronets-würde (⏑⏑..) f ⓖ baronetcy.
Baronie (⏑⏑¹) f ⓖ barony.
Baronin (⏑¹⏑) f ⓖ (Freifrau) baroness.
baroniſieren (⏑⏑⏑¹⏑) ⚯ **I** v/a. **1.** to make a baron of. — **II** v/n. (h.) **2.** (als Baron leben) to live in baronial (fig. great) style. — **3.** fig. co. (keine Beſchäftigung haben) to walk the streets, to lounge about, F co. to inspect the pavement.
Barons-titel (⏑⏑..) m ⓖ baronial title.
Baroſkop ⚯ (⏑⏑¹) [grch.] n ⓖⓒ. phys. (chemiſches Wetterglas) baroscope.
Barre (⏑⏑) [fr.,*flt.] f ⓖ (Metallſtange, Schranke, Sandbank, ♩ Taktſtrich, her., ⚓) bar; ~ Gold, Silber ingot, bullion.
Barren (⏑⏑) m ⓖ **1.** = Barre. — **2.** Turnerei: parallel bar(s pl.).
Barren-form (⏑⏑⏑) ✧ f ⓖ ingot-mould; **=förmig** a. ⓖⓖ ingot-shaped; **=gold** ♀ n bar gold; **=turnen** n parallel bar exercises pl.; **=zufuhr** ✧ f bullion supply.
Barri-ere (⏑(⏑)¹⏑) f ⓖ (Sperre) [fr.] (jetzt: Schranke) gate; Landſtraße: turnpike; Sport: über eine ~ ſetzen to take a fence.
Barri-eren-riff ♀ (⏑..) n ⓖ Barrier Reef; **=trakta't** m (zw. Holland u. England gegen Frankreich 1709) Barrier Treaty; **=wärter** 🚂 m gateman.
Barrikade ✕ (⏑⏑¹⏑) [fr.] f ⓖ (Straßenſperrung) barricade; **~n-kampf** (⏑..) m ⓖ, **=krieg** ✕ m barricade-fighting.
barrikadieren ✕ (⏑⏑⏑¹⏑) [fr.] v/a. ⓖ (mit Barrikaden verſchanzen) to barricade.
Barring ⚓ (⏑⏑) f ⓖ (Deckbalkengerüſt zw. Fock- u. Großmaſt) barring. [(Perca).]
Barſch¹ (¹) [ndd.] m ⓖⓐ. ichth. perch
barſch² (¹) a. ⓖⓖ **1.** (of an) unpleasant (taste), tart. — **2.** fig. (rauh) rude (to a p.), harsh, rough; offhandish; (mürriſch) gruff; e-n 2 anfahren to talk sharply (or roughly) to a p., to snub a p.
Bar-ſchaft (¹⏑) f ⓖⓖ ready money, cash; meine ganze ~ all my cash; **☉ klingende**, a. bereite ~ ready cash.

Barſch-heit (¹-) f ⓖⓖ gruffness, offhandishness,, ſtärker: rudeness (to a p.).
Bar-ſendung mſt ⚫ (¹..) f ⓖ cash remittance, große: specie consignment.
Bär-ſpinner (¹..) m ⓖ = Bären-2.
barſt (¹) impf. von berſten (ſ. bd.).
Bart¹ [ahd.: beard] m ①ⓑ. **1.** beard; einen ~ bekommen to get one's whiskers, to show signs of a beard; ſich den ~ wachſen laſſen to grow (co. to sport) a beard or one's whiskers. — **2.** bei Fiſchen, Pflanzen: barb, beard; eines Hahns: wattle. — **3.** ~ (Dieb) am Lichte waster; F thief; ⚙ Gießerei: (Gußnaht) seam; ~ e-s Schlüſſels bit; ⚓ (Seegras 2c., das am Schiff feſtſitzt) crust of filth. — **4.** fig. e-m (liebkoſend) den ~ ſtreicheln, um den ~ gehen to wheedle round, to cajole a p., to curry favour with a p.; in den ~ brummen to mumble, to mutter to oneself; in den ~ hinein (unverſchämt) lügen to tell impudent (F big) lies; e-m e-n ~ (von Stroh) m. (ihn betrügen) to cheat (F to diddle) a p.; ſich um des Kaiſers ~ (unnötig, kleinlich) ſtreiten to quarrel about (mere) bagatelles.
Bart-becken (¹..) n ⓖ shaving-dish or basin; **=bürſte** f shaving-brush.
Bärtchen (¹⏑) n ⓖ (dim. v. Bart) little beard. [broad axe.]
Barte¹ (⏑⏑) [ahd.] f ⓖ (Breitbeil)
Barte² (¹) [ndd.] = Bärte (pl. v. Bart)] f ⓖ (Fiſchbein) (whole) whalebone.
Bartel (⏑⏑) f ⓖ ichth. (fadenförmige Hautbildung am Maule vieler Fiſche) barb(el).
Barten-wal (⏑⏑¹) m ⓖ zo. right-whale (Balae'na mystice'tus).
Bart-faden (¹..) m ⓖ, **=faſer** f, zo. beard, barb(el); **=finne** f = flechte a; **=fiſch** m: a) ichth. = Barbe 1; b) zo. = Walfiſch; **=flechte** f = a) med. barber's itch, ⚯ sycosis; b) ♀ beard-moss (U'snea barba'ta); **=geier** m, orn. bearded vulture (Gypaë'tos barba'tus); **=gerſte** ♀ f = Pfauengerſte; **=gras** ♀ n beard-grass (Andropo'gon Ischae'mon); **=gras** ♀ ✧ f beard-grass (Andropo'gon Ischae'mon); **=grundel** f, ichth. loach (Cobi'tis barba'tula); **=haar** n hair of a beard.
Barthel (⏑⏑) [Bartholomäus] [hebr.] npr/m. ⓖⓐ. ⓖⓖ (Vn.) Sprichw. er weiß, wo ~ den Moſt holt (kennt die Schliche) he knows his business or what he's about; F he knows the ropes.
Bartholomä-us (⏑⏑⏑¹⏑) [hebr.] npr/m. ⓖγ. (Vn.) (St.=)~ (St.) Bartholomew.
Bartholomäus-nacht (⏑⏑⏑¹..) f ⓖ hist. (Pariſer Blutʜochzeit, 24. Auguſt 1572) (Massacre of) St. Bartholomew.
Bär-tierchen (¹..) n ⓖ zo. (Art Spinnentiere) ⚯ tardigrade.
bärtig (¹⏑) a. ⓖⓖ bearded, whiskered, ♀ u. zo. auch: barbed u. barbate.
Bart-kratzer F (¹..) m ⓖ barber, contp. shaver, chin-scraper; **=kuckuck** m barbet (Bucco); **=länge** f length of a beard; **=lappen** m, **=läppchen** n: a) shaving napkin: b) unter dem Schnabel der Hühner: gill; ⚯los a. ⓖⓖ von jungen Leuten auch ♀: beardless; **=loſe(r)** m ⓖ lack-beard; **=loſigkeit** f beardlessness; **=moos** ♀ n beard-moss (Phascum); **=nelke** ♀ f sweet-william (Dia'nthus barba'tus); **=putzer** F m = Barbier.
Bartſch ♀ (¹) m ⓖⓐ. = Wieſenbärenklau.

Bart-ſcheren (¹..) n ⓖ clipping of the beard; **=ſcherer** F m = Barbier; **=ſeife** f shaving-soap; **=wichſe** f cosmetique (for the moustache).
Barutſche (⏑⏑⏑) [it.] f ⓖ (zwei- ob. vierrädriges Fuhrwert) barouche.
Bar-vorrat mſt ⚫ (¹..) m ⓖ = **=beſtand**; ~ der (Königlichen) Bank bullion at the Bank. [athama'nticum).]
Bär¹-wurz ♀ (¹⏑) f ⓖ spignel (Me'um
Barymetrie (⏑⏑⏑¹) [grch.] f ⓖ (Schweremeſſung) barymetry.
Baryt ⚯ (⏑¹) [grch.] m ⓖⓒ. min. baryta; chm. anhydrous barium oxide (BaO); **Baryt-erde** (⏑..) f ⓖ = Baryt; **=haltig** a. ⓖⓖ barytiferous, barytic; **=hydra't** n, chm. (Ätzbaryt) caustic baryta.
☞ **Baryton** ♩ (⏑⏑⏑) 2c. = Bariton 2c.
Barytonon (⏑¹⏑⏑) [grch.] n ⓖ grch. Grammatik: (Wort mit unbetonter letzter Silbe; ant. Oxytonon) barytone.
Baryt-waſſer (⏑..) n ⓖ baryta-water.
Baryum ⚯ = Barium.
bary-zentriſch (⏑⏑⏑⏑) [grch.=It.] a. ⓖⓖ (auf den Schwerpunkt bezüglich) barycentric.
Bar-zahlung mſt ⚫ (¹..) f ⓖ cash-payment, money paid down; nur gegen ~ terms pl. strictly (for) cash.
Bas (¹) [ndl.] m ⓖⓐ. (Herr, Hausvater, Meiſter) governor, bſd. Am. boss.
Baſalt ⚯ (⏑¹) [lt., *äg.] m ⓖⓑ. min. (Geſtein in prismatiſchen Säulen) basalt.
Baſalt-bruch (⏑..) m ⓖ basalt quarry.
baſalten ⚯ (⏑⏑⏑) a. ⓖⓖ (of) basalt, basaltic. [≈haltig a. basaltic.]
baſalt-förmig (⏑⏑..) a. ⓖⓖ basaltiform;
Baſanit (⏑⏑¹) [grch.] m ⓖⓒ. min. (olivenartiger Baſalt; Probierſtein) basanite.
Baſar (⏑¹) [perſ.] m ⓖⓒ. fancy-fair, Wohltätigkeits≈ bazaar, sale of work; einen ~ veranſtalten to hold a bazaar.
Bä-ſchaf (¹..) n ⓖ Kinder: baa-sheep.
Bäschen (¹⏑) n ⓖ, dim. v. Baſe¹.
Baſchi-Bosuk(s) ✕ (⏑⏑¹⏑) [türk.] m/pl. ⓖ (türk. irreguläre Truppen) Bashi-bazouks pl. [Frauenkappe) bashlik, bashlyk.]
Baſchlik (⏑¹) türk. Kopfſling m ⓖ (Art
Baſe¹ (¹⏑) [ahd.] f ⓖ (weibliche Verwandte) kinswoman, engſ.: a) aunt; b) (female, lady) cousin; v. Mädchen a.: girl cousin.
Baſe² ⚯ (¹⏑) (Baſis) f meiſt chm. (ant. Säure) alkali, base.
Baſel ♀ (¹⏑) [grch. königlich] npr/n. ⓖⓐ. Basle, (fr.) Bâle, auch Basel.
Baſ(e)ler (¹(⏑)⏑) **I** m ⓖ, **~in** f ⓖ native (inhabitant) of Basle. — **II** a., inv. of (or belonging to) Basle; ~ Friede (1795) Treaty of B.
baſen²-bildend ⚯ (¹..) a. ⓖⓖ, chm. basigenous; **=bild(n)er** m ⓖ basifier.
baſenhaft (¹⏑⏑) a. ⓖⓖ gossip-like.
baſieren (-¹⏑) [grch.] ⓖ **I** v/a. (begründen) to base or found (up)on. — **II** v/n. (h.) to be based or founded (up)on, to rest (up)on.
Baſili-e ♀ (⏑¹(⏑)⏑) [grch.] f ⓖ, **~n-kraut** (⏑..) n ⓖ (common or sweet) basil (O'cymum basi'licum).
Baſilika ♀ (⏑¹⏑⏑) [grch.] f ⓖ anat. und arch. basilica. [= Baſilie.]
Baſilikum ⚯ ♀ (⏑¹⏑⏑) [lt., *grch.] n ⓖ
Baſilisk (⏑⏑¹) [grch.] m ⓖ myth. u. ehm. ✕ basilisk, zo. auch: cockatrice. [glance.]
Baſilisken-(an)blick (⏑..) m ⓖ basilisk

Signs (see page XVII): F familiar; P vulgar; F flash; ↖ rare; † obsolete (died); * new word (born); ++ incorrect; ♩ music;

[Basis] — 147 — [bauchen]

Basis ⚭ (‿⌣) [grch.] f ⑲ arch., math., ♉, &c.: base, basis.
basisch ⚭ (‿⌣) a. ⑯ chm. (ant. sauer) basic, radical; ⚴es Salz, a. subsalt.
basisch-essigsaures Blei (‿⌣⌣‿⌣‿⌣") subacetate of lead.
Basizität ⚭ (‿‿‿⌣) [lt.] f ㊻ chm. basicity.
Baske ♀ (‿) m ㊹, **Baskin** ♀ (‿) (Pyrenäenvolk), **baskisch** a. ⑯ Basque.
Bäslein (⌣‿) n ㉓, dim. v. Base¹. [relief.]
Bas-relief (ba-r⁴-lĭĕ'f) [fr.] n ㊿ sculp. bas-
Baß¹ ♪ (⌣) [it.] m ⑧a. (tiefste Stimme und tiefstönendes Instrument) bass; (Menschenstimme) bass voice; erster ~ (tiefer Tenor) baritone; zweiter oder tiefer ~ contrabass; begleitender (gebundener, obligaʼter) ~ continued bass; den ~ streichen to play contrabass.
baß² (⌣) [ahd.: besser] adv. 1. jetzt als Positiv: = sehr, ungemein. — 2. mst poet. = besser, mehr. (Pascha) pasha.)
Bassa (⌣) [türk.] m ㊼ und ㊹ (Bassen)
Baß¹-bläser ♪ (⌣‿) m ㊻ (Fagottist) bassoon(ist); **-brummer** m in Orgeln: bombard (= Bombart).
Basselisse (baß-li'ß) [fr.] f ㊽ (Figurentapete) low warp, figured tapestry.
Basset ♀ (⌣‿) [engl.] m ㊿ (Hunderasse) basset. [Tenor u. Baß] bassetto.)
Bassett ♪ (‿⌣) [it.] m ⓫b. (Stimme zwischen
Bassett-horn ♪ (‿⌣‿) n ㉒ basset-horn.
Baß¹-geige ♪ (⌣‿) f ㉒: kleine ~ (Cello) bass-viol, violoncello; große ~ (Kontrabaß) contrabass.
Bassin (ba̠ß̌) [fr.] n ㉓ großes: reservoir, tank, kleines: basin; vgl. Becken. [ment.]
Baß-instrument ♪ (⌣‿‿) n ㉒ bass instru-
Bassist ♪ (‿⌣) [Baß] m ㊷ bass(-singer); (e-r der zweiten Baß singt) contrabass.
Baß-note ♪ (⌣‿) f ㉒ bass note.
Basson ♪ (‿ba̠) [fr.] m ㊿ = Baßpfeife.
Baß-pfeife ♪ (⌣‿) f ㉒ (Fagott) bassoon; **-pfeifer** m bassoon(ist); **-saite** f bass-string; **-sänger** m = Bassist; **-schlüssel** m bass clef; **-spieler** m violoncellist; **-stimme** f bass voice or part, s. Baß¹.
Baß-straße ♀ (⌣‿‿) [engl. Seefahrer Bass 1797] npr/f. ㊺ Meer-enge zw. Australien u. Tasmanien: Bass Strait.
Bast (⌣) [ahd.: bast, bass] m (n) ⑪ (⑦)b. 1. ♀ (abziehbare Haut unter der Rinde) bast, inner bark; ~ der Kokosnüsse coco-nut fibre; (bei anderen Pflanzen, z.B. Flachs, die äußere Haut) harl. — 2. hunt. am neuen Hirsch- u. Reh-gehörn: fraying. — 3. (Haut an den Händen zc.) (scarf-)skin, ⚭ cuticle.
basta (‿⌣) [it. genug] I int. that will do!, stop!; und damit ⚄! (and) now you know!, (and) that's enough! — II ~ m ㊿ (f ㊺) = Baste.
Bastard (⌣‿) [mhd.; *fr. bâtard] m ⑪b. 1. bastard; (uneheliches Kind) illegitimate child. — 2. ♀ u. zo. (Mischling) cross (breed). [hybrid species.]
Bastard-art (⌣‿‿) f ㊶ cross breed, ⚭ **bastardieren, bastardieren** (⌣‿‿‿) ㊸ v/a. u. sich ⚄ v/refl. to mix, to cross, ⚭ to hybridize (= verbastarden).
Bastard-(er)zeugung (⌣‿‿‿) f: ⚭ hybridism; **-hund** m mongrel (dog), **-klimmer**; **-klee** m f ♀ bastard clover (Trifoʼlium hyʼbridum); **-pflanzen** ♀ f/pl. (Mischlinge, Blendlinge) hybrids, crossings, crossed species pl.

Bastardschaft (⌣‿‿‿) f ㊻ bastardy, v. Hunden: mongrelism, ♀ u. zo.: crossing, ⚭ hybridism. [Solo; Treff-As im Lomber)basto.)
Baste (⌣‿) f ㊻ Trumpfkarte: (Grün-oder im
Bastei (‿⌣) [it.] f ㊻ ⚔ und fig. bastion; bulwark (s. Bastion).
basteln, bästeln F (‿⌣) v/a. u. v/n. (h.) ㉒a. to be careful (or fussy) about trifles.
basten (⌣‿) [Bast] a. ⑯ (made) of bast, weitS. auch: (made) of bark.
Bast-hut (⌣‿) m ㉒ chip-hat.
Bastion ⚔ (⌣‿⌣) f ㊻ ⚔ a. m u. ⓬c. bastion; mit ~en versehen bastioned.
Bästling ♀ (‿⌣) m ⑪d. (männl. Hanfpflanze) male (or fimble-)hemp.
Bast-matte (⌣‿) f ㉒ bast mat.
Bastonade (‿⌣‿) [fr.] f ㊽ bastinado; eine ~ erhalten to be bastinadoed.
Bast-seide ♀ (⌣‿) f ㉒ Indian half silk; Persian sarsenet; **-seil** n bast rope.
bat (⌣), **bäte** (⌣) impf. v. bitten (f. ds.).
Bataille ⚔ (bä-tä'l-jᵉ) [fr.] f ㊽ battle.
Bataillon ⚔ (bä-täl-jō'n) [fr.] n ⓬c. Truppenkörper: battalion.
Bataillons-adjutant (‿‿‿) m ⓬ adjutant of the battalion; **-bureau** n orderly-room; **-kommandeur** m commander (or commanding officer) of a battalion; **-tambour** m drum-major.
Batate ♀ (⌣‿⌣) [span.] f ㊻ 1. (süße Kartoffel) batata, sweet potato (Ipomoeʼa Bataʼtas). — 2. = Erdbirne (Topinambur).
Bataver (⌣‿⌣⌣, r-r ‿‿‿⌣⌣) m ㉒, **-in** (‿⌣‿‿) f ㊼ Batavian. [tavia.)
Batavien (⌣‿⌣⌣(⌣)) npr/n. ㉓a. Ba-
batavisch (⌣‿⌣⌣) a. ⑯ Batavian.
Batengel ♀ (‿‿⌣) [P aus lt. betoniʼcula: Betonie] m ㉒ = Gamander (echter).
Bathometer (⌣‿‿‿) [grch.] n (m) ㉒ phys. (Tiefenmesser) bathometer.
Bathseba (‿‿‿⌣‿‿) [hebr.] npr/f. (Weib des Uria u. David, Mutter Salomos) Bathsheba.
Bathybius ♀ (⌣‿‿‿) [grch. Tiefenwesen] m, inv. bathybius.
☛ **Bäting** ⚓ (‿⌣) zc. s. Beting zc.
Batist ⚚ (‿⌣) [fr.] m ⓫b. cambric.
batisten (‿⌣‿) a. ⑯ (of) cambric.
Batrachier (⌣‿⌣‿) [grch.] m/pl. (froschartige Tiere) batrachians pl.
Batrachomyomachie (⌣‿⌣‿⌣‿‿") [grch.] f ㊽ = Froschmäusekrieg.
batten provc. (‿⌣‿) [ahd.] v/n. (h.) ⑨ (helfen, nützen) to be useful.
Batterie (‿‿⌣, F ‿⌣) [fr.] f ㊽ 1. ⚔ (Geschütze) battery, ordnance; ⚓ tier (of guns); e-e ~ auffahren lassen to bring up a battery; e-e ~ zum Schweigen bringen to silence a battery; fahrende, reitende ~ mounted b.; eine ~ aufwerfen to raise (or mount) a battery. — 2. phys. battery; galvanische ~ galvanic battery; e-e ~ laden to charge a battery; die beiden Pole e-r ~ verbinden to short-circuit a battery. — 3. ⚙ mach. (zſ-wirkende Geräte) battery; Pochstempel-⚄ battery of stamps.
Batterie-deckung ⚔ (‿‿‿) f ㊻ cover(ed position) for a battery; **-entladung** f phys. discharge of a battery; **-führer** ⚔ m leader of a battery; **-geschütz** n piece of ordnance.
Batzen (⌣‿) [mhd.] m ㉓ 1. (zſ-backende Masse) caked mass, heavy lump. — 2. (ehm. obd., schwz. Münze = 4 Kreuzer)

batz(en) (= about one penny); F er hat keinen ~ he hasn't a farthing or a sou or a penny.
Bau¹ (⌣) [ahd.] m ⓬c. (pl. mst Bauten) 1. a) das Bauen; b) kunstvolles Zusammenfügen; c) das Gebäude, meist: building, construction; zu c auch: structure. — 2. (Art des Baues) oft: style; organischer Körper: organism, frame; besonders zum Bewohnen errichteter ~ structure, unvollendeter: premises pl. in course of erection or construction, vollendeter: building, prachtvoller: edifice, auch: pile; weitS. bsß. fig. fabric, e-s Bühnenstücks zc.: framework; ⚒ working. — 3. (auf Ertrag von Früchten und Mineralien zielende Arbeit) agr. ~ (des Feldes) cultivation (of the field), tillage (of the soil); ⚒ exploitation. — 4. (Wohnung wilder Tiere) lair, ⚭ habitat; hunt. earth, der Biber: lodge, dam; der Bienen: structure of wax cells; der Dachse, Füchse zc.: kennel; unterirdischer ~ der Kaninchen zc.: warren, burrow; den Fuchs zc. in den ~ treiben (jagen, verfolgen) to run ... to earth (or to ground); im ~ liegen (oder hausen) to kennel; zu ~ kriechen to burrow, vom Fuchs zc.: to come to earth. — 5. fig. immer in seinem ~ sitzen (F to stick) for ever at home, F to sit in one's den all day.
bau² (⌣) int. 1. (Hundegebell) ⚄ ⚄! bowbow! — 2. baff, ⚄! bang!, clap!, pop!
Bau-abstand (⌣‿‿) m ⓬ vom Gebäude des Nachbars: distance from the neighbouring house (to be kept in building); **-akademie** f school (or academy) of architecture; **-amt** n board of works; **-anschlag** m, arch., ⚓ particulars pl. of construction, builder's estimate; **-art** f structure; oft: = Stil (s. ds.); **-aufseher** m surveyor (or overseer, clerk) of the works, (Werkführer) foreman; **-bedarf** m building material (s pl.); **-beflissene(r)** m architect('s pupil).
Bauch (⌣‿) [ahd.] m ⑦c. 1. (a. Unterleib, b. Magen, c. Gebärmutter, d. fig. hervortretende Wölbung, innerer hohler Raum) meist: belly; zu d auch: bilge, arch. bulge; einen ~ bekommen ob. sich zulegen F to get a big belly or a corporation; seinem ~e frönen to worship one's belly, to lead a life of gluttony; bibl. fauler ~ sluggard, P lazy guts pl.; Sprichw. voller ~, leerer Kopf a fat belly, a lean brain; den ~ betr., zum ~ gehörig ⚭ ventral. — 2. a) (Unterleib) anat. = abdomen; b) (Magen) F stomach, co. pouch, paunch, F co. periphery; ein rundes Bäuchlein haben to have a portly (or round) stomach; sich den ~ halten vor Lachen to hold one's sides (with laughter). — 3. ♪ ~ e-r Geige zc. body; ⚓ ~ e-s Schiffes bottom; fig. (Inneres) bosom.
Bauch-arterie (⌣‿‿) f ㉒ anat. = **-aufschlitzen** n (japanischer Selbstmord) hara-kiri; **-beschwerden** f/pl. path. abdominal (or gastric) complaint(s pl.); **-binde** f belly-band; **-diener** m glutton, bisw. a. gastrolater.
☛ **Bauche, Bäuche** zc. s. Beuche zc.
Bäuchelchen (⌣‿‿) n ㉓ dim. v. Bauch.
bauchen (⌣‿) I v/a., v/n. (sn) und sich ⚄ v/refl. ㊸ = aus⚄. — II ~ n ㉓

⚭ scientific; ♀ botanical; ♁ geography; ⊕ machinery; ⚒ mining; ⚔ military; ⚓ marine; ⬛ commercial; ✉ postal; 🚂 railway.

[Bauchfell] — 148 — [baulustig]

Bauchung 1. — III ge-baucht p.p. u. a. 66 = bauchig.
Bauch-fell (˝ch...) n 62 anat.: ☞ peritoneum; -fell-entzündung f, med.: ☞ peritonitis; -finne f, -floſſe f, ichth. ventral fin; -floſſer m/pl., ichth. abdominal fish pl.; ꝛförmig a. 66 belly-shaped, bulged; -füß(l)er m/pl., zo.: ☞ gastropods pl., -grimmen n, med. (Kolik) gripes pl., P belly-ache; -gurt m des Pferdegeſchirrs: belly-band, girth; -höhle f, anat.: ☞ abdominal cavity.
bauchig (ˡch◡) a. 66 bellied; (geſchwollen) inflated, (gewölbt) convex; ↯ ventricose, ⊙ ² werden to bulge; ...² (...˝◡) a. 66, z.B. dick² big-bellied.
Bauch-kneifen (ˢch...) n 62, -kneipen n = -grimmen; -krampf m, med. colic; -krankheit f ſ. -beſchwerden.
Bäuchlein (˝ch) n 23, dim. v. Bauch (ſ. bſ. 2 b).. [belly, in a prone position.]
bäuchlings (ˡ◡) adv. lying on one's Bauch-muskel (˝ch...) m 62 abdominal muscle; -nerv m, anat. abdominal nerve; -öffnung f, surg. gastro(s)tomy; -rede-kunst f ventriloquist's art; -redner m ventriloquist; -rednerei f ventriloquism; ²rednerisch a. ventriloquial; -riemen m = -gurt; -rutscher m, contp. crawler; -schmerz F m belly-ache; -schnitt m, surg. ☞ laparotomy, gastrotomy; -speichel-drüse f, anat.: ☞ pancreatic gland; -stich m, surg. abdominal puncture, ☞ paracentesis; -stoß ⚔ m, fenc. ehm. seconde; -stück n: a) piece of the belly; b) ↓ floor-timber; -tiere n/pl. zo.: ☞ mollusks pl.
Bauchung (ˡch◡) f 46 1. swelling, inflation. — 2. convexity.
Bauch-wassersucht (˝ch...) f 62 med.: ☞ ascites; -weh n stomach-ache; weitS. = -grimmen; -wolle ⊙ underlocks pl.; -würmer m/pl. intestinal worms pl., ☞ ascarides pl.; -zange f für Schmelztiegel: crucible-tongs pl.
Baude prov. (ˡ◡) f 48 (Hütte) hut.
Bau-direktor (˝...) m superintendent (or manager) of works.
bauen (ˡ◡) [ahd.] 68 I v/a. u. ſich ² v/refl. 1. ein Haus, Schiff, eine Straße, Eisenbahn (a. fig. F e-n Rock) ² to build, to construct; vom Körper: schön ob. gut (schlecht) gebaut (gewachsen) well- (ill-)shaped or proportioned; bſd. fig. auf Felsen (Sand) ² to build on rocks (sand), fig. Luftschlösser ² to build castles in the air; sich arm ² to impoverish o.s. by building. — 2. (errichten) to erect; einen Altar ² to raise...; ſein Nest ² to make one's nest (auch F fig.); fig. ſein Urteil auf et. ² to base (or rest) one's judgment (or opinion) (up)on something. — 3. agr.: das Land ² (beſtellen) to cultivate ..., to till ...; Getreide ꝛc. ² to grow ...; ⚒ eine Grube ꝛc. ² to work ...; Silber ꝛc. ² (gewinnen) to extract ... from a mine, abs. auf Silber ꝛc. ² to dig for ... — 4. bibl. (aufrichten, fortpflanzen) to raise up. — II v/n. (ħ.) 5. to build. — 6. an et. ² to be (engaged in) building something. — 7. auf e-n, et. ² (ſich verlaſſen) to rely on somebody, something; auf mein gutes Recht ²b trusting in the justice of my cause. — III ~ n 23 8. = Bau 1–3.

Bau-entwurf (˝...) m 62 = -plan.
Bauer¹ (ˡ◡) [ahd.; *bauen] m 22 constructor (of a ship, &c.), builder (of a house), cultivator (of a field).
Bauer² (ˡ◡) [†(ahd.) Geᵇ v.~³] m 36 1. (Landbewohner) peasant, countryman; engS. (Beſitzer e-s Bauerngutes) peasant-proprietor, farmer, squire, (Pächter) tenant or farmer; fig. (plumper Kerl) rustic, boor, churl; Sprichw. was versteht der ~ vom Gurkensalat? etwa: what does he know about it?, he knows as much about it as a crow does about Sunday; ein ~ bleibt ein ~ what's bred in the bone will come out in the flesh; ja, ~, das iſt ganz was anderes! (wenn zwei dasselbe tun, gilt es nicht dasselbe) that's quite a different matter, F that's a different pair o' breeches! — 2. im Kartenspiel: knave; Schach: pawn. [cage = Vogelbauer.)
Bauer³ (ˡ◡) [ahd.: bower] m(n) 62 bird-
Bauer-arbeit (˝◡...) f 62: a) farming, farmer's work; husbandry, tilling the land; b) rough labour; -bengel m, b.s. hobbledehoy; -bursche m country-lad.
Bau-erde (˝...) f 62 arable soil.
Bauer-dirne (˝◡...) f 62 country-lass.
Bauerei (-◡ˡ) f 46 1. (Mauerarbeit) masonry. — 2. = Bauſucht.
Bauer-flegel (˝◡...) m 62 = -lümmel; -frau f ſ. Bauern-; -freund m peasants' friend; -gut m = Bauer(n)hof.
bauerhaft (ˡ◡◡) a. 22 = bäurisch.
Bauer-hof (˝◡...) m ſ. Bauern-; -hund m mastiff. [countrywoman.)
Bäuerin (ˡ◡◡) f 47 peasant woman,
bäuerisch (ˡ(◡)◡) a. 66 ſ. bäurisch.
Bauer-junge (˝◡...) m 62 = -bursche; -kittel m smock(-frock); -knecht m farmer's boy, farm-servant or -hand.
Bau-erlaubnis (˝...) f 62 concession (or permission) for building.
Bauer-leh(e)n (˝◡...) n 62 ploughman's fee, † soc(c)age. [yokel, rustic.)
Bäuerlein (ˡ◡◡) n 23 dim. von Bauer
bäuerlich (ˡ◡◡) a. 66 (ländlich) rural, rustic; von ²er Herkunft ſein to come (or descend) from a peasant stock or a country family; ²e(r) Abgeordnete(r) country (or rural) member.
Bauer-lümmel (˝◡...) m 62 countrybumpkin; -mädchen n country-girl.
Bauern-art (˝◡...) f 62 countryman's ways pl.; -aufruhr m, -aufstand m peasant rising; -bund m peasant league; -bursche ſ. Bauer-; -fang m = -fänger; -fänger m cheat, F confidence man; im Spiele: professional gambler; -fängerei f F take-in, confidence-trick; -fest n rural fête; -frau f farmer's wife; -freund m = Bauer-...; -frone f statute labour; -gut n (ant. Rittergut) peasant farm; -haus n farm-house, cottage; -hochzeit f country wedding, rustic nuptials pl.; -hof m farm (-yard); -krieg m Peasant(s') War; -lied n rustic ditty; -regel f country-people's saying, engS. rule of weather-experts.
Bauer(n)schaft (ˡ◡◡) f 62 peasantry; the inhabitants pl. of a village or hamlet.
Bauern-schenke (˝◡...) f 62 village ale-house; -senf ⚘ m = Ackersenf; -sohn m peasant's son, rustic; -sprache f peasant (or country) dialect; -stand m

farmer's calling or vocation, coll. peasantry; -stolz m countryman's (fig. foolish) pride; ²stolz a. stupidly proud; -tabak ⚘ m Indian tobacco (Nicotia'na ru'stica); -tanz m country-dance; -tochter f peasant's daughter; -tracht f peasant-dress.
Bauer(n)tum (ˡ◡...) n 25 (o.pl.) condition (or property) of peasants, rustic life.
Bauern-verstand (˝◡...) m 62 untutored mind; -volk n country-folk or -people; -weib n country-woman, vgl. Bäuerin.
Bauer-pferd (˝◡...) n 62 farm-horse, -regel f = Bauern-...
Bauerschaft ſ. Bauernschaft.
Bauers-frau (˝◡...) f 62 ſ. Bauern-; -sitten (˝◡...) f/pl. 66 rural customs, rustic habits pl.
Bauers-mann, pl. -leute = Bauer² 1.
Bauer-tölpel (˝◡...) m 62 clod-hopper, -wesen n: a) rustic household; b) bäurisches Wesen b.s. boorishness; -wirtschaft f farm, weitS. agriculture.
Bau-fach (˝...) n 62 architecture, building trade; ²fähig a. 66 agr. arable, ⚒ workable; ²fällig a. (ant. bauhaft, baulich 2) out of repair, dilapidated, crumbling away, going to wreck and ruin; -fälligkeit f dilapidated (or tumble-down) state or condition; stärker: decay; ²fest a. solid, substantial; -flucht f alinement; -fuhre f carriage (or cartage) of building material(s); -führer m: a) = -leiter; b) als Titel etwa: junior architect; -gefangene(r) m convict; -gerüst ⊙ n scaffold(ing); -gewerbe, -gewerk n building (or builder's) trade; -gewerkschule f, etwa: art(isan) school, (builders') technical school; -grube f foundation-trench or -ditch, excavation; -grund m: a) building plot; b) foundation; c) weitS. = -stelle. [workable.)
bauhaft ⚒ (ˡ◡) a. 66 (ant. baufällig)
Bau-handwerker (˝...) m 62 workman (or mechanic) in (or belonging to) the building trade; -herr m: a) owner (of a house in course of construction); b) contractor; -hof m builder's (building-)yard; -holz ⊙ n timber, (zugerichtetes) Am. lumber; -holzfäller m Am. lumberer; -hütte f (hut serving as the) foreman's office in a building-yard; -inspektor m = -aufseher; -kasten m für Kinder: box of bricks; -klotz m für Kinder: architectural block; -kontrakt m builder's contract; -kosten pl. cost of building, building expenses pl.; -kosten-anschlag m builder's estimate; -kunst f architecture; -künstler(in f) m architect; -leiter m (head) manager (or superintendent) of building operations; -leute pl. ſ. -mann.
baulich (ˡ◡) a. 66 1. (den Bau betreffend) architectural. — 2. arch. u. ⚒ (ant. baufällig) in dem Stande erhalten to keep in (good) repair or condition.
Baulichkeit (ˡ◡...) f 46 1. (Gebäude) building; größere ~ premises pl., structure, edifice, pile. — 2. (zu baulich 2) (good) state of repair.
Bau-linie (˝...) f 62 einer Straße: alinement; -lust f fondness for building; ²lustig a. 66 fond of building.

Zeichen (ſ. S. XVII): F familiär; P Volkssprache; ⸝ Gaunersprache; ⸜ ſelten; † alt (auch geſtorben); * neu (auch geboren); ‡ unrichtig;

[**Baum**] | — 149 — | [**bauschig**]

Baum (¹) [ahd.: beam, boom] m ⓉC.
1. ♀ tree, ⚲ arbor. — 2. Sprichw. es ist
dafür gesorgt, daß die Bäume nicht in
den Himmel wachsen, etwa: even the
mightiest shall be curbed in their
pride; allg. everything has its limits;
er sieht vor lauter Bäumen den Wald
nicht *lit.s.* he does not see the wood
for trees, *fig.* he does not see the main
point; zwischen ~ und Borke sitzen, etwa:
to be between hammer and anvil;
F das geht über die Bäume!, etwa: that's
too much of a good thing!; man
kennt den ~ an seiner Frucht a tree is
known by its fruit. — 3. ⊕, &c.: ~
e-s Hafens: boom; e-s Wagens: shaft; e-r
Presse: beam, arbor; zum Schließen eines
Tores: bar; am Pfluge, Krane, Webstuhle:
beam; Gerberei: currier's beam; Häute
auf dem ~e strecken to beam … — 4. ⚓
boom; großer ~ main boom.
Baum-abdruck (″…) m ⓶ auf Steinen: ⚲
arborization; =**achat** m, min. mit baum-
ähnlicher Zeichnung: ⚲ arborescent agate,
dendrachate; ♀**ähnlich** a. ⓰ tree-like,
⚲ arboreal, arboreous, arborescent,
dendroid; =**ähnlichkeit** f: ⚲ arbores-
cence; =**allee** f avenue; =**aloe** ♀ f agave;
=**ameise** ♀, ent. horse-ant (*Formi'ca rufa*).
Bau-mann (″…) m ⓶, bsp. pl. =**leute** (men
pl. of) the building trade, workmen pl.
baum-artig (″…) a. ⓰ = ♀**ähnlich**; =**artigkeit** f ⓶ = =ähnlichkeit. [material(s pl.).⟩
Bau-material (″…) n ⓶ building⟨
Baum-auster (″…) f zo. tree-oyster
(*O'strea arbo'rea*); =**bast** ♀ m = Bast 1;
=**blatt** n leaf of a tree; =**blüte** f blos-
som(ing) of a tree; =**brand** m blight
of trees; =**bruch** m trees pl. uprooted
(or wood blown down) by a storm.
Bäumchen (ᴸ⌣) n ⓶ *dim. v.* Baum: small
tree; junges ~ (a. *fig.*) young sapling
or shoot; Spiel: „Verwechselt das ~!"
„Puss in the corner!"
baum-dick (″…) a. ⓰ (as) big as a tree;
=**efeu** ♀ m (n) = Efeu.
Bau-meister (″…) m ⓶ architect.
Baumel F (ᴸ⌣) f ⓰ (Hängelocke) bob; (Ohr♀)
pendant, drop.
baumeln (ᴸ⌣) v/n. (h.) ⓰ a. to dangle, to
hang down, to bob (up and down);
mit den Armen ♀ to swing one's arms
about; die Beine 2c. ♀ lassen to dangle
one's legs, &c.; Verwünschung: ich möchte
ihn lieber ♀ sehen I should see him
hanged first. [a tree.⟩
baumen (ᴸ⌣) v/n. ⓰ hunt. to climb up⟨
bäumen (ᴸ⌣) [boom³] ⓰ I v/a., agr. (mit
dem Wiesbaume befestigen) ein Fuder Heu 2c.
♀ to wind up … (with the beam); ⊕
Weberei: Kette ♀ to beam … — II sich ♀
v/refl. von Pferden: to rear, to prance,
fig. (sich widersetzen) to resist, to put up
one's back; *man.* (störrisch sein) to jib,
to take head. — III ~ n ⓶ v. Pferden:
rearing, prancing; jibbing.
Baum-ente (″…) f ⓶ orn. widgeon;
=**falke** m, orn. hobby (*Falco subbu'teo*);
=**farn** ♀ m tree-fern; =**feldwirtschaft** f
arboriculture in conjunction with
farming; ♀**fest** a. ⓰ F (as) firm as a
rock; =**flechte** ♀ f tree-lichen; =**förmig** a. tree-shaped, ⚲ arboriform;
=**fraß** ♀ m (dry) rot, canker; =**frevel**

m damaging of trees; =**gang** m avenue (of trees); =**bedeckter** ~ covered
walk; =**gans** f, orn. barnacle (*Berni'cla*);
=**garten** m orchard, für die Baumzucht:
nursery; =**gärtner** m nursery man, ⚲
arboriculturist; =**gärtnerei** f arboriculture; a. = =zucht; =**geländer** n, hort.
espalier, planted hedge; ♀**gerade** a.
(as) straight as a dart, (as) stiff as a
post or a poker; =**gruppe** f clump of
trees; =**hacker** m, orn. nuthatch (=
Kleiber 2); =**harz** n gum, resin; =**hecke** f
hedge-row; =**heide** ♀ f brier (*Eri'ca arbo'-
rea*); ♀**hoch** a. (as) tall as a tree, (as) big
as a house, *fig.* gigantic; =**holz** n forest
timber; =**huhn** n, orn.: ⚲ alector (*Crax
ale'ctor*); =**kahn** m der Wilden canoe;
=**kante** ⊕ f, carp. rough edge; ♀**kantig**
⊕ a., carp. rough-edged; =**kauz** m, orn.
screech-owl (*Sy'rnium alu'co*); =**kenner** m:
⚲ dendrologist, arborist; =**kitt** m
glue for injured trees; =**krätze** f der
Bäume: (disease of trees caused by)
parmelia; =**kuchen** m pyramid cake;
=**kultur** f = =zucht; =**kultus** m, rel.
worship of trees, ⚲ dendrolatry;
=**kunde** f: ⚲ dendrology; ♀**lang** a. F
fig. as tall (F long) as a lamp-post;
=**läufer** m, orn. common creeper (*Ce'r-
thia familia'ris*); =**laus** f, ent. wood- or
tree-louse (*Aphis*); =**leiter** f (wooden)
steps pl., trestles pl.; =**lerche** f woodlark (*Alau'da arbo'rea*); ♀**los** a. tree-less;
=**marder** m, zo. pine-marten (*Muste'la
martes*); =**messer**: a) n, hort. pruning-
knife; b) m: ⚲ dendrometer; =**nachtigall**
f, orn. hedge-sparrow (*Acce'ntor*);
=**nymphe** f, myth. hamadryad; =**öl** n
olive-oil, sweet oil; ♀**ölen** v/a. ⊕⚹⚹*
to lubricate with sweet oil; =**pfahl** m
prop, support; =**pflanztag** m, Am. u.
Australien: arbor-day; =**pflanzung** f nursery, plantation; =**pflaster** n = =wachs;
=**pieper** m, orn. tree-pipit (*Anthus arbo'-
reus*); =**räude** f scurf (of trees), vgl. =krätze;
=**rauhe** ⊕ f rasp; ♀**reich** a. abounding
in trees, well wooded; =**rinde** f bark
(of a tree); =**saft** m sap; =**säge** f
pruning-saw; =**schere** ⊕ f (garden-)
shears pl.; =**aberuncator** ⊕ m,
paint. foliage(-painting); =**schnitt** m,
hort. lopping (off the branches), pruning; =**schröter** m, ent. stag-beetle (=
Hirschkäfer); =**schule** f, hort. nursery
(-garden), von gepfropften Stämmen: nursery of grafted trees; =**schutzkorb** m
(grobes Geflecht aus Weiden 2c. zum Schutz
der Bäume) osier, &c. basket (or casing)
for the protection of trees; =**schwamm**
♀ m agaric; =**seide** ♀ f bombazin(e);
=**specht** m, orn. = =läufer; ♀**stark** a. (as)
stout as a tree, of powerful build; mst
fig. (as) strong as a horse; =**stein** m,
min.: ⚲ dendrite; =**stock**, =**strunk** =
=stumpf; =**stumpf** m stump (of a tree);
=**tau** ⚓ n guess-rope or -warp; =**ver-
steinerung** f: ⚲ dendrolite; =**wachs** n,
hort. grafting-wax; mummy; =**wanze**
f, ent. forest-bug, wood-bug (*Penta'toma
ru'fipes*); =**wärter** m nursery-man;
(Förster) forester; =**werk** n: a) = =gruppe;
b) (Reisig) brushwood.
Baum-wolle mst (″…) f ⓶ cotton; rohe
(a. med. entfärbte) ~ cotton-wool; kurz-,

lang-staplige ~ short(-staple), long
(-staple) cotton; F *fig.* ein Kind 2c. in ~
wickeln (verhätscheln) to coddle a child.
baum-wollen (″…) a. ⓰ 1. (made of)
cotton, cottony. — 2. ⚹ *fig. v.* Stoffen 2c.:
fragile.
Baumwoll(en)-batist (″…⌣…) m ⓶ cotton
cambric; =**baum** ♀ m (silk) cotton-
plant or -tree (*Bombax*); ♀**erzeugend** a.
cotton-growing or -producing; (großer)
=**fabrikant** m cotton-lord; =**garn** n
cotton-yarn, twist; =**gaze** f tarlatan;
=**knopf** m twist button; atlasartiger
=**köper** ⊕ m satin jean; =**molton** ⊕ m
beaverteen; =**pflanze** ♀ f = =staude;
=**raupe** f, ent. cotton-worm (*Ale'tia
xyli'na*); =**samen-öl** n cotton-oil, nigger-
oil; =**sam(me)t** m velveteen; =**spinnerei**
f cotton-manufacture; cotton(-manu-)
factory or -mill; =**staude** f cotton-plant
(*Gossy'pium*); =**tüll** ⊕ m bobbinet, bobbin-
net; =**waren** f/pl., =**zeuge** n/pl. cotton
goods, cottons pl., cotton cloth(s pl.),
calico(es pl.); =**zwirn** m cotton (thread).
Baum-wuchs (″…) m ⓶ timber-growth;
=**wunde** f injury to (or injured part of)
a tree; =**würger** ♀ m staff-tree (*Cela'strus
scandens*); =**wurzel** f = =wurzler; =**wurzler** m sucker;
=**zucht** f growing of (fruit-)trees, fruit-
growing, ⚲ arboriculture; =**züchter** m
grower of (fruit-)trees.
Bau-ordnung (″…) f ⓶ building regulations pl.; =**plan** f = =entwurf, =riß,
=zeichnung; architect's plan or sketch;
=**platz** m = : a) =hof; b) =grund; c) =stelle;
=**rat** m, etwa: government surveyor
(of works); =**recht** n right to build;
♀**reif** a. ⓰: ♀es Terrain land ready
for building purposes.
bäurisch (ᴸ⌣) a. ⓰ 1. *g.s.* rustic, peasant-
like; ♀es Werk rustic work. — 2. *fig. b.s.*
(roh) clownish, churlish; (ungebildet) boorish, homely, F countrified. [sketch.⟩
Bau-riß (″…) m ⓶ architect's plan or⟨
☞ **Baus**-…, ♀… f. Paus-…, ♀-…
Bau-sand (″…) m ⓶ sand for building
purposes or for (mixing with) mortar.
Bausch (¹) [mhd. Schlag, Beule] m ⓉC. 1. (et.
Wulstiges, Gepolstertes) pad, bolster,
(small) cushion, am Ärmel: puff(ing),
v. Falten im Kleide: gathering (Schwulst)
puff, (Bündel) bunch. — 2. *surv.* (Aus-
buchtung; ant. Bogen, Einbuchtung)
convexity, bend; *fig.* in ~ und Bogen
in a lump, in the bulk, all together,
on an average; ⊕ in ~ und Bogen kaufen
F to buy (in) the lot, to buy in the
lump or bulk, to purchase wholesale.
Bausch-ärmel (″…) m ⓶ puffed (or F
leg-of-mutton) sleeve, bell-sleeve.
Bäuschchen (ᴸ⌣) n ⓶ (*dim. von* Bausch)
small pad or bolster or cushion.
Bausche (ᴸ⌣) f ⓰ 1. *surg.* compress. —
2. = Bausch. — 3. (Pausche) lump, bundle.
Bau-schein (″…) m ⓶ = =erlaubnis.
bauschen (ᴸ⌣) ⓰ I v/n. (h.) u. sich ♀ v/refl.
(sich schwellend ausdehnen) to swell (or
bulge) out, to bag. — II v/a. to puff
(out), to inflate; gebauschtes Haar
fluffy hair. — III ~ n ⓶ = Bauschung.
Bausch-hosen (″…) f ⓶ wide trousers
pl.; für Damen: bloomers.
bauschig (ᴸ⌣) a. ⓰ puffy, puffed out,
baggy, (aufgeblasen) inflated.

♪ Musik; ⚲ Wissenschaft; ♀ Pflanze; ⚱ Geographie; ⊕ Technik; ⚔ Bergbau; ⚔ Militär; ⚓ Marine; ⚫ Handel; ✉ Post; 🚂 Eisenbahn.

[Bauschkauf] — 150 — [beaufsichtigen]

Bausch-kauf ♀ (″...) m ㉜ purchase in the lump, buying a large parcel.
Bäuschlein (⌣′) n ㉓ = Bäuschchen.
Bau-schlosser (″...) m ㉜ builder's locksmith; weitS. builder's ironmonger.
Bausch-summe ♀ (″...) f ㊻ (Pauschsumme) lump sum, total.
Bau-schule (″...) f ㊷: a) = -gewerkschule; b) † = technische Hochschule (s. ds).
Bauschung (⌣′) f ㊻ inflation, bagginess.
Bau-schutt (″...) m ㉗c. rubbish; **-schwindel** m etwa: jerry-builder's operations pl.; wildcat building scheme.
Bause(=...), **bausen**¹ s. Pause ꝛc.
bausen² (⌣′) [: booze] v/n. ㉙ = zechen.
Bau-stein (″...) m ㉜ building stone; brick (auch für Kinder); (Sandstein) freestone; fig. ~e pl. zu // material (& bricks pl.) for //; **-stelle** f (building site); **~n zu verkaufen** (building) land to be sold in plots; vgl. a. **-grund**; **-stil** m (architectural) style; **-stoffe** m/pl. building materials pl.; **-sucht** f building mania, auch: brick-and-mortarism.
Baute (⌣′) [uhd.] f ㊻ (mst ~n als pl. zu Bau 1); öffentliche ~n pl.: a) public buildings pl.; b) public works pl.
Bau-tischler ☉ (″...) m ㉜ (builder's) carpenter; **-tischlerei** ☉ f ㊻ (builder's) carpentry work; **-unternehmer** m builder; **-verständig** a. ㊺ conversant with (or skilled in, F well up in) building matters or architecture; **-werk** n building, s. Werk 2; **-wesen** n (things pl. relating to or principles pl. of) architecture, building matters; **-winde** ☉ f lifting jack; **-wissenschaft** f architectural science or knowledge; **-würdig** ⚒ a. workable, payable; ♀e Ader paying lode or shoot.
Bauxit (bo-kßit') [fr. v. *Les B(e)aux bei Arles] m ㉗c. min. bauxite(Al_2O_3. $2H_2O$).
bauz (⌣′) int. bang!, bash!, dash!, smash!; ♀, flog die Tür zu! slam went the door! [building site).]
Bau-zaun (″′) m ㉗d. fence (round a}
bauzen F (⌣′) v/n. ㉙ to bounce (F to go bang) against; to dash (or go smash) into.
Bau-zweck (″′) m ㉗c.: zu ~en for architectural (or building) purposes.
Bayer (⌣′) (Bajo-(Bojer)wa'rier (Männer)] m ㊹. **~in** f ㊼ Bavarian.
bayerisch (⌣′) s. bayrisch.
Bayer-land ♀ (⌣⌣′) n ㉗c., **Bayern** (⌣′) npr/n. ㉓α. Bavaria.
bayrisch (⌣′) a. ㊺ Bavarian, of Bavaria; ♀(es) Bier, oft: lager(-beer).
bazillär ⚕ (⌣tß⌣′) [lt.] a. ㊺ bacillary.
Bazillarie ⚕ (⌣tß⌣′(⌣)⌣) f ㊸ (Stab-alge) bacillaria.
Bazillus ⚕ (⌣tß⌣⌣) [lt. Stäbchen] m ㉗ Biologie: (Spaltpilz) bacillus, weitS. germ.
Bch. abbr. = Buch. [of disease.]
Bd., **Bde.** abbr. = Band, Bände.
Bdellium (⌣⌣⌣) [lt.; grch.; *hebr. bedolach] n ㊵ (Gummiharz) bdellium.
be-... (⌣...) [ahd.: be... = bei] Vorsilbe in Bssgn mit verbs, immer untrennbar (*); hat folgende Bed.: **1.** aus e-m v/n. macht sie ein v/a., zB. aus „auf etwas achten" sie ein v/a. „etwas beachten": to attend to a th."; et. beachten to pay heed to a th. — **2.** aus e-m s. macht sie ein v/a., zB.: a) aus „Absicht intention": beabsichtigen to intend; b) Verwendung des s. als Ziel des v., zB aus „Schuh shoe": beschuhen to (put on a) shoe. — **3.** aus einem a. bildet sie ein v/a., zB. aus „frei free": befreien to (set) free. — **4.** in Verbindung mit einem einfachen v. bezeichnet be- oft: **a)** die Beziehung der durch das v. ausgesprochenen Tätigkeit auf die ganze Oberfläche des Gegenstandes, zB. aus „malen to paint": bemalen to paint all over, oder **b)** Vollendung, Verdoppelung, Häufigkeit dieser Tätigkeit, zB. aus „fragen to ask": befragen to question. — **5.** auch ganze Redensarten können durch be- zu einem v/a. werden, zB aus „ins Werk stellen": bewerkstelligen to put into execution.

be-absichtig/en (⌣⌣⌣⌣) v/a. ㊽* et. ♀ to intend (or purpose) doing a th., to have a th. in view, to contemplate (doing) a th., to aim at a th.; ich b/e ihn zu besuchen I mean (or intend) to call on him; (nichts) Böses ♀ to have (no) evil intentions; das B/te the object in view; es liegt darin et. B/tes there is some (distinct) purpose in it.

be-acht/en (⌣⌣cht⌣) I v/a. ㊽** to heed, to consider, to pay attention (or heed) to; im warnenden Sinne: to take care that; to mind that; (gewahren) to notice, to observe; e-n, et. ♀ (berücksichtigen) to take into account or consideration; j-s Rat (nicht) ♀ to follow (to disregard, to set aside) somebody's advice; nicht ♀ auch: to overlook. — **II ~n** ㉓ = Beachtung.

be-achtens-wert (⌣⌣cht⌣...) a. ㊺, **-würdig** worthy (or deserving) of notice or consideration, remarkable, noteworthy, noticeable; kaum ♀ trifling.

Be-achtung (⌣⌣cht⌣) f ㊻ attention, notice, (Berücksichtigung) consideration, regard.

be-ackern (⌣⌣⌣) agr. I v/a. ㉒a* to till, cultivate, ein Brachfeld ♀ to fallow. — **II ~** ㉓ tilling, tilth, cultivation.

Be-amte (⌣⌣⌣) m ㊲ **1.** (Staatsdiener) meist: (government) official, civil-servant, höherer: (high state-)functionary; Post ꝛc. auch: officer; politischer: officeholder, placeman; co. Jack-in-office; **~r sein** to be in the civil service, to hold a government appointment. — **2.** weitS. (Angestellter) employé, Polizei ꝛc.: officer; richterlicher **~r** magistrate.

Be-amten-beleidigung (″...) f ㊻ insult (offered) to an official (in the performance of his duty); **-herrschaft** f bureaucracy; **-konferenz** f meeting of officials (or officers); **-personal** n, coll. staff (of officials).

Be-amtenschaft (⌣⌣⌣⌣) f ㊻ (the) civil (or public) service, contp. officialdom.

Be-amten-stand (⌣⌣⌣⌣) m ㉗ civil servants pl., civil service; **-stolz** m official pride. [Beamtenschaft.)

Be-amtentum (⌣⌣⌣⌣) n ㉗d. (ohne pl.) =

Be-amten-wirtschaft (⌣⌣⌣⌣) f ㊻, **-zopf** m (official) red-tape, red-tapism.

Be-amtete†(⌣⌣⌣⌣)m,f㊲,*Be-amtin (⌣⌣⌣) f ㊻ = Beamte.

be-ängsten ⚘ (⌣⌣⌣) ㊽* = beängstigen.

be-ängstig/en (⌣⌣⌣⌣) I v/a. ㊽* to alarm, to fill with anxiety or anguish, stärker: to harass, to frighten; ♀♀ von Nachrichten, oft: alarmist. — **II ~n** ㉓ und

Be-ängst(ig)ung (⌣) f ㊻ alarm, anxiety.

be-anlagt (⌣⌣⌣) p.p. u. a. ㊹: gut ♀er Mensch (highly) gifted person.

be-ansprüch/en (⌣⌣⌣⌣) I v/a. ㊽* et. ♀ (von) to demand a th. from, als ein Recht: to claim a th. from a p., to lay claim to a th.; Fleiß, Sorgfalt: to require; Zeit: to occupy, to take. — **II ~ n** ㉓ u. **Be-anspruchung** f ㊻ claim (to a th.).

be-anstand/en (⌣⌣⌣⌣) v/a. ㊽* to object to, e-e Forderung ꝛc.: to demur to, eine Wahl ꝛc.: to oppose — **II B/ung** f ㊻ v. Waren refusal of goods.

be-antrag/en (⌣⌣⌣⌣) I v a. ㊽* = antragen II. — **II ~ n** ㉓ u. **B/ung** f ㊻ = Antrag 1.

be-antwort/en (⌣⌣⌣⌣) I v/a. ㊽* eine Frage ꝛc. ♀ to answer (or to reply to) a question, &c.; das b/et sich leicht (von selbst) that admits of an easy (requires no) answer; et. schwer zu ~des F a poser. — **II ~ n** ㉓ u. **B/ung**.

Be-antworter (⌣⌣⌣⌣) m, **~in** f ㊼ one who answers a question, &c., who replies to a p., a letter, &c.

Be-antwortung (⌣) f ㊻ answer(ing); schlagfertige: repartee; in~Ihres Schreibens in reply (or response) to …

Be-antwortungs-schreiben (″...) n ㉜, **-schrift** f (written) reply (to).

be-arbeit-bar (⌣⌣⌣⌣) a. ㊺ capable of being wrought or fashioned; workable.

be-arbeit/en (⌣⌣⌣⌣) I v/a. ㊽* **1.** (so m., wie man etwas haben will) meist: to work (auch ⚒, man. u. fig.); (Form geben) to model, to fashion; fig. **~ n** ♀ (zu bereden suchen) to use one's power of persuasion with a p. — **2.** et. nach abgeändertem Plane ♀ to recast a th.; e-n Stoff ꝛc. (wissenschaftlich) ♀ to elaborate …, to treat …; dieses Buch ist nach dem Englischen bearbeitet … has been adapted from the English (original); nach den neuesten Quellen ♀ to bring up to date; neu bearbeitete Auflage revised edition; ein Werk neu ♀ to re-edit (or re-write) …; ein Wörterbuch ♀ to compile … — **3.** ☉ = agr. to till; auf der Drehscheibe ♀ to turn; Steine: to hew, cut. — **4.** co. (durchprügeln) to belabour, cudgel, thrash. — **II ~ n** ♀ **5.** = B/ung.

Be-arbeiter (⌣⌣⌣⌣) m ㉒, **~in** f ㊼ one who works, &c. a th. (s. bearbeiten); v. Büchern: adapter, editor, compiler, reviser.

Be-arbeitung (⌣⌣⌣⌣) f ㊻ **1.** work(ing), fashioning. — **2.** elaboration, treatment; adaptation. — **3.** ☉ (auch fig.): cultivation (of the soil); auf der Drehscheibe: turning; mit dem Meißel: hewing. — **4.** ☉ ~ der Rohstoffe manufacture (or working up) of raw material. — **5.** geistige ~ editing; in ~, oft: in preparation; (Umarbeiten) recast(ing), gediegene ~ solid workmanship.

be-argwöhn/en (⌣⌣⌣⌣) I v/a. ㊽* e-n e-r Sache ♀: a) aus Mißtrauen: to suspect a p. (of a th.); b) aus Klugheit: to credit a p. (with a th.). — **II ~ n** ㉓ und **B/nung** f ㊻ suspicion (against a. p.).

Beatifikation (⌣⌣⌣⌣tß⌣′) [lt.] f ㊻ = Seligsprechung. [seligsprechen.]

beatifizieren (⌣⌣⌣⌣⌣′) [lt.] ㊽* = }

Beatrice (⌣⌣′tß⌣) [it.] f ㊸ß., **Beatrix** (⌣′⌣) [lt.] ㊴⑥γ. npr/f. Beatrice.

be-aufsichtig/en (⌣⌣⌣⌣⌣) I v/a. ㊽* e-n, et. ♀ to watch over (or to control, to

---

Signs (see page XVII): F familiar; P vulgar; ꟾ flash; ⚘ rare; † obsolete (died); * new word (born); ++ incorrect; ♪ music;

[Beaufsichtiger] — 151 — [bedecken]

be-aufsichtigen supervise a p., a th.; (genau prüfen) to inspect. — II ~ n ⓘ = B/ung.
Be-aufsichtiger (‿‿‿) m ⓘ controller; supervisor; superintendent; inspector.
Be-aufsichtigung (..) f ⓘ control, supervision; inspection; unter polizeilicher ~ under surveillance, on ticket-of-leave.
be-auftrag/en (‿‿‿) I v/a. ⓘ* e-n mit et. ⓘ to charge a p. with a th.; bsb. ⓘ: to commission a p. to do a th.; bei der Verwaltung: to authorize a p. to do a th. — II ~ n ⓘ = B/ung. — III be-auftragt p.p. u. a. ⓘ: ⓘ von by order of; Ler Richter judge in charge of a case; ~e(r)m f ⓘ p. commissioned (to do a th.), agent; (Bevollmächtigter) mandatory; (Abgeordneter) deputy. — IV Be-auftragung (f. I) f ⓘ commission, authorization, mandate.
be-äugeln F (‿‿‿) v/a. ⓘa* to ogle, to eye; schielend: to leer at; verliebt: to cast side-glances (or make sheepish eyes) at.
be-augenscheinigen (‿‿‿‿) I v/a. ⓘ* to view, to (have a) look at, to inspect. — II ~ n ⓘ u. Be-augenscheinigung f ⓘ view, review, (close) inspection.
be-baken ↓ (‿‿) v/a. ⓘ* (mit Baken versehen) to mark off with buoys.
be-bändern (‿‿‿) v/a. ⓘa* to deck (or adorn, trim up) with ribbons; be-bändert beribboned, arch. with ribbon ornaments.
be-bartet (‿‿‿) a. ⓘ bearded.
be-bau/en (‿‿‿) I v/a. ⓘ* 1. agr. u. fig. = anbauen 1; nie bebautes Land virgin soil. — 2. ⚒ to work. — 3. (mit Bauwerken besetzen) to build upon (a plot), F to cover (a plot) with brick and mortar. — II ~ n ⓘ 4. = B/ung.
Be-bauer (‿‿) m ⓘ 1. = Anbauer. — 2. p. who erects buildings on (a plot).
Be-bauung (‿‿) f ⓘ 1. (zu bebauen 1) = Anbau 1. — 2. (zu 3) covering (plots or land) with buildings.
Be-bauungs-plan (‿‿‿) m ⓘ plan for erecting dwellings on a building site.
beben (‿‿) [ahd.] I v/n. (h.) ⓘ 1. (vor Zorn) to quiver (with rage). — 2. das Herz bebt mir my heart throbs; vor Freude ⓘ to thrill with joy; vor Furcht ⓘ to quiver (or tremble) with fear; vor Kälte ⓘ to shiver with cold. — II ~ n ⓘ 3. zu I: trembling, shivering. — 4. ♪ (Zittern) tremolo.
Beber-esche ⚘ (‿‿‿‿) f ⓘ = Zitterpappel.
Bebe-zug ♪ (‿‿‿) m ⓘ der Orgel tremor, tremolo-stop. [cover) with pictures.)
be-bildern (‿‿‿) v/a. ⓘa* to adorn (or
be-binden (‿‿‿) v/a. ⓘ* ⓘ mit to tie round with, to wrap up in. [veneer.)
be-blatten ⊕ (‿‿‿) v/a. ⓘ* (furnieren) to
be-blättern (‿‿‿) I v/a. u. v/refl. ⓘa*: (sich) ⓘ to cover (o.s.) with foliage. — II be-blättert p.p. und a. ⓘ furnished with leaves; leafy; ⚘ foliate.
be-blümt (‿‿) a. ⓘ flowery.
be-bohlen (‿‿‿) v/a. ⓘ* to plank over, to cover with boards.
be-brillen (‿‿‿) v/a. ⓘ* to provide (or arm) with spectacles (or glasses); bebrillt spectacled, wearing glasses; bebrilltes Gesicht P goggle-eyes pl.
be-brüten (‿‿‿) I v/a. ⓘ* to hatch; aber: bebrütetes Ei egg that has been sat on; addled egg. — II ~ n ⓘ und Be-brütung f ⓘ incubation.
Bebung ♪ (‿‿) f ⓘ tremolo.
be-buscht (‿‿) p.p. u. a. ⓘ bushy.
Becher (‿‿) [ahd.: beaker; lt.; *grch.] m ⓘ 1. (Trinkgeschirr) (drinking-)cup, beaker, goblet; (Kirche) chalice; weitS. (Trinkglas) tumbler. — 2. ~ zum Würfeln dice-box. — 3. (Maß) etwa: pint. — 4. ⚘ = (Napf) der Eicheln cup(ule).
Becher-blume ⚘ (‿‿‿) f ⓘ = -kraut.
Becherchen (‿‿‿) n ⓘ (dim. von Becher) small goblet or cup.
Becher-druse ⚒ (‿‿‿) f ⓘ min. quartz; -flechte ⚘ f cup-moss (Lichen pyxidatus); -förmig a. ⓘ cup- (or goblet-)shaped; ⚘ cyathiform; ⚘ der Gallapfel cup-gall; -früchtler ⚘ m/pl. = ⚘ cupuliferæ pl.; -glas n cup-shaped glass, tumbler, chm. beaker; -hülle ⚘ f: ⚘ cupule; -klang m jingling of glasses; unter fröhlichem ~, etwa: amid (gay) revelry or carousing; -kraut ⚘ n garden (or salad) burnet (Sanguisorba minor).
Becherlein (‿‿‿) n ⓘ = Becherchen.
Becher-moos ⚘ (‿‿‿) n ⓘ cladonia (Cladonia pyxidata). [to booze, to lush up.)
bechern (‿‿) v/n. (h.) ⓘa. to tipple, F u. P
Becher-pilz ⚘ (‿‿‿) m cup-mushroom (Peziza); -qualle f: ⚘ calycozoan; -spiel n der Taschenspieler cup-and-balls; -werk ⊕ n chain-pump work.
Beck † (‿) [ahd.] m ⓘc. = Bäcker.
Becken (‿‿) [ahd., *mlt.] n ⓘ 1. (flaches rundes Gefäß): a) basin (auch ⚘ u geol.); b) anat. (knöchernes Gerüst des Unterleibes): ⚘ pelvis. — 2. ♪ ~ pl. cymbals pl.
Becken-arterie (‿‿‿‿) f ⓘ ⚘ hypogastric artery; -bein n pelvic bone; -förmig a. basin-shaped; -höhle f pelvic cavity; -knochen m = -bein; -messer m Geburtshilfe: ⚘ pelvimeter; -messung f pelvimetry; -schläger ♪ m cymbal-player.
Becquerel-strahlen (bä-k'räl...) [Henry B. 1896, fr. Physiker, * 1852] m/pl. ⓘ ⚘ Becquerel (or uranium) rays.
be-dach/en (‿‿‿) I v/a. ⓘ* (ant. abdachen) to (cover with a) roof. — II ~ n ⓘ = B/ung I. — III be-dacht¹ p.p. roofed (in).
be-dacht² (‿‿) I 1. p.p. v. bedenken. — II a. ⓘ 2. (überlegt) thoughtful, wary. — 3. (achtsam) mindful of, intent on; auf seinen Vorteil sehr ⓘ sein to be bent on benefiting o.s., to be keenly alive to one's own interest, to take good care of o.s., F to look well after number one.
Be-dacht³ (‿) m ⓘb. (ohne pl.) (Überlegung) reflection, consideration; (Vorsicht) caution, forethought; mit gutem ~ after mature deliberation; mit ~ handeln to act deliberately; ~ nehmen auf et. to have (or pay) regard to a th., to take a th. into account, to consider a th.
Be-dachte(r) m f (‿‿‿) ⓘ jur. (j. dem ein Vermächtnis ausgesetzt ist) legatee.
be-dächtig (‿‿‿) a. ⓘ 1. (mit Bedacht handelnd) cautious, circumspect, thoughtful; ⓘ(sich) zu Werke gehen to go about a th. warily. — 2. (langsam u. abgemessen) slow and deliberate; mit Ler Schnelle with moderate speed; mit Len Schritten with measured steps.
Be-dächtigkeit (‿‿‿‿) f ⓘ 1. cautiousness, circumspection, (Überlegung) thoughtfulness. — 2. (Langsamkeit) slowness, (Abgemessenheit) deliberateness.
be-dachtsam (‿‿‿...) a. ⓘ inconsiderate, unthinking; -losigkeit f ⓘ inconsiderateness, thoughtlessness; -nahme f (auf) regard (to).
be-dachtsam (‿‿‿) a. ⓘ lost in thought; (bedächtig) thoughtful, circumspect.
Be-dachtsamkeit (‿‿‿--) f ⓘ thoughtfulness, circumspection. [2. roof.)
Be-dachung (‿‿‿) f ⓘ 1. roofing. —
be-danken (‿‿‿) ⓘ* I sich ⓘ v/refl. 1. to render thanks; sich bei e-m für et. ⓘ to thank a p. for a th.; sich bei e-m ⓘ, auch: to express one's thanks (or gratitude) to a p.; rel. sich bei Gott ⓘ to return thanks to the Almighty. — 2. iro. (abweisen) to decline (or refuse) a th.; ich bedanke mich dafür F I'm much obliged, but I would rather not; auch: I would rather be excused. — II ⓘ v/a. 3. nun sei bedankt, mein lieber Schwan! now let me thank you, dearest swan!
be-darf¹ (‿‿) pres. ind. von bedürfen.
Be-darf² (‿‿) m ⓘb. (o. pl.) ⓘ (Bedürfnis, Mangel an) want (or lack) of; ⓘ demand (or inquiry) for; bei ~ if required, if inquired for; je nach ~ according to requirement; seinen ~ in et. decken to supply deficiencies (in one's stock), to stock an article. — 2. (Vorrat an et.) supply, stock; ich habe m-n ~ (gedeckt) I have purchased all that I require.
Be-darfs-fall (‿‿‿...) m ⓘ: im ~ in case of necessity or need; -haus n für Beamte civil-service stores pl.
be-dauerlich (‿‿‿) a. ⓘ (von Sachen) regrettable, to be regretted; stärker: deplorable, lamentable, sad; es ist sehr ⓘ, daß // it is a great pity that //.
be-dauern (‿‿‿) [mhd.] I v/a. ⓘa* 1. einen wegen etwas ⓘ to sympathize with a p. in a th.; e-n ⓘ, auch: to pity (or to feel pity for) a p.; j-s Unglück ⓘ to feel (or be) sorry for a p.'s ..., stärker: to deplore a p.'s ... — 2. e-n Vorfall ꝛc. ⓘ to regret (stärker: to deplore or lament) an occurrence, &c. — II ~ n ⓘ 3. zu I: über e-n Verlust: regret; wir haben mit ~ vernommen, daß // we regret to hear (or to be informed) that//; we have heard with regret that //.
be-dauerns-wert (‿‿‿...) a. ⓘ. ⓘ würdig in Bezug auf einen Verlust: to be pitied, pitiable, stärker: deplorable.
Bede † (‿‿) [ndd.: bieten] f ⓘ = Abgabe.
be-deck/en (‿‿‿) I v/a. u. v/refl. ⓘ* 1. (sich) mit et. ⓘ to cover (o.s.) with a th.; bitte, ⓘ Sie sich! pray be covered!, please put on your hat!; mit bedecktem Haupte with one's hat (or cap) on; bedecktes (bewohnbares) Boot houseboat. — 2. (verhüllen) to clothe, ⚔ to mask; ⚔ bedecktes Gelände broken (or difficult, intersected) ground; (verheimlichen) to cloak; den Tisch mit einem Tuche ⓘ to spread a cloth over the table; der Himmel bedeckte sich (mit Wolken) the sky was overcast; bedeckte (belegte) Stimme F ropy voice. — 3. (schützen) to protect; ⚔: eine Stadt ⓘ to cover ...; das Gepäck ⓘ (begleiten) to escort the baggage. — 4. ⊕ mit e-m Mauerwerke ⓘ to wall in (or

⚘ scientific; ⚘ botanical; ⚘ geography; ⊕ machinery; ⚒ mining; ⚔ military; ↓ marine; ⓘ commercial; ⓘ postal; ⓘ railway.

up). — 5. fig. mit Ehre (Schande) ≈ to load with honours (shame). — II ~ n ㉓ 6. = B/ung 1 u. 2.
be-deckt=ſamig ♀ (◡́◡̇◡̇) a. ⓖ ⚘ angiospermous, angiospermatous; ≈e Pflanze(n f/pl.)(Hüllſamer) angiosperm(ia pl.).
Be-deckung (◡́◡) f ㊻ 1. covering. — 2. protection. — 3. (das zur ~ Dienende) cover(ing). — 4. (Bekleidung) clothing. — 5. meiſt ⚔ (Begleitmannſchaft) guard, safeguard, escort; zur ~ dienen to escort; ⚓ (~ſchiff) convoy. — 6. ast. e-s Sterns: occultation.
Be-deckungs=mannſchaft(◡́...) f ㊻, =ſchiff ⚓ n, =truppen f/pl. convoy, escort.
be-denken (◡́◡) ㊻* I v/a. 1. (erwägen) et. ≈ to reflect about (or to consider) a th., ſtärker: to ponder on a matter; (überlegen) to think over; vorher ≈ to premeditate; die Folgen ≈ to weigh the consequences; ich gebe es Ihnen zu ≈: a) I leave it to your consideration; b) drohend: think (or mind) what you are doing!; ≈, daß to bear in mind that; und wenn man bedenkt, daß // to think that //. — 2. e-n ≈ (für ihn ſorgen) to provide for a p.; e-n mit et. ≈ (verſorgen) to supply a p. with a th.; e-n in ſ-m Teſtamente ≈ to remember a p. (or to put a p. down) in one's will; to leave (or bequeath) a p. s.th. in one's will; von der Natur, vom Glücke gut bedacht ſein to be highly favoured by ... — II ſich ≈ v/refl. 3. (ſich beſinnen) to reflect, to deliberate; ſich eines ander(e)n od. eines Beſſer(e)n ≈ to change (or alter) one's mind; to think better of it. — 4. (erwägend zögern, et. zu tun) to hesitate before doing a th., to waver in one's resolution. — 5. (an ſich denken) to think of oneself or self. — III ~ n ㉓ 6. (zu 1:) consideration; (zu 3:) reflection; (zu 4:) hesitation; ~ tragen, et. zu tun to shrink (back) from (doing) a th.; das hat kein ~ there is no objection to that; er wird kein ~ tragen (hegen) F he won't stick at that, he'll have no compunction about it; er macht ſich wenig ~ darüber he does not let it trouble him, he feels little concern about it. — 7. (Zweifel, Anſtandnahme) doubt, scruple; ~ bei e-m über et. erregen to cast (or instil) doubts into a p.'s mind (or to fill a p. with suspicion) about a th.; ohne ~ without hesitation, unhesitatingly, (zuverſichtlich) confidently; voller ~ hesitating, diffident; scrupulous. — IV **be-dacht** p.p. u. a. ⓖ 8. ſ. 2 u. bſd. Art.
be-denklich (◡́) a. ⓖ 1. (Bedenken erregend) doubtful, ſtärker: serious, critical, grave; (heikel) delicate, precarious, ticklish; das war oder ſchien ihm ≈ that was a grave matter to him, it made him think twice. — 2. (Bedenken hegend) full of doubts or scruples, scrupulous.
Be-denklichkeit (◡́◡◡) f ㊻ 1. = bedenken 7; Sie kennen ſeine ~(en) you know his objections. — 2. (mißliche Beſchaffenheit) e-r Krankheit: seriousness, gravity; e-r Lage: precariousness.
Be-denk=zeit (◡́◡) f ㊻ time for reflection, breathing-time; e-m ~ geben to grant a p. a (few days') respite.

be-deut/en (◡◡́) I v/a. ⓖ* 1. a) mſt. (einen beſtimmten Sinn haben) to signify; was bedeutet dieſes Wort? what is the meaning of this word?; die Bretter, die die Welt ≈ (SCH.) the boards which represent the world; b) (von Wichtigkeit ſein) der Mann (die Sache) bedeutet et., hat (et)was oder viel zu ≈ he is a man (it is a matter) of great consequence or import(ance); das hat nichts zu ≈ it does not matter, it is of no consequence; von e-m begangenen Fehler: there is no harm (done); es hat wenig zu ≈ it matters little, it does not much signify; tadelnd: was hat das zu ≈? what's the meaning of that?; c) (andeuten) to indicate, to suggest; (bezeichnen) to point to; das bedeutet nichts Gutes that bodes (or augurs) no(thing) good, it means mischief; F das hat was zu ≈, oft: there's something (or some intention) in that; d) (e-n Wink geben) e-m ob. e-r Ś. (zu mit inf.) to intimate (or point out) to a p. (a th. or that he should mit inf.); laſſen Sie ſich ≈ be advised (in time), take my advice; er will ſich (dat.) nicht ≈ laſſen he won't listen to reason; e) (erklären) to declare to a p.; belehrend: to explain to a p. — II ~ n ㉓ 2. = B/ung 1. — III ≈d p.pr. u. a. ⓖ 3. Beb. des inf. — 4. (ſ. 1 a u. b) significant. — 5. (Geltung habend) important; (die Blicke auf ſich ziehend) distinguished; (bemerkenswert) notable, remarkable; ≈ oder Gewinn, Verluſt a considerable gain, heavy loss; adv. considerably, by far, &c.
Be-deutenheit (◡◡́◡) f ㊻ importance; eines Talents ꝛc.: superiority, greatness.
be-deutſam (◡◡́) a. ⓖ significant, fraught with meaning, suggestive, pregnant, expressive; **~keit** (◡◡́◡◡) f ㊻ significance, (Wichtigkeit) import(ance).
Be-deutung (◡◡́◡) f ㊻ 1. (zu bedeuten 1 a:) signification; (zu 1 b:) importance; (zu 1 d:) intimation; (zu 1 e:) declaration. — 2. (zu 1 a:) eine ~ haben (für) to signify (to); in des Wortes verwegenſter ~ in the fullest (or boldest) sense of the word; zu b: (Wichtigkeit) importance; von geringer ~ of little account or consequence, unimportant; ~ gewinnen bei // to become important (or an important factor) in //, to gain in importance for //; von ~ ſein (für e-n, für et.) to be (a matter) of consequence (to a p., for a th.); e-m, einer Sache eine höhere ~ verleihen to attribute greater importance to a p., a th.; zu c: indication. — 3. mſt gr.: acceptation; bildliche (eigentliche) ~ e-s Wortes figurative (proper) meaning (or sense) ...; (zu 1b:) (Wert) value; (Tragweite) import; (zu 1 c:) v. ſchlimmer ~ of evil augury, ominous; (zu 1 d:) (Abſicht) et. mſt ſagen to say a th. pointedly.
be-deutungs-leer (◡◡́◡...) a. ⓖ, =los a., oft: insignificant, ſtärker: void of meaning or importance, of no account; =loſigkeit f ㊻ insignificance, unmeaningness; ≈reich a.: a) fraught with meaning; b) admitting (of) various interpretations; ≈ſchwer, ≈voll a.: a) weighty, of

great consequence or moment, momentous; b) für die Zukunft: portentous; c) full of meaning, ſ. bedeutſam.
Be-dielen ⊙ (◡́◡) ⓖ* ꝛc. = dielen ꝛc.
be-dienen (◡́◡) ⓖ* I v/a. 1. e-n, et. ≈, meiſt: to serve a p., a th.; e-n Kranken ≈ to wait (or attend) on a patient, to nurse an invalid; die Tafel (oder bei Tiſche) ≈ to wait at table. — 2. fig. iro. ich habe ihn tüchtig bedient I have cajoled him, F I've buttered him up; die (ärztliche) Praxis ≈ to attend to one's patients; ⚔ ⚓ ein Geſchütz ≈ to work a gun or piece of ordnance. — 3. faſt † (bekleiden) ein Amt ≈ to fill one's post. — 4. (Kartenſpiel) Farbe ≈ to follow suit. — II ſich ≈ v/refl. 5. ſich einer Sache (gen.) ≈ to avail o.s. of (or to use) a th., to make use of a th.; bei Tiſche: bitte, ≈ Sie ſich! please help yourself (pl. yourselves)! — III ~ n ㉓ 6. = Bedieung 1 u. 2.
be-dienſten (◡◡́◡) v/a. ⓖ* e-n ≈ to give employment (or a situation) to a p.
Be-dienſtete([r] m) (◡◡́◡) f ㊻ employé; die Be-dienſteten pl., oft: the staff; (Dienſtboten) establishment (of servants).
Be-diente(r) (◡◡́◡) m ⓖ gewöhnlich: (Dienſtbote) serving-man; in vornehmen Häuſern: lackey, footman, valet; boy in buttons.
be-dientenhaft (◡◡́◡◡) a. ⓖ contp. flunkey-like; servile; **~igkeit** (◡◡́◡◡◡) f ㊻ contp. flunkeyism, servility.
Be-dienten=kleidung(◡◡́◡...) f ㊻, =livree f livery; =pack n, etwa: footman and butlers pl.; =ſeele f flunkey, lackey, weit S. cringing nature; =ſitz m (hinten am Wagen) dicky; =ſtand m (class of) serving-men, men-servants pl.; =tracht f footman's livery; =zimmer n servants' hall.
Be-dienung (◡◡́◡) f ㊻ 1. (Aufwartung) service, attendance; ⚔ artill. ~ eines Geſchützes service (or working) of a gun; in dieſem Wirtshauſe iſt die ~ ſchlecht one gets badly waited (up)on ... — 2. (Kartenſpiel) following suit; ~ iſt nötig you must follow suit. — 3. coll. (Dienerſchaft) servants, domestics pl.
Be-dienung(s-mannſchaft) ⚔ (◡́...) f ㊻, artill. eines Geſchützes: gunners pl.
Be-ding † (◡́) m, n ⓑ. = Bedingung 2.
be-ding/en (◡́◡) v/a. u. v/refl., 1 u. 2. ⓖſt* 3 u. 4: ⓖ* 1. (durch Vertrag ꝛc. feſtſetzen) et. ≈, meiſt: to agree upon a th., ſtärker: to stipulate (or settle) a th.; e-e Ware ≈ (feilſchend behandeln) to bargain (or haggle) about (or for) the price of goods; ein Schiff ≈ (befrachten) to charter ... — 2. (beſchränkend feſtſetzen) = ausbedingen 2. — 3. ⚲ (beſchränken) to restrict; bedingt werden durch to be dependent on, to depend on. — 4. mit ſachlichem Subjekt: et. bedingt et. (erheiſcht es, erfordert es, bringt es mit ſich) s.th. must result in a th., s.th. involves (the necessity of) a th. — II ~ n ㉓ 5. = B/ung 1. — III **bedingt** p.p. u. a. ⓖ 6. (eingeſchränkt) limited (by certain conditions); ≈e Feſtſetzung ⚔ jur. (Subſtituierung) qualified (or conditional) stipulation; gram. ≈e Form conditional (mood); jur. ≈e Verurteilung qualified ſentence, verdict with a recommendation to mercy.

Be-dingt-heit f, **Be-dingt-sein** (⌣–) n limitation (by), restrictedness.
Be-dingung (⌣⌣) f 1. (zu bedingen 1:) agreement; (zu 3:) restriction. — 2. condition; ~en stellen to lay down one's conditions, to make one's terms; ● ~en einreichen to tender for ...; unter der ~, daß // on condition (or with the understanding) that //; unter billigen ~en on easy terms; unter k-r ~ on no account, not on any terms, not at any price.
be-dingungs-los (–⌣...) a) a. (auch als s. =lose(s) n) (the) absolute; b) a. und adv. unconditional(ly); =losigkeit f absoluteness; unconditionalness; =satz m, gram. hypothetical sentence or clause; ~weise adv. conditionally.
be-dräng/en (⌣⌣) I v/a. (bedrücken) to (op)press, to press hard (upon); (quälen) to vex; (betrüben) to distress, to afflict; von Feinden, Gläubigern ꝛc. bedrängt harassed by ...; in bedrängter Lage, in bedrängten Umständen sein to be in great distress or straits, F to be hard up or P broke(n). — II ~ n, **Be-drängnis** (⌣⌣-) f, n, **Bedrängtheit** (⌣⌣-) f, **Be-drängung** (⌣⌣-) f: a) materiell: embarrassment, (Not) trouble, pinch (of poverty), stärker: distress; b) geistig: (Betrübnis) vexation, stärker: tribulation, affliction; downcast state, rel. soreness of spirit.
be-dräuen † ob. poet. (⌣–) = bedrohen.
be-droh/en (⌣⌣) I v/a. e-n (mit et.) ≤ to threaten (or menace) a p. (with a th.). — II ~ n = B/ung.
be-drohlich (-) a. threatening to.
Be-drohung (-) f threat or menace (to a p.), threatening (a p.).
be-drucken (⌣⌣) v/a. to print over or on; to cover with printed matter.
be-drück/en (⌣⌣) I v/a. to press (heavily) upon, b.s. to oppress, s. bedrängen I; mit Steuern ≤ to grind down (with taxes). — II ~ n = B/ung. [of, tyrant over.)
Be-drücker (⌣⌣) m, ~in f oppressor;
Be-drückung (⌣⌣) f oppression of, tyranny over, s. Bedrängnis.
Beduin/e (-⌣⌣) [ar.] m, B/in f (Wüstenaraber[in]), b/isch (-⌣⌣) a. Bedouin.
be-dünken I v/n. (h.) u. v/impers. = dünken I; es will mich (ob. mir) ≤, daß // it appears to me that //, I have an idea that //. — II ~ n opinion, belief; meines ~s, nach meinem ~ in my opinion, to my way of thinking.
be-dürfen (⌣⌣) v/a., v/n. (h.) u. v/imp. ich bedarf etwas oder e-r Sache (gen.) I am in need (or want) of a th.; sie bedarf einiger Unterstützung she wants (or requires) a little assistance; es bedurfte nur eines Wortes it needed (or required) but a (or one) word; das bedarf einer Erklärung that requires or calls for) an explanation; es bedarf keiner Überlegung there is no need for deliberation, you need not consider the matter.
Be-dürfnis (⌣⌣) n († f) lack, want, stärker: need; es ist mir ein ~ zu sagen // I feel it my (bounden) duty to say //, I cannot help (or forbear) saying //;

seine Bedürfnisse befriedigen to satisfy one's wants; er hat große Bedürfnisse his necessities (or requirements) are great; F euph. ein ~ verrichten to relieve o.s., to ease nature; F to do s. th.
Be-dürfnis-anstalt (⌣...) f (water-)closet (abbr. W. C.); für Herren auch: lavatory; für Damen: cloak-room; ≤los a. having no wants or requirements; (mäßig) frugal; =losigkeit f absence of needs or wants; (Mäßigkeit) frugality.
be-dürftig (⌣⌣) a. (arm) poor, necessitous, (notleidend) indigent, needy; e-r Sache (gen.) ≤ in need (or want) of a th., needing (or wanting, requiring) a th.
Be-dürftigkeit (⌣⌣-) f 1. (das Bedürfen) need, necessity. — 2. (Not) indigence, stärker: destitution, distress, misery.
be-duseln P (⌣⌣) ≈ a* I v/a. to make drunk or tipsy; beduselt tipsy, half seas-over, fuddled, muddled. — II sich ≤ v/refl. F to get fuddled or boozy.
Beefsteak T (bi'f-ſtēt) n (beef-)steak; auf dem Rost gebratenes ~ roast steak; gut durch=(nur halb=)gebratenes ~ well done (underdone) steak.
be-ehren (⌣⌣) * I v/a. e-n mit et. ≤ to honour (a p. with a th., ● mit Briefen, Aufträgen ꝛc.: to favour; einen Wechsel ≤ to honour a draft or bill; ≤ Sie uns bald mit einem Besuche kindly favour us with (or do us the favour of) an early call; das Vertrauen, mit dem (ob. womit) Sie uns beehrt haben the confidence which you have reposed in us. — II sich ≤ v/refl. ich beehre mich, Ihnen mitzuteilen I beg (amtlich ob. feierlich: I have the honour) to inform you.
be-eiden (⌣⌣) *, **be-eidigen** (⌣⌣⌣) * I v/a. 1. et. ≤ to confirm a th. by (an) oath, to take an oath upon a th.; be-eidigte Aussage: a) mündliche: sworn evidence, evidence (confirmed) by oath; b) schriftliche: affidavit. — 2. = vereid(ig)en I. — II ~ n u. **Be-eid(ig)ung** f 3. (zu 1:) confirmation (of a th.) by oath; (zu 2:) = vereid(ig)en II.
be-eifer/n (⌣⌣⌣) I sich ≤ v/refl. ≈ a* sich ≤ zu tun (make (great) efforts to, to do one's utmost in order to, to endeavour to. — II ~ n u. B/ung f zeal(ous effort), endeavour, assiduousness.
be-eilen (⌣⌣) * I v/a. seine Schritte ≤ to hasten one's steps. — II sich ≤ v/refl. tc make haste, to hasten (zu to //) ohne inf.: to hurry, F to put one's best leg forward, Am. to hustle; beeile dich! make haste!, look sharp!, look alive!, F u. P buck up!
be-einflussen (⌣⌣⌣) I v/a. to influence, to have influence with; (einwirken auf) to work upon, to affect; ~ gegen to prejudice against. — II ~ n u. **Be-einflussung** f influence, ...ing; using one's influence with a p., being influenced by a p. or a th.
be-einträchtig/en (⌣⌣⌣⌣⌣) [Eintrag tun] I v/a. e-n, et. ≤ (benachteiligen) to injure, to impair a p., a th.; to wrong a p., (j-s Rechte verletzen) to prejudice a p.('s interest), to encroach upon a

p.'s rights. — II ~ n u. B/ung f = (von // oder gen.) injury (or wrong) inflicted on (or done to) //.
be-eisen[1] (⌣⌣) [Eis] v/a. * a. v/refl. (mit Eis bedecken) to cover (over) with ice; sich ≤ to become frozen over.
be-eisen[2](-)[Eisen] v/a. * to shoe a horse; to case in iron, to cover with iron.
Beelzebub (⌣⌣-,⌣⌣-) [hebr. Herr der Fliegen (bösen Geister) 2. Kön. 1,2ff] m ● a. Beelzebub.
be-enden (⌣⌣) *, mst **be-endigen** (⌣⌣⌣) * I v/a. to finish, to put an end to, to bring to a conclusion, to terminate; das Fest mit Feuerwerk ≤ to wind up (or conclude) ... with fireworks. — II ~ n u. **Be-end(ig)ung** f finish(-ing), termination, conclusion.
be-engen (⌣⌣) I v/a. to narrow (down), (beklemmen) to oppress, to cramp (up), stärker: to choke; fig. (einschränken) to confine, restrain, straiten; sich beengt fühlen to feel oppressed or confined. — II ~ n, **Be-engt-heit** (⌣⌣-) f, **Be-engung** f narrowness, der Brust: oppression, tightness (on the chest); fig. confinement, restraint.
be-erben (⌣⌣) I v/a. e-n ≤ to inherit (or to be heir to) a p.('s property), F to come into a p.'s money. — II be-erbt p.p. und a. (mit Erben versehen) leaving successors or (direct) heirs (to one's estate). [heiress to ...]
Be-erber (⌣⌣) m, ~in f heir,)
Beer-blau (⌣⌣) n und ≤ a. turnsole (or vegetable) blue; =blume ♀ f Malabar nightshade (Base'lla rubra).
be-erdigen (⌣⌣⌣) I v/a. to bury, inter. — II ~ n u. **Be-erdigung** f burial, interment; funeral.
Be-erdigungs-feier (⌣...) f funeral, obsequies pl.; =kasse f (funds pl. of a) burial society; =konto n undertaker's (or funeral furnisher's) business; =kosten pl. funeral expenses pl.; =platz m burial-ground, cemetery; =recht n right of burial; =schein m certificate of death, Am. burial-permit. — Vgl. auch Begräbnis..., Grab=..., Leichen=..., Toten=...
Beere ♀ (⌣⌣) [ahd.: berry] f berry, ♁ bacca; ~n suchen u. ≤n ● to gather berries, F to go a berrying.
beeren-ähnlich (⌣⌣⌣...) a., ≤artig a. like (or resembling) a berry, vgl. auch ≤förmig; =blau n = Beerblau; ≤förmig a. berry-shaped; ♁ & bacciform; ≤fressend a. orn.: ♁ baccivorous; =fresser m/pl., orn. baccivorous birds pl.; =frucht & f berry; =obst n ♁ bacciform fruit; =tang ♀ m gulf-weed (Sarga'ssum bacci'ferum); ≤tragend ≈ a. berry-bearing, ♁ bacciferous.
Beer-grün ♀ (⌣...) n = Immergrün; =melde ♀ f = Erdbeerspinat; =most m rape-wine; =raute ♀ f = Raute[1] Biest.)
Beest (⌣) [ndd.: *It. bēʹstia f] n b. =)
Beet (⌣) [= Bett] n ●c. agr., hort. bed; schmales ~ (Rabatte) border, narrow bed; schräges ~ shelving bed; (Mist=)~ hotbed; in ~en wachsend bedded.
Beete ♀ (⌣) f. Bete. [flower-bed.)
Beet-einfassung (⌣...) f border of)
beeten (⌣⌣; Hom. beten) v/a. ● agr. die Felder ≤ to arrange the fields in strips or beds.

♪ Musik; ⚛ Wissenschaft; ♀ Pflanze; ♁ Geographie; ⊕ Technik; ⚒ Bergbau; ✕ Militär; ⚓ Marine; ● Handel; ✉ Post; 🚂 Eisenbahn.

[beet=weise] — 154 — [befestigen]

beet-weise (‿⊥‿) *adv. agr.* in beds or small lots.
be-fähigen (‿⊥‿‿) ⓢ* **I** *v/a.* to enable; to qualify (or capacitate) for ... — **II** sich 2 *v/refl.* sich zu et. 2 to qualify (or be fit) for a th. — **III be-fähigt** *p.p.* und *a.* ⓖⓖ capable of, fit for.
Be-fähigung (‿⊥‿‿) *f* ⓖⓖ ability, qualification, capacity, fitness, competence; zu e-r Kunst 2c.: aptitude, (Gabe) gift, talent, taste; (Geschick) skill, cleverness; ~s-**nachweis** (⊥...) *m* ⓖⓖ proof of ability or proficiency; einen ~ liefern to prove one's fitness or competence (for); ~s=**zeugnis** *n* certificate of capacity or proficiency or fitness (for a post).
be-fahl (‿⊥) *impf. von* befehlen (s. bs).
be-fahrbar (‿⊥‿) *a.* ⓖⓖ passable; Weg: practicable, Gewässer: navigable.
be-fahr/en[1] (‿⊥‿) **I** *v/a.* ⓖb* **1.** (fahrend passieren) e-e Straße, e-n Weg: to ride (or drive) on or through ... in a vehicle); oft 2 to frequent; sehr 2e Straße much frequented road. — **2.** ⚒ einen Schacht 2 to go down (or descend) into a pit. — **3.** ♒ e-n Fluß 2 to navigate (on) ..., to ply ... (in boats), die Küste(n) 2 to sail along the coast, to (hug the) coast. — **4.** (fahrend bedecken) to cart upon; eine Landstraße mit Kies, ein Feld mit Dünger 2 to shoot gravel on a highway or road, to unload manure on a field. — **5.** ✱ die Märkte sind stark 2 the markets are well stocked (with goods), there is a glut of goods (in the market). — **II** *p.p.* u. *a.* ⓖⓖ (D 9) **6.** Beb. des *inf.* — **7.** ♒ (weit gereist) well-seasoned, experienced (in navigation). — **III** ~ *n* ⓖ **8.** = B/ung. [fürchten.]
be-fahren[2] (~) [: fear] *v/a.* ⓖ* = be=]
Be-fahrung (‿⊥‿) *f* ⓖⓖ (zu befahren 1:) ⚒ Weges: passing of (or along) ...; (zu 2:) ⚒ descent into ...; (zu 3:) ♒ e-s Gewässers: navigation on ...; (zu 4:) cartage; ~ eines Weges mit Kies carting (or shooting) gravel on a road.
be-falbeln (‿⊥‿‿) *v/a.* ⚘a* Damenschneiderei: to flounce, to furbelow.
be-fallen (‿⊥‿) *v/a.* u. *impers.* ⓖa* **1.** von et. Schlimmem: (angreifen) to attack; (überfallen, packen) to surprise, to take unawares, suddenly to come upon; vom Fieber 2 sein to be seized (or taken) with (a) fever; ⚘ v. Meltau 2 blighted; vom Sturme 2 w. to be overtaken by a storm; *v/imp.* es befiel ihn eine plötzliche Angst he was suddenly seized with alarm. — **2.** von äußerlichen Dingen: to fall upon a p. or a. th.
be-fangen (‿⊥‿) **I** *v/a.* ⓖb* **1.** ♰ = umfangen. — **2.** *fig.* to embarrass, einschüchternd: to intimidate; in Vorurteilen 2 sein to be steeped in prejudice; in e-m Irrtume 2 sein to labour under a mistake; von falschem Wahn 2 sein to labour (or be) under a delusion. — **II** *p.p.* u. *a.* ⓖⓖ (D 9) **3.** (sich nicht freifühlend) entangled, confined, constrained, *fig.* embarrassed, intimidated; (verwirrt) confused, stärker: perplexed; 2er Kopf narrow mind; (eingeschüchtert) nervous; (parteiisch) partial; (eingenommen für, gegen) prejudiced, biassed.

Be-fangenheit (‿⊥‿‿-) *f* ⓖⓖ embarrassment, constraint, stärker: perplexity, entanglement; (Schüchternheit) timidity, nervousness; (Eingenommenheit): a) des Geistes: preoccupation (of the mind), b) der Seele: foreboding (of the heart); (Parteilichkeit) partiality, weitS. prejudice, bias.
be-fassen (‿⊥‿) ⓖⓞ* **I** *v/a.* = anfassen I. — **II** *v/refl.* sich mit et., mit e-m 2 (beschäftigen) to concern (or occupy) o.s. with, (zu tun haben) to have dealings (or to meddle in) with a th., a p.; sich mit Dingen 2, wovon man nichts versteht to dabble in things (that) one knows nothing about. — **III** ~ *n* ⓖ = anfassen III; das ~ mit dieser Sache ist mir unangenehm it is unpleasant for me to have anything to do with (or to have to meddle in) this matter.
be-fehd/en (‿⊥‿) **I** *v/a.* und *v/rpr.* ⓖ* ⚬ to make war upon; (angreifen) to attack; sich 2 to be at (or to carry on a) feud with one another. — **II** ~ *n* ⓖ = B/ung.
Be-fehdung (~) *f* ⓖⓖ (hostile) attack upon; ~ j-s feud (or hostilities *pl.*) carried on against a p., inroad made into a neighbour's country or territory.
Be-fehl (‿⊥) *m* ⓖc. **1.** a) (Gebot) *allg.* command, besonderer: ⚔ order, injunction; der Eltern oder Erzieher: precept; ⚔ mündlicher (schriftlicher) ~ command by word of mouth (in writing), auch: spoken (written) order; auf ~ von e-m hin by order of a p.; seinem ~e gemäß at his bidding or command, in compliance with his order; auf ~ des Königs in the name (or by order) of the king; auf wessen ~? by whose orders or injunction?; es wurde der ~ gegeben, daß // orders were given that //; e-n ~ ausführen (ausrichten) to carry out (or to execute) an order; bis auf weiteren ~ until (or till) further orders; b) (Macht über et. zu befehlen) command, authority; den ~ führen (über //) to have command (of //) or authority (over //); den ~ übernehmen über // to take (over) the command of //; c) Höflichkeitssätze: ich stehe (Ihnen) zu ~ I am at your service or disposal; haben Sie noch weitere ~e? what are your further orders?; was steht zu ~? what is your pleasure? — **2.** *jur.* injunction; e-n ~ gegen e-n erlassen to issue a writ (or a warrant) against a person; die Regierung oder Obrigkeit erließ einen ~, daß // published a decree or decreed that //.
be-fehlen (‿⊥‿) [ahd.] **I** *v/a.* u. *v/n.* (h.) ⓖc* **1.** a) (ein Gebot kundtun) *allg.*: to command a p. to; (Wünsche kundgeben) to order a p. to, to enjoin upon a p.; von seiten e-r Obrigkeit: to decree that; (heißen) to tell (or bid) a p. to; er befahl mir, es zu tun he bade me do it (*passiv*): I was bidden by him to do it); wir haben ihm befohlen zu schweigen we enjoined silence on him (*passiv*: he was enjoined silence by us); er befahl mir, den Schatz zu behüten he charged me to guard the treasure; ich lasse mir nichts von ihm 2 I won't be ordered about (or dictated to) by him; er hat uns nichts zu 2 he is not our master; wer hat

hier zu 2? who is (lord and) master here?, who gives orders here?; die Weiber 2 hier we are under petticoat-government; 2 über (acc.) to command; über eine große Heerschar 2 (gebieten) to command (or lead) a great host; b) Höflichkeitssätze: wenn Sie 2 if you wish it; wie Sie 2 as you please; was 2 Sie? what can I do for you?, what is your pleasure?; ⚘ was 2 Sie sonst noch? what may (or shall) be the next thing?; 2 Sie noch etwas Suppe? may I help you to ...?; Sie haben nur zu 2 you have only to say; wie 2 Sie? please?, auch: I beg your pardon, weniger höflich: what did you say?; c) et., e-m 2 (beordern) to give orders for ... or that; j-e Pferde 2 to have one's horses put to. — **2.** fast † (zur Verwahrung übergeben) seine Seele Gott 2 to resign one's soul or to commend one's spirit) to God; *bibl.* s-e Wege Gott 2 to commit one's ways unto the Lord; Abschiedsformel: Gott befohlen! adieu! good bye! — **II** ~ *n* ⓖ **3.** command(ing), &c. (vgl. a. Befehl). — **III** 2d (‿⊥‿) *p.pr.* u. *a.* ⓖⓖ **4.** (herrisch) imperious, dictatorial; ein 2er Ton tone of command.
be-fehlerisch (‿⊥‿‿) *a.* ⓖⓖ = befehlshaberisch.
be-fehligen (‿⊥‿‿) *v/a.* ⓖⓞ* a) ein Heer 2c. (unter seinem Befehle haben) to command (to lead); von europäischen Offizieren befehligt officered (or led) by ...; under the command of ...; b) = befehlen 1c; er wurde befehligt zu // he was commanded or commissioned (or he received orders) to //.
Be-fehls-erteilung ⚘ (‿⊥‿...) *f* ⓖⓑ giving (or issuing) a command; =**form** *f*, *gram.* imperative (mood); =**haber** ⚔ commander, commanding officer; erster (oberster) ~ commander-in-chief; **2haberisch** *a.* ⓖⓖ imperious, lordly, domineering, dictatorial; =**haberstab** *m* staff of command; field-marshal's baton; =**haberstelle** *f* command(ership); =**übermitt(e)lung** ⚔ *f* passing on the (word of) command; **2weise** *adv.* imperatively, by way of command; =**wort** *n* word of command, injunction.
be-feilen (‿⊥‿) *v/a.* ⓖ* to file.
be-feinden (‿⊥‿) *v/a.* ⓖ* u. ~ ⓖ u. **Be-feindung** *f* ⓖⓖ = anfeinden I u. II.
be-festig/en (‿⊥‿‿) **I** *v/a.* u. *v/n.* (h. u. su) ⓖ** **1.** einen Gegenstand an etwas 2 to fix (or fasten, attach) a th. to a th. — **2.** an=ea. 2 to couple; mit Klammern 2 to fasten with clamps (or cramps) to, to clamp (or to cramp) to; (nieten) to rivet to; (festkleben) to stick to. — **3.** ⚔ (verschanzen) Festungswerke, Orte, Stellungen: to fortify, to strengthen, to make secure; ein Lager 2 to entrench a camp; ⚔ b/te Feldstellung fortified (or strongly secured) position. — **4.** ♒ (durch Ankerstich) 2 to clinch (a cable). — **5.** a. *v/refl.* (sichern) to secure; ein Reich: to consolidate; Macht: to establish (firmly); sich 2 to grow strong(er), to gain (in)strength; ✱ die Preise haben sich befestigt prices (or quotations) have hardened or stiffened or show (greater) strength; *fig.* das Band der Freundschaft wieder

Signs (see page XVII): F familiar; P vulgar; ⌐ flash; ⟍ rare; † obsolete (died); * new word (born); ⁺⁺ incorrect; ♪ music;

[Befestigung] — 155 — [Befragung]

⚬ to draw closer the bonds of friendship. — II ~ n ㉓ 6. = Befestigung.
Be-fe̱ſtigung (⌣⌣⌣) f ㊻ (zu befeſtigen 1:) fixing, fastening; (zu 2:) ⊕ coupling; (zu 3:) ⚔ fortification, entrenchment; (zu 4:) ⚓ clinching; (zu 5:) (Sicherſtellung) a. der Geſundheit ꝛc.: strengthening, weiteS. consolidation, (firm) establishment.
Be-fe̱ſtigungs-arbeiten (⌣...) ⚔ f/pl. defensive operations pl.; **=bauten** f/pl. defensive works pl.; **=kunſt** f (art of) fortification; **=pfahl** m (Schanzpfahl) palisade; **=tau** ⚓ n (Knebeltropp) becket; **=werk** n defences pl. — Vgl. Feſtungs=...
be-feuchten (⌣⌣⌣) I v/a. ㊽* to moisten, to damp, ſtärker: to wet; (bewäſſern) to irrigate. — II ~ n ㉓ u. **Be-feuchtung** f ㊻ moistening, damping, ſtärker: wetting; (Bewäſſerung) irrigation.
be-feuern (⌣⌣⌣) v/a. ㊾a* to fire, inflame.
Be-feuerung (⌣⌣⌣) f ㊻ = der Küſte (Verſehen mit Leuchttürmen, Feuerſchiffen und Leuchttonnen) lighting up (of) ...
Beffchen (⌣⌣) [ndd.] n ㉓ = der proteſtant. Geiſtlichen (clerical) band.
be-fiedern (⌣⌣⌣) I v/a. u. v/refl. ㊽a* to furnish with feathers; **ſich** ⚬ (Federn bekommen) to become fledged, to show (the first) feathers. — II ~ n ㉓ u. B/ung. — III **be-fiedert** p.p. u. a. ㊻ von Vögeln: fledged; von Pfeilen: feathered; ⚲ von Blättern: ⚬ pennate. **[**ting) plumage.**]**
Be-fiederung (⌣⌣⌣) f ㊻ der Vögel: (get-f
be-fiehl (⌣⌣) imper.; ⚬ (f) t pres. v. befehlen.
be-fiel (⌣⌣) impf. v. befallen.
be-finden (⌣⌣⌣) ㊽* I v/a. 1. (finden, merken) to find; die Nachricht iſt (als) wahr befunden worden ... has proved true, (es) für gut ⚬ (dafürhalten) to deem (or think) (it) right, to think proper; er iſt für ſchuldig befunden worden he was found (or brought in) guilty; bibl. zu leicht befunden found wanting or too light in the scales. — II **ſich** ⚬ v/refl. 2. ſich an einem Orte, in einer Lage ⚬ (ſein) to be (found) ...; ſich in der Notwendigkeit ⚬ zu // to be under the necessity of //; Sie ⚬ ſich im Irrtume you are mistaken or labouring under a mistake. — 3. vom Geſundheitszuſtande: wie ⚬ Sie ſich?: a) how do you do?, F how are you?; b) an einen Kranken: how do you feel?, F how are you getting on?; ich befinde mich (nicht ganz) wohl I am (not quite) well. — III ~ n ㉓ 4. (f. 1) (Gut-achten) opinion, (Schätzung) estimation; nach ~ der Umſtände according to circumstances; abs. nach ~ (Gutdünken) as you (may) think fit. — 5. (f. 2) condition (or state) of a p., ꝛc. — 6. (f. 3) state of a p.'s health; ſich nach j-s ~ erkundigen to inquire (or make inquiries) after a p.'s health.
be-findlich (⌣⌣⌣) a. ㊻ to be found, in existence, being (in a place); die in ſeiner Bibliothek ⚬en Bücher the books (contained) in his library; die im Zuge ⚬en Paſſagiere the passengers in (or travelling by) the train; irgendwo ⚬ ſein to be (or exist) somewhere.
be-flaggen (⌣⌣⌣) v/a. ㊽* to dress (or deck, adorn) with flags; die Stadt war bunt beflaggt, oft: the town was gay with bunting.

be-flechten (⌣⌣⌣) v/a. ㊽b* to plait (or braid) round, to cover with plaiting or wickerwork; Stühle mit Stroh (wieder) ⚬ to cane chairs (afresh).
be-flecken (⌣⌣⌣) ㊽* I v/a. 1. auch v/refl. (beſchmutzen) to soil, spot, stain; (beſudeln) to defile, pollute; (anſtecken) to contaminate, vitiate; mit Fett ⚬ to grease; mit Tinte: to ink, to blot; fig. j-s Ruf ꝛc.: to stain, ſtärker: to sully; j-s Ruhm: to tarnish; mit Blut befleckt stained (or polluted, defiled) with blood. — 2. ⊕ Schuhm.: Schuhzeug ⚬ to heel, to put a pair of (fresh) heels to ... — II **ſich** ⚬ v/refl. 3. ſ. 1; bſd. fig. to soil o.s. (or one's hands). — 4. ſich ſelbſt ⚬ to practise self-pollution; path. to masturbate. — III ~ n ㉓ u. **Be-fleckung** f ㊻ 5. (zu 1:) defilement, pollution; (zu 2:) ⊕ heeling, putting on (fresh) heels to; (zu 4:) med. masturbation, bibl. onanism.
be-fleißen ⚲ (⌣⌣⌣) ㊽a*, meiſt **be-fleißigen** (⌣⌣⌣⌣) ㊽* I **ſich** ⚬ v/refl. ſich e-r Sache (gen.) ⚬ to apply o.s. to (or to study) a th.; to bestow pains upon a th.; to aim at a th.; ſich der Rechtswiſſenſchaft ⚬ to study (or follow) the law; ſich der Medizin (als Student) ⚬ to be a medical student, auch: to walk the hospitals; ich will mich der Kürze ⚬ I will (endeavour to) be short or brief, F I'll cut it short. — II ~ n ㉓ u. **Be-fleißigung** f ㊻ application (to one's studies), studiousness; (Eifer) zeal, devotion. — III **be-fliſſen** p.p. u. a. ㊻ (D9) mit gen. studious, engaged in; (fleißig) diligent in, (eifrig) zealous in, devoted to; in Zſſgn, zB. dienſt⚬obliging; ~e(r) m, ~e f ㊼ ~er der Rechte (der Medizin) law (medical) student; ſ. a. Bau=, Handlungs=⚬e(r).
be-fließen (⌣⌣⌣) v/a. ⊕d* to flow over, (berieſeln) to irrigate. **[**fleißen (ſ. ds).**]**
be-fliß (⌣⌣) impf., **be-fliße** subj. von be=⌐
be-fliſſen (⌣⌣⌣) p.p. v. befleißen (ſ. ds III).
~**heit** (⌣⌣⌣~) f ㊻ = befleißen II;
⚬**tlich** (⌣⌣⌣⌣) adv. assiduously; (abſichtlich) intentionally (— gefliſſentlich).
be-flittern (⌣⌣⌣) v/a. u. v/refl. ㊽a* to bespangle, to tinsel over; **ſich** ⚬ to cover o.s. with tinsel, weiteS. to dress (o.s.) up in flimsy (or gaudy) clothes.
be-flogen (⌣⌣⌣) p.p. v. befliegen u. a. ㊻ (D9) 1. for. covered with young shoots. 2. hunt. = flügge.
be-floren (⌣⌣⌣) [Flor] v/a. u. v/refl. ㊽* to wrap in gauze, oft auch fig. to veil (in); als Trauerzeichen: **ſich** ⚬ (den Hut ⚬) to put crape on (round one's hat), to wear a mourning-(hat)band.
be-flügeln (⌣⌣⌣) I v/a. ㊽a* to give (or add) wings to; fig. (eilen machen) to accelerate; ſ-e Schritte ⚬ to make haste, to hasten one's steps, to quicken one's pace, F to put one's best leg foremost. — II ~ n ㉓ = B/ung.
be-flügelt (⌣⌣⌣) p.p. u. a. ㊻ winged. **[**ation.**]**
Be-flüg(e)lung (⌣⌣(⌣)⌣) f ㊻ fig. acceler-f
be-fluten ⚓ (⌣⌣⌣) v/a. ㊽* (unter Waſſer ſetzen) to flood. **[**p.p. v. befehlen.**]**
be-föhle subj. impf., **be-fohlen** (⌣⌣⌣)f
be-folgen (⌣⌣⌣) v/a. ㊽* j-s Rat ꝛc.: to follow, to take, ein Beiſpiel, auch: to imitate; eine Regel, ein Geſetz: to ob-

serve, to obey; rel. die Gebote: to keep. — II ~ n ㉓ = Befolgung.
be-folgens-wert (⌣⌣⌣...) a. ㊻, ⚬**würdig** a. worth following, &c.
Be-folgung (⌣⌣⌣) f ㊻ durch ~ Ihres Rates by following (or taking) your advice; Zſ=... = befolgens=...
Be-förderer (⌣⌣⌣⌣) m ㊷, **Be-förd(r)erin** f ㊼ 1. (zu befördern 2:) one who hurries on, promoter; (zu 3:) ~ der Künſte patron of arts; (zu 4:) ~ v. Frachtgütern forwarding agent. — 2. meiſt b.s. ~ von et. Verwerflichem: abettor (of evil).
be-förderlich (⌣⌣⌣⌣) a. ㊻ (ant. nachteilig) conducive or contributing (zu et. to a th.), weiteS. useful (for).
be-fördern (⌣⌣⌣) I v/a. ㊽a* 1. to forward. — 2. (in ſchnellerem Gang bringen) to accelerate; (beſchleunigen) to hasten, expedite, hurry (forward); (ſchnell abmachen) to dispatch; (anreizen) to stir (up). — 3. (begünſtigen) to favour, ſchützend: to support; helfend: to further; die Künſte ⚬ to patronize ... — 4. (hinſchaffen) to convey; 🚂 (per Bahn) ⚬ to forward; dieſer Zug befördert keine Güter ... takes no goods. — 5. e-n (in eine höhere Stellung bringen) to promote (to a higher) post; befördert w. to get a promotion, to (get a) rise, F to take a step up(wards). — 6. b.s. e-n in die andere Welt ⚬ to dispatch a p., P to do for a p.; (hinrichten) to launch into eternity. — II ~ n ㉓ und **Be-förderung** f ㊻ 7. (zu 2:) acceleration, dispatch; (zu 3:) furtherance, patronage; (zu 4:) conveyance; (zu 5:) promotion; ⚔ f-e ~ zum Major erhalten to be promoted to major, to receive one's majority.
Be-förderungs-gebühr (⌣⌣⌣...) f ㊷ =**koſten**; **=geſuch** n petition for promotion or a rise; **=koſten** pl. charges pl. for conveyance or carriage; 🚂**railway**-charges pl.; **=mittel** n: a) allg.: means of conveyance; b) von Fuhrwerken: vehicle; c) ⚲ : des Schalles ꝛc. medium of, (Antrieb) stimulant for; der Verdauung: med. peptic; des Schlafes: med. soporific, opiate, hypnotic; **=vorſchlag** m proposing a p.'s promotion.
be-fracht/en (⌣⌣⌣t/n) I v/a. ㊽* e-n Wagen ꝛc.: to load ...; ⚓ ein Schiff ⚬ to charter ..., to freight — II ~ n ㉓ = B/ung 1.
Be-frachter (⌣⌣) m ㉖ ⚓ (Verſender) consignor; ⚓ (Mieter) charterer, freighter.
Be-frachtung (⌣⌣) f ㊻ 1. loading (a. ⚓); ⚓ charter(age), freight(age).
2. (Fracht) charges pl., freight.
be-fragen (⌣⌣⌣) ㊽* (⫶ ㊽b*) I v/a. e-n um (über, nach, wegen) et. ⚬, allg.: to ask a p. about (or concerning) a th.; (um Rat fragen) to consult; (ausfragen) to question, to query; (verhören) to examine, to interrogate (ſämtlich wie to ask konſtruiert); ich habe ihn (über, nach, wegen) et. befragt I inquired (or made inquiry) of him about (or concerning, respecting, &c.) a th. — II **ſich** ⚬ v/refl. ſich bei e-m nach (um) et. ⚬ to seek information (at the hands) of a p. about a th. — III ~ n ㉓ u. **Be-fragung** f ㊻ zu I u. II: question(ing), inquiry; ~ durch den Richter: examination,

⚲ scientific; ⚘ botanical; ⊕ geography; ⊕ machinery; ⚒ mining; ⚔ military; ⚓ marine; 💼 commercial; ✉ postal; 🚂 railway.

[befransen] — 156 — [begegnen]

interrogatory; auf mein ~ antwortete er on my questioning him he replied.
be-fransen (◡◡) **I** v/a. ⑩* to (be)fringe. — **II be-franst** (◡◡) p.p. und a. ⑥ fringed, ⌒ laciniate.
be-freien (◡⌣◡) [frei] **I** v/a. u. v/refl. ⑱*
1. (ſich) ⌒ to free or deliver (o.s.) (von e-m, et. from a p., a th.); e-n aus Gefangenſchaft ꝛc. ⌒ to set a p. free, to release a p., durch Löſegeld: to ransom; ſich ⌒ von to rid o.s. of, to get rid of. — **2.** aus et. Läſtigem: ſich aus j-s Macht ⌒ to escape (or slip) from ...; aus Schwierigkeiten ⌒ to disentangle (or extricate) from ...; ⚔ aus gefährlicher Lage ⌒ to disengage (a body of troops); ſein Gewiſſen von einem Vorwurf ⌒ to unburden (or ease) one's conscience of a reproach, einen Sklaven ⌒ to set free (weitſ. to emancipate) ... — **3.** von et. Drohendem: e-n von der Strafe (die ihn treffen ſollte)⌒ to save a p. from punishment; aus der Not, Bedrängnis ꝛc. ⌒ to rescue (or extricate) from ... — **4.** e-n von et. ⌒: a) von e-r Verpflichtung ꝛc. ⌒ to release (or exempt, relieve, excuse) a p. from ...; auch: to dispense with a p.'s services; b) von e-r Schuld, v. Tadel ꝛc. ⌒ to exonerate a p. from ...; c) von e-r Gewohnheit, Krankheit ꝛc. ⌒ to cure a p. of ... — **II** ~ n ㉓ **5.** = Befreiung.
Be-freier (◡◡) m ㉒, ~**in** f ㊼ deliverer, liberator, emancipator.
Be-freiung (◡◡) f ㊻ (von, aus from) **1.** (zu befreien **1**:) deliverance, release; (zu **2:**) escape; ~ aus der Leibeigenſchaft ꝛc. emancipation; (zu **3:**) aus e-r Gefahr: rescue; (zu **4:**) exemption, relief, exoneration. — **2.** a) ~ von Laſten, Abgaben: immunity from ...; b) (Entlaſſung v. Gefangenen) (jail-)delivery, discharge, release.
Be-freiungs=kampf (⌣...) m ㉒, **=krieg** m ⓱ war of deliverance or liberation; (Freiheitskrieg) fight for freedom.
be-fremd/en (◡◡◡) **I** v/a. ⑱* das befremdet mich I think it strange (that he or you should //), I am surprised (ſtärker: astonished) at it; es muß ihn ⌒, daß // he must wonder that //. — **II** ~ n ㉓ = B/ung. — **III** ⌒d p.pr. surprising; ein ⌒der Anblick a strange (or striking, curious) sight.
be-fremdlich (◡◡◡) a. ⑥ e-m ⌒ surprising to a p.; auch strange, odd, queer, curious, striking (appearance, &c.).
Be-fremdung (◡◡◡) f ㊻ surprise, astonishment, amazement.
be-freund/en (◡⌣◡) **I** v/a. u. ſich ⌒ v/refl. ⑱*
1. e-n mit e-m ⌒ to bring about a p.'s friendship with a p.; ſich mit e-m ⌒ to make friends (or to strike up a friendship, to form a friendly alliance) with a p. — **2.** (vertraut machen) ſich mit einem Gedanken ⌒ to get reconciled (or to reconcile o.s.) to ...; ſie kann ſich nicht damit ⌒ she does not take kindly to it, ſtärker: she disapproves of it. — **II** ~ n ㉓ **3.** = B/ung. — **III be-freundet** p.p. u. a. ⑥ **4.** friendly or on friendly terms (mit with); eng ⌒ mit in close friendship with, intimate; ſie ſind ſehr eng ⌒ F they are thick friends or great chums or they are as thick as thieves; pol. ⌒e

Mächte pl. allied powers; ⊛ eine ⌒e Firma a business connexion; **Be-freundete**([r] m) f ㊻ friend, ally.
Be-freundung (◡⌣◡) f ㊻ friendly alliance, springing up of a friendship.
be-frieden (◡⌣◡) v/a. ⑱* **1.** = einfrieden(ig)en. — **2.** faſt = befriedigen **I**.
be-friedig/en (◡◡◡◡) **I** v/a. ⑱* **1.** (zufriedenſtellen) e-n ⌒ to satisfy a p.; ſchwer zu ⌒(d) difficult to satisfy, hard to please. — **2.** j-n Hunger, j-n Rachedurſt ⌒ to appease, gratify ...; ſeine Luſt an et. ⌒ to indulge in (or to give the rein[s] to) one's passion; ſ. a. Bedürfnis. — **3.** (beruhigen) to pacify, to assuage; ſein Gewiſſen ⌒ to soothe ... — **II** ~ n ㉓ **4.** = B/ung. — **III** ⌒d p.pr. ⑯ **5.** satisfactory.
Befried(ig)ung (◡⌣(◡)◡) f ㊻ **1.** satisfaction; zu befriedigen **2**: ~ der heftigen Begierden gratification, indulgence; zu **3**: pacification. — **2.** ⊛ (Zahlung) payment; ~ der Gläubiger compromise (or making terms) with one's creditors.
be-frieren (◡⌣◡) v/n. (ſn) ㈚c* to become frozen over or covered with ice.
be-fruchten (◡◡◡(ich)*) **I** v/a. ⑱* to fructify, (ſchwängern) to impregnate, ⌒ zo. to fecundate; die Felder ⌒ to enrich the soil; (düngen) to fertilize. — **II** ~ n ㉓ **4.**
Be-fruchtung f ㊻ fructification, impregnation, fecundation, fertilization.
Be-fugnis (◡⌣◡) f ⑱(n⑰) authority; (Berechtigung) privilege; j-e Befugniſſe überſchreiten to go beyond (or exceed) one's authority or powers or warrant; jur. competence, ...y, legality; power (to act).
be-fugt (◡⌣) p.p. u. a. ⑥ authorized (or empowered, entitled, licensed) to; ⌒er Richter competent judge.
be-fühlen (◡⌣◡) v/a. ⑱* to touch, einen Stoff: to handle; mit den Fingern ⌒ to finger; von Blinden: to feel all over.
Be-fund (◡⌣) m ⓫b. state (or condition) in which a th. is found; (Beſtand, Verzeichnis) inventory; (je) nach ~ according to circumstances, as the case may be; nach (dem) ~ der Sachverſtändigen according to the finding (or report) of the experts. [inventory.)
Be-fund=buch ⊛ (◡⌣...) n ㉕ stock-book,)
Be-funds=beſcheinigung (◡⌣...) f ㊷ auditor's (or inspector's) certificate.
Be-fund=ſchein (◡⌣...) m ㊷ certificate attesting the real state of affairs or stating the actual things found.
be-fürchten (◡⌣◡) **I** v/a. ⑱* et. ⌒ to fear (or to be afraid) that (or lest) something might happen; das Schlimmſte iſt zu ⌒ we must be prepared for the worst; herannahende Gefahren ⌒ to be apprehensive of (or to apprehend, to dread) approaching dangers; ein neuer Anfall iſt nicht zu ⌒ there is no fear (or danger) of a new attack. — **II** ~ n ㉓, mehr gbr. **Be-fürchtung** f ㊻ fear, apprehension, misgiving.
be-fürworten (◡⌣◡◡) **I** v/a. ⑱* et. ⌒ to speak up for a th., to advocate a th., to back a th.; eine Bitte ⌒ to support ...; (empfehlen) to (re)commend; ich be-fürworte ausdrücklich, daß // I strongly urge that //, I deem (or think) it most advisable that //. — **II** ~ n ㉓ u. **Be-fürwortung** f ㊻ (re)commendation.

Beg (¹) [türk.] m ㊿ (Titel) bey.
be-gab/en (◡⌣◡) **I** v/a. ⑱* e-n mit et. ⌒ (ausſtatten) to bestow a th. upon a p., bſd. von Naturgaben: to endow a p. with a th. — **II** ~ n ㉓ = B/ung **1.** — **III be-gabt** p.p. u. a. ⑥ gifted, talented, (very) able; ein hoch ⌒er Dichter a highly gifted poet, a poet of conspicuous talent; ~**heit** f ㊻ = B/ung **2.**
Be-gabung (◡) f ㊻ **1.** endowment. — **2.** gift, talent(s pl.), ability, capacity.
be-gaffen (◡◡◡) v/a. ⑱* = angaffen.
be-gangen (◡◡◡) p.p. von begehen (ſ. ds).
Be-gängnis (◡◡◡) n ⑰ (Leichen-⌒) funeral.
be-gann (◡⌣) impf. von beginnen (ſ. ds).
Begard (-⌣) [ſ. Begine] m ㊷ eccl. (Kloſterbruder o. Gelübde, Bettelmönch) Beghard.
be-gatt/en (◡⌣◡) [: beget] **I** v/recip. ⑱*
ſich ⌒: a) allg. von Tieren: to pair, to copulate; b) hunt. nur von ㉓: to mate, weitſ. to breed. — **II** ~ n ㉓ = B/ung.
Be-gattung (◡) f ㊻ pairing, mating, physiol. copulation; v. Menſchen: cohabitation, sexual intercourse.
Be-gattungs=trieb (⌣...) m ㉒ sexual craving or passion; =**zeit** f coupling- (von Vögeln ꝛc. auch:) breeding-) time.
be-gaunern (◡⌣◡) v/a. ⓬a* to cheat, F to gull; er ließ ſich ⌒ he was fleeced.
be-gebbar (◡⌣◡) a. ⑥ Wechſel: negotiable.
be-geben (◡⌣◡) ⑯c* **I** ſich ⌒ v/refl. **1.** (wohin gehen) to proceed to, to betake o.s. to, to repair to. — **2.** ſich **an die Arbeit** ⌒ (ſie beginnen) to set to work; ⚓ ſich an Bord (e-s Schiffes) ⌒ to go on board (ship), to join a vessel; ſich **auf die Flucht** ⌒ to take to flight; ſich auf das Land ⌒ to go into the country; ſich auf die Reiſe, den Weg ⌒ to set out or start (on one's journey); ſich **in** den Eheſtand ⌒ to enter the married (or matrimonial) state; ſich in Gefahr ⌒ to run into danger; ſich **unter** j-s Schutz ⌒ to place o.s. under the protection (F wings) of a p.; ſich **zu** Bett (zur Ruhe) ⌒ to go to bed, to retire to rest or to one's couch, F co. to go to roost; ⚔ ſich zu ſ-m Korps ⌒ to join one's corps. — **3.** meiſt v/impers. (ſich ereignen) to happen, to occur, to come to pass, to take place. — **4.** ſich eines Rechtes (gen.) ⌒ (darauf verzichten) to waive one's right, to renounce (or resign) one's claim, to forego one's share; ſich ſ-r Machtſtellung ⌒ to divest o.s. of one's power, to resign one's high position. — **5.** ⚓ (aus den Fugen weichen) to break up, weitſ. to go to pieces. — **II** v/a. **6.** (an den Mann bringen, verkaufen) to sell, to dispose of, eine Anleihe: to issue, Waren: to clear off, Wechſel: to negotiate; die Anleihe an ein Konſortium ⌒ to delegate the loan to (or to put it into the hands of) a syndicate; e-n Wechſel an e-n andern (durch Unterſchrift auf dem Rücken) ⌒ to endorse a bill. — **III** ~ n ㉓ **7.** = Begebung.
Be-gebenheit (◡⌣◡) f ㊻, **Be-gebnis** (◡⌣◡) n ⑰ event, occurrence; (Abenteuer) adventure; (Unfall) accident.
Be-gebung (◡⌣◡) f ㊻ (zu begeben **4**:) renunciation; (zu **6**:) ⊛ issue, negotiation.
be-gegn/en (◡⌣◡) ⌒ ⑥b* **I** v/n. (ſn, h.), ſich (dat., bisw. auch acc.) od. **ea.** ⌒

Zeichen (ſ. S. XVII): F familiär; P Volksſprache; ⌒ Gaunerſprache; ⌒ ſelten; † alt (auch geſtorben); * neu (auch geboren); ⸫ unrichtig;

[Begegnis] — 157 — [Begleitstimme]

v/rpr. 1. e-m ⁂ to meet a p., durch Zufall: to come upon a p., to run across a p.; to chance upon a p.; j-s Wünschen ⁂ to anticipate a p.'s ...; sich ob. ea. ⁂ to meet, v. Briefen: to cross. — 2. (e-m zustoßen) to befall a p.; mir ist ein Unglück begegnet I met with (or I had) an accident. — 3. (sich gegen e-n benehmen) to behave towards a p.; e-m höflich ⁂ to act politely towards a p., to show civility to a p.; einem unartig ⁂ to treat a p. rudely or roughly or with discourtesy. — II v/n. (h.) 4. (bekämpfend entgegentreten) to encounter, (vorbeugen) to obviate; Unglücksfällen ⁂ to prevent, avert ...; e-m Fehler ꝛc. ⁂, oft: to make good ... — III ~ n ⓘ 5. = B/ung 1.
Be-gegnis (⌣⌢⌣) n ⑰ (/⑱) 1. (das Begegnen) meeting. — 2. (Vorgang) occurrence, event; (Unglück) mishap, accident.
Be-gegnung (⌣) f ⑯ 1. (zu begegnen 1:) meeting; (zu 3:) treatment. — 2. (Zs.-kunft) interview; feindliche ~ encounter, collision, ⚔ auch: engagement.
Be-gegnungs-gefecht ⚔ (⌣...) n ⑫ (accidental) encounter of hostile forces.
be-geh(e)n (⌣⌢(⌣) I v/a. ⑳* 1. e-n Weg ꝛc. ⁂ to pass (or walk, go, march) along ...; hunt. ein Revier ⁂ (abjuchen) to beat a cover. — 2. (feiern) to celebrate, to commemorate. — 3. (tun; ant. unterlassen) ein Verbrechen, e-n Frevel ⁂ to commit (or perpetrate) ... (an e-m against a p.); e-n Fehler ꝛc. ⁂ to make ...; er hat eine große Dummheit begangen he committed a great folly, he acted very foolishly, he did a very silly thing; ein Unrecht ⁂ to do wrong, to commit an injustice. — II ~ n ⓘ 4. = Begehung.
Be-gehr (⌣⌢) m u. n ⓒ c. demand or inquiry (nach // for //), was ist sein ~? what is his desire?, what does he wish (for) or want?; ⚝ für Wolle sprach sich ein regerer ~ aus there was a stronger (or brisker) demand for wool; ein starker ~ für Diamanten a boom in ...; weitS. = Begehrung.
be-gehren (⌣⌢⌣) [mhd.: yearn] I v/a. u. v/n. (h.) ㉘* 1. (fordern) et. von einem ⁂ to ask a p. for a th. or a th. of a p.; stärker: to demand (or request) a th. of a p.; zur Ehe, zur Frau ⁂ to ask in marriage, to claim for (or as) a wife; weitS. to propose to. — 2. (wünschen) to wish for, to desire a th., stärker: to hanker after, to crave for, rel. to covet a th. — 3. ⚝ begehrt sein to be in request or demand; Kartoffeln sind sehr begehrt there is a great demand (or a good market or a ready sale) for potatoes. — 4. (sich sehnen nach etwas) to long (or yearn) for a th. — II ~ n ⓘ 5. = Begehrung.
be-gehrens-wert (⌣⌢...) a. ⑯, ⁂würdig a. desirable, auch: to be coveted.
be-gehrlich (⌣⌢⌣) a. ⑯ (begehrend) passionately desiring (or longing) for, (lüstern) greedy after or of, rel. covetous.
Be-gehrlichkeit (⌣⌢⌣...) f ⑯ strong desire for, greed(iness) after, of; fleischliche, sinnliche ~ carnal, sensual appetite or lust; mst. rel. concupiscence.
Be-gehrung (⌣⌢⌣) f ⑯ 1. (zu begehren 1:) demand. — 2. (zu 2:) wish, stärker: craving, lust, greed, rel. covetousness.

be-gehrungs-los (⌣⌢⌣...) a. ⑯ without greed; =vermögen n ⑫ appetitive faculty or power; vgl. a. begehrens...
Be-gehung (⌣⌢⌣) f ⑯ (zu begehen 2:) celebration; (zu 3:) commission, perpetration. [sins pl. of commission.]
Be-gehungs-sünden (...) f/pl. rel.)
be-geifern (⌣⌢⌣) v/a. ⑳a* to beslaver; fig. (verleumden) to backbite, slander.
Be-geiferung (⌣⌢⌣) f ⑯ fig. backbiting, slander(ing), aspersion.
be-geistern (⌣⌢⌣) v/a. u. v/refl. ⑳a* to fill with enthusiasm (for or about a th.), dichterisch: to inspire (with); die Hörer: to electrify; (entzücken) to enrapture; sich ⁂ to feel inspired, weitS. to warm up to one's theme, to be full of enthusiasm; für Musik ꝛc.: to be devoted to ..., to be an enthusiastic lover of ...
be-geistert (⌣⌢⌣) a. ⑯ enthusiastic, F gushing, dichterisch, religiös: inspired; dithyrambic; ein ⁂er Empfang a rapturous welcome; in ⁂en Worten in spirited (or fiery) words, F in heroics.
Be-geisterung (⌣⌢⌣) f ⑯ 1. inspiration. — 2. enthusiasm (for or about). — 3. dichterische ~ poetic vein; stärker: poetic ecstasy or frenzy or rapture.
Be-gier (⌣⌢) f ⑯ (o. pl.) immoderate desire (or appetite); s. a. Begierde 1.
Be-gierde (⌣⌢⌣) f ⑯ 1. b.s. = Gier(de); (Gelüst) sensual appetite, bsd. rel. cupidity. — 2. (Verlangen) eagerness for, stärker: passionate longing for; greed after; avidity to ... (inf.); ich brannte vor ~, es ihm zu sagen I burnt to tell him.
be-gierig (⌣⌢⌣) a. ⑯ eager for or after, stärker: with a passionate longing for after or desire for; nach Ruhm u. Ehre ⁂ thirsting after ...; nach Schätzen ⁂ covetous of ...; ich bin ⁂ zu erfahren I am anxious (or longing) to hear.
be-gieß|en (⌣⌢⌣) I v/a. ⑳d* 1. Blumen ⁂ to water ...; Gras ⁂ to sprinkle ..., den Braten ⁂ to baste ...; (schwemmen) to flush; (befeuchten) to moisten, to damp. — 2. ein abgeschlossenes Geschäft ⁂ to drink on the conclusion of (F co. to wet) a bargain. — 3. F co. (sich) die Nase ⁂ to wet one's whistle, to lubricate one's throat, e-n ⁂, e-m das Kleid ⁂, v/refl. sich ⁂ to wet (or splash) a p.'s dress, o.s.; stärker: (übergießen) to drench (mit with). — II ~ n ⓘ 4. = B/ung. — III begossen p.p. u. a. (D 9) 5. wie ⁂ wet to the skin; F fig. wie ein ⁂er Pudel abziehen to retire discomfited or abashed or crestfallen.
Be-gieß-löffel (⌣⌢...) m ⑫ Kochkunst: basting-ladle. [s. begießen I.]
Be-gießung (⌣⌢⌣) f ⑯ watering, &c.,)
Begine (⌣⌢⌣) [[Lambert le) Bègue, 12/13. sae.] f ⑱ (Klosterfrau ohne Gelübde) Beguine.
Be-ginn (⌣⌢) [ahd.] m ⓑ b. (o. pl.) beginning (s. Anfang u. Anbeginn).
be-ginnen (⌣⌢⌣) [ahd.: begin] I v/a. u. v/n. (h.) ㉘a* to begin (= anfangen, das mehr F ist); (unternehmen) to venture, set on foot, start; den Kampf ⁂ to engage the enemy or foe (in combat); Sprichw. frisch begonnen, halb gewonnen a good beginning makes a good ending. — II ~ n ⓘ (zu I:) beginning, commencement; venture; b.s. ein

schändliches ~ a disgraceful enterprise or deed, a shameful proceeding.
be-gipsen (⌣⌢⌣) v/a. ⑳* to plaster (over), to overlay with plaster (of Paris).
be-glänzen (⌣⌢⌣) v/a. ⑳* 1. to illuminate, to shed a lustre on; beglänzt resplendent with, shining with. — 2. (glänzend färben) to give a brilliant colour to.
be-glasen (⌣⌢⌣) v/a. ⑳* to glaze, Fenster ꝛc.: to provide with panes.
be-glauben †(⌣⌢⌣), jetzt mst be-glaubig|en (⌣⌢⌣) I v/a. ㉘* 1. et. ⁂ to prove a th. to be true, to substantiate (or corroborate) a th., stärker: to testify to a th.; etwas durch Zeugen, Unterschrift ⁂ to attest, to certify a th. by ..., weitS. to speak to (the truth of) a th.; ein Schriftstück ⁂ to authenticate ..., to verify ...; amtlich, gerichtlich ⁂ to legalize; eine gut beglaubigte (festgestellte) Tatsache a well attested (or well established) fact. — 2. e-n Gesandten bei e-m ⁂ to accredit ... to (or at) a court. — II ~ n ⓘ u. Be-glaubigung (⌣⌢⌣) f ⑯ 3. attestation, legalization; ~ eines Gesandten ꝛc. credentials pl., accreditation; jur. zur ~ dessen habe ich // in witness (or testimony) whereof I have // — Vgl. auch bestätigen und Bestätigung.
Be-glaubigungs-eid (⌣...) m ⑫ confirmation upon (or testimony by) oath, weitS. affidavit; =schreiben n eines Gesandten ꝛc.: credentials pl. (vgl. Kreditiv). [(= ausgleichen 3).)
be-gleichen ⚝ (⌣⌢⌣) v/a. ⑳ast* to balance)
be-gleit|en (⌣⌢⌣) [be- u. geleiten] I v/a. ⑱* 1. to accompany, zB. e-m ein Lied ⁂, e-n auf dem Klavier ⁂ to accompany (or to play the accompaniment to) a p. on the piano; bsd. ⚔ ⚓ to escort, to (protect by) convoy. — 2. e-n bis an einen Ort ⁂ to conduct a p. (⚔ to give a p. safe-conduct) to a place; e-n nach Hause, bis an die Tür ⁂ to see a p. (safely) home, to the door; ⁂ Sie den Herrn die Treppe hinab see the gentleman downstairs; Damen in Gesellschaften ꝛc. ⁂ to chaperon ..., to play the chaperon to ...; ♪ ⁂de Stimme = Begleitstimme; phls., &c. die ⁂den Umstände the attendant (or accessory, concomitant) circumstances; med. die ⁂den Symptome ⚕ the assident signs or symptoms. — II ~ n ⓘ 3. = B/ung 1.
Be-gleiter (⌣⌢⌣) m ⑫, ~in f (Gefährte) travelling, &c. companion to or of; (Gesellschafterin) (lady) companion to or of; (Diener) attendant to or of. — 2. ~ = Dame protector; b.s. (Zuhälter) bully; ~in f (Anstandsdame) chaperon to or of. — 3. ♪ accompanist. — 4. ast. (Trabant) satellite. — 5. ⚓ = Begleitschiff.
Be-gleit-erscheinung (⌣⌢...) f ⓒ phys. attendant phenomenon, symptom; =mannschaft ⚔ f escort; =schein ⚝ m (Frachtbrief) bill of carriage; (Lieferungsschein) bill of delivery; (Zollfreischein) pass-bill; permit; =schiff ⚓ convoy; tender; =schreiben ⚝ n letter of advice; zu andern Schriftstücken: covering letter; =stimme ♪ f accompanying voice (in part-singing), weitS. accompani-

[Begleitung] — 158 — [begründen]

ment; eine ~ zu e-r Melodie setzen to harmonize.
Be-gleitung (⌣́⌣) f ⊕ 1. (das Begleiten) accompaniment (a.♪); (Bedeckung)bsd.⚔.↯ escort, convoy; safeconduct. — 2. in ~ von: a) accompanied (or attended) by; b) in the company of; (Gefolge) suite (attendant upon //), attendance.
Be-gleitungs-mannschaft ⚔ u. ↯ (‿...) f ⑫ escort; **=schiff** ↯ n = Begleitschiff; **⚓weise** adv. for companionship; ⚓ mit e-m reisen to keep a p. company in (or whilst) travelling.
Be-gleit-wort (⌣́‿...) n ⑫ word of explanation, explanatory remark; gr. attributive adjective; **=zettel** ✼ m bill of lading; auch: way-bill.
be-glück-en (⌣⌣́) I v/a. ⑱* e-n ⚓ to make a p. (feel) happy; (mit Erfolg krönen) to prosper; mit etwas beglückt werden to be favoured with s.th.; Gott beglückte ihn mit// God blessed him with //; hoch beglückt highly favoured, most fortunate. — II ~ n = B/ung.
Be-glücker (⌣⌣́) m ②, **~in** f ⑰ giver of blessings; benefactor m, ... tress f.
Be-glückung (⌣⌣́) f ⑯ durch die ~ s-s Volkes by making his people happy; **~s-theorie** (‿...) f ⑫ theory as to promoting (people's) happiness.
be-glückwünsch-en (⌣⌣́‿) I v/a. ⑨* e-n ⚓ to congratulate a p., to offer a p. one's congratulations (zu etwas, wegen einer Sache on a th.), to wish a p. joy of ... — II ~ n ⑬ u. B/ung f ⑯ congratulation, felicitation.
be-gnad-en (⌣⌣́) v/a. ⑱* e-n mit et. ⚓ (ihm als Gnade gewähren) mercifully to grant a th. to a p., to bless (or endow, favour) a p. with a th.
be-gnadigen (⌣⌣́⌣) I v/a. ⑱* (gnädig behandeln) to be merciful (or gracious) to, to show mercy to; (von Strafe freisprechen) to pardon, to let off, to (grant a) pardon to; bei Todesstrafen: to recommend to mercy; wegen politischer Vergehen: to amnesty, to grant an amnesty to. — II ~ n ⑬ = B/ung.
III **Be-gnadigte**([r]m) f ⑰ jur. pardoned (or amnestied) person or prisoner.
Be-gnadigung (⌣⌣́⌣) f ⑯ pardon; wegen politischer Vergehen: amnesty; strafmildernde ~ reprieve; **~s-gesuch** (‿...) n ⑫ petition for mercy or for a redress of justice, bei Todesurteilen: petition for a commutation of the sentence; **=recht** ⑫ (royal) prerogative of mercy, weit.S. right of granting(free) pardon(s).
be-gnüg-en (⌣⌣́) [be-u. Genüge]⑱* I sich ⚓ v/refl.: sich mit (oder an) etwas ⚓ to content o.s. (or to put up) with a th., to be satisfied (or content) with a th. — II v/n. (h.) († = genügen) sich (dat. ob. acc.) an ob. mit et. ⚓ lassen I. — III ~ n ⑬ contentment.
be-gnügsam (⌣⌣́‿) a. ⑯, **~keit** (⌣⌣́‿‿) f ⑯ = genügsam, Genügsamkeit.
Begoni-e ⚘ (⌣⌣́⌣)⌣) [neutl.] f ⑯ (Schiefblatt) begonia (Bego'nia); **⚓n-artig** (‿...) ⚘ a. ⑯ begoniaceous.
be-gönne (⌣⌣́) subj. impf., **be-gonnen** p.p. von beginnen (s. ds).
be-gönnern (⌣⌣́) v/a. ⑫a* (protegieren) to patronize.

be-graben (⌣⌣́) v/a. und sich ⚓ v/refl. ⑥b* 1. to bury, to inter, to commit to the grave; vgl. beerdigen. — 2. die Wellen haben sie ⚓ the waves have engulfed (or swallowed) them; der Schutt hält sie ⚓ they lie ontombed in the ruins; P damit können Sie sich ⚓ lassen! (das taugt nichts), etwa: F that won't do for me!, P that won't wash!; fig. das Kriegsbeil, die Streitaxt (nach Indianerweise) ⚓ to bury the hatchet; Sprichw. da liegt der Hund ⚓ (daran stößt sich die Sache) there's the rub, that's the (main) point. — 3. fig. sich ⚓ (sich verbergen) to live (or lead) a secluded (or retired, solitary) life.
Be-gräbnis (⌣⌣́‿) n ⑰ 1. (Beerdigung) burial, interment; (Leichenbegängnis) funeral; (feierl. Bestattung) obsequies pl. — 2. (Grabstätte) tomb, bibl. sepulchre.
Be-gräbnis-feier(lichkeit) (⌣⌣́‿‿) f ⑫ = Beerdigungsfeier; **=gebühren** f/pl. burial-fee; **=kosten** pl. funeral expenses or charges, cemetery dues pl.; **=pl.tz** m burial-ground (or -place), (Friedhof) cemetery; **=schmaus** m burial-feast, in Irland: wake; **=tag** m day of the funeral.
be-gradigen ⊙ (⌣́⌣⌣) [gerade] v/a. ⑱* Wege, Wasserläufe ⚓ (geradelegen) to level...
be-gras-en (⌣⌣́) I v/a. und v/refl. Land ⚓ to (cover with) grass, to turf, weit.S. to turn into meadow-land; sich ⚓ to run into grass; begrast grassy, covered with grass. — II v/a. v. Tieren: to browse, graze (= abgrasen).
be-graut (⌣⌣́) p.p. u. a. ⑯ grey-haired.
be-greifbar (⌣⌣́‿) 2c. f. begreiflich 2c.
be-greif-en (⌣⌣́) ⑥bst* I v/a. 1. (befühlen) to handle, (betasten) to touch, finger. — 2. mst fig. (einschließen) to include, imply, contain; mit (ein)⚓ to comprise; er ist dabei mit (ein)begriffen he is among the number. — 3. fig. (geistig erfassen) to apprehend; (auffassen) to comprehend; (verstehen) to understand, conceive, grasp; schnell (schwer) ⚓ to be quick (or slow, dull) of apprehension; das ist nicht zu ⚓ that is incomprehensible, (rätselhaft) inconceivable; ich kann nicht ⚓, was er damit sagen) will I cannot think (or make out) what he is driving at; wir können (den Sinn davon) nicht ⚓ that is beyond us or a puzzle to us; es läßt sich leicht ⚓, daß // it is easy to understand that //, it is obvious that //. — II sich ⚓ v/refl. 4. (zu begreifen sein) das begreift sich leicht that is easily understood. — III ~ n ⑬ 5. = B/ung.
IV **be-griffen** p.p. 6. a) auf dem Marsche ⚓ sein to be on the march; b) in etwas ⚓ (mitten darin) sein to be engaged in (or busy doing) a th.; in der Ausführung ⚓ in a fair way of being carried (through); im Bau ⚓ in the course of construction, being built, building; im Entstehen ⚓ (still) forming, (a)rising, chm. nascent; im Steigen ⚓ (in the act of) ascending.
be-greiflich (⌣⌣́‿) a. ⑯ (ant. un⚓) comprehensible, (denkbar) conceivable, (verständlich) intelligible; e-m et. ⚓ machen to make a p. understand a th.. to make the matter clear to him; ⚓er

weise adv.: a) (leicht zu begreifen) as may be easily understood or conceived; b) (natürlich) evidently, obviously; (as a matter of) course; **~keit** f ⑯ comprehensibility, (Verständlichkeit 2c.) intelligibility; (Augenscheinlichkeit) obviousness.
Be-greifung (⌣⌣́‿) f ⑯ apprehension, comprehension, conception; **~s-kraft** (‿...) f ⑫, **=vermögen** n = Begriffs...
begrenzbar (⌣⌣́‿) a. ⑯ limitable.
be-grenz-en (⌣⌣́) I v/a. ⑨⁰* (mit Grenzen versehen) to mark off by (or with) boundary-lines; to delimit, (die Grenze von et. bilden) to form the boundary (or frontier) of ..., to border on. weit.S. to divide, to separate; fig. (beschränken) to confine, limit, circumscribe; b/ter Gesichtskreis horizon. — II ~ n ⑬ = B/ung. [limitation. fig. narrowness.]
Be-grenzt-heit (⌣⌣́‿) f ⑯ limitedness,)
Be-grenzung (⌣⌣́‿) f ⑯ delimitation, (forming the) boundary (of).
Be-griff (⌣́) m ⑪b. 1. (Vorstellung) idea, (Wissen von et.) notion; verallgemeinter ~ abstraction; nach unsern ⚓en, oft: from (or according to) our point of view; das geht über (od. übersteigt) alle ~e that is beyond all comprehension, that beats everything (hollow); man macht sich keinen ~ davon people have no idea of it. — 2. (Verständnis) conception, insight; das ging über seine ~e that was beyond him or his horizon, it was more than he could grasp. — 3. (vgl. begreifen 6b.) im ~(e) sein, etwas zu tun to be about to do a th., to be thinking of doing a th.; er ist im ~ abzureisen he is ready (or going) to start, he is on the point of leaving, F he is now off.
be-griffen (⌣⌣́‿) p.p. v. begreifen (s. ds, bsd. 6.)
be-grifflich (⌣⌣́‿) a. ⑯ notional; rein ⚓ abstract; ⚓ (adv.)bestimmen to define.
Be-griffs-ähnlichkeit (⌣́‿...) f ⑫ synonymy; **=bestimmung** f definition; **=bildung** f abstraction; **=fach** n category; **=kraft** f, **=vermögen** n intelligence, power of apprehension, apprehensive faculty or power; **=lehre** f ideology; **=name** m abstract noun; **=schrift** f ideography; **=verwechs(e)lung** f, **=verwirrung** f confusion (of ideas), P jumble.
be-gründ-en (⌣⌣́) I v/a. ⑱* 1. a) to found or base (auf et. on a th.); einen Bau ⚓ to lay a solid foundation to ...; fig. (stiften) ein Geschäft ⚓ to establish a business; von neuem ⚓ to re-establish; ✼ eine neue Firma ⚓ to set up a new firm, to start a new (house of) business; eine Aktiengesellschaft ⚓ to form (or promote) a joint-stock company; b) e-n ⚓ (in feste Stellung bringen) to establish a p., to start (or set up) a p. in business; c) einen Satz ⚓ (mit Gründen unterstützen) to substantiate ... by; to give reasons for ...; e-n Antrag ⚓ to speak in support of ...; e-e Anklage ⚓ to sustain ...; ⚓d causal, causative. — 2. ⚓ e-n (a. v/refl.)⚓ in e-r Wissenschaft ⚓ (sicher m.) to initiate a p. (o.s.) in ..., to make a p. (o.s.) a thorough master of ... — II ~ n ⑬ 3. = B/ung.
III **be-gründet** p.p. u. a. ⑯ 4. substantiated, well founded, established.

Signs (see page XVII): F familiar; P vulgar; ℙ flash; ↘ rare; † obsolete (died); * new word (born); +* incorrect; ♪ music;

[Begründer] — 159 — [Behandlung]

Be-gründer (⌣⌢⌣) m ㉒, **~in** f ㊻ founder (f foundress), originator; ● e-r Aktiengesellschaft: promoter, e-s Geschäftes, auch: starter; (Anstifter) prime mover.

Be-gründung (⌣⌢⌣) f ㊻ foundation, establishment; initiation, feste ~ consolidation; (Angabe der Gründe) argumentation), reasoning, weit S. proof (s pl.), bisw. auch: motivation; zur ~ e-s Antrages 2c. in support of …; ~ e-s Entschlusses, e-r Handlung reason(s) adduced for a decision, an action.

be-grünen (⌣⌢⌣) ⊛* I v/a. to cover with (or clothe in) verdure. — II v/n. (zu), sich ≈ v/refl. to grow green, Bäume: to burst into leaf or into foliage.

be-grüßen (⌣⌢⌣) I v/a. ⊛⁰* 1. to greet, salute, welcome; durch Verneigung: to bow to; im Orient: to salaam; durch Hutabnehmen: to doff (or take off) one's hat (or cap) to; als Sieger 2c. ≈ to hail as … — 2. F e-n um et. ≈ (angehen) to apply to a p. for (leave of) a th., to do a p. the honour of asking him for a th. — II ~ n ㉓ = Begrüßung.

Be-grüßung (⌣⌢⌣) f ㊻ greeting, salutation of; **~s-rede** (⌢…) f ㊷ address of welcome; **~s-schuß** m salute (in honour of).

be-gucken F (⌣⌢⌣) v/a. ⊛* to have a look (or peep) at, to eye, to gaze at.

be-günstigen (⌣⌢⌣⌣) I v/a. ⊛* 1. to favour. — 2. (fördern) to promote; to forward (a p.'s interest); (unterstützen) to countenance, support, patronize; (bevorzugen) to push forward (a candidate or candidature); von den Umständen begünstigt favoured by (or by the favour of) circumstances. — II ~ n ㉓ 3. = Begünstigung.

Be-günstiger (⌣⌢⌣⌣) m ㉒, **~in** f ㊻ supporter, promoter; Sport, a. pol. backer; (Helfershelfer) accomplice, abettor.

Be-günstigte([r] m) f (~) ㊺ favourite (a. im Sport), auch allg.: (fr.) protégé(e f).

Be-günstigung (⌣⌢⌣⌣) f ㊻ 1. promotion; support or countenance (given to), (Bevorzugung) auch: favouritism (auch Sport), der Verwandten: nepotism; ~ e-s Vergehens: complicity (in). — 2. (Gunst) favour (shown) to.

Begünstigungs-zoll (⌢…) m ㊷ preferential duty. [et. with a th.); to belt.

be-gürten (⌣⌢⌣) v/a. ⊛* to (be)gird (mit

Be-guß (⌣⌢) m ⊛ a. sprinkling (or watering) of, (Schwemmen) flushing of.

be-gut-achten (⌣⌢⌣⌣) I v/a. ⊛* et. ≈ to give (or express) one's opinion upon (or about) a th.; et. ≈ lassen to submit a th. to (or to lay it before) a competent judge. — II **Be-gut-achtung** f ㊻ judgment pronounced upon a th., expert opinion.

be-gütern (⌣⌢⌣) I ⸺ v/a. ㉒a* e-n ≈ to bless a p. with riches. — II **be-gütert** p.p. und a. ㊻ owning (or being possessed of) landed estates or landed property; weit S. wealthy, opulent, well-to-do; er ist in Schlesien ≈ he has (large) estates (or property) in Silesia.

be-gütigen (⌣⌢⌣⌣) v/a. ⊛* to soothe (with kind words); to quiet, calm, appease, pacify, propitiate.

be-haaren (⌣⌢⌣) I sich ≈ v/refl. ⊛* 1. to become hairy. — II **behaart**

p.p. u. a. ㊻ 2. hairy; am ganzen Körper ≈ with hair all over the body. — 3. ⚘ ⚘ pilose, crinite; rauh ≈ hirsute, weich (ob. flaumig) ≈ pubescent, villous. — III **Be-haarung** f ㊻ 4. hair, hairiness, ⚘ ⚘ hirsuteness, &c. (f. II).

be-haben ⸺ (⌣⌣) [mhd.: behave] I v/refl. ⊛*(o.impf.) sich ≈ als (mit flgb. nom.) to behave as or like. — II ~ n ㉓ behaviour.

be-häbig (⌣⌢⌣) [: heavy] a. ㊻ v. Sachen: snug, cozy; allg.: comfortable; (wohlhabend) well off; (beleibt) pretty stout, plump; **~keit** f ㊻ snugness, coziness, comfort; stout(ish)ness, plumpness.

be-hacken (⌣⌢⌣) I v/a. ⊛* 1. ⊙ Holz ≈ to chop …; to square …; Bäume ≈ to lop … — 2. agr. die Erde ≈ (mit der Hacke lockern) to hoe …, to loosen … (round the roots). — II **Be-hackung** f ㊻ 3. chopping, &c. (f. I).

be-haften* (⌣⌢⌣) v/a. ⊛* jur. e-n ≈ (haftbar m.) to make a p. liable, to hold a p. responsible for a th.

be-haftet (⌣⌢⌣) a. ㊻ mit (bisw. a. von) et. (Lästigem, Üblem) ≈ sein to be afflicted or infected (schwächer: affected) with …; mit der Fallsucht ≈ subject to epileptic fits; mit der Luftröhrenentzündung ≈ bronchial; mit Schulden ≈ loaded (or burdened, encumbered) with debt.

be-hagen (⌣⌢⌣) [mhd.: *Hag] I v/n. (h.) ⊛* 1. et. behagt mir a th. suits me, stärker: it pleases me; das hat ihm schlecht behagt it was not to his taste; wie behagt Ihnen das? how do you like (or relish) it?; er ließ sich das Essen ≈ he did full justice to … — II ~ n ㉓ 2. comfortable feeling, gratification; ~ an et. finden to find pleasure in a th., to be gratified by (or pleased with) a th. — 3. et. mit großem ~ tun to delight in doing a th., to do a th. with great gusto or zest or delight. to relish a th.; wir konnten uns nach ~ gütlich tun we could take our ease or have our comfort(s).

be-haglich (⌣⌢⌣) a. ㊻ 1. (Behagen empfindend) at one's ease; ≈ (adv.) leben to lead an easy (or a comfortable) life; er fühlte sich nur wenig ≈, auch oft: he did not feel (or was not) himself. — 2. (Behagen erweckend) cozy, snug; (bequem) comfortable; der Ort snuggery; machen Sie sich's ≈! make yourself (pl. yourselves) quite at home!, take your ease!

Be-haglichkeit (⌣⌢⌣⌣) f ㊻ ease, comfort(ableness); coziness, snugness.

be-halmt (⌣⌢) a. ㊻ bladed (= halmig).

be-haltbar (⌣⌢⌣) a. ㊻ easy to retain.

be-halten (⌣⌢⌣) v/a. ⊛a* 1. to keep, für die Dauer: to retain; ≈ auf Lager ≈ to keep in stock. — 2. die Fassung, die Geistesgegenwart ≈ to retain (or preserve) one's self-possession, one's presence of mind; F den Kopf oben ≈ not to lose one's head; to remain calm; das Leben ≈ to save one's life; e-n lieb ≈ to continue one's affection for a p.; er kann nichts ≈ he cannot retain (or remember) anything, he forgets everything; die Oberhand ≈ to get the upper hand (or the better) of; recht ≈ to be right in the end;

weit S. to gain one's cause; ich habe et. übrig ≈ I have s.th. over or left; wenn wir dieses Wetter ≈ if this weather continues, if there is no change in the weather; wohl zu ≈! (you must) bear in mind!, mark that!; ≈ Sie dies (Geld 2c.) für sich (⌣ ⌢) this is (or shall be) for you; Pläne für sich ≈ to keep one's own counsel; e-e Sache (ein Geheimnis) für sich ≈ to keep … secret or dark or to oneself; e-n et. im Andenken, Gedächtnis ≈ to keep a p. a th. in mind, to preserve the memory of a p.; et. im Auge ≈ to keep a th. in view, not to lose a th. out of sight; Arithmetik: im Sinne ≈ to carry. — 3. † ob. ⚓ = (in gutem Stande) erhalten (f. d. 1); noch gebr. im p.p.: ≈e Ankunft (= wohl ≈e A.) safe arrival; ≈e Güter n/pl. goods pl. in a perfect state (of preservation); wohl≈: a) well preserved, in good repair or condition; b) safe and sound; uninjured.

Be-hälter (⌣⌢⌣) m ㉒ 1. meist: reservoir. — 2. = Behältnis 1.

Be-hältnis (⌣⌢) n ㉗ 1. (Gelaß) receptacle, (store-)cupboard, chest, mit Verschluß: locker. — 2. tank, für Fische: pond.

be-haltsam (⌣⌢⌣) a. ㊻ retentive; **~keit** (~⌢) f ㊻ retentiveness.

be-hämmern ⊙ (⌣⌢⌣) v/a. ㉒a* to hammer; behämmert hammer-dressed.

be-handeln (⌣⌢⌣) I v/a. ㉒a* 1. to treat (auch chm., ⊙ u. fig.): a) e-n als Freund ≈ to treat a p. like (or as) a friend, b) erschöpfend ≈ to treat exhaustively or thoroughly; et. oberflächlich ≈ to deal superficially with a th., to touch only the surface of a th., to skim a th.; der zu ≈de Gegenstand the subject to be discussed. — 2. (verfahren mit) to use; e-n grob (nachsichtig) ≈ to deal harshly (gently or leniently) with a p.; rauh ≈ to use (or treat, handle) roughly; schlecht ≈ to maltreat; tyrannisch, rücksichtslos ≈ to tyrannize, to brutalize, F to bully; Pferde, Hunde 2c.: to manage; schwer zu ≈(d) difficult to deal with, stärker: unmanageable. — 3. et. ≈ (darum feilschen) to haggle (or bargain) about a th. — 4. welcher Arzt behandelt ihn? who is his medical man?, what doctor attends (or treats) him?; ⊙ Erze im Hochofen 2c. ≈ to work (or smelt) … — II ~ n ㉓ 5. = Behandlung 1.

be-händig/en (⌣⌢⌣) I v/a. ⊛* e-m et. ≈ to hand over a th. to a p., to deliver a th. into a p.'s hand; jur. e-m e-e Vorladung ≈ to serve a summons on a p. — II ~ n ㉓ u. **B/ung** f ㊻ delivery.

Be-händigungs-schein (⌢…) m ㊷ jur. receipt (on delivery of deeds, &c.).

Be-handler (⌣⌢⌣) m ㉒ 1. one who treats, &c. (vgl. behandeln). — 2. phys. one who works (or manipulates) ath.

Be-handlung (⌣⌢⌣) f ㊻ (zu behandeln 1:) treatment; (zu 2:) brutality; v. Pferden, Hunden 2c.: management; (zu 4:) medical attendance or treatment. — 2. e-m freundliche (schlechte) ~ angedeihen lassen to use a p. well (ill), to accord kind (bad) treatment to a p.; schlechte ~ maltreatment, ill-usage.

⚘ scientific; ⚘ botanical; ⚲ geography; ⚙ machinery; ⚒ mining; ⚔ military; ⚓ marine; ● commercial; ✉ postal; 🚆 railway.

[Behandlungsart] — 160 — [behindert]

Be-handlungs-art (⌣⌣⌣...) f 62, =**weise** f manner of treatment, way (or method) of dealing with a th.; *chm.* die ätherische ~ the ether treatment.

Be-hang (⌣⌣) m ⑦b. 1. hanging, appendage to; (Faltenwurf) drapery. — 2. *hunt.* (Schlappohren des Jagdhundes) (long) lop-ears *pl.*

Be-hänge (⌣⌣) n 22 (Schmuck) ornaments *pl.*, adornments *pl.*, F the get-up.

be-hangen (⌣⌣) I .†. v/a. 69b* = behängen. — II *p.p. u. a.* 66 (D9) covered with.

be-hängen (⌣⌣) 88* I v/a. 1. mit et. 2 to hang with a th.; einen Saal 2 to drape (or festoon) a hall, e-e Wand mit Bildern 2 to cover ... — II sich 2 v/refl. 2. sich mit Bändern ec. 2 to adorn o.s. with ..., to trim o.s. up (or to deck o.s. out) with ... — 3. sich mit et. (Lästigem) 2 to encumber o.s. with a th., to take s.th. on one's shoulders.

Be-hänge-zeit (⌣⌣-) f 46 *hunt.* season for training (or entering) hounds.

be-harr/en (⌣⌣) I v/n. (h., ⚓ ju) 88* 1. to persevere in a th.; *a. abs.* im Guten 2 to persevere. — 2. auf ob. bei et. 2 to persist in (doing) a th.; auf seinem Rechte ec. 2 to insist on ..., to stand out for ...; auf einer Behauptung, bei e-r Aussage 2 to adhere to ..., F to stick to ...; auf seinem Sinne 2 to show o.s. determined; bei f-m Vorsätze 2 to hold on to one's purpose; steif und fest auf et. 2 to hold out unflinchingly for a th., to insist on a th. with fixed determination. — II~n 23 3. = B/ung.

be-harrlich (⌣⌣) *a.* 66 persevering, (beständig) constant; (fest) determined, inflexible, unflinching; sein Les Stillschweigen his persistent (or continuous) silence; 2 bei der Arbeit plodding (or assiduous) in one's work, bent on (performing) one's task; ~**keit** (⌣⌣-) f 46 (*o. pl.*) perseverance, constancy, determination, inflexibility, persistence, continuance, assiduity.

Be-harrung (⌣⌣) f 46 1. persevering in. 2. = Beharrlichkeit.

Be-harrungs-mut (″...) m 62 endurance; =**vermögen** n, *phys.* law of continuity, inertia; =**zustand** m permanence, permanent state, power of resistance.

be-haubt (⌣⌣) *p.p. u. a.* 66 *orn.* crested; ♀ cassideous. [breathe upon a th.]

be-hauchen (⌣⌣) v/a. 88* et. 2 to)

be-hauen (⌣⌣) I v/a. 88c* 1. to hew. — 2. ⊙ *arch., &c.*: a) Bretter: to chip; b) Holz, Steine: aus dem groben 2 rough-hew; Bildhauerei: to chisel, rechtwink(e)lig 2 to square; c) e-n Stein 2 to ... — 3. e-n Baum 2, einem Baume die Äste 2 to lop a tree, to clip the branches of(f) a tree. — 4. ⚔ ein Gestein 2 (durch Anhauen die Härte erproben) to test ... — II~n 23 5. = B/ung.

be-häufe(l)n (⌣⌣) v/a. 88* (2a)* Pflanzen 2 (mit Erdhäufchen umgeben) to hill ...

be-haupt/en (⌣⌣) I v/a. 89* 1. *auch v/refl.* (et. festhalten) to maintain; (stützen) to uphold; sich 2 (geltend machen) to assert o.s., to stand one's ground, to hold one's own, *weits.* to make one's influence (or power) felt. — 2. seinen Rang 2 to keep one's rank; ⚔ die Kurse 2 sich, Preise sind behauptet prices are steady or firm or maintained; ⚔ das (Schlacht-)Feld 2 to remain master of the field; den Sieg 2 to carry the day, to gain the victory. — 3. (aussprechen) eine Meinung: to allege, assert, contend, state; (als sicher darstellen) to affirm; (vorgeben) to pretend (that a th. is true or a th. to be true); er behauptet steif und fest, daß // he is positive (or he positively declares) that //; es wird behauptet, daß er tot sei he is reported to be dead; er behauptet ihn gesehen zu haben he pretends (or feigns) to have (or having) seen him. — II~n 23 4. = B/ung 1. III 2d *p.pr. u. a.* 66 5. Bed. des *inf.* — 6. *gr.* 2der Satz affirmative sentence.

Be-hauptung (⌣⌣) f 46 1. maintenance, assertion, contention, statement; ⚔ ~ e-r Stellung holding (or maintaining) a position, stärker: stubborn defence of a point. — 2. das ist eine bloße ~, etwa: that is a mere conjecture; eine unwahre ~ a false statement.

be-hausen (⌣⌣-) [Haus] I v/a. 90* e-n 2 = beherbergen. — II **Be-hausung** f 46 dwelling(-place), lodging; domicile, F diggings; Sie finden mich in meiner ~ you (will) find me at home.

Be-hausungs-ziffer (⌣⌣-...) f 46 (Zahl der Personen, die auf 1 Haus entfällt) average (number) of occupants (in a house).

be-häuten (⌣⌣-) [Haut] v/a. 89* to cover with a hide or a skin. [f. behauen I.)

Be-hauung f 46 hewing, chipping, &c.,)

be-heben (⌣⌣) v/a. 9b* 1. öst. ⚔ ♀ Geld 2 to draw money. — 2. F (heben) Hindernisse 2 to clear away obstacles; die Schwierigkeit ist noch nicht behoben the difficulty is not yet removed.

be-heizen ⊙ (⌣⌣) v/a. 89* ein Haus 2 to heat ..., (mit Öfen versehen) to provide ... with fire-places or stoves.

Be-helf (⌣⌣) m ⓪b. 1. (was einem hilft) help, resource, expedient; bes. *jur.* remedy; (Vorrichtung) appliance, contrivance; (Ausflucht) device. — 2. (womit man sich behilft) makeshift, shift.

be-helfen (⌣⌣): sich 2 v/refl. ⓪b* 1. (durchkommen) to make shift; (sich durchschlagen) to make both ends meet, to have a hard struggle, to be in needy (or straitened) circumstances. — 2. sich mit et. 2 to make a th. do; sich ohne et. 2 to go (or do) without a th.; sich mit wenigem 2 to manage with little, to cut and contrive. [bridge.]

Be-helfs-brücke ⚔ ⊙ (⌣⌣...) f 62 spare-}

be-helligen (⌣⌣⌣) I v/a. 89* e-n mit et. 2 to importune (or annoy, molest) a p. with a th., ich will Sie nicht länger 2 I won't trouble (or bother) you any longer. — II ~ n 23 u. **Be-helligung** f 46 importunity, annoyance.

be-helmt (⌣⌣) *p.p. u. a.* 66: a) helmeted; b) ♀ galeate.

Behen ♀ (⌣⌣) [ar., pers.] m 50 be(he)n; saw-leaved centaury (*Centaurea Behen*).

be-hende (⌣⌣) [mhd. ♀ Hand] *a.* 66 (flink) nimble, agile, light (on one's feet); (geschwind) quick; (gewandt) smart, handy.

Be-hendigkeit (⌣⌣-) f 46 nimbleness, agility; quickness; smartness.

Behen-nuß (″...) f 62 ben(-nut); (nuß-)**baum** m ben(-tree) (*Moringa oleifera*); =**öl** n ben-oil; =**säure** f, *chm.* benic acid ($C_{22}H_{44}O_2$); =**wurzel** f, *pharm.* be(he)n.

be-herberg/en (⌣⌣⌣) I v/a. 88* to harbour, house, lodge; e-n Freund 2, oft: to take in (or accommodate, receive, put up) ... — II ~ n 23 u. **B/ung** f 46 housing, lodging; e-n um ~ bitten to ask for a p.'s hospitality, *weits.* to seek shelter (or accommodation) at a p.'s house.

be-herrschen (⌣⌣⌣) 69* I v/a. 1. ein Volk 2 to rule (over) ..., (die Herrschaft ausüben) to govern (over), to sway, *b.s.* to domineer over, P to boss it over. — 2. *fig.* f-e Leidenschaft ec. 2 to master ..., to (keep in) check ..., to (keep under) control ...; f-n Gegenstand, e-e Sprache 2 to be master (or to have full mastery) of ...; er beherrscht das ganze Fach he is fully conversant (or acquainted) with ..., he has a thorough grasp of ...; von f-n Leidenschaften beherrscht werden to be a slave to one's passions. — 3. (örtlich überragen) die Ebene ec. 2 to tower above ..., to look down (up)on ..., ⚔ *frt. auch:* to command; 2de Höhe ⚔ commanding height. — II sich 2 v/refl. 4. sich (selbst) 2 to restrain o.s.; er kann sich nicht 2 he has no command (or control) over himself or his passions, he is without self-control. — III ~ n 23 5. = Beherrschung.

Be-herrscher (⌣⌣⌣) m 23, ~**in** f 47: ~ e-s Landes ec. ruler (or governor) over (or of) ..., sovereign over (or of) ...; *fig.* ~(in) f-r (ihrer) Leidenschaften ec. master (mistress) over (or of) ...

Be-herrschung (⌣⌣⌣) f 46 1. government, (self-)control. — 2. sway (over a nation, &c.), ruling (a country, &c.).

be-herzigen (⌣⌣⌣) [uhd.] I v/a. 88* to take to heart, schwächer: to take into consideration; (erwägen) to weigh (in one's mind; 2s=**wert** *a.*, 2**würdig** *a.* 66 worthy of consideration; 2e Tatsache notable (or remarkable) fact. — II **Be-herzigung** f 46 taking a th. to heart; (Erwägung) reflection, consideration.

be-herzt (⌣⌣) *a.* 66 courageous, bold, plucky, stout-hearted; e-n 2 m. to instil courage in a p.; (entschlossen) determined; sein Les Auftreten his resolute demeanour; (kühn) daring; 2e Antwort spirited reply; ~**heit** (⌣⌣-) f 46 courage, pluck, spirit; (Entschlossenheit) resolution; (Kühnheit) daring.

be-hexen (⌣⌣) I v/a. 88* 1. to bewitch. — 2. (bezaubern) to enchant, to charm; wie behext dastehen to be spell-bound, to stand transfixed. — II ~ n 23 u. **Be-hexung** f 46 3. enchantment, charm.

be-hilflich (⌣⌣) *a.* 66 helpful, (nützlich) useful, serviceable; sei ein bißchen 2 F lend (us) a hand; e-m sein 2 to render a p. assistance; e-m bei et. 2 sein to aid (or assist, help) a p. (in doing) a th.; e-m zu et. 2 sein to help a p. to a th., to put a p. in the way of (obtaining or getting) a th.

be-hindern (⌣⌣⌣) I v/a. 2a* = hindern. — II **be-hindert** *p.p. u. a.* 66 delayed, checked, obstructed; 2e Atmung heavy (or hard) breathing.

[behobeln] — 161 — [beibringen]

be-hobeln ⊙ (⌣⌣⌣) v/a. ⓐ* to plane, to smooth; *fig.* e-n Satz ⚭ to polish ...
be-hoben (⌣⌣) p.p. *von* beheben.
be-holmen ⊙ ⚓ (⌣⌣⌣) v/a. ⓐ* die Pfähle ⚭ to cap the piles.
be-holz/en (⌣⌣⌣) ⓐ* **I** v/a. **1.** *for.* einen Wald ⚭: a) to afforest ...; b) beholzt wooded, planted with woods or trees. — **II** sich ⚭ v/refl. **2.** (Äste ansetzen) to branch out, to form branches; (in Holz wachsen) to run into wood. — **3.** to become covered with trees. — **III** ~ n ㉓ u. **Be-holzung** f ㊻ **4.** zu I, zB.: afforestation. — **5.** nur B/ung: (Holzbestand) (growth of) timber.
Be-holzungs-recht (⌣⌣⌣⌣⌣) n ㊷ right of cutting timber or wood.
Be-hör ⚓ (⌣⌣) n(m) ⓑc. (o.pl.) = Zubehör.
be-horchen (⌣⌣⌣) v/a. ⓐ* to spy out, to listen to; to overhear.
Be-hörde (⌣⌣⌣)[mhd.18.sae.v.behören,provc. = gehören] f ㊻ (Obrigkeit) (competent) authority, (government-)board; städtische ~ town (or municipal) authorities pl.; vgl. Magistrat; in kleineren Ortschaften: local board; vorgesetzte ~ superior (oft auch: senior) officer(s pl.) or clerk(s pl.), official(s pl.), &c.
be-hördlich (⌣⌣⌣) a. ㊻ official, authoritative (= amtlich).
be-hosen (⌣⌣⌣) v/a. ⓐ* to put into trousers or breeches; behost wearing trousers or breeches, auch: trousered.
Be-huf (⌣⌣) [mhd.: behoof; * beheben († = erhalten)] m ⓑc. (Gebrauch) use; (Nutzen) behoof; zu diesem ~ for this purpose; zum ~(e) behufs.
be-hufs (⌣⌣) *prp.* mit *gen.* in (or on) behalf of; with the intention of; ⚭ Übernahme des Geschäfts for the purpose of taking over (or with a view to the transfer of) the business.
be-huft (⌣⌣) a. ㊻ zo. hoofed.
be-hügelt (⌣⌣⌣) a. ㊻ hilly.
be-hüten (⌣⌣⌣) v/a. ⓐ* **1.** *agr.* ein Feld ⚭ to put (or turn out) cattle into ... — **2.** (in f-e Hut nehmen) to look after, guard, watch over; e-n vor et. ⚭ to preserve (or keep, shield) from ...; behüt' dich Gott! God keep (or bless) you!, *feierlich:* God be with you!; *weitS.* Farewell! — **3.** (verhüten) *ell.* (Gott) behüte! on no account!, God forbid!
be-hutsam (⌣⌣-) a. ㊻ (vorsichtig) careful, cautious, (bedächtig) wary; du mußt ⚭ zu Werke gehen you must be on your guard; ~keit (⌣⌣--) f ㊻ care(fulness), cautiousness, caution, wariness.
Be-hütung ⚓ (⌣⌣⌣) f ㊻ looking after, guarding, watch(ing), &c., f. behüten ⚭.
bei¹ (⌣) [ahd.: by] **I** auch **nahe bei** *prp.* mit *dat.* **1.** örtliche Nähe: near (to) ...; ⚘ Schöneberg bei Berlin ... near Berlin; in persönlichen Verhältnis zu e-m: with ..., (f. 2 c, e, f); dicht bei close to ... — **2.** a) Örtlichkeit: er schlug sie bei Azincourt ⚘ ... at Agincourt; etwas bei der Hand haben to have s. th. at hand; ⚔ Schlacht bei Leipzig ⚘ battle of ...; bei e-m sitzen to sit by (or beside) a p.; dicht bei dem Hause close to the house; b) Aufenthalt: bei Hofe at (the) court; Gesandter bei der Königin ambassador to ...; c) Wohnort, Sitte ⚭., oft: with; er wohnt bei mir, bei s-m Bruder ... with me, at his brother's; bei uns zulande with us, in our country; ich lese bei Horaz ... in Horace; es war Sitte bei den Griechen ... among (or with) the Greeks; das kommt selten bei ihm vor that's a rare thing (or occurrence) with him; das steht bei Ihnen it rests (or remains) with you; d) (Bei-sich-tragen in der Tasche ⚭c.) meist: about (one), on (one); ich habe kein Geld bei mir ... about me; man fand e-n Brief bei ihm a letter was found on him, on his person; oft nicht zu übersetzen: ich hatte e-n Stock, e-n Dolch bei mir I carried a stick, a dagger; e) Begleitung, meist: with: er hatte einen Bedienten bei sich ... with him; f) persönliches Verhältnis: bei Gott ist alles möglich with God all things are possible; bei diesem Lehrer lernt man viel from (or with) a master like him ...; bei wem haben Sie Stunden? of whom do you take lessons?; bei e-m anfragen, anklopfen to inquire of a p., to knock at a p.'s door; ⚔ bei der Artillerie dienen to serve with the artillery or as a gunner; ⚓ bei der Marine dienen to serve in the navy; bei e-m im Dienste stehen to be in the service of a p.; Kommis bei e-m Kaufmann a merchant's clerk. — **3.** Zeit, Umstände: bei seiner Abreise on his departure; bei s-m Aufenthalte: a) (gelegentlich) on the occasion of his visit; b) (zur Zeit) during his stay; beim Essen at dinner; bei erster Gelegenheit on the first opportunity, bei günstiger Gelegenheit at a favourable time or opportunity; bei hellem Tage in broad daylight, stärker: in the (full) glare of noon; bei seinen Lebzeiten in (or during) his lifetime; bei Lichte betrachtet on thorough examination, bei dieser Nachricht on receiving this news; bei(m) Ostwind with an easterly wind, while the wind is in the east; bei jedem Schritte at each step; beiseite (bsd. Artikel); bei Tage in (the) day-time, by day; bei Tische at table; ⓗ bei Verfall zahlen ... at maturity, ... when due; ⓗ bei Vorzeigung (des Wechsels), bei Sicht on presentation of the bill); bei günstigem Wetter if the weather permits, in fine weather; bei dem schönen Wetter in such fine weather, while this fine weather lasts; bei diesen Worten at these words; beizeiten (bsd. Artikel). — **4.** Rückbeziehung: ich dachte bei mir selbst I thought to myself. — **5.** Zustände: bei Appetit sein to have a healthy (or good) appetite; bei der Arbeit sein to be at work; bei näherer Bekanntschaft (Erkundigung) on closer acquaintance (examination); bei Gelde (auch Kasse) sein to be in funds, to be flush of money; nicht bei Gelde sein to be short of cash or money, to be hard up or F in low waters; bei guter Gesundheit in good health, hale and hearty; schon bei Jahren sein to be advanced (F well on) in years; bei Kräften robust; bei Licht, bei einer Lampe arbeiten to work by candle- (or lamp-)light; bei offenem Fenster schlafen to sleep with open windows; das Beste bei der Sache ist the best of it is; mir ist nicht wohl bei dieser Sache I don't feel at ease over this business; bei Sinnen, bei Verstande, bei sich sein to be in one's right senses or right mind; nicht bei Sinnen (bei Verstande) sein to be out of one's mind; ⓗ bei dem heutigen Stande der Kurse at present prices or quotations; bei Strafe // on pain of //; bei Todesstrafe upon pain of death; mit substantiviertem Verbum: beim Aufwachen on awaking. — **6.** Anhaltspunkte: bei der Hand fassen, führen, halten to grasp, lead, hold by the hand; bei den Haaren ziehen to pull by the hair. — **7.** Vergleichung, Einräumung: a) bei so vielen Schwierigkeiten considering the (or in the face of so) many difficulties; b) mit folgendem all (= trotz): bei all seiner Klugheit ist er betrogen worden despite (or with all) his prudence ...; bei alle(m) dem, bei dem allem (,+ alten) for all that. — **8.** bei Schwüren, meist: by; beim Himmel! by Jove!, feierlich: by heaven!; bei den Göttern! by the powers (above)!; bei meiner Seele (Ehre)! upon my soul (honour)!; schwören bei // to swear by //. — **9.** Maß: er ist bei weitem reicher ... richer by far; bei einem Haare by a hair's breadth, F by a mere shave; einen bei Heller und Pfennig bezahlen ... to the last farthing or penny. — **10.** Zahlangabe: bei Tausenden erscheinen sie ... by (or in) thousands. — **11.** ⚓ beim Winde segeln to sail close to the wind. — **II** bisw. als adv. **12.** (ungefähr) bei vierhundert Jahre about ..., nearly ... — **13.** F (in der Nähe) meist mit beigefügtem *adv.*: hier bei near (or close) by.
Bei² (⌣) [türk.] m ㊿ u. ⓑc., Titel ㊴ ⓖ ~ von Tunis bey of Tunis.
Bei-..., **bei-**... (⌣...) Vorsilbe in Zssgn: **I** mit *verbs,* die immer trennbar (**) sind und oft ein Dativ-objekt haben, bezeichnet Nähe, zB.: ⚭binden (f. a. bfd. Art.) to tie to(gether); dem Texte ⚭drucken to print by the side of (or with) the text. — **II** m. u. a.: **1.** Beistand, zB.: Beikoch (f. a. bfd. Art.) m assistant cook. — **2.** Nebensache, zB.: Beiwerk (f. a. bfd. Art.) n accessory parts pl. [neben⚭ incidentally.⟩
...**bei** (...⌣) in Zssgn, zB.: an⚭ herewith;⟩
bei-an F (⌣) *adv.* close by, near by.
bei-behalten (⌣⌣⌣⌣) **I** v/a. ⓐ*/* to keep up or on; er behielt die Gewohnheit bei he kept to (or retained) the custom. — **II** ~ n ㉓ u. **Bei-behaltung** f ㊻ retention; ⓗ unter ~ unserer Firma while continuing (the name of) our firm.
bei-biegen (⌣⌣⌣) v/a. ⓐ** Kanzleisprache u. ⓗ in Briefen: to enclose, to annex.
bei-binden (⌣⌣⌣) v/a. ⓐ** to tie (or bind) to(gether with); e-m Buche ⚭ to bind up with a book; vgl. a. beigebunden.
Bei-blatt (⌣⌣) n ⓑc. supplement (to a periodical, &c.), (Extrablatt) supplementary (or extra) sheet, extra edition of a (news)paper.
bei-bringen (⌣⌣⌣) **I** v/a. ⓐ** **1.** = bringen. — **2.** (vorbringen) to bring forward; Beweise ⚭ to produce ...; Gründe

[Beibuch] — 162 — [beikommen]

♃ to allege ...; Gewährsmänner ♃ to cite ..., to quote ... — 3. e-m et. ♃: a) mst in feindlichem Sinne: to administer a th. to a p.; einem Arznei, Gift ♃ to give (or administer) ...; e-m eine Niederlage, e-n Verlust ♃ to inflict ... upon a p.; e-n Stoß ♃ to deal a p. a blow; b) (zu wissen tun) to impart (or convey) a th. to a p.; to instil (knowledge) in a p.; (gewandt) ♃, mst b.s. to insinuate a th. to a p.; e-e schlimme Nachricht schonend ♃ to break bad news to a p. — 4. (verständlich machen) to make clear to a p., to explain to a p., mit Mühe: F to drum (or drive) into a p.; (lehren) to teach a p. a th.; (einprägen) to inculcate a th. in(to) a p. — II ~ n 23 u. **Bei-bringung** f 46 5. (zu 2:) production, allegation; (zu 3:) administration, insinuation.

Bei-buch ❀ (⁻ˡˡ) ⒟d. counter- (or retail-) book; (Buch des Arbeiters für die Abrechnung mit dem Fabrikherrn) etwa: workman's journal or entry book.

Bei-chaise ❀ (⁻ˡʃã'-ʃᵉ) f 48 extra carriage or coach (= Beiwagen).

Beichte (ˡ⌣) [† Be-jicht (ahd.) = Bekenntnis] f 48 eccl. confession (auch fig.); † shrift; ~ ablegen to confess (o.s.); e-m die ~ abnehmen to confess († to shrive) a p.; zur ~ geh(e)n to go to confession; zur ~ gehörig confessionary.

beichten (ˡ⌣) [mhd.: * Beichte] 69 eccl. I v/a. seine Sünden ♃ to confess ... — II v/n. (h.) to confess (o.s.) (bei e-m to a p.); fig. to make a(n open) confession, to make a clean breast of it.

Beicht-formel (ˡˡ...) f 62 formula of confession; ≈geheimnis n secret of the confessional; ≈geld n, ≈groschen m confessor's (weitS. priest's) fee; ≈gänger m penitent (sinner), bisw. confessant, weitS. parishioner.

Beichtiger (ˡ⌣⌣) m 22, ~**in** f 47 eccl. 1. = Beichtvater. — 2. Cath. (nicht gemarterter Heiliger) confessor.

Beicht-kind (ˡˡᵈ) n, **Beichtling** (ˡ⌣) m ⒟d. = Beichtgänger.

Beicht-opfer (ˡˡ...) n 62, ≈**pfennig** m = ≈geld; ≈schein m = ≈zettel; ≈siegel n seal of confession, weitS. seal of secrecy; ≈stuhl m confessional (box or chair); ≈vater m (father) confessor, † ghostly father; ≈zettel m register of sins, ticket of confession.

beid (ˡ) [ahd.: both] a/numer. 66 (C.), mst pl. ♄e both; ♄es both things; wir (F zwei) ♄e both of us, we both; ♄en the two of us, we two; alle ♄e both of them; einer (oder jeder) von ♄en either of the two; e-s von ♄en one of the two, either; eines von ♄en genügt either will do; ♄e(s) nicht, keiner (keines) von ♄en neither of the two; welcher (welches) von ♄en? which of the two?; sind das die ♄en? are these the two?; ♄e Brüder both (or the two) brothers; in ♄en Fällen in either case; ♄er Geschlechter of either sex, gr. of common gender; seine ♄en Pferde both his horses; ich sah die Sache von ♄en Seiten an I looked at it both ways.

beider-hand (ˡˡ...) adv. left and right, on either hand; ♄lei (ˡ⌣) a. inv. (of) both kinds, (of) either sort; rel. Safra-

ment in ♄ Gestalt sacrament in both kinds; auf ♄ Art (in) both ways; ♄ Geschlechts vgl. beid u. beidgeschlechtig. ♄seitig a. 66, ♄seits adv.: a) on both sides, on either side, mutual(ly); b) (auf zwei Personen 2c. bezüglich) zum ♄seitigen Nutzen for (their) common (or mutual) profit; c) (gegenseitig) reciprocal; durch ♄seitige Übereinkunft by mutual consent or agreement.

Beider=wand ❀ (ˡˡ⌣) [Bidar, St.i.Ost-I.] f 40 od. n ⒪c. (o. pl.) (halbwollener Stoff) linsey-woolsey.

beid-geschlechtig ❀ (ˡˡ...) a. 66: ♄ epicene; ≈händig a. a) written with both hands; b) (mit beiden Händen geschickt) ♄ ambidexter, ambidextrous; ≈lebig a. ♄ u. zo. amphibious (a. fig.).

beid-recht ❀ (ˡˡᵈ) α. 66 leinwandartig gewebte Stoffe: (auf beiden Seiten gleich) reversible.

bei-drehen (⌣ˡ) v/a. u. v/n. (h.) 88** (ein Segel ♃ to bring (or to round) to.

bei-drucken (ˡˡ⌣) v/a. 88** f. bei=... I.

bei-drücken (ˡˡ⌣) v/a. 88** sein Siegel ♃ to affix one's seal to.

beid-schattig (ˡˡ...) a. 66 ♄ amphiscian.

bei-ein-ander (⌣⁻ˡ⌣⌣) adv. (all or both) together, keeping one another company.

Bei-er (ˡ⌣) m 22 = Bär², Eber).

Bei-erbe (ˡˡ⌣⌣) m 44 jur. joint heir, coheir.

bei-ern (ˡ⌣) [ndd.] v/n. (h.) ♃a. to chime.

Bei-essen (ˡˡ⌣⌣) n 23 Kochkunst: side-dish, (Nebengericht) entrée, entremets pl.

beif. abbr. = beifolgend.

Bei-fall (ˡˡᵈ) m ⒪c. (o. pl.) (Beistimmen) assent; (Billigung) approval, approbation; (billigende Kundgebung) durch Händeklatschen: applause; durch ♄klatschen (loud) cheers pl.; stürmischer ~ (loud) peals pl. of applause; ~ finden, ~ haben: a) to meet with approval; b) bjS. thea. to earn or get (stärker: to evoke) applause (ant. Abfall 6); thea. stürmischen ~ finden to bring down the house; e-m ~ zollen (klatschen) to applaud (or clap) a p.

bei-fallen (ˡˡᵈ⌣) v/n. (jn) 86a** 1. e-m ♃ (ins Gedächtnis kommen) to occur to a p.; das Wort fällt mir nicht bei I cannot remember (or recall) the word, it has slipt from my memory, it has gone out of my head. — 2. (= einfallen 5) lassen Sie sich nicht ♃ zu schreiben! don't you think of writing!

bei-fällig (ˡˡᵈ⌣) a. 66 assenting, assentient; approving; (günstig) favourable (ant. abfällig 3); adv. etwas ♃ (huldvoll) aufnehmen to receive a th. graciously.

Beifall-klatschen (ˡˡᵈ⌣⌣) n 62: (donnerndes) ~ round of (or thundering) applause; ≈klatscher m one who claps (an actress, &c.), thea. bezahlter ~, bisw. a. clapper [eine gewerbsmäßige Claque ist in England unbekannt!].

Beifalls=bezeigung (ˡˡᵈ⌣⌣...) f 62 applause, weitS. mark of approval or approbation; ≈geschrei n = ≈rufen; ≈liebe f approbativeness; ≈ruf m acclamation; ≈rufen n cheering (a p.), shouts pl. of applause; ≈sturm m round (or burst, thunder) of applause, ringing cheers pl.; ≈wert, ≈würdig a. 66 worthy of approval or applause; von Vorschlägen: plausible. [between two furrows.]

B(e)i-fang (ˡ⌣) [ahd.] m ⒪c. agr. ridge

bei-folgen (ˡˡᵈ⌣) I ♄ v/n. (jn) 88** to follow with. — II ♄d p.pr. u. a. 66 (B*) (a. adv.) annexed under cover; ♄d (im Briefe) empfangen Sie you will find enclosed, you receive herewith.

Bei-fracht ♃ (⁻ˡˡ) f 46 = Beilast.

bei-fügen (ˡˡᵈ⌣) I v/a. 88** to add, stärker: to append. — II ~ n 23 = B/ung 1. — III **bei-gefügt** p.p. und a. 66 enclosed.

Bei-fügung (ˡˡᵈ⌣) f 46 1. addition, appendage; unter ~ der Zeugnisse (in or while) enclosing ... 2. gr. apposition.

Bei-fuß (ˡˡᵈ) (ahd.) m ⒪a. 1. ♄ (o. pl.) mugwort (Artemisia). — 2. ♄ (Racк parrel (of a yard). [Zugabe).]

Bei-gabe (ˡˡᵈ⌣) f 48 addition to // (=

Beige¹ (ˡ⌣) (ahd.) f 48 (aufgeschichteter Haufen) stack (of hay,) pile (of wood).

beige² (bä̅G)(fr.) a. 66 (naturfarben) natural

beigeb. abbr. = beigebunden. I (wool. &c.).

Bei-geben (ˡˡᵈ⌣) v/a. 88* 1. to add to; e-m e-n Gehilfen ♃ to give (or allow) a p. an assistant; e-r Gesandtschaft ♃ to attach to ... — 2. Kartenspiel: eine Karte ♃ to throw down (or away) ..., klein ♃ to play low (cards), abs. F fig. to give in, F to sing small, pol. to climb down.

bei-gebunden (ˡˡᵈ⌣⌣) [p.p. v. beibinden] a. 66 (D9) s.th. bound in with (s.th. else).

bei-geh(e)n (ˡˡᵈ⌣) v/n. (jn) 88** (in den Sinn kommen) es (od. der Gedanke) geht mir bei it strikes me (= beifallen 1).

beigen (ˡ⌣) [Beige¹] v/a. 88 (aufschichten, bjS. Heu, Holz) to stack, to pile up.

Bei-geordnete(r) (ˡˡᵈ⌣⌣) [beiordnen] m 67 (♃ Bürgermeister) second burgomaster, in England: deputy-mayor.

Bei-gericht (ˡˡᵈ⌣) n ⒟c. = Beiessen.

bei-geschlossen (ˡˡᵈ⌣⌣) p.p. v. beischließen.

Bei-geschmack (ˡˡᵈ⌣) m ⒪c. (ohne pl.) peculiar (or strange) flavour or taste (nach of), nach taste: after-taste; fig. e-n ~ haben von oder nach // to have a relish (or taste) of //, to taste (slightly) of //.

bei-gesellen (ˡˡᵈ⌣⌣) 88*/* I v/a. 1. einen einem ♃: a) to associate (or put) a p. with a p.; b) im Amte: to attach a p. as an assistant (or junior) to a p. — II sich ♃ v/refl. 2. to associate (o.s.) with a p. — 3. beim Gehen: ich gesellte mich ihnen (wieder) bei I (re)joined them.

Bei-gesellung (ˡˡᵈ⌣⌣) f 46 association or aggregation with, attachment to.

bei-her (⌣⁻ˡ) adv. = nebenher; in Zssgn mit v. meist: beside, by the side of ..., zB.: ≈schwimmen (ˡˡ...) v/n. ⒟a(b)** (h. u. jn) to swim by the side of.

Bei-hilfe (ˡˡᵈ⌣) f 48 1. für Bedürftige: assistance; für Schwache: aid, help, support; unter ~ (durch Vermittelung) von through (or by) the instrumentality of. — 2. (Beisteuer) subsidy, succour. — 3. jur. (dem Täter geleistete Hilfe) aiding and abetting the culprit.

bei-holen (ᵍˡ⌣) v/a. 88** 1. ♃ die Segel ♃ to haul home ... — 2. jur. to request.

Bei-klang (ˡˡᵈ) m ⒪c. accompanying sound. [gum) (on to).]

bei-kleben (ˡˡᵈ⌣) v/a. 88 ** to paste (or

Bei-koch (ˡˡᵈ) m ⒪d. under-cook.

bei-kommen (ˡˡᵈ⌣) v/n. (jn) 88** 1. e-m ♃ (et. anhaben) to attack a p.; ihm ist nicht beizukommen one cannot get at (or lay hold of) him, he is inacces-

Signs (see page XVII): F familiar; P vulgar; ſ flash; ⌐ rare; † obsolete (died); * new word (born); ++ incorrect; ♪ music;

[Beil] — 163 — [beinfelt]

sible or unapproachable, F he's not to be got at. — 2. *prov.* bisw. mit „und": er kam bei und legte wieder Geld hin so he (came and) once more put down his money. — 3. (nahe kommen) **a)** örtlich: e-m, e-r Sache ⁋ to get near (or up to) a p., a th.; **b)** *fig.* (gleichkommen) to approach a th., stärker: to equal a p., a th. — 4. (erlangen) e-r Sache ⁋ to obtain a th.; seinem Schaden ⁋ (ihn ersetzen) to make good one's loss(es). — 5. sich (*dat.*) et. ⁋ (einfallen lassen) to take s.th. (or a fancy) into one's head, to have some new idea (crossing one's mind). **Beil** (⁀) [ahd.] *n* ⓐc. **1.** hatchet, des Fleischers ꝛc.: chopper, größeres: axe; durch das ~ hinrichten to cut off a p.'s head (or to execute a p.) with an axe, weitS. to behead a p. — **2.** ~ der Guillotine knife; ⊕ (Hohlbeil) adze. **beil.** *abbr.* = beiliegend. **Bei-lage** (⁀⌣) *f* ⓘ **1.** (Beigefügtes) piece joined on to; addition. — **2.** ~ e-s Briefes: enclosure, s.th. enclosed; ~ e-r Zeitung supplement to (or extra edition of) a daily paper; Gemüse mit ~ meat with vegetables; Schlächterei: bones *pl.* sold with the meat, makeweight. **Bei-lager** (⁀⌣) *n* ⓐ ehm. (eheliches ~) solemnization (engS. consummation) of marriage; nuptials *pl.*; das ~ halten ob. vollziehen to consummate the marriage. **Bei-last** ⌄ (⁀⌣) *f* ⓘ **1.** (eigenes Gepäck der Seeleute) adventure. — **2.** extra freight. **Bei-läufer** (⁀⌣) *m* ⓐ (Laufbursche) foot-boy, errand-boy; (Bote) messenger. **bei-läufig** (⁀⌣) **I** *a.* ⓘ **1.** (nebensächlich) casual; (gelegentlich) occasional; ⁋e Frage incidental question. — **II** *adv.* **2.** incidentally in a casual way, by way of parenthesis; (da ich davon spreche) by the way; ⁋ gesagt by the by. — **3.** bsd. südd., öst. (ungefähr) about. **Beil-brief** (⁀...) *m* ⓑ: **1.** ⌄ † (Schiffszertifikat) ship's register. — **2.** schwz. (Hypothekenschein) mortgage on an estate. **Beilchen** (⁀⌣) *n* ⓓ (*dim.* von Beil) small hatchet or chopper or axe. **bei-legen** (⁀⌣) ⓖ⌄ **I** *v/a.* **1.** (hinzufügen) et. einer Sache ⁋ to add a th. to (or to enclose a th. with) a th. — **2.** (zuschreiben) e-m, e-r Sache et. ⁋ to attribute (or assign, impute) a th. to a p., to a th.; et-m *in* Namen ꝛc. (als Titel) ⁋ to confer (or bestow) ... on a p.; einer Sache Wert ⁋ to attach (some) value to a th.; *gr.* beigelegt attributive. — **3.** (beseitigen) einen Streit ⁋ to settle ..., to arrange ..., weitS. to put an end to ...; die Sache ist beigelegt the matter has been made up or adjusted or compromised (F squared). — **4.** ⌄ die Segel ⁋ = einreffen; ein Schiff ⁋ to bring ⁋ to. — **II** *v/n.* (h.) **5.** ⌄ to come (or lay) to. — **III** ~ *n* ⓓ u. **Beilegung** *f* ⓘ **6.** (zu 1): addition, enclosure; (zu 3): settlement, adjustment, gütliche ~ eines Rechtsstreites compromise. **bei-leibe** (-⁀⌣) *adv.* etwas ⁋ nicht tun to take good care not to do a th.; ⁋ nicht! on no account!, not for the world! **Bei-leid** (⁀⁀) *n* ⓓd. (*o. pl.*) condolence, weitS. sympathy; e-m sein ~ bezeigen to condole (or sympathize) with a p.

Beileids-besuch (⁀...) *m* ⓑ visit of condolence; ⁋ **bezeigend** *a.* ⓖ condolatory, weitS. sympathetic; **bezeigung** *f* condolence; ⁀**brief** *m* letter of condolence; ⁀**karte** *f* card of condolence; ⁀**schreiben** *n* = ⁀brief. **Beil-eisen** (⁀...) *n* ⓑ axe-head; ⁋**fertig** ⌄ *a.* ⓖ (fertig bis auf das Tafeln) ready for rigging; ⁋**förmig** *a.* ⓖ axe-shaped, ⁊ securiform; ⁀**hieb** *m* stroke of an axe. **beilen** (⁀⌣) [mhd.] *v/a.* ⓖ *hunt.* (Wild) ⁋ (zum Stehen bringen) to bring ... to bay. **bei-liegen** (⁀⌣) *v/n.* (h.) ⓖ** **1.** (dabei liegen) to lie (enclosed) with; ⁋**d** enclosed (herewith); ⁋**de** Muster *n/pl.* the enclosed (or annexed) samples *pl.* — **2.** e-r Person (zum Beischlafe): to lie with ..., to have sexual intercourse with. — **3.** ⌄ to lie to; vor Topp und Tafel ⁋**d** a-hull. **Beilke** (⁀⌣) [ndd.] *f* ⓖ, *a.* ~⁀**spiel** (⁀⌣⁀) *n* ⓑ, ⁀**tafel** *f* shovel-board, truck-table. **Beil-kraut** (⁀...) *n* ⓑ = Kronwicke; ⁀**picke** *f* pickaxe; ⁀**stein** *m, min.* ⊕ (Axinit) ax(e)-stone, jade, (Nephrit) nephrite; ⁀**stiel** *m* helve (of an axe or a hatchet), handle of an axe. **Bei-luft** (⁀⌣) *f* ⓞ: die Zigarre hat ~ the cigar has a flaw, it lets in air. **beim** (⁀) [mhd. = bei dem (s. bei)] bsd. vor substantiertem *inf.*, z.B. es ⁋ alten lassen to leave things (just) as they are; ⁋ Einpacken in packing. **bei-mengen** (⁀⌣) ⓖ** = beimischen. **bei-messen** (⁀⌣) *v/a.* ⓖ** **1.** = beilegen 2. — **2.** e-r Sache ob. Person (*dat.*) Glauben ⁋ to put faith in ... **bei-mischen** (⁀⌣) **I** *v/a.* ⓖ** einer Sache (*dat.*) et. ⁋ to mix a th. with a th. (*a. chm.*). — **II** ~ *n* ⓓ u. **Bei-mischung** *f* ⓘ admixture of; mit e-r geringen ~ von with a dash (or sprinkling, touch) of. **Bein** (⁀) [ahd.: bone] *n* ⓐc. **1.** *anat.* (Körperteil) leg (auch eines Tisches und Stuhles); von Tieren, Geräten ꝛc. auch: foot; nur v. Menschen: ~e F *co.* understandings *pl.*; das dicke ~ thigh; *iro.* dünne ~e thin legs, F *co.* broomsticks, drumsticks *pl.*; schwach auf (ob. in) den ~en weak on one's legs or F pins; die ~e übereinanderschlagen to cross one's legs. — **2.** (Knochen) bone; ⊕ in ~ arbeiten to work (or manufacture) in bone; *fig.* es geht einem durch Mark und ~ it sends a shiver (or a thrill) through one, stärker: it cuts one to the quick; die Kälte drang mir durch Mark und ~ the cold chilled me to the bone, numbed me; es friert Stein und ~ (zusammen) it is freezing hard, there is a black frost; Stein und ~ (b. i. auf Altar u. Reliquie) schwören to take a most solemn oath. — **3.** Redensarten: F *fig.* et. ans ~ **binden: a)** (verloren geben) to give s.th. up as lost; **b)** (e-n Verlust verschmerzen) to get over a loss; er hat ~e **bringen** to set going, ⚔ ein Heer: to raise; F ~e **haben** (flint sein) to be light on one's legs or F pins, to be nimble; junge ~e haben to be young and nimble; alles, was ~e hat all who can walk or run, young and old; das hat lange ~e (lange Zeit) there is plenty of time for that; e-m (wieder)

auf die ~e **helfen** to set a p. on his legs (or feet), F to give him a lift; wieder auf die ~e **kommen** to recover, F to pick o.s. up again; F e-m ~e **machen** (e-n antreiben) to urge (or drive) a p.; ich will ihm schon ~e m. F I'll make him find his legs; lange ~e m. to hurry (or speed) along, F to put one's best leg forward; sich auf die ~e m. to start (on one's journey), to be off; F *co.* die ~e in die Hand **nehmen** (davonlaufen) to take to one's heels, to run (away), to fly; auf den ~en **sein** (nicht zu Bett) to be up; sind Sie früh auf den ~en? are you an early riser (F bird)?; noch gut auf den ~en sein to be firm on one's legs or F pins or ist gut auf den ~en he is a good walker; sie ist ewig auf den ~en she is for ever on her legs (F on the move); immer auf den ~en sein auch: to be always about, to be never off one's legs; noch fest auf den ~en **steh(e)n** (trotz großer Verluste) to keep one's head above water; er konnte (vor Müdigkeit) auf keinem ~e mehr steh(e)n he was so tired that he could not stand, P he was dead beat; e-m ein **stellen** to trip a p. up; et. ans~**streichen, wischen** = et. ans ~ **binden** (s. ds). — **4.** (Bein-ähnliches) ~ e-r Bank ꝛc. support. **Bein-ader** (⁀...) *f* ⓘ crural blood vessel. **bei-nahe** (-⁀⌣) (F *a.* **beinah**, ⁀⌣) *adv.* nearly, almost, all but; within an ace of; ich wäre ⁋ umgekommen I was very near (or I narrowly escaped) being killed, I had a narrow escape (F shave); das Haus ist (auch wäre) ⁋ abgebrannt the house was very nearly (or within a little of being) burnt down; sie sind ⁋ am Verhungern F they are next door to (or on the verge of) starvation; es ist ⁋ eine Million it is little short of a million; ⁋ dasselbe, ⁋ einerlei much the same thing, F much of a muchness; ⁋ unmöglich next to impossible. **bein-ähnlich** (⁀...) *a.* ⓖ = beinartig. **Bei-name** (⁀⌣) *m* ⓐ (*a.* ~**n** ⓓ) **1.** der (Bekenner) the surname (of Confessor); *v. grch.* Göttern: epithet; Wilhelm mit dem ~n des Großen William surnamed (or called) the Great. — **2.** nickname (= Spitzname). **Bein-arbeiter** (⁀...) *m* ⓑ turner (or worker) in bone; ⁋**artig** *a.* ⓖ bonelike; resembling a leg, ⊕ (knochenartig) osseous; ⁀**asche** *f* (Knochenasche) bone-ash (*es pl.*) or -earth; ⁀**brech** *n* *c.*: **a)** ♀ = ⁀heil; **b)** *min.*: ⊕ osteocolla; ⁀**brecher** *m, orn.* osprey (*Haliaëtos*); ⁀**bruch** *m, surg.* fracture of a leg, broken (or fractured) leg; *fig.* das ist kein ~ (kein großer Schaden) that's no great misfortune or disaster; ⁋**brüchig** *a.* ⓖ with broken bones or a broken leg. **Beinchen** (⁀⌣) *n* ⓓ (*dim.* von Bein) zB. (zu Bein 1): small leg; (zu 2): small bone, ⊕ ossicle (s. *a.* Knöchelchen). **Bein-drechsler** (⁀...) *m* ⓑ = ⁀arbeiter. **beinern** (⁀⌣) *a.* ⓖ bony, (made) of bone. **Bein-fäule** (⁀...) *f* ⓖ (Knochenfraß) ⊕ caries; ⁀**feile** *f* ⊕ scalping iron, *surg.* raspatory. [mitred.]
be-infelt ⌄ (⌣⌣) [Infel, Inful] *a.* ⓖ

───

⊕ scientific; ♀ botanical; ⚲ geography; ⊕ machinery; ⚔ mining; ⚔ military; ⌄ marine; ⊕ commercial; ✉ postal; 🚆 railway.

[Beingeſchwulſt] — 164 — [Beißer]

Bein=geſchwulſt (⏑⏑…) f ⓬ a) swelling in the legs; b) med.: ☞ exostosis; **=harniſch** m ehm.⚔ cuisses, cuish(es pl.), cuissarts, greaves pl.; **=hart** a. ⓺ as hard as a bone; **=haus** n charnel-house; **=haut** f, anat.: ☞ periosteum; **=heil** & m bog-asphodel (Narthe'cium ossi'fragum); **=höhle** f, anat. osseous cavity, ☞ cotyle; **=holz** & n = Liguster.
beinicht (⏑⏑) a. ⓺ osseous, hard as bone.
beinig (⏑⏑) a. ⓺ 1. F (gut auf den Beinen; munter) with a good pair of legs, nimble; brisk, alert. — 2. in Zſſgn. (Beine, Füße habend) with legs, feet; z.B.: vier=⏒ four-legged, -footed.
Bein=kleid (⏑…) [nhd. 17 sae.] n ⓬ (Hoſen) trousers pl.; co. unmentionables pl.; **kurzes** ~ (short) breeches, knickerbockers pl., bſd. ehm. auch: small clothes; **=kleiderſtoff** m trousering; **=lade** f, surg. splint(s pl.) (or cradle) for a fractured leg; **=leder** n (Lederſchaft an Stiefeln) leather shaft (to top-boots).
Beinling (⏑⏑) m ⓭d. (oberer Strumpf) (ant. Füßling) leg (of a stocking).
bein=los (⏑…) a. ⓺: a) boneless; ☞ exosseous; b) without legs; **=rüſtung** f = harniſch; **=ſäge** f bone-saw, surgical saw; **=ſchellen** f/pl. shackles, fetters pl.; **=ſchiene** f a) surg. = lade; b) ehm.⚔ cuisse, vgl. =harniſch; **=ſchwarz** n bone-black, ivory-black; **=ſtellen** n Fußball: tripping; **=ware** f bone (or ivory) goods or articles; **=weh** n pain in the legs; **=well** & m, ⓭c. consound (Sy'mphytum); großer ~ comfrey (S. officina'le); **=wunde** f leg-wound; **=wurz** & f = well.
bei-ordnen (⏑⏑⏑) I v/a. ⓫b** 1. (beigeben) to adjoin to. — 2. (an die Seite ſtellen) to co-ordinate (auch gr.); beigeordnet p.p. co-ordinate, vgl. Bei=geordnete(r). — II ~ n ㉓ u. **Bei=ordnung** f ⓮ 3. co-ordination.
bei-packen (⏑⏑⏑) v/a. ⓬** to pack up with, to put into the same package.
Bei-pferd (⏑⏑) n ⓭c. = Handpferd.
bei-pflichten (⏑⏑⏑) I v/n. (h.) ⓬** (bei=ſtimmen) to agree with, to assent to, e-r Anſicht ꝛc.: to espouse, to acquiesce in. — II **Bei-pflichtung** f ⓮ agreement, assent, acquiescence.
Beiram (⏑⏑) [türk.] m u. n ⓮, **~feſt** (⏒…) n ⓬ (türkiſche Oſtern) Bairam.
Bei-rat (⏑⏑) m ⓭d. 1. o. pl. advice. — 2. mit pl. (beiratende Perſon) legal adviser; spiritual director; counsellor; literariſcher ~ e-s Verlags ꝛc. literary adviser.
be-irren (⏑⏑⏑) v/a. ⓬* to confuse, to mislead; er läßt ſich nicht ⏒ he is not easily diverted from his purpose or talked out of a th.
bei-ſammen (⏑⏒⏑) adv. together; dicht ⏒ close to (or by) each other; (in traulicher Gemeinſchaft) cheek by jowl; halt deine Gedanken ⏒! keep (all) your wits about you!; **~ſein** (⏒⏒) n ㉓ being together; meeting.
Bei-ſaß (⏑⏒) [mhd.] m ㊷, **Bei-ſaſſe** (⏑⏒⏑) m ㊹ in Deutſchland bis 1848: (Schutz=verwandte(r) denizen.
Bei-ſatz (⏑⏒) m ⓭a. 1. addition; (Bei=miſchung) admixture; von Geringerem, bib. metall. alloy (auch fig.), (Anflug) dash, tinge. — 2. gram. adjunct; apposition.

Bei-ſchiff ⚓ (⏑⏒) n ⓭c. 1. (kleines Boot) cockboat. — 2. (Begleitungsſchiff) tender.
Bei-ſchlaf (⏑⏒) m ⓭⓭d. cohabitation.
Bei-ſchläfer (⏑⏒⏑) m ㉒, **~in** f ㊷ (Schlafgenoſſe, Schlafgenoſſin) bedfellow.
Bei-ſchlag (⏑⏒) m ⓭d. 1. norddtſch. arch. (Vorplatz e-s Hauſes) area. — 2. mint. faſt †: base coin; weitS. fig. (Wertloſes) rubbish.
bei-ſchlagen (⏑⏒⏑) Ib** I v/a. = bei=ſchließen. — II v/n. (h.) hunt. von Jagdhunden: to follow the same scent.
bei-ſchließen (⏑⏒⏑) v/a. ⓭d** (einſchließend beifügen) to enclose, append; die beigeſchloſſenen Muſter the enclosed samples, the samples enclosed herewith.
Bei-ſchluß (⏑⏒) m ⓭a. enclosure; letter, &c., enclosed; im ~ herewith enclosed; durch ~ under cover.
Bei-ſchlüſſel (⏑⏒⏑) m ㉒ = Nachſchlüſſel.
Bei-ſchmack (⏑⏒) m ⓭c. = Beigeſchmack.
bei-ſchreiben (⏑⏒⏑) I v/a. ⓮** e-r Sache ꝛc. ⏒ to write s.th. by the side of a th., to add a note (or a remark) on the margin of a th. — II ~ n ㉓ letter accompanying another letter.
Bei-ſchrift (⏑⏒) f ㊻ (marginal) note; (Gloſſe) annotation, ☞ gloss. [stay-sail.]
Bei-ſegel ⚓ (⏑⏒⏑) n ㉓ studding-sail,]
Bei-ſein (⏑⏒) n ㉓ presence; im ~ der Eltern in the presence of (or before)…; ohne ſein ~ without his being present or there, in his absence.
bei-ſeite (⏑⏒⏑) adv. apart; (ein) ~ n ㉒ thea. (an) aside; Scherz ⏒! (all) joking apart! — ⏒(=)**bringen** (⏒…) v/a. ⓮** to abstract, to put (or spirit) away; **⏒legen** v/a. ⓬** (vgl. Seite 2) to put by; **⏒ſchaffen** v/a. ⓬** = ⏒bringen; **=ſchaffung** f abstraction; b.s. purloining; **=ſchiebung** f pushing (a th.) aside, weitS. removal; den Anſtand ⏒**ſetzen** v/a. ⓺** to set aside all (rules of) propriety; **=ſetzung** f neglect; ~ der Ehrerbietung want of respect; mit ~ von without heeding (or paying regard) to; ⏒**ſteh(e)n** v/n. (h.) ⓬*** to stand aside; ⏒**treten** v/n. (ſn) ⓭d* to step aside.
bei-ſeits ⚓ (⏑⏒) adv. = beiſeite. [aside.]
Beiſel öſt. (⏑⏑) n ⓬ pub (= Kneipe).
bei-ſenden (⏑⏒⏑) v/a. ⓮a** to send (along) with, to enclose in a parcel.
bei-ſetzen (⏑⏒⏑) I v/a. ⓮** 1. Verſtorbene: to put by (the coffin or body) in a tomb or vault; (beerdigen) to bury, entomb, inter. lay to rest. — 2. Speiſen, den Topf ⏒ to put … on (the fire). — 3. ⚓ Segel: to unfurl; alle Segel ⏒ to crowd (or clap on) all sail or canvas. — II ~ n ㉓ u. **Bei-ſetzung** f ㊻ 4. burial; ⚓ durch ~ vieler Segel by carrying a (full) press(ure) of sail, by crowding sails. [justice or in a council).]
Bei-ſitz (⏑⏒) m ⓭a. seat (in a court of)
bei-ſitzen (⏑⏒⏑) v/n. (h.) ⓭*** to sit (close) by; bſd. jur. to sit (in a court of justice) as assistant judge.
Bei-ſitzer (⏑⏒⏑) m ㉒ assessor; junior barrister; **~amt** (⏒…) n ⓬ office (or duties pl.) of an assistant judge.
Bei-ſpiel (⏑⏒) [mhd.: spell, gospel] n ⓭d. example; zum ~ (abbr. z.B.) for instance, for example [auch abbr. e. g. = exempli gratia]; ich z.B. I for one; wie zum ~ as for instance, such as; als

~ anführen to quote as a case in point, to (give as an) instance, jur. to quote as precedent; ein ~ an e-m aufſtellen to make an example of a p.; als ~ aufgeſtellt w., zum ~ werden to be put up (or to serve) as a pattern or model; nimm dir ein ~ an ihm: a) als Muſter: take him for a model, take a leaf out of his book; b) als Warnung: let him be a warning (or a lesson) to you; mit gutem ~ vorangeh(e)n to set a good example to others; to practise what one preaches; Sprichw. böſe ~e verderben gute Sitten bad examples (bibl. evil communications) corrupt good manners.
bei-ſpiel-los (⏑⏒…) a. ⓺ unexampled, unprecedented, unparalleled; matchless; ein ⏒es Verfahren a.: a most extraordinary proceeding; **=loſigkeit** f ⓬ singularity; matchlessness.
bei-ſpiels=halber (⏑⏒…), **⏒weiſe** adv. for (or by way of) example, for instance.
bei-ſpringen (⏑⏒⏑) v/n. (ſn.) ⓭f** e-m ⏒ to hasten (or run) to a p.'s assistance, weitS. to assist (or help) a p.
Beiß=beere & (⏑…) f ㊷ cayenne (pepper) = Pfeffer (ſpaniſcher).
beißen (⏑⏑) [ahd.: bite] I v/a., v/n. (h.) u. v/refl. ⓭a. 1. to bite (auch fig.); nach e-m ⏒ to snap at a p.; ſich auf die Lippen, die Zunge ⏒ to bite one's lips, one's tongue; F fig. ins Gras ⏒ to bite the dust; to die, F to kick the bucket; da beißt die Maus keinen Faden ab the thing is done or perfect. — 2. (nagen) to gnaw, to nibble; ich kann das Fleiſch nicht ⏒ (tauen) I cannot chew the meat; F I cannot get my teeth through it; um ſich ⏒ to snap at everybody or everything; ſich (herum=)⏒ to bite one another; fig. to wrangle, to squabble; to be (for ever) bickering and biting; fig. ſie haben nichts zu ⏒ noch zu brechen they have nothing to eat, they are starving or famishing; in einen ſauren Apfel ⏒ to swallow a bitter (or nasty) pill, auch: to grin and bear it. — 3. (ſtechen) von Inſekten ꝛc.: to sting, to bite. — 4. (beizen, ſtechen) to smart; (brennen) to burn; der Pfeffer, Senf beißt mir auf der (ob. mich auf die) Zunge is hot, burns, has a pungent (or sharp) taste; impers. es beißt mich I am (or feel an) itching; der Rauch beißt mir in den ob. in die (oder mich in die ob. in den) Augen … makes my eyes smart. — 5. fig. ein ⏒der Schmerz a tormenting (or gnawing) pain. — 6. fig. (tief verletzen) to sting (to the quick); (verſpotten) to sneer at. — II ~ n ㉓ 7. biting, bite, (Stechen) sting(ing), (Jucken) itching. — III ⏒d p.p.r. u. a. ⓺ 8. Bed. des inf. — 9. ⏒de Bemerkung sarcastic (or satirical) remark, sarcasm, ⏒e Erwiderung smart (or cutting, poignant) reply; ⏒e Kälte nipping cold; er hat einen ⏒en Witz he has a caustic (or keen) wit; vgl. 5.
Beißer (⏑⏑) m ㉒ 1. biter; snappish dog; fig. (a. **~in** f ㊷) quarrelsome (or litigating) person; brawler. — 2. Kinderſpr.: ~, dim. **~chen**, **~lein** n ⓬ (Zahn) (little) tooth, toothlet.

Zeichen (ſ. S. XVII): F familiär; P Volksſprache; Γ Gaunerſprache; ⚓ ſelten; † alt (auch geſtorben); * neu (auch geboren); ⚞ unrichtig;

Beißker (⌣́) [tschech.] m 🄶 ichth. loach (*Cobi'tis*).

Beiß-kohl ♀ (⁗...) m 🄶 beet (= Bete¹); **-korb** m (Maulkorb) muzzle; **-zahn** m incisor, cutting tooth; **-zange** f obb. (pair of) pliers pl. or nippers pl.

Bei-stand (⁗́) m ⑦c. 1. (o. pl.) (Hilfe) assistance; help, succour; (Schutz) protection; (Stütze) support; e-m ~ leisten to render (or lend) assistance (or to give aid) to a p.; ohne ~ unaided. — 2. (mit pl.) (Helfer) person who assists or helps; weitS. supporter, backer; vor Gericht: counsel; (Gehilfe) assistant.

bei-stechen ⚓ (⁗́⌣) v/n. (h.) 🄰a** to sail close to the wind or close-hauled.

bei-stecken (⁗́⌣) 🄶** = einstecken 1.

bei-steh(e)n (⁗́(⌣)) v/n. (h.) 🄶** 1. e-m ~ to render aid or assistance to a p.; (zur Seite stehen) to side with, to back up; mit Reden: to plead (or speak up) for; mit Trost: to comfort; mit Geld xc.: to succour; to relieve (the poor, the distressed); Gott steh(e) mir bei! God (or the Lord) be merciful unto me!, Heaven defend me! — 2. ⚓ (dabei-stehen) nur p.pr. die **Bei-stehenden** pl. the bystanders, the lookers-on pl. — 3. ⚓ alle Segel ⚓ lassen to crowd on the canvas. [or aids (= Beistand 2.)]

Bei-steher (⁗́) m 🄶 one who assists

Bei-steuer (⁗́) f 🄶 contribution, subsidy, von Geld: pecuniary aid; (Geldsammlung) collection (of funds for).

bei-steuern (⁗́) v/n. (h.) 🄰a** zu et. ⚓ to contribute to(wards) a th.; eine kleine Summe zu et. ⚓ to give a small contribution (or to contribute one's small share) in aid of a th.; abs. ⚓ (zf.-legen) to club together; to collect a fund; ⚓d contributing, ...ory, ...ive to.

bei-stimmen (⁗́⌣) I v/n. (h.) 🄶** to agree to or with, to concur with; dem Urteile oder der Ansicht j-s ⚓ to fall (or chime) in with a p.'s view(s) or opinion; (einwilligen in) to consent (or accede, assent) to; vgl. beitreten 1. — II ~ n 🄶 = Beistimmung.

Bei-stimmer (⁗́) m 🄶, **~in** f 🄵 assentor, assenting party.

Bei-stimmung (⌣) f 🄶 agreement (or concurrence) with; consent (or assent) to.

Bei-strich (⁗́) m ⑦d. gram. comma.

Beitel ⚓ (⌣́) [ndd.] m 🄶 (Meißel) chisel.

Bei-töne ♪ (⁗́⌣) m/pl. ⑦d. seconds pl.

Bei-trag (⁗́) m ⑦d. 1. contribution. — 2. (Anteil) portion, bei Geldsammlungen auch: share, quota; Versicherungs-wesen: premium (of insurance); Steuer-wesen: verhältnismäßiger ~ payment pro rata. — 3. schriftliche Beiträge liefern zu write (articles) for, to contribute to; j. der regelmäßige Beiträge liefert regular contributor; geschichtliche, kritische Beiträge historical, critical essays pl.

bei-tragen (⁗́⌣) v/a. u. v/n. (h.) 🄶b** zu et. ⚓ to contribute to(wards) a th.; to be instrumental in accomplishing a th.; fördernd: to promote a th.; zur Gesundheit ⚓ to be conducive to health; zur Verdauung ⚓ to aid (or improve) digestion; es wird viel zur Hebung des Handels ⚓ it will in a large measure help to improve trade.

bei-treiben (⁗́⌣) I v/a. 🄰** eine Zahlung ⚓ to recover a debt; to exact payment; Abgaben: to collect; ⚓ e-e Kriegssteuer ⚓ to levy a contribution. — II ~ n 🄶 u. **Bei-treibung** f 🄶 recovery; exaction; collection; ⚓ requisition.

bei-treten (⁗́⌣) v/n. (fn.) 🄶d** 1. e-m ⚓ (beistimmen) to take sides with a p.; to back up a p.('s opinion); e-r Ansicht auch: to assent to, to concur with; to espouse; e-m Vorschlage xc.: to accede to (a proposal); to co-operate in (an enterprise). — 2. einer Gesellschaft: to join; einer Partei: to go over to, to side with.

Bei-tritt (⁗́) m ⑦c. siding (or concurrence) with; accession to; co-operation in; zu einer Gesellschaft: enrolment; **~s-erklärung** (⁙...) f 🄶 declaration of accession or adhesion.

Bei-wache ⚓, **-wacht** ⚓ ⚓ † (⁗́(⌣)) f campfire (= Biwak).

Bei-wagen ⚓ (⁗́⌣) m 🄶 extra coach; supplementary (or extra) carriage.

Bei-weg (⁗́) m ⑦d. by-way, by-path; branch of the main road.

Bei-werk (⁗́) n ⑦c, accessory (part), accessories pl.

bei-wohnen (⁗́⌣) I v/n. (h.) 🄶** 1. einem Vorgange ⚓ to be (present at); e-r Versammlung: to attend. — 2. e-m Weibe: to cohabit (or lie) with. — 3. e-m wohnt et. bei (ist in ihm wirksam) s.th. is inherent (stärker: born) in him; mit aller ihr zu den List with all the shrewdness that she was endowed with; with all her native (or natural) cunning. — II ~ n 🄶 u. **Bei-wohnung** f 🄶 4. presence, attendance, inherence; (Beischlaf) cohabitation, sexual intercourse.

Bei-wort (⁗́) n ⑦c. 1. gram. adjective; (Zusatz) epithet. — 2. (Titel) title.

bei-wörtlich (⁗́⌣) a. 🄶 epithetic, gram. adjectival; adv. adjectively.

bei-zählen (⁗́⌣) v/a. 🄶** to number (or count) among; to reckon with; er wird den Radikalen beigezählt he is classed with the Radicals.

Beiz-brühe ⊕ (⁗...) f 🄶 corrosive fluid.

Beize (⌣́) [ahd.] f 🄶 1. meist ⊕ (Gebeizt-werden) corrosion; Gerberei: mastering; med. cauterization. — 2. ⊕ (Beizmittel) caustic (auch med.); Färberei: mordant, stain, strong fluid for staining; Gerberei: oozing; Kupferstecherei: aquafortis. — 3. hunt. (Falkenjagd) hawking; baiting (the hawk).

Bei-zeichen (⁗́⌣) n 🄶 1. mark; (accessory) sign. — 2. ♪ diesis (♯). — 3. ⚓ (Gegenzeichen) countermark. — 4. her. accident, rühmliches: rebatement.

bei-zeiten (-⌣́) adv. 1. (frühzeitig) early, betimes; ⚓ zu Bette geh(e)n to keep good hours, to retire at an early hour. — 2. (rechtzeitig) in (good) time.

beiz/en (⌣́) [ahd.: beißen] I v/a. 🄶 1. (v/n.) (ätzen) to corrode. — 2. Fleisch xc. in Essig: to pickle; surg. to cauterize; Färberei: (fixieren) to mordant. — 3. ⊕ Gerberei: to steep (in ooze); to curry; mit Lohe: to tan; Metalle: to etch, dip, pickle; join.: to stain; schwarz ⚓ to ebonize; Tabak: to sauce. — 4. hunt. [beißen m.]: a) (anködern) to bait; b) (jagen) to fly. — II ⚓d p.pr. u. a.

⊕ 5. corrosive; surg. caustic. — III ~ n 🄶 6. = B/ung. [mordant dyes pl.]

beizen-färbend (⁗́⌣) a. 🄶 ⚓ Farbstoffe

Beiz-hund (⁗́) m 🄶 hunt. pointer.

Beiz-kraft (⁗́...) f 🄶 corrosive strength or power; **-lüfe** f Gerberei: tan-vat; **-mittel** n corrosive; Färberei: mordant.

Beizung (⌣́) f 🄶 corrosion; surg. cauterization; hunt. baiting, hawking.

Beiz-vogel (⁗́...) m 🄶 hunt. hawk; **-wasser** ⊕ n ⚓ brühe; join. stain; f. Beize 2.

be-jagen (⌣⌣́) v/a. 🄶** ein Revier ⚓ to shoot over (an estate); to hunt in (a preserve).

be-jah/en (⌣⌣́) I v/a. 🄶** to affirm, to answer in the affirmative; to say 'yes' to (a question); Sprichw. wer schweigt, bejaht silence gives consent. — II ⚓d p.pr. und a. 🄶 (in the) affirmative. — III ~ n 🄶 = B/ung.

be-jahrt (⌣⌣́) a. 🄶 aged, advanced (F well on) in years, elderly. [great) age.]

Be-jahrtheit (⌣⌣́) f 🄶 advanced (or)

Be-jahung (⌣⌣́) f 🄶 affirmative reply.

Be-jahungs-fall (⁙...) m 🄶 affirmative; im ~e if the answer be (in the) affirmative; **-satz** m affirmative sentence; **-weise** adv. affirmatively; **-wort** n, gr. adverb of affirmation, with. consent.

be-jammern (⌣⌣́⌣) v/a. 🄰a* to bewail, bemoan, deplore, lament; ⚓**-wert**, **-würdig** (⁙...) a. 🄶 deplorable, lamentable; pitiable; **~s-würdigkeit** f 🄶 deplorable (or lamentable) state or condition; deplorableness; (utter) misery.

be-jauchzen (⌣⌣́⌣) 🄶a* v/a., **be-jubeln** (⌣⌣́⌣) 🄶a* v/a. to greet with shouts of triumph; to exult over; to cheer.

be-kaien ⚓ (⌣⌣́⌣) v/a. 🄶** die Besa'n ⚓ to shift the mizzen; f. kaien.

Be-kaier ⚓ (⌣⌣́⌣) m 🄶 (Niederholer, Geitau) downhaul(er). [lime or chalk, to chalk.]

be-kalken (⌣⌣́⌣) v/a. 🄶** to cover with

be-kalmen ⚓ (⌣⌣́⌣) v/a. 🄶* ein Schiff (durch Abfangen des Windes) ⚓ to becalm ...

be-kämpf/en (⌣⌣́⌣) I v/a. 🄶** to combat, to resist; to fight (or struggle, strive) against; einen Antrag ⚓ to oppose; Wut, Zorn xc.: to keep in check or under control. — II ~ n 🄶 = B/ung.

Be-kämpfer (⌣⌣́⌣) m 🄶 antagonist.

Be-kämpfung (⌣) f 🄶 resistance (offered) to; struggle (carried on) against.

be-kannt (⌣⌣́) I 1. p.p. von bekennen. — II a. 🄶 2. e-m ⚓ (well) known to a p.; der Kerl ist mir als (ob. für e-n) Dieb ⚓ I know the fellow to be a (notorious) thief. — 3. (allgemein) ⚓ notorious, renowned, noted; es ist ⚓ it is (well) known; es dürfte Ihnen wohl ⚓ sein, daß // you are undoubtedly aware that //; ⚓ geben = ⚓machen; sich ⚓ machen to make o.s. known (vgl. a. ⚓machen); als ⚓ voraussetzen to take for granted, ⚓ (ruchbar) werden to get abroad, to come to light, to transpire; wenn es ⚓ wird when it comes to be known. — 4. mit et. ⚓ (vertraut) familiar (or conversant) with a th., versed in a th.; nicht ⚓ mit unfamiliar with; ⚓ wie ein bunter Hund F known all over the place; an einem Orte ⚓ sein to know (one's way about) a place; ich bin hier wenig ⚓ I am strange (or a

stranger) in this town; e-n mit et. 2 machen to initiate a p. in a th.; sich mit et. 2 machen to familiarize o.s. with a th. — 4. mit e-m genau 2 sein to be (intimately) acquainted with a p.; stärker: to be on intimate terms with a p.; oberflächlich 2 sein mit to know slightly or superficially, auch: to be on nodding (or bowing) terms with; e-n (sich) mit einem 2 machen to introduce a p. (o.s.) to a p.; mit e-m 2 werden to make the acquaintance of a p.; F to fall in with a p.; mit e-m 2 tun to claim a p.'s acquaintance; F b.s. to thrust o.s. on a p. — III adv 5. ❦ Stoffe in 2 vorzüglichen Qualitäten materials of acknowledged excellence. — IV ~e(r) m, ~e f ⑰ 6. acquaintance; ein guter ~er von mir a great friend (F a great chum) of mine; ~e pl. acquaintances pl.; F pals pl.; ein alter ~er F an old crony; feiner von unseren ~en none of our acquaintance(s), not one of our friends.
be-kannte (⌣⌣) impf. von bekennen.
Be-kannten-kreis (⌣⌣⌣...) m ⑫ circle of acquaintances or friends.
be-kannter-maßen (⌣⌣⌣⌣...) = bekanntlich.
Be-kanntheit (⌣⌣) f ⑰ (o.pl.) 1. notoriety. — 2. ~ mit et. knowledge of a th.
Be-kanntin ⟋ (⌣⌣) f ⑰ = Bekannte (f. bekannt IV.)
be-kanntlich (⌣⌣⌣) adv. as everybody knows; 2 ist er ... he is known to be ...
be-kannt-machen (⌣⌣...) v/a. ⑱** : e-m et. 2 to acquaint a p. with or of a th.; (öffentlich) 2 to publish; to blazon forth; in der Zeitung ꝛc.: to advertise; rühmend: to puff (up); durch Anschlagezettel: to post up; to placard (about), to bill; Geheimes 2 to reveal ..., to divulge ... (vgl. a. bekannt 2, 3 u. 4); **=macher**(in f ⑰) m ⑫ p. who publishes (or divulges) a th.; in Zeitungen: advertiser, ❦ puffing tradesman; **=machung** f ⑯ publication; feierliche: proclamation; v. Gesetzen: promulgation; in Zeitungen advertisement; der Obrigkeit: (public) notice; **=machungsschreiben** n ⑳ written notice; (Rundschreiben) circular (letter).
Be-kanntschaft (⌣⌣⌣) f ⑯ acquaintance; bei näherer ~ on closer acquaintance; j-s (ob. mit e-m) ~ machen u. mit e-m ~ haben = mit einem bekannt (f. ob II 4) werden und sein; vertraute ~ mit familiarity with, intimate knowledge of.
Be-kannt-werden (⌣⌣...) n ⑫, **=werdung** f publicity (given to a report).
be-kanten ⊙ (⌣⌣) v/a. ⑱* carp. Balken 2 to blunt (or round) the edges of timber; to square timber.
be-kappen (⌣⌣) I v/a. ⑱* 1. hort. to lop (trees). — 2. to provide (a p.) with a cap; hunt. to hood (a falcon). — 3. ⊙ Schuhe: to top (boots). — 4. ⚔ Feuerwerker: die Zünder 2 to cap the fuses. — 5. arch. (bedachen, bekrönen) to cope (a wall). — II **be-kappt** p.p. u. a. ⑯ 6. capped; hooded; ⚔, zo. ꝛc. cucullated).
Bekasse (⌣⌣) [fr.] f ㊽ = Waldschnepfe.
Bekassine (⌣⌣⌣) [fr.] f ㊽ orn. (common) snipe, jack-snipe (Sco'topax galli'nula).
Be-kehr-... (⌣⌣...) ⑫ = Bekehrungs-...
be-kehrbar (⌣⌣) a. ⑯ rel. convertible.

be-kehr/en (⌣⌣) I v/a. u. v/refl. ⑱* meist rel. die Heiden ꝛc. (zu ...) 2 to convert ... (to ...); weitS. to proselyt(iz)e ...; sich nach e-m lasterhaften Leben 2 to turn over a new leaf, to mend one's way(s); e. bekehrter Sünder a converted (or reclaimed) sinner. — II ~ n ㉓ = 2/ung.
Be-kehrer m ⑫ p. who converts (others); rel. missionary; evangelist.
Be-kehrte(r) (⌣⌣) m, **Be-kehrte** f ⑰ convert; bisw. neophyte; proselyte.
Be-kehrung (⌣⌣) f ⑯ conversion (zu to); zum Christentum: christianization; evangelization; e-s Sünders reclaiming.
Be-kehrungs-anstalt (⌣⌣⌣...) f ⑯ mission(ary establishment); **=bote** m missionary; **=eifer** m missionary zeal; vgl. **=sucht**; **=gesellschaft** f missionary society; Cath. eccl. propaganda; **=sucht** mania for converting (people), proselytism; propagandism; **=versuch** m attempted conversion; missionary effort; **=wesen** n missionary matters pl.; evangelization; **=wut** f = **=sucht**.
be-keicht ⟋ (⌣⌣) a. ⑯. ⚂ calycate.
be-kenn/en (⌣⌣) ⑯b* I v/a. 1. a) rel. Christum 2 to profess (the faith of) Christ; b) f-e Fehler, Sünden 2 (gestehen) to confess (or avow) ...; (zugestehen) to own, admit, acknowledge. — 2. Karten Farbe 2 to follow suit; nicht 2 to revoke; fig. 2 Sie Farbe (seien Sie offen)! make a clean breast of it!, be open with me! — II sich 2 v/refl. 3. sich zu etwas (als Anhänger, Parteigänger) 2 to espouse (a cause); to profess (a religion); to attach o.s. (or adhere) to (a party); to follow (a method); (eingestehen) to own up; vgl. 1 b. — 4. sich (als ob. für) schuldig (ob. als den Schuldigen) 2 to confess one's fault or having done a th.; gerichtlich: to plead guilty. — 5. sich zum Empfange eines Briefes 2 to acknowledge the receipt of a letter. — III ~ n ㉓ 6. = 2/ung.
Be-kenner (⌣⌣) m ⑫ person who confesses; Eduard der ~ (englischer König, 1042-66) Edward the Confessor.
Be-kenntnis (⌣⌣) n ⑰ († f ⑱) 1. = Bekennung. — 2. rel. (Glaubens-)~ creed; (religiöse Gemeinschaft) (religious) denomination; vgl. A. B., H. B.
Be-kenntnis-bücher (⌣...) n/pl. ⑫ rel. symbolic books pl.; **=feier** f, rel. the Lord's Supper; **=schein** m receipt, acknowledgment; **=schrift** f (book containing a p.'s) confessions pl.
Be-kennung (⌣⌣) f ⑯ profession; confession; avowal; (Empfangsanzeige) acknowledgment (of receipt).
be-kichern (⌣⌣) v/a. ⑫a* et. 2 to giggle (or titter) at a th.
be-klagen (⌣⌣) ⑱* I v/a. e-n, ein Unglück ꝛc. 2 to lament over ...; to deplore ...; j-s Schicksal: to bewail, bemoan; (bemitleiden) to commiserate, pity; die Tat ist sehr zu 2 ... much to be regretted, ... most deplorable. — II sich 2 v/refl. to make (a) complaint; sich über et. 2, sich bei e-m über et., e-n 2 to complain about (or of) a th., a p. to a p.; Sie können sich nicht 2 you have no reason to complain or nothing to complain of; ich kann mich über ihn,

sein Benehmen nicht 2 I have nothing to say against ...
be-klagens=wert (⌣⌣...) a. ⑯, **=würdig** a. Person: (much) to be pitied; Sache: lamentable, deplorable, pitiable.
Be-klagte([r] m) f (⌣⌣) ⑰, f a. **Beklagtin** ㊼ (Angeklagte(r) (the) accused; im Zivilprozeß: defendant.
be-klatschen (⌣⌣) v/a. ⑱* 1. bsd. thea. e-n, ein Stück: to applaud, to clap. — 2. to talk (or gossip) about; (verleumden) to backbite, slander, defame.
be-klauben (⌣⌣) v/a. ⑱* to pick about; to handle, thumb, finger.
be-kleben (⌣⌣) v/a. ⑱* to paste over with; eine Wand mit (Papier-)Tapete 2 to paper ...; Pakete mit Zetteln 2 to label parcels; eine Wand mit Zetteln 2 to stick bills on (or all over) ...
Be-klebe-zettel (⌣⌣⌣...) m ⑫ poster, placard; für Gepäck: label; way-bill.
be-klecken ⑱*, **be-kleckern** ⑫a*, **be-klecksen** ⑳*(⌣⌣⌣) v/a. und v/refl. to blot, to blotch; mit Schmutz: to bespatter; mit Farbe: to daub (over).
be-kleiben † ob. poet. (⌣⌣) v/n. (in) ⑱* (Wurzel fassen) to take root.
be-kleiden (⌣⌣) I v/a. u. v/refl. ⑱* 1. (sich) to dress or clothe (o.s.); schmückend: to array, attire; verhüllend: to drape; ⊙ to cover (over), to (en)case in, mit Rasen: to turf, mit Täfelwerk: to wainscot; join. (furnieren) to veneer; (ausfüttern) to line, coat, face; ⚓ ein Schiff 2 to plank. — 2. fig. ein Amt 2 to hold (or have) a (responsible) position, von Ministern: to be in office, to hold office; e-e Stelle 2 to occupy (or fill) a situation or post or berth; mit Vollmacht 2 to vest (full) authority in. — II ~ n ㉓ 3. = Bekleidung 1.
Be-kleidung (⌣⌣) f ⑯ 1. dressing, &c.; ~ mit e-m Amte instalment; investiture; e-s Amtes: tenure (of office). — 2. dress, clothing, garment, attire; drapery; ⚔ accoutrement, clothing; outfit; uniform, regimentals pl.; ⊙ lining, facing, coating, casing; ⚓ v. Schiffen: planking; (side-) planks; (Furnier) veneer; (Tapete) paper (hangings pl.), arch., &c ~ e-r Böschung revetment of a slope or bank.
Be-kleidungs-amt ⚔ (⌣...) n ⑫ clothing depot; **=gegenstände** m/pl. articles pl. of clothing; wearing apparel; (Putz) finery; **=künstler** m, co. tailor (= Schneider); **=mauer** f, arch. retain-wall; **=stücke** ⚔ n/pl. soldiers' wearing apparel or clothing; **=wesen** ⚔ n clothing department, matters pl. concerning soldiers' uniforms or accoutrement.
be-kleistern (⌣⌣) v/a. ⑫a* = bekleben.
be-klemmen (⌣⌣) I v/a. ⑱* (zs.-pressen) (p.p. oft: beklommen f. b.) to confine; to oppress or tighten (the chest); 2d oppressive, v. d. Luft auch: sultry; fig. er ist in e-r ⟋den Lage he is in great straits. — II ~ n ㉓ u. **Be-klemmung** f ⑯ confinement; der Brust: tightness (of the chest), heavy breathing; fig. an ~ leiden to feel in (great) anguish, to be (very) uneasy.
be-klommen (⌣⌣) [p.p. v. † beklimmen] a. ⑯ anxious, uneasy; oppressed.

Signs (see page XVII): F familiar; P vulgar; ℱ flash; ⟋ rare; † obsolete (died); * new word (born); ‡ incorrect; ♪ music;

[Beklommenheit] — 167 — [belappen]

Beklommenheit(‿‿‿)*f* ㊻ = Beklemmung; ~ der Luft: sultriness, oppressiveness.
be-klopfen (‿‿) *v/a.* ㊹* to test by knocking or beating; *med.* zur Erforschung e-s kranken Körperteils: to percuss.
be-klotzen (‿‿) I *v/a.* ㊹* to pave with (squares of) wood. — II ~ *n* ㉓ u. **Be-klotzung** *f* ㊻ (laying) wood pavement.
be-flunkern F(‿‿‿) *v/a.* und *v/refl.* ㉒a* sein Kleid, sich ≗ to bedraggle o.s.
be-knabbern, be-knappen P (‿‿‿) *v/a.* ㉒a* to nibble (or gnaw) at.
be-kneipen (‿‿) [Kneipe] ㉘* burschikos: I *v/a.* e-n ≗ (besuchen) to give (a p.) a look-up. — II sich ≗ *v/refl.* F to get tipsy or fuddled or muddled or boozed; bekneipt tipsy, the worse for drink, half seas-over.   [to recover.]
be-kobern F (‿‿): sich ≗ (erholen) *v/refl.*
be-kommen (‿‿) ㊽* I *v/a.* 1. to receive, obtain, get; wir werden Regen ≗ we shall have rain; er hat Erlaubnis ≗ zu // he obtained leave to //, he was given permission to //; wieviel ≗ Sie? what is your due?, what do I owe you? — 2. a) mit *s., a. ob. adv.*: Angst ≗ to grow (F to get) anxious; e-n Bart ≗ to have whiskers growing; der Baum hat Blätter ≗ the tree is in (full) leaf or has burst into leaf; Blüten ≗ to (begin to) bloom or blossom; to (burst into) flower; Durst ≗ to grow (or become) thirsty; et. fertig ≗ to accomplish a th.; er hat es nicht fertig ≗ he could not do (or accomplish) it; Fieber ≗ to catch (or contract) a fever; et. auf die Finger ≗ to get a rap on the knuckles; Furcht ≗ to get (F to get) frightened; nasse Füße ≗ to get one's feet wet; Geschmack an et. ≗ to acquire a taste (or liking) for a th.; zu Gesicht ≗ to espy, discover, to get a sight of; ⚓ to descry (land); Hunger ≗ to grow (or feel) hungry; Junge ≗ to have young ones; *fig.* e-n Korb ≗ to meet with a refusal or a rebuff; eine Krankheit ≗ to catch a disease or complaint, to be taken ill; ⚓ ein Leck ≗ to spring a leak; Luft ≗ zu to feel inclined to, to have a good mind to; e-n Mann ≗ to get a husband; Mut ≗ to take courage; e-n, et. satt ≗ to grow weary (or tired) of a th.; F to be(come) sick of a th.; Schnupfen ≗ to catch a cold (in the head); *fig.* von et. Wind ≗ to get wind of a th.; Wurzeln ≗ to strike root; Zähne ≗ to cut one's teeth; er hat es zurück ≗ he got (or had) it back, besser: he had it returned to him; b) mit *p.p.*: ich habe es geborgt ≗ I had it lent me; ich bekomme sie zugeschickt I have them sent (on) to me; c) mit *inf.*: das ist hier nicht zu ≗ that's not to be had here; ich kann ihn nicht zu sprechen ≗ I cannot find an opportunity (or I have not been able) to speak to him, I cannot gain access to him. — II *v/n.* 3.(*n*): e-m (gut, schlecht) ≗ to agree (well, ill) with a p.('s health); die Reise ist mir gut ≗ I feel all the better for the journey; (ist es Ihnen) gut ≗? did it agree with you?, has it benefited you or done you good?; wie ist ihm

die Arz(e)nei ≗? how did the medicine agree with him?; wohl bekomm's (euch)! I trust it may do you good!, *iro.* I hope you'll like it!; es wird ihm schlecht ≗, wenn er //he will rue the day on which he //. — III sich (ob. ea.) ≗ *v/recip.* 4. *v.Liebespärchen*: to get married.
be-kömmlich (‿‿‿) *a.* ㊺ 1. (zuträglich) beneficial. — 2. *(erhaltbar) e-e schwer ≗ Ware an article difficult to obtain.
be-komplimentieren (‿‿‿‿‿) *v/a.* ㊸* to compliment; a. *v/recip.* sich (ob. ea.) ≗ to exchange compliments.
be-köstigen (‿‿‿) I *v/a. u. v/refl.* ㊸* to board, victual, feed; sich selbst ≗ to keep o.s. — II **Be-köstigung** *f* ㊻ boarding, board, food; weitS. maintenance, keep; ohne ~ without board or meals.
be-kräftigen (‿‿‿) I *v/a.* ㊸* to confirm, corroborate, make good (an assertion, a statement); (beteuern) to vouch for; eidlich ≗ to take an oath upon; *jur.* to take (or make) swear an affidavit upon; ≗d confirmatory, corroborative. — II ~ *n* ㉓ u. **Be-kräftigung** *f* ㊻ confirmation, corroboration; zur ~ der Beweise in support of...   [matory oath.)
Be-kräftigungs-eid (¨...) *m* ㉒ confir-/
be-kränzen (‿‿‿) I *v/a. u. v/refl.* ㊹* (sich) ≗ to crown (o.s.) with wreaths or garlands; mit Lorbeer bekränzt crowned (or wreathed) with laurel; Wände usw. ≗ to festoon ... — II **Be-kränzung** *f* ㊻ crowning with wreaths, &c., *s.* I.
be-kratzen *v/a.* ㊹* to scrape.
be-kreisen *v/a.* ㊹* *hunt.* e-n Wald ≗ to beat (or go) round ...
be-kreuzen (‿‿‿) ㊹* I *v/a.* to mark with a cross, to cross. — II sich bekreuz(ig)en *v/refl.* ㊺(㉘)* to cross o.s.; *fig.* sich vor et. ≗ to shrink back from a th.
be-kriechen (‿‿‿) *v/a.* ㉓dṣ* et. ≗ to crawl on (or creep over) a th.
be-kriegen (‿‿‿) *v/a.* ㊸* to make war upon, to fight against.
Be-krittelei F (‿‿‿) *f* ㊻ fault-finding.
be-kritteln (‿‿‿) I *v/a.* ㉒a* to censure, criticize; to carp (or cavil) at; to find fault with. — II ~ *n* ㉓ und **Be-krittelung** (‿‿‿) *f* ㊻ censure; von Schriften: slashing critique or review.
Be-krittler (‿‿‿) *m* ㉒, ~**in** *f* ㊵ fault-finder; caviller; severe critic.
be-kritzeln (‿‿‿) *v/a.* ㉒a* eine Wand usw. ≗ to scribble (or scrawl) on ...
be-krönen (‿‿‿) *v/a.* ㊸* to crown. — II **Be-krönung** *f* ㊻ *arch.* (oberer Abschluß) crowning part of a building; (Giebel) gable; ☉ an Möbeln usw. ornamental top; (Gesims) moulding, cornice.
be-krusten (‿‿‿) I *v/a. u. v/refl.* ㊹* to (en)crust. — II ~ *n* ㉓ u. **Be-krustung** *f* ㊻ incrustation.
be-kümmern (‿‿‿) ㉒a* *v/a.* 1. e-n ≗ to cause grief (or trouble) to a p.; to grieve (or distress, afflict) a p.; tief bekümmert deeply grieved, in deep affliction or sorrow. — 2. *bfd. neg.* u. fragend: das bekümmert mich nicht that does not concern me; was bekümmert's euch? what do you care? — II sich ≗ *v/refl.* 3. sich über et. ≗ to be grieved (or concerned, troubled, distressed) about a th., to grieve over a th., to

take it to heart. — 4. sich um et. ≗ to trouble o.s. (or one's head) about a th., to attend to a th.; ≗ Sie sich nicht um meine Sachen, ≗ Sie sich um sich (selbst)! don't meddle with my affairs, mind your own business!
Be-kümmernis(‿‿‿) *f* ⑱ (⚓ *n* ⑰) grief, trouble, distress, affliction.
be-kunden (‿‿‿) *v/a.* ㊸* 1. (aussagen) to state; vor Gericht: to give evidence of or about, to depose. — 2. (dartun) to manifest, demonstrate, evince; (auch *v/refl.* sich ≗ als //) to show (o.s.) //; sich als ein(en) Ehrenmann ≗ to prove (o.s.) a man of honour; ⚖ die Börse bekundet eine feste Haltung the stock-market shows a firm tone.
be-lächeln (‿‿‿) ㉒a*, **be-lachen** (‿‿ᚷ) ㊸* *v/a.* to smile (or laugh) at.
be-lachens-wert (‿‿‿...) *a.* ㊺, ≗**würdig** *a.* laughable, ridiculous.
be-laden (‿‿) I *v/a. u.* (sich) *v/refl.* ㊹b* mit et. ≗ to burden or load (o.s.) with a th.; (belasten) to charge, weigh down. encumber. — II *p.p.* mit Ruhm ≗ covered with glory; schwer ≗ heavily laden; vgl. befrachten.
Be-lag (‿‿) *m* ⑦c. 1. ~ der Zunge fur (on the tongue); ~ e-s Spiegels foil (or foiling, covering) of a mirror. — 2. ✢ = Beleg 2 (s. ds.).
Be-lagerer (‿‿‿) *m* ㉒ beleaguerer.
be-lagern ⚔ (‿‿‿) I *v/a.* ㉒a* to besiege, beleaguer, lay siege to; *fig.* e-n mit et. ≗, belagert halten to importune (or beset) a p. with a th. — II ~ *n* ㉓ u. **Be-lagerung** (‿‿‿) *f* ㊻ siege; regelmäßige ~ regular siege or investment; die ~ aufheben (aushalten) to raise (to endure, to be subjected to) a siege.
Belagerungs-arbeiten (‿‿‿‿...) *f/pl.* ⚔ siege-operations *pl.*, vgl. ≗**werfe** = ar**tillerie** *f*, **batterie** *f*, **geschütz** *n* battering-train; siege-artillery or -guns *pl.* or -park; **heer** *n* beleaguering army; **kranz** *m* röm. Alt.: obsidional crown; **maschine** *f* der Alten: battering-engine; **park** *m* siege-park, heavy ordnance and requisites for siege-operations; **train** *m* train of siege-guns; **werke** *n/pl.* siege-works, approaches *pl.*; **zustand** *m* state of siege; der kleine ~ the minor state of siege; in ~ versetzen to declare in a state of siege; den ~ verhängen über to proclaim a state of siege in, to put under martial law.
Be-lang (‿‿) *m* ⑦b. import(ance); von ~ important; nicht von ~ of no consequence.
be-langbar (‿‿‿) *a.* ㊺ *jur.* actionable.
be-lang/en (‿‿‿) I *v/a.* ㊸* *jur.* e-n gerichtlich ≗ to sue a p.; to bring an action (or to take proceedings) against a p. — II *v/impers.* = an(be)langen. — III ~ *n* ㉓ = ≗/ung.
be-lang-los (‿‿...) *a.* ㊻ insignificant, of no account; ≗**reich** *a.* considerable; of great import(ance) or moment.
Be-langung (‿‿‿) *f* ㊻ action; legal proceedings *pl.* (against a p.).
be-lappen (‿‿‿) *v/a.* ㊸* *hunt.* e-n Wald ≗ to hang rags (a)round ...(for the purpose of frightening back the game)

㊼ scientific; ♀ botanical; ⚲ geography; ⊕ machinery; ⚒ mining; ⚔ military; ⚓ marine; ⚖ commercial; ✉ postal; 🚂 railway.

[belassen] — 168 — [Beleidigung]

be-lassen (⌣⌣)[obb.] v/a.⊕a* et. ² to leave a th. in its place; *fig.* to put up with a th.; alles beim alten ² to leave things unchanged or just as they were.

be-last/en (⌣⌣) **I** v/a.⊕⁸* **1.** (a. sich ² v/refl.) (beladen) to load (or charge) with a burden; *fig.* a. to saddle (with a th.; *jur.* (beschuldigen) to accuse; (schuldig m.) to incriminate; mit Schulden belastet loaded with (or deep in) debt; *med.* erblich belastet with a hereditary disposition; *vgl.* beladen. — **2. ⊕** j-s Konto (ob. e-n) mit et. ² to put a th. to a p.'s debit, to debit (or charge) a th. to a p.'s account. — **II** ~ *n* ㉓ **3.** = B/ung.

be-lästigen (⌣⌣⌣)[nhd.] **I** v/a.⊕⁸* to molest, importune, bother, pester, annoy a p.; ich will Sie nicht ² I won't trouble (or incommode, inconvenience) you; ²d troublesome; annoying. — **II** ~ *n* ㉓ u. **Be-lästigung** f ㊻ molestation, bother, botheration, annoyance.

Be-lastung (⌣⌣) f ㊻ load(ing), burden, burdening; ⊕ strain; ⊕ debit(ing); ⚓ (Tragkraft) carrying power of a ship; **~s-fähigkeit** ⊕ f ㊷ loading capacity, bearing (or straining) power; **~s-zeuge** m witness for the prosecution.

be-latten ⊕ (⌣⌣) v/a.⊕⁸* *carp.* to fit with laths or lattice-work; to lath.

be-lauben (⌣⌣) **I** v/a. u. v/refl.⊕⁸* **1.** (sich) ² to clothe (o.s.) in foliage; sich ² auch: to produce fresh leaves, to put on new foliage, to burst into leaf; sich ²d ⚘ frondescent. — **2. ⊕** Meiler ² (mit Laub bedecken) to cover ... with foliage. — **3.** *hort.* Maulbeerbäume ² (Laub abpflücken) to strip mulberry-trees (of their foliage). — **II be-laubt** *p.p.* u. a. ㊺ **4.** in leaf, covered with foliage, ⚘ frondose; leafy (wood).

be-lauern (⌣⌣) v/a. ⊕²a* to lie in wait for; to watch for, to spy (out).

Be-lauf (⌣¹) *m* ①c. (o. *pl.*) amount (of a sum); bis zum ~e von to the amount of, amounting to.

be-laufen (⌣⌣) ⊕aft* **I** v/a. **1.** e-n Raum ² to run over ..., to traverse ...; besichtigend: to inspect, view, survey. — **2.** mit sächlichem Subjekt: to run (or roll, flow) across. — **II** sich ² v/refl. **3.** (sich beziffern) to amount to, ⊕ to figure up to, to come to; wie hoch beließ sich die Rechnung? what did the account come (or run up, total up) to?, F how much was the bill?

be-lauschen (⌣⌣) v/a. ⊕¹* to spy out.

Belche (⌣⌣) [ahd.: lt. *fu'lica*] f ⊕ *orn.* (Wasserhuhn) coot (*Fu'lica atra*).

be-leben (⌣⌣) **I** v/a. u. v/refl.⊕⁸* **1.** (sich) ² to call into (or come to) life; (sich) wieder ² to restore (or to come back) to life; to revive; ²des Mittel restorative. — **2.** (anfeuern) to liven (or cheer) up; to enliven, to rouse or stimulate (to action); to put fresh life (or new heart) into; to electrify, galvanize; j-s Hoffnung ² to raise a p.'s hopes. — **II** ~ *n* ㉓ **3.** = Belebung.

Be-leber (⌣¹⌣) *m* ㉒, **~in** f ㊼ reviver; resuscitator; regenerator.

belebt (⌣¹) *p.p.* u. *a.* ㊺ alive, (lebhaft) animated, enlivened, lively, (all) alive, brisk, spirited; (bevölkert) populous,

v. Straßen: (much) frequented, full of life (and bustle), (very) crowded, bustling; ²e Motoren living agencies *pl.*; ²e Wesen living beings *pl.*

Be-lebt-heit (⌣¹⌣) f ㊺ (o. *pl.*) animation; (Lebhaftigkeit) liveliness, briskness, vivacity; der Straßen: crowded state.

Be-lebung (⌣¹⌣) f ㊺ vivification, (Auferweckung) resuscitation, (Aufmunterung) enlivenment, stimulation, (Neu)~ des Verkehrs, der dramatischen Kunst ꝛc. revival of trade, of dramatic art, &c.; **~s-mittel** (⌣...) *n* ㊷ restorative; **~s-versuch** *m* attempt at resuscitation; attempted restoration or revival.

be-lecken (⌣⌣) v/a. ⊕⁸* to lick; von der Kultur beleckt having a mere surface polish, (overlaid) with a thin veneer (or coating) of culture.

be-ledern ⊕ (⌣⌣) **I** v/a. ⊕²a* Klavierhämmer ꝛc.: to (cover with) leather; Billardstock: to tip (with leather). — **II Be-lederung** f ㊺ leathering, &c., *f.* I.

Be-leg (⌣¹) *m* ⓒc. **1.** † ob. ⊕ = Belag. — **2.** (Beweisstück) (authentic) record, proof, evidence; (Beispiel) illustration, example; (Zitat) quotation, (Urkunde) document, deed, voucher; (Quittung) receipt; zum ~(e) für in proof of; ~e zu et. liefern to furnish positive proofs of (or to verify, exemplify) s.th.

be-legbar (⌣¹⌣) a. ㊺ coverable; (beweisbar) provable.

be-legen¹ (⌣¹⌣) [: belay] **I** v/a. ⊕⁸* **1.** (bedecken) to overlay (or cover) with; (einfassen) to face with. — **2.** Redensarten: mit Abgaben ² to impose (or lay, F put or clap) taxes (or duty) on; mit Arrest ² to arrest; mit e-m Namen ² to give a name to; (nick)name; mit (e-r) Strafe ² to visit with punishment, to inflict a punishment upon. — **3.** ⊕ am Rande mit et. ² to border with s.th.; mit Rasen ² to (cover with) turf; Butterbrot mit Schinken ² to make ham-sandwiches. — **4.** (bestellen, sichern, füllen) f-n Platz ² to mark ...; e-n Platz ² to book, engage, secure (beforehand) a seat or a place or a berth (on board ship) or a stall (in a theatre); ein belegter Platz a reserved seat; ein Kolleg ² to subscribe to a course of lectures; to enter one's name (in the register); ⚔ e-e Stadt mit Truppen ² to quarter (or billet) soldiers upon a town. — **5.** (a. v/refl.) sich ² to get (or become) coated; seine Zunge ist belegt his tongue is coated or furred; ♪ belegte Stimme husky ...; er ist belegt (heiser) F he is ropy or hoarse. — **6.** e-n mit et. ² (belasten) to charge, load, burden a p. with a th.; *f.* Bann **2**; *jur. f.* Beschlag **3**. — **7.** (beweisen) to prove (or illustrate) by quotations; *jur.* durch Urkunden: to support by documentary evidence. — **II** ~ *n* ㉓ **8.** = Belegung.

be-legen² (⌣¹⌣) [*p.p. v.* †beliegen] Kanzleistil: situated; wo ² sein (liegen) to lie (or be situated) somewhere; die am Rhein ²en Schlösser the castles situated (or bordering) on the Rhine.

Be-leger (⌣..) *m* ㉒, **~in** f ㊷ p. who covers, faces, &c.; Spiegelfabr.: silverer.

Be-leg-exemplar (⌣¹¹...) *n* ㊽ author's copy; **~klampe** f, **~nagel** *m* ⚓ belaying-cleat, belaying-pin.

Be-legschaft ⚒ (⌣¹⌣) f ㊺ (Mannschaft e-s Bergwerks) set of men, party (or gang) of pitmen or miners.

Be-leg-stelle (⌣¹¹...) f ㊷ illustrative quotation; authoritative passage.

Be-legung (⌣¹⌣) f ㊺ **1.** imposition (of taxes); infliction (of punishment); booking or reservation (of a seat); ⚔ der Quartiere: quartering. — **2.** ⊕ tinfoiling or quicksilvering (of a mirror); *phys.* coating (of a Leyden jar); armature (of an electric machine).

Be-legungs-fähigkeit (⌣...) f ㊺ ⚔ e-r Stadt accommodation for the quartering (or billeting) of soldiers; die Irrenanstalt hat e-e ~ für 800 Kranke the lunatic asylum can accommodate (or house, receive) 800 patients.

be-lehn/en (⌣¹⌣) **I** v/a. ⊕⁸* Feudalwesen: e-n mit et. ² to invest a p. with a fief, to enfeoff. — **II** ~ *n* ㉓ = B/ung.

Be-lehner (⌣¹⌣) *m* ㉒ feoffor, liegelord.

Be-lehnte(r) (⌣¹⌣) *m* ㉖ Feudalwesen: feoffee, liegeman, vassal. [feudation.)

Be-lehnung (⌣¹⌣) f ㊺ investiture, in-)

be-lehren (⌣¹⌣) **I** v/a. v/refl. ⊕⁸* **1.** e-n (sich) von et. ² (unterrichten) to instruct (or inform) a p. (o.s) about a th.; e-n über et. ² to apprise a p. of a th.; e-n über et. ² to enlighten a p. on a subject. — **2.** er läßt sich gern ² he gladly listens to reason; he is open-minded or willing to take advice; e-n (über et.) e-s ander(e)n, e-s Besser(e)n ² to set a p. right (with regard to a th.); to disabuse (a p.'s mind); to undeceive (or correct) a p. — **II** ~ *n* ㉓ **3.** = B/ung. — **III** ²d *p.pr.* u. a. ㊺ **4.** Bed. des *inf.* — **5.** instructive; (lehrhaft) didactic.

Be-lehrung (⌣¹⌣) f ㊺ instruction, information, correction (of a p.'s views); er nimmt keine ~ an he won't listen to reason, he won't be advised.

be-leibt (⌣¹) a. ㊺ corpulent. stout; (stattlich) portly; (prall) plump; **~heit** f ㊻ (o. *pl.*), **~sein** *n* ㉓ (⌣¹⌣) corpulence, stoutness, portliness; plumpness; (*fr.*) *embonpoint*; *co.* rotundity.

be-leidigen (⌣¹⌣) v/a. ⊕⁸* **1.** to offend, to give offence to; stärker: to affront, (beschimpfen) to insult; (verletzen) to hurt or injure (a p.'s feelings); tätlich ² to assault; ²d offensive. insulting. — **2.** sich durch et. für beleidigt halten ob. beleidigt fühlen to take offence (or umbrage) at a th.; diese Musik beleidigt das Ohr ... jars (or grates) on the ear; diese grelle Farbe beleidigt das Auge ... is offensive to (or hurts) the eye.

Be-leidiger (⌣¹⌣) *m* ㉒, **~in** f ㊼ offender; person who offends, &c. others.

be-leidigt (⌣¹⌣) *p.p.* ㊺: der ²e Teil (auch die ²e Person), der **~e** ㊷ the offended person, the injured party.

Be-leidigung (⌣¹⌣⌣) f ㊺ offence, affront; insult; injury (stärker: outrage) to a p.'s feelings; ich verzeihe dir deine (ob. meine) ~ (beides = daß du mich beleidigt hast) I'll forgive you your offence; zu groben ~en schreiten to become (most) insulting or abusive; *vgl.* einstecken **2**.

Zeichen (f. S. XVII): F familiär; P Volkssprache; Г Gaunersprache; ⧵ selten; † alt (auch gestorben); * neu (auch geboren); ⁺⁺ unrichtig;

[beleihen] — 169 — [bemächtigen]

be-leihen (⌣⌣́) v/a. ⊛* 1. † = belehnen. — 2. ⚓ (auf et. als Pfand leihen) to (grant a) loan on. 【with ledges.}
be-leisten ⊙ (⌣⌣́) v/a. ⊛* to furnish}
be-leitern ⚒ (⌣⌣́) v/a. ⊛a* e-n Schacht: to provide with ladders.
be-lemmern (⌣⌣⌣́) [ndd., ndl.] v/a. ⊛2a* 1. ⚓ (behindern) to encumber (the ship). — 2. (verwirren) to confuse.
Belemnit ⚒ (⌣⌣́) [grch.] m ⊛42 geol. (Donnerkeil) belemnite, F finger-stone.
be-lesen (⌣⌣́) I v/a. ⊛2a* Linsen ꝛc.: to pick; ⊙ Tuchm.: (noppen) to burl. — II a. ⊛66 (D9) (in Büchern bewandert) well-read; scholarly; F bookish; sehr ⸗er Mensch, oft: p. of great (or vast) reading or erudition; F hard reader; er ist in den Klassikern sehr ⸗ he has made a thorough study of the classics; ~heit f ⊛46 (knowledge acquired by extensive) reading; book-learning.
Bel-etage (⸗⌣⌣́) [⸗⸗ fr. *le bel* ⟨r-r. *le premier*⟩ *étage*] f ⊛48 first floor, first story; die ~ bewohnen to live on the first floor.
be-leuchten (⌣⌣́) I v/a. ⊛* 1. to light up; festlich: to illuminate. — 2. fig. to throw light on (or to elucidate) a subject; (näher) ⸗ (prüfen) to examine closely. — II ~ n ⊛23 u. **Be-leuchtung** (⌣⌣́) f ⊛3. lighting (up) the streets, &c.; illumination, elektrisch: electric lighting; paint. helle, dunkle ~ light, dark tints or shades pl.; (un)günstige ~ e-s Bildes (un)favourable light; freie ~ und Heizung free gas and coals. — 4. fig. elucidation; examination.
Be-leuchtungs-apparat (⌣⌣⌣́...) m ⊛2, ⸗körper m, med. zu künstlicher Beleuchtung: s.th. used for lighting (or illuminating) purposes; ⸗kosten pl. cost of lighting (or illuminating) a town, &c.; ⸗materialien n/pl. substances pl. used for lighting or illumination.
be-leum(un)det ⚒ (⌣⌣⌣́) p.p. u. a. ⊛6: gut ⸗ (held) in good repute, reputable; übel ⸗ (held) in evil repute, ill-famed, disreputable.
belfern (⌣⌣́) [ndd.] v/n. (h.) ⊛2a. v. Hunden: to yelp; v. Menschen: to bawl; (schelten) to scold, to grumble.
Belfried ⚒ (⌣⌣́) m ⊛d. = Bergfried.
Belge(n pl.) (⌣⌣́) m ⊛44 hist. (die alten Belgier) Belgæ, (ancient) Belgians pl.
Belgi-en ⚧ (⌣⌣⌣́) npr/n. ⊛3α. Belgium.
Belgi-er ⚧ (⌣⌣⌣́) m ⊛2, ~in f ⊛40 Belgian.
belgisch (⌣⌣́) a. ⊛6 Belgian; auf die Belgen in Cäsars Tagen bezüglich, meist: Belgic.
Belgrad ⚧ (⌣⌣́) npr/n. ⊛3α. Belgrade.
Belial (⌣́⌣⌣) [hebr.] m ⊛6 (sibonischer Gott) (= Teufel) Belial; ~s-kind (⸗́...) m ⊛2 bibl. child of B., weitS. (Sünder) sinner.
be-lichten ⊙ (⌣⌣́) I v/a. ⊛9* phot. to expose to the solar rays or light; zu lange ⸗ to solarize. — II **Be-lichtung** f ⊛46 exposure (to the solar rays or light); übermäßige ~ solarization.
be-lieben (⌣⌣́) I v/a. u. v/n. (h.) ⊛8* 1. mir beliebt (gefällt) et. I am pleased with s.th. — 2. (wollen) ⸗ Sie Bier od. Kaffee? do you take ...?; was ⸗ die Herrschaften sonst noch? (have you) any further orders?, im Laden auch: is there anything else I can show (or do for)

you?; what is the next thing? — 3. (geruhen zu) Sie ⸗ (wohl nur) zu scherzen you are joking; ⸗ Sie einzutreten! please step in! — II v/impers. (h.) 4. es beliebte ihr nicht zu antworten she did not condescend (or choose) to reply; nehmen Sie **was** Ihnen beliebt take whatever you like, höflicher: you may have your choice; was beliebt Ihnen? what's your pleasure?; **wenn's** beliebt if you please; in der Zukunft: whenever you (may) feel inclined to; **wie's** Ihnen beliebt as you please; wie beliebt? I beg your pardon! excuse me, (I did not quite understand); rel. wie es Gott beliebt as God wills, as Heaven ordains. — III ~ n ⊛23 (o. pl.) 5. oft: liking, pleasure; nach ~ (so viel wie man will) as much as one likes; ⸗ u. F ad lib(itum), s. beliebig; nach Ihrem ~ as you feel inclined, as you like; iro. at your own sweet will, at your discretion; es steht in Ihrem ~ it rests with you; ich stelle es ganz in Ihr ~ I leave it entirely to you(r discretion); handeln Sie nach ~ please yourself; do as you like.
be-liebig (⌣⌣⌣́) a. ⊛66 optional; to one's liking; e-e ⸗e Anzahl any (or an indefinite) number; eine (F ꝛ:) ⸗e Linie any line (whatever or whatsoever); wählen Sie jedes ⸗e Kleid ... any dress (that) you like; F ... any dress you please; in jeder ⸗en Menge to any amount, F ad lib [abbr. von lt. ad libitum]; jeder ⸗e Mensch, jeder ⸗e anybody (whoever he may be); zu jeder Ihnen ⸗en Zeit at any time (that may be) convenient to you, whenever it may suit you.
be-liebt (⌣́) p.p. von belieben und a. ⊛6 a) von Personen: (much) liked; popular; stärker: beloved; sich bei e-m ⸗ machen to ingratiate o.s. with a p.; bei e-m ⸗ sein to be a favourite (or in good odour) with a p.; allgemein ⸗ sein to be a general favourite; b) von Sachen: favourite; in vogue, fashionable, ⚓ in (great) request or demand; ⸗ werden to rise in favour; **~heit** f ⊛46, **~heit** n ⊛23 (⌣⌣́) popularity; (being in) vogue or favour or fashion.
Belisar (⌣⌣́) [weißer Zar] npr/m. ⊛α. (byzantinischer Feldherr, 505—65) Belisarius.
be-listen (⌣⌣́) v/a. ⊛* e-n ⸗ to deceive (or dupe, cheat, overreach) a p.
Belladonna ⚘ (⌣⌣⌣́) [it. schöne Frau] f ⊛49 = Tollkirsche.
Belle-Alliance ⚧ (⸗⌣-⌣-la͞a-ß): die Schlacht bei ~ (18.6.1815) the battle of Waterloo.
bellen (⌣⌣́) [ahd.: bawl, bell] I v/n. (h.) ⊛6 († ⊛b.) to bark or bay (auch fig. von Menschen); v. Füchsen ꝛc.: to yelp; hunt. (anschlagen) to open; to give tongue; fig. ein ⸗der Magen an empty (or a hungry) stomach; ⸗de Hunde beißen nicht barking dogs do not bite. — II ~ n ⊛23 barking.
Beller (⌣⌣́) m ⊛2 barker, barking dog.
Belletrist (⌣⌣⌣́) [ndh. 1750; *fr. belles-lettres*] m ⊛42 person cultivating polite (or light) literature; engS. literary man; ~**erei** (⌣⌣⌣́) f ⊛46 contp. literary fagging, novel-scribbling; ~**ik** (⌣⌣́)

f ⊛46 polite (or light) literature; (fr.) belles-lettres pl.; **Lisch** (⌣⌣⌣́) a. ⊛66 (schönwissenschaftlich) referring to popular writers or works, auch: belletristic.
Bellevue (⌣⌣wǘ) [fr. schöne Aussicht] f ⊛48 (⊛6) fair prospect, belvedere (= Belvedere).
Bell-hammel (⸗́...) [ndd.] m ⊛62 (Leithammel) bell-wether.
Belmontyl-öl ⊙ (⌣⌣⌣⌣́l) n ⊛62 belmontin(e).
be-lob(ig)en (⌣⌣́(⌣)⌣) I v/a. ⊛8* e-n ⸗ to eulogize a p.; et. ⸗ to praise (or commend) a th. — II ~ n ⊛23 = B/ung.
Be-lob(ig)ung (⌣⌣́(⌣)⌣) f ⊛46 eulogy; praise; commendation; honourable mention; ~**s-schreiben** (⸗́...) n ⊛62 letter in praise of a p.; commendatory epistle.
belog(en) (⌣⌣́(⌣)) impf. (p.p.) v. belügen.
be-lohnen (⌣⌣́) v/a., v/refl., v/impers. ⊛* e-n für et. ⸗ to reward a p. for ...; mit Geld: to remunerate for; nach Gebühr belohnt duly recompensed; mit Undank ⸗ to serve (or repay, requite) with ingratitude; es belohnt sich der Mühe (nicht) it is (not) worth the trouble, it repays (does not repay) one.
be-lohnens-wert (⸗́...) a. ⊛6 worthy of recompense, deserving a reward.
Belohner (⌣⌣́) m ⊛2, ~**in** f ⊛40 p. who rewards, &c. (s.belohnen); remunerator.
Be-lohnung (⌣⌣́) f ⊛46 1. (das Belohnen) rewarding. — 2. (Lohn) reward; remuneration; recompense (für ... for ...); eine schlechte ~ a poor return.
Belsazar (⌣⌣́⌣) npr/m. ⊛α. (letzter babyl. Kg., † 538 v. Chr.) Belshazzar.
Belt ⚧ (⌣́) npr/m. ⊛b. der Große (der Kleine) ~ (Meer-engen bei Dänemark) the Great (the Little) Belt.
be-luchsen (⌣⌣́⌣) v/a. ⊛* (betrügen) to deceive by deep cunning, to entrap.
be-lügen (⌣⌣́) [mhd.: belie] v/a. ⊛d*: e-n ⸗ to tell a p. a falsehood (F a story or a crammer), to deceive a p. by lies; er hat sie frech belogen F he told them a pack of lies; jedermann ⸗ to impose on everybody.
be-lustig-en (⌣⌣́⌣) I v/a. u. v/refl. ⊛8* 1. sich ⸗ mit ob. an to amuse or divert (o.s.) with; der Scherz wird ihn ⸗ the joke will tickle his fancy; er belustigte sich auf m-e Kosten he disported himself (or made merry) ad my expense; sich den ganzen Abend ⸗ to keep it up all the evening; ⸗d amusing, merry; auf ⸗de Art in an entertaining manner; amusingly. — 2. sich ⸗ über to make sport of. — II ~ n ⊛23 3. = B/ung.
Be-lustigung (⸗́...) f ⊛46 amusement; merrymaking; entertainment; sport(s pl.); ⸗en im Freien outdoor amusements pl.; ~**s-ort** (⸗́...) m ⊛62 place of entertainment; pleasure-gardens, recreation-grounds pl.
Belutsche (⌣⌣́) [pers. balū́tschi] m ⊛44, **Belutschin** f ⊛47 Bewohner[in] von Belutschistaⁿ) Baluchi, Belooch(e).
Belutschistan ⚧ (⌣⌣⌣́) npr/n. ⊛α. (Land, südöstl. Teil v. Iran; Alt.: Gedrosien) Baluchistan, Beloochistan. [belvedere.]
Belvedere (⌣⌣⌣́) [it.] n ⊛6 (schöne Aussicht)}
Bem. abbr. = Bemerkung.
be-mächtigen (⌣⌣⌣́) I v/refl. ⊛8* sich j-s, e-r Sache (gen.) ⸗ to seize (upon) or occupy a th.; to take possession of

♪ Musik; ⚒ Wissenschaft; ⚘ Pflanze; ⚧ Geographie; ⊙ Technik; ⚒ Bergbau; ⚔ Militär; ⚓ Marine; ⊛ Handel; ⚑ Post; 🚂 Eisenbahn.

[bemäfeln] — 170 — [benehmen]

a th.; to secure (a prisoner, a prize); to lay (or get) hold of; sich des Throns widerrechtlich ⁀ to usurp the throne. — II **Be-mächtigung** f ⓐ seizure; occupation; usurpation.
be-mäkeln (⌣⌢⌣) v.a. ⓐa* = befritteln.
be-malen (⌣⌢⌣) v.a. ⓐ* 1. auch v/refl. (sich) ⁀ to paint (o.s.) (all) over; thea. to make (o.s.) up; (anstreichen) to daub over; (schmücken) to decorate with paintings. — 2. ⋏ (mit e-m Male, Merkzeichen versehen) to mark.
be-mängeln (⌣⌢⌣) I v/a. ⓐa* to find fault with, to cavil at. — II ~ n ㉓ und **Bemäng(e)lung** (⌣⌢(⌣)⌣) f ⓐ fault-finding, cavilling, vgl. befritteln.
be-mannen ↓ (⌣⌢⌣) I v/a. ⓐ* ein Schiff: to man; (in Dienst stellen) to commission; to equip (for sea-service); ungenügend bemannt undermanned. — II ~ n ㉓ = Bemannung 1.
Be-mannung ↓(⌣)f ⓐ 1. manning; commissioning; equipment. — 2. Mannschaft ausschließl. d. Offiziere, Beamten u. Passagiere) (ship's crew, ship's company.
be-mänteln (⌣⌢⌣) I v/a. ⓐa* 1. to (cover with a) cloak. — 2. fig. (beschönigen) to palliate, extenuate, gloss over, varnish over; (verbergen) to cloak, disguise, hide. — II ~ n ㉓ u. B/ung f ⓐ 3. palliation; extenuation; disguise.
be-masten ↓ (⌣⌢⌣) I v/a. ⓐ* to mast, to furnish with masts. — II ~ n ㉓ = Bemastung 1.
Be-mastung ↓ (⌣⌢⌣) f ⓐ 1. masting. — 2. (die Masten, Rahen ꝛc.) the (ship's) masts, spars, yards, booms pl.
be-mausen F (⌣⌢⌣) v/a. ⓐ* to rob of trifles; to pilfer (or filch, F pinch, nick) from. [(or chip) with a chisel.]
be-meißeln ⊙ (⌣⌢⌣) v/a. ⓐa* to work]
be-meistern ⊙ (⌣⌢⌣) v/a. u. v/refl. ⓐa* to master or sway or subdue (one's passions); er kann sich nicht ⁀ he cannot contain (or control) himself; he has no control over himself; sich e-r Sache (gen.) ⁀ to make o.s. master of a th.; to get control over a th.
be-meldet (⌣⌢⌣) a. ⓐ = besagt, erwähnt.
be-mengen ⋏ (⌣⌢⌣) v/refl. ⓐ*: sich mit et., mit e-m ⁀ b.s. = befassen II.
be-merkbar (⌣⌢⌣) a. ⓐ perceptible, observable, visible; sich ⁀ m. to make o.s. conspicuous; ⁀keit f ⓐ perceptibility, perceptibleness; conspicuousness.
be-merken (⌣⌢⌣) I v/a. ⓐ* 1. (wahrnehmen) to perceive, observe, notice; (sehen) to see. — 2. (bezeichnen) to mark. — 3. (aufzeichnen) to note down. — 4. (erwähnen) to observe, remark, mention; er bemerkte folgendes he made the following remark(s) or observation(s); nebenbei bemerkt by the by. — II ~ n ㉓ 5. observation, &c. (f. 4); er schloß mit dem ~ he concluded by saying.
be-merkens-wert (⌣"...) a. ⓐ remarkable (durch for); worthy of notice or observation; not(ice)able, observable.
be-merklich (⌣⌢⌣) a. ⓐ observable; sich ⁀ machen to make o.s. conspicuous.
Be-merkung (⌣⌢⌣) f ⓐ observation, notice; (Aufzeichnung) note; (Ausspruch) observation, remark, utterance, comment; kritische ~en strictures pl.; ~en

machen über to make (or pass) remarks upon, to comment upon.
be-messen (⌣⌢⌣) I v/a. ⓐ* to measure (= messen). — II p.p. u. a. ⓐ (D10) measured; (carefully) adjusted; ~heit f ⓐ carefulness; exactness; proportion(ateness).
be-mitleiden (⌣⌢⌣⌣) I v/a. ⓐ* to pity, to commiserate; to take compassion (or pity) on. — II ~ n ㉓ = B/ung.
be-mitleidens-wert (⌣"...) a. ⓐ, ⁀würdig a. worthy of commiseration or compassion, to be pitied, pitiable; v. e-r Lage a. deplorable. [tion; compassion.]
Be-mitleidung (⌣⌢⌣) f ⓐ commisera-]
be-mittelt (⌣⌢⌣) a. ⓐ well off, with plenty of means; (wohlhabend) wealthy; well-to-do; in easy (or good, comfortable) circumstances.
Bemmchen (⌣⌣) n ㉓ dim. u. **Bemme** (⌣⌣) [Schul-sl.* grch. bamma] f ⓐ slice of bread and butter.
be-mogeln F (⌣⌢⌣) [F] v/a. ⓐa* to trick.
be-moosen (⌣⌢⌣) I v/n. u. v/refl. (fn.) ⓐ* to be(come) clad in moss; sich ⁀ to gather moss. — II be-moost (⌣⌢⌣) p.p. u. a. ⓐ moss-grown; (sehr alt) hoary; burschitos: Les Haupt, etwa: senior student; veteran; F (jolly) old boy or buck.
be-mörteln ⊙ (⌣⌢⌣) v/a. ⓐa* to plaster (over); to rough-cast (a wall).
be-mühen (⌣⌢⌣) ⓐ* I v/a. e-n ⁀ to trouble a p. (um for). — II sich ⁀ v/refl. to take pains or trouble; bitte, ⁀ Sie sich nicht! pray don't trouble (about it)!; Sie ⁀ sich umsonst you labour in vain; you have your trouble for nothing; sich ⁀, zu to endeavour to; sich für e-n um et. ⁀ to exert o.s. on behalf of a p.; sich um et. ⁀ to strive (or try) hard for a th.; sich um j-s Gunst, Liebe ⁀ to seek a p.'s ~; wenn Sie sich zu mir ⁀ wollen if you will come (round) to see me; F if you do not mind giving me a call; bitte, ⁀ Sie sich herauf, herunter! please step up!; please come down!; bitte, ⁀ Sie sich in das Zimmer please step (or walk) into the room; eifrig für et. bemüht sein to make great endeavours towards obtaining a th.
Be-mühung (⌣) f ⓐ trouble, pains sg., labour; exertion, endeavour; vergebliche ~ useless effort, fruitless endeavour.
be-müßigen (⌣⌢⌣) v/a. ⓐ* e-n ⁀, et. zu tun to oblige a p. to …; sich bemüßigt sehen et. zu tun to feel (in duty) bound to do a th.
be-muttern (⌣⌢⌣) v/a. ⓐ* to be like a mother to; junge Damen: to chaperon.
be-nachbart (⌣⌢⌣)-⌣) a. ⓐ 1. neighbouring, close (at hand). — 2. (angrenzend) adjacent to, adjoining, contiguous to.
be-nachrichtigen (⌣⌢⌣⌣⌣) v/a. ⓐ* e-n von et. ⁀ to inform (or advise) a p. of a th., to acquaint a p. with a th.; im voraus: to give a p. warning (or notice) of a th.; wir müssen ihn sofort ⁀ (, daß //) we must at once send him word or let him know (that //).
Be-nachrichtiger (⌣) m ㉒ person giving information; informant.
Be-nachrichtigung (⌣) f ⓐ information; notification; warning, notice; öffentliche: advertisement; um ~ bitten to

ask for advice or instructions; ~s-schreiben (⌣"...) n ㉒ letter of advice.
be-nachteiligen (⌣⌢⌣-⌣⌣) I v/a. ⓐ* e-n ⁀ to wrong (or injure, damage, prejudice) a p.; das wird ihn sehr ⁀ that will be a great detriment (or loss) to him. — II ~ n ㉓ u. **Be-nachteiligung** f ⓐ wrong or injury (inflicted on a p.), damage (done to a p.).
be-nageln (⌣⌢⌣) v/a. ⓐa* 1. (aufnageln) to fasten with nails to, to nail to. — 2. (mit Nägeln versehen) to furnish (or provide) with nails.
be-nagen (⌣⌢⌣) I v/a. ⓐ* to gnaw at; Knochen ꝛc.: to pick. — II be-nagt p.p. u. a. ⓐ gnawed, &c.; ⅋ eroded.
be-nähen (⌣⌢⌣) v/a. ⓐ* mit Packtuch ꝛc: to sew up in …; (säumen) to hem.
be-nahm (⌣⌢) impf. von benehmen (f. ds).
be-nam(s)en, fast † (⌣⌢⌣) ⓐ(⓺)* to name, to dub (= benennen).
be-nannt (⌣⌢) p.p. von benennen (f. ds).
be-narbt (⌣⌢) p.p. ⓐ scarred, med.: ⊘ cicatrized; agr. mouldy.
be-naschen (⌣⌢⌣) v/a. ⓐ* to taste or sip (dainties); to pick or pilfer (sweets).
be-nässen (⌣) v/a. ⓐ* to wet. [string.]
Bendel obb. (⌣) [ahd.; *Band] m, n ㉓]
bene F (⌣⌢) [lt.] adv. sich ⁀ tun to feast sumptuously; F to have a good (or fine, jolly) time of it; e-m ein Bene antun to give a p. a (great) treat.
be-nebeln (⌣⌢⌣) I v/a. ⓐa* 1. to (cover with) fog; to cloak in mist or haze. — 2. fig. (trüben) den Blick ꝛc.: to dim, cloud, obfuscate. — II be-nebelt p.p. u. a. ⓐ 3. in a fog, cloudy; F fig. (betrunken) tipsy, fuddled, (blind) drunk.
be-nebst † (⌣⌢) prp. = nebst.
benedei-en (⌣⌣⌢⌣) [mhd.; *lt. běnědī'cere] eccl. I v/a. ⓐ u. ⓑ (segnen) to bless. — II~n㉓ u. **Benedei-ung** f ⓐ benediction.
Benedikt (⌣⌣⌢) [lt.] npr/m. ⓓα. Benedict (dim. Bennet); ~a (⌣⌣⌢⌣) f ⓕⓕα. Benedicta; **~en-kraut** ⅋ (⌣⌣⌢...) n ㉖: a) (Cni'cus benedi'ctus); b) = Nelkenwurz (echte); ~rose ⅋ f = Pfingstrose (echte); ~wurz ⅋ f = ~en-kraut.
Benediktiner (⌣⌣⌢⌣) [der heil. Benedikt von Nursia, 480—543] m ㉒, **~in** f ⓰ Benedictine (monk, nun); ~(-liför) ("...) m ㉖ Benedictine; **~mönch** m, **~nonne** f = ~(in); **~orden** m Benedictine order; **~schnaps** m = -liför.
Benefiz (⌣⌣⌢) [lt. běněfi'cium] n ①a. benefit (night or performance); **~iant** (⌣⌣-(⌣)⌢), bff.: **~iat** (⌣⌣-⌣⌢) [lt.] m ㉒ beneficiary; auch = Stipendiat; **~ium** (⌣⌣⌢⌣) n ㉘ (Wohltat) benefit; **~vor-stellung** (⌣"...) f = Benefiz.
be-nehmen (⌣⌢⌣) [ahd.] ⓐa* I v/a. 1. e-m, e-r Sache et. ⁀ (entziehen) to take a th. away from …; das benimmt mir den Appetit it takes away (or spoils) my appetite; e-m den Atem ⁀ to put a p. out of breath; die Aussicht ⁀ to obstruct the view; e-m alle Hoffnung ⁀ to deprive a p. of all hope, to nip a p.'s hopes in the bud; das hat ihm die Lust dazu benommen it sets him against it; e-m den Mut ⁀ to dishearten (or discourage) a p., to take (all) the heart out of a p.; e-m seinen Zweifel ⁀ to remove a p.'s doubts. — 2. e-m

Signs (see page XVII): F familiar; P vulgar; ⌒ flash; ⋏ rare; † obsolete (died); * new word (born); ⁘ incorrect; ♪ music;

[beneiden] — 171 — [bequem]

Kopf 2 (betäuben) to make a p.'s head swim; von Getränken: to affect a p.'s head; benommen stupefied, giddy, benumbed. — **II ſich** 2 v/refl. 3. (ſich verhalten) to behave (o.s.); to conduct (or demean) o.s.; ſich anſtändig, fein 2 to show o.s. a gentleman or a lady; ſich feig 2 to play the coward; wir müſſen uns dort gut 2 we must be on our best behaviour there; er weiß ſich nicht zu 2 he has no manners; er hat ſich nicht gut (ob. ſchön) gegen ſie benommen he did not act properly towards (or deal fairly with) them; ſich 2 wie ein dummer Junge to behave like a (or to play the) stupid boy. — 4. ſich mit e-m 2 (verſtändigen) to agree with a p. — **III ~** n 23 c. 5. behaviour, conduct, demeanour; manner (of acting); (Haltung) bearing, carriage, deportment; feines ~ gentlemanly (ladylike) ways or manners pl.

be-neiden (◡⊥◡) v/a. ⊛* e-m et., e-n um et. 2 to envy (or begrudge) a p. his luck; to feel envious at a p.'s good fortune; er wird allgemein beneidet he is universally envied, he is an object of universal envy.

be-neidens-wert (⊥…) a. ⊛, 2würdig a. enviable, to be envied.

be-nennbar (◡⊥◡) a. ⊛ nameable.

be-nennen (◡⊥◡) **I** v/a. ⊛b* to name, denominate, weitS. to call, term; er wurde nach ſeinem Oheim benannt he was named (or christened) after his uncle. — **II ~** n 23 u. **Be-nennung** (◡⊥◡) f ⊛ name, denomination; title; term; falſche ~ misnomer; arith. Brüche auf gleiche ~ bringen to bring (or to reduce) fractions to a common denominator. — **III be-nannt** p.p. u. a. ⊛ (sur)named, called; arith. 2e Zahl concrete number or quantity.

be-netz/en (◡⊥◡) **I** v/a. ⊛* to moisten, sprinkle, wet, ſtärker: to soak, wash, water; mit Tau: to bedew; mit Tränen benetzt bathed in (or wet with) tears. — **II B/ung** f ⊛ moistening, &c., ſ. I.

Bengalen ♀ (◡⊥◡) npr/n. 23 α. (Provinz Oſt-indiens) Bengal.

bengaliſch (◡⊥◡) a. ⊛ Bengal; 2es Feuer, 2e Flamme Bengal fire or light; ♀ ~er Golf Bay of Bengal.

Bengel (⊥◡) [mhd.] m ⊛ 1. F obd. (Knüttel) cudgel, club. — 2. ⊕ typ. (Preß-)bar; ~ (Klöppel) e-r Glocke: clapper; ~ (Schwengel) am Brunnen: sweep. — 3. (Pa.⊛) fig. (derber Burſche) clumsy (or uncouth, rude) fellow; churl, boor, F impudent (or saucy) rascal; großer: great booby or lout; kleiner: little urchin.

Bengelei (◡◡⊥) f ⊛ churlishness; boorishness; (böſer Streich) clownish trick.

bengelhaft (⊥◡◡) a. ⊛ churlish, boorish.

be-nieſen (◡⊥◡) v/a. ⊛* 1. to sneeze at. — 2. to confirm by sneezing.

Benjamin (⊥◡⊥) [hebr.] npr/m. ⊛α. (Bn.) Benjamin, dim. Ben(ny).

Benne jüdd.(◡⊥) [: bin; it.; *flt.] f ⊛ a) (Korbwagen) basket-carriage; b) (Wagenkaſten) body of a carriage.

be-nommen (◡⊥◡) p.p. von benehmen (ſ. bſd. 2); **~heit** f ⊛ (o. pl.), **~ſein** n 23 stupor; giddiness; numbness.

be-nötigen (◡⊥◡◡) v/a. ⊛* et. 2, mehr gbr. einer Sache (gen.) 2 ob. **benötigt ſein** to be (or stand) in need (or in want) of a th.; benötigtenfalls in case of need; das benötigte Geld the necessary money, the required funds pl.

benſchen(◡◡) [jüd.; *lat. bĕnĕdīcere] v/a. ⊛ (ſegnen) to bless. [to number.]

be-nummern ⚘ od. öſt. (◡⊥◡) v/a. ⊛a*]

be-nutzbar (◡⊥◡) a. ⊛ available, useful, utilizable; (anwendbar) adaptable; **~keit** f ⊛ (o. pl.) availableness, availability, usefulness, adaptability.

be-nutz/en, be-nützen (◡⊥◡) **I** v/a. ⊛* 1. (anwenden) to use, utilize, employ; to avail o.s. of; to make the best of; mit Vorteil: to profit by; to take advantage of; to turn to (good) account; die Gelegenheit 2 to embrace the opportunity; to improve the occasion by. — 2. (ſich dienſtbar machen) to lay (or place) under contribution. — **II ~** n 23 u. **Be-nutzung** f ⊛ 3. use, utilization, employment; mit (ob. unter) ~ von with the aid of, making use of; unter vorſichtiger ~ ſeiner Hilfsmittel cautiously drawing upon his resources; einen Park ꝛc. zur öffentlichen ~ freigeben to open … to (or for the free use of) the public.

Benz-aldehyd ⚗ (◡⊥-⊥) m(n) ⊛ c. chm. (Bittermandelöl) benzaldehyde (C_7H_6O).

Benzin (◡⊥) [Benz(oe) u. lt. Endung -in] n ⊛ c. chm. (flüſſiger Kohlenwaſſerſtoff) petrol, ⚘ benzine; **~droſchke** (⊥…) f ⊛ benzine motor-cab; **~motor** m benzine motor; **~reſervoir** n benzine tank.

Benzo-e ⚗ (◡⊥◡) [14. sae.* ar.(lu)ban Java Weihrauch v. 3.] f ⊛ benzoin(e), benjamin-gum; **~äther** (⊥…) m ⊛ chm. benzoic ether ($C_7H_5O_2 \cdot C_2H_5$); **~baum** ⚘ m benjamin (or benzoine-)tree (Styrax Be'nzoin); **~ſalz** ꝛc. n, **2ſaures** Salz ⚗ m. benzoate; **~ſäure** f, chm. benzoic acid ($C_7H_6O_2$). [Benzoebaum.]

Benzo-in[1] ⚗ ⚙ (⊥-) [fr.] m ⊛ c. =]

Benzo-in[2] ⚗ (◡⊥) n ⊛ c. chm. benzoin, bitter-almond-oil camphor ($C_{14}H_{12}O_2$).

Benzol ⚗ (◡⊥) n ⊛ c. (o. pl.) (Steinkohlenbenzin) benzene. (C_7H_5O).

Benzo-yl ⚗ (◡◡⊥) n ⊛ c. chm. benzoyl.

Benzyl- alkohol ⚗ (◡⊥-⊥…) m, ⊛ benzyl (-ic) alcohol (C_7H_8O); **~äther** m, chm. benzyl(ic) ether.

be-ob-acht/en (◡⊥◡◡) mſt ◡⊥-b…) **I** v/a. ⊛* 1. (betrachten) to observe (aB. aſt., ⚓, ⚔); genau: to examine, study, watch; **ſich** 2 v/refl. u. v/recip. to examine o.s.; to look at each other. — 2. (wahrnehmen) to perceive, notice, see. — 3. (befolgen) to follow, to obey, to comply with. to act up to; med. (eine) Diät 2 to diet o.s.; den Anſtand 2 to act with propriety or decorum; Stillſchweigen 2 to keep silence. — **II ~** n 23 4. = **B/ung**. — **III 2d** p.pr. u. a. ⊛ 5. observing, &c.; die Formen ängſtlich 2d formal; 2de Haltung obſervant attitude; (forſchend) speculative; zu 2de Dinge rules pl. (for a p.'s guidance); (lt.) observanda pl.

Be-ob-achter (…⊥…) m ⚙, **~in** f ⊛ observer; controller; (Zuſchauer) spectator.

Be-obachtung (…⊥…) f ⊛ observance (a. aſt., ⚓ u. ⚔); (Befolgung) observance of, com-

pliance with; des Anſtandes: propriety. — **Be-obachtungs-gabe** (⊥…) f ⊛, **~geiſt** m power (or gift) of observation; **~heer** ⚔, **~korps** n army of observation; **~poſten** ⚔ m post of o., lookout, scouting picket; **~ſtation**, **~warte** f observatory.

be-ohrt (◡⊥) a. ⊛ having ears, ⚘ zo. ⚗ auriculate(d); fein, zart 2 quick of hearing, with sharp ears.

be-ordern (◡⊥◡◡) **I** v/a. ⊛a* e-n zu et. 2 (bſd. ⚔) to order (or command) a p. to do a th.; beordert werden to receive an order or a command; ⚘ (beſtellen) to order, commission, write for. — **II ~** n 23 u. **Be-orderung** (◡⊥◡◡) f ⊛ order(ing), command(ing).

be-packen (◡⊥◡) v/a. ⊛* to pack (or charge) with a load or burden, to load (or encumber) with luggage or baggage.

be-panzern (◡⊥◡) **I** v/a. ⊛ u. v/refl. to arm (o.s.) with a cuirass or a coat of mail; ⚓ to loricate; ⚓ Schiffe 2 to coat … with armour-plate(s); bepanzerter Kreuzer armoured cruiser; bepanzertes Schiff ironclad (ship).

be-pelzt (◡⊥) a. ⊛ covered with fur, fur-coated, furred.

be-perlen (◡⊥◡) v/a. ⊛* to set in pearls, to adorn with pearls; to pearl.

be-pfählen (◡⊥◡) **I** v/a. ⊛* to pale in, to enclose with palisades; to fence off with stakes; Weinſtöcke ꝛc. 2 to prop, to stake. — **II ~** n 23 u. **Be-pfählung** f ⊛ palisading, enclosure, fencing.

be-pflanzen (◡⊥◡) v/a. ⊛* to plant (with flowers, &c.); e-n Wald wieder mit Holz 2 to restock a forest (with trees).

be-pflaſtern (◡⊥◡◡) v/a. ⊛a* 1. e-e Gaſſe: to pave. — 2. Wunden: to (cover with a) plaster, to put a plaster on.

be-pflügen (◡⊥◡) v/a. ⊛* to plough.

be-pinſeln (◡⊥◡) v/a. ⊛* = pinſeln.

be-planken (◡⊥◡) **I** v/a. ⊛* to plank, to line with planks or boards. — **II Beplankung** f ⊛ planking.

be-platten ⊕ (◡⊥◡) v/a. ⊛* 1. die Hausflur ꝛc.: to tile. — 2. ⚓ ein Schiff: to plate, to case in armour-plate(s).

be-plaudern (◡⊥◡◡) v/a. ⊛a* to talk (or chat, gossip) about.

be-polſtern (◡⊥◡◡) v/a. ⊛a* = polſtern.

be-pudern (◡⊥◡◡) v/a. ⊛a* to (be)powder with; ⚗ bepudert pulveraceous.

be-quartieren ⚔ (◡◡⊥◡) v/a. ⊛* Soldaten 2 to quarter (or billet) soldiers.

be-quem (◡⊥) [ahd. = bekömmlich] a. ⊛ 1. (behaglich) commodious, comfortable, snug, easy; machen Sie es ſich 2 take your ease; ich machte mir's 2 I made myself quite at home; es e-m 2 machen to make a p. comfortable; to ease a p.'s work; to set a p. at ease; der Rock ſitzt 2 the coat fits well or comfortably; 2e Schuhe easy(-fitting) boots pl. — 2. (geeignet) convenient, suitable; (zur Hand) handy; 2 zu handhaben, zu tragen easy to handle, convenient to carry; wann es Ihnen 2 iſt whenever it may suit you, at your convenience; wie es Ihnen 2 iſt just as you can make it convenient. — 3. (träge) indolent, easy-going; ſtärker: lazy, slothful; er iſt ſehr 2 he won't bestir himself or put himself (much)

⚗ scientific; ⚘ botanical; ♀ geography; ⊕ machinery; ⚒ mining; ⚔ military; ⚓ marine; ⚘ commercial; ✉ postal; 🚂 railway.

[bequemen] — 172 — [bereden]

out; zu ~ sein, um // F to be too easy-going to //.
be-quemen (⌣´⌣) sich ~ v/refl. ⊛* **1.** abs. to yield to circumstances. — **2.** (sich fügen) to submit to, to put up with, to make the best of; sich nach den Umständen ~ to adapt (or accommodate) o.s. to (existing) circumstances; ihr müßt euch nach der Zeit ~ you must conform (or go) with the time(s pl.); ich mußte mich (wohl oder übel) dazu ~ I had to comply (whether I liked it or not); er wollte sich nicht dazu ~ he would not condescend to do it.
be-quemlich (⌣´⌣) a. ⓖⓤ u. adv. = bequem 1.
Be-quemlichkeit (⌣´⌣) f ⓕ **1.** (Behaglichkeit) comfort(ableness), snugness, ease; zu (oder nach) Ihrer ~ at your convenience or pleasure; Sie finden jede ~ dort you will find there every convenience or accommodation. — **2.** (Trägheit) indolence; laziness, sloth. **~s-liebe** (⌣´…) f ⓖ love of ease or of comfort.
Be-quemung (⌣´⌣) f ⓕ accommodation.
be-rändeln ⓑ*, **-randen** ⊛*, **-rändern** ⓑ* (⌣´⌣) **I** v/a. **1.** to (provide with a) margin, border, edge, rim; Münzen: to mill. — **II be-randet** p.p. u. a. ⓖⓤ **2.** Bed. des inf. — **3.** ♃ ⚹ marginate.
be-ranken (⌣´⌣) v/a. ⊛* to cover (or entwine) with tendrils. [casting.]
Be-rapp ⊙ (⌣´) m ⓑb. Maurerei: rough-⌐
be-rappen¹ ⊙ (⌣´⌣) [rappen] v/a. ⊛* **1.** Maurerei: (rauh verputzen) to plaster or rough-cast (a wall). — **2.** for. to rough-hew or baulk (trees or timber).
be-rappen² (⌣´⌣) [F* Rappen] v/a. ⊛* **1.** ⚹ (mit Geld versehen) to supply with money; berappt (gut bei Kasse) sein to be flush of money. — **2.** (bezahlen) to pay, F to fork out, dub up.
be-rasen (⌣´⌣) ⓖⓐ* **I** v/a. to (cover with) turf; beraster Platz greensward; lawn. — **II** sich ~ v/refl. to form (into) a lawn.
be-raspeln (⌣´⌣) v/a. ⓑ* to rasp.
be-rat/en (⌣´⌣) **I** v/a., v/n. (h.) u. sich ~ v/refl. ⓖⓐ* **1.** e-n ~ to advise (or counsel) a p., to give a p. advice; gut (schlecht) ~ sein to be well (ill) advised. — **2.** fast † (ausrüsten) Gott berate euch! God help you!; auch v/refl. sich mit et. ~ to provide o.s. with a th.; noch jur.: Le (bei Lebzeiten der Eltern durch eine gewisse Summe [Beratung] abgefundene) Kinder children who received their portion (of the inheritance) during their parents' lifetime. — **3.** ⚹ e-n ~ (um Rat fragen) to consult a p. — **4.** et. ~, v/n. über et. ~: a) (erwägen) to deliberate on a th. b) auch v/refl. sich über et. mit andern ~ to take counsel (or compare notes) about s.th. (or to confer) with others. — **5.** sich ~ (beschließen) to resolve. — **II ~** n 23 **6.** = B/ung. — **III** ~d p.pr. u. a. ⓖⓤ **7.** ⓛde Versammlung ꝛc. deliberative assembly. — **8.** (Rat suchend) consultative. — **9.** (Rat gebend) advisory.
Be-rater (⌣´⌣) m ㉒, **~in** f ㊼ **1.** (Ratgeber[in]) adviser, counsellor. — **2.** (Fürsorger[in]) patron(ess), protector (f protectress, protectrix).
be-ratschlag/en (⌣´⌣) **I** v/n. (h.) u. sich ~ v/refl. ⊛* = beraten 4; sich heimlich

mit⸗ea. ~ to be in secret conference or close consultation, to be closeted together. — **II** ~ n 23 u. **B**/ung = deliberation; consultation; conference.
Be-ratung (⌣´⌣) f ㊻ advice, counsel; (Beratschlagung) deliberation; der Ärzte: consultation; (Konferenz) conference; ein Plan ist in ~ a scheme is under consideration; jur. f. beraten 2; **~s-saal** (″…) m ⓺² council-chamber; **-stimme** f deliberative voice; vote in council; **-zimmer** n eines Arztes: consulting-room.
be-rauben (⌣´⌣) [: bereave] ⊛* **I** v a. e-n ~: a) mit gen. to deprive or despoil (stärker: to rob or strip) of; (entblößen) to denude of; (entkleiden) to divest of; eines Besitzes: to dispossess of …; des Thrones: to dethrone; des Wahlrechts: to disfranchise; b) meist ohne gen.: to rob, plunder, strip; to pillage or sack (a town); to rifle (a p.'s) pockets; fig. to fleece a p.; des Gatten beraubt bereft of her spouse; widowed. — **II** sich ~ v/refl. to deprive o.s. of a th.; sich eines Vergnügens ~ to deny o.s. (or to forego) a pleasure. — **III** ~ n 23 = B/ung.
Be-rauber (⌣´⌣) m ㉒, **~in** f ㊼ despoiler, robber; einer Kasse: embezzler.
Beraubung (⌣´⌣) f ㊻ deprivation; spoliation; denudation; divestiture; robbery; (Unterschlagung) embezzlement, peculation.
be-räuchern (⌣´⌣) v/a. ⓑ* to perfume (with incense, &c.); fig. to flatter or adulate. [fumigation; fig. adulation.]
Be-räucherung (⌣´⌣) f ㊻ perfuming;⌐
Be-rauh⸗wehrung ⚓ ⊙ (⌣″…) f ㊻ (Uferbedeckung mit Strauchholz u. Flechtwerk) fortification of a bank by means of faggots and wicker-work.
be-rauschen (⌣´⌣) ⓑ¹* **I** v/a. to intoxicate, to inebriate; to make drunk or tipsy; ⓛd intoxicating; ⓛdes Getränk, auch: alcoholic liquor; ⓛder Wein heady wine; berauscht intoxicated (a. fig.), drunk, nur fig.: overflowing (with joy, &c.). — **II** sich ~ v/refl. to drink to excess; F to get drunk or tipsy or boozy. — **III** ~ n 23 u. **Be-rauschung** f ㊻ intoxication; drunkenness; tipsiness; bsd. fig. inebriation.
Berber (⌣´⌣) **I** m ㉒, **~in** f ㊼ (Bewohner[in] der Berberei) Berber, Moor. — **II** a. inv. Berber, of (the) Barbary (States), Barbaresque.
Berberei ♀ (⌣´⌣) npr/f. ㊻a. (Nordwesten von Afrika) chm. Barbary (States pl.).
Berberin¹ (⌣´⌣) f ㊼ f. Berber.
Berberin² ♃ (⌣´⌣) [lt.] n ⓒc. chm. berberine ($C_{20}H_{17}NO_4$). [Berberitze.]
Berberis (⌣´⌣) ♃ (⌣″…) [neult., *ar.] f, inv. =⌐
berberisch (⌣´⌣) a. ⓖⓤ = Berber II.
Berberitze ♀ (⌣´⌣) [Berberis] f ㊽, **~=baum** (″…) m ㉒, **-beere** f, **-strauch** m (Sauerdorn) barberry (Be'rberis).
Berber⸗pferd (⌣″…) n ㉒, **-roß** n Barbary horse or steed, barb. [(over).]
be-rechen ⊙ (⌣´⌣) v/a. ⊛* agr. to rake⌐
be-rechenbar (⌣´⌣) a. ⓖⓤ calculable, computable; ♪ appreciable; ♃ math. genau ~ (rational) rational.
Be-rechenbarkeit (⌣´⌣⌣) f ㊻ calculability; computability; math. rationality.

be-rechn/en (⌣´⌣) ⓑa* **I** v/a. **1.** to calculate (auch fig.); (zf.-zählen) to sum (or cast, total) up; (überschlagen) to compute; (abschätzen) to value (or estimate) at; allg.: to reckon; auf Erregung der Leidenschaften berechnet calculated (or adapted) to rouse the passions (⊛) fremde Münzen ꝛc. auf einheimische ~ to reduce … — **2.** ✡ = anrechnen 1; als Schuld: to debit; wir ~ Ihnen nur 200 Mark we charge you only £ 10. — **II** sich ~ v/refl. **3.** ✡ sich mit e-m ~ to balance (or settle) accounts with a p.; et., das sich nicht ~ läßt s.th. beyond calculation. — **III** ~ n 23 **4.** = B/ung. — **IV** ~d p.pr. u. a. ⓖⓤ **5.** in den Bed. des inf. — **6.** fig. ⓛder Mensch calculating (stärker: cold-hearted, scheming) person.
Be-rechner (⌣´⌣) m ㉒, **~in** f ㊼ calculator, computer, reckoner; accountant.
be-rechnet (~) p.p. u. a. ⓖⓤ **1.** Bed. des inf. — **2.** (vorausbedacht) premeditated; wohl ~ well calculated or thought out; darauf ~ zu calculated (or purposing) to.
Be-rechnung (⌣´⌣) f ㊻ calculation; reckoning; bsd. ✡ account; bei billigster ~ on most moderate terms, at the lowest quotation or price; (Umrechnung) reduction; falsche ~ miscalculation; ungefähre ~ rough estimate; math. Lehre von der ~ der Dreiecke trigonometry; typ. in ~ arbeiten to do piece-work, to work by the piece, to be on lines; **~s-weise** f ⓺² mode (or method) of calculation.
be-rechtig/en (⌣´⌣) **I** v/a. ⓑ* e-n zu et. ~ to give a p. a right (or to entitle a p.) to (do) a th.; (bevollmächtigen) to authorize or empower a p. (to do a th.); to warrant a p. (in doing a th.); was berechtigt Sie zu der Meinung, daß //? what makes you think that //?; er berechtigt zu großen Erwartungen great things may be expected of him, he bids fair to have a great future. — **II** ~ n 23 = B/ung. — **III be-rechtigt** p.p. u. a. ⓖⓤ entitled (or qualified) to, justified in; jur. able, capable, competent to; ⓛe Hoffnung legitimate hope; **~e(r)** m, **~e** f ⓺⁷ person entitled (or authorized) to.
Be-rechtigung (⌣´⌣) f ㊻ authorization to; right (or title) to; qualification for; bürgerliche ~ civil (or civic) rights pl.; franchise; das Gerücht hat keine ~ is groundless or without foundation; ~ e-r Lehranstalt für den Militärdienst ꝛc. privilege attaching to a (state-)school; **~s-grund** (″…) m ⓺² title; **-schein** m, **-zeugnis** n qualifying certificate, für den Militärdienst ꝛc.: certificate of admission for one year's service, &c.).
be-red/en (⌣´⌣) **I** v/a. u. v/refl. ⊛* **1.** et., e-n ~ to speak (or talk) of a th. or a p. — **2.** et. ~ (beraten) to discuss (stärker: to debate) a th.; v/refl. sich mit e-m über et. ~ to confer with a p. about a th.; sie haben sich mit⸗ea. beredet they have concocted it between them. — **3.** e-n (trügerisch, listig) ~ to impose upon a p.; bsw. ~ in e-m einer ⓛde (gen.) ~, e-m et. ~ to make a p. believe (a lie). — **4.** (überreden) e-n zu et. ~, e-n et. zu tun ~ to prevail (up)on a p. to do

Zeichen (s. S. XVII): F familiär; P Volkssprache; Γ Gaunersprache; ⚹ selten; † alt (auch gestorben); * neu (auch geboren); ⧺ unrichtig;

[beredsam] — 173 — [bergen]

a th., to persuade (or induce) a p. to do a th. — II ~ n 23 5. = B/ung.
be-redsam (⌣⌣⌣) a. 66 eloquent (= beredt); **~keit** (⌣⌣⌣) f 46 eloquence; readiness (or fluency) of speech.
be-redt (⌣⌣) a. 66 eloquent; auf das 2(e)ste most eloquently; Ler Sprecher fluent speaker; adv. sich 2 ausdrücken to have a good flow of speech, F to have the gift of the gab. [conference.
Be-redung (⌣⌣⌣) f 46 discussion, debate,
be-regnen (⌣⌣⌣) 2 b* 1. et. wurde beregnet s.th. was moistened by (or wet with) rain. — 2. fig. (bedecken) e-n mit Blumen 2 to shower flowers upon a p. or to smother a p. with flowers.
be-regt (⌣⌣) a. 66 Kanzleisprache: aforesaid; der Le Gegenstand the subject mentioned or alluded to or in question.
Be-reich (⌣⌣) m, n @c. reach; (Umgebung) environs pl.; e-s Schlosses 2c.: purlieu; e-r Kunst, Wissenschaft 2c.: department, sphere, domain; ⚔ im ~e (aus dem ~e) der Geschütze within (beyond the) range of the guns; das gehört nicht in meinen ~ that is beyond my province or out of my range (F line); im ~ meines Gesichtskreises within my ken; außer dem ~e der Menschenaugen poet. far from mortal ken.
be-reichern (⌣⌣⌣) 2 a* I v/a. to enrich; fig. den Geist mit Kenntnissen 2 to store the mind with ... — II sich 2 v/refl. to enrich o.s., to acquire (great) wealth, F to make one's pile. — III ~ n 23 u. **Be-reicherung** f 46 enrichment.
be-reifen[1] ⊙ (⌣⌣⌣) [Reisen] v/a. 68* Böttcherei: ein Faß 2 to hoop ...
be-reifen[2] (⌣⌣⌣) [Reif, gefrorner Tau] I v/a. 68* to cover with hoar-frost; bereift hoary; ✿, zo. pruinous, pruinose. — II ~ n 23 u. **Be-reifung** f 46 hoar-frost.
be-reinigen (⌣⌣⌣⌣)v/a.68*(ins reine bringen) to clear up, to settle (an account, &c.).
be-reisen (⌣⌣⌣) I v/a. 68* 1. ein Land 2c.: to travel (over or across), to visit (or see, cross) as a traveller or on one's travels, to journey (or walk. drive, ride) through; Meere: to navigate; Messen 2 to frequent fairs. — II bereist p.p. und a. 66 2. Des Land ... known to travellers. — 3. Ler (weit gereister) Mann one who has travelled much, great traveller.
Be-reisung (⌣⌣⌣) f 46 travelling over, &c.; (Besichtigung) inspection.
be-reit (⌣⌣) [mhd.: ready] a. 66 prepared or ready (for a th., to do a th.); (zu et. geneigt) disposed to; schnell 2 prompt; sich 2 finden lassen zu to show an inclination to; et. 2 machen to prepare (or get ready) for a th.; 2 steh(e)n, sich 2 halten to keep ready (or in readiness) for.
be-reiten[1] (⌣⌣⌣) [bereit m.] I v/a. u. v/refl. 69* 1. ein Mahl 2c.: to prepare, to make (or get) ready. — 2. (machen) a) to make; Tee, Punsch, a.: to brew; Leder: to curry, to dress; b) mit abstr. Objekt: e-m Kummer 2 to grieve a p.; die Last hat er sich selbst bereitet the burden is of his own making; e-m Unannehmlichkeiten 2 to cause a p. annoyance; e-m den Untergang 2 to work (or bring about)

a p.'s ruin; e-m Vergnügen (Verdruß, e-e Überraschung) 2 to give a p. pleasure (trouble, a surprise); ✿ e-m Wechsel eine gute Aufnahme 2 to honour a bill. — II ~ n 23 3. = Bereitung.
be-reiten[2] (⌣⌣⌣) [reiten] I v/a. 69b* 1. eine Gegend, bsd. besichtigend 2 to inspect ... on horseback; 2 to ride across ... — 2. man. ein Pferd 2 to break in a horse. — II **be-ritten** p.p. u. a. 66 (D 9) 3. mounted; 2 machen (mit Reitpferden versehen) to (re)mount or horse (cavalry, &c.); Ler Schutzmann mounted constable; Le engl. Landwehr yeomanry.
Be-reiter[1] (⌣⌣⌣) [bereiten[1]] m 23 one who prepares, &c.; ⊙ (Zurichter) des Leders leather-dresser, currier; ~ (Appretierer) des Tuches cloth-dresser.
Be-reiter[2] (⌣) [bereiten[2]] m 23 1. (Beamter) mounted inspector. — 2. man. riding-master; (Zureiter) horse-breaker, rough-rider; für Rennpferde: trainer; Zirkus: equestrian.
be-reit-legen (⌣⌣...) I v/a. 68** = 2 stellen; II ~ n 23: ⚔ ~ der Munition holding ready the ammunition.
be-reits (⌣⌣) adv. already; previously.
Be-reitschaft (⌣⌣⌣) f 46 (o. pl.) readiness, preparedness; in~haben (oder halten) to keep in readiness, Geld: to keep in hand, to have (or hold) ready; sich stets in~halten to be (or stand) on the alert; in~setzen to prepare, to equip; ~s-aufstellung ⚔ (⌣...) f 46 position taken up in anticipation (of an action, &c.).
be-reit-stellen (⌣⌣...) v/a. 68*** to keep ready, to prepare (for action, &c.).
Be-reitung (⌣⌣⌣) f 46 preparation; ✿ manufacturing, manufacture; making. [manner of preparing.
Be-reitungs-art (⌣⌣⌣...) f 46. **~weise** f
be-reit-willig (⌣⌣⌣⌣) a. 66 ready or willing (to do a th.); (dienstfertig) obliging; (eifrig) eager, zealous, prompt; adv. et. 2 tun to do ... willingly or gladly (stärker: with all one's heart).
Be-reitwilligkeit (⌣⌣⌣⌣~) f 46 readiness, willingness; obligingness; eagerness, zeal, promptitude.
Berenike (⌣⌣⌣⌣) [äg.; *grch. Phereníke Siegbringerin] npr/f. 39 48 3. ast. Haar der ~ Berenice's hair (Coma Berenices).
be-rennen (⌣⌣⌣) I v/a. 9b* e-e Festung: a) (einschließen) to invest; einen Hafen: to blockade; b) (angreifen) to assault, to make an assault upon. — II ~ n 23 und **Be-rennung** f 46 investment; blockade; assault.
be-reu/en (⌣⌣⌣) I v/a. 68* to repent (of) a th.; schwächer: to regret having done a th.; to be sorry for (having done) a th.; das soll er 2! he shall rue (or smart for) it! — II ~ n 23 = B/ung
be-reuens-wert (⌣⌣⌣⌣...) a. 66, 2**würdig** a. worthy of repentance or regret.
Be-reuung (⌣⌣⌣) f 46 repentance, (feeling) regret; (Buße) penitence.
Berg (⌣) [ahd.: barrow] m@b. 1. mountain; mit folgendem npr. meist: mount, 3B.: Mount Ætna; feuerspeiender ~: volcano; hoher, spitzer ~: peak (3B. of Teneriffe); den ~ hinan, hinab up (the) hill, down (the) hill; zu ~ fahren: a) (SCH.) to ascend (or climb) the moun-

tains; b) ⚓ to go up the river. — 2. fig.: gold(e)ne ~e versprechen to promise wonderful (or impossible) things; hinter dem ~e halten to keep one's own counsel; hinter dem ~e wohnen auch noch Leute there are others as clever as you; da sich(e)n die Ochsen am ~e there we (they) are stuck in the mud or at our (their) wits' end; there is the rub; er ist über alle ~e, über ~ und Tal he is out of reach; he has vanished or taken to his heels; über den ~ (über Schwierigkeiten hinaus) sein to be round the corner or out of the wood; wir sind noch nicht über den ~ we have not come to the end of it yet; das Haar stand ihm zu ~e his hair stood on end.
berg-ab (⌣⌣) adv. down hill; fig. es geht mit ihm 2 allg.: he is on the decline. vom Alter: F he's on the shady (or wrong) side (of forty, &c.); im Geschäft: he is going down; **~abhang** (⌣⌣⌣) m 62 mountain-slope; hillside; **~abhänge** mountain-sides pl.: 2**abwärts** (⌣⌣⌣) adv. = 2 ab; 2**ader** ⚒ (⌣⌣...) f mineral vein; **~ahorn** ✿ m sycamore (Acer pseudoplatanus); **~akademie** ⚒ f in Deutschland 2c.: university for students of mining; **~akademiker** m student of mining; **~alaun** m. min. rock-alum.
Bergamott-baum ✿ (⌣⌣⌣...) [Bergamo, it. St.] m 62 bergamot (Citrus berga'mea).
Bergamotte (⌣⌣⌣⌣) [türk. beg armu'di Fürstenbirne] f 48 bergamot (pear).
Bergamott-öl ✿ (⌣⌣⌣...) n 62 v. B.-baum: bergamot oil, essence of bergamot.
Berg-amsel (⌣⌣...) f 62 orn. ring-ousel (Turdus torqua'tus); **~amt** ⚒ n in Sachsen 2c.: mine-office; board of mines; 2**an** (⌣⌣) adv. up hill; 2 steigend ascending, acclivous; ⚓ 2 fahrend going upstream; **~arbeit** ⚒ (⌣...) f mining; **~arbeiter** ⚒ m miner; 2**auf** (⌣⌣⌣) adv. = 2 an; **~bahn** ✿ (⌣...) f mountain- (or alpine-) railway; **~bau** ⚒ m mining (industry); working of a mine or pit.
Bergbau-berechtigung (⌣⌣...) f 62 right of mining; **~gebiet** n mining-district; **~kunde** f science of mining; **~kundige(r)** m mining expert; mineralogist; **~verein** m mining association.
Berg-beamte(r) ⚒ (⌣...) m 62 manager (or officer) of a mine; **~behörde** f = **~amt**; **~beschreibung** f: ⚒ orography; **~bewohner(in /)** m mountaineer; **~blau** n, chm. (Farbe) mountain-blue; lapis lazuli; **~bohrer** ⚒ m zu Sprenglöchern: terrier; **~braun** n (Malerfarbe) umber; **~butter** f, min. rock-butter; **~dorf** n mountain- (or mining-) hamlet; **~durchstich** m tunnel. [country or ground.
Berge ⚒ (⌣⌣) f (unhaltiges Gestein) barren
Berge[1]**-geld** ⚓ (⌣⌣...) [bergen] n 62 = **~lohn**; **~gut** n salvage(-goods pl. or -stock); **~hafen** m harbour of refuge.
berge[2]**-hoch** (⌣⌣) [Berg] a. 66 mountainhigh, as high (or big) as a mountain.
Berg-eisen ⚒ (⌣...) n 62 miner's pickaxe.
Bergelchen (⌣⌣⌣) n 23 (dim. von Berg) = Berglein. [or charges pl.
Berge[1]**-lohn** ⚓ (⌣⌣...) m 62 salvage (money)
bergen (⌣⌣) [ahd.: bury] I v/a. u. v/refl. b. (sich) 2 to save or shelter (o.s.) from danger; to secure (o.s.) against in-

♪ Musik; ⚒ Wissenschaft; ✿ Pflanze; ⚓ Geographie; ⊙ Technik; ⚒ Bergbau; ⚔ Militär; ⚓ Marine; ✿ Handel; ✉ Post; 🚂 Eisenbahn

[Bergenge] — 174 — [Bericht]

jury; to protect (o.s.) against enemies; es ist (gut) geborgen it is safely stowed away or ↓ safely landed; er ist gut geborgen he is quite safe or secure; ↓: gestrandete Güter ⚑ to recover salvage (-goods); jur. Eigentümer einer geborgenen Ladung salvagee; Segel ⚑ to take in (or shorten) ...; fig. er ist ein geborgener Mann he has plenty to live on, he is well off or F in clover; die Erde birgt in ihrem Schoße // the earth conceals (or contains) in its womb //. — II ~ n ㉓ = Bergung.
Berg=enge (ˊ…) f ㉖ (narrow) defile.
Berger ↓ (ˊ…) m ㉒ sa(l)ver, wrecker.
Bergere (vGˊv) [fr.] f ㊽ (breiter tiefer Polsterstuhl) comfortable stuffed (arm-)chair. 〔right of salvage.〕
Berge=recht ↓ u. ✹ (ˊ…) [bergen] f ㉒〕
Berg=erz (ˊ…) n ㉒ crude ore.
Berges=hang (ˊ…) m ㉒ mountain-slope; =**höhe** f, =**wand** f = Berg=...
Berg=fach (ˊ…) n ㉒ mining (profession); =**fahrer** ✕ m superintendent of a mine or the miners; =**fahrt** f: a) mountain-climbing; b)↓der Flußschiffe: up-passage; =**fall** m land-slip; =**farbe** f (durch metallische Beimischung gefärbte Erde) (natural) mineral dye; (Oder) ochre; ²**fertig** ✕ a. ㊻ incapacitated for mining (work); =**feste** ✕, =**festung** f mountain-fort (-ress); =**fex** m(amateur)mountaineer; alpinist; =**fink** m, orn. brambling (Fringi′lla montifringi′lla); =**flachs** m, min. mountain-flax, amianthus; =**freiheit** ✕ f right of mining; =**fried** m belfry; =**gang** ✕ m lode (of ore). mineral vein; =**gebrauch** m miners' custom; =**gegend** f mountainous region, upland; =**gegenschreiber** ✕ m controller of mines; =**geist** m mountain-goblin, gnome; =**gelb** n, min. yellow ochre; =**gesetze** n/pl. mining regulations pl.; =**gewerk(schaft)** f) n ✕ miners' union; =**gezäh**, =**gezeug** n ✕ miner's tools pl.; =**gipfel** m mountain-top; =**gold** n gold produced from a mine; =**grat** m mountain-ridge; =**grün** n (Malerfarbe) mountain-green; =**gut** ✕ n ore minerals, fossils pl.; =**halde** f mountain-slope, hillside, barrow; =**harz** n, min. (fossil) bitumen; =**haue** ✕ f miner's pick; =**hauptmann** m head manager (or director) of mines; als Titel etwa: (Government) Chief Inspector of Mines; ²**hin=ab** (ˊ…) adv. = ²**ab**; ²**hoch** (ˊ…) a. = bergehoch; =**höhe** f: a) height of a mountain; b) summit of a mountain; =**hoheit** ✕ f ownership (or supreme control) over (or of) a mine; =**höhle** f mountain-cave(rn); =**holz** n, min. (Holz=asbest) rock-wood; [von bergen v/a.] ↓ großes ~ mainwale; =**hund** ✕ m miner's truck or tram; =**hütte** f: a) chalet, alpine hut; b) ✕ pit-roof, cover of a pit or mine.
bergicht, **bergig** (ˊ…) a. ㊻ mountainous, hilly, covered with mountains.
Berg=ingenieur (ˊ…) m ㉒ mining engineer; =**junge** m miner's boy; =**kamm** m crest; =**kappe** f miner's cap; =**kegel** m cone-shaped mountain, conical peak; =**kessel** m deep gorge or hollow; =**kette** f chain of mountains,

mountain-range; =**kiesel** m, min. rockflint, ⚘ petrosilex; ²**kieselartig** a., min. ⚘ petrosiliceous, =**kluft** f ravine, chasm; =**knappe** ✕ m miner, pitman; =**knappschaft** ✕ f corporation (or staff) of miners; =**kork** m, min. (Art Asbest) mountain-cork or -leather; =**krankheit** f beim Ersteigen hoher Berge: alpine climber's malady, complaint due to the rarefaction of the air in elevated regions; =**krägler** F m = =fex; =**kristall** m, min. rock-crystal; =**kübel** ✕ m miner's bucket; =**kunde** f: ⚘ orology; =**kupfer** n, min. native copper; =**kuppe** f dome-shaped summit; =**land** n hill(y) (or mountainous) country; highland; =**lauch** ♀ m carinate garlic (A′llium carina′tum); ²**läuf(t)ig** ✕ a. u. adv. after the fashion of miners; =**leder** n, min. = =fex; =**lehne** f mountain-side.
Berglein (ˊ…) n ㉓ (dim. von Berg) tiny hill, small mountain.
Berg=leute (ˊ…) ㉖ pl. v. =mann; =**luft** f mountain-air; =**mann** m (pl. =leute): a) mountaineer; b) ✕ miner; Kohlenbergwerk: collier, pitman; =**männchen** n = =geist; ²**männisch** a. ㊻ relating to (or customary among) miners, vgl. ²üblich); =**mannsausdruck** m term used by miners; =**mannsleder** n miner's apron; =**mannstracht** f miner's dress; =**mehl** n, ⚚ bergmehl, min. infusorial earth; =**meister** ✕ m mining surveyor; =**melisse** ♀ f = Kalaminthe; =**messer** n miner's knife; =**milch** f, min. rock-milk; fossil farina; =**minze** ♀ = Feldkalaminthe; =**naphtha** f, min. = =öl; =**nelke** ♀ f sheep's-bit (Iasi′one monta′na); =**nymphe** f, myth. oread; =**öl** n, min. petroleum; vgl. =pech; =**ordnung** ✕ f mining regulations pl.; =**partei** f, hist. im französischen Konvent: the Mountain; =**paß** m mountain-pass; =**pech**, min. (vgl. =teer) asphalt(um), bitumen; =**pfad** m mountain-path; =**predigt** f: a) sermon for miners; b) bibl. the Lord's) Sermon on the Mount (Matth. 5,1 2c.); =**rat** m: a) board of a mining company; b) (Mitglied dieses Rates) director of a mining company; =**recht** ✕ n: a) right to work a mine; b) miners' (code of) laws; ²**rechtlich** ✕ a. according to the laws and statutes on mining; =**regal** ✕ n mining royalty; =**reise** f mountain-tour; =**revier** ✕ n mining-district; =**rot** n, min. red ochre, (Rötel) red chalk; =**rücken** m mountain-ridge or -crest; =**rutsch** m landslip; =**sachen** ✕ f/pl. mining concerns pl.; =**salz** n, min. rock-salt; =**schicht** ✕ f miner's overtime (shift); =**schlitten** m mountain- (or ✕ miner's) sledge; =**schloß** n mountain-castle; =**schlucht** f mountain-gorge, ravine, glen; =**schotte** m. =**schottin** f Scotch Highlander; =**schreiber** ✕ m clerk of a mine; =**schule** f mining-school; school for miners; =**schüler** m pupil (or student) of a mining-school or -academy; =**schwaden** ✕ m fire-damp; =**schwefel** m, min. native sulphur; =**see** m mountain-lake; =**segen** ✕ m mining produce, output of a mine or pit; =**seife** f, min. (Art Ton) mountain-soap; =**spitze** f

mountain-top; summit; peak; =**steigen** n mountain-climbing; =**steiger** m: a) mountain-climber; b) ✕ foreman of miners; =**stock** m: a) alpenstock; mountaineer's climbing pole (with iron point); b) massive rock; =**straße** f: a) mountain-road; b) ♀ id. (range of hills between Darmstadt and Heidelberg); =**strom** m mountain-stream; torrent; =**stufe** ✕ f ore mixed with dead rock; =**sturz** m landslip; =**sucht** ✕ f miner's pulmonary disease; =**teer** m a) mineral tar; b) asphalt; =**tracht** f mountaineer's (or miner's) garb; =**trift** f (Alm) alpine meadow; ²**üblich** ✕ a. usual among miners, vgl. ²männisch; =**ulme** ♀ f witch-elm (Ulmus monta′na); = **und Tal=bahn** f switchback.
Bergung (ˊ…) [bergen] f ㊻ bsd. ↓ salvage.
Bergungs=korps (ˊ…) n ㉒ bei Feuersbrünsten: salvage-corps.
berg=unter (ˊ…) adv. down hill.
Berg=versatz (ˊ…) m ㉒ filling-up; gobbin(g); =**verwalter** ✕ m administrator of a mine; =**verwaltung** ✕ f administration of mines; =**volk** n: a) mountain-tribe or -race; b) ✕ (body of) miners pl.; =**wage** f, surv. (Böschungswage) batter-level; =**wand** f: a) precipitous side of a mountain, steep mountain-side; b) ✕ (taube Wand) dead wall; attle, rubbish; =**wand(e)rer** m alpine tourist; =**wand(e)rung** f alpine (or mountain-)tour or excursion; =**wardein** ✕ m assayer of a mine; ²**wärts** adv. towards the mountains, mountainward; =**wasser** n mountain-stream; ✕ water in a mine; =**weide** f mountain-pasture; =**welt** f alpine world; =**werk** ✕ n mine; (Kohlengrube) pit.
Bergwerks=aktie ✕ (ˊ…) f ㉖. =**anteil** m share in a mining property; =**aktienmarkt** m Börse: mining market; =**arbeiten** f/pl. mining operations pl.; (Schürfarbeiten) prospecting; =**bahn** in Bergwerken: (underground) railway in a mine or pit; =**gesellschaft** f mining company; =**kunde** f metallurgy; science of mining; =**produkte** n/pl. = Bergsegen; =**unternehmer** m prospector; mining adventurer or lessee.
Berg=wesen ✕ (ˊ…) n ㉒ mining (affairs or concerns pl.); =**wissenschaft** f = =werkskunde; =**zehent(e)** ✕ m tithe (or royalty) on the profits of a mine; =**zinnober** m. min. native cinnabar; =**zwiebel** ♀ f = =lauch.
Beriberi (ˊvˊvv) [ind. große Schwäche] f ㊻ path. beriberi.
Be=richt (vˊ) [mhd.*richten] m ⓤb. report (to a superior); eingehender: detailed account, full particulars pl.; statistischer: (official) returns pl.; (Protokoll) minutes pl.; in Zeitungen: kurzer (Tages=)~ short summary (of the day's news); ~ abstatten, erstatten to give an account, to hand in a (full) statement (of the facts); ~ über den Stand e-r Sache vorlegen to report progress; 🕮 ~ von Kaufleuten (market-)report; laut ~ as per advice, as previously stated; ohne ~ without advice or further news; es ist ~ über ein Schiff eingelaufen the vessel has been reported or sighted.

Signs (see page XVII): F familiar; P vulgar; ⌐ flash; ↘ rare; † obsolete (died); * new word (born); ‡ incorrect; ♪ music;

be-richten (◡◡́◡) *v/a.* [89]*: **a**) e-m et. (a. *v/n.* [h.] über et.) ≈ to (hand in a) report to a p. about a th.; ausführlich: to give full particulars, to make a detailed statement to; ſchriftlich: to send in a written notice to; amtlich: e-m et. ≈ to notify a p. of a th.; wie oben berichtet (as) previously mentioned; **b**) (melden) to advise (or inform, acquaint, apprise) a p. of a th.; to let a p. know a th., to send a p. word (that s.th. has happened); es ward ihm ſofort berichtet he at once received intelligence of it; gut, falſch berichtet well informed, misinformed.

Be-richt-erſtatter (◡◡̋...) *m* [62] reporter; informant; für Zeitungen a.: correspondent, als Ausfrager a.: interviewer; bei Wahlen u. in Gerichtshöfen: returning officer; **-erſtattung** *f* (making a) report (= Bericht).

be-richtig/en (◡◡́◡◡) [richtig machen] **I** *v/a.* [88]* **1.** Irrtümer: to rectify, set right, adjust; (Schreib-, Druck-)Fehler &c.: to correct. — **2.** ein Geſchäft ≈ (in Ordnung bringen) to arrange, put right; (abſchließen) to settle, dispatch; e. Schuld &c.: to pay (or clear, square) a debt; to settle (or adjust) an account. — **II** ~ *n* [23] **3.** = B/ung.

Be-richtiger (◡◡́◡◡) *m* [22] corrector; *typ.* (Korrektor) (proof-)reader.

Be-richtigung (~) *f* [46] rectification, adjustment; correction; arrangement; settlement; ~ eines Textes: ⚗ emendation; ☿ die ~ der Rechnung beſcheinigt N. N. received in (full) settlement of my account, N. N.

be-riechen (◡–́◡) *v/a.* und *v/rpr.* [75]c* to smell at; (beſchnüffeln) to sniff at; eine Spur: to scent; F to nose.

be-rief (◡–́) *impf.* von berufen.

be-riefe(l)n (◡–́◡) [ndd.] *v/a.* [88] ([92]a)* to groove (= riefe(l)n).

be-riemen (◡–́◡) *v/a.* [88]* to provide (or furnish, fit up) with leather straps.

be-rieſeln (◡–́◡) **I** *v/a.* [92]a* bſd. *agr.* to irrigate; weitS. to canalize (a country). — **II** ~ *n* [23] u. **Be-rieſelung** (◡–́◡◡) *f* [46] irrigation; canalization.

Be-rieſelungs-anlage (≈̋...) *f* [62]. **-anſtalt** *f* irrigation-works *pl.*

be-rinden (◡◡́◡) **I** *v/refl.* [89]* **ſich** ≈ to put on (or become covered with) a bark or rind. — **II be-rindet** *p.p.* u. *a.* [66] barky; ≈es (unbehauenes) Holz unhewn (or rough) timber.

Be-ring (◡◡́) *m* [11]b. (Umkreis) circumference; purlieu; im ~(e) der Stadt in the environs of the town.

be-ringen (◡◡́◡) [Ring] *v/a.* [88]* to furnish (or fit, adorn) with rings or a ring; beringter Finger ... covered with rings.

Bering(s)-ſtraße 🌐 (–̋◡...) [Bering, 1728, dän. Seefahrer] *f* [62] (Meerenge zw. Aſien u. Nord-amerika) Bering Strait.

be-rippt ⚘ (◡◡́) *p.p.* u. *a.* [66] nerved.

Be-rippung ⚘ (◡◡́◡) *f* [46] nervation.

Be-ritt (◡◡́) *m* [11]b. **1.** district of a mounted inspector (vgl. Bereiter[2] 1). — **2.** ⚔ Kavallerie: (subdivision of a) squad; troop.

be-ritten (◡◡́◡) *p.p.* von bereiten[2] (ſ. ds II).

Berkan ☿ (◡́◡) [mhd., fr., *ar.] *m* [56] (dicker Stoff) berracan.

berlicke-berlocke (◡◡́-◡◡́) [fr.] *adv.* (Hals über Kopf) helter-skelter.

Berlin 🌐 (◡–́) [ſlaw.] *npr/n.* [51]α. Berlin.

Berline (◡–́◡) *f* [48] (ehm. vierſitziger Reiſewagen) berlin(e); coach.

Berliner (◡–́◡) **I** *m* [22], **~in** *f* [47] native of Berlin, Berliner. — **II** *a. inv.* of (or coming from) Berlin; ein ~ Kind a true Berliner; *chm.*: **~-blau** *n* (1704) Prussian blue, ⚗ ferrocyanide of iron; ~ Blauſäure Prussic acid.

berlinern F (◡–́◡) *v/n.* (h.) [92]a to speak the Berlin dialect or with a Berlin accent.

berliniſch F (◡–́◡) *a.* [66] = Berliner II.

Berlocke (◡◡́◡) [fr. *breloque*] *f* [48] (Uhrgehänge) trinket, charm, watch-suspender.

Berme ⚔ (◡́◡) [fr., *dtſch] *f* [48] *frt.* (Böſchungsabſatz) berm(e).

Bern 🌐 (◡́) [Verona] *npr/n.* [51]α. (Kanton u. Hauptſtadt der Schweiz) Bern(e).

Berner (◡́◡) **I** *m* [22], **~in** *f* [47] native of Berne, Bernese. — **II** *a. inv.* Bernese, zB. ~ Alpen 🌐 Bernese Alps *pl.*; das ~ Oberland the Bernese Uplands or Highlands *pl.*

berneriſch (◡́◡◡) *a.* [66] = Berner II.

Bernhard (◡́◡) [= bärenſtark] *npr/m.* [51]α. Bernard; der heilige ~ Saint Bernard; 🌐 (Alpen) der Große (Kleine) St. ~ the Great (Little) St. Bernard.

Bernhardiner (◡◡–́◡) **I** *m* [22], **~in** *f* [47] **1.** Bernardine or Cistercian (monk, nun). — **2.** = Bernhardinerhund. — **II** *a. inv.* **3.** Bernardine.

Bernhardiner-hund (◡◡–̋◡...) *m* [62] *zo.* St. Bernard('s) dog; **-kloſter** *n*, *eccl.* Bernardine convent; **-orden** *m*, *eccl.* Bernardine (or Cistercian) order.

bernhardiniſch (◡◡–́◡) *a.* [66] = Bernhardiner II.

Bernhards-krebs (◡̋◡...) *m* [62] *zo.* soldier-crab (*Pagu'rus bernha'rdus*).

Bernikel-gans (◡–̋◡...) [fr.; *dim.* zu *lt. *perna* Schinken] *f* [62] *zo.* (weißwangige Gans) barnacle (*Berni'cla leuco'psis*).

berniſch (◡́◡) *a.* [66] = Berner II.

Bernſtein (◡́-) [ndd.: burn = Brennſtein] *m* [11]d. (o. *pl.*) *min.* amber; ſchwarzer ~ (Gagat) jet.

Bernſtein-arbeiter (≈̋...) *m* [62] worker in amber; ≈**artig** *a.* [66] (like) amber, ⚗ succinous; **-drechſler**, **-dreher** *m* amber-worker.

bernſteine(r)n (◡́-◡) *a.* [66] (made of) amber.

Bernſtein-fang (◡̋-...) *m* [62] fishing for (or picking up) amber; **-farbe** *f* amber colour, amber; **-firnis** *m* amber-varnish; **-fiſcherei** *f* = -fang; **-korallen** *f/pl.* amber beads *pl.*; **-lack** *m* amber-lacquer; **-öl** *n* amber-oil; **-perlen** *f/pl.* = -korallen; ≈**ſauer** *a.*, *chm.*: ⚗ succinated; ≈ſaures Natron sodium succinate; allg.: ≈ſaures Salz succinate; **-ſäure** *f*, *chm.*: ⚗ succinic acid ($C_4H_6O_4$); **-ſchmuck** *m* amber ornaments *pl.*; **-ſchnur** *f* string of amber beads; **-ſpitze** *f* amber mouthpiece (of a pipe); amber cigar-holder;

be-roch (◡◡́ch) *impf.* und **be-rochen** (◡◡́ch◡) (*p.p.*) von beriechen.

be-rohren ⚙ (◡–́◡) *v/a.* [88]* Maurerei: to cover with reed(s), to reed.

be-roſten (◡◡́◡) *v/n.* (ſn) [89]* to grow rusty, to be(come) coated with rust.

Berſch(ling) (◡́(◡) *m* [11]a(d). *ichth.* = Barſch[1].

Berſerker (◡◡́◡) [ſkand. Bärenkleid] *m* [22] nord. *myth.* (wild ſtürmender Krieger) Berserk(er), fierce (or frantic); ≈**haft** *a.* [66] furious; madly courting danger; **~-wut** *f* [46] (ohne *pl.*) warlike frenzy; weitS. ungovernable fury or rage.

Berſich (◡́◡) *m* [11]d. *ichth.* = Barſch[1].

berſten (◡́◡) [ndd. u. md. (*LU.*): burst] **I** *v/n.* (ſn) [73]e, a. [75]b. od. [88] (*pres.* du, er birſt) to burst (asunder); (platzen) to explode; von Kleidern: (Riſſe bekommen) to split; von der Haut auch: to chap; to crack; (ſpringen) vom Glas: to fly; (ſich ſpalten) to split; *fig.*: vor Ärger ≈ (wollen) to be in a tearing passion; vor Neid ≈ (wollen) to burst with envy; vor Lachen ≈ (wollen) to split (one's sides) with laughing. — **II** ~ *n* [23] burst(ing), &c. (ſ. I); disruption; explosion.

Berta (◡́◡) [die Glänzende] *npr/f.* [56][57]α. (Bn.), *dim.* **Bertchen** *n* [23]α. Bertha, *dim.* Berty.

Berte (◡́◡) [fr. berthe; *dtſch. Berta] *f* [48] (Spitzenkragen) lace collar.

Bertram[1] (◡́◡) [ahd. Glanzrabe] *npr/m.* [51]α. (Bn.) Bertram.

Bertram[2] ⚘ (◡́◡) [lt.; *grch. *py'rĕthrŏn* Feuerwurz] *m* [51] **1.** römiſcher ~ pellitory of Spain (*Ana'cyclus*). — **2.** deutſcher ~ = Sumpfgarbe.

berüchtigt (◡◡́◡) *p.p.* u. *a.* [66] (verrufen) in ill (or bad) repute, ill-famed; notorious.

be-rück/en (◡◡́◡) [rücken] **I** *v/a.* [88]* **1.** *hunt.* Vögel: to (en)snare; allg.: to (en)trap. — **2.** (überfallen) to (take by) surprise; bſd. *fig.* ſie hat ſein Herz berückt she has captivated his heart or charmed him; ≈d fascinating, bewitching. — **3.** (überliſten) to entice, allure, inveigle, beguile; (prellen) to cozen; er hat ſich ≈ laſſen he fell into the trap (that was set for him); F he was taken in (nicely). — **II** ~ *n* [23] **4.** = B/ung.

be-rückſichtigen (◡◡̋◡́◡◡) **I** *v/a.* [88]* to take into consideration; to pay regard (or heed) to; to bear in mind; (in Anſchlag bringen) to allow (or make allowance) for; j-s Dienſte ≈ to take account of (or to acknowledge) a p.'s ...: nicht ≈ to take no notice of, to leave out of consideration, to overlook. — **II Be-rückſichtigung** *f* [46] (taking into) consideration; aus (oder in) ~ ihrer Notlage out of consideration for (or due regard to) their distress; in ~ daß considering that; unter ~ der Umſtände under (or in consideration of) the circumstances.

Be-rückung (◡◡́◡) *f* [46] (ſ. berücken) entrapping; fascination; enticement, allurement; cozenage; F take-in.

Be-ruf (◡–́) *m* [11]c. **1.** (Tätigkeit) (daily) occupation; (Geſchäft) trade, business; (Amt) office; (Fach) department; F line, shop; höherer ~ profession; ein Mann höheren ~es a professional man; den ~ e-s Arztes ausüben to follow the medical profession, to practise as a doctor; das bringt mein ~ mit ſich it is (a) part of my (daily) duty or routine; einen ~ ergreifen to go into a trade; to enter a profession; ſ-m ~e nachgehen, obliegen to attend to one's business or (professional) duties, to follow one's profession; in der Ausübung ſeines ~s

[berufen] — 176 — [besamen]

sterben to die in harness; von ~ by profession, by trade. — 2. innerer: calling; vocation; seinen ~ verfehlen to mistake one's vocation. — 3. (Neigung) disposition; keinen ~ zu et. haben to be disinclined to do a th.

be-rufen (‿‿́‿) Sb* I v/a. 1. e-n ℒ to send for a p.; to summon a p. — 2. das Parlament ꝛc. ℒ to convoke, assemble, summon …; e-e Versammlung ℒ, a.: to convene or to call (together) …; rel. Gott hat hat ihn zu sich ℒ God has called (or taken) him to his heavenly home. — 3. e-n zu et. ℒ to appoint a p. (to a post); bibl. s. auserwählt. — 4. et. ℒ (beschreien) to cause ill luck to a th. — 5. fast †: a) e-n, et. ℒ to bring a p., a th. into notice; g.s. to extol a p., a th.; b.s. to cry down; b) e-n um (ob. wegen) et. ℒ (zur Rede stellen) to call a p. to account or F to book. — II sich ℒ v/refl. 6. sich auf e-n, et. ℒ: a) (beziehen) to refer to a p., a th.; sich auf einen Präzedenzfall ℒ to cite (or allege) a precedent; sich auf sein Recht ℒ to stand on one's right; sich auf seine Unschuld ℒ to protest (or plead) one's innocence; b) (appellieren) to appeal to. — III p.pr. u. a. ⑥ 7. in den Bed. des inf. — 8. zu etwas ℒ sein to have a call for a th., to be fitted (or qualified) for s.th.; ich fühle mich (nicht) dazu ℒ I feel a (no) vocation (or call) for it. — 9. (berühmt) famous, celebrated; (berüchtigt) notorious. — IV ~ n ㉓ 10. = Berufung 1.

Be-ruf-kraut ♀ (‿‿‿…) [berufen 4] n ㉖ fleabane (Erigeron).

be-ruflich (‿‿́‿) a. ⑥ (u. adv.) professional(ly).

Be-rufs-arbeit (‿‿́‿…) f ㉖ professional work or labour; -art f kind of trade or profession, ㊉ line of business; -eifer m professional zeal; -fach = -geschäft a; -freudigkeit f pleasure derived from (the discharge of) one's daily duties; -genosse m colleague; die gesamten ~n the profession; the trade; -genossenschaft f co-operative association; (Genossenschaft der Arbeitgeber, Unternehmer-verband) employers' association; -geschäft n: a) profession, trade; ㊉ (line of) business; b) professional (or official) duties pl.; -krankheit f disease caused by the exercise of a trade; -leben n professional (or business) activity; ℒmäßig a. professional; et. ℒ betreiben, tun to make a business (or trade) of a th.; nicht ℒ amateurish; -offizier m officer by profession; -pflicht f professional duty; -reise f professional (or official) tour; -soldat m soldier by profession; -tätigkeit f = -leben; -treue f devotion to one's professional work; -wahl f choice of a profession or vocation; ℒwidrig a. unprofessional.

Be-rufung (‿‿́‿) f ㊻ 1. summons to; convening or convocation (of an assembly); appointment (to a post); (Beruf) calling. — 2. (Verweisung) reference to; jur. (Appellation) appeal (to a higher court); ~ einlegen (appellieren) to give notice of (or to lodge an) appeal against.

Be-rufungs-beklagte([r] m) f (‿‿́‿…) ㊻ defendant in a court of appeal, vgl. Appellat; -gericht n, court of (first, second) appeal; -klage f appeal; -kläger(in f) m plaintiff in a court of appeal, vgl. Appellant; -recht n a) right of appeal; b) (Ernennungsrecht) patronage; der Minister hat das ~ zu dieser Stelle the appointment is in the patronage of …

be-ruhen (‿‿́‿) v/n. (h.) ⑧* 1. auf et. (dat.) ℒ to rest (be or be founded) on a th.; to be attributable to a th.; (von et. ob. e-m abhängen) to depend (up)on a th.; das beruht auf einem Irrtum it is (due to or caused by) a mistake; auf Gegenseitigkeit ℒd mutual, reciprocal. — 2. ℒ bleiben to remain unchanged; et. auf sich ℒ lassen: a) to leave a th. as (or where) it is; b) (es aufgeben) to let it (severely) alone; to acquiesce in it; lassen wir das auf sich ℒ we'll let it rest (there), we won't pursue it any further or dwell on it any longer; ich will's dabei ℒ lassen I'll let the matter rest, I'll leave it alone.

be-ruhigen (‿‿́‿‿) I v/a. u. v/refl. ⑧* 1. (sich) ℒ to calm down, to set (to be) at ease; (trösten) to (take) comfort; (mit Vertrauen erfüllen) to reassure (o.s.), to quiet (o.s.); ℒ Sie sich! compose yourself!; make yourself easy!; be calm!; vgl. beschwichtigen I. — 2. sich bei et. (dat.) ℒ (zufrieden geben) to put up with a th., to acquiesce in it, to get reconciled to it. — 3. ein Land: to pacify. — II ℒd p.pr. u. a. ⑥ 4. in den Bed. des inf. — 5. soothing, sedative; ℒd wirken to soothe (or steady) the nerves; med. ℒdes Mittel soothing medicine or draught, sedative, vgl. Beruhigungsmittel.

Be-ruhigung (‿) f ㊻ calming (down), &c.; composure; e-s Landes: pacification; das wird zu seiner ~, zur seines Gemütes beitragen that will give him great comfort or restore his peace of mind or ease his mind; ~s-grund (ℒ…) m ㊂ cause for reassurance; ~s-mittel n, ~s-tropfen m/pl. soothing or quieting, composing draught (for the nerves), sedative.

be-rühmen (‿‿́‿) v/a., v/refl. u. v/n. ⑧* to praise, glorify (~rühmen).

be-rühmt (‿‿́) a. ⑥ renowned (wegen e-r Sache for a th.); stärker: celebrated, illustrious, famous; far-famed; sich ℒ m. to gain renown or repute or fame; to become celebrated; to make a (great) name (for o.s.), to distinguish (or signalize) o.s.; ~heit f ㊻ renown, fame, (great or world-wide) reputation; illustriousness (of a name); (berühmte Person) celebrity, illustrious or eminent) person, famous man, F (great) star, lion (f lioness) of the day.

be-rühren (‿‿́‿) I v/a. u. sich ℒ v/refl. ⑧* 1. to touch; leicht: to graze, brush, skim; to brush against (an et. stoßen) to border on, to meet; (anfassen) to finger, to handle; sich ℒ to meet. — 2. (erwähnen) to touch (lightly) upon, to mention by the way; to allude to; der berührte Gegenstand … referred to. — 3. e-n ℒ (nahe angehen) to affect a p.('s interest or welfare); die Sinne (un)angenehm ℒ to cause (un)pleasant sensations; das Stück, der Anblick berührt unangenehm … jars upon (or shocks) one's feeling(s), offends the eye; Worte, die (nicht) angenehm ℒ words which have a(n un)pleasant effect. — 4. e-n Ort auf einer Reise ℒ to pass through a town, to reach a place. — II ~ n ㉓ 5. = Berührung. — III ℒd p.pr. u. a. ⑥ 6. touching, concerning, (angrenzend) contiguous, adjoining math. die eine Kurve ℒde Linie tangent (to a curve).

Be-rührung (‿) f ㊻ touch(ing); contact; contiguity, math. v. Kurven: ⚷ osculation; (Zusammenhang) connection with, reference to; mit e-m in ~ kommen to come in(to) contact with (or to meet) a p., F to knock against a p.; tel. von Drähten: mit der Erde in ~ kommen to make (contact with the) earth.

Be-rührungs-ebene (‿‿́‿…) f ㊻ math. tangent-plane; -elektrizität f, phys. voltaic electricity, galvanism; -fläche f surface of contact or friction; -linie f tangent; -punkt m point of contact.

be-rupfen (‿‿́‿) ⑧* to pluck (= rupfen).

be-rußen (‿‿́‿) v/a. u. sich ℒ v/refl. ⑨* (sich) ℒ to begrime (o.s.); to besoot.

Beryll ⚷ (‿‿́) [grch., *ind.] m ⓐb. min. (Edelstein) beryl, aquamarine; ~-erde (ℒ…) f ㊻ chm.: ⚷ glucina (BeO).

Beryllium (‿‿́(‿)‿) [grch.] n ⓝ chm. (Berylmetall) beryllium (Be).

bes. abbr. = besonders.

be-sabbern F (‿‿́‿) v/a. u. sich ℒ v/refl. ⓐ* e-n (sich) ℒ to beslobber a p. (o.s.).

be-säen (‿‿́‿) v/a. ⑧* 1. agr. einen Acker mit ℒ to seed … with s.th.; to sow seeds in … 2. fig. mit et. ℒ (bedecken) to crowd (or stud) with s.th.; besät studded; ein mit Sternen besäter Himmel a starry sky, a sky bespangled with stars.

be-sagen (‿‿́‿) I v/a. ⑧* 1. (angeben) to announce, notify; to say; die Briefe ℒ das Nähere … give full particulars; der Paragraph besagt (lautet), daß // … is to the effect that //. — 2. (bedeuten) to purport, mean, indicate, signify, imply. — 3. (ausmachen) das will nicht viel ℒ it is of no great consequence; das will wenig ℒ it little matters or goes for little. — II be-sagt p.p. u. a. ⑥ 4. (vorher erwähnt) before-mentioned, aforesaid; um (wieder) auf ℒen Hammel zu kommen to return to our subject or F to our muttons.

be-sagter-maßen (‿‿́‿‿ ‿‿) adv. as previously stated or mentioned; in the aforesaid manner. [ℒ to (re)string.]

be-saiten (‿‿́‿) v/a. ⑧* e-e Geige (wieder)]

be-salben (‿‿́‿) ⑧* = salben.

be-samen (‿‿́‿) I v/a. u. v/refl. ⑧* 1. von Pflanzen: (sich) ℒ to (run to) seed vgl. besäen. — 2. sich ℒ (fortpflanzen) propagate (o.s.) by seed; to multiply. — 3. (befruchten) to fructify, impreg-

Zeichen (f. S. XVII): F familiär; P Volkssprache; ῀ Gaunersprache; ⟋ selten; † alt (auch gestorben); * neu (auch geboren); ⁎ unrichtig;

[Beſan] — 177 — [beſcheiden]

nate. — II ~ n u. **Be-ſamung** f 4. seeding; propagation; fructification; impregnation; *for.* seeds, seedlings *pl.*, vgl. Aufſchlag 8.

Be-ſan ⊥ (‿‿) [ndl. *bezaan*; *it. *mezzana* Mittel-] m ⚓c. (halbes Segel) mizzen; **~baum** (⸗…) m ⚓ spanker-boom.

be-ſanden (‿‿‿) v/a. ⚓* to (strew with or cover with) sand.

be-ſänftig/en (‿‿‿) I v/a. u. v/refl. ⚓* to soften (down); Stürme: to appease, calm, pacify, lull; Leiden: to assuage, soothe, mitigate; **ſich** 2 to calm down. — II ~ n u. **Be-ſänftigung** f appeasement; mitigation.

Be-ſänftigungs-mittel (⸗…) n ⚓ med. palliative, composing (or soothing) draught, sedative.

be-ſang (‿‿) *impf.* von beſingen.

Beſan-mars ⊥ (‿‿…) m ⚓ mizzen-top.

be-ſann (‿‿) *impf.* von beſinnen.

Beſan-ſchote ⊥ (‿‿‿) f ⚓ spanker-boom sheet; **-ſtag** ⊥ n mizzen-stay.

be-ſaß (‿‿) *impf. v.* beſitzen.

be-ſät (‿‿) *p.p.* von beſäen.

Be-ſatz (‿‿) [beſetzen] m ⚓a. 1. am Kleide: trimming, border, edging; loſer: flounce. — 2. ⊕ v. Pudellöfen: fettling. — 3. einer Alpenweide: grazing cattle.

Be-ſatz-band (‿‿…) n ⚓ (ribbon for) trimming, flouncing; (Küche) ruche; **-ſchnur** f (Gimpe) gimp, binding; **-teich** m Fiſcherei: stock-pond.

Be-ſatzung (‿‿‿) f ⚓ 1. ⚔ garrison; eine Stadt mit einer ~ verſehen to garrison … — 2. ⊥ (Mannſchaft e-s Kriegsſchiffs) crew of a man-of-war.

Be-ſatzungs-truppen ⚔ (⸗…) f/pl. ⚓ troops in (or forming a) garrison.

be-ſaufen P (‿‿) **ſich** 2 v/refl. ⌘f* to get drunk; f. beſoffen.

be-ſäumen ⊕ (‿‿‿) v/a. ⚓* to hem, border, edge; *carp.* beſäumt squared.

Be-ſä-ung (‿‿‿) f ⚓ sowing, seeding.

be-ſchädig/en (‿‿‿‿) I v/a. u. v/refl. ⚓* 1. von Sachen: to damage, injure, do harm to; (zerſchlagen) to batter (or knock) about; (ſchlechter m.) to deteriorate; von Pflanzen: durch Meltau 2 to blight; ſtark beſchädigt greatly damaged or injured, ⊥ v. Schiffen: disabled; ⚖ beſchädigte Ware spoilt (or damaged) goods *pl.*; durch Waſſer ob. Feuer auch: salvage-stock. — 2. von Perſonen: (ſich) 2 to hurt (o.s.), to injure (o.s.), to (receive a) wound; *fig.* j-s Ruf, Ausſichten 2 (verderben) to blast (or impair) a p.'s reputation, prospects. — III ~ n u. **Be-ſchädigung** f ⚓ 3. damage, injury (suffered); deterioration; hurt; ⊥ v. Seeſchiffen: average. — [son who damages, &c.]

Be-ſchädiger (‿‿‿‿) m ⚓, **~in** f ⚓ person.

be-ſchaff/en (‿‿‿) [ſchaffen] I v/a. 1. to procure, provide, get, supply; ⚖ Geld 2 auch: to find the money (for s.th.), es iſt nicht zu 2 it is not to be had (for love or money). — 2. (ins Werk ſetzen) to effect, do, perform. — II ~ n 3. = B/ung. — III 2 *a.* (†*p.p.*) ⚓ (D 9) 4. (geartet) constituted, qualified, conditioned; gut 2 in good condition; er iſt von Natur ſo 2 such is his nature or constitution. his character or disposition; wie iſt es damit 2? how does the matter stand?; anders 2 als ich mir dachte different from what I thought.

Be-ſchaffenheit (‿‿‿‿) f ⚓ 1. state (or condition) of a th. — 2. (Eigenſchaft) quality; (Anlage) character, disposition; nature; des Körpers: constitution; (je) nach ~ der Umſtände according to circumstances; as the case may be.

Be-ſchaffung (‿‿‿) f ⚓ providing, supply; ⚖ ~ von Geldern, auch: finding the cash or the means (for carrying on a business. &c.).

be-ſchäften ⚔ (‿‿‿) v/a. ⚓* = ſchäften.

be-ſchäftigen (‿‿‿‿) I v/a. u. v/refl. ⚓* 1. (ſich) 2 to occupy (o.s.) with a th.; ſich mit et. 2 to work at a th.; to apply o.s. to a th.; to have a th. in hand, to be engaged in a th.; er beſchäftigt ſich mit Dante he has taken up Dante. — 2. dies beſchäftigt ihn (nimmt ihn in Anſpruch) that preoccupies him, engrosses his attention; ganz beſchäftigt mit entirely absorbed in. — 3. Arbeiter 2 to employ (or give employment to) …; bei e-m beſchäftigt ſein to be in the employ of a p., to work for a p. — II **beſchäftigt** *p.p.* u. *a.* ⚓ 4. Bed. des *inf.* — 5. (ſtark) 2 (deeply) engaged, (very) busy; er iſt augenblicklich ſehr 2 his time is fully occupied (or taken up) just now; ein ſehr 2er Zahnarzt a dentist with a large practice or connexion.

Be-ſchäftigung (‿‿‿‿) f ⚓ occupation, work; preoccupation; employment; pursuit; keine ~ haben: to lead an idle life; b) to be out of employment or work, to have no work to do.

Be-ſchäftigungs-art (⸗…) f ⚓ mode of employment; **-los** *a.* ⚓ without occupation or work; **-loſigkeit** f want of occupation or employment; unemployment; **-neuroſe** f, *med.* neurosis (or nervous complaint) arising from a p.'s employment. [stud.]

Be-ſchäl-anſtalt (‿‿…) f ⚓ für Pferde:

be-ſchalen ⊕ (‿‿‿) [Schale] v/a. 1. Meſſer ꝛc. 2 to put handles to …, to haft … — 2. (mit Brettern, Latten bekleiden) to plank, to board up; to lath.

be-ſchälen[1] (‿‿) [Schale] v/a. ⚓* Bäume ꝛc.: to bark, to peel.

be-ſchälen[2] (‿‿) [Schäl(hengſt)] v/a. ⚓* vom Hengſt: to cover (the mare).

Be-ſchäler (‿‿‿) [beſchälen[2]] m ⚓ (Deckhengſt) stallion, stud-horse.

be-ſchämen (‿‿‿) I v/a. ⚓* 1. to (put to) shame; (ſchamrot machen) to put to the blush; (verwirren) to confound, to confuse; Höflichkeitswendung: Sie 2 mich durch Ihre Güte you overwhelm me with (your) kindness; 2d, *oft:* mortifying; beſchämt abashed; er ſah beſchämt aus he looked ashamed (of himself). — 2. (weit übertreffen) to outshine, to eclipse. — II **Be-ſchämung** f ⚓ 3. putting to shame; confounding; confusion; (feeling of) shame; abashment; ich konnte mich vor ~ nicht faſſen I was utterly ashamed or confounded, I could have sunk into the ground for shame.

character or disposition; **be-ſchatten** (‿‿‿) I v/a. ⚓* 1. to shade, to cast (or throw) a shadow on; *bibl.* (überſchatten) to overshadow. — 2. *fig.* (beſchirmen) to protect, screen, cover. — II ~ n u. **Be-ſchattung** f ⚓ 3. shading; protection.

☛ **be-ſchatzen** (‿‿‿) ꝛc. = ſchatzen ꝛc.

be-ſchau/en (‿‿‿) I v/a. ⚓* 1. to look (or gaze) at, to eye; mit Muße: to view, to contemplate. — 2. (prüfen) to examine, to inspect; (durchſuchen) to search (into). — II ~ n 3. = B/ung.

Be-ſchauer (‿‿‿) m, **~in** f ⚓ 1. p. who views a th., weitS. spectator. — 2. inspector; surveyor, ~ von Leichen: coroner, von Waren: examiner, sorter (of goods).

be-ſchaulich (‿‿‿) *a.* ⚓ contemplative, meditative; 2es Leben life of meditation; **~keit** f ⚓ contemplativeness; *rel.* heart-searching.

be-ſchäumen (‿‿‿) v/a. ⚓* to cover with foam; beſchäumt foamy.

Be-ſchauung (‿‿‿) f ⚓ view, viewing, contemplation; examination, inspection; von Leichen: coroner's inquest; Alt.: ~ der Opfertiere hieroscopy.

Be-ſcheid (‿‿) [ſcheiden] m ⚓c. 1. decision; abſchlägiger ~ negative reply, refusal; (Anweiſung) instruction; bis auf weiteren ~ until further orders. — 2. *jur.* (gerichtliche Entſcheidung) judgment, decree, sentence, award; ~ geben to pronounce sentence. — 3. meiſt ohne *art.:* (Auskunft) intelligence; e-m ~ geben to give a p. information; e-m ~ ſagen (auch zukommen) laſſen to send a p. word; e-m gehörig ~ ſagen to give a p. a bit of one's mind; auf alles ~ wiſſen to be well informed on everything; to be never at a loss for an answer; in einem Hauſe ~ wiſſen to know one's way about a house; in e-r Sache ~ wiſſen to know the ins and outs of a th.; to be well posted up in it; ich weiß hier keinen ~ I am a stranger here. — 4. e-m (trinkend) ~ tun to pledge a p. (in drinking).

be-ſcheiden[1] (‿‿‿) [ahd.] Beſt* I v/a. 1. e-m et. 2 (zuteilen) to apportion (or allot, assign) s.th. to a p., to mete (or dole) s.th. out to a p.; von Naturgaben: to endow a p. with (natural gifts), to bestow (a talent) on a p.; mir iſt et. beſchieden s.th. has fallen to my lot, I am destined to … — 2. e-n 2 to instruct (or inform) a p. on a th.; ſ. abfällig 3; e-n abſchlägig 2 to give a p. a refusal; er ward abſchlägig beſchieden he had a refusal (ſtärker: a rebuff) given him; he met with a refusal; e-n eines Beſſer(e)n 2 to undeceive a p., to open a p.'s eyes; to enlighten a p. on a th.; er iſt dahin beſchieden worden, daß//he received notice that//; *jur.:* die Parteien 2 to appoint a day for …; e-n wohin 2 (kommen heißen) to bid a p. appear somewhere; er beſchied mich auf den Nachmittag he told me to come (back) in the afternoon; vor Gericht 2 to summon (before a court of law); ⚔ e-n Soldaten zum Regiment 2 to order … to join his regiment. — II **ſich** 2 v refl. 4. (Maß

[bescheiden] — 178 — [Beschlagung]

halten) to moderate o.s. or one's pretensions; to resign o.s. (to one's fate); to be resigned; er weiß sich zu ℒ he assumes nothing, F he knows his place; ich will mich m-s Urteils, m-r Ansicht ℒ I keep my own counsel, reserve my opinion; sich mit et. ℒ to rest content (or satisfied) with a th., to acquiesce in a th.

be-scheiden² (⌣⌣́⌣) [nhd., †p.p.] a. ⊕ (D9) 1. (Maß haltend) moderate (auch ⚭ von Preisen); discreet, reserved; ℒe Mittel limited means pl. — 2. modest; (anspruchslos) unassuming, unpretentious, unobtrusive; (demütig) humble; (sittsam) coy, demure; ℒe Ansprüche machen to make no large pretensions.

Be-scheidenheit (⌣⌣́⌣⌣) f ⊕ (o.pl.) 1. moderation, discretion. — 2. modesty, unassumingness, unpretentiousness, unobtrusiveness; (Demut) humility.

be-scheidentlich (⌣⌣́⌣⌣) adv. modestly.

be-scheinen (⌣⌣́⌣) v a. ⊕* to shine (or cast one's rays) (up)on; to illuminate; von der Sonne beschienen lit up by the sun, sunlit.

be-scheinigen (⌣⌣́⌣⌣) v a. ⊕* to certify, to attest; (beglaubigen) to vouch (for the truth of); den Empfang von et. ℒ to acknowledge the receipt of a letter, &c.; von Geld: to give a receipt for money paid; to receipt a bill. [&c.

Be-scheiniger (~) m ⊕ p. who certifies,

Be-scheinigung (~) f ⊕ certificate, attestation, voucher; für Empfangenes: acknowledgment, receipt.

be-scheißen P derb (⌣⌣́⌣) v/a. ⊕a* (betrügen) to cheat, bamboozle, diddle.

be-schenken (⌣⌣́⌣) I v/a. ⊕* e-n ℒ to make a present to a p.; e-n mit et. ℒ to present a p. with s.th., to make a p. a gift of s.th.; reichlich ℒ to load with presents; Kellner ꝛc.: F to tip; der, welcher einen beschenkt donor. — II ~ n ㉓ = IV. — III Be-schenkte(r)m f ㊼ p. to whom a present (or gift) has been made, auch donee. — IV Be-schenkung f ⊕ present(ation), bestowing a gift upon; v. Kellnern ꝛc.: F tipping.

be-scheren¹ (⌣⌣́⌣) [: shear] v/a. ⊕a. (a.⊕)* Menschen: to shave; Tiere: to shear; von Schafen auch: to clip (the fleece).

be-scher/en² (⌣⌣́⌣) [ahd.: share] I v/a. ⊕* e-m et.: (schenken) to give (as a) present (or); to bestow (as a gift) on; to confer on; was hat Ihnen das Christkindchen beschert? what Christmas presents (bei Dienstboten: Christmas boxes) had you or did you get?; solches Glück ward mir nie beschert such good fortune was never allotted (or meted out) to me or never meant for me; et. von Gott (vom Zufall) Beschertes a godsend (a windfall). — II ~ n ㉓ = B/ung 1.

Be-scherung (~) f ⊕ 1. presentation of gifts; bestowal of presents; (Weihnachtsgeschenke) Christmas present(s pl.), für Dienstboten: Christmas box(es pl.). — 2. iro.: das ist die ganze ~! that is all!, F that's the (whole) affair!; da haben wir die ~! there we are!, there's a bother!, what a pickle (or mess) to be in!; eine schöne ~ das! a fine business this!, a pretty kettle of fish!

be-schick/en (⌣⌣́⌣) I v/a. ⊕* 1. e-n Landtag, ein Konzil ꝛc. ℒ to send a deputation (or delegates) to …; ⚭ Märkte, Messen ℒ to send (or forward) goods to the markets, the fairs. — 2. a) fast † (besorgen) to do, to arrange; sein Haus ℒ to put one's house (or affairs) in order; b) ⊕ metall. den Hochofen, den Schmelztiegel mit Erz ℒ to charge (or feed) the furnace, the crucible; Metalle ℒ (legieren) to alloy …; Erze ℒ (gattieren, mollern) to mix the ores with flux. — II ~ n ㉓ 3. = B/ung.

Be-schickung (~) f ⊕ (dispatch of a) delegation to; representation at; charging or charge (of a furnace); mixing (of ore and flux); ~s-boden ⊕ (⌣́…) m ⊕ metall. für Erze: mixing-shed; =regel f, arith. (Mischungsregel) rule of alligation.

be-schielen (⌣⌣́⌣) p.p. von beschielen¹.

be-schielen (⌣⌣́⌣) v/a. ⊕* to squint at.

be-schienen¹ (⌣⌣́⌣) p.p. von bescheinen.

be-schienen² ⊕ (⌣⌣́⌣) [Schiene] I v/a. ⊕* Stellm.: e. Rad ℒ to bind (or tire, rim) …, to fit with bands or tires; ⚒ to lay rails on (the sleepers); surg. ℒ to splinter (broken limbs) or to put (them) in splints. — II ~ n ㉓ u. Be-schienung f ⊕ binding, &c. (i. I).

be-schieß/en (⌣⌣́⌣) I v/a. ⊕c(ej)t* ⚔ to fire upon, to cannonade; mit Bomben: to bombard; mit Granaten: to shell; ein Hügel, von dem aus sich eine Stadt ℒ läßt a hill commanding a town; vgl. bestreichen 4. — 2. fast †: ein Gewehr ℒ (probieren) to test a gun. — 3. hunt. ein Revier ℒ to shoot over … — II ~ n ㉓ u. Be-schießung f ⊕ 4. cannonading; bombardment.

be-schiffbar ⛵ (⌣⌣́⌣) a. ⊕ navigable.

be-schiff/en ⛵ (⌣⌣́⌣) I v/a. ⊕* to navigate, to sail on or across (the sea). — II ~ n ㉓ u. Be-schiffung f ⊕ navigation; eines Flusses auch: river traffic.

be-schilden (⌣⌣́⌣) v/a. ⊕* to (provide or arm or cover with a) shield.

be-schilft (⌣⌣́⌣) p.p. u. a. ⊕ overgrown with reeds; reedy.

be-schimmeln (⌣⌣́⌣) v/n. (sn) ⊕a* to grow (or turn) mouldy or fusty.

be-schimpf/en (⌣⌣́⌣) I v/a. ⊕*1. (mit Schande bedecken) to disgrace, dishonour, cover with shame. — 2. (beleidigen) to affront, to insult; stärker: to outrage; durch Nachreden: to traduce; ℒ der Ausdruck abusive term. — II ~ n ㉓ 3. = B/ung.

Be-schimpfer (⌣⌣́⌣) m ㉒, ~in f ㊼ p. who disgraces, affronts, insults, &c.

Be-schimpfung (~) f ⊕ staining (of) a p.'s honour, disgrace; affront or insult (offered to a p.); stärker: outrage (on a p.'s honour), indignity (heaped on a p.).

be-schindeln (⌣⌣́⌣) ⊕a* ⚒ schindeln.

be-schinden (⌣⌣́⌣) ⑲* = schinden.

be-schirm/en (⌣⌣́⌣) v/a. ⊕* 1. et. ℒ to put a th. under cover, to house a th. (safely). — 2. e-n ℒ (beschützen) to protect (or shield, screen) a p. from; (verteidigen) to defend a p. against. — II ~ n ㉓ 3. = Beschirmung.

Be-schirmer (⌣⌣́⌣) m ㉒, ~in f ㊼ protector m, …tress f; defender; supporter; e-r Dame: cavalier m, chaperon f.

Be-schirmung (~) f ⊕ protection; defence.

be-schlabbern F (⌣⌣́⌣) v/a. u. v/refl. ⊕a* = besabbern.

be-schlaf/en (⌣⌣́⌣) v/a. ⊕a* 1. ein Lager ℒ to lie on … — 2. F fig. et. ℒ (sich überlegen) to sleep upon a th.; to put off a th. for the morrow, to consider a th. over night; weitS. to take counsel with one's pillow.

Be-schlag (⌣⌣́) m ⊕c. 1. ⊕ u. ⚓ (iron) binding or hoop or band; ironwork; e-s Buches: (metal) clasp; e-r Flinte ꝛc.: mounting; e-s Pferdes: shoeing; e-s Rades: tire, tyre; am Stock: ferrule; Beschläge am Wagen, an Fenstern u. Türen ꝛc.: (metal) fittings pl. — 2. (feuchter Anflug) dew(-drops pl.); moisture or damp or steam (flying to a cold surface); chm. efflorescence; auf Metallen: oxidized surface; (Schimmel) mould(iness); von Pflanzenteilen: ⚘ pruina. — 3. jur. (Festnehmung) seizure, attachment; et. in ~ nehmen, et. mit ~ belegen, auf et. ~ legen (lassen): a) (ergreifen) to seize, attach, lay hands upon; b) (wegnehmen) to confiscate or stop or impound (goods or effects); Möbel: to levy a distress on; to distrain; ⚓ ein Schiff: to put (or lay) an embargo on, to embargo; weitS. Plätze: to secure (beforehand). [shoeing-block or stand.

Be-schlag-bock ⊕ (⌣́…) m ㉒ (farrier's)

Be-schläge ⊕ (⌣⌣́) n ㉒ = Beschlag 1.

be-schlag/en (⌣⌣́⌣) [ahd.] ⊕b* I v/a. 1. mit et. ℒ to cover (or overlay) with metal work, planks, &c.; mit Eisen ℒ to brace (or tip. head) with iron; mit eisernen Reifen ℒ to hoop, to bind with iron; mit Eisen, Silber ℒer Stock iron-tipped, silver-mounted stick; mit Nägeln: to stud; to spike; ein Pferd: to shoe; scharf ℒes Pferd rough-shod horse; ein Rad ℒ to tire a wheel; e-e Retorte mit Kitt ℒ to lute a retort; ⚓ ein Schiff mit Kupfer ℒ to cover (or arm, sheathe) a ship's bottom with (sheeted) copper. — 2. fig. in et. (gut, wohl) ℒ sein (Bescheid wissen) to be conversant (or well acquainted) with a th., skilled (or well versed) in a th., F (thoroughly) well up in a th., a good hand at a th. — 3. jur. (ergreifen) to seize, to attach, arrest. — 4. ⚓ die Segel ℒ (an der Rahe befestigen) to furl … — II v/n. (sn) u. v/refl. 5. sich ℒ (sich mit hauchartigem Anfluge bedecken) to become dimmed or hazy; die Fenster sind ℒ … steamed, covered with moisture; das Silber ist ℒ (angelaufen) … tarnished; die Wände sind ℒ … are sweating; chm. to effloresce; (schimmeln) to grow mouldy or fusty. — III ~ n ㉓ = B/ung.

Be-schlag-legung (⌣́…) f ⊕ = -nahme; =leine ⚓ f furling-line; =nahme, =nehmung f jur. = Beschlag 3; ~ des Vermögens sequestration, confiscation; ⚓ embargo; ✕ ~ von Zeitungen, Telegrammen ꝛc., um Aufschlüsse zu erhalten: interception, capture. [sequestration.

Be-schlags-befehl (⌣́…) m ⊕ detainer;

Be-schlags-schmied (⌣́…) m ㉒ farrier.

Be-schlags-verwalter (⌣́…) m ㉒, verweser m sequestrator; =verwaltung f sequestration. [ing: e-s Pferdes: shoeing.

Be-schlagung (⌣⌣́⌣) f ⊕ mit Reifen: hoop-

Signs (see page XVII): F familiar; P vulgar; ℱ flash; ⟩ rare; † obsolete (died); * new word (born); ✝ incorrect; ♪ music;

[Beſchlagzange] — 179 — [beſchreien]

Be-ſchlag-zange ⊕ (‿ᵊ...) f ⓰ farrier's tongs pl.; **=zeug** n farrier's tools pl.
be-ſchleichen (‿⊥‿) **I** v/a. ⓰a* e-n ⚶ to sneak (or steal) up to a p., to surprise a p.; das Reh ⚶ to stalk the deer; die Angſt beſchlich uns fear came over us, crept upon us, seized us. — **II** ~ n ⓳ u. **Be-ſchleichung** f ⓮ stealthy approach; des Wildes: deer-stalking.
be-ſchleunig/en (‿⊥‿‿) **I** v/a. ⓰* to hasten, accelerate, quicken (the speed); (fördern) to (hurry) forward, dispatch, expedite, urge on; die Schritte ⚶ to double one's pace, F to put one's best leg foremost; phys. beſchleunigte Bewegung accelerated motion; ⚔ mittels beſchleunigter Märſche by forced marches. — **II** ~ n ⓳ = B/ung. — **III** ⚶d p.pr. u. a. ⓰ accelerative.
Be-ſchleunigung (‿) f ⓮ acceleration; quickening; increased speed. [chen.
be-ſchlich(en) (‿⊥(‿)) impf. (p.p.) v. beſchlei=
be-ſchlief (‿⊥) impf. von beſchlafen.
be-ſchließen (‿⊥‿) **I** v/a. ⓰d* 1. et. (zu tun) ⚶ to decide (to do a th.), to determine (upon a course); abs. to resolve; to arrive at a decision; parl. oft: to vote a th.; to carry (a motion); to pass (a bill); et. bei ſich ⚶ to make up one's mind about a th.; et. mit=ea. ⚶ to agree upon a th.; die Sache iſt feſt beſchloſſen... finally settled or definitely arranged. — 2. gerichtlich ⚶ to decree. — 3. (umſchließen) das Gebirge beſchließt den Horizont... bounds (or limits) the horizon. — 4. (be=endigen) to close, conclude, terminate; ſeine Tage in Frieden ⚶ to end one's days in peace; das Feſt wurde mit Tanzen beſchloſſen the fête (was) wound up (or finished) with a dance, it ended in a dance. — **II** ~ n ⓳ 5. = Beſchluß.
Be-ſchließer (‿) m ⓲, **~in** f ⓱ keeper; caterer; steward(ess); (lady) housekeeper; (Kellermeiſter) butler.
Be-ſchließer-amt (⚶...) n ⓲ stewardship; housekeeper's place or situation.
Be-ſchließung (‿⊥‿) f ⓮ = Beſchluß 1.
be-ſchloß (‿ᵊ) impf., **be-ſchloſſen** (‿ᵊ‿) p.p. von beſchließen.
be-ſchloſſener=maßen (‿ᵊ‿‿⊥‿) adv. as previously resolved (or determined, decided) upon, in accordance with our (their, &c.) resolution or decision.
be-ſchlug (‿⊥) impf. von beſchlagen.
Be-ſchluß (‿ᵊ) m ⓲a. 1. decision, resolution, determination; decree; parl. einen ~ annehmen to adopt (or pass) a resolution; et. zu einem ~ erheben to vote (or carry) a motion; e-n ⚶ faſſen to resolve, to decide upon. — 2. (Ende) conclusion, termination, close; zum Beſchluſſe in conclusion, in the end, finally, last of all; to conclude (with); den ~ machen to be (or come) last.
be-ſchluß-fähig (‿⊥) a. ⓰ parl. sufficient in number to discuss (or pass) a resolution; forming a quorum or a house; ⚖ die Anzahl quorum; **=fähigkeit** f ⓮ legal capacity (of an assembly for transacting business); quorum (required for a debate); **=faſſung** f, **=nahme** f (coming to a) decision (= Beſchluß 1); ⚶reif a. mature(d) for decision; parl. fully (or sufficiently) debated, thoroughly thrashed out.
be-ſchmaddern F (‿ᵊ‿) ⓰a* = beſchmieren.
be-ſchmeißen F (‿⊥) v/a. 1. ⓰a* = bewerfen. — 2. ⓰* = beſudeln.
be-ſchmier/en (‿⊥) **I** v/a. und v/refl. ⓰* 1. (beſtreichen) to (be)smear, to grease or ⚓ to pay (with fat, tallow, &c.); to daub over (with paint, &c.). — 2. Brot mit Butter ⚶ (gewählter: beſtreichen) to spread... with butter, to butter ...; mit Fett ⚶ to grease; mit Honig ⚶ F to lay (or dab) the honey on thick; mit Teer ⚶ to tar. ⚓ ein Schiff: to pay. — 3. (beſudeln) (ſich) ⚶ to bespatter (F mess) (o.s.); fig. Papier ⚶ to waste paper (with scrawling or scribbling). — **II** ~ n ⓳ B/ung (‿⊥‿) f ⓮ 4. besmearing, &c. (ſ. I).
be-ſchmutz/en (‿⊥‿) **I** v/a. und v/refl. ⓰* (ſich) ⚶ to dirty or F to muck (o.s.); to soil (one's hands or face); (beſchmieren) to grease or begrime (o.s.), ſtärker: to befoul (o.s.); fig. (entweihen) to pollute (or sully) a p.'s fair fame. — **II** ~ n ⓳ u. B/ung f ⓮ pollution; blemish.
be-ſchnauſen (‿⊥‿) ⓰* = beſchnüffeln.
be-ſchneidbar (‿⊥⊥) a. ⓰ tonsile.
Be-ſchneide-bank ⊕ (‿⊥‿...) f ⓰ Buchbinderei: dressing-bench; **=brett** n reglet; **=hobel** m plough-knife, edge-tool; **=maſchine** f paper-cutting machine; **=meſſer** n =hobel.
be-ſchneid/en (‿⊥) **I** v/a. ⓰c* 1. Haare, Flügel ꝛc.: to clip (a. von Gold); to cut (off or short); Nägel: to pare; Bücher mit beſchnitt(e)nem Rande books with cut edges. — 2. agr. Bäume ꝛc.: to lop, to prune; Hecken: to trim; Reben: to dress; Bienenſtöcke ⚶ to take out (honey and wax) from ...; ⊕ am Rande ⚶ to edge, Münzen: to clip; carp. vierkantig ⚶ to square. — 3. rel. bei Juden und Mohammedanern: ein Kind ⚶ to circumcise ...; die Beſchnittenen m/pl. the circumcised pl. — 4. fig. (einſchränken) to reduce, curtail, diminish, lessen. — **II** ~ n ⓳ 5. = B/ung.
Be-ſchneide-preſſe (‿⊥‿) f ⓮ cutting-press.
Be-ſchneider (‿⊥‿) m ⓲ 1. **~(in** f ⓱) p. who clips, &c. — 2. rel. circumciser. — 3. (Inſtrument) cutting-tool.
Be-ſchneide-werkzeug ⊕ (‿⊥‿...) n ⓲ = Beſchneidemaſchine.
Be-ſchneidung (‿⊥‿) f ⓮ clipping, &c. (ſ. beſchneiden I); rel. circumcision; fig. reduction (or curtailment) of expenses, &c.
be-ſchneien (‿⊥‿) v/a. u. v/n. (ſn) ⓰* to cover (or get covered) with snow; beſchneite Gipfel snow-clad (poet. snow-capped) peaks.
be-ſchneiteln (‿⊥‿‿) ⓰* = ſchneiteln.
be-ſchnipfeln, **be-ſchnippeln**, **be-ſchnippern** alle drei ⓰a*, **be-ſchnipſen** ⓰*, **be-ſchnitzeln** ⓰a*, **be-ſchnitzen** ⓰* (alle ‿⊥‿) v/a. to clip, to pare, to snip.
be-ſchnitt (‿ᵊ) impf., ⚶en (‿ᵊ‿) p.p. von beſchneiden; **~e(r)** ſ. beſchneiden 3.
be-ſchnüffeln, **be-ſchnuppern** (‿⊥‿‿) v/a. ⓰a* to smell (or sniff) at; fig. er beſchnüffelt alles he puts (or thrusts, F pokes) his nose into everything.
be-ſchnüren (‿⊥‿) ⓰* 1. (mit Schnüren beſetzen) to (trim with) braid. — 2. (mit Stricken umwickeln) to (tie with) string or cord; to bind (or fasten) with cords.

Be-ſcholtenheit (‿⊥⊥‿) f ⓮ jur. stained reputation, blemish(ed character).
be-ſchönen † (‿⊥‿) ⓰* = beſchönigen.
be-ſchönig/en (‿⊥‿‿) **I** v/a. ⓰* fig. to palliate; to gloss over, varnish, cloak; es läßt ſich nicht ⚶ there is no excuse for it, F we must not mince the matter. — **II** ~ n ⓳ = Beſchönigung. — **III** ⚶d p.pr. u. a. ⓰ palliative.
Be-ſchöniger (‿⊥‿‿) m ⓲, **~in** f ⓱ person who glosses over (faults).
Be-ſchönigung (‿⊥‿‿) f ⓮ palliation, glossing over, extenuation.
be-ſchoſſen (‿⊥‿) p.p. von beſchießen.
be-ſchottern ⊕ (‿⊥‿) **I** v/a. ⓰a* Wege: to gravel, to ballast (vgl. aufſahren 8). — **II** ~ n ⓳ u. **Be-ſchotterung** f ⓮ gravel(ling), ballast(ing).
be-ſchränk/en (‿⊥‿) **I** v/a. und v/refl. ⓰* 1. to limit, to bound; to confine (within certain limits), to circumscribe; ſich auf et. ⚶ to restrict (or confine) o.s. to s.th. — **II** ~ n ⓳ 2. = B/ung. — **III** ⚶d p.p. u. a. ⓰ 3. in den Beb. des inf. — 4. restrictive. — **IV** **be-ſchränkt** p.p. u. a. ⓰ 5.: a) limited; confined; (SH.) cribbed and cabined; ⚶e Anſichten f/pl. narrow views pl.; ein ⚶er Raum a confined space; in ⚶em Sinne in a restricted sense; in ⚶en Verhältniſſen leben to live in straitened circumstances, to have limited means; b) ⚶er Verſtand weak understanding; narrow-mindedness; ⚶er Kopf p. of poor intellect, dullard, F duffer.
Be-ſchränkt-heit (‿⊥-) f ⓮ 1. des Raumes: limitedness, confinement; b. Zeit: shortness. — 2. fig. des Geiſtes: narrowness (or meanness) of mind; ſtärker: weakness of intellect, thick-headedness.
Be-ſchränkung (‿⊥‿) f ⓮ limitation, confinement; circumscription; restriction.
be-ſchreib/en (‿⊥) **I** v/a. ⓰d* 1. Papier ꝛc.: to cover (or fill) with writing, to write upon; beſchrieb(e)ne Steintafeln inscribed tablets pl. — 2. fig. et. ⚶ to describe (or set forth) s.th.; (ſchildern) to depict, to sketch; (alles) umſtändlich ⚶ to give a minute description of, to go into (or to give) full details. — 3. beſ. ⚷ math.: einen Kreis ꝛc. ⚶ to describe a circle; e-e Figur aus gegebenen Stücken: to construct; ein Dreieck in (um) e-n Kreis ⚶ to inscribe (circumscribe) a triangle in (about) a circle. — **II** ~ n ⓳ 4. = B/ung. — **III** ⚶d p.pr. u. a. ⓰ 5. Beb. des inf. — 6. descriptive, graphic.
Be-ſchreiber (‿⊥‿) m ⓲ describer, p. who describes, &c. (ſ. beſchreiben); depicter (of morals, &c.), delineator (of life, &c.).
Be-ſchreibung (‿⊥‿) f ⓮ 1. inscription. — 2. (Darſtellung, Schilderung) description; graphic art; delineation; (Erzählung) detailed narrative; et. das jeder ~ ſpottet s.th. that defies (or beggars) description; über alle ~ ſchön fair beyond (all) description. — 3. math. construction; ast. ~ e-r Planetenbahn ꝛc.: course, motion (round the sun, &c.); vgl. a. Erd-, Orts-⚶ ꝛc.
Be-ſchreibungs-gabe (‿⊥⊥...) f ⓰ descriptive (or graphic) power(s pl.).
be-ſchrei-en (‿⊥) v/a. ⓰* 1. v. Neugeborenen: die vier Wände ⚶ to utter the first

---

⚡ scientific; ⚘ botanical; ⚢ geography; ⊕ machinery; ⚒ mining; ⚔ military; ⚓ marine; ⚭ commercial; ✉ postal; 🜚 railway.

cry. — 2. einen ~ (verschreien) to decry (or disparage, abuse) a p. — 3. (durch Schreien verhexen) to bewitch; man muß es nicht ~! we must not crow too soon!

be-schreiten (◡́◡) v/a. ⓢb* 1. to put one's foot (or to stop) on (land or shore, &c.), (besteigen) to bestride; das Verdeck ~ to walk on deck; den Altar ~ to go up to the altar. — 2. *fig. jur.* den Rechtsweg ~ to go to law, to take legal proceedings. [*schreiben.*]

be-schrieb(en) (◡́◡(◡)) *impf.* (*p.p.*) von be-]

be-schriebener-maßen (◡́◡◡◡́◡) *adv.* as previously described or set forth.

be-schritten(en) (◡́◡(◡)) *impf.* (*p.p.*) von be-schreiten. [edges) off, to edge, rim.]

be-schroten ⊕ (◡́◡) v/a. ⓢ* to clip (the]

be-schuhen (◡́◡) I v/a. u. v/refl. ⓢ* to shoe (meist im *p.p.* shod); man muß ihn neu ~ he must be newly shod; sich ~, oft: to provide o.s. with (new) boots, to put (a pair of) boots on one's feet; schlecht beschuht ill shod, F out at heels. — II **Be-schuhung** f ⓡ (Fußbekleidung) shoes and boots *pl.*; weitS. covering for the feet, auch: footgear, footwear.

be-schuldig/en (◡́◡◡) I v/a. ⓢ* e-n e-r Sache (*gen.*) ~ to accuse a p. of a th., to impute a th. to a p.; to lay the blame of a th. on a p.; *jur. a.*: to charge a p. with a th., *abs.* to inculpate (or incriminate) a p. — II ~ n ⓩ = B/ung.
Be-schuldiger (◡́◡◡◡) m ⓺, accuser. *jur. a.*: prosecutor m, …trix f.
Be-schuldigte([r] m) f (◡́◡◡◡) ⓡ the accused; *jur.* the defendant; Kriminalrecht: the prisoner (in the dock).
Be-schuldigung (◡́◡◡◡) f ⓡ accusation, imputation, charge.

be-schummeln F (◡́◡◡) [obd.] v/a. ⓢa*: e-n ~ (im Spiele ꝛc. betrügen) to cheat (or trick) a p. (um et. out of a th.); F to bilk (or diddle, do, take in) a p.

be-schuppen (◡́◡◡) [ndd.] v/a. ⓢ* 1. to furnish (or cover) with scales. — 2. = abschuppen. — 3. a. **be-schupsen** ⓢ* P = beschummeln.

be-schürfen ⚒ (◡́◡) v/a. ⓢ* e-n Gang ~ to discover (or find, strike) a lode.

be-schürzt (◡◡́) a. ⓡ aproned.

Be-schuß-anstalt ⊕ (◡◡́…) f ⓡ testing-shed or yard for small arms.

be-schütten (◡́◡) v/a. u. v/refl. ⓢ* 1. e-n mit et. ~ to pour (or throw) s.th. on (or over) a p.; mit Blumen ~ to cover (stärker: to smother) with flowers; sich mit Sauce ~ to spill gravy over one's clothes. — 2. ⊕ mit Erde, Sand ~ to shoot (or cart) earth, sand (up)on; mit Kies ~ to gravel (= beschottern).

be-schütz/en (◡́◡) I v/a. ⓢ* to protect (or guard, safeguard, shelter) from; (verteidigen) to defend against. — II ~ n ⓩ = B/ung.
Be-schützer (◡́◡◡) m ⓺, ~in f ⓻ protector, protectress; Schirmer; ~ des Glaubens (Titel englischer Könige seit Heinrich VIII.) Defender of the Faith (*fi'dei defe'nsor, abbr.* F. D.).
Be-schützung (◡́◡◡) f ⓡ protection of; giving shelter to; defence of.

be-schwänzt (◡◡́) *p.p. u. a.* ⓡ tailed.

be-schwatzen F (◡́◡) v/a. ⓢ* 1. et. ~ to talk of (or about) a th. — 2. einen ~ (überreden) to talk a p. over; er ließ sich dazu ~ he was talked (or coaxed)

into it, he was prevailed upon to do it, he yielded to (their) persuasion in the matter.

be-schweift (◡◡́) a. ⓡ tailed.

be-schweißen (◡́◡) I v/a. ⓢ* 1. to cover (or mark) with sweat. — 2. *hunt.* [Schweiß = Blut] to mark with blood. — II **be-schweißt** *p.p. u. a.* ⓡ 3. sweaty; *hunt.* blood-stained.

Be-schwer ↘ (◡́) f ⓡ = Beschwerde 1.
Be-schwerde (◡́◡) [mhd.] f ⓡ 1. (Bürde) burden, hardship, (Mühseligkeit) trouble, vexation; bother, worry; (Unannehmlichkeit) unpleasantness; annoyance, discomfort; (Körperleiden) complaint; das Atmen macht ihm große ~ he suffers much from shortness of breath; Schweinebraten macht ihm (bei der Verdauung) ~ roast pork disagrees (or does not agree) with him; das macht ihm wenig ~ that does not trouble him much. — 2. (Klage) complaint; den ~n abhelfen to redress grievances; bei einem über et. ~ führen to lodge a complaint with a p. about a th., to complain of a th. to a p.

Be-schwerde-buch (◡́◡…) n ⓬ book for entering complaints of travellers or passengers; =**führer(in** f) m *jur.* complainant; =**führung** f statement of grievances; =**punkt** m subject of complaint, grievance; =**schrift** f petition (for the redress of grievances), mit kreisförmig geordneten Unterschriften: round-robin; =**weg** m: den ~ gegen e-n einschlagen to make complaints about a p.

be-schweren (◡́◡) I v/a. und v/refl. ⓢ* (*ant.* erleichtern) 1. to weigh (or rest) heavily on; Käse beschwert den Magen F cheese lies heavy on the stomach; (beladen) to load (or burden, encumber) with a th.; with a ⊕ Hypothek ~ to mortgage. — 2. (belästigen) to incommode, inconvenience, trouble, molest, annoy; *path.* to disturb (the system). — 3. sich ~ (beklagen) to complain to *p.* about a th.; sich laut ~ über to cry out against. — II ~ n ⓩ 4. = Beschwerung.

be-schwerlich (◡́◡) a. ⓡ burdensome or onerous (task); (ermüdend) fatiguing or difficult (road); (belästigend) annoying, troublesome, bothersome; (unbequem) inconvenient (hour); hard (life); e-m ~ sein oder fallen to cause trouble (or inconvenience) to a p.; durch f-e Gegenwart: to incommode (or bore) a p.; ~**keit** (◡-) f ⓡ onerousness (of a task); difficulty (of a road); troublesomeness (or bothersomeness) (of an affair or a p.); inconvenience (of time or place); hardship (of a toiler's life).

Be-schwerniß (◡́◡) 1. f ⓲ (Beschwerlichkeit) troublesomeness. — 2. n ⓱ (et. Beschwerliches) hardship, trouble.

Be-schwerte([r] m) f ⓬ (◡́◡) *jur.* (*ant.* Bedachte(r)) p. who has to pay a legacy.

Be-schwerung (◡́◡) f ⓡ load(ing), burden(ing), molestation, annoyance, disturbance; *jur.* ~ (Pfandbelastung) encumbrance; mortgage.

be-schwichtig/en (◡́◡◡) [ndd.] I v/a. ⓢ* to (put to) silence; to quiet, to pacify; to still or hush (the waves), (beruhigen) to appease (anger), to calm or lull

(a storm), to allay (fear); (lindern) to assuage, soothe, soften (down); sein Gewissen ~, auch: to beguile (or quiet) one's conscience; vgl. beruhigen 1; 2b calming, soothing, comforting, conciliatory. — II ~ n ⓩ = B/ung.
Be-schwichtigung (◡́◡◡◡) f ⓡ silencing; appeasement; assuagement; conciliation; zur ~ m-s Gewissens (in order) to quiet (or to allay the pangs of) my conscience. [money.]
Be-schwichtigungs-geld (◡…) n ⓩ hush-]
be-schwindeln F (◡́◡◡) v/a. ⓢa* to swindle (or humbug, cheat) a p. out of a th.; ich lasse mich nicht ~ F I won't be done.
be-schwingen (◡́◡) v/a. ⓢ* to wing.
be-schwingt (◡́) a. ⓡ winged, on wings.
be-schwor (◡◡́) *impf.,* **be-schworen** (◡́◡) *p.p.* von beschwören.
be-schwör/en (◡́◡) I v/a. ⓢb* 1. (durch Eid bekräftigen) to confirm by oath, to swear to, to take one's oath (*jur. auch:* one's affidavit) upon. — 2. (durch Zauberworte bannen) die Geister ~ to raise (or conjure, call up) the spirits (of the deep); böse Geister ~ (wegbannen) to exorcize …; e-n Sturm ~ to lay … — 3. (anflehen) e-n um des Himmels willen ~ to adjure a p. for heaven's sake; wir ~ Sie auf den Knien we implore you on our knees. — II ~ n ⓩ 4. = B/ung.
Be-schwörer (◡́◡) m ⓶, ~in f ⓻ (von Geistern) conjurer; exorcist.
Be-schwörung (◡́◡) f ⓡ (confirmation by) oath; der Geister: raising (of spirits); exorcism; (Anflehen) adjuration.
Be-schwörungs-formel (◡…) f ⓬, =**kunst** f formula, art of exorcism.

be-schwur (◡◡́) *impf.* von beschwören.

be-seel/en (◡́◡) [Seele; vgl. beseligen] I v/a. ⓢ* to give animation (or life) to; *fig.* to inspire; er war von dem Wunsche beseelt // he was filled (or animated) with a desire to (mit *inf.*). — II ~ n ⓩ u. **Be-seeltheit** f ⓡ, **Be-seeltsein** n ⓩ, **Be-seelung** f ⓡ animation; inspiration.

be-segeln ↓ (◡́◡) v/a. ⓢa* 1. (segelnd befahren) to sail upon or navigate (a sea, a lake); vgl. beschiffen. — 2. (mit Segeln versehen) to furnish (or rig) with sails.

be-sehen (◡́◡) v/a. u. v/refl. ⓢa* 1. to look at, to view; prüfend: to inspect; (besuchen) to visit; sich im Spiegel ~ to look at (*co.* to admire) o.s. in the glass; sich (*dat.*) et. genau ~ to examine a th. minutely or closely; bei(m) Lichte *p.p.* on closer inspection, when looked at in the proper light; sich eine Stadt gut ~ to take a good look round a town, F to do the sights of a town. — 2. F (bekommen) hier ist wenig zu ~ there is little to be had (F got) here; Prügel ~ to get (or receive) a good beating.

be-sehens-wert (◡́◡…) a. ⓡ, ~**würdig** a. worthy of inspection, worth seeing or inspecting. — Vgl. a. sehens-…

be-seitigen (◡́◡◡) [erst nhd.] I v/a. ⓢ* 1. to lay (or set) aside, to do away with, (absondernd) to eliminate, ausstreichend: to expunge; Hindernisse ~ to remove, clear away; Schwierigkeiten: to brush aside, smooth over; *tel.* Störungen ~ to remove faults (or flaws) in the circuit; Verdacht: to clear up. — 2. (erledigen)

[**beseligen**] — 181 — [**besitzen**]

to get (a task or job) done or out of the way, to finish (a job); Streit: to settle, arrange, accommodate. — **II** ~ n ⌂ u. **Be-seitigung** ꝏ 3. (zu 1:) laying (or brushing) aside, removal; elimination; (zu 2:) settlement; accommodation.

be-seligen (◡´◡◡) [selig] **I** v/a. ⊛* to make happy, to fill with bliss or happiness; (entzücken) to enrapture; beseligt, auch: happy; in raptures pl. — **II** ⌂d p.pr. u. a. ⊛ rapturous; ⌂der Gedanke delightful thought. — **III** B/ung f ⊛ bliss(ful state); delight; rel. beatitude.

Besemschon ⚘ (◡´◡◡) [ndl.] m(n) ⊕d. (Abzug für das, was beim Ausleeren v. Waren an der Umhüllung hängen bleibt) allowance for loss sustained in unpacking (goods).

Besen (´◡) [ahd.: besom] m ⌂ **1.** broom, bisw. besom; kleiner (Hand-)~ handbrush; Sprichw. neue ~ kehren gut new brooms sweep clean. — **2.** (Feder-)~ feather brush; (Stroh-)~ whisk. — **3.** burschikos: (Magd) servant, F slavey; (Weib) woman, wench.

Besen-binder (´◡◡◡) m ⌂ broom-maker, fig. f. laufen 1; ⌂förmig a. ⊛ broom-shaped, ⚘ scopiform; =ginster ⚘ m common broom (Sarotha'mnus ob. Cy'tisus scopa'rius); =heide ⚘ f = Heidekraut; =kraut ⚘ n: a) = Feldbeifuß; b) = =ginster; =raufe ⚘ f flix-weed, fine-leaved hedge-mustard (Sisy'mbrium So'phia); =reis n, =reisig n birch(en) twig; =stiel m broom-stick; steif wie ein ~ as stiff as a poker; -winde ⚘ f broom-bindweed (Convo'lvulus scopa'rius).

be-sessen (◡◡´◡) **I** p.p. von besitzen. — **II** a. ⊛ (D9) vom Teufel ⌂ possessed of a devil; distracted, frantic; schreien wie ⌂ to shout like mad or like a maniac; er ist darauf wie ⌂ he has a mania (or craze) for it; F he is mad (or crazy) after it. — **III** ~e(r) m, ~e f ⊛ one possessed; demoniac, co. crazy Jack. **Be-sessen-heit** f ⊛, =sein n ⌂ (◡´◡◡) possessed state; frenzy; craziness.

be-setzen (◡◡´◡) [:beset] **I** v/a. ⊛* **1.** mit et. ⌂ to put (or place, set) one th. on another. — **2.** (ausstatten) mit Bäumen, Hecken ⌂ to plant with ...; mit Fischen, Geflügel ⌂ to stock with ...; mit Einwohnern ⌂ to (fill with) people; ⚔ eine Stadt mit Soldaten ⌂ to garrison ...; vgl. 4; mit Spitzen, mit Pelz ⌂ to trim (or border) with lace, to line (round) with fur; ⊕ ein Straßenpflaster ⌂ (mit der Handramme ebenen) to level the pavement by ramming it (down). — **3.** ein Amt ꝛc. ⌂ to fill up an appointment or a vacancy; er (die Krone) hat die Stelle zu ⌂ the post is in his appointment (in the gift of the crown); die Stellen in e-m Bureau ⌂ to staff an office: thea. die Rollen (auch ein Stück) ⌂ to cast the parts (for a play); die Rolle ist gut besetzt the part is well supported; die Rollen waren gut besetzt there was a good (or strong) cast; f-e Stunden sind besetzt his time is fully engaged or taken up; der Wagen ist besetzt, die Stühle, Sitze sind besetzt all seats are taken or engaged; tel. eine gut besetzte Linie a busy circuit. — **4.** (in Besitz nehmen) to occupy,

im Zug ꝛc.: (hier ist alles) besetzt! engaged!, taken!, F full up!; ⚔ eine Anhöhe ꝛc. ⌂ to seize (or occupy) ... — **5.** Spiel: to stake (or put) money on a card, &c. — **II** ~ n ⌂ **6.** = Besetzung.

be-setzt (◡´) p.p. u. a. ⊛ **1.** in den Bed. des inf. besetzen; von Häusern, Zimmern ꝛc.: occupied, tenanted; ⚔ ⌂ halten to hold (a position). — **2.** (gedrängt voll; vgl. auch besetzen 4) crowded, F crammed (full); mit Diamanten ⌂ studded with diamonds; eine gut ⌂e Tafel a well-spread board, a richly furnished table, F a good spread. — **3.** ♀ vom Lande ⌂ (eingeschlossen) land-locked; ⚓ ⌂ sein mit Land (im Sturm eine Küste unter dem Winde haben) to be drifted to (or embayed on) the lee-shore.

Be-setzung (◡´◡◡) f ⊛ stocking, filling, &c.; e-r Stelle: appointment, eccl. presentation; v. Rollen: cast(ing); ⚔ occupation; einer Karte: stake (put on a card).

Be-setzungs-recht (´◡◡◡) n ⌂ right of nomination (zu besetzen 3); bsd. parl. in England: patronage; eccl. auch: advowson.

be-seufzen (◡´◡◡) v/a. ⊛* to sigh (or groan) at or over, to bemoan.

be-sichtig·en (◡◡´◡◡) **I** v/a. ⊛* et. ⌂ to view a th.; (prüfend besehen) to inspect, examine; ein Hospital ꝛc.: to visit; (vermessen) to survey (a country); ⚔ to inspect, muster. — **II** ~ n ⌂ = B/ung.

Be-sichtiger (◡◡´◡◡) m ⌂, ~in f ⊛ p. who views, &c.; inspector; visitor; surveyor; (Sachverständiger) expert.

Be-sichtigung (◡◡´◡◡) f ⊛ view; inspection; visit; survey; e-r Leiche: (coroner's) inquest; nach genauer ~ after a close search; ⚔ inspection, muster.

Be-sichtigungs-gebühren (´◡◡◡◡) f/pl. ⊛ inspector's (or surveyor's) fees pl.; =reise f tour of inspection.

be-siedeln (◡◡´◡) v/a. ⊛a* to colonize. — **II Be-sied(e)lung** f ⊛ colonization.

be-siegbar (◡´◡◡) a. ⊛ conquerable; =keit (◡´◡◡◡) f ⊛ conquerableness.

be-siegeln (◡◡´◡) **I** v/a. ⊛a* to seal a deed, to affix (or put) one's seal to a document; fig. die Wahrheit mit dem Tode ⌂ to bear witness to the truth with one's life; seinen Glauben mit dem Blute ⌂ to die a martyr to one's faith; das wird ihr Los, ihr Schicksal ⌂ that will seal their fate or doom. — **II** ~ n ⌂ u. **Be-sieg(e)lung** (◡◡´◡◡) f ⊛ sealing, &c. (s. I).

be-sieg·en (◡◡´◡) **I** v/a. u. v/refl. ⊛* **1.** (sich) ⌂ to conquer (o.s.); (schlagen) to beat, to defeat, to get the better of, to overthrow; (unterwerfen) to subdue (a nation, one's passion); der besiegte Feind the vanquished foe; fig. Schwierigkeiten ⌂ to overcome (or surmount, get over) difficulties. — **2.** Spiel: to beat a p., to win a game of (or from) a p.; sich für besiegt erklären to declare o.s. beaten; to give in. — **II** ~ n ⌂ **3.** = B/ung.

Be-sieger (◡◡´◡) m ⌂, ~in f ⊛ conqueror; vanquisher, victor; winner.

Be-siegelung (◡◡´◡◡) f ⊛ s. Besiegelung.

Be-siegung (◡◡´◡) f ⊛ conquest (of a country); defeat (of the enemy).

Be-sing ⚘ (´◡) [ndd.: Beere] m ⊕d. bsd. schwarze ~e = Heidelbeeren.

be-singen (◡◡´◡) v/a. ⊛* to sing of; to chant; (preisen) to praise (in song); ⌂-wert (´◡...) a. ⊛, ⌂-würdig a. ⊛ glorious; worthy of a poet's song, worthy to be set forth in song.

be-sinn·en (◡◡´◡) **I** sich ⌂ v/refl. ⊛* **1.** (sich zu erinnern suchen) to try to recollect. — **2.** (ins Gedächtnis zurückrufen) to call (back) to one's memory or mind; to remember, to recollect; ich besinne mich nicht, daß ich ihn gesehen habe I do not remember having seen him; ich konnte mich nicht darauf ⌂ I could not hit upon it; wenn ich mich recht besinne if I recollect rightly; unless I be mistaken. — **3.** (auf den Gedanken kommen) to bethink o.s. of; sich e-s ander(e)n (oder Besser(e)n) ⌂ to change one's mind, to think better of it. — **4.** (nachdenken) sich über et. ⌂ to reflect (or deliberate) on a th., to consider a th.; stärker: to puzzle about s. th.; ohne sich (lange zu) ⌂ without a moment's consideration; on the spur of the moment; sich hin und her ⌂ to rack one's brain about a th. — **II** ~ n ⌂ **5.** recollection; reflection; nach kurzem ~ after a moment's hesitation; was hilft das (lange) ~? what is the use of considering (so long)? — **III be-sonnen** p.p. **6.** s. bs.

Be-sinnung (◡◡´◡◡) f ⊛: die ~ verlieren: a) to lose consciousness; b) (die Fassung verlieren) to be disconcerted, to falter, to get flurried; (wieder) zur ~ kommen: a) to recover one's senses, F to come to; b) to come to (or to recover one's) reason; zur ~ bringen: a) to restore to life; b) to bring back to one's senses; er ist nicht bei ~ he is not in his right senses; ~s-kraft (´◡...) f ⊛ power of recollection; memory; ~s-los a. ⊛ insensible, unconscious; ~s-losig-keit f insensibility, unconsciousness.

Be-sitz (◡´) m ⊕a. **1.** (das Besitzen) possession; (Anwesen) property; des Staates: domain; (Landgut) manor, (landed) estate; (Möbel) goods and chattels pl.; rel. unser irdischer ~ our worldly belongings pl. — **2.** in den ~ von etwas gelangen oder kommen to obtain (or gain, get) possession of a th.; ~ nehmen oder ergreifen to take possession of a th.; to appropriate a th.; von einem Gute: to enter upon an estate; im ~e von et. sein to be possessed (or in possession) of a th., to have (or hold) a th. in one's possession; e-n (wieder) in den ~ von et. setzen to put a p. in(to) possession of a th.; in ~ treten to enter into possession of a th. — **3.** e-n aus dem ~e bringen (setzen oder treiben) to dispossess (or expropriate) a p.; jur. (austreiben) to eject (or evict, oust) a p.; ⚔ im ~ e-r Stellung bleiben to remain master of (or to maintain) a position.

be-sitz-anzeigend (◡´◡...) a. ⊛ gram. possessive (pronoun, adjective).

be-sitzen (◡◡´◡) **I** v/a. ⊛* **1.** to possess, to be possessed (or in possession) of; to own; to have; Ausdauer, Kraft ꝛc. ⌂ to be endowed (or gifted, armed) with ... — **2.** (innehaben) to occupy, hold, own,

---

♪ Musik; ⚘ Wissenschaft; ⚘ Pflanze; ♀ Geographie; ⊕ Technik; ⚒ Bergbau; ⚔ Militär; ⚓ Marine; ✆ Handel; ✉ Post; 🚂 Eisenbahn.

[Besitzentziehung] — 182 — [besprechen]

gute Gesundheit ꝛc. ♎ to enjoy ...; die 2den Klassen the propertied (or moneyed) classes. — II ~ n ㉓ 3. = Besitz 1. [session, expropriation.]
Be-sitz-entziehung (⌣ˊ⌣...) f ㉖ dispos-
Be-sitzer (⌣ˊ⌣) m ㉒, ~**in** f ㊼ occupier; (Eigentümer) owner; von Häusern ꝛc. auch: proprietor; e-s Geschäftshauses ꝛc.: principal; e-s Hotels ꝛc.: keeper; e-s Wechsels ꝛc.: holder; den ~ wechseln to change hands; unrechtmäßiger ~ usurper, intruder.
Be-sitz-ergreifer (⌣ˊ...) m ㉒ person who takes possession of a th.; Am., &c. (von Staatsland) squatter; b.s. claim-jumper; **=ergreifung** f taking possession of ...; jur. auch: seizin(g), seizure; widerrechtliche: usurpation; Am., &c. von Land: squatting; b.s. claim-jumping; vgl. =**nahme**; **=fall** m, gram. possessive case, genitive; **=los** a. without property, stärker: destitute, pennyless; die =lose Menge the proletariat; die =losen the destitute, pol. die non-haves, the disowned pl.; **=losigkeit** f (total) lack of means; **=nahme** f appropriation, occupation; e-r Erbschaft: entrance upon (an inheritance), vgl. =ergreifung; **=nehmer** m occupant, e-s Pachtgutes: incoming tenant; **=recht** n right of occupation; legal possession; **=stand** m: a) ownership; b) ⚭ assets pl.; **=störung** f interference with (rights of) ownership; **=stück** n piece of property; **=titel** m, title, title-deed.
Be-sitztum (⌣ˊ⌣-) n ②d. property; vgl. Besitz 1. [(⌣ˊ...) = Besitz...]
Be-sitzung (⌣ˊ⌣) f ㊻ = Besitz 1; ~**s-**...
Be-sitz-urkunde (⌣ˊ...) f ㉖ = =titel.
be-socken (⌣ˊ⌣) v/a. ㊽* to put socks on a p.'s feet; to new-foot stockings.
be-soden (⌣ˊ⌣) v/a. ㊽* eine Böschung ♎ (mit Rasen belegen) to turf ...
be-soffen P (⌣ˊ⌣) p.p. v. besaufen u. a. ㊅ (D9) drunk, in liquor, F tipsy, tight; schwer ♎ helplessly (F blind) drunk; ~**heit** f ㊻ drunkenness, F tipsy state.
be-sohlen ⊕ (⌣ˊ⌣) v/a. ㊽* Schuhmacherei: to sole, to put (a pair of) soles on boots, shoes; wieder (oder neu) ♎ to re-sole, to new-sole.
be-solden (⌣ˊ⌣) I v/a. ㊽* to keep in one's pay; ⚔ Truppen ꝛc.: to pay; Beamte ꝛc.: to pay a salary (or stipend) to; Dienstboten, Arbeiter: to pay wages to. — II ~ n ㉓ payment of salary. — III **be-soldet** p.p. u. a. ㊅ salaried; stipendiary (magistrate, &c.).
Be-soldung (⌣-) f ㊻ pay (⚔ of soldiers); salary or stipend (of officials); wages pl. (of servants); ~**s-erhöhung** (⌣ˊ...) f ㊷ increase of pay; **=verhältnisse** n/pl.; amount of salary; **=zulage** f ~~=erhöhung.
be-sonder (⌣ˊ⌣) ㊅ (D9) I a. meist: particular, (außergewöhnlich) special (object); specific (quality); (eigentümlich) peculiar (circumstances), individual (taste); (vereinzelt) singular (case), separate (volume); (befremdend) strange or odd (manner); er hat seine ♎(e)n Ansichten he has opinions of his own; er hat keine ♎(e)n Fähigkeiten his abilities are very ordinary or commonplace. — II **Be-**

sond(e)re(s) n ㊇ das Allgemeine und das Besond(e)re generals and particulars pl., vgl. allgemein III; etwas, nichts Besond(e)res something, nothing special or out of the common; (des Fachs) speciality; insbesondere adv. in particular; severally; im besonder(e)n specially; (für sich) apart (for itself); separately; individually.
Be-sonderheit (⌣ˊ⌣-) f ㊻ particularity; speciality; peculiarity; individuality; singularity; strangeness; ~**en** pl. details pl.
be-sonders (⌣ˊ⌣) I a. prädikativ: die Sache ist nicht gerade ♎ ... nothing out of the common, F not up to much. — II adv. particularly, (e)specially; (namentlich) above all; distinctly; (hauptsächlich) chiefly, principally; steigernd: ♎ gut particularly (or exceptionally) good; es gefällt mir nicht ♎ I am not over-pleased with it; sie spielte nicht ♎ (schön) she played indifferently or not very (or particularly) well.
be-sonnen¹ (⌣ˊ⌣) [Sonne] v/a. ㊽* to (expose to the rays of the) sun; besonntes Land sunny country, land bathed in sunshine.
be-sonnen² (⌣ˊ⌣) [besinnen] a. ㊅ (bedacht) thoughtful, considerate; (vorsichtig) circumspect, cautious, wary; prudent; (kaltblütig) cool-headed; (zurückhaltend) discreet; ~**heit** (⌣ˊ⌣-) f ㊻ thoughtfulness, considerateness; circumspection, cautiousness, caution, wariness, prudence; cool-headedness; discretion; (Geistesgegenwart) presence of mind.
be-sorg/en (⌣ˊ⌣) I v/a. ㊽* 1. (fürchten) to apprehend, fear; to be apprehensive (or afraid) of; wir haben nichts von ihm zu ♎ we have nothing to fear from him or to dread on his part; Unheil ♎ to apprehend some accident, to fear lest s.th. (untoward) might happen; auch v/n. (h.): wir besorgten für sein Leben we trembled for his life. — 2. (Sorge tragen für) to attend (to), to take care of, Kinder, Kranke ♎ to nurse (or mind) ...; den Laden ꝛc. ♎ to look after ...; to superintend ...; die Wirtschaft ♎ to keep house. — 3. (tun) to do, perform, execute, carry out; ich will Ihnen das ♎ I will see to that for you; einer kann es leicht ♎ one (person) can easily manage it, it is an easy job for one (person); e-e Arbeit ♎ to do a piece of work; e-n Auftrag, ein Geschäft ♎ to do a commission, to transact business for a p.; e-e (neue) Ausgabe ♎ to (re-)edit or (re)publish a book; die Küche ♎ to do (or look after) the cooking; F der ist besorgt und aufgehoben (SCH.) he is dispatched and safely stored, einfacher: he is safely disposed of. — 4. e-m etwas ♎ (verschaffen) to get (or procure) a th. for a p.; Lebensmittel ♎ für // to cater for //. — 5. (befördern) Briefe ꝛc. ♎ to post, forward, send off —. II ~ n ㉓ 6. = B/ung.
Be-sorger (⌣ˊ⌣) m ㉒, ~**in** f ㊼ person who looks after a th.; provider, furnisher, von Speisen: caterer, (Bote) messenger, commissionaire.

be-sorglich (⌣ˊ⌣) a. ㊅ 1. f. besorgt 2. — 2. (zu befürchten) alarming, disquieting.
Be-sorglichkeit (⌣ˊ⌣-) f ㊻ 1. (Angst) apprehensiveness, anxiousness. — 2. (Sorgfalt) solicitude, carefulness, attentiveness.
Be-sorgnis (⌣ˊ⌣) f ⑱ apprehension (or fear, concern) about; (Befangenheit) disquietude, misgiving; in ~ geraten to get alarmed; wir hegen ~, daß // we are apprehensive (or in fear) that or lest //. [alarm, alarming.]
be-sorgnis-erregend (⌣ˊ...) a. ㊅ causing
be-sorgt (⌣ˊ⌣) p.p. u. a. ㊅ 1. in den Bed. des inf. besorgen. — 2. in aktivem Sinne: apprehensive for; (beängstigt) anxious about, solicitous for; concerned about; für seine Gesundheit (stark) ♎ sein to bestow (great) attention (or care) on ...; to study ... (carefully). [concern) about.]
Be-sorgtheit (⌣ˊ⌣-) f ㊻ uneasiness (or
Be-sorgung (⌣ˊ⌣) f ㊻ care (or attention) bestowed on; superintendence exercised over; e-m et. zur ~ überlassen to entrust (or leave) s.th. to a p.'s solicitude or management; (Auftrag) commission; ~**en** ausrichten to go on errands, to do commissions (vgl. besorgen).
be-spannen (⌣ˊ⌣) I v/a. ㊽* 1. den Wagen mit Pferden ♎ to put the horses to; mit zwei Pferden bespannt drawn by ... — 2. ein Instrument mit Saiten ♎ to string ... — 3. mit den Fingern ♎ to span. — II **Be-spannung** f ㊻ 4. pair (\draught) of (carriage-)horses; team of draught- (or cart-)horses.
be-speien (⌣ˊ⌣) ⑪(⑧)* = anspeien.
be-spicken (⌣ˊ⌣) ㊽* = spicken.
be-spiegeln (⌣ˊ⌣) I sich ♎ v/refl. ㉑a* to look (or gaze) at o.s. (F to admire o.s.) in the glass. — II ~ n ㉓ und **Be-spieg(e)lung** (⌣ˊ(⌣)-) f ㊻ reflection in the mirror.
be-spinnen (⌣ˊ⌣) v/a. ㉒a* to spin over; to cover with weft; besponnene Saiten wire- (or silk-)spun chords pl.; besponnener Knopf cloth (or silk) button.
be-spitzt (⌣ˊ⌣) p.p. u. a. ㊅ (leicht berauscht) a little the worse for drink, F slightly (or just a bit) on.
be-sponnen (⌣ˊ⌣) p.p. von bespinnen.
be-spornen (⌣ˊ⌣) v/a. ㊽* Stiefel ♎ to put spurs on ...; besspornt spurred.
be-spötteln ㉒a*, **be-spotten** ㊽* (⌣ˊ⌣) I v/a. to rail (stärker: to mock, scoff, sneer) at; to ridicule, deride; F to chaff. — II ~ n ㉓ u. **Be-spöttelung**, **Be-spottung** f ㊻ raillery; mockery, sneer(ing); ridicule, derision; F chaff.
be-sprach (⌣ˊ⌣), **be-sprang** (⌣ˊ⌣) impf. von besprechen, bespringen.
be-sprechen (⌣ˊ⌣) ㉒a* I v/a. 1. = bereden 1 u. 2. — 2. (verabreden) to agree upon, to arrange (a marriage); to settle (the terms of a contract). — 3. (durch Zaubersprüche heilen, beschwören) to cure by magic, to charm away by magic (words). — 4. (rezensieren) to review, criticize, comment upon. — II v/refl. 5. sich mit e-m über et. ♎ to converse (or talk confer) with a p. about a th.; (unterhandeln) to negotiate; (sich verabreden) to come to an understanding or agreement; sich da-

Signs (see page XVII): F familiar; P vulgar; ℉ flash; ⚲ rare; † obsolete (died); * new word (born); ⁒ incorrect; ♪ music;

[Besprecher] — 183 — [bestallen]

hin 2, daß // to settle (or agree) that //. — III ~ 23 6. = Besprechung.
Be-sprecher (◡◡◡) m 22. **~in** f 40 person who heals by magic (formula or spell); von Büchern: reviewer; weitS. (Kunstrichter) art-critic.
Be-sprechung (◡◡◡) f 46 discussion, lebhafte: debate; zur ~ kommen to become a subject of deliberation; (Verabredung) agreement, understanding; (Beschwörung) incantation, (Zauberspruch) (magic) charm; (Beurteilung) criticism; (Rezension) review, (literary) notice; (Unterhandlung) negotiation; (Zusammenkunft) conference, interview; ~ des Manövers ꝛc.: criticism (or comment) passed upon …; sich auf e-e ~ mit e-m einlassen to enter into parley (or negotiations) with a p.; **~s-formel** (◡◡◡) f 40 magic formula or spell; charm.
be-sprengen (◡◡◡) I v/a. 68* mit einer Flüssigkeit 2 to (be)sprinkle with …; eccl. mit Weihwasser: to asperse. — II ~n 23 u. **Be-sprengung** f 46 sprinkling; eccl. aspersion.
be-springen (◡◡◡) v/a. 68t* to leap (or spring) upon; to mount with a leap.
be-spritzen (◡◡◡) I v/a. 90* to squirt (or splash) with water, &c.; (besprengen) to (be)sprinkle; eccl. to asperse; mit Blut 2 to stain with blood; von oben bis unten mit Kot 2 to bespatter (with mud) from head to foot; v/refl. sich mit Kot 2 to bedraggle o.s. — II **Be-spritzung** f 46 sprinkling; eccl. aspersion.
be-sprochen (◡◡◡) p.p. von besprechen.
be-sprudeln 2a*, **be-sprühen** 68* (◡◡◡) v/a. = bespritzen.
be-sprungen (◡◡◡) p.p. von bespringen.
be-spucken F (◡◡◡) 68* = anspeien.
be-spülen (◡◡◡) v/a. 68* to wash (the shore, the banks); to beat against (the rocks); poet. to lave (the silver sands, &c.); surg. to bathe (a wound).
be-spunden, be-spünden (◡◡◡) v/a. 68* to bung up (a cask, a barrel).
Bessarabi-en ♀ (◡◡◡◡) [Bessen (Volk)] npr/n. 23a. (russische Provinz) Bessarabia; **Bessarabi-er(in** f 40) m 22, **bess-arabisch** a. 66 Bessarabian.
Bessemer-apparat T ⊕ (◡◡◡…) [Bessemer, engl. Ingenieur, 1813—98] m 62, **=birne** f Bessemer converter; **=prozeß** m Bessemer process (for converting iron into steel); **=stahl** m Bessemer steel; **=werk** n B. works pl. or plant.
besser (◡◡) [ahd.: better] I a. 66 (D 9) u. adv. (comp. von gut a. und von wohl adv.) 1. better; es geht ihm 2, es steht 2 mit ihm he is going on better or more satisfactorily; es geht ihr immer 2 she is steadily improving or progressing; danke, es geht mir 2 thanks, I am better; er hat es 2 (aus ihr 2 daran) als // he is better off than //; desto (ob. um so) 2! so much the better! um so 2 als // all the better since //; Sprichw. 2 spät als niemals better late than never. — 2. du bliebest 2, wo du bist you had better remain where you are! das kommt ja immer 2 (toller) that is going from bad to worse; es sollte noch 2 (schlimmer) kommen worse (things) followed; 2 machen to (make) better,

to improve; das macht's nicht 2 that won't mend (or improve) matters; er macht's 2 als sie he does better than she, F he takes the shine out of her; 2 sein als // to excel (or outshine) //; in et. 2 sein to be stronger (or more apt) in a th.; das wäre noch 2! that would crown (or beat) all!; what next?; 2 werden to improve (in quality); to recover (from an illness); vom Wetter: to brighten up. — 3. P (mehr, stärker) 2 laufen to run faster; 2 unten! further below! — 4.* F als negative Steigerung von schlecht: eines der ~(e) Rührstücke one of the better (or less sensational) melodramas; Zeitungsanzeige: 2e Köchin gesucht a superior cook required; ✉ eine 2e Ware a better class of goods. — II **~es** n 67 5. that which is better or preferable or more to the purpose; es ist das 2e, daß (= 2, daß) it is better that //; in Ermangelung e-s ~(e)n in default of s.th. better; e-n ~(e)n belehren f. besehren 2; sich e-s ~(e)n besinnen f. besinnen 3; Sie könnten nichts ~es tun als / you could not do better (or you might do worse) than /; eine Wendung zum ~(e)n nehmen to take a turn for the better; Sprichw. das ~e ist des Guten Feind, leave (or let) well alone; auch: you might go farther, and fare worse; good is good, but better is better.
bessern (◡◡) [ahd.] 2a. I v/a. 1. to (make) better; to improve, to make improvements in; to mend (matters, morals); to ameliorate (a state of things); to correct (faults); to reform (habits); nicht zu 2(d) past mending; incorrigible. — 2. = aus2. — II sich 2 v/refl. 3. to grow (or to change for the) better; es hat sich manches gebessert there have been many improvements, F things are looking up; sittlich: to mend or reform (one's ways); to turn over a new leaf; gesundheitlich: to recover, improve, gain strength; vom Wetter: to brighten (or clear) up; ✉ vom Kurse: to advance, rise, gain, go up, go better; ✉ Börse: die Aktien konnten sich schließlich wieder bis auf 20 2 the shares finally rose again (or improved) to 20, the shares recovered at the close and finished off at 20.
Besserung (◡◡◡) f 46 mending, amelioration; correction; reform(ation); recovery; improvement; ✉ advance, rise, gain; von Kranken: es ist ~ eingetreten a favourable change has set in, there is a decided improvement; auf dem Wege der ~ on the road (or way) to (or towards) recovery; sittlich: reforming; allg.: F on the mend; gute ~! good (or better) health to you!; I trust you may (or will) soon be better!; **~s-anstalt** (◡◡◡…) f 62, **=haus** n house of correction, reformatory; **=fähig** a. 66 improvable, mendable; rel. reclaimable; **=mittel** n corrective.
Besser-wissen (◡◡…) n 23, **=wisserei** (◡◡◡◡) f 46 priggishness; learned conceit; **=wisser(in** f 40) m 22 one who professes to know everything better (than others); prig.

best (◡) [ahd.: best] sup. v. gut a. u. v. wohl adv. I adv. 1. best: a) inv. nur in Zsgn mit s. u. a., bsd. part., s. Bietend ꝛc.; b) 2ens, aufs (oder **auf das**) 2e, zum 2en: in the best manner (possible or conceivable); to the best of one's ability; wir werden das 2ens besorgen we shall give it our best attention; ich danke Ihnen 2ens (I) thank you very much!, many thanks!, (I am) much obliged (to you)!, alles ist aufs 2e eingerichtet … arranged for the best; er hält seine Leute nicht zum 2en he treats his men indifferently well or rather badly; ist es uns gelungen not done overwell, far from (being) a success; ✉ 2ens Börse: at the best price or figure; c) am 2en: es ist am 2 (oder das 2e ist), du gehst selbst the best thing for you to do is to go yourself; es wäre wohl am 2en für ihn, zu // his best course would be to //; aufhören, wenn es am 2en schmeckt to leave off with an appetite. — II a. (als s. der. die **~e**) 67 2. (the) best; er ist der ~e in der Klasse he is at the head (or top) of the class; das 2e Obst the choicest fruit; mein 2er Herr dear sir; m-e ~e my dear (or good) lady. — 3. im 2en Alter, in den 2en Jahren in the prime of life; im 2en Arbeiten hard at work; im 2en Falle at best; at the most; der 2e Mensch von der Welt the best fellow alive; im 2en Schlafe in a sound (or profound) sleep; nach m-m 2en Wissen to the best of my knowledge. — 4. der erste (oder nächste) 2e the first comer; the first p. (that) one may chance to meet or to run against. — III **~e(s)** n 67 (oft auch klein geschrieben) 5. the best (thing); das ~e ist für ihn gut genug the best is good enough for him; F (Auserlesenes) the cream or élite (of society); the pick (of the basket, of the troops); the flower (of chivalry); ich halte es für das ~e I think it best; es würde das 2e sein, wenn // it would be best for him to //; sein ~es (möglichstes) tun to do one's utmost, to use every effort (so as to). — 6. (Nutzen, Heil) das gemeine ~e the common good or weal; für das allgemeine ~e for the good of all; zum ~en der Armen for the benefit of the poor; ich tue es zu deinem ~en I do it for your good or to further your interest; zum ~en raten to advise for the best) — 7. e-n zum 2en haben: a) (hänseln, to make game (or sport) of; to chaff (or tease); b) (hinhalten) to put off (with fine promises); zum 2en kehren, lenken, wenden to give the most favourable turn to, to turn to the best advantage. — 8. e-m et. zum 2en geben to treat a p. to (a dinner); F to stand a p. (a drink); er gab uns ein Lied zum 2en he favoured us with a song.
be-stach (◡◡) impf. von bestechen.
be-stahl (◡◡) impf. von bestehlen.
be-stallen (◡◡◡) [.+ aus bestallt, † p.p. v. bestellen] I v/a. 68* (ernennen) to appoint to; (einsetzen) to install in; feierlich: to invest with; neu bestallt

⚛ scientific; ♀ botanical; ⊕ geography; ⊕ machinery; ⚒ mining; ⚔ military; ⚓ marine; ✉ commercial; ✉ postal; 🚂 railway.

[Bestallung] — 184 — [besteigen]

newly appointed, recently installed. — II **Be-stallung** *f* ⊕ appointment; installation; investiture.
Be-stallungs-brief (ˊ…) *m* ⊕, **-urkunde** *f* diploma; parchment; letters *pl.* patent; **-recht** *n* right of investiture.
be-stand[1] (ˇˇ) *imp.* von bestehen.
Be-stand[2] (ˇˇ) *m* ①b. **1.** (Bestehen) existence; (Fortbestehen) continuance, duration; (Dauerhaftigkeit) stability, durability; (Beharren) consistency; von ~ sn, ~ haben to continue, to last, to be of long duration; vom Wetter: keinen ~ haben to be unsettled or changeable; der Friede wird f-n ~ haben peace will not last, it will be of short duration. — **2.** (Vorhandenes, Vorrat) stock, store; ~ eines Forstes amount (or stock) of timber; ~ (Vieh, Wild) e-s Gutes live stock; ⚔ e-s Regiments: actual strength; ⊕ ~ der Kasse: cash (or balance) in hand; ~ der Waren: goods *pl.* on hand. — **3.** *prov.* öst. ein Gut in ~ (Pacht) geben to let out a farm or an estate.
Be-stand-buch ⊕ (ˊ…) *n* ⊕ inventory.
be-standen (ˇˇ) *p.p.* von bestehen.
be-ständig (ˇˇˇ) *a.* ⊕ **1.** (Bestand habend) stable; vom Wetter: settled; (anhaltend) permanent; (dauerhaft) durable, lasting; invariable; (ausdauernd) persevering; steadfast; (un-aufhörlich) incessant; *math.* ⊇e Größe constant (value); ⊕ ⊇e Nachfrage steady inquiry or demand. — **2.** (un-unterbrochen) continuous, stärker: persistent; perpetual; *adv.* er ist ⊇ leidend he is for ever ailing.
Be-ständigkeit (ˇˇˇˇ) *f* ⊕ (o. *pl.*) stability; settled state; permanency; durability; perseverance, constancy; continuousness; persistency.
Be-stand-liste (ˇˇ…) *f* ⊕ = -buch; ⊇los *a.* ⊕ without duration; unstable; (unbeständig) inconsistent; **-losigkeit** *f* instability, inconsistency; **-teil** *m* ingredient; wesentlicher ~ essential part; einen wesentlichen ~ von et. bilden to be part and parcel of a th., to enter largely into the composition of a th.; *chm.* constituent, component; unzerlegbarer ~ element; **-vertrag** *m* öst. = Miet-, Pacht-v.; **-verzeichnis** *n* = -buch.
be-stärken (ˇˇˇ) I *v/a.* ⊕* to confirm; e-n in seinem Glauben, seiner Ansicht ⊇ to fortify (or strengthen) a p.'s belief; to support a p.'s opinion. — II ~ *n* ⊕ u. **Be-stärkung** *f* ⊕ confirmation.
be-stätig/en (ˇˇˇˇ) I *v/a.* u. *v/refl.* ⊕* **1. a)** (bekräftigen) to corroborate, e-e Nachricht: to confirm; to substantiate (facts); to endorse (an opinion); to uphold (a sentence or judgment); (billigen) to approve; ⊕ indem wir unser früheres Schreiben ⊇ confirming our previous letter; **b)** (als richtig bartun) to verify (statements); to bear out (assertions); to establish (the truth of a th.); **c)** den Empfang eines Briefes ⊇ to acknowledge the receipt…; e-n Vertrag: to ratify; Handlungen: to sanction; obrigfeitlich ⊇ to authorize; **d)** die Nachricht bestätigt sich … is confirmed or holds good; f-e Worte h. sich nicht bestätigt… have not come true, … have proved false. — II ~ *n* ⊕ **2.** = Bjung. —

III ⊇d *p.pr.* u. *a.* ⊕ **3.** Bed. des *inf.* — **4.** confirmatory, corroborative.
Be-stätigung (ˇˇˇˇ) *f* ⊕ confirmation, corroboration; substantiation; endorsement; verification; ratification; sanction; authorization.
Be-stätigungs-order ⚔ (ˊ…) *f* ⊕ further order confirming a previous one; **-urkunde** *f* deed confirming an appointment, a settlement, &c.; bei Erwerbungen: title-deed; **-urteil** *n* confirmatory sentence; summary judgment.
be-statten (ˇˇˇ) ⊕* = beerdigen I; durch Verbrennen: to cremate.
be-stätten ⊕ (ˇˇˇ) I *v/a.* ⊕* Güter ⊇ to convey … (from a railway-station to the consignee's address). — II ~ *n* ⊕, **Be-stätterei** u. **Be-stättung** *f* ⊕ carting, conveyance (of goods).
Be-stattung (ˇˇˇ) *f* ⊕ funeral = Beerdigung; durch Verbrennen: cremation.
be-stauben (ˇˇˇ) *v/n.* (sn) ⊕* to become dusty, to collect dust.
be-stäuben (ˇˇˇ) I *v/a.* ⊕* to cover with dust; mit Puder ⊇ to powder. — II **be-stäubt** *p.p.* u. *a.* ⊕ dusty; ♃ *u.ent.*: ⚹ pruinose, …ous. [⚹ pruina.]
Be-stäubung (ˇˇˇ) *f* ⊕ dustiness;
be-stauden ♃ (ˇˇˇ) I sich ⊇ *v/refl.* ⊕* von Kohl ⁊c.: to form a stalk or head, to tillow. — II **Be-staudung** *f* ⊕ tillowing. [astonished at.]
be-staunen (ˇˇˇ) *v/a.* ⊕* to look ⟩
best-bietend (ˊˇˇ) *a.* ⊕ making the highest (or best) bid.
☞ **beste** ⁊c. f. best.
be-stechbar (ˇˇˇ) *a.* ⊕ = bestechlich.
be-stechen (ˇˇˇ) I *v/a.* ⊕a* **1.** ☉ Buchbinderei, Schuhmacherei ⁊c.: to stitch; Näherei: to button-hole the edges; e-n Saum ⊇ to overcast a seam; ⚔ Zimmerung, Gang (prüfend) ⊇ to sound the timber-work, the lode. — **2.** *fig.* e-n ⊇ (erkaufen) to bribe (or corrupt) a p.; F to grease a p.'s palms; Zeugen, auch: to suborn; (für sich einnehmen) to ingratiate o.s. with a p.; ⊇d attractive, taking; specious; ein ⊇des Äußere an attractive appearance; *b.s.* a showy outside; Richter, der sich nicht ⊇ läßt incorruptible … — II ~ *n* ⊕ **3.** = Bestechung.
Be-stecher (ˇˇˇ) *m* ⊕, ~in *f* ⊕ von Knopflöchern: button-holer; *fig.* (durch Geld) briber, corrupter; suborner.
be-stechlich (ˇˇˇ) *a.* ⊕ open to bribery, corruptible; (käuflich) venal; **~keit** *f* ⊕ corruptibility, …leness; venality.
Be-stech-naht ☉ (ˇˇˇ…) *f* ⊕ flat seam; **-presse** *f* Buchbinderei: head-band press; **-stich** *m* herring-bone stitch.
Be-stechung (ˇˇˇ) *f* ⊕ stitching; bribery; corruption; subornation; attractiveness; **~s-system** *n* ⊕ system of corruption; *pol. a.*: jobbery; **~s-versuch** *m* attempt at bribery.
Be-steck (ˇˇ) *n* ①c. **1.** chirurgisches, mathematisches ~ case of surgical, mathematical instruments. — **2.** (silbernes) (Eß-, Tafel-)~ (silver) knives, forks and spoons *pl.* — **3.** F burschikos: schnurriges ~ (Individuum) queer fellow; F rum old codger. — **4.** ♃ **a)** (Schiffbauentwurf) scheme (or plan) for the

laying-down of a ship; **b)** (Punkt auf der Seekarte, der den Ort des Schiffes bezeichnet) reckoning; ship's place on the chart; das ~ machen to prick the chart; mit dem ~ voraus (zurück) sein to be behind (ahead of) one's reckoning.
be-stecken (ˇˇˇ) *v/a.* ⊕* to prick (or stick) with pins; mit Blumen ⊇ to trim (or deck, plant) with flowers.
Be-steck-macher (ˇˇˇ…) *m* ⊕ surgical, &c. instrument-maker.
Be-steck-reder ♃ (ˇˇˇ) [*ndd.*] *m* ⊕ owner of a ship which is being built or in the course of construction.
Be-steg ⚔ (ˇˇ) *m* ⓐc. bed of loam between two bodies of ore.
be-steh(e)n (ˇˇˇ) ⊕a* I *v/a.* **1.** to pass (or go) through; Abenteuer ⊇ to meet with …; Gefahren siegreich ⊇ to overcome …; e-e Operation: to undergo; e-e Probe (glücklich) ⊇ to stand a test (well); e-e Prüfung ⊇ to pass an examination; mit Ehren: to pass with (or in) honours; nicht ⊇ to fail, to be plucked or floored; ♃ einen Sturm ⊇ to weather (out) … — **2.** von (oder mit) Gesträuchen bestanden sn to be planted (or covered) with shrubs. — II *v/n.* (sn u. h.) **3.** von Flüssigem: ⊇ bleiben (fest werden) to coagulate, to congeal. — **4.** (dauernd dasein) to exist, subsist, continue, last; er kann bei seinem Gehalte nicht ⊇ he cannot live on his salary; er kann nur kärglich ⊇ he can only just struggle along or make two ends meet; mit et. ⊇ (sich zufrieden geben) to tolerate (or endure) a th.; nicht mit ⁊c. ⊇ können to be incompatible or inconsistent. — **5.** in e-r Probe, Prüfung ⊇ to come off successfully or victoriously; im Kampfe gegen e-n (standhalten) to stand one's ground (or hold one's own) against a p.; vor e-m ⊇ to show (or prove) o.s. a match for a p. — **6.** auf e-r Sache ⊇ (beharren) to insist on a th.; auf f-m Kopfe ⊇ stubbornly to adhere to one's opinion. — **7. a)** aus etwas ⊇ (zf.-gesetzt sein) to be composed (or to consist) of …; **b)** in etwas ⊇ (sein Wesen haben) to consist in … — III ~ *n* ⊕ **8.** *p.pr.* (sn) (Dasein) existence; (Unterhalt) subsistence; (Dauer) continuation, …nce, duration; langjähriges ~ old standing; auf et.: insistence on a th.; auf f-m Kopfe: stubborn adherence (or attachment) to an opinion. — IV **be-stehend** *p.pr.* u. *a.* ⊕ **9.** Bed. des *inf.* — **10.** für sich ⊇d absolute; gesetzlich ⊇d established by law; die ⊇de Obrigkeit those (placed) in power or in authority; ⊕ ⊇de Preise *m/pl.* ruling (or prevailing) prices *pl.*; das ~de the existing (or prevailing) order of things.
be-stehlen (ˇˇˇ) *v/a.* ⊕d* to rob a p. a th.; er hat mich darum bestohlen he stole it from me; Schriftsteller, Bücher ⊇ (ausschreiben) to plagiarize (from) authors, books.
be-stehn ⁊c. f. besteh(e)n ⁊c.
Be-stehung (ˇˇˇ) *f* ⊕ = besteh(e)n III.
be-steigen (ˇˇˇ) I *v/a.* ⊕d* to mount (a ladder, a pulpit); to ascend (a mountain, the throne); to go (or climb) up

Zeichen (f. S. XVII): F familiär; P Volkssprache; ⌐ Gaunersprache; ⚹ selten; † alt (auch gestorben); * neu (auch geboren); ⚹⚹ unrichtig;

[**Besteiger**] — 185 — [**Bestmann**]

(a hill); to scale (a wall); ein Pferd: to mount, bisw. a. to bestride; ein Schiff: to go on board (ship), to embark. — II ~ n 23 = Besteigung.

Be-steiger (⌣́⌣) m 22, ~**in** f 47 v. Bergen: (mountain-)climber; der Alpen: alpinist.

Be-steigung (⌣) f 46 mounting; ascent; des Thrones: accession (or coming, succeeding) to the throne.

be-stellbar (⌣́⌣-) a. 46 **1.** ⚓ deliverable; Bureau für nicht ℒe Briefe Returned († Dead) Letter Office. — **2.** agr. cultivable. für den Pflug: tillable, arable.

Be-stell-buch 🏛 (⌣́⌣...) n 62 order-book.

be-stell en (⌣⌣) I v/a. 8⃝* **1.** den Tisch mit Speisen ℒ to set out … (with dishes). — **2.** (einrichten) to arrange; sein Haus ℒ to set one's house in order, weitS. to arrange domestic matters, to put one's affairs in order; die Wirtschaft ℒ to attend to the housekeeping or household; v/impers. es ist gut, schlecht **um** (oder **mit**) etwas bestellt a th. is in a good, bad condition or state; es ist schlecht um ihn (sein Geschäft) bestellt he (his business) is in a sad plight (or pickle or F in a shaky condition); mit seiner Algebra ist es schwach bestellt his … is weak, he is weak in … — **3.** (be-arbeiten) ein Feld: to cultivate, till, plant; den Boden ℒ, auch: to dress the surface soil. — **4.** (besorgen) to carry out; Aufträge ℒ to do errands or commissions; Briefe ℒ to deliver; e-m Grüße von e-m ℒ to make (or deliver) a p.'s compliments to a p.; to give a p.'s love to a p.; haben Sie etwas an ihn zu ℒ? have you any message to (or for) him? — **5.** (einen Auftrag geben) to order a th. from a p.; Zucker beim Kaufmann ℒ to order … at the grocer's; bestellte Arbeit (Ware) bespoke work (goods pl.); order in hand; Plätze ℒ to book (or engage, secure) seats; sich (dat.) beim Schneider e-n Rock ℒ to give the tailor an order for a coat. — **6.** e-n (kommen heißen) to send for a p.; to make an appointment with a p. (for a certain day); ich will ihn auf 7 Uhr ℒ I will appoint to see him at seven. — **7.** (anstellen; vgl. bestallen I) to install; e-n zum Richter, Vormund ℒ to appoint a p. as judge, as guardian; e-n über etwas ℒ to set a p. over s. th. — II ~ n 23 &. = B/ung.

Be-steller (⌣⌣⌣) m 22, ~**in** f 47 one who attends to (or does) a th., von Briefen, Grüßen ꝛc.: deliverer.

Be-stell-gebühren (⌣⌣⌣...) f/pl. 42, -**geld** n carrier's (or messenger's) fee(s pl.); ⚓ carriage, postage; -**kontor** 🏛 n order-office; bespoke-department.

Be-stellung (⌣⌣⌣) f 46 arrangement; des Bodens: cultivation, tillage; ⚓ von Briefen: delivery; e-r Zeitung ꝛc.: sub-scription (to a periodical); (Abrede) appointment with a p.; (Auftrag) order, commission; ~en m. to give orders to; auf ~ gemacht made to order, bespoke(n); ~**s-brief** (⌣⌣...) m 62 (Urkunde für die Anstellung eines Konsuls) letters patent containing (the provisions of) a consular appointment; ~**s-buch** 🏛 n order-book.

Be-stell-zeit (⌣⌣...) f 62: **a)** ⚓ time of delivery; **b)** agr.tilling season, time for sowing or tilling; -**zettel** 🏛 m note containing an order; gedruckt: order form.

be-stempeln (⌣⌣⌣) 8⃝a* = stempeln.

besten-falls (⌣́⌣) adv. in the best possible case, under the most favourable conditions (possible).

bestens (⌣⌣) adv. s. best Ib.

be-sternt (⌣⌣) a. 46 **1.** beset (or adorned, bespangled) with stars; (bestirnt) starry (sky); (ordentragend) decorated with orders (and stars). — **2.** Schriftum, typ.: marked with an asterisk (*).

be-steuer n (⌣́⌣) I v/a. 8⃝a* **1.** to impose (or lay, put) taxes on the people; to tax the people; so und so hoch ℒ to assess (or tax) at a certain amount. — **2.** ⚓ on Schiff: to steer. — II ~ n 23 **3.** = B/ung. — III **Be-steuerte(r** m) f 67 **4.** p. assessed; tax-payer.

Be-steu(e)rung (⌣́⌣⌣) f 46 imposition of taxes; taxation; assessment; ⚓ ~ eines Schiffes (art of) steering a ship; ~**s-recht** (ℒ...) n 62 right of imposing (or levying) taxes or duty.

best-gehaßt (⌣́...) a. 46 most hated (of all); der ℒe Mann Europas the best hated man in Europe; **~gelegen** a. best situated; **~gemeint** done with the best intention; well-meant; ℒer Rat advice given with the best intention; **~gut** 🏛 n 62 best tobacco leaves; **~haupt** n Lehnsrecht: heriot.

bestialisch (⌣́(⌣)⌣) [it. f. Bestie] a. 46 (viehisch) bestial; brutal; **Bestialität** (⌣́(⌣)⌣-⌣⌣́) f 46 bestiality, brutality.

be-sticken (⌣⌣) v/a. 8⃝* to embroider, to adorn with embroidery.

Besti-e (⌣́(⌣)⌣) [it. bē'stiă] f 46 (ferocious) beast or brute (auch fig. von Menschen).

be-stieben (⌣⌣) 8⃝ = bestäuben.

be-stiefelt (⌣⌣) a. 46 booted.

be-stieg(en) (⌣⌣́) impf. (p.p.) v. besteigen.

be-stielen (⌣⌣) v/a. 8⃝* to fit with a handle, Werkzeuge a.: to helve.

be-stielt (⌣⌣) a. 46 fitted with a handle; ♀, zo., &c. petiolate; Blüte: pedunculate.

be-stimmbar (⌣⌣⌣) a. 46 determinable; definable; (abschätzbar) appreciable; **~keit** f 46 determinability, definability.

be-stimmen (⌣⌣⌣) I v/a. 8⃝* **1.** e-n zu etwas ℒ (veranlassen) to induce (or to prevail upon) a p. to do a th.; sich zu etwas ℒ lassen to be talked into a th.; stärker: to be led away; v/refl. sich ℒ to determine, to resolve; s. **5.** — **2.** (entscheiden) to decide a th.; (festsetzen) Zeit und Ort ℒ to fix (or appoint) time and place; den Preis, die Bedingungen ℒ to state (or fix) … — **3.** gram. näher ℒ to qualify, to modify; phls. einen Begriff: to define; med. eine Krankheit: to diagnose; chm. e-n Stoff ℒ to analyse (the ingredients of) s. th.; Naturgeschichte: to determine or recognize (plants, insects, &c.); math. Winkel, den Flächen-inhalt ℒ to measure angles, the area; die geographische Breite ℒ to ascertain (or find) the latitude of a place. — **4.** (an-ordnen) to regulate a th.; über e-n, etwas (nach Belieben) ℒ to dispose of …; ℒ, daß // to arrange that //; hierüber ward nichts bestimmt this point was not settled; die Gesetze ℒ daß // the laws prescribe (or provide) that //; der Himmel hat es so bestimmt Heaven so ordained (or ordered) it (to be). — **5.** a. v/refl. (ausersehen) (sich) für et., zu et. ℒ to choose a vocation, to devote (o.s.) to a purpose; er ist zu hohen Dingen bestimmt he is destined (or cut out) for great things; Cromwell bestimmte s-n Sohn Richard zu s-m Nachfolger … designated … as his successor. — II **2d** p.pr. u. a. 46 **6.** determinant; decisive; gram. qualifying; das ~de dabei war für uns // what decided us was //. — III **be-stimmt** (⌣⌣) p.p. u. a. 46 **7.** (entschlossen) decided, determined, resolute; (stark ausgeprägt) pronounced; ℒer Befehl peremptory order; ℒe Leugnung categorical denial; ℒer Ton firm tone; ℒe Weigerung positive (or distinct) refusal; sich ℒ (aufs Leste) weigern to refuse pointblank. — **8.** (genau) precise, exact; ℒer Begriff definite notion; ℒes Gehalt fixed salary; für e-n ℒen Zweck for a set (or well-defined) purpose; gram. der ℒe Artikel the definite article; sich ℒ ausdrücken to express o.s. distinctly, to make o.s. clearly understood; e-m et. ℒ (adv.) vorschreiben, zur ℒen Vorschrift m. to give a p. strict injunctions (or explicit orders) about a th. — **9.** (gewiß) (auch adv.) certain(ly), sure(ly); (festgesetzt) precise(ly); exact (-ly); von der Zeit ꝛc.: fixed; zu e-r ℒen Stunde at an appointed hour; ich glaube (weiß) ℒ, daß // I am confident (positive) that // — **10.** ⚓ ℒ nach bound (or making) for (a certain port).

Be-stimmt-heit (⌣⌣-) f 46 (Entschiedenheit) decision, determination; firmness; positiveness; distinctness; (Genauigkeit) precision, exactness; (Gewißheit) certainty; mit ~ wissen to know for certain or for a certainty or positively.

Be-stimmung (⌣⌣⌣) f 46 (s. bestimmen) decision; appointment; definition; gram. modification; med. ~ e-r Krankheit: diagnosis; chm. analysis; math. measurement; (Anordnung) regulation, arrangement, disposition, settlement; e-s Vertrages: stipulation; (Verordnung) provision, prescription; order; (Zukunft) destination; (Ernennung) designation; ~ über etwas treffen to come to a decision about …; to settle a point; ~ (Geschick) des Menschen destiny, fate; (Beruf) vocation, mission; Allerhöchste ~en His, Her Majesty's, &c. (gracious) commands; 🏛 es wird um nähere ~ hierüber gebeten kindly favour us with your specifications (or full instructions) respecting this point.

Be-stimmungs-grund (ℒ...) m 62 motive; **=hafen** ⚓ m port of destination; port for which a ship is bound; **=mensur** f v. Studenten: duel arranged between members of different 'Corps'; **=ort** m (place of) destination; **=wort** n gram. determinative word; demonstrative.

be-stirnt (⌣⌣) (Stern) a. 46 starred, starry.

Best-mann ⚓ (⌣́⌣) m 62 fully qualified mariner or boatman.

♪ Musik; ⚗ Wissenschaft; ✿ Pflanze; ⚱ Geographie; ⊕ Technik; ⚒ Bergbau; ⚔ Militär; ⚓ Marine; 🏛 Handel; ✉ Post; 🚂 Eisenbahn.

[bestmöglich] — 186 — [betäuben]

best-möglich (⌣́⌣) *a.* ⑥ best possible; *adv.* in the best manner possible.
be-stochen (⌣⌣́) *p.p.* von bestechen.
be-stocken (⌣⌣́) I *v/a.* ⑧*: mit Reben ⸺ to plant with vines; bestocktes Holz fully matured (or grown) wood. — II **Be-stockung** *f* ㊻ (Bildung v. Seitensprossen) formation of fresh shoots or branches. [put on (or to show) a stem.]
be-stöken (⌣⌣́): sich ⸺ *v/refl.* ⑧* *agr.* to
be-stohlen (⌣⌣́) *p.p.* von bestehlen (f. ds).
be-stöpseln (⌣⌣́) *v/a.* ㉒a* to cork.
be-stoßen (⌣́⌣) *v/a.* ㉒a* 1. (berühren) to knock (or push) against. — 2. ⊙ (abhobeln) to rough-plane; *typ.* to trim. — 3. (beschädigen) *a. v/rpr.* to hurt or damage (one another).
Be-stoß-feile ⊙ (⌣"..) *f* ㉒ planing-file, Schriftgießerei: justifier; =**hobel**=smoothing- (or jack-) plane; Schriftgießerei: dresser: **zeug** *n. typ.* dressing-rod.
be-straf|en (⌣⌣́) I *v/a.* ⑧* to punish a p. (for an offence); mit Worten: to reprimand; to rebuke; mit Schlägen: to chastise; die Fehler der Kinder ⸺ to correct the faults of ...; *rel.* (heimsuchen) to visit (the sins of the fathers on the children). — II ~ *n* ㉓ = B/ung.
Be-strafer (⌣⌣́) *m* ㉒, **~in** *f* ㊼ p. who punishes. &c.: inflicter of punishment.
Be-strafung (⌣⌣́) *f* ㊻ (f. bestrafen) (infliction of) punishment; reprimand, chastisement; correction; *rel.* visitation (of heaven).
be-strahlen (⌣⌣́) I *v/a.* ⑧* to shine (or beam) upon; ⋄ to (ir)radiate. — II ~ *n* ㉓ *u.* **Be-strahlung** *f* ㊻ *opt.*: ⋄ (ir)radiation, (ir)radiancy.
be-streb|en (⌣⌣́) I sich ⸺ *v/refl.* ⑧* sich ⸺ zu to endeavour (or strive to); to make an effort to; (versuchen) to attempt (or try) to; sich um etwas ⸺ to strive (or seek) after a th., to aspire to a th. — II ~ *n* ㉓ und **B/ung** *f* ㊻ endeavour, effort; exertion; es wird mein ~ sein, zu ⸺ I shall make it my study to; eifriges ~ zeal; ziellose B/ung aimless pursuit.
be-streichen (⌣⌣́) I *v/a.* ㉖aft* 1. to spread over (= beschmieren 1 u. 2). — 2. ↓ fahrend die Küste ⸺ to hug the shore. — 3. (streifen) to glide (or pass) across; to brush (past); leise: to graze; mit der Hand: to stroke, to rub (gently); mit e-m Magnet ⸺ to magnetize. — 4. ✕ die Ebene ⸺ (beschießen) to sweep (or scour; weits. to command) the plain: bestrich(e)ner Raum space swept by guns, shells. &c.; zone under fire, fire-swept zone, fire-zone; längsweise ⸺ to enfilade; von der Seite ⸺ to flank; ⸺des Feuer (*a.* **Be-streichfeuer** *n*) enfilading fire. — II **Be-streichung** *f* ㊻ 5. spreading over, &c., f. I; mit dem Magnet: magnetization; ~ des Geländes mit Granaten sweeping the country with shells or shellfire, shelling the open ground.
be-streitbar (⌣⌣́) *a.* ⑥ contestable, debatable, disputable. **~keit** *f* ㊻ contestableness, debatableness.
be-streit|en (⌣⌣́) I *v/a.* ㉖b* 1. *bibl.*, &c., mit Waffen: to make war on. — 2. mit Worten: to contest; das will

ich nicht ⸺ (in Abrede stellen) I won't dispute (or contradict, deny) it; die Tatsache läßt sich ⸺ the fact is open to controversy or argument. — 3. Ausgaben, Kosten ⸺ (aufbringen) to defray (or bear, meet) the expense, to supply (or furnish) the means or funds, F to find the cash; wir können es nicht ⸺ we cannot afford it. — II ~ *n* ㉓ 4. = B/ung.
Be-streiter (⌣⌣́) *m* ㉒ 1. *bibl.* combatant. — 2. disputant; *bsd.* jur. contestant.
Be-streitung (⌣⌣́) *f* ㊻ 1. contesting, &c. (zu bestreiten 2). — 2. (zu 3:) defraying the expense(s); supply of money; zur ~ der Unkosten (in order) to pay off (or to clear) expenses.
be-streuen (⌣⌣́) I *v/a.* ⑧* mit Blumen ꝛc.: to (be)strew (or [be]sprinkle) with ...; mit Kies: to gravel; mit Mehl: to dredge; mit Pulver: to powder; mit Samen: to (stock with) seed; mit Sand ⸺ to (strew with) sand; mit Zucker ⸺ to sugar, Gebäck: to frost. — II **Be-streuung** *f* ㊻ (be)strewing, gravelling, &c., f. I. [von bestreichen.]
be-strich (⌣⌣́) *impf.*, **be-strichen** (⌣⌣́) *p.p.*]
be-stricken¹ (⌣⌣́) [stricken] *v/a.* ⑧* to knit over; im Ball: to cover with netting.
be-stricken² (⌣⌣́) [Strick] I *v/a.* (festbinden) to (tie with) cord; *fig.* e-n ⸺ to ensnare, entrap, entangle; (fesseln) to captivate; ⸺d *p.pr.* ⑥ captivating, fascinating, charming, enthralling. — II ~ *n* ㉓ *u.* **Be-strickung** *f* ㊻ cording; entanglement; captivation, fascination, enthralment.
be-stritt(en) (⌣⌣́) *impf.* (*p.p.*) von bestreiten. [vgl. bespülen.]
be-strömen (⌣⌣́) *v/a.* ⑧* to flow over,]
be-stücken ↓ (⌣⌣́) I *v/a.* ⑧* ein Schiff ⸺ to arm (or mount) ... with guns or cannon; mit Kanonen bestückt carrying guns. — II **Be-stückung** *f* ㊻ (ship's) armament, guns (or gunning), torpedoes, &c. (of a man-of-war).
Be-stuhlung (⌣⌣́) *f* ㊻ (Ausstattung einer Kirche mit Sitzplätzen) fitting up (of) a church with pews and seats.
be-stürm|en (⌣⌣́) I *v/a.* ⑧* 1. = auf et. anstürmen. — 2. *fig.* mit Besuchen ⸺ to molest (or bore) with one's visits; mit Bitten ⸺ to solicit, to implore; mit Fragen ⸺ to ply (or besiege) with questions. — II ~ *n* ㉓ 3. = B/ung.
Be-stürmer (⌣⌣́) *m* ㉒ assailant.
Be-stürmung (⌣⌣́) *f* ㊻ storming, assault, *fig.* molestation; solicitation; ✱ ~ e-r Bank run on (or besieging) a bank.
be-stürz|en (⌣⌣́) I *v/a.* ⑨* = bestürzt machen (f. II). — II **Be-stürzt** *p.p. u. a.* ⑥ (außer sich) disconcerted; (entsetzt) alarmed, horrified, dismayed; (erstaunt) amazed, astounded, F taken aback; (ratlos) perplexed; (sprachlos) dumbfounded; (verblüfft) F flummuxed, flabbergasted; (verwirrt) confused, upset; (beschämt) abashed; ⸺ machen to ⸺e Miene machen to look alarmed, perplexed. — III **Be-stürztheit**, **Be-stürzung** *f* ㊻ alarm, dismay; consternation, perplexity, confusion; abashment; in Bestürzung geraten to get alarmed, dismayed.

Be-such (⌣⌣́) *m* ⑬c. 1. visit, call; ich bin hier auf ~ I am on a visit; e-n ~ abstatten, m. to pay a visit to, auf e-n Weilchen: to (make a) call on, F to drop in on; *bsd.* in Geschäften: to have an interview with, to interview. — 2. (Gäste) er hat ~ he has visitors; zahlreichen ~ bekommen to receive a good deal of company; ~ (bei sich) haben to have company (staying at the house). — 3. ~ e-s Ortes frequentedness of a place; der Kirche, e-r Versammlung: attendance (at church, at a meeting).
be-suchen (⌣⌣́) *v/a.* ⑧* 1. to go to see a p.; to come to visit (or pay a visit to) a p.; auf e-e kurze Weile: to call on, F to drop in upon; ich habe ihn besucht I have been to see (geschäftlich *a.*: to interview) him, F I've given him a look-up; sie besucht gerne die Läden she is fond of shopping. — 2. einen Ort: to visit; eine Versammlung: to attend; die Kirche, Schule ꝛc. ⸺ to go to (or attend a) church, school, &c.; öfters ⸺ to frequent, meist *b.s.* to haunt; besuchter Vergnügungsort popular resort.
Be-sucher (⌣⌣́) *m* ㉒, **~in** *f* ㊼ visitor, caller; der Kirche: church-goer; (j. der öfters kommt) frequenter (of a place); ✱ customer; regelmäßiger ~ e-s Wirtshauses (Stammgast) ordinary (or daily) guest of ...; (fr.) habitué(e *f*) *m*.
Be-such(s)-karte (⌣"⌣(⌣)..) *f* ㉒ (visiting-) card; =**recht** *n* ⇃⇂ right of visitation; =**tag** *m* (regular) visiting-day; der Damen, auch: at-home (day); =**zimmer** *n* drawing- (or reception-)room.
be-sudeln (⌣⌣́) I *v/a. u. v/refl.* ㉒a* (sich) ⸺ (beschmutzen) to dirty (o.s.), soil (o.s.), begrime (o.s.); *fig.* (beschmutzen) to pollute, sully, defile; mit Blut besudelt stained with blood or gore, gory. — II **Be-sud(e)lung** *f* ㊻ dirtying, &c.; (Entweihung) pollution, defilement.
be-täfelt (⌣⌣́) *a.* ⑥ wainscoted.
be-tagt (⌣⌣́) *a.* ⑥ 1. (bejahrt) aged, stricken in years. — 2. ✱ Wechsel: due.
Beta-in ⸱⸱⸱ (⁻⌣⌣́) [Bete¹] *n* ⑬c. *chm.* betain(e) ($C_5H_{11}NO_2$)
betakeln ↓ (⌣⌣́) I *v/a.* ㉒a* to rig. — II **Be-tak(e)lung** *f* ㊻ (ship's) rigging.
be-tasten (⌣⌣́) I *v/a.* ⑧* to touch, feel, finger, handle. — II **Be-tastung** *f* ㊻ touching, feeling, &c. (f. I).
be-tätig|en (⌣⌣́) [erst nhd. tätig erweisen] I *v/a. u. v/refl.* ⑧* 1. seine Freundschaft ꝛc. ⸺ to prove ... (through one's actions); to exemplify ...; mit sachlichem Subjekt: sich ⸺ to become evident or manifest; sich als treuer Freund ⸺ (bewähren) to prove (o.s.) a true friend; sie betätigt sich am liebsten in der Küche she likes best being busy (F pottering about) in the kitchen. — 2. sich bei et. ⸺ (beteiligen) to participate in s.th. — II ~ *n* ㉓ *u.* **Be-tätigung** *f* ㊻ 3. manifestation or exemplification or practical proof (of one's feelings); participation (in an enterprise); (Tätigkeit) activity.
be-täub|en (⌣⌣́) I *v/a.* ⑧* 1. to deafen. — 2. (wirr m.) durch Getöse, einen Schlag ꝛc. to stun; to stupefy. — 3. (starr m.) to

---

Signs (see page XVII): F familiar; P vulgar; ℉ flash; ⸜ rare; † obsolete (died), * new word (born); ⁺⁺ incorrect; ♩ music.

[Betäubtheit] — 187 — [Betreff]

(be)numb; (einschläfern) to lull (or send) to sleep; to make unconscious; *surg.* to narcotize (with ether, chloroform, &c.); die Nerven: to calm, to dull; (abstumpfen) to deaden (a. *fig. v.* Gewissen). — II ~ *n* 23 4. = B/ung 1. — III 2d *p.pr.* u. *a.* 66 5. in den Bed. des *inf.* — 6. *med.* 2d(es Mittel), 7 narcotic, anæsthetic. — IV be-täubt *p.p. u. a.* 46 7. stupefied; (be)numbed; dizzy; torpid. [Betäubung 2.]
Be-täubtheit *f* 46, **Be-täubt-sein** *n* 23 =
Be-täubung (⌣́⌣) *f* 46 1. deafening, &c. (f. betäuben I). — 2. stupor, numbness; dizziness; dumpfe: lethargy, torpor. [narcotic, anæsthetic.
Be-täubungs-mittel (⌣́...) *n* 62:
be-tauen (⌣́⌣) [: bedew] *v n.* (jn.) *v a.* u. *v/refl.* 68* (sich) 2 to bedew; to (become) wet with dew.
be-taumeln (⌣́⌣) *v/a.* 2a* to make dizzy or giddy. [bigot; *iro.* saint.]
Bet-bruder (⌢⌣...) *m* 62 devotee, bisw./
Bete¹ ? (⌣́⌣) [ndd.; *lt. beta*] *f* 48 (Runkel-rübe) beet(-root) (*Beta vulga'ris*); rote ~ common (or red) beet.
Bete² (⌣́⌣; mit bét) [fr. *bête*] *f* 48 Kartenspiel: ~ *m.* (*w.*) to win (to lose) the game.
be-teeren ⊖ (⌣́⌣) *v/a.* 68* to tar (over).
Beteigeuza, ...ze (⌣́⌣) [ar.] *m* 9 *ast.* (Stern α im Orion) Beteigeuse.
be-teilig/en (⌣́⌣⌣) 68* I *v/a.* e-n bei etwas 2 to give a p. a share (or an interest) in a th.; 7 to make a p. a partner in s.th. — II *v/refl.* sich an (oder bei) etwas 2 to participate (or share, co-operate) in a th.; to be interested (or concerned) in (a business); to take part in (a discussion). — III ~ *n* 23 = B/ung. — IV **Be-teiligte[r]** *m* 67 interested party; ⊛ shareholder, partner.
Be-teiligt-sein (⌣́⌣⌣) *n* 23 being interested (or having a share) in.
Be-teiligung (⌣́⌣) *f* 46 participation or share or co-operation or interest in; ohne seine ~ hätte sie es nicht gewagt without his assistance ...; unter zahlreicher ~ des Publikums amid a large concourse of people; before a numerous audience; die Sache fand schwache (allgemeine) ~ ... met with little (universal) support.
Betel ? (⌣́⌣) [jft.] *m* 22 betel(-pepper) (*Piper Betle*); (Kaumittel) betel; **~nuß**(⌢...) *f* 62 betel- (or areca-)nut; **-palme** ? *f* cashew-nut tree; **-pfeffer** *m* = Betel.
beten (⌣́⌣) [ahd.] 69 I *v/n.* (h.) 1. (zu Gott) 2 to pray (to God); *abs.* sie betet she is praying or saying her prayers; mit-ea. 2 to unite in one's prayers or devotions. — 2. vor (nach) Tische 2 to say grace before (after) a meal or before (after) meat. — II *v/a.* 3. (betend hersagen) to offer up (a prayer or one's devotions); ein Vater-unser 2 to say (or repeat) the Lord's Prayer; den Rosenkranz 2 to count (or tell) one's beads. — 4. ↘ e-n lebendig 2 to (re-)call a p. to life by one's prayers; *v/refl.* sich in den Himmel 2 to gain access to heaven by one's devotions. — III ~ *n* 23 5. prayer; (sich) zum ~ hinknien to kneel down to prayer.

Beter (⌣́⌣) *m* 22, **~in** *f* 47 p. who prays.
Be-teu(e)rer (⌣́(⌣)⌣) *m* 22, **~in** *f* 47 person who protests, &c.
be-teuern (⌣́⌣) I *v/a.* 2a* to protest, assert, asseverate; to declare solemnly; eidlich 2 to assert on (or to confirm by) oath; to swear to. — II ~ *n* 23 u.
Be-teu(e)rung (⌣́(⌣)⌣) *f* 46 protestation; assertion; asseveration; solemn declaration; confirmation (by oath); profession (of faith); **~s-formel** *f* 62 (den Eid ersetzende Formel) affirmation.
Bet-fahrt (⌢...) *f* 62 (Wallfahrt) pilgrimage; **-gang** *m* procession.
Bethani-en ♀ (⌣⌣̇⌣) [hebr. Haus der Armen] *npr/n.* 23 *a.* (Flecken bei Jerusalem) Bethany. [to) Bethany.
bethanisch (⌣⌣̇⌣) *a.* 66 of (or belonging/
Bet-haus (⌢...) *n* 62 house of prayer; für engl. Dissid'nten: chapel, tabernacle; Juden: synagogue; Moslems: mosque.
Bethlehem ♀ (⌣̇⌣⌣) [hebr. Haus d. Brotes] *npr/n.* 50 *a.* Bethlehem; **~iter(in** *f* 47) *m* 22, **-itisch** *a.* 66 Bethlehemite; **-itischer** Kindermord massacre of the innocents. [Antertau) bitts *pl.*]
Beting ⌇ (⌣́⌣) *m* 9d., *f* 18 (Winde für das/
Beting-balken (⌢...) *m* 62 cross-beam of the bitts. [silly (or stupid) action.]
Betise (⌣́⌣) [fr. *bêtise* Dummheit] *f* 48/
be-titeln (⌣́⌣) I *v/a.* u. *v/refl.* 2a* 1. to give a title (or name) to; to confer a title on; das Buch war betitelt : the book bore the title // — 2. (nennen) to call, to style, name; sie 2 ihn „Graf" they address him as "count". — II **Be-titelung** *f* 46 3. title, name; falsche ~ misnomer.
Bet-kapelle (⌢...) *f* 62 = Bethaus.
be-tölpeln (⌣́⌣) *v/a.* 2a* to dupe, befool, bamboozle, beguile, cheat; er ließ sich 2 F he was taken in.
Beton (-tŏ') [fr.] *m* 9 *arch.* (Grobmörtel) concrete; mit ~ bauen to build with c.
be-ton/en (⌣́⌣) I *v/a.* 68* Silbe: to lay stress upon, to accent(uate); Wort: to emphasize. — II ~ *n* 23 = B/ung.
Betoni-e ? (−⌣́⌣⌣) [it.] *f* 48 betony: rote ~ wood (or common) betony (*Betonica officinalis*). [with concrete.]
betonieren (⌣⌣́⌣)[Beton]*v/a.*63 to build/
Be-tonung (⌣́⌣) *f* 46 stress, accent, accentuation; emphasis; schwebende ~ level stress. [foundation.]
Beton-unterlage (-tŏ...) *f* 62 concrete/
be-tören (⌣́⌣) [Tor *m*] I *v/a.* 68* (verblenden) to befool, delude, mislead, infatuate; F to make a fool of a p.; (betrügen) to deceive, dupe, impose upon. — II ~ *n* 23 = Betörung.
Be-törer (⌣́⌣) *m* 22, **~in** *f* 47 deceiver.
Bet-ort (⌢...) *m* 62 = Bethaus.
Be-törtheit (⌣́⌣) *f* 46 (o. *pl.*) folly.
Be-törung (⌣́⌣) *f* 46 delusion; deception, imposition (practised upon).
Bet-platz (⌢...) *m* 62 = Bethaus; **-pult** *n* (*m*) praying- (or kneeling-)desk.
betr. *abbr.* = betreffend, betreffs.
Be-tracht (⌣́⌣t) [nhd.] *m* 9b. (o. *pl.*) (Erwägung) mst mit *prp.* : etwas außer ~ lassen to leave a th. out of consideration or account; (mit) in ~ kommen to be taken into consideration, to be of some account, to count; nicht in ~

kommen to be of no account or importance, to have no weight; die Kosten kommen nicht in ~ the expense (or money) is no consideration or plays no part; dieser Punkt kommt dabei nicht in ~ ... need not be considered; et. in ~ (nehmen ob.) ziehen to take a th. into consideration or account.
be-tracht/en (⌣́⌣t) [ahd.] I *v/a.* 69* 1. to consider, to regard; körperlich: to look at, to inspect; nachdenkend: to contemplate; to reflect on; et. von e-m anderen Standpunkte aus 2 to see a th. from another point of view; die Dinge in rosigem Lichte 2 to look at the best side of things; (beobachten) to observe. — 2. (halten für) wir 2 es als ein Unglück, daß // we think (or consider) it a misfortune that //. — II ~ *n* 23 3. = B/ung.
be-trachtens-wert (⌢...) *a.* 66. 2 **würdig** *a.* worthy of consideration or of inspection. [beholder; spectator./
Be-trach/er (⌣́⌣) *m* 22, **~in** *f* 47 viewer./
be-trächtlich (⌣́⌣) *a.* 66 considerable, important; 2e Kosten *pl.* heavy costs; um ein 2es (very) considerably, very much. [ableness; importance./
Be-trächtlichkeit (⌣́⌣~) *f* 46 consider-/
Be-trachtung (⌣́⌣t) *f* 46 consideration; inspection; view; observation; contemplation, meditation, reflection; ~en über et. anstellen to meditate (or reflect) on a th.; tiefen (düsteren) ~en nachhängend plunged into (or lost in) deep (gloomy) meditation or speculation.
be-traf (⌣́⌣) *impf. von* betreffen.
Be-trag (⌣́, ↘ ⌣́⌣) *m* 9c. amount; (Gesamtsumme) (sum) total; ein kleiner ~ a small sum; im ~e von amounting to, F to the tune of; bis zum ~e von (up) to the amount (or value) of; zu jedem (beliebigen) ~e to any amount or extent; at any price; Quittung: ~ erhalten received (in payment), paid.
be-tragen (⌣́⌣⌣) ⊛ *b** I *v/n.* (h.) *von* Geld: to amount (F to run up) to; ⊛ die Rechnung beträgt 200 Mark ... comes to £10; wieviel beträgt das Ganze? how much does it total up to? — II sich 2 *v/refl.* = benehmen 3. — III ~ *n* 23 behaviour = benehmen III.
be-trank (⌣́⌣) *impf. von* betrinken.
be-tränt (⌣́⌣) *a.* 66 (bathed) in tears.
be-trat (⌣́⌣) *impf. von* betreten.
be-trauen (⌣́⌣) I *v/a.* 68* e-n mit et. 2 to confide (or entrust) a th. to a p.; ⊛ wir sind damit betraut (worden) we have been entrusted with it or commissioned to do it; we are in charge of the business. — II **Be-traute(r** *m*) *f* 67 (Vertraute[r]) confidant, bosom-friend; ⊛ agent (acting on behalf of others); *jur.* trustee.
be-trauern (⌣́⌣) *v/a.* 2a* to bemourn a p., to mourn for a p.; weitS. to lament (or deplore) the loss of a p. or a th.
be-träufe(l)n (⌣́⌣) *v/a.* 68 (62a)* to drip water, &c. on; (besprützen) to besprinkle; Braten mit Fett 2 to baste meat.
Be-treff (⌣́⌣) *m* 9c. meist als *prp.* in 2 ob. ~, *a.* 23 e-r Sache (*gen.*) with (or in) regard to (or respecting, in respect of) a th.; in dem ~ in that respect, as to that, as for that (vgl. Anbetracht).

be-treffen (‿´‿) I v/a. ᗕa* (impf. betraf) **1.** to come (suddenly) upon a p.; e-n **auf** ob. **über etwas** ⚄ (ertappen) to catch (or surprise) a p. in the (very) act or on the (very) spot; bei einem Morde: to catch a p. red-handed. — **2.** ein Unglück, e-e Krankheit hat ihn betroffen (befallen) … has befallen him or stricken him down. — **3.** = angehen 9: das betrifft Sie it relates to you, it concerns (or touches, affects) you; was mich betrifft as far as I am concerned, as for me; es betrifft deine Ehre … is at stake; es betrifft nur die paar Groschen it's only a matter of a few pence. — II ⚄ p.pr. und a. ᗕ **4.** das ⚄e Wort (Geschäft) the word (the business) in question or referred to; die ⚄e Behörde the competent authority; die ⚄en Leute the people (or F parties) concerned. — **5.** als prp. mit acc.: concerning, regarding, respecting. — III **be-troffen** p.p. u. a. ᗕ (D9) **6.** in den Beb. des inf. — **7.** (verwirrt) struck (with amazement), thunderstruck, perplexed, confused, F (quite) taken aback, flummuxed.

be-treffs (‿ˢ) prp. (abbr. betr.) s. Betreff.

be-treiben (‿´‿) ᗕ* I v/a. **1.** die Felder mit Vieh ⚄ to take cattle out to pasture, to graze the cattle. — **2.** (beschleunigen) to hasten, to urge (forward); ein Geschäft mit Schwung ⚄ to push …, to keep … going (in fine style); einen Prozeß eifrig ⚄ to push on (or fight out) a case. — **3.** ein Handwerk, e-n Beruf ⚄ (ausüben) to carry on a business, a trade; to follow a profession; to pursue a calling; ein Bergwerk, eine Fabrik ꝛc.: to work; to manage; Künste u. Wissenschaften: to cultivate; Studien: to prosecute; England betreibt e-n bedeutenden Handel mit Indien England carries on an important trade (or has large commercial dealings) with India. — II ‿ n ᗕ **4.** = Betreibung; auf sein ‿ hin at his instigation or urgent request.

Be-treiber (‿´‿) m ᗕ, ‿in f ᗕ (s. betreiben 2 und 3) urger; eines Geschäftes: manager (for life and soul) of a business.

Be-treibung (‿´‿) f ᗕ grazing (the cattle); carrying on (a trade); exercise (of a profession); management (of a business, a mine, &c.); cultivation (of arts); prosecution (of studies).

be-tret/en (‿´‿) I v/a. ᗕd* **1.** to tread (or step, set one's foot) upon; unbefugt ⚄ to trespass upon a p.'s premises, &c.; den Kampfplatz ⚄ to enter the arena or the lists; die Kanzel ⚄ to mount the pulpit; ich werde seine Schwelle nicht wieder ⚄ I shall not cross his threshold again; das Ufer, die Küste ⚄ to step (or set one's foot) on land, on shore. — II ⚄ p.p. u. a. ᗕ (D9) **2.** Beb. des inf. — **3.** Ler (viel beschrittener) Weg (much) frequented thoroughfare, wellworn road, beaten path. — **4.** (verlegen) embarrassed, F flummuxed, auch = betreffen 7. — III ‿ n ᗕ **5.** = Ajung; als Plakat: das ‿ dieser Wiese ꝛc. ist verboten trespassers will be prosecuted.

Be-tretenheit (‿´‿-) f ᗕ (Verlegenheit) embarrassment, confusion, perplexity.

Be-tretung (‿´‿) f ᗕ entrance.

Be-tretungs-fall (‿´‿…) m ᗕ gerichtlich: im ‿e (ob. auf den ‿) if caught (or taken) in the act; if arrested on the spot or near the scene of the crime.

be-treuen prov. (‿´‿) v/a. ᗕ* (beschützen, bewahren) to take care of.

Be-trieb[1] (‿´‿) m ᗕc. **1.** = Betreibung. — **2.** (Führung e-s Geschäfts ꝛc.) management. — 🚆 (passenger- and goods-)traffic; die Bahn ist seit Ostern im ‿e the line was opened at Easter; in vollem ‿e in full working order; mach. a. in full action; at full speed; außer ‿ setzen: a) 🚆 to close (a line); to discard (old engines, &c.); b) Maschinen: to put out of gear or action, to ungear; c) Fabriken ꝛc.: to close the works; to stop a mill; to shut down a furnace or a mine; dem ‿e übergeben to open for traffic, for public use, &c.); (elektrischer ‿: a) electric traffic or traction; b) electric works pl. [von betreiben.]

be-trieb[2] (‿´‿) impf. u. ⚄en (‿´‿) p.p.

be-triebsam (‿´‿-) a. ᗕ industrious, active, busy. [activity.]

Be-triebsamkeit (‿´‿--) f ᗕ industry,

Be-triebs-amt 🚆 (‿´‿…) n ᗕ traffic manager's office; ꞊**anlage** f plant (of an establishment); ꞊**art** f, for., agr. method of management; ꞊**aufseher** m: a) 🚆 inspector of the line; b) 🏭 traffic manager; superintendent (or working manager); ꞊**direktor** 🚆 m managing director, a. = ꞊aufseher b; ꞊**gebäude** n business premises pl.; (Fabrik) works pl.; ꞊**geheimnis** n business (or manufacturer's) secret; ꞊**inspektor** m = ꞊aufseher b; ꞊**jahr** n working-year; in Jahresberichten auch: financial year; ꞊**kapital** n working capital; money employed (or sunk) in a business; stock-in-trade; ꞊**kosten** pl. working expenses pl.; ꞊**krankenkasse** f sick- (or provident) fund for workmen; ꞊**leitung** f (internal) management (of a business, of works, &c.); ꞊**material** n, ꞊**mittel** n/pl. 🚆 rolling-stock; Fabrik: working machinery, stock (of materials, &c.); ꞊**personal** n staff; ꞊**stockung**, ꞊**störung** 🚆 f interruption of the traffic; obstruction or break-down on the line; ꞊**vorschriften** 🚆 f/pl. regulations pl. for the traffic; ꞊**zeit** f working-period, ⊕ e-s Ofens ꝛc.: campaign.

be-trinken (‿´‿) v/refl. ᗕt* sich ⚄ to drink to excess; to get drunk, vgl. betrunken.

be-troffen (‿´‿) s. betreffen III.

Be-troffenheit (‿´‿-) f ᗕ amazement, perplexity, confusion.

be-trog (‿´) impf., **be-trogen** p.p. von betrügen (s. ba). [v/a. = beträufeln.]

be-tröpfeln ᗕa*, **be-tropfen** ᗕ* (‿´‿)

be-trüben (‿´‿) v/a. und v/refl. ᗕ* (sich) ⚄ to grieve; das betrübte ihn sehr that greatly distressed (or afflicted) him, it grieved him to the heart; nur refl. sich ⚄ to be (or feel) (ag)grieved or distressed or afflicted or F cut up (über et. about a th. or at a th.).

Be-trübnis (‿´‿) f ⑱ grief, distress, affliction; disappointment, dejectedness, sadness, sorrow.

be-trübt (‿´) p.p. u. a. ᗕ (ag)grieved, schwächer: distressed, afflicted; (enttäuscht) disappointed; (niedergeschlagen) dejected, cast down; (bestürzt) dismayed; eine ⚄e Geschichte a sad (or sorrowful) tale; ⚄ aussehen to make a sad (F to pull a long) face.

Be-trübtheit (‿´‿) f ᗕ = Betrübnis.

be-trug[1] (‿´) impf. von betragen.

Be-trug[2] (‿´) m ⑦c. deception; in größerem Umfange: fraud; (Überlistung) cheating, sharp practice; (Schwindel) imposition; F swindle, take-in; frommen ‿ üben to practise pious fraud (upon the public); fig. ‿ der Sinne delusion.

be-trüge(n[1] pl.) (‿´‿) impf. subj. v. betragen.

be-trügen[2] (‿´‿) I v/a. u. v/refl. ᗕd* (täuschen) to deceive, dupe, gull, bamboozle; (anführen) to defraud (wholesale); to cozen, dupe, F diddle; (hinters Licht führen) to mystify, hoax; (beschwindeln) to impose upon, swindle, F take in; er hat mich um mein Hab und Gut betrogen he has tricked (or cheated, F done) me out of all (that) I possessed; sich ⚄ to be deceived or mistaken or out of one's reckoning; in s-n Hoffnungen betrogen werden (a. sich in seinen Hoffnungen ⚄) to be disappointed in one's hopes; der von ihnen Betrogene their victim or dupe. — II ‿ n ᗕ = Betrug[2].

Be-trüger (‿´‿) m ᗕ, ‿**in** f ᗕ (s. betrügen[2] I) deceiver, cozener; impostor, swindler, trickster, cheat; (Gauner) rogue, sharper; der betrog(e)ne ‿ F the biter bit.

Be-trügerei (‿‿´‿) f ᗕ deceit, imposture, roguery; roguishness; (List) ruse.

be-trügerisch (‿´‿‿) a. ᗕ deceitful, roguish, knavish, tricky; ⚄er Bankrott fraudulent bankruptcy; ⚄e Versprechungen f/pl. false promises pl.; adv. ⚄ handeln to practise fraud, to (have) resort to sharp practices.

be-trügerischer-weise (‿´‿‿‿´‿) adv. by fraud(ulent means), deceptively.

be-trüglich (‿´‿) a. ᗕ **1.** betrügerisch. — **2.** (die Sinne täuschend) deceptive, fallacious, illusory, delusive.

Be-trüglichkeit (‿´‿-) f ᗕ deceptiveness, fallaciousness, delusiveness.

be-trunken (‿´‿) I p.p. von betrinken u. a. ᗕ (D9) the worse for (or under the influence of) drink, intoxicated; schwer ⚄ helplessly drunk — II **Betrunk(e)n(er)** m f ᗕ drunken (or intoxicated) p., p. under the influence of drink.

Be-trunkenheit (‿´‿-) f ᗕ drunkenness, intoxicated (or drunken) state.

Bet-saal ("…) m ᗕ hall for prayer-meetings; eccl. oratory; ꞊**schemel** m (kneeling) stool, hassock.

Betschuane(n pl.) (‿‿´‿) [afr.] m ᗕ (Bantu-volk Südafrikas) Bechuana(s pl.)

Bet-schwester ("…) f ᗕ (female) devotee; saintly (F a. goody-goody) lady; ꞊**stuhl** m praying-chair; ꞊**stunde** f hour of prayer; prayer-time; e-e ‿ (ab)halten to hold a prayer-meeting.

Bett (⁵) [ahd.: bed] n ᗕb. **1.** (Ruhestätte) bed; weites ⚄ couch; ‿ mit Rollen truckle-bed; zweischläf)iges ‿ double bed; (Strohsack) pallet; ‿en pl., oft: bedding; zu Füßen des ‿es at the foot of the bed; ein ‿ aufschlagen to put (o make) up a bed; ein Kind zu ‿ bringen

[Bettag] — 189 — [beugungsfähig]

to put ... to bed; zu ~(e) gehen, sich zu ~(e) legen to go to bed, Kindersprache: to go to bye-bye; F to turn in between the sheets; krankheitshalber: to take to one's bed; das ~ hüten (krank sein) (to have) to keep in bed or to one's couch, to be confined to one's bed; im ~ liegen to be (lying) in bed; to lie a-bed; ~en machen to make beds; am ~ sitzen to sit by (or at) the bedside; ein ~ (frisch) überziehen to put (fresh) sheets (on a bed). — 2. e-s Flusses: bed, channel. — 3. hunt. ~(e) e-s Hoch- oder Reh-wildes: lair. — 4. ⚔ (Schicht) layer, bed. — 5. ⚘ (Fruchtboden) thalamus.

Bet=tag (⁂...) m ⓫ day of prayer, day devoted to prayer.

Bett=bank (⁂...) f ⓮ (zj.-legbare Bettstelle) folding bed(stead); =**behang** m an der Seite: valance; =**behänge** m/pl. = =**vorhang**; =**bezug** m (leinener Überzug) bed-linen, sheets pl. and pillow-case(s pl.).

Bettchen (⁂) n ⓯ (dim. von Bett) small bed; chair-bedstead; für Kinder: crib.

Bett=decke (⁂...) f ⓮ coverlet; gesteppte: quilt, counterpane; mit Eiderdaunen: eiderdown (quilt); wollene: blanket.

Bette (⁂) n ⓰ † ob. hunt. s. Bett 3.

Bettel (⁂) [mhd.] m ⓮ (o. pl.) **1.** begging (= Bettelei 1). — 2. F contp. (Plunder) trash, rubbish; trifle; das ist der ganze ~ that's the whole (paltry) concern; ich kann nicht an jeden ~ denken I cannot think of every detail; der ganze ~ ist das nicht wert the whole (trumpery) lot is not worth it.

bettel=arm (⁂...) a. ⓰ (as) poor as a church-mouse or as Job; (wholly) destitute; ²e Leute (mere) beggars, paupers pl.; =**armut** f ⓮ extreme poverty; destitution; vgl. =**wesen**; =**brief** m begging letter or petition; =**brot** n beggarly living, paltry pittance; das ~ essen to eat the bread of charity, to live on alms or charity; =**bruder** m professional beggar, mendicant; =**bube** m beggar-boy.

Bettelei (⁂) f ⓮ **1.** begging; beggar's trade; mendicancy; gewerbsmäßige: F cadging. — 2. (lästiges Bitten) bothersome (or importunate) begging or petitioning or soliciting; importunity.

Bettel=frau (⁂...) f ⓮ beggar-woman; =**geld** n: a) alms, money obtained by begging; b) ich habe es für ein ~ gekauft I bought it for a mere song; =**gesindel** n = =**volk**.

bettelhaft (⁂) a. ⓰ beggarly, (elend) wretched, miserable; ~**igkeit** (⁔⁓) f ⓯ beggarliness; wretchedness, misery.

Bettel=handwerk (⁂...) n ⓫ begging; F cadging; das ~ treiben to live on alms; =**herberge** f tramps' (or beggars') lodging-house; =**junge**, =**knabe** m = =**bube**; =**kram** m trash (= Bettel 2); =**leute** pl. = =**volk**; =**mann** m (poor) beggar, mendicant; F cadger; =**mönch** m mendicant friar, im Orient: dervish, fakir; =**mönchs=orden** m = =**orden**.

bettel=n (⁂) [ahd.] wa. I v/n. (h.) **1.** u. v/a. to go (a-)begging or F cadging; to beg (alms), to solicit alms; Sprichw. Kunst geht nicht ², etwa: skilled hand finds work in every land. — II v/refl. sich durch

England ² to beg one's way through England. — III ~ n ⓯ = Bettelei 1.

Bettel=orden (⁂...) m ⓫ order of mendicant friars; =**pack** n = =**volk**; =**sack** m (beggar's) wallet or pouch or scrip; =**staat** m tawdry adornment; =**stab** m beggar's staff; fig. beggary, mendicity; e-n an den ~ bringen to reduce a p. to beggary or destitution; to pauperize a p.; an den ~ kommen to become a beggar or pauper; auch: to (have to) go to the workhouse; to come upon the parish; =**stolz** m beggar's (or beggarly) pride; =**tanz** m uproarious merriment; fig. useless fuss; =**vogt** m (workhouse-)beadle; =**volk** n (crowd of) beggars or paupers or mendicants pl.; beggarly (or ragged) mob or brigade or crew; =**weib** n = =**frau**; =**wesen** n mendicity; pauperism.

bett=en (⁂) ⓰ I v/n. (h.) **1.** (Betten machen) to make (the) beds; ⚔ e-m ² to make up a bed for a p. — II v/a. u. v/refl. **2.** e-n ² to put a p. to bed; (unterbringen) to sleep a p., to give a p. a bed for the night; sich ² to go to bed, to retire to rest; sich zusammen ² to sleep together. — 3. Sprichw. er ist nicht auf Rosen gebettet he is not lying (or he does not rest) on a bed of roses; his is not a very pleasant life; wie du dir (s. 1) ob. dich (s. 2) bettest, so schläfst du, a.: wie man sich bettet, so schläft man as you make your bed, so you must lie on it. — III ~ n ⓯ 4. = B/ung 1.

Bet=teppich¹ (⁂⁔) m ⓫ der Mohammedaner prayer-rug.

Betteppich² (⁂⁔) [Bett=teppich] m ⓫ bedside rug or carpet.

Bett=flasche (⁂...) f ⓮ hot-water bottle; =**gerät** n bed-furniture; =**gestell** n bedstead; ~ und Bett bed and bedding; =**himmel** m canopy; tester.

Betti, =**na** (⁂, ⁔⁂) [(Elisa)beth] npr/f. ⓯ ⓰ α. Betty, Bets(e)y, Bessie.

Bett=kasten (⁂...) m ⓫ press-bed; =**kopf=kissen** n pillow; =**lade** f wooden bedstead; =**lägerig** a. ⓰ lying in bed, bed-ridden; er ist ~, auch: he is confined (or a prisoner) to his couch; =**lägerigkeit** f confinement to bed; weitS. invalid (or prostrate) state; =**laken** n sheet.

Bettler (⁂) m ⓫, ~**in** f ⓯ beggar(-man, -woman), mendicant, F cadger; (Landstreicher[in]) tramp; unverschämter ~ sturdy beggar; ~**bande** (⁂...) f ⓫ band of beggars; weitS. beggarly (or F ragamuffin) crew or tribe; =**herberge** f = Bettelherberge; =**leier** f = Drehleier; =**sprache** f beggars's cant; =**stolz** m beggar's (or beggarly) pride.

Bett=linnen (⁂...) n ⓫ bed-linen; =**nässen** n, path. wetting the bed, ⚗ enuresis (nocturna); =**pfanne** f warming-pan; =**pfosten** m bed-post; =**pfühl** m u. n bolster; =**sack** m (Strohsack) palliasse; =**schirm** m bed-screen; =**schwere** F f: die nötige ~ haben (genug getrunken h.) etwa: to have taken in sufficient for a week, to be full up; =**sponde** f, =**statt**, =**stätte**, =**stelle** f = =**gestell**; =**stollen** m bed-post; =**stroh** n bed-straw; =**stuhl** m bed-chair for invalids; =**überzug** m pillow-slip, bolster-case.

Bett=tuch (⁂⁄ch) [Bett=tuch] n ⓫ sheet.

Bettung (⁂) f ⓯ **1.** making up a bed. — 2. mech. bedding, framework; ⚙ (Unterlage) von Fässern u. dgl.: rest, support; Wasserbaukunst: bed (or frame) of a sluice; ⚔ von Geschützen: platform.

Bett=vorhang (⁂...) m ⓫ bed-hangings pl., bed-curtain; =**vorlage** f, =**vorleger** m = Bettteppich²; =**wanze** f, ent. (common) bug (Aca'nthia lectula'ria); =**wärmer** m warming-pan; =**wäsche** f, =**zeug** n bed-linen or -clothes pl.; bedding; reine(s) ~ clean sheets pl.; =**zieche** f = =**bezug**; =**zwil(li)ch** m bedtick(ing).

be=tuchen, **be=tucht** (⁔⁄ch, ⁔⁄cht) [hebr.] a. ⓰ **1.** (Vertrauen habend) having confidence. — 2. (wohlhabend) well-to-do, wealthy.

be=tulich F (⁔⁄) [tun] a. ⓰ handy.

be=tun (⁔⁄) ⓰* I v/a. F = tun. — II sich ² v/refl. = sich betätigen.

be=tünchen (⁔⁔) v/a. ⓰* to put (the last coating of) whitewash (or plaster) on.

be=tüpfe(l)n, **-tupfen** (⁔⁄) I v/a. ⓰ (⓮a)* **1.** to dab (or touch gently) with s.th. — 2. (mit Flecken, Punkten versehen) to spot, to dot; betüpfelt dotted, speckled. — II ~ n ⓯ dabbing, &c. (s. I); von Zündhölzchen mit der Zündmasse: dipping.

be=turbant (⁔⁂) a. ⓰ turbaned.

Bet=woche (⁂...) f ⓮ eccl. (Himmelfahrtswoche) Rogation Week.

Betzel provc. (⁂) [mhd.] m ⓮, f ⓮ (Kopfbedeckung, Haube) headgear, (woman's) cap.

Beuche (⁔⁄) [ahd.: buck] f ⓮ (Lauge z. Waschen) buck, lye; (Bealösung) soda-water.

beuchen (⁔⁄) v/a. ⓰ Wäsche: (in Lauge einweichen) to buck; (put in) soak.

Beuch=faß (⁂...) n ⓫ bucking tub.

beug† (⁄) imper. v. biegen.

beug' (⁄) (beuge) imper. v. beugen.

beugbar (⁄⁔) a. ⓰ **1.** (biegbar) flexible. — 2. (nachgiebig) of a yielding disposition.

Beuge (⁄⁔) f ⓮ (Krümmung) bend(ing).

Beuge=fall (⁄⁔...) m ⓫ gram. (oblique) case; =**muskel** ⚗ m, anat. bending muscle, flexor (ant. Streckmuskel).

beug=en (⁄⁔) [ahd.] I v/a. u. sich ² v/refl. ⓰ **1.** (sich) ² to bend or bow (down); fig. den Kopf vor Gott ² to bow (down) before God; den Nacken (oder sich) vor einem ² to humble o.s. before a p., to submit humbly to a p.; j-s Stolz ² to humble a p.'s pride; sich zur Erde ² to stoop to the ground; sich tief ² to stoop (or bowdown) low. — 2. gram. (abwandeln) to inflect; (deklinieren) to decline. — II ~ ² n 3. = B/ung. — III ge=beugt p.p. und a. ⓰ **4.** mst fig. (tief) ² crushed (by misfortune), prostrate with grief; vom Alter ² bowed down or bent, stooping, with age; (niedergeschlagen) cast down, dejected.

Beuge=sehne (⁄⁔...) f ⓮ des Pferdes: bending (or flexing) sinew.

beugt 2. P., **beugt** 3. P. pres. ind. a) † v. biegen, b) v. beugen.

Beugung (⁄⁔) f ⓮ bend(ing), &c. (s. beugen); des Knies: genuflexion; phys. des Lichtes, Schalles &c.: diffraction; gram. inflexion; (Fall-²) declension.

beugungs=fähig (⁄⁔...) a. ⓰ gram. capable of inflexion; (deklinierbar) declinable; =**silbe** f ⓮ gram. inflexional suffix or syllable or increment.

[Beule] — 190 — [bevorzugt]

Beule (⌣‐) [ahd.: boil] f ⓐ 1. (Höcker) hump. — 2. *path.* bump, swelling, *durch Schlagen verursacht*: bruise; (Geschwür) boil, ulcer, *tiefer liegend*: tumour; (Frost=)~ chilblain; e-m eine ~ schlagen to raise a bruise (or a wale) on a p. — 3. (Verzierung an Metallsachen) boss.

Beulen-pest (‐ʹ⌣) f ⓑ *path.* bubo-pest.

beulig (⌣‐) a. ⓑ formed like a boss, boss-shaped; full of boils or bumps; bruised.

Beunde (⌣‐) [ahd.] f ⓐ land set apart for the special use of the landowner; (Einfriedigung) fenced-in plot of land.

be-unruhig/en (⌣⌣‐⌣) I v/a. u. v refl. ⓑ* 1. e-n ⁓ to disturb (or disquiet) a p.('s peace of mind); *stärker:* to alarm (or upset) a p.; ⁜ a. to harass (the enemy); sich über et. ob. wegen j-s ⁓ to feel alarmed (or troubled, uneasy) about a th. or a p.; F to put o.s. out about a. th. or a p. — 2. e-n ⁓ (verwirren) to trouble, upset, worry, unsettle a p.; (aufregen) to excite (or agitate) a p. — II ~ n ⓒ u. **Be-unruhigung** f ⓓ 3. disquieting, harassing, &c. (f. I). — 4. *nur B/ung* (Unruhe) disquietude; alarm; uneasiness, trouble, worry; (state of) agitation.

be-urkund/en (⌣⌣‐⌣) I v/a. ⓑ* 1. to prove by documentary evidence; to authenticate, to verify. — II ~ n ⓒ u. **Be-urkundung** f ⓓ 2. documentary proof of a th.; authentication, verification of a fact. — 3. B/ung des Personenstandes civil register.

be-urlaub/en (⌣‐⌣) ⓑ* I v/a. e-n ⁓ to give (or grant) a p. leave of absence; *in Geschäftshäusern:* to give a p. (a week's, &c.) holiday; ⁜ to furlough; (entlassen) to dismiss, discharge; Söldner: to disband. — II sich ⁓ v/refl. (ver-abschieden) to take leave of a p.; to bid a p. farewell. — III ~ n ⓒ u. B/ung. — IV **be-urlaubt** p.p. u. a. ⓑ (absent) on leave, home on (sick-)leave; ⁜ on (a six weeks', &c.) furlough; ~en-stand m ⓑ col. soldiers pl. on leave of absence (or home) on furlough.

Be-urlaubung (⌣‐⌣) f ⓓ granting of a (sick-)leave or a holiday; furlough(ing); (Entlassung) discharge.

be-urteil/en (⌣⌣‐⌣) I v/a. ⓑ* 1. e-n, et. ⁓ to judge of a p., a th., to pronounce a judgment upon; e-n nach seiner Kleidung, Manier ⁓ to judge a p. by his clothes, his manners; (abschätzen) to estimate (by a certain standard); to gauge; falsch ⁓ to misjudge. — 2. scharf, streng ⁓ to censure, to criticize, to cavil (or carp) at; e-n zu streng ⁓ to be too hard on a p.; ein Buch &c.: to review ...; *tadelnd:* to condemn, F to slate. — II ~ n ⓒ 3. = B/ung. [critic; reviewer.]

Be-urteiler (~) m ⓑ, **~in** f ⓓ judge;

Be-urteilung (~) f ⓓ judging, judgment; censure, criticism; v. Schriften: critique, review(ing); ~s-gabe (⌣‐⌣...) f ⓑ, ‐kraft f, ‐vermögen n power of judgment; discernment; critical faculty.

beust † (‐ʹ) f.‐ für bestie = bietest.

beut † (‐ʹ) poet. für bietet; biete. (s. bieten).

Beute¹ (⌣‐) [ndd.: booty] f ⓐ 1. der Soldaten: booty; auf ~ ausgeh(e)n to go out marauding or plundering; reiche ~ m. to capture (or gather in) rich spoils or a large booty. — 2. *v. wilden Tieren:* prey; victim; das Lamm ist den Wölfen zur ~ geworden ... fell a(n easy) prey to the wolves; den Flammen zur ~ w. to be consumed by (or to perish in) the flames. — 3. ↓ prize; als gute ~ erklären to declare a lawful prize.

Beute² (⌣‐) [ahd.] f ⓐ 1. (Backtrog) wooden trough. — 2. (Bienenstock der Waldbienen) bee-hive in a forest-tree.

beute¹**-gierig** (‐ʹ⌣...) a. ⓑ keenly bent on (or eager after) plunder; von Raubtieren &c. auch: predatory.

Beute²**-honig** (‐ʹ⌣...) m ⓑ wild honey.

Beutel¹ (⌣‐) [ahd.: *biutel] m ⓑ 1. (Säckchen) small bag or pouch. — 2. (Geld-)~ purse; (Tabaks-)~ tobacco-pouch; arm am ~ impecunious; F low in funds; bei leerem ~ with an empty purse or pocket; bei vollem ~ with a purse full of money; das greift den ~ (sehr) an it tells (heavily) upon one's purse; den Knopf auf dem ~ (das Geld in Händen) haben to hold the purse-strings; sich (dat.) den ~ gut spicken to line one's pocket (well); aus anderer Leute ~ ist gut zehren it is easy to live on other people's money; aus einem ~ zehren to share each other's expenses; den ~ ziehen to loosen (or undo) one's purse-strings. — 3. Türkei: (bag of) 500 piastres pl. — 4. zo. (Tasche der Beuteltiere) pouch. — 5. Billard: pocket; ⊕ Müllerei: bolter, bolting-bag.

Beutel² ⊕ (⌣‐) [ndd.: beetle (beat)] m ⓑ (Meißel) chisel.

Beutel¹**-bär** (‐ʹ⌣...) m ⓑ zo. Australian bear, koala (*Phascola'rctus cine'reus*); ‐dachs m, zo. marsupial badger, ⚥ perameles; ‐faul a. ⓑ loath to spend money; ‐förmig a. ⓑ purse-shaped; ‐hase m, zo. = Känguruh.

beutel²**ig** (‐ʹ(⌣)‐) a. ⓑ v. Kleidern: baggy; v. e-r Naht &c.: puckered; ⁓ w. = beuteln I.

Beutel³**-kammer** ⊕ (‐ʹ⌣...) [beuteln 2] f ⓑ, ‐kasten m bolting-house, -room; bolting-chest; ‐marder m, zo. ⚥ dasyure; ‐maschine, ‐mühle f bolting-mill.

beuteln (⌣‐) ⓑ a. I v/n. (h.) u. sich ⁓ v/refl. 1. (Falten werfen) to crease; (sich aufbauschen) to bag, bunch, swell out; von der Naht: to pucker. — II v/a. 2. (rütteln) to shake (up) ⊕ Müllerei: to bolt (or sift) flour. — 3. Flachs ⁓ (klopfen) to beat flax.

Beutel¹**-ratte** (‐ʹ⌣...) f ⓑ zo. opossum (*Dide'lphys virginia'na*); ‐schneider m cut-purse, pick-pocket; ‐schneiderei f arch-roguery; picking pockets; ‐schnur f purse-string; ‐sieb n bolting-sieve, bolter; ‐star m, orn. crested oriole (*Ca'ssicus*); ‐tiere n/pl. zo. marsupials or ...ia pl.; ‐tuch ⊕ n bolting cloth; tamine; ‐wahl n, co. das ~ h. to have an empty purse, to be short of cash; ‐wolf m, zo. phalanger, ⚥ thylacine (*Thylaci'nus cynoce'phalus*).

beuten (⌣‐) v/a. ⓑ (mit wilden Bienen besetzen) to stock (a hive) with wild bees.

beute¹**-schwer** (‐ʹ⌣...) a. ⓑ laden with (one's) booty or plunder; ‐zug m ⓑ marauding (or plundering) expedition.

Beut-heie (‐ʹ⌣) [ndd.] f ⓐ (Böttcherschlegel) cooper's mallet.

Beutler (⌣‐) m ⓑ glover.

Beutner (⌣‐) m ⓑ keeper of wild bees.

beutst † (‐ʹ) poet. für bietest (s. bieten).

be-völker/n (⌣⌣‐⌣) I v/a. u. v/refl. ⓑ a* to (fill with) people; sich ⁓ to become inhabited, to grow (more and more) populous; dicht (schwach) bevölkert densely (sparsely) populated; stark bevölkert populous. — II ~ n ⓒ = B/ung 1.

Be-völkerung (⌣⌣‐⌣) f ⓓ 1. peopling. — 2. (Einwohnerschaft) population; inhabitants, people pl.; ~s-dichtigkeit (‐ʹ...) f ⓑ, ‐stand m, ‐zunahme f density, state, increase of population.

be-vollmächtig/en (⌣⌣‐⌣) I v/a. ⓑ* e-n zu et. ⁓ to authorize a p. to do a th.; to give a p. (or to invest a p. with) full power(s) to act. — II ~ n ⓒ = B/ung.

Be-vollmächtigte ⚥ (⌣⌣‐⌣) m ⓑ (Auftragsgeber) constituent; (Kunde) customer.

be-vollmächtigt (⌣⌣‐⌣) p.p. u. a. ⓑ authorized; jur. having (or holding) power of attorney: Diplomatie: der Minister plenipotentiary; ~e([r] m) f ⓑ authorized agent, mandatory; (Vertreter) proxy; ⚥ assignee, trustee.

Be-vollmächtigung (⌣⌣‐⌣) f ⓓ authorization; mandate; durch ~ by proxy, jur. by power of attorney.

be-vor (⌣‐ʹ) [ahd.: before] cj. before, ere; ⁓ er krank wurde previous (or prior) to his falling ill, before he fell ill.

be-vormund/en (⌣⌣‐⌣) I v/a. ⓑ* 1. to act as guardian to a p.; *fig.* (be-aufsichtigen) to hold a p. in tutelage; to act as (or to play) a p.'s mentor and adviser; streng bevormundet F (kept) in leading-strings. — 2. to set a guardian over a p.; to place a p. under the care of a guardian. — II ~ n ⓒ u. B/ung f ⓓ 3. guardianship; *fig.* tutelage.

be-vorrecht/en (⌣⌣‐⌣) I v/a. ⓑ* 1. to grant privileges or prerogatives to; b/ete Stände m/pl. privileged classes, pl. — II B/ung f ⓓ 2. granting privileges, &c. to. — 3. (Vorrecht) privilege, prerogative; monopoly.

bevor-steh(e)n (⌣⌣‐ʹ(⌣)) I v/n. (h.) ⓑ** to be at hand or in prospect, *stärker:* to be imminent, to impend; es steht uns eine Hungersnot bevor a famine is threatening us or F staring us in the face; der strenge Winter steht uns bevor the hard winter is (close) at hand or fast approaching; es steht ihm eine Freude bevor ... is in store for him; die ⁓de Jahreszeit the (forth)coming, ensuing, approaching season; ⁓de Gefahr impending (*stärker:* imminent) danger. — II ~ n ⓒ prospect, perspective; der Gefahr &c.: imminence.

be-vorteilen (⌣⌣‐⌣) &c. s. übervorteilen.

be-vorworten (⌣⌣‐⌣) v/a. ⓑ* 1. ein Buch ⁓ to (provide with a) preface. — 2. (im voraus erklären) to declare beforehand.

be-vorzug/en (⌣‐⌣) I v/a. ⓑ* to prefer, to show (a) preference for; (begünstigen) to favour; e-n im Testament ⁓ to make special provision for a p. in one's will. — II ~ n ⓒ = B/ung. — III **be-vorzugt** (⌣‐ʹ) p.p. u. a ⓑ (specially) favoured; der v. e-m ~e a p.'s favourite or protégé.

Signs (see page XVII): F familiar; P vulgar; F̶ flash; ⟍ rare; † obsolete (died); * new word (born); ǂ incorrect; ♪ music;

Be-vorzugung (⌣⌴⌣) f ⓺ preference (given to a p.); favour(itism).
be-wachen (⌣⌵⌵) I v/a. ⓼* to (keep) watch over, to guard, to keep one's eye upon a p., a th.; streng bewacht in close custody or confinement; e-n ⌵ lassen to set spies (or a watch) over a p., durch Geheimpolizisten: to shadow a p. — II ~ n ⓻ = Bewachung.
be-wachsen (⌣⌵⌵) ⓈB(ej)t* I v/a. Moos bewächst das Dach moss is growing (or spreading) over the roof. — II v/n. (fn) mit Moos ⌵ to be(come) grown (all over) with ...
Be-wachung (⌣⌵⌵) f ⓺ watching; watch; custody; supervision; polizeiliche auch: espionage.
be-waffnen (⌣⌵⌵) I v/a. u. v/refl. ⓶b* (sich) ⌵ to arm (o.s.), to provide (o.s.) with arms or a weapon. — II ~ n ⓻ = B/ung. — III **be-waffnet** p.p. u. a. ⓺ mit ⌴er Faust, Hand by force of arms, with sword in hand; ⌴e Macht armed force; ~e(r) m ⓺ armed person, ehm. ⚔ man-at-arms.
Be-waffnung (⌣⌵⌵) f ⓺ armament; equipment; eines Magnets: armature.
Be-wahr-anstalt (⌣⌵⌵...)/⓺ für kleine Kinder: nursery(-school); kindergarten.
be-wahren (⌣⌵⌵) [ahd.; *wahren] I v/a. und v/refl. 1. (beschützen) to guard (or shield) from evil; (sicherstellen) to (make) secure; vor der Nässe ⌵ to keep from (or protect against) the wet; Aufschrift: vor Nässe zu ⌵!: to be kept dry!; der Himmel möge uns vor Feuer ⌵ Heaven save us from fire; fig. den Schein ⌵ to keep up appearances; besser bewahrt wie beklagt prevention is better than cure; sich vor et. ⌵ to guard (or provide) against danger; to keep out of mischief; ei, bewahre!, Gott soll mich ⌵! Heaven forbid!, oft: never!, oh dear, no! — 2. = aufbewahren I. — II ~ n ⓻ 3. = Bewahrung.
be-währen (⌣⌵⌵) [mhd.; *wahr] I v/a. u. v/refl. 1. (bestätigen) to confirm, aver, verify, substantiate; sich ⌵ v/refl. to prove true; dieser Satz wird sich stets ⌵ ... will always hold good. — 2. (als gut erweisen) j-n Ruf, sich ⌵ to stand the test; F to be (fully) up to the mark; sich nicht ⌵ to prove a failure; sich schlecht ⌵ to answer badly; die Erfindung hat sich trefflich bewährt ... has turned out well; sich ⌵ als (mit nom. od. acc.) to show o.s. a friend, &c., to prove (to be) a good man, a genuine article, &c. — II ~ n ⓻ 3. = Bewährung.
Be-wahrer (⌣⌵⌵) m ⓶, ~in f ⓻ guard (-ian), keeper, custodian; preserver.
be-wahrheiten (⌣⌵⌵) [erst nhd. 18. sae.] I v/a. ⓼* to verify und II **Be-wahrheitung** f ⓺ = bewähren 1 u. 3.
be-währt p.p. u. a. ⓺ well tried or seasoned; trustworthy; genuine; ⌴er Freund true ...; ⌴es System approved, sound, thoroughly good system; ~heit f ⓺ trustworthiness, genuineness, soundness; thoroughness.
Be-wahrung (⌣⌵⌵) f ⓺ guard (kept over a th.); protection; preservation.
Be-währung (⌣⌵⌵) f ⓺ confirmation; verification; proof; trial.

Be-wahrungs-mittel (⌣⌵...) n ⓺ preservative (vor, gegen against).
be-walden (⌣⌵) v/a. u. v/refl. ⓼* to afforest; sich ⌵ to become covered with woods; bewaldeter Hügel woody (or well-wooded) hill.
be-waldrechten ⊕ (⌣⌵⌵) v/a. ⓼* carp. to rough-hew (timber in the forests).
Be-waldung (⌣⌵⌵) f ⓺ afforestation; state (or number) of forests; woodiness.
be-wall/en (⌣⌵⌵) I v/a. ⓼* 1. to construct banks (for a canal). — 2. Hopfen: to hill. — II B/ung f ⓺ 3. embankment.
be-wältigen (⌣⌵⌵) I v/a. ⓼* Arbeit: to accomplish; Hindernisse: to conquer, to overcome; e-n Stoff: to master; (unterwerfen) to subdue. — II ~ n ⓻ u. **Be-wältigung** f ⓺ accomplishment; (Unterwerfung) subjugation.
be-wandert (⌣⌵⌵) p.p. u. a. ⓺ fig. in et. ⌵ (erfahren) sein to be well acquainted with, skilled (or experienced) in a th.; in einer Kunst, Wissenschaft: versed in, conversant with; ~heit (⌣⌵⌵) f ⓺ (intimate) acquaintance (with a subject); skill (or experience) (in a handicraft or in arts); thorough knowledge (of languages, &c.).
be-wandt (⌣⌵) a. ⓺ (vgl. bewenden) es ist um (od. mit) et. so ⌵ the matter stands thus; the state of affairs is this; bei so ⌴en Umständen this being the case, under these circumstances.
Be-wandtnis (⌣⌵⌵) f ⓲ († n ⓱) state (or position) of affairs; es hat mit der Sache eine (ganz) andere ~, als Sie glauben things are (quite) different from what you think; es hat damit e-e ganz eigene ~, die Sache hat ihre (ganz) eigene ~ it is a (most) peculiar matter, a (very) curious case; oft co. thereby hangs a tale; damit hat es folgende ~ the case (or the state of affairs) is as follows.
be-wangen ⌄ (⌣⌵⌵) v/a. ⓼* (beschalen) to fish (a mast).   [bewerben.
be-warb, be-warf (⌣⌵) impf. v. bewerben.⌋
be-wässerbar (⌣⌵⌵) a. ⓺ irrigable.
be-wässern (⌣⌵⌵) I v/a. ⓼* to water (plants), agr. ⊕ to irrigate (land). — II ~ n ⓻ u. **Be-wässerung** (⌣⌵⌵) f ⓺ watering, agr. ⊕ der Felder irrigation.
Be-wässerungs-anlage ("....) f ⓺, =anstalten ⓺ f/pl. irrigation-works pl., catch-work; =graben m, =kanal m, =rinne f ⊕ irrigation-channel, canal, feeder, catch.
be-wegbar (⌣⌴⌵) a. ⓺ movable.
Be-wegbarkeit (⌣⌴⌵-) f ⓺ movability.
be-wegen (⌣⌵⌵) I v/a. u. v/refl. ⓼a 1. (sich) ⌵ to move (on or away); er will sich nicht von der Stelle ⌵ F he won't budge. — 2. (rühren, rücken) (sich) ⌵ to stir; der Wind bewegt die Blätter ... stirs (or moves) the leaves; von Maschinenteilen: sich auf und nieder ⌵ to work up and down; sich auf et. hin ⌵ to move towards (F to make for) a th.; sich (viel) in freier Luft ⌵ to take (much) open-air (or outdoor) exercise; sich im Kreise um et. ⌵ to revolve (or to move in a circle) round s.th.; fig. sich in feinen Kreisen ⌵ to move (or mix) in good society, in aristocratic circles. — 3. (erregen) to agitate; ⌄

von der See: heftig bewegt rough, stärker: stormy; fig. ein bewegtes Leben führen to lead a roaming (or an adventurous) life, to have a chequered career — 4. (aufregen) to excite, agitate, rouse, stir; (erweichen) to move (or soften) a p.'s heart; (beunruhigen) to disquiet a p.'s mind; fig. bewegt (gerührt) touched; mit bewegter Stimme with trembling voice, in a voice thrilled with emotion; bewegte Zeiten stirring (or eventful troubled, troublous) times; sich ⌵ lassen to be moved with pity, &c.; (nachgeben) to give way, to yield. — II v/a. ⓼b* 5. et. ⌵ zu et. ⓺ (bestimmen) to induce a p. to do a th.; ich bewog ihn fortzugehen I prevailed upon him to leave; das hat mich dazu bewogen, es zu glauben that was the reason for my believing it; er fand sich nicht bewogen, es zu tun he did not feel inclined (or would not condescend) to do it, he saw no reason (or necessity) for doing it; er ließ sich durch nichts dazu ⌵ nothing could bring (or get) him to do it; hierdurch bewogen influenced by these motives. — III ⌵d p.pr. u. a. ⓺ 6. moving, mech. locomotive, dynamic (force, &c.); sich selbst ⌵ self-acting, automatic, von Wagen: self-propelled, durch elektr. Strom: electrically driven or propelled.
Be-weger (⌣⌵⌵) m ⓶ mover, &c. (s. bewegen); phys., ⊕ motor, motive force.
Be-weg-grund (⌣⌵...) m ⓺ motive; inducement; =kraft f motive (or locomotive, motor) force; moving power; (electric) motor.
be-weglich (⌣⌵⌵) a. ⓺ 1. = bewegbar; (behende) agile, mobile, nimble, sprightly. — 2. jur. ⌴e (ant. liegende) Güter personal property, goods and chattels pl.; furniture; ⊕ ⌴e Rolle moving pulley. — 3. (rührend) touching; in ⌴em Tone, mit ⌴er Stimme in a tone of entreaty, with (or in) a tremulous voice.
Be-weglichkeit (⌣⌵⌵-) f ⓺ 1. agility, mobility, nimbleness, sprightliness. — 2. earnestness or urgency (of an entreaty), tremor (of the voice).
be-wegt (⌣⌵) p.p. u. a. ⓺ s. bewegen 3, 4; ⌴e Wellen stormy waves, tempestuous billows; ~heit f ⓺ emotion, agitation.
Be-wegung (⌣⌵⌵) f ⓺ 1. movement; unruhige: stir, bustle, commotion; (Ortswechsel) locomotion; ~ mit den Armen, dem Kopfe ꝛc.: gesture, unwillkürliche: action; er ist immerfort in ~ he is constantly astir or always on the move; er macht sich keine (viele) ~ he takes no (plenty of) exercise; ❀ die Kurse zeigten wenig (auch die Börse blieb ohne) ~ prices were the market was flat or lifeless; F there was little doing on 'Change. — 2. phys. &c. meist: motion; gleichförmig beschleunigte (verzögerte) ~ uniformly accelerated (retarded) motion; rückläufige ~ retrograde movement, ast. auch: ⚵ retrogradation; schwingende, wellenförmige ~ oscillating, undulatory movement; oscillation, vibration; ~ e-s Körpers um e-n Mittelpunkt rotatory movement, rotation, Lehre von der ~:

⚵ scientific; ❀ botanical; ♁ geography; ⊕ machinery; ⚒ mining; ⚔ military; ⌄ marine; ❀ commercial; ✉ postal; 🚂 railway.

[Bewegungsachse] — 192 — [bewogen]

⚡ kinematics; et. in~ erhalten to keep a th. going or in working order; Maſchinen in (außer) ~ ſetzen to throw ... into (out of) gear, to start (to stop) ...; der elektriſche Wagen, der Zug iſt in ~ the electric car, the train is moving; et. in ~ ſetzen to put a th. in(to) motion, to set a th. going. — 3. (Gemüts-)emotion, heftige: agitation; in ~ verſetzen to stir, move, touch, agitate.

Be-wegungs-achſe (⌣–́⌣...) f ⓰ axis of rotation; =empfindung f. physiol. (Muſkelſinn) ⚡ kinæsthesia; =fähig a. ⓰ capable of (loco)motion; vgl. bewegbar; =fähigkeit f (loco)motivity; vgl. Bewegbarkeit; =kraft f motor force, motive power; =krieg ⚡ m (Feldkrieg) war (-fare) in the open country; =lehre f: ⚡ kinematics; dynamics, mechanics; =los a. motionless, immovable; =loſigkeit f immobility; fixity; =mittelpunkt m centre of motion; =torpedo m, self-propelling torpedo; =vermögen n faculty of (spontaneous) motion.

be-wehren (⌣–́⌣) ⓮* ꝛc. ſ. bewaffnen ꝛc.; **be-wehrt** (⌣–́) p.p. u. a. ⓰ armed (a. her.).

be-weiben (⌣–́⌣) v/a. und v/refl. ⓮* to provide with a wife; ſich ⚓ to get married or wedded, to take a wife.

be-weinen (⌣–́⌣) v/a. ⓮* e-n, et. ⚓ to lament, deplore, weep over (the loss of) a p..a th.; ⚓=wert, ⚓würdig a. ⓰ lamentable, deplorable; (elend) pitiable.

Be-weis (⌣–́) m ⓫a. 1. proof of; zum Beweiſe deſſen dient // it is proved (or supported) by (the fact that) //; den ~ für et. liefern to furnish proof of a th., jur. to produce (legal) evidence of a fact; das bedarf keines weiteren Beweiſes there is no further proof needed (for it), that's self-evident or obvious. — 2. ~(=grund) argument; ſchlagender, unumſtößlicher ~ conclusive (or striking) proof, incontestable (or forcible) argument; ⚡ log. u. math. den ~ eines Satzes führen to prove (or to demonstrate the truth of) a proposition. — 3. (Kundgebung) manifestation, mark, sign, token of; ein rührender ~ ſeiner Liebe a touching instance of his love.

Be-weis-antretung (⌣–́⌣...) f ⓰ jur. production of (legal) evidence; =aufnahme f argument(ation).

be-weisbar (⌣–́-) a. ⓰ capable of proof or demonstration; provable, demonstrable; ~keit (~-) f ⓰ provableness, demonstrableness, demonstrability.

be-weis-dienlich (⌣–́...) a. ⓰ useful as an argument, demonstrative.

be-weiſen (⌣–́⌣) v/a. u. ſich ⚓ v/refl. ⓫* 1. to prove; to establish the truth of a th., one's claim, &c.; to make out a case; einen Satz ⚓ to prove (or demonstrate) a proposition; eine Behauptung ⚓ to make good (or substantiate) a statement; ſich als wahr ⚓ to come (or prove) true; das will nichts ⚓ that's no proof; das iſt noch zu ⚓ that remains to be proved; ⚓d concluſive. — 2. e-m ſ-e Achtung ⚓ (erzeigen) to show one's esteem (or respect) for a p.; e-m viel Aufmerkſamkeiten ⚓ to pay great attentions to a p.; große Teilnahme für et. ⚓ (kundtun) to evince great interest in a th.; das beweiſt für mich it speaks (or tells) in my favour; ſich dankbar, freundlich gegen e-n ⚓ to show o.s. grateful, kind to a p.; ſich e-m als Freund (nom. ob. acc.) ⚓ to prove a friend to a p.

Be-weis-friſt (⌣–́...) f ⓰ adjournment for (further) collection of evidence; =führer(in f) m person who conducts a proof or produces evidence; =führung f =demonstration (of the truth of s.th.); argument(ation) of a p. on s.th.; =grund m (valid) argument; =kraft f argumentative power of a p., demonstrative (or conclusive) force of a statement; ⚓kräftig a. ⓰ conclusive; (überzeugend) convincing; =laſt f burden of (the) proof; =mittel n means of proving a th.; evidence; =pflicht f =laſt; =ſatz m jur. (Gegenſtand des Beweiſes) theorem; =ſchrift f =ſtück.

be-weißen (⌣–́⌣) ⓰* = weißen.

Be-weis-ſtelle (⌣–́...) f ⓰ passage (quoted) in support of a th., authority (adduced) for a statement; =ſtück n legal instrument (or document) in support (of a case); =verfahren n adjudging the proofs (before passing judgment).

be-wenden (⌣–́⌣) I v/n. (ſn) ⓰a* es bei (oder mit) et. ⚓ laſſen to acquiesce in a th., to put up with a th.; wir laſſen es beſſer dabei ⚓ we had better let the matter rest there or leave it as it is or do nothing more in it; vgl. bewandt. — II ~ n ⓴ dabei hat es (oder behält es) ſein ~ there the matter must reſt or end (for the present).

be-werben (⌣–́⌣) I ſich ⚓ v/refl. ⓰b* 1. ſich um et. ⚓ to seek to obtain a th.; ſich um ein Amt ⚓ to apply (or sue) for an appointment; F to try (or put in) for a post; ſich um ein Mädchen ⚓ to court (or woo) ..., to pay (one's) court (or one's addresses) to ...; ſich um Stimmen ⚓ to canvass for votes. — 2. ſich gemeinſchaftlich um den Preis ⚓ to compete (als Schütze auch: to shoot) for the prize; ☉ ⚘ ſich um e-e Lieferung ⚓ to tender for a contract. — II ~ n ⓴ 3. = Bewerbung.

Be-werber (⌣–́⌣) m ⓬, ~in f ⓱ applicant (or candidate) for a post; suitor to (or of) a lady; competitor for a prize; pretender to the throne; aspirant to power; ☉ ⚘ p. tendering for a contract.

Be-werbung (⌣–́⌣) f ⓰ application; courtship; competition (vgl. bewerben).

be-werfen (⌣–́⌣) I v/a. ⓰b* 1. e-n mit et. ⚓ to pelt a p. with s.th.; to fling (F to pitch) s.th. at him; e-n mit Kot, mit Schmutz ⚓ to pelt (ſtärker: to bombard) a p. with mud; e-n mit Steinen ⚓ to throw stones at a p. — 2. Maurerei: mit Mörtel ⚓ to plaster, grob: to rough-cast. — II **Be-werfung** f ⓰ 3. pelting (ſ. 1.) plastering (ſ. 2).

be-werkſtellig/en (⌣–́⌣⌣) [nhd. 17/18. ſæc.] I v/a. ⓰* to (carry into) effect; (ausführen) to achieve, accomplish, perform, bring about (ſ. a. be=... 5); die Sache iſt ſchwer zu ⚓, läßt ſich ſchwer ⚓ ... is difficult to carry out or of accomplishment. — II ~ n ⓴ u. **B-ung** f ⓰ carrying into effect; achievement, accomplishment, performance.

be-werten ⚘ (⌣–́⌣) I v/a. u. v/refl. ⓰* to price; (abſchätzen) to assess, to value; ſich ⚓ auf to amount to. — II **Be-wertung** f ⓰ assessment, valuation.

Be-wetterung ⛏ (⌣–́⌣⌣) f ⓰ (Lüftung der Bergwerke) ventilation of (the underground workings of) a mine or pit.

be-wickeln (⌣–́⌣) I v/a. ⓰a* to wrap (in cloth), to wrap round (with straw), to wrap (or fold) up (in paper). — II **Be-wick(e)lung** (⌣–́⌣) f ⓰ wrapping (up or round); wrap(per).

be-wies (⌣–́) impf., **be-wieſen** (⌣–́⌣) p.p. von beweiſen.

be-willigen (⌣–́⌣⌣) I v/a. ⓰* 1. to grant, to allow; Rechte ꝛc.: to concede; parl. Geld ⚓ to vote supply or the estimates. — 2. (zugeſtehen) to agree, to consent to; Sie werden ⚓, daß // you will allow (or admit) that //; eine Bitte ⚓ to comply with a request. — II ~ n ⓴ 3. = Bewilligung.

Be-willigung (⌣–́⌣⌣) f ⓰ granting, allowance; concession, parl. (carrying of a) vote; ☉ Ihre ~ vorbehalten subject to your approval or assent; ~s-recht (⌣́...) n ⓰ parl. right of voting (or to vote) supply.

be-willkomm(n)en (⌣–⌣⌣) I v/a. ⓰(⓬b)* to welcome (home); to receive kindly or hospitably. — II ~ n ⓴ u. **Be-willkomm(n)ung** f ⓰ welcoming (home), welcome (held out to a p.); kind (or hospitable) reception (of a p.).

be-wimpeln ⚓ (⌣–́⌣⌣) v/a. ⓰a* ein Schiff ⚓ to hoist the pennant on a man-of-war; to dress a ship with pennants.

be-wimpert ⚘ (⌣–́⌣) a. ⓰ ⚡ ciliated.

be-winden (⌣–́⌣) ⓰* = bewickeln.

be-wirkbar (⌣–́-) a. ⓰ practicable, feasible, manageable, realizable.

be-wirken (⌣–́⌣) v/a. ⓰* to effect, cause, bring about; (hervorrufen) to produce, to call forth; (veranlaſſen) to occasion, ſtärker: to provoke.

be-wirt/en (⌣–́⌣) I v/a. ⓰* to receive (or entertain) hospitably; mit Speiſe und Trank: to feast, to regale (with eating and drinking); F to treat (to a dinner, &c.). — II ~ n ⓴ u. **B-ung**.

Be-wirter (⌣–́) m ⓬, ~in f ⓱ host(ess).

be-wirtſchaft/en (⌣–́⌣⌣) I v/a. ⓰* agr. den Acker ⚓ to till the land, to cultivate the soil; to work a farm; ein Gut ⚓ (verwalten) to manage (or superintend) an estate. — II ~ n ⓴ u. **B-ung**.

Be-wirtſchafter (⌣–́⌣⌣) m ⓬ manager, steward, bailiff (of a farm).

Be-wirtſchaftung (⌣–́⌣) f ⓰ tilling the land, &c. (ſ. bewirtſchaften); management (or superintendence) of an estate.

Be-wirtung (⌣–́⌣) f ⓰ (hospitable) reception or entertainment; F treat; (Koſt) cheer, fare; die ~ iſt hier gut the attendance here is good; here one is well looked after; die ~ beſorgen to wait upon the guests.

be-witzeln (⌣–́⌣⌣) v/a. ⓰a* to joke (ſtärker: to sneer) at, to (turn into) ridicule; to make game (or sport or fun) of.

be-wog(en) (⌣–́-) impf. (p.p.) u. **be-wöge** impf. subj. von bewegen.

Zeichen (ſ. S. XVII): F familiär; P Volksſprache; ⌐ Gaunerſprache; ⤬ ſelten; † alt (auch geſtorben); * neu (auch geboren); ⁺⁺ unrichtig;

be-wohnbar (⌣-́) *a.* (in)habitable, von Häusern auch: fit to live in, comfortable; nicht 2 uninhabitable; ein Haus ꝛc. 2 machen to put ... into habitable repair; **~keit** *f* (ohne *pl.*) habitableness, habitable state.

be-wohn/en (⌣-́⌣) I *v/a.* to inhabit, live in a (house, country); to reside in (a town); to occupy a (dwelling, flat, suite of rooms). — II ~ *n* = B/ung.

Be-wohner (⌣-́⌣) *m*, **~in** *f* inhabitant, resident, occupier; (Bürger) citizen, weitS. denizen; (Mieter) tenant, von Zimmern: lodger; **~schaft** *f* inhabitants or residents *pl.*; (Eingeborne) natives *pl.* [residency, occupancy.)

Be-wohnung (⌣-́⌣) *f* inhabiting, &c.;

be-wölken (⌣⌣́⌣) I *v/a.* u. *v/refl.* (sich) 2 1. to cloud; *fig.* to darken, to obscure; der Himmel bewölkt sich the sky is becoming cloudy, looks overcast or lowery; das Wasser bewölkt sich ... is getting turbid. — II **Be-wölkung** *f* 2. clouding. — 3. (Bewölktheit) cloudiness. [v. be-werben, -werfen, -winden.)

be-worben, -worfen, -wunden (⌣-́⌣) *p.p.*

Be-wund(e)rer (⌣-́(⌣)⌣) *m*, **Be-wund(r)erin** *f* (male, female) admirer.

be-wundern (⌣-́⌣) *v/a.* to admire; **2~wert** ꝛc.] **s.** bewunderungs-...

Be-wunderung (⌣-́⌣⌣) *f* admiration; **2~wert** (*„...*) *a* 2, **~würdig** *a.* admirable, wonderful, marvellous.

Be-wurf (⌣́⌣) *m* ⒯b. Maurerei: plaster, plastering; grober: rough-cast.

be-wurzeln (⌣-́⌣⌣) *v/n.* (in) u. sich 2 *v/refl.* to take (or strike) root (a. *fig.*), be-wurzelt rooted.

be-wußt (⌣-́) *a.* 1. subjektiv: (wissend) ich bin mir e-r Sache (*gen.*) 2 I am conscious (or aware, cognizant) of a th.; er war sich dessen wohl 2, daß // he was quite alive to the fact that //, he knew perfectly well that //; ich bin mir keiner Schuld 2 I have nothing to reproach myself with; ich bin mir des Vorfalls nicht klar 2 I have no clear recollection of the occurrence; er w ir f-r selbst nicht (mehr) 2 he was unconscious, he had lost (all) consciousness. — 2. objektiv: (bekannt) die Sache ist mir 2 the matter is known to me; soviel mir 2 (ist) as far as I know; for aught (that) I know; das 2e Buch the aforesaid ..., the ... referred to or in question.

Be-wußtheit (⌣-́-) *f* 1. intimate knowledge. — 2. (bewußtes Sein) self-consciousness; vgl. Bewußtsein.

be-wußt-los (⌣-́...) *a.* (ohne Wissen) without knowledge; (instinktmäßig) instinctive, *adv.* instinctively; (ohnmächtig) unconscious, insensible; 2 w. to lose consciousness; **-losigkeit** *f* unconsciousness, insensibility; **-sein** *n* (full) knowledge; es wurde mir zum klaren ~ gebracht, es kam mir zum ~ it came (or was brought) home to me; it (suddenly) dawned upon me; das ~ verlieren to lose (all) consciousness; zum ~ bringen to bring round; (wieder) zum ~ kommen to return to (or to recover) consciousness; F to come to.

Bey *f.* Bei².

bez. *abbr.* = bezahlt; bezüglich.

be-zackt ⊕ (⌣-́) *a.* jagged, indented.

be-zahlbar (⌣-́⌣) *a.* payable.

be-zahl/en (⌣-́) I *v/a.* u. *v/n.* (h.) 1. (zahlen) to pay; e-m et. 2 to pay a p. (for) s.th.; Ärzte ꝛc. 2 to (pay a) fee to ...; sie werden schlecht bezahlt they are badly paid, underpaid or ill remunerated; e-e Rechnung 2 to settle ...; Schulden 2 to clear off (or discharge) ...; ich mußte die Zeche 2 I had to find the money or F to pay the piper, to stand treat. — 2. e-n nach Gebühr 2 to give a p. his due (reward), fully to compensate him; e-n mit gleicher Münze 2 to pay a p. back in his own coin, to give a p. tit for tat; nicht mit Gold zu 2(b) not to be bought (for money); invaluable; ⦿ das macht sich bezahlt oder *v/refl.* bezahlt sich (bringt Geld ein) that repays one, it pays, it's a paying business, it's worth doing; er hat sich bezahlt gemacht he has repaid (or reimbursed) himself. — II ~ *n* 3. = B/ung.

Be-zahler (⌣-́⌣) *m*, **~in** *f* payer; ein guter ~ one who pays well, auch: a good paymaster.

be-zahlt *p.p.* u. *a.* paid; (besoldet) salaried; *b.s.* (bestochen) bribed; hired (for money); vgl. bezahlen.

Be-zahlung (⌣-́⌣) *f* payment; (full) settlement; (doctor's, &c.) fee; (soldier's, &c.); pay; (clerk's) salary; nur gegen bare ~ for cash (or ready money) only; F strictly on cash terms; **~s-schein** (*„...*) *m* receipt.

be-zähmbar (⌣-́⌣) *a.* tamable; *fig.* controllable; **~keit** (*~*) *f* tamableness.

be-zähm/en (⌣-́) I *v/a.* u. *v/refl.* to tame; *fig.* (sich) 2 to restrain (o.s.); to subdue or control or master (one's passions); to check or curb or bridle or moderate (one's desires). — II ~ *n* = taming, &c. (f. I).

Be-zähmer (⌣-́⌣) *m*, **~in** *f* tamer (of lions, &c.); f. bezähmen.

Bezähmung (⌣-́⌣) *f* = bezähmen II.

be-zahnt ⊕ (⌣-́) *a.* toothed, indented.

Be-zaub(e)rer (⌣-́(⌣)⌣) *m*, **Be-zaub(r)erin** *f* enchanter (f enchantress), sorcerer (f sorceress), charmer.

be-zauber/n (⌣-́⌣) I *v/a.* to charm, enchant (= behexen ꝛc.); 2d *p.pr.* u. *a.* *fig.* charming, enchanting, bewitching. — II B/ung (⌣-́⌣) *f* charm(ing), enchantment. (casting a) spell (over).

be-zäumen (⌣-́⌣) * to zäumen.

be-zechen (⌣-́⌣), meist sich 2 *v/refl.* to get the worse for drink; bezecht drunk, tipsy, in liquor; bezecht machen to make drunk, to ply with liquor.

be-zeichn/en (⌣-́⌣) [: betoken] b* I *v/a.* 1. to mark sheep, &c.; to label goods. — 2. mit e-m Akz'nt 2 to accent(uate); mit Punkten: to dot. — 3. (ausdrücken) to express, designate, denote; Begriffe mit Worten 2 to clothe ideas in words. — 4. e-m et 2 (andeuten) to indicate, signify out a th. to a p. — 5. (kennzeichnen) to characterize, stamp, qualify as. — 6. e-e Wand 2 to cover ... with drawings. — II sich 2 *v/refl.*

7. (sich darstellen) to appear (to the eye); du hast dich als meinen Freund bezeichnet you described yourself as my friend. — III 2d *p.pr.* u. *a.* 8. Bed. des *inf.* — 9. (bedeutsam) expressive (or significant) of; (eigentümlich) characteristic, distinctive. — IV ~ *n* 10. = B/ung.

Be-zeichnung (⌣-́⌣) *f* mark(ing); designation; indication; characterization; *chm.* u. *math.* notation; **~s-zettel** (*„...*) *m* label, ticket.

be-zeigen (⌣-́⌣) b* I *v/a.* Freude ꝛc. 2 to show (or express, give signs of) ...; (bekunden) to manifest, testify; f-n sein Beileid 2 to condole with a p. (in his bereavement); e-m f-n Dank für et. 2 to show o.s. grateful (or to render thanks, to express one's gratitude) to a p. for s.th. — II *v/refl.* sich 2 to show o.s., to prove (to be). — III ~ *n* u. **Be-zeigung** *f* show(ing); manifestation. [bezichtigen.)

be-zeihen ⌕ (⌣-́⌣) *v/a.* b* = zeihen.

be-zeptert (⌣-́⌣) *a.* sceptred.

be-zetteln ⦿ (⌣-́⌣) *v/a.* 2a* to label.

be-zeug/en (⌣-́⌣) I *v/a.* b* 1. to bear witness (feierlicher: testimony) to, to testify; *a.* to attest a fact; to witness a deed; vor Gericht: er bezeugte, daß er es gesehen habe he deposed to having seen it. — 2. (beweisen) to prove (by documents); (bescheinigen) to certify; (feststellen) to establish the truth. — II ~ *n* u. **Be-zeugung** *f* 3. testimony; attestation; (legal) proof or evidence; certifying; certificate.

be-zicht(ig)en (⌣-́(⌣)⌣) I *v/a.* (beschuldigen) to accuse a p. of a th.; to charge a p. with a th. — II **Be-zichtigung** *f* accusation, charge.

be-ziehbar (⌣-́⌣) *a.* 1. (bewohnbar) (in)habitable. — 2. ⦿ obtainable; nur bar 2 (to be had) for cash only.

be-zieh/en (⌣-́⌣) b* I *v/a.* u. *v/refl.* 1. ein Haus 2 to move (or go) into ..., to take possession of ...; die Märkte, die Messen 2 (besuchen) to frequent the markets, the fairs; eine Schule, Universität 2 to enter (or go to) a school, (a) college, a university (auch: to go to Eton, to Oxford, &c.). — 2. *typ.* den Deckel 2 to cover the tympan; ⚔ ein Lager 2 to go (or move) into a camp; einen Posten 2 to occupy a post; die Wache 2 to mount guard; ⚔ die Winterquartiere 2 to take up one's winterquarters. — 3. (sich) 2 (bedecken) mit to cover (get covered) with; der Himmel bezog sich (mit Wolken) the sky was overcast or became cloudy, F it came over lowery. — 4. et. mit 2 (überziehen) to spread s.th. over a th., to cover over (or case) a th. with s.th.; — *abs.* ein Bett 2 to make up ..., to put (new) sheets on ...; ♪ e-e Geige ꝛc. mit Saiten 2 to string ...; — 5. ⦿ e-n 2 (einen Wechsel auf ihn ziehen) to draw on a p. (for a certain sum). — 6. et. von woher 2 (kommen lassen) to obtain (or procure, F to get) from Paris, to order of (or from) a wholesale firm; Einkünfte, Gehalt ꝛc. 2 to receive ... — 7. et. auf et. 2 to connect a th. with a th.; er hat es auf sich bezogen he

applied it to himself, he thought it referred to (or was meant for) him. — II sich ~ v/refl. 8. f. 3. — 9. sich auf et. 2 to refer (or relate) to a th.; to bear upon a subject; sich auf e-n, et. 2 (berufen) to refer (or make reference) to a p., a th.; Sie dürfen sich auf mich 2 you may mention (or use) my name (as reference). — III ~ n ② 10. = B/ung 1.
be-ziehentlich (⌣‿⌣‿) a. u. adv. = bezüglich, beziehungsweise.
Be-zieher ⊕ (⌣‿⌣) m ②, ~in f ④: ~ e-s Wechsels drawer (or giver) of a bill (ant. Bezogene(r); * = Abonnent.
Be-ziehung (⌣‿⌣) f ④ 1. moving (or going) into (a house); entering (college); mounting (guard); receipt (of a sum of-money, &c.). — 2. (f. beziehen 7 u. 9) connexion with; reference (or relation) to; auf et. ~ h. to bear upon, to refer to a th.; in ~ zu e-m steh(e)n to stand in (a certain) relation(ship) to a p.; to be connected with a p.; freundschaftliche ~en zu e-m unterhalten to keep up friendly relations (or intercourse) with a p.; in dieser ~ in this connexion or respect; in ~ auf with regard (or reference) to, in relation to, concerning (or regarding, respecting); in finanzieller ~ in matters of (or as regards, as to) finance; in jeder ~ in every respect, from every point of view, to all intents and purposes; ⊕ unter ~ auf unsere frühere Mitteilung referring to our previous communication.
Be-ziehungs-begriff (⌣‿⌣‿...) m ② relative idea; =fürwort n, gr. relative pronoun; ²weise adv. respectively, (⁎⁎ statt „oder") or; =wort n, gram. relative (term).
be-zielen (⌣‿⌣) v/a. ⊕* to aim at.
be-ziffern (⌣‿⌣) ②a* I v/a. to mark with figures or numbers; ♪ bezifferter Baß figured bass. — II sich 2 v/refl., südd. a. 2 v/n. (h.) (sich) so und so hoch 2 to amount (or F total up, come) to so much; ⊕ auch: to figure (or run) up to. — III Bezifferung math. v. ♪ (⌣‿⌣) f ④ (numeral) notation. [timber.
be-zimmern ⊕ (~) v/a. ②a* carp. to⌋
be-zinnt (⌣⁸) [Zinne] a. ⊕ arch. castellated; ⚔ frt. crenel(l)ated, embattled.
Be-zirk (⌣⁸) [mhd. *be-u. *lt. circus Kreis] m ⓓc. (Stadt-, Land-)² (urban, country-)district; parl. für Wahlen: borough, county; allg.: electoral district; Am. auch: electoral precincts pl.; e-s Beamten zc.. circuit, e-s englischen Richters: venue; ~ einer Stadt (für städtische Wahlen zc.) ward; innerhalb eines (Gerichts-)~s within the jurisdiction of a court; fig. das liegt außerhalb meines ~s that is (or lies) beyond my department or range or province, F that's not in my line.
Be-zirks-amt (⌣⁸...) n ② = =gericht; =anstalt f für öffentliche Armenpflege workhouse, poor-house, union; =arzt m medical officer of a district; =gericht n district-court, (englisches Grafschaftsgericht) county-court; (Polizeigericht) police-court; =kommandeur ⚔ m commanding officer of a district, local commander; =kommando ⚔ n

(Behörde, die das Ersatzgeschäft besorgt) military depot (for recruiting purposes); =polizei-wache f police-station; =schulinspektor m, =schul-rat m inspector of schools in a district or county; =versammlung f district-council, ländliche: rural council; =vorsteher m guardian of the poor; police-officer (of a district); ²weise adv. by districts or wards.
Bezoar (‑tz⁻⌣¹) [pers. bād-sahr Gegengift] m ⓓc. (Ballen im Magen von Wiederkäuern) bezoar(-stone); ~mittel (⌣...) n ② pharm. (chm. als Gegengift dienend) bezoardic; =säure f, chm. bezoardic acid; =stein m bezoar(-stone); =ziege f zo.bezoar-goat.paseng(Capraaegagrus).
be-zog (⌣¹) impf., **be-zogen** (⌣⌣) p.p.v. beziehen. [drawee (ant. Bezieher(in).⌋
Be-zogene(r m) f (⌣‿⌣) ④⌥ bei Wechseln:⌋
be-zollen (⌣‿⌣) v/a. ⊕* to lay (or impose, put) a duty (or toll) on.
be-zuckern (⌣‿⌣) v/a. ②a* to sugar (over).
Be-zug (⌣¹) m ⓓc. 1. (Überzug) von Betten, Möbeln zc.: covering, case, casing; ~ von Saiten set of strings. — 2. = Beziehung 2; in ² (od. ~) auf, mit ~ auf with regard (or reference) to, in relation to, vgl. bezüglich II; ~ haben auf to relate (or refer) to, to be connected with, to bear upon; auf et. ob. e-n ~ nehmen to refer to a th. or a p.
be-züglich (⌣‿⌣) I a. ⊕ relative (auf et. to a th.); gram. ⚐es Fürwort relative pronoun. — II prp. mit gen. regarding, respecting, concerning, as to.
Be-zugnahme (⌣‿⌣‿) f ④ reference to; mit ~ auf et., unter ~ e-r Sache with reference (or regard) to a th., referring to a th.; respecting a th.
Be-zugs-anweisung (⌣‿⌣‿) f ② (vgl. beziehen 6) order (for delivery); =bedingungen f/pl. terms (or conditions) pl. of delivery; =ort m, =platz m, =quelle f source of supply; unsere beste =quelle ist Paris our best market for buying (or to buy in) is Paris; =spesen pl. charges pl. for delivery; =tag ⊕ m Börse: day appointed for the delivery of stock (previously purchased).
bezw. abbr. = bzw.
be-zwang (⌣⁸) impf. von bezwingen.
be-zwecken (⌣‿⌣) v/a. ⊕* 1. to have in view, to aim at; (beabsichtigen) to intend, purport, purpose; was will er damit ²? what can be his object in that? what is he aiming at? — 2. ⊕ Schuhm.: (benageln) to fasten with pegs.
be-zweifelbar (⌣‿⌣‿) a. ⊕ questionable, open to doubt, doubtful.
be-zweifeln (⌣‿⌣) I v/a. ②a* to doubt, to (call into) question; j-s Ehrlichkeit ², auch: to suspect a p.'s ...; die Sache ist nicht zu ² the matter is unquestionable or beyond doubt. — II Bezweif(e)lung f ④ doubting, &c. (f. I).
be-zwingbar (⌣‿⌣) a. ⊕ conquerable.
be-zwingen (⌣‿⌣) v/a. u. v/refl. ⓓst* (bewältigen) to master, overcome; sich ² to restrain (or check) o.s., to govern one's passions; (besiegen) to conquer, to vanquish, to get the better (or the upper hand) of; (untertänig machen) to subdue; (knechten) to enslave; seinen Schmerz ² to suppress ...; fig. ihr habt

das Herz mir bezwungen (SCH.) you have conquered (or melted) my heart.
Be-zwinger (⌣‿⌣) m ② conqueror.
be-zwinglich (⌣‿⌣) a. ⊕ conquerable.
be-zwingt (⌣⁸) p.p. u. a. ⊕ (mit Zwingen versehen) (provided) with a ferrule.
Be-zwingung (⌣‿⌣‿) f ④ mastering; conquest; subjugation.
be-zwungen (⌣‿⌣) p.p. von bezwingen.
Bf. abbr. = Brief; **Bg.** = Bogen.
BGB. abbr. = Bürgerliches Gesetzbuch.
Bibel (⌣¹) [mhd.; *grch. bibli'a pl. Bücher] f ④ die ~ the Bible, (the) Holy Scripture(s pl.); die ~ betreffend biblical.
Bibel-abschnitt(⌣...) m ② section of the Bible, anglikan. Kirche: lesson (to be read in the service); =anstalt f = =gesellschaft; =ausdruck m biblical (or scriptural) expression or term; =ausgabe f edition of the Bible; =auslegung f =erklärung f interpretation of the Holy Word; ⚋ exegesis; ²fest a. ⊕ thoroughly acquainted with (or firmly believing in) the Scriptures, auch: scripture-proof; =gesellschaft f society for the propagation of the Bible, Bible Society; ²gläubig a. believing in the Bible; =kenner m person deeply versed in the Bible; =kunde f scriptural knowledge; ²mäßig a. scriptural; =sprache f biblical (or scriptural) language; =spruch m verse (taken) from the Bible; bsd. für Predigten: (scriptural) text: =stelle f passage (chosen) from the Bible; =stunde f bible- (or scripture-)lesson; =text m scriptural text; =übersetzung f translation of the Bible; neue englische ~ Revised Version; =vers m verse of the Bible; =werk n Reference Bible; =wort n = =stelle.
Biber (⌣‿) [ahd.: beaver] m ② a) zo. (a. ~in f ④) beaver (Castor Fiber), biswl. castor; b) a. n (a. = ~fell, =haar, =hut) beaver; ⊕ (dickes Tuch) beaver; duffel; =bau (⌣‿...) m ② beaver-dam; beaver's den or lodge; =baum ⊕ m magnolia (Magno'lia); =eisen n, =falle f beaver-trap; =fänger m (beaver-) trapper; =fell n beaver(-skin); =geil n ⓓd. pharm.: ⚋ castoreum; =haar n beaver(-hair); =hut m beaver(-hat); =jagd f beaver-hunting; =jäger m = =fänger; =klee ⚘ (⌣) = Fieberklee.
Bibernell(e f (⌣‿‿‿⌣) [urspr. aus fr. pimpinelle] f ④ (⚘) a) burnet saxifrage (Pimpine'lla); b) welsche ~ = Becherkraut.
Biber-schwanz (⌣‿...) m ②: a) beaver's tail; b) arch. flat tile.
Bibi¹ P (⌣¹) m ⑭ (Hut) hat, F tile.
Bibi² (⌣¹) f ⑩ (Frau) Suaheli woman.
Bibliograph (⌣‿‿⌣f) [grch.] m ② (Bücherkenner) bibliographer; =ie (‑‿‿‿f) f ④ bibliography; periodical list of books; ²isch (‑‿‿‿f⌣) a. ⊕ bibliographical, weitS. bookish.
Bibliomane (‑‿‿⌣‿) [grch.] m ⑭ (Büchernarr, =wurm) bibliomaniac; F bookworm; **B/ie** (‑‿‿⌣¹) f ④ bibliomania.
Bibliophile (‑‿‿f⌣) [grch.] m ⑭ (Bücherfreund) bibliophile, lover of books.
Bibliothek (‑‿‿⌣¹) [grch.] f ④ (Bücherei) library; städtische ~ town library; ~ar (‑‿‿‿⌣¹) m ⓓc. librarian; ~arin

---

Signs (see page XVII): F familiar; P vulgar; ⌈ flash; ⚮ rare; † obsolete (died); * new word (born); ⁺⁺ incorrect; ♪ music;

[biblisch] — 195 — [Bigamist]

(-⌣⌣--(⌣)⸚) n ⓔc. librarianship, librarian's office; Larifch (-⌣⌣-⸣⌣) a. ⓕ concerning librarians or libraries.
biblisch (⸍⌣) a. ⓕ biblical, scriptural; ²c Geschichte Scripture History.
Biblist (-⸍) m ⓬ rel. scripturalist.
Bi-chlorid ⚛ (⸌⸍-⸍) [grch.] n ⓔc. chm. (Doppelchlorid) bichloride.
Bick-beere ⚘ (⸌⸍-) f ⓭ = Heidelbeere.
☞ **Bicke** (⸌⌣) ꝛc. f. Picke.
Bickel (⸌⌣) m ⓶ (Karst) mattock.
bieder (⸍⌣) [ndd.] a. ⓕ (ehrenhaft) honest, honourable, upright; (edelmütig) generous; (o. Falsch) straightforward, plainspoken; (treu) loyal, true.
Biederkeit (⸍⌣-) f ⓭ honourable (or upright)character; straightforwardness, plainspokenness; loyalty; integrity.
Bieder-leute (⸍⌣...) pl. honest folk pl.; **mann** m honourable (gentle)man; iro. good (old) fellow, (old) fool, F duffer; **meier** m good and honest, but humdrum fellow, **meier-stil** m arch. jejune (or plain, unadorned) style of (German) middle-class houses; **sinn** m = Biederkeit.
biegbar (⸍-) a. ⓕ flexible, pliable.
Biege (⸍⌣) f ⓭ 1. bend, curvature. — 2. ⓯ zum Biegen von Reifen: bender.
Biege-fall (⸍⌣...) m ⓮ = Biegungsfall; **flinge** ⊕ f Nadlerei: bending-plate; **maschine** ⊕ f bending-machine; **muskel** m, anat. flexor (muscle).
bieg/en (⸍⌣) [ahd.] Majt I v/n. (sn) 1. = bugen I; um die Ecke ² to turn (round) the corner. — II v/a. u. v/refl. 2. (sich) ² to bend, (trümmen) to curve; wieder gerade ² to bend straight again; es läßt sich ² it is flexible, it bends, F it gives; gebogen p.p. u. a. ⓕ (D 9) bent, crooked. — 3. fig. sich schmiegen und ² to bow low (or to cringe, to crawl) before people; es muß ² oder brechen, etwa: they must either yield or succumb; it must be settled either one way or the other; we must do it by hook or by crook; besser ² als brechen better to yield than to perish. — 4. ⊕ sich krumm ² to warp. — 5. gr. (abwandeln) to inflect. — III ~ n ⓳ 6. = B/ung.
biegsam (⸍-) a. ⓕ pliable, pliant, bendable, ductile, flexible; (geschmeidig) supple, lithe; fig. yielding, tractable; manageable; **~keit** (⸍--) f ⓮ pliability, pliancy; flexibility; suppleness, litheness; tractableness.
Biegung (⸍⌣) f ⓕ 1. bending, &c. (f. biegen); phys. deflexion; des Lichtes: diffraction; gr. inflexion; declension. — 2. (Krümmung) curvature; phys. flexure; ~en pl. e-s Flusses: windings, meanderings pl.; e-s Weges: turnings pl.; ~en m. to wind, to meander. [case.]
Biegungs-fall (⸍⌣...) m ⓬ gram. (oblique)
Bieg-walzwerk ⊕ (⸍⸍...) n ⓕ = Biege-maschine. [(or young) bee.]
Bienchen (⸍⌣) n ⓳ (dim. v. Biene little)
Biene (⸍⌣) [ahd.: bee] f ⓮ ent. (hive or honey-)bee (Apis melli/ica); männliche ~ drone; so geschäftig (so munter) wie e-e ~ as busy (as brisk) as a bee; Sprichw. jede ~ hat ihren Stachel bees have stings in their tails; den Bien null, etwa: necessity has no law.

Bienen-bau (⸌⌣...) m ⓬ = zucht; **baum** ⚘ m = Feldahorn; **blume** f, deren Blüten den Bienen Nahrung gibt: flower rich in honey; **brot** n (Nahrung junger Bienen) bee-bread, a. hive-dross; **brut** f larvæ pl.(or young stock) of bees; **dreck** m f. After² 2; **fleiß** m, fig. assiduity; **fresser** m bee-eater, mudwall (Merops apia'ster); **garten** m bee-garden; **harz** n (Stopfwachs zum Zellenbau) bee-glue; **haube** f cap with veil (worn by bee-keepers when cutting honeycombs); **haus** n bee-house, bee-shed, apiary; **käfer** m bee-wolf (Tricho'des apia'rius); **kappe** f (=haube; **königin** f, ent. queen-bee; **korb** m bee-hive; in den ~ (aus dem ~) treiben to (un)hive; **kraut** ⚘ n = Thymian; **kunde** f bee-lore, ⚛ apiarian knowledge; **laus** f (Braula caeca) bee-louse; **linie** f (Luftlinie, kürzeste Entfernung) bee-line; **motte** f bee-moth (Galle'ria mellone'lla); **orchis** ⚘ f bee-flower (Ophrys api'fera); **saug** ⚘ f. Bienaug; **schwarm** m swarm of bees; **stand** m stock of bees; **stock** m bee-hive; **vater** m = züchter; **wachs** n bees' wax; **wolf** m = a) fresser, b) käfer; **zelle** f cell in a hive, ⚛ alveolus; **zucht** f bee-rearing, keeping of bees, ⚛ apiculture; **züchter** m bee-keeper, hiver, ⚛ apiarist.
Bienlein (⸍-) n ⓳ = Bienchen.
Bi-ennium (⸌⸍(⌣)⸍) [lt.] n ⓶ (Zeitraum von zwei Jahren) biennium. [nessel.]
Bien-saug ⚘ (⸍⸍) m, n ⓔc., f ⓮ = Taub/
Bier (⸍) [ahd.: beer] n ⓔc. beer; malt liquor; (helles) englisches ~ Bass's (pale) ale, dunkles englisches ~ stout; porter; bayrisches ~ lager(-beer), Bavarian beer or ale; ~ vom Faß draught ale; ~ auf Flaschen gezogen bottled beer or ale; ~ (aus)schenken to sell beer (on the premises); (geben Sie mir) ein Glas ~! please a glass (or half a pint) of bitter (ale), stout, &c.!; zu ~(e) gehen F to go to the pub or beer-shop.
Bier-bank (⸌⸍...) f ⓬ tap-room bench; auf der ~ sitzen to spend one's time at the bar, to sit in the pub; **baß** m hoarse bass voice; **bauch** m (beer-drinker's) paunch; **bottich** m beer-vat; **brauen** n brewing of ale; **brauer** m brewer; **brauerei** f brewery; **bruder** m one fond of his pot of beer, tipper; **druck-apparat** ⊕ m = pumpe; **essig** m vinegar made of (stale) beer; **faß** n: a) (empty) beer-barrel [ein Faß Bier = a barrel (or cask) of beer]; b) fig. = bauch; **fiedler** m ale-house fiddler; **flasche** f beer-bottle; **füll-maschine** f beer-bottling machine; **garten** m beer-garden; open-air restaurant; **geld** n: a) beer-money, money spent on beer; b) = Trinkgeld; **glas** n beer-glass; **hahn** ⊕ m tap; **halle** f, Am., &c. beer-saloon; **haus** n = schenke; **hefe** f yeast; **hefe-pilz** ⚛ m yeast-plant (Saccharomy'ces cerevi'siae); **kaltschale** f = Kaltschale; **kanne** f pewter (ale-)pot; **keller** m beer-cellar; **kellner** (in f) m barman (F pot-man, pot-boy), barmaid; **kneipe** f F pot-house; **krug**

m beer-jug; **probe** f sampling (or tasting) the beer; **pumpe** ⊕ f beer-engine or -machine or -fountain; Griff der ~ (beer-)pull; **reise** F f beer-crawl; **schank** m: a) licence for (retailing) beer; b) = schenke; **schenk** m = wirt; **schenke** f ale-house, F beer-shop, pub(lic house), contp. pot-house; **schröter** m brewer's man; **seidel** n pint-mug or -glass [ein Seidel Bier = a pint of beer]; **steuer** f duty on ale or malt liquor; **stube** f tap-room, public (or private) bar; **suppe** f beer-soup; **tonne** f beer-vat; fig. very stout man, big-bellied person; **verlag** m brewer's agency; **verleger** m brewer's agent; cellar-man; **wage** ⊕ f beer-gauge; **wagen** m brewer's cart or van; dray-cart; **wirt** m ale-house keeper, publican; licensed victualler; **wirtschaft** f ale-house, F beer-shop, contp. pot-house; **würze** f beer-wort.
Biese ⚔ (⸍⌣) f ⓕ (Schnur am Beinkleid ꝛc. v. Soldaten) piping, braiding, cord.
biesen (⸍⌣) I v/n. (h.) ⓳ to madden (as by the sting of a gadfly). — II ~ n ⓳ frenzy, rage, mad(dened) state.
Bies-fliege (⸍⌣-) f ⓕ ent. gadfly (=Breme) (Taba'nus). [(= Bestie).]
Biest¹ P (⸍) [lt. bé'stia] n ⓥb. beast
Biest² (⸍) [ahd.: beest(ings)] m ⓥb. (o.pl.), **~milch** (⸌⸍) f ⓕ agr. (erste Milch der Kuh nach dem Kalben) beestings mst pl.
bieten (⸍⌣) [ahd.: bid] I v/a. und v/refl. ⓕa. 1. to offer; (zeigen) to show; eine Blöße ² to expose o.s. to attack; das bietet Schwierigkeiten it has its difficulties. — 2. sich (dar-)² to offer o.s.; es bot sich Gelegenheit dazu the opportunity (for it) presented itself. — 3. einem die Hand ꝛc. ² (darreichen) to (pr)offer (or hold out) one's hand to a p. (auch fig.); die Hand (zur Hilfe) ² to stretch out a helping hand, to, to offer (or tender) one's aid to; dem Glücke die Hand ² to try one's luck; F to take a plunge; einem e-n guten Morgen ² to bid (or wish) a p. .... — 4. 💰 bei Versteigerungen: to bid; zuerst ² to make the first bid; (weniger) ² als ein anderer to outbid (to underbid) another person; bietet keiner mehr? (is this the) highest bid?, no higher bid? vgl. feilbieten, meistbietend. — 5. einem et. ² (zumuten) to expect (or exact) s.th. from a p.; das darf mir niemand ² I shan't stand that from anybody; das läßt er sich nicht ² he won't swallow (or put up with) that. — 6. (entgegenhalten) die Stirn, die Spitze, es e-m ² to make a bold stand against a p.., to offer resistance to a p.; e-m Hohn, Trotz ² to defy a p., to set a p. at defiance; Schach ² to give check (to the king). — II ~ n ⓳ 7. offer(ing), &c. (f. I), vgl. a. Angebot.
Bieter (⸍⌣) m ⓶, **~in** f ⓕ bidder.
Bifang (⸍-) m ⓔc. = Beifang.
Bifurka'tion ⚛ (-⌣⌣-⸍⸍) [lt.] f ⓕ (Zwei-teilung) bifurcation. [bigamy.]
Bigamie (⸌⌣⸍) [lt.arch.] f ⓮ (Doppelehe)
bigamisch (⸌⸍⌣) a. ⓕ bigamous.
Bigamist (⸌⌣⸍) m ⓬ bigamist.

⚛ scientific; ⚘ botanical; ⚲ geography; ⊕ machinery; ⚒ mining; ⚔ military; ⚓ marine; 💰 commercial; ✉ postal; 🚂 railway.

[Bignonie] — 196 — [Bildungstrieb]

Bignoni-e f ? (⌣⌣⌣) [Abbé Bignon, 1662—1743] f ⊕ trumpet-flower (*Bigno'nia*).
bigott (-⌣) [fr.; *btſch b(e)i Gott!] a. ⓺ (frömmelnd) bigoted; saintly. [ness.|
Bigotterie (-⌣⌣⌣) f ⊕ bigotry; saintli-⌐
Bijou (⌣Gu⌣) [fr.] m ⓾ (Juwel, Kleinod) jewel, gem; (costly) trinket.
Bijouterie=waren (⌣Gu⌣⌣...) f/pl. ⓺ jewelry *sg.*, trinkets *pl.*
Bikarbonat ⌐ (⌣⌣⌣) [lt.] n ⓚc. chm. (doppeltkohlensaures Salz) bicarbonate.
bikonkav ⌐ (⌣⌣f) [lt.] a. ⓺ biconcave.
bikonvex ⌐ (⌣⌣m⌣) [lt.] a. ⓺ biconvex.
Bilander ⌘ (⌣⌣⌣) [ndl. Binnenländer] m ⓶ (einmastiges Schiff) bilander.
Bilanz ⓺ (⌣⌣, oft ⁀⁀ bi-lą̆'ʦ) [it. *bila'ncia f* Wage, fr. *balance f*, *bilan m*] f ⓺ (Abrechnung) balance; rohe (reine) ~ rough (net) balance; die ~ ziehen to strike the balance. [to balance accounts.|
bilanzieren ⓺ (⌣⌣L⌣) v/n.(h.) ⓺ (abrechnen)
Bilanz-konto (⌣f...) n ⓺, =**rechnung** f balance-account.
Bilch (⌣) [ahd.] f ⓲, ~**maus** f ⓺ zo. (Siebenschläfer) dormouse (*Myo'xus glis*).
Bild (⌣) [ahd.] n ⓫b. **1.** (Abbild) image; ganz ihr ~! (it's) the image of her! — **2.** (Ölbild) oil-painting; (Zeichnung) drawing, sketch; (Kupfer=, Stahlstich) engraving; in Büchern ꝛc.: illustration; (Porträt) picture, portrait, likeness; (Spielkarte) court-card; (Lichtbild) photograph; positives, negatives ~ positive, negative; durchscheinendes ~ transparency; ~ von Erz, ehernes ~ bronze statue; gegossenes ~ cast; *bibl.* graven image; (Götzen=) ~ idol; im ~e verbrannt burnt in effigy; *typ.* = ⓼ Buchstabenface. — **3.** *fig.*: a) ein ~ des Elends a picture of misery; die Stadt bot ein ~ der Verlassenheit dar the town was a picture (or scene) of desolation; ein ~ von e-m (ein bildschönes) Mädchen quite a picture, a real (or perfect) beauty of a girl, a beautiful (or lovely) girl; es bietet ſich ein an=d(e)res ~, Frrr! ein ander ~! the scene changes; ein trübes ~ gewähren to be (or offer) a melancholy sight; (Redefigur) figure of speech, metaphor; in ~ern ſprechen … figuratively, metaphorically; b) (Schilderung) ein ~ von et. entwerfen to give a description (or sketch) of a th.; c) (Vorstellung) ſich ein (klares) ~ von et. machen to have a (clear) notion of a th.; to realize a th.; er gab mir ein richtiges (falsches) ~ davon … correct (false) idea of it. — **4.** = Gleichnis.
Bild-arbeit (⌣...) f ⓺ = Bildhauerarbeit.
bildbar (⌣-) a. ⓺ = bildsam.
Bildchen (⌣⌣) n ⓶ (*dim.* von Bild) little image or picture.
bilden (⌣⌣) [ahd.; *Bild] **I** v/a. u. v/refl. ⓹ **1.** (ſich) ⓶ to form; einen Kreis ⓶ to form (or to arrange o.s. in) a circle; ⚔ ein Karree ⓶ to form a square; ſich ⓶ auch: to arise, to spring up; es hat ſich eine neue Gesellſchaft gebildet … has been founded, has sprung up; die größere Hälfte ⓶ (ſein) von to constitute the larger half of; ⚔ den Nach=trab ⓶ to bring up the rear. — **2.** (formen) to shape, mould, fashion; den Geiſt ⓶ to cultivate (or improve, train) the mind; nach dem Muſter der Antike

⓶ to construct after the classical model. — **3.** neu ⓶ (ſchaffen) to create (anew); (einrichten) to organize, set up, establish; ein Kabinett, ein Miniſterium ⓶ to form a cabinet, a ministry; von neuem ⓶ to reconstitute, reconstruct; ſich ⓶ (unterrichten) to instruct o.s.; to initiate o.s. in (the ways of the world); to acquire polish. — **4.** *gram.* Iupiter bildet den Dativ Iovi: the dative of *Iupiter* is *Iovi*, *Iupiter* has (or becomes) *Iovi* in the dative. — **II** ~ n ⓺ **5.** = Bildung 1 u. 2. — **III** ⓶d *p.pr.* u. *a.* ⓺ **6.** (zum Bilden dienend) formative, plastic; (ʒſ.=ſetzend) component, constituent; (belehrend) instructive; ⓶ die Künſte plastic (or graphic) arts. — **IV** ge=**bildet** *p.p.* u. *a.* ⓺ **7.** ein (körperlich) wohlgebildeter Menſch a well shaped or made or built person. — **8.** geiſtig ⓶ civilized, cultivated; educated, well instructed; (aufgeklärt) enlightened, well informed; ſein ⓶ accomplished, refined, cultured; ⓶er Menſch, als *s.*: ~**e**(r m) f ⓱ educated (or well-bred) person; die ~en the educated (classes), cultured people *pl.*
Bilder (⌣⌣) **I** *pl.* v. Bild. — **II** [ahd.] faſt † m ⓶ = Bildner.
Bilder-acha't (⌣⌣...) m ⓺ *min.* figurate agate; =**anbeter** m idolater, image-worshipper; ⌐ iconolater; =**anbetung** f idolatry, image-worship; ⌐ iconolatry; =**beſchreibung** f: ⓶ iconography; =**bibel** f illustrated (or pictorial) Bible; =**blende** f, *arch.* = niſche; =**bogen** m sheet of pictures; =**buch** n picture-book.
Bilderchen (⌣⌣⌣) *pl.* von Bildchen.
Bilder-dienst (⌣⌣...) m ⓶ = anbetung; =**fibel** f illustrated primer; =**galerie** f picture-gallery; =**handel** m trade in pictures or paintings; =**händler** m picture-dealer, dealer in oil-paintings, &c.; =**kabinett** n = ſammlung; =**liebhaber** m lover of pictures; =**marmor** m = Bild-m.; =**niſche** f, *arch.* niche for (paintings or) statuary, *vgl.* Apoſtelhäuschen; =**rahmen** m picture-frame; =**rätſel** n rebus; ⓶**reich** a. ⓺ rich in pictures; *rhet.* flowery, abounding in metaphor(s); =**reichtum** m der Rede: floweriness, ornate style; =**ſaal** m picture-gallery; =**ſammlung** f collection of pictures or paintings; =**ſchmuck** m artistic ornamentation, adornment by way of pictures; =**ſchrift** f hieroglyph(ic)s *pl.*; =**ſprache** f figurative (or metaphorical) speech; =**ſtürmer** m iconoclast; =**ſtürmerei** f iconoclasm; ⓶**ſtürmeriſch** a. iconoclastic; =**telegraphie** ⌐ f telephotography; =**verehrung** f = anbetung; =**werk** n (richly) illustrated work.
Bild-fläche (⌣...) f ⓺ *paint.* perspective plane; *fig.* auf der ~ erſcheinen to appear on the scene; von der ~ verſchwinden to disappear (from the scene), to vanish, to drop out of existence; =**former** m modeller; =**geſtell** n pedestal; =**gießer** m bronze- (or statue-) founder; =**gießerei** f bronze- (or statue-) foundry; art of casting statues; =**hauer(in** f) m sculptor, statuary; =**hauer-arbeit** sculpture, statuary, carved work; tracery(-work); =**hauerei**

f statuary, sculptor's art; =**hauer-kunſt** f (art of) sculpture.
Bildlein (⌣⌣) n ⓶ = Bildchen.
bildlich (⌣⌣) a. ⓺ **1.** pictorial; et. ⓶ und ſchriftlich erklären to illustrate a th. by word and picture. — **2.** *rhet.* figurative, metaphorical; (ſinnbildl.) allegoric(al), emblematic(al); ⓶e Darſtellung, auch: typical …; ⓶er Sinn (auch) ~**keit** f ⓺ figurative, &c. sense.
Bild-marmor (⌣...) m ⓺ *min.* figured marble; =**meß-kunſt** f (Meſſung durch photographiſche Aufnahme) ⌐ photogrammetry.
Bildner (⌣⌣) m ⓶, ~**in** f ⓺ **1.** \ (Schöpfer[in]) creator. — **2.** = Bildhauer(in).
Bildnerei (⌣⌣⌣) f ⓺ **1.** allg.: creation, formation. — **2.** = Bildhauerarbeit.
Bildnis (⌣⌣) n ⓱ **1.** ~ einer Perſon portrait, likeness. — **2.** (Abbildung) image; auf Münzen: effigy (vgl. Bildſeite). — **3.** ⚓ am Schiffsbug, bſd. ehm.: figure-head.
bildſam (⌣-) [nhd. 18. *sae.* (W.)] a. ⓺ easy to fashion or shape, shapable; plastic; *fig.* ⓶er Menſch docile person (ſ. bildungsfähig); ⓶e Sprache flexible …
Bildſamkeit (⌣--) f ⓺ plasticity; docility, flexibility (ſ. Bildungsfähigkeit).
Bild-ſäule (⌣...) f ⓺ statue; zu Pferde: equestrian statue; büſtenartige: bust; =**ſchnitzer** m (wood-)carver; sculptor; =**ſchnitzerei** f (wood-)carving, sculpture; ⓶**ſchön** a. ⓺ of rare (or dazzling) beauty; lovely (girl) (vgl. Bild 3); =**ſeite** f e-r Münze: obverse, F head (ant. tail); =**ſtein** m, *min.* = a) ⌐ lithoglyphite; b) (chineſiſcher Speckſtein) soapstone, ⌐ agalmatolite; =**ſtock** m (hölzerner Pfeiler mit Kruzifix) shrine with crucifix by the roadside.
Bildung (⌣⌣) f ⓺ **1.** (Geſtaltung) formation; (Gebilde) growth; *chm.* ~ von Kriſtallen crystallization; *gram.* ~ von neuen Wörtern coinage of … — **2.** (Aus=) ~ angeborener Gaben training, instruction, schooling. — **3.** (das Gelernte) information, (bookish) knowledge; höhere ~ accomplishments *pl.*; weitS. (intellectual) culture; allgemeine, klaſſiſche, feine ~ general, classical, polite education; (Gelehrſamkeit) learning, scholarship; von feiner ~ well-bred, well educated; von hoher ~ highly cultured. — **4.** (feine Sitte) refinement, polish, good breeding; ohne ~ uneducated, uncultured, unrefined; ill-bred; Mann von feiner ~ (well-bred) gentleman.
Bildungs-anſtalt (⌣⌣...) f ⓺ educational establishment; school, seminary; (Penſiona't) boarding-school; ⓶**fähig** a. ⓺ fit for (or capable of) education or intellectual training; cultivable; =**fähigkeit** f fitness for education; =**gang** m course of instruction or education; =**gewebe** ⚕ n (Teilungsgewebe) formative tissue, ⌐ meristem; =**grad** m degree of culture or refinement; =**hunger** m thirst for knowledge, desire for culture; =**kraft** f formative power; =**mittel** n means of instruction; =**ſchule** f, =**ſtätte** f training-school; =**ſilbe** f, *gram.* formative syllable; =**ſtufe** f = =grad; =**trieb** m desire for learning or improvement; Naturwiſſenſchaft: creative force;

Zeichen (ſ. S. XVII): F familiär; P Volkſſprache; ⌐ Gaunerſprache; \ ſelten; † alt (auch geſtorben); * neu (auch geboren); ⁀⁀ unrichtig;

[Bildweberei] — 197 — [Bindestrich]

Bild=weberei (⌣…) f ⓲ fancy-weaving: **=werk** n carved work, carving, sculpture; **=wirker(in** f) m tapestry-worker, damask-weaver; **=zauber** m (Zauber ausgeübt am Bilde e-r Person) charm practised on a p.'s likeness or image.
Bileam (⌣⌣⌣) [hebr.] npr/m. ⓧ a. Balaam; **=s Esel** Balaam's (speaking) ass.
Bilge ⚓ (⌣⌣) [ndd.] f ⓳ (Raum über den Kielplatten oder dem inneren Boden des Schiffes) bilge.
Bill ⚖ (⌣) f ⓰ parl. (Gesetzesvorschlag) bill.
Billard (bi'l-järt) [nhd. 1815, *fr.] n ⓪ d. (⓰) 1. (Spiel) billiards; ~ **spielen** to play (at) billiards. — 2. (Balltafel zum ~spielen) billiard-table.
Billard=ball (⌣…) m ⓰, **=kugel** f (billiard-)ball; in England geflechte(r) ~ spot(ball); **=kellner, =marför** m marker; **=loch** n pocket; **=queue** n = **=stock**; **=saal** m billiard-room; **=spiel** n (game of) billiards pl.; **=spieler** m billiard-player; **=stock** m cue; **=überzug** m billiard-cloth; **=zimmer** n billiard-room.
Bille ⊙ (⌣⌣) [ahd.] f ⓱ (Beil zum Schärfen d. Mühlsteine) millstone-dresser.
billen (⌣⌣) v/a. ⓰ to dress millstones.
Billetdoux (bi(l)-je-bü') [fr.] n ⓯ (Liebesbriefchen) billet-doux.
Billett (bi'l-jè't) [fr.] n ⓪ c. (⓰) 1. (Zettel) bill; (Briefchen) note. — 2. 🚂, &c. ticket (= Fahrkarte f. db).
Billetteur (bi'l-jè-tö'r) m ⓪ d. u. **Billetteuse** (…tö'…) f ⓯ [+ + fr.] (Schalter-beamter, =beamtin) (female) ticket-clerk.
billettieren (…⌣⌣⌣) v/a. ⓯ (mit Zetteln versehen) to label.
billig(⌣⌣)[ahd. aus † **Bill** (f. Unbill) u. **=lich**] a. ⓰ 1. (gerecht) just, fair; (dem Recht gemäß) equitable, right; (vernünftig) reasonable; **wenn wir ℒ sein wollen** if we want to be just; **das ist nicht mehr als ℒ** that's only fair or nothing more than proper; Sprichw. **was dem e-n recht ist, ist dem andern ℒ** what's good for the goose is good for the gander; we must treat all alike. — 2. (wohlfeil) cheap, inexpensive; **für ℒes Geld, zu ℒem Preise kaufen** to buy at a moderate (or low) price, cheaply; **ℒ aber schlecht** cheap and nasty; **sehr ℒ** dirt-cheap; **sehr ℒ** (adv.) **kaufen** to buy for a mere song; **sehr ℒer Kauf** great bargain; **ziemlich ℒ** not at all dear, reasonable (in price); **ℒe Lebensweise** economical mode of life; **man kann es nicht ℒer** (adv.) **tun** it can't be done more cheaply.
billig=denkend (⌣⌣…) a. ⓰ fair-minded, just, reasonable, sensible.
billig/en (⌣⌣⌣) [nhd.] I v/a. ⓰ to approve (of) a th., to consent to a th.; (genehmigen) to agree to a proposal, to sanction an accomplished fact; **j-s Verhalten ℒ** (loben) to applaud a p.'s conduct. — II ~ n ㉓ = ℬ/ung.
Billiger (⌣⌣⌣) m ⓰, ~**in** f ⓱ approver.
billiger=maßen (⌣⌣⌣⌣), **ℒweise** adv. fairly, justly, in (all) fairness; **ℒweise sollte er mehr geben** (if he wanted) to be fair he should give more.
Billigkeit (⌣⌣⌣) f ⓱ 1. justice, fairness, equity; **nach** ~ according to (the rules of) equity; **nach Recht und** ~ according to right and justice. — 2. moderateness (or reasonableness) of prices; cheapness (or low price[s pl.]) of goods.
Billigkeits=gefühl (⌣⌣…) n ⓰ = **=sinn; =gericht** n court of equity; **=grund** m: **aus =gründen** from reasons of fairness; **=sinn** m fair-mindedness.
Billigung (⌣⌣⌣) f ⓯ approval (or approbation) of, consent (or agreement) to.
Billigungs=zeichen (⌣…) n ⓰ sign of approbation.
Billion (bil-jō'n) [fr., *it. (Marko Polo 1300)] f ⓯ (= 1 000 000 × 1 000 000) billion.
Billon (bi-jō') [fr.] m, n ⓯ (minderwertiges Silber) inferior silver.
Bilse ❦ (⌣⌣) [ahd.] f ⓱, **schwarzes ~=kraut** (⌣…) n ⓰ henbane, hog's-bean (Hyoscyamus niger).
bimbam (⌣⌣ ob. ⌣⌣) int. ding-dong.
Bimetallismus (⌣⌣⌣⌣⌣) [it.] m ㉗ Münzwesen: (Doppelwährung) bimetallism, gold-and-silver currency.
Bimetallist (-⌣⌣⌣) m ⓰ (Anhänger der Doppelwährung) bimetallist. [(ist)ic.)
bimetallistisch (-⌣⌣⌣⌣) a. ⓰ bimetall-
Bimmel F (⌣⌣) f ⓱ (Glöckchen) (ding-dong) bell, F tinkler.
bimmeln F (⌣⌣) ⓶ a. I v/n. (h.) (klingen) to tinkle; (läuten) **es bimmelt** the bells are ringing. — II v/a. to set ringing. — III ~ n ㉓ tinkling; ringing of bells, F tintinnabulation. [~stein.)
Bims ⚒ (⌣) [ahd.; *it. pūmex] m ⓪ a. =
bimsen ⊙ (⌣⌣) v/a. ⓰ to (rub with) pumice-stone, to pumicate.
Bims=stein (⌣⌣) [f. **Bims**] m ⓪ d. (erhärteter Lavaschaum) pumice-stone; **ℒ=artig** (⌣…) a. ⓰ pumiceous, pumiciform; ~ **pulver** n ⓰ pounce; ~ **seife** f pumice-soap. [pres. ind. v. sein; ich ℒ I am.)
bin (⌣) (ahd.: be(en)) ⓰ a. 1. Person sg.)
binär ⌣, **binar(isch)** a/r (-⌣(⌣)) [it.] a. ⓰ (auf zwei beruhend) binary. [(f. **Binde**).)
Bindchen (⌣⌣) n ㉓ dim. small band, &c.)
Binde (⌣⌣) [ahd.; *binden] f ⓰ 1. (schmaler Streifen) mst: (narrow) band; surg. (Verband) bandage, dressing, roller; **den Arm in e-r ~ tragen** to carry one's arm in a sling; ⚔ Sanitätskorps: **rote ~** red badge or band; anat. (Sehnen)~ ⚕ fascia; ⚔ Schiedsrichter: **weiße ~** ber white badge or band; bursch.: **e-n auf Säbel ohne ~n und Bandagen fordern** to call a p. out to a sword-duel without (protective) wraps and bandages. — 2. **um den Leib:** sash. — 3. **Augen=, Stirn=)~** bsd. im Altertum: fillet; **e-m e-e ~ vor die Augen tun** to blindfold a p.; fig. **e-m die ~ von den Augen nehmen** to open a p.'s eyes, to undeceive a person; fig. **die ~ fällt mir von den Augen** my eyes have been opened, I begin to see through it. — 4. (Hals=)~ tie, necktie; steife: cravat, von Frauen: necker-chief, necklace; fig. **einen (Schluck Bier, Schnaps ꝛc.) hinter die ~ gießen** F to put away (or pour down) the liquor or stuff, to wet one's whistle.
Binde=balken ⊙ (⌣⌣…) m ⓰ tie- (or bind-)beam, girder; (Stützbalken) architrave; **=band, =bändchen** n an Hauben ꝛc. (bonnet-)string; **=bogen** ♪ m slur (~ oder ⌢); **=draht** ⚒ m zum Binden: (soft) wire for binding; **=gewebe** n anat. connective tissue; **=gewebs=**
entzündung f: 🩺 phlegmon; **=glied** n connecting link; **=haut**/des Auges anat.: ⚕ conjunctiva; **=haut=entzündung** f des Auges path.: ⚕ conjunctivitis.
Bind=eisen ⊙ (⌣⌣…) n ⓰ der Glasmacher: blowing-iron (for bottle-work, &c.).
Binde=mittel (⌣⌣…) n ⓰ binding (or sticking) substance, ⚕ agglutinant; (Zement) cement.
bind en (⌣⌣) [ahd.: bind] ⓪ I v/a., v/n. (h.), v/refl. 1. to bind; (festknüpfen) to tie (fast) or fasten (an to); (befestigen) to attach to a th.; fenc. **die Klingen vor Beginn des Schlagens ℒ** to bind the swords; **mit Stricken ℒ** to cord; **ihm sind die Hände gebunden** (bsd. fig.) his hands are tied; **sich** (dat.) **etwas um den Hals ℒ** to tie (or put) s.th. round one's neck; Kochkunst: **sich ℒ** (verdicken) to thicken. — 2. **Ballen:** to pack; **Besen:** to make; **Heu:** to bundle; **vom Korn: in Garben ℒ** (auch **sich in Garben ℒ lassen**) to bind (or make up) in sheaves; **ein Pferd ꝛc. an einen Pfahl ℒ** to tether —; **Sträuße ℒ** to make (up) nosegays; gram. **ℒ** (zs.=hängend aussprechen) to bind (or draw) together; ♪ **Noten ℒ** (schleifen) to slur. — 3. fig. **du mußt ihm nicht alles auf die Nase ℒ** F you must not let out everything to him; **e-m et. aufs Gewissen, auf die Seele ℒ** to urge (or enjoin) a th. most earnestly (or earnestly) upon a p.('s conscience); **sich** (dat.) **selbst eine Rute ℒ** to make a rod for one's own back. — 4. ⊙ Böttcherei: **ein Faß ℒ** to hoop…; Buchbinderei: **in Franzband ℒ** to bind in calf; **der Mörtel bindet** (zieht an)… takes. — 5. ⚓ (mit einer Seifing befestigen) to lash, to seize. — 6. fig. abs. **sich ℒ** to bind (or engage) o.s.; **e-n ant. ℒ** (fesseln) to bind a p. to perform a promise; to oblige (or compel) a p. to adhere to a th.; **ℒd** obligatory; **ein ℒdes Versprechen** a binding promise. — II v/refl. 7. f. 1 und 6. — III ~ n ㉓ = ℬ/ung. — IV **ℒd** p.pr. ⓰ 9. f. 6. — V **gebunden** p.p. u. a. ⓰ (D 9) 10. bound, &c. (f. I); **an die Scholle ℒ** tied to the spot; **an die Stunde ℒ** tied for time. — 11. **durch eine Erklärung ℒ** committed by a declaration; chm. **an ein anderes Element ℒ** combined (or in combination) with another element; phys. **ℒe Wärme** latent heat; gram. **in ℒer Rede** in metrical language, in verse; ⊙ Buchbinderei: **in Leinwand, Franzband ℒ** in cloth covering, in calf binding.
Binder (⌣⌣) m ⓰ 1. (a. **~in** f ⓱) person who binds, ties, &c. (f. binden); binder, (Faß=)~ cooper. — 2. ⊙ arch. (Bindebalken) principal (or main) girder, bind-beam. [**Binder 2.**)
Binder=balken ⊙ (⌣⌣…) m ⓰ carp. =
Binderei (⌣⌣⌣) f ⓰ (Blumenbindekunst) (art of) arranging flowers or making (up) wreaths.
Binder=lohn (⌣⌣…) m ⓰ a) für Faßbinder: cooperage; b) für Buchbinder: binding (expense), charge for binding.
Binde=satz (⌣⌣…) m ⓰ gram. conjunctional clause; **=sohle** f sandal; **=stein** m, arch. bond-stone, bonder, bisw.: perpend(er); **=strich** hyphen,

♪ Musik; ⚕ Wissenschaft; ❦ Pflanze; 🌐 Geographie; ⊙ Technik; ⚒ Bergbau; ⚔ Militär; ⚓ Marine; ⚖ Handel; ✉ Post; 🚂 Eisenbahn.

dash (-); vgl. =bogen; **weide** f osier (twig); =**wort** n, gram. conjunction; =**wörterhäufung** f, gram. ⚹ polysyndeton; =**ziegel** ⊕ m, arch. buttress-brick. — Vgl. a. Bund=.

Bind=faden (⸗...) m ⚷ twine, (pack-)thread; string; F der Regen fiel wie in ~ it was raining cats and dogs; =**fadenrolle** f reel of twine, &c.; =**gerte** f = Bindeweide. [soil or land.]

bindig (⸗⸗) a. ⚷ agr. der Boden binding

Bindsel ↓ (⸗⸗) n ⚷ lashing, seizing.

Bindung (⸗⸗) f ⚷ binding, tying, &c.; gram. binding (fr. liaison) of words, glide, ⚹ synepy; ⸗ slurring (or ligature) of notes; ⊕ hooping of casks; binding (or covering) of books.

Bindungs=... (⸗⸗) = Binde=...

Binge ⚒ (⸗⸗) f ⚷ (trichterförmige Grube) funnel- (or kettle-) shaped pit.

Bingel=kraut ♀ (⸗⸗⸗) [nhd.] n ⚷ mercury (Mercuria'lis).

binnen (⸗⸗) [ndb.: ben = be(i)-innen] prp. (mit gen. u. dat.) — innerhalb; zeitlich: ⚶ e=s Jahres within a twelvemonth (from to-day); F u. ⚶ this day twelvemonth; ⚶ heute (auch hier) und Ostern between this (day) and Easter; ⚶ kurzem shortly, ere (or before) long.

Binnen=achtersteven ↓ (⸗⸗...) m ⚷ inner post; ⚶**bords** ↓ adv. (im Schiffsraume) inboard; =**deich** m inner dam; =**dock** n inner dock; =**gewässer** n inland water; =**hafen** ↓ m inner (basin of a) harbour or port; =**handel** m inland (or home) trade; =**klüver** ↓ m inner jib; =**land** n inland region, country without seaboard; in England: midland counties pl.; =**länder** ↓ m = Bilander; =**länder** m person living inland or in the interior of a country; ⚶**ländisch** a. ⚷ (situated) inland; (in the) interior; weitS. continental; =**meer** n land-locked (or inland) sea; =**schiffahrt** f inland (or fresh-water) navigation; =**see** m inland lake; =**staat** m inland state; =**stadt** f inland (in England auch: midland)town; =**verkehr** m inland (or home) traffic; =**wasser** n (in Niederungen sich sammelndes Wasser) stagnant water in low-lying inland districts; =**zoll** m inland duty.

Binokel (⸗⸗) [fr. binocle m] n ⚷ (Augenglas, Kneifer) (double) eyeglass.

binokular ⚹ (⸗⸗⸗⸗) [lt.] a. ⚷ (für zwei Augen bestimmt) binocular.

Bi-nom ⚹ (⸗⸗) [lt.-grch.] n ⚷c. math. (zweigliedriger Ausdruck) binomial.

binomisch (⸗⸗⸗) a. ⚷ binomial; ⚶er (Lehr=)Satz binomial theorem.

Binse ♀ (⸗⸗) [ahd.] f ⚷ (bul)rush (Iuncus) a. = Sime (Scirpus); graue ~ hard rush (I. glaucus); sparrige =moos=, heath-rush (I. squarro'sus); von ~n bewachsen rush-grown, rushy, fig. in die =n gehen (zunichte werden) to fall to the ground, to come to nothing, F to go to pot.

binsen=ähnlich (⸗⸗...) a. ⚶=**artig** a. rush-like; =**büschel** m, n ⚷ rush-bed, bed of rushes; =**korb** m rush-basket, junket; =**lager** n bed (or couch) (made up) of rushes; =**licht** n rush-light or -candle; =**matte** f rush-mat; =**quecke** ♀ f rushy wheat-grass (Tri'ticum iu'-

ceum); =**seide** ♀ f = Wollgras; =**stuhl** m rush-bottomed chair; =**wahrheit** f (Gemeinplatz) commonplace (saying), well-worn truism.

Binsicht[1] (⸗⸗) n ⚶d. = Binsenbüschel.

binsicht[2], **binsig** (⸗⸗) a. ⚷ 1. covered with (or full of) rushes, rushy, rush-grown; (schilfig) sedgy. — 2. rushlike.

Bio-graph ⚹ (⸗⸗⸗f) [grch.] m ⚷ biographer; ~**ie** (⸗⸗⸗⸗) f ⚷ (Lebensbeschreibung) biography; ~**ie** von Pitt Life of Pitt; 2**isch** (⸗⸗⸗⸗) a. ⚷ biographical.

Bio-log ⚹, ~**e** ⚹ (⸗⸗⸗) [grch.] m ⚷,⚷ biologist; ~**ie** (⸗⸗⸗f) f ⚷ (Lebenskunde) biology; ~**isch** (⸗⸗⸗⸗) a. ⚷ biological.

Bio-skop (⸗⸗⸗) [grch.] n ⚷c. bioscope.

Bi-peden ⚹ (⸗⸗⸗) [lt.] pl. (Zweifüßer) bipeds n.

Bi-quadrat ⚹ (⸗⸗⸗) [lt.] n ⚷c. math. (4. Potenz) biquadratic; fourth power; 2**isch** (⸗⸗⸗⸗) a. ⚷ biquadratic.

Bireme ↓ (⸗⸗⸗) [lt.] f ⚷ Alt. (Zweiruderer) bireme. [von bergen.]

birg. 2ft, 2t (⸗) imper., 2. u. 3. Pers. pres.

Birke ♀ (⸗⸗) [ahd.: birch] f ⚷ (weiße) ~ birch(-tree) (Be'tula).

birken (⸗⸗) a. ⚷ (D9) birch(en).

birken=artig ♀ (⸗⸗⸗) a. ⚷ birchlike; =**baum** ♀ m ⚷ = Birke; =**besen** m birch-broom; =**hänschen** n birch-rod; co. Dr. Birch; =**holz** n birch-wood; =**öl** n birch-oil; =**reis** n = =rute; =**rinde** f birch-bark; =**rute** f birch(-rod); =**saft** m birch-juice; =**teer** m birch-tar; =**wald** m birch-grove; =**wäldchen** m = Birficht; =**wasser**, =**wein** m birch-water, -wine.

Birk=hahn (⸗...) m ⚷ orn. heath-cock; =**henne** f.orn.heath-hen; =**huhn** n=wild.

Birficht (⸗⸗) n ⚷d. (Birkenwäldchen) wood of birch-trees, birch-grove.

Birkling ♀ (⸗⸗) n ⚷d. (Birkenschwamm) rough boletus (Bole'tus scaber).

Birk=wild (⸗...) n ⚷ blackgame (Te'trao tetrix); =**wildjagd** ♀ f, hunt. grouse-shooting on the Scotch moors.

Birma ♀ (⸗⸗) npr/n. ⚷a. (Reich in Hinterindien) Burma. ~**ne** (⸗⸗⸗) m ⚷, ~**nin** f ⚷, 2**isch** a. ⚷ Burmese, Burman.

Birn=baum ♀ (⸗...) m ⚷ pear-tree (Pi'rus [commu'nis]).

Birnchen (⸗⸗) n ⚷ dim. v. Birne.

Birne ♀ (⸗⸗) [ahd.; roman. pira; *lt. pirum n; *grch. api(s)on] f ⚷ 1. pear (a. fig. = birnförmiger Gegenstand). — 2. = Birnbaum. — 3. ⊕ f. Bessemerbirne; ~ des elektrischen Glühlichts (pear-shaped) electric glow-lamp.

birn(en)=förmig (⸗⸗...) a. ⚷ = pear-shaped; ⚹ pyriform.

Birn=moos ♀ (⸗...) n ⚷ thread-moss (Bry'um arge'nteum); =**most** m = =wein; =**pflaume** f pear-plum; =**quitte** ♀ f pear-quince (Cydo'nia oblo'nga); =**wein** m perry.

▶ **Birsch** (⸗) 2c. f. Pirsch 2c. [v. bersten.]

birst (⸗) 2. u. 3. Person pres. ind. u. imper.

Birutsche (⸗⸗⸗) [it.] f ⚷ = Barutsche.

bis (⸗) [Hom. biß] [ahd. aus bi (bei) u. az=: engl. at] **I** prp. (ant. von) **1.** zeitlich (ant. seit); till, until; ⚶ jetzt up to the present, up to now, hitherto; ⚶ heute (⚶ a. ⚶ dato) up to this day; F up to date; wartet ⚶ morgen ... until to-morrow; ⚶ dahin up to that time, till then; ⚶ wann wird es dauern? how long (or

up to what time) ...?; ⚶ **auf** weiteres until further orders, for the present; ⚶ **gegen** Mittag till (F up to) about noon; ⚶ **in** sein hohes Alter till he was quite old; ⚶ um zehn Uhr till ten o'clock; ⚶ **vor** wenigen Jahren until some few years back; ⚶ **zu** Ende (right) to the end; to the last; ⚶ zum Tode until (bibl. even unto) death; ⚶ zu s-m Tode until (the time of) his death; ⚶ zu Ende des Prozesses pending the trial. — **2.** räumlich: as far as; von (f. dß 7) L. **2** B. from L. to B.; ⚶ dahin as far as that place, up to there; ⚶ hierher up to here, thus far; ⚶ wohin how far?; ⚶ wie weit? up to what point?; ⚶ **ans** Knie up to the knee; ⚶ **auf** den Gipfel right to the top, to the very top; er kam ⚶ auf zehn Meter heran he came to within ten yards; ⚶ **in** das Haus right into the house; ⚶ in den Himmel up to the sky; f. a. Puppe 3; von hier ⚶ **nach** Japan from here to Japan; ⚶ **über** den Kopf ins Wasser gehen ... out of (or beyond) one's depth; fig. ⚶ über die Ohren in Schulden stecken, verliebt sein to be over head and ears in debt, in love. — **3.** Zahl=angabe: sieben ⚶ acht Tage from seven to eight days; F bei unteilbaren Dingen: or, z.B.: fünf ⚶ sechs Elefanten five or six elephants; ⚶ zu hundert as many as a hundred; ⚶ auf das letzte Stück to the very last piece; f. a. drei 2. — **4.** Grad: ⚶ aufs höchste to the utmost, in the highest degree; f. a. Blut 3; ⚶ ins kleinste (down) to the minutest details; ⚶ zu Tränen gerührt moved (even un)to tears; f. a. äußerst III; ⚶ zur Wut gereizt goaded into fury; ⚜ Kredit geben ⚶ zu 200 Mark to give credit up to (or for not more than) £ 10. — **5.** Ausnahme: except; alle ⚶ auf einen all but one; ⚶ auf die Knochen: a) all except the bones; b) einschließend: to the very bones. — **II** cj. **6.** ⚶ (daß) till, until; warte, ⚶ // wait till //; geh nicht (eher) fort, ⚶ (P .+ ⚶ nicht) // do not leave before (or until) //; ⚶ er Kaiser wurde until (or up to the time that) he became emperor.

Bisam (⸗⸗) [ahd.; *hebr. besem Wohlgeruch] m ⚷c. musk (= Moschus); nach ~ duftend scented with musk, musky.

bisam=artig (⸗⸗...) a. ⚷ musk-like, musky; =**duft** m = =geruch; =**eibisch** ♀ m = Abelmosch; =**ente** f, orn. musk-duck (Cairi'na moscha'ta); =**geruch** m musk-scent; muskiness. [artig.]

bisamicht, bisamig (⸗⸗⸗) a. ⚷ f. bisam=

Bisam=körner ♀ (⸗⸗...) n/pl. ⚷ = Abelmoschus=f.; =**kraut** ♀ f = musk-root, moschatel (Ado'xa moschatelli'na); =**kugel** f musk-ball; =**ratte** f. zo. musk-rat (Fiber zibe'thicus); =**rose** ♀ f musk-rose (Rosa moscha'ta); =**rüßler** m, =**spitzmaus** f, zo. = Rüsselmaus. Vgl. a. Moschus ...

bisch F (⸗) = bst!, pst!

Bischof (⸗⸗⸗) [ahd.; *grch. epi'skopos Aufseher] m ⚷d. eccl. Catholic, Anglican, ⚶ ⚷d. bishop [Anrede in England: My Lord (Bishop); als 3. Person: The Right Reverend, the Lord Bishop]; ~ **in** par'tibus bishop in foreign parts.

[**bischöflich**] — 199 — [**bittersüß**]

bischöflich (ˊ–◡) a. ⊕ (u. adv.) episcopal; ℓ Gesinnte m/pl., a. ℓe Partei Episcopalians pl. (in England a.: Church Party, Anglicans pl.); ℓer Ornat s. Bischofsornat; ℓer Sprengel bishopric, diocese; Ew. ~e Gnaden in England: Your Lordship.

Bischof(s)=amt (ˊ◡…) n ⊕ episcopal office or dignity, episcopate; **=hut** m: a) (bishop's) mitre (auch zo. Art Schnecke); b) ⚘ = Sockenblume; **=mütze** f = =hut; **=ornat** m episcopal robes pl. (in England auch: lawn-sleeves and bishop's apron); **=sitz** m episcopal see; **=stab** m crosier; **=stuhl** m = =sitz; **=würde** f = =amt.

Bise schwz. (ˊ–) [ahd.] f ⊕ (Nordostwind) bise. [geschlechtig) bisexual.)

bisexuell ⚕ (◡◡◡ˊ) [lt.] a. ⊕ (zwei-)

bisher (◡ˊ) adv. hitherto, up to the present (day), till (or up to) now, as yet, so far; wie ℓ as in the past.

bisherig (◡ˊ◡) a. ⊕ hitherto prevailing, existing; die ℓen Nachrichten the news received up to now or F up to date; sein ℓes Glück the (good) luck (which) he has had all along or so far; his (good) luck in the past; das ℓe Ministerium the outgoing (or retiring) ministry; das ~e what has happened up to now, the state of things existing hitherto; im ℓen (im obigen) in the above, thus far; vgl. seitherig.

Biskaya ♁ (◡ˊ◡) npr/n. ⊕α. (baskische Provinz Spaniens) Biscay.

biskayisch ♁ (◡ˊ◡) a. ⊕ ~er Meerbusen Bay of Biscay.

Biskuit (◡twiˊt) [fr.] n ⊕c. (⊕) (Zwieback, Zuckerbrot; unglasiertes Porzellan) biscuit; **~ofen** (ˊ…) m ⊕ zum Tonbrennen: biscuit-oven; **=porzellan** n b.(-ware).

bislang ⚓ (◡ˊ) [mhd.] adv. = bisher.

Bismarck ♂ [Bi(schof)s=Mart] npr m. ⊕α. (Fürst) ~ (Prince) Bismar(c)k; **~archipel** ♁ (ˊ…) m ⊕ (melanesische Inselgruppe) Bismarck Archipelago; ℓisch (◡◡ˊ) a. ⊕ Bismarckian.

Bison (ˊ◡) [grch.; lt.; *dtsch. Wisent] m ⊕ zo. bison (Bos americaˊnus).

biß¹ (ˊ) Hom. bis) impf. von beißen.

Biß² (ˊ) [ahd.: bit] m ⊕a. biting, bite; ~(=stelle, =wunde) bite (of a dog); sting (of a snake), allg.: wound caused by a bite or a sting.

Bißchen¹ (ˊ◡) n ⊕ dim. v. Bissen u. Biß.

bißchen² (ˊ◡) a. inv., adv., (a. n ⊕ a little; F a (little) bit; ein (F ganz) flein ℓ a (very) little bit, F (just) a wee-bit; F auch nicht ein ℓ F not the least bit; not an atom, not a particle; fein ℓ Brot not a morsel (or crumb) of bread (to eat); ein ℓ Geld a trifling sum, a few pence, some little money. F one or two coppers; ein ℓ Latein a smattering of Latin; unser ℓ Mobiliar F our few sticks (of furniture); das ℓ Vergnügen the little pleasure; mein ℓ Vermögen my few belongings pl., what little I have; wart' ein ℓ wait a moment (P abbr. mo') or a second (P abbr. sec); ein ℓ höher a little (F a little bit) higher; ein ℓ zu dunkel a shade too dark; ein ℓ zu niedrig a trifle (or somewhat) too low; rather low; F ein ℓ viel a trifle too much;

F das ist ein ℓ zu stark! that's a bit too strong!, that's rather strong!

bisse (ˊ◡) impf. subj. von beißen.

bissel südd. (ˊ◡) = bißchen.

Bissen (ˊ◡) [ahd.] m ⊕ 1. (Mundvoll) mouthful; schmackhafter: tit-bit, (dainty or toothsome or savoury) morsel; getunkter: sop. — 2. (Speise) food; er hat heute noch keinen ~ gegessen he has not eaten (or touched) a morsel today; e-m jemdm ~ geben to dole (or mete) out small portions to a p.; e-m f-n ~ gönnen to grudge a p. every crust of bread; ein saurer ~ hard earnings pl., money well earned.

bissen=weise (ˊ◡…) adv. (doled out) in mouthfuls, by bits.

bissig (ˊ◡) a. ⊕ fond of (or given to) biting; von Hunden u. fig. von Menschen: snappish; ℓe Bemerkung cutting remark; er hat einen ℓen Stil he has a caustic (F slashing) style.

Bissigkeit (ˊ◡–) f ⊕ snappishness.

Biß=stelle (ˊ…) f, **=wunde** f ⊕ s. Biß².

bist (ˊ) 2. Person sg. pres. ind. v. sein; du ℓ thou art. [bistre.)

Bister (ˊ◡) [fr.] m, n ⊕ paint. (Rußbraun))

Bistouri (◡tu'◡) [fr.; *lt. bastum Stock] m, n ⊕ surg. (Klappmesser) bistouri.

Bistum (ˊ–) [ahd. Bi(schof)stum] n ⊕d. bishopric, diocese.

bisweilen (◡ˊ◡) adv. sometimes, at times, occasionally; (dann und wann) from time to time, now and then, now and again, between whiles.

Bithyni-en (◡ˊ(◡)◡) npr/n. ⊕α. Alt.: (Landschaft in Kleinasien) Bithynia; **Bithyner** (in f ⊕) m ⊕, **bithynisch** (◡ˊ◡) a. ⊕ Bithynian.

Bitt=brief (ˊ◡) m ⊕ = =schreiben.

Bitte (ˊ◡) [ahd.] f ⊕ prayer, petition; ich habe (noch) e-e Bitte an Sie zu richten I want to ask you for s.th. (or for one more favour); (Anliegen) request, demand; auf seine ~ hin at his request; e-m f-e ~ gewähren to grant a p.'s wish or petition; (Einladung) invitation; die sieben ~n des Vaterunsers the seven petitions of the Lord's Prayer.

bitten (ˊ◡) [ahd.] I v/a. ⊕ 1. e-n bitten, et. zu tun to beg of (or to ask, stärker: to beseech, to implore) a p. to do a th.; ich bat ihn, er möge Geduld haben I begged of (stärker: I entreated) him to be patient; für e-n ℓ to intercede on behalf of a p., to plead for a p.; e-n um et. ℓ to ask a th. of a p., to ask (nicht to pray!) a p. for a th.; ich bat ihn um Erlaubnis, mich zu entfernen I asked him for leave to withdraw; um Frieden ℓ to sue for peace; um Gnade ℓ to beg (or plead) for mercy; er bat sie um Hilfe he solicited (stärker: implored) their help; höflich: darf ich um Ihre Photographie ℓ? may I ask you to favour me with your photo(graph)?; e-n demütig um Verzeihung ℓ to crave (or implore) a p.'s pardon; um Aufträge ℓ to solicit orders; ℓd begging, petitioning, soliciting. — 2. Redewendungen: noch etwas Suppe, wenn ich ℓ darf may I trouble you (or I will thank you) for a little more soup;

bitte, reichen Sie mir den Hut please pass me the hat; bitte, sagen Sie uns doch// pray tell me /; bitte um Verzeihung! I beg your pardon! Antwort: granted!, pray don't mention!; bitte doch sehr! (ich gebe es nicht zu) allow me to differ!; ich bitte Sie! (bin erstaunt) you don't say so!, is that so?; Spiel: bitte! play! — 3. (einladen) e-n zu Tische, zu sich ℓ to ask (förmlicher: to invite) a p. to dinner, to one's house. — II ~ n ⊕ 4. = Bitte; zu J: nach vielem od. auf vieles ~ after a good deal of entreaty; ihr flehentliches ~ her urgent entreaties or appeals pl.; — III **~de(r)** m, **~de** f ⊕ 5. petitioner (soft: the fair petitioner), (Einladende(r)) person who invites, host, F founder of the feast.

Bitter¹ (ˊ◡) m ⊕, **~in** f ⊕ = bitten III.

bitter² (ˊ◡) [ahd.: bitter; * beißen] I a. ⊕ (D⊕) 1. bitter; ℓ schmecken to have a bitter taste. — 2. ℓe (scharfe) Kälte biting cold. — 3. fig. ℓer Ernst fixed determination; es ist ℓer Ernst it is only too true; es ist sein ℓer Ernst he is in bitter (or thoroughly in) earnest; ℓer Feind deadly foe; ℓer Groll rancour; ℓer Kummer sore grief; ℓe Not: a) severe (or sore) distress; b) (Zwang) sheer necessity; ℓe Wahrheit sad truth; ℓe Worte sharp words pl. or rebuke; das ist bitter it's hard to bear or galling; das hat ihn ℓ gekränkt, geschmerzt it cut him to the quick. — 4. F co das ist nicht ℓ (nicht übel)! that's not bad! — II ~ n ⊕ (o. pl.) 5. bitter (essence). — III **Bitt(e)re(r)** m ⊕, 6. in Zssgn: **=bitter** m ⊕ e-n Bittern (Schnaps) trinken F to take a drop of (bitter liqueur). — IV **Bitt(e)re(s)** n ⊕ 7. bitter substance; bitter taste; bitterness.

Bitter²=bier (ˊ◡…) n ⊕ bitter ale or beer; F bitter; ℓböse a. ⊕: a) (aufgebracht) very wroth or cross; extremely angry; b) (boshaft) very malicious or wicked; **=erde** f, chm.: ⚕ magnesia; ℓfeind a. very hostile; **~gurke** ⚘ f = Koloquinte; **~holz** ⚘ n quassia(-wood); **=holzbaum** ⚘ m quassia (Quaˊssia amaˊra).

Bitterich ⚘ (ˊ◡◡) m ⊕d. yellow succory (Piˊcris hieracioiˊdes).

Bitter²=kalk (ˊ◡…) m ⊕, min. dolomite, magnesian limestone; **=kalt** a. ⊕ bitterly cold, F bitter; F ℓer Tag bleak day; ℓer Wind bitterly cold wind.

Bitterkeit (ˊ◡–) f ⊕ 1. bitterness (a. fig.). — 2. fig. severity, sharpness; (Hohn) sarcasm; ~en sagen to say bitter things.

Bitter²=klee (ˊ◡…) = Fieberklee; **=kleesalz** n, chm. +. = Sauerkleesalz; **=kraut** ⚘ n = Bitterich; **=kresse** ⚘ f = Schaumkraut (bitteres).

bitterlich (ˊ◡◡) a. ⊕ bitterish, somewhat bitter; adv. ℓ weinen to cry bitterly.

Bitterling ⚘ (ˊ◡◡) m ⊕d. yellow-wort (Chlora perfoliaˊta). [bitter-almond oil.)

Bitter²=mandel-öl (ˊ◡◡ˊ◡…) n ⊕ chm.)

Bitternis (ˊ◡◡) f ⊕ bitterness.

Bitter²=salz (ˊ◡…) n, chm. Epsom salts pl., sulphate of magnesia (Mg SO₄); **=säure** f, chm. picric acid; **=spat** m, min. magnesite; **=stoff** m, chm. vegetable bitter; ℓsüß a. ⊕ bitter-sweet; von der Miene: half smiling, half crying;

⚕ scientific; ⚘ botanical; ♁ geography; ⊕ machinery; ✕ mining; ⚔ military; ⚓ marine; ● commercial; ✉ postal; 🚂 railway.

[**Bitterſüß**] — 200 — [**Bläſer**]

=**ſüße** bitter-sweet, woody nightshade (*Solanum Dulcama'ra*); =**waſſer** n mineral water (containing magnesia salts, &c.); =**wurzel** ℣ f = Enzian (gelber).
Bitt-gang (ᵛ...) m ❷ eccl. procession (offering up prayers for s. th.); =**geſuch** n petition; an Behörden: memorial.
Bittre (ᴗᴗ) m, n f. bitter III u. IV.
Bitt-ſchreiben (ᵛ...) n ❷, =**ſchrift** f petition an e-e Behörde: memorial; e-e ſchrift bei e-m einreichen to petition (or memorialize) a p.; =**ſteller**(in f) m petitioner; jur. auch: suitor; ⁎**weiſe** adv. by way (or in form) of a prayer or request; =**wort** n (word of) entreaty.
Bitumen ᴁ (⁻⁻) [lt.] n ❷❸ (o. pl.) min. (Erdpech) bitumen; **Bituminiſierung** (ᴗ‿ᴗᴗ⁻) f ⓮ chm. (Behandlung mit ober Verwandlung in Erdpech) bituminization; **bituminös** (ᴗ‿ᴗ⁻) a. ⓮ bituminous; bituminöſer Schiefer bituminous slate.
Biwak meiſt ✕ (⁻ᴗ) [fr.; *dtſch Beiwacht] ⓮e. (⓮) (Feldnachtlager) bivouac; ~**dienſt** (⁻....) m ❻ b. duty; =**feuer** n b. fire.
biwakieren (⁻ᴗ⁻ᴗ) v/n. (h.) ⓮ to bivouac; to camp out.
bizarr (ᴗ⁻) [fr.] a. ⓮ (ſeltſam) strange, odd, eccentric; ~**erie** (ᴗᴗᴗ⁻) f ⓮ (Seltſamkeit) strangeness, oddity, eccentricity.
Bl. *abbr.* = Blatt.
Blach-feld† *bibl. od. poet.* (⁻ᵃ...) [mhd.] n ❷ (raised) open country or field, plain. [cuttle- (or ink-)fish (*Se'pia*):]
Black-fiſch (ᵃᵃ) [ndd. Tintenfiſch] m ❷ ᴁ zo.
blaff (ᵛ) [lautm.] *int.* (Hundegebell) bow-wow.
blaffen, bläffen (ᴗᴗ) [lautm.] v/n. (h.) ⓮ (bellen) to bark.
Blaffer, Bläffer (ᴗᴗ) m ❷ barking dog.
Blage *provc. N.W.* (⁻ᴗ) [ndd. Plack] f ⓮ (läſtiges Kind) burdensome child, brat.
Blahe (⁻ᴗ) [mhd.] f ⓮ (Wagendecke) tarpaulin, awning, tilt.
bläh-en (⁻ᴗ) [ahd.] v. blow: lt. *flare* blaſen] ⓮ I v/a. und ſich ᴗ v/refl. to blow (o.s.) out; *fig.* ſich ᴗ to puff o.s. up, to assume a pompous air; ſich mit et. ᴗ to boast of s. th. — II v/n. (h.) *path.* to cause flatulency or F windy spasms; ⁎**des Gericht** dish which makes a p. flatulent or F fills him with wind. — III ~ n ❷❸ *fig.* puffing, pomposity; *path.* = B/ung.
Bläh-ſucht (⁻...) f ❷ *path.* flatulency; ⁎**ſüchtig** a. ⓮ flatulent.
Blähung (⁻ᴗ) f ⓮ *path.* wind(iness), flatulence; windy spasm; von Säuglingen· an ~en leiden F to suffer from (or to be troubled with) the wind; ~s-**mittel** (⁻...) n ❷ ᴁ carminative.
Blak (⁻) [ndd.] m ❷ⓒ.(Rauch vom Lampendocht) sooty smoke from a charred wick.
blaken (⁻ᴗ) v/n. (h.) ⓮ to burn with a smoky flame, to smoulder, smoke.
Blaker (⁻ᴗ) m ❷ ⁎**wall-lamp with reflector.**
blak[e]rig (⁻(ᴗ)ᴗ) a. ⓮ beſ. von Speiſen: smoky, smoked, tasting of smoke.
Blamage (ᴗ⁻ᴁ) f ⓮ [++ fr.] (ärgerliche Bloßſtellung) public exposure, disgrace; ſich e-e ~ zuziehen to expose o.s.
blamieren F (ᴗ⁻ᴗ) [(++) fr.] v/a. u. v/refl. ⓮ (bloßſtellen) to expose publicly, to show up before the world; ſich ᴗ to make o.s. ridiculous, to expose o.s. to ridicule; to commit o.s.; er hat ſich tüchtig blamiert he made a great fool

of himself, he has become the general laughing-stock; du haſt dich wieder (ſchön) blamiert! you were sold again!
Blancmanger (blᾱ-mᾱ-Geʹ) [fr.] n ⓮ Kochkunſt: blancmange.
blank (⁻) [ahd.: blank] a. ⓮ 1. (blinkend) shining, bright, glittering; zehn ᴗe Dukaten ten shining ducats; in ᴗem Gelde bezahlen F ... in (ready) cash; ᴗ machen, ᴗ polieren, ᴗ reiben (beſ. Metallſachen) to furbish (or polish) up; to scour; in ᴗer Rüſtung in polished armour; die Stiefel ᴗ putzen to polish (F to shine) up the boots; ᴗer putzen to give more polish to; ᴗe Waffen *pl.* (*ant.* Feuerwaffen) weapons for cutting or thrusting. — 2. (glatt) smooth; (wohlgenährt) sleek, plump. — 3. (bar, bloß) bare, naked; *fig.* pure, mere; ᴗ ziehen to draw the sword; F ſich bin ᴗ (ohne Geld) I am pennyless, F cleaned out. — 4. ᴗer Wein white wine. — 5. mit e-m ᴗ ſteh(e)n (feind ſein) to be at enmity (F at daggers drawn) with a p.
Blanka (⁻ᴗ) [ſpan., *got.] npr/f. ⓮ ⓮ a. (Vorname) Blanche.
Blänke (⁻ᴗ) f ⓮ (Waldblöße) glade.
Blankett (ᴗ⁻) [fr., *dtſch] n ⓮ b.(⓮) (unbedingte Vollmacht) (fr.) carte blanche; ⓮ ~ (unausgefülltes Formular) zu e-m Bankſchein blank cheque.
Blank-leder (ᵛ...) n ❷ sleek(ed) leather; =**machen** ⓮ n furbishing (or polishing) up, F shining up (boots, metal. &c.).
blanko ⓮ (⁻ᴗ) [it., *dtſch] a. *inv.* in ᴗ (unbeſchrieben) in blank; in ᴗ (ohne verfügbare Mittel) akzeptieren, indoſſieren to accept, endorse in blank; in ᴗ (unausgefüllt) laſſen to leave void; in ᴗ traſſieren to draw in blank.
Blanko-abgabe (⁻...) f ❻ sale of stock which one does not hold, bearish operation; =**akzept** n blank acceptance; =**formular** n blank form; =**giro** n blank endorsement; =**kredit** m blank (or unlimited) credit; =**wechſel** m blank bill.
Blank-polieren (ᵛ...) n ❷ = =**machen**; =**ſcheit** [(P) fr. *planchette*] n (Fiſchbein im Korſett) busk; =**vers** † m engl. Verskunſt: blank verse.
Bläschen (⁻ᴗ) n ❷❸ *dim.* small bubble or blister or bladder; beſ. *path.*: pustule, pimple; ℣ (Schlauch) utricle.
Blaſe (⁻ᴗ) [ahd.] f ⓮ 1. (Luft-)~ bubble; ~n aufwerfen to bubble up; (Schaum) froth. — 2. *path.* (Waſſer-)~ auf der Haut: blister, pustule, pimple. ᴁ vesicle; mit ~n an den Füßen with blistered feet, foot-sore; ~n verurſachen, ziehen to cause, raise blisters, to blister the skin. — 3. (Harn-)~ bladder; f. Schwimm- ᴁ (Tabaksbeutel) (tobacco-)pouch. — 4. ⓮ (hohler Raum) im Stahl ꝛc.: blister, flaw; in Edelſteinen ꝛc.: flaw; beſ. im Glas: bleb. — 5. (Deſtillier-)~ still; ehm. alembic. — 6. F die ganze ~ (Sippe) the whole set or gang.
Blaſe-balg ⓮ (⁻ᴗ...) m ❷ der Orgel: bellows *pl. u. sg.*; ein ~ a pair of bellows; den ~ treten to blow the organ; =**balgröhre** f bellows-pipe or -nozzle; =**balgtreter** m organ- (or bellows-) blower; =**balken** ⬇ m wash-boards *pl.* under the cheeks; =**inſtrument** ♪ n f.

Blas-i.; =**maſchine** ✕ f (Sprengzylinder) blast-engine.
blaſen (⁻ᴗ) [ahd.] I v/n. (h.) u. v/a. ⓮ a. 1. to blow (a. ⓒ beſ. v. Glas); woher bläſt der Wind? in what quarter is the wind?; er bläſt aus e-m kalten Loch it blows from a cold quarter; der Wind bläſt in die Segel ... fills (or expands) the sails; e-m et. in die Ohren ᴗ to whisper s. th. into a p.'s ear; keuchend ᴗ to be puffing and blowing. — 2. ♪ das Horn ob. auf dem Horn ᴗ to wind (or blow) the horn; die Flöte, Klarinette ꝛc. ᴗ to play (on) the flute, the clarionet, &c.; das Hifthorn ᴗ to sound the bugle; ✕ zum Angriff, Rückzuge, Aufſitzen ᴗ to sound the charge, the retreat, to horse. — 3. Damenſpiel: einen Stein ᴗ to buff a man. — 4. Sprichw. in e-m Horn ob. aus demſelben Ton mit e-m ᴗ (einverſtanden ſein) to play into each other's hands, to be hand and glove (together), to act in concert with a p.; das läßt ſich nicht gleich ᴗ (fertig machen) it cannot be done in a moment or in a twinkle; F ich will ihm was ᴗ (er kann lange warten) I'll see him at Jericho first; e-m Staub in die Augen ᴗ (et. vorſchwatzen) to throw dust in a p.'s eyes. — II ~ n ❷❸ 5. blowing; (Hauch) breath. — 6. ♪ winding, blowing, &c. (ſ. 2).
blaſen-ähnlich ℣ (⁻...) [Blaſe] a. ⓮ vesicular, ...ous; =**arterie** ᴁ ❷ *anat.* cystic artery; ⁎**artig** a.: bladdery, ᴁ ampullate; =**ausſchlag** m, *path.*: ᴁ pemphigus; =**baum** ℣ m = -ſtrauch; =**entzündung** f, *path.* inflammation of the bladder; =**farn** ℣ m bladder-fern (*Cysto'pteris fra'gilis*); ⁎**förmig** *a.,* *anat.*: ᴁ ampullaceous; =**fuß** m, *ent.* thrips; =**füßer** m/pl., *ent.*: ᴁ physopoda *pl.*; =**galle** f, *physiol.* cystic bile; =**gang** m, *anat.* vesicular duct; =**grieß** m, *path.* gravel; =**grün** ⓒ n bladder-green, sap-green; =**käfer** m, *ent.* Spanish fly; =**katarrh** m, *path.* cystic catarrh; =**kirſche** ℣ f = Juden-ᴗ; =**krampf** m, *path.* spasm in the bladder; =**kupfer** ⓒ n, *metall.* blister-copper; =**pflaſter** n blister(ing-plaster), ᴁ vesicant; ein ~ auflegen to (put on a) blister; ᴁ to vesicate; =**räumer** m, *surg.* scoop; =**ried** ℣ n = ſegge; =**robbe** f, *zo.* bladder - nose (*Cysto'phora crista'ta*); =**ſchlag-ader** f = ſegge; =**ſchlauch** m bladdery carex (*Ca'rex vesica'ria*); =**ſenne** ℣ f = -ſtrauch; =**ſonde** f, *med.* catheter; =**ſtahl** ⓒ m, *metall.* (Zementſtahl) blister-steel; =**ſtein** n., *path.* stone (in the bladder), ᴁ cystic calculus; =**ſteinſchnitt** m = Steinſchnitt; =**ſtrauch** m bladder- (or bastard-)senna (*Colu'tea*); =**tang** ℣ m bladder-kelp, ᴁ fucus (*Fucus vesiculo'sus*); =**vesication**; ⁎**ziehend** a.: raising blisters; ᴁ epispastic; des Mittel: vesicant. [blowing-furnace.]
Blaſe-ofen ⓒ (⁻ᴗ...) m ❷ Glasfabrikation:
Bläſer (⁻ᴗ) m ❷, ~**in** f ⓮ 1. ♪ person who blows (or plays) a wind-instrument; bugler, trumpeter. — 2. ⓒ Glasfabrikation: blower; (Luftklappe) ventilator. — 3. *orn.* = Kropftaube.

Zeichen (ſ. S. XVII): F familiär; P Volksſprache; Г Gaunerſprache; ⬆ ſelten; † alt (auch geſtorben); * neu (auch geboren); ⁎⁺ unrichtig;

[Blaserohr] — 201 — [Blattzinn]

Blaſe-rohr (⁻ᵘ...) n ⊕: a) zum Schießen: pea-shooter; b) Glasfabrikation: blowpipe; c) ⊙ metall. blast-main; d) = Blasrohr b; ⸗**werk** n e-r Orgel: bellows. — Vgl. auch Gebläſe=...
blaſicht (⁻ᵘ) a. ⊕ bladdery. ſ. blaſig.
blaſiert (⸌⸍) [fr.] a. ⊕ surfeited, jaded, (fr.) blasé; ⸗**heit** f ⊕ surfeit (or indifference) caused by pleasure or enjoyment; (fr.) blasé state.
blaſig (⁻ᵘ) a. ⊕ like (or full of) blisters; ⚘ vesicular; ⚘ ampullate; ⊙ Gießerei: blistered. honeycombed; min. flawy.
Blas-inſtrument ♪ (⁻ᵘ...) n ⊕ windinstrument; Kapelle von ⸗en brassband; Muſik von ⸗en = Blechmuſik.
Blaſius (⸌ᵘ⸍) npr/m. ⊕ γ. (Bn.) Blase, co. Herr ~ (Blaſewind) (Mr.) Blowhard.
Blas-muſik ♪ (⁻ᵘ...) f ⊕ = Blechmuſik.
blaſonieren (⌣⌣⸍) [fr. blasonner] v/a. ⊕ (mit Wappen ſchmücken) to (em)blazon.
Blasphemie (⸌⸍) [grch.] f ⊕ (Läſterung) blasphemy; ⸝**ren** (⸌⁻⸍) v/a. u. v/n. (h.) (läſtern) to blaspheme; **blasphem(iſt)iſch** (⸌⸍, ⸌⌣⸍) a. ⊕ (läſterhaft) blasphemous.
Blasrohr (⁻ᵘ...) n ⊕: a) = Blaſerohr; b) 🜨 der Lokomotive, das den auspuffenden Abdampf in den Schornſtein leitet: eduction-pipe.
blaß [ahd.] a. ⊕ (D 3, 10) pale, (bleich) blanch(ed), pallid, (fahl) sallow; (abgezehrt) haggard, wan; ⸝ wie der Tod (as) white as a sheet, deadly (or ghastly) pale; F ich hatte keine blaſſe Ahnung davon ... not the slightest notion (or the least idea) of it.
Bläß (⸍) m ⊕ = Bleſſe.
blaß-blau (⸍⸍) a. ⊕ pale (or delicate, light) blue.   [Gazella albifrons.
Bläß-bock (⸍...) m ⊕ zo. blesbok;
Bläſſe (⸍⸍; f. Bleſſe) f ⊕ paleness, pallor, (Fahlheit) sallowness; ſ. aufränkeln.
blaß-grün (⸍⸍) a. ⊕ pale (or delicate, light) green.   [bald coot.]
Bläß-huhn (⸍...) n ⊕ orn. (Waſſerhuhn)
bläßlich (⸍⌣) a. ⊕ palish, pallid.
blaß-rot (⸍⸍) a. ⊕ reddish, (light) pink.
Blaſt prov. (⸍) [ahd.: blast] m ⊕ b. (scharfer Wind) cold blast. cutting wind.
Blatt (⸍) [ahd.: blade] n ⊕ b. (doch vgl. 2 u. 6) 1. leaf of a tree; blade of grass; e-r Blütenkrone: petal; e-s Kelches: sepal; e-s Pilzes: gill, plate, e-r lamella; ent. Wandelndes ⸝ ⸝-heuſchrecke; der Baum bekommt (verliert) ſ-e Blätter the tree is putting forth (is shedding or loosing) its leaves. — 2. ⊕ 6. ~ e-s Buches: leaf; das ~ umdrehen to turn over the leaf; ~ (e-s) Papier(bogens): sheet (of paper); ⸝ typ. (Probe-)~ proof (-sheet); ♪: vom ~ (e) (unvorbereitet) ſpielen to play at sight; Singen vom ~(e) sight-singing. — 3. (Zeitung) journal, (news)paper; in e-m ~(e) drucken laſſen, veröffentlichen to insert, publish in a (daily) paper; öffentliche Blätter, auch: public prints pl.; (Wochenſchrift) weekly (paper or publication). — 4. (Zeichnung) drawing; (Holzſchnitt) print; (Kupferſtich) engraving; (Spielkarte) card. — 5. ⊙ (Platte) plate; an der Säge, am Schwert und Ruder: blade; am Tiſche: leaf. — 6. ⊕ 6. ♣ ~ (Bahn) von Zeug: ſ. ~breite. — 7. anat. (Schul-

ter-)~ blade- (or shoulder-)bone; hunt. shoulder-blade; fore-leg. — 8. 🜨 (ſ.-geſchrumpfter Gang) fissure. — 9. fig. ein neues ~ (im Buche des Lebens) beginnen to turn over a new leaf, to make a fresh start; kein ~ vor den Mund nehmen to speak out (plainly), not to mince the matter; das ſteht auf e-m andern ~e (hat hiermit nichts zu tun) that's quite another (or a different) thing or story or F another pair of breeches; das ~ umwenden to turn the tables; das ~ wendet ſich (die Dinge ändern ſich) things are taking a new (or different) turn.   [foliaceous.
blatt-ähnlich (⸍ᵘ...) a. ⊕ leaf-like, ⚘]
Blattang (⸌ᵘ⸍) [Blatt-tang] m ⊕: ⚘ laminaria; zu den ⸗en gehörig ⚘ laminarian.
Blatt-anſatz ⚘ (⸍ᵘ...) m ⊕: ⚘ stipule.
⸝**artig** ⚘ (⸍ᵘ...) = ⸝ähnlich; ⸗**auge** ⚘ n leafbud, ⚘ gemma; ⸗**bildung** f leafing (of plants), ⚘ foliation; ⸗**blume** ⚘ f (Euphorbiaceae) ⚘ phyllanthus; ⸗**breite** f e-s Zeuges: width of cloth.
Blättchen ⚘ (⸍ᵘ⸍) n ⊕ (dim. v. Blatt) 1. small leaf, leaflet; ⚘ foliole. — 2. anat. ~ des Gehirns: ⚘ membrane. — 3. min. (Plättchen): ⚘ lamina; (Gold-)~ leafgold, gold foil or leaf.
Blättchen-pulver ⚔ (⸍ᵘ...) n ⊕ (rauchſchwaches Pulver) leaf- (or flake-) powder.
blatten (⸍ᵘ) v/a. ⊕ agr., hort. to pluck off (or thin out) the leaves of trees, vines. &c.   [bildung.]
Blatt-entwick(e)lung (⸍ᵘ...) f ⊕ = Blatt-]
Blatter (⸍ᵘ) [ahd.: bladder; * blähen] f ⊕ path. 1. (Hautbläschen) (Hitz-)~ pimple, ⚘ pustule. — 2. ~ n pl. (Pockenkrankheit) small-pox sg., ⚘ variola sg.   [leaf.
Blätter-abfall (⸍ᵘ...) m ⊕ fall of the]
Blätterchen (⸍ᵘ...) pl. zu Blättchen.
Blätter-dach (⸍ᵘ...) n ⊕ = ⸝ſchmuck;
⸗**erz** n, min. lamellar virgin silver;
⸗**fülle** f leafiness, abundance of foliage;
⸗**gebäck(e)(s)** n puff-paste; ⸗**gold** n = Blattgold.
Blätter-grube (⸍ᵘ...) f ⊕ = ⸗narbe.
Blätter-grün (⸍ᵘ...) n ⊕ = Blattgrün.
blatt(e)rig (⸍ᵘ⸍) [Blatter] a. ⊕ path. pimpled, ⚘ pustulated; auch: papular, papulous, papulose.
blätt(e)rig (⸍ᵘ⸍) [Blatt] a. ⊕ 1. ⚘ leafy, foliate(d); bſd. in Zſſgn. ⸝B. vier-⚘ four-leaved, ⚘ von der Blumenkrone: four-petaled. — 2. min. (ſich ſpaltend) ⚘ laminated, lamellar.
Blätter-knoſpe ⚘ (⸍ᵘ...) f ⊕ leaf-bud;
⸗**kohle** f, min. slate- (or slaty) coal; paper-coal; ⸝**kondenſator** m, elect. condenser consisting of alternate layers of paraffined paper and tinfoil.
Blätter-lymphe (⸍ᵘ...) f ⊕ med.: ⚘ vaccine.
Blätter-magen (⸍ᵘ...) m ⊕ zo. der Wiederkäuer: manyplies, ⚘ omasum, psalterium; ⸗**magnet** m, elect. lamellar magnet; ⸗**meldung** f newspaper report.
blättern (⸍ᵘ) a. I v/n. (h.) in e-m Buche ⚘ to turn over the leaves of a book. — II v/a. (und ſich ⚘ v/refl.) Bäckerei: ⚘ to make a light (or flaky) crust, (to rise like puff-paste); min.: ⚘ to exfoliate.
Blatter-narbe (⸍ᵘ...) f ⊕ pock-mark, pit.

blatter-narbig (⸍ᵘ...) a. ⊕ marked by (or pitted with) small-pox.
Blattern-epidemie (⸍ᵘ...) f ⊕ smallpox epidemic; ⸗**gift** n vaccine virus;
⸗**impfung** f vaccination, inoculation of the small-pox. — Vgl. a. Pocken⸗...
Blätter-paſtete (⸍ᵘ...) f ⊕ pie (made) with puff-paste; ⸗**pilz** ⚘ m agaric (Agaricus); ⸗**pilz-artig** a.: ⚘ agaricoid;
⸝**reich** a. ⊕ leafy, with luxuriant foliage; ⚘ foliose, frondous; ⸗**ſchimmel** ⚘ m (Meltau) blight; ⸗**ſchmuck** m, poet. leafy garb (or adornment, roof) of trees; ⸝**ſchwamm** ⚘ m = ⸗pilz; ⸝**ſtand** ⚘ m foliation; foliage; ⚘ frondescence.
Blätter-ſtein (⸍ᵘ...) m ⊕ min.: ⚘ variolite.
Blätter-tabak ⚘ (⸍ᵘ...) m leaf tobacco,
⸗**teig** m, ⸗**teig-kruſte** f puff-paste, flaky crust; ⸗**tellur** n, min. foliated tellurium, ⚘ nagyagite; ⸗**ton** m, geol. slaty clay;
⸝**tragend** ⚘ a.: ⚘ foli(i)ferous; ⸝**treibend** ⚘ a. bursting into leaf; ⚘ frondescent; ⸝**trieb** ⚘ m leaf-bud; ⸝**werk** n, arch. leaf-work; ⸝**wuchs** ⚘ m =
⸝ſtand; ⸝**zahn** m scaly tooth; vgl. Blatt⸗...
Blatt-feder ⊙ (⸍ᵘ) f ⊕ plate-spring,
⸝**federchen** ⚘ n (Knöspchen der keimenden Pflanze): ⚘ plume, plumule; ~ des Gerſtenkeims: ⚘ acrospire; ⸝**förmig** a. ⊕ leaf-shaped; mit zen Beinen leaflegged; ⸝**füßer** m: ⚘ phyllopod; ⸝**gewächs** ⚘ n = ⸗pflanze; ⸝**gold** n gold foil or leaf, unechtes: Dutch gold or metal; ⸝**grün** ⚘ n: ⚘ chlorophyll;
⸝**heuſchrecke** f, ent. walking leaf (Phyllum siccifolium); ⸝**horn(käfer** m) n: ⚘ lamellicorn; ⸝**hüter** ⊙ m, typ. catchword; ⸝**käfer** m: ⚘ chrysomel; ⸝**keim** m = ⸝federchen; ⸝**keimer** m (pl.) dicotyledon(s pl.); ⸝**kugelblume** ⚘ f globedaisy (Globularia vulgaris); ⸝**knoſpe** ⚘ f = ⸗auge; ⸝**kupfer** n sheet-copper;
⸝**laus** f, ent. plant- (or tree-)louse, vine-grub; ⚘ aphis; ⸝**los** a. leafless; ⚘ von Pflanzen: aphyllous, von Blüten: apetalous; ⸝**loſe** ⚘ f = Mauerpfeffer;
⸝**loſigkeit** f leaflessness;
⸝**metall** n leaf- (or sheet-)metal; ⸝**naſe** f, zo. (Art Fledermaus): ⚘ phyllostome;
⸝**pflanze** f foliage-plant; ⸝**reich** a. leafy, with rich foliage, ⚘ foliose.
blattrig, blättrig (⸍ᵘ...) ſ. blatt(e)rig 2c.
Blatt-rippe ⚘ (⸍ᵘ...) f ⊕ rib or nerve, (vein) of a leaf; ⸝**roller** m, ent. leafroller, tortricid which rolls up the leaves; ⸝**ſalat** m young lettuces pl.;
⸝**ſcheide** ⚘ f sheath; ⸝**ſchuß** m, hunt. shot in the shoulder-blade; ⸝**ſeite** f (a) side of a leaf; in e-m Buche: page;
⸝**ſilber** n leaf-silver, silver leaf, silver foil; ⸝**ſtahl** m spring-steel plates pl.; ⸝**ſtand** ⚘ m foliation; ⸝**ſtändig** ⚘ a. (auf Blättern wachſend): ⚘ epiphyllous; ⸝**ſtellung** ⚘ f: ⚘ phyllotaxis; ⸝**ſtiel** ⚘ m leaf-stalk, ⚘ petiole; zwiſchen ⸝en ſtehend ⚘ interpetiolar; ⸝**ſtück** ⸝ n, carp. capping-piece; wall-plate; ⸝**vergoldung** ⊙ f leaf-gilding; ⸝**weiſe** adv. leaf by leaf; ⸝**wender** ⊙ m turnover,
⸝**weſpe** f, ent. saw-fly (Familie Tenthredinidae); ⸝**wickler** m, ent. = ⸝roller;
⸝**winkel** ⚘ m: ⚘ axil(la); ⸝**winkelſtändig** a. axillar(y); ⸝**zeichen** n bookmark; tassel; ⸝**zinn** ⚘ n tinfoil.

♪ Muſik; ⚘ Wiſſenſchaft; ⚘ Pflanze; ⚱ Geographie; ⊙ Technik; 🜨 Bergbau; ⚔ Militär; ⚓ Marine; ⚖ Handel; ✉ Poſt; 🜨 Eisenbahn.

[blau] — [bleiben]

blau (ˊ) [ahd.: blue] **I** a. ⊕ 1. blue; ⁀eAugen blue eyes pl.; ⁀ angelaufenes Auge black eye; ⁀ färben, ⁀ machen, ⁀ anlaufen lassen to blue; ⁀ vor Kälte blue with cold; ⁀er Vitriol (Kupfervitriol) blue vitriol. — 2. fig. mit e-m ⁀en Auge davonkommen to come (or get) off with a trifling loss or injury; F to get off cheaply; vgl. Auge 1; es wird mir grün und ⁀ vor den Augen I (begin to) feel quite dizzy; F I see stars (before my eyes); von ⁀em Blut (adelig) blue-blooded. of blue blood; ⁀e Bohne, ⁀es Korn (Flintenkugel) blue pill; e-n braun und ⁀ schlagen to beat a p. black and blue; e-m ⁀en Dampf od. Dunst, Nebel (Flunkereien) vormachen to fog (or mystify) a p., to cast a haze before a p.'s eyes, F to bamboozle (or humbug) a p.; ⁀e Flecken (von Schlägen) bruises pl.; ⁀en (Montag) machen (feiern) F to go on the spree; wir wollen heute ⁀ machen F we'll knock off work today, we'll make a (merry) day of it, we'll have a jolly day; ↓ ⁀er Peter (Abfahrtssignal) Blue Peter; sein ⁀es Wunder sehen to see wonders, to be taken aback (with amazement); P(na) so ⁀! (wer wird so dumm sein) I am not so silly (F such a fool, so green) as all that!, catch me doing (such a silly thing as) that! — **II** ⁀ n, ⁀e(s) n ⊕ 3. blue (colour or dye); in ⁀ gekleidet dressed in blue; mit ⁀ bemalt painted blue; das ⁀ des Himmels the azure sky; im ⁀ zerfließen to melt (or dissolve) in bluish tints; s. Berliner II. — 4. fig. das ⁀e vom Himmel herunterschwören (lügen) to swear black and blue (to a th.); das ⁀e vom Himmel heruntersingen to sing like an angel, iro. to scream one's lungs out; ins ⁀e hinein at hazard, at random; ins ⁀e hinein schwatzen to talk at random; ins ⁀e hinein blicken, stieren to gaze, stare into vacancy.

Blau-amsel (ˊˊ...) f ⊕ orn. blue-thrush (Monti'cola cya'nea); ⁀ad(e)rig a. ⊕ with blue veins; ⁀äugig a. blue-eyed; =bart m blue-beard; =beere ⊕ f (Heidelbeere) bilberry (Vacci'nium Myrtil'lus); ⁀blütig a. fig. (adelig) with (or of) blue (or aristocratic) blood, of noble extraction; =bock m, zo. (Schimmelantilope) blaubok, blue buck (Hippo'tragus equi'nus); =buch ⊤ n der engl. Regierung: Blue book; =drossel f, orn. = =amsel.

Bläue (ˊˊ) f ⊕ blueness; blue colour; ⁂ (Waschblau) blue.

Blau-eisen-erde (ˊˊˊ...) f ⊕ min. blue phosphate of iron; =eisen-erz n, min. ⊘ vivianite.

blauen, meist ⊕ (ˊˊ) v/n. (h.) und sich ⁀ v/refl. ⊕ to be (or appear) blue or bluish; (blau w.) to become (or turn) blue; poet. soweit der Jura blauet, etwa: where Jura fades in azure tints.

bläuen (ˊˊ) v/a. ⊕ to (make or dye) blue.

Blau-farbe (ˊˊ...) f ⊕ blue-colour or dye; =farben-glas n ⊕ (Schmalte) smalt; =farben-werk ⊕ n smalt-house or -works pl.; =färber m dyer in blue; =felch(e[n m] f) m, ichth. blue char (Salmo lavare'tus); =fuchs m, zo. (Eisfuchs) arctic fox; =fuß m, orn. (Würgfalk) lanner (Falco lania'rius); ⁀grau a. ⊕ bluish grey, slate-coloured; livid; ⁀grün a. bluish green, ⊘ glaucous; =holz(baum ⊕ m) ⁂n logwood, Campeachy-wood (Haemato'xylon campechea'num); =jacke ⊤ ↓ f (Matrose) bluejacket; =kehlchen n, orn. bluethroat (Eri'thacus cyane'culus); =kohl ⊕ m red cabbage; =küpe ⊕ f Färberei: blue vat.

bläulich (ˊˊˊ) a. ⊕ bluish; das ⁀e bluishness; ⁀=gelb (ˊˊ...) a. ⊕ bluish yellow, ⁀=grau a. bluish grey.

Blau-licht ↓ (ˊˊ) n ⊕c. (Signallicht zum Herbeirufen eines Lotsen) blue light.

Bläuling, **Bläuling** (ˊˊ) m ⊕d. ichth. = **Blaufelche**.

Blau-meise (ˊˊ...) f ⊕ orn. blue-bonnet, blue tit(mouse) (Parus caeru'leus); ⁀rot a. bluish red, purple blue; ⁀sauer a., chm. ⊘ prussic; ⁀saures Salz: ⊘ prussiate; =säure f, chm.: ⊘ prussic (or hydrocyanic) acid (HCN); =säureverbindung f, chm.: ⊘ cyanide; =scheck(e f) m dapple-grey (horse); =schimmel ⊕ m bluish grey (horse); =schreiber ⊕ m, tel. ink-writer, Morse-printer; ⁀schwarz a. blue-black; =spat m, min.: ⊘ lazulite; =specht m, orn. (Spechtmeise) nuthatch, nutjobber (Sitta); =stern ⊕ m blue bell (Scilla); =strumpf ⊤ (1750) m (gelehrte Frau) blue-stocking; =strumpfigkeit f learned pedantry of women; =sucht f, path.: ⊘ cyanosis; ⁀süchtig a., path.: ⊘ cyanochroic; =werden n der Milch 2c.: turning blue.

Blech (ˊ) [ahd.; *bleich] n ⊕c. 1. sheet-metal; weißes ~, verzinntes ~ tinned iron(-plate), tin, tin-plate; schwarzes (Eisen)~ black iron-plate; zu ~ schlagen to plate iron, &c.; zu ~ walzen to roll into sheets. — 2. (aus Blech Gefertigtes) tin (plate). — 3. F co. (Geld) money, F tin. — 4. F fig. das ist reines ~ (dummes Zeug) F it's all rubbish or bosh or P (tommy)rot, it's pure twaddle.

Blech-abfälle (ˊˊ...), =abschnitte (ˊˊ...) m/pl. ⊕ shavings (or shreds, filings, chips) pl. of sheet-metal; =arbeit f tin-work; =arbeiter m worker in tin; ⁀artig a. ⊕ tin-like; =beschlag m tin-plating; sheet-metal covering; =büchse f tin (canister or box); in ~n verpackt tinned (meat, &c.); =dach n iron-plate roof.

blechen[1] F (ˊˊ) [nhd. 18. sae.; *F Blech Pfennig] v/a. u. v/n. (h.) ⊕ (zahlen) to pay (up), F to put down the tin, to fork out the cash.

blechen[2] †, meist **blechern** (ˊˊ) a. ⊕ (of) tin, made of tinned iron; ⁀e Gießkanne tin water-can.

Blech-gefäß (ˊˊ...) n ⊕ tin(-plate, -vessel); =geschirr n: a) = =gefäß; b) coll. tins, tin(ned) kitchen utensils pl.; =hammer ⊕ m: a) (Werkzeug) (steam-)hammer for plating; b) (Werkstatt) sheet-iron forge or works pl.; =haube f = =kappe; =hütte ⊕ f = =hammer b; =instrument ⁂ n brass instrument; =kanne f tin can; =kappe f skull-cap; =kasten m tin box; =kuchen m shortcake; =lehre ⊕ f metal-gauge; mit Fühlhebel: lever-gauge; =löffel m tin spoon; =münze f (dünne Münze) Mittelalter: brac-

teate; =musik ♪ f music of brass instruments, (music of a) brass-band.

Blechner provc. (ˊˊ) m ⊕ = **Klempner**.

Blech-ofen (ˊˊ...) m ⊕ light movable stove; =schere ⊕ f plate-(or tin-)shears pl.; =schläger, =schmied m tin-worker (or -smith or -man); =topf m tin pot; =verzinnung ⊕ f tinning of plate; =walzwerk ⊕ n sheet-iron works pl.; =ware f tin goods.

blecken (ˊˊ) [ahd. blicken lassen] v/a. ⊕ die Zähne ⁀ to show one's white teeth, F to sport one's ivories.

Blei[1] (ˊ) [ndd.] m ⊕c. ichth. bream (A'bramis Brama).

Blei[2] (ˊ) [ahd.] n ⊕c. 1. (Metall) lead (a. = Senkt); chm. plumbum (Pb), chm. saturn; gedieg(e)nes, gereinigtes, gewalztes ~ native, refined, rolled lead; gehachtes ~ slugs pl.; hunt. (Kugel) bullet; Pulver und ~ powder and shot; ⊕ typ. auf dem ~ lesen to correct (or read) type; Angelsport: ~ an der Angel plumb, sinker. — 2. fig. es liegt mir wie ~ in den Gliedern I feel as heavy as lead; F ~ im Munde (eine schwere Zunge) haben to be heavy of tongue, to have a thick speech.

Blei-abfall (ˊˊ...) m ⊕ scrap-lead; =abgang, =abstrich, =abzug m lead-scum or -dross; =antimonglanz m, min. zinkenite; =arbeit f: a) plumber's work, plumbing; b) lead-smelting; =arbeiter m plumber; =arsenglanz m arsenical lead; ⁀artig a. ⊕ lead-like, ⊘ plumbeous; =asche f lead-ash(es pl.), oxide of lead; =auflösung f, chm. lead solution; vgl. =wasser; =baum m lead-tree, (it.) arbor Saturni; =bedachung f = =dach.

bleiben (ˊˊ) [ahd.: (be)leave; *Leib, Leben] **I** v/n. (sn) ⊕ 1. to remain; (verweilen) to stay, abide, rest, sojourn; er blieb ein halbes Jahr in Paris he stayed (or stopped) six months in Paris; ich blieb zum Mittagessen bei ihm I stayed to dinner (F auch ohne to) with him. — 2. (verharren) to continue; ernsthaft ⁀ to preserve one's gravity, to keep one's countenance; fern ⁀ to keep away or aloof; fest ⁀ to stand firm; gesund ⁀ to continue in good health, to remain well; sich gleich ⁀, sich getreu ⁀ to be always the same; es bleibt jetzt hell bis sieben it is now light till seven; neutral ⁀ to remain neutral; ruhig (a. gelassen) ⁀ to remain calm, to keep one's temper (under control); tot ⁀: a) to remain dead, not to revive; b) (umkommen) to perish; unbelohnt, unbestraft ⁀ to go unrewarded, unpunished; unverheiratet ⁀ to remain single, als Junggeselle: to be(come) a confirmed old bachelor, als alte Jungfer F to remain on the shelf. — 3. mit Verben: hangen ⁀ to remain hanging; er blieb mit dem Rock am Nagel hangen the nail caught his coat; leben ⁀ to remain alive; to survive, to outlive others; liegen ⁀ to remain lying, nach e-m Falle to remain on the ground, not to get up, vgl. 6; sitzen ⁀ to keep one's seat, to remain (or keep) seated; bleib(t) sitzen! keep your seat(s), don't get up (yet)!; Mädchen, das auf dem

Signs (see page XVII): F familiar; P vulgar; ⁀ flash; ⁀ rare; † obsolete (died); * new word (born); ÷ incorrect; ♪ music;

[Bleibergwerk] — 203 — [blenden]

Ball ſitzen bleibt F wallflower; ſtecken ⟨2⟩ to stick in the mud or mire; in der Rede: to break down in the middle; ſteh(e)n ⟨2⟩ to stand still, to stop walking; to continue standing; wo ſind wir (beim Leſen) ſteh(e)n geblieben? where did we leave off?; meine Uhr iſt ſich(e)n geblieben … has stopped (going). — 4. mit präpoſitionalen Redensarten: am Leben ⟨2⟩ to remain alive; am ſelben Orte ⟨2⟩ to stay (or abide) in the same place; bei et. ⟨2⟩ to persevere in (F to stick to) a th.; es bleibt alles beim alten things remain as they were, F we go on in the old style or way; er bleibt bei ſeiner Ausſage he adheres to his statement or evidence; es bleibt dabei! that's settled!; es kann nicht dabei ⟨2⟩! it won't rest there!; bei der Entſcheidung muß es ⟨2⟩ it is a final decision; es bleibt bei unſer(e)m Handel! (we are) agreed!; bei der Sache ⟨2⟩ to keep to the subject or the point; bei der Wahrheit ⟨2⟩ to keep (F to stick) to the truth; für ſich ⟨2⟩ to keep to o.s.; ⟨2⟩ Sie mir weg ⟨2⟩ to keep the field; ⟨2⟩ Sie mir weg mit dieſen Dingen!, ⟨2⟩ Sie mir mit dem Unſinn vom Halſe! don't trouble me with such rubbish!, keep those things to yourself!; das bleibt unter uns this is quite between ourselves or strictly confidential. it must not go any further; von e-m, et. (fern=) ⟨2⟩ to keep away from a p., a th.; zu Hauſe ⟨2⟩ to stay (or stop) at home. — 5. (übrigbleiben) to be left, to remain; (Arithmetik) vier von ſieben ⟨2⟩ drei take four from seven and three remain, auch: four from seven leaves three; es blieb ihm nichts auf der Welt (übrig) he had nothing left in the world. — 6. (umkommen) to perish, to be killed; es blieben 2000 Mann auf der Walſtatt (liegen) two thousand bodies were left on (or covered) the battlefield; geblieben killed, slain, dead. — 7. (ausbleiben) to stay away, tarry, linger; wo biſt du ſo lange geblieben? where have you been all this time?; ich weiß nicht, wo er geblieben iſt … where he has gone to or what has become of him. — 8. et. ⟨2⟩ laſſen (unterlaſſen) to leave (or let) a th. alone; laß das ⟨2⟩! don't do it!, leave (or let) it alone!. leave off!, stop that (noiſe. F row, &c.)!; das ſollen Sie mir wohl ⟨2⟩ laſſen! I defy you to do it again!; das werde ich wohl ⟨2⟩ laſſen! I shall do nothing of the kind. — II ~ n ⟨23⟩ 9. stay; hier iſt meines ⟨2⟩s nicht mehr. hier ~ für mich I cannot stay (or abide) here any longer. I could not stop (or hold out) here (much longer). — III ⟨2⟩d p.pr. u. a. ⟨6⟩ 10. Bed. des inf. — 11. (immerwährend) lasting, enduring; ein ⟨2⟩der Ausſchuß a standing committee; ⟨2⟩de Farbe fast colour; keine ⟨2⟩de Stätte h. to have no permanent (or fixed) abode or residence.

Blei=bergwerk ⚒ (⁂ …) n ⟨62⟩ lead mine.
bleich (⁂) [ahd.: bleak] a. ⟨66⟩ (vgl. blaß) von Farben: faint, faded; ⟨2⟩ werden to turn (or grow) pale, ⌀ to etiolate.
Bleich=anſtalt (⁂ …) f ⟨⁂⟩ = Bleiche 3.

Bleichart (⁂) m ⓢd. light red wine.
Bleiche (⁂) f ⟨⁂⟩ 1. (Bläſſe) paleness, pallor. — 2. = Bleichung. — 3. (Bleichanſtalt. Bleichplatz) bleaching-ground, bleaching-yard, bleachery.
bleich/en (⁂) [ahd.: bleach] I v/n. (h. n. ſn) Gaſt. a. ⌀ to bleach. blanch. fade; to turn pale or white. v. Pflanzen a. ⌀ to etiolate. — II v/a. ⟨⁂⟩ Leinwand ꝛc.: to bleach, blanch, whiten. — III ~ n ⟨23⟩ = B/ung. ⁂ f auch: laundress.
Bleicher (⁂) m ⟨⁂⟩, ~in f ⟨⁂⟩ bleacher;
Bleich=erde (⁂ …) f ⟨⁂⟩ bleaching clay.
Bleichert (⁂) [ahd.] m ⓢd. = Bleichart.
bleich=farbig (⁂ …) a. ⟨66⟩ of a faint hue or tint; **=flüſſigkeit** f ⟨⁂⟩ bleaching-liquor; **=geſicht** † n ⟨⁂⟩ (European) pale face; white man; **=kalk** ⊙ m bleaching powder; (Chlorkalk) chloride of lime; **=kraft=meſſer** m, chm. für Chlorkalk: ⌀ blanchimeter; **=mittel** n ⌀ decolorant; **=platz** m = Bleiche 3; **=pulver** n bleaching powder. [chloride (Pb Cl₂).⟩
Blei=chlorid ⊙ (⁂ …) n ⟨⁂⟩ lead (or plumbic)
Bleich=ſoda (⁂ …) f ⟨⁂⟩ bleaching soda; **=ſucht** f. path. green-sickness; ⌀ chlorosis; physiol.. ⁂: ⌀ etiolation; **=ſüchtig** a. ⟨66⟩ ⌀ chlorotic; (blutarm) anæmic.
Bleichung (⁂) f ⟨⁂⟩ (vgl. bleichen) bleaching, ⌀ decoloration.
Bleich=waſſer (⁂ …) n ⟨⁂⟩ = **=flüſſigkeit**; **=waſſerſucht** f = Hautwaſſerſucht.
Blei=dach (⁂ …) n ⟨⁂⟩ leaden roof or covering; hist. **=dächer** pl. (Kerker) zu Venedig (the) leads pl. of Venice; **=draht** m spun lead.
Bleie (⁂) f ⟨⁂⟩ ichth. = Blei¹. [tracery.⟩
Blei=einfaſſung (⁂ …) f ⟨⁂⟩ arch. lead⟩
bleien¹ (⁂) v/a. ⟨⁂⟩ (mit Blei verſehen, beſchweren) to (load with) lead, to plumb.
bleien² †, mſt **bleiern** (⁂) a. ⟨66⟩ leaden, of lead; fig. heavy (as lead), very dull or slow.
Blei=erz (⁂ …) n ⟨⁂⟩ lead-ore; **=eſſig** m, pharm. (baſiſch eſſigſaure Bleilöſung) extract of lead. Goulard's extract; **=farben** a. ⟨66⟩, **=farbig** a. lead-coloured, leaden; **=feder** f lead pencil; **=gelb** n, min. yellow-lead; (gelbes Bleioxyd) massicot; **=gewicht** n an einer Angelſchnur lead bob; fig. wie ein ~ (as) heavy as lead, (like) a dead weight; **=gießen** n, zum Weisſagen: (foretelling the future by) casting the lead; **=gießer** m plumber; **=gießer=arbeit** f = **=arbeit**; **=gießerei** f lead-works pl.; **=glanz** m, min. natürliches Schwefelblei, Pb S) lead-glance. galena; **=glas** n crystal- (or flint-)glass; **=glätte** f (gelblich=rotes Bleioxyd) litharge, **=grau** n leaden grey; **=grau=kryſtall** grey; **=graupe** f lead crystal; **=grube** f lead-mine; **=haltig** a. containing lead, ⌀ plumbiferous.
Bleihe (⁂) f ⟨⁂⟩ ichth. = Blei¹.
Blei=herd (⁂ …) m ⟨⁂⟩ lead-refining hearth; **=holz** ⚓ n u.s. leatherwood, rope-bark (Dirca palustris); **=horner** n: native chloride of lead. ⌀ phosgenite; **=hütte** f lead-works pl.
bleiig (⁂) a. ⟨66⟩ = bleie(r)n.
Blei=jodid (⁂ …) n ⟨⁂⟩ lead iodide (Pb J₂); **=kammer** / a = **=dach**; b) ⊙ Schwefelſäurefabrikation ꝛc.: lead chamber; **=klumpen** m lump of lead; **=kolik** f. path. lead- (or

painter's) colic; **=könig** m. metall. regulus of lead, chm. (lt.) regulus Saturni; **=kugel** f lead(en) ball or bullet; **=laſur** min.: ⌀ linarite; **=lot** n. arch. &c. plumb (-line), plummet; mit dem ~ richten to plumb; **=lötung** lead-solder(ing); **=mantel** ⚔ m der Geſchoſſe lead(en) casing or covering. lead-coat; ⊙ elect. e-s Kabels lead casing; **=mulde** f lead pig = muſm m, min. friable galena; **=nagel** m lead nail; ⚓ scupper-nail; **=ocker** m, min. (natürliches Bleioxyd) lead-ochre; **=oxyd** n, chm. &c. lead (or plumbic) oxide; rotes ~ (Mennige) minium; **=pflaſter** n, pharm. lead-plaster; **=platte** f sheet of lead; **=probe** f lead-assay; **=rauch** ⚒ m lead-fumes pl.; **=rohr** n, **=röhre** f lead(en) pipe; **=rohr=kabel** ⊙ n. elect. lead-cased cable; **=rot** n red-lead, (Mennige) minium; **=ſalbe** f, pharm. lead-ointment; **=ſalz** n, chm. salt of lead; **=ſchaum** m, **=ſchlacke** f = **=abgang**; **=ſchnur** f plumb-line, sounding-line; **=ſchrot** n lead shot; **=ſchweif** m compact galena; **=ſchwer** a. ⟨66⟩ (as) heavy as lead; **=ſicherung** f, elect. leaden casing; **=ſiegel** n leaden seal. ⚓ leads pl.; **=ſoldat** F m (r-r Zinn=ſ.) Kinderſpielzeug: lead (or tin) soldier; **=ſpat** m. min. black-lead spar; roter, weißer: red, white lead-ore; **=ſteg** m, typ.: ~e pl. lead furniture; **=ſtift** m, n lead pencil; mit ~ geſchrieben pencilled; **=ſtift=halter** m, **=hülſe** f pencil-case; **=ſtift=ſchneider**, **=ſtift=ſpitzer** m (Werkzeug) pencil-pointer or -sharpener; **=ſtift=zeichen** n pencilmark; **=ſtift=zeichnung** f pencil-drawing; **=ſulfid**, **=ſulfuret** n (Schwefelblei) sulphide of lead; plumbic sulphide (Pb S); vgl. **=glanz**; **=ſuper=oxyd** plumbic dioxide or peroxide (Pb O₂); **=tafel** f = **=platte**; **=vergiftung** f, path. lead poisoning; **=verſchluß** m Zollamts: leading; unter ~ leaded; **=wage** f plumb(-line). level, levelling instrument; **=waſſer** n, pharm. (aus Bleieſſig u. Waſſer für Umſchläge hergeſtellt) Goulard water; **=weiß** n, chm. white lead, ⌀ ceruse; **=weiß=fabrik** f white-lead works pl.; **=weiß=farbe** f white paint; **=weiß=ſalbe** f, pharm. white-lead ointment; **=wurf** ⚓ m heave of the lead; **=wurz** ⚘ f leadwort (Plumbago); **=zucker** m. chm. (eſſigſaures Blei) sugar (or acetate) of lead. plumbic acetate.
Blende (⁂) f ⟨⁂⟩ 1. (Blendung, Bedeutung:) opt. diaphragm. a. = Blendglas; (Scheuleder) blinker(s pl.); bſd. ⚔ (Blendlaterne) dark lantern; (ſpaniſche Wand) folding-screen; frt. = Blendung 2. — 2. (Blendwerk) arch. (Wandvertiefung) niche, recess; (blindes Fenſter. blinde Tür) sham window, door. — 3. ⚓ (blinde Lute) dead-light. — 4. min. ⚒ (Zink ⟨2⟩) blende. mock-lead, false galena, native sulphide of zinc. — 5. prov. Schneiderei: trimming (cut crosswise).
blende=haltig (⁂ …) a. ⟨66⟩ min.: ⌀ blendous.
blenden (⁂) [ahd.: blind] I v/a. ⟨69⟩ 1. (blind machen) körperlich, fig. u. ⚔ to blind; geblendet. auch: struck with blindness; e-n ⟨2⟩ (der Augen berauben) to put (or burn. gouge) a p.'s eyes out. weiſ. to deprive a p. of his sight. — 2. vorübergehend: ⟨2⟩ to dazzle,

⌀ scientific; ⚘ botanical; ⊕ geography; ⊙ machinery; ⚒ mining; ⚔ military; ⚓ marine; ⊛ commercial; ✉ postal; 🚆 railway.

[Blendfenster] — 204 — [blitzen]

daze; *fig.* (verwirren) to confuse; (täuschen) to deceive, delude; (bezaubern) to fascinate; 2des Licht glaring (or brilliant) light; *adv.* 2d hell dazzling, glary. — 3. (gegen Licht schützen) to darken, screen, shade; to protect against the light. — 4. (des Glanzes berauben) to tarnish (metal). — II ~ n ⌀ 5. blinding, dazzling, &c.; des Lichtes: glarishness, brilliancy; (Täuschung) delusion.

Blend-fenster (ᵂ…) n ⓬ blind window; **=glas** n dark(ening)-glass; **=laterne** f dark lantern, bull's-eye; **=leder** n = Scheuklappe.

Blendling (ᴸᵛ) [nhd.] m ①d. (Mischling) cross-breed; mixed breed, mongrel, bastard.

Blend=nische (ᵂ…) ⓬ f s. Blende 2; **=rahmen** ⊕ m, arch., paint. blind frame; **=scheibe** f s. Blende 2; **=stein** ⊕ m, arch. facing stone.

Blendung (ᴸᵛ) f ⓮ 1. = blenden II. — 2. ⊕ Optik. (Okular) eye-piece or -glass; (Blendscheibe) diaphragm; ⚔ frt. (Gewehr gegen Geschosse) blind(age), für Geschützmannschaft 2c.: mantelet.

Blend=werk (ᵂ…) n ⓬ blind, deception; (Sinnestäuschung) (optical) delusion, illusion; (Bezauberung) fascination; (Taschenspielerei) jugglery; *phys.* (Luftspiegelung) (fr.) mirage, (it.) *fata Morgana*; *fig.* das ist lauter (eitel) ~ that's nothing but a fraud; all is vanity; **=ziegel** ⊕ m, arch. facing-brick.

Blennorhöe ⊘ (ᵛᵛᴸ) [grch.] f, path. ⊕ (Eiter-, Schleim-fluß) blennorhoea.

Bleß=… (ᵛ…) ⓬ = **Bläß=…**

Blesse (ᴸᵛ) [mhd.] f ⓮ (weißer Stirnstreifen) blaze; white spot on the forehead; Pferd mit einer ~ horse with a blaze.

blessieren † (ᵛᴸᵛ) [fr.] v/a. ⓯ (verwunden) to wound; ⚔ blessierter Soldat, (auch) **Blessierte(r)** † m ⓭ wounded soldier.

Blessur † (ᵛᴸ) [fr.] f ⓮ wound (or injury) received in war.

Bletz (ᵛ) m ⓐa. (Flicklappen) patch; ⚒ (Keil) miner's wedge.

Bleuel (ᴸᵛ) m ⓮ (Schlegel) mallet; bsd. für die Wäsche: beetle(r); copper-stick; **~=stange** (ˈ…) f ⓮ pole for turning (or stirring) the clothes in the copper.

bleuen (ᴸᵛ) [ahd.: blow] ⓮ v/a. to beat, to trash. [(f. bs.)]

blich (ᵛ) (2e subj.) impf. von bleichen/

Blick (ᵛ) [ahd.] m ⓫b. 1. look; flüchtiger: glance (or peep) at, glimpse of; böse ~ the evil eye, s. a. am Schluß; e-n flüchtigen ~ auf etwas werfen, von et. erhaschen to catch a glimpse of a th.; durchbohrender, durchbringender ~ piercing, penetrating glance; er hat e-n scharfen ~ he has a sharp (or quick) eye; ein umfassender ~ a comprehensive view; *fig. auch:* large views *pl.*; mit unverwandten Blicken with a steady gaze; vielsagende ~e *pl.* telling glances *pl.*; auf den ersten ~ at the first glance, at first sight; auf einen ~, mit einem ~ at a glance, in the twinkling of an eye; er ließ mich einen tiefen ~ tun in he gave me a deep insight into or a good idea of; e-m e-n bösen ~ zuwerfen to cast a cross look at a p. — 2. ⊕ metall. (Silber-)~ shine, ⊘ coruscation. [(*Alburnus, Blicca*).]

Blicke (ᵛ) f ⓮ ichth. ablet, bleak/

blicken (ᴸᵛ) ⓮ I v/n. (h.) 1. to look at, to cast a glance (or glances) at; scharf 2: a) to pierce with a glance; b) to have a quick eye; so weit das Auge blickt as far as the eye reaches; von der Sonne, dem Monde: durch die Wolken 2 to break through the clouds. — 2. (aussehen) sanft 2 to have a gentle look or appearance; finster 2d scowling; finster 2de Augen sinister eying. — 3. sich 2 lassen to show o.s.; to appear on the scene; er darf sich hier nicht wieder 2 lassen he dare not show his face here again; das läßt tief 2 that is an eye-opener, it gives one a deep insight, F it tells a tale. — 4. (leuchten) to shine. — II v/a. 5. to show by one's looks. — 6. mit prp. Friede in j-s Seele 2 to soothe (or calm) a p.'s mind with one's glances.

Blick=feuer (ᵛ…) n ⓬, **=signal** n auf Leuchttürmen: revolving light; **=silber** n pure (or refined, lightened) silver.

blieb (ᴸ) (2e subj.) impf. von bleiben (s. ds.)

blies(ᴸ) (**bliese** subj.) impf. von blasen (s.ds.)

blind (ᵛ) [ahd.: blind] a. ⓮ 1. blind (a. *fig.*); sightless; ganz, vollständig 2 (auch stock-2) stone-blind, (as) blind as a bat; auf einem Auge 2 blind of one eye; sie ist 2 für seine Fehler she shuts her eyes to his faults; sie sind 2 gegen sein Verdienst they are blind to his merits; von Scheiben 2c.: (trüb, angelaufen) dim, dull, v. Metall a.: tarnished. — 2. *fig.* 2er Gehorsam, Glaube implicit (or blind) obedience, faith; 2es Glück mere chance, hazard (of the die); ein 2es Werkzeug a blind (or willing) tool in a p.'s hands; *adv.* 2 schießen to fire blank cartridges; 2 drauflosschlagen (schießen) to strike (to shoot) in the air or at random; 2 drauflosgehen, draufzufahren to go blindly at a th. — 3. (unsichtbar, versteckt) hidden, concealed; ⚓ 2er Anker anchor without buoy; 2e Klippe sunken rock; 2er Passagier F: a) ⚓ stowaway, b) 🚂 deadhead; im ~en tappen to grope in the dark (a. *fig.*). — 4. (falsch, täuschend) feigned, fictitious; 2es Gefecht sham-fight; 2er Kauf sham purchase; 2e Mauer, Wand (ohne Fenster und Türen) dead wall; ⚓ 2e Patrone (ohne Kugel) dummy, blank cartridge; ⚓ 2e Rahe sprit(-sail)yard; 2er (ant. scharfer) Schuß blank shot, shooting with a blank cartridge. — 5. (inhaltslos) 2er Eifer schadet nur too great zeal does nothing but harm; 2er Lärm false alarm.

Blind=boden (ᵛ…) m ⓬ false bottom; **=darm** m, anat. blind-gut, ⊘ cæcum; **=darm=entzündung** f appendicitis, ⊘ (peri)typhlitis.

Blinde (ᴸᵛ) I ~(r) m, ~ f ⓮ 1. blind man, blind woman; Sprichw. bei (auch unter) den ~n ist der Einäugige König, the one-eyed is king in the land of the blind. — 2. Whist: mit dem ~n (zu Dreien mit dem Strohmann) spielen to play with dummy; nehmen Sie den ~en? will you take dummy? — II ~ f ⓬ 3. ⚓ = Blendung 2; (blinde Lute) dead light; ⚓ große ~ sprit(-)sail.

Blinde-kuh (ᵛᴸ…) f, *inv.* Spiel: blindman's buff; ~ spielen to play (or to have a game at) blindman's buff.

Blinden=anstalt (ᵛᵛ…) f ⓬ institution (or home) for the blind; or blind-asylum; **=druck** m printing for the blind; **=schule** f school for the blind.

Blind=gänger ⚔ (ᵛ…) m ⓬ a) nicht geplatzte Granate) blind shell; b) (versagender Schuß) miss-fire; 2geboren a. ⓮(D9) born blind; **=gebor(e)ne(r)** m(f) ⓭ (wo)man blind from her (his) birth.

Blindheit (ᵛᴸ) f ⓮ 1. blindness; mit ~ geschlagen struck blind. — 2. *fig.* er ist wie mit ~ geschlagen he must be blind, he is under a delusion.

Blind=holz ⊕ (ᵛ…) n ⓬ join. wood for veneering.

blindlings (ᴸᵛ) adv. blindly; ich könnte es 2 tun I could do it blindfold; (aufs ungewisse) at random, at hazard; (unbedingt) unconditionally, with implicit faith, with heart and soul; e-m 2 ergeben passionately devoted to a p.; **~=spiel** (ˈ…) n ⓬ Schach: blindfold game of chess.

Blind=maus (ᵛ…) f ⓬ zo. mole-rat (*Spalax typhlus*); **=schleiche** [ahd.] f, zo. slow-(or blind-)worm (*Anguis fragilis*); *fig.* (tückische Person) snake in the grass.

blink (ᵛ) [nbd.: blink] a. ⓮: 2 und blank glittering and shining.

blinke(r)n (ᴸᵛ) v/n. (h.) ⓮(⓯a.) (leuchten) to glitter, sparkle, gleam, shine; von Sternen: to twinkle; mit den Augen 2 = blinzeln. [intermittent light.]

Blink-feuer ⚓ (ᵛᴸ…) n ⓬ der Leuchttürme/

blinze(l)n (ᴸᵛ) [nhd.] I v/n. (h.) ⓮(⓯a.) blink, to wink with one's eyes; *physiol.*: ⊘ to nict(it)ate. — II ~ n ⓫ blinking; *physiol.* (krampfhaftes) ~: ⊘ nictitation.

Blinz(e)ler (ᴸᵛ)(ᵛ) m ⓬, **~in** f ⓮ (Kurzsichtige[r]) blinker, bisw. blinkard.

Blitz (ᵛ) [mhd.: *Blick*] m ⓐa. 1. beim Gewitter: (forked) lightning (ant. sheet-lightning Wetterleuchten); vom ~ getroffen struck by l.; der ~ hat ins Dach eingeschlagen the lightning has struck the roof; gegen ~ geschützt lightning-proof. — 2. (~strahl) flash of lightning, *auch:* thunderbolt; ein ~ aus heiterem Himmel a bolt from the blue. — 3. *fig.* (schnell) wie der ~ quick as lightning, vgl. blitzschnell; wie vom ~ getroffen thunderstruck; *Fluch:* der ~ schlage drein! the deuce (take it)!

Blitz=ableiter (ᵛ…) m ⓬ lightning-rod or -conductor; lightning-discharger or -arrester or -protector; **=ableiterspitze** f lightning-point; 2ähnlich a. ⓮, 2artig a. like lightning; **=auge** n flashing eye; 2blank a. spick and span, shining like gold; 2blau (und donnergrün) F a. (beaten) black and blue, F in all the colours of the rainbow.

blitzen (ᴸᵛ) ⓰ I v/n. u. v/impers. (h., bei 4 auch sn) 1. es blitzt it lightens; *fig.* von Augen: vor Zorn 2 to flash with anger. — 2. = blinken. — 3. *fig.* (fluchen) und wettern F to swear till all is blue. — 4. (sich blitzschnell bewegen) es ist mir ein Gedanke durch die Seele geblitzt a

Zeichen (s. S. XVII): F familiär, P Volkssprache, Γ Gaunersprache, ⟋ selten; † alt (auch gestorben); * neu (auch geboren); ⁓⁓ unrichtig,

[**Blitzzeile**] thought flashed through my mind. — II v/a. 5. to strike (down) like lightning; e-n zu Boden 2 to look a p. down. — III ~ n 23 6. (flashes pl. of) lightning; der Bajonette: gleam (of bayonets).

Blitzes=eile od. **=schnelle** (⌣…) f 62 rapidity of lightning; mit =eile with lightning-speed; as quick as (or like a flash of) lightning.

Blitz=häuschen (⌣…) n 62 phys. thunderhouse; **=junge**, **=kerl** F m bewundernd: smart (or capital) lad, fellow; devil of a boy, of a fellow; fine chap, brick; **=licht** n, phot., &c. magnesium light; **=mädchen**, **=mädel** n: a) smart (or buxom, nimble) girl or lass, F (a) treasure (or trump) of a girl; b) co. (Telegraphistin) telegraph-girl; **=pulver** n (Bärlappmehl) vegetable sulphur; witch-meal; **=röhre** f: a) min. durch den Blitz im Sandboden erzeugt: sand-tube, ⌒ fulgurite; b) phys., elect. zum Überspringenlassen elektrischer Funken: luminous tube; **=schlag** m = Blitz 2; auch: thunder-clap; **=schnell** a. 66 swift (or quick) as lightning, with lightning-speed; adv. er eilte 2 davon F he was off like a shot; **=röhre** s = **=röhre** a; **=stoff** m electric fluid, electricity; **=strahl** m flash of lightning; wie ein ~ aus heiterm Himmel like a bolt out of the blue; **=tafel** f, phys. luminous plate or pane; **=wenig** a. very little; **=zug** 🚂 m very fast train, express (train), F flier, flyer.

Block (⌣) [ndb.: block] m ⓒc., aber (Abreiß=)~ (s. ds) a. ⊛ 1. (Klotz, auch zum Fleischhacken, zur Hinrichtung u.) block; auf den ~ (aufs Schafott) bringen to take (or lead) to the block; kleinerer: log (of wood); ~ Blei, Eisen pig of lead, iron; ~ Seife bar of soap; ⊛ (Zwangblock) für Gefangene stocks pl.; in den ~ legen to put in the stocks; Schuhmacherei: tree, last. — 2. geol. erratischer ~ (Wanderstein) erratic block, boulder (=stone). — 3. fig. über Stock und ~ jagen to ride (or race) across country, (spornstreichs) to rush off at full speed or in mad career. — 4. ⊛ mech. und ⚓ (Rollkloben) pulley-block; ⚓ der ~ läuft auf dem Herd the sheave runs foul. — 5. (Spieleinsatz, Stammbete) pool. — Vgl. a. Abreiß=, Häuser=2, en bloc.

Blockade (⌣⌣) [+ fr.; *dtsch. Block] f 48 1. ⚓ blockade, (close) investment; die ~ durchbrechen, aufheben to run, raise the blockade. — 2. ⊛ typ. letter turned upside down, turned letter.

Blockade=brecher ⚓ (⌣⌣…) m ⊛ (Schiff) blockade-runner; **=geschwader** n blockading-squadron; **=zustand** m: einen Hafen ꝛc. in ~ erklären to declare the blockade of a port, &c.

Block=blei ⊛ (⌣…) n 62 metall. pig-lead; **=buch** n, mit Holzplatten gedruckt: block-book. [block, &c.]

Blöckchen (⌣…) n 23 [dim. v. Block] small]

Block=decke ⚓ (⌣…) f 62 cullion-head; **=druck** ⊛ m für Kattun ꝛc.: block-printing; **=eis** n ice in blocks; **=eisen** ⚓ n als Ballast: kentledge.

blocken¹ (⌣⌣) v/n. (h.) 88 von Raubvögeln: hunt. (sitzen) to perch (or sit) on a tree.

— 205 —

blocken², **blöcken** ⊛ (⌣⌣) v/a. 88 e-n Hut 2 (auf den Block spannen) to block…; Stiefel 2 to put (or stretch) boots on the boot-tree or the block, to block boots.

Block=haus (⌣…) n 62: a) arch. log-house- or hut; b) × frt. (Bollwerk aus Stämmen) block-house; **=holz** n log-wood; **=holzfloß** n, Am. log-raft.

blockieren (⌣⌣⌣) [fr.] I v/a. 88 ⚓ × eine Stadt ꝛc. 2 (einschließen) to blockade, to invest; ⊛ blockiertes Kapital money locked up (or invested) in business; Billard: e-n Ball 2 (ins Ceßloch schnellen) to pocket a ball; ⊛ typ. 2 (umgekehrt setzen) to set (type) upside down, to turn a letter. — II ~ n 23 u.

Blockierung f 66 blockade.

Block=karren (⌣…) m 62: ⊛ (heavy) cart, timber-wagon; (Handwagen) truck; **=lafette** × f, artill. (Geschützproße) devil-carriage; **=nagel** ⊛ m a) wooden peg; b) ⚓ pin of the block; **=rolle** ⊛ f pulley, block-sheave; **=säge** ⊛ f log- or pit-saw.

Blocks=berg ♀ (⌣…) npr/m. ⓒc. (Brocken, myth. Hexentanzplatz) Brocken.

Block=schiff ⚓ (⌣…) n 62 hulk of an old man-of-war (used as school-ship, hospital, guardship, &c.); **=schlitten** n Am. log-sledge; **=schrift** f, typ. = Egyptienne; **=(signal=)system** 🚂 n (Absperrsystem) block-system; **=strecke** 🚂 f (bestimmter Strecken zw. 2 Zügen) block; **=stück** × n (Rohmetall) pig; **=verband** m, arch. old English block-bond; **=wagen** m 🚂 (offener Güterwagen) lowry, truck; **=zinn** m blocktin.

Blöd=auge (⌣…) n 62 a) weak (or feeble, dim) sight, weak-eyed (or shortsighted) person; b) zo. ⌒ typhlops (Typhlops vermicula'ris); **=äugig** = **=sichtig**.

blöde (⌣⌣) [ahd.] a. 66 1. (schwach, zart) weak, delicate; 2 Augen haben to be weak- (or dim-) sighted. — 2. (zaghaft) ant. dreist) timid, shy; (ängstlich) nervous; (verschämt) abashed, bashful.

Blödigkeit (⌣⌣…) f 66 1. weak- (or dim-) sightedness. — 2. timidity, nervousness, bashfulness, diffidence.

blöd=sichtig (⌣…) a. 66 weak- (or dim-, short-)sighted, blear-eyed; purblind; **=sichtigkeit** f 66 weak- or short-)sightedness; fig. dulness of intellect; **=sinn** m imbecility, stärker: idiocy; (Unsinn) nonsense, absurdity; höherer ~ the height of folly, egregious (or pure) nonsense; reiner ~ F all rubbish or bosh; **=sinnig** a. imbecile, stärker: idiotic.

blöken (⌣⌣) [ndb.] v/n. (h.) 88 v. Rindern: to bellow, to low; v. Schafen: to bleat.

blond (⌣) [fr., *dtsch.] a. 66 fair(-haired), of (or with) fair (or light) hair (and complexion), fair-complexioned, bisw. blond(e); co. impertinent 2 red-haired, F ginger, sandy-coloured.

Blonde (⌣⌣) f 48 1. ⊛ ~n pl. (Spitzen) blond- (or silk-)lace. — 2. = Blondine. — 3. berlin. F co. fühle ~ (Weißbier) pint of white beer. [**=haarig** a. fair-haired.]

blond=gelockt (⌣…) a. 66 = ²lockig;

Blondin (⌣bg·) m 50, ~e (⌣⌣) f 48 fair (or light-haired) man (f woman); nur f (blondes Mädchen) fair-haired girl or woman, bisw. a. blonde.

[**Blüette**] **Blond=kopf** (⌣…) m 62 fair-haired child; ²lockig a. 66 with fair (or light) curls.

bloß (⌣) [ahd.] I a. 66 1. (weiter nichts als) plain, simple; im 2en Unterröckchen with nothing on but a petticoat; der 2e Anblick, Gedanke the mere (or very) sight, thought; die 2e Darstellung der Tatsachen the unvarnished statement of the facts; auf der 2en Haut tragen to wear next to the skin; 2er Neid pure envy; das 2e Schwert the naked sword. — 2. (unbedeckt) uncovered, (nackt) naked; mit 2em Auge with the naked …; auf der 2en Erde schlafen to sleep on the bare ground; mit 2en Füßen with bare feet, bare-footed; mit 2em Halse gehen, sich 2 tragen (von Frauen) to wear low (-necked) dresses pl.; mit 2em Haupte bare-headed; auf 2em Pferde (o. Sattel) reiten to ride bare-backed; bin nun selbst der Sünde (dat.) bloß (bloßgestellt) (G.) now my own sin has been laid bare. — 3. (bar) von aller Hilfe 2 deprived of all aid. — 4. mit Verben s. ²decken, ²legen ꝛc. — II adv. 5. (nur) simply, solely, barely; ich habe ihn 2 berührt I only just touched him; ich tue es 2 Ihnen zu Gefallen I do it only to please you or for your pleasure; F das ist 2 Spaß von ihm. (a. 2 sein Spaß) he is merely (or only) joking, F that's only (or nothing but) his fun; nicht 2 //, sondern auch // not only //, but also //; vgl. nur.

bloß=decken (⌣…) v/a. (u. v/refl. sich) ⊛** to uncover (o.s. or one's body).

Blöße (⌣⌣) f 48 1. (Nacktheit) nakedness, nudity (a. fig.); 2 (Mangel) bareness, (de)privation. — 2. (unbedeckte Stelle) × space exposed to (artillery-)fire, fire-zone; fenc., &c. unprotected (weit s. undefended) part; sich e-e ~ geben to lay o.s. open (to attack); to show one's weak side or point or part; gib dir keine ~! be on your guard!; fig. j-s ~ aufdecken to lay bare a p.'s faults, to expose (or unmask) a p. F to show a p. up.

bloß=füßig (⌣…) a. ⊛ wienerisch: barefooted; sich ²geben v/refl. ⊛c** to expose o.s.; fig. to commit o.s., F to give one's game away; ²legen v/a. ⊛** to lay bare; fig. Übelstände ꝛc. 2 to expose … (to the public gaze), to unearth, F to show up …; ~ n 23 exposure; **=liegen** n exposure; es liegt bloß am Tage it is manifest, clear; ²stellen v/a. ⊛** to put in an exposed position, to expose; ⊛ die Flanke 2 to expose one's flank (to the enemy); sich der Gefahr 2 to run into danger; sich dem Gelächter von … 2 to make o.s. the laughing-stock of …; wir haben den Schurken bloßgestellt we have unmasked the scoundrel; **=stellung** f 66 exposure; behufs Gelderpressung mit ~ bedrohen to blackmail.

blubbern F (⌣) [lautm.: blubber] v/a. (h.) 2 a. (hastig und verworren reden) to splutter; (gluckend fließen wie aus einer Flasche) to gurgle.

Blüette (⌣⌣) [fr.] f 48 (kleines witziges Bühnenstück) dramatic trifle, light farce, als Vorspiel: curtain-lifter.

♪ Musik; ⚛ Wissenschaft; ✿ Pflanze; ♀ Geographie; ⊛ Technik; × Bergbau; × Militär; ⚓ Marine; ⊛ Handel; ✉ Post; 🚂 Eisenbahn.

[blühen] — 206 — [Blut]

blühen (⌣́) [ahd.: blow] **I** v/n. (h.) ⊛ 1. to bloom, blossom, flower; (sich entfalten) to blow; die Kirschbäume ⌣ ... are in flower or in (full) bloom, show blossom; *fig.* der Handel ꝛc. blüht trade, &c. flourishes; ihr ⌣ vier Söhne she is blessed with four youthful sons; ihm hat das Glück wie wenigen geblüht, *etwa*: fortune lavished her favours (or smiled) upon him, he was fortune's minion. — 2. *bisw. v. Farben*: to be bright or brilliant; ⌣de Gesichtsfarbe florid complexion; *chm.* (auswittern): ⚬ to effloresce. — **II** ⌣ n ⊛ 3. bloom(ing), blossom(ing), flowering (season); *chm.*: ⚬ efflorescence. — 4. *fig.* prosperity. — **III** ⌣d *p.pr. u. a.* ⊛ 5. blooming, &c. (f. I); *fig.* flourishing; f. a. 2; e-e ⌣de Stadt a prosperous or thriving town; in ⌣sten Alter in the prime of life; in ⌣der Gesundheit in robust (or vigorous) health, hale and hearty, F in fine form. [nip.]

blüh-weiß (⌣́⌣) *a.* ⊛ Wäsche: (as) white as

Blümchen (⌣́⌣) *n* ⊛ *dim.* little flower, tiny blossom, floweret; *a.* = Blume 2e; ⌣**-kaffee** (ˊ...) *m* ⊛ weak coffee.

Blume (⌣́) [ahd.: bloom] *f* ⊛ **1.** flower (*a. fig.*), weitS. flowering plant; ⌣n malen, sticken auf // to diaper (up)on //; künstliche ⌣ artificial flower. — **2.** (Blumenartiges): **a)** (Duft feiner Weine) aroma(tic flavour), (fr.) bouquet; **b)** *fig.* (Auserlesenes) flower of chivalry, élite of society, pick of the army, best of the bunch; **c)** (Schaum) froth; ⌣ beim Biertrinken: ich komme dir meine ⌣! (den ersten Schluck), *etwa*: my first draught to you(r health)!; **d)** *chm.* † (fein Verteiltes): Schwefel-, Zink-⌣n *pl.* flowers of sulphur, of zinc; **e)** (weißer Fleck) f. Blesse; **f)** (Redensfloskel) flourish, flowery language, metaphor; *rhet.* trope, flower (or figure) of speech. — **3.** durch die ⌣ (verblümt) sprechen to speak figuratively or by the card. — **4.** *hunt.* **a)** beim Hasen: (Schwanz) tail; **b)** bei Wolf u. Fuchs: (Schwanzspitze) tip of the brush. — **5.** ⊛ Wollhandel: softest fleece.

Blümelei ⟍ (⌣⌣́) *f* ⊛ *rhet.* florid style.

Blüm(e)lein (⌣́⌣) *n* ⊛ *dim.* (pretty) little flower, vgl. Blümchen.

blümeln (⌣́) *v/n.* (h.) ⊛ *a.* **1.** to pick flowers; von Bienen ꝛc.: to flit from flower to flower. — **2.** *fig.* to speak (or write) in flowery language; to use flourishes or figures of speech.

blümen (⌣́) *v/a. u. v/refl.* ⊛ **1.** (sich) ⌣ to adorn (o.s.) with flowers. — **2.** *paint. u. Weberei*: to diaper.

Blumen-ampel (⌣́ˊ...) *f* ⊛ hanging (or pendant) flower-basket; ⌣**asch** *m* flower-pot; ⌣**ausstellung** *f* flower-show; ⌣**bau** *m* cultivation (or growing [of]) flowers, ⚬ floriculture; ⌣**beet** *n* flower-bed; ⌣**binde** *f* festoon; ⌣**binderei** *f* = Binderei; ⌣**binse** ⚘ *f* = Schwanenblume; ⌣**blatt** *n* leaf of a flower; (Kronenblatt) ⚘ petal; ⌣**blatt-los** *a.* ⊛: ⚬ apetalous; ⌣**brett** *n* shelf for flowers; vor dem Fenster: window-box; weitS.: flower-stand; ⌣**decke** *f*: ⚬ perianth; ⌣**duft** *m* fragrance (or perfume, scent) of flowers; ⌣**erde** *f* mould (for flowers);

⌣**fabrik** *f* artificial-flower factory; ⌣**fabrikant(in** *f*) *m* flower-maker; ⌣**fest** *n* flower-fête; ⌣**fliege** *f*, *ent.* ⚬ anthophilous fly; ⌣**flor** *m* show of flowers, weitS. flowering-season; ⌣**flur** *f*, *poet.* flowery meadow or field; ⌣**förmig** *a.* flower-shaped, ⚬ floriform; ⌣**freund** (-in *f*) *m* lover (or cultivator) of flowers, flower-fancier; ⚬ floriculturist; ⌣**garten** *m* flower-garden; ⌣**gärtner** *m* florist, horticulturist; ⌣**gehänge** *n* festoon, garland of flowers; ⌣**gestell** *n* flower-stand; ⌣**gewächs** *n* flowering plant; ⌣**gewinde** *n* = ⌣gehänge; ⌣**göttin** *f* goddess of flowers, Flora; ⌣**griffel** ⚘ *m*: ⚬ pistil; ⌣**händler(in** *f*) *m* florist; ⌣**honig** ⚘ *m* nectar; ⌣**hülle** *f* = Blüten-h.; ⌣**käfer** *m*, *ent.* ⚬ anthobian; ⌣**kelch** ⚘ *m*: ⚬ calix; ⌣**kenner** *m* (good) judge of flowers; ⌣**kohl** [nhd. 1600 vgl. Karfiol] ⚘ *m* cauliflower (Bra'ssica olera'cea botry'tis); ⌣**korb** *m* flower-basket; *arch.* corbel; ⌣**korso** *m* battle of flowers; ⌣**kranz** *m* wreath of flowers, chaplet; ⌣**krönchen** ⚘ *n* corollule, corollet; ⌣**krone** *f* crown of flowers, ⚘ corolla; ⌣**kübel** *m* tub (for a large plant or shrub); ⌣**lese** *f*: **a)** gathering (or picking) of flowers; **b)** *fig.* ⌣ aus Schriftstellern: selection, anthology; ⌣**liebhaber(in** *f*) *m* = ⌣freund(in); ⌣**liebhaberei** *f* fondness for flowers; ⌣**los** *a.* flowerless; ⌣**mädchen** *n* flower-girl; ⌣**maler(in** *f*) *m* painter of flowers; flower-painter; ⌣**malerei** *f* painting of flowers; ⌣**monat** *m* month of flowers, May; ⌣**muster** *n* floral pattern; ⚘ Stoff mit ⌣ figured material; ⌣**pfad** *m* flowery path, *poet. a.*: primrose path; ⌣**polyp** *m*, *zo.*: ⚬ anthozoon (Anthozo'um); ⌣**qualle** *f*, *zo.* ⚬ anthomedusa; ⌣**reich** *a.* abounding in flowers; *fig.* ⌣e reiche Sprache flowery (or high-flown) language; ⌣**reich** *n* kingdom of flowers; ⌣**reichtum** *m* flowerinesss; ⌣**rohr** ⚘ *n.* (indisches) ⚬ Indian cane (Canna i'ndica); ⌣**same** ⚘ *m* flower-seed; ⌣**sammlung** *f* collection of flowers; ⌣**scheide** ⚘ *f* sheath, ⚬ spathe, spatha; mit e-⌣ ⚬ versehen: ⚬ spathaceous; ⌣**scherbe(n** *m*) *f* = ⌣topf; ⌣**schirm** ⚘ *m*: ⚬ umbel; ⌣**schlacht** *f* = ⌣korso; ⌣**schmuck** *m* floral decoration; *arch.* floral work; ⌣**schnur** *f* festoon; ⌣**spiel** *n* floral game; ⌣**sprache** *f* language of flowers; ⌣**stab** ⚘ *m* = Stock a; ⌣**stand** ⚘ *m* inflorescence; ⌣**ständer** *m* = ⌣gestell; ⌣**staub** ⚘ *m*: ⚬ = Blüten-...; ⌣**stengel**, ⌣**stiel** ⚘ *m* stalk of a flower, ⚬ peduncle; ⌣**stielchen** ⚘ *n*: ⚬ pedicle; ⌣**stock** *m*: **a)** zum Anbinden v. Pflanzen: flower-stick; **b)** plant (or flower) in a pot; ⌣**strauß** *m* bunch (or bouquet) of flowers, nosegay; ⌣**stück** *n*: **a)** *hort.* flower-bed; **b)** *paint.* flower-piece; ⌣**tai** *n*, *poet.* vale of flowers, flowery vale; ⌣**tee** ⚘ *m* imperial tea; ⌣**tisch(en** *n*) *m* flower-stand; ⌣**topf** *m* flower-pot; ⌣**tragend** *a.* bearing flowers, blossoming, ⚬ floriferous; ⌣**vase** *f* flower-vase; ⌣**welt** ⚘ *f* flora; ⌣**werk** *n*, *arch.* floral work; ⌣**festons** *pl.*; ⌣**wut** *f* mania for flowers; ⌣**zeit** *f* flowering-time; ⌣**zieher** *m* florist; ⌣**zierat** *m* = ⌣schmuck; ⌣**zucht** *f*

floriculture; ⌣**zwiebel** ⚘ *f* flower-bulb. — Vgl. auch Blüten:...

blümerant F (-⌣⌣́) [fr. bleu mourant] *a.* ⊛ pale blue; mir ward ganz ⌣ vor den Augen I felt faint, I became quite dizzy.

blumicht, **blumig** (⌣́⌣) *a.* ⊛ (bunt von Blumen) gay with flowers, flowery.

blumieren ⊛ ⚘ (-⌣⌣́) [dtsch=lt.] *v/a.* ⊛ (mit Blumenmustern versehen) to work in flowery patterns.

Blumist (-⌣́) [dtsch=lt.] *m* ⊛, ⌣**in** *f* florist; ⌣**ik** (-⌣́) *f* ⊛ = Blumenzucht.

Blümlein (⌣́⌣) *n* ⊛ = Blümelein.

Blunder-büchse ehm. ⚔ ⚒ (ˊ⌣⌣́...) [ndl.] *f* ⊛ blunderbuss.

Bluse (⌣́) [fr. blouse] *f* ⊛ **a)** Damenoberkleid) blouse; **b)** (Kittel) smock.

Blüse ⚓ (⌣́) [dän.] *f* ⊛ (Feuerzeichen), (Leuchtturm) lighthouse, beacon; ⚬ lighthouse.

Blusen-mann (⌣́⌣...) [Bluse] *m* ⊛ labourer (in a smock), peasant.

Blust *provc. u. poet.* (⌣́) [ahd.: blossom: lt. flōs] *m* ⊙ b. = Blüte.

Blut[1] (⌣́) [ahd.: blood; *blühen] *n* ⊙ c. (o. pl.) **1.** blood; geronnenes ⌣ coagulated or clotted blood, gore (a. *poet.* allg. für Blut); *med.* cruor; da lag er in f-m ⌣ ... (swimming) in a pool of blood, covered with blood; es machte ihm das ⌣ in seinen Adern erstarren, gerinnen it made the blood curdle in his veins; das ⌣ stieg ihm ins Gesicht the blood rushed (or rose) to his face, flushed his face; ⌣ speien to spit blood; er tauchte seine Hände in ⌣ (a. *fig.*) he steeped ... in gore; Wangen wie Milch u. ⌣ cheeks like lilies and roses; *anat.* ⌣ führend ⚬ sanguiferous; zo. von ⌣ lebend ⚬ sanguivorous. — **2.** *fig.* (Sinnesart) das macht böses ⌣ it breeds ill blood or creates a bad feeling; er hat heißes ⌣ he has hot blood, a passionate (or hot) temper(ament); in mit kaltem ⌣e in cold blood; immer ruhig ⌣! don't be (too) hasty!, keep your temper!; sein ⌣ empörte sich (kochte) his blood was up (boiled); ⌣ schwitzen vor Angst ob. Unruhe: to be on hot irons or in dreadful suspense. — **3.** (das Leben) für et. mit seinem ⌣e einsteh(e)n to shed or give one's blood (or to lay down one's life) for a th.; Gut und ⌣ opfern to sacrifice everything; e-n bis aufs ⌣ peinigen to torment (or worry) a p. to death; sie schlugen ihn bis aufs ⌣ they beat him to within an inch of his life; in Fleisch und ⌣ (wirklich lebendig) umherwandeln F (auch co.) to walk in the flesh. — **4.** *bibl.* Fleisch und ⌣ (der biblische, sinnliche Mensch) flesh and blood. — **5.** (Totschlag) es ging nicht ohne ⌣ ab it did not end without bloodshed. — **6.** (Bluts-verwandtschaft, -verwandte[r]) Bande des ⌣es blood-relationship, family-ties *pl.*; von edlem (gutem) ⌣e of noble (good) blood or stock; sein eigenes Fleisch und ⌣ his own child or flesh and blood; vgl. Fleisch 1; das liegt im ⌣e it runs in the blood or in the family; Sprichw. das ⌣ verleugnet sich nicht, *etwa*: blood is thicker than water; Tierzüchterei: blood, breed, f. Vollblut. — **7.** (Person, mst mit *a.*) sie ist

Signs (see page XVII): F familiar; P vulgar; ꟾ flash; ⟍ rare; † obsolete (died); * new word (born); ⁒ incorrect; ♪ music;

[blut...] — 207 — [Blutreinigung]

noch ein junges ~ (Mädchen) F she is but a young creature, an innocent thing; das arme ~! F the poor dear! — 8. ~ (Saft) der Reben grape-juice.

blut²... (¹...) [blutt] f. Arm, Jung 2c. **Blut¹-abgang** (ᴵᴵ...) m ⓶ loss of blood; =**achat** m, min. blood-coloured agate, ⟨⟩ hemachate; =**acker** m, bibl. field of blood, Aceldama; =**ader** f vein; =**ähnlich** a. ⓺ =artig; =**ampfer** ⚘ m blood-wort (Rumex sangui'neus); =**andrang** m, path. congestion of blood to the head, &c.; =**apfelsine** ⚘ f blood-orange; =**arm** a.: path. of poor blood, stärker: bloodless; ⟨⟩ anæmic; ²**arm** (¹ˢ) a. (sehr arm) wretchedly poor, as poor as Job or as a church-mouse, (utterly) destitute; =**armut** (ᴵᴵ...) f, path. poorness (or deficiency) of blood, ⟨⟩ anæmia; ²**artig** a. blood-like, ⟨⟩ hematoid; =**auffrischung** f introduction of fresh blood into a stock (of cattle, &c.); =**auge** n a) path. bloodshot eye, ⟨⟩ hemophthalmia; b) ⚘ finger-fern (Co'marum palu'stre); ²**ausleerend** a. med.; ⟨⟩ depletive; =**austritt** m, med.: ⟨⟩ extravasation of blood; =**auswurf** m, path. spitting (or discharge) of blood, ⟨⟩ hemoptysis; =**bad** n, fig. carnage, butchery, massacre, slaughter; =**bann** m ehm. penal judicature; judicial power over life and death; =**baum** ⚘ m = Blauholzbaum; ²**bedeckt**, ²**befleckt** a. blood-stained, gory; =**behälter** m blood-vessel; ²**bespritzt** a. bespattered with blood; =**bewegung** f (Kreislauf) circulation of the blood; ²**bildend** a. physiol. forming blood, ²**es** Mittel blood-forming substance, ⟨⟩ sanguifier; =**bildner** m, physiol. (Eiweißkörper) albuminoid; =**bildung** f, physiol. formation of blood, ⟨⟩ hematosis, sanguification; =**blase** f bloodblister, path. encysted blood, ⟨⟩ hematocystis; =**blume** ⚘ f blood-flower (Haema'nthus); =**brechen** n, path. vomiting (or eruption) of blood, ⟨⟩ hematemesis; =**bruch** m, path.: ⟨⟩ hematocele; =**buche** ⚘ f copper-beach (Fagus sangui'nea); =**bühne** f scaffold (for executions).

Blütchen (¹ᴸ) n ⓶ dim. v. Blüte.

Blut-durst (ᴵᴵ...) m ⓶ blood-thirstiness; ²**dürstig** a. ⓺ bloodthirsty, sanguinary, murderous.

Blüte (¹ᴸ) [ahd.; * blühen] f ⓺ 1. ⚘, min. u. fig. meist: flower, bsd. v. Bäumen: blossom; in ~ stehen (ant. abblühen) to be in flower or bloom or blossom, to be flowering or blossoming; ⚘ auf ~en bezüglich floral. — 2. fig. flourishing (or prosperous, thriving) condition or state, prosperity; ~ des Alters vigour of (wo)manhood; in der ~ seines Glücks at the height (or summit) of his fortune; in der ~ der Jahre in the prime of life; ~ der römischen Jugend the flower (or élite, pick) of Roman youth(s). — 3. (Blütezeit) flowering-season, florescence; in der ~ geknickt nipped in the bud (a. fig.). — 4. path. (Bläschen) pimple, (Ausschlag) eruption.

Blut¹-egel (ᴵᴵ...) m ⓶ zo. leech, ⟨⟩ sanguisuge (Hiru'do medicina'lis); Familie der ~ ⟨⟩ bdelloidea; e-m ~ ansetzen to apply leeches to a p.; fig. bloodsucker, vampire; =**einflößung** f infusion (or transfusion) of blood.

bluten (¹ᴸ) [ahd.] ⓼ I v/n. (h.) 1. to bleed; an der Stirn, aus e-r Wunde ⟨⟩ to bleed from the forehead, from a wound; aus der Nase ⟨⟩ to bleed at the nose; ihr ⟨⟩ die Füße her feet are bleeding; fig. mir blutet das Herz bei diesem Anblick my heart bleeds (within me) at the sight of it; mit ²dem Herzen with a sore heart, deeply grieved. — 2. fürs Vaterland ⟨⟩ (sterben) to die (or to shed one's blood) for one's native land. — 3. fig. (Verluste erleiden) to suffer losses; er wird ⟨⟩ müssen ... have to pay or to suffer or to bleed; er soll mir dafür ⟨⟩! ... smart (or pay) for it! — II v/a. u. v/refl. 4. das Bett voll ⟨⟩ to fill the bed with (a pool of) blood; sich zu Tode oder tot ⟨⟩ to bleed (o.s.) to death. — III ~ n ⓶ 5. = Blutung.

Blüten-auge ⚘ (¹ᴸ...) f ⓺ =**knospe**; =**blatt** n: ⟨⟩ petal; =**boden** m receptacle; =**büschel** m tuft of flowers; =**decke** f: ⟨⟩ perianth; =**duft** m perfume of flowers; =**honig** m honey of blossoms and flowers; =**hülle** f: einfache ⟨⟩ perigone, von Doldenblüten 2c.: ⟨⟩ involucre; =**kätzchen** n catkin; =**kelch** ⚘ m ⟨⟩ calix; =**knospe** flower-bud; =**lese** f, fig. = Blumenlese; =**stand** m ⟨⟩ inflorescence; ²**ständig** a. ⓺ floral; =**staub** m: ⟨⟩ pollen; des Hopfens: ⟨⟩ lupulin(e); =**stecher** m, ent. (Käfer): ⟨⟩ anthonomus; =**stengel**, =**stiel** m flower-stalk, ⟨⟩ peduncle; ²**stiel-ständig** a. ⟨⟩ pedunculate; =**traube** f: ⟨⟩ raceme.

blut¹-entleerend (ᴵᴵ...) a. ⓺, ²**entziehend** a., =**entleerung** f ⓶, =**entziehung** f bleeding. [(violent) hemorrhage.]

Bluter (¹ᴸ) m ⓶ path. predisposed to

Blut¹-ergießung (ᴵᴵ...) f ⓶, =**erguß** m, path. effusion (or extravasation) of blood; ⟨⟩ hemorrhage.

Bluter-krankheit (¹ᴸ...) f ⓶ path. (Veranlagung zu gefährlichem Blutverlust) predisposition to (dangerous) hemorrhage, ⟨⟩ hem(at)ophilia.

blut¹-erzeugend (ᴵᴵ...) a. ⓺ = ²**bildend**; =**erzeugung** f = =**bildung**.

Blüte-zeit (¹ᴸ...) f ⓶: a) = Blüte 3; d) fig. ~ des Lebens spring of life.

Blut¹-farbe (ᴵᴵ...) f ⓶ blood-colour, (dark) crimson; ²**farben** a. ⓺, ²**farbig** a. = ²**rot**; =**farbstoff** m. chm.: ⟨⟩ hemochrome; =**fehde** f blood-feud; =**feind** m mortal foe, deadly enemy; =**fink** m, orn. bullfinch (Py'rrhula vulga'ris); =**flagge** ⚓ f red-flag, ⚓ bloody ancient; =**fleck** m blood-stain; ~en m/pl. bei Fieberkrankheiten path.: petechiæ, =**flecken-krankheit** f: a) path. purples pl., ⟨⟩ purpura; b) vet. der Pferde: ⟨⟩ petechial fever; =**fluß** m, path.: hemorrhage; ²**fremd** (¹ˢ) a. quite (or utterly) strange; eine ²**e** Person quite a (or a perfect) stranger; =¹**fülle** (ᴵᴵ...) f richness of blood, sanguineness, ⟨⟩ plethora; =**gefäß** n, anat. blood vessel; ²**gefäß** a. sanguiferous vessel; =**gefäßlehre** f, anat.: ⟨⟩ angiology; =**geld** n traitor's (or murderer's) wage or fee, bibl. price of blood; zur Sühne e-s Totschlages: fine for homicide, bei den Angelsachsen: weregeld, wergild; =**gericht** n = =**bann**; =**gerüst** n = =**bühne**; =**geschwür** n, path. blood(y) tumor, boil, ⟨⟩ furuncle, phlegmon; =**gier**(**igkeit**) f = =**durst**; ²**gierig** a. ⓺ = ²**dürstig**; =**hänfling** m, orn. linnet (Fringi'lla lino'ta); =**harnen** n, path. ⟨⟩ hematuria; =**herrschaft** f reign of blood; =**hirse** ⚘ f finger-grass (Pani'cum sanguina'le); =**hochzeit** f, hist. Pariser ~ (24.8.1572) (the Massacre of) St. Bartholomew; =**holz** ⓸ n Färberei: = Blauholz; =**hund** m: a) (Schweißhund) bloodhound; b) fig. (blutdürstiger Wüterich) sanguinary (or bloodthirsty) tyrant; =**husten** m coughing up blood, hemoptysis.

blutig (¹ᴸ) a. ⓺ 1. bloody, wegen seiner Verwendung als Fluchwort im feinen Stile zu ersetzen durch: blood-stained or -covered, bleeding, gory; wenig gebraten: half-raw, underdone (meat); ⟨⟩ machen to stain with blood; ⟨⟩ ein ⟨⟩ schlagen (beißen) to beat (bite) a p. till the blood flows or comes, till he bleeds. — 2. (blutgierig) sanguinary, bloodthirsty; ²**e** Schlachten, Taten sanguinary battles, deeds pl.; engl. hist. die ~e Marie Bloody Mary (1553–1558). — 3. fig. es war ihm ²**er** Ernst he was in deadly (or thorough) earnest; ²**e** Tränen weinen to shed bitter tears or (poet.) tears of blood. [hot-blooded.)

...**blütig¹** (...¹ᴸ) [Blut] a. ⓺, 3B. heiß-²)

...**blütig²** (...¹ᴸ) [Blüte] a. ⓺, 3B. lang-² flowering (or blossoming, in bloom) for a long time or period.

Blut-igel P (ᴵᴵ...) m ⓶ ⁂ = Blut-egel.

blutig-rot (¹ᴸ...) a. ⓺ blood-coloured, red as blood; f. a. blutrot.

blut²-jung (¹ˢ) a. ⓺ very young; =¹**klumpen** (ᴵᴵ...) m ⓶ = =**kuchen**; =**koralle** f red coral; =**körperchen** n blood-corpuscle, vgl. = =**kügelchen**; =**kraut** ⚘ n (blutstillende od. blutrote Pflanze) sanguinary (3B. amaranth), ⟨⟩ =**kreislauf** m, physiol. circulation of the blood; =**kuchen** m, physiol. clot of blood, ⟨⟩ crassamentum; =**kügelchen** n, physiol. blood-globule; =**lassen** n, surg. blood-letting; =**lauf** m = =**fluß**; =**laugensalz** n, chm.: gelbes ~ (Ferroxyantalium) potassium ferrocyanide (K4 Fe[CN]₆); rotes ~ (Ferrixyantalium) potassium ferricyanide (K₆Fe₂[CN]₁₂); ²**leer** a. = ²**arm** a.; =**leere** f, =**leerheit** f = =**armut**.

...**blütler** ⚘ (...¹ᴸ) [Blüte] m ⓶, 3B. Lippen-²; ⟨⟩ labiate.

Blütling ⚘ (¹ᴸ) m ⓭ (Pilz) orange agaric (Aga'ricus delicio'sus).

blut-los (ᴵᴵ...) a. ⓺ bloodless; =**losigkeit** f ⓶; =**mangel** m = =**armut**; =**masse** f mass of blood; =**mehl** n (powdered) dry blood; =**mensch** m = =**hund** b; =**rache** f revenge for homicide or murder; weitS. murderous revenge, (it.) vendetta; =**rächer** m avenger of murder or bloodshed; =**regen** m (durch eine Alge, Palme'lla prodigio'sa, veranlaßt) blood-rain; =**regierung** f = =**herrschaft**; ²**reich** a. path. sanguine, ⟨⟩ plethoric; ²**reinigend** a. med. purifying the blood; =**reinigung** f, med. purification

⟨⟩ scientific; ⚘ botanical; ⚲ geography; ⊖ machinery; ⚒ mining; ⚔ military; ⚓ marine; ⊛ commercial; ⚒ postal; 🚂 railway.

[Blutreinigungsmittel] — 208 — [Bocksprung]

of the blood; =reinigungs=mittel n, med. purifier of the blood, ⚕ depurative medicine, abluent, purgative; =richter m criminal judge; =rinne ⚔ f an Stoßwaffen: fullering; ²rot a. red as blood, blood-red, crimson, sanguineous, poet. incarnadine; =rot n, physiol. ⚕ hemochrome; =ruhr f, path. dysentery; ²rünftig a. running with blood, bleeding; e-n ⚔ schlagen to deal a p. blows which draw blood or cause blood to flow; ²sauer (¹·ᵘ·) a. fig. most difficult or laborious, es sich ⚔ w. l. to drudge like a slave, F to work like a nigger; F to sweat at a th.; =sauger (¹·...) m blood-sucker (a. fig.); vgl. a. =egel u. Vampir; =saugerei f bloodsucking (auch fig.); vampirism; (Erpressung) extortion; =schande f incest; =schänder(in f) m incestuous person; =schänderisch a. incestuous; =schlag m. path. (Schlagfluß) apoplectic fit; =schuld f blood-guiltiness; eine ~ auf sich laden to commit (or make o.s. guilty of) homicide; =schwamm ⚔ m hepatic fistulina (Fistuli'na hepa'tica); =schwäre (n m) f = =geschwür; =schweiß m, bibl. bloody sweat; ²²selten (¹·ᵘ·) a. u. adv. very rare(ly), of very rare occurrence.
Bluts=freund (¹·...) m 𝔐² kinsman; =freundin f kinswoman; =freundschaft f blood-relationship, consanguinity.
Blut¹=spat (¹·...) m 𝔐² vet. blood-spavin; =speien, =spucken n = =auswurf; =spur f track (or mark) of blood; =stätte f scene of bloodshed or of a murder; =stein m, min. (Roteisenerz) blood-stone; (red) hematite; ²stillend a. med. stanching blood, ⚕ styptic, hemostatic; ²es Mittel styptic; =stockung f stagnation of blood; =strieme(n m) f wale, red bruise, ⚕ suggillation; =strom m stream (or flow) of blood.
Bluts=tröpfchen ⚘ (¹·...) n 𝔐² pheasant's-eye (Ado'nis autumna'lis); =tropfen m: a) drop of blood; b) ent. (Dämmerungsfalter) burnet-moth or -fly (Zygae'na).
Blut¹=sturz (¹·...) m 𝔐² path. eruption of blood, hemorrhage, einen ~ haben, oft: to break a blood vessel.
bluts=verwandt (¹·...) a. 𝔐² (closely) related to; consanguineous; ~e(r) m, e~ 𝔐⁷ = =freund(in); ~schaft f 𝔐² kinship, vgl. =freundschaft.
blutt prov. (ᵛ) [ahd.] a. 𝔐² (nackt) ²und bloß naked and bare, in a state of nudity.
Blut=tat (¹·...) f 𝔐² deed of blood, sanguinary act; =taufe f baptism of blood, blood baptism; ⚔ das Regiment erhielt seine ~ the regiment was blooded; ²triefend a. 𝔐² dripping (or reeking) with blood; =überfüllung f physiol.: ⚕ hyperæmia; ²überströmt a. covered (or streaming) with blood, vgl. ²triefend; =umlauf m (Kreislauf des Blutes) circulation of the blood.
Blutung (¹·ᵛ) f 𝔐⁶ bleeding (a. v. Pflanzen u. fig.); loss (or flow) of blood, path.: ⚕ hemorrhage.
blut¹=unterlaufen (¹·...) a. 𝔐² path. suffused with blood, bloodshot; =unterlaufung f 𝔐² path. extravasation of blood, ⚕ ecchymosis; =urteil n

sentence of death; =vergießen n bloodshed, vgl. =bad; ohne ~ without bloodshed, bloodless (victory); =vergiftung f, path. blood-poisoning, ⚕ pyæmia; =verlust m loss of blood; =wärme f (ca. 37,5⁰ C.) bloodheat; =wasser n, physiol.: ⚕ lymph, serum; =wassergefäße n/pl. lymphatic ducts, serous vessels pl.; ²wässerig a. lymphatic, serous; =wässerigkeit f serosity; =weiderich ⚘ m purple loosestrife (Lythrum Salica'ria); =welle f rush of (the) blood, eine zarte ~ flog ihr über das Gesicht a slight flush suffused (or passed across) her countenance; ²²wenig (¹·ᵘ·) a. wretchedly little or few; =wolle f 𝔐 carrion- (or fell-)wool; =wurst f black-pudding; =wurz ⚘ f blood-wort or -dock (Potenti'lla tormenti'lla); =zeuge m, =zeugin f martyr; =zwang m, path. dysenteric spasm.
B=Moll (¹·ᵘ·) n f. B. (Ruhr) dysentery.
Bö ⚓ (¹) [ndd.] f 𝔐⁶ sudden squall.
Boa (¹·ᵛ) [it., *brasil.] f 𝔐⁶: a) zo. (Schlange) boa, bsd. boa constrictor; b) a. m 𝔐 (Damenhalsbekleidung) boa.
Boberell ⚘, ~e (·⚔·) [tschech.] f 𝔐⁶ = =Judentirsche.
Bobine ⚔ (¹·ᵛ) [fr.] (Spule) bobbin, drum.
Bobinet ⚔ (¹·ᵛ·) [engl.] m 𝔐 Weberei: bobbinet, bobbin-net.
Bochara ⚓ (·ᵗ·ᵛ·) [türk.] npr/n. 𝔐 a. (Stadt und Khana't in Turkesta'n) Bokhara.
Bock¹ (ᵛ) [ahd.: buck] m 𝔐b. 1. zo. (Männchen von Kaninchen, Hasen, Rehen etc.) buck; von Ziegen: he-goat, F billy-goat; von Schafen: ram; fig. den ~ zum Gärtner machen, setzen to set a fox (or wolf) to mind the geese or sheep. — 2. F fig. steifer ~ clumsy person, awkward fellow, F clumsy Dick; vgl. bocksteif; co. (Schneider) snip; weinen, schluchzen, daß einen der ~ stößt oder als ob einen der ~ stieße (stoßweise, krampfhaft) to cry (or sob) violently or convulsively, F to blubber one's heart out. — 3. (Purzelbock) (heavy) fall, F cropper; einen ~ schießen: a) (purzeln) to fall, tumble, sprawl, to turn a somersault; b) [nhd. ("Verstoß": der ~ stößt)] fig. (ein Versehen m.) to make a mistake, to blunder, to go on the wrong track, F to get into hot water, to put one's foot in (it). — 4. (erhöhter Sitz) high stool; (Kutschersitz) box, driver's (or coachman's) seat; vom ~ aus fahren to drive from the box or two- (four-, &c.) in-hand; per ~ (als blinder Fahrgast) mitfahren to get a drive (or ride) for nothing, bsd. ebm. to play the buck. — 5. ~ zu Turnübungen: (wooden) horse; ~ springen über eines andern Rücken: to play leap-frog. — 6. ⚒ (Stoßmaschine) (Sturm)~ (battering-)ram, (Ramm)~ rammer, (Gestell) platform, jack; für Wäsche, Kleider: clothes-horse; (Brückenbock) trestle; (Feuerbock) andiron; ⚒ Billard: (Krücke oder Handstellung zur Stütze des Stoßtockes) bridge; carp.: (Hänge)=truss; zum Sägen: saw-frame or gate; jack; (Winde für Lasten) capstan, windlass. — 7. ehm. (Folterwerkzeug) e-n in den ~ spannen, legen to put a p. in(to) the

stocks, to tie a p.'s arms and legs together; to buck a p.
Bock² F (ᵛ) m 𝔐b, 6. = Bockbier (s. ds).
bock¹=beinig (ᵛ·...) a. 𝔐 goat-footed, bow- (or bandy-) legged; fig. stubborn.
Bock²=bier (ᵛ·...) [nhd. 19.sae. „aus (Ein)beck", St.] n 𝔐² kind of strong lager- (or Bavarian) beer, ⚔ bock-beer.
Bock¹=brücke ⚒ (ᵛ·...) f 𝔐² trestle-bridge.
Böckchen (¹·ᵛ) n 𝔐b. [dim. von Bock] kid.
Bock¹=decke ⚒ (ᵛ·...) f 𝔐² einer Kutsche: hammer cloth.
bocken (¹·ᵛ) [mhd.] v/n.(h.) ⚒ 1. (stark riechen oder schmecken) to have a goaty (or ⚕ a hircine) smell or taste, to smell (or taste) after (or like) a goat. — 2. (Bocksprünge machen) to skip like a goat; von Pferden: to capriole, (den Kopf senken und hinten ausschlagen, bsd. v. Prairiepferden Am.) to buck, to butt. — 3. fig. v. Menschen: (trotzen) to show o.s. refractory, (schmollen) to sulk. — 4. ⚓ v. Schiffen: (stampfen) to pitch, to heave.
Bock¹=fell (ᵛ·...) n 𝔐² goatskin; =geruch m goatish smell, vgl. Bocks=g.; =gestell ⚒ n Wagenbau: body (or frame) of a coach; ⚔ frt. für Faschinen: chandelier; =hochsprung m Turnerei: high jump on the horse; =hüpfen n = =springen.
bockig (¹·ᵛ) a. 𝔐 1. (stinkend) having a goaty (or ⚕ hircine) smell, vgl. böckisch. — 2. = bock=steif, bocks=ähnlich. — 3. (störrisch) stubborn.
böckisch (¹·ᵛ) a. 𝔐 rammish, ⚕ hircinous, vgl. bockig 1.
Bock¹=käfer (ᵛ·...) m 𝔐² ent. capricorn beetle (Cera'mbyx); longicorn; =kasten ⚒ m coach-boot; =kissen n e-s Wagens: box-cushion; =leder n goat's leather, dressed goatskin; ²ledern a. made of goat's skin or goatskin; fig. pedantic, dry; =leiter f double ladder, (pair of) steps pl.; =mühle f German windmill on trestles; =pfeife ⚔ f bagpipe.
bocks=ähnlich (ᵛ·...) a. 𝔐, ²artig a.: ⚕ hircine, ⚘ u. zo. a.: ⚕ hircinous; =bart m 𝔐 goat's beard ⚘ goat's-beard, salsify (Tragopo'gon); =beutel m: a) [oben] (lederne Weinflasche) pouch-shaped wine-bottle; b) [corr. aus ndd. = Buch(s)=beutel (Bibeltasche)] F (Schlendrian) old-fashioned custom or form; easy jog-trot; =beutelei F f fondness for antiquated observances; ²beutelig F a. old-fashioned, pedantic; =distel f ⚘ =dorn m = Tragant. [sulphuretted hydrogen.]
böcksein (¹·ᵛ·) v/n. 𝔐a. v. Wein: to taste of⟩
Böcker (¹·ᵛ) m 𝔐² (nach Schwefelwasserstoff schmeckender junger Wein) newly fermented wine tasting of sulphuretted hydrogen or rotten eggs.
Bocks=geile(n m) f 𝔐² ⚘ (¹·...) ⚘ (Orchis=art) satyrion (Saty'rium); =geruch m rank (or ⚕ hircine) smell; =horn n goat's horn; fig. e-n ins ~ jagen (einschüchtern) to intimidate (F to bully) a p.; to scare a p. (out of his wits).
Bock¹=spiere ⚓ (ᵛ·...) f 𝔐² sheer-leg; =springen n leap-frog; vgl. Bock 5; =sprung m skipping, v. Pferden: buck-jump, bucking, als Spiel: leap-frog; von Menschen: =sprünge tun, machen to cut capers (in the air), to gambol (like a young kid).

Zeichen (s. S. XVII): F familiär; P Volkssprache; Γ Gaunersprache; ⚔ selten; † alt (auch gestorben); * neu (auch geboren); ⊹⊹ unrichtig.

[bockſteif] — 209 — [Bogenſchutz]

bock¹-ſteif (ˇ...) F a. ⓖ as stiff as a poker; -verſtellung ⊕ f, arch. scaffolding-trestle; -windmühle ⊕ f = -mühle.
Boden (⌣) [ahd.: bottom: lt. fundus] m mit ⑳, bff. ㉓ 1. (Grund unter den Füßen) ground, soil; ſich auf den ~ legen to lie down on the ground; auf dem ~ liegen to lie on the ground; auf Gottes (Erd-)~ here below, on this earth; auf dem bloßen ~ ſchlafen oder übernachten to sleep on the bare ground or floor; Zimmer auf eb(e)nem ~ ... on the ground-floor; (feſten) Boden faſſen to get a (firm) footing; dem (Erd-)~ gleich machen to raze to the ground, to (make) level with the ground. — 2. (Land) Grund und ~ beſitzen to have landed property, to own real estate; fruchtbarer, unfruchtbarer, jungfräulicher ~ fertile, barren, virgin soil. — 3. (untere Fläche) ~ eines Faſſes bottom of a cask or barrel; dem Faſſe den ~ ausſtoßen to knock the bottom out of (or to stave in) a cask, fig. to take all the strength (or life) out of a th.; to put an end to a th.; einem Faſſe den ~ einſetzen to head (or bottom) a cask; kegelförmiger ~ einer Flaſche kickup of a bottle; (Fuß-)~ einer Stube aus Brettern boarded floor; getäfelter ~ inlaid floor; aus Stein: stone floor; mit Moſaikverzierung: tessellated floor; ~ e-s Schiffes ship's bottom; Koch.: ~(teig) e-r Paſtete bottom- (or under-)crust; Gefäß ꝛc. mit flachem ~ flat-bottomed ... — 4. nordd. (Raum unter dem Dache) top room, loft, vgl. ~kammer; fig. Korn auf dem ~ haben to have something put by (for a rainy day), to be well off or in clover. — 5. fig. e-m ~ abgewinnen to gain on a p., to outrun (or outstrip) a p.; der ~ brennt ihm unter den Füßen (er kann nicht dort bleiben) the place (or it) is getting too hot for him (there), he is burning to get away; e-n unter den ~ (ins Grab) bringen to carry a p. into his grave, to bury a p.; ſich auf den ~ des Geſetzes ſtellen to put o.s. under the protection (or to keep within the bounds) of the law; ~ gewinnen, verlieren to gain, to lose ground; (Standpunkt) point of view; (Grundlage) foundation; base, basis; einer Behauptung den ~ entziehen to knock the bottom out of a statement; auf dem ~ der Erfahrung on the basis of experience; auf dem ~ der Wiſſenſchaft in the realm of science; Sprichw. Handwerk hat gold(e)nen ~, etwa: a trade to lie on the ground, to hold gold in every land. — 6. in (auch aus) Grund und ~ (ganz und gar) gut, ſchlecht thoroughly (or extremely) good, bad; in Grund und ~ faul rotten to the core; zu ~ (nieder) drücken to press down; fig. to overwhelm; zu ~ ſchlagen to knock down; fig. to crush, overpower; es ſchlug ſ-e Hoffnungen zu ~ it upset, destroyed his hopes; die Augen zu ~ ſchlagen to cast down one's eyes; zu ~ ſinken to sink down, to fall to the ground, to topple over; zu ~ ſtrecken, werfen to knock (or bowl) over, F to floor.

Boden-art (⌢...) f ⓖ nature of the soil; -bearbeitung f cultivation of the soil, husbandry; -beſchaffenheit f quality of the soil; -beſitz m landed (or real) property; -(beſitz)reform f agrarian reform; -beſtandteile m/pl. chm. constituents pl. (or components pl.) of the soil; -bildung f (geological) formation of the soil; -blütig a. ⓖ: ℒe Pflanzen ♀ thalamiflorous plants pl.; -druck m e-r Flüſſigkeit upward pressure; -erhebung f rising (or elevated) ground; ⚓ frt. (Geländewelle) (fr.) rideau; -ertrag m produce of the soil; -fenſter n top-room (or attic-)window; -geſchoß n, arch.: a) ground-floor; b) (Dach-etage) top floor; -holz ⊕ n Böttcherei: heading; -kammer f garret, attic; -kredit m credit on landed property; -kreditanſtalt f, -kreditbank f land-mortgage bank; -kunde f knowledge of the properties of the soil; -loch n = -fenſter; ℒlos a. bottomless, fig. unfathomable; excessive; ℒloſe Tiefe abysmal depth, abyss, chasm, bibl. (Hölle) bottomless pit; fig. ℒloſer Jammer untold (or indescribable) misery; ℒloſer Leichtſinn boundless levity; adv. ℒ dumm exceedingly (or unutterly) stupid; ℒ unwiſſend ignorant beyond measure; -luke f = -fenſter; -melioration f (Umwandlung in Kulturland) amelioration of the soil, bringing land under the plough; -müdigkeit f (Verſagen eines Bodens für beſtimmte Pflanzenarten) exhaustion of the soil; -raum m garret, loft; -reform f = -beſitzreform; -rente f ground-rent; -riegel ⊕ am Wagen, -rippe ⚓ e-s Schiff bottom bar; -ſatz m, chm. &c. sediment; (Kaffeeſatz ꝛc.) grounds pl. of coffee, &c.; (Hefe) feculence; dregs, lees pl. of beer, wine, &c., dunder of cane-sugar; -ſchicht f, geol. lowest stratum, bottom layer; -ſee ♀ [Bodman, chm. Kaiſerpfalz] n pr./m. Lake of Constance; ℒſtändig a.: a) v. d. Bevölkerung: (ſeßhaft) permanent; b) ♀ receptacular, ⚓ hypogynous; -ſtein ⊕ m e-r Mühle: nether millstone, bedder, bedstone; ℒſtet ♀ a. v. Pflanzen: (ausſchließlich auf beſtimmten Bodenarten zu finden) peculiar to certain kinds of soil; -ſtück ⊕ n Böttcherei: bottom piece; ⚔ artill. (hinterer Teil der Geſchützrohre mit dem Verſchluß) breech-piece; -teig m ſ. Boden 3; -treppe f stairs leading to a loft or an attic, garret-staircase; -ventil ⊕ n, mach. foot-valve, bottom blow-valve; -verhältniſſe n/pl. conditions pl. of the soil or of landed property; weitS. rural affairs pl.; -wohnung f rooms pl. (or apartments pl.) on the top floor; attic floor; -zacken ⊕ m metall. bottom-plate.
bodmen, böbmen (⌣) [Boden] v/a. ⓑ.
1. ⊕ ein Faß ꝛ. to bottom, to head.
2. ⚓ ein Schiff ♀ (verpfänden) to raise money on bottomry.
Bodmerei ⊕ u. ⚓ (-⌣) [nbd.: bottom-ry] f ⓖ (Schiffsverpfändung) bottomry, gross adventure, jur. ~ auf die Schiffs-ladung (loan in) respondentia pl.; Geld auf ~ geben, außtun to advance, to lend money on bottomry.

Bodmerei-brief (-⌣...) m ⓖ bottomry-bond or -letter; letter (or bill) of bottomry; -prämie f premium of bottomry; -vertrag m = -brief.
Boſiſt ♀ (⌣) [nbd. Bubenfiſt] m ⓒ. puff-ball (Lycope'rdon bovi'sta); grauer ~ (Bovi'sta plu'mbea).
bog (¹) (u. böge subj.) impf. von biegen.
Bögelchen (⌣⌣) u. Bög(e)lein (¹(ˇ)-) n ㉓ dim. v. Bogen.
Bogen (⌣) [ahd.: bow;* biegen] m, oft ⑳, bff. ㉓ (vgl. 7) 1. (Gebogenes) bow, bend, (Krümmung) curvature, curve (d line); e-s Fluſſes ꝛc.: bend, turning, winding; Schlittſchuhlauf: ~ ſchlagen, ſchneiden, fahren to cut (or make) figures (on the ice). — 2. math. e-s Kreiſes: arc, allg. curve; einen ~ von 60⁰ ſchlagen, beſchreiben to describe (or construct) an arc of 60 degrees; ſpitz, ſtumpf-winf(e)liger ~ arc containing an acute, obtuse angle. — 3. ehm. Waffe: bow; langer: long-bow; vgl. Armbruſt; (Flitz-)~ boy's bow; mit Pfeil und ~ ſchießen to shoot with bow and arrows; den ~ ſpannen to bend (or draw, pull) the (long-)bow; fig. den ~ hoch ſpannen to aim high; mehr als eine Sehne zu ſ-m ~ haben to have many strings to one's bow. — 4. ⊕ arch. arch, vault; (Spitzbogen) ogive; überhöhter ~ stilted arch; ~ einer Brücke arch of a bridge; (ſich) als ~ wölben to arch. — 5. ⊕ ~ am Sattel (saddle-)bow; ~ e-r Brille bridge; elektriſcher ~ Voltaic arc. — 6. ♪ (Fiedel-)~ (violin-)bow, co. fiddlestick; mit dem ~ ſpielen to play with the) bow. — 7. ⒵6. (abbr. Bg.) ~ Papier sheet of paper; ein halber ~ half a sheet. — 8. in Bauſch und ~ ſ. Bauſch 2.
bogen-artig (⌣⌣...) a. ⓖ arched, bow-shaped, arch-like; ⚗ arcuate; (gewölbt) vaulted; -bezeichnung f ♪, typ. = -zahl; -bohrer ⊕ m bow-drill; -brücke ⊕ f, arch. arched (or arch-)bridge, bridge built with arches; viaduct; -dach n arched roof; -decke f vaulted ceiling.
Bog(e)ner ♔ ⊕ (¹(ˇ⌣)) m ㉒ = Bogen-macher; poet. (Bogenträger) ſ. Silber2.
Bogen-fenſter (⌣⌣...) n ⓖ bay-, bow-window; -form f, arch. arched shape; vault; ⚗ arcuation; ℒförmig a. — ℒartig; -führung ♪ f bowing, handling (or management) of the bow; er hat e-e gute ~ he bows well; -gang m, arch. arcade; (Verbindungsgang) archway; -gerüſt n centring, scaffold for vaulting; -gewölbe n (arched) vault; -größe f ⓑ Buches: folio (size); -gang = instrument n instrument played with a bow, weitS. string-instrument; -laube f arched arbour; -(licht)lampe f, -licht n ⊕ elect. arc-lamp, arc-light; -linie f circular line, curved (or sinuous) line; -macher ⊕ m bowyer; -maß n, math. circular measure of an angle; -pfeiler m, arch. arched (or flying) buttress, arch-pier; -rippe f rib (or nerve) of a vault; -ſäge ⊕ f bow-saw; -ſchießen n archery; -ſchlegel m Hutm. bow-bat; -ſchluß m, arch. keystone; -ſchreiber m copyist; -ſchutz m bow-

♪ Muſik; ⚗ Wiſſenſchaft; ♀ Pflanze; ♁ Geographie; ⊕ Technik; ⚒ Bergbau; ⚔ Militär; ⚓ Marine; ⚖ Handel; ✉ Poſt; 🚂 Eiſenbahn.

[bogig] — 210 — [Bolzen]

shot; =artill. (Steilfeuer) high-angle fire; =schußweite f bow-shot range; =schütz(e) m ebm. archer; bowman; =schützenkunst f (art of) archery; =schützenverein m archery- (or toxophil(it)e) club; =sehne f bowstring; =seite ⊕ f, typ. folio page; =spanner m bender; =sprung m, man. (kurzer Galopp) curvet, pannade; =stellung f, arch. arcade; ⚔ arcuation; =strebe f, arch. arch-brace; =strich ♪ m = führung; =sturz m, arch. arched cap-piece; =tür f, arch. arched (or vaulted) door; ♀weise adv.: a) arch. in arches, archwise; b) von Papier: by the sheet; =werk n = =stellung; =zahl f, =zeichen n, typ. signature; =zirkel ⊕ m bow compasses pl.; =züge ⚔ m/pl. curved rifling sg.

bogig (⸗⸍) a. ⓖ arched; curved.

Böglein f. Bögelein f. Bogener.

Bohle ⚓ (⸗⸍) [udd. (mhd.): bole Baumstamm] f ⊛ (5-10 cm dick; ant. Brett) thick plank or board; (eichene Planke zum Schiffbau ꝛc.) oaken board, thick stuff, (fr.) madrier; mit ~n belegen od. **bohlen** (⸗⸍) v/a. ⊛ to plank. to board.

Bohlen=belag ⊕ (⸗⸍…) m ⑭ carp. planking, e-s Rostes: plank-bottom of a grate; =bogen m (Bogenträger einer Decke) curbplate; =dach n plank-roof; =wand f timber-wall(ing); =weg m plank-way.

Bohl=werk (⸗⸍) n ⓖ (Bollwerk) mound (or dyke) supported by powerful planks and piles, am Strande a sea-defence.

Böhme (⸗⸍) m ⓚ. **Böhmin** f ⓚ Bohemian. [Österreichs] Bohemia.]

Böhmen ♀ (⸗⸍) npr/n. ⓚα. (Kronland)

Böhmer=wald ⚓ (⸗⸍…) m (Gebirge) Bohemian Forest or Mountains pl.; (böhm.) Bœhmerwald.

böhmisch (⸗⸍) a. ⓖ Bohemian; eccl. ~e Brüder m/pl. Bohemian (or United) Brethren pl.; vgl. a. Mährische Brüder u. Herrnhuter; die ⚔e (r-r tschechische) Sprache the Czech language; fig. das sind mir ⚔e Dörfer F that's Greek (or double Dutch) to me.

Bohn=axt ⊕ (⸗⸍…) f ⓖ smoothing-axe; =bürste f rubbing- (or polishing-)brush.

Böhnchen (⸗⸍) n ⓐ. dim. v. Bohne.

Bohne¹ ♀ (⸗⸍) ⊛ ⓚ. ♢ bean; gemeine oder welsche ~ kidney-bean (Phaseolus vulga'ris); türkische ~ French bean, scarlet runner (Ph. multiflo'rus). — 2. hort. Kocht. … grüne ~n French beans pl.; dicke ~n (Saubohnen) broad beans pl. (von Vi'cia Faba); (trockene) weiße ~n haricot beans pl.; fig. keine ~ wert F not worth a straw or a rush or a farthing. — 3. (Bohnenförmiges) fig. blaue ~ (Flintenkugel) ⚔ co. blue pill.

Bohne² ♀ (⸗⸍) [ar. bunn(i) Kaffee²] f ⊛ Kaffee in ~n ungground coffee(-berries).

bohnen ⊕ (⸗⸍) [udd.: Bühne] v/a. ⊛ join. to polish, to varnish; den Fußboden ♀ to wax (or polish) the floor.

Bohnen=baum ♀ (⸗⸍…) m ⊛ (Goldregen; =erz n. min. = =Bohn=erz; =fest n am Dreikönigstag: bean-feast; =hülse f bean-pod; =kraut ♀ n savory, beantressel (Sature'ia horte'nsis); =kuchen m Twelfth(night) cake; =lied n: das geht übers ~ (ist zu arg) that's too much of a good thing, that's beyond all

bounds; =mehl n bean-flour or -meal; =ranke f bean-stalk; =stange f beanpole; F fig. (lange dürre Person) F lamppost, maypole. longshanks; =strauch ♀ m = Goldregen; =stroh n bean-straw; fig. grob wie ~ very rude or coarse; =suppe f haricot-soup.

Bohner ⊕ (⸗⸍) m ⓖ. ~in f ⓖ polisher (or waxer) of floors.

Bohn¹**=erz** (⸗⸍…) [Bohne¹] n ⓖ (törniger Toneisenstein) pea- (or bean-)ore.

Bohn²**=lappen** (⸗⸍…) [bohnen] m ⓖ flannel rag for polishing the floor; =wachs n rubbing-(or polishing-)wax.

Bohr (⸗⸍) m ⓒ. = Bohrer.

Bohr=arbeit (⸗⸍…) f ⓖ boring (operations pl.); =bank f: a) Büchsenm.: boring bench; b) Drechslerei: drilling lathe; c) der Bohrmaschine: drilling bench; =brunnen m Artesian well; =eisen n boring or auger-)bit.

bohren (⸗⸍) [ahd.: bore: lt. (per)fora're] ⊛ I v/a. u. v/refl. 1. to bore, to drill; einen Tunnel ♀ to drive a tunnel, to tunnel; Käfer ♀ sich in das Holz ... bore (or work their way) into the wood; ♣ ein Schiff in den Grund ♀ to sink (or scuttle) a ship; e-m den Dolch durch den Leib ♀ to run one's dagger through a p.('s body); fig. er mag feine harten Bretter ♀ he likes easy work or his ease. — II v/n. (h.) 2. Würmer ♀ in der Erde ... bore (or dig) in the earth; er bohrt gern in der Nase he is fond of picking his nose. — 3. fig. (quälen) an e-m ♀ to worry (or bore) a p.; die Sachen ♀ mir im Kopfe ... are never out of my head, ... are (for ever) worrying me; ihre Worte bohrten sich ihm tief in die Seele her words sank deep down into his soul or went right home; ♀der Schmerz gnawing pain. — III ~ n ⓤ 4. = Bohrung 1.

Bohrer (⸗⸍) m ⓖ 1. Person: borer. — 2. ⊕ Werkzeug: borer; großer ~ (ground-)auger; (Erd=)~ terrier; langer ~ (Ratsch=)~ lever-brace, ratchet-drill; (Schnecken=)~ screw-auger; (Schneide=)~ broach, (Stech=eisen) piercer; med. (Kopf=) trepan, perforator.

Bohr=käfer (⸗⸍…) m/pl. ⓖ ent.: ⚔ ptinidæ pl.; =kurbel f crank-brace, wimble; =lade f boring-frame or -clamp; =loch n boring, auger-hole; (Sprengloch) blasthole; ⚔ von Minen: bore-hole; =maschine f boring (or drilling) engine or machine; mit Kurbel: drilling frame, rock-drill; =mehl n boring-dust; drillings pl.; =mühle f boring-mill; =muschel f, zo. stone-borer, pholad, pholas; ~n pl.: ⚔ lithophagi; =pflug m drill-plough; =pfriem m wimble; Gewehrfabr. a.: gunpicker; =schlitten m boring-carriage; =schmied m bore-smith; =seil n aus Gußstahl: steel rope for boring.

Bohrung (⸗⸍) f ⓖ 1. boring, drilling, driving tunnels; ⚔ ⚒ u. Schießen blasting. — 2. bore(-hole); ⚔ artill. (Seelendurchmesser) bore or caliber.

Bohrungs=… (⸗⸍…) ⓖ = Bohr=…

Bohr=versuch (⸗⸍…) m ⓖ experimental (or trial) boring; =(werk)zeug n boringtools pl., zum Sprengen: blasting-tools

pl.; =wurm m. ent., &c. (Holz anbohrendes Insekt ꝛc.) borer; vgl. =käfer; =zeug n boring-tools pl.

Boi ⊛ u. ⊕ (⸗⸍) [ndl.; *fr. boie f] ⊛ ⓖc. Weberei: (Art Fries od. Flanell) baize.

boien ⊛ u. ⊕ (⸗⸍) a. ⓖ (made of) baize.

böig (⸗⸍) [Bö] ⚓ a. ⓖ squally.

Boi=salz (⸗⸍…) n ⓖ f. Baisalz; =weber ⊛ m baize-maker.

Bojar (⸗⸍) [slaw. Mann] m ⓖ, ~in f ⓖ (rumänische[r] Adlige[r], bsd. Gutsherr[in]) boyar. [rule.]

Bojaren=wirtschaft (⸗⸍…) f ⓖ boyar]

bojarisch (⸗⸍) a. ⓖ boyar.

Boje ⚓ (⸗⸍) [ndl.; *lt. Fessel] f ⓖ buoy; float; f. Ankerboje; eine ~ auslegen to place a buoy; die ~ strömen (über Bord werfen) to stream the buoy; an e-r ~ verteien to fasten (or moor) to a buoy.

bojen ⚓ (⸗⸍) v/a. ⓖ to buoy (up).

Bojer ⚓ (⸗⸍) [Boje] m ⓖ vessel used for laying buoys; (Dutch) singlemasted vessel.

Boje=reep ⚓ (⸗⸍…) n ⓖ buoy-rope.

boken (⸗⸍) v/a. ⊛: Flachs ♀ to beat (or beetle) flax.

Bol (⸗⸍) m ⓒc. **Bolar=erde** (⸗⸍⸗⸍) f ⓖ = Bolus; min. (Siegel-erde) bolus.

Bolch (⸗⸍) m ⓖ ⊛ ichth. = Kabeljau.

Boleine ⚓ ⚓ (⸗⸍) f ⓖ bowline; die ~n anholen to haul tight the bowlines.

Bolero (⸗⸍…) [span.] m ⓖ (span. Nationaltanz) a. ~jäckchen n bolero.

Boleslaw (⸗⸍) npr/m. ⓖα. (Pn.) Boleslaw.

Bolivia ♀ (⸗⸍w⸍) [Simon Boli'var, südamerik. Staatsmann, 1783–1830] ⓚα. auch **Bolivi=en** (⸗⸍) npr/n. ⓚα. Bolivia.

boliv(ian)isch (⸗⸍…) a. ⓖ, **Boliv(ian)=er(in f** ⓖ) m ⓖ Bolivian. [to bleat.]

bölken (⸗⸍) [ndd.: lautm.] v/n. ⓖ (blöken)]

boll † (⸗⸍) impf. v. bellen.

Bolle ♀ (⸗⸍) f ⊛ ⓖ 1. [ahd.] (Wurzelknollen) bulb. — 2. nordd. [P nach it. cipolla, Zwiebel] onion (A'llium Cepa).

bölle † (⸗⸍) impf. subj. v. bellen.

Bollen=beißer (⸗⸍…) m ⓖ orn. bullfinch; =gewächs n bulb(ace)ous plant.

Böller ⚔ (⸗⸍) [mhd. „Wurf"maschine] m ⓖ (kleiner Mörser) small mortar.

böllern (⸗⸍) v/n. (h.) ⓖα. 1. (poltern) to rumble. — 2. ⚔ to shoot with a mortar.

Böller=schuß (⸗⸍…) m ⓖ mortar-shot; e-n mit =schüssen empfangen to salute a p. with a salute of guns.

bollig (⸗⸍) a. ⓖ: a) (knollenartig) bulbous; b) (spröde) brittle.

Boll=werk (⸗⸍) [ndd.; *Bohle] n ⓒc. 1. ⚔ frt. bastion; fig. (Schutzwehr) ᛏ bulwark, stronghold. — 2. (Seewehr) quay.

Bologneser (⸗⸍nj⸍…) m ⓖ od. ~ (a., inv.) Hund (Seidenpudel) Bologna dog; =fläschchen n Bologna phial.

Bolus (⸗⸍) [lt. *grch.] m, inv. bolu_

bolus=artig (⸗⸍…) a. ⓖ bolar.

Bolz fast † (⸍) [ahd.: bolt] m ⓒa. = Bolzen.

Bolzen (⸗⸍) m ⓖ 1. (Armbrust=)~ bolt, shaft for the cross-bow; ~ mit Widerhaken barb-bolt; fig. alles zu ~ drehen to use every possible device, to leave no stone unturned; e-m die ~ fiedern (Beistand leisten) to give a p. a lift, to assist (or succour) a p.; feine ~ verschießen to empty one's quiver. — 2. ⊕ (zylindrisches Eisen zum Verbinden) iron

Signs (see page XVII): F familiar; P vulgar; ⸗ flash; ⚓ rare; † obsolete (died); * new word (born); ⁒ incorrect; ♪ music;

[Bolzenbüchse] — 211 — [Bordiamant]

peg or pin; mit viereckigem Kopf: dog-bolt; mit Vorstecker: eye-bolt; ⚔ artill. (Hafen=) ~ lip-head bolt; ↓ ~ der Kettenschäkel (Schäkelbolzen) shackle-bolt. — 3. ~ (des Plätteisens) heater (of a flat-iron). — 4. ⊕ (Keil) wedge. — 5. ⊕ (senkrechter Balken) upright prop; gerade wie ein ~ bolt-upright, as straight as a dart.

Bolzen-büchse (ᵇ⁻…) f ⊕ air-gun; ⁰ge= rade a. ⊕ s. Bolzen 5; =kopf m bolthead; =schloß n cylindrical padlock; =schrau= be f bolt-screw; =schraubenschneide= maschine f bolt-screw cutting machine.

Bölzung ⚔ (ᵇ⁻) f ⊕ (vorübergehende Holz= bekleidung der Seitenwände) provisional timbering of the walls.

bomätschen ↓ provc. Elbe (-ᴵ⌣) v/a. ⊕ (treideln) to tow (along).

Bombarde (ᵇᵇ⌣)[fr.;*Bombe]f ⊕ 1. ehm. (Steingeschütz) bombard. — 2. ↓ (Bomben= schiff) bomb-ketch or -vessel, mortar-vessel. — 3. ♪ = Bomhart.

Bombardement ⚔ (⌣⌣⌣mᵃ‘) [fr.] n ⊕ bombardment (a. fig.), shelling.

Bombardier ⚔ (ᵇ⁻…) [fr.] m ⊕c. 1. (Bombenwerfer) bombardier. — 2. artill. (Obergefreiter) corporal in the artillery.

bombardier/en ⚔ (ᵇᵇᴵ⌣) [fr.] I v/a. ⊕ (be= schießen) to bombard (a. fig.), to shell; fig. e-n mit Briefen 2 to bombard (or pester) a p. with letters. — II ~ n ⊕ = B/ung.

Bombardier-galeo'te ↓ (ᵇᵇᴵᴵ…) f ⊕ = Bombarde 2; =käfer m, ent. bombar= dier-beetle (Brachi'nus cre'pitans).

Bombardierung ⚔ (ᵇᵇᴵ⌣) f ⊕ bombard= ment of, throwing shells at. [käfer.)

Bombardist (ᵇᵇᴵ⌣) m ⊕ = Bombardier=)

Bombardon ♪ (ᵇᵇgᵃ‘) [fr.] n ⊕ (großes Blasinstrument) bombardon.

Bombasin ⊕ u. ⊕ (ᵇᵇᴵ) ⊕c., a. (ᵇᵇgᵃ‘) ⊕ [fr. v. mlt. bombax Baumwolle] m, Weberei: (leichter wollseidener Stoff) bombasine.

Bombast ⸋ (ᵇᵇ oᵇ. ᵇ⁻) [engl. s. Bombasin] m ⊕b. (Wortschwall) bombast, fustian, F gas; inflated style.

bombastisch (ᵇᵇᴵ⌣) a. ⊕ (schwülstig) bom= bastic, inflated, stilted, F gasy; ²e Redeweise F tall (or big) talk.

Bombe ⚔ (ᵇᵇ⌣) [fr., it., *grch. lautm.] f ⊕ ehm. artill. shell, bomb shell; mit ~n beschießen, bewerfen to shell, to ply with shells, to bombard; fig. wie e-e ~ hereinplatzen to rush in like a steam-engine; die ~ ist geplatzt (das Erwartete ist geschehen) it (or the event) has come off, v. et. überraschendem: F it came upon us like a bomb shell.

Bomben-attentat (ᵇᵇ…) n ⊕ bomb out= rage, attempt with bombs; =eleme"nt! int. damn it!, hang it all!, good gra= cious!; =erfolg m decided (or rattling, striking) success; ²fest a. bomb- or shell-proof, F fig. das steht ² that's quite certain, it's a positive (or solid) fact, that's as sure as eggs, it's as as sure can be; =kiste f tumbril; als Mine: bomb-chest; =schiff ↓ n = Bom= barde 2; ²sicher a. (as) safe as a house; ⚔ 2 einbeten to make bomb-proof; =splitter m, =stück n splinter of a (bomb-) shell; =werfer m bomb-thrower, or -flinger, vgl. Bombardier 1.

bombieren ⊕ (ᵇᵇᴵ⌣) [fr.] v/a. ⊕ (wölben, schweifen) to curve, chamfer, flute.

Bomhart ♪ (ᵇᵇ) [fr. bombarde] m ⊕c. (Baßbrummer in Orgeln) bombard.

Bommel F (ᵇᵇ⌣) f ⊕ und **Bommelage** F (ᵇᵇ⌣gᵃ) f ⊕ = Bammel².

Bon ⊕ (ᵇg) [fr.] m ⊕ promissory note.

bona fide (ᴵ⌣ ᴵᴵ⌣) [lt. im guten Glauben] adv. bona fide, in good faith.

Bonaparte (-⌣⌣⌣) [it.] m ⊕α. Bonaparte; ehm. Spitzname: Boney.

Bonapartist (-⌣⌣ᴵ) m ⊕ Bonapartist.

Bonapartismus (ᴵ⁻…) m ⊕ Bonapartism.

bonapartistisch (-⌣⌣ᴵ⌣) a. ⊕ Bonapartist.

Bonbon (bᵍ-bᵍ‘) [fr.] m, n ⊕ sweet (-stuff), sugar-plum, sugar-tablet; mit Zitronen= saft: acid drop; ~s pl. confectionery, sweetmeats pl.; (Knall-)~ cracker.

Bonbon-laden (…) m ⊕ sweet-shop.

Bonbonniere (bᵍ-(⌣)ᴵ⌣) [fr.] f ⊕ box of sweets, leere: sweetmeat-box.

Bongert ⸋ (ᴵ⌣) m ⊕c. = Bangert.

Bön-hase F (ᴵᴵ⌣) [ndd. Bühnhase] m ⊕ 1. (Pfuscher) quack, cobbler, botcher. — 2. ⊕ (Winkelmakler) small broker.

bön-hasen F (ᴵᴵ⌣) v/n. (h.) ⊕* to botch.

Bonifaz ⊕ γ., **Bonifatius** ⊕ γ. (-ᴵ, -ᴵ⌣…) [it. ⌣⌣…] npr/m. (Apostel der Deutschen, † 755) Boniface.

Bonifikation (-⌣⌣-tᵊ(⌣)ᴵ) [lt. ⌣⌣…] f ⊕ (Vergütung) compensation, allowance.

bonifizieren (-⌣⌣-) [lt. ⌣⌣⌣] v/a. ⊕ to make good, to allow (or compensate) for.

Bonis (ᴵ⌣) [lt.] jur. nur in: ~ zedieren to assign (or surrender, hand over) the bankrupt estate to the creditors.

Bonität ⊕ (-⌣ᴵ) [lt.] f ⊕ (superior) quality of goods; value of an article.

Bonite (⌣ᴵ⌣) [span.] m ⊕ ichth. bonito (Pe'lamys). [chäger] valuer, appraiser.}

Boniteur (-⌣-tᵊ'r) [+.+ fr.] m ⊕d. (Ab=)

bonitieren (-⌣ᴵ⌣) [neu=lt.] agr. I v/a. ⊕ to value (or appraise) the quality of the) soil. — II ~ n ⊕ u. **Bonitierung** f ⊕ valuation (or appraisement) of (the productivity) of arable land.

Bonkal ⊕ (ᵇ⌣) m ⊕ Gewicht in Ost=J.: buncal.

Bonmot (bᵍ-mᵒ‘) [fr.] n ⊕ joke, pun.

Bonne (ᵇ⌣) [fr.] f ⊕ nursery-governess.

Bonnett (⌣ᴵ) [fr.] n ⊕b. ⊕, ~e f ⊕ 1. ⚔ frt. (Brustwehrkappe) bonnet; durch ein(e) ~ geschützt bonneted. — 2. ↓ (Verlängerung des unteren Segels) bonnet, eking-piece, (kleines Hilfssegel) drabbler.

Bonvivant (bᵍ-wi-wᵃ') [fr.] m ⊕ (Lebemann) man of pleasure, (fr.) bon-vivant.

Bonze (ᵇ⌣) m, **Bonzin** (ᵇ⌣) f ⊕ [japan.] (buddhistischer Priester) bonze, weitS.priest.

Boot (ᴵ) [ndd.] n ⊕c., a. ⊕c. boat; (Fischer-)~ fishing-smack, (Fähr-)~ ferry(-boat), (Barke) barge, (Baumkahn) canoe; das große ~ (Pinasse) eines Dampfers long-boat, pinnace, das kleine ~ (Jolle) jolly-boat; ein seegehendes, seetüchtiges ~ a sea-going, seaworthy craft; im ~ fahren to go (or travel) by boat; ein ~ niederlassen to lower a boat; ein Riemen ins ~ tun to ship the oars; im ~ übersetzen to ferry across; zu ~ befördern to carry by boat.

Bo-otes ⊕ (-ᴵ⌣) [grch.] m ⊕γ. ast. Stern= bild: Boötes.

Boot-fahrt (ᴵᴵ…) f ⊕ boating; F a row (in a boat), a sail; ²förmig a. ⊕ boat-shaped, ⊕ cymbiform.

Böoti-en ⊕ (-ᴵ(⌣)⌣) [grch.] npr/n. ⊕α. alte hist. Boeotia; **Böotier** (in f ⊕) m ⊕ Boeotian. fig. dullard.

böotisch (-ᴵ⌣) a. ⊕ Boeotian.

Boot-klampen (ᴵᴵ…)f/pl.⊕ boat-cleats pl.

Boots-anker ↓ (ᴵᴵ…) m ⊕ boat's anchor, grapnel; =eigentümer m barge-master; owner of a boat; =führer m boatman, waterman, bargeman, bargee; =haken m boat-hook; =haus n boat-house; =knecht m: a) =führer; b) (Schiffsmann) sailor; =leute pl. coll. crew; s. =mann b; =mann m: a) (Aufsicht über die Boote ɛc. führender Offizier) (pl. =männer) boat-swain; b) (Matrose) (pl. =leute) sailor; =mannschaft f = =volk; =manns-maat m boatswain's mate; =manns-pfeife f boatswain's whistle or call; =schuppen m = =haus; =seil, =tau n boat's painter or rope; =volk n crew (of a boat or a barge), sailors pl.

Boot-wettfahrt (ᴵᴵ…) f ⊕ boat-race; =zieher ↓ m hauler; (Kabeltau) hawser.

Bor ⊕ (ᴵ) [Borax] n ⊕c. (o. pl.) chm. boron (B).

Borat (-ᴵ) [Bor] n ⊕c. ⊕ chm. (Bor= säuresalz) borate.

Borax (ᴵ⌣) [ar.] m ⊕a., auch inv., chm. borax ($Na_2B_4O_7 + 10H_2O$); roher (ob. natürlicher) ~ aus Tibet: tincal.

Borax-säure (ᴵᴵ…) f ⊕ = Borsäure; =spat m = Borazit. [($Mg_7Cl_2B_{16}O_{30}$).)

Borazit ⊕ (-⌣ᴵ) m ⊕c. min. boracite)

Borch (ᴵ) [ahd.] m ⊕b. castrated male hog. [(BCl_3).)

Bor-chlorid ⊕ (ᴵᴵ…) n ⊕ boron chloride)

Bord¹ (ᴵ) [ndd. (ahd.): Borte] m ⊕b. (Rand) border, edge, rim; ↓ (Rand e-s Schiffes, das Schiff selbst) Kommando: an ~! come on board, come aboard!; an ~ bringen to ship, embark, take on board, take aboard; an ~ geh(e)n to go on board (a ship); ⚔ das Schiff hat 30 Kanonen an ~ the ship carries (or is armed with) thirty guns; ⊕ frei an ~ geliefert (abbr. Fob.) quoted free on board (abbr. f. o. b.); ~ an ~ liegen to lie side by side, alongside; an ~ nehmen s. o. bringen; an ~ sein to be on board (a ship); ~ gegen ~ aboard of each other; über ~ fallen, werfen to fall, to throw over board; Mann über ~! man over-board!; ein Schiff von hohem (niedrigem) ~ a ship high above (deep in) the water; ⊕ frei vom ~ verkaufen to sell free from board.

Bord² (ᴵ) [ndd.: board = Brett] n ⊕b. (Brett, Bücher²) (book-)shelf.

Bord-brett (ᴵ…) n ⊕ oben an Fenstern für Vorhänge: curtain-pole.

Borde (ᴵ) f ⊕ = Bord¹ 1; s. a. Borte.

Börde (ᴵ⌣) [ndd.] f ⊕ fertile plain.

Bordeaux (-dᵒ‘) [fr. St.] ⊕ m ⊕ = ~wein; =rot n u. ²rot a. dark red; =wein m Bordeaux wine, roter: claret.

Bordell (-ᴵ) [it.; *Bord²] n ⊕b. brothel, disorderly house, P knocking-shop.

Bördel-maschine ⊕ (ᵇ…) f ⊕ zum Um= biegen von Rändern an Blecharbeiten: turn-overmachine (for tinware).

bördeln ⊕ (ᴵ⌣) v/a. ⊕α. Blechränder 2 (umbiegen) to turn over …

borden ↓ (ᴵ⌣) v/a. ⊕ to board. [boron.)

Bor-diamant (ᴵ…) m ⊕ crystallized)

⚔ scientific; ⚜ botanical; ⚘ geography; ⊕ machinery; ⚒ mining; ⚔ military; ↓ marine; ⊕ commercial; ⊕ postal; 🚂 railway.

[bordieren] — 212 — [böse]

bordier/en (⌣´⌣)[fr.; *dtjch Bord¹] **I** v/a. ⑬ (mit Borten befetzen) to trim, edge, braid; Hüte: to bind. — **II** ~ n ㉓ = B/tung.
Bordierer (⌣´⌣) m ㉒ trimmer, edger.
Bordierung (⌣´⌣) f ㊻ trimming, &c. (f. bordieren I); edge, border.
Bording ⌄ (´⌣) m ⓐd. lighter.
Bord=linie ⌄ (´...) f ㉖ eines Schiffes: water- (or floating-)line; **=ſchicht** f eines Daches: barge- (or verge-)course; **=ſtein** m e-r Goſſe: kerbstone, cheek- (or edge-)stone; **=uhr** ⌄ f, täglich nach der geogr. Länge berichtigt: ship's chronometer.
Bordüre (⌣´⌣) [f. bordieren] f ㊻ = trimming, braiding; für Hüte: binding.
Bord=wand ⌄ (´⌣) f ㉖ (Außenwand des Schiffes) ship's side.
Boreade (⌣⌣´⌣) m ㊹ myth. (Sohn des Boreas) Boread. [northern.]
boreal(iſch) (⌣´⌣(⌣)) [grch.] a. ㊻ boreal,
Boreas (´⌣⌣) [grch. „Berg"wind] m ⑮γ. myth. (Gott des Nordwindes) Boreas.
➤ **Bore(t)ſch** ⌄ (´⌣) ꝛc. ſ. Borretſch ꝛc.
Bor=fluor (´⌣...) n ㊱ borofluoride, boron fluoride (BF₃); **=fluorwaſſerſtoff** m hydrofluoboric acid (HBF₄).
Borg¹ (´) [mhd.] m ⓑb. (o. pl.) credit; (Borgen) borrowing, loan; **auf** ~ geben, nehmen to give, to take (or buy) on credit or F on tick; **vom** ~ leben to live on credit, to run up bills (with everybody), F to live on tick.
Borg² (´) m ⓑb. = Borch. [braces pl.]
Borg=braſſen ⌄ (´...) f/pl. ㊲ preventer-
borgen (´⌣) [ahd.: borrow; *bergen]
I v/a. ⓐ **1**. (auf Borg nehmen) to take on credit; et. von (ob. bei) e-m ⌣ to borrow a th. of a p.; arith.: beim Subtrahieren ⌣ to borrow. — **2**. (auf Borg geben) to credit, advance, lend; hier wird nicht geborgt! terms (strictly) cash!, (for) cash (or ready money) only! — **II** ~ n ㉓ **3**. (ſ. 1) borrowing Sprichw. ~ macht Sorgen he who goes borrowing goes sorrowing, he that his money lends loses both coin and friends. — **4**. (ſ. 2) crediting, &c.
Borger (´⌣) m ㉒, **~in** f ㊸ (vgl. borgen) **1**. borrower. — **2**. ⌣ lender.
Borgis ⊕ (´⌣) [Bourgeois] f, inv. typ. (Schriftgattung von 9 Punkten) bourgeois.
Borg=tau ⌄ (´...) n ㉖ preventer(-rope); **=weiſe** adv. on credit, on trust, F on tick.
Borium ⌂ (´⌣⌣) n ㊱ = Bor. [(B₆C).]
Bor=karbid ⌂ (´...) n ㊱ boron carbide
Borke (´⌣) [ndd.: bark] f ㊻ **1**. (Rinde) bark (a. ⊖ Gerberei); fig. ſ. Baum **2**. — **2**. path. (Schorf auf Wunden) scab.
Bork(en)=dach (´⌣...) n ㊱ bark roof; **=käfer** m, ent.: bark-boring beetle (Bo'strichus); **=tier** n, zo. Steller's sea-cow (Rhy'tina Ste'lleri).
borkig (´⌣) a. ㊻ **1**. bark(y), (made) of bark. — **2**. path. (ſchorfig) full of scabs.
Born nordd., bibl., poet. (´) [ndd. = Brunnen] m ⓑb. **1**. spring, well; ⊖ (Salz)~ salt springs pl., salt-pit. — **2**. (Quell) fountain.
Borneo ♀ (´⌣⌣) npr/n. ⓐα. (größte der Sunda-inſeln) Borneo. **~=kampfer** (´...) m ㊲ Borneo camphor; **=kampfer=öl** n, chm. borneene (C₁₀H₁₆).
borniert (⌣´) [fr.] a. ㊻ (beschränkt) narrow-minded, of limited (or weak) understanding; **~heit** (⌣´...) f ㊻ narrow-mindedness; vgl. Beſchränktheit 2.
Bornu ♀ (´⌣) npr/n. ⓐα. (Negerreich im Suda'n) Born(o)u, Bornoo.
Borrago ♀ (⌣´⌣) [lt., *ar.] m ⓢ. **Borretſch** ♀ (´⌣) m ⓐa. borage (Borra'go officina'lis); **⌣=artig** a.: boragin(ac)-eous; **⌣e** Gewächſe ⌒ boraginaceæ.
Börs (´) m ⓐa. ichth. = Barſch¹.
bor=ſauer (´...) a. ㊺ bor(ac)ic; **=ſäure** f ㊻ (Hydriumborat) bor(ac)ic acid (H₃BO₃); **=ſäure=anhydri'd** n boron trioxide (B₂O₃).
Borsdorfer (´⌣⌣) [Borsdorf, Dorf bei Leipzig] a. inv. u. m ㉒ (Apfel, etwa: Blenheim orange, pippin; Backen wie ~ Äpfel, cheeks like (two) rosy apples.
Börſe (´⌣) [mlt. bursa; *grch. byrsa Fell] f ㊺ **1**. [fr.] purse; vgl. Beutel **2**. — **2**. [ndl.] ⊕ (Verſammlungsort der Kaufleute) Lo.: the (Royal) Exchange, the Stock-exchange; ausländiſche: bourse; weits. (money-)market; auf der ~ on 'Change, in the (money-)market.
Börſen=baron (´⌣...) m ㊸ great financier or operator, Stock-exchange magnate; **=bericht** m: a) list of (official) quotations; b) money-article, market-report; **=beſuch** m attendance at the (Stock-)exchange or on 'Change; der Woll(ꝛc.)-händler: going to the wool-, &c. exchange; **=blatt** n: a) =bericht a; b) financial (news)paper; **=brauch** m usage of the stock-exchange; **=buch** m: a) manual of (or guide to) the stock-exchange; b) stockbroker's or (or note-)book; **=drucker** ⊕ m (telegr. Typendruckapparat mit ſelbſttätig ſich abrollendem Papierſtreifen) tape-machine; **=effekten** pl. stock-exchange securities pl., (scrip of) bonds or shares pl.; **=fähig** a. ㊻ admitted to the stock-exchange; **=er Makler** sworn (ant. outside) broker, **=e Papiere** marketable (or negotiable) values pl.; **=fürſt** m = =baron; **=gängig** a. quoted (or current) on 'Change; **=gebäude** n, the Exchange; **=gericht** n Committee of the Stock-exchange; **=gerücht** n stock-exchange (or market) rumour; **=geſchäft** n stock-exchange transaction; **=halle** f (hall of) the Exchange; **=kommiſſionsgeſchäft** n firm of stockbrokers; **=makler** m (stock-)broker, stock-jobber; **=manöver** n stock-exchange manœuvre or stratagem, rigging the market; **=mäßig** a. customary on 'Change, in conformity with the rules of the Stock-exchange; **=ordnung** f stock-exchange regulations pl.; **=papiere** n/pl. stock(s pl.); **=ſchwindel** m = =ſpiel; **=ſpekulant** m = Börſianer; **=ſpiel** n stock-exchange gambling or F operating; market-rigging; **=ſpieler** m = Börſianer; **=ſteuer** f tax on stock-exchange dealings; **=ſtrömung** f tendency of the money-market; **=ſtunden** f/pl. = =zeit; **=uſance** = =brauch; **=zeit** f official hours pl. for stock-exchange business; **=zettel** m = =bericht a.
Börſianer (⌣⌣´⌣) [dtſch.-lt.] m ㉒ stock-exchange operator or speculator or wirepuller, (fr.) boursier.
borſt¹ ⌄ (´) impf. v. berſten (ſ. b§).

Borſt² (´) [berſten] m ⓑb. (Riß) crack, chink; einen ~ bekommen to crack.
Borſte (´⌣) (ahd.: bristle, bur] f ㊸ bſb. des Schweines: bristle; (⚥ langes, ſteifes Haar) ⌒ chæta, seta.
borſte (´⌣) impf. subj. v. berſten.
borſten¹ (´⌣) a. ㊻ (aus Borſte) made of bristles. [von Igeln ꝛc.: to bristle up.]
borſten² (´⌣) v/n. (h.) u. ſich ⌣ v/refl. ⑰
borſten=ähnlich (´⌣...) a. ㊻, **=artig** a. bristly, bristle-like; ⚥ ⌒ setaceous; **=beſen** m ㉒ hair-broom; **=förmig** a. bristle-shaped; vgl. =ähnlich; **=gras** ⚥ n matweed (Nardus); **=hering** m, ichth. bristle-herring (Chaetoe'ssus); **=hirſe** f = Fench; **=igel** m, zo. auf Madagaskar: centetid (Cente'tes); **=pinſel** m painter's brush (made of bristles); **=ſimſe** ⚥ f least club-rush (Scirpus seta'ceus); **=tragend** a. bristle-bearing; ⌒ chætophorous, chætiferous, setiferous; **=vieh** n bristle-bearing animals pl.; **=wurm** m, zo. ⌒ chætopod, setiger. [nitride (BN).]
Bor=ſtickſtoff (´⌣...) ㊱ boric (or boron)
borſtig (´⌣) a. ㊻ **1**. bristly, ⚥ setaceous. — **2**. F fig. (mürriſch) surly, sour-tempered, F grumpy, huffy, waxy; ⌣ (zornig) werden to fire up, to fly into a temper.
Borſtigkeit (´⌣⌣) f ㊻ (vgl. borſtig) bristliness; F fig. surliness.
Borſt=ſimſe ⚥ (´⌣...) f ㊷ ſ. Borſten-ſ.
Borte (´⌣) [ahd.: border] f ㊸ trimming, edging, border; (Treſſe) gold braiding or lacing, galloon; mit ~n beſetzt gold-braided, gallooned; **~n=macher** (´...) m ㊲, **=weber**, **=wirker** m braid- (or lace-)maker; **~n=weberei**, **=wirkerei** f braid- (or lace-)making.
bortieren (⌣´⌣) = bordieren.
Boruſſe (⌣´⌣) [neu-lt.] m ㊹, **Boruſſin** ㊵ poet. ſ. Preuße ꝛc.
boruſſifizieren (⌣⌣⌣´⌣) [dtſch.-lt.] v/a. ㊹ to prussianize.
Bor=wiſch (´⌣) m ⓐa. (Kehrwiſch mit langem Stiele) long-handled broom or brush.
bös (´) [ſ. D] (D10) ſ. böſe; **⌣=artig** (´´...) a. ㊻ ill-natured, wicked, malicious; bſb. von Tieren: vicious; von Krankheiten: malignant, virulent; **=artigkeit** f ㊻ ill-nature, wickedness, viciousness; von Krankheiten: malignancy, virulence.
böſchen ⊕ (´⌣) Straßenbau ꝛc.: **I** v/a. ⑰ slope, bſb. ⚔ frt.: to escarp. — **II** ~ n ㉓ = Böſchung 1.
Böſchung (´⌣) [nhd. 16. sae.] f ㊻ **1**. sloping; ⚔ frt. escarping. — **2**. slope, scarp, talus. [angle of elevation.]
Böſchungs=winkel (´⌣...) m ㊲ gradient,
böſe (´⌣) [ahd.] (ant. gut) **I** a. ㊻ **1**. bad, evil, (böswillig) wicked, malicious; ⌣ Feind ob. Geiſt, ⌣s Weſen (Satan, Teufel) evil spirit, (foul) fiend; the Evil One; in Märchen: ⌣r Geiſt goblin, demon; F e-e ⌣ Geſchichte an unpleasant affair; ⌣s Gewiſſen evil (or bad) conscience; ⌣ Nachricht bad (piece of) news; ſich (dat.) e-n ⌣n Namen machen to get a bad (or an ill) name; in ⌣n Ruf bringen to bring into ill repute or into disrepute; e-m e-n ⌣n Streich ſpielen to play a p. a mean (or F nasty) trick; ⌣ Sieben, ⌣s Weib vixen, dragon (of a woman); ⌣r Vorſatz, ⌣r Wille ill-will, evil intention, malice; ⌣e Zeiten f/pl. hard (or bad)

Zeichen (ſ. S. XVII): F familiär; P Volksſprache; F̄ Gaunerſprache; ⌣ ſelten; † alt (auch geſtorben); * neu (auch geboren); ⁺⁺ unrichtig;

[**Bösewicht**] — [**Boxeraufstand**]

times pl. — 2. adv. ich habe es nicht 2 gemeint I meant no harm; sie haben ihm 2 mitgespielt F ... treated him very·shabbily. — 3. (trant) troublesome (tooth, &c.), bad (foot, &c.); 2s Ding (Nagelgeschwür) whitlow; ein 2r Hals a sore throat; 2 Säfte m/pl. bad (or peccant) humours pl.; 2s Wesen epilepsy. — 4. (schädlich) hurtful; (verderblich) pernicious; 2 Dünste m/pl. noxious vapours or effluvia pl.; ⚒ 2s Wetter chokedamp; vgl. Blick 1. — 5. (zürnend) angry, F out of temper; e-n 2 machen to make a p. angry or cross; auf (ob. über) e-n (a. e-m) 2 sein to be angry (or cross, offended) with a p.; sie sind sich (dat.) 2. sie sind 2 mit·ea. they are at variance or F at loggerheads; warum bist du ihm 2? oft: what have you against him?; sich 2 stellen, 2 tun to feign anger; 2 werden to grow angry with a p. — II ~e(r) m, ~e (-n) 6. bad (or wicked) person, die ~n the wicked pl.; rel. der ~ = der 2 Feind (s. 1). — III ~(s) n ⊕ 7. evil; e-m et. ~s antun to do a p. harm or an injury; ~s beabsichtigen, im Schilde führen to be bent on mischief; das ~ bringt manchem Gutes it's an ill wind that blows nobody any good; ~s mit Gutem vergelten to return good for evil; e-m ~s zufügen to inflict an injury on a p., to harm (or injure, wrong) a p. — 8. (Unheil) mir schwant ~s (SCH.) I have an evil presentiment; das läßt mich ~s ahnen that appears ominous to me, I have strange misgivings, my heart misgives me.

Bösewicht (⁻ᵕ⁻) m ⓐc., ⓓc. villain, wretch, bad fellow, (wicked) scoundrel; stärker: miscreant; (Schuldiger) culprit; der kleine ~ the little scamp or rogue.

bös·gelaunt (⁻ᵕ⁻) a. ⓖ ill-humoured.

boshaft (⁻ᵕ) a. ⓖ 1. malicious; 2er Gedanke, Plan mischievous thought, plan. — 2. bsb. bibl. wicked, (gottlos) ungodly. — 3. (zornig) wrathful; (tückisch) spiteful, bsb. v. Tieren: vicious.

Boshaftigkeit (⁻ᵕ⁻) u. **Bosheit** (⁻ᵕ) f ⓖ (s. boshaft) 1. malice; mischievousness, wickedness; wrath, spite, spitefulness; aus reiner ~ from sheer wantonness or spite. — 2. (böse Tat) wicked deed, bibl. auch: (deed of) iniquity. — 3. fast † (Grimm) rage, fury; s-e ~ an e-m auslassen to vent one's anger on a person.

Bosheits·sünde (⁻ᵕ⁻...) f ⓖ sin of malice.

Boskett (ᵕ⁻) [fr., it.; *dtsch Busch] n ⓐb. (Gebüsch) shrubbery, boscage, bosket.

Bös·kraut ♀ (⁻ᵕ⁻) n ⓖ scorching-fennel (Tha'psia).

böslich (⁻ᵕ) [böse] a. ⓖ (u. adv.) wicked(-ly), malicious(ly); jur. 2e Verwahrlosung der Kinder wilful neglect ...

Bösling ♀ (⁻ᵕ) m ⓐd. (weibliche Hanfpflanze) female hamp.

Bosniake (ᵕᵕ⁻ᵕ) m ⓐⓐ = **Bosnier**; **Bosni·en** ♀ (⁻ᵕᵕ) npr/n. ⓑ α. Bosnia. **Bosni·er** (⁻ᵕᵕ) m ⓐⓐ, ~in f ⓐⓖ, **bosnisch** (⁻ᵕ) a. ⓖ Bosnian, Bosniac.

Bosporus ♀ (⁻ᵕᵕ) [grch. Ochsfurt] m ⓒ γ. (Meerenge) Bosp(h)orus.

Boß (⁻) m ⓐⓑa. (Kloß, auf dem der Pflugbaum ruht) wooden rest for the plough-beam.

Boße (⁻ᵕ) [ahd.] m ⓖⓖ, f ⓖ (Flachsbündel) bundle of flax.

Bossekel s. **Possekel**.

Bossel (⁻ᵕ) m ⓖ (Kegelkugel) bowl.

bosselieren (ᵕᵕ⁻ᵕ) v/a. ⓖ = bossieren 1.

bosseln¹ provc. (⁻ᵕ) v/a. ⓖa* to play (at) bowls or ninepins.

bosseln² (⁻ᵕ) [fr.: boss; * bosseln¹] v/a. ⓖa. (ausbessern) to patch up; (aus weicher Masse formen) to mould.

Bossen (⁻ᵕ) m ⓖ (der nicht oder nur ganz roh bearbeitete Teil eines Werksteinblockes) (sculpturer's) block in its raw or half-finished state.

Bossier·arbeit ⊕ (⁻ᵕ⁻...) f ⓖ (getriebene Arbeit) embossed work; embossing; =bein n embossing-bone or -stick.

bossieren ⊕ (ᵕ⁻ᵕ) [fr.] v/a. ⓖ 1. (erhabene Arbeit machen) to emboss. — 2. (modellieren) to mould in wax, &c.

Bossierer ⊕ (ᵕ⁻ᵕ) m ⓖⓐ embosser.

Bossier·holz, ·hölzchen (⁻ᵕ⁻...) n = =bein; =kunst f embossing (or embosser's) art.

Boston·presse (⁻ᵕ...) f ⓖ typ. jobbing hand-press, lever-press.

böswillig (⁻ᵕ...) a. ⓖ malevolent, ill-intentioned; mit 2er Absicht with evil intention; jur. 2er Schaden wilful damage; ~keit f ⓖ malevolence; evil intention or design. [summons.]

Bot¹ (⁻) [: Gebot] n ⓐc. (Vorladung)

bot² (⁻) impf. ind. von bieten (s. ds).

Botanik (ᵕ⁻ᵕ) [grch.: pers. bostán Garten] f ⓖ (Pflanzenkunde) botany.

Botaniker (ᵕ⁻ᵕᵕ) m ⓐⓐ botanist.

botanisch (ᵕ⁻ᵕ) a. ⓖ botanical; 2er Ausflug botanical excursion.

botanisieren (ᵕᵕᵕ⁻ᵕ) v/n. (h.) ⓖ (Pflanzen sammeln) to go botanizing; **Botanisier·büchse** (ᵕᵕᵕ⁻ᵕ...) f ⓖ, **=trommel** f botanizing-box, specimen-box.

Bötchen (⁻ᵕ) n ⓖ (dim. v. Boot) small boat, canoe, F co. nutshell.

Bote (⁻ᵕ) [ahd.: bode; * bieten] m ⓖⓐ (f s. Botin). 1. messenger; (Dienstmann) commissionaire, a. porter; (Laufbursche) errand-boy; ~n laufen to go (or run) on errands, to deliver messages; (Fuhrmann) carrier; (Kurier) express, courier; reitender: mounted messenger; bisw. a. (fr.) estafette; (Amts·)~ des Gerichts: messenger of the court, bisw. bailiff. — 2. der hinkende ~, etwa: bad news, unfavourable report; die zwölf ~n (Apostel) the twelve apostles.

Böte¹ (⁻ᵕ) pl. von **Boot** (s. ds).

böte² (⁻ᵕ) impf. subj. von bieten (s. ds).

Boten·amt (⁻ᵕ...) n ⓖ, =dienst m post (or duties pl.) of a messenger; =frau f woman going on errands or doing commissions; =gang m errand, commission; =gänger, =läufer m runner, vgl. Bote 1; =laufen n running on errands; =lohn m (n) messenger's (or porter's) fee, carriage of a letter; =schild n messenger's (or porter's) badge.

Botin (⁻ᵕ) f ⓖ = **Botenfrau**.

bot·mäßig (⁻ᵕ⁻ᵕ) [Bot¹] a. ⓖ 1. (gebietend) sovereign, lordly. — 2. (gehorsam) obedient; (untertänig) subject; (zinspflichtig) tributary.

Botmäßigkeit (⁻ᵕ⁻ᵕ) f ⓖ sovereign power, sway, dominion; unter s-e ~ bringen to bring under one's sway or

dominion, weit. to reduce to submission or subjection, to subdue.

Botryolith ⚒ (ᵕᵕ⁻) [grch. Traubenstein] m ⓖ min. botryolite.

Botschaft (⁻ᵕ) [ahd.; * Bote] f ⓖ 1. message; auf ~ gehn (Botendienst tun) to do (or go on) errands; e-e ~ ausrichten to deliver a message, to bring word. — 2. (Nachricht) news, communication, tidings pl., die neueste ~ (Kunde) the latest intelligence. — 3. (Gesandtschaft) embassy (auch das Gebäude).

Botschafter (⁻ᵕᵕ) [nhd. 17. sae.] m ⓐⓐ, ~in f ⓐ (Gesandter ersten Ranges) ambassador m, bisw. a. ...dress f; ~ des Papstes (it.) nuncio, bsb. ehm. papal legate.

Böttcher ⊕ (⁻ᵕ) [Bottich] m ⓐⓐ (Faßbinder) cooper; ~=arbeit (⁻...) f ⓖ: a) cooper's work or trade; b) = =ware; =beil n cooper's adze.

Böttcherei ⊕ (⁻ᵕᵕ⁻) f ⓖ cooperage.

Böttcher·hammer (⁻ᵕ...) m = =schlegel; =handwerk n coopering, vgl. =arbeit a; =holz n cooper's wood; (Faßholz) staves pl.; =lohn m (n) cooperage; =meister m master cooper; =schlegel m cooper's mallet; =ware f coopery, cooperage; =werkstatt f cooper's workshop.

Botte (⁻ᵕ) m, **Bottin** f ⓐⓖ (Bewohner[in] von Botten) Bothnian.

Bottelier ↓ (⁻ᵕᵕⁱ⁻) [ndl.] m ⓖ steward.

Botten ♀ (⁻ᵕ) npr/n. ⓑ α. (Küstenland am Bottnischen Meerbusen) Bothnia.

Bottich (⁻ᵕ) [ahd.: body] m ⓐⓓ. tub, vat; ein ~ voll a tubful; Bierbr.: (Maisch=)~ mash(ing)·tub or -tun or -vat. [room or office.]

Bottlerei ↓ (⁻ᵕᵕ⁻) [ndl.] f ⓖ steward's

bottnisch ♀ (⁻ᵕ) a. ⓖ Bothnian, Bothnic; ~er Meerbusen zwischen Schweden u. Rußland: Gulf of Bothnia.

boucherisieren ⊕ (ᵕᵕᵕ⁻ᵕ) [Boucherie, franz. Chemiker, † 1871] v/a. ⓖ (Holz mit Kupfervitriol tränken) to boucherize.

Boudoir (bu-ˈdŏā'r) [fr.] n ⓖⓓ. (Damenzimmer) boudoir; lady's dressing-room.

Bouillon (būl-jō') [fr.·m Aufwallendes] f ⓖ (Fleischbrühe) (meat·)broth, beef-tea or -gravy, clear soup; ~ mit Ei beef-tea (beaten up) with an egg.

Bouillon·kapseln (...ᵕ...) f/pl. ⓖ portable soup; =löffel m gravy-spoon; =tafeln f/pl. = =kapseln.

Boule·arbeit (būl·l...) [Boul(l)e (++Buhl), fr. Kunsttischler, 1642—1732] f ⓖ buhl(·work).

Boulevard (būl·ᵕ·wār) [fr.; *dtsch Bollwerk] m ⓖ boulevard.

Bourbone (būr·⁻ᵕ) [fr.] m ⓐⓐ (fr. Königshaus) Bourbon (king, prince).

Bourgeois (būr·ˈgŏā') m ⓐⓐ = **Borgis**.

Boutcille (bu·tē'l·j̆) [fr.] / ⓖ (Flasche) bottle.

Bowie·messer ⬚ (bō'·ᵉ..., oft ·..·) [amer. Oberst B., † 1836] n ⓖ bowie knife.

Bowle ⬚ (bō'·l·ᵉ) [engl.] f ⓖ 1. (Schale, Schüssel, Terrine) bowl, tureen. — 2. (gewürzter Wein) mulled (or spiced) wine, kalt: claret·cup; (Punsch·)~ (hot) negus.

boxen ⬚ (⁻ᵕ) [engl.] v/n. (h.) u. sich v/refl. ⓖ to box, (to have a) fight; zu 2 anfangen to come to fisticuffs.

Boxer (⁻ᵕ) m ⓐⓐ 1. boxer. (prize·)fighter; pugilist. — 2. (chines. Empörer) Boxer; ~=aufstand (⁻ᵕ...) m ⓖ (Chinese) Boxer rising or movement (1900).

♪ Musik; ⚚ Wissenschaft; ♀ Pflanze; ♁ Geographie; ⊕ Technik; ⚒ Bergbau; ⚔ Militär; ↓ Marine; ⬚ Handel; ⬚ Post; 🚂 Eisenbahn.

Boxerei (∸⏑⏑) *f* [W] box(ing), (prize-) fight(ing); pugilism; es kam zu e-r ~ they came to blows, it ended in a (hand-to-hand) fight *or* scuffle.
Box-kunst (∸...) *f* [G] (the art of) boxing, *co.* the noble art of self-defence.
Boyer ✱ *m* (friesartiger Stoff) baize (= Boi).
Boykott ⊤ (bȯi'⏑) [engl., Kapitän Boycott, 1880] *m* [U]c. (Verruf) boycott.
boykottieren (bȯi⏑∸⏑) *v/a.* [B] to boycott.
br (∸) *int.* = burr.
br. *abbr.* = broschiert.
brach[1] (∸ch) *impf.* von brechen (s. bs).
brach[2] (∸ch) [nhd.; *Brache] *a.* [G] *agr.* von Feldern: 2(-)liegen to lie fallow, to remain untilled *or* uncultivated; auch *fig.* von Personen u. Sachen: to lie idle, to remain unoccupied *or* unemployed *or* unused; von Kunst und Wissenschaft: to lie neglected, to remain stagnant.
Brach-acker (...) *m* [G] fallow (ground); **-distel** ⚘ *f* field fever-wort, eryngo (*Ery'ngium campe'stre*).
Brache (...) [ahd.; * brechen] *f* [W] *agr.* 1. (Brachliegen) fallowness; *fig.* stagnant state. — 2. = Brachacker.
bräche (∸⏑) *subj. impf.* v. brechen.
brachen (...) [ahd.; * Brache] *v/n.* (h.) u. *v/a.* [B] *agr.* (den Brachacker aufbrechen) to break up (*or* work) the fallow land; Sumpfland 2 to turn marshes into arable land.
Brach-feld (...) [ahd.] *n* [G] fallow soil; **-käfer** *m*, *ent.* (Johanniskäfer) fern-beetle (*Scarabae'us solstitia'lis*); **-land** *n* fallow land; **2liegen** *v/n.* s. brach[2]; ~ *n* fallowness; **-männchen** ⚘ *n* (Champignon) field-agaric (*Aga'ricus campe'stris*); **-monat** [ahd.] *m* (month of) June; **-pilz** ⚘ *m* = -männchen.
Brachs (...) *m* [U]a. s. Brachse.
Brach-schnepfe (...) *f* [G] *orn.* = -vogel a.
Brachse (...) [ahd.] *f* [W], **Brachsen** (...) *m* [B] *ichth.* bream (*A'bramis Brama*).
Brachsen-farn (...) *m* [G], **-kraut** ⚘ *n* Merlin's-grass (*Isoe'tes lacu'stris*).
Brach-sinnau ⚘ (...) *m* [G] field lady's-mantle (*Alchemi'lla arve'nsis*). [bringen.]
brachte (...) (u. **brächte** *subj.*) *impf.* v.
Brach-vogel (...) [nhd.] *m* [G] *orn.*: a) großer ~ common curlew (*Nume'nius arcua'tus*); b) kleiner ~ (Art Regenpfeifer) dotterel (*Eudro'mias Morine'llus*); **-zeit** *f* fallow(ing) season.
Brack[1] (∸) [ndd. braken = brechen] *n* [U]b. ✱ (Ausschuß) refuse, trash; sweepings *pl.* bsd. (geringwertiges Pelzwerk) inferior [fur.]
Brack[2] (∸) *m* [G] *hunt.* = Bracke[1].
Brack[3] (∸) [: brackig] *n* [O]b. (natürliche Salzlecke) (pool of) brackish water.
Brack-bank (...) *f* ⊙ = Bracktisch.
Bracke[1] (∸⏑) [ahd.: brach] *m* [W] u. *f* [W] *hunt.* † kind of lime-hound (used by huntsmen of former centuries).
Bracke[2] ✱ (∸⏑) *f* [W] (Ausschuß zur Prüfung auszusondernder Waren, Vieh 2c.) board of inspection for testing marketable goods, cattle, &c.
bracken (⏑) *v/a.* [B] 1. ✱ (aussondern, vgl. Bracke[2]) to sort inferior goods *or* cattle. — 2. = braken.
Bracker ✱ (∸⏑) *m* [B] sorter (of goods).
Brack-gut ✱ (...) *n* [G] s(p)oiled (*or* cast-off) goods *pl.*; vgl. Brack[1].
brackig ⚓ (∸⏑) *a.* [G] (süßsalzig) brackish.
Bräckin (∸⏑) *f* [W] *hunt.* s. Bracke[1].
brackisch (∸⏑) *a.* [G] *min.* 2e Bildung, 2es Gestein sedimentary formation in brackish water.
Brack-kaffee ✱ (...) *m* [G] coffee spoilt by seawater; **-schaf** *n* cast-off sheep; **-tisch** *m* sorting table for goods; **-vieh** *n* cast-off cattle; **-ware** ✱ *f* = -gut; **-wasser** ⚓ *n* (süßsalziges Wasser) brackish water. [(Gott) Brahma.]
Brahma (∸⏑) [skt. ...] *npr/m* [U]a. (ind.)
Brahmane (-∸⏑) [skt.] *m* [W] Brahmin.
Brahmanin (⏑) *f* [W] Brahminee.
brahmanisch (-∸⏑) *a.* [G] Brahmin(ic).
Brahmanismus (--∸⏑) *m* Brahminism.
Brahmaputra ♀ (-⏑∸⏑) *npr/m.* [U]a. (Strom in Ost-J.) Brahmapootra.
Brahmine 2c. s. Brahmane 2c.
Brake (∸⏑) [ndd. s. braken] *f* [W] (Flachsbreche) flax-brake *or* -break.
braken ⊙ (∸⏑) [ndd.: brake = brechen] *agr.* Flachs 2 to beat .... to brake ...
Brakteat ⊘ (⏑⏑∸) [lt.] *m* [W] *num.* (Münze 13. u. 14. *sae.*) bracteate.
Bram[1] (∸) [ahd.: broom] *m* [U]c. 1. ⚘ a) = Ginster; b) = Brombeere. — 2. a. **Bräm** = Brame 2.
Bram[2] ⚓ (∸) [ndl.] *m* [U]c. = Bramstenge.
Bramah-... ⊤ ⊙ (...) [Bramah, engl. Mechaniker 1749–1814] [G]: **~-presse** *f* (hydraulische Presse) Bramah press; **~-schloß** *n* Schlosserei: Bramah lock.
Bramarbas (-∸⏑) [nhd. 1710, dän.. *span.] *m* [U] braggart, swaggerer, bully.
bramarbasieren (-⏑⏑∸⏑) *v/n.* (h.) [B] to brag, swagger, bully. [mon broom.]
Bram[1]**-besen** (...) *m* [G] aus Ginster: com-
Bram[2]**-brasse** (...) *f* [G] (Tau an beiden Enden der Bramstenge) topgallant brace.
Brame (bsd. 1), **Bräme** (bsd. 2) (∸⏑) [: brim] *f* [W] 1. (Wiesen- oder Feldrand mit Buschwerk) border (*or* edge) of a meadow (*or* field) planted with bushes. — 2. ⊙ Kürschnerei = Verbrämung.
Bram[2]**-fall** (...) *n* [G] (Aufziehtau des Bramsegels) topgallant halyard; Oberblock *m* des ~es jack-block.
Bramling, Brämling (∸⏑) *m* [U]d. *orn.* (Bergfink) bramble-finch, brambling.
Bram[2]**-rahe** (...) *f* [G] topgallant yard; **-segel** *n* topgallant sail; **-(segel-)schote** *f* topgallant sheet; **-segel-fall** *n* = -fall; **-stenge** *f* (zweite Mastverlängerung) topgallant mast.
Branche bsd. ✱ (brg'-sch) [fr. Zweig] *f* [W] branch, department, F line (of business).
Brand (∸) [ahd.: brand; von *brennen] *m* [O]b. (s. aber 2 u. 5) 1. (Brennen) combustion; die Zigarre hat einen guten ~ the cigar burns (*or* draws) well; (Feuersbrunst) conflagration, (great) fire; (Flamme) blaze; in ~ geraten to catch fire, to blaze up; in ~ stecken od. setzen to (set on) fire, to set fire to, to set ablaze, to ignite; ein Land mit Mord u. ~ heimsuchen to ravage (*or* lay waste) a country(side) with fire and sword; *jur.* ~ (an)stiften to commit arson. — 2. ⊙ ~ des Kalkes, der Ziegel burning of lime, bricks, tiles; ~ der Töpferware baking of pottery; ⚒ (Reinigung des Silbers) refining (of) silver; vgl. Brandprobe u. Brandsilber; [O]b. (gebrannte Masse, Satz) batch, baking, charge of the furnace. — 3. *surg.* cauterization; *vet.* (Einbrennen e-s Mals) marking with a hot iron, branding; (das Mal selbst) mark; ✱ (Marke) brand (auch die also bezeichnete Ware). — 4. (Hitze) heat; (Dürre) dryness; (Durst) parched throat, thirst; (Glut) ardour; (Liebesglut) burning passion of lovers; (Rausch) intoxication; F in ~ (Geldverlegenheit) sein to be short of money, to be hard up (for money), P to be stone-broke. — 5. auch [O]b. (brennender Körper) (fire-) brand. — 6. *agr.* (wüste Stelle) barren plot *or* tract, (ausgerodete Stelle) bare spot (from which underwood and weeds have been removed by fire). — 7. ⚘ u. *agr.* ~ (durch Brandpilze verursachte Krankheit) der Getreide-arten 2c.: mildew, blight, rust (= Meltau); (Holz-, Wundfäule) rot. — 8. ⊘ *path.* (Absterben durch Entzündung) heißer ~ gangrene; kalter ~ mortification, ⊘ sphacelus; (Knochen-)~ necrosis, (Knochenfraß) caries. — 9. ⊙ Büchsenm.: ~ (Schmutz) im Gewehre remains *pl.* of (the) gunpowder; vom Gewehr: guten ~ haben (scharf schießen, mit gutem Pulver geladen sein) to have superior quick-firing qualities.
brand-artig (...) *a.* [G] *path.*: ⊘ sphacelate(d), gangrenous; **-assekuranz** *f* [G] = Feuerversicherung; **-blase** *f* blister raised by burning; **-bock** ⊙ *m* andiron; **-bolzen** *m*, **-bombe** ✱ *f*, *artill.* round carcass; **-brief** *m*: a) letter from an incendiary (threatening with arson); b) *fig.* urgent petition, letter asking for money *or* demanding payment; **-direktor** *m* superintendent (*or* head) of a fire-brigade; **-eisen** *n* (zum Einbrennen von Zeichen) branding iron.
Brandel ⚔ öst. (∸⏑) *m*, *n* [B] percussion-tube (= Schlagröhre).
branden (∸⏑) [ndd.] I *v/n.* (h.) [B] 1. ⚓ von Wellen: to surge, to break (*or* dash) against the rocks, to roll up to the beach *or* shore. — 2. *fig.* (toben) to rave, rage; auf den Straßen brandet ein gewaltiges Leben a mighty torrent of life sweeps (*or* rushes, surges) along the streets. — II ⚓ ~ *n* [B] 3. = Brandung 1.
Brand-ente (...) *f* [G] *orn.* sheldrake (*Tado'rna vulpa'nser*).
Brander (∸⏑) [ndl.] *m* [B] 1. ⚓ (Brandschiff) fire-ship. — 2. = Brandfuchs d. — 3. ⚔ (auch **Bränder**[1]) fuse(e).
Bränder[2] (∸⏑) *pl.* von Brand 5.
Brand-erz (...) *n* [G] *min.* a) (bituminöser Schieferton) bituminous shale; b) (Quecksilberlebererz) hepatic mercurial ore; **-fackel** *f* incendiary('s) torch; *fig.* torch of war; **-faß** ⚔ *n* fire- (*or* thundering-)barrel; **2fest** *a.* [G] fire-proof; **-fieber** *n* (Entzündungsfieber) inflammatory fever; **-fleck(en)** *m*: a) singed spot, mark left by burning; burn: b) *path.* gangrenous spot; **2fleckig** *a.* stained by fire, with marks of burning *or* scalding; **-fuchs** *m*: a) *zo.* brant-fox (*Canis alo'pex*) b) (fuchsrotes Pferd) sorrel horse; c) F (Rothaariger) F ginger(-pate), bsd. ehm. P sorrel-pate; d) burschikos.

[Brandgasse] — 215 — [Bratkartoffeln]

junior (student), freshman (in his second term); =gase ⚔ n/pl. inflammatory (or explosive, foul) gases pl.; =gasse f fast † narrow alley (as safeguard against the spreading of fire); =geruch, =geschmack m burnt smell, taste; =geschoß ⚔ n, artill. fire-ball; =geschwür n, path. gangrenous abscess or ulcer; =giebel m, arch. parting-wall between housetops, ehm. common gable; =glocke f tocsin, fire-bell; =granate ⚔ f = =kugel; =haken m für Feuersbrünste: fire-hook.

brandicht, mst brandig (⌣⌣) a. 1. having a burnt smell or taste; von Korn, Mehl ꝛc.: (dumpfig) musty, smutty. — 2. ♃ agr. (vgl. Brand 7) mildewed, blighted, rusty. — 3. ⚕ path. (vgl. Brand 8) mortifying, gangrenous.

Brand-kasse (⌣…) f ⊕: a) fund to provide against losses by fire; b) fire (-insurance) office; =korn ♃ n blighted corn; =kugel ⚔ f, ehm. artill. carcass of a howitzer; fire-ball; =laden m iron shutter; =leder n leather for inner soles; =leger m incendiary; =legung f incendiarism, arson; =leiter f fire-ladder; =loch n: a) ⊕ am Hochofen: (Flammloch) fire-hole; b) ⚔ an Hohlgeschossen: fuse(e)-hole; =mal n: a) =fleck a; b) bsd. ♃ mark made with a hot iron; bei Verbrechern auch: brand; nur fig.: stigma; =malerei f poker-painting or -picture, pokerwork, ♃ pyrography; ⚕marken v/a. ⊕*₋* to mark with a hot iron, to brand; nur fig. to stigmatize; to fasten (or cast) a stigma (or reproach) upon a p., to show up (before the world); er war für zeitlebens gebrandmarkt he (or his character) was blasted (or ruined) for life, he was a marked man; =mauer f fire-proof wall; (Grenzmauer) partition-wall, party-wall; =maus f, zo. (long-tailed) field-mouse (Mus agra'rius); =mehl n flour of blighted grain; =meise f, orn. great titmouse (Parus maior); =meister m head of a fire-brigade, bsd. Am. fire-ward(en); =mittel n, med. remedy for burns and scalds; =opfer n burnt-offering, der Juden auch: holocaust; =ordnung f (firemen's) regulations pl. for the extinction of fire; =pfahl m ehm. stake at which martyrs, heretics, &c. were burnt, burning stake; am~enden, umkommen to perish (or be burnt) at the stake; =pfeil ⚓ m ehm. fire-arrow; =pflaster n, med. plaster for burns and scalds; =pilz ♃ m rust, blight (Ustila'go); =probe f des =silbers ⚔. fire-test; =rakete ⚔, artill. Congreve (or war-, carcass-) rocket; =röhre f fuse(e) (of a bomb); =rose f, path.: ⚕ gangrenous erysipelas; =rot a. red like fire, of a burning red (colour); =röte f red glow of fire; =salbe f, med. ointment (or salve) for burns and scalds; =satz ⚔ m, ehm. artill. carcass-composition; =schaden m injury (or damage, loss) caused by fire; a. = =wunde; ⚕schatzen (⌣⌣) v/a. ⊕*₋* eine Stadt ꝛc. ⚕ to lay ... under contribution, to levy a contribution on ...; to exact the sinews of war from ..., (ausplündern) to sack, ravage, pillage, plunder a province, &c.; fig. einen ⚕ to extort money from a p., F to drain (or fleece) a p.; ~ n ⚕ u. =schatzung f ⊕ (imposing or raising a) contribution; contribution levied (or laid) on a town; sacking, pillage, plunder; extortion of money from a p.; =schiff ⚓ n (Brander) fire-ship; =schorf m, path. gangrenous scab or crust; ⚕schwarz a. jetblack; =silber ⊕ n, metall. refined silver; =sohle ⊕ f Schuhmacherei: inner sole, welt; =spritze f fire-engine; =stätte, =stelle f scene of a fire or conflagration, =stein m (fire-) brick; =steuer f: a) (Steuer zum Besten Abgebrannter) contribution to a fund for people who have suffered by fire; b) fire-insurance premium; =stifter(in f) m incendiary; =stiftung f incendiarism, jur. arson; (angelegtes Feuer) incendiary fire; =stiftungs-trieb m: ⚕ pyromania; =tür f (iron) fire-proof door.

Brandung ⚓ (⌣⌣) [ndd.] f ⊕ surging sea; surge (of the sea), surf; (heavy) wash (or roll) of the sea; breakers pl.; Ruf: ~ voraus! breakers ahead!

Brandungs-boot (⌣…) n ⊕, =fahrer m zum Landen von Passagieren u. Waren: surf-boat; =welle f surging billow, breaker.

Brand=versicherung (⌣…) f ⊕ fire-insurance; =wache f fire-watch, ⚓ a. = Wachtschiff; =weizen m blighted wheat; =wunde f burn, scald; =zeichen n, bsd. ♃ u. der Gestüte ==mal b; =zeug ⚔ n: a) allg.: inflammable substance; b) = =satz.

Brane (⌣) [: Brame] f ⊕ (Waldsaum) outskirt(s pl.) of a forest.

Branke (⌣⌣) f ⊕ s. Pranke.

brannte (⌣⌣) impf., ind. von brennen (f. d§).

Brannt-wein (⌣⌣) [brennen] m ⊕c. allg.: spirits pl., alcohol(ic liquor); (Korn-) ~ whisky; (Franz-)~ brandy; (Wacholder) gin; ~ brennen to distil spirits; im Wirtshaus: ein Glas ~ heiß mit (Wasser und) Zucker a glass of hot brandy (whisky, &c.) with sugar; ein Gläschen ~ für den Appetit oft: a pick-me-up.

Branntwein-blase (⌣…) f ⊕ still, ehm. alembic; =brenner m distiller; =brennerei f: a) (Brennen) distilling; b) (Betrieb) distillery; =flasche f brandy-bottle or -flask; =haus n, =laden m, =schenke f gin-shop or -palace; =monopol n monopoly for the sale of spirits; =schärfe f alcoholic solution of substances of pungent taste; =spülicht ⊕ m (Schlempe) distiller's wash; =steuer f excise (or duty) on spirits; =trinker m person who drinks spirits, bisw. dram-drinker, F one who is fond of his (f her) drops; =wage ⊕ f alcoholometer.

branstig provc. (⌣⌣) a. ⊕ = brandicht 1.

Brante (⌣⌣) [it.] f ⊕ hunt. paw (of a bear, lion, &c.).

Brasilianer (⌣-(⌣)⌣) ꝛc. s. Brasilier ꝛc.

Brasili-en (⌣⌣(⌣)⌣) [port. Rothoß] npr/n. ⊕ α. (früheres Kaiserreich, seit 1889 Republik in Südamerika) Brazil; ~holz (⌣…) n ⊕, Brazil- (or log-)wood (Caesalpi'nia echina'ta) ; =nüsse f/pl. Brazil-nuts pl.; Brasili-er (⌣⌣⌣) m ⊕, ~in f ⊕, brasilisch (⌣⌣⌣) a. ⊕ Brazilian.

Braß (⌣) [: prasseln] m ⊕a. 1. F co., contp. (Gerümpel) lumber. — 2. (geschälter Reis) husked rice.

Brasse[1] (⌣⌣) [ndl., *fr.] f ⊕ (Tau an den Raaen) brace; große ~ main brace.

Brasse[2] (⌣⌣) [ndd. = hd. Brachse(n)] m ⊕ f ⊕ ichth. bream (A'bramis).

Brasselett (⌣⌣⌣) [fr. bracelet] n ⊕b. (Armband) bracelet.

Brassen[1] (⌣⌣) [ndd.] m ⊕ = Brasse[2].

brassen[2] ⚓ (⌣⌣) [Brasse[1]] v/a. ⊕ e-e Rahe ⚕ (die Brassen anholen) to brace a yard; ins Kreuz ⚕ to brace square; in den Wind ⚕ to brace sails; scharf beim Winde gebraßt close-hauled.

brät (⌣) 3. Pers. sg. pres. ind. von braten.

Brat-aal (⌣⌣…) m ⊕ spitch-cock; =apfel m: a) zum Braten: baking apple, b) gebraten: baked (or roasted) apple; =bock m bsd. ehm. (Gestell für den Bratspieß) jack-frame, spit-rack; vgl. Bratenwender.

Brätchen (⌣⌣) n ⊕ dim. von Braten[2].

braten[1] (⌣⌣) [ahd.] I v/n. (h.) u. v/a. ⊕a. 1. Fleisch ꝛc.: to roast on a spit or a meat-jack (s. Bratenwender); to bake in the oven; to grill on a gridiron; to broil by the open fire; to fry in a pan; Äpfel ⚕ to bake apples; zu wenig (zu start) gebraten underdone (overdone); gerade genug gebraten done to a turn, done (or cooked) just enough. — 2. fig. (große Hitze leiden) in der Sonne ⚕ to be baking (or roasting, scorching, F frizzling) in the sun. — 3. Sprichw. da bratet's und siedet's alle Tage (there) they feast daily; Schlaraffenland, wo einem die gebrat(e)nen Tauben in den Mund fliegen fool's paradise; er meint, die gebrat(e)nen Tauben werden ihm in den Mund fliegen he thinks fortune will come to him in his sleep, he expects to find everything just as he wishes it; nach dem Manne brät man die Wurst (man macht Unterschiede), etwa: people are served according to their station or means; let each man have his due. — II ~ n ⊕ 4. roasting (a. ⊕ metall.), &c. (s. I). — III Gebrat(e)ne(s) n ⊕ 5. roast (or baked) meat; s.th. fried or grilled or baked or broiled.

Braten[2] (⌣⌣) [ahd.: brawn] m ⊕ 1. roast meat; joint (of meat); den ~ mit Fett begießen to baste the joint; den ~ umwenden to turn the joint. — 2. fig. ein fetter ~ für die Advokaten a fat morsel for the lawyers; den ~ riechen (Witterung bekommen) to smell a rat.

Braten-brühe (⌣…) f ⊕ (meat-)gravy; =fett n dripping; =löffel m baster; =rock m, co. (best) Sunday-coat, (Gehrock) frock-coat, (Feiertagskleid) holiday-garment; =saft m gravy (from the joint), juice of roast meat; =schmalz n = =fett; =schüssel f dish for serving up joints; =wender m ehm., Person: turnspit; jetzt Vorrichtung: meat-jack.

Brater (⌣⌣) m ⊕, ~in f ⊕ person who attends to the roasting (of the joints); im Hotel, etwa: chef in the grill-room.

Brat-fisch (⌣…) m ⊕: a) fish for frying; b) fried fish; =herd m, metall., &c. hearth for roasting; =hering m fried herring; =huhn n roast fowl; =kartoffeln f/pl. fried potatoes pl.

⚕ scientific; ♃ botanical; ⊕ geography; ⊕ machinery; ⚔ mining; ⚔ military; ⚓ marine; ⚚ commercial; ✉ postal; 🚂 railway.

[Brätling] — 216 — [Braurecht]

Brätling (´‿) m ⓓd. ichth. = Breitling.
Brat-ofen (″...) m ⓶ a) oven (for baking and frying); **-pfanne** f frying-pan; zum Einschieben in den Bratofen: baking-tin; **-röhre** f frying-tube; **-rost** m gridiron, grill.
bratsch (´) int. (Krachen nachahmend) crash!
Bratsche ♪ (´‿) [it. vio'la di bra'ccio] f ⓸⓼ (bass-)viol, alto-viola; **~(n)-spieler** (´‿...) m ⓶ (alto-)violinist. | spieler.
Bratschist ♪ (-´) m ⓶ = Bratsche(n)=
Brat-spieß (″...) m ⓶: a) bfd. ehm. broach, spit (for roasting); er schrie, als ob er am ~ stäke he yelled as if he was being murdered, he cried for dear life; an den ~ stecken to spit; b) F co. (Schwert) sword, ↓ hanger; F co. cheesetoaster; **-spieß-bock** m = -bock; **-spieß-dreher** m turnspit; **-spill** ↓ n windlass.
brätst (´) 2. Perf. sg. pres. ind. v. braten.
Brat-wurst (″...) f ⓸⓶: a) sausage for frying; b) fried sausage.
Brau, nft **Bräu** ☉ (´) [:bree] ⓓc. u. ⓼ 1. m = Brauer(ei), Brauhaus. — 2. n u. m (Gebräude) brew(ing), malt liquor brewed at one time; in Zsgn, zB.: Löwen-₂ (beer from the) Lion brewery.
brau-berechtigt (″...) a. ⓶⓶ having a brewer's licence; **-bottich** ☉ m ⓶ brewing- (or ale-, beer-)vat or tub.
Brauch (´ch) [ahd.] m ⓘc. usage, ⓼ auch: usance; kirchlicher ~ rite; nach altem ~ according to old (or time-honoured) custom, jur. by (ancient) prescription; das ist so der ~ hier, das ist hier so ~ that's the custom (or usual thing) here.
brauchbar (´ch-) a. ⓶⓶ serviceable, of (great) service, fit for use, handy, v. Kleidungsstücken: fit for wear, wearable, von Personen auch: up to the mark, able, fit, efficient; (nützlich) useful, of (good or great) use, apt; ₂er Mensch useful (or practical, stärker: smart) fellow, a. handy man; ✕ (dienstfähig) fit for service, able-bodied; **~keit** (´ch-) f ⓸⓶ serviceableness, fitness; usefulness, aptitude, smartness.
brauchen (´ch) [ahd.: brook ertragen: It. früi genießen] ⓼ I v/a. mit acc. u. gen. 1. (r-r- ge₂) to use, to make use of; (anverwenden) to employ, apply; Arznei ₂ to take medicine or physic; eine Brunnenkur ₂ to take the waters, to go to a spa; Gewalt ₂ to use force; bist du nicht willig, so brauch' ich Gewalt (G.) if you resist I shall use my strength; eine Kur ₂ to go through a cure or a course of treatment; wir ₂ Sie jetzt nicht we have at present no employment for you; er, es ist nicht zu ₂ he, it is of no use, useless; gram. diese Präposition wird mit dem Dativ gebraucht ... is used with (or governs) the dative; er läßt sich von ihnen zu allem ₂ he is a tool in their hands; das Eisen läßt sich zu vielem ₂ iron lends itself to many purposes; ☉ gebrauchte Bücher, Möbel second-hand books pl.; furniture. — 2. (bedürfen) to be in want (or need) of ...; wir ₂ 200 M. für Kleider we require (or want, need) £ 10 for clothing; ein Dampfschiff braucht drei Tage für die Reise ... takes three days for the voyage, F can do it in three days;

wie lange wird er ₂? how long will he take or F be, how much time will it take him?; man braucht mit der Nähmaschine zwei Stunden, um es fertig zu machen it takes two hours (to do) on the sewing-machine; **wozu** ₂ (erfordern) sie all das? what do they want all that for? — 3. ₂ zu (mit inf.): das einzige, was sie zu wissen ₂ (nötig haben) the only thing that they need know; was braucht er mich zu schimpfen? why need he abuse me?; darauf braucht man nicht stolz zu sein it's nothing to be proud of; Sie ₂ nicht ans Aufstehen zu denken you must not think of getting up; man braucht sich darüber nur wenig zu (ver)wundern it is but little to be wondered at; man braucht ihn nur anzusehen one need only look at him; er hätte nicht hinzugeh(en) ₂ (statt: gebraucht) there was no occasion (or necessity, F call) for him to go there. — 4. (verbrauchen) to use up, wear out, consume, expend. — **II** v/impers. 5. was braucht es so viel(er) Umstände? why all this fuss (or ceremony)?; das braucht es nicht there is no need for it; braucht es noch besserer Beweise? are better proofs required, does it need (or require) better proofs (than these)?
Braue (´‿) [ahd.: brow: grch. ὀphrÿ's] f ⓸⓼ eyebrow (= Augenbraue).
Brau-eigner (″...) m ⓶ owner (or master) of a brewery.
brauen (´‿) [ahd.: brew] ⓼ I v/a. 1. auch v/impers. Hexen ₂ Sturm witches send forth (or let loose) the storm; fig. ₂ (im Schilde führen) to hatch a scheme, to brew mischief; es braut ein Ungewitter there is a thunderstorm brewing or gathering. — 2. ☉ Bier: to brew; Punsch 2c. ₂ to mix (or brew) a bowl of punch, &c.; Essig ₂ to manufacture (or make) vinegar. — **II** v/n. 3. (dampfen(d emporsteigen)) die Berge ₂ Nebel the mountains are sending forth mists; Nebel ₂ mists are rising.
Brauer (´‿) m ⓶, **~in** f ⓸ brewer.
Brauerei (-´‿) f ⓸ 1. (art of) brewing, brewer's trade. — 2. Gebäude: brewery; brew-house; brewer's premises pl.
Brauer-gilde (″...) f ⓶, **-innung**, **-zunft** f company (or guild) of brewers.
Brau-gerät (″...) n ⓶ brewing implements pl.; **-gerechtigkeit** f = -recht; **-haus** n, **-hof** m brewery; **-herr** m brewer, vgl. -eigner; **-kessel** ☉ m brewer's copper, boiler for brewing; **-knecht** m brewer's man; (Bierfahrer) drayman; **-kufe** ☉ f = -bottich; **-meister** m master brewer.
braun (´) [ahd.: brown; * brennen] I a. ⓶⓶ 1. brown; ₂es Mädchen dark girl. bism. (fr.) brunette; ₂ färben, ☉ beizen to brown; ₂ werden to become (F to get) brown. — 2. ₂ und blau (geschlagen) black and blue, in all the colours of the rainbow; ₂e Butter fried butter; in Butter ₂ braten to brown up in butter; ₂e Gesichtsfarbe tanned (or sun-burnt, tawny) complexion; ₂es Pferd bay horse; schwarz-braunes: dun(-coloured) horse; Zucker ₂ machen (bräunen) to burn sugar. —

II (das) ~ n, **~e(s)** n ⓶ (o.pl.) 3. brown (colour). — **III** **~e(r)** m, **~e** f ⓶ 4.: a) (Person) dark person, p. with a dark (or tawny) complexion; b) (Pferd) bay (or dun) horse; c) der **~e**, nst als n/pr. Braun in der Tierfabel: (Bär) Bruin.
braun-äugig (″...) a. ⓶⓶ brown-eyed; **-zen** n ⓶ browning, bronzing; **-bier** n brown beer; **-bleierz** n pyromorphite.
Bräune (´‿) f ⓸ 1. [mhd: braun] brown colour. — 2. [it. prüna kohle] † path. auch vet. u. ♀ (Hals-)~: 🜨 angina, mit Entzündung: quinsy; häutige ~ croup.
bräune-artig a. ⓶⓶ quinsy-(or croup-)like.
Braun-eisen-erz (´‿...) n ⓶, **-eisen-stein** m, min. brown clay iron-ore; limonite.
Braunelle (-´‿) f ⓸ 1. ♀ = Wiesenknopf (großer). — 2. orn. (Waldflüevogel) hedgesparrow (Acce'ntor modula'ris).
bräunen (´‿) [mhd.] I v/n. (h.) u. sich ₂ v/refl. to grow (or become) brown, von der Haut: to tan, to bronze. — **II** v/a. to make (or dye, colour) brown; Kochkunst: to brown the meat, &c.; den Zucker ₂ to burn ~.
Braune(r), **Braune(s)** s. braun II u. III.
Braun-fisch (″...) m ⓶ porpoise (Phocae'na); **-fleckig**, **-gefleckt** a. ⓶⓶ with brown spots or speckles; **-gelb** a. yellowish brown, fallow; (fr.) feuille-morte; **-grün** a. brownish green; **-haarig** a. brown-haired; **-heil** ♀ n = Braunelle; **-holz** n Brazil-wood.
Braunit 🜨 (-´) n ⓓc. chm. 🜨 braunite, manganese sesquioxide ($Mn_2 O_3$).
Braun-kehlchen (″...) n ⓶ orn. whinchat (Prati'ncola); **-kohl** ♀ m red cabbage; **-kohle** f, geogn. browncoal; 🜨 lignite, lose: peat-coal (Torf) peat; **-kohlen-formation** f † = Tertiär-f.; **-kohlen-haltig** a.: 🜨 lignitic, ligniteferous; **-kohlen-sandstein** m, min. brown-coal grit.
Bräunlein ♀ (´‿) n ⓶ nigritella (Nigrite'lla angustifo'lia).
bräunlich (´‿) a. ⓶⓶ brownish; tawny; (graubraun) dun; **-gelb** a. (″...) ⓶⓶ brownish yellow, v. Pferden: isabel; **-weiß** a. brownish-white.
Bräunling (´‿) m ⓓd. 1. s.th. brown, brown apple, &c. — 2. ent. (Schmetterling) (common) brown, pierid.
braun-rot (″...): a) a. ⓶⓶ brown-red, russet; b) ~ n ⓶: spanisches ~ (Art Oder) almagra; **-scheckig** a. piebald; **-schimmel** m irongrey horse; **-schwarz** a. brownish black, tawny.
Braunschweig ♀ (´‿) [ahd. 861; *mlt. Bruno'nis vicus] npr/n. ⓓa. (St. u. Land) Brunswick; **~er(in** f ⓸) m ⓼, Lisch (a. ~er inv.) a. ⓶⓶ Brunswickian; ~er-grün n Brunswick green; ~er Wurst Brunswick sausage.
Braun-spat (″...) m ⓶ min. (eisenhaltiger Dolomit) brown-spar; **-stein** m, min. manganese (dioxide) ($Mn O_2$); **-stein-erz** n manganese ore; graues: 🜨 pyrolusite; **-stein-kiesel** m: 🜨 photizite; **-wurz** f brownwort (Scrophula'ria); **-wurz-blütenkäfer** m, ent. carpet beetle or bug (Anthre'nus scrophula'riae).
Brau-ordnung (″...) f ⓶ brewing regulations pl.; **-pfanne** f brewer's copper; **-recht** n right (or privilege) of brewing.

Zeichen (s. S. XVII): F familiär; P Volkssprache; Γ Gaunersprache; ↘ selten; † alt (auch gestorben); * neu (auch geboren); ⁒ unrichtig;

[Braus] — 217 — [brechen]

Braus (¹) [mhd.] m ⓐ a. 1. ⚔ bustle, uproar. — 2. Saus und ~ (Schwelgerei) revelry, riotous (or gay, wild) life; in Saus und ~ (üppig) leben to lead a life of pleasure or enjoyment or a riotous life; F to live on (or off) the fat of the land.

Brausche (¹⌣) [mhd.: bruise] f ⓑ bump on the forehead, bruise; surg. contusion; (Blutbeule) carbuncle.

Brause (¹⌣) [mhd.] f ⓑ 1. effervescence, (Gärung) fermentation; das Bier ꝛc. ist in der ~ … is fermenting, F …is working, is up. — 2. (durchlöcherter Aufsatz einer Gießkanne ꝛc.) rose of a watering-can, &c. — 3. weitS. (Gießkanne) watering-can or -pot; (Tropfbad, Dusche) = ~=bad.

Brause=bad (¹⌣…) n ⓑ shower-bath, (fr.) douche; **=kopf** m impetuous (or hot-headed) person, hotspur; ⚔ **köpfig** a. impetuous, hot-headed, -tempered, hasty; **=limonade** f effervescent lemonade; sherbet.

brausen (¹⌣) [mhd.] ⓑ I v/n. (h. u. ſn.) u. v/impers. 1. (rauschen) to roar, to rush; (summen) to hum, buzz, whiz. — 2. es braust mir in den Ohren there is (or I have) a singing or buzzing in my ears. — 3. (aufwallen) to effervesce, F to fizz; (schäumen) to foam; (gären) to ferment. — 4. (ſn) (voranstürmen) to come along with a roar or rush; die Limonade ist aus der Flasche gebraust the lemonade rushed out of (or bubbled over from) the bottle. — 5. to take a shower-bath or douche. — II v/a. 6. das Pferd braust (stöß) Dampf aus der Nase … breathes steam (poet. fire) from its nostrils. — 7. (besprengen) to water, to sprinkle with water. — III ~ n ⓑ 8. roar(ing), &c. (ſ. I u. II); ~ in den Ohren singing in the ears. — 9. effervescence; boisterousness. — IV ⓑ p.pr. u. a. ⓑ 10. in den Beb. des inf. — 11. effervescent (water); boisterous (wind); impetuous (youth).

Brause=pulver (¹⌣…) n ⓑ effervescent powder; abführendes englisches ~ Seidlitz powder; **=wein** m sparkling wine; **=wind** m: a) roaring wind; b) fig. (flatterhafter Mensch) light-hearted person, F harum-scarum; vgl. =kopf.

braust (¹) 1. 2. (a. brausest) u. 3. (a. brauset) Person sg. pres. v. brausen (ſ. ds 2 u. 6). — 2. Person sg. pres. v. brauen.

Brau=steuer (¹⌣…) f ⓑ tax on brewer(ie)s, brewer's license.

Braut (¹) [ahd.: bride] f ⓓ 1. (Verlobte) betrothed, affianced, (fr.) fiancée; seine ~, auch: his intended, his young lady; (Neuvermählte am Hochzeitstage) bride. — 2. fig., rel. des Himmels ~ (Nonne) nun, bisw. the Lord's spouse and consort; Sprichw. wer das Glück hat, führt die ~ heim, etwa: the lucky one gains the prize or wins the fair lady, fortune favours the brave. — 3. ⚘: ~ in Haaren = Schwarzkümmel (türkischer).

Brau=tag (¹⌣…) m ⓑ brewing day.

Braut=altar (¹⌣…) m ⓑ marriage-(poet. hymeneal) altar; **=anzug** m = **=kleid**; **=ausstattung** f (wedding-)trousseau; vgl. Aussteuer; **=bett** n bridal bed or couch.

Bräutchen (¹⌣) n ⓑ dim. little (or young) bride.

Braut=fahrt (¹⌣…) f ⓑ = **=schau**; **=führer** m bride's (best) man; **=führerin** f bridesmaid; **=gemach** n = **=kammer**; **=geschenk** n wedding-present.

Bräuti=gam (¹⌣⌣) [Braut u. =gam: lt. homō Mann] m ⓓ. (ⓑ) betrothed, (fr.) fiancé; ihr ~ auch: her intended, F her young man; (Neuvermählter am Hochzeitstage) bridegroom.

Braut=jungfer (¹⌣…) f ⓑ bridesmaid; **=kammer** f nuptial (or bridal) chamber; **=kleid** n bridal gown, bride's dress; wedding-dress or -garment; **=kranz** m, bridal wreath; **=kuß** m nuptial kiss; **=lauf** m = **=zug**; **=leute** pl. betrothed (or affianced, engaged) couple; am Hochzeitstage: newly married couple, bridal pair.

bräutlich (¹⌣) a. ⓑ bridal, nuptial.

Braut=lied (¹⌣…) n ⓑ nuptial (or wedding-) song or hymn, ⚘ epithalamium; **=mahl** n wedding-feast; **=mutter** f bride's mother; **=nacht** f nuptial night; **=paar** n = **=leute**; **=ring** m wedding-ring.

Brautschaft (¹⌣) f ⓑ = Brautstand.

Braut=schatz (¹⌣…) m ⓑ (Mitgift) dowry; marriage-portion; **=schau** f inspection of the bride; auf die ~ geh(e)n to go to see (or propose to) the lady of one's choice; to be on the look-out for a wife; **=schleier** m bride's veil; **=schmuck** m bride's jewelry; **=staat** m bride's adornment; **=stand** m (time of) engagement; **=steuer** f = **=schatz**; **=tag** m wedding-day; **=vater** m bride's father; den ~ machen to give the bride away; **=wagen** m bridal carriage, wedding-coach; **=werber** m (der für e-n andern wirbt) match-maker; **=werbung** f match-making; **=zug** m bridal procession.

Brau=wesen (¹⌣…) n ⓑ brewing trade; **=wirt** m brewer, licensed victualler.

brav (¹f) [mhd. 17. sae.; *fr.; it.] I a. ⓑ (D1, ſübd. D2) 1. (wacker, bieder) honest, upright; ein 2er Kerl, Mensch a good (F a brick of a) fellow, P a (regular) trump; es ist 2 von Ihnen, daß Sie gekommen sind it is good (or kind) of you to have come; er hat sehr 2 (adv.) gehandelt he acted very honourably, he has done the right thing. — 2. (artig) well-behaved; good child. — 3. ⚓ (beständig) steady. — II F adv. 4. (sehr) well; sehr 2! well done!

Bravade (⌣⌣¹⌣) [fr.] f ⓑ (Prahlerei) bravado, boast, swagger.

Bravheit (¹f⌣) f ⓑ (Biederkeit) honesty, uprightness; (Artigkeit) good behaviour.

bravo (¹⌣) [it.] I int., gesteigert: **bravissimo** (⌣⌣¹⌣⌣) (Beifallsruf) 1. bravo!, well done! — II **Bravo** ⓑⓑ 2. ~=**rufen** ⓑ) n shouts of bravo, cheers pl. — 3. m (Meuchelmörder) bravo.

Bravour (⌣wū'r) [fr.] f ⓑ (pl. ~=**stücke**) (Mut) bravery, valour; **~=arie** (⌣…) f ⓑ ♪ bravura (air), (it.) aria di bravura; **~=stücke** pl. acts of bravery, valiant (or daring) feats pl.

Break ⚑ (brēt) [engl.] m ⓑ (vierrädriger Wagen) break; (fr.) char-à-banc.

Breccie ⚘ (brē't=sch) [it. pl.] f ⓑ min. (Brodengestein) breccia; **~n=marmor** (²⌣…) m ⓑ min. brecciated marble.

Brech=arz(e)nei (¹⌣…) f ⓑ = =mittel a; **=bank** f der Bäcker zum Brechen des Teiges: kneading-bench or -board.

brechbar (¹⌣) a. ⓑ 1. breakable, fragile, frangible; (von Glas ꝛc. auch:) brittle. — 2. opt. ⚡ refrangible.

Brechbarkeit (¹⌣⌣) f ⓑ 1. frangibility; brittleness. — 2. opt. refrangibility.

Brech=bohnen (¹⌣…) f pl. ⓑ Kocht.: French beans pl.; **=durchfall** m. path. cholerine (cho'lera nostras); diarrhœa with vomiting. [von Flachs und Hanf) brake.]

Breche ⓞ (¹⌣) f ⓑ Spinnerei: (zum Brechen)

Brech=eisen (¹⌣…) n ⓑ crow(bar).

brechen (¹⌣) [ahd.: break] I v/a., v/n. (ſn) u. v/refl. ⓑa. (ſ. aber 6) 1. meist: to break, crack, crush, gewaltsam: to smash (or shatter, shiver) to pieces or atoms, als v/n. a.: to be (F to get) broken, shattered, smashed; Bahn 2 vgl. Bahn 1; das Joch 2 to throw off the yoke, to break one's chains; fig. eine Lanze mit e-m (für e-n) 2 to break a lance with (for) a p.; to enter the lists with a p.; den Stab über e-n (od. e-m) 2: a) jur. to pronounce the death-sentence upon a p.; b) fig. to condemn a p.; to judge him severely; Sprichw. er hat nichts zu beißen und zu 2 he hasn't a crust of bread to eat, he is pinched or starving; Not bricht Eisen necessity knows no law; vgl. a. Krug. — 2. von Gliedern und Organen des Menschen: sein Arm ist gebrochen his arm is broken; sich (dat.) den Arm, das Bein, den Hals 2 to break one's arm, leg, neck; ein gebroch(e)nes Bein, Glied a broken (or fractured) leg, limb; von Sterbenden: die Augen 2 ihm his eyes grow dim; e-m das Kreuz 2 to break a p.'s back; einer Flasche den Hals 2 to crack a bottle; fig. der Kummer hat ihm das Herz gebrochen grief has broken his heart; er spricht gebrochen(es) Deutsch he speaks broken German; ein gebroch(e)ner Mann a broken (or crushed, ruined) man; mit gebroch(e)ner Stimme (von Sterbenden) with a broken (or dying) voice. — 3. den Eigensinn, Trotz, widerspenstigen Geist eines Kindes 2 (beugen) to break down a child's obstinate (or stubborn) spirit; ihre Kraft, Macht war gebrochen their power was broken or destroyed or gone. — 4. (abweichen von, übertreten) to transgress; die Ehe, das Ehegelübde 2 to commit adultery; die Fasten, ein Gelübde 2 to break one's fast, one's vow; das Gesetz 2 to infringe (or break) …; gebroch(e)ne (nicht gerade) Linie broken line; die Treue, sein Wort 2 to break one's pledged word; phys. Lichtstrahlen 2 to refract rays of light; vgl. 5. — 5. (teilen) ein Wort 2 to divide …; arith. gebroch(e)ne Zahl fractional number or value, fraction; phys. Lichtstrahlen 2 to split up rays of light into their prismatic colours. — 6. ⚘ agr. Flachs 2 ſ. Flachs; Hanf 2 (p.p. gebrecht ⓑ) (brafen) to dress (or peel) …; den Acker 2 to break (or turn) up the soil; ⚓ ⚑ die Ladung 2 to break bulk. — 7. (zu Ende gehen,

♪ Musik; ⚘ Wissenschaft; ⚘ Pflanze; ⚘ Geographie; ⓑ Technik; ⚒ Bergbau; ⚔ Militär; ⚓ Marine; ⓑ Handel; ⚐ Post; ⚑ Eisenbahn.

bringen) der Faden der Geduld bricht mir my patience is coming to an end. — 8. (falten) ein Blatt Papier ≈ to fold ...; einen Rand ≈ to make (or leave) a margin; ⊕ *typ.* die Spalten ≈ to make up (or adjust) the columns. — 9. (nachlassen, sich ändern) to relax, to change; die Kälte hat sich gebrochen the cold has abated or is breaking up; die Krankheit bricht sich ... is taking a turn (for the better); s-e Stimme bricht sich (beim Mannbarwerden) ... is breaking. — 10. (pflücken, losreißen) Blumen, Früchte ≈ to gather (or pluck, pick) ...; ⊕ Erze ≈ to dig (or break) ore; ein Schloß von der Tür(e) ≈ to take (or wrench) a lock off the door; Steine ≈ to pick (or break) stones in a quarry; to quarry; *fig.* einen Streit mit e-m vom Zaune ≈ to pick a quarrel with a p. — 11. v/n. mit *prp.*, oft von e-m *adv.* begleitet: **aus dem Hinterhalte** (hervor) ≈ to burst (or sally forth, rush forth) from an ambush; die Tränen ≈ ihm aus den Augen (hervor) the tears burst (or gush) from his eyes; **durch** feindliche Scharen (hindurch=) ≈ to force (or fight) one's way through hostile troops; die Sonne bricht durch die Wolken ... breaks through (or pierces) the clouds; **in** ein Haus (ein=) ≈ to break into a house, als Dieb auch: to commit a burglary; **mit** e-m (ein Verhältnis ab=) ≈ to break (or fall out) with a p., to sever (or break off) one's connexion with a p.; **über** e-n herein=≈ to come down upon a p. — 12. (sich) brechen (erbrechen) to vomit, to bring up one's food; zu ≈ einnehmen to take an emetic. — II ~ *n* ② 13. break(ing), smash(ing), &c. (f. 1, 2, 3); von Gesetzen, Verträgen *etc.*: breach, infraction, violation; e-r Zahl: fraction; e-s freundschaftlichen Verhältnisses: rupture. — 14. *med.* vomiting; zum ~ einnehmen to take an emetic; ~ erregend vomitive, ...ory; das ist zum ~ (ekelhaft) that's nauseous or enough to make one sick, F it's a sickener.
Brecher (ˊ˘) *m* ② 1. (a. ~**in** *f* ④) p. who breaks, &c. (f. brechen); breaker of the law, &c., smasher of crockery, &c. — 2. ✠ (Sturzsee) breakers *pl.*, heavy sea.
Brech=körner (ˊ˘...) *n/pl.* ② (Früchte der Rizinuspflanze) castor beans *pl.*; =**maschine** ⊕ *f* breaking- (or crushing-)machine or mill; =**mittel** *n*: a) *med.* emetic, vomitive; b) *fig.* F sickener, (lästiger Kerl) bore; =**nuß** *f*, *pharm.* (Samen von *Strychnos nux vo'mica*) (it.) nux vomica (auch als homöopathisches *etc.* Mittel), bisw. vomic nut; =**pulver** *n*, *med.* emetic powder; =**punkt** *m*, *phys.* point of refraction; =**reiz** *m. path.* sickly feeling; (Würgen) retching; =**ruhr** *f*, *path.* cholerine, (mild form of) cholera; =**stange** ⊕ *f* Bauw.: crowbar, (Hebestange) handspike; =**trank** *m*, *med.* emetic draught or potion.
Brechung (ˊ˘) *f* ② 1. = brechen 13; *opt.* ~ des Lichts refraction. — 2. *gram.* f. S. XXXIII Mitte.
Brechungs=ebene (ˊ˘...) *f* ② plane of refraction; =**exponent** *m* (Verhältnis des

Sinus d. Einfallwinkels zum S. des B.=winkels) index of refraction; =**fläche** *f* = =ebene; =**winkel** *m* angle of refraction.
Brech=veilchen ⊕ (ˊ˘...) *n* ② = =wurzel; =**weinstein** *m*, *chm.* (Antimonyl-kalium-tartrat, $C_4 H_4 Sb KO_7$) tartar emetic; =**wurzel** ⊕ *f* ipecacuanha (Wurzel v. *Cephae'lis Ipecacua'nha*); =**zange** ⊕ *f* pincers *pl.*; =**zeug** ⊕ *n* implements *pl.* for breaking doors,&c. open; burglar's (set of) tools *pl.*
bregeln mb. (ˊ˘) v/a. u. v/n. (h.) ② a. = braten.
Bregen nordd. (ˊ˘) [udd.: brain] *m* ② bsd. Kochkunst: brain; F = Gehirn.
Brei (ˊ) [ahd.] *m* ② *c.* 1. für Kinder: pap; (Kleister) size; (Gallerte) jelly; ② Papierfabr.: pulp; von Gips, Amalgam: paste; Kocht.: (Erbsen=)~ pease-pudding; (Kartoffel=)~ mashed potatoes *pl.*; ~ aus Äpfeln, Birnen *etc.* stewed apples, pears, &c.; (Grütze) porridge; das Fleisch ist ganz zu ~ gekocht ... is boiled to a pulp or to rags; in ~ verwandeln (to turn into) pulp, Kartoffeln *etc.*, to mash. — 2. *fig.*: F einen langen ~ v. et. machen to tell a long rigmarole (or yarn) about a th.; P zu ~ schlagen to knock (or break) to pieces, to beat into a jelly, to pound, to smash up; derb: e-m den ~ ums Maul schmieren (Schönes vorspiegeln) to buoy a p. up (with false hopes); den ~ verschütten to spoil a th., F to make a hash of it. — 3. Sprichw. er geht wie die Katze um den heißen ~ he is beating about the bush; (zu) viele Köche verderben den ~ too many cooks spoil the broth.
Brei=apfelbaum ⊕ (ˊ˘...) *m* ② naseberry-tree, sapodilla (*Achras Sapo'ta*); =**artig** *a.* ② like pap; pulp-like; pulpy; mashed; ≈**e Beschaffenheit**, das ~e ⊕ pulpiness; mashed condition.
brei-icht, breiig (ˊ˘) *a.* ② = breiartig.
Brei=löffel, =**napf** *m* ② pap-spoon, -boat.
breit (ˊ) [ahd.: broad] **I** *a.* ② 1. meist: broad; er ist ebenso lang als ≈ he is as long as he is broad; mit den Schultern broad-shouldered; ohne Rücksicht auf die Länge: wide; zwei Ellen (Meter) ≈ two yards (metres) wide; drei Zoll lang und vier Zoll ≈ three inches by four; *fig.* (weitschweifig) diffuse, prolix, verbose. — 2. nicht e-n Finger ≈ not a finger's breadth, oft: not an inch; es fehlt kein Haar(=)≈ daran not a hair's breadth is missing or wanting; ≈er m., w. to broaden, to widen; Buch mit ≈em Rande ... with a wide (or large) margin. — 3. da liegt es groß und ≈ (in die Augen fallend) it strikes one at a glance, it is palpable or evident; **weit** und ≈ far and wide. — 4. *fig.* die Sache ist so ≈ wie (sie) lang (ist) (es läuft auf dasselbe hinaus) it's as broad as it's long; sich ≈ machen: a) (viel Raum einnehmen) to take up much room, F to spread o.s out; b) (sich brüsten) to put on (or give o.s.) airs, F to do the grand, to raise a great dust; sich mit et. ≈ machen to make a great show with a th.; Malerei: e-n breiten Pinsel führen to have a bold (or vigorous) style. — **II** ~**e**(**s**) *n* ② 5. ins ≈ gehen to widen (out), weiteS. to extend, expand, spread; des langen und ≈en at

full length, in detail; ein langes und ≈es plaudern, schwatzen to have a good long talk or chat; to spin a long yarn; sich des ≈en über et. auslassen to enlarge (or expatiate) on a th.; des ≈er(e)n darlegen to enlarge (or dilate) upon.
Breit=axt (ˊˊ...) *f* ②, =**beil** *n* ⊕ broad (or chip-)axe; =**beinig** *a.* with legs wide(ly) apart, (sperrbeinig) straddle-legged; =**blätt(e)rig** ♀ *a.* broad-leaved; ~**latifoliate**; =**brüstig** *a.* broad-chested or -breasted; =**drücken** v/a. ⊕** to flatten (or widen, spread) out; ≈**gedrückte Nase** flat(tened) nose.
Breite (ˊ˘) *f* ② 1. breadth (a. ⚓ = des Schiffes); width (f. breit 1); 10 Ellen in die ~ ten yards wide or in width; in die Länge und ~ in length and breadth; der ~ nach broadwise; v. Band, Spitzen *etc.*: depth; ⚓ ~ (Tiefe) e-r Flagge, e-s Segels: hoist; ⚔ ~ (Mächtigkeit) e-s Ganges thickness, width. — 2. ♀ u. *ast.* (Winkelabstand vom Äquator, von der Ekliptik) latitude; in 5° 12′ nördlicher ~ in 5° 12′ north latitude; hohe (niedere) ~n high (low) latitudes *pl.*; ⚓ ~ machen to run down latitude. — 3. (weit ausgedehntes Feld) broad acres *pl.*; open (range of) country. — 4. *fig.* ~ (Weitschweifigkeit) diffuseness, prolixity, verbosity.
breiten (ˊ˘) v/a. u. v/refl. ⊕ 1. (sich) ≈ to spread out, extend, expand; ⊕ Eisen *etc.* ≈ (strecken) to hammer (or beat, flatten) out. — 2. eine Serviette *etc.* aus=ea.=≈ to unfold ...; ⚓ die Segel ≈ to brace ... — 3. (breittreten).
Breiten=grad (ˊ˘...) *m* ② ♀, *ast.* degree of latitude; =**kreis** *m* ♀, *ast.* (mit dem Äquator parallel gezogener Kreis) parallel (or circle) of latitude; =**streuung** ⚔ *f* lateral spread.
Breit=fock ⚓ (ˊ˘...) *f* ② (viereckiges Segel kleiner Fahrzeuge) squaresail; =**füßig** *a.* ② flat-footed, with flat feet; *anat.*: ~ **platycnemic**; =**füßigkeit** *f* ② flat-footedness; ~ **platycnemia**; =**gesichtigkeit** *f*: ~ **brachyprosopy**; =**gestirnt** *a.* with a broad forehead; broad-browed; =**hammer** ⊕ *m* (Streckhammer) flattening-hammer; =**händig** *a.* broad-handed; =**kirchliche** *m/pl.* members of the **Broad** Church; =**köpfig** *a. anat.*: ~ **platycephalous**; =**krempig** *a.* broad-brimmed. [sprattus.]
Breitling (ˊ˘) *m* ② *d. ichth.* sprat (*Clu'pea*
breit=mäulig (ˊˊ...) *a.* ② broad-mouthed; =**nasen** *f/pl.* ② *zo.* Familie der Affen: ~ **platyrrhines** *pl.*; =**nasig** *a.* flat-nosed, *zo.*, &c.: ~ **platyrrhine**, ...ian; =**randig** *a.* = =krempig; =**rückig** *a.* broad-backed; =**saat** *f* f. =**wurf**; =**schlagen** v *a.* ⑤**: a) = =drücken; b) F *fig.* einen (zu et.) ≈ to coax a p. (into a th.); =**schnäb(e)lig** *a.* broad-billed, broad-beaked; ~ **latirostrous**; =**schult(e)rig** *a.* broad-shouldered, square-built; =**seite** ⚓ *f* e-s Schiffes: broadside; =**spurig** *a.*: a) 🚂 broad-gauge (line); b) *fig.* von Personen: overbearing; F bumptious; =**spurigkeit** *f* meist *fig.* overbearing conduct; F bumptiousness; =**stirnig** *a.* = =gestirnt; =**treten** v/a. ⊕**** *fig.* et. ≈ (ausdehnen) to spin out a th.; to give a circumstantial account of it;

[Breitwimpel] — 219 — [Brennweite]

=wimpel ↓ des Dtsch. Kaisers (das höchste Kommandozeichen der dtsch. Marine) Imperial broad pennant; —wurf m. agr. broadcast (sowing); =würfig a. u. adv.: ~ säen to sow broadcast; =zähnig a. zo.: broad-toothed, ⚗ latidentate.

Brei=umschlag (″...) m ⚙ poultice: =umschläge um et. machen to poultice a th.; =weich a. 🌕 (as) soft as pulp or pap; succulent; fig. sentimental, F soft; ~ schlagen to smash to pulp.

Breme (⌣) f 🌕 ent. ⚗ oestrus; (Familie der) ~n pl.: ⚗ oestridæ pl.

Bremer (⌣) I bisw. a. **Bremenser** (-⌣) m ⚙, ~in f 🌕 native (or inhabitant) of Bremen. — II a. inv., a. **bremisch** a. 🌕 of B.; Malerei: **Bremer=blau** n B. blue; Bremer Stadtmusikanten travelling musicians pl., German band sg.

Bremmer ⚒ (⌣) m ⚙ shaft with resting-places or landing-stages.

Brems ⊕ (⌣) m ⓐa. = **Bremse**².

Brems=achse (″...) f ⚙ = =welle; =backen m der Backen- od. Klotzbremse: brake-block; =berg m self-acting inclined plane; =dynamometer m dynamometrical (or Prony's friction-)brake.

Bremse¹ (⌣) [ndd.: breeze] f 🌕 ent. (Rinds-)~ gadfly, breeze, bot- (or burrel-)fly (Taba'nus bovi'nus); ~n (Familie) ⚗ tabanidæ pl.

Bremse² ⊕ (⌣) [mhd., ndd., *ndl.] f 🌕 1. (Hemmschuh) meist: brake; für Fuhrwerke 2c. auch ⊕ drag(-wheel); 🚂, auch: carriage-lock; selbstwirkende ~ self-acting brake; die ~ anlegen 🚂, &c.: to apply the brake, bei Karren: to put on the drag. — 2. Hufschmiede: (Nasenkrebel für Pferde u. Bullen) barnacle.

bremsen ⊕ (⌣) v/a. ⚙ 1. (f. Bremse² 1) to apply (or put on) the brake or the drag or the lock, to lock. — 2. ein Pferd ⚒ to barnacle. [sting of a gadfly.)

Bremsen=stich (⌣...) [Bremse¹] m ⚙

Bremser 🚂 (⌣) m ⚙ brakesman.

Brems=fliege (″...) f ⚙ = Breme; =hebel m brake-lever; =flosz m = =backen; =rad n br.-wheel; =schuh m br.-shoe, auch = =backen; =schwengel m: a) br.(-handle or -bar); b) = =backen; =vorrichtung f br.-arrangement or -mechanism; brake; =wagen 🚂 m br.-van; =welle f br.-shaft; =winkel=eisen n der Lokomotive: br.-angle plate of the engine.

Brenke prov. (⌣) f 🌕, ~l n ⚙ (Holzgefäsz zum Unterseten beim Zapfen) wooden vessel to catch up the drippings from the tap; ~l=bier (″...) n ⚙ drippings pl. from the tap of a beer-barrel.

Brenn=apparat ⊕ (″...) m ⚙ a.) surg.: = Brenneisen; b) surg. galvanocaustic apparatus; c) Brandmalerei: implement for (making) poker-pictures.

brennbar (⌣-) a. 🌕 combustible, (leicht entzündlich) inflammable; ⚡e Luft = Wasserstoffgas; ⚡es Mineral f. Brenz 1.

Brennbarkeit (⌣--) f 🌕 (f. brennbar) combustibility; inflammability.

Brenn=berge (″...) f ⚒ (kohlenstoffhaltige Schiefertone zw. Kohlenflözen) carboniferous shale between seams of coal; =blase f Branntweinbrennerei: distilling- (or distillery-)apparatus, still; ehm. alembic; =bündel n faggot; =eisen n: a) zum Zeichnen

von Tieren, ehm. a. Sträflingen: marking- (ehm. a. branding-)iron; b) vet. firing-iron; c) Friseur: curling-iron or -tongs pl.; d) surg. cauterizing iron, cautery.

brennen (⌣) [ahd.: burn] v/n. (h.), v/a. u. v/refl. ⚙ b. I v/n. (h.), a. v/impers. 1. to burn; med. auch: to cauterize; es brannte ein Feuer im Kamine there was a fire (or a fire was burning) in the grate; das Haus brennt ... is on fire; das Dorf brennt lichterloh ... is all ablaze; es brennt in der Stadt there is a fire in the town; als Ruf: es brennt! fire!; brennt das Gas? is the gas burning or alight?; ihr Kleid brannte ... (had) caught fire; fig. mir brennt (glüht) der Kopf my head is burning, is as hot as fire; ihm ⚡ die Augen his eyes smart; die Wunde brennt ... burns or smarts. — 2. fig.: a) (heftig begehren) to desire ardently or keenly; sie ⚡ (vor Verlangen), ihn zu sehen they are burning (with a desire) to see him; er brennt auf die (nach der) Ehre, Sie kennen zu lernen he is eagerly desiring the honour of your acquaintance; b) das brennt ihm wie Feuer in den Adern that makes his blood boil; es (od. das Feuer) brennt ihm auf die Nägel he is hard driven; es brennt ihm unter den Sohlen he wants to be off, the place is (getting) too hot for him; das Geld brennt ihm in der Tasche (es läszt ihm keine Ruhe, bis er's ausgegeben hat) the money is burning a hole in his pocket; c) Kinderspiel: es brennt (man ist dem Ziele nahe)! (now) it's hot!, it burns! — II v/a., oft auch ohne Objekt: 3. to burn (up); Holzgefäsze. Vieh 2c. ⚡ (zeichnen) to mark (or brand) ... with a hot iron; Sprichw. ein gebranntes Kind scheut das Feuer a burnt child dreads the fire; once bit(ten) twice shy. — 4. (empfindlich stechen, jucken) die Sonne brennt ... is scorching (hot); die Nessel brennt the nettle stings; fig. das Geheimnis brennt ihm auf der Zunge F he is itching (or burning, F dying) to let out the secret; mich brennt's wie Feuer, bis ich es weisz I am most anxious to know it. — 5. (in Brand stecken) sengen und ⚡ to put a country to fire and sword, to burn and ravage. — 6. e-m eins auf den Pelz (od. aufs Leder) ⚡ (aufe-n schieszen) to shoot (F to pot) at a p. — 7. ⊕ (mit Feuer zubereiten) Holz zu Asche ⚡ to reduce wood to ashes; die Haare ⚡ to curl the hair; Erze, Kaffee 2c. ⚡ to roast ...; Kartoffeln 2c. zu Spiritus, Branntwein ⚡ to distil spirits out of potatoes, &c.; Kalk ⚡ to burn lime; Kohlen in Meilern ⚡ to char coal, to make charcoal; gebrannte (geglühte) Magnesia (Magnesiumoxyd) burnt (or calcined) magnesia; Porzellan ⚡ to fire or bake, burn) china or porcelain; Ziegel ⚡ to burn (or bake) bricks (or tiles); gebrannte Töpferware baked earthenware, (it.) terracotta; ↓ ein Schiff (fürs Kalfatern rein-) ⚡ to bream (it.); metall. Silber ⚡ to refine ...; Stahl ⚡ to (an)neal ...; Erze ⚡ (rösten) to calcine ...; agr. den Rasen ⚡ to fire the grass or turf. — III sich ⚡ v/refl. 8. to burn o.s. — 9. F

fig.: a) (sich irren) da brennst du dich! you are (greatly) mistaken there!; b) sich weisz, rein ⚡ (wollen) to (try to) exculpate or exonerate or clear o.s. —

IV ~ n ⚙ 10. burning, &c. (f. I u. II); fire; v. Augen, Wunden: smarting (pain); der Sonne: scorching (heat); ~ und Sengen devastation or havoc wrought by warfare; ⊕ ~ v. Schnaps: distillation; ~ (Rösten) von Erzen 2c. calcination ...; med. ~ der Haut heat or itching; ~ im Magen (Sodbrennen) heart-burn; surg. ~ (Ätzen) cauterization, cautery; mittels des galvanischen Stromes: galvanocauterization, galvanocautery. —

V ⚡ p.pr. und ⚡ 11. (f. I u. II) burning; ⚡es Haus house in flames, on fire; ⚡ de Sonnenglut parching (or scorching) heat of the sun. — 12. ⚡ (adv.) rot of a fiery red, (as) red as fire; ⚡ de Farbe glaring (F loud, startling) colour; ⚡ der Schmerz stinging (or smarting) pain. — 13. fig. hot, fervent; ⚡ de Liebe ardent love; ~de Liebe 🌺 scarlet lychnis (Lychnis chalcedo'nica); ⚡ de Tagesfrage burning (or urgent, pressing) question.

Brenner (⌣) m ⚙ 1. (Branntwein=) distiller. — 2. ⊕ (Ziegel=)~ burner, brick-maker or -manufacturer. — 3. ⊕ (Gas=)~ (gas-)burner, (gas-)light. — 4. ⊕ (Ofen=) furnace. — 5. ↓ = Brander 1. — 6. 🌿 schwarzer ~ d. Weinstocks: ⚗ anthracnose.

Brennerei (⌣″) f ⚙ a.) für Branntwein: distillery; b) für Ziegel 2c.: kiln.

Brennessel 🌿 (⌣⌣) [Brenn=nessel] f 🌕 stinging nettle (Urti'ca). [nen (f. ds).)

brenn(e)te (⌣(⌣)) impf. subj. von bren-)

Brenn=glas (″...) n ⚙ phys. burning-glass or -lens; =haus n ⚙: a) distillery; b) metall. casting-house; =helm m top of the still; =herd m, metall. für Silber: refining-hearth or -furnace; =hitze f very high temperature, intense heat; =holz n fire-wood, weiszS. fuel; =kapsel ⊕ f: a) cap for dynamite fuse; b) Porzellanfabr.: saggar; =kegel m, med. bsd. im Orient gbr.: moxa; =kolben m =blase; =kraft f der Heizmaterialien: calorific force; =linie f, phys. caustic (curve); =linse f = =glas; =material n = =stoff; =messer n, vet. firing-iron; =mittel n, surg. caustic; =nessel 🌿 f f. Brennessel; =ofen m: a) metall. refining-furnace; b) für Ziegel 2c.: kiln; c) Töpferei: (burning) oven; =öl n n oil for lighting purposes, engS. lamp-oil; =palme 🌿 f Ost-Indien: ⚗ caryota (Caryo'ta urens); =pfanne f Glasm. 2c.: melting-pot or -pan; =punkt m, phys. u. fig. focus; in dem ~ sammeln, vereinigen to focus; =punkts=abstand m = =weite; =schere f =eisen c; =silber n amalgam for silvering copper; =spiegel m. phys. burning-mirror or -reflector; =spiritus m (methylated) spirits pl. of wine for burning; =stahl m, metall. cemented (or converted) steel; =stahl=bereitung f cementation, converting of steel; =stahl=ofen m, metall. cementing-furnace; =stift m Brandmalerei: burin for doing poker-drawings; =stoff m combustible (matter); für Öfen: fuel; =weite f, phys. focal

⚗ scientific; 🌿 botanical; 🌐 geography; ⊕ machinery; ⚒ mining; ⚔ military; ↓ marine; 💰 commercial; ✉ postal; 🚂 railway.

[Brennwert] — 220 — [Briefpost]

distance; **=wert** *m* value as fuel; *phys.* calorific capacity; **=zeug** *n* distilling utensils *pl.*; **=ziegel** *m* fire-brick; **=zünder** ⚔ *m*, *artill.* time-fuse.

Brenz (⌣) [brennen] ⓐ*a.* **1.** *n* (brennbares Mineral) combustible, ⚚ empyreuma. — **2.** *m, prov.* = Branntwein. [C₆H₄(OH)₂.]

Brenz-catechin ⚚ (⌣...) *n* ⓑ₂ pyrocatechin;
brenzeln (⌣⌣) *v/n.* (h.) ⓐ*a.* to smell (or taste) of burning or like burnt.

brenzlicht ⚄, *mſt* **brenzlig** (⌣⌣) *a.* ⓒ₆ *chm.* smelling (or tasting) of burning or like burnt, *min. u. chm.* empyreumatic; auch = Brenz-..., z. B. ⸗e Säure pyro-acid; ⸗er Geruch: ⚚ empyreuma; ⸗e Holzsäure (Holz-eſſig) pyroligneous acid. [oils *pl.*; **=säure** *f* pyro-acid.]

Brenz-öle (⸗...) *n/pl.* ⓑ₂ empyreumatic)

Bresche ⚔ (⌣⌣) [fr. *brèche*; *dtſch brechen*] *f* ⓑ₈ breach; ~ schießen in ... to make (or effect, form) a breach in ..., to breach ...; *fig.* sich in die ~ stellen, in die ~ springen to fill up the gap, to come to the rescue.

Bresch(e)-batterie ⚔ (⌣(⌣)...) *f* ⓑ₂ breaching-battery or -train.

Bresling ⚘ (⌣⌣) *m* ⓐ*d.* **1.** (rote Beere) red berry. — **2.** = Knackelbeere.

Brest(e) (⌣⌣) *m* ⓑ*b.* ⓒ₄ (Fehler, Gebrechen) defect, infirmity. [infirm, decrepit.]

bresthaft ⚄ (⌣⌣) *a.* ⓒ₆ (gebrechlich) invalid,)

Bretagne ♀ (brĕ-tä'n-je) *npr/f.* ⓑ*a.* (fr. Landſchaft) Brittany; **~er(in** *f* ⓐ₇) *m* ⓑ₂, **bretagniſch** (⌣⌣) *a.* ⓒ₆ Breton.

Bretone (⌣⌣) *m* ⓒ = Bretagner; **bretoniſch** *a.* ⓒ₆ = bretagniſch.

Brett (⌣) [ahd.: Bord] *n* ⓐ*b.* **1.** (Holztafel von weniger als 5 cm Stärke; *ant.* Bohle) board, plank; (Diele) deal board; zollſtarkes (2¹/₂ cm ſtarkes) ~ inch-board or -plank; mit ⸗ern auslegen, beſchlagen, vernageln to board (up), to plank; (täfeln) to panel, to wainscot. — **2.** ſchwarzes ~ (für Bekanntmachungen) notice-board; am ſchwarzen ~ anſchlagen to (publish on the) board; auf dem ſchwarzen ~ ſteh(e)n (bei e-m Schulden haben), etwa: to be in debt with (or to owe a debt to) a p. — **3.** (Präſentierteller) tray. — **4.** (Bücher-)~ shelf. — **5.** a) (Dambrett) draught-board; *fig.* bei e-m einen Stein im ⸗e haben to be a favourite (or in favour) with a p., F to be in a p.'s good books; b) (Zähl-, Rechen-brett) counting-board, ehm. abacus. — **6.** (Tiſch) table, board; (Werktiſch der Handwerker) (work-)bench; et. auf einem ⸗e (auf einmal) bezahlen to pay down in a lump sum, F to plank down. — **7.** (grüner Ratstiſch) council-board or -table; vors ~ kommen (vorgefordert werden) to (have to) go before the board or to appear in court; *fig.* hoch ans ~ kommen (in der Welt ſteigen) to attain (great) distinction, to reach the top of the tree or ladder; (hoch) am ⸗e ſein, ſitzen (hochgeſtellt ſein) to be in power or at the helm or in a high position. — **8.** (Schaubühne) boards *pl.*, stage; über die ⸗er geh(e)n (aufgeführt w.) to be put (or acted) on the stage; *poet.* to sweep the tragic boards; die ⸗er (als Schauſpieler) beſteigen to mount (or step upon) the boards, to walk the stage; die ⸗er betreten (Schauspieler w.) to go on the stage; auf den ⸗en, die bedeuten (*SCH.*), etwa: upon the boards which represent the world. — **9.** *fig.* Redensarten: er kann durch ein ~ (ſehr ſcharf) ſehen he can see through a brick wall; ein ~ vor den Augen (vor dem Kopfe) h. F to be blind (blockheaded, dense, obtuse); ein ~ vor dem Munde haben to keep one's mouth shut; mit ⸗ern vernagelt ſein to be very dull or slow (of comprehension); da iſt die Welt mit ⸗ern vernagelt there's no thoroughfare (here)!, that's a blind alley; e-m das ~ unter den Füßen wegziehen (ſo daß er fallen muß) to trip up a p., to bring about a p.'s fall.

Brett-baum ⓞ (⸗...) *m* ⓑ₂ tree, block for making (or cutting into) planks; **=bohle** *f* sawn plank.

Brettchen (⌣⌣) *n* ⓐ₄ *dim.* small board; Spiel mit bunten ~ Chinese puzzle.

Bretter-bude (⸗⌣...) *f* ⓑ₂ booth; **=bühne** *f* platform; **=dach** *n* plank-roof; (Schindeldach) shingle-roof; **=gerüst** *n* scaffolding made of planks; **=haus** *n*, **=hütte** *f* Alpen ꝛc. chalet.

brettern (⌣⌣) *a.* ⓒ₆ (made) of boards or planks; Les Dach boarded or planked ...; Les (Fachwerk-)Haus frame-house.

Bretter-verſchlag (⸗⌣...) *m* ⓑ₂, **=wand** *f* ⓞ partition (made of boards or planks); **=werk** ⓞ *n* boarding, planking; boards, planks *pl.*; **=zaun** *m* wooden fence; ⓞ hoarding.

Brett-mühle (⸗...) *f* ⓑ₂ saw-mill; **=nagel** *m* plank- (or board-)nail; **=säge** *f* plank- (or pit-)saw; **=säger** *m* sawyer; **=schaukel** *f* seesaw; **=schneider** *m* = ⸗säger; **=spiel** *n* game played on a board; (Dambrett) (game of) draughts *pl.*; (Puffſpiel) backgammon; **=stein** *m* Damſpiel: man (or piece) (at draughts, &c.); **=verkleidung** *f* boarding.

Breve (⌣*lw*) [it.] *n* ⓐ₆, ⓒ₃ (päpſtliches Sendſchreiben) papal brief.

Breviarium (-w⌣(⌣)⌣) [it.] *n* ⓐ₈ (kurze Überſicht) summary, brief extract.

Brevier (-w*l*) [it.] *n* ⓐ*c. Cath. eccl.* (lat. Gebetbuch der Prieſter) breviary.

brevi manu (*lw*-*ll*-) [lat.] *adv.* (kurzer hand) on the spot. at once, offhand.

Brezel (⌣*l*) [ahd. **it.*] *f* ⓐ₈ etwa: hard biscuit in B shape; beſ. auch: (light) bretzel. [*ind.* von brechen (ſ. b).]

brich (⌣) *imper.*, **brichſt, bricht** (⌣) *pres.*

Bricke (⌣⌣) [ndd.] *f* ⓐ₈ *ichth.* (Neunauge) lamprey (*Petromy'zon*).

Brief (*l*) [ahd.; **it.* (*li'tera*) brĕ'*vis*] *m* ⓐ*c.* **1.** letter; eingeſchriebener ~ registered letter; beſ. *bibl. u.* F epistle (ganz kurzer ~ (short) note; ⸗e auf die Poſt geben to post letters; mit e-m ⸗e wechſeln to correspond with a p.; war der ~ frankiert? was the letter paid (for)?; ich ſchrieb ihm e-n ganz kurzen ~ F I dropt him a few lines or a line; ⓞ wir haben Ihren geehrten ~ empfangen your (esteemed) favour (has come) to hand; unſere früheren ⸗e our previous communications; in unſerm letzten ⸗e bemerkten wir wie remarked in our last; in Erwiderung Ihres ⸗es vom 20. d. M. in answer to your lines (kürzer: to yours, höflicher: to your favour, to your communication) of the 20th inst. — **2.** (ſchriftliche Urkunde) (written) document; ~ und Siegel über et. geben to give s.th. in writing or under one's hand and seal; weiß. to bind o.s. by an agreement to do a th.; ~ und Siegel über et. haben, etwa: to have s.th. in writing; *jur.* to possess documentary proof(s); *fig.* to be sure of (or positive about) a th. — **3.** ⓞ ~ (Wechſel) bill (of exchange), draft; im Kurszettel: (angeboten; *abbr.* **B(r)**.) offered, for sale, seller, paper. — **4.** ⸗e von England ꝛc. kommende ⸗e, *oft*: the English, &c. mail; Bureau für unbeſtellbare ⸗e Returned († Dead) Letter Office. — **5.** (briefartig gefaltetes Papier) paper (folded) in form of a letter; ein ~ Nadeln a packet of needles or pins.

Brief-abfertigung ⚚ (⸗*ll*...) *f* ⓑ₂ dispatch of the mail(s); **=abholung** *f* collection of letters (by postmen); von poſtlagernden Briefen: calling for letters (at the post-office); **=adel** *m* (title of) nobility (conferred) by letters-patent; **=annahme** *f* receiving of letters; **=annahme(-ſtelle)** receiving-house (for letters); **=aufgabe** *f* posting (of) a letter; **=aufſchrift** *f* address (or direction) of a letter; **=ausgabe** *f* postal delivery; **=beſchwerer** *m* letter- or paper-)weight; **=beſtellung** *f* delivery of letters, postal delivery; **=beutel** *m* letter- (or mail-)bag; **=bogen** *m* sheet of note-paper; **=bote** *m* = ⸗träger; **=buch** ⓞ *n* letter-(copy)book.

Briefchen (⌣⌣) *n* ⓐ₃ *dim. v.* Brief.

Brief-decke (⸗*ll*...) *f* ⓑ₂ = ⸗umſchlag; **=einwurf** *m* (slot of a) letter-box, vgl. =kaſtenspalt; **=fach** *n* pigeon-hole; der Sortierer: sorting-case; **=fell-eiſen** *n* mail-(bag), dispatch-box; **=form** *f*: a) letter-form; in ~ in the form (or shape) of a letter; b) = ⸗ſtil; **=geheimnis** *n* inviolability (or privacy) of letters; **=halter** *m* letter-rack or -clip; **=hülle** *f* envelope; **=karte** *f* letter-card; **=kaſten** *m* letter-box; *Engl.*: rot lackierter ſäulenförmiger ~ pillar-box; **=kaſtenleerung** *f* clearance of the letter-box; **=kaſtenſpalt** *m* slot of the letter-box; **=klemmer** *m* = ⸗halter; **=kopf** *m, typ.* head of a letter, letter-head; **=kuvert** *n* envelope.

Brieflein (*l*-) *n* ⓐ₃ *dim. v.* Brief.

brieflich (*l*⌣) *a.* ⓒ₆ *u. adv.* by letter, weiß. in writing; ⚚ epistolary; mit e-m verkehren to keep up a (or to be in) correspondence (or to correspond) with a p.

Brief-mappe (*ll*...) *f* ⓑ₂ portfolio, writing- (or blotting-)case; **=marke** *f* (postage-)stamp; **=marken-album** *n* stamp-album; **=marken-kunde** *f:* ⚚ philately; **=marken-liebhaber, =marken-ſammler** *m* stamp-collector; ⚚ philatelist; **=marken-ſammlung** *f* stamp-collection; **=muſter** *n* model letter; **=nadeln** *f/pl.* paper- or sheet-pins *pl.*; **=papier** *n* note-(or letter-) paper; gelblich geripptes: cream-laid paper; dünnes: foreign (note-)paper; **=porto** *n* (fee for) postage; **=poſt** *f* letter mail; (ba-

Zeichen (ſ. S. XVII): F familiär; P Volksſprache; Γ Gaunerſprache; ⚄ ſelten; † alt (auch geſtorben); * neu (auch geboren); ⧾ unrichtig;

[Briefpostsachen] — 221 — [bringen]

mit beladener Wagen) mail-coach; mit der nächsten ~ by the next mail or post; =**postsachen** f/pl. articles pl. conveyed (or carried) by letter-post; =**presse** f letter-press.
Briefschaften (⸍⸤⸥) f/pl. ㊻ letters pl.; correspondence; weitS. papers deeds, documents pl.
Brief-schalter (⸍...) m ㊷: a) letter-box (in a wall or window); b) receiving-office; =**schluß** m conclusion (or finishing sentences pl.) of a letter; =**schrank** m cupboard (or safe) for letters; =**schreibe-kunst** f art of letter-writing, ♫ epistolography; =**schreiber** m letter-writer; =**schulden** f/pl. arrears pl. of correspondence; =**sortierer** m letter-sorter; =**steller** m: a) =**schreiber**; b) (Anleitungsbuch) epistolary guide; polite letter-writer; =**stellerei** f letter-writing, ♫ epistolography; =**stempel** m post-mark; =**stil** m epistolary style; =**streicher** m (Falzbein) paper-knife or -folder; =**tabak** ✿ m tobacco in packets; =**tasche** f: a) pocket-book; b) = **mappe**; =**taube** f, orn. carrier- (or messenger-) pigeon (Colu'mba li'via tabella'ria); =**taxe** f rate of postage for letters; =**träger** m postman; letter-carrier; =**umschlag** m envelope, cover; =**verkehr** m: a) zwischen Personen: exchange of letters, correspondence; b) in e-m Lande: total (number) of letters (carried within a certain period); =**wage** f letter-balance or -scales pl.; =**wechsel** m =verkehr a; e-n ~ mit einem anfangen (unterhalten) to open (to carry on) a correspondence with a p.; mit e-m im ~ steh(e)n to exchange letters (or to correspond) with a p.
Brieschen (⸍⸥) n ㉓ = Bröschen.
briet (⸍) impf. von braten (s. ds).
Brigade (⸍⸤⸥) [fr., it.] f ㊷ (Truppenverband aus zwei Regimentern derselben Waffengattung) brigade; =**adjuta'nt** (⸍...) m ㊷ aide-de-camp to a brigadier-general; =**exerzieren** n brigade-drill; =**genera'l** m = Brigadier; =**kommandeur** m general officer commanding a brigade, brigadier; =**majo'r** m brigade-major.
Brigadier ⚔ † (⸤⸥) [fr.] m ㊷ brigadier (-general); chief of a brigade.
Brigant (⸍) [it.] m ㊷ (Räuber) brigand; ~**entum** (⸍⸤⸥) n ㉒ d. brigandism.
Brigantine ⚓ (⸤⸥) [it.] f ㊺ (Briggschoner) brigantine, two topsail-schooner, brig-schooner.
Brigg ⚓ (⸍) [engl.] f ㊺ (Zweimaster mit Rahsegeln) brig.
Brigg-kutter (⸍...) m ㊷ brig-cutter; =**schoner** m f. Brigantine; =**takelung** f brig-rigging.
Bright † (brāīt) [engl.] npr/m., med. ~**sche** Nierenkrankheit Bright's disease.
Brigitte (⸤⸥) [schwd.] npr/f. ㊴ ㋚. (Vn.) Bridget.
Brikett (⸤⸥) [fr. briquette f] n ⓒ. (㊽) (Preßkohle) briquette, patent fuel.
brikolieren (⸤⸥⸍) [fr. bricoler] v/n. (h.) ㊸ Billard: (to make a) back-stroke.
Brikol-schuß † ⚔ (⸤⸥⸍) m ㊷ rebound.
brillant¹ (bril-jä'nt) [fr.] a. ㊺ (glänzend) brilliant, splendid; (vorzüglich) first-rate, first-class, F A-one, A 1.

Brillant² (bril-jä'nt) [fr.] m ㊷ (als Doppelpyramide geschliffener Diamant) brilliant, diamond cut in(to) facets.
Brillant-feuer (⸍...) n ㊷ Feuerwerk: bouquet of fire, aigret(te); =**nadel** f breastpin (set) with a brilliant; =**schnitt** m facet-cut(ting) of jewels.
Brille (⸍⸥) [mhd. 1300 aus *Beryll(e pl.)] f ㊺ (pair of) spectacles pl., glasses pl.; F co. specks, barnacles pl.; der Automobilisten: goggles pl.; mit einer ~ bewaffnet, versehen spectacled, P goggle-eyed; eine ~ tragen to wear spectacles; (sich dat.) die ~ aufsetzen to put on one's glasses; fig. einem eine ~ aufsetzen (et. vorspiegeln) to impose on a p., to dupe (F to gull) a p.; et. durch die richtige ~ sehen to see things in the right light; et. durch eine (fremde) ~ ansehen to see things with other eyes.
brillen-ähnlich (⸍⸥...) a. ㊻ spectacle-shaped; =**bogen** m bridge (or bow) of (a pair of) spectacles; =**einfassung** f spectacle-frame; =**futteral** n spectacle-case; =**glas** n spectacle-glass or -lens; =**glas-schleifer(in** f) m spectacle-glass cutter; =**händler** m spectacle-maker, weitS. optician; =**kaiman** m, zo. spectacled alligator (Alliga'tor scleroʹps); =**macher** m = händler; =**schanze** ⚔ f =**werf**; =**schlange** f. zo. spectacle-snake, cobra (de capello) (Naia tripu'dians); =**schleifer(in** f) m = glasschleifer(in); =**tragend** a. wearing spectacles, spectacled, P goggle-eyed; =**träger(in** f) m p. wearing glasses; =**werk** ⚔ n lunette.
brillieren (bril-jī'⸥) v/n. (h.) ㊼ (glänzen) to shine; ~ mit of //, to make a (great) show with or of //, to show off (to advantage).
Brimborium F ⚠ (⸤⸥⸍⸥) [fr., it.] n ㉘ (unwesentliche Zutat) odd trifle, knick-knack; (läppisches Zeug) stuff, trash.
Brindisi ⚠ (⸍⸤⸥) *ich bring' dir sie (die Gesundheit)!] n ㊿ (I drink to) your health; ♪ (Trinklied) drinking song.
bringen (⸍⸥) [ahd.: bring] v/a. ㊿ **1.** (befördern) to convey, to take; (tragen) to carry; e-n nach Hause ⸺ to es-cort) a p. home; ☉ Güter per Achse (per Bahn) von e-m Orte zum andern ⸺ to carry (or transmit) goods by road (by rail) ... — **2.** (zu einem, bsd. zum Sprechenden, befördern) to bring; ⸺ Sie mir die Schlüssel bring me ...; eine Antwort ⸺ to bring (or come back with) an answer; er brachte mir Bescheid he brought me word; was bringt Sie (zu mir) her? what (business) brings you here?; nun, was ⸺ Sie? F well, what's up?, what is it you want?, höflicher: what is your pleasure? — **3.** (darbringen) to offer; e-m ein Geschenk ⸺ to make a p. a present; e-m Hilfe ⸺ to render a p. assistance, to come to a p.'s aid; to succour a p.; (große) Opfer für e-e Sache ⸺ to make (great) sacrifices for a cause; e-m ein Ständchen (e-n Toast) ⸺ to serenade (to toast) a p. — **4.** (bereiten) Ehre ⸺ in r Familie ꝛc. Ehre ⸺ to do honour (or credit) ...; e-m Gewinn ⸺ to yield a profit to a p., to be profitable to a p.; das hat ihm Glück (Unglück) gebracht it has brought him good (bad or ill) luck; das wird ihm wenig Nutzen

Vorteil ⸺ that will be of little avail (or advantage, use) to him; einem Schaden ⸺ to cause injury (or detriment) to a p.; e-m Schande ⸺ to bring (or reflect) disgrace upon a p.; to cover a p. with shame; das hat ihm den Tod gebracht it has caused (or been) his death; Zinsen ⸺ to bear (or yield) interest; Sprichw. Wahrheit bringt Haß truth engenders hate; Zeit bringt Rat time will show the way; Zeit bringt Rosen all (will come) in good time. — **5.** (erzeugen) to bear (or bring forth) ...; Junge zur Welt ⸺ to give birth to (F to drop) young (ones). — **6.** (bieten) die Zeitungen ⸺ wenig Neues there's little news in the papers; was ⸺ Sie Neues? what news have you? what is the (latest) news? — **7.** mit adv. (zugleich oft mit es) etwas **auf**(=) ⸺ (F [⸺friegen) to get a th. open; einen **dahin** ⸺, daß er // oder es **dahin** ⸺, daß j. // to induce (or persuade) a p. to (inf.); ich kann ihn nicht dahin (oder dazu) ⸺ oder seine Pflicht tut I cannot prevail upon (F get) him to do his duty; wir werden es (noch) dahin ⸺, daß wir sie bändigen we shall (yet) manage (or contrive) to subdue them; einen **heim**=⸺ to conduct (or see) a p. home; was bringt ihn **her**? what is he doing here?; bring (zeig') einmal her! F let me have a look!; er soll es **heraus** ⸺, **hinaus** ⸺ he shall take (or carry) it out, remove it; et. **herein** ⸺, **hinein** ⸺ to get in a th.; vgl. a. herab=⸺, hinab=⸺, herauf=⸺, hinauf=⸺, herüber=⸺, hinüber=⸺, hinunter=⸺ ꝛc.; sein Leben **hoch** ⸺ to attain (or live to) a ripe, old age; er hat's hoch gebracht he has made his way (F has got up high) in the world; dem Untergange **nahe** ⸺ to bring to the brink of ruin; Schüler **vorwärts** ⸺ to push (F to get) on ...; es in j-m Fache **weit** (od. **hoch**) ⸺ to attain great proficiency (stärker: a high eminence) in one's department; von Schülern: er hat es im Latein nicht weit gebracht he is not very strong (or advanced) in Latin; er hat es nie weiter gebracht he never advanced a step (or any) further, F he never got beyond that; Geld **zusammen** ⸺ to amass ...; ⚔ ein Heer zj.=⸺ to collect ...; et. **zuwege** ⸺ to accomplish (or achieve, effect) a th. — **8.** in Verbindung mit prp. (fehlende Wendungen s. unter dem eingeklagten s.) **an**: etwas **an** sich ⸺ to acquire (or take possession of) a th.; Leute an=ea.=⸺ (hetzen) to set people by the ears; vgl. Bettelstab, Galgen; et. **an** den Mann ⸺: a) (e-m mitteilen) to make a th. known to a p., to show off one's knowledge before a p.; b) (loswerden) to get rid (or clear) of a th.; ✿ Waren: to dispose of goods; er weiß seine Ware an den Mann zu ⸺ he is a good salesman; c) seine Tochter an den Mann ⸺ to find a husband for ..., F to get ... (married) off; einen an den Rand des Verderbens ⸺ very nearly to ruin a p., F to be nearly the ruin of a p.; vgl. nahe ⸺ (unter 7.); et. an den Tag ⸺ to bring a th. to light; **auf**: math. Brüche

♪ Musik; ⚛ Wissenschaft; ❀ Pflanze; 🜨 Geographie; ☉ Technik; ⚒ Bergbau; ⚔ Militär; ⚓ Marine; ✿ Handel; ⚐ Post; 🚂 Eisenbahn.

[bringen] — 222 — [Bringer]

ꝛc. auf den einfachsten Ausdruck 2 to reduce ... to the simplest denomination; ſ. äußerſt III, Bahn 1; einen auf die Beine 2 to put a p. on his legs (a. *fig.*); e-n wieder auf die Beine 2 (i-s Verhältniſſe aufbeſſern) to set up a p. anew or afresh; ✕ ein Heer auf die Beine 2 to raise (or levy) an army; ein Stück auf die Bühne 2 to put ... on the stage, to produce (or act) ...; ſ. Fährte; e-n auf den Gedanken od. Einfall (od. auf et.) 2 to suggest (or insinuate) a th. to a p., to put a p. in mind of a th.; das brachte mich wieder darauf that reminded me of it; e-n auf e-n Einfall 2 to put an idea into a p.'s mind, to suggest a th. to a p.; e-n auf andere (auf böſe) Gedanken 2 to divert (to poison) a p.'s mind; *math.* Brüche auf einen gemeinſamen Nenner 2 to reduce fractions to a common denominator; et. aufs Höchſte 2 to attain the highest degree of perfection in a th.; to carry a th. to its highest pitch or level; ſein Leben od. es (bis) auf 80 Jahre 2 to live to (the age of) eighty, to reach eighty; auf die Nachwelt 2 to hand down to posterity; Briefe ꝛc. auf die Poſt 2 to take (or carry) ... to the post(-office); to post ...; 🞸 e-m et. auf Rechnung 2 to put s.th. to a p.'s account, to debit a th. to a p.; ſ-n Sohn auf die Schule 2 to put (or send) ... to school or college; et. ob. einen auf die Seite (beiſeite) 2 to push s.th. or a p. aside, to remove a th. or a p.; e-n auf ſeine Seite 2 to draw (or win) a p. over to one's side; *hunt. u. fig.* auf die Spur 2 to put on the (right) scent or track; et. aufs Tapet 2 to bring a th. on the carpet or on the tapis; e-n auf ein (beliebtes) Thema 2 to start a (favourite) subject with a p.; Kochk.: warm auf den Tiſch zu 2! to be served up hot!; ich will ihn (ſchon) auf den Trab 2 I will hurry him on, F I'll make him trot or find his legs; e-n auf den rechten Weg 2 to put a p. on the right path, *fig.* to lead a p. in(to) the right way; ein Kind (a. *fig.* Geiſteserzeugniſſe) auf die Welt 2 to bring ... into the world, to give birth to ...; **aus:** Streitende aus=ea.=2 to separate disputants; *fig.* e-n aus der (ob. außer, vgl. unten) Faſſung (F aus dem Häuschen) 2 to disconcert (or upset) a p.; e-m et. aus den Gedanken, aus dem Kopfe 2 to put (or drive) a th. out of a p.'s mind or head; es iſt nichts aus ihm (heraus=) zu2 there is nothing to be drawn (F got) out of him, F he won't be drawn; **außer:** *fig.* e-n außer Faſſung, außer ſich 2 to put a p. out of countenance, to disconcert (or flurry, upset) a p., ſtärker: to exasperate a p.; **bei:** beiſeite 2 to put away or out of sight; **bis (zu):** er hat es bis zum Major gebracht he attained the rank of major; **hinter:** e-n hinter Schloß u. Riegel 2 to lock a p. up; **in:** in Achtung 2 to secure esteem (or respect) for; ſ. Anſchlag 7; in Anwendung (ob. Gebrauch) 2 to put to practical use or account;

to apply; to employ; in Aufnahme 2 to bring into vogue or fashion, to introduce; in Aufregung 2 to excite, stir, rouse; 🞸 Buchführung: in Ausgabe, Einnahme 2 to enter (as) expenditure, receipts; in ſ-n Beſitz 2 to put o.s. in possession of; et. in Bewegung 2 to put a th. in motion; et. in Blüte (Flor) 2 to make a th. prosper or thrive; in (großes) Elend 2 to reduce to (abject) misery; in Erfahrung 2 to learn, to ascertain, F to get to know; e-m et. in Erinnerung, ins Gedächtnis 2 to jog a p.'s memory about a th.; to remind a p. of a th.; in Fäſſer 2 to put into casks, to cask; ſ. Fluß 5, Gang 4; in Galopp, Trab 2 to put at a gallop, at a trot; in Gefahr 2 to expose to danger, to hazard, to jeopardize; ſich ins Gerede 2 to make o.s. the talk of the town; F to get into people's mouths; e-n, et. in ſeine Gewalt 2 to make o.s. master of a p., a th.; ins **gleiche** 2 to arrange; in Harniſch 2 to irritate; et. in e-n (hinein=) 2, einem etwas in den Kopf (hinein=) 2 to drive a th. into a p.'s head; in eine böſe Lage 2 to get (in)to great straits; Licht in et. 2 to clear up a matter; Mannigfaltigkeit in et. 2 to vary a th.; in Mode 2 to bring into fashion; in Ordnung 2 to set in order; einem in Rechnung 2 to place (or put) to a p.'s account or debit; ins reine 2 to settle; e-n, et. in guten (üblen) Ruf 2 to bring a p., a th. into good (ill) repute; ſ. Schäfchen; e-n in Schweiß 2 to make a p. perspire, durch Arznei: to send a p. into a perspiration; in Sicherheit 2 to (make) secure, to put in a place of safety or out of harm's way; mit ins Spiel 2 to implicate; ſ. Tinte, Umlauf, Unordnung; in Verdacht 2 to throw suspicion upon; in Verlegenheit 2 to embarrass; F to put out; in Verruf 2 to bring into discredit or disrepute; in Verſe 2 to versify; e-n in Wallung 2 to make a p.'s blood boil; in Wegfall 2 to suppress; in Wut 2 to enrage; in Zug 2 to set going; **mit:** es mit ſich 2, daß // to require (or necessitate) that //; die Sache bringt (auch die Umſtände 2) es ſo mit ſich the circumstances call for it or make it unavoidable; e-n Fehler ꝛc. mit ſich auf die Welt 2 to be born with a defect, &c.; Ausgaben, die ein Geſchäft mit ſich bringt, incidental business expenses: **nach:** e-n nach Hauſe 2 ſ. 1; **über:** e-n über die Grenze 2 to take a p. across the frontier; ich kann es nicht übers Herz 2 zu // I cannot prevail upon myself (F get myself) to //; über die Lippen 2 to utter; Unglück über e-n 2 to bring down misfortune upon a p.; **um:** e-n um et. 2 to make a p. lose a th.; (berauben) to rob a p. of a th.; (betrügen) to defraud a p. of a th., to cheat (or F do, diddle) a p. out of a th.; ſie ſind um alles gebracht worden, auch: they have been utterly ruined, F they've been done out of everything; e-n ums Leben 2 to kill (or slay) a p.; ſich ſelbſt ums Leben 2 to take one's

own life, to commit suicide; das hat ihn um den Verſtand gebracht that deprived him of his reason, it drove him mad; **unter:** ſ. Botmäßigkeit; unter Dach (und Fach) 2 to store away, to house, ein Haus: to roof in; e-n unter die Erde 2 to commit a p. to the grave; *fig.* to cause (or be) the death of a p.; unter ſeine Gewalt 2 to get into one's power; ein Mädchen unter die Haube 2 F to get ... married off or wedded; unter die Leute 2: a) Geld: to spend freely; b) Gerüchte: to set afloat, to spread (abroad, to circulate); **von:** e-n, et. vom Fleck, von der Stelle to remove ...; er iſt nicht vom Fleck zu 2 he won't stir or F budge; es bringt mich faſt von Sinnen it almost maddens me or drives me mad; *fig.* vom (rechten) Wege (ab=) 2 to lead away (from the right path); ſ. davonbringen; **vor:** Fremde (bis) vor das Haus 2 to take strangers (right) up to the house; et. vor ſich 2 to accomplish a task, to get on with a th.; er wird et. vor ſich 2 he will get on (or make his way) in the world, auch: he will make a mark; **zu:** zur Abſtimmung 2 to put to the vote; e-n (wieder) zu Anſehen, zu Ehren 2 to (re-)establish a p.'s credit, honour; e-n zur Beſinnung 2 to bring a p. to his senses; e-m et. zum Bewußtſein 2 to make a p. conscious (or aware) of a th.; einen dazu 2, et. zu tun to induce (or decide) a p. to do a th.; zu Ende 2 to bring to a close, (vollenden) to achieve, to finish; etwas zur Entſcheidung 2 to bring ... to a head; e-n zu Fall(e) 2 to be the cause of a p.'s fall; zum Gehorſam 2 to force into submission; zum (als) Geſchenk 2 to present; e-n zum Geſtändnis 2 to wring a confession from a p.; einem zur Kenntnis 2 to bring to a p.'s knowledge; e-n (wieder) zu Kräften 2 to give (new) strength to a p., to (re-)invigorate a p.; einen zum Lachen, Lächeln, Weinen 2 to make a p. laugh, smile, cry; zu Markte 2 to take to market, to offer for sale; et. zu Papier 2 to put s.th. down on (or to commit s.th. to) paper; einen zur Ruhe, zum Schweigen 2 to calm, to silence p.; e-n wieder zu ſich 2 to restore a p. to consciousness, F to bring a p. round or to (himself); et. zur Sprache, zur Erörterung 2 to bring a th. on the carpet, to broach a subject; et. zuſtande, zuwege 2 to bring about (or accomplish) a th.; zum Stehen 2 to bring to a stand(still), to arrest (a th. in its progress); e-n zur Vernunft 2 to bring a p. to his senses; einen zur Verzweiflung 2 to drive a p. to despair; zu hoher Vollendung, Vollkommenheit 2 to carry a p. to great perfection; zum Weichen 2 to force a p. to yield or to give in; ✕ den Feind: to shatter the enemy's ranks; zur Welt 2 to bring into the world, to bring forth; es zu et. 2 to gain (or attain) a position (in life); es zu nichts 2 to fail (in life). **Bringer** (⏑‿) *m* ㉒, **~in** *f* ㊶ 1. p. who brings; carrier; einer Botſchaft: mes-

Signs (see page XVII): ⌐ familiar; P vulgar; ⌐ flash; ⟍ rare; † obsolete (died); * new word (born); ⁺⁺ incorrect; ♪ music;

[Bringeschuld] — 223 — [Brotgelehrsamkeit]

senger. — 2. (Überbringer) eines Briefes ꝛc.: bearer.
Bringe-schuld (⌣⌣) f ⊕ debt which the debtor has to discharge to the creditor in person. ⟦(Grashügel) grassy mound.⟧
Brink *prov.* (⌣) [ndd.: brink] m ⓤb.
brisant (-́) [fr., *dtsch] a. ⊕ ♆e Stoffe explosives pl. (= Sprengstoffe).
Brisanz-geschosse ♆ (-⌣́...) n/pl. ⊕ explosive projectiles pl.
Brise ⌁ ⚓ (⌣́⌣) [engl., fr.] f ⊕ (gentle) breeze or gale; es weht eine frische ~ F there's a fresh breeze on.
Britannia-metall ⊕ (⌣⌣́⌣⌣...) n⊕(Zinn, Antimon u. Kupfer) Britannia-metal.
Britanni-en (⌣⌣́⌣⌣) [It. ſ. Brite] npr/n. ⊕α. Alt. Britain, *poet.* Britannia.
britannisch (⌣⌣́⌣) a. ⊕ = britisch.
Brite (⌣⌣) [klt. Tätowierter] m ⊕, **Britin** f ⊕ Englishman, f Englishwoman; richtiger: Briton (auch *hist.*); *Am.* Britisher; *poet.* Son of Albion.
britisch (⌣́⌣) a. ⊕ English, British.
Britisch=Nord=Amerika ⚓ (⌣⌣́⌣...) npr/n. ⊕ British (North) America; **=Indien** npr/n. British India.
Britsche (⌣́⌣) f ⊕ = Pritsche.
Britschka (⌣́⌣) [russ.] f ⊕⊕(Wagen) britzka.
br. m. *abbr.* = brevi manu, ſ. kurzer-hand (ſ. h.). ⟦little morsel; crumb.⟧
Bröck(e)lig (⌣́⌣) a. ⊕ easily crumbled, crumbling (away); (zerbrechlich) brittle; **~keit** (~) f ⊕ liability to crumble.
bröckeln (⌣́⌣) ⊕a. I v/a. Brot ꝛc.: to crumb(le) ..., to break (up) ... into small pieces. — II v/n. (ſn) sich ⚓ v/refl. to crumble (away), to come off in (small) bits.
Brocken¹ (⌣́⌣) [ahd.; *brechen] m ⊕ 1. von Brot ꝛc.: crumb; (Teilchen) fragment, bit; übrig gebliebene ~ pl. von Speisen: scraps pl.; broken meat; (Abfälle) odd bits, odds and ends pl.; *fig.* lateinische ~ scraps pl. of Latin. — 2. ♆ (abge-sprungenes Gestein) shiver, block; ~ pl. (Würfelkohlen) cobbles, nuts pl. — 3. (Speise) morsel (= Bissen 2).
Brocken² ⚓ (⌣́⌣) npr/m. ⊕ (o. pl.) (Gipfel des Harzgebirges) (the) Brocken.
brocken³ (⌣́⌣) v/a. ⊕ = bröckeln I; *fig.* er hat nichts zu beißen und zu ♆ he has nothing to eat, he is starving or famishing; er kann was in die Suppe ♆ he has plenty to live on, he is in comfortable (or easy) circumstances.
Brocken²-blume ⚘ (⌣́⌣...) f ⊕ alpine windflower(*Anemo'ne alpi'na*); **=²gespenst** n, *phys.* (opt. Täuschung) the Brocken spectre; **=¹gestein** n, *min.* = Breccie; **=²haus** n inn of the Brocken; **=¹stahl** ⊕ m, *metall.* steel in bars; **⚓¹weise** *adv.* bit by bit, in lumps, piecemeal.
Bröcklein (⌣́⌣) n ⊕ = Bröckchen.
bröcklig, ~keit ſ. bröckelig ꝛc.
Brod=¹perle (⌣́⌣...) [fr. barod] f ⊕ (schief-runde Perle) ragged pearl.
Brodel (⌣́⌣) [: broth] m ⊕ = Brodem.
brodeln (⌣́⌣) I v/n. (h., ⚓ ſn) ⊕a. a) (auf-wallen) to bubble (up), to effervesce; heftig: to wallop; von schäumenden Wellen: to foam; in Fett ꝛc.: to simmer; *fig.* in ſ-m Kopfe brodelte es wirr durcheinander his head was all in a whirl or a fog.

— II ~ n ⊕ bubbling (up), effervescence; ebullition (a. *fig.*).
Brodem (Broden) ⊕ (⌣́⌣) (ahd.: breath) m ⊕ (hot) steam, vapour; (Qualm) (reeking) fumes pl., (Ausdünstung) effluvia pl.; ♆ (metallische Ausdünstung) metallic fumes pl., (Grubengas) choke-damp.
Brod=winner ⚓ ſ. Brotwinner.
Brokat ⚘ (⌣́) [fr. brocart; *it. broccato] m ⊕c. (mit Gold und Silber durchwirkte Seide) brocade; in ~ gekleidet brocaded.
Brokatell ⚘ (⌣⌣́) [it.] n ⊕b. (nachgeahm-ter Brokat) brocatel(le); tinsel.
Brokat(ell)=marmor (⌣́...) m ⊕ *min.* brocatine, brocatelle.
brokaten (⌣⌣́⌣) a. ⊕(D 9) brocaded.
Brokkoli ⚘ (⌣́⌣⌣) [it.] m/pl. (Spargelkohl) broccoli (*Br'assica olera'cea botry'tis*).
Brom ♆ (⌣́) [grch. übler Geruch] n ⊕c. *chm.* bromine (Br); *phot.* mit ~ behandeln to bromize.
Brombeer-busch ⚘ (⌣́⌣...) m ⊕ = staude.
Brom=beere ⚘ (⌣́⌣) [ahd.: bramble; *Bram(e)] f ⊕ 1. (Frucht) blackberry; **~n suchen, pflücken** to go blackberry-ing. — 2. = Brombeerstrauch.
Brombeer=gesträuch ⚘ (⌣́⌣...) n ⊕, **=hecke** f brambles pl., brier, brake; **=staude** f, **=strauch** m blackberry- (or bramble-) bush (*Rubus frutico'sus*). ⟦print.⟧
Brom=druck (⌣́...) m ⊕ *phot.* bromide
Bromid (⌣⌣́) n ⊕c. *chm.* bromide (...ic dem Namen des Metalls beizufügen).
Bromit ♆ (-́) m ⊕c. *min.* (rohes Brom-silber) bromite, bromyrite.
Brom=kalium ⚛ (⌣́⌣⌣) n ⊕c. *chm.* bromide of potassium (KBr); **=metall** n (me-tallic) bromide; **²sauer** a. ⊕ bromic; **²saures Salz** bromate; **=säure** f bromic acid (HBrO₃); **=silber** n bromide of silver (AgBr); **=silber=gelatine=papier** n f, *phot.* gelatino-bromide (paper).
Bromür ♆ (-́) n ⊕c. bromide (...ous dem Namen des Metalls beizufügen).
Brom=verbindung (⌣́...) f ⊕ bromide; **=wasserstoff=säure** f hydrobromic (or bromhydric) acid (HBr); **=cyanür** n Goldindustrie: bromo-cyanide.
Bronchial=katarrh ⚕ (⌣⌣⌣́...) [grch.] m ⊕ *path.* bronchial catarrh or cold.
Bronchi-en ⚕ (⌣́⌣⌣) [grch.] f/pl. *inv.* anat. (Luftröhren-äste) bronchia (l ways) pl.
Bronchitis ⚕ (⌣⌣́⌣) [grch.] f, *inv. path.* (Luftröhren-entzündung) bronchitis.
Bronn ⚘ (⌣́) ⊕b., **~en** m ⊕ *poet.* spring, fountain (= Born).
Bronze ⊕ (⌣̊ᵘ, ⌁⊕ fr. brɒ'-ẽ̄) [fr. bronze (brɐj) u. it. bronzo m] f ⊕ bronze, für Bildgewebe: statue-metal.
Bronze-arbeit (⌣́...) f ⊕ bronze-work; **=arbeiter** m br.-worker; **=farbe** f br.- (or gold-)paint; **²farben** a. ⊕ br.-coloured, (sonnenverbrannt) auch; bronzed; **=gießer** m br.-founder; **=krankheit** f, *path.* Addison's disease.
bronzen ⊕ (⌣) a. ⊕ (D9) (of) bronze; weitS. (ehern) bsd. *bibl.* brazen.
Bronze=waren ⊕ (⌣́⌣) f/pl. ⊕ bronze ware or articles pl.; **=waren=fabrikant** m bronze (ware) manufacturer; **=zeit-alter** n Archäologie: br. period.
bronzieren ⊕ (⌣⌣́⌣) I v/a. ⊕ to bronze (over). — II ~ n ⊕ = Bronzierung.
Bronzierer ⊕ (⌣⌣́⌣) m ⊕ bronzer.

Bronzier=salz (⌣⌣́...) n ⊕ (Chlor-antimon) bronzing-salt. ⟦bronze-gilding.⟧
Bronzierung (⌣⌣́⌣) f ⊕ bronzing,
Bronzier=vergoldung (⌣⌣́⌣...ſ. o.) f wash- (or water-)gilding.
Brosam (⌣́) [ahd.; *brechen] m. n ⊕d., **Brösämchen** (⌣́⌣) n ⊕ *dim.*, **Brosame** (⌣́⌣) f ⊕ (mſt pl. ~n) u. **Brosämlein** (⌣́⌣⌣) n ⊕ *dim.* crumb (of bread); weitS. bit, scrap.
brosch. *abbr.* = broschiert. ⟦brooch.⟧
Brosche (⌣́⌣)[fr. broche] f ⊕(Vorstecknadel)
Bröschen (⌣́⌣) n [: brisket] n ⊕ Kocht. (calf's) sweet-bread.
Broschier=faß ⊕ (⌣⌣́⌣...) n, **=lade** f ⊕ Weberei: lathe with drop-box for broché-goods.
broschieren (⌣⌣́⌣) ⊕ [fr. brocher] I v/a. ⊕ Buchbind.: to stitch, to sew; Web.: (blümen mustern) to figure; Lederfabrik: (auswaschen) to cleanse (glacé kid). — II **broschiert** *p.p.* u. a. ⊕ Buchb.: in paper (or loose) cover; steif: in stiff cover, in boards; ♆e Gewebe (Art Bildgewebe) broché-goods pl.
Broschur ⊕ (⌣⌣́) f ⊕ Buchbinderei: (das Heften) stitching (the sheets).
Broschüre (⌣⌣́⌣) f [fr. *brochure*] f ⊕ 1. book in loose cover, stitched book. — 2. (Streitschrift) pamphlet; **~(n)=schreiber** (⌣́...) m ⊕ pamphleteer.
Brösel (⌣́⌣) n ⊕ = Brosämlein.
bröseln (⌣́⌣) ⊕a. to crumb(le).
Brot (⌣́) [ahd.: bread; *brauen] n ⊕c. (Pa.⊕c..⊕c., vgl. 2) 1. bread; alt(backen)es (friſches) ~ stale (new) bread; haus-backenes ~ home-made bread; schwarzes ~ brown (or wholemeal) bread; feines ~ fancy bread; auf Wasser u. ~ (ſetzen) to put) on bread and water; der versteht mehr als ~ eſſen he knows on which side his bread is buttered, F he knows a thing or two. — 2. ⊕⊕. ein ~ Zucker a loaf of sugar. — 3. (Erwerb, Unterhalt) unſer tägliches ~ our daily bread, auch: bread and cheese; mehr Schläge als ~ bekommen to get more kicks than half-pence; ſein gutes ~ haben to have (or make) a comfortable income or a competency, to receive good wages or good money; ſein ~ verdienen to earn a living or a livelihood; ſein eig(e)nes ~ eſſen to be one's own master; fremdes (auch fremder Leute) ~ eſſen to serve (other people); in j-s (Lohn u.) ~ in a p.'s service; um das trockene ~ arbeiten to earn barely sufficient to live upon, F to work hard for one's bread and cheese; e-n um ſein ~ bringen to take the bread out of a p.'s mouth.
Brot=backen (⌣́...) n ⊕ baking of bread; **=bäcker** m baker; **=bank** f bread-stall; **=beutel** m bread-bag, ♆ haversack; **=brechen** n, *bibl.* breaking of (the) bread.
Brötchen (⌣́⌣) n ⊕ (*dim.* v. Brot) small loaf, (French) roll; belegtes ~ meat-sandwich.
Brot=erwerb (⌣́...) ⊕m making a living, gaining a livelihood; als ~ as a trade, professionally; **=frucht** f bread-fruit; vgl. **=getreide**; **=frucht=baum** ⚘ m bread-(fruit) tree (*Artoca'rpus*); **=gelehr-samkeit** f professional knowledge or

---

⚗ scientific; ⚘ botanical; ⚓ geography; ⊕ machinery; ♆ mining; ♆ military; ⚓ marine; ✽ commercial; ✉ postal; 🚃 railway.

[Brotgelehrter] — 224 — [Bruder]

scholarship; =gelehrte(r) m one who uses his learning as a means of subsistence; =getreide n bread-stuffs pl.; =herr m e-s Arbeiters ꝛc. employer, master; e-s Handlungsdieners ꝛc.: principal; =kammer f: a) pantry; b) ⚓ =raum; =korb m bread-basket; fig. e-m den ~ höher hängen, etwa: to put a p. on short commons, to treat a p. less indulgently; =krume f, =krümchen n crumb of bread, bread crumb; =kruste f crust of bread; geraspelte ~, bsd. für Schinken: bread-raspings pl.

Brötlein (¹⁻) n ⓩ — Brötchen.
brot=los (ᴜ...) a. ⓖ breadless, weitS. out of employment; ˜lose Kunst unremunerative (or unprofitable) art; =losigkeit f ⓖ² destitution; want of employment; =messer n bread-knife; =neid m professional jealousy; =pflaster n bread-poultice; =pudding m bread-pudding; =raum ⚓ m bread-bin; =rinde f — =kruste; =röster m toasting-fork; =schau f inspection of bread; =schaufel f baker's peel; =scheibe f slice of bread, geröstete: (piece of) toast; =schneidemaschine f bread-cutter; =schnitte f slice of bread; =schrift f od. Werkschrift (Typengattung, mit der der laufende Text gedruckt ist) f, typ. body-type, text-type, ordinary type for books and newspapers; =sonntag m — Lätare; =spende f distribution of bread; =studium n professional reading or study; =suppe f bread soup; =teig m dough (for bread); =teller m bread-platter or -tray; =(ver)wandlung f Cath. eccl. transubstantiation; =wasser n für Kranke: toast-and-water; =winner ⚓ m (Segel) ring-tail; =wissenschaft f — =gelehrsamkeit; =wurzel ⚹ f cassava; =zucker m (Hutzucker) clay-sugar.
Brouillon (brū(l)-iǫ') [fr.] n ⓭ 1. (Entwurf) rough draft or sketch. — 2. ⚯ (Kladde) memorandum. [German beer.
Broyhan (¹⁻) [~ npr.] m ⓛⓒ. a light brr! int. whir; f. burr.
Bruch¹ (⚹⅍) [ahd.: brook] m ⓞc., n ⓞⓒ. (morastiges Land) marsh(y land); bog, moor, fen, morass, quagmire.
Bruch² (Ꞩ) [ahd.: breach; * brechen] m ⓞc. 1. (Brechen) des Brotes, der Siegel ꝛc.: breaking; surg. v. Knochen: fracture; einen ~ einrichten to set a broken limb; path. ~ (Ortsveränderung) v. Eingeweiden: rupture, ⚕ hernia; mit einem ~ behaftet ruptured, ⚕ hernious; (Riß) e-r Mauer ꝛc.: crack, crevice, chink; ⚔ (Einsturz) falling-in, caving-in, im Grubenbau: choke; zu ~e bringen, werfen to bring down; metall. im Guß: flaw, blemish; ⚯ v. Porzellanwaren: breakage; fig. in die Riff' und Brüche treten to fill up a breach or a gap. — 2. ⚯† — Bank(e)rott. — 3. ~ (Verletzung) breach; ~ e-s Vertrages, Gesetzes violation of a treaty, infringement of a law; f. a. Brüche. — 4. (Abbrechen e-r Verbindung) breach; es ist zwischen ihnen zu einem ~e gekommen it has come to a rupture between them; ein ~ mit der Vergangenheit leaving off one's former habits, turning over a new leaf. — 5. ~ (Biegung) in Papier,

Tuch ꝛc.: crease, fold; Brüche bekommen to get creased. — 6. arith. (gebrochene Zahl) fraction; (un)echter ~ (im)proper fraction; gemischter ~ (zB. 3²/₅) mixed number; gemeiner (a. gewöhnlicher) ~ vulgar (ant. decimal) fraction; einen ~ heben to reduce a fraction (to its lowest terms); abs. to cancel; Brüche auf einen Generalnenner bringen to bring (or reduce) fractions to a least common denominator. — 7. (Stein=)~ quarry. — 8. (Zerbrochenes) breakage, wreckage; (Stücke v. Felsen ꝛc.) fragments pl.; (Geröll) debris pl. — 9. min. (innere Schichtung) blätteriger, förniger, muscheliger~ foliated, granular, conchoidal fracture. — 10. hunt. (nach erfolgreicher Jagd angesteckter Zweig) green bough worn by a huntsman (after a day's successful sport).

Bruch¹=ampfer ⚹ (²⅍¹..., ²⅍²...) m ⓖ — Sauerklee; ²artig a. ⓖ marshy, boggy, fen-like; =²band n, surg. (hernial) truss or bandage; =¹beere ⚹ f — Trunkelbeere; =²binde f bandage (or sling) for a fracture(d limb); =²dach n, arch. curved roof.
Brüche † (⚹⅍) f ⓘ (Frevel, Strafe) nur noch: in die ~ fallen, geh(e)n, geraten, kommen („in Strafe verfallen") to fall to the ground, to come to nought, to lead to nothing, to prove a failure.
Bruch²=einklemmung (²⅍...) f ⓖ² path. strangulation of a rupture; =eisen ⊕ n old (or broken) iron, scrap-iron; ²fällig a. ⊕ von Häusern: falling (or crumbling, tumbling) to pieces; ²fest a. resisting pressure; not liable to break; tough; =festigkeit f ability to resist pressure on a (breaking) strain; toughness; =fläche f, min. (surface of) fracture; ²frei c.: a) path. free from rupture; b) ⚯ without breakage(s); =glas n broken glass. [boggy.
bruchig, bruchicht (⚹⅍) [Bruch¹] a. ⓖ
brüchig (⚹⅍) [Bruch²] a. ⓖ 1. (leicht brechbar) fragile; (spröde) brittle; (bröckelig) apt to crumble; metall. (kalt=)⚯ cold-short (iron, &c.). — 2. (zerbrochen) broken; (geborsten) cracked, burst, split; von Tuch ꝛc. auch: damaged; full of holes. — 3. path. (an e-m Bruch leidend) ruptured, ⚕ hernious. [one's word.
...brüchig (...⚹⅍) ⚯B. wort² breaking
Bruch²=kraft ⊕ (²⅍...) f — breaking-strain or -tension; =kraut ⚹ n rupture-wort (Hernia'ria); =kupfer ⊕ n shroff-copper; =¹land n boggy soil, fen-country; =²pflaster n, pharm. hernia-plaster; =rechnung f (calculation involving) fractions; in der Schule auch: fraction sum; =schnitt m, surg.: ⚯ celotomy, herniotomy; =stein m quarry-stone; behauener ~ dressed ashlar; kleine ~ rubble-stones pl., zum Straßenbau: road-metal; =stein-mauerwerk n quarry-stone work; =stück n fragment (auch einer Schrift); weitS. piece, scrap, aus ~en zs.=gesetzt fragmentary, scrappy; ²stückweise adv. piecemeal, vgl. auch ²weise; =teil m fraction; verschwindender ~ insignificant percentage; jur. (Quote) e-r Erbschaft, e-s Grundstücks portion of an inheritance, of a plot; =trag-

band n, surg. suspensor, suspender; =¹wasser n peat-water; =²weide ⚹ f crack-willow, brittle willow (Salix fra'gilis); graue ~ grey willow (Salix cine'rea); ²weise adv. in fragments, in shreds; =zahl f fraction(al number); =ziffer f fraction; typ. zs.=gegossene ~ whole fraction; zs.=zusetzende ~ split-fraction, piece-fraction.
Brucin ⚗ (-tʃ̣-) [lt.] n ⓝⓒ. (starkes Pflanzengift, bsd. in der Brechnuß, f. Strychnin) brucin(e) ($C_{23}H_{26}N_2O_4$).
Brücke (⚹⅍) f ⓖ a) bridge; * Prügel f ⓖ 1. bridge (a. fig. — Mittelstück e-r Brille); (Viadukt) viaduct; fliegende ~ flying bridge; hängende ~ suspension br.; schwimmende ~ floating br.; stehende ~ permanent br.; eine ~ über einen Fluß schlagen to throw (or build) a br. across a river; mit einer ~ überspannen to span (with a) bridge; e-e ~ abbrechen to break (or take) down a br.; fig. alle ~n hinter sich abbrechen to cut o.s. off from all means of escape, fig. to burn one's (own) ships; Sprichw. fliehenden Feinden bau' goldene ~n build golden bridges for the flying foe. — 2. fig. als ~ (Bindeglied) dienen to form a connecting link with. — 3. ⊖ — einer ~wage platform of a weigh-bridge; elect. elektrische ~ zur Messung des Stromwiderstandes: Wheatstone's bridge; typ. ~ an der Presse till, shelves pl.
brücken (⚹⅍) ⓖ I v/a. to bridge (over), to provide with a bridge. — II sich ² v/refl. to form a br.; to span a chasm, &c.
Brücken=bahn (⚹⅍...) f ⓖ roadway of (or across) a bridge; =balken m girder, joist (or beam) of a bridge; =bau m bridge-building, building (or construction) of a bridge; allg.: bridge-building; =baum m — =balken; =belag m (wooden) flooring (or pavement) of a br.; =bock m trestle of a br.; =bogen m arch of a br.; =bohle f plank (in the flooring) of a br.; =feld n span (or bay) of a br.; =geländer n railing (or parapet) of a br.; =geld n bridge-toll; =geld=einnehmer m — Brückner; =haus n für den Aufseher: bridge-house; =joch n pier (or support) of a wooden bridge; =kahn ⚓ m pontoon; =kopf ⚔ m head of a bridge; =lehne f — =geländer; =meister m bridge-master; weitS. controller of bridges; =pfeiler m pier; =schanze f — =kopf; =schiff n pontoon; =schlag(en) m — =bau; =train ⚔ m pontoon-train; =wage f (1822) weigh-bridge, weighing-machine; =zoll (=einnehmer) m — =geld (=einnehmer).
Brückner (⚹⅍) m ⓰ ehm. (Brückengeld-einnehmer) tollman of a bridge.
Brückung ⊖ (⚹⅍) f ⓖ a) — Brückenbau; b) laying down a stable-floor; wooden flooring of a stable; c) (Gerüst e-r Sägemühle) frame of a saw-mill.
brudeln (¹⁻) v/n. (h.) ⓖa. — brodeln.
Bruder (¹⁻) [ahd.: brother: lt. fra'ter] m ⓘⓔ. ⓖ⑥ 1. brother; wie Brüder zs.=leben to live like brothers; gleich einem ~ brotherlike; mein leiblicher ~ my own br.; so viel ist's unter Brüdern wert, etwa: it's fully worth that, it's a

Zeichen (f. S. XVII): F familiär; P Volkssprache; ℐ Gaunersprache; ⚹ selten; † alt (auch gestorben); * neu (auch geboren); ⁒ unrichtig;

bargain at that price; wir (Menschen) sind alle Brüder all men are brothers or brethren. — 2. (Ordens=)~ friar, monk; dienender ~ lay brother; Mährische Brüder *pl.* Moravian brethren *pl.* — 3. (Amts=)~ colleague ; (Waffen=)~ brother-in-arms ; in Apoll(o) brother poet or minstrel; *rel.* Brüder *pl.* in Christo brethren *pl.* in Christ. — 4. (Genosse) comrade, F mate, chum, pal; lustige (Zech=)Brüder jolly (or boon-)companions *pl.*; a merry set (or band) of fellows; du bist der beste ~ auch nicht *iro.* you are a nice (or a queer) sort, you are not the man for me or F for my money; Sprichw. gleiche Brüder, gleiche Kappen, etwa: (you must) do as your friends do. — 5. mst *co.* vor Eigennamen, die aus s. und a. gebildet sind: ~ Leichtfuß, ~ Liederlich, ~ Lustig *m* 64, etwa: gay (young) fellow; F jolly (or giddy) old boy; ~ Studio *m* 64 (merry) student; ~ Zimperlich, etwa: bashful (or shy, timid) young man.
Bruder=art (⸗⸗...) *f* 62 brotherly manner or way; nach ~ fraternally, brotherlike; **=band** *n*, **=bund** band of brothers; brotherly union; confraternity.
Brüderchen (⸗⸗⸗) [dim. v. Bruder] *n* 23 little brother; *fig.* ~! (my) dear fellow!, F dear old chap!
Bruder=gemein(d)e (⸗⸗...) *f* 2 *eccl.* der Herrnhuter: (community of) Bohemian (or Moravian) Brethren *pl.*
Bruder=herz (⸗⸗...) *n* 62 etwa: brother love; **=krieg** *m* fratricidal war; **=kuß** *m* brotherly (or brother's) kiss.
Brüderlein (⸗⸗⸗) *n* 23 = Brüderchen.
brüderlich (⸗⸗⸗) *a.* 66 brotherly, fraternal; F m=e 2e Liebe my (dear) brother! *adv.* like brothers, fraternally.
Brüderlichkeit (⸗⸗⸗) *f* 46 brotherliness, brotherly affection or tie or feeling; weitS. fraternity.
Bruder=liebe (⸗⸗...) *f* 2 brotherly love, Christian charity; **=mord** *m*, **=mörder** (=in *f*) *m*, **=mörderisch** *a.* fratricide.
Brüderschaft (⸗⸗⸗) *f* 46 1. (brüderl.Verhältnis) brotherhood, zw. Freunden: good fellowship; ~ *m.* (a. schließen) to enter into a brotherly bond with; to fraternize with; ~ trinken to hobnob (over a glass of beer or a bottle of wine). — 2. a. **Bruderschaft** (Genossenschaft) community, fraternity; *rel. a.* congregation.
Bruders=frau (⸗⸗...) *f* 62 brother's wife, sister-in-law; **=kind** *n* brother's child; nephew *m.* niece *f.*
Brudertum (⸗⸗⸗) *n* 2d. = Brüderschaft 1.
Bruder=volk (⸗⸗...) *n* 62 people of the same race; von Amerikanern 2c. oft: (our) kinsfolk (across the sea); **=zwist** *m* quarrel between brothers.
Brügge ♀ (⸗⸗) npr/n. 2 *a.* alte Handelsstadt in Belgien) Bruges; **~r(in** *f*) *m* 62 native of Bruges.
Brühe (⸗⸗) [mhd.] *f* 2 1. Kochk.: (Fleisch=) ~ beef-tea, gravy-soup, (mutton-) broth; (Tunke) sauce, gravy. — 2. (Obst- und Fleisch=saft) juice (of apples, roast meat, &c.). — 3. ⊙ Färberei: (warme) (hot) dye; ~ (Beize) für Tabak: sauce. — 4. *fig.*: in der ~ (Verlegenheit) sitzen (ob.

stecken) F to be in a pretty pickle or a nice mess; eine lange ~ (großen Wortschwall) über et. machen to tell a long rigmarole (or tale, yarn) about a th.; ich mußte die ganze ~ (Zeche) bezahlen I had to pay (for) all or F for the lot; Sprichw. die ~ (Zutat) kommt teurer als die Brocken the little extras are more (expensive) than the main item(s).
brühen (⸗⸗) [mhd.] *v/a.* 88 1. Geflügel, Gemüse 2c. ♀ to scald ... (in boiling water). — 2. ⊙ die Wäsche 2c. ♀ (beuchen) to soak ... (in soda-water, &c.).
Brüh=erz (⸗⸗...) *n* 62 yellow copper-ore; **=faß** ⊙ in Zuckfabr.: scalding-tub; **=futter** *n*, *agr.* scalded (or boiled) food; **=heiß** *a.* 66 = siedend=heiß. [succulent.]
brühig (⸗⸗) *a.* 66 full of juice, juicy,⌋
Brüh=kartoffeln (⸗⸗...) *f/pl.* 62 (steamed) potatoes mashed up with meat-broth.
Brühl (⸗) [ahd. (* Bruch¹), *flt.] *m* 11c (Wiesenbusch) marsh (or bog) overgrown with grass and shrubs.
Brüh=napf (⸗⸗...) *m* 62, **=näpfchen** *n* gravy- (or sauce-)dish or boat; ♀ (siedend=)heiß, ♀**warm** *a.* 66 scalding (or boiling) hot; mir war's ♀warm F I felt (or was) red-hot or boiling; *fig.* quite fresh; *adv.* einem et. ♀warm (wieder=) erzählen, mitteilen to retail news to a p. immediately (or post-haste) after receiving it. [monkey (*Myce'tes*).]
Brüll=affe (⸗⸗...) *m* 62 howler, howling⌋
brüllen (⸗⸗) [mhd. ☉ brawl] 88 I *v/n.* (h.) 1. von Rindern: to bellow; von Kühen *a.*: to low; von Löwen 2c.: to roar; von Menschen: to bawl (with a thundering voice); to vociferate; (heulen) to howl; (plärren) to blubber. — II *v/a.* 2. e-m Beifall ♀ to give ringing cheers for a p., to cheer a p. vociferously or to the echo. — III ~ *n* 23 3. bellowing, &c. (i. 1). — 4. roar(ing) of a lion, of thunder, &c.; roll(ing) of thunder; bawl(ing or vociferation) of people; mit lautem ~ vociferously.
Brüll=frosch (⸗⸗...) *m* 62 bullfrog (*Rana mu'giens*); **=ochs** *m* (Zuchtstier) bull.
Brumm=bär (⸗⸗...) *m* 62: a) *zo.* (growling) bear; b) F *fig.* grumbler, growler; **=bart** F *m* = daß ~ *m* =baß; **=baß** *m*: a) strong bass (voice); b) (Art Baßtuba) bombardo(n); c) (Orgelpfeife) (fr.) bourdon.
Brumm=eisen (⸗⸗...) *n* 62 (Maultrommel) Jew's-harp, a. jews' harp.
brummeln, brümmeln (⸗⸗) *v/n.* (h.) u. *v.a.* ♀ *a.* (ein wenig brummen) to growl (or grumble) a little; (murmeln) to mutter.
brummen (⸗⸗) [mhd.: lt. *fre'mere*] I *v/n.* (h.) *u. v/a.* 88 1. vom Bär: to growl; von Hummeln: to hum, buzz, drone; von einer Glocke: to ring forth its deep notes; mir brummt der Kopf davon, etwa: my head is dizzy (or quite aches) with the noise. — 2. von Menschen: (murren) to growl, grumble, mutter, F in den Bart ♀ to mutter (or mumble) to o.s. — 3. [mhd. 19. *sae.,* *F*] (eingesperrt sitzen) to be in safe quarters, to sit (or be) in jail, F to do time. — II ~ *n* 23 4. growl(ing). &c. (i. 1). — 5. von Menschen: growls *pl.*; er ist ewig am ~ he is always grumbling.

Brummer (⸗⸗) *m* 22 1. (*a.* ~**in** *f* 47) = Brummbär b. — 2. *zo.* (brummendes Tier) = Brummfliege. — 3. (Kanone) (big) cannon with a deep roar; ♪ = Brummbaß.
Brumm=fliege (⸗⸗...) *f* 2 *ent.* blue-bottle, meat-fly (*Musca vomito'ria*).
brummig (⸗⸗) *a.* 66 (fond of) grumbling or growling, F grumpy.
Brumm=kater (⸗⸗...) *m* 62 = =bär b; **=kreisel** *m* humming top; **=laut** *m* (m) hum(ming sound); **=ochs**, **=ochse** *m*, *zo.* parish-bull; **=schädel** F *m* headache caused by tippling; F *co.* hot coppers *pl.*; e-n ~ haben, *a.*: to feel seedy (after a drinking-bout).
Brunelle ♀ (⸗⸗⸗) *f* 2 1. self-heal, heal-all (*Brunel'la vulga'ris*). — 2. = Prünelle.
brünett (⸗⸗) [fr.] I *a.* 66 dark(-haired), of dark (stärker: of swarthy) complexion. — II ~**e** *f* 2 (dunkelhaariges Mädchen, Weib) girl, woman with dark hair or complexion; dark(-haired or -skinned) woman or lady, (fr.) brunette.
Brunft (⸗) [mhd.; *brummen*] *f* 10 hunt., &c. heat, ruttishness, sexual desire, ♀ oestrus; ♀ig (⸗⸗) *a.* 66 in heat.
Brunft=zeit (⸗⸗...) *f* 2 rutting-time.
Brünier=eisen ⊙ (⸗⸗...) *n* 62 = =stahl.
brünieren ⊙ (⸗⸗) [fr.; *dtsch* braun] *v/a.* 93 1. (Gold-, Silberzeug 2c. glänzend *m.*) to burnish, polish. — 2. (Stahl, Flintenläufe 2c. bräunen) to brown (vgl. *a.* bronzieren).
Brünier=gold ⊙ (⸗⸗...) *n* 62 Goldarbeit: burnished gold; **=salz** *n* = Bronzier=s.; **=stahl** *m* (Polierstahl) burnishing-stick, burnisher; **=stein** *m* (Glättstein) burnishing-stone; agate.
Brunn (⸗) *m* poet. = Brunnen 1.
Brunne ⚒ (⸗⸗) *f* 2 (Gesteinsfurche) fissure (or break) in a lode.
Brünne (⸗⸗) [ndd. *flt.] *f* 2 ehm. *u.* noch *poet.* (Panzer) mail-coat, cuirass.
Brunnen [ahd.: b(o)urn(e); ndd.Born] *m* 23 1. (unterirdische, natürliche Quelle) (natural) well or spring; source; (Pumpe) pump. — 2. (Mineralquelle, Gesundbrunnen) mineral water(s *pl.*) or spring(s *pl.*); spa (*a.* Kur=ort), (Bade=ort) (inland) watering-place; (den) ~ trinken (*a.* brauchen) to take (or drink) the waters. — 3. (künstliche Quelle) mit hervorsprudelndem Wasser: fount(ain); abessinischer, artesischer, gebohrter ~ Abyssinian. Artesian, bored well; ⊙ *mach.* heißer ~ der Luftpumpe hot well; einen ~ bohren to bore a well; einen ~ graben to sink (or dig) a well. — 4. *fig.* wie in den ~ gefallen quite lost or puzzled; meine Pläne sind in den ~ gefallen (vereitelt) ... have fallen to the ground, have utterly failed; Sprichw. Wasser in den ~ tragen (überflüssiges tun) to carry coals to Newcastle; den ~ zudecken, wenn das Kind ertrunken ist, etwa: to lock the stable-door, when the steed is stolen; to shut the stable-door, when the horses are stolen.
Brunnen=ader (⸗⸗...) *f* 62 vein of a well; **=anstalt** *f*: a) (Trinkhalle) pump-room; b) (Bade=ort) spa, watering-place; **=arzt** *m* (appointed) physician at a watering-place; **=bau** *m* sinking of a well or of wells; **=becken** *n* basin of a fountain or well; **=behälter** *m*

♪ Musik; ⚛ Wissenschaft; ⚘ Pflanze; ♀ Geographie; ⊙ Technik; ⚒ Bergbau; ⚔ Militär; ⚓ Marine; ⚖ Handel; ✉ Post; ⚐ Eisenbahn.

[Brunnenbeschlag] — 226 — [Brut]

reservoir (or cistern) of a fountain or well; vgl. =ſchale; **beſchlag** m pump-gear; =**bohrer** ⊕ m: a) Arbeiter: well-sinker or -digger; b) Werkzeug: (sinking-)auger (or borer, drill) for well-sinkers; =**brüſtung** f parapet of a well; =**dach** n, =**deckel** m roof (or shed), cover (or lid) of a well; =**eimer** m (well-)bucket; pail; =(**ein**)**faſſung** f well-curb; enclosure of a well; =**gaſt** m visitor of a watering-place; =**geländer** n railing of a well; =**gräber** m well-digger; =**haus** n well-house; =**kaſten** m water-cistern; =**kreſſe** ⚥ f water-cress, F u. Pauch: water-cresses pl. (*Nastu'rtium [officina'le]*); =**kur** f mineral-water cure; e-e ~ (ge)brauchen to take (or use) the waters (medicinally); =**loch** n pit (or mouth) of a well; =**macher** m: a) =bohrer a; b) pump-maker; =**meiſter** m: a) inspector of wells; b) e-s Babe-ortes: manager (or master) of the pump-room; =**ort** m watering-place; =**rand** m edge (or rim) of a well; =**röhre** f pump(ing)-barrel or -cylinder; =**ſchale** f vase (or basin) of a fountain; =**ſchwengel** m draw-beam of a well; pump-handle; =**ſeil** n, =**ſtange** f rope, pole of a draw-well; =**vergiftung** f poisoning of wells or a well; =**waſſer** n spring- (or well-, pump-) water; =**zeit** f season for taking the waters. [small well or fount(ain).} **Brünnlein** (⸗) n ㉓ (*dim.* von Brunnen)ʃ **Brunn-quell(e** f) m (⸗...) ⓶ fountain-head (of a spring or well).

Brunſt (⸍) [ahd.; *brennen] f ⑩ 1. *fig.* (innere Glut) ardour; (Gier) fiery (or violent, hot) passion. — 2. von Tieren: = Brunſt.

brünſtig (⸍⸌) *a.* ⓮ 1. 2 (2lich *adv.*) ardent(ly), eager(ly), in hot passion; (ſinnlich) sensual, F u. P hot. — 2. = inbrünſtig.

Brünſtigkeit (⸍⸌⸍) f ㊻ = Inbrunſt.

Brunſt-zeit (⸍...) f ⓶ = Brunſt b.

Brüſch ⚥ (⸍) [fr. *brusc*] m ⓵a. prickly butcher's-broom (*Ruscus aculea'tus*).

Brüschen (⸍⸌) n ㉓ = Bröschen.

brüſk (⸍) [fr. *brusque*] *a.* ⓮ (barsch) rude, offhandish; (fr.) brusque.

brüſkieren (⸍⸌⸍) *v/a.* ⓮ to snub, to treat cavalierly or offhandishly or brusquely, (fr.) to brusque.

Brüſſel ⚥ (⸍) npr/n. ⓶ a. Brussels.

Brüſſeler (⸍⸌⸌), **Brüßler** (⸍⸌) I m ⓶, ~**in** f ㊵ inhabitant of Brussels. — II *a.*, *inv.* (of) Brussels; ~ Spitzen *pl.*, Teppich Brussels lace, carpet.

Bruſt (⸍) [ahd.: breaſt] f ⑩ 1. breast; (Bruſt-kaſten ob. -höhlung u. -organe) chest; *anat.*: ☤ thorax; eine breite ~ haben to have a large (or wide, broad) chest; e-e gute, ſtarke ~ haben to have a good, strong chest; er hat es auf der ~, ſeine ~ iſt verſchleimt he has a cold (or much phlegm) on his chest; an der ~ leiden to have a delicate (or to be delicate on the) chest; to be weak-chested; die ~ betr., zur ~ gehörig, *anat.*: ☤ pectoral, thoracic. — 2. e-n an ſeine ~ drücken (umarmen) to press a p. to one's bosom, to hug a p.; ſich in die ~ werfen (brüſten) to put (or throw, F puff, P chuck) out one's chest; *fig.* to give o.s. airs, to assume an air of

importance. — 3. (weiblicher Buſen) breast, bosom; e-m Kinde (ſäugend) die ~ geben to give the breast to (or to suckle) a baby or child; ein Kind an der ~ an infant at the breast, a suckling baby; ohne ~ aufziehen to bring up by hand; (von der ~) entwöhnen to wean; *anat.* zur weiblichen ~ gehörig ☤ mammary. — 4. *fig.* frei von der ~ (ober Leber) weg reden to speak one's mind freely; in der heimlichen ~ verwahren to lock up in the depth of one's bosom or breast, to conceal in one's inmost heart; Seufzer ſchwellen ſeine ~ sighs heave up from his aching heart. — 5. Schlächterei, Kocht. ~(=ſtück) brisket of beef, &c.; (Hammels-, Kalbs-)~ breast of mutton, of veal; ~ einer Gans ꝛc. breast(-bone) of a goose, &c. — 6. (Teil eines Kleidungsſtücks) body of a dress; *auch*: stomacher; (shirt-, coat-)front.

Bruſt-ader (⸍...) f ⓶ = =gefäß; =**angſt** f = =beklemmung; =**arte'rie** f, *anat.*: ☤ thoracic (or mammary) artery; =**atmung** f chest-breathing; =**arz(e)nei** f, *balſam* m medicine, balm for the chest or lungs; pectoral remedy; =**band** n: a) lace (or string) for stays; b) *surg.* bandage for the breast or chest; =**baum** m Weberei: breast-beam; =**beer-baum** ⚥ m: a) roter ~ (common) jujube-tree (*Zi'zyphus vulga'ris*); oſtindiſcher ~ Indian jujube-tree (*Z. juju'ba*); b) ſchwarzer: sebesten (*Co'rdia myxa* und *C. latifo'lia*); =**beere** f: a) rote: jujube; b) ſchwarze: sebesten (plum); =**bein** n, *anat.* breastbone, ☤ sternum; eines Huhns *auch* hism.: merrythought; =**beklemmung**, =**beſchwerde** f oppression, affection of the chest, chest complaint; =**beule** f, *vet.* der Zugpferde: tumour in the chest (of a draught-horse); =**bild** n, *paint. u. phot.*: half-length portrait or photograph; *sculp.* bust; =**binde** f = =band b; =**blatt** n: a) *anat.* breastbone; b) ⊕ = =riemen; =**bohrer** ⊕ m breast-borer or -drill; =**bonbon** m, n pectoral lozenge or jujube, cough-drop; =**bräune** f, *path.*: ☤ (lt.) angi'na pe'ctoris; =**brett** ⊕ n eines Drillbohrers: breast-board or -plate of a drill.

Brüſtchen (⸍⸌) n ㉓ (*dim. v.* Bruſt) 1. small breast. — 2. (Leibchen) small bodice.

Bruſt-drüſe (⸍...) f ⓶ *anat.* ☤ mammary gland; vom Kalbe: sweetbread; =**drüſen-entzündung** f, *path.*: ☤ mastitis; =**eiſen** n (Blanſcheit) busk.

brüſten (⸍⸌) ſich 2 v/refl. ⑩ (proudly) to hold up one's head, to give o.s. airs; ſich mit et. 2 to pride (or plume) o.s. on a th., to glory in a th., F to make a (great) show with (or of) a th.

Bruſt-entzündung (⸍...) f ⓶ *path.* inflammation of the chest or lungs; =**fell** n, *anat.*: ☤ pleura; =**fell-entzündung** f, *path.*: ☤ pleurisy; =**fell- u. Herzbeutel-entzündung** f ☤ pleuropericarditis; =**finne** f = =floſſe; =**fleiſch** n e-s Rebhuhns ꝛc.: breast; =**floſſe** f, *ichth.* pectoral fin; =**floſſer** m/pl., *ichth.* thoracic fish pl.; =**gang** m, *anat.*: ☤ thoracic duct; =**gefäß** n, *anat.* thoracic (blood-)vessel; =**geſchwür** n, *path.* ulcer in the breast or chest; =**glas** n (Milchpumpe) breast-

glass or -fountain; =**grube** f, *vet.* e-s Pferdes: counter; =**gurt** ⊕ m = =riemen; =**hammer** ⊕ m Schmiede: lift-hammer; =**harniſch** ⚔ m breast-plate, cuirass; ²**hoch** *a.* ⓮ breast-high; =**höhe** f breast-height; =**höhle** f, *anat.*: ☤ thoracic cavity. [narrow-chested.}

...**brüſtig** (...⸌⸍) in Zſſgn, z.B. eng=ʃ

Bruſt-kaſten (⸍...) m ⓶ chest, *anat.*: ☤ thorax; =**kern** m Schlächterei ꝛc.: brisket; =**knochen** m = =bein; =**knorpel** m, *anat.* ☤ sternal cartilage; =**krampf** m, *path.* pectoral spasm; asthma; ²**krank** *a.* ⓮ suffering from (an affection of) the chest, (ſchwindſüchtig) consumptive; =**krankheit** f, *path.* disease (or affection) of the chest or lungs, chest-disease, pectoral complaint; =**kügelchen** n, *pharm.* = =bonbon; =**latz** m (Mieder) bſd. ehm. stomacher; =**leder** n leather apron; *fenc.* plastron; =**lehne** f, *arch.* balustrade; vgl. =wehr; =**leiden** n = =krankheit; ²**leidend** *a.* = ²krank; =**leier** ⊕ m =bohrer; =**meſſer** n, *med.*: ☤ stethometer, thoracometer; =**mittel** n, *med.* pectoral (remedy); =**platte** ⊕ m = =brett; ²**reinigend** *a.* ⓮, *med.*: expectorant; =**riegel** ⊕ m, *carp.* breast-rail; =**riemen** ⊕ n am Pferdegeſchirr: breast-collar, -part or -plate; des Tornisters: breast-strap; =**ſchild** n breast-plate; des jüd. Hohenpriesters: pectoral; von Inſekten: ☤ thorax; =**ſchleier** m e-r Nonne: wimple; =**ſchmerz** m pain in the chest; =**ſeuche** f, *vet.* contagious pneumonia with pleurisy; =**ſtiche** m/pl. stitches in the chest; =**ſtimme** ♪ f voice from the chest, chest-voice; =**ſtück** n: a) = =bild; b) ⚔ = =harniſch; c) = Bruſt 5; =**taſche** f breast- (or bosom-)pocket; =**tee** m, *med.* pectoral herb-tea; =**ton** ♪ m chest-note; *fig.* laryngeal tone; *fig.* ~ der Aufrichtigkeit, der Überzeugung true ring of sincerity, of conviction. [wehr.}

Brüſtung (⸍⸌) f ㊻ parapet; ſ. Bruſt=ʃ **Brüſtungs-geſims** (⸍⸌...) n ⓶ e-s Fensters: breast-moulding; =**mauer** f breast-wall.

Bruſt-verſchleimung (⸍...) f ⓶ phlegm on the chest, bronchial catarrh; =**warze** f, *anat.* nipple, ☤ papilla; =**waſſerſucht** f, *path.* pectoral dropsy, water on the chest; ☤ hydrothorax; =**wehr** f, *arch.* u. ⚔ *frt.* breast-work or -wall; parapet; =**wehr-kappe** ⚔ f, *frt.* bonnet; =**wehrturmſchiff** ⚓ n breast-work turret-ship; =**weite** f width of (or across the) chest; =**werk** n ♪ in der Orgel: (in der Mitte aufgeſtelltes Pfeifenwerk) front (or centre) of an organ; =**wurz** ⚥ f wood angelica (*Ange'lica silve'stris*).

Brut (⸍) [ahd.: brood; *brühen] f ㊻ 1. (Brüten) hatch(ing), ☤ incubation; die Vögel ſind in der ~ ... are hatching or sitting. — 2. (Neſt voll Junge) brood, (nestful of) young ones. — 3. (Nachkommenſchaft bſd. eierlegender Tiere) offspring, progeny; ~ (Same) der Seidenwürmer silkworms' eggs; ~ der Bienen stock of young bees; ~ (Laich) von Fiſchen fry, spawn(ing); die Fiſche ſetzen ~ (laichen) ... are spawning. — 4. *fig. b.s.* von Menſchen: rabble; von Kindern: small fry; brats *pl.*; böſe ~ bad se

Signs (see page XVII): F familiar; P vulgar; ⚡ flash; ⚞ rare; † obsolete (died); * new word (born); ✢ incorrect; ♪ music

[brutal] — 227 — [Bücherweisheit]

(or F lot) of people. — 5. (ungeschliffene Edelsteine) uncut gems pl.
brutal (-́) [fr.] a. ⓖⓖ (roh, ungeschliffen) brutal, brutish; rude, savage, churlish; Ђer Kerl brute (F beast) of a fellow.
Brutalität (--́ˇ) f ⓖⓖ brutality; rudeness, savageness, churlishness.
Brut-amme (″...) f ⓖⓖ v. Bienen: bee-nurse; **-apparat** m incubator; **-biene** f drone.
Brüt-ei (″...) n ⓖⓖ: a) egg for hatching; b) egg partially hatched; egg spoiled by being sat on, addled egg.
brüten (-́) [ahd.] v/n. (h.) u. v/a. ⓖⓖ 1. to sit on (or to cover) eggs; to hatch (a. fig.), künstlich: to incubate. — 2. fig. über et. (dat. ob. acc.) ⚥ (nachsinnen) to brood over a th.; to muse (or meditate, ponder) on a th.; Unheil ⚥ to brood (or hatch out) mischief. — II~ n ⓖⓖ 3. hatching, künstl.: incubation; fig. brooding, meditation.
Brut-, meist **Brüt-haus** (″...) n ⓖⓖ house (or shed) for hatching chickens.
Brut-henne (″...) f ⓖⓖ hen sitting on eggs, sitting hen; eine gute ~ a.: a good sitter; **-hitze** f = -wärme.
brütig (-́) a. ⓖⓖ 1. von Hühnern: wanting to sit. — 2. Џes Ei = Brütei b.
Brut-kasten (″...) m ⓖⓖ, **-kiste** f Fischzucht: spawn-hatcher; **-knospe** ⚥ f = -zelle b.
Brüt- od. **Brut-maschine** (″...) f, **-ofen** m hatching apparatus; incubator; **-ort** m: a) breeding-place; b) path. für Krankheiten: seat of infection. ⚥ nidus.
Brut-stätte (″...) f ⓖⓖ: a) breeding-place, fig. hotbed (of disease, revolution, &c.); b) Fischzucht: spawning-ground; **Brüt-stätte** f = Brütort.
Brut-teich (″...) Fischzucht: spawning-pond.
brutto (-́) [it.] (ant. netto) I adv. ⚥ (mit Verpackung) wiegen to weigh in the gross. — II ~ n ⓖⓖ = Bruttogewicht.
Brutto-betrag (ˇ...) m ⓖⓖ gross amount; **-einnahme** f, **-ertrag** m, **-gewinn** m gross receipts or earnings pl.; **-gewicht** n gross weight; **-preis** m gross price. — Vgl. auch Roh-...
Brut-wärme (″...) f ⓖⓖ temperature required (or heat necessary) for incubation; = (ob. **Brüt-)zeit** f hatching-time; **-zelle** f: a) Bienen: brood-cell; b) ⚥ Algen &c.: ⚥ gonidium. [rübe.}
Bryoni-e ⚥ (ˇ́-ˇ-ˇ) f [grch.] f ⓖⓖ = Zaun-}
bst (́) int. ⚥! hush!, 'sh!, a. hist!
Bt(t)o. abbr. = brutto.
Bübchen (-́) n ⓖⓖ dim. von Bube.
Bube (-́) [mhd.: boy, baby] m ⓖⓖ 1. bfd. südd. (Knabe) boy; a (kleiner Junge) oft: (little) urchin; P nipper; b) oft poet. (kräftiger Jüngling) strong youth or lad; (Liebhaber, Schatz) lover, sweetheart; böser, unartiger ~ bad (or mischievous, troublesome) boy. — 2. Kartenspiel: knave of hearts, &c. — 3. (Schimpfname) knave, villain, rogue, rascal. [like.}
buben-haft, ⚥ **-mäßig** (″...) a. ⓖⓖ **-urchin-**
Buben-streich (″...) m ⓖⓖ, **-stück** n, **-tat** f boy's trick; (Gaunerstück) knavish trick, knavery, villainy, (piece of) roguery. [act.}
Büberei (-ˇ-́) f ⓖⓖ knavery, villainous}
Bübin (-́) f ⓖⓖ (artful) vixen; jade; F hussy; baggage; allerliebste kleine ~ charming little rogue.

bübisch (-́ˇ) a. ⓖⓖ mischievous; (schurkisch) knavish, villainous, roguish.
Bubo(n) (-́-) [lt.] m ⓖⓖ path. (Pestbeule) bubo; ⚥ = Steinepppich.
Bubo(nen)-pest (-́ˇˇ-́ˇ...) f ⓖⓖ Indien &c.: bubo- (or bubonic) plague or disease.
Buch[1] (-ch) [ahd.: book; *Buche] n ⓖⓖ&c. (f. aber 5) 1. book; ein ~ herausgeben, verlegen to edit, publish a book; immer über den Büchern sitzen, hocken, liegen to be for ever poring over books; fig. er spricht wie ein ~ he talks like a book, he is well spoken; wie es im ~(e) steht quite as it should be; da muß man das ~ zumachen nothing more can be said about it. — 2. ⚥ die Bücher führen to keep the books or the accounts, to do the bookkeeping; ins ~ eintragen, zu ~ bringen to enter in the books, to book; (genau) ~ und Rechnung führen über et. to keep an (exact) account of a th.; zu ~ schlagen (sich bezahlt machen) to pay well, to yield a (good) profit; hoch zu ~ steh(e)n to stand at a high price. — 3. (Band) Buchhandel: ~ in Folio, Quart(o), Oktav(o) folio-, quarto-, octavo-volume. — 4. (Abschnitt) bibl. das erste ~ der Könige (the) First Book of the Kings; 1., 2., 3., 4., 5. ~ Mosis (ob. Mose) Genesis, Exodus, Leviticus, Numbers pl., Deuteronomy, die 5 Bücher Mose the Pentateuch; das letzte ~ der Æneide the last book of the Æneid. — 5. ⚥ 6. (Maßeinheit), f. ⚥. XXXIX, III) zehn ~ Papier ten quires (= ½ ream) of paper; drei ~ (zu 12 bis 25 Blättern) Blattgold three books of leaf-gold. — 6. ein ~ Karten a (full) pack of cards; ⚥ mit &c. auch: a suit. — 7. zo. = Blättermagen.
Buch[2]... (-ch...) [ahd.] [Buche] ⓖⓖ f. Buch-ecker &c.
Buch[1]**-adel** (-ch...) m ⓖⓖ = Briefadel.
Bucharei ⚥ ⚥ (-ˇ(-́)) / Bochara/ npr./ ⓖⓖ a. die ~ (LandOstasiens) Bucharia, Bukhara.
Buch[1]**binder** (-ch́ˇ) m ⓖⓖ bookbinder; **-beschneidehobel** (́...) m ⓖⓖ ploughknife; **-ei** ⚥ (-ch́ˇˇ) f ⓖⓖ = -handwerk, -werkstatt; **-geselle** (-ch́ˇˇ) m ⓖⓖ journeyman bookbinder; **-handwerk** n book-binding (trade); **-kattun** m -leinwand; **-kunst** f bookbinding; **-leinwand** f bookbinder's calico, cloth; **-waren** f/pl. stationery (goods pl.); **-werkstatt** f bookbinder's workshop, bisw. a. bindery. [printed matter.}
Buch[1]**druck** (-ch́ˇ) m ⓖⓖ printing of books;
Buch[1]**drucker** (-ch́ˇ-) m ⓖⓖ: a) allg.: printer; b) (Pressendrucker) (letter-press) printer, pressman; c) (Schriftsetzer) compositor; typographer, F comp.
Buch[1]**druckerei** (-ch́ˇ-ˇ-́) f ⓖⓖ = Buchdrucker-werkstätte u. -kunst; **-besitzer** m proprietor of a printing-office or -establishment, master printer.
Buch[1]**drucker-faktor** (-ch́ˇ-ˇ-...) m ⓖⓖ master printer; **-farbe** f = Buchdruckfarbe; **-gehilfe** m journeyman printer; **-junge** m printer's apprentice, (Laufbursche) F printer's devil; **-lehrling** m = -junge; **-presse** f printing- (or letter-) press; **-schriften** f/pl. printing-types pl.; **-schwärze** f = Buchdruckfarbe;

-stock m vignette, head-piece; **-werkstätte** f printing-office; **-zeichen** n printer's (or publisher's) monogram.
Buch[1]**druck-farbe** (-ch́ˇ...) f ⓖⓖ printer's ink; **-presse** f = Buchdruckerpresse.
Buche ⚥ (-́ch) [ahd.: beech: lt. fā'gus] f ⓖⓖ beech (Fagus).
Buch[2]**-ecker** (-ch́...) [Bucheckernöl = Buchöl.] f ⓖⓖ, **-eichel** f, **Buchel** (-ch́ˇ), **Büchel** (-́) [mhd.] f ⓖⓖ beech-nut.
Büchelchen F (-́ˇˇ) n ⓖⓖ (dim. von Buch[1]) (tiny) little book; bisw. booklet.
buchen[1] ⚥ (-́ˇ) [Buch[1]] I v/a. ⓖⓖ to book, to enter (or pass) into the books; gleichlautend oder gleichförmig ⚥ to book (or note, pass) in conformity. — II ~ n ⓖⓖ = Buchung. [beech(en).}
buchen[2] (-́ch) [Buche], **büchen** (-́) a. ⓖⓖ (D9)}
Buchen-allee (-́ch...) [Buche] f ⓖⓖ, **-gang** m avenue of beeches; **-hain** m beech-grove or -wood; **-holz** n beech-wood; **-(spring-)rüßler** m, ent. beech-hopper (Orche'stes fagi); **-wald** m beech-forest; **-wäldchen** n = -hain.
Bücher-abschluß ⚥ (-́ˇ...) [Bücher, pl. v. Buch[1]] m ⓖⓖ balancing (or closing) of the books; **-ankündigung** ⚥ f notice (or advertisement) of books published or appearing; **-auktio'n** f Buchhandel: trade-sale; **-beschreiber** m = -kenner; **-beschreibung** f = -kenntnis; **-bestellzettel** ⚥ m = -zettel; **-brett** n book-shelf or -stand; weitS. (set of) book-shelves pl.
Bücherchen (-́ˇ) n/pl. ⓖⓖ v. Büchelchen.
Bücherei (-́ˇ-́) [mhd. 17. sae.] f ⓖⓖ library; vgl. Büchersammlung.
Bücher-freund (-́ˇ...) m ⓖⓖ lover of books, ⚥ bibliophile; **-gestell** n f. -brett, -schrank; **-halter** m book-clamp; **-handel** m (second-hand) book-trade, bookseller's business; **-händler** m dealer in books, (Antiquar) second-hand bookseller; **-kenner(in** f) m bibliographer; **-kenntnis** f bibliography; **-kram** m = -handel; **-kunde** f = -kenntnis; **-kundige(r)** m = -kenner(in); **-laden** m book-stall or -store; **-laus** f, ent. book-louse (Troctes oder A'tropos); **-liebhaber** m = -freund; **-macher** m = -schmierer; **-mappe** f satchel; **-marke** f = Buchdruckerzeichen; **-mensch** m bookish person; **-milbe** f = -laus; **-nachdruck** m F piracy; **-narr** m: a) bibliomaniac; **-re(g)al** n = -brett; **-revisor** ⚥ m (Sachverständiger der Buchführung) auditor (who examines the books), chartered accountant; **-saal** m library; **-sammler** m collector of (rare) books; **-sammlung** f, **-schatz** m collection of (valuable) books; **-schmierer** m, contp. scribbler (of books), bookwright; F bookseller's hack; **-schmuck** m adornment of books; **-schrank** m bookcase; **-skorpio'n** m, zo. book-scorpion (Che'lifer cancro'ides); **-sprache** f bookish (weitS. literary, choice) language or phraseology; **-stand** m book-stall; **-ständer** m: drehbarer ~ revolving book-case; **-staub** m dust of books; **-stube** f library; eines Gelehrten: study; **-wut** f = -tasche f satchel; **-trödel** m = -handel; **-verleiher** m p. who keeps a circulating library; **-verzeichnis** n catalogue of books; **-weisheit** f wis-

⚥ scientific; ⚥ botanical; ⚥ geography; ⊕ machinery; ⚒ mining; ⚔ military; ⚓ marine; ⓖ commercial; ✉ postal; ⚋ railway.

[Bücherwesen] — 228 — [buckelig]

dom derived from books, bookish knowledge; =**wesen** n literature; =**wurm** m: a) ent. = Skorpion; b) fig. bookworm; v. Schülern: plodding boy; =**wut** f bookishness, ◇ bibliomania; =**zeichen** n book-plate, (lt.) ex-libris; =**zettel** m (offene, gedruckte Bestellung ob. Angebot v. Büchern ꝛc.) printed order for (or offer of) books, &c.; bookseller's circular.

Buch²=**esche** ♀ (″ch…) f ⓔ = Weißbuche; =**fink** m, orn. chaffinch (Fringi'lla cae'lebs).

Buch¹=**forderung** (″ch…) f ⓔ jur. claim proved by the books, vgl. Schuld; =**form** f, =**format** n, typ. size of a book; =**führen** n, =**führung** ⚹ f = =**halten**, =**haltung**; =**führer** ⚹ m = =**halter**; =**gelehrsamkeit** f erudition; vgl. =**wissen**; =**gläubiger** m book-creditor; =**gold** ⊖ n leaf-gold; =**halten** n = =**haltung**; =**halter** ⚹ m bookkeeper; =**halterei** f bookkeeping; =**haltung** ⚹ f bookkeeping, einfache (doppelte): by single (double) entry; =**handel** ⚹ m bookselling (trade), book-trade.

Buch²=**händler** (″ch…) m ⓔ: a) (Verleger) publisher; b) (Sortimenter) (discount-)bookseller; fliegende(r)~ flying stationer; 🚂 railway-bookseller; ~**börse** f Lo.: Stationer's Hall; Lisch ⓐ a. ⓒ connected with the book-trade, bibliopolic(al); ~**korporation** f Lo.: Stationer's Company; ~**messe** f booksellers' fair; ~**preis** m, =**währung**, =**zahlung** f booksellers' value.

Buch¹=**handlung** (″ch…) f ⓔ bookseller's shop or business.

Buchholtz (″ch…) [Schatzmeister Friedrichs b. Gr., 1706—98] npr/m. 👑γ. F dazu hat ~ kein Geld we have no money for that; da kennen Sie ~en schlecht then you don't know me, him, &c.

Buch¹=**laden** (″ch…) m ⓔ = =**handlung**.

Büchlein (¹-) n ㉓ (dim. v. Buch¹) little book, booklet.

Buch¹=**leinen** (″ch…) n ⓔ, =**leinwand**, =**linnen** n ⓒ book-linen; =**macher** ⊺ m Wettrennen: bookmaker, F penciller; =**macherei** f manufacture of books (a. b. s.); =**magen** m, zo. = Blätter=m.

Buch²=**mast** (″ch…) f ⓔ für Schweine: beech-mast; =**nuß** ♀ f = =**ecker**; (=**nuß**)=**öl** n beech-nut oil.

Buch¹=**post** ⚹ (″ch…) f ⓔ book-post; =**rechnung** ⚹ f account in the books.

Buchs ♀ ⚘ (ʲch…) [ahd., *grch. py'xos] m ⓐ a. = ~baum.

Buchsbaum (ʲch…-¹) m ⓔ box(-tree) (Buxus sempe'rvirens); ~**einfassung** (¹…) f hort. der Beete: box-edge; ⚘**en** a. ⓒ (made) of box-wood; ~**holz** n box-wood.

Büchschen (ʲch…) n ㉓ dim. v. Büchse.

Buch¹=**schreiber** (″ch…) m ⓒ einer Oper: librettist, author of the words; =**schrift** f, typ. book-face; =**schuld** ⚹ f book-debt.

Büchse ⊖ (ʲch…) f ⓒ = Büchse 5.

Büchse (ʲch…) [ahd., *grch. pyxi's] f ⓔ 1. (cylindrical) box; (Spar=)~ money-box; aus Blech: tin (box or canister); in ~en eingemachtes Fleisch ꝛc. tinned (or potted) meat, &c.; für Salben ꝛc., a.: pot, (china) jar; Alt.: ◇ pyxis, mint. ~ mit Probemünzen: pyx. — 2. fig. v. klugen, aber kleinen Menschen: kleine ~n, gute Salben

good things are packed (up) in small parcels; in die ~ blasen (Strafe zahlen) to (have to) pay a fine. — 3. [14/15. sae.] ehm. (allg.: Schießgewehr) fire-arm; später: (tragbares Feuergewehr) blunderbuss; jetzt: (gezogenes Gewehr; ant. Flinte) rifle(d gun). — 4. ♀ (Moos)~: ◇ pyxis, theca. — 5. ⊖ (Hülse) socket; (zylindrische Bekleidung e-s Maschinenteils) wheel-box or -cap; (Stopf=)~ einer Dampfmaschine piston-rod collar; stuffing-box.

büchsen ⊖ (ʲch…) [Büchse] v/a. ⑨⓪ to (protect with a) box or cap.

Büchsen= (Büchse 5 auch: **Büchsen**=**bohrer** (ʲch…) m ⓔ gun-borer; =**fleisch** n ⓒ tinned (or preserved) meat; ⚂**förmig** a. ⓒ boxshaped, ◇ pyxidate; =**futter(al)** n gun-case; =**gemüse** ⚹ n tinned or preserved, Am. canned vegetables pl.; =**kugel** f rifle-ball; =**lauf** m rifle-barrel; =**licht** n good light for rifle-practice; =**macher** ⊕ m ehm.: blunderbuss-maker; jetzt: gunsmith, gun-maker; =**macherei** f, =**macher**=**handwerk** n; =**kunst** f ehm.: blunderbuss-making, jetzt: gun-making; =**meister** m ehm. 💥 artill.: master-gunner; =**öffner** m tin-opener; =**pulver** n (feinstes Schießpulver) rifle-powder; =**ranzen** m (Jagdtasche) hunting; =**schaft** m gun-stock; =**schäfter** ⚹ m gun-stocker; =**schießen** n rifle-practice; =**schloß** n rifle-lock; =**schmied** m gunsmith; =**schuß** m Sc. rifle-shot; =**schütze** ⚹ m ehm.: (h)arquebusier, jetzt: rifleman; =**spanner** m, hunt. Jäger, der f-s Herrn Gewehr spannt) gun-charger, (gun-)loader; =**wettschießen** n rifle-match or competition.   [rifle and gun.]

Büchs=**flinte** ⚹ (ʲch…) f ⓔ combined

Büchslein (ʲch…) n ㉓ = Büchschen.

Buch²=**stabe** (″ch-¹) [ahd. buchener Stab] m ⓔ 1. Handschrift, typ., &c.: letter; großer ~ capital (letter), kleiner ~ small letter; in ~n (ausgeschrieben) at full length; mit ~n bezeichnen to letter; nach dem ~n, dem ~n nach literally; vgl. buchstäblich; fig. am ~n hangen, kleben to adhere to the letter, to cling to the literal meaning (of the words); bibl. der ~ tötet, aber der Geist macht lebendig the letter killeth, but the spirit giveth life. — 2. (Schriftzug) mit lateinischen ~n schreiben … in Latin character(s). — 3. ⊖ typ. type (vgl. a. 1).

Buch²=**staben**=**ausdruck** (″ch-¹…) m ⓔ math. algebraic expression; =**folge** f alphabetic(al) order; =**gleichklang** m, pros. alliteration; =**gleichung** f, arith. algebraic equation; =**krämer**, =**mensch** m literalist; worshipper of the letter; =**rätsel** n: ◇ logogram; =**rechnung**, =**rechenkunst** f math. algebra; =**schloß** n letter-keyed (or alphabetical) lock; =**schrift** f (ant. Hieroglyphenschrift) alphabetical writing; =**spiel** n: ◇ anagram; =**versetzung** f, =**wechsel** m: a) = =**spiel**; b) gram. transposition of letters, ◇ metathesis.   [book.]

Buchstaben=**buch** (″ch-¹…) n ⓒ spelling-

buchstabier=**en** (″ch-¹…) I v/a. to spell; falsch 2 to misspell. — II ~n ㉓ = B/ung.

Buchstabier=**methode** (″ch-¹…) f ⓒ (ant. Lautiermethode) alphabetical method.

Buchstabierung (″ch-¹…) f ㊻ (art of) spelling, ◇ orthography.

buchstäblich (″ch-¹…) a. ⓒ literal; adv. literally, in the literal (or strictest) sense of the word. bisw. (it.) literatim; eine Stelle 2 nehmen to take … in its literal meaning; (allzu) 2 übersetzen to cling (too much) to the letter; 2 wahr perfectly (or absolutely) true; ~**keit** (″ch-¹…) f ⓒ literalism, literalness; (close) adherence to the letter.

Bucht (ʲch…) [ndd.: bight; *biegen] f ⓔ 1. † allg.: curvature. — 2. (Meeres=) (kleine Bai) (small) bay (or inlet) of the sea; (Schlupfhafen) bight; kleine ~ creek, cove. — 3. ndd. P (Bett) bed; (sofiger Winkel) snug corner; (Abteilung im Schweinestall) box, partition. — 4. ⚓ ~ (Biegung der Taue ꝛc.: bight; eines Innenholzes: knuckle. — 5. (Winkelbogen) arc, ◇ sinus.

buchten (ʲch…) ⊖ I v/a. to scallop. — II sich 2 v/refl. to form a bay or a creek or an inlet; von einem See, Fluß auch: to widen (out) into a bay. — III ~ n ㉓ (f. II) das Sich=2 formation of a bay or creek, &c.; f. Bucht 2.

buchtig (~) [Bucht] a. ⓒ 1. von e-r Küste: (well) indented or cut up; full of bays or creeks. — 2. ♀ von Blättern: ◇ sinuate.

Buch=**titel** (″ch…) m ⓔ title of a book.

Buchung ⚹ (″ch…) f ⓒ booking; entry.

Buch²=**weizen** ♀ (″ch-¹…) [ndd.: *Buche] m ㉓ buckwheat (Poly'gonum Fagopy'rum); ~**grütze** f ⓒ buckwheat-groats pl.

Buch¹=**wissen** (″ch…) n ⓒ bookish knowledge; book-learning or -lore; =**zeichen** n book-mark(er); =**zwang** m in Deutschland ꝛc.: compulsory registration of (every plot of) land. — Vgl. auch Bücher=…   [taur.]

Bucintoro (-tich…-¹-) [it.] m ⓔ Bucen-

Buckel¹ (²-) [mhd.; *fr. boucle] f ⓒ 1. (Hervorragung) convexity. — 2. a. m ⓔ (erhabene Metallverzierung) boss; (Knauf) knob, stud; am Pferdegeschirr ꝛc.: knuckle; (Schnalle) buckle. — 3. ~n pl. (Ringe) der Locken ringlets, curls pl.

Buckel² (²-) [Buckel¹, P: bücken] m ㉒ 1. (Auswuchs) (camel's) hump or hunch; (Höcker) hump(back), hunch(back), ◇ cyphosis; ♀ von Früchten: (out)growth, excrescence; Knorren: knot. — 2. arch. die Mauer macht einen ~ the wall bellies (or bulges) out. — 3. fig. sich einen ~ (a. schief, krumm) lachen to split (one's) sides with laughing; vgl. buckelig 1; e-n ~ machen (sich verneigen) to bow (low). — 4. F (Rücken) back; einen ~ machen to stoop, to bend one's back, to bow down; von einer Katze: sie macht einen krummen ~ she puts (or sets, P rides) up her back; e-m den ~ voll schlagen oder prügeln, den ~ schmieren F to tan (or curry) a p.'s hide, to leather a p.; ein ~ voll Schläge a sound thrashing or drubbing; F a good hiding or licking; fig. er hat einen breiten ~ he has a broad back, he can bear a large burden, P steig mir den Buckel 'nauf! etwa: go and be hanged!

buck(e)licht ~, mst **buck(e)lig** (²(~)-) I a. ⓒ 1. hunched, hunchbacked, humpbacked; ◇ gibbous; er ist 2, oft: F has a hump; fig. sich 2 lachen (wollen) F to

Zeichen (s. S. XVII): F familiär; P Volkssprache; ⌐ Gaunersprache; ↘ selten; † alt (auch gestorben); * neu (auch geboren); ₊₊ unrichtig;

buckeln (ˇ⌣) [Buckel²] v/n.(h.) ⓐa.(e-n Buckel m.) to crook (or put up) one's back.
Buckel²=ochs (ˇ⌣...) m ㉒ zo. = Zebu.
Buckelorum (⌣⌣ˊ⌣) [dtsch.=lt.] m ㊵ hunchback(ed person), humpback.
bucken ✕ (ˇ⌣) v/n. (h.) ⓘ artill. vom hinteren Teil des Geschützrohrs beim Schießen: (hochspringen) to bounce.
bücken (ˇ⌣) [mhd.; *biegen] ⓘ I v/a. 1. to bend; (neigen) to incline; gebückt geh(e)n to stoop in walking; vor Alter gebückt.bent (down) with (old) age. — II sich ⚳ v/refl. 2. to bow down; er bückte sich danach he stooped to pick it up. — 3. sich vor e-m ⚳ (verbeugen) to bow to a p., stärker: to bow and scrape (untertänig: to cringe and crawl) before a p.
Bücking (ˇ⌣) [ndd.; *Bock¹] m ⓘd. (geräucherter Hering) bloater; red herring.
bucklicht, bucklig (ˇ⌣) a. ⓖⓖ = buckelig.
Bückling¹ (ˇ⌣) [pökeln] m ⓘd. = Bücking.
Bückling² F (ˇ⌣) [bücken] m ⓘd. (Verbeugung) bow; von Damen ehm., jetzt noch bei Tänzen: curtsy; einen ~ machen to (make a) bow; ~(e)macher m ㉒ one who bows and scrapes before people; (Kriecher) cringer.
Buckskin ⟙ ⚔ u. ⊕ (ˇ⌣) [engl.] m ㊵ (Tuch) buckskin; Hosen, Gamaschen f/pl. aus ~ buckskin breeches, leggings pl.
buddeln F (ˇ⌣) ⓘ I v/n. (h.) to dig (in the earth, &c.). — II v/a. agr. Kartoffeln ⚳ (ausmachen) to dig up (or lift) potatoes.
Buddha (ˇ⌣) [fkr. der Erweckte] (6. sae. v. Chr.) npr/m. ⓐa. rel. Buddha.
Buddh(a)ismus (⌣ˇ⌣ˊ⌣) m ㉗ (in Ostasien verbreitete Religion der Buddhaverehrer) Buddhism; **Buddhist** (⌣ˇ⌣) m ⓐ und **buddhistisch** (⌣ˇ⌣) a. ⓖⓖ Buddhist.
Bude (ˊ⌣) [ahd.: booth] f ⓐ (Kram=, Meß=)~ booth, stall; (Laden) shop; F co. (Zimmer) room, lodgings, F diggings (abbr. digs) pl.; e-m auf die ~ rücken to visit a p. at his lodgings, to intrude upon a p. (at his house or apartments); F fig. Leben in die ~ bringen to put (new) life into a th., to cause a stir, F (Am.) to make things hum; es kommt Leben in die ~ things are beginning to look (more) lively.
Buden=geld (ˊ⌣...) n ㉒ stall-rent or -money; **=leute** pl. stall-keepers pl. (at a fair); **=stand** m (room for a) stall or stand; **=zins** m = =geld.
Budget ⟙ (fr. bü-dGe') [engl.; *fr. bougette Ränzel] n ㉒ parl. (Staatshaushalts-voranschlag) budget, (yearly) estimates pl.; das ~ vorlegen to introduce the budget; to bring in the estimates; das ~ (die Jahresausgaben) bewilligen to grant supply.
Budget=beratung (ˊ⌣...) f ㉒ debate on the budget; **=kommission** f (in Engl.) für die Voranschläge: Committee of Supply; für die Deckungsmittel: Committee of Ways and Means.

Budike F (⌣ˊ⌣) [fr. boutique; *grch. Apotheke] f ⓐ (kleiner Laden, Garküche) small (eating-)shop; P grub(bing)-shop or grubbing-ken (f. Bums¹); **~er(in** f ㊸) m ㉒ (low) eating-house keeper.
Büdner nordb. (ˊ⌣) [Bude] m ㉒ small peasant-proprietor, cottager.
Büfett (⌣ˊ⌣, a. noch fr. bü-fe') [fr. buffet] n ⓐb. 1. (Schenktisch) als Möbel: side-board; side-table; im Schenkzimmer: bar. — 2. (Schenkzimmer) refreshment-room.
Büfett=abendbrot (⌣ˊ...) n ㉒ stand-up supper; light refreshments pl.; **=mamsell** f barmaid; **=zimmer** n, thea., &c. refreshment-room.
☞ **Buff** (⌣) ꝛc. f. Puff ꝛc.
Büffel (ˇ⌣) [fr. buffle; lt. bu'balus] m ㉒ 1. zo. buffalo (Bos Bu'balus); amerikanischer: bison; bonasus. — 2. fig. ein wahrer ~ (grober Mensch) a rude or coarse, rough, uncouth fellow, a regular boor. — 3. a) (~leder) buff; b) (Lederkoller, bsd. ✕ ehm.) buff(-coat).
Büffelei (⌣⌣ˊ) f ⓐ 1. = büffeln II. — 2. (Roheit) rudeness. uncouthness.
Büffel=haut (ˇ⌣...) f ㉒ buffalo-hide or -skin; **=horn** n buffalo-horn; **=jagd** f, **=jäger** m buffalo-hunt(ing), -hunter; **=koller** n = Büffel 3 b; **=kopf** m, fig. blockhead; **=leder** n buff.
büffeln F (ˇ⌣) [nhd. 16.sae.] ⓘ I v/n. (h.) ⓐa. bursch.: to study hard; F to cram (or grind, bisw. swot) for an examination. — II ~ n ㉓ hard study or reading; F cramming, grinding.
Büffel=rock (ˇ⌣...) m ㉒, **=wams** n bsd. ✕ ehm. buff-coat.
Büffler (ˇ⌣) [büffeln] m ㉒ hard reader; F plodder, ⟍ swotter; dagegen: crammer = Lehrer, der für Prüfungen vorbereitet!
Bug¹ (ˊ) [ahd.; *biegen, bough] m ⓘc. 1. (Beingelenk) joint of the leg; (Hechse, Knieflechse) hock, hough, ham; bsd. bei Pferden: (Vorder-)~ (Schulterblatt) shoulder-blade. — 2. ⟰ (Schiffsvorderteil) bow; breiter, schmaler, überhangender ~ bold, lean, flaring bow; am ~ forward; mit dem ~ gegen ein Schiff laufen to foul a ship with the bow; über den andern ~ geh(e)n, auf e-n andern ~ wenden to tack (about).
Bug² (ˊ) [mhd.; *biegen] m ⓘc. bend, bow.
Bug¹=anker ⟰ (ˊˊ...) m ㉒ bow-anchor, bower; **=band** ⟰ n breast-hook.
Bügel (ˊ⌣) [nhd. = bail; *biegen] m ㉒ 1. bent (piece of) wood or metal. — 2. (Steig=)~ stirrup; von Reitern: ~ an ~ (riding or F lying) close(ly) together. — 3. ⊕ mech. bridle; ~ (Henkel) am Eimer ꝛc.: bail; an der Gabeldeichsel: holdback; am Flintenschloß: trigger-guard; am Geldbeutel: (outside) casing; mach. des Mannlochdeckels: bow; fenc. des Säbels: bow; ⟰ ~ (Doppelring zum Aufhängen) des Kompasses gimbals pl., über den Luken: batten of the hatch; ⟰ (Kuppelungs=) ~ am Waggon: shackle.
Bügel=brett (ˊ⌣...) n ㉒ ironing-board; **=dohne** f, hunt. (Schlinge) gin, springe; **=eisen** n box- or flat- (bisw. smoothing- or pressing-)iron, heater; **=fest** a. firm in one's stirrups; **=horn** ✕ n bugle; **=los** a. without stirrups.

bügeln (ˊ⌣) [nhd. 17. sae.] ⓐa. I v/a. 1. ⊕ Wäsche ⚳ (plätten) to iron ...; Schneiderei: to press (or smooth) with a flat-iron; Nähte ⚳ to press seams with a hot iron or a heater; fig. geschniegelt und gebügelt looking very neat and prim. — 2. F e-n ⚳ (trinken) F to have a glass or a drop. — II v/n. (h.) man. (die Vorderfüße beim Traben auswärts werfen) to throw out the forelegs in trotting.
Bügel=riemen (ˊ⌣...) m ㉒ man. stirrup-strap; **=säge** f bow-saw; **=stahl** m heater (of a flat-iron); **=tuch** n ironing-cloth. -blanket; vgl. Plätt=, Steigbügel=.
Bug¹=figur ⟰ (ˊ...) f ㉒ = Galjon; **=flagge** f = Gösch; **=geschütz** n bowgun or -piece; **=gording** ⟰ f buntline; **=lahm** a. ⓖⓖ v. Pferden: splay-should-ered; ein Pferd ⚳ m. to splay a horse's shoulder; **=lähme** f, **=lahmheit** f, **=lähmung** f sprain(ing) of the shoulder, vet. strain; **=leine** ⟰ f = Boleine.
Bügler (ˊ⌣) m ㉒, **~in** f ㊸ ironer.
Bug¹=pforte ⟰ (ˊ...) f ㉒ (Ladeöffnung e-s Kriegsschiffes) bridle-port.
Bugsier=... (⌣ˊ⌣...) ⟰ = Schlepp=...
bugsieren ⟰ (⌣ˊ⌣) [ndl.] v/a.㉓= schleppen.
Bug¹=spriet ⟰ (ˊ...) [ndl.] n (m) ⓘd. (schräger Mast am Bug) bowsprit.
Bugspriet=backen ⟰ (ˊˊ...) f/pl. ㉒, **=klampen** f/pl. cheeks pl. of the bowsprit, bo.-bees pl.; **=fischung, =gat** f bo.-bed; **=wanten** f/pl. (Taue) bo.-shrouds pl.; **=wuhling** f (Tauring zum Festhalten des Bugspriets) gammoning of the bo.
Bug¹=stag ⟰ (ˊ...) n ㉒ shroud of the bow-sprit; **=stück** n Schiffsschlerei: shoulder-piece.
Bugt(=...) ⟰ (ˊ, ˊ...) = Bucht 4.
Bug¹=welle ⟰ (ˊ...) f ㉒ (v. e-m Schiff in Fahrt aufgeworfene Wassermenge) bow-wave; **=zelt** n forecastle awning.
Büh(e)l ⟍ obb. (ˊ) [ahd.; *biegen] m ㉒ (ⓘc.) = Hügel.
Buhl=dirne (ˊ...) f ㉒ = Buhle f.
Buhle (ˊ⌣) [mhd.] m ㊹, f ㊽ jetzt meist b.s. paramour; g.s. (G.) seine ~ his sweetheart, his beloved.
buhlen (ˊ⌣) I v/n. (h.) ⓐ 1. mst b.s. to carry on a love-affair or an intrigue with a p. — 2. poet. (lofen) to caress (gently or fondly). — 3. um et. ⚳ to strive for a th.; um j-s Gunst ⚳ to court a p.'s favour, to woo a p. — 4. an Schnelle ꝛc. mit e-m (um die Wette) ⚳ to try to outdo (or outstrip) a p. in speed, &c., to compete (or vie) with a p. in speed, &c. — II ~ n ㉓ 5. = Buhlerei.
Buhler (ˊ⌣) m ㉒, **=in** f ㊸ paramour; **~m** ads: lover, sweetheart, (Hofmann) suitor, wooer; **=in** f a.: courtesan, gay woman, (Kokette) coquette.
Buhlerei (⌣⌣ˊ) f ㊻ 1. (Liebesverhältnis) courtship; b.s. intrigue, illicit intercourse. — 2. weitS. ~ um et. striving (or competing, competition, rivalry) for a th. — 3. (Gefallsucht) coquetry.
buhlerisch (ˊ⌣) a. ⓖⓖ (verliebt) amorous; gallant; (gefallsüchtig) coquettish.
Buhlin (ˊ⌣) f ㊸ = Buhle f.
Buhlschaft ⟍ (ˊ⌣) f ㊻ (Liebschaft) love-affair, (amorous) intrigue.
Buhne ⊕ (ˊ⌣) [ndd. = Bühne] f ㉒ 1. Wasserbau: (Deich) dike; zum Schutz des Ufers, an der See: sea-wall, sea-defence (works

pl.); am Meer ob. an Flüssen: breakwater, groin, groyne. — 2. *arch.* (Ufermauerwerk) quay; wharf. — 3. (Fischzaun) crawl; (durchlöcherter Fischbehälter) well (or tank) of a fishing-boat. — 4. ↓ ※ (Warenhof am Hafen) (bonded) warehouse.
Bühne (⁻‿) [mhd. Latte] *f* ⊕ 1. (Schaubühne) stage; weitS. theatre (beide auch *fig.*); the boards *pl.*; auf der ~, auch: before the footlights; auf die ~ bringen to (put on the) stage, to produce; die ~ betreten, auf der ~ auftreten to appear on the stage, to tread the boards; über die ~ geh(e)n: a) vom Schauspieler: to walk the stage; b) von Theaterstücken: to be put on the stage; Romane für die ~ bearbeiten to dramatize ..., to adapt ... for the stage. — 2. (Brettergerüst) scaffold; (Tribüne) platform, *pol. a.* hustings *pl.*; für Journalisten: gallery. — 3. ※ (Absatz im Schacht) platform, sollar. [a floor. — 2. ※ to line a shaft.]
bühnen ⊕ (⁻‿) *v/a.* ⊛ 1. (bielen) to board)
Bühnen-anweisung (⁻‿‿) *f* ⊕ stage-direction; **=aussprache** *f* pronunciation of the stage; **=ausstattung** *f* stage-scenery or -appointments *pl.*; **=dekoration** *f* setting (or fitting) up of the scenery, scenery; **=dichter(in** *f*) *m* playwright; dramatist; **=dichtung** *f* stage-play; dramatic poetry; **=diener** *m* scene-shifter; **=effekt** *m* stage-effect; **⚥fähig** *a.* ⊛ suitable (or adapted) for the stage; Les Stück acting-play; **=fähigkeit** *f* suitability (or fitness) for the stage; **⚥gerecht** *a.*, **=gerechtigkeit** *f.* ⚥fähig *a.*; **=held(in** *f*) *m* stage-hero (-ine); **=kenntnis** *f* knowledge of (or familiarity with) the stage; **⚥kundig** *a.* well acquainted with (the routine of the) stage; **=künstler(in** *f*) *m* player, dramatic artist; **=leiter** *m* stage-manager; **=maler** *m* scene-painter; **=malerei** *f* scene-painting; **⚥mäßig** *a.*: a) scenic; F *contp.* stagey; b) = ⚥fähig.
Bühnen-meister (⁻‿‿) *m* ⊕ master of the quay, wharfinger.
Bühnen-streich (⁻‿‿) *m* ⊕ stage-trick; **=stück** *n* piece, (theatrical) play, drama; vgl. =dichtung; **=veränderung** *f* scene-shifting; **=vorhang** *m* (drop-)curtain; **=wand** *f* side-scene; **=werk** *n* = ⚥fähiges Stück; **=werkmeister** *m* stage-carpenter; theatrical machinist; **=weijung** *f* stage-direction; **=wesen** *n* theatrical affairs *pl.*; **=zubehör** *n* stage- (or theatrical) property.
Bühn-loch ※ (⁻‿) *n* ⊕ in das Gestein eingehauen zur Aufnahme von Tragstempeln: hollow (or gap) cut into the rock for receiving the shaft-timbering.
buk (⁻) (u. büke *subj.*) *imp.f. v.* backen (f. ds.).
Bukanier (‿⁻‿) [fr. *farib.*] *m* ⊕ (*westind.* Seeräuber des 17. *sae.*) buccaneer.
Bukett (‿⁻) [fr. *bouquet m*; *dtsch.* Busch] *n* ⊕b. 1. (Blumenstrauß) nosegay, bouquet; fürs Knopfloch: button-hole. — 2. (Duft, Blume) (fine) aroma of wine.
Bukett-halter (‿⁻‿) *m* ⊕ bouquet-holder; button-hole fastener.
Bukolika (‿⁻‿‿) [grch. Hirtenlieder] *n/pl. inv.* bucolics *pl.* of Theocritus, Virgil, &c.
Bukoliker (‿⁻‿‿) [fr.] *m* (Idyllendichter) bucolic poet.

bukolisch (‿⁻‿) *a.* ⊛ bucolic; Les Lied bucolic (or pastoral) song.
Bulette (‿⁻‿) [fr. *boulette*] *f* ⊕ (Fleischklößchen) meat-ball.
Bulgare (‿⁻‿) *m* ⊕ Bulgar(ian).
Bulgarei ♀ (‿‿⁻) *npr/f.* ⊕, die ~, *mft.* **Bulgari-en** (‿⁻(‿)) *npr/n.* ⊕α. (Balkanstaat) Bulgaria.
bulgarisch (‿⁻‿) *a.* ⊛ Bulgarian.
Bulge[1] ※ *u. prov.* (⁻‿) [ahd.: bilge, bulge] *f* ⊛ (Ledersack, Schlauch) leather bag.
Bulge[2] ※ † (*LU.*) (⁻‿) [mhd.: billow] *f* ⊛ (Welle) billow; vgl. Bilge.
Bulin(e ↓ (‿⁻(‿) [= Bug-leine] *f* ⊛(⊕) = Boleine. [beißer.]
Bull-dogg(e *m, f*) *m* (⁻‿...) ⊕ = Bullen-)
Bulle[1] (⁻‿) [ndd.] *m* ⊕ zo. 1. (männliches Zuchttier) bull. — 2. ※ = ~nbeißer.
Bulle[2] (⁻‿) [mhd. *·lt. bulla*] *f* ⊕ 1. (Siegel) seal (on a deed). — 2. (Urkunde) bull; *bsd.* päpstliche ~ papal bull.
Bullen ↓ (⁻‿) *m* ⊕ (Kiel(e)ichter) pontoon for careening ships, sheer-hulk.
Bullen-beißer (⁻‿‿) *m* ⊕ zo. bulldog, mastiff; **=hatz**, **=hetze** *f* bull-baiting. **=kalb** *n*, zo. bullcalf. [bullary.]
Bullen[2]**-sammlung** (⁻‿‿) *f* ⊕ der Päpste)
Bullen-tau ↓ (⁻‿‿) *n* ⊕ zum Festhalten e-s Segelbaums: sheer-line, guy of a boom.
bullerig F (⁻‿‿)*a.* ⊛ boisterous. [rumble.]
bullern F (⁻‿) [lautm.] *v/n.* (h.) ⊛a. to)
Bulletin (bü·l·tä') [fr.] *n* ⊕ (kurzer ärztlicher, militärischer ec. =Tages=Bericht) bulletin.
Bull-ochs (⁻‿...) *m* ⊕ bullock.
Bullrich-salz (⁻‿⁻) *n* ⊕ *pharm.* (doppelt-kohlensaures Natron) bicarbonate of soda.
Bülte (⁻‿) *f* ⊕, **Bulte(n** (⁻‿) *m* ⊕(⊛) (Hügel) hillock, (fester Boden im Moor) solid part of a bog or swamp, *schott. hag.*
bum (⁻) *int.* boom!; (slap-)bang!, bounce! vgl. *a.* [bim]bam).
Bumerang (⁻‿‿) [⁺⁺ austral.] *m, n* ⊕d. (Wurfwaffe) boomerang.
Bummel F (⁻‿) [ndd.] *m* ⊕ 1. (am Kleide ec. lose Herabhangendes) *s. th.* loosely hanging down one's dress, vgl. Bammel[2]. — 2. *bsd. burch.* stroll; lounge; jaunt; auf den ~ gehen to stroll (or lounge) about, F to go on the spree.
Bummelei F (⁻‿‿) *f* ⊛ (Umherschlendern) lounging (or sauntering, loafing, loitering) about; *weitS.* laziness; vgl. Bummelleben.
bumm(e)lig F (⁻‿) f. bummlig.
Bummel-leben (⁻‿...) *n* ⊕ lazy or idle, inactive) life; vagabond('s) existence; F loafing.
bummeln F (⁻‿) [ndd.] **I** *v/n.* (h.) ⊛a. 1. = baummeln. — 2. (umherschlendern) to lounge (or saunter, F *u.* P mooch) about; (müßiggehen) to lead a lazy (or idle, inactive) life, to gad (or loaf) about. — 3. (säumig sein) to lag, loiter, dawdle. — **II** ~ *n* ⊕ 4. = Bummelei.
Bummel-zug 🚂 (⁻‿...) *m* ⊕ slow (or parliamentary) train; F crawler.
Bummler (⁻‿) [: bummer] *m* ⊕, **~in** *f* ⊕ 1. loafer, loiterer, F *u.* P moocher, *co.* inspector of the pavement. — 2. (Landstreicher) tramp, vagabond. — 3. *weitS.* careless (or heedless, dissolute) person, dawdler, idler.
bummlig F (⁻‿)*a.*⊛ loitering; dawdling; lazy, idle. Les Leben = Bummelleben.

Bums[1] P (⁻) *m* ⊕a. (Speisehaus niederen Ranges) low(-class) eating-house or dining-room(s *pl.*) or restaurant.
bums[2] (⁻) *int.* pop!, smash!, dash!; vgl. bum. [bang or crash; to dash into.)
bumsen (⁻‿) *v/n.* (h.) ⊛a. (to fall with a))
Bums[1]**-keller** P (⁻‿‿) *m* ⊕ = Bums[1].
bums[2]**-still** F (⁻‿) *a.* ⊛ stock-still, motionless.
Bund[1] (⁻) [mhd.; *binden] *m* ⊕b. 1. *allg.* (Bündnis) union, alliance; im ~e mit e-m sein (ob. stehen) to be in league with a p.; einen ~ mit e-m schließen to enter into a compact (or an alliance) with a p.; im ~e mit seiner Frau jointly with (*weitS.* with the aid of) his wife. — 2. *pol.* confederacy, confederation; zu Schutz und Trutz: league; coalition; *hist.* ~ der schottischen Presbyterianer gegen König Karl I. (1643) Solemn League and Covenant; der Deutsche, der Schweizer ~ the German, the Swiss Confederation; *pol.* ~ dreier Staaten (Dreibund) Triple Alliance; die Staaten e-s ~es (a. die zu e-m ~e vereinigten Staaten) federal (or confederate) states; *bibl.* der Alte und der Neue ~ the Old and (the) New Testament. — 3. (Binde) band(age); truss; (Gurt) girdle; (waist)band; (Knoten) knot; Orient. (türkischer) ~ turban. — 4. ⊙ Glaserei: lead frame of a pane; Schmiede: iron band or brace; ♪ ~ (Griff) an Saiteninstrumenten: fret.
Bund[2] (⁻) [mhd.; *binden] *n* ⊕b, ⊛. 1. *allg.:* bundle (3B. Hanf, Tafelglas, Papiere ec.); packet, bunch, als Maßeinheit für Garn s. S. XXXIX, III. — 2. ~ Flachs bobbin of flax; ~ Heu bottle (or bundle) of hay; ~ Reiser, Reisig faggot, ⚔ *frt.* fascine; ~ (Pott ⁺⁺ *m*) Schlüssel bunch of keys; ~ Seide skein (or hank) of silk; ~ Stroh truss (or bundle) of straw.
bund[2]**-artig** (⁻‿...) *a.* ⊛ in (the) shape of a bundle, packet, faggot, &c. (f. Bund[2]); ⚔ fasciculate(d).
Bund[1]**-axt** (⁻‿...) *f* ⊕ (Zimmerart) smoothing-axe; **=bruch** *m* ⊕ violation of a treaty, breach of a contract; **⚥brüchig** *a.* ⊛ breaking (or violating) a compact or treaty; *weitS.* faithless, treacherous.
Bündchen (⁻‿) *n* ⊛ *dim. v.* Bund.
Bündel (⁻‿) [mhd.: bundle] *n* (*m*) ⊛ 1. bundle(vgl. Bund[2]); ~ Pfeile (24 Pfeile) sheaf of arrows; ~ Stahlstäbe (30 Stäbe) sheaf of steel; ~ (von) Aften, Ruten (*bsd. hist.* der röm. Liktoren) ⚔ fascicle, fasces *pl.* — 2. ⚔ packet, parcel; in ~ packen to make up in packages, to make packages of. — 3. (Gepäck) luggage; F sein ~ schnüren to pack up one's traps, to be off.
bündel-förmig (⁻‿‿) *a.* ⊛ in shape of a bundle or parcel; ⚔ fasciculate(d), fascicular.
bündeln F (⁻‿) *v/n.* (h.) ⊛a. *b.s.* to form a (secret) league or society; (sich verschwören) to plot, to form a conspiracy.
Bündel-pfeiler (⁻‿‿) *m* ⊛, **=säule** *f*, **=schaft** *m*, *arch.* bundle-pillar, clustered column; **⚥weise** *adv.* in bundles or packets or parcels.
Bundes-angelegenheit (⁻‿‿‿)[Bund[1]] ⊕ matter concerning a confederation;

[Bundesartifel] — 231 — [Bürgerheer]

federal concern; =artikel m/pl. U.S. hist. (1787) Articles of Confederation; =behörde f: a) federal government; b) ~n pl. federal authorities pl.; =beschluß m ehm.: resolution (or decision) of the German Diet or Confederation; =bruch m violation of a compact or treaty, weitS. treachery; ≈brüchig a. = bundbrüchig; =bruder m confederate; ally; =feldherr m commander-in-chief of the federal troops; =festung ✗ f ehm. fortress of the German Confederation; =fürst m prince of one of the confederate states; =genosse m ally, engS. confederate, associate; =genossenkrieg alte hist. Social War; =genossenschaft f: a) confederacy; alliance; b) allies, confederates pl.; ≈genössisch a. federal; belonging to an ally; =gericht n federal court or tribunal; =kanzler m ehm. Chancellor of the North-German Confederation; =lade f, bibl. Ark of the Covenant; ≈mäßig a. federal; =mitglied n: a) ally, confederate; b) = staat b; =präsident m der Schweiz President of the Swiss Confederacy; =rat m federal council; Schweiz: Federal Government; =regierung f = =behörde a; =staat m: a) confederation; b) (einzelner Staat) federal (or confederate) state; =tag m federal diet; ehm.: deutscher ~ German(ic) Diet; =truppen ✗ f/pl. federal troops; =verfassung f federal constitution; =versammlung f federal assembly; =vertrag m treaty of confederation; ≈verwandt a. allied, confederate; =völker n/pl. (con)federate nations pl. — Vgl. auch Bund=...

bund²-förmig (ˇ...) a. = ≈artig; =holz n ⊕ faggot-wood; (fire-)wood in bundles.

bündig (ˇ) [mhd.] a. ⊕ 1. (bindend) binding, valid; (verpflichtend) obligatory, compulsory. — 2. (beweisend) demonstrative, stärker: conclusive, clenching (argument). — 3. vom Stil: (knapp, gedrängt) concise, terse, curt; succinct, (genau) precise; kurz und ≈ plain and concise, (very) telling; adv. sich kurz und ≈ ausdrücken to speak briefly and to the point.

Bündigkeit (ˇ) f ⊕ 1. validity. — 2. conclusiveness. — 3. conciseness.

bündisch (ˇ) a. ⊕ confederate.

Bündler (ˇ) m ⊕ b.s. member of a secret society; plotter, intriguer, schemer.

Bündner (ˇ) [Bund¹] m ⊕, ~in f ⊕ 1. (Bundesgenosse) ally, confederate. — 2. ⚲ (Graubündner) (native of) Grison.

Bündnis (ˇ) n ⊕ = Bund¹ 1.

Bund²-schuh (ˇ...) [mhd.] m ⊕: a) kind of peasant's boot; b) hist. peasants' rebellion in the middle ages; =steg ⊕ m, typ. gutter(-stick); side-stick; ≈weise adv. in bundles or faggots.

Bunge (ˇ) [ahd.] f ⊕ 1. ⚲ brook-weed (Sa'molus Valera'ndi). — 2. (Reuse) drum-net.

Bunker ⚓ (ˇ) [ndd.] m ⊕ (Kohlenraum auf Dampfschiffen) bunker.

Bunsen (ˇ) npr/m. ⊕ α. (dtsch. Chemiker 1811—99); ~brenner (ˇ...) m ⊕ Bunsen burner; ≈isch (ˇ...) a. ⊕: elect. ~sches Element Bunsen cell.

bunt (ˇ) [mhd.; *lt. pu'nctus] I a. ⊕ 1. (vielfarbig) of many colours, variegated, or many-coloured, ⛵ multicoloured; bibl. Der Rock coat of many colours; ≈ gewürfelt chequered; ≈ gewürfeltes (sog. schott.) Wollenzeug tartan; ≈ (scheckig) mottled (soap), party-coloured (garb), piebald (horse). — 2. (farbig) coloured; Des Glas, Papier stained ...; ≈e Karten court- (or picture-)cards pl. — 3. (lebhaft) ≈e Farbe bright (or light) ...; sie kleidet sich gern ≈ (adv.) she is fond of (wearing) gay (or F loud) attire or colours; dort herrscht ein ≈es Leben there is a great deal of life there, the place is brimful of (or astir with) life. — 4. fig. (allerlei enthaltend) mixed; ≈e Menge motley crew; ≈es Allerlei = ≈ II; (verwirrt) confused; ≈ durch=ea. in thorough confusion; F higgledy-piggledy; ≈ durch=ea=werfen ob. =mischen to jumble together or up; es geht bei Ihnen ≈ zu F they are all at sixes and sevens; es ging ≈ (dort) zu F there were strange goings-on; er treibt es sehr (auch gar zu) ≈ he is acting very strangely; he goes too far; die Sache wird mir zu ≈ it's (becoming) too much for me; es wird immer ≈er things are getting worse and worse. — 5. (abwechselnd) ≈e Reihe ladies and gentlemen pl. arranged in couples or pairs. — II ~e(s) n ⊕ 6. in Zeitungen ꝛc.: miscellaneous news, miscellanies pl.

Bunt-bleiche ⊕ (ˇ...) f ⊕ Indigofärberei: branning; =bock m, zo. Süd-afrika= bontebok (Bu'balis pyga'rga); =druck ⊕ m printing in colours, chromatic (or coloured) printing, lithographischer ~ chromolithography; das Bild: chromolithograph; =färben ⊕ n (Beizen) staining; =färber ⊕ m stainer; ≈farbig a. = bunt 1; ≈fiedrig a. ⊕, ≈gefiedert a. of gay plumage; ≈fleckig, ≈gefleckt, ≈gesprenkelt a. speckled; spotted, motley; mottled (soap).

Bunt-heit (ˇ...) f ⊕ variegated (or motley) appearance; bright colour.

Bunt-kupfererz (ˇ...) n ⊕ min. purple copper-ore; =papier n coloured paper; nur auf e-r Seite gefärbt: stained paper; =sandstein m, min. variegated (or New Red) Sandstone; ≈scheckig a. spotted, piebald; ≈schillernd a. opalescent; =specht m, orn.: large spotted woodpecker, French pie (Picus maior); =stift m coloured pencil; ≈streifig a. with light(-coloured) stripes; =weberei f ⊕ coloured weaving.

☞ Bunze(n) ꝛc. f. Punze(n) ꝛc.

Bur (ˇ) [ndl. Bauer] m ⊕e. (Süd-afrikaner von holl. Abkunft) Boer.

Bürde (ˇ) [ahd.: burdan; * (ge)bären tragen] f ⊕ 1. (zu tragende Last) burden (a. fig.); (aufgeladene Last) load; e-m eine schwere ~ auflegen to put (or impose) a heavy burden on a p. — 2. Maßeinheit: (s. Bund² 2 u. Bündel 1) bundle, &c.

bürden (ˇ) v/a. ⊕ to load.

Büre (ˇ) [ndd.] f ⊕ = Bettüberzug.

Bureau (bü-rō') [fr.; *dtsch Büre] n ⊕ 1. (Geschäftszimmer) office; eines Anwalts: chambers pl. — 2. (Schreibtisch) desk.

Bureau-ausgaben (ˇ...) f/pl. ⊕ office-expenses pl.; =beamte(r) m official; -clerk; =diener m office-boy or -lad; messenger.

Bureaukrat (bü-rē-krā't) [fr.=grch.] m ⊕ (Attenmensch) red-tapist, narrow-minded official; F jack-in-office; ~entum (ˇ...) n ⊕c, ~ie (ˇ...) f ⊕ (Beamtenherrschaft) red-tapism, bureaucracy; ≈isch (ˇ...) a. ⊕ bureaucratic.

Bureau-mensch (bü-rō"...) m ⊕ etwa: government (or office) drudge; =stunden f/pl. office-hours pl.; =vorsteher m head of the office; head clerk; im Ministerium: head of a department.

Buren-freund (ˇ...) [Bur] m ⊕ pro-Boer; =krieg m Boer-war.

Bürette (-ˇ) [fr.] f ⊕ chm. (Meßröhre) small dropping-glass; ~ mit Quetschhahn burette with clip.

Burg (ˇ) [ahd.: borough, burgh; *bergen] f ⊕ 1. † fortified place or town. — 2. (festes Schloß) strong castle; (baronial) manor; stronghold, citadel; mit e-r gekrönt castellated. — 3. fig. (Zuflucht) (place) of refuge; (Beschirmer) protector; eine feste ~ a rock of ages.

burg-artig (ˇ...) a. ⊕ castle-like; =bann m ehm. jurisdiction (or precincts, surroundings pl.) of a (baronial) castle.

bürge¹ (ˇ) impf. subj. v. bergen.

Bürge² (ˇ) [ahd.; *borgen] m ⊕, Bürgin f ⊕ 1. für Zahlung: security; gerichtlich meist: bail, surety; e-n ~n stellen, sich ~n verschaffen to find bail for a certain sum; ~ werden für to stand bail for, vgl. 2. — 2. bsd. jur. guarantor; sponsor; sicherer, tauglicher = substantial (or good) security; (Geisel) hostage; für e-n ~ werden to make o.s. responsible (or answerable) for a p. [=meister.]

Burge-meister † (ˇˇˇ...) ⊕ = Bürger-

bürgen (ˇ) [mhd.; *Bürge] v/n. (h.) ⊕ 1. für einen, etwas ≈ (haften) to become security (gerichtlich: to stand bail) for a p., for a sum of money. — 2. für die Güte von etwas ≈ (einstehen) to guarantee (or warrant) the quality of a th.; für die Wahrheit: to vouch for its truth.

Bürger (ˇ) [ahd.; *Burg] m ⊕, ~in f ⊕ 1. † inhabitant of a fortified town (f. Burg 1). — 2. (Stadt-)~ burgher, freeman; co. cit; bisw. ~in citizeness; als Wähler: burgess; (Stadtbewohner) ant. Bauer: townsman (bisw. f. townswoman), pl. townspeople, townsfolk, townsmen; weitS. inhabitant; ~ werden to be put on the municipal roll or register; weitS. to be admitted to (the rights of) citizenship; als Ehren=≈: to be presented with (or to receive) the freedom of a city. — 3. (Staats-)~ citizen (of a state); (Welt-)~ denizen (of the world), ⛵ cosmopolite. — 4. (ant. Adeliger) commoner; contp. plebeian; (ant. Militär) civilian.

Bürger-adel (ˇ...) m ⊕: a) patriciate; b) coll. patricians pl.; =amt n municipal (or town) office; =ausschuß m (select) committee of townsmen; =buch n burgess-roll; =eid m civic oath; =frau f citizen's wife; woman (or lady) of the middle classes; =garde ✗ =wehr; =gardi'st m Engl.: volunteer; militia-man; =gerechtsame f/pl. privileges pl. of citizenship; =heer n Engl.

⛵ scientific; ⚘ botanical; ⚲ geography; ⊕ machinery; ⚒ mining; ✗ military; ⚓ marine; ● commercial; ✉ postal; 🚂 railway.

[**Bürgerfrieg**]

seit 1907 territorial army; =**krieg** m civil (or domestic) war; =**krone** f ehm. civic crown; =**kunde** f sociology.
bürgerlich (⌐⌐) I a. ⊕ 1. (dem Bürgerstande angehörig) middle-class (folk); (ant. adelig) (person) without title, contp. plebeian (origin); (ant. militärisch) civilian (population); 2 (adv.) gekleideter Offizier officer in plain clothes. — 2. (das Bürgertum betr.): ~es Gesetzbuch civil code; Des Gericht civil court; Des Recht civil law; Der Tod civil death; thea. Des Schauspiel domestic (ant. historical) drama; jur. (ant. kriminal): Der Klagefall civil action; De Rechtsstreitigkeiten civil lawsuits pl. — 3. (De Ämter, Ehren, Pflichten betr.) civic (honours, duties). — 4. fig. (einfach) unpretentious (style), frugal (living); De Gewohnheiten f/pl., Küche, Sitten f/pl. plain (or simple, homely) habits pl., cooking, manners pl. — II =**e(r)** m, ~e ⊕ 5. = Bürger 4. — 6. coll., bsd. parl. the ~en pl. the commonalty.
Bürgerlichkeit (⌐⌐-) f ⊕ middle-class manners pl.; unpretentiousness, frugality, plainness, homeliness, &c.; vgl. bürgerlich 4.
Bürger=mädchen (⌐⌐...) n ⊕ (respectable) girl of the middle classes; =**meister** [nhd. 15/16. sae. †+ ft. † Burg(e)meister] m ⊕ England: (für ein Jahr gewählter Alderman) mayor, schott. provost; in großen Städten: Lord Mayor (f Lady Mayoress), schott. Lord Provost; Holland und Deutschland: burgomaster; =**meisteramt** n mayorship, mayoralty, mayor's office or dignity; =**meisterei** f: a) mayorship; b) mayor's official residence; Lo. City: Mansion House, schott. provostry; =**meisterin** f mayoress; vgl. =meister; =**meister=stelle**, =**würde** f = =meister=amt; =**pack** n, b. s. etwa: riff-raff, mob; =**pflicht** f citizen's (or civic) duty; =**recht** n in einer Stadt: municipal (or urban) citizenship; freedom (bisw. auch livery) of a city; im Staate, bsd. parl.: franchise; einem das ~ verleihen to enfranchise a p.; einem Fremden, auch fig. einer Sache: to naturalize an alien, a custom, &c.; einem das ~ entziehen to disfranchise a p., to deprive a p. of his civic rights; =**rolle** f = =buch.
Bürgerschaft (⌐⌐) f ⊕ coll. the citizens, ~ the middle classes f. (ant. Adel) the commoners pl., the commonalty.
Bürger=schule (⌐⌐...) f ⊕ middle-class school; higher elementary school.
Bürgers=frau (⌐⌐...) f ⊕ s. Bürgerfrau; =**haus** n citizen's house, private residence.
Bürger=sinn (⌐⌐...) m ⊕ loyal spirit of a citizen, (local) patriotism, public spirit; =**kind** n ⊕ citizen's child, (respectable) child of the middle classes; =**mann** m (pl. =**leute**) citizen, townsman; =**Bürger=soldat** (⌐⌐...) m ⊕ citizen-soldier, Engl.: volunteer; =**stand** m: a) citizenship; b) coll. (respectable) citizens, middle classes pl., (ant. Adel) common(er)s pl., commonalty; =**steig** m pavement, footpath, bsd. Am. side-walk; =(s)**tochter** f (respectable) citizen's daughter; vgl. =mädchen; =**stolz** m civic

(or middle-class) pride; **tugend** f civic virtue or excellence.
Bürgertum (⌐⌐-) n (d. 1. Bürgerschaft. 2. (bürgerliches Wesen) condition of a citizen; citizenship; civil estate. s& civilian life.
Bürger=versammlung (⌐⌐...) f ⊕ meeting of townsmen or burgesses or citizens (für Parlamentswahlen a. of borough constituents); =**wache**, =**wehr** f volunteer corps or force; militia; Mittelalter, bsd. Lo.: (city) train-bands pl.; Frankreich ehm.: national guard; vgl. =heer.
Burg=flecken (⌐...) m ⊕ borough, burgh; =**frau** f lady of the castle or manor; =**fräulein** n, etwa: baron's daughter, high-born damsel; =**friede(n)** m: a) =**bann**; b) peace within the precincts of the castle; =**gericht** n baronial court; =**graben** m castle-moat or -ditch; =**graf** m, =**gräfin** ehm.: burgrave, burgravine; =**grafschaft** f burgraviate; =**hauptmann**, =**herr** m governor, lord of a (feudal) castle; =**hof** m castle-yard.
Bürgin (⌐⌐) f s. Bürge.
Burg=keller (⌐...) m ⊕ =verlies; =**lehen** n tenure of a castle with the adjoining land; =**mann** m (pl. =**leute**) ehm.: vassal of a (baronial) castle; =**richter** m justiciary of the castle and its borough; =**saß** m = =mann.
Bürgschaft (⌐⌐) f ⊕ 1. allg. (Unterpfand) pledge; e-m als ~ für die Zukunft, für j-s redliche Absicht dienen to serve a p. as a pledge (or a guarantee) for the future, of someone's good faith. — 2. für Zahlung = Bürge 1; sichere ~ good (or substantial) bail; ~ **leisten** (a. **stellen**) für e-n, et. = bürgen 1; auf ~ freigelassen let out on bail; ⅍ ~ für die Güte von etwas: guarantee, warrant; ⚓ ~ für ein Schiff bottomry-bond.
Bürgschafts= brief (⌐⌐...) m ⊕ warrant(y), (written) guarantee; jur. bond (for bail); 9**fähig** a. ⊕ able to give security; jur. bailable; =**leistung** f: a) pledging one's word for; b) jur. (giving or F going) bail for.
Burg=stall (⌐...) m ⊕: a) (kleine Burg) small castle; b) hunt. (Erhabenheit i. d. Fährte) raised ground in the trail of a stag. &c.; =**tor** n castle-gate.
Burgund ♀ (~ᵈ) npr/n. ⊕ α. (fr. Provinz u. altes Königreich) Burgundy; ~**er(in** f ⊕) m ⊕, =**Lifch** a. ⊕ Burgundian; ~(Wein), a. =Lifcher Wein Burgundy (wine).
Burg=verlies (⌐...) n ⊕ dungeon (or keep) of a castle; =**vogt** m, =**vögtin** f warden, steward(ess) of a castle; bisw. castellan; =**vogtei** f stewardship of a castle, bisw. castellany; =**warte** f watch-tower of a castle.
burlesk (~ᵈ) [fr., *it.] I a. ⊕ (possenhaft) burlesque, farcical. — II =**e** f ⊕ thea. (Posse) burlesque, farce.
Burnus (⌐⌐) [ar.] m ⊕, a. inv. (Beduinenmantel, Damenmantel) burnous.
burr (~ᵈ) [lautm.] int. whir; zum Pferde (halt!) who(a) (back)!; (schwirren b. Käfer 2c.) buzz...., (lauter Schall) bang!, plump!
burren (~⌐) v/n. (h. u. fn) ⊕ von Kutschern: to say (gee-)who(a); (schwirren) to whiz, von Käfern 2c.: to buzz, hum. |**läufer**|
Burr=hahn (⌐⌐) m ⊕ orn. = Kampf=

[**Bürzel**]

Bursch (⌐⌐) m ⊕, a. ⊕ Bursche (wb. 2).
Bürschchen (⌐⌐) n ⊗ (dim. von Bursche) (kleiner Schelm) young rogue or F Turk, (mischievous) young dog, F pickle.
Bursche (⌐⌐) [nhd. 17. sae. aus Burse (s. ds)] m ⊕ 1. youth, lad, stripling, contp. youngster; F young nipper or shaver; die jungen ~(n) the young fellows or F chaps pl.; mein lieber ~ (Kamerad) F my dear (old) fellow or boy, old cock! — 2. (Student) student (of a German university). — 3. (Lehrling) apprentice; (Lauf=)~ errand-boy. — 4. (Aufwärter) waiting boy; (boy in) buttons; ⚓ ~ e-s Offiziers officer's man or attendant, auch: soldier-servant. — 5. (Kerl) fellow; ehrlicher, gutmütiger ~ honest, good-natured fellow; entschloffener ~ F determined (young) rascal, co. Sie sind mir ein netter, sau(b)e(r)er ~! F you are a nice fellow or a fine chap; ein strammer ~ (auch von Weibern) F a (regular) whacker or bouncer or strapper.
Burschen=brauch (⌐⌐...) m ⊕ students' (Englands: college-) custom or usage.
burschenhaft (⌐⌐⌐) a. ⊕ 1. like a youth; student-like. — 2. = burschikos.
Burschen=herrlichkeit (⌐⌐...) f ⊕, etwa: (the) glorious college-days pl.; =**leben** n university-life, Englands: college-life.
Burschenschaft (⌐⌐⌐) f ⊕ "Burschenschaft" (German Students' Association founded in 1815 for patriotic purposes, in opposition to the 'Corps'); ~(**l)er** (⌐⌐⌐) m ⊕ member of a B.; =**lich** (⌐⌐⌐) a. ⊕ relating to a B.
Burschen=sitte (⌐⌐...) f ⊕ = =brauch. **Burschentum** (⌐⌐-) n ⊕ d. 1. students' life. — 2. = Burschenschaft.
burschikos (⌐⌐⌐ˢ) [dtsch-grch.] a. ⊕ (D10) 1. (studentenhaft) student-like. — 2. (munter, zwanglos) jovial, gay, merry; unconventional, unceremonious, unrestrained, F free and easy; ...ſes Wesen jovial nature or manners pl., jollity, mirth.
Bürschlein (⌐⌐-) n ⊕ = Bürschchen.
Burse† (⌐⌐) [mhd.; *mlt. bursa (= Börse)] f ⊕ German students' inn or hall or hostelry or lodging-house.
Bürstchen (⌐⌐-) n ⊕ dim. v. Bürste.
Bürste (⌐⌐) [mhd.; *Borste] f ⊕ brush; zum Wichsen: blacking-brush, zum Fegen: whisk; (Tischbesen) crumb-brush.
bürsten (⌐⌐) I v/a. to brush; sich (dat.) den Rock tüchtig 2 to give one's coat a good brush; ich habe mir die Zähne, die Nägel gebürstet I have brushed (or cleaned) my teeth, nails. — II Fv/n. (h.) (rennen) to brush (or rush) along.
Bürsten=abzug ⊕ (⌐⌐...) m ⊕ typ. brush-proof; 9**artig** a. ⊕ brush-like; brush-shaped; =**binder** ⊕ m brush-maker, F fig. er kann laufen (saufen) wie ein ~ he can run like a hare (drink like a fish); =**binderei** ⊕ f brush-making; =(**binder=)waren** f/pl. brushes and brooms pl.; =**fabrik** ⊕ f brush-(manu)factory; 9**förmig** a. ⊕ =artig; =**händler(in** f) ⊕ m brush-seller; =**macher** m = =binder; =**rad** ⊕ n brush-wheel.
☛ **Burzel** (⌐⌐) 2c. s. Purzel 2c.
Bürzel (⌐⌐) [nhd.] m ⊕ (Vogelsteiß) rump, Kochkunst: F parson's (or pope's) nose.

[Busch] — 233 — [Butterblume]

Busch (ᵛ) [ahd.: bush] m ①a. **1.** bush; (Strauch) shrub; (kleines Gehölz) copse, thicket; weitS. (Wald) wood. — 2. *hunt.* anf den ~ klopfen (um das Wild auszutreiben) to beat (game out of) a bush or thicket; *fig.* (bei e-m leise nachforschen) to beat about the bush; to sound a p.'s (opinion); to feel a p.'s pulse; F sich (seitwärts) in die Büsche schlagen to run (F to slip) away; P to slope off; *fig.* hinter die Büsche (Schule) geh(e)n to play the truant; hinter dem ~e halten (mit etwas), lange um den ~ geh(e)n to hesitate, to be a long time (doing a th.). — **3.** (Büschel) ~ v. Blättern, Blumen, Haaren ꝛc. tuft, bunch of ...; ~ von Federn (als Helmschmuck ꝛc.) plume.
Büschchen (ᵛᵛ) n ㉓ *dim.* von Busch.
Büschel (ᵛᵛ) [nhd.; *Busch] m, n ㉒ **1.** = Busch 3; ~ Stroh wisp of straw, (Quaste) tassel. — **2.** ~ von Blättern, Blüten, Kirschen ꝛc.: cluster; ♀ fascicle; ♀ (Rispe) panicle; ♀ (Doldentraube) corymb; in ~n wachsend clustered, ♀ fasciculate(d). — **3.** ~ (Schopf) von Vögeln ꝛc.: crest, tuft; (Feder-)~ (als Kopfschmuck) aigrette; *phys.* elec'trische (Strahlen-)~ *pl.*: electric aigrettes *pl.* — **4.** ~ (Bündel) Reisholz (small) faggot.
büschel-artig (ᵛᵛᵛ) *a.* ⓺ = ♀förmig; **-boden** ⊕ m ㉒ (Haarsiebgewebe für Brauereizwecke) fine hair-sieve used by brewers.
Büschelchen (ᵛᵛᵛ) n ㉓ *dim.* von Büschel.
büschel-förmig (ᵛᵛᵛ...) *a.* ⓺ tufted, bunchy; ♀: fascicular (rispenförmig) paniculate(d), (doldentraubenförmig) corymbiate(d), clustered.
büsch(e)licht, büsch(e)lig (ᵛ(ᵛ)ᵛ) *a.* ⓺ = büschel-artig, ♀förmig.
Büschel-kiemer (ᵛᵛ...) m ⓰ *ichth.*: ⚓ lophobranch(iate); **-nelfe** ♀ f = Nelke (rauhe); ♀tragend *a.*: a) ♀ corymbiferous; b) *orn.* crested; ♀weife *adv.* in tufts or bunches or clusters. [S. XXXIX, III.]
Büschen¹ öft. ⓫ (ᵛᵛ) m ㊱. Maßeinheit f.]
buschen² (ᵛᵛ): sich ᒾ *v/refl.* ㉑ to grow in bushes or tufts or shrubs.
Busch-gras ♀ (ᵛ...) n ㉒ tussock-grass (*Dac'tylis caespito'sa*); **-holz** n brushwood, copsewood, underwood; thicket; **-huhn** n, *orn.* brush-turkey (*Talega'lla Latha'mi*).
buschicht, mft **buschig** (ᵛᵛ) *a.* ⓺ **1.** tufted, bunchy; Haar: shaggy. — **2.** (mit Gebüsch bewachsen) covered with bushes, bushy.
buschieren (ᵛᵛᵛ) [dtsch-lt.] *v/n.* (h.) *hunt.* (mit Vorstehhunden im Holz Wild aufsuchen) to scour the bushes (or to shoot in covert) with dogs.
Busch-klepper (ᵛ...) [ndl.] m ⓺ (Strauchdieb) bush-ranger; foot-pad.
Büschlein (ᵛᵛ) n ㉓ *dim.* von Busch.
büschlicht, büschlig f. büschelicht ꝛc.
Busch-mann (ᵛ...) [ndl.] m ⓺, **-männin** f (niedere Menschenrasse, Süd-afrika) Bushman, Bushwoman; **-mensch** m = Orang-Utan; **-neger** m West-indien ꝛc.: maroon; **-streu** f litter (made up) of dry leaves; **-wald** m undergrowth, copse; **-werk** n bushes, shrubs *pl.*, shrubbery; **-windröschen** ♀ n wind-plant (*Anemo'ne nemoro'sa*). [small fishing-smack.]
Büse ⚓ (ᵛᵛ) [: buss; *nbl.] f ⓺ (Herings⚓)
Busen (ᵛᵛ) [ahd.: bosom] m ㉓ **1.** (Brust, bsd. e-s Weibes) bosom, breast; weitS.

auch in der Kunst: bust. — **2.** *fig.* im tiefsten ~ in the depth (or at the bottom) of one's heart; in den eig(e)nen ~ greifen to dive into (or to search) one's own heart or bosom; ein Geheimnis im (stillen) ~ verwahren to hold ... enshrined in one's bosom. — **3.** ♀ (Meer-)~ gulf, bay, bight.
Busen-freund(in f) m (ᵛᵛ...) ⓺ bosom-friend; *pl.* auch oft: sworn (or intimate) friends; **-kind** n (SCH.) favourite (or pet) child; darling; **-krause** f am Mannshemde, bsd. ehm.: shirt-frill; **-latz** m ehm. stomacher; **-nadel** f breast- (or scarf-)pin; **-schleier** m e-r Nonne wimple; **-schleife** f bosom-knot; **-krause** f; **-sünde** f, *theol.* besetting sin; **-tuch** n neckerchief.
...busig (...ᵛᵛ) *a.* ⓺: a) -bosomed, ʒB. hoch-♀ high-bosomed; b) ♀ vom Küstenlande: reich-♀ rich in gulfs or bays.
Buß südd. (ᵛ) m ⓸a. = Bufferl.
Bussard (ᵛᵛ) [fr. busard] m ⓬d., a. **Buß-aar** (ᵛ..¹) m ⓬ *orn.* buzzard (*Falco bu'teo*).
Buß-bank (ᵛᵛ...) f ⓬ *eccl.* ehm. stool of repentance; Heilsarmee jetzt: penitent form; **-buch** n penitentiary.
Buße (ᵛᵛ) [ahd.: boot; *baß, besser(n)] f **1.** penitence; (Reue) repentance; (Sühnung) atonement; (Genugtuung) satisfaction, compensation; *rel.* in Sack und Asche ~ tun to do penance in sackcloth and ashes; für et. ~ tun (sühnen) to atone (weitS. to make amends) for (a wrong, an injury); auf die ~ bezüglich, zur ~ gehörig penitential, penitentiary. — **2.** (Strafe, Geldstrafe) fine; e-m eine ~ von 5 Mark auferlegen to impose a fine of 5 shillings on a p., to fine a p. (or to mulct a p. in) 5 s.; ~ zahlen to pay a fine, to be mulcted (in a fine); zu e-r schweren ~ verurteilt werden to be heavily fined.
büßen (ᵛᵛ) [Buße] ⓰ **I** *v/a.* u. *v/n.* (h.) **1.** to atone (or propitiate) for an offence, weitS. to make amends (or to give satisfaction) for a wrong; ein Verbrechen ♀ to expiate a crime; er wird es (ob. dafür) ♀ müssen he will have to suffer (or smart) for it, he shall pay for it. — **2.** et. mit Geld ♀ to be fined (weitS. to have to pay) for ...; einen Schaden ♀ to make good a loss. — **II** nur *v/n.* (h.) **3.** (Buße tun) to do penance. — **III** nur *v/a.* **4.** ʃ-e Lust ♀ (befriedigen) to satisfy one's desire, stärker: to indulge one's passion. — **5.** ⊕ = ausbessern; *fig.* die Lücke ♀ to stop a gap (vgl. Lückenbüßer). — **IV** ~n ㉓ **6.** atonement, expiation; penance, penitence. — **V** ~de(r) m ⓺ = Büßer(in).
Büßer (ᵛᵛ) m ⓬, ~in f ⓬ *eccl.* penitent (sinner); **-gewand** n ⓬ = Bußhemd.
Busse(r)l südd. (ᵛᵛ) n ㉒ (Kuß), ⚓ buss.
Büßer-orden (ᵛᵛ...) m ⓬ *eccl.* order of Penitents.
buß-fällig (ᵛ...) *a.* ⓺ ehm. *jur.*: subject to a fine, punishable; ♀fertig *a.* penitent or repentant (sinner); contrite (heart); ~e *pl.* penitent sinners *pl.*; **-fertigkeit** f ⓬ penitence, repentance; **-gebet** n, *eccl.* prayer of repentance; **-gewand** n ehm. = -hemd.
bußhaft (ᵛᵛ) *a.* ⓺ penitent.

Buß-hemd (ᵛ...) n ⓬. Kleid n penitential garment. [female hemp.]
Büßling ♀ (ᵛᵛ) m ⓬d. (weibl. Hanfpflanze).
Bussole ⚓ (ᵛᵛᵛ) [fr. boussole; *it. Büchschen] f ⓬ (Seekompaß) (nautical) compass; mit Wasserwage: ⚓ eclimeter.
Buß-prediger (ᵛ...) m ⓬ *eccl.* preacher of penitence, engS. Lent preacher; **-predigt** f penitential sermon, engS. Lent sermon; **-psalm** m penitential psalm; **-tag** m day of penance or penitence or humiliation; **-übung** f penitential exercise; ~ und Bet-tage *m/pl.* days *pl.* of fasting and prayer; Heilsarmee auch: self-denial week.
Büßung (ᵛᵛ) f ⓬ = büßen IV.
Buß-werke (ᵛ...) *n/pl.* ⓬ *eccl.* penitential works *pl.*, works *pl.* of repentance; ~ verrichten to do penance; **-zeit** f time of repentance; **-zelle** f penitentiary (cell), in Klöstern: dark cell.
Büste (ᵛᵛ) [fr. buste m] f ⓬ bust.
buten nbd., ⚓ (ᵛᵛ) *adv.* (außen) outside.
Butike(r) (-ᵛᵛ) = Budike(r).
But-luv ⚓ (ᵛᵛ) m ⓬c. (kleiner Kran an jeder Seite des Schiffsbugs) bumkin.
Butt (ᵛ) [ndd.] m ⓭b. *ichth.* **1.** (Glatt-)~ brill (*Rhombus laevis*). — **2.** (Stein-)~ turbot (*Rhombus ma'ximus*). — **3.** (Scholle) flounder (*Pleurone'ctes*).
Butte¹ (ᵛᵛ) f ⓬ **1.** *ichth.* = Butt. — **2.** ♀ (Knospe) bud; (Hage-)~ hip.
Butte², mft **Bütte** (ᵛᵛ) [ahd.; *grch. pyti'nē] f ⓬ (Faß) butt, vat; (Zuber) tub; eine ~ voll a vatful, a tubful; kleinere ~, auch: kit; (Kübel, Tragmulde) hod; *fig.* Geld in der ~ steh(e)n haben to have money in the bank, to have put by some money. [(Flasche) bottle.]
Buttel ⚓ F (ᵛᵛ) [ndd., *engl.] f ⓬
Büttel (ᵛᵛ) [ahd.: beadle; *bieten] m ⓬ **1.** (Gerichtsdiener) sheriff's officer, *contp.* (bum)bailiff. — **2.** (Henker) hangman, executioner, *contp.* Jack Ketch.
Büttelei (ᵛᵛᵛ) f ⓬ (Gefängnis) jail. [glass.]
Buttel-glas ⊕ n ⓬ (Flaschenglas) bottle-
buttein (ᵛᵛ) *v/a.* (h.) ㉑a. **1.** (glucken) to gurgle. — **2.** F (a. *v/a.*) = buddeln.
Bütten-papier (ᵛᵛ...) n ⓬ hand-made paper (ant. Maschinenpapier).
Butter (ᵛᵛ) [ahd., *grch.] f ⓬, obb. m ⓬ **1.** butter; zum Kochen: cooking butter; frische, ranzige, gesalzene ~ fresh, rancid, salt b.; künstliche ~ margarine; ein Klümpchen ~ Klumpen ~ a pat, lump of butter; ein Stück ~ a roll of butter; ~ aufs Brot schmieren to spread butter on the bread, to spread the bread and b.; mit ~ bestreichen, schmieren to butter. — **2.** (Kakao-)~ cacao-butter; *chm.* (Spießglanz-)~ (Chlor-antim'on) butter of antimony; *physiol.* (Augen-)~ secretion from the eye(s), gum. — **3.** *fig.* e-m die ~ vom Brot(e) nehmen to deprive a p. of the sweets of life; sich die ~ vom Brote nehmen lassen to allow o.s. to be robbed or cheated.
butter-ähnlich (ᵛᵛ...) *a.* ⓺, ♀artig *a.* (buttery); ⚓ butyric, butyr(ace)ous; **-äther** m ⓬ butyric ether or ethyl butyrate ($C_4H_7O_2 \cdot C_2H_5$); **-baum** m = butter- (or shea-)tree (*Ba'ssia butyra'cea, Pentade'sma* ꝛc.); **-bemme** f = -brot; **-birne** f butter-pear; **-blume** P ♀ f (Name

♪ Musik; ⚓ Wissenschaft; ♀ Pflanze; ♁ Geographie; ⊕ Technik; ⚒ Bergbau; ⚔ Militär; ⚓ Marine; ⓭ Handel; ✉ Post; 🚂 Eisenbahn.

[Butterbrief] — 234 — [Cäsarianer]

gelber Blumen) bjd.: (Löwenzahn) dandelion; (Dotterblume) marsh-marigold; (Hahnenfuß) buttercup; **=brief** m Cath. eccl. license for eating butter during Lent; **=brot** n (slice of, piece of) bread and butter; belegtes **~** mit Butter, F fig. für ein **~** faufen F to buy dirt-cheap or for a mere song; Spiel: **~** auf dem Wasser werfen to play (at) ducks and drakes; **=brühe** f butter-sauce; **=büchse, =dose** f butter-dish; **=faß** n: a) butter-tub or -barrel; b) zum Butterstoßen: churn; **=form** f butter-mould, -stamp; **=frau** butter-woman; **=gebäck(e)ne(s)** n light pastry; **⚥gelb** a. butter-coloured, auch: (as) yellow as a guinea or a saffron-bag; **=geschäft** n butter-shop; **⚥haltig** a. containing butter; ⚗ butyr(ace)-ous; **=handel** ☉ m butter-trade, trade in butter; **=händler(in)** f m butter-(wo)man; **=handlung** f butter-shop, dairy; **⚥herzig** a. fig. soft-(or tender-)hearted; **=hose** f butter-tub.

butt(e)richt †, **butt(e)rig** (⌣⌣⌣) a. ⓖ = butter-ähnlich, ⚥haltig.

Butter=kammer (⌣⌣⌣...) f ⓑ dairy; **=kühler** m, **=kühl=glocke** f butter-cooler; **=land** ⚓ n fog-bank (or misty form) resembling land; **=markt** m b.-market; **=messer** ☉: a) n butter-knife; b) m zur Ermittelung des Buttergehaltes: ⚗ butyro-meter; **=milch** f butter-milk.

buttern (⌣⌣) v.n. (h.) u. v a. ⓦa. **1.** to churn butter or milk. — **2.** (mit Butter bestreichen) to butter. — **3.** nur v/n. to turn to butter; F fig. das will nicht ⚥ it is useless (trouble); F that won't do (it), it won't wash.

Butter=öl (⌣⌣...) n ⓒ chm. ⚗ butyric oil; **=säure** f, chm. butyric acid ($C_4H_8O_2$); **=säure=äthyl** = **=äther**; **=säure=gärung** f ⚗ butyric fermentation; **=schnitte** f = **=brot**; **=ständer** m b.-tub; **=stempel** m = **=stößel**; **=stößel** m churn-staff; **=stulle** P [ndd.] f = **=brot**; **=teig** m puff-paste; **=tonne** f = **=faß** a; **=topf** m irdener: butter crock (Topf mit Butter) stone jar (filled) with butter; **=ver=fälschung** f adulteration of butter; **=vogel** m: a) = Kohlweißling; b) prove. (Tagschmetterling) butterfly; **=weck(e/n)** m Gebäck: bun, scone; **=weich** a. (as) soft as butter; **=wurz(el)** ♀ f = Fettkraut.

Butt=fisch (⌣⌣) m ⓑ ichth. = Butt.

buttig prove. (⌣⌣) a. ⓑ (kurz und dick) podgy, dumpy, stumpy, thick(-set).

Büttner [Bütte] m ⓑ = Küfer.

buttricht, buttrig f. butterichtt, butterig.

Butyl ⚗ (⌣⌣) [grch.] n ⓒ c. chm. chem. Radikal: butyl (C_4H_9).

Butyl=aldehy'd ⚗ (⌣⌣⌣...) m (n) ⓒ butyl aldehyde (C_4H_8O); **=a'lkohol** m butyl alcohol ($C_4H_{10}O$). [lene (C_4H_8).|

Butylen ⚗ (⌣⌣⌣) [grch.] n ⓒ c. chm. buty-|

Butyl=wasserstoff (⌣⌣...) m ⓑ butyl hydride (C_4H_{10}). [Buzenmann.|

Butz(e) ¹ (⌣⌣) [(mhd.: beat) m ⓑ (44/37) —|

Butz², **~e²**, **~en** (⌣⌣) [mhd. 16. sae.] m ⓑ, 𝔇 **1.** (Kloß, Klümpchen) clod, clot, (c)lump; ⚔(Ernest) pocket. — **2.** am Lichte: thief. — **3.** im Obstgehäuse, Obste: core. — **4.** ⓒ Kronglasfabr.: Mitte der Scheibe) bull's eye.

Butzen¹=mann (⌣⌣...) m ⓑ (Schreckgespenst) bogy, bugbear; **=scheibe** ☉ f Kronglas-fabr.: (Mondglas) bull's-eye glass.

Butz=kopf (⌣⌣) m ⓑ zo. (Schwertfisch) grampus (Orca gladiator).

Buxen † P nordd. (⌣⌣) [buckskin] f/pl. ⓑ = Hosen.

Buzentaur (⌣⌣⌣) [grch.] m ⓑ myth. mit menschl. Oberkörper u. Stierleib: Bucentaur.

Buzephalus (⌣⌣⌣⌣) [lt., *grch. Stierkopf] m, ⓖγ.(Leibpferd Alexanders d. Gr.) Bucephalus.

Byssus ⚗ (⌣⌣) [grch.] m, inv. Alt.: (feines Gewebe) byssus; a. zo. (Muschelseide) sea-silk; **~kleid** n byssus garment.

Bythometrie ⚓ (⌣⌣⌣⌣) [grch.] (Meeres-tiefenmessung) deep-sea sounding.

Byzantiner (⌣⌣⌣⌣) m ⓑ, **~in** f ⓑ, **by=zantinisch** a. ⓑ Byzantine.

Byzantinismus (⌣⌣⌣⌣⌣) m ⓑ (Griechen-tum des Mittelalters) byzantinism.

Byzanz ☉ (⌣⌣) npr/n. ⓖγ. grch. Alt.: (jetzt Konstantinopel oder Stambul) Byzantium.

Bz. ⚗ abbr. = Brennzünder.

bzw. abbr. = beziehungsweise (f. ds).

C

C, c (tße') n, inv. **1.** (Buchstabe) C, c. — **2.** ent. (Falter) species of vanessa and other genera; kleines weißes C white vanessa (Vane'ssa C a'lbum).

C, c ♪ (⌣) n, inv. C; **C-Dur** C major; **C-Moll** C minor; **C-Schlüssel** (Diskant-, Alt-, Tenor-f.) C cleff.

C abbr. — **1.** ⚗ [lt. carbo] chm. Symbol für Kohlenstoff. — **2.** = Celsius. — **3.** ☒ = Konstruktion; zB. C/73 (b. i. 1873). **ca.** abbr. = circa (f. ds).

☞ **Ca...** f. auch **Ka...**

Cab † (käb) [engl., abbr. von Kabriolett] n ⓑ (4räderige, 4sitzige Droschke) cab.

Cab=wagen (⌣...) m ⓑ motor cab.

Cachenez (käsch-ne') [fr. m] n ⓑ wrap (for the throat), comforter.

Cachou¹ (kä-schū) [(+,) fr. (fr. re'glisse); *tamul.] n ⓑ (Katechu-pillen) cachou.

Cachou²=baum ♀ (⌣...) [fr. acajou; *ind.] m ⓑ = Akajou²; **=nuß** f cashew-nut.

Cäcili-e (tß=tß⌣⌣) [lt. Blinde] npr/f. ⓦ Ⓑß. (Bn.) Cecil(y); die heilige **~** St. Cecilia.

Cabre (kä'br) [fr.] m (n) ⓑ = Kader¹.

Café (⌣) [fr.] n ⓑ (Kaffeehaus) coffee-house or -shop, feines: café; **~** chantant (pl. **~** s ...õ) (Tingeltangel) music-hall.

Cafetier (tä-f-tiē') [fr.] m ⓑ coffee-shop keeper, proprietor of a café.

Caisson ⚓ (tä-ßõ') [fr.] m ⓑ (Senkkasten) caisson. [⓶γ. röm. Alt. = Caius.|

Cajus (t⌣) [lt. Caius, bff. Gaius] npr/m.|

Calamit (⌣⌣) ♀ m ⓑ geol. (vor-weltlicher Schachtelhalm) calamite.

☞ **Calc...** f. Kalz... [Kalauer.|

Calembour (tä-lą-bū'r) [fr.] m ⓑ =|

Camaïeu (tä-mä-ö') [fr.] m, sg. inv., pl. **~**x ⓑ, auch: **~=gemälde** n ⓑ (ein-farbiges Bild) camaieu.

Camera (t⌣⌣) [lt.] f (sg. inv., pl .... rae) phys., phot.: **~** lu'cida (Hellkammer) camera lucida; **~** obscu'ra (Dunkelkammer) camera obscura; bisw.: (Schurke) hand camera; für Blitz-aufnahmen: detective c., *kodak.

Cameralia (t⌣⌣⌣⌣) = Kameralien zc.

Camphin ⚗ (t⌣⌣) [Kampfer] n ⓒ c. chm. camphene, **~ine** ($C_{10}H_{16}$). [($C_{10}H_{14}$).|

Camphogen ⚗ (t⌣⌣⌣) n ⓒ c. chm.|

Camphren ⚗ (t⌣⌣) n ⓒ c. camphrene ($C_9H_{14}O$). [Petroleums] canadol.|

Canadol ⚗ (t⌣⌣) n ⓒ c. (Bestandteil des|

Canaille (tä-nä'l-j⌣) [fr. Hundepack] f ⓑ **1.** coll. the lowest of the populace, the scum of the earth, the dregs of the people, rabble, mob; auch: (fr.) canaille. [tiger Tanz] cancan.|

Cancan (tą-tą', tą'-tän) [fr.] m ⓑ (unzüch-|

cand. abbr. = Kandidat, zB. **~** med. Kandidat der Medizin.

Cantharidin ⚗ (t⌣⌣⌣) [grch.] n ⓒ c.(Kantha-ridenkampfer) cantharidin(e) ($C_{10}H_{12}O_4$).

caprin=sauer ⚗ (t⌣⌣) [lt. căpră Ziege] a. ⓑ chm. capric; **⚥saures Salz** caprate; **=säure** f ⓒ capric acid ($C_{10}H_{20}O_2$).

Capron=fett ⚗ (t⌣...) n ⓒ chm. caprone; **⚥sauer** a. ⓒ caproic; **⚥saures Salz** caproate; **=säure** f caproic acid ($C_6H_{12}O_2$); **=säure** f ⓒ caprylic acid ($C_8H_{16}O_2$).

Capuchon (tä-pü-schą') [fr.] m ⓑ (Mantel mit Kapuze) lady's cloak with a hood.

Caput mortuum ⚗ † (t⌣⌣ ⚥⌣⌣) [lt. Toten-kopf] n, inv. chm. (Destillationsrückstand) caput mortuum, ⊕ colcothar.

Carapa=öl ♀ (t⌣...) [guayan. karā'pa öl] n ⓒ Seifenfabrikation: carap-oil.

Carbamid ⚗ (t⌣⌣) [lt. carbo Kohle] n ⓒ c. chm. (Harnstoff) carbamide.

Carbamin=säure ⚗ (t⌣⌣⌣...) f ⓒ chm. carbamic acid ($CO\ NH_2\ HO$).

Carotin ⚗ (t⌣⌣) [Karotte] n ⓒ c. chm. (gelber Farbstoff der Mohrrübe) carotin(e).

Carreau (tä-rō') 2c. f. Karo 2c.

Carte blanche (tärt blä'nsch) [fr.] f (Voll-macht) carte blanche, full power(s pl.).

Carvol ⚗ (t-w⌣) [lt.] n ⓒ c. chm. (im Kümmel-öl enthaltene Flüssigkeit) carvol ($C_{10}H_{14}O$).

Cäsar (tß⌣⌣) **I** npr/m. ⓦ⚥a. (römischer Feldherr u. Staatsmann, 100—44 v. Chr) Caesar. — **II** m ⓑ (Kaiser) cæsar, emperor.

Cäsaren=herrschaft (tß=⌣⌣...) f ⓑ (a. **=tum** n ⓑd. Cæsarean rule, weitS. Cæsarism, imperialism, autocracy, autocratic government; **=wahn(sinn)** m Cæsarean madness.

Cäsareopapismus ⚥ (⌣⌣⌣⌣⌣⌣⌣) [neut.] m ⓑ (Kaiserherrschaft über die Kirche, Unter-ordnung der Kirche unter das Oberhaupt des Staates) Cæsaropapism.

Cäsarewa (⌣⌣⌣⌣) [lt..ruff.] f ⓑ (ruff. Kaiserin) Tsesarewa; **Cäsarewitsch** (⌣) m ⓑ (ruff. Thronfolger) Tsesarevitch.

Cäsarewna (⌣) f ⓑ (Gemahlin d. ruff. Thronfolgers) Tsesarevna.

Cäsarianer (tß=⌣⌣⌣) [lt.] m ⓑ (An-hänger Cäsars), **cäsarisch** (tß=⌣⌣) a. ⓑ (kaiserlich) Cæsarean.

Signs (see page XVII): F familiar; P vulgar; ꜰ flash; ＼ rare; † obsolete (died); * new word (born); ⁒ incorrect; ♪ music;

[Cäsarismus] — 235 — [Charakteristik]

Cäsarismus (tß-⌣⌣) [lt.] m ㉗ (Alleinherrschaft) Caesarism; autocracy.

Cäsar=pfählchen ⚔ (tß⁻⌣…) n (pl.) (dicht neben=ea. in den Erdboden gesteckte, oben zugespitzte Holzpfähle) palisades, pickets pl.

Cassius¹ (t⌣(⌣)⌣) [lt.] npr/m. ㉖γ. (Verschwörer gegen Cäsar) Cassius.

Cassius² (~) npr/m.㉖γ.(dtsch.Arzt, 17. sae.): ~(scher Gold)purpur z. Porzellanmalerei: purple of Cassius, cassius (purple).

Cästus (tß⁻ʻ⌣; vgl. Cestus) [lt.] m ⑯ Alt. (Schlagriemen, Fechthandschuh) cestus.

Catechin (t⌣⌣⁻) n ⑪c. (Katechusäure) catechin (e) ($C_{19}H_{18}O_8$).

Causerie (to⌣⁻⌃) [fr.] f ㊽ (Plauderei) chit-chat, tittle-tattle, sociable talk; in Zeitschriften:(literary, theatrical, &c.) gossip.

Causeuse (to-ß⁻-f⌣) [fr.] f ㊽ (kleines „Plauder"sofa) small sofa, (fr.) causeuse.

cbkm, cbm, ccm, cdcm abbr. = Kubikfilometer, =meter, =zentimeter, =dezimeter.

C=Dur (tße"…) n ㊽ d. f. C.

☞ **Ce…** s. a. Ze… u. Ke…

Cedille (ß⁻-dī'l-jə) [fr.; *grch. zeta (ζ)] f ㊽ gram. (Häkchen am c = ß) cedilla.

Celleporen (tß⌣⌣⌣) [ncu=lt. celli'pora] f/pl. ㊿ zo. (Zellenkorallen) Celleporæ pl.

Cellist ♪ (tsch⁻) [it.] m ㊷ (violon)-cello-player; (violon)cellist.

Cello ♪ (tscho⁻) [it.] n ㉝, ㊽ (violon)-cello; ~=spieler („…) m ㊷ = Cellist.

Celsius ⚭ (~) npr/m. (schwedischer Astrono'm, 1701-44): ~(sches) Thermome'ter (mit 100 gradiger Skala zw. Gefrier= u. Siedepunkt) Celsius (or centigrade) thermometer.

Celte ⚔ ꝛc. s. Kelte.

Cent (ß⌣; a. tßʻ) [it.] m ㊿ (kleine Münze: a) in Holland [= $^{1}/_{100}$ Gulden]; b) in Nordamerika [= $^{1}/_{100}$ Dollar]) cent.

Centime (ßᴀ=tī'm) [fr.] m ㊽, ㊿ (0,01 Frank) centime = nearly half-a-farthing].

Cera=in ⚛ (tß=⌣⁻) [lt. cerā Wachs] n ⑪c. chm. im Bienenwachs: cerain.

Cerasin ⚛ (tß⌣⌣⁻) [lt.] n ⑪c. (Schleimstoff im Kirschgummi) cerasin ($C_6H_{10}O_5$).

Cerat (tß⁻) [lt.]n⑪c.pharm.(Wachssalbe) cerate. [(fossiles Widderhorn) ceratite.]

Ceratit ⚛ (tß⌣⌣⁻) [grch. Horn…] m㊷ zo.

Ceres (tßʻ⁻⌣) [lt.] npr/f. inv. myth. Göttin des Getreidebaues u. ast. Asteroid: Ceres; ~=feste n/pl. = Zerealien 1.

Cerin ⚛ (tß⁻⌣) [lt.] n ⑪c. chm. cerin(e); ~=säure f ㊷ (Wachssäure) ceric acid.

cerise (ß⁻rī'z) [fr.] a. inv. (kirschfarbig) cerise.

Cerium ⚛ (tß⁻⌣) [Planet Ceres] n ㊽ chm. (1803 entdeckt) = Zer; ~=oxy'd, ~=oxy'du'l n ㊷ ceric, cerous oxide.

Cerosin ⚛ (tß⌣⌣⁻) [lt.; *grch. Wachs…] n ⑪c.chm.(wachsartiger Stoff aus dem Zuckerrohr) cerosin(e) ($C_{24}H_{48}O$).

Ceroten ⚛ (tß⌣⁻) [lt.] n ⑪c. chm. cerotene ($C_{27}H_{54}$).

Cerotin ⚛ (tß⌣⌣⁻) n ⑪c. = Cerylalkohol; ~=säure f ㊷ cerotic acid ($C_{26}H_{52}O_2$).

Certe=partie ⚓ (ß⌃ʻt⁻⌃) [+⁺ fr.] f ㊽ = Chartepartie.

Cerussit ⚛ (tß⌣⌣⁻) [lt. Bleiweiß…] m ⑪c. min. Weißblei=erz) cerus(s)ite ($PbCO_3$).

Ceryl=alkohol ⚛ (tß⁻⌣…) m ㊷ (aus chines. Wachs hergestellte weiße feste Substanz) cerotin, cerylic alcohol ($C_{26}H_{54}O$).

Ces ♪ (tßⁿ) n, inv. C flat.

Cestus (tßʻ⁻⌣; vgl. Cästus) [lt.; * grch. kestó's] m⑯(Gürtel[d.Venus])girdle.belt.

cetera (tßⁿ⁻⌣⌣) [lt. das übrige] adv.: et cetera (abbr. etc. oder &c.) and the rest, and so on, and so forth.

Cetin ⚛ (tß⁻⌣) [lt.] n ⑪c. chm. (Walratfett) cetin(e) ($C_{32}H_{64}O$); ~=säure f cetic acid.

Cetyl ⚛ (tß⁻⌣) [lt.=grch.] n ⑪c. chm. cetyl, cetyle; ~=alkohol m ㊷ = Äthal.

Ceylon ♀ (tß⁻⌣) npr/n. ⓐa. (gewürzreiche Insel im Indischen Ozean) Ceylon; aus ~ Bewohner(in) ~s Cingalese; ~=kaffee („…) m ㊷, ~=tee m Ceylon coffee, tea.

cf. abbr. = lt. confer(atur): (man) vergleiche (s. vergleichen).

C=Falter (tße"…) m ㊷ s. C, c 2.

cg (öft. **cg**) abbr. = Zentigramm (s. ds).

☞ **Ch…** s. auch K(h)… und Sch…

Chabasit ⚛ (ch⌣⁻) [grch.] m ⑪c. min. (Würfelzeolith) chabasite.

Chagrin (schā-grā') [fr.; *pers.] m ㊽ Gerberei: (genarbtes Leder) shagreen (leather); ~=arbeiter m ㊷ (Ledernarber) shagreen-maker; ~=leder n — (Chagrin) Ziert (ch⌣⌣⁻) shagreened, granulated.

Chaine (schän) [fr. chaîne] f ㊽ Kontertanz: chaine (anglaise or des dames), auch: right and left. [chaise.]

Chaischen (schä'ß⌣) n ㉓ small pony-

Chaise (schä-f⌣) [fr.] f㊽(Halbkutsche)chaise; mit Ponies bespannte ~ pony-chaise

Chaldäa ♀ (t⌣⌣) npr/n. ⓐa. Alt.: (südlicher Teil von Babylo'nien) Chaldea.

Chaldäer (t⌣⌣⁻) m ㊷, ~=in f ㊸, chaldä=isch a. ㊻ Chaldean; die chaldäische Sprache, das Chaldäi(sch)e n ㊼ Chaldaic, Chaldean, Chaldee.

Chalkothy'pie ⊕ (ch⌣⌣⌣) [grch.] f ㊽ (Kupferdruck) chalcotype.

Chalzedon (t⌣⁻)[Chalke'don, St. in Kleinasien: Kadiköi] m ⑪c. min. chalcedony; ~=artig, ~=haltig („…) a. ㊻ chalcedonic.

Chamäleon (t…, ch⌣⌣⁻) [grch.] n ㊿ zo. chameleon (Chamae'leon vulga'ris); wie ein ~ die Farbe wechseln to change colour rapidly, bisw.: to chameleon-ize; ~=artig a. ㊻ chameleon-like.

Chambre garnie (schā'brə=⌣") [fr.] f (pl. …s =s) furnished apartments pl.

Chambregarnist (schā'brə=⌣⁻) [+⁺ fr.] m ㊷ one who lives in lodgings or furnished apartments, lodger.

chamois (schā'm=sā) [fr.; *dtsch. Gemse] a. u. n ~ ㊻ (braungelb(e Farbe)) buff, tan.

Champagner (schām-pā'n=jⁿr) [fr.] (la Champagne, nördliche Provinz Frankreichs) m ㊷ (Schaumwein) champagne (wine), sparkling wine, F fiz; deutscher ~ sparkling hock or moselle; ~ in Eis iced champagne; ein Dutzend Flaschen ~ a dozen (bottles) of champagne.

Champagner=bowle („…) f ㊷ champagne-cup; =flasche f, =glas n ch.-bottle, -glass; =pfropfen, =stöpsel m tampion; =wein m = Champagner.

champagnern (~) v/n.(h.)㊽(in Champagner zechen) to drink champagne, F u. P to polish off the fizz.

Champignon (schā'm=pīn-jɔ)[fr.]m㊷(Pilz) field-agaric, (common) mushroom, fairy-ring mushroom (Aga'ricus od. Psallio'ta campe'stris, Mara'smus ore'ades, (fr.) champignon; kleine unerschlossene ~ button-mushrooms, buttonspl.; ~=sauce f ㊷ mushroom ketchup or -catchup.

Champion ᛏ (schä'm=pjⁿ) [engl.; fr.; *dtsch Kämpe] m ㊽ (Preiskämpfer ꝛc.) champion.

Chance (schāʻ⁻ß⌣) fr.] f ㊽ F die reine ~ (Glücksfall) a pure accident or chance; er hat ~ (Aussicht) he has a chance, he has good prospects or chances, he is in luck's way; ihre ~n waren gleich their chances were even, they had the same prospects.

chancen=voll ⚭ („…) a. ㊻ Börse: offering a good (or fair) chance, hopeful, promising. [= Tauschgeschäft.]

Change (schā'g=G⁻) [fr.] f ㊽ u. Buchhandel

changeant (schā=G⌣) [fr.] a. ㊻ (farbenschillernd) iridescent, opalescent.

changieren (schā=G⌣⌣⁻) [fr.] v/n. (h.) ㊽ 1. allgemein: (wechseln, tauschen) to change; bsd. man. to change hands or sides. — 2. ♉ (schillern) to change colours, to be iridescent; Seidenfabr. ꝛc.: 2d a. ㊻ (schillernd) shot-coloured, chatoyant.

Chansonette (schā=G⌣⌣⁻) [fr.] f ㊽ 1. short song, ballad, (fr.) chansonette. — 2. [+⁺ fr.] (Sängerin) ballad-singer.

Chaos (t⌣⁻ ob. ch⌣⁻) [grch.] n ⑯ chaos.

chaotisch (t⌣⁻ ob. ch⌣⁻) [grch.] a. ㊻ (verworren) chaotic; weitS. confused.

Chapeau claque (schā=pⁿ⁻tlāʻt) [+⁺ fr.] m (pl. …x …[ß]) (folding) opera-hat.

chaptalisieren (schⁿ⌣⌣⌣⁻) [fr. Chaptal, fr. Chemiker, 1756—1832] v/a. ㊽ Wein (=most) 2 (mit Zucker versetzen) to treat grape-juice according to Chaptal('s method), weitS. to doctor up wine.

☞ **Char=…** (tⁿ⁻…) s. Kar=…

Charaban (schār-ⁿ=bⁿʻ) [fr. char à banc(s)] m ㊽ char-à-banc = Kreuzer.

Charakter (t⌣⌣⁻) [mhd.; *grch. Gepräge] m⑪c. 1. (Gemütsart, Wesen) character, nature, disposition; ein Mann von ~ a man of (pronounced) character, a man who knows his own mind; ein Mensch von gefährlichem ~ F a dangerous character; ohne ~ unprincipled, vgl. 2los; von verschiedenem ~ of a different stamp or type; Krankheit v. bösartigem ~ malignant disease. — 2. (Rolle) e-n neuen ~ annehmen to assume a new part or rôle. — 3. (Rang) oft: capacity; ⚔ mit dem ~ (Titel) als Oberst with the (brevet) rank of a colonel.

charakter=ähnlich (t⌣⌣⁻…) a. ㊻ similar in character; =ähnlichkeit f ㊽ similarity (or analogy) of character; =bild n portrait, =buchstabe m characteristic (letter); =fehler m fault (or defect) in a p.'s character; 2fest a. ㊻ of firm character, of solid (or stanch) principles, steady; =festigkeit f firmness of ch., stanchness, steadiness; ohne ~, oft: F without backbone.

charakterisieren (t⌣⌣⌣⌣⁻) [grch.] I v/a. ㊽ 1. to characterize; diese Worte 2 (kennzeichnen) den Mann … show the character (or are characteristic) of the man. — 2. (beschreiben) to depict, describe, delineate; (hervorheben) to point out the salient features. — II **charakterisiert** p.p. u. a. ㊻ brevet rank; 2er Oberst brevet colonel.

Charakteristik (t⌣⌣⌣⁻) [grch.] f ㊽ 1. (Schilderung) description (or delineation) of the character (or features) of a th.; ~ e-r Person (life-like) portrait. —

⚛ scientific; ♀ botanical; ♀ geography; ⊕ machinery; ⚒ mining; ⚔ military; ⚓ marine; ⚭ commercial; ✉ postal; 🚂 railway.

2. *math.* (Kennziffer eines Logari'thmus) characteristic.

Charakteristiker (k◡◡◡´◡◡) *m* ㉒ = Charakterzeichner.

charakteristisch (k◡◡◡´◡) **I** *a.* (66) characteristic. — **II** ~e(s) *n* (67) character; das ~e an der Sache the characteristic (or distinctive) feature of (or in) a th.; ihr Gesicht hat nichts ~es her face lacks (or is devoid of) expression, there is no character in her face.

charakter=los (k◡´◡…) *a.* (66) without character or principle, unprincipled, of wavering (or weak) character; **=losigkeit** *f* (62) lack of principle, fickleness of character; F want of backbone; **=maske** *f* fancy-costume or -dress; **=schilderung** *f* character-sketch, delineation of character; **≗schwach**, **≗stark** *a.* of weak, strong ch.; weak-minded, strong-minded; **=schwäche**, **=stärke** *f* weakness, strength of ch.; **=zeichner** *m* delineator of character(s); **=zug** *m* (distinguishing) trait in a p.'s ch., characteristic (feature).

Charge (sch´◡) [(⁺₊)fr.] *f* ㊽ **1.** allg.: (Anstellung) office, appointment, post; ⚔ (Dienstgrad) rank; Person: official, officer, dignitary; (Hof=)~n *pl.* Officers (or Servants) *pl.* of the Royal Household. — **2.** ⚔ (Angriff, Salve) charge.

Chargen=pferd *n* (62) (Dienstpferd) charger.

chargier/en ↘ (sch◡´◡) [fr.] **I** *v/a.* (93) **1.** ⚔ † (stürmen) to charge, to storm. — **2.** ⚙ = laden²2, beschicken 2b. — **3.** *thea.* = karikieren. — **II** ~ *n* ㉓ **4.** = Ch/ung.

Chargier=schritt ⚔ † (sch◡″…) *m* (62) (Sturmschritt) double-quick step.

Chargierte(r) (sch◡´◡) *m* (67) **1.** ⚔ ehm. Chargierte *m/pl.* officers and non-commissioned officers *pl.* — **2.** studentisch: officer of a (students') club (Korps 2c.).

Chargierung (sch◡´◡) *f* ㊻ charging; ⚙ feeding.

Charis (ch´◡) [grch. ´◡] *f* (*sg. inv.*, *pl.* Chariten: ch◡´◡) *myth.* und *poet.* meist *pl.*: (Grazien) (the three) Graces.

Charité (sch◡◡´) [fr.] *f* (56) (öffentliches Krankenhaus) infirmary.

Charitin (ch◡´◡) [grch.] *f* ㊼ = Charis.

Charivari (sch◡◡w´◡) [fr.] *m*, *n* (53) (buntes Durcheinander) jumble, confusion; (Katzenmusik) caterwauling; (Heidenlärm) infernal noise or row, F u. P hullabaloo.

Charlotte (sch◡´◡) [fr.; *dtsch. Karl] **I** *npr/f.* ㊴㊽β. (Vn.) Charlotte. — **II** ♀ *f* ㊽ = Schalotte.

Charte=partie ⚓ ❀ (schă'rt=◡″) [fr.] *f* ㊽ (Vertrag[s=Urkunde] zwischen Reeder und Befrachter) charter(-party).

chartern ⚲ ⚓ (sch´◡) [engl.] *v/a.* (93) ein Schiff ≗ (befrachten) to charter …

Chartreuse (schăr-trȫ'-s(ᵉ)) [fr.] *f* ㊽ a) (Kartäuserkloster u. b) P *m* (Likör) Chartreuse.

Chartum ♁ (k´◡, r-r ch´◡) *npr/n.* (51)α. (ägyptische Stadt) Khartoum.

Charybdis ♁ (ch◡´◡) [grch.] *npr/f. inv.* Alt.: (gefährlicher Strudel in der Meerenge von Messina) Charybdis; Sprichw. aus (oder von) der Szylla in die ~ (aus einer Gefahr in die andere, größere) fallen od. geraten od. kommen, etwa: to fall from the frying-pan into the fire.

Chassepot=gewehr ⚔ (schă″ß-(ᵉ-)po…) [fr. 1866] *n* (62) chassepot (gun).

Chasseur ⚔ (schă-ßȫ'r) [fr. Jäger] *m* ⑪d(51) *chasseur*, in Engl.: rifleman.

chassieren (sch◡´◡) [fr.] *v/n.* (sn) (92) Tanz: to advance and retire; (fr.) to *chassé*.

Chassis=tuch ❀ (scha-ßi″=´ch) [fr. *châssis* Streichkasten] *n* (62) (Siebtuch) sieve-cloth.

Chätopoden ⚘ (ch-◡´◡) [grch.] *m/pl.* ㊹ *zo.* (Borstenwürmer) chætopods *pl.*

Chatterton=komposition ⚲ ⚙ (tschä″t-ᵉʳ-tᵉn…) [engl.] *f* (62) (Isoliermasse für Telegraphenkabel aus Guttapercha, Harz u. Holzteer) Chatterton's compound.

Chauffeur* (scho-fȫ'r) [fr. Heizer] *m* ⑪d. (Automobilführer) chauffeur (of a motor-car).

Chaussee (schö-ße') [fr.] *f* ㊽ highway, causeway, mit Schlagbaum: turnpike-road; (Steinschutt=)~ macadam(ized) road.

Chaussee=arbeiter (schŏ-ßĕ″…) *m* (62) road-maker; vgl. =wärter; **=bau(ten** *pl.*) *m* road-making, construction (or building) of highways; macadamizing; **=geld** *n* (in England fast †) turnpike-toll; **=(geld=)einnehmer** *m* turnpike-man, toll-collector; **=graben** *m* ditch along a highway; **=haus** *n* toll-house; **=inspektor** *m* road-surveyor; **=pappel** ♀ *f* = Pyramiden=p.; **=schmutz**, **=staub** *m* mud, dust of the roads; **=stein** ⚙ *m* broken stone (for road-making); ~e *pl.* (Beschotterung) (road-)metal; **=walze** ⚙ *f* street-roller, road-leveller; **=wärter** *m* road-man, road-mender.

chaussieren (schö-ß´◡) [fr.] *v/a.* u. *v/n.* (h.) (93) to build (or construct) roads; mit Steinschutt: to macadamize.

Chauvinismus (scho-w◡´◡) [fr.] *m* ㉗ (übertriebener Vaterlandseifer) chauvinism, in Engl. seit den 80er Jahren: jingoism.

Chauvinist (scho-w◡´) [fr.] *m* ㊷, **≗isch** *a.* (66) chauvinist, in England: jingo.

Chef (schĕf) [fr.] *m* chief, head; ❀ auch: (Geschäfts=inhaber) principal; (Teilhaber) partner (in the firm); (Verwalter) (head) manager; ⚔ ~ des Generalstabs Chief of the Staff; ⚓ ~ der Admiralität First Lord of the Admiralty.

Chef=d'œuvre (schæ-dȫ'wr) [fr.] *n*, *inv.* od. (51) (Meisterstück) masterpiece, (fr.) *chef-d'œuvre*.

Chef=redakteur (schĕ″f…) *m* (62) chief editor.

Chemie ⚘ (ch-´) [s. Alchimie] *f* ㊽ chemistry; (an)organische ~ (in-)organic ch.; angewandte, landwirtschaftliche ~ applied or practical, agricultural chemistry; ~ lebender Wesen ⚘ biochemistry.

Chemigraphie ⚘ (ch-◡◡f´) *f* ㊽ = Chemitypie.

Chemikali-en ❀ (ch-◡´(◡)◡) [grch.] *n/pl.* ㉙ chemicals, chemicals drugs *pl.*

Chemiker (ch´◡◡) [grch.] *m* ㉒ (scientific or analytical) chemist.

chemisch (ch´◡) [grch.] *a.* (66) chemical; ≗es Element elementary body, (chemical) element; ≗e Fabrik ch. works *pl.*; ≗e Verbindung, Wirkung chemical compound, action; *adv.* ≗ bleichen to bleach chemically; nach ≗en Grundsätzen heilend ⚘ iatrochemical.

Chemisett (sch◡◡´) [fr.] *n* ⑪c., (51), **~e** (sch◡◡´◡) *f* ㊽ (Vorhemd) shirt-front.

Chemismus ⚘ (ch-´◡) [grch.] *m* ㉗ (chem. Kraft) chemical force, ⚘ chemism.

Chemist (ch-´) [grch.] *m* ㊷ scientific chemist, chemical investigator.

Chemitypie ⚘ ⚙ (ch-◡-´) [grch.] *f* ㊽ (chem. Herstellung v. Reliefdruck) chemitypy.

…chen (…'ch◡) [(mhd.) ndd.] *dim.*=Endung, zB. Lämmchen lambkin, *dim.* von Lamm lamb.

Chenille ❀ (schᵉ-nĭ'l-jᵉ) [fr. Raupe] *f* ㊽ (Art Sammetschnur) chenille.

Chersones ♁ (ch´◡″) [grch. *f*] *m* ⑪a. Alt.: (Halbinsel) Chersonese.

Cherub (ch´◡ od. k´◡) [hebr., *assyr. *kᵉrûb* Flügelwesen; vgl. Greif] *m* (51) (*pl.* a. ~im: -◡´) cherub; **≗(in)isch** (-◡´◡, -´◡) *a.* (66) cherub, cherublike.

Cherusker (ch◡´◡) *m* ㉒, **~in** *f* ㊼, **cheruskisch** *a.* (66) dtsch. Alt.: Cheruscan.

Chester=käse ⚲ ❀ (t)sch´◡…) [Chester, engl. St.] *m* Cheshire cheese.

chevaleresk (sch◡w◡◡´) (ritterlich) *a.* (66) chivalrous, …ric, …resque; (gala'nt) galla'nt.

Chevalier (schᵉ-wă-lie') [fr.] *m* (51) (Ritter) knight, cavalier, (fr.) chevalier.

Cheviot ⚲ ❀ (sch´w(◡)◡) [engl. v. ~schaf aus den ~bergen] *m* (51) (dicker Wollstoff) cheviot.

Chiasmus (ch-´◡) [grch.] *m* ㉗ (Kreuz=(X=)stellung) *gr.*, *rhet.* chiasmus, decussation.

Chibou=baum ♀ (sch″-…) *m* (62) s. =harz; **=harz** *n*, vom Chiboubaum, *Bu'rsera gummi'fera*, stammend: cachibou.

Chiffon (schĭ-fŏ') [fr.] *m* (51) (dünnes Gazegewebe zum Besatz v. Kleidern, Hüten 2c.) chiffon.

Chiffonnier (e *f* ㊽) *m* (51) (sch◡◡nie', sch◡◡(◡)´◡) (kleiner Seitenschrank) chiffonier.

Chiffre (schĭ'f-ᵉʳ) [fr., *ar. (: Ziffer)] *f* ㊽ **1.** (Geheimschrift) cipher; in ~n schreiben to (write in) cipher. — **2.** Anzeige: **unter der ~** (Initiale) *ll* under the initial *ll*.

Chiffre(n)=schlüssel (schĭ″-fᵉʳ(n)…) *m* (62) cipher-key or -code; **=schreiber** *m*: ⚘ cryptographer; **=schrift** *f* cipher-writing, ⚘ cryptography; **=sprache** *f*: ⚘ cryptology; **=telegramm** *n* cipher- (or code-)telegram.

Chiffreur (schĭ-frȫ'r) [fr.] *m* ⑪d. one who knows (or operates with) a code of ciphers.

chiffrieren (sch◡´◡) [fr.] *v/a.* u. *v/n.* (h.) (93) (in Chiffren schreiben) to cipher.

Chiffrierer (~) *m* ㉒ cipherer, a. = Chiffreur.

Chiffrier=kunst (sch◡″…) *f* (62) art of cipher-writing, ⚘ cryptography.

Chignon (schĭ-niŏ') [fr.] *m* (51) (Haartracht der Frauen) knot of hair twisted behind; bsd. von falschem Haar: chignon.

Chile ♁ (tsch´◡) *npr/n.* (51)α. (süd=amerikan. Republik) Chili, Chile.

Chilene (tsch◡´◡) *m* ㊹, **Chilenin** *f* ㊼; **chilenisch** *a.* (66) Chilian, bisw. a. Chilese.

Chiliade (ch-◡´◡) [grch.] *f* ㊽ (ein Tausend; Jahrtausend) chiliad, millennium.

Chiliasmus (ch-◡´◡ od. k-◡´◡) [grch.] *m* ㉗ *theol.* (Lehre vom tausendjährigen Reiche Christi) millenarianism; **Chiliast** (ch-◡´ od. k-◡´) *m* ㊷ millenarian.

Chili=salpeter (tsch″◡…) *m* (62) *chm.* (salpetersaures Natron) Chili saltpetre, nitrate of soda.

Chimära (ch◡´◡) [grch.] *f* (56) *myth.* (Alt.: Ungeheuer mit Löwenkopf, Ziegenleib u. Schlangenschweif) Chimera; *fig.* s. Schimäre.

Chimborasso ♁ (t)sch◡◡´◡) [mex.] *npr/m.* (51)α. (Berg in Ecuador) Chimborazo.

China¹ ♁ (ch´◡) [engl., malai. *Tjen, chin. Küstenprovinz] *npr/n.* (51)α. China.

China²=baum ♀ (″…, a. k″◡…) [peru. *kina* Rinde] *m* (62) (Fieberrindenbaum) Peruvian bark tree (*Cincho'na*); **≗baumartig** *a.* (66)

[Chinaessenz] — 237 — [Chorege]

∂ cinchonaceous; ≈esse'nz f, ≈extra'tt n tincture, extract of (Peruvian) bark. **China¹-fahrer** (ch"...) ↓ m ship bound for China, Chinaman; ≈gras n, ≈hanf m, ≈nessel f ♀ China-grass, grass-cloth plant (Boehme'ria ob. Urti'ca ni'vea).

China²-rinde (℞..., a. t"...) f ⚕ pharm. china- (or Peruvian, Jesuits') bark (Cortex chinae); in aufgerollten Stücken: quillbark vom ≈baum; ♀**sauer** a. chm.: ∂ kinic, quinic; ♀**saure** f, chm.; ∂ kinic acid (C₇H₁₂O₆).

China¹-silber ⊙ n ⚙ (Art Neusilber) China-silver, electro-plate(d ware); ≈**wurzel** ♀ (Bodenwurzel) china-root (Smilax china).

Chinchilla (tschin-tschi'l-ja) [span., *am.] I n ⚘ zo. (Wollmaus) chinchilla (Chinchi'lla lani'gera). — II f ⚘ u. m ⚘, ~**pelz** ⚘ m ⚙ chinchilla-fur.

Chinese (ch-⌣-̄) [China¹] m ⚙, **Chinesin** f ⚘ Chinese, iro. oft: John Chinaman, f Chinese woman or lady.

chinesisch (ch⌣-̄ ⌣) a. ⚙ I Chinese; ♀ der Hanf ≈Chinagras; ♀ ℒe Nelke China-pink (Dia'nthus sine'nsis); die ℒe Mauer the Great Wall of China; der Porzellanton china-clay, kaolin(e); ℒe Seide china-silk; die ℒe Sprache = II; ~e Tusche Indian ink; der ℒ-japanische Krieg the Chino-Japanese War (1894—95). — II ~ n, inv. das ~e ⚙ the Chinese (language); des ~en Kundiger: ∂ chinologist, sinologist.

Chinicin (ch-⌣ťs⌣) n ⚘c. chm. quinicine. [dine (C₂₀H₂₄N₂O₂ + O₂H).)

Chinidin (ch-⌣-̄ ⌣) n ⚘c. chm. quini-/

chinieren (sch⌣-̄ ⌣) [fr. *China¹] v/a. ⚙ Weberei: (flammig mustern) to cloud.

Chinin (ch-̄ ¹, t-̄ ¹) n ⚘c. [China²] n ⚘c. chm. (Hauptalkaloid der Chinarinde, Fiebermittel) quinine (C₂₀H₂₄N₂O₂); schwefelsaures ~ sulphate of quinine.

Chinolin (ch, t-⌣ ¹) n ⚘c. chm. quinoline (C₉H₇N). [quinone (Benzo² C₆H₄O₂).)

Chinon (ch-̄ ¹, t-̄ ¹) n ⚘c. chm. kinone,/

Chinova (ch-̄ -̄ ⌣) [China² nova ∂ Kaskarillrinde] f ⚘, ~**bitter** n ⚘ chm. kinova (C₃₀N₄₈O); ♀**sauer** a. ⚘ kinovic; ♀saures Salz kinovate; ~**säure** f kinovic acid.

Chiragra ∂ (ch-̄ ⌣ ⌣) [grch. Handgicht] n ⚘ path. gout in the hands, ∂ chiragra.

Chirognomie ∂ (ch-̄ ⌣-̄ ⌣) f ⚘ (Handlesekunst) chirognomy.

Chiromant ∂ (ch-̄ ⌣-̄ ⌣) [grch.] m ⚘, ~**in** f ⚘ (Handwahrsager[in]) chiromancer; ~**ie** (ch-̄ ⌣ ⌣-̄ ¹) f ⚘ palmistry, ∂ chiromancy.

Chirurg (ch-̄ ⌣ ¹) [grch. -̄ ¹] m ⚘ surgeon; ~**ie** (ch-̄ ⌣-̄ ¹) f ⚘ surgery; ♀**isch** (ch-̄ ⌣-̄ ⌣) a. ⚘ surgical; Verfertiger v. ℒischen Instrumenten surgical instrument-maker.

chladnisch (t̄⌣-̄ ⌣) (Chladni, Naturforscher, 1756—1827] a. ⚘ phys., ♪ ℒe Klangfiguren fpl. Chladni's (acoustic) figures pl.

Chlamys ∂ (ch-̄ ⌣ ¹) [grch. -̄ ⌣ ¹] f, inv. grch. Alt.: (Männermantel) chlamys.

Chlodwig (t-̄ ⌣ ¹) [= Ludwig] npr/m. ⚙ ⚙ ⚙ ℵ.(erster Frankenkönig, 465—511) Clovis.

Chlor ∂ (t-̄ ¹) [grch. gelblichgrün] n ⚘c. chm. chlorine (gas) (Cl); mit ~ behandeln to treat with chlorine, to chlorinize.

Chloral ∂ (t-̄ ⌣ ¹) [Chlor-Al(kohol)] m] n ⚘c. chm.(Liebig, 1832) chloral (C₂HCl₃O); ~**hydrat** (℞...) n ⚘ (Schlafmittel) chloral hydrate (C₂HCl₃O.H₂O).

Chlor=alum (t"...) n ⚙ chm. (Bleichmittel) chlor-alum; =**alumi'nium** n chloride of aluminium, aluminium chloride (Al₂Cl₆); =**ammo'nium** n (Salmiak) ammonium chloride, sal ammoniac (NH₄Cl); =**antimo'n** n (Antimonchlorid) chloride (or butter) of antimony.

Chlorat ∂ (t-̄ ¹) [grch.] n ⚘c. chm. (Chlorsäuresalz) chlorate.

Chlor=äther ∂ (t"...) m ⚙ ethyl chloride (C₂H₅Cl); =**azety'lsäure** f chloracetic acid; =**ba'rium** n baric chloride (BaCl₂); =**blei** n plumbic chloride (PbCl₂); =**bleiche** f (1785) chemical bleaching; =**bromsilber** n chloro-bromide of silver; =**entwicklungs-apparat** m apparatus for making chlorine; =**gas** n = Chlor; ♀**haltig** a. containing chlorine, chlorid.

Chlorid ∂ (t-̄ ¹) [grch.] n ⚘c. chm. chloride; als chlorreichere Verbindung mit ...**ic** bz., zB.: Quecksilber-♀ mercuric chloride (HgCl₂). — Vgl. Chlorür.

chlorieren ⊙ (t-̄ ⌣ ¹) v/a. ⚙ chm., metall. (mit Chlor behandeln) to chlorinate.

chlorig (t-̄ ⌣) [Chlor] a. ⚘ chlorous; ℒe Säure chlorous acid (HClO₂).

Chlorig-säure-anhydri'd ∂ (℞...) n ⚙ chlorous anhydride (Cl₂O₃).

Chlorit ∂ (t-̄ ¹) [grch.] m ⚘c. min. chlorite; ♀**artig**, ♀**haltig** a. ⚘ chloritic, ...ous; ~**schiefer** m ⚙ chlorite slate.

Chlor=kalium ∂ (t"...) n ⚙ chloride of potassium, potassium chloride (KCl); =**kalk** m (1798) (mit Chlor gesättigter Ätzkalk) chloride of lime; =**kalzium** n calcic chloride, chloride of calcium (CaCl₂); =**kleesäure** f chloroxalic acid; =**kohlenoxy'd-gas** n chloro-carbonic acid (COCl₂); =**kohlenstoff-äther** m chlorocarbonic ether; =**magne'sium** n chloride of magnesium; =**messer** m chlorometer; =**messung** f (Bestimmung des Chlorgehaltes in Chlorkalk) chlorometry; =**meta'll** n (metallic) chloride; =**na'trium** n (Kochsalz) chloride of sodium, sodic chloride (NaCl); ♀**natriumhaltig** a. ⚘ containing salt, saliferous.

Chloroform ∂ (t-̄ ⌣-̄ ¹) [grch.-lt.] n ⚘b. chm. (betäubende Flüssigkeit) chloroform (= chloride of formyl CHCl₃).

chloroformieren (t-̄ ⌣ ⌣-̄ ¹) v/a. ⚙ to (put under) chloroform, to chloroformize.

Chlorometrie ∂ (t-̄ ⌣-̄ ¹) [grch.] f ⚘ = Chlormessung.

Chlorophyll ∂ (t-̄ ⌣-̄ ¹) [grch.] n ⚘b. (Blattgrün) chlorophyll; ~ enthaltend chlorophyllaceous, ...ic.

Chlorose ∂ (t-̄ ⌣ ¹) [grch.] f ⚘ path. (Bleichsucht) chlorosis.

Chlor=räucherung (t"...) f ⚙ chlorine fumigation; ♀**sauer** a. chloric; ♀**saures** Kali chlorate of potash, potassium chlorate (KClO₃); ♀**saures** Salz chlorate; =**säure** f chloric acid (HClO₃); =**säure-anhydri'd** n chloric anhydride (Cl₂O₅); =**säuresalz** n chlorate (= Chlorat); =**silber** n chloride of silver (AgCl); =**silbergelatinepapier** n, phot. gelatino-chloride paper; =**stickstoff** m chloride of nitrogen (NCl₃).

Chlorür ∂ (-̄ ¹) n ⚘c. chm. chloride; als chlor-ärmere Verbindung durch ...**ous** bz., zB.: Quecksilber-♀ mercurous chloride (Hg₂Cl₂). — Vgl. Chlorid.

Chlor=wasser (t"...) n ⚙ chlorine water; =**wasserstoff-säure** f (Salzsäure) hydrochloric or chlorhydric (ehm. auch muriatic) acid (gas) (HCl); =**zink** n (Zinkchlorid) chloride (or butter) of zinc (ZnCl₂).

Chok ℛ ℞.(sch¹) [fr. choc] m ⚙ ℛ u. path. (Angriff, Anprall) shock, attack.

chokant (sch⌣-̄ ¹) [fr. choquant] a. ⚘ (anstößig, verletzend) shocking.

chokieren (sch⌣-̄ ⌣) [fr. choquer] v/a. ⚙ to shock, to offend.

Cholera ∂ (t-̄ ⌣ ⌣) [grch. -̄ ⌣ ⌣] f, inv. cholera; asiatische ~ Asiatic (or Indian, oriental) cholera, ∂ cholera asiatica; einheimische ~ European cholera, ∂ cholera nostras; ~ der Kinder (children's) intestinal catarrh, ∂ cholera infantum; von der ~ angesteckt, befallen werden to be infected, seized with cholera.

cholera-ähnlich (t-̄ ⌣-̄ ⌣...) a. ⚘, ♀**artig** a. ⚘ choleraic; =**anfall** m ⚙ attack of cholera, cholera attack; =**bazillus** m cholera-bacillus; =**epidemie** f cholera epidemic; =**gift** n choleraic virus; =**kranke(r)** s. cholera patient; =**mittel** n remedy for (or against) cholera; =**tropfen** m/pl. cholera-drops pl.

Choleriker (t-̄ ⌣-̄ ⌣) [grch.] m ⚙ p. of choleric (or irascible) temper(ament).

Cholerine ∂ (t-̄ ⌣-̄ ⌣) [fr.] f ⚘ path. (choleraähnliche Krankheit) cholerine.

cholerisch (t-̄ ⌣-̄ ⌣) a. ⚘ physiol. (gallblütig) choleric; weitS. (jähzornig) irascible.

Choleste(a)rin (t-̄ ⌣-̄ (⌣)¹, t-̄ ⌣-̄ ⌣) n ⚘c. chm. (Gallenfett) cholesterin (C₂₇H₄₅.OH).

choliambisch (ch-, t-̄ ⌣ ⌣) a. ⚘ choliambic.

Choliambus (ch-̄ ⌣ ⌣, a. t-̄ ⌣ ⌣) [grch.] m ⚙ pros. (iambischer Hinkvers) choliamb.

chol-sauer (t"...,ch"...) [grch. chôlè' Galle] a. ⚘ chm. cholic; ♀**saures** Salz cholate; =**säure** f ⚙ (Gallensäure) cholic acid.

Chondrin ∂ (ch-̄ ⌣ ¹) [grch.] n ⚘c. chm. (Knorpelleim) chondrin(e).

Chor (t-̄ ¹; Hom. for. Körps) [grch. f. Chorus] I m ⊙c. 1. ~ im Drama: chorus; ♪ ~(-gesang) chorus(-singing); im ~ einfallen, singen to sing (or join) in chorus; ~! (alle!) tutti! — 2. (Sänger-)~ in Kirchen u. Konzerten: choir; zum ~ gehörig, vom ~ ausgeführt choral. — 3. F fig. ~ der Rache, etwa: set of demons, hellet loose, ragged brigade, rag-tag and bobtail. — II n ⚘c. 4. arch. (Empokirche) choir; (Sing-)~ chancel.

Chorage ∂ (t-̄ ⌣-̄ ⌣) ℞.= Chorege ℞.

Choral ∂ (t-̄ ¹) [lt.] m ⚘c. choral (song), sacred song, anthem, hymn; (einfache Weise) plain chant or song or tune; simple melody; weitS. sacred music; ♀**artig** a. ⚘ hymn-like; resembling sacred music; =**buch** n ⚙ hymn-book.

Choralist (t-̄ ⌣-̄ ¹) [it.] m ⚙ chorister.

choral-mäßig (t-̄ ¹...) a. ⚘ = ♀artig.

Chor=altar (t"...) m ⚙ high altar; =**amt** n cathedral (or full choir-) service; ♀**artig** a. ⚘ choral; =**bischof** m (Weihbischof) suffragan (bishop). [chord.)

Chorde (t-̄ ⌣) [grch.] f ⚘ ♪, math., path./

Chor=dienst (t"...) m ⚙ choir-service; =**direktor**, =**dirigent** m = Führer.

Chordometer ♪ (t-̄ ⌣-̄ ⌣ ⌣) [grch.] n (m) ⚙ (Saitenmesser) chordometer.

Chorege ∂ (t-̄ ⌣-̄ ¹) [grch.] m ⚙ (Chorführer) choragus; leader of the chorus.

[choregisch] — 238 — [chronometrisch]

choregisch ⚔ (t⌣⌢) a. 🌐 choragic.
chore-isch (⌣) [grch.] a. 🌐 = trochäisch.
Choreographie ⚔ (t⌣⌣⌣f⌢) [grch.] f 🌐 (Ballettkunst) choreography.
choreographisch ⚔ (t⌣⌣f⌢) a. 🌐 (die Ballettkunst betr.) choreographic.
Chore-us (t⌣f⌢) [grch.] m 🌐 pros. (Trochäus) choreus, trochee (Versfuß: -⌣).
Chor-führer (t⌢⌢) m 🌐 leader of the chorus or the choir; eccl. choir-master; **-gang** m, arch. aisle; **-gesang** m choral (or choir) singing or song; chorus; Alt.: choric song; **-gesangbuch** n antiphonary; **-gitter** n choir-screen, chancel; **-hemd** n surplice, alb; der Bischöfe: rochet; **-herr** m canon, prebendary.
choriambisch ⚔ (t⌣⌣⌣⌣, a. t⌣⌣⌣⌣) [grch.] a. 🌐 pros. choriambic.
Choriambus ⚔ (t⌣⌣⌣⌣, a. t⌣⌣⌣⌣) [grch.] m 🌐 pros. choriamb(us)(Versfuß: -⌣⌣-).
chorisch (t⌣f⌢) [grch.] a. 🌐 choral. choric.
Chorist (t⌣f⌢) [grch.] m 🌐, **~in** f 🌐 (ant. Soli'st) chorister; thea. chorus-singer, f a. chorus-girl.
Choristen-rolle (t⌢⌣⌢) f 🌐 chorus (or inferior) part, part of a chorus-girl.
Chor-knabe (t⌢⌢) m 🌐 chorister, choir-boy; **-nische** f, arch. apsis, apse.
Chorograph (ch-⌣f⌢, t⌣f⌢) [grch.] m 🌐 (Landbeschreiber) chorographer; **~ie** (ch⌣, t⌣f⌢) f 🌐 chorography; **Lisch** (ch⌣, t⌣f⌢) a. 🌐 chorographic(al).
Chor-pult (t⌢⌢) n 🌐 reading-desk; **-rock** m cope; **-sänger(in** f) m (female) chorus-singer; eccl. member of the choir, chorister; **-schranke** f = **-gitter**; **-schüler** m = **-knabe**; **-stuhl** m stall; **-stunden**, **-übungen** f/pl., thea. rehearsal(s pl.) of the chorus; eccl. choir-practice.
Chorus, meist F (t⌣) [lt., * grch. chŏrŏ's Reigentanz] m(sg.inv., pl.Chöre) = Chor I.
chor-weise (t⌢⌢) adv. in chorus, (it.) tutti.
Chose F (sch⌣) [fr.] f = Sache, Ding.
Chrestomathie ⚔ (t⌣⌣⌣) [grch.] f 🌐 (Blütenlese) anthology, selection(s pl.).
Chri-e (t⌢⌢) [grch.] f 🌐 rhet. theme; dissertation on appointed topics.
Chrisam (t⌣⌢) [grch.] n 🌐 (a. Chrisma (t⌣⌢) n 🌐) eccl. (Salb-öl, Salbung) chrism.
Christ (t⌢) [ahd.;* grch. christŏ's Gesalbter] I npr/m. 🌐 b. 1. bisw. = Christus. — 2. der Heilige ~ (Weihnachten) Christmas, bsd. = Christbescherung. — II [erst nhd. Kürzung aus lt. christia'nus] m 🌐, **~in** f 🌐 3. rel. Christian (man m, woman f); einem guten ~ geziemend becoming a good Christian, Christian-like; zum **~en machen** to Christianize.
Christ-abend (t⌢⌢) m 🌐 Christmas Eve; **-baum** (nhd. 18. sae.) m Christmas tree; **-bescherung** f (giving) Christmas presents pl.; **-dorn** ♀ m Christ's thorn (Zi'zyphus spina Christi) vgl. Christusdorn.
Christel (t⌢⌢) npr/f. 🌐 α.(Bn.)Christina.
christeln (t⌢⌢) v/n. 🌐 α. (christliche Gesinnung heucheln) to affect Christianity, to pretend to be a (good) Christian.
Christen-gemeinde (t⌢⌣⌢) f 🌐 Christian community; **-glaube** m Chr. faith; **-heer** n Christian host or army.
Christenheit (t⌣⌢) f 🌐 (Gesamtheit der Christen) Christendom, Christian world; die ganze ~ all Christendom, all Christian people, all Christians pl.

Christen-kind (t⌢⌢) n 🌐 (anders: Christfind) Christian (child); **-lehre** f Chr. doctrine, vgl. Christologie; **-leute** pl. Chr. people or folk; **-liebe** f Chr. charity; **-mensch** m = **-seele**; **-menschen** pl. = **-leute**; **-pflicht** f Chr. duty; **-seele** f Chr. (soul or person); es war keine ~ (niemand) da not a soul was there; **-sinn** m Chr. spirit.
Christentum (t⌢⌢) n 🌐 d. Christianity, Christian religion or faith; das ~ annehmen to accept (or embrace) Christianity; zum ~ bekehren to convert to Christianity, to Christianize.
Christen-verfolgung (t⌢⌢) f 🌐 persecution of Christians; **-volk** n Christian nation or people.
Christ-fest (t⌢⌢) n 🌐 Christmas(-tide); personifiziert als: Old Father Christmas; **-geschenk** n bsd. für englische Dienstboten usw.: Christmas box.
Christian (t⌢(⌣)-) [lt.] npr/m. 🌐 α., **~e** (t⌣(⌣)⌣) npr/f. 🌐 β. (Bn.) Christian(a).
Christin (t⌢⌢) f 🌐 f. Christ II.   [tina.⌐
Christine (t⌢⌢) npr/f. 🌐 β. (Bn.) Chris-
Christ kind(chen) (t⌢⌢) n 🌐, **-findlein** n the (holy) child Jesus; the Infant Jesus; als Bringer von Weihnachtsgeschenken in Engl.: F Santa Claus.
christlich (t⌢⌢) a. 🌐 Christian; 2 gesinnt thinking as a Christian, Chr.-minded; 2 leben to lead a Christian life; das 2 Bekenntnis the Christian faith; mit dem Mantel der Liebe bedecken to cover with the cloak of Chr. charity; 2 Zeitrechnung Chr. era.
Christlichkeit (t⌢⌢) f 🌐 Christian character or nature or charity; Christianity.
christlich-sozial (t⌢⌢) a. 🌐 Christian socialist(ic).   [socialist.
Christlich-Soziale(r) (t⌢⌢) s. 🌐 Chr./
Christ-markt (t⌢⌢) m 🌐 Christmas fair; **-messe** f, **-mette** f, Cath. eccl. Christmas matins pl.; **-monat** m (month of) December; **-nacht** f night before Christmas, Christmas Eve.
Christologie ⚔ (t⌣⌣⌢) f 🌐 (Lehre von Christus) Christology.
christologisch (t⌢⌢) a. 🌐 Christological.
Christoph (t⌢⌢) f) [grch. Christo'-phoros Christusträger] npr/m. 🌐 α. (Bn.) (dim. Stoffel usw.) Christopher.
Christophs-kraut ♀ (t⌢⌢) n 🌐 baneberry, Herb Christopher (Actaea spicata).
Christ-rose ♀ (t⌢⌢) f 🌐; **-wurz**; **-tag** m Christmas Day.
Christus (t⌢⌢) [grch. Gesalbter (= Messias)] npr/m. 🌐, 🌐 γ. Christ; vor Christi Geburt before Christ (abbr. B.C.); im Jahre 596 nach Christo (reiner nach ~) in (the year) 596 of our Lord (abbr. A. D. = anno domini), um Christi willen for Christ's (or Jesus' sake); Brüder in Christo brethren in Christ.
Christus-akazie ♀ (t⌢⌢) f 🌐 honey-locust, three-thorned acacia (Gleditschia triaca'nthus); **-auge** ♀ n Christ's eye (I'nula O'culus Christi); **-bild** n image of Christ (rel. of our Lord), am Kreuze: crucified Christ; **-dorn** ♀ m Weinrose, vgl. Christdorn; **-kopf** m Christ's head; weit ¾. divine face or countenance; **-lehre** f Christology.

Christ-woche (t⌢⌢) f 🌐 Christmas-week; **-wurz** ♀ f = Nieswurz (schwarze).
Chrom ⚔ (t⌢) [grch. Farbe] n 🌐 c. (ohne pl.) chm. chrome, chromium (Cr).
Chrom-alaun ⚔ (t⌢⌢) m 🌐 chrome alum ($Cr_2 \cdot 3 SO_4, K_2 SO_4 + 24 H_2O$).
Chromat ⚔ (t⌣⌢) [grch.] n 🌐 c. chm. (chromsaures Salz) chromate.
Chromatik ⚔ (t⌣⌢) [grch.] f 🌐 phys. u. ♪ (Farbenlehre) chromatics.
chromatisch (t⌣⌢) a. 🌐 phys. (farbig) u. ♪ chromatic; 2e Tonleiter, in halben Tönen auf- u. absteigend: chromatic scale.
Chromatrop ⚔ (t⌣⌢) [grch.] n 🌐 phys. (Farbenspiel) chromatrope.
Chrom-chlorid ⚔ (t⌢⌢) n 🌐 chm. chromic chloride ($Cr_2 Cl_6$); **-chlorür** n chromous chloride ($Cr Cl_2$); **-eisenstein** m, min. chromite, chrome ore or iron-stone ($Fe O Cr_2O_3$); **-gelb** n chromsaures (i. d.) Blei; **-grün** n chromegreen; ♂haltig a. 🌐 chromic, chromiferous; **-hydroxyd** n hydrated chromic oxide, chromic hydroxide ($Cr_2 H_6 O_6$).
Chromolithograph ⚔ ⊙ (t⌢⌣f⌢) [grch.] m 🌐 (lithographischer Farbendrucker) chromolithographer; **~ie** (t⌢⌣⌣f⌢) f 🌐 (farbiger Steindruck) chromolithography; **Lieren** (t⌢⌣⌣⌢) v/a. 🌐 to chromolithograph; **Lisch** (t⌢⌣f⌢) a. 🌐 chromolithographic.
Chrom-oxyd (t⌢⌢) n 🌐 chromic (or chromium) oxide ($Cr_2 O_3$); **-oxyd-hydrat** n = **-hydroxyd**; **-rot** n chrome red, red chromate of lead; ♂sauer a. 🌐 chromic, ♂saures Blei (Bleichroma't) chrome- (or Paris) yellow, yellow chromate of lead ($Pb Cr O_4$), ♂saures Salz chromate, saures ♂saures Kali bichromate of potash or potassium ($K_2 Cr_2 O_7$); **-säure** f chromic acid ($H_2 Cr O_4$); **-säure-anhydrid**, **-trioxyd** n chromic anhydride, chromium trioxide ($Cr O_3$).
Chronik (t⌣⌢) [grch. ⌣⌣⌢...] f 🌐 1. chronicle, in eine ~ eintragen to chronicle. — 2. Pa'rische ~ Arundel Marbles pl.
Chronika (t⌣⌣) [grch.] f 🌐 = Chronik; bibl. Bücher der ~ (Book of) Chronicles pl., ♂ Paralipomena pl.
Chroniken-schreiber (t⌢⌢) m 🌐 chronicler, annalist.
chronisch (t⌣⌢) [grch.] a. 🌐 path. (langwierig, schleichend) chronic (disease).
Chronist (t⌣⌢) [grch.] m 🌐 chronicler.
Chronogramm (t⌣⌣⌢) [grch.] n 🌐 b. (Zeitinschrift) chronogram; **Latisch** (t⌣⌣⌢) a. 🌐 chronogrammatic(al), ...ic.
Chronograph ⚔ (t⌣⌣f⌢) [grch.] m 🌐 (Meßapparat für Zeitteilchen) chronograph; **~ie** (t⌣⌣f⌢) f 🌐 (Geschichtsschreibung) chronography; **Lisch** (t⌣⌣f⌢) a. 🌐 (in zeitlicher Reihenfolge) chronographic(al).
Chronolog, **~e** (t⌣⌣f⌢) [grch.] m 🌐, 🌐 (Zeitforscher) chronologist, ...er; **~ie** (t⌣⌣f⌢) f 🌐 chronology; **Lisch** (t⌣⌣f⌢) a. 🌐 (der Zeit nach geordnet) chronologic(al).
Chronometer (t⌣⌣⌢) [grch.] n 🌐 🌐 phys., ast., ♪, ♪ (Zeitmesser, Uhr) chronometer; time-keeper; meine Uhr geht wie ein ~ my watch keeps chronometer-time or excellent time.
Chronometr/ie (t⌣⌣⌢) f 🌐 chronometry, **ch/isch** (t⌣⌣⌢) a. 🌐 chronometric(al).

Signs (see page XVII): F familiar, P vulgar, ♭ flash, ⚔ rare; † obsolete (died); * new word (born); ¡+ incorrect; ♪ music;

[Chronoskop] — 239 — [Croup]

Chronoskop ⚗ (t͞u-ˌ) [grch.] n ⑪c. phys. (Zeitmesser) chronoscope.
Chrysalide ⚗ (ḱh-ˬ-ˌˬ) [grch. gold(gefleckte) f ⑱ ent. (Schmetterlingspuppe) chrysalis.
Chrysanthem ⚗ ♀ (ḱh-ˬˌˬ) n ㉕, ~**um** (ḱh-ˬˬ) [lt.; *grch. Goldblume) n ㉘ (pl. ~en, ḱh-ˬˌˬ), ⑬ (Wucher=blume, Winter=after) chrysanthemum (*Chrysa'nthemum*).
Chryſoberyll ⚗ (ḱh-ˬˬˬˋ) [grch.] m ⑪b. min. chrysoberyl (Be Al₂O₄).
Chryſo=idin (ḱh-ˬˬˋ) n ⑪c. chm. (gelbe Anilinfarbe) chrysoidine.
Chryſolith ⚗ (ḱh-ˬˬˋ) [grch.] m ⑪c., ㊷ min. chrysolite; olivine.
Chryſopras ⚗ (ḱh-ˬˬˋ) [grch.] m ⑪ ㊺a. min. chrysoprase.
Chryſoſtomos, ...**us** (ḱh-ˬˬˬ) [grch. Gold= mund] npr/m. ⑯γ. Chrysostom.
chthonisch (ḱhˬˋ) (ton) a. ⑯ myth. Alt.: 2e (unterirdische) Götter m/pl. chthonian gods pl.
Chur ♀ (tˋ; Hom. Cour, Kur) npr/n. ⑬α. (St. in Graubünden) Coire.
chur=welsch (tˬˋ) a. ⑯ of (or belonging to) the Grisons; die 2e Sprache, das ~(e) n ㊿ Romansh, the Rhæto-Romanic language or dialect; ~**e**[**r**] m) f ㊻ (Graubündner) Grison.
Chylus ⚗ (ḱh-ˬˋ) [lt., *grch.] m ㊳ physiol. (Milchsaft, Speisesaft) chyle.
Chymus ⚗ (ḱh-ˬˋ) [lt., *grch.] m ㊳ physiol. (Speisebrei im Magen) chyme.
☞ **Ci...** s. auch Zi... und Ki...
Cicero (tˬ=ˌ tsˋ) [lt. ˬˌˬ] **I** npr/m. ⑬ ㊴α. (römischer Redner, 106—43 v. Chr.) Cicero. — **II** ⊕ f ㊾ typ. pica.
Cicerone (tʃ-tʃˬˋˬˬ) [it.] m, ⑱, (Fremdenführer) cicerone, guide.
Ciceronianer (tstsˬ-ˬ(ˬ)ˌˬ) [Cicero] m ㊴ (Nachahmer Ciceros); **ciceron(ian)isch** (ts ˬˬˬ ˌˬ, ts-tsˬˌˬ) a. ⑯ Ciceronian.
Cicero=schrift (tsˌˬll ˬˬˬˋ...) f ㊷ = Cicero II.
Cicutin (tsˬ tˋ) [lt.] n ⑪c. (Alkaloid des Wasserschierlings) cicutin(e).
Cid (tsi̇̂t) [span.; *ar. Herr] npr/m. ⑬α. (spanischer Held, † 1099) Cid.
Cimbern (tsˋ, r=r; lt.) m/pl. (germanischer Volksstamm) Cimbri, Cimbrians pl.; **cimbrisch** a. ⑯ Cimbric.
Cimolit ⚗ (tʃˬˋlt) [lt.; *Ki'mōlos ♀ grch. Inſel] m ⑪c. min. (Ton) cimolite.
Cinchona ♀ (tsˬtʃˌˬ) [span.; *Gräfin Chin=chon, Gemahlin des Vizekönigs von Peru, 1638] f ㊶ (Fieberrindenbaum) cinchona.
Cinchonin ⚗ (tsˬtʃ-ˌ) [Cinchona] n ⑪c. (ohne ⑤) chm. pharm. (Alkaloid der Chinarinde) cinchonin(e)(C₁₉H₂₂N₂O); ~**=ver=giftung** (ˬˌ...) f ⑪ cinchonism.
Cinnamomin ⚗(tʃˋ...) [neu=lt. Zimt=...] n ⑪c. (o. pl.) chm. = Styrol.
Cinquecentiſt (tʃˬktʃˬ=tʃˬˬˌ) [it.] m ㊷ (it. Künstler od. Dichter des 16. sae.) cinque=centist.   [marmor.] cipolin.]
Cipollin(tʃˌ=ˬ) [it.] m ⑪c. min. (Zwiebel=
circa (tsˬˋt=) [lt.] adv. (meift abbr. **ca.**) about, nearly = ungefähr.
Circe (tsˋˬtsˬ) npr/f. ⑲ ㊼β. (Zauberin, die den Odysseus zu fesseln suchte) Circe (= Kirke).
Cirriped(ien pl.) ⚗ (tsˬ=ˬ(ˬ)ˋ) [lt.] (Rankenfüßer) cirriped(s pl.).
Cis ♪ (tsˬˋs) n, inv. C sharp; ~=**Dur** C sharp major; ~=**Moll** C sharp minor.
Citracon=säure (tsˬˋtsˬ=ˌˬˬll) [Zitronen=] f ㊷ chm. citraconic acid (C₅H₆O₄).

City ⸸ (sˬˌ=tˬ) [engl.] f ⑮ (pl. a. **Cities**) (Stadt, bfd. Lo. Altstadt) city, (the) City.
☞ **Cl...** s. auch Kl...
cl (öft. **cl**) abbr. = Zentiliter.
Clair=obscur (klär=ˬbsˌkˌr) [fr. Helldunkel] n ㊿ ⊕ typ., &c. (Holzschnittdruck) light and shade, (it.) chiaroscuro.
Clan ⸸ (klän) [klt.] m ⑳ (Stamm) clan.
Clanschaft ⸸ (klä'n=) f ㊻ clanship.
Claque [fr.] **I** (klat) m ⑳ (Chapeau) opera=hat. — **II** (kla't=ˬ) f ㊷ thea. etwa: hired applauders pl., bisw. clappers pl., (fr.) claque.
Claqueur (klä=kˋr) [Claque II] m ⑪d. (㊿) thea. claquer, bisw. auch: (hired) clapper (im engl. Theater unbekannt).
Clique (klit=) [fr.] f ㊻ (Sippschaft) clique, set, b.s. gang, ring, coterie.
Cliquen=wesen (ˌˬ...) n ㉒, ~**wirtschaft** f (Spaßmacher) cliquism.
Clown ⸸ (klaun, F auch klōn) [engl.] m ⑳ thea.
cm (öft. **cm**) abbr. = Zentimeter.
cm², **cm³** öft. abbr. = Quadrat=, Kubik=zentimeter; **cmm** = Kubikmillimeter.
C=Moll (tsˬˋll) n ㉒ ♪ C.
☞ **Co...** s. auch Ko...
Co. abbr. für Compagnon u. Compagnie (s. Kompagnon, Kompanie).
Cochenillin ⚗ † (tˬ=ʃ=nˋl=[j]ˬn) [Koschenille] n ⑪c. chm. cochenilline (= Karmin).
Cocytus s. Kozytus.   [min.]
Code (kōd) [fr.; *lt. caudex, codex] m ⑬ (Gesetzbuch) code; ~ civil civil code.
Coeur (kṓr) [fr. Herz] n, inv. ob. ⑳ Kartenspiel: hearts pl.; ~ ist Trumpf hearts are trumps; ~=**as** (ˌ...) n ㉒ ace of hearts; =**dame** f queen of hearts.
Coiffeur (kᵘä=fōˋr) [fr.] m ⑪d. (Haarkünstler) hairdresser.
Colchicin ⚗ (t=ˬˋ) [Co'lchicum ♀ Herbst=zeitlose] n ⑪c. chm. Alkaloid: colchicin(e).
Cölestiner (tsˬ=ˬˋ) [Papst Cölestinus V., 1294/6] m ㊴, ~**in** f ㊵ (auch =**mönch** m, ~**nonne** f) Celestine (monk m. nun f).
Colombier (kō=lɔ̄ŋ=bīˋēˋ) [fr.] n ㊿, ~=**papier** n ㉒ columbier. [Metall: columbium (Cb).]
Columbium ⚗ (ˬˬˬˬ) [...] n ⑪c. chm.
Comer=see ♀ (tˬˬˌˬ) [Como, it. St.] npr/m. ㉒ Lake Como, (it.) Lago di Como.
☞ **Comité** (tˬ=ˬˋ) 2c. s. Komitee 2c.
Commis voyageur (kō=mi'=vᵘä=ſa=ĝū"r) [fr.] m ㊿ commercial traveller, F bagman.
☞ **Compagn...** s. Kompa(g)n...
Compound=lokomotive ⸸ ⊕ (kō"m=paund=...) [engl. Verbund=...] f ㊷ compound locomotive or engine; ~=**maschine** f compound machine, a. = Dynamo=
comptant (kō=tā') [fr. bar] s. kontant.
Comptoir (kō=tᵘäˋr) [± += fr.] n ⑪c. 2c.
☞ **Conc...** s. auch Konz...
Concordia (tˬˌˬ) 2c. f ⑰. Konkordia 2c.
Condom (kō=dɔ̄') [fr.; *~, Erfinder] m ㊿ (Schutzmittel) French letter.
conj. abbr. = Konjunktiv.
Consecutio temporum (tˬˌllˬˋˬˬ) [lt. Zeitenfolge] f (lt.) gr. sequence of tenses.
Consilium abeundi (tˬˬˋ ˬˬˌˬ) [lt.] (Rat, v. d. Schule od. d. Universität abzugehen) warning to a student previous to rustication; das ~ erhalten to be rusticated, F to be sent down from college.
☞ **Contre...** s. Konter...
contumacia (tˬˬˋˬ(ˬ)ˬ) [lt.]: in 2m verurteilen s. Kontumaz, kontumazieren.

Convoi (kō=wäˋ) [fr.] m ㊵ (Schutzgeleit) convoy.   [Zubäa.]
Coquito=palme ♀ (tō=tˌ=tō...) f ㊷ =
Cornelia, ...**lius** npr. s. Kornelia, ...lius.
☞ **Cou...** s. auch Ku...
Couleur (tū=lȫr) [fr.] f ㊸ univ. Students pl. (Korpsstudenten c.) who wear the same colour(s); ~=**student** m student wearing the colours of a (certain) corps.
Coulomb (tu=lɔ̄ˋ) [fr. Ingenieur, 1736—1806] **1.** npr.: ~=**sche Drehwage** phys. Coulomb's torsion=balance. — **2.** = ⑮. (elektrische Maß=einheit: die bei 1 Ampere in 1 Sekunde gelieferte Elektrizität) coulomb.
Coup (tū; Hom. Kuh) [fr. Schlag] m ㊿ stroke, feat, ec. coup.
Coupé (tu=peˋ) [fr.] n ㊿ **1.** ⚙, &c. (fr.) coupé. — **2.** 🚂 = Abteil.
Couplet (tu=pleˋ) [fr.] n ㊿ couplet; thea. (die Zeitverhältnisse behandelndes Lied oder Gedicht) topical song or lines pl. or verses pl.; song of the day, music=hall song; ~=**dichter** (ˌ...) m ㊷, =**schreiber** m song=writer; music=hall poet.
Coupon (tu=pɔ̄ˋ) [fr.] m ㊿ (Abschnittschein) coupon, (Zinsschein) dividend=warrant.
Coupon=abschneidemaschine (ˬ...) f ㊷ coupon=cutter; =**bogen** m c.=sheet; =**numeriermaschine** f machine for numbering coupons; =**steuer** f tax on coupons.
Cour (kūr; Hom. Chur, Kur) [fr. Hof] f ㊻ **1.** es ist große ~ (Versammlung bei Hofe) the King or Queen is holding a Drawing Room or Levee. — **2.** e=r Dame die ~ machen oder F schneiden to pay one's courtship to a lady; sie läßt sich gern die ~ machen she is fond of being courted (by men); weits. she is a great flirt or coquette.
Courage F (tu=rāˋ=ǰ) [fr. Mut] f ㊸ pluck, plucky spirit.
cour=fähig (kūˋr ...) a. ⑯ (hoffähig) presentable at court, enjoying the right to appear at court; =**machen** n ㊷ courtship (paid to a lady); flirtation (carried on with a lady); vgl. Cour 2; =**macher** m gallant; weits. ladies' man, beau; einer ihrer ~ one of her admirers or worshippers.
Courtage (kūr=tāˋ=ǰ) [fr.] f ㊸ (Makler=gebühr) brokerage.
Courtoisie (kūr=tᵘä=ſīˋ) [fr.] f ㊻ (Höflichkeit) courtesy, courteousness, politeness.
Cousin (tū=ʒa') [fr.] m ㊿ (Vetter) (male, gentleman) cousin; ~**e** (tuˌ) f ㊸ (Base) (female, lady) c.; (Bäschen) girl c.
cpt. abbr. = comptant (bar).
☞ **Cr...** s. auch Kr...
Cracovienne (trä=tō=wiäˋn) [fr.] f ㊸ (Tanz Krakowiak] und Musik dazu) cracovienne.
Creme (träm, [fr. *crème*]) f ㊿ Kocht. (hier P oft m: Rahmspeise) u. fig. (hier nur f: das Beste) cream; ~=**farbe** f ㊷ (Mattgelb) creamcolour; ⨂(=**farben**) a. ㊹ cream=coloured; ~=**torte** f cream(=)tart.
☞ **Crêpe** 2c. f. Krepp 2c.
crescendo ♪ (trĕ=ʃeˋn=bo) [it. zunehmend] adv. u. **Crescendo** n ㊿ crescendo.
Crete ⚔ (tˬˋ) [fr. *crête*] f ㊷ frt. crest.
Crocin ⚗ (tˬˬˋ) [lt.; *Krokus] n ⑪c. chm. (Farbstoff) crocin(e) (C₅₈H₈₆O₃₁).
☞ **Croquet** s. Krocket.   [frorieren.]
☞ **croquieren, Croquis** s. Kroki,
Croup ⸸ (trūp) [engl.] m ㊿ = Krupp.

⚗ scientific; ♀ botanical; ⚘ geography; ⊕ machinery; ⚒ mining; ⚔ military; ⚓ marine; ✉ commercial; ⚘ postal; 🚂 railway.

[Croupier] — 240 — [dabei]

Croupier (tru-pie') [fr.] m (Bankwart) [croupier.]
☞ **Cruci...** f. Kruzi...
C=Schlüssel ♪ [tsē"...] m C.
☞ **Cu...** f. auch Ku...
Cumalin (t-‿́) [Kumarin] n C. chm. (aus der Apfelsäure gewonnener Stoff) cumalin(e).
Cuminol (t-‿́) [neul.] n C. chm.
Cunninghamia ⚥ ⚲ (kŏn-ing-hăm′ĭa) f (Spießbaum) broad-leaved chinafir (Cunningha'mia verticilla'ta).
Curaçao (kü-räˈzō') [∼♀, ndl. Kariben=insel] m Likör: curaçao.

Curcumin ⚥ (t-t-‿́) [neul.-lt.] n C. (Kurkumagelb) curcumin(e) ($C_{10}H_{10}O_3$).
Curry ⊤ (tŏŏ′n-ə) [engl.; * tamul. kāri] n (ind. Gewürz) curry; mit ∼ zubereitetes Huhn curried fowl.
☞ **Cy...** f. auch Ky... und Zy...
Cyan-amid ⚥ (t-‿́) [grch.] n C. chm. cyanamide ($CN.NH_2$); vgl. Zyan(=...).
Cyanit ⚥ (tsh-‿́) [grch.] m C. min. (blauer Schörl) cyanite (= Disthe'n).
Cyanur-säure ⚥ (tsh-‿‿́...) f C. chm. (brenzliche Harnsäure) cyanuric acid ($C_3N_3O_3H_3$, polyme′r mit Zyansäure, f. ds).

Cybele (tsh-‿́-) [grch. t-‿-] npr f. myth. (phrygisch-kretische Erdgöttin) Cybele.
Cymol ⚥ (tsh-‿́) [lt.] n C. chm. (Kohlenwasserstoff des Kümmel=Öls) cymol ($C_{10}H_{14}$).
cyrillisch (tsh-‿‿́) [Cyrillus, Slawen-apostel, 863/9] a. C: Ꞇe Schrift cyrillic script.
Cyrillus (tsh-‿́-) npr m. C. Cyril(lus).
Cyropädie (tsh-‿-‿́-) [grch.] f (Werk Xe'nophons über (Jugend und) „Erziehung des Cy'rus") cyropædia.
Cyrus (tsh-‿́-) npr/m. C. γ. (altpersische Könige, 559—529 und 424—401 vor Chr.) Cyrus.
☞ **Cz...** f. Tsch... u. Z...

D, d (‿́) n, inv. (Buchstabe) D, d.
D, d ♪ n, inv. (Note u. Saite) D; **D=Dur** D major; **D=Moll** D minor.
d. abbr. = a) der, die das, vgl. d. Ä., d. Gr., d. J., d. O., d. h., d. i.; b) dieses, vgl. d. J., d. M.
D. abbr. a) = Doktor der ev. Theologie, vgl. Dr.; b) ☿ = Debet; c) ☍ = Durchgangszug; d) ⚡ = dringendes Telegramm. [tilgt," man streiche.]
∫ abbr. = deleatur „es werde gedu abbr. öft. = Dezjar.
da¹ (‿́) [mhd.; * dar] adv. I Ort: 1. mst there; hier und da here and there; der Mann (das Haus) da the man (the house) there or yonder; da draußen (drinnen, droben, drüben) out (in, up, over) there; da herum, da in der Nähe thereabouts, close by (there); da vorn das Tor the gate there in front; da, wo (jetzt) die Kirche steht there (or in the same spot, in the same locality) where (now) the church stands; von da (aus) from there, from thence, from that point, from yonder spot; F was ist da nur los? what is the matter there?; es ist da und da geschehen it happened at such and such a place; ⚥ wer da? who goes there? — 2. (hier) here; da und dort here and there; ich bin da, da bin ich I am here, here I am; ich bin (so)gleich wieder da I shall be back in a minute; wer ist da gewesen? who has been here. F who has called or been?; beim Überreichen: da hast du es!, da nimm's! here it is!, there take it!, F here you are! — 3. (vorhanden, gegenwärtig) in existence, present; es war niemand da there was nobody present; wenn er nicht da ist when he is not there, in his absence; das ist noch nie da'=gewesen! such a thing never happened before!; (das ist) alles schon da'gewesen! (sagt Ben Aki'ba) there is nothing new under the sun! (says B. A.) — 4. Redensarten: da haben wir es! there we are!, unwillig: a fine business!, a nice mess (or pickle) to be in!; da hast du es! there you are!, (hab' ich dir's nicht gesagt?) did I not tell you?; da komme ich schön an! I have put my foot in it nicely!, I am in a fine mess!; da sehen Sie //! you see now //! — 5. Ausruf: sieh da! look (there)!; feierlich: behold!;

nichts da! by no means!, on no account! — 6. Füllwort: als da sind such are (for instance); da ist keiner, der nicht // there is nobody but //; als ich ihn sah, da lachte er when I saw him he laughed; was da kreucht und fleugt (sch.) every creeping and flying thing; was da nur Beine hatte // all that had legs //; wer da (nur) will // whoever likes to //; bibl. wer da suchet, der findet he that seeketh findeth. — II Zeit: 7. (dann, damals) then, at that time (of day, at this juncture); da gab es (noch) keine Eisenbahnen there were ... then; da lachte nun jeder aus then (or thereupon) everybody laughed at him; da werde ich nicht mehr leben I shall not be alive then; **da erst** only then, not till then; **von da an, von da ab** from that time (forward), thenceforward, since then. — 8. ⚥ relativisch: der Tag da (an dem) du erschienst the day on which (weniger gut: when) you appeared; jetzt da nun that; zu der Zeit da // at the time when //. — III Umstand: 9. (unter solchen Verhältnissen) in that case, this being so, then; was läßt sich da machen? what can be done in such a case?; da irren Sie sich! you are mistaken there or in that matter!; da wäre ich (doch) dumm! that would be silly of me!; da wird man sich (wohl erst) besinnen müssen that requires thinking over (first); iro. (und) da ... (noch), zB. und da wagt man (noch) zu sagen and yet people venture to say; *da u. dort hie(r) u. ba) now and again.
da² (‿́) conj. 1. Zeit: (als, indem, während) as, when, while; da alles vorüber war when all was over; da er hereinkam, ging ich hinaus as he entered ... (so lange) er am Leben ist as long as he is alive. — 2. Grund: (weil) because; da er taub war, hörte er es nicht as he was deaf (stürzer: being deaf) he did not hear it; **da nun einmal, da doch, da ja** now since, since indeed; whereas; (in Erwägung, daß //) considering that //; da dem so ist such being the case. — 3. Gegensatz: **da aber, da (je)doch** but since, but considering that //; **da hingegen** whereas //.
da... ("‿́") Vorsilbe in Zssg. 1. mit v., immer trennbar (**), bz. Gegenwärtiges,

Vorhandenes, zB. 2behalten to keep back, to retain, to make stay; 2bleiben to stay (there); von Schülern: to be kept in; zum Essen 2bleiben to stay (for) dinner; vgl. dasteh(e)n. — 2. (vor Vokalen **dar**) mit prp. statt der 3. Person des personal pron. und des demonstrative pron. mit sächlicher Beziehung. zB. 2gegen contrary to that, 2mit therewith; 2zwischen between (them); **dar=unter** among them, &c.
d. Ä. abbr. = der Ältere sen(ior).
da-behalten (‿‿́‿‿) v/a. C a*/* f. da=... 1.
da-bei (-‿́, die Sache betonend: ‿́-) adv. 1. örtliche Nähe: **a)** meist: near (at hand), near by; therewith; wir sind ganz nahe 2 we are quite close to it; 2=sitzen, =steh(e)n (‿‿‿‿, ‿‿‿‿) to be sitting, standing close by, dagegen: 2 sitzen, steh(e)n (‿‿‿‿, ‿‿‿‿) to be sitting, standing all (or during) the time; **b)** (gegenwärtig, bsd. als Teilnehmer) present, there; waren Sie (mit) 2? did you take part in it?; wollen Sie 2 sein? will you join the party or us?; er ist immer gleich dabei, wenn // he is always one of the first when //; oft iro. da müßte ich auch 2 sein I should also have a word to say in the matter; **c)** (anstoßend) ein Haus und ein Garten (auch: mit einem Garten) 2 a house with a garden attached to it. — 2. zeitliche Nähe: ich war gerade 2 zu packen I was just then going to pack; nahe 2 sein, etwas zu tun to be on the point of doing a th. — 3. allg. Beziehung auf etwas: ich befinde mich ganz wohl 2 I feel quite happy (or comfortable) with (or over or in the midst of) it (all); vgl. bewenden; 2 bleiben (‿́‿ ‿‿) (verharren) to persist in a th., not to budge (from one's assertion or opinion); dagegen: 2=bleiben (‿‿‿‿́‿) (sich nicht trennen) to remain (true to a th.), not to sever o.s. (from old friends or associations); er bleibt 2 (bei dem Früheren) he persists in it, he keeps (or adheres, sticks) to it; es bleibt 2 (bei der Abmachung)! (it is) settled!, (we are) agreed, done!; 2 blieb's (bei dem) that the matter ended; 2 soll's bleiben! so it shall be (henceforth)!; ich habe mir nichts Böses 2 gedacht I meant no harm (in doing it); er erwarb sich ein Vermögen 2 he made a

[dabeibleiben] — 241 — [dafür]

fortune by it or over it or through that; ich kam schlecht ≈ weg, verlor ≈ I got off badly, lost over it; ≈ kommt nichts heraus nothing is (to be) gained by it; er läuft keine Gefahr ≈ he runs no risk with it or through it; es ist ein Haken ≈ there is a little obstacle in the way; es ist nichts ≈ there is nothing (or no harm) in it; it does not (much) matter; was ist denn ≈? what harm is there in that?, what of that?, F what's in that?; was ist (auch viel) ≈, wenn // what is there so wonderful if //. — 4. Zusatz (außerdem) besides; (dazu, ferner) moreover; er ist gelehrt und ≈ (⊥-) bescheiden he is learned and modest withal; sie sind reich und ≈ (trotzdem) nicht stolz they are rich and yet not proud. [bei 3.]
dabei-bleiben (⌣⌣⌣) v/n. (sn) ⑪** f. da-
dabei-sitzen (⌣⌣⌣) v/n.(h.) ⑭** f. dabei 1.
dabei-steh(e)n (⌣⌣⌣) v/n. (h.) ⑭** f. dabei 1; die Dabeistehenden ⑰ the bystanders, the onlookers pl.
da-bleiben (⌣⌣) v/n. (sn) ⑪** f. da-... 1.
da capo (- t⌣-) [it.], da capo; thea., &c. (fr.) encore!; ≈ rufen (ob. verlangen) to call for an encore, to (call) encore; ≈ singen to encore a singer or a song; ≈ singen to sing an encore or a second time.
Dach [ahd.: thatch; *decken] n ②c. 1. ~ eines Hauses, Wagens ꝛc.: roof (auch fig. = Haus 1); flaches, spitzes (oder altdeutsches) ~ flat, pointed roof; mit Ziegeln (Schiefer, Stroh) gedecktes ~ slated (tiled, thatched) roof; ein Haus unter ~ bringen to roof in ...; ein ~ decken to cover a roof; unter demselben ~e wohnen to live under (or to share) the same roof. Sprichw. besser ein Sperling in der Hand als zehn (ob. als eine Taube) auf dem ~e a bird in hand is worth two in the bush; f. Spatz. — 2. ~ und Fach (Obdach) (place of shelter); ein Haus in ~ und Fach (in gutem Stande) erhalten to keep ... in (good) repair; fig. unter ~ (und Fach) (in Sicherheit) bringen, sein to put, to be under cover or in a safe place or in safe keeping. — 3. F fig. (Kopf des Menschen) bei ihm ist gleich Feuer im ~e he soon fires up or boils over, he's hot-headed, he is easily put out; e-m auf dem ~e sitzen (aufpassen) to watch a p. very closely or narrowly, to keep an eye on him; bei ihm ist's unter dem ~e (auch: im ~ stübchen, vgl. ~stube) nicht ganz richtig he has a bee in his bonnet, he is wrong in his head; e-m aufs ~ (zu ~e) steigen (zu Leibe gehen) to call a p. to account or F to book, F to come (or pounce) down upon a p. — 4. anat. (Schädel-)~ (Hirnschale) cranium. — 5. ⚒ (das über dem Gange liegende, deckende Gestein) roof of a seam.
Dach-balken (⌣⌣...) m ⑫ roof-beam; =**binder** m tie-beam; =**boden** m loft; =**brücke** f tiler's scaffolding; =**decker** m mit Ziegeln: tiler, mit Schiefer: slater, mit Stroh: thatcher, mit Schindeln: shingler; auch: roofer; =**decker-arbeit** f, =**deckerei** f roofing; =**deckung** f tiling, &c.
Dächelchen (⌣⌣⌣) n ㉓; dim. v. Dach small roof, bisw. rooflet.

dachen (⌣ch⌣) [Dach] ⓼ **I** v/a. to (cover with a) roof. — **II** sich ≈ v/refl. (sich abdachen) to (form a) slope. — **III** ~ n ㉓ = Dachung.
Dach-fahne (⌣ch⌣...) f ⑫ (Wetterfahne) vane, weathercock; =**fenster** n top-room (or attic) window; =**fette** f = =balken; =**filz** m felt for covering a roof, roofing-felt; =**first** m, f ridge of a roof; ≈**förmig** a. ⓺ roof-shaped; =**gebälk** n timbering of a roof; =**geschoß** n top story, attic, garret-floor; =**gesims** n cornice of a roof; =**gesparr(e)** n roof-truss, rafters pl. (or joists pl. or body of a roof; =**giebel** m gable(-end); =**hase** m, co. (Katze als Hasenbraten ausgegeben) cat served up as roast hare.
dachig ⚓ (⌣ch⌣) a. ⓺ roof-like, sloped; bsd. ♀ (dachziegel-artig) imbricated.
Dach-kamm ⊕ (⌣ch⌣...) m ⑫ arch. crest; =**kammer** f = =stube; =**luke** f: a) opening in the roof; b) dormer-window; =luthern, vgl. =fenster; =**neigung** f slope (or angle, pitch) of a roof; =**pappe** f asphalt for roofing, roofing-felt; =**pfanne** f pantile; =**pfette** f = =balken; =**reiter** m (kleiner Turm) (ridge-) turret, belfry; =**rinne** f gutter; eaves pl.; =**röhre** f gutter-pipe.
Dachs (⌣ch⌣) [ahd.: grch. (Archi)tekt] m ⑪⑦ a. 1. zo. (f f. Dächsin) (common) badger (Meles taxus ob. vulga'ris); einen ~ aus s-m Bau graben to dig up (or unearth) a b. — 2. fig. er schläft wie ein ~ F he sleeps like a top or like a dormouse. — 3. hunt. = ~hund.
Dachs-bau (⌣ch⌣...) m ⑫ badger's burrow or hole or earth or lodge; =**beil** ⊕ n = Dexel; ≈**beinig** a. ⓺ bow-(or bandy-) legged.
Dach-schalung ⊕ (⌣ch⌣...) f ⑫ roof-boarding. [small (or young) badger.]
Dächschen (⌣ch⌣⌣) n ㉓ (dim. v. Dachs)
Dach-schiefer ⊕ (⌣ch⌣...) m ⑫ slate for roofing; roof-slate; =**schindel** f shingle; =**schwelle** f lower beam of a roof; pole-plate.
Dachs-eisen (⌣ch⌣...) n ⑫ = =falle.
Dächsel (⌣ch⌣) m ⑫ 1. hunt. = Dachshund. — 2. ⊕ (a. n) carp. = Dexel.
dächseln (⌣⌣) v/a. ⓼ a. 1. hunt. to hunt a badger. — 2. ⊕ carp. = dexeln.
Dachs-falle (⌣ch⌣...) f ⑫ hunt. badger-gin or -trap; =**fell** n badger's skin; =**fett** n badger-grease; =**graben** n drawing (or unearthing) a badger; =**haarpinsel** m badger's hair brush; =**hund** m, hunt. badger-dog, terrier, T dachshund (Canis ve'rtagus). [badger.]
Dächsin (⌣ch⌣) [Dachs] f ㊸ female
Dachs-jagd (⌣ch⌣...) f ⑫ badger-baiting, badger-hunting.
Dächslein (⌣ch⌣-) n ㉓ = Dächschen.
Dach-span (⌣ch⌣...) m ⑫ = =schindel; =**sparren** m, carp. rafter (of the roof). =**Dachs-pinsel** (⌣ch⌣...) m = =haarpinsel.
Dach-spitze (⌣ch⌣...) f ⑫ = =first; =**stein** m = =ziegel; =**stroh** n thatch; =**stube** f, dim. =**stübchen** n toproom (nearest the roof), garret, attic; fig. es ist bei ihm im =stübchen nicht richtig he is queer in his attic; he is wrong in his upper story; vgl. Dach 3; =**stuhl** m (Zimmerwerk unter den Sparren) frame-work (or

supports pl., timber) of a roof; vgl. =gesparr(e); =**stuhl-brand** m fire (which has arisen) in the timbering of the roof.
Dachs-weibchen (⌣ch⌣...) n ⑫ = Dächsin.
Dacht prove.(⌣ch⌣) m (n) ⑪ b.(a.f⑱) = Docht; Wortspiel mit „dachte": ~e sind keine Lichte you should know, not think. [denken.]
dachte (⌣ch⌣) (**dächte** [⌣⌣] subj.) impf. v.
Dachtel P (⌣⌣) [nhd. Denkzettel ob. = Dattel] f ㊽ (Ohrfeige) box on the ear.
Dach-traufe (⌣ch⌣...) f ⑫ eaves pl.; =**traufen-ziegel** m gutter-tile; =**trespe** ♀ f roof broomgrass (Bro'mus tecto'rum).
Dachung (⌣ch⌣) f ⑫ 1. (das Dachen) roofing. — 2. (Abdachung) slope.
Dach-werk (⌣ch⌣...) n ⑫ roof, roofing, roof-work; =**wohnung** f garret; =**ziegel** m tile for roofing; =**ziegelartig**, =**ziegelförmig** a. ⓺ tile-shaped, ♀ imbricated; =**zimmer** n = =stube.
dädalisch (-⌣⌣) [grch. Dä'dalos npr.] a. ⓺ 1. (kunstvoll) artistic, ingenious. — 2. (verschlungen) intricate (maze), mazy (path. walk); Dædal(ian), dedal.
da-durch (-⌣, die Sache betonend: ⌣⌣) adv. 1. (durch diesen Ort; auch da durch) through there; that (or this) way; ≈ (⌣⌣) müssen alle gehen all must pass through that way or through it. — 2. (durch dieses Mittel, auf solche Weise) by that means, in that way or manner; thereby; thus. — 3. ≈, daß Rom die Welt eroberte // Rome, by conquering the world, //; ≈, daß er gewann, verlor ich through (or owing to, by) his winning I lost; as he won I lost; ≈, daß er sich für uns bemüht hat thanks to his efforts on our behalf.
da-fern ⚓ (-⌣) cj. = wofern, (in)sofern.
da-für (-⌣, die Sache betonend: ⌣⌣) adv. 1. (als Ersatz für et.) in return for it; instead of it; as a compensation; ≈ (⌣-) bekommen Sie es nicht. ≈ (⌣-) kann ich es nicht geben you won't get it for that, I cannot sell it at that price or figure; sie ist häßlich, aber ≈ reich ... but proportionately rich. or: but (then), she is very rich; ist dies mein Lohn ≈? is this my reward (or return) for it?; als Belohnung ≈ in recompense for it. — 2. ≈ daß: wir straften ihn ≈, daß (weil) er nicht kam ... for (his) not coming or because he did not come; er erhielt die goldene Medaille zum Dank ≈, daß er so viele gerettet hat ... in recognition of his saving so many lives. — 3. (zugunsten einer Sache; ant. dagegen, dawider): ≈ und dagegen sprechen to speak for and against (a th.); es läßt sich vieles ≈ und dawider sagen there are two sides to it, F it has its pros and (its) cons; sind Sie ≈? are you in favour of it?; ich bin (ob. stimme) ≈, daß Sie abreisen I advise you to depart, I am of opinion that you should leave; ≈ gibt es kein Mittel there is no remedy for that, F there's no cure (or help) for it. — 4. (in Beziehung auf etwas) with regard (or in reference) to a th.; ich bürge (Ihnen) dafür I'll be answerable (to you) for it; er wird (schon) ≈ sorgen he will see (or attend) to it or see it carried out; sie werden ≈ sorgen,

♪ Musik; ⚓ Wissenschaft; ♀ Pflanze; 🜨 Geographie; ⊕ Technik; ⚒ Bergbau; ⚔ Militär; ⚓ Marine; ⊛ Handel; ✉ Post; 🚂 Eisenbahn.

daß er nicht entkommt they will take care that he does not escape. — 5. ∼ können: ich kann nichts ∼ (bin nicht schuld daran) it is not my fault or my doing; ich konnte nicht(s) ∼ (tat's nicht mit Fleiß) I conld not help it; I did not do it on purpose; wer kann ∼? whose fault is it?, who is reponsible for it?
da-für-halten (-ʺ-ʹ‿) I *v/n.* (h.) [86]a** to be of opinion, to deem, ↖ to opine. — II ~ *n* [23]: meines ~s, nach m-m ~ in my opinion or estimation, (according) to my way of thinking, as far as I can see; nach meinem bescheidenen ~ in my humble opinion or judgment.
da-gegen (-ʹ‿, die Sache betonend: ʹ-‿) I *adv.* (s. da-... 2) 1. ich stieß mit dem Fuße ∼ I knocked (with) my foot against it. — 2. (*ant.* dafür 3) seine Gründe ∼ his objections to it; er blieb taub ∼ he turned a deaf ear to it or to these words; ich habe nichts ∼ (einzuwenden), **daß** du spielst I have no objection to (or nothing to say against) your playing; wenn Sie nichts ∼ (einzuwenden) haben if you have no objection, oft auch: if you are agreeable to it; with your permission; wir handeln (verstoßen) ∼ we are acting contrary to (or in contravention of) it; ∼ hilft nichts there's nothing to stop it, there's no help (or remedy) for it; ∼ sein to be of a different (or contrary) opinion; to be adverse to it; ∼ stimmen to vote (or declare) against it; 10 Stimmen waren dafür, 12 ∼ there were ten ayes (or votes for it) and twelve noes (or votes against it); er sträubt sich ∼ zu zahlen he refuses to pay, he objects to paying. — 3. Vergleich: in comparison with (or to) it; er litt viel, mein Leiden ist nichts ∼ ... nothing compared with it; ∼-halten (erwidern) to compare, contrast, confront; to put side by side. — II *cj.* 4. Gegensatz: er fuhr, wir ∼ gingen ... we, on the contrary (or on the other hand), went; sie schlief, er ∼ wachte ... whereas (or whilst) he watched. — 5. (Tausch, Ersatz) in exchange for it; ☿ per count; er zahlt und will die Kuh ∼ ... in return (for his money). [s. dagegen 3.]
da-gegen-halten (-ʺ‿-ʹ‿) *v/a.* [86]a**
Daguerreotyp † (da-gä'-rō̆ʺ) [fr.-grch. *Daguerre, Erfinder, 1838/9] *n* [11]c. *phot.* (Art Lichtbild) daguerreotype.
da-heim (-ʹ) I *adv.* 1. (zu Hause) at home, at my (your, his &c.) house; (*ant.* im Freien) indoors; (in der Heimat) in my (your, his, &c.) native land or country or place; Sprichw. ∼ ist's am besten there is no place like home. — 2. *fig.* in einer Wissenschaft ∼ sein to feel at home in ..., to be conversant with ... — II ~ *n* [11]c. 3. home; house and hearth; weitS. domestic circle.
da-her (-ʹ, die Sache betonend: ʹ-) I *adv.* 1. Ort: (from) thence, from that place or spot; ∼ (ʹ-) kann er nicht kommen ... that way or from there. — 2. Ursache: ∼ (ʹ-) kommt (stammt) die Verwirrung hence (arises) the confusion; ∼ kam es, daß // thus (or so, in that way) it happened (or came about) that //; ich kannte ihn ∼, weil ich ihn früher gesehen hatte I knew him through (or because of) my having seen him before. — 3. ↖ relativisch: (= woher) whence. — II *cj.* (-ʹ) 4. (demgemäß) accordingly; ich war krank, ∼ (folglich) blieb ich im Bett ..., consequently (or for that reason), I stayed in bed; er stottert, ∼ spricht er auch nur wenig ... that also explains his speaking (or that's the reason why he speaks) so little.
da-herab (ʹ‿ʺ, die Sache betonend: ʺ‿ʹ) *adv.* a. getrennt: da vom Hügel herab down (there) from the hill.
da-herauf (ʺ‿ʺ) *adv.* a. getrennt: da vom Tal herauf up (there) from the valley.
da-heraus, da-herein (ʹ‿ʺ u. ʺ‿ʹ) *adv.* a. getrennt: da zur Tür heraus, herein out of (or in at) the door.
da-her-brausen (-ʺ...) *v/n.* (sn) [90]** to rush (along); ∼**bringen** *v/a.* [97]** to bring, to carry along with one.
da-herein s. daheraus.
da-her-fahren (-ʺ...) *v/n.* (sn) [85]b**, ∼gefahren kommen to come along driving or riding (in a carriage) or cycling; ∼**fliegen** *v/n.* (sn) [76]a**, ∼**geh(e)n** *v/n.* (sn) [94]** to walk (or march) along; ∼**kommen** *v/n.* (sn) [84]** to come along, to draw near; oft mit *p.p.*, zB. ∼gelaufen, ∼getrippelt kommen to come running, tripping along; vgl. auch ∼fahren, ∼ziehen; ∼**rauschen** *v/n.* (sn) [91]** to come roaring (or rushing) along; ∼**reiten** *v/n.* (sn) [80]b**, ∼geritten kommen to come riding along (on horseback, &c.); ∼**schleichen** *v/n.* (sn) [80]ast** to sneak along; ∼**schlendern** *v/n.* (sn) [92]a** to stroll (or saunter) along; ∼**schreiten** *v/n.* (sn) [80]b** to stalk along; ∼**sprengen** *v/n.* (sn) [88]** to gallop along; ∼**stolzieren** *v/n.* (sn) [93]*/* to strut along.
da-herüber (ʺ‿ʺ‿) *adv.* a. getrennt: da vom Walde herüber from the wood yonder.
da-herum (ʺ‿ʺ) *adv.* thereabouts; (i. d. Umgegend) about the neighbourhood.
da-herunter (ʺ‿ʺ‿) *adv.* down there.
da-her-wanken (-ʺ...) *v/n.* (sn) [88]** to totter along; ∼**ziehen** *v/n.* (sn) [76]b**, ∼gezogen kommen to come travelling along.
da-hier (-ʹ) *adv.* here, at this place; Kanzleistil: in this town or borough; Briefaufschrift: Local [mst mit Angabe der Stadt!].
da-hin (-ʹ, die Sache betonend: ʹ‿) *adv.* 1. räumliches Ziel: thither, to that place, there; er ist gestern ∼ gefahren, **gereist** he started for that place (or town) ..., he went there ...; ∼ und dorthin hither and thither, here and there, weitS. in every direction; es ist weit (bis) ∼ it is a long way (to travel), it is a long distance (or journey) from here. — 2. zeitliches Ziel: **bis** ∼ until then; Sprichw. bis ∼ läuft noch viel Wasser den Rhein hinab, etwa: a great deal of water will flow into the sea before that (time comes), many things may happen meanwhile or in the meantime or between this and that. — 3. (immer ʹ‿, wo nichts bsd. bemerkt ist) Ziel im allgemeinen, Zweck, Grad: ∼ **arbeiten** daß // to endeavour (or make every effort) to // (*inf.*); es ∼ **bringen** to arrive at that point; ich habe es noch nicht ∼ (zustande) gebracht I have not attained my object yet, I have not succeeded yet; ∼ hat er es gebracht he has come (F got) to that; es ∼ bringen, daß // to bring it about that //; to carry matters so far that //; sie haben ihn ∼ gebracht, daß // they have induced (or prevailed upon) him to // (*inf.*); vgl. a. bringen 7; man hat sich ∼ **geeinigt** (a. **vereinigt**) daß // it has been agreed upon to // (*inf.*), matters have been so far settled that //; meine Meinung **geht** ∼ (ist folgende) my opinion is this; das **gehört** nicht ∼ (-ʹ) that is in no way connected (or has nothing to do) with it; man **kommt** ∼ (ʹ‿), daß man jeden meidet one gets so far as to shun everybody; ist es ∼ gekommen? has it come to that?; ist es ∼ mit ihm gekommen? have things come to such a pass with him?; seine Worte **lauten** ∼ his words are to that effect; s-e Sorge ∼ **richten**, daß // to take care that //; ∼ **streben**, ∼ **wirken**, ∼ **zielen**, ∼ **zwecken** to strive to (*inf.*), to aim at. — 4. (immer -ʹ) *ell.* (Verschwundensein bezeichnend) away, past, over; vgl. dahinbrausen 2c.
da-hinab (ʹ‿ʺ, die Sache betonend: ʺ‿ʹ) *adv.* down there; a. getrennt: da den Berg hinab down that mountain.
da-hinauf (ʺ‿ʺ) *adv.* up there; mst getrennt: da die Treppe hinauf up those stairs.
da-hinaus (ʺ‿ʺ) *adv.* out there, out that way; getrennt: da zum Tor hinaus out of that gate; *fig.* will er ∼? (ʺ‿ʹ) is that what he is aiming (or driving) at?
da-hin-brausen (-ʺ...) *v/n.* (sn) [90]** to rush on; ∼**eilen** *v/n.* (sn) [88]** to pass by swiftly; to hurry along.
da-hinein (ʹ‿ʺ u. ʺ‿ʹ) *adv.* in there; a. getrennt: da ins Haus hinein into the house yonder.
da-hin-fahren (-ʺ...) *v/n.* (sn) [85]b** to move (or drive) along; zeitlich: to pass away; *fig.* to die; ∼**fließen** *v/n.* (sn) [75]d** to flow on; -**gabe** *f* [48] ~ (an et.) (entire) devotion to a th. (= Hingabe); ∼**geben** *v/a.* [82]c** to give up, to abandon.
da-hingegen ↖ (ʹ‿ʺ‿) *adv.* on the contrary (s. dagegen 4).
dahin-geh(e)n (-ʺ...) *v/n.* (sn) [94]** to pass (away), to pass on; (verschwinden) to vanish; vgl. dahin 3; ∼**gleiten** *v/n.* (sn) [80]b** to glide along; ∼**haben** *v/a.* [70]b** to have (received) one's share; *bibl.* sie h. ihren Lohn dahin they have their reward; ∼**raffen** *v/a.* [88]** to snatch away; *fig.* to carry (or cut) off, to kill; ∼**reißen** *v/a.* [80]a** to carry away; ∼**rauschen** *v/n.* (sn) [91]** to rush on; ∼**rollen** *v/n.* (sn) [88]** to roll along; ∼**scheiden** *v/n.* (sn) [81](e)st** to expire; ∼**schießen** *v/n.* (sn) [75]c(es)t** to shoot (or dash, dart) along; ∼**schwinden** *v/n.* (sn) [71]** to dwindle away; ∼ (fort) **sein** *v/n.* (sn) [70]a** to be lost or gone; ihre Jugend ist dahin the days of her youth have flown; die alten Freunde sind dahin ... are dead (and

[dahinsiechen] — 243 — [damit]

gone); die Zeiten sind dahin those are days of the past; those times are past and gone; ⁓siechen v/n. (ſn) ⊕** to waste away; ⁓ſinken v/n. (ſn) ⊕ſt** to sink (down), to droop; ⁓ſprengen v/n. (ſn) ⊕** to gallop (or dash) along; ⁓ſteh(e)n v/n. (h.) ⊕** to be uncertain; es ſteht noch dahin, ob // it is not yet decided whether //; ⁓ſtellen v/a. ⊕**: ⁓geſtellt ſein laſſen to leave uncertain or undecided; es mag ⁓geſtellt bleiben, ob // it is open to doubt whether //.

da-hinten (⌣⌣) adv. behind (there); ⁓bleiben v/n. (ſn) ⊕** to remain behind, to be left (behind); ⁓laſſen v/a. ⊕a** to leave behind, to forsake.

da-hinter (⌣⌣, die Sache betonend: ⌣⌣) adv. behind that or it; fig. of it, was ⁓ iſt ... what it means; es könnte doch et. ⁓ ſein there might be something (or some truth) in it; es iſt bei ihm nichts ⁓ he is not (at all) well off, he has nothing to boast of; ⁓kommen v/n. (ſn) ⊕a** to find out (a secret). to get to the bottom of (a th.); ſich ⁓ machen to set to work; ⁓ her ſein to be after a th.; es ſteckt (od. iſt) et. ⁓ there is something at the bottom of it, F there's s.th. in it; ich möchte wiſſen, was ⁓ ſteckt I should like to know the real truth (or to get to the bottom of it.

da-hinüber (⌣⌣⌣, die Sache betonend: ⌣⌣⌣) adv. over there; a. getrennt: da die Kluft hinüber in (or by) crossing that chasm.

da-hinunter (⌣⌣⌣ und ⌣⌣⌣) adv. down there; auch getrennt: da den Abhang hinunter down that slope yonder.

da-hinwärts (⌣⌣) adv. thitherward.
da-hin⁓welken (⌣⌣...) v/n. (ſn) ⊕** to fade (or wither) away.
Dahl-bord ⚓ (⌣⌣) m ⚔ (Schanz)deck) gunwale, gunnel; thole-board. [dally.]
dahlen prov. ⚓ u. P (⌣⌣) v/n. (h.) ⊕a. to]
Dahli-e ⚘ (⌣⌣) [Dahl, ſchwed. Botaniker] f dahlia; ſ. Georgine. [Dyaks pl.]
Dajak ⚘ (⌣⌣) m/pl. inv. Volk auf Borneo:]
Dak Oſt-J. (⌣) f ⚐ (Poſt) dawk.
Dakapo (⌣⌣) [da capo] n ⚐, ⁓ruf m ⚐ call for an encore; ⁓zeichen n repeat.
Daktyliothek ⚓ (⌣⌣⌣) [grch.] f ⚐ Fingerring- u. Gemmen-ſammlung dactyliotheca.
daktyliſch ⚓ (⌣⌣) [grch.] a. ⚐ pros. dactylic; Das Versmaß dactylics.
Daktylus ⚓ (⌣⌣) [lt. * grch. Finger] m ⚐ pros. dactyl Versfuß: -⌣⌣).
dal ndd. (⌣) (talwärts) adv. down.
Dalai-Lama (⌣⌣⌣) [mongol. Prieſterozean] m ⚐ ⊕ Dalai Lama.
dalbern P (⌣⌣) v/n. (h.) ⊕a. to dally.
Dale ⚘ ſchwz. (⌣) f ⚐ = Kiefer² (gem.).
dalen ⚓ (⌣⌣) [dal] v/n. (h.) ⊕ die Sonne dalt ... is on the decline or downgrade, ... has passed the meridian.
Dallen ⚓ (⌣⌣) [ndd.] m ⚐ = Dückdalbe.
Dalles P (⌣⌣) [hebr.] m, inv. (Geldlemme) impecuniosity; im ⁓ ſein to be hard up (for money), P to be stone-broke.
Dalmati-en ⚐ (⌣⌣tſ(y⌣)) [alban. del(me) Schaf] npr/n. ⚐a. Dalmatia.
Dalmati-er ⚐ (⌣⌣⌣⌣), **Dalmatiner** (⌣⌣⌣⌣) m ⚐, ⁓in f ⚐, **dalmat(in)iſch** (⌣⌣, ⌣⌣) a. ⚐ Dalmatian.

Dalmatika (⌣⌣⌣) [Dalmatien] f ⚐ eccl. (Art Tunika) dalmatic.
Daltonismus (⌣⌣⌣) [1798 John Dalton, engl. Chemiker] m ⚐ (Rotblindheit) daltonism.
Dam¹ (⌣; Hom. Damm)(ahd. *lt. dām(m)ā f (m) Reh, Gemſe] m ⚐c. = Damhirſch.
Dam²... (⌣...) [Dame] f. ⁓brett, ⁓ſpiel ꝛc.
da-malig (⌣⌣) a. ⚐ of that time or period or day; der Le Beſitzer the then owner; in, zu Ler Zeit at that time (of day), in those days, then; ſein Les Verſprechen the promise which he then gave, the promise then given by him.
da-mals (⌣) I adv. at that time; die ⁓ herrſchenden Sitten the customs prevailing in those days; erſt ⁓ only then, not till then; ſchon ⁓ even then. — II ⁓ n, inv. wenn man das Jetzt mit dem ⁓ vergleicht comparing the present with the (things of the) past.
Damaskus ⚐ (⌣⌣) [aram. bunt durchwirkt] npr/n. inv. (St. in Syrien) Damascus.
Damaſt ⚐ (⌣⌣) [fr., it. v. *Damaſkus] m ⚐ (großmuſtriges Gewebe) damask; auf ⁓(art) weben to damask.
Damaſt-arbeit (⌣...) f ⚐ damask-work; ⁓artig a. ⚐ like damask.
damaſten (⌣⌣) a. ⚐ (D 9) (of) damask; Les Tafelzeug oder Tiſchgedeck damask table-linen or tabling.
Damaſt-fabrik (⌣⌣, ⌣⌣...) f ⚐ damask-factory or -works pl.; ⁓leinwand f damask-linen; ⁓ſtuhl m d.-weaver's loom; ⁓weber m d.-weaver; ⁓weberei f d.-weaving; ⁓wirker(ei) = ⁓weber(ei).
Damaszener (⌣⌣⌣)[Damaſkus] I npr/m. ⚐, ⁓in f ⚐ Damascene, inhabitant of Damascus.— II m ⚐ = ⁓Klinge (ſ. III). — III a., inv. damask; ⁓ Klinge ⚔ Damascus (or damask) blade; ⁓ Pflaume ⚘ damson (Prunum damascenum); ⁓ Roſe ⚘ damask rose (Rosa damascena); ⁓ Stahl ⚔ damask steel.
damaszeniſch (⌣⌣⌣) [Damaſkus] a. ⚐ damask, Damascene.
damaszier-en (⌣⌣⌣⌣) [fr.v.*Damaſkus] I v/a. ⚔ metall. (tauſchieren) to damask(een), to damascene; b/ter Flintenlauf damask-barrel, gewundener: Damascus twist. — II ⁓n ⚐ D/ung. [worker.]
Damaszierer ⚔ (⌣⌣⌣⌣) m ⚐ damask-]
Damaszierung (⌣...) f ⚐, **Damaszier-kunſt** f ⚐ damask(een)ing, damascening.
Dam¹-bock (⌣) m ⚐ fallow-buck.
Dam-brett (⌣⌣) n ⚐ draught-board.
Dämchen (⌣⌣) n ⚐ (dim. v. Dame) little lady, young damsel.
Dame (⌣⌣) [fr. *lt. dŏmĭnā] f ⚐ 1. (ant. Herr) lady; gentlewoman by birth; große (a. vornehme) ⁓ great lady, lady of position or rank; adlige ⁓ titled lady; ſein gebildete ⁓ (highly) accomplished lady; ſie iſt keine feine ⁓ she is not a lady; wie eine feine ⁓ ladylike; die vornehme ⁓ ſpielen to act (F to put on) the fine lady; bei öffentlichen Anreden: meine Herren und ⁓ Ladies and Gentlemen! — 2. Damſpiel: (aufgedamte) ⁓ king; eine ⁓ machen to crown (or get) a king; die ⁓ ziehen, ⁓ ſpielen to play (at) draughts; Kartenſpiel, Schach: queen.
Damel F (⌣⌣) m ⚐, ⁓(j)ack F (⌣⌣) m ⚐ (derb) simpleton; F silly fellow, noodle,

duffer; ⁓ei F (-⌣⌣) f ⚐ stupidity, foolishness, silly conduct; ⁓ich (⌣⌣) a. ⚐ f. dämlich. [have (or talk) foolishly.]
dämeln F (⌣⌣) v/n. (h. u. ſn) ⊕a. to be-]
Damen=abteil 🚂 (⌣⌣...) m ⚐ ladies' compartment; ⁓brett n = Dambrett; ⁓coupé n = ⁓abteil; ⁓garderobe f, thea., &c. (ladies') cloak-room; ⁓gürtel m lady's girdle or belt or waist-band; ⁓handſchuh m lady's glove; ⁓held m ladies' man or pet; beau; lady-killer, b.s. gay Lothario; ⁓hut m runder mit Krempe: lady's hat; an den Kopf ſich anſchließender: lady's bonnet; ⁓kleid n lady's dress; ⁓kleidermacher m ladies' tailor; ⁓kragen(mantel) m lady's cape; ⁓mantel m lady's cloak; ⁓mäßig a. ⚐ lady-like; ⁓putz m lady's finery; ⁓reitanzug m od. ⁓reitkleid n lady's ridinghabit; ⁓ſattel m lady's (or side-)saddle; ⁓ſchneider m ladies' tailor; ⁓ſpiel n draughts pl.; ⁓ſtein m = Damſtein; ⁓ſtiefel m/pl. lady's (kid) boots pl.; ⁓täſchchen n lady's (little) bag; ⁓toilette f = ⁓zimmer; ⁓überwurf n lady's wrap; ⁓welt f the ladies pl., the fair sex; ⁓zimmer n, 🚂, thea., &c. ladies' waiting- (or cloak-)room. Vgl. a. Frauen... und Weiber-...
Dame-ſpiel (⌣⌣) n ⚐ = Damenſpiel.
Dam¹-geiß (⌣...) f ⚐ doe (of a fallow-deer); ⁓hirſch(bock) m ⚐ fallow-buck (Cervus dama); vgl. ⁓wild; ⁓hirſchkuh f = ⁓geiß; ⁓hirſchleder n buck-leather, buckskin.
dämiſch F ſüdd. (⌣⌣) a. ⚐ 1. (ſchwindlig) giddy, dizzy; (ohne klares Bewußtſein) unconscious. — 2. = dämlich.
da-mit (-⌣, die Sache betonend: ⌣⌣) I adv. (ſ. da⁓...2) 1. therewith, herewith, with that or it; thereby, by that or it; was fange ich ⁓ an? what am I to do with it?, what can I use it for?; was macht er ⁓? what does he do with it?; ich bin ⁓ zufrieden I am satisfied with it; er iſt ⁓ einverſtanden he agrees to it. — 2. Redensarten: es iſt nichts ⁓ it (or the thing) is useless; ⁓ (⌣⌣) iſt es aus (noch nicht vorbei) oder es iſt (noch) nicht vorbei ⁓ (⌣⌣) it (or the affair) is all over (not at an end yet); ⁓ wird er nichts ausrichten he will effect (or do) nothing in that way; ⁓ hat es nichts zu bedeuten that means nothing, that's of no consequence; ⁓ iſt mir nicht (a. ſchlecht) gedient that does not serve my purpose, F that won't do for me; ich bin ⁓ (-⌣) ob. (⌣⌣) bin ich einverſtanden I am agreeable to it, I agree (or consent) to it, agreed!; es wird ſich ⁓ geben that will be all right (presently); ⁓ geht's nicht that's of no use, (es läßt ſich nicht tun) it's impracticable; heraus ⁓! out with it!, make a clean breast of it!; laſſen Sie mich ⁓ in Ruhe! P ⁓ können Sie mir geſtohlen bleiben! leave that alone!, don't talk about that!; ⁓ iſt alles geſagt in saying that I have said all; that is (really) all; was will er ⁓ ſagen? what does he mean by it?; wie ſteht es ⁓? how do matters stand there?; ⁓ baſta! (oder genug!, gut!, Punktum!) that's enough!, there's an

⚓ scientific; ⚘ botanical; ⚐ geography; ⊕ machinery; ⚒ mining; ⚔ military; ⚓ marine; ⚐ commercial; ✉ postal; 🚂 railway.

[Damkalb] — 244 — [Dampfdruckmesser]

end of that! — 3. bei folgender Ergänzung oft nicht zu übersetzen: ich fing 2 (ᴸᵛ) an, ihm zu sagen I began by telling him; sie gehen 2 um zu verreisen they are thinking of travelling, they intend starting on a tour. — 4. † relativ = womit. — II (nur -ᵛ) cj. 5. Absicht: (in order) that; (in order) to ... (inf.); 2 ... nicht lest; ich winkte, 2 er mich sähe ... so that he might see me; ich hielt ihn, 2 er nicht sinke ... lest he might drop; 2 ich es kurz mache to be brief, to put it in very few words, F to cut it short. [the fallow deer.)

Dam¹=kalb (ᵍ...) n ⓥ, **=kitze** f fawn (of
Dämlein (ᴸᵛ) n ㉓ = **Dämchen**.
dämlich F (ᴸᵛ) [ndd.] a. ⓥ 1. (dumm) stupid, foolish, silly. — 2. = **dämisch**.
Dämlichkeit F (ᴸᵛ⁻) f ⓥ 1. stupidity, foolishness. — 2. F co. ~en = **Damen**.
Damm (ᵍ; Hom. Dam¹) [ndd.: dam] m ⓥb. 1. (Deich) dam, dike; barrier; (Eisenbahn=) bank, embankment; (Hafen=) jetty, mole; als Schutzmauer auch: breakwater, groin, sea-wall; (erhöhter Fahrweg) causeway, carriage-road; e-n ~ aufwerfen (od. aufschütten) to throw up a mound; fig. e-r Bewegung xc.: einen ~ entgegensetzen to stem the (rising) tide. — 2. Redensarten: F fig. e-n auf den ~ (auf die rechte Bahn) bringen to put a p. on the right way or track; das hat ihn wieder auf den ~ gebracht x. set him right (or on his feet, on his legs) again; wieder auf den ~ kommen (genesen) to recover (from an illness); (wieder in Aufnahme kommen) to come in vogue again. — 3. ⓥ a) **~grube**, b) an Schmelzöfen: dam (or wall) for banking up the smelted matter (in a foundry-furnace). — 4. anat. (Mittelfleisch) ⓧ perineum.
Dammara ⓥ (ᵍᵛᵛ) [malai. dammar Harz; Licht, Fackel] n 𝔐 Dammar resin or gum, dammarin(e).
Dammara=baum (ᵍᵛᵛ...) m ⓥ, **=fichte** f ♀: a) dammara-pine (A'gathis Da'mmara); b) kauri, southern dammara (Da'mmara austra'lis); **=firnis**, **=lack** ⓥ m Dammar varnish; **=harz** n = **Dammara**; **=säure** f, chm. ⓧ dammaric acid.
Damm=arbeit(en pl.) ⊕ (ᵍ...) f ⓥ earth-works pl.; **=arbeiter** m banker, digger, navvy; **2artig** a. ⓥ like a dam or dike; mound-shaped; **=aufseher** m dike-inspector; bsd. ehm. dike-reeve; **=balken** m (Versatzholz für Schleusen) slide, sliding timber; **=bau(meister)** m construction (constructor) of dikes; **=böschung** f slope of a dike, gradient of an embankment; **=bruch** m a) bursting of a dam, breach in a dike or dam; b) [Damm 4] surg. rupture of the perineum; **=riß**.
dämmen (ᵛ) [Damm] I v/a. ⓥ 1. (gegen Fluten beschützen) to dike (or dam) in or up, to protect by an embankment or by earthworks; fig. (hemmen) to check, restrain, stop, hold back; (zügeln) to bridle, to curb; (unterdrücken) to repress. — 2. (mit einem Straßenpflaster versehen) to pave. — II ~ n ㉓ 3. = **Dämmung**.
Dämmer¹ (ᵛ) [dämmen] m ⓥ = Dammarbeiter, Dammsetzer.

Dämmer² fast † (ᵛᵛ) [ahd.: dim] m ⓥ (mattes Licht) subdued (or dim, faint) light, glimmer; dusk, twilight.
Damm=erde (ᵍ...) f a) agr. (innige Vermengung der Humussubstanzen mit den Bodenkrümeln) mould, vegetable earth, surface soil; b) ⓥ earth for (making) dams; Gießerei: pit-sand.
Dämmerer F⤴ (ᵛᵛ) m ⓥ dreamer.
dämmerhaft (ᵛᵛ), **dämmerig** (ᵛᵛ) a. ⓥ 1. dusky; dim (light); cloudy (sky). — 2. fig. uncertain or vague (form); (träumerisch) dreamy (mood), dreaming.
Dämmer=licht (ᵛ...) n ⓥ grey dawn of day, ast. ⓧ crepuscular light.
dämmern (ᵛᵛ) [nhd.; * Dämmer²] Wa. I v/n. (h.) 1. to spread a feeble (or dim, uncertain) light, to diffuse faint rays of light; v/impers. es dämmert (schon) it is growing dusk; der Morgen dämmert the day breaks or dawns; it dawns; der Abend dämmerig night sets in or is closing in; in 2der Frühe in the early dawn (of day). — 2. fig. es dämmert mir in der Seele I have a vague presentiment or foreboding; eine 2de Hoffnung a faint (gleam of) hope. — 3. (sich in einem Halbschlafe, in Träumen wiegen) to be in a dreamy, somnolescent state. — II sich 2 v/refl. 4. (dämmernd verblassen) to fade away (in the distance), to be evanescent. — III ~ n ㉓ 5. = **Dämmerung**. — 6. vague presentiment, dreamy state, somnolescence; faint (or dim) light or apparition; evanescence.
Dämmer=schein (ᵛᵛ...) m ⓥ =licht; **=stunde** f hour of dawn or twilight, F blind man's holiday; (Abend=) nightfall; in der ~ in the dusk (of the evening), F between the lights.
Dämmerung (ᵛᵛ) [nhd.] f ⓥ twilight, gloaming, ⓧ crepusculum; (Morgen=) ~ dawn, break of day, grey of the morning; (Abend=) ~ nightfall; in der ~ in the dusk, F between the lights; (morgens früh) at daybreak. — Vgl. dämmern III.
Dämmerungs=falter (ᵛᵛᵛ...) m ⓥ ent. hawk-moth (Sphinx); **=kreis** m. ast.: ⓧ crepuscular circle; **=licht** n dim (or faint) light; **=schmetterling** m = =falter; **=strahlen** m/pl. faint rays of light; **=vogel** m = =falter.
Dämmer=zeit (ᵛᵛ...) f ⓥ =stunde; **=zustand** m (Trübung des Bewußtseins) semiconscious state.
Damm=gegend (ᵍ...) f ⓥ anat. ⓧ perineal region; **=geld** n quay- (or harbour-)dues pl.; **=grube** f ⓥ moulding-hole, casting-pit, foundry-pit; **=inspektor** m = =aufseher; **=riß** m, anat.: ⓧ perineal rupture; **=schüttung** f (throwing up of an) embankment; **=setzer** m (Pflasterer) paver, paviour; **=stein** m ⓥ Gießerei: (Wallstein eines Hochofens) dam-stone; **=straße** f = =weg; **=stürzung** f taking down (the upper part of) a dike. — Vgl. a. Deich=.
Dämmung (ᵛᵛ) [dämmen] f ⓥ diking, embanking, embankment; (Hemmung) check(ing), restraint. [way.)
Damm=weg (ᵍ¹) m ⓥ causeway, high-
Damnifikant ⓧ (ᵛᵛᵍ) [lt.] m ⓥ jur. (Übeltäter) offender.

Damnifikat (ᵛᵛᵛᴸ) [lt.] m ⓥ (Beschädigter) injured person.
Damno ⓥ (ᵍᵛ) [++ it. danno u. lt. damnum] m, n 𝔐 loss; ~ machen to suffer a loss; to sell under cost-price.
Damokles (ᴸᵛᵛ) [grch.] npr/m. ⓥ γ. Alt.: (Höfling des Diony'sios von Syraku's) Damocles; **~schwert** (ᵛ...) n ⓥ (oft fig.: stets drohende Gefahr) sword of Damocles, Damocle(si)an sword.
Dämon (ᴸᵛ) [grch. dai'mōn] m 𝔐 Alt.: (höheres Wesen) demon.
Dämonen=beschreibung (−ᵘ...) f ⓥ demonography; **=glaube** m demonism; **=lehre** f demonology.
dämonisch (−ᴸᵛ) [grch.] a. ⓥ demoniac, demoniacal, b.s. demon-like; (teuflisch) diabolical. [Dämonenlehre.)
Dämonologie (−ᵛᵛᵛᴸ) [grch.] f ⓥ =
Dampf (ᵍ) [ahd.: damph] m ⓥb. 1. (Dunst) vapour, steam; aufsteigender auch: (the rising) damp; (Ausdünstung) exhalation; chm., metall., &c. fumes pl.; (Rauch) smoke. — 2. mach. gesättigter, überhitzter ~ saturated, overheated steam; ~ von hoher, niedriger Spannung high-pressure, low-pressure steam; den ~ anlassen, ablassen (absperren) to put the steam on, to let off (to cut off) the steam; ~ aufmachen to get up the steam; mit vollem ~ fahren to go at full speed; phys., &c. in ~ verwandeln to vaporize, to steam off; fig.: es geht mit ~ it goes like steam; die Maschine hat ~ auf the steam (of the engine) is on or up; mit ~ arbeiten to work at full speed. — 3. F fig. Hans ~ (in allen Gassen) giddy fellow, bragging (or vapouring) fool, F harum-scarum; e-m den ~ (Verdruß) antun to vex (or annoy) a p. — 4. (Engbrüstigkeit) asthma, vet. = Dämpfigkeit.
Dampf=ableitungsrohr (ᵍ...) n ⓥ ⊕ mach. blow-off pipe, waste-steam pipe; **=absperrung** f cutting off (the) steam; **=absperr=ventil** n stop-valve; **=apparat** m steam-apparatus; **=aufzug** m steam-mudheaver, vgl. =bagger; **=ausgang** m exhaust-passage; **=auslaß=rohr** n od. **=auslassungs=rohr** n escape- (or waste-steam=)pipe; **=austritts=öffnung** f exhaust-port; **=bad** n vapour- (or steam-)bad; **=bagger** ↓ m steam-dredger.
dämpfbar a. ⓥ quenchable.
Dampf=barkasse ↓ (ᵍ...) f ⓥ steam-launch.
Dämpfbarkeit (ᵍ⁻⁻) f 46 quenchableness.
Dampf=barometer (ᵍ...) n (m): ⓧ elaterometer; **=behälter** ⊕ m steam-vessel; **=beiboot** ↓ n steam-launch; **=betrieb** ⊕ m working (or manufacture) by steam; **=bildung** f formation of steam; **=bläschen** n little steam-bubble; **=blech=schere** f ⊕ steam plate-shears pl.; **=bleiche** f bleaching by steam; **=boot** n steamboat; **=boot=bremse** f steam-brake; **2bringend** a. ⓥ vaporiferous; **=brot** n steam-(made) bread, machine-made bread; **=büchse** ⊕ f e-r Dampfmaschine slide-box, steam-chest; **2dicht** a. st.-proof or -tight; **=dichte** f density (or specific gravity) of steam; **=droschke** f steam-propelled cab; **=druck** m steam-pressure; **=druckerei** f steam-printing (works pl.); **=druck=messer** ⊕ m steam-

Zeichen (s. S. XVII): F familiär; P Volkssprache; F Gaunersprache; ⤴ selten; † alt (auch gestorben); * neu (auch geboren); ++ unrichtig;

[**Dampfdynamo**] — 245 — [**danach**]

gauge, manometer; =**dynamo** ⊕ m, mach. u. elect. steam-dynamo.

dampfen (⌐∪) [erſt nhd.] 🞼 **I** v/n. (ſn) 1. to rise in the shape of steam, fumes, smoke, &c. (ſ. Dampf 1). — 2. (durch Dampfkraft ſich fortbewegen) to steam away or off; die Lokomotive dampft über die Brücke ... is steaming (or puffing) across the bridge. — **II** v/a. u. v/n.(h.) 3. to emit (or exhale, throw up) steam, fumes, smoke, &c.; vom Dünger ꝛc.: to reek; von Sümpfen: to emit (or give forth) vapours; ∫de Pferde ∾ profusely sweating; von Rauchern: eine Pfeife ∾ to send forth clouds (or puffs) of smoke from a pipe; paſſend: to puff at one's pipe. — 4. meiſt poet. die Fluren ∾ würzigen Geruch the fields give forth (or exhale) ... — **III** ∼ n ㉓ 5. emission of steam, &c., exhalation.

dämpfen (⌐∪) [ahd.] **I** v/a. 🞼 **1.** (unter= drücken) to suppress, to check; die Feuersglut ∾ to quench (or put out, extinguish) the (blazing) fire; Flam= men ∾ to smother flames; ⊕ den Hoch= ofen ∾ to damp (or stop) the furnace; fig. (abſtumpfen) to blunt, (einſchränken) to restrain, (einſchläfern) to hush, to lull; einen Aufſtand ∾ to quell (or stamp out, put down) an insurrection; Leidenſchaften ∾ to calm passions, j-s Mut ∾ to damp a p.'s courage or spirits; j-s Schmerz, Wut ∾ (lindern, ſtillen) to soothe (or assuage) a p.'s pain, wrath. — 2. einen (hellen) Ton ∾ (dumpf m.) to deaden ...; ge= dämpfter Ton muffled sound; eine Geige ∾ to apply a mute to a violin; e-e Trommel ∾ to muffle a drum; mit gedämpfter Stimme with (or in) a low voice, in an undertone; e-n Farbenton ∾ to soften (down) a colour; in ge= dämpften Farben in dull (or sombre) hues, in neutral tints or colours; ein gedämpftes (mattes) Licht a subdued (or soft) light. — 3. (den Atem beklemmen) to suffocate, stifle, choke, smother. — 4. Kochkunſt: Fleiſch ∾ (ſchmoren, dünſten) to stew ...; ⊕ Kattundruckerei: Zeuge ∾ to steam ... — **II** ∼ n ㉓ 5. = Dämpfung.

Dampf=entwäſſerungs=apparat ⊕ (⌐...) m steam-drying apparatus.

Dampfer ⌘ (⌐∪) m ⑫ steamship; mit Hinterrad: stern-wheeler; ∼ in unregel= mäßiger („wilder") Fahrt tramp steamer; ſ. Dampfſchiff.

Dämpfer (⌐∪) m ⑫ **1.** person who sup= presses, &c. (ſ. dämpfen) fig.: (Licht=)∾ (Freund der Finſternis) darkling, obscur= antist; e-n ∾ aufſetzen to put a damper on; to damp (a p.'s ardour or joy). — 2. (Löſchvorrichtung) extinguisher (= Löſch=horn); 🜨 (Tondämpfer) für Geigen: mute, sordine; am Klavier: damper; ⊕ (Klappe) damper; phys.: e-r Magnetnadel damper.

Dampfer=flotte ⌘ (⌐∪...) f ⑫ = Dampf=f.; =**geſellſchaft** f steamship company; =**linie** f line of steamers, steamship line, steamer service; =**ſubvention** f sub= sidizing (or subsidy paid to) a line of steamers; =**wege** m/pl. communication by (means of a line of) steamers, auch: steam-communication, vgl. Dampfweg.

dampf=erzeugend ⊕ (⌐∪...) a. 🞼 pro= ducing steam, vaporific; =**erzeuger** m ⑫ steam-generator; =**erzeugung** f pro= duction of steam; =**eſſe** f e-s Dampfers ꝛc. chimney(-shaft), smoke-pipe; =**fähre** f steam-ferry; =**fahrkunde** f (science of) steam - navigation; =**färberei** f steam-colouring; =**faß** n Zeugdruckerei: drum for colour-fixing.

Dämpf=feuer (⌐∪...) n ⑫ chm. smoulder= ing fire; **fleiſch** n Kocht.: stew(ed meat).

Dampf=flotte ⌘ (⌐∪...) f ⑫ steam-fleet; =**fördermaſchine** ✕ f steam-winch or windlass; =**förmig** a. 🞼 like vapour or steam, ⚶ vaporiform; =**fregatte** ⌘ f steam-frigate; =**gebläſe** n steam-blast or -blower; =**geſchütz** ✕ n. artill. steam- (or machine-)gun; =**getriebe** n steam-mechanism; =**göpel** m steam-whim, machine-winch.

Dämpf=gording ⌘ (⌐∪...) f ⑫ (Geitau der Gaffelſegel) leech-line.

Dampf=hammer (⌐∪...) m ⑫ steam-hammer; =**heizung** f heating by steam (-pipes); =**hemd(e)** n = Mantel.

dampfig (⌐∪) [Dampf] a. 🞼 steamy, vaporous, full of vapour, steam, &c.

dämpfig (⌐∪) [Dampf 4] a. 🞼 (kurz=atmig) asthmatical, pursy; vet. brokenwinded, chest-foundered.

Dampfigkeit (⌐∪–) f ㊶ (ſ. dampfig) steaminess, vaporousness.

Dämpfigkeit (⌐∪–) f ㊶ vet. broken-wind (-edness), roaring; Pferd, das die ∼ hat, auch: roarer, F co. musical horse.

Dampf=jacht ⌘ (⌐∪...) f ⑫ steam-yacht; =**kaffee** m coffee roasted by steam; =**kammer** f, faſten m 🆘 steam-room or -chest; =**keſſel** m (steam-)boiler, steam-generator; ∼ mit Hochdruck high-pressure boiler; =**keſſel=exploſion** f (steam-)boiler explosion; =**keſſel=kohle** f = kohle; =**keſſel=ſpeiſe=apparat** m boiler-feeder; =**klappe** f steam-valve; =**koch=topf** m steam-cooking appara= tus, F steamer; für hohe Berge: Papin's digester; =**kochung** f cooking by steam; =**kohle** f steam-coal; =**kolben** m (steam-)piston; =**kolben=liederung** f piston-packing; =**kolben=ſtange** f pis= ton-rod; =**kraft** f steam-power; =**kran** m st.-crane; =**krumpe** f steaming of cloth; =**küche** f steam-kitchen; =**kugel** f, phys. (Hohlkugel, aus welcher Dämpfe aus= ſtrömen): ⚶ æolipile; =**leitung** f steam-conduit; =**loch** n steam-hole or -port; =**mantel** m (Zylindermantel) steam-jacket or -case, cylinder-jacket; =**marine** ⌘ f steam-navy; =**maſchine** f steam-engine; mit Balancier: beam-engine; mit Hoch=(bzw. Nieder=)druck: high- (low-) pressure engine; =**maſchinen=gebäude** n engine-house or -shed; =**maſchinen=weſen** n steam-engineering; =**meſſer** m = Druckmeſſer; =**mühle** f steam-mill; =**öffnung** f steam-port; =**omnibus** m steam-propelled (omni)bus; =**paket=boot** ⌘ n steam-packet. [ing-pan.]

Dämpf=pfanne (⌐...) f ⑫ Kocht.: stew-]

Dampf=pfeife (⌐∪...) f ⑫ steam-whistle; =**pflug** m, agr. steam-plough; =**pinaſſe** ⌘ f steam-pinnace; =**poſt=verbindung** f packet-steamer service; =**preſſe** f steam-press; steam-printing-machine;

=**pumpe** f steam-pump; =**ramme** f steam-ram, locomotive for pile-driving; =**raum** m = kammer; =**regu=lator** m steam-regulator; =**röhre** f steam-pipe; =**roß** n, co. (Lokomotive) steam-horse; =**ruder** ⌘ n steam-rudder; =**ſägewerk** n steam-saw works pl.; =**ſchieber** m steam-distributor; =**ſchiff** ⌘ n steam-boat, st.-vessel, steamer; =**ſchiffahrt** ⌘ f steam-navigation; (einzelne Fahrt) voyage (or passage) by steamer; (Ausflug) excursion by steam-boat; =**ſchiff(ahrt)s=verbindung** ⌘ f steam-communication; =**ſchlepp=ſchiff** ⌘ n steam-tug; =**ſchneidemühle** f steam-saw mill; =**ſchornſtein** m = eſſe; =**ſchraube** ⌘ f an Schraubendampfern steam-propeller; =**ſpannung** f tension of steam; =**ſpritze** f (Feuerſpritze) steam fire-engine; =**ſteu(e)rung** f = ſchieber; =**ſtrahl=gebläſe** n injector for the manufacture of steel; =**ſtrahl=pumpe** ⌘ f steam-jet bilge-pump; =**ſtraßen=bahn** f steam-tramway.

Dämpf=topf (⌐∪...) m ⑫ Kocht.: stew-pot.

Dampf=tranſport (⌐∪...) m ⑫ steam-conveyance, carriage by steam(er); =**turbine** f steam-turbine.

Dämpfung (⌐∪) f ⑫ **1.** in den Bed. des inf. (ſ. dämpfen). — 2. suppression; extinction of fire; lowering of the voice; softening of light; (Erſticken) suffocation; Kochkunſt: stewing.

Dampf=verteiler (⌐∪...) m ⑫ = ſchieber; =**wagen** m steam-carriage or -car; 🚂 locomotive (engine); =**walze** f steam-roller; =**waſch=anſtalt** f steam-laundry; =**weg** m st.-passage; =**zeiger** m st.-indicator; =**zylinder** m st.-cylinder.

Dam¹=ſchaufler (⌐...) m ⑫ fallow buck with palmated antlers; =**²ſpiel** (⌐...) n = Damen=ſpiel; =**¹ſpießer** m young fallow deer, fawn; =**¹ſtein** m man (at draughts); =**¹tier** n = geiß u. hirſch; =**wild** n fallow deer.

da-nach (⌐–ch, die Sache betonend: ¹–ch) adv. 1. after that, thereupon, upon that, (nachher) subsequently, later on; bald ∾ soon after; ich habe ihn ∾ gefragt I as= ked (or questioned) him about it; ich frage nichts ∾ I don't trouble about it, I pay no heed to it; er trägt Verlangen ∾ he has a desire for it; ∾ (¹–) ſieht ſein Streben that's what he is aiming at. — 2. mit folgender Ergänzung, oft nicht zu überſetzen: ich ſehnte mich ∾ zurück=zukehren I longed to return; er trachtet ∾, berühmt zu werden he is making great efforts to become famous. — 3. nach Maßgabe von etwas: according (or conformably) to that or it; dies iſt mein Wunſch, nun handelt ∾ ... now act ac= cordingly; ich kann nichts kaufen, die Zeiten ſind nicht ∾ ... do not allow it; der Hut iſt billig, aber er iſt auch ∾ ... but it's worth no more; iro. er ſieht (auch) ∾ aus he quite looks it; er hat es ∾ gemacht, daß // he so managed (or behaved) that //; alles läßt ſich ∾ an, als ob // everything seems to indi= cate that // — 4. bezüglich, a. hinweiſend (wie, alſo) accordingly; ∾ es ſich trifft just as it may happen; Sprichw. ∾ die Arbeit, ∾ der Lohn as the work, so

🎵 Muſik; ⚶ Wiſſenſchaft; 🜨 Pflanze; ⚤ Geographie; ⊕ Technik; ✕ Bergbau; ✕ Militär; ⌘ Marine; 🆘 Handel; ⚒ Poſt; 🚂 Eiſenbahn.

[Danaer] — 246 — [dann]

the wages; 2 sich einer führt. 2 wird einem as you sow, so you will reap.
Dana-er (⌣‿) [grch.] m/pl. ㉒ Alt. (Griechen) Danai, Greeks pl.; =geschenk n, etwa: fatal (or deceitful) gift; snare.
Dana-ide (‿⌣⌣) [grch.] npr/f. ㊽, mst im pl.: die ~n myth. (50 Töchter des Danaos) the Danaides; ~n-arbeit (‿...) f ㊷ (fruchtloses Bemühen) sieve of the Danaides, vain efforts pl.
Däne (⌣‿) m ㊹, **Dänin** f ㊼ Dane.
da-neben (⌣‿⌣) adv. **1.** beside (or by the side of) it or that, near (or next to) it or that; dicht 2, gleich 2 close (F hard) by. — **2.** fig. 2-geh(e)n, von Personen: to miss one's way, to go on a wrong track; von Sachen: to go amiss; 2-gießen to spill; 2-schießen to miss one's mark. — **3.** (außerdem) besides, moreover; in addition to that; arm, 2 (auch) blind poor and blind withal.
Dänemark ♀ (⌣⌣‿) npr/n. (skand. Königreich) Denmark. [people, Danes pl.]
Dänen (⌣‿) npr/pl. ㊹ (Volk) Danish]
Dane-werk (⌣‿) n ㊷ (Grenzwall) Danework, Danorum Vallum.
dang (‿) (u. **dänge** subj.) impf. v. dingen.
da-nieden†, noch poet. (⌣‿⌣) adv. **1.** down there. — **2.** bibl. (hienieden) here below.
da-nieder (⌣‿⌣) adv. down, on (or to) the ground or floor or earth; in Verbindung mit verbs: 2 beugen to bend, to weigh down, fig. to depress; 2 drücken to oppress; 2 fallen to fall to the ground; 2-liegen to lie down, to lie on the ground; von Kranken: to lie (ill or sick) in bed; to be laid up (with an illness); fig. to be depressed or prostrate or ruined; das ~-liegen des Handels the depression in trade; 2 schlagen, 2 werfen to knock over or down, to upset. — Vgl. auch nieder=...
Daniel (⌣‿⌣) [hebr. Richter Gottes] npr/m. ㊾ ㊵α. bibl. (550 v. Chr.) Daniel, dim. Dan, Danny; ~ in der Löwengrube Daniel in the lions' den.
dani-elisch (bäˈn-ĭʹlĭsh) a. ㊺ [John F. Daniell, engl. Physiker, 1790—1854] Des Element elect. (Zink-Kupfer-element) Daniell's cell.
Dänin (⌣‿) f ㊼ s. Däne.
dänisch (⌣‿) a. ㊺ Danish; die 2e Sprache, das 2 ㊶ the Danish language, Danish; ⊛ 2es Handschuhleder Danish skin or leather; der ~-deutsche Krieg (1864) the Danish-German War.
danisieren (⌣⌣‿⌣) [dtsch.-lt.] v/a. ㊺ (dänisch machen) to make Danish.
Dank (‿) [ahd.: thank] I m (2—6:) ⓐb. (o.pl.),(vgl.1 u.7) ㉕ b.† (Denken, Gedanke) noch gbr. in: gegen, wider j-s ~ (Willen) against a p.'s wish; einem et. zu ~(e) (nach Wunsch) machen to do a th. to a p.'s liking; man kann es ihr nie zu ~e machen ... never please (or satisfy) her. — **2.** (Dankbarkeit) meist: gratitude (towards a p. gegen einen); wir sind ihm großen ~ dafür schuldig we owe him a great debt of gratitude for it; ich weiß dir's (ob. dir dessen) keinen ~ I don't thank you for it; er wird es uns schlechten ~ wissen ... not think it kind of us; einem ~ für et. wissen to feel grateful to a p. for a th.; mit ~ annehmen (anerkennen) to accept (to acknowledge) gratefully; Sie würden mich zu (großem) ~ verpflichten you would (greatly) oblige me. — **3.** (Anerkennung) thanks pl.; e-m ~ erstatten, sagen, zollen to return (or render) thanks to a p.; e-m ~ schulden to owe a debt of gratitude to a p., to be under an obligation to a p.; ich statte Ihnen dafür meinen besten ~ ab I thank you most heartily for it, I am very much obliged to you for it; es bedarf keines ~es you need not thank me for it. — **4.** Redensarten: m-n ~! ob. haben Sie ~! thanks!; bsd. in Briefen: accept my (kindest) thanks!, stärker: allow me to thank you!; großen ~!, schönen ~!, vielen ~!, tausend ~! many thanks!, (I) thank you very (or so) much! — **5.** (Lob, Preis) Gott (ob. dem Himmel) sei ~ dafür! God (or Heaven) be praised (or thanked) for it!; let us give praise to the Lord for it!; eingeschaltet: das ist, Gott sei ~, nicht der Fall! thank God (F thank Goodness), that's not the case! — **6.** (Lohn) reward; er hat doch dessen keinen ~ he gets no return for it, he has his pains for nothing; ist das der ~ für meine Mühe? is that the return for (all) my trouble?; schlechten (F des Teufels) ~ mit etwas verdienen, davon bekommen to be ill repaid (or requited) for a th.; zum ~ für seine Dienste // as an acknowledgment for his services //; arbeiten, ohne ~ zu ernten to labour for nothing. — **7.** ⓐb. † bei Turnieren: (Kampflohn, Siegespreis) prize; den ~, Dame, begehr' ich nicht (SCH.) poet. the guerdon, lady, I do not claim. — II 2 prp. mit gen. ob. dat.: **8.** 2 f-m Fleiße (ob. j-s Fleißes) thanks (or owing) to his industry.
Dank-adresse (‿...) f ㊷, etwa: address (gratefully acknowledging a p.'s services); (Dankesvotum) vote of thanks; =altar m altar for thank-offerings.
dankbar (‿⌣) a. ㊺ **1.** innerlich, auf die Dauer: grateful; äußerlich, vorübergehend: thankful (für et. for a th.), adv. (~-2-lich[st]) auch: from gratitude; ich bin Ihnen äußerst 2 I feel (or am) exceedingly grateful (or greatly indebted, much obliged) to you for it; ich wäre Ihnen 2, wenn Sie // I would thank you if you //; was wir 2 (adv.) anerkennen which we gratefully acknowledge; sich 2 gegen e-n erweisen to show o.s. grateful to a p. — **2.** (lohnend) profitable, remunerative, advantageous, lucrative; 2e Aufgabe, Rolle grateful (or pleasant) task, part.
Dankbarkeit (‿‿‿) f ㊷ gratitude, gratefulness, thankfulness (vgl. dankbar 1); s-e ~ bezeigen, an den Tag legen to show (or manifest, give proof of) one's gratitude; aus reiner ~ out of (or from) sheer gratitude; vgl. Dank 2; ~s-bezeigung f ㊷ mark (or token) of (one's) gratitude, showing o.s. grate-
dankbarlich(st) ⌣ (‿⌣‿) s. dankbar 1. [ful.]
dank-beflissen (‿...) a. ㊺, 2begierig a. eager to show (or desirous of proving) one's gratitude; =begier(de) f ㊷ desire of showing o.s. grateful; =bezeigung f manifestation (or mark, proof of (one's) gratitude; =brief m letter of thanks or of (grateful) acknowledgment; 2durchdrungen a. = erfüllt.
danken (‿⌣) [ahd.] ㊸ **I** v/n. (h.) **1.** e-m für et. 2 to thank (or return thanks to) a p. for a th.; bibl. er nahm das Brot, dankte und brach's ... and when he had given thanks, he brake it; danke schön! many (or my best) thanks!; seid gedankt allow me to (or let me) thank you!; er ließ mir aufs herzlichste dafür 2 he sent me his kindest acknowledgments for it; Quittungsformel: 2d erhalten received with thanks. — **2.** ablehnend: to decline with thanks; wir 2 Ihnen bestens für Ihr Anerbieten, aber // we thank you very much for your (kind) offer, but //; wollen Sie noch ein Glas Wein? Ich danke! may I give you another glass of wine? No(t any) more, thank you!; iro. da danke ich! thanks, I would rather not!; na, (ich) danke! no, not I; erstaunt: I never (heard of such a thing)! — **3.** e-m 2 (einen Gruß erwidern) to return a p.'s bow. — **II** v/a. **4.** (lohnen) e-m et. 2 to recompense a p. for a th.; e-m schlecht 2 to make a p. a poor return; das danke dir Gott! may Heaven bless you for it!; niemand wird es mir 2 no one will commend (or thank) me for it. — **5.** (verdanken) er hat dir das Leben zu 2, er dankt dir das Leben he owes his life to you; ihm 2 wir, daß // we owe it to him that //, it is due to him that //. — **III** ~ n ㉓ **6.** returning (of) thanks, expression of gratitude; über dem ~ vergißt er, daß // whilst thanking he forgets that //.
dankens-wert (‿‿⌣) a. ㊺ worthy of thanks or of acknowledgment.
dank-erfüllt (‿...) a. ㊺ filled with (or full of) gratitude.
Dankes-kirche (‿⌣...) f ㊷ votive (or thanksgiving) church; =tafel f votive tablet; =worte n/pl. words of gratitude.
Dank-fest (‿...) n ㊷ thanksgiving (day); =gebet n prayer of thanks, thanksgiving; =gefühl n feeling of thankfulness; =gottesdienst m thanksgiving service; =lied n hymn (or song) of thanksgiving; 2los a. thankless; =opfer n thank-offering; =predigt f thanksgiving sermon; =psalm m psalm of praise or thanksgiving; =rede f grateful words pl., speech expressing thanks; =sage f = sagung.
danksag/en (‿⌣‿) I v/a. ㊸** ich sage Dank I express my thanks, s. Dank 3. — II v/n. (h.) ㊸*.* bibl. du danksagest thou thankest. — III ~ n ㉓ = Dtung 1.
Danksagung (‿...) f ㊶ **1.** expressing one's thanks, returning thanks, grateful acknowledgment. — **2.** = Dank 3; e-n mit ~en (schönen Worten) bezahlen to repay a p. with fine words. — ~s-schreiben n = Dankbrief; ~s-tag m = Dankfest.
Dank-tag (‿...) m ㊷ = =fest; 2vergessen a. ㊺ ungrateful.
dann (‿) [ahd.: then] adv. **1.** (in einer darauf folgenden Zeit) then; (nachher) after that, afterwards, thereupon; (in dem Falle) in that case; wie 2?, und (was) 2? how then?, and what next?; selbst

Signs (see page XVII): F familiar; P vulgar; F flash; ⟍ rare; † obsolete (died); * new word (born); ⥉ incorrect; ♪ music;

[dannen] — 247 — [darauflegen]

⟳, wenn es wahr wäre even suppose it to be true. — 2. (außerdem) besides, moreover; ⟳ läßt sich noch sagen it may further be said. — 3. ⟳ und wann, zeitlich: now and then; räumlich: at intervals; (nach Laune) by fits and starts; ⟳ und ⟳ (zu der u. der Zeit) at such and such a time. — 4. ✠, oft in Fragen = denn.

dannen (⟨⟩) adv. 1. von ⟳ (von da fort) (from) thence, from there; von ⟳ geh(e)n, ziehen to go away, to be off, to start (or on a journey); er ritt von ⟳ he left (or started) on horseback. — 2. bibl. von ⟳ (wo) er wiederkommen wird from thence he shall come again.

dantesk (⟨⟩), **dantisch** (⟨⟩) [Dante Alighieri, it. D. 1265—1321] a. ⟳ Dantesque, Dantean, in Dante's style or manner.

Danzig ⚷ (⟨⟩) [slaw.] npr/n. ⛭a. (Handelsstadt an der Ostsee) Dan(t)zig.

Danziger (⟨⟩) I m ⓶, ~in ⓶ inhabitant of Dan(t)zig. — II a., inv. of D.; ~ Goldwasser (Likör) D. water.

dar (¹) [ahd.: there] adv. I ⟳... in Zssgn mit prp., die vokalisch anfangen, = da=... 2. — II Vorsilbe in Zssgn mit v/a., stets trennbar (**) bz. ein überreichen, Vorlegen, zB. ⟳geben to present.

dar-an (⟨-⟩, die Sache betonend: ⟨-⟩) I adv. F **dran** (⟨⟩) 1. thereat, at it, at that; near (or by, on) it or that; ⟳ erkennst du ihn thereby (or by that) you may know him; der Knopf ist schon ⟳ ... is already on it; ein neues Kleid mit Bändern ⟳ ... with bows (fastened) to it; ein Hut und ein Band ⟳ with a ribbon round it; ein Hemd, aber kein Kragen ⟳ ... without a collar to it; es fehlen fünf Mark ⟳ (an dem Gelde) it was five shillings short of the amount; er nimmt keinen Anstoß ⟳ he takes no offence at it; er ist nicht schuld ⟳ it is not his fault; F he is not to blame for it; ich zweifle nicht ⟳, daß er gewinnen wird I have no doubt (about it) that he will win, F I don't doubt but what he'll win. — 2. mit folgender Ergänzung, oft nicht zu übersetzen: ich habe nie ⟳ gedacht, ihn zu beleidigen I never meant to offend him. — 3. in Verbindung mit andern adverbs: **drauf und dran** on the point of doing a th.; wenn es drauf und dran kommt when(ever) it (really) comes to pass; (wenn es gilt) when it comes to the point (F to the pull); es war drauf und dran, daß sie abgereist wäre she was on the point of leaving; ⚔ drauf und dran! (auf den Feind!) advance to the attack!, at them!, on then!, F give it them!, go it!; F alles was **drum und dran** ist (oder hängt) everything connected with it; F the whole lot or shoot; **nahe ⟳** close by; sie waren nahe ⟳ zu weichen ... just on the point of yielding or F just about to yield; **neben ⟳** next door, adjoining; **hinten (unten, oben) dran** behind (below, above) it. — II ~ n, inv. 4. s. darum 8. — III in Verbindung mit s.. v. (immer trennbar**) u. a.: 5. ~**gabe**(⟨...⟩) f ⓶ earnest-money; s. a. Aufgeld. ⟳**geben** (⟨⟩) v/a. ⛭c** to give up or over; er wird ⟳ müssen ... have to abandon

it; ⟳**geh(e)n** (⟨⟩) v/n. (ſn) ⛭** to set to (work), F to fall to; =**geld** (⟨⟩) n ⓶ =**gabe**; ⟳ **glauben** (⟨⟩) to believe in it; er hat ⟳ glauben (sterben) müssen he had to yield, he succumbed, he perished; er wird ⟳ glauben müssen he is doomed or lost; sich **halten** (⟨⟩) v/refl. ⛭a** to keep (F to stick) to one's work, &c.; (⟨⟩): du mußt dich ⟳ (an die Abmachung) halten you must abide by it; ⟳**kommen** (⟨⟩) v/n. (ſn) ⛭** to come to it; jetzt komme ich daran (an die Reihe) now it is my turn (Kricket: it's my innings); jeden ⟳ lassen to give each (one) his turn; ⟳ **liegen** (⟨⟩) to import, to signify; was liegt mir ⟳? what does it matter to me?; es liegt mir viel (wenig, nichts) ⟳ it is of great (little, no) consequence to me; es lag uns (sehr) ⟳ zu // we deemed it (most) important to //; ⟳**liegend** (⟨⟩) a. ⛭** adjacent; sich **machen** (⟨⟩) v/refl. ⛭** = ⟳**gehen**; ⟳**müssen** (⟨⟩) v/n. (h.) ⛭** er muß ⟳ he must take his turn or submit to it; er muß schwer (a. tüchtig) ⟳ he has to work hard, F he is kept well (or hard) to it; ⟳**nehmen** (⟨⟩) v/a. ⛭a** to take in hand or to task; ⟳**sein** (⟨⟩) v/n. (ſn) ⛭a**: a) ⟳ (an der Reihe) sein to take one's turn; Kricketspiel 2c.: to have one's innings; wer ist ⟳? whose turn is it?; die Partei, die ⟳ ist beim Kricketspiel 2c.: the ins pl.; b) es ist etwas (Wahres) ⟳ there is s.th. (or some truth) in it; es ist nichts (Gutes) ⟳ it is worthless; c) er ist gut (übel) ⟳ he is well (badly) off, he is in good (poor) circumstances; wie ist er mit Kleidern ⟳? how is his stock of (F how is he off for) clothes?; wie bist du mit ihm ⟳? how do you get on (or on what terms are you) with him?; man weiß nicht, wie (ob. wo) man mit ihm ⟳ ist ... what to make of him; d) ⟳ ⟳ (im Begriffe) sein zu // to be ready to //; wir sind eifrig ⟳ zu säen we are very busy sowing; er war (nahe) ⟳ zu // he was just going to //; ⟳**setzen** (⟨⟩) v/a. ⛭** to venture; sein Leben (alles) ⟳ to stake (or hazard, risk) one's life (all); ⟳ **stoßen** (⟨⟩) to knock against a th.; ⟳**stoßend** (⟨⟩) a. adjoining; ⟳ **tun** (⟨⟩): er hat gut ⟳ getan he acted wisely (in doing it); du würdest wohl ⟳ tun zu schreiben it would be well for you to write; er würde besser ⟳ tun nachzugeben it would be better for him to yield, he had better give in; ⟳**wachsend** ⚘ (⟨⟩) a. ⚙ adnascent; ⟳**wollen** (⟨⟩) v/n. (h.) ⛭**: er will nicht (gern) ⟳ he has no wish (or mind) to do it, F he fights shy of it.

dar-auf (⟨-⟩, die Sache betonend: ⟨-⟩), F **drauf** (⟨⟩) adv. I räumlich: 1. (up)on it (or that); there(up)on; hier ist ein Stuhl, setz' dich ⟳! ... sit down on it!; ein Helm und ein (oder mit einem) Federbusch ⟳ a helmet with a crest on it; eine Kirche, aber kein Turm ⟳ a church but no (or without a) steeple to it; stolz ⟳ sein to be proud of it; er ist darauf versessen he is mad(ly bent) on it. — 2. mit anderen adverbs:

drauf und dran s. daran 3; frisch ⟳! (auch drauf!) at it (or at them) with a will!, on! on! gerade ⟳ zu straight up to it; ⟳ **hin**, ⟳ **los**, ⟳ **zu** (gehen to go) straight for (or towards) it; (wacker) ⟳ hin (oder los) arbeiten to work away at it, F to set to like mad; ⟳ wollte ich **hinaus** that's what I was aiming at. — II zeitlich: 3. after it or that, afterwards; das Jahr ⟳ the next (or following) year; ein Jahr ⟳ the year after (that); den Tag ⟳ the day after, on the morrow (of that day). — 4. mit andern adverbs: **drauf und drauf** (immerfort) for ever; **bald ⟳** soon after (that), a little later; **gleich ⟳** directly after(wards). — III allgemein bestimmend und hinweisend: 5. er beharrt ⟳, daß // he adheres to his statement that //; ⟳**hin** mied er uns in consequence of that he shunned us. — 6. oft nicht zu übersetzen, bsd. mit folgender Ergänzung: ich lege kein Gewicht ⟳, daß er ein Fremder ist I lay no stress on his being a stranger; ich wollte ⟳ schwören, daß er der Schuldige ist I could swear to his being the culprit; Sie dürfen ⟳ rechnen, daß er kommen werde you may rely (or depend) on my coming. — IV in Verbindung mit s., v. (immer trennbar**) a. u. adv. 7. ⟳ **ankommen** (⟨-⟩) to be of consequence; ⟳ soll es mir nicht ankommen I shall not mind that; ⟳ kommt alles an all depends on that; ⟳ **ausgeh(e)n**, ⟳ **aussein** (⟨-⟩) to aim at a th., vgl. ausgehen 10; ich kann mich nicht ⟳ **besinnen** (⟨-⟩) I cannot (re)call it to mind or remember it; ⟳ **besteh(e)n** (⟨-⟩) to insist upon it; ⟳ **dringen** (⟨-⟩) to insist upon it; sich ⟳ **einlassen** (⟨-⟩) to venture upon a th.; er will sich nicht ⟳ einlassen he won't have anything to do with it; ⟳ **fallen** (⟨-⟩): fig. ⟳ wird niemand (ver)fallen that (idea) won't strike anybody; ⟳**folgend** (⟨-⟩) a. ensuing; ~**gabe** (⟨⟩) f ⓶ earnestmoney, s. a. Aufgeld; (Handgeld) ⟳**geben** a) (⟨⟩) v/a. ⛭c** to pay earnest-money (or a deposit) on a th.; b) ⟳ **geben** (⟨-⟩) ich gebe nichts (nicht viel) ⟳ I attach no (great) importance to it; ⟳ **gefaßt** (⟨-⟩) sein to be prepared for it; ⟳**geh(e)n** (⟨⟩) v/n. (ſn) ⛭** to be lost or consumed; es geht viel Zeit ⟳ it takes (or wastes) much time; es sind viele Menschen ⟳**gegangen** ... have perished or died; er läßt viel Geld ⟳**gehen** he spends (or lavishes) ...; =**geld** (⟨⟩) n deposit, vgl. =gabe; ⟳ **halten** (⟨-⟩) to lay stress upon it; er hält viel ⟳ he thinks highly (or a great deal) of it; er hält sehr ⟳, daß // he is very particular that //; e-m ⟳**helfen** (⟨⟩) v/n. (h.) ⛭b** to help a p. to remember a th.; ⟳**hin** (⟨⟩) adv. thereupon, on the strength of it, vgl. darauf 2 u. 5; ⟳ **kommen** (⟨-⟩) to hit upon an idea; wie sind Sie ⟳ gekommen? how came you to think of it?; ⟳**legen** (⟨⟩) v/a. ⛭** to lay (or put) on (the top of) it; fig. u. ⚙ to superpose; ⟳(steigen

⟲ scientific; ⚘ botanical; ⚷ geography; ⛭ machinery; ⚔ mining; ⚔ military; ⚓ marine; ⛭ commercial; ✉ postal; 🚂 railway.

[daraus] — 248 — [Darrling]

ꝛc.)=müssen (⸗⸗⸗) v/n. (h.) ⬚** to be compelled to mount it; ⸗schlagen (⸗⸗⸗) v/n. (h.) ⬚b** to add to it; ⸗setzen (⸗⸗⸗) v/a. u. v/refl. sich ⸗setzen to sit down (or seat o. s.) on it; ⬚** to put (or seat) on it; ⸗sollen (⸗⸗⸗) v/n. (h.) ⬚** to be obliged to mount it; ⸗steh(e)n (⸗⸗⸗) v/n. ⬚** a) (h. u. sn) to stand on it; b) (⸗⸗⸗) (h.) es steht Todesstrafe ⸗ it is a capital offence or it is a hanging matter; Sie können sich (fest) ⸗ verlassen (⸗⸗⸗), daß // you may (safely) rely (or depend) upon it that //; ⸗ warten (⸗⸗⸗) to wait for a th.; ⸗ wetten (⸗⸗⸗), daß // to (lay a) wager that //.

dar-aus (⸗⸗, die Sache betonend: ⸗⸗), F **draus** (⸗) adv. therefrom, from there; (from) thence; die Bibel od. e-e Stelle ⸗ ... a passage taken from it; es folgt ⸗, daß // hence it follows that //; ⸗ wird nichts nothing will come of it; it cannot be done, it is unfeasible; was ist ⸗ geworden? what has become of it?; was wird (schließlich) ⸗ werden? what will be the result (or end) of it?; es mag ⸗ werden, was da will come (of it) what may; ich mache mir nichts (oder wenig) ⸗ I care (or trouble) little about it, I don't mind (it); ich mache mir nichts ⸗, ob // it does not (much) matter to me whether //; ich kann nicht klug ⸗ werden I cannot make it out, F I can't make head or tail of it.

darben (⸗⸗) [ahd.] I v/n. (h.) ⬚ to suffer (great) want; stärker: to starve; ⸗ I. to (let) starve; freiwillig ⸗ to submit to (or suffer) voluntary privation, to pinch o.s. — II ~ n ⬚ want; starvation; privation; destitution.

dar-bieten (⸗⸗⸗) I v/a. (u. sich ⸗ v/refl.) ⬚a** to offer or present (o.s.); es bieten sich Schwierigkeiten dar there are difficulties (or obstacles) in the way; sollte sich eine Gelegenheit ⸗ should an opportunity present itself, should an occasion arise. — II **Dar-bietung** f ⬚ (Vortrag u. Spiel an einem Festabend) recitation, recital; weitS. entertainment, performance.

dar-bring/en (⸗⸗⸗) I v/a. ⬚** to present; als Opfer: to offer (up), to sacrifice; huldigend ⸗ to pay one's homage to. — II ~ n ⬚ = D/ung. **Dar-bringer** m ⬚, ~in f ⬚ p. who presents, offers, &c. (s. dar-bringen). [offering, sacrifice.] **Dar-bringung** f ⬚ presentation;

Darbysten (⸗⸗⸗) m/pl. ⬚ rel. Brüdergemeinde; Plymouth Brethren pl.

Dardanellen (⸗⸗⸗) npr/pl. ⬚, a.: ~=straße (⸗⸗) f ⬚ the Dardanelles pl.; chm. the Hellespont. [Darjeeling.]

Darbschiling (⸗⸗⸗) npr n. ⬚. Ost-J.]

dar-ein (⸗⸗, die Sache betonend: ⸗⸗), F **drein** (⸗) adv. 1. therein(to), in(to) it or that; obendrein into the bargain. — 2. in Verbindung mit verbs, z.B.: ⸗blicken (⸗⸗⸗), ⸗schauen; sich ⸗ (er)geben (⸗⸗⸗⸗) (od. finden, fügen, schicken) to submit to it, to acquiesce in it; ich kann nicht

nicht ⸗ finden I cannot get reconciled to it; ⸗fahren (⸗⸗⸗) v/n. (sn) ⬚b** to interfere (or talk) roughly, (oben) ⸗geben (⸗⸗⸗) v/a. ⬚c** to give into the bargain; die Handschuhe sollen (mit) ⸗geh(e)n (⸗⸗⸗) v/n. (sn) ⬚** the gloves shall go with it or be included; sich ⸗legen (⸗⸗⸗) od. ⸗mengen ⬚**, ⸗mischen (⸗⸗⸗) ⬚** v/refl. vermittelnd: to mediate, intervene, interpose; eingreifend: to interfere (or meddle) with (other) people's affairs; F to put in one's spoke; ⸗mischung f ⬚ s. Einmischung; ⸗reden (⸗⸗⸗) v/n. (h.) ⬚** to put in a word; to interrupt a p.'s speech; er hat nichts ⸗zureden he has nothing to (F he has no) say in the matter; ⸗schauen ⬚** od. ⸗sehen ⬚a** (⸗⸗⸗) v/n. (h.) to look (on); die Ritter schauten mutig drein (G.) the knights put on a defiant look; ⸗schlagen (⸗⸗⸗) v/n. (h.) ⬚b** to strike out (in all directions), to lay about one; ⸗sprechen (⸗⸗⸗) v/n. (h.) ⬚a** = ⸗reden; ⸗willigen (⸗⸗⸗) to consent to a th.

Darg (⸗) [fries.] m ⬚b. (Moorboden unterm Klei) marshy soil below the clay; (Torf) peat.

Dari ? (⸗⸗) [türk.] n ⬚ = Durra.

dar-in (⸗⸗, die Sache betonend: ⸗⸗), F **drin** (⸗) adv. 1. therein, in it or that; within; ein Käfig und zwei Vögel ⸗ a cage with two birds in(side) it; ein Beutel und kein Geld ⸗ a purse without any money (in it); was ist ⸗? what is inside (it)?; ⸗ (⸗⸗) irren Sie sich there you are mistaken; es liegt et. Schönes ⸗, daß // there is s.th beautiful in the fact (or the thought) that //; mit ⸗ begriffen included with (or in) it. — 2. bei folgender Ergänzung oft nicht zu übersetzen: er sucht etwas (od. seine Freude) ⸗, andern zu helfen he takes a delight in assisting others; die Weisheit des Sokrates bestand ⸗, daß er seine Fehler eingestand the wisdom of Socrates consisted in his acknowledging his faults.

dar-innen (⸗⸗⸗) adv. within, inside (it); bibl. u. poet. a. bezüglich: das Land, ⸗ sie wohnen the land wherein they dwell.

dar-legen (⸗⸗⸗) I v/a. ⬚** to display, show, exhibit; to lay open; fig. (auseinandersetzen) to expose, explain, expound, interpret; offen ⸗ to set forth; Punkt für Punkt, umständlich ⸗ to particularize, to (state in) detail. — II ~ n ⬚ = Darlegung.

Dar-leger (⸗⸗⸗) m ⬚, ~in f ⬚ person who displays, &c. (s. darlegen), exhibitor; fig. expositor, interpreter.

Dar-legung (⸗⸗⸗) f ⬚ display, exposition, explanation, (detailed) statement; durch ~ aller Umstände by going into full details or particulars.

Darleh(e)n (⸗⸗) n ⬚ (⬚c.) loan; e-m ein ~ geben oder machen to grant a p. a loan, to advance (or lend) a p. money, to make an advance (or to lend money) to a p.; ~=gesellschaft f, ~=kasse f, ~=(kassen)verein m (⸗) ⬚ (mutual) loan-society.

dar-leih/en (⸗⸗⸗) I v/a. ⬚** to lend (out); Geld a. to advance. — II ~ n ⬚ = D/ung.

Dar-leiher (⸗⸗⸗) m ⬚, ~in f ⬚ (money-)lender, one who advances (money, &c.)

Dar-leihung (⸗⸗) f ⬚ lending, advance.

Darm (⸗) [ahd.] m ⬚b. 1. anat. intestine, intestinal canal, F gut; der große od. dicke (der dünne) ~ the large (the small) intestine, (Mast-)~: ⬚ rectum; Därme pl. auch: bowels pl.; die Därme betr. intestinal, enteric. — 2. (Wursthülle) skin of a sausage.

Darm-ausleerung (⬚...) f ⬚ physiol. relief (of the bowels); stool, motion; ⬚ defecation, (alvine) evacuation; ⸗bein n, anat.: ⬚ ilium; ⸗bein-muskel m: ⬚ iliac muscle; ⸗beschreibung f, anat.: ⬚ enterography; ⸗bewegung f, beim Verdauen: peristaltic motion; ⸗blutung f intestinal hemorrhage, ⬚ enterohemorrhage; ⸗bruch m, surg. rupture of the intestines, intestinal hernia, ⬚ enterocele.

Därmchen (⸗⸗) n (dim. v. Darm) small intestine or gut.

Darm-drüse (⬚...) f ⬚ anat.: intestinal gland; ⸗entzündung f inflammation of the bowels, ⬚ enteritis; ⸗fell n Bauch-f.: ⸗fistel f, path. intestinal fistula; ⸗geschwür n, path. ulcer in the bowels; ⸗gicht, ⸗grimmen n colic; ⸗krebs m, path. intestinal cancer; ⸗krankheit f, ⸗leiden n intestinal complaint; ⸗lähmung f, path. paralysis of the bowels; ⸗netz n, anat.: ⬚ epiploon, omentum; ⸗saite f bsd. ♪catgut, (gut-)string; ⸗saiten-macher m gut-spinner; ⸗schnitt m, surg.: ⬚ enterotomy; ⸗schwindsucht f, path. consumption of the bowels, ⬚ tabes of the intestines; ⸗stein m: ⬚ enterolith, coprolith; ⸗verschlingung f twisting of the bowels; ⸗verschluß m intestinal obstruction, constipation; ⸗wurm m = Spul-w.; ⸗zotte f (meist pl.) anat.: ⬚ villus, pl. villi; ⸗zwang m: ⬚ tenesmus = Stuhl-z. ☛ **dar-nach** (⸗⸗u. ⸗⸗), **dar-neben** (⸗⸗⸗), **dar-nieder** (⸗⸗⸗) adv. = da-nach ꝛc.

darob (⸗⸗), F **drob** (⸗) adv. on that account, because of that, for that reason.

Darr-arbeit (⬚...) f ⬚ drying operations pl.; ⸗boden m = ⸗kammer.

Darre (⸗⸗) [ahd.: dürr, dörren] f ⬚ 1. ⬚ Brauerei: a) kiln-drying; b) = Darrhaus od. ⸗kammer. — 2. path. von Vögeln: pip, roup; bisw. ? (Ausdorren) withering of plants or trees.

dar-reich/en (⸗⸗⸗) I v/a. ⬚** to present, hand, tender, offer, hold forth; med. Arznei, eccl. das Sakrament ⸗ to administer ... — II ~ n ⬚ u. **Dar-reichung** f ⬚ presentation; med., eccl. administration of medicine, of the sacrament.

darren ⬚ (⸗⸗) [Darre] I v/a. ⬚ 1. (trocknen) to dry; Brauerei: to kiln-dry (malt). — 2. metall. Kupfer ⸗ (seigern) to liquate (or smelt) copper. — II ~ n ⬚ 3. Brauerei: kiln-drying; metall. liquation.

Darr-fieber (⬚...) n ⬚ path. hectic fever; ⸗gekrätz(e) ⬚ n. metall. dross of copper, washing-slag; ⸗haus n dry(ing-)house, kiln-house; ⸗kammer f drying-room, -kiln.

Darrling (⸗⸗) [darren 2] m ⬚d. metall. (gedarrtes Kupfer) copper reduced (or refined) by liquation.

Zeichen (s. S. XVII): F familiär; P Volkssprache; ⚡ Gaunersprache; ~ selten; † alt (auch gestorben); * neu (auch geboren); ++ unrichtig;

[Darrmalz] — 249 — [das]

Darr-malz (⁵...) n ⓬ kiln-dried malt; **-ofen** m (drying-)kiln; ☉ **metall.** (Seiger-ofen) liquation-hearth or -furnace; **-staub** m malt-dust; **-stube** f = -kammer; **-sucht** f, path. tubercular disease of the mesenteric glands; **-süchtig** a. ⓺ consumptive, ⚓ atrophic. [floating wet dock.)

Darsena ⚓ (⌣⌣⌣) [it.; *ar. Werft] f ⓭

dar-stellbar (⌣⌣-) a. ⓺ fit for representation or delineation, representable; thea. actable, fit to be acted, fit (or suitable) for the stage.

dar-stellen (⌣⌣⌣) I v/a. u. sich ⌣ v/refl. ⓺** 1. (vor die Augen führen) to present (o.s.); (vorzeigen) to show, produce, exhibit; sich ⌣ als (mit nom. od. acc.) to appear as; sich gut ⌣ (erweisen) to prove good, to show o.s. good; abs. das stellt sich (jedem von selbst) dar that's self-evident or obvious. — 2. chm. ein Meta'll ⌣: a) to find out a (new) metal; b) to prepare (or produce) a metal. — 3. (ver-anschaulichen, bsd. durch die Kunst) to represent, sketch, delineate; durch Gebärden: to mimic; falsch ⌣ to misrepresent; (schildern) to describe, to depict; er stellt es anders dar he gives a different account of it, he puts a different complexion on it; thea. to perform (or act) a piece or a part, to personate (or take, support) a character. — 4. weitS., allg. (bilden, sein) to form, to be. — II ⌣d p.pr. u. a. ⓺ 5. in den Bed. des inf. — 6. etwas ⌣d representative of s.th.; ⌣de Geometrie descriptive geometry; ⌣de Künste a) (bildende Künste) pictorial (or graphic) arts; b) (Schauspielkunst) dramatic (or mimic) art.

Dar-steller (⌣⌣⌣) m ⓶, **~in** f ⓭ 1. p. who presents, &c. (s. darstellen I); exhibitor. — 2. thea. performer, actor (actress f), player, a. mime.

Dar-stellung (⌣⌣⌣) f ⓺ 1. presentation, exhibition, &c. (s. darstellen 1). — 2. chm. preparation, production. — 3. durch die Kunst ⁊c.: representation, delineation; description; thea. performance of a play; personation of a character. — 4. jur.: ~ des Tatbestandes full statement of the facts; ~ der Zeugen production of witnesses.

Darstellungs-art (⌣⌣⌣...) f ⓬ manner (or style) of representation; chm. preparation; **-gabe** f, **-kraft** f descriptive (or graphic) gift or power or talent, des Schauspielers: mimic art; **-kunst** f descriptive art; vgl. Darstellung 3; **-talent** n = -gabe; **-weise** f = -art.

dar-strecken (⌣⌣⌣) v/a. ⓺** 1. = dar-reichen. — 2. = darleihen.

dar-tun (⌣⌣) I v/a. ⓺** (erweisen) to prove, to substantiate; to make good (a statement); anschaulich ⌣ to demonstrate, to show clearly. — II ~ n ⓴ und **Dar-tu-ung** f ⓺ proof, substantiation; demonstration.

dar-über (⌣⌣⌣, die Sache betonend: ⌣⌣⌣), F **drüber** (⌣⌣) adv. I Raum: 1. over that or it; eine Tür und ein Schild ⌣ ... with a signboard over (or above) it; es ist keine Brücke ⌣ gebaut, keine Brücke führt ⌣ no bridge is built across it, leads across it; er fuhr mit dem Nachen ⌣ he crossed it in a boat; als sie den Wagen sahen, fielen sie ⌣ her ... they fell upon it; er machte sich eiligst ⌣ (her) he set to work quickly; er ist ⌣ (an der Arbeit) he is (now) doing it or at it; eine Halle mit einem Glasdach ⌣ ... surmounted by a glass-roof. — 2. mit andern adv.: ⌣ **hin** (fahren to glide) along it; ⌣ **hin-aus**, ⌣ **hinweg** beyond (or past) it; er ist ⌣ (über Kleinigkeiten) weit hinaus he is far above that; wir sind ⌣ (über die Schwierigkeit) hinweg we have got over it, we are (safely) out of it; **drunter und drüber** (all) upside-down, topsy-turvy, es geht bei ihnen alles drunter und drüber they are at sixes and sevens; alles drunter und drüber geh(e)n lassen to let things go anyhow. — II Zeit: 3. during that time; es unterblieb, weil er ⌣ starb ... he died (in the) meanwhile or in the attempt; ⌣ (⌣⌣⌣) werden Jahre hingehen years will elapse before that, it will take years. — III Grund: 4. on that account; er ist ⌣ zugrunde gegangen he was ruined by it; ich freue mich ⌣ I am glad to hear it; ich (⌣⌣) lasse ich mir kein graues Haar wachsen that doesn't trouble me in the least; ⌣ längs Gras gewachsen that is an old forgotten story. — IV Hinweisung: 5. alles was ich ⌣ (über das Erwähnte) weiß all that I know about it. — 6. bei folgendem Zusatz oft nicht übersetzt: er beklagt sich ⌣, daß er bestohlen worden sei he complains of having been robbed. — V Überschuß, Vorzug: 7. es ist ein Viertel ⌣ it is a quarter past (the hour); es waren 2 Pfund ⌣ there were two pounds over or more; nicht ⌣ oder darunter, nicht drüber noch drunter neither more nor less; das geht noch ⌣ that tops (or beats) it. — 8. ⌣ geht nichts there is nothing like (or to beat) it; es ging ihm nichts ⌣ (G.) he prized (or cherished) it above everything; ich setze dies noch ⌣ I prefer this to it. — VI in Verbindung mit verbs immer trennbar (**), z.B. ⌣-**liegen** (⌣⌣⌣...) v/n. (h.) ⓺** to lie on top of it; ⌣-**setzen** v a. ⓺** to put (or set) above (or over) it or atop of it, fig. u. ⚓ to superpose.

darum (⌣⌣, die Sache betonend: ⌣⌣) I adv., F **drum** (⌣) 1. ⌣ (herum) (a)round it or that; ich band ein Seil ⌣ I tied a rope round it; das Schloß und die Dörfer ⌣ the castle and the villages around it or the surrounding villages; fig. es hängt viel **drum und dran** there is a good deal connected with it, much depends on it; s. dar-an 3. — 2. about it or that; er hat sich (sehr) ⌣ bemüht he tried (hard) for it; ich bat ihn inständigst ⌣ I implored him to do it; niemand kümmert sich ⌣ ... troubles about it; es sei ⌣! then let it be so!; es steht schlecht ⌣, etwa: it's (or things are) in a bad way; es ist mir ⌣ zu tun, ihn zu beschämen it is my object to ..., I desire to ... —

3. bei folgender Ergänzung oft nicht übersetzt: es handelt sich ⌣ zu wissen, ob // the point is to know whether // — 4. ⌣ (⌣⌣), auch cj. (deshalb) for that (reason), therefore; ⌣ hat er es getan that's what he has done it for, that's why he did it; ⌣ eben sollst du hingehen that's just (the reason) why you should go there, for that very reason you are to go; ⌣ **daß**, ⌣ **weil** because. — 5. (trotzdem) er ist nicht klüger geworden he has grown no wiser for (all) that. — II ~ n ⓴ 6. (Grund) ich habe mehr als ein ⌣ I have more than one reason (for it). — 7. das ganze ~ (-s) und Dara'n everything connected with it, all the surroundings pl. — III in Verbindung mit verbs, meist Verlust anzeigend: ⌣-**bringen** (-⌣⌣⌣) v/a. ⓺** to deprive of a th.; man hat mich ⌣ gebracht I have been robbed of it; ⌣-**kommen** (-⌣⌣) v/n. (sn) ⓺** to lose a th.

dar-unter (-⌣, die Sache betonend: ⌣⌣), F **drunter** (⌣⌣) I adv. 1. thereunder, under(neath) it or that, beneath it or that; (there) below; ein Brett ⌣ legen to put ... underneath (it); lassen Sie Ihren Namen ⌣ (unter den Brief) put your signature to it; ⌣ hervor from underneath; fig. ⌣ steckt et. there is s.th. at the bottom of it, there is some mystery about it. — 2. **drunter und drüber** s. darüber 2. — 3. (weniger) 60 Mark und ⌣ three pounds (£3) and less; von zwei Jahren und ⌣ two years old and under; ⌣ ich kann es nicht ⌣ (billiger) geben I cannot let it go cheaper or for less; ⌣ tun sie es nicht they won't do it for less or go below that. — 4. (unter der Zahl) es sind viele ⌣ there are many among them; mitten ⌣ in the midst of them; er gehört (mit) ⌣ (unter sie) he belongs to them or is one of them; ich finde keinen Unterschied ⌣ (dazwischen) ... no difference between them. — 5. (dadurch) thereby; er leidet ⌣ he suffers under (or through) it; was versteht er ⌣? what does he mean by it? — II in Verbindung mit verbs immer trennbar (**): sich ⌣-**mischen** (-⌣⌣⌣) v/a. und v/refl. ⓺** to mix with them, to go among them; ⌣-**setzen** v/a. ⓺** to put underneath; ⌣-**steh(e)n** v/n. (h.) ⓺** to stand below or beneath.

Darwinismus ⚓ (⌣⌣⌣) [Charles Robert Darwin, englischer Naturforscher, 1809—82] m ⓴ Darwinism.

Darwinist (⌣⌣⌣) m ⓬, **darwinistisch** (⌣⌣⌣) a. ⓺ Darwinist.

dar-zählen ⚓ (⌣⌣⌣) v/a. ⓺** to count down, to enumerate. [show, display.)

dar-zeigen ⚓ (⌣⌣⌣) v/a. ⓺** to exhibit.)

☞ **dar-zu** f. dazu.

das (⁵, Hom. daß) [ahd.: that] neuter von der in allen Bedeutungen. I definite art. ① 1. (F u. poet. abbr. 's) ⌣ Buch the book. — II dem. pron. ⓺ A 2 b. 2. that; das, was er sagt what he says; statt dessen instead of that; ⌣ ist es that's what it is, that is it; alles ⌣, was ich geschrieben habe all that I have written; ⌣ heißt (abbr. **d.h.**) that means, that is to say (abbr. i.e. — it.

[dasein] — 250 — [dauern]

id est); 2 heißt doch noch arbeiten that's what I call working; 2 ist (abbr. d. i.) 2 sind it (or that) is, they (or those) are; 2 sind mir schöne Geschichten! fine doings, these!, those are pretty goings-on!; 2 wären zwei (nette Kerle)! two fine birds!; 2 wäre! oder 2 muß wahr sein! you don't mean it!; wenn dem so ist if it (really) be the case, if such be the fact or the state of affairs. — 3. als Ersatz e-s vorhergehenden inf. od. part.: er hat studiert, 2 hast du nicht ... which you have not; er ward bestraft, und 2 (und zwar) von Rechts wegen ... and that was as it should be. — 4. als Ersatz des Prädikats, oft nicht zu übersetzen: er ist reich, 2 bin ich nicht he is rich, I am not. — 5. Bezeichnung des Subjekts in Neunsätzen mit s. ob. pron. als Prädikat: 2 war ein Neger, 2 waren Chinesen it (or that, he) was a negro, they were Chinese; 2 waren herrliche Zeiten! those were glorious times!; 2 bin ich it is (F it's me); 2 sind Sie it is you; 2 schienen Weiber (zu sein) they appeared to be women; mit Auslassung von ist, sind: schändlicher Mensch 2! what an infamous fellow! — F von Personen, zi.-fassend: ich höre Kinder gern, 2 lärmt und lacht den ganzen Tag ... they shout and laugh all day; 2 denkt wie ein Seifensieder (SCH.) such people (as these) are narrow-minded. — III rel. pron., deklиniert wie II, zB. das Mädchen, dessen Bruder du kennst ... whose brother you know.
da-sein (⌣́⌣) I v/n. ⓐa** to be there, f. da¹ 7 u. 3. — II ~ n ㉓ existence; f. Kampf; ein früheres (künftiges) ~ a previous (future) life.
Da-seins-berechtigung (⌣́⌣⌣...) f ㊷ right to exist; **=kampf** m struggle for existence or for life.
da-selbst (⌣⌣́) adv. there, in that place.
dasig (⌣́⌣) [nhd. 16. sae.] (ant. hiesig) a. ⓐ unichön = dortig.
das-jenige (⌣́⌣⌣⌣) n von derjenige (f. ds).
daß (⌣́; Hom. das) [= das] I cj. 1. that; so 2 so that; nicht 2 not that; es sei denn 2 unless; ich weiß, 2 Blücher ein Held war I know (that) Blücher was a hero or B. to have been a hero, f. 2; ich hörte, 2 er krank sei I heard (that) he was ill; es tut mir leid, 2 Sie abreisen I am sorry (that) you leave. — 2. oft nicht zu übersetzen: wir glauben, 2 Homer blind war ... Homer to have been blind; der Mann, von welchem wir glauben, 2 er ihr Vater ist ... whom we believe to be her father; er entschuldigte sich, 2 er spät kam he apologized for being late; was ist ihr, 2 sie so lacht what (is it that) makes her laugh so?; ich wundere mich, 2 er nicht kommt I wonder at his not coming or (that) he has (or does) not come; im Fall, 2 er ruft in case of his calling; ich wünsche, 2 er ginge! I wish he would go! — 3. mit prp. und adv.: auf 2 in order that; bei gleichem Subjekt: in order to (mit inf.); außer 2 sie reich ist, hat sie Talent besides being rich, ...; er sagte uns nichts, außer 2 ... except that; **dadurch** 2, **dafür** 2, **daran** 2, **ohne** 2 meist durch das engl. Gerundium auszudrücken, zB.

dadurch 2 die Russen Moskau in Brand steckten owing to the Russians setting fire to Moscow; er fiel, ohne 2 ich es merkte ... without my noticing it; nur 2 nicht // provided that // — 4. er ist zu dumm, als 2 er lernen könnte he his too silly to learn; es ist leichter, 2 er es tue, als 2 ich it is easier for him (to do) than for me. — 5. in unvollständigen Sätzen: ach, 2 es (doch) wahr wäre! oh, would (or I wish) it were true!; 2 Gott erbarm'! God be merciful!, F Lord a mercy me!; 2 mir gerade das passieren muß! that such a thing should happen to me!; 2 Sie auch gar nicht hören! why do you not listen?; nicht 2 ich wüßte! not that I know of!, not as far as I know; befehlen: 2 du dich nicht rührst! don't (you) move! — II ~ n, inv. 6. ein ~ ist mehr als ein Wie a fact is (or weighs) more than a motive.
Dassel-beule (⌣́⌣...) f ㊷ swelling caused by the sting of a gadfly; **=fliege** f, ent. gadfly, breeze (= Bremse).
das-selb(ig)e (⌣⌣(⌣)⌣) I a. f. derselb(ig)e. — II s. the same thing.
da-steh(e)n (⌣́⌣) v/n. (h.) ⓐ** 1. to be there; to stand there. — 2. fig. jetzt steht er ganz anders da now he is in quite a different position; er steht in der Geschichte unerreicht da he stands forth in history unparalleled or unrivalled; einzig, schuldlos ꝛc. 2 to stand unique, blameless, &c.; einzeln, frei 2d standing alone, isolated, Haus a.: detached.
Dasymeter (⌣⌣́⌣⌣) [grch.] n (m) ㉒ (Luftdichtigkeitsmesser v. Guericke, 1650) dasymeter. [tier) dasypode, dasypodine.)
Dasypus (⌣́⌣⌣) [grch.] m ⓐ zo. (Gürtel-)
Dasyurus (⌣⌣́⌣) [grch.] m ⓐ zo. (Beutelmarder) dasyure. [schrieben.)
dat. abbr. = datum [it. gegeben, ge-)
Data, Daten (⌣́⌣) n/pl., inv. [it.] 1. pl. von Datum. — 2. (Tatsachen, Angaben, Stoff) (actual) facts, realities pl.. evidence, math., &c. (it.) data pl.
datieren (⌣⌣́⌣) [fr.] ⓐ I v/a. (das Datum beisetzen) to date; früher, später 2 to antedate, to postdate. — II (sich) 2 v/refl. und v/n. (h.) (zeitlich stammen, herrühren von) to date from; das datiert noch von der Sintflut her that dates from olden times, F it has come out of the Ark, it's as old as the hills.
Dativ(us) (⌣́⌣-f. ⌣́⌣⌣v⌣) [lt. Gebe-...] m ⓐc.⑬ gr. (3. Fall. Wemfall) dative (case); weit 2. (a. ~objekt n ㉒) indirect object formed by means of the preposition 'to'; **~endung** f dative termination or suffix.
dato ⚹ (⌣́⌣) [it. gegeben] adv. to date; bis 2 till now, up to the present; a 2 from this date (forward); per Wochen 2 ... after date. [after date.)
Dato-wechsel (⌣́⌣...) m ㉒ bill (due)
Dattel ⚹ (⌣́⌣) [nhd.; *grch. da'ktylos m Finger] f ㊸ (Frucht des Dattelbaumes) date.
Dattel-baum m (⌣́⌣...) m ㉒ date-palm or -tree (Phoenix dactyli fera); **=farben** a. ⓐ date-coloured, ⚹ spadiceous; **=hain** m = **=wald**; **=fern** m = date-stone, kernel of the date; **=muschel** f. zo. stone-borer (Pholas da'ctylus); **=palme** ⚹ f = **=baum**; **=pflaume** (n=baum) f = date-

plum, persimmon (Diospy'ros lotus); **=wald** m grove (or forest) of date-palms; **=wein** m date-wine.
Datum (⌣́⌣) [mhd.; *lt. Gegebenes] n ㉘ u. ⓑ 1. (Angabe von Zeit u. Ort) date; ohne ~ without date, not dated; ein Brief von dem und dem ~ a letter of such and such a date; von welchem ~ ist der Brief? of what date is ...?, how is ... dated? — 2. (Monatstag) was für ein ~ ist (es ob. haben wir) heute? what day of the month is it? — 3. pl. Daten (f. ds).
Datum-anzeiger (⌣́⌣...) m ㉒ date-box; **=eier** n/pl. (fowls') eggs pl. bearing the date on which they were laid; **2los** a. ⓐ dateless, undated; **=stempel** m date-stamp; **=(s)uhr** f clock (or watch) showing the date.
Datura ⚹ (⌣⌣́⌣) [ar., *pers., ssft.] f ㊾ = Stech-apfel. [(ar.,*pers.,sft.] daturine.)
Daturin ⚹ (⌣⌣́⌣) n ⓐc. chm. (Alkaloid des)
Daturin=säure (⌣⌣́...) f ㊷ daturic acid.
Dau ↓ (⌣́) [ar., *ind. m Fahrt] f ㊻ Schiffsart: dhow.
Daube ⊕ (⌣́⌣) [fr. douve; mlt. doga; *grch. dōchē] f ㊾ Böttcherei: stave; die ~n eines Fasses einschlagen to stave in a cask. [staves pl.)
Dauben-holz (⌣́⌣...) n ㉒ staff-wood;
☞ **däuchten** (⌣́⌣) f. deuchten.
Dauer (⌣́⌣) [dauern¹] f ㊽ (o. pl.) 1. (Zeitraum) duration, length of time; immerwährende, ununterbrochene ~ continuity, perpetuity; ein Vertrag von zehnjähriger ~ ... for a term of ten years; von kurzer ~ of short duration; von lang(jährig)er ~ of long standing, lasting many years, long-lived. — 2. abs. (lange Zeit) auf (auch für) die ~ for a permanency, permanent(ly); das kann ich auf die ~ nicht ertragen I cannot stand it for any length of time or for long. — 3. (Dauerhaftigkeit) von ~ sein to last well, von Stoffen u. Farben: to wear well; auf die ~ (dauerhaft) gearbeitet made to last or to wear, made for wear, solidly made.
Dauer-apfel (⌣́⌣...) m ㉒. **=birne** f winter-apple, -pear; **=brenner** ⊕ m oven (or furnace) with slow - burning fire; **=feuer** ⚔ n continuous firing; **=gewächs** ⚹ n perennial (plant); **=gänger** m walkist, indefatigable walker.
dauerhaft (⌣́⌣⌣) a. ⓐ durable, lasting; 2 gemacht substantial(ly built), solid(ly constructed); stout(ly manufactured); vgl. Dauer 3; 2e Farbe fast (or permanent) dye, colour that wears well; 2er Friede lasting peace; 2e Gesundheit robust health.
Dauerhaftigkeit (⌣́⌣⌣⌣-) f ㊻ durability, durableness, lastingness; solidity; stoutness; vgl. a. Dauer 3.
Dauer=lauf (⌣́⌣...) m, **=marsch** m etwa running-exercise or -practice.
dauern¹ (⌣́⌣) [mhd.; *lt. dura're] I v n. (h.) ⓐa. 1. (fortbestehen) to last, to continue; ewig 2 to continue for ever; Äpfel 2 bis März apples keep ...; es kann in der Hitze nicht 2 it cannot stand the heat or keep in hot weather. — 2. (vorhalten) wie lange dauert Ihnen das Holz? how long do you make the wood last?; nichts dauert ewig nothing

Signs (see page XVII): F familiar; P vulgar; 🗲 flash; ↘ rare; † obsolete (died); * new word (born); .+. incorrect; ♪ music;

[dauern] — 251 — [dazu]

is made for ever; länger 2 als to last longer than, to outlast. — 3. (währen) auch v/impers. das soll nicht lange 2 it won't be (for) long; es wird lange 2, ehe (ob. bis) die Arbeit zustande kommt it will take a long time (or while) to finish the work; es wird nicht lange 2, so kommen sie zurück they will return before long, F it won't be long before they are back; wie lange dauert es, bis Sie gebadet haben? how long will you be bathing?, how long will it take you to have a bath?; es dauert mir zu lange it is too long for my liking, I find it too tedious. Sprichw. alles dauert nur e-e gewisse Zeit everything comes to an end (at last). — II 2d p.pr. u. a. ⓖ⓴ 4. in den Bed. des inf. — 5. durable, enduring, permanent; firmly established; ein 2des Denkmal a lasting monument; das ganze Jahr 2d ⚘ perennial.

dauern² (⌣́) [mhd.: *teuer] v/a. ⓖa. 1. (bedauern) to regret, to grieve at. — 2. (rühren) to move to pity; du dauerst mich I feel (sorry) for you, I pity you; mich dauert sein Unglück I am sorry (or grieved) to hear of his misfortune. — 3. auch v/impers. sich (dat.) weder Mühe noch Geld 2 (verdrießen) lassen to grudge neither the trouble nor the money; mich dauert mein Geld nicht I do not consider (or regret) the money.

Dauer-pflanze (⌣́⌣⌣) f ⓖ₂ =gewächs; **=ritt** m ride without halt or stop, endurance ride, *= Distanzritt; **=speise** f = Konserve; **versuch** m ⚔, ⚓, ⚙ endurance test, severe trial; **=wurst** f sausage that keeps well.

Daulas † ⚙ (⌣́) [engl.] n, inv. (grobe Leinwand) dowlas(s).

Däumchen (⌣́) n ⓖ₂ dim. v. Daumen.

Daumen (⌣́) [ahd.: thumb] m ⓖ₂₃ 1. thumb (auch am Handschuh); ohne ~ thumbless. — 2. F fig. einem den ~ halten (Stütze gewähren) to support (or back up, side with) a p.; e-m den ~ aufs Auge halten (ihn bändigen) to have a p. under one's thumb, to keep an iron rod (or a tight hand) over a p. — 3. ⚙ am Hobel: handle; mach. (Hebe-)~ cam, tappet.

Daumen-ballen (⌣́...) m ⓖ₂ anat. ⚔ thenar (muscle); **=beuger** m, anat.: ⚔ flexor (muscle) of the thumb; ⓞ**breit** a. ⓖ⓴ of the width of (or as wide as) a thumb; **=breite** f thumb's width, inch; ⓞ**dick** a. (as) thick as a thumb; **=drücker** m ⚙ Schlosserei: (Türklinke mit Drücker) thumb-latch; **=klapper** f castanet; **=klopfer** m, anat. abductor (of the thumb); **=leder** m = Däumling 1; ⓞ**los** a. thumbless; **=rad** ⚙ n cam-wheel; **=ring** ⚙ m cam-ring; **=scheibe** f ⚙ thumb-plate; **=schraube** f = Daumschraube; **=schützer** m thumb-protector; ⓞ**=dick** f. ⓞ**dick**; **=strecker** m, anat. extensor (muscle) of the thumb; **=welle** f, mach. cam-shaft.

Daum-kappe f ⓖ₂ thumb-stall.

Däumling (⌣́) m ⓓ₅ 1. (Leder ꝛc. zum Schutz für den Daumen) thumb-stall; s. auch Daumenschützer. — 2. (kleine Person) F hop-o'-my-thumb, in Kindermärchen: F (Little) Tom Thumb; myth. pygmy.

Daum=schraube (ⁿ⌣) f ⓖ₂ thumb-screw (ehm. Folterwerkzeug, jetzt noch fig.).

Daun ⚘ (¹) m ⓖc. hemp-nettle (Galeo'psis); bunter ~ bee-nettle (G. specio'sa).

D(a)une (⌣́) [ndd., *isl.] f ⓖ (Flaumfeder) down; (wie) auf ~n gebettet resting on a bed of ease.

D(a)unen=bett (⌣́...) n ⓖ₂ eiderdown- (or feather-)bed, soft bed.

daunenhaft (⌣́⌣⌣), **daunicht**, **daunig** (⌣́) a. ⓖ₆ downy, like (or as soft as) down.

Daus¹ (¹) [ahd.; fr.; *lt. duo(s)2] n ⓖa. Würfel: (Zwei) deuce; Karten: (As) ace.

Daus² (¹) [mlt. du'sius, lt. deus] m ⓖa., dim. Däuschen (⌣́) n ⓖ₂₃ F ei (auch was) der ~ F what the deuce!; ein Junge wie ein ~ a smart lad, F a trump (or brick, devil) of a boy; geputzt wie ein ~ F as smart as a new pin.

David (⌣́ⁿ) [hebr. Geliebter] npr/m. ⓖ ⓖ ⓖ₅₄a. (jüd. König 1040—1000) David.

Davids=gerste (⌣́...) f ⓖ₂, **=korn** n ⚘ many-rowed spring-barley (Ho'rdeum caele'ste).

Davis=quadrant ⚓ (dē″-wiß...) [Seefahrer Davis 1550—1605] m ⓖ back-staff, Davis's quadrant or staff; **=straße** ⚓ npr/f. ⓖ zwischen Grönland u. Baffinsland: Davis Strait (entdeckt 1585).

Davit ⚓ † (dē″-wit) [engl.; fr.; *David] m ⓖ (beweglicher Kran) davit.

da-von (-ⁿ⌣, die Sache betonend: ⁿ⌣́) I adv. 1. thereof, therefrom, of (or from) it or that; 2 ist nicht die Rede we are not talking about (or of) that; nichts mehr 2!, still 2! be quiet (F hold your tongue) about it!; ein andermal 2! we'll discuss that another time!; habe ich et. 2?, was habe ich 2? do I gain anything by it?, what is the use of it to me?; ich habe nichts 2 I am none the better off (for it), F I make nothing by it; ich halte nicht viel 2 I don't think much of it; infolge 2 in consequence thereof, owing to that (fact); 2 (⌣́⌣) habe ich nur Verdruß it brings me nothing but vexation; das kommt 2 that's the result (or end) of it; nicht weit 2 not far off. — 2. bei folgender Ergänzung oft nicht zu übersetzen: man redet 2, Rußland wolle Krieg they say Russia wants war; das kommt 2, wenn man nicht aufpaßt that's the consequence of (people) being careless; man redet 2, daß er sie heiraten will they say he is going to marry her. — 3. ⚙ ⚓ 2 ab (abzuziehen) fünf Prozent deduct (or take away) five per cent. — 4. (fort, weg) sie sind (auf und) 2! they are gone or flown!; auf und 2! let's be off! — II. in Verbindung mit verbs immer trennbar (**) und stets -ᵉ-...), bsd. mit v. der Bewegung, entsprechend denen mit fort-... und weg-..., z.B.: 2=bleiben (-ᵉ-...) (⌣́) ⓖ⚙** to keep off (or clear of) a th.; bleib davon! leave it alone!; 2eilen v/n. (sn) ⓖ⚙** to hasten away, to hurry off; 2fahren v/n. (sn) ⓖb** to drive away (in a carriage or a motor, a boat, &c.); 2fliegen v/n. (sn) ⓖa** to fly off or away; 2geh(e)n v/n. (sn) ⓖ⓴** to go off; heimlich: to run away, to vanish; 2helfen v/a. ⓕb**: e-m 2 to help a p. to get away, (et. abnehmen) to relieve a p. of a thing;

2huschen v/n. (sn) ⓖ₁** to slip away; 2jagen v/a. ⓖ₈** to drive (or chase) away, F to turn off; v/n. (sn) to gallop away; 2kommen v/n. (sn) ⓖ₄** to get off; mit blauem Auge (mit genauer Not) 2 to have a lucky (a narrow) escape; ohne Schaden (mit dem bloßen Schrecken) 2 to come off unhurt (with a mere fright); 2laufen v/n. (sn) ⓖast to run away, to scamper off; to take to one's heels; ⚔ to desert; einem 2 to give a p. the slip; es ist um zu-laufen (auch zum ~)! it is enough to drive one mad, F to make a saint (or a parson) swear; 2machen v/refl. ⓖ⚙** sich (auf und) 2 to take to one's heels, F to make off, to clear out; 2müssen v/n. (h.) ⓖ⚙** to be obliged to leave or start; 2reiten v/n. (sn) ⓖb** to depart (or start) on horseback; 2schleichen v/n. (sn) ⓖast und sich 2 v/refl. to sneak (or slink) away or off; 2sprengen v/n. (sn) ⓖ⚙** to gallop off; 2stieben v/n. (sn) ⓖast** to rush away; 2tun v/a. ⓖ⚙** to take off; 2traben v/n. (sn) to trot off; 2tragen v/a. ⓖb**, to carry away or off; fig. eine Krankheit: to catch; den Preis (Sieg) 2 to carry (or gain) the prize (the victory); to bear off the palm; to come off with flying colours; Schande 2 to disgrace o.s.; 2ziehen v/n. (sn) ⓖb** to set out (on one's journey), to go away, to move (to other quarters).

da-vor (-ⁿ⌣, die Sache betonend: ⁿ⌣́) adv. 1. Ort: in front of it or that; ein Schloß 2 legen to put a padlock to it. — 2. Verhältnis: from it or that; ich habe e-n Abscheu 2 I have a horror of it; 2 (⌣́⌣) fürchte ich mich nicht I am not afraid of it; sei (ob. behüt') uns Gott 2!, da sei Gott (ob. der Himmel) vor! God (or Heaven) forbid. — 3. provc. u. P = dafür. [stand in front of it.]

da-vor=steh(e)n (ⁿ⌣-⌣́) v/n. (h.) ⓖ⚙** to]

Davysch (dē″-wᵉiʃ) [Davy, engl. Chemiker, 1778—1829] a. ⓖ ⚒ ~e (Sicherheits=)Lampe (1815) Davy's lamp.

da-wider (-ⁿ⌣, die Sache betonend: ⁿ⌣́) adv. against it or that; ich habe nichts (a. bin nicht) 2 I have nothing to say against it. I don't object to (or oppose) it; dafür und 2 for and against, oft: pro and con.

da-zu (-ⁿ⌣, die Sache betonend: ⁿ⌣́) I adv. 1. Ort: thereto; to (or near) it or that; man kann nicht 2 (zu dem Fleck) gelangen oder kommen one cannot get there or to it. — 2. Zweck: for it or that; er ist 2 abgerichtet he is trained for that purpose; 2 gehört Geld u. Zeit that requires ...; er zeigt wenig Lust 2 he shows little inclination for it; ich riet ihm (sehr) 2 I (strongly) advised him to do it; er ist nicht der Mann 2 he is not the (right) man for it, he's not one that could do it or would stand it. — 3. allg. Bezeichnung: wie kommen sie 2? how do they come by it?; ich kann nicht 2 (⌣́⌣) kommen auszugehen ob. daß ich ausgehe I cannot find time to go out or for going out; 2 (dahin) wird es nie kommen it will never come to that or get so far; was

⚘ scientific; ⚘ botanical; ⓖ geography; ⓞ machinery; ⚒ mining; ⚔ military; ⚓ marine; ⚙ commercial; ⚐ postal; ⚒ railway.

[dazugeben] — 252 — [decken]

fagft du 2? ... to (or about) it? — 4. (Hinzufügung): (noch) 2 in addition (to it or that); arm und alt 2 poor and old besides; Meffer und Dolch 2 ... to boot or in(to) the bargain; gehört der Bogen auch dazu (zu der Violine)? 2 (-) .he bow go (along) with it?; 2 (-) fommt, daß // it must be added that // or and, moreover, //. — 5. Begleitung: er arbeitet und fingt 2 ... and sings at the same time. — II (-"...) in Verbindung mit verbs, auch a. u. fubft. Inf., zB.: 2geben (-"...) v/a. 2c* to contribute to(wards) it; 2gehören v/n. (h.) B**/* to belong (or appertain) to it; vgl. 4; 2gehörig a. 66 belonging to it; forming part of it; 2fommen v/n. (fn) 64** to come upon s.th. by accident or by surprise; ich kam gerade dazu, als fie fchoffen I happened to come up or to arrive on the spot when they were shooting; vgl. 1, 3 u. 4; 2fommen n 23, bisw. a. -funft f 60 accidental meeting; addition(al arrival); sudden arrival; 2legen v/a. 68*** to put (or lay) with it.

da-zumal (1-) adv. at (or about) that time, in those days, then; f. Anno.

da-zu-rechnen (-"...) 2b**, 2tun 65**, 2zählen 68** v/a. to add to the number; -tun n 23: ohne fein ~ without his intervention.

da-zwifchen(-"-") I adv. 1. between them; Hügel und Schluchten 2 hills intersected by ravines; wählen Sie 2 choose between (them); es ift der Unterfchied 2, daß // there is this difference (between them) that // . — II in Verbindung mit verbs (immer trennbar**), p.pr. u. fubft. Inf., zB.: 2 einschalten (_"..._), einschieben (_"1..._) v/a. to put in between, to insert; 2 bfd. aft.: to intercalate; in die Schriften anderer: to interpolate; 2fahren ("1-) v/n. (fn) Bb** to rush in between; 2fommen ("2-) v/n. (fn) 64** to come between, to intervene; wenn nichts 2fommt if nothing (unforeseen) happens (in the) meanwhile, unless there be some obstacle or hindrance; -fommen ("...) n 23, -funft f 60 intervention. interposition; 2legen ("2...) v/a. 68*** to lay between, to interpose; 2liegen ("1-) v/n. (h.) 64** to lie between; 2liegend ("1-) p.pr. u. a. 66 interjacent or intermediate (space), intervening (time); 2reden ("1-) v/n. (h.) 69** to put in a word (or two); e-m 2 to interrupt a p.; fich 2fchlagen ("1-) v/refl. 5b** = 2treten; 2fchreiben ("1-) v/a. 2b** to write between the lines; 2feten ("1-) v/a. 60** to interpose; 2fteh(e)n ("1-(-)) v/n. (h.) 94** to stand between; 2ftellen ("1-) v/a. 68** to put between; 2treten ("1-) v/n. (fn) 2d** to step in between; fig. to intercede, interfere, interpose, intervene; -treten n 23 intercession, intervention; 2werfen ("...) v/a. 2b** to throw in among.

d. c. abbr. = da capo.

dca. deg. del. dem = Dezi-ar. -gramm.

d. d. abbr. = de dato (vom Tage der Ausftellung) after date; from to-day.

DDr. abbr. = Doftoren.

deballieren (-"1-) [fr.] v.a. 93 to unbale; to unpack. | (Ausladen) unloader.

Debardeur ↓ (-"bö'r) [fr.] m ⓓd. (50)

Debatte (-") [fr.] f 49 (Verhandlung) debate on; zur ~ bringen to bring on a discussion of; die ~ eröffnen to open the debate; vgl. Diskuffion; 2-los adv. parl. es wurde 2los genehmigt it was agreed to without any discussion; ~-fchrift f 62 parl. (fehr gefürzte Stenographie) parliamentary short-hand.

debattieren (-"1-) [fr.] v/a. 93 et. 2 on a subject, to discuss a th.; nach allen Seiten hin: (thoroughly) to thrash out a matter, a subject.

Debet (-"") [lt. er fchuldet] n 50 (Soll ant. Kredit, Haben) debit; im ~ fteh(e)n to be on the debit- (or debtor-)side.

Debet-poften (-"...) m 62 entry on the debit-side; -feite f im Hauptbuche: debit- (or debtor-)side.

Debit ⚹ (de-bi') [fr.] m ⓓc. (Warenabfat) sale (of goods), market.

debitieren (-"1-) [fr.] v/a. 93 1. [f. Debit] (Waren 2c. verfchleißen) to dispose of (goods, &c.). — 2. [f. Debet] e-n mit et. 2 (belaften) to charge s.th. to a p.'s account, to debit a p. with s.th.

Debit-maffe (de-bi'...) [f.] f 49 Konkurs-m. [= Konkurs-...]

Debitor ⚹ (-"-) [lt.] m 31 (Schuldner) debtor.

Debit-verfahren ⚹ (de-bi"[t]...) n 62

deblofieren (-"1-) [fr.] v/a. 93 1. ⚓ to raise the blockade of. — 2. typ. to invert turned letters. [bibl. Deborah.]

Debora (-"-) [hebr. Biene] npr/f. 56 ⓣa.

debouchieren ⚹ (de-bu-fch"-) [fr.] I v/n. (fn) (aus e-m Defilee herausmarchieren) to debouch. — II ~ n 23 debouchment.

Debüt (-bü") [fr.] (m u.) n 50 (erftes Auftreten) first appearance on the stage, &c., (fr.) debut, début; ~ant(in f 40) m 2 (-"-") beginner, (fr.) debutant(e f) m; 2ieren (1-"-") v/n. (h.) 93 to make one's first appearance or one's debut, to come out; thea. to act for the first

☞ Dec... f. Def... und Dez... [time.]

☞ Dechant (-") m 42 2c. f. Defan 2c.

Decharge ⚹ (-fch"G") [fr.] f 48. ~-erteilung f 46 (Entlaftung) discharge; e-m erteilen to grant a p. a (full) discharge for to release a p.) from all obligations.

dechargieren (-fch"G"-) [fr.] v/a. (entlaften, entlaffen) to discharge. to release.

Decher (-") [lt. decu'ria] m. u. n 22 (Gefamtheit von 10 Stück, bfd. Fellen) bale of ten (ehm. dicker, daker of) hides.

dechiffrieren (-fch"1-) [fr.] v/a. 93 (entziffern) to decipher; **Dechiffrierer** m 22 (Entzifferer) decipherer.

☞ Deci.. f. Dezi...

Deck[1] (-") [ndd.] n ⓤb. 1. ⚓ deck; oberes (unteres) ~ upper (lower) deck; glattes (lofes) ~ flush- (preventer-)deck; auf ~ on deck; vom feindlichen Gefchüt: das ~ beftreichen to sweep the deck. — 2. outside (seat) or top of an omnibus, &c.

Deck[2]... (-"...) [decken] ⓕ f. Deckbett 2c.

Deck[1]**-balfen** ⚓ ("...) m 62 (deck-)beam.

deckbar ("-) a. 66 coverable; ⚹ der Schaden ift (nicht) ~ the damage can(not) be covered or made good.

Deck[2]**-bett** ("...) n 62 coverlet, (eiderdown) quilt; **-blatt** n: a) ⚹ bract(ea); b) von Zigarren: outside (leaf), wrapper; c) = Textur; **-blatt-ähnlich** ⚹ a. 66 bracteiform; **-blättchen** ⚹ n 23 bracteole.

Deckchen (-") n 23 dim. v. Decke.

Decke (-") [ahd.] f ⓤ 1. cover(ing); (Fuß-)~ floor-cloth; (Kutfchbock-)~ hammer-cloth; (Pferde-)~ horse-rug, -cloth; (Reife-)~ travelling rug, (Stepp-)~ quilt, (Tifch-)~ table-cloth; (Wagen-)~ (Plane) awning, tilt. geteerte: tarpaulin; wollene (Bett-, ⚹ Pferde-)~ blanket; gehäfelte ~ (auf Möbeln zur Schonung) antimacassar, tidy; fig. die ~ des Himmels the vault of heaven. — 2. fig.: fich nach der ~ ftrecken to live within one's income; to cut one's coat according to one's cloth; unter einer ~ mit e-m ftecken to be in league (or in collusion) with a p., to conspire (or connive) with a p. — 3. (Haut) anat. coat(ing); hunt. (Haut, Fell) coat, skin; ⚹ integument. — 4. ~ von Saiteninftrumenten: (Refona'nzboden) sounding board. — 5. ⓞ (deckende Schicht) top layer; Zuckerbäckerei: ~ von Zucker coating of sugar, icing; arch. e-s Zimmers: ceiling; Buchbind.: (Umfchlag) loose cover(ing), wrapper.

Deckel (-") [erft nhd.; * Decke] m 22 1. lid of a kettle, a pot, a saucepan, &c.; aufzufchraubender ~ screw-cap; mit e-m ~ verfehen capped, covered. — 2. F fig. Topf und ~ (Paar) a (well-matched) couple; Darby and Joan. — 3. F (Kopfbedeckung) headgear, cap, (Hut) hat, tile, chimney-pot; ⚹ zo. ~ von Moostapfeln, Schnecken 2c.: operculum; e-m ~ verfehen: operculated. — 4. ⓞ Buchbind.: cover; typ. ~ e-r Druckerpreffe tympan, der Handpreffe: outer tympan; metall. ~ der Gußrinne cover.

deckel-ähnlich (-"...) a. 66 lid-like, operculiform; **-becher** m 22. **-fanne** f goblet, pitcher with a lid; **-fapfel** ⚹ f: ⚹ pyxidium; **-forb** m covered basket; **-frug** m tankard.

deckeln (-") ⓐa. I v/a. to cover (or provide) with a lid. — II F v/n. (h.) to take off (F to doff) one's cap or hat.

Deckel-fchnecke (-"...) f zo. ⚹ operculate snail; **-fpinne** f, zo. trap-door spider (= Minierfpinne); **2tragend** a.: ⚹ operculiferous; **-ventil** ⓞ n = -flappe.

decken (-") [ahd.: lt. te'gere; vgl. Dach] I v/a. v/refl. 68 1. meift: (fich) 2 to (put o.s.) under ⓐ cover; ⚓ Schach 2c.: e-e Stellung (e-e Figur) 2 to cover (or protect) a position (a piece); fenc. fich 2 to take (up) one's guard; gedeckter Weg covered way, unterirdifcher: subway; ⚹ e-n (i-s Koften) 2 to cover (or reimburse) a p., to make remittances to a p.: ift gedeckt ... secured (against losses); bfd. ⚓ den Rückzug 2 to cover one's retreat; gedeckt (adv.) feuern to fire under cover; hunt. die Hunde 2 das Schwein (halten es feft) ... hold (or attack) the boar; von ⚹ 2 gegen to protect o.s. from or against. — 2. den Tifch 2. a. abs. 2 to lay the cloth or the table; es ift gedeckt dinner is ready or served. — 3. ⚹ Ausgaben 2 to cover (the) expenses; ein Defizit, e-n Schaden 2 to make good a deficiency, a loss; e-n

Zeichen (f. S. XVII): F familiär, P Volksfprache, F Gaunerfprache, ⚹ felten, † alt (auch geftorben), * neu (auch geboren), +⁺ unrichtig,

[Deckenbalken] — 253 — [dehnen]

Wechsel 2 to give security for a bill. — 4. ⊕ Zuckerfabr.: den Zucker 2 to clay ...; arch., &c. ein Dach mit Schiefer, Stroh, Ziegeln 2 to slate, thatch, tile a roof. — 5. math. eine Figur deckt eine andere ... coincides with another; die Dreiecke 2 sich ... coincide (with one another) or are equal in all respects; fig. sich 2 to be identical. — II ~ n 23 6. covering, &c. (s. I). — 7. = Deckung.

Decken-balken ⊕ (ᵕ...) m 62 arch. joist; =feld n, arch. panel of a ceiling; =flechter m mat-maker; =gemälde n ceiling-piece; 2hoch a. 66 up to (or as high as) the ceiling; =macher m = =flechter; =maler m fresco-painter; =putz m plastering (or moulding) of ceilings; =stück n: a) = =gemälde; b) thea. bewegliche =stücke pl. flies, heavens pl.

Decker (ᵕ) m 22 1. = Dachdecker. — 2. ♌ v. Tabak: ein guter (schlechter) ~ a good (bad) outside brand.

Deck²-farbe (ᵕ .) f 62 paint. body- (or opaque) colour; =federn f/pl. orn. coverts, ⚔ tectrices pl.; =firniß m, paint. (top coating of) varnish; cream; =flügler m/pl. ent. (Käfer): ⚔ coleoptera; ²-gang ⚔ m, frt. covert way; =garn n, hunt. fowler's net; =glas n Mikroskopie: cover-glass; =haut f ♀ integument, anat. coat(ing), lining; =klärsel n Zuckerfabr.: fine-liquor; =kraft f, paint. body (or covering-power) of a colour; =¹ladung ⚓, =last f (auf dem Oberdeck untergebrachte Ladung) cargo stowed on the upper deck, a. deck-load; =²lünse f Wagenbau: linch-pin; =mantel m mst fig. cloak (of piety, &c.), pretence or veil (of truth); unter dem ~ der Freundschaft, a.: under the mask of friendship; =name m assumed name, pseudonym; = Schriftstellers auch: (fr.) nom de plume; =¹offizier ⚓ m (Portepee-unteroffizier) warrant-officer; =passagier ⚓ m deck-passenger; =planken ⚓ f/pl. deck-planks pl.; =²platte ⊕ f covering (or top) slab; cover-plate; arch. capping, coping; =rasen m facing-sod; =rohr n common reed (for roofing).

Decks-... (ᵕ...) in Zsgn s. Deck²...

Deck²-samenpflanzen ♣ (ᵕᵕᵕ..) f/pl. 62 = Hüllsamer; =¹schwabber ⚓ m mainstaysail; =²schwelle ⊕ f, carp. e-s Pfahlrostes: coping-piece; =stroh n thatch; =¹stütze ⚓ f deck-pillar or -stanchion.

Deckung (ᵕ) f 46 1. cover, shelter, protection; ⚔, fenc. (Parade) guard. — 2. ⚔ ~ e-s Rückzuges covering a retreat; hinter et. ~ suchen to take up a fortified position (auch: to entrench or ensconce o.s.) behind s.th. — 3. ✸ reimbursement (of costs); genügende ~ ample security; ohne ~ without cash in hand, unsecured; ~ anschaffen to provide funds, to send (or make) remittances; ~ finden to be covered or secured; ~ senden to remit the necessary funds or the amount required; wir werden für rechtzeitige ~ sorgen we shall see that due provision (for the bill) is made. — 4. Schach: einer Figur die ~ nehmen to leave a piece uncovered. — 5. math. (Kongru'nz) equality in all respects, perfect equality.

Deckungs-gräben (ᵕᵕ...) m/pl. ⚔ sheltering trenches pl., trenches serving as cover; =linie ⚔ f line of defence, coverline; =mannschaft f escort, covering party; =mittel ✸ n/pl. funds pl. for reimbursement, cover; ⚔ (Sand, Holz, Mauern) covering material.

Deck²-wachs ⊕ (ᵕ...) n 62 bei Ätzungen: bordering-wax; =werk ⚔ n, frt. blind (-age); =wrange ⚓ f deck-transom.

decouragieren (-tu̯ᵕᵕ̯) [fr.] v/a. 93 (entmutigen) to discourage.

decrescendo ♪ (dĕ-trĕ-sche̯'n-bo) [it.] adv. (abnehmend; ant. crescendo) decrescendo. 〚date, from this day.〛

de dato (᷼ ᵕ) [lt.] (abbr. d. d.) after

Dedikation (-ᵕᵕtᵕ̯)ᵕ) [lt.] f 46 (Widmung) dedication; ~s-exemplar (ᵕ...) n 62 e-s Buches presentation-copy.

dedizieren (-ᵕᵕᵕ) [lt.] v/a. 93 (widmen) to dedicate or inscribe to; F e-m et. 2 (schenken) to present s.th. to a p.

Deduktion ⚔ (-ᵕtᵕ̯)ᵕ) [lt.] f 46 phls. (Schluß vom Allgemeinen zum Besonderen; ant. Induktion) deduction; ~s-verfahren (ᵕ...) n 62 deductive method.

deduktiv (-ᵕᵕᵕf) [lt.] a. 66 phls. (das Besondere aus dem Allgemeinen herleitend; ant. induktiv) deductive.

deduzieren ⚔ (-ᵕᵕᵕ) [lt.] v/a. 93 phls. (herleiten) to deduce; weit S. to infer.

de facto (᷼ ᵕ ᵕ) [lt.] als adv. (tatsächlich) de facto, in fact.

Defekt¹ (᷼ ᵕ) [lt.] a. 66 (mangelhaft) defective, incomplete; (beschädigt) damaged; 2es Buch (a. Exempla'r) imperfect copy; ⊕ typ. der Buchstabe od. die Type battered letter; vgl. Defektbuchstabe.

Defekt² (᷼ ᵕ) [lt.] m ①b. defect; ⊕ typ. &c. imperfection; ✸ (Fehlbetrag) deficiency; es ergab sich ein (Kassen-)~ von 200 Mark there was (found to be) a deficit of ten pounds; ~e pl., typ. (mangelhafte Schrift) imperfect type or fount, auch sorts pl.

Defektarius (-ᵕᵕ(ᵕ)ᵕ) [lt.] m 27 pharm. chemist's laboratory-assistant.

Defekt-bogen ⊕ (᷼ ᵕᵕ...) m 62 typ. imperfect (or defective) sheet; =buchstabe m imperfection; batter.

defektieren ✸ (-ᵕᵕ) [lt.] v/n. (h.) 93 (um Nachsendung ersuchen) to ask for missing letters, &c. to be forwarded.

defektiv (-ᵕᵕf) [lt.] a. 66 gr. (unvollständig) defective; ~um (-ᵕᵕᵕᵕ) n 50 (pl. a. ~e) gram. defective noun or verb or word.

Defekt-kasten (᷼ ᵕ...) m 62 typ. case of batter, case of imperfect type.

Defektur ⚔ (-ᵕᵕ) [lt.] f 46 pharm. laboratory-work; vgl. Defektarius.

Defekt-zettel (᷼ ᵕ...) m 62 bill of the incomplete fount. 〚gung) defence.〛

Defension ⚔ (-ᵕ(ᵕ)ᵕ) [lt.] f 46 (Verteidi-)

defensiv (-ᵕᵕf) [lt.] a. 66 (ant. offensi'v) sich 2 verhalten to be on the defensive.

Defensive (-ᵕᵕᵕᵕ) [fr.] f 48 (Verteidigung) in der ~ beharren, bleiben to stand on the defensive; die ~ ergreifen to act on the defensive.

Defensiv-krieg ⚔ (-ᵕᵕf...) m 62 defensive war; =stellung f = Defensive.

Defilee (Défilé 50) (-ᵕᵕᵕ) [fr.] n 26 1. (Hohlweg) defile, (narrow) pass. — 2. ⚔ = Defiliermarsch.

Defilement ⚔ (-᷼-(ᵕ)ᵕmg̯) n 80 frt. (Deckung der inneren Werte) defilading.

defilieren ⚔ (-᷼᷼ᵕᵕ) [fr.] v/n. (h. u. sn) u. v/a. 93 (paradenmäßig vorbeimarschieren) to defile, to march past.

Defilier-marsch ⚔ (-᷼᷼-ᵕ᷼) m 62 (Vorbeimarsch) defile, march past.

definierbar (-ᵕᵕ᷼ ᵕ) a. 66 (erklärbar) definable. 〚(bestimmen) to define.〛

definieren (-᷼᷼ᵕᵕ) [lt.] v/a. 93 (begrifflich)

Definition (-᷼᷼-tᵕ̯)ᵕ) [lt.] f 46 definition.

definitiv (-᷼᷼-ᵕf) [lt.] a. 66 (endgültig) definite; 2 abgemacht finally settled.

Defizit ✸ (ᵕᵕᵕ) [lt.] n Me., 50 (Fehlbetrag) deficit; ein ~ decken to make good a deficiency; ~ am Gewicht short(ness) of weight.

Defraudant (---ᵕ) [lt.] m 42 defrauder.

Defraudation (---tᵕ̯)ᵕ) [lt.] f 46 (Unterschlagung) embezzlement; (Steuer-)defraudation (of the revenue).

defraudieren (---ᵕᵕ) [lt.] v/a. u. v/n. (h.) 93 (unterschlagen) to defraud (the revenue), (schmuggeln) to smuggle.

deftig (᷼ᵕ) [udd. (: hd. tüchtig): deft] a. 66 sturdy, strong, stout, robust.

Degen¹ fast † (ᵕᵕ) [ahd.: thane: grch. te'knön Kind] m 23 bsd. ehm. warrior, hero; jetzt meist: F alter ~ old soldier.

Degen² [nhd. 15/16. sae.: dagger; *fr. dague Dolch] m 23 (Hieb- und Stoßwaffe) sword; zum ~ greifen, den ~ ziehen to draw the sword.

Degen²-band (ᵕᵕ...) n 62 sword-knot.

Degeneration (-᷼ᵕᵕtᵕ̯)ᵕ) [lt. génér-] f 46 (Entartung) degeneracy, degeneration.

degenerieren (---ᵕᵕ) [lt.] v/n. (sn) 93 (entarten) to degenerate.

Degen²-fisch (ᵕᵕ...) m 66 ichth. hairtail (Trichiu'rus); =fläche f flat (side) of a sword; =förmig a. 66 sword-shaped, ⚔ ensiform; =futter n = =scheide; =gefäß n = =griff; =gehenk n sword-belt or -girdle; =geklirr n clashing of swords; =griff m sword-handle or -hilt; =klinge f sword-blade; =knopf m pommel; fig. alter ~ old warrior; =koppel f = =gehenk; =quaste f sword-knot or -tassel; =scheide f scabbard (or sheath) of a sword; =schlucker m Artist: sword-eater or -swallower; =stock m sword-stick; =stoß m. fenc. thrust with a sword.

Degradation ⚔ (-ᵕ-tᵕ̯)ᵕ) [lt.] f 46 (Herabsetzung im Rang) degradation.

degradieren (-ᵕᵕᵕ) [fr.] I v/a. 93 to degrade; ⚔ zum Gemeinen 2 (herabsetzen) to reduce to the ranks. — II ~ n 23 u. **Degradierung** f 46 degradation.

Degras ⊕ (dĕ-gra') [fr.] n, inv. (Gerberfett) degras, stuff.

dehnbar (᷼ᵕ) a. 66 1. phys. dilatable, extensible; (streckbar) ductile; Leder 2c. supple; ⊕ metall. durch Hämmern: malleable; 2 flüssiger Körper elastic fluid. — 2. fig. vague, wide; 2es Gewissen elastic (or flexible) conscience; (zweideutig) ambiguous.

Dehnbarkeit (᷼ᵕᵕ) f 46 (s. dehnbar) dilatableness, extensibility, ductility; suppleness; malleability; elasticity; fig. vagueness; ambiguousness; ~s-messer (᷼...) m ⚔ ductilimeter.

dehnen (᷼ᵕ) [ahd.: lt. te'ndere: grch. tei'nein] v I v/a. u. sich 2 v/refl. 93 1. to

♪ Musik; ⚔ Wissenschaft; ♣ Pflanze; ⊕ Geographie; ⊕ Technik; ⚒ Bergbau; ⚔ Militär; ⚓ Marine; ✸ Handel; ✉ Post; 🚂 Eisenbahn.

[Dehnung] — 254 — [Dekoration]

extend, to stretch; (aufblasen) to distend; ⊕ metall. (hämmern) to malleate; phys. sich 2 to expand, to dilate; (sich) in die Länge, Breite 2 to lengthen, widen. — 2. fig. beim Lesen ob. Sprechen: to draw out; to drawl (out); gedehnte Sprache drawling tone or voice, drawl; pros. gedehnte Silben long syllables pl. — II ~ n 23 u. **Dehnung** f 46 3. (f. I) extension, expansion, dilatation; pros. einer Silbe: lengthening, ⚬ diastole.
Dehnungs-h (⌣⌢⌣...) n 2 Lautlehre: h serving to lengthen a (preceding) vowel; =**messer** m ⚬ extensometer, Luftpumpe: ⚬ elaterometer; =**muskel** m, anat. ⚬ extensor; =**werkzeug** ⊕ n stretcher; =**zeichen** n, pros. sign denoting a long syllable; gr. circumflex.
Deich (⌣) [ndd. (:hd. Teich): dike, ditch] m ⑯c. (Hochwasserdamm) dike, dam, bank; zur Seite e-s Flusses: embankment; einen ~ aufführen to raise (or throw) up (or to construct) a dike.
Deich-amt (⌣⌢...) n 2 board of dikes, dike-office; =**anfer** m foundation of a dike; =**arbeiter** m diker, ditcher; bsd. ⚓ navy; =**aufseher** m = =eidige(r); =**bau** m diking; embankment; =**baumeister** m dikebuilder; =**beamte(r)** m dike-official; =**bruch** m breach in (or breaking of) a dike; =**damm** m small dam (protecting a dike); =**eidige(r)** m (sworn) inspector of a dike.
deichen (⌣⌢) I v/a. 88 to raise up (or build) a dike or dikes; to repair a dike. — II ~ n 33 = Deichung.
Deicher (⌣⌢) m 22 = Deich-arbeiter.
Deich-gräber (⌣⌢...) m 2 = =arbeiter; =**graf**, =**gräfe**, =**hauptmann** m bsd. ehm. dike-grave or -reeve; =**kamm** m, =**koppe** f ridge of a dike; =**land** n (low-lying) district protected by dikes, dikeland; =**meister** m surveyor (or master) of a dike; =**pflicht(igkeit)** f obligation to keep up a dike; =**rat** m, etwa: member of a board of dikes; =**recht** n dike-laws pl.; =**richter** m dike-judge; =**schleuse** f dike-lock; =**schoß** md. =rates pl.
Deichsel[1] ⊕ (⌣tß⌣) [ahd.: thill] f 46 am Wagen 2c. shaft (or pole, beam) of a carriage, &c.; (Gabel=)~ thill. [= Deißel.]
Deichsel[2] † (~) [ahd.] f 46 (kurzstielige Axt).
Deichsel-arm ⊕ (⌣tß⌣...) m 2 shaft-bar; =**blech** n pole-, beam-plate; =**bolzen** m pole-pin; =**eisen** n einer Schiene: leg-piece of a rail; =**hafen** m pole-hook; =**kuppelung** f thill-coupling; =**nagel** m shaft-bolt; =**pferd** n shaft- (or thill- or wheel-horse); =**riemen** m shaft- (or pole-)strap; =**ring** m pole- (or thill-)ring; =**stütze** ⚔ f, artill. pole-prop.
Deich-ufer (⌣⌢...) n 2 dike-bank.
Deichung (⌣⌢) f 46 diking; construction (or maintenance) of dikes.
Deich-vogt (⌣⌢...) m 2 = =meister; =**weg** m dike-way or -path; =**wesen** n matters pl. relating to dikes, diking; =**zwang** m dike-judicature.
dein (⌣) [gen. v. du] I gen. von du ⑯ A1 1. geh. Spr. = deiner[2]; wir gedenken 2 we think of thee. — 2. bei den verbs bleiben, fühlen, glauben, machen, nennen, scheinen, sein, werden 2c., F a. bei ge-

hören = 2 Eigentum: ich bin 2 I am thine (üblicher: yours; F es gehört 2 it belongs to thee (üblicher: to you). — II ~ [ahd.: thy, thine; * 2 I] a. und possessive pron. ⑯C. 3. poet. thy (üblicher: yours); 2e Mutter (poet. die Mutter 2) your mother; dieser 2 Freund this friend of yours; 2 bißchen Englisch the little English that (or what little English) you know. — III a) 2er[1] m, 2e f, 2es n ⑯ A2; b) mit dem bestimmten art. der (die, das) 2(ig)e ⑯ 4. poet. thine, üblicher: yours; als s.: ewig der (die) ~(ig)e ever yours; die ~(ig)en your family or folk or people; das ~(ig)e (what is) yours; der Dank der ~(ig)en the gratitude of your people; ich bin der ~(ig)e I am yours; du hast das ~(ig)e getan you have done your best or your duty. — IV n, inv. 5. das Mein und ~ mine and thine, (lt.) meum and tuum.
deiner[2] (⌣⌢) gen. von du (vgl. dein I) ⑯ A1; sie ist 2 nicht wert she is not worthy of you; 2=**seits** (⌣⌢⌣) adv. on your part.
deines=gleichen (⌣⌣⌢⌣⌣) pron. inv. of thy (üblicher: your) kind, the like of you, one of your sort; your equals pl.
deinet=halben (⌣⌢...), 2**wegen**, 2**willen** for thy (üblicher: your) sake; um 2**willen** on your behalf.
deinige (⌣⌢⌣) f. dein III b. [swell.]
Deining ⚓ (⌣⌢) f 46, m ⑯d. ground-
dei(n)sen ⚓ (⌣⌢) [bz. tanzen] 90 I v/n. (h.) (rückwärts gehen) to have sternway (n), to fetch sternway, to go (or fall) astern. — II ~ n 23 sternway.
Deinung ⚓ (⌣⌢) f 46 = Deining.
deisen d (⌣⌢) f. deinsen.
deisig ↓ (⌣⌢) a. 66 = diesig.
De-ismus † (⌣⌢⌣) [neu=lt.] m 27 rel. (reiner od. natürlicher Gottesglaube) deism.
Deißel (⌣⌢) f 46, m, n 2 carp. (Dexel) adze; 2**n** v/a. 92 a. to adze, to dub.
De=ist † (⌣⌢) [neu=lt.] m 42, =**in** f 47 rel. deist; 2**erei** F (⌣⌣⌢) f 46 deism; 2**isch** (⌣⌢) a. 66 deistic, deistical.
Deizel F (⌣⌢) [corr. = Teufel] m 2 (o. pl.) deuce; zum ~! the dickens!
Dejeuner (-ʒö-'ne') [fr.] n 50 (Frühstück) breakfast; zweites ~ (gegen Mittag) lunch(eon). [breakfast; to lunch.]
dejeunieren (-ʒö-') [fr.] v/n. (h.) 93 to
Dekade (⌣⌢⌣) [grch. dě'ka zehn] f 46 (Reihe von zehn Dingen) decade.
dekadisch (⌣⌢⌣) a. 66 consisting of tens; 2es Zahlensystem decimal system of numeration or numbers.
Deka-eder ⚬ (⌣⌢⌣⌣) [grch.] n (m) 2 math. (Zehnflach) decahedron.
Deka-gramm (⌣⌢⌣) [fr., *grch.] n 2 (10 Gramm; abbr. **dkg**) decagram(me); =**liter** n (m) (10 Liter; abbr. **dkl**) decalitre.
Dekalo ⚓ (-⌣⌢) [it.] n 50 (Verlust) short(-ness) of weight caused by shrinkage.
Dekalog (⌣⌢⌣) [grch.] m ⑯c. rel. (10 Gebote) decalogue; the Ten Commandments.
Dekameron (⌣⌢⌣⌣) [it., *grch. 10 Tage] n 50 (Boccaccio, 1352) The Decameron.
Deka=meter (⌣⌢⌣⌣) [fr., *grch. dě'ka 10] n (m) 2 (10 Meter; abbr. **dkm**) decametre.
Dekan (-⌣⌢) vgl. Defhan [lt., *grch.] m ⑯c. (Vorsteher e-r Fakultät ob. Cath. ecl. e-s Kapitels) dean; ~**at** (-⌣⌢) [lt.] n ⑯c. deanery, deanship.

Dekandria ⚬ ♀ (⌣⌣⌢⌣) [grch.] f 46 (zehnte Klasse nach Linné) decandria.
dekandrisch ♀ (⌣⌣⌢⌣) a. 66 (zehnmännig: mit 10 Staubgefäßen) decandrous.
dekantieren ⊕ (-⌣⌢⌣) [fr.] v/a. 93 chm., pharm. (abgießen) to decant, to pour off.
dekapieren ⊕ (-⌣⌢⌣) [fr.] v/a. 93 Metall (von Oryd 2c. befreien) to clear of rust or oxides, to polish, to furbish.
Dekar (⌣⌢) [fr.] n (m) ⑯c,6. = 10 Ar.
dekartieren † ⚬ (-⌣⌢⌣) [fr.] v/a. 93 = entkarten. [(10 Kubikmeter) decastere.]
Deka=ster schwz. (⌣⌢⌣) [fr., *grch.] n (m) 2
dekatier/en ⊕ (-⌣⌢⌣) [fr. décatir den Preßglanz (cati) nehmen] Tuchm.: I v/a. 93 to hot-press, to steam; (krimpen) to sponge, shrink. — II ~ n 23 = D/ung.
Dekatierer ⊕ (-⌣⌢⌣) [fr.] m 22 Tuchm. hot-presser; (Krimper) sponger.
Dekatier=maschine ⊕ (-⌣⌢"...) f 42 Tuchm. sponging machine.
Dekatierung (-⌣⌢⌣) f 46 hot-pressing.
Dekhan ♀ (⌣-; vgl. Dekan) [sst. rechts, d. i. südlich] npr/n. ⑯α. (süd-indisches Tafelland) Deccan.
Deklamation (-⌣-tß(⌣)⌢) [lt.] f 46 (Vortrag) declamation; in Schulen: recitation.
Deklamator (-⌣⌢⌣) [lt.] m ⑪ reciter, contp. spouter.
deklamatorisch (-⌣-⌢⌣) a. 66 declamatory, rhetorical; pathetic, pathetical.
deklamieren (-⌣⌢⌣) [lt.] I v/a. u. v/n. (h.) 93 to recite, to deliver (or utter) with rhetorical effect, to speak with great emphasis or pathos; contp. to spout. — II ~ n 23 = Deklamation.
Deklaration ⚓ (-⌣-tß(⌣)⌢) [lt.] f 46 (Angabe) declaration, entry; ~**s-schein** (⌣"....) m 2 bill of entry; dispatch-note.
deklarieren, bsd. ⚓ (-⌣⌢⌣) [lt.] v/a. 93 (Verzollbares angeben) to enter (at the custom-house); zu wenig 2 to enter short; haben Sie etwas zu 2? have you anything (dutiable) to declare?
Deklination ⚬ (-⌣-tß(⌣)⌢) [lt.] f 46 1. gr. ([Fall=]Abwandlung) declension. — 2. ast., phys., &c. (Abweichung) declination.
Deklinations=busole ↓ (⌣"...) f 42 = Deklinatorium; =**instrument** n, ast. declinator; =**nadel** f declination-needle.
Deklinatorium ↓ (-⌣-⌢(⌣)⌢) [lt.] n 2 (Kompaß, der die horiz. Abweichung der Magnetnadel anzeigt) declination-compass.
deklinierbar ⚬ (-⌣⌢⌣) [lt.] a. 66 gr. declinable; ~**keit** (..⌢) f 46 declinability.
deklinieren (-⌣⌢⌣) [lt.] v/a. u. v/n. (h.) 93 1. gr. (abwandeln) to decline, to inflect (nouns or adjectives). — 2. ast., phys., &c. (abweichen) to deviate, swerve.
Deklino-graph ⚬ (-⌣⌢f) [lt.=grch.] m 42 (Fueß 1881) (Vorrichtung zur Selbstaufzeichnung der Deklinationsunterschiede) declinograph; =**meter** (-⌣⌢⌣) n 22 phys. declinometer.
Dekokt ⚬ (-⌢) [lt.] n ⑯b. pharm. (Abkochung) decoction.
dekolletiert (-⌣⌣⌢) [fr.] a. 66 Kleid: low-necked; Dame: bare-shouldered.
Dekorateur (-⌣-⌣tö'r) [fr.] m ⑯d. decorator; painter; thea. scene-painter.
Dekoration (-⌣-tß(⌣)⌢) [lt.] f 46 (Verzierung und Orden) decoration, als Orden a. badge conferred on a p. as a mark of honour; star, cross, medal; arch. ornament; thea. scenery; bewegliche ~ shift-scene.

Signs (see page XVII): F familiar; P vulgar; ⚡ flash; ⚬ rare; † obsolete (died); * new word (born); ++ incorrect; ♪ music;

[Dekorationsmaler] — 255 — [dengeln]

Dekorations-maler (-⏑-tẞ(ᵛ)ʰ...) m ⓑ house-painter; *thea.* scene- (or stage-) painter; **-malerei** *f* decorative painting; *thea.* scene- (or stage-)painting; **-pflanzen** *f pl.* ornamental plants *pl.*

dekorativ (-⏑-ᴸí) [lt.] *a.* ⓖⓖ decorative.

dekorieren (-⏑-ᴸᵛ) [lt.] *v/a.* ⓖⓖ (schmücken) to decorate (a. mit Orden); to adorn.

Dekort ⓖ (-ᴸ) [fr. *décourt*] *m* ⓑ. (Abzug) deduction, abatement.

dekortieren ⓖ (-⏑-ᴸᵛ) *v/a.* ⓖⓖ to deduct (as discount), to abate. [decorum.]

Dekorum (-ᴸ⏑) [lt.] *n* ⓖⓖ (*o. pl.*) (Anstand)

dekrepitieren ⓖ (-⏑-ᴸᵛ) [lt.] **I** *v/n.* u. *v/a.* ⓖⓖ *chm.*, &c. (ab-, verknistern) to decrepitate. — **II** *~ n* ⓖⓖ decrepitation.

Dekret (-ᴸ) [lt.] *n* ⓑ. (Verfügung) decree. [decretal.]

Dekretale (---ᴸᵛ) [lt.] *f* ⓖⓖ *Cath. eccl.*

dekretieren (---ᴸᵛ) [lt.] *v/a.* u. *v/n.* (h.) ⓖⓖ *jur.* (verfügen) to decree, to order.

Dekuri-e (-ᴸ(ᵛ)ᵛ) [lt.] *f* ⓖⓖ röm. Alt.: (Abteilung v. Zehn) decury. [neu) decurion.]

Dekurio (-ᴸ(ᵛ)-) [lt.] *m* ⓖⓖ,ⓖⓖ (*pl.* Dekurio'-)

del. *abbr.* **1.** = *delea'tur* (s. ds). — **2.** (unter Kupferstichen) = *delinea'vit* [lt. er hat gezeichnet] he has signed (it).

deleatur (-⏑-ᴸᵛ) [lt. es werde getilgt!] *abbr.* **del.** *od.* **d.**)

Deleatur-zeichen (ʺ...) *n* ⓖⓖ *typ.* dele.

Delegat (---ᴸ) [lt.] *m* ⓖⓖ (Abgeordneter) delegate. [ⓖ assignment (of a debt).]

Delegation (---ẞ(ᵛ)ᴸ) [lt.]*f* ⓖⓖ delegation;

delegieren (---ᴸᵛ) [lt.] *v/a.* ⓖⓖ (abordnen) to delegate; (vertreten) to substitute.

Delegierte(r) (---ᴸᵛ) *m* ⓖⓖ = Delegat.

delektieren (---ᴸᵛ) [lt.] *v/a.* ⓖⓖ (ergötzen, laben) to fill with delight.

Delfter (ᴸᵛ) [Delft, holl. Stadt] *a. inv. ~* Fayence Delft- (or Dutch) ware, delf.

Deli-er (ᴸ(ᵛ)ᵛ) *m* ⓖⓖ, **~in** *f* ⓖⓖ [Delos, grch. Insel] Delian (auch = Apo'llo).

delikat(-⏑-ᴸ)[fr.]*a.*ⓖⓖ(zart)delicate;(wählerisch) particular, nice; (lecker) delicious.

Delikatesse (-⏑-ᴸᵛ) [fr.] *f* ⓖⓖ (Zartgefühl) delicacy; nicety; (Leckerbissen) delicious morsel, dainty bit; *~n pl.* dainties, F tit-bits *pl.*; **~n-händler** *m* ⓖⓖ Italian ware-houseman, provision-merchant; **~n-handlung** *f,* Italian warehouse, provision-store. [crime, offence.]

Delikt (-ᴸ) [lt.] *n* ⓑ. *jur.* (Verbrechen)

Delinquent (-⏑-ᴸ) [lt.] *m* ⓖⓖ, **~in** *f* ⓖⓖ (Verbrecher[in]) delinquent, offender.

Delirium ⓖ (-ᴸ(ᵛ)-) [lt.] *n* ⓖⓖ *path.* (Fieberwahnsinn) delirium; *~ tre'mens* (Säuferwahnsinn) delirium tremens.

delisch (ᴸᵛ) [Delos] *a.* ⓖⓖ Delian; der *~ed* Gott (Apo'llo) the Delian God; vgl. Delier. [delicious.)

deliziös (-⏑(ᵛ)ᴸ)[fr.]*a.* ⓖⓖ (D 10) (köstlich)

Delkredere ⓖ (ᵛᴸᵛᵛ) [it.] *n* ⓖⓖ (Bürgschaft) guarantee; *~ steh(e)n,* das *~* übernehmen to stand surety or bail, &c.

Delle (ᴸᵛ) [ndd.] *f* ⓖⓖ (Vertiefung) hollow, depression, notch.

delogieren ⓖ (-ᵛGᴸᵛ) [fr.] (vertreiben, zum Abzug veranlassen) *v/a.* ⓖⓖ to dislodge.

Delphi-er(ᴸᵛᵛ)[Delphi, grch.St. mit Orakel des Apo'llo] *m* ⓖⓖ, **~in** *f* ⓖⓖ Delphian.

Delphin (ᵛᴸ) [mhd., * grch.] *m* (ⓖ n) ⓑ.ⓖⓖ *zo.* dolphin (*Delphi'nus delphis*).

Delphinin ⓖ (ᵛᴸ) [*Delphi'nium ℞ Ritter-* sporn]*n*ⓑ.*chm.*delphinine($C_{31}H_{49}NO_7$).

delphisch (ᴸᵛ) [Delphi] *a.* ⓖⓖ Delphian, Delphic; Des Orakel Delphian oracle.

Delta (ᴸᵛ) [grch. Buchstabe: Δ] *n* ⓖⓖ delta; **-förmig** (ᴸᵛ...) *a.* ⓖⓖ deltoid; **~-land** *n* ⓖⓖ (Anschwemmung zwischen Flußmündungen) delta; **-metall** ⓖ *n* (56 Kupfer, 40 Zink, 1 Eisen, 1 Blei) delta-metal; **-muskel** *m, anat.* (Oberarmmuskel) deltoid (muscle).

Delto(id-dodeka)eder ⓖ (ᵛᴸʺ-ᵛᵛᴸᵛᵛ) [grch.] *n* ⓖⓖ *min.* deltohedron.

dem (ᴸ) (*dat. v. der od. das*) ① **I** *art.* unbetont: ℒ Buche to the book. — **II** *dem. pron.* ⓖⓖ A2 (betont): bei (trotz) alleℒ with (despite) all that; es ist nicht an ℒ there is no truth in it, it's not the case; wenn ℒ so ist if that be true; wie ℒ auch sei, ℒ sei wie ihm wolle however that may be, be that as it may; bei folgender Ergänzung oft nicht zu übersetzen: ℒ zufolge, was er sagt according to ...; er fügte ℒ, was sie schrieb, nichts bei he added nothing to ... — **III** *rel. pron.* (= welchem): to whom, to which.

Demagog (-⏑ᴸ) [grch.] *m* ⓖⓖ (Volksführer) demagogue; popular leader, tribune of the people; **~en-hetze** *f* ⓖⓖ persecution of demagogues; **~entum** (-⏑ᴸᵛ) *n* ⓑ., **~ie** (-⏑-ᴸ) *f* ⓖⓖ (grch.) *a.* ⓖⓖ demagogic(al); ℒische Wühlerei dem. agitation.

Demant (-ᴸ) [mhd.; fr.; * grch. *ada'mant* = unbesiegbar: Stahl] *m* ⓑ. = Diamant; **~en** (-ᴸᵛ) *a.* ⓖⓖ (D 9) = diamanten.

Demarkations-linie (-⏑-tẞ(ᵛ)ʺ...) [fr.] ⓖⓖ (Grenzlinie) line of demarcation.

demaskieren (-⏑-ᴸᵛ) [fr.] *v/a.* u. *sich* ℒ *v/refl.* ⓖⓖ to unmask (o.s.).

Dementi (-ᵛ-. bĕ-mᵍ-ti') [fr.] *n* ⓖⓖ (Lügenstrafen) denial, (flat) contradiction; e-m ein *~* geben to give the lie to a p.

dementieren (-⏑-ᴸ. -mᵍᴸ-) [fr.] *v/a.* ⓖⓖ (ableugnen) to contradict, to deny.

dem-entsprechend (ᴸᵛᵛ) *adv.* accordingly, proportionately.

dem-gemäß (ᴸᵛᵛ *oder* -ᵛᴸ) *adv.* u. *a.* according to (or in conformity with) that or it; corresponding(ly).

Demimonde (b'mi-mᵍ'd) [fr.] *f* ⓖⓖ = Halbwelt.

Demission *zc.* [fr.] = Dimission.

Demi-urg ⓖ (-ᵛᴸ) [grch.] *m* ⓖⓖ *phls.* (Weltschöpfer) demiurge, creator.

dem-nach (ᴸᴸ) *adv.* **1.** Muster: according to that, accordingly. — **2.** Folge: consequently, therefore, hence.

dem-nächst (ᴸᴸ) *adv.* **1.** (nächstens) shortly, soon; in a short time. — **2.** (darauf) after (or next to) that; thereupon.

dem-nächtig (ᴸᴸᵛ) *a.* ⓖⓖ impending, approaching, imminent; (baldig) early.

demobilisieren ⓖ (-⏑-⏑-ᴸᵛ) [fr.] **I** *v/a.* ⓖⓖ u. **II** *~ n* ⓖⓖ *D/ung f* ⓖⓖ = abrüsten, Abrüstung.

Demokrat (-⏑-ᴸ) [grch.] *m* ⓖⓖ democrat; **~ie** (-⏑-⏑-ᴸ)*f* ⓖⓖ(Volksherrschaft) democracy; ℒisch (-⏑-ᴸᵛ) *a.* ⓖⓖ democratic(al).

Demokrit (-⏑-ᴸ), **~os** (ᴸ-⏑-⏑) *npr. m.* ⓑ. γ. (grich. Phil. 465-365) Democritus.

demolier/en (-⏑-ᴸᵛ) [fr.] **I** *v/a.* ⓖⓖ (zerstören) to demolish; destroy; F to smash. — **II** *~ n* ⓖⓖ *D/ung,* **Demolition** (-⏑-tẞ(ᵛ)ᴸ) [fr.] *f* ⓖⓖ demolition, destruction.

Demonstration ⓖ und ⓖ (-⏑-tẞ(ᵛ)ᴸ) [lt. --ᴸ-] *f* ⓖⓖ (Kundgebung)demonstration; eine *~* veranstalten to hold a dem.

demonstrativ (-⏑-ᴸⓘ) [lt.] *a.* ⓖⓖ demonstrative; **~(um)** *n* ⓑ.ⓖⓖ.(59); **~-pronomen** *n* ⓖⓖ demonstrative (or distinguishing)pronoun (or adjective). [strate.)

demonstrieren (-⏑-⏑-ᴸᵛ) *v/a.* ⓖⓖ to demon-

demontieren bsd. ⓖ (-mᵍᴸᵛ) [fr.] *v/a.* ⓖⓖ to unhorse cavalry; to disable (or dismount, silence) a battery.

Demoralisation (---ẞ(ᵛ)ᴸ) *f* ⓖⓖ demoralization. [sittlichen) to demoralize.)

demoralisieren(---⏑-ᴸᵛ)[fr.]*v/a.* ⓖⓖ (ent-

Demos (-ᵛ) [grch.] *m* ⓖⓖ Alt.: (Stadtgemeinde) demos, deme; weitS. (Volk*) people: in Zeitungen oft: demos.

demosthenisch (-⏑-ᴸᵛ) [Demo'sthenes, grch Redner 383—322 v. Chr.] *a.* ⓖⓖ of Demosthenes. Demosthenic.

dem-unerachtet, ℒungeachtet (ᴸᵛᵛᵛᵛ)*adv.* despite it, nevertheless, for all that.

Demut (ᴸ-) [ahd. Die(ner)-(ge)müt] *f* ⓖⓖ humility, meekness, stärker: lowliness; (Unterwürfigkeit) submissiveness.

demütig (ᴸᵛᵛ) [mhd.] *a.* ⓖⓖ humble, meek, stärker: lowly; (unterwürfig) submissive; Des Flehen supplication; *adv.*: ℒ bitten to supplicate; ℒst most humbly, in all humility.

demütigen (ᴸᵛᵛᵛ) **I** *v/a.* u. *sich* ℒ *v/refl.* ⓖⓖ to humble (o.s.), to humiliate (o.s.); (herabwürdigen) to abuse; (kränken) to mortify; sich ℒ (herablassen) to stoop low, F to eat humble-pie; sich ℒ (unterwerfen) to submit. — **II** *~ n* ⓖⓖ u. **Demütigung** *f* ⓖⓖ (s. I) humiliation; abasement; mortification; F setdown; tiefe *~* erleiden to suffer deep humiliation; e-m eine *~* zuteil w. Lto humble a p.('s pride), F to take a p. down a peg. [voll *a.* ⓖⓖ = demütig.)

Demut(s)-sinn (ᴸʺ...) *m* ⓖⓖ humility;

dem-zufolge (ᴸᵛᴸᵛ) *adv.* = demnach.

den (ᴸ) ① **1.** *acc. sg.* von *der* (s. ds) in allen Bdgn: an ℒ Tisch to the table; F ah! hören Sie doch ℒ! now, just listen to him! hark at him! — **2.** *dat. pl.* von *der, die, das (definite art.)* to the; in ℒ Wäldern in the woods; ℒ Geistern to the spirits.

Denar (-ᴸ) [lt. Zehner] *m* ⓑ. (älteste röm. Silbermünze, seit 269 v. Chr.) denar(ius).

denaturier/en ⓖ (---ᴸᵛ) [lt.] *v/a.* ⓖⓖ (ungenießbar m.) to debase, to make undrinkable; d/ter Spiritus methylated (or debased) spirits *pl.*

Dendrit ⓖ (-ᴸ) [grch.] *m* ⓖⓖ *min.* dendrite; ℒisch (-ᴸᵛ) *a.* ⓖⓖ dendritic.

Dendrolith ⓖ (-⏑-ᴸ) *m* ⓑ.ⓖⓖ (versteinerter Baumstamm) dendrolith.

Dendrologie ⓖ (-⏑-⏑ᴸ) [grch.]*f* ⓖⓖ (Baumkunde) dendrology.

Dendrometer ⓖ (-⏑-ᴸᵛ) [grch.] *n (m)* ⓖⓖ (Baummesser) dendrometer.

denen (ᴸᵛ) ⓖⓖ2b *dat. pl.* von *der, die, das* **I** *dem. pron.* to them; allen ℒ, die es angeht to all (those) whom it concerns. — **II** *rel. pron.* to whom, to which.

Dengel-hammer ⓖ (ᴸᵛ...) *m* ⓖⓖ *agr.* scythe-hammer.

dengeln ⓖ (ᴸᵛ) [mhd. *ding*] *v/a.* ⓖⓖ a. (hämmern) to hammer; die Sense ℒ to sharpen the scythe by hammering it.

⚗ scientific; ♁ botanical; ♁ geography; ⚙ machinery; ⚒ mining; ⚔ military; ⚓ marine; ✲ commercial; ✉ postal; 🚆 railway.

Dengel-zeug ⊙ (⁻ᵘ⁻) *n* 🅶 sharpening-tools *pl.* for scythes.

Dengue (ᵍᵉ) [span.] *f* 🅵, **~fieber** *n* 🅶 *path.* Westindien ꝛc. dengue, dandy-fever.

Denk-art (ᵘ⁻) *f* 🅶 mode (or way, manner) of thinking; s. Denkungsart.

denkbar (ᵘ⁻) *a.* 🅶 conceivable; es ist wohl 2, daß // it may be imagined that //; in der 2 kürzesten Zeit in the shortest time imaginable or possible; **~keit** (ᵘ²⁻) *f* 🅶 conceivableness.

Denk-brot (ᵘ⁻) *n* 🅶 jüd. rel. Schaubrot; **=buch** *n* memorandum-book.

denken (ᵘ⁻) [ahd.: think] 🅶 **I** *v/a., v/n.* (h.) und *v/refl.* **1.** ohne Objekt: **a)** to think; nachzusinnen, to reflect; vernunft-gemäß: to reason; 2de Wesen *n/pl.* rational beings *pl.*; (überlegen, erwägen) to meditate, to contemplate; ich sollte (doch wohl) 2! I should think so(, indeed)!; das gibt e-m zu 2 that is s.th. to think about, it sets one thinking; sie ist älter als wir 2 she is older than we imagine; solange ich 2 (mich erinnern) kann as long as (or as far back as) I can remember; **b)** (beabsichtigen) Sprichw. der Mensch denkt, Gott lenkt man proposes, God disposes; **c)** (der Ansicht sein) to be of opinion; ich denke mir, daß // I am of opinion that //, I consider that //; machen Sie es, wie Sie 2 do as you please or think right; einschaltend: das ist, denke ich, zu viel I think (or fancy) that's too much; **d)** mit *adv.*: edel, rechtschaffen 2 to have noble, honest sentiments, to be high-minded, honourable; hoch hinaus 2 to have lofty ideas, to aim high; laut 2 to think aloud; nicht gering von sich 2 to have a good idea of o.s., F to think no small beer of o.s.; wo 2 Sie nur hin? what are you thinking about or of?, vgl. **4**; zurück-2 to carry one's thoughts back to, to recall to one's mind; **e)** im *imperative*: 2 Sie nur, denk' (mal einer) an! only (or just) think or fancy! — **2.** mit Objekt: **a)** allgemeines *pron.*: wer hätte das 2 (sich vorstellen) können? who could have thought (or foreseen) that?; ich kann mir's schon 2 ... easily imagine (or conceive) it; das hätte ich mir nie gedacht I should never have imagined it or given it a thought; ich hatte mir das so schön gedacht I had taken such a rosy view of it; wart'!, ich denk' es dir! wait!, I'll repay you for it!; auch *v/refl.* das läßt sich leicht 2 that's easily understood; ~ es denkt sich schön an stillem Orte, etwa: a quiet spot gives scope to meditation; vgl. **c**; **b)** mit *adjektiv. s.*: Arges, Böses 2 (sinnen) to have evil designs, to brew (or be bent on) mischief; er denkt immer das Schlimmste he looks at the blackest side of everything; **c)** sich (*dat.*) e-n, et. 2 (vorstellen) to imagine a p., a th., to picture a p., a th. to o.s.; das habe ich mir gedacht that's what I expected; ich kann es mir gar nicht 2 I cannot realize (or conceive) it; es läßt sich 2 that is very likely!, bisw.: of course!; vgl. **a**. — **3.** mit abhängigem Satze: **a)** in indirekter Rede: ich dachte, er sei einer von Ihren Freunden I thought him (to be) one of your friends; man sollte 2, er wäre ein Narr you would think (that) he was mad; ich kann mir gar nicht 2, von wem es kommt I have no idea from whom it comes; er denkt Wunder, wer er ist (auch sei) he thinks himself a very important person, F he thinks a mighty deal of himself; 2 Sie sich nur, er will nach Japan! just think (or fancy) he wants to go to Japan; ich dächte, wir setzten unsere Reise fort I was thinking it would be best (for us) to continue our journey; **b)** mit *inf.* und **zu**: er denkt (hat die Absicht oder hofft) mich zu betrügen he intends (or hopes) to cheat me; ich denke (hoffe) meinen Prozeß zu gewinnen I hope to (or I trust that I may) win my case; **c)** mit *acc. u. p.p. ob. a. als* Prädikat: ich dachte mich von m-m Ohr getäuscht I imagined (that) my ears had deceived me; er dächte sich verlassen, wenn // he would consider himself abandoned, if //. — **4.** mit abhängiger *prp.*: **an** e-n, et. 2 to think of a p., a th.; er denkt zuviel an sich F he thinks too much of number one, he is too much wrapt up in himself; denke daran! think of it!, don't forget!; er denkt aus Heiraten he thinks of marrying, he intends getting married; ihr sollt an uns 2! you shall remember us!; er soll daran 2! he shall suffer for (or rue) it!; ich dachte nicht weiter daran I had dismissed it from my thoughts; ich will daran 2 I will consider it or turn it over in my mind; es ist nicht daran zu 2 it is not to be thought of, it is out of the question; F (ich) denk' nicht dran I should not dream of it; woran 2 Sie?, wie können Sie daran 2? what are you thinking of?, how can you think of such a thing?; 2 Sie sich an seine Stelle put yourself in his place; 2 Sie ernstlich daran, ein Automobil zu kaufen? are you seriously thinking of buying a motor-car?; wir 2 nicht daran, eins zu kaufen we have no intention of buying one; **auf** et. 2 (sinnen) to plan a th.; to revolve a th. in one's mind; auf Mittel (und Wege) 2 to devise means (and ways); wir müssen darauf 2, wie wir es machen we must consider how to do it; et. **bei** et. 2: wir 2 uns nichts Böses (dabei) we don't mean any harm (by it); **für** einen 2 to think (or take counsel) for a p.; **in** seinen Sack (auf seinen Vorteil) 2 to study one's (own) interest, F to look after number one; **über** etwas (nach-)2 to reflect (or meditate) on a th.; was 2 Sie darüber? what is your opinion about it?; **von** e-r Person od. Sache Gutes (Böses) 2 to have a good (bad) opinion of a p. or a th.; was werden Sie von mir 2? ... think of me? — **II** ~ *n* 🅶 **5.** thinking, &c. (s. I); des ~s fähig capable of thinking or reasoning, rational. — **6.** (Nachdenken) reflection, meditation; vernunftgemäßes ~, (logical) reasoning; (Forschen) speculation. — **III** ge-dacht *p.p. u. a.* 🅶 **7.** Bed. des *inf.* — **8.** (erwähnt, genannt) der Herr the aforesaid gentleman.

Denker (ᵘ⁻) *m* 🅶, **~in** *f* 🅶 thinker; engs. speculator, philosopher.

Denkerei (⁻⁻⁻ᴵ) *f* 🅶 b. s. useless (or frivolous) thinking.

Denk-fähig (ᵘ⁻) *a.* 🅶 able to think, capable of reasoning; rational; **=fähigkeit** *f* 🅶 thinking capacity, capability of reasoning; rationality; 2faul *a.* too lazy to think (for o.s.), weit S. slow of comprehension; **=freiheit** *f* freedom of thought or opinion, weit S. free interchange of ideas; **=gesetz** *n*, *log.* law of thought, logical rule; **=kraft** *f* thinking- (or brain-)power, intellectual capacity; vgl. **=fähigkeit**; **=kunst** *f*, **=lehre** *f* logic; **=mal** *n* ② ⓓ. ~ für einen monument raised to the memory of a p.; ein bleibendes ~ an // a lasting memorial of //; **=mäler** *pl.* antifer Kunst antique works *pl.* of art; **=münze** *f* (commemorative) medal; 2richtig *a.* logical; **=säule** *f* commemorative column or pillar; (Bildsäule) statue; **=schrift** *f* memorial; eine ~ bei e-r Behörde ꝛc. einreichen to memorialize; (kurze Abhandlung) memoir; **=spruch** *m* aphorism; (Grundsatz) maxim; (Sinnspruch) motto; apophthegm; **=spruchartig** *a.* sententious, apophthegmatical; **=stein** *m* memorial-stone; **=übung** *f* mental exercise.

Denkungs-art (ᵘ⁻) *f* 🅶 = Denkart; von edler (gemeiner) ~ high- (low-) minded; im Schatten kühler ~, etwa: in (the shade of) sober meditation.

Denk-vermögen (ᵘ⁻) *n* 🅶 = **=kraft**; **=vers** *m* commemorative line or verse or rhyme; **=weise** *f* = **=art**; 2würdig *a.* 🅶 (ewig ever) memorable, notable; **=würdigkeit** *f* memorableness, (bedeutendes Ereignis) memorable event; ~en *pl.* memoirs *pl.*; **=zeichen** *n* token (of remembrance), keep-sake; **=zettel** *m*: a) note to remind a p. of s.th.; (short) memorandum; F reminder; b) jüd. rel. phylactery; c) (leichte Strafe) light punishment, correction; e-m e-n ~ geben to give a p. a (severe) lesson, to make a p. smart.

denn (ᵉ) [ahd. (= dann): then, than] *cj.* **1.** begründend: for; because, since; 2 er hat es ja gesagt inasmuch as (or considering that) he said so; tonlos: dies zeigt uns 2 **doch** // this, surely, shows us //. — **2.** nach *comp.* fast †, jetzt bsd. statt e-s zweiten **als**: kein anderer 2 ich none but I (F me); mehr 2 einmal more than once; mehr als Abenteurer 2 als Gesandter (a.) more as an adventurer than as an ambassador; pleonastisch: *poet.* ehe 2 ich sterbe ere I die. — **3.** tonlos = also; bsd. in Frage- u. Wunschsätzen: wo ist er 2? well, where is he?; ist er 2 so arm? is he, indeed, so poor?; was ist 2 **nur** (los)? what can be the matter?; wieso 2? how so?; so mag es 2 dabei bleiben! then, let it be so!; (wohl)auf 2! up, then!; well, then!; P (na) 2 nicht!, etwa: leave it if you don't like it! — **4.** tonlos = schließlich; in der Tat; es ist ihm 2 doch gelungen then he has succeeded after all; ich

[dennoch] — 257 — [dermaßen]

schalt ihn, was er sich 2 auch zu Herzen nahm ... and, indeed, he took it to heart. — 5. tonlos (= außer wenn, wofern nicht, ohne daß) mit e-m *subj*.: but that, if not, unless; wir lassen dich nicht los, du singest uns 2 ein Lied ... unless you sing us a song; es sei 2, daß er krank ist except he be ill.

dennoch (ᴗ́ᴗ) [denn noch] *adv. cj.* yet, still, however, nevertheless; es ist 2 wahr! it is true all the same or for all that, yet it is the truth, schwächer: it is true though. 　　　[dental.

dental (ᴗ́) [lt.] *a.* ⓰ (die Zähne betreffend)

Dentalis (ᴗ́ᴗ) *f*, *sg. inv.*, *pl.* Dentales, **Dental-laut** (ᴗ́ᴗᴗ) *m* ⓶, *gram.* (Zahnlaut) dental sound.

Dentist (ᴗ́) [fr.] *m* ⓷ (Zahnkünstler) dentist, dental surgeon.

Denunziant (ᴗᴗᴗ́) [lt.] *m* ⓷, **~in** *f* ⓸ denouncer, informer (= Angeber 3); ⚖ *jur.* (Strafantragsteller) prosecutor.

Denunziation (ᴗᴗᴗ-tsᴗ́) [lt.] *f* ⓯ = Angeberei. 　　　[nounce = angeben 2).

denunzieren (ᴗᴗᴗ́) [lt.] *v/a.* ⓰ to de-

Departement (-ᴗᴗmaᴗ́) [fr.] *n* ⓹ (Abteilung, Geschäftskreis ꝛc.) department; Ministerium: ~ der inneren (äußeren) Angelegenheiten, in England: Home (Foreign) Office.

Dependenz (-ᴗᴗ́) [lt.] *f* ⓰ (*pl. a.* ~ien) (abhängiges Gebiet) dependency.

Depesche (-ᴗᴗ) [fr. *dépêche*] *f* ⓰ dispatch; telegraphische ~ telegraphic message, telegram, wire, Kabel-2: cable message.

Depeschen-beförderung ⚓ (-ᴗᴗ...) *f* forwarding of dispatches; **=formular** *n* message- (or telegraph-) form; **=reiter** *m* mounted messenger or courier; **=tasche** *f* dispatch-box; **=weg** *m*: im ~e drahtlich.

depeschieren (-ᴗᴗ́) [fr.] *v/n.* (h.) ⓰ to send dispatches; to telegraph, to (send a) wire, mittels Kabels: to cable.

Deplacement ⚓ (-ᴗᴗ(ᴗ́)-maᴗ́) [fr.] *n* ⓹ ~ (Wasserverdrängung e-s Schiffes) displacement. 　　　[marschieren) to deploy.

deployieren ⚔ (-pla-ᴗ́-) [fr.] *v/a.* ⓰ (auf-

Deponens (-ᴗ́) [lt.] *n* ⓷⓪, ⓹⓽ *gram.* (lt. Zeitwort mit passiver Form, aber aktiver Bedeutung) deponent (verb).

Deponent (-ᴗᴗ́) [lt.] *m* ⓷⓶, **~in** *f* ⓸ 1. *jur.* (aussagender Zeuge) witness giving evidence. — 2. ⚖ (Hinterleger) depositor.

deponieren (-ᴗᴗ́) [lt.] *v/a.* ⓰ 1. (gerichtlich aussagen) to state in evidence, to depose. — 2. ⚖ (hinterlegen) to deposit furniture, money, &c.; to put money in a bank, &c.

Deportation (-ᴗ-tsᴗ́) [lt.] *f* ⓰ von Verbrechern: transportation; deportation.

deportieren (-ᴗᴗ́) [lt.] *v/a.* ⓰ to transport, to deport.

Deportierte([r] *m f* (-ᴗᴗ́) ⓸ (transport-)

Depositar (-ᴗᴗ́) [lt.], **Depositär** [fr.] *m* ⓬, **~in** *f* ⓸ (Verwahrer[in]) depositary, trustee (*ant.* Deponent 2).

Depositen-bank (-ᴗᴗ...) *f* ⓶ (deposit-) bank; **=gelder** *n/pl.* money in trust; in Banken: deposits *pl.*; **=kasse** *f* trust-funds *pl.*, trust-money; **=schein** *m* banker's receipt for a deposit.

Depositorium (-ᴗᴗᴗ́-) [lt.] *n* ⓲ (Hinterlegungsstelle) depository.

Depositum (-ᴗ́ᴗ-) [lt.] *n* ⓲, ⓹⓽ (Hinterlegtes) deposit(ed funds *pl.*), trust money.

depossedieren (-ᴗᴗᴗ́) [fr.] *v a.* ⓰ *jur.* (aus dem Besitz vertreiben) to dispossess.

Depot (de-vṓ) [fr.] *n* ⓹⓪ 1. *a)* ⚔ repository, für Waren: stores *pl.*, store-house, für unverzollte Waren: bonded warehouse; *b)* ⚓ depot, (fr.) *dépôt* — 2. = Depo'situm.

Depot-platz ⚓ (‴...) *m* ⓶ depot; **=wechsel** ⚖ *m* change of storage.

Depression ⚓ (-ᴗ(ᴗ)ᴗ́) [lt.] *f* ⓰ ⚔, *ast., path., phys.* depression; ~ des Horizonts dip of the horizon.

Depressions-winkel (-ᴗ(ᴗ)ᴗ́...) *m* ⓶ angle of depression (*ant.* Elevationswinkel).

deprimieren (-ᴗᴗ́) [lt.] *v/a.* ⓰ 1. (herabdrücken) to depress. — 2. *fig.* (niederschlagen) to depress, deject, discourage.

Deputat (-ᴗ́) [lt.] *n* ⓳c. (Gehaltszulage in Naturalien) allowance (or emolument) in kind; **~getreide** *n* ⓶ all. of corn.

Deputation (-ᴗᴗ-tsᴗ́) [fr.] *f* ⓰ (Absendung, *coll.* Abgesandte) deputation. 　　　[depute.

deputieren (-ᴗᴗ́) *v/a.* ⓰ (abordnen) to

Deputierte([r] *m f* (-ᴗᴗ́) ⓺ (Abgeordnete) deputy. 　　　[of deputies.

Deputierten-kammer (ᴗ́...) *f* ⓶ chamber

der (ᴗ́) [ahd.: the(re)] *m*, **die** (ᴗ́) *f*, **das** (ᴗ́) *n* I *def. art.* ①, ⓰ⒷB 1. the; der Wolf frißt das Schaf the wolf eats the sheep; oft auch durch das *poss. pron.* oder gar nicht übersetzt, zB.: ich wusch mir das Gesicht I washed my face; er kam mit dem Hut in der Hand ... with his hat in his hand, F ... hat in hand. — 2. mit ausgelassenem *s*. (= derjenige; vgl. 4) mein zur und der des Gastes ... that of the guest. — II *dem. pron. u. a.* ⓰ⒶⒷ 3. (dieser, jener) der Mann hier this man; dieser und der dies one and that one; der, die mit der Brille! the one with the glasses (on)!; der und der (die und die) Mr. (Mrs.) So and So; an dem u. dem Tage on such and such a day; Possen das! (it's) tomfoolery!; sind das Ihre Bücher? are those ...?; mein einziger Trost ist der, daß ihr hier seid my only comfort is that you are (or your being) here; elliptisch mit und, meist *iro.* der und so baden gehen? go bathing?, not he!. — 4. auf e-n Relativsatz bezüglich = derjenige (*gen. pl.* derer); der(jenige), welcher he who; auch der ist zu loben, der (welcher) // also he is to be praised who //; Gott hilft denen, die andern helfen God assists those who help others. — III *rel. pron. u. a.* ⓰ⒶⒷ 5. who, which, that; das Mädchen, mit dem (mit dessen) Vater) ich sprach the girl to whom (to whose father) I spoke; ich, der ich Zeuge davon war I who witnessed it; die Soldaten, denen (deren Hauptmann) wir begegneten the soldiers whom (whose captain) we met; am Rhein ist kein Ort, **der nicht** seine Sage hätte on the Rhine there is not a spot but (F but what) has its legend.

derangieren (be-rg-Ǵᴗ́) [fr.] *v/a.* ⓰ (stören) to derange, disarrange, upset.

der-art (ᴗ́ᴗ) *adv.* in such a manner or way, to such a degree; (so sehr) so much; er prahlt 2, daß // he brags to such an extent that //.

der-artig (ᴗ́ᴗᴗ) *a.* ⓰ such; etwas (nichts) 2es s.th. (nothing) of the kind.

derb (ᴗ́) [nbd. (ahd.)] *a.* ⓰ 1. (fest gefügt) compact, solid, firm; der Stoff stout substance. — 2. (kräftig) sturdy; robust; ein 2er Geselle a powerful (F whacking) fellow; ein 2es Weib (sbild) F a buxom wench; e-n 2 (*adv.*) durchprügeln F to give a p. a good hiding. — 3. (rauh) rude; (grob, roh) rough, coarse; (schwer, massig) heavy, weighty, ✕ *min.* massive, in (irregular) lumps; (plump) clumsy; (unverblümt) blunt; 2er Kuß hearty kiss; 2e Lüge downright lie; 2e (Tracht) Prügel sound thrashing or beating, hard blows *pl.*; 2e Wahrheiten *f/pl.* home thrusts or truths *pl.*

Derbheit (ᴗ́-) *f* ⓰ (s. derb) 1. compactness, solidity, firmness; stoutness. — 2. sturdiness, robustness. — 3. rudeness, roughness, coarseness, bluntness.

der-einst (ᴗᴗ́) [nbd.] *adv.* 1. Zukunft: (a. 2ens, 2mals) some (future) day, in days (or years, times) to come. — 2. Vergangenheit: (in days) of old or of yore.

der-einstig (ᴗᴗ́ᴗ) *a.* ⓰ future, intended.

deren (ᴗ́ᴗ) ⓰ⒶⒷ2b. *gen. sg. f u. gen. pl.* (unbetont) von der (die, das) 3 u. 5.

derent-halben (ᴗᴗ́ᴗ), **2wegen** (ᴗᴗ́ᴗ), um **2willen** (ᴗᴗ́ᴗ) 1. *dem.* for her, their, &c. sake; on her, their, &c. account or behalf. — 2. *rel.* for the sake (or on behalf, on account) of whom (or which; die Leute, um 2willen er sich bemühte the people on whose behalf (or for whom) he exerted himself; die Kinder, 2halben er sich ins Feuer stürzte the children for whose sake (or for whom) he rushed into the fire.

derer (ᴗ́ᴗ) *gen. pl.* (betont) von der (die,)

deret-halben ꝛc. *f. derent=*. 　　　[das] 4.

der-gestalt (ᴗᴗ́ᴗ) *adv.* = derart.

der-gleichen (ᴗᴗ́ᴗ) *a., inv.* 1. bezüglich: (welcher Art) Dinge, 2 ich nimmer sah things the like of which (or things such as) I never saw (before). — 2. hinweisend: (von solcher Art) such; 2 Leute people of that kind; in 2 Fällen, bei 2 Gelegenheiten in such (like) cases, on occasions of that sort; dies und 2 (mehr) (*abbr.* u. dgl. [m.]) and the like, and so forth; nichts 2 nothing of the kind, nothing like it, no such thing; nichts 2 tun (F nichts merken lassen) to pretend (or appear) not to notice (or mind) a th., to make no response.

Derivat ⚗ (--wᴗ́) [lt.] *n* ⓳c. *chm.* (abgeleiteter Körper) derivat(iv)e.

derivativ (-ᴗ-wᴗ́) [lt.] *a.* ⓰ derivative.

Derivativum ⚗ (--wᴗ́ᴗ-) [lt.] *n* ⓹⓽ (*pl. a.* ...i've) *gr.* (abgeleitetes Wort) derivative.

der-jenige (ᴗ́ᴗᴗ) *m*, **die-jenige** (ᴗ́ᴗᴗ) *f*, **das-jenige** (ᴗ́ᴗᴗ) *n* ⓰ⒸⒷ 2 u. ⓸ 1 *dem. pron.* he who, she who; that which; derjenige ist glücklich, welcher // happy is he who //. — 2. *dem. a.* (derselb(ig)e, jener) derjenige Mann, welcher // the (same) man that //; diejenigen Leute, welche // those (same) people who //.

derlei (ᴗ́-) *a., inv.* = dergleichen.

der-mal-einst(ig) (ᴗᴗ-ᴗ́) = dereinst(ig).

der-malen (ᴗ́-) *adv.* (just) at present, actually; erzählend: at that time, then.

der-malig (ᴗ́ᴗᴗ) *a.* ⓰ present, actual; der 2e König the (now) reigning king.

der-maßen (ᴗ́-ᴗ) *adv.* = derart.

[dermatisch] — 258 — [Detonation]

dermatisch ⚯ (⌣⌢⌣) *a.* ⓺ dermatic.
Dermatologie ⚯ (⌣⌣⌣⌢) [grch.] *f* ⓸ (Lehre von der Haut) dermatology.
dero Kanzleistil (⌢⌣) *gen.* = deren, derer, jetzt nur noch gbr. in der Anrede von Fürsten: (↘ 2. Person) Your; (3. Person) His, Her.
dero-halben† (⌢⌣⌣), ⚥**wegen** (⌢⌣⌣) *adv.* = deshalb I.
Deroute ⚔ (-rū⌣) [fr.] *f* ⓸ (jähe wilde Flucht) rout, precipitous flight; ⚒ Börse: (Kurssturz) sudden fall, panic, scare.
der-selbe *m*, **die-selbe** *f* (⌢⌣⌣), **das-selbe** *n* (⌢⌣⌣) *dem. pron.* ⓺ C 2, B¹ **1.** Einerleiheit bezeichnend: the same; **eben-**⚥ (auch ganz ⚥, genau ⚥) just (or quite, exactly) the same; the very same; ein und derselbe the very same (man, &c.); es ist alles ein(s) und dasselbe it is all the same (thing), it comes to the same thing (in the end); **ein und dasselbe**, ein und dieselbe Sache one and the same thing; vgl. selb. — **2.** ⚡ zurückverweisend, tonlos, statt er, sie, es und diese(r, s): er will dieselben (sie, die Schulden) nicht bezahlen he does not want to pay them; eine Klausel derselben (Urkunde) one clause of it; vgl. Höchstdieselben. [selbe ꝛc.]
der-selbige ꝛc. (⌢⌣⌣) † ob. *bibl.* = der-
der-weil ↘ (⌣⌢), **⚥e(n)** (⌣⌢) = dieweil; ⚥ ich eben lad' (U.) whilst I am loading.
Derwisch (⌢⌣) [pers. Armer (= Fakir)] *m* ⓵a. (mohammedan. Mönch) dervish.
der-zeit (⌢⌣) *adv.*, ⚥**ig** (⌢⌣⌣) *a.* ⓺ = dermalen, dermalig.
des¹ (⌢) **1.** ① *gen.* von der. — **2.** † = dessen; *bibl.* der Wille des, der mich gesandt hat the will of Him that sent me.
Dos² ♪ (⌢) *n, inv.* D flat.
desarmieren ⚔ (-⌣⌢⌣) [fr.] *v/a.* ⓸ (entwaffnen) to disarm.
desavouieren (-⌣⌣⌢⌣) [fr.] *v/a.* ⓸ (ableugnen) to disavow.
Deserteur ⚔ und ⚓ (-⌣⌢r) [fr.] *m* ⓵d. (Ausreißer) deserter, runaway (soldier).
desertieren (-⌣⌢⌣) [fr.] *v/n.* (in) to desert (the colours), to run away (from one's regiment). — **Desertion** (-⌣tz(⌣)⌢) *f* ⓸ (Fahnenflucht) desertion (of the colours); absence without leave.
des-falls (⌢⌣) *adv.* **1.** (für den Fall) in that case. — **2.** (deshalb) on that account, on that score; therefore.
des-fallsig (⌢⌣⌣ ob. ⌢⌢⌣) *a.* ⓺ Kanzleiwort (den Fall angehend) eventual.
des-gleichen (⌣⌢⌣) **I** *a. inv.* **1.** bezüglich (wie) such as, like. — **2.** hinweisend: some such = dergleichen; *adv.* likewise; und die übrigen ⚥ also do (or did, &c.) the rest. — **II** *cj.* **3.** ⚥ daß // just as //.
des-halb (⌢⌣ u. ⌣⌢) **I** *adv.* (deswegen) on that account, for that reason, therefore; (für den Zweck) for that purpose; eben ⚥ for that very reason; ich achte ihn ⚥ (trotzdem) nicht weniger ... none the less (for it); ⚥ ist er doch mein Freund he is my friend nevertheless or all the same. — **2.** vor weil ꝛc. oft nicht zu übersetzen: ich tat es nur ⚥, weil // I did it only because //; er schrieb ⚥, damit wir // he wrote so that we //; weshalb kam er? ⚥ um //, ⚥ weil // why did he come? in order to //, because //. — **II** *cj.* **3.** that is (the reason) why.

Desiderat ⚯ (--⌣⌢) [lt.] *n* ⓵c. *phls.* (Vermißtes; Lücke) desideratum, pl. ...ta; ~**ivum** (--⌣⌢⌣w) *n* ⓹⓺ *gr.* desiderative verb; ~**um** *n* ⓹⓺ = Desiderat.
designieren (-⌣⌢⌣) [lt.] *v/a.* ⓽⓷ (bezeichnen) to designate as successor, for a post.
Desinfektion (-⌣⌣tz(⌣)⌢) [fr.] *f* ⓸ (Entseuchung) disinfection; deodorization; ~⚥**mittel** (″...) *n* ⓺⓶ disinfectant.
desinfizier/en (-⌣-⌢⌣) [fr.] **I** *v/a.* ⓽⓷ (von Ansteckungsstoffen reinigen) to disinfect; (geruchlos m.) to deodorize. — **II** ⚥**b** *p.pr.* u. *a.* ⓺⓺ disinfecting, ...ant. — **III** ~ *n* ⓹⓷ u. **D/ung** *f* ⓸ disinfection; (Geruchlosmachung) deodorization.
Desintegrator ⚯ (-⌣⌣⌢⌣) [fr.=lt.] *m* ⓷⓵ (Maschine zum Zerkleinern) chopping (or mincing, pounding) machine.
Desman (⌣⌢) *m* ⓹⓵ *zo.* (Bisamspitzmaus) Russian musk-rat (Myo′gale moscha′ta).
Desmologie (-⌣⌣⌢) [grch.] *f* ⓸ *anat.* (Lehre von den Gelenkbändern) desmology.
desolat (-⌣⌢) [lt.] *a.* ⓺⓺ (vereinsamt) desolate, dreary, lonely; (traurig) sad.
Desorganisation (-⌣⌣⌣-tz(⌣)⌢) *f* ⓸ (Zerrüttung) disorganization.
desorganisieren (-⌣⌣⌣-⌢⌣) [fr.] *v/a.* ⓽⓷ (auflösen) to disorganize.
Desoxydation (-⌣⌣⌣-tz(⌣)⌢) *f* ⓸ *chm.* (Sauerstoffentziehung) deoxidation, deoxygenation.
desoxydieren (-⌣⌣⌣⌢⌣) [fr.] *v/a.* u. *v/refl.* ⓽⓷ *chm.* (des Sauerstoffs berauben) (sich) ⚥ to deoxidate, to deoxidize, to deoxygenate.
despektierlich (-⌣⌣⌢⌣) [lt. u. dtsch.-lich] *a.* ⓺⓺ (unehrerbietig) disrespectful, disdainful.
Despot (⌣⌢) [grch.] *m* ⓷⓶ (Willkürherrscher) despot, tyrant; ~**ie** (⌣-⌢) *f* ⓸ (Willkürherrschaft) despotic rule; ⚥**isch** (⌣⌢⌣) *a.* ⓺⓺ despotic(al), tyrannical; ⚥**isieren** (-⌣⌢⌣) *v/a.* ⓽⓷ to despotize, tyrannize, to domineer over; ~**ismus** (⌣-⌣⌢) *m* ⓷⓷ despotism, tyranny, absolutism.
des-selben (⌢⌣⌣) *gen. sg.* v. derselbe.
des-selb(ig)en-gleichen ↘ (⌣⌢(⌣)⌣⌣″) *a. inv.* = desgleichen.
dessen (⌢⌣) *gen. sg.* v. der (das) **II** u. **III** ⓺⓺ A 2 b. **1.** hinweisend: of him, of it, of that; ⚥ (= desjenigen), der // of him who //. — **2.** bezüglich: whose, of whom, of which; der, die in ⚥ Hause ... in whose house; das Dorf, in ⚥ Nähe ... in the vicinity of which, near (or close to) which.
dessent-halben (⌢⌣...), ⚥**wegen** *adv.* = deshalb I; um ⚥**willen** **1.** hinweisend: on that account. — **2.** bezüglich: on account of which.
dessen-ungeachtet (⌢⌣...″) *adv.* despite all that, nevertheless, notwithstanding that, for all that. [dessert.]
Dessert (⌣⌢r) [fr.] *n* ⓹⓵ (Nachtisch)
Dessert-gabel (″...) *f* ⓺⓶, ⚥**löffel** *m*, ⚥**messer** *n*, ⚥**service** *n*, ⚥**teller** *m* dessert-fork, -spoon, -knife, -service, -plate; ⚥**serviette** *f* doily. [pattern.]
Dessin (⌣⌢ā′) [fr.] *n* ⓹⓵ (Muster) design,
Dessinateur (⌣-⌣⌢r) *m* ⓶ (Musterzeichner) designer, pattern-drawer. [inery.]
Dessin-maschine ⚯ *f* ⓺⓶ figuring-mach-
Destillat ⚯ (⌣-⌢) [lt. f. destillieren] *n* ⓵c. *chm.*, &c. (durch Kühlung von Dämpfen Hergestelltes) distillate, fluid obtained by distilling; ⚯ abstraction.

Destillateur (⌣-⌣-tš⌢r) [⁺⁺ fr.] *m* ⓵d. distiller; dealer in spirits.
Destillation (⌣-⌣-tz(⌣)⌢) [lt.] *f* ⓸ **1.** *chm.* (Abziehen durch Abdampfen und Kühlung) distillation, distilling; trock(e)ne ~ destructive (or dry) d.; wiederholte ~ redistilling, rectification. — **2.** (Branntweinbrennerei) distillery; (Schnapsschenke) a. **P Destille** (⌣⌢⌣) *f* ⓸ gin-shop.
Destillier-apparat ⊕ (⌣-⌢″...) *m* ⓺⓶ still.
destillierbar (⌣-⌢″...) *a.* ⓺⓺ *chm.* distillable, weit S. volatil(izabl)e. [*chm.* alembic.]
Destillier-blase (⌣-⌢″...) *f* ⓺⓶ *chm.* retort,
destillier/en (⌣-⌢⌣) [lt. de-stilla′re] *v/n.* herabträufeln u. *fr. distiller*] *v/a.* ⓽⓷ *chm.* (abziehen) to distil, bis w. to abstract; d/tes Wasser distilled water; mehrmals d/t redistilled, rectified.
Destillier-gefäß ⊕ (⌣-⌢″...) *n* ⓹⓶ *chm.* = ⚥**blase**; ⚥**helm**, ⚥**hut** *m* helm of a retort or still; ⚥**kolben** *m* still-(head); ⚥**kunst** *f* art of distilling; ⚥**rückstand** *m* residuum of a distillation.
desto (⌢⌣) [mhd.] *adv. mit comp.* the (more so); ⚥ schlimmer (that's) all the worse; (nun) ⚥ besser well, all the better; je mehr, ⚥ besser the more the better, the more the merrier; er hat es nur ⚥ lieber he likes it all the more or the better; vgl. nichts⚥weniger.
des-ungeachtet (⌢⌣⌣⌣) *f.* dessen=u....
des-wegen (⌢⌣⌣, ⌣⌢⌣), um des-willen (⌢⌣⌣) *adv.* = deshalb I, dessentwillen.
Deszendent (-⌣⌢) [lt.] *m* ⓸⓶ (Nachkomme, Abkömmling) descendant.
Deszendenz (-⌣⌢) *f* ⓸⓶ (Nachkommenschaft) descendants *pl.*, offspring; ~**theorie** *f* theory of transmission (by descent).
Detachement ⚔ (dĕ-tă-sch(⌣)-mā′) [fr.] *n* ⓹⓶ (Kommando, Abteilung) detachment; draft; kleines ~ squad.
detachieren (-⌣sch⌣⌢) [fr.] *v/a.* ⓽⓷ (abkommandieren, entsenden) to detach; to draft off.
Detail (dĕ-tă′(i)′t) [fr.] *n* ⓹⓵ **1.** (Einzelheit) detail; ins ~ eingeh(e)n to enter into particulars, F to go into detail. — **2.** ⚒ (Einzelverkauf) retail; en détail, im ~ (verkaufen to buy (sell) by retail.
Detail-bericht (″...) *m* ⓺⓶ detailed statement; einen ~ über et. abstatten to give a circumstantial account of a th.; ⚥**geschäft** *n*, ⚥**handel** *m* ⚒ retail business; ⚥**händler** *m* = Detaillist.
detaillier/en (dĕ-tăl-ji′⌣) [fr.] **I** *v/a.* ⓽⓷ (einzeln anführen) to detail, particularize; to specify; ⚒ (im kleinen verkaufen) to (sell by) retail; detailliert with full details, in detail. — **II D/ung** *f* ⓸ specification; [händler] retail dealer.
Detaillist ⚒ (dĕ-tăl-ji′ßt) [fr.] *m* ⓺⓶ (Klein-
Detail-verkauf *m* ⓺⓶ selling by retail, retailing; ⚥**verkäufer** ⚒ *m* = Detailli′st.
Detektiv(e) † (⌣⌢f, ⌣-⌢⌣w) [am., *lt.] *m* ⓵⓴ (Geheimpolizist) detective, P† teck.
Determinante ⚯ (-⌣-⌢⌣) [lt.] *f* ⓸⓶ *math.* determinant.
Determinismus ⚯ (-⌣-⌢⌣) [neu=lt.] *m* ⓶⓻ *phls.* (Lehre von den Einflüssen auf den menschlichen Willen) determinism.
determinier/en ⚯ (-⌣-⌢⌣) [lt.] **I** *v/a.* ⓽⓷ (festsetzen) to determine. — **II b/t** *p.p.* u. *a.* ⓺⓺ (entschlossen) determined, firmly resolved, resolute. [fung] detonation.
Detonation (-⌣-tz(⌣)⌢) [lt.] *f* ⓸⓺ (Verpuf-

Signs (see page XVII): F familiar; P vulgar; ⌐ flash; ↘ rare; † obsolete (died); * new word (born); ⁺⁺ incorrect; ♪ music;

[detonieren] — 259 — **[Diagonalstoff]**

detonier/en (-⁻ᷝ⌣) [lt.] **I** v/n. (h.) ⊛ ♩ to intonate wrongly. — **II** ~ n ㉓ und **Detonierung** f ㊻ ♩ wrong intonation; *chm.* = Detonation.

detto öft. (⌣-) [it.] f. dit(t)o.

deucht (⌣) 3. Person *sg. pres.* (bff. dünkt) u. ℒe *impf.* v. dünken (f. b). [**Luppe.**

Deul(ing) ⊛ ⊕ (⌣⌣) m ⓒ(d). *metall.* =⌋

Deus ex machina (⌣⌣ ⌣ ⁻ᷝ⌣) [lt. Gott aus e-r Maschine] m *deus ex machina*; *fig.* (unverhoffter, wunderbarer Retter) unexpected (or miraculous) deliverer.

Deut (⌣) [ndl., *†fand.] m ⓒc. (Scheidemünze = 2 Pf.) doit; *fig.* er hat f-n ~ F he hasn't (or he's not worth) a farthing.

deutbar (⌣-) *a.* ㊺ explicable.

Deutelei F (-⌣⌣) f ㊺ subtle (or far-fetched, strained) interpretation; F quibble (on words).

deuteln (⌣⌣) **I** v/a. ⓐa. to interpret (or explain) with great nicety, to twist the meaning of words; (zergliedern) to analyse (minutely). — **II** ~ n ㉓ = Deutelei.

deuten (⌣⌣) [ahd.: deutsch] ⊛ **I** v/n. (h.) 1. auf et. (ob. nach et.) hin:ℒ to point at a thing, weit:ℒ to show (or indicate, point out) a th. — 2. *fig.* (vorhersagen) to point to, to prognosticate; alles deutet auf Stürme (hin) everything forebodes stormy weather. — **II** v/a. u. sich ℒ v/*refl.* 3 = I; sich ℒ (anzeigen) to appear, to announce o.s. — 4. (ausdeuten) to interpret, explain, construe; die Sterne ℒ to read in the stars. — 5. et. schlecht, übel ℒ (auslegen) to put a bad (or an ill) construction (up)on a th.; et. zum guten ℒ to put a kindly construction upon a th., to put a th. in a favourable light, to take a th. in good part.

Deuter (⌣⌣) *m* ㉒, ~**in** f ㊷ interpreter.

Deuterei (-⌣⌣) f ㊺ = Deutelei.

...deutig (...⌣⌣) ㊺ in Zssgn., z. B. zwei-ℒ ambiguous. [pettifogger.⌋

Deutler (⌣⌣) *m* ㉒, ~**in** f ㊷ quibbler,⌋

deutlich (⌣⌣) [deuten] *a.* ㊺ (leicht unterscheidbar) distinct, marked; (verständlich) clear, intelligible, plain; lucid (style); (einleuchtend) evident; ℒe Handschrift legible (hand-)writing; ℒ (*adv.*) lesen to read intelligibly; e-m et. klar und ℒ sagen to tell a p. the plain truth of a th.; ich sehe ℒ I see plainly; ~**keit** (⌣⌣-) f ㊺ distinctness, clearness; plainness; des Stils: lucidity, perspicuity; der Handschrift: legibility.

deutsch (⌣) [ahd.: Dutch = völkisch] **I** *a.* ㊺ 1. German; das ~e Reich, der ~e Bund the German Empire, Confederation; der ℒe Kaiser the German Emperor, a.: der Kaiser; f. Meile; ℒe Schrift German character(s *pl.*); ~ (das ~e) reden to speak German; er spricht gut ~ he speaks good German; *fig.* ℒ (offen) mit e-m sprechen (vgl. 3) to talk plain English to a p. — 2. das ~e Meer the North Sea, the German Ocean; *hist.* der ~e Orden the Teutonic Order; ℒe Spracheigenheit, Wendung Germanism; der ℒe (Volks=)Stamm the Germanic (or Teutonic) race. — 3. *fig.* das heißt auf gut ~ that means in plain language; er hat ℒen Sinn, ein ℒes Herz he is straightforward; ℒ mit

e-m sprechen (ihm deutlich die Wahrheit sagen) to tell a p. the plain truth; ℒ heraus, (um es ℒ zu sagen to speak plainly; der ℒe Michel, etwa: clumsy German. — **II** ~**e(r)** *m*, ~**e** f ㊻ 4. German; was ist des ~en Vaterland? which is the German('s) Fatherland?; die alten ~en the Germani(cs) *pl.*, the ancient Germans or Teutons *pl.* — **III** ~ *n*, *inv.*, das ~**e** n ㊻ 5. (ℒe Sprache) German, the G. language; auf ℒ, im ~en in G.; er kann (fein) ~ he knows (no) G.; ich lerne ~ I am learning G.; er schreibt, spricht ~ (ob. das ~e) he writes, speaks G.; ein ℒ geschriebener Brief a letter written in G., a G. letter.

Deutsch=amerikaner(in f) *m* (⁻⌣...) ㊷ German American; ℒ**(en)=feindlich** (⁻⌣...) *a.* ㊺ anti-German; ~**freundlichkeit** f liking for Germans; kind(ly) feeling towards Germany; ~**zösisch** *a.* Franco-German (vgl. französisch=deutsch), aber: ℒes Wörterbuch German-French dictionary.

Deutschheit (⌣-) f ㊺ German origin or nationality; weit:ℒ. G. character or nature. [like German.⌋

deutsch=klingend (⁻⌣...) *a.* ㊺ sounding⌋

Deutschland ♀ (⁻⌣) [nhd.] *npr/n.* ⓑα. Germany; *alte* ~ ancient Germany.

Deutsch=Lothringen ♀ (⁻⌣⌣⌣ u. -⌣⌣) *npr/n.* ㉓α. German Lorraine.

Deutsch=meister(tum n) *m* (⁻...) ㊷ Grand-Master(ship) of the Teutonic Order; ℒ**österreichisch** *a.* Austro-German; ℒ**redend** *a.* German-speaking; ~**sprechen** *n* speaking G., G. speech.

Deutschtum (⌣-) n ㉔. (deutsches Volkstum) German nationality or patriotism; (deutsche Sitten) G. customs *pl.*; vgl. Deutschheit. [stärker: teutomania.⌋

Deutschtümelei (⌣-⌣⌣) f ㊺ teutonism,⌋

deutschtümeln (⁻⌣⌣) v/n. (h.) ⓐa. to affect (or show off) German manners or ways.

Deutschtümler (⁻⌣⌣) *m* ㉒, ~**in** f ㊷, etwa: one who displays a love for Germans or German things. [tically German.⌋

deutschtümlich (⁻⌣⌣) *a.* ㊺ characteris-⌋

Deutsch=verderber (⁻...) *m*, ~**in** f ㊷ one who corrupts (or speaks bad) German.

Deutung (⌣⌣) [deuten] f ㊺ interpretation, explanation; einer Sache eine richtige (falsche) ~ geben to put a right (a wrong) construction upon a th.

deutungs=voll (⁻⌣⌣) *a.* ㊺ significant, full of meaning; suggestive; (Unglück verheißend) ominous, portentous.

Devise (-w-⌣⌣) [fr.] f ㊸ 1. (Wahl-spruch) device, motto. — 2. ♣ (Wechsel auf ausländische Plätze) foreign bill (of exchange); ~**n=geschäft** (-w⌣⌣...) business (done) in foreign bills.

devonisch ♀ (-w-⌣⌣) [englische Grafschaft Devonshire] *a.* ㊺ *geol.* Devonian.

devot (-w-⌣) [lt.] *a.* ㊺ 1. (fromm) devout. — 2. (ergeben) devoted. — 3. (demütig) humble. [heit, Andacht) devotion.⌋

Devotion (-w-tſ(⌣)⌣) [lt.] f ㊺ (Ergeben-⌋

Dexel ⊕ (⌣⌣) *m, n* ㉒ *carp.* (Art Beil) adze. [an) adze.⌋

dexeln ⊕ (⌣⌣) v/a. ⓐa. to (shape with⌋

Dextrin ♀ u. ⊕ (-⌣⌣) [lt. rechts] *n* ⓒc. *chm.* dextrin(e), starchgum ($C_6H_{10}O_5$); ~**zucker** (-⌣⌣...) *m* ㉒ starch-sugar.

Dextrose (-⌣⌣) [lt.] f ㊸ (Traubenzucker) dextrose, dextroglucose.

Dezem (⌣⌣) [lt.] *m* ⊛ 1. (Zehnte) tithe. — 2. F e-m f-n ~ geben to pay a. p. back (or home) in his own coin.

Dezember (⌣⌣⌣) [lt. „zehnter" Monat der alten Römer] *m* ㉒ December; ~**frost** D. frost; ℒ**lich** (⌣⌣⌣) *a.* ㊺ December-like.

Dezemvir (⌣⌣⌣⌣) [lt.] *m* ⊛ röm. Alt.: (Mitglied e-s Zehnmännerrates) decemvir; ~**at** (⌣⌣⌣⌣) *n* ⓒc. decemvirate, ...ship.

Dezennium (⌣⌣⌣⌣) [lt.] *n* ㉓ (Jahrzehnt) decade; space of ten years.

dezent (⌣⌣) [lt.] *a.* ㊺ (ehrbar) decent.

Dezentralisation (-⌣-⌣-tſ(⌣)⌣) [fr.] f ㊺ (Ent-einheitlichung) decentralization.

dezentralisieren (-⌣-⌣-⌣⌣) [fr.] v/a. ㊺ (enteinheitlichen) to decentralize (a. *pol.*).

Dezenz (⌣⌣) [lt.] f ㊺ decency.

Dezernat (-⌣⌣) [lt.] *n* ⓒc. (Geschäftskreis) administrative department.

Dezernent (-⌣⌣) *m* ㊷ head of a department (with whom decisions rest).

Dezi=ar (⁻⌣...) [fr.] *n* (*m*) ㊷ ($1/10$ Ar; *abbr.* **dca**, öft. *da*) deciare; ~**gramm** n ($1/10$ Gramm; *abbr.* **dcg**, öft. *dg*) decigram; ~**liter** n (*m*) ($1/10$ Liter; *abbr.* **dcl**, öft. *dl*) decilitre.

Dezimal=bruch (⌣⌣⌣...) *m* ㊷ decimal fraction; ~**maß** n decimal measure; ~**rechnung** f d. numeration; engS. decimal fraction, sum; ~**stelle** f d. (figure); ~**system** n, ~**zahl** f decimal system, d. number; ~**wage** f decimal balance.

Dezime ♩ (⌣⌣) [lt.] f ㊸ (zehnter Ton v. Grundton aus) tenth.

Dezi=meter (⁻⌣...) [fr.] *n*(*m*) ㊷ ($1/10$ Meter; *abbr.* **dcm**, öft. *dm*) decimetre.

dezimieren ⚔ (-⌣⌣⌣) [lt.] **I** v/a. ㊺ (den 10. Mann hinrichten) to decimate. — **II** ~ *n* ㉓ u. **Dezimierung** f ㊺ decimation.

Dezi=ster (⁻⌣...) [fr.] *n*(*m*) ㊷ ($1/10$ Kubikmeter; *abbr.* **dg** *abbr.* öft. = **Dezigramm**. [decistere.⌋

dgl. *abbr.* = bergleichen 2.

d. Gr. *abbr.* = der Große the Great.

d. h. *abbr.* = das heißt that is to say.

d. i. *abbr.* = das ist it (or that) is.

Diabas ♀ (-⌣⌣) [grch.] *m* ⓐ. *min.* diabase, greenstone. [(Harnruhr) diabetes.⌋

Diabetes ☤ (-⌣⌣⌣) [grch.] *m*, *inv. path.*⌋

diabolisch (-⌣⌣⌣) [grch.] *a.* ㊺ (teuflisch) diabolic, diabolical, fiendish.

Diachylon=pflaster (⌣⌣⌣...) *n* ㊺ (erweichendes Bleipflaster) diachylon plaster.

Diadelphia ♀ ♀ (-⌣⌣f(⌣)⌣) [grch.] f ㊸ (17. Klasse nach Linné) diadelphia.

diadelphisch ♀ (-⌣⌣f⌣) *a.* ㊺ (zweibrüderig: mit Staubfäden in 2 Bündeln) diadelphian.

Diadem (⌣⌣⌣) [grch.] *n* ⓒc. (Stirnband) diadem, royal headband; coronet.

Diagnose ☤ (-⌣⌣⌣) [grch.] ㊸ *path.* [Krankheits-]Erkennung) diagnosis; e-e ~ stellen, **diagnosieren** (-⌣⌣⌣⌣) v/a. ㊺ to diagnose a patient; **diagnostisch** (⌣⌣⌣⌣) *a.* ㊺ diagnostic; **diagnostizieren** (⌣⌣⌣⌣⌣) v/a. ㊺ to diagnose, diagnosticate. [(schräg) diagonal.⌋

diagonal ☤ (⌣⌣⌣⌣) [grch.] *a.* ㊺ *math.*⌋

Diagonale ☤ (⌣⌣⌣⌣) [grch.] f ㊸ *math.* diagonal (line); ⚔ diagonal drift.

Diagonal=kraft (⌣⌣⌣⌣⌣...) f ㊷ *mech.* resultant (of two forces); ~**maßstab** ⊕ *m* diagonal scale; ~**stoff** ✻ *m* (schräg kariertes Zeug) diagonal cloth.

⚔ scientific; ♀ botanical; ♀ geography; ⊕ machinery; ⚒ mining; ⚔ military; ⚓ marine; ♣ commercial; ✉ postal; 🚂 railway.

Diagramm ⌐ (⏑⏑⏔) [grch.] *n* ⓒ. (graphische Darstellung ꝛc.) diagram.
Diagraph ⌐ (⏑⏑f) [grch.] *m* ㊷ (Werkzeug zu perspektivischen Aufnahmen) diagraph.
Diakon [⏑⏑²] [grch. Diener] *m* ⓐd., ㊷ *eccl.* deacon; ~at (⏑⏑⏑²) *n* ⓒc. deaconry; ~ei (⏑⏑⏑f) *f* ㊻, ~en=haus *n* ㊷ deaconry.
Diakonisse (⏑⏑⏑⏑) [grch.] *f* ㊹, **Diakonissin** *f* ㊸ *eccl.* deaconess, sister of charity; **Diakonissen=anstalt** (⏗..) *f* ㊷ home for deaconesses. [= Diako'n.
Diakonus (⏑⏑⏑⏑) [lt., *grch.] *m* ⓐ, ㉒]
diakritisch (⏑⏑⏑⏑) [grch.] *a.* ㊻ *typ.* (zur Unterscheidung dienend) diacritical.
Diakustik † ⌐ (⏑⏑⏑⏑) [grch.] *f* ㊻ *phys.* (Schallfortpflanzungslehre) diacoustics.
Dialekt [grch.] *m* ⓑ. (Mund=art) dialect; ~=forschung *f* study of dialects.
Dialektik ⌐ (⏑⏑⏑⏑) [grch.] ㊻ (*g.s.* logische, *b.s.* sophistische Disputierkunst) dialectics; ~er (⏑⏑⏑⏑⏑) *m* ㉒ dialectician.
dialektisch ⌐ (⏑⏑⏑⏑) [grch.] *a.* ㊻: a) (mundartlich) dialectal; b) (die Dialektik betr.) dialectic, dialectical.
Dialog (⏑⏑²) [grch.] *m* ⓒc. (Zwiegespräch) dialogue; **≈isch** (⏑⏑⏑²) *a.* ㊻ colloquial, ⌐ dialogic(al), dialogistic; **Lisieren** (⏑⏑⏑⏑²) *v/a.* ㊽ to treat (or arrange) in form of a dialogue, ⌐ to dialogize.
Dialyse ⌐ (⏑⏑⏑) [grch.] *f* ㊸ *chm.* (Trennung durch Osmose) dialysis.
dialytisch ⌐ (⏑⏑⏑⏑).[grch.] *a.* ㊻ dialytic.
Diamagnetismus ⌐ (⏑⏑⏑⏑⏑) *m* ㉗ diamagnetism.
Diamant (⏑⏑²) [mhd.; fr.; *grch. s. Demant] *m* ㊷ 1. diamond; *fig.* (Symbol des Harten ꝛc.) auch: adamant, roher ~ fassen, schleifen, facettieren to set, cut, facet a d. — 2. ⓒ Glaserei: — ~=spitze. — 3. ~ *f, inv. typ.* — =schrift.
Diamant=abfall (⏑⏑⏔⏑..) *m* ㊷ =bort a; **≈artig** *a.* ㊻ diamond-like; *fig.* adamantine; **=bort** ⓕ *m:* a) d.-bort; b) =pulver.
diamanten (⏑⏑⏑⏑) *a.* ㊻ (D9) 1. diamond, (made) of diamonds; a. = diamantartig. — 2. *fig.* Le Hochzeit diamond (or sixtieth anniversary of a) wedding.
Diamanten=..(..)㉒= Diama'nt=..
Diamant=fasser (⏑⏑⏔⏑..) *m* ㊷ diamond-setter; **=(en)feld** *n* d.-field; **Sförmig** *a.* ⓒ d.-shaped; **=gewicht** *n* carat; **=gräber** *m* diamond-digger or -miner; **=grube** *f* d.-mine; **=pulver** ⓒ *n* d.-powder or -dust; **=ring** *m* d. ring; **=schleifen** *n* d.-cutting; **=schleifer** *m* d.-cutter; **=schliff** *m* Glasfabr.: facet-cut; **=schmuck** *m* d. ornaments *pl.*, set of diamonds; **=schneider** *m* — =schleifer ⓒ *f*, **=schrift** ⓒ *f*, *typ.* (vier (engl. 4½) Punkte groß **diamond**(-type), kem: **=spat** *m*, *min.* corundum; **=spitze** ⓒ *f* Glaserei: diamond pencil; **=spitzfeder** *f* diamond-tipped nib or pen.
Diameter ⌐ (⏑⏑²⏑) [grch.] *m* ㊷ *math.* (Durchmesser) diameter.
diametral(isch) (⏑⏑⏑²⏑)(⏑), **diametrisch** (−⏑²⏑) *a.* ㊻ (in der Richtung des Durchmessers) diametrical, transverse; *adv. fig.* ꝛ entgegengesetzt diametrically opposed.
Diana (⏑²⏑) [lt.] *npr/f.* ㊺㊸, a. (v. Diane) ㊵ *röm. myth.:* (jungfräuliche Göttin der Jagd, Schwester Apollos) Dian(a), (gr.) Artemis.
Diandria ⌐ ♀ (⏑²⏑⏑) [grch.] *f* ㊾ (zweite Klasse nach Linné) diandria.

diandrisch ⌐ ♀ (⏑²⏑⏑) *a.* ㊻ (zweimännig: mit 2 Staubfäden) diandrian.
Dianen=baum (⏑²⏑..) *m* ⓒhm. (baumförmige Silberbildung) (lt.) arbor Dianæ.
Diapason ♪ (⏑⏑⏑²) [grch. durch alle] *m*, *n* ⓒ, (ⓜ) (Oktave, Umfang e-r Stimme) diapason.
diaphan ⌐ (⏑⏑f) [grch.] *a.* ㊻ *phys.* (durchscheinend) diaphanous; **≈bild** *n* ㊷, **≈ie** (⏑⏑f⏑) *f* ㊸ (Leuchtbild) transparency.
Diärese ⌐ (⏑²⏑⏑) [grch.] *f* ㊸, **Diäresis** (⏑²⏑⏑) *f* ㊺ *gr.* (getrennte Aussprache zweier zusammenstehender Vokale, auch das Zeichen ‥) diæresis.
Diarium (⏑²(⏑)⏑) [lt.] *n* ㉘ (Tage=, Notiz=buch) diary, note-book; (Klabbe) waste-book.
Diarrhöe (⏑⏑rö') [grch.] *f* ㊸ *path.* (Durchfall) diarrhœa.
Diaspor ⌐ (⏑⏑²) [grch.] *m* ⓒc. (o. *pl.*) *min.* (Ton=erde=hydra't) diaspore (Al₂H₉O₄).
Diaspora (⏑²⏑⏑) od. (⏑⏑⏑²) [grch.] *f* ㊵ dispersion; Christen in der ~ Christian communities *pl.* in pagan lands.
Diastase ⌐ (⏑⏑²⏑) [grch.] *f* ㊸ *chm.* (Malzbildner) diastasis. [s. ~en *pl.*/
Diät¹ † (⏑²) [lt. *di'es* Tag] *f* ㊻ (Tagung),)
Diät² (⏑²) [fr., *diète;* * grch. *d'iaita*] I *f* ㊻ (Lebensordnung) diet, dietary; strenge ~ (Enthaltsamkeit) beobachten to observe a strict diet or regimen; auf (knappe) ~ setzen to (put on a low) diet. — II **diät** *adv.:* ꝛ (streng) leben to diet o.s., to be very strict in one's diet.
Diätar(ius) (⏑²⏑(⏑)⏑) [**Diät¹**] *m* ⓒc. (㉗, ㊳) (auf Zeit Angestellter) p. with a temporary engagement, one who is engaged by the day; (Hilfsarbeiter) supernumerary.
Diäten (⏑²⏑) [**Diät¹**] *f/pl. inv.* (Tagegelder) daily allowance or remuneration or fee; ~ (a. **=gelder**) *pl.* der Abgeordneten: payment of members (of parliament).
Diätetik ⌐ (⏑²⏑⏑) [grch.] *f* ㊻ (Gesundheitslehre) dietetics; **=er** (−−²⏑⏑) *m* ㉒ dietetist; **diätetisch** (⏑²⏑⏑⏑) *a.* ㊻ dietetic(al), dietary. [slip) in matters of diet.]
Diät=fehler (⏑²⏑..) *m* ㊷ mistake (F
Diätist (⏑²⏑²) [lt.] *m* ㊷ — Diätar.
diatherman ⌐ (⏑⏑²⏑) [grch.] *a.* ㊻ *phys.* (Wärme durchlassend) diathermanous; **≈ität** (⏑⏑⏑²²) *f* ㊸ diathermancy.
Diatomeen ⌐ ♀ (⏑⏑⏑²⏑) [grch.] *pl.* (Spalt=, Stäbchen=algen) diatomaceæ *pl.*
diatonisch ♪ (⏑⏑²⏑) [grch.] *a.* ㊻ (nach der Tonleiter fortschreitend) diatonic.
Diät=vorschrift (⏑²..) *f* ㊷ dietary (prescription).
Diazo=amidobenzol (⏑²..) *n* ㊷ diazo-amido-benzol (C₁₂H₁₁N₃); **=benzol** *n* diazo-benzol (C₆H₅ . NN . OH).
dibbeln ⚨ (⏑⏑) [engl.] *v/a.* ㊽a. *agr.* (mit dem Pflanzstock pflanzen) to dibble.
dibbern (⏑²⏑) [⚨ hebr.] *v/n.* (h.) ㊽a. (leise reden) to speak softly.
Dibrachys ⌐ (⏑²⏑⏑) [grch.] *m, inv. pros.* dibrachys (⏑⏑).
dich, in Briefen ꝛc.: **Dich** (⏑) (ahd.: thee) *acc.* von du ㊶ A1(3†): thee; you; ꝛ selbst yourself; beruhige ꝛ! calm yourself!; ease your mind! setze ꝛ! sit down!
Dichro=ismus ⌐ (⏑⏑⏑⏑) [grch.] *m* ⓒ *opt.* (Zweifarbigkeit) dichroism.
dicht¹ (⏑) [mhd. (ndd.): tight] I *a.* ㊻ 1. (für Luft, Wasser ꝛc. undurchdringlich) (air-, water-, &c.) tight; *phys.* dense; *geol.* &c. impervious; Les Schiff tight(ly built) ship; Les Zeug stout (or thick) cloth. — 2. (eng zs.=gedrängt) close(ly packed); compact; Le Bevölkerung dense population; im Lesten Schlachtgetümmel in the thickest of the fight(ing) or the fray; Ler Wald dense forest; schreiben Sie nicht so ꝛ! do not cram your writing so much! — II *adv.* 3. ꝛ (nahe) an et. next (or close) to a th.; ꝛ an=ea. close together; cramped; ↓ ꝛ an der Küste segeln to hug the shore; ↓ ꝛ am Lande sein to lie close in shore; ↓ ꝛ anliegend tight(ly fitting); ꝛ bei e-m ob. et. close to (or by) a p. or a th.; ↓ ꝛ beim Winde halten (laufen) to go (or sail) close to the wind; ꝛ dabei close (or hard) by; ꝛ daneben close (or next door) to it; ꝛ hinter e-m her close at a p.'s heels; ↓ ꝛ gerefft close-reefed; ⚔ in ꝛ geschlossenen Reihen in serried ranks or files. [ꝛc.; vgl. Dichtungs=..]
Dicht²=... (⏑..) [dichten²] ㊷ *f.* ~kunst]
dicht¹=belaubt (⏑²..) *a.* ㊻ with dense (or thick) foliage.
Dichte ⚨ (⏑⏑) *f* ㊻ = Dichtheit.
Dicht¹=eisen ⊕ (⏑²..) *n* ㊷ a) ↓ zum Kalfatern: calking-iron; b) ⊕ = =meißel.
Dichtelei ⚨ (⏑⏑²) *f* ㊻ = Reimerei.
dichten¹ (⏑⏑) [dicht¹] I *v/a.* ㊽ (dicht m.) to tighten; etwas ꝛ to make a th. fit tightly; (zs.=drängen) to condense; *chm.* mit Kitt ꝛ to lute; ⊕ Maurerei: Fugen ꝛ (ausstreichen) to flush the joints; ↓ (kalfatern) to calk. — II *n* ㉓ = Dichtung 1.
dichten² (⏑⏑) [ahd.; * lt. *dicta're*] I *v/a.* u. *v/n.* (h.) ㊽ 1. (sinnen) auf et. ꝛ und trachten to turn (all) one's thoughts to a th. — 2. (mittels der Einbildung schaffen) to compose a poem, &c., to create a character &c.; weitS. to write, produce, devise; zu den alten Sagen dichtet das Volk stets neue hinzu the people constantly add new legends to the old ones.—3.(vorspiegeln) to feign, invent, sham. — II ~ *n* ㉓ 4. (s. 1): darauf geht sein ganzes ~ und Trachten all his thoughts and desires are bent that way; that's what he has set his heart upon.—5. = Dichtung² 1 u. 2.
Dichter (⏑⏑) [dichten²] *m* ㉒, **=in** *f* ㊴ poet(ess *f*), weitS. bard, minstrel.
Dichterei (⏑⏑⏑²) *f* ㊻ mst *contp.* making (jingling) rhymes, writing (indifferent) poetry.
Dichter=ader (⏑⏑⏑..) *f* ㊷ poetic vein; **=art** *f* manner of poets; nach ~ in a poet's way; **=flug** *m*, **=glut** *f* poetic inspiration or fire; **=gabe** *f* poetic gift; **=greis** aged poet.
dichterisch (⏑⏑⏑⏑) *a.* ㊻ poetic(al); Le Freiheit *f* poetic license. [poet.]
Dichter=jüngling (⏑⏑⏑..) *m* ㊷ youthful/
Dichterling ⨍ (⏑⏑⏑) *m* ⓐd. *contp.* petty (or wretched) poet, poetaster, rhymster.
Dichter=quell(e *f*) *m* (⏑⏑..) ⓒ oft: Hippocrene; **=roß** *n* Pegasus; **=volk** *n* tribe of poets, poetic tribe; **=werk** *n* poetical work; **=wort** *n* (famous) saying of a poet.
dicht¹=gefügt (⏑²..) *a.* ㊻ close-grained; **≈gewebt** ⊕ *a.* close-webbed, -woven.
Dicht=heit ⚨ (⏑²), mst **Dichtigkeit** (⏑⏑⏑²⏑) *f* ㊸ (s. dicht¹) tightness; density; imperviousness; closeness, compactness.

Zeichen (f. S. XVII): ⨍ familiär; ⚨ Volkssprache; ⨍ Gaunersprache; ⚨ selten; † alt (auch gestorben); * neu (auch geboren); ⁺⁺ unrichtig.

[Dichtigkeitsmesser] — 261 — [dielektrisch]

Dichtigkeits=messer (˘˘-...) *m* ⓺ phys. für Flüssigkeiten: areometer; **=messung** *f* des spez. Gewichts v. Flüssigkeiten: areometry.

dicht¹=förnig (˘...) *a.* ⓺ = ⌾gefügt.

Dicht²=kunst (˘...) *f* ⓺ (art of) poetry; poetic art.

Dicht¹=meißel ⊙ (˘...) *m* ⓺ driver; ⌾fäulig *a.* ⓺ arch.: ☊ pycnostyle.

Dichtung¹ (˘˘) *f* ⓺ (f. dichten¹ 1) (Liederung) tightening; condensation; *chm.* (Verkittung) lutation; Maurerei: flushing; ↓ calking.

Dichtung² (˘˘) *f* ⓺ 1. (f. dichten² 2) composition of verse, &c.; Körners vaterländische ~en K.'s patriotic poetry or minstrelsy. — 2. (f. dichten² 3) fiction, invention. — 3. poem; weitS. poetic production, romance, work of fiction.

Dichtungs=art (˘˘...) *f* ⓺ kind (or style) of poetry; **=gabe, =kraft** *f*, **=vermögen** *n* poetic gift or power.

Dicht¹=werg ↓ (˘...) *n* ⓺ oakum.

Dicht²=werk (˘...) *n* = Dichterwerk.

dick (˘) [ahd.: thick] *a.* ⓺ 1. (ant. dünn) thick, big; (umfangreich) bulky, voluminous; (bir Band a stout volume; als Maß: einen Meter 2 sein to be one metre thick or in thickness; das 2e Ende eines Gewehres ⁊c. the butt-end. — 2. F (beleibt) big, stout, corpulent; (fett) obese, fat; (schwanger) big with child, pregnant, F in the family-way; (brall) plump; ziemlich 2 oft *a.*: F of a tidy size, pretty sizable; 2er Bauch big (F pot-) belly, paunch; 2es (pausbäckiges) Gesicht chubby (or plump) face; 2e Person stout (or corpulent) person; eine große und 2e Person F a strapping (or whacking) fellow (*f* wench or woman), a strapper or whacker; 2 und fett werden to grow fat and stout. — 3. (angeschwollen) swollen, swoln (cheek, nose, eyes *pl.*, &c.); 2e Lippen (thick) pouting lips; *v.* Negern ⁊c.: blubber-lips *pl.* — 4. (undurchdringlich) er hat ein 2es Fell, eine 2e Haut he has a thick skin; einen 2en Kopf haben: a) von Eigensinnigen: .. a hard head; b) von Dummen: .. a thick head. — 5. (reichlich, dicht) 2es Haar thick (F good head of) hair; 2e Luft close air; 2er (drückender) Nebel dense (or thick) fog; in 2en Strömen in large volumes; im 2sten Walde in the densest (or thickest) part of the forest. — 6. von Flüssigkeiten: 2es (geronnenes) Blut clotted blood; 2e (geronnene) Milch curdled milk; 2 werden (gerinnen) to coagulate; das ~e (der Bodensatz) the grounds *pl.* of coffee, the yeast of wine. — 7. meist F *fig.* Redensarten: durch 2 und dünn through thick and thin; durch 2 und dünn für e-n gehen to go through fire and water for a p.; das 2e Ende kommt nach the worst is yet to come; sich 2 (satt) essen to eat (or have) one's fill; sie sind sehr 2e Freunde they are very thick (friends), F they are as thick as thieves; er hat es rasch 2 (satt) bekommen he soon grew tired (F got sick) of it; etwas 2 haben (überdrüssig sein) to have enough (F to be sick and tired) of a thing, P to be fed up with

a th.; er hat es 2 hinter den Ohren he is not as simple as he looks, F he is a deep card; das Griechische sitzt bei ihm nicht sehr 2 he is not very strong in (or F not overstocked with) Greek; vgl. a. dictum.

dick=bäcig (˘...) *a.* ⓺ (pausbäckig) chubby-cheeked; ⌾bändig *a.* voluminous; **=bauch** *m* ⓺ = wanst; ⌾bäuchig *a.* = 2wanstig, **=bein** *n* (Schenkel) thigh; ⌾beinig *a.* big-legged, **=blatt** ⚘ *n* (Fettpflanze) ☊ crassula (Cra'ssula rubens); ⌾blätt(e)rig *a.* thick-leaved, ☊ crassulaceous; ⌾blütig *a.* thick-blooded, **=darm** *m. anat.* large intestine, F great gut.

Dicke (˘˘) *f* ⓺ (f. dick) thickness, bigness; bulk(iness); stoutness; einer Person auch: corpulency, plumpness (ant. Dürre); e-r Flüssigkeit: consistency; ~ (Größe) einer Erbse size of a pea.

Dicke(r) (˘˘) *m*, **Dicke** (˘˘) *f* ⓺ meist F: stout(ish) man, woman (f. dick 2).

Dicke=milch *f* ⓺ curdled milk (f. dick 6).

dick=fäustig (˘...) *a.* ⓺ club-fisted; **=fellig** *a.* ⓺ thick-skinned; *zo.* von Elefanten ⁊c.: ☊ pachyderm(at)ous; *fig.* (unempfindlich) auch: case-hardened, callous; **=felligkeit** *f* ⓺ *fig.* callousness; ⌾flüssig *a.* thick, stärker: viscid; **=fuß** *m*: a) *orn.* stone-curlew or -plover (Oedicne'mus); b) ⚘ crassiped pontederia (Ponteded'ria cras'sipes); ⌾füßig *a. zo.*: ☊ pachypod; ⌾halsig *a.* thick-necked, **=häuter** *m, zo.*: ☊ pachyderm; ⌾häuter-artig, ⌾häutig *a.* ☊ pachydermoid; vgl. 2fellig.

Dickicht (˘˘) [dick] *n* ⓺ *d.* thicket.

Dick=kopf (˘...) *m* ⓺ a) big head; b) *fig.* (eigensinniger Mensch) stubborn fellow; (Dummkopf) blockhead; c) *ichth.* chub (Squa'lius ce'phalus); **=kopf-falter** *m/pl. ent.* skippers (Hespe'ridae) *pl.*; ⌾köpfig *a.* ⓺ big-headed; *fig.* (eigensinnig) stubborn, F pig-headed; (dumm) blockheaded, F thick-skulled; **=köpfigkeit** *f fig.* stubbornness; ⌾leibig *a.* corpulent (vgl. dick 2); von Bänden: bulky, stout; **=leibigkeit** *f* corpulency; bulkiness, stoutness; ⌾lippig *a.*, ⌾mäulig *a.* thick-(F blubber-)lipped; **=milch** *f* f. Dicke-milch; ⌾nasig *a.* thick-(F bottle-) nosed; ⌾rindig *a.* thick-coated; von Käse: thick-rinded; ⌾schalig *a.* thick-shelled; ⌾schnäb(e)lig *a.* thick-billed, ☊ pachyrhynchous; **=tuer** *m* braggart; **=tuerei** *f* bragging, swagger, F big talk; ⌾tuerisch *a.* bragging, boastful; ⌾tun *v'n.* (h.) ⑤** to brag, F to talk big; mit et. 2 to boast of a th., to make a great fuss about a th.; **=wanst** *m* big belly, paunch; ⌾wanstig *a.* big-bellied, vgl. dick 2; **=zirkel** ⊙ *m* callipers *pl.*

☛ **Dict...** f. Dikt...

Didaktik (˘˘˘) [grch.] *f* ⓺ (Unterrichtslehre) didactics; **~er** (˘˘˘˘) *m* ⓶ didactician; **didaktisch** (˘˘˘) *a.* ⓺ didactic.

dideldum(dei) (-˘˘, ˘˘˘˘) *int.* (lustiger Ausruf) etwa: heyday; tweedledumdee!

Didynamia ⚘ ⚘ (˘˘˘˘) [grch.] *f* ㊾ (14. Klasse nach Linné) didynamia.

didynamisch ⚘ ⚘ (˘˘˘˘) *a.* ⓺ (zweimächtig: mit zwei längeren und zwei kürzeren Staubgefäßen) didynamian.

die (¹) [ahd.: the(y)] ①, ⓺B *f/sg. u. nom. u. acc. pl.* von der, die, das.

Dieb (¹) [ahd.: thief] *m* ⓒ., **~in** *f* ㊼ 1. thief, F cross-cove, buzzer, napper; ~in female thief, feinere: lady thief; (Mauser) pilferer, F prig(ger); (Räuber) robber; (Einbrecher) burglar, F cracksman; (Laden-)~ F shop-lifter; (Taschen-)~ pick-pocket; feiner: swell mobsman; ~e *pl. auch*: (the) light-fingered gentry, fein gekleidete: swell mob; Ausruf: ein ~!, haltet den ~! stop thief!; Sprichw. die kleinen ~e hängt man, die großen läßt man laufen, etwa: petty thieves are hanged, the great ones go free; Gelegenheit macht ~e opportunity makes the thief. — 2. *fig.* am Lichte: thief, F guest.

Diebel (¹˘) *m* ㉒ = Dobel.

Dieberei (-˘¹) *f* ㊻ thieving, pilfering.

Dieb(e)s=bande (¹(˘)...) *f* ㊷ set (or gang, pack) of thieves, *co.* long-fingered tribe, F happy family; (feine Gauner) swell mob; **=gehilfe, =genoß, =gesell(e)** *m* = ⌾helfer; **=gesindel** *n* = ⌾bande; **=glück** *n* undeserved (good) luck; **=gut** *n* stolen goods *pl.*; **=haken** *m* = Dict(e)rich; **=handwerk** *n* thief's (or thieves') trade; **=hehler** *m* receiver of stolen goods; **=helfer** *m* thief's accomplice; **=herberge, =höhle** *f* den of thieves, F slum(ken); **=kniffe** *m/pl.*, **=künste** *f/pl.* thievish tricks or dodges *pl.*; **=laterne** *f* dark lantern; **=nest** *n* = ⌾herberge; **=schlüssel** *m* skeleton-key, picklock; ⌾sichere Schränke burglar-proof safes *pl.*; **=sinn** *m* Phrenologie: organ (F bump) of acquisitiveness; **=sprache** *f* thieves' Latin or cant or slang, flash language; **=wirt** *m* harbourer of thieves, keeper of a thieves' inn or lodging-house.

Diebin (¹˘) *f* ㊼ f. Dieb.

diebisch (¹˘) *a.* ⓺ 1. thievish. — 2. *fig.* (verstohlen) furtive, *adv. a.* stealthily, by stealth; on the sly.

diebischer=weise (¹˘˘˘˘˘) *adv.* thievishly, by (way of) theft.

Diebs=... (¹...) in Zssgn f. Diebes=...

Diebstahl (¹-) [mhd.: *Dieb und stehlen*] *m* ⓘd. 1. theft; mit Einbruch: burglary, (burglarious) robbery; bisw.: housebreaking; es wurde ein großer ~ bei einem Juwelier verübt a great robbery was committed at a jeweller's; meist jur. (heimlicher) ~ ohne Gewalt larceny; kleiner, großer ~ petty, grand larceny. — 2. literarischer ~ plagiarism, von Buchhändlern, oft: piracy.

die=jenige (¹˘˘˘) *f* von derjenige (f. ds).

Diele (¹˘) [ahd.: *deal*: lt. *te'llus*] *f* ㊵ 1. (Brett für Fußböden) deal board (for floors), ~n *pl. auch*: deals *pl.*; stärkere: deal plank; (Eichen-)~ oak plank. — 2. (gedielter Fußboden) floor(ing); niedsächs. (Dreschtenne) barn- (or thrashing-)floor; auf der ~ schlafen to sleep on the floor or on the bare boards; man möchte von der ~ speisen (es war so sauber) you could eat your dinner off the floor. — 3. ndd. (Hausflur) (entrance-)hall, vestibule; (Gang) passage.

di-elektrisch (˘˘˘˘) [lt.-grch.] *a.* ⓺ elect. (nicht leitend) dielectric.

[dielen] — 262 — [Dienstleute]

dielen ⊕ (˘ˇ) **I** v/a. ⊛ to board, to plank; to floor (with boards). — **II** ~ n ㉓ = **Dielung** 1.

Dielen=kopf (ˇˇ...) m ㊆ arch. dorischer Säulen; ⚔ mutule; **=lager** n boarding- (or bridging-)joist; **=säge** ⊕ f long-saw, pit-saw.

Dieler ⊕ (˘ˇ) m ㉒ floorer.

Dielung (˘ˇ) f ㊻ 1. boarding, planking; flooring. — 2. floor.

Dieme nordd. (˘ˇ) [nbd.] f ㊽, ~n m ㉓ agr. rick = (Getreide=)Schober.

dienen (˘ˇ) [ahd.] ⊛ **I** v/n. (h.) 1. mst. to serve; dem Vaterlande 2 to s. one's country; Gott 2 (gehorchen) to s. God; bibl. zween Herren 2 to serve two masters; dem Mammon, den Götzen ꝛc. 2 to serve (or worship) Mammon, idols, &c.; ⚔ bei der Artillerie 2 to serve in the artillery; als gemeiner Soldat 2 to serve in the ranks, to be a private (soldier); von der Pike (oder von unten) auf 2 to s. from the ranks; ein vom Gemeinen auf gedienter Offizier officer who has served from the ranks, ⚔ auch: ranker; gedienter Soldat (seasoned) veteran; ⚓ zur See 2 to serve before the mast. — 2. e-m mit seiner Börse 2 (beistehen) to assist a p. with one's purse; ist Ihnen damit gedient, wenn //? will it be of service (or of use) to you, if //? — 3. höfliche Wendungen: Ihnen zu 2 (I am) at your service; zu 2, oft: right (you are), sir!; womit kann ich Ihnen 2 (aufwarten)? what is your pleasure?; ⊛ in Läden: what can I do for you (or show you), madam?; damit kann ich 2 it is at your command; ⊛ I have just the article (or goods) that you want. — 4. abs. von Dienstboten: to be in service; die ⒧e Klasse (domestic) servants, domestics pl., weit S. menials, attendants pl.; er dient (schon) zwanzig Jahre he has (full) twenty years' service or character. — 5. (sich verwenden lassen als, zu, für) als Mittel zum Zwecke 2 to serve (or to be used) as a means to an end; das soll ihm als Warnung 2 that shall be a warning to him; damit würde ihm nur schlecht gedient (geholfen) sein that would hardly answer (or serve) his purpose; das dient nicht zur Sache that is beside the purpose, that has nothing to do with it; Kleider 2 zum Schutze des Körpers clothes serve (or are useful) as a protection for (or to protect) the body; er wird ihnen zum Spotte 2 they will make sport of him or mock him; das würde zu nichts 2 that would be of no (or not be of any) use; es könnte nur dazu 2 (beitragen), ihn zu reizen it could only serve (or tend) to irritate him. — 6. ⊛ Gegenwärtiges dient, Ihnen mitzuteilen the object (or purpose) of these lines (or of the present) is to inform you, we purpose by these lines to advise you. — 7. e-m auf etwas 2 (antworten) to retort upon a p., F to give a p. as good as he sent. — **II** ~ n ㉓ 8. serving, &c. (f. I); des =s müde tired of service; f. Dienst.

Diener (˘ˇ) m ㉒, **~in** f ㊼ 1. domestic; (man-, maid-)servant; (Bedienter) footman, valet; contp. lackey; rel. ~(in) des Herrn a servant before the Lord; bibl. auch: f the Lord's handmaid; ~ des göttlichen Wortes minister of the Gospel or of God's holy word; ~ der Götzen idolater. — 2. in Redensarten: Ihr gehorsamster (oder ergebenster) ~ your very obedient servant; als Briefschluß auch: Yours most obediently; gegen e-n den gehorsamen ~ machen to play the humble servant to a p. — 3. (Beamter) official; ~ des Staates government official. — 4. F (Verbeugung) bow; e-m einen ~ machen to (make a) bow to a p. — 5. fig. stummer ~ (Nebentischchen) dumb-waiter.

Diener=... (ˇˇ...) in Zssgn = Bedienten=...

dienerhaft, dienerisch (beide: ˘ˇˇ) a. ㊅ servant-like; contp. flunkey-like.

dienern (˘ˇ) v/n. (h.) ㉒a. to bow (and scrape); to make a bow; tief 2 d bowing low, b.s. cringing (and crawling).

Dienerschaft (˘ˇˇ) f ㊻ establishment of servants; (domestic) servants, domestics pl.; (kgl. Hofstaat) His or Her Majesty's Household; bei der ~, in England: below-stairs.

dienlich (˘ˇ) a. ㊅ e-m 2 serviceable, useful, expedient to a p., F handy; (heilsam) salutary; (zuträglich) suitable; der Gesundheit: wholesome; ⊛ wenn Sie es für 2 erachten if you approve of it; **~keit** (˘ˇˇ) f ㊻ (f. dienlich) serviceableness, usefulness, expediency; suitability.

Dienst (´) [ahd.; * dienen] m ㊂a(b). 1. (Arbeit für andere) service; e-m einen guten ~ erweisen, leisten to render a p. a good service, F to do a p. a good turn; der Rock hat mir gute ~e geleistet ... has done me good service, has lasted well; was steht zu Ihren ~en? what orders (or commands) have you?; what is your pleasure?; im Laden: what can I do for you?; Sprichw. ein ~ ist des andern wert one good turn deserves another. — 2. v. Beamten, a. ⚔, ⚓: (Amtsleistung) function, official duty; ~ im Felde field-duty; im (außer) ~ on (off) duty; den (feinen) ~ haben to be on (off) duty; ~ bei Hofe haben to be in ordinary at court; ~ tun to officiate; von Kriegsschiffen: im ~e, in ~ gestellt in commission; außer ~ gestellt laid up in ordinary; Offizier vom ~ officer on duty. — 3. (Stelle) situation, post; außer ~ out of employment, F out of a berth, without a job, ⚔ off duty; e-m den ~ aufsagen to give a p. notice or warning; e-n in ~ nehmen to engage a p.; ~e nehmen, in ~ treten to enter service, ⚔ to join (or go into) the army, to enlist, to join the ranks; ⚔ ~ bei der Fahne active service; Hauptmann außer ~ (abbr. a. D.) retired captain, half-pay captain. — 4. e-m auf den ~ passen to keep a strict watch over a p., to watch a p. closely. — 5. got. arch. (Säulchen) (small) respond.

Dienst=ablösung (ˇˇ...) f ㊆ relief; **=abteil** ⚒ m service-compartment; **=abzeichen** ⚔ n (official) badge, von engl. Unteroffizieren, Polizisten ꝛc.: stripe; **=adel** m (title) of nobility obtained in return for (military, &c.) services.

Diens=tag (´ˇ) [nbd. * Thingsus (*Ding 7)] m ⓓd. Tuesday; vgl. Sonntag.

Dienst=alter (ˇˇ...) n ㊅ (Ancientität) length (or years pl.) of service, seniority; **=anerbieten** n offer (or tender) of services; **=angelegenheit** f = =sache; **=antritt** m installation; beim ~ on taking up one's post; **=anweisung** f instruction(spl.); **=anzug** m =kleid a; **=auszeichnung** f distinction earned by good services; ⚔ long-service medal.

dienstbar (˘ˇ) a. ㊅ 1. (untertänig) subject; (zinspflichtig) tributary; sich (dat.) and(e)re 2 machen to make others subservient to one's own ends, to make people serve one's purpose. — 2. (unterwürfig) submissive, (sklavisch) servile; ⒧er Geist bibl. ministering spirit or angel; fig. factotum; F co. (Magd) maid-of-all-work, F slavey.

Dienstbarkeit (˘ˇˇ) f ㊻ (f. dienstbar) subjection; servitude; submissiveness.

Dienst=bedürfnis (ˇˇ...) n ㊆ requirements pl. of the service; **⒧beflissen** a. ㊅ officious, zealous; **⒧beflissenheit** f officiousness, zeal; **⒧berechtigt** a. entitled to claim (certain) services; **⒧bereit** a. ready to serve; obliging; **=beschädigung** ⚔ f, im Dienst erlittene: injury received in the discharge of one's official duties; **=bote** m domestic (servant); **=boten=not** f scarcity of (domestic) servants; **=boten=treppe** f, etwa: backstairs pl.; **=buch** n für Gesellen und Gesinde (in Engl. unbekannt) service-book or -register; **=eid** m official oath; **=eifer** m: a) officiousness; b) = =fertigkeit; ⒧eifrig a.: a) officious; b) = ⒧fertig; **=einkommen** n official salary, income earned in the (public) service; **=enthebung** f suspension from (active) duty or service; **=entlassung** f dismissal (or discharge) from service, ⚔ cashiering; **=entsetzung** f (Kassation) removal from office; **=erfahrung** f experience gained in the service; **=erweisung, =erzeigung** f service (rendered); kindness (shown); **=fähig**(**keit** f) a. = =tauglich(keit); ⒧**fertig** a. ready to serve, weit S. kind, obliging; **=fertigkeit** f readiness to serve, weit S. kindness, obligingness; ⒧**frei** a. (ohne Dienst) off duty; **=führung** f, conduct of public affairs, official routine; **=gang** m a) method of carrying on the (public) service; b) dispatch of business; **=geber** m employer; ⒧**gefällig** a. complaisant; **=gehilfe** m assistant; **=geschäft** n official business; **=gewalt** ⚔ f: (Mißbrauch der) ~ (abuse of) military authority; **=grad** m ⚔ (Charge) rank; ⒧**habend** a. ⚔ on duty, bei Hofe: in waiting = ⒧**tuend**; **=herr** m master, principal; employer; **=herrschaft** f master, f mistress; **=jahr** n year of service; **=jubiläum** n jubilee; **=kleid**(**ung** f) n a) ⚔ uniform; b) livery; **=knecht** m serving man; **=leistung** f service (rendered), (Funktion) function; **=leute** pl. v. =mann b u. c.

Signs (see page XVII): F familiar; P vulgar; ⚡ flash; ⚙ rare; † obsolete (died); * new word (born); ‡ incorrect; ♪ music;

[dienstlich] — 263 — [Diktatur]

dienstlich (⸚) a. ⑯ (amtlich) official; 2e Angelegenheit = Dienstsache.
Dienst-lohn (″…) m (n) ⑫ wages pl.; =lokal n office; =mädchen n, =magd f servant-girl or -maid; =mann m: a) ㉕c. liege-man, vassal, retainer; b) pl. =leute domestics pl.; vgl. Dienerschaft; c) ②c. pl. a. =leute (Gepäckträger) (licensed) porter; (Bote) messenger, commissionaire; F handy (or jobbing) man; =mannschaft f: a) corps of missionaires; b) ⚔ (Präsenzstärke) effectives pl., effective strength; =mütze f, in Deutschland: cap worn by officials; =ordnung f official regulations pl.; =personal n: a) staff of officials; b) (Dienerschaft) attendants pl.; =pferd ⚔ n service-horse; =pflicht f: a) (Pflicht eines Dienenden) official duty; ⚔, ⚓ military (naval) duty; b) (Verpflichtung zu dienen) obligation to serve; ⚔ allgemeine ~ compulsory (system of) military service; seiner ~ genügen to serve one's time in the army; =pflichtig a. ⑯ obliged (or bound) to serve; ⚔ auch: liable to be called to the colours; im 2en Alter of an age liable to (military) service; =pflichtige(r) ⚔ m ⑰ p. liable to serve or to be called out; conscript; =reise f official tour; =rock m = =kleid a; =sache f official business, matter relating to the (public) service; =sprache f official language; =stand m menial condition; =stellung ⚔ f (Funktion) official function; =stunden f/pl. hours pl. of duty; official (business) hours pl.; =tauglich a. fit for service, ⚔ auch: effective; =tauglichkeit f fitness for service, ⚔ auch: effectiveness; =treue f loyalty; =tüchtig (keit f) a. = =tauglich(keit); =tuend a.: a) doing (official) duty, officiating; b) (Tagesdienst versehend) on duty; 2er Kammerherr … in attendance; =unbrauchbar, =unfähig, =untauglich, =untüchtig a. unfit to serve or for service; bsd. ⚔ durch Krankheit 2c.: invalided, disabled; durch Alter: superannuated; =unbrauchbarkeit, =unfähigkeit, =untauglichkeit, =untüchtigkeit f unfitness (or incapacity) for service; superannuation; =unterricht m (theoretical) instruction; =vergehen n disciplinary offence; breach of duty; delinquency; =verhältnis n domestic service; =verhältnisse pl. conditions pl. attaching to the public service; =vernachlässigung f derelication (or neglect) of duty; =verrichtung f (official) function; =vertrag m contract between master (or employer) and servant (or employe[e]); =volk n servants pl.; =vorschrift f official rule or order; =weg m official way; =widrig a., contrary to official rules; =willig(keit f) a. = =fertig(keit); =wohnung f official residence; =zeit f e-s hohen Beamten: term of office; e-s Dienstboten, Soldaten 2c.: time (or years pl.) of service; ⚔ seine ~ aushalten to serve one's time; =zeugnis n certificate; für Dienstboten: (written) character; =zwang m compulsory service; =zweig m branch of the service.

dies (⸍) abbr. v. dieses ⑯ A2a (f. dieser 3).
dies-bezüglich (″⸍⸍) a. ⑯ referring (or relating) (t)hereto; 2e Worte words to that effect.
Di-ese¹ ♪ (⸍⸍) [fr. *dièse*, f. * Diesis] f ㊽ (Erhöhungszeichen) diesis, sharp (♯).
diese² (⸍⸍) ⑯ A2a f u. pl. v. dieser.
die-selb(ig)e (⸌⸌⸍) f. derselb(ig)e.
dieser (⸍⸍) [ahd.: this, these] m, dem. pron. ⑯ A2a, B*. 1. adjektivisch: this, pl. these; 2 selbe Punkt this same point; 2 mein Kamerad F this chum of mine; diese guten Leute these good people; diese seine (unsere) Söhne these sons of his (of ours); diese paar Sachen these few things; dieser Tage: a) (Vergangenheit) a day or two ago; the other day; b) (Zukunft) one of these days, on some future day. — 2. substantivisch: sg. this one, pl. these (ones); 2 ist (diese sind) es this is (these are) the (right) one(s); 2 und jener this one and that (one), the one and the other; (auserlesene Leute) people of all sorts; Verwünschung: hol' dich 2 und jener! the deuce take you!; ell. ⚘ den Dritten dieses (Monats) on the third instant (abbr. inst.); der Schreiber dieses (Briefes) the writer of these lines or of the present; Vorzeiger dieses the bearer of this (letter). — 3. die(se)s n this, that; dies ist (sind) meine Schwester(n) this is (these are) my sister(s); vor diesem (ehemals) before (or ere) this or now; once; at one time; vgl. ohnedies, überdies.
dieser-halb † (″⸍⸍) adv. = deshalb, 2seits ⸌, 2wärts (″⸍⸍) adv. on this side; thitherwards; 2wegen † (″⸍⸍) = deswegen. [case.]
dies-falls (″⸍) adv. in this (or that) [case.]
diesig provc. (⸍⸍) [ndd.] a. ⑯ (trüb, unklar) turbid, muddled, (töricht) silly.
Di-esis ♪ (⸍⸍) [grch.] f ㊽ = Diese.
dies-jährig (″⸍⸍) a. ⑯ of this (or of the present) year, this year's (f. heurig).
dies-mal (″⸍) adv. this time, on this occasion, for (this) once.
dies-malig (″⸍⸍) a. ⑯ taking place this time; present, actual.
dies-seit (″⸌) f. diesseits.
dies-seitig (″⸍⸍) a. ⑯ 1. (situated) on this side of a river, &c. — 2. (unser) die 2en Truppen our troops; der 2e (unser Land vertretende) Gesandte the Ambassador of this (or our) country.
dies-seit(s) (″⸌) I adv. u. prp. mit gen. on this side; 2 und jenseits on this side and on that (vgl. 3is-…). — II ~ n, inv. das ~ und das Jenseits this life and the life hereafter, the life here (below) and the life to come.
Diet(e)rich¹ ⊙ (⸍(⸍)⸍) [mhd.; Dietrich²] m ⑯d. Schlösserei: (Sperrhaken) picklock, (Nachschlüssel) skeleton-key, (Hauptschlüssel) master-key; ein Schloß mit e-m ~ aufbrechen to pick a lock.
Dietrich² (⸍⸍) npr/m. ⑮ ⑯x. (Bn.) Derrick; (Ostgotenkönig, † 526) Theodoric.
die-weil, fast † (⸌⸍) [: while] I adv. (in the) meanwhile. — II cj. (weil) because; whereas; (während) while, whilst, as long as.
Diffamation ☿ jur. (⸌⸌⸌tʃ(⸍)⸍) [lt.] f ㊻ (Verleumdung) defamation.

diffamatorisch ☿ (⸌⸌⸌)a. ⑯ defamatory.
differential (⸌⸌⸌⸍) [lt.] I a. ⑯ ⚙ u. math. (unterscheidend) differential. — II ~ n ⑫c. math. differential, fluxion.
Differential-flaschenzug (⸌⸌⸌⸌tʃ(⸍)″…) m ⑫ mech. differential block; =galvanometer n differential galvanometer; =getriebe n Automobilwesen 2c.: differential gear; =gleichung f, math. differential equation; =größe f, math. differential; =koeffizient m. math. differentiate; =methode f Fernsprechwesen: (Gegensprechen) differential principle; =quotient m differential quotient; =rechnung f differential calculus; =schaltung f, elect. differential system (of switching); =tarif ⚘ m differential tariff; =thermometer n (m) differential thermometer; =zoll m (Begünstigungszoll) differential duty. — Vgl. a. Differenz-…
differentiieren ☿ (⸌⸌⸌tʃ(⸍)⸍) [lt.] v/a. ⑬ math. (scheiden) to differentiate.
Differenz (⸌⸌⸍) [lt.] f ㊻ 1. (Unterschied) difference; ⚘ (Überschuß) surplus, excess, balance. — 2. (Mißhelligkeit) misunderstanding, difference of opinion.
Differenz-geschäft (⸌⸌⸌…) n ⑫, =handel m ⚘ business done on the basis of (periodical settlement of) differences; gambling in futures; time-bargain.
differenzieren (⸌⸌⸌⸍) [neult.] v/a. ⑬ to differentiate. [Differentialzoll.]
Differenz-zoll ⚘ (⸌⸌⸌…) m ⑫ =)
differieren (⸌⸌⸍) [lt.] v/n. (h.) ⑬ (sich unterscheiden) to differ, to diverge.
diffizil (⸌⸌⸍) [lt.] a. ⑯ 1. (schwierig) difficult. — 2. a. Personen: (schwer zu behandeln) difficult to deal with or to manage; (empfindlich) sensitive.
digerieren ☿ (⸍⸍⸍) [lt.] v/a. ⑬ chm. (durch Wärme erweichen) to digest.
Digesten ☿ (⸍⸌) [lt.] n/pl., inv., Gesetzsammlung Justinia'ns: Digest.
Digestiv-salz (⸍″…) n ⑫ chm. (Chlorkalium) digestive salt, potassium chloride. [(Topf) (Papin's) digester.)
Digestor ☿ (⸍⸌) [lt.] m ㉛ phys. (papinscher)
Digitalin ☿ (⸍⸌⸍) [lt. Digitalis ⚕ (⸍⸌⸍) Fingerhut] n ⑫c.chm. (Alkaloid von *Digita'lis purpu'rea*) digitaline ($C_{25}H_{40}O_{18}$).
Digitalin-salz ☿ (⸍⸌⸍…) n ⑫ digitalic salt. [schlitz) diglyph.]
Diglyph ☿ (⸍⸍) [grch.] m ⑪c. arch. (Doppel-)
di-hexa-edrisch ☿ (⸍⸌⸍⸍) [grch.] a. ⑯ cryst. (doppeltsechsflächig) dihexahedral.
Diiambus ☿ (⸍⸍⸌⸍) [lt., *grch.] m ㉒ pros. diiamb(us) (⸌⸌⸌). [Propatria.]
Difasterial (format) ☿ (⸍⸍⸌(⸍)⸌) n ⑫c. =)
Dikasterium ☿ (⸍⸌⸌(⸍)⸌) [lt., *grch.] n ㉘ grch. Alt.: (höherer Gerichtshof) dicastery.
diklinisch ☿ ⚘ (⸍⸌⸍) [grch. zweibettig] a. ⑯ (nur Staubgefäße oder nur Stempel tragend) diclinous.
Dikotyledone(n pl.) ☿ ⚘ (⸌⸌⸌⸌⸍) [grch.] f ㊽ (Blattkeimer) dicotyledon(s pl.).
dikotyledonisch (⸌⸌⸌⸌⸍) a. ⑯ (zweisamenlappig) dicotyledonous. [Diptam.]
Diktam ☿ ⚘ (⸍⸍) [lt., *grch.] m ⑫d. =)
Diktat (⸍⸍) [lt.] n ⑫c. dictation; nach dem ~ schreiben to write from (or under) dictation or as dictated. [tator.)
Diktator (⸍⸌⸍) [lt.] m ㉛ (Gebieter) dic-)
diktatorisch (⸍⸌⸍⸌) a. ⑯ dictatorial.
Diktatur (⸍⸌⸍) [lt.] f ㊻ dictatorship.

☿ scientific; ⚘ botanical; ♆ geography; ⊕ machinery; ⚒ mining; ⚔ military; ⚓ marine; ⚘ commercial; ✉ postal; 🚂 railway

diktieren (⌣́⌣) [lt.] v/a. ⑬: (in die Feder) ⚲ to dictate; ich schrieb, wie er diktierte I wrote as he dictated or to (or from) his dictation.

Diktion ⚇ (⌣tz(⌣)́) [lt.] f ㊻ (Schreibart) diction, style; rhet. (Ausdrucksweise) elocution.

Diktionär ⚋ (⌣tz(⌣)⌣́) [fr. dictionnaire] n ⑪c.(Wörterbuch) dictionary. [dilatory.]

dilatorisch (-⌣́⌣) [lt.] a. ㊿ jur. (aufschiebend)

Dilemma ⚇ (⌣⌣́⌣) [grch.] n ㉝ (㉖) log. (Doppelschluß), fig. Zwiespalt) dilemma.

Dilettant (-⌣́) [it.] m ⑭, ~**in** f ㊼ (Kunstliebhaber[in]) amateur, f lady amateur; (Sportliebhaber) gentleman (ant. professional) player, rider, &c.; Lenhaft (-⌣⌣⌣) a. ㊿ amateurish; Len-mäßig (-⌣⌣́...) a. ㊿ amateurish; ~**en-theater** n ㉒ private theatricals pl.; ~**entum** (-⌣⌣...) n ②d. amateurishness, amateurship, dilettantism; ~**en-vorstellung** (-⌣⌣́...) f ㊷ amateur performance; **Lisch** (-⌣⌣́) a. ㊿ amateurish, unprofessional; ~**ismus** (-⌣⌣́⌣) m ㉗ = Dilettantentum.

dilett(ant)ieren (-⌣(⌣)⌣́⌣) [it.] v/n. (h.) ⑬ thea. to play (or act) as an amateur (performer).

Diligence (-⌣Gā̆⌣z) [fr.] f ㊽ stage-coach.

Dill ⚢ (-⌣́) [ahd.: dill] m ⑪b., auch ~**e**¹ (⌣́⌣) f ㊽ dill (Ane'thum grave'olens).

Dille² (⌣́⌣) f ㊽ f. Tülle.

dillen (⌣́⌣) v/a. ㊽ (Fische fangen durch Aufspießen unter dem Eis) to catch fish by spearing them under the ice.

Dilleni-e ⚢ (⌣⌣́(⌣)⌣) [Dille'nius, dtsch. Botaniker, 1687—1747] f ㊽ (Rosen-apfel) syalite (Dille'nia specio'sa).

Dill-öl (⌣́...) n ㉒ chm. anethol.

Diluvial-bildung ⚇ (--w(⌣)́...) f ㉒ diluvial formation.

diluvianisch ⚇ (--w(⌣)́⌣) [lt.] a. ㊿ geol. (angeschwemmt) diluvial, (sintflutlich) ...n.

Diluvium ⚇ (-⌣̄w(⌣)⌣) [lt.] n ㉘ 1. (Sintflut) deluge. — 2. geol. (uralte Anschwemmung) diluvium. [dimension.]

Dimension (-⌣(⌣)⌣́) [lt.] f ㊻ (Ausdehnung)

Dimethyl-anilin ⚇ (⌣⌣⌣́⌣-⌣⌣́) n ⑪c. chm. dimethyl aniline ($C_6H_5 \cdot N[CH_3]_2$).

diminutiv ⚇ (--⌣⌣́f) [lt.] I a. ㊿ (verkleinernd) diminutive. — II ~(**um**) (⌣, --⌣⌣́w) n ⑭e. ㊾ gr. diminutive.

Dimission (-⌣(⌣)́) [it.] f ㊻ (Entlassung) dismissal; s-e ~ einreichen to hand (or send) in one's resignation. [to resign.]

dimissionieren (-⌣(⌣)⌣⌣́⌣) [lt.] v/n. (h.) ⑬

Dimissoriale (-⌣-(⌣)⌣́⌣) n㉙, **Dimissorium** (-⌣́(⌣)⌣) n ㉘ eccl. dimissorial, dimissory letter. [dimorphous, dimorphic.]

dimorph ⚇ (-⌣́f) [grch.] a. ㊿ (zweigestaltig)

Dimorphie ⚇ (-⌣f) f ㊽, **Dimorphismus** (-⌣f⌣́⌣) m ㉗ chm., &c. dimorphism.

dinarisch ⚢ (-⌣́⌣) a. ㊿: ~e Alpen zwischen Dalma'tien u. Bo'snien: Dinaric Alps pl.

Diner (-nē') [fr.] n ㉘ (Mittagsessen) dinner; ein ~ geben to give a dinner party.

Ding (⌣́) [ahd.: thing] n ⑪b. (F auch ④) 1. meist. thing; vor allen ~en above all things; first and foremost, in the first place; phls. das ~ an sich (Kant) the thing-in-itself. — 2. (Gegenstand) object; unbedeutendes ~ trifling object, trifle. — 3. (Angelegenheit, Sache) er hat and(e)re Dinge zu besorgen

other matters to attend to; ich habe and(e)re ~e im Sinn(e) ... other fish to fry; bei so gestalteten ob. bewandten ~en (Umständen) under these circumstances, such being the case, things being as they are; im gewöhnlichen Lauf der ~e in the ordinary course of things or of events; wie die ~e jetzt steh(e)n as matters now stand, as things now are. — 4. Redensarten (mit ~ in ganz allg. sachlicher Bed.): bei Gott ist kein ~ (nichts) unmöglich with God nothing is impossible; Sprichw. aller guten ~e sind drei, etwa: all good things go by threes, three is a good number; ich habe ganz and(e)re ~e erlebt ... seen greater marvels (or more curious things) than these; das ist ein ander ~ that's quite different; Sprichw. geschehen ~ ist nicht zu ändern what's done can't be undone, F it's no use crying over spilt milk; geschehene ~e (accomplished) facts pl.; sie halten große ~e von ihm they think highly of him; Sprichw. gut ~ will Weile haben slow and sure wins the race; more haste less speed; jedes ~ hat s-e zwei Seiten everything has its two sides, there are two sides to every question; es ist ein köstliches ~ um e-n Freund it is a precious thing to have a friend; es geht nicht mit rechten ~en zu (es ist Spuk dabei) F there's some hocus-pocus (or devilry, jugglery) about it; das müßte nicht mit rechten ~en zugehen it would be wonderful if that were not the case; das sind mir schöne ~e (Geschichten)! fine doings these!, (that's) a pretty (or nice) state of affairs!; es wäre kein übles ~, wenn // it would not be bad if //; ein ~ der Unmöglichkeit an (utter) impossibility; unverrichteter ~e abziehen to leave without having attained one's end; was ist das für ein ~? what is this? — 5. (et., das ~ich nöher bezeichnen läßt) oft dim.:
~**elchen**; pl. ~**er(chen)**: a) von leblosen Gegenständen: thing, concern; path. das böse ~ (Fingerwurm) whitlow; b) von Tieren: die kleinen ~er (zB. Kätzchen)! the (dear) little mites or creatures; c) von Personen, bsd. jungen Mädchen: sie ist nur ein kleines ~ ... only a little thing or F a chit (or little bit) of a girl; das arme ~! the poor thing or creature!; artige ~er (Kinder) well-behaved little ones, good little mites pl.; das dumme ~ the silly girl or goose, F the flat or fool (of a girl); ein naseweises ~ an inquisitive (or forward) creature; ein niedliches ~ a nice (or pretty) little thing or girl; iro. (was für ein ~ von Brief! what a (thing of a) letter! — 6. guter ~e (guten Mutes) sein to be of good cheer or in high glee or in good temper; seid guter ~e! cheer up! — 7. †, noch prov. (Gericht, Gerichtsverhandlung) (popular) court of justice, law-proceedings pl.

dingbar (⌣́-) a. ㊿ that may be hired, &c. (s. dingen 1); von Personen: mercenary.

Dingelchen (⌣⌣́⌣) n ㉓ dim. von Ding 5.

dingen (⌣́⌣) [ahd.] ⑪ (㊽) ist ob. hat I v/a.1. von Sachen u. Tieren, meist: to hire a carriage,

a donkey, &c. (bisw. auch von Personen, zB. ein gedung(e)ner Mörder a hired assassin); Arbeiter, Dienstboten, Ladendiener &c.: to engage; für bestimmte Zeit durch Vertrag: to indenture; ⚓ Matrosen ⚲ (heuern) to ship seamen; b.s. falsche Zeugen ⚲ to suborn false witnesses. — 2. ⚓ ein Schiff ⚲: to charter. — II v/n. (h.) 3. (feilschen) to haggle or bargain (um about); er läßt nicht mit sich ⚲ he won't be bargained with. — III ~**n** ㉓ 4. (s. I) hiring, hire; engagement. — 5. (s. II) haggling, bargain(ing).

Dinger¹ (⌣́⌣) [dingen] m ㉒ one who hires, engages, &c.

Dinger² (⌣́⌣) pl. von Ding (s. ds, bsd. 5).

Dingerchen (⌣́⌣⌣) dim. pl. von Ding 5.

Dingerich (⌣́⌣⌣) m ob. n ⑪d. ~**s-hausen** (⌣⌣́⌣⌣) n ob. n ㊿ = Dingsda.

ding-fest (⌣́⌣) [Ding 7] a. ㊻: a) † fixed by law; b) weitS. = fest; einen ⚲ m. to arrest a p.; =**hof** m ㉒ court of justice.

Dingi ⚓ (⌣́-) [bengal.] n ㊿ (kleines Beiboot) dinghy, a. ding(e)y. [thing.]

Dinglein (⌣́-) n ㉓ (dim. v. Ding) little

dinglich (⌣́⌣) a. ㊿ jur. real. [rights pl.]

Dinglichkeit (⌣́⌣-) f ㊻ reality, real

Dingo (⌣́-) [austral.] m ㊺ zo. (wilder Hund) dingo (Canis dingo). [recently, of late.]

...**dings** (...⌣́) in Zssgn, zB. neuer⚲ lately,

Dings (⌣́) [gen. sg. von Ding] m, n. inv. F für ein Wort, das einem nicht einfällt: Herr, Frau ~(=**da**) F Mr., Mrs. Thingum(aj)y. Thingum(y)bob, What-you-may-call-him; das ~(=**da**) F that thingamitum; in ~**da**, ~**hausen** ob. ~**kirchen** F at what-ye-may-call-it.

Ding-statt (⌣́...) [Ding 7] f ㊷, =**stätte** †, =**stelle** † f meeting-place for the court; =**wort** [Ding 1] n, gr. noun, substantive.

dinieren (-⌣́⌣) [fr.] v/n. (h.) ⑬ to dine.

Dinkel ⚢ obb. (⌣́⌣) [ahd.] m ㉒ (auch ~**weizen** m) spelt (Tri'ticum Spelta).

Dinosauri-er ⚇ (-⌣⌣́⌣⌣) [grch.] m ㉒ geol. fossiles Reptil dinosaurian.

Dinotherium ⚇ (-⌣⌣́⌣⌣) [grch.] n ㉙ geol. fossiles Rüsseltier: dinotherium.

☞ **Diöc...** s. Diöz...

Diokletian (⌣⌣-tz(⌣)́) npr/m. ㊿ ㊼ α. Alt. (römischer Kaiser, 284—305) Diocletian.

diokletianisch (⌣⌣-tz(⌣)́⌣) a. ㊿ of Diocletian; die ~e Verfolgung (der Christen) the persecution (of Christians) under Diocletian. [Fliegenfalle.]

Dionäa ⚇ ⚢ (⌣⌣́⌣) [grch.] f ㊽ =

Dionys (⌣⌣́), **Dionysius**, ~**ios** (⌣⌣́(⌣)⌣) [grch.] npr/m. ⑯γ. (Bn.) Dionysius; Dennis. (Bacchusfest) Dionysia pl.

Dionysien (⌣⌣⌣́⌣) [grch.] pl. Alt.

dionysisch (⌣⌣́⌣) [grch.] a. ㊿ grch. myth. Dionysian, Bacchic.

diophantisch ⚇ (⌣⌣f⌣́⌣) [Diopha'ntos, grch. Math., 4. sae. n. Chr.] a. ㊿ math. ⚲e (unbestimmte) Gleichung Diophantine (or indeterminate) equation.

Diopter ⚇ (⌣⌣́⌣) [grch.] n ㉒ surv. (Sehspalte) diopter, sight-vane; ~(**=lineal**) (⌣...) n ㉒ math. alidad(e); ⚲**brechungslehre** f ㊽ dioptrics; ⚋ anaclastics.

Dioptrik (⌣⌣́⌣) [grch.] f ㊻ phys. (Lichtbrechungslehre) dioptrics; ⚋ anaclastics.

dioptrisch (⌣⌣́⌣) a. ㊿ dioptric.

Diorama ⚇ (⌣⌣́⌣) [grch. Durchsicht] n ㉘ (Rundschaubild) diorama.

dioramisch (⌣⌣⌣́⌣) a. ㊿ dioramic.

[Diorit] — 265 — [disponieren]

Diorit ⌑ (⏑‑́) [grch.] *m* ⓜ*c. min.* diorite.
Dioskuren (⏑‑⌣‑́) [grch.] *m/pl., inv., myth.* (Zwillinge Kastor u. Pollux) Dioscuri *pl.*
Diözesan (⏑‑‑́) [grch.] *m* ⓥ *eccl.* (Einwohner e-s Sprengels) diocesan. [clergy.]
Diözesan=geistlichkeit (‑‑‑...) *f* ⓥ diocesan
Diözese (⏑‑́⌣) [grch.] *f* ⓥ *eccl.* (Sprengel) diocese; Geistlichkeit der ~ f. Diözesan-g.
Diözia ⌑ § (⏑‑́(⌣)) [grch.] *f* ⓥ (22. Klasse) clergy. [nach Linné) diœcia.]
diözisch ⌑ § (⏑‑́‑) [grch.] *a.* ⓥ (zweihäufig: mit männlichen u. weiblichen Blüten auf verschiedenen Stämmen) diœcian, ...ous.
Diphenyl=amin ⌑ (⏑f‑‑‑́) [grch.] *n* ⓜ*c. chm.* diphenylamine (NH(C₆H₅)₂).
Diphtherie ⌑ § (⏑‑́), mst ⁺⁺ **Diphtheritis** (⁵f⌣‑⏑́) *inv.* [grch.] (Schleim=)Haut] *f*, *path.* (brandige od. häutige Bräune, Rachenbräune) diphtheria.
diphther(it)isch (⏑f(⌣)‑‑⏑/a. ⓥ) diphtheric, ...itic.
Diphthong ⌑ (⏑f‑) [grch.] *m* ⓜb., ⓥ *gram.* (Doppelvoka'l) diphthong; **Lieren** (⏑f‑‑‑) *v/a.* ⓥ to diphthongize.
Dipleidoskop ⌑ (⏑‑‑‑) [grch. Doppelbildseher] *n* ⓜ*c.* (1844) *opt. ast.* dipleidoscope.
Diplom (⏑‑́) [grch. „doppelt" gefalteten (Papier)] *n* ⓜ*c.* ((Bestallungs=)Urkunde) diploma; e-s engl. Elementarlehrers: parchment.
Diplomat (⏑‑‑‑́) [fr.] *m* ⓥ (Staatsmann) diplomatist; **~ie** (⏑‑‑‑́) *f* ⓥ (Staatsverhandlungskunst) diplomacy; **~ik** (⏑‑‑́‑) [grch.] *f* ⓥ (Urkundenlehre) diplomatics; **~iker** (⏑‑‑‑‑) *m* ⓥ (Urkundenkenner) expert in diplomatics; **Lisch** (⏑‑‑‑́) [grch.] *a.* ⓥ a) (in der Verhandlungskunst gewandt, *fig.* schlau) diplomatic; b) (gesandtschaftlich) ambassadorial; das ⏑e Korps the diplomatic body.
Dipodie ⌑ (⏑‑‑́) [grch.] *f* ⓥ *pros.* (zweifüßiges Versglied) dipody.
Dippel (⏑‑) *m* ⓥ 1. *vet.* (Drehkrankheit der Schafe) staggers. — 2. ⓞ = Dübel.
Dippel=hafer § (⏑‑‑‑...) *m* = Taumellolch.
Diptam § (⏑‑́) [grch.] *m* ⓜ*c.* (ⓥ) dittany (*Dicta'mnus albus*). [= Dipteros.]
Dipteral=tempel (⏑‑‑‑́) [it.‑grch.] *m* ⓥ
Dipteren (⏑‑‑́) [grch.] *pl., ent.* (Zweiflügler) diptera, dipterans *pl.*
Dipteros ⌑ (⏑‑‑⌣) [grch.] *m, inv.* (Tempel mit zwei Säulenreihen) dipteral temple.
Diptychon ⌑ (⏑‑‑) [grch.] *n* ⓥ Alt.: (zf.‑legbare Schreibtafel) diptych.
dir, in Briefen: **Dir** (‑́) *personal pron., dat. v.* du ⓐA1 (3t) 1. to thee, to you; hat er ⏑ geschrieben? has he written to you?; ⏑ lächelt das Glück fortune smiles upon you; haft du ⏑ weh(e) getan? did you hurt yourself?; gibst du ⏑ Mühe? do you take pains?; *fig.* mir nichts, ⏑ nichts with great indifference, very coolly; without much ado. — 2. als *dati'vus e'thicus* meist nicht zu übersetzen: das ist ⏑ eine wahre Lust it is (, you may believe me,) a real pleasure.
direkt (‑‑́) [lt.] *a.* ⓥ (u. *adv.*) direct(ly); in ⏑er Linie in a straight line; ⏑e Abstammung lineal descent; er kam ⏑ nachher he came immediately after (-wards); ⏑er Schaden positive injury or loss; ⓞ*mach.* ⏑ wirkend direct-acting; ⏑e Steuern *pl.* direct taxation *sg.*; ⏑e Verbindung, ⏑er Verkehr direct (or through=)communication; ⏑er Wagen, Zug through-carriage, -train; ⏑e Waren

⏑ beziehen to get ... direct (from the producer; Ware) to buy ... (at) first hand.
Direktion (‑‑tz(⌣)‑́) [lt.] *f* ⓥ 1. (Richtung) direction; (Verwaltung) management, administration. — 2. *coll.* (Vorstand) board (of directors, managers, governors).
Direktions=linie (‑‑...) *f* ⓥ line of direction; *math.*: ⌑ directrix; **=mitglied** *n* member of the board.
Direktive ⌦ (‑⌣‑⌣) [fr.] *f* ⓥ (Richtschnur) general instructions *pl.*
Direktor (‑‑‑́) [lt.] *m* ⓥ, **~in** (‑‑‑́‑) *f* ⓥ: a) e-r höheren Schule: headmaster; principal; ~in e-r Töchterschule head mistress, head governess; b) e-s Geschäfts, Theaters, einer Gesellschaft 2c.: (head) manager, managing director; ~in (mst Direktrice) manageress, lady manager; c) ⏏ u. ⊙ technischer ~ chief (or head) engineer, auch: acting manager; d) der Bank von England, e-s Zuchthauses 2c.: governor.
Direktor=amt (‑‑⌣...) *n* ⓥ, **Direktorat** (‑⌣‑‑́) [lt.] *n* ⓜ*c.* directorship, directorate; manager's post; in e-r Schule: head(master)ship. [managerial.]
direktorial (‑‑⌣(⌣)‑́) [lt.] *a.* ⓥ directorial.
Direktorium (‑‑⌣(⌣)‑) [lt.] *n* ⓥ board of directors, managing (or governing) board; *fr. hist.* das ~ (1795) the Directory.
Direttrice (‑‑tz‑⌣) [fr.] *f* ⓥ f. Direktor b.
Dirigent (‑‑⌣́) [lt.] *m* ⓥ (Leiter) director; manager of a business; head of a firm; conductor of an orchestra; leader of a band.
dirigieren (‑‑⌣‑‑́) [fr.] I *v/a.* ⓥ (leiten) to direct, to manage; ♪ to conduct. — II ~ *n* ⓥ direction, management.
Dirk ⌑⌦ [ndd.] *m* ⓜb. (Talje am äußern Ende des Besanbaums) derrick; (Kranleineblock) topping-lift block.
Dirk=läufer ⌦ (‑‑‑...) *m* ⓥ derrick-fall.
Dirnchen (⏑‑‑) *n* ⓥ, sübd. **Dirnd(e)l** (‑́(‑)) *n* ⓥ *dim. v.* Dirne.
Dirne (⏑‑́) [ahd.] *f* ⓥ girl, lass; F (young) damsel; faule ~ lazy wench; *b.s.* feile, gemeine ~ common wench or prostitute, strumpet; F (low) hussy, baggage; leichtfertige, liederliche ~ oft: lady of easy virtue; F fast creature, loose character.
Dis ♪ (‑́) *n, inv.* D sharp; ~‑Dur D sharp major, ~‑Moll D sharp minor.
⏏ disc... f. dis⏑... und diß...
Disharmonie (‑‑‑‑‑́) [grch.] *f* ⓥ 1. ♪ disharmony, want of harmony; unharmonious chord; (Mißklang) dissonance (auch *fig.*). — 2. *fig.* (Uneinigkeit) disunion, discord; ⏏ disharmony.
disharmonisch, mst ♪ (‑‑‑‑́‑) *a.* ⓥ unharmonious, dissonant.
disjunktiv (‑‑‑‑́) [lt.] *a.* ⓥ *gr., log.* (gegensätzlich) disjunctive conjunction, &c.
Diskant ♪ (⏑‑‑́) [it.] *m* ⓥ*b.* descant; üblicher: treble, soprano (a. = ~sänger); hoher (tiefer) ~ first (second) treble; **~bratsche**, **~flöte**, **~hoboe** *f* treble-viol, -flute, -hoboe. [sänger.]
Diskantist ♪ (⏑‑‑‑́) [it.] *m* ⓥ = Diskant=
Diskant=sänger (‑‑⌣...) *m* ⓥ soprano (singer); **=schlüssel** *m* treble-clef; **=stimme** *f* treble (or soprano) voice; canto.
Diskont ⏏ (⏑‑‑́) [it.] *m* ⓜb. (Abzug, Rabatt) discount; abzüglich 5%/₀ ~ deducting (or less) five per cent. discount.
diskontierbar ⏏ (⏑‑‑‑́) *a.* ⓥ discountable; **~keit** (⏑‑‑‑) *f* ⓥ discountability.

diskontieren ⏏ (⏑‑‑‑́) [it.] *v/a.* ⓥ (gegen Rabatt einwechseln) to discount a bill, &c.
Diskontierer ⏏ (⏑‑‑‑‑) *m* ⓥ (bill‑)discounter; (Wechselmakler) bill-broker.
Diskonto (⏑‑‑́) *m* ⓥ (⁵⁸) = Diskont 2c.
Diskont(o)=bank ⏏ (⏑‑‑‑...) *f* ⓥ discount-bank; *vgl.* =haus; **fuß** *m* rate of discount; **=geschäft(e** *pl.*) *n* discounting (business); **haus** *n*, **=kasse** *f* discounting house; **=Kommanditgesellschaft** *f* discount credit-bank; **=satz** *m* = =fuß.
diskreditieren (⌣‑⏑‑‑́) [fr.] *v/a.* ⓥ (in Mißkredit bringen) to (bring into) discredit or disrepute; ⏏ to depreciate. [creet.]
diskret (⏑‑‑́) [lt.] *a.* ⓥ (verschwiegen) discreet.
Diskretion (⏑‑tz(⌣)‑́) [lt.] *f* ⓥ (Verschwiegenheit) discretion; nach ~ (nach eigenem Ermessen) at one's discretion, as one feels inclined or disposed; **~s=jahre** *n/pl.* years *pl.* of discretion; **~s=tage** ⏏ *m/pl.* (Verzugstage) days *pl.* of grace or respite. [discriminant.]
Diskriminante ⌑ (⌣‑⌣‑‑́) [lt.] *f* ⓥ *math.*
Diskurs (⏑‑‑́) [lt.] *m* ⓜ*a.* (Gespräch) discourse, conversation; einen langen ~ halten mit to have a long talk with.
Diskus (⏑‑) [lt.] *m, inv.* Alt.: (Wurfscheibe) disk, discus.
Diskussion (⌣⌣(⌣)‑́) [lt.] *f* ⓥ (Verhandlung) discussion, debate.
Diskus=werfer (⏑‑‑...) *m* ⓥ ⌑ discobolus.
diskutierbar (⏑⏑‑́) *a.* ⓥ discussable.
diskutieren (⏑⏑‑‑́) [lt.] *v/a.* und *v/n.* (h.) ⓥ über et. ⏑ to discuss (or debate) a th.
Dislokation ⌑ (⏑‑‑tz(⌣)‑́) [lt.] *f* ⓥ⌦, *surg. geol.* (Verteilung) dislocation.
dislozier/en (⏑‑⏑‑‑́) [lt.] I *v/a.* ⓥ (verlegen, verteilen, *surg.* verrenken) to dislocate (a. ⌦ u. *surg.*), displace, remove; ⓥ to convey goods, &c. — II ~ *n* ⓥ *u.* D/ung (⏑‑) ⓥ dislocation, displacement, removal.
Dispache ⌦ ⏏ (⌣‑(⌣)‑́) [fr.] *f* ⓥ (Seeschadenberechnung) adjustment (or statement) of average; **Dispacheur** (‑‑‑‑(⌣)‑́) *m* ⓜ*d.* ⓥ (Strandrichter) arbitrator of averages.
Dispens (⏑‑‑́) [lt.] *m* ⓜ*a.*, **Dispensation** (⏑‑‑tz(⌣)‑́) [lt.] *f* ⓥ (Lossprechen) dispensation, (special) license.
Dispensations=gericht (⏑‑‑tz(⌣)‑‑...) *n* ⓥ *eccl.* Court of Faculties; **=recht** *n*, **=vollmacht** *f* dispensing power.
Dispensatorium ⌑ (⏑‑‑‑(⌣)‑) [lt.] *n* ⓥ, **Dispensier=anstalt** (⏑‑‑‑...) *f* ⓥ *pharm.* dispensary. [dispensable.]
dispensierbar (⏑⏑‑́) [lt.] *a.* ⓥ (erläßlich)
dispensieren (⏑⏑‑‑‑) [lt.] *v/a.* ⓥ 1. (verteilen) to distribute. — 2. *pharm.* (bereiten) to prepare. — 3. e-n v. et. ⏑ (entbinden) to dispense (or exempt) a p. from s. th.
Disponent ⏏ (⏑‑‑‑́) [lt.] *m* ⓥ (Geschäftsführer) (head) manager, managing clerk.
disponibel (⏑‑‑‑́) [fr.] *a.* ⓥ (verfügbar) disposable; mst available; at (one's) disposal; ⏏ in hand; ⓥ unattached.
Disponibilität (⏑‑‑‑‑‑́) [fr.] *f* ⓥ availability, availableness; ⓥ in ~ versetzen to put (or place) on the retired list or on half-pay; **~s=gehalt** ⓥ *n* half-pay.
disponieren (⏑‑‑‑) [lt.] ⓥ I *v/a.* (anordnen) to arrange. — II *v/n.* (h.) über etwas ⏑ (verfügen) to dispose of a th. — III **disponiert** *p.p. u. a.* ⓥ gut (übel) ⏑ (gestimmt, gesinnt) well (ill) disposed

[Disposition] — 266 — [Docke]

Disposition (⌣⌣⌣tʃ(ᵛ)ᴸ) [lt.] *f* ⑥ (Anordnung) arrangement; neue ~en treffen to adopt (or take) new measures; ⚔ zur ~ der Ersatzbehörden (*abbr. z. D.*) liable to be called (out) by the military authorities; (Stimmung, Neigung) disposition; frame of mind; e-m zur ~ steh(e)n (stellen) to be (to place) at a p.'s disposal; ⚭-**fähig** (⌣...) *a.* ⑥ (fully) capable of disposing of one's property; *jur.* = **geschäftsfähig**; ⚭-**recht** *n* ⑥ right of disposal (or to dispose of) an estate, of one's property, &c.
Disput (⌣ᴸ) [fr.] *m* ⑪c. (Streit) dispute.
Disputant (⌣⌣ᴸ) [lt.] *m* ⑫ (Streitender) disputant; (Gegner) opponent.
Disputation (⌣⌣tʃ(ᵛ)ᴸ) [lt.] *f* ⑥ (Wortkampf) disputation, controversy; ~**s-satz** *m* auf Hochschulen, bes. ehm.: ⌒ thesis.
disputieren (⌣⌣ᴸᵛ) [lt.] **I** *v/n.* (h.) ⑨ über et. ⌒ to dispute (stärker: to squabble) about a th., to debate (or argue) a th. — **II** ~ *n* ⑫ dispute, debate, argument.
Disputierer (⌣⌣ᴸᵛ) [lt.] *m* ⑫ disputant.
Disputier-kunst (⌣⌣ᴸ...) *f* ⑥ art of debating, dialectics; ⚭-**süchtig** *a.* ⑥ argumentative; ⚭-**übung** *f* disputation; exercise in debating.
Disqualifikation (⌣⌣⌣⌣-tʃ(ᵛ)ᴸ) *f* ⑥ Rennsport: (Untauglichkeit) disqualification.
Dissertation (⌣⌣⌣-tʃ(ᵛ)ᴸ) [lt.] *f* ⑥ (Abhandlung) dissertation, treatise; gelehrte ⌒ thesis.
dissertieren (⌣⌣ᴸᵛ) [lt.] *v/n.* (h.) ⑨ über et. ⌒ to discuss (or argue) a th.
Dissident (⌣⌣ᴸ) [lt.] *m* ⑫, ~**in** *f* ⑥ *eccl.* (Andersgläubige(r)) one of a different faith; in Engl.: (nicht-anglikanische(r) Protestant(in)) Dissenter, Nonconformist.
Dissonanz (⌣⌣ᴸ) [lt.] *f* ⑥ ♪, *rhet.,* &c. (Mißklang) dissonance; *fig. a.* discord.
dissonieren (⌣⌣ᴸᵛ) [lt.] *v/n.* (h.) ⑨ to jar (or grate) upon the ear; ⌒d discordant.
Distanz (⌣ᴸ) [lt.] *f* ⑥ (Abstand) distance, Rennsport: (Strecke von 200 Meter [240 yards zw. Ziel u. ⚭pfahl; *vgl.* bs.) interval.
distanzieren (⌣⌣ᴸᵛ) *v/a.* ⑨ Rennsport: to distance; *d/tes* (hinter dem Distanzpfahl zurückgebliebenes) Pferd distanced horse.
Distanz-messer ⊕ (⌣⌣...) *m* ⑫ für Fußgänger: ambulator; für Schüsse ⌒c., rangefinder; ⚭-**pfahl** *m* Sport, beim Probereiten: distance-post; *vgl.* Distanz; ⚭-**reiten** *n*, ⚭-**ritt** *m* Sport: long-distance ride; ⚭-**richter** *m* Sport: distance-judge; *vgl.* distanzieren; ⚭-**signal 🚂** *n* (Einfahrtzeichen) distance-signal. **I** (*Cirsium u. Carduus*.)
Distel ♀ (⌣ᵛ, a. ᴸᵛ) [ahd.] *f* ⑥ thistle.
Distel-falter (⌣ᵛ...) *m* ⑫ *ent.* painted-lady, thistle-butterfly (*Vanessa cardui*); ⚭-**fink** *m* ⑬ *orn.* goldfinch (*Fringilla carduelis*).
distelig (⌣ᵛᵛ oder ᴸᵛᵛ) *a.* ⑥ thistly.
Distel-vogel (⌣ᵛ...) *m* ⑫ = **-falter**; ⚭-**wolle** *f* thistle-down.
Disthen ⌓ (⌣ᴸ) [grch.] *m* ⑪c. *min.* disthene; blauer ~ cyanite, kyanite.
Distichon ⌓ (⌣ᵛᵛ) [grch.] *n* ⑱ (⑲) *pros.* (zweizeilige Strophe) distich.
distinguiert (⌣⌣ᵍᴸ) [fr.] *p.p. u. a.* ⑥ (vornehm) distinguished, (fr.) *distingué(e)f.*
distributiv (⌣⌣⌣ᴸf) [lt.] *a.* ⑥ (verteilend) distributive; ~-**zahl** *f* gr. d. number.
Distrikt (⌣ᴸ) [lt.] *m* ⑪b. (Bezirk) district; ~**s-arzt** *m* ⑫ (district) medical officer.

Disziplin (⌣⌣ᴸ) [lt.] *f* ⑥ 1. (Wissenszweig) branch of knowledge. — 2. (⚔ Mannszucht, *eccl.* Geißelung) discipline; streng auf ~ halten, die ~ streng handhaben to keep good discipline, to be a strict disciplinarian; F to be very strict, to rule with an iron rod.
Disziplinar-bestrafung (⌣⌣-ᴸᴸ...) *f* ⑥ disciplinary punishment; ⚭-**fall** *m* infraction of discipline. [ciplinary.)
disziplinarisch (⌣⌣-ᴸᵛ) [lt.] *a.* ⑥ dis-)
Disziplinar-kammer (⌣⌣-ᴸᴸ...) *f* ⑥ court (or board) for disciplinary offences of civil servants, &c.; ⚭-**untersuchung** *f*, ⚭-**verfahren** *n* disciplinary offence; d. investigation or proceedings *pl.*; ⚭-**weg** *m*: auf dem ⌒e by way of disciplinary correction or censure.
disziplinier/en (⌣⌣⌣ᴸᵛ) [lt.] *v/a.* ⑨ (in Zucht halten) to (accustom to good) discipline; ⚔ gut *d/t* well disciplined.
dithionig ⌓ (⌣ᴸᵛ)[grch.] *a.* ⑥ *chm.:* ⌒e (unterschweflige) Säure hyposulphurous acid ($H_2S_2O_3$). [dithionic acid ($H_2S_2O_6$).)
Dithion-säure ⌓ (⌣ᴸᴸ...)[grch.] *f* ⑥ *chm.*)
Dithyrambe (⌣ᴸᵛ) *f* ⑥, **Dithyrambus** *m* ⑰ [lt.,* grch.] *bes.* Alt.: (urspr. Bacchuslied, allg.: begeisterter Gesang) dithyramb(us).
dithyrambisch *a.* ⑥ dithyrambic.
dito (ᴸᵛ), **ditto** (ᵛᵛ) *adv.* (*abbr.* **do.**) *bes.* ⑨ (besgleichen) ditto; the same.
diuretisch ⌓ (⌣ᴸᵛ) [grch.] *a.* ⑥ *med.* (harntreibend); ⌒(es Mittel) diuretic.
Diva (ᴸᵛᵛ) [lt. Göttliche] *f* ⑥ (erste Sängerin) diva, star artiste, primadonna.
divergent ⌓ (⌣ᵛᴸᵛ) [lt.] *a.* ⑥ (abweichend) divergent. [divergence, divergency.)
Divergenz (⌣ᵛᴸᵛ) [lt.] *f* ⑥ (Abweichung))
divergieren ⌓ (⌣ᵛᴸᵛ) [lt.] *v/n.* (h.) ⑨ (abweichen) to diverge from (*auch* *fig.*); *math.* ⌒de Linien divergent lines.
divers ⌓ (⌣ᵛ) [lt.] *a.* ⑥ (D10) sundry; diverse Dinge, Artikel *etc.* sundries *pl.*
Diversion (⌣ᵛᵛ(ᵛ)ᴸ) [lt.] *f* ⑥ ⚔, *fenc.* (Ablenkung[s-angriff]) diversion.
Dividend (⌣ᵛᵛᴸ) [lt.] *m* ⑫ *arith.* (zu teilende Zahl) dividend.
Dividende ⊕ (⌣ᵛᵛᴸ) [lt.] *f* ⑥ (Gewinnanteil) dividend; bonus; eine ⌒-festsetzen, verteilen to declare a dividend; ⚭-**papier** *n* Börse: dividend-paying stock; ⌒n-**schein** *m* dividend-warrant.
dividieren (⌣ᵛᵛᴸᵛ) [lt.] *v/a.* ⑨ *arith.* (teilen) to divide (durch by), *abs.* to do (or work) a division (sum).
Dividivi (⌣ᵛᵛᵛ) [amer.] *pl.* ♀ *u.* ⊕ Gerberei: dividivi (*Caesalpinia coriaria*).
Divination (⌣ᵛᵛ--tʃ(ᵛ)ᴸ) [lt.] *f* ⑥ (Weissagung) divination; ⌒**s-gabe** (⌣...) *f* ⑥ prophetic gift. **I** (Bindestrich) hyphen.)
Divis ⊕ (⌣ᴸ) [lt.] *n, inv. ob.* ⑪a. *typ.*)
Division (⌣ᵛᵛ(ᵛ)ᴸ) [lt.] *f* ⑥ *arith.,* ⚔, ⚓ division; ~**är** ⚔ (⌣ᵛ(ᵛ)ᴸ) [fr.] *m* ⑪c. = ⚭-**general**.
Divisions-befehl ⚔, ⚓ (⌣...) *m* ⑫ order issued to a division; ⚭-**exempel** *n, arith.* division sum; ⚭-**general** ⚔ *m,* ⚭-**kommandeur** *m* general (or commander) of a division; ⚭-**weise** ⚔, *a.* ⚓ *adv.* by (or in) divisions. [divisor.)
Divisor (⌣ᴸᵛ) [lt.] *m* ⑫ *arith.* (Teiler))
Diwan (ᴸᵛ) türk., *perf.-*ᴸ) *m* ⑪c. 1. (türk. Staatsrat) Divan. — 2. (Sofa, Ruhelager) divan, sofa, couch.

d. J. *abbr.* = a) dieses Jahr(es) (of) this (or the present) year; b) der Jüngere junior, *abbr.* jun.
dkg, dkl, dkm (öft. *dkg, dkl, dkm*) *abbr.* = Deka-gramm, -liter, -meter.
dl, dm öft. *abbr.* = Dezi-liter, -meter. dm^2, dm^3 öft. *abbr.* = Quadrat-, Kubik-dezimeter. [month, inst. (= instant).)
d. M. *abbr.* = dieses Monats of this)
Dnjepr, Dnjestr ♀ (ᴸ) *npr/m.* ⑨ ⚓. (Flüsse in Südrußland) Dnieper, Dniester.
do. *abbr.* = dito (s. bs). [mentioned.)
d. O. *abbr.* = der Obige the above-)
Dobber ⚓ (ᴸᵛ) *m* ⑫ buoy of a fishing-net.
Döbel (ᴸᵛ) [nbd.] *m* ⑫ 1. ⊕ (Holzpflock) dowel, peg, plug. — 2. *ichth.* dobule, chub (*Squalius cephalus*).
dobeln, döbeln ⊕ (ᴸᵛ)[Döbel 2] *v/a.* ⊕ to dowel, to fasten with pegs.
☞ **Doc..**, s. Doz.
doch (ᵛᵛ) [ahd.: though] *cj. u. adv.:*
A. betont: **1.** (dennoch) however, yet, still, for all that; ich sah es (aber) ⌒ ... nevertheless. — **2.** (je⌒): ich hat ihn, ⌒ er wollte nicht ... but he would not do it. — **3.** a) nach verneinter Frage: Siehst du's nicht? ⌒ (ja), ich sehe es! ... yes, I do (see it)!; hat er (denn) kein Geld? ⌒!, ... yes, he has!; b) freilich ⌒!, ja ⌒!, yes, indeed!; of course!; nicht ⌒! not indeed!, oh no!, certainly not! — **B.** unbetont: **4.** (gewiß, wirklich) Sie wissen ⌒, daß er ‖ you surely know that he ‖; das ist ⌒ Unsinn! it's nonsense, I am sure!; was ⌒ nur der Grund sein mag? whatever can be the reason?, I wonder what the cause may be; er ist ⌒ nicht etwa schwindsüchtig? he is not consumptive, I hope?; er ist (denn) ⌒ noch immer sehr arm he is undoubtedly still very poor; das ist ⌒ (gar) zu arg! that is really too bad!; er hat es ⌒ selbst gesagt why, he said so himself; sah euch ⌒ niemand kommen since (or as) nobody saw you come; das kann dir ⌒ nicht(s) schaden it surely can't hurt you. — **5.** auffordernd: kommen Sie ⌒ herein! do come in!, pray step in!; komm ⌒ mit! come with us (F come along), do!; sei ⌒ nur geduldig! do have a little patience!, be patient, will you! — **6.** wünschend: wäre es ⌒ erst jetzt! if it were only light!; ach, wenn er ⌒ (nur) käme! oh, if he would only come!; would that he might come!; hätt'st du's ⌒ gleich gesagt! had you only (or I wish you had) said so from the first! [or a lamp.)
Docht (ᵛᵛt) [ahd.] *m* ⑪b. wick of a candle)
Docht-garn (ᴸ...) *n* ⑫ wick-yarn; ⚭-**halter** *m* burner of a lamp, wick-holder.
Dock ⚓ ↓ (ᵛ) [engl.] *n* ⑪d., ⊕ dock, dockyard; (Hafenbecken) basin; nasses (trockenes) ~ wet (dry) dock; schwimmendes ~ floating dock; ins ~ bringen to (put into) dock; aus dem ~ bringen to take out of dock.
Dock-arbeiter ⚓ ↓ (ᵛ...) *m* ⑫ docklabourer, docker; ⚭-**aufseher** *m* = ⚭-**meister**; ⚭-**bänke** *f/pl.* dock-banks *pl.*; ⚭-**beamte(r)** *m* dock-official.
Docke (ᵛᵛ) [ahd.] *f* ⑥ dock Stummel, duck Puppe) *f* ⑥ 1. ⊕ (kleiner dicker Pfeiler)

Signs (see page XVII): F familiar; P vulgar; F flash; ⚹ rare; † obsolete (died); * new word (born); ⁺⁺ incorrect; ♪ music;

[docken] — 267 — [Dominostein]

short stout pillar; upright, post, column; des Geländers: baluster; (Drehbankspindel) mandrel; Drehbank mit ~ chuck-lace. — 2. 🟤 (Bündel) skein of yarn; bundle of hemp, tobacco-leaves, &c. — 3. (Spielpuppe) doll. — 4. ⚓ = Dock.
docken[1] ⚓ (ˇ͜ˇ) [Docke 2] v/a. ⚙ Garn: to wind (up) in skeins; Flachs: to bind; Seide ⚓ (in Strähne legen) to sleave ...
docken[2] ⚓ (ˇ͜ˇ) [Dock] v/a. ⚙ Schiffe: to (lay up in) dock, to put into dock.
Docken-geländer ⊕ (ˇ͜ˇ...) [Docke 1] n ⚙ arch. balustrade.
Dock-futtür (ˇ͜ˇ) f ⚙ dock-gate; =gebühr f dock-duty or -rent; ~en pl. auch: dock-dues pl., dockage; =geld n = =gebühr; =meister m dock-master; =stufen f/pl. = =bänke; =winde f dockblock; =zins m = =gebühr.
Dodeka-eder ⚗ (ˇ͜ˇˇ) [grch.] n ⚙ math., cryst. (Zwölfflach) dodecahedron.
dodeka-edrisch (~) a. ⚙ dodecahedral.
Dodekandria ⚗ ♀ (ˇ͜ˇˇˇ) [grch.] f ⚙ (11. Klasse n. Linné) dodecandria.
dodekandrisch ⚗ ♀ (ˇ͜ˇˇˇ) a. ⚙ (zwölfmännig: mit 12 Staubgefäßen) dodecandrian.
dodonäisch (--ˇ͜ˇ) [Dodo'na, grch. St. in Epirus mit altem Orakel] a. ⚙ Dodonæan.
Dogaressa (-gˇ͜ˇˇ) [it.] f ⚙ hist. (Frau des Dogen) dogessa, dogaressa f.
Dog-boot ⚓ (⸚˙) n ⚙ = Dogger.
Doge (mst. ˊGˇ) [it. do'bGě] m ⚙ (ehm. in Venedig und Genua: Haupt der Republik) doge; zum ~n gehörig ducal.
Dogen-amt (ˮGˇ...) n ⚙ hist. dogeship, dog(e)ate; =palast m palace of the doges, ducal palace; =würde f = =amt.
Dogge ꕗ (ˇ͜) [engl.] f ⚙, a. m ⚙ bulldog; deutsche ~ great Dane; englische ~ (Bullenbeißer) mastiff; ~n-paar n ⚙ couple of bull-dogs. [dogger(-boat).]
Dogger ⚓ (ˇ͜ˇ) [ndl.] m ⚙ Herings-(2c.)fang:
Dogger-bank ♀ (ˇ͜ˇ...) f ⚙ große Sandbank der Nordsee: Dogger(-)Bank; =boot ⚓ n ⚙ = Dogger. [in a dogger-boat.]
doggern (ˇ͜ˇ) v/n. (h.) ⚙ a. to go fishing
Dögling (ˊˇ) m ⚙ d. zo. (Entenwal) bottle-nosed whale (Hypero'odon bidens).
Dogma ⚗ (ˇ͜ˇ) [grch.] n ⚙, ⚙ phls. u. bsd. theol. (Glaubenssatz) dogma, article of faith; ~tik (ˇ͜ˇ) f ⚙ (Glaubenslehre) dogmatics, dogmatic theology; ~tiker (ˊˇˇ) m ⚙ dogmatist; ⚓tisch (ˊˇ) a. ⚙ dogmatic(al); ⚓tisieren (ˊˇˇˇ) v/n. (h.) ⚙ to dogmatize; ~tismus (ˊˇˇ) m ⚙ (Festhalten an Lehrsätzen) dogmatism.
Dogmen-geschichte ⚗ (ˇ͜ˇ...) f ⚙ theol. history of Christian doctrines or dogmatic theology.
(ˊˇ) Hom. Dole) [ahd.: daw] orn. h, daw. jackdaw (Corvus mone'dula).
Dohne (ˊˇ) [ahd.] f ⚙ Vogelfang: (Schlinge) springe, noose, gin; ~n stellen to lay snares for birds, to snare birds.
Dohnen-fang (ˮˇ...) m ⚙ noosing (or snaring) of birds; =strich m springe-line.
doktern F (ˊˇ) [it.] v/n. (h.) ⚙ a. 1. to practise as a doctor; to give medical advice; to physic. — 2. to be under a doctor('s care); to take medical advice; to physic (or to cure, F doctor) o.s.
Doktor (ˇ͜ˇ) [nhd. 1500, *lt.] m ⚙ (P ⚙, als Titel ⚙), ~in f ⚙ r. 3 1. doctor; ~ der Gottesgelahrtheit (ob. Gottesgelehrsam-

keit, Theologie, abbr. Cath. **Dr. theol.**, ev. **D.**) Doctor of Divinity (D. D.); ~ der Medizin (**Dr. med.**) Doctor of Medicine (M. D.); ~ der Philosophie (**Dr. phil.**) D. of Philosophy (in Engl.: Master of Arts ob. M. A.); ~ der Rechte (**Dr. jur.**) Doctor of Laws (LL. D.); ~ werden, den ~ machen to pass (or take) one's doctor's degree; e-n zum ~ machen to make a p. a doctor, to bestow the doctor's degree (or title) upon a p. — 2. engS. (Arzt) medical man, doctor. — 3. ~in f: a) female doctor, lady doctor; F doctoress; b) doctor's wife; als Titel der Frau nicht zu übersetzen: Frau ~(in) N. Mrs. N.
Doktorand (ˇ͜ˇˇ) [lt.] m ⚙ candidate for a doctor's degree.
Doktorat (ˇ͜ˇˇ) [lt.] n ⚙c. doctor's degree or title, doctorate. [ploma.]
Doktor-diplom (ˇ͜ˇ...) n ⚙ doctor's di-
Doktoren-... (ˇ͜ˇˇ) ⚙ = Doktor-...
Doktor-examen (ˇ͜ˇ...) n ⚙ examination for a d.'s degree; F doctor (or M. D.) exam(ination); das ~ bestehe(e)n to graduate as a doctor of medicine, to pass one's M. D.; =fisch m, ichth. doctor-fish (Acanthu'rus); =grad m doctor's degree, doctorate. =hut m doctor's cap.
doktorieren F (ˇ͜ˇ˘ˇ) [lt.] v/n. (h.) ⚙ to take one's doctor's degree.
Doktorin (ˇ͜ˇ, ˇ͜ˇˇ) f ⚙ f. Doktor 3.
Doktor-ingenieur (ˇ͜ˇ...) m ⚙ (abbr. Dr.-Ing.) Doctor of Engineering; =mantel m doctor's gown; ⚓mäßig a. ⚙ doctoral; =miene f solemn (or dignified) air or look; =promotion f promotion to a d.'s degree; =schmaus m dinner given by a newly promoted doctor; =titel m d.'s title; =würde f = =grad; die ~ erhalten to receive one's doctor's diploma or degree.
Doktrin (ˇ͜ˇ) [lt.] f ⚙ (Lehre) doctrine.
doktrinär (ˇ͜ˇˮ) [fr.] **I** a. ⚙ theoretical, (fr.) doctrinaire. — **II** ~ m ⚙c. (polit. Theore'tiker) doctrinaire, political theorist. [bisw. doctrinarianism.)
Doktrinarismus ⚓ (ˇ͜ˇ-ˇ͜ˇ) [lt.] m ⚙
Dokument (ˇ͜ˇˊ) [lt...] n ⚙b. (Urkunde) document, deed, (legal) instrument; ⚓arisch (ˇ͜ˇˊ) a. ⚙ documentary; ⚓ieren (ˇ͜ˇˊˇ) v/a. ⚙ to prove by documents or documentary evidence.
Dolch [nhd. 16. sae. *slaw.] m ⚙b. dagger, poniard; schottischer ~ dirk, kleiner ~ (it.) stiletto; mit dem ~ verwunden, erstechen to stab, kill with a dagger. to pierce with a poniard.
dolch-förmig (ˇ͜ˇ...) a. ⚙ dagger-like; =messer n ⚙, oft: poniard-shaped knife; Am. (Sagbmesser) bowie-knife; =spitze f point of a dagger; =stich m stab with a poniard; dagger-wound; ⚓Worte sind (wie) ~e his words are like (or he speaks) daggers; =stock m dagger-cane, sword-stick; =stoß m = =stich.
Dolde ♀ (ˇ͜) [ahd.: Tolle] f ⚙ umbel.
dolden-artig ♀ (ˇ͜ˇ...) a. ⚙, ⚓förmig a. ⚙ umbelliform; =blume f, =blüte f umbellate flower; ⚓blütig a. umbellate(d); =gewächse n/pl., =pflanzen f/pl. umbellate (or umbelliferous) plants, umbelliferæ pl.; ⚓ständig a. umbellate(d); ⚓tragend a. umbelliferous; =traube f

corymb(us); ⚓traubig a. corymb(ifer)ous. [umbelliferous.]
doldig ♀ (ˇ͜ˇ) a. ⚙ umbellate, umbellar,
Dole (ˊˇ) Hom. Dohle) [ahd.] f ⚙ (Kanal, Abzugsgraben) drain(-pipe), sewer.
Dollar ꕗ (ˇ͜ˇ) [amer.; *dtsch. Taler] m ⚙. (= 4,1979 Mark) dollar.
Doll-bord ⚓ (⸚...) m ⚙ (Schan[z]beck[el] e-s Bootes) gunwale. thole-board.
Dolle ⚓ (ˇ͜) [ndd.: thole] f ⚙ (Ruderpflock) thole(-pin).
Dolman (ˇ͜ˇ) [türk.] m ⚙e. (⚙) (⚒ Husarenjacke [jetzt: Attila], Damenmantel 2c.) dolman.
Dolmen (ˇ͜ˇ) [klt. dol Tafel u. men Stein] m ⚙ (altes Steingrabmal) dolmen.
Dolmetsch (ˇ͜ˇ) [mhd., *türk.] m ⚙, interpreter; Levante: dragoman.
dolmetschen (ˇ͜ˇˇ) **I** v/n. (h.) u. v/a. ⚙ to interpret, to act as interpreter. — **II** ~ n ⚙ interpretation.
Dolmetscher (ˇ͜ˇˇ) m ⚙, ~in f ⚙ = Dolmetsch; vgl. a. Ausleger 1 a; ~-posten m ⚙ interpretership; dragoman's post.
Dolomit (ˇˇˊ) [Dolomieu, fr. Geolog, † 1801] m ⚙c. min. (Bitterkalt) dolomite; bitter-spar, magnesian limestone; in ~ verwandeln ⚗ to dolomize; ~-bildung (ˮ...) f ⚙ geol. dolom(it)ization.
dolomitisch (ˇˇˊˇ) a. ⚙ dolomitic.
dolos (ˇˊ) [lt.] a. ⚙ (D10) jur. = arglistig.
Dolus (ˊˇ) [lt. ˘ˇ Trug] m, inv. jur. cunning, deception, malice.
Dom[1] (ˊ) [fr.] ⚙ ⚙c. 1. [lt. dō̆mus (de'i)] (Hauptkirche) cathedral (church); auch: minster (zB. York M.). — 2. (fr. dôme) arch. (Kuppeldach) dome, cupola; fig. der ~ des Himmels (Dampfhaube) the canopy (or vault) of heaven. — 3. ⊕ ⚙ (Dampfhaube) dome.
Domäne (ˇˊˇ) [fr.] f ⚙ (Kron-, Kammergut) domain, crown-land, bsb. jur. demesne.
Domänen-gut (ˇˊˇ...) n ⚙ = Domäne; =pächter, =verwalter m farmer, bailiff (or manager) of a (royal) domain.
Dom-bauverein (ˮ...) m ⚙, etwa: association for the completion of the Cologne cathedral; =chor m ⚙ cathedral choir; =dechant m dean of a cathedral; =frau f canoness; =herr m canon, prebendary; ⚓herrlich a. canonical; weitS. capitular; =herrn-pfründe, =stelle, =würde f = =pfründe; =herrn-schmuck m canonicals pl.
Dominante ♪ (ˇ͜ˇˇ) [it.] f ⚙ (Quinte des Grundtons) dominant.
dominieren (ˇ͜ˇˇ) [lt.] v/n. (h.) u. v/a. ⚙ to domineer, F to lord it over a person.
Dominik(a f) m (ˊˇ, ˇ͜ˇ) npr/m. ⚙ ⚙ (f ⚙⚙)a. (Bn.) Dominic(a).
Dominikaner (ˇ-ˇˊˇ) [lt. 1215 * Dominikus b] m ⚙, ~in f ⚙ rel. dominican (friar, f nun), a. preaching (or predicant), friar, in England ehm. black friar; ~-kloster (ˮ...) n ⚙, ~orden m Dominican convent, order.
Dominikus (ˇ͜ˇˇ) npr/m. ⚙γ. a) (Bn.) b) der heilige ~ (1170—1221) Dominic.
Dominium (ˇˊ(ˇ)) [lt.] n ⚙ = Domäne.
Domino (ˊˇ) [lt.] ⚙ ⚙ 1. (Kleidung eines do'mini [Geistlichen]) m (Maskentracht) domino. — 2. n Spiel: dominoes pl.; ~ spielen to play (at) dominoes.
Domino-maske (ˊˇˇ...) f ⚙ domino; =spiel n: a) = Domino 2; b) (=steine) set of dominoes; =stein m domino,

⚗ scientific; ♀ botanical; ♁ geography; ⊕ machinery; ⚒ mining; ⚔ military; ⚓ marine; ● commercial; ✉ postal; 🚂 railway.

[Domit] — 268 — [Doppeltschwefeleisen]

piece; Kasten mit ~en box of dominoes, bisw.: domino-box. [domite.]
Domit ⚇ (—ᴸ) m ⓂC. min. (Art Trachyt)
Domizil (⌣ᴸ) [lt.] n ⓂC. (Wohnung) domicile (● Zahlungsort e-s Wechsels) (Wohnsitz) residence; weitS. address.
domizilier/en (⌣⌣ᴸ–) [lt.] ⓑ I v/n. (in) (wohnen) to be domiciled; to reside. — II v/a. (a. ● e-n Wechsel) ⓔ to domicile. — III ~ n ⓑ u. D/ung f ⓐ taking up one's domicile or residence.
Domizil=veränderung (⌣⌣ᴸᴸ–) f ⓑ change of residence; =wechsel m: a) =veränderung; b) ● domiciliated bill.
Dom=kapitel (ᴸ–) n ⓑ chapter of a cathedral; =kirche f cathedral church.
Dommel (⌣⌣) f ● orn. f. Rohr=⌐.
Domper ↓ (⌣⌣) m ● (Tau als Stütze) martingale.
Dom=pfaff(e) (ᴸ–) m ● orn. bullfinch (Py'rrhula vulga'ris); =pfründe, =stelle f canonry, canonicate, prebendary-ship; =propst m provost of a cathedral; =schule f bsd. im Mittel=alter: cathedral-school; =stift n cathedral-chapter.
Don (ᴸ) [span. Herr] m ⓈD (Titel ⓑ ⓑ) don; ~ Juan, ~ Quichotte (Quijote) Don Juan, Don Quixote. [lay brother.]
Donat¹ (—ᴸ) [lt.] m ⓑ(Laienbruder im Kloster)
Donat² (—ᴸ) m ⓂC. (lt. Grammatit des A'lius Dona'tus, 4. sae.) ehm. Donatus.
Donatar (——ᴸ) [lt.] m ⓂC. = Beschenkte(r).
Donation (——ᴸ) [lt.] f ⓐ = Schenkung.
Donator (——ᴸ) [lt.] m ⓑ jur. = Schenker.
Donau ♀ (ᴸ–) [fkt.] npr/f. ⓓα. Danube; ~fürstentümer n/pl. (Moldau u. Walachei, jetzt: Rumänien; a. Serbien u. Bulgarien) Danubian Principalities pl.; ~tiefland n Danubian plain or lowland (s pl.).
donisch (ᴸ⌣) [Don, ♀ ruff. Fl.] a. ⓑ ☓ ~e Kosaken m/pl. Don Cossacks pl.
Don Juan (ᴸ ᴸ⌣) [span.] Don Juan; fig. (Verführer, Wüstling) gay Lothario, lady-killer, debauchee.
Donner (⌣⌣) [ahd.: thunder] m ⓑ thunder; der ~ (g)rollte, krachte the th. was roaring, there were (loud) peals (or claps) of th.; unter ~ und Blitz amid th. and lightning; fig. wie vom ~ gerührt thunderstruck; ~ der Geschütze thunder (or booming) of cannon, peals pl. of artillery; ~ und Doria! (SCH.) hang (or damn) it all!, the deuce (take it)!, confounded nuisance!
Donner=bart ♀ (⌣⌣–) m ⓑ = Hauswurz (echte); =büchse ☓ f ehm. blunderbuss.
Donnerer (⌣⌣–) m ⓑ = Donnergott.
Donner=gebrüll (⌣⌣–) n ⓑ, =gekrach, =gepolter, =geroll, =getöfe n rolling (or crashing, rumbling) of thunder, thundering noise, peals pl. of thunder; =gott m (Zeus, Thor ꝛc.) the Thunderer; (blitz=blau und) =grün F a. ⓑ f. blitzblau; =hall m = =gebrüll; =keil m thunderbolt; geol.: ⚇ belemnite; =maschine f, thea. thundering-machine; arch. Alt.: bronteon, ...um; =mäßig a. thunderlike, adv. F dencedly, confoundedly.
donnern (⌣⌣) ⓐa. I v/n. (h.) u. v/impers. to thunder; von Geschützen auch: to boom; es donnert it thunders; die See donnert ... is roaring; an die Tür ⚇ to storm against the door; to hammer (or pound) away at the door; fig. (wettern)

to fulminate; to shout and roar; ⟨des Gelächter roaring (or loud roars, peals pl. of) laughter. — II v/a. (laut erschallen lassen) e-n aus dem Schlafe ⚇ to rouse a p. by loud rumbling (noises); mit Kanonen donnert er die Antwort he replies with roaring (peals) of cannon. — III ~ n ⓑ f. Donner=gebrüll, =schlag.
Donner=schlag (⌣⌣–) m ⓑ peal (or burst, F crack) of thunder, thunderclap; † thunder-stroke; wie ein ~ F like a bolt from the blue.
Donners=tag (⌣⌣–) [Donar (Donnergott)] m ⓑ Thursday; grüner ~ Maundy-Th.
Donner=stimme (⌣⌣–) f ⓑ thundering voice; voice of thunder; =strahl m flash of lightning, F thunderbolt; =wetter n thunderstorm, thunder and lightning, a.: electric storm; (zum) ~! damn (or confound) it!, hang it (all)!; =wolke f thunder-cloud; =wort n word of terror, crushing (or terrible) sentence.
Donquichot(t)erie (⌣⌣ᴸ⌣–) f ⓑ, Donquichot(t)ismus (⌣ᴸ⌣ᴸ⌣) m ⓑ [Don Quichotte (Quijote) de la Mancha: Held e-s span. Romans v. Cerva'ntes] quixotism, quixotry. [(form or warrant or bill).]
Doppel ● (⌣⌣) n ⓑ (Duplikat) duplicate
Doppel=adler (⌣⌣–) m ⓑ auf Wappen ꝛc.: double eagle; =axt f twibill; =B ♪ n double flat (♭♭); =bahn 🚆 f double-line or -track; =becher m: a) double cup; b) (Würfelbecher) dice-box; =bewußtsein n double consciousness; =beziehung f double relationship; =bindung f, chm. double combination; =boden m double (or false) bottom; =brechung f, opt. double refraction; =bruch m: a) surg. compound fracture or rupture; b) math. compound fraction; =büchse f do.-barrelled rifle; =buchstabe m do.-letter, ligature; =ci'cero ⓒ f, typ. (24 Punkte) double-pica; ⚇deutig a. ⓑ = ⚇sinnig; =draht m double wire; =dreizack ♃ m (Triglo'chin mari'tima) sea arrow-grass; =druck m, typ. mackle; =ehe f bigamy.
Dopp(e)ler (⌣⌣⌣) m ⓑ 1. Karbätschemm.: double-carder. — 2. (falscher Spieler) cheat at cards, professional gambler.
Doppel=fall (⌣⌣–) m ⓑ alternative; =fehler m Tennis: double fault; =fenster n double window; =fernrohr n binocular telescope; =flinte f do.-barrelled gun; =flöte ♪ f der Orgel: double flute; =gänger(in f) m double, second self; =geleise 🚆 n do.-rail or -way; f. =bahn; ⚇g(e)leifig ⓐ a. do.-railed; ⚇e Bahn = =bahn; =gesang n duet; =gestirn n = =stern; =gleis n = =geleise; ⚇gleisig a. = ⚇geleisig; ⚇glied(e)rig a. path. rickety; =griff ♪ m Violinspiel: double stop or fingering; =häuer ☓ m miner (or pitman) doing a double shift; =kinn n double chin; =knöpfe m/pl. link-buttons pl.; =kolonne ☓ f double column; =köper ● m fancy-tweel; =köpfig a. do.-headed; =kreuz ♪ n (zur Erhöhung e-r Note um zwei halbe Töne) do.-sharp (𝄪); =krone f German gold coin of twenty marks, German sovereign; ⚇läufig a. do.-barrelled (gun); =laut m, gr. diphthong; ⚇lebig a.

amphibious; =leiter f trestles pl.; =maschine f, typ. double frame; =mittel ● f, typ. a) Schrift: (28 Punkte, etwa): double English, two-line English; b) Presse: two-feeder machine.
doppeln (⌣⌣) [mhd.; *fr. doubler] I v/a. 1. (verdoppeln) to double. — 2. ● u. ↓ (füttern) to line; (beschlagen) to sheathe. — II v/n. (h.) 3. (beim Spiel betrügen) to cheat in playing. — III ~ n ⓑ 4. (f. 1) doubling. — 5. ● u. ↓ (f. 2) lining; sheathing. — 6. (f. 3) cheating; card-sharping.
Doppel=natur (⌣⌣–) f ⓑ double nature; =okta've f double octave, bisdiapason; =paarig a. ⓑ: = bigeminate, ...al; =posten ☓ m double sentry; =punkt m, gr., &c. colon; =reihe f double row, lane; ⚇reihig a. do.-rowed; =salz n, chm. double salt; =satz ● m, typ. double; =schattern (Tropenbewohner), ⚇schattig a.: ⚇ amphiscian; =schlag m: ♪ turn; =schleiche f amphisbæna; =schlitz m, arch.: ⚇ diglyph; ⚇schluß m, log.: ⚇ dilemma; =schraube f d.-thread(ed) screw; =schraub(en=dampf)er ↓ m twin-screw steamer; =sichtigkeit f = Doppeltsehen; =sinn m double meaning; b.s. (fr.) double entente; ⚇sinnig a. ambiguous, equivocal; =sinnigkeit f ambiguousness; ambiguity; vgl. =sinn; =spat m, min. (wasserheller Kalkspat) Iceland spar; =spiel n: a) ♪ duet; b) (doppelte Rolle) double part, fig. double-dealing; c) Tennis: four-handed game; =spielfeld n Tennis: double court; =sprech=apparat m, tel. = =telegra'ph; =stern m, ast. double star; =stück n duplicate.
doppelt (⌣⌣) [uhd.; *fr. double] I a. ⓑ u. adv. (zwiefach) double, twofold; adv. doubly, twice; ⚇ so alt als ich double my age; ⚇ so groß als sie double her size; ⚇ so hoch (of) double (or twice) the height; ⚇ so viel(e) twice as much (many); double the quantity (the number); ⚇ so viel (Geld) bezahlen to pay double the price or do. the money; ⚇ sehen to see do.; in ⚇er Abschrift in duplicate; ⚇er Adler = Doppeladler; mit ⚇em Boden double-bottomed; ⚇e Buchführung book-keeping by double entry; fig. mit ⚇er Kreide aufschreiben to charge exorbitantly, F to pile it on (thick); to run up a long (or heavy) bill; ein ⚇es (falsches) Spiel spielen to play a double (or false) game; ⚇e Verneinung: ⚇ litotes; Sprichw. ⚇(er Vorspann) reißt nicht store is no sore, it's better to make (doubly) sure or to be on the safe side. — II ~e(s) n ⓑ (the) double; das ~e der Zahl od. davon double the number. [telegraph.]
Doppel=telegra'ph (⌣⌣–) m ⓑ duplex-
doppelt=fied(e)rig (⌣⌣–) a. ⓑ (doppelt gefiedert): ⚇ bipinnatifid; =gefiedert ♃ a.: ⚇ bipinnate(d); ⚇gepaart ♃ a.: ⚇ bigeminate; ⚇hochrund a. phys.: ⚇ convexo-convex, biconvex; ⚇hohl a. phys.: ⚇ concavo-concave, biconcave; ⚇kohlen=sauer: ⚇kohlensaures Natron chm. bicarbonate of soda (NaHCO₃).
Doppel=triller (⌣⌣–) m ⓑ double shake.
Doppelt=schwefel=eisen (⌣⌣–) n ⓑ disulphide of iron, iron pyrites (FeS₂).

Zeichen (f. S. XVII): F familiär; P Volkssprache; Γ Gaunersprache; ☓ selten; † alt (auch gestorben); * neu (auch geboren); ⁺⁺ unrichtig;

[**Doppeltfehen**] — 269 — [**dozieren**]

=sehen *n, path.* double-sight, seeing double, ⚕ diplopia.
Doppel=tür (ᵍ⌣) *f* ㊷: a) double-door; b) (Flügeltür) folding-door(s *pl.*).
Dopp(e)lung (ʸ(⌣)⌣) *f* ㊻ = doppeln III.
doppelt=wirkend (ᵍᵈ…) *a.* double-acting (engine,&c.); **=zusammengesetzt** *a.*: ⚕ decompound; **=zweizählig** ♀ *a.* ⚕ gepaart.
Doppel=verhältnis (ᵍ⌣…) *n* ㊷ *math.* duplicate ratio; **=vers** *m, pros.* distich; **=vokal** *m* = =laut; **=währung** *f* double standard, bimetallism; **=zentner** *m* (*abbr.* **dz**, öft. *q*) f. S. XXXIX, II; **=züngig** *a.* double-dealing or =tongued; **=züngigkeit** *f* do.-dealing, duplicity; **=züngler** *m.* do.-dealer.
Doppler, Dopplung f. Doppeler, Dop=pelung.
Dora (ᴸ⌣) [grch.] *npr/f.* ㊺㊱α. (Vn.) Dora; Doll(y).
Dorado (–ᴸ⌣) [span. „Gold"land] *n* ㉛ El Dorado.
Dorant ♀ (–⌣) *m* ㉛ b. = Taubnessel.
Dorchen (ᴸ⌣) *n* ㉔ *dim. v.* Dora. [Dort.
Dordrecht ♀ (ᴸ⌣) *npr/n.* ㊱α. (ndl. St.)
Dorf (ᴸ) [ahd.: thorp: lt. *turba*] *n* ㉝ b. village; hamlet; auf (ob. in) e-m ~e wohnen to live in a village; *fig.* das find ihm böhmische Dörfer it's all Greek (or double Dutch) to him.
Dorf=bengel (ᵍ…) *m* ㊷ village-lad, country-bumpkin; **=bewohner(in** *f*) *m* villager, rustic, *pl.* auch =leute.
Dörfchen (ᴸ⌣) *n* ㉔ (*dim. von* Dorf) small village or hamlet.
Dorf=geistlicher (ᵍ…) *m* ㊷ village- (or country-) clergyman or parson; **=gemeinde** *f* rural parish or community; *coll.* the villagers *pl.*; **=gemeinderat** *m* parish- (or rural) council; **=geschichte** *f* rusticale, story of country-life; **=junker** *m* village-squire; **=krug** *m* = =schenke; **=leben** *n* village- (or country-) life.
Dörflein (ᴸ⌣) *n* = Dörfchen. [ner(in).
Dörfler (ᴸ⌣) *m* ㉒, ~**in** *f* ㊹ Dorfbewoh=
Dorf=leute (ᵍ…) *pl.* ㊷ village-folk, villagers, rustics *pl.*
dörflich (ᴸ⌣) *a.* ㊻ relating to a village.
dorf=mäßig (ᵍ…) *a.* ㊻ like a village, (ländlich) rustic, rural; **=pfarrer** *m* ㊷, **=prediger** *m* village-parson; **=roman** *m* novel of village-life.
Dorfschaft (ᵍ⌣) *f* ㊺ = Dorfgemeinde.
Dorf=schenke (ᵍ…) *f* ㊺ country-inn; **=schule** *f* village-school; **=schulmeister** *m* village-schoolmaster; **=schulze** *m* village chief or magistrate, headman of a village. — Vgl. auch Bauer(n)=.
Doria (ᴸ(⌣)⌣) [it.] *npr.* f. Donner am Schluß.
Dor(i)er (ᴸ(⌣)⌣) *m* ㉒, ~**in** *f* ㊹ grch. Alt.: (Bewohner[in] v. Doris) Dorian.
dorisch (ᴸ⌣) I *a.* ㊻ grch. Alt.: a) zur Landschaft Doris gehörig: Dorian; b) den Dorierstamm, seine Sitten und Sprache betr.: Doric; ㉓e Säulenordnung *arch.* Doric order; ㉓e Spracheigentümlichkeit od. ⚕ dorism. — II ~(e) *n* ⓪ (b. dorische Mundart) Doric, the Doric dialect.
Dorment (–⌣) [lt.] *n* ㉛b., **Dormitorium** (⌣⌣ᴸ(⌣)⌣) *n* ㉘ (Schlafsaal) dormitory.
Dorn (ᴸ) [ahd.: thorn] *m* ㊳ b. u. ㉛b. 1. thorn, (Stachel) prickle; ♀ spine; ~ tragend ⚕ spiniferous, spinigerous; *bibl.* etliches fiel unter die ~en some fell among thorns. — 2. ⊕ Schlofferei 2c.; mandrel; ber Türangel: bolt, an der Drehbank: pike; ~ (Heftzapfen) einer Klinge tang of a blade; ~ (Stachel) einer Schnalle tongue of a buckle; (Locheisen) punch(eon); *anat.* ~ (=fortsatz) e-s Wirbels spinal process, ⚕ acantha; Dörner *pl., metall.* (Rückstände) waste, residue *sg.* — 3. ein ~ im Auge an eyesore; er ist mir ein ~ im Auge … a thorn in my side; keine Rose ohne ~en no rose without thorns; no joy without toil. [apfel.
Dorn=apfel ♀ (ᵍ…) *m* ㉓ datura (=Stech=
dorn=artig (ᵍ…) *a.* ㊻ thorn-shaped; ♀ acanthaceous, spiniform, spinous, …se; **=busch** *m* ㊷ thorn- (or bramble-) bush; *bsd. poet.* brake, brier; **=butt(e** *f*) *m, ichth.* turbot (*Rhombus ma'ximus*).
Dörnchen (ᴸ⌣) *n* ㉔ (*dim. von* Dorn) small thorn, ♀ ⚕ spinule.
Dorn=dreher (ᵍ…) *m* ㊷ *orn.* red-backed shrike (*Enne'ctonus collu'rio*); **=eidechse** *f zo.* stellion (*Ste'llio*).
dornen (ᴸ⌣) [ahd.] *a.* ㊻ of thorns.
Dornen=hecke (ᵍ…) *f* ㊷ thorn- (or thorny) hedge, hedge of thorns; **=krone** *f* crown of thorns; **=los** *a.* thornless; **=pfad** *m* thorny path; **=voll** *a.* beset with thorns (auch oft *fig.*).
dorn=förmig (ᵍ…) *a.* ㊻ = ⚕artig; **=fortsatz** *m* = Dorn 2 *anat.*; **=gebüsch, =gesträuch** *n* = =busch; **=grundel** *f, ichth.* loach; **=hai** *m, ichth.* pricked dog-fish, dorn-hound (*Squa'lius, Aca'nthias* u. verwandte Fischarten); **=hecke** *f* = Dornenhecke. [=Dornbusch).
Dornicht[1] (ᵍ…) *n* ⓪d. thorn-bush (=
dornicht[2] ⚕, mst **dornig** (ᴸ⌣) *a.* ㊻ 1. (mit Dornen versehen u. *fig.* mühselig) thorny. — 2. = dorn-artig und dornenvoll.
Dorn=röschen (ᵍ…) *n* ㉔ im Märchen: Sleeping Beauty; **=rücken** *m, ichth.* thornback, dorn (*Raia clava'ta*); **=schloß** ⊕ *n* Schlofferei: pipe-keyed lock; **=schwänzig** *a.* ㊻ *zo.* von Eidechsen: thorn-tailed; **=stein** *m* Salzwerk: thornstone; **=strauch** *m* = =busch; **=tragend** *a.* thorny; ⚕ spinigerous; **=wand** *f* Salzwerk: (e-s Grabierwerkes) thorn-wall, graduation-wall; **=wicke** ♀ *f* = Zaun=w.
Dorothea, Dorothee (–⌣ᴸ⌣) [grch.] *npr/f.* ㊺α., ㊻β. (Vn.) Dorothy.
dorren (ᴸ⌣) [ahd.: lt. *torre're*] *v/n.* ㉛ to (become) dry, in ber Sonne: (fn) parch; (welten) to fade.
dörren (ᴸ⌣) [nhd.; *darren*] *v/a.* ㉛ to dry; or to desiccate, im Ofen: to bake, to roast; to kiln-dry; (röften) to scorch, parch, swelter; ⊕ *metall.* to calcine; Malz: to cure; gedörrtes Obst, auch **Dörr=obst** (ᵍᵈ) *n* ㊲ dried fruit.
Dorsch (ᴸ) [ndd.: torsk] *m* ㊳(⑦)a. *ichth.* cod(fish) (*Gadus mo'rrhua*); (junger Kabeljau) codling.
Dorsche ♀ ⚕ (ᴸ⌣) [ahd.: grch. Thyrsos] *f* ㊺ (Stengel)stalk, (Kohlftrunk) cabbage-stalk.
dort [ahd.; *dar*] *adv.* (ant. hier) 1. ⚕, bisw. auch ㉓en there, yonder. in that place, over there; nach ㉓ that way, thither; er kommt von ㉓ (her) … from there, (from) thence; da und ㉓ here and there. — 2. *fig.* (im künftigen Leben) hereafter, beyond the grave, in the life to come. — 3. mit anderen *adv.*: ㉓ herum round (about) there, there about(s); ㉓ oben (unten) up (down) there or yonder; ㉓ hinein (hinaus) in (out) there; vgl. dort=her, dort=hin.
Dörthe *f* [Dorothea] *npr/f.* ㊺β. little Dorothy.
dort=her (ᵍᴸ) *adv.* (von) ㉓ from there, (from) thence, from that place.
dort=hin (ᵍᴸ) *adv.* thither, there; er hat fich ㉓ gewandt he applied there or at that address; bis ㉓ as far as (or up to) there or that place.
dortig (ᴸ⌣) *a.* ㊻ of that place or town or locality; unfere ㉓en Freunde our friends there or in that neighbourhood or in that town; er hält fich in England auf, um das ㉓e Leben kennen zu lernen … to study the life of the people there or of the English people.
Döschen (ᴸ⌣) *n* ㉓ *dim. v.* Dofe. [Dofis.
Dofe[1] (ᴸ⌣) [Dofis] *f* ㊺ *pharm.*, &c. =
Dofe[2] (ᴸ⌣) [ndl.] *f* ㊺ box; (Schnupf=tabaks=) snuff-box; Sprichw., v. kleinen Leuten: in den kleinsten ~n find die besten Salben the best things are packed in the smallest parcels.
Döse ⊕ (ᴸ⌣) [ndl. = Dofe[2]] *f* ㊺ = Gärbottich. [schlummern) to doze (off).
dösen F (ᴸ⌣) [ndd.: doze] *v/n.* (h.) ㊿ (ein=
Dosen=bild (ᴸᴸ…) *n* ㊷ painting on a snuff-box; **=deckel** *m* lid of a box; **=schildkröte** *f zo.* box-turtle or =tortoise (*Cistu'do caroli'na*); **=schnecke** *f, zo.* trumpet-shell; **=stück** *n* = =bild.
dofieren (ᴸ⌣ᴸ⌣) ⊕ *v/a.* ㊿ *pharm.* to dose.
dofig (ᴸ⌣) [ndd.] *a.* ㊻ (schläferig, dämlich) sleepy-headed, dull, silly.
Dofis (ᴸ⌣) [grch. ⚕ Gabe] *f* ㊺ *med., pharm.,* &c. dose; zu große ~ overdose.
doffieren (–ᴸ⌣) [fr.] I *v/a.* ㊿ to slope. — II ~ *n* ㉓, **Doffierung** ⊕ *f* ㊻ 2. (Abböfchung) slope, slant; ⚒ talus. — 3. [fr. *doucis*] (Glasschleifen) ~ der Spiegelgläfer, Metallflächen 2c. second grinding or polishing.
Doft ♀ (ᴸ) [ahd.] *m* ⑪b., ~**e** *f* ㊺, ~**en** *m* ㉓ origan; echter ~ wild marjoram (*Ori'ganum vulga're*).
Dotation (–⌣ᴸ⌣) [lt.] *f* ㊹ *jur.* (Schenkung) dotation; endowment.
dotieren (–ᴸ⌣) [lt.] *v/a.* ㊿ to endow; to present with an endowment.
Dotter (ᴸ⌣) [ahd.: dodder, dot] 1. *m* (*n*) ㊷ yolk (of an egg); *zo.* u. ♀: ⚕ vitellus. — 2. ♀ *m* ㉒ od. *f* ㊺ gold-of-pleasure (*Cameli'na*).
Dotter=blume ♀ (ᵍ…) *f* ㊷ marsh-marigold (*Caltha palu'stris*); **=gelb** *a.* ㊻ as yellow as the yolk of an egg, bisw. yolk-coloured, ⚕ luteous; **=sack** *m* des Embryos: yolk-sac or =bag; **=weide** *f* yellow willow (*salix vitelli'na*).
Douane (du=ᴸ⌣) [fr., it.] *f* ㊹ custom-house. [house officer.
Douanier (du=ä=nje') [fr.] *m* ㊷ custom=
Doublette, Douche 2c. f. Dublette, Dufche. [(Trinkgeld) tip.
Douceur (du=ßö'r) [fr. Süßigkeit] *n* ⓶e.㊳.
Do-ut-des=Politik (ᴸ⌣ᴸ…) [lt.] *f* ㊷ policy based on the principle of "give and take" or of mutual advantage.
Doxologie (⌣⌣⌣ᴸ) [grch. Lobpreifung] *f* ㊹ doxology. [teacher or lecturer.
Dozent (–ᴸ) [lt. ⌣⌣…] *m* ㊷ university=
dozieren (–ᴸ⌣) [lt. *doce're*] *v/a.* u. *v/n.* (h.) ㊻ to teach, to lecture.

♪ Musik; ⚕ Wissenschaft; ♀ Pflanze; ♁ Geographie; ⊕ Technik; ⚒ Bergbau; ⚔ Militär; ⚓ Marine; ⚖ Handel; ⚘ Post; 🚂 Eisenbahn

Dr. (jur., med., phil., techn., theol.) abbr. = Doktor (der Rechte, der Medizin, der Philosophie, (st.) der technischen Wissenschaften, der Theologie, vgl. D).
Drache (˘˘) [ahd.; *grch.] m ④, ~n m ㉓ 1. dragon (auch fig.); her. a. wyvern. — 2. zo. flying-lizard (Draco). — 3. (papierener) ~ (Spielzeug) kite; einen ~n steigen lassen to fly a kite. — 4. (feurige Lufterscheinung) dragon; fireball. — 5. fig. (böses Weib) termagant.
Drachen-anker (˘˘...) m ㉒ grapnel (= Dregg); ²artig a. ⑥ ²förmig; =baum ⁹ m: a) dragon-tree (Dracae'na Draco); b) = Elsbeere; =blatt n dragon's leaf (Dracophy'llum); =blut n, pharm. u. ⁹ Pflanzenharz: dragon's-blood; =blut-baum ⁹ m = ‑baum a; =brut f, horrid imps pl., infernal crew; =fisch m, ichth. dragonet (Callio'nymus lyra); ²förmig a. dragonish, ⚔ dracontine; =kopf m: a) ⁹ dragon's-head (Dracoce'phalum); b) arch. (Wasserspeier) gargoyle; c) ichth. ⚔ scorphænoid; =kraut n ⁹ dragon-wort (Draco'ntium); =nest n, dr.'s lair; fig. (Räuberhöhle) den of thieves, robbers' den; =saat f des Kadmus, myth. dr.'s teeth; =schwanz, =schweif m dr.'s tail; =töter m dr.-slayer; =wurz ⁹ f = =kraut.
Drachme (˘˘) [grch.] f ⑥ 1. grch. Alt.: (Münze) drachma. — 2. Apothekergewicht: ⅛ Unze = 3,75 g) dram. **[Dolmetscher.**
Dragoman (˘˘˘) [türk.; ar.] ⓦe.,㊿ =
Dragon ⁹ (˘˘) m, n ㊿ = Estragon.
Dragonade (˘˘˘˘) [fr. dragonnade] f ⑥ hist. (gewaltsame Protestantenbekehrung durch Dragoner unter Ludwig XIV., seit 1681) (a. fig. Gewaltmaßregel) dragonade.
Dragoner (˘˘˘) [fr.] m ⑳ 1. ⚔ dragoon; fluchen wie ein ~ to swear like a trooper. — 2. fig. wahrer ~ F whacker, (derbes Frauenzimmer) virago, F horse-god-mother, (regular) strapper.
Dragonne (˘˘˘) f zo. (südamerikan. Krokobi'leidechse) dragonet (Thori'ctis dracae'na).
Dragun ⁹ (˘˘) [fr.] m, n ㊿ s. Dragon.
Draht (¹) [ahd.: thread Faden; * drehen] m ⓒc. 1. wire; mit ~ binden, (be)flechten, bewickeln to wire; ~ ziehen to draw wire, to wiredraw; gleich ~, (so zäh und fest wie ~ wiry. — 2. = Telegraph(en-draht); per ~ antworten to reply by wire or by telegraph, to wire (or telegraph) back. — 3. P (Geld) F chink, brass, the ready.
Draht-antwort (¹...) f ㉒ telegraphic reply, F answer by wire; =arbeit f wire-work; Goldschmiede: filigree (-work); ²artig a. ⑥ like wire; fig. (sehr zähe) wiry; =bahn f = =seilbahn; =band n wire-ribbon; =bank f = =zieh-bank; =bauer m (n) = =käfig; =bericht m telegraphic information; F wire(d intelligence); =boden m eines Siebes: sieve-bottom; =bogen m Schriftguß: bow; =bürste f wire-brush. **[wire.**
Drähtchen (¹˘) n ㉓ small (or thin)
Draht-eisen ⊕ (¹...) n ㉒ = =zieheisen.
drahten¹ (¹˘) v/a. ⑥ 1. tel. to telegraph, wire. — 2. ⊕ Buchbind.: (mit Draht heften) to fasten with wire.
drahten², **drähtern** (¹˘) a. ⑥ (D9) (made) of wire.

Draht-falle (¹...) f ㉒ wire-trap; =feder f wire-spring; Schriftgießerei: bow; =fenster n wire-gauze-window; =gaze f wire-gauze: fine wire-netting; =geflecht n plaited wirework (for fences, mats, mattresses, &c.); =gewebe n wire-cloth or -gauze; =gitter n wire-(trellis)work, wire-grating; =glocke f für Speisen: wire-gauze (cover); =hammer m = ‑mühle; =haube ⊛ f der Lokomotive: cowl; =heftmaschine f Buchb. wire-stitching machine; =hemd ⚔ n ehm. mail-shirt made of wire netting; =hindernis ⚔ n, frt. wire entanglement; =hütte f = ‑mühle; =käfig m wire-cage; =kommo'de f, co. (Klavier) piano; =leitung f, elect. conducting wire; tel. telegraph line or wire.
drahtlich (¹˘) a. ⑥ u. adv. telegraphic (-ally); ²e Mitteilung wired message, F wire; er wurde ² abgerufen he was away by wire or by a telegram; auch: he was telegraphed (or wired) for; ⊛ ² bestellte Waren goods pl. wired for.
draht-los (¹...) a. ⑥ (D 10) ²lose Telegraphie wireless telegraphy; ² (adv.) telegraphieren to send a wireless message; =maß n ㉒, =messer m wire-gauge; =mitteilung f wire-message; =mühle f wire-works pl., wire-drawing mill; =nachricht f telegraphic message or news, F wire; =netz n wire-netting; =panzer n = =hemd; =puppe f, =püppchen n puppet; =rädchen ⊕ n zum Aufwickeln von Draht: bobbin for wire; =rolle f coil of wire; =saite ♪ f metal-string; =schere f wire-shears pl.; =schirm n Kamin: wire-fender or -guard; =schleife f wire-noose; =segge ⁹ f smaller panicled sedge (Carex teretius'cula); =seil n wire-rope; Künstler auf dem schlaffen ~ performer on the slack-wire; =seilbahn f wire-tramway(-line), cable-railway; elektrische: telpher-way; =seilbrücke f wire-bridge; =sieb n wire-sieve; =stift m wire-tack.
Drahtung (¹˘) [drahten¹ 1 u. Draht 2] f ⑥ tel. wire-message, telegram.
Draht-wehr ⚔ (¹...) f ⑥ wire-enclosure; =werk n = =mühle; =wurm m, zo.: a) hair-worm, wire-eel (Go'rdius); b) (Käfer) wire-worm; =zaun m wire-fence; =zieh-bank f wire-drawing frame or bench or machine; =ziehe-eisen n wire-drawing plate; =ziehen n wire-drawing; =zieher m wire-drawer; =zieherei f: a) wire-drawing; b) =mühle; =zugbarrie're ⊛ f movable wire-barrier.
☞ **Drain** ꝛc. s. Drän ꝛc.
Draisine (˘¹˘) [Drais, bad. Forstmeister, 1817] f ⑥ a) ⚙ velocipede; b) ⊛ trolly.
Drake (¹) [ndd.] m ④ orn. drake.
drakonisch (˘¹˘) [Drako, strenger athe'n. Gesetzgeber, um 624 v. Chr.] a. ⑥ Draconic; ²e Strenge Draconic severity.
drall¹ (¹) [ndd.: drillen] a. ⑥ 1. Faden: tight(ly twisted). — 2. fig. (fest, derb) firm, robust; ²es Bauernmädchen buxom (F strapping) country-lass.
Drall² ⚔,⊕ (¹) m ⓑb. (Drehung der Züge in Feuerwaffen) spiral of the grooves; ~winkel m angle of the spiral.

Drama (¹˘) [grch.] n ㉘ (Schauspiel) drama; zu einem ~ umgestalten to dramatize; ~tik (˘¹˘) f ㊻ dramatic poetry or art; ~tiker (˘¹˘˘) m ㉒ dramatic author, dramatist, F playwright.
dramatisch (˘¹˘) [grch.] a. ⑥ (u. adv.) dramatic(ally); ²er Dichter dramatist; ein ²er Auftritt a dramatic scene.
dramatisieren (˘˘˘¹˘) [fr.] v/a. ⑱ (für die Bühne bearbeiten) to dramatize, to adapt for (or to put on) the stage.
Dramaturg (˘˘¹) [grch.] m ㊱,㊷ 1. stage- (or theatrical) critic. — 2. (Kenner der Schauspielkunst) dramatic (or scenic) expert; dramaturgist.
Dramaturgie (˘˘˘¹) [grch.] f ⑱, **Dramaturgik** (˘˘¹˘) f ㊻ (theory of) dramatic (or scenic) art; dramaturgy.
dramaturgisch (˘˘¹˘) a. ⑥ relating to (the principles of) dramatic (or scenic) art; dramaturgic. **[or play.}**
Dramolett (˘˘¹) [fr.] n ⓑb. short drama;
dran F (¹) adv. s. daran.
Dran- F (¹...) s. Daran-...
Drän ⁅ (¹) [engl.] m ㊿ agr. (Entwässerungs-röhre, -kanal) drain.
Dränage (˘¹ɢ˘) [engl.] f ⑮ agr. drainage; ~ ziegel m ⊛ = Dränziegel.
drang¹ (¹) impf. v. dringen (s. ds).
Drang² (¹) [mhd.: throng] m ⓑb. 1. (gedrängter Haufen) throng, crowd. — 2. (Bedrängnis) oppression; (Not) need, distress; im ~ des Augenblicks on the spur of the moment; der ~ der Geschäfte the pressure (or wear and tear) of business; im ~ der Not, der Verhältnisse from (sheer) necessity, under the stress of circumstances. — 3. (Antrieb) impetus, impulse; (Eifer) zeal; (heftiges Verlangen) intense desire, passionate longing, craving (for or after). — 4. path. (Stuhlzwang) ⚔ tenesmus.
drängeln P (¹˘) v/n. (h.) ⑫a. mst co. = drängen, bsd. 1, 5 und 6.
drängen (¹˘) [mhd.: dringen] ⑫ I v/a. 1. (zs.-drücken) to squeeze, to press (together); (stoßen) to push; fig. e-n in die Ecke ² to drive a p. into a corner. — 2. fig. (bedrängen) to oppress; (plagen) to harass, worry, vex; (mahnen) to press, Schuldner: to dun; (verfolgen) to persecute. — 3. (jagen) to drive, urge, hustle, hurry; eine Lustbarkeit drängte die andere the festivities followed (each other) in rapid succession, one entertainment followed close upon the other. — 4. v/impers. es drängt mich (oder mich drängt's) zu // I am longing (or eager) to //, I burn to //. — II sich ² v/rpr. und v/refl. 5. to push (or jostle) one another; alles drängte sich dahin the people flocked (or crowded) there; man drängte sich fürchterlich an den Türen there was a terrible crush at the doors. — 6. sich **an**-ea. ² to press closely together; sie drängten sich dahin they crowded (or flocked, swarmed) to the place; sich **durch** die Menge ² to force (or elbow) one's way through the crowd; sich **in** eine Ecke ² to crouch in a corner; sich **um** e-n ² to crowd (or press) around a p.; sich ⁹ Scharen: to swarm round a p.; sich

---

Signs (see page XVII): F familiar; P vulgar; F flash; ⟋ rare; † obsolete (died); * new word (born); ⁒ incorrect; ♪ music;

unter die Menge ⚲ to push one's way among (or to mix with) the mob; es ⚲ sich viele **zu** dem Amte there are many (keen) competitors for the post; sich **zwischen** die Streitenden ⚲ to separate the disputants. — **III** v/n. (h.) 7. to be pressing or urgent; die Sache drängt the matter brooks no delay; die Zeit drängt time presses, the time is short; auf et. ⚲ (bringen) to urge (or insist on) a thing; ein ⚲der Fall an urgent case. — **IV ~** n ㉓ 8. (f. 1) squeezing, &c.; (f. 2 u. 3) oppression, vexation; hurry; (f. 4) longing, eagerness (f. 5 u. 6) jostling, crowding; crowd, crush; (f. 7) pressure, urgency, insistence; auf sein ~ (hin) at his instigation. — 9. ~ und Treiben bustle, pressing and pushing, running and rushing. — **V gedrängt** p.p. u. a. ㊻ 10. in den Bed. des inf. — 11. der Saal ist ⚲ voll the hall is crammed full or crowded or closely packed; sie standen, fochten in dicht ⚲en Reihen they stood, fought in (closely) serried ranks. — 12. vom Stil: terse, succinct; ⚲ schreiben: a) von der Handschrift: to write closely together; b) vom Stil: to write concisely or tersely.
Dränger (⚲~) m ㊷, **~in** f ㊵ p. who pushes, &c. (f. drängen); oppressor.
Drangsal (⚲–)[nhd. 15. sae.] n ⑪d., a. f ⑱ affliction, distress; viel ~ erdulden to suffer much hardship or tribulation.
drangsal(ier)en (⚲–, ⚲–⚲–) v/a. ⑱⑲ to afflict, to (op)press; (plagen, quälen) to plague, vex, torment, worry.
dränier/en † (–⚲–) [engl.] agr. **I** v/a. ⑱ to drain. — **II ~** n ㉓ = D/ung.
Dränierer (~) [engl.] m ㊷ agr. drainer.
Dränier=graben (–⚲–...) m ㊷ draining-ditch; **=maschine** f dr.-mill or -engine.
Dränierung (–⚲–) f ㊻ drainage.
Dränier=ziegel (–⚲–...) m = Drän=z.
Drän=röhre (⚲–...) f ㊷ drain(-pipe); **=ziegel** m draining-tile.
Draperie (⚲⚲–) [fr.] f ㊻ drapery.
drapier/en (⚲/⚲–) [fr.] **I** v/a. ㊽ Kunst: (in Falten legen) to drape. — **II ~** n ㉓ u. D/ung f ㊻ (Faltenwurf) drapery.
drasch (⚲) impf. von dreschen (f. ds).
drastisch (⚲–) [grch.] a. ㊻ (heftig) drastic.
Drau ♀ (⚲) npr/f. ㊻ die ~ (Fluß) the Drave. [drohen.]
dräuen † ob. poet. (⚲–) v/n. (h.) ⑱ =⎫
drauf f ⚲ **I** adv. f. darauf; ⚲ und dran sein zu geh(e)n to be on the point of going. — **II** int. (nun,) ⚲ los! (now,) for it!, at it!, F go it!; (haut zu!) F give it (or pitch into) them!
Drauf=gabe F (⚲–...) f ㊷ f. Darauf=; **=gänger** F m one who goes recklessly ahead, go-ahead fellow, dare-devil, reckless spirit; Sport und Börse: plunger (liederlicher Mensch) rake, fast fellow; **=gängertum** n recklessness, fast (or profligate) living; ⚲**geh(e)n** v/n. (ſu) ㊻** er läßt viel ⚲ he spends a great deal (of his substance), he is most lavish (with his money); **=geld** n f. Darauf=...; **Drauflos=fahren, =reiten** n reckless driving, riding.
Dräume ㊻ (⚲–) [: thrum] pl. (Garn=abfälle) ends pl. of yarn.

draus F (⚲) [mhd.] adv. f. daraus.
dräuschen prov. (⚲–) v/n. (h.) ⓶ Regen 2c.: to patter, to pelt; es dräuscht it is pouring, F it's raining cats and dogs.
draußen (⚲–⚲) [bar=außen] adv. (ant. drinnen) 1. outside; ⚲ und drinnen without and within; (im Freien) out of doors, in the open (air). — 2. (in der Fremde) abroad, out in the world.
drawidisch (–⚲–) [Drawida, ind. Rasse] a. ㊻ Dravidian.
Drechsel=bank ⊕ (⚲tx...) f ㊻ (turning-)lathe; turner's bench; **=mühle** f turning-mill. — Vgl. Drechsler=...
drechseln ⊕ (⚲tx⚲) [mhd.; *drehen] **I** v/a. u. v/n. (h.) ㉛a. to turn on a lathe; fig. to do with great care; wie gedrechselt very exact(ly); highly finished; nicely done; F just so. — **II ~** n ㉓ turning; turner's (fig. careful) work.
Drechsler ⊕ (⚲tx⚲) [mhd.] m ㊷ turner.
Drechsler=arbeit ⊕ (–⚲...) f ㊻ turner's job, turning; **=bude** f = **=werkstatt**.
Drechslerei ⊕ (⚲tx⚲–) f ㊻ 1. (art of) turning, turner's craft. — 2. = Drechslerwerkstatt.
Drechsler=lehrling (⚲tx⚲...) m ㊷ turner's apprentice; **=meister** m master turner.
drechslern (⚲tx⚲) v/n. (h.) ㉛a. to amuse o.s. with a lathe or with turning.
Drechsler=ware (⚲tx⚲...) f ㊻ turnery (-ware); **=werkstatt** f turner's shop or workroom or workshop.
Dreck ㊻ [mhd.] m ⑪c. 1. (Schmutz) dirt, filth, F muck; (Straßenkot) mud, mire; in den ~ fallen to fall in(to) the mud; (Exkre'mente) excrements pl., von Tieren: dung; (Fliegen=)~ fly-dirt. — 2. f. fig.: wir sind aus dem dicksten ~ heraus we are (F we've got) over the worst, we are nearly out of the wood; ich mache mir e-n ~ daraus F I don't care a snap (of my fingers); da sitzen wir nun im ~ F now we are in a nice mess or pickle; im ~ stecken bleiben to stick in the mud; sie haben ihn aus dem ~ gezogen they pulled (or dragged) him out of the mire. — 3. contp. von et. Wertlosem: (mere) dirt; rubbish, trash; Geld ist (nur) ~ money is muck.
Dreck=bürste (⚲...) f ㊻ scrubbing- (or mud-)brush; **=fink, =hammel** m F fig. a) (Straßenfeger) scavenger; b) (Schmutzkerl) dirty (or filthy) fellow, F muck-worm.
Dreck=käfer (⚲...) m ㊷ = Mist=k., fig. = **=fink** b; **=karren** m scavenger's (or contractor's) cart; (Mistkarren) dung-cart; **=kerl** m = **=fink** b; **=lilienwurzel** ♀ f, pharm. asphodel root; **=orange** ♀ f mock-orange; **=sack** m = **=fink** b; **=saum** m e-s Kleides: draggle-tail; **=seele** f = **=fink** b; **=treter** m/pl., co. mudboots pl.; **=winkel** m dirty (or filthy) corner or hole.
Dreesch (⚲) m ⑪a. (zeitweilig als Weide benutztes Ackerland) arable land serving temporarily for grazing purposes.
Dregg ⚓ (⚲) m ㉕b., auch **~e** (⚲–) f ㊻, **Dregg=anker** (⚲...) m ㊷ grapnel.
dreggen ⚓ (⚲–) v/a. ㊽ (baggern) to dredge; e-n Fluß (mit e-m Schleppnetz) ⚲ to drag the bottom of (or to sweep) a river.

Dregg=haken (⚲...) m ㊷ drag; **=tau** n (Ankertau) mooring-rope.
Dreh=achse ⊕ (⚲...) f ㊷ mech. axis of rotation or revolution; **=bahn** ⊕ f Seilerei: rope-walk; **=ball** m Tennis: twist-ball; **=bank** ⊕ f (turning or turner's) lathe; **=schlitten** m slide-rest; **=bank=spindel** ⊕ f mandrel.
drehbar (⚲–) a. ㊻ capable of being turned; rotatory; **~keit** (⚲––) f ㊻ capability of being turned.
Dreh=basse ⚓ (⚲...) f ㊻ (ehem.: leichtes drehbares Schiffsgeschütz) pederero; **=baum** m: a) mech. revolving beam; b) = **=kreuz**; c) ⚓ (Hebebaum) crab-bar; **=bohrer** m breast-drill; **=bolzen** ⚔, artill. pivot-bolt; **=brett** n (Glücksspiel) dial, wheel of fortune; **=brücke** f pivot- (or swing-, swivel-) bridge; **=eisen** n = **=stahl**.
drehen (⚲–) [ahd.] ⊕ **I** v/a. und fig. ⚲ v/refl. 1. to turn; sich (im Kreise) ⚲ to twist (or twirl, whirl) round; sich ⚲ und wenden (a. winden) (ehe man et. beginnt) to be undecided, to shuffle, to waver irresolutely; es dreht sich darum, daß (ob. ob) // it is only a question whether //, the point is whether //; das, worum (oder die Sache, um die) es sich dreht the point in question, the main point, that upon which the matter hinges; es dreht sich alles um ihn everything depends on him; ⚓ Börse (sich) ⚲ (von der Baisse zur Hausse übergehen ob. umgekehrt) to change one's tactics (from bearing to bulling or vice versa). — 2. (wenden) die Füße auswärts ⚲ to turn one's toes out; fig. den Mantel nach dem Winde ⚲ to trim one's sails to the wind, to go with the times; e-m den Rücken ⚲ to turn one's back upon a p.; et. zu f-m Vorteil ⚲ to turn s.th. to good account, to profit by s. th.; sie wußte es so zu ⚲ (und zu wenden), daß // she knew how to arrange (or turn) things (so) that //; eine Stelle ⚲ und deute(l)n to twist (or wrench) the meaning of a passage (vgl. II). — 3. e-m et. aus der Hand ⚲ (winden) to wrest (or wrench) a th. out of a p.'s hand; fig. e-m eine Nase ⚲ to make a fool of a p., to hoax (or gull) a p. — 4. ⊕ vgl. drechseln; Seide ⚲ (zwirnen) to twist silk; Seile ⚲ (spinnen) to make ropes; aus Litzen Taue ⚲ to strand cables; Tüten ⚲ to make paper bags; eine Zigarette ⚲ to make (or roll up) a cigarette; ⚓ das Schiff ⚲ to tack, to veer (round); das Schiff in den Wind ⚲ to stay ... — 5. (herumwirbeln) meist v/refl.: to spin round, ⊙ to gyrate; um eine Achse ⚲ to rotate, to turn round its axis; die Erde dreht sich um die Sonne ... revolves round the sun; der Kreisel dreht sich (spinnt) the top spins (round); es dreht sich mir alles wie ein Mühlrad im Kopfe (herum) my brain reels, my head swims. — **II** v/n. (h.) 6. an einem Gesetze ⚲ to twist (or put a new construction upon) a law; ⚓ Wind: to veer (round), to shift. — **III ~** n ㉓ 7. = Drehung. — **IV** (sich) ⊙ pp. u. a. ㊻ 8. Bed. des inf. — 9. (f. 5) revolving; sich um die Achse ⚲d rota(to)ry, ⊙ gyratory.

⚓ scientific; ♀ botanical; ♀ geography; ⊕ machinery; ⚒ mining; ⚔ military; ⚓ marine; ⚫ commercial; ✉ postal; 🚂 railway.

Dreher (⌐ᴸᵛ) m ☉ **1.** p. who turns, &c. (f. drehen); (Drechsler) turner; (Töpfer) potter, thrower. — **2.** ☉ (Kurbel) crank, winch. — **3.** (Ländler) slow waltz. — **4.** vet. (mit Drehkrankheit behaftetes Schaf) sheep suffering from the staggers. **Dreh=feuer** (ᵘ...) n ☉ eines Leuchtturms: revolving light; **=gelenk** n cup-and-ball joint; **=hals** m, orn. wryneck (= Wendehals); **=herb** ⚔ m rotating huddle; **=käfer** m, ent. whirligig (-beetle) (Gyri'nus nata'tor); **=kraft** f, mech. torsional (or rotary) force; **=kran** ☉ m rota(to)ry crane; **=krank** a., vet. bsd. von Schafen: suffering from (the) staggers; **=krankheit** f, vet. staggers pl.; sturdy; **=kraut** ♃ n hartwort (Tordy'lium); **=kreis** ↓ m turning circle, tactical diameter; **=kreuz** n (revolving) turnstile; **=lade** f founder's lathe; **=leier** f (Bettlerleier) hurdy-gurdy.

Drehling ☉ (ᴸᵛ) m ⊕d. **1.** a) handle of a wheel; b) = Dreher 2. — **2.** ☉ mach. (Stockgetriebe, Trilling) spring-wheel, trundle-wheel, lantern-pinion.

Dreh=maschine (ᵘ...) f ☉ ☉ slide-rest lathe; **=meißel** ☉ m turning-chisel; **=moos** ♃ n funaria (Funa'ria hygrome'trica); **=muskel** m, anat.: ☉ rotator; **=orgel** f barrel-organ; **=pistole** f = Revolver; **=punkt** m turning-point; mech. centre of rotation; (Angelpunkt) pivot, (Stützpunkt) fulcrum; **=rad** ☉ n turning- (or cord-)wheel; **=ring** ☉ m swivel; **=rolle** f: a) swivel-pulley; b) (Mange(l) mangle; **=rost** ☉ m revolving grate; **=scheibe** f: a) 🜨 turning platform, turn-rail or -table; b) ☉ Drahtzieherei: table for wiredrawing; c) Töpferei: potter's lathe or wheel; c) (Ziel fürs Wettschießen) turning target; **=seide** ♃ (gezwirnte Seide) twisted silk; **=sessel** m revolving arm-chair; **=späne** m/pl. des Drechslers: turnings pl.; **=spiegel** m cheval- (or swing-)glass; **=stahl** m turner's chisel or tool; **=stock** m Töpferei: turning-staff, **=strom** m, elect. (verkettete Wechselströme) polyphase electric current; **=strom=betrieb** m polyphase electric installation; **=stuhl** m a) für Klavierspieler: music-chair; b) ☉ für Uhrmacher ꝛc.: turn(ing)-bench; **=tisch** m revolving table; **=turm** ↓ m auf Panzerschiffen: revolving turret.

Drehung (ᴸᵛ) f ☉ **1.** turning, &c. (f. drehen I). — **2.** im Kreise: ☞ gyration, um e-e Achse: rotation; um e-n Körper: revolution. — **3.** ☉ (Windung) turn; twist; torsion.

Drehungs=achse (ᵘ...) f ☉ axis of rotation; **=ellipso=i'd** n spheroid; **=festigkeit** f torsional strength or force; **=geschwindigkeit** f velocity of rotation, speed of revolution; **=halbmesser** m radius of rotation, ☞ radius of gyration; **=körper** m solid of revolution; **=messer** m ☉ gyrometer; **=vermögen** n rotary capacity or power.

Dreh=wage (ᵘ...) f ☉ phys. torsionbalance; **=würfel** m Spielzeug: teetotum; **=wurm** m, vet. der Schafe: ☞ cœnure (Coenu'rus cerebra'lis); **=zange** f tweezers pl.; **=zeug** n turning- or twisting-gear.

drei (ᴸ) [ahd.: three: lt. tres] numer. **I** card. numb. ☉ A₃† (o. s. ofst ♩e); gen. ♩er; dat. ♩en) **1.** three; ♩und zwanzig twenty-three; sie waren zu ♩en, es waren ihrer ♩(e) there were three of them; Tennis: Spiel zu ♩en three-handed game; je ♩, ♩ und ♩, ♩ zu ♩ three and three, by (or in) threes; es ist halb ♩, ♩ Viertel auf zehn ... half past two, a quarter to ten; ♩ Jahre dauernd, jede ♩ Jahre sich wiederholend triennial; bibl. die (heiligen) Könige the wise men of the East, the three Magi; ⚓ ♩ Mann tief three deep. — **2.** fig. ich hielt mir ihn ♩ Schritt von Leibe I kept him (three yards) off me; ehe man ♩ zählen konnte before one could say Jack Robinson; in a trice; er kann nicht (bis) ♩ zählen he does not know a B from a bull's foot; vgl. Ding 4. — **3.** math., &c. aus ♩ (Einheiten) bestehend: ☞ ternary. — **II** (die Zahl) **Drei** f ☉ (number) three.

Drei=achteltakt ♪ (¹⁻⁸ᶜʰᵗ⁻ᵘ⁴) m ☉ threequaver measure; **=akter** (ᵘ...) m, ♩aktig a. ☉ three-act (play); **=armig** a. three-armed; **=basisch** a., chm. tribasic, zB. ♩e Phosphorsäure tribasic phosphoric acid (H₃PO₄); **=beinig** a. three-legged or -footed; **=blatt** ♃ n triplet; (Klee) trefoil; der Fren: shamrock, vgl. Klee; b) arch. (lanceolated or round) trefoil; c) Kartenspiel: three-card trick; ♩blätt(e)rig a. three-leaved, trifoliate; ♩blumen=blättrig ♃ a. three-petaled; ♩brachen v/a., agr. to three-fallow, to thrifallow; **=bund** m, pol. Triple Alliance; **=decker** ehm. ↓ m three-decker; ♩drähtig a. = ♩fädig; **=eck** n, geom. triangle; ♩eckig a. threecornered, geom. triangular; **=ecks=lehre**, **=messung** f ☉ geom. trigonometry; ♩einig a., theol. triune, (being) three in one; **=einigkeit** f, theol. Trinity; **=einigkeits=bekenner** m Trinitarian; **=einigkeits=lehre** f Trinitarianism.

Dreier (ᴸᵛ) m ☉ ehm. (coin of) three pfennige (= 1½ farthings); weitS. half-penny; small copper coin.

dreierlei (¹⁻⁻) a. inv. of three kinds or sorts; auf ♩ Art in three (different) ways.

drei=fach (ᵘ...) a. ☉ threefold, treble, triple, triplicate; ♩e Krone des Papstes triple crown, tiara; ♃ ♩ fiederspaltig, gefiedert, gerippt ☞ tripinnatifid, tripennate, trinervate; das ♩e e-r Zahl three times (or thrice) the number; ♩fäch(e)rig ♃ a. three-celled, ☞ trilocular; **=fachheit** f triplicity; **=fädig(er Zwirn)** a. three-cord; ♩fältig(keit) f a. = ♩fach(heit), ♩einig(keit); **=fältigkeits=blümchen** ♃ n = Siebenstern; **=farben=druck** m, typ. three-colour print(ing); ♩farbig a. three-coloured; ♩e Fahne Frankreichs the tricolo(u)r (flag); **=felder=wirtschaft** f, agr. three-fallowing; triennial rotation of crops; ♩flächig a. geom trihedral; **=furchig** ♃ a.: ☞ trisulcate; **=fuß** m tripod, trivet; ♩füßig a. three-footed, ☞ tripedal; ♩gab(e)lig a. ☞ trifurcated; **=gesang** ♪ m trio; ♩gestrichen ♪ a.: ♩e Oktave thrice-accented octave; ♩geteilt a. tripartite; vgl. ♩teilig; ♩glied(e)rig a. math. trinomial (value), cryst. rhombohedral. [= Dreieinigkeit.]

Dreiheit (¹⁻) f ☉ **1.** triad. — **2.** theol.

Drei=herr(scher) (ᵘ...) m ☉ triumvir; **=herrschaft** f triumvirate; ♩hörnig a. ☞ tricorn, ☞ tricornigerous; ♩hundert numer., a. three hundred; **=hundertel** n three-hundredth; ♩hundertjähriges Jubiläum tercentenary; ♩jährig a. three years old; ein ♩es Kind a three-year-old child; ♩jährlich a. triennial; ♩kantig a. three-edged; ♩kapselig ♃ a. three-capsuled; **=käsehoch** m hop-o'-my-thumb, Tom Thumb, F bit of a boy; ♩klang ♪ m triad; ♩klappig a. three-valved; ☞ trivalvular; ♩knotig ♃ a. ☞ trinodal; **=königs=fest** n, **=tag** m Twelfthday, eccl. Epiphany; **=königs=kuchen** m bsd. ehm. twelfth-cake; ♩köpfig a. three-headed; (f. köpfig 2); ♩körnig a. three-grained; ♩lappig ♃ a. three-lobed, ☞ trilobate; **=laut** m, gram. triphthong; ♩mähdig a., agr. producing three crops. [of three units or parts.]

Dreiling fast† (ᴸᵛ) m ⊕d. s. th. consisting **drei=mal** (ᵘ...) adv. three times, thrice; ♩malig a. ☉ occurring three times, thrice repeated; ♩männ(er)ig ♃ a. (mit drei Staubgefäßen) ☞ triandrian, triandrous; **=master** m ☉: a) ↓ three-master; b) (Hut) three-cornered hat; ♩mastig ↓ a. three-masted; ♩monatlich a.: a) (taking place) once in three months, quarterly; b) lasting three months; three-monthly; **=monats=tratte** f ☉ three months' draft.

drein F (¹) adv. f. darein ꝛc.

drei=paarig ♃ (ᵘ...) a. ☉ tergeminal, ...ate; **=paß** m ☉ arch. round trefoil; **=pfünder** ⚔ m three-pounder; ♩phasig a., elect.: ♩er Strom three-phase current; ♩prozentig ☞ a. bearing three per-cent.; ♩e Papiere three-per-cents pl.; **=rad** n tricycle, zweifitziges: sociable; ♩räd(e)rig a. three-wheeled; ♩er Wagen, a.: three-wheeler; **=rad=fahrer** m tricyclist; ♩reihig a. (placed) in three rows or lines; ♃ ☞ trifarious; ♩rippig ♃ a. three-nerved, ☞ trinervate; **=ruderer** ↓ m Alt.: trireme; ♩rud(e)rig ↓ a. with three rows of oars; ♩es Schiff grch. Alt.: trireme; ♩saitig ♪ a. three-stringed (instrument); **=satz** m, arith. rule of three; **=schlag** m: a) triple (time), b) man. amble; **=schlitz** m, arch. triglyph; ♩schlotig ↓ a.: ♩er Kreuzer three-funnel(led) cruiser; **=schnitt** m, math. trisection; ♩schürig a., agr. von Wiesen: annually producing three crops of hay; ♩seitig a. three-sided, trilateral; vgl. ♩kantig; ♩silbig a., gram. trisyllabic; **=sinnige(r)** (blinde(r) Taubstumme(r)) one possessed of only three senses; blind deaf-and-dumb; ♩sitzig a. with three seats; ♩spaltig a. three-cleft, ☞ trifid; **=spänner** m three-horse vehicle; ♩spännig a. with (or drawn by) three horses; yoked with three oxen; **=spiel** ♪ n trio; ♩spitzig a. three-pointed; ♪ ☞ tricuspid(ate); ♩sprachig a. in three languages, trilingual; **=sprung** m Turnerei: hop, step, and jump.

dreißig (ᴸᵛ) [drei u. †zig = zehn] numer. **I** card. numb. inv. thirty; im Alter von ♩ (Jahren) at the age of thirty; Tennis: zu ♩ thirty all. — **II** (die Zahl) ~ f ☉

[Dreißiger] — 273 — [drinnen]

(number) thirty; grch. hist. (Athen 404 u. 403 v. Chr.) die ~ the Thirty (Tyrants); in die ~ kommen to approach the (age of) thirty. — III 2er a. inv. in den 2er Jahren in the thirties; ~er(in f ⑩) m ㉒ man (f woman) of thirty (years of age) or aged (or turned) thirty; in den ~ern sein to be past (or over) thirty; er ist in den ~ern = a man turned (or of about) thirty.

dreißig-fach (⁻ᵛ...) a. ⑥, ⁀fältig a. thirtyfold; ⁀jährig a. lasting (or of) thirty years; hist. der ~e Krieg the Thirty Years' War (1618–1648), Engl.: the Wars of the Roses (1455–1485).

dreißigste (¹ᵛᵛ) ord. numb. ⑥ thirtieth; den (a. am) 2n (30.) März on the thirtieth of March or on March the thirtieth; 2l a. inv. u. ~l n ㉒ thirtieth (part); 2ns adv. in the thirtieth place.

dreist (¹) [ndd.] a. ⑥ 1. (kühn; ant. blöde 2) bold, daring; unabashed. — 2. (keck) audacious, F saucy; (frech) impudent, F cheeky; ich darf 2 (adv.) behaupten I make bold to say; sein gutes Glück wird ihn noch 2er machen his good fortune will make him bolder still or embolden him still more.

Drei-stab (⁻¹) m ㉒ Kricket: wicket.

Dreistigkeit (¹ᵛ-) f ㊻ (s. dreist) boldness, daring; audacity; impudence; F sauciness, cheek; mit edler ~ with wonderful coolness or assurance or F cheek.

drei-stimmig ♪ (⁻¹...) a. ⑥ for three voices; ⁀stöckig a. three-storied; ⁀stündig a. of three hours(' duration); ⁀stündlich a. happening every three hours; ⁀tägig a.: a) lasting three days; three days old; b) coming (or happening) once in three days; med. 2es Fieber tertian (ague); ⁀tausend numer. a. three thousand; ⁀tausendste(r) a. three thousandth; ⁀teilig a. in three parts; ⁊ tripartite, trichotomous; ⁎ = ⁀spaltig; 2er Ausdruck math. trinomium; ⁼teiligkeit f ㊻ bsd. theol. ⁊ trichotomy; ⁼viertel-geige ♪ f three-quarter violin; ⁼viertel-profil n three-quarter profile; ⁼viertelspieler m Fußball: three-quarter back; ⁼viertel-takt ♪ m measure of three crotchets; ⁀weibig ⁎ a. (mit drei Griffeln) trigynian; ⁎...ous; ⁀wertig a., chm. trivalent; 2es Element triad; ⁼wertigkeit f, chm. trivalence; ⁀wink(e)lig a. triangular; vgl. ⁀eckig; ⁼zack m: a) bsd. Mil.: trident; b) Walfischerei: eel-prong; c) ⁎ arrow-grass (Triglo'chin); ⁀zackig a. = ⁀zinkig; ⁼zahl f triad; ⁀zählig a. ternary, ⁎ ternate; ⁼zahn ⁎ ⁎ m: liegender ~ heather-grass (Trio'dia decu'mbens); ⁀zehig a. vom Faultier 2c.: three-toed, ⁊ tridactylous.

dreizehn (⁻¹) numer. I card. numb. inv. thirteen; co. 2 (Kinder 2c.) a baker's dozen. — II (die Zahl, Ziffer) ~ f ㊻. ~er m ㉒ (number) thirteen; die böse ~ the unlucky (or ill-starred) thirteen; 2-jährig (⁻¹...) a. ⑥ thirteen years old.

dreizehnte (⁻¹ᵛ) ord. numb. ⑥ thirteenth; Ludwig XIII. (der ~) Louis XIII (the Thirteenth); 2l a. inv. u. ~l n ㉒ thirteenth (part); 2ns adv. in the thirteenth place.

drei-zeilig (⁻¹...) a. ⑥ = ⁀reihig; ⁀ziff(e)rig a., arith. of three digits; ⁀zinkig a. three-pronged or-forked; ⁀zöllig a. three-inch(ed); ⁀züngig a. three-tongued; vgl. ⁀sprachig; ⁼zylindermaschine ⊕ f three-cylinder machine.

Drell ⁎ (¹) [ndd.] m ⑪b. = Drillich.

Drempel (⁻ᵛ) [ndd.: trampeln] m ㉒ ⊕ carp. little jamb; ⚓ (port-)sill.

Dresch-boden (⁻¹...) m ㉒, **-diele** f thrashing-floor. [threshing (a. = Prügel 2).}

Dresche F (⁻ᵛ) f, agr. ⑥ thrashing,}

dreschen (¹) [ahd.: thrash] I v/a. u. v/n. (h.) ⚘e. (a. ⑪b)(e)st 1. agr. to thrash, to thresh; fig. leeres Stroh 2 (sich vergebens bemühen) to waste one's words, to lose one's labour; F to flog a dead horse. — 2. (prügeln) to thrash, beat, cudgel; auf e-n los 2 F to give a p. a good hiding or licking; F (mit der Zunge) to (klatschen) to wag one's tongue. — 3. fig. Akten 2 (durcharbeiten) to pore over deeds (all day long); Phrasen 2 to spin out fine sentences. — II ~ n ㉓ 4. thrashing, threshing.

Drescher (⁻ᵛ) m ㉒ agr. thrasher; er (fr)ißt wie ein ~ he eats like a wolf or a cormorant, he gorges (himself).

Drescher-lohn (⁻ᵛ...) m ㉒ agr. (daily) wages pl. paid for thrashing.

Dresch-flachs (⁻¹...) m ⊕ unthrashed flax; ⁼flegel m flail; ⁼maschine ⊕ f thrashing-machine; ⁼tenne f = ⁼boden; ⁼wagen m, bibl. (Jes. 41,15) sharp threshing instrument; ⁼walze ⊕ f thrashing-roller; ⁼zeit f, agr. thrashing-season.

Dressier-band (⁻ᵛ¹...) n ㉒ (Halsband für Hunde) training-collar for dogs.

dressieren (⁻ᵛ¹) [fr.] ⑱ I v/a. (abrichten) to train; (zureiten) to break in; Jagdhunde 2c. auch: to enter; von Menschen: gut dressiert well drilled or coached. — II ~ n ㉓ = Dressur.

Dressierer (⁻ᵛ¹ᵛ) [fr.] m ㉒ trainer.

Dressier-leine (⁻ᵛ¹...) f ㊻ training-lash.

Dressierung (⁻ᵛ¹ᵛ) f ㊻ = Dressur.

Dressur (⁻¹) [fr.] f ㊻ training; breaking in of horses; coaching of pupils; ich finde nicht die Spur von e-m Geist, u. alles ist ~ (G., Faust) I find no trace of wit, and all is drill and polish.

Driesch (¹) m, n ⑪a. = Dreesch; 2 a. ⑥ agr. (brach) fallow. [fallow.}

drieschen (⁻¹ᵛ) v/a. ⑨¹ agr. (brachen) to}

drieseln (⁻¹ᵛ) [ndd.; * drehen] v/a. u. v/n. (h.) ⚘a. to turn (or spin, twirl) round.

Drift¹ ⊕ (¹) [ndd.] m ⑪b. 1. (schlechter Torf) inferior peat. — 2. Färberei: (Küvennetz) dyer's net-ring.

Drift² T (¹) [engl.] f ㊻ (auch n ⑪b.) 1. geol. (Treibeisströmung) (glacial) drift. — 2. ⚓ (oft Trift, auf dem Wasser Treibendes) drift; (Wrackgut) flotsam and jetsam.

Drift-strömung ⚓ (⁻¹...) f drift-current.

Drilch ⁎ (¹) m ⑪b. = Drillich.

Drill¹ (¹) m ⑪b. = Drillich. [drill(ing).}

Drill² ⚔ (¹) [drillen 3] m ⑪b. (Übung)}

Drill-bogen ⊕ (⁻¹...) m ㉒ e-s Drillbohrers, drill-bow; ⁼bohrer ⊕ m drill(-borer), wimble, auger.

drillen (¹) [ndd.; * drehen] ⑧ I v/a. 1. meist: to turn (rapidly); v/refl. sich 2 to twirl (or spin) round. — 2. ⊕ Fäden 2 (winden) to twist ...; agr. ⁊ Samen 2 (in Reihen ausstreuen) to drill ... — 3. ⚔ ⚒ Rekruten 2 F to drill (or train) recruits. — 4. weit S. (plagen) to harass. — 5. ⚓ ein Schiff 2 to tow ... by a rope with a single block. — II v/n. (h.) 6. mit dem Ruder 2 to steer.

Driller ⊕ (⁻ᵛ) m ㉒ = Drillbohrer.

Drillich ⁎ (⁻ᵛ) (⁻ᵛ) [P aus lt. trili'cium] m ⑪d. tick(ing), (grober Damast) huck-aback; ⚔ ~anzug (⁻ᵛ...) m ㉒ canvas frock and trousers.

Drilling¹ (⁻ᵛ) [drei] m ⑪d. one of triplets, one of three children born at a birth; (dreiläufiges Gewehr) three-barrelled gun.

Drilling² ⊕ (⁻ᵛ) [drillen] m ⑪d. (Getriebe) spring-wheel, lantern(-wheel).

Drillings¹-geburt (⁻ᵛ...) f ㊻ birth of triplets; ⁼rolle f arbor of a lantern; ⁼walzen f/pl. trio-rolls pl.

Drill-maschine ⊕ (⁻ᵛ...) f ㊻ agr. drill (-harrow); ⁼meister ⚔ m drill-sergeant, -instructor; ⁼pflug m, agr. drill-plough.

drin F (¹) adv. s. darin.

Dr.-Ing. abbr. = Doktor-ingenieur.

dringen (¹) [ahd., vgl. Drang] I v/n. ⑩t: a) (zu) 1. durch etwas 2 (sich hindurch-arbeiten) to force (or work) one's way through, to get (or squeeze) through; durch die Menge 2, auch: to push (one's way) through the crowd; fig. es drang mir durchs Herz, als //, etwa: it cut me to the quick when //. — 2. aus et. 2 to break forth (⚔ to sally) from s. th.; bis in das Innere der Erde 2 to penetrate into the very (or right into the) bowels of the earth; das Gerücht ist bis zu ihm gedrungen ... reached (even) him, F ... got to his ears; in ein Geheimnis 2 to fathom (or to get to the bottom of) a secret; die Nachricht wird in die Öffentlichkeit 2 ... get abroad, spread about, F ooze out; ⚔ in eine Stadt 2 to enter ... (by force); zum Herzen 2 to go straight to the heart. — b) (h.) 3. abs. (drängen) auf et. 2 to insist on a th., to demand a th., mit Bitten in e-n 2 to entreat (or solicit) a p.; sie drang mit Fragen in ihn she plied (or besieged) him with questions; sie drang in ihn, daß er nachgebe she urged (or pressed) him to give in. — II 2d p.pr. u. a. ⑥ 4. urgent, pressing; 2de Gefahr imminent danger; 2de Gründe cogent reasons pl.; 2de Geschäfte, Notwendigkeit urgent (or pressing) business, need; 2der Verdacht strong suspicion; adv. 2d bitten to plead (or beg) hard; wir haben es 2d nötig we are in urgent need of it, F we want it badly. — III ge-drungen p.p. u. a. ⑥ (D9) 5. in den Bed. des inf. — 6. ich fühle mich 2 zu klagen I feel (myself) compelled (or obliged) to complain. — 7. Gestalt: square-built, thick-set, F squat; Stil: concise, terse; vgl. drängen V.

dringentlich (⁻ᵛᵛ) adv. urgently.

dringlich (⁻ᵛ) a. ⑥ pressing, urgent.

Dringlichkeit (⁻ᵛ⁻) f ㊻ urgency, pressure (of circumstances); ~s-antrag m, ~s-erklärung f motion, declaration of urgency. [within (= darinnen).}

drinnen (⁻ᵛ) adv. (ant. draußen) inside,}

[drisch] — 274 — [drücken]

drisch (´) imper., **drisch(e)st** (´‿), **drischt** (´) sg. pres. ind. von dreschen. [Flegel.]
Drischel † (´‿) [ahd.] m ② = Dresch-
dritt (´) [ahd.: third: lt. *tertius*] ord. numb. ⑭ 1. third; ℒens, zum ℒen adv. thirdly, in the third place; ich habe es aus ℒer Hand I heard it from another source; am (oder den) ℒen Juni on the third of June; ℒe Person third person or party, als Begleiterin eines Pärchens: lady propriety; als Schieds-richter: umpire; immer den ℒen Tag every third day; Heinrich III. (der ~e) Henry III (the Third); *math*. in die ℒe Potenz erheben to raise to the third power, to cube; *fig*. das ist sein ℒes Wort that's his favourite (or pet) saying. — 2. wir waren zu ℒ (drei) there were three of us, we were three. — 3. ⑭ der Wechsel ist in ℒer (anderer) Hand the bill has been passed on (by endorsement); ✱ für Rechnung e-s ~en for account of the third party.
drittehalb (´‿‿) f. dritthalb.
Dritteil fast † (´‿) [mhd. dritte Teil] *n* (m) ② = Drittel.
Drittel (´‿) [Dritteil] *n* ② und *a. inv.* third (part); zwei ~ two(-)thirds; eine ℒ Meile one-third of a mile; ~(geviert) *n*, *typ*. thick space.
dritteln (´‿) *v/a.* ②a. to divide into three parts.
drittens (´‿) adv. f. dritt 1.
dritt-halb (´‿) *a. inv.* two and a half; ℒ Jahre two years and a half, two and a half years; ℒletzt *a*. last but two; *gr*. ℒe Silbe antepenult.
drob F (´) adv. f. darob, darüber.
droben (´‿) [bar oben] adv. (ant. drunten) above, up there; (up) aloft; (eine Treppe hoch) upstairs; (im Himmel) on high, in heaven (above).
Droge ⚹ (´‿) [nhd. 18. sae.; *fr. *drogue*] *f* ⑭ (Arzneiware) drug.
Drogen-geschäft ⚹ (´‿...) *n* ⑫ whole-sale druggist's (business); **=handel** *m* drug-trade; **=händler** *m* wholesale druggist; **=handlung** *f* druggist's (shop); **=waren** *f/pl.* drugs *pl.*
Drogerie (‿´‿) *f* ⑭ = Drogenhandlung; ~;... (‿‿´) ⑫ f. Drogen-...
Drogett ⚹ (‿´) [fr.] *m*, *n* ⑪b. (grobes Wollzeug) drugget; **~fabrikant** *m* dr.-maker.
Drogist, meist ⚹ (‿´) *m* ⑭ (wholesale) druggist (= Drogenhändler).
Droh-brief (´´...) *m* ⑫ threatening note, letter of intimidation.
drohen (´‿) [ahd.] I *v/n.* (h.) ⑭ to threaten, to menace; e-m (etwas oder mit etwas) ℒ to threaten a p. with a th.; das Haus droht einzustürzen ... is bound to tumble (before long), is doomed to ruin; uns droht ein Sturm we are threatened with a storm; Sprichw. wer droht, macht dich nicht tot threats kill nobody; barking dogs seldom bite; strong words break no bones; *v/imp*. es droht mit Regen it's threatening with rain, it (or the sky) looks lowering; ℒd threatening; *jur. a.*: ⚔ comminatory; e-n ℒd (adv.) an-blicken to cast threatening glances at a p., to frown at a p.; ℒde Gefahr imminent danger; der ℒde Untergang

des Reiches the impending ruin of the empire. — II ~ *n* ㉓ = Drohung.
Droher (´‿) *m* ② one who threatens.
Drohne (´‿) [ndb.: drone] *f* ⑭ ent. (männliche Biene) drone; F *fig.* idler.
dröhnen (´‿) [ndb.: drone] I *v/n.* (h.) ⑭ 1. to rumble; vom Donner: to roar, to roll; v. Geschützen auch: to boom. — 2. (erschüttern) to quake, to shiver. — II ~ *n* ㉓ 3. rumbling, &c. (f. I). — 4. roar(ing) (or rolling) of thunder; boom of cannon; thud of a falling body.
Drohnen-schlacht (´´...) *f* ⑫ im Bienen-korbe: slaughter of the drones.
Droh-note (´´...) *f* ⑫ =brief.
Drohung (´‿) *f* ⑭ threat(ening), geh.Spr.: menace; jur. auch: commination; leere, prahlerische ~ idle threat, bravado.
Droh-wort (´´⸗) *n* ㉓ (word of) threat.
Drolerie (‿´‿) [fr.] *f* ⑭, **Drollerei** (‿‿´) *f* ⑭ drollery; funny action, fun.
drollicht ⚺, mst **drollig** (´‿) [ndb.: droll] *a.* ⑭ nur *fig.* droll; funny, ludicrous; (witzig) facetious; (komisch) comical, quaint; ℒer Kerl queer fellow, F odd-ity, cure, caution.
Dromedar (‿‿´, auch ´‿‿) [grch.] *n* ⑪c. 1. *zo.* (einhöckeriges Kameel) dromedary (*Camelus dromedarius*). — 2. *fig.* block-head, dullard, stupid fellow, F duffer.
Drommete (‿´‿) *f* ⑭ *poet.* = Trompete.
Dronte ⚺ (´‿) [fr.] *f* ⑭ *orn.* (ausgestor-bener Riesenvogel) dodo (*Didus ineptus*).
drosch F (´) (**drösche** *subj.*) *impf. v.* dreschen.
Droschke (´‿) [nhd., poln., *russ.] *f* ⑭ (Mietwagen) hackney-carriage; vierräderige ~ cab, fly, F four-wheeler, F growler; zweiräderige ~ (Lo.) hansom (-cab); (mit der) ~ fahren to drive in a cab, F to cab it; eine ~ mieten oder nehmen to engage (or hire, take) a cab.
Droschken-besitzer (´‿...) *m* ② cab-owner; **=fahrgeld** *n* cab-fare; **=fuhr-mann** *m* = =kutscher; **=halte-platz** *m* stand for hackney-carriages, F cab-stand; **=kutscher** *m* cab-driver, cab-man; F cabby, *co*. Jehu; **=pferd** *n* cab-horse; **=tarif** *m*, **-taxe** *f* table of cab-fares. [= drieseln.]
dröseln (´‿) [ndb.: *drehen] *v/n.*(h.) ㉓a.
Drossel¹ (´‿) [ahd.: throstle, thrush: lt. *turdela*] *f* ⑭ *orn.* thrush, throstle (*Turdus*); (Sing-)~ mavis (*Turdus musicus*). [f ⑭ = Kehle 1.]
Drossel² † ob. *hunt.* (´‿) [ahd.: throat]
Drossel²-ader (´´...) *f* ⑭ *anat.* jugular vein; **=bart** *m*: König ~ King Blue-beard; **=klappe** ⊕ *f* Dampfm.: throttle.
drosseln (´‿) *v/a.* ⊕a. Dampfm.: to throttle; gedrosselter Dampf throttled steam.
Drossel²**-stuhl** ⊕ (´‿...) *m* ⑫ (Waterspinn-maschine) throstle; **=ventil** ⊕ *n* = =klappe, a. throttle-valve; **Hebel des ~s** throttle-lever, water-spinning frame.
Drost (´) [mlt.; *nbd. = Truchseß] *m* ⑪b. u. ⑫ ehm. i. Niedersachsen: (Landrat) bailiff; **~ei** (‿´) *f* ⑭ circuit of a bailiff.
D. R. P. *abbr.* = Deutsches Reichs-patent German (Imperial) patent.
drüben F (´‿) adv. over there, yonder; hüben u. ℒ (on) this side and (on) that.
drüber F (´‿) adv. f. darüber.
Druck¹ (´) [ahd.; *drücken] *m* ⑪b.1.(Drücken) pressing, pressure; der Hand: squeeze

(or grip) of the hand. — 2. (Last) weight; burden of taxation; oppression by government; ~ im Magen pressure on (F heaviness of) the stomach; *fig.* ~ ausüben auf to put pressure upon. — 3. ⑭ ~ (niedriger Stand) der Preise depression (or depressed state) of the market, low level of prices. — 4. *phys.*, *mech.* (downward) pressure, com-pression; (Schwerkraft) (force of) grav-ity; ~ von Gasen expansive (or elastic) force of gases.
Druck² ⊕ (´) [drucken] *m* ⑪b. 1. *typ.* a) (Drucken) printing, putting (or set-ting up) in type; im ~(e) befindlich in (or passing through) the press; in (den) ~ geben to put in(to) print; to send to press; b) (Gedrucktes) print (auch ⚹ von Stoffen); impression; (Abzug) copy, proof; bunter ~ coloured impression (a. ⊕ v. Stoffen); kleiner, großer ~ small, large type; unreiner ~ slurred (or foul) copy; einen ~ abziehen to pull off a proof. — 2. Buchhandel: (Ausgabe) issue; zweiter ~ reimpression; ~ und Verlag von L., Berlin L., Printers and Publishers, Berlin.
druckbar (´‿) *a.* ⑭ fit to be printed.
Druck-berichtiger (´‿...) *m* ② *typ.* printer's (or publisher's) reader; (Korrektor) proof-reader; **=berichtigung** *f* correction (for the press); (Korrektur-lesen) proof-reading; **=besorger** *m* (supervising) editor; **=bewilligung** *f* permission to print; (lt.) imprimatur; **=bogen** *m*, *typ.* printed sheet; **=buchstabe** *m* type, character, (printed) letter.
Drückeberger F (´‿‿‿) *m* ② one who shirks work (or his duty) or who shuns danger; poltroon; sneak.
drucken (´‿) [nhd. 1462] *v/a.* ⑭ bsd. ⊕ *typ.* 1. to print, to put in type; ich ließ es ℒ I had (F got) it printed; wir lassen das Buch ꝛc. (jetzt) ℒ we are (now) going to press; laß (es) nicht zu rasch ℒ! don't rush into print!; wieder ℒ to reprint. — 2. *fig.* er lügt wie ge-druckt he tells the most plausible lies or tales; ⚺ he lies like truth.
drücken (´‿) [ahd.] ⑭ I *v/a.* 1. (pressen) to press; to squeeze (or grip) a p.'s hand; e-n an die Wand ℒ to push a p. against the wall; e-n in die Arme, ans Herz ℒ to clasp a p. in one's arms, to one's heart; to hug a p.; e-m ein Geldstück in die Hand ℒ to slip a coin in(to) a p.'s hand; den Hut tief(er) ins Gesicht ℒ to pull one's hat over one's eyes; das Siegel auf etwas ℒ to put (or impress) one's seal upon a thing. — 2. breit, platt ℒ to squash, to flatten; tot ℒ to squeeze to death; vom Sattel ꝛc.: ein Pferd wund ℒ to chafe (or gall) a horse; sich (*dat.*) den Fuß wund ℒ to rub one's foot sore; zu Boden ℒ to weigh down, to crush. — 3. meist *fig.* (belästigen, bedrängen) to oppress, to molest; es drückt ihn, daß // it weighs on his mind that //, it troubles him that //; der Alp drückt ihn he has (or suffers from) night-mare; die armen Leute ℒ to be hard on the poor; schwer auf das Volk ℒ to weigh (or press) heavily upon the

Signs (see page XVII): F familiar; P vulgar; ꟾ flash; ⚺ rare; † obsolete (died); * new word (born); ⁒ incorrect; ♪ music;

[Drucker] — 275 — [Ducht]

people; sein böses Gewissen drückt ihn his bad conscience pricks him; der Hunger drückt sie hunger pinches them; meine Stiefel 2 mich ... hurt me; ⬤ den Markt, die Preise 2 to depress the market, to bring down prices; Sprichw. jeder weiß, wo ihn der Schuh drückt everybody knows where his own shoe pinches; e-e 2de Luft an oppressive air. — II v/n. (h.) 4. die Bohnen 2 ihr im Magen ... press (or lie heavy) on her stomach; an einer, auf eine Feder 2 to press (or touch) a spring; etwas drückt (lastet) auf seinem Herzen he has a heavy burden on his heart. — III sich 2 v/refl. und v/recip. 5. (f. I) sich an=ea. 2 to push against one another. — 6. das Obst hat sich gedrückt ... is (slightly) spoilt or damaged. — 7. sich in die Ecke 2 to crouch (or huddle) in a corner; (sich bucken) to cringe (and crawl). — 8. F u. hunt. (sich bucken, heimlich entfliehen) to decamp, to make o.s. scarce, to sneak away, F to hook it. — IV ~ n 9. pressure, squeezing, &c. (f.I); impression of a seal; vgl. auch Druck. — V ge=drückt p.p. u. a. ⬤ 10. in den Beb. des inf. — 11. er ist in 2er Lage ... in straitened circumstances, in straits; ⬤: 2e Preise low prices; die Börse war 2 the stock-market was depressed or dejected or flat or lifeless.

Drucker (⌣⌢) [nhd.] m ⬤ 1. typ. one who prints, &c. (f. drucken); bsb. (Buch=)~ printer, ⚔ typographer; an der Presse: pressman; ~ und Verleger (firm of) Printer(s) and Publisher(s). — 2. * paint. part of the picture set off by strong shades or lights.

Drücker (⌣⌢) m ⬤ 1. one who presses, &c. (f. drücken). — 2.⬤(Klinken=) latch, latch-key; thumb-latch. — 3.⬤Büchsenm.: (Abzug) trigger of a gun. [beam.

Drucker=baum ⊕(⌣⌢...)m,typ. printer's

Druckerei (⌣⌢‼) f ⬤ 1. ⊕: a) = Buch= druckerei; b) printing-works pl. = Zeugdruckerei. — 2. F printing.

Drückerei (⌣⌢‼) [drücken 1 u. 9] f ⬤ squeezing; (Durchbrennen) decamping, sneaking away, taking one's hook.

Drucker=farbe (⌣⌢...) f ⬤ printer's ink.

Druck=erlaubnis (⌣...) f ⬤ =bewilligung.

Drucker=lohn (⌣⌢...) m ⬤ printer's wages pl.; =marke f trade-device; =saal m press-room, printing-office, -room.

Drücker=schloß ⊕(⌣⌢...) n ⬤ Schlosserei: thumb- (or latch-)lock. [ter's ink.

Drucker=schwärze ⊕(⌣⌢...) f ⬤ prin=

druck²=fähig (⌣...) a. ⬤ typ. ready for printing; =fehler m ⬤ misprint, printer's (or typographical) error; pl. meist. (lt.) errata; =fehler=verzeichnis n (list of) errata; ²=fertig a. ready for the press, ready to go to press; 2 erklären to sign for press; =firma f (publisher's or printer's) imprint; =form f printing-block; =formular n printed form; =freiheit f freedom of the press; =hebel m, mech. downward-acting lever; =jahr n year (or date) of impression; =kattu'n ⬤ m print(ed goods pl.), (3itz) chintz; =¹knopf m, elect. e-s Weckers 2c., bell-push; =²kosten pl.

printing expense(s pl.); =¹kraft f = Druck¹ 4; =kugel ⚔ f (überladene Mine) globe of compression; =linie f, arch. thrust-line; =luft ⊕ f als Kraftmittel: compressed air; =²maschine f (Schnell=presse) printing-machine; mit Reliefwalzen: surface p.-m.; =¹messer m, mach. pressure-gauge; manometer; =²ort m e-r Schrift: place of publication; =papier n printing-paper; =presse f printing-press; =probe f specimen, proof; =¹pumpe f, mach. pressure- (or forcing-) pump; ²=reif a. ²=fertig; =sache f ⬤ Aufschrift: printed matter; book-post; =schrift f print(ed work); (Type) (printing-)type; =seite f (printed) page; pl. auch bisw.: pages of letterpress.

drucksen F (⌣⌢) v/n. (h.) ⬤ (zögern) to waver, hesitate; **Druckser** m⬤waverer; **Druckserei** (⌣⌢‼) f ⬤ wavering.

Druck¹=stange (⌣...) f ⬤ mach. forcing-lever; =stempel m am Brunnen, mach. piston of a forcing-pump, forcer; =²telegraph m, tel. printing- (or type-setting) telegraph; =¹verband m, surg. compress; =²verbot n prohibition to print a book, &c.; =verfahren n Zeug=druckerei: printing-process; =walze f: a)¹ mach. pressing-roller, presser; b)² typ. printing-roller; =²waren f/pl. printed goods pl.; =werk n: a) mach. pressure-engine; b) typ. printed work; vgl. auch Drucker=... und Buchdrucker=...

Drude (⌣⌢) f ⬤ 1. (Hexe) witch. — 2. = Druide.

Druden=baum (⌣⌢...) m ⬤ witches' tree; =fuß m (Zaubersiegel gegen Hexerei) pentacle. — Vgl. auch Hexen=...

Dru=ide (⌣⌢⌣) [klt.] m ⬤, **Dru=idin** f ⬤ hist. (Priester[in] der Kelten) druid(ess f).

Dru=iden=denkmal (⌣⌢⌣...) n ⬤ cromlech, cairn, dolmen; =dienst m druidism; =steine m/pl., =tempel m druidic circle.

Dru=identum (⌣⌢⌣) [klt.] n ⬤d. druidism (= Druidendienst).

dru=idisch (⌣⌢⌣) [klt.] a. ⬤ druidic(al).

drum F (⌣) adv. f. darum.

drunten F (⌣⌢) [dar unten] adv. (ant. droben) below, down there; im Hause: down-stairs.

drunter F (⌣⌢) adv. f. darunter; 2 und drüber topsy-turvy; vgl. darüber.

Drusch (⌣) m ⬤(⊤)a. 1. = dreschen II. — 2. number of sheaves thrashed.

Drüschen (⌣⌢) n ⬤ (dim. von Drüse) anat.: ⚔ glandule.

Drüschling ♇ (⌣⌢) m ⬤d. = Dreeschling.

Druse (⌣⌢) [nhd.; *Drüse] f ⬤ 1. ⚒ min. (Kristall)~ ♇ druse, crystallized ore. — 2. vet. glanders (or strangles) of horses. — 3. anat. = Drüse. — 4. ~n pl. (Weinhefe) lees pl. of wine.

Drüse (⌣⌢) [ahd.] f ⬤ anat. gland; kleine ~ = Drüschen; path. an den ~n (Stro'feln) leiden to suffer from scrofula, to be scrofulous.

drusen (⌣⌢) [nbd.: drowse] v/n. (h.) ⬤a. to be drowsy, to doze, to slumber.

Drusen subd. (⌣⌢) [ahd.] f, inv. = Druse 4.

drüsen=artig (⌣⌢...) a. ⬤ anat. = ²för=mig; =beschreibung f ⬤ physiol. = ²=lehre f; =beule f bubo; =entzündung f, path.: ⚔ adenitis.

drusen=förmig (⌣⌢...) a. ⬤ min.: ⚔ drusy;

drüsen=förmig (⌣⌢...) a. ⬤: ⚔ glandiform, glandular, ...ous; =geschwulst f ⬤ swelling of the glands, am Halse auch: mumps pl.; =krankheit f affection (or disease) of the glands; =kunde, =lehre f, physiol.: ⚔ adenology.

Drüsen=lehre (⌣⌢...) f ⬤ = Drüsenkunde; =marmor m, min. shell-marble.

Drüsen=schmerz (⌣⌢...) m ⬤ path.: ⚔ adenalgia; =schnitt m, surg.: ⚔ adenotomy; ²tragend ⚔ a. glanduliferous; =verhärtung f, path.: glandular induration, ⚔ scirrhosity.

drusicht, drusig (⌣⌢) a. ⬤ min.: ⚔ drusy; crystallized.

drüsicht, drüsig (⌣⌢) a. ⬤: a) = drüsen=förmig; b) path. scrofulous. [(hohle)

Drüs=wurz ♇ (⌣⌢) f ⬤ = Pferdesaat.

Dryade (⌣⌣⌢) [grch.] f ⬤ myth. (Baum=, Wald=nymphe) dryad. [Jubbulpore.

Dschabalpur ⬤ Ost=J. (⌣⌢⌣) npr/n ⬤a.)

Dschagannath (⌣⌣⌢) [ift. Herr der Welt] npr/m. ⬤a. myth. Juggernaut.

Dschaipur ⬤ Ost=J. (⌣⌢⌣) npr/n ⬤a. Jaipur.

Dschangel (n pl.) (⌣⌣) [indisch] f ⬤, m ⬤ (Schilfmoor) jungle(s pl.).

Dschengis=Khan (⌣⌢⌣) npr/m. ⬤a hist. (mongol.Herrscher,1154-1227) Jengis-Khan.

Dschiggeta-i ⚔ (⌣⌢⌣) [mongolisch] m ⬤ zo. (Halb=esel) dziggetai (Equus hemi'onus).

Dschonke ⚓ (⌣⌢) [chin.] f ⬤ (großes flaches Flußboot) (Chinese) junk.

Dtzd. abbr. = Dutzend.

du, Du (⌣) [ahd.] pron.: lt. tū] I person. pron. der 2. Person ⬤ A 1, 3† 1. vertraulich unter Freunden, Kindern und Verwandten: you, bis in SH.'s Tage a. thou; in Gebeten und Gedichten noch jetzt: thou (früher auch unter Quäkern gebr.); du selber hast's gesagt you said so yourself. — 2. mit e-m auf Du und Du steh(e)n, bsb. ehm. to thou a p.; weitS. to be on intimate terms with a p., to hobnob with a p. — 3. nach rel. pron. nie zu übersetzen: du, der du mein Freund bist you who are my friend; o Gott, der du mein Herz kennst Thou (Lord) that knowest my heart. — 4. nach dem Imperativ unvor e-m Vokativ selten und nur zur besonderen Hervorhebung der 2. Person zu übersetzen: du das nicht don't (you) say that!; setz dich! sit down!; du Narr! fool that you are! — II n, inv. 5. dein anderes Du your other self, your (lt. a.) alter ego.

Dual ⚔ (⌣⌢) [lt.] m ⬤c., ~is (⌣⌢) m gr. (Zweizahl) dual (number); ~ismus (⌣⌣⌢⌣) m ⬤ phls. dualism; ~ist (⌣⌣⌢) m ⬤ dualist; **²istisch** (⌣⌣⌢⌣) a. ⬤ dualistic; ~ität (⌣⌣⌢) f ⬤ phls. duality.

Dübel (⌣⌢) m ⬤ dowel-pin, wooden plug (for a wall).

Dublette (⌣⌢) [fr. doublet m] f ⬤ (Doppel=stück) duplicate, double (specimen).

dublieren (⌣⌢) [fr. doubler] v/a. ⬤ 1. Billard: to (cannon off) the cushion. — 2. ⊕ a) Spinnerei: (mehrfach zs=zwirnen) to twine; b) Weberei: Stoffe 2 (auf die halbe Breite zs=legen) to fold ... double.

Dublone (⌣⌢) [span.] f ⬤ (span. Gold=münze, etwa 21 Mart) doubloon (=100 reals).

Ducht (⌣) [nbd.] f ⬤ 1. ⚓ (Querbank) thwart; die ~en einheben (auslegen) to (un)ship the thwarts. — 2. ⬤ ~ (Litze) e-s Taues strand.

⚔ scientific; ♇ botanical; ⚱ geography; ⊕ machinery; ⚒ mining; ⚔ military; ⚓ marine; ⬤ commercial; ✉ postal; 🚂 railway.

[Dückdalbe] — 276 — [Dunggrube]

Dückdalbe ❂ ⚓ (⌣⌣⌣) [(⁺⁺ P *duc d'Albe*) nbd. Dief= (Deich=)ballen] f ㊽ Wasserbaukunst: bollards *pl.*, posts *pl.* joined obliquely for mooring ships in the harbour; **~n=stich** (⌣…) m ㉒ bowling-knot.

Ducke *prov.* (⌣⌣) f ㊽ = Dücker¹.

ducken F (⌣) [mhd. (nbd.): duck; *tauchen] ⑱ **I** v/a. (senken) to lower; *fig.* (demütigen) to humble. — **II sich** ⚲ v/refl. to bow one's head; to stoop; ausweichend: to duck one's head.

Ducker¹ (⌣⌣) m ㉒ zo. (Antilope) duyker-(bok), impoon (*Cephalo'lophus mergens*).

Ducker², bff. **Dücker¹** ❂ (⌣⌣) [lt. (*aquae*) *ductus*] m ㉒ Wasserbau: siphon.

Dücker² (⌣⌣)[: duck] m ㉑ *orn.* (Tauch=ente) sea-duck.

Duck=mäuser F (⌣⌣⌣) m ㉒ (Schleicher) sneak; (Scheinheiliger) hypocrite; **~ei** (⌣⌣⌣⌣) f ㊽ sneaking; hypocrisy; **2ig** (⌣⌣⌣) a. ㊻ sneaking, hypocritical; **2n** (⌣⌣⌣) v/a. ㊷a. to (play the) sneak.

Duck=stein *prov.* (⌣⌣) m ㉒ (Tuff, Traß) (calcareous) tuff.

Dudeldei (⌣⌣⌣) n ㊿ tweedledee, tweedle-dum; **dudeldum(dei)** vgl. bideldum(dei).

Dudelei F (⌣⌣⌣) f ㊽ tootling, wretched music of wind-instruments; **Dud(e)ler** (⌣⌣⌣) m ㉒ tootler, wretched musician; **dudeln** [poln.] (⌣⌣) v/n. (h.) ㊷a. to tootle; to play on the bagpipe; to make hideous music.

Dudelsack ♪ (⌣⌣⌣) m ㉒ bagpipe, schott. bagpipes *pl.*; Sprichw. den Himmel für einen **~** (ob. eine Baßgeige) ansehen, etwa: to be overjoyed or in raptures; **~(s)=pfeifer** m ㉒ bagpipe (player).

Dudler F (⌣⌣) m ㉒ f. Dudeler.

Dudu F (⌣⌣) m ㊾ *orn.* = Dronte.

Du=ell (⌣⌣) [fr., *lt. (Zweikampf)single combat, duel (auf Pistolen, Degen with pistols, swords); ein **~** auskämpfen, bestehen to fight a duel; zum **~** herausfordern, bsd. ehm. to call out, to challenge;

Du=ellant (⌣⌣⌣) [lt.] m ㉒ duellist, combatant; principal in a duel.

du=ellieren (⌣⌣⌣⌣) [lt.] **sich** ⚲ v/refl. ㊹ to (fight a) duel; sich mit e-m ⚲, to fight (a duel with) a p., † to go out with a p.

Duell=regeln (⌣⌣⌣) f/pl. ㊽ laws *pl.* of duelling. [(Anstandsdame) duenna.)

Duenja, öft. **Duenna** (⌣⌣jä) [span.] f ㊽ ㊾)

Du=ett ♪ (⌣⌣) [it.] n ⑪b. (Zweigesang) duet.

duff (⌣) [nbd.] a. ㊻ (matt, glanzlos) dull.

Düffel T (⌣) m ㉒ (dickes langhaariges Wolltuch) duffle, stout hairy cloth.

Duft¹ (⌣) [ahd.] m ①b. **1.** (Dunst) exhalation; vapour, haze; (Beschlag von Obst) bloom, ⚳ pruinescence; *phys.*, &c. (ausströmender Hauch) aura. — **2.** (angenehmer Geruch) scent, perfume, aroma, fragrance, (sweet) odour.

Duft² † = Ducht. [f. Tüftelei, tüfteln.)

☛ **Düftelei** F (⌣⌣⌣), **düfteln** F (⌣⌣))

duften (⌣⌣) **I** v/n. ⑱ **1.** (fn) to rise as vapour. — **2.** (h.): **a)** meist v/impers.: es duftet um den See there is a haze (a)round the lake; die Wände ⚲ (schlagen aus) the walls are clammy, F the walls sweat; **2b** damp, moist; **b)** (angenehmer riechen) to give forth scent or perfume. *a.v/impers.*: es duftet lieblich nach Blumen there is sweet perfume of flowers. — **II ~ n** ㉓ **3.** = Duft 2.

duftig (⌣⌣) *a.* ㊻ **1.** (f. Duft¹ 1) vaporous, hazy. — **2.** (f. Duft¹ 2) scented, perfumed, aromatic, fragrant, sweet-smelling, ⚳ odor(ifer)ous.

Duftigkeit (⌣⌣⌣) f ㊽ haziness.

duft=los (⌣⌣) *a.* ㊻ inodorous, scentless; **2reich** *a.* scented, perfumed.

Dugong (⌣⌣) [malai.] m ⑪c. ⚷ zo. ducong, duyong, sea-cow (*Hali'core Dugong*).

du jour ⚔ ✝ (bü Gu'r) [fr. des Tages] *inv.* (vom Dienst) on (special) duty, on guard.

Dukaten (⌣⌣⌣) [mhd. 12. sae.; *Dukas npr.* It. Kaiser=familie] m ㉓ (Goldmünze, etwa 9,55 Mark) ducat; **~=gold** n ㊷ fine gold.

Düker ❂ (⌣) [nbd. Taucher] m ㉒ **1.** = Dücker¹. — **2.** ⚓ (Nagel ohne Kopf) sprig.

duktil (⌣⌣) [it.] *a.* ㊻ (dehnbar) ductile; **~ität** (⌣⌣⌣⌣) f ㊽ ductility.

duldbar (⌣⌣) *a.* ㊻ tolerable, sufferable.

dulden (⌣⌣) [ahd.] ⑱ v/a. u. v/n. (h.) (leiden) to tolerate, to suffer; (ertragen) to endure, to bear; (aushalten) to submit to, to put up with, to stand; ich kann es nicht ⚲ (zulassen) I cannot allow (or permit) it; das duldet keinen Aufschub it brooks no delay.

Dulder (⌣⌣) m ㉒, **~in** f ㊵ (patient) sufferer, a. martyr; Kranke[r] invalid.

duldsam (⌣⌣) *a.* ㊻ enduring, long-suffering; in Glaubenssachen ꝛc.: tolerant; **~keit** (⌣⌣⌣) f ㊽ endurance; tolerance.

Duldung (⌣⌣) f ㊽ toleration, sufferance, (Nachsicht) indulgence; endurance.

☛ **Dulle** ⚓ f. Dolle. **Dülle** = Tülle.

Dult fübd. (⌣) [ahd.] f ⑱ (Jahrmarkt) fair.

Dulzinea F (⌣⌣⌣) [span. Dulcinea del Toboso, Geliebte des Don Quichotte] f ㊽ (㊾) *co.* lady love, sweetheart.

dumm (⌣) [nbd.: dumb] **I** *a.* ㊻ (D 2, 7) **1.** (stumpfen Geistes) stupid, dull (of comprehension), slow (of understanding); (einfältig) silly, foolish, simple-minded, F thick-headed; (schwachsinnig) imbecile, idiotic; 2er (unwissender) Bauer ignorant clod-hopper; 2e Gans silly goose; 2er Kerl, Mensch blockhead, simpleton; er ist nicht so ⚲, wie er aussieht ... such a fool as he looks; *iro.* du bist nicht ⚲! you are no fool!, F you know a thing or two!; fo ⚲ bin ich nicht I am not so (F such a) silly as that!; ⚲ machen, oft.: to stupefy, to stun; *adv.* etwas ⚲ angreifen to begin (or do) a th. clumsily or awkwardly. — **2.** (Geistesarmut verratend) 2e Handlung ob. Rede, 2er Schnack tomfoolery; 2er Streich silly action, F stupid thing to do; 2es Zeug nonsense, silly stuff, idle talk, als Ausruf auch: rubbish!, stuff!; 2es Zeug reden, vorbringen to talk nonsense (F twaddle, bosh). — **3.** (unangenehm) das ist eine 2e Geschichte ... an awkward (or unpleasant) matter. — **4.** (schwindelig) es wird mir ganz ⚲ im Kopfe my head feels quite giddy or dizzy. — **5.** fast †: a) von Eßwaren: (abgestanden) stale, insipid; das Gewürz ist ⚲ geworden ... has lost its flavour; *bibl.* wo nun das Salz ⚲ (taub) wird (Matth. 5, 13) but if the salt have lost his savour; b) v. Körperteilen: (empfindungslos) numb. — **II ~ e(r** m) f ㊷ **6.** stupid (or silly) one, fool; (f. der sich prellen läßt) dupe, jay; die ~en h. das meiste Glück ob. die dümmsten Bauern h. die größten Kartoffeln the biggest fools have the most luck; F fools for luck; die ~en w. nicht alle fools will never die out; damit fängt man die ~en that's (the bait) to catch fools with.

Dumm=bart (⌣⌣) m ㉒ = =kopf; **2dreift** *a.* foolhardy, impertinent, F saucy, cheeky; **=dreistigkeit** f foolhardiness, impertinence, F sauciness, cheek.

Dummerjan (⌣⌣⌣) m ⑪e. stupid fellow, numskull, dunce; F noodle; vgl. dumm II.

Dummheit (⌣⌣) f ㊽ **1.** (Dummsein) stupidity; foolishness; imbecility; mit der **~** kämpfen Götter selbst vergebens (*SCH.*) with folly even gods combat in vain. — **2.** (dummer Streich) stupid (or foolish) act, blunder, eine **~** begeh(e)n to commit a foolish action.

Dumm=kopf (⌣⌣) m ㉒ blockhead; F duffer; **2köpfig** *a.* ㊻ blockheaded; **=koller** m, *vet.* sleepy staggers.

Dummrian (⌣⌣) m ⑪e. = Dummerjan.

dumm=stolz (⌣⌣) *a.* ㊻ stupidly proud.

Dum=palme ♀ (⌣⌣⌣) f ㊽ gingerbread-tree, doom-palm (*Hyphae'na theba'ica*).

dumpf (⌣) *a.* ㊻ [nbd. „gedämpft": thump, dump] **1.** vom Ton: hollow, dull, deep-sounding; 2es Rollen des Donners ꝛc. rumbling … — **2.** von der Luft: close, heavy, sultry; von e-m Zimmer: close, confined, (muffig) fusty, stuffy; (feucht) damp. — **3.** fast † von Menschen = dumm 1; mir wird ganz ⚲ im Kopf I (begin to) feel quite stupefied or dazed. — **4.** 2es (bedrücktes) Schweigen oppressive silence.

Dumpfheit (⌣⌣) f ㊽ (f. dumpf), hollowness of sound; closeness of air; fustiness of a room; stupor of the senses.

dumpfig (⌣⌣) *a.* ㊻ f. dumpf 2; (schimmelig) mouldy, musty; **~keit** (⌣⌣⌣) f ㊽ fustiness, mould(iness).

dun F (⌣) *a.* ㊻ tipsy; dick u. ⚲ full up, crammed with food.

Düna ♀ (⌣⌣) *npr./f.* ㊽ a. (ruff. Fluß) Dvina.

Dune (⌣⌣) f ㊽ = Daune.

Düne (⌣⌣) [(nhd. 1400) nbd.: down] f ㊽ (sandiger Strand) sandy beach; F sands *pl.*; (Sandhügel) downs *pl.*

Dünen=hafer ♀ (⌣⌣⌣) m ㉒ (Sandrohr) beach-grass (*Ammo'phila*); **=rose** f ㊽ Scotch rose (*Rosa spinosi'ssima*); **=sand** m sea-sand. [Dünger.)

Dung¹ (⌣) [ahd.: dung] m ⑪b. *agr.* =)

dung² (⌣⌣), **dünge** (⌣⌣) ⚓ u. *poet. impf.* v. dingen. [=mittel n = Dung=mittel.)

Dünge=jauche (⌣⌣⌣) f ㊽ liquid manure;)

düngen (⌣⌣) ⑱ **I** v/a. *agr.* to manure, to fertilize the soil. — **II** v/n. (h.) to serve as manure, to have fertilizing properties. — **III ~ n** ㉓ = Düngung.

Dünger (⌣⌣) [Dung] m ㉒ *agr.* manure, fertilizer; (Mist) dung; F muck; (Kunst)**~** artificial manure, (Stall=)**~** stable-manure.

Dung=erde (⌣⌣) f ㊽ vegetable earth; rich mould; vgl. Dünger=erde.

Dünger=erde (⌣⌣⌣) f ㊽ compost, (garden=)mould, vgl. Dung=erde; **=haufen** m dung-heap, dunghill, manure-heap, F muckheap.

Dung=fliege (⌣⌣) f ㊽ *ent.* dung-fly (*Scato'phaga*); **=gabel** f d.-fork; muck-rake; **=grube** f d.-hole; manure-pit;

Zeichen (f. S. XVII): F familiär; P Volkssprache; Γ Gaunersprache; ⚲ selten; † alt (auch aeftorben); * neu (auch geboren); ⁺⁺ unrichtig;

=käfer m, ent. dung-beetle (Apho'dius); =mittel n fertilizer; (Jauche) liquid manure; =streuen n spreading (of) manure; =streuer ⊕ m, agr. manure-spreader or -distributor. — Vgl. auch Dünge=..., Dünger=...

Düngung (◡◡) f ⊕ manuring, fertilization of the soil; (Obenauf=)~ top-dressing of a field; ~s..f. Dung=, Dünge=.

dunkel (◡◡) [ahd.: dun] I a. ⊕ (D 8, 9) 1. (ant. hell) dark; (finster) gloomy; (düster) dusky; (trübe) murky; ein Zimmer ⊆ machen to darken ...; es wird ⊆ it is growing (F getting) dark or dusky; als es (ganz) ⊆ war when (the) night had set in, after dusk. — 2. (trüb) dim; es wird mir ⊆ vor den Augen my eyes grow dim; adv. die Lampe brennt ⊆ ... sheds a feeble (or gives a bad) light or burns dim(ly) or faintly. — 3. von Farben: dark, sombre; dunkler m. to deepen the colour; dunkles Schwarz deep (or jet-)black. — 4. fig. (unklar) obscure; (unverständlich) abstruse; (geheimnisvoll) deep, mysterious; (unbestimmbar) vague; e-e dunkle Erinnerung a faint recollection; von dunkler (unbekannter) Herkunft of unknown (or obscure) origin; eine dunkle Vorstellung a confused (or hazy) notion; das dunkle Zeitalter (Mittel=alter) the Dark Ages pl. — II ~ n ⊕ 5. darkness, gloom, dusk, fig. obscurity; im ~ der Nacht in the depth of night. — III Dunkle(s) n ⊕ 6. im ~n in the dark, in the shade; f. a. munkeln; fig. im 2n in obscurity; e-n im 2n lassen (im ungewissen) l. to leave a p. in the dark or in ignorance; im 2n leben to live in obscurity, to lead an obscure life or existence; Farbe: ins Dunkle spielend of a dark(ish) hue or shade.

Dünkel (◡◡) [nhd.; *dünken] m ⊕ (Selbstüberschätzung) conceit; (Anmaßung) presumption; (Hochmut) haughtiness, pride, F bumptiousness; er hat einen gewaltigen ~ he thinks much (or has a good opinion) of himself.

Dunkel=arrest ⚔ (◡◡...) m ⊕ dark cell, black hole; =äugig a. ⊕ dark-eyed; =blau a. da.-blue; =braun a. da.-brown; Pferd: bay(-coloured); Hautfarbe: tanned, tawny; =farbig a. da.(-coloured), of a deep dye; =haarig a. da.-haired.

dünkelhaft (◡◡◡) a. ⊕ (f. Dünkel) conceited, presumptuous, haughty, proud, F bumptious; ~igkeit ⊕ = Dünkel.

Dunkelheit (◡◡~) f ⊕ = dunkel II; die ~ der Nacht the gloom (poet. the shades pl.) of night; bei anbrechender ~ at nightfall, at dusk; bei völliger ~ in perfect darkness, when it is quite dark, in the depth of night.

Dunkel=kammer (◡◡...) f ⊕ phot. dark-room, (it.) camera obscura; =mann m hist. u. pol. obscurantist.

dunkeln (◡◡) 2a. I v/n. (h.) u. sich ⊆ v/refl. (dunkel werden) to grow dark or dim; (dunkler w.) to darken; a. v/impers. es dunkelt it is growing dark or dusky. — II v/a. eine Farbe ꝛc.: to darken, to make darker, fig. to obscure.

Dunkel=werden (◡◡...) n ⊕ darkening; vor dem ~ before it gets dark, ere (or before) nightfall.

dünken (◡◡) [ahd.: think] ⊕ I v/n. (h.) u. v/impers. to seem; (erscheinen) to appear; es dünkt (deucht) mich (ob. mir), daß //, als ob //, als wenn // it seems to me (fast † methinks) that //, as if //, as though //; Fit runs in my head that //; ich tue was mir gut dünkt I do as I think fit or right; es dünkt ihm lächerlich he thinks (or deems) it ridiculous, it appears ridiculous to him. — II sich ⊆ v/refl. ich dünke mich (ob. mir) glücklich (zu sein) I esteem (or think) myself happy; sich etwas (Großes) ⊆ to have a high opinion of o.s. or of one's importance; F to fancy o.s. (somebody); sie dünkt sich schön she thinks (that) she is beautiful, she thinks (or fancies) herself good-looking; er dünkte sich krank he imagined that he was ill.

Dünkirchen ♀ (◡◡~) npr/n. ⊕ a. (fr. Stadt) Dunkirk, (fr.) Dunkerque.

dunkle(...) f. dunkel.

dünn (◡) [ahd.: thin; lt. te'nuis; *] (D 7) 1. (ant. dick) thin; (schmächtig) slender, slim; (mager) thin, lean; (locker) flimsly; ⊆e Beine thin legs; ⊆er Faden slender thread; durch dick und ⊆ f. dick 7; ⊆ machen to (make) thin; F fig. sich ⊆ machen to make o.s. scarce; ⊆e Finger thin (or tapering) fingers pl.; typ. ⊆es Spatium hair-space. — 2. (zerstreut) scattered; ⊆e Bevölkerung sparse population; ⊆es Haar thin (or fine) hair; ⊆er Nebel slight haze or mist; adv.: ⊆ bevölkert thinly (or sparsely) inhabited; ⊆ säen to sow wide apart. — 3. v. Flüssigkeiten: weak (tea), dilute(d) (alcohol); ⊆es Blut poor (or serous) blood; ♅ phys. ⊆e Luft rarefied air; fig. in ⊆e Luft zerrinnen to dissolve in thin air.

dünn=bäckig (◡◡...) a. ⊕ hollow-cheeked; =beil ⊕ n ⊕ carp. chip-axe; ⊆beinig a. thin- (F spider-)legged; =bier n weak (bisw. small) beer; ⊆blätt(e)rig ♃ a. thin-leaved, ⚘ tenuifolious; =darm m small intestine.

Dünne (◡◡) f ⊕ = Dünnheit.

dünn=häutig (◡◡...) a. ⊕ thin-skinned.

Dünn=heit (◡◡) f ⊕ (f. dünn) thinness, slenderness; leanness; flimsiness of material; weakness of a fluid; poorness of blood; rarefaction of the air.

dünn=leibig (◡◡...) a. ⊕ lank(-bodied); ⊆lippig a. thin-lipped; ⊆schalig a. von Eiern: thin-shelled; von Apfelsinen ꝛc.: thin-skinned; =schliff m ⊕ Mikroskopie: transparent section; ⊆schnäb(e)lig a. orn.: ⚘ tenuirostral; =schnäbler m, orn.: ⚘ tenuiroster, pl. ...res; =stein m table-diamond. [des Wildes) flank.)

Dünnung (◡◡) f ⊕ hunt. mst pl. (Flanke)

dünn=wabig (◡◡...) a. ⊕ spindle-legged.

dunsen (◡◡) I faft + v/n. (fn) ⊕ = anschwellen. — II ge=dunsen p.p. f. bsd. Art.

Dunst (◡) [ahd.: dust] m ⊕ a(b). 1. exhalation; (Dampf) vapour, steam; (Rauch) smoke; dichte (starke) Dünste dense (strong) fumes pl.; schädliche Dünste noxious effluvia pl.; ⚒ in Schachten: choke-damp. — 2. fig. (Schein) (mere) show, (false) appearance; blauer ~ smoke (and puff); F gas; e-m (einen) blauen ~ vormachen to cast a mist before a p.'s eye, to bamboozle (or gammon, humbug) a p.; leerer ~ (mere) fancies or phantoms or bubbles pl.; alles ging in ~ und Rauch auf, wurde zu ~ it all dissolved into thin air, F all went to nothing. — 3. hunt (Vogel=)~ (feines Schrot) small (or fowling-)shot.

dunst=artig (◡...) a. ⊕ vapour-like; gaseous; =bad n ⊕ vapour-bath; =bläschen n steam-bubble, -globule; =druck m tension of the vapour in the air.

dunsten, dünsten (◡◡) ⊕ I v/n. (h.) to evaporate, to (rise as) steam; to exhale vapour or steam; es dunstet it is damp(ing) or misty. (zu Gas w.) to volatilize; (rauchen) to smoke, reek; (schwitzen) to perspire. — II v/a. Kocht.: (dämpfen) to stew. — III ~ n ⊕ evaporation; steaming; volatilization; perspiration.

Dunst=flinte (◡...) f ⊕ fowling piece; =gebilde n misty shape, hazy form; fig. vision, phantom; =hülle f = =kreis.

dunstig (◡◡) a. ⊕ (f. Dunst) 1. vaporous; filled with steam or fumes; (gasförmig) gaseous; (neblig) hazy, misty. — 2. = dumpf 2. — 3. path. v. der Haut: moist (with perspiration); P sweaty.

Dunst=kreis (◡◡...) m ⊕ atmosphere; =kugel f, phys. = Dampfkugel; =loch ⊕ n, arch. air-hole; =obst n stewed fruit; =rohr ⊕ n, arch. ventilating tube.

Dünung (◡◡) ⚓ [= Deining) f ⊕ (bewegte See) ground-swell, surf.

Dunzel F südd. (◡◡) [fr. donzelle; *it.] f ⊕ (Mädchen) damsel; girl.

Duo ♪ (◡◡) [it.] n ⊕ duo (a. = Due'tt).

Duodez (◡◡◡) [it.] n ⊕ a. typ. duodecimo (abbr. 12mo, 12⁰); halfsheet of twelves; Buch in ~ book in twelves.

Duodez=band (◡◡◡...) m ⊕ duodecimo (-volume); =fürst m petty prince or sovereign; bisw. princelet; =fürstentum n petty principality.

duodezimal (◡◡◡◡◡) [it.] a. ⊕ duodecimal; =maß (◡...) n ⊕, =system n duodecimal measure(ment), system.

Duodezime ♪ (◡◡◡◡◡) [it.] f ⊕ (Intervall v. Oktave u. Quinte) twelfth, duodecimo.

düpieren (◡◡◡◡) [fr.] v/a. ⊕ (betrügen) to dupe; der, die von ihnen Düpierte ⊕ their dupe or victim. [telegraphy.)

Duplex=telegraphie (◡◡tg...) f⊕ duplex)

duplieren (◡◡◡◡) [it.] v/a. ⊕ typ. to mackle; duplierter Druck (Doppeldruck) mackle; = dublieren.

Duplik (◡◡) [fr.] f ⊕ ehm. jur. rejoinder.

Duplikat (◡◡◡◡) [it.] n ⊕ c. (Abschrift) duplicate, identical copy; ⊕ Wechsel in ~ bill in sets or in duplo; =ur (...)¹ [it.] f ⊕ (doppelte Lage) double layer.

duplizieren (◡◡◡◡) [it.] v/a. ⊕ ehm. jur. to rejoin; **Duplizität** (◡◡◡◡) f ⊕ (Zweideutigkeit) ambiguity; (Falschheit) duplicity.

duplo (◡◡) [it.] adv.: in ⊆ (doppelt) in duplicate or in duplo. [major.)

Dur ♪ (◡) [it.] n, inv. (ant. Moll²))

durch (◡) [ahd.: th(o)rough] I prp. mit acc. 1. Ort: through; ⊆ ... hin through-out; ⊆ die Luft fliegen to fly through the air; ⊆ die Nase reden to speak through the nose; (quer oder mitten) ⊆ across; ⊆ das Zimmer schreiten to stride across the room; ⊆ die Wälder (hindurch) across the forests; vgl. ⊆-

einander; *fig.* e-m ⌾ die Finger sehen to overlook (or wink at) a p.'s fault(s); das ging mir ⌾ den Kopf it came (or flitted) across my mind, it occurred to me; das ging mir ⌾ Mark und Bein it sent a shiver (or a thrill) right through me or through my body. — 2. Mittel oder Ursache: through (the instrumentality of); by, by means (or dint) of; ⌾ einen Dolmetscher sprechen to speak through an interpreter; ⌾ sein Eingreifen through (or owing to) his intervention; ⌾ die Post by (or per) post or mail; through (the medium of the post; ⌾ den Regen ist der Weg schmutzig geworden through (or in consequence of) the rain the road has become muddy; ⌾ seine hohe Stellung by virtue of his high position; ⌾ Überanstrengung from over-exertion; ⌾ Zufall through accident, by chance. — 3. Zeitdauer: ⌾ das ganze Leben (**hindurch**) throughout (or during) life or a (whole) life-time. — **II** *adv.* immer nach dem *s.*: 4. mst zeitlich, bisw. räumlich: wir reisten die ganze Nacht ⌾ we travelled all night long; er ging die ganze Reihe ⌾ he went along the whole line. — 5. oft *ell.* für ein mit „durch" zs.-gesetztes *v.* der Bewegung. er ist ⌾: a) (vorbeigegangen) he has gone by; b) (durchgekommen) he has (safely) got through or escaped, he is out of danger; c) (durchs Examen) he has passed (his examination), F he got through (his exam); F seine Schuhe sind ⌾ (gerissen) … worn (out) or F on the ground; F unten ⌾ (verloren) sein … utterly lost or ruined. — 6. **durch und durch** from end to end; completely; ⌾ und ⌾ faul utterly (or thoroughly) rotten; ⌾ und ⌾ ehrlich honest to the backbone; ⌾ und ⌾ naß wet (or drenched) to the skin; ein Ehrenmann, ein Schurke ⌾ und ⌾ a thorough gentleman, an out-and-out (or arch-) villain; ich kenne es ⌾ und ⌾ I know it inside and out.

durch-… (⌾… ob. ⌾…) Vorsilbe in Zssgn mit *v.* **I** immer trennbar (**): 1. (hindurch): durchschimmern (⌾⌾) to shine through. — 2. (bis zu Ende) alle Stücke durchspielen (⌾⌾) to play all the pieces (right) through. — 3. (vollkommen): ein Zimmer durchheizen (⌾⌾) to heat a room thoroughly. — 4. *fig.* (mit Anstrengung) sich durchschlagen (⌾⌾) to fight one's way through. — **II** immer untrennbar (*): 5. (anfüllen): durchschimmern (⌾⌾) to fill with light. — 6. (befahren): alle Meere durchschiffen (⌾⌾) to navigate every sea. — 7. (hastig abmachen): e-n Brief durchfliegen (⌾⌾) to take a (hasty) glance at … — 8. (verbringen): die Nacht durchseufzen (⌾⌾) to spend … in groaning.

durch-ächzen (⌾⌾) *v/a.* ⌾* to spend in groaning, to sigh away hours or days.

durch-ackern (⌾⌾) *v/a.* ⌾a* **1.** völlig: to finish ploughing. — **2.** gehörig: (mst ⌾⌾ ⌾a*) to plough thoroughly or all over, *fig.* to search thoroughly or throughout; to work out with care.

durch-ädert (⌾⌾) *a.* ⌾ interveined, veiny, full ғf veins, ⌾ streaky.

durch-arbeiten (⌾⌾) ⌾** **I** *v/a.* **1.** (zu Ende arbeiten) to finish, complete; (⌾⌾) ⌾* (gehörig bearbeiten) to work through or thoroughly; *v.* Teig: to knead well. — **2.** geistig: to elaborate; to study (or examine) thoroughly; to digest. — **3.** (durchbringen) to get (or force) through. — **4.** sich (*dat.*) die Hände ⌾ to work one's hands sore. — **II** sich ⌾ *v/refl.* **5.** to work one's way through or up; to (w)edge (one's way) through a crowd; to toil through a dense wood; to wade through a bog, *fig.* to pull through great difficulties, a long illness, &c. — **6.** (den Weg bahnen) to pave (or make) one's way by dint of hard work; sich durch den ganzen Shakespeare (hin) ⌾ to plod (or F wade, plough) through the whole of Sh.('s works). — **III** ~ *n* ⌾ u. **Durch-arbeitung** *f* ⌾ **7.** (f. 2) elaboration, thorough study or examination. — **8.** (f. 5) toilsome (or laborious) crossing or passage.

durch-atmen (⌾⌾) *v/a.* ⌾b* (atmend durchdringen) to fill (or impregnate) with one's breath or odour, to scent.

durch-ätzen (⌾⌾) *v/a.* ⌾* to corrode (thoroughly); to etch (through).

durch-aus (⌾⌾, mit Nachdruck a. ⌾⌾) *adv.* **1.** (vollständig) thoroughly, throughout, completely, entirely, in every way; ⌾ richtig quite (or perfectly) correct; er wünscht ⌾ nicht, Sie zu hindern he has not the least desire to prevent you. — **2.** (unbedingt) absolutely; positively, by all means; ⌾ nicht not at all, not in the least; er ist ⌾ nicht reich he is by no means rich, he is far from rich; er will ⌾ reisen he is (thoroughly) bent on travelling.

durch-backen *v/a.* **1.** (⌾⌾) ⌾b (⌾)** (völlig backen) to bake through or thoroughly. — **2.** (⌾⌾) ⌾b (⌾)* (backend vermischen) mit Rosinen ⌾ to mix in baking (mit with).

durch-baus(ch)en *s.* durchpausen.

durch-beben (⌾⌾) *v/a.* ⌾* to cause to vibrate or to shiver or to shake; *fig.* to thrill, to fill with emotion.

durch-beißen (⌾⌾) ⌾a** **I** *v/a.* (a. ⌾⌾ ⌾a*) to bite (or eat) through, to crush between the teeth. — **II** *v/n.* (h.) to get through by (means of) biting. — **III** sich ⌾ *v/refl.* to work one's way by biting; *fig.* to fight a th. through or out; to attain one's end by fighting.

durch-beizen (⌾⌾) *v/a.* ⌾* = durchätzen. [(or pass) through an opening.

durch-bekommen (⌾⌾) *v/a.* ⌾*/* to get*/*

durch-beraten (⌾⌾) **I** *v/a.* ⌾a*/* (carefully) to deliberate upon a th.; *parl.*, &c. to discuss (or debate) a bill, &c. thoroughly, F to thrash a matter out. — **II** ~ *n* ⌾ u. **Durch-beratung** *f* ⌾ complete (or lengthy) discussion.

durch-beten *v/a.* **1.** (⌾⌾) ⌾* die Nacht ⌾ to spend the night in prayer. — **2.** (⌾⌾) ⌾** to say a prayer from beginning to end; to go through a litany, &c.

durch-betteln **I** (⌾⌾) *v/a.* ⌾a* ein Land ⌾ to beg one's way through … — **II** (⌾⌾) sich ⌾ *v/refl.* ⌾a* to support o.s. (or to keep o.s. alive) by begging;

sich bis in die Stadt ⌾ to beg one's way into the town. [bolt flour.]

durch-beuteln (⌾⌾) *v/a.* ⌾a** to

durch-bewegen (⌾⌾⌾) *v/a.* ⌾*/* to move through. [*tel.* Leitungsdraht: to sag.]

durch-biegen (⌾⌾) sich ⌾ *v/refl.* ⌾a**

durch-bilden (⌾⌾) **I** *v/a.* ⌾ u. sich ⌾ *v/refl.* ⌾** to form (or educate) perfectly or thoroughly; sich ⌾ to complete (or perfect) one's education; durchgebildet (highly) educated, accomplished; ein technisch durchgebildeter Mann a man with a thorough(ly good) technical education or training. — **II** ~ *n* ⌾ und **Durch-bildung** *f* ⌾ thorough (or complete) education.

Durch-binder ⌾(~) *m* ⌾ *arch.* through-/

Durch-blasen *v/a.* **1.** (⌾⌾) ⌾a** a) to blow through; b) ♪ to play over (or through) on a wind-instrument. — **2.** (⌾⌾) ⌾a* to fill (or move) with one's breath.

durch-blätter/n (⌾⌾ u. ⌾⌾) **I** *v/a.* ⌾a* u. ** to turn over the leaves (or to run over the pages) of a book, &c.; to glance (cursorily) at a periodical, &c., to skim a treatise, &c., to peruse a document, &c. — **II** ~ *n* ⌾ u. D/ung *f* ⌾ (f. I) cursory glance at a periodical, &c., hasty perusal of a book, &c.

durch-bleuen (⌾⌾) *v/a.* ⌾** (durchprügeln) to thrash, to beat soundly, to drub.

Durch-blick (⌾⌾) *m* ⌾d. peep (through), glance across; *fig.* penetrating glance, penetration, quick eye; *paint.* perspective; vista.

durch-blicken **I** (⌾⌾) *v/n.* (h.) ⌾** **1.** (hindurchblicken) to peep (or look) through, to glance across. — **2.** *fig.* (erscheinen) to become visible; to appear (below the surface or behind the clouds); to transpire; ⌾ lassen to make (it) apparent; to hint, to suggest; to give a p. to understand. — **II** (⌾⌾) *v/a.* ⌾* **3.** (durchschauen II) to look through; to see through, to penetrate.

durch-blinken (⌾⌾) *v/n.* (h.) ⌾** to gleam through; to twinkle across.

durch-blitzen **I** (⌾⌾) *v/n.* (h.) ⌾** to flash across, to gleam across (like a flash of lightning). — **II** (⌾⌾) ⌾*/to traverse with lightning-speed; ein Gedanke durchblitzte sein Gemüt a thought flashed through (or suddenly crossed) his mind.

durch-bohr/en (⌾⌾) *v/a.*, *v/n.* (h.) u. sich ⌾ *v/refl.* ⌾** **1.** to bore (or dig, pierce) through; sich ⌾ to work (or bore) one's way through, von Würmern 2c.: to pierce the wood, &c. — **II** (⌾⌾) *v/a.* (und sich ⌾ *v/refl.*) ⌾* **2.** to pierce (o.s.), to stab (o.s.) with a dagger; to run (o.s.) through with a sword; vom Stier: to gore with his horns; *fig.* mit den Blicken ⌾ to pierce with one's glances, F to look daggers at; f. nicht s 4. — **3.** (durchlöchern) to perforate; *surg.* den Schädel ⌾ to trepan the skull; ⌾ durchbo"hrt perforate(d), zo., &c. ⌾ foraminated. — **III** ~ *n* ⌾ u. D/ung *f* ⌾ **4.** boring through, &c. (f. I u. II); perforation; *surg.* trepanning.

durch-braten (⌾⌾) **I** *v/a.* (gut ob. recht) ⌾ to roast (a. F to cook) thoroughly; gut (schlecht) du"rchgebraten well

[durchbrausen] — 279 — [durchfallen]

done (underdone). — II v/n. (ſu) to be roasting (or cooking, doing) well.

durch-brauſen I (ᵝᴸ⌣) v/n. (ſn) ⓐ** to rush (or roar) through, vom Zug auch: to steam (or whiz) through. — II (ᵝ⌣⌣) v/a. ⓐ* to fill with a roar (-ing noise); Stürme ꝶ den Wald storms roar (or howl, whistle) through …

durch-brechbar (ᵝ⌣- u. ᵝᴸ⌣) a. ⓖ breakable, pierceable; fragile.

durch-brechen I (ᵝ⌣⌣) 1. v/a. ⓖa** und v/refl. einen Stock ꝛc.: to break through, to snap; ein Loch ꝶ to bore (or make) a hole (or an opening) through; eine Straße ꝶ to make (or cut, build) a street through or across; ſich ꝶ to break through; v. Gefangenen: to break loose, to break out of (or escape from) jail. — 2. v/n. (h.) to break through, to force one's way out; von Blattern: to break (or come) out; von Blumen: to spring forth, to open, to unfold; von Tränen: to burst forth; von Zähnen: to break (or cut) through the gums. — II (ᵝ⌣⌣) v/a. 3. ⓖa** to pierce; ⚔ eine Blockade ꝶ to run a blockade; ⚔ die feindlichen Glieder, Reihen ꝶ to break (or to cut one's way) through the enemy's ranks; (durch-löchern) to perforate; durchbro'ch(e)ne Arbeit pierced work; der Goldschmiede: filigree(-work); Näherei: pinked work, open work; arch. fretwork, carved work. — III ~ n ⓔ 4. (ſ. I) breaking through, &c.; escape from jail; cutting of teeth. — 5. (ſ. II) piercing, &c.; running of a blockade. [Lochen: puncheon.

Durch-brech=meißel (ᵝᴸ⌣ …) m ⓔ zum **durch-brennen** I (ᵝ⌣⌣) v/a. ⓖb** und v/n. (ſn) 1. (durch u. durch brennen) to burn (a hole) through; F fig. (heimlich durch-gehen) to run away, to abscond; F to levant, bolt, walk off; P to (do a) bunk; mit e-m Mädchen ꝶ to elope with a girl; er ist mit der Kaſſe du"rchge-brannt he appropriated the money and vanished, F he made off with the cash. — II (ᵝ⌣⌣) v/a. ⓖb* 2. (brennend durchbringen) to burn through, to pierce by burning. — 3. to heat.

Durch-brenner (ᵝ⌣⌣) m ⓔ runaway; bſd. ſchuldenhalber: F levanter; Sport: welsher.

durch-bringen (ᵝ⌣⌣) ⓖ** I v/a. 1. e-n durch e-e Stadt ꝛc. ꝶ to take (or see) a p. (safely) through … — 2. fig. to get (or pull) a p. through a difficulty or an illness; to deliver (or save) a p. from danger or out of the jaws of death; e-n im Examen ꝶ to pass a person (through an examination); ein Geſetz ꝶ to pass a bill; Kinder ꝶ (großziehen) to bring (or rear) up children. — 3. (zu Ende bringen) to bring to an end; ſein Vermögen ꝶ to dissipate, squander, spend, waste; er hat alles, all ſein Geld, ſein Hab und Gut du"rch-gebracht he has made ducks and drakes of his money, he has run through everything. — 4. * (ᵝ⌣⌣) ⓖ** (verbri'ngen) ich durchbra"chte e-e ſchlafloſe Nacht I passed a sleepless night. — II ſich ꝶ v/refl. 5. to find one's way through (or out of) a difficulty, &c.; engS. ſich kümmerlich ꝶ ſ. durchſchlagen 5 b. —

III ~ n ⓔ 6. (ſ. 2) deliverance from danger. — 7. (ſ. 3) dissipation of property.

Durch-bringer (ᵝ⌣⌣) m ⓔ, ~in f ⓐ (Verſchwender[in]) spendthrift; rake.

durch-brochen (ᵝ⌣⌣) p.p. ſ. durchbrechen 3.

Durch-bruch (ᵝ⌣) m ⓞd. 1. = durch-brechen II. — 2. fig. zum ~ kommen to break through, to burst forth, to come into full display or full operation; theol. Gnade: to take (full) effect, to work a (complete) conversion (or regeneration) of the sinner. — 3. (Lücke) opening, aperture, gap; einer Mauer a. breach; e-s Dammes: bursting, rupture; ☉ = Durchbrechungel.

Durch-bruch=arbeit (ᵝᴸ⌣ …) f ⓔ Weberei: open work; ⚕ Bluſe mit ~ open-work (or openwork) blouse.

Durch-bruchs=gefecht ⚔(ᵝᴸ⌣ …)n ⓔ breaking through the enemy's line of battle.

durch-dacht (ᵝ⌣⌣cht) ſ. durchdenken II.

durch-dampfen (ᵝ⌣⌣) v/a. ⓖ** to fill with vapour or steam or fumes.

durch-dauern (ᵝ⌣⌣) v/n. (h.) ⓖa* to last through days or years.

durch-denken I (ᵝ⌣⌣) ⓖ** u. (ᵝᴸ⌣) ⓖ* v/a. to think over, to revolve (or turn over) in one's mind, to make a deep (or thorough) study of. — II **durch-dacht** (ᵝ⌣⌣cht) p.p. u. a. ⓖ (reiflich erwogen) well weighed, well thought out; ein wohl ꝶer Plan a well-considered (or -contrived) plan.

durch-dienen (ᵝᴸ⌣) v/n. (h.) ⓖ** to serve one's (full) time.

durch-drängen (ᵝ⌣⌣) v/a. u. v/refl. ⓖ** ſich ꝶ to squeeze (or wedge one's way) through the crowd.

durch-dreſchen (ᵝ⌣⌣) v/a. ⓖe.(a. ⓖb)**, agr. to thrash thoroughly; F fig. to beat soundly; ein Thema: to thrash out.

durch-dring/en I (ᵝ⌣⌣) v/n. (ſn) ⓞſt** to press through, von Flüſſigkeiten: to ooze through, to permeate; fig. (zum Ziele gelangen) to attain one's end, to prevail; er iſt damit durchgedrungen he has carried his point; er wird da-mit ꝶ he will succeed (in the end). — II (ᵝ⌣⌣) ⓞſt* (ganz erfüllen) to penetrate, permeate, pervade; (ſättigen) to impregnate; ꝶde Kälte piercing (or biting) cold; ꝶder Verſtand keen understanding, searching intellect; von et. durchdrungen ſein to be fully convinced of a th., to be impressed with a belief. — III ~ n ⓔ = D/ung.

durch-dringlich (ᵝ⌣⌣) a. ⓖ penetrable, permeable, pervious; ~keit (⌣) f ⓖ penetrability, permeability, perviousness.

Durch-dringung (ᵝ⌣⌣) f ⓐ (ſ. durch-dringen II) penetration, permeation; impregnation.

durch-drücken (ᵝ⌣⌣) ⓖ** I v/a. 1. to press (or squeeze) through; ⚔ die Knie ꝶ to straighten the knees; fig. (durchſetzen) to force through, to enforce. — 2. (wund machen) to rub sore, to gall. — II ſich ꝶ v/refl. 3. to squeeze one's way through the crowd. &c. — 4. F = durchſchlagen 4 b. [dringen II.

durch-drungen (ᵝ⌣⌣) p.p. von durch-

durch-duften, durch-düften (ᵝ⌣⌣) v/a. ⓖ** to (fill with) perfume or scent.

durch-dünſten I (ᵝ⌣⌣) v/a. ⓖ* to fill with vapour or steam. — II (ᵝ⌣⌣) (h.)ⓖ** to escape as vapour or steam.

durch-dürfen (ᵝ⌣⌣) v/n. (h.) ⓖ** to be allowed to pass through.

durch-eilen I (ᵝ⌣⌣) ⓖ** v/a. u. (ᵝᴸ⌣) ⓖ** v/n. (ſn) to hurry (or hasten through or across, to travel quickly across; fliegend: to flit (or fly) across; reitend: to cross rapidly on horseback. — II ~ n ⓔ hasty journey (or flight, passage) through or across.

durch-ein-an-der (ᵝ-ᵝ⌣) I adv. confusedly, pell-mell, F higgledy-piggledy; bunt ꝶ promiscuously, at sixes and sevens, F anyhow, in a thorough muddle, all of a jumble. — II ~ ⓔ confusion, disorder, medley; F omniumgatherum, muddle, jumble.

Durch-ein-an-der-liegen (ᵝ⌣…) = n ⓔ disarrangement, disorder; ꝶmengen v/a. ⓖ** to mix up (in a heap), to throw into confusion, to disarrange, F to muddle (or jumble) up; ~ n confused mixture; ꝶreden ⓔ** u. ꝶſprechen ⓖa** v/a. to talk at the same time, to speak all at once, to create a regular Babel; ~ n ⓔ simultaneous talking, confused (din of) voices pl.; F hubbub; co. confusion of tongues, regular Babel; ꝶwerfen v/a. ⓖb** u. ~ n ⓔ = =mengen.

durch-eitern (ᵝᴸ⌣) v/n. (h.) ⓖa** to fester through. — II (ᵝ⌣⌣) v/a. ⓖa* to saturate with pus or matter.

durch-fahrbar (ᵝᴸ-) a. ⓖ passable.

durch-fahren I (ᵝᴸ⌣) v/n. (ſn) ⓖb** to pass (or drive, ride, cycle) through a place; unter e-r Brücke ꝶ to shoot a bridge; ⚓ to sail (or steam) through; vgl. durcheilen. — II (ᵝ⌣⌣) v/a. ⓖb* to cross (or pass through) rapidly; ein Schau(d)er durchfu"hr ſeine Glieder oder ihn a shudder thrilled his frame or F went through him; ⚔ das Gebirge ꝶ to intersect (or cut across) the rock.

Durch-fahrt (ᵝᴸ) f ⓖ 1. (Hindurchfahren) passing (through); hier iſt keine ~! no thoroughfare!; vgl. Durchreiſe. — 2. (Ort) passage, thoroughfare (Tor) gate(-way); (Kanal) channel.

Durch-fahrts=geld (ᵝᴸ…) n ⓔ = =zoll; =recht n right of passing or of way; =zoll, m toll paid by passing ships, carriages, &c., transit-duty. — Vgl. auch Durch-fuhr=… und Durchgangs=…

Durch-fall (ᵝ⌣)m ⓞc. 1. falling through; fig. im Examen, bei einer Wahl ꝛc.: failure, rejection. — 2. path. diarrhœa, looseness(or relaxation) of the bowels.

durch-fallen I (ᵝ⌣⌣) v/n. (ſn) ⓖa** 1. to fall through; im Examen ꝛc.: to fail, to be rejected, F to be plucked or ploughed; bei Wahlen auch: to be unsuccessful; von Entwürfen: to fall to the ground; thea. von Stücken: to fall flat; phys. vom Licht: ꝶd: ⚗ transmitted; du"rchge-fall(e)ner Kandidat rejected (or unsuccessful) candidate. — 2. F die Nacht ꝶ (durchſchwärmen) to make a night of it, to be out (on the spree) all night. — II (ᵝ⌣⌣) v/a. ⓖa* 1. einen Raum ꝶ to traverse (or to drop through) … — III ~ n ⓔ 4. = Durchfall 1.

⚗ scientific; ♃ botanical; ⚱ geography; ⊕ machinery; ⚔ mining; ⚔ military; ⚓ marine; ⚕ commercial; ✉ postal; 🚂 railway.

[durchfechten] — 280 — [durchgehen]

durch-fechten (⌣‿) 79b** **I** v/a. 1. to fight out a matter, to battle through difficulties; fig. eine Meinung ⁓ to carry one's opinion or one's point. — **II** sich ⁓ v/refl. 2. to fight one's way; to struggle along. — 3. v. Handwerksburschen = durchbetteln 2.

durch-fegen v/a. 1. (⌣‿) ⊛** to sweep thoroughly or from end to end. — 2. (⌣‿) ⊛* (durchstreifen) vom Sturme ꝛc.: to sweep across or through.

durch-feilen (⌣‿) v/a. ⊛** to file through; fig. bsd. Schriften: to polish, to give the last finish(ing touches) to.

durch-feuchten I (⌣‿) v/a. ⊛* (mit Feuchtigkeit erfüllen) to moisten (or damp) well, to soak. — **II** (⌣‿) v/n. (h.) ⊛** von Feuchtigkeit: to penetrate.

durch-feuern I (⌣‿) 1. v/a. ⊛a** einen Ofen: to heat well. — 2. v/n. (h.) (hindurchschießen) to fire through a window, &c. — **II** (⌣‿) v/a. ⊛a* 3. to (fill with) heat; fig. (entflammen) to fire, rouse, incite, inflame, kindle.

durch-finden (⌣‿) v/n. (h.) und sich ⁓ v/refl. ⊛** to find one's way through; fig. sich in einem Prozeß, einer Wissenschaft ⁓ to make o.s. thoroughly familiar with ...

durch-fischen (⌣‿) v/a. ⊛* ein Gewässer: to clear of fish.

durch-flammen (⌣‿) v/a. ⊛* to flash through; vgl. durchfeuern II.

durch-flattern (⌣‿) v/n. (ʃn) ⊛a** und (⌣‿) v/a. ⊛a* to flutter through.

durch-flechten (⌣‿) v/a. ⊛b* to intertwine; das Haar mit Blumen ⁓ to dress ... with flowers; durchflo"cht(e)ne Arbeit interlaced work; fig. mit Redeblumen ⁓ to interlard (or interweave) with flowers of speech.

durch-fliegen I (⌣‿) v/n. (ʃn) ⊛aft** to fly through. — **II** (⌣‿) v/a. ⊛aft* to fly (or pass rapidly) through; die Lüfte ⁓ to fly (or flit, sail) through the air, to float through space; fig. e-n Brief: to glance through, skim over; s. durch- 7.

durch-fließen I (⌣‿) v/n. (ʃn) ⊛d** to flow through, in Tropfen: to trickle through. — **II** (⌣‿) v/a. ⊛d* to water (or irrigate) a plain. [durchschimmern.]

durch-flimmern (⌣‿) u. (⌣‿) ⊛a** u. * =]

durch-flochten (⌣‿ch¡·) a. ⊛ p.p. v. durchflechten; ꝛc.: to float through.]

durch-flößen (⌣‿) v/n. (ʃn) ⊛d** von Holz

Durch-flucht (⌣‿) f ⓾, **Durch-flug** (⌣‿) m ⓓd. flight through a place.

Durch-fluß (⌣‿) m ⓼a. flowing through; passage (or course) across a country, &c.

durch-fluten (⌣‿) v/n. (ʃn) ⊛** u. v/a. ⊛* to flow (or stream) through.

durch-forschen (⌣‿) ⓵** und (⌣‿) ⓵* **I** v/a. to search through, to examine (thoroughly), to make an exhaustive study of, im einzelnen: to scrutinize; ein Land: to explore. — **II** sich ⁓ v/refl. to examine o.s., to dive into one's heart. — **III** ⁓ n ㉓ u. **Durch-forschung** f ㊻ (s. I) search through, (thorough) examination; scrutiny; exploration.

durch-forst/en I v/a. (⌣‿) ⊛*, (⌣‿) ⊛** for. e-n Wald: to manage according to the rules of forestry. — **II Ⅾ/ung** f ㊻ proper management of woods and forests; afforestation of a country.

durch-fragen I (⌣‿) ⊛ (+‿⊛b) * (fragend durchziehen): er hat die ganze Stadt nach dir durchfra"gt the went round the town inquiring for you; e-n Prüfungsgegenstand ⁓ (erschöpfen) to go deeply into (or to exhaust) a subject. — **II** ⊛ (+‿⊛b)**: sich ⁓ v/refl. to find one's way by asking (questions).

durch-fressen I (⌣‿) v/a. u. sich ⁓ v/refl. ⊛³** 1. von Insekten ꝛc.: to eat (or gnaw, nibble) one's way through a thing; ätzend: to corrode. — 2. F von Personen: sich ⁓ (schmarotzen) to sponge on others. — **II** (⌣‿) v/a. ⊛* 3. = 1; von Motten, Rost, Würmern (path. vom Krebs) ꝛc. moth-, rust-, worm- (cancer-)eaten; vom Scheidewasser ⁓ corroded (or eaten away) by aquafortis.

durch-frieren I (⌣‿) v/n. (ʃn) ⓒ** to freeze (or chill) right through, to get thoroughly frozen or chilled. — **II** (⌣‿) v/a. ⓒ* to chill right through; to congeal fluids; F to nip up (or numb) living beings. — **III durch-froren** (⌣‿) p.p. (s. II) u. a. ⊛ (D9) frozen through, thoroughly chilled or numbed.

durch-frösteln (⌣‿) v/a. ⊛a* (fröstelnd durchbringen) (slightly) to chill.

durch-fühlen (⌣‿) ⊛** **I** v/a. to feel through s.th. else; fig. er scheint es nicht durchzufühlen he seems not to notice (or feel) it or F to see through it — **II** sich ⁓ v/refl. to grope (or feel) one's way along.

Durch-fuhr (⌣‿) f ㊻ 1. = Durchfahrt 1. — 2. ⁓ (von Waren) ⊛ transit of goods; vgl. Durchgang ⑤...).

durch-führbar (⌣‿) a. ⊛ practicable, feasible; v. Plänen auch: workable; **~keit** (⌣‿) f ㊻ practicability, feasibility.

durch-führ/en I v/a. ⊛** 1. to lead (or take, convey) through or across; ⊛ du"rchgeführte Ware goods pl. in transit. — 2. fig. to carry through or out; to accomplish, perform, achieve; to execute in detail; eine Rolle ⁓ to sustain (or support) one's part to the end; ♪ eine Fuge ⁓ to develop ... — **II** ⁓ n ㉓ 3. = Ⅾ/ung. [trade.]

Durch-fuhrhandel (⌣‿...) m ㉒ transit-]

Durch-führung (⌣‿) f ㊻ (s. durchführen 2) accomplishment, performance, achievement; execution. [duty.]

Durch-fuhr=zoll (⌣‿...) m ㉒ transit-]

durch-furchen (⌣‿) v/a. ⊛* to furrow, to mark with furrows; den Boden ⁓ (aufreißen) a. to plough (or tear) up the ground; die See ⁓ to plough the deep; durchfu"rchte Stirn furrowed (or wrinkled) brow.

durch-futtern, bff. -füttern **I** (⌣‿) v/a. ⊛a** 1. e-n Rock mit Pelz ⁓ to line a coat with fur throughout. — **II** (⌣‿) v/n. (h.) ⊛a** 2. Vieh: to feed through the winter; to hibernate. — 3. Menschen: to board, feed; (ernähren) to keep.

Durch-gang (⌣‿) m ⓓc. 1. (Durchgehen) passing through; ⎈ ~ (Durchfahrt) durch einen Tunnel crossing a tunnel; ast. ~ durch den Mittagskreis passing the meridian, ⚷ culmination; ~ der Venus durch die Sonnenscheibe transit of Venus. — 2. ⊛ = Durchfuhr 2. — 3. (Ort) way through, passage, gate

(-way); ⊕ einer Schleuse: flood-gate; ⚔ frt. (Ausfallspforte) postern; enger ~ defile; (hier ist) kein ~! no thoroughfare!, private road!

Durch-gänger F (⌣‿) m ㉒ (s. durchgehen 4): a) v. Pferden: bolting horse; b) v. Personen: (a. **~in** f ㊼) absconder; (s. der mit einer Kasse durchgeht) one who absconds with the cash, defalcator, embezzler (who flies from justice).

durch-gängig (⌣‿) a. ㊻ und adv. general(ly), universal(ly), usual(ly); Mäuse sind ⁓ kleiner als Ratten mice, on an average (or as a rule, ordinarily speaking), are smaller than rats.

Durch-gangs=abgabe ⚔ (⌣‿...) f ㊻ =Durchfuhrzoll; **=bescheinigung** f = =schein; **=fernrohr** n, ast. transit-instrument; **=gut** n, =güter n/pl. goods pl. in transit; **=handel** m = =verkehr; **=punkt** m point of intersection; passage, crossing; **=recht** n right to pass through, right of way; **=schein** m permit (of transit); **=ton** m passing-note; **=verkehr** m transit-trade, through-traffic; **=wagen** ⎈ m corridor-carriage, Pullman car; **=zug** ⎈ m corridor-train, train with corridor-carriages or Pullman cars. — Vgl. a. Durchfahrts=..., Durchfuhr=...

durch-geh(e)n (⌣‿) ⊛** **I** v/n. (ʃn) 1. to pass (through); der Hieb, Schuß ging durch das Fleisch durch ... went right through (or penetrated) the flesh; von Gesetzen und Vorschlägen: to pass, to be carried or passed or adopted or agreed to; parl. nicht ⁓ to be dropped or rejected, to fall through; phys. das Licht ꝛc. ⁓ lassen to transmit ...; fig. das geht (mit) durch, das mag so mit ⁓ that may pass, F it will do; et. ⁓ lassen to allow a th. to pass; sie ließen es ihm ⁓ they overlooked (or excused) his fault or mistake; sie lassen ihm nichts ⁓ they don't spare (or spoil) him in any way, they are very hard on him. — 2. darf ich ⁓? may I pass (or go) through?; Wasser kann nicht ⁓ (durchbringen) ... cannot get through; der Zug geht durch ... passes through, does not stop. — 3. durch alle Teile ⁓ (sich erstrecken) to go right through, to extend from end to end. — 4. von Pferden ꝛc.: to run away, to bolt; von Personen auch: to abscond, von zwei Liebenden: to elope. — 5. fig. er geht gerade durch (handelt entschieden) he acts straightforwardly; (greift durch) he carries it (right) through. — **II** v/a. 6. die Schuhe ⁓ (verschleißen) to wear out one's boots (by walking); sich (dat.) die Füße ⁓ to walk one's feet sore; etwas ⁓ to take ... right through; Schriften auch: to peruse. — 7. (auch ⌣‿(⌣) ⊛*) fig. eine Rechnung ꝛc. ⁓ (prüfen) to examine, inspect, go through ...; genau ⁓ to search closely; noch einmal ⁓ (überarbeiten) to work (or do) over again; to overhaul; literarisch: to revise; bessernd: to repolish. — **III** ⁓ n ㉓ 8. = Durchgang 1. — 9. ⁓ eines Vorschlages passing, adoption. — 10. ⁓ ⚔ 4: ⁓ eines Liebespaares elopement. — 11. (s. 7) ⊛ bei(m) ⁓ Ihrer Faktur ... on looking over (or examining) your

Zeichen (s. S. XVII): F familiär; P Volkssprache; ⌜ Gaunersprache; ⁒ selten; † alt (auch gestorben); * neu (auch geboren); ⁒⁒ unrichtig;

[durchgehend] — 281 — [Durchlaucht]

invoice ... — **IV durch-gehend** *p.pr.* u. *a.* ⊕ **12.** in den Bed. des *inf.* — **13.** 🚂 Les Billet through-ticket; *typ.* Le Breite full measure; Le Linie through- (or main) line; 🚂 Ler Wagen. Zug through-carriage, -train. — **14.** Le Waren transit-goods *pl.* [*adv.*]

durch-gehends (⁸ᴸ⌣) *adv.* = durchgängig)

durch-geist(ig)en (⁸ᴸ''⌣) *v/a.* ⊛(⊛)* to intellectualize, to spiritualize.

durch-gerben ⊖ (⁸ᴸ⌣) *v/a.* ⊛** to tan well; *fig. auch:* to thrash soundly.

durch-gießen (⁸ᴸ⌣) *v/a.* ⓓ** to pour through; to strain, to percolate.

durch-glänzen (⁸ᴸ⌣) *v/n.* (h.) ⊛** to shine (or sparkle) through. — **II** (⁸ᴸ⌣) *v/a.* ⊛* to fill with brilliant light.

durch-gleiten (⁸ᴸ⌣) *v/n.* (fu) ⓑ(⊛)** u. (⁸''⌣) *v/a.* ⓑ(⊛)* to glide (or slide, slip) through.

durch-glühen *v/a.* **1.** (⁸ᴸ⌣) ⊛** to heat well (in a furnace); to keep at red heat; ⊕ Blech, Draht ꝛc.: to anneal; *chm.* to calcine. — **2.** (⁸''⌣) ⊛* *fig.* to inflame (or fire) with passion.

durch-graben I (⁸ᴸ⌣) *v/a.* u. *v/refl.* ⓑ** Löcher ‿ to dig holes through; sich ‿ to dig one's way through a hill, &c. — **II** (⁸''⌣) *v/a.* ⓑ** to cut through (or to pierce) by digging; to excavate; e-n Berg ‿ to tunnel a mountain.

durch-greifen (⁸ᴸ⌣) **I** *v/n.* (h.) ⓑ** **1.** to pass one's hand(s) through or across. — **2.** *fig.* (entscheidende Maßregeln ergreifen) to take energetic (or decisive) measures, to carry a th. (through) with a strong hand. — **II** ‿d *p.pr.* u. *a.* ⊕ **3.** (f. 2) energetic (step), vigorous (action); decisive (measures); thorough (-going) (change); sweeping (reform).

durch-grübeln (⁸ᴸ⌣) u. (⁸''⌣) *v/a.* ⊛* u. ** to meditate deeply on; to think out well; to examine (or study) carefully.

durch-gucken F (⁸ᴸ⌣) *v/n.* (h.) ⊛** to peep (or look, spy, glance) through.

Durch-guß (⁸ᴸ) *m* ⓐ. **1.** (f. durchgießen) pouring through; percolation. — **2.** (Gußstein) sink. — **3.** (Seihtuch) strainer.

durch-haben F (⁸ᴸ⌣) *v/a.* ⓑ** Buch: (durchgelesen h.) to have read ... through.

durch-hacken (⁸ᴸ⌣) *v/a.* ⊛** to chop through (with a hatchet, &c.).

durch-hallen (⁸ᴸ⌣) *v/a.* ⊛** to fill with loud (or echoing, ringing) sound(s).

durch-halten (⁸ᴸ⌣) *v/a.* ⊛** **1.** (aushalten) to hold out (to the end); (durchführen) to carry right through.

durch-hämmern (⁸ᴸ⌣) *v/a.* ⊛** **1.** to hammer thoroughly, to forge well. — **2.** to perforate (or pierce) by means of hammering.

Durch-hau (⁸ᴸ) *m* ⓓ. **1.** *for.* glade, path cut through a wood. — **2.** ⚔ cross-cutting, intersection.

durch-hauen (⁸ᴸ⌣) *v/a.* ⓒ** **1.** ein Loch ‿ to cut an opening through; einen Weg ‿ to cut a road across; ein Nebel so dick, daß man (nicht) mit dem Säbel ‿ kann a fog so thick that one cannot cut it with a knife, a very dense fog. — **2.** (auch: ⁸''⌣ ⓒ**) (spalten) to hew, cleave, split; (entzweihauen) to cut in two; den gordischen Knoten ‿ to cut the Gordian knot. — **3.** e-n ‿ (sich ‿

v/refl.) to get a p. (to cut one's way) through sword in hand. — **4.** einen ‿ (schlagen) to give a p. a beating.

Durch-haus (⁸ᴸ) *n* ⓐ. house with a thoroughfare (leading through it).

durch-hecheln (⁸ᴸ⌣) **I** *v/a.* ⊛** **1.** ⊖ to hatchel thoroughly. — **2.** *fig.* to criticize, to find fault with; F to pull to pieces, to handle severely, to slate. — **II** ~ n ⊛ u. **Durch-hech(e)lung** *f* ⊛ **3.** *fig.* (sharp) criticism, fault-finding.

durch-heizen *v/a.* f. durch-... 3.

durch-helfen (⁸ᴸ⌣) ⓑ** **I** *v/n.* (h.) und bisw. *a. v/a.* e-m ‿ to help (or get) a p. through danger, &c., weit⊖. to help a p. out of a difficulty; Gott wird uns ‿ God will carry us through all our trouble; e-m durch eine Krankheit ‿ to save a p. from (F to pull a p. through) an illness. — **II** sich ‿ *v/refl.* to make one's way (F to get) through the world; sich mit Betteln ꝛc. ‿ to save (or support) o.s. by means of begging, &c.; sich kümmerlich ‿ f. durchschlagen 5b.

Durch-hieb (⁸ᴸ) *m* ⓓ. = Durchhau 1.

durch-hin (⁸⌣) *adv.* all (or right) through.

durch-hören (⁸ᴸ⌣) *v/a.* ⊛* **1.** to hear through a partition. — **2.** to hear out.

durch-huschen F (⁸ᴸ⌣) *v/n.* (fu) ⊛** to slip (or glide, flit) through or across.

durch-irren (⁸''⌣) *v/a.* ⊛* den Wald ꝛc. ‿ to roam (or ramble, range, rove, stray, wander) through ...

durch-jagen (⁸ᴸ⌣) ⊛** **I** *v/n.* (fu) **1.** to hurry (or gallop) through. — **II** *v/a.* **2.** den Feind durch das Tor ‿ to drive (or chase) the foe through the gate. — **3.** (auch: ⁸''⌣ ⊛*) das Land ‿ to hunt across country; *fig.* ein Buch ‿ to rush through ..., to devour ...

durch-jauchzen ⊛*, **durch-jubeln** ⓐ* (⁸ᴸ⌣) *v/a.* **1.** to fill with jubilant sounds or with (sounds of) rejoicing. — **2.** die Nacht ‿ to spend ... in noisy revelry or in rioting and shouting.

durch-kälten (⁸''⌣) *v/a.* ⊛* to chill (right) through, to (be)numb; Getränk: to ice; vgl. durchfrieren II. [thoroughly.]

durch-kämmen (⁸ᴸ⌣) *v/a.* ⊛*(*) to comb)

durch-kämpfen (⁸ᴸ⌣) *v/a.* ⊛* u. sich ‿ *v/refl.* = durchfechten 1 u. 2.

durch-kauen, -käuen (⁸ᴸ⌣) *v/a.* ⊛** to chew (or masticate) well or thoroughly; *fig.* to ponder (or ruminate) on.

durch-klettern I (⁸ᴸ⌣) *v/n.* (fu) ⓐ** to climb (or scramble) through. — **II** (⁸''⌣) *v/a.* ⓐ* to climb (or scramble) all over.

durch-klimmen (⁸ᴸ⌣) *v/n.* (fu) und (⁸''⌣) *v/a.* ⓐ(⊛)** u. * = durchklettern.

durch-klingen (⁸ᴸ⌣) ⓓf** u. * *v/n.* (h.) u. *v/a.* to fill with sound.

durch-klopfen (⁸ᴸ⌣) *v/a.* ⊛** **1.** to knock (a hole) through. — **2.** to beat well.

durch-klüftet (⁸ᴸ⌣) *p.p.* und *a.* ⊕ full of chasms or fissures; rifted.

durch-kneten (⁸ᴸ⌣) u. (⁸''⌣) *v/a.* ⊛** und * to knead well or thoroughly.

durch-kochen (⁸ᴸ⌣) *v/a.* ⊛** to boil meat, &c. well (through) or thoroughly.

durch-kommen (⁸ᴸ⌣) [ahd.] **I** *v/n.* (fu) ⊛** **1.** to come (or pass) through a town, &c. — **2.** *fig.* mit Mühe: to (manage to) get through difficulties; to make shift with small means; durch Gefahr: to have (a

lucky) escape; durch eine Krankheit auch: to recover; to get over it; es ist nicht du"rchzukommen there is no (such) getting through or no way out; kümmerlich ‿ to scrape through; so (gerade) ‿ to make both ends (just) meet; damit (mit der Ausrede) wird er nicht ‿ that (excuse) will not avail (or save, serve) him; ich kann damit (mit dem Gelde) nicht ‿ I cannot subsist (or live) on that, I cannot make the money do. — **3.** im Examen: to pass (successfully), to get through. — **4.** ↘ (zu Ende bringen) to get (or toil) through a book, a piece of work, &c. — **II** ~ n ⊛ (f. 1) coming (or passing) through, &c. — **6.** (f. 2) (lucky) escape; (Genesung) recovery.

durch-komponiert (⁸''⌣) *a.* ⊛ (composed) with a different air to each verse.

durch-können (⁸ᴸ⌣) *v/n.* (h.) ⊛** to be able to pass (or get) through.

durch-kosten (⁸ᴸ⌣) *v/a.* ⊛** (nach=ea.) ‿ to taste in succession; alle Freuden ‿ to enjoy every pleasure in life.

durch-kratzen (⁸ᴸ⌣) ⊛** **I** (a. ⁸''⌣ ⊛*) *v/a.* to scratch through or open; to make sore by scratching. — **II** *v/refl.* sich ‿ (wund kratzen) to scratch o.s. sore; sich ‿ (sich kratzend durchgraben) to scratch one's way through.

durch-kreuzen (⁸''⌣) **I** *v/a.* und sich ‿ *v/refl.* ⊛* **1.** (sich) ‿ to cross, to traverse, F to run crossways; sich ‿ auch: to intercross; von Absichten, Unternehmen ꝛc.: to clash (with each other), to come into collision; durchkreu"zt ✝, &c.: decussate. — **2.** *fig.* Pläne ‿ to thwart (or frustrate) a p.'s designs, to balk his schemes, to cross his purposes. — **II** ~ n ⊛ u. **Durch-kreuzung** *f* ⊛ **3.** 🚂 &c.: crossing; †, *math.* &c. gegenseitige Durchkreuzung ⚡ decussation. — **4.** *fig.* (f. 2) thwarting, frustration.

durch-kriechen (⁸ᴸ⌣) ⓓf** **I** *v/n.* (fu) to creep (or crawl) through. — **II** *v/a.* (a. ⁸''⌣ ⓓf*) to creep all over a place, to crawl into every nook and corner.

Durchl. *abbr.* = Durchlaucht.

durch-lärmen (⁸''⌣) *v/a.* ⊛* to fill with uproar; to drown.

Durch-laß (⁸ᴸ) *m* ⊛(⊕)ₐ. **1.** letting a p. or a thing through. — **2.** (narrow) passage; outlet; opening; ⊕ *arch.* (Abzugskanal) conduit; 🚂 für Wasser(läufe) unter Eisenbahndämmen: culvert.

durch-lassen (⁸ᴸ⌣) **I** *v/a.* ⊛ₐ** **1.** to let a p. or a th. through, to allow to pass. — **2.** der Stoff läßt kein Wasser durch ... is waterproof; *phys.* Licht ꝛc. ‿ to transmit ...; das Licht (nicht) ‿d (im)pervious to light. — **3.** im Examen: to (let) pass. — **4.** (durchseihen) to strain. — **II** ~ (⁸ᴸ⌣) = Durchlassung.

durch-lässig (⁸ᴸ⌣) *a.* ⊛** fit (or able) to pass through; pervious, permeable; ~keit (⌣‿) *f* des Bodens: perviousness.

Durch-laß-posten ⚔ (⁸ᴸ...) *m* ⊛ picket stationed (at an entrance) to examine persons before entering; ‿rohr ⊛ Wasserbau: (Abflußrohr) discharge-pipe.

Durch-lassung (⁸ᴸ⌣) *f* ⊛ (durchlassen 2:) transmission; (3:) passing of candidates.

Durch-laucht (⁸⌣) [mhd. (lt. *illu'stris*)] *f* ⊛ *abbr.* **Durchl.** (fürstlicher Titel) steht

unter „Hoheit“, über „Erlaucht“) (Serene) Highness; Anrede: Eure (Ew.), Ihre ~! Your (Serene) H.!; ≗ig(st) (ˊ˝⌣ u. ˝ˊ⌣) *a.* [66] meist von regierenden Fürsten: most serene, august; der ~igste Herzog His Most Serene Highness.

Durch-lauf (˝ˊ) *m* [7]d. **1.** running (or passage) through. — **2.** = Durchlaß 2. — **3.** *path.* = Ruhr.

durch-laufen I (˝ˊ⌣) *v/n.* (sn) [87]aft** to run (or move quickly) through; to flow (or filter) through. — **II** (ˊ˝⌣) *v/a.* [87]aft* to run (or hurry) through; to pass hastily through; e-e Bildergalerie ≗ to take a hasty glance at …; die Rechnungen ≗ to run through the accounts; *phys.* die Lichtwellen ≗ den Raum in raschem Fluge the waves of light travel through space at a rapid rate; er hat alle Länder der Welt ≗ (durchreist) he has trotted (or travelled) all round the globe.

durch-leben (˝ˊ⌣) [88]** u. (ˊ˝⌣) [88]* *v/a.* to live through a period; er hat glücklichere Tage durchle″bt (mitgemacht) he has seen better days; et. selbst ≗ to go (or pass) through a th. o.s.

durch-lesen (˝ˊ⌣) [82]a** **I** (a. ˊ˝⌣ [82]a*) *v/a.* to read (carefully) through; to read with attention; to peruse; flüchtig: to glance at, to skim (over). — **II sich ≗** *v/refl.* to work (or go) through a book from beginning to end. — **III** ~ *n* [23] und **Durch-lesung** *f* [46] (careful) reading, (hasty) perusal.

durch-leuchten I (˝ˊ⌣) *v/n.* (h.) [89]** to shine through; *fig.* (sich kund-geben oder -tun) to come to light, to show o.s. — **II** (ˊ˝⌣) *v/a.* [89]* to fill with light, to illuminate; mit Röntgenstrahlen, Radium rc. ≗ to light up with Röntgen rays, radium, &c.

durch-liegen (˝ˊ⌣): **sich ≗** *v/refl.* [74]** *path.* a. sich (*dat.*) die Haut ≗ to become bed-sore (or to contract bed-sores) by lying (too long).

durch-lochen ⚙ (ˊ˝ch⌣) *v/a.* [88]* to perforate, to punch (a. 🚂 e-e Fahrkarte ≗).

durch-löchern (ˊ˝⌣) **I** *v/a.* [92]a* to make holes (or openings) through, to perforate; 🚂 Fahrkarten rc.: to punch; ⚔ von Kugeln durchlö″chert riddled with bullets. — **II** ~ *n* [23] u. **Durch-löcherung** (ˊ˝⌣⌣) *f* [46] perforation.

durch-lüften (ˊ˝⌣) **I** *v/a.* [89]* to air well; to ventilate. — **II** ~ *n* [23] u. **Durch-lüftung** *f* [46] airing; ventilation.

Durch-lüftungs-gewebe ⚘ (″≗…) *n* [62] ventilating tissue.

durch-lügen (˝ˊ⌣): **sich ≗** *v/refl.* [76]d** to make one's way by lying or fraud.

durch-machen (˝ˊch⌣) *v/a.* [88]** **1.** = durchlöchern I. — **2.** (bis zu Ende tun) to pass through; alle Klassen ≗ (lassen) to go (to put) through a whole school-course. — **3.** (erleiden) to suffer hardship, to undergo fatigue, to experience changes; e-e Krankheit ≗ to go through (or to have) an illness; er hat schon viel Bitteres und Schweres du″rchgemacht he has had many bitter and unpleasant experiences.

Durch-marsch, bsd. ⚔ (˝ˊ) *m* [7]a. march(-ing) through; beim ~ von Truppen on the passing through of troops.

durch-marschieren (˝⌣ˊ⌣) *v/n.* (sn) [93]*/* to march through.

durch-mengen (˝ˊ⌣) *v/a.* [88]*(*) = durchmischen I.

durch-messen (˝ˊ⌣) *v/a.* [83]** **1.** to measure (right) through. — **2.** (meist ˊ˝⌣ [83]*) (durchschreiten) to pass (or walk, journey) through; to traverse.

Durch-messer (˝ˊ⌣) *m* [22] *math.* diameter; äußerer, innerer ~ outside, inside diameter; ⚔ *artill.* (Seelen-)~ caliber; *opt.* ~ eines Fernglases aperture of a telescope.

durch-mischen *v/a.* **I** (˝ˊ⌣) [91]** to mix (up) thoroughly, to blend well. — **II** (ˊ˝⌣) [91]* mit et. ≗ to mix up with s.th.

durch-müssen (˝ˊ⌣) *v/n.* (h.) [98]** to be obliged to pass (or go, travel) through.

durch-mustern (˝ˊ⌣) [92]a** u. (ˊ˝⌣) [92]a* *v/a.* to (pass in) review; to search through, to examine (or inspect, scan) closely, to scrutinize.

durch-nagen (˝ˊ⌣ u. ˊ˝⌣) *v/a.* und **sich ≗** *v/refl.* [88]** u. * to gnaw (or nibble, eat) one's way through, to make a hole by gnawing.

durch-nähen *v/a.* **1.** (˝ˊ⌣) [88]**: sich (*dat.*) die Finger ≗ to sew (or stitch) one's fingers sore. — **2.** (ˊ˝⌣) [88]* to quilt; durchnä″hte (gesteppte) Arbeit quilting.

durch-nässen (˝ˊ⌣) [90]** **I** (a. ˊ˝⌣ [90]*) *v/a.* to wet through, stärker: to soak, to drench; bis auf die Haut durchnä″ßt wet (or drenched) to the skin. — **II** *v/n.* (h.) to let the wet through.

durch-nehmen (˝ˊ⌣) *v/a.* [73]a** **1.** to go through a book; to get up Cæsar; to take the syntax through; to plod through Euclid; in der Klasse et. ≗ to treat (or deal with) s.th in class; Vergil mit Schülern ≗ to work with pupils through Virgil, to expound (or explain) Virgil to students. — **2.** *fig.* = durchhecheln 2.

durch-netzen (ˊ˝⌣) = durchnässen.

durch-örtern ⚒ (ˊ˝⌣) = durchfahren II.

Durch-paß, bsd. ⚔ (˝ˊ) *m* [8]a. defile.

durch-passieren (˝⌣ˊ⌣) *v/n.* (sn) [93]*/* to pass (or travel) through a place.

durch-pausen (˝ˊ⌣) *v/a.* [90]** to pounce; (durchzeichnen) to trace (through).

durch-peitschen (˝ˊ⌣) [91]** **I** *v/a.* **1.** to whip (or flog) well or soundly. — **2.** *fig.* (hastig durchnehmen) to hurry (or rush, fly) through; Geschäfte ≗ to dispatch … quickly. — **3.** (ˊ˝⌣) [91]* Regen durchpei″tscht die Luft rain is sweeping the air. — **II** ~ *n* [23] u. **Durch-peitschung** *f* [46] **4.** *parl.* ~ des Etats toiling through (or thrashing out) the budget.

durch-pfeifen (˝ˊ⌣) [80]b** **I** *v/a.* to whistle a tune (right) through). — **II** *v/n.* (h.) Wind: to blow through.

durch-pflügen (˝ˊ⌣ u. ˊ˝⌣) *v/a.* [88]** u. * to plough all over (= durchackern).

durch-pilgern (˝ˊ⌣) *v/n.* (h.) [92]a** u. (ˊ˝⌣) *v/a.* [92]a* to journey through.

durch-pressen (˝ˊ⌣) [90]** **I** *v/a.* to press through an opening. — **II sich ≗** *v/refl.* to squeeze one's way through.

durch-probieren (˝⌣ˊ⌣) *v/a.* [93]*/* **1.** to examine (or test) thoroughly, to try one after another. — **2.** ♪ = einüben 1. — **3.** = durchkosten.

durch-prügeln (˝ˊ⌣) *v/a.* [92]a**: e-n ≗ to beat (or thrash, tan, drub) soundly.

durch-queren (ˊ˝⌣) **I** *v/a.* [88]* to cross, to traverse (from end to end). — **II** ~ *n* [23] u. **Durch-querung** *f* [46]: ~ Afrikas journey(ing) across Africa.

durch-quetschen (˝ˊ⌣) *v/a.* [91]** to squeeze through, Kochk.: to strain through.

durch-radeln (˝ˊ⌣) *v/n.* (sn) [92]a** to cycle through, to pass (or ride) through on a cycle.

durch-rasen (˝ˊ⌣) [90]** **I** *v/n.* (sn) to run madly (or furiously) through. — **II** (mst ˊ˝⌣ *v/a.* [90]*) to race frantically through; to dispatch in mad haste; nach rasch durchra″stem Tanze (*G.*) after a fast and furious dance.

durch-rasseln (˝ˊ⌣) *v/n.* (sn) [92]a** to rumble (or rattle) through.

durch-räuchern (˝ˊ⌣) [92]a** u. (ˊ˝⌣) [92]a* *v/a.* to smoke meat thoroughly; bsd. behufs Desinfizierung: to fumigate a room.

durch-rauschen I (˝ˊ⌣) *v/n.* (h. u. sn) [91]** to rustle (or rush) through. — **II** (ˊ˝⌣) *v/a.* [91]* vom Winde: to pass through with a rustling sound, to rustle through, to rush (or sweep) through.

durch-rechnen (˝ˊ⌣ u. ˊ˝⌣) *v/a.* [92]b** u. * to calculate (or count) through; noch einmal ≗ to recast an account.

durch-regnen (˝ˊ⌣) [92]b** **I** *v/n. impers.* (h.) **1.** es regnet überall durch the rain is coming through everywhere. — **2.** es hat die ganze Nacht du″rchgeregnet it has rained all night. — **II** (a. ˊ˝⌣ [92]b*) *v/a.* **3.** ich bin ganz durch(ge)regnet the rain has soaked (or wetted) me through; sich ≗ lassen to expose o.s. to the soaking (or drenching) rain.

durch-reiben (˝ˊ⌣) *v/a.* [81]** **1.** to rub through; to wear out with rubbing or by friction; (reibend wund m.) to chafe the skin, to gall a horse, to rub one's hands, &c. sore; Kochkunst: to strain, to mash; durchgeriebene Kartoffeln mashed potatoes. — **2. sich ≗** *v/refl.* to rub (or ride) o.s. sore. — **3.** (a. ˊ˝⌣ [81]*) to rub all over; (massieren) to massage.

durch-reichen (˝ˊ⌣) [88]** **I** *v/a.* e-m et. ≗ to hand (or pass) across (or through) an opening. — **II** *v/n.* (h.) durch den Winter ≗ to suffice for (or to last through) the winter; damit werden wir ≗ we shall make that do, that will be sufficient (F will do) for us.

Durch-reise (˝ˊ⌣) *f* [48] journey (or travelling) through; auf unserer ~ durch Köln on our passing (or our way) through Cologne.

durch-reisen I (˝ˊ⌣) *v/n.* (sn) [90]** to journey (or pass, travel) through a town. — **II** (ˊ˝⌣) *v/a.* [90]* to traverse (or cross, explore, travel all over) a country. — **III** ~ *n* [23] = Durchreise. — **IV ≗d** *p.pr.* u. *a.* [66] passing through; **~de([r]** *m*) *f* [67] (through-)passenger.

durch-reißen (˝ˊ⌣) [80]a** **I** (a. ˊ˝⌣ [80]a*) *v/a.* to tear (or rend) asunder or in two; to break a thread. — **II** *v/n.* (sn) to tear (or be torn) asunder; to come in two (or apart); to break.

durch-reiten A. (˝ˊ⌣) [80]b** **I** *v/n.* (sn) to pass through (or to cross, to traverse) on horseback; to ride through. —

[durchrennen] — 283 — [Durchschnittsrechnung]

II v/a.: a) ein Pferd ⁂ to gall a horse by riding; Beinkleider: to wear out by riding; b) ein Pferd ⁂ (zureiten) to break in (or train)…; gut du"rchgeritten well (or thoroughly) broken in. — **III** sich ⁂ v/refl. (sich wund reiten) to chafe o.s. by riding. — **B.**(⁂)⊛b* **IV** v/a. to cross (or traverse) a country on horseback.

durch-rennen (⁂)⊛b** **I** v/n. (sn) 1. to run (or race) through a place. — **II** v/a. (a. ⁂⊛b*) 2. to run all over a place. — 3. mit e-r Waffe: to run a p. through with a lance or a spear or a sword.

durch-rieseln I (⁂) v/n (sn) ⊛a** 1. to glide (or flow) through with a bubbling sound or a soft murmur like a stream. — **II** (⁂) v/a. ⊛a* 2. to cross with a bubbling (or gurgling) noise. — 3. v/impers. es durchrieselt mich kalt I am seized with cold shivers; F I feel a cold shiver (or shudder) running through me or all over me.

durch-rinnen (⁂) v/n. (sn) ⊛b(a)** und (⁂) v/a. ⊛b(a)* = durchfließen.

Durch-ritt (⁂) m ⊛c. ride through.

durch-rollen A. (⁂) ⊛** **I** v/n (sn) to roll through the gate. — **II** v/a. Wäsche ⁂ to mangle… — **B.**(⁂) ⊛* **III** v/n. (h.) der Donner durchro"llt die Wolken the thunder rolls through …

durch-rücken (⁂) v/n. (sn) ⊛** von Truppen: to move (or march) through.

durch-rudern (⁂) ⊛a* **I** v/n. (sn) to row (or scull) through. — **II** v/a. sich (dat.) die Hände ⁂ to make one's hands sore with (or to rub off the skin of one's hands in) rowing or sculling.

durch-rütteln (⁂ u. ⁂) v/a. ⊛a** u.* to shake (up) well, to jolt well.

durchs (⁂) = durch das.

durch-sägen (⁂ u. ⁂) v/a. ⊛** u.* to saw through or across.

durch-salzen (⁂ u. ⁂) v/a. ⊛* u. * to salt thoroughly or well.

durch-säuern (⁂ u. ⁂) v/a. ⊛a** u. * 1. to make (thoroughly) sour; chm. to acidify, to make (or to mix with) acid. — 2. Teig: to leaven.

durch-säuseln (⁂) v/a. ⊛a* to murmur (or whisper) through.

durch-sausen (⁂ u. ⁂) v/n. (sn) u. v/a. ⊛** u. * = durchbrausen.

durch-schaben (⁂ u. ⁂) v/a. ⊛** u. * to scrape (or shave) through or sore.

durch-schaffen (⁂) v/a. ⊛** to convey (or get, carry, lug) through.

durch-schallen (⁂ u. ⁂) v/n. (sn) und v/a. ⊛ u. ⊛a** u. * = durchtönen.

durch-schauen I (⁂) v/n. (h.) ⊛** to look (or peep) through; vgl. durchblicken 1. — **II** (⁂) v/a. ⊛* to see through a p.; j-s Absichten auch: to read …; (herausfinden) to find out, to detect, discover, (un)fathom; to notice; ich kann seine Kniffe ⁂ I can see through his tricks or F what he is up to; vgl. durchblicken II.

durch-schauern (⁂) v/a. ⊛a* to fill (or thrill) with a shudder, to thrill.

durch-scheinen (⁂) v/n. (h.) ⊛** to shine (or let light) through; ⁂ transparent, translucent, diaphanous; schwach ⁂ semidiaphanous. — **II** (⁂) v/a. ⊛* to fill with (sun)light; vom Sonnenlicht durchschie"nen transfused with (or bathed in) sunlight, sunlit. **III** ~ n ⊛ (f. I) transparency, translucence, ⁂ diaphanousness, …eity.

durch-scherzen (⁂) v/a. ⊛* to spend one's time in jesting or joking.

durch-scheuern (⁂) v/a. ⊛a** = durchreiben. [(or forward) through.]

durch-schicken (⁂) v/a. ⊛** to send/

durch-schieben (⁂) v/a. ⊛c** to push (or shove) through; fig. (ausführen, fördern) to carry out, to push (forward).

durch-schießen I (⁂) v/n. ⊛c(es)t** 1. (h.) mit dem Gewehr ⁂ to shoot (or fire) through or across. — 2. (sn) (sich schnell hindurchbewegen) to pass rapidly through; vgl. durchblitzen I. — **II** (⁂) v/a. ⊛c(es)t* 3. to shoot through, to pierce with a dart or shot; von vielen Kugeln durchscho"ssen riddled with bullets. — 4. = durchblitzen II. — 5. ⊕ Buchbind.: mit Papier ⁂ to interleave, interfoliate; typ. (gesperrt drucken) to space out, to lead; vgl. durchschossen.

durch-schiffen I (⁂) v/n. (sn) ⊛** to sail (or navigate, steam) through. — **II** (⁂) v/a. ⊛* to traverse (or cross, navigate) the sea; to sail across the ocean; die Lüfte ⁂ to plough (or navigate) the air; vgl. durch…6.

durch-schimmern I (⁂) v/n. (h.) ⊛a** to (let a) glimmer through, to shine (or gleam) through; vgl. durch…1. — **II** (⁂) v/a. ⊛a* f. durch…5.

durch-schlafen (⁂ u. ⁂) v/a. ⊛a** u. * to sleep the night through; to sleep away a whole day; v. Tieren: den Winter ⁂ to hibernate.

Durch-schlag (⁂) m ⊕d. 1. ⊕ Werkzeug zum Lochen: punch(eon); Schlosserei: mandrel; vgl. Dorn 2. — 2. Kochkunst: (Sieb) colander, strainer. — 3. (Öffnung) opening, aperture; breach; for. cut (across); (Lichtung) glade.

Durch-schlag-eisen ⊕ (⁂) n ⊕ punch(eon); piercer; (Lochmeißel) mortise-chisel.

durch-schlagen I (⁂) v/a. (h.) u. v/refl. ⊛a** *. 1. to break (or pass) through; to penetrate; die Tinte ⁂ schlägt durch … soaks (or gets, wets) through; F das Papier schlägt durch … blots, runs; Papier, das nicht durchschlägt (glazed) paper which does not run. — 2. von Arzneien: pharm. to have effect; to operate on (or to open) the bowels. — 3. fig. to prove efficacious, to take effect; ⁂ efficacious, effective, powerful; e-n ⁂den Erfolg h. to have a telling (or decided) effect. — 4. (durchseihen) to strain (through); du"rchgeschlagene Kartoffeln mashed potatoes pl. — 5. sich ⁂ v/refl.: a) to fight (or battle) one's way through (the world); F to (have to) rough it; f. durch-…4; b) eng. sich kümmerlich (durchs Leben) ⁂ to earn (F to pick up) a scanty living; to lead a precarious existence, F to have an uphill fight; to support (F to shift for) o.s. — **II** (⁂) v/a. ⊛a* 6. to knock (a hole) through; to break through a wall; to pierce; e-n Faßboden ⁂ to stave in a cask; vgl. durchlöchern I. — **III** (⁂) ~ n ⊛ 7. (f. 1) das ~ der Nässe the getting through of the wet. — 8. (f. 2) das ~ e-r Arznei the good effect of …; e-s Planes: the (thorough) success of …

Durch-schlag-hammer (⁂…) m ⊛ drift.

Durch-schlags-kraft ⁂ f ⊕ eines Geschosses force of percussion, perforating effect.

durch-schlängeln I (⁂) v/a. ⊛a** to cross in a serpentine line. — **II** (⁂) sich ⁂ v/refl. ⊛a* to wind through; von Flüssen ⁊c. auch: to meander.

durch-schleichen I (⁂) v/n. (sn) u. sich ⁂ v/refl. ⊛a** to steal (or slink, sneak) through. — **II** (⁂) v/a. ⊛a* to pass (or convey) furtively through a place.

durch-schleppen (⁂) ⊛** **I** v/a. to drag (or pull) through (auch fig.). — **II** sich ⁂ v/refl. to drag o.s. along.

durch-schlingen v/a. **A.** (⁂) ⊛ft** einen Faden ⁂ to pass (or twist) a thread through. — **B.** (⁂) ⊛ft* to intertwine, to interlace (a. fig.).

durch-schlüpfen (⁂) v/n. ⊛** to slip through; (entwischen) to slip away, to get off; F to give people the slip; mit genauer Not ⁂ to have a narrow escape or F a narrow squeeze.

durch-schmecken (⁂) ⊛** **I** v/n. (h.) to (be discoverable by the) taste. — **II** v/a. to (discover by the) taste.

durch-schmettern (⁂) v/a. ⊛a* to fill with trumpet- (or bugle-)sound.

durch-schmuggeln (⁂) v/a. ⊛a** to smuggle through the custom-house.

durch-schneiden (⁂) ⊛c* **I** (mst ⁂ ⊛c**) v/a. 1. to cut across or through or in two; to sever (with a knife); mit der Säge: to saw through; fig. das durchschni"tt ihm das Herz it cut him to the very heart or to the quick. — 2. (kreuzen) to cross, traverse; ⁊ von Schienensträngen durchschni"tten intersected by railway-lines; math. eine Linie ⁂ to cut (or intersect) a line; ⚓ die Wellen ⁂ to cleave (or plough) the waves; ⁂ durchschni"tt(e)nes Gelände broken (or rough, uneven) ground. — **II** 3. sich ⁂ v/recip. to cross or intersect (one another). — **III** ~ n ⊛ u. **Durch-schneidung** f ⊛ 4. (f. 1) cutting through, &c. — 5. (f. 2) crossing; intersection.

durch-schneien (⁂) v/impers. ⊛** to snow through the chimney, &c.

Durch-schnitt (⁂) m ⊛c. 1. = durchschneiden III. — 2. = ~s-punkt. — 3. = Durchmesser. — 4. ⊕ (Lochmaschine) puncher, puncheon, punching machine. — 5. arch. (Riß) section, profile, plan. — 6. ⁂ (Mittelwert) average (amount); mean (between extremes); im ~ on an average; taking one with another; ⁂ in the lump, by the bulk.

durch-schnittlich I a. ⊛ average; of medium size or quality. — **II** adv. on an average, ordinarily (speaking).

Durch-schnitts-ansicht (⁂…) f ⊛ arch. profile; section(al drawing or view); -einkommen n, -ertrag m average income or revenue; -fläche f, geom. plane of intersection; -linie f, geom. line of intersection; -mensch m commonplace (or ordinary, every-day) person; -preis m average price; -prozente ⁂ n/pl. von Treffern beim Schießen: average percentage; -punkt m, math. point of intersection; -rechnung f, arith. (rules

pl. for finding) averages *pl.*; =ſatz *m* (rule for) finding the average, account of averages; =ſumme *f* average (sum); mean amount; =verhältnis *n* mean proportion; =wert *m* average (or mean) value; =zahl *f* average (number); mean (value); =zeichnung *f* =anſicht. [*v*/*a*. ⓐ*(*) to sniff (out).)

durch-ſchnüffeln,-ſchnuppern(ᵍᵒᵘ u. ᵒᵘ)

durch-ſchoſſen (ᵒᵘ) *a*. Ⓖ (D9) u. *p.p.* von durchſchießen II: Leß Buch interleaved ...; *typ.* Ler Satz spaced-out type.

durch-ſchreiten I (ᵍᵒᵘ) *v/n.* (ʃn) ⓑ** to stride (or step) through; ich bin du"rch=geſchritten I walked (or stepped) across. — **II** (ᵒᵘ) *v/a.* ⓑb* to cross (or traverse) on foot or with measured steps; ⚔ (†paſſieren) to pass (or march) through; ich habe den Fluß durch=ſchri"tten I waded through the river. — **III ~ *n*** ㉓ march (or walk) across.

Durch-ſchuß ⊕ ⓐ* [durchſchießen]*m* ⑧a.
1. Weberei: (Einſchlag) woof, weeft. —
2. *typ.* (leerer Raum zw. 2 Zeilen) interlinear space or blank; **~=kaſten** *m*, *typ.* lead-and-slug case; **~** (auch **~=linie** *f*, **~=ſtück** *n*) space-line, (pieced) leads *pl.*

durch-ſchüttel/n(ᵍᵒᵘ)*v/a.* ⓐa*(*)to shake (up) well; *fig.* vom Fieber, Froſt d/t (ᵒᵘ) shivering with fever, with cold.

durch-ſchütten (ᵍᵒᵘ) *v/a.* ⓑ** to pour through; (ſeihen) to strain (through).

durch-ſchüttern (ᵍᵒᵘ u. ᵒᵘ) *v/a.* ⓐa** u.* to shake (or agitate) violently.

durch-ſchwärmen (ᵍᵒᵘ) *v/n.* ⓑ** **1.** (ʃn) to swarm through. — **2.** (h.) e-e Nacht ⓛ to spend a night in revelry; to feast (or carouse, F booze) all night through.

durch-ſchweben (ᵍᵒᵘ) *v/n.* (ʃn) (ᵒᵘ) *v/a.* ⓑ* to float through.

durch-ſchweifen(ᵒᵘ)*v/a.* ⓑ** to roam (or range) through the country, &c., to ramble about the wood, &c., to cross a plain, &c. in all directions.

durch-ſchwelgen (ᵍᵒᵘ u. ᵒᵘ) *v/a.* ⓑ** u. ** to spend in feasting.

durch-ſchwimmen I(ᵍᵒᵘ)*v/n.*(ʃn)ⓐa(b)** to swim (von Dingen: to float) through or across. — **II** (ᵒᵘ) *v/a.* ⓐa(b)* to cross by (or in, while) swimming or floating, to swim across a river.

durch-ſchwirren I(ᵒᵘ)*v/a.*ⓑ** to fill with chirping (sounds) or with buzzing (noises); Gerüchte ⓛ die Luft rumours are filling the air, reports are being whispered about. — **II** (ᵍᵒᵘ) *v/n.* (ʃn) ⓑ** to whiz through.

durch-ſchwitzen (ᵍᵒᵘ) ⓐ** **I** *v/n.* (h.) ⓛ sweat through, ⚗ to transude; *fig.* v. Neuigkeiten ꝛc.: to ooze out. — **II** *v/a.* auch: (ᵒᵘ) ⓐ* to wet (or soak) with perspiration; durch(ge)ſchwitzt perspiring profusely or from every pore.

durch-ſegeln ⚓ (ᵍᵒᵘ) *v/n.* (ʃn) ⓐa** und (ᵒᵘ) *v/a.* ⓐa* to sail through or across; alle Meere ⓛ (ᵒᵘ) to navigate ...

durch-ſehen (ᵍᵒᵘ) ⓐa*. **I** *v/n.* (h.) ⓛ to see (or look) through; mit unperſönlichem Subjekt: die Ellenbogen ſehen durch ... are through; bei ihm ſehen die Ellenbogen durch he is out at elbows. — **II** (a. ᵍᵘᵒᵘ ⓐa*) *v/a.* prüfend: to look (or run) over; to examine; leſend: to read over, to peruse; bſd. *typ.* to revise;

verbeſſernd: to correct, to read the proofs; beſichtigend: to inspect; flüchtig: to glance over. — **III ~ *n*** ㉓ (ʃ. II) looking over; examination; perusal; revision (or correction) of proofs; inspection of papers, books, &c.

durch-ſeih/en (ᵍᵒᵘ) ⓑ** **I** *v/n.* (ʃn) = durchſickern 1. — **II** (a. ᵒᵘ ⓑ**) *v/a.* to strain (through), filter, percolate. — **III ~ *n*** ㉓ u. D/ung *f* ⓖ (ʃ. II) straining, filtering, filtration, percolation.

Durch-ſeiher (ᵍᵒᵘ) *m* ⓐ strainer, filter.

durch-ſein (ᵒᵘ) *v/n.* (ʃn) ⓐa** ſ. durch 5.

durch-ſenken ⚒ (ᵒᵘ) = durchſinken II.

durch-ſetzen A. (ᵍᵒᵘ) ⓖ** **I** *v/a.* **1.** (zu Ende führen) to carry through or out. —
2. *fig.* (durchführen) to (carry into) effect, mit Mühe oder Gewalt: to enforce; ich habe es du"rchgeſetzt I carried the day, I effected my purpose; ein Geſetz ꝛc. ⓛ to carry, to pass (or push) through; ſein Vorhaben ⓛ to achieve one's object, to carry one's point; ſeinen Willen mit Macht ⓛ to sweep everything before one; er wird (es) ⓛ, daß etwas geſchieht he will see that s.th. shall be done or insist on s.th. being done. —
3. *arch.* ein Haus ⓛ (durch eine Querwand teilen) to partition (off) by a wall; ⚒ Erz ⓛ (durch das Sieb ob. den Schmelzofen durchgehen I.) to screen the ore for smelting. — **II** *v/n.* (ʃn u. h.) **4.** to gallop (or hurry) through a place; ſchwimmend (watend): to swim (to wade) across.— **III ~ *n*** ㉓ **5.** = Durchſetzung.—

B. (ᵒᵘ) ⓖ** **IV** *v/a.* **6.** to mix; ⚒ durch-ſe"tzt (well) mineralized; interspersed with ore; das Geſtein iſt durchſe"tzt mit // the rock is interspersed with //; die Luft iſt mit Fäulniſſtoffen durchſe"tzt the air is vitiated with putrid matter.

Durch-ſetzung (ᵍᵒᵘ) *f* ⓖ carrying (through); enforcement; (Vollendung) achievement; accomplishment.

durch-ſeucht (ᵒᵘ) *a.* ⓖ vitiated, tainted.

durch-ſeufzen (ᵍᵒᵘ) *v/a.* ⓑ** ſ. durch=...8.

Durch-ſicht (ᵍᵒᵘ) *f* ⓖ **1.** view, perspective, vista. — **2.** = durchſehen III; ⚜ zur gefälligen ~ for your kind perusal or inspection, on approval.

durch-ſichtig (ᵍᵒᵘ) *a.* ⓖ transparent, pellucid; *phys.* pervious to light, ⚛ diaphanous; *fig.* (hell) clear, lucid; **~keit** (ᵍᵒᵘ=) *f* ⓖ transparency, pellucidity; ⚛ diaphanousness, diaphaneity; *fig.* clearness, lucidity.

Durch-ſichtigkeits-meſſer (ᵍᵒᵘ=...) *m* ⓖ für die Luft: ⚛ diaphanometer.

durch-ſickern (ᵍᵒᵘ) *v/n.* (ʃn)ⓐa** **1.** to ooze (or come, filter, trickle) through; to percolate. — **2.** *fig.* to ooze out.

durch-ſieben (ᵍᵒᵘ u. ᵒᵘ) ⓑ** u.* to sift, to (pass through a) sieve; Kohlen ꝛc.: to screen; Mehl: to bolt.

durch-ſingen (ᵍᵒᵘ) *v/a.* ⓑfſ** to sing through or to the end.

durch-ſinken I (ᵍᵒᵘ) *v/n.* (ʃn) ⓑfſ to sink through. — **II** (ᵒᵘ) *v/a.* ⓑ* ⚒ einen Schacht ⓛ to sink a shaft.

durch-ſinnen (ᵍᵒᵘ u. ᵒᵘ) ⓑ** u.* to think over; ein wohl durchſo"nnener Plan a well thought-out scheme.

durch-ſintern (ᵍᵒᵘ) *v n.* (ʃn) ⓑa** to ooze through (= durchſickern 1).

durch-ſitzen (ᵍᵒᵘ) ⓐ** **I** *v/a.* **1.** to wear out trousers by sitting. — **2.** to sit through a concert; eine Nacht (beim Spiel ꝛc.) ⓛ to sit up all night gambling. — **II** ſich ⓛ *v/refl.* **3.** to sit o.s. sore, to make o.s. sore with sitting.

durch-ſollen (ᵍᵒᵘ) *v/n.* (h.) ⓑ** *ell.* to be obliged (or to have) to pass through.

durch-ſonnen¹ (ᵍᵒᵘ) ⓑ* **I** *v/a. phot.* Platten ⓛ to solarize plates. — **II** ſich ⓛ *v/refl.* to bask in the sun(shine).

durch-ſonnen² (ᵍᵒᵘ) *p.p.* v. durchſinnen (ſ. dß). **I** = durchforſchen.

durch-ſpähen (ᵍᵒᵘ u. ᵒᵘ) *v/a.* ⓑ** u. *

durch-ſpalten (ᵍᵒᵘ u. ᵒᵘ) *v/a.* ⓑ** u. * to split in two; durchſpa"ltet riven.

durch-ſpellen (ᵍᵒᵘ) ⓑ** = durchſpalten

durch-ſpicken (ᵍᵒᵘ u. ᵒᵘ) *v/a.* ⓑ** u. * Kochkunſt: to interlard (auch *fig.*).

durch-ſpielen *v/a.* **A.** (ᵍᵒᵘ) ⓑ** **1.** to play through or from beginning to end (a. ♪); ♪ ein Stück zur Übung ⓛ to play a piece over; *thea.*, &c. eine Rolle ⓛ to play (or support, keep up) one's part to the end; Kartenſpiel: wir wollen noch einmal ⓛ let us have one round more; vgl. auch durch=... **2.** — **B.** (ᵒᵘ) ⓑ* **2.** to spend the night in (or to sit up all night) playing or gambling. — **3.** *poet.* ein ſanfter Hauch durchſpie"lt die Blätter a gentle breath whispers through the leaves. [to (pierce with a) spear.)

durch-ſpießen (ᵍᵒᵘ u. ᵒᵘ) *v/a.* ⓑ** u. *

durch-ſprechen (ᵍᵒᵘ) *v/a.* ⓐa** **1.** to speak (or talk) through; Fernſpr.: to (speak through the) telephone. — **2.** ein Gebet ꝛc. ⓛ to say (or repeat) ... to the end. — **3.** auch: (ᵒᵘ) ⓐa* (beſprechen) to discuss a th. (thoroughly), to debate a scheme, to talk matters over.

durch-ſprengen A. (ᵍᵒᵘ) ⓑ** **I** *v/n.* (ʃn)
1. to gallop through.— **II** *v/a.* ⊕ ⓛ **2.** einen Tunnel ⓛ to hollow out a tunnel by blasting. — **B.** (ᵒᵘ) ⓑ** **III** *v/a.* **3.** eine Strecke ⓛ to cross ... at full gallop or at full speed. — **4.** mit etwas ⓛ to besprinkle with s.th.; engS. (bunt m.) to variegate with s.th.

durch-ſpringen I (ᵍᵒᵘ) *v/n.* (ʃn) ⓑfſ**
1. durch einen Reifen ⓛ to skip (or leap, jump) through a hoop. — **2.** (einen Riß bekommen) to split, crack, burst (asunder). — **II** (ᵒᵘ) *v/a.* ⓑfſ* **3.** to cross with a leap or at one bound.

durch-ſpüren (ᵍᵒᵘ) *v/a.* ⓑ** **1.** (a. ᵍᵒᵘ ⓑ*) to search thoroughly (= durch-forſchen); *hunt.* to scour (or search) the wood for game. — **2.** = durchfühlen I.

durch-ſtechen A. (ᵍᵒᵘ) ⓑa* **I** *v/a.* = durchbohren II; mit dem Meſſer: to pierce; to run through; mit e-r Nadel: to prick through; durchſtochenes Muſter pricked drawing or pattern; ⊕ einen Damm ⓛ to cut (or dig through) a dike; der Damm wird durchſto"chen the dike is being cut; *agr.* Getreide ⓛ (mit der Schaufel umwenden) to turn over the grain. —

B. (ᵒᵘ) ⓐa** **II** *v/a.* eine Nadel durch et. ⓛ to pass a needle through a th.; die Nadel wird du"rchgeſtochen the needle is passed (or stuck) through; eine Zeichnung ⓛ (durchpauſen) to prick (or trace) a design. — **III** *v/n.* (h.) die Spitze ſticht durch the point passes

[Durchstecherei] — 285 — [durchwichsen]

(or has passed) through or goes (right) through; F faſt † mit-ea. ♃ to conspire (or plot) together; fig. (sich bemerklich machen) to become noticeable: ein fauliger Geruch sticht durch a putrid smell is to be noticed. — **IV** ~ n ㉓ (s. I) das ~ der Landenge von Suez the cutting of the isthmus of Suez.

Durch-stecherei F (⸗⸗‿‿) f ㊻ fig. (s. durchstechen III F) plotting, intriguing, sharp practices pl.; jur. collusion; mit e-m ~ treiben to play into a p.'s hands; to plot (or intrigue) with a p.

Durch-stechung (⸗‿)f㊻= durchstechen IV.

durch-stecken (⸗‿) v/a. ⓼** to pass (or put, run, stick) through.

durch-stehlen (⸗‿): sich ♃ v/refl. ㊲d** to steal (or sneak, slip) through.

durch-steigen I (⸗‿) v/n. (sn) ㉑** to get (or enter) through a window; to step through (or to enter; stärker: to storm) a breach. — **II** (⸗‿) v/a. ㉑* to cross (or pass through) in mounting.

durch-steppen (⸗‿ u. ‿⸗) v/a. ⓼** u. * to quilt (right through).

Durch-stich (⸗‿) m ⓽d. 1. = durchstechen IV. — 2. Straßenbau ꝛc.: (durchstochene Stelle) cut(ting), passage; excavation; 🚆 tunnel; (Graben) trench.

durch-sticken (⸗‿ u. ‿⸗) v/a. ⓼** u. * to cover with embroidery.

durch-stöber/n (‿⸗‿) **I** v/a. ⓶a * to ransack a house, to hunt through every corner, to scour the country; eine Schublade ♃ to rummage a drawer. — **II** ~ n ㉓ u. D/ung f ㊻ ransacking, &c., s. I.

durch-stochen (⸗‿ch) p.p. u. a. ㊽ (D9) v. durchstechen I.

durch-stopfen (⸗‿) v/a. ⓼** to stuff through, to ram (or press) through.

Durch-stoß ⊕(⸗‿) m ⓽a. = Durchschnitt 4.

durch-stoßen I (⸗‿) v/a. ⓶a** 1. to push (or thrust) through; to knock a hole through. — 2. Kleider durch langes Tragen: to wear out (at the bottom). — **II** (‿⸗‿) v/a. ⓶a** 3. = durchbohren II.

durch-strahlen I (⸗‿) v/n. (h.) ⓼** to radiate (or shine) through. — **II** (‿⸗‿) v/a. ⓼* to fill with radiant light; von der Sonne durchstrahlt resplendent (or lit up) with sunlight.

durch-streichen (⸗‿) v/a. ⓺aſt** 1. (a. ⸗‿) ⓺aſt* to strike out (= ausstreichen 1); durchgestrichen struck out. — 2. = durchstreifen 1; er hat das ganze Land durchstri"chen he travelled (or roamed) all over the country. — 3. die Lüfte ♃ das Tal the breezes blow through (or waft across) the valley; vom Winde durchstri"chen swept by the wind.

durch-streifen (⸗‿ u. ‿⸗) v/a. ⓼** u. * 1. to roam (or rove, wander, range) freely through a country. — 2. (mit Streifen versehen) to stripe; durchstrei"ft striped, streaked; ♣, ꝛo., &c. striate(d).

Durch-strich (⸗‿) m ⓽d. 1. [durchstreichen 1] stroke through a passage or a word. — 2. [durchstreichen 2] passage of birds.

durch-strömen I (⸗‿) v/n. (h.) ⓼** to flow (or run) through in a stream, to stream through. — **II** (‿⸗‿) v/a. ⓼* to flow across, weitS. to water (or irrigate) a plain; fig. v. Menschen ꝛc.: to crowd through (in dense masses).

durch-studieren (⸗‿‿) v/a. ⓽** 1. to study (or examine) thoroughly. — 2. die Nacht ♃ to spend the night in study, to study (or read) all night.

durch-stürmen I (‿⸗‿) v/n. (sn) ⓼** to storm (or rush) through. — **II** (‿⸗‿) v/a. ⓼** = I; von heftigen Winden durchstü"rmt swept by violent gales or storms; fig. von Leidenschaften durchstü"rmt agitated by stormy passions.

durch-stürzen (⸗‿) v/n. (sn) ⓽** to tumble (or fall) through.

durch-suchen (⸗‿ch u. ‿⸗ch) **I** v/a. ⓼** u. * 1. to search through; to examine (closely); vgl. durchstöbern. — 2. hunt. ein Revier ♃ to beat a cover. — **II** ~ n ㉓ = Durchsuchung. [searcher.]

Durch-sucher (⸗‿) m ㉒, ~in f ㊼

Durch-suchung (‿⸗‿ch) f㊻ search, searching, (close) examination; polizeilich: eines Hauses, oft: domiciliary visit; richterlicher Befehl dazu: search-warrant; ~s-recht n ㊷ right of search(ing).

durch-tändeln (⸗‿) v/a. ⓶a* to spend in dallying or toying; to trifle away.

durch-tanzen A. (⸗‿) ⓽** **I** v/n. (h. u. sn) to dance across a room. — **II.** v/a. einen Tanz ♃ to go through ...; sich (dat.) die Sohlen ♃ to wear out one's soles with dancing. — **B.** (‿⸗‿) ⓽** **III** v/a. to spend the night in dancing, to dance (all) through the night.

durch-taumeln I (⸗‿) v/n. (sn) ⓶a** to tumble through. — **II** (⸗‿) v/a. ⓶a* to spend in romping (about).

durch-teufen ⚒ (‿⸗‿) = durchsinken II.

durch-toben (‿⸗‿) v/a. ⓼* to pass (or spend) in a rage; die Nacht ♃ to rave all night.

durch-tönen (⸗‿) v/n. (h.) ⓼** to sound (or be audible) through a wall. — **II** (‿⸗‿) v/a. ⓼* to fill with sound.

durch-tosen (‿⸗‿) v/a. ⓽* to fill with roaring (sounds) or with uproar.

durch-tränken (‿⸗‿) v/a. ⓼*: mit et. ♃ to impregnate (or soak, steep) with s.th.

durch-träumen (⸗‿ u. ‿⸗) v/a. ⓼** u. * to dream away the time; to pass the hours in dreaming or in dreams.

durch-treiben I (⸗‿) v/a. ⓽** Vieh ♃ to drive cattle through; einen Pflock ♃ to run a plug through. — **II** (⸗‿) v/n. (sn) ⓽* † (durchstreifen) to roam; **durch-trieben** (‿⸗‿) p.p. u. a. s. bsd. Artikel.

durch-treten (⸗‿) ⓽d** **I** v/a. (abnutzen) to wear shoes through; (durchlöchern) to break through the ice, &c. by treading on it. — **II** v/n. (sn) (hindurchtreten) to step through; ⚔ (bem Vordermann folgen) to file (up) well; to cover each other in file. [through a funnel.]

durch-trichtern (⸗‿) v/a. ⓶a** to pour

Durch-trieb (⸗‿) m ⓽d. (right of) driving cattle through.

durch-trieben (‿⸗‿) a. ㊻ (D9) b.s. cunning, crafty, artful, smart, F knowing; ein Geselle sly fox; ♃er Schelm artful dodger, F deep card; (spitzbübisch) roguish, knavish; ~heit (‿⸗‿) f ㊻ cunning, craftiness, artfulness, smartness; roguery, knavery.

durch-triefen (⸗‿) ⓼e (㊼) ſt** u. **durch-tropfen** (⸗‿) ⓼** v/n. (sn) to drip (or trickle) through, to ooze (or sweat) through a wall.

durch-üben (⸗‿) v/a. ⓼** to practise (right) through; thea. to rehearse.

durch-wachen (⸗‿ u. ‿⸗‿) ⓼** u. * to watch through the night; bang durchwa"chte Zeit time of anxious watching, anxious vigil.

durch-wachsen A. (⸗‿) ⓼b** **I** v/n. (sn) to grow through a crevice, &c. — **B.** (‿⸗‿) ⓼b** **II** v/a. to mix thoroughly with; bsd. im p.p. und als a., z.B.: mit Fleisch ♃er Speck streaky bacon. — **III** p.p. u. a. ㊻ s. **II**; ♃ mit streaked with; ♣ perfoliate(d). [physis.]

Durch-wachsung (‿⸗‿) ♣ f ㊻ ⚭ dia-

durch-wagen (⸗‿): sich ♃ v/refl. ⓼** to venture (to pass) through a place.

durch-walken ⊕ (⸗‿ und ‿⸗) v/a. ⓼** u. * Tuchfabr.: to full (or mill) well; F fig. = durchprügeln.

durch-wallen I (⸗‿) v/n. (sn) ⓼** to wander through. — **II** (⸗‿) v/a. ⓼* to cross (or visit) on one's pilgrimage.

durch-wamsen F (⸗‿) v/a. ⓽** F to give a p. a (good) jacketing or hiding.

durch-wandeln (⸗‿ u. ‿⸗) v/n. (sn) u. v/a. ⓶a** u. * to walk (or pass, go) through.

durch-wandern I (⸗‿) v/n. (sn) u. (‿⸗‿) v/a. ⓶a** u. * to wander (or ramble, journey) through or across, to cross on foot. — **II** ~ n ㉓ und **Durch-wanderung** f㊻ rambles pl. (or journey) through; bisw. auch: peregrination.

durch-wärmen (⸗‿ u. ‿⸗‿) ⓼** u. * to warm through or thoroughly.

durch-waschen (⸗‿) ⓼b** 1. to wash one after another; F du"rchgewaschen (durchnäßt) F soaked through. — 2. sich (dat.) die Hände ♃ to wash one's hands sore, to make one's hands sore with washing. — 3. (a. ‿⸗‿) ⓼b*) bsd. im p.p., z.B.: von den Wellen durchwa"schen wave-tossed.

durch-wässern (⸗‿) v/a. ⓶a* 1. to water (or irrigate) well; Fleisch ꝛc.: to soak. — 2. (mit Wasser verdünnen) to mix with water, to dilute.

durch-watbar (⸗‿) a. ㊻ fordable.

durch-waten (⸗‿) v/n. (sn) u. (‿⸗‿) v/a. ㉑** u. * to wade through, to ford.

durch-weben v/a. (⸗‿) ⓼.㊲b** bsd. fig. to interweave, interlace, intermix (mit with); mit Redeblumen: to interlard.

Durch-weg¹ (⸗‿) m ⓽d. passage (or way) through. [(gewöhnlich) ordinarily.)

durch-weg² (⸗‿ u. ‿⸗) adv. through-out;

durch-wehen (⸗‿) **I** v/n. (h.) to blow through. — **II** v/a. (⸗‿ u. ‿⸗) ⓼* to fill with one's breath or blast; von Stürmen durchwe"ht swept by storms; fig. to pervade, inspire, instil.

durch-weichen (⸗‿ u. ‿⸗) ⓼** u. * **I** v/n. (sn) to become soft(ened) or wet. — **II** v/a. Wachs ꝛc.: to soften; durch Nässe: to soak, to wet through.

durch-weinen (⸗‿ u. ‿⸗) ⓼** u. * to spend in crying or weeping; kummervoll durch(ge)weinte Nacht night of sorrowful tears.

durch-werfen (⸗‿) ⓼b** to cast through; to hurl across.

durch-wettert (‿⸗‿) a. ㊻ weather-worn, -proof; well-seasoned; inured to rough weather. [durchprügeln.]

durch-wichsen F (⸗‿ch) v/a. ⓽** =

♪ Musik; ⚛ Wissenschaft; ❦ Pflanze; ♁ Geographie; ⊕ Technik; ⚒ Bergbau; ⚔ Militär; ⚓ Marine; ⚫ Handel; ✉ Post; 🚆 Eisenbahn.

[**durchwimmern**] **durch-wimmern** (ᛋᛋ᛫) v/a. ⓶a* to spend in moaning or whining.
durch-winden A. (ᛋᛋ᛫) ⓵** I v/a. to wind through. — **II.** ſich ⓶ v/refl. to work (or edge) one's way through a crowd; to struggle through a difficulty. — **B.** (ᛋᛋ᛫) ⓵* III v/a. to intertwine with.
durch-wintern (ᛋᛋ᛫) ⓶a** I (a. ᛋᛋ᛫ ⓶a*) v/a. to keep cattle, &c. through the winter; to winter plants, ⁊ to hibernate. — **II** v/n. (h.) to (pass the) winter. — **III** ~ n ㉓ u. **Durch-winterung** f ㊻ wintering, ⁊ hibernation.
durch-wirken I (ᛋᛋ᛫) v/a. ⓺** **1.** (durchweben) to interweave (mit et. with s.th.). — **2.** (durchbringen) to imbue (or saturate) with. — **II** (ᛋᛋ᛫) v/n. (h.) ⓺** **3.** (völlig wirken) to act well, to have good (or complete) effect.
durch-wischen F (ᛋᛋ᛫) ⓺** v/n. (ſn) to escape (durchſchlüpfen).
durch-wittert (ᛋᛋ᛫) p.p. u. a. ⓺ min. interspersed (or intermixed) with efflorescent minerals.
durch-wollen F (ᛋᛋ᛫) v/n. (h.) ⓺** to be wishing to pass (or go, get) through.
durch-wühlen (ᛋᛋ᛫) ⓺** I (a. ᛋᛋ᛫ ⓺*) v/a. to rake (or tear, grub, root) up the ground. — **II** ſich ⓶ v/refl. to burrow (or dig) through s.th.
Durch-wurf (ᛋᛋ᛫) m ⓵c. **1.** (ſ. durchwerfen) casting through. — **2.** ⊕ (grobes Sieb) screen, riddle; (Kornſieb) cribble.
durch-würzen (ᛋᛋ᛫) v/a. ⓺* to (fill with) perfume or scent, to make fragrant or aromatic, Speiſen: to spice well.
durch-zählen (ᛋᛌ᛫ u. ᛋᛌ᛫) I v/a. ⓺** u. * to count over, to enumerate. — **II** ~ n ㉓ enumeration.
durch-zechen (ᛋᛋ᛫ u. ᛋᛌ᛫) v/a. ⓺** u. * to spend in carousing; die Nacht ⓶ to drink (F booze) through the night.
durch-zeichn/en (ᛋᛌ᛫) I v/a. ⓶b** to trace (through transparent paper). — **II** ~ n ㉓ u. **D/ung** f ㊻ tracing; Papier zum ~ tracing-paper.
durch-ziehen A (ᛋᛌ᛫) ⓵b** I v/a. **1.** durch ein Loch: to draw (or pass) through a hole; einen Faden ⓶ to thread a needle; durch einen Raum bewegen: to pull (or drag) across … — **2.** e-e Linie ⓶ to draw a line through or across, to cross. — **3.** fig. e-n, etwas ⓶ = durchhecheln 2. — **II** ſich ⓶ v/refl. **4.** to extend (or run) through; to pervade. — **III** v/n. (ſn) **5.**: a) mit belebtem Subjekt: to pass (or travel) through a country; b) mit unbelebtem Subjekte: et. ⓶ (durchbringen) to penetrate (or soak) into a th. — **IV** ~ n ㉓ **6.** (ſ. IIIa) passage; ſ. Durchzug 2. — **B** (ᛋᛌ᛫) ⓵b* **V** v/a. **7.** (ſich durch et. hinziehen) to traverse; Wälder ⓶ das Land forests run through (or cover) the land. — **8.** (durchreiſen) to travel (or pass, march) through or across; ſie haben ganz Italien durchzo˝gen they travelled all through Italy. — **9.** faktitiv: mit et. ⓶ (durchbringen) to saturate (or soak through) with something; mit Furchen, mit Gräben ⓶ to furrow, to trench; Seidenzeug mit Gold- und Silber-fäden ⓶ to brocade silk. — **10.** a. v/refl.: das Papier durchzieht ſich mit Öl … soaks in (or absorbs) the oil.

durch-zittern (ᛋᛋ᛫) v/a. ⓶a* to (cause to) vibrate; bſd. fig. to thrill.
durch-zogen (ᛌᛌ᛫) p.p. von durchziehen B.
Durch-zoll (ᛋᛋ᛫) m ⓵c. = Durch-fuhr-zoll.
durch-zucken (ᛋᛋ᛫) v/a. ⓺* to flash through; bſp. fig. to convulse.
Durch-zug (ᛋᛌ᛫) m ⓵d. **1.** (zu durchziehen 1:) drawing through, &c. — **2.** (zu IV:) burch ein Land: journey (or march) through. — **3.** arch. (burchgezogener Balken) ⊕ girder, summer, ⁊ architrave.
Durchzugs-recht (ᛋᛌ᛫…) n ㉒ right of travelling (or passing, journeying) through; ⚔ right to march troops through a neighbouring country.
durch-zwängen ⓺**, **-zwingen** ⓵ft** (ᛋᛌ᛫) I v/a. to force through. — **II** ſich ⓶ v/refl. to squeeze o.s. through.
dürfen (᛫ᛌ᛫) [ahd.] I v/n. (h.) ⓺ **1.** (wagen) to dare, to venture to; ich darf es nicht tun I dare not do it. — **2.** (das Recht, die Erlaubnis haben) to have the power (or right) to; to be allowed to; to be at liberty to; wir ⓶ nicht we must not; darf ich Ihnen noch etwas Fleiſch anbieten? may I help you to a little more meat?; ich habe nicht ausgeh(e)n ⓶ I have not been allowed (or I had no permission) to go out; wenn ich bitten darf, a. darf ich bitten? please!; pray will you (kindly) …!; wenn ich ſo ſagen darf if I may so express myself; darf ich m-n Augen trauen? may I trust (or can I believe) my eyes?; Aufſchrift: hier darf nicht geraucht werden! smoking is not allowed, no smoking (allowed)!; ell. es darf niemand herein! no admission (except on business)!; F der Deckel darf nicht ab the lid must not come off. — **3.** mit Verneinung oder „nur" und inf.: ſie ⓶ ihn nicht fragen, weil ſie es ſchon wiſſen they have no need to ask him …; wir ⓶ es nur wünſchen, ſo geſchieht es we need only wish for it, and it is done; Sie ⓶ nur klatſchen, ſo kommt er ſchon if you only clap your hands he will come; er hätte nur telegraphieren ⓶ he need only have telegraphed, F if he had only sent a wire; wir ⓶ nur winken, ſo geſchieht's we have only to nod, and it is done. — **4.** (Grund haben) ſie ſich darüber ⓶ Sie ſich nicht wundern you must not be astonished at that; wir ⓶ es bezweifeln we have reason to doubt it. — **5.** (mögen, können) höflich einleitend: das dürfte kaum ſo leicht ſein, wie er ſagt it's probably (or I dare say it is) not quite as easy as he says; man darf wohl erwarten, daß // it is to be expected that // — **II** ~ n ㉓ **6.** permission. [**dürfen**.]
dürfte ind., **dürfte** subj. (ᛌ᛫) impf. von
dürftig (ᛌ᛫) [ahd.] a. ⓺ **1.** (barbend) indigent, needy, necessitous. — **2.** fig. (ungenügend) insufficient, inadequate; (gering) scanty, paltry, insignificant, F poor; e-s Ergebnis a meagre result.
Dürftigkeit (ᛌ᛫…) f ㊻ (ſ. dürftig) **1.** indigence, need(iness), penury, want. — **2.** insufficiency, inadequacy; scantiness; meagreness.

Dürlitz(e) ⚘ (᛫ᛌ(᛫)) [ſlaw.] f ㊻ (㊽) = Hartriegel.
dürr (᛫) [ahd.: Darre, dorren] a. ⓺ **1.** (trocken, welk) dry (wood); parched (soil); arid (zone); barren (land); withered (plant); dead (tree); poet. sear (leaf). — **2.** (mager) lean, thin, fleshless, F (long and) lanky; (eingeſchrumpft) shrunken (form), shrivelled (up) (hag); weazen (face); ⓶e Beine F (pair of) broomsticks pl.; ⓶e Perſon, F ⓶es Gerippe (mere) skeleton, (nothing but) skin and bones. — **3.** fig. bare, unadorned; mit ⓶en Worten in plain words or language; plainly, bluntly.
Durra ⚘ (᛫) [ar.] f ㊻, a. ~-**gras** n ⓺ (Mohrenhirſe) d(h)urra (Sorghum vulgare).
Dürre (ᛌ᛫) [ahd.] f ㊻ (ſ. dürr) **1.** (ant. Feuchtigkeit) dryness, aridness, aridity; barrenness; (Regenmangel) drought. — **2.** (ant. Dicke) leanness, shrunkenness.
Dürr-erze ⚒ (᛫…) n/pl. dry silver-ores pl.; **-futter**, **-heu** n dry fodder, hay; ⓶leibig a. ⓺ = dürr 2; **-ſucht** f, path. ⁊ atrophy; **-wurz** ⚘ f ㊻ conyza (Inula Conyza); blaue ~ = Berufskraut.
Durſt (᛫) [ahd.: thirst; * dürr] m ⓵b. thirst(iness); path. krankhafter ~: dipsosis; ~ haben to be thirsty; ~ auf ein Glas Bier haben to thirst (or long) for a glass of beer; ſeinen ~ löſchen to quench (or slake) one's thirst; e-m Durſt machen to make a p. thirsty; gern einen über den ~ trinken to be addicted to drink or fond of one's drops or fond of tippling; fig. ~ nach Ehre thirsting after glory; ~ nach Ruhm craving for glory.
durſten, bſſ. **dürſten** (ᛌ᛫) v/n. (h.) ⓺ to be thirsty; v/impers. es dürſtet mich ober mich dürſtet I feel thirsty; fig. to be thirsting (or longing, hankering) for; bibl. nach Gerechtigkeit ⓶ to thirst after righteousness.
durſtig (ᛌ᛫) [ahd.] a. ⓺ **1.** thirsty; ⓶e Seele, ⓶er Bruder, oft co.: thirsty soul; tippler; ⓶ ſein = dürſten; faktitiv: ⓶es (durſt-erregendes) Wetter thirsty weather. — **2.** fig. (begierig) thirsting after or for, eager for, longing for.
durſt-löſchend (᛫…) a. ⓺, ⓶**ſtillend** a. quenching the thirst; **-löſcher** m thirst-quencher. [major key, scale.]
Dur-ton-art (᛫…) f ㉒, **-tonleiter** f
dus (᛫) [: dusk: düſter] a. ⓺ **1.** (trüb) dull. — **2.** (leiſe, ſchüchtern) gentle, timid.
Duſch-bad (ᛌ᛫) n, **Duſche** (ᛌ᛫) [fr. douche] f ㊻ douche, shower-bath; vgl. Brauſe.
duſchen (ᛌ᛫) [Duſche] v/a. u. v/n. (h.) ⓶ to douche, v/n. a. to have a douche.
Düſe ⚒ (ᛌ᛫) f ㊻ (Blaſrohr bei Schmelzöfen) blast-pipe of a smelting furnace.
Duſel F (ᛌ᛫) [nbb.: dizzy, doze] m ㉒ (Schwindel) dizziness; (Halbſchlaf) stupor, (Träumerei) dreaminess; burſch. (unverbientes Glück) pure luck, windfall; ~-ei F (᛫᛫᛫) f ㊻ (Schläfrigkeit) sleepiness; (Gedankenloſigkeit) thoughtlessness; ⓶ig F (ᛌ᛫…) a. (träumeriſch) dreamy, sleepy; (dumm) silly, stupid; (betäubt) dizzy; ~-igkeit F (ᛌ᛫…) f ㊻ silliness.
duſeln F (ᛌ᛫) v/n. (h.) ⓶a. (ſ. Duſel) to be dizzy, sleepy or stupid.
düſig (ᛌ᛫) a ⓺ = dieſig.

Signs (see page XVII): F familiar; P vulgar; Γ flash; ⚹ rare; † obsolete (died); * new word (born); ++ incorrect; ♪ music;

Duft (´) [ndd.] *m* [11]b. (Staub) dust.

düster (´˘) [ndd.] **I** *a.* [66] (D9) **1.** (finster, dunkel, trübe) dark, gloomy, dusky. — **2.** *fig.* (traurig) sad, sullen, mournful, melancholy; (trübe) dim; ≗e Farben *f/pl.* dull (sombre) colours *pl.*; sich ≗e Gedanken machen to have sad thoughts; ≗es Schweigen gloomy silence. — **II** ~ *n* [22] **3.** darkness, gloom, dusk.

Düster(n)heit, Düsterkeit (´˘-) *f* [46] darkness, gloom = düster II; *fig.* sullenness, melancholy.

düstern (´˘) *v/n.* (h.) [92]a. to be (or grow) dark or dusky; auch *v/impers.* **es** düstert schon the dusk is setting in.

Düsternis (´˘˘) *f* [18] darkness.

☞ **Düte** (´˘) **rc.** s. Tüte rc.

Dutte bayr. (´˘) [ahd.] *f* [48] (Zitze) teat.

Dutzend (´˘) [mhd.; * fr. *douzaine f*] *n* [11]e, 6. dozen; ein ~ Gläser a dozen (↘ of) glasses; ein ~ guter Stahlfedern (*gen.*) kostet (od. ein ~ gute St. [*nom.*] **kosten**) 20 ₰ a dozen good nibs cost twopence halfpenny; zwölf ~ machen ein Gros twelve dozen make a gross.

dutzende=mal (´˘˘´) *adv.* (several or some) dozens of times.

Dutzend=gesicht (´˘...) *n* [62] ordinary face; ≗**mal**: ein ≗ a dozen times; =**mensch** *m* average person, ordinary individual, commonplace fellow; =**preis** *m* price by the dozen; ≗**weise** *adv.* by the dozen.

Duumvir (-´w˘) [lt.] *m* [36] Alt.: duumvir; ~**at** (-˘w˘´) [lt.] *n* [11]c. duumvirate.

Duz=bruder (´´...) *m* [62] friend whom one addresses with "thou", weitS. (boon-) companion; ⸢ chum, pal.

duzen (´˘) [mhd.; * du] *v/a.* (u. **sich** ≗ *v/recip.*) [90] to call a p. (one another) „thou"; ehm.: to (thee and) thou.

Duz=fuß (´´...) *m* [62] (boon-)companionship indicated by "thou"; auf dem ~(e) steh(e)n to be on intimate terms; =**schwester** *f* lady friend addressed with "thou"; vgl. =bruder.

dwars ⚓ (´) *adv.* (quer) athwart; ≗ See liegen to stand athwart the waves; ~=**kurs** † *m* loxodromic course; ~=**saling** ⚓ *f* (Querbaum) cross-tree.

Dwei(de)l ⚓ (´˘) [ndd. = Zwehle: towel] *m* [22] mop, swab.

Dyade ⚗ (-´˘) [grch.] *f* [48] (Zweiheit, Zweizahl, *chm.* zwei-atomiges Element) dyad.

Dyas ⚗ (´˘) [grch.] *f* (*sg. inv., pl.* Dya'den) *chm.* dyad (= Dyade); ~=**formation** (´´˘...) *f* [62] *geol.* Permian formation.

Dyn ⚗ (´) *n* [11]c. = Dyne.

Dynamik ⚗ (˘´˘) [grch.] *f* [46] *phys.*, &c. (Kraft=, Bewegungs-lehre) dynamics; **dynamisch** (˘´˘) *a.* [66] dynamic, dynamical.

Dynamit (˘˘´) [(Nobel, 1867) grch.] *n* († *m*) [11]c. *chm.* u. ⚙ (Sprengstoff) dynamite.

Dynamit=attentat (´´...) *n* [62] dynamite attempt; =**bombe** *f* dynamite bomb; =**fabrik** *f* dyn. works *pl.*; =**ladung** *f* dyn. charge; =**patrone** *f* dyn. cartridge; =**verbrechen** *n* dyn. outrage; =**verbrecher** *m* dynamiter. [schine.)}

Dynamo (´˘-) *m* [51] dynamo (= ~=ma-}

Dynamo=haus ⚙ (´´˘-... u. ´˘-...) *n* [62] dynamo shed; =**maschine** *f* (Siemens, 1867) dynamo-electric machine, dynamo (machine); =**meter** *n* (*m*) *phys.* (Kraftmesser) dynamometer; ≗**metrisch** *a.* [66] dynamometric, dynamometrical; =**technik** *f* dynamo technics.

Dynast (˘´) [grch.] *m* [42] (Herrscher) dynast, ruler; ~**ie** (˘˘´) *f* [48] (Herschergeschlecht) dynasty; ≗**isch** (˘´˘) *a.* [66] dynastic(al).

Dyne ⚗ (´-) [grch.] *f* [48] (Kraft-einheit, in England: Fußpfund) *mech.* foot-pound, ⚗ dynam, dyne.

Dysenterie ⚗ (˘˘˘´) [grch.] *f* [48] *path.* (rote Ruhr) dysentery.

dz *abbr.* = Doppelzentner, s. S. XXXIX.

D=Zug *abbr.* = Durchgangszug (s. ds).

E

E, e[1] (´, s. S. X) *n, inv.* (a. [51]) (Buchstabe) E, e. [E=Moll E minor.}

E, e ♪ *n, inv.* E, e; E=Dur E major;}

e[2] (´) *int.* = ä und eh[1].

Eau de Cologne (o-d'kŏ-lŏ'nj) [fr.] *f, n* = Kölnisch(es W.)=wasser.

Ebb=... ⚓ (´...) [62] s. Ebbe=...

Ebbe ⚓ (´˘) [ndd.: ebb] *f* [48] (*ant.* **Flut**) ebb(-tide); ~ und Flut high tide and low tide, ebbing and flowing tide, *fig.* ebb and flow; vgl. Nippflut; es tritt ~ ein the tide is going out or receding; es ist ~ the tide is out or down, it is low tide or water; Fluß, Hafen mit ~ und Flut tidal river, harbour; *fig.* es ist ~ in seinem Geldbeutel his funds are very low or at a low ebb, ⸢ he's in low waters. [anchor.}

Ebb(e)=anker ⚓ (´(˘)...) *m* [62] ebb-}

ebben (´˘) *v/n.* und *v/impers.* (h.) [88] **1.** ⚓ das Meer (oder **es**) ebbt it is ebb-tide or low water, the tide is (going) out or receding or subsiding or low. — **2.** *fig.* (sich verlaufen) to run down, to ebb away, to subside.

Ebb(e)=tor (´(˘)...) *n* [62] (inneres Tor einer Schleuse in Seehäfen) tail-gate, aft-gate; =**zeit** ⚓ *f* ebb-tide.

ebd. *abbr.* = ebenda(selbst).

eben[1] (´˘) [ahd.: even] **I** *a.* [66] (D9) **1.** even, uniform; (glatt) smooth; (flach) level, plain; *math.* plane (angle, geometry, &c.); (zu) ≗er Erde on the ground-floor; ≗en Fußes on the same floor or level; ≗es Gelände level ground, flat surface; ≗es Land open country; ≗ machen to level (down). — **2.** *fig.* (passend) convenient, fit, suitable, agreeable; kein Mensch ist ihm ≗ nobody is to his liking. — **II** *adv.* **3.** (gerade) er kam ≗ recht he came at the (very) nick of time; ⸢ ... just right or in time; ≗ wie just like; vgl. ≗da..., ≗der(=die)selbe, ≗dieser, ≗so. — **4.** (genau, just) exactly, precisely; das wollte ich ≗ (sagen) that's just what I wanted (to say); das (wohl nun) ≗ nicht! not exactly that!, not quite so!; ich will ≗ nicht versprechen I won't really promise; das will er (ja) ≗ vermeiden that's just what he wants to avoid; schwach verstärkend: nicht ≗ frisch, allzugut, allzuviel not very (or not particularly) fresh, good, much; vgl. ≗deshalb, ≗deswegen. — **5.** (knapp reichend) barely; nur so ≗ only just (enough). — **6.** zeitlich: ≗ damals just at that time; ≗ erst only just now, just a minute ago; da kommt er ≗ there he comes, he is just coming; er ist (so) ≗ gekommen he has only just come; ≗ wollte ich ihn rufen I was just going to call him; ein Knabe, der ≗ die Schule verlassen hat a boy fresh from (or who has just left) school; ≗ genannt s. ≗=genannt.

Eben[2]**=baum** (´´˘...) [ahd.; * hebr. *eben* Stein] *m* [62] = Ebenholzbaum.

Eben[1]**=bild** (´´˘...) *n* [62] (exact) likeness, bsd. *bibl.* image; **das** ~ der Mutter the very picture ...; ≗**bürtig** *a.* [66] of equal birth or rank; er ist ihm nicht ≗ ... not his equal or his peer. ⸢ ... not a patch on him; =**bürtigkeit** *f* equality of birth or rank; ≗**da(selbst)** at the very (same) place, (lt.) *ibidem*; ≗**daher** (≗**dahin**) *adv.* from (to) the very (same) place; ≗**der=**, ≗**die=**, ≗**das(selbe)** *dem. pron.* the very same (person, thing); ≗**deshalb**, ≗**deswegen** *adv.* on that (very) account, for that (very) reason; ≗**dieser** *dem. pron.* this very person, this same individual.

Ebene (´˘˘) [ahd.] *f* [48] ♁ plain, level (or flat) ground; *math.* plane (surface); schiefe ~ inclined plane; in gleicher ~ mit on a level with, ⚙ flush with.

ebenen (´˘˘) [88] s. ebnen.

ebener=maßen s. ebnermaßen.

eben[1]**=falls** (´´˘´) *adv.* likewise, also; ≗**genannt** *a.* [66] previously mentioned.

Ebenheit (´˘-) [s. eben[1]] *f* [46] evenness, uniformity, &c. (s. eben[1]).

Eben[2]**holz** (´´˘´) *n* [62]: a) ebony wood; b) *fig.* (Neger) bit (or piece) of ebony; ≗=**artig** *a.* [66] like ebony; ~=**baum** ⚘ *m* [62] ebony(-tree) (*Diospy'ros e'benum*); ~=**kiste** *f* ebony case or box; ~=**tischler** *m* ebonist, weitS. cabinet-maker; ≗**en** *a.* of ebony.

ebenieren (-˘´˘) [Eben(holz)] *v/a.* [93] Kunst: to inlay with ebony.

Eben[1]**=maß** (´´˘...) *n* [62] symmetry, harmony, right proportion; ins ~ bringen to harmonize; ≗**mäßig** *a.* [66] symmetrical, proportionate.

ebenso (´´˘´) (mit *a.* getrennt, mit *adv.* zs.=geschrieben) just so; sie ist ≗ (in demselben Grade) reich als schön she is as rich as she is fair; es ist ganz ≗ (in derselben Weise) wie // it is just the same as if //; das wäre ≗ **gut** it would do quite as well; ≗=**lange** just as long; ≗=**oft** just as often; ≗=**sehr**, ≗=**viel** just as much; es kostet ≗ viel it costs just as much, the price is just the same; ≗ **viele** *pl.* just as many; ≗=**wenig(e** *pl.*) just as little (few); ≗=**wohl** quite as well.

⚗ scientific; ⚘ botanical; ♁ geography; ⚙ machinery; ⚒ mining; ⚔ military; ⚓ marine; ⚜ commercial; ✉ postal; 🚂 railway.

[Ebenstrauß] — 288 — [Edelschule]

Eben-strauß (⌣⌢⌣⌣) m = Doldentraube.
Ebnung (⌣⌣) f. Ebnung.
Eber (⌣⌣) [ahd.: lt. *aper*] m ⓶ wild boar (*Sus scrofa*); junger ~ a. boar-pig.
Eber-esche ⚘ (⌣⌣...) [nhd.] f ⓶ mountain-ash (*Sorbus aucuparia*); zahme ~ = Speierling; **-fleisch** m brawn; **-hard** (⌣⌣) npr/m.⓵⓺α., ⓹⓸α.(Bn.) Everard; **-jagd** f boar hunt; **-raute** f, **-reis** n southern wood (*Artemisia abrotanum*); **-wurz** ⚘ f carline thistle (*Carlina*); **-wurz-öl** n carline-oil.
ebnen (⌣⌣) v/a. und sich ⓶ v/refl. ⓶b. to level, to flatten; to roll a path, to smooth (down) obstacles; Bauholz ꝛc. to square; Steine: to face; *fig.* e-m die Bahn ⓶ to pave (or smooth) the way for a p.
ebner-maßen (⌣⌣⌣⌣) *adv.* likewise.
Ebnung (⌣⌣) f ⓸⓺ levelling. [ebonite.]
Ebonit a (⌣⌢⌣) [It.:*Eben(holz)] n ⓶c.chm.
☛**Ebräer** (⌣⌢⌣) ꝛc. f. Hebräer ꝛc.
Ebresche ⚘ (⌣⌣) f ⓶ = Eberesche.
Echelon (⌣ʃʃ⌃ɪQ⌣) [fr.] m ⓶⓰ (Staffel)echelon.
echelonieren ⨯⨯ (⌣ʃʃ⌣⌣⌣) v/a. ⓸⓺ (staffeln) to draw up in echelon formation.
Echinit a (⌣⌢⌣) [grch.] m ⓶c. u. ⓶ *geol.* (versteinerter See-igel) echinite. [häuter.]
Echinodermen a (⌣⌣⌣⌣) *pl.* = Stachel-
Echinokokkus a (⌣⌣⌣⌣) [lt., *grch.] m ⓶⓻ (Bandwurm) echinococcus (*Taenia echinococcus*). [oval moulding.]
Echinus a (⌣⌣) [grch.] m, *inv. arch.*
Echo (⌣⌣) [grch.-¹] n ⓺⓪ (Widerhall) echo (a. ♪ u. *fig.*); ein ~ (er)wecken to awaken an echo; ein ~ geben to (re-)echo.
echo-artig (⌣...) a. ⓺⓺ u. *adv.* echo-like.
echo-en (⌣⌣⌣) v/n. (h.) ⓸⓼ to (re-)echo; to reverberate, to resound.
Echo-zug ♪ (⌣⌣...) m ⓶ einer Orgel: echo-key. [f zo. lizard.]
Echse (⌣tʃ⌣) [+v.Often 1836 aus (Gi-d)echse]
echt (⌣) [nhd.: eh-haft; * Ehe] a. ⓺⓺ genuine; (wahr) true; (unverfälscht) unadulterated, pure; (wirklich) real; 2er Diamant real (or pure) diamond; 2er Erbe legitimate heir; 2er Freund stanch friend; 2es Gold sterling gold; 2e Urkunde authentic deed; 2er Wert intrinsic value or merit; ⓾ der 2e Artikel, *oft*: F the real thing or stuff; ein 2er Engländer a regular (in geh. Spr.: a true-born) Englishman; 2es (ant. falsches) Haar natural hair; ihr Haar ist 2 it is her own hair, she wears no false hair; von 2em Schrot und Korn thoroughly genuine or reliable, *pol.* very loyal, true blue.
Echt-blau (⌣⌣...) n ⓺⓻ chm. Anilinfarbe: induline; **-gelb** n Azofarbe: fast yellow.
Echt-heit (⌣⌣) f ⓸⓺ (f. echt) genuineness; purity, pureness; sterling quality; authenticity; ⓾ die ~ von et. verbürgen to guarantee (or warrant) a th. as a genuine (or the real, the true) article.
Echt-rot (⌣⌣...) n ⓺⓶ chm. Azofarbe: fast red, Roccellin; **-scharlach** m chm. Meister's scarlet, *auch*: scarlet G.
Eck (⌣) [f. Ecke] n ⓶c. 1. in Zssgn, z.B. Vier-2 quadrangle; Sechs-2 hexagon. — 2. *adv.* über ~: a) across; F crosswise: b) et. über ~ bringen (fortschaffen) to get a th. out of the way.
Eck-balken ⊙ (⌣⌣...) m ⓶ *carp.* corner-post or -beam; **-ball** m, Fußball: corner-

kick; **-blatt** n, *arch.* base-edge ornament; **-brett** n bracket, (corner-)shelf.
Eckchen (⌣⌣) n ⓶⓷ (*dim. von* Ecke) little nook or corner.
Ecke (⌣⌣) [ahd.: edge] f ⓸⓼ 1. (spitzer Punkt) angle; (Kante) edge; (Winkel) corner (a. i. Fußballspiel); e-r Stube *auch*: nook; Mauer:) ~ *arch.* quoin; (Ende) end; um die ~ biegen to turn (round) the corner; biegen Sie rechts um die erste ~ take the first turning to the right or on your right; sich in eine ~ drücken to crouch in(to) a corner; die ~ e-s Blattes umschlagen to turn down the corner of a leaf. — 2. *math.* körperliche oder räumliche ~ (wo drei oder mehr Ebenen zs.-treffen) solid angle. — 3. *fig.* bläst der Wind aus der ~? is that how matters stand?; is that the way the wind blows?; sie kamen von allen ~n und Enden they came from every quarter; F einen ob. et. um die ~ bringen to put a p. or a th. out of sight or out of the way; F um die ~ (zugrunde) geh(e)n to perish, F to go to the dogs; F ich traue ihm nicht um die ~ I don't trust him out of my sight. — 4. (kurzer Weg) short distance; (a) little way; ich will eine ~ mit Ihnen geh(e)n I'll see you to the (next) corner.
ecken (⌣⌣) v/a. ⓸⓺ to shape like (or to form into) an angle.
Ecken-rundstoßmaschine ⊙ (⌣⌣...) f ⓶ Buchbinderei: cornering-machine; **-steher** m man at the corner, corner-man; (Dienstmann) commissionaire, runner; (Träger) porter; (Bummler) loafer.
Ecker (⌣⌣) [ndd.: acorn] f ⓸⓼ 1. = Buch-ecker, Eichel(mast *coll.*). — 2. ~n *pl.* Kartenspiel: clubs *pl.*
Ecker-..., ecker-... (⌣⌣) in Zssgn = Eichel-...
Eck-fenster (⌣...) n ⓺⓶ corner-window; **-first** ⊙ m, f, *carp.* corner-rafter; **-hip; -flügler** m, *ent.* a vanessa; **-haus** n corner-house; **-hölzer** n/pl. (Kantholzer) square(d) timber *sg.*
eckig (⌣⌣) a. ⓺⓺ 1. angular (vgl. drei- ꝛc. 2; in Zssgn *auch*: ...gonal, z.B. sechs-2 hexagonal; vgl. Eck); *bsd.* F cornered (*auch in* Zssgn, z.B. fünf-2 five-cornered); *typ.* 2e Klammer bracket. — 2. *fig.* (unbeholfen) awkward, clumsy, stiff; (ungeschliffen) uncouth, unpolished.
Eckigkeit (⌣⌣) f ⓸⓺ (f. eckig) angularity; *fig.* awkwardness; uncouthness.
Eck-kegel (⌣...) m ⓶ Kegelspiel: corner-pin; **-knollen** m, *arch.* = **-blatt; -laden** m corner-shop.
Eck-lein (⌣⌣) n ⓶⓷ = Eckchen.
Eck-loch (⌣...) n ⓺⓶ corner-hole, Billard: pocket; **-pfeiler, -pfosten** m, **-säule** f ⊙ *arch.* corner-pillar, quoin, *vgl.* **-balken; -schrank** m, **-schränkchen** n, **-spind(chen)** n corner-cupboard, cupboard fitted in(to) a corner; **-schupper** m, *ichth.* a ganoid; **-stein** ⊙ m, *arch.* corner-stone; (Preßstein) curbstone; (Grenzstein) boundary-stone; Kartenspiel: diamond; ~ Dame queen of diamonds; **-stollen** ⊙, *carp.* corner-foot; **-stoß** m = **-ball; -stube** f, **-stübchen** n = **-zimmer; -zahn** m canine tooth; **-zierat** ⊙ m (f), *arch.* corner-ornament; **-zimmer** n corner-room, (Erker) alcove.

ed. *abbr.* = edidit [lt. hat (es) herausgegeben] published by //.
Ed. *abbr.* = editio [lt. Ausgabe] edition.
Edamer (⌣⌣) [Edam ⚑ ndl. St.] a. *inv.* ~ Käse Edam (weitS. Dutch) cheese.
Edda (⌣⌣) [isländ.Urgroßmutter] f⓺⓺(Sammlung altnordischer Sagen) Edda; **-lieder** (⌣⌣...) n/pl. ⓺⓶ songs *pl.* of the Edda; zur ~ gehörig (a. **eddisch** a. ⓺⓺) Eddaic.
edel (⌣⌣) [ahd.; *Adel] I a. ⓺⓺(D 8, 9) 1. noble; von edler Abstammung, von edelm Blut of noble (or high) descent or birth, of gentle blood; ein Pferd von edler Rasse a thorough-bred horse, &c.; von edelm Gemüte, Sinn noble-minded; edle Sinnesart lofty (or magnanimous) mind. — 2. ✕ ein edler Gang a rich lode; *physiol.* die edle(re)n Körperteile the vital organs *pl.* (of the body); *chm.* edle (bei Oxydation widerstehende) Metalle n/pl. precious metals *pl.* — II **Edle([r]** m) f ⓺ 3. nobleman (f lady of noble birth or titled lady); die Edeln (Edlen) the nobility; (der niedere Adel) the gentry; Edler von ... (öst. Titel) bleibt unübersetzt, etwa dem engl. Titel "Sir" entsprechend. — 4. die Edel(st)en (Vornehmsten) der Stadt the first (or foremost) men ... — 5. *fig.* noble-hearted (or -minded) (wo)man; *auch*: gentle-(wo)man. — III das **Edle** ⓺ 6. nobleness (of the mind); das Edle an seiner Handlung the noble trait in his action.
Edel-bürger(in f) m (⌣⌣...) ⓶ patrician (lady); **-bürtig** a. ⓺⓺ of noble birth; **-dame** f = **-frau; -denkend** a. noble-minded; magnanimous; high-souled; generous(-hearted); **-erz** n rich ore; **-falke** m, *orn.* (trained) falcon, falcon used for hawking; **-fäule** f der Trauben rotting of the grapes on the vine; **-fink** = Buchfink; **-fische** m/pl. *ichth.*: a physostomi *pl.*; **-frau** f lady of noble rank, titled lady, peeress, noblewoman; **-fräulein** n spinster of noble birth, titled spinster; **-früchte** f/pl. choice (kinds of) fruit; **-gas** n (neu entdeckte Gase in der Luft: Argon, Neon, Xenon, Helium, Krypton) rare constituent of our atmosphere; **-geboren** a. nobly- (or high-)born; **-gesinnt** a. = **-denkend; -gestein** n, *fast* †: precious stones *pl.*; **-herzig** a. = **-denkend; -hirsch** m, zo. stag, red deer (*Cervus elaphus*); **-hof** m (nobleman's) country-seat or estate or manor, *bsd. ehm.* baronial hall.
Edeling (⌣⌣) m ⓾d. nobleman, bei den Angelsachsen: atheling.
Edel-kamille ⚘ (⌣⌣...) f ⓶ = Kamille (römische); **-knabe** m page; **-knappe** m, **-knecht** *ehm.* squire; knight's serving man; **-koralle** f red coral (*Corallium rubrum*); **-mann** m (*pl.* **-leute**) nobleman (*pl.* noblemen, nobility); **-männisch** a. ⓺⓺ becoming (or appertaining to) a nobleman; **-marder** m, zo. marten (*Mustela*); **-metall** n (Gold, Silber, ꝛc. Platin ꝛc.) precious metal; **-mut** m = **-sinn; -mütig** a. = **-denkend; -raute** f Schweizer Alpen: icy (or yellow) wormwood (*Artemisia glacialis, A. Mutellina*); **-reis** ⚘ n, *hort.* slip for grafting; **-rost** m patina; f, m = Salbei (echte); **-schule** f, *hort.* nursery-garden for graft-

Zeichen (f. S. XVII): F familiär; P Volkssprache; P Gaunersprache; ↘ selten; † alt (auch gestorben); * neu (auch geboren); ⨯⨯ unrichtig;

ing (trees); =**finn** m noble-mindedness, magnanimity, generosity; ⚥**finnig** a. = ⚥denkend; =**ſitz** m nobleman's country-seat, vgl. =hof; =**ſtein** m precious stone, jewel (a. fig.); geſchnittener: gem; künſtlicher: artificial gem; in Gold gefaßter ~ jewel set in gold.

Edelſtein=faſſer (ˊ—…) m ⓶ setter of jewels or gems; =**händler** m (wholesale) jeweller, dealer in gems; =**ſchleifer**, =**ſchneider** m lapidary.

Edel=tanne ⚘ (ˊ—…) f ⓶ = Weißtanne; =**weiß** n lion's foot (Gnapha'lium leontopo'dium), auch: ⚘ edelweiss; =**wild** n, hunt., coll. (Rotwild) fallow-deer; weitS. (Hochwild) large game.

Eden (ˊ—) [hebr. Garten (1. Moſ. 2,8)] n ⓷ bibl. (garden of) Eden; Paradise.

edeniſch (–ˊ—) [Eden] a. ⓺ Eden-like.

edieren (–ˊ—) [lt.] v/a. ⓽: ein Buch ⚥ (verlegen) to edit (or publish) …

Edikt (–ˊ) [lt.] n ⓵b. (Erlaß) edict, decree; ein ~ erlaſſen, widerrufen to issue, to revoke a decree.

Edikt(al)=ladung (–ˊ, –ˊˊ…) f ⓶, =**zitation** f = Vorladung (öffentliche).

Edinburg ⚥ (ˊˊ) [König Edwin (616—33)] npr/n. ⓵a. (ſchott. Hauptſtadt) Edinburgh; bisw.: the Athens of the North; ~**er**(**in** f ⓶) m ⓶ inhabitant of Edinburgh.

edle(r) 2c. ſ. edel. [mund, dim. Ned.⎫

Edmund ⚘ (ˊˊ) npr/m. ⓵⓶⓷⓸a. Ed-⎭

Edomiter (–ˊˊ—) [Edom (Eſau) „der Rote", Sohn Iſaaks] m ⓶ bibl. Edomite.

edomitiſch (–ˊˊ—) a. ⓺ Edomitish (= idumäiſch). [(Vn.) Edward.⎫

Eduard ⚘ (ˊˊˊ) [fr., *engl.] npr/m. ⓵a.⎭

Edukt ⚥ (–ˊ) [lt.] n ⓵b. chm. (im Rohſtoff ſchon Enthaltenes, bei der Fabrikation 2c. Ausgeſchiedenes) educt.

E=dur ♪ (ˊˊ) n, inv. ſ. E♪.

Efendi (—ˊ—) [türk. Herr; ſ. grch.] m ⓶ (Titel, nachgeſtellt) Effendi.

Efeu ⚘ (ˊ—) [ahd.: ivy] m (n) ⓷ ivy (He'dera Helix); mit ~ bekleidet ivy-clad.

efeu=ähnlich (ˊˊ—…) a. ⓺, ⚥**artig** a. ivy-like, ⚥ hederaceous; ⚥**bekränzt** a. ivy-crowned; ⚥**bewachſen** a. ⓺ ivy-grown; =**bitter** n ⓷ chm. ⚥ hederine; =**blatt** n ivy-leaf; =**harz** n ivy-resin; =**ranke** f ivy tendril or branch; ⚥**umhüllt**, ⚥**umrankt** a. ivy-mantled, entwined with ivy.

Effeff (ˊˊ) n, inv. aus dem ~ (FF) thoroughly, well; etwas aus dem FF verſtehen to know the ins and outs of a th.

Effekt (–ˊ) [lt.] m ⓵b. (Wirkung) effect; ~ **machend** effective; mech. (Arbeitseinheit) unit of work.

Effekten (–ˊ—) [lt.] n/pl. ⓶1. (Habſeligkeiten) effects, goods and chattels pl.; (Gepäck) luggage, F traps pl.; ⚔ baggage; ⚔ u. ⚓=**kit.** — 2. ⚫ (Wertpapiere) stock(s pl.), securities pl., bonds pl., scrip.

Effekten=börſe ⚫ (–ˊˊ…) f ⓶ Stock Exchange; =**handel** m dealing in stocks; =**händler** m stockbroker; ſpekulierender: stock-jobber; =**markt** m market for stocks.

Effekt=haſcherei (–ˊˊ…) f ⓶ straining after effect, thea. playing to the gallery; showing off.

effektiv (–ˊˊ) [lt.] I a. ⓺ (wirkungsvoll) effective; ⚔ ſ. wirklich. — II ~ n ⓷ effects pl.; (Beſtand) (actual) amount or number. — III adv. really, in reality, in fact, actually.

Effektiv=beſtand (–ˊˊ…f…) m ⓶ = ſtand; =**einnahme** ⚫ f actual receipts or takings pl.; =**geſchäft** ⚫ n money-(F cash-) transaction; =**kraft** ⊕ f effective force; =**preis** ⚫ m F cash-price; =**ſtand** m ⚔ u. ⚓ effectives pl., effective strength; =**wert** m actual value; =**zahl** f actual (or real) number. [effectual.⎫

effekt=los (–ˊˊ) a. ⓺ without effect, in-⎭

effektuieren ⚫ (–ˊˊ—) [fr.] v/a. ⓽ (ausführen) to effect (or execute, carry out) orders, sales, &c. [taking.⎫

effekt=voll (–ˊˊ) a. ⓺ effective; (anziehend)⎭

Effet (–ˊ) [fr.] ⓷ ⚽ Billard: dem Ball ~ geben to put screw into the ball.

Effuſion ⚥ (–ˊˊˊ) f ⓸ phys. (Entweichung) bſd. v. Gaſen: escape, leakage.

egal F (–ˊ) [fr.] a. ⓺ (gleich) alike, the same; (einerlei) indifferent; (unaufhörlich) es regnet ⚥ it is for ever raining.

Egalität (–ˊˊˊ) f ⓺ sameness, likeness.

Egart ⚥ (ˊ—) f ⓶ agr. (Grasland) pasturage, pasture-land; ~(**en**)**wirtſchaft** ⚥ f ſübd. (geregelte Feldgraswirtſchaft) cultivation of grazing-land or pastures.

Egel (ˊ—) [ahd.] m ⓶ (Blut=egel) leech.

Egel=ſeuche ⚥ (–ˊˊ…) f ⓶ vet. (Leber=egelkrankheit) disorder (of sheep) arising from gourd-worms; =**wurm** m, vet. gourd-worm.

Egge ⚥ (ˊˊ) [udd. = Eck(e)] f ⓶ 1. agr. harrow, größere: brake; dreieckige für ſchweren Boden: drag. — 2. Tuchmacherei: (Salband) selvedge, selvage.

eggen ⊕ (ˊˊ) v/a. u. v/n. (h.) ⓶ den Boden ⚥ (aufreißen) to harrow … (a. fig.).

Eggen=ſchlitten ⊕ (ˊˊ—…) m ⓶ harrow-sledge; drag.

Egger ⊕ (ˊˊ) m ⓶ agr. harrower.

ego ⚥ (ˊˊ) [lt. ˊˊ ich]: alter ⚥ second self.

Ego=ismus (–ˊˊˊ) [lt.] m ⓶ (Selbſtſucht) selfishness; egotism.

Ego=iſt (–ˊˊ) m ⓶ selfish person; (ſ. der immer von ſich ſelbſt ſpricht) egotist.

ego=iſtiſch (–ˊˊ—) a. ⓺ selfish, self-seeking, self-centred; egotistic(al).

egrenieren ⚫ (–ˊˊ—) [fr. égrener] v/a. ⓽ (entkörnen) to clean (or gin) cotton.

Egyptienne (–ˊˊˊˊˊ) [fr.] f ⓸ typ. (Blockſchrift) fette = **egyptian**; halbfette ~ clarendon type.

eh[1] (ˊ) [fr.] int. ah!, oh!

eh[1] (ˊ) = ehe[1].

ehe[1] (ˊ—) [mhd. aus * eher]: ⚥ daß ere; ⚥ (bevor) er kam before (or ere) he came, ⚥ previous (or prior) to his coming; geh nicht hin, ⚥ (bis) er ſchreibt! do not go there until (or unless) he writes!; comp. eher; sup. eheſte (ſ. ds).

Ehe[2] (ˊ—) [ahd.(: ewig, je, echt): lt. aevum] f ⓸ matrimony, wedded (or married) state, married life; ~ aus Liebe love-match; (un)glückliche ~ (un)happy union; wilde ~ concubinage; ſich in den Stand der ~ begeben to enter the matrimonial state, to marry; eine ~ ſchließen to contract a marriage; Kind aus erſter ~ child by the first wife or husband; außer der ~ geboren born out of wedlock, illegitimate; Sprichw. die ~ n werden im Himmel geſchloſſen marriages are made in heaven.

Ehe[2]=**band** (ˊˊ—…) n ⓶ marriage-tie, bond of wedlock; =**betrug** m (Ehe-erſchleichung) marriage by false pretences; =**bett** n marriage-bed, nuptial couch; ⚥**brechen** v/n. (nur im inf.) to commit adultery; =**brechen** n ⓷ adultery (vgl. =bruch); =**brecher**(**in** f m adulterer, f adulteress; ⚥**brecheriſch** a. ⓺ adulterous; =**bruch** m adultery; jur. auch: criminal conversation; =**bund** m, =**bündnis** n matrimonial union or alliance. [mals).⎫

ehe[1]=**dem** (ˊˊˊ) adv. before, ere (of old ⎭

Ehe[2]=**feind** (ˊˊ—…) m ⓶; ⚔ misogamist; ⚥**feindlich** a. ⓺ anticonnubial; =**frau** f married woman or lady; (lawful) wife, consort; =**freuden** f/pl. connubial joys pl., vgl. ⚥**glück**; =**gabe** f marriage-portion; =**gatte** m, =**gattin** f, =**gemahl**(**in** f) m, =**genoß** m, =**genoſſin** f = =mann, =frau; =**geſpons** m (n) co. = =mann.

ehe[1]=**geſtern** ⚥ 2c. (ˊˊ—) adv. = vorgeſtern 2c.

Ehe[2]=**glück** (ˊˊ—…) n ⓶ connubial bliss (oft iro.); =**gott** m, myth. Hymen; =**gut** n (Vermögen e-r Ehefrau) wife's private estate; =**güterrecht** n law relating to married people's property; =**haften** ⚥ pl. lawful impediments pl. to non-appearance in court; =**hälfte** F f better half; =**herr** m (her) lord (and master); ⚥**herrlich** a. ⓺ = ⚥männiſch; =**hindernis** n obstacle to a p.'s marriage; =**irrung** f, euph. = =bruch; =**joch** n marriage-yoke; =**kontrakt** m = =vertrag; =**kreuz** n: a) troubles pl. of married life; b) F (böſe Frau) termagant; =**krüppel** F m impotent husband; (old) family-man; =**leben** n married (or wedded) life; ⚥**leiblich** ✝ a.: ⚥e (i. d. Ehe geborene) Kinder children pl. born in wedlock; =**leute** pl. married people or folk(s) pl.; husband and wife.

ehelich (ˊˊ—) a. ⓺ 1. conjugal, matrimonial, connubial; vgl. ehemänniſch; in ⚥er Gemeinſchaft leben to live as man and wife; ⚥es Leben married (or wedded) life; adv. ⚥ verbinden to join in wedlock; ſich ⚥ verbinden to marry, to get married; F co. to take a partner for life. — 2. (in der Ehe geboren) born in wedlock, legitimate; ⚥ erklären, machen to legitimate to legitim(at)ize.

ehelichen (ˊˊˊ—) v/a. ⓶ to marry.

Ehelichkeits=erklärung (ˊˊˊˊ…) f ⓶ von Kindern: legitim(iz)ation.

Ehe[2]=**liebſte**(**r** m) f (ˊˊ—…) ⓶ F = =mann, =frau; ⚥**los** a. ⓺ unmarried, single; ⚥**loſer Stand** unwedded state, co. single blessedness; =**loſigkeit** f celibacy; ⚥**luſtig** a. inclined to marry.

ehe[1]=**malig** (ˊˊˊ—) a. ⓺ former; old; ſein ⚥er Herr his late master.

ehe[1]=**mals** (ˊˊˊ) adv. formerly; of old; in the past; in past times; in days of yore.

Ehe[2]=**mann** (ˊˊ…) m ⓶ married man; (her) husband or spouse or F goodman; ⚥**männiſch** a. ⓺ marital; ⚥**mündig** a. marriageable; =**mündigkeit** f marriageableness, marriageable age; =**paar** n married (or wedded) couple; =**paften** pl. marriage-settlement; =**pfand** n pledge; child; =**pflicht** f conjugal duty; =**prozeß** m matrimonial lawsuit.

eher (ˊ—) [ahd.: ere, early; vgl. ehe[1]] I adv. 1. (früher) earlier, sooner; drei

[Eherecht] — 290 — [Ehrenzeichen]

Tage 2 als seine Flucht three days before (or previous to, prior to) his flight; er war 2 da als du he was there before you; je 2, desto besser, je 2, je lieber the sooner the better; desto 2, um so 2 all the sooner or the faster; vgl. 4. — 2. (lieber, vielmehr) rather, F sooner; 2 wollte ich // I would rather //. — 3. (leichter) more easily; er kann es 2 tun als ich he can do it more conveniently than I (can); das läßt sich 2 hören (glauben, tun) that sounds better, that's more feasible; 2 fiele der Himmel ein sooner the heavens would fall. — 4. desto 2, um so 2 all the more (easily or probably); er wird es um so 2 tun he will be (all the) more likely to do it. — 5. abs. (vordem) formerly.

Ehe²-recht (⸺...) n ⓺ matrimonial law(s pl.) or right; 2rechtlich a. ⓺ u. adv. relating to the marriage-laws.

ehern (⸺) [ahd.: ore: lt. aer-(aes)] a. ⓺ brazen (auch fig.); (of) bronze; bibl. die 2en Säulen the pillars of brass; fig. mit 2er Stirn brazen-faced.

Ehe²-scheidung (⸺...) f ⓺ divorce; =scheidungsklage f divorce-suit; 2scheu a. ⓺ loath to marry; =scheu f aversion to matrimony, ⚚ misogamy; =schliessung f contracting marriage; =segen m nuptial blessing; fig. (Kinderschar) (numerous) offspring; =stand m wedded state, married life, matrimony.

eheste (⸺) [sup. v. ehe¹] a.⓺: ich war am 2n hier I was here first; des 2n, mit 2m, 2r Tage, 2ns at the earliest (date); as soon as possible; schreiben Sie mir mit 2r Post ... by the earliest post, at your earliest convenience; er kann 2ns (adv.) morgen hier sein he cannot be here before (or until) to-morrow.

Ehe²-steuer (⸺...) f ⓺ dowry; =stifter (in f) m match-maker; =streit(igkeit f) m matrimonial dispute; =teufel m matrimonial fiend; destroyer of matrimonial happiness, Asmodeus; (böses Weib) termagant; =trennung f (judicial) separation; =verächter m = =feind; =verbindung f matrimonial alliance; vgl. =bund; =verlöbnis n betrothal, engagement; =versprechen n promise of marriage; =vertrag m marriage-contract or -deed or -settlement; =weib n = =frau; =werbung f matrimonial suit; courting, wooing.

Ehr-abschneider(in f) m (⸺...) [Ehre] ⓺ (Verleumder[in]) slanderer; =abschneiderei f slander, defamation.

ehrbar (⸺) a. ⓺ honourable; (anstandsgemäß) respectable, decent; decorous (conduct); modest (behaviour); ~keit (⸺⸺) f ⓺ honourableness; respectability, decency; decorousness; modesty.

Ehr-begier(de) (⸺...) f ⓺ coveting honour (and glory); 2begierig a. ⓺ covetous of honour or fame; =beraubung f = =abschneiderei; =durst m thirst(ing) for honour.

Ehre (⸺) [ahd.: lt. aes(tima'ri) f ⓺ 1. (persönliche Würde und die ihr gezollte Achtung) honour; (Ansehen) reputation, repute, credit, (fair) fame; (Auszeichnung) distinction; (Ruhm) glory. — 2. Redewendungen: es sich zur ~ anrechnen oder schätzen to consider it an honour to; e-m (große) ~ antun, erweisen to do a p. (great) honour, to show him (every) respect; ⚔ mit militärischen ~n begraben w. to be buried with (full) military honours; et. mit ~n besteh(e)n to acquit o.s. creditably at a th.; ein Examen auch: to pass an examination with distinction, to obtain honours; einen (wieder) zu ~ bringen to raise (to restore) a p. to an honourable position; ~ einlegen mit oder durch to gain credit by; es macht ihm (alle) ~, es gereicht ihm zur ~, daß // it does him credit that //; der ~ halber f. 2n-halber; (ängstlich) auf seine ~ halten (jealously) to guard one's honour; in ~n halten to hold in esteem, to pay (due) honour to; ein Geschenk: to lay great store by; sein Amt mit ~n verwalten to perform one's duties creditably; das ist aller ~n wert it deserves great credit; von Anerbietungen: that's a fair offer, it's most acceptable; seine ~ darein setzen (oder darin suchen) zu ... to make it a point of honour to do a th., to take a pride in doing a th.; wir tun es ihm zu ~n we do it in honour of him. — 3. Höflichkeitsformeln, brieflich: ich habe die ~ zu sein, zu verbleiben I have the honour to be, to remain; ich werde mir die ~ geben zu // I shall do myself the honour to //; mit wem habe ich die ~ (zu sprechen)? whom have I the honour (or the pleasure) to address? — 4. Beteuerungen u. Sprichw.: auf ~!, bei meiner ~! upon my honour!; ~ dem ~ gebührt honour to whom honour is due; einen Kuß in ~n kann niemand verwehren an innocent kiss comes never amiss; Ihr Wort in ~n! (ich denke anders) with due deference to you!

ehren (⸺) [ahd.] v/a. ⓺ 1. (ant. entehren) to honour (durch od. mit by or with); to pay honour to; Sprichw. wer den Pfennig nicht ehrt, ist des Talers nicht wert take care of the pence, and the pounds will take care of themselves. — 2. (hoch-achten) to esteem, to respect; brieflich: Geehrter Herr! (Dear) Sir (nicht: honoured Sir); parl. der geehrte Redner the Honourable Member. — 3. e-n 2 (e-m huldigen) to do (or render) homage to a person.

Ehren-akzept (⸺...) n ⓺ =annahme; =amt n honourable (ohne Gehalt: honorary) post; pl. =ämter dignities pl.; =annahme ⓺ acceptance upon honour; =benennung f =titel; =besuch m ceremonial (or official) visit; =bett n bed of state; =bezeigung f mark of respect; e-n mit ~en überschütten to shower honours upon a p.; =bezeugung (en pl.) ⚔ f military salute; =bürger m honorary freeman or burgess; =bürgerrecht n freedom of a city; =dame f Lady of the Bedchamber, Lady in Waiting; =degen m sword of honour; =denkmal n statue (or monument) raised to a p.; =dienst m bei Hofe: duty of a Lord (or Lady) in Waiting; =erklärung f reparation of honour, oft: (fr.) amende honorable; 2fest † a. ⓺ (thoroughly) honourable; =fräulein n maid of honour; =gabe f honourable gift, vgl. =geschenk; =gast m (the most) honoured guest, chief guest; =gefolge, =geleit n retinue, suite; =gehalt n pension; =gericht n court of honour; 2gerichtlich a. referring to a court of honour; =geschenk n presentation (made to a p.); testimonial (presented to a p.); =grabmal n mausoleum; =grad m honorary degree. ehrenhaft (⸺) a. ⓺ (ant. ehrlos) honourable; high-principled; vgl. ehrbar; ~igkeit (⸺⸺) f ⓺ honourable character, integrity; vgl. Ehrbarkeit. [sake.]
ehren-halber (⸺) adv. for honour's) Ehren-halle (⸺...) f ⓺ hall of honour, pantheon; =handel m = =sache; =hold † m (Herold) herald; =klage f libel-suit, action for libel; =kleid n robe of honour, ceremonial (or festive) gown or dress; =kränkung f injury inflicted on a person's honour; (defamatory) libel; =kranz m wreath of honour; =krone f crown of honour or glory; =legion f, in Frankreich: Legion of Honour; =lohn m honorarium, vgl. =sold; =mahl n banquet given in honour of a p.; =mal n monument (raised to a p); =mann m man of honour; =mitglied n honorary member; =münze f commemorative coin; =pforte f triumphal arch; =platz m seat of honour; =posten m a) = =amt; b) ⚔ = =wache; =preis m: a) prize; b) n ⚘ speedwell (Vero'nica); =punkt m point of honour; =rat m court of honour; =raub m defamation; vgl. =kränkung; =räuber m defamer, detractor; =recht n honorary privilege; Verlust der bürgerlichen ~e loss of civic rights; 2reich a. ⓺ rich in (or loaded with) honours; =retter m apologist; =rettung f vindication of a p.'s honour; rehabilitation of a p.'s character; 2rührig a. defamatory, libellous; =rührigkeit f defamatory (or libellous) character; =sache f affair of honour; (Duell) duel; =salve ⚔ f salute of guns; =säule f commemorative column; vgl. =denkmal; =schänder m = =räuber; 2schänderisch a. = 2rührig; =schändung f = =kränkung; =schein m note of hand whereby a p. pledges his honour; =schießen, =schüsse = =salve; =schuld f debt of honour; =sitz m = =platz; =sold m wage of honour; vgl. =lohn; =staffel f = =stufe; =stand m honourable vocation or profession; =stelle f position of honour or trust; vgl. =amt; =strafe f degrading punishment; =stufe f degree of honour; =tag m day of glory; memorable day; ⚭ ~e pl. = Respekttage; anniversary of a glorious day; =tempel m = =halle. ehrent-halben, -halber = ehrenhalber. Ehren-titel (⸺...) m ⓺ honorary title; =trunk m toast in honour of a p.; 2voll a. ⓺ honourable, glorious; 2e Erwähnung honourable mention; =wache f, =wacht f ⚔ guard of honour; 2wert a. respectable; =wort n word of honour; Gefangene auf ihr ~ entlassen to release prisoners on parole; =zeichen n decoration; (war-)medal; weitS.: mark (or badge) of distinction.

Signs (see page XVII): F familiar; P vulgar; ⌐ flash; ⟍ rare; † obsolete (died); * new word (born); ⁺⁺ incorrect; ♪ music;

[ehrerbietig] — 291 — [Eiderente]

ehr-erbietig (⁻...) a. ⓡ respectful; reverential, deferential; **-erbietigkeit** f ⓔ, **erbietung** f respect(fulness); reverence, deference; **-furcht** f veneration; ~ einflößen to (strike with or inspire with) awe; ⚡**furcht-einflößend**, **-gebietend** a. awe-inspiring; ⚡**fürchtig** a. reverential; **-furchts-bezeigung** f (rendering) homage; ⚡**furchtsvoll** a. respectful; **-gefühl** n sense of honour; **-geiz** m ambition; ⚡**geizig** a. ambitious; **-gier(ig** a.) f = begier(ig).

ehrlich (⁻ᵥ) a. ⓡ 1. honest; im Handel, beim Spiel: fair, fair-dealing; (ohne Trug) reliable; (ohne Falsch) true, loyal; plain-dealing or -spoken, candid; (ohne Schimpf) of fair (or good) repute; vgl. ehrbar. — 2. Redewendungen: sein Les Auskommen haben to make an honest living; Les Begräbnis decent burial; gestehen Sie es ⎯ (adv.) ein! make a clean breast of it!; ⬤ Ler Handel bona-fide bargain; F gute Le Haut good(-natured and open-hearted) fellow, easy-going person; in Lem Kampfe in (a) fair (or stand-up) fight; Ler Leute Kind son (or daughter) of respectable parents; er meint es ⎯ (adv.) mit uns he means well by us, his intentions towards us are good; Ler Name good name or character, fair repute; e-n wieder ⎯ m. to make a respectable man (or woman) of a p., to rehabilitate a p.('s character); ⎯ (adv.) zu Werke gehen to go openly to work; to be fair-dealing; Sprichw. ⎯ währt am längsten honesty is the best policy. — 3. (tüchtig) meist iro.: F er lügt was ~es zusammen he tells awful lies or F fine fibs; F das soll was ~es (a. ein Les Sümmchen) kosten it will cost a good round sum or F a pretty penny.

Ehrlichkeit (⁻ᵥ⁻) f ⓔ (i. ehrlich) honesty; reliability; loyalty; plain dealing; fair repute; vgl. Ehrbarkeit; **~⁐erklärung** (⁻ᵥ...) f ⓔ rehabilitation (of a p.'s character), reinstatement. [rettung.]

Ehrlich-machung (⁻ᵥ∫⁻) f = **Ehren-**

Ehr-liebe (⁻ᵥ...) f ⓔ love of honour; ⚡**liebend** a. ⓡ loving honour, seeking honour; ⚡**los** a. void (or destitute of (all sense of) honour; dishonourable, stärker: infamous; **-losigkeit** f dishonourableness, stärker: infamy.

ehrsam (⁻ᵥ) a. ⓡ (jetzt meist als Titel) decent; respectable; Le Jungfer modest maid; **~keit** (⁻ᵥ⁻) f ⓔ respectability.

Ehr-sucht (⁻ᵥ...) f ⓔ = **-durst**; ⚡**füchtig** a. ⓡ pursuing honour. [a p.)

Ehrung (⁻ᵥ) f ⓐ honour conferred on) **ehr-vergessen** (⁻ᵥ...) a. ⓡ unmindful of (the dictates of) honour; base(-minded); **-vergessenheit** f ⓔ base-mindedness, villainy; **-verlust** m jur. loss of (all) civic rights; pol. disfranchisement; ⚡**widrig** a. contrary to honour; **-würden**: Euer (Ew.) ~! Your Reverence!; ⚡**würdig** a. venerable, reverend.

ei¹ (⁻) int. ah!; ⎯ das wäre!, ⎯ warum nicht gar! indeed!; you don't say so!; ⎯ freilich!, ⎯ ja doch!, ⎯ jawohl! why, of course!; aye, to be sure!; ⎯ sieh da!; lo, behold!, there, now!; ⎯ der Tausend the deuce (take it)! ⎯ was! oh, nothing of the kind!; you don't mean it!

Ei² (⁻) [ahd.: egg: lt. ōvum] n ④c. 1. egg (auch anat.), ⚘, physiol., &c.: ⚑ ovum; ~er legende Tiere ⚑ oviparous animals pl.; altes, frisches, rohes ~ stale, new-laid, raw egg; faules ~ rotten (or bad, addled) egg; Kocht.: hart (weich) gesott(e)nes ~ hard (soft) boiled egg; vgl. Spiegeleier. — 2. Redensarten (mſt F): (wie) auf ~ern gehen to walk upon hot coals; aus dem ~ kriechen ob. schlüpfen to creep out of the egg, to peep out of the shell; kaum aus dem ~ gekrochen F a mere chicken, a young greenhorn; einander gleichen wie ein ~ dem andern to be as (like one another as) two peas; das ~ will klüger sein als die Henne don't teach your grandmother how to suck eggs; sich um ungelegte ~er kümmern to trouble about things not (yet) in existence or which do not concern us; er sieht aus wie aus dem ~geschält ob. gepellt he looks as if he came out of a bandbox; man muß mit ihm um gehen wie mit einem rohen ~ he has to be handled very carefully or tenderly.

eiapopeia! (⁻ᵥ⁻ᵥ⁻) [mhd., *grch.] I int. lulla(by)! hush-a-by! — II ~ n ⓔ (Wiegenlied) lullaby (song).

Eibe ⚘ (⁻ᵥ) [ahd.: yew] f ⓧ (a. **~n-baum** m ⓔ) yew(-tree) (Taxus bacca'ta); ⎯ n a. ⓔ of yew(-wood). **~n-holz** n yew-wood.

Ei-bildung (⁻ᵥ...) f ⓔ im tierischen Körper: ⚑ ovulation.

Eibisch ⚘ (⁻ᵥ) [ahd.: *lt. hibī'scum n] m ⓐa. 1. althæa, marsh-mallow (Althae'a officina'lis). — 2. eßbarer ~ edible hibiscus (Hibi'scus escule'ntus). — **~saft** (⁻ᵥ⁻) m ⓔ marsh-mallow syrup, **-tee** m marsh-mallow tea, **-wurzel** f marsh-mallow root. [office.]

Eich²-amt (⁻ᵥ⁻) [eichen³] n ⓔ gauging)

Eich¹-apfel ⚘ (⁻ᵥ⁻) [Eiche¹] m ⓔ gall; vgl. Gallapfel. **-baum** m = Eiche¹; **-blatt** n ſ. Eichenblatt.

Eiche¹ ⚘ (⁻ᵥ) [ahd.: oak] f ⓧ oak(-tree) (Quercus); junge ob. kleine ~ oakling.

Eiche² (⁻ᵥ) [mhd.; *eichen³] f ⓧ 1. gauging; vgl. eichen³ II. — 2. = Eichmaß.

Eichel ⚘ ⚑ (⁻ᵥ) [ahd., *Eiche¹] f ⓧ 1. (Frucht der Eiche) acorn; im Kartenspiel: **~n** pl. clubs. — 2. ⚘ u. anat.: ⚑ glans.

Eichel-becher (⁻ᵥ...) m ⓔ = **-napf**; **-entzündung** f, path.: ⚑ balanitis; **-ernte** f = mast; ⚡**förmig** a. ⓡ glandiform; **-häher** m, orn. jay (Garrulus glanda'rius); **-kaffee** m (beverage made of) roasted acorns; **-kappe** f, **-kelch** m = **-napf**; **-lese** f glandage; **-mast** f mast of acorns, jur. pannage; **-napf** m, **-näpfchen** n ⚘ acorn-cup; ⚡(n)-tragend ⚘ a.: ⚑ gland(ul)iferous.

Eichen¹ (⁻ᵥ) n ⓑ (dim. v. Ei²) tiny egg, ⚑ ovulum, ovule.

eichen² (⁻ᵥ) [Eiche¹] a. ⓡ (D9) oaken, made (or built) of oak.

eichen³ (⁻ᵥ) [mhd.] I v/a. Hohlmaße: to gauge; Gewichte: to adjust; to measure, test. — II ~ n ⓔ = Eichung.

eichen-artig (⁻ᵥ⁻) [Eiche¹] a. ⓡ oaky; **-ast** m ⓔ branch of an oak; **-baum** m = Eiche¹; ⚡**beschattet** a. shaded with oak-trees; **-blatt** n oak-leaf; **-borke** f = **-rinde**, **-diele** f oak plank or board; **-farn** ⚘ m oak-fern (Phego'pteris, Dryo'pteris); ⚡**fest**, ⚡**hart** a. hard (or solid) as oak; **-gall-wespe** f, ent. gall-fly or-wasp (Cynips); **-hain** m oak-grove; **-holz** n oak-wood or -timber; **-kern-holz** n heart of oak (oft fig.); **-klotz** m oak-block; **-kranz** m oaken garland; **-laub** n oak-leaves pl.; **-lohe** f, **-mehl** n ground (or powdered) oak-bark; **-rinde** f oak-bark; **-rose** f = Gallapfel; **-spanner** m, ent. oak-beauty (Biston prodroma'ria); **-stamm** m trunk of an oak(-tree); **-wäldchen** n small oak-wood, vgl. Eichwald; **-zweig** m oak(or oaken) branch.

Eicher (⁻ᵥ) [eichen³] m ⓔ gauger.

Eich²-gebühr (⁻ᵥ...) f ⓔ, **-geld** n gauger's fee, charge for gauging.

Eich¹-hase ⚘ (⁻ᵥ...) m ⓔ: a) zo. = **-hörnchen**; b) branchy boletus (Bole'tus ramosi'ssimus; Poly'porus umbella'tus).

Eich¹-horn, mst **-hörnchen** (⁻ᵥ(⁻) [ahd.] n ⓔ zo. squirrel (Sciu'rus), sibirisches ~ miniver (a. dessen Pelz); **~arten** (⁻...) f/pl. ⚑ sciurines pl.; ⚡**artig** a. ⓡ ⚑ sciurine. **~fell** n squirrel-skin; **~jagd** f squirrel-shooting.

Eich¹-kätzchen (⁻ᵥ...) n ⓔ, **-katze** f = **-horn**; **-mast** f = Eichel-m.

Eich²-maß (⁻ᵥ...) n ⓔ gauge; standard measure of capacity, &c.; in England auch: gauge-point; vgl. **-stab**, **-meister** m gauger, adjuster; **-pfahl** m (Merkpfahl) water-mark (post); **-stab** m gauging-rod or -rule; standard-yard; **-stempel** m für Hohlmaße: gauging-stamp; **-strich** m gauging-line.

Eichung (⁻ᵥ) [eichen³] f ⓔ gauging; adjustment; **~s-...** (⁻ᵥ...) ſ. Eich²-...

Eich¹-wald (⁻ᵥ) m ⓔ oak-wood or -forest; vgl. Eichenwäldchen.

Eid (⁻) [ahd.: oath] m ⓔc. oath; einen ~ auf et. ablegen, leisten, schwören to take an (or one's) oath upon a th., to swear to a th.; e-m einen ~ abnehmen, e-n einen Eid schwören lassen to administer an oath to a p.; to put a p. on his oath; e-n Beamten &c.: to swear ... in; in ~ und Pflicht genommen w. to be sworn in (on taking office); einen falschen ~ schwören to commit perjury, to perjure o.s.; an ~es Statt instead (or in lieu) of an oath; Versicherung an ~es Statt affirmation.

Eidam fast (⁻ᵥ) [ahd.: *Eid] m ⓓd. (Schwiegersohn) son-in-law.

Eid-brecher (⁻ᵥ...) m ⓔ, **-brüchige(r)** m perjurer; **-bruch** m breaking (of) an oath, perjury; ⚡**brüchig** a. ⓡ perjured; forsworn; ⎯ werden to break one's oath; **-bürge** m bail upon oath; **-bürgschaft** f sworn bail.

Eidechse (⁻ᵥ⁻) [ahd.] f ⓧ zo. lizard (Lace'rta); grüne ~ green lizard (L. vi'ridis); graue ob. gemeine ~ sand-lizard (L. a'gilis); Familie der ~n: ⚑ saurians pl.; ⚡**n-artig** (⁻ᵥ...) a. ⓡ lizard-like, ⚑ lacertine; **~n-kunde** f ⓔ saurology.

Eider (⁻ᵥ) [isld.] m ⓔ u. f ⓧ = **-gans**; **~d(a)unen** (⁻ᵥ...) f/pl. ⓔ coll. (a. ⬤) eiderdown sg.; **-ente**, **-gans** f, orn. eider-duck (Somate'ria molli'ssima).

⚑ scientific; ⚘ botanical; ⚘ geography; ⊕ machinery; ⚒ mining; ⚔ military; ⚓ marine; ⬤ commercial; ✉ postal; 🚂 railway.

[**Eides-abnahme**] — 292 — [**eigentlich**]

Eides-abnahme (‒‿…) [Eid] f ② administration of an oath; **-bruch** m = **Eidbruch**; **-formel** f form (or wording) of an oath; **-helfer** m jur. cojuror, ehm. compurgator; **-leister** m one who takes an oath, jur.: juror; **-leistung** f taking an oath; jur. schriftlich: (swearing an) affidavit; **-statt** f = **Eides Statt**, i. Eid; **stattlich** a. ⑥: Le Versicherung affirmation; **zuschiebung** f jur. tendering an oath to a p.

Eid-genoß (″…) m ② confederate; **-genossenschaft** f confederation, league; (Staatenbund) (the Swiss, &c.) Confederacy; **-genössisch** a. ⑥ federal; eng S. Swiss, Helvetian.

eidlich (⸌‿) a. ⑥ u. adv. sworn; Le Aussage sworn deposition or evidence; adv. ⸚ aussagen (bekräftigen, erhärten) to declare upon (to confirm or testify by) oath. [egg, ⸚ vitellus.]

Ei²-dotter (″…) m (n) ② yolk of an **Eid-schwur** (″…) m ② = Eid; **vergessen** a. ⑥ = **brüchig**; **verweigerer** m, bsd. engl. hist.: (Jakobi't) non-juror.

Eier-apfel (‒‿…) [Eier, pl. v. Ei²] ♀ m ② (Frucht der Eierpflanze) egg-apple; **-becher** m egg-cup; **-bier** n egg-flip.

Eierchen (⸌‿‿) [dim. pl. v. Ei²] small (or tiny) eggs, ⸚ ovules pl.

Eier-frucht ♀ (″…) f ② = **-apfel**; **-händler** m egg-dealer, dealer in eggs; **-käse** m egg-cheese; white curds pl.; **-klar** n = Eiweiß; **-kocher** m egg-boiler or **-poacher**; **-kuchen** n omelet(te), mit Gelee: sweet-omelet; **-kunde** f ⸚ oology; **-legen** n egg-laying; ~ der Insekten ⸚ ovipositing; **legend** a. ⑥ laying eggs, ⸚ oviparous; Le Henne laying fowl, (good) layer; **-löffel** m egg-spoon; **-öl** n, physiol. yolk-oil; **-pflanze** ♀ f egg-plant (Sola'num melo'ngena); **-pflaume** ♀ f egg-plum; **-prüfer** m egg-tester, ⚫ auch: candler; **-rahm** m custard; **-sauce** f egg-sauce; **-schale** f egg-shell; **-schalen-porzellan** ⚫ n egg-shell china, egg-shells pl.; **-schnee** n (froth of) beaten-up egg(s pl.); **-speise** f dish prepared with (or made of) eggs, custard; **-stab** m, arch. egg-moulding; egg-and-anchor; **-ständer** m egg-stand; **-stock** ⚫ f, anat.: ⸚ ovary; **-tanz** m egg-dance; **tragend** a. egg-bearing, ⸚ oviferous; **-uhr** f egg-boiler, egg-glass.

Eifer (⸌‿) [nhd. LU.] m ② 1. zeal, eagerness; stärker: ardour, fervour; ([heftiges] Verlangen) (passionate) desire, (earnest) longing; mit ~ betreiben to pursue eagerly, to conduct zealously or with zeal; Sprichw. s. blind 5. — 2. (Aufregung) agitation; (Unwille) indignation; (Zorn) wrath; anger; in ~ bringen to exasperate; in ~ geraten to become angry or heated, stärker: to fly into a (violent) passion.

Eiferer (⸌‿‿) m ㉒, **Eiferin** (⸌‿‿) f ㊼ zealot; zealous adherent or friend, fanatical (or keen) partisan.

Eifer-geist (″…) m ② zeal(otism).

eifern (⸌‿) I v/n. (h.) ⓐa. 1. (heftig streben) to show zeal for, to be eager (or to long) for or after. — 2. (sich mitbewerben) to compete (or vie) with a p. for a th. — 3. (sich aufregen) to grow heated or passionate or violent (über et. about a th.); to declaim (or to raise an outcry) against, to fire up at. — II ~ a ㉓. 4. fit of anger, passion; eagerness; rivalry, rivalship.

Eifer-sucht (″…) f ② jealousy (auf e-n of a p.); von Nebenbuhlern: rivalry between; **-süchtelei** f petty rivalry; jealous feeling; **-süchteln** v/n. (h.) ⓐa. to nourish a petty jealousy towards a p.; **-süchtig** a. ⑥ jealous (auf e-n of a p.); **-sucht(s)-toll** a. mad with jealousy.

Ei²-form (″…) f ② egg- (or oval) shape; **-förmig** a. ⑥ egg-shaped, oval; ⸚ oviform; ♀ ovate.

Eierin (⸌‿‿) f ㊼ s. Eierer.

eifrig (⸌‿) a. ⑥ u. adv. (s. Eifer) 1. zealous(ly), eager(ly), keen(ly); stärker: ardent(ly), fervent(ly), earnest(ly); sich ⸚ bemühen to make strenuous efforts; ⸚ mit et. beschäftigt keenly intent (or bent) upon a th.; sich aufs Äste einer Person, Sache annehmen to show the tenderest solicitude for a p., a th., to interest o.s. most keenly for a p., in a th. — 2. bibl. = eifersüchtig.

Ei²-gelb (″…) n ② = Eidotter.

eigen (⸌‿) [ahd.: own] I. a. ⑥ (D9) 1. (ant. fremd2) own; aus Lem Antriebe of one's own accord; spontaneously; etwas auf Le Faust (od. Hand) tun to do a th. on one's own authority; sein Ler Herr sein to be one's own master; auf Le Kosten at one's own expense; durch Les Verschulden through one's own fault; aus Ler Wahl of one's own (free) choice; zu ⸚ haben to have in one's possession; sich (dat.) et. zu ⸚ machen to make a th. one's own; sich einen Gedanken zu ⸚ machen, auch: to adopt (or utilize) an idea; sich eine Sprache zu ⸚ machen, auch: to make o.s. master (or mistress) of a language; zu ⸚ nehmen to appropriate (to o.s.); Sprichw. (ein) Ler Herd ist Goldes wert there's no place like home; ⚫ für Le Rechnung for one's own account, at one's sole risk. — 5. (zugehörend) das ist mein ⸚, das gehört mir ⸚ od. zu ⸚ that is my (property), it is mine, it belongs to me. — 3. von Personen: = leibeigen. — 4. ⚫ Ler (od. trockener) Wechsel bill drawn on o.s.; promissory note; zum Len Verbrauch for home consumption. — 5. (besonder) particular, singular; mein Ler Besitz my private property; er hat dafür ein Les Haus he has a special (or separate) house for it; er hat seine Le Meinung he has opinions of his own; der Mensch hat nichts so ⸚ nothing is so thoroughly (or characteristically) human. — 6. (sonderbar) strange, peculiar; (seltsam) odd, singular; ein Ler Mensch a queer (F rum) fellow. — 7. (streng) exact, exacting, precise, accurate; er ist sehr ⸚ in diesen Dingen he is very strict (or particular) in these matters. — II adv. 8. = eigens. — III ~ s. 9. m ㊼ meine ~sten my nearest kinsfolk, auch oft: my own flesh and blood. — 10. n ㉓ = Eigentum.

Eigen-ansicht (″…) f ②: a) (eigne Meinung) private opinion; b) (eigne Besichtigung) autopsy; **-art** f peculiarity; **⸚artig** a. ⑥ of a special (or particular) kind, (urwüchsig) original; Ler Reiz peculiar charm; **-bericht** m e-r Zeitung: special report, original correspondence; **-besitz** m jur. (one's own) property, private estate; **-brödler**, **-brötler** m: a) (schwäbisch: single man keeping house for himself; b) (sonderling) person of singular (or strange) habits or tastes; **-dünkel** m = Dünkel; **-gewicht** n dead weight, ⚫ net weight; **-gut** n ehm.: allodium; jetzt: freehold; b) literar hist: (the author's) own ideas pl. or invention; **-handel** m self-conducted business, business of one's own; **⸚händig** a. u. adv. with (or under) one's own hand; von Briefen eines Fürsten ꝛc.: autograph; ⸚ übergeben to deliver personally.

Eigenheit (⸌‿‿) f ㊻ singularity, peculiarity; (particular or special) feature; (Seltsamkeit) strangeness, oddity, queerness; ⸚ idiosyncrasy; ~ einer Sprache idiom(atic peculiarity).

Eigen-lehner (⸌‿…) m ② a) (der auf eigner Lehne baut) peasant-proprietor, b) ⚒ ✝ = **-löhner**; **-liebe** f self-love, love of self; self-complacency; **-lob** n self-praise or commendation; **-löhner** ⚒ m miner who works a mine on his own account; **⸚mächtig** a. ⑥ u. adv. by one's own power, on one's own authority; arbitrar(il)y; ⸚ verfahren to act arbitrarily or without consideration for others; **-mächtigkeit** f arbitrariness; **-name(n)** m proper name or noun (a. gr.), (Familienname) family-name, ⸚ cognomen; **-nutz** m = Eigennützigkeit; **⸚nützig** a. self-interested, self-seeking, selfish; avaricious; **⸚nützigkeit** f self-interest(edness); selfishness; (Habsucht) avarice.

eigens (⸌‿) adv. expressly, purposely, on purpose; particularly.

Eigenschaft (⸌‿‿) f ㊻ 1. quality; (Merkmal) attribute, property; (Wesen) nature; gute, schlechte ~en pl. good, bad points pl.; auszeichnende ⸚ (distinctive) feature, character(istic); phys., chm. &c. ~en pl. des Eisens physical, chemical, &c. properties pl. of iron. — 2. in meiner ~ (Stellung) als Vormund in my position (or capacity) as (a) guardian. [adjective.]

Eigenschafts-wort (⸌‿…) n ② gram.

Eigen-sinn (⸌‿…) m ② (s. ⸚sinnig) caprice, peevishness; waywardness, wilfulness, obstinacy, stubbornness, F co. kleiner ~, etwa: troublesome young Turk; **⸚sinnig** a. (wunderlich) capricious, peevish; (unlenksam) wayward, wilful, unmanageable; (hartnäckig) obstinate, stubborn, headstrong; **⸚süchtig** a. self-seeking, selfish, F bent on self.

eigentlich (⸌‿‿) I a. ⑥ 1. = eigen 5. — 2. (wirklich) true, real; (wesentlich) essential; (genau) proper, precise; im ⸚(st)en Sinne (oder Verstande) des Wortes in the (most) literal sense of the word; Ler (innerer) Wert intrinsic 'value or merit. — II adv. 3. (besonders) specially, particularly; (wirklich) really; (ausdrücklich) expressly; (genau) exactly, properly speaking; Buckingham hieß ⸚ Villiers

[Eigentum]

the real (or original) name of B. was V.; er hat 2 recht he is decidedly (or really) right; Swift war recht 2 ein Menschenfeind S. was, in the true sense of the word, a misanthropist.

Eigentum (⌣-) n ②d. (o. pl.) meist: property; (Gut) estate, landed property; das Geld ist mein ~ the money is mine or my own; die Bücher sind sein ~ the books are his (property); co. mein biß= chen ~ my few goods and chattels pl., what little I have or possess; sein ~ verschwenden to waste one's substance; kleines ~ (Erspartes) savings pl.

Eigentümer (⌣⌣-⌣) m ㉒, ~in f ㊵ proprietor, f proprietress; owner; (Haus= wirt, Gutsherr) landlord; ~ e-s Ritter= gutes lord of the manor; die ~ coll. auch: the proprietary.

eigentümlich (⌣⌣⌣⌣) I a. ⑥ 1. (zugehörig) own, proper; es gehört ihm 2 zu it is his own (property). — 2. = eigen 6. — II 3. das ~e ㊳ (an) der Sache the peculiar (or characteristic) feature of the affair, the strangest part of it.

Eigentümlichkeit (⌣⌣⌣-⌣) f ㊻ property (f. eigen 2); characteristic (feature); ⚛ idiosyncrasy; vgl. Eigenheit; berech= tigte ~en pl. legitimate distinctions or peculiarities pl.

Eigentums=herr (⌣⌣-...) m ㉒ lord of the estate or manor; vgl. Eigentümer; =recht n ownership, proprietorship; literarisch: copyright; =steuer f pro= perty-tax; =vergehen n offence (or crime) against (the rights of) pro= perty; trespass(ing); =vorbehalt m jur. reservation of the owner's rights.

eigen=warm (⌣⌣-...) a. ⑥ von Tieren: ⚛ idiothermic; =wille m ㉒ (strong) self-will, wilfulness; ⚖willig a. ⑥ self-willed, wilful, obstinate; vgl. Eifsinnig.

☞ **eigne** (⌣⌣) = eigene, f. eigen.

eignen (⌣⌣) [eigen] ⓑb. I sich 2 v/refl. (brauchbar sein) to be suitable or fit; sich zu et. 2 to be (well) adapted (or qualified) for a th. — II ge=eignet p.p. u. a. ⑥ suitable, fit, (well) adapted or qualified; nicht geeignet zu not cal= culated to. — III ↘ v/n. (h.) e-m 2 (gehören) to belong to a p.

eigner¹, eignes (⌣⌣) = eigener, eigenes f. eigen. [tümer(in).]

Eigner² (⌣⌣) m ㉒, ~in f ㊵ = Eigen=∫

Eignung * (⌣⌣) f ㊻ qualification; ~ zur Ausübung der Praxis professional qu.

eigtl. abbr. = eigentlich.

Ei=land (⌣⌣) [nd.] n ②c. poet. island; isle; **Ei=länder** (⌣⌣⌣) m ㉒ islander.

Eil=bestellung (⌣⌣-...) f ㊻ † express de= livery; =boot ↓ n fast boat; =bote m express (messenger), courier.

Eile (⌣⌣) [ahd.] f ㊻ haste; (Flinkheit) promptness, promptitude; (Schnellig= keit) speed; große ~ precipitancy; ⚔ auf Meldekarten: keine ~ (X), ~ (XX), große ~ (XXX) no hurry, hurry, great hurry; in (aller) ~ in (great or hot) haste, with (great) dispatch; die Sache hat (keine) ~ ... is (not) urgent, F ... can(not) wait; ich habe (keine) ~ I am (not) in a hurry, I am (not) pressed for time; damit hat es keine ~ there is plenty of time for that; mit möglichster

~ as speedily (or as fast) as possible; F post-haste, at the top of one's speed; Sprichw. zu große ~ bringt Weile, ~ mit Weile the more haste the less speed.

Ei=leiter ⚛ (⌣⌣-⌣) f ㊳ anat. ⚛ oviduct.

eilen (⌣⌣) [ahd.] I v/n. u. sich 2 v/refl. ⑱: a) (in) to make haste; b) (h.) abs. to hasten (forward), to hurry (on); er hat sich nicht (damit) geeilt he did not bestir himself; he took a long time (about it); wir müssen uns 2 we must be quick; beim Gehen: we must put our best leg forward; er ist nach Hause geeilt he hurried (or made for) home; e-m zu Hilfe 2 to hasten to a p.'s aid; seinem Verderben entgegen 2 to rush headlong into destruction; eilt euch damit! be quick about it!, make haste!; die Sache eilt, a. v/impers. es eilt it is an urgent matter, it needs dispatch. — II 2d p.pr. u. a. ⑥ speedy, hasty, quick; precipitate; 2den Fußes with hasty step, at a quick pace.

eilends (⌣⌣) adv. speedily, quickly, hur= riedly; in (hot) haste.

eilf † (⌣, meist ělf) numer. = elf.

eil=fertig (⌣⌣...) a. ⑥ hasty; stärker: pre= cipitate; =fertigkeit f ㊻ hastiness; precipitancy; =fracht, =fuhre f, =gut ⊞ n express goods, dispatch-goods pl. sent by passenger-train; vgl. =sendung.

eilig (⌣⌣) a. ⑥ u. adv. 1. (dringend) re= quiring haste or speed; pressing (or urgent) business; es 2 haben, 2 sein to be in a hurry or in haste. — 2. (schnell) speedy, quick, prompt, fast; wohin so 2?, where are you hurrying to?, geh. Spr. whither so hurriedly?; wozu so 2? why do you hurry so?, F what's your hurry?; er ging 2(st) davon he went off in (great) haste, he rushed off (headlong), F he was off like a shot.

Eiligkeit (⌣⌣-⌣) f ㊻ = Eile.

Eil=marsch ⚔ (⌣⌣...) m ㉒ forced march; dem Feinde durch =märsche zuvorkom= men to steal a march upon the enemy; =post ⚒ f mail; f.=wagen; =schritt m quick step or march; =sendung f quick(est) dispatch or conveyance (= =fracht).

Eilung ↓ (⌣⌣) f ㊻ gust of wind before a thunderstorm.

Eil=wagen ⚒ (⌣⌣...) m ㉒ mail-coach; bsd. ehm. stage-coach; =zug ⊞ m fast (or express) train.

Eimer (⌣⌣) [ahd.] m ㉒ pail; bucket (a. ⊙); für Schmutzwasser: slop-pail.

Eimer=kette ⊙ (⌣⌣-...) f ⑫ chain-pump, chain of buckets; =kunst f ⊙ pater= noster-pump or -work; =voll m pail= ful; bucketful; =weise adv. by buckets, in pailfuls; =werk n = =kunst.

ein (⌣) [ahd.: one, a(n): lt. unus] I card. numb.: ein m, eine f, ein n ① u. ⑥ C; abs. o. s. Name: eine, eine, ein(es) A 2; be= ziehungslos (meist klein geschrieben): eins inv. 1. one; in einem (numer.) und einem (art.) halben Jahre (with)in eighteen months; als s.: (Zahl) Eins f ㊻ (number) one; hundertundein(s) one hundred and one; einundfünfzig(st) fifty-one (fifty-first); eins und zwei macht drei one and two make three; dreimal eins ist drei three times one are three; mit dem Schlage eins, Punkt eins on (or at)

[ein]

the stroke of one, F at one sharp; es schlägt eins it is striking one; um halb eins at half-past twelve; ein Viertel auf eins a quarter past twelve; ein viertel vor eins a quarter to one; in eins, zwei, drei (im Nu) in a trice; **Eins** f ㊻ auf Karten, Würfeln ꝛc.: ace. — 2. immer betont: (ant. alle, viele ꝛc.) es gibt nur einen Gott there is but one God; die Sache hat ein Gutes there is one good thing in it; der eine Mann that one man (alone); einer von beiden either; nur eins von beiden only one of the two (things); ein für allemal once for all (times); dies eine Mal this once; einer für alle und alle für einen, etwa: all for each and each for all; jointly and severally; ihr ein und alles her one and all, all her belongings pl.; in einem Zuge at one draught; in einem fort ob. weg without stopping or a break, on and on, F at a stretch; das eine, was not tut the one thing needed; vgl. abwechseln 6, Decke 2. — 3. in Bezug zu „der andere": einer ist so schlecht als der andere one is as bad as the other; einer nach dem andern one after another, each (one) in his turn; die einen lachen, die andern weinen some laugh, others cry; die einen hassen die andern the one set hate(s) the other; they hate each other or one another; eins ins andere gerechnet reckoning (or taking) one (thing) with another; die Brüder lieben einer den andern ... love one another. — 4. (der=, die=, das=selbe) immer betont: ein und derselbe one and the same; the very same; ein(e) und dieselbe Frau the very same woman; in einem und demselben Jahre in the very same (or in that very) year; sie sind eins (ganz einig) they are of one mind or thorough= ly agreed; sie wurden eins, das zu tun they agreed ...; das ist alles ein Ding, ein Tun, (ganz) eins, es ist alles eins it is all the same (thing); das ist mir eins it's the same (or quite indifferent) to me; es kommt auf eins heraus, es läuft auf eins hinaus it (all) comes to the same thing; das Sagen und Schießen war eins to say this and (to) fire was the work of an instant. — II indefinite art. ① 5. mst: a, an; one; einen Bart haben to have whiskers or a beard; sie ist eine Eng= länderin she is an Englishwoman, F she is English; es ist (eine) Tatsache, daß // it is a fact that //; das war ein Jam= mern there was (a) lamentation; die Beredsamkeit eines Burke the eloquence of a man like B.; wie ein Fürst leben to live like a prince; einer meiner (seiner) Freunde a friend of mine (of his); F eine vierzehn Tage one (or a) fortnight; prädikativ: die dort verbrachte Stunde war für ihn eine selige the hour spent there was to him a happy one or one of bliss; ein jeder each one; solch (F a. so) ein Mann such a man; welch ein, was für ein Glück, Unglück what luck, what a misfortune; ein (besser: etwas) Weiteres something further, s.th. else. — 6. F ell. ohne s.

(meist klein geschr.): einen (Trunk) nehmen, eins trinken F to have a glass or a drop; j-m eins geben, versetzen to deal (or strike, F fetch) a p. a blow; F e-m eine (eine Ohrfeige) stechen to give a p. a box on the ear; eins darfst du nicht vergessen one thing you must not forget; noch eins! one thing (or word) more!; mit eins (zugleich, plötzlich) all at once, all of a sudden. — **III** *indefinite pron.* **7.** (man, jemand, etwas) einer von euch someone among you; wie kann einer so dumm sein? how can (any) one be so stupid?; manch einer many a one; unsereiner, unsereins people like us, any of us; F (any of) our sort?; was für einer? which one?, what (kind of) man?; ein(e)s muß ich dir sagen I must tell you something or one thing. — **8.** als obliquer Kasus v. „man": das tut einem wohl it does one good; man muß Leute wählen, die einem ehrlich dienen one (or we) must choose people who serve one (or us) honestly; Sprichw. was man nicht weiß, macht einem nicht heiß what is concealed from us does not much worry us, vgl. heiß 2.

...ein (¹) [ahd.] *adv.* f. aus 7; querfeld=2 across the fields, right across country. [mon(o)..., uni...}

Ein¹-..., ein¹-... (one-..., ⁊) **ein²-...** (˝...) Vorsilbe (meist = der *prp.* in) in Zssgn mit *verbs*, stets trennbar (**) bz.: **1.** (*ant.* aus-...) ein Hineinbringen, Hineinkommen, Bergen, Ordnen, z.B. 2führen to introduce, 2treten to step in, 2wickeln to wrap up, 2richten to put in order; ein und aus geh(e)n (⌞⌟) to go in and out, to pass to and fro; vgl. aus 11. — **2.** Zerstörung, Untergang, z.B. 2äschern to reduce to ashes, 2stürzen to fall to pieces. — **3.** Abnahme, z.B. 2büßen to lose. — **4.** Erwerbung, z.B. 2kaufen to purchase. — **5.** Inschlafbringen, z.B. 2ullen to lull to sleep. — **6.** Wirkung auf das Gemüt, z.B. 2schüchtern to intimidate. [monaxial.]

ein¹-achsig ⊓ (˝...) *a.* ⑥ *u. min., cryst.*

ein²-ackern (˝˘˘) *v/a.* ⑳a** *agr.* (unterpflügen) to plough in, to cover (up) in ploughing, to turn in; *fig.* bursch. sich in etwas 2 (einarbeiten) to work o.s. into a th., to get up a subject.

ein¹-ad(e)rig (˝...) *a. elect.:* 2es Kabel single-core cable; 2aktig *a.* in one act; 2es Stück (F =akter *m* ㉒) one-act play.

ein²-altern (˝˘˘) *v/n.* (sn) ⑳a** durch langes Bestehen: to grow obsolete or rusty; eingealtertes System obsolete system.

ein¹-ander (-˘˘) [ahd.: another] *adv.* **1.** one another, each other; fie find 2 im Wege ... in each other's way; sich (*dat.*) 2 helfen (schaden) to assist (to injure) one another; oft, bsd. F a. mutual(ly); sie gewannen 2 lieb they formed a mutual attachment, they became mutually attached (to each other). — **2.** mit *prp.* s. an=, auf=, aus=, bei=, durch=, gegen=, hinter=, in=, mit=, nach=, neben=, über=, von=, zu=; sich vor= 2 fürchten to be afraid of one another.

ein²-ankern (˝˘˘) *v/a.* ⑳a** to (cast the) anchor; (vertäuen) to moor a buoy, &c.

ein²-arbeiten (˝˘˘) *v/a. u. sich 2 v/refl.* ⑲**: e-n (sich) in et. 2 to initiate a p. (o.s.) in a thing, to make a p. (o.s.) acquainted (or familiar) with a thing; er hat sich in die Geschäftsroutine eingearbeitet he has worked himself into (or familiarized himself with or mastered) the business-routine.

ein¹-armig (˝...) *a.* ⑥ one-armed or -branched; *mech.:* 2er Hebel mit der Kraft zwischen Stützpunkt u. Widerstand: one-armed lever, lever of the second kind; 2artig *a.* of one kind or sort or species; (gleichförmig) uniform.

ein²-äschern (˝˘˘) **I** *v/a.* ⑳a** to reduce (or burn) to ashes or to cinders, Stadt: to burn down; *chm.* to calcine, incinerate. — **II** ~ *n* ㉓ *u.* **Ein²-äscherung** *f* ㊻ burning to ashes; *chm.* calcination, incineration. [fit to breathe.]

ein²-atembar (˝˘˘˘) *a.* ⑥ breathable,}

ein²-atmen (˝˘˘) **I** *v/a.* ⑳b** (*ant.* ausatmen) **I** to inhale, to breathe; etwas frische Luft 2 F to get a breath (or a 'sniff) of fresh air; vgl. ausatmen II. — **II** ~ *n* ㉓ *u.* **Ein²-atmung** *f* ㊻ inhalation, breathing; respiration.

ein²-ätzen (˝˘˘) *v/a.* ⑳** to etch in.

Ein¹-auge (˝...) *n* ㉖ cyclops; 2äugig *a.* ⑥ one- (F boss-)eyed; ⊓ monocular.

Ein¹-back (˝˘) *m* ①ⓒ. (*ant.* Zwieback) s. th. baked only once, ordinary baking or baker's ware.

ein²-backen (˝˘˘) ⑤b. (+ ⑧)** **I** *v/a.* Mandeln in e-n Kuchen 2 to bake ... into a cake. — **II** sich 2 *v/refl.* to bake (or get baked) into bread, &c.

ein²-ball(ier)en ⊛ (˝˘˘, ˝˘˘˘) **I** *v/a.* ⑳**(⑳*/*) to pack (or to make up, to consign) in bales. — **II** E/ung *f* ㊻ packing (or consignment) in bales.

ein¹-bällig ⊙ (˝...) *a.* ⑥ Schuhmacherei: made to fit one foot only; 2e Schuhe *m/pl.* a. rights and lefts *pl.*

ein²-balsamier/en (˝˘˘˘˘) **I** *v/a.* ⑳*/* to embalm, to mummify; einbalsamierte Leiche mummy. — **II** ~ *n* ㉓ *u.* E/ung *f* ㊻ embalming, mummification.

Ein²-balsamierer (…) *m* ㉒ embalmer.

Ein²-band ⊙ (˝...) *m* ⑦ⓒ. Buch: binding; cover; (Ausstattung) F get-up of a book; ~=decke *f* ㉖ cover (and back) of a book.

ein²-bändig (˝˘˘) *a.* ⑥ in one volume.

ein²-bansen (˝˘˘) *v/a.* ⑳** *agr.* to store in a barn, to garner. [⊓ monobasic.}

ein¹=basig, =basisch (˝...) *a.* ⑥ *chm.* Säure:}

Ein²-bau ⊙ (˝...) *m* ⑦ⓒ. *arch.* interior (of a building); interior structure.

Ein¹-baum ↓ (˝...) *m* ㉒ (Boot aus einem Baumstamm) monoxyle, dug-out, canoe.

ein²-bauen (˝˘˘) ⑧** **I** *v/n.* (h.) *u.* sich 2 *v/refl.* to build within s.th.; *fig.* sich wo 2 (einnisten) to put up (or hide away) somewhere; to make one's home (or to settle down) in a place. — **II** *v/a.* to enclose with buildings or walls; (eindeichen) to dam (or dike) up; ⚒ Pumpen 2 to put up pumps.

ein²-bedingen (˝˘˘˘) *v/a.* ⑳fi*/* (mit) 2 to comprise (or include) in a bargain.

Ein¹-beere ⚘ (˝...) *f* true-love, oneberry (*Paris quadrifo'lius*).

ein²-begreifen (˝˘˘˘) **I** *v/a.* ⑳b*/* (mit) 2 to comprise (include, imply) in a

th. — **II** (mit) (e)in-begriffen *p.p. u. a.* ⑥ (D9) (material, &c.) included, including or inclusive of (costs, &c.).

ein²-behalten (˝˘˘˘) *v/a.* ⑳a*/* to keep back, detain, retain; j-s Lohn 2 to dock (F to dock) a p.'s wages.

ein¹-beinig (˝˘˘) *a.* ⑥ one-legged.

ein²-beißen (˝˘˘) ⑳a** **I** *v/n.* (h.) in etwas 2 to bite into s.th. — **II** *a.* sich 2 *v/refl.* von Insekten ⁊c.: sich in die Haut 2 to bite through (or pierce) the skin.

ein²-beizen (˝˘˘) *v/a.* ⑳** to etch into a copper plate; to vein wood, &c.

ein²-bekommen (˝˘˘˘) *v/a.* ⑳a*/* ⑧ **1.** Geld 2 to get in ... — **2.** F (einholen) to catch up.

ein²-berufen (˝˘˘˘) **I** *v/a.* ⑳b** to call soldiers in or out; to call (or convene, convoke) a meeting; to summon parliament. — **II** ~ *n* ㉓ = E/ung.

Ein²-berufer (˝˘˘˘) *m* ㉒ person who calls or summons; summoner; *parl.* whip. ehm.: whipper-in.

Ein²-berufung (˝˘˘˘) *f* ㊻ call(ing in); convention, convocation; ⚔ ~ der Reserven, eines Jahrganges calling in of the reserve, of the year's conscripts; ~s-order ⚔ † = Gestellungsbefehl.

ein²-betten (˝˘˘) ⑳** **I** *v/a.* **1.** to put in(to) a bed; im Kalf, Sande eingebettet embedded in lime, sand. — **2.** eine Fluß 2 = eindämmen. — **II** sich 2 *v/refl.* **3.** to get a bed (or a night's lodging) at a p.'s house.

ein²-biegen (˝˘˘) ⑥aft** **I** *v/a. u.* sich 2 *v/refl.* to bend inward(s), to turn down the corner of a leaf. — **II** *v/n.* (sn) in die Straße links 2 to take the turning (or to turn) to the left, wieder in den Weg 2 to turn back to (or to resume) one's way. — **III** ~ *n* ㉓ = V. — **IV ein²-gebogen** *p.p. u. a.* ⑥(D9) bent inward(s), turned in at the edge; ⚘ inflected; (buchtig) sinuous; 2e Beine *n/pl.* a. bent (F bow-) legs *pl.* — **V Ein²-biegung** *f* ㊻ inward bend, curvature, ⊓ incurvation; *phys., &c.* inflexion.

ein²-bilden (˝˘˘) **I** *v/a.* ⑲** **1.** sich (*dat.*) etwas 2 (vorstellen) to conceive a th.; mittels der Phantasie: to imagine (or fancy) a thing; ich bilde mir nicht ein was Rechts zu wissen (G.) I do not pretend to (have) any real knowledge; sich 2, ein Kenner zu sein, oft: to pose as a connoisseur; sich allerlei 2 to have all sorts of vain imaginings; sich etwas steif und fest 2 to be firmly convinced of a thing. — **2.** sich viel 2 (dünken) to be conceited or full of conceit, to presume too much; F to think too much of o.s.; er bildet sich nichts Geringes ein he has high notions (F he thinks no small beer) of himself, F he fancies himself somebody; sich etwas auf etwas 2 to pride (or pique) o.s. on a thing. — **II ein²-gebildet** *p.p.* und *a.* ⑥ **3.** (f. 1) imaginary, fancied, fanciful: chimerical. — **4.** (f. 2) conceited; vainglorious; (anmaßend) presumptuous

Ein²-bildung (˝˘˘˘) *f* ㊻ **1.** (zu einbilden 1:) imagination, fancy; (Trugbild) illusion, chimera. — **2.** (zu 2:) conceit, vaingloriousness; presumption.

Signs (see page XVII): F familiar; P vulgar; ⌐ flash; ⟋ rare; † obsolete (died); * new word (born); ⁺⁺ incorrect; ♪ music;

Ein²-bildungs-kraft (⏑́⏑…) f [E] (power of) imagination, imaginative (or inventive) faculty or power; dichterische ~ poetic fancy or phantasy or conceit.
ein²-binden (⏑́⏑) v/a. [D]** 1. to (wrap and) tie up; seinem Paten etwas ℒ to make a present to a godchild at the christening. — 2. ⚙ Buchbinderei: to bind a book; Stellmacherei: ein Rad ℒ (beschienen) to rim (or case, tire) a wheel; ⚓ die Segel: to furl; ein Reff ℒ to take in a reef; ✱ Waren: to bale up, to embale; hort. junge Bäume zum Schutz ℒ to tie up … with straw, &c.
ein²-blasen (⏑́⏑) v/a. [B]a** 1. to blow (or breathe) into a th. — 2. fig. e-m etwas ℒ (einraunen) to whisper a th. to a p. or into a p.'s ear; fig. to suggest (or insinuate, prompt) a th. to a p.
Ein²-bläser (⏑) m [22] fig. prompter; secret adviser; **Ein²-bläserei** (⏑-⏑́) f [46] fig. suggestion, insinuation prompting.
Ein²-blasung (⏑) f [46] med. ⚗ insufflation.
Ein¹-blatt ✿ (⏑́) n [E] grass of Parnassus (Parna'ssia vulga'ris); -**blattdruck** m, typ. (nur auf einer Seite bedrucktes Blatt) broadsheet; ℒ**blätt(e)rig** ✿, bff. ℒ**blattig** a. [66] one leafed, ⚗ monophyllous.
ein²-bläuen (⏑́⏑) v/a. [B]** Wäsche: to blue.
ein²-bleuen (⏑́⏑) v/a. [B]**: e-m et. ℒ (einschärfen) to inculcate a thing in(to) a p.; durch Prügel: to knock (or drub, drum) a th. into a p.
Ein²-blick (⏑́) m [U]c. insight (F look) into; e-m einen ~ in etwas geben, gewähren to give (or allow) a p. an insight into a th.; ich verschaffte mir einen ~ in die Sache I (thoroughly) looked (or F went) into the matter.
ein¹-blumig ✿ (⏑́⏑) a. [66] one-flowered, ⚗ uniflorous.
ein²-bohren (⏑́⏑) [B]** I v/a. ein Loch in ein Brett ℒ to bore a hole into a plank. — II v/n. (h.) und sich ℒ v/refl. to bore (one's way) into a th., to pierce a th.
ein²-brechen (⏑́⏑) [D]a** I v/a. 1. ein Loch in etwas ℒ to break an opening into a th.; eine Tür: to break (or force) open; eine Mauer: to pull down. — II v/n. (sn) 2. (einsinken) to break (or sink) in; to give way under a load. — 3. in ein Haus (gewaltsam) ℒ to break into a house, to enter forcibly, von Dieben auch: to commit a burglary; es ist bei ihm eingebrochen worden he has had (the) burglars in his house; ⚔ in ein Land ℒ to invade (or to make an inroad into) a country; in die feindliche Stellung ℒ to rush (or to make an incursion into) the enemy's position; fig. das über uns ℒde Verhängnis the fate befalling us. — 4. (plötzlich erscheinen) to appear (or approach) suddenly; bei ℒder Nacht at the approach of night, at nightfall, when night sets in. — III ~ n [23] 5. (s. 1 u. 2) breaking in or open. — 6. (s. 3) forcible entrance; burglarious attempt, burglary; ⚔ incursion, invasion, inroad. — 7. (s. 4) sudden appearance or approach; der Nacht: nightfall. [burglar.]
Ein²-brecher (⏑́⏑) m [22] housebreaker,

ein²-brennen (⏑́⏑) [M]b** I v/a. 1. to burn in(to); ein Zeichen ℒ to mark (or brand) with a hot iron; ⚙ Farben ℒ to anneal colours; eingebrannte Wachsmalerei encaustic (painting); die Glasur ℒ to bake the glaze; surg. to cauterize a wound, &c. — 2. Fässer ꝛc. mit Schwefel ℒ to (fumigate with) sulphur … — II v/n. 3. (h.) to burn in(to). — 4. (sn) (brennend einsinken) to drop (or collapse) in burning. — III ~ n [23] 5. (s. 1) burning in, branding; cauterization; surg. ⚙ der Glasur: glaze-baking. [art.]
Ein²-brenn-kunst (⏑́⏑) f [E] encaustic
ein²-bringen (⏑́⏑) I v/a. [D]** 1. to introduce; to get in(to); parl. to bring in a bill, to propose a resolution; Gefangene: to bring in; Getreide (in die Scheune): to gather in(to the barn); to house (safely); eingebrachtes Gut (von der Frau eingebrachtes Vermögen) marriage-portion, dowry; (Ausstattung) (wedding-)trousseau. — 2. etwas ℒ (eintragen) to bring in money, to yield a profit or good returns; to endow with riches or honour; sein Geschäft bringt nur wenig ein his (weekly) returns are but small; wieviel mag das Amt ℒ?, oft: how much may the post be worth? — 3. (nachholen) to make good, to retrieve; die versäumte Zeit wieder ℒ to make up for lost time; ⚙ typ. eine Zeile ℒ (eng setzen; ant. ausbringen 5) to set up … (more) closely; to get in; weitS. to save … — II ~ n [23] und **Ein²-bringung** f [46] 4. (s. 1) introduction; bringing in, &c.; der Ernte: (gathering in of the) harvest, harvesting.
ein²-brocken (⏑́⏑) v/a. [B]** 1. to crumble bread into the broth. — 2. F fig. er hat etwas einzubrocken he is well off or in comfortable circumstances; e-m etwas (oder eine Suppe) ℒ to do a p. an ill turn, F to serve a p. a nasty trick; vgl. auch ausessen.
ein²-bröseln (⏑́⏑) v/a. [B]a** Kochk.: (panieren) to cover with bread-crumbs.
Ein²-bruch (⏑́) m [D]d. = einbrechen III; ~(s)-**dieb(stahl)** (⏑́…) m [22] burglar(y); ~s-**stelle** ⚔ f point of irruption, convenient spot for an incursion or invasion.
ein¹-brüd(e)rig ✿ (⏑́…) a. [66] (Staubfäden zu einem Bündel verwachsen): ⚗ monadelphous; ℒ Pflanze: ⚗ monadelph.
ein²-brühen (⏑́⏑) v/a. [B]** to scald.
Ein²-buchtung (⏑́⏑) f [46] inlet; indenture; (small) bay, bight, creek; ~s-**winkel** m [22] re-entering angle. [in.]
ein²-buddeln F (⏑́⏑) v/a. [B]a.** to dig
ein²-bürgern (⏑́⏑) [B]a** I v/a. to admit as citizen(s) or to the rights of citizenship; weitS. to naturalize, pol. to enfranchise; fig. auch: to adopt foreign words or customs; eingebürgert naturalized; adopted. — II sich ℒ v/refl. to become naturalized (auch fig.); to settle down in a foreign land; fig. auch: to be(come) adopted, to gain currency. — III ~ n [23] u. **Ein²-bürgerung** (⏑́⏑⏑) f [46] naturalization, enfranchisement; settlement; fig. adoption. [loss; forfeiture.]
Ein²-buße (⏑́⏑) f [46] damage, injury;

ein²-büßen (⏑́⏑) v/a. [B]** to suffer the loss of; to lose; to forfeit (vgl. ein-… 3).
ein²-dämm|en (⏑́⏑) I v/a. [B]** to dam up or in, to (em)bank a river; ⚙ Gießerei: die Form ℒ to ram down the mould; fig. (einschränken) to check, to restrain. — II ℒ**ung** f [46] embankment; fig. check, restriction put upon.
ein²-dämmern F (⏑́⏑) v/n. (sn) [B]a** to (fall into a) slumber, to doze off.
ein²-dampfen (⏑́⏑) v/n. (sn) [B]** = abdampfen 1. [dämpfen 1 u. 2.]
ein²-dämpfen (⏑́⏑) v/a. [B]** = ab-
ein²-decken ⚙ (⏑́⏑) I v/a. u. v/n. (h.) [B]** 1. arch. to (put on the) roof; das Dach ℒ to cover up the roof. — 2. Weinstöcke: to (hill up with) earth, to cover up with straw. — II ~ n [23] und **Ein-deckung** f [46] 3. (s. 1) roofing; ⚔ covering in (of) the entrenchments.
ein²-deichen (⏑́⏑) v/a. [B]** = eindämmen.
ein¹-deutig (⏑́…) a. [66] (ant. zweideutig) having but one meaning.
ein²-deutschen (⏑́⏑) v/a. [D]** to make German, to Germanize.
ein²-dicken (⏑́⏑) I v/a. [B]** Kochk.: to thicken gravy, &c.; chm.: ⚗ to inspissate; eingedickte Milch condensed milk. — II ~ n [23] u. **Ein-dickung** f [46] thickening; condensation; ⚗ inspissation.
ein²-docken ⚓ (⏑́⏑) v/a. [B]** = docken².
ein²-dorren (⏑́⏑) v/n. (sn) [B]** to dry up; in der Sonne: to be parched up.
ein¹-drähtig ⚙ (⏑́…) a. [66] single-threaded or -wired.
ein²-drängen (⏑́⏑) [B]** I v/a. to squeeze (or push, thrust) in. — II sich ℒ v/refl. to squeeze (or force, push) one's way in; to intrude; to obtrude o.s. upon. — III ~ n [23] squeezing in; intrusion.
ein²-drillen F (⏑́⏑) v/a. [B]** 1. Rekruten ꝛc.: to drill (well). — 2. fig. e-m et. ℒ to drill (or ground) a p. in a th.
ein²-dringen (⏑́⏑) I v/n. (sn) [D]t** 1. to enter forcibly or by force, to break (or burst) in(to); auf e-n ℒ to fall (or rush) upon a p.; bei e-m ℒ to enter forcibly (or to force one's way into) a p.'s house; ⚔ als Feind in ein Land ℒ to invade a country; vgl. eindrängen II. — 2. v. Flüssigkeiten: to soak in or through; to penetrate; ⚗ to infiltrate. — 3. fig. in ein Geheimnis, in das Wesen e-r Sprache ℒ to fathom (or dive into) a mystery, the depths of a th.; ℒd searching. — II ~ n [23] 4. = Eindringung.
ein²-dringlich (⏑́⏑) a. [66] intrusive; penetrative; (eindrucksvoll) impressive, stirring, emphatic, striking; (rührend) touching, pathetic; (gewaltig) forcible, urgent. [intruder; interloper.]
Ein²-dringling (⏑́⏑) m [U]d. invader.
Ein²-dringung (⏑) f [46] 1. (zu eindringen 1:) forcible entry; irruption; inroad, invasion. — 2. (zu 2:) infiltration.
Ein²-druck (⏑́) m [D]c. 1. = eindrücken III. — 2. (hinterlassene Spur) imprint(ed mark), impress(ion). — 3. fig. impression; dauernder (vorübergehender) ~ lasting (fugitive) impression; er macht den ~ eines höflichen Lebemannes he makes the impression of being (or

⚗ scientific; ✿ botanical; ♀ geography; ⚙ machinery; ⚒ mining; ⚔ military; ⚓ marine; ✱ commercial; ✉ postal; 🚂 railway.

[eindrucken] — 296 — [einfassen]

he impresses one as) a courteous man of the world; e-n (un)angenehmen ~ auf e-n machen to make a(n un)favourable impression upon a p., to impress (or strike) a p. (un)favourably; er hat den ~, als ob // he has an impression (or idea) that //.

ein²-drucken (⁻'⌣⌣) ⊛** typ. (dem Druck einverleiben) to insert into the letterpress; Buch mit eingedruckten Holzschnitten ... illustrated by woodcuts.

ein²-drück/en (⁻'⌣⌣) ⊛** I v/a. 1. to press (or squeeze) in(to); to insert; man. die Sporen 2 to dig in the spurs. — 2. (einprägen) to imprint, impress, print upon. — 3. (platt drücken) to compress. to flatten (down); (zermalmen) to crush (in), squash. — II sich 2 v/refl. 4. to be(come) imprinted upon. — III ~ n 23 5. = E/ung. — IV ein-gedrückt p.p. u. a. ⊛ 6. in den Bed. des inf. — 7. 2e Nase flat (or pug-)nose; ⚭ von Blättern: ⚹ retuse.

ein²-drücklich (⁻'⌣⌣) a. ⊛ = eindringlich.

Ein²-drückung (⁻'⌣⌣) f ⊛ 1. (zu eindrücken 1:) insertion. — 2. (zu 3:) flattening (down), crushing (in).

ein²-drucks-fähig (⁻'⌣...) a. ⊛ impressi(ona)ble; -fähigkeit f ⊛ impressi(ona)bility; 2los a. unimpressive; 2voll a. impressive; urgent; effective. powerful. [to doze off.)

ein²-duseln F (⁻'⌣⌣) (in Schlummer fallen)/

ein²-eb(e)nen (⁻'⌣(⌣)⌣) v/a. ⊛a(⊛)** to (make) level; to flatten; to make even (with the ground); to smooth.

ein²-eggen (⁻'⌣⌣) v/a. ⊛** to work in(to the ground) with the harrow, to turn in with the harrow, vgl. eineggen.

ein²-eisen (⁻'⌣⌣) [Eis²] v/a. ⊛** to hem in with ice; ⚓ eingeeist p.p. icebound, ice-locked.

einen (⁻'⌣) v/a. u. v/refl. ⊛ = einigen.

ein²-engen (⁻'⌣⌣) v/a. ⊛** to (make) narrow; to confine, compress, cramp (up); (einschließen) to hem in, enclose; (einpferchen) to pen in; sehr eingeengt narrowly confined, very cramped.

einer (⁻'⌣) I card. numb. abs. f. ein I. — II Einer m ⊛ arith. (einstellige Zahl) unit, figure of one dimension or below ten.

einer-lei (⁻⌣⌣́) I a. inv. of one (or the same) kind or sort or description; identical; (gleichgültig) indifferent, immaterial; es ist ziemlich ~ it is as broad as it's long; es ist mir ganz 2 it is all the same (or all one) to me. — II ~ n ⓒc. sameness, uniformity, (Einförmigkeit) monotony, monotonous round, dull routine; immer das ewige ~! the same thing (F the same old story) over and over again!

Einer-lei-heit (⁻⌣⌣́⁻) f ⊛ identity; sameness, uniformity.

ein²-ernten (⁻'⌣⌣) I v/a. ⊛*. 1. agr. to reap; vgl. ernten. — 2. fig. Ruhm von (ob. für) et. 2 to earn (or gather) fame by a th. — II ~ n ⊛ 3. reaping; harvest. [the one hand.)

einer-seits, eines-teils (⁻⌣⌣́) adv. on)

ein²-exerzieren ⚔ (⁻'⌣⌣*) I v/a. ⊛*,* to drill (or train) well; to practise; to exercise. — II ~ n ⊛ drilling; (military) training; practice, exercise.

ein¹-fach (⁻'⌣ch) I a. ⊛ simple (auch math.); single (sheet of paper, ticket, railway-line, &c.); plain (dress, food, style, &c.); homely (manner); private (soldier, citizen); frugal (repast); ⚹ ⚯ incomposite; math. indivisible (value); simple (fraction); ⚘ 2e Buchführung bookkeeping by single entry; arith. 2e Zahl (Primzahl) prime number; vgl. einglied(e)rig; phys. 2e Farben primitive (or prismatic, elementary) colours pl.; chm. 2er Körper element(ary body), simple (or uncombined) substance; ⚘ 2e Fahrkarte 3. Klasse single third-class ticket. — II adv. sie war 2 angezogen she was simply (or plainly) dressed; F sie sah 2 (ganz) wie ein Engel aus she looked a perfect angel; du gehst 2 (ohne weiteres) hin und // you shall go there without further ado and //.

Ein¹-fachheit (⁻'⌣⁻) f ⊛ simplicity; homeliness; im Essen: frugality.

ein¹-fach=wirkend ⚯ (⁻'⌣ch...) a. ⊛ mach. single-acting.

ein²-fädeln (⁻'⌣⌣) v/a. ⊛a** to thread a needle; fig. ein Gespräch: to start; e-e Sache: to contrive; sie hat die Sache schlau eingefädelt she cleverly manœuvred the matter, she set to work most ingeniously; vgl. anzetteln 2.

ein²-fahren (⁻'⌣⌣) ⊛b** I v/n. (ſn) 1. to enter in a carriage; to drive in(to); ⚓ to sail (or steam) in(to port); ⚒ to descend (into the shaft); hunt. (in den Bau kriechen) to go to earth. — II v/a. 2. to cart in; to carry (or bring) in by vehicle; Getreide: to get in. — 3. (fahrend einstoßen) to drive into; to run (or dash) into with a carriage, motor, &c.; einen Weg 2 to cut up a road. — 4. Pferde 2 to train (or break in) carriage-horses; sich 2 v/refl. to practise driving. — III ~ n ⊛ 5. (f. 1) entrance, driving in; ⚒ descent; ⚓ beim ~ on sailing into (or on entering) a port, a strait, &c. — 6. (f. 4) training of carriage-horses.

Ein²-fahrer ⚒ (⁻'⌣⌣) m ⊛ inspector of mines.

Ein²-fahrt (⁻'⌣) f ⊛ 1. = einfahren 5. — 2. (Ort) gateway, doorway; drive.

Ein²-fahrt(s)-signal (⁻'⌣...) n ⊛, =zeichen ⊛ n station- (or distance-)signal.

Ein²-fall (⁻'⌣) m ⓒc. 1. (Hineinfallen) fall(ing in). — 2. ⚔ ~ in ein Land inroad (or incursion, irruption) into (or invasion of) a country; descent upon a (hostile) shore; feindlicher ~ hostile invasion; einen ~ abwehren to repel (or beat back) the invader or the invading host. — 3. (Einsturz) falling down, (down)fall; stärker: (utter) collapse; vgl. einfallen 6. — 4. phys. des Lichtes; ⚹ incidence. — 5. (Gedanke) (sudden flash of) thought; ich geriet auf den ~ the idea (or it) suddenly struck or occurred to) me; F I took it into my head; lustiger ~ merry thought or conceit; jocose (or facetious) remark; witziger ~ sally (of wit), witticism; wunderlicher ~ curious idea or fancy; strange caprice or whim; was für ein ~! what an idea!, what a curious fancy or notion!

ein²-fallen (⁻'⌣⌣) I v/n. (ſn) ⊛a** 1. to fall in(to); phys. 2de Lichtstrahlen incident rays of light. — 2. (plötzlich kommen) to appear suddenly; hunt. (niederfliegen) to alight on the ground; ⚔ in ein Land 2 to invade (or overrun) a country; vgl. Einfall 2. — 3. ♪ to chime in; die Flöten sind (a. haben) zur rechten Zeit eingefallen the flutes joined (or struck) in at the right time. — 4. (in die Rede fallen) to interrupt (or cut short) a p.'s speech. — 5. (in den Sinn kommen) to strike (or occur to) a p.; dabei fällt mir gerade ein it just comes (in)to my mind, I am just thinking; es fiel mir eben plötzlich ein it suddenly flashed upon my mind; der Name will mir nicht 2 I cannot remember the name; the name has dropt from my mind; fällt mir nicht (einmal) ein!, das würde mir im Traume nicht 2 I should never dream of (F catch me doing) such a thing!; das hätte ich mir nie 2 lassen that would never have entered my head; das laß dir nie 2! you must never think of such a thing!; was fällt Ihnen (nur) ein? what are you thinking (or dreaming, talking) of. — 6. (einstürzen) to fall (in), tumble (down), stärker: to collapse. — 7. (zs.-sinken) to drop, give way, waste (away); eingefall(e)ne Wangen f/pl. sunken (or hollow) cheeks pl. — 8. sich (dat.) et. 2, zB. sich den Schädel 2 to break one's head by a fall or by falling. — II ~ n ⊛ 9. = Einfall 1 bis 4. — 10. (f. 4) interruption of a speech.

Ein²-falls-ebene (⁻'⌣⌣...) f ⊛, =punkt, =winkel m, phys. plane, point, angle of incidence.

Ein²-falt (⁻'⌣) [ahd.] f ⊛: a) Kunst: simplicity of style; b) (Schlichtheit) simpleness; ingenuousness; (Unschuld) innocence; single-heartedness; (Dummheit) silliness; c) (einfältige Person) simpleton; simple-minded (country-)girl; (leicht Betrogene[r]) F jay.

ein²-falten (⁻'⌣⌣) v/a. ⊛** to fold, plait; to wrap up. [or fold.)

ein¹-faltig (⁻'⌣⌣) a. ⊛ with one plait)

ein¹-fältig (⁻'⌣⌣) a. ⊛ simple (-minded); ingenuous, innocent; silly, foolish; F soft; 2es Zeug rubbish, nonsense, trash; ~keit (⁻'⌣⌣⁻) f ⊛ = Einfalt b.

Ein¹-falts=pinsel (⁻'⌣...) m ⊛ dunce, silly fellow, blockhead, simple Simon. simpleton, F noodle, ninny.

ein²-falzen ⚯ (⁻'⌣⌣) I v/a. ⊛b** Buchb.: to fold in or up; carp.: to rabbet planks; Böttcherei: (tröseln) to groove.

Ein¹-familien=haus (⁻⌣⁻(⌣)⌣⁻) n ⊛ house for one family (only).

ein²-fangen (⁻'⌣⌣) I v/a. ⊛b** to catch and seize; to capture, apprehend, secure, Verbrecher ꝛc.: to take into custody, to arrest. — II ~ n ⊛ capture. apprehension.

ein¹-farbig (⁻'...) a. ⊛ one-coloured; plain, ⚹ monochromatic; 2es Bild ⚹ monochrome; =farbigkeit f sameness (or plainness) of colour.

ein²-fass/en (⁻'⌣⌣) I v/a. ⊛** 1. mit et. 2 (umrändern) to border (or edge, von

Zeichen (f. S. XVII): F familiär; P Volkssprache; ſ Gaunersprache; ⟋ selten; † alt (auch gestorben); * neu (auch geboren); ⫽ unrichtig;

[Einfasser] — 297 — [Einführung]

Kleidern ıc. auch: to bind or trim) with s.th.; mit Franſen eingefaßt bound (round) with fringe; mit Blumen ≈ to border with flowers; rings (im Kreiſe) ≈ to encircle. — 2. ⊕ e-n Brunnen ≈ to curb a well; hort. mit Buchs ıc. ≈ to border (or edge) ...; Juwelier: mit Edelſteinen ≈ to enchase, to set with precious stones; mit Gold ≈ to mount in gold; arch. mit Mauern ≈ to enclose (or encompass) with walls; mit Perlen ≈ to hem (around) with pearls; in e-n Rahmen ≈ to (put in(to) a) frame; typ. to edge (off). — 3. Bier ıc. ≈ (in Fäſſer füllen) to barrel ıc., to put ... in casks or barrels; Bienen (in einen Korb): to (put into a) hive. — II ~ n ㉓ 4. = E/ung 1. [von Diamanten: mounter.]
Ein²-faſſer (ᴵᴵ◡◡) m ㉒ edger, trimmer.
Ein²-faſſung (ᴵᴵ◡◡) f ㊻ 1. (ſ. einfaſſen 1) border(ing), edging, edge, binding, (lace-, &c.) trimming. — 2. ⊕ (ſ. einfaſſen 2) curb of a well; hort. bordering, edging; Juwelier: setting; arch. enclosure; (Tür-, Fenſter-rahmen) door-, window-frame; einer Brille: mounting.
ein²-feilen ⊕ (ᴵᴵ◡) ⊛** to file into; to mark (or notch, groove) with a file. [to drive ... a cornig.]
ein²-femen (ᴵᴵ◡) v/a. ⊛**: Schweine ≈
ein²-fetten (ᴵᴵ◡◡) I v/a. ⊛** to grease; ⊕ mach. (ſchmieren) to lubricate. — II ~ n ㉓ und Ein-fettung f ㊻ greasing; ⊕ mach. lubrication.
ein²-feuchten (ᴵᴵ◡◡) v/a. ⊛** to moisten, to damp; ſtärker: to wet, to soak.
ein²-feuern (ᴵᴵ◡) v/n. (h.) ⊛a** to make up (or light) a fire; fig. e-m (a. v/a. e-n) ≈ to egg (or urge) a p. on, to kindle (or inflame) a p.'s passion.
ein²-finden (ᴵᴵ◡◡) I ſich ≈ v/refl. ⊕** to appear (on the scene); vor Gericht: in court); to arrive; es fanden ſich nur wenige ein only a few appeared (on the scene) or were present or put in an appearance; wird er ſich bei uns ≈? will he come to see us?, will he present himself at our house? — II ~ n ㉓ appearance, arrival; presence.
ein²-flechten (ᴵᴵ◡◡) ⊛b** I v/a. 1. to interlace; die Haare ıc. ≈ to plait (or braid) the hair, &c.; Rohr in Stühle ≈ to cane chairs; Bänder ins Haar ≈ to dress the hair with ribbons. — 2. fig. to put in a word; to insert a note; to introduce a jest, to intersperse fine phrases; Zitate in eine Rede ≈ to interlard (or interweave) a speech with quotations; eingeflocht(e)ne Lieder songs woven in or dispersed through the book. — II ~ n ㉓ u. Ein-flechtung f ㊻ 3. (ſ. 1) plaiting, &c. — 4. (ſ. 2) fig. insertion; introduction; interspersion.
ein²-flicken (ᴵᴵ◡◡) v/a. ⊛** ein Stück ≈ to put a patch in; vgl. einflechten 2.
ein²-fliegen (ᴵᴵ◡) v/n. (ſn) ⊕aft** to fly in; aus- und ≈ to fly in and out.
ein²-fließen (ᴵᴵ◡) I v/n. (ſn) ⊕d** 1. to flow in(to); wo die Ströme ins Meer ≈ ... flow in (or empty) into (or join) the sea. — 2. fig. von Geldern: to come (or be paid) in, to be received. — 3. fig. Worte mit ≈ laſſen to put (or slip) in a few words; (casually) to make (or drop) a remark; to join in (a discussion). — II ~ n ㉓ 4. inflow, influx; von Geld: receipt.
ein²-flößbar (ᴵᴵ◡-) a. ㊻ infusible.
ein²-flößen (ᴵᴵ◡) I v/a. ⊛⁰** to cause to flow into; to instil a conviction, to inspire confidence, to infuse courage, to excite a desire (e-m in a p.); e-m Bewunderung, Mitleid(en) ≈ to call forth (or evoke, rouse) a p.'s admiration, pity; einem Liebe ≈ to fill (ſtärker: to transfuse) a p. with love; e-m Verdacht ≈ to rouse (or excite) a p.'s suspicion. — II ~ n ㉓ und Ein²-flöß/ung f ㊻ instillation; inspiration; infusion.
Ein²-flug (ᴵᴵ) m ⑧d. entrance to a hive.
ein¹-flüg(e)lig (ᴵᴵ◡(◡)◡) a.㊻ one-winged, ⌁ monopteral.
ein²-fluß (ᴵᴵ◡) m ⑧a. 1. (Einfließen) flowing in; influx. — 2. Ort: ~ des Mains in den Rhein confluence of the Main and the Rhine. — 3. fig. influence with; ascendency (or sway) over; guter (ſchlimmer) ~ influence for good (for bad); perſönlicher ~, auch: interest with; großen (ausgedehnten) ~ haben to have a great (wide-spread) influence or authority; ~ ausüben, haben auf to exercise, to have (an) influence over or on or with; ſeinen ~ geltend machen to make one's influence felt; ſein Leiden hat ~ auf ſein Gemüt his malady affects (or tells upon) his mind; das hat keinen ~ auf ihn that has no weight with him; das hat keinen ~ darauf that has no connexion with it, no bearing upon it; er hat großen ~ bei Hofe he is a great favourite at court; er ſtand unter ihrem ~ he was under her influence or F thumb.
ein²-fluß-los (ᴵᴵ◡) a. ㊻ uninfluential; ≈reich a. influential; ≈e Leute influential people, F great guns, bigwigs; ≈rohr ⊕ n ㉖, ≈röhre ⊕ f, mach. inlet-pipe.
Ein²-flüſterei (ᴵᴵ◡◡◡) f ㊻ = einflüſtern II.
Ein²-flüſterer (ᴵᴵ◡◡◡) m ㉒ prompter.
ein²-flüſter/n (ᴵᴵ◡◡) I v/a. ⊛a** e-m et. ≈ to whisper s.th. in a p.'s ear; vgl. einblaſen 2. — II ~ n ㉓ u. E/ung f ㊻ whispering; prompting; suggestion.
ein²-fordern (ᴵᴵ◡◡) I v/a. ⊛a** 1. to call (or get) in money; to demand payment of a debt; Steuern ıc. to collect. — II ~ n ㉓ und Ein-forderung f ㊻ 2. calling in, &c. (ſ. 1). — 3. demand for payment; collection of taxes, &c.
ein¹-förmig (ᴵᴵ◡◡) a. ㊻ (und adv.) uniform(ly); vgl. eintönig. [vgl. Eintönigkeit.]
Ein¹-förmigkeit (ᴵᴵ◡◡◡) f㊻ uniformity.
ein²-forſten (ᴵᴵ◡◡) v/a. ⊛** for. to afforest; to plant afresh (with trees).
ein²-freſſen (ᴵᴵ◡◡) I v/a. ⊛** 1. (freſſen) to devour; fig. to swallow one's grief. — 2. (ätzend zerſtören) chm., &c. to corrode. — II v/n. (h. u. ſn) und ſich ≈ v/refl., chm., &c. 3. to eat into a substance; Scheidewaſſer frißt (ſich) in die Platte ein aquafortis attacks the copper plate. — III ~ n ㉓ chm. &c. 4. corrosion.
ein²-fried(ig)en (ᴵᴵ◡(◡)◡) I v/a. ⊛(⊛)** to hedge (or fence, rail) in; to enclose. — II ~ n ㉓ = E/ung 1.

Ein²-fried(ig)ung (ᴵᴵ(◡)◡) f ㊻ 1. fencing in; railing. — 2. hedge, fence, enclosure; (Pfahlzaun) paling, ⚔ palisade.
Ein²-fried(ig)ungs=mauer (ᴵᴵ...) f ㉖ boundary-wall, enclosure-wall.
ein²-frieren (ᴵᴵ◡◡) v/n. (ſn) ⊕c** to freeze in or fast; eingefroren frozen in, von Schiffen ıc.: ice-bound.
ein¹-früchtig ⚘ (ᴵᴵ◡◡) a. ㊻: ⌁ monocarpous, monocarpellary.
ein²-fuchſen F (ᴵᴵ◡tʃ◡) v/a. ⊛⁰** e-m et. ≈ (einbrillen) F to drub a th. into a p.
ein²-fugen ⊕ (ᴵᴵ◡◡) I v/a. u. ſich ≈ v/refl. ⊛⊛** to fit (or let) in; in ein Käſtchen: to encase, to enchase; in e-n Falz: to rabbet. — II ~ n ㉓ u. Ein²-fugung f ㊻ fitting in, &c. (ſ. I).
ein²-fügen (ᴵᴵ◡◡) ⊛** I v/a. 1. ⊕ to dovetail; ⊥ to splice; hort. (okulieren) to inoculate; med. Adern: ⌁ to inosculate. — 2. a. fig. to insert; (einſpiden) to interlard. — II ſich ≈ v/refl. 3. to fit in (well); fig. auch: to adapt o.s. to the surroundings, to be adapted or suitable. — III ~ n ㉓ u. Ein²-fügung f ㊻ 4. fitting in; hort. inoculation; med.: ⌁ inosculation; auch fig insertion.
Ein²-fuhr ⚓ (ᴵᴵ◡) f ㊻ import(ation); ~ und Ausfuhr imports and exports pl.
Ein²-fuhr-artikel ⚓ (≈...) m (pl.) ㉖ article(s pl.) of import(ation); imports.
ein²-führbar (ᴵᴵ◡-) a. ㊻ (zuläſſig) admissible; ⚓ importable.
Ein²-führbarkeit (ᴵᴵ---) f ㊻ admissibility; ⚓ fitness for importation; admissibleness as an import.
ein²-führ/en (ᴵᴵ◡) I v/a. (u. ſich ≈ v/refl.) ⊛** 1. (ſ. ein=... 1) to introduce (o.s.), to establish (o.s.); in den Magen ≈ to receive into the stomach; et. ſanft in e-e Wunde ıc. ≈ gently to insert a th. into a wound, &c.; eine Sitte ≈ to introduce (or set up) a custom; eine Mode ≈ to start (or set) a (new) fashion; bei e-m ≈ to introduce at (or into) a p.'s house; in eine Geſellſchaft ≈ to introduce into a company; bei Hofe ≈ to present at court; beim Publikum ≈ to bring before (or make known to) the public; es iſt bei uns eingeführt, daß // it is the custom with us that //; in ein Zimmer (anmeldend) ≈ to usher in(to a room); ⚓ Waren ≈ to import goods; ⚓ neu eingeführte Artikel: a) newly imported goods pl.; b) new fashions, novelties pl. — 2. fig. in et. ≈ (einweihen) to initiate in a th.; in ein Amt ≈ to install, feierlich: to inaugurate. — 3. in Erzählungen ıc.: einen redend ≈ (darſtellen) to reproduce a p.'s speech, to quote his (very) words. — II ~ n ㉓ 4. = E/ung.
Ein²-führer (ᴵᴵ◡) m ㉒, ~in f ㊻ 1. von Perſonen: introducer; (Zeremonienmeiſter) Gentleman Usher; von Gebräuchen ıc.: originator. — 2. ⚓ importer.
Ein²-fuhr-handel ⚓ (ᴵᴵ...) m ㊅ import trade; ≈liſte f, ⊥ list of arrivals or imports, register of a ship's cargo; ≈prämie ⚓ f bounty on imports; ≈regiſter n = ≈liſte.
Ein²-führung (ᴵᴵ◡) f ㊻ 1. (zu einführen 1:) introduction; presentation; ⚓ importation. — 2. (zu 2:) initiation; installation, inauguration.

Ein²-führungs-feierlichkeit (⁻ᴵ⌣...) f ⓬ inaugural ceremony, inauguration; **=gesetz** n law supplementing a larger legislative measure.

Ein²-fuhr-verbot (⁻ᴵ...) n ⓬ prohibition to import goods, in Engl. auch: order (passed) in Council (against the importation of cattle, &c.); **=waren** f/pl. imported goods pl.; **=zoll** m import-duty, duty paid on imports.

ein²-füllen (⁻ᴵ⌣) I v/a. ⓬** to fill (or put, pour) into casks, &c.; in Fässer, Flaschen ≈, auch: to barrel (off, up), to bottle. — II ~ n ㉓ u. **Ein-füllung** f ⓬ filling into, barrelling, &c. (f. I).

ein¹-füßig (⁻ᴵ⌣) a. ⓬ one-footed.

Ein²-gabe (⁻ᴵ⌣) f ⓬ 1. ~ e-r Bittschrift ⅽ.: presentation. — 2. (Gesuch) petition; address; eine ~ machen to present a memorial; eine ~ bei einem machen to petition (or memorialize) a p.; der eine ~ Machende the memorialist.

Ein²-gang (⁻ᴵ) m ⓪c. 1. (Eintreten) entering, entry; Ort: entrance; way in; mouth of a cave; beim ~ on entering; ihr ~ und Ausgang, feierlich: their ingress and egress, bisw.: their exits and their entrances (sh.); e-m den ~ gestatten to grant a p. admission; sich (dat.) ~ verschaffen to gain admission; Aufschrift: verbotener ~! no admittance! — 2. ~ (Aufnahme) finden to find favour, to meet with a favourable reception; es fand keinen ~, oft: it did not take (with the public); einer Sache ~ verschaffen to bring a th. into vogue or fashion, to introduce a th.; ~ to set a custom going. — 3. ~ (Beginn) opening, preamble; ♪ prelude; e-s Dramas: prologue; e-r Rede: exordium; im ~e = ≈s. — 4. ⚭ ~ (Ankunft) von Waren arrival (or entry) of goods; ~ einer Summe payment of a sum; beim ~ des Wechsels on receipt of the draft; ~ der Zahlung besorgen to see that the amount is paid, to procure payment. — 5. Eingänge pl. a) ⚭ (eingegangene Waren) goods received; b) pol. (ant. Ausgänge) receipts pl., revenue sg.

Ein¹-gänger (⁻ᴵ) hunt. = Einsiedler.

ein²-gangs (⁻ᴵ) adv. at the beginning or commencement; ≈ erwähnt aforesaid, above-mentioned, previously alluded (or referred) to.

Ein²-gangs-artikel ⚭ (⁻ᴵ...) m ⓬ article of importation; **=buch** ⚭ n book of entries or arrivals; **=deklaration** ⚭ f bill of entry; **=halle** f entrance hall; **=journal** ⚭ n = =buch; **=stück** ♪ n prelude; einer Oper: overture; **=tor** n entrance-gate; **=zoll** ⚭ m import-duty.

ein²-geben (⁻ᴵ⌣) I v/a. ⓬c** 1. einem Arznei ≈ to administer medicine to a p., to give a p. physic; einem ein Abführmittel ≈ to purge a p. — 2. fig. einem et. ≈ (einreden) to put s.th. in(to) a p.'s mind; vgl. einblasen 2. — II ~ n ㉓ 3. = Eingebung 1.

ein²-gebildet (⁻ᴵ⌣) p.p. f. einbilden II.

Ein²-gebildet-heit (⁻ᴵ⌣-) f ⓬ (Dünkel) (self-)conceit(edness); vaingloriousness; presumption. [for binding.]

Ein²-gebinde (⁻ᴵ⌣) n ㉒ charge(s pl.)

ein²-gebogen (⁻ᴵ⌣) p.p. f. einbiegen III.

ein¹-geboren (⁻⌣⌣) a. ⓬(D9): Der Sohn Gottes, a. s.: der ~e the only-begotten (Son of the Heavenly Father).

ein²-geboren (⁻ᴵ⌣)[†eingebären]a.⓬(D9) 1. (einheimisch), a. **Ein-gebor(e)ne**([r] m) f ⓬ native; ~e pl., a. aborigines. — 2. (v. Natur eigen) inborn, innate; indigenous; (anhaftend) inherent. [bringen 1.]

Ein²-gebrachte(s) (⁻ᴵ⌣ᴵt) n ⓬ f. ein-]

Ein²-gebung (⁻ᴵ⌣) f ⓬ 1. (f. eingeben 1.) administration. — 2.fig. = einflüstern II; eine göttliche ~ a divine inspiration; nach der ~ des Augenblicks handeln to act on the impulse of the moment.

ein²-gebürgert (⁻ᴵ⌣) p.p. f. einbürgern 1.

Ein²-geburt (⁻ᴵ⌣) f ⓬ u. ~s-recht (⁻ᴵ⌣ᴵ) n ⓬ right(s pl.) of a native.

ein²-gedenk (⁻ᴵ⌣) a. ⓬ (meist mit sein, bleiben, werden) einer Sache (gen.) ≈ sein (bleiben) to bear (to keep) a th. in mind, to be (to remain) mindful of a thing; er ward seines Versprechens ≈ he remembered his promise.

ein²-gedickt, -gedrückt, -gefallen (⁻ᴵ⌣) p.p. f. ein-dicken I, -drücken IV, -fallen (3, 7).

ein-gefleischt (⁻ᴵᴵ) [(incarna'tus)] p.p. u. a. ⓬ incarnate; der Säufer, Schurke inveterate drunkard, arch-rogue, thorough scamp. [f.-frieren,-gehen.]

ein-gefroren(⁻ᴵ⌣),**-gegangen**(⁻ᴵ⌣)p.p.]

ein²-geh(e)n (⁻ᴵ(⌣) ⓬** I v/n. (fn) 1. (antommen) to arrive; ~ es sind Aufträge, Briefe eingegangen orders, letters have dropped in or come to hand; ≈de Ausstände debts recovered; alles Eingegang(e)ne (Geld) all receipts (or F incomings) pl., all money paid (or coming) in. — 2. auf et. ≈ (sich einlassen) to give one's consent to a th., to agree to a th.; auf j-s Ansicht ≈ to enter into (or to chime in with) a p.'s idea(s); auf eine Frage ≈ to go (or enter) into a question; er ging eifrig auf unsern Vorschlag ein he eagerly accepted (or acceded to) our proposal; auf et. näher (a. des näheren) ≈ to sift (or dive into) a matter. — 3. rel. in die ewige Ruhe, zum ewigen Leben ≈ (sterben) to go to one's last resting-place or eternal home. — 4. (in den Sinn gehen) F das geht ihm glatt ein: a) (hört er gern) he likes to hear it; b) (faßt er leicht) he quickly grasps (or understands) it. F he readily takes it in. — 5. (aufhören) to cease; (abkommen) to be out of use or fashion; (aus-, ab-sterben) to die out, to wither, to decay; hunt. vom Wild u. v. Jagdhunden: to die, to succumb; (erlöschen) to become extinct; ≈ lassen to discontinue; v. Zeitungen: to cease to appear; er ließ das Blatt ≈, a. he dropped the paper, he allowed it to drop; ♦ die Firma ist eingegangen the firm has ceased to exist; ein Geschäft ≈ lassen to give up (a) business, F to shut up shop. — 6. (zs.-schrumpfen) to shrink, to shrivel (up). — II v/a. 7. (h. und fn) eine Ehe ≈ to contract a marriage, to enter (into) matrimony; e-n Handel ≈ to make (or strike) a bargain; einen Vergleich ≈ to come to an arrangement, to make a compromise; einen Vertrag ≈ to enter into an agreement; eine Wette ≈ to (lay a) wager, F to (make a) bet; ich will jede Wette ≈, daß // I'll bet you anything (you like) that //. — III ~ n ㉓ 8. (f. 1) arrival; recovery (or payment) of debts; receipt of money. — 9. (f. 2) consent (or agreement) to. — 10. (f. 5) cessation; discontinuance of a newspaper, &c.; extinction of a firm, &c.

ein²-gehend (⁻ᴵ⌣) a. ⓬ adv. in detail; searching; aufs, auf das eingehendste in detail, with full particulars; (gründlich) thoroughly, exhaustively, searchingly; ≈d behandeln to enter into full particulars; ≈de Prüfung, Untersuchung thorough (or exhaustive) examination, close investigation.

Ein²-geladene([r] m) f (⁻ᴵ⌣⌣) [einladen 2] ⓬ invited guest.

ein²-gelegt(⁻ᴵ⌣)p.p. f. einlegen. [railed.]

ein¹-g(e)leisig 🚂 (⁻ᴵ(⌣)ᴵ) a. ⓬ single-]

Ein²-gemachte(s) (⁻ᴵ⌣ᴵt) [einmachen 2] n ⓬ in Zucker: preserve(d fruit); jam; in Essig: pickles pl.

ein²-gemeinden (⁻ᴵ⌣ᴵ) v/a. ⓬** to incorporate into a parish or=commune.

ein²-genommen (⁻ᴵ⌣) I p.p. f. einnehmen (f. dß). — II a. ⓬(D9) 2. (befangen) prejudiced (or prepossessed or biassed) against or in favour of; ganz ≈ für, a.: infatuated (or in love, F taken, smitten) with; von sich ≈ (self-)conceited, wrapped up in o.s.; self-opinionated. — 3. der Kopf ist mir ≈ (schwer) my head feels heavy or dull.

Ein²-genommenheit (⁻ᴵ⌣⌣-) f ⓬ (f. eingenommen) prejudice, prepossession, bias; infatuation, great love for; (self-)conceit; self-opinion(atedness); des Kopfes: heaviness, dulness.

Ein²-gesandt (⁻ᴵ⌣) n ⓬ f. einsenden I.

ein¹-geschlechtig (⁻ᴵ⌣) a. ⓬ unisexual; ♀ (mit getrennten Geschlechtern) diclinous.

ein²-geschlossen (⁻ᴵ⌣) f. einschließen IV; ~heit ⚭ (⌣-) f ⓬ confinement.

ein²-geschnitten (⁻ᴵ⌣) p.p.v.einschneiden; ~ne(s) n ⓬ Kochk.: stew, hash(ed meat).

ein²-geschossen (⁻ᴵ⌣) p.p. v. einschießen.

ein²-geschränkt (⁻ᴵ⌣) f. einschränken IV.

Ein²-geschränktheit (⁻ᴵ⌣) f ⓬ limitedness, restrictedness, restriction; fig. straitened circumstances pl.

ein²-geschrieben (⁻ᴵ⌣) f. einschreiben III.

ein²-gesessen (⁻ᴵ⌣) I a. ⓬(D9) resident, residentiary, domiciled. — II ~e(r) s. ⓬ resident, inhabitant; dweller of the soil.

ein²-gesprengt (⁻ᴵ⌣) p.p. von einsprengen.

ein²-gestandener-maßen (⌣-⌣⌣-) adv. admittedly, confessedly. [nis.]

Ein²-geständnis (⁻ᴵ⌣⌣) n ⓬ f. Geständ-]

ein²-gesteh(e)n (⁻ᴵᴵ(⌣) v/a. ⓬*/* to admit, confess, own (up), vgl. gestehen.

ein¹-gestrichen ♪ (⁻ᴵ⌣) a. ⓬(D9) ≈e Note quaver; ≈e Oktave once-accented octave.

ein²-gestrichen (⌣) p.p. von einstreichen.

ein²-getragen (⁻ᴵ⌣) p.p. von eintragen.

Ein²-geweide (⁻ᴵ⌣) [mhd.* Weide²] n ㉒ bowels pl., F u. P inside; anat. intestines pl., ⚕ viscera pl.; bsd. des Viehs: entrails, P guts pl.; auf die ~ bezüglich intestinal, ⚕ visceral; das ~ ausnehmen to draw a fowl, to gut or clean a fish, to disembowel slaughtered cattle. &c.

[Eingeweidebeschauer] — 299 — [Einheitlichkeit]

Ein²-geweide-beschauer (ᴵᴵ˘ᴵ˘…) m ⓺² röm. Alt.: ⚔ haruspex; **=bruch** m hernia, ⚔ enterocele; **=lehre** f: ⚔ splanchnology, enterology; **=nerv** m: ⚔ splanchnic (nerve); **=schlag=ader** f, anat. celiac artery; **=schmerz** m intestinal pain; F gripes pl.; **=würmer** m/pl. intestinal worms, ⚔ entozoa, enthelminthes pl.; ~ austreibend ⚔ anthelmintic.

Ein²-geweihte([r]m) f (ᴵᴵ˘ᴵ˘) [einweihen] ⓺⁷ initiate(d person) (pl. meist: the initiated), adept; F knowing one.

ein²-gewöhnen (ᴵᴵ˘ᴵ˘) I v/a. und sich ⌇ v/refl. ⓺⁸*/* (sich) ⌇ to accustom (eleganter: to habituate) (o.s.) to, an einen Ort: to acclimatize (o.s.); er wird sich rasch ⌇ F he will soon get used to it; sich in et. ⌇ to familiarize o.s. with a th., to adapt o.s. to one's surroundings or circumstances. — II ~ n ㉓ u. **Ein²-gewöhnung** f ⓺⁶ acclimatization.

ein²-gezogen (ᴵᴵ˘ᴵ˘) p.p. von einziehen (s. ds) u. a. ⓺⁶ (D9) 1. Beb. des inf. — 2. (zurückgezogen) retired, secluded; (einsam) solitary; ⌇ (adv.) leben to lead a secluded life, to live by o.s. or in seclusion; ⌇es Leben (a. ~heit f ⓺⁶) (life of) retirement or seclusion or privacy.

ein²-gießen (ᴵᴵ˘ᴵ˘) I v/a. ⓺d** to pour in(to); ✹ mit Blei ⌇ (festmachen) to (fasten with) lead; fig. to infuse, to inspire. — II ~ n ㉓ und **Ein²-gießung** f ⓺⁶ pouring in; infusion (auch surg.); fig. inspiration.

ein²-gittern (ᴵᴵ˘ᴵ˘) v/a. ⓺²a** to rail off, to enclose with railings, to fence in.

ein¹-gleisig 🚆 (ᴵᴵ˘ᴵ˘) a. ⓺⁶ single-railed.

ein¹-glied(e)rig (ᴵᴵ˘(˘)˘) a. ⓺⁶ math. of one term, ⚔ monomial.

ein²-graben (ᴵᴵ˘ᴵ˘) ⓺b** I v/a. 1. to dig in(to the ground); (unter die Erde bringen) to put into (or hide in) the earth; bsd. Tote: to inter, inhume, bury; Furchen ⌇ to furrow, to trench. — 2. (einmeißeln) to chisel in; in Metall ꝛc. eingegraben incised; in Stahl (fig. ins Gedächtnis) ⌇ to engrave in steel (in the memory). — II sich ⌇ v/refl. 3. vom Fuchse ꝛc.: to burrow, to go to earth; ⚔ (sich verschanzen) to entrench o.s. — 4. fig. sich in seine Bücher ꝛc. ⌇ to bury o.s. in one's books, &c. — III **Ein²-grabung** f ⓺⁶ 5. (f. 1) interment, burial; (f. 2) incision; engraving.

ein²-gravieren ✹ (ᴵᴵ˘w ᴵ˘) v/a. ⓺*/* to engrave; vgl. eingraben 2.

ein²-greifen (ᴵᴵ˘ᴵ˘) I v/n. (h.) ⓺b** 1. v. Personen: in et. ⌇ to put one's hands in(to) a th.; ♪ in die Saiten ⌇ to touch the chords. — 2. von Sachen: in=ea. to fit into one another; ✹ to interlock, to catch (into); mach. von Zahnrädern: to gear into or together; in die Achse ⌇ to be geared to the shaft; ⚓ der Anker greift nicht ein … does not bite; fig. die Teile greifen gut in=ea. ein … interlink well, ✹ mach. … are well geared or connected; in=ea. ⌇d (a. fig.) dovetailed, interwining; (zs.-wirkend) co-operating. — 3. fig. (einmischen) in et. ⌇ to intervene in a th., to (inter-)meddle (or interfere) with a th. — 4. fig. in j-s Rechte ⌇ (übergreifen) to encroach upon a p.'s rights or privi-

leges; to infringe (upon) a p.'s patent (rights), to invade a p.'s domain. — II ~ ㉓ 5. (f. 2) (perfect) fit; ✹ interlocking, gearing, connexion. — 6. fig. (f. 3) intervention, interference; in j-s Rechte: encroachment, infringement. — III ⌇d p.pr. und a. ⓺⁶ 7. in den Beb. des inf. (f. auch 2). — 8. (wirksam) efficacious, effective.

ein²-grenzen (ᴵᴵ˘ᴵ˘) v/a. ⓺⁰** to set bounds (or limits) to; vgl. einfriedigen I.

Ein²-griff (ᴵᴵ˘) m ⓺c. = eingreifen II.

Ein²-guß (ᴵᴵ˘) m ⓺a. 1. = eingießen II. — 2. ✹ (Gießform) ingot-mould.

Ein²-gußröhre (ᴵᴵ˘…) f ⓺², **=trichter** m funnel (or jet) of the ingot-mould.

Ein²-gut (ᴵᴵ˘) n ⓺d. (beweg. Besitz) movable property, goods and chattels pl.

ein²-haken (ᴵᴵ˘ᴵ˘) ⓺⁸** I v/n. (h.) in et. ⌇ to cut (or hew) into a thing; fig. sie hackten alle auf mich ein they all attacked me, F each one had a cut (or hit) at me. — II v/a. Kochkunst: Fleisch ⌇ to chop up (or mince, hash) meat.

ein²-häkeln ⓺²a**, **=haken** (ᴵᴵ˘) v/a., v/n. (in) u. sich ⌇ v/refl. to hook (or catch) into; to fasten (with a hook); to clasp; (einklinken) to clench; to latch; ⚓ f. einhängen.

Ein²-halt (ᴵᴵ˘) m ⓺c. (Unterbrechung) interruption, stop, check; (Pause) break; einer Sache (dat.) ~ tun, gebieten to put a stop (or stoppage) to a th., to check (or stop) a th.; Mißbräuchen ꝛc. auch: to suppress (or to put an end to, to do away with) abuses, &c.

ein²-halten (ᴵᴵ˘ᴵ˘) ⓺a** I v/a. 1. (hemmen) to stop, arrest, check; (zügeln) to rein in; (mäßigen) to moderate; (verbieten) to prohibit. — 2. fig. (pünktlich beobachten) to observe punctually or strictly, to fulfil (or keep, adhere) to the letter; e-e Frist, die Zeit ⌇ to be punctual (in one's time); ✹ seine Zahlungen ⌇ to keep up one's payments. — 3. beim Nähen: (in Falten legen) to gather (or take) in. — II v/a. u. sich ⌇ v/refl. 4. to keep in(doors) or at home; sich ⌇ a. to stay in(doors) or at home. — III v/n. (h.) 5. (aufhören) to stop, to leave off, to cease; bei e-m Unternehmen ꝛc. ⌇, auch: to hold one's hands; mit dem (a. im) Lesen ⌇ to stop (or discontinue or pause in) reading; halt ein! stop (there)!, hold your tongue!, P shut up! — IV ~ n ㉓ u. **Ein²-haltung** f ⓺⁶ 6. (f. 1) stopping, stoppage, &c.; prohibition. — 7. fig. (f. 2) punctual observance of.

ein²-handeln (ᴵᴵ˘ᴵ˘) v/a. ⓺²a** et. ⌇ to (make a) purchase; to buy; gegen et. anderes ⌇ to barter (P to swop) for s.th. else; mit ⌇ to include in a bargain.

ein²-händig (ᴵᴵ˘) a. ⓺⁶ one-handed; fig. single-handed.

ein²-händigen (ᴵᴵ˘˘) I v/a. ⓺⁸** e-m et. ⌇ to hand a th. (over) to a p., to remit (or deliver) a th. into a p.'s hands; jur. to serve a summons upon a p. — II ~ n ㉓ u. **Ein²-händigung** f ⓺⁶ handing (over), remission, delivery.

Ein²-händigungs=schein (ᴵᴵ˘…) m ⓺² bill (or receipt) of delivery.

Ein¹-hands=gut (ᴵᴵ˘…) n ⓺² jur. (Sondergut) private property of a married p.

ein²-hängen (ᴵᴵ˘ᴵ˘) v/a. ⓺⁸** to hang in(to); (aufhängen) to hang (up), to suspend; die Tür ist schlecht eingehängt the door is badly hung; die Hemmkette ⌇ to put on the skid or drag or brake; ⚓ das Steuer ⌇ (einhaken) to ship the rudder; arch. ⌇des (auch: einhängiges) Dach pent-roof.

ein²-hauch/en (ᴵᴵ˘ch˘) I v/a. ⓺⁸** (einatmen) to breathe life into a p.; fig. (einflößen) to instil a th. into a p., to inspire a p. with a thing. — II ~ n ㉓ u. **⌇ung** f ⓺⁶ breathing into; fig. instilment, inspiration; (Wint) suggestion.

ein²-hauen (ᴵᴵ˘ᴵ˘) I v/n. (h.) 1. to hew (or cut) in(to); to fall (or rush) upon; ⚔ auf den Feind ⌇ to charge the enemy with swords (in hand), to mow down the enemy (with sabres). — 2. fig. wacker ⌇ (essen) to eat heartily, F to play a good knife and fork, to clear the dishes, P to have a good tuck-in. — II v/a. 3. ✹ ein Loch ⌇ to knock (or dig) a hole in a th.; eine Figur ꝛc. in den Stein ⌇ to engrave … on the stone. — 4. (aufbrechen) to break (or cut, chop) open with an axe, a pick-axe, &c. — 5. Schlächterei: Fleisch ⌇ to cut up meat. — 6. bursch. e-n ⌇ to train a p. in fencing or in the use of the rapier; sich ⌇ v/refl. to practise fencing.

ein²-häufig (ᴵᴵ˘ᴵ˘) ♀ a. ⓺⁶ (mit männl. und weibl. Blüten auf derselben Pflanze): ⚔ monœcian, monœcious.

ein²-heben (ᴵᴵ˘ᴵ˘) v/a. ⓺(⓻)b** eine Tür ⌇ to put … on hinges; ✹ typ. die Form ⌇ to lift (or put) the form (in the press), to lay on form(e).

ein²-heften (ᴵᴵ˘ᴵ˘) v/a. ⓺⁹** to sew (or stitch) in(to); to fix the lining, &c. with stitches; (lose zs.-nähen) to baste (together); Buch: to sew (or stitch) a book.

ein²-hegen (ᴵᴵ˘ᴵ˘) v/a. ⓺⁸**, ~ n ㉓ u. **Ein²-hegung** f ⓺⁶ = einfriedigen; E/ungs= recht n ⓺² jur. right of enclosure.

ein²-heimisch (ᴵᴵ˘) a. ⓺⁶ native, indigenous (a. ♀); home (produce, &c.); med. endemic (disease); ⌇e (innere) Zwistigkeiten domestic feuds pl.; ich bin in dieser Stadt ⌇ I am a native of this town; ⌇ machen to naturalize; ⌇ werden to become a resident (or to settle down) at a place.

ein²-heimsen (ᴵᴵ˘ᴵ˘) v/a. ⓺⁰** 1. agr. to garner (or get) in; to house corn, &c. 2. fig. to make (or F net) large profits.

ein²-heiraten (ᴵᴵ˘˘) ⓺⁹**: v/refl. sich in e-e Familie ⌇ to marry into a family.

Ein²-heit (ᴵ˘) f ⓺⁶ 1. unity, union; phys. ~ des elektrischen Widerstandes unit of electrical resistance. ohm; ⚔ taktische ~ tactical unit. — 2. (übereinstimmung) uniformity, identity; agreement, conformity.

ein¹-heitlich (ᴵ˘˘) a. ⓺⁶ united, undivided; (nach Einheit strebend) unionist (-ic); (gleichmäßig) homogeneous, coherent; ⌇er Plan symmetrical (or uniform) plan; ⌇e Regierung central (or centralized) government; **~keit** (ᴵ˘˘) f ⓺⁶ undividedness; unionism; symmetry, uniformity; centralization.

⚔ scientific; ♀ botanical; 🜨 geography; ✹ machinery; ⚒ mining; ⚔ military; ⚓ marine; ✉ commercial; ✉ postal; 🚆 railway.

[Einheitsbestrebung] — 300 — [Einkerkerer]

Ein¹heits=bestrebung (¹⁻...) f ⑫, **=bewegung** f centralizing (or unionist) tendency, movement; **=gläubige(r)** s. eccl. unitarian; **=mangel** m lack of uniformity; incoherence; **=zeit** f central (or uniform) time for Europe, &c.

ein²-heizen (ᴗᴗ) v/n. (h.) ⑩** to make (or light) a fire in a room, &c.; ich ließ ⵌ I had a fire lit (in my room, &c.); F fig. e-m tüchtig ⵌ (zusetzen) F to give it a p. hot and strong; gehörig ⵌ (trinken) to drink hard, F to lush up.

Ein²-heizer (ᴗᴗ) m ⑫ stoker; fireman; vgl. a. Heizer.

ein²-helfen (ᴗᴗ) v/n. (h.) ⑬b**: e-m ⵌ to help a p. in; fig. to assist a p.('s memory) in speaking; to prompt a p.

Ein-helfer (ᴗᴗ) m ⑫ prompter.

ein¹-hellig (ᴗᴗ) a. ⑯ unanimous; adv. auch: with one accord, by common consent; **~keit** (ᴗᴗ) f ㊻ unanimity; concord, agreement, harmony.

ein²-hemmen (ᴗᴗ) v/a. ⑱** to lock a wheel; to put the brake on. [handle.]

ein¹-henk(e)lig (ᴗ(ᴗ)ᴗ) a. ⑯ with one⌋

ein²-her-... (¹ᴗ...) adv. mit v/n., die meist eine Bewegung auf den Sprechenden zu andeuten, stets trennbar (**), z. B.: **ⵌfahren** ⑤b**, **ⵌfliegen** ⑥aſt**, **ⵌjagen** ⑤b***, **ⵌreiten** ⑩b**, **ⵌschlendern** ②a** to come driving, flying, galloping, riding, sauntering along; oft mit dem Nebenbegriff des Feierlichen: **ⵌgeh(e)n** ⑭**, **ⵌschleichen** ⑥aſt**, **ⵌschreiten** ⑪b**, **ⵌstolzieren** ⑬*/*, **ⵌtrippeln** ②a**, **ⵌziehen** ⑭b** to walk, sneak, stride, strut, trip, move along; er geht wie ein Bettler einher he goes about like a beggar.

ein²-hetzen (ᴗᴗ) v/a. ⑩** hunt. Hunde ⵌ to enter or train (young) hounds.

ein²-hieven ↓ (ᴗᴗ) v/a. ⑱** to heave in.

Ein²-hilfe (ᴗᴗ) [einhelfen] f ㊽ prompting; reminder; (Wint) suggestion, hint; ↓ assistance.

ein²-hol/en (ᴗᴗ) I v/a. ⑱** 1. (entgegengehen) to go to meet. — 2. (erreichen) to catch up, to come up with, to join, to overtake (auch ↓ ein Schiff und fig.). — 3. das Versäumte (wieder) ⵌ (nachholen) to make up for lost time. — 4. (herbeiholen) to go and fetch; ⌘ Futter ⵌ to forage, to go foraging. — 5. j-s Befehle, Anweisungen ⵌ (erbitten) to ask for (or take) a p.'s orders, instructions; j-s Erlaubnis, Genehmigung ⵌ to apply for (or to get) a p.'s permission, consent; Nachricht über et. ⵌ (einsammeln) to gather (or collect) information about (or respecting) a th.; Stimmen ⵌ to solicit votes. — 6. ↓ Flaggen, Rahen ⵌ to strike ...; ein Tau, ein Geschütz ⵌ to haul home ...; Segel ⵌ (reffen) to reef ..., to take in ... II ~ n ㉓ 7. = ⵌ/ung. [inhaul(er).]

Ein²-holer ↓ (ᴗᴗ) m ⑫ e-s Gaffelsegels:⌋

Ein²-holung (ᴗᴗ) f ㊽ (feierliche) ~ (ceremonious or official) reception; von Nachrichten: collection of news.

Ein¹-horn (ᴗᴗ) n ⑫c. fabelhaftes Tier: unicorn; **~fisch**, **=wal** m ⑫ zo. narw(h)al, sea-unicorn (Mo'nodon mono'ceros).

Ein¹-hufer (ᴗᴗ) m ⑫ zo.: ☉ soliped, solidungulate; **ⵌhufig** a. ⑯ wholehoofed, ☉ solipedous, solidungulate.

ein²-hüll/en (ᴗᴗ) I v/a. u. sich ⵌ v/refl. ⑬** 1. (sich) in et. (dat. ob. acc.) ⵌ to wrap (o.s.) up in a th., wärmer: to muffle (o.s.) up (in a th.); (einwickeln) to wrap round with, to tuck up in; eine Leiche: to (wrap in a) shroud, (umschließen) to (en)case in; in Nebel, Rauch, Staub ꝛc. eingehüllt enveloped (or hidden) in fog, smoke, dust, &c.; math. ⵌde Kurve ⚭ envelope; med. ⵌes Mittel: ☉ emollient. — 2. fig. (verbergen) to hide; to shroud in mystery. — II ~ n ㉓ u. ⵌung f ㊻ 3. (f. I) wrap(ping); envelopment, encasement. [hundred.]

ein¹-hundert (ᴗᴗ) numer. one (or a)⌋

einig¹ (¹ᴗ) [ahd.] a. ⑯ (übereinstimmend) in agreement or harmony or concord; united, unanimous; on good (or friendly) terms; sie leben ⵌ (adv.) zusammen ... unitedly (or amicably) together; (wieder) ⵌ machen to make (to restore) peace between; ⵌ sein mit to be at one (or of one mind) with; ⵌ werden über to agree about; wir sind darüber ⵌ geworden we have settled (or arranged) it; mit sich selbst nicht ⵌ undecided; mit sich ⵌ werden to make up one's mind.

einig² (¹ᴗ) [ahd.: any] indef. pron. u. a. ⑯ (A3†) I a. (sg. fast † = etwas; mst pl. = etliche; wenige): ⵌe Bücher several books; ⵌe der Bücher ob. von den Büchern some (or a few) of the books; vor ⵌen Tagen some (few) days ago, the other day; ⵌe gute Leute a (or some) few good people; ⵌe (etwa) zwanzig Jahre twenty odd years, some twenty years; ⵌe Male several times. — II ⵌes n something; ⵌe pl. a (or some) few; ⵌe von ihnen some of them; ⵌe ..., and(e)re ... some ..., others ...

einige=mal (ᴗᴗᴗ¹) adv. sometimes.

ein(ig)en (¹(ᴗ)ᴗ) I v/a. u. sich ⵌ v/refl. ㊽ to unite, to unify, to form into one (body); sich ⵌ auch: to come to an agreement or to terms; (versöhnen) to conciliate. — II ~ n ㉓ = Ein(ig)ung.

Einiger (¹ᴗᴗ) m ⑫ peace-maker.

einiger-maßen (ᴗᴗᴗᴗᴗ) adv. in some degree or measure, to some extent; somewhat; (nicht sehr gut) after a fashion.

Einigkeit (¹ᴗᴗ) f ㊻ (f. einig¹) agreement, harmony, concord; un(anim)ity; Sprichw. ~ macht stark union is strength.

Ein(ig)ung (¹(ᴗ)ᴗ) f ㊻ un(ific)ation; agreement, conciliation, harmony.

Ein(ig)ungs-amt (¹(ᴗ)ᴗᴗ...) n ⑫ etwa: arbitration-court (for disputes), in Lohnangelegenheiten ꝛc.: board for settling labour disputes, board of conciliation (and arbitration).

ein²-impf/en (ᴗᴗ) I v/a. ⑱** med. e-m einen Krankheitsstoff ⵌ to inoculate a virus into a p.; e-m die Kuhpocken ⵌ to vaccinate a p.; fig. to engraft, to implant. — II ~ n ㉓ = ⵌung.

Ein²-impfer (ᴗᴗ) m ⑫ med. inoculator, vaccinator; engrafter.

Ein²-impfung (ᴗᴗ) f ㊻ med. inoculation, vaccination.

ein²-jagen (ᴗᴗ) v/a. ⑱** 1. to drive (or chase) in(to). — 2. hunt. = einhetzen. — 3. fig. e-m Angst, Schrecken ⵌ to alarm (or frighten, scare, terrify) a p.; to strike terror into a p.'s breast.

ein¹-jährig (ᴗᴗ) a. ⑯ of one year; one year old; lasting one year; ⵌes Kind one-year-old child; ♀ ⵌe Pflanze annual; ⌘ **~e(r)** m ⑰, **~=Freiwillige(r)** m ⑲ soldier serving one year (at his own expense).

ein²-jochen (ᴗᴗ) v/a. ⑱** agr. Ochsen ⵌ to (put to the) yoke.

ein²-fachelnt F (ᴗᴗ) v/a. ②a** (gehörig) ⵌ to make a good (stärker: a roaring) fire.

ein²-falken ⊕ (ᴗᴗ) v/a. ⑱** to put (or steep, lay) in lime(-water).

Ein¹-kammer-system (¹ᴗᴗ„ᴗ¹) n ⑫ pol. single-chamber system. [capsular.]

ein¹-kapselig ♀ (¹ᴗᴗᴗ) a. ⑯ ⚭ uni-⌋

ein²-kapseln (ᴗᴗ) v/a. ②a** to enclose in a capsule or case; path. eingekapselte Trichinen encysted trichinæ.

ein²-kassier/en ⊛ (ᴗ¹ᴗ) I v/a. ⑬*/* to get (or call) in money, to (en)cash a bill, to collect outstanding debts. — II ~ n ㉓ u. ⵌung f ㊻ getting in, &c. (f. I); encashment; collection.

Ein²-kauf (ᴗᴗ) m ⑪ 1. purchase; Ein- und Verkauf buying and selling; Einkäufe machen to go shopping or marketing. — 2. ⊛ = ⵌsgeld.

Ein²-kauf-... (ᴗᴗ...) ⑫ s. Einkaufs-...

ein²-kaufen (ᴗᴗ) I v/a. ⑬** 1. to buy (or purchase) goods, &c. (f. ein-... 4); abs. to make purchases, to do shopping; ⊛ neue Vorräte, frische Waren ⵌ to lay (or take in) a fresh stock (of goods); das von ihm Eingekaufte his purchase(s pl.). — II v/a. (u. sich ⵌ v/refl.) to buy a p. (o.s.) in; e-n (sich) in eine Anstalt ⵌ to get (admission for) a p. (o.s.) into a home by payment. — III ~ n ㉓ (f. I) buying, purchase; shopping.

Ein²-käufer (ᴗᴗ) m ⑬, **~in** f ㊽ buyer (a. ⊛ im Großhandel), purchaser, von Lebensmitteln auch: caterer, f cateress.

Ein²-kaufs-buch (ᴗᴗ...) n ⑫ purchase-book; **=geld** n purchase-money; **=kommissionär** m buying agent, (wholesale) buyer; **=konto** n buying-account; **=preis** m original price, actual (or prime) cost, cost-price; zum ⵌpreise at first cost; **=rechnung** f bill of invoice; **=zeit** f season for buying. [fehlen I.]

ein²-fehlen ⊕ (ᴗᴗ) v/a. ⑱** = aus-⌋

Ein²-kehr (ᴗᴗ) f ㊺ 1. stay(ing) with a p., putting up at a hotel. — 2. Ort: resting-place (for travellers), (public) resort; (Nacht-) shelter; (Wirtshaus) public(-)house, inn, bsd. ehm. hostelry. — 3. fig. (In-sich-gehen) self-communion, rel. heart-searching.

ein²-kehren (ᴗᴗ) v/n. (sn) ⑱** 1. bei e-m, in einem Gasthofe ⵌ to stay (F to turn in) with a p., to put up (or alight) at a hotel; bald wird der Lenz (wieder) bei uns ⵌ ... (re)visit us. — 2. fig. in sich ⵌ to commune with o.s., to examine o.s.; reuig: to feel remorse, to repent; to reform.

ein²-keilen ⊕ (ᴗᴗ) v/a. ⑱** to wedge (or drive) in; typ. to quoin up.

ein²-kellern (ᴗᴗ) v/a. ②a** to put (or lay up or store) in a cellar, to cellar.

ein²-kerb/en (ᴗᴗ) I v/a. ⑱** to indent, jag, notch; to score, tally. — II ⵌung f ㊻ indentation, notching.

Ein²-kerkerer (ᴗᴗᴗ) m ⑫ incarcerator.

Zeichen (s. S. XVII): F familiär; P Volkssprache; ⌐ Gaunersprache; ⍀ selten; † alt (auch gestorben); * neu (auch geboren); ⁺⁺ unrichtig;

[einkerkern] — 301 — [einlassen]

ein²-kerker/n (‖◡◡) **I** v/a. Ⓢa** to incarcerate, to shut up in jail or in a dungeon; to imprison. — **II ~** n Ⓘ u. Ⓔ/ung f ⓌⒺ incarceration; imprisonment.

ein²-kesseln ⚔ (‖◡◡) v/a. Ⓢa** to hem in on all sides.

Ein¹-kindschaft (‖◡◡) f ⓌⒺ jur. marriage-contract allotting equal portions to children of different mothers.

ein²-kitten (‖◡◡) **I** v/a. Ⓢ** to (fix with) cement; ⊙ Glaserei: to (fasten with) putty. — **II ~** n Ⓘ u. **Ein²-kittung** f ⓌⒺ cementing, cementation.

ein²-klagbar (‖‒‿) a. ⓌⒺ jur. actionable; **~keit** (‿‒) f ⓌⒺ actionableness.

Ein²-klage (‖◡◡) f ⓌⒺ action for (the recovery of a) debt.

ein²-klagen (‖◡◡) v/a. Ⓢ** jur. e-e Schuld: to take legal proceedings for (the recovery of a) debt.

ein²-klammer/n (‖◡◡) **I** v/a. Ⓢa** **1.** to fasten with clamps or cramps. — **2.** gram., math., ⊙ typ. to bracket, to enclose in brackets or crotche(t)s; to put a word in (a) parenthesis, auch: to parenthesize; eingeflammert, bes. in der Rede, auch: parenthetic(al). — **II ~** n Ⓘ u. Ⓔ/ung f ⓌⒺ **3.** bracketing, &c. (s. 2). — **4.** Ⓔ/ung (Eingeflammertes) parenthesis (pl. parentheses).

Ein¹-klang ♪ (‖◡◡) m Ⓞc. unison, accord (a. fig.); in ~ bringen to bring in(to) accord with, to harmonize with, to reconcile with; im ~ stehen mit to be consonant (or consistent) with, to chime in with.

ein¹-klappig (‖◡◡) a. ⓌⒺ ♀ u. zo. single-valved, ☞ univalvular.

ein²-kleben (‖◡◡) v/a. Ⓢ** to stick in; mit Kleister: to paste in(to); mit Leim: to glue in(to); mit Gummi: to gum in(to).

ein²-kleiden (‖‒‿) **I** v/a. u. sich Ⓛ v/refl. Ⓢ** **1.** (sich) Ⓛ (ausrüsten) to accoutre (o.s.), to clothe (o.s.), F to rig (o.s.) out; einen Mönch, eine Nonne: to hood, to veil; sich Ⓛ lassen to take the hood or the veil; ⚔ Rekruten: to provide with uniforms. — **2.** fig. in Worte Ⓛ to put into (bisw. auch to clothe in) words, to word; to express. — **II ~** n Ⓘ u. **Ein-kleidung** f ⓌⒺ **3.** (f. 1) accoutrement, clothing, &c. — **4.** fig. (f. 2) wording (or expression) of a thought.

ein²-kleistern (‖◡◡) v/a. Ⓢa** to paste in(to), to stick in with paste.

ein²-klemm/en (‖◡◡) **I** v/a. Ⓢ** to pinch, to squeeze (or wedge, jam) in(to); surg. eingeklemmter Bruch strangulated hernia. — **II** Ⓔ/ung f ⓌⒺ pinching, jamming; surg. strangulation.

ein²-klingen ♪ (‖◡◡) v/n. (sn) Ⓓft** to chime in; to harmonize.

ein²-klinken (‖◡◡) v/a. u. v/n. (sn) Ⓢ** to (put down the) latch; to clench; die Tür war nur eben eingeklinkt the door was (only just) on the latch.

ein²-klopfen (‖◡◡) v/a. Ⓢ** **1.** Nägel ꝛc.: to knock (or drive) in. — **2.** bie Wände ꝛc. Ⓛ (einstoßen) to knock (or ram) in …

ein²-kneifen (‖◡◡) v/a. Ⓢb** to fasten with a pinch or a (tight) squeeze.

ein²-kneten (‖◡◡) v/a. Ⓢ** to knead (or work) into the dough.

ein²-knicken (‖◡◡) Ⓢ** **I** v/a. to fold, to double (up); to turn down the corner of a page; eingeknickt, oft: bent double. — **II** v/n. (sn) to bend (inwards), to give way, to droop.

ein²-knöpfen (‖◡◡) v/a. Ⓢ** to button up.

ein²-knüpfen (‖◡◡) v/a. Ⓢ** to tie up.

ein²-kochen (‖◡◡) **I** v/n. (sn) to grow thick (or condensed) by boiling. — **II** v/a. to boil down, to steam off; to thicken, condense, chm. to inspissate; in Gelee eingekochter Saft juice boiled down to a jelly. — **III ~** n Ⓘ condensation; boiling down; chm. inspissation.

ein²-kommen (‖◡◡) **I** v/n. (sn) Ⓢ** **1.** persönlich: bei der Behörde Ⓛ (ein Gesuch einreichen) to make an application, to (present a) petition, to memorialize the authorities; beim Minister um Gehaltserhöhung Ⓛ to petition the minister for an increase of salary; mit e-r Klage Ⓛ to lodge a complaint; gegen etwas Ⓛ to (raise a) protest against a th. — **2.** sachlich: a) vom Getreide ꝛc.: to be gathered (or got) in; to get home (safely); b) von Geldern ꝛc.: to come in, to be paid in; c) fig. (in den Sinn kommen) to occur to a p.; vgl. einfallen 5. — **II ~** n Ⓘ **3.** (s. 1) application, petition. — **4.** (s. 2a) produce. — **5.** (s. 2b) pl. meist Einkünfte (s. Einkunft) (annual) income, emoluments pl., proceeds pl.; revenue; e-s Geistlichen auch: living; ein englischer Richter hat ein (Jahres-)~ von 100000 Mark … (a salary of) five thousand (pounds) a year; Einkommensteuer/veranlagungskommission f (assessors pl.) of income-tax.

ein²-koppeln (‖◡◡) v/a. Ⓢa** = einfriedigen I.

Ein¹-korn ♀ (‖‿) n Ⓘ one-grained wheat (Triticum monoco'ccum).

ein²-krallen (‖◡◡): sich Ⓛ v/refl. Ⓢ** to fasten one's claws (or fangs) into.

ein²-kramen ● (‖◡◡) v/a. Ⓢ**: ausgestellte Waren Ⓛ to pack up show-goods, to take in goods exposed for sale.

ein²-kratzen (‖◡◡) v/a. Ⓢ** to scratch in(to); vgl. eingraben 2.

ein²-kreisen (‖◡◡) v/a. Ⓢ** to encircle, encompass, surround.

ein²-kriechen (‖◡◡) v/n. (sn) Ⓓft** **1.** to creep in(to). — **2.** ⊙ (einschrumpfen) to shrivel up (to shrink (away).

ein²-kriegen F provc. (‖◡◡) v/a. Ⓢ** to get in(to) (= einbekommen).

ein²-krimpen ⚓ (‖◡◡) Ⓢ** **I** v/a. **1.** Tuchfabr.: to shrink cloth. — **II** v/n. (sn) **2.** eingehen 6. — **3.** ⚓ der Wind krimpt ein the wind is going down or abating or slackening.

ein²-kritze(l)n (‖◡◡) v/a. Ⓢ(a)** Worte, Namen ꝛc. to scrawl (or scratch) … into.

Ein²-kunft ↘ (‖‿) f [einkommen] f ⓌⒺ, mst pl. **Ein-künfte** (‖◡◡) revenue; (Auskommen) competency; (Pachtzins) rent(al); (Zinsregister) rent-roll; vgl. Einkommen 5.

ein²-kürzen (‖◡◡) v/a. Ⓢ** to (draw in and) shorten; paint. to foreshorten.

Ein²-lade-… (‖‿…) Ⓔ = Einladungs-…

ein²-laden (‖◡◡) **I** v/a. Ⓢb** **1.** Waren: to load (into); ⚓ to take cargo on board; to ship. — **2.** (pres. a. [ursprgl. nur] Ⓢ**) in sein Haus, zu Tisch (zum Essen, zur Mahlzeit), zum Ball Ⓛ to invite (or ask) to one's house, to dinner, to a ball; sie waren nicht eingeladen, bes. im höheren Stile: they were not bidden; e-n ein für allemal Ⓛ to give a p. a general (or standing) invitation; e-n e-e Woche voraus (ob. vorher) Ⓛ to give a p. a week's invitation; zu e-r Versammlung Ⓛ (berufen) to summon (to a meeting), to convoke; ich lud ihn dringend ein, sich's bequem zu machen I urged (or pressed) him to take his ease; er ließ mich durch f-n Bruder freundlich zum Essen Ⓛ he sent me through his brother a kind invitation to dinner. — **II** Ⓛd p.pr. und a. ⓌⒺ **3.** in den Bed. des inf. — **4.** (verlockend) enticing, tempting; (reizend) attractive.

Ein¹-lader ⚔ (‖‒‿) m Ⓘ (ant. Mehrlader) single loader.

Ein²-lader (‖‒‿) m Ⓘ, **~in** f ⓌⒺ one who invites; bisw. auch: inviter, bidder.

Ein²-ladung (‖‒‿) f ⓌⒺ **1.** (s. einladen 1) loading, lading; shipment. — **2.** (s. einladen 2) invitation, F invite; förmlich: bidding; summons.

Ein²-ladungs-karte (‖‒‿…) f ⓌⒺ card of invitation; **-platz** m place for loading; ⚓ wharf, quay; **-schreiben** n letter of invitation; **-schrift** f oft: program(me).

Ein²-lage (‖‒‿) f ⓌⒺ **1.** (Einlegen) laying in; ⊙ (Einpacken) packing (up). — **2.** (Eingelegtes) matter enclosed in a letter or parcel, enclosure; in der (auch unter) ~ enclosed (herewith), under cover; thea. (Gesangs-)~ topical song. — **3.** ~ e-r Zigarre (ant. Deckblatt) inside leaves pl., filler; e-r Krawatte: stiffening. — **4.** ⊙ ground protected by a dike. — **5.** ● von Geld: money (or capital) put in(to a concern), investment; in e-r Sparkasse ob. Bank: deposit; beim Spiel: stake; auch = Einlagegeld.

Ein²-lage-buch (‖‒‿…) n ⓌⒺ bei Sparkassen: savings-bank (or depositor's) book; **-kapita'l** n capital invested; money sunk (in a business).

ein-lagern (‖‒‿) v/a. u. sich Ⓛ v/refl. Ⓢa** **1.** ● to store up (or warehouse) goods. — **2.** ⚔ Truppen Ⓛ to quarter (or billet) soldiers; sich Ⓛ to take up (one's) quarters. — **3.** geol., &c. eingelagert embedded, ☞ interstratified.

Ein²-laß (‖‒) [: inlet] m Ⓘa. **1.** (Hineinlassen) letting-in; admission; ~ begehren, finden to desire, to gain admittance. — **2.** inlet (Pförtchen); (small) gate; wicket; entrance(-gate).

Ein²-laß-billett (‖‒‿…) n Ⓘ = -karte.

ein²-lass/en (‖◡◡) **I** v/a. Ⓢ** **1.** (zulassen) to let in, to admit; sie wollten uns nicht Ⓛ they refused us admittance. — **2.** mach. Dampf Ⓛ to let in steam; Wasser in ein Gefäß Ⓛ to let water flow into a vessel, to turn on water to fill a vessel; carp. (einfügen) to insert wood, to dovetail the parts. — **3.** Tuch Ⓛ (einlaufen lassen) to shrink. — **II** sich Ⓛ v/refl. **4.** sich in, auf et. Ⓛ (damit abgeben) to enter into (or to engage in) a th.; to embark in an enterprise; er will sich darauf nicht Ⓛ he will have nothing to do with it; sich in ein

♪ Musik; ⚙ Wissenschaft; ♀ Pflanze; ⚱ Geographie; ⊙ Technik; ⚒ Bergbau; ⚔ Militär; ⚓ Marine; ● Handel; ✉ Post; 🚂 Eisenbahn.

[Einlaßgeld] — 302 — [einmachen]

Gespräch mit e-m ‿ to enter into conversation with a p., to have a talk with a p.; jur. vom Beklagten: sich auf e-e Klage ‿ to defend a charge; sich auf ein Wagnis ‿ to engage in a bold venture. — 5. sich mit e-m ‿ to have dealings with a p.; heimlich: to plot (or scheme, intrigue) with a p.; laß dich mit ihm nicht ein! don't have anything to do with him! — III ~ n ⓔ 6. = E/ung.

Ein²-laß-geld (ᴵᴵ‿...) n ⓔ entrance- (or gate-)money; **=karte** f ticket, card of admission; voucher; **=klappe** ⊙ f inlet- (or induction-)valve.

ein²-läßlich ⟨ᴵᴵ‿⟩ a. u. adv. detailed, in detail; des ‿ten with full particulars or details, most minutely.

Ein²-laß-pforte (ᴵᴵ‿...) f ⓔ = Einlaß 2; **=preis** m = geld; **=rohr** n, **=röhre** f ⊙ inlet-pipe; **=tor** n, **=tür** f = Einlaß 2.

Ein²-lassung (ᴵᴵ‿‿) f ⓔ 1. = Einlaß 1. — 2. ⊙ (zu einlassen 2:) letting in; insertion. — 3. (zu 4:) engagement in a th.; jur. defence to a charge.

Ein²-laß-venti'l ⊙ (ᴵᴵ‿...) n ⓔ = =klappe.

Ein²-lauf (ᴵᴵ) m ⓓd. Kanzleistil: (eingelaufenes Schriftstück) document received.

ein²-laufen (ᴵᴵ‿) ⓔaft** I v/n. (ſn) 1. to come in, to arrive, to enter; ⚓ to enter (or sail into) a harbour, to touch (or call) at a port, schutzsuchend: to put into a port for shelter; vgl. eingehen 1. — 2. es sind Klagen darüber eingelaufen complaints have been received (or sent in) about it; sobald die Nachricht einlief as soon as the news arrived; ☞ die ‿ten Bestellungen the orders (which have come) to hand. — 3. einige Worte mit ‿ (einfließen) lassen to put in a few words. — 4. v. Geweben: (einschrumpfen) to shrink. — 5. (einrennen) to run in(to); fig. e-m das Haus ‿ to besiege a p.'s house. — III ~ n ⓔ 6. (ſ. 1) coming in, arrival. — 7. (ſ. 4) shrinkage of cloth.   I(gun).)

ein²-läufig (ᴵᴵ‿) a. ⓔ single-barrelled

ein²-laugen (ᴵᴵ‿) I v/a. ⓔ** to steep (or soak) in lye or in soda-water. — II **Ein²-laugung** f ⓔ steeping, &c.

ein²-läuten (ᴵᴵ‿) v/a. ⓔ** to ring in, to announce by ringing the bells.

ein²-leben (ᴵᴵ‿): sich ‿ v/refl. ⓔ** to accustom o.s. to a new mode of life or living; sich an e-m Orte ‿ to become familiar(ized) with a place; sich in et. ‿ to make o.s. (thoroughly) at home in (or conversant with) a th.

Ein²-lege-brettchen ⊙ (ᴵᴵ‿...) n, carp. ⓔ veneer; **=holz** n = =brettchen; **messer** n clasp-knife.

ein²-leg/en (ᴵᴵ‿) I v/a. (u. v/refl. sich) ⓔ** 1. to lay (or put) in; to enclose in a letter, &c.; Soldaten bei e-m ‿ to quarter (or billet) ... on a p.; sich bei e-m ‿ to take up one's lodgings with a p. — 2. Kocht.: Fleisch ꝛc. ‿ to put meat, &c. in pickle; Früchte ꝛc. ‿ (einmachen) to preserve fruit, &c.; in Fäſſer ‿ to barrel; in Töpfe ‿ to put in(to) jars or pots, to put; ein Meſſer ꝛc. ‿ to fold (up) ...; Reben ‿ (senken) to lay vines, to provine; ⚓ Spaken ‿ to rig the capstan; Wein ‿ (in den Keller) to lay up ... (in the cellar), to cellar ...; ein Zitat ꝛc. (in ein Werk) ‿ to insert ... — 3. ⊙ mit Elfenbein, Metall ꝛc. ‿ to inlay with ...; eingelegte Arbeit inlaid (gewürfelte a.: chequered) work; (Mosai't) marquetry, (fr.) marqueterie; typ. Schrift ‿ to lay type. — 4. chm. eine Lanze ‿ to couch ∞, fig. e-e Lanze für e-n ‿ to champion a p.'s cause; hunt. Hirsch: (mit vorgestrecktem Geweih den Jäger oder Hund annehmen) to stand at bay (in a position of defence). — 5. fig. jur. Berufung ‿ to (lodge an) appeal against; für e-n eine Fürbitte, ein gutes Wort ‿, auch sich für einen ‿ to intercede on a p.'s behalf; willst du ein gutes Wort für mich ‿? will you put in a word for me?; Verwahrung ‿ to (enter or raise a) protest against. — 6. Ehre mit et. ‿ to gain honour (or credit) by a thing. — II ~ n ⓔ 7. = E/ung.

Ein²-leger (ᴵᴵ‿) m ⓔ 1. in Sparkassen ꝛc.: depositor. — 2. hort., &c. (Steckling, Absenker) layer, cutting.

Ein²-lege-sohle (ᴵᴵ‿...) f ⓔ für Schuhe: (cork-, &c.) sock.

Ein²-legung (ᴵᴵ‿) f ⓔ (s. einlegen) 1. laying in, &c.; enclosure. — 2. pickling, &c.; insertion. — 3. ⊙ inlaying, marquetry. — 4. fig. intercession.

ein²-leimen (ᴵᴵ‿) v/a. ⓔ** to glue in(to), to stick in with glue.

ein²-leit/en (ᴵᴵ‿) I v/a. ⓔ** 1. e-n ‿ to lead (or usher) a p. in(to); chm. Gase ‿ to pass gases into a fluid, &c. — 2. et. ‿ (beginnen) to initiate (or start, introduce, prepare) a th.; to set a th. on foot; to arrange a matter; ein Buch mit einigen Bemerkungen ‿ to preface a book by a few remarks; ♪ ein Lied ꝛc. ‿ to prelude a song, &c.; Verhandlungen ‿ to open negotiations; jur. ein Kriminalverfahren, eine gerichtliche Untersuchung ‿ to institute criminal proceedings, a judicial inquiry; e-n Prozeß ‿ to take legal proceedings, to go to law. — II ‿d p.pr. u. a. ⓔ 3. Bed. des inf. — 4. (s. 2) initiatory, introductory, preparatory; prefatory; ‿de Schritte m/pl. preliminary steps, preliminaries pl.

Ein²-leitung (ᴵᴵ‿) f ⓔ introduction; preliminary (step); preface to a book; exordium of a speech; ♪ prelude, overture; jur. ~ des Strafverfahrens institution of criminal proceedings, criminal procedure; parl. ~ e-s Gesetzentwurfs preamble to a bill (of parliament); die nötigen ~en zu et. treffen to make the necessary arrangements (or preparations) for a th.; mit einer ~ versehen to preface, to preamble.

Ein²-leitungs-satz (ᴵᴵ‿...) m ⓔ, **=spiel** n ⓔ introductory movement.

ein²-lenk/en (ᴵᴵ‿) ⓔ** I v/n. (h.) in den Weg ‿ to turn the right way; fig. wieder ‿ to come back to the main point, to return to the subject; (nachgeben) to give in, to come round, to waver. — II sich ‿ v/refl., anat. von Knochen: to articulate, to be articulated. — III ~ n ⓔ E/ung f ⓔ turning, &c.; anat. E/ung articulation, joint.

ein²-lernen (ᴵᴵ‿) v/a. ⓔ** 1. to learn thoroughly, to get up (by heart). — 2. F e-m et. ‿ to drill (or drub, inculcate) a th. into a p.

ein²-lesen (ᴵᴵ‿) ⓔa** I v/a. to gather (or get) in, to pick. — II sich ‿ v/refl. to read o.s. into a book, to study an author, to read (or get) up a subject; er hat sich gut eingelesen (auch: er ist gut eingelesen) he is well read, F he has the subject at his fingers' ends; he is well up in it, he has familiarized himself with it.

ein²-leuchten (ᴵᴵ‿) I v/n. (h.) ⓔ** to be evident or clear or obvious; das leuchtet mir (nicht recht) ein I can't (quite) understand (or F see through) it; das muß jedem ‿ that must be intelligible (or clear) to everybody. — II ‿d p.pr. und a. ⓔ evident, clear, obvious; intelligible (account), plausible (reason).

ein²-liefern (ᴵᴵ‿) I v/a. ⓔ** to deliver (up); ✉ Briefe ‿ to post letters; vgl. abgeben 1. — II ~ n ⓔ u. **Ein²-lieferung** f ⓔ delivery.

Ein²-lieferungs-schein (ᴵᴵ‿...) m ⓔ receipt (or certificate) of delivery; **=zeit** f time of delivery.

ein²-liegen (ᴵᴵ‿) I v/n. (ſn) ⓔ** 1. to be enclosed in a letter, &c. — 2. Person: to lodge with, ⚔ to be quartered on. — II ‿d p.pr. u. a. ⓔ 3. enclosed.

Ein²-lieger (ᴵᴵ‿) m ⓔ 1. cottager (working for his landlord). — 2. bedfellow, lodger.

Ein¹ling (ᴵ‿) m ⓓd. (Einsiedler) hermit, recluse; (Sonderling) peculiar person, eccentric (or queer) fellow, F oddity.

ein¹-lippig (ᴵᴵ‿) a. ⓔ one-lipped, ♀ unilabiate.

ein²-lochen (ᴵᴵ‿) v/a. ⓔ** 1. ⊙ to hole, to perforate; carp. mit Zapfenloch: to mortise. — 2. P (einsperren) to lock up, F to lay by the heels, P to put in quod.

ein²-löffeln (ᴵᴵ‿) v/a. ⓔa** to take (or give, administer) by spoonfuls or with (or in) a spoon.

ein²-logieren (ᴵᴵG‿) v/a. u. sich ‿ v/refl. ⓔ*/* (sich) ‿ to take lodgings (or rooms) for a p. (o.s.); to lodge with a p.

ein²-lösbar (ᴵᴵ‿-) a. ⓔ redeemable; **~keit** (ᴵᴵ---) f ⓔ redeemableness.

ein²-lös/en (ᴵᴵ‿) I v/a. ⓔ** to redeem a pledge, a mortgage (auch fig. one's promise), to take s.th. pledged out of pawn, to discharge (or pay) a bill, an account; to cash coupons, &c.; to ransom a prisoner. — II ~ n ⓔ u. **Ein²-lösung** f ⓔ redeeming, redemption; discharge, payment; ransom(-ing).

Ein²-lösungs-frist ⚔ (ᴵᴵ‿...) f ⓔ date of redemption; **=kasse**, **=stelle** f branch-bank for paying off banknotes, &c.

ein²-loten ⊙ (ᴵᴵ‿) v/a. ⓔ** to set vertical or vertically; to (test with a) plumb-line; ⚓ die Spanten ‿ (lotrecht stellen) to balance the frames.

ein²-löten ⊙ (ᴵᴵ‿) v/a. ⓔ** to solder in.

ein²-lotsen ⚓ (ᴵᴵ‿) v/a. ⓔ** to pilot in(to port), to pilot inward.

ein²-lullen (ᴵᴵ‿) v/a. ⓔ** to lull asleep or (in)to sleep (ſ. ein=... 5).

Ein²-mach(e)-büchse (ᴵᴵ(‿)...) f ⓔ, **=glas** n tin, glass for preserving.

ein²-machen (ᴵᴵ‿) v/a. ⓔ** 1. to put in(to); to do up in. — 2. Kochkunst:

[einmähdig] — 303 — [einordnen]

Früchte 2 to preserve fruit; Gurken zc. in Essig: to pickle; in Blechbüchsen, Töpfen eingemacht tinned, potted; in Zucker eingemacht (kandiert) candied; vgl. Eingemachte(s). — 3. (kneten) to knead dough, &c.; to mix (or temper) lime, &c. with water. [one crop of hay.]

ein¹-mähdig (⎯‿) a. 🙢 agr. yielding

ein²-mahlen (⎯‿) 🙢** I v/a. to grind corn for storage. — II sich 2 v/refl. to lose (or waste) in grinding.

ein²-maischen ⊕ (⎯‿) v/a. 🙢** Brauerei: das Malz 2 to mash the malt.

ein¹-mal adv. A. (⎯‿) 1. once; 2 blau, 2 grün now ..., now ...; 2 dies, 2 das sagen ... different things at different times; 2 (erstens) weil ..., sodann weil first because ..., then (again) because ...; auf 2 all at once; alle, alles auf 2, mit einem Mal all, everything at the same time; ein für allemal once for all; nicht 2, sondern zehnmal not once, but ten times (vgl. 6); noch 2 once more; (over) again; er ist noch 2 so alt als ich ... twice (or double) my age; noch 2 so viel(e) as much (many) again; Sprichw. 2 ist keinmal once does no harm, once does not count; wer 2 lügt, dem glaubt man nicht, und wenn er auch die Wahrheit spricht a liar is not believed even when he speaks the truth. — B. (⎯‿) oft auch einfach F mal) 2. (ehemals) once (upon a time); in times (or days) past; sie waren früher 2 reich at some former period they were rich. — 3. (bereinst, zukünftig) at some future time, one day; er wird es wohl noch 2 bereuen müssen some day he will yet (have to) repent it. — 4. et. Unabänderliches bezeichnend: es ist nun 2 so (geschehen) what is done cannot be undone; das ist nun 2 so in der Welt that's the way of the world, such is life; ich bin (nun) 2 so I cannot help being as I am; da (nun) doch 2 alles verloren scheint now that all seems irretrievably lost; ist es 2 erst fort when once he is really gone. — 5. beim imper.: komm 2 her!, kommen Sie doch 2 her! come here, please!, do, come here!; stellen Sie sich (nur) 2 ihre Not vor! (only) just think of their distress! — 6. nicht 2 not even; er wollte mich nicht 2 anhören he would not so much as listen to me.

Ein¹maleins (⎯‿‿) n, inv., arith. multiplication-table, Schul-sl. tables pl.

ein¹malig (⎯‿) a. 🙢 happening (but) once; nach 2em Durchlesen after one perusal; 2e Ehe monogamy; nach 2em Rufen after a single call.

ein¹-männ(er)ig, ⎯männisch ? (⎯‿...) a. 🙢 (mit einem Staubgefäß): ⚥ monandrous.

ein²-marinieren (⎯‿‿⎯‿) v/a. 🙢*/* to cure fish, to pickle herrings, salmon &c.

ein²-marken (⎯‿) v/a. 🙢** to mark off with boundary-stones; to enclose.

ein²-markten (⎯‿) v/n. 🙢** to go marketing, to buy in, to purchase.

Ein²-marsch, bsd. ⚔ (⎯‿) m ⑦a. marching in, entry.

ein²-marschieren, bsd. ⚔ (⎯‿‿⎯‿) v/n. (in) 🙢*/* to march in(to a town, &c.), to enter marching.

Ein¹-master ⚓ (⎯‿‿) m 🙢 onemasted ship; cutter.

ein²-mauern ⊕ (⎯‿) v/a. 🙢a** to wall in; to enclose with(in) walls; fig. to immure; eingemauert, auch: pent up.

ein²-meißeln (⎯‿) v/a. 🙢a** to chisel in(to), to engrave with a chisel.

ein²-meng/en (⎯‿) 🙢** I v/a. to mix (up) with. — II sich 2 v/refl. to (inter-)meddle (or interfere) in a p.'s affairs; vermittelnd: to interpose (or intercede) in a dispute; sich unberufen 2, oft: to intrude; to pry; sie mengt sich in alles ein she thrusts (F pokes) her nose into everything. — III ~ n ㉓ = E/ung.

Ein²-mengsel (⎯‿) n ㉓ admixture; (Gemengsel) mess, medley.

Ein²-mengung (‿) f 🙢 (s. einmengen II) meddling; interference.

ein²-messen (⎯‿) 🙢** I v/a. to measure in(to). — II sich 2 v/refl. to lose (or decrease, shrink) by measurement.

ein²-miet/en (⎯‿) I v/a. u. sich 2 v/refl. 🙢** 1. to find (or take) lodgings or a dwelling(-house) for a p. (for o.s.); vgl. einlogieren. — 2. agr. [Miete Schober]: Kartoffeln, Rüben zc.: to stack up, to put away (in sheds). — II ~ n ㉓ = E/ung.

Ein²-mieter (‿) m ㉒ ⚥ inquiline, pl. ...æ (Gallwespe, die Eier in die Gallen anderer Wespenarten legt). [lodgings.]

Ein²-mietung (⎯‿) f 🙢 taking (up)

ein²-misch/en (⎯‿) I v/a. u. sich 2 v/refl. 🙢** = einmengen; Lotterie: die Lose 2 (mischen) to shake up the lots. — II E/ung f 🙢 interference, interposition.

ein¹-monatlich (⎯‿‿) a. 🙢 of one month('s duration), one month's.

ein²-mumme(l)n F (⎯‿) v/a. u. sich 2 v/refl. 🙢(🙢a)**: e-n (sich) to muffle (or wrap) a p. (o.s.) up.

ein²-münd/en (⎯‿) I v/n. (h.) 🙢** 1. in das Meer: to empty (or discharge, flow) into the sea. — 2. anat. von Gefäßen: to inosculate with; ⊕ von Röhren zc.: to fit (or run) into. — II ~ n ㉓ u. E/ung f 🙢 3. discharge of a river, &c.; anat. inosculation of vessels. [of discharge.]

Ein²-mündungs-winkel (⎯‿‿‿‿) m 🙢 angle

ein²-münz/en (⎯‿) I v/a. 🙢** to convert bullion into coin; to (re)coin money. — II E/ung f 🙢 (re)coinage.

Ein¹-muskler ⚥ (⎯‿‿) m 🙢 zo. Muscheltier: monomyarian.

ein²-mustern ⚔ (⎯‿) v/a. 🙢a** to enrol (or enlist) as soldier(s).

ein¹-mütig (⎯‿) a. 🙢 unanimous; ~keit (⎯‿‿) f 🙢 unanimity (= einhellig zc.).

ein²-nageln (⎯‿) v/a. 🙢a** to nail in(to), to fasten with nails.

ein²-nähen (⎯‿) v/a. u. sich 2 v/refl. 🙢** 1. to sew (or stitch) in(to); Blumen in Spitzen 2 to embroider flowers on lace, to diaper lace. — 2. eine Nähmaschine 2 to put a sewing-machine into working order (by using it). — 3. (verengern) to take in (or shorten) by sewing; sich 2 v/refl. to grow shorter (or to shrink) in sewing.

Ein²-nahme (⎯‿) [einnehmen] f 🙢 1. ⚔ e-r Stadt: taking (possession) of a town; capture; e-s Landes: occupation, conquest. — 2. 🙢 (ant. Ausgabe) receipts, proceeds pl.; in ~ bringen, stellen to enter (or book) as cash (or value) received. — 3. (Jahres=)~ revenue, (annual, yearly) income.

Ein²-nahme-buch (⎯‿‿...), =journal n 🙢 book for entering receipts; =posten ♣ m sum received; =quelle f source of income or revenue; =stube f receiver's (or tax-collector's) office.

ein²-nehmbar (⎯‿) a. 🙢 liable to be taken, easy of capture; pregnable.

Ein²-nehme-löffel (⎯‿‿‿) m 🙢 für Arznei zc.: spoon for taking medicine, &c., medicine-spoon.

ein²-nehmen (⎯‿) I v/a. 🙢a** 1. to take in (z.B. ⚓ ballast, a cargo); ⚓ Fracht, Güter 2 to freight, to ship goods; Kohlen, Mundvorrat, Wasser 2 to coal, victual, water; Segel 2 to furl (or reef, take in) sails. — 2. (genießen) to take medicine; to have (or eat) one's dinner; to partake of a meal. — 3. Geld: to receive; Steuern: to collect; ♣ er nimmt wenig ein his receipts (F takings) are small. — 4. ⚔ to take possession of; ein Land: to occupy or conquer; Städte: to take or capture; Stellungen: to carry; mit Sturm: to (take by) storm. — 5. eine Stelle 2 to fill a post; j-s Stelle 2 to act as a p.'s substitute; seinen (zu viel) Platz 2 to take up one's position or stand (too much room); denselben Rang 2 wie // to be of (or to have) the same rank as //, to be on the same level with //. — 6. fig. für sich 2 (gewinnen) to prepossess in one's favour; ihre Anmut nimmt jeden für sie ein ... captivates (or charms) everybody; er wird sie gegen uns 2 he will prejudice (or set) them against us; sich für etwas (nicht) 2 lassen to take a(n) un)favourable view of a th. — 7. die Leidenschaft nimmt ihn ein (erfüllt ihn) ... sways (or possesses) him; e-m den Kopf 2 (benebeln) to affect a p.'s head; to stupefy (or overcome) a p.; die Sinne 2 to benumb the senses. — II ~ n ㉓ 8. taking in, &c. (s. I u. vgl. Einnahme). — 9. (s. 6 u. 7) = Eingenommenheit. — III 2 p.pr. u. a. 🙢 10. Bed. des inf. — 11. fig. (s. 6) prepossessing, captivating, F taking; 2des Wesen engaging (or winning) manners or ways pl. — IV ein-genommen p.p. u. a. 12. f. bs.

Ein²-nehmer (⎯‿) m 🙢, ~in f ㊼ von Einkünften, Steuern zc.: receiver; (rate-, tax-) collector; (tax-)gatherer.

Ein²-nehmerei (⎯‿‿⎯‿) f 🙢 (rate-, tax-) collector's office; rate-office.

ein²-netzen (⎯‿) v/a. 🙢** to moisten.

ein²-nicken F (⎯‿) v/n. (in) 🙢** to nod (or doze) off; vgl. einschlummern.

ein²-nieten (⎯‿) v/a. 🙢** to rivet.

ein²-nisten (⎯‿) sich 2 v/refl. 🙢** to nest(le); fig. to settle down (or F to get a footing) in or at a place; to quarter o.s. on a p.; to gain (a hold on) a p.'s favour.

ein²-nötigen (⎯‿‿) v/a. 🙢**: e-m e-e Tasse Kaffee, e-n Teller Suppe 2 to press ... upon a p. [solitude, wilderness.]

ein¹-öde (⎯‿) [P ⁑: öde] f 🙢 desert,

ein²-ölen (⎯‿) v/a. 🙢** to oil.

ein²-ordnen (⎯‿‿) I v/a. 🙢b** to arrange (in proper order); klassenweise

⚓ scientific; ♀ botanical; 🜨 geography; ⊕ machinery; ⚒ mining; ⚔ military; ⚓ marine; ♣ commercial; ✉ postal; 🚂 railway.

[Einordnung] — 304 — [einreichen]

to classify. — II ~ n 23 u. **Ein-ord-nung** f 46 arrangement; classification.
ein²-pack|en (ᵘᵈᵛ) 68** I v/a. 1. to pack (up); to (em)bale goods; to do up parcels; to make up bundles or packages; in Fässer 2 to barrel (up); in Kästchen, Kisten 2 to put (up) in boxes, cases; in Papier, Stroh ꝛc. 2 to wrap up in paper, straw, &c. — 2. F (essen) F to pack (or put) away the food; to clear the dishes; abs. to cram o.s., to gorge. — II v/n. (h.) 3. zur Reise 2 to pack (one's trunk, F one's things). — 4. F (sich trollen) to pack and be off; to trundle (one's way); F er mußte 2 he had to hold his tongue or withdraw (or retire. — III sich 2 v/refl. 5. to muffle o.s. up. — IV ~ n 23 6. = S/ung.
Ein²-packer ⚥ (ᵘᵈᵛ) m 22, ~in f 47 packer.
Ein²-packung (~) f 46 packing (up), &c. (s. einpacken I u. II); Wasserkur: nasse ~ wrapping (or packing) the body in wet sheets (and a blanket over them).
ein²-pappen (ᵘᵈᵛ) v/a. 68** 1. to paste in(to), F to stick in. — 2. F to seal.
ein²-paschen (ᵘᵈᵛ) 68** = einschmuggeln.
ein²-passen (ᵘᵈᵛ) 68** I v/n. (h.) to fit in. — II v/a. to fit (or fix) in(to); to accommodate; ⊕ to adjust; (einfalzen) to rabbet. — III **Ein²-passung** f 46 accommodation; adjustment.
ein²-passieren (ᵘᵛᴸᵛ) I v/n. (s.) 63*/* to pass in, to enter. — II ~ n 23 entry, entrance; ⚓ inward passage.
ein²-pauken F (ᵘᴸᵛ) v/a. 68**: e-m etwas 2 F to drub (or drive) a th. into a p., to coach (or grind) a. p. in a th.
Ein²-pauker (~) m 22 für Prüfungen: F coach; crammer; für Sport: trainer.
ein²-peitschen (ᵘᴸᵛ) v/a. 68** to whip (or beat, drub) learning, &c. into a child; Hunde 2 to whip in dogs.
Ein²-peitscher (~) m 22 parl. (party-)whip, ehm. whipper-in.
ein²-pfähl|en (ᵘᴸᵛ) I v/a. 68** to fence in with stakes; ⚓ to stockade, to palisade. — II ~ n 23 = S/ung 1.
Ein²-pfählung (ᵘᴸᵛ) f 46 1. fencing in, &c. — 2. fence; enclosure; ⚓ stockade, palisade, pale.
ein²-pfarren (ᵘᴸᵛ) I v/a. 68** to incorporate with (or assign to) a parish. — II **Ein-gepfarrte**(r) m) f 67 parishioner, member of a parish.
ein²-pfeffern (ᵘᴸᵛ) v/a. 92a** to pepper.
ein²-pferchen (ᵘᴸᵛ) v/a. 68** to pen (or fold) sheep; fig. eingepfercht huddled (or cooped) up, crammed (or crowded) together, densely packed.
ein²-pflanzen (ᵘᴸᵛ) 68** I v/a. 1. Bäume ꝛc. 2 to plant ... — 2. fig. e-m et. 2 to implant (or inculcate, engraft) a th. in(to) a p.; tief eingepflanzte Gewohnheit ineradicable (or deep-rooted, inveterate) habit. — II sich 2 v/refl. 3. to be(come) implanted (auch fig.).
ein²-pflöcken (ᵘᴸᵛ) v/a. 68** to peg (or plug) in(to); to fix with pegs.
ein²-pflügen (ᵘᴸᵛ) v/a. 68** agr. to plough in; vgl. einackern.
ein²-pfropfen (ᵘᴸᵛ) I v/a. 68** hort. to engraft or inoculate (auch fig.); vgl. einpflanzen 2. — II ~ n 23 u. **Ein²-pfropfung** f 46 engrafting, inoculation.

Ein¹-pfünder ⚥ (ᵘᴸᵛ) m 22 artill. ehm. one-pounder; ⊕ pfündig a. 66 one-pound.
ein¹-phasig (ᵘᶠᴸᵛ) a. 66 elect.: Der Strom single-phase current.
ein²-pichen (ᵘᴸᵛ) v/a. 68** to pitch (over); to fix (or fasten) with pitch.
ein²-pökeln (ᵘᴸᵛ) v/a. 92a** to pickle, brine, cure, salt, souse; eingepökeltes (gekochtes u. gesalzenes) Rindfleisch corned beef; F fig. wie die Heringe eingepökelt packed like (or as close as) sardines.
ein²-prägen (ᵘᴸᵛ) v/a. u. sich 2 v/refl. 68** 1. to impress, to imprint. — 2. fig. to impress a th. on a p.'s mind; e-m et. scharf 2 strongly to enjoin (or urge) a th. upon a th.; sich dem Gedächtnisse 2 to become fixed (or engraved) in one's memory; ich habe mir (a. es hat sich mir) das tief (in die Seele) eingeprägt it left a deep impression upon me, it engraved itself on my mind, it sank deep into my soul.
ein²-predigen (ᵘᴸᵛ) v/a. 68** to inculcate by preaching, to preach into.
ein²-pressen (ᵘᴸᵛ) v/a. 90** to press (or squeeze) in; to compress.
ein²-prob(ier)en (ᵘᴸᵛ, ᵘᵍᴸᵛ) v/a. 68** (63*/*) to try (to fit in); to rehearse a play, &c., F to try over a song, &c.
ein²-prügeln (ᵘᴸᵛ) v/a. 92a** = einbleuen.
ein²-pudern (ᵘᴸᵛ) v/a. 92a** to powder.
ein²-pumpen (ᵘᴸᵛ) v/a. 68** to pump in(to); fig. e-m et. 2 F to drive (or force, drub) a th. into a p.
ein²-puppen (ᵘᴸᵛ) I sich 2 v/refl. 68** to become (or be transformed into) a chrysalis, to change into a pupa, to enter (into) the chrysalis (or pupa) state. — II ~ n 23 (change into the) chrysalis state.
ein²-quartieren (ᵘᴸᵛᴸᵛ) I v/a. u. sich 2 v/refl. 93*/* (sich) 2 to quarter (o.s.) upon (a. ⚓); sich bei e-m 2 to take up one's quarters (⚓ a.: to billet) with a p. — II ⚓ ~ n 23 u. **Ein-quartierung** f 46 quartering (or billeting) of soldiers; ⚓ ~ bekommen to have soldiers quartered on one, weitS. to (have to) receive (unwelcome) guests at one's house; wir haben ~... soldiers quartered (or billeted) on us. (billet.)
Ein²-quartierungs-zettel (ᶻ...) m 62
ein²-quellen (ᵘᴸᵛ) v/a. 68** to soak, to steep; to swell by soaking.
ein²-quetschen (ᵘᴸᵛ) v/a. 91** (durchQuetschen hineinbringen) to squeeze (or jam) in(to).
ein²-quirlen (ᵘᴸᵛ) v/a. 68** (quirlend hineinbringen) to twirl in(to).
ein²-rahmen (ᵘᴸᵛ) v/a. 68** to (put in a) frame; Bilder, Photographien 2 to mount pictures, photo(graph)s.
ein²-rammen ⊕ (ᵘᴸᵛ) v/a. 68** to (c)ram in(to) or down; Pfähle 2 to drive in piles; vgl. einpressen.
ein²-rangier|en (ᵘᴸᵛ, ᵘʳᵃᵍᴸᵛ) v/a. 93*/*, ~n 23 u. S/ung f 46 = einreihen I u. II.
ein²-räuchern (ᵘᴸᵛ) I v/a. 92a** to (fill with) smoke; to fumigate; für gesundheitliche Reinigung a.: to disinfect. — II ~ n 23 u. **Ein-räucherung** f 46 fumigation.
ein²-räumen (ᵘᴸᵛ) I v/a. 68** 1. to put in order; Möbel ꝛc. 2 to move furniture, &c. into a room; Zimmer 2 to furnish (one's) rooms;

Waren ꝛc. 2 (aufs Lager bringen) to store ..., to stow (away) ..., to warehouse ... — 2. (abtreten) to yield (or give) up one's place to a p.; to concede a right; (zugestehen) to admit, grant, allow; ⚥ e-m gewisse Vorteile 2 to grant a p. certain facilities; 2d concessive. — II ~ n 23 und **Ein-räumung** f 46 3. furnishing, &c. (s. 1); storage of goods, &c. — 4. (s. 2) concession of a right; admission, allowance, favour.
Ein²-räumungs-satz (ᵘᴸᵛ...) m 62 gram. concessive sentence; 2weise adv. by way of concession.
ein²-raunen (ᵘᴸᵛ) 68** s. einblasen 2.
ein²-rechnen (ᵘᴸᵛ) v/a. 92b** to include in one's (or to take into) account; ⚥ Kosten mit eingerechnet including (or inclusive of) expenses; all costs (or expenses) included.
Ein²-rede (ᵘᴸᵛ) f 46 objection; (Widerspruch) contradiction; remonstrance; eine ~ erheben to remonstrate; jur. eine ~ vorbringen to put in a plea.
ein²-reden (ᵘᴸᵛ) 68** I v/a. 1. e-m et. 2 to talk a p. into a th., to talk a p. over to do a th.; e-m Mut, Vertrauen 2 to inspire a p. with courage, confidence; e-m Vernunft 2 to reason with a p.; das lasse ich mir nicht 2 I won't believe (or credit) that; das hat er sich so eingeredet he has taken that into his head. — II v/n. (h.) 2. e-m (gute Worte geben) to try to persuade a p. — 3. in etwas 2 (sich einmischen) to put in one's spoke in anything; man darf ihm nicht 2 (widersprechen) one dare not contradict (or oppose) him. — III ~ n 23 4. (s. 1 u. 2) inspiration; persuasion. — 5. (s. 3) = Einrede.
ein²-reffen ⚓ (ᵘᴸᵛ) v/a. 68** to reef (or clew down) a sail.
ein²-registrier|en (ᵘᵛᴸᵛ) I v/a. 93*/* to (enter in a) register, to (put on) record. — II ~ n 23 u. S/ung f 46 registration, (keeping a) record.
ein²-regnen (ᵘᴸᵛ) 92b** I v/n. (h.) 1. v/impers. es regnet hier ein the rain comes in here. — 2. fig. auf e-n 2 to pelt down on a p.; die Schläge regneten auf ihn ein blows were showered upon him. — II v/a. 3. Passiv: eingeregnet sn to be detained (or kept in) by the rain.
ein²-reib|en (ᵘᴸᵛ) I v/a. 91** 1. Brot ꝛc. in eine Schüssel 2 to crumble ... into a dish. — 2. (a. sich 2 v/refl.): to rub in(to); mit Fett 2 to grease; sich mit Opodeldok 2 to rub o.s. with opodeldoc; sich (dat.) den Arm mit Kampferöl 2 to rub one's arm with camphor-oil; eingerieb(e)ner Glasstöpsel ground-in stopper. — II ~ n 23 3. = S/ung.
Ein²-reibe-salbe (ᵘᴸᵛ...) f 46 liniment.
Ein²-reibung (ᵘᴸᵛ) f 46 1. rubbing (in), friction; med. mit Knetung: massage. — 2. ~(s-mittel n 62) f, med. embrocation; vgl. Einreibesalbe.
ein²-reichen (ᵘᴸᵛ) v/a. 68** to hand in, to deliver; e-e Beschwerde (Klage) 2 to prefer a complaint (to bring an action) against a p.; seine Entlassung 2 to tender one's resignation; ein Gesuch, eine Bittschrift ꝛc. 2 to present (or send up) a petition, a memorial,

[Einreichung] — 305 — [Einsatzstück]

&c. to a p. — II ~n ⓔ u. **Einreichung** f ⓐ delivery; presentation.

ein²-reifeln (ˡˡ‿) v/a. ⓑa** ⚔ artill. = einriefen.

ein²-reih/en (ˡˡ‿) I v/a. ⓑ** 1. to put in a row or line, to (ar)range; to insert; ⚔ to enrol (or enlist) recruits. — 2. Näherei. to fix; vgl. einheften. — II ~n ⓔ u. E/ung f ⓐ 3. (ar)ranging; insertion; ⚔ enrolment of recruits.

ein¹-reihig (ˡˡ‿) a. ⓖ v. Kleidungsstücken: single-breasted; ⚕ ⚛ unilateral.

ein²-reiß/en (ˡˡ‿) ⓑa** I v/a. 1. to rend a garment; to pull down (or demolish) a house; ⚔ (schleifen) to raze a fort; (über den Haufen werfen) die Wälle e-r Festung 2 to dismantle a fortress; fig. to upset or disconcert a scheme. — 2. paint. (in Umrissen zeichnen) to trace. — II v/n. (fn) 3. (Risse bekommen) to rend, tear, split; to be rent or torn. — 4. fig. (sich verbreiten) to spread (more and more); to prevail; bsd. b.s. to take root, to gain ground; es war Lockerheit der Sitten eingerissen laxity of morals had set (or crept) in; tief eingerissene Übel deeply seated evils pl. — III ~n ⓔ u. E/ung f ⓐ 5. (f. 1) rending; demolition. — 6. fig. (f. 4) spreading; prevalence.

ein²-reiten (ˡˡ‿) ⓑb** I v/n. (fn) 1. to ride in(to), to enter on horseback. — II v/a. 2. Pferde 2 to break in ...; (nicht) eingeritt(e)ne Pferde (un)broken horses pl. — 3. et. 2 to ride down (or over) a th., to smash (or break) a th. in riding. — III ~n ⓔ 4. = Einritt.

ein²-renk/en (ˡˡ‿) I v/a. ⓑ**, bsd. surg. to set (or reduce) dislocated joints or bones; fig. die Sache ist wieder eingerenkt (in Ordnung) the matter has been set right (again). — II v/n. ⓔ E/ung.

Ein²-renker (ˡˡ‿) m ⓑ, ~in f ⓓ v. Gliedern, mst nicht ein Arzt: bone-setter.

Ein²-renkung (ˡˡ‿) f ⓐ (f. einrenken) setting, reduction; surg.: ⚛ taxis.

ein²-rennen (ˡˡ‿) ⓑb** I v/n. (fn) to run in(to); auf=ea. 2 to dash against each other. — II v/a. die Tür ꝛc. 2 to break open ... with a rush; sich (dat.) den Schädel 2 to break one's head by running against a wall, &c.; F man kann Wände mit ihm 2 he is thick-headed or thick-skulled or blockheaded.

ein²-richt/en (ˡˡ‿) ⓑ** I v/a. 1. (f. ein² ...1) (ordnen) to arrange, to (put in) order, to organize; to regulate; ich will es so 2, daß // ... so manage (or contrive) that //; nach e-m Muster 2 to adapt to a (given) pattern or sample; ⚔ militärisch eingerichtet with a military organization. — 2. sein Haus 2 to fit up ...; Schulen ꝛc. 2 to set up (or organize, establish, found) ... — 3. e-n (sein Haus) 2 to furnish a p.'s house, F to set a p. up. — 4. arith. e-e gemischte Zahl 2 to reduce a mixed number to a(n) improper) fraction. — 5. surg. to set broken limbs. — 6. ⓔ to put machinery right. — II sich 2 v/ref. 7. to establish o.s.; er hat sich nett eingerichtet he has a nicely furnished house; sich einzurichten wissen to adapt o.s. (to circumstances); to cut one's garments according to one's cloth;

sich auf et. 2 to prepare for a thing; sich nach et. 2 to accommodate o.s. to a th.; wir müssen uns danach 2 we must arrange accordingly; man muß sich so 2, daß // one must so manage that //. — 8. abs. (sparsam sein) to live economically. — III ~n ⓔ 9. = E/ung 1-3.

Ein²-richter (ˡˡ‿) m ⓑ (f. einrichten) p. who arranges, &c.; organizer; regulator.

Ein²-richtung (ˡˡ‿) f ⓐ (f. einrichten) 1. arrangement; organization; adaptation. — 2. arith. reduction. — 3. surg. setting; v. Verrenkungen a.: ⚛ diorthosis. — 4. e-s Hauses: (household-)establishment; furniture; e-s Ladens: fittings pl.; einer Fabrik ꝛc.: plant; e-r Maschine: mechanism; (Anordnung) disposition; (Bau-art) structure; ⚔ militärische ~en military customs and regulations pl., military system sg.; ⚔ ~en im Gelände (Gräben, Wälle ꝛc.) military works pl.; zweckmäßige ~, oft: suitable provision; (die nötigen) ~en treffen für // to make (the necessary) preparations for //.

ein²-riefen ⚔ (ˡˡ‿) v/a. ⓑ**: ein Geschützrohr 2 to rifle the barrel of a gun.

ein²-riegeln (ˡˡ‿) v/a. u. sich 2 v/refl. ⓑa** (sich) 2 to bolt (o.s.) up in a place.

Ein²-riß (ˡˡ‿) [einreißen] m ⓐ a. rent.

Ein²-ritt (ˡˡ‿) [einreiten] m ⓒc. ride (or riding) into; entry on horseback.

ein²-ritzen (ˡˡ‿) v/a. ⓑ** 1. to scratch the skin. — 2. ⓔ to engrave (or cut) a name into metal, stone, &c.

ein²-rollen (ˡˡ‿) I v/a. u. sich 2 v/refl. ⓑ** (sich) 2 to roll (o.s.) up; to wrap (o.s.) up; (sich) am Rande 2 to curl (up); ⚕ eingerollt: ⚛ involute. — II ~n ⓔ u. **Ein²-rollung** f ⓐ rolling; curling; ⚕ ⚛ involution.

ein²-rosten (ˡˡ‿) v/n. (fn) ⓑ** to rust in, to become rusty or fixed by rust.

Ein²-rück(e)- und Aus²-rück(e)-Hebel ⓔ (ˡˡ(‿)...) m ⓑ, -zeug n, mech. engaging- and disengaging-gear.

ein²-rücken (ˡˡ‿) I v/a. 1. to insert in(to) s.th.; eine Anzeige in die Zeitung 2 (lassen) to put (or insert) an advertisement in(to) the paper. — 2. ⓔ mach. to throw into gear, to set going; typ. eine Zeile 2 (ant. ausrücken) to indent a line. — II v/n. (fn) 3. in j-s Stelle 2 to (under)take a p.'s place or post, to succeed a p.; ⚔ von Truppen: to march in(to); to enter a town; in die Reihe 2 to join ranks; to fall in. — III ~n ⓔ u. **Ein²-rückung** f ⓐ 4. (f. 1) insertion. — 5. ⓔ (f. 2) throwing into gear, &c. — 6. ⚔ (f. 3) marching in; entry.

Ein²-rückungs-gebühren (ˡˡ‿ ...) f/pl. ⓑ cost sg. of insertion or advertising.

ein²-rühren (ˡˡ‿) v/a. ⓑ** 1. to stir (up) and mix; Eier: to beat (up). — 2. F fig. e-m etwas 2 = einbrocken 2.

ein²-rußen (ˡˡ‿) v/a. ⓑ** to cover (or blacken) with soot.

Eins (ˡ) f ⓐ, eins f. ein I; ~-sein (ˡˡ‿) n ⓔ union, unity; identity; ~-werden (ˡˡ‿) n ⓔ unification; coming to terms with one another; agreement.

Ein²-saat (ˡˡ) f ⓐ agr. 1. (Säen) sowing. — 2. (Saatkorn) seed.

ein²-sacken (ˡˡ‿) v/a. ⓑ** 1. Korn ꝛc. 2 to put ... into sacks or bags, to sack (or bag) ... — 2. F (einsäckeln) to pocket.

ein²-säen (ˡˡ‿) I v/a. ⓑ** agr. to sow the seed; to put seed into the ground; das Feld 2 to (stock with) seed. — II ~n ⓔ = **Einsäung**.

ein²-sägen (ˡˡ‿) v/a. ⓑ** = ansägen.

ein¹-saitig ♪ (ˡˡ‿) a. ⓖ with one chord.

ein²-salben (ˡˡ‿) I v/a. ⓑ** to rub with ointment; to anoint; mit Pomade 2 to (dress with or grease with) pomade. — II ~n ⓔ und **Ein²-salbung** f ⓐ anointment.

ein²-salzen (ˡˡ‿) I v/a. ⓑ** to salt; Fische 2 (und räuchern) to cure fish; eingesalz(e)nes Rindfleisch salt beef; vgl. einpökeln. — II **Ein²-gesalz(e)ne(s)** n ⓖ salt provisions pl., salt beef, fish, &c. — III ~n ⓔ = **Einsalzung**.

Ein²-salzer (ˡˡ‿) m ⓑ salter; Heringsfischerei: (fish-)curer, bsd. ehm. drysalter.

Ein²-salzung (ˡˡ‿) f ⓐ salting; curing.

ein¹-sam (ˡ‿) [nhd.] a. ⓖ (verlassen) solitary or forsaken or isolated (spot), lonely (place or person); (abgelegen) sequestered, secluded; ein 2es Leben führen to lead a retired life; zo. 2-lebendes Tier hermit; adv. (ganz) 2 leben to live in (strict) seclusion or privacy or retirement.

ein¹-samenlappig ⚕ (ˡˡ‿‿) a. ⓖ: ⚛ monocotyledonous; -samig ⚕ (ˡˡ‿) a. one-seeded; ⚛ monospermous.

Ein¹-samkeit (ˡ‿‿) f ⓐ solitude; isolation; loneliness; seclusion; privacy.

ein²-sammeln (ˡˡ‿) I v/a. ⓑa** to gather (in) the harvest; to pick cherries, &c.; to glean ears of corn; Beiträge, Geld 2 to collect subscriptions, money; mit dem Hute Geld 2 to pass the hat round (for contributions); Kenntnisse 2 to acquire knowledge; fig. Lorbeeren 2 to win (one's) laurels. — II ~n ⓔ = **Einsammlung**.

Ein²-sammler (ˡˡ‿) m ⓑ, ~in f ⓓ gatherer; picker; collector of money, &c.

Ein²-sammlung (ˡˡ‿) f ⓐ (f. einsammeln 1) gathering; collection.

ein²-sargen (ˡˡ‿) v/a. ⓑ** to (put into a) coffin, to screw down in a coffin.

ein²-satteln (ˡˡ‿) I sich 2 v/refl. ⓑa** von Bergpässen: ꝛc form a depression or dip. — II **Ein²-satt(e)lung** f ⓐ depression, (saddle-shaped) pass.

Ein²-satz (ˡˡ‿) m ⓓa. 1. (das Eingesetzte) an Eßtischen: leaf; bei Kleidern: insertion; krauser ~ am Mannshembde: frilled shirtfront; vgl. ~-stück; beim Spiele: stake(s pl.), der ganze ~, a. oft: pool; den ganzen ~ gewinnen to sweep the stakes, to win the pool; den ~ verdoppeln to double one's stake(s). — 2. ~ von Bechern, Schachteln ꝛc. von abnehmender Größe: set (or nest) of cups, boxes, &c. — 3. (Behälter für Fische) fish-pond. — 4. ♪ ~ einer Stimme chiming in; intonation. — **Ein²-satz-becher** (ˡˡ‿‿) m ⓑ, =gewicht n one of a set of cups, weights; =härtung ⓔ f, metall. case-hardening; =preis m bei Versteigerungen: starting price; =rennen n sweep-stake; =schachtel f one of a set of boxes; =schenkel m e-s Zirkels: screw-leg; =streifen m, =stück

♪ Musik; ⚛ Wissenschaft; ⚕ Pflanze; ⓕ Geographie; ⓔ Technik; ⚔ Bergbau; ⚔ Militär; ⚓ Marine; ⓑ Handel; ✉ Post; 🚂 Eisenbahn.

[Einsatzteich] — 306 — [einschlagen]

n an Frauenwäsche: stripe, piece let in(to other material), (worked) insertion; =teich *m* storepond; =zeichen ♪ *n* signal to start (singing or playing).
ein²=sauen (ᴵᴵᴸ◡) *v/a.* ⓖ** to befoul.
ein²=säuern (ᴵᴵᴸ◡) *v/a.* ⓖa** 1. Brot ⌒ to leaven bread. — 2. Kochkunst: to pickle meat, fish, &c. (in vinegar).
Ein²=sauge=gefäß (ᴵᴵᴸ◡...) *n* ⓖ² *anat.* absorbent(vessel), lymphatic duct; =mittel *n* means of absorption; *med.* absorbent.
ein²=saug/en (ᴵᴵᴸ◡) ⓣc(88)** I *v/a.* to suck (in or up); to absorb; Flüssigkeiten: to draw in, to imbibe; *fig.* etwas mit der Muttermilch ⌒, etwa: to be bred (or nurtured) in a th. from infancy; fähig, geneigt einzusaugen absorptive; *med.* ⌒d absorbent. — II sich ⌒ *v/refl.* to attach (or fasten) o.s. by suction; von Farben ꝛc.: to soak in. — III ~ *n* ㉓ = ⌒/ung. 【tube.
Ein²=sauge=rohr *n* (ᴵᴵᴸ◡...) *n* ⓖ² suction-
Ein²=saugung (ᴵᴵᴸ◡) *f* ⓖ⁶ suction, absorption; imbibing.
ein²=säumen (ᴵᴵᴸ◡) *v/a.* ⓖ** to hem.
Ein²=säung (ᴵᴵᴸ◡) *f* ⓖ⁶ (f. einsäen) sowing.
ein¹=säurig (ᴵᴵᴸ◡) *a.* ⓖ⁶ *chm.* monacid.
Ein²=sauung (ᴵᴵᴸ◡) *f* ⓖ⁶ befouling.
ein²=schachtel/n (ᴵᴵᴸ◡) ⓖa** I *v/a.* to put into (or enclose in) a box or case; to encase; *fig.* eingeschachtelte Sätze involved sentences *pl.* — II sich ⌒ *v/refl. co.* to box o.s. up in a confined space, to be jammed together. — III ~ *n* ㉓ *u.* ⌒/ung *f* ⓖ boxing up; ⌒ encasement; *v.* Sätzen: involution. 【⌒ univalvular.
ein¹=schalig (ᴵᴵᴸ◡) *a.* ⓖ⁶ with one shell,
ein²=schalt/en (ᴵᴵᴸ◡) I *v/a.* ⓖ** to put (or throw) in; Worte ꝛc.: to insert; Tage im Kalender: to intercalate; et. nicht Hingehöriges: to interpolate; eingeschaltete Bemerkung incidental remark; eingeschaltete Tage intercalary days *pl.*; in eine Erzählung Eingeschaltetes episode, incident; *elect.* (ant. ausschalten) to connect, elektrisches Licht ꝛc.: to switch on. — II ~ *n* ㉓ = ⌒/ung.
Ein²=schalter (ᴵᴵᴸ◡) *m* ⓖ² interpolator.
Ein²=schaltung (ᴵᴵᴸ◡) *f* ⓖ⁶ (f. einschalten) insertion; intercalation; interpolation (auch *math.*); *elect.* connexion; ~s= zeichen (ᴸ...) *n* *typ.* (it.) caret (∧).
ein²=schanzen ⚔ (ᴵᴵᴸ◡) *v/a.* ⓖ** to entrench, to fortify by trenches.
ein²=schärfen (ᴵᴵᴸ◡) I *v/a.* ⓖ** e-m et. ⌒ to inculcate a th. in(to) a p. — II ~ *n* ㉓ und Ein²=schärfung *f* ⓖ inculcation, injunction, urgent (or strict, stringent, impressive) order.
ein²=scharren (ᴵᴵᴸ◡) *v/a.* ⓖ** to put in(to) the earth, to bury; *a.* sich ⌒ *v/refl.* von Tieren: to go to earth.
ein¹=schattig (ᴵᴵᴸ◡) *a.* ⓖ⁶ (2e Völker *n/pl.*): ⌒ heteroscians (*pl.*).
ein²=schätz/en (ᴵᴵᴸ◡) *v/a.* ⓖ** Steuerwesen: to assess; *fig.* (besser: schätzen) to value; sie h. seine Fähigkeiten richtig eingeschätzt they have formed a correct estimate of his abilities. — II ~ *n* ㉓ = ⌒/ung.
Ein²=schätzung (⌒) *f* ⓖ⁶ assessment; ~s=kommission (ᴸ...) *f* ⓖ² in England: assessors *pl.* of taxes.
ein²=schaufeln (ᴵᴵᴸ◡) *v/a.* ⓖa** to shovel in; to bury with a shovel.

ein²=schaukeln (ᴵᴵᴸ◡) *v/a.* ⓖa** (in den Schlaf wiegen) to rock (off) to sleep; to (lull to sleep in a) cradle.
ein²=schenken (ᴵᴵᴸ◡) *v/a.* ⓖ** to pour out or in(to a glass); e-m Wein, Tee ⌒ to help a p. to a glass of wine, a cup of tea; *fig.* e-m reinen (auch klaren) Wein ⌒ to tell a p. the whole (or plain, unvarnished) truth.
ein²=scheren ⚓ (ᴵᴵᴸ◡) *v/a.* ⓖ** ein Ende ⌒ to reeve a rope or a cable.
ein²=scheuern (ᴵᴵᴸ◡) [Scheuer] *v/a.* ⓖa** *agr.* to put in(to) the barn.
ein²=schichten (ᴵᴵᴸ◡) *v/a.* ⓖ** to arrange (or put up, pile up) in layers; *geol.* eingeschichtet: ⌒ (inter)stratified.
ein¹=schichtig (ᴵᴵᴸ◡) *a.* ⓖ⁶ (allein, ledig) single, unmarried, unwedded.
ein²=schicken (ᴵᴵᴸ◡) *v/a.* ⓖ** to send in to a p.; *amtlich:* to present; vgl. einsenden.
Ein²=schiebe=bild (ᴵᴵᴸ◡) *n* ⓖ² für die Zauberlaterne: slide; =gericht *n* Kocht.: extra dish, (fr.) entremets *pl.*, entrée; =leiste ⊕ *f*, *carp.* clamp.
ein²=schieb/en (ᴵᴵᴸ◡) ⓣc** I *v/a.* 1. to push (or slip) in, F to shove in; Bäckerei: das Brot ⌒ (einschießen) to put ... in(to) the oven. — 2. (einschalten) to insert, to put between; einen Satz ⌒ to intercalate, heimlich: to interpolate; vgl. einschalten I. — 3. e-n (in eine Stelle) ⌒ to appoint (or promote) a p. over the heads of others, F to push a p. forward. — II sich ⌒ *v/refl.* 4. to slip in(to), F to push o.s. forward. — III *v/n.* 5. *hunt.* Schwarzwild: (sich niederlegen) to settle down. — IV ~ *n* ㉓ 6. ⌒/ung 1.
Ein²=schieber (ᴵᴵᴸ◡) *m* ⓖ² (f. einschieben) one who pushes in, inserts, &c.; vgl. Einschalter.
Ein²=schiebe=satz (ᴵᴵᴸ◡...) *m* ⓖ² *gr.* intercalation, parenthesis; insertion; =tisch *m* telescope-table.
Ein²=schiebsel (ᴵᴵᴸ◡) *n* ⓖ⁶ s.th. slipped in or inserted; in Schriften *a.* parenthesis; interlinear note; intercalation, *b.s.* interpolation.
Ein²=schiebung (⌒) *f* ⓖ⁶ 1. pushing in, &c. (f. einschieben I). — 2. = Einschiebsel.
Ein¹=schienen=bahn 🚋 (ᴵᴵᴸ◡⌴) *f* ⓖ⁶ monorail line. 【mono-line system.
ein¹=schienig 🚋 (ᴵᴵᴸ◡) *a.* ⓖ⁶: ⌒es System
ein²=schieß/en (ᴵᴵᴸ◡) ⓣc(ef)t** I *v/a.* 1. ⚔ to shoot (or batter) down with musketry or cannon; to breach a wall. — 2. ⚔ (auch sich ⌒ *v/refl.*) (sich) ⌒ to instruct in (to practise) shooting. — 3. ⚔ ein Gewehr ⌒ to try (or prove, test, season) a gun. — 4. (mit einschieben) to slip in with; Brot ⌒ f. einschieben 1; ↓ Ballast in ein Schiff ⌒ to (shoot) ballast; *typ.* die Form ⌒ to lift the form(e) into the press; ⊕ Weberei: den Eintrag ⌒ to shoot the weft. — 5. ⊛ Geld (in die Kasse) ⌒ to pay in money, F to put down the cash; eingeschossene Kapitalien capital *sg.* invested in (or put into) a concern. — II sich ⌒ ⚔ *v/refl.* 6. f. 2. — III ~ *n* ㉓ 7. f. 1. (1) battering down with gunshot, demolition by artillery. — 8. (f. 2) gun-practice. — 9. (f. 3) trial of a gun. — 10. ⊛ (f. 5) investment.
ein²=schiffen ⚓ (ᴵᴵᴸ◡) ⓖ** I *v/a.* (ant. ausschiffen) to ship goods; to put (or take) on board; auch 🚋 ⚓: to embark. — II sich ⌒ *v/refl.* to embark, to go on board; to take ship (nach for); sich in Liverpool nach New York ⌒ to take passage from Liverpool to New York; sich wieder ⌒ to re-embark. — III ~ *n* ㉓ *u.* Ein²=schiffung *f* ⓖ⁶ shipment of goods; embarkation.
ein²=schirren (ᴵᴵᴸ◡) *v/a.* ⓖ** to (put into) harness; weit S. to yoke to.
ein²=schlachten (ᴵᴵᴸ◡chi) *v/a.* ⓖ** Schwein ꝛc.: to kill for home consumption.
ein¹=schlächtig (ᴵᴵᴸ◡) *a.* ⓖ⁶ = einartig.
ein²=schlafen (ᴵᴵᴸ◡) *v/n.* (ſn) ⓖa** 1. to fall asleep, to drop off (or to go) to sleep; to doze off; über (*a.* bei) einer Sache ⌒ to go to sleep over a th.; ich konnte vor Müdigkeit nicht ⌒ I was too tired to (go to) sleep. — 2. *fig.* (sanft sterben) to pass away gently, to die peaceably; vom Eifer ꝛc.: (nachlassen) to slacken, abate, subside; von Sitten ꝛc.: (in Verfall geraten) to die out, to decay; to go (or get) out of use. — 3. von Gliedern: (gefühllos werden) to go to sleep, to become numb; mir ist Bein eingeschlafen I have pins and needles in my leg. 【schläfig.
ein¹=schläf(e)rig (ᴵᴵᴸ(◡)◡) *a.* ⓖ⁶ = ein-
ein²=schläfern (ᴵᴵᴸ◡) I *v/a.* ⓖa** 1. e-n ⌒ to lull (F to send) a p. to sleep, to make a p. (feel) sleepy or drowsy; *fig.* to lull into security; künstlich: ⌒ to narcotize; to hypnotize; den Schmerz ⌒ to deaden (or assuage, soothe) the pain; ⌒d: producing sleep, ⌒ soporific, narcotic. — 2. (unempfindlich machen) to (be)numb. — II ~ *n* ㉓ *u.* Ein=schläf(e)rung *f* ⓖ 3. lulling a p. to sleep, &c. (f. I); ⌒ soporification, narcotization; hypnotization; ~s=mittel (ᴸ...) *n* sleeping draught; ⌒ soporific, narcotic. 【(bed).
ein¹=schläfig (ᴵᴵᴸ◡) *a.* ⓖ⁶ ⌒es (Bett) single
Ein²=schlag (ᴵᴸ) *m* ⓣd. 1. = einschlagen IV. — 2. e-s Patents ꝛc.: wrapper, cover. — 3. Weberei: woof = Einschuß 2; (Maschinengarn) machine-made twist; *hort.* (provisorische Pflanzung) nursery for young trees; * *fig.* das Land weist trotz seiner slawischen Bevölkerung einen starken deutschen ~ auf the country, despite its Slav population, shows a strong percentage (or contingent) of Germans; ein Dichter, der seinen Idealen einen ~ von lebendiger Wirklichkeit gibt a poet who gives his ideals a touch (or colouring) of living realism; in Kette und ~ verwandte Geister minds akin in warp and weft.
Ein²=schlag(e)=dolch (ᴵᴵᴸ(◡)...) *m* ⓖ² claspdagger; =garn *n* Weberei: machine-spun yarn, weft-yarn; =messer *n* clasp-knife.
ein²=schlagen (ᴵᴵᴸ◡) ⓖb** I *v/a.* 1. ⚔ Nagel ꝛc.: to knock (or drive, force, thrust) in; fest ⌒ to drive home. — 2. Löcher ⌒ to make ... by knocking; auch: to punch out ... — 3. (zerbrechen) to demolish, to break (or smash) window-panes; to break open doors; j-s Schädel ⌒ to break a p.'s skull, to brain a p.; einem Fasse den Boden ⌒ to stave in a cask (vgl. ausschlagen 8).

Signs (see page XVII): F familiar; P vulgar; F flash; ⟋ rare; † obsolete (died); * new word (born); ++ incorrect; ♪ music;

[Einschlagepapier] — 307 — [einschränken]

— 4. (einwickeln) to wrap (or do) up in paper, &c., to tie up in a cloth; to pack in cases; *agr.* und *hort.* to (cover with) earth. — 5. Näherei: (kürzer m.) to tuck in; to turn in at the edge; (übernähen) to overcast (vgl. a. einnähen 3); Web.: Fäden ≈ to pass in threads. — 6. e-n falschen Weg ≈ to take a wrong turning or route; *fig.* to pursue (or strike out) a wrong course; den Weg der Güte ≈ to apply (or adopt) gentle (or conciliatory) measures; die von ihm eingeschlag(e)ne Laufbahn the career which he entered upon, the career chosen by him. — 7. (fechtend einüben) (bsd. sich ≈ v/refl.) to perfect (o.s.) in fencing; sich ≈ auch: to practise fencing. — II v/n. 8. (h.): a) ⚒ (schürfen) to commence digging (operations); b) auf e-n ≈ to belabour a p. with a stick, &c.; c) (eindringen) to fall (or rush) upon; der Blitz hat (auch es hat) in das Haus eingeschlagen the lightning has struck the house; d) in ein Fach ≈ (gehören) to belong to a department, to come within one's province; das schlägt (nicht) in mein Fach ein, auch oft: F that's (not) in my line; e) (in j-s Hand) ≈ to shake hands (with a p.); schlagen Sie ein! we'll shake hands (over it); eingeschlagen! agreed!, done! — 9. (in) (gut, schlecht ≈) (geraten) to turn out (well, ill); er schlägt (gut) ein he is in a fair way (towards success); ⬢ die Artikel schlagen nicht ein ... do not take or are unsaleable. — 10. *paint.* Farben:(den Glanz verlieren) to turn dull. — III sich ≈ v/refl. 11. f. 7. — IV ~ n 🖃 12. knocking in, &c. (f. I u. II); durch das ~ dieser Methode by the adoption of this method; beim ~ des Blitzes when the lightning strikes or struck.

Ein²-schlag(e)-papier (ᵁᴸˇ...) n ⬢ packing-paper;-seide f shot-silk, tram.
ein²-schlägig (ᵁᴸˇ) a. ⬢ belonging (or appertaining, referring, corresponding) to; die ≈en Verhältnisse the surrounding (or concomitant) circumstances pl. [schlagen IV.]
Ein²-schlagung (ᵁᴸˇ) f ⬢ = ein-]
ein²-schleichen (ᵁᴸˇ) v/n. öfter: sich ≈ v/refl. ⬢a** to creep (or slip, sneak, steal) in(to), to find one's way into; *fig.* die sich etwa ≈den Irrtümer mistakes which may creep in.
ein²-schleiern (ᵁᴸˇ) v/a. ⬢a** to veil a nun; sich ≈ lassen to take the veil.
ein²-schleifen¹ (ᵁᴸˇ) v/a. ⬢** to drag in (on a sledge); to smuggle (in).
ein²-schleifen² ⊕ (ᵁᴸˇ) v/a. ⬢b** Bilder ≈ to engrave (or cut) ... in(to) glass, &c.
ein²-schleppen (ᵁᴸˇ) I v/a. ⬢** to drag in; schmuggelnd: to smuggle (in); eine Krankheit: to import. — II ~ n 🖃 und Ein-schleppung f ⬢ importation.
ein²-schließ/en (ᵁᴸˇ) ⬢d** I v/a. 1. (a. sich ≈ v/refl.) to lock (o.s.) in or up; to shut (o.s.) up; eingeschlossen (put or kept) under lock and key; in eine Stube eingeschlossen confined (or pent up) in a room. — 2. (umgeben) to enclose with walls; mit einem Gitter (einer Hecke): to rail (to hedge) in; rings von e-m Zaune eingeschlossen fenced in all round; ⚔ den Feind: to hem in, to surround; eine Stadt: to invest, besiege, blockade; von Eis, Schnee eingeschlossen ice-bound, snow-bound. — 3. (einlegen) to put into; to enclose in a letter, &c. — 4. *fig.* in Klammern ≈ to enclose (or put) in brackets. — 5. *fig.* (in sich begreifen) to include, comprise, embrace; in sein Gebet (mit) ≈ to pray for; ≈d inclusive. — II sich ≈ v/refl. 6. f. 1. — III ~ n 7. = S/ung. — IV ein-geschlossen p.p. u. a. ⬢(D9) 8. Beb. des *inf.*; vgl. 1 u. 2. — 9. ⬢ Verpackung mit ≈ including (or inclusive of) package.

ein²-schließlich (ᵁᴸˇ) a. ⬢ (mst mit *gen.*) inclusive of; including, included, comprising; *adv.* inclusively of, with (the) inclusion of.
Ein²-schließung (ᵁᴸˇ) f ⬢ 1. (f. einschließen 1) locking up; confinement. — 2. ⚔ investment, siege, blockade; ⚔ ~s-linie f line of investment.
ein²-schlingen (ᵁᴸˇ) v/a. ⬢f** 1. to (put into a) sling. — 2. to swallow (up) greedily, F to gobble up, to put away.
ein²-schlitzen (ᵁᴸˇ) v/a. ⬢** to slit.
ein²-schlucken (ᵁᴸˇ) v/a. ⬢** to gulp down; F to bolt; vgl. einschlingen 2.
ein²-schlummern (ᵁᴸˇ) v/n. (jn) ⬢a** to (fall into a) slumber.
ein²-schlüpfen (ᵁᴸˇ) v/n. (jn) ⬢** to slip in(to), heimlich: to steal into.
ein²-schlürfen (ᵁᴸˇ) v/a. ⬢** to sip.
Ein²-schluß (ᵁˇ) m ⬢a. 1. inclusion; mit ~ von inclusive(ly) of; ⬢ mit ~ der Kisten cases included, including cases. — 2. (Einlage) letter (or sample, &c.) enclosed, enclosure.
Ein²-schluß-klammer (ᵁᴸ...) f ⬢, -zeichen n, *typ.*, &c. crotch(et), ([]), bracket.
ein²-schmeicheln (ᵁᴸˇ) ⬢a** I v/a. e-m et. ≈ to coax a p. into a th. — II sich ≈ v/refl. to ingratiate (or insinuate) o.s. (or to curry favour with a p.; to wheedle o.s. into a p.'s good graces. — III ≈d p.pr. u. a. ⬢ insinuating; winning, engaging. — IV ~ n 🖃 u.
Einschmeich(e)lung (ˢ¹(ᵛ)ˇ) f ⬢ ingratiation, insinuation. [werfen 1 u. 2.]
ein²-schmeißen F (ᵁᴸˇ) v/a. ⬢a** = ein-]
ein²-schmelzen ⊕ (ᵁᴸˇ) I v/n. (jn) ⬢b** to melt down. — II sich ≈ v/refl. ⬢** to be reduced (or lost) in (s)melting, to melt away. — III v/a. ⬢** to smelt, melt down; (ausseigern) to liquate.
ein²-schmieden (ᵁᴸˇ) v/a. ⬢** to hammer chains together; to put convicts, prisoners in iron(s) or chains.
ein²-schmiegen (ᵁᴸˇ): v/refl. sich ≈ ⬢** to ingratiate o.s.
ein² schmieren (ᵁᴸˇ) I v/a. ⬢** 1. mit et. ≈ to (be)smear (or bedaub) with s.th.; mit Fett, Öl, Pomade ≈ to grease, oil, pomade; ⊕ *mach.* to lubricate. — 2. (hineinschmieren) to rub grease, &c. into; *fig.* e-m et. ≈ (vorkauen) to drub a th. into a p. — 3. F (schlecht einschreiben) to scrawl (or scribble) into a book. — II ~ n 🖃 4. u. Ein-schmierung f ⬢ greasing; lubrication.
ein²-schmuggeln (ᵁᴸˇ) ⬢a** v/a. ≈ to smuggle in; eingeschmuggelte Ware smuggled goods pl., ⚔ contraband (of war). — II sich ≈ v/refl. f. sich einschleichen. — III ~ n 🖃 smuggling of goods, bsd. ⚔ contraband (trade).
ein²-schmutzen (ᵁᴸˇ) v/a. ⬢** = beschmutzen. [(down or in).]
ein²-schnallen (ᵁᴸˇ) v/a. ⬢** to buckle]
ein²-schnappen (ᵁᴸˇ) ⬢** I v/a. Luft ≈ to gasp for air, to draw in (or inhale) air. — II ⊕ v/n. (jn) v. Federn: to catch.
ein²-schneiden (ᵁᴸˇ) ⬢c** I v/a. 1. to indent; to incise, to notch, to indent; to make an incision into; ⊕ die Zähne e-s Rades ≈ to cog a wheel; ⬢ eingeschnitten incised. — 2. seinen Namen ≈ to carve one's name in(to); Brot in die Suppe ≈, die Suppe ≈ to cut up bread into the soup; ⊕ *carp.* ein Zapfenloch ≈ to mortise; ⚔ *frt.* † Schießscharten ≈ (einkerben) to cut (or make) embrasures; ⚔ * eingeschnitt(e)n(e Batterie, Schützenlinie) dug-in (battery, marksmen) — 3. *agr.* Korn ≈ (a. *abs.*) to cut corn. — II v/n. 4. (h.) to cut into; to hurt; die Feile schneidet ein the file bites; *surg.* ins Fleisch ≈ to cut to the quick; *fig.* ≈d incisive; trenchant: *fig.* tief ins Herz, in die Seele ≈d heart-rending or -piercing; eine tief ≈de Maßregel a step of very incisive (or powerful) effect. — III sich ≈ v/refl. 5. to cut into. — IV ~ n 🖃 6. (f. 1) incision, indenture. [handsaw.]
Ein²-schneide-säge (ᵛ...) f Buchbinderei:]
ein¹-schneidig (ᵁᴸˇ) a. ⬢ one-edged.
ein²-schneien (ᵁᴸˇ) v/a. ⬢** to cover with (or to bury in) snow; sie waren im Gebirge eingeschneit they were snowed up in the mountains; eingeschneiter Zug snow-bound train.
Ein²-schnitt (ᵁᴸˇ) m ⬢c. incision, cut; *pros.* im Verse: cæsura; (Kerbe) indentation, notch; (Schlitz) slit; 🜊, &c. (Erd-)~ cutting; ⊕ Schlosserei: (Zapfenloch) mortise; ⚔ *frt.* (Schießscharte) embrasure. (Geschützdeckung) covering for artillery.
Ein²-schnitt-meißel ⊕ (ᵁᴸ...) m ⬢ jagger; -messer n, *surg.*: ⚔ bistoury.
ein²-schnitze(l)n (ᵁᴸˇ) v/a. ⬢(⬢a)** to carve (or cut, engrave) in(to). [up.]
ein²-schnupfen (ᵁᴸˇ) v/a. ⬢a** to sniff]
ein²-schnür/en (ᵁᴸˇ) I v/a. u. sich ≈ v/refl. ⬢** (sich) ≈ to lace (o.s.); sie schnürt sich zu sehr ein she laces (or draws herself in) too tightly; ein Paket: to tie (or cord) up; 🜊, &c. eingeschnürt strangulated; *surg.* strictured. — II ~ n 🖃 u. E/ung f ⬢ lacing; ⚕ &c. strangulation; *surg.* stricture.
ein²-schöpfen (ᵁᴸˇ) v/a. ⬢** to draw and pour water, &c. into a vessel.
ein²-schränk/en (ᵁᴸˇ) I v/a. und sich ≈ v/refl. ⬢** 1. (sich) ≈ to restrict (o.s.) to confine (o.s.) (auf et. to s.th.); seine Ausgaben ≈ to reduce (or retrench, curtail) one's expenses; wir müssen uns ≈, auch oft: F we must draw in. — II ~ n 🖃 2. = S/ung. — III ≈d p.pr. u. a. ⬢ 3. Beb. des *inf.* — 4. restrictive; (mildernd) mitigative. — IV ein-geschränkt p.p. u. a. ⬢ 5. Beb. des *inf.* — 6. limited, dem Raume nach: cramped (or pinched) for room or space; in ≈em Maße leben to live in a qualified sense; (*adv.*) leben to live economically or

⚡ scientific; ⚘ botanical; ⚲ geography; ⊕ machinery; ⚒ mining; ⚔ military; ⚓ marine; ⬢ commercial; ✉ postal; 🚂 railway.

[Einschränkung] — 308 — [einsetzen]

sparingly or in a humble style or F in a poor way. — V **Ein-schränkung** (ᴵᴵᵛ) f ㊻ 7. restriction; retrenchment, curtailment; limitation, qualification; ohne ~ (Vorbehalt) without reservation, unreservedly; unconditionally; vgl. Eingeschränktheit.
ein²-schrauben(ᴵᴵᵛ)v/a. ㊿c** to screw in(to); to fix with screws or bolts.
Ein²-schreibe-amt (ᴵᴵᵛ...) n ㊷ registry-office; =**brief** m registered letter; =**bureau** ⚬ n booking-office; =**gebühr(en** pl.) f, =**geld** n registration-(or booking-) entrance-)fee.
ein²-schreib/en (ᴵᴵᵛ) I v/a. ㊿** 1. to enter (or write down) in a book; bsd. ⓢ to book (down); ⚬ to register a letter, &c.; Namen in eine Liste: to inscribe; seinen Namen ⁼ lassen, sich ⁼ v/refl. to enter (or give in) one's name, to enrol o.s.; als Student: to matriculate; in ein Register: to register. — 2. in das Gedächtnis ⁼ to impress on one's memory; in das Protokoll ⁼ to enter in the minutes. — 3. math. to inscribe; ein Dreieck in einen Kreis ⁼ to inscribe a triangle in a circle. — II ~ n ㉓ 4. = E/ung, auch = Einschreibebrief; als Briefaufschrift: registered. — III **ein=geschrieben** p.p. u. a. ㊺ (D9) 5. Bed. des inf.
Ein²-schreiber (ᴵᴵᵛ) m ㉖, ~**in** f ㊵ registrar, recorder.
Ein²-schreibe-sendung ⚬ (ᴵᴵᵛ...) f ㊷ registered parcel; =**stelle** f = =bureau.
Ein²-schreibung (ᵉᴵᵛ) f ㊻ entering, &c. (f. einschreiben I); registration; inscription; enrolment; matriculation; entry; ~s=... (″...) ㊷ = Einschreibe-...
ein²-schreiten (ᴵᴵᵛ) I v/n. (fn) ㊺** 1. to step (or stride, walk) in(to); fig. (sich einmischen) to interfere; vgl. einmengen II. — 2. gerichtlich: to proceed against a p.; kriminell: to prosecute a p.; streng ⁼ to take severe measures against a p. — II ~ n ㉓ 3. fig. interference; interposition; gerichtlich: (legal) proceedings pl.; prosecution.
ein²-schroten ⊕ (ᴵᴵᵛ) v/a. ㊿**: Fässer ⁼ to haul (or let)... down into the cellar.
ein²-schrumpfen (ᴵᴵᵛ) v/n. (fn) ㊺**, to shrink (or shrivel) up; von der Haut: to become wrinkled, to show wrinkles, to wrinkle; (verwelken) to wither.
Ein²-schub (ᴵᴵ, F ᴵᴵᵛ) m ㊇d. e-s Tisches: additional leaf; vgl. Einschiebsel.
ein²-schüchter/n (ᴵᴵᵛ) I v/a. ㊺** (f. ein²) to intimidate, F to bully; durch Blicke: to browbeat; er läßt sich nicht leicht ⁼ he is not easily frightened; eingeschüchtert, auch: cowed down. — II ~ n ㉓ E/ung (ᴵᴵᵛ) f ㊻ intimidation, F bullying; E/s=**system** (″...) n ㉖, =**versuch** m systematic (attempted) intimidation; F system of (attempt at) bullying.
ein²-schulen (ᴵᴵᵛ) I v/a. ㊺** 1. to school; vgl. abrichten 1. — 2. (e-r Schule zuweisen) to put a boy to school; to enter (or place) him at a school. — II ~ n ㉓ u. **Ein²-schulung** f ㊻ 3. schooling, training, practising.
Ein¹-schur (ᴵᴵᵛ) f ㊷ von Schafen: wool of the first shearing; =**schürig** a. ㊺: a) Schafe: once shorn; b) agr. Wiesen: annually producing one crop of hay.

Ein²-schuß (ᴵᴵᵛ) [einschießen] m ㊇a. 1. ⚫ an Geld: capital (or sum) invested in a business, money sunk in a concern; investment; ~ leisten to pay down money (on account). — 2. ⊕ Weberei: (Fadengruppe, die die Kette kreuzt) woof, weft, filling (auch fig. = Einschlag 3). — 3. ⚔ hunt. (Stelle, wo die Kugel eindrang) spot where the bullet entered. — 4. vet. (Entzündungsgeschwulst) inflammatory swelling (of cows, &c.), ⚕ phlegmon.
ein²-schustern F (ᴵᴵᵛ) v/n. (h.) ㉒a** to lose (or fail) in business, to come down in the world, to be down on one's luck.
ein²-schütten (ᴵᴵᵛ) v/a. ㊺**: Korn ꝛc. ⁼ to pour... into a sack or mill, &c.
ein²-schwärzen (ᴵᴵᵛ) v/a. ㊿** 1. to blacken. — 2. = einschmuggeln I.
Ein²-schwärzer (ᴵᴵᵛ) m ㉖ smuggler; bsd. ⚙ contraband trader, contrabandist. [schmuggeln III.]
Ein²-schwärzung (ᴵᴵᵛ) f ㊻ = ein=}
ein²-schwatzen (ᴵᴵᵛ) ㊿** I v/n. (h.) mit (hin)⁼ to put a word in. — II v/a. et. ⁼ to talk a p. into (doing) a th., to make a p. believe a th. — III sich ⁼ v/refl. = einschmeicheln II.
ein²-schwefeln (ᴵᴵᵛ) v/a. ㊿a** to (strew with) sulphur, ⊕ to sulphurize.
ein²-schwenken ⚔ (ᴵᴵᵛ) v/n. (h.) ㊺** to wheel in(to) or inward; aus der Kolonne in Linie ⁼ to form from column into line.
ein²-schwingen (ᴵᴵᵛ) v/n. (fn) ㊹fi** hunt. v. Auer- u. Birkwild: (sich auf Bäume niederlassen) to perch (on trees).
ein²-segeln ⚓ (ᴵᴵᵛ) v/n. (fn) ㉒a** to sail in (under full press of canvas); in den Hafen ⁼ to sail into port.
ein²-segnen (ᴵᴵᵛ) rel. I v/a. ㉒b** 1. to bless, to give one's blessing (or benediction) to; Brot u. Wein: to consecrate. — 2. Geistliche: to ordain. — 3. Kinder ⁼ (konfirmieren) to confirm; e-e Wöchnerin: to church. — II ~ n ㉓ und **Ein²-segnung** f ㊻ 4. (f. 1) blessing, benediction; consecration; (f. 2) ordination; (f. 3) confirmation.
ein²-sehen (ᴵᴵᵛ) ㉒a** I v/n. (h.) 1. ⚑ in et. ⁼ to look (or glance) into a th. — 2. mit e-m (ins Buch) ⁼ to look over (the same book) with a p. — II v/a. 3. to look (or search) into; to investigate, inspect, examine. — 4. (begreifen) to understand, to comprehend, to see (the drift of); ich kann den Grund davon leicht ⁼ (fassen) I can easily conceive (or see, perceive) the reason of it; er will seinen Irrtum nicht ⁼ he won't acknowledge (or see) his mistake; sie will seine Fehler nicht ⁼ she shuts her eyes to his faults. — III ~ n ㉓ 5. looking (or glancing) into or over, &c. (f. I). — 6. (f. 3) search; investigation. — 7. (f. 4) ein ~ (Einsicht) h. ob. nehmen to have (or show) consideration; er sollte ein~ h. he should be reasonable or listen to reason.
ein²-seifen (ᴵᴵᵛ) v/a. ㊺** to soap; fig. (betrügen) to humbug; sich ⁼ v/refl. to lather (or soap) one's chin or face.
ein¹-seitig (ᴵᴵᵛ) a. ㊺ one-sided; ⚑, &c.: ⚕ unilateral; (eingenommen) partial, bias(s)ed; (oberflächlich) superficial; (ausschließlich) exclusive; adv. auch: from one

point of view only; (beschränkt) narrow-minded; ⚕er Friede separate peace.
Ein¹-seitigkeit (ᴵᴵᵛ) f ㊻ one-sidedness; partiality, bias; exclusiveness; narrow-mindedness, narrowness.
ein²-send/en (ᴵᴵᵛ) I v/a. ㉒a** to send in, forward, remit; an Zeitungen: to communicate, contribute; **Eingesandtn** (private) contribution or correspondence; insertion. — II ~ n ㉓ = E/ung.
Ein²-sender (~) m ㉒, ~**in** f ㊵ one who sends in, &c.; remitter; an Zeitungen: contributor, (occasional) correspondent. [(f. I einsenden); remittance.}
Ein²-sendung (~) f ㊻ sending in, &c.}
ein²-senk/en (ᴵᴵᵛ) I v/a. u. sich ⁼ v/refl. ㊺** 1. to sink, to let (down) into the ground; (begraben) to inter, bury; (eintauchen) to dip, immerse; eingesenkt interred; immersed; v. Boden: depressed. — 2. hort. to lay (or set, plant) cuttings or slips. — II ~ n ㉓ 3. = E/ung 1.
Ein²-senkung (~) f ㊻ 1. sinking, letting down. — 2. des Bodens: depression.
Einser (ᴵᵛ) m ㉒ = Einer.
Ein²-setz-... (ᴵᴵᵛ...) ㊷ = Einsatz-...
ein²-setz/en (ᴵᴵᵛ) ㊿** I v/a. 1. to put (or set) in (its place); e-n ⁼ (einsperren) to put a p. in jail or prison, to imprison a p.; hort. Bäume ⁼ to plant trees. — 2. ein Blatt in ein Buch ⁼ to insert a leaf; ⊕ den Boden in ein Faß ⁼ to head a cask; Fische in e-n Fluß ⁼ to stock a river with fish; ⚓ e-n Mast ⁼ to set up a mast; Scheiben in ein Fenster ⁼ to put in panes; ⊕ die Speichen in ein Rad ⁼ to spoke a wheel; dem Pferde die Sporen ⁼ to set spurs to the horse; Vögel (in e-n Käfig ⁼ to put birds in(to) a cage, to cage (up) birds; Zähne ⁼ to put in (false) teeth.; ⊕ e-e Anzeige ⁼ lassen to insert an advertisement. — 4. (aufs Spiel setzen) in die Lotterie ⁼ to put into the lottery; sein Ehrenwort zum Pfande ⁼ to pledge one's word of honour; seine beste Kraft ⁼ to work (or try) with all one's might; sein Leben ⁼ to stake one's life. — 5. (einführen) ein Fest ꝛc. ⁼ to appoint (or institute) a feast-day or holiday, &c.; in ein Amt, eine Würde ⁼ to install (in one's office, dignity); bsd. ehm.: to invest (with the insignia of one's office); wieder ⁼ to reinstall, reinstate, rehabilitate; e-n in f-n früheren Besitz, f-e früheren Rechte wieder ⁼ to restore a p.'s (or to reinstate a p. in his) possessions, rights; e-n zu seinem Erben (zum Richter) ⁼ (ernennen) to make (or appoint, constitute) a p. one's heir (a judge); eccl. e-n englischen Bischof feierlich ⁼ to enthrone... — II v/n. (h.) 6. (eintreten) to set in; ⚓ die Brise setzt wieder ein the breeze is springing up again; jetzt setzte die Flutwelle ein then high tide set in; * allg. (beginnen) die Bautätigkeit setzt im März ein building operations begin (or are resumed) in March; ⚫ Börse: die Spekulation, die in Paris eingesetzt hat speculation which is reviving (or showing activity) in Paris. — III sich ⁼ v/refl. 7. ⚑ sich (in einen Wagen ꝛc.) (hin)⁼ to

Zeichen (f. S. XVII): F familiär; P Volkssprache; Ϝ Gaunersprache; ⚑ selten; † alt (auch gestorben); * neu (auch geboren); ⚌ unrichtig;

[Einsetzung] [einstecken]

take (up) one's seat (in a carriage, &c.). — 8. mit sachlichem Subjekt: (sich festsetzen) to take root, to become established. — IV ~ *n* 23 und **Ein²-setzung** *f* ⊕ 9. (f. 1) putting in; imprisonment, &c. — 10. (f. 2 u. 3) insertion of a leaf, of an advertisement. — 11. (f. 5) appointment, institution, installation; investiture; (re)instalment; restoration; constitution; bishop's enthronement. — 12. (f. 8) establishment. — 13. ⊕ (Einsatzhärtung) case-hardening.
Ein²-setzungs-worte (ᵘᴸ⌣...) *n|pl.*, *eccl.* des Abendmahls: sacramental words *pl.* — Vgl. auch Einsatz...
Ein²-sicht (ᵘᴸ) [einsehen] *f* ⊕ 1. inspection, (Untersuchung) examination; wir legen es Ihnen zur geneigten ~ (Ansicht) vor we submit it for your kind inspection. — 2. (Verständnis) insight, understanding, discernment; viel ~ haben to have great judgment, to be highly intelligent; mit (ohne) ~ handeln to act with(out) judgment, (in-)judiciously; ~ von etwas gewinnen, nehmen to gain (or get) an insight into a th., to take cognizance of a th.; nach m-r ~ (Ansicht) in my opinion, to my mind. — 3. ~ nehmen s. einsehen 7.
ein²-sichtig (ᵘᴸ⌣) *a.* ⊕ = einsichtsvoll.
Ein²-sicht-nahme (ᵘᴸ⌣ᴸ⌣) *f* ⊕ = Einsicht 1.
ein²-sichts-los (ᵘᴸ⌣) *a.* ⊕ injudicious, unintelligent; **-losigkeit** *f* 62 injudiciousness, lack of intelligence, want of understanding; **-voll** *a.* judicious, intelligent; (verständig) sensible.
ein²-sickern (ᵘᴸ⌣) *I v|n.* ⊕a** in den Sand *ꝛc.* ⌾ to soak (or ooze) into ...; to infiltrate into... — II ~ *n* 23 u. **Ein²-sickerung** *f* ⊕ infiltration.
Ein¹-siedel (ᵘᴸ⌣) [ahd.] *m* 22 hermit.
ein²-siedelei (ᴸ⌣ᵛᴵᴵ) *f* ⊕ hermitage.
ein²-sieden (ᵘᴸ⌣) *v|a.*, *v|n.* (fn) u. *sich* ⌾ *v|refl.* ⊕e** u. ⊕** to boil down (= einkochen).
Ein¹-siedler (ᵘᴸ⌣) [mhd.] *m* 22, ~**in** *f* 47 hermit(ess *f*); anchorite; recluse.
ein¹-siedlerisch (ᵘᴸ⌣) *a.* ⊕ anchoretic; weitS. solitary or retired (life); *zo.* von Strahlentierchen: ⫶⫶ monozoan.
Einsiedler-krebs (ᵘᴸ⌣...) *m* ⊕ *zo.* hermit- (or soldier-)crab (*Pagu'rus*); **-leben** *n* hermit's life, anchoretism.
ein²-siegeln (ᵘᴸ⌣) *v|a.* ⊕a** to seal up, to fasten with a seal.
ein¹-silbig (ᵘᴸ⌣) *a.* ⊕ gram. of one syllable. ⫶⫶ monosyllabic (word, language); *fig.* (wortkarg) sparing of words, taciturn, (man) of few words; ~**keit** (⌣ᴸ⌣) *f* ⊕ gram.: ⫶⫶ monosyllabism; *fig.* taciturnity.
ein²-singen (ᵘᴸ⌣) ⊕fi** *I v|a.* to sing to sleep; vgl. einlullen. — II *sich* ⌾ *v|refl.* to practise (or perfect o.s. in) singing.
ein²-sinken (ᵘᴸ⌣) *I v|n.* (fn) ⊕fi** 1. to sink (or break) in(to a pool, &c.); to be swallowed up by the earth, to be engulfed by the waves; *fig.* eingesunkene Augen sunken (or hollow) eyes *pl.* — 2. vom Erdboden *ꝛc.*: to subside, give way, cave in. — II ~ *n* 23 3. sinking in; subsidence of the soil; landslip.
ein³-sitzen (ᵘᴸ⌣) ⊕e** *v|n.* (fn) to stay

(much) at home. — II *v|a.* etwas ⌾ to press a th. down by sitting on it.
ein¹-sitzig (ᵘᴸ⌣) *a.* ⊕ single-seated.
eins-mals (ᵘᴸ) *adv.* = einst(mals).
ein¹-sohlig (ᵘᴸ⌣) *a.* ⊕ with one sole.
ein²-sommern (ᵘᴸ⌣): *sich* ⌾ *v|refl.* ⊕a** to accustom o.s. to the summer-heat.
ein²-spannen (ᵘᴸ⌣) *v|a.* ⊕*** 1. Zeug in einen Rahmen ⌾ to frame ... — 2. Pferde, metonymisch: den Wagen ⌾ (a. *abs.* ⌾) to put (or yoke) the horses to (the carriage). — 3. ⤳ *fig.* ihr, ihr dort draußen in der Welt, die Nasen eingespannt! (*SCH.*) ye people yond in foreign lands, don't put your noses up!
Ein¹-spänner (ᵘᴸ⌣) *m* 22 one-horse carriage; **-spännernatur** *f* 62 one who likes to do everything himself; ⌾**spännig** *a.* ⊕ drawn by one horse (only).
ein²-speichern (ᵘᴸ⌣) *v|a.* ⊕a** to store up, lay in, (ware)house, put by.
ein²-sperren (ᵘᴸ⌣) *I v|a.* u. *sich* ⌾ *v|refl.* ⊕*** 1. to shut in (between four walls, to shut (or lock) up; Hühner *ꝛc.*: to coop up; eingesperrt imprisoned, (*SH.*) cribbed and confined, F boxed up; vgl. einschließen 1. — 2. ⚔ in Arrest ⌾ to put under arrest; ins Gefängnis ⌾ to lock up (in jail); P to put in quod; in e-n Käfig ⌾ to cage (up). — II ~ *n* 23 u. **Ein²-sperrung** *f* ⊕ 3. imprisonment; confinement.
ein²-spielen (ᵘᴸ⌣) *I v|a.* to practise a piece well. — II *sich* ⌾ *v|refl.* to practise playing; gut eingespielt sein to be in good practice, meist to be an accomplished player or performer.
ein²-spinnen (ᵘᴸ⌣) ⊕a** *I v|a.* to spin into, to draw into (or enclose in) one's web (auch *fig.*). — II *sich* ⌾ *v|refl.* von Seidenraupen *ꝛc.*: to (spin a) cocoon; eingesponnene Seidenraupe silkworm in its chrysalis state, cocoon; *fig.* (sich absondern) to lead a secluded (or solitary) life.   [— 2. = Einspruch.]
Ein²-sprache (ᵘᴸ⌣) *f* ⊕ 1. = Einrede.
ein²-sprechen (ᵘᴸ⌣) ⊕a** *I v|n.* (h.) 1. to take part in a conversation; a. *v|a.* ein Wort mit ⌾ to put in a word. — 2. für e-n ⌾ (sich verwenden) to intercede on behalf of a p. — 3. bei e-m ⌾ to call on a p.; to go to stay with a p. — II *v|a.* 4. einem Mut ⌾ to instil courage into a p., to inspire a p. with courage; e-m Trost ⌾ to speak (words of) comfort to a p., to console a p.
ein²-sprengen (ᵘᴸ⌣) ⊕*** *I v|a.* 1. to hollow out a rock, &c. by blasting, to burst open a door. — 2. mit Wasser, mit Salz ⌾ to sprinkle with water, with salt; Buchbinderei *ꝛc.*: eingesprengt (v. Schnitt: gesprenkelt) marbled. — 3. (einstreuen) to intersperse; geol. eingesprengt (eingeschichtet) ⫶⫶ interstratified; in das Gestein eingesprengtes Gold gold interspersed in the rock. — II *v|n.* 4. (fn) to (make a) dash at; (hin)⌾ to gallop in(to); ⚔ auf den Feind ⌾ to charge the enemy with cavalry. — III ~ *n* 23 u. **Ein²-sprengung** *f* ⊕ 5. bursting open, &c.; geol. interstratification; ⚔ cavalry charge.
Ein²-spreng-maschine (ᵘᴸ⌣ᴸ⌣...) *f* 62 bei der Appretur: sprinkling-engine.

ein²-springen (ᵘᴸ⌣) *v|n.* (fn) ⊕fi** 1. to jump (or leap) in; auf etwas ⌾ to leap (or spring) at a th.; F fig. mit Geld ⌾ to put in cash; (eintreten) to join a club, &c. — 2. auf die Mensur ⌾, von Sekundanten: to intervene; to order a pause. — 3. (sich einbiegen) to bend in or inward; ⦷der Winkel re-entering angle. — 4. ⊕ von Federn, Schlössern *ꝛc.*: to catch, to snap. — 5. F *fig.* (aushelfen) to assist, to come to the rescue.
ein²-spritzen (ᵘᴸ⌣) *I v|a.* ⊕*** to inject, squirt in(to), syringe (alle a. *med.*) — II ~ *n* 23 = Einspritzung.
Ein²-sprit-hahn ⊕ (ᵘᴸ⌣...) *m* 62, **-röhre** *f.* injection-cock, -pipe.
Ein²-spritzung (ᵘᴸ⌣) *f* ⊕ injection, syringing; *med.* des Darms: ⫶⫶ enema.
Ein²-sprit-venti'l (ᵘᴸ⌣ᴸ) *n* ⊕ injection-valve.
Ein²-spruch (ᵘᴸ⌣) *m* ⊕d.opposition,(Verwahrung) objection, protest; (Beschwerde) reclamation, ~ erheben, tun to object (or raise an objection) to, to enter a protest against; to put one's foot down, *bsd. jur. auch*: to demur; *eccl.* gegen die Eheschließung: to forbid the banns; *jur.* gegen Geschworene: to challenge the jury; *Fußballspiel*: appeal.
ein²-spünden (ᵘᴸ⌣) *v|a.* ⊕** to bung.
ein¹-spurig ⦶ (ᵘᴸ⌣) *a.* ⊕: (⌾e Bahn) single-line (railway).
Eins-sein (ᵘᴸ) *n* 23 f. eins.
einst (ᴸ) [ahd.: once] *I adv.* 1. (vormals) once (upon a time); at one time, in days past or gone by; of yore. — 2. (künftig) some (or one) day, at some future time, in days to come, one of these days. — II ~ *n*, *inv.* 3. (f. I) das ~ the past; the (distant) future.
ein²-stallen (ᵘᴸ⌣) *v|a.* ⊕** vom Vieh: (put into a) stable; eingestallt stabled.
ein²-stampfen (ᵘᴸ⌣) *I v|a.* ⊕** 1. in et. ⌾ to stamp (or ram) into a thing; den Boden: to stamp down. — 2. Akten, Papiere *ꝛc.* ⌾ I. to put ... into the paper-stamp, to repulp...; Glas *ꝛc.* ⌾ I. to break up (or pulverize)... by stamping. — II ⌾ung *f* ⊕ 3. stamping (down); pulverization.
Ein²-stand (ᵘᴸ) *m* ⊕c. 1. installation (into an office); entering on one's duties; coming into one's rights. — 2. (Geld zur Aufnahme) entrance-fee; seinen ~ bezahlen, geben to pay one's footing. — 3. *Tennis*: deuce.
Ein²-stands-geld (ᵘᴸ⌣...) *n* 62 entrance-fee = Einstand 2; **-mann** ⚔ *m* = Einsteher; **-schmaus** *m* installation-dinner (= Antrittsschmaus).
ein²-stänkern F (ᵘᴸ⌣) ⊕a** to fill with stench or offensive smells.
ein²-stauben (ᵘᴸ⌣) *v|n.* (fn) ⊕** to collect (or to become covered with) dust.
ein²-stäuben (ᵘᴸ⌣) *v|a.* ⊕** to cover (or sprinkle) with dust or powder.
ein²-stauen ⚓ (ᵘᴸ⌣) *v|a.* ⊕** to stow.
Ein²-stech-bogen (ᵘᴸ⌣...) *m*, *typ.* ⊕ (Abziehbogen) tympan-sheet.
ein²-stechen (ᵘᴸ⌣) *v|a.* ⊕a** to perforate; to stick (or thrust, dig) in a sharp tool; to pierce with a pin, &c.; Löcher ⌾ to cut (or punch) out ...; ⊕ *typ.* in die Punkturspitzen ⌾ to prick.
ein²-stecken (ᵘᴸ⌣) *I v|a.* ⊕** 1. to put (F stick) in; in die Tasche ⌾ to

♪ Musik; ⫶⫶ Wissenschaft; ❦ Pflanze; ⚲ Geographie; ⊕ Technik; ⚒ Bergbau; ⚔ Militär; ⚓ Marine; ⚫ Handel; ✉ Post; ⦶ Eisenbahn.

[Einsteckkamm] — 310 — [einteilig]

pocket; Stecknadeln in Briefe 2 to paper pins; ⚔ das Schwert 2 to sheathe the sword; *abs.* F e-n 2 (einsperren) to put (F to clap) a p. in jail, F to put a p. away; er wurde vom Schutzmann eingesteckt, oft F he was run in by the policeman. — 2. *fig.* eine Beleidigung (ruhig) 2 (hinnehmen) to put up with (F to pocket, to swallow) an affront or insult. — II ~ n 23 3. = S/ung.

Ein²-steck-kamm (ᴵᴸ…) m 62 high comb, dress-comb; **=leiter/**Art Feuerleiter) fire-escape; **=schloß** n Schlosserei: mortise-lock; stock-lock.

Ein²-steckung (ᴵᴸᴗ) f 46 putting in, &c. (f. einstecken 1); imprisonment.

ein²-steh(e)n (ᴵᴸ(ᴗ) v/n. (fn) 94** für e-n 2 to take a p.'s place; to act (or serve) as a p.'s substitute; für e-n, etwas 2 (Gewähr leisten) to make o.s. answerable (or responsible) for a p., a th., to be (or become, stand) security for a p., a th.; (sich wehren) für seine Rechte 2 to stand up for one's rights; Sprichw. jeder muß für sich selbst 2 every tub must stand on its own bottom.

Ein²-steher ⚔ (ᴵᴸᴗ) m 22 ehm. substitute. [sich einschleichen.]

ein²-stehlen: sich 2 v/refl. 94** =}

Ein²-steig(e)-brunnen m = =schacht.

ein²-steigen (ᴵᴸᴗ) I v/n. (fn) 91** 1. to step (or F get, jump) into a carriage, &c.; ⚓ to embark in (or go on board) a vessel; 🚂 &c. Ruf vor der Abfahrt: 2! take your seats, please, ⚓ all aboard!; nach Boston 2! *Am.* 🚂 all aboard for B.! — 2. in ein Haus (als Dieb) 2 to enter (or break into) …; zum Fenster, durchs Dach 2 to get in at the window, through the roof. — II ~ n 23 3. ⚓ embarkation, 🚂 entering a carriage.

Ein²-steig(e)-platz (ᴵᴸ(ᴗ)…) m 22 starting-place, 🚂 departure-platform; **=schacht** ⊕ m e-r Rohrleitung: manhole.

ein²-stell/en (ᴵᴸᴗ) 98** I v/a. 1. to put in (its place); to set right; einen Apparat 2 to adjust …; in Fernrohr, die Kamera ꝛc. in den Brennpunkt 2 to focus …; ⊕ Wasserbau: die Schützen 2 to stop the flood-gates. — 2. Leute 2 (in Arbeit nehmen) to engage workmen; ⚔ Rekruten 2 to enlist recruits. — 3. (zum Stillstand bringen) to discontinue, to leave off, to stop; die Arbeit 2 to suspend work, to (go on) strike; den Betrieb 2 to stop operations or work; ⚔ Feindseligkeiten, das Feuer(n) 2 to suspend hostilities, to cease firing; Mißbräuche 2 to abolish abuses; 💲 Zahlungen 2 to stop (or suspend) payment. — II sich 2 v/refl. 4. = sich einfinden; *phot.* sich (gut, schlecht) 2 to focus well, badly; sich selbst 2d self-focusing. — III ~ n 23 5. = S/ung.

ein¹-stellig (ᴵᴸᴗ) a. 66 *arith.* of one figure or dimension.

Ein²-stellung (ᴵᴸᴗ) f 46 (f. einstellen 3) discontinuance, stoppage, suspension, cessation; abolition of abuses; quashing (of) legal proceedings; der Arbeit: strike; ⚔ ins Heer enlistment.

ein²-stemmen (ᴵᴸᴗ) v/a. 98** 1. to support against; die Arme 2 to rest one's arms on one's hips, bsd. ⚓ to stand with one's arms a-kimbo. — 2. ⊕ to chisel out a hole.

einstens (ᴵᴸ) adv. = einst.

ein²-steuern (ᴵᴸᴗ) v/a. 92a** to assess (for purposes of taxation), to tax.

ein²-sticken (ᴵᴸᴗ) v/a. 98**: Blumen in Tuch 2 to embroider … into cloth.

einstig (ᴵᴸ) a. 66 1. Vergangenheit: former. — 2. Zukunft: future, (in times) to come, that is to be.

ein²-stimmen ♪ (ᴵᴸᴗ) v/n. (h.) 98** 1. to (be in) accord with, to harmonize with. — 2. (mit) 2 to chime (or join) in; im Chore 2 to sing in chorus; to swell the chorus; *fig.* in etwas 2 to agree (or assent) to a th.; mit e-m 2 to coincide with a p.

ein¹-stimmig (ᴵᴸᴗ) a. 66: a) ♪ (set) for one voice; 2es Lied solo (song); b) = einhellig; 2 (adv.) gewählt chosen unanimously, elected without a dissentient voice; **~keit** (ᴵᴸᴗ) f 46 = Einhelligkeit.

Ein²-stimmung (ᴵᴸᴗ) f 46 accord; agreement, assent. [eintunken.)

ein²-stippen F (ᵇᴠ) v/a. 98 = eintauchen.)

einst-mals (ᴵᴸ) adv. = einst.

ein¹-stöckig (ᴵᴸᴗ) a. 66 one-storied (house).

ein²-stopfen (ᴵᴸᴗ) v/a. 98** to stuff (or cram) in; die Bettücher 2 to tuck in.

ein²-stoßen (ᴵᴸᴗ) I v/a. 92a** 1. to push (or knock, force, thrust, drive) in; ⚔ eine Ladung 2 to ram down a charge. — 2. (zerbrechen) to knock in; to smash a pane, to stave in a cask; to knock down the walls; sich (dat.) die Zähne 2 to break one's teeth (against s.th.). — II **Ein²-stoßung** f 46 3. pushing (or knocking) in, ramming down, &c., f. I.

ein²-streichen (ᴵᴸᴗ) 94at** I v/a. 1. to rub into; Mörtel in die Fugen 2 to plaster the joints, to fill up the commissures. — 2. in ein Netz 2 to sweep into a net; Geld in die Tasche) 2 to pocket …; im Spiele ꝛc.: alles 2 to sweep the board. — 3. Manuskript 2 (streichend kürzen) to condense (or F to cut down) manuscript by striking (out) or deleting. — II v/n. 4. (fn) *hunt.* die Lerchen streichen ein … go into the nets or springes. — III ~ n 23 5. rubbing into, pocketing, &c. (f. I).

ein²-streuen (ᴵᴸᴗ) I v/a. 98** 1. to strew in(to); Samen ꝛc. 2 to scatter … broadcast; Stroh für Vieh: to litter a stable. — 2. *fig.* (einmischen) to intersperse, intermix, throw in; to interlard a speech with quotations. — II ~ n 23 3. = Ein²-streuung. [matter.)

Ein²-streusel (ᴵᴸᴗ) n 22 interspersed/

Ein²-streuung (ᴵᴸᴗ) f 46 *fig.* (f. einstreuen 2) interspersion, intermixture.

Ein²-strich (ᴵᴸ) m ⓐd. 1. (Einstreichen) rubbing-in; pocketing. — 2. ✕ =e pl. (Querhölzer) cross-beams, traverses pl.

ein²-stricken (ᴵᴸᴗ) v/a. 98** to knit new heels, &c. into socks, stockings, &c.

ein²-ström/en (ᴵᴸᴗ) I v/n. (fn) 98** to stream (or flow) in(to); *fig.* v. Menschen: to crowd (or flock) in. — II ~ n 23 2. S/ung 46 streaming, &c. (f. I); admission of steam, &c.; *fig.* influx of people.

ein²-stück(e)ln (ᴵᴸᴗ) v/a. 98 (92a)** einen Flicken in et. 2 to put a patch (or a new piece) in(to) a th.

ein²-studieren (ᴵᴸᴸᴗ) v/a. 98*/* to study well, to learn by rote; *thea.* auch: to rehearse a play, to get up a part; einstudierte Rede set (or prepared) speech.

ein²-stürmen (ᴵᴸᴗ) v/n. (h. u. fn) 98** 1. to rush in(to); auf e-n 2 to rush upon a p., *fig. auch:* to assail a p. — 2. auf seine Gesundheit 2 to wreck (or ruin) one's health.

Ein²-sturz (ᴵᴸ) m ⓐa. (down)fall, collapse, tumble, crash, overthrow; zum ~ bringen to cause to fall, to overthrow; ein Haus ꝛc.: to bring down (with a crash), to demolish.

Ein²-sturz-beben (ᴵᴸᴗᴸᴗ) n 62 (Erdbeben) destructive earthquake.

ein²-stürzen (ᴵᴸᴗ) 98** I v/n.(fn)1.(f. ein²-...2) to fall (or tumble) down or to pieces, to collapse; to crumble (away); *fig.* to come to grief; f. drohen I. — 2. (a. sich 2 v/refl.) = einstürmen. — II v/a. 3. to knock (or pull) down; to demolish, F to smash up. — III ~ n 23 4. = Einsturz.

Ein²-sturz-krater (ᴵᴸ…) m 22 e-s Vulkans: crumbling (or sinking) crater.

einst-weilen (ᴵᴸᴗ) adv. und cj. meanwhile, in the meantime; (vorläufig) for the present, for a while, for the time being, temporarily; *jur.* in the interim.

einst-weilig (ᴵᴸᴗ) a. 66 temporary, provisional (orders, &c.); interim (arrangements, &c.); der 2e Schriftführer the secretary for the time being or (lt.) *pro tem.* or *p. t.* [= *pro tempore*].

ein²-sudeln (ᴵᴸᴗ) v/a. 98** to soil.

Eins-werden (ᴵᴸᴗ) n 23 f. eins.

ein¹-tägig (ᴵᴸᴗ) a. 66 of (or lasting) one day, 🔬 ephemeral; 2es Fieber *path.:* 🔬 ephemera.

Ein¹-tags-blume ♀ (ᴵᴸᴸ…) f 62: 🔬 ephemeral flower; **=fieber** n, *path.* 🔬 ephemera; **=fliege** f, *ent.* day-fly (*Ephe'mera*); **=geschöpf** n ephemeral being, 🔬 ephemeron.

ein²-tanzen (ᴵᴸᴗ) : sich 2 v/refl. 98** to practise (or acquire skill in) dancing.

ein²-tauchbar (ᴵᴸ-) a. 66 immersible.

ein²-tauchen (ᴵᴸᴗ) 98** I v/a. to dip (or plunge) in(to), immerse, duck; (eintunken) to soak, steep, sop; die Feder 2 to dip one's pen; *fig.* to put (one's) pen to paper; eingetauchter Bissen sop. — II v/n. (fn) to plunge (or dive) in. — III ~ n 23 = Eintauchung.

Ein²-taucher ⊕ (ᴵᴸᴗ) m 22 dipper.

Ein²-tauchung (ᴵᴸᴗ) f 46 dip(ping in), &c. (f. eintauchen I); immersion.

Ein²-tausch (ᴵᴸ) m ⓐa. exchange, (Tauschhandel) barter, bartering, truck.

ein²-tauschen (ᴵᴸᴗ) v/a. 98** to exchange (or barter) for a th., to give (or take) in exchange for a th.

ein²-teeren (ᴵᴸᴗ) v/a. 98** to tar.

ein²-teil/en (ᴵᴸᴗ) I v/a. 98** 1. to/divide; weiter 2 to subdivide; (interpunktieren) ♪ u. *gr.:* to punctuate; in zwei, vier Teile: to halve, to quarter; in Grade: to graduate; ⚔ in Sektionen: to squad; (trennen) to separate. — 2. (verteilen) to distribute, to parcel out; in Klassen: to class(ify); seine Zeit gut 2 to make good use of one's time. — II ~ n 23 3. = Einteilung.

ein¹-teilig (ᴵᴸᴗ) a. 66 *math.* = 2gliederig.

Signs (see page XVII): F familiar; P vulgar; ⚓ flash; ↘ rare; † obsolete (died); * new word (born); ++ incorrect; ♪ music;

[Einteilung] — 311 — [einwalken]

Ein²-teilung (⁻ᴸ◡) f ⓺ 1. division; punctuation; graduation; separation. — 2. distribution; classification. — 3. ~ e-ß Thermometers ꝛc. thermometer, &c. scale of graduation.

Ein²-teilungs-grad (⁻ᴸ◡⁻) m ⓺ am Thermometer ꝛc.: degree (⁰); **zahl** f, gram. distributive number.

ein¹-tönig (⁻ᴸ◡) a. ⓺ monotonous; (langweilig) tedious; **~keit** (⁻ᴸ◡⁻) f ⓺ monotony; tediousness.

ein²-tonnen (⁻ᴸ◡) v/a. ⓺** to barrel; to put into barrels or casks or tuns.

Ein¹-tracht (⁻ᴸcht) [mhd.] f ⓺ harmony; union; accord; in ~ united(ly); sie (Mann und Frau) leben in voller ~ they live in perfect accord, they agree (F they hit it off) well together, they are a very united couple; Sprichw. ~ macht stark union is strength.

ein¹-trächtig (⁻ᴸ◡) a. ⓺ united (= einhellig); **~keit** f ⓺ = Einhelligkeit.

Ein¹-trachts-Göttin (⁻ᴸ◡⁻...) f ⓺ Concordia.

Ein²-trag (⁻ᴸ◡) m ⓸d. 1. (Eintragen und Eingetragenes) entry in a book or register; registration. — 2. ⊕ = Einschuß 2. — 3. (Abbruch) prejudice; disparagement; (Schaden) harm, damage, detriment; e-m ~ tun to be prejudicial to a p., to damage (or injure) a p.; j-s Ansehen ~ tun to be derogatory (or detrimental) to a p.'s reputation.

Ein²-trag-... (Einträge- u. Eintrags-...)

ein²-tragbar (⁻ᴸ◡⁻) a. ⓺ registrable.

Ein²-trage-buch (⁻ᴸ◡⁻...) n ⓺ book of entry; register; ⬤ account-book.

ein²-tragen (⁻ᴸ◡) I v/a. ⓺b** 1. to carry in(to); abs. die Bienen tragen ein ... are bringing in the honey. — 2. a) in ein Buch, Register ꝛc. 2 to enter in(to) ...; to record; eingetrag(e)ne Genossenschaft ꝛc. registered association, &c.; ⬤ in die Bücher 2 to enter in(to) ..., to carry into ...; irrig 2 to make a wrong entry; alles bis auf den heutigen Tag 2 to post everything up to date; vgl. einschreiben 1; **b)** Linien ꝛc. 2 (einzeichnen) to draw ... — 3. (einbringen) to produce, yield, bring in; Geschäft, das wenig (viel) einträgt unprofitable (lucrative) business. — **II** ~ n ⓹ 4. = Eintragung.

ein²-träglich (⁻ᴸ◡) a. ⓺ (f. eintragen 3) productive, profitable, lucrative; ⬤ paying (concern); (lohnend) remunerative; eine 2e Stelle a good berth, F a fine screw. [tivity, profitableness.]

Ein²-träglichkeit (⁻ᴸ◡⁻) f ⓺ produc-]

Ein²-trag(s)-faden ⊕ (⁻ᴸ◡...) m ⓺ shoot; **-rolle** ⬤ ⊕ für das Urheberrecht: register (or record) of patent-rights; **-spule** f pirn. [entry, amtliche: registration.]

Ein²-tragung (⁻ᴸ◡) f ⓺ (f. eintragen 2)]

Ein²-tragungs-amt (⁻ᴸ◡⁻...) n ⓺ registry; registration-office.

ein²-tränken (⁻ᴸ◡) v/a. ⓺** 1. to soak, steep, impregnate. — 2. fig. e-m et. (gehörig, tüchtig) 2 to pay a p. out (well) for a thing; ich will es ihm schon 2 I'll give him tit for tat.

ein²-träufeln (⁻ᴸ◡) v/a. ⓺a** med., &c. to administer a fluid by drops.

ein²-treffen (⁻ᴸ◡) I v/n. (sn) ⓺a** (impf. traf ein) 1. (ankommen) to arrive (at the right time or place). — 2. fig. (in Erfüllung gehen) to come true, to be realized or accomplished; die Voraussagung ist nicht eingetroffen ... has not been fulfilled; die Waren sind glücklich hier eingetroffen the goods have reached us safely. — **II** ~ n ⓹ 3. arrival; fig. realization, accomplishment.

ein²-treib-bar (⁻ᴸ⁻) a. ⓺ recoverable.

ein²-treiben (⁻ᴸ◡) ⓺** I v/a. 1. Nägel ꝛc. 2 to drive in ...; F einen Hut 2 to crush (F to bash in) the crown (of) a hat. — 2. Vieh: to drive home. — 3. Schulden, Steuern: to collect; Zahlung auf gesetzlichem Wege 2 to enforce payment by legal proceedings; schwer einzutreiben difficult to get in or to recover. — **II** v/n. 4. (sn) to drift into a river, &c. — **III** ~ n ⓹ 5. driving in or home; collection; recovery (vgl. I).

Ein²-treiber (⁻ᴸ◡) m ⓺ driver-in; collector of rents, taxes, &c.

Ein²-treibung (⁻ᴸ◡) f ⓺ = eintreiben III.

ein²-treten (⁻ᴸ◡) ⓺d** I v/n. (sn) 1. (f. ein ... 1) to enter; to step (or go, walk) in(to); bitte, treten Sie ein! please step in(to the room)!; ⬤ als Teilhaber in ein Geschäft 2 to join (or enter) a firm as partner, to become partner in a firm; fig. in eine Stelle 2 to enter upon one's duties; ⚔ ⚓ ins Heer, in die Flotte 2 to join the army (als Gemeiner: the ranks), to enter the navy; jur. in j-s Rechte 2 to succeed to a p.'s rights; von Arbeitern: in einen Streik 2 to (enter upon a) strike; parl. in eine Verhandlung 2 to open a discussion. — 2. fig. für e-n, et. 2 = einstehen. — 3. (sich ereignen) to happen, to come to pass, to take place; es ist kaltes Wetter eingetreten the cold (weather) has set in; 2den-falls (adv.) should the case arise; bei 2der Flut (Nacht) with the rising tide (at nightfall); bei 2der Gelegenheit when the opportunity offers (or presents) itself; eingetret(e)ner Hindernisse halber owing to intervening obstacles or unforeseen circumstances; f. Umschwung. — **II** v/a. 4. Tritte in den Schnee ꝛc. 2 to impress (or make) foot-prints in ...; et. in die Erde 2 to stamp a th. into the ground; sich (dat.) e-n Dorn 2 to run ... into one's foot. — 5. Schuhe 2 to run one's boots down at the heels. — 6. (einstürzen m.) to kick in or over. — **III** ~ n ⓹ 7. entry; stepping in; beim ~ on entering.

ein²-trichtern (⁻ᴸ◡) v/a. ⓺a** to pour in(to a bottle, &c.) through a funnel; F fig. e-m etwas 2 to drub (or drive) a th. into a p.('s head).

ein²-trinken (⁻ᴸ◡) v/a. ⓺f** to drink (in), to imbibe (auch fig.).

Ein²-tritt (⁻ᴸ◡) m ⓺c. 1. entry, entrance; freier ~ free admission; beim ~ ins Leben on coming into the world, at the threshold of life; ⚔ (freiwilliger) ~ ins Heer joining the ranks, enlistment; ast. ~ in den Schatten e-s Gestirns immersion, ingress. — 2. (Anfang) beim ~ der Regenzeit at the beginning of the rainy season; when the rainy season set(s) in; nach ~ der Dunkelheit after (or as soon as it is) dark.

ein²-tritts-fähig (⁻ᴸ◡...) ⓺ a. admissible; **-fähigkeit** f admissibility; **-geld** n entrance- (or gate-) money; F admission; **-karte** f card (or ticket) of admission; **-termin** m time (or date) of admission.

ein²-trocknen (⁻ᴸ◡) ⓺b** I v/n. (sn) 1. to dry up, to be parched up. — 2. (einschrumpfen) to shrink (or shrivel) in drying. — **II** v/a. 3. to dry, to parch (up); chm.: ⚗ to desiccate. — **III** ~ n ⓹ 4. drying (up); ⚗ desiccation.

ein²-tröpfeln (⁻ᴸ◡a**, **-tropfen** ⓺** (⁻ᴸ◡) I v/n. (sn) to fall in (or by) drops, to drip into. — **II** v/a. to pour in by drops; ⚗ to instil; weitS.: to infuse. — **III** ~ n ⓹ u. **Ein²-tröpf(e)lung** f ⓺ falling (or pouring in) by drops; ⚗ instillation; weitS.: infusion.

ein²-tun (⁻ᴸ◡) v/a. ⓺** to put in(to); in einen Gewahrsam 2 to lock up in prison, to put into jail.

ein²-tunken (⁻ᴸ◡) v/a. ⓺** to dip in(to); to sop bread, &c.; vgl. eintauchen.

ein²-üben (⁻ᴸ◡) I v/a. u. sich 2 v/refl. 1. ein Lied ꝛc. 2 to practise (or study) ... — 2. e-n 2 to train (or drill) a p. in a th. — **II** ~ n ⓹ u. **Ein²-übung** f ⓺ 3. practice; study; training; drill(ing).

ein¹-und-ein-halb (⁻ᴸ◡⁻⁻) numer. a. (1½) one and a half.

ein¹-und-zwanzig (⁻ᴸ◡⁻◡) numer. a. (21) twenty-one, a.: one-and-twenty.

ein²-verleib/en (⁻ᴸ◡⁻/* I v/a. to embody in, to incorporate with, to annex to; 2de Sprache polysynthetic language. — **II** sich 2 v/refl. physiol., &c. to assimilate or amalgamate) with. — **III** ~ n ⓹ und **2ung** f ⓺ incorporation, e-s Staates: annexation; physiol. assimilation.

Ein¹-vernehmen (⁻ᴸ◡⁻◡) n ⓹ = Einverständnis; in gutem ~ on friendly terms; herzliches ~ cordial agreement, pol. auch: (fr.) entente cordiale.

ein¹-verstanden (⁻ᴸ◡⁻) a. ⓺(D9) (vgl. einverstehen) of the same mind; sind Sie (a. erklären Sie sich) damit 2? do you assent (or F are you agreeable) to it?; ich bin damit 2 I agree (or consent) to it; einverstanden! agreed!, (all) right!, be it so!

Ein¹-verständnis (⁻ᴸ◡⁻) n ⓱ agreement; secret understanding, intelligence with the enemy (vgl. Eintracht und Einvernehmen); strafbares ~ jur. collusion, connivance; sich in ~ mit e-m setzen to put o.s. in communication (or to come to an agreement) with a p.; zu einem ~ mit e-m kommen to come to a friendly understanding (or to terms) with a p.

ein¹-versteh(e)n ↺ (⁻ᴸ⁻(◡)): sich 2 v/refl. ⓺*/* to come to an understanding (or agreement) with each other.

ein²-vetter(michel)n (⁻ᴸ◡(◡)⁻): sich 2 v/refl. ⓺a** = einschmeicheln II.

ein²-wachsen (⁻ᴸ◡tr) v/n. (sn) ⓺b(e)t** ins Fleisch ꝛc. 2 to grow into the flesh, &c.; fig. = einwurzeln.

Ein²-wage ⬤ (⁻ᴸ◡) f ⓺ loss suffered in weighing (out). [in(to).]

ein²-wägen (⁻ᴸ◡) ⓺b** v/a. to weigh]

ein²-walken (⁻ᴸ◡) v/a. ⓺** Tuchmacherei: I v/a. to full thoroughly or closely. —

⚗ scientific; ⚘ botanical; ⊕ geography; ⊕ machinery; ⚒ mining; ⚔ military; ⚓ marine; ⬤ commercial; ✉ postal; 🚂 railway.

[einwalzen] — 312 — [Einzahlungssumme]

II v/n. (ſn) und **ſich** ~ v/refl. (einlaufen) to shrink in (the process of) fulling.
ein²-walzen (ᴗᴗ) v/a. ⊕** agr. to roll in(to the ground); to roll down gravel, &c.
Ein²-wand (ᴗᴗ) [einwenden] m ⑦c. objection; vgl. Einspruch.
Ein²-wanderer (ᴗᴗᴗ) m, **Einwanderin** f ㊼ immigrant.
ein²-wandern (ᴗᴗᴗ) **I** v/n. (ſn) ㉒a** to immigrate into; von Handwerkern ꝛc. bisw.: to travel (or pass) through. — **II** ~ n ㉓ u. **Ein-wanderung** (ᴗᴗᴗ) f ㊻ immigration.
ein²-wand-frei (ᴗᴗ‿ᴵ) a. ㊅ free from objection; (unanfechtbar) incontestable, indisputable; (tadellos) immaculate, nicht ~ objectionable.
Ein²-wandrer(in), **Ein²-wandrung** ſ. Einwanderer, Einwanderung.
ein²-wärts (ᴗᴗ) adv. inward(s); ~ geh(e)n, die Füße ~ ſetzen to walk with one's toes turned in, to turn one's toes in; mit ~ gebogenen Knien (x-beinig) knock-kneed; ~ kehren, wenden to turn in(ward), ⚕ to introvert; ↯ ~ gerollt: ⚕ involute; anat. ~ ziehender Muskel = Einwärtszieher.
Ein²-wärts-zieher (ᴗᴗ‥) m ㉖ anat.: ⚕ adductor (muscle).
ein²-wäſſern (ᴗᴗᴗ) v/a. ㉒a** to steep (or lay, soak) in water; vgl. einweichen.
ein²-weben (ᴗᴗ) v/a. ㉓b** u. ㉘** 1. ⊙ to weave (or work) in(to); Blumen (in ein Zeug) ~ to figure, to damask; eingewoben woven in, inwoven. — 2. fig. in et. ~ to interweave (or interlace, insert) in a th.; geſchickt eingewob(e)ne (a. eingewebte) Lieder songs cleverly interwoven or interspersed or interlarded; vgl. einflechten 2.
ein²-wechſeln (ᴗᴗᴗtᶻᴗ) v/a. ㉒a** to give (or get, take) in exchange; Banknoten ~ to cash (or change) banknotes; vgl. eintauſchen. — **II** ~ n ㉓ u. **Ein-wechſ(e)lung** f ㊻ (ex)change.
ein²-wehen (ᴗᴗ) v/a. ㉘** to blow in.
ein¹-weibig ♀ (ᴗᴗ) a. ㊅ (mit einem Griffel): ⚕ monogynian, …ous; ~e Pflanze(n pl.): ⚕ monogyn(ia pl.).
ein²-weichen (ᴗᴗ) **I** v/a. Wäſche ꝛc. to (lay in) soak, to steep, to soften by immersion; chm., pharm. to infuse, ⚕ to macerate. — **II** ~ n ㉓ u. **Ein²-weichung** f ㊻ soaking; immersion; infusion; ⚕ maceration.
ein²-weihen (ᴗᴗ) **I** v/a. ㉘** 1. rel. to consecrate a church; to dedicate a holy offering; to bless the Lord's servant; to ordain a priest. — 2. fig. to open a railway, to inaugurate a new building, F einen Rock ꝛc. ~ (zum erſtenmal tragen) to wear (or F to sport) a coat, &c. for the first time. — 3. e-n ꝛu etwas ~ to consecrate a p. for some (holy) purpose. — 4. e-n in et. ~ to initiate a p. in a th.; e-n in ein Geheimnis ~ to let a p. into a secret; gut eingeweiht thoroughly initiated, F well posted up; vgl. Eingeweihte(r). — **II** ~ n ㉓ u. **Ein²-weihung** f ㊻ 5. (ſ. I) consecration; dedication; ordination; opening, inauguration; initiation. — 6. ~ einer neuen Wohnung (durch einen Schmaus): (giving a) housewarming.

Ein²-weihungs-feierlichkeit (ᴗᴗᴗ…) f ㉖, **-feſt** n inaugural ceremony or fête; **-predigt, -rede** f inaugural sermon, address; **-tag** m day of inauguration or opening.
ein²-weiſen (ᴗᴗ) **I** v/a. ㉛** e-n ~ to install (or introduce) a p. in his office, to instruct a p. in his duties; jur. e-n in einen Beſitz ~ to give a p. the full control over his property. — **II** ~ n u. **Ein-weiſung** f ㊻ installation, introduction.
ein²-wenden (ᴗᴗ) **I** v/a. ㉖a** to object to a th., to oppose a th., to protest against a th.; es läßt ſich nichts dagegen ~ there is nothing to be said (or urged) against it, there can be no objection to it. — **II Ein²-wendung** f ㊻ objection, opposition, protest; (Erwiderung) reply, jur. rejoinder; gegen et. ~en m. to raise objections to (or against) a th., to protest (F to kick) against a th., to demur to a th.
ein²-werfen (ᴗᴗ) **I** v/a. ㉝b** 1. to throw in(to); to put a letter in(to) the box; e-n (ins Gefängnis) ~ to throw (or cast) a person in(to) prison; vgl. einſtecken 1. — 2. (zertrümmern) Fenſter ~ to smash (or break) windows by throwing stones, &c. — 3. Geld (in eine Kaſſe, ein Geſchäft) ~ (einſchießen) to contribute money (to a fund), to put (or pay) money (into a concern). — 4. fig. (einwenden) to object. — **II** ~ n ㉓ 5. throwing in(to), &c. (ſ. 1. u. 2). — 6. fig. (ſ. 4) (Einwurf) objection.
ein¹-wertig (ᴗᴗ) a. ㊅ chm.: ⚕ monovalent; ~es Element ⚕ monad; **~keit** (~ʹ) f ㊻: ⚕ monovalence.
ein²-wichſen (ᴗᴗtᶻ)v/a. ⊕** to blacken (or polish) boots; to wax the floor.
ein²-wickeln (ᴗᴗ) **I** v/a. u. **ſich** ~ v/refl. ㉒a** (ſ. ein²-…1) to wrap (up), in Wollbecken ꝛc.: to tuck up; mſt. fig. to envelop; wickeln Sie ſich gut ein! wrap (or muffle) yourself up well!; in Papier ~ to roll up in paper; ein Kind ~ to swathe o.s., to put … in swaddling-clothes; die Haare ~ to put … in(to) curling-papers. — **II** ~ n ㉓ u. **Ein²-wick(e)lung** f ㊻ wrapping up; envelopment; rolling up; ⚕ involution.
ein²-wiegen (ᴗᴗ) v/a. ㉘** to rock to sleep; in falſche Hoffnungen ~ to lull (or soothe, buoy up) with false hopes.
ein²-willigen (ᴗᴗᴗ) **I** v/n. (h.) und v/a. ㉘** in etwas ~ to consent (or assent, agree, accede) to a th., to approve of a th.; to acquiesce in a th.; to sanction a th. — **II** ~ n ㉓ und **Ein²-willigung** f ㊻ consent, assent, approval, acquiescence; sanction.
ein²-winden (ᴗᴗ) v/a. und **ſich** ~ v/refl. ⑲** (einhüllen) to wind (o.s.) in(to); to wrap (o.s.) up in; in ein Leintuch ~ to wind round with a sheet; ⚓ den Anker mit dem Gangſpill ~ to weigh the anchor with the capstan.
ein²-wintern (ᴗᴗᴗ) ㉒a** **I** v/n. (ſn) 1. = einfrieren. — 2. to be overtaken by the winter(y cold). — **II ſich** ~ v/refl. 3. to get inured to the winter. — **III** v/impers. 4. es wintert ein (the) winter is approaching or coming.

ein²-wirken (ᴗᴗ) ㉘** **I** v/a. = einweben 1 und einkneten. — **II** v/n. (h.) auf e-n, etwas ~ to act (or operate) upon a person, a thing; to make an impression upon a p., a th.; to influence a p., a th. — **III** ~ n ㉓ und **Ein-wirkung** f ㊻ action, operation; impression; influence.
ein¹-wöchentlich (ᴗᴗᴗ) a. ㊅ weekly, ⚕ hebdomadal; ~wöchig, ~wöchig a. lasting a (one) week, one week's.
ein²-wohnen (ᴗᴗᴗ) ㉘** **I** v/n. (h.) 1. bei e-m ~ to live (or lodge) with a p. — 2. einer Sache (dat.) ~ (anhaften) to be inherent (or to inhere) in a th.; ~ inherent. — **II** v/a. (zugrunde richten) to damage (or spoil) a dwelling. — **III ſich** ~ v/refl. to get accustomed to one's dwelling(-place); to begin to feel at home. — **IV** ~ n ㉓ = ㊂ung.
Ein²-wohner (ᴗᴗᴗ) m ㉒, **~in** f ㊼ inhabitant (or resident) of a town; occupant of a house; **~melde-amt** (ᴸ…) n ㉖, etwa: office for registration of removals; **~reservate** n/pl. der deutſchen Schutzgebiete: reservations pl. for the natives; **~ſchaft** (ᴗᴗᴗ) f ㊻ (sum total of) inhabitants pl., entire population; **~zahl** f number of inhabitants, (total) population; **~zählung** f census (of the population).
Ein²-wohnung (ᴗᴗᴗ) f ㊻ (ſ. einwohnen I) (taking a) lodging with a p.; (Anhaften) inherence, inherency; rel. bisw.: indwelling (or presence) of the Holy Ghost.
ein²-wölben ⊙ (ᴗᴗᴗ) v/a. ㉘** to arch.
ein²-wollen (ᴗᴗᴗ) v/n. (h.) ⑨** 1. to want to go in or to enter or to get inside. — 2. das will mir nicht ein I don't understand (or grasp, F see) it, F that won't go down with me, I can't swallow that.
ein²-wühlen (ᴗᴗᴗ) v/a. ㉘** (a. **ſich** ~ v/refl.) to grub (or wallow) in.
Ein²-wurf (ᴗᴗ) m ⑦c. 1. (Einwerfen) fig. objection (raised), reply (made); bſd. jur. auch: rejoinder; e-n ~ abweiſen, widerlegen to refute a plea or an argument; e-n ~ gegen et. erheben to take exception to; vgl. Einſpruch. — 2. am Briefſchalter: slot (or aperture) of the letter-box.
ein²-wurzeln (ᴗᴗᴗ) **I** v/n (ſn) und **ſich** ~ v/refl. ㉒a** to take (or strike) root; fig. to become deeply rooted; tief eingewurzelt deep-rooted (evil), inveterate (habit); (wie) eingewurzelt ſteh(e)n to stand (as if) rooted to the ground or spell-bound. — **II** ~ n ㉓ u. **Ein-wurz(e)lung** f ㊻ taking (deep) root (auch fig.); ⚕: ⚕ radication.
ein²-zacken (ᴗᴗᴗ) v/a. ㉘** = einkerben.
Ein¹-zahl (ᴗᴵ) f ㊻ singular (number).
ein²-zahlbar (ᴗᴗᴗ) — a. ㊅ payable.
ein²-zahlen ⊛ (ᴗᴗᴗ) v/a. ㉘** to pay in(to); voll eingezahlte Aktie fully paid-up share; ⚑ 40 Mark ~ to take out a post-office order for £ 2.
ein²-zählen (ᴗᴗᴗ) v/a. ㉘** 1. to count in(to). — 2. (einrechnen) to include.
Ein²-zahlung ⊛ (ᴗᴗᴗ) f ㊻ payment of a call made on shares, &c.; eine neue ~ ausſchreiben to make a fresh call on shares; **~s-ſumme** f ㉒ instalment.

Zeichen (ſ. S. XVII): F familiär; P Volksſprache; ⌐ Gaunerſprache; ⚹ ſelten; † alt (auch geſtorben); * neu (auch geboren); ⁒ unrichtig,

ein²-zahn/en, ein-zähn/en (⊓∪) **I** v/a. ⊛** = einferben. — **II** = E/ung f ⊛ indentation.

ein²-zapf/en (⊓∪) **I** v/a. ⊛** 1. to draw off wine, &c. in bottles. — 2. ⊕ carp. to join (or bind) timber, to mortise in(to). — **II** ~ n 23 u. E/ung f ⊛ 3. drawing off wine, &c.; ⊕ carp. (binding by means of a) mortise joint.

ein²-zäun/en (⊓∪) **I** v/a. ⊛** to hedge (or fence) in; eingezäuntes Feld, Land close, enclosure. — **II** ~ n und E/ung f ⊛ hedging in; enclosure.

ein¹-zehig (⊓∪) a. ⊛ zo. one-toed, ⌀ monodactylous.

ein²-zeichn/en (⊓∪) **I** v/a. ⊛ b** 1. to draw (or sketch) in. — 2. weitS. = einfchreiben 1. — **II** ~ n 23 und Ein-zeichnung f ⊛ 3. = einfchreiben II.

ein¹-zeilig (⊓∪) a. ⊛ one-lined, in one row, ⌀ monostichous, uniserial.

Einzel-arrest (⊓∪...) m ⊛ = -haft; -aufzählung f (single) enumeration; -ausbildung ⚔ f individual training; -ausgabe f separate edition; -beschreibung f monograph(y); -ding n individual (object); -fall m particular case; -feuer ⚔ n individual firing, skirmishing; -gabe f, med. (single) dose; -haft f solitary (or single) confinement.

Einzelheit (⌐∪) f ⊛ 1. (ant. Gesamtheit) singularity, individuality. — 2. (Einzelnes) isolated fact; mit allen ~en with full particulars or details; die kleinsten ~en the minutest details pl.

Einzel-kampf (⊓∪...) m ⊛ single combat, hand-to-hand fight; -kopie f single copy; -leben n solitary (or individual) life.

ein¹-zellig (⊓∪) a. ⊛ one-celled, ⌀ monocellular, unicellular.

einzeln (⌐∪) [ahd. ⊛ A³ + I a. single; (besonder) particular; (für sich allein) individual; isolated; uncoupled; (abgetrennt) separate, detached; ⌐er Band, Schuh 2c. odd volume, shoe, &c.; die ⌐en Glieder, Teile the several members, parts pl.; die ⌐en Umstände full details pl.; die ⌐en Umstände individually, (f. I). — **II** adv. singly, individually, (f. I). — ⌐ angeben, betrachten to particularize, individualize; Dorf mit ⌐ stehenden Häusern straggling village; ⊛ ⌐ verkaufen to sell by retail. — **III** ⌐e(r), der ⌐e individual (man, ⌐ woman); jeder ~ each one in particular. — **IV** ~e(s) n ⊛ ⌐es (einiges) hat mir gefallen some (parts) I liked; bis ins ⌐(f)te (down) to the minutest (or most trifling) particulars; f. Einzelheit 2; im ⌐en = ⌐ **II**, auch: (taken) in detail.

Einzel-spiel (⊓∪...) n ⊛ Tennis: single-handed game; -spielfeld n single-court; -staaten m/pl. confederate states pl.; ⌐stehend a. ⊛ standing alone, solitary, detached; -stimme ♪ f solo (voice); -tanz m solo dance; -verkauf ⊛ m sale by retail, retail trade; -wesen n individual (being).

ein-ziehbar (⊓∪) a. ⊛ 1. physiol., &c.; ⌀ introversible, retractile. — 2. von Geldern: recoverable. — 3. von Gütern 2c.: forfeitable, seizable.

ein-zieh/en (⊓∪) ⊛ b** **I** v/a. 1. räumlich: to draw (or pull) in(to); die Hörner, Krallen ⌐ to draw in one's horns, claws; den Kopf, die Schultern ⌐ to sit (or stand) with drooping head, with round shoulders. — 2. ⊕ arch. e-e Mauer ⌐ (nach oben verjüngen) to taper (off) ...; ⌂ die Flagge ⌐ (streichen) to strike one's colours; die Segel ⌐ (einreffen): a) to furl (or to shorten, to take in) ...; b) fig. einfach: ⌐ (nachgeben) to give in, to yield; ⊕ typ. eine Zeile ⌐ (einrücken) to indent. — 3. gefänglich ⌐ (verhaften) to arrest, to apprehend; (einsperren) to put in jail, to lock up. — 4. Ausstände 2c. ⌐ (eintreiben) to call in (or collect) ...; Wechsel: to cash. — 5. jur. (mit Beschlag belegen) to seize, confiscate; eingezog(e)ne Güter n/pl. auch: escheated (or forfeited) estates pl. — 6. ⚔ Landwehr, Reserve ⌐ to call out (or in) reserves; einen Posten ⌐ to vacate a post. — 7. Erkundigung, Nachrichten ⌐ (sammeln) to gather (or collect) information; to make inquiry after. — 8. = einsaugen I. — 9. (einschränken) (auch fich ⌐ v/refl.) to retrench (one's expenses); ⌐ to reduce (one's household); F to draw in; f. eingezogen 2. — 10. (abschaffen) ein Amt, eine Stelle ⌐ to abolish (or to do away with) an office, a post; Münzen: to call in, to withdraw from circulation. — **II** fich ⌐ v/refl. 11. f. 9. — **III** v/n. (fn) 12. bei e-m ⌐ to take lodgings (or to take up one's quarters) with a p.; ⚔ in eine Stadt ⌐ to march into (or enter) a town; in eine Wohnung ⌐ to move into a house; bei e-m ⌐ to go to live with a p. — 13. v. Flüssigkeiten: to soak in(to). — **IV** ~ n 23 u. E/ung f ⊛ 14. drawing in, &c. (f. **I**). — 15. (f. 3) apprehension. — 16. ⊛ (f. 4) collection of book-debts; cashing of a draft. — 17. (f. 5) seizure, confiscation. — 18. (f. 10) abolition; withdrawal; 🚂 ~ von Zügen reduction of trains. [einstreu.]

ein¹-ziff(e)rig (⊓∪) a. ⊛ arith. =]

einzig (⌐∪) [mhd.] **I** a. ⊛ 1. only (child); sole (heir); single (witness); (einsam) alone; (unteilbar) one; nicht ein ⌐es, nur ein ⌐es Mal never once, but once; adv. ⌐ und allein solely, purely, entirely; das ⌐ Richtige the only correct thing (to do). — 2. (ohnegleichen) unique, unmatched, unparalleled; in f-r Art matchless, peerless; ⌐artig a. unique (of its kind). — **II** ⌐e(r) m, ⌐e f, ⌐e(s) n ⊛ 3. the only one, (the) only thing; das ⌐e, was er tun kann all that he can do; das ⌐e (+ Inf.) wäre, zu // the only thing (to be done) would be to //; ein ⌐er one man only, a single person.

Einzler (⌐∪) m ⊛ (Fuhrwerkunternehmer mit einem Wagen) private owner of a hackney-carriage.

ein¹-zollig, ⌐²zöllig (⊓∪...) a. ⊛ one-inch.

ein-zucker/n (⊓∪) v/a. ⊛ a** to sugar.

Ein-zug (⊓∪) [einziehen] m ⊕ d. 1. entry, entrance; ⊛ ~ halten to enter (in state). — 2. in eine Wohnung: moving in.

Ein-zug(s)-schmaus (⊓∪...) m ⊛ house-warming; =spesen ⊛ pl. expenses incurred by cashing a draft, &c.

ein-zwängen (⊓∪) v/a. u. sich ⌐ v/refl. ⊛** to wedge (or force) (o.s.) in.

ein-zwingen (⊓∪) v/a. ⊛i** 1. in etwas ⌐ to force into a th. — 2. e-m etwas ⌐ to force a p. to take physic, &c.

Ein-zylinder-maschine ⊕ (⌐∪∪...) f mach. one-cylinder engine.

ei-rund (⊓∪) a. ⊛ ⌐förmig, & verkehrt ⌐: ⌀ obovoid, obovate, oboval.

Eis¹ (⌐) gen. sg. v. Ei².

Eis² (⌐) [ahd.: ice] n ⊛a. (o. pl.) 1. ice; schwimmendes ~ floating ice, floe; es hat ~ gefroren there has been ice on the ground, we have had a (hard) frost; zu ~ gefrieren to freeze, to congeal; v. Flüssen: mit Eis geh(e)n, ~ treiben to carry ice; das ~ trägt the ice bears; von ~ eingeschlossen ice-bound, ice-locked; v. Fischen, Wein 2c.: in ~ bewahrt, gestellt kept in ice, iced; fig. e-n aufs ~ (in Versuchung) führen to tempt (or entice) a p. by questions, &c.; das ~ brechen to break the ice; Sprichw. f. Esel 2. 2. ein Glas, e-e Portion ~ (Gefrorenes) an ice (pl. ices).

E-is³ ♪ (⌐∪) n, inv. E sharp (E ♯).

Eis²-appa'rat ⊕ (⌐∪...) m ⊛; — -maschine; ⌐artig a. ⊛ ice-like, icy, glacial; -axt f ice-axe; -bahn f skating-ground or -rink; Kanada: (Rutschbahn) toboggan-slide; -bank ⌂ f bank of ice; vgl. -feld; -bär m polar bear (Ursus mari'timus); ⌐bedeckt a. covered with ice; -beere & f snowberry (Chioco'cca); ⌐begrenzt a. ice-bound; -bein n [ndl. *ft. = i'schium] pig's pettitoes pl.; -berg m zu Lande: glacier; zur See: ⌂ iceberg; -beutel m zum Kühlen eis-bag; -blink m (Widerschein des Eises) ice-blink; -block m block of ice; -blume f: a) am Fenster: ice-fern; pl. auch: flowers pl. of ice; b) &; -fraut; -bock m starling; -bruch m = -gang; -creme f (Gefrorenes) ice-cream; -decke f sheet of ice; -eimer m ice-pail; cooler.

eisen¹ (⌐∪) [Eis] **I** v/a. 1. to (turn into or to) ice. — 2. to clear of ice. **II** v/n. (h.). 3. (unter dem Eise fischen) to fish under the ice. — 4. v/impers. es eist it is freezing (hard), there is ice on the ground.

Eisen² (⌐∪) [ahd.: iron] n ⊛ 1. iron; chm. ferrum (Fe); gegossenes, geschmiedetes, gewalztes, hämmerbares ~ cast, wrought, rolled, malleable iron; mit ~ beschlagen to rivet with iron; p.p. auch: iron-bound or -cased or -shod; fig. von ~ (eiserner Gesundheit) sein to have an iron constitution or frame, to be made of iron; Sprichw. man muß das ~ schmieden, solang (oder dieweil) es noch warm ist strike the iron while it is hot; Not bricht ~ necessity knows no law. — 2. (Werkzeug) iron tool or implement; (Huf-)~ horseshoe; surg. glühendes ~ hot iron for cauterizing. — 3. in ~ (Fesseln) legen to put in irons. — 4. altes ~ (broken) iron; fig. auch: old rubbish; zum alten ~ werfen to cast (or put) away as lumber.

[Eisenabfälle] — 314 — [Eisfuchs]

Eisen-abfälle ⊕ (ᴵᵛ...) m/pl. ⊕, **-abgang** ⊕ m scrap-iron; **-ader** ⚒ f lode of iron-ore; **-alaun** m, chm. iron-alum; **-arbeit** ⊕ f work(ing) in iron; ~en pl. iron-work sg.; **-arbeiter** ⊕ m iron-worker, worker in iron; **-artig** a. ⊕ iron-like, ⚹ ferruginous; **-arz(e)nei** f, med. preparation of iron, steel medicine; vgl. -tropfen; **-asbest** m fibrous silica; **-auflösung** f, chm. iron-solution.
Eisenbahn ⊞ (ᴵᵛ⁻ᴵ) f ⊕ railway, Am. railroad; atmosphärische, elektrische, unterirdische ~ pneumatic, electric, underground railway; mit der ~ by rail(way); vgl. Bahn 4.
Eisenbahn-abteil ⊞ (ᴵᵛ...) m ⊕ railway-compartment; **-aktie** f r.-share; **-anleihe** f r.-loan; **-anschluß** m connexion (of trains); (Station) junction; **-arbeiter** m r.-labourer, navvy; **-bau** m building (or construction) of a railway; **-beförderung** f forwarding (or transmission) by railway; **-betriebsdirektor** m traffic-manager; **-betriebsmittel** n/pl. rolling-stock sg.; **-coupé** n =-abteil; **-damm** m f. Damm 1; **-direktorium** n = -verwaltung. [man.]
Eisenbahner ⊞ (ᴵᵛ⁻ᴵᵛ) m ⊕ railway-
Eisenbahn-fahrkarte ⊞ (ᴵᵛ⁻ᴵ...) f ⊕ railway-ticket; **-fahrplan** m time-table; **-fahrt** f r.-journey or -trip; **-fracht** f r.-freight; **-gesellschaft** f r.-company; **-karte** f r.-map; **-krankheit** f r.-spine; **-kursbuch** n r.-guide; **-netz** n system of railways, network of r.-lines; **-perron** m = Bahnsteig; **-postanstalt** ⚹ f = Bahnpost; **-postwagen** ⚹ m post-office carriage, Am. mail-car; **-projekt** n r.-scheme; **-regiment** ⚒ n, etwa: r.-corps or -regiment; **-schaffner** m r.-guard; **-schiene** f rail; **-schlafwagen** m sleeping-car(riage); **-schwellen** f/pl. r.-sleepers pl.; **-signal** n r.-signal; **-station** f r.-station; größere auch: terminus; **-system** n r.-system; **-tarif** m r.-tariff or rates pl.; **-transport** m carriage by rail(way); vgl. -beförderung; **-truppen** ⚒ f/pl. r.-battalion; **-unfall** m, **-unglück** n r.-accident; **-unternehmer** m r.-contractor; **-verbindung** f r.-connection; **-verwaltung** f: a) r.-management; b) (Verwaltungsrat) managing board of a r.(-line); **-wagen** m r.-carriage, Am. car; für Güter: luggage-van; truck; **-wesen** n r.-affairs pl.; **-zerstörung** ⚒ f destruction of railways; **-zug** m r.-train.
☛ Das hier Fehlende f. unter Bahn-...
Eisen-band ⊕ (ᴵᵛ...) n ⊕ iron-band or -brace; **-baron** m great (or rich) iron-master, iron-lord; **-barren** ⊕ m bar-iron; **-bau** m iron-structure; **-beize** ⊕ f iron-liquor; **-bergwerk** n = -grube; **-beschlag** ⊕ m iron mounting or fastenings pl.; **-beschläge** pl., auch: iron fittings pl. or furniture; **-blau** ⚒ n blue iron-ore; **-blausauer** a. ⊕ chm.: ferrocyanic; **-blausaures** Salz ferro cyanate; **-blausäure** f, chm. ferro cyanic acid ($H_4 Fe Cy_6$); **-blech** ⊕ n sheet-iron; gewelltes: corrugated iron-plate; verzinntes: tinned iron (-plate); verzinktes: galvanized (sheet-)iron; vgl. a. Blech 1; **-blechtafel** ⊕ f

sheet of rolled iron; **-blüte** f, min. (Aragonit) aragonite; **-bronze** f iron bronze; **-bruch** ⚒ m = -grube; **-chlorid** ⊕ n, chm. ferric chloride (Fe_2Cl_6); **-chlorür** ⊕ n, chm. ferrous chloride ($FeCl_2$); **-draht** ⊕ m iron-wire; **-drahtarbeiter** m iron-wire drawer; **-drahtmühle** f iron-wire drawing-mill; **-drahtseil** n iron-wire cable; **-druse** ⚒ f crystallized iron-ore; **-erde** f iron-earth; ⚹ ferruginous earth; **-erz** n, min. iron-ore; **-erzeugung** f production of iron; **-farbe** f iron-grey; **-farbig** a. iron-coloured; **-feil(icht)** n, **-feile** f, **-feilspäne** m/pl. ⊕ iron filings pl.; **-fest** a. (as) hard as iron; **-fleck(en)** m iron-mould or -stain; **-fleckig** a. iron-moulded, spoiled by iron-mould; **-fresser** F m, fig. fire-eater, bully, (Prahler) braggart; **-frischschlacke** ⊕ f, metall. finery-cinders pl. or -slag; **-gang** ⚒ m iron-lode; **-ganz** ⊕ f, metall. iron-pig; **-gehalt** m richness in iron; Erz von geringem ~... containing a small quantity of iron; **-gerät**, **-geschirr** n iron-tools or utensils pl.; **-gießer** ⊕ m iron-founder; **-gießerei** ⊕ f iron-foundry; **-gitter** n iron railing or fence; **-glanz** m iron-glance; **-glimmer** m, min. micaceous iron-ore; **-grau** a. iron-grey; **-grube** ⚒ f iron-mine or -pit; **-guß** ⊕ m iron-casting; **-gußwaren** f/pl. cast-iron (or iron-foundry) goods pl.; **-haltig** a. containing iron, ⚹ ferruginous, ferriferous; **-haltigkeit** f des Bodens, eines Erzes ꝛc.: richness in iron; **-hammer** m: a) (Werkzeug) sledge-, forge-hammer; b) (Fabrik) iron-works pl.; forge; der Gang nach dem ~ (SCH.) the Walk to the Forge; **-handel** ⚹ m iron-trade; vgl. -kram a.; **-händler(in)** f m ironmonger, dealer in hardware; **-holz** (**-baum** m) n ⚛ iron-wood (tree) (Sideroxylon, Xylia, &c.); **-hut** m: a) ehm. skullcap; b) ⚛ = Sturmhut; **-hütchen**, **-hütlein** n: a) ⚛ = -hut b; b) her. vair; **-hütte** ⊕ f = -hammer b; **-hütten-besitzer** m iron-master, vgl. -baron; **-hüttenkunde** f, -**wesen** n metallurgy of iron; ⚹ siderotechny; **-hydroxyd** ⚹ n, chm. ferric hydrate ($H_6 Fe_2 O_6$), min. brown iron-ore or hematite; **-hydroxydul** ⚹ n ferrous hydrate ($H_2 Fe O_2$); **-industrie** f iron-industry or -manufacture; **-industrielle(r)** m iron-master; **-ixie** ⚛ f hardwood-tree (Ixia ferrea); **-kalk** min. calcined iron; **-karbid** n iron carbide; **-kette** f iron chain; **-kies** m, min. = Schwefelkies; **-kiesel** m, min.: ⚹ ferruginous quartz; **-kitt** ⊕ m iron-rust cement; **-kram** m: a) ⚹ hardware-trade; b) ⚹ ironmonger's shop; c) ⊕ =-abfälle; **-krämer** ⚹ m dealer in hardware; vgl. -händler; **-kraut** ⚛ n vervain (Verbena officinalis); **-kuchen** (Waffel) m gofer, wafer; **-kur** f, med. iron-treatment; **-lack** m lacquer for iron goods; **-laden** ⚹ m ironmonger's shop; **-lot** n iron-solder; **-mal** n = -fleck; **-mine** ⚒ f = -grube; **-mohr** m, chm. black oxide of iron; **-niederschlag** m precipitate of iron; **-ocker** m, min. iron (or blue) ochre; **-ofen** m: a) iron stove; b) ⊕ metall. iron- (or smelt-

ing-)furnace; **-oxyd** ⚹ m, chm. ferric oxide (Fe_2O_3); **-oxydhydrat** ⚹ n = -hydroxyd; **-oxydsalze** ⚹ n/pl. (Ferrisalze) ferric salts pl.; **-oxydul** ⚹ n, chm. ferrous oxide (FeO); **-oxyduloxyd** ⚹ n, chm. magnetic oxide (Fe_3O_4); **-oxydulsalze** ⚹ n/pl. (Ferrosalze) ferrous salts pl.; **-panzer** ⚔ m coat of mail, ⚓ iron armour; **-platte** f iron plate; **-pflock** m iron bolt; **-präparate** n/pl. iron drugs pl., ⚹ chalybeates pl.; **-quelle** f fountain rich in iron, ⚹ chalybeate spring; **-rahm** m, min. iron-froth; **-ring** m iron-ring; **-rost** m: a) rust(ed iron) b) (Gatterwerk aus Eisen) iron grate; **-salz** n, chm. iron-salt (vgl. oxyd[ul]salze; **-sau** ⊕ f, metall. pig of iron, iron-pig; **-säuerling** m = -wasser; **-säure** ⚹ f, chm. ferric acid ($H_2 FeO_4$); **-schiene** ⚒ f iron-rail; **-schimmel** m (Pferd) iron-grey horse; **-schlacke** f fining-slag; **-schmelze**, **-schmelzhütte** ⊕ f iron-foundry; **-schmied** m blacksmith; **-schmiede** ⊕ f (iron-)forge; **-schneidemühle** ⊕ f = -spaltwerk; **-schröter** ⊕ m slitter of iron; **-schüssig** a. ⊕ ⚹ ferruginous; **-schwarz** n: a) powdered black-lead; b) = -schwärze; **-schwärze** f: a) min. specular iron-ore, black-lead; b) ⊕ = -beize; **-spaltwerk** ⊕ n slitting-mill or -rollers pl.; **-späne** m/pl. = -feilicht; **-spat** m, min. sparry (or spathic) iron(-ore); **-stab** m iron bar or rod; **-stein** m, min. iron-stone; **-stufe** ⚒ f (block of) iron-ore.
[Hareldα glacialis.)
Eis²-ente (ᴵᵛ⁻ᴵᵛ) f ⚒ zo. winter-duck;
Eisen-teilchen (ᴵᵛ...) n ⊕ particle of iron; **-ton** m, min. iron-clay; **-tropfen** m/pl., med. steel- (or iron-)drops pl.; **-vitriol** m (n), chm. iron (or green) vitriol; ⚹ (Ferrosulfat) ferrous sulphate (FeSO₄); **-walzwerk** ⊕ n, metall. (iron-)rolling-mill, iron-rollers pl.; **-ware** ⚹ f iron-ware, hardware; **-waren-handlung** f, **-warenladen** m ⚹ = -laden; **-wasser** n: a) chalybeate water; **-werk** ⊕ n: a) =-beschlag; b) = -hammer b; **-wurz** ⚛ f ⚹ black centaury (Centaurea scabiosa); **-zeit** f ⊕ age of iron, iron age; **-zeug** n = -gerät; **-zyan(ür)-zyanid** n, chm. (Berlinerblau) Prussian blue.
eisern (ᴸᵛ) a. ⊕ 1. (made of) iron (auch fig.); Der Geldschrank iron-safe; (aus Eisen erbaut) iron-built. — 2. fig. stern, unwavering; ⊕ Der Bestand einer Kasse permanent fund; ⚓ Der Bestand (an Vorräten) permanent stock or store; Der (unermüdliche) Fleiß unwearying industry; Des (unerbittliches) Herz heart of steel or as hard as flint; der ~ Kanzler (Bismarck) the Iron Chancellor; das ~e Kreuz (1813, 1870/71) the Iron Cross; von Der Natur wiry (vgl. Eisen 1 fig.); Le Stirn brazen face. — 3. jur. (unveränderlich) unalterable; (unveräußerlich) inalienable. — 4. das ~e Tor ⚓ n⁕ (Stromenge der Donau) the Iron Gates pl.
Eis-fahren (ᴸᵛ...) n ⊕, **-fahrt** f: a) journey across the ice; b) skating, sledging; **-feld** n ice-field; **-fischerei** f durch ein -loch ice-fishing; **-fläche** f = -decke; **-frei** a. ⊕ free from (or clear of) ice; ice-free (harbour); **-fuchs** m, zo. arctic

Signs (see page XVII): F familiar; P vulgar; Γ flash; ⟍ rare; † obsolete (died); * new word (born); ⸗ incorrect; ♪ music;

[Eisgang] — 315 — [Elefantenführer]

fox (Canis lago'pus); =**gang** m drifting (or floating, breaking up) of the ice; =**gebirge** n: a) =berg; b) arctic mountains pl.; =**gefror(e)nes** n = =creme; =**gegend** f arctic region, frigid zone; =**gewächs** ❀ n = =kraut; =**glas** n = frosted glass; ♁**grau** a. hoary (with age); =**griff** ⊕ m am Hufeisen calk(in); =**grube** = =höhle; =**händler** m iceman, dealer in ice; =**höhle** f ice cav(ern); =**huf-eisen** ⊕ n ice-shoe.

eisig (⌣‿) a. ❀ icy, covered with (or as cold as) ice; chilly; fig. freezing. **Eisigkeit** (⌣‿-) f ❀ iciness, chilliness. **Eis²-jacht** (ⁿ...) f Sport: ice-yacht or -boat; ♁**kalt** (ⁿd, oft: ‿⌣) a. ❀ (as) cold as ice, icy, frosty; =**kälte** f ❀ icy cold, iciness, frostiness; =**kammer** f, =**kasten** m ice-box or -chamber or -closet, refrigerating chamber; =**keller** m ice-cellar or -house or -pit; =**kluft** f, ♁**klüftig** a. for. frost-cleft; =**klumpen** m lump of ice; =**kraut** ⚕ n ice-plant (Mesembrya'nthemum crysta'llinum); =**lauf** n skating; =**läufer** m skater; =**loch** n (Lume) ice-hole for fishing, &c.; =**lotse** ⚓ m ice-master; =**maschine** ⊙ f freezing-apparatus or -machine; freezer; =**masse** f mass of ice; =**meer** ♀ n polar sea; nördliches, südliches ~ Arctic, Antarctic Ocean; =**möwe** f glaucous gull (Larus glaucus); =**nagel** ⊕ m am Hufeisen frost-nail; =**nebel** m frosty fog; =**papier** n ice-paper; =**perio'de** f = =zeit; =**pfahl**, =**pfeiler** ⊕ m = =bock; =**pflanze** f = =kraut; =**pflug** ⊙ m ice-plough; =**picke** f ice-pick; =**punkt** m, phys. freezing-point; =**punsch** m iced punch; =**regen** m icy shower, sleet; =**rinde** f crust of ice (auch fig.); =**scharbe** f, orn. cormorant; =**schimmer** m = =blink; =**scholle** f floating ice, floe; =**schrank** m ice-screen; refrigerator; =**schuh** m skate; =**spat** min. = Adular; =**spiel** n game (played) on the ice, vgl. =sport; =**spind** n = =schrank; =**sporn** ⊕ m = =nagel; =**sport** m sport on the ice, skating and sleighing; =**sprießel**, =**sprießen** m, =**sprosse** f, hunt. (Geweih-ende im 4. Jahre) bez-antler, bay; =**stauung** f blockage of floating (or drifting) ice; =**stein** m cryolite; =**strom** m glacier; =**sturmvogel** m, orn. fulmar (Fu'lmarus glacia'lis); =**taucher** m, orn. ember-goose, ice-loon (Coly'mbus glacia'lis); =**theorie** f glacial theory; =**treiben** n drifting of the ice; =**vogel** m, orn. kingfisher, halcyon (Alce'do), orn. ⚕ limenitis; =**wermut** ⚕ m icy wormwood (Artemi'sia glacia'lis); =**zacken**, =**zapfen** m icicle; =**zeit** f, geol. glacial period or age; =**zone** ♀ f frigid (or arctic) zone.

eitel (⌣‿) [ahd.: idle] a. ❀ (D8 und 9) 1. vain; a. idle (talk); futile (effort); vainglorious (boast); flimsy (pretext); coquettish (woman); rel. worldly or frivolous (mind); eitler Dunst, Tand empty show; eitler Geck conceited fop; rel. es ist alles ♁ auf der Welt all is vanity in this world. — 2. meist inv. (nichts als, lauter) nothing but; ♁ Brot essen ... dry bread; ♁ Gerede idle talk, mere twaddle; ♁ Gold pure gold; eitle Possen silly tricks pl., mere rubbish, nonsense.

Eitelkeit (⌣‿-) f ❀ (s. eitel 1) vanity; futility; vaingloriousness; coquettishness; frivolity; conceit(edness).

Eiter (⌣‿) [ahd.] m ❀ path. (purulent or festering, ⚕ suppurative) matter, ⚕ pus; ~ erzeugen to fester, to ulcerate, ⚕ to suppurate; ~ ziehen to gather. **Eiter-abfluß** (ⁿ...) m ❀, =**abgang** m discharge of pus; =**ansammlung** f collection of matter or pus, gathering, ⚕ empyema; ♁**artig** a. ❀: ⚕ purulent, pyoid; =**ausfluß** m = =fluß; =**befördernd** a.: ⚕ suppurative; =**beule** f abscess, boil; ulcer; ♁**bildend** a. producing pus, ⚕ pyogenic; =**bläschen** n, =**blatter** f: ⚕ pustule; =**blase** f = =sack; ♁**erzeugend** a. festering; =**fluß** m discharge of matter; =**fraß** m corrosive ulcer; =**geschwulst** f, =**geschwür** n festering boil or tumour, gathering. **eiterhaft, eit(e)richt, eit(e)rig** (⌣‿) a. ❀ resembling pus or matter; ⚕ path. purulent; (eiternd) festering, ulcerating. **Eiter-jauche** (ⁿ...) f ❀: ⚕ ichor. **eitern** (⌣‿) path. I v/n.(h.) ❀a. to fester, to ulcerate, ⚕ to suppurate; to discharge (or secrete) pus or matter; ♁b, ⚕ rankling.—II~ ❀ ❀ = Eit(e)rung. **Eiter-pilz** ⚕ (ⁿ...) m ❀ micrococcus found in pus or festering matter (Microco'ccus pyo'genes); =**pflock**, =**pfropf** m core (of a boil, &c.); =**sack** m: ⚕ cyst (of an abscess); encysted tumour; =**stock** m = =pflock.

Eit(e)rung (⌣(⌣)-) f ❀ festering, ulceration, ⚕ suppuration; zur ~ bringen to bring to a head. [glair, ❀ albumen.) **Ei²-weiß** (ⁿd) n ❀a. white of an egg, **eiweiß-artig** (ⁿd...) a. ❀, ♁**haltig** a.: ⚕ albuminous, ⊕ glairy; =**harnen** n, path.: ⚕ albuminaria; =**körper** m ❀ physiol.: ⚕ albuminoid, endosperm; =**papier** n albuminized paper; =**stoff** m, chm.: ⚕

Ei-zelle (ⁿ...) f ❀ egg-cell. [albumin.**Ejektor** (⌣‿-) [it.] m ❀ (Dampfstrahlpumpe zum Entleeren e-s Behälters) ejector.

Ekel¹ (⌣‿) [ndb.: irk] m ❀ 1. sickly feeling, nauseousness; ⚕ nausea. — 2. (Widerwillen) disgust, loathing; (Abneigung) aversion, dislike, repugnance; (Überdruß) surfeit; einem ~ einflößen, erregen to disgust a p.; einen ~ vor et. empfinden, haben to have an aversion to a th., to loathe a th.; die Sache ist ihm zum ~ (geworden) he has taken a dislike to it. F he is sick of it, P he's fed up with it; (bis) zum ~, oft: (lt.) ad nauseam. — 3. F (etwas Widerliches) loathsome (F nasty) p. or th. **ekel²** (⌣‿) a. ❀ (D8 und 9) 1. es ist mir ♁ (übel) I feel sick or F qualmish. — 2. (leicht Ekel empfindend) squeamish, (empfindlich, heikel) fastidious, particular, nice, sensitive; (wählerisch) hard to please, im Essen: dainty. **ekelhaft** (⌣‿) a. ❀ disgusting, loathsome, nauseous; v. Gerüchen offensive. **Ekelhaftigkeit** (⌣‿-) f ❀ loathsomeness, nauseousness; offensiveness. **ekelig** (⌣‿) a. ❀ = eklig. **ekeln** (⌣‿) ❀a. I v/n. (h.) etwas ekelt mir ... makes me heave or (feel) sick. — II v/impers. u. v/refl. es ekelt mich ob. mir, mich ob. mir ekelt vor e-m Ding, ich

ekle mich vor (ob. an) e-m Ding. poet. auch: e-r Sache (gen.) I feel a loathing (or dislike) for a th.; I am disgusted at (or with) a th., stärker: it makes me (feel) sick, it sickens me.
Ekel-name (ⁿ...)[ndb.] m ❀ nick-name.
Eklaireur (⌣‿-) † (è-klä-rö'r) [fr.] m ⚔d.(❀) = Aufklärer.
Eklat (e-tla') [fr.] m ❀ (glänzendes Auftreten, Glanz) eclat, splendour; striking (ing, dazzling) effect. [ing, dazzling.) **eklatant**(-⌣⌣)[fr.] a. ❀ brilliant, strik-) **Eklektiker** ⚕ (⌣‿⌣) [grch.] m ❀ phls., **eklektisch** (⌣‿) a. ❀ eclectic. **Eklektizismus** (⌣‿⌣⌣) [grch.] m ❀ eclecticism. **eklig** (⌣‿) (Ekel) a. ❀ (ekelhaft) disgusting; weitS. (unangenehm) unpleasant, nasty. **Eklipse** ⚕ (⌣‿) [grch.] f ❀ ast. (Verfinsterung) (solar, lunar) eclipse. **Ekliptik** (⌣‿) f ❀ math., ⚕ ast. (Sonnenbahn), **ekliptisch** (⌣‿) a. ❀ ecliptic. **Ekloge** (⌣‿-) [grch.] f ❀ (Hirtengedicht) eclogue, pastoral (or bucolic) poem. **Eklogen-dichter** (z...) m ❀ pastoral (or bucolic) poet. [eclogite.) **Eklogit** ⚕ (⌣‿⌣)[grch.]m ❀c.min.(Gestein) **Ekrü-seide** ❀ (ⁿ...) [fr. soie écrue] f ❀ Weberei: ecru silk.
Ekstase ⚕ (⌣‿-) [grch.] f ❀ (Verzückung) ecstasy; in ~ geraten F to go into ecstasies or raptures. [ecstatic(ally).) **ekstatisch** ⚕ (⌣‿) a. ❀ (u. adv.) (verzückt)) **Ektasis** ⚕ (⌣⌣-) [grch.] f, metr., pros., rhet. (Dehnung e-r kurzen Silbe) ectasis.
Ekzem ⚕ (⌣‿) [grch.] n ❀c. (nässende Hautflechte) eczema.
Elaborat (---‿) [lt.] n ❀c. (Ausarbeitung, Aufsatz) composition, essay, theme.
Ela-idin ⚕ (---‿) [grch.] n ❀c. chm. elaidin(e) $(C_8H_{33}O)_3 C_3H_5O_3$.
Ela-in (---‿) [grch.] n ❀c. = Olein.
Elastik † (‿⌣) [engl.] f ❀, n ❀ (Gummiband) elastic.
elastisch (-‿‿) [grch.] a. ❀ (federnd) elastic; springy, rebounding; das Eis ist ♁ ... yields, F gives; fig. ♁e Naturen buoyant natures pl.; phys. ♁e Flüssigkeit fluid, ♁-flüssig a. ❀ gaseous.
Elastizität (---‿‿) f ❀ elasticity; springiness; fig. buoyancy.
Elb-Athen ♀ (ⁿ...) n ❀ fig. Dresden; =**Florenz** ♀ n fig. Dresden; =**kahn** m, =**schiff** n boat plying on the Elbe; F co. =**kähne** pl. large boots, F co. beetle-crushers pl.; =**schiffahrt** f navigation on the Elbe; =**strom** ♀ m (the river) Elbe.
Elch (d) m ⚕b. ⚕c. zo. = Elen ⚕c.
Eldorado(⌣-‿-)[span.] n❀(fabelhaftes Goldland) Eldorado, El Dorado (= Dorado).
Eleasar (⌣‿⌣‿)[hebr.]npr.⚕.⚕a.Eleazar. **eleatisch** (⌣⌣‿) [E'lea, grch. St. in Luka'nien, Unteritalien] a. ❀ Alt. = phls. ♁e Schule (540–460 v. Chr.) (des Parme'nides, Ze'no(n) 2c.) Eleatic School.
Ele-er (⌣‿-) [Elis, grch. Landschaft im westl. Peloponnes] m ❀, ~**in** f ❀ Elean.
Elefant (⌣⌣‿) [ahd., grch., *ind.] m ❀ zo. elephant (E'lephas); ~ mit guten Stoßzähnen, auch: tusker; fig. aus e-r Mücke e-n ~en machen to make a mountain (out) of a mole-hill.
elefanten-artig (-‿⌣...) a. ❀ elephantine; =**führer** m ❀ Ost-J.: cornac;

[Elefantenjagd] — 316 — [Ellbogen]

=jagd f el.-hunting; =laus ⚥ ⚭ f cashew-nut; =lausbaum ⚥ m cashew, acajou (Anaca'rdium occidenta'le); =lausfrucht, =nuß f anacard, cashew-nut; =rüssel m elephant's trunk or proboscis; =spitzmaus f, zo. elephant-shrew or =mouse (Macrosce'lides ty'picus); =zahn m tusk of an elephant.

Elefantiasis ⌐ (-⌣⌣⌶⌣⌣) f inv. path. elephantiasis, elephant-leg.

elegant(-⌣⌶)[fr.] I a.⦿ elegant or stylish (dress), fashionable (lady, world), F swell or smart (company). — II ~ (-⌣ga') m ㊺ beau, fop; F swell, don, masher.

Eleganz (-⌣⌶) [fr.] f ㊻ elegance, fashionableness, F swellishness, smartness, stylishness.

Elegiambus (⌣⌣(⌣)⌶⌣) [grch.] m ㉗ pros. elegiambic verse.

Elegie (⌣⌣⌶) [grch.] f ㊽ (Klagelied) elegy.

Elegien=dichter, Elegiker (⌣⌶⌣⌣) m ㉒ writer of elegies, elegiac poet.

elegisch (⌣⌶⌣) a. ⦿ elegiac; Le Verse, oft: elegiacs pl.; weitS. (klagend) plaintive, mournful, doleful.

Ele-ison (⌣⌶⌣⌣) [grch.] n ㊵ s. Kyrie ~

Elektoral=rasse (-⌣⌶⌶...) [lt. kurfürstlich (sächsisch)] f ㊷ zo. electoral breed or race (of sheep); =wolle ⚥ f electoral wool.

Elektriker (-⌶⌣⌣) m ㉒ electrician.

elektrisch (-⌶⌣) [grch. ele'ktron Bernstein] a.⦿ electric(al); ⚲ machen to electrify; Le Anlage electric installation or plant; Ler Funken, Le Klingel, LeS Licht, Ler Schlag, Strom electric spark, bell, light, shock, current; Ler Lokomotivbetrieb electric (locomotive-)traction; Le Schnellbahn electric high-speed railway; adv. ⚲ beleuchtet electrically lighted, lit up with electric light or by electricity.

elektrisierbar (-⌶-⌶-⌶) a. ⦿ electrifiable.

elektrisieren (-⌶-⌶⌶) [grch.] I v/a. ⑨ phys. to electrify, ⌐ to electrize. — II ~ n ㊷ electrification, ⌐ electrization.

Elektrisierer (-⌶-⌶⌶⌣) m ㉒ electrifier.

Elektrisier=maschine (-⌶-⌶⌶...) f ㊷ electrical machine.

Elektrisiert=sein (⌶...) n ㉓, =werden n electrification = elektrisieren II.

Elektrizität (-⌶-⌶⌶⌶) [grch.] f ㊷ phys. (positive, negative) electricity; galvanische ~ galvanism; mit ~ laden to electrify; ⊕ von ~ getrieben, fortbewegt electrically driven, propelled.

Elektrizität(s)=entwicklung⊕(-⌶-⌶⌶⌶...) f ㊷ production (or excitement) of electricity; =erreger m: ⌐ electromotor; =erregung f: ⌐ electromotion; =leiter m conductor of el.; =messer m: ⌐ electrometer; =sammler m, =strom m, =werke n/pl. electric condenser, current, works pl.; =wage f = =messer; =zähler m electric indicator; =zeiger m: ⌐ electroscope; galvanometer.

Elektro=automobil (-⌶⌣...) n ㉓ electric motor(-car); =chemie f, ⚲chemisch a. electro-chemistry, -chemical; =chemiker m electro-chemist.

Elektrode (-⌣⌶⌣) [grch.] f ⊕ elect. (Polende e-r galvanischen Kette) electrode.

Elektro=dynamik (-⌣⌶...) f ㊷ electrodynamics; ⚲dynamisch a. ⦿ e.-dynamic; ⚲galvanisch a. e.-galvanic; =lyse

f ⊕ electrolysis; =magnet m electromagnet; ⚲magnetisch a. e.-magnetic; =magnetismus m e.-magnetism; =meter n (m) electrometer; =mobil n = =automobil; mo'tor m, ⚲moto'risch a. electromotor. [atom] (1904) electron.

Elektron ⌐ (-⌣⌶.] n ㉓ (Elektrizitäts-)

elektronisch ⌐ (-⌣⌶⌣) a. ⦿ electronic.

Elektro=phor ⌐ (-⌣⌶...) m ⑪c. electrophorus; =skop n electroscope; =technik f ㊷ electrical engineering; =techniker m electrical engineer; ⚲technisch a. ⦿ electro-technical; =therapie f electrotherapeutics.

Element (⌣⌣⌶) [mhd.;*lt.] n ⑪b.1.(Grundstoff) element; fig. in (außer) s-m ~e sein ... in one's element (like a fish out of water). — 2. ~e pl. (Anfangsgründe) elements, rudiments pl. — 3. in Flüchen: Blitz~! the deuce!, hang it all!

elementar (⌣⌣⌣⌶) [lt.] a. ⦿ elementary, rudimentary; Le Kräfte elementary (or primitive) forces pl.

Elementar=buch (⌣⌣⌣⌶⌣) n ㉓ primer; auch oft: first steps pl. in grammar, &c.

elementarisch (-⌣⌣⌶⌣) a. ⦿ = elementar.

Elementar=gewalt (⌣⌣⌣⌶⌣...) f ㊷ elementary force; =klasse f junior form; =lehrer(in f) m elementary teacher; =schule f elementary (or provided) school; =stoff m elementary (or simple) substance; =unterricht m elementary instruction; auch oft: the three R's; =werk n elementary treatise.

Elemi ⚥ (-⌶⌣, ⌶⌣ ⌶⌣) [mlt.: * ar.] n ㊵ (Ölbaumharz, =gummi) (gum) elemi.

Elen (⌣⌶) [lit.: Elch] m u. n ㉓ zo. elk (Cervus alces), amerit.: orignal; ~antilo'pe f ㊷ zo. eland (Ore'as canna); ~haut f elk-skin; ~hirsch m, ~tier n = Elen.

Elend¹ (⌣⌶) [ahd. Ausland: else] n ⑪c. misery; wretchedness; (Mißgeschick) adversity, calamity; (Not) need, distress; (Armut) indigence, penury; ins ~ bringen, stürzen to bring (or reduce) to misery; ins ~ geraten, versinken to come to (or sink into) poverty; to come to want; F to come down (low) in the world; F graues ~ the blues pl.

elend² (⌣⌶) I a. ⦿ miserable, forlorn, wretched; (in Not, sehr arm) distressed, indigent, needy; Le (tägliche) Ausflucht paltry excuse; Le (jämmerliche) Lage pitiful (or sorrowful) condition or plight; ⚲ (krank) aussehen to look very ill or F poorly. — II ~e(r) s. ⦿ wretch. — III adv. (a. elendig(lich)) miserably, wretchedly; pitifully. [m = Elen.]

Elen=haut (⌶...) f ㊷ elk-skin; =hirsch

Elen=tier (⌶...) n ㉓ = Elen. [Eleanor.]

Eleonore (-⌣⌣⌶) npr/f. ㊴ ⦿β. (Bn.)

eleusinisch (⌣⌣⌶⌣) [Eleu'sis, att. St. mit Demetertempel] a. ⦿ Eleusinian; die Len Geheimnisse od. Mysterien m/pl. the Eleusinian mysteries pl.

Elevation ⚥ (-⌣w-tß(⌣)⌶) f ㊸ elevation (= Erhöhung).

Elevator (-⌣w⌶⌣) [lt.] m ㉑ (Aufzug) lift,

Eleve (⌣⌶w) m ㊹, Elevin f ㊵ [fr. Schüler(in)] pupil, scholar, student.

Elf¹ ⚥ (⌶) m ⑫ myth. = Elfe.

elf² (⌶) [ahd. einleven] numer. I ohne s. auch Le card. number, inv. (bisw. pl. elfe) eleven. — II Elf f ㊷ (number) eleven.

elfe¹ (⌣⌶) wenn nichts folgt = elf.

Elfe² ⚥ (⌣⌶) [engl.] f ㊸ myth. elf, fairy; weitS. goblin.

Elf=eck (⌶...) n ㉓ math.: ⌐ hendecagon.

Elfenbein (⌶⌣⌶) [ahd. Elef(ant)en=bein] n ⑪d. ivory; ⚭ gebranntes ~ (Beinschwarz) bone-black.

Elfenbein=arbeiten (⌶⌣⌶...) f/pl. ivory work or articles pl.; =arbeiter, =drechsler m iv.-worker, -turner; =artig a. ⦿ ivoried, ivory(like); =händler m ivory-trader; =jäger m iv.-hunter; =küste ⚥ npr/f. West=afrika: Ivory Coast; =nuß ⚥ f u. ⦿ (Frucht der =palme) iv.-nut; =palme ⚥ f ivory-palm (Phyte'lephas macroca'rpa); =papier n (feines Druckpapier) iv.-paper; =schnecke f, zo. ⌐ eburna.

elfenbeine(r)n (⌶⌣⌶⌣) a. ⦿ (of) ivory.

elfenhaft (⌶⌣⌶) a. ⦿ fairy-like.

Elfen=könig(in f) m (⌶⌣...) ㉒ king of the elves (f fairy-queen); =reigen, =tanz m dance of the fairies; =ringe m/pl. fairy-rings pl.; =reich n fairy-land.

Elfer (⌣⌶) m ㉒ (Gesamtheit v. elf Dingen) group of eleven units. [sorts.]

elferlei (⌶⌣⌶) adv. (of) eleven kinds or

elf²=fach (⌶...) a. ⦿ u. adv. eleven-fold; ⚲jährig a. eleven years old; Ler Knabe eleven year-old boy; ⚲mal adv. eleven times; ⚲silbig a.: ⌐ hendeca-syllabic; ⚲stündig a. lasting eleven hours.

elfte (⌣⌶) ord. numb. ⦿ I a. eleventh; am 2ten März on the eleventh of March; der ~ (des Monats) the eleventh (day of the month); fig. in der 2n (letzten) Stunde at the eleventh hour. — II der, die, das ~: Ludwig XI. (der Elfte) Louis XI (the Eleventh).

elfte=halb (⌶⌣...) a. inv. ten-and-a-half.

Elftel (⌣⌶) n ㉓ u. ⚲ a. inv. eleventh (part).

elftens (⌣⌶) adv. in the eleventh place.

Elger ⚭ (⌣⌶) (Aal=Ger) m ㉒ fishgig.

Elias (-⌣⌶) [hebr. Eli-ja(hu)] npr/m. ⑯γ. (1. Könige 17,1) Elijah.

elidieren (⌣⌣⌶⌣) [lt.] v/a. ⑨ gr. (ausstoßen) to elide. [⦿α. bibl. Eleazar.]

Elieser (-⌣⌶⌣) [hebr. Gotthilf] npr/m. ㊵

Elimination ⌐ (--⌣-tß(⌣)⌶) [lt.] f ㊸ elimination (a. math.); ⚲s=verfahren n ㉓ eliminating process; eliminieren (--⌣⌶⌣) v/a. ⑨ (absondern) to eliminate.

Elisa [hebr.] I (--⌶) npr/m. ⑯⦿α. (1. Kön. 19,16) Elisha. — II (-⌶⌣) npr/f. ⑯⦿α. (Bn.) = Elise.

Elisabeth (-⌶⌣⌣)[hebr. Gottgeweihte] npr/f. ⑯⦿α. (Bn.) Elizabeth, abbr. Betsy; ⚲a'nisch a.⦿Elizabethan(age,drama,&c.)

elisch (⌣⌶) [Elis, grch. Landschaft; vgl. Ele-er] a. ⦿ Alt.: Eliac, Elean.

Elise (-⌣⌶) [Elisabeth] npr/f. ⑯⦿α. (Bn.) Eliza, abbr. Lizzy, Lizzie.

Elision ⌐ (--(⌣)⌶) [lt.] f ㊷ gr. (Ausstoßung eines Vokals oder einer Silbe) elision.

Elite (⌣⌶) [fr. élite Auswahl] f ⦿ the pick or flower of an army; the élite or cream of society, &c.; ~=truppen f/pl. picked troops pl., crack regiment.

Elixier (-⌣⌶) [ar.] n ⑪c. (Heiltrank) elixir.

Elk (⌶) [ndd.] m ⑪b. zo. = Elch.

Ell=bogen (⌣⌶⌣) [ahd.: elbow] m ㉓ elbow; den ~ krümmen to crook (or bend) the elbow; mit den ~ stoßen to elbow; sich mit den ~ den Weg (durch die Menge) bahnen to elbow one's way

(through the crowd); am ~ zerrissen out at elbows (auch *fig.*); die ~ frei haben to have elbow-room; ~=**bein** *n* [62] *anat.*: ⚗ ulna, cubit; ~=**gelenk** *n* el.-joint; ~=**lehne** *f*, ~=**polster** *n* elbow-rest or -cushion; ~=**muskel**, ~=**nerv** *m*, *anat.*: ⚗ cubital muscle, nerve.

Elle (ˊ˘) [ahd.: ell] *f* [48] (ehm. deutsches Längenmaß von ca. 2/3 Meter) in engl. Maße etwa: seven-tenths (or 7/10) of a yard; *fig.* e-m mit gleicher ~ messen to pay a p. back in the same (or his own) coin; *co.* er hat eine ~ verschluckt (ist kerzengerade) he has swallowed a poker.

Ellen=bandmaß (ˊ˘...) *n* [62] yard-measure; =**bogen** *m* = Ellbogen; ≗**lang** *a.* [66] one yard (or ell) in length; *fig.* very long; =**maß** *n* yard-measure, -rod; =**reiter**, =**ritter** F *m*, *contp.* counter-jumper; =**stock** *m* = =maß; =**waren** *f/pl.* drapery(goods *pl.*); =**waren=händler** *m* draper; =**weise** *adv.* by the yard or ell.

Eller ⚘ (ˊ˘) [ndd.: alder] *f* [48] alder (= Erle).

Ellipse ⚗ (˘ˊ˘) [grch.] *f* [48] 1. *gr.* (Auslassung) ellipsis. — 2. *math.* ellipse; ≗**n=artig**, ≗**n=förmig** *a.* [66] elliptic, elliptical; ~**n=form**, =**gestalt** *f* [62] ellipticity; ~**n=zirkel** *m* ellipsograph, elliptograph, trammel.

Ellipso-id ⚗ (ˊ˘–ˊˊ) [grch.] *n* [ü]c. *math.* (Körper, dessen Schnittflächen Ellipsen sind) ellipsoid; ≗**isch** (˘ˊ–ˊˊ˘) *a.* [66] ellipsoidal.

elliptisch ⚗ (˘ˊ˘) [grch.] *a.* [66] elliptic(al), *adv.* elliptically.

Elliptizität (ˊ˘–˘ˊˊ) [grch.] *f* [46] ellipticity.

Elms=feuer (ˊˊ˘) [it. *S.* Er[as]mo] *n* [62] *phys.* Sankt ~ (elektrische Erscheinung an Mast- &c.-spitzen) corposant.

Eloah (–ˊ), *pl.* **Elohim** (––ˊ) [hebr. der Mächtige] *m inv.* (Gott) Elohim.

Eloge (–ˊG˘) [fr.] *f* [48] (Lob) eulogium.

Elongation (–˘–tß(˘)ˊ) [lt.] *f* [46] *ast.* (Abstand der Sonne von einem Planeten) elongation.

Elritze (ˊ˘˘) [ndd.] *f* [48] *ichth.* minnow (*Phoxi'nus laevis*).

Elsa (ˊ˘) [Ilsa; Elisa] *npr/f.* [66][57]α. Elsa, Eliza (= Elsbeth).

Elsaß ♁ (ˊ˘) [ahd. Ausland] *npr/n.* (*m*) [16][17]α. Alsace; ~=**Lothringen** (ˊ...) *n* [23]α. Alsace-Lorraine.

Elsässer (ˊ˘˘) *m* [22], ~**in** *f* [47] (a. **elsässisch** [66]) *a. inv.* Alsatian.

Els=beer=baum (ˊˊˊ) *m* [62] service-tree (*Pirus* od. *Sorbus tormina'lis*); **Els=beere** ⚘ (ˊˊ˘) [ndd.] *f* [62] service-berry.

Elsbeth F (ˊ˘) [Elisabeth] [66][57]α., **Else**[1] F (ˊ˘) [39][48]β. *npr/f.* (Vn.) Betsy, Elsie.

Else[2] ⚘ (ˊ˘) [ndd.] *f* [48] = Eller, Erle.

Else[3] (ˊ˘) *f* [48] *ichth.* = Alse.

Else-beere ⚘ (ˊ˘–ˊ˘) *f* [62] = Elsbeere.

Elster (ˊ˘) [ahd.] *f* [48] *orn.* magpie (*Pica*); schwatzen wie eine ~ to chatter like a magpie or like a parrot; ~(**n**)=**auge** *n* [62] an den Zehen corn; bunion.

elterlich (ˊ˘˘) *a.* [66] parental.

Eltern (ˊ˘; *Hom.* ältern) [ahd. *älter] *pl. inv.* parents *pl.*; von guten (nicht von schlechten) ~ sein to be of good parentage, F *fig.* (sehr gut sein) to be first-rate or A 1; ~=**liebe** *f* [62] parents' (or parental) love; ≗=**los** *a.* [66] without parents; orphaned; =**mord**, =**mörder** *m* parenticide; parricide.

elysä-isch (––ˊ˘), **elysisch** (–ˊ˘) [grch.] *a.* [66] *myth.* elys(ä)ische Gefilde Elysian fields *pl.*; Elysäische Felder in Paris: (Champs) Elysées; **Elysium** (–ˊ(˘)˘) *n* [53], [28] (Wohn-ort der Seligen) Elysium.

Elzevir (ˊ˘w–) [holl. Buchdrucker 16./17. *sae.*] ~=**ausgabe** *f* [62], ~=**format** *n* Elzevir edition, size; ~=**schrift** *f*, *typ.* old French style (of printing).

Email (ĕ-ma'(l)j) *n* [51] (P ++ ~**le** (-mä'l-jᵉ,) *f* [48]) ⚙ [fr. *émail m*; *dtsch. Schmelz] (Schmelzglas) enamel; ~=**arbeiter** *m* [62] enameller; ~=**farben** *f/pl.* enamel (or vitrifiable) colours or pigments *pl.*; ~=**gemälde** *n* enamelled painting; ~=**geschirr** *n* enamelled (iron)ware.

Emaillier=ofen ⚙ (-mäl-ji'r...) *m* [62] enamel(ling)-furnace.

emaillieren ⚙ (-mäl-ji'˘; s. Email) *v/a.* [93] to enamel; (verglasen) to vitrify; ✱ emaillierte Ware enamelled (iron) goods *pl.*; **Emaillierer** *m* [22] enameller.

Email=malerei (-mä'(l)j...) *f* [62] enamel-painting.

Emanation ⚗ (–––tß(˘)ˊ) [lt.] *f* [46] *phys.*, &c. (Ausströmen) emanation; **emanieren** (––ˊ˘) *v/n.* (sn) [93] to emanate.

Emanuel (˘ˊ˘˘) [port. = Immanuel] *npr/m.* (meist Vn) [51][54]α. Emmanuel.

Emanzipation (–˘˘–tß(˘)ˊ) [lt.] *f* [46] (Freimachung) emancipation.

emanzipieren (–˘˘–ˊ˘) *v/a.* [93] (freimachen) to emancipate, to liberate; emanzipierte Frauen *f/pl.* emancipated (or strong-minded) women *pl.*, free womanhood, *coll.* a. F *co.* the new woman.

Emballage ✱ (a˘ˊG˘) [fr.] *f* [48] (Verpackung) packing; ~=**kosten** *pl.* (charge for) package; **emballieren** (a˘ˊ˘) *v/a.* [93] to pack (or bale) up; ✉, &c. to (make up the) mail.

Embargo ⚓ (˘ˊ˘) [span.] *m* u. *n* [51] embargo; vgl. Beschlag 3.

Emblem (˘ˊ) [grch.] *n* [ü]c. (Sinnbild) emblem; ≗**atisch** (˘–ˊ˘) *a.* [66] emblematic.

Embryo ⚗ (ˊ˘–) [grch.] *m* [51] (*pl.* a. Embryo'nen [31]) (Keim) embryo; ≗**nen=artig** *a.*, ≗**nisch** (˘˘ˊ˘) *a.* [66] embryonic; *fig.* auch: in the earliest (or first) stage.

Embuskade ⚔ (a-büß-ˊ˘) [fr.] *f* [48] = Hinterhalt; **embuskieren** (...ˊ˘) (sich in e-n Hinterhalt legen) to lay an ambush.

Emendation ⚗ (–ˊ–tß(˘)ˊˊ) [lt.] *f* [46] (Verbesserung) emendation; **emendieren** (–ˊ–ˊˊ˘) *v/a.* [93] to emend(ate) texts, &c.

Emerit (–˘ˊ) [lt.] *m* [42] (in den Ruhestand Versetzter) pensioner; ~**en=anstalt** *f* [62] home for retired teachers, &c.

emeritieren (–˘˘ˊ˘) [lt.] *v/a.* [93] (am Schluß der Dienstlaufbahn in den Ruhestand versetzen) to pension off, to put on the retiring-list; emeritierter Professor, Geistlicher (a. **Eme'ritus** *m* [58]) retired professor, clergyman.

Emeute (˘mö'˘) [fr.] *f* [48] (Aufstand, Meuterei) rising, mutiny.

Emigrant (–˘ˊ) [fr.-lt.] *m* [42], ~**in** *f* [47] (Auswanderer[in]) emigrant; ~**entum** (––ˊ˘–) *n* [2]d emigration.

Emigration (–˘–tß(˘)ˊ) [lt.] *f* [46] emigration; **emigrieren** (–˘ˊ˘) *v/n.* (sn) [93] (auswandern) to emigrate to a country.

Emil (ˊ–) [fr., *lt. od. grch.] *npr/m.* [15][16]α. Emil(ius), auch: Emile.

Emili-e (–ˊ˘˘) *npr/f.* (Vn.) [39][48]β., a. *dim.* **Emilchen** *n* [23]α. Emily, *dim.* Em(mie).

eminent (–˘ˊ) [lt.] *a.* [66] (hochstehend) eminent, distinguished, renowned; **Eminenz** *f* [46] (Kardinalstitel) Eminence.

Emir (–ˊ, F ˊ–) [ar.] *m* [ü]c. (*pl.* a. Omrah) (Fürst) emir, ameer, zB. the Ameer of Afghanistan; ~**at** (––ˊ) [lt.] [ü]c. emirate, ameership.

Emissar (–˘ˊ) [lt.] *m* [ü]c. (unterirdischer (Ableitungs)kanal) underground drain-pipe.

Emissär (–˘ˊ) [fr.] *m* [ü]c. (Sendling) emissary.

Emission ✱ (–˘(˘)ˊ) [lt.] *f* [46] (Ausgabe) issue of shares, &c.; ~**s=kurs** *m* [62] v. Anleihen &c.: rate of issue, issue price.

Emittent ✱ (–˘ˊ) [lt.] *m* [42] issuer.

emittieren ✱ (–˘ˊ˘) [lt.] I *v/a.* [93] to issue shares, banknotes, &c. — II ~ *n* [23] u. **Emittierung** *f* [46] issue.

Emmentaler (ˊ˘ˊ˘) *a. inv.* ~ Käse Emmental cheese.

Emmerich (ˊ˘˘) [Heinrich] *npr/m.* [15][16]α. (Vn.) Emery.

E=moll ♪ (ˊˊ) s. E♪.

Emolument (–˘˘ˊ) [lt.] *n* [ü]b. mst *pl.* ~**e** (Einkünfte) emoluments *pl.*; income.

empfahl (˘ˊ) *impf.* von empfehlen.

empfand (˘ˊ) *impf.* v. empfinden.

Empfang (˘ˊ) *m* [7]b. 1. von Personen: reception; e-m einen guten (schlechten) ~ bereiten to give a p. a kind (cold) reception or welcome; am engl. Hofe: King's Drawing-room. — 2. von Geld &c.: receipt; bei ~ on receipt, ✱ von Waren: on delivery; vor ~ dieses (Briefes) ere this (may reach you); indem ich Ihnen den ~ Ihres Geehrten vom 6. d. M. anzeige in acknowledging the receipt of your favour of the 6th inst.; den ~ von et. bescheinigen to (acknowledge the) receipt of s. th.; in ~ nehmen to receive; to accept.

Empfang=... (˘ˊ...) [62] s. Empfangs=...

empfangen (˘ˊ˘) [entfangen] [66]b* I *v/a.* 1. Personen: to receive, freundlich: to welcome; e-n gut (übel) ≗ to give a p. a good (bad) reception. — 2. et. ≗ to receive s. th.; von e-m Befehle ≗ to take (one's) orders from a p.; mit Dank ≗ to accept with thanks; Quittung: (bar und richtig) ≗ *p.p.* (payment duly) received; paid. — II *v/n.* (h.) 3. (befruchtet w.) to conceive; to become pregnant.

Empfänger (˘ˊ˘) *m* [22], ~**in** *f* [47] 1. receiver, mehr gebr.: recipient of gifts, &c.; e-s Briefes auch: addressee; ✱ v. Waren: consignee; eines Wechsels: acceptor. — 2. *tel.* (Empfangs-apparat) receiver, receiving instrument.

empfänglich (˘ˊ˘) *a.* [66] susceptible of, responsive to; alive to; für Eindrücke: impressi(ona)ble; ~**keit** (˘ˊ˘–) *f* [46] susceptibility; impressi(ona)bility.

Empfang=nahme (˘ˊˊ˘) *f* [48] receipt of money; reception of guests.

Empfängnis (˘ˊ˘) *f* [18] *physiol.*: ⚗ conception.

Empfangs=anzeige (˘ˊ...) *f* [62] acknowledgment of receipt); bitte um gütige ~ please acknowledge receipt; =**apparat** *m tel.* receiver, s. Empfänger 2; =**bekenntnis** *n*, =**bestätigung** *f* = =anzeige; =**berechtigte(r)** s. p. authorized to receive money; =**bescheinigung** *f*, =**schein** *m* ✱ receipt for; vgl. =anzeige;

[Empfangsstation] — 318 — [Enaksjohn]

=ſtation f receiving station; =zimmer n reception-room, drawing-room.
Empfehl ⟨⟩ (⌣´) m ⓜc. = Empfehlung.
empfehlbar (⌣´⌣) a. ⓖ recommendable.
empfehlen (⌣´⌣) [entfehlen] I v/a. u. ſich ⟵ v/reſl. ⓦc* 1. (ſich) ⟵ to commend (o.s.); ich kann dir meinen Schneider ⟵ I can recommend you ...; es empfiehlt ſich, daß // it is (re)commendable to // (inf.); dieſe Farben ⟵ ſich dem Auge ... please the eye; ſich (dat.) etwas emp= fohlen ſein laſſen to pay great atten= tion to a th.; ⓢ empfohlen durch // in= troduced by //; Ihr Empfohl(e)ner, oft: your protégé. — 2. Höflichkeitsfor= meln: (ich) empfehle mich Ihnen! (I wish you a) good day, morning, evening!, farewell!; ⟵ Sie mich Ihrem Herrn Vater make my kind regards (or re= member me kindly) to your Father; mein Bruder läßt Sich Ihnen beſtens ⟵ ... sends you his best respects or compli= ments. — 3. ſich ⟵ (Abſchied nehmen) to bid farewell to one's friends; F (ſich davon= machen) to take French leave. — II ⟵d p.pr. u. a. ⓖ 4. Beh. des inf. — 5. ⟵des Äußere prepossessing (or pleasing) appearance.
empfehlens=wert (–⌣´⌣) a. ⓖ, ⟵würdig a. (re)commendable, von Leuten auch: deserving, F worthy.
Empfehlung (⌣´⌣) f ⓟ recommenda= tion; auf ſeine ⟵ (hin) upon his r.; gute ⟵en h. to be highly recommended; Höflichkeitsformel: machen Sie ihm meine ⟵(en), mit beſten ⟵en an ihn make (or with) my best respects (or regards) to him; ⟵s=brief m ⓥ, ⟵=ſchreiben n letter of recommendation or intro= duction; ⟵s=karte ⓢ f business-card; ⟵s=wert, =würdig a. = empfehlenswert; ⟵s=würdigkeit f recommendableness.
empfiehl (⌣´⌣) 2c. ſ. empfehlen.
empfindbar (⌣´⌣) a. ⓖ perceptible; ſen= ſible; ⟵keit (⌣´⌣–) f ⓟ perceptibility.
Empfindelei F (⌣⌣⌣ⁿ) f ⓟ ſenti= mentalism.
empfindeln (⌣⌣⌣) v/n. (h.) ⓑa* b.s. to sentimentalize, to affect sentiment or delicate feelings.
empfinden (⌣´⌣) [ahd. ent=finden] ⓦ* I v/a. u. v/n. (ſn) to feel; (gewahren) to perceive; (erfahren) to experience a sensation, &c.; et. ſehr übel ⟵ to take a th. very ill; ich empfand es peinlich, ſchmerzvoll it pained me; ein ⟵des Weſen a sentient being; aufrichtig empfund(e)nes Mitleid sincere pity; nochmal empfund(e)ne Freude twice felt joy, renewed pleasure; tief emp= fund(e)r Kummer heartfelt grief. — II ⟵ n ⓥ = Empfindung.
Empfindler ⟨⟩ (⌣⌣⌣) m ⓥ, ⟵in f ⓟ ſenti= mentalist, p. affecting fine feelings.
empfindlich (⌣´⌣) a. ⓖ 1. sensible to light, &c.; (zart empfindend) sensitive (a. phot. von Platten); delicate (auch von Inſtrumenten); von Perſonen: (fein fühlend) of tender feelings or notions; (leicht verletzt) touchy, easily offended; eine ⟵e Stelle a tender part; ⟵ gegen Kälte sensitive to cold, (acutely) suf= fering from the cold (weather); phot. Platten ⟵ (für chemiſch wirkſame Strah=

len) machen to sensitize plates; fig. ſeine 2te Stelle (od. Seite) his sore point or weak side; ⟵es Weſen sensitiveness. peevishness. — 2. (ver= letzend, ſchmerzlich) severe or biting (cold), grievous (loss), sharp or acute (pain); adv. ſich ⟵ beleidigt fühlen to feel grievously hurt.
Empfindlichkeit (⌣´⌣–) f ⓟ (ſ. emp= findlich) 1. sensibility; sensitiveness; touchiness. — 2. severity, griev= ousness of a loss, sharpness of a pain.
empfindſam (⌣´⌣)a.ⓖ of delicate feeling, tender-hearted, sentimental, vgl. empfindlich; ⟵keit (⌣´⌣–) f ⓟ delicacy of feeling, tender-heartedness, senti= mentality, vgl. Empfindlichkeit.
Empfindung (⌣´⌣) f ⓟ feeling, per= ception, sensation; (Gemütsſtimmung) sentiment; frame of mind.
Empfindungs=eigenheit (⌣´⌣...) f ⓥ: ⟵ idiosyncrasy; ⟵erreger m, physiol. ⟵ æsthesiogen; =erregung f ⟵ æsthesiogeny; ⟵fähig a. ⓖ physiol. capable (or susceptible) of im= pressions, ⟵ sensitive, sentient, per= ceptive; =fähigkeit f perceptive (or sensitive) faculty; ⟵ sentiency, per= ceptivity; =laut m, gr. interjection; ⟵leer, ⟵los a. ⓖ without sensation; (ge= fühllos) unfeeling, apathetic; (regungs= los) torpid, dead; =loſigkeit f insensi= bility; lack of feeling, unfeeling= ness; apathy; torpor; =ſitz m seat of the sensitive faculty; physiol.: ⟵ sensor= ium; =vermögen n = =fähigkeit; ⟵voll a. (full of) feeling; adv.feelingly, tend= erly; pathetically; =wort n = =laut.
empfing (⌣´) impf. von empfangen.
empföhle (⌣´⌣) subj. impf. u. empfohlen (⌣´⌣) p.p. von empfehlen.
empfunden (⌣´⌣) p.p. von empfinden.
Emphaſe (⌣´–) [grch.] f ⓟ (Nachdruck) emphasis; emphatiſch a. ⓖ (und adv.) emphatic(ally); pointed(ly); im= pressive(ly). [geſchwulſt] emphysema.)
Emphyſem ⟵ (⌣⌣–) [grch.] nⓒc. path. (Luft=)
Empire=ſtil (a-pi´´r=) m ⓥ aus der Zeit Napoleons I.: Empire style.
Empirie ⟵ (⌣–´) ⓟ, Empirik (⌣´⌣) f ⓟ [grch.] f empiricism. [falber] quack.)
Empiriker (⌣´⌣⌣) m ⓥ empiric; Quack=)
empiriſch a. ⓖ (und adv.) (erfahrungsmäßig) empirical(ly); Empirismus (⌣⌣–´⌣) m ⓥ empirism. [= geſchütz=einſchnitt.]
Emplacement ⟵ (a-pla=ßma´) [fr.] n ⓥ)
empor¹ (⌣´) [ahd. in bore in die (der) Höhe] adv. in unechten Zſsgn mit v. (immer trennbar**) und s. bezeichnet ſtets eine Richtung nach oben: ſich ⟵arbeiten v/reſl. ⓖ** to work one's way up; ⟵blicken v/n. (h.) ⓖ** to look up to; ⟵bringen v/a. ⓕ** to raise (auch fig.). [= =kirche.]
Empor²=bühne (⌣´⌣) [⟵] (Empore) f ⓟ)
Empore (⌣´–) [nhd.] f ⓟ = Emporkirche.
empören (⌣´⌣) [ahd.] I v/a. und ſich ⟵ v/reſl. ⓖ** 1. to drive into revolt, to stir up, goad on, agitate; ſich ⟵ to (rise in) revolt against a th., to rebel. — 2. (aufbringen) to rouse a p.'s anger or indignation; empört ſein über et. to be indignant at a th. — II ⟵de(s) n ⓔ 3. indignity. [vgl. Aufrührer.]
Empörer (⌣´⌣) m ⓥ rebel, insurgent;)

empöreriſch (⌣´⌣⌣) a. ⓖ rebellious; insurrectionary; vgl. aufrühreriſch.
empor¹=fahren (⌣´´...) v/n. (ſn) ⓖb** to start up. [story.]
Empor²=geſchoß (⌣´´...) n ⓥ upper)
empor¹=halten (⌣´´...) v/a. ⓖa** to hold (or prop) up; ⟵heben v/a. ⓖ(⑦)b** to lift (up), to raise, fig. auch: to elevate; =hebung f ⓟ Cath. eccl. elevation of the host; e-m ⟵helfen v/n. (h.) ⓖb** to help a p. up.
Emporium ⟵ (⌣⌣´⌣) [lt., * grch.] n ⓥ (Markt, Stapelplatz) emporium of commerce; staple(-place), mart. [choir or gallery.]
Empor²=kirche (⌣´´...) f ⓟ arch. (church-)
empor¹=kommen (⌣´´...) v/n. (ſn) ⓖ** to rise, to get up, v. Gewächſen ꝛc.: to come (or spring) up; =kommen n ⓥ rising; =kömmling m ⓓd. b.s. upstart; g.s. fortune's minion; ſich ⟵raffen v/reſl. ⓖ** to raise o.s. with an effort; ⟵ragen v/n. (h.) ⓖ** (über et.) to tower (above a th.); ⟵richten v/a. ⓖ** to raise (up); ⟵ſchauen ⓖ**, ⟵ſehen ⓖa** v/n. (h.) = ⟵blicken (⌣); ⟵ſchnellen (⌣–) v/n. (ſn) ⓖ** to jerk up(wards); ſich ⟵ ſchwingen v/reſl. ⓖſt** to soar up, to rise rapidly; j. der ſich ⟵geſchwungen hat b.s. upstart, g.s. self-made man; ⟵ſteigen v/n. (ſn) ⓖ** to climb up; to rise (to the surface); ⟵ſtreben v/n. (h.) ⓖ** to strive (or tend) upwards; fig. to aspire to; ⟵ſtrecken v/a. ⓖ** to stretch forth, to raise; ⟵treiben v/a. ⓖ** to drive (or urge) up(wards); chm. to sublimate.
Empörung (⌣´⌣) f ⓟ 1. rebellion, insur= rection; vgl. Aufruhr 2. — 2. (Unwille) (feeling of) indignation, resentment.
Empörungs=geiſt (⌣´⌣...) m ⓥ spirit of revolt, seditious spirit; ⟵ſüchtig a. ⓖ seditious; vgl. aufrühreriſch.
empor¹=wachſen (⌣´´...) v/n. (ſn) ⓖb(e)ſt** to grow up; raſch: to shoot (or spring) up; ⟵ziehen v/a. ⓕb** to rear; aus der Niedrigkeit: to raise from the dust or the gutter. [Dienſteifer.]
Empreſſement (a=präß=ma´) [fr.] n ⓥ =)
empyre=iſch (⌣´–⌣) [grch.] a. ⓖ (himmliſch, erhaben) empyreal, ⟵an; Empyre=um (⌣) n ⓥ, 28 (höchſter Himmel) empyrean.
Emſe (⌣´–) [ndd.: emmet] f ⓟ = Ameiſe.
Emſer (⌣´–) [Bad Ems ⓟ] a. inv. Kongreß (1786) Ems Conference.
emſig (⌣´⌣) [ahd.] a. ⓖ (fleißig) diligent, industrious; hardworking; (flink) quick (at work); (tätig) active, busy, assiduous; (unermüdlich) indefatigable, laborious, plodding; (eifrig) eager, keen; adv. ⟵ arbeiten to work hard or diligently, to be hard at (or to keep close to) one's work, to plod on.
Emſigkeit (⌣´⌣–) f ⓟ (ſ. emſig) diligence, industry; activity, assiduity; labori= ousness, eagerness, keenness.
Emu (⌣´–) [auſtral.] m ⓦ orn. emu (Dromae´us Novae Holla´ndiae).
Emulſin ⟵ (⌣´–) [lt.] n ⓒc. chm. emulsin, amygdalin.
Emulſion ⟵ (⌣–⟨⌣⟩⌣) [lt.] f ⓟ chm. und pharm. (milchähnliche Flüſſigkeit) emulsion.
Enakiter (⌣–´⌣⌣) [hebr.] m ⓥ, Enaks= kind ⟨⌣´´...⟩ n ⓥ, =ſohn m (5. Moſe 9,2) son (or child) of Anak; giant.

Signs (see page XVII): F familiar; P vulgar; ⌐ flaſh; ⟨ rare; † obsolete (died); * new word (born); +* incorrect ♪ muſic;

[Enanthem] — 319 — [Enge]

En-anthem ⚕ (⌣́) [grch.] n ⓛc. path. (innerer Ausschlag) enanthema.

en avant (ä-nä-wą́) [fr.] = vorwärts.

en bloc (ą ⁀) [fr.] (in Bausch u. Bogen) in a lump. [enchanted, charmed.

enchantiert (a-tschą¹) [fr.] a. ⓕ (entzückt)

encouragieren (a-tu⌣G⌣) [fr.] v/a. ⓩ (ermutigen) to encourage.

End-absicht (ʃ...) f ⓕ ultimate object, final aim; **-bahnhof** 🚂 m terminal station, terminus; **-bescheid**, **-beschluß** m bsj. jur. final sentence, decision; **-buchstabe** m final letter.

Endchen (⌣) n ⓒ (dim. von Ende) short (or fag-) end; (Bißchen) bit; ich will dich ein ~ begleiten I will accompany you a little (or short) way or distance.

End-durchsicht (ʃ...) f ⓕ final revision.

Ende (⌣) [ahd.: end] n ⓩ 1. (ant. Anfang, f. ds) end; am letzten ~, am ~ aller ~n at the fag-end; at the end of all things; das ~ vom Liede, etwa: the conclusion, the finale, F the upshot of it all; zu ~ bringen to (bring to an) end, to terminate; zu ~e geh(e)n (sich zu ~e neigen) to come (to draw) to an end; von der Zeit auch: to run out; auch v/impers. es geht mit ihm zu ~ a) von e-m Sterbenden F he is going fast or sinking; ⚙ b) it's all up with him; fig. zu ~ geh(e)n lassen to bury; einen Brief zu ~ lesen, schreiben to finish (reading, writing) ...; einer Sache ein ~ machen to put an end to a th.; Sprichw. ~ gut, alles gut all's well that ends well (SH.). — 2. Ablauf von Zeiträumen: am ~ der Woche at the end (or close) of the week; bis ans ~ to the (very) last; Klagen ohne ~ endless (F everlasting) lamentations pl.; ich würde kein ~ finden, wenn // I should never come to an end if //; mit e-m ein ~ machen oder zu ~ kommen to have done with a p.; ein schlimmes ~ nehmen to come to a bad end, to turn out badly; mit s-m Latein, seiner Kunst zu ~ sein to be at one's wits' end; das ist jetzt zu ~ it's over now. — 3. (Ergebnis) result; etwas zu e-m glücklichen (guten) ~ führen to bring s.th. to a happy issue or conclusion. — 4. am ~ in the end; in the long run; (hinterbrein) after the fair; (alles erwogen) taking everything into account; es ist am ~ (schließlich) doch besser it is perhaps better after all; ich kann mir am ~ (in der Tat) vorstellen I can, indeed, imagine; am ~ kommt er gar nicht mehr wieder he may not return after all. — 5. ... und kein Ende ... without end; Shakespeare und kein ~! Shakespeare, and nothing but Shakespeare! — 6. (Zweck) zu dem ~ for that purpose, to (attain) that end; zu dem ~, daß // in order that //. — 7. räumlich: ~ e-s Stockes ꝛc. (extreme) end ...; am ~ der Straße at the bottom of the street; das obere (untere) ~ der Tafel the head (bottom) of the table; äußerstes ~ extreme point, extremity; ⚙ Schraube ohne ~ endless screw; fig.: an allen Ecken und ~n on all sides; all over the country, F all over the place;

bis ans ~ der Welt to the end of the world, poet. to the confines of the earth; das dick(st)e ~ kommt noch (ob. nach) the worst is yet to come; es ist ein ganzes ~ (e-e gute Strecke) bis dahin it's a good long way (F a tidy distance) from here; vgl. anfassen I. — 8. hunt.: ~n pl. am Geweih: antlers pl. — 9. ↓ (Tau-)~ rope, rope's end. [angle.

End-ecke (ʃ...) f ⓕ cryst. terminal]

Endemie ⚕ (⌣́) f ⓕ path. endemic (or local) complaint or malady.

endemisch ⚕ (⌣) [grch.] a. ⓕ path. (an bestimmten Orten vorherrschend) endemic(al).

enden (⌣) [ahd.] ⓕ I v/a. 1. = beenden I. — II v/n. (h.) und sich ~ v/refl. 2. to finish, terminate, end; mit etwas ~ (fertig werden) to come to an end with s.th., to conclude a th. — 3. gr. (sich) ~ auf to terminate in. — 4. (aufhören) to cease; (verscheiden) to expire (auch von Zeiträumen); v/impers. es endet mit ihm his end is approaching or drawing near. — III ~ n ⓩ 5. completion, finish(ing), termination, end(ing); conclusion. [sixteen-ender.|

..ender (..."⌣) in ßffgn. ₃B. Sechzehn-~]

End-ergebnis (ʃ...) n ⓕ final result.

Endes-bezeichnete(r) (⌣⌣...) s. ⓕ, **-unterfertigte(r)**, **-unterschriebene(r)**, **-unterzeichnete(r)**: (ich)~ (I) the undersigned.

en detail ⓖ s. Detail.

End-fläche (ʃ...) f ⓕ cryst. terminal face; **-geschwindigkeit** f, phys. terminal velocity; **-gültig** a. ⓕ final, ultimate conclusive; ~er Abschluß definite conclusion; ~ entscheiden to give a final decision, jur. to pronounce the final verdict (from which there is no appeal); **-gültigkeit** f conclusiveness, finality.

endigen (⌣) v/a. u. v/n. ⓕ = enden.

Endigung (⌣) f ⓕ = enden III.

Endivie ⚘ (⌣⌣) [nhd. 1500; it.] f ⓕ endive (Cichorium endivia); ~n-salat m lettuce(s pl.); weiß S. (green) salad.

End-knospe ⚘ (ʃ...) f ⓕ terminal bud; **-land** ⚘ n (narrow) tongue of land).

endlich (⌣) [mhd.] I a. ⓕ 1. (begrenzt) limited; phls. finite. — 2. (den Schluß bildend) final, ultimate; (unumstößlich) conclusive. — 3. (spät eintreffend) late. — II ~e(s) n ⓕ 4. phls. the finite; rel. das ~e the transient things pl. of this world. — III adv. 5. (s. 2) finally, ultimately, in the end. — 6. (s. 3) at last, at length; so sind Sie ~ doch gekommen! so you have come after all!

Endlichkeit (⌣⌣-) f ⓕ limitedness, limitation; phls.: finiteness.

end-los (ʃ...) a. ⓕ(D10) never ending, endless (a. ⚙); (unbegrenzt) unbounded, boundless, infinite; **-losigkeit** f ⓕ endlessness; boundlessness.

endogen ⚘ (⌣⌣́) [grch.] a. ⓕ (von innen heraus wachsend) endogenous.

Endosperm ⚘ (⌣⌣́) [grch.] n ⓛb. (Nährgewebe im Samenkorn) endosperm.

endossieren (a⌣L⌣) [fr.] = indossieren.

End-pfeiler (ʃ...) m, arch. main-abutment; **-punkt** m extreme (or farthest) point, (Ziel) goal, e-r Reise: destination; **-reim** m end-rhyme.

Endschaft (⌣) f ⓕ end, conclusion; s-e ~ erreichen to come to a close.

End-schraube ⚙ (ʃ...) f ⓕ Sattler-pad-screw; **-silbe** f final syllable; **-spiel** n Schach ꝛc.: final game; **-station** 🚂 f terminus; **-stück** n end-piece.

Endung (⌣) f ⓕ ending, termination.

End-ursache (ʃ...) ⓕ final cause; **-urteil** f final judgment; **-ziel** n, **-zweck** m final aim, ultimate object.

Energie (⌣⌣́) [grch.] f ⓕ (Tatkraft) energy; vigour; phys. aktuelle ~ (lebendige Kraft) actual (or effective, kinetic) energy; potentielle ~ (Spannkraft) potential en.; ~-los a. ⓕ(D10) lacking (or wanting in) energy, lackadaisical; **-losigkeit** f ⓕ lack (or want) of energy; **-strom** m ⓕ flow of energy.

energisch (⌣⌣́) [grch.] a. ⓕ (u. adv.) energetic(ally), vigorous(ly); ~e Sprache strong (or pithy, vigorous) language; ~ handeln, oft: to put one's shoulder to the wheel.

Enfilement ⚔ (a⌣mą́)[fr.] n ⓕ(Bestreichung mit Geschützen) enfilading, longitudinal firing, weit S. raking fire.

enfilieren ⚔ (a⌣L⌣)[fr.] v/a. ⓕ (der Länge nach beschießen) to enfilade, to sweep with longitudinal firing.

eng (⌣) [ahd.] a. ⓕ (ant. weit) 1. narrow, of limited space; bibl., ꝛc. bisw.: strait; in ~em Gewahrsam in close custody; adv. ~ sitzen (stehen) to sit (stand) closely together, to be huddled together; ⚔ ~e Quartiere close quarters pl.; ~e Wohnung cramped (or small) lodgings pl. — 2. (dicht anschließend) tight (breeches, ꝛc.); die Schuhe sind mir zu ~, auch: ... pinch me; adv. von Kleidern: sich ~ anlegen to fit tightly or like a glove; ~(er) machen to tighten, to narrow down; von Kleidern a.: to take in. — 3. fig. ~er Ausschuß select committee; im ~eren Sinne in a restricted (or narrower) sense; sein ~eres Vaterland his native district, in England: his native county; zur ~eren Wahl schreiten to proceed to the final election or ballot; adv. ~ verbunden intimately connected, closely allied; aufs (auf das) ~ste most closely or narrowly.

engagieren (a⌣gä-G⌣) [fr.] v/a. ⓕ ([an-]werben) to engage; zum Tanzen ~ to engage for the next dance; sehr engagiert (in Anspruch genommen) sein to be largely engaged or very busy; ⓒ engagiertes Kapital locked-up (auch: dead) capital; money sunk.

eng-anschließend (ʃ...) a. ⓕ tight(ly fitting); **-beleibt** a. very intimate; **-brüstig** a. short-winded, asthmatic(-al), vet. broken-winded; **-brüstigkeit** f ⓕ shortness of breath; asthma; vet. broken-windedness.

Enge (⌣) f ⓕ 1. (Engsein) narrowness, closeness, tightness. — 2. fig. (schwierige Lage) straits pl., embarassment, difficult position; e-n in die ~ treiben to drive a p. into a corner, to press (or push) him hard. — 3. (enger Ort) narrow pass(age); vgl. Engpaß, und Meer-enge.

⚕ scientific; ⚘ botanical; ⚲ geography; ⚙ machinery; ⚒ mining; ⚔ military; ↓ marine; ⓒ commercial; ✉ postal; 🚂 railway.

[Engel] — 320 — [entblößen]

Engel (ˇ) [ahd.; grch.; *pers. Bote] m ⓶ angel (✶ ~in f ㊼, etwa: angelic woman or being); liebkosend: pet, love, darling; *fig.* die ~ im Himmel pfeifen hören, etwa: to see stars; F es fliegt ein ~ durchs Zimmer (die Unterhaltung stockt) there is a dead stop in the conversation, the room is hushed in silence.

Engel=... (ˇ...) ⓶ vgl. Engels=...; =ähnlich *a.* ㊿ angel-like, angelic, seraphic; =brot n ⓶ angel's food; bfd. *rel.* (heavenly) manna.

Engelchen (ˇ..) n ㉓ (*dim. v.* Engel) little angel or cherub.

Eng(e)lein (ˇ(-)-) n ㉓ = Engelchen.

Engel=fisch (ˇ...) m *ichth.* angelfish (*Squati'naangelus*); =gleich a. ㊿ = =ähnlich.

engelhaft (ˇ..) a. ㊿ angelic.

Engel=hai (ˇ..) m ⓶ = =fisch; =macher(in f) m F *b.s.* baby-farmer; =macherei F f baby-farming; =mild a. ㊿, =rein a. (as) gentle (pure) as an angel.

Engels=angesicht (ˇ...) n ⓶, =bild n angel's image, angelic form; =burg f in Rom San (or St.) Angelo.

Engel=schar (ˇ...) f ⓶ choir (or host) of angels.

Engels=geduld (ˇ...) f ⓶ patience of an angel or of Job or of a lamb; =gesicht n = =bild; =gruß m, *eccl.* (Ave|=Maria) Angelic Salutation (Lut. 1,28); =güte f angelic kindness; =kind = =bild; =kopf m (, =köpfchen n little) angel's (or cherub's) head; =nähe f: ihre ~ her angelic presence.

Engel(s)=speise (ˇ...) f ⓶ = Engelbrot; =stimme f angel's voice.

Engel=füß ⁂ (ˇ...) n ⓶ (Tüpfelfarn): ⊕ polypody (*Polypo'dium vulg.*); =(§)zunge f angel's tongue.

Engel=taler (ˇ...) m ⓶ ehm. fl. Goldmünze: angel(ot); =wurz § f: ⊕ archangel (*Archange'lica offcina'lis*).

engen (ˇ) v/a. (und sich ꝛ v/refl.) ⓼ to (grow) narrow (= einengen).

Engerling (ˇ..) m ⓶ d. ent. (Larve des Maikäfers) larva (or grub) of the cockchafer.

Enger=werden (ˇ-ˇ-) n ㉓ growing narrower; tightening; shrinkage.

eng=halsig (ˇ...) a. ㊿ von Flaschen ꝛc.: narrow-mouthed; §herzig a. narrowminded; (genau) strait-laced; =herzigkeit f ㊻ narrow-mindedness.

England ⓺ (ˇˇ) [9.sae. Angel(n)=Land] npr/n. ⓷a. England.

Engländer (ˇˇ..) m ⓶, (~in f ㊼) Englishman (*pl.*...men), f Englishwoman (*pl.*...women); *coll.* die ~ *pl.*, the English (people); ~ei F (ˇˇ..ʲ) f ㊻ Anglomania.

Englein (ˇ..) n f. Eng(e)lein.

englisch¹ (ˇ..) (ˇ) [Engel] *a.* ㊿ = engelähnlich; der ꝛe Gruß = Engelsgruß.

englisch² (ˇˇ) [aus England] ⓺⓺ I a. English; ꝛe Kirche Anglican church, als Titel: Church of England; *path.* ꝛe Krankheit rickets; ꝛes Pflaster court-plaster; ꝛe Sprachwendung anglicism; *co.* sich ꝛ empfehlen to take French leave; *man.* ꝛ (sich) traben to go at a light trot. — II das ~(e) ⓺ a) (die ꝛe Sprache) English, the English language; ꝛ lernen, sprechen to learn, to speak English; das ~e radebrechen to murder the King's English; b) (das ꝛe Wesen) English ways (or customs, habits, ideas) *pl.*

englisch=amerikanisch (ˇˇ...) *a.* ㊿, =deutsch *a.* Anglo-American, -German, aber: ꝛes Wörterbuch English-German dictionary; =leder ⊕ n ⓶ (engl. Baumwollgewebe) sateen, satinet; =pflaster n f. englisch² I; =rot n (Eisenoxyd, das als Farbe ꝛc. dient) English red, colcothar.

englisieren (ˇˇˇˇ) ⓺⓺ = anglisieren 2.

Eng=paß (ˇˇ) m ⓶ (narrow) pass or strait, ⚔ defile.

en gros (ag̱ro') [fr.] adv. wholesale, in a large way, on a big scale.

Engros=geschäft ⓺ (g-grō'...) n ⓶, =handel m wholesale business; =händler, Engrossi'st m ⓶ wh. merchant or dealer; =preis m wh. price.

eng=spurig ⊕ (ˇ...) *a.* ㊿ narrow-gauge (line); =weg m ⓶ narrow path.

enharmonisch ♪ (ˇˇˇˇ) [grch.] *a* ㊿ (dem Klang, nicht Namen, nach gleich) enharmonic.

Enkaustik ⊕ (ˇˇˇˇ) f ㊻ (eingebrannte Wachsmalerei) encaustic painting.

enkaustisch ⊕ (ˇˇˇˇ) [grch.] *a.* ㊿ (u. *adv.*) encaustic(ally)

Enke¹ ⊕ (ˇ(-)) f ㊾ *hort.* = Absenker; ~ am Pfluge: plough-peg. [ploughboy.\

Enke² ⊕ (ˇ) m ㊹ (Ackerknecht) farm-hand,\

Enkel¹ (ˇˇ) [ahd. *dim.* zu Ahn] m ㊹, ~in f ㊼ (=sohn) grandson, f (=tochter) granddaughter, (=kind) grandchild; *coll.* die ~ (Nachkommen) descendants *pl.*

Enkel² nbb., mb. (ˇˇ) [ahd.: ankle] m ㊹ (Fußknöchel) ankle.

Enklave (a-k̄laˇˇ) [fr.] f ㊽ (von fremdem Gebiete umgebener Landesteil) enclave.

Enklitika ⊕ ㉗ (ˇˇˇˇˇˇ) [grch.] f ㊾, Enklitikon n ㉘(⑻) *gram.* (anhängbares Wort), **enklitisch** (ˇˇˇˇ) *a.* ㊿ enclitic.

Enlevage ⊕ (g-w-l-Q˘) [fr.] f ㊽ (Ätzbeuche) Zeugdruckerei: (chemical) discharge.

Enneandria ⊕ ♀ (ˇˇˇˇˇˇ) [grch.] f ㊾ (neunte Klasse nach Linné) enneandria; **enneandrisch** (ˇˇˇˇˇ) *a.* ㊿ (neunmännig: mit 9 Staubgefäßen) enneandrious.

ennuyant (g-nü-i-a') [fr.] a. ㊿ tiresome.

ennuyieren (ˇˇˇ-ˇˇ) [fr.] v/a. ㊿ (langweilen) to tire, to weary, F to bore.

enorm (-ˇ) [fr.] *a.* ㊿ (u. *adv.*) (ungeheuer) enormous(ly), huge(ly); ~ität (-ˇˇˇˇ) f ㊻ enormity. [by the way.\

en passant (ā̱ˇa') [fr.] adv. in passing,\

Enquete (g-t̄ˇˇ) [fr.] f ㊽ (amtliche Untersuchung) official inquiry.

enragiert (g-raG̱¹) [fr.] a. ㊿ (erbost) enraged; (begierig) eager.

Ensemble (a-ḇa'bl) [fr.] n ㉑ (das Ganze) ensemble, the whole, F the altogetherness.

ent=... (ˇ...) [ahd.: it. a'nte, grch. anti'] ㊷ Vorsilbe in Zssgn. mit *verbs*, immer untrennbar (*), bz. **1.** Beraubung, Befreiung, Trennung meist in transitiven, aus Dingwörtern gebildeten v., z.B. entfärben to discolour, entlarven to unmask. — **2.** Entfernen, Entweichen, z.B. entführen to carry off, entlaufen to run away. — **3.** Werden, Hervorkommen, Anfang, z.B. entsprießen to sprout forth.

ent=adeln (ˇˇˇ) v/a. ⓶a* to strip a p. of his noble rank; weits. to degrade.

ent=arten (ˇˇˇ) ⓶⓵* I v/n. (ʃn) und sich ꝛ v/refl. to degenerate; to deteriorate;

entartet degenerate, debased; sittlich. depraved. — II. ~ n ㉓ u. **Ent=artung** f ㊻ degeneration, degeneracy; deterioration; depravation, depravity.

Entase ⊕ (ˇˇˇ) ㊵, **Entasis** (ˇ-ˇˇ) ㊿ [grch.] f, *arch.* (Anschwellung eines Säulenschaftes) entasis, slight inflation of the shaft.

ent=äußer/n (ˇˇˇˇ) I v/a., mehr gbr. sich ꝛ v/refl. ⓶a* sich einer Sache (gen.) ꝛ to divest o.s. of a th., to part with a th., to discard (jur. to alienate) a th. — II =~ n ㉓ u. **E/ung** f ㊻ divestiture; jur. alienation; (Entsagung) renunciation.

e=t=band (ˇˇ) *impf. v.* entbinden.

entbehren (ˇˇˇˇ) [ahd.] v/a. ⓶* **1.** etwas ꝛ, a. einer Sache (gen.) ꝛ to miss (or lack) a th., to be deprived (or in want) of a th. — **2.** etwas freiwillig ꝛ to do (F to go) without a th., to forego a th.; to dispense with a th.; wir wollen es gern ꝛ we'll gladly make shift without it; wir können ihn nicht ꝛ we cannot spare him or part with him.

ent=behrlich (ˇˇˇˇ) *a.* ㊿ dispensable; needless; (überflüssig) superfluous; ~keit (ˇˇˇ-) f ㊺ dispensableness; needlessness; superfluousness.

Ent=behrung (ˇˇˇˇ) f ㊻ privation, want; =s=lohn m ⓶ co. interest = Zins(Zinsen).

ent=bieten (ˇˇˇˇ) v/a. ⓶a* **1.** e-m et. ꝛ (befehlen) to enjoin a th. on a p.; (zu wissen tun) to notify a th. to a p.; f-n Gruß ꝛ to send a p. one's kind regards. — **2.** e-n zu sich ꝛ (bescheiden) to summon a p. to one's presence, to send for a p.

ent=binden (ˇˇˇˇ) I v/a. u. sich ꝛ v/refl. ⓺* **1.** e-n von etwas ꝛ to dispense (or absolve) a. p. from a th.; e-n eines Eides, Versprechens ꝛ to release a p. from an oath, a promise. — **2.** vom Geburtshelfer, von der Hebamme: to deliver a woman of a child, to attend to a woman (in childbed) as accoucheur, as midwife; Wöchnerin: entbunden werden to be (safely) delivered of a child; von Zwillingen entbunden w. to give birth to twins, to be confined of twins. — **3.** chm. (freimachen) to disengage. — II. ~ n ㉓ u. **Ent=bindung** f ㊻ **4.** (f. 1) dispensation, release. — **5.** (f. 2) delivery, confinement; (fr.) accouchement. — **6.** (f. 3) disengagement.

Ent=bindungs=anstalt (ˇˇˇ...) f ⓶ lying-in hospital; =anzeige f announcement of a birth; =kunst f: ⊕ obstetric art, obstetrics; =zange f: ⊕ obstetrical forceps. — vgl. auch Gebär=...

ent=blätter/n (ˇˇˇˇ) ⓶a* I v/a. to strip (or denude) of leaves, ⊕ to defoliate; ꝛ e/t: ⊕ defoliate(d), denudate. — II sich ꝛ v/refl. to shed the leaves. — III ~ n ㉓ u. **Ent=blätt(e)rung** f ㊻: ⊕ defoliation, effoliation.

ent=blöde/n (ˇˇˇˇ) sich ꝛ v/refl. ⓶* **1.** ✶ (sich erdreisten) to be so bold as to //, not to be ashamed (or abashed) to //. — **2.** (sich scheuen) sie ꝛ sich nicht zu // they have the effrontery to //.

entblößen (ˇˇˇˇ) I v/a. u. sich ꝛ v/refl. ⓶* **1.** (sich) ꝛ to denude (o.s.), to divest (o.s.); das Haupt ꝛ to uncover (or bare) one's head; entblößt bare, nude; entblößten Hauptes bare-headed,

Zeichen (f. S. XVII): F familiär; P Volkssprache; ⎾ Gaunersprache; ✶ selten; † alt (auch gestorben); * neu (auch geboren); ⁺⁺ unrichtig;

[entbot] — 321 — [entflammen]

uncovered; ⚔ seine Flanken ≳ to expose one's flank (to an attack). — 2. fig. (sich) von etwas ≳ to strip or deprive (o.s.) of a thing; aller Mittel (von Geld) entblößt without any means (any money); destitute, F hard-up. — II ~ n ㉓ u. **Ent-blößung** f ㊻ 3. (f. 1) denudation; divestment; (Nacktheit) nudity. — 4. fig. (f. 2) deprivation; (Mangel) destitution.

ent-bot (⌣⌢) (u. **ent-böte** [⌣⌣⌣] subj.) impf., **ent-boten** (⌣⌣⌣) p.p. von entbieten.

ent-brach (⌣⌢ch) (u. **ent-bräche** [⌣⌣⌣] subj.) impf. v. entbrechen.

ent-brannt (⌣⌢) p.p., ≳e impf. v. ent-brennen. [⓶ a* = sich enthalten.

ent-brechen, fast † (⌣⌣⌣): sich ≳ v/refl.

ent-brennen (⌣⌣⌣) v/n. (fn) ⓶ b* to be inflamed, to blaze up; fig. to burn (vor with); to be kindled (auch vom Krieg 2c.). [p.p. v. entbrechen, entbinden.

ent-brochen (⌣⌣ch), **ent-bunden** (⌣⌣⌣)

Entchen (⌣⌣) n ㉓ [dim. von Ente] duckling, little (or young) duck; F liebkosend: duckie. [christianize.

ent-christlichen (⌣⌣⌣⌣⌣) v/a. ⓶ 8* to de-

ent-decken (⌣⌣⌣) I v/a. u. sich ≳ v/refl. ⓶ * 1. to discover a new country or fact; to find out the truth; to detect a crime, a mistake; to unravel (or un)fathom a mystery; to descry land. — 2. (kundtun) to reveal, to disclose; sich e-m ≳ to make o.s. known to a p.; e-m sein Herz ≳ to open one's heart (or to unbosom o.s.) to a p. — II ~ n ㉓ 3. — IV. — III **Ent-decker** (⌣⌣⌣) m ㉒, ~in f ㊵ 4. discoverer. — IV **Ent-deckung** (⌣⌣⌣) f ㊻ 5. (zu 1:) discovery; detection. — 6. (zu 2:) relevation.

Ent-deckungs-reise (⌣⌣⌣) f ㊻ voyage of discovery, exploring tour; **-reisende(r)** explorer.

Ente (⌣⌣) f [ahd. † t. a'năt- (ănăs)] f ㊻ 1. (weibliche) ~ (female) duck, ⚕ anas; vgl. Enterich; junge ~ = Entchen (f. d⸱s); vgl. a. Bisam-≳; schnattern, watscheln wie eine ~ to quack, to waddle like a duck; fig. wie eine bleierne ~ schwimmen to swim like a leaden duck or a stone. — 2. [nhd. 16. sae. P Lüg-≳ von Legende] (falsche Nachricht) false report (of the papers), (newspaper-)invention, hoax, fudge, (fr.) canard.

ent-ehren (⌣⌣⌣) I v/a. u. sich ≳ v/refl. ⓶ * 1. (sich) ≳ to disgrace (o.s.); to degrade (o.s.); to bring shame upon (o.s.); er steht entehrt da he stands dishonoured, his character is blasted. — 2. (in Verruf bringen) (sich) ≳ to bring (o.s.) into disrepute, to disparage. — 3. (schänden) to ravish, dishonour, take advantage of, seduce. — II **Ent-ehrer** (⌣⌣⌣) m ㉒, ~in f ㊵ 4. one who disgraces a p.; (Verleumder) defamer; (Schänder) ravisher, seducer. — III **Ent-ehrung** (⌣⌣⌣) f ㊻ 5. disgracing, degradation; (Verleumdung) defamation; (Schändung) rape, seduction.

ent-eignen (⌣⌣⌣) ⓶ b* I v/a. to expropriate, to dispossess. — II sich ≳ v/refl. sich e-r Sache ≳ to divest o.s. of a th., to part with a th. — III ~ n ㉓ u. **Ent-eignung(s-verfahren** n ㉒) f ㊻ (process of) expropriation.

ent-eilen (⌣⌣⌣) I v/n. (fn) ⓶ 8* to hasten (or hurry) away; (entfliehen) to escape, to run away; von der Zeit 2c.: to slip, to glide away (rapidly), to pass quickly. — II ~ n ㉓ flight, escape.

ent-eisen (⌣⌣⌣) [Eis] v/a. ⓿ * to free from (or to clear of) ice.

Enten-adler (⌣⌣⌣...) m ㉒ orn. osprey, sea-eagle; **-artig** a. ⓺ duck-like; **-beize** f duck-shooting; **-braten** m roast duck; **-dunst** m hunt. duck-shot; **-ei** n duck's egg; **-fang** m capture (or decoying) of (wild) ducks; **-flinte** f duckinggun; **-floß, -flott** n, **-grieß** m, **-grün** n, **-grütze** f ⚕ (Wasserlinse) duck-meat or -weed (Lemna); **-hagel** m, hunt. duckshot; **-herd** m decoy-(pond); **-jagd** f duck-shooting; **-muschel** f, zo. a) = Teichmuschel; b) barnacle (Lepas anatifera); **-pfuhl** m duck-pond; **-schlag** m duck-hunting.

Entente (a-ta-t⸱) [fr. Einverständnis] f ㊻ agreement; friendship; **Entente cordiale** cordial agreement or understanding; close friendship.

Enten-teich (⌣⌣⌣) m ㉒ duck-pond.

Enter (⌣⌣) [ndd.] m, n ㉒ (1jähr. Pferd) yearling, one-year-old.

Enter-beil ⚓ (⌣⌣...) n ㉒ boarding-axe.

ent-erben (⌣⌣⌣) I v/a. ⓶ * to disinherit, F to cut off with a farthing. — II ~ n ㉓ = IV — III **Ent-erbte([r]** m) f (⌣⌣⌣) ㊸ disinherited child or relative or person; die Enterbten the disinherited pl., the outcasts pl. of society. — IV **Ent-erbung** f ㊻ disinheritance, jur. bisw.: ⚖ exhereditation.

Enter-haken ⚓ (⌣⌣...) m ㉒ grapnel, grappling-irons pl.

Enterich (⌣⌣⌣) [ahd.: drake] m ⓶d. (männliche Zucht-ente) drake.

Enter-luken ⚓ (⌣⌣...) f/pl. boarding-scuttles pl.

enter/n ⚓ (⌣⌣⌣) [holl.; span.; *lt. intra're] I v/a. ⓶a. ein Schiff ≳ to grapple (or board) ... — II ~ n ㉓ = ㊵-ung.

Enter-netz ⚓ (⌣⌣⌣...) n ㉒, **-pike** f boarding-net, -pike. [ing.)

Enterung (⌣⌣⌣) f ㊻ grappling, board-

ent-fachen (⌣⌣ch) v/a. ⓶ * to set ablaze, to kindle (a. fig.); vgl. a. anfachen.

ent-fahren (⌣⌣⌣) v/n. (fn) ⓶b* to escape; to slip from (or out of) one's hands; Worte ≳ lassen to drop (or let slip) words.

ent-fallen (⌣⌣⌣) v/n. (fn) ⓶a* 1. to fall (or slip, drop) from a p.'s hands, &c.; fig. ihr Name ist mir ≳ ... has slipped (from) my memory, I cannot recall (or remember) ...; dir könnte der Mut ≳ your courage might give way or fail (you). — 2. es ≳ auf jeden 100 Mark £ 5 fall (or are apportioned to) each one('s share).

ent-falten (⌣⌣⌣) I v/a. u. sich ≳ v/refl. ⓺ *. 1. to unfold; (aufrollen) to unroll; (ausbreiten) to expand; die Stirn ≳ to unknit (or smooth) one's brow; von Blüten: sich ≳ to (burst) open, to bloom; voll entfaltet full-blown. — 2. (sich) ≳ (entwickeln) to develop (o.s.), to display (o.s.); (bilden) to form (o.s.). — II ~ n ㉓ u. **Ent-faltung** f ㊻ 3. (f. 1) unfolding; expansion. — 4. (f. 2) development, display, formation.

ent-färben (⌣⌣⌣) I v/a. u. sich ≳ v/refl. ⓶ * to discolour; ⓿ to decolorate; sich ≳ to lose (or change) colour; (bleichen) to grow pale or livid; (verblassen) to fade; vor Schreck entfärbte sie sich she turned pale with fright; sein Haar entfärbt sich (wird grau, weiß) his hair is turning (grey, white). — II ~ n ㉓ u. **Ent-färbung** f ㊻ discolouring; ⓿ decolor(iz)ation; change of colour; (Blässe) pallor, paleness; lividness.

ent-fasern (⌣⌣⌣) v/a. ⓶a* to divest of fibres; von Stoffen: to ravel out.

ent-fernbar (⌣⌣-) a. ⓺ removable.

ent-fernen (⌣⌣⌣) ⓶ * I v/a. 1. to remove (auch fig. from a post, an office); to put away or aside; aus dem Register ≳ (streichen) to strike off the register. — II sich ≳ v/refl. 2. to absent o.s.; to retire, withdraw; (verreisen) to depart, leave; (abweichen) to deviate from; sich heimlich ≳ to steal (or slip, sneak) away. — III ~ n ㉓ 3. = ㊵-ung.

ent-fernt (⌣⌣) a. ⓺ 1. removed; (entlegen) remote, distant, far (away); math. gleich weit ≳: ⓿ equidistant; fig. ich bin weit davon ≳ zu behaupten, daß // I am far from asserting that //; e-n von sich ≳ halten to keep a p. at a distance. — 2. ich habe nicht die Leste (geringste) Ahnung davon ... the least (or remotest, faintest) idea of it; adv.: ≳ verwandt distantly related; nicht im Lesten not in the least, not in the slightest (or faintest) degree.

ent-fernter-weise (⌣⌣-⌣⌣⌣) adv. remotely.

Ent-fernt-heit (⌣⌣-) f ㊻, **Ent-ferntsteh(e)n** (⌣⌣⌣¹(⌣)) n ㉓ remoteness.

Ent-fernung (⌣⌣⌣) f ㊻ 1. removal. — 2. absence, retirement, withdrawal; deviation; (Ferne) remoteness; (Abstand) distance; die ~ von Tokio bis Paris ist ganz bedeutend it is a far cry from T. to P.; ⚔ unerlaubte ~ absence without leave; ⚔ ~ eines Offiziers aus dem Heere cashiering; ast. größte (kleinste) ~ e-s Planeten von der Sonne: ⚕ aphelion (perihelion); auf kurze, weite ~ at a short, long range.

Ent-fernung=schätzen ⚔ (⌣⌣...) n ㉓ estimating distances.

ent-fesseln (⌣⌣⌣) I v/a. u. sich ≳ v/refl. ⓶a* (sich) ≳ to unchain (o.s.), to unfetter (o.s.); weitS. to release (o.s.); der entfesselte Prometheus Prometheus unbound; fig. die Kriegsfurie ≳ to kindle war, geh. Spr.: to unleash (sH. to let slip) the dogs of war. — II ~ n ㉓ u. **Ent-fesselung** (⌣⌣⌣⌣) f ㊻ unchaining, &c. (f. I); (Befreiung) release.

ent-festigen (⌣⌣⌣) v/a. u. sich ≳ v/refl. ⓶a* to dismantle a town.

ent-fetten ⓿ (⌣⌣⌣) v/a. ⓶ * to ungrease, to free from fat or grease or oil; to scour wool. [~=kur f = Bantingkur.)

Ent-fettung (⌣⌣⌣) f ㊻ ungreasing, &c.;

ent-fiedern (⌣⌣⌣) v/a. ⓶a* to pluck, to strip (or deprive) of feathers. [fallen.)

ent-fiel (⌣⌢) ind. u. ≳e subj. impf. v. ent-

ent-flammen (⌣⌣⌣) I v/a. (anzünden) to set alight or ablaze; fig. to inflame, to kindle; er entflammte ihren Mut he fired (or roused) their courage; von Wut entflammt incensed with rage;

♪ Musik; ⚕ Wissenschaft; ⚘ Pflanze; 🜨 Geographie; ⓿ Technik; ⚒ Bergbau; ⚔ Militär; ⚓ Marine; ❀ Handel; ✉ Post; 🚂 Eisenbahn.

[entfleischen] — 322 — [Enthaltsamkeit]

ₒd inflammatory (speech, &c.). — II v/n. (jn) u. sich ₂ v/refl. fig. to be(come) inflamed or incensed, to fire up.

ent-fleischen (⌣́⌣) v/a. ⓐ* to strip of flesh; entfleischt auch: fleshless; entfleischte Knochen bare bones. [away.]

ent-fliegen (⌣́⌣) v/n. (jn) ⓜa†* to fly/

ent-fliehen (⌣́⌣) v/n. (jn) ⓜb* to flee (or escape) from; F to make off, to take to one's heels; die Zeit ist entflohen the time has (or is) gone by.

ent-fließen (⌣́⌣) v/n. (jn) ⓜd* to flow away or off; in Tropfen: to trickle away or down; in Strömen: to gush forth.

ent-flog (u. -flöge), -flogen, -floh (u. -flöhe), -flohen, (⌣́(⌣) -floß (u. -flöße), -flossen (⌣́⌣) impf. (subj.) u. p.p. von entfliegen, entfliehen, entfließen.

ent-fremd/en (⌣⌣́) v/a. ⓐ* I v/a. e-m etwas ₂, etwas von e-m ₂ to estrange (or alienate) a p. from a th.; sich (dat.) das Herz j-s ₂ to alienate a p.'s heart. — II sich ₂ v/refl. to become a stranger to. — III ~ n ㉓ u. ₂/ung f ㊻ estrangement, alienation; v. Eigentum: larceny, pilfering; embezzlement.

ent-führen (⌣́⌣) I v/a. ⓑ* to carry off; mit Einwilligung der Entführten: to elope (or run away) with a girl, &c.; mit Gewalt: to abduct (or kidnap) a child, &c.; ₂ und heiraten to make a runaway match with a girl, &c. — II ~ n ㉓ = Entführung. [napper.]

Ent-führer (⌣́⌣) m ㉒ abductor, kidnapper/

Ent-führung (⌣́⌣) f ㊻ (s. entführen) elopement; runaway match; abduction.

ent-fuseln (⌣́⌣) v/a. ⓐa* Branntwein ₂ to free ... from fusel(-oil).

ent-galt (⌣⸥) ind. u. **ent-gälte** (⌣⌣⸥) subj. impf. v. entgelten. [lost or missed.]

Ent-gang (⌣⸥) m ⓪b. (Verlust) loss, s.th./

ent-gangen (⌣⌣⸥) p.p. v. entgehen.

ent-gegen (⌣⌣⸥) [abb.: again] I adv u. prp. mit dat. in opposition to; j-m Befehl ₂ contrary to (or despite) his injunction; auf, Gesellen, dem Feind ₂! up, boys, to meet the foe!; ↓ der Wind war uns ₂ we had a contrary wind, we faced the gale. — II als prädikatives a. = entgegengesetzt, vgl. sein. — III in Verbindung mit verbs (stets trennbar **), die meist den dat. regieren, und mit verbalem s., z. B.: e-m, e-r Sache ₂-arbeiten (₂...) v/n. (h.) ⓖ** to work against (or to oppose) a p., a th.; to thwart a person('s plans); (das) ~ n ㉓ gegen (the) opposition made against or offered to; ₂blicken v/n. (h.) ⓖ** to look forward to a th.; ₂bringen v/a. ⓕ** to carry a th. towards a p., fig. to meet a p.('s wishes) half-way; ₂duften v/n. (h.) ⓖ**: die Rosen duften uns entgegen the roses breathe (or waft) their (sweet) fragrance towards us; ₂eilen v/n. (jn) ⓖ** to hasten towards a p.; der Gefahr: to run into danger; dem Untergang: to rush (head-long) into destruction; ₂fahren v/n. (jn) ⓜb** to go to meet a p. by carriage or rail or boat or (bi)cycle, &c.; ₂geh(e)n v/n. (jn) ⓜa** to go to meet a p.; der Gefahr: to face (or brave, court) danger; die Dinge geh(e)n einer

Lösung entgegen matters are approaching a solution; ₂gesetzt a. ㊺ (gegenüberliegend) opposite; fig. contrary; (widerstrebend) repugnant; ich bin ₂er Meinung I am of the contrary (or of a different) opinion; in ₂er Ordnung in the reverse order; ₂enfalls adv. in the contrary case; ₂halten v/a. ⓐa** to hold out; vgl. ₂strecken; fig. (einwenden gegen) to object to; (in Gegensatz bringen zu) to contrast with; ₂handeln v/n. (h.) ⓖ** to act in opposition to; e-r Regel: to contravene (or infringe) a rule; vgl. ₂arbeiten, ~ n ㉓ contravention (or infringement) of a rule; ₂jauchzen ⓖ**, ₂jubeln ⓖa** v/n. (h.) to hail (or greet) a p. with jubilant sounds or with jubilation; ₂kommen v/n. (jn) ⓜ** to come to meet a p.; fig. to meet a person('s wishes) half-way; ₂d obliging, accommodating, compliant, kindly disposed; ~ n ㉓ obligingness, accommodating spirit; friendly advance; j-s ~ erwidern to respond to a p.'s advances; ₂laufen v/n. (jn) ⓜa**: a) to run towards (or up to) a p.; b) fig. von Meinungen: to run counter to, to clash with; ₂nahme f ㊺ reception; ₂nehmen v/a. ⓜa** to take s.th. offered, to receive; (annehmen) to accept; ~ n ㉓ acceptance; vgl. ₂nahme; ₂reisen ⓖ** (₂reiten ⓜb**) v/n. (jn) to go to meet a p. by rail, &c. (on horseback, &c.); ₂rücken v/n. (jn) ⓖ** to move (or push) towards; ₂ dem Feinde ₂ to march against the foe; ₂sehen v/n. (h.) ⓐa** to look forward to a th.; dem Tode ruhig ₂, oft: to look death calmly in the face; ⊙ einer baldigen Antwort ₂d awaiting an early reply; ₂sein v/n. (jn) ⓜa** to be opposed to a th.; ₂setzen v/a. ⓖ** to set against, to oppose; sich ₂ v/refl. to offer opposition to; ~ n ㉓ u. ₂setzung f ㊻ opposition; rhet.: ₂ antithesis; ₂steh(e)n v/n. (h., ↘ jn) ⓐa** to be opposed to; ₂stellen v/a. ⓖ**: a) = ₂setzen; b) = ₂halten fig.; ~ n ㉓ und ₂stellung f ㊻ = ₂setzung; ₂strecken v/a. ⓐa** to stretch out one's arms, hands towards; ₂treten v/n. (jn) ⓜd** to step up to; fig. to set o.s. (or one's face) against a p., a th.; ₂wirken v/n. (h.) ⓖ**, ~ n ㉓ = ₂arbeiten; ₂ziehen v/n. (jn) ⓜb** to advance (or march) towards.

ent-gegnen (⌣⌣⸥) I v/n. (h.) ⓑb* to reply, to answer; schlagend: to retort. —

II **Ent-gegnung** f ㊻ reply, answer; (schlagende Antwort) retort, repartee.

ent-geh(e)n (⌣́(⌣) v/n. (jn) ⓜa* 1. subjektiv mit dat.: to escape from danger, to elude (or get away from) one's pursuers; to avoid death. — 2. objektiv mit acc. ₂ lassen to let slip (from one's grasp or clutches); die Gelegenheit ₂ lassen to miss one's opportunity; sich (dat.) etwas nicht ₂ lassen to make sure of a th.; das Wort, der Fehler ist ihm entgangen ... escaped his observation or notice. — 3. v/impers. es kann ihm nicht ₂, daß // he cannot fail to notice that //, he cannot but perceive that //.

ent-geistern (⌣⌣⸥) v/a. ⓐa* to deprive of life or vitality; entgeistert lifeless, without animation, devitalized.

ent-geistigen (⌣⌣⸥) v/a. ⓐ* to strip (or deprive) of intellectual (or spiritual) qualities; entgeistigt void of intellectual (or spiritual) power.

Ent-gelt (⌣⸥, ⸥⸥) n (m) ⓪b. equivalent, (lt.) quid pro quo; (Lösegeld) ransom; (Lohn) remuneration, recompense; (Ersatz) compensation; gegen ~ for a consideration; ohne ~ without compensation or remuneration, gratuitously.

ent-gelten (⌣⌣⸥) I v/a. ⓜe(a)* etwas ₂ to suffer (or atone) for a th.; er soll es mir ₂ he shall smart (or F pay) for it; e-n etwas ₂ lassen to make a p. suffer for a th., F to pay him out for it. — II ~ n ㉓ u. **Ent-geltung** f ㊻ atonement; vgl. Entgelt.

ent-geltlich (⌣⌣⸥) a. ㊺ jur. ₂er Vertrag contract involving monetary considerations. [gehen.]

entging (⌣⸥) ind. u. ₂e subj. impf. v. ent-/

Ent-glasung (⌣⌣⸥) f ㊻ (Kristallitenbildung im Glasfluß) devitrification.

ent-gleis/en 🚆 (⌣⌣⸥) I v/n. (jn) ⓖ* to run off the line or the rails, to derail. — II ~ n ㉓ u. ₂/ung f ㊻ derailment.

ent-gleiten (⌣⌣⸥) v/n. (jn) ⓜb* to slip from one's hands; to glide past.

ent-glimmen (⌣⌣⸥) v/n. (jn) ⓜa* to begin to glow; to catch fire.

ent-glitt (⌣⸥) ind., ₂e subj. impf. u. ₂en (⌣⸥) pp. v. entgleiten.

ent-glomm (⌣⸥) ind. impf., ₂en p.p. u. **ent-glömme** subj. impf. v. entglimmen.

ent-glühen (⌣⌣⸥) v/n. (jn) ⓜa†* to burn (or flare) up; vgl. entglimmen.

ent-gölte (⌣⌣⸥) subj. impf., **ent-golten** (⌣⌣⸥) p.p. von entgelten.

ent-göttern (⌣⌣⸥) v/a. ⓐa* (der Götter berauben) to deprive of gods or deities.

Ent-granner ⊙ (⌣⌣⸥) m ㉒ agr. für Gerste ₂c.: hummeller, hummelling-machine.

ent-gräten (⌣⌣⸥) v/a. ⓐ* to bone fish.

ent-gürten (⌣⌣⸥) v/a. ⓐ* to ungird, unbelt, to take the belt off a p.

ent-haaren (⌣⌣⸥) I v/a. ⓐ* to strip of hair, ↗ to depilate. — II ~ n ㉓ u. **Ent-haarung** f ㊻ depilation; ₂smittel ("...") n ㉒: ↗ depilatory.

ent-halftern (⌣⌣⸥) v/a. ⓐa* to unhalter (or to loosen the halter of) a horse.

ent-halten (⌣⌣⸥) ⓐa** (p.p. ₂) I v/a. to contain; (in sich fassen) to hold, comprise, comprehend; in et. mit ₂ sein to be included in a th.; wie oft ist 4 in 12 ₂? how many times does 4 go into 12?, Schule a. how many fours make twelve? — II sich ₂ v/refl. to abstain from a th.; sich der Abstimmung ₂ to refrain from voting; sich der Tränen ₂ to keep back one's tears; ich muß mich des Urteils darüber ₂ ... defer (or postpone) my judgment upon it; ich kann mich nicht ₂ zu kritisieren I cannot help (or forbear) criticizing.

ent-haltsam (⌣⸥⸤) a. ㊺ im Essen u. Trinken: abstemious, frugal; bisw.: abstentious, abstinent; (nüchtern) sober; (mäßig) moderate, im Trinken: temperate; ~**keit** (⌣⸥⸤⸤) f ㊻ abstemiousness, frugality; sobriety; moderation; im Trinken

---

Signs (see page XVII): F familiar; P vulgar; Ⲡ flash; ↘ rare; † obsolete (died); * new word (born); +⁺+ incorrect; ♪ music;

[Enthaltung] — 323 — [Entleiher]

temperance; v. allen geistigen Getränken: (total) abstinence; F teetotalism.

Ent-haltung (⌣‿⌣) f ⊕ (f. enthalten II) abstention from voting, &c.; abstinence in eating and drinking; forbearance; j. der ~ übt abstainer, a. abstentionist.

ent-haupten (⌣‿⌣) I v/a. ⊕* to behead, decapitate. — II ~ n ㉓ u. **Ent-hauptung** f ⊕ beheading, decapitation.

ent-häuten (⌣‿⌣) I v/a. ⊕* to skin; hunt. to uncase; ☛ to excoriate. — II ~ n ㉓ u. **Ent-häutung** f ⊕ skinning; ☛ excoriation.

ent-heben (⌣‿⌣) I v/a. u. sich ⚖ v/refl. ⓑ (⑦)b* e-n (sich) e-r Sache (gen.) ob. von et. ⚖ to free (or deliver) a p. (o.s.) from a th.; von etwas Lästigem: to exonerate (or exempt) from a th.; vgl. entbinden 1; e-n j-s Amtes ⚖ to remove (or dismiss) a p. from his post or situation, to suspend a p.; enthebe dich! be gone!, bibl. get thee hence! — II ~ n ㉓ u. **Ent-hebung** f ⊕ (f. I) deliverance; exoneration, exemption; removal, dismissal, suspension.

ent-heilig/en (⌣‿⌣) I v/a. ⊕* to desecrate, profane. — II ~ n ㉓ = ⚖ung. **Ent-heiliger** (⌣‿⌣) m ㉒, ~in f ㊼ desecrator, profaner. [profanation.] **Ent-heiligung** (⌣‿⌣) f ⊕ desecration,}

ent-hielt (⌣‿) ind., ⚖e subj. impf. v. enthalten. — **ent-hob** (⌣‿) ind. impf., ⚖en (⌣‿⌣) p.p., **ent-höbe** (✱ **ent-hübe**) subj. impf. von entheben.

ent-hüll/en (⌣‿⌣) I v/a. u. sich ⚖ v/refl. ⊕* (sich) ⚖ to uncover (o.s.); ein Denkmal (feierlich) ⚖ to unveil a monument; fig. to reveal, to disclose. — II ~ n ㉓ u. ⚖ung f ⊕ uncovering, &c. (f. I); fig. revelation; disclosure.

ent-hülsen (⌣‿⌣) v/a. ⊕* = aushülsen; Kaffeebohnen: to pulp; **Ent-hülser** ⊕ m ㉒, **Ent-hülsungs-maschine** f ⑫ hulling- (für Kaffee: pulping-)machine.

ent-hüpfen (⌣‿⌣) v/n. (fn) ⊕* to hop (or skip, jump) away.

enthusiasmieren (⌣‿(⌣)⌣‿) [grch.] ⊕ to fill with enthusiasm; to enrapture.

Enthusiasmus (⌣‿(⌣)⌣‿) [grch.] m ㉗ (Begeisterung) enthusiasm.

Enthusiast (⌣‿(⌣)⌣‿) m ㉒ enthusiast.

enthusiastisch (⌣‿(⌣)⌣‿) a. ⊕ (u. adv.) (begeistert) enthusiastic(ally).

Enthymem ☛ (⌣‿⌣) [grch.] n ①c. log. (abgekürzter Vernunftschluß) enthymeme.

Entität ☛ (⌣‿‿) [spät-lt.] f ⊕ phls. (Sein, Wesen) entity, being, essence.

ent-joch/en (⌣‿⌣) I v/a. ⊕* Ochsen ⚖ to unyoke...; fig. ein Volk ⚖ to deliver... — II ⚖ung f ⊕ unyoking; deliverance.

ent-kam (⌣‿) ind., **ent-käme** (⌣‿⌣) subj. impf. v. entkommen.

ent-keimen (⌣‿⌣) v/n. (fn) ⊕* to germ, germinate, sprout, spring up; *v/a. to sterilize = sterilisieren].

ent-kernen (⌣‿⌣) v/a. ⊕* = auskernen.

ent-kleid/en (⌣‿⌣) I v/a. u. sich ⚖ v/refl. ⊕* 1. to undress, disrobe, strip; sich ⚖ to undress (o.s.), to take off one's clothes. — 2. fig. einer Sache (gen.) ober von et. ⚖ to divest (or denude, deprive) of a th. — II ~ n ㉓ u. **Ent-kleidung** f ⊕ 3. undressing, disrobement; fig. divestiture.

ent-knospen (⌣‿⌣) v/n. (fn) u. sich ⚖ v/refl. ⊕* to unfold, to (break) open.

ent-kohlen (⌣‿⌣) I v/a. ⊕* chm. to decarbonize. — II ~ n ㉓ u. **Ent-kohlung** f ⊕ chm. decarbonization.

ent-kommen (⌣‿⌣) I v/n. (fn) (p.p. ⚖) ⊕* = entgehen 1; mit genauer Not ⚖ F to escape by the skin of one's teeth. — II ~ n ㉓ escape; an ein ~ war nicht zu denken flight was out of the question.

ent-koppeln (⌣‿⌣) v/a. ⊕* hunt. Jagdhunde ⚖ to unleash hounds.

ent-korken (⌣‿⌣) v/a. ⊕* eine Flasche to uncork a bottle. [⚖ to gin cotton.]

ent-körnen ⊕ (⌣‿⌣) v/a. ⊕* Baumwolle} **Ent-körner** ⊕ (⌣‿⌣) m ㉒ von Baumwolle: ginner. [embody.}

ent-körpern (⌣‿⌣) v/a. ㉒a* to dis-}

ent-kräft(ig)en (⌣‿(⌣)⌣‿) ⊕(⊕)* I v/a. u. sich ⚖ v/refl. 1. (sich) ⚖ (schwächen) to weaken (o.s.), enfeeble, debilitate (o.s.); (entnerven) to enervate (o.s.); (abnutzen) to wear (o.s.) out, to exhaust (o.s.); fig. (mildern) to extenuate; Beweise ⚖ (widerlegen) to refute ... — 2. jur. (ungültig m.) to invalidate a decree; to quash a verdict. — II ~ n ㉓ u. **Entkräft(ig)ung** f ⊕ 3. (f. I) weakening, enfeeblement, debilitation; enervation; exhaustion; extenuation; refutation; path. debility, ☛ inanition. — 4. (f. 2) invalidation.

ent-kriechen (⌣‿⌣) v/n. (fn) ⓑdf* to creep (or crawl) out (of or from).

ent-kroch (⌣‿) ind. impf., ⚖en (⌣‿⌣)p.p., **ent-kröche**(⌣‿⌣) subj.impf. von entkriechen.

ent-kuppeln ⊕ (⌣‿⌣) v/a. ㉒a* mach. to uncouple, disconnect, ungear.

ent-laden (⌣‿⌣) ⊕b* (p.p. ⚖) I v/a. = ausladen 1. — 2. ⚔ u. phys. to discharge. — II sich ⚖ v/refl. 3. vom Gewitter: to burst, to break; von Feuerwaffen: to go off; von Sprengstoffen: to explode. — III ~ n ㉓ 4. = Entladung.

Ent-lader ⊕ (⌣‿⌣) m ㉒ elect. discharger, discharging-rod.

Ent-ladung (⌣‿⌣) f ⊕ (f. entladen I u. II) discharge; explosion.

ent-lang (⌣‿) [ndd.] adv. u. prp. mit vorangehendem acc. oder an mit dat.: den Fluß ⚖ (ob. an dem Flusse ⚖) along (or by the side of) the river; dem, das Ufer ⚖ along the bank; denselben Weg ⚖ by the same route; an e-m Felde ꝛc. ⚖ geh(e)n (fahren, reiten) to skirt a field, &c.; ↓ der Küste ⚖ fahren to sail along the coast, to hug the shore.

ent-larv/en (⌣‿⌣) I v/a. u. sich ⚖ v/refl. ⊕* to unmask (auch fig.). — II ~ n ㉓ u. **Ent-larvung** f ⊕ unmasking.

ent-lass/en (⌣‿⌣) v/a. ⊕a* (p.p. ⚖) 1. to dismiss, discharge, pay off; Dienstboten a. to give notice to, to part with; Beamte: to remove; (fortschicken) to send away (F adrift), to turn off; stärker: F to (give the) sack; ⚖ werden to be dismissed or discharged, F to get the sack. — 2. Beamte ꝛc. ⚖ (pensionieren) to pension ... off; ⚔ ↓ Mannschaften ⚖ to discharge men, ↓ to pay off the crew; Offiziere: to put on the retired-list, mit Halbsold: on half-pay, strafweise: to cashier; Sklaven: to set free, to emancipate; Sträflinge: to discharge, to release; ⚔ Truppen: to disband; Soldaten als dienstuntauglich⚖ to invalid soldiers; als dienstuntauglich ⚖ p. p. invalided.

Ent-lassung (⌣‿⌣) f ⊕ (vgl. entlassen:) 1. dismissal, discharge; removal (from office); F sack(-ing). — 2. retirement; emancipation; release; von Sträflingen auch: jaildelivery; seine ~ einreichen to send in (or to tender) one's resignation; j-e ~ nehmen to resign (one's office); to throw (or give) up one's appointment; to retire (from a post).

Ent-lassungs-gesuch (⌣‿⌣...) n ㉒ (tendered) resignation; =schein m dischargepaper, -ticket; für vorläufig entlassene Sträflinge: ticket-of-leave; =schreiben n dismissory (letter); =zeugnis n = =schein.

ent-last/en (⌣‿⌣) I v/a. ⊕* 1. to unburden, unload, discharge; sich ⚖ v/refl. fig. to exonerate o.s. — 2. ⚖ e-n für eine Summe ⚖ to credit a p. for a certain amount; to put a sum to a p.'s credit. — II ~ n ㉓ u. ⚖ung f ⊕ 3. discharge; exoneration; ⚖crediting.

Ent-lastungs-bogen ⊕ (⌣‿⌣...) m arch. discharging-(or relieving-)arch; =zeuge m witness for the defence.

ent-lauben (⌣‿⌣) v/a. u. sich ⚖ v/refl. ⊕* = entblättern I u. II; die Buchen ⚖ sich the beeches are shedding their leaves or their foliage; **Ent-laubt-sein** (⌣‿,⌣) n ㉓ leaflessness; vgl. entblättern III.

ent-lauf/en (⌣‿⌣) I v/n. (fn) ⓑaft* (p.p. ⚖) to run away (f-n Eltern from one's parents); F to give a p. the slip; von Soldaten: to desert from the army; vgl. entfliehen. — II ~ n ㉓ u. ⚖ung f ⊕ running away; desertion; escape.

ent-ledigen (⌣‿⌣) I v/a. u. sich ⚖ v/refl. ⊕* (freimachen ob. =setzen) to (set) free, deliver, discharge, release; der Fesseln ⚖ to unfetter, to unchain; sich j-s, e-r Sache ⚖ to rid o.s. of a p., a th.; sich e-s Auftrages ⚖ to execute (or F do) a commission; sich seiner Pflicht ⚖ to acquit o.s. of a duty; sich der Sorge ⚖ to cast (or throw) off care; sich einer Verbindlichkeit ⚖ to discharge (or perform) an obligation. — II ~ n ㉓ u. **Ent-ledigung** f ⊕ (f. I) deliverance, discharge, riddance, execution; acquittance; discharge; performance.

ent-leer/en (⌣‿⌣) I v/a. ⊕* = ausleeren; physiol. to eject, void, emit. — II ⚖ung f ⊕ emptying; ejection, emission.

ent-legen (⌣‿⌣) a. ⊕(D9) distant, remote; far away; far off; ⚖e Örter out-of-the-way places; ~heit (⌣‿⌣‿) f ⊕ (long) distance from, remoteness.

ent-lehnen (⌣‿⌣) v/a. ⊕* e-m et. ob. et. von e-m ⚖ to borrow a th. of (or from) a p.; schriftstellerisch: b.s. to plagiarize; fig. (herleiten) to drive from. — II ~ n ㉓ = ⚖ung. [aus Büchern: b.s. plagiarist.} **Ent-lehner** (~) m ㉒, ~in f ㊼ borrower,}

Ent-lehnung (~) f ⊕ borrowing; loan; plagiarism; (Herleitung) derivation.

ent-leib/en (⌣‿⌣) I mst sich ⚖ v/refl. ⊕* to slay (or make away with) o.s.; to commit suicide. — II **Ent-leibung** f ⊕ (Selbst-)⚖ung suicide.

ent-leihen (⌣‿⌣) v/a. ⊕* = entlehnen.

Ent-leiher (~) m ㉒, ~in f ㊼ borrower.

☛ scientific; ⚘ botanical; ♁ geography; ⊕ machinery; ⚒ mining; ⚔ military; ↓ marine; ⊛ commercial; ✉ postal; 🚆 railway.

[Entleihung] — 324 — [entscheidbar]

Ent-leihung (⌣⌢⌣) f ⑯ = Entlehnung.
Entlein (⌣⌢) n ㉓ = Entchen.
ent-lieh (⌣⌢) ind., ₂e subj. impf. u. ₂en p.p. v. entleihen. [lassen.]
ent-ließ (⌣⌢) ind., ₂e subj. impf. v. ent-⌡
Ent-lobung (⌣⌢⌣) f ⑯ F co. (ant. Verlobung) breaking off an engagement.
ent-locken (⌣⌢⌣) ⑱*: e-m etwas ₂ to draw (or elicit, wheedle) a th. from a p. by flattery, &c.; vgl. ablocken.
ent-lodern (⌣⌢⌣) ⑱a* = auflodern.
ent-lohnen (⌣⌢⌣) v/a. ⑱* Arbeiter ₂ to pay off ...
Ent-lüftungs=ventil ⊕ (⌣⌢⌣...) n ㉖ für Pumpen, Dampfmäntel ꝛc.: ventilating valve (for letting off foul gases).
ent-mannen (⌣⌢⌣) I v/a. ⑱* to castrate; fig. to emasculate, enervate, unman, undo, unnerve; (schwächen) to enfeeble. — II ~ n ㉓ u. **Ent-mannung** f ⑯ castration, emasculation, enervation.
ent-masten ↓ (⌣⌢⌣) v/a. ⑱* to unmast, dismast, unrig, to deprive of masts; entmastet without masts or a mast.
ent-menschen (⌣⌢⌣) I v/a. ⑱* to divest of human attributes or feeling, to dehumanize, stärker: to brutalize; entmenscht inhuman. — II ~ n ㉓ u. **Ent-menschung** f ⑯ brutalization; **Ent-menschtheit** f ⑯ inhumanity.
ent-mündigen (⌣⌢⌣) I v/a. ⑱* e-n ₂ to declare a p. incapable of managing his affairs. — II ~ n ㉓ u. **Ent-mündigung** f ⑯ interdiction.
ent-mutigen (⌣⌢⌣) I v/a. ⑱* to discourage, to dishearten; entmutigt despondent; ✕ demoralized. — II ~ n ㉓ u. **Ent-mutigung** f ⑯ discouragement; despondency; demoralization.
ent-nahm (⌣⌢) ind. impf. v. entnehmen.
Ent-nahme ⊕ (⌣⌢⌣) f ⑯ bei ~ v. 2 Pfund on taking (or purchasing) two pounds.
ent-nähme (⌣⌢⌣) subj. impf. v. entnehmen.
ent-nehmen (⌣⌢⌣) v/a. ⑱a* 1. (entlehnen) to take (or draw, borrow) from; ⊕ auf e-n (durch eine Tratte) ₂ (sich auf e-n erholen) to draw upon a p. for a certain sum. — 2. fig. = abnehmen 5; ⊕ wir aus Ihrem Briefe we understand (or gather) from your letter.
Ent-nehmer ⊕ (⌣⌢⌣) m ⑳ drawer of a bill.
Ent-nehmung (⌣⌢) f ⑯ drawing (or borrowing) from; ⊕ drawing upon a p.
ent-nerv/en (⌣⌢⌣) I v/a. ⑱* to enervate, to unnerve; entnervt enervate(d). — II ~ n ㉓ u. **E/ung** f ⑯ enervation; weakening of the nerves.
ent-nommen (⌣⌢⌣) p.p. v. entnehmen.
ent-nüchtern (⌣⌢⌣) v/a. ⑱ a* = ernüchtern.
ent-ölen (⌣⌢⌣) v/a. ⑱* to unoil; to free cocoa, &c. from (its) oil.
Entomolog, ~e ⌧ (⌣⌢⌣⌣) [grch.] m ⑫, ⑭ entomologist; ~ie (⌣⌣⌣⌢) f ⑯ (Insektenkunde) entomology; ₂isch ⌧ (⌣⌢⌣⌣) a. ⑲ entomological.
Entozo-en ⌧ (⌣⌣⌢⌣) [grch.] n/pl. zo. (Eingeweidewürmer) entozoa(ns), intestinal worms pl.
ent-puppen (⌣⌢⌣): sich ₂ v/refl. ⑱* ent. vom Schmetterling: to break (or burst) the cocoon, to change from a pupa or chrysalis (into a butterfly); fig. to throw off one's disguise or mask

ent-quellen (⌣⌢⌣) v/n. (fn) ⑬b* to gush (or bubble, burst) forth from a rock, &c.
ent-quoll (⌣⌢) ind. impf., ₂en (⌣⌢⌣) p.p. u. **ent-quölle** subj. impf. von entquellen.
ent-raffen (⌣⌢⌣) v/a. ⑱*: e-m etwas ₂ to snatch a th. from a p.
ent-raten fast † (⌣⌢⌣) v/a. u. v/n. (h.) ⑬a* (p.p. ₂) et. (acc.) ob. e-r Sache (gen.) ₂ to dispense with a th.; f. entbehren 2.
ent-rätsel/n (⌣⌢⌣) I v/a. ⑱a* to decipher manuscripts, writings; to unriddle dark sayings; to unravel (or to clear up, to disentangle) a mystery; to solve a problem. — II **E/ung** f ⑯ decipherment, unravelling, disentanglement.
Entrechat (ątr-schā') [fr.] m ⑲ (Kreuzsprung) beim Tanzen: cut(ting); pl. mst: capers.
ent-rechten (⌣⌢⌣) v/a. ⑱* Verbrecher ꝛc. ₂ (der bürgerlichen Rechte berauben) to deprive of (civic or civil) rights.
Entrée (ą-trē') [fr.] f ⑤, n ⑪ 1. f (Eintritt, Zugang) entrance. — 2. n (P m) (Vestibül, Korridor) entrance-hall. — 3. f (Vorspeise) first dish (nicht: entrée). — 4. n (Eintrittsgeld) entrance- (or gatе-) money; (fee of) admission.
ent-reißen (⌣⌢⌣) v/a. ⑱a* 1. e-m et. ₂ to snatch (or wrest) a th. from a p.('s grasp); weitS. (wegnehmen) to take a th. away from a p.; er ward ihr entrissen he was torn from her; vgl. entringen. — 2. der Gefahr ₂ to save (or rescue) from danger; der Vergessenheit entrissen saved from oblivion.
entre nous (ątr-nū') [fr.] between ourselves, between you and me.
Entrepôt (ątr-pō') [fr.] n ⑪ 1. (Lagerhaus) bonded store or warehouse; in ~ geben (to put in) bond. — 2. a. ~=platz m ⑫ (Stapelplatz) (fr.) entrepôt.
Entrepreneur (ątr-pr²-nö'r) [fr.] m ⑭d. (⑪) (Unternehmer) (building-, &c.) contractor ⑭ (⑪): undertaker.
Entreprise (⌣prī'-ʒ⌣) f ⑯ (Unternehmen) undertaking, enterprise; (Verdingung e-r Arbeit) contract.
Entresol (ątr-zō'l) [fr.] m, n ⑲ (Zwischengeschoß) intermediate story. [view.]
Entrevue (ątr-mü') [fr.] f ⑯ (Zusammenkunft) inter-⌡
ent-richt/en (⌣⌢⌣) I v/a. ⑱* e-m et. ₂ to pay a p. (for) s.th., to discharge a debt to a p., to render thanks to a p.; Zoll auf et. ₂ to pay duty on s.th. — II ~ n ㉓ u. **E/ung** f ⑯ payment, discharge.
ent-riegeln (⌣⌢⌣) v/a. ⑱a* = aufriegeln.
ent-rieseln (⌣⌢⌣) v/n. (fn) ⑬a* to ripple from; vgl. entquellen. [v. entraten.]
ent-riet (⌣⌢) ind., ₂e (⌣⌢⌣) subj. impf.⌡
ent-ringen (⌣⌢⌣) ⑬f* I v/a. to wring (or wrench) from a p.('s hands). — II sich ₂ v/refl. to break forth, escape.
ent-rinnen (⌣⌢⌣) I v/n. (fn) ⑬b(a)* 1. to run (or flow) from; von der Zeit: to slip (or pass) away. — 2. (entfliehen) to escape, to flee; vgl. entgehen 1. — II ~ n ㉓ 3. (f. 2) escape, flight.
ent-rippen ⊕ (⌣⌢⌣) v/a. ⑱* = ausrippen.
ent-riß (⌣⌢) ind. impf., **ent-risse(n** p. p.) subj. impf. v. entreißen.
ent-rollen (⌣⌢⌣) I v/n. (fn) to roll down (or away) from; von Tränen: to stream (or trickle down) one's eyes; von Wagen: to roll away. — II v/a. sich ₂ v/refl. = aufrollen 6; ein Bild

von etwas ₂ to unfold (or sketch) a (graphic) picture of s.th.
ent-ronnen (⌣⌢⌣) p.p. von entrinnen.
Entropie (⌣⌣⌢) [grch.] f ⑯ phys. (innere Wärme-energie) entropy.
ent-rück/en (⌣⌢⌣) I v/a. und sich ₂ v/refl. ⑱* to remove from; to put beyond the reach of; sich den Blicken ₂ (entziehen) to withdraw from public view; geh. Spr.: sterblichen Augen entrückt moved (or wafted) out of (human) sight; poet. beyond mortal ken; irdischen Sorgen entrückt beyond the reach (or grasp) of earthly cares. — II ~ n ㉓ u. **E/ung** f ⑯ removal; withdrawal.
ent-rüst/en (⌣⌢⌣) [mhd.] I v/a. sich ₂ v/refl. ⑱* 1. (in Unwillen versetzen) to fill with indignation; sich ₂ to become indignant. — 2. (erzürnen) to provoke, irritate, rouse; sich ₂ to grow angry; (heftig) entrüstet in (great) anger or wrath; in a (towering) rage. — II **Entrüstung** f ⑯ 3. indignation; (Zorn) anger, wrath, rage; e-n Schrei der~ erheben to raise a cry of indignation or an outcry.
ent-sag/en (⌣⌢⌣) I v/a. ⑱* e-r Sache (dat.) ₂ to renounce worldly pleasures, to abandon (or waive) a claim, to resign (or throw up) a good position; to abdicate the throne; to give up beer, spirits, wine; ein geistigen Getränken ~der an abstainer. — II ~ n ㉓ und **E/ung** f ⑯ (f. I) renunciation; resignation; abdication of the throne.
ent-sandt (⌣⌢) p.p., ₂e ind. impf. von entsenden.
ent-sank (⌣⌢) ind., **ent-sänke** (⌣⌢⌣) subj. impf. v. entsinken.
ent-sann (⌣⌢) ind., **ent-sänne** (⌣⌢⌣) subj. impf. v. entsinnen.
Ent-satz ✕ (⌣⌢) m ⑬a. relief, (Entsetzung) raising the siege of a town; zum ~ e-s Heeres ꝛc. kommen to come to relieve (or succour) an army, &c.
Ent-satz=heer (⌣⌢...) n ⑫, =truppen f/pl. relief-column, succour.
ent-säuer/n (⌣⌢⌣) I v/a. ⑱* chm. to free from acid, durch Wasser: to sweeten, ⌧ to edulcorate; durch Basen: to neutralize. — II ~ n ㉓, **E/ung** f ⑯ chm. neutralization; a..: ⌧ deacidification.
Entsch. abbr. = Entscheidung.
ent-schädig/en (⌣⌣⌣) I v/a. und sich ₂ v/refl. ⑱* to indemnify (or compensate) a p. for a loss; to reimburse a p. for money spent; to make amends to a p. for an injury or insult; to remunerate a p. for services rendered; sich für et. ₂ to cover (or make up) a loss; to recoup (or reimburse) o.s. for s.th. — II **E/ung** f ⑯ (f. I) indemnification, compensation; reimbursement; amends pl.; remuneration; gegen ~, auch: for a consideration; vor Gericht ~ erhalten (verlangen) to recover (to claim) damages.
Entschädigungs=anspruch(⌣...) m ⑫ claim for damages, =betrag m indemnity, amount of damages; =klage f action for damages, =summe f = =betrag.
Ent-scheid (⌣⌢) m ⑫c. decision (arrived at); jur. judgment (given), sentence (pronounced).
ent-scheidbar (⌣⌢-) a. ⑲ determinable.

Zeichen (s. S. XVII): F familiär; P Volkssprache; ⌐ Gaunersprache; ⌧ selten; † alt (auch gestorben); * neu (auch geboren); ✛ unrichtig;

[entscheiden]   — 325 —   [entspringen]

ent-scheiden (⌣́⌣) I v/a. u. sich ⁀ v/refl. ⑨(e)fit* 1. (sich) ⁀ to decide, to determine; durch e-n Spruch ⁀ to pass (or pronounce) a judgment upon; auch: to pronounce upon; als Schiedsrichter: to arbitrate upon disputes; sich für (gegen) e-n ⁀ to decide for (against) a p.; es muß sich jetzt ⁀ it must now be decided (or settled). — II ⁀d p.pr. und a. ⑥ 2. in den Beb. des inf. — 3. (endgültig) decisive, conclusive, final; im ⁀den Augenblick at the critical moment; ⁀de Stimme (des Vorsitzenden) casting vote (of the chairman). — III 4. ent-schieden p.p. u. a. f. bs. — IV Ent-scheidung f ⑥ 5. (arriving at a) decision; determining, determination; jur. (final) judgment or sentence; arbitration; der Geschworenen: verdict; path., &c. crisis; eine ⁀ treffen to come to a decision, to take one's choice; wenn's zur ⁀ kommt when it comes to the point or the push.

Ent-scheidungs=grund (⌣⌣́…) m ⑫ motive; final reason; =punkt m critical (or turning-)point, crisis; =schlacht f decisive battle; =stimme f casting vote; =stunde f critical (bisw. supreme) hour; ⁀voll a. ⑥ decisive, fatal, big with fate; =zeichen n, med. critical symptom. [v. entscheiden.

ent-schied (⌣́) ind., ⁀e (⌣́⌣) subj. impf.]
ent-schieden (⌣́⌣) I p.p. in den Beb. des inf. entscheiden. — II a. ⑥(D9) (ent-schlossen, bestimmt) determined, resolute; firm, positive; eine ⁀e Antwort a straightforward (or decided) answer; das ist ein ⁀er (a. adv. ⁀ ein) Gewinn that's a decided (or that's decidedly a) gain; ⁀er Ton peremptory (stärker: authoritative) tone.

Ent-schiedenheit (⌣́⌣-) f ⑥ (f. ent-schieden II) determination, resoluteness; firmness; peremptoriness.

Entschl. abbr. = Entschließung.

ent-schlafen (⌣́⌣) v/n. (fn) ⑨a* (p.p. ⁀) 1. to drop off to sleep; vgl. einschlafen 1. — 2. (sterben) to expire, to breathe one's last, to die, to depart this life; rel. im Herrn ⁀ to go to one's heavenly home; die ⁀en pl. the departed pl.

ent-schlagen (⌣́⌣): sich ⁀ v/refl. ⑨b* (p.p. ⁀) to get rid of a th.; sich e-s Gedankens ⁀ to dismiss (or banish) a thought (from one's mind). [friechen.

ent-schleichen (⌣́⌣) v/n. (fn) ⑨a*f = ent-
ent-schleiern (⌣́⌣) v/a. ⑨a* to unveil (a. fig.), to uncover; vgl. enthüllen I.

ent-schlich (⌣́) ind., ⁀e (⌣́⌣) subj. impf. u. ⁀en (⌣́⌣) p.p. von entschleichen.

ent-schlichten ⊕ (⌣́⌣) [Schlichte] v/a. ⑨* Gewebe: ⁀ (waschen u. spülen) to take (or wash) the dressing out of …

ent-schlief (⌣́) ind., ⁀e (⌣́⌣) subj. impf. v. entschlafen.

ent-schließen (⌣́⌣) ⑨d* I sich ⁀ v/refl. 1. to decide (stärker: to determine or resolve) on a th.; sich anders ⁀ to change one's mind; ich kann sich nicht dazu ⁀ he cannot make up his mind for it or to do it; er entschloß sich zu reisen he resolved (or decided) 1. to travel. — II ⁀ v/a. 2. = aufschließen 1.

Ent-schließung (⌣́⌣) f ⑥ = Entschluß.

ent-schlossen (⌣́⌣) p.p. u. a. ⑥ (D9) (vgl. entschließen) determined, resolved; kurz ⁀ of quick resolve, prompt (in acting); fest ⁀ zu heiraten bent on marrying, determined to get married; ⁀heit (⌣́⌣-) f ⑥ 1. = Entschiedenheit. — 2. (Tatkraft) energy, pluck.

ent-schlug (⌣́) ind., ent-schlüge (⌣́⌣) subj. impf. v. entschlagen.

ent-schlummern (⌣́⌣) v/n. (fn) ⑨a* to fall into a slumber, to doze off.

ent-schlüpfen (⌣́⌣) v/n. (fn) ⑧* to slip (or glide) away from; vgl. entgehen.

Ent-schluß (⌣́) m ⑧a. decision, resolution, resolve, determination; einen ⁀ fassen, zu e-m Entschlusse kommen to form (or come to) a resolution, to resolve; er kann zu keinem Entschlusse kommen he cannot make up his mind; mein ⁀ ist gefaßt I have made up my mind, auch: my mind is (thoroughly) made up. [strip) of shoes or boots.)

ent-schuhen (⌣́⌣) v/a. ⑧* to divest (or)
ent-schuldbar (⌣́-) a. ⑥ excusable.

ent-schuldigen (⌣́⌣) v/a. u. sich ⁀ v/refl. ⑧* (sich) ⁀ to excuse (o.s.), to exculpate (o.s.); sich bei e-m ⁀ to plead an excuse with a p., to apologize to a p.; sich mit Unwissenheit ⁀ to plead ignorance, &c.; Höflichkeitsphrase: ⁀ Sie! I beg your pardon!, accept my apologies!; bitte, ⁀ Sie mich! I beg to be excused!; es läßt sich nicht (auch ist nicht zu) ⁀ there is no excuse for it, it is inexcusable.

Ent-schuldigung (⌣́⌣⌣) f ⑥ (f. entschul-
digen) excuse, exculpation, plea, apology; (Ausflucht) subterfuge; leere, gute ⁀ lame, valid excuse; es bedarf keiner ⁀ there is no apology needed or required, it does not require (or call for) an apology; als ⁀ für et. vorbringen to plead as an excuse for (or in excuse of) a th.; e-n um ⁀ bitten to beg a p.'s pardon, to offer an apology to a p.

Ent-schuldigungs=grund (⌣́⌣⌣…) m ⑫ plea, (ground for an) excuse; =schreiben n letter of excuse or apology. [pen I.)

ent-schuppen (⌣́⌣) v/a. ⑧* = abschup-
ent-schweben (⌣́⌣) v/n. (fn) ⑧* poet. to hover (or soar, float) away from.

ent-schwefeln (⌣́⌣) I v/a. ⑨a* chm.: ⁀ to desulphurate. — II ⁀ n ㉓ u. Ent-schwef(e)lung f ⑥ desulphuration.

ent-schweißen (⌣́⌣) v/a.⑨* Wolle: to scour.

ent-schwinden (⌣́⌣) v/n. (fn) ⑨* to disappear (or vanish) from sight; v. Tönen: to die away; dem Gedächtnisse ⁀ to fade (or drop) from one's memory.

ent-schwommen, ent-schwunden (⌣́⌣) p.p. von entschwimmen, entschwinden.

ent-seelen (⌣́⌣) v/a.⑧* (ant. beseelen) to deprive of life; entseelt lifeless, inanimate; die Entseelten the dead pl.

ent-senden (⌣́⌣) v/a. ⑨a* to send off (or forth) from; to dispatch letters.

ent-setzbar (⌣́-) a. ⑥ removable.

ent-setzen (⌣́⌣) [ahd.] I v/a. und sich ⁀ v/refl. ⑨* 1. e-n e-r Sache (gen.) ⁀ to dispossess a p. of a th.; e-n e-s Amtes ⁀ to dismiss a p. from his post, bsd. pol. to turn a p. out of office, zeitweilig: to suspend a p.; des Thrones ⁀ to dethrone, to depose. — 2. (erschrecken) to frighten, scare, startle; er war entsetzt darüber he was quite alarmed (or terrified, horrified) at it. — 3. ✕ eine Festung ⁀. ⁀ to relieve (or succour) …; to raise the siege of … — II ⁀ n ㉓ 4. (f. 1) dispossession; dismissal, suspension. — 5. (f. 3) (bringing) relief, raising the siege of a fortress, a town. — 6. (f. 2) fright; alarm, terror, horror.

ent-setzlich (⌣́⌣) a. ⑥ awful, frightful, horrible, horrid, dreadful, shocking; (gräßlich) atrocious; fast F: ⁀er (großer) Aufwand F tremendous expense; adv. ⁀ reich F awfully rich; ⁀ lange Zeit F unconscionable time.

Ent-setzlichkeit (⌣́⌣-) f ⑥ awfulness.

Ent-setzung (⌣́⌣) f ⑥ = entsetzen 4 u. 5.

ent-sichern ✕ (⌣́⌣) v/a. ⑨a* ein Gewehr ⁀ to release the safety-catch of …

ent-siegel/n (⌣́⌣) I v/a. ⑨a* Briefe: to unseal; weits. to (break) open. — II ⁀ung f ⑥ unsealing, removal of seals. [to sink (down), vgl. entfallen.)

ent-sinken (⌣́⌣) v/n. (fn) ⑨fit* to drop,)
ent-sinnen (⌣́⌣): sich ⁀ v/refl. ⑨* sich e-r Sache (gen.) ⁀ to remember (or recollect) a th.; to recall it to one's mind; soviel ich mich ⁀ kann as far as I can remember or recollect, as far as my recollection goes.

ent-sittlich/en (⌣́⌣⌣) I v/a. ⑧* to deprave, to demoralize. — II ⁀ n ㉓ u. ⁀ung f ⑥ depravation, depravity, demoralization. [p.p. von entsinnen.)

ent-sonne (⌣́⌣) subj. impf., ent-sonnen (⌣́⌣) p.p. von entsinnen.
ent-spann (⌣́) ind. impf. v. entspinnen.
ent-spinnen (⌣́⌣) ⑨a* I v/a. to start, originate, begin; (Böses) to scheme. — II sich ⁀ v/refl. to arise, originate, begin; es entspann sich ein Streit there ensued a quarrel, a dispute arose.

ent-spitzen (⌣́⌣) v/a. ⑨* junge Pflanzen ⁀ (die Triebspitze ausknipsen) to pinch the top shoots off …

ent-spönne (⌣́⌣) subj. impf., ent-sponnen (⌣́⌣) p.p. von entspinnen.

ent-sprach (⌣́-) ind., ent-spräche (⌣́⌣) subj. impf. v. entsprechen.

ent-sprang (⌣́) ind., ent-spränge (⌣́⌣) subj. impf. v. entspringen.

ent-sprechen (⌣́⌣) I v/n. (h.) ⑨a* 1. e-r Sache (dat.) ⁀ to correspond to a th.; to answer a purpose; j-s Erwartungen (nicht) ⁀ to come up to (to fall short of) a p.'s expectations; j-s Wünschen ⁀ to conform (or comply) with (or to meet) a p.'s wishes; j-s Zwecken ⁀ to serve a p.'s purpose or turn. — II ⁀d p.pr. und a. ⑥ 2. in den Beb. des inf. — 3. ⁀de (angemessene) Belohnung adequate reward; (dem Klima) ⁀de Kleidung suitable (or proper, appropriate) clothing; Sofa mit den ⁀den Stühlen … with chairs to match or to correspond; f-m Vorschlage ⁀ in accordance (or in conformity) with his proposal; f-n Wünschen ⁀ agreeable to his wishes; dem ⁀ accordingly, conformably; correspondingly.

ent-sprießen (⌣́⌣) v/n. (fn) ⑨d* von Pflanzen: to sprout (or spring) forth, to shoot up; a. fig. = abstammen 1.

ent-springen (⌣́⌣) v/n. (fn) ⑨fit* 1. aus dem Gefängnisse ⁀c. ⁀ to escape from

♪ Musik; ⚛ Wissenschaft; ♣ Pflanze; ⚲ Geographie; ⊕ Technik; ✕ Bergbau; ⚔ Militär; ⚓ Marine; ⚖ Handel; ✉ Post; 🚂 Eisenbahn.

(or to break out of) jail, &c.; entsprung(e)ner Sträfling convict at large. — 2. von Quellen: to rise (or come, descend, originate, spring) from; der Rhein entspringt auf den Alpen ... has its source in the Alps. — 3. fig. to arise (or proceed) from; to originate in; es wird Unglück daraus ♀ it will breed (or bring forth) mischief, it will be a source of trouble.
ent-sprochen (⌣⌣⌣) p.p. von entsprechen.
ent-sprossen (⌣⌣) I v/n. (ſn) ⑩* = entsprießen. — II p.p. von entsprießen.
ent-sprungen (⌣⌣⌣) p.p. von entspringen u. a. ⑥ (D9) ~e([r] m) f ⑰ aus dem Tollhause ~(r) escaped lunatic.
ent-staatlich/en (⌣⌣⌣) I v/a. ⑧* to disestablish a church. — II E/ung f ⑯ disestablishment. [ſtammen 1.]
ent-stammen (⌣⌣) v/n. (ſn) ⑧* = ab-]
ent-stand (⌣⌣) ind., ent-stände subj. impf. u. ent-standen (⌣⌣⌣) p.p. von entstehen.
ent-steh(e)n (⌣⌣(⌣) I v/n. (ſn) ⑭* to (a)rise, to spring (or come) into existence, to take birth; to form; (verurſacht werden, hervorgehen) to be caused (or engendered) by, to result from; (geſchehen) to occur, happen, arise; vgl. entspringen 3; von einem Aufſtande, Feuer ꝛc.: to break out; große Dinge ♀ oft aus kleinen Anfängen ... often spring from ...; was auch daraus ♀ mag come of it what may; was wird daraus ♀? what will be the end (or upshot) of it (all)?; die dadurch entſtand(e)ne Verzögerung the delay caused by it or due to it. — II ~ n ㉓ u. Ent-stehung f ⑯ (f. I) rise, birth, formation, origin, beginning; ⌑ genesis, nascence; im ~ (begriffen) still forming, in its first beginning, budding; ⌑ nascent.
Ent-stehungs-art (⌣⌣⌣...) f ⑫ (manner of) birth or origin; -geschichte f, oft: ⌑ genesis, -weise f = -art; -zustand m, chm., &c.: ⌑ nascent state.
ent-steigen (⌣⌣⌣) v/n. (ſn) ⑧* e-r Sache (dat.) ♀ to rise (or emerge) from s. th.; weitS. to emanate from a th.
ent-stell/en (⌣⌣) I v/a. u. sich ♀ v/refl. ⑧* 1. (sich) ♀ to disfigure (o.s.); (verunstalten) to deface, deform (verſtümmeln) to maim, mutilate; entstellte (verzerrte) Züge distorted features pl. — 2. fig. to misrepresent (or misstate) facts; to twist (or colour) the true meaning. — II ~ n ㉓ u. E/ung f ⑯ 3. (f. I) disfigurement; defacement; mutilation, misrepresentation; misstatement.
ent-stieg (⌣⌣) ind., ♀e (⌣⌣⌣) subj. impf. u. ♀en (⌣⌣) p.p. von entsteigen.
ent-strömen (⌣⌣⌣) v/n. (ſn) ⑧* to flow (in streams) from; vgl. entquellen.
ent-stünde (⌣⌣⌣) subj. impf. v. entstehen.
ent-stürzen (⌣⌣⌣) v/n. (ſn) u. sich ♀ v/refl. ⑩* to rush (or tumble) from.
ent-sühn/en (⌣⌣), ent-sündig/en (⌣⌣⌣) I v/a. u. sich ♀ v/refl. ⑧* to purge (or clear) from sin; sich ♀ to expiate (or atone for) one's offences or crime. — II ~ n ㉓ u. E/ung f ⑯ purgation; expiation, atonement.
ent-sunken (⌣⌣⌣) p.p. v. entsinken.
ent-täusch/en (⌣⌣⌣) I v/a. u. sich ♀ v/refl. ⑩* (sich) ♀ to undeceive (o.s.); to

disabuse (or disillusion) a p.'s mind; er hat sich (auch: er ist) enttäuscht he is disappointed; his hopes are dispelled or dashed to the ground. — II E/ung f ⑯ disillusionment; disappointment.
ent-thron/en (⌣⌣⌣) I v/a. ⑧* to dethrone. — II E/ung f ⑯ dethronement.
ent-tröpfeln ⑫ a*, ent-tropfen ⑧* (⌣⌣) v/n. (ſn) to trickle (or drip) down.
Ent-vogel (g...) m ⑫ (männliche Ente) drake.
ent-völker/n (⌣⌣⌣) I v/a. u. sich ♀ v/refl. ⑫ a* to unpeople, to depopulate; sich ♀ to decrease in population; entvölkert sparsely(or thinly) inhabited, desolate, deserted. — II E/ung f ⑯ depopulation.
ent-wachsen (⌣⌣⌣) v/n. (ſn) ⑥ b* (p.p. ♀) 1. von Pflanzen: dem Boden ♀ to grow (or sprout) from the soil. — 2. ſ-n Kleidern ♀ to outgrow (or grow out of) one's clothes; sie ist den Kinderſchuhen, der Schule ♀ she is no longer a child, a school-girl; er ist der Rute ♀ he has outgrown the rod.
ent-waffn/en (⌣⌣⌣) I v/a., v/n. (h.) ⑨ b* to disarm. — II ~ n ㉓ und Ent-waffnung f ⑯ disarmament.
ent-währen (⌣⌣⌣) I v/a. ⑧* 1. entwehren: (außer Beſitz ſetzen) to dispossess, evict. — 2. (nicht mehr als Währung gelten l.) to withdraw from circulation, to demonetize, invalidate, vgl. entwerten. — II Ent-währung f ⑯ 3. dispossessment, eviction; invalidation.
ent-wald/en (⌣⌣⌣) I v/a. ⑨* to clear of woods; (abholzen) to deforest. — II ~ n ㉓ u. E/ung f ⑯ deforestation.
ent-wand (⌣⌣) ind., ent-wände (⌣⌣⌣) subj. impf. v. entwinden. [wenden.]
ent-wandt (⌣⌣) p.p., ♀e impf. v. ent-]
ent-warf (⌣⌣) impf. v. entwerfen.
ent-wässer/n (⌣⌣⌣) I v/a. ⑫ a* agr. to drain a field, a bog; ⌑ to desiccate a substance; chm. Alkohol ♀ to rectify ... — II ~ n ㉓ u. E/ung (⌣⌣⌣) f ⑯ (f. I) draining, drainage; ⌑ desiccation, chm. rectification. [f ⊕ agr. drain.]
Ent-wässerungs-kanal(l...) m ⑫, -röhre]
ent-weder (⌣⌣⌣) [ahd.] cj. mit folgendem „oder": either ... or; ♀ ſagſt du es ihm oder ich (ſage es ihm) either you tell him or I (shall); ♀, oder! (you must do) either one thing or the other!, take it or leave it!; ♀ alles oder nichts! neck or nothing!
ent-wehren (⌣⌣⌣) ⑧* I v/a. = entwähren 1. — II sich ♀ v/refl. (sich erwehren) mit gen.: to ward off; entwehrt euch der Sorge! guard against care!
ent-weich/en (⌣⌣) v/n. (ſn) ⑩ a*† allg.: to escape (a. ⨁ v. Gas ꝛc.); (verschwinden) to disappear, von Perſonen: to flee, to abscond, F to make o.s. scarce, to vanish; in längſt entwich(e)nen Zeiten in times long past, in days gone by long ago; ⊖ (dämpfen) der ♀e Dampf the exhaust-steam; vgl. entgehen 1. — II ~ n ㉓ u. E/ung f ⑯ (f. I) escape; disappearance, flight; E/ungs-klappe ⊖ f discharge-valve.
ent-weih/en (⌣⌣) I v/a. ⑧* 1. Priester: to degrade. — 2. heilige Orte: to desecrate, to profane; (ſchänden) to pollute. — II ~ n ㉓ u. E/ung.
Ent-weiher (⌣⌣⌣) m ⑫ desecrator.

Ent-weihung (⌣⌣⌣) f ⑯ degradation; desecration, profanation; pollution.
ent-wend/en (⌣⌣⌣) I v/a. ⑫ a* (heimlich nehmen) to abstract; diebisch: to misappropriate, pilfer, filch, purloin; Kaſſengeld: to embezzle. — II ~ n ㉓ = E/ung.
Ent-wender (⌣⌣⌣) m ⑫ pilferer; purloiner; (Kaſſendieb) embezzler.
Ent-wendung (⌣⌣⌣) f ⑯ (ſ. entwenden I) abstraction; misappropriation; pilfering; embezzlement.
ent-werf/en (⌣⌣⌣) I v/a. ⑨ b* 1. to trace out a design; flüchtig: to sketch, draft, (rough)draw, outline; to make a rough sketch (or draft) of. — 2. fig. Pläne ♀ (ausdenken) to devise (or contrive, concoct, lay out) schemes or plans. — II ~ n ㉓ 3. = E/ung.
Ent-werfer (⌣⌣⌣) m ⑫ designer; fig. v. Plänen: contriver, concocter, schemer.
Ent-werfung (⌣⌣⌣) f ⑯ tracing; sketch(ing), draft(ing), &c. (ſ. entwerfen I).
ent-wert/en (⌣⌣⌣) I v/a. ⑧* to depreciate; to debase; to reduce in value; (außer Kurs setzen) to call in, to withdraw; ⑨ to demonetize; ⌑ Briefmarken: to deface, to cancel; entwertet, auch: reduced in value. — II ~ n ㉓ u. E/ung f ⑯ depreciation, debasement; ⑨ demonetization; ⌑ defacement; E/ungs-stempel m ⑫ für Briefmarken: defacing stamp.
ent-wick/eln (⌣⌣⌣) I v/a. u. sich ♀ v/refl. ⑫ a* 1. (sich) ♀ to develop (o.s.); phot. eine Platte ♀ to develop a plate; sich aus e-r Puppe zu einem Schmetterling ♀ to be(come) transformed from a pupa or chrysalis into a butterfly; von Gaſen: to evolve, disengage; fig. der sich ♀e Geiſt eines Kindes the dawning (or growing) intellect of a child. — 2. (aufrollen) to unroll, unfurl; (entfalten) to unfold; ⚔ to deploy, to form; fig. im Drama: to unravel a plot. — 3. j-s Anlagen ♀ (bilden) to develop (or cultivate, form) a p.'s talents; seine Gedanken ♀ (aus-ea. ſetzen) to evolve, elucidate, set forth ... — 4. Tatkraft ♀ (an den Tag legen) to show ..., to give proof of ... — II ~ n ㉓ und Entwick(e)lung f ⑯ 5. (f. I) development; growth; evolution; ⚕ Lehre von der ~ der Pflanzen ⌑ phytonomy. — 6. (f. 2) ⚔ deployment, formation; im Drama bisw.: (fr.) dénouement, im Trauerſpiel: catastrophe. — 7. (ſ. 3) elucidation, exposition.
ent-wick(e)lungs-fähig (⌣⌣⌣⌣...) a. ⑯ capable of development or growth; -flüssigkeit f ⑫ phot. developing solution, developer; -gang m course of development; phls. evolution; -gefäß n, phot. developing dish; -geschichte f: ⌑ ontogenesis, ontogeny; -krankheit f, path. älterer Leute climacteric disease; -lehre f theory of evolution; -periode f junger Leute (age of) puberty; -prozeß m phot., &c. process of development; -stufe f stage of dev.; -theorie f = -lehre; -verfahren n, -vorgang m process of development.
ent-winden (⌣⌣⌣) v/a. und sich ♀ v/refl. ⑪* to wring (or wrench) from; vgl. entreißen 1; sich ♀ to escape o.s. from.

[entwirren] — 327 — [epigraphisch]

ent-wirren (⌣⌣) I v/a. ⑱* to disentangle or unravel a skein; fig. to puzzle out a problem; fig. to disembroil. — II ~ n ㉓ u. Ɛ**ung** f ㊻ disentanglement, unravelling, &c.

ent-wischen F (⌣⌣) I v/n. (ſn) ⓺* to slip (or steal away) from; to (make one's) escape; F to get away or off, to make tracks; er iſt uns entwiſcht he has given us the slip. — II ~ n ㉓ (ſ. I) slipping, &c.; (Flucht) flight, escape.

ent-wöhn/en (⌣⌣) I v/a. ⑱* to wean a child (from the breast); e-r Sache (gen.) oder von etwas ⌒ (auch ſich ⌒ v/refl.) to break a p. (o.s.) of a habit; ſich ⌒, a. to leave off smoking, &c.; der Arbeit entwöhnt disaccustomed from (mehr gbr.: unaccustomed to) work. — II~n ㉓ u. Ɛ**ung** f ㊻ weaning; disuse.

ent-wölken (⌣⌣) v/a. u. ſich ⌒ v/refl. ⑱* to uncloud; der Himmel entwölkte ſich the sky cleared (or brightened) up; entwölkt unclouded, cloudless.

ent-worfen (⌣⌣) p.p. von entwerfen.

ent-wuchs (⌣⌣ſz) ind., **ent-wüchſe** (⌣⌣ſz) subj. impf. v. entwachſen.

ent-wunden (⌣⌣) p.p. von entwinden.

ent-würdig/en (⌣⌣) I v/a. ⑱* to degrade, to disgrace. — II ~ n ㉓ und Ɛ**ung** f ㊻ degradation, disgrace.

Ent-wurf (⌣⌣) [entwerfen] m ⓯b. 1. (Zeichnung) (rough) sketch, outline, (first) draft, design; parl. ~ eines Geſetzes bill. — 2. (Plan) design, plan, project, scheme. — 3. (Konzept) rough draft or sketch or outline or copy.

ent-würfe (⌣⌣) subj. impf. v. entwerfen.

ent-wurzel/n (⌣⌣) I v/a. ⑫a* to uproot, to root out, to tear (or pull) up by the roots; fig. to extirpate, eradicate; nicht zu ⌒ not to be uprooted, ineradicable. — II ~ n ㉓ und Ɛ**ung** f ㊻ fig. extirpation, eradication.

ent-zaubern (⌣⌣) I v/a. ⑫a* to disenchant. — II ~ n ㉓ und **Ent-zauberung** f ㊻ disenchantment.

ent-zieh/en (⌣⌣) I v/a. u. ſich ⌒ v/refl. ⑯b* 1. e-m et. ⌒ to withdraw (or withhold) a th. from a person; to take s.th. away (or to abstract s.th.) from a person; (rauben) to rob (or deprive) a p. of a th.; e-m den Boden (oder den Halt) ⌒ to cut the ground from under a p.'s feet; ſich (dat.) den Schlaf ⌒ to go short (or to deprive o.s.) of sleep; surg. e-m Blut ⌒ to bleed a p. — 2. ſich einer Sache (dat.) ⌒ to withdraw (or retire) from a th.; ſich der Gerechtigkeit ⌒ to fly from justice, to abscond, F to make tracks; das entzieht ſich aller Berechnung it baffles (or defies) all calculation; er entzog ſich raſch ihren Blicken he fled (or vanished) from their sight. — II ~ n ㉓ und Ɛ**ung** f ㊻ 3. withdrawal; (de)privation; (Wegnahme) abstraction; des Wahlrechtes: disenfranchisement; chm. von Sauerſtoff, Schwefel: deoxidation, desulphuration.

Ent-ziehungs-diät, -kur (⌣...) f ㊷ low diet, starvation-cure. [(lesbar) legible.

ent-zifferbar (⌣⌣⌣-) a. ㊿ decipherable;

Ent-zifferer (⌣⌣⌣) m ㉒ decipherer.

ent-ziffer/n (⌣⌣⌣) I v/a. ⑫a* to decipher writing; tel. to decode; fig. to solve,

unpuzzle, clear up, unravel. — II ~ n ㉓ und Ɛ**ung** f ㊻ deciphering; tel. * decodification; Ɛ**ungs-kunſt** f ㊷ art of deciphering.

ent-zog (⌣⌣) ind., **ent-zöge** (⌣⌣) subj. impf., **ent-zogen** (⌣⌣) p.p. von entziehen.

ent-zück/en (⌣⌣) I v/a. ⑱* to charm, enchant, enrapture; er war entzückt über die Blumen he was delighted (or charmed) with …; ⌒d charming, delightful. — II ~ n ㉓ u. Ɛ**ung** f ㊻ enchantment, rapture; delight; ſtärker: ecstasy; in ~ geraten to go into raptures, to be charmed or delighted.

ent-zügeln (⌣⌣) v/a. ⑫a* Pferde: to unbridle; fig. p.p.: entzügelt unbridled, unrestrained, licentious; riotous.

ent-zündbar (⌣⌣-) a. ㊿ inflammable (auch fig.), combustible, ignitable; ~**keit** (⌣⌣--) f ㊻ inflammability (auch fig.).

ent-zünd/en (⌣⌣) ⑱* I v/a. to kindle, ignite, light, set on fire; fig. to inflame (or fire, kindle) passions, &c. — II ſich ⌒ v/refl. to kindle, ignite, catch fire, flare up; path. und fig. to be(come) inflamed or irritated; es wird ſich ein Krieg ⌒ a war will be kindled or break out. — III ~ n ㉓ = Ɛ**ung**.

Ent-zünder (⌣⌣) m ㉒, ~**in** f ㊷ inflamer, kindler, p. who lights (or fires) a th.

ent-zündlich (⌣⌣) a. ㊿ inflammatory = entzündbar.

Ent-zündung (⌣⌣) f ㊻ kindling, ignition, &c. (ſ. entzünden I); path. u. fig. inflammation, irritation; ⚗ oft durch das grch. Suffix …itis wiedergegeben, zB. ~ der Aorta ⚗ aortitis, ~ der Eingeweide ⚗ enteritis; ~s-fieber n ㉓, -**krankheit** f inflammatory fever, complaint.

ent-zwei (⌣⌣) [ahd. in-zwei] I adv. in two, asunder, F in half; (zerriſſen) torn; (zerbrochen) broken (to pieces), shattered, F smashed. — II in Verbindung mit verbs, ſtets trennbar (*) zB. ⌒**beißen** v/a. ⑯a* to bite in two; ⌒**berſten** v/n. (ſn) ⓺e** to burst asunder.

ent-zweien (⌣⌣) ⑱* I v/a. to disunite, to set at variance; (entfremden) to estrange; entzweit, a. divided, at variance, F at loggerheads. — II ſich ⌒ v/refl. to fall out with one another.

ent-zwei-fallen (⌣⌣...) v/a. ㊺a** to fall and break; ſich (dat.) einen Arm ꝛc. ⌒ to break an arm. &c. in falling; ⌒**geh(e)n** v/n. (ſn) ⓺* to go (or fall, tumble) to pieces, to break, F to go to smithereens; (ſich ſpalten) to split in two; ⌒**hauen** v/a. ⓺c** to hew (or cut) asunder; ⌒**reißen** v/a. u. v/n. (ſn) ㊿a** to tear asunder or to rags; fig. bald riß ſein Wahn ⌒ his dream was soon dispelled; ⌒**ſchlagen** v/a. ⓺b** to knock to pieces, to break asunder; ⌒**ſchneiden** v/a. ⓺c** to cut in two or to pieces; ⌒**ſein** v/n. (ſn) ⓺a* to be torn or broken or F smashed.

Ent-zweiung (⌣⌣) f ㊻ (ſ. entzweien) disunion, discord, division; estrangement; (Zank) quarrel.

enumerieren (-⌣⌣⌣) [lt.] v/a. ㊾ (aufzählen) to enumerate.

en vogue (a wo'g) [fr.] adv. in vogue.

Enzian (⌣⌣) [lt.] m ⓭c. gentian (Gentia'na); gelber ~ yellow gentian

(G. lu'tea); ſtengelloſer ~ gentianella (G. acau'lis); ~**bitter** n, chm. gentianin(e).

Enzyklika (⌣⌣⌣) [grch.] f ㊾ (Rundſchreiben des Papſtes) encyclical letter;

enzykliſch (⌣⌣⌣) a. ㊿ encyclical.

Enzyklopädie ⚗ (⌣⌣⌣-⌐) [grch.] f ㊺ (Wiſſenſchaftskunde, Sachwörterbuch) (en)cyclopædia; **enzyklopädiſch** (⌣⌣⌣⌐⌣) a. ㊿ (en)cyclopædic; **Enzyklopädiſt** (⌣⌣⌣-⌐) m ㉒ (en)cyclopædist.

E-os (-⌐) [grch. -⌐ Morgenröte] npr/f. inv. Eos; poet. oft: (rosy-fingered) Aurora.

E-osin ⚗ (-⌣⌐) [grch.] n ⓭c. chm. (rote Anilinfarbe) eosin.

E-ozän ⚗ (-⌣⌐) [grch.] n ⓭c. u. ⌒ a. ㊿ geol. (früheſte Tertiä'rbildung) eocene.

epagogiſch ⚗ (⌣⌐⌣⌣) [grch.] a. ㊿ log. u. rhet. (vom einzelnen zum Allgemeinen) epagogic, inductive.

Epakte ⚗ (⌣⌐⌣) [grch.] f ㊸ ast. (Unterſchied zw. Sonnen- u. Mond-Jahr) epact.

Eparch (⌣⌐) [grch. Statthalter] m ㊷ eparch; **Eparchie** (⌣⌣⌐) f ㊺ eparchy.

Epaulett (⌣⌣⌐, ſd. (-po⌐) [fr.] n ⓭c., ~**e** (⌣⌐) f ㊺ shoulder-knot, epaulet(te).

Epentheſe ⚗ (⌣⌐⌣) [grch.] f ㊺, **Epentheſis** (⌣⌐⌣) f ㊿ (pl. a. …ſes) gr. (Einſchaltung v. Buchſtaben) epenthesis;

epenthetiſch (⌣⌣⌐⌣) a. ㊿ gr. (eingeſchaltet) epenthetic(al).

Epexegeſe ⚗ (⌣⌣⌐⌣) [grch.] f ㊺ (Erklärung) epexegesis. [getic(al).

epexegetiſch (⌣⌣⌣⌐⌣) a. ㊿ epexe-

Ephebe (⌣f⌐) [grch. e'phebòs Jüngling] m ㊹ Altertum: (Greek) youth or young man (from 18 to 20 years old).

ephemer ⚗ (⌣f-⌐) [grch.] a. ㊿ (eintägig, vergänglich) ephemeral, …ous, transitory, transient. [zo. ephemera, …is, …id.)

Ephemere ⚗ (⌣f-⌐⌣) f ㊺ (Eintagsfliege)

Ephemeriden ⚗ (⌣f-⌣⌐⌣) f/pl. ㊸: a) ast. (Tagestafeln, Kalender) ephemeris, almanac; b) (liter. Tageserſcheinungen) daily papers, periodicals pl.

ephemeriſch ⚗ (⌣f-⌣⌐) a. ㊿ = ephemer.

Epheſer (⌣f⌐) [Epheſus, grch. St.] m ㉒, ~**in** (⌣f⌐-) f ㊷, **epheſiſch** (⌣f⌐-) a. ㊿ Ephesian; a. auch Ephesine.

Ephor (⌣f⌐) m ㉒, ~**us** (⌐f⌣-) m ㉒ [grch. Aufſeher] ephor; overseer; eccl. superintendent; ~**at** n ⓭c., ~**ie** (⌣⌣⌐) f ㊺ (Fünfmänner-rat in Sparta) ephoralty; eccl. eldership; superintendent's office.

Epidemie ⚗ (⌣⌣⌣⌐) [grch.] f ㊺ path. (Seuche) epidemic, infectious malady.

Epidermis ⚗ (⌣⌣⌐⌣) [grch.] f ⓯㊻ ⚖ anat. (Oberhaut) epidermis, F top (or outside) skin. [epidote.)

Epidot (⌣⌣⌐) [grch.] m ㊷ min.)

Epigone ⚗ (⌣⌣⌐⌣) [grch.] m ㊹ (Nachkomme) descendant (of old worthies); ~**n-kampf, -krieg** m ㊷ myth. war of the epigones; ~**n-perio'de** f (⌣⌣⌐⌣**ntum**) n ⓬d. decadence (or decay) in literature, &c.

Epigramm ⚗ (⌣⌣⌐) [grch.] n ⓭b. (Sinnſpruch, treffendes Wort) epigram; ~**atiker** (⌣⌣⌣⌐⌣⌣) m ㉒ epigrammatic speaker or writer; coiner of epigrams; **-atiſch** (⌣⌣⌣⌐⌣) a. ㊿ epigrammatic; pithy, terse; ~**atiſt** (⌣⌣⌣⌐) m ㊷ (auch ~**n-dichter** m ㉒ epigrammatist.

Epigraph ⚗ (⌣⌣⌐) [grch.] n ⓭c. (Inſchrift) epigraph; ~**ik** (⌣⌣⌐⌣) f ㊻ epigraphics; **-iſch** (⌣⌣⌐⌣) a. ㊿ epigraphic(al).

Epik (⌣⌣) [grch.] f ㊻ (erzählende Dichtkunst) epic poetry; **~er** (⌣⌣) m ㉒ epic poet.

Epikure-er (⌣⌣⌣) (Epiku'ros), grch. Philosoph, 341—270 v. Chr.] m ㉒ (Genußmensch) Epicure(an); (epikureischer Philosoph) Epicurean philosopher; **epiku-r(e-)isch** (⌣⌣⌣⌣) a. ㊻ fig. (genußsüchtig) Epicurean; self-indulgent; **Epikur(e)ismus** (⌣⌣-(-)⌣⌣, ⌣⌣-⌣⌣) m ㉗ Epicur(ean)ism.

Epilepsie (⌣⌣⌣⌢) [grch.] f ㊽ path. (Fallsucht) epilepsy, falling sickness; **Epileptiker** (⌣⌣⌣⌣) m ㉒, **epileptisch** (⌣⌣⌣⌣) a. ㊻ epileptic; an den Anfällen leiden, oft: to be subject to epileptic fits.

Epilog (⌣⌣⌢) [grch.] m ⓐc. (Schlußwort) epilogue; after-speech; **~isch** (⌣⌣⌣) a. ㊻ (schlußwort-artig) epilogistic.

Epiphania (⌣⌣f⌢(⌣)⌣) [grch.] f ㊾ **~s-**, **Epiphanien-fest** n eccl. (Dreikönigstag, 6. Januar) Epiphany.

Epiphora ⌣ (⌣f⌣⌣) [grch.] f, inv. rhet. (Wortwiederholg. am Satzende) epiphora.

Epiphyt(en pl.) ⌣ (⌣⌣f(⌢)⌣) [grch.] m ㊷ (Luftpflanze(n) epiphyte(s).

Epirot (⌣⌣⌢) [Epi'ros, nordgrch. Landschaft] m ㊷, **~in** f ㊼ Epirot(e); **Lisch** (⌣⌣⌣) a. ㊻ Epirotic. [Der Sagenkreis epic cycle.]

epish (⌣⌢) [grch.] a. ㊻ (erzählend) epic;

episkopal (⌣⌣⌣⌢) [grch.] a. ㊻ (bischöflich) episcopal; **~ismus** (…⌣⌣) m ㉗ episcopalism; **~kirche** f ㉒ Episcopal (in England auch: Anglican) Church; **Episkopat** m u. n ⓐc. (Bischofstum) episcopate.

Episode (⌣⌣⌢⌣) [grch.] f ㊽ (Zwischenfall) episode; **episodisch** a. ㊻ episod(ic)al.

Epistel (⌣⌢⌣) [grch.] f ㊽ epistle; fig. e-m die **~** lesen to give a p. a (good) talking-to or F a (long) lecture.

Epitaph(ium) ⌣ (⌣⌣f([⌣]⌣) [grch.] n ⓐc. (㉘) (Grabschrift) epitaph.

Epithalamium ⌣ (⌣⌣⌣f(⌣)⌣) [grch.] n ㉘ Alt. (Hochzeitslied) epithalamium.

Epithelium ⌣ (⌣⌣⌢(⌣)⌣) [lt., *grch.] n ㉘ (oberste Zellenschicht der Haut) epithelium.

Epitheton ⌣ (⌣⌢⌣⌣) [grch.] n ㊾ rhet., &c. (Beiname; ursprl. in Homer) epitheton.

Epitomator (⌣⌣⌣⌢⌣) [lt.] m ㉛ (Verfasser eines Auszuges) epitomist, epitomizer.

Epitome (⌣⌢⌣⌣) f ㊽ epitome. summary.

Epizeuxis ⌣ (⌣⌢⌣⌣) [grch.] f ㊽ rhet. (nachdrückliche Wiederholung) epizeuxis.

epizön ⌣ (⌣⌣⌢) [grch.] a. ㊻ gr. v. Tiernamen: (zweigeschlechtig) epicene.

Epizoon (⌣⌣⌢⌣) [grch.] n ㉘ ⓐ (Schmarotzertier auf der Haut) epizoon.

Epizykl-oide ⌣ (⌣⌣f⌣⌣⌢) [grch.] f math. (Kurve, welche ein Punkt einer Kreisperipherie beschreibt, die auf der Außenseite e-s anderen Kreises vorrandollt) epicycloid.

Epoche (⌣f⌣⌣) [grch.] f ㊽ (Zeit-abschnitt) epoch; period. [ing.]

epoche=machend (⌢…) a. ㊻ epoch-mak-**Epode** (⌣f⌣) [grch.] f ㊽ Altertl.: (Schlußgesang) epode; **epodisch** a. ㊻ epodic.

Epopöe (⌣⌣⌢⌣) f ㊽, **Epos** (⌣⌢) n ㉗ [grch. ⌢⌣] n (Heldenlied) epic (poem).

Eppich ⌣ (⌣f⌣) [ahd.; *lt. a'pium] m ⓐd.: a) P = Sellerie; a. Scharbockskraut; b) poet. = Efeu.

☛ Equi-.. s. a. Aqui-...

Equipage (-t(w)⌣⌣G⌣) [fr. m] f ㊽: a) [+fr.] (elegant) carriage; sich e-e **~** halten to keep one's own carriage; b) ⚓

(Schiffsmannschaft) (ship's) crew; c) ⚓ = Equipierung.

equipier/en (-t(w)⌣⌣) [fr.] I v/a. u. sich ⌣ v/refl. bsd. ⚔ (sich) ⌣ (ausrüsten) to equip (o.s.), to fit (o.s.) out; F to rig (o.s.) out. — II **~** n ㉓ = Ɛ/ung.

Equipierung (⌣) f ㊻ equipment, outfit; F rig-out; **~s-gelder** n/pl. ㉖, **=kosten** pl. allowance (or charges pl.) for outfit, cost of equipment or outfit.

er (⌢) [ahd.] I personal pron. der 3. Person ㊻ A 1, 3 +. **1. a)** von männlichen Personen u. Tieren: he; er selbst he himself; ist er's?, is it he?; er wird selber kommen he will come himself; **b)** von Dingen mst: it; selten personifizierend: he, z.B. wo ist mein Hut? da ist er where is my hat? there it (co. auch: he) is. — 2. bsd. ehm. in der Anrede an Untergebene: you (zweite Person pl.); er behauptet also you then assert. — II **Er** inv. **3.** s/m. von Personen u. Tieren: der Er und die Sie the he and the she, the male and the female. — **4.** s/n. das veraltete Er: ich verbitte mir das Er, etwa: I won't be addressed like a valet, I must ask you to address me properly.

er... (⌣…) [ahd.] Vorsilbe, in Zssgn mit verbs, immer untrennbar (*) **1. bz.** Anfang der Handlung, z.B. **erblühen** to begin to blossom. — **2. bz.** Erwerbung, Auswirkung, z.B. **erschreiben** to gain by writing. — **3. bz.** Töten, Sterben durch die im v. ausgedrückte Handlung, z.B. **erschlagen** to slay; **erfrieren** to die of cold. — **4. bz.** Aufwärtsbewegung, z.B. **erstehen** to rise from the ground. — **5. bz.** Verstärkung des Ausdrucks, z.B. **erwägen** to weigh (in one's mind). — **6.** bildet Zeitwörter aus Adjektiven, z.B. **erleichtern** to make easy aus „leicht easy".

er-achten (⌣⌣⌣) I v/a. ⓧ* = **achten 1**; etwas für dienlich, nötig ⌣ to deem (or consider) a th. useful, necessary. — II **~** n ㉓ judgment; meines **~s**, nach m-m **~** in my opinion, to my way of thinking, in my estimation, F as I take (or look upon) it.

er-arbeiten (⌣⌣-⌣) v/a. ⓧ* to gain (or achieve) by (one's) work or labour.

erasmisch (⌣⌣⌣) [Erasmus von Rotterdam 1466—1536] a. ㊻ Erasmian.

Erb-adel (⌢…) m ㊷ hereditary nobility; **=amt** n h. office; **=anfall** m legacy.

er-bangen ⌣ (⌣⌣⌣) v/n. (sn) ⓧ* poet. to tremble with fear, to be full of anxiety.

Erb-anspruch (⌢…) m ㊷ claim to an estate or inheritance; **=anteil** m = =teil.

er-barmen (⌣⌣⌣) ⓧ* I sich ⌣ v/refl. und v/impers. sich j-s, über e-n ⌣ to take pity on a p., to have commiseration with (or compassion on) a p.; es erbarmt mich j-s I feel pity for a p.; Ausruf: daß (sich od. es) Gott erbarme! (the) Lord be merciful!, F Good gracious!, ehm.: God-a-mercy! — II v/a. er erbarmt mich I pity (or commiserate) him; iro. sie singen, daß Gott erbarme they sing pitifully, miserably. — III **~** n ㉓ pity, commiseration, compassion; ohne **~** without mercy, pitiless; zum **~** piteous, pitiful, (much) to be pitied; das Frühstück war zum **~** the breakfast was wretchedly bad.

er-barmens-wert (⌣⌣…) a. ㊻, **=würdig** a. deserving pity, piteous.

Er-barmer (⌣⌣⌣) m ㉒, **~in** f ㊼ pitiful (or merciful) p.; rel. God of mercy.

er-bärmlich (⌣⌣⌣) a. ㊻ (täglich) pitiable; (elend) miserable, wretched, deplorable; (abscheulich) detestable; (kleinlich) paltry, mean; ein Der Mensch a despicable (or contemptible) fellow; **~keit** f ㊻ pitiableness; miserable state, wretchedness; paltriness, meanness.

Er-barmung (⌣⌣⌣) f ㊻ = erbarmen III. **er-barmungs-los** (⌢…) a. ㊻ devoid of compassion, merciless, pitiless, callous, **=reich**, **=voll** a. merciful, compassionate, **=wert**, **=würdig** = erbarmens-wert. [v. erbitten.]

er-bat (⌣⌢) ind., **er-bäte** (⌣⌢⌣) subj. impf.]

er-bau/en (⌣⌢⌣) I v/a. ⓧ* **1.** to build (up), construct, raise (up); to erect a building, a monument, e-e Stadt oft: to found; Sprichw. Rom ist nicht in einem Tage erbaut Rome was not built in a day. — **2.** rel. fig. (a. sich ⌣ v/refl.) to edify; to be edified by a th.; solche Dinge ⌣ (ergötzen) mich wenig such things give (or afford) me (but) little pleasure or satisfaction. — II **~** n ㉓. = Ɛ/ung. [tor; erl.Stadt: founder.]

Er-bauer (⌣⌢⌣) m ㉒ builder, construc-**er-baulich** (⌣⌢⌣) a. ㊻ fig. edifying; rel. devotional; **~keit** (⌣⌢⌣) f ㊻ edifying nature; edification afforded by a th.; rel. devotional character.

Erb-auseinandersetzung (⌢…) f ㉒ liquidation of an estate.

Er-bauung (⌣⌢⌣) f ㊻ construction; foundation; rel. fig. edification.

Er-bauungs-buch (⌣⌢…) n ㉒, **=schrift** devotional book, (religious) tract; **=stunde**, **=übung** f devotional hour, exercise of devotion; **=vortrag** m religious address.

Erb-begräbnis (⌢…) n ㉒ family tomb or vault; **=berechtigt** a. ㊻ entitled to an inheritance, qualified to enter upon an inheritance; **=berechtigung** f = =recht; **=besitz** m hereditary property; family estate; weitS. freehold (land); **=bestand** m = =pacht; **=bibel** f family bible.

Erbe (⌣⌣) [ahd.] I m ㊹, **Erbin** f ㊼ heir, f heiress; successor; bsd. jur. a.: inheritor (f …ress, …rix) legatee; lachende **~n** laughing (or joyful) heirs pl.; e-n zum **~n** einsetzen to appoint (or make) a p. one's heir(ess); ohne leibliche **~n** without progeny or offspring or direct issue, childless. — II **~** n ㉖ (Nachlaß) inheritance, inherited estate; bsd.in geh.Spr.: heritage.

er-beben (⌣⌢⌣) I v/n. (h. u. sn) ⓧ* to shake (or tremble) with fear; stärker: to quake, to quiver. — II **~** n ㉓ shaking, &c. (f. I); (Angst) dread.

erb-eigen (⌢…) a. ㊻ hereditary, inherited; **=eigentum** n ㊷ = =besitz; **=eigentümer** m owner of a family estate; **=eigentümlich** a. ㊻ = =ein-gesessen a. living on one's patrimony or inherited estate, vgl. **=gesessen**; **=einsetzung** f appointment of an heir.

erben (⌣⌢) ⓧ* I v/a. etwas von e-m ⌣ to inherit s.th. from a p.; j-s (ganzes) Vermögen ⌣ to come into a p.'s (whole)

fortune; to succeed to a p.'s estate or property. — II v/n. (ſn), mehr gebr. ſich ○ v/refl. to be transmitted (or handed down) by inheritance (von Krankheiten ꝛc.: by heredity); to descend (from generation to generation).
er-beten¹ (◡◠◡) v/a. ⓖ* to obtain by one's prayer(s) or petition.
er-beten² (◡◠◡) p.p. von erbitten.
er-betteln (◡◠◡) v/a. ⓐ* to obtain by begging or soliciting, to beg for.
er-beuten (◡◠◡) v/a. ⓖ* to take (or secure) as booty; to capture, to carry off (as prize); **Er-beuter** m ⓑ captor.
erb=fähig (◡...) a. ⓖ capable of succeeding (to an estate); **=fähigkeit** f ⓑ capability of succession; **=fall** m (case of) succession; heritage; ♀**fällig** a. due by right of inheritance, of succession; **=fehler** m hereditary fault, vice or defect; **=feind** m foe, sworn (or mortal) enemy; **=feindſchaft** f hereditary (or mortal) enmity; **=folge** f right of succession; **=folge-krieg** m war of succession; **=folger** m successor; **=folge-recht** n = =folge; **=fürſt**(in f) m hereditary prince(ss); **=genoß** m jointheir; **=gerichts-herr** m bſd. ehm. justiciary of a court-baron; weitS. lord of the manor; **=geseſſen** a. possessing real property, vgl. Eingeſeſſen; **=grind** m, path. hereditary scab; (Grindkopf) P scald-head; **=grund** m, **=gut** n inherited estate; (ancestral) manor; vgl. **=beſitz**; **=herr** m lord of the manor, owner of the estate; ♀**herrlich** a. manorial; **=herrſchaft** f hereditary possession; **=huldigung** f oath of fealty to the hereditary prince.
er-bieten (◡◠◡) I ſich ○ v/refl. ⓐ* to offer (o.s.) to do a thing, freiwillig: to volunteer (or to declare one's readiness or willingness) to do a th. — II ~ n ⓒ u. **Er-bietung** f ⓖ (voluntary) offer.
Erbin (◡◡) f ⓖ ſ. Erbe I.
er-bitten (◡◠◡) v/a. ⓐ* 1. et. von e-m ○ to ask (ſtärker: to solicit or to petition) a p. for a th.; ☀ umgehende Antwort wird erbeten an answer by return will greatly oblige; ſich (dat.) eine Gunſt ○ to beg for a favour. — 2. (erlangen) to obtain by entreaty. — 3. e-n ○ (bewegen) to move a p. by one's entreaties; er läßt ſich nicht ○ he won't flinch or yield, he is inexorable.
er-bittern (◡◠◡) I v/a. ⓐ* to embitter; ſtärker: to irritate, nettle, provoke, exasperate; auf e-n erbittert bitter against a p. — II **Er-bitterung** (◡◠◡) f ⓖ irritation, exasperation.
er-bittlich (◡◠◡) a. ⓖ flexible, yielding (to entreaty).
Erbi-um ⚗ (◡◡) [(Ytt)erby in Schweden] n ⓑ chm. (Metall) erbium (Er ob. E).
Erb-krankheit (◡...) f ⓖ hereditary disease; **=land** n hered. estate or land or property; die kaiſerlichen ~e the Emperor's patrimonial dominions pl.
er-blaſſen (◡◠◡) v/n. (ſn) ⓖ* 1. (erbleichen) to grow (or turn) pale (vor Zorn with anger); von Farben auch: to fade (away), to pale, F to fly; ○ machen to make pale, to (cause to) fade, to blanch. — 2. fig. (ſterben) to die, expire, pass

away; poet. du ſollſt am Kreuze ○(SCH.) thou shalt perish on the cross.
Erb-laſſer(in f) m (○...) ⓑ testator, f testatrix; **=leh(e)n(s-gut)** n hereditary estate or fief, jur. auch: fee-simple; entail; **=leh(e)ns-herr** m = =herr.
er-bleichen (◡◠◡) v/n. (ſn) ⓑaft(a. ⓖ)* = erblaſſen; er iſt erblichen he has passed away, he is dead.
er-blich¹ (◡◠) impf. von erbleichen, ○e subj. u. ○en (◡◠◡) p.p. von erbleichen.
erb-lich² (◡◠) a. ⓖ hereditary, (ererbbar) inheritable; **~keit** f ⓖ hereditariness; physiol. auch: heredity.
er-blicken (◡◠◡) I v/a. ⓖ* to behold, view, perceive; (entdecken) to discover, to espy; to catch sight (or to get a glimpse) of; to descry (or sight) a sail, &c.; das Licht der Welt ○ to come into the world, to be born; *ich erblicke (beſſer: ſehe) darin einen großen Nachteil I see a great drawback in that. — II ~ n ⓒ view; espying; sight(ing).
er-blinden (◡◠◡) I v/n. (ſn) ⓖ* to grow (F to go) blind, to lose one's sight. — II ~ n ⓒ u. **Er-blindung** f ⓖ loss of (one's) sight.
erb-los (◡◠) a. ⓖ(D 10): a) (ohne Erben) heirless, without an heir; b) (der Erbſchaft beraubt) disinherited.
er-blühen (◡◠◡) v/n. (ſn) ⓖ* to (come into) flower; vgl. er=... 1.
Erb-nehmer (○...) m ⓑ = Erbe I; **=onkel** m (=tante f) wealthy uncle (aunt) whose property one hopes to inherit; **=ordnung** f order of succession.
er-borgen (◡◠◡) v/a. ⓖ* to borrow from; erborgt borrowed or second-hand (phraſes, &c.); (künſtlich) artificial, assumed; fig. erborgtes Licht reflected light.
er-boſen (◡◠◡) [mhd.] I v/a. u. ſich ○ v/refl. ⓖ* (ſich) ○ to make (to grow) angry; erboſt ſein to be vexed or angry. — II **Erboſtheit** u. **Erboſung** f ⓖ anger, passion, wrath.
er-bot ind., **er-böte** (◡◠◡) subj. impf. u. **er-boten** (◡◠◡) p.p. von erbieten.
er-bötig (◡◠◡) a. ⓖ; zu etwas ○ subj. impf. (or willing) to do (or to perform) a th.
Erb-pacht (○...) f ⓖ hereditary tenure (of land); (Lehnsgut) copyhold; **=päch-ter**(in f) m hereditary tenant; copyholder; **=prinz(eſſin** f) hereditary prince(ss). [impf. von erbrechen.]
er-brach (◡◠◠) ind., **er-bräche** (◡◠◡) subj.)
er-bracht p.p., ○e (◡◠◠) impf. von erbringen.
er-brauſen (◡◠◡) v/n. (ſn) ⓖ* to (begin to) roar; vgl. brauſen I.
er-brechbar (◡◠◡) a. ⓖ easily broken open or into, auch: easy to break open.
er-brechen (◡◠◡) ⓐ* I v/a. = aufbrechen 1. — II v/a. u. ſich ○ v/refl. to vomit (or bring up) one's food; ſich ○ wollen to heave, to feel nauseous or sick; to retch. — III ~ n ⓒ vomiting, bisw. vomition; Neigung zum ~ nausea, sick(ly) feeling; ~ erregend nauseous, emetic, ♀ anacathartic; F sickly (taste).
Erb-recht (○...) n ⓖ hereditary right; right of inheritance or succession.
Er-brechung (◡◠◡) f ⓖ = erbrechen III.
Erb-register (○...) n ⓑ rent-roll; **=reze'ß** m jur. = =vergleich.

er-bringen (◡◠◡) v/a. ⓖ* 1. = einbringen 2. — 2. jur. e-n Beweis ○ to produce (legal) evidence or proof; *die erbrachten (beſſer: die angeführten) Beiſpiele the examples quoted or mentioned.
er-brochen (◡◠◡) p.p. von erbrechen.
Erbs=...., erbs=... (○...) ⓑ = Erbſen=...
Erb-ſaß, =ſaſſe (○...) m ⓑ lord of the manor; hereditary proprietor; **=ſatzung** f, jur. will, bequest.
Erbs-brei (○...) m ⓑ ſ. Erbſen=...
Erb-ſchaden (○...) m ⓑ = =fehler.
Erbſchaft (◡◠) f ⓖ inheritance; (Vermächtnis) legacy; vgl. Erbe II; e-e ~ antreten to enter upon an inheritance, to come into a legacy; er hat eine reiche ~ gemacht he had a large fortune left him; der ~ verluſtig m. to disinherit.
erbſchaftlich (◡◠◡) a. ⓖ relating to an inheritance or a legacy or a bequest.
Erbſchafts-anfall (○d...) m ⓑ devolution of an inheritance; **=angelegenheit** f = =ſache; **=anſpruch** m claim to an inheritance or a succession; **=anteil** m = Erbteil; **=forderung** f = =anſpruch; **=gericht** n court of probate; **=klage** f lawsuit about an inheritance; **=maſſe** f estate to be divided among the heirs; **=ſache** f matters pl. (gerichtlich: action) relating to an inheritance; **=ſteuer** f probate-duty, ſeit 1894: estate duty.
Erb-ſchleicher(in f) m (○...) ⓑ legacyhunter; **=ſchleicherei** f legacy-hunting; **=ſchuld** f encumbrance on an (inherited) estate.
Erbſe (◡◡) [ahd. ſt. e'rvum] f ⓑ pea (Pisum sati'vum); enthülſte ~n pl. split (or shelled) peas; kocht. gequetſchte, durchgeſchlagene ~n pl. pease-pudding.
Erbſen-acker (○...) m ⓑ agr. field of peas; ♀**artig** a. ⓖ peashaped, ⚭ pisiform; **=bau** m cultivation of peas; **=baum** ♀ m =ſtrauch; **=beet** n bed of peas; **=brei** m pease-pudding; **=brot** n pease-bread; ♀**förmig** a. = ♀artig; **=gericht** n dish of peas; ♀**groß** a. as large as a pea; ♀**grün** a. pea-green; **=hülſe** f pea-shell; **=käfer** m, ent. peabeetle or -weevil (Bruchus pisi); **=mehl** n pea-meal; **=ſchote** f pea-pod; **=ſtrauch** ♀ m Siberian pea-tree (Caraga'na); **=ſtroh** n pease-straw; **=ſuppe** f pea-soup; **=wicke** ♀ f pea-shaped vetch (Ervum pisifo'rme).
Erbs-ſtroh (○...) n ⓑ = pease-straw.
Erb-ſtiftung (○...) f ⓑ = =lehen; **=ſtück** n heirloom; **=ſünde** f, rel. original sin.
Erbs-wurſt (○...) f ⓑ sausage made of (thick) pease-pudding.
Erb-tante (○...) f ⓑ ſ. =onkel; **=teil** m (n) (share of an) inheritance; **=teilung** f division of an inheritance; **=tochter** f daughter who is to come into a fortune, oft a. (rich) heiress.
er-buhlen (◡◠◡) v/a. ⓖ* to gain by courtship or by amatory intrigues; j-s Gunſt ○ to curry favour with a p.
erb= und eigentümlich (◡◡ ◡◠◡◡) a. ⓖ acquired (or one's own) by heredity or inheritance.
Erb-verbrüderung (○...) f ⓑ mutual agreement of succession; **=vergleich** m jur. settlement of claims to an inheritance; **=vermächtnis** n legacy;

♪ Muſik; ⚛ Wiſſenſchaft; ♣ Pflanze; ♀ Geographie; ⚘ Technik; ⚒ Bergbau; ⚔ Militär; ⚓ Marine; ✉ Handel; ✉ Poſt; 🚂 Eiſenbahn.

[Erbvermögen] — 330 — [Erdreich]

bequest; =vermögen n patrimony; =vertrag m testamentary contract or deed; =verzicht m waiving (one's claim to) an inheritance; =zins m quit-rent, ground-rent; =zins-gut, =leh(e)n n copyhold.

Erd-achse (⌣…) f ⓐ axis of the earth.
er-dacht (⌣⌣̆) p.p., ⌢e (⌣⌣̆) ind. u.
er-dächte (⌣⌣̆) subj. impf. von erdenken.
Erd-alkalimetalle (⌣…) n/pl. ⓐ (Barium, Strontium, Kalzium) metals pl. of the alkaline earths; =apfel m provc. a) = Kartoffel; b) = birne; =arbeiten ⓐ f pl. earthworks pl.; =arbeiter m excavator, bsd. ⚒ navvy; =art f sort of earth; agr. (kind of) soil or mould; ⚒ geol., &c. mineral formation; ⌢artig a. ⓐ earth-like, earthy; =aufschüttung f, =aufwurf m. mound, =bahn f, ast. orbit of the earth (vgl. Erdenbahn); =ball m ♀ terrestrial globe or sphere; =balsam m mineral oil, naphtha; =bank f bank of earth, embankment; =bau m earth work; underground structure; =beben n vibration of the earth, earthquake, ⌢ seismic disturbance or tremor; =beben-kunde, -lehre f ⌢ seismology; =beben-messer m ⌢ seismometer; =beben-warte f ⌢ seismic observatory; =beben-welle f earth-wave. [berry-tree (A'rbutus une'do).]
Erd-beer-baum ♀ (⌣¹…) m ⓐ straw-
Erd-beere ♀ (⌣¹⌣) [ahd.] f ⓐ a) (Frucht) strawberry; b) (Pflanze) strawberry-plant (Fraga'ria).
Erdbeer-fingerkraut ♀ (⌣¹…) n barren strawberry (Potenti'lla ste'rilis); =klee ♀ m strawberry-trefoil (Trifo'lium fragi'ferum); =kraut v., pflanze f = Erd-beere b; =spinat m blite (Blitum); =staude f, =stock, =strauch m = Erd-beere b; =suche f picking of strawberries, strawberry-gathering.
erd-beschreibend (⌣…) a. ⓐ geographical; =beschreiber m ⓐ geographer; =beschreibung f geography; =be-wegung* ⓐ f (Fortschaffung von Erde) removal of earth; =bewohner m inhabitant of the globe, dweller on earth, poet. (earth-born) mortal; =biene f, ent. bumble-bee, ⌢ andrena; =bildungs-lehre f: ⌢ geogeny, geology; =birne ♀ (Batate) f Jerusalem artichoke, topinamber (Helia'nthus tube-ro'sus); =boden m soil, (surface of the) earth; dem ⌢ gleich machen to level with the ground; auf Gottes ⌢ in the (wide) world, on God's earth; =bogen ⓐ m, arch. dry-arch; =bohrer m ⚒ earth-borer or -drill, terrier; miner's borer; =brand ⚒ m subterraneous fire; =bruch m subsidence of the soil; =brustwehr f ⚔ earth-work; =damm m embankment, dike; =durchmesser m diameter of the earth.
Erde (⌣⌣) [ahd.: earth] f ⓐ (pl. ⌢n (§. 2) = Erdarten) 1. earth, (Welt) world, globe; zur ⌢ gehörig, aus der ⌢ kommend terrestrial; auf der ⌢ liegend lying on the ground, prostrate; im Schoße der ⌢ in the womb (or depth) of the earth; unter der ⌢ befindlich underground, subterraneous; über der ⌢ above ground, overground (railway,

&c.); bsd. rel. auf ⌢n on (this) earth, here below; f. bloß 2; mit fig. e-n unter die ⌢ bringen (j-n Tod bewirken) to be the death of a p. — 2. (Boden-art) (kind of) soil or ground or mould; lehmige ⌢ clayey soil, clay; rote ⌢ red ochre; vegetabilische ⌢ vegetable mould; (wieder) zu ⌢ werden to be reduced (or to fall, rel. to return) to dust; ⌢n pl. min.: earths, earthy minerals pl., chm.: oxides, chlorides and fluorides pl. of light metals.
Erde-essen (⌣⌣…) n ⓐ: ⌢ geophagy; ⌢essend a. ⓐ: ⌢ geophageous; =esser m: ⌢ geophagist.
Erd-eichel ♀ (⌣…) f ⓐ a) arachis, earth-nut, peanut (A'rachis hypogae'a); b) = nuß b.
Erden¹ (⌣⌣) f, inv., poet., bibl. = Erde 1.
erden² ⚒ (⌣⌣) a. ⓐ = irden.
Erden-bahn (⌣…) f poet. (man's) journey on this earth, (our) earthly travels pl. or course (vgl. Erdbahn); =bürger m earthly (or sublunary) being or creature, dweller on (this) earth, mortal (man); =freude f earthly joy.
Erd-enge (⌣…) f ⓐ ♀ (Land-enge) isthmus.
Erden-geschöpf (⌣…) n ⓐ = =bürger; =glück n earthly happiness; =güter n/pl. earthly possessions pl., rel. the treasures pl. of this earth.
er-denkbar (⌣⌣̆) a. ⓐ = erdenklich.
er-denken (⌣⌣̆) I v/a. ⓐ* 1. to think out, contrive, devise, conceive. — 2. b.s. Unwahres: to invent, forge, fabricate; das hat er sich (dat.) bloß so er-dacht that's only his invention, it's (a story of)'his own fabrication. — II ⌢ n ⓐ 3. contrivance, device; invention, fabrication.
Erden-kind (⌣⌣…) n ⓐ = =bürger.
er-denklich (⌣⌣̆) a. ⓐ imaginable, (begreiflich) conceivable; sich (dat.) alle ⌢e Mühe geben to take the greatest pains possible or imaginable.
Erden-kloß (⌣⌣…) m ⓐ clod (of earth); fig. mortal man; =last f, rel. burden of this life; =leben n. rel. (our) earthly existence, the life here below; =lei-den n earthly suffering; =not f toil in this life or world; =ruhm m earthly glory, glory of this world; =rund n = Erdrund; auf dem weiten ⌢ in the whole wide world; =schoß m womb of the earth; =sohn m = =bürger; =sorge f earthly care; =traum m earthly dream; (the short dream of) human life.
Erd-entstehung(s-lehre) (⌣…) f ⓐ: ⌢ geogeny. — Erden-wallen (⌣⌣…) n ⓐ (our) earthly pilgrimage; =wurm m poet. earthborn worm or creature.
Erd-enzian ♀ (⌣…) m ⓐ gentianella (Gentia'na acau'lis); =erschütterer m, poet. myth. (Poseidon) earth-shaker; =erschüt-terung f vibration (or concussion) of the earth, schwächer: earth-tremor; vgl. =beben; ⌢fahl a. ⓐ, ⌢falb a. earth-coloured, (of an) earthy grey, livid; =fall m landslip, landslide, subsidence of (or cavity in) the earth; =farbe f earthy colour; (Farbstoff) mineral colour; ⌢farben, ⌢farbig a. = ⌢fahl; =ferkel n, zo. earth- (or ground-) hog (Oryete'ropus cape'nsis); =ferne f,

ast.: ⌢ apogee; =fläche f surface of the earth; =floh m, ent. flea-beetle (Ha'ltica); =forschung f: ⌢ geology; =früchte f/pl. fruits pl. of the earth; =gallert(e f) n ♀ star-jelly (Nostoc commu'nis); =gang m ⚒, ⚙, arch. drive, adit, gallery, tunnel; =gans f, orn. sheldrake (Tado'rna); =gas n natural gas; ⌢geboren a. earth-born or-bred, ⌢ terrigenous; =gebor(e)ne(r) m f earth-born being, earthly creature, mortal; =gegend f region (of the earth); =geist m gnome; =gelb n, min. yellow ochre; =geruch, =geschmack m earthy smell, taste; =geschoß n ground-floor, basement; =gleicher ⚙ ⌢ equator; =grube f, hort. zur Überwinterung v. Gemüsen ɛc.: earth-pit; =grün n, paint. verditer; =gürtel m ♀ zone; =halbmesser m radius of the earth, =hälfte f ♀: ⌢ hemisphere; ⌢haltig a. containing earth; =harz n, min. asphalt(um), bitumen, ⌢ ampelite; ⌢harzig a. asphaltic, bituminous; =haufe(n) m heap of earth; =höhle f underground cave; =hügel m hillock, (earth-)mound.
erdicht ⚒ (⌣⌣̆) a. ⓐ = erdig.
er-dichten (⌣⌣̆)[mhd.]v/a.ⓐ* = erdenken 2; sich (dat.) Ruhm ⌢ to win fame as a poet or by rhyming or by one's verses; erdichtet, oft: fictitious (name, p. &c.).
Er-dichter (⌣⌣̆) m ⓐ fabricator.
Er-dichtung (⌣⌣̆) f ⓐ 1. invention. — 2. (ant. Wahrheit) b.s. fiction, fabrication;(Märchen) (fairy) tale;(Sage) legend.
erdig (⌣̆) a. ⓐ earth-like; earthy (smell, taste); adv. ⌢ riechen to smell earthy.
Erd-karte (⌣…) f ⓐ ♀ map of the world; =floß, =klumpen m = Erden-floß; =kluft f crack (or gap) in the ground; =kobalt m, min. earthy cobalt, schwarzer: black cobalt-ochre, roter: arseniate of cobalt; =kohle f, min.: (brown) lignite; =körper m a) earthly b) (die Erde als Weltkörper) terrestrial globe (or terrestrial) body; =kreis m: der (ganze) ⌢ the whole world; =kruste = -rinde; =kugel f ♀ = =ball; =kunde f geography; =kundige(r) m geographer; ⌢kundlich a. geographical; =lage f = =schicht; =leitung f, tel. earth-connexion; =licht n = =schein; =magnetismus m, phys. terrestrial magnetism; =maus f, zo. field-vole (Arvi'cola); =messer m land-surveyor; =meßkunst, =messung f land-survey (-ing); =metalle n/pl. chm., deren Oxyde die Erden sind: metals pl. of the earths; =mittelpunkt m ⓐ centre of the earth; =moos n = Bärlapp; =nähe f, ast.: ⌢ perigee; =natur-beschreibung f: ⌢ physiography; =nuß ♀ f: a) = Knollen-fümmel; b) earth-mouse or -nut (La'thyrus tubero'sus); c) = eichel; =oberfläche f = =fläche, =rinde; =öl n, min.: a) petroleum; b) ⌢ naphtha.
er-dolchen (⌣⌣̆) v/a. u. sich ⌢ v/refl. ⓐ* (sich) ⌢ to stab (o.s.) with a dagger.
Erd-pech (⌣…) n ⓐ asphalt(um); =platte f, tel. earth-plate; =pol m pole of the earth; =rauch ♀ m fumitory (Fuma'ria); =räumer ⚒ m (miner's) drag or shovel; =reich n: a) earth, soil, ground, b) bibl. (the) Earthly Kingdom.

Signs (see page XVII): F familiar; P vulgar; ꟾ flash; ⚒ rare; † obsolete (died), * new word (born); ⁓ incorrect; ♪ music;

er-dreisten (⌣´⌣): sich 2 v/refl. @@* sich 2 zu // (inf.), sich einer Sache (gen.) 2 to venture (or hazard) to //, to be so bold as to //, stärker: to have the audacity (F the cheek) to //.

er-dreschen (⌣´⌣) v/a. @b. = dreschen.

Erd-rinde (´...) f @ earth's crust; =riß m = =kluft. [= dröhnen 1.)

er-dröhnen (⌣´⌣) v/n.(h.) @@* to resound)

er-drosch ⌣ (⌣´) ind., **er-drösche** subj. impf., **er-droschen** p.p. v. erdreschen.

er-drosseln (⌣´⌣) I v/a. @@a* to throttle, strangle, garrotte. — II ~ n @ und **Er-drosselung**, **Er-droßlung** f @ throttling, strangulation, garrotting.

Erd-rücken¹ (´...) m @ = Bergrücken.

er-drücken² (⌣´⌣) I v/a. @@* to squeeze to death; to smother, stifle, suffocate; mit 2der Mehrheit by an overwhelming majority. — II ~ n @ und **Er-drückung** f @ smothering, &c. (f. I); zum ~ voll crowded to suffocation; F crammed. [⊕ terrestrial globe.]

Erd-rund (´...) n @ face of the earth;)

Er-drusch (⌣´) [erdreschen] m ⊕a. quantity of corn thrashed.

Erd-rutsch (´...) m @ = =fall; =sack ⚒ m earth-bag; =schanze ⚒ f earthworks pl.; =schatten m, ast. shadow of the earth; =scheibe ⚒ f = Alpenveilchen; =schein m, ast. des unbeleuchteten Mondteils: earth-light or -shine; =schicht f layer of earth; untere: subsoil; =schlegel m clod-beater; =schluß m = =rutsch; =schluß m, elect. earth; =schluß-anzeiger m, elect. earth-indicator; =schlüsselblume ⚒ f primrose (Pri'mula acau'lis); =schnecke f, zo. slug(-snail (Limax agre'stis); =scholle f clod; =schwamm ⚒ m mushroom, champignon (Aga'ricus campe'stris); =schwein n, zo. tamandua (Myrmeco'-phaga tetrada'ctyla), auch = =ferkel; =spalte f chasm; vgl. a. =kluft; =spitze f ⚒ neck of land; =stern ⚒ m earth-star (Gea'ster stella'tus); =stoß m shock of earthquake, ⚘ seismic shock; =strich m region, ⚒ zone; =strom m, elect. terrestrial current; =stufe f terrace; =sturz m = =fall; =teer m, min. mineral tar, auch = =harz; =teil m part of the world, ⚒ continent; =dung f @ = =dulden ꝛc.)

er-dulden (⌣´⌣) @@*, ~ n @ u. **Erdul-** **Erd-umfang** (´...) m ⚒ circumference of the earth; =umschiffer m circumnavigator of the globe; =umschiffung f circumnavigation of the globe; =umsegler ꝛc. f. =umschiffer ꝛc.

er-dursten (⌣´⌣) v/n. (fn) @@* to die of (or to suffer from) thirst.

Erd-viertel (´...) n ⚒ quarter of the globe; =wachs n, min. native paraffin, ⚘ ozocerite; =wall m = =damm; =wand f mudwall; =wärme f mean temperature of the earth; =wärts adv. earthward(s); =weite f, ast.: mean distance between the earth and the sun; =werk n earthwork; =winde ⚒ f ♃ capstan; =wolf m zo. hyena-dog; earth-wolf (Pro'teles Lala'ndii); =zittern n earth-tremor; =zone f = =strich; =zunge f = =spitze.

er-eifer/n (⌣´⌣) I sich 2 v/refl. @a* 1. = eifern 1. — 2. (in Feuer geraten) to fire up,

to be(come) heated or excited, stärker: to fly into a passion; F to boil over; sich wegen e-r Kleinigkeit 2 to be put out by a(ny) trifle; 2 Sie sich nicht! don't fire up (so)!, don't excite yourself!, keep cool! — II ~ n @ u. E/ung f @ 3. excitement, passion, F heat.

er-eignen (⌣´⌣)[adv.:*Auge] sich 2 v/refl. @b* to happen, occur, chance, take place; bisw. to betide; sollte es sich 2 daß // should it come to pass that //.

Er-eignis (⌣´⌣) [nhd. 16. sae.] n ⑰ event; (Vorfall) occurrence, incident; (Unfall) accident; welches ~! F what an event!; auf alle Ereignisse gefaßt ready for any emergency; 2=los a. uneventful; 2=reich, 2=voll a. @ eventful; full of (important) events.

er-eilen (⌣´⌣) v/a. @@* to overtake, to catch (F to fetch) up, to come up with; fig. der Tod hat ihn mitten im Schaffen ereilt death overtook (or surprised) him in the midst of his work.

Eremit (⌣⌣´) [grch.] m @, ⌣ =in f @ hermit, anchorite; ~age (⌣⌣´⌣⌣) [fr.] f @ hermitage; 2=enhaft (⌣⌣´⌣⌣), 2=isch (⌣´⌣) a. hermit-like; secluded.

Er(e)n west-dtsch. (´(⌣) m @ (Flur) f. Haus 2.

er-erben (⌣´⌣) v/a. @@* = erben I.

er-fahren (⌣´⌣) [mhd.] I v/a. @b* 1. durch Hören: to hear, learn, understand; to come to know; von wem hat er es 2? from whom did he hear (or get to know) it or get the news? — 2. durch Erproben: to (know from) experience, to make the experience of; to go through; er hat viel Unglück erfahren (erlitten) he has suffered (or undergone) a great deal of misfortune; viel Widerwärtiges 2 to meet with great unpleasantness. — II p.p. u. a. @ (D 9) 3. in den Bed. des inf. — 4. aktivisch: in Geschäften: experienced; in Künsten: expert, skilled; in den Dingen der Welt: shrewd, practical; ein 2er Mann a man of (practical) experience; ~e(r m) f @ experienced person, expert. — 5. in et. 2 (geübt) well versed in (or conversant with, well acquainted with) a th.; er ist wenig 2 in solchen Dingen he has little knowledge of such things. — III ~ \ n @

Er-fahrenheit (⌣´⌣⌣) f @, **Er-fahren-** **sein** (⌣´⌣⌣) n @ = Erfahrung 1.

Er-fahrung (⌣´⌣) f @ 1. experience, practical (⚘ empirical) knowledge; aus ~ wissen to know from (practical) exp.; Sprichw. ~ ist die beste Schule, durch ~ wird man klug, etwa: practice makes perfect; ~ kommt mit den Jahren experience grows with the years. — 2. in ~ bringen (hören) to learn, ascertain, hear; to come to know; ich habe in ~ gebracht, daß // I have found out that //, I understand that //; ich habe böse ~en damit (mit ihm) gemacht I made (or had) some unpleasant experiences with it (with him); ich habe durch ihn in ~ gebracht, daß // I was told by him that //, he gave me to understand that //. — 3. (Übung, Fertigkeit) (practical) routine or skill.

Er-fahrungs-arzt (⌣´⌣⌣...) m ⊕: ⚘ empiric; =begriff m, phls. ⚘ inductive

notion; =beweis m experimental proof; 2=gemäß = 2=mäßig, =kunde, =lehre f: ⚘ empiricism; 2=los a. @ inexperienced; =losigkeit f lack of experience; 2=mäßig a. (u. adv.) experimental(ly), ⚘ empirical(ly); adv. 2 wissen wir, daß // we know from experience that //; 2=reich a. experienced; =satz m principle founded on experience; =seelen-kunde, =lehre f ⚘ empirical psychology; =weg m: auf dem ~ by (way of) experiment, experimentally; =wissen(schaft f) n ⚘ empirical knowledge. [v. erfinden.)

er-fand (⌣´) ind., **er-fände** (⌣´⌣) subj.impf.)

er-faßbar (⌣´⌣) a. @ graspable.

er-fassen (⌣´⌣) v/a. @@* to grasp (auch fig.), to seize (hold of), to clutch; plötzlich: to snatch; fig. to comprehend; den günstigen Augenblick 2 to seize the right moment or the opportunity; et. Neues mit Begier 2 eagerly to seize (upon) ...; to rush upon ..., F to catch at ..., to catch (or lay) hold of ...

er-fechten (⌣´⌣) v/a. @b* to obtain by fighting; den Sieg 2 to gain the victory, to carry (or win) the day; ein schwer erfochtener Sieg a dearly bought victory.

er-finden (⌣´⌣) I v/a. @* 1. to invent; to find out, contrive, devise, conceive; (schaffen) to create, dichterisch: to think out, to plot (out), to make up; er hat das Pulver nicht erfunden he won't set the Thames on fire, he is no genius. — 2. b.s. = erdenken 2. — 3. fast †: e-n treu 2 to find a p. faithful. — II ~ n @ 3. = Erfindung 2.

Er-finder (⌣´⌣) m @, ~in f @ inventor (f oft: inventress), contriver, deviser; (Urheber[in]) author(ess f).

er-finderisch (⌣´⌣⌣) a. @ inventive; (scharfsinnig) ingenious, fertile in (or full of) resource, resourceful; (phantasievoll) imaginative, fanciful; creative; Sprichw.: Not macht 2 necessity is the mother of invention.

Er-finder=schutz (⌣´⌣...) m @ patent of invention; =wahn m = Erfindungs-w.

er-findsam (⌣´⌣) a. @ = erfinderisch.

Er-findung (⌣´⌣) f @ 1. (Erfinden und Erfundenes) invention, (Vorrichtung) contrivance, device. — 2. b.s. = Erdichtung 2; das ist seine eigene ~ that's his own make-up or story.

Er-findungs=gabe (⌣´⌣⌣...) f @ inventive faculty, (power of) imagination; =geist m inventive genius; =kraft f = =gabe; =patent n patent of invention; 2=reich, 2=voll a. @ = erfinderisch; =wahn m inventive mania.

er-flehen (⌣´⌣) v/a. @@* et. 2 to obtain s.th. by entreaty; to implore (or beg hard) for a th., to crave (or solicit) a th.

er-focht (⌣´⌣t) (**er-föchte** ⌣´⌣ subj.) impf., **er-fochten** (⌣´⌣t) p.p. von erfechten.

Er-folg (⌣´) m @b. result; (Ausgang) outcome, issue, end; (Wirkung) effect; abs. (glücklicher) ~ success; (keinen) ~ haben to succeed (to fail); (schlechten) ~ erzielen to prove (un)successful; von ~ gekrönt crowned with success; der ~ übertraf meine Erwartung the result surpassed my expectations.

⚘ scientific; ⚘ botanical; ⚒ geography; ⊖ machinery; ⚒ mining; ⚒ military; ♃ marine; ⚘ commercial; ⚘ postal; 🚂 railway.

[erfolgen] — 332 — [ergeben]

er-folgen (⌣⌣) v/n. (ſn) Ⓢ* **1.** to ensue, to follow, als Wirkung: to result; was wird daraus ⚲? what will be the upshot of it or come of it? — **2.** (ſtatt-finden) to take place; die Antwort iſt noch nicht erfolgt ... has not yet arrived or come to hand; es iſt nichts weiter darauf erfolgt the matter has not been further proceeded with; ⁂ die Zahlung wird bei Ablieferung ⚲ payment will be made on delivery.

erfolg-los (⌣⌣ ...) a. Ⓢ unsuccessful, fruitless, adv. in vain; **=loſigkeit** f ⓺ unsuccessfulness, fruitlessness; **⚲reich** a. successful, effective.

er-forderlich (⌣⌣⌣) Ⓢ **I** a. requisite, necessary; zu dieſer Arbeit iſt Zeit ⚲ this work requires (F takes) time; ⚲enfalls in case of need or necessity, if need be, if any necessity arose. — **II** das **⁓e** ⓺ the thing(s pl.) required or needed, F all necessaries pl.; das zum Leben ⁓e the necessaries pl. of life, enough to live upon, a sufficient income. — **⁓keit** (⌣⌣⌣⌣) f ⓺ requisiteness.

er-fordern (⌣⌣) **I** v/a. Ⓢa* to require, necessitate, demand; raſches Handeln ⚲ to call for prompt action; viel Zeit ⚲ to take up much time; gram. Zeitwörter, die den Dativ ⚲ verbs which govern the dative. — **II** ⁓ n ㉓ und **Er-forderung** f ⓺, mehr gbr. **Er-fordernis** n ⑰ exigency (or necessity) of the case; die dringenden Erforderniſſe unſerer Zeit the pressing demands (or requirements) pl. of our time.

er-forſchbar (⌣⌣-) a. Ⓢ explorable.

er-forſch/en (⌣⌣) Ⓢ* **I** v/a. **1.** to explore (= ausforſchen I). — **2.** (ergründen) to fathom; (durchſchauen) to penetrate (or F get to the bottom of) a th.; to dive into a matter. — **II** ſich ⚲ v/refl. **3.** to examine o.s. — **III** ⁓ n ㉓ **4.** = ⚲ung.

Er-forſcher (⌣⌣) m ㉒ explorer, investigator; von gelehrten Dingen: student.

er-forſchlich (⌣⌣) a. Ⓢ investigable; (ergründlich) fathomable; vgl. erforſchbar.

Er-forſchung (⌣⌣) f ⓺ exploration, &c., e-s Gelehrten: research; vgl. ausforſchen II.

er-fragen (⌣⌣) v/a. Ⓢ (⁓Ⓢb)* to (try to) find out by inquiry; to ascertain; im Bureau ⚲ inquire at the office!; bei Herrn N. zu ⚲ apply to Mr. N.

er-frechen (⌣⌣): ſich ⚲ v/refl. Ⓢ* to have the audacity (F the face or cheek) to // (inf.), to dare // (inf.).

er-freuen (⌣⌣) **I** v/a. **1.** to gladden, to give pleasure to, ſtärker: to delight; (befriedigen) to gratify; wann ⚲ Sie mich mit Ihrem Beſuche? when will you favour me with a call?; ich bin darüber erfreut I am glad of it, pleased (or charmed) to hear it; ich bin ſehr erfreut, Sie zu treffen I am delighted (or very pleased) to meet you. — **II** ſich ⚲ v/refl. **2.** ſich an et. (dat.) ⚲, ſich e-r Sache (gen.) ⚲ to find pleasure in a th. — **3.** ſich e-r Sache (gen.) ⚲ (ſie genießen) to enjoy (or possess) a th.

er-freulich (⌣⌣) a. Ⓢ pleasing, pleasant, delightful, gratifying, charming; (günſtig) favourable; ⚲er Bericht satisfactory report; das ⁓ſte für ihn iſt // what pleases him most is //.

er-freulicher-weiſe (⌣⌣⌣⌣⌣⌣) adv. to my (our) great joy, fortunately.

er-frier/en (⌣⌣) **I** v/n. (ſu) Ⓢc* **1.** to die of (or to perish from) cold; das Kind iſt erfroren ... was frozen to death; die Bäume ſind erfroren the frost killed (or nipped) ..., ... were frostbitten. — **2.** ich bin ganz erfroren I am quite (be)numbed (with cold) or thoroughly frozen; er hat erfrorne Hände ꝛc. he has chilblains on his hands, &c., his hands, &c. are frostbitten. — **II** ⁓ n ㉓ u. ⚲ung f ⓺ death (or perishing) from cold or frost.

er-friſchen (⌣⌣) **I** v/a. und ſich ⚲ v/refl. Ⓢ* **1.** (ſich) ⚲ to refresh (o.s.). — **2.** weitS. (erquicken) to comfort (or regale) with; F to set up (afresh); (beleben) to give new life to, to revive; (abtühlen) to cool; das Auge ⚲ to relieve the eye; ⚲d refreshing, comforting. — **II** ⁓ n ㉓ und **Er-friſchung** f ⓺ **3.** (ſ. I) refreshment; comfort.

Er-friſchungs=mittel (⌣ ...) n ㉒ refreshment, collation; (Trunk) refreshing draught; **=ſtation** ⛁ f station providing (passengers with) refreshments; **=zimmer** n refreshment-room or -bar.

er-fror (⌣⌣) (**er-fröre** ⌣⌣⌣ subj.) impf. u. **er-froren** (⌣⌣) p.p. von erfrieren.

er-fuhr (⌣⌣) ind., **er-führe** (⌣⌣⌣) subj. impf. v. erfahren.

er-füll/en (⌣⌣) **I** v/a. Ⓢ* **1.** to fill one with admiration, &c., to imbue (or inspire) one with sound faith, hope, &c., to strike with terror, &c.; mit et. ganz ⚲ to penetrate with s.th.; bis zum Rande erfüllt von brimful of; ganz von Gedanken erfüllt engrossed (or deeply absorbed) in thought; von Wut, von Zorn erfüllt boiling over (or inflamed, fired) with rage, anger. — **2.** j-s (auch e-m ſeine) Bitte ⚲ to comply with (or accede to) a p.'s request; von Gott: to grant (or hear) a p.'s prayer or petition; ein Gelübde ⚲ to keep (or fulfil) one's vow; eine Pflicht ⚲ to perform a duty; eine Verbindlichkeit ⚲ to meet an obligation; ein Verſprechen ⚲ to make good (or redeem) a promise; e-n Vertrag ⚲ to perform (or carry out) an agreement; ſ-n Zweck ⚲ to accomplish an object. — **II** ſich ⚲ v/refl. **3.** v. Weisſagungen ꝛc.: to come true, to take effect; ſeine Hoffnungen h. ſich (nicht) erfüllt ... have been realized (have failed or miscarried). — **III** ⁓ n ㉓ **4.** = ⚲ung.

Er-füllung (⌣⌣) f ⓺ compliance with a request; fulfilment of a vow; performance of a duty; redemption of a promise; accomplishment of an object; realization or consummation of a hope.

Er-füllungs=ort ⁂ (⌣ ...) m ㉒ place where a contract is to be fulfilled or to come into effect; **=tag** settling (or pay-)day.

er-funden (⌣⌣) p.p. von erfinden.

Erg ⚲ (⌣) [grch. érgon Wert] n ⓺ (dynam. Maßeinheit der Arbeitsgröße erg(on).

erg. abbr. = ergänze! [ergeben.]

er-gab (⌣⌣) (**er-gäbe** ⌣⌣⌣ subj.) impf. v. ſ

er-gangen (⌣⌣) p.p. von ergehen.

er-gänz/en (⌣⌣) Ⓢ* **I** v/a. **1.** to complete; (erſetzen) to supply, make up, supplement; to fill up gaps in; eine verſtümmelte Bildſäule (auch einen Text). to restore, F to patch up; ⚔ das Heer, ein Korps ⚲ to recruit the army, to complement a corps; math. ein Winkel von 30⁰ ergänzt den von 60⁰ zu einem rechten an angle of 30⁰ is complementary (or serves as complement) to one of 60⁰ — **II** ſich ⚲ v/refl. **2.** to be supplemented, restored, &c. (ſ. I); auch ea. ⚲ v/rpr. to supplement one another; die beiden Dinge ⚲ ſich ob. ea. ... are supplementary (or serve as supplements) one to the other. — **III** ⁓ n ㉓ **3.** = ⚲ung **1.** — **IV** ⚲d p.pr. u. a. Ⓢ **4.** in den Bed. des inf. — **5.** supplementary, supplemental, complementary; (zum Ganzen gehörend) integral.

Er-gänzer (⌣⌣) m ㉒ von Kunſtwerken ꝛc.: restorer, eines Textes auch: emendator.

Er-gänzung (⌣⌣) f ⓺ **1.** completion; restoration; recruiting; zur ⚲ dienend = ergänzend (ſ. ergänzen IV). — **2.** (das Ergänzte) supplement, complement; math. ſ. ⚲winkel.

Er-gänzungs=band (⌣⌣ ...) m ㉒ supplement(ary volume); **=blatt** n, **=bogen** m Buchhandel: supplement(ary sheet); waste (or imperfect) sheet; **=farben** f/pl., phys. (gelb und violet, orange und blau, rot und grün) complementary colours pl.; **=heft** n Buchhandel: supplement(ary number); **=kredit** m, parl. supplementary credit; **=mannſchaft** ⚔ f reserve (or complement) to a body of troops; in England auch: feeding-battalion, feeder, draught; **=parallelogramm** n, math. complement; **=pferde** ⚔ n/pl. remount(s pl.); ~ kaufen, ſtellen to remount; **=ſteuer** f additional tax; **=ſtück** n supplement; **=teil** m integral part; **=vorrat** m reserve store(s pl.); **⚲weiſe** adv. by way of supplement; **=werk** n supplement; **=winkel** m, math. a) zu e-m Rechten: complement (ſ. ergänzen 1); b) zu zwei Rechten: supplement; **=wörterbuch** n supplement to a dictionary.

er-gattern F (⌣⌣) v/a. Ⓢa* to obtain by sharp practices; to ferret out a secret, &c.

er-gaunern (⌣⌣) v/a. Ⓢa* to obtain by roguery or by roguish means.

er-geben (⌣⌣) Ⓢc* **I** ſich ⚲ v/refl. **1.** mſt ⚔: to surrender (or submit, yield) to the victor; ⚔ auf Gnade und Ungnade: to surrender at discretion. — **2.** ſich e-m, e-r Sache ⚲ (widmen) to devote o.s. (or to give o.s. up or over) to a p., a th.; ſich e-m ganz zu Willen ⚲ to place o.s. at a p.'s disposal; ſich dem Studium ⚲ to apply o.s. to study; ſich dem Laſter, dem Trinken ⚲ to indulge in vice; to take to drink(ing); er hat ſich ſchlechten Gewohnheiten ⚲ he has contracted (or is addicted to) bad habits. — **3.** ſich in et. ⚲ (fügen) to acquiesce in a th.; ſich in ſein Schickſal ⚲ to resign o.s. to one's fate; in ſein Schickſal ⚲ (p.p.) resigned to one's fate. — **4.** (aus et. folgen) to follow (or result) from a th.; hieraus ergibt ſich // (w)hence it follows //; weitS. (ſich ereignen) es ergibt ſich, daß // it happens that //; ſollten ſich Hinderniſſe ⚲ should obstacles arise

---

Zeichen (ſ. S. XVII): F familiär; P Volksſprache; Ⲅ Gaunerſprache; ⚲ ſelten; † alt (auch geſtorben); * neu (auch geboren); ⁑ unrichtig;

[Ergebenheit] — 333 — [erhalten]

or accrue; die sich hieraus Oden Verdrießlichkeiten the vexations pl. arising (or resulting) therefrom. — II v/a. 5. die Felder 2 (liefern) gutes Korn ... yield (or produce) good corn; das Verhör hat seine Unschuld 2 the trial has clearly proved (or brought out) his innocence. — III p.p. und a. ⑥(D9) 6. in den Bed. des inf.; einer Sache mit Leib und Seele 2 loyally attached (auch: wedded) to a cause; vgl. a. 3. — 7. in Höflichkeitsphrasen: Ihr 2ster (ob. ganz 2er) Diener your most devoted (or your humble) servant; in Briefen mst: Yours obediently or faithfully or very truly; ich bitte Sie 2st, zu // I most humbly (or respectfully) beg (of) you to //; ❀ wir teilen Ihnen ganz 2st mit we have the honour of informing you, we beg to tell you; unser ~stes our (previous) letter, auch: our respects pl.

Er-gebenheit (⌣⌣⌣) f ⑥ 1. devotion, devotedness, (loyal) attachment. — 2. ~ in den Willen Gottes resignation to God's will.

Er-gebnis (⌣⌣⌣) n ⑰ result; (Ausgang) issue; conclusion (or F upshot) of an affair; e-r Ernte: yield; math. result, answer; in Addition, Multiplikation, Subtraktion, Division: sum, product, remainder, quotient; zu keinem ~ führen to give (or yield) no result, to lead to nothing, to prove a failure.

Er-gebung (⌣⌣⌣) f ⑥ surrender, submission, resignation.

er-geh(e)n (⌣⌣(⌣) ⑧* I sich 2 v/refl. 1. zur Erholung: to walk (or stroll) about; to take (walking) exercise; fig. s-e Blicke 2 sich über // his eyes wander across (or survey) //. — 2. fig. sich in et. 2 to indulge in hopes, &c.; erzählend: to expatiate on a th.; schmähend: to break out (or launch forth) in invectives; to pour forth abuse; ratend: to make (shrewd) guesses. — II v/n. (ſn) 3. von Schriftſtücken: to be published; es ist ein Gesetz ergangen a law has been passed or promulgated; e-n Befehl, eine Einladung 2 lassen to issue an order, an invitation; ein Urteil 2 lassen to pronounce a judgment or sentence. — 4. et. über sich 2 lassen to submit to (or bear, suffer) a thing patiently; Gnade für Recht 2 lassen to let mercy take the place of justice, to temper justice with mercy. — 5. v/impers. es ergeht (geht) ihm gut, schlecht he fares (or is doing) well, badly; es würde ihm übel 2 he would come off badly or fare ill; so übel war es mir nie ergangen I had never been in such a parlous (or wretched) condition, things had never gone (or fared) so ill with me; wie mag es ihm 2? what may have become of him?; so möge es allen Dieben 2! may all thieves be served like that! — III ~ n⑳ 6. (f.5) condition (or luck, state of health) of a p.

er-geizen (⌣⌣⌣) v/a. ⑨* to hoard up riches, to amass wealth; F to scrape together (by screwing and pinching).

er-giebig (⌣⌣⌣) [ergeben] a. ⑥ yielding (much), productive, (fruchtbar) prolific, fertile, fruitful; (reich) rich or abounding (an in); ein 2es Geschäft a lucrative (or paying) business; 2e Regengüsse copious (or abundant) showers pl.

Er-giebigkeit (⌣⌣⌣-) f ⑥ yieldingness, productiveness; prolificness, fertility; richness, abundance; lucrativeness.

er-gießen (⌣⌣⌣) I v/a. und sich 2 v/refl. ⑥d* 1. to pour forth or out (auch fig.); sich 2 to flow forth, ([sich] ausbreiten) to spread; der Fluß ergießt sich ins Meer ... discharges (or empties) itself (or falls, flows) into the sea; die Gewässer 2 sich über das Land the waters overflow (or submerge) the land; die sich über ihre Wangen 2de Röte the blush which suffused (or spread over, coloured) her cheeks. — 2. fig. sich in Tränen 2 to burst into tears. — II ~ n⑳ u. **Er-gießung** f ⑥ 3. (f.I) pouring forth; spread(ing); discharge; fig. von Gefühlen: effusion, outpouring, overflow(ing), F gush.

er-ging (⌣⌣) ind., 2e subj. impf. v. ergehen.

er-glänzen (⌣⌣⌣) v/n. (ſn) ⑨* to shine forth, to beam; (funkeln) to sparkle.

er-glimmen (⌣⌣⌣) v/n. (ſn) ⑥a(⑧)* to begin to glimmer or glow. [er-glimmen.]

er-glomm (⌣⌣) impf., 2en (⌣⌣⌣) p.p. von]

er-glühen (⌣⌣⌣) v/n. (ſn) ⑧* to (begin to) glow; für e-n, et. 2 to be an ardent supporter of a p., a th.

er-goß (⌣⌣) ind., **er-göſſe** (⌣⌣⌣) subj. impf., **er-goſſen** (⌣⌣⌣) p.p. von ergießen.

er-gößen (⌣⌣⌣) [mhd. vergeſſen m.] I v/a. u. sich 2. ⑨* to divert, to entertain; to make glad, to gladden; die Augen, die Sinne 2 to please the eye, to flatter the senses; sich 2 to enjoy o.s.; er wird sich höchlich darüber 2 he will be highly amused (or delighted) at (or with) it. — II ~ n⑳ u. **Er-gößung** f ⑥ 4. das ~e the sublime, the grand, &c (f. 2); vom ~en zum Lächerlichen ist nur ein Schritt it's but one step from the sublime to the ridiculous.

Er-habenheit (⌣⌣⌣-) f ⑥ (f.erhaben) elevation; saliency; prominence, loftiness; phys. convexity; (Hervorragendes) protuberance; fig. sublimeness, sublimity, eminence, grandeur; superiority.

er-hallen (⌣⌣⌣) v/n. (ſn) ⑧* to resound.

er-haltbar (⌣⌣⌣) a. ⑥ (f.erhalten) 1. preservable, maintainable. — 2. obtainable.

er-halten (⌣⌣⌣) I v/a. und sich 2 v/refl. ⑥a* 1. (bewahren) to keep, preserve, uphold; (unterstützen) to support, assist, maintain, keep up; am Leben 2 to keep alive; möge ihn Gott am Leben 2 may God spare him; Gott erhalte den König! God save the King!; in gutem Stande 2 to keep in good repair; das Gemälde, Manuskript ist gut (ob. hat sich gut) 2 ... is in a good state of preservation, ... is in good condition; ❀: ich will mich bestreben, mir Ihr Vertrauen zu 2 ... to retain your confidence; die Wolle hat sich im Preise 2

♪ Musik; ⚛ Wissenschaft; ⚘ Pflanze; 🜨 Geographie; ⚙ Technik; ⚒ Bergbau; ⚔ Militär; ⚓ Marine; ⚖ Handel; ✉ Post; 🚆 Eisenbahn.

[Erhalter] — 334 — [Erhörung]

... has remained firm; von Preisen: sich 2 to rule (or keep) steady. — 2. sich 2 (ernähren) to keep (or support, maintain) o.s.; to earn (or make) a living; sich von etwas 2 to live on s.th., to make a living out of a th. — 3. (bekommen) Erlaubnis zu et. 2 to obtain (P to get) permission (or leave) for a th.; ich habe gestern Kunde, Nachricht von ihm 2 I received (or had) news, intelligence from him yesterday; *parl.*, &c. das Wort 2 to catch the Speaker's eye, to obtain possession of the House, weit. to be allowed to speak or to make a speech; ich habe es zugeschickt 2 I had it sent on to me; ❊: einen besseren Preis 2 to secure (or get) a higher price; ich bescheinige, 100 Mark 2 zu h. I acknowledge the receipt of five pounds; Wert 2 (*p.p.*) value received. — 4. (hervorbringen) to produce; Salz läßt sich aus dem Salzwasser 2 salt can be obtained (or made) from salt water. — II ~ *n* ㉓ 5. = Erhaltung.

Er-halter (◡˘◡) *m* ㉒, **~in** *f* ㊵ (f. erhalten 1) keeper, preserver, upholder; supporter; (Hauptstütze) mainstay.

er-hältlich (◡˘◡) *a.* ㊻ (zu erhalten) obtainable; (zu kaufen) purchasable; nicht 2 not to be bought or had.

Er-haltung (◡˘◡) *f* ㊻ keep(ing), preservation, support, maintenance; *phys.* ~ der Kräfte conservation of forces.

Er-haltungs-brille (◡˘◡...) *f* ㊷ eye-(or sight-)preservers *pl.*; =mittel *n/pl.* means *pl.* of subsistence or support; =trieb *m* preservative instinct; instinct of self-preservation.

er-handeln (◡˘◡) *v/a.* ㉒a* 1. Vermögen: to acquire (F make) ... by trade. — 2. Waren 2 to purchase goods.

er-häng/en (◡˘◡) I *v/a.* (u. sich 2 *v/refl.*) ⓫* to hang (o.s.). — II ~ *n* ㉓ = E/ung. **Er-hängte**([r] *m* *f* (◡˘◡) ㊷ p. hanged. **Er-hängung** (◡˘◡) *f* ㊻ hanging.

er-harschen ⓵*, **er-harten** ⓺* (◡˘◡) *v/n.* (in) to grow harsh, hard.

er-härt/en (◡˘◡) I *v/a.* ⓫* *fig.* (bekräftigen) to corroborate, to confirm; (beweisen) to prove; eidlich 2 to affirm on (or to substantiate by) oath. — II ~ *n* ㉓ und E/ung *f* ㊻ corroboration, confirmation; proof; affirmation.

er-haschen (◡˘◡) *v/a.* ⓫* to catch, seize, lay hold of; to snatch, F grab; erhaschte Freuden *f/pl.* snatches *pl.* of joy.

er-heben (◡˘◡) ⓰(⑦)b* I *v/a.* 1. (in die Höhe bringen) to raise, to lift; mit Mühe: to heave; die Augen 2 to cast (or lift) up one's eyes; 2b elevating (auch *fig.*). — 2. *fig.* ein Geschrei, die Stimme 2 to raise a shout, one's voice; Klagen 2 to utter lamentations, to wail, to lament; Schwierigkeiten 2 to raise difficulties or objections; einen Streit 2 (anfangen) to start a dispute, to pick a quarrel; *jur.* eine Klage 2 gegen // to bring an action against //. — 3. (erhöhen) to elevate; j-s Verdienst 2 (preisen) to exalt a p.'s merit; in den Adelsstand 2 to raise to the peerage, to give noble rank to, to make a peer (or a nobleman)

of; in den Himmel 2 to extol (or laud, praise) to the skies; zum Königreiche 2 to erect into a kingdom; zum Gesetz 2 to pass (into law), to put on the statute-book; zum Ritter: to knight; zum System 2 to make a system of; *math.* zum Quadrat, Kubus 2 to square, to cube; zu e-r höheren Potenz, zu der *x*ten Potenz 2 to raise to a higher power, to the xth power. — 4. Gelder 2c. 2 (in Empfang nehmen) to raise money, to levy (or collect) taxes, to draw one's salary, to receive a legacy; Geld bei e-r Bank 2 to draw money at (or out of) a bank. — 5. *jur.* 2 (feststellen) to make (an) inquiry, to investigate. — II sich 2 *v/refl.* 6. to (a)rise, to raise o.s.; plötzlich: to start (or spring) up; von Vögeln 2c. to soar (or fly) up. — 7. sich gegen e-n 2 to rebel (or rise, revolt) against a p.; sich über et. 2 to surmount a th., to tower above a th.; sich über andere 2 (proudly) to look down upon others; *fig.* sich nie über das Alltägliche 2 never to soar above the commonplace; sich mit der Stimme nicht über ein Flüstern 2 not to raise one's voice (or not to speak) above a whisper.

er-heblich (◡˘◡) *a.* ㊻ considerable, (wichtig) important, weighty; of (great) consequence or importance; (bedeutlich) grave, serious; *adv.* 2 (viel) größer considerably larger, much greater; **~keit** *f* ㊻ considerableness, importance, weightiness; gravity.

Er-hebung (◡˘◡) *f* ㊻ 1. raising (or elevation) to the throne, &c.; des Bodens 2c.: upheaval, (Hügel) swelling (or rising) ground; eminence. — 2. promotion; exaltation, laudation; *math.* zu einer Potenz: ⟶ involution. — 3. von Geldern: raising, levying; collection of taxes, &c. — 4. *jur.* (official) inquiry. — 5. rebellion, rising, revolt.

er-heiraten (◡˘◡) *v/a.* ⓫* ein Vermögen 2 to obtain (or acquire, get) ... by (or through) marriage, F to marry ...

er-heischen (◡˘◡) ⓵* = erfordern I.

Er-heiterer (◡˘◡) *m* ㉒ cheerer.

er-heiter/n (◡˘◡) *v/a.* ⓫a* u. ~ *n* ㉓, E/ung *f* ㊻ = aufheitern 2c.

er-heizen (◡˘◡) I *v/a.* ⓫* to heat well or thoroughly. — II ~ *n* ㉓ u. Er-heizung *f* ㊻ heating; firing.

er-hellen (◡˘◡) ⓺* I *v/a.* to light up a room, to illuminate a town, to brighten a colour; *fig.* to elucidate a matter, to clear up (or throw light upon) a question; das Nordlicht erhellt die Nächte Lapplands the northern light illuminates (or lends brightness to) the nights of Lapland; vom Monde erhellt lit up by moonshine, moon-lit. — II *v/n. impers.* to be(come) clear or apparent; hieraus erhellt, daß // from that it is (or becomes) evident that //. — III ~ *n* ㉓ u. Er-hellung *f* ㊻ lighting up, illumination.

er-heucheln (◡˘◡) *v/a.* ㉒a* 1. to obtain by hypocrisy or false professions. — 2. (fälschlich vorgeben) to feign, pretend, affect, profess, simulate; F to sham, to put on; erheuchelt pretended, affected, hypocritical, F sham (piety, &c.).

er-hielt (◡˘) (2e *subj.*) *impf. v.* erhalten.

er-hitzen (◡˘◡) I *v/a.* und sich 2 *v/refl.* ⓮* to heat, to make hot; *fig.* to fire the imagination; sich 2 to get heated, to grow hot; *fig.* to become heated or animated or angry, F to fire up; zu sehr 2 to overheat; erhitzt aussehen to look (over-)heated. — II ~ *n* u. Er-hitzung *f* ㊻ (f. I) heat(ing), firing; ⟶ calorification.

er-hob (◡˘) *ind.*, **er-höbe** (◡˘◡) *subj. impf.* u. **er-hoben** (◡˘◡) *p.p.* von erheben.

er-hoffen (◡˘◡) *v/a.* ⓺* to hope for; der erhoffte Gewinn the hoped-for (or expected) gain, the profit looked for.

er-höhen (◡˘◡) I *v/a.* und sich 2 *v/refl.* ⓺* 1. to raise; vgl. erheben 3; *bibl.* wer sich selbst erhöhet, der wird erniedrigt werden he that exalteth himself shall be abased. — 2. (steigern) to raise, increase, enhance, heighten; erhöhte Geschwindigkeit accelerated speed; erhöhter Lohn higher (or better) pay or wages; erhöhte Preise advanced (or higher) prices; erhöhte Tätigkeit increased activity; erhöhter Zoll additional duty; den Wert von etwas 2 to improve the value of a thing; *arith.* auf das Doppelte, Dreifache, Vierfache 2 to double, treble, quadruple; auf das Hundertfache, Vielfache 2 to centuple, to multiply. — 3. ♪ to sharpen a note. — II ~ *n* ㉓ u. Er-höhung *f* ㊻ 4. (f. 1) raising; (Anhöhe) elevation; vgl. Erhebung 1 u. 2. — 5. (f. 2) enhancement; increase; auch acceleration of speed; rise of wages; advance (or improvement) of prices.

Er-höhungs-grad (◡˘◡...) *m* ㉒, =winkel ✕ *m* eines Geschützes degree, angle of elevation; **=zeichen** ♪ *n* sharp (#).

er-holen (◡˘◡): sich 2 *v/refl.* ⓺* 1. to recover from an illness or a loss; to come to (or come round) after a faint(ing fit); sich wieder 2 to gain (or gather) new strength; nach der Arbeit: to take recreation or rest, to rest o.s.; nach dem Studium: to unbend (or relax) one's mind; ❊ die Preise haben sich erholt prices have recovered or rallied. — 2. sich bei e-m Rats 2 to seek a p.'s advice. — 3. ❊ sich auf e-n (auch an e-m) 2 für et. to reimburse o.s. (durch Wechsel) to draw) upon a p. for s.th.

Er-holung (◡˘◡) *f* ㊻ (f. erholen I) recovery; *med.*: ⟶ analepsis; recreation, rest, relaxation; ich ging zu meiner ~ in die Schweiz I went to Switzerland for a change; er gönnt sich keine ~ he does not give himself any rest.

Er-holungs-reise (◡˘◡...) *f* ㊷: pleasure-trip; (Ausflug) outing, excursion; weit. change of air; **=stunde**, **=zeit** *f* für Schüler recreation- (or play-)time, break between the lessons.

er-hör/en (◡˘◡) I *v/a.* ⓺* e-n (oder j-s Bitte) 2 to listen (or give ear) to (stärker: to grant) a p.'s request; nicht 2 to turn a deaf ear to; *rel.* Gott hat sie erhört ... heard her prayer. — II ~ *n* ㉓ und E/ung *f* ㊷: listening to, &c. (f. I); (feine) ~ finden to meet with a favourable (with no) response.

Signs (see page XVII): F familiar; P vulgar; ꝉ flash; ↘ rare; † obsolete (died); * new word (born); ⁺⁺ incorrect; ♪ music;

[erhub] — 335 — [Erklärung]

er-hub subst. (⌣́) ind. u. **er-hübe** (⌣́⌣) subj. impf. v. erheben.

Erich (⌣́) [schwd.] npr/m. ⑮⑯α. (Bn.) Eric. [(Heidekraut) heather (*Erica*).]

Erika ♀ (-⌣́⌣, P₊₊ ⌣́⌣) [grch.] ♀ ㊺ u. ㊻

Er-inner ⌢ (⌣́⌣⌣) m ㉒ monitor.

er-innerlich (⌣́⌣⌣) a. ㊿ within one's memory or recollection, present to one's mind; das ist mir (ganz) ♀ I remember it (well), I (fully) recollect it; soviel mir ♀ ist as far as I can remember, to the best of my recollection.

er-innern (⌣́⌣⌣) [nhd.] ㉑a* I v/a. 1. e-n an etwas (*poet.* auch einer Sache gen.) ♀ to remind a p. of a th., to call (or bring) a thing back to a p.'s mind; ich muß ihn oft daran ♀ I have often to refreshen (F brush up) his memory; ♀d an commemorative of. — 2. et. (mahnend, tadelnd ꝛc.) ♀ to mention s.th. by way of admonition, reproach, &c.; ich habe nichts dabei zu ♀ ... nothing to say (or no objection) to it; im Vorbeigehen will ich daran ♀, daß // I may just observe in passing that //. — II sich ♀ v/refl. 3. sich einer Sache (gen.), j-s oder an et., e-n ♀, auch: sich (dat.) et. ♀ to remember (or recollect, bear in mind) a th., a p.; soviel ich mich ♀ kann as far as I (can) recollect or my recollection goes; sie ♀ sich dessen nicht mehr they have no recollection of it. — III ♀d p.pr. u. a. ㊿ 4. in den Bedeutungen des inf. — 5. commemorative of.

Er-innerung (⌣́⌣⌣) f ㊺ 1. reminder; (Mahnung) admonition; ich kann es nicht aus der ~ bringen I cannot forget it or eradicate it from my memory; e-m et. in ~ bringen to remind a p. of a th.; to recall a th. to a p.'s mind. — 2. remembrance, recollection; von längst Vergangenem: reminiscence of the past; zur ~ an // in commemoration (or memory, remembrance) of //.

Er-innerungs-buch (⌣́⌣⌣⌣) n ㊻ memorandum-book; =fest n commemoration(-day), commemorative fête or festival; =kraft f power of recollection; memory; =schreiben n monitory letter; =schrift f memorial; =tafel f commemorative tablet; =vermögen n = =kraft; ♀weise adv. by way of a reminder; =zeichen n souvenir, keepsake; token of love, &c.).

Erinnye (⌣⌣́⌣) f ㊽, **Erinnys** (⌣́⌣⌣) [grch. *Erī'nys*] f ㊾ myth. (Rachegöttin) Erin(n)ys, pl. oft: Furies.

Eris (⌣́) [grch.] npr/f.inv., myth. (Göttin der Zwietracht) Eris; ~apfel m ㊷ apple of discord; cause of (a) dispute.

er-jagen (⌣⌣́) v/a. ㉑* 1. ein Wild ♀ to hunt up game. — 2. to catch up (or overtake) in running; *fig.* to secure, lay hold of, snatch, F grab; das Glück zu ♀ suchen to hunt (or race) after fortune.

er-kalt/en (⌣⌣́) I v/n. (fn) ㉑* to cool down (auch *fig.*), to grow cold or chilly; in seinem Eifer ♀, auch: to abate in one's zeal. — II ~ n ㉓ = ♀ung.

er-kälten (⌣⌣́) I v/a. u. sich ♀ v/refl. ㉑* to chill; meist: sich ♀ to catch (or take) (a) cold or a chill; sich leicht ♀ to be susceptible to cold; erkältet

having a cold or a chill. — II ~ n ㉓ = ♀kältung.

Er-kaltung (⌣⌣́⌣) f ㊺ cooling down, &c. (f. erkalten I); *fig.* (a. growing) coolness, coldness; abatement of zeal.

Er-kältung (⌣⌣́⌣) f ㊺ path. cold, chill, catarrh; an e-r starken ~ leiden to suffer from a severe (F to have a nasty) cold.

er-kämpfen (⌣⌣́⌣) v/a. ㉑* to gain (or obtain) by fighting or battling.

er-kannt (⌣⌣́), ♀e(⌣⌣́⌣) impf. v. erkennen.

er-kauf/en (⌣⌣́) I v/a. ㉑* 1. = kaufen: et. mit (od. durch) sein Leben ꝛc. ♀ to purchase a th. at the price of one's life, &c. — 2. ein günstiges Urteil durch Bestechung ♀ to obtain a favourable judgment by bribery or corruption; e/ter Mörder, Zeuge hired assassin, suborned witness. — II ~ n ㉓ = ♀ung.

er-käuflich (⌣⌣́⌣) a. ㊿ ꝛc. = käuflich 2.

Er-kaufung (⌣⌣́⌣) f ㊺ 1. purchase. — 2. bribery, corruption, subornation.

er-kecken (⌣⌣́): sich ♀ v/refl. ㉑* to make bold to, to be so bold as to (mit inf.).

er-kennbar (⌣⌣́) a. ㊿ 1. (kenntlich) recognizable; *phls.* knowable. — 2. (wahrnehmbar) perceptible, discernible.

Er-kennbarkeit (⌣⌣́--) f ㊺ (f. erkennbar) 1. recognizability. — 2. perceptibility, discernibility.

er-kennen (⌣⌣́) ⑮b* I v/a. 1. to recognize; (wahrnehmen) to discern, perceive, notice; e-n an der Stimme ꝛc. ♀ to know a p. by his voice, &c.; sich seinen Freunden zu ♀ geben to make o.s. known (or to discover o.s.) to one's friends; e-m et. zu ♀ geben to signify (or notify) s.th. to a p.; sich nicht zu ♀ geben to keep one's incognito; er ließ sich nicht ♀ he was not recognizable; es läßt sich leicht ♀ it is easily understood that //; es läßt sich nicht ♀, ob // it is impossible to know whether //; *bibl.* an ihren Früchten sollt ihr sie ♀ by their fruits ye shall know them; Sprichw. den Freund erkennt man in der Not a friend in need is a friend indeed. — 2. *jur.* über (ob. in) etwas ♀ to pronounce judgment upon a th.; auf Todesstrafe ♀ to pass a death-sentence; in seinem Prozeß ist noch nicht erkannt worden in his suit judgment has not yet been pronounced. — 3. ♀ für eine Summe ♀ to credit a p. for a sum of money. — 4. *bibl.* fleischlich ♀ to know a woman. — II sich ♀ v/refl. 5. to (begin to) understand o.s.; erkenne dich selbst! know thyself!; sich schuldig ♀ to confess one's guilt, vor Gericht: to plead guilty; vgl. a. 1. — III ~ n ㉓ 6. = ♀ung. [kennen.]

er-kenn(e)te (⌣⌣́⌣) subj. impf. von er-]

er-kenntlich (⌣⌣́⌣) a. ㊿ a) easily recognized; b) (dankbar) grateful for; ich bin Ihnen dafür sehr ♀ I am greatly obliged to you for it; ~keit (⌣⌣́⌣) f ㊺ gratefulness, (sense of) obligation.

Er-kenntnis (⌣⌣́⌣) I f ⑱ knowledge; (Wahrnehmung) perception; (Einsicht) discernment, intuition; (Verständnis) understanding, *phls.* cognition; e-n zur ~ (seines Irrtums ꝛc.) bringen, oft: to disabuse (or disillusion) a p., to

bring a p. to his senses; zur ~ gelangen, kommen to recognize (or see) one's mistake; *bibl.* der Baum der ~ the tree of knowledge. — II n ㉗ *jur.* ~ (Spruch) e-s Gerichts: judgment, sentence, (final) decision; der Geschworenen: verdict given by the jury.

Er-kenntnis-grund (⌣⌣́⌣...) m ㊷ foundation of knowledge; criterion; =kraft f perceptive faculty, intellect(ual power); =kreis m circle of knowledge; =vermögen n = =kraft.

Er-kennung (⌣⌣́⌣) f ㊺ 1. recognition; vgl. Erkenntnis. — 2. *bibl.* (f. erkennen 4) carnal knowledge of a woman. — 3. *med.* einer Krankheit: ⚗ diagnosis.

Er-kennungs-marke (⌣⌣́⌣...) f ㊷ bsd. ⚔ identity-disk; =szene f scene of recognition; =vermögen n = Erkenntniskraft; =wort n bsd. ⚔ watchword, (Parole) password; =zeichen n sign of recognition; distinctive mark; *med.* diagnostic symptom.

Erker (⌣́⌣) [nhd.; *mlt. arcora*] m ㊷ *arch.* projecting room or story; (Eckzimmer) alcove, ehm.: oriel; (Altan) balcony.

Erker-fenster (⌣́⌣...) n ㊶ bay- (or bow-) window; bisw. a. jut-window; =säule f jutty-column; =stübchen, =zimmer n turret-chamber, corner-room.

er-kiesen geh. Spr. (⌣⌣́⌣) v/a. ㉑* (*impf. ꝛc.* f. "erkor) to choose, elect. [erklingen.]

er-klang (⌣⌣́) (**er-klänge** subj. impf. von]

er-klärbar (⌣⌣́-) a. ㊿ explainable, interpretable, accountable, explicable; es ist mir nicht erklärbar, warum // it is inexplicable to me why //; ~keit (⌣⌣́--) f ㊺ accountableness, interpretableness, explicableness.

er-klären (⌣⌣́⌣) I v/a. und sich ♀ v/refl. ㉑* 1. (auseinandersetzen) to explain; (aufklären) to elucidate, illustrate, clear up; (deuten) to interpret dreams; to comment upon a passage; ausführlich: to expound the scriptures, &c.; Begriffe, Worte ♀ to define notions, words; das erklärt sich leicht it is easily accounted for; ♀d explanatory; illustrative; bsd. *jur.* declarative. — 2. sich ♀ (aussprechen) to declare; sich deutlich ♀ to speak plainly. — 3. f. Acht²; eine Stadt in Belagerungszustand ♀ to proclaim (martial law or a state of siege in) a town; e-n für einen Betrüger ♀ to call a p. a cheat; etwas für null und nichtig ♀ to declare a th. null and void, to invalidate (or annul) a th.; Krieg ♀ to declare war against; er wurde für schuldig erklärt he was pronounced (or found) guilty, f. vogelfrei. — 4. sich für, gegen e-n ♀ to declare for, against a p.; sich für besiegt ♀ to acknowledge o.s. defeated. — II **er-klärt** p.p. u. a. ㊿ 5. Bed. des *inf.* — 6. (entschieden) avowed, professed.

Er-klärer (⌣⌣́⌣) m ㉒, ~in f ㊵ interpreter, commentator, expounder.

er-klärlich (⌣⌣́⌣) a. ㊿ = erklärbar; leicht ♀ easily accounted for, easy of explanation, quite comprehensible.

Er-klärung (⌣⌣́⌣) f ㊺ 1. (vgl. erklären) explanation, elucidation, illustration; interpretation, commentary; exposition, definition; kritische: ⚗

⚗ scientific; ♀ botanical; ♀ geography; ⊕ machinery; ⚔ mining; ⚔ military; ⚓ marine; ● commercial; ✉ postal; ⛟ railway.

[Erklärungsart] — 336 — [erleichtern]

exegesis; es bedarf keiner ~ it requires no explanation or comment; e-e genügende ~ über et. abgeben to give a satisfactory account of a th. — 2. declaration of war, &c.; öffentliche ~ public statement; politische (it.) manifesto; vor Gericht: deposition, evidence.
Er-klärungs-art (‿́‿…) f ⑫ manner (or method) of explanation; =kunst f: ⚥ exegetics; =schrift f commentary; =versuch m attempted explanation.
er-klecklich (‿‿‿) a. ⑥ considerable; einen ~en Gewinn m. to make a substantial profit; F to be a large gainer; das kostete ihn ein ~es that cost him a good deal (of money).
er-klettern ⑨a*, **er-klimmen** ⑨a (⑱)* (‿‿‿) I v/a. to climb (or swarm) up a tree; to scale a wall, to ascend a mountain; to mount up a ladder; F to scramble up a hillside. — II ~ n ㉓ climbing up, &c. (f. I); ascent of a mountain, mounting (of) a ladder.
er-klingen (‿‿‿) v/n. (fn) ⑰f* to resound; laut ~ to ring out.
er-klirren (‿‿‿) v/n. (fn) ⑧* to (begin to) rattle; von Schwertern: to clash.
er-klomm (‿‿) (**er-klömme** subj.) impf., **er-klommen** (‿‿‿) p.p. v. erklimmen.
er-klügeln (‿‿‿) v/a. ⑨a. to puzzle out, to discover by (deep) meditation.
er-klungen (‿‿‿) p.p. von erklingen.
er-kor (‿‿) ind., **er-köre** (‿‿‿) subj. impf., **er-koren** (‿‿‿) p.p. von erkiesen.
er-kranken (‿‿‿) I v/n. (fn) ⑧* to fall (or be taken) ill; an den Masern ~ to fall sick of the measles; gefährlich erkrankt dangerously ill. — II ~ n ㉓ u. **Er-krankung** f ⑯ being taken ill, &c. (f. I); wegen plötzlicher ~ owing to sudden indisposition, through sudden illness; im ~s-falle in case of illness (occurring).
er-kühnen (‿‿‿) I sich ~ v/refl. ⑧* schwächer als sich erdreisten to make bold to, to venture to; sich e-r Sache (gen.) ~ ob. sich ~ et. zu tun to attempt s. th. bold. — II ~ n ㉓ u. **Er-kühnung** f ⑯ boldness, daring; venture(someness).
er-kunden (‿‿‿) I v/a. ⑧* to find out by inquiry; to spy out; to ascertain; ✕ (rekognoszieren) to reconnoitre. — II ~ n ㉓ = Erkundung.
er-kundigen (‿‿‿‿): sich ~ v/refl. ⑧* sich nach (ob. über) et. ~ to inquire after (or about) a th. (bei e-m of a p.); hast du dich nach der Zeit erkundigt? did you ask (or inquire) the time or what the time was?
Er-kundigung (‿‿‿‿) f ⑯ inquiry; ~ einziehen über et. to make inquiry (or to gather information) about a th., to inquire into a th.; ~s-bureau (‿…) n ⑫ (Auskunftei) inquiry-office.
Er-kundung (‿‿‿) f ⑯ finding out; ascertainment; ✕ reconnaissance.
er-künsteln (‿‿‿‿) I v/a. ⑨a* to affect; weit.S. = erheucheln 2. — II ~ n ㉓ u. **Er-künst(e)lung** f ⑯ affectation, pretence, F sham(ming). I (⑨*) to choose, elect.
er-küren geh. Spr. (‿‿‿) [erfor] v/a. ⓜd*J
Erl. abbr. = Erlaucht.   [= laben.J
er-laben (‿‿) v/a. u. sich ~ v/refl. ⑧*J
er-lag (‿‿) (**er-läge** subj.) impf. v. erliegen.

er-lahm/en (‿‿‿) I v/n. (fn) ⑧* to grow lame; fig. to be paralysed; to grow weary; to flag (or relax, slacken, droop) in one's efforts; sein Eifer ist erlahmt, er ist in seinem Eifer erlahmt his zeal has abated, he has cooled down (in his enthusiasm). — II **E/ung** f ⑯ lameness (setting in); paralysis.
er-langbar (‿‿‿) a. ⑥ attainable, procurable; ~keit (‿‿‿‿) f ⑯ attainableness.
er-langen (‿‿‿) I v/a. ⑧* etwas ~ (erreichen) to reach (meist fig. to attain) a th.; (sich verschaffen) to procure, obtain, get; (erwerben) to acquire; Zutritt ~ to gain admission; wieder ~ to recover; schwer zu ~ difficult of attainment. — II ~ n ㉓ u. **Er-langung** f ⑯ (f. I) reaching; attainment; acquisition, acquirement; recovery.
er-las (‿‿) (**er-läse** subj.) impf. v. erlesen.
Er-laß (‿‿) m ⓫(öst. a. ⑧) a. 1. (Lossprechung) dispensation, (Erleichterung) remission of taxes, sins &c.; relief; gänzlicher: exemption, acquittance, release; ⊛ (Rabatt) reduction, deduction, abatement. — 2. (Schreiben, Verordnung) issue of an order, enactment of a law; writ of parliament; öffentlicher ~ edict, proclamation, decree.
er-lass/en (‿‿‿) I v/a. ⑧a* (p.p. ~) 1. e-n Befehl, Gesetze ꝛc. ~ (ergehen lassen) to publish (or issue) an order, &c.; to enact laws, &c. — 2. e-m e-e Schuld, e-e Verbindlichkeit ~ to remit a p.'s debt; to release (bisw. acquit) a p. from an obligation; to let a p. off; (verzeihen) to pardon a p. (for) a th. — II ~ n ㉓ = E/ung.
er-läßlich (‿‿‿) a. ⑥ remissible, pardonable; ~e Sünde, **Er-laß-sünde** f ⑯ rel. venial (or slight) offence.
Er-lassung (‿‿‿) f ⑯ 1. publication, issue, enactment of sins. — 2. = Erlaß 1.
Er-lassungs-brief (‿‿‿…) m ⑫ letter of remission or dispensation; =jahr n = Ablaßjahr; =sünde f venial offence.
er-lauben (‿‿‿) [ahd.: leave] v/a. ⑧* 1. to allow (or permit) a p. to do a th.; to give a p. leave (or permission) for (or to do) a th.; gesetzlich erlaubt legal; Redensarten: ~ Sie! allow me!, als Einwurf: pardon me!; wenn Sie es ~ if you are agreeable to it; wir ~ uns zu bemerken we beg …; es ist ihm (nicht) erlaubt auszugehen he is allowed (forbidden) …; er wollte uns nicht ~ zu rauchen he would not let us smoke, he objected to our smoking; meine Mittel ~ mir das I can afford it; wenn das Wetter es erlaubt wind and weather permitting; ⊛ durch Gegenwärtiges ~ wir uns, zu // herewith (or with the present) we beg to //, we purpose by these lines to //. — 2. sich (dat.) etwas ~ (herausnehmen) to take liberties, to take upon o.s. to; to make free of; stärker: to make bold to do a th.
Er-laubnis (‿‿‿) f ⑱ permission; leave; eccl. license, dispensation; mit Ihrer ~ with your permission, by your leave; mit j-s stillschweigender ~ with a p.'s tacit consent; er bat um ~, zu // he begged leave to //; ~karte f ⑫, ~schein m license, pe'rmit; pass.

er-laucht (‿‿t) [mhd. aus erleucht(et) = mlt. illu'stris] I a. ⑥ illustrious, noble; (erhaben) augu'st. — II (‿‿) ~ f ⑯ v. fürstlichen Personen: Se. (Seine) ~ der Reichsgraf His Highness the Count.
er-lauern (‿‿‿) v/a. ⑨a* den günstigen Augenblick ~ to (be on the) watch for the favourable moment, to seize (or snatch) one's opportunity. [listening.J
er-lauschen (‿‿‿) v/a. ⑨* to learn byJ
Er-läuterer (‿‿‿‿) m ㉒, **Er-läut(r)erin** f ⑯ elucidator, interpreter.
er-läutern (‿‿‿) I v/a. ⑨a* to elucidate, interpret, make clear; durch Beispiele: to exemplify; (erklären) to explain. — II ~ n ㉓ u. **Er-läuterung** f ⑯ (f. I) elucidation, exemplification; explanation; gram. (Umschreibung) paraphrase.
Erle ♀ (‿‿) [ahd.: alder] f ⑯ alder (-tree) (Alnus); ⊕ (Metallplatte unter der Schale des Taschenmessers) metal plate in the handle of a penknife.
er-leben (‿‿‿) v/a. ⑧* 1. to live to see; wir werden noch ~, daß Menschen fliegen we shall yet live to see people fly; hat je einer so was erlebt? did ever anyone witness the like?; was man nicht (alles) erlebt! what strange things we experience! — 2. sein achtzigstes Jahr, ein hohes Alter ~ (erreichen) to live (up) to one's eightieth year, to a good old age; die zehnte Auflage ~ to go (or run) through ten editions. — 3. (erfahren) to experience; to meet with, to pass through, Schlimmes: to undergo; das von ihm in Afrika Erlebte his experiences pl. in Africa, his African adventures pl.
Er-lebnis (‿‿‿) n ⑰ personal experience, event (or occurrence) in a p.'s life; scene witnessed by a p.; (Abenteuer) adventure, unangenehmes: misadventure.
er-ledigen (‿‿‿‿) I v/a. u. sich ~ v/refl. ⑧* 1. sich einer Sache (gen.) ~ (entledigen) to free o. s. from a th., to rid o. s. of a th. — 2. (beseitigen, beendigen) to dispatch, discharge, settle, terminate; to set at rest; Fragen: to answer; einen Streit: to adjust; Zweifel: to remove; hiermit erledigt sich die Sache that settles (or finishes) the matter, this brings the matter to a close. — II ~ n ㉓ 3. = IV — III **er-ledigt** p.p. u. a. ⑥ 4. in den Beb. des inf. — 5. von Ämtern: vacant; vacated. — III **Er-ledigung** f ⑯ 6. (f. 2) dispatch of business; settlement of a question; answer to an inquiry; adjustment of a difference. — 7. (f. 4) vacancy.
er-legen[1] (‿‿‿) [: allay] I v/a. ⑧* 1. to pay (or put) down a sum; to discharge taxes, &c.; als Zurückzahlung: to refund. — 2. (erschlagen) to slay, kill. — II ~ n ㉓ 3. = Erlegung.
er-legen[2] (‿‿‿) p.p. von erliegen (f. bs).
Er-legung (‿‿‿) f ⑯ (zu erlegen 1:) payment, discharge; (zu 2:) killing of game.
er-leichter/n (‿‿‿‿) I v/a. u. sich ~ v/refl. ⑨a* (ant. beschweren) to make easy; to lighten a burden, to relieve (or alleviate) distress, to facilitate a task; to soothe a pain; sein Gewissen ~ to ease (or clear) one's conscience; sein Herz ~ to disburden one's heart; F seinen Bauch ~,

Zeichen (f. S. XVII): F familiär, P Volkssprache, Ր Gaunersprache, ⟍ selten; † alt (auch gestorben); * neu (auch geboren); ⁒ unrichtig,

[Erleichterung] — 337 — [Ernährung]

sich ⁇ to relieve o.s., F to make o.s. comfortable. — II ~ n ⁇ = E/ung. **Er-leichterung** (⌣⌣⌣) f ⁇ relief, alleviation; facility; ease; clearance; ⚔ ~en auf dem Marsche allowances pl. made on the march; ❀ ~en pl. im Zahlen ꝛc.: facilities pl.; ~s-mittel (⌣...) n ⁇ soothing (or comforting) remedy, relief. **er-leiden** (⌣⌣) v/a. ⁇* 1. = erfahren 2; e-e Niederlage, e-n Verlust ⁇ to sustain (or suffer) a defeat, a loss; eine Veränderung ⁇ to undergo a change. — 2. (ertragen) to bear; gebulbig: to endure, tolerate, put up with.
erlen (⌣⌣) [Erle] a. ⁇ (of) alder-wood. **Erlen-baum** ♀ (⌣...) m ⁇ = Erle; =busch m, =gebüsch n ⁇ alder-bush or -brake; =fink m orn. = Zeisig; =holz n alder-wood; =könig m = Erl=k.; =wald m alder-forest. [quirable.]
er-lernbar (⌣⌣⌣) a. ⁇ learnable, acquirable.
er-lern/en (⌣⌣) I v/a. ⁇* to learn a trade, to acquire (or master) an art, a language, &c.; das mühsam von uns Erlernte what we learnt by dint of hard study, the knowledge laboriously acquired by us. — II ~ n ⁇ = E/ung. [learning or acquiring.]
er-lernens-wert (⌣⌣⌣⌣) a. ⁇ worth
Er-lernung (⌣⌣⌣) f ⁇ learning, acquirement, acquisition; apprenticeship.
er-lesen (⌣⌣⌣) I v/a. ⁇a* to select = auslesen 1. — II p.p. u. a. ⁇ (D 9) select = auserlesen II.
er-leucht/en (⌣⌣⌣) v/a. ⁇* u. ~ n ⁇ = beleuchten; rel. der Erleuchtete the inspired one, one full of the divine light; E/ung f ⁇ illumination.
Erlicht (⌣⌣) [Erle] n ⁇d. = alder-grove.
er-liegen (⌣⌣⌣) v/n. (fn) ⁇* to succumb; unter e-r Last ⁇ to sink under a burden; er ist s-n Wunden erlegen he succumbed to (or died from) his wounds.
er-lies (⌣⌣) imper. von erlesen.
er-ließ (⌣⌣) (⌣e subj.) impf. v. erlassen.
er-lisch (⌣⌣) imper., **er-lisch(e)st** (⌣⌣⌣), **er-licht** (⌣⌣) pres. ind. von erlöschen.
er-listen (⌣⌣⌣) v/a. ⁇* to obtain by artifice or cunning or (wily) stratagems; et. von e-m ⁇ to cheat (F diddle, do) a p. out of a th.
er-litten (⌣⌣⌣) p.p. von erleiden.
Erl-könig (⌣⌣⌣) [H. ✝ aus dän. ellerkonge Elsenkönig] m ⁇ King of the elves.
er-log (⌣⌣) ind. u. **er-löge** (⌣⌣⌣) subj. impf., **er-logen** (⌣⌣⌣) p.p. von erlügen.
Er-lös (⌣⌣) m ⁇a. amount realized by (or net proceeds from) a sale.
er-losch (⌣⌣) ind., **er-lösche** subj. impf., **er-löschen** (⌣⌣⌣) p.p. v. erlöschen.
er-löschen (⌣⌣⌣) I v/n. (fn) ⁇b* to be extinguished, to go out; to die away; von Geschriebenem ꝛc.: to be(come) effaced or obliterated; von Farben: to fade (away); von Augen: to grow dull or dim; erloschen dull(ed), dim(med), obscure(d), lifeless; vom Feuer ꝛc.: dead; fig. von Verträgen ꝛc.: to expire; ein Gesetz ist erloschen ... has fallen into disuse; ❀ die Firma ist erloschen ... has ceased to exist. — II ~ n ⁇ und **Er-löschung** f ⁇ (f. I) extinction; effacement; fig. expiration.
er-losen (⌣⌣) v/a. ⁇* to obtain by lot.

er-lös/en (⌣⌣⌣) I v/a. ⁇* to save, redeem, release; (loskaufen) to ransom; (freimachen) to deliver, to free, aus der Gefahr: to rescue from danger. — II ~ n ⁇ = Erlösung.
Er-löser (⌣⌣⌣) m ⁇, ~in f ⁇ deliverer, liberator; rel. Redeemer, Saviour.
Er-lösung (⌣⌣⌣) f ⁇ redemption (auch rel.), release; deliverance, rescue; theol. salvation by Christ; ~s-stunde (⌣...) f ⁇ hour of deliverance or rescue; =weg m rel. road to salvation; =werk n, rel. work of redemption.
er-lügen (⌣⌣⌣) v/a. ⁇d* to invent, fabricate, forge; to obtain by lying; erlogen fabricated, false, mendacious; erlogene Geschichte made-up story.
er-lustigen (⌣⌣⌣⌣) v/a. ⁇*, ~ n ⁇ und **Er-lustigung** f ⁇ = belustigen ꝛc.
er-mächtig/en (⌣) I v/a. ⁇* to empower, authorize. — II ~ n ⁇ = E/ung.
Er-mächtigung (⌣) f ⁇ (full) power, authorization, authority; ~s-schreiben n letter granting an authority to act; (Vollmacht) power of attorney.
er-mahn/en (⌣⌣⌣) I v/a. ⁇* to exhort, admonish; (erinnern) to remind; (zurechtweisen) to reprimand, lecture, sermonize; (warnen) to warn; ⌣b exhortatory, admonitory. — II ~ n ⁇ = E/ung.
Er-mahner (⌣⌣⌣) m ⁇ admonisher, (ad)monitor; (friendly) counsellor.
Er-mahnung (⌣⌣⌣) f ⁇ exhortation, admonition; reminder; reprimand; (fair) warning; ~s-rede f ⁇, =schreiben n admonitory speech, letter.
er-mangeln (⌣⌣⌣) I v/n. (h.) ⁇a* 1. to be wanting in, to be deficient in, to be in want of; sie ⁇ der nötigen Tatkraft they are lacking in (stärker: devoid of) energy; ich will es an nichts ⁇ lassen I will spare nothing or no trouble or no pains; a. v/impers. es ermangelt mir an Geld I am short of (stärker: without) money. — 2. ich will nicht ⁇ zu // (inf.) I will not fail (w omit) to // (inf.). — II ~ n ⁇ u. **Er-mang(e)lung** (⌣⌣(⌣)⌣) f ⁇ 3 want, deficiency, lack; failure; in ~ von et. Besser(e)m ob. eines Besser(e)n in default (or for want) of s.th. better; in ~ von Beweisen (Zeugen) in the absence of proofs, (witnesses); as no proofs (witnesses) are forthcoming.
er-mann/en (⌣⌣) I sich ⁇ v/refl. ⁇* to sum(mon) up courage, to pluck up heart; to stand up like (or to show o.s.) a man, to make a bold stand; to recover (one's) strength; ermanne dich! be (or show yourself) a man! — II ~ n ⁇ u. E/ung f ⁇ summing up (or taking) courage; &c., f. I. [messen.]
er-maß (⌣⌣) (**er-mäße** subj.) impf. v. er-
er-mäßig/en (⌣⌣⌣) I v/a. ⁇* to moderate, lessen, abate; to lower prices; zu ermäßigtem Preise at a reduced price, at a lower (or special) rate. — II ~ n ⁇ u. **Er-mäßigung** f ⁇ moderation, abatement, reduction.
er-matten (⌣⌣⌣) ⁇* I v/a. to weary, to tire; durch Arbeit: to fatigue; (entkräften) to weaken; (erschöpfen) to exhaust, F to fag (out); ⌣b wearisome, ermattend weary, jaded; worn out,

F fagged (out), knocked up. — II v/n. (fn) to grow weary or tired or fatigued or faint; to feel exhausted or F fagged out; (nachlassen) to flag (in one's energies). — III ~ n ⁇ u. **Er-mattung** f ⁇ weariness; fatigue; lassitude; weakness; exhaustion; (Ohnmacht) faintness.
er-messen (⌣⌣⌣) I v/a. ⁇* (p.p. 2) 1. to measure (out). — 2. geistig: to estimate, judge, consider; (berechnen) to calculate; (erwägen) to weigh, to balance; das läßt sich leicht ⁇ that is easily understood or imagined. — II ~ n ⁇ 3. (f. 2) estimate, judgment; nach meinem ~ in my estimation or opinion; nach eigenem ~ at one's own discretion; je nach s-m ~ according as he may think fit.
er-mittelbar (⌣⌣⌣) a. ⁇ ascertainable, discoverable, durch Nachspüren: traceable.
er-mitteln (⌣⌣⌣) I v/a. ⁇a* to find out, ascertain, discover. — II ~ n ⁇ u. **Er-mitt(e)lung** (⌣⌣(⌣)⌣) f ⁇ ascertainment, discovery; (Abschätzung) valuation; ~(en) über et. anstellen to make inquiry (or to collect information) about a th., to inquire into a th.
er-möglichen (⌣⌣⌣) I v/a. ⁇* et. ⁇ to make a th. possible, to render it feasible; (nicht) zu ⁇(b) (im)possible, (un)feasible. — II **Er-möglichung** f ⁇ making a th. possible.
er-mord/en (⌣⌣⌣) ⁇* I v/a. to murder, meuchlerisch: to assassinate; (niedermetzeln) to butcher, massacre, slaughter. — II sich ⁇ v/refl. to commit suicide. — III ~ n ⁇ u. E/ung f ⁇ murder, (Meuchelmord) assassination; (Niedermetzelung) massacre, slaughter.
er-müd/en (⌣⌣⌣) v/a. u. v/n. (fn) ⁇* und ~ n ⁇, E/ung f ⁇ = ermatten ꝛc.
Er-munt(e)rer (⌣⌣⌣) m ⁇ instigator.
er-muntern (⌣⌣⌣) I v/a. u. sich ⁇ v/refl. ⁇a* 1. vom Schlafe: (sich) ⁇ to rouse (o.s.). — 2. (erheitern) to cheer F to liven) up, to enliven. — 3. (anregen) to stir up, urge, encourage; (anfeuern) to fire, to rouse; zum Lernen ⁇ to incite (or exhort) to study. — II ~ n ⁇ = E/ung (⌣⌣⌣) f ⁇ 4. rousing, &c. (f. I); encouragement; incitement.
Er-munterungs-mittel (⌣⌣⌣...) n ⁇ stimulant, F rouser; =rennen n Sport: race for the encouragement of untried horses or competitors.
er-mutig/en (⌣⌣⌣) I v/a. u. sich ⁇ v/refl. ⁇* to encourage; sich ⁇ zu // to summon up courage to //. — II ~ n ⁇ u. E/ung f ⁇ encouragement.
er-nährbar (⌣⌣⌣) a. ⁇ nourishable.
er-nähr/en (⌣⌣⌣) I v/a. u. sich ⁇ v/refl. ⁇* 1. (sich) ⁇ to nourish (o.s.) to feed (o.s.), F to keep (o.s.) in food. — 2. (sich) ⁇ (am Leben erhalten) to keep (o.s.), to support (o.s.); er muß sich durch seiner Hände Arbeit ⁇ he has to work for his living; seine Familie ⁇ to maintain one's family. — II ~ n ⁇ = E/ung.
Er-nährer (⌣⌣⌣) m ⁇, ~in f ⁇ person who feeds others; (Stütze) support, e-r Familie: bread-winner.
Er-nährung (⌣⌣⌣) f ⁇ 1. nourishment, feeding; physiol.: nutrition, alimen-

♪ Musik; ⚛ Wissenschaft; ❦ Pflanze; 🜨 Geographie; ⊕ Technik; ⚒ Bergbau; ⚔ Militär; ⚓ Marine; ⚖ Handel; ✉ Post; 🜚 Eisenbahn.

[Ernährungskunde] — 338 — [Erpichtheit]

tation, zur ~ dienend nourishing, nutritive. — 2. support; maintenance.
Er-nährungs-kunde (◡◡´◡◡) f ⓶: ⓷ dietetics; =**organ** n organ of nutrition; =**störung** f derangement of the alimentary functions. [nennen.]
er-nannt (◡´) p.p., ⓶e (◡´◡) impf. v. er=
er-nennbar (◡´◡) a. ⓺⓺ qualified for an appointment; fit to be appointed.
er-nennen (◡´◡) v/a. ⓺⓺b* to appoint; (vorschlagen) to nominate (or designate for an appointment; jur.: Geschworene ⓶ to impanel a jury; e-n zu seinem Erben ⓶ to appoint (or constitute) a p. one's heir; er wurde zum Minister ernannt he was made (or appointed) Minister.
Er-nenner (◡´◡) m ⓶, ~**in** f ⓸⓻ nominator.— [ernennen.]
er-nenn(e)te (◡´(◡)◡) subj. impf. von
Er-nennung (◡´◡) f ⓸⓺ appointment; nomination, designation; (Beförderung) promotion to; seine ~ zum Direktor his appointment as manager; bei seiner ~ zum Richter on his appointment to a judgeship, on his being raised to the Bench.
Er-nennungs-brief (◡´◡...) m ⓶ letter of appointment; a. parchment; =**recht** n right of appointment, pol. u. eccl. oft: patronage; =**urkunde** f = =**brief**.
er-neuen (◡´◡) ⓺⓶* ⓶c. = erneuern ⓶c.
er-neuer/n (◡´◡) ⓶⓶a* I v/a. to renew, to renovate; (ausbessern) to repair; (neu beleben) to revive; (auffrischen) to freshen up; e-n Angriff, e-e Anklage ⓶ to return to the charge; s-e Tätigkeit ⓶ to resume one's activity; mit erneu(er)ter Kraft with fresh strength. — II sich ⓶ v/refl. to be renewed or revived. — III ~ n ⓶⓷ = E/ung.
Er-neu(e)rer (◡´(◡)◡) m ⓶, ~**in** f ⓸⓻ renovator of a house; pol. innovator.
Er-neu(e)rung (◡´(◡)◡) f ⓸⓺ renewal, renovation; revival; resumption; ~**s-schein** m (Talon) certificate of renewal.
er-niedrig/en (◡´◡◡) I v/a. u. sich ⓶ v/refl. ⓺⓶* 1. to lower (or reduce) prices, &c.; fig. (sich) ⓶ (herabwürdigen) to degrade (o.s.); (bemütigen) to humble (o.s.); bibl. wer sich selbst erhöhet, der soll erniedrigt werden he that exalteth himself shall be abased; sich ⓶, auch: to condescend, to stoop; ⓶d abasing, humiliating (task, &c.), degrading (work, &c.); erniedrigt degraded, her. abaissé. — 2. ♪ e-e Note ⓶ to flatten (or depress) a note. — II ~ n ⓶⓷ u.
Er-niedrigung (◡´◡◡◡) f ⓸⓺ 3. lowering, &c.; reduction; fig. degradation, humiliation, abasement. — 4. ♪ depression of a note by means of a flat.
Er-niedrigungs-grad (◡´◡◡...) m ⓶ degree of debasement, &c.; =**zeichen** ♪ n mark of depression, mehr gbr.: flat (♭).
Ernst[1] (´) npr/m. ⓯ ⓰α. Ernest.
Ernst[2] (´) [ahd.: earnest] m ⓵a. (o. pl.) (ant. Scherz) 1. seriousness; der ~ des Lebens the serious side of life; ist das Ihr ~?, auch: ist es Ihnen ⓶ damit? are you in earnest?, do you really mean it?; es war sein bitterer ~ he was in bitter (or real) earnest; das ist wohl nicht Ihr ~? F you don't (really) mean it?, you don't say so?;

alles (ob. allen) ~es in good (or full) earnest; (all) joking apart; wenn es ~ wird when it comes to the point; aus dem Spiele wird ~ the affair is becoming serious; vgl. bar 3 fig. — 2. ~ aus (ob. mit) einer Sache machen to treat a matter seriously or in a serious light; aus dem Scherze ~ machen to turn a jest (or joke) into bitter earnest; im ~ seriously; mit ~ (Anstrengung) an e-r Sache arbeiten, et. in vollem ~e treiben to work with heart and soul (F with a vengeance) at a th. — 3. (Strenge) severity; sternness of character; rigour of the law; (Würdigkeit, Wichtigkeit) gravity.
ernst[3] (´) [nhd.] a. ⓺⓺ (ant. heiter) serious; earnest; (feierlich) solemn; (strenge) severe, stern; (wichtig) grave; ich nehme die Sache ⓶ I treat the matter seriously or in a serious light; es ist mein ⓶er Wunsch, daß // it is my earnest desire or sincere(st) wish that //.
Ernst-fall (´...) m ⓶: im ~e when things become serious, ⚔ in case of war.
ernsthaft (´◡) [ahd.] a. ⓺⓺ serious; earnest; mit ⓶er Miene, auch: with a grave (or stern) countenance; ~**igkeit** (´◡◡) f ⓸⓺ seriousness; earnestness; stärker: gravity, sternness.
ernst-komisch (´...) a. ⓺⓺ serio-comic.
ernstlich (´◡) a. ⓺⓺ u. adv. 1. earnest(ly); (eifrig) fervent(ly), ardent(ly); es ⓶ meinen to be in earnest about a th. ?; beleidigt deeply offended. — 2. es ist mein ⓶er (ausdrücklicher) Wille, daß // it is my express wish that //; ⓶er (entscheidender) Schritt serious (or decisive) step.
Ernte (´◡) [earn] f ⓸⓺ harvest (-time); gathering of the harvest; (Ertrag) crop (a. fig.); ~ auf dem Halme standing crop; die ~ einbringen to gather (or garner) in the harvest or the crops; eine reiche ~ halten to hold a rich harvest; Sprichw. wie die Saat, so die ~ as you sow so you reap.
Ernte-arbeit (´◡...) f ⓸⓺ harvest-work or -operations pl.; =**arbeiter(in** f) m reaper, harvester; a. harvest-(wo)man; =**dankfest** n, eccl. h.-thanksgiving; =**ertrag** m yield of the harvest, crop; =**fest** n harvest-feast or -home; =**göttin** f, myth. Ceres; =**kranz** m harvest-wreath; =**lied** n h.-song; =**mahl** n h.-feast; =**maschine** ⓰ reaping-machine; =**monat** m August.
ernten (´◡) [ahd.: earn] v/a. ⓺⓽ to reap (the harvest, fig. the fruit of one's labour, the reward for one's services, &c.); to gather (in), get in; wenig Dank für seine Mühe ⓶ to receive small thanks for one's labour; fig. Wind säen und Sturm ⓶ to sow the wind and reap the whirlwind.
Ernte-puppe (´◡...) f ⓶ harvest-doll, schott. kern-baby; =**schmaus** m = =**mahl**; =**segen** m rich harvest; =**wagen** m waggon (or wain, cart) for (getting home) the crops; =**zeit** f harvest-time; time for (reaping) the harvest.
er-nüchter/n (◡´◡◡) I v/a. ⓺⓶a* to make sober; fig. to disenchant, to disillusion. — II sich ⓶ v/refl. to become sober, to sober down. — III ~ n ⓶⓷

u. E/ung f ⓸⓺ becoming sober; fig. disenchantment, disillusionment.
Er-oberer (◡´◡◡) m ⓶, **Er-ob(r)erin** f ⓸⓻ conqueror, vanquisher, one who captures or takes a town, &c. (a. ⚔).
er-obern (◡´◡) [mhd.] I v/a. ⓶a*: etwas von e-m ⓶ to conquer a th. from a p.; ⚔ to take (or capture, carry) a fortress; mit Sturm ⓶ to (take by) storm (a. fig.). — II ~ n ⓶⓷ u. **Er-oberung** (◡´◡◡) f ⓸⓺ conquest; capture; auf Eroberungen ausgeh(e)n to be bent on conquest, fig. to try to captivate (men's hearts); eine große Eroberung machen to make a great capture.
Er-oberungs-durst (◡´◡◡...) m ⓶, =**gelüste** n thirst (or eagerness) for conquest; =**krieg**, =**plan** m war, scheme of conquest; =**sucht** f lust of conquest; ⓶**süchtig** a. ⓺⓺ desirous of conquest; ⓶es Weib coquette, flirt; =**zug** m warlike expedition; invasion of a country.
er-öffnen (◡´◡) I v/a. und sich ⓶ v/refl. ⓺⓶b* 1. to open; feierlich: to inaugurate; den Ball ⓶ to open the ball (a. fig.); e-e Besprechung: to open, start, begin; ein Geschäft: to open, start, commence, establish; ⚔ das Feuer, die Schlacht ⓶ to open fire, the battle; ⓸ ein Konto ⓶ to open an account; es ⓶ sich gute Aussichten the prospects are brightening. — 2. e-m etwas ⓶ (tunbun) to disclose (or reveal) a th. to a p.; förmlich: to notify (or communicate) a th. to a p., geschäftsmäßig: to advise (or acquaint, inform) a p. of a th. — II v/n. (h.) 3. ⓰ Börse: italienische Werte ⓶ abgeschwächt Italian securities open weak or flat. — III ~ n ⓶⓷ u. **Er-öffnung** f ⓸⓺ 4. (s. 1) opening; inauguration; beginning; commencement; e-s Testamentes: opening (or reading) of a will. — 5. (s. 2) disclosure, revelation; notification, communication; jur. ~ eines Urteils publication of a judgment or sentence.
Er-öffnungs-feier(lichkeit) (◡´◡◡...) f ⓶ opening fête, day of inauguration; =**gedicht** n introductory poem; =**rede** f opening (or inaugural) speech or address, thea. prologue.
er-örter/n (◡´◡◡) [mhd.] I v/a. ⓶a* to discuss, argue, debate; gründlich: to thrash out; vor Gericht: to plead; die Sache läßt sich ⓶ the matter is open to discussion. — II ~ n ⓶⓷ u. **Er-örterung** (◡´◡◡◡) f ⓸⓺ discussion, argument(ation), debate, ⓷ disquisition.
er-örterungs-fähig (⓶...) a. ⓺⓺ open to (or fit for) discussion, debatable.
Eros (◡´) [grch.⟶] npr/m. (sg. inv., pl. Ero'ten) myth. (Liebesgott) Eros, Cupid; (god of) Love.
Erosion ⓷ (--(◡)´) [lt.] f ⓸⓺ geol. (Auswaschung, Zerklüftung) erosion.
Erotiker (◡´◡◡) [grch.] m ⓶ (Dichter von Liebesliedern) erotic poet.
erotisch (◡´◡) [grch.] a. ⓺⓺ erotic.
Erpel m [ndd.] m ⓶ (Enterich) drake.
er-picht (◡´) a. ⓺⓺ intent (or bent) upon, stärker: mad (or crazy) after, passionately fond of; aufs Geld ⓶ eager (or greedy) after money; ~**heit** (◡´◡) f ⓸⓺ eagerness (or greediness) after a th.

Signs (see page XVII): F familiar; P vulgar; ⌐ flash; ⟍ rare; † obsolete (died); * new word (born); ‡ incorrect; ♪ music:

er-preff/en (⏑⏑́⏑) I *v/a.* [90]* to extort from = auspressen 2. — II ~ *n* [23] = E/ung.
Er-presser (⏑⏑́⏑) *m* [22], **~in** *f* [47] extortioner, bisw. exactor; F bloodsucker.
Er-pressung (‿) *f* [46] extortion, exaction, durch Drohungen 2c.: blackmailing.
er-proben (⏑⏑́⏑) *v/a.* [88]* to experience, to try, to (put to the) test; erprobt experienced, well tried or tested; wohl erprobtes Mittel highly approved remedy. [[88]* u. ~ *n* [23] = erfrischen.]
er-quicken (⏑⏑́⏑) [ahd.] *v/a.* u. **sich** ℒ *v/refl.*
er-quicklich (⏑⏑́⏑) *a.* [66] refreshing, comforting, enjoyable; recreative; (angenehm) pleasant; (kühlend) cooling.
Er-quickung (⏑⏑́⏑) *f* [46] = Erfrischung; **~s-mittel** *n* [62] = Erfrischungsmittel.
er-raffen (⏑⏑́⏑) *v/a.* [88]* to snatch (up), seize, grasp; to attain by (dint of) great efforts or exertions. [erringen.]
er-rang (⏑⏑́) (**er-ränge** *subj.*) *impf.* v.
Errata (⏑⏑́⏑) s. Erratum.
er-ratbar (⏑⏑́–) *a.* [66] easy to guess or to divine; guessable; conjecturable; et. leicht ~es an easy guess.
er-raten (⏑⏑́⏑) I *v/a.* [86]a* (*p.p.* ℒ) to guess, divine, conjecture; to hit upon the answer; to solve a riddle; schwer zu ℒ(d) a hard nut to crack; j-s Gedanken, Vorhaben ℒ to read a p.'s thoughts, to see through his intentions. — II ~ *n* [23] guessing, divining; solution.
Er-rater (⏑⏑́⏑) *m* [22], **~in** *f* [47] one who guesses or divines; a.: guesser, diviner.
erratisch ⚗ (⏑⏑́⏑) [lt.] *a.* [66] *geol.* ℒe (zerstreut liegende) Blöcke *m/pl.* erratic blocks.
Erratum (⏑⏑́⏑) [lt. Irrtum] *n* [59] *typ.* mst *pl.* Errata (Druckfehler) errata, misprints *pl.*
Er-ratung (⏑⏑́⏑) *f* [46] = erraten II.
er-regbar (⏑⏑́–) *a.* [66] excitable (*a. path.*), irritable; (jähzornig) irascible; (leidenschaftlich) passionate, fiery, hot-headed; (empfindlich) sensitive.
Er-regbarkeit (⏑⏑́––) *f* [46] excitability (*a. path.*), irritability; passionate nature; sensitiveness.
er-reg/en (⏑⏑́⏑) I *v/a.* [88]* to excite, irritate, agitate, stir; Angst ℒd alarming; s. Anstoß 4; den Appetit ℒ to sharpen (or whet) the appetite; Appetit ℒd appetizing; Bedenken ℒ to meet with objections; Besorgnis, Erstaunen ℒ to cause anxiety, surprise; j-s Bewunderung ℒ to excite (or rouse) a p.'s admiration; Lachen ℒ to provoke laughter; j-s Mitleid ℒ to move a p.'s pity; *med.* ℒd irritant, stimulating; ℒdes Mittel stimulant, excitant; Schrecken ℒ to inspire terror; Schrecken ℒd terrific; einen Sturm ℒ to raise a storm; heftig erregt greatly excited or agitated. — II ~ *n* [23] = E/ung.
Er-reger (⏑⏑́⏑) *m* [22], **~in** *f* [47] p. who excites, stirs, &c. (s. erregen); agitator.
Er-regtheit (⏑⏑́–) *f* [46] excitement.
Er-regung (⏑⏑́⏑) *f* [46] irritation, agitation, stir(ring); provocation; inspiration; *med.*, &c. stimulation; voll ~ full of excitement, greatly agitated.
Er-regungs-mittel (⏑⏑́⏑...) *n* [62] *med.* stimulant, excitant.
er-reichbar (⏑⏑́–) *a.* [66] within reach, F *co.* come-at-able; für die Stimme: within call; bsd. *fig.* attainable.
Er-reichbarkeit (⏑⏑́––) *f* [46] attainability.
er-reich/en (⏑⏑́⏑) I *v/a.* [88]* 1. to reach; nicht zu ℒ(d) out of one's reach; bsd. *fig.* to attain; (verschaffen) to procure; seine Absicht (nicht) ℒ to accomplish (to fail in) one's purpose; ein hohes Alter ℒ to live to a great age; ⚓ das Land zu ℒ suchen to make (for) land; die off(e)ne See ℒ to gain (or reach) the offing. — 2. den höchsten Grad, den Höhepunkt von et. ℒ to attain the highest (degree of) perfection in s.th.; sein Ziel, s-n Zweck ℒ to gain (or encompass) one's end, to secure one's object. — 3. (einholen) to catch up, to come up with; *fig.* to match, equal, come up to. — II ~ *n* [23] u. **E/ung** *f* [46] 4. reaching, &c. (s. I); attainment; accomplishment; nach ~ eines solchen Alters after living to such an age.
er-reiten (⏑⏑́⏑) *v/a.* [80]b* to reach (or catch up or overtake) on horseback.
er-rettbar (⏑⏑́–) *a.* [66] savable.
er-retten (⏑⏑́⏑) I *v/a.* [89]* to save, rescue, deliver, (set) free; e-n vom Tode ℒ to save a p.'s life, *rel.* to deliver a p. from death, to redeem a p. — II ~ *n* [23] = Errettung.
Er-retter (⏑⏑́⏑) *m* [22], **~in** *f* [47] person who saves; deliverer; *rel.* Saviour.
Er-rettung (⏑⏑́⏑) *f* [46] saving, rescue, deliverance; *rel.* salvation.
er-richtbar (⏑⏑́–) *a.* [66] erectable; capable of being erected, &c.; s. errichten.
er-richten (⏑⏑́⏑) I *v/a.* [89]* = aufrichten 3; ⚔, ⚙ Erdwerke ℒ to throw up earthworks; *math.* ein Lot ℒ to raise a perpendicular; ✱ ein Handlungshaus ℒ to set up (or establish, found) a house of business. — II ~ *n* [23] und **Er-richtung** *f* [46] erection; ✱ establishment, foundation.
er-riet (⏑́) (ℒe *subj.*) *impf.* v. erraten.
er ringen (⏑⏑́⏑) *v/a.* [71]st* to obtain by a great effort or struggle; e-n Erfolg 2c. ℒ to achieve a success; den Preis, den Sieg ℒ to carry off the prize, to gain the victory; ein schwer errung(e)ner Sieg a victory won at a heavy sacrifice or by severe exertion.
er-ritt (⏑⏑́) *ind.* u. **ℒe** (⏑⏑́⏑) *subj. impf.*, **ℒen** (⏑⏑́⏑) *p.p.* von erreiten.
er-röt/en (⏑⏑́⏑) I *v/n.* (sn) [89]* to redden with anger; to blush, F to colour up (über at); ihr e/etes Antlitz her flushed countenance. — II ~ *n* [23] u. **E/ung** *f* [46] blush(ing). [reach of one's voice.]
er-rufbar (⏑⏑́–) *a.* [66] within call, within
er-rufen (⏑⏑́⏑) *v/a.* [87]b* to reach with a call or with one's voice.
er-rungen (⏑⏑́⏑) *p.p.* von erringen.
Er-rungenschaft (⏑⏑́⏑⏑) [erringen] *f* [46] acquisition, achievement; die ~en der Forschung the conquests *pl.* (or attainments *pl.*, progress) of (scientific) research; *jur.* joint property acquired by husband and wife.
Er-rungenschafts-gemeinschaft (⏑⏑́...) *f* [46] *jur.* (married couple's) joint ownership of acquired property.
er-sann (⏑⏑́) *impf.* v. ersinnen.
er-sättig/en (⏑⏑́⏑⏑) I *v/a.* [88]* to satiate. — II ~ *n* [23] u. **E/ung** *f* [46] satiation.
er-sättlich (⏑⏑́⏑) *a.* [66] satiatable.
Er-sättlichkeit (⏑⏑́⏑–) *f* [46] satiability.
Er-satz (⏑⏑́) *m* [7]a. (o. *pl.*) (Vergütung) compensation; amends; e-m (einen) ~ für et. leisten to compensate (or indemnify) a p. for s.th.; to make amends for a th.; (Schadloshaltung) indemnification; (Gegenwert) equivalent; (Genugtuung) reparation; (Wieder-erstattung) restitution; zum ~e (dagegen) in return (for it); F (intended) to make up (for it); ✱ als ~ für beschädigte Ware as a set-off for damaged goods; ⚓ ~ Preußen vessel to replace the 'P.'
Er-satz-bataillo'n ⚔ (⏑⏑́...) *n* [62] für Indien 2c.: linked battalion, feeder; **-erbe** *m* substitute of an heir; **-geschäft** ⚔ *n* recruiting; **-leistung** *f* indemnification; **-mann** *m* substitute, deputy; *jur.* auch: proxy; (Aushelfer) odd man; **-mannschaft** ⚔ *f* fresh recruits *pl.*, new levy; **-mittel** *n* substitute; **-pferde** *n/pl.* relay of horses; **-pflicht** *f* liability to compensation; **ℒpflichtig** *a.* [66] liable to (pay) damages or compensation; **-rad** ⚙ *n* change-wheel; **-rahe** ⚓ *f* spare yard; **-rese'rve** ⚔ *f* reserve (troops *pl.*); ⚓ supernumeraries *pl.*; **-reservi'st** ⚔ *m* man belonging to the reserve; in Engl. auch militiaman; ⚓ supernumerary; **-stoff** *m* (Surrogat) substitute; **-stück** *n* duplicate; ⚓ preventer; **-summe** *f* compensation, indemnity; **-truppen** ⚔ *f/pl.* reserve forces *pl.*; **-wahl** *f*, *parl.* by-election.
er-saufen P (⏑⏑́⏑) *v/n.* (sn) [75]f* derb: (ertrinken) to be (or get) drowned; ⚒ (sich mit Wasser anfüllen) to be(come) submerged.
er-säufen P (⏑⏑́⏑) [88]* derb: (ertränken) I *v/a.* to drown a dog, &c.; (unter Wasser setzen) to submerge, to flood. — II **sich** ℒ *v/refl.* to drown o.s., F *co.* to make a hole in the water.
er-schaffbar (⏑⏑́–) *a.* [66] producible.
er-schaffen (⏑⏑́⏑) I *v/a.* [85]a* (*p.p.* ℒ) to create; (erzeugen) to produce, to make. — II **~e([r]** *m*) *f* [67] creature. — III ~ *n* [23] = Erschaffung.
Er-schaffer (⏑⏑́⏑) *m* [22], **~in** *f* [47] (Schöpfer) creator; (Produzent) producer, maker.
Er-schaffung (⏑⏑́⏑) *f* [46] creation; production; ⚗ genesis.
er-schallen (⏑⏑́⏑) *v/n.* (sn) [75]a* 1. to (re-)sound (or ring) with; es erscholl ein lautes Gelächter a roar of laughter was heard. — 2. (bekannt w.) to spread (abroad), to become known; es erscholl ein Gerücht a rumour was set afloat.
er-schaudern (⏑⏑́⏑) *v/n.* (sn) [92]a* to shudder, to be thrilled with horror.
er-schauen (⏑⏑́⏑) *v/a.* [88]* to see, perceive, notice; von ferne: to espy.
er-schauern (⏑⏑́⏑) *v/n.* (sn) [92]a** to shiver; *poet.* die Blätter ℒ im Nachtwinde the leaves tremble in the night-breezes; seine Seele erschauert bei dem Gedanken his soul shudders (or is horrified) at the thought.
er-scheinen (⏑⏑́⏑) I *v/n.* (sn) [81]* 1. to appear, F to put in an appearance; Buchhandel: to appear, to come out; soeben erschienen just published, just out; ℒ lassen to publish, to bring out; (geschehen) to happen; (sich zeigen) to show o.s.; (sich offenbaren) to reveal o.s.; in

[Erscheinung] — 340 — [ersetzen]

e-m andern Lichte 2 lassen to put in a new light, to throw a new light upon. — 2. es ist ihm ein Gespenst erschienen he has seen a ghost; zum ersten Male in Gesellschaft 2 to make one's first appearance (or F one's entrée or debut) in society; junge Dame, die zum ersten Male bei Hofe ꝛc. erscheint (fr.) debutante. — 3. Gerichtswesen: vor Gericht 2 to appear in court; auf eine Vorladung nicht 2 to make default. — 4. impers. es erscheint wünschenswert it seems (stärker: it is obviously) desirable. — II ~ n ㉓ 5. (f. I) appearance (auch vor Gericht); eines Gespenstes: apparition; e-s Buches: publication.

Er-scheinung (ᴗ́ᴗ) f ㊻ 1. sight, spectacle; (Natur=)~ phenomenon; (Luft=)~ meteor; (Traumgesicht) vision; (Gespenst) ghost, spectre; zur ~ bringen to present (bodily), to make manifest; ~en haben to see visions; zur ~ kommen to appear, to become visible or manifest; in die ~ treten to come to light or to the surface or into existence. — 2. äußere ~ outward appearance; sie ist eine liebliche ~ she is a lovely creature; ihre majestätische ~ her majestic presence or bearing; es ist eine eigentümliche (seltsame) ~ (Tatsache), daß // it is a curious (strange) fact that //; (Krankheits=) ~ (pathological) symptom. — 3. eccl. ~ Christi (Feast of) Epiphany, Twelfth-day.

Er-scheinungs-form (ᴗᴗᴗ...) f ㊷ outward shape, embodiment, manifestation; ⚤ phase; =tag m Börse: (von Wertpapieren) day of issue.

er-schien (ᴗ́) ind., 2e (ᴗ́ᴗ) subj. impf. und 2en (ᴗ́ᴗ) p.p. von erscheinen.

er-schießen (ᴗ́ᴗ) ⓢc(e)ß* I v/a. 1. (totschießen) to shoot (dead), to kill by a shot, with a bullet, with an arrow, &c.; mir wurde das Pferd unter dem Leibe erschossen my horse was shot under me; ⚔ e-n Deserteur ꝛc. 2 (mit Pulver und Blei hinrichten) to shoot a deserter, &c. by martial law. — 2. (durch Schießen erwerben) sich (dat.) einen Preis 2 to carry off a prize for (good) shooting; ⚔ (durch Schießen kennen lernen) to ascertain by shooting; die erschossene Entfernung the distance found out by (experimental) firing. — II sich 2 v/refl. 3. to shoot o.s., to blow out one's brains. — III ~ n ㉓ a. **Er-schießung** f ㊻ 4. shooting death by (a) gunshot; ⚔ military execution; F das ist zum ~ that's enough to aggravate a saint; F co. zum ~ (lustig) uncommonly merry, F awfully jolly.

er-schlaffen (ᴗᴗ́) ㊸* I v/n. (sn) to relax, languish, droop; (nachlassen) to slacken, give way, flag; (die Spannkraft verlieren) to lose one's vigour or elasticity; (verweichlichen) to grow effeminate or enervated. — II v/a. (f. I) to relax, weaken, effeminate, enervate; to unstring (or unbrace) a p.'s nerves. — III ~ n ㉓ u. **Er-schlaffung** f ㊻ relaxing, &c. (f. I u. II); effeminacy, enervation; path. debility, ⚤ atony; stärker: prostration. — IV er-schlafft p.p. relaxed (a. path.); languid.

er-schlagen (ᴗᴗ́) I v/a. ⓢb* (p.p. 2) e-n 2 to slay (or kill) a p.; der Blitz hat ihn 2 he was killed by lightning; die vom Blitz 2en Schafe the sheep killed (or destroyed) by lightning. — II ~e([r]m) f ⑰: man fand ihn unter den ~en he was found among the slain.

er-schleich/en (ᴗᴗ́) I v/a. ⓢaft* to obtain surreptitiously; sich (dat.) j-s Gunst 2 to sneak into a p.'s favour; erschlich(e)nes Besitztum property obtained by surreptitiously (or underhand) means. — II ~ n ㉓ u. Ɛ/ung (ᴗ́ᴗ) f ㊻ fraudulent acquisition.

er-schlich (ᴗ́) ind., 2e (ᴗ́ᴗ) subj. impf. u. 2en (ᴗ́ᴗ) p.p. von erschleichen.

er-schließbar (ᴗ́=) a. ⓺ capable of being (or fit to be) unlocked, F unlockable.

er-schließen (ᴗ́ᴗ) v/a. u. sich 2 v/refl. ⓢd* 1. bsd. fig. (sich) 2 to unlock, open; (zugänglich m.) to make accessible. — 2. fig. (folgern) to infer, conclude.

er-schloß (ᴗ́) ind., **er-schlösse** (ᴗ́ᴗ) subj. impf., **er-schlossen** (ᴗ́ᴗ) p.p. v. erschließen.

er-schlug (ᴗ́) ind., **er-schlüge** (ᴗ́ᴗ) subj. impf. v. erschlagen.

er-schmeicheln (ᴗᴗ́ᴗ) v/a. ⓶a* to obtain by flattery or coaxing; et. von e-m 2 to wheedle (or coax) a th. out of a p.; sich (dat.) j-s Gunst 2 to wheedle o.s. into a p.'s favour.

er-schnappen (ᴗᴗ́ᴗ) v/a. ⓶* to snatch (away), to catch up.

er-sch;äuffeln (ᴗᴗ́ᴗ) v/n. (h.) ⓶a* to sniff out; fig. to ferret (or F furrage) out.

er-scholl (ᴗ́) ind., **er-schölle** (ᴗ́ᴗ) subj. impf. u. **er-schollen** (ᴗ́ᴗ) p.p. v. erschallen.

er-schöpf/en (ᴗ́ᴗ) I v/a. u. sich 2 v/refl. ⓶* (sich) 2 to exhaust (o.s.), to wear (o.s.) out; to spend (one's strength); vgl. ermatten I; erschöpft spent with fatigue, tired out, F dead-beat, knocked up; meine Mittel sind erschöpft my means are exhausted, I have run short of cash; völlig erschöpft (thoroughly) drained, F played out. — II ~ n ㉓ = Ɛ/ung. — III 2d p.pr. u. a. ⓺ a. exhaustive; adv. ein Thema 2d abhandeln to treat a subject exhaustively.

er-schöpflich (ᴗᴗ́ᴗ) a. ⓺ exhaustible.

er-schöpftheit (ᴗᴗ́=) f [erschöpft p.p. von erschöpfen] f ㊻ = Erschöpfung.

Er-schöpfung (ᴗᴗ́ᴗ) f ㊻ exhaustion; weariness; fatigue; path. inanition.

er-schoß (ᴗ́) ind., **er-schösse** (ᴗ́ᴗ) subj. impf. u. **er-schossen** (ᴗ́ᴗ) p.p. v. erschießen.

er-schrak (ᴗ́) ind. u. **er-schräke** (ᴗ́ᴗ) subj. impf. v. erschrecken.

er-schrecken (ᴗᴗ́ᴗ) I v/a. ⓶* to frighten, terrify, horrify; plötzlich: to alarm; to startle; du erschreckst ihn you alarm him. — II v/n. (sn) ⓶a*u. sich 2 v/refl. ⓶* to be frightened, terrified. horrified. to take fright (über et. at a th.); du erschrickst (selbst) you are alarmed! 2 Sie nur nicht! don't be alarmed! — III ~ n ㉓ fright, terror, alarm.

er-schreck/lich (ᴗᴗ́ᴗ) a. ⓺ = schrecklich.

er-schreiben (ᴗᴗ́ᴗ) v/a. ⓢl* to gain by writing; to earn with one's pen.

er-schrick imper., =ſt, 2t (ᴗᴗ́) pres. ind. von erschrecken II.

er-schrieb (ᴗ́) ind., ~e (ᴗ́ᴗ) subj. impf. u. 2en (ᴗ́ᴗ) p.p. von erschreiben.

er-schrocken (ᴗᴗ́ᴗ) p.p. von erschrecken II; ~heit (ᴗᴗ́=) f ㊻ fright, terror, alarm.

er-schroten ⚔ (ᴗ́ᴗ) v/a. ⓶*: Lagerstätten ꝛc. 2 = erschürfen.

er-schuf (ᴗ́) ind. u. **er-schüfe** (ᴗ́ᴗ) subj. impf. v. erschaffen.

er-schürfen ⚔ (ᴗᴗ́ᴗ) v/a. ⓶* (durch Schürfen auffinden) to discover (or lay open) by digging.

er-schütter/n (ᴗᴗ́ᴗ) [nhd.] I v/a. ⓶a* to shake (up), stärker: to convulse the universe, &c.; ⚔ eine Truppe durch heftiges Feuern 2 to harass (or unnerve) troops; fig. e-m das Zwerchfell 2 to make a p.('s sides) shake with laughter; einen 2 (rühren) to stir a p.'s emotions; eine 2de Szene an affecting (or agitating) scene; seine erschütterte Gesundheit his shattered health; ihre Nerven sind heftig erschüttert her nerves are terribly shaken or unstrung. — II ~ n ㉓ und Ɛ/ung f ㊻ shaking; concussion; violent motion; (Stoß) shock; convulsion; (Rührung) emotion.

er-schwang (ᴗ́) u. **er-schwänge** (ᴗᴗ́ᴗ), **er-sah** (ᴗ́) u. **er-sähe** (ᴗ́ᴗ), **er-sann** (ᴗ́) u. **er-sänne** (ᴗ́ᴗ), **er-saß** (ᴗ́) u. **er-säße** (ᴗ́ᴗ) ind. u. subj. impf. v. er-schwingen, ersehen, ersinnen, ersitzen.

er-schweren (ᴗᴗ́ᴗ) I v/a. ⓶* 1. to make heavy or heavier. 2. fig. to render (more) difficult; den Fortschritt 2 to impede (or obstruct) progress; Fehler ꝛc. 2 (verschlimmern) to aggravate ...; jur. 2de Umstände aggravating circumstances pl. — II ~ n ㉓ u. **Er-schwerung** f ㊻ 3. aggravation. — 4. (auch **Er schwernis** f ⑱) impediment to.

er-schwindeln (ᴗᴗ́ᴗ) v/a. ⓶a* to obtain by swindling or humbug(ging).

er-schwingen (ᴗᴗ́ᴗ) v/a. ⓢft* (mit Mühe erreichen, aufbringen) to attain by a great effort, to supply (or buy) with difficulty; ich kann es (a. die Ausgabe) nicht 2 I cannot afford it; nicht zu 2(d) unattainable, von Ausgaben: beyond one's means, ruinous.

er-schwinglich (ᴗᴗ́ᴗ) a. ⓺ attainable; within one's reach or means.

Er-schwingung (ᴗᴗ́ᴗ) f ㊻ bsd. ⚖ der Kosten covering (of) the expenses.

er-schwungen (ᴗᴗ́ᴗ) p.p. von erschwingen.

er-sehen (ᴗᴗ́ᴗ) [nhd.] v/a. ⓶a* (p.p.2) 1. aus et. 2 (entnehmen) to learn (or understand, infer) from a th.; soviel ich daraus 2 kann as far as I can judge from it; aus Ihrem Schreiben 2 wir we see (or gather) from your letter. — 2. die Gelegenheit 2 (erspähen) to espy one's opportunity; to bide one's time. — 3. (aus 2) to choose, to select. — 4. F e-n, et. nicht 2 können to be(come) disgusted with a p., a th.

er-sehnen (ᴗᴗ́ᴗ) v/a. ⓶* to long (or yearn) for, to have a great desire (or wish) for; to hanker after.

er-sessen (ᴗᴗ́ᴗ) p.p. von ersitzen.

er-setzbar (ᴗᴗ́=) a. ⓺ capable of being replaced, replaceable; von Schaden ꝛc.: reparable (wrong), retrievable (loss).

er-setzen (ᴗᴗ́ᴗ) I v/a. ⓶* 1. to replace; (vertreten) to take the place of, to serve (as substitute) for; to supply s.th. missing; et. durch et. and(e)res 2 to

Zeichen (f. S. IX): F familiär; P Volkssprache; ſ Gaunersprache; ⚹ selten; † alt (auch gestorben); * neu (auch geboren); ⁺⁺ unrichtig;

[**erſetzlich**] — 341 — [**erſteiglich**]

substitute (or put) one thing for another; Talent durch Fleiß ~ to supplement talent by industry; vgl. auch ergänzen 1. — 2. (vergüten) to make good a loss. to make amends (or reparation) for wrong, to pay compensation for damage; Geſtohlenes ꝛc. ~ (herausgeben) to restore ...; einem et. ~ to indemnify (or refund) a p. for a th.; et. erſetzt erhalten, bſd. gerichtlich: to recover damages. — II ~ n 23. = Erſetzung.
er-ſetzlich (⌣⌣) a. 66 = erſetzbar.
Er-ſetzung (⌣⌣) f 46 1. replacement; substitution; supplement(ing). — 2. reparation; compensation; restoration; indemnification.
er-ſichtlich (⌣⌣) a. 66 visible; (augenſcheinlich) evident, manifest, apparent, obvious; (klar) plain, clear (to the mind); es iſt daraus ~, daß // hence it appears (or is evident) that //.
Er-ſichtlichkeit (⌣⌣-) f 46 visibleness; (clear) evidence, manifestness.
er-ſingen (⌣⌣) v/a. 😀t* to gain by singing, to earn with one's voice.
er-ſinnen (⌣⌣) v/a. 😀²* to contrive, to devise; vgl. ausdenken I.
er-ſinnlich (⌣⌣) a. 66 conceivable; durch jedes ~e Mittel by every imaginable (or possible) means.
erſiſch (⌣⌣) a. 66 (gäliſch) Erse (dialect).
er-ſitzen (⌣⌣) v/a. 😀* to obtain by long sitting; von Schülern: ſich (dat.) ein Zeugnis ~ to secure ... by spending the required time in a class; jur. (durch 10jährigen Eigenbeſitz erwerben) to acquire land, &c. by prescription or usucaption.
er-ſoff (⌣⌣) ind., **er-ſöffe** (⌣⌣) subj. impf. u. **er-ſoffen** (⌣⌣) p.p. von erſaufen.
er-ſönne (⌣⌣) subj. impf. u. **er-ſonnen** (⌣⌣-) p.p. von erſinnen.
er-ſpähen (⌣⌣)v/a. 😀³* to espy; am Horizonte ~ to descry on the horizon.
er-ſpar/en (⌣⌣) I v/a. 😀* to save, to economize; e-m Mühe, Koſten ~ to save a p. trouble, expense; mir eine Kummer wurde mir erſpart I was spared that one grief. — II ~ n 23 = E/ung.
Er-ſparnis (⌣⌣) f 46 a): = Erſparung, a. retrenchment; der ~ halber for economy's sake; Erſparniſſe eintreten laſſen to economize, retrench, reduce expenses, F to draw in; b) (a. n 27) = erſpartes Geld savings pl.
Er-ſparung (⌣⌣) f 46 saving, economy.
er-ſpielen (⌣⌣) v/a. 😀*: ſich (dat.) et. ~ to win s.th. at cards, by gambling, &c.
er-ſprießen (⌣⌣) v/n. (ſn) 😀d* 1. = aufſprießen. — 2. aus etwas ~ (hervorgehen) to arise (or originate, take its rise) from a th.
er-ſprießlich (⌣⌣) a. 66 useful, profitable; (vorteilhaft) advantageous; (heilſam) beneficial, salutary.
Er-ſprießlichkeit (⌣⌣-) f 46 usefulness; profitableness; advantage.
er-ſproß (⌣⌣) ind., **er-ſpröſſe** (⌣⌣) subj. impf. u. **er-ſproſſen** (⌣⌣) p.p. von erſprießen.
erſt¹ (´, prov. ᷉) [ahd., sup. von eher] adv. 1. (zuerſt) at first; (anfänglich) at the commencement or outset, originally; ~ wollte er nicht at first he would not do it, he first of all refused. — 2. (vorher) previously; ich muß ~ Briefe ſchreiben ... write letters before that; F ~ abwarten (und dann Tee trinken)! oder ~ ſehen! that remains to be seen, F let's see (or wait) first!; für ihn muß eine Frau ~ noch geboren werden his wife has yet to be born or has to be specially made for him; Sprichw. ~ das Geſchäft und dann das Vergnügen business before pleasure; ~ gehen, dann laufen F before you can run you must walk. — 3. (vorhin) ich glaubte ~, ihn zu hören I thought I heard him just now. — 4. (bloß) only (just); ich habe ~ 10 Seiten geleſen I have not read more than ten pages; (nicht früher) not before; (nicht ſpäter) not later than; not till; ~ damals not till then; ~ geſtern erfuhr ich // I heard only (or but) yesterday //; er iſt (eben) ~ angekommen he has just (this minute) arrived; ~ vor drei Tagen only three days ago; ~ in drei Tagen not for another ...; er kam ~ als alles vorbei war he did not come till ... — 5. ſteigernd: wenn er nun ~ (einmal) Oberſt ſein wird if ever he becomes a colonel; wenn ich ~ in Paris bin! when once I am ...!; nun ~ recht nicht now all the less or not at all! — 6. wünſchend: wäre ich ~ wieder daheim! if only I could get back home!
Erſt² prov. (~) f 46 in der ~, für die ~ (anfangs) at first, to begin with.
er-ſtach (⌣⌣) ind., **er-ſtäche** (⌣⌣) subj. impf. v. erſtechen.
er-ſtand (⌣⌣) ind., **er-ſtände** subj. impf. u. **er-ſtanden** (⌣⌣) p.p. v. erſtehen.
er-ſtarb (⌣⌣) ind. impf. v. erſterben.
er-ſtark/en (⌣⌣) I v/n. (ſn) 😀* to grow strong or firm or robust, to gather (or gain) strength. — II E/ung f 46 growing stronger, &c., ſ. I.
er-ſtarr/en (⌣⌣) 😀* I v/n. (ſn) to stiffen, to grow stiff; von Gliedern oft: to grow numb or torpid; ſtärker: to lose all power, to be paralysed; erſtarrt numb, torpid; ~ machen to benumb; phys. (gerinnen) to congeal, to coagulate; (gefrieren) to freeze, to turn to ice. — II v/a. (ſ. I) to stiffen; to benumb. — III ~ n 23 und E/ung f 46 (ſ. I) stiffness; numbness, torpor, torpidity; phys. congelation, coagulation; allmähliches ~, auch: torpescence.
er-ſtatt/en (⌣⌣) I v/a. 😀* 1. to restore, to return; weits. = erſetzen 2. — 2. e-m etwas (als Lohn) ~ to recompense (or to make a return to) a p. for a th. — 3. Bericht ~ to make (or send in) a report; die ihm erſtatteten Dienſte, Wohltaten the services rendered (to) him, the benefits bestowed on him. — II ~ n 23 und E/ung f 46 3. compensation; restitution; return; e-s Berichts: sending in (or delivery) of a report.
Erſt-aufführung* (-...) f 62 thea. first-night(er), (fr.) première.
er-ſtaunen (⌣⌣) 😀* I v/n. (ſn) to be surprised, ſtärker: to be astonished, amazed (über et. at a th.). — II v/a. to astonish; erſtaunt struck with amazement. — III ~ n 23 surprise; astonishment; amazement; zu meinem (höchſten) ~ to my (utter) surprise; in ~ ſetzen to astonish; ſtarr vor ~ thunderstruck, F taken aback (with astonishment), dumbfounded.
er-ſtaunens-wert (⌣⌣...) a. 66, ~würdig a. = erſtaunlich.
er-ſtaunlich (⌣⌣) a. 66 surprising, astonishing, amazing; (gewaltig) prodigious, stupendous, colossal; das ~e dabei iſt // the marvellous (or wonderful) part of it is //; ~keit (~-) f 46 stupendousness, marvellousness.
Erſt-ausgabe* (~..) f 62 first edition.
erſt-beſte (⌣⌣) a. 66 = erſte (ſ. ds) beſte.
erſte (´⌣, prov. ᷉⌣) [ſ. erſt] I ord. numb. 66. 1. first; Karl der ~ Charles the First (Charles I); der 2 Mai the first of May; am ~n des (fünften) Monats on the first of next month or 🌑 proximo; mit der ~n Poſt by the earliest mail; der ~ beſte first come first served; im ~n Stock (eine Treppe hoch) wohnen ... on the first floor; der ~ beſte the first comer; zum ~nmal ob. ~n Male for the first time. — 2. (vorzüglich) die ~n Geiſter, der ~ Redner jener Zeit the greatest minds, the first (or chief) orator ...; die ~ Klaſſe: a) e-r engl. Volks- ober Bürgerſchule: the First Form; b) eines engl. College the Sixth Form; thea. ~r Liebhaber leading man; ~ Liebhaberin leading lady; der ~ Miniſter the Prime Minister, the Premier; ⚓ Offizier senior officer; das ~, was ihm auffiel the first thing that struck him; der ~ (Primus) in der Klaſſe the first (or head, top) boy of the class; bibl. die ~n werden die Letzten ſein the first shall be the last; die ~n der Stadt the leading men (F the bigwigs) ...; das ~ und das Letzte the first thing and the last; 💰 von ~r (beſter) Qualität first-rate, of prime quality; aus der ~n Hand kaufen ... (at) first-hand. — 3. wenn von zweien die Rede iſt: der erſtere, der letztere the former, the latter. — 4. adv. mit prp.: am ~n kommen to arrive first; fürs († vors) ~: a) = erſtens; b) (für den Anfang) at first, for the present, for the moment, for the time being; mit ~m (nächſtens) on (or by) the first opportunity; zum ~n in the first place, to begin with. — II ~ f 46 5. = Erſt.
er-ſtechen (⌣⌣) v/a. 😀a* to stab (or run through, pierce) with a knife or dagger, &c.
er-ſteh(e)n (⌣⌣) 😀⁴* I v/a. bei Verſteigerungen: to buy (or purchase) at an auction. — II v/n. (ſn) to arise, to rise (from the ground); wieder ~ (auch vom Tode) to rise again or anew. III ~ n 23 u. **Er-ſtehung** f 46 (ſ. II) purchase; (ſ. II) rel. resurrection.
er-ſteiglich (⌣⌣) a. 66 = erſteiglich.
er-ſteigen (⌣⌣) I v/a. 😀* 1. = erklettern I. — 2. fig. die höchſten Stufen der Ehre ~ to attain (to) the highest honours. — II ~ n 23 = Erſteigung.
Er-ſteiger (⌣⌣) m 22, ~in f 47 (mountain-)climber; vgl. Beſteiger.
er-ſteigern (⌣⌣) 😀a* = erſtehen I.
er-ſteiglich (⌣⌣) a. 66 climbable, ascendable; v. Mauern: scalable; (wegſam) practicable; von Gipfeln: accessible; nicht ~ inaccessible.

♪ Muſik; ⚛ Wiſſenſchaft; ♣ Pflanze; 🏆 Geographie; ⊙ Technik; ⚒ Bergbau; ⚔ Militär; ⚓ Marine; 💰 Handel; ✉ Poſt; 🚂 Eiſenbahn.

[Ersteigung] — 342 — [erwachsen]

Er-steigung (⏑⏑) f climbing up; ascent; *fig.* attainment (of or to).
er-stellen* (⏑⏑) [obd.] v/a. (fertigstellen, herbeischaffen) to provide, to (carry into) effect, to procure.
erstens (⏑⏑) adv. first, in the first place, to begin (or start) with.
erster (⏑⏑) comp. von erste (f. d. 3).
er-sterben (⏑⏑) I v/n. (fn) 1 to die (slowly), to expire; *fig.* to die away or out, to become extinct; (das Gefühl verlieren) to grow numb or torpid; das Wort erstarb auf seinen Lippen he could not utter the word, F the word stuck in his throat. — 2. ehm. in Briefschlüssen: ich ersterbe in tiefster Ehrfurcht Ihr // I remain (for ever) your most humble and obedient //. — II ~ n 3. (slow) death; dying out, extinction.
erstere(r) f. erste 3.
erst-geboren (⏑...) a. (D9), ~e f first-born, bsd. bibl. first-begotten.
Erst-geburt (⏑...) f a) (Erstgeborene[r]) the first-born (child); b) jur. primogeniture. bibl. birth-right; ~s-recht n jur. right of primogeniture.
erst-gedacht (⏑...) a., ~gemeldet a., ~genannt (⏑...) a. afore-mentioned, aforesaid; previously named.
er-sticken (⏑⏑) [abd.] I v/n. (fn) 1. to suffocate, to choke (an et. with a th.); (gewürgt w.) to be smothered (f. II). — II v/a. 2. to suffocate; durch Verstopfen der Luftröhre: to choke; durch äußeres Hemmen der Atmung: to smother; durch giftige Gase: to asphyxiate; die Luft stifling atmosphere. — 3. *fig.* einen Aufstand (unterbrücken) to suppress (or smother) a rebellion; im Keime to nip in the bud. — III ~ n und **Er-stickung** f 4. suffocation; choking; smothering; ☾ asphyxia; es ist eine Hitze zum ~ the heat is enough to suffocate (or stifle) one.
Er-stickungs-anfall (⏑...) m choking fit; ~tod m death from suffocation or asphyxia. [en (⏑⏑) p.p. v. ersteigen.]
er-stieg (⏑) ind., ~e (⏑⏑) subj. impf. u.]
erst-klassig* (⏑...) a. first-rate, first-class a. prime, F A 1, A one. [erst.]
erstlich (⏑⏑) adv. = 1. erstens. — 2. zu-]
Erst-ling (⏑⏑) m d. first fruit(s pl.), first production; von Menschen u. Vieh: first-born; v. Früchten: ~e der Jahreszeit first fruit of the season, fruit which has just come in; der ~ seiner Muse his first poetic attempt; ~s-reise ↓ ("...) f maiden trip; ~s-versuch m first (or earliest) attempt.
erst-malig* (⏑...) a. = erste; ~mals* (⏑...) adv. (zum erstenmal) for the first time; auch = zuerst.
er-stochen (⏑⏑) p.p. von erstechen.
er-storben (⏑⏑) p.p. von ersterben.
erst-rangig* (⏑...) a. ~es Hotel hotel of the first rank, high-class hotel.
er-streben (⏑⏑) I v/a. 1. (anstreben) to endeavour to obtain; to aspire to or after; to pursue. — 2. (erreichen) to attain. — II ~ n 3 u. **Er-strebung** f 3. aspiration to or after; pursuit of.
er-strecken (⏑⏑) I sich v/refl. to extend, reach, spread, stretch (bis zu

up to, as far as); sich längs der Küste ℒ to run along(side) the coast, to skirt (or follow) the coast-line; so weit ℒ sich die Aufzeichnungen nicht ... do not go so far; s-e Fähigkeiten ℒ sich nicht so weit his abilities are (or he is) not equal to it, it is beyond his capacity; seine Angaben ℒ (beziehen) sich nur auf Rom ... refer (or relate) only to Rome. — II ~ n u. **Er-streckung** f extension, extent.
er-streiten (⏑⏑) v/a. b*: sich (dat.) ℒ to obtain by disputing or fighting.
er-stritt (⏑) ind., ℒe (⏑⏑) subj. impf. u. ℒen (⏑⏑) p.p. von erstreiten.
er-stünde (⏑⏑) subj. impf. von erstehen.
er-stunken (⏑⏑) [p.p. von † erstinken] F *fig.* es ist ℒ und erlogen it is an abominable (or impudent) lie.
er-stürbe (⏑⏑) subj. impf. von ersterben.
er-stürmbar (⏑⏑) a. assailable.
er-stürmen ⚔ (⏑⏑) I v/a. b* to take (or carry) by storm or assault, to force (or storm) a position, &c. — II ~ n u. **Er-stürmung** ⚔ f (taking by) assault, storming a fortress, &c.
er-suchen (⏑⏑) I v/a. b* to ask (or request, desire, entreat) a p. to do a th.; man hat mich dringend darum ersucht I have been urged to do it; vgl. ansuchen I. — II ~ n = ansuchen II; auf sein ~ at his request or desire.
er-sungen (⏑⏑) p.p. von ersingen.
er-tappen (⏑⏑) I v/a. b* to surprise, catch, detect; auf der Tat ℒ to take in the (very) act; beim Stehlen ℒ to catch stealing; er hat sich dabei ℒ lassen he was caught at it. — II ~ n und **Er-tappung** f catching, &c. (f. I); detection.
er-teil/en (⏑⏑) I v/a. b* to bestow (or confer) on; to dispense, to administer the sacrament, &c. (bewilligen) to grant permission, &c.; man hat mir den Auftrag erteilt zu // I have been entrusted with a commission to //; e-m Geschäftsmanne e-n Auftrag ℒ to give a tradesman an order; e-m den gemessenen Befehl ℒ, zu // to give a p. strict orders to //; man hat mir den Rat erteilt, zu // I have been advised to //; Unterricht ℒ to give (or impart) instruction. — II ~ n = e/ung.
Er-teiler (⏑⏑) m, ~in f dispenser.
Er-teilung (⏑⏑) f bestowal, conferring, grant(ing).
er-tönen (⏑⏑) v/n. (fn) b* = erschallen 1; s-e Stimme ℒ lassen to raise ...
er-töten (⏑⏑) I v/a. b* *fig.* to deaden; (vertilgen) to exterminate; *rel.* die Begierden ℒ to mortify the flesh; die Leidenschaften ℒ to subdue (or curb) the passions. — II ~ n u. **Er-tötung** f deadening; extermination; *rel.* mortification of the flesh.
Er-trag (⏑) m c. fruits pl. of the earth, of one's labour; yield of the soil; produce of land, &c.; return pl. of a business; output of a mine; (Einnahme) receipts pl.; (Einkommen) revenue; reichen ~ einbringen to yield high returns, to bring in good profits; reiner ~ net proceeds pl. or gain; clear profit.
er-trag/en (⏑⏑) I v/a. b* (p.p. ℒ) to

(for)bear, endure, tolerate; vgl. auch aushalten 2. — II ~ n = e/ung.
ertrag-fähig, **~keit** f. ertrags-...
Er-trag-gebend (⏑...) a. yielding profit; profitable.
er-träglich (⏑⏑) a. 1. bearable, endurable, tolerable, sufferable. — 2. (ziemlich gut) passable; adv. er schreibt ℒ (gut) he writes pretty (or fairly, tolerably) well.
Er-träglichkeit (⏑⏑⏑) f endurableness, tolerableness.
er-trag-los (⏑⏑) a. unproductive.
Er-trägnis (⏑⏑) n = Ertrag.
er-trags-fähig (⏑...) a. productive; **~keit** f productiveness.
Er-trag-steuern (⏑...) f/pl. taxes on the (assessed) value of profits.
Er-tragung (⏑⏑) f forbearance, endurance, toleration.
er-trank (⏑) ind., **er-tränke** (⏑⏑) subj. impf. von ertrinken.
er-tränken (⏑⏑) b* I v/a. to drown. — II sich ℒ v/refl. to drown o.s. — III **Er-tränkung** f drowning.
er-träumen (⏑⏑) v/a. b* to dream of, to imagine; erträumt imaginary; nie erträumt undreamt (or never dreamt) of.
er-trinken (⏑⏑) I v/n. (fn) b* to be drowned; Sprichw. der ~de greift nach einem Strohhalm a drowning man will catch at a straw; ertrunken drowned. — II ~ n drowning.
er-trotzen (⏑⏑): v/a. b* von e-m etwas ℒ to get s.th. from a p. by a defiant attitude or by stubborn pertinacity.
er-trug (⏑) ind., **er-trüge** (⏑⏑) subj. impf. v. ertragen.
er-trunken (⏑⏑) p.p. v. ertrinken.
er-übrig/en (⏑⏑⏑) [übrig] b* I v/a. (übrig behalten, zurücklegen) to save, to lay by. — II v/n. (h.) (übrigbleiben) to remain, to be left or over; mst v/impers: a) es erübrigt (mir) nur noch hinzuzufügen, daß // there remains nothing (for me) to add but that //; b) oft ++ = III. — III* sich ℒ v/refl. (übrig, überflüssig w.) dies zu beweisen erübrigt sich wohl there is no need to prove it, no proof is required. — IV **Er-übrigte(s)** n, **Er-übrigung** f savings pl.
eruieren ⚔ (-⏑⏑⏑) [lt.] v/a. = ermitteln. [bruch) eruption.]
Eruption ⚔ (-⏑t(y)⏑) [lt.] f (Aus-]
Erve ♀ (⏑⏑) [lt.] f bitter-vetch (*Ervum*), rape (*Oroba'nche rapum*).
Erven-würger ♀ (⏑...) m broom-]
er-wachen (⏑⏑ch) I v/n. (fn) b* to (a)wake, plötzlich: to start up; *fig.* der Tag erwacht day breaks; sein Gewissen erwacht ... is roused or awakened; die Liebe erwachte in ihr love dawned upon her. — II ~ n awakening.
er-wachsen (⏑⏑ch) I v/n. (fn) b* 1. von Pflanzen und Menschen: to grow (or spring) up; der Knabe ist zu einem Manne ℒ the boy has grown to man's estate or has reached manhood; ℒ p.p. (D9) grown-up, adult; (ausgewachsen) full-grown, fully developed; (mündig) of age; ℒer Mensch = II; ℒes Mädchen young woman, F big girl. — 2. aus et. ℒ (entstehen) to arise (or proceed, spring) from a th.; es ist ihm

Signs (see page XVII): F familiar; P vulgar; F flash; ⟋ rare; † obsolete (died); * new word (born); ++ incorrect; ♪ music;

[erwägen] — 343 — [erwuchs]

eine große Last daraus 2 it put him to (or caused him) great inconvenience; die daraus 2den Übel the evils accruing (or resulting) from it; ◉ die Kosten, die daraus ... attending it. — II~e([r]m/f⊕grown-up person, adult. — III~heit f⊕ adult state; puberty.
er-wägen (⌣⌊⌣) v/a. ⊕a (⌣ ⊕)* to weigh or balance (in one's mind); (überlegen) to consider, to ponder (over); to reflect (or deliberate) upon; (prüfen) to examine; alles wohl erwogen all things considered, after due deliberation, after all.
Er-wägung (⌣⌊⌣) f ⊕ consideration; reflection, deliberation; in ~ ziehen to take into consideration; nach reiflicher ~ on mature consideration; in ~, daß // considering that //.
er-wählen (⌣⌊⌣) I v/a. ⊕* to choose, to make choice of; durch Abstimmung: to elect, to vote for; er ward zum König erwählt he was elected (as) king; der erwählte Präsident the president elect; zum Vorsitzenden 2 to vote into the chair. — II Er-wählte[r] m/f ⊕ = auserwählt. — III ~ n ⊕ u. Erwählung f ⊕ choice, election.
er-wähnen (⌣⌊⌣) I v/a. ⊕* et. oder einer Sache (gen.) 2 to mention (or refer to) a th., to make mention of a th.; es sei ferner erwähnt, daß // it is further to be noticed (or observed) that //; oben erwähnt above-mentioned, aforesaid; er-wähnter-maßen adv. as previously mentioned. — II Er-wähnung f ⊕ mention(ing); e-r Sache ~ tun to make mention of a th.
er-warb (⌣⌊) ind. impf. v. erwerben.
er-warmen (⌣⌊⌣) v/n. (sn) ⊕* to grow warm, to get heated (auch fig.).
er-wärmen (⌣⌊⌣) ⊕* I v/a. to (make) warm. — II sich 2 v/refl. to (grow) warm; für eine Sache: to take a warm (or lively) interest in a matter. — III ~ n ⊕ = Erwärmung.
Er-warmung (⌣⌊⌣) f ⊕ growing (or getting) warm.
Er-wärmung (⌣⌊⌣) f ⊕ making warm, warming, ⚙ calefaction; ~s-kraft f ⊕ heating (⚙ caloric) power or force.
er-warten (⌣⌊⌣) I v/a. ⊕* to wait for, to await; to expect (von e-m from a p.); er kann es kaum 2, daß // he can barely abide (or await) the time until //; he is eagerly looking forward to the time when //; es war nicht zu 2 (hoffen), daß // it was not to be expected that //; das hatte ich nicht erwartet (befürchtet) I was not prepared for that; ich habe nicht viel Gutes zu 2 (hoffen) I have not much to look forward to; es steht zu 2 (ist anzunehmen), daß // it is to be supposed that //. — II ~ n ⊕ über (wider) ~ beyond (contrary to) expectation.
Er-wartung (⌣⌊⌣) f ⊕ expectation; voller (a. in gespannter) ~ on the tip-toe of exp.; sein Fleiß berechtigt zu guten ~en ... gives a fair promise for the future; in seinen ~en getäuscht w. to be disappointed (in one's hopes), to see one's expectations blighted; brieflich: in ~ Ihrer Antwort awaiting

your reply; in der festen ~, daß // being fulling confident that //.
er-wartungs-voll (⌣⌊⌣...) a. ⊕ full of expectation or hope; expectant; =wert m ⊕ agr. for. an Erträgen: expected yield (of crops, timber, &c.).
er-wecken (⌣⌊⌣) I v/a. ⊕* 1. to awaken, to rouse; vom Tode: to resuscitate, to raise from the dead, to recall to life; fig. zum Fleiße, zur Tugend 2c. 2d inciting to (or encouraging) industry, virtue, &c. — 2. fig. (erregen) to create (or excite) envy, suspicion; to cause fear; to inspire confidence, courage; to raise hopes; wieder ~ to revive faith, &c. — II ~ n ⊕ 3. = Erweckung.
Er-weckung (⌣⌊⌣) f ⊕ (s. erwecken I) awakening; vom Tode: resuscitation; fig. incitement; encouragement; inspiration; des Glaubens: revival; ~s-prediger (⌣⌊⌣...) m ⊕ rel. revivalist.
er-wehren (⌣⌊⌣): sich 2 v/refl. ⊕* to defend o.s. against; sich der Hunde, Diebe 2c. 2 to keep (or ward) off ...; sich der Tränen 2 to restrain (or suppress) one's tears; ich konnte mich des Lachens nicht 2 I could not help laughing.
er-weichbar (⌣⌊⌣) a. ⊕ capable of softening or being softened; mollifiable.
er-weichen (⌣⌊⌣) ⊕* I v/a. 1. Wachs 2c. 2 to soften, vgl. aufweichen I. — 2. fig. e-n 2 to mollify a p.; (rühren) to touch, to move to tears; j-s Herz 2 to melt a p.'s heart. — II v/n (sn) u. sich 2 v/refl. 3. to soften, to grow soft; fig. (a. sich 2 lassen) to relent. — III ~ n ⊕ 4. = S/ung. — IV 2d p.pr. u. a. ⊕ 5. Bed. des inf. — 6. med. 2d(es Mittel). ⚙ emollient, lenitive.
Er-weichung (⌣) f ⊕ softening; mollification; chm., &c.: ⚙ emollescence; ~s-mittel n ⊕: ⚙ emollient, demulcent.
Er-weis ⌣ (⌣⌊) m ⊕a. = Beweis.
er-weis/en (⌣⌊⌣) ⊕b* I v/a. 1. = beweisen 1. — 2. (erzeigen) e-m Dienste, Ehre 2 to render a p. services, to do a p. honour; e-m die letzte Ehre 2 to pay a p. the last tribute of respect; e-m eine Gunst, Wohltat 2 to confer (or bestow) a favour, benefit upon a p. — II sich 2 v/refl. 3. to show o.s.; sich dankbar 2 to prove (o.s.) grateful; sich als treuer (a. treuen) Freund 2 to prove (or behave as) a true friend; er erwies sich als mein alter Schulkamerad he turned out to be my old school-fellow. — III ~ n ⊕ 4. = S/ung.
er-weislich (⌣⌊⌣) a. ⊕ = beweisbar; 2ermaßen adv. evidently, manifestly.
Er-weisung (⌣⌊⌣) f ⊕ = Beweis.
er-weitern (⌣⌊⌣) I v/a. u. sich 2 v/refl. ⊕a* 1. ⊕ u. arch. to enlarge, to widen; v. e-m Kleide auch: to let out; fig. den Riß 2 to widen the breach; sich 2 to grow larger or wider, to widen. — 2. (ausdehnen) (sich) 2 to extend, expand, dilate. fig. a.: to amplify; fig. sein Ansehen 2 to extend (or increase) one's authority; s-n Blick, s-en Gedankenkreis 2 to enlarge (or widen) one's horizon; path. von der Pupille: erweitert dilated; in erweitertem Sinne in a wider (or larger) sense. — II ~ n ⊕ u. Er-weiterung (⌣⌊⌣) f ⊕ 3. enlar-

gement; extension, expansion; path. dilatation of the pupil. Er-weiterungs-bau (⌊...) m ⊕ additional building or wing; enlargement of premises.
Er-werb (⌣⌊) m ⊕b. 1. (das Erwerben) acquisition. — 2. (Gewinn) gain, profit, return(s pl.); (Lohn) wage(s pl.); pay; (Unterhalt) livelihood, living, weits. income. — ~... s. Erwerbs-...
er-werben (⌣⌊⌣) I v/a. ⊕b* to acquire wealth, knowledge, &c.; durch Arbeit: to earn, to gain; sich (dat.) sein Brot 2 to earn one's (daily) bread or a living; sich j-s Achtung 2 to gain a p.'s esteem; sich Verdienste um das Vaterland 2 to deserve well of one's country; erblich erworben inherited, hereditary; teuer erworben dearly bought; erworb(e)ne Kenntnisse, Fertigkeiten f/pl. attainments, accomplishments pl. — II ~ n ⊕ = Erwerb.
Er-werber (⌣⌊⌣) m ⊕, =in f ⊕ acquirer; jur. (s. der Rechte übernimmt) transferee.
er-werbsam ⌣ (⌣⌊⌣) a. ⊕ industrious; ~keit f ⊕ industriousness, industry.
er-werbs-fähig (⌣⌊...) a. ⊕ capable of making a living; =fähigkeit f ⊕ ability to earn a livelihood; =fleiß m ⊕ industry; =genossenschaft f, =gesellschaft f ⊕ cooperative association; =mittel n, =quelle f means of living; resource; =sinn m Phrenologie: acquisitiveness; =tätigkeit f ⊕ industry; trade; 2unfähig a. unable to earn one's (or to make a) living; =unfähigkeit f inability to support o.s.; =urkunde f jur. title-deed, transfer-deed; =zweig m (means of earning a) livelihood; branch of industry or trade, F line of business. [Erwerb(s-...)]
Er-werbung(s-...) (⌣⌊⌣...) f ⊕ (⊕) =)
er-widern (⌣⌊⌣) I v/a. ⊕a* 1. to return; (vergelten) to requite; to reciprocate a p.'s friendship, &c.; e-m Gleiches mit Gleichem 2 (vergelten) to give a p. tit for tat, to retaliate upon a p.; j-s Besuch, Gruß, 2 to return a p.'s call, bow; j-s Liebe, Neigung 2 to reciprocate (or return) a p.'s love or affection. — 2. auch abs. (antworten) to reply to a letter, a question, &c.; to answer a note, an inquiry, &c. = entgegnen I. — II ~ n ⊕ Er-widerung (⌣⌊⌣...) f ⊕ 3. (s. 1) return; reciprocation; retaliation; (s. 2) (Antwort) answer, reply; (quick) retort; in ~ auf //, auch: in response to //; Er-widerungs-schrift f jur. rejoinder.
Er-wiedern (⌣⌊⌣) 2c. ehm. = erwidern 2c.
er-wies (⌣⌊) ind., er-wiese (⌣⌊⌣) subj. impf. v. erweisen.
er-wiesener-maßen (⌣⌊⌣⌣⌊⌣)adv. according to evidence (produced), as previously proved. [effect; vgl. auswirken 2.)
er-wirken (⌣⌊⌣) v/a. ⊕* to (carry into)
er-wischen (⌣⌊⌣) v/a. ⊕* to catch (P to cop) a thief, &c.; sich 2 lassen to be caught (in a trap), vgl. ertappen I.
er-wog (⌣⌊) ind., er-wöge (⌣⌊⌣) subj. impf., er-wogen (⌣⌊⌣) p.p. v. erwägen.
er-worben (⌣⌊⌣) p.p. v. erwerben.
er-wuchern (⌣⌊⌣) v/a. ⊕a* to gain (or get, earn, acquire) by usury.
er-wuchs (⌣⌊ ts) ind., er-wüchse (⌣⌊⌣ ts) subj. impf. v. erwachsen.

⚙ scientific; ⚘ botanical; ⚲ geography; ⊕ machinery; ⚒ mining; ⚔ military; ⚓ marine; ⚛ commercial; ✉ postal; 🚂 railway.

[erwünschen] — 344 — [Erzscheidekunst]

er-wünschen (⌣⌣⌣) I v/a. ®* 1. = wünschen. — 2. to obtain by wishing. — II **er-wünscht** p.p. u. a. ⑱ 3. in den Beb. des inf. — 4. desirable; (willkommen) welcome; die Ꙋe Gelegenheit the desired opportunity; es kam sehr Ꙋ (adv.) it came most opportunely or F in the nick of time. [dice.]

er-würfeln (⌣⌣⌣) v/a. ⓶a* to win at

er-würgen (⌣⌣⌣) ®* I v/a. to strangle, throttle, garrotte; (ersticken) to suffocate; weitS. (umbringen) to kill, to massacre; ihn magst du, entrinn' ich, Ꙋ (SCH.) him you may slay if I escape. — II v/n. (zu) to choke with s. th. — III ~ n ㉓ = Erwürgung.

Er-würger (⌣⌣⌣) m ㉒ strangler, garrotter; weitS. slayer; murderer.

Er-würgung (⌣⌣⌣) f ㊻ (s. erwürgen I) strangulation; suffocation; weitS. slaughter, massacre.

Erythräa ♀ (⌣-⌣) [grch.] npr/n. ⓶a. (it. Kolonie am Roten Meere) Erythrea.

Erythrin ⚗ (⌣-⌣) [grch.] n ⓶c. chm. (roter Farbstoff der Flechten) erythrin ($C_{20}H_{22}O_{10}$).

Erz¹ (⌣, a. ⌣) [ahd.] n ⓶a. 1. min. (metallhaltiges Gestein) ore; mineralized stone or ground. — 2. (Metall) metal; (Kupferzint, Messing) brass; (Bronze) bronze; aus ~ gefertigt brazen, bronze; aus ~ gefertigte Sachen brazen articles, bronzes pl.

Erz²-..., **erz²-...** (⌣-..., a. ⌣-...) [ahd.; *grch. archi...] I von Titeln und Würden meist: arch(-)... — II e-n hohen Grad bezeichnend, oft b.s. in Schimpfwörtern ꝛc., meist: arch-..., arrant..., thorough..., consummate..., &c. [liferous) vein or lode.]

Erz¹-ader (⌣...) f ㊵ mineral (or metal-)

er-zählbar (⌣-⌣) a. ⑱ fit to be (re)told, fit for narration; ~keit (⌣-⌣-) f ㊻ fitness for narration.

er-zähl/en (⌣-⌣) [mhd.: tell] I v/a. ®* to tell, relate, recount; berichtend: to report, kunstvoll: to narrate, umständlich: to retail; ein langes und (ein) breites Ꙋ to spin a long yarn; ich habe mir Ꙋ lassen, man hat mir erzählt I have been told; man erzählt sich, daß // people say (or it is reported, the story goes) that //; er kann et. davon Ꙋ (an viel erlebt) he can tell some marvellous tales, he has seen something, F he knows a thing or two; er kann schnurrige Geschichten Ꙋ he knows (or can tell) some funny tales; Ꙋd narrative; Ꙋdes Gedicht narrative poem, epic tale. — II ~ n ㉓ = E/ung.

er-zählens-wert (⌣-⌣...) a. ⑱ worth (re)telling, deserving to be retold.

Er-zähler (⌣-⌣) m, ~in f ㊵ narrator, v. Geschichten: story-teller [a. = Lügner!], als Schriftsteller: writer of tales, author of fiction, novelist.

Er-zählung (⌣-⌣) f ㊻ narration, narrative; report; mit Einzelheiten: detailed account; (Geschwätz) talk, gossip; (Geschichte) story, tale; (Erdichtetes) fiction, romance, invention; ~s-art (⌣⌣...) f ㊷, ~s-weise f narrative style, manner of telling tales; Ꙋs-weise² adv. in (the) form of a tale or a story, in narrative form, narratively.

Erz²-amt (⌣...) n ㉒ hist. im Deutschen Reiche: elector's office; =¹**anflug** ⚒ m

slightly mineralized stone; =**arbeit** f bronze-work; =**arbeiter** ⊕ m bronze-worker; Ꙋ**arm** ⚒ a. yielding poor (or little) ore; =**art** ⚒ f kind (or species) of ore; Ꙋ**artig** a. metallic; brazen; Ꙋ**beschlagen** a. brass-bound; =²**betrüger** m = =gauner; =¹**bild** n bronze statue; bibl. brazen image; =²**bischof** [ahd.] m archbishop; Ꙋ**bischöflich** a. ⑱ archiepiscopal; =**bistum** n archbishopric; =**bösewicht** m, =**bube** m thorough villain; vgl. =gauner; =¹**bruch** ⚒ m mine; pit; =²**diakon** m archdeacon; =**dieb** m incorrigible (F awful) thief; =¹**druse** f crystallized ore; =²**dumm** a. ⑱ thoroughly (F fearfully) stupid, exceedingly silly; =**dummkopf** F m regular blockhead or idiot.

er-zeig/en (⌣-⌣) ®* I v/a. 1. = zeigen. — 2. = erweisen 2. — II sich Ꙋ v/refl. 3. = erweisen II. — III ~ n ㉓, E/ung f ㊻ 4. show(ing); v. Ehren: doing honour; e-r Wohltat: conferring a charity, bestowing a benefit.

erzen¹ (⌣, a. ⌣) [Erz¹] a. ⑱ = ehern.

erzen² F (⌣) [er 2] v/a. ⑩ to address a subordinate in the third person.

Erz²-engel (⌣...) m ㉒ archangel.

er-zeugbar (⌣-⌣) a. ⑱ producible; chm. &c. auch: ⚗ generable; ~keit (⌣-⌣-) f ㊻ producibleness, producibility.

er-zeug/en (⌣-⌣) ®* I v/a. 1. = zeugen. — 2. (hervorbringen) to produce, durch Wachstum: to grow; (bilden) to form; fig. to engender; chm., &c.: ⚗ to generate gases, &c.; path. to breed a fever, &c.; der in Rußland erzeugte Weizen the wheat grown in Russia or of Russian growth; in rechtmäßiger Ehe erzeugt lawfully begotten. — II sich Ꙋ v/refl. 3. (f. 2) to be produced; to form, arise. — III ~ n ㉓ 4. = E/ung. — IV 5. **Er-zeugte([r]** m) f ⑰ offspring.

Er-zeuger (⌣-⌣) m ㉒ I (a. ~**in** f ㊵) procreator; (male, female) parent. — II ⊕ (Dampfapparat) steam-generator.

Er-zeugnis (⌣-⌣) n ㉗ (natural) produce; landwirtschaftliche Erzeugnisse pl. agricultural produce sg.; ~ des Geistes, der Kunst ꝛc.: production, creation; ⊕, chm., &c. product; (Gewächs) growth.

Er-zeugung (~) f ㊻ procreation; generation; weitS. production; formation.

Er-zeugungs-kosten ⊕ (⌣ᵘ...) pl. f ㊷ cost of production; =**kraft** f procreative (or generative) force.

Erz¹-farbe (⌣...) f ㊷, Ꙋ**farbig** a. ⑱ bronze-colour(ed); =**faß** ⚒ n ore-tub; Ꙋ²**faul** a. excessively idle, bone-lazy; =**feind** m ⑱ arch-enemy or -foe; =**flegel** m rude (or brutal, coarse) fellow; F regular bear or brute; =¹**förderung** ⚒ f output of ore; Ꙋ**führend** a. geogn. carrying (good) ore, ore-bearing; =**gang** ⚒ m (mineral) lode; =²**gauner** m arrant knave, thorough rogue, arch-villain; consummate cheat or rascal; expert swindler; F awful scoundrel; =¹**gebirge** n: a) metalliferous mountain-range; b) ♁ (sächsisches) ~ (Saxon) Erzgebirge; =**gießer(ei** f) m ⊕ brass-founder(-foundry); =**gräber** ⚒ m miner, digger; =**grobian** m = =flegel; =¹**grube** f mine, pit, digg-

ing; =**guß** m bronze cast; =**halde** ⚒ f heap of dead ore; Ꙋ**haltig** ⚒ a. containing ore, metalliferous; =²**herzog** (=in f) m archduke (f archduchess); Ꙋ**herzoglich** a. archducal; =**herzogtum** n archduchy; =**heuchler** m arch-hypocrite; =¹**hütte** ⚒ f smelting-house or -shed.

er-zieh/en (⌣-⌣) I v/a. ⑱b* to educate, to rear (or bring) up; gut (schlecht) erzogen, oft: well- (ill-) bred; in der Schule des Unglücks erzogen schooled by misfortune, trained (or reared, nurtured) in the school of adversity; vgl. aufziehen 6. — II ~ n ㉓ = E/ung.

Er-zieher (⌣-⌣) m ㉒, ~**in** f ㊵ educator; pedagogue; (Lehrer) teacher, (private) tutor, f lady teacher; in Schulen ꝛc.: master, f governess.

er-zieherisch (⌣-⌣⌣) a., **er-ziehlich** (⌣-⌣) a. ⑱ educational; pedagogic(al).

Er-ziehung (⌣-⌣) f ㊻ education; breeding; rearing (up); er hat eine gute (schlechte) ~ genossen he has had a good (bad) education, he was well (badly) brought up or educated or taught.

Er-ziehungs-anstalt (⌣-⌣ᵘ...) f ⑫ educational establishment, school; =**art** f educational method or system; =**fach** n = =kunst, =**kunst**, =**kunde** f (art of) education, ⚗ pedagogics; Ꙋ**los** a. uneducated; =**rat** m educational council or board; =**schriftsteller** m educational writer; =**wesen** n educational matters pl.; =**wissenschaft** f science of education, ⚗ pedagogics, pedagogy.

er-zielen (⌣-⌣) I v/a. ⑱b* (erstreben) to aim at; (erreichen) to obtain, to attain one's end; to achieve success; damit läßt sich nichts Ꙋ nothing can be gained (or accomplished) by that; ⚒ erzielter Gewinn profit realized or made or secured; die erzielten Preise pl. the prices pl. obtained. — II ~ n ㉓ und **Er-zielung** f ㊻ attainment; achievement; ⚒ realization.

er-zittern (⌣-⌣) v/n. (zu) ⓶a* to begin to tremble or to shake or to shiver.

Erz²-jude (⌣...) m ㉒ (=**jüdin** f) thorough Jew(ess); =**kämmerer**, =**kanzler** m in Engl.: Lord High Chamberlain, Chancellor; Ꙋ**katholisch** a. ultra-Catholic; =**ketzer(ei** f) m arch-heretic (-heresy); =**knauser** m, =**knicker** m confirmed miser; =**kokette** f arch-coquette, F desperate (or awful) flirt; =¹**kunde** f metallurgy; =**kundige(r)** m metallurgist; =**lagerstätte** ⚒ f deposit of ore, shoot; =²**lügner** m arch-liar, infernal story-teller; =**lümmel** m common lout, hooligan; =**marschall** m ehm. Grand Marshal of the German Empire; =**mundschenk** m = =schenk; =**narr** m, =**närrin** f downright fool; =¹**ofen** ⚒ m smelting-furnace.

er-zog (⌣-⌣) impf., Ꙋ**en** (⌣-⌣) p.p. v. erziehen.

Erz¹-pochen ⚒ (⌣...) n ㉒ pounding (or crushing) of ore; =²**priester** m high priest; Cath. eccl. arch(i)presbyter; Ꙋ**priesterlich** a. ⑱ Cath.eccl. archipresbyteral; =¹**probe** ⚒ f assaying (of) ore, assay; Ꙋ**reich** ⚒ a. rich (or abounding) in ore; =²**schalk** m arch-wag; =¹**scheidekunst** ⊕ f sorting (or picking) of ore;

Zeichen (s. S. XVII): F familiär; P Volkssprache; ſ Gaunersprache; ⧵ selten; † alt (auch gestorben); * neu (auch geboren); ₊* unrichtig;

[Erzscheider] — 345 — [essen]

metall.: ⚒ docimastic art; =**scheider** ⚒ *m* ore-picker; =**schelm** *m* = =gauner; =**schenk** *m*, *hist.* im Deutschen Reiche: arch-butler or -cupbearer; =¹**schicht** ⚒ *f* twenty-four hours' shift or smeltings *pl.*; =**schlich** ⚒ *m*, *metall.* slick; crushed ore; =**schürfer** ⚒ *m* (miners') foreman; =²**schurke** *m* = =gauner; =**spitzbube** *m* = =dieb; =¹**staub** ☉ ⚒ *m* ore-dust; =**stufe** *f* (kleines Stück Erz) lump of ore; =**teufe**, =**tiefe** ⚒ *f* depth of the (richest) ore-level; =²**tölpel** *m* thorough duffer; F clumsy Jack; =¹**trog** ⚒ *m* buddle; *vgl.* =faß; =²**truchseß** *m* archdapifer; =**tugend** *f* cardinal virtue; =¹**umschient** ⚔ *a*. armed with metal greaves.

er-zürnen (‿‿) ⊛* **I** *v/a.* 1. to make angry; (aufreizen) to provoke, irritate. — **II** *v/n.* (jn) u. **sich** ⟲ *v/refl.* 2. to grow angry at a th.; F to get cross; to lose one's temper over a th. — 3. sich mit einem ⟲ to fall out with a p., to be angry with a p.

Erz²-vater (‸...) *m* ⓖ (väterlich *a.* ⓖ) patriarch(al); =**verschwender** *m* reckless spendthrift; =¹**wage** ⚒ *f* scales *pl.* for weighing ore.

er-zwang (‿‿) *impf. v.* erzwingen.

Erz¹-wäsche ⚒ (‸...) *f* ⓖ, *metall.*: a) washing of ore; b) (Anstalt) dressing- (or washing-) floor or -room, washer; =**wäscher** ⚒ *m* ore-washer, streamer.

er-zwingbar (‿‿) *a.* ⓖ enforceable.

er-zwing/en (‿‿) **I** *v/a.* ⊛ft* to force, enforce; et. von e-m ⟲ to obtain a th. by force (stärker: to extort a th.) from a p.; es kann sich nicht ⟲ that cannot be forced or done by force. — **II** ~ *n* ⓖ u. Ɛ/ung *f* ⓖ enforcement; extortion.

Erz²-wucherer (‸...) *m* ⓖ (cruel) extortioner, pitiless or heartless) usurer.

er-zwungen (‿‿) *p.p.*, *a.* (D9) 1. forced, f. erzwingen. — 2. (unnatürlich) affected; (erheuchelt) feigned, simulated.

es¹ (♂ u. ♀), *abbr.* '**s** [ahd.: it: lt. *id*] ⓖ **A** 1. *personal pron.*, *neuter* von er. **I** als Objekt: 1. it; er nimmt es, hat es genommen he takes it, has taken it; auf das Folgende hinweisend: ich halte es für unnütz, ihn zu fragen I deem it useless ...; 2. in stehenden Wendungen, oft nicht zu übersetzen: f. absehen 5; aufnehmen 3; aushalten 2; bieten 6; bringen 7 u. 8; bunt 4; er hat's dick hinter den Ohren he is very sly or artful, he is not as simple as he looks; es gut haben to be well off or well treated or happy; es mit e-m halten to side with a p. — **II** als *gen.* statt seiner oder dessen: 3. ich hab' es (bin des Dinges) satt I am sick (or tired) of it. — **III** als Ersatz oder Ergänzung des Prädikats: 4. er ist jm, wir sind es auch ..., so are we; sind Sie die Mutter des Kindes? — ja, ich bin es ... yes, I am; waren das die Mädchen? — nein, sie waren es nicht ... no, they were not (the ones); sind Sie es? nein, ich bin's (wir sind es) is it you? no, it is I or F me (it is we or F us); sie waren es, die // it was they who //; er ist's, war's it is he, it was he. — **IV** als Subjekt or *v/impers.*: 5. it (darf nicht fehlen, auch wenn es deutsch ausgelassen

ist, *z.B.*: wenn sich findet, daß // if it be found that //); es gibt Leute, die // there are people who //; es regnet it rains, it is raining; es kamen drei Wagen there came ...; es lebe der König! long live the king!; es wird gespielt they are playing, the play is going on; es läßt sich nicht glauben, daß // it is not creditable that //. — 6. mit **sein**: a) vor *a.*, mit Bezug auf Folgendes oder Vorhergehendes, *z.B.*: es ist offenbar, daß Sie recht haben it is evident that you are right; auch: you are right, that is evident; b) vor *s.* mit *art.*, &c., *z.B.*: es ist eine arme Frau it is, ist nicht mein Haus, es ist das m-r Mutter ... it is my mother's; es ist (nicht mehr) Zeit it is (there is no) time; es sind ihrer nur wenige there are but few of them. — 7. meist *poet.*: (ein unbeschreibliches Etwas, *z.B.*: es riß mich hinunter, etwa: a something drew me down. — **V** Es *n, inv.*: 8. das unbestimmte the indefinable "It".

Es² ♪ (♩) *n, inv.* E flat. [= Jesaias.]

Esaias (‸‿‿) *npr/m.* ⓖ γ. *bibl.* Isaiah

Esau (‸‿) *npr/m.* ⓖ ⓖα. *bibl.* Esau.

☛ **Esc...** f. Esk...

Esch *prov.* (‸) [ahd.] *m,* n ⓖa. (bebaute Flur) (large plot of) ploughland.

Esche ♀ (‸‿)[ahd.: ash] *f* ⓖ ash(-tree) (*Fra'xinus*); echte~ common ash (*F. exce'lsior*).

Eschel ♀ (‸) *m* ⓖ *chm.* (feinste Schmalte, Kobaltfarbe) kind of powder-blue; zaffer.

eschen (‸‿) [Esche] *a.* ⓖ ashen, of ash.

eschen-artig (‸‿...) *a.* ⓖ ash-like; =**baum** *m* ⓖ = Esche; =**holz** *n* ⓖ ash-wood; =**wald** *m* ash-grove, forest of ash-trees.

Esdragon f. Estragon.

Esel (‸‿) [ahd.: *lt. a'sinus*] *m* ⓖ, ~**in** *f* ⓖ 1. *zo.* ass (*Equus a'sinus*); donkey; *co.* neddy, P moke; männlicher ~ he-ass, jackass; weiblicher ~ ob. ~**in** she- (or jenny-)ass; wilder ~ wild ass (*Equus o'nager*); *fig.* als Schimpfwort: (jack)ass, donkey, duffer, dunce; der ~ schreit the donkey brays. — 2. Redensarten: ein ~ nennt den andern Langohr (it's like): the pot calling the kettle black; vom Pferde auf den ~ kommen to come down in the world; den Sack schlagen und den ~ meinen to say (or do) one thing and mean another; wenn dem ~ zu wohl wird, geht er aufs Eis (tanzen) a wanton fool grows reckless, too much luck makes us foolhardy. — 3. ehm. (hölzernes Pferd als Strafmittel *rc.*) wooden horse. — 4. ⊕ *arch.* rammer; *typ.* horse.

Eselchen (‸‿‿) *n* ⓖ (dim. von Esel) *zo.* little (or young) donkey.

Eselei (‿‸) *f* ⓖ stupid act or conduct.

Eselein (‿‿) *n* ⓖ = Eselchen.

Esel-füllen (‸‿‿) *n* ⓖ ass's colt, foal.

eselhaft (‸‿) *a.* ⓖ donkey-like, asinine; (dumm) stupid; (halsstarrig) stubborn; sich ⟲ benehmen to make an ass of o. s.

Eselin (‸‿) *f* ⓖ f. Esel.

Esels-arbeit (‸‿...) *f* ⓖ drudgery; =**brücke** *f, fig.*: a) (Übersetzung für Schüler) crib; b) *math.* bridge of asses (lt. *pons asinorum*); =**distel** ♀ *f* Scotch thistle (*Onopo'rdon Aca'nthium*); =**geschrei** *n* bray(ing) of an ass; ⟲**grau** *a.* ⓖ grey

as a donkey; =**haupt** ⚓ *n* (Klotz zwischen Mast und Stenge) cap (of a mast); ein ~ aufsetzen to get a cap over, to cap; =**kinnbacken** *m bibl.*, &c.: jawbone of an ass; =**kopf** *m, fig.* blockhead, dunce; =**milch** (*f* a) asses' milk; b) leafy spurge (*Eupho'rbia e'sula*); =**ohr** *n* donkey's ear; *fig.* (Kniff in e-m Buche) dog's ear; mit ~**en** dog's-eared. — **Esel-stall** *m* stable for donkeys; =**treiber**(**in** *f*) *m* donkey-driver, driver of donkeys.

Eskader öft. ⚓ (‿‸‿), **Eskadre** (ĕ-ḵṭā'dr) [*fr.*] *f* ⓖ (Geschwader) squadron.

Eskadron ⚔ (‿‿‸) [*fr.*] ⓖ (Schwadron) squad(ron); ~**s-chef** *m* ⓖ leader of a squad(ron). [er) conjurer, juggler.]

Eskamoteur (‿‿‿tö'r)[*fr.*]*m*⊕ⓖ.(Gaukler)

eskamotieren (‿‿‿‸‿) [*fr.*] *v/a.* ⓖ (fortzaubern) to conjure away.

Eskarpe ⚔ (‿‸‿) [*fr.*: *dtsch.* scharf] *f* ⓖ *frt.* (innere Grabenböschung) escarp; ~**n-galerie** *f* ⓖ escarp-gallery.

Eskimo (‸‿‿) [indian. Rohfleisch-esser] *m* ⓖ Esquimau, *pl.* ...x, Eskimo.

eskomptieren, **eskontieren** ⊕ (‿‿‸‿)[*fr.*] *v/a.* ⓖ, ~ *n* ⓖ und **Eskomptierung**, **Eskontierung** *f* ⓖ *rc.* = diskontieren *rc.*

Eskorte ⚔ (‿‸‿) [*fr.*] *f* ⓖ (Bedeckung) escort; ⚓ u. ⚔ convoy.

eskortieren (‿‿‸‿) [*fr.*] *v/a.* ⓖ ⚔ to escort; ⚓ u. ⚔ to convoy.

Esoteriker ⚒ (‸‿‿‿) [*grch.*] *m* ⓖ *phls.* (in Geheimlehren Eingeweihter) esoteric, *pl.* oft: the initiated; **esoterisch** (‿‸‿) *a.* ⓖ esoteric; initiated.

Esparsette ♀ (‿‿‸‿) [*fr.*, *span.*] *f* ⓖ cockshead, sainfoin (*Ono'brychis sati'va*).

Esparto(=**gras**) ♀ (‿‸‿) [*span.*] *n* ⓖ ⓖ esparto-grass (*Stipa tenaci'ssima*).

Espe ♀ (‸‿) [ahd.: asp] *f* ⓖ aspen-tree, asp, trembling-poplar (*Po'pulus tre'mula*); **espen** (‸‿) *a.* ⓖ of asp.

Espen-baum ♀ (‸‿...) *m* ⓖ = Espe; =**laub** *n* foliage of asps, aspen-leaves *pl.*; wie ~ zittern to tremble like an aspen-leaf; to shake in every limb.

esquilinisch (‿‿‸‿) [lt. *Esquili'nus mons*, einer der sieben Hügel Roms] *a.* ⓖ Alt.: ~**er** Hügel ob. Berg (Mount) Esquiline.

Esra (‸‿) [hebr.] *npr/m.* ⓖ ⓖα. (458 v. Chr., Wiederhersteller d. jüd. Staates) Ezra.

Essäer (‿‸‿) [hebr.] *m* ⓖ Essene.

Essäismus (‿‿‸‿) *m* ⓖ Essenism.

eßbar (‸‿) *a.* ⓖ eatable, fit to eat; edible; (genießbar) ⟲ esculent; Ɛ Dinge eatables *pl.*, P grub; ~**keit** (‸‿...) *f* ⓖ eatableness, edibility.

Eß-begier (‸‿...) *f* ⓖ = Eßgier.

Esse¹ (‸‿) [ahd.] *f* ⓖ (Rauchfang) chimney, flue; (Schlot) funnel; (Herd) hearth; (Schmiede) forge.

Esse² *f* (‸‿) [lt.] *n, inv.*: in seinem ~ sein to be at (one's) ease.

essen (‸‿) [ahd.: eat; lt. *e'dere*] **I** *v/a.* ⓖ 1. to eat; weits. to feed (or live) upon; gut ⟲ und trinken to live well, *bibl.* to fare sumptuously; wenig (viel) ⟲ to be a small (a great) eater; zu viel ⟲ to overeat o.s., F to gormandize, to stuff o.s.; ⟲ Sie gern Obst? do you like (or are you fond of) fruit?; was haben Sie gegessen? what have you had to eat?, what had you for dinner (or supper, &c.)?; bei uns

[Essenaufsatz] — 346 — [etwas]

wird viermal am Tage gegessen we eat (or have) four meals a day; wir 2 im Speisehaus we take our meals at a restaurant; wer nie sein Brot mit Tränen aß (G.) he whose bread was never wet with tears; iro. er hat die Weisheit mit Löffeln gegessen, etwa: he thinks himself extremely clever. — 2. mit Zeitbestimmung: zu Mittag, zu Abend 2 to dine, to sup; to have dinner, supper; ⚔ to mess; gut zu Mittag, zu Nacht 2 to eat a good (or hearty) dinner, supper. — 3. mit Angabe der Wirtung; a. v/refl.: e-n arm 2 to eat a p. out of house and home; die Schüssel leer 2 to empty (or clear) the dish; den Bauch (ob. sich) voll 2 to fill one's belly; sich krank (satt) 2 to eat o.s. ill (one's fill); das Fleisch läßt sich gebraten 2 ... eats well roasted; Pfannkuchen 2 sich am besten heiß pancakes are best (or should be) eaten hot. — II ~ n ⚙ 4. eating; weitS. feeding. — 5. (Speise) food, meat; (Gericht) dish; (Mahlzeit) meal, repast; dinner, supper; (Schmaus) feast, banquet; einfaches ~ plain food or diet or living; ihm schmeckt das ~ nicht he does not enjoy (or relish) his food or meal(s); e-n zum ~ einladen to invite a p. to dinner or supper.

Essen-aufsatz (ᵊᵛ...) [Esse¹] m ⚙ chimney-pot.

Essener (ᵛᴸᵛ) m ⚙ ꝛc. = Essäer ꝛc.

Essen=feger, =kehrer (ᵊᵛ...) m ⚙ (chimney-)sweep(er).

Essens=zeit (ᵛᴸ...) f ⚙ time for mealing or dinner or supper; vgl. Eßzeit.

Essenz (ᵛᵛ̆) [It.] f ⚙ pharm. (Auszug) essence; (ätherisches Öl) essential oil.

Esser (ᵋᵛ) m ⚙, ~in f ⚙ eater; schwacher ~ poor eater; er ist ein starker ~ he plays a good knife and fork; ~ei (ᵛᴸⁱⁱ) f⚙ feasting, gorging, F stuffing.

Eß=feige ⚘ (ᵛ...) f ⚙ common fig-tree (*Ficus ca'rica*); **=gelage** n feast, banquet; **=geschirr** n dinner-service; **=gier** f greediness, voracity; gluttony; ²**gierig** a. ⚙ greedy, voracious.

Essig (ᵛᵛ) [ahd.; *lt. ăcē'tum n] m ⚙d. 1. vinegar; ~ an et. tun to season a th. with vi.; in ~ einlegen to pickle (or preserve) in vi.; sauer wie ~ sour (or sharp) as vi. — 2. fig. es ist ~ damit, das ist ~ it's a failure; F it's no go; zu ~ werden to come to nothing.

Essig=älchen (ᵊᵛ...) n ⚙ = Aalterchen; **=äther** m, chm. acetic ether ($C_2H_3O_2$. C_2H_5); **=baum** ⚘ m tanner's sumac(h) (*Rhus coria'ria*); **=bildung** f, chm.: acetification; **=brauer** m vinegar-maker or manufacturer; **=brauerei** f vi.-works pl.; **=essenz** f 2 concentrated vinegar; **=fabrik** f vi.-factory; **=faß** n vi.-cask, mit Essig: cask of vi.; **=flasche** f vi.-bottle or -cruet; **=früchte** f/pl. mixed pickles pl.; **=gärung** f, chm.: = Azeton; **=gurke** f pickled cucumber; **=handel** m vi.-trade; **=händler** m vi.-merchant; **=hefe** f vi.-dregs pl.; **=honig** m, pharm.: ⚗ oxymel; **=messer** m ⚙ acetometer; **=mutter** [ndb. Moder] f, **=pilz** m vi.-plant (*Mycode'rma ace'ti*); **=rose**

f French rose (*Rosa ga'llica*); 2**säuer** a. as sour as vinegar; chm.: ⚗ acetic; 2**säures** Kali potassium acetate ($KC_2H_3O_2$), vgl. basisch...; **=säure** f, chm.: ⚗ acetic acid ($C_2H_4O_2$); **=säure-anhydrid** n: ⚗ acetic anhydride ($C_4H_6O_3$); **=säuresalz** n acetate = Azetat; **=säure-Äthyl-äther** m = -äther; **=sieder** m ꝛc. = -brauer ꝛc.; **= und Öl-ständer** m cruets pl., cruet-stand.

Eß=kastanie ⚘ (ᵛ...) f eatable chestnut; **=korb** m hamper; basket for (or with) provisions, F prog-basket; **=löffel** m table-spoon; ein ~l. voll a table-spoonful; **=lust** f appetite; ²**lustig** a. inclined to eat; **=saal** m, **=stube** f dining-room or -hall; **=stunde** f dinner-hour; **=tisch** m dining-table; **=waren** f/pl. eatables, victuals, provisions pl.; **=zeit** f dinner- (or meal-)time; co. feeding-time, vgl. Essenszeit; **=zimmer** n = -saal.

Estafette (ᵛᵛᴸᵛ) [Fr.] f ⚙ = Stafette.

Este (ᴸᵛ) m ⚙, **Estin** f ⚙ Esthonian.

Ester ⚗ (ᴸᵛ) [engl.] m ⚙ chm. (abgekürzter Äther, ätherartige Verbindung) ester.

Esther f [hebr.] npr/f. ⚙⚙ α. Esther.

Estland ⚘ (ᴸᵛ) npr/n. ⚙ Esthonia.

Estländer (ᴸᵛᵛ) m ⚙, **~in** f ⚙; **estländisch** a. ⚙ Esthonian.

estnisch (ᴸᵛ) a. ⚙ = estländisch.

Estrade (ᵛᴸᵛ) [fr.] f ⚙ (erhöhter Platz) estrade, stage, platform.

Estragon ⚘ (ᵛᵛᵍᵛ) [fr.] m ⚙ tarragon (*Artemi'sia dracu'nculus*) (= Dragun).

Estrich (ᴸᵛ) [ahd., *grch...] m ⚙d. arch. (Fußboden) floor; (Gipsboden) plaster floor; gegossener ~ cast plaster floor.

etablieren (-ᵛᴸᵛ) [fr.] v/a. u. sich 2 v/refl. ⚙: e-n (sich) 2 to establish a p. (o.s.); sich 2 auch: to set up (or start) a business. [ment.]

Établissement (-ᵛᵛᵇmᵍ') n ⚙ establish-⎦

Étage (-ᴸᴳᵛ) [fr. *étage* m] f ⚙ (Stockwerk) story, als Mietwohnung: flat; die erste ~ bewohnen to live on the first floor; **~n-keffel** ⚙ m double-story boiler.

Étagere (-ᵛᴳᴸᵛ) [fr.] f ⚙ (Stufengestell) bracket; (Bücherbrett) set of book-shelves.

Etamin ⚘ (ᵛᴸᵛ) [fr. *étamine* f] n (m) ⚙c. (Siebtuch) estamin, tamin(e), taminy.

Etappe ⚔ (-ᴸᵛ) [fr. *étape*; *ndd. Stapel] f ⚙ halting-place; day's march or provisions pl.; **~n-kommandant** (⚔...) m ⚙ commandant of a halting-place; **~n-platz** m halting-place; **~straße** f military road or route.

État (-ta') [(⚔) fr. *état*] m ⚙ ⚙ (Abschluß) balance-sheet, (periodical) statement; parl. (Voranschlag) estimate(s pl.), budget; den ~ aufstellen to bring in the estimates; ⚔ &c. auf dem ~ stehen to be on the establishment, (zum Regiment gehören) to be on the strength.

etatisieren (---ᵛᴸᵛ) v/a. ⚙ ⚙ to balance the accounts, parl. to draw up the estimates, to make up the budget.

etat=mäßig (-ta'...) a. ⚙ in accordance with the estimates.

Etats=beratung (-ta'β...) f ⚙ discussion of the estimates, budget debate; **=buch** ⚙ n ledger; **=jahr** n financial (or fiscal) year; ²**mäßig** a. = etat=m.; **=rat** m counsellor of state; **=rede** f

budget speech; **=stärke** ⚔ f ⚙ estimated strength or number (of troops).

etc. abbr. = et cetera [lt. und so weiter] etcetera (abbr. etc.; &c.).

Etesien (-ᵛᴸ(ᵛ)ᵛ) [grch. *Jahres...*] pl. (Passatwinde) etesian winds pl.

Ethik ⚗ (ᴸᵛ) [grch.] f ⚙ phls. (Sittenlehre) ethics, moral philosophy; **ethisch** a. ⚙ ethic, ethical.

ethnisch (ᴸᵛ) [grch.] a. ⚙ = heidnisch.

Ethnograph ⚗ (ᵛᴸᵛf) [grch.] m ⚙ ethnographer; **~ie** (ᵛᵛᴸⁱⁱ) f ⚙ (Völkerbeschreibung) ethnography; ²**isch** (ᵛᵛᴸⁱᵛ) a. ⚙ ethnographic(al).

Ethnolog ⚗ (ᵛᴸᵛ) [grch.] m ⚙, **~e** m ⚙ ethnologist; **~ie** (ᵛᵛᴸⁱⁱ) f ⚙ (Völkerkunde) ethnology; ²**isch** a. ⚙ ethnological.

Etikett=... (ᵛᵛᴸⁱⁱ...) in Zssgn f. Etiketten=...

Etikette (ᵛᵛᴸᵛ) [fr. *étiquette* f; dtsch. Stecl (brief)] f ⚙ 1. (Förmlichkeit) etiquette; auf ~ halten to stand upon ceremony. — 2. ⚙ (P a. **Etikett** (ᵛᵛᴸᵛ) n ⚙,⚙d.) label, ticket; (Schutzmarke) trade-mark.

Etikett(en)=druck (ᵛᵛᴸᵛ...) m ⚙ typ. label printing; **=schutz** ⚙ m (Markenschutz) protection of trade-marks; **=streit** m dispute about matters of etiquette or of ceremony.

etikettieren ⚙ (ᵛᵛᴸᵛ) [fr.] v/a. ⚙ to (mark with a) label; Waren: to ticket.

etlich (ᴸᵛ) [ahd.] indef. pron. ⚙(A 3 †), mst pl. 2**e** some, a few; 2**e** gute Leute some good people; 2**e** Tage several days; dreißig und 2**e** Jahre thirty odd years; 2**e** Male (a 2**emal** adv.) several (or sundry) times; 2**es** a few things, some few matters pl.; bibl. 2**es** fiel unter die Dornen some fell among thorns.

Etmal ♃ (ᴸᵛ) [ndb., ndl.] n ⚙c. day's reckoning, 24 hours' run.

Etruri-en ⚘ (ᵛᴸ(ᵛ)ᵛ) [It.] npr/n. ⚙α. röm. Alt.: (nord-italisches Land) Etruria.

Etruri-er (ᵛᴸ(ᵛ)ᵛ), **Etrusker** (ᵛᴸᵛ) m ⚙, **~in** f ⚙, **etrurisch** (ᵛᴸᵛ), **etruskisch** (ᵛᴸᵛ) a. ⚙ Etrurian, Etruscan.

etsch¹ F (ᴸ) int. = ätsch.

Etsch² ⚘ (ᴸ) [lt. *A'thesis*] npr/f. inv. ⚙ die ~ (Fluß Nord-italiens) the Adige; **~tal** n ⚙ valley of the Adige.

Etter sübb. (ᵛᵛ) [ahd.] m ⚙ (Grenze) boundary, auch: Zaun, Hecke.

Etüde (-ᴸᵛ) [fr.] f ⚙ ♪ u. Kunst: study.

Etui (-tä') [fr.] n ⚙ (Behälter) case.

etwa (ᴸᵛ) [ahd.], bisw. 2**n** (ᴸᴸ) adv. 1. (ungefähr) about, nearly; 2 300 Leute about (or some) three hundred people; 2 so somewhat like this; ist dies so 2 recht? is this about right? — 2. (vielleicht) perhaps, perchance; (möglicherweise) possibly; (zufällig) accidentally; nicht 2, daß // not as if //; denken Sie nicht 2 don't perhaps think; soll das 2 bedeuten (ob. heißen), daß //? do you mean to imply (or am I to understand) that //?; wenn ich 2 sterben sollte in case I should die; Spiel: sollte er 2 aus sein should he happen to be out.

etwaig, fast †**etwanig** (ᵛᴸᵛ) a. ⚙ eventual; contingent; 2**e** Ausgaben incidental...; 2**en=falls** adv. eventually.

etwas (ᵛᵛ) [ahd.] I indef. pron. inv. (oft abbr. **was**) ⚙ 1. substantivisch (mst klein gschr.): 2 sehen to see something; so 2

[etwelch] — 347 — [Ev.]

von ritterlicher Kühnheit a dash of ...; ohne 2 (a. irgendwas) zu sagen without saying anything; ich habe so 2 nie gehört I never heard the like or anything like it; hast du nicht 2 gesehen? did you not see something?; das ist doch 2 there is something in that; es ist doch 2! well, it is (a) something!; das wäre 2 für dich that's what you want, it's quite your taste; daraus kann 2 werden something may come out of that; aus ihm wird 2 he is getting on, he will be somebody (soon); so 2 will ausgesonnen sein these things want thinking out; F ach, hat sich was! (warum nicht gar) you don't say so!; F nein, so was, so 2 gibt's nicht! who would believe it?, did you ever (hear of such a thing)?; ein gewisses ~ a(n indefinable) something. — 2. abjektivisch: 2 Geld some money; gibt es 2 Neues? is there any news?; 2 and(e)res something different, s.th. else; a different thing; es ist 2 Schönes um die Liebe there is something beautiful about love; es ist etwas Schwärmerisches an ihm he is something of an enthusiast. — II adv. (ein bißchen) a little; er ist 2 ruhiger he is somewhat calmer; 2 jung rather young, F youngish. — III ~ n inv., phls. (ant. Nichts): ✡ entity.
etwelch ↘ (⌣´) indef. pron. ⓖ = etlich; 2e alte Schriften a few old writings pl.
Etymolog ✡ (⌣´⌣⌣) [grch.] m ㉗, ~e m ㊹ etymologist; ~ie (⌣⌣⌣´) f ㊽ (Ableitung der Wörter) etymology; 2isch (⌣⌣´⌣) a. ⓖ etymological; 2isieren (...´⌣) v/a. ㉓ to etymologize.
Etymon (⌣´⌣) [grch.] n ㊾ gr. (Wurzel) etymon, root.
Et-zeichen (´⌣´⌣) [lt. et und] n ㉓ typ. (Zeichen &) ampersand.
Etzel (´⌣) [mhd. (got.) f. Attila] npr/m. ⓖⓐα. (Hunnenkönig) Attila.
etzlich † (´⌣) indef. pron. ⓖ = etlich.
euch [ahd.: you] in Briefen ⁊c.: **Euch** (´) ⓖ (A 1) acc. u. dat. pl. von du: you, to you; reflexiv: ihr betrügt 2 you deceive yourselves; setzt 2! sit down!
Eucharistie (⌣⌣⌣´) [grch. Danksagung] f ㊽ (Abendmahlsfeier) eucharist.
Eudiometer ✡ (⌣⌣´⌣⌣) [grch.] n (m) ㉒ phys. (Luftgütemesser) eudiometer.
euer [ahd.: your] ⓖ (A 1) in Briefen ⁊c.: **Euer** (´⌣) I personal pron. (gen. pl. v. du) of you; ich gedenke 2 I think of you, I have you in my thoughts, I bear you in mind; 2 waren zehn there were ten of you, you were ten. — II possessive pron. m. u. n ⓖ(C.) **eu(e)re, Eu(e)re** f u. pl. your; unser und 2 Feld our field and yours; der, die, das **Eu(e)re (Eurige)** yours; ist das Haus 2? is the house yours?; vor Titeln: **Eure** (abbr. Ew.) Hoheit Your Highness.
euert-... (´⌣...) in Zssgn = euret-...

Eugen (⌣´, ´⌣, ⸚ ¹⌣—) [grch. wohlgeboren] npr/m. ⓖⓐα., **~ius** (⌣´(⌣)⌣) ⓖγ. (Vn.) Eugene; Prinz ~ (ſt. Feldherr, 18. sae.) Prince Eugene; **~ie** (⌣´(⌣)⌣) npr/f. ⓖⓐβ. (Vn.) Eugenia, Eugenie.
Eukalyptus ✡ ♀ (⌣⌣´⌣) [grch.] m, inv. ob. ㉗ eucalyptus, gum-tree.

Euklid (⌣´) [grch.] npr/m. ⓤα. (alexandrinischer Mathematiker, um 300 vor Chr.) Euclid; 2isch a. ⓖ Euclidean (geometry). [1 u. 2).]
Eulchen (´⌣) n ㉓ dim. v. Eule (s. das]
Eule (´) [ahd.: owl] f ㊽ 1. orn. owl (Strix); kleine ~ owlet. — 2. ent., auch **Eulchen** (Nachtfalter) noctuid (No'ctua). — 3. fig. Sprichw. ~n nach Athen tragen (überflüssiges tun) to carry coals to Newcastle; des einen ~ ist des andern Nachtigall there is no accounting for tastes; ⚓ eine ~ fangen (den Wind von vorn bekommen) to be taken aback, to face the gale. — 4. (Vorwisch) soft broom.
Eulen-affe (´⌣...) m ㉒ zo. douroucouli (Nyctipithe'cus); **2artig** a. ⓖ owl-like, owlish; **-falter** m = Eule 2; **-geschrei** n screeching of owls; **-loch, -nest** n owl's nest; **-spiegel** m [wisch' (f. Eule 4) den Spiegel!] als npr. Till ~ (Schalksnarr, 14. sae., u. Volksbuch) Eulenspiegel, ehm. a. Owlglass; weit S. wag; **-spiegelei** f, **-spiegel-streich** m buffoonery, tomfoolery, practical joke; waggery.
Eumenide (⌣⌣´⌣) [grch.] f ㊽ myth. Alt.: meist ~n pl. Eumenides; Furies pl. (= Eri'nnyen); ~n-chor m ㉗ in der grch. Tragödie: chorus of the Eumenides.
Eunuch (⌣´ch) [grch. Bettbüter] m ㊷ (Haremswächter) eunuch; **~en=(wirt) schaft** f ㊽ eunuchism.
Euphemismus ✡ (⌣-f-⌣´) [grch.] m ㉗ (beschönigender Ausdruck) euphemism; **euphemistisch** (⌣-f-⌣´) a. ⓖ (beschönigend) euphemistic. [(klang-, laut) euphony.]
Euphonie ✡ (⌣-f-´) [grch.] f ㊽ (Wohl-]
euphonisch ✡ (⌣-f-´) [grch.] a. ⓖ (wohlklingend) euphonic(al), euphonious.
Euphorbiaze-e (⌣⌣-f-⌣´⌣) [grch.=lt.] f ㊽ (Wolfsmilch-gewächs) euphorbiaceous plant; ~n euphorbiaceae pl.
Euphorbi-e ♀ (⌣-f´(⌣)⌣) [grch.] f ㊽ (Wolfsmilch) spurge (Eupho'rbia); **2n = artig** a. ⓖ wolfsmilch-artig) euphorbiaceous.
Euphrat ♀ (´⌣) npr/m. ⓤα. (Fluß Asiens) Euphrates; **~bahn** ⛁ (´⌣´) f ㊷ Euphrates Railway.
Eurasi-en ✡ (-´(⌣)⌣) [Eur(opa)=Asien] n ㉓α. Eurasia, **Eurasi-er** (~) m ㉒ u. **eurasisch** (-´⌣) a. ⓖ Eurasian.
eure, Eure (´⌣) ⓖ f. **euer** II und **eurig**.
eurer (´⌣) 1. gen. u. dat. sing. (f) u. gen. pl. von **euer** II. — 2. oft ⸚ f. **euer** I.
eurer-seits (´⌣⌣´) adv. on your part.
eures-gleichen (´´⌣´⌣) pron. inv. the likes of you, F (people of) your sort.
euret-halben (´⌣...), **2wegen, (um) 2willen** adv. for your sakes, on your account, because of you.
eurig, Eurig (´⌣) possessive pron. ⓖⓖ der (die, das) ~e yours; in Briefen: ganz ⸚ Yours truly (vgl. Ihrig); die ~en your people pl., your family.
Europa (⌣´⌣) [grch.] npr. I f ⓖⓐα. myth. (Tochter des Age'nor) Europa. — II ♀ n ⓤα. (der a. Europens) Erdteil Europe.
Europäer (--´⌣) m ㉒, **~in** f ⓖ European; **~tum** n ㉔d. Europeanism.
europäisch (--´⌣) a. ⓖ European; 2es Gleichgewicht balance of power in Europe; weit S. European Concert.
europäisier/en (1---´⌣) I v/a. ㉓ (europäisch machen) to Europeanize. — II S./ung f ㊽ Europeanization.

europa-müde (-´´⌣...) a. ⓖ tired (or F sick) of Europe; die ~n people tired of Europe.
eustachisch (⌣-´ch) [Eustachio, ital. Anatom, † 1574] a. ⓖ: 2e Röhre anat. zwischen Ohr und Nase: Eustachian tube.
Eustachius (⌣-´ch⌣) [lt.] npr/m. ⓖγ. (Patron der Jäger 20/9.; Vn.) Eustace.
Euter (´⌣) [ahd.: udder] n (m) ㉒ udder, P dug; mit vollem ~ full-uddered.
eutern (⌣~) v/n. (h.) ♀a. v. Kühen: to have full udders, to give milk.
ev. abbr. = evangelisch, eventuell.
Ev. abbr. = Evangelium.
Eva (´⌣⌣, a.: -´⌣) [hebr.] npr/f. ⓖⓐα. ⓖⓐβ.: a) bibl. (Adams Weib) Eve; b) (Vn.) Eva (f. a. Evchen); **~=tochter** f ⓖ (Weib) daughter of Eve.
Evakuation ✡ (-⌣´⌣-tz(⌣)´) [lt.] f ㊽ bsd. ⚔ med. (Räumung) evacuation.
evakuieren (⌣-⌣´⌣) v/a. ㉓ to evacuate.
Evangeli-en-harmonie (⌣⌣´(⌣)...) f ㊷ theol.: ✡ diatessaron. [gelization.]
Evangelisation (⌣⌣⌣⌣⌣-tz(⌣)´) f ㊽ evan-]
evangelisch (⌣⌣⌣´⌣) [grch.] a. rel. I a. ⓖ evangelical; die 2e Kirche the Protestant Church; 2e Lehre teaching of the gospel, gospel- teaching; (protestantisch) Protestant. — II **~e([r] m)** f ⓖ, meist pl.: die ~en Protestants.
evangelisieren (⌣⌣⌣⌣´⌣) [grch.] I v/a. ⓖ to evangelize. — II n ㉓ u.
Evangelisierung f ㊽ evangelization, spreading of the gospel. [gelist.]
Evangelist (⌣⌣⌣⌣´) [grch.] m ㊷ evan-]
Evangelium (⌣⌣⌣´(⌣)⌣) [ahd.-grch. eu-ange'lion frohe Botschaft] n ㉘ (abbr. Ev.) gospel, bisw. evangel; ~ St. Matthäi ⁊c. the Gospel according to St. Matthew, &c.; er schwört darauf wie aufs ~ he swears to it as if it were gospel-truth or the gospel.
Evas-tochter (´⌣ ob. ¹⌣...) f ⓖ fig. (Weib) daughter of Eve, woman.
Evchen (´⌣) n ㉓α. (dim. von Eva a) little Eve, (kosend für Liebchen) love, darling.
Evens-kind (´⌣⌣...) n ⓖ fig. (Mensch) child of Eve; mortal (man).
Eventualität (⌣⌣⌣-´⌣⌣⌣-) f ㊽ (Möglichkeit) event(uality), contingency.
eventualiter (⌣⌣⌣⌣-⌣⌣⌣⌣) [lt.] adv. (meist abbr. event.) eventually.
eventuell (⌣⌣⌣⌣´) [fr.] a. ⓖ u. adv.: ● (wenn der Fall) if so, if such be the case; (wenn nötig) if need be, in case of need; (gegebenenfalls) eventually; 2er Verlust possible (or eventual) loss; (möglicherweise) possibly; gerichtlich: er wurde zu einer Geldstrafe von 60 Mark, 2 zwölf Tagen Haft verurteilt his sentence was a fine of three pounds or (auch: with the option of) twelve days' jail.
evident (-⌣´) [lt.] a. ⓖ u. adv. (augenscheinlich) evident(ly).
Evidenz (-⌣´) [fr.] f ㊽ evidence.
Evolute (-⌣´⌣) [lt.] f ㊽ math. (abgewickelte Linie) evolute of a curve.
Evolution (-⌣-tz(⌣)´) [lt.] f ㊽ ⚔, phls., math., &c. (Abz, Entwicklung) evolution. [(Abwickelungskurve) involute.]
Evolvente (-⌣´⌣) [lt.] f ㊽ math.]
evolvierend (-⌣⌣´⌣) a. ⓖ math. evolvent. [stät Your Majesty.]
Ew. abbr. = Euer, Eure(r); Ew. Maje-]

✡ scientific; ♀ botanical; ♀ geography; ⊕ machinery; ⚒ mining; ⚔ military; ⚓ marine; ● commercial; ✉ postal; ⛁ railway.

[Ewer] — 348 — [Experiment]

Ewer ↓ (L∨) [ndl.] *m* ⓶ (einmastiges offenes Boot) lighter, barge, wherry(-boat).
Ewer=führer ↓ (‿...) *m* ⓶ lighterman, waterman, wherryman.
ewig (L∨) [ahd.: Ehe] **I** *a.* ⓺ **1.** (ohne Anfang und Ende) eternal; (ohne Ende) everlasting, endless; (fortdauernd) continuous, continual, unceasing, stärker: perpetual; (unsterblich) immortal; *adv.* auf ≈ for ever(more), to the end of time; immer und ≈ for ever and ever; daraus wird ≈ nichts that will never come to pass or come to anything; seit ≈(en Zeiten) since the beginning, from all eternity. — **2.** Der Haß implacable hatred; der ≈ Jude (Ahasve'r) the wandering Jew; *rel.* Des Leben life eternal, eternal life; ≈e Liebe undying love; ≈er Schnee perpetual snow; ≈e Verdammnis everlasting damnation; das ≈ Weibliche the eternal feminine. — **II** *adv.* **3.** (immer und) ≈ for ever (-lasting), perpetually, stärker: eternally; das ist ≈ (sehr) schade that's a great pity, stärker: a thousand pities; da kann ich ≈ warten I may wait till doomsday or for everlasting. — **III** *s.* der ~e ⓺ **4.** (Gott) the Eternal.
Ewigkeit (L∨-) *f* ⓺ (s. ewig) eternity; everlastingness; perpetuity; von ~ her from all eternity, from time(s) immemorial; bis in alle ~ to all eternity, to the end of days; *eccl.* von ~ zu ~ world without end; man hat Sie seit e-r ~ nicht gesehen we have not seen you for an age or for ages or for ever so long; das glaube ich in ~ nicht I shall never believe that.
ewiglich † *od. bibl.* (L∨-) *adv.* = ewig 3.
Ex=... (∂...) [lt.] ⓶ ex-..., former ...
exakt (∨∂) [fr.] *a.* ⓺ (genau) exact.
Exaktheit (∨∂-) *f* ⓺ exactness, exactitude. — [spannt) eccentric.)
exaltiert (∨∨∂) [lt.] *p.p. u. a.* ⓺ (über=
Examen (∨∠∨) [lt.] *n* ⓺⓪ (Prüfung) examination, F exam; mündliches (schriftliches) ~ oral or viva voce (written) examination; im ~ durchfallen to fail (in an examination), F to be plucked or ploughed; (schriftliche) ~=arbeit, =aufgabe *f* ⓺ examination-paper.
Examinand (∂-∨∂) [lt.] *m* ∠ [Prüfling) examination-candidate. [examiner.]
Examinator (∂-∨∨) *m* ⓷ (Prüfender)
examinieren (∂-∨∨) [mhd., *lt.] *v/a.* ⓽ (prüfen) to examine; to test.
Exanthem ⚙ (∂-∨∂) [grch.] *n* ⓵c. *path.* (Haut=ausschlag) eruption, ⚙ exanthem(a).
Exarch (∨∂) [grch.] *m* ⓶ Mittelalter: (byzantinischer Statthalter) exarch.
Exarchat (∂-∨∂) *n* ⓵c. exarchate.
Exartikulation ⚙ (∂-∨-∨tß(∨)ⁿ) [lt.] *f* ⓺ *surg.* (Glied=ablösung) exarticulation.
Exaudi (∨-L∨) [lt.erhöre! (Psalm 27,7)] (6. Sonntag nach Ostern) sixth Sunday after Easter.
☞ **Exc..., exc...** s. **Erz...**, **erz**...
Exegese ⚙ (∨-L∨) [grch.] *f* ⓺ (Auslegung der Bibel 2c.) exegesis, exegetics; exposition of the Scriptures.
Exeget ⚙ (∨-L∨) *m* ⓶ (Erklärer) expounder, interpreter; ~ik (∂-L∨) *f* ⓺ = Exegese; ≈isch (∨-L∨∨) *a.* ⓺ *(adv.)* exegetical(ly).
exekutieren (∨-L∨∨) [lt.-fr.] *v/a.* ⓽ (ausführen) hinrichten) to execute.

Exekution (∨-L-tß(∨)ⁿ) [fr., *lt.] *f* ⓺ *jur.* (Zwangsvollstreckung, Vollstreckungshandlung) execution; eine ~ vollstrecken to put in an execution; to levy (a) distress upon a p.('s goods and chattels); *öft.* (Eintreibung von Steuern) collection of taxes.
Exekutions=befehl (‿...) *m* ⓶, **=mandat** *n* warrant of distress; **=verfahren** *n*, **=vollstreckung** *f* execution, seizure of goods.
exekutiv (∨-L∨∂) [lt.-fr.] *a.* ⓺ (vollziehend) executive; ~e (∨-L-∨∨) *f* ⓺ (vollziehende Gewalt) executive; ~=gewalt (∨-L∂...) *f* ⓺ executive power; **=prozeß** *m* summary proceedings *pl.*
Exekutor (∨-L∨∨) [lt.] *m* ⓷ executor; (Gerichtsvollzieher) (court-)bailiff; ≈isch (∨-L-∨∨) *a.* ⓺ (vollstreckend) executive, executory; ≈e Gewalt power to act.
Exempel (∨-L∨) [mhd., *lt.] *n* ⓶ **1.** = Beispiel; ein ~ an einem statuieren to make an example of a p. — **2.** (Rechen=) (arithmetical) sum or problem; ein ~ rechnen to work (F to do) a sum (in arithmetic).
Exemplar (∂-∨L) [lt.] *n* ⓵c. **1.** (Muster) sample, pattern. — **2.** *typ.* (einzelner Abdruck) copy; e-r Zeitschrift 2c.: number; weggeschenktes ~ eines neuen Werkes: presentation-copy.
exemplarisch (∂-∨L∨)[lt.]*a.*⓺exemplary; *adv.* e-n ≈ bestrafen to punish a p. in an exemplary manner or severely.
Exequatur (∂-∨L∨∨) [lt.] *n* ⓾ *jur.* (amtliche Beglaubigung) exequatur.
Exequien (∨-L∨∨) [lt.] *s/pl., inv.* (Totenfeier, Leichenbegängnis) obsequies *pl.*, funeral ceremony.
exerzieren ⚔ (∨-L∨∨) [lt.] ⓽ **I** *v/a.* ⚔ to drill (or train) recruits. — **II** *v/n.* (h.) to practise (drilling); er ließ die Rekruten, Soldaten ≈ he put ... through their facings. — **III** ~ *n* ⓶ drilling (practice); *weiteres.* exercises *pl.*
Exerzier=knochen ⚔ (‿...) *m* ⚔, *med.* ossification of the muscle caused by (excessive) drilling; **=meister** *m* drill-sergeant or -instructor; **=patrone** *f* blank cartridge used for drilling, dummy (cartridge); **=platz** *m* drill (or drilling)-ground; **=reglement** *n* army regulations *pl.*
Exerziti=en=buch (∨-L∨(∨)...) *n* ⓶, **=heft** *n* exercise- or lesson-)book.
Exerzitium (∨-L∨tß(∨)∨) [lt.] *n* ⓶ ⚔, Schule 2c.: exercise; *rel.* (Andachtsübung) devotional exercise; ein schriftliches ~ machen to do an exercise.
Exil (∨L) [lt.] *n* ⓵c. (Verbannung) exile, banishment; im ~ in exile.
exilieren (∨-L∨) *v/a.* ⓽ to exile.
eximieren (∨-L∨∨) [lt.] *v/a.* ⓽: von et. ≈ (befreien) to exempt from a th.; eximiert exempt; privileged.
Existenz (∨-L∂) [fr.] *f* ⓺ (Dasein) existence; feine (deine) ~ haben to lead a precarious existence, to have no reliable (source of) income; *fig.* verfehlte ~en (Leute, die nichts geworden sind) failures *pl.* (in life).
Existenz=bedingung (∨-L∂...) *f* ⓶ condition of existence; **=berechtigung** *f* right to exist; ≈fähig *a.* ⓺ able to exist or to live; ⚙ paying (one's way); **=minimum** *n* living wage.

existieren (∨-L∨∨) [lt.] *v/n.* (h.) ⓽ (bestehen) to exist; (leben) to subsist, to live.
exkl. *abbr.* = exklusive. [to exclude.]
exkludieren (∂-L∨∨) [lt.] *v/a.* ⓽ (ausschließen)
Exklusion (∂-L-(∨)ⁿ) [lt.] *f* ⓺ exclusion.
exklusiv (∂-L∂) *a.* ⓺, ≈e (∂-L-∨∨) *adv.* (ausschließlich) exclusive(ly).
Exklusivität (∂-L-∨-∂) *f* ⓺ exclusiveness.
Exkommunikation (∨∂-∨-∨-tß(∨)ⁿ) [lt.] *f* ⓺ (Kirchenbann) excommunication.
exkommunizieren (∨∂-∨-∨L∨∨) *v/a.* ⓽ to excommunicate; *weiteres* : to exclude (from a community), to cast out, to expel.
Ex=könig (∂L∨) *m* ⓶ ex-king.
Exkrement (∂-L∂) [lt.] *n* ⓵c. (Auswurfstoff) *mst* ~e *pl.* excrements, ⚙ fæces *pl.*
Exkurs ⚙ (∨∂) [lt.] *m* ⓵a. (beigegebene Abhandlung) appendix; (Abschweifung) digression. [sion, outing, tour, trip.]
Exkursion (∂-L-(∨)ⁿ) *f* ⓺ (Ausflug) excur=
Exlibris* (∂L...) [lt. aus den Büchern] *n*, *inv.* (Bücherzeichen) ex-libris, book-plate.
Exmatrikulation (∂-∨-∨-tß(∨)ⁿ) [lt.] *f* ⓺ *univ.* removal of a student's name from the register.
exmatrikulieren (∂-∨-∨L∨∨) [lt.] *v/a.* ⓽ Studenten: to strike off the register.
Exmission (∂L∨(∨)ⁿ) [lt.] *f* ⓺ *jur.* (Austreibung) eviction (or ejection, ejectment) of a tenant.
exmittieren (∂L∨∨) [lt.] *v/a.* ⓽ to evict (or eject) a tenant, F to turn a p. out (of house and home).
exorbitant (∂-∨-L∂) [lt.] *a.* ⓺ (übertrieben) exorbitant, excessive.
Exorzismus (∂-∨L∂) [grch.] *m* ⓶ (Austreibung böser Geister) exorcism.
exoterisch ⚙ (∂-L∨∨) [grch.] *a.* ⓺ *phls.* (öffentlich, populär) exoteric; *vgl.* esoterisch.
exotisch ⚙ (∨-L∨∨) [grch.] *a.* ⓺ (ausländisch) exotic (plants, &c.).
Expansion ⚙ *u.* ⨁ (∂-∨(∨)ⁿ) [lt.] *f* ⓺ *bsf. phys.* (Spannung) expansion.
Expansions=(dampf)maschine ⚙ *u.* ⨁ (∂-∨...) *f* ⓶ expansion-engine; **=geschoß** *n* expanding bullet.
expansiv ⚙ *und* ⨁ (∂-∨∂) *a.* ⓺ (ausdehnungsfähig) expansive.
Expansiv=kraft (‿...) *f* ⓶ *phys.* expansive force, power of expansion.
Expedi=ent ⚕ (∂-L∨∂) [lt.] *m* ⓶ (dispatching) clerk; manager.
expedieren (∂-L∨∨) [lt.] *v/a.* ⓽ (abfertigen) to dispatch, forward, expedite; to send off by post, &c.
Expedition (∂-L-tß(∨)ⁿ)[lt.]*f*⓺(Reise, Zug) expedition; (Unternehmen) enterprise; (Zeitungs=) (publishing-)office; ⚕ forwarding department; *s. a.* Güter≈.
Expeditions=armee ⚔ (∂-L-tß(∨)ⁿ...) *f* ⓺ expeditionary army; **=gebühr** *f* forwarding (agent's) charges *pl.*; **=geschäft** ⚕ *n* commission-business; **=korps** *m*, **=mannschaft** *f* expeditionary force; **=lokal**, **=zimmer** *n* dispatch-office; e-r Zeitung: publishing-office.
expektorieren (∂-L∨∨) [lt.] **I** *v/a. u. sich* ≈ *v/refl.* ⓽ (hustend auswerfen) to expectorate; *fig.* sich ≈ to unbosom o.s... to pour out one's heart to a p. — **II** ~ *n* ⓶ *u.* **Expektoration** (∂-∨-tß(∨)ⁿ) *f* ⓺ expectoration; *fig.* disclosure.
Experiment (∂-∨L∂) [lt.] *n* ⓵b. (Versuch) experiment, trial.

Zeichen (s. S. XVII): F familiär; P Volkssprache; ℱ Gaunersprache; ⚙ selten; † alt (auch gestorben); * neu (auch geboren); ⁺⁺ unrichtig;

[experimental] — 349 — [Fabrikarbeit]

experimental a. (u. adv) experimental(ly); tentative(ly).
Experimental-chemie f, **-physik** f experimental chemistry, physics.
experimentieren [lt.] I v/n.(h.) to experiment(alize), to make (or try) experiments upon or with a th. or a p. — II ~ n experiment(aliz)ing. — III ~de(r) m (auch **Experimentator** m) experimenter, ...alist; experimenting philosopher.
expert [lt.] a. (erfahren) expert; ~(e) m (Sachverständiger) expert.
Explikation [lt.] f (Erklärung) explanation; **explizieren** v/a. (erklären) to explain.
explodierbar [lt.] a. explosive; ~keit f explosiveness.
explodieren [lt.] v/n. (n u. h.) (platzen) to explode, to burst; F to go off; chm. a.: to detonate, fulminate.
Explosion [lt.] f explosion, F burst-up; chm. a. detonation.
explosions-fähig a. explosive; **-stoff** m (Sprengstoff) explosive.
explosiv a. explosive; ~stoffe m/pl. chm. explosives pl.
Exponent [lt.] m math. einer potenzierten Größe: index.
Exponential-gleichung f, **-größe**, **-reihe** f, math. exponential equation, quantity, series.
exponieren [lt.] v/a. u. sich 2 v/refl. (sich) 2 (aussetzen) to expose o.s.
Export [lt.] m (Ausfuhr) export (-ation); pl. ~en = Ausfuhrwaren.
Exporteur [fr.] m d. exporter.
exportieren v/a. to export (nach ... to ...); a.: to sell abroad.
expreß [lt.] I a. (D 10) (eigens) express(ly adv.), als adv. auch: purposely, on purpose. — II **Expresse(r)** m (Eilbote) express (messenger), courier.
Expreß-zug m express-train, express.
Expropriation [lt.] f (Enteignung) expropriation; **exproprieren** v/a. to expropriate.

exquisit [lt.] a. (auserlesen) exquisite; select, picked, choice.
Exspektant [lt.] m = Anwärter.
Exspektanz [lt.] f = Anwartschaft.
Extirpation [lt.] f (Ausrottung) extirpation. [tirpator.]
Extirpator m agr. ex-f
extirpieren v/a. to extirpate.
Exsudat [lt.] n physiol., med. (Ausschwitzung, Erguß) exudation.
Extemporale [lt.] n (pl. auch ...lia) Schule: (in der Klasse anzufertigende Aufgabe) extempore (exercise).
ex tempore [lt.] adv. (aus dem Stegreif) extempore, off-hand.
extemporieren [lt.] v/n. (h.) u. v/a. to extemporize, to speak (or play) extempore; (aus dem Stegreif dichten) to improvise. [= necken.)
extern[1] mb., nordd. (ndd.) v/a. a.)
extern[2] I a. (auswärtig) external, foreign. — II ~e(r) m (Tagschüler[in]) day-pupil or -scholar.
Externat [lt.] n (Tagschule) day-school.
extra [lt.] adv. (besonders) extra, specially; (außerdem) besides; P a. als n: das ist et. ganz ~es that's something quite special.
Extra-ausgabe f extra (or additional) expense; sundry expenses pl.; **-beilage** f, **-blatt** n special (or extra)edition or supplement; **-fahrt** f excursion(-train); **-fein** a. extra-fine, superfine, of special quality.
extrahieren [lt.] v/a. (ausziehen) to extract, to draw out of; jur. = wirken [pl.; sundries pl.)
Extra-kosten pl. extra charges)
Extrakt [lt.] b. (Auszug): a) m, n, chm. aus Stoffen: extract; b) m, aus Büchern; auch: abstract.
Extraktiv-stoff m chm. extractive matter or principle.
Extra-liegetage m/pl. days pl. of demurrage; **-post** f postchaise, special mail; ~ nehmen to travel with post-horses, to post;

-spesen pl. = kosten; **-stunden** f/pl. Schule: extra lessons pl.; Fabrik 2c.: over-time.
extravagant [lt.] a. (maßlos) extravagant.
Extravaganz f extravagance.
extravagieren v/n. to exceed the bounds, to outstep the mark.
Extra-würstchen n fig. something (quite) special; **-zug** m (Sonderzug) special train; excursion-train.
extrem [lt.] I a. (u. adv.) (äußerst) extreme(ly); einer Len Richtung angehören to belong to an advanced school of thinkers, &c. — II ~ n extreme; fig.: die ~e berühren sich extremes meet; von einem ~ ins andere fallen to go from one extreme to another; in ~e verfallen to go to extremes or extremities.
Extremität [lt.] f (Hände und Füße) mst ~en pl. extremities pl.
exzellent [lt.] a. (ausgezeichnet) excellent.
Exzellenz [fr.] f (Titel bjd. der Gesandten und Statthalter — nicht der engl. Minister!) Excellency; in der Anrede: ~ brauchen nur zu befehlen Your Excellency's orders shall be obeyed.
exzellieren v/n.(h.) to excel.
Exzenter n (m), **Exzentrik** n, f mach.(Steuerungsscheibe) eccentric.
exzentrisch [lt.] a. eccentric (auch fig.); Le Scheibe = Exzentrik; fig. Les Wesen eccentricity. [(auch fig.).)
Exzentrizität f eccentricity)
exzeptionell [fr.] a. u. adv. (ausnahmsweise) exceptional(ly).
exzerpieren v/a. ein Buch 2 (ausziehen) to extract ...
Exzerpt [lt.] n (Auszug) extract; vgl. auch Ausschnitt 4.
Exzeß [lt.] m (Übermaß) excess; (Ausschreitung) extravagance.
Exzitatorium [lt.] n (Erinnerung) admonitory decree or notice.
Ezechi-el [hebr.] npr/m. α. bibl. (Prophet) Ezekiel.

F, f (ef) n, inv. (Buchstabe) F, f.
F, f ♩ n, inv. (vierte Note) F; F-Dur F major; F-Moll F minor; F-Schlüssel (Baß-schlüssel) bass clef.
F abbr. auf Thermometern = Fahrenheit.
f. abbr. = für; folgende Seite; fein.
f. ♩ abbr. = forte. [(vgl. ff.).)
Fabel (lt.) [nbd., * lt.] f (Dichtung) fable; die äsopischen ~n Æsop's fables pl.; (Erdichtung) fiction; legend; eine leere ~ an idle story or tale, F a fib.
Fabel-buch n fable-book; volume of fables; **-dichter** m writer (or author) of fables, fabulist, vgl. -schmied.
Fabelei f 1. = fabeln II. — 2. (Gefabeltes) fabulous account or story, nursery-tale; (leeres Geschwätz) idle talk.
fabelhaft a. fabulous, mythical; prodigious, incredible; adv.: 2

reich immensely rich; 2 billig wonderfully cheap; ans ~e grenzen to border (or verge) on the fabulous.
Fabel-land n fabulous country, vgl. Fabelreich.
fabeln [lt.] I v/a. u. v/n. (h.) a* to tell a fable, to tell stories or (fabulous) tales; to spin yarns; (irre reden) to talk at random; (faseln) to drivel. — II ~ n telling fables or stories, &c. (f. I).
Fabel-reich n mythical country, fairy-land; **-sammlung** f collection of fables; **-schmied** m inventor (or forger) of fables; story-teller; **-welt** f fabulous (or mythical) world; **-werk** n (work containing) fabulous tales; bloßes ~ mere fables, idle tales pl.; **-wesen** n fabulous being.

Fabian npr/m. α. Fabian.
Fabi-er npr/m/pl. Altert.: (röm. Patriziergeschlecht) (the) Fabii pl.
Fabius npr/m. γ. f. Kunkta'tor.
Fabler m = Fabeldichter, Fabelschmied.
Fabrik [fr.] f (manu)factory, größere: works pl.; (Baumwoll-, Seiden-)~ (cotton-, silk-)mill.
Fabrik-anlage f putting up a factory; (das zu e-r Fabrik Gehörige) manufacturing-plant.
Fabrikant [fr.] m manufacturer, maker, vgl. Fabrik-herr.
Fabrik-arbeit f manufacture, work in a factory; manufactured article or goods pl.; **-arbeiter(in** f) m factory-worker or -hand (f a. -girl, -woman); operative.

[Fabrikat] — 350 — [Fadenpilze]

Fabrikat ❋ (⌣́) [lt.] n ⓑc. (Erzeugnis) manufacture(d article); eig(e)nes ~ one's own make; deutsche ~e German-made goods pl.; (Gewebe) (textile) fabrics pl.; **~ion** (⌣⌣-tz̆⌣́), **~ur** (⌣⌣-́) f ⓑ (Herstellung) manufacturing, making; **~ions-zeugnis** ❋ n ⓑ certificate of origin.

Fabrik-aufseher(in f) m (⌣̇-...) ⓑ inspector (or overseer) of a factory, fore(wo)man; **-besitzer** m = -herr; **-betrieb** m working of a (manu-)factory; **-direktor** m working manager of a factory; **-gebäude** n premises pl. of a (manu)factory; auch: the works pl.; **-gegend** f manufacturing district; **-geschäft** n = Fabrik-; **-herr, -inhaber** m owner (or proprietor) of a (manu)factory; manufacturer; mill-owner; **-inspektor** m factory inspector; **-mädchen** n factory-girl; **-mäßig** a. ⓑ (like) manufactured; **-ordnung** f factory regulations pl. or laws pl.; **-ort** m manufacturing town; **-preis** m m.-price.

Fabriks-... öft. (⌣̇-...) = Fabrik-...

Fabrik-stadt (⌣́-...) f ⓑ = -ort; **-ware** f manufactured goods pl. or article; **-wesen** n manufacturing-concerns pl. or -industry; **-zeichen** n (manufacturer's) trade-mark; **-zeichen-schutz** m protection of trade-marks.

fabrizieren (⌣⌣́⌣) [lt. ⌣́⌣] v/a. ❋ to manufacture, make, produce; ❋ in Deutschland fabriziert German-made, made in Germany; im Lande (selbst) fabriziert home-made.

fabulieren (⌣⌣́⌣) ⓑ = fabeln I.

Face (⌣́fv) [fr.] f ⓑ arch. (Vorder-ansicht) [face, front.] facen f. abfacen.

Facette ⊕ (⌣bź⌣) [fr.] f ⓑ Steinschleiferei, a. zo., anat., geol. facet(te).

Facett(en)-auge (⌣bz̆⌣̇(⌣)...) n ⓑ (Netzauge) ent. compound (or faceted) eye; **-steg** m, typ. stereo-catch, plate-clip, claw.

facettieren (⌣bz̆⌣́⌣) [fr.] v/a. ❋ to facet, to cut in facets.

Fach (⌣̆ch) [ahd.; * fahen] n ⓑc. (❋ ⓑc., als Maß ⓑ6) 1. (Abteilung) compartment, division; ❋, anat., &c.: cell, ⌣ locule; in einem Schranke: partition; im Stalle auch: stall; im Schreibtisch: pigeon-hole; geheimes ~ secret case or drawer; im Bücherschranke: shelf; typ. im Schriftkasten: box; Hutmacherei: (Schlagholz) bat, auch = Fach-bogen; **join.** (Feld) panel; arch. (Mauerfeld) pane of a wall; vgl. Dach 2. — 2. fig. (abgegrenztes Feld) branch, province, department; (Gegenstand) subject; spezielles ~ speciality; Geschäft: trade, F line (of business); Mann von ~ specialist; Musiker ꝛc. von ~ ... by profession; sein ~ verstehen to understand one's business; das schlägt nicht in mein ~ that's out of my province, F that's not in my line; F co. ❋ simpeln to talk shop.

...fach [mhd.] in Zssgn: ...times, -fold, ⅃B. zehn-fach ten times, tenfold; vgl. ein-, zwei-, drei-, mehr-, viel-(ꝛc.)fach.

Fach-ausdruck (⌣̆ch-...) m ⓑ technical term or expression; **-baum** m ⓑ der Mühle: (oberster Balken eines Wehrs) chief

sill of a weir, saddle-beam sill; **-bildung** f professional training; **-bogen** ⊕ m hatter's bow.

fächeln (⌣̆⌣) [nhd.; * Fächer] v/a. u. sich ⌣ v/refl. ⓑa. to fan (o.s.). [anfachen.]

fachen¹ (⌣̆ch) [lt. focus Herd] v/a. ⓑ = fachen² (⌣̆ch) [Fach] v/a. ⓑ (in Fächer teilen) to partition off, to form into compartments; ❋ Hut- u. Tuchmacherei: to plank wool with a bow.

Fächer (⌣̆⌣) [nhd.17.sae.;*fachen¹] m ⓑ fan; eccl.flabellum;indischer(Feder-)~punkah. **fächer-artig** (⌣̆⌣-...) a. ⓑ = -förmig; **-brenner** m ⓑ für Gas: fantail- (or batwing-)burner; **-fabrikant** m fan-maker; **-fenster** n fan-light; **-flügler** m/pl. ent. ⌣ strepsiptera pl.; **-förmig** a. fan-like or -shaped; ⅌: ⌣ flabelliform; **-frucht-tang** ⅌ m gulf-weed, sargasso (Sarga’ssum bacci’ferum); **-gas-brenner** m = -brenner; **-gewölbe** n, arch. fan-vaulting.

fäch(e)rig (⌣̆⌣(⌣)⌣) I a. ⓑ divided into compartments, ⅌ locular. — II ... **fäch(e)rig** oft in Zssgn mit Zahlen, ⅃B. zwei-⌣ with two compartments, &c.

fächern (⌣̆⌣) [Fächer] v/a. ⓑa. to fan.

Fächer-palme (⌣̆⌣-...) f ⓑ fan-palm (Chamae’rops hu’milis); **-schwanz** m, orn. Austr.: fantail (Rhipidu’ra); mit ~ versehen fan-tailed; **-werk** n, arch. fan-shaped tracery.

Fach-gelehrte(r) (⌣̆ch-...) m ⓑ savant by profession; (learned) specialist; **-genosse** m colleague; **-lehrer** m teacher of a special subject; **-leute** pl. v. -mann.

fachlich (⌣̆ch) a. ⓑ special, professional, belonging to a special branch.

Fach-mann (⌣̆ch-...) m ⓑ expert, specialist; **-männisch** a. ⓑ professional; ⅌es Urteil expert opinion; **-mäßig** a. professional; **-ordnung** f classification.

fächrig (⌣̆⌣) f. fächerig.

Fach-schule (⌣̆ch-...) f ⓑ (professional) training-school; **-simpel** m one who is fond of talking shop; **-simpelei** f talking shop (vgl. Fach am Schluß); **-spaltig** ⅌ a. ⓑ ⌣ loculicidal; **-studium** n professional study or training; **-wand** ⊕ f, arch. (ant. Steinwand) lath-and-plaster wall; partition-wall; **-weise** adv. by compartments or divisions; **-werk** ⊕ n, arch. framework; panel- (or bay-)work; **-werk(s)-bau** m timber framework; **-werk-brücke** f truss-bridge; **-werk-haus** n frame-house; **-wissenschaft** f speciality; special (scientific) branch; **-zeitschrift** f technical (or professional) journal, trade-journal.

Fackel (⌣̆⌣) [ahd.; * spät-lt. fa’cula] f ⓑ torch, ehm.: link, von Wachs: (fr.) flambeau; fig. firebrand; die ~ des Krieges anzünden to light the torch of war.

Fackel-beleuchtung (⌣̆⌣-...) f ⓑ = -licht; **-distel** f: a) (Säulenkaktus) torch-thistle (Ce’reus [peruvia’nus]); b) opuntia, Indian fig (Opu’ntia ficus i’ndica).

Fackelei (...⌣⌣́) [fackeln 2] f ⓑ fibbing, prevarication, story-telling.

Fackel-feuer ⅃ (⌣̆⌣-...) n ⓑ blue lights pl.; **-fliege** f, ent. lantern-fly (Fulgo’ra lanterna’ria); **-jagd** f hunting by torch-light; **-licht** n torch-light.

fackeln (⌣̆⌣) v/n. (h.) ⓑa. 1. [Fackel] (auch fn) vom Lichte: to flicker, to flare (up). — 2. [: fickle] F fig. (zaudern) to hesitate, waver, vacillate; da heißt's nicht lange gefackelt there is no time for delay, F it's no use making a long fuss; (flunkern) to fib, prevaricate, tell stories, throw the hatchet.

Fackel-schein (⌣̆⌣-...) m = -licht; **-ständchen** n torch-light serenade; **-tanz** m torch-dance; **-träger** m torch-bearer, ehm. a. link-boy; Alt.: ⌣ lampadary; **-zug** m torch-light procession.

Fädchen (⌣́⌣) n ⓑ (dim. v. Faden) little (or thin, feeble) thread; an einem ~ hangen to hang by a thin thread.

fad(e) (⌣́(⌣)) [fr.] a. ⓑ (geschmacklos) tasteless, insipid; (schal) stale; (geistlos) flat, dull, silly; fader Mensch humdrum fellow; fades Zeug silly (or F poor) stuff, trash, F bosh.

fädeln (⌣́⌣) ⓑa. I v/a. einen Faden in eine Nähnadel ⌣ to thread a needle. — II v/n. (h.) u. sich ⌣ v/refl. von ganzen Flüssigkeiten: to grow stringy or ropy.

Faden (⌣́⌣) [ahd.: fathom] m ⓑ (hoch vgl. 3) 1. thread (auch von tierischem Gewebe); ein ~ Seide, Zwirn a thread of silk, twist; gezwirnter ~ twine; der ~ ist gerissen the thread is broken (auch fig.); v. Flüssigkeiten: sich in Fäden ziehen to string, to be stringy; Fäden ziehend stringy, ropy. — 2. F ich hatte keinen trocknen ~ am Leibe I hadn't a dry thread on me, I was wet to the skin; fig. es ist kein guter ~ an ihm he hasn't a single good (or redeeming) quality (in him); sein Leben hing an einem ~ his life hung by a thread; den ~ einer Geschichte ꝛc. wieder aufnehmen to take (F to pick) up the thread ...; das zieht sich wie ein roter ~ durch das ganze Buch hindurch that runs (or may be traced) right through the book. — 3. ⓑ6. Längenmaß: (Klafter) fathom.

fäden (⌣́⌣) a. ⓑ (consisting of) thread(s), in threads; stringy.

Faden-abschneider (⌣́⌣-...) m ⓑ ⊕ der Nähmaschine thread-cutter; **-ähnlich** a. ⓑ thread-like; thready; **-alge** ⅌ f conferva, **-artig** a. = -ähnlich; **-artigkeit** f threadiness; **-dreieck** n im astron. Fernrohr: ⌣ reticule; **-dünn** a. (as) thin as a thread; vgl. -ähnlich; **-feder** f, orn. thread-feather; **-flosser** m, ichth. thread-fin (Polyne’mus); **-förmig** a. thread-shaped; ⌣ filiform; **-gerade** a. in a straight line; (as) straight as a die; **-gold** n gold thread; **-heft-maschine** ⊕ f Buchbinderei: book-sewing machine.

...fädenig (...⌣⌣́) [Faden]: in Zssgn, ⅃B. grob-⌣ coarse-threaded.

Faden-klee ⅌ (⌣́⌣-...) m ⓑ lesser yellow trefoil (Trifo’lium minus); **-kraut** ⅌ n cotton-rose (Fila’go); **-kreuz** n ast. reticule, cross-wires pl.; **-leiter** ⊕ f Spinnerei: thread-guide; **-mühle** f loom for spinning gold (or silver) thread; **-nackt** a. stark-naked; **-nudeln** f/pl. vermicelli; **-nudel-fabrikant** m v.-maker; **-öler** ⊕ m, mach. thread-oiler; **-pilze** ⅌ m/pl. ⌣ hyphomycetes pl.;

Signs (see page XVII): F familiar; P vulgar; ⌐ flash; \ rare; † obsolete (died); * now word (born); ✛ incorrect; ♪ music.

[Fadenprobe] — 351 — [fahren]

=probe f Zuckerfabr.: string-test; ⚚recht a. = gerade; ⚚scheinig a. vom Tuche: (worn) threadbare, shiny, shabby; =schlag m Schneiderei: basting; =seide f dodder (Cu'scuta); =silber n silver thread; =skorpion m, zo. whip-scorpion, vinegar-maker (Thely'phonus); =weise adv. thread by thread; =wichs=appara't ⊕ m der Nähmaschine thread-waxer; =wurm m, zo. threadworm (Oxyu'ris); hairworm (Go'rdius); f. a. Askariden; =zähler ⊕ m Weberei: thread-counter.

Fahheit (⸗) [fad(e)] f ⓬ tastelessness; insipidness; staleness; flatness.

...fadig ⸜, ...fädig ⸜ (⸗) f. fädenig.

Fädlein (⸗) n ⓫ = Fädchen.

Fagott ♪ (⸗◡) [it.] n ⓴b. (Baßpfeife) bassoon; ~ist (◡◡) m ⓬ bassoon(-player), bassoonist.

Fäh ⚚ (⸗) [ahd. bunt] n ⓴c. Kürschnerei: (Fell des sibirischen Eichhörnchens ꝛc., Grauwert) miniver, calabar skin(s pl.).

Fähe (⸗) [f. Fäh] f ⓬ 1. hunt. bitch, female of a small beast of prey, (Füchsin) vixen. — 2. = Fäh.

fahen † u. poet. (⸗) [ahd.] v/a. ⓮ = fangen, fahnden.

Fäh-händler (⸗...) m ⓬ = Kürschner.

fähig (⸗) [uhd. 16. sae.; *fahen] a. ⓰ 1. capable of doing a th.; able (or competent, fit) to do a th.; qualified for (doing) a th.; passiv: susceptible of; liable (or subject, apt) to; abs. (talentvoll) able, gifted; ein ⸗er Kopf a clever head; a man of ability or of parts; ⸗ machen to enable to, to fit (or capacitate) for; sich zu et. ⸗ machen to qualify (o.s.) for a th. — 2. meist b.s. zu allem (zu allen Schandtaten) ⸗ capable of anything (of any deed of infamy); er (sie) ist nicht ⸗ dazu he is not the man (she is not the woman) to do such a thing, he (she) is not made for it.

Fähigkeit (⸗) f ⓬ (f. fähig) capability; ability; fitness, qualification; (Anlage) capacity; geistig: aptitude, talent, faculty, gift(edness); physisch: fitness; das reicht über seine ~en hinaus that is beyond his capacity or strength, F that's beyond him; ~s=diplom n certificate of capacity; diploma.

fahl (⸗) [ahd. (ndd.) =falb] a. ⓰ v. Farben: fallow; (verschossen) faded; (grau-braun) dun; (blau-grau) livid; ⸗e Gesichtsfarbe sallow (stärker: livid) complexion; fig. e-n auf dem ⸗en (a. faulen) Pferde (auf Unerlaubtem) ertappen to catch a p. in the (very) act or F on the hop or tripping.

Fahl=band ⚒ (⸗...) n ⓬ (Erzlagerstätte ✝) fahlband; ⸗ braun a. ⓰ dun; =erz n, min. grey copperore, ✝ fahlerz; ⸗gelb a. ⓰ fallow; ⸗grau a. ⓰ greyish; (bleifarben) livid.

Fahlheit (⸗) f ⓬ sallowness; lividity.

Fahl=leder ⊕ (⸗...) n ⓬ Gerberei: skins pl. for upper leathers, dressing-hides pl.; upper (or shaft-)leather; =rot a. ⓰ fawn-coloured.

Fähnchen (⸗) n ⓫ 1. dim. von Fahne.— 2. ⚓ (Wimpel) pennant, pennon.—3. F=Frauenkleid.—4. ♪ (Schwanz einer Note) pennant of a note. — 5. (Verweisungszeichen) reference-mark.

fahnden (⸗) [ahd. v/a. u. v/n (h.) ⓰ (auf) e-n, nach e-m ⸗ to (endeavour to) seize; (verfolgen) to pursue.

Fähndrich ⚚ (⸗) ꝛc. f. Fähnrich ꝛc.

Fahndung (⸗) f ⓬ pursuit.

Fahne (⸗) [ahd.: vane] f ⓬ 1. bes. ⚚ colour(s pl.), flag; poet. streamer (Banner) banner, for Reiterei: standard; für Fußvolk, bsd. Alt.: ensign; ⚚ weiße ~ (der Parlamentäre) white flag; mit fliegenden ~n with flying colours; zu den ~n berufen werden to be called to the colours; bei der ~ sein to serve with the colours; mit fliegenden ~n und klingendem Spiel with colours flying and drums beating; die ~n schwenken (senken) to wave (to lower) the colours.—2. (Fahnen-ähnliches): a) am Federkiele: beard of a quill; b) (Schwanz des Jagdhundes) tail of a hound; c) hunt. (Frauenkleid) dress; ~n pl. (Putz) fine (silk) dress; F adornments pl.; d) typ. (Abzug) proof(-slip), vgl. Fahnenabzug; e) ⚘ ~ (Schmetterlingsblüte) ⚚ vexil(lum); f) bei Edelsteinen: (Trübung) cloud.

Fahnen=abzug ⊕ (⸗...) m ⓬ typ. proof-sheet, proof in slips, (rough) proof; ⚚artig a. ⓰ flag-like, ⚓: =vexillary; =band n colour-belt; =eid m military oath; =flucht ⚚ f desertion (from the colours); ⚚flüchtig a.: ⸗ werden to desert the colours; =flüchtige(r) ⚚ m deserter; =junker ⚚ m: a) ehm.: standard-bearer, ensign, der Reiterei: cornet; b) jetzt: († Avantageur) (gentleman) cadet; =korrektur f, typ. correction of proofs; =schmied m farrier to a squadron or battery; =schuh m colour-rest, -sheath; =stange f, =stock m flag-staff; =träger ⚚ m standard-, colour-bearer; vgl. =junker; =unteroffizier ⚚ m colour-sergeant; =wache f standard- (or colour-)guard; =weihe f presentation of the colours; ⚚weise adv. in companies or squad(ron)s.

Fähnlein (⸗) n ⓳: a) = Fähnchen; b) ehm. ⚚ ein ~ (Trupp) Soldaten, Reiter a troop (or squad) of soldiers, horsemen.

Fähnrich ⚚ (⸗) m ⓴d. 1. ehm. Kavallerie: cornet; Infanterie: ensign; vgl. Fahnenjunker.—2. jetzt: († Portepee-⸗) ensign; ~ zur See ⚓ († Seekadett) midshipman.

Fähnrich(s)=presse (⸗...) f ⓬ army-crammer's establishment; =stelle f cornetcy; ensign's post, ensigncy.

Fahr=bahn (⸗...) f ⓬ carriage-way; 🚆 (railway-)line.

fahrbar (⸗) a. ⓰ v. Wegen: passable, practicable; ⚓ v. Flüssen: navigable; ~keit f ⓬ passableness, practicability; ⚓ navigableness, navigability.

Fahr=betrieb 🚆 (⸗...) m ⓬ traffic; =betriebsmittel n/pl. rolling-stock.

Fähr=boot ⚓ (⸗...) n ⓬ = Fähre.

Fahr-, Fähr=brücke ⊕ (⸗...) f ⓬ flying-bridge; f. a. Auflauf 3.

Fahr=bühne ⚒ (⸗...) f ⓬ sollar; =damm m dike (or road) for vehicles; carriage-road. [(= Dampffähre).

Fähr=dampfer (⸗...) m ⓬ steam-ferry

Fährde ⚚ (⸗) f ⓲ a) (Gefahr) in Nöten und in ~n (U.) in (time of) distress and danger; b) (List) ohn' alle ~ (G., U.) (aufrichtig) without any artifice or guile.

Fahr=dienst 🚆 (⸗...) m ⓬ train-service.

Fähre ⚓ (⸗) [mhd.] f ⓭ ferry(-boat); fliegende ~ flying-bridge; in einer ~ übersetzen to cross (over) in a ferry, to ferry over or across.

fahren (⸗) [ahd.: fare (f. ⸗ 5)] ⓰b. I v/n. (sn) 1. (sich rasch bewegen) to move (or shift, proceed) from place to place; e-m an den Kopf ⸗ to fly at a p.'s head, von Personen: (a. auf e-n zu ⸗) to rush upon (or at) a p.; an= (ob. auf=) ea. (los) ⸗ to clash; auf die Alp ⸗ to go up the mountains; aus dem Bette ⸗ to start (up) from (one's) bed; das Messer fuhr mir aus der Hand ... slipped from my hand; vor Ungeduld (fast) aus der Haut ⸗ (almost) to burst with impatience; der Speer fährt durch die Wand ... goes through (or pierces) the wall; der Schreck fuhr mir durch (a. in) alle Glieder I was terrorstricken, I shook in every limb; es ist ihm etwas durch den Kopf gefahren a thought flashed across his mind; gen Himmel ⸗ to go (up) to heaven; fahre hin, Mammon depart thou hence, ...; mit der Hand hin und her ⸗ to pass one's hand to and fro; in die Grube ⸗: a) ⚒ to descend into the shaft; b) fig. ins Grab ⸗ to go down into one's grave; e-m in die Haare ⸗ to pull a p. by the hair; weits. to fall upon a p.; in die Höhe ⸗ to start up; was ist in den Menschen gefahren? what has possessed (or come over) the fellow?; es ist ein böser Geist in sie gefahren an evil spirit has laid (or seized) hold of them; in die Stiefel ⸗ to slip into one's boots; mit dem Löffel in den Topf ⸗ to dip the spoon into the pan; nach et. ⸗ to snatch at a th.; mit der Hand über die Haare ⸗ to pass one's hand over the hair; um e. Ecke ⸗ to turn (round)...; er fuhr unter sie he rushed (in) among them; unter die Säue ⸗ to enter (into) the swine; vom Stuhle ⸗ to start (up) from one's chair; zu Berg ⸗ to mount uphill; bibl. zur Hölle ⸗ to descend into hell; zu den Vätern (a. von hinnen) ⸗ to depart this life, to join the majority; weiter ⸗ to continue (on) one's way. — 2. ⸗ lassen (loslassen) to let go, to drop; (aufgeben) to abandon, to give up, to renounce; eine Gelegenheit ⸗ (entschlüpfen) l. to let an opportunity slip; alle Sorgen ⸗ lassen to banish (or dismiss) all care; zornige Worte ⸗ l. to drop ...; a. 3.—3. auf e-m Fuhrwerk ob. Fahrzeug: statt zu gehen, muß er immer ⸗ ... he must always drive (or ride) in a carriage; sehr schnell ⸗ to shoot or race, ⚓: to boom) along; mit dem Automobil ⸗ (to go by) motor, to travel by (or in a) motor-car, to go motoring; Kahn, Nachen ⸗ to go boating or sailing; erster Klasse ⸗ to travel (or go) first-class; ⚓ die Küste entlang ⸗ (to hug the) coast; über Land ⸗ to go across country; einen Omnibus, Zug ꝛc. ⸗ lassen to run an omnibus, a train, &c.; mit der Post, dem Schiff, dem Zug, dem Wagen ⸗ to travel (or go) by

---

⚚ scientific; ⚘ botanical; ⛢ geography; ⊕ machinery; ⚒ mining; ⚚ military; ⚓ marine; ⚛ commercial; ✉ postal; 🚆 railway.

[Fahrer] — 352 — [faktisch]

stage-coach, by boat, by train, by coach or in a carriage; Schlitten 2 to drive (or go) in a sledge; mit der elektrischen Straßenbahn 2 to travel by (or to take the) electric tram; auf dem Zweirad 2 to ride (on) a bicycle, to (use a) bicycle, F to bike. — 4. von Fuhrwerken u. Fahrzeugen: der Wagen, das Boot, der Zug ꝛc. fährt zweimal den Tag ... runs (or goes, leaves) twice a day; ↓ es 2 Dampfer zwischen L. u. M. steamers ply ...; den Strom aufwärts (zu Tal) 2 to sail (or steam) up-(down-) stream. — 5. fig. gut (schlecht) bei oder mit et. 2 (sich befinden, stehen) to fare (or do) well (ill) at (or with) a th.; to succeed (to fail) in a th.; er ist sehr gut (schlecht) dabei gefahren he came off very well (badly); he got the best (the worst) of it; fahre (pl. fahrt) wohl farewell, a. poet. fare thou (pl. ye) well. — II v/a. 6. a. abs. ob. v/n. (h.) auf einem Fahrzeuge oder Fuhrwerke: to drive, convey, take; gut 2 to drive well, to be a good whip; er hat uns gut gefahren he drove us at a good pace; selbst 2 to handle the ribbons, Automobil: to drive one's own motor or car, in a (one's own)chauffeur; Steine ꝛc. 2 to cart ...; e-n spazieren 2 to take a p. (out)for a drive; e-n über den Fluß 2 to ferry a p. across the river. — 7. mit Angabe der Wirkung: entzwei(über den Haufen) 2 to smash (to knock down) in driving; ein Kind tot 2 to run over (and kill) ...; ein Pferd zuschanden 2 to work ... to death (with driving); ↓ ein Schiff in Grund und Boden 2 to run down ...; v/refl. sich fest 2 to stick fast (in the mud or sand, in marshy land, &c.); ↓ to run aground, sich müde 2 to tire o.s. with driving, riding, cycling, &c. — III v/refl. (sieh auch 7) 8. sich selbst 2 to drive o.s.; v/impers. hier fährt es sich gut it's easy (or good) driving here. — IV ~ n 23 9. mit Wagen: coaching, mit Rad: cycling, mit Automobil: motoring; er versteht das ~ gut he understands driving, he knows how to handle the ribbons, he is a good whip; sie kann das ~ nicht vertragen she cannot stand the riding in a carriage, &c.; das ~ (der Wagenverkehr) auf der Straße the carriage-traffic. — V 2d p.pr. u. a. 66 10. Bed. des inf. — 11. Der (umherschweifender) Ritter knight-errant, 2de Spielleute strolling (or roaming) minstrels pl.; 2des Volk, 2de Leute vagrants, tramps pl. ehm. 2de Schüler (Baganten) travelling scholars pl.; 2de Habe (Möbel) movable property, goods and chattels pl. — VI ~de(r) 66 12. vagabond, tramp; wandering (or itinerant) gipsy or juggler.
Fahrer (¹ᵥ~) m 62 driver; **~ei** (~ᵥ¹) f 46 driving (about); coaching (sport).
Fahr=gast (¹¹...) m 62 passenger; **=gebühr** f, **=geld** n = =preis.
Fähr=geld (¹¹...) n 62 ferriage; fare (for crossing a ferry).
Fahr=gelegenheit (¹¹...) f 62 conveyance; (railway-, &c.) connexion; **=geleise** n track for carriages / rut made by wheels; **=geschwindigkeit** f (running-)speed.

=güter n/pl., **=habe** f jur. = fahrende Habe, s. fahren 11; **=handschuhe** m/pl. driving- gloves pl.
fahrig (¹ᵥ) a. 66 (unbeständig) fickle; (zerfahren) giddy, unsettled; **~keit** f 46 fickleness; giddiness, unsettledness.
Fähr=kahn ↓ (¹¹) m = Fähre.
Fahr=kappe ⚒ (¹¹...) f 62 miner's cap or headgear.
Fahr=karte 🚂 (¹¹∪) f 62 ~ 1., 2., 3. Klasse first-, second-, third-class ticket; durchgehende ~ through-ticket; ~ für die Hin- und Rück=fahrt return ticket; eine ~ nach London lösen to book for ...; am Schalter: einfache ~ zweiter Klasse nach Köln: second single to Cologne!; ~n ausgeben, einsammeln to issue, collect tickets.
Fahrkarten=abgabe 🚂 (¹¹∪...) f 62: die ~ findet in N. statt tickets to be given up at N.; **=ausgabe** f: a) issue of tickets; b) = **=kasse**; **=ausgeber** m ticket-(or booking-)clerk; **=einnehmer** m ticket-collector; **=kasse** f = =schalter; **=kontrolleur** m inspector; **=schalter** m ticket- (or booking-)office.
Fähr=knecht ↓ (¹¹∪) m 62 ferryman's assistant; bargee.
Fahr=korb ⚒ (¹¹...) m 62 cage; **=kunst** f: a) driving, als Sport: coachmanship; b) ⚒ miner's cage; **=lässig** a. 66 (sorglos) careless, inattentive; (nachlässig) neglectful, negligent; (saumselig) remiss; 2e Tötung homicide caused by negligence; **=lässigkeit** f carelessness; neglect; remissness; grobe ~ culpable neglect.
Fährlichkeit (¹ᵥ~) f 46 (Gefahr) peril.
Fahr=loch ⚒ (¹¹ʌ) n (Mannloch am Dampfkessel) man-hole of a boiler.
Fähr=mann (¹¹...) m (¹¹) 62 ferryman, waterman; **=meister** m master of a ferry.
Fahrnis (¹ᵥ) f 18 ob. n 17 I ↘ (Gefahr) hazard, risk, danger. — II (fahrende Habe) goods and chattels pl.
Fahr=plan (¹¹...) m 62 🚂, &c. time-table; 2**plan=mäßig**(er Zug) regular (train); **=post** f für Gepäck ꝛc.: mail-coach; **=preis** m für Personen: fare; für Güter: freight; **=rad** n cycle, F auch: machine; zwei-, dreirädriges bicycle (F bike), tricycle; ~ mit pneumatischen Reifen pneumatic (cycle); Ausflug auf dem ~(e) cycling tour or trip; **=radfabrik** f cycle works pl.; **=rad=fabrikant** m cycle-maker or -manufacturer; **=schacht** ⚒ m climbing-shaft; **=schein** m 🚂, &c. ticket; vgl. Billett 2.
Fähr=schiff ↓ (¹¹) n 62 ferry-boat.
Fahr=schule (¹¹∪) f 62 school for driving or coachmanship.
Fähr=seil ↓ (¹¹) n 62 ferry-rope.[chair.
Fahr=sessel (¹¹...) m 62 Bath- (or rolling) **fährst** (¹) 2. P. sg. pres. von fahren.
Fahr=straße (¹¹...) f 62 carriage-way; weitS. (Heerstraße) highway; **=stuhl** m: a) = =sessel; b) (Aufzug) lift, elevator.
Fahrt (¹) [ahd. * fahren] f 46 1. (Reise) journey, tour; (Ausflug) trip, excursion; im Wagen: drive, ride; zur See: voyage, passage; vgl. Bootfahrt. — 2. eine ~ zu Lande, zu Wasser machen to travel (or cross) by land, by water; er ist immer auf der ~ F ... for ever on

the move; eine tolle ~ a mad (or desperate) run or race; hier endete seine tolle ~ here ended his mad career. — 3. ↓: a) (Kurs) course; von der ~ abkommen to get off (or to deviate from) one's course; die Fahrt nehmen nach // to stand to (!; die ~ machen to make headway; die ~ nach Norden richten to shape one's course northward; b) (Geschwindigkeit) run of the ship; eine gute (a. schnelle) ~ h. to make a good (or quick) run; in voller ~ sein to be going (at) full speed. — 4 ⚒: a) (Einfahren) descent into the shaft or pit; b) miner's ladder.
fährt (¹) 3. P. sg. pres. v. fahren.
Fahr=tarif (¹¹...) m 62 tariff; scale of fares; **=taxe** f = =preis.
Fahrt=ball ↓ (¹¹ᵥ) m 62 etwa: speed-ball.
Fährte (¹ᵥ) f [nhd., pl. v. Fahrt] f 48 hunt. track, trace, trail, print; kalte ~ cold scent; auf die ~ kommen to get the scent; von der ~ abkommen to lose the scent, to be at fault; der ~ folgen, die ~ verfolgen to follow the scent, to track one's game; fig. e-n auf die richtige, falsche ~ bringen to put a p. on the right, wrong scent or track; auf der falschen ~ sein to be on the wrong scent or track.
Fahrten=liste (¹¹ᵥ...) f 62 der Stadtwagen time-table; **=plan** = Fahrplan; **=schwimmer** m long-distance swimmer.
Fahrt=haken (¹¹...) m 62, **=haspe** ⚒ f hook for attaching the ladder; **=moment** ↓ n eines Schiffes: momentum of a ship's motion; **=unterbrechung** f break(ing of the journey).
Fahr=vorschrift (¹¹...) f 62 rule of the road; **=wasser** ↓ n navigable water, fairway, road, course; offenes ~ open channel, clear passage; fig. in s-m ~ sein to be in one's element; **=weg** m = =bahn; **=wind** m favourable (or fair) wind; **=zeit** f running-time; (Abfahrtszeit) starting-time; ⚒ working-time (in mines or pits); **=zeitüberschreitung** f lateness of a train, &c.; **=zeug** [nhd.] n: a) ↓ vessel, craft; b) ↘ (Fuhrwerk) vehicle, conveyance; ↘ der Bagage: baggage-waggon.
Fäh=werk (¹¹ᵥ) [Fäh(e)] n 62 = Fäh.
Faiseur (fä-sö'r) [fr.] m ⓓd. (Macher, Anstifter, a. b. s.) wirepuller, instigator.
fäkal ⚒ (¹ᵥ) [lt.] a. 66 (auf den Auswurf bezüglich) physiol. fecal; **~i=en** (~¹(ᵥ)~) n/pl. inv. **~=dünger** m 62 agr. fecal manure; **~=stoffe** m/pl. physiol. (Auswurfstoffe) fecal substances, fecals, excrements pl.
Fakir (¹¹) [ar. Armer (= Derwisch)] m ⑪(50) (mohammedanischer Bettelmönch) fakir.
Faksimile (¹¹ᵥ) [lt.] n 61 (Nachbildung) facsimile; **faksimilieren** (ᵥ~ᵥ¹)v/a.93 to make a facsimile (or faithful copy) of.
Faktage ⚒ (¹ᵥ¹∪) [fr.] f 48 (Paketbestellung) dispatch of parcels, parcel-post duties pl.
Fakten (¹ᵥ) n/pl. v. Faktum.
Faktion (ᵥ¹ᵥ∪¹) [lt.] f 46 (Partei) faction **faktiös** (ᵥ¹ᵥ∪¹) a. 66(D 10) factious.
faktisch (¹ᵥ) [lt.] a. 66 (tatsächlich) effective, real, founded on fact; adv. in fact, really; jur.: der 2e Inhaber the actual (or de facto) owner.

Zeichen (s. S. XVII): F familiär; P Volkssprache; Γ Gaunersprache; ↘ selten; † alt (auch gestorben); * neu (auch geboren); ⁺⁺ unrichtig;

[faktitiv]

faktitiv ⚤ (ˬ‿ᵘf) [lt.] *gram.* **I** *a.* ⑯ (bewirkend) factitive, causative. — **II** ~ *n* ⑪c. (Bewirkungswort): tränken ist das ~ des Zeitworts trinken to drench is the factitive of the verb to drink.

Faktor (ˬ‿) [lt.] *m* **I** ㉛ **1.** *math.* factor (a. *fig.*); der größte gemeinschaftliche ~ the greatest common factor or measure, *abbr.* g. c. m.; in ~en zerlegen to split (up) into factors, to factorize. — **II** (oft: ‿⊥ ⓓd) **2.** ⑭ (Geschäftsführer) manager, managing clerk. — **3.** ⑭ (Werkmeister) foreman (of a workshop), *typ.* foreman (or overseer) of a printing-office.

Faktorei ⚤ (ˬ‿ᵘ) [lt.] *f* ㊻ (Handelsniederlassung) factory, trading company, foreign settlement; **~handel** (ˮ...) *m* ㉒ foreign agency.

Faktor=substitu't (ˬ‿ˬ...) *m* ㊷ *typ.*, &c. foreman's assistant; **=zimmer** *n* foreman's room.

Faktotum (‿⊥ˬ) [lt. *fac totum* mach' alles!] *n* ㊹ factotum; jack-of-all-trades.

Faktum (ˬ‿) [lt.] *n* ㊾ (Tatsache) fact.

Faktur (ˬ⊥) [lt.] *f* ㊻, *a.:* **~a** (ˬ‿) *f* ㊾ (Warenrechnung) invoice; laut ~ as per invoice; ~ geben to invoice.

Faktura=, Faktur(en)=buch ⚤ (ˬ‿ᵘ...) *n* ㊷ invoice-book; **=preis** *m* invoiced price; prime cost.

fakturieren ⚤ (ˬ‿⊥ˬ) *v/a.* ⑭ to invoice.

Fakturist ⚤ (ˬ‿⊥) *m* ㊷ invoice clerk.

Fakultas (ˬ‿ˬ) [lt.] *f* (*sg. inv., pl.* **Fakultä'ten**) (Befähigung) qualification; *Facultas doce'ndi* für Mathematik &c. teacher's certificate (or parchment) for mathematics, &c.

Fakultät (ˬˬ⊥) [lt.] *f* ㊻ *univ.* theolo'gische (medizi'nische, juri'stische, philoso'phische) faculty of divinity (of medicine, law, arts); **~s=stu'dium** (ˮ...) *n* ㊷ university (or professional) studies *pl.*

fakultativ (ˬˬ‿⊥) [lt.] *a.* ㊻ (freigestellt, *ant.* obligato'risch) optional (subject).

falb (ˬ) [*s. fahl*] **I** *a.* = fahl; bsd.: (graugelb) (u. **II=e(r)** *m* ㊿) Pferd: cream-coloured (horsc). — **III ~c** *f* ㊻ pale tint.

Falbel (ˬ‿) [lt.] *f* ㊽ (Faltensaum) furbelow, flounce; mit ~n besetzt furbelowed.

fälbeln (ˬ‿) (ˬ‿) ⓐa. to furbelow, flounce.

Fälber ⚥ (ˬ‿) *m* = Felber.

Falerner (ˬ‿ˬ) [lt.] *a. inv.* röm. Alt.: ~ (Wein) *m* ㉒ Falernian (wine).

Falke (ˬ‿) [ahd.] *m* ㊹ **1.** *orn.* falcon (*Falco*) ~; hawk; den ~n steigen lassen to fly a hawk; *fig.* er hat Augen wie ein Falke he has eagle's eyes. — **2.** [fahl] = Falbe(r) (Pferd).

Falken=auge (ˬ‿ˬ...) *n* ㉒: a) falcon's eye; b) *fig.* hawk's (or eagle's) eye; mit ~n eagle- (or keen-)eyed; **=beize** *f, hunt.* hawking, falconry; **=blick** *m, fig.* eagle's glance; **=haube** *f, hunt.* hood of a falcon; **=haus** *n* mew.

Falkenier (ˬ‿⊥) [fr.] *m* ⑪c. *hunt.* ehm.: falconer; hawker; **~=kunst** (ˮ...) *f* ㊷ falconry; hawking.

Falken=jagd (ˬ‿...) *f* ㉒; **=beize; =jäger** *m* falconer; **=meister** *m, hunt.* ehm.: falconer; keeper of (the) hawks; **=riemen** *m, hunt.* leash; **=wärter** *m* = **=meister; =weibchen** *n* female hawk; **=würger** *m, orn.* falconet (*Falcu'nculus*).

falkieren (ˬ‿⊥) [fr. *falquer*] *v/a.* ⑲ *man.* (zierliche Sprünge m.) to make falcades.

Falkner (ˬ‿) [mhd.] *m* ㉒ = Falkenier; **~ei** (ˬ‿⊥) *f* ㊻ *hunt.* falconry.

Falkonier (ˬ‿⊥) *m* ⑪c. = Falkenier.

Fall¹ (ˬ) [ahd.: fall] *m* ⑦b. **1.** fall, F tumble; einen schweren ~ tun to have a heavy fall, F u. Sport: to come a cropper; *fig.* Hochmut kommt vor dem ~ pride comes before (or will have) a fall; e-n zu ~e bringen to cause a p.'s downfall or ruin; ein Mädchen: to ruin (or seduce) a girl; zu ~e kommen to be ruined; *adv.* Knall und ~ on the spot; there and then. — **2.** ~ der Blätter fall of the leaf; ~ des Wassers, Barometers &c.: fall, drop; (Wasser=)~ waterfall; kleiner: cascade, großer: cataract; falls *pl.* of Niagara, &c. — **3.** (Senkung) decline, fall; ⚒ gradient. — **4.** (Sterben des Viehes) mortality of cattle. — **5.** (Glückswechsel) reverse, (Unglück) mishap, stärker: catastrophe; (Unfall) accident; ⚥ e-r Firma: failure, bankruptcy. — **6.** (Vorfall) case; ein dazu passender oder dahin gehöriger ~ a case in point; **auf alle Fälle, auf jeden ~** at all events, in any case, at any rate; by all means; auf alle Fälle gefaßt sein to be prepared for all emergencies; auf keinen ~ on no account, in no case, by no means; das ist auch **mein** ~ it's the same with me, I am in the same position or predicament; das ist nicht mein ~ oder nicht bei mir der ~ that's not my case, it does not apply to me; vgl. eintreten 3; f. erforderlichen=falls; gesetzt den ~ oder gesetzt den(e)s supposing that; im ~(e), auf den ~, daß (oder falls) dies geschähe in case this should happen; im gleichen ~e sein to be in the same boat; im ~e f-s Ausbleibens, Todes &c. failing him; im ~ der Not (auch nötigenfalls) in case of need or of emergency; außer im ~e, daß // except if //; ich bin (oder befinde mich) im ~e (in der Lage) zu // I am able (or so situated as) to //; wenn ich in den ~ kommen sollte, zu // if I should happen to //; im ~e eines Unglücks in case of misfortune; im schlimmsten ~e, schlimmsten=falls in the worst case, if the worst comes to the worst, vgl. ...falls; **von ~ zu** ~ entscheiden to decide each case according to its (individual) merits, to judge each case on its own merits; Politik von ~ zu ~ policy (without general principles) which acts according to circumstances, or: opportunism. — **7.** *gram.* (Kasus) case; der erste (zweite &c.) ~ the nominative (genitive, &c.) case. — **8.** ⚒ (Kluft) crack, fissure, crevasse.

Fall² ⚓ (ˬ) [ndd.] *n* ⑤b. (Tau zum Auf= u. Niederbringen der Segel, Rahen &c.) ~ e-r Rahe halyard of a yard.

Fall¹=abwand(e)lung (ˬ‿...) *f* ㉒ *gram.* (Deklination) declension.

Fäll=axt (ˬ‿...) *f* ㉒ axe for felling trees.

fällbar (ˬ‿) *a.* ⑯: a) *for.* fellable, ready for felling; b) *chm.* precipitable, fit for precipitation, easily precipitated.

[fallen]

Fall¹=baum (ˬ‿...) *m* ㉒ (Schlagbaum) turnpike; ⚔ frt. portcullis; **=beil** *n* guillotine; **=beugung, =biegung** *f* = **=abwandelung; =block** ⊙ *m* pile-driver, pile-driving engine; **=brett** *n* falling-board; am englischen Galgen: drop; (Laden) shutter; **=brücke** *f* (Zugbrücke) drawbridge; (Sturzbrücke) bridge with bascules.

Falle (ˬ‿) [ahd.] *f* ㉒ ⚤ trap; (Schlinge) snare; e-m eine ~ stellen to set a trap (or lay a snare) for a p.; in die ~ geh(e)n to fall into a trap, to take the bait; in eine ~ geraten to be caught in a trap; in die ~ locken to ensnare, to entice; *fig.* es ist nur eine ~F it's only a catch or trap; wir sitzen in der ~ we are (en)trapped or F sold.

fallen (ˬ‿) [ahd.: fallt] ⑯a. **I** *v/n.* (sn) **1.** to fall; et. ~ lassen to let a th. fall, to drop a th. (vgl. a. 11); auf den Boden ~ to fall on the ground; der Länge nach auf die Erde ~ to tumble down (at) full length, to topple over; ins Wasser ~ to fall into the water, v. Personen auch: to get a ducking; über einen Stein ~ to stumble over ...; vom Pferde, Fahrrad &c. ~ to fall off one's horse, cycle, &c.; e-m zu Füßen ~, vor e-m auf die Knie ~ to fall at a p.'s feet; *fig.* an e-n ~ (erblich übergehen) to come to a p. (by inheritance); e-m in die Hände ~ (geraten) to fall into a p.'s hands; unter die Räuber ~ to fall among thieves; der Würfel ist gefallen the die is cast. — **2.** (eintreten) den Fest fällt auf Sonntag ... falls on a Sunday. — **3.** (gehören) das fällt in dieselbe Kategorie it comes under (or belongs to) ...; in diese Zeit ~ seine Hauptwerte ... belong to that period. — **4.** Redensarten: er ist nicht **auf** den Kopf, auf den Mund (F aufs Maul) gefallen he is no fool, not tongue-tied; **aus** allen f-n Himmeln ~ to become disillusioned; aus der Rolle ~ to forget (or not to keep up) one's part; er war (wie) aus den Wolken gefallen ... as if he had dropt from the clouds; ins Gewicht ~ to be of consequence or of great weight; mit der Tür ins Haus ~ (herausplatzen mit et.) to speak out bluntly (without any ceremony or introduction); to blurt out a th.; **in** Ohnmacht ~ to faint (away), to swoon; einem in die Rede, ins Wort ~ to interrupt a p.'s speech; ⚔ dem Feind in den Rücken, in die Flanke ~ to attack the enemy in the rear, to turn the enemy's flank; das ist ihm (ohne sein Zutun) in den Schoß gefallen it came to him by sheer luck, it was a windfall (to him); bei einem in Ungnade ~ to lose a p.'s favour, to incur a p.'s displeasure; dem Pferde in die Zügel ~ to seize a horse by the bridle; **über** einen her ~ to fall upon a p.; sie fiel ihm **um** den Hals she fell on (or round) his neck; *fig.* **von** der Bank ~ (unehelich geboren werden) to be born out of wedlock; mir ist e-e Last vom Halse (e. Stein vom Herzen) gefallen a burden has been taken off my shoulders; e-m **zur** Last ob. lästig (zur Beschwerde ob. beschwerlich) ~ to become (or be) a burden (a trouble) to a p.;

♪ Musik; ⚤ Wissenschaft; ⚘ Pflanze; ⚯ Geographie; ⊙ Technik; ⚒ Bergbau; ⚔ Militär; ⚓ Marine; ⚥ Handel; ⚬ Post; 🜚 Eisenbahn.

[**fällen**]   — 354 —   [**Falschheit**]

der Gemeinde zur Laſt ⁓ to be thrown (or to come) upon the parish; ſ. a. Apfel 1; Sprichw. kein Meiſter fällt vom Himmel (a. es iſt noch kein Gelehrter vom Himmel gefallen), etwa: there is no royal road to learning. — 5. (plötzlich ſterben) to die suddenly; er iſt auf dem Platze gefallen he died on the spot, he fell down dead; durchs Schwert ⁓ to die by the sword; die Gefall(e)nen those who perished (in der Schlacht: who fell); abs. von Tieren = krepieren. — 6. (ſinken) to fall, sink, abate; das Barometer (das Waſſer) fällt ... is falling (is subsiding) ♣ die Aktien, Preiſe ⁓ ... are going down or falling or receding or drooping; die Kurſe ſind ſtark gefallen prices have greatly declined or gone down or have had a severe drop; wieder ⁓ to relapse; fig. ein gefallener Engel, ein gefall(e)nes Mädchen a fallen angel, a ruined girl. — 7. (wahrnehmbar werden) in die Augen, die Sinne ⁓ to strike the eye, the senses; dieſe Farbe fällt ſtark in die Augen ... is very glaring or F loud; es fällt ins Grüne (nähert ſich dem Grün) it has a greenish tint; ins Lächerliche ⁓ to border (or verge) on the ridiculous; ſein Auge fiel auf ſie he fixed his glance upon her. — 8. (ſein, werden) die Arbeit fällt ihm ſchwer ... comes hard (or difficult) to him; es fiel mir ſchwer, es abzuſchlagen I refused with great reluctance; ✗ der Gang fällt ſenkrecht ... runs perpendicular(ly). — 9. (gehört werden) es fiel ein Schuß a shot (or the report of a gun) was heard; es ⁓ beleidigende Reden offensive speeches are made. — 10. (hervorgehen) to come forth; von Tieren: (geboren werden) to be born, F to drop; weiß. wie es fällt (auch endg) just as it may happen; es falle wie es wolle come (or let happen) what may; das Los fiel auf mich the lot fell upon me. — 11. ⁓ laſſen: a) e-e Maſche ⁓ laſſen to drop a stitch; thea. den Vorhang ⁓ laſſen to drop (or to ring down) the curtain; b) e-e Bemerkung, Worte ⁓ laſſen (vorbringen) to make a remark, to drop (or utter) words; c) ſeine Anſprüche ⁓ laſſen (aufgeben) to drop (or relinquish) ... — 12. ♩ aus dem Schiffe ins Boot ⁓ (ſteigen) to man the boat. — II v/a. u. ſich ⁓ v/refl. mit Angabe der Wirkung: 13. e-n tot ⁓ to kill a p. by (or in) one's fall; ſich den Arm aus dem Gelenke ⁓ to put one's arm out of joint; to dislocate one's arm; ſich lahm ⁓ to be lamed by a fall. — III ⁓ n ㉓ 14. (ſ. 1) meiſt = Fall¹ 1; ₫B.: beim ⁓ in falling; (ſ. 5) klar zum ⁓ clear. — 15. (ſ. 5) sudden death; mortality of cattle. — 16. (ſ. 6) abatement; subsidence; ♣ fall (or decline) of prices; downward movement of the market. — IV ⁓b p.pr. u. a. ⓺ 17. Bed. des inf. — 18. math. ⁓de Reihe descending series; path. die ⁓de Sucht: ⚕ epilepsy.

fällen ♣ [ahd.] fell fallen machen] I v/a. ⓼ 1. Holz: to fell, to cut (or hew) down. — 2. ✗ das Bajonett ⁓ to fix bayonets; fällt's Bajonett! charge bayonets!; mit gefälltem Bajonett einnehmen, erſtürmen to take (or carry) at the point of the bayonet. — 3. Tiere ⁓ (töten) to kill beasts, game. — 4. chm. (als Niederſchlag aus e-r Löſung ausſcheiden) to precipitate. — 5. math. eine Senkrechte auf eine Gerade ⁓ to drop a perpendicular on a straight line; von e-m Punkte eine Senkrechte auf eine Gerade ⁓ from a point to draw a line at right angles to a straight line. — 6. jur. ein Urteil ⁓ (ausſprechen) to pronounce (or give) judgment, to pass sentence; weitS. to give one's opinion upon a subject. — II ~ n㉓ 7. felling, &c. (ſ. 1). — 8. chm. (ſ. 4) precipitation. — 9. jur. (ſ. 6) passing of a sentence.

Fall¹-endung (ˢ⌣...) f ⓺ gram. casetermination.   [hunt. trapper.)

Fallen-leger (ˢ⌣...) m ⓺2, ⁼ſteller m,)

Fall¹-fenſter (ˢ...) n ⓺2 sash-window; ⁼gatter ✗ n, frt. herse, sarrasin(e); vgl. ⁼baum ✗; ⁼geſchwindigkeit f, mech. velocity of falling bodies; ⁼geſetze n/pl., mech. laws pl. of falling bodies or of gravitation; ⁼gitter ✗ n, frt. portcullis, vgl. ⁼gatter; ⁼grube f, hunt. pit(fall); ⁼höhe f, mech. altitude of fall; ⁼holz n, for. windfall(en wood).

fallieren ♣ (⌣⌣) [it.] v/n. (h.) ⑬ to fail (in business), to become bankrupt or insolvent; F to break, to go to smash.

fällig ♣ (ˢ⌣) a. ⓺ (verfallen) due; längſt ⁓ overdue; (zahlbar) payable; v. Wechſeln ꝛc.: wenn ⁓ werden to fall due, to expire; wenn ⁓ when due, at maturity.

Fälligkeit (⌣⌣-) f ⓺ von Wechſeln ꝛc.: maturity, expiration.

Falliment ♣ (⌣⌣⌣) [it.] n ⓫b., **Falliſſement** (⌣⌣ᵇᵐᵍ') [+,+ fr.] n ⑤ (ſ. fallieren) failure (in business), bankruptcy, insolvency, F smash.

fallit, Fallit ♣ (⌣⌣) [fr., it.] a.⓺ u. m⓶: der Kaufmann, ⁓ insolvent (or bankrupt, F broken) tradesman, bankrupt.

Falliten-gericht ♣ (⌣⌣⌣...) n ⓺2 bankruptcy-court; ⁼maſſe f bankrupt('s) estate, assets pl. of a bankrupt.

Fallit-erklärung ♣ (⌣⌣...) f ⓺2 declaration of insolvency; jur. filing a petition in bankruptcy.

Fall¹-klappe (ˢ...) f ⓺ trap-door; ⁼klinke ⊙ f (falling) latch; ⁼maſchine f, phys. (Atwood's) falling-machine.

Fäll-mittel (ˢ...) n ⓺2 chm. precipitant.

Fall¹-obſt (ˢᵈ⌣) n ⓺2 dropped fruit, windfall(en fruit), windfalls pl.

fallopiſch ⚕ (⌣⌣⌣) [Fallo'pia, ital. Anatom, 1523-62] a. ⓺ anat. die Gänge, die Röhren (im Schläfenbein) Fallopian ducts pl.

Fall¹-raum (ˢ...) m ⓺2 mech. space traversed by a falling body; ⁼reep ♩ n gangway; ⁼reeps-luſe f, ⁼reeps-tau n, ⁼reeps-treppe f ♩ entering-port, entering-rope, ⁼ladder.

falls (ˢ) [Fall¹] cj. in case (that); provided (that); in the event that; ⁓ er kommen ſollte if he should come, in the event of his coming, vgl. Fall¹ 6. ...falls(⌣⌣...) in ⓲ſſan, ⓰ kleineſtfalls under no circumstances.

Fall¹-ſchirm (ˢ...) m ⓺2 der Luftſchiffer: parachute; ⁼ſilber n, chm., &c. silver-precipitate, precipitated silver.

fällſt (ˢ⌣) 2. Perſ. sg. pres. von fallen.

Fall¹-ſtoß (ˢ...) m ⓺2 Fußballſpiel: punt; ⁼ſtrick m snare, noose, gin; (Hinterhalt) ambush; (auch fig.) einem ⁓e legen to lay a snare (or set a trap) for a p.; ⁼ſucht f, path. falling sickness, ⚕ epilepsy; ⁼ſüchtig a. ⓺, ⁼ſüchtige(r) ⓺₇; ⚕ epileptic.   [fallen.]

fällt (ˢ; Hom. Feld) 3. Perſ. sg. pres. von)

Fall¹-tor (ˢ...) n ⓺2, ⁼tür(e) f trap-door; ⁼treppe f trap-stairs pl.

Fällung (⌣⌣) f ⓺ = fällen II.

Fall¹-verſchluß (ˢ...) m ⓺2 phot. dropshutter; ⁼werk ⊙ n zum Stanzen und Prägen: stamp; ⁼winkel ✗ m (Neigungswinkel) eines Ganges dip (or incline) of a lode; ⁼zeit f time of fall.

Fäll¹-zeit (ˢᴸ) f ⓺ for. season for cutting down trees or felling timber.

falſch (ˢ) [mhd.] I a. ⓺(D 6) 1. (unrichtig) wrong(place), mistaken (idea), incorrect (sum), erroneous (opinion); ♪ der Aſ⸗fo'rd, ⁓e Note false chord, note; gram. der Ausdruck wrong expression; ſ. Fährte; von Bildern: in einem ⁓en Lichte hängen to hang in a bad light; adv. ein Wort ⁓ ausſprechen to pronounce badly or wrongly; to mispronounce ...; die Uhr geht ⁓ ... keeps bad time, is wrong, goes badly; ⁓ ſchreiben (ſprechen) to write(to speak) incorrectly or badly; ♪ ⁓ ſingen (ſpielen) to sing (to play) out of tune; Tennis: ⁓! fault!, not up. — 2. (unecht, nachgemacht) ⁓e Banknote forged banknote; der Diamant false (or imitation) diamond; ⁓es Geld counterfeit (or bad, base) coin; ⁓e Zähne false (or artificial) teeth pl. — 3. (betrügeriſch) false, deceitful; (doppelzüngig) double-dealing; ⁓es Herz false heart; der Menſch false (or treacherous) person, F deep card; unter ⁓em Namen under a fictitious (or false) name, v. Schriftſtellern: under an adopted name or a pseudonym; ⁓es Spiel foul play; auf dem ⁓en Wege ſein to be on the wrong road or track, fig. to be out of one's reckoning; ⁓e Würfel loaded dice pl.; adv. ⁓ anführen to misquote; ⁓ ſchwören to forswear (or perjure) o.s. — 4. ⚓ auf e-n ⁓ (böſe) w. to be cross (or angry) with a p. — II ~ m ⓶ n⓲ a. 5. (ſ.3) falsehood, deceit(fulness); es iſt kein ~ in ihm there is no cunning (or guile) in him, he is perfectly candid; ohne ~ without guile, guileless, harmless, singlehearted; open.

fälſchen (ˢ⌣) [mhd.] I v/a. ⑭ to falsify; Karten: to mark; Lebensmittel ꝛc.: to adulterate; Geld ꝛc.: to counterfeit, debase, forge; Wein ꝛc.: F to doctor; die Bücher ⁓ to tamper with ...; gefälſchte Rechnungen false (F doctored or cooked) accounts. — II ~ n ㉓ (ſ. I) falsification; adulteration; counterfeiting, forgery. Vgl. a. verfälſchen.

Fälſcher (ˢ⌣) m ⓶, ~in f ⓺ (ſ. fälſchen) falsifier; forger of banknotes, &c.

falſch-gläubig (ˢ...) a. ⓺ theol. ⚕ heterodox; (ketzeriſch) heretic.

Falſchheit (ˢ⌣) f ⓺ (ſ. falſch 3) falseness, falsehood, deceit(fulness); perfidiousness; duplicity, double-dealing; artfulness, cunning, F depth.

Signs (see page XVII): F familiar; P vulgar; ♭ flash; ⚓ rare; † obsolete (died); * new word (born); ⁺ incorrect; ♪ music;

falsch-herzig (*...) *a.* false-hearted; **≈klingend** ♪ *a* dissonant, discordant.

fälschlich (*...) *a.* u. *adv.* (als *adv.* auch **≈er-weise**) false(ly), wrong(ly), (irrtümlich) erroneous(ly); by mistake; ≈ vorgeben to pretend; to sham.

Falsch-münzer (*...) *m* (false) coiner; coiner of base money; forger; **münzerbande** *f* gang of (false) coiners or forgers; **münzerei** *f* false coining; weitS. forgery; **netzflügler** *m/pl. ent.*: ⚛ pseudoneuroptera *pl.*; **schmuck** *m* imitation jewellery; **schreibung** *f* misspelling; **schwörer** *m* perjurer; **spieler** *m* cheat (or one who cheats) at cards, card-sharper, (professional) gambler.

Fälschung (*...) *f* 1. = fälschen II. – 2. forged document.

Falsett ♪ (*...) [it.] *n* ⊕b., ~**stimme** (*...) *f* (Fistel) falsetto (voice).

Falsifikat (*...) [it.] *n* ⊕c. forgery.

Falsum (*...) [lt.] *n* jur. fraud; ein ~ begeh(e)n to commit a forgery.

faltbar (*...) *a.* foldable, pliable.

Falt-boot ⚓ (*...) *n* collapsible boat.

Fältchen (*...) *n* *dim.* von Falte.

Falte (*...) [ahd.: fold] *f* 1. fold; in der Haut: wrinkle; im Tuche: plait, pleat; (Knitter, Kniff) crease; (Bulst) bunch, pucker; die Stirn in ~n ziehen to knit one's brow(s). – 2. ⊕ Gerberei: eine ~ herunterlassen to take out a tuck; in ~n legen to fold, to plait; Schneiderei: to gather (in); sich in ~n legen (oder werfen) to crease, bunch, pucker (up); das Kleid wirft keine ~n the dress shows (or has) no creases, is a perfect fit. – 3. *fig.* die geheimsten ~n des Herzens the innermost (or most secret) recesses of the heart.

fälteln (*...) [mhd.] *v/a.* und sich ≈ *v/refl.* ⊕a. to plait, crease; (kräuseln) to frill.

falten (*...) [ahd.: fold] I *v/a.* und sich ≈ *v/refl.* ⊕ (+⊕a.; aber noch *p.p.* f. 2) 1. e-n Brief 2c.: to fold; Tuch auch: to plait; (träufeln) to frill, to ruffle; von Stoffen: sich ≈ (trumpeln) to crease, to crumple; gefaltet ⚘, zo., anat.: ⚛ plicate(d); mit gefalteter Stirn with wrinkled brow. – 2. die Hände ≈ to join (or clasp, fold) one's hands; mit gefalteten Händen with folded (or clasped) hands. – II ~n ⊕ 3. folding,&c.(i.1);⚛plication.

Falten-kapitell (*...) *n* arch. indented capital; **≈kleid** *n* plaited gown; **≈leger** ⊕ *m* plaiter (a. Werkzeug); an der Nähmaschine: plaiting-attachment; folder; **≈leg-maschine** ⊕ *f* = ≈leger; **≈los** *a.* without folds or plaits; von Kleidern auch: without a crease, close-fitting; **≈magen** *m*, zo. = Blättermagen; **≈morchel** ⚘ = Herbstmorchel; **≈rand** *m* am Bett valance; **≈reich** *a.* full of folds or creases; **≈rock** *m* plaited gown; **≈saum** *m* = ≈rand; f. a. Falbel; **≈voll** *a.* = ≈reich; **≈weise** *adv.* in folds or plaits; **≈werfung** *f*, **≈wurf** *m* Kunst: (arranging the) drapery.

Falter (*...) [nhd. 18. sae.] *m* ent.: ⚛ lepidopter; (bsd. Tagfalter) butterfly; **~-blume** ⚘ *f* ⚛ durch Schmetterlinge bestäubt: flower fertilized by butterflies.

faltig (*...) *a.* in plaits, plaited, braided, ⚛ plicate(d); von der Stirn: wrinkled; (bauschig) puckered.

...fältig (*...) *...)* in Zssgn, zB. vielfältig multiple, aber Dreifaltigkeit trinity.

Fältlein (*...) *n* *dim.* von Falte.

Falt-stuhl (*...) *m* folding-chair, camp-stool.

Faltung (*...) *f* = falten II. [stool.]

Falz ⊕ (*...) [mhd.: falzen] *m* ⊕a. arch., carp., &c. (längliche Vertiefung) groove, notch; fold; (Fuge) rabbet; an einer Säule, an Möbeln 2c.: fluting, channel; Buchbinderei: guard.

Falz-bein ⊕ (*...) *n* (paper-)folder, folding-stick or -bone, paper-cutter or -knife; **≈brett** *n* Buchbinderei: folding-board. [Falz.)

Falze ⊕ (*...) *f* arch. (Säulenrinne) =

falzen (*...) [ahd.] *v/a.* 1. e-n Brief 2c.: to fold; ⊕ Buchbinderei: Bogen ≈ to sheet paper; ein Brett 2c.: to rabbet, join. to groove; arch. (ausreisen) to flute. – 2. ⊕ Gerberei: Häute ≈ (schaben) to shave hides; Leder ≈ to pare leather.

Falzer ⊕ (*...) *m*, **~in** *f* ⊕ folder.

Falz-hobel (*...) *m* ⊕ join. rabbet- (or grooving-)plane; fillister (plane).

falzicht, falzig (*...) ⊕ *a.* arch., &c. grooved, fluted; like grooves or flutes.

Falz-maschine (*...) *f* ⊕ rabbeting- (or folding-)machine; book-folder; **≈säge** *f*, join. rabbet-saw; **≈schiene** *f* tramrail; **≈schienenweg** *m* tramway; **≈zange** ⊕ *f* Klempnerei: pliers *pl.* used in folding; **≈ziegel** *m* grooved tile, gutter-tile.

Fama (*...) [lt.] *npr/f.*, *inv.* (o. *pl.*), myth. (the goddess of) Fame; weitS. (oft: die ~) fame; die ~ sagt, daß // it is (commonly) reported that //; the report goes that //.

familiär (*...) [fr.] *a.* (vertraut) familiar, intimate; ≈ tun to take liberties, to make o.s. at home.

familiarisieren (*...) *v/a.* ⊕ (vertraut machen) to familiarize. [familiarity.)

Familiarität (*...) *f* (Vertrautheit)

Famili-e (*...) [fr., *lt.] *f* 1. family (a. ⚘ u. zo.); das liegt in der ~ it runs in the family or blood; die ganze ~, oft: the whole tribe or stock; seine ganze ~ (Verwandtschaft) his whole kith and kin, all his people or relations; von guter ~ sein ... of good parentage or well connected; f. Schoß³. – 2. keine ~ (Kinder) haben to have no children or no family.

Famili-en-ähnlichkeit (*...) *f* family likeness; **≈angelegenheit** *f* fa. affair; **≈anzeigen** *f/pl.* = ≈nachrichten; **≈bad** *n* mixed bathing; **≈bande** *n/pl.* family ties *pl.*; **≈begräbnis** *n* fa. grave; **≈fehler** *m* fa. defect; **≈gemälde** *n* fa. picture or portrait; sketch of domestic life; **≈glück** *n* domestic happiness; **≈gut** *n* fa. estate; **≈haupt** *n* head of the family; **≈haus** *n* tenement-house; **≈krankheit** *f* fa. disease, hereditary malady; **≈kreis** *m* fa. circle; **≈leben** *n* fa. life; **≈nachrichten** *f/pl.* (Zeitungsrubrik) births, deaths, and marriages; F co. (column of) hatches, matches, and dispatches *pl.*; **≈name** *m* fa. name, surname, ⚛ cognomen; **≈rat** *m* family council; **≈rücksichten** *f/pl.* fa. considera-

tions *pl.*; **≈sitz** *m* fa. seat or mansion; *vgl.* ≈gut; **≈stiftung** *f* fa. settlement; **≈stolz** *m* fa. pride; **≈stück** *n* (Vererbtes) fa. heirloom; **≈vater** *m* father of a family, oft auch (lt.) paterfamilias; **≈vertrag** *m* fa. compact; **≈wohnung** *f* fa. residence; large commodious dwelling; **≈zwist** *m* family quarrel.

famos F (*...) [lt.] *a.* ⊕(D 10) famous; (ausgezeichnet) excellent; famoser Kerl, Spaß capital fellow, prime (or jolly) fun; famose Geschichte bang-up affair.

Famulus (*...) [lt. Diener] *m* ⊕ u. ⊕ (Gehilfe e-s Gelehrten) (lt.) amanuensis; (professor's) assistant.

Fanal (*...) [fr., it.] *m* u. *n* ⊕d. 1. ship's lantern. — 2. ↓ (Leuchtfeuer) beacon. — 3. (Leuchtturm) lighthouse.

Fanatiker (*...) *m* ⊕, **~in** *f* ⊕ (Schwärmer[in]) fanatic; **fanatisch** (*...) *a.* ⊕ fanatical; **fanatisieren** (*...) *v/a.* ⊕ bisw. to fanaticize; **Fanatismus** (*...) *m* ⊕ fanaticism.

Fanchon(=**zeck**) (*...) *n* Kinderspiel: game at catching. [fandango.)

Fandango (*...) [span.] *m* ⊕ (Tanz)

fand (*...) u. **fände** (*...) *subj. impf. v.* finden.

Fanfare ⚔ (*...) [fr.] *f* ⊕ (Trompetengeschmetter) flourish of trumpets.

Fang (*...) [ahd.] *m* ⊕b. 1. (o. *pl.*) (das Fangen, das Gefangene) capture, catch (-ing); (Beute) prey, booty; v. Fischen a. draught, take, beim Angeln: basket; einen guten ~ tun to have (a. to make) a good catch or a large haul or a good basket. – 2. (Falle, Schlinge) trap, snare. – 3. (mst im *pl.*) Fänge des Wildschweins ⚛ tusks *pl.*; der Raubvögel: fangs, claws, talons *pl.* — 4. hunt. einem Rehbock den ~ geben to dispatch a buck with the hunting-knife.

Fang-apparat ⚔ (*...) *m* ⊕ catching- (or safety-) apparatus; **≈ball** *m* Spiel: catch-ball; *fig.* (Spielball) toy; **≈becher** (=**spiel** *n*) *m* cup-and-ball; **≈damm** ⊕ *m* Wasserbau: coffer-dam; **≈eisen** *n*, hunt.: a) (iron or steel) trap; b) = ≈messer.

fangen (*...) [nbd.: hd. fahen] ⊕b. I *v/a.* 1. to catch (or take) fish, &c.; to capture (or seize) fugitives; mit der Angel: to hook; in der Falle: to (en)trap; im Netze: to net; mit der Schlinge: to gin; mit dem Schleppnetze: to drag; bsd. vom Jäger: to bag; Katzen ≈ Mäuse ... catch ...; sich ≈ lassen to allow o.s. to be caught, to go into a trap, to run one's neck into a noose; *fig.* er läßt sich nicht leicht ≈ he is not easily caught or tripped up. — 2. Feuer ≈ to catch fire (auch *fig.*), *fig.* leicht Feuer ≈ to be of an excitable nature, to fall easily in love; Grillen ≈ to brood over one's troubles; eine Krankheit ≈ to catch a disease. — 3. Sprichw. wer den ≈ will, muß früh aufsteh(e)n it would take a smart fellow to catch him; F he won't be caught napping; mit einem Schurken muß man einen andern ≈ set a thief to catch a thief; mit gefangen, mit gehangen, etwa: rogues of a gang on one gibbet must hang; f. a. Maus¹. — II sich ≈ *v/refl.* 4. passivisch: to be caught; Wasser: to catch (in a passage, &c.), *vgl.* 1; *fig.* sich in seinen eigenen

⚛ scientific; ⚘ botanical; ⚱ geography; ⊕ machinery; ⛏ mining; ⚔ military; ⚓ marine; ⊛ commercial; ✉ postal; 🚂 railway.

[**Fänger**] **Worten** ⁂ to be caught in one's own words or net. — III~ n ⊕ 5. = Fang 1.
Fänger (⁂) m ⊕ 1. one who catches; capturer, captor. — 2. hunt. Hirschfänger. — 3. pl. zo. = Fangzähne. — 4. ⊕ (Vorrichtung) catch.
Fang-garn (⁂...) n ⊕ (landing-)net; vgl. =strict; =geräte, =gestelle n/pl. hunt. traps, gins, snares pl.; =grube f, hunt. pitfall; =haken ⊕ m grab, catching-hook; =heuschrecke f, ent. praying-cricket (Mantis religio'sa).
fängisch (⁂) a. ⊕ hunt. v. e-r Falle: ready (for trapping or snaring), set.
Fang-laterne (⁂...) f ⊕ zum Fangen von Insekten: lamp for insect-catching; =leine f: a)↓ e-s Bootes: painter; b) hunt. für Hunde: leash, =messer n hunting-knife, hanger; =netz n = =garn.
Fango-bäder (⁂...)[it.]n/pl.=Schlamm-.
Fang-schlinge (⁂...) f ⊕, =seil n lasso; =strick m snare, noose.
fängst, fängt (⁂) pres. von fangen.
Fang-tau ⊥ (⁂...) n ⊕ short piece (or end) of rope, rope's end; =tuch ⊥ n tinder; =vorrichtung ⚡ f safety-catch of a cage; =weise f manner of catching (or snaring) birds, &c.; =zähne m/pl. zo. fangs, tusks pl.
Fanni (⁂) npr/f. ⊕⊕α. Fanny.
Fant (⁂) [ndd.] m ⓐb. (Gec) fop, dandy; coxcomb; (bes. ehm. a. lockerer Bursche) loose (or fast) young fellow; eitler ~ conceited youngster or puppy.
Farad ⊤ ⊕ (⁂) [Faraday, engl. Physiker, 1791—1867] n ⊕ 6. elect. (Einheit der elektrischen Kapazität) farad; ~isation (⌣⌣⌣-⁀)(⌣)¹] f ⊕ med. (elektrische Behandlung) faradization; **isieren** (⌣⌣⌣⁀) v/a. ⊕ physiol. (elektrisieren) to faradize. [dye.]
Farb-brühe ⊕ (⁂...) f ⊕ colour-liquor.]
Farbe (⁂) [ahd.] f ⊕ 1. colour, Am. color; hue; (Schattierung) tinge, tint, shade; (Gesichts-)~ complexion; die ~ verändern to change colour; ~n betreffend chromatic; ~n erzeugend colorific, ⊕ chromatogenous. — 2. fig. die ~ halten to stick to one's colours; (sich bewähren) to prove stanch, to remain faithful; die ~ (Partei) wechseln to change sides; vgl. 3 u. 4. — 3. ⊕ (Anstrich) colouring, mit Ölfarbe: paint (-ing); die ~ ist noch frisch it's fresh paint, the paint is still wet; typ. printer's ink; (Farbstoff) echte ~ (die gut hält) fast colour; fig. a. true blue; schlechte ~ inferior dye, fugitive colour; typ. ~ auftragen to distribute the ink; fig. die ~n stark auftragen to exaggerate, F to lay it on thick. — 4. Kartenspiel: suit; welche ~ ist Trumpf? what is trumps?; vgl. bedienen 4, bekennen 2; fig. mit der ~ herausrücken to express o.s. freely or candidly.
Färbe (⁂) f ⊕ (Färben) dyeing.
Färbe-bad ⊕ (⁂...) f ⊕ = =flotte.
Farbe-ballen (⁂...) m ⊕ typ. ink-ball; =behälter m, typ. ink(ing)-trough.
Färbe-faß ⊕ (⁂...) n ⊕ = =küfe; =flotte f dye(r's)-bath; =flüssigkeit f dye-fluid or -liquor.
farbe-haltend (⁂...) a. ⊕, ⊕haltig a. keeping colour; dyed in the grain.
Färbe-holz ⊕ (⁂...) n ⊕ dyewood.

Farb-eisen ⊕ (⁂...) n ⊕ typ. slice.
Farbe-kasten (⁂...) m ⊕ typ. ink-duct or -fountain, ductor; Zeugdruck: colour-box; =kissen n zum Stempeln: ink(ing)pad.
Färbe-küfe (⁂...) f ⊕, =küpe f dyeing-coffer or -tub, or -vat, dye-beck; =lack m zum Rotfärben: lac-dye.
...farben (...⁂) ⊕(D9) in Zssgn: gold~ of golden colour.
färben (⁂) ⊕ I v/a. to colour; mit Blut ⁂ to stain with blood; ⊕ to dye wool, cloth, &c.; ⁂ to stain glass, paper; in der Wolle ⁂ to dye in (the) grain; fig. ein in der Wolle gefärbter Radikaler a thorough (or stanch) Radical. — II sich ⁂ v/refl. to colour; (erröten) to colour (up), to blush; sich grün &c. ⁂ to turn green, &c.; hunt. (Haarwechseln) to shed the coat; auch = bluten, schwitzen. — III ~ n ⊕ = Färbung 1.
Farben-abstufung (⁂...) f ⊕ = =stufe; =auftrag m, paint. laying on (of) colours or (of) the paint; =bild n, phys. (coloured) spectrum; ⊕blind a. ⊕ colour-blind; =blindheit f c.-blindness; =brechung f, phys. refraction of colours; =brett n, paint. palette; =buchdruck ⊕ m, typ. chromotyp(o-graph)y; =dreieck n, opt. chromatic triangle; =druck ⊕ m colour-(or chromatic) printing; Bild: chromo-type; engS. = =buchdruck, =steindruck; =druckpresse f chromatic printing-press; ⊕echt a. dyed in the grain; =fabrikant m colour-striker; ⊕froh a. fond of colour(s); =gebung f, paint. application of colours, coloration; =glanz m brilliancy of colours; =handel m colour-trade; =händler m (oil-and-)colour-man, oilman, oil-merchant; =harmonie f chord of colour, harmonious blending of colours; =kleckser m (schlechter Maler) dauber; =körper m colouring body, ⊕ pigment; =kreisel m, opt. colour-top; =kunde f, phys. science of colours, ⊕ chromatics; chromatology; =kundige(r) m colourist; =lehre f = =kunde; =maßstab m ⊕ chromatometer; =mischung f mixing (or blending) of colours; mixed (or mixture of) colours; =mühle ⊕ f colour- (or paint-)mill; =muschel f c.-shell; =näpfchen n c.-saucer; =reibmaschine f = Farbe-reiber; =reibstein ⊕ m, typ. inkblock; =reich(tum m) a. rich(ness) in colour(s); =ringe m/pl. opt. Newton's rings pl.; =scheibe f, opt. colour-disk, Newton's disk; ⊕schillernd a. phys.: ⊕ iridescent; Seidenfabrikation: shot-coloured; =schmelz m enamel(ling); =sehen n, path.: ⊕ chromatopsy; =sinn m sense of colour, physiol. colour-sense; =skala f scale of colours; colour-chart; =spektrum n = =bild; =spiel n: ⊕ iridescence, opalescence; chroma-trope; =steindruck ⊕ m Verfahren: chromolithography; Bild: chromolithograph; =steindrucker m chromolithographer; =stift m coloured crayon or pencil; =stoff m = Farbstoff; =stufe f gradation of colours or shades; =tafel f, =täfelchen n (cake of) paint; =theorie f theory of colours; =ton m tone (of colour), hue; =topf m paint-pot, ⊕ typ.

[**Farin**]
ink-pot; =walze f, typ. ink-roller; =wechsel m change (or variegation) fo colour(s); =werk ⊕ n dye-works pl.; =zelle f, physiol.: chromatophore; =zerstreuung f, opt. chromatic aberration.
Färber (⁂) m ⊕, ~in f ⊕ dyer; ~al'anna ⊕ f ⊕ dyer's-alkanna or -bugloss (Anchu'sa tincto'ria); =baum ⊕ m = Perückenb.; =distel ⊕ f = Saflor.
Färberei ⊕ (⌣⌣⌣⁀) f ⊕ (Kunst) dyer's art or trade; (Werkstatt) dyer's works pl.
Farbe-reiber (⁂...) m ⊕ colour-grinder; (Maschine) brayer, muller, colour-grinding machine.
Färber-eiche ⊕ (⁂...) f ⊕ dyer's-oak (Quercus tincto'ria); =flechte ⊕ f dyer's-moss, orseille-weeds pl. (Rocce'lla tincto'ria); =geselle m d.'s (journey-)man; =ginster ⊕ m d.'s-broom (Geni'sta tincto'ria); =kamille ⊕ f yellow camomile (A'nthemis tinct'oria); =knöterich ⊕ f dyer's-knotgrass (Poly'gonum tincto'rium); =meister m master-dyer; =röte ⊕ f (Krapp) dyer's-madder (Ru'bia tincto'rium); =scharte ⊕ f sawwort (Serra'tula tincto'ria); =waid ⊕ m d.'s-woad (I'satis tincto'ria); =wau ⊕ m d.'s-weed (Rese'da lute'ola); =wurzel ⊕ f = =röte. [slice.]
Farbe-spachtel (⁂...) f, m ⊕ typ. ink-
Färbe-stoff (⁂...) m ⊕ = Farbstoff.
Farbe-teller (⁂...) m ⊕ typ. ink-disc; =tisch m, typ. ink(ing)-table; =walze f ink(ing)-roller.
Farb-holz (⁂...) n ⊕ dye(r's)-wood; =holz-raspelmaschine ⊕ f rasping mill.
...farbig (...⁂) a. ⊕ mst ... coloured, z.B. viel-⁂ many-coloured; ⊕ a. ...chromatic, z.B. ein-⁂ monochromatic.
farbig (⁂) I (⊕ =farbig) a. ⊕ coloured, stained, variegated; ⊕ Zer Holzschnittdruck chromoxylography. — II ~e(r) m/f ⊕ (ant. Weiße(r)) coloured man (f woman); pl. coloured people.
Farb-kuchen ⊕ (⁂...) m ⊕ dye-cake; ⊕los a. ⊕ colourless (auch fig. vom Stil &c.); (blaß) pale; phys.: ⊕ achromatic; fig., pol., &c. indifferent, neutral; =losigkeit f colourlessness; pallor; ⊕ achromatism; fig. indifference; =schreiber ⊕ m, tel. ink-writer; =spachtel = Farbespachtel; =stein m, typ. block, inking-stone; =stoff m, ⊕ substanz f colouring matter; ⊕ pigment; =stoff-mangel m = Albinismus; =tisch m, typ. ink-slab.
Färbung (⁂) f ⊕ 1. colouring, dyeing. — 2. = Farbe 1; eine neue ~ annehmen to change colour; fig. to assume a new complexion or aspect.
Farb-waren ⊕ (⁂...) f/pl. colours, dyes, paints pl.; =warenhändler m = Farbenhändler; =warenhandlung ⊕ f oil-(and-colour-)shop; ⊕wechselnd a. changing colour; (schillernd) iridescent; =werk ⊕ n inking apparatus; ⊕ typ. inking cylinder, ductor-roller.
Farce (⁂) [fr.] f ⊕ 1. Kochkunst: (Füllsel) stuffing. — 2. thea. (Posse) burlesque; (kleineres Lustspiel) farce.
farcieren (⌣⁀) [fr.] v/a. ⊕ Kochkunst: (füllen) to stuff; farciertes Fleisch forcemeat; stuffing.
Farin ⊕ (⌣⁀) [it. Mehl] m ⓐc., ~ade (⌣⌣⁀) f ⊕ moist sugar.

Zeichen (s. S. XVII): F familiär; P Volkssprache; Γ Gaunersprache; ⚡ selten; † alt (auch gestorben); * neu (auch geboren); ⁺⁺ unrichtig;

[Farinzucker] — 357 — [Faßschnecke]

Farin=zucker (⌣⌣⌣) m ㉒ = Farin.
Farm ⚓ (′ und ′) [engl.] f ㊻ ([Pacht=]Gut) farm; **~=besitzer** m ㊷ owner of a farm; **Farmer** (⌣⌣) m ㉔ (Landwirt) farmer. [bracken (Filix).]
Farn ♃ (′) (ahd.: fern) m ⑪ b. fern,
Farn=gebüsch (′...) n ㊷ fern-brake.
Farnicht (′⌣) [Farn] n ⓪d. (Farngebüsch) fern-brake; künstlich gepflanztes: fernery.
Farn=kraut ♃ (′...) n ㊷ = Farn; **♃=kraut=ähnlich**, **♃=krautartig** a.: ⚲ filiciform, pteroid; **=kraut=anlage** f fernery; **=samen** m fern-seed.
Faröer(inseln) ♀ (fä′r⌣⌣...) npr/f/pl. ㊹ Faroe Islands pl.
Farre obb. ob. bibl. (′⌣) m ㉔ (Zuchtstier) bull. [Kuh) heifer.]
Färse (′⌣; Hom. Ferse) [ndd.] f ㊻ (junge
Fasan (⌣′) [ahd., grch., *Phasis (fl.)] m ㉓c. orn. pheasant; junger ~, **Fasänchen** n ㉔ dim. pheasant pout.
Fasanen=braten (⌣′⌣⌣) m ㊷ roast pheasant; **=garten** m, **=gehege** n ph.-walk; **=hahn** m ph.-cock; **=haus** n ph.-house; **=hof** m =garten; **=huhn** m ph.-hen, hen-pheasant; **=jagd** f ph.-shooting; **=wärter** m, **=zucht** f keeper, breeding of pheasants.
Fasanerie (⌣⌣′⌣) [Fasan] f ㊹ pheasantry; pheasant-preserve.
Fäschen (′⌣) n ㉔ (dim. von Fase²) thin (or slender) thread.
Faschine (⌣′⌣) [fr. fascine] f ㊹ ⚔ frt. u. ⊕ Wasserbau: fascine; faggot-bundle
Faschinen=bekleidung (⌣′⌣...) f ㊸, **=blendung** f fascine-revetment; **=messer** ⚔ n billhook, hedging-bill; rifle-sword; **=werk** n fascine-work.
Fasching südd. (′⌣) [mhd.: Fastnacht] m ⓪d. carnival; **~s=scherz** (′⌣...) m ㊷ fun (or merriment) of carnival; (Mummenschanz) mummery; fancy-dress fête or ball; **~s=zeit** f Shrovetide, carnival (time or festivities pl.).
faschinieren ⚔ (⌣⌣′⌣) [lt.=fr.] I v/a. ㊽ to fascine; to protect with fascines or faggots. — II ~ n ㉓ u. **Faschinierung** f ㊻ fascine-work.
Fase¹ (′⌣) f ㊸ (abgeschrägte Kante) bevelled (or chamfered) edge.
Fase² (′⌣; Hom. Phase) [ahd.] f ㊸ thread.
Fasel (′⌣) [ahd.] m ㉔ 1. = Fase². — 2. (Fortpflanzung) propagation.
Fasel=bock (′⌣...) [Fasel 2] m ㊷ ram.
Faselei (-⌣′) f ㊻ (Narretei) craziness, giddiness; tomfoolery; (Geschwätz) silly talk, twaddle, babble, drivel.
Faseler (′⌣⌣) m ㉒, **Fasel=hans** m ㊵㊶ F crazy Jack, F harum-scarum.
Fasel=hengst (′⌣...) [Fasel 2] m stallion.
faselig (′⌣⌣) **faselhaft** (′⌣⌣) a. ㊿ crazy, giddy; twaddling, drivelling (talk); (unbesonnen) thoughtless; (flatterhaft) F (highty-) flighty; **Faselhaftigkeit** f ㊺ craziness, giddiness; thoughtlessness, F (highty-)flightiness.
Fasel=liese F (′⌣⌣...) [faseln] f ㊷ crazy (or giddy) woman or girl.
faseln (′⌣) v/n. (h.) ㊺a. (umherschwärmen) F to go (ab)out pleasuring, to gad about; weitS. (Scherz treiben) to have (great) fun, F to skylark; (phantasieren) dumm reden) to ramble, to talk at random, to (talk) twaddle, to drivel.

fäseln (′⌣) = fasern.
Fasel=vieh (′⌣...) n ㊷ breeding-cattle.
fasen¹ (′⌣) v/a. ㊾ (abschrägen) to bevel, to chamfer.
Fasen² (′⌣) m ㉓ thread = Fase².
fasen=nackt (′⌣⌣) a. ㊿ stark naked.
Faser (′⌣) [mhd.] f ㊸ (Faden) thread; von Bohnen ꝛc.: string; von Fleisch ꝛc.: (a. anat.) fibre; ♃ auch: ⚲ filament; ~n pl. an Wolle und Baumwolle: pile sg.
faser=artig (′⌣⌣) a. ㊿ fibrous.
Fäserchen (′⌣⌣) n ㉓ (dim. von Faser) small fibre; (Muskel= ꝛc.)~: ⚲ fibril, fibrilla, funicle.
Faser=gewebe (′⌣...) n ㊷ ♃ u. anat. fibrous tissue, ⚲ prosenchyma; **=gips** m = =kalk.
faserig (′⌣⌣) a. ㊿ stringy, thready; ⚲ fibrous, filamentous, filaceous.
Faser=kalk (′⌣...) m ㊷ min. fibrous gypsum, limestone; **=kiesel** m, min. fibrolite, fibrous quartz; **=los** a. fibreless, v. Bohnen ꝛc.: not stringy.
fasern (′⌣) v/a. u. sich ^ v/refl. ㊺a. to ravel (out); gefasert: ⚲ fibrillate(d).
faser=nackt (′⌣...) a. ㊿ = fasennackt; **=pflanze** ♃ f ㊷ thread-plant; **=stoff** m, chm.: ⚲ fibrin(e), ♃ vegetable fibrin(e); **=stoffhaltig** a.: ⚲ fibrinous; **=wurzel** f fibrous (or fibrillated) root.
fasig (′⌣) = faserig.
Faß (′) [ahd.: vat] n ③a, 6. (als Maß pl. inv.) 1. cask; kleines ~ (small) barrel; kilderkin; für Heringe ꝛc.: keg; für Talg ꝛc.: firkin; großes ~ butt, hogshead, tun; (Bütte) vat, tub; ~ Butter tub of butter; vgl. anstechen 2; ein ~ aufsetzen ob. binden to hoop a cask; nach dem Fasse schmecken to taste of the cask; Bier vom ~ draught ale or stout; Wein vom ~ wine from the wood; in Fässer füllen, packen to barrel, to cask. — 2. fig. so dick wie ein ~ as big as a butt or a tub; vgl. ausschlagen 8 und Boden 3.
Fassade (⌣′⌣) [fr. façade] f ㊸ arch. (Vorderseite) front(side), (fr.) façade.
Faß=band (′...) n ㊷ hoop.
faßbar (′-) a. ㊿ seizable, ⚲ prehensible; fig. geistig: comprehensible.
Faß=bier (′...) n ㊷ (ant. Flaschenbier) draught beer or ale or stout; **=binder** (=lohn) m cooper(age) (s. Böttcher=...); **=boden** ⊕ m bottom (or head) of a cask; **=bohrer** ⊕ m Böttcherei: piercer, gimlet; **=brücke** f (Tonnenbrücke) cash-bridge; **=butter** f (ant. Stückenbutter) tub-butter; inferior butter.
Fäßchen (′⌣) n ⓪b. dim. v. Faß (f. d§ 1).
Faß=daube ⊕ (′...) f ⊕ Böttcherei: stave; **=daubenholz** n wood for staves.
fassen (′⌣) [ahd.] ⊕ I v/a. 1. to seize, to take (or lay) hold of; Fußballspiel: to tackle; mit der ganzen Hand, mit der Faust: to clutch, to grasp; (fangen) to catch (hold of); (festnehmen) to arrest; an der Hand ^ to take by the hand; beim Kragen ^ to take (by the) collar. — 2. fig. Abneigung gegen ein ^ to take a dislike to a p.; ins Auge ^ to fix one's glance upon; fig. to have in view; e=n scharf ins Auge ^ to look a p. straight in the face; e=n bei der Ehre ^ to appeal to a p.'s honour;

to rouse a p.'s ambition; f. Fuß 2; einen Gedanken ^ to form (or conceive) an idea; sich (dat.) ein Herz ^ to take heart (of grace); eine Meinung ^ to form an opinion; Mut ^ to summon up courage, einen Vorsatz ^ to form a resolution, to resolve; e=n beim Worte ^ to take a p. at his word; Wurzel ^ to take root, Zuneigung zu e=m ^ to conceive an affection for a p.; ☿ Brot, Geld ꝛc. ^ (empfangen) to receive ..., to take ... — 3. Bier, Wein ꝛc. ^ (in ein Faß ꝛc. füllen) to put in(to); bibl. Most in alte Schläuche ^ to put new wine into old bottles. — 4. ⊕ = einfassen I; fig. in schöne Worte ^ to couch (or put, frame) in fine words. — 5. (aufnehmen können) to hold; der Saal faßt hundert Menschen the room holds (or accommodates) a hundred people; fig. in sich ^ to include, comprise, embrace. — 6. (begreifen) den Sinn einer Stelle ^ to seize (or F catch) the meaning of a passage; der Knabe faßt leicht ... is quick (of comprehension). — 7. (ausdrücken) f=e Meinung klar, bestimmt, knapp ^ to express one's opinion clearly, definitely, briefly; seine Meinung (ob. v/refl. sich) kurz ^ to sum up (or summarize, compress) one's view(s) in a few words, to be brief; bitte, ^ Sie sich kurz! F please cut it short!; um die Sache kurz zu ^ to put the whole thing in a nutshell. — II sich ^ v/refl. 8. f. 7. — 9. sich mit e=m (beim Ringen) ^ to grapple with a p. — 10. (sich zs.=nehmen) to contain (or collect, restrain) o.s.; sich in Geduld ^ to resign o.s.; er konnte sich vor Freude nicht ^ he was beside himself with joy; ^ Sie sich! compose yourself! — 11. etwas faßt sich, läßt sich ^ ... can be (easily) understood. — III v/n. (h.) 12. ⊕ v. Maschinenteilen: in=ea. ^ to catch, to clench. — IV ~ n ㉓ = Fassung 1. — V **ge=faßt** p.p. u. a. ㊿ 13. in den Beb. des inf. — 14. (ergeben) resigned; (ruhig) calm; (besonnen) cool(-headed); auf etwas (vorbereitet) sein to be prepared (or ready) for a th.; auf alles ^ resigned to whatever may (or might) happen.
fässer=weise (′⌣...) adv. in casks or barrels or kegs, f. Faß 1.
Faß=geschmack (′...) m ㊷ taste of the cask; **=hahn** ⊕ m tap of a cask; spigot; **=holz** n cask- (or staff-)wood, staves pl.
fässig (′⌣) a. ㊿ ?es Bier beer fit for the cask, beer ready to be casked.
Fäßlein (′-) n ㉓ dim. v. Faß (f. d§ 1).
faßlich (′⌣) a. ㊿ comprehensible, conceivable, vgl. begreiflich; **~keit** (′⌣...) f ㊻ comprehensibility, conceivableness.
Fasson (fä=ßŋ′) [fr. façon] f ㊿, öst. a. (Form) shape, pattern, fashion, make, aus der ~ out of shape; F ohne ~ (Umstände) without ceremony or ado; **~=eisen** ⊕ n, metall. figured iron.
fassonieren ⊕ (⌣ßŋ⌣′⌣) [fr. façonner] v/a. (gestalten) to shape, to fashion; a. **fassoniert** (geblümt) figured; **fassonierte Artikel** fancy articles or goods pl.
Faß=pech (′...) n ㊷ cooper's pitch; **=reif**, **=reifen** m hoop (of a cask or barrel); **=schnecke** f, zo.

♪ Musik; ⚲ Wissenschaft; ♃ Pflanze; ♀ Geographie; ⊕ Technik; ⚒ Bergbau; ⚔ Militär; ⚓ Marine; ⚖ Handel; ✉ Post; 🚂 Eisenbahn.

[**Faßspund**] — 358 — [**Faust**]

tun (*Do'lium*); =**spund** *m* bung (of the cask). [faffen.]
faßt (˘; *Hom.* faft) 2. u. 3. Perf. pres. von
Faſſung (ˬ) *f* ⓰ 1. seizure; capture. 2. eines Schmuckes: mounting; einer Rede ꝛc.: wording, style, diction; schriftlich: draft, drafting. — 3. (f. faffen 10) (Gemütsruhe) contentment, resignation, calmness; ganz außer ~ quite beside o.s., thoroughly upset; aus der ~ bringen to disconcert, to upset; durch Anstieren: to stare out of countenance; (nicht) aus der ~ kommen to lose (to retain) one's self-control or self-command; ohne aus der ~ zu kommen without being upset or put out; die ~ verlieren to lose one's head.
Faſſungs=gabe (ˬ...) *f* ⓰, =**kraft** *f* (power of) comprehension, mental capacity; das geht über meine =kraft it passes my comprehension, F that's beyond me; =**los** *a.* ⓰ disconcerted; =**losigkeit** *f* disconcertedness; =**vermögen** *n* = =gabe.
Faß=waren ⚓ (ˬ...) *f/pl.* ⓰ goods *pl.* in casks or barrels; =**weise** *adv.* by the cask, in casks or barrels.
faſt (˘; *Hom.* faßt) [ahd. = feſt] *adv.* = beinahe; ~ nichts scarcely (or hardly) anything; ~ nie hardly ever; ~ nur (noch) almost entirely, barely; ~ unmöglich well-nigh impossible; ich möchte ~ glauben, daß // I could almost (or I feel inclined to) believe that //.
Faſttage, r-r. Fuſttage (ˬ'ˬ) [+ fr.] *f* ⓰ Böttcherei: cooperage.
Faſte † (ˬ) [ahd.] *f* ⓰ = **Faſten**¹.
Faſten¹ (ˬ) [ahd.: faſt] *f/sg.* und *pl. inv.* 1. fast(ing); f. faſten II. — 2. (die 40 Tage vor Oſtern) Lent; ~ halten to keep Lent.
faſten² (ˬ) [ahd.: faſt] **I** *v/n.* (h.) ⓰: a) (nichts eſſen) to fast, to abstain from food; b) (kein Fleiſch eſſen) to abstain from (or to eat no) meat. — **II** ~ *n* ⓰ fasting; abstention, abstinence.
Faſten=donnerſtag (ˬ...) *m* ⓰ eccl. Sacramental Thursday; =**mahlzeit** *f* bfd. ehm. lenten fare or feast; =**mäßig** *a.* lenten; =**prediger** *m*, =**predigt** *f* Lent-preacher, -sermon; =**ſonntag** *m* Sunday in Lent; =**ſpeiſe**, =**ſuppe** *f* bfd. ehm. lenten dish, soup; =**zeit** *f* Lent.
Faſter (ˬ) *m* ⓰, ~**in** *f* ⓰ one who fasts, fasting (wo)man, bisw. faster.
Faſt=nacht (ˬ·cht) [mhd.] *f* ⓰ (o.*pl.*) Shrovetide; a. =ˬ=**dienſtag**; (Faſching) carnival.
Faſtnachts=dienſtag (ˬ...) *m* ⓰ Shrove Tuesday; =**kleid** *n* carnival-dress or -garb; =**luſtbarkeit**, =**poſſe** *f*, =**ſcherz** *m*, =**ſpiel** *n*, =**ſpuk** *m*, etwa: carnival-sport or -fun or -merriment; masquerade, mummery; =**zeit** *f* = Faſtnacht.
Faſt=tag (ˬ) *m* ⓰ eccl. (ant. Fleiſchtag) fast(ing)-day; ↓ banian-day.
Faſzikel (ˬˬ) [lt.] *m* ⓶ (Bündel Papier) bundle of deeds, file of papers.
faſzinieren (ˬˬˬ) [lt.] *v/a.* ⓰ (behexen, bezaubern) to fascinate, bewitch.
Fata (ˬ) [it.] *f* = **Fee**; *phys.*: ~ **Morgana** *f* ⓶ ⓰ (Luftſpiegelung) Fata Morgana, mirage.
fatal (˘ˊ) [lt.] *a.* ⓰ (widerwärtig) disagreeable, vexatious, annoying; ~e Geſchichte F awkward affair; ~**ismus**

(˘ˬˬ) *m* ⓶ (Verhängnisglaube) fatalism; ~**iſt** (˘ˬˬ) *m* ⓴ fatalist; **Liſtiſch** (˘ˬˬ) *a.* ⓰ fatalistic; ~**ität** (˘ˬˬˊ) (Verhängnis) fatality; F (böſer Zufall) mishap, mischance; unpleasant business or incident; F nasty accident.
Fatum (ˊˬ) [lt.] *n* ⓳ (Verhängnis) fate, fatality; (Geſchick) destiny, lot. [fool.]
Fatzke F (ˬ) [ndd.] *m* ⓮ u. ⓰ simpleton.]
fauchen (ˊˬ) [mhd.] **I** *v/n.* (h.) ⓰ Katze ꝛc.: to spit (after the manner of a cat); die Lokomotive the whizzing (or hissing) engine. — **II** ~ *n* ⓰ spitting (like a cat); das ~ des Zuges the whizzing (or hissing) of the train.
faul (ˊ) [ahd.: foul] **I** *a.* ⓰ 1. (ant. friſch) rotten, putrid, (zerſetzt) decomposed, putrefied, v. Steinen ꝛc.: mouldering, crumbling; ~ werden to rot, putrefy, decay; ~es Ei rotten (or bad) egg; ~es Fleiſch rotten (or tainted, bad) meat; *path.* in Wunden: proud flesh; ~e Gärung putrefaction; ~er (bröckeliger) Zahn decayed (or carious) tooth; ↓ ~e Küſte unhealthy coast. — 2. *fig.* ~e Fiſche, ~e Redensarten (leere Vorwände) hollow pretexts, lame excuses, artful shifts *pl.*; ~er Fleck sore point; ~er Junge, ~er Kopf good-for-nothing, P rotter; ~er Kram rotten affair; ~er Kunde fishy (or slippery) customer; e-n auf dem ~en Pferde finden f. fahl *fig.*; ~e Sache queer (F rotten) affair; ~e Witze *m/pl.* bad jokes *pl.*; ~er Zauber humbug; ~e Zuſtände corrupt (or rotten) state of affairs; *adv.* es steht ~ mit der Sache things are in a bad way. — 3. ~ (ſchlecht) inferior, of low quality; von Wechſeln ꝛc.: worthless. — 4. (träge) lazy, indolent, slothful; (müßig) idle; gräßlich (ob. stinkend) ~ bone-lazy; sich auf die ~e Haut (ob. Seite) legen to lead an idle life, to lounge about; ~er Kerl, Menſch, Strick lazy fellow, idle vagabond; F lazybones *fig.*; er, nicht ~ (ohne zu warten), sprang auf sie los he, without a moment's hesitation, rushed at them. — **II** ~**e**(**s**) ⓰ 5. rotten (or decayed) substance. — **III** ~(**[r**] *m*) *f* ⓰ 6. sluggard; f. Faulenzer 1.
faulbar (ˊˬ) *a.* ⓰ corruptible; putrescible; ~**keit** (ˊˬ) *f* ⓰ corruptibility.
Faul-baum ⚘ (ˊ...) *m* ⓮ black alder(-tree) (*Fra'ngula Alnus*); =**beere** ⚘ *f* (Frucht des ~baumes) black alder-berry; =**bett** *n* bed of ease, idle couch; =**bruch** ⊕ *m* des Schmiedeeiſens: shortness (or brittleness) of wrought iron; =**brut** ⚯ Bienenkrankheit: foul-brood.
Fäule (ˊˬ) *f* ⓰ rot(tenness); f. Fäulnis.
faulen (ˊˬ) **I.** *v/n.* (h.) ⓰ ⓲ to rot, decay, putrefy; vom Fleiſche ꝛc.: F to turn (or go) bad; ~d rotting, ~ putrescent; vom Fleiſche: tainted, high. — **II** ~ *n* ⓳ rotting, decay, putrefaction; *fig.* corruption; ~ putrescence.
fäulen (ˊˬ) *v/a.* ⓰ (faul machen) to rot, decay, make putrid.
faulenzen (ˊˬˬ) [mhd. 16. sae.] *v/n.* (h.) ⓰ to lead an idle life; ~ to idle (away one's time); to be idle (or lazy); to spend a life of idleness or indolence; (umherlungern) to lounge (F to lazy, P to hang-slang or rot) about.

Faulenzer (ˊˬˬ) *m* ⓶ 1. (auch ~**in** *f* ⓰) sluggard, idler, idle (or lazy) person, lounger, F lazybones; ~**leben** *n* = Faulenzerei 1. — 2. comfortable chair; (Polſter) ottoman, (soft) couch, cushion.
Faulenzerei (ˊˬˬˬ) *f* ⓰ 1. lazy (or idle, useless) life or existence; (Umherlungern) lounging (F lazying) about. — 2. = Faulheit.
Faul-fieber (ˊ...) *n*, *path.* putrid fever; *co.* (fit of) idleness, lazy fit; =**fleck** *m* putrid spot, auf Obſt ꝛc.: speck; ⁰**fleckig** *a.* ⓰ with putrid spots.
Faulheit (ˊˬ) *f* ⓰ idleness, laziness, indolence, sloth, slothfulness; lazy (or indolent) ways or habits *pl.*
faulicht, **faulig**, **fäulig** (ˊˬ) *a.* ⓰ rotten, decayed, putrid; (faulend) rotting, ~ putrescent; faulige Gärung ~ putrefactive fermentation.
Fäulnis (ˊˬ) *f* ⓲ rottenness, putrefaction; (Verweſung) corruption, decay; (Zerſetzung) decomposition, rotting, ~ putrescence; des Holzes: dry-rot; *path.* der Knochen: ~ caries; *fig.* ſittliche ~ moral corruption; in ~ geraten, übergehen to rot, putrefy, decay; ~ bewirkend causing decay, ~ septic; ~ hindernd preventing decay, ~ antiseptic.
Fäulnis-prozeß (ˊ...) *m* ⓮ process of decomposition or decay; =**widrig** *a.* ⓰ staying decay, ~ antiseptic.
Faul-pelz (ˊ...) *m* ⓮ = Faulenzer 1; =**tier** *n*: a) zo. sloth (*Bra'dypus*); b) = Faulenzer 1.
Faulung (ˊˬ) *f* ⓰ = faulen II.
Faul-weizen ⚘ (ˊ...) *m* ⓮ smut-fungus or -ball (*Tille'tia ca'ries*); =**werden** *n* decay, putrefaction, ~ putrescence.
Faum (ˊ) [mhd.: foam] *m* ⓮ foam, froth = **Feim**¹ (Schaum).
Faun (ˊ) [lt.] *m* ⓮c., ~**in** *f* ⓰ *myth.* (Waldgott) Faun; *fig.* (lüſterner Menſch) grossly sensual person.
Fauna (ˊˬ) [lt.] *f* ⓱ (Geſamtheit der Tiere eines Landes) fauna.
faun(en)=artig (ˊ(ˬ)...) *a.* ⓰ = fauniſch; =**blick** *m* lascivious glance.
fauniſch (ˊˬ) [Faun] *a.* ⓰ faun-like; (lüſtern) lascivious, lecherous, sensual.
Fauſt¹ (ˊ) [ahd.: fiſt] *f* ⓴ 1. fist; *co.* große ~ (Hand) F big paw; F ballen 1; aus der ~ eſſen to have an impromptu meal; sich mit Fäuſten schlagen to come to fisticuffs, F to have a (free) fight; mit dem Schwert in der ~ (with) sword in hand; mit eiſerner ~ with a mailed fist, with an iron grip; e-m eine ~ machen, mit der ~ drohen to shake one's fist at a p. — 2. *fig.* et. auf eigene ~ tun to do a th. on one's own responsibility or F on one's own hook; aus freier ~ (aus dem Stegreif) extempore; (ſich) in die ~ (auch ins Fäuſtchen) lachen (ſich heimlich freuen) to laugh in one's sleeve; eine ~ im Sacke machen (f-n Zorn verbergen) to conceal one's anger, to chafe inwardly; von der ~ weg ſchreiben ... with ease; das paßt (ob. reimt ſich) wie die ... aufs Auge that's hardly suitable for the purpose (in view); they are as different as chalk from (*iro.* as like as chalk and) cheese; vgl. Auge 5 unter auf.

Signs (see page XVII): F familiar; P vulgar; Ƒ flash; ⚹ rare; † obsolete (died); * new word (born); ₊₊ incorrect; ♪ music;

Faust² (´) *npr/m.* [15][16] [S][A]α. 1. [lt. *faustus* glücklich] Doktor ~ Doctor Faustus; ~ (Drama von Goethe, Oper ꝛc.) Faust. — 2. Johann ~ = Fust.
Faust²=ausgabe (´´...) *f* [62] edition of (Goethe's) Faust.
Fäustchen (´⌣) *n* [23] (*dim.* von Faust¹) small fist; sich ins ~ lachen s. Faust¹ 2.
faust¹=dick (´´⌣) *a.* [66] (as) big as a fist; er hat es 2 hinter den Ohren he is a sly fox *or* F a sly-boots *or* up to snuff; he isn't such a fool as he looks; F es kam 2 F it came all of a heap.
Fäustel ⚒ (´⌣) *n* [22] miner's hammer.
Faust¹=griff (´´...) *m* [62] grip (of one's fist); 2**groß** *a.* [66] (as) big as a fist, F *co.* no bigger than two twopenny loaves; =**handschuh** *m* mitten; =**hobel** ⚙ *m* small smoothing-plane.
faustisch (´⌣) [Faust²] *a.* [66] like (*or* after the manner of) Faust.
Faust¹=kampf (´´...) *m* [62] pugilistic encounter *or* contest *or* fight; boxing-match; F fisticuffs *pl.*; =**kämpfer** *m* pugilist; vgl. Boxer.
Faust²=legende (´´...) *f* [62] legend (*or* story, myth) of Doctor Faustus.
Fäustlein (´⌣) *n* [23] = Fäustchen.
Fäustling (´⌣) *m* [G]d. = Fausthandschuh.
fäustlings (´⌣) *adv.* with the fist(s).
Faust¹=pfand (´´...) *n* [62] *jur.* dead pledge; =**recht** *n* law of the strongest, right of the stronger; club-law; =**riemen** ⚔ *m* der Kavallerie: sword-knot.
Faust²=sage (´´...) *f* [62] = =legende.
Faust¹=schlag (´´...) *m* [62] blow (*or* stroke) with the fist; cuff, F punch.
Faustus (´⌣) *npr/m.* [16]γ. = Faust².
Faust¹=voll (´´⌣) *f, inv.* handful.
Fauteuil (fo-tö'j) [fr.; *dtsch. Faltstuhl] *m* [S] easy chair, arm-chair.
Faut=fracht ⚓ (fō''⌣cht) [fr.-dtsch.] *f* [62] (Fehlfrachtvergütung) dead freight.
Fauxpas (fō'-pā) [fr. falscher Schritt] *m* [55] (Fehltritt; Verstoß) false (*or* wrong) step, (fr.) *faux pas.*
favorisieren (⌣w⌣´⌣) [fr.] *v/a.* [93] (begünstigen) to favour, to patronize.
Favorit (⌣w⌣´) *m* [42], **~e** *f* [48], **~in** *f* [47] [fr. *favori(te)*] (Günstling) favourite; *contp.* minion; **~=sulta'nin** (´...) *f* [62] favourite sultana.
Faxe (´⌣) [nhd. 18. *sae.*] *f* [48], **~rei** (´⌣´´) *f* [46] trick(ery), farce, (tom)foolery, buffoonery; ich lasse mir keine ~n vormachen I won't be imposed upon; **~n=macher** (´⌣=´⌣) *m* [62] buffoon, wag, clown, bisw. (fr.) farceur.
Fayence (⌣jä'ß(*)) [fr. *faïence*; *it. Faë'nza 🌐 St.] *f* [48] (Halbporzellan) common china (-ware), bisw. faience; holländische ~ bsd. ehm.: Delft-ware; **~=geschäft** *n* [62] (Geschirrladen) china-shop.
Fazies 🔬 (´(⌣)⌣) [lt.] *f, inv. anat.*, 🌐, *geol.* (Angesicht, Oberfläche) face.
Fazit (´⌣) [lt. *fa'cit* es macht] *n* [U]e., [S] *arith.* u. *fig.* result, answer; 💰 amount; das ~ ziehen aus to sum up the results of.
F.D.O. ⚔ *abbr.* = Felddienstordnung.
Feber *provc.* (´⌣) *m* [22] = Februar.
Februar (´⌣⌣) [lt.] *m* [16]d. February.
fechsen südd. (´⌣) *v/n.* (h.) [90] (Reben senken) to provine, to lay a vine-shoot in the ground; *hcrt.* (Sämereien ꝛc. ziehen) to grow plants from seeds. [vine-shoot.]
Fechser ⚘ (´⌣) *m* [22] (Senkrebe) provine,
Fechsung (´⌣) *f* (s. fechsen): Samen eigener ~ (Zucht) self-grown seeds *pl.*
Fecht=art (´...) *f* [62] manner (*or* style) of fencing; =**boden** *m* fencing-school *or* -room *or* -loft; =**bruder** F *m* beggar, F cadger; =**degen** *m* zum Stoßen: foil; zum Hauen: rapier.
fechten (´⌣) [ahd.: fight] [S]b. **I** *v/n.* (h.) ⚔ 1. (kämpfen) to fight (with a sword). — 2. *fenc.* to fence, to handle the sword, to practise swordsmanship; auf den Hieb, den Stoß 2 to strike, to thrust. — 3. mit den Händen 2 (hin u. herfahren) to spar (with one's hands), to move (*or* throw) one's hands about; to gesticulate — 4. von Handwerksburschen: (betteln) to go begging *or* F cadging. — **II** *v/a.* 5. ⚔ ein Gefecht 2 to fight a battle; *fenc.* e-n Gang 2 to fight one round. — **III** ~ *n* [23] 6. (s. 1) fight(ing); combat; (s. 2) fencing; swordsmanship; ~ auf Hieb und Stoß cut and thrust.
Fechter (´⌣) *m* [22] 1. fighter, fencer, swordsman; (Faustkämpfer) pugilist. — 2. röm. Alt.: gewerbsmäßiger ~ gladiator.
Fechter=abstand (´...) *m* [62] *fenc.* ⚔ (Mensu'r) (measured) distance of swordsmen; =**gang** *m*, *fenc.* fencing-match; a. assault of arms, onset; bout; =**kampf** *m* swordsmen's contest, sword-fight; =**kunst** *f*: a) = Fechtkunst; b) (List e-s Fechters) swordman's trick *or* knack; 2**mäßig** *a.* [66] according to the laws of swordsmanship; =**spiele** *n/pl.* röm. Alt.: gladiatorial games *pl.*; =**sprung** *m* (fencer's) leap backwards, =**stellung** *f* swordsman's (*or* fencing) attitude *or* posture; sich in ~ halten to take (up) one's guard *or* position.
Fecht=handschuhe (´...) *m/pl.* [62] fencing-gloves *pl.*; =**kunst** *m* (art of) fencing; swordsmanship; =**lehrer**, =**meister** *m* fencing-master; =**platz** *m*: a) (Kampfplatz) scene of combat *or* action, arena; b) = =boden; =**saal** *m* = =boden; =**schule** *f* fencing-academy; vgl. =boden; =**schüler** *m*: a) pupil of a fe.-academy; b) F young cadger; =**stock** *m* fencing-(*or* single-)stick; =**stunde** *f* fe.-lesson; =**übung** *f* fe.-practice; =**unterricht** *m* instruction in fencing *or* swordsmanship; er hat ~ gehabt, auch: he has learnt fencing. — Vgl. auch Fechter=...
Feder (´⌣) [ahd.: feather] *f* [48] 1. eines Vogels: feather; (Flaum=)~ down; (Schmuck=)~ plume; kleine Feder a. plumelet, 🔬 plumule; e-m Vogel die ~n ausrupfen to strip a bird of its feathers, to pluck a bird; *fig.* sich mit fremden ~n schmücken to adorn o.s. with (*or* to appear in) borrowed plumes; er liegt noch in den ~n he is still in bed *or* F between the sheets. — 2. (Schreib=)~ pen; (Gänse=)~ quill-pen; e-e ~ schneiden to make a pen; s. Stahl=2; die ~ führen to wield the pen; ein Werk unter der ~ haben to have a work in hand; Mann von der ~ man of the pen, writer, literary (gentle-) man; von der ~ leben to live by one's pen; *fig.* e-m et. in die ~ diktieren to dictate s.th. to a p. — 3. ⚙ (Sprung=)~ spring; (Uhr=)~ watch-spring; auf ~n ruhen to rest (*or* balance) on springs; Wagen auf ~n spring-carriage *or* -cart *or* -van. — 4. ⚘ (Samen=)~: 🔬 gemmule.
feder=ähnlich (´´...) *a.* [66] = 2artig; =**alaun** *m* [62] *min.* plume- (*or* feather-) alum, 🔬 halotrichite; =**arbeiter(in** *f*) *m* plume-maker; feather-cleaner; 2**artig** *a.* feather-like, feathery, downy; 🔬 plumose; ⚙ (federnd) springy, elastic; =**artigkeit** *f* springiness, elasticity; =**ball** *m* shuttlecock; =**ballspiel** *n* battledore and shuttlecock; =**besen** *n* feather-brush *or* -broom *or* -duster, whisk; =**bett** *n* feather-bed; (Deckbett) quilt; =**bleiche** *f*, =**bleicher** *m* feather-bleaching, -bleacher; =**büchse** *f* pen(cil)-case; =**busch**, =**büschel** *m* tuft of feathers, plume, *orn.* a. crest, 🔬 plumicorn; (Reiherbusch) aigret(te).
Federchen (´⌣⌣) *n* [23] = kleine Feder.
Feder=deckbett (´´...) *n* [62], =**decke** *f* eiderdown (*or* feather) quilt; =**erz** *n*, *min.* feather-ore, 🔬 heteromorphite; =**fächer** *m* f.-fan; 2**förmig** *a.* [66] f.-shaped, 🔬 penniform; =**fuchser** *m* F quill-driver, ink-spiller, scribbler; *Am.* ink-slinger; =**fuchserei** *f* F quill-driving; scribbling; 2**füßig** *a. orn.*: 🔬 plumiped; =**geistchen** *n* = =motte; =**gips** *m*, *min.* striate gypsum; =**gras** ⚘ *n* feather-grass (*Stipa penna'ta*); =**halter** *m* penholder; =**handel**, =**händler** *m* feather-trade, -merchant; 2**hart** *a.* springy, elastic; =**härte** *f* des Stahls springiness; =**harz** *n* India rubber, caoutchouc; **harz=baum** ⚘ *m* caoutchouc-tree (*Sipho'nia ela'stica*); =**haus** *n* e-r Uhr: spring-barrel; =**held** *m* knight of the quill; =**hut** *m* hat adorned with (ostrich-, &c.) feathers.
federicht, **federig** (´⌣⌣) *a.* [66] feather-like, feathery; vgl. feder=artig.
Feder=kasten (´´...) *m* [62] pen(cil)-box *or* -case; =**kiel** *m* quill; =**kissen** *n* (eider)down-cushion *or* -pillow; =**kleid** *n* der Vögel: plumage; =**kraft** *f* springiness, elasticity; =**krieg** *m* paper-war, literary feud; =**krone** ⚘ *f* pappus; =**kupfer** ⚒ *n* feathershot; 2**leicht** *a.* [66] (as) light as a feather.
Federlein (´⌣⌣) *n* [23] = Federchen.
Feder=lesen (´´...) [mhd.] *n* [62] picking of feathers; *fig.* nicht viel ~s (Umstände) machen to make short work of (F no bones about) a th.; 2**los** *a.* [66] plumeless, without feathers, plumes *or* springs; *orn.* (nicht flügge) unfledged; =**matra'tze** *f* spring-mattress; =**messer** *n* penknife; =**motte** *f*, *ent.* plume-moth (*Ptero'phorus*).
federn (´⌣) [S]a. **I** *v/n.* (h.) 1. to shed (one's) feathers; die Betten 2 (sehr) ... are (fast) losing their down. — **II** *v/n.* u. **sich** 2 *v/refl.* 2. *orn.* (mausern) to moult, to mew. — 3. ⚙ (Federkraft haben) to be springy *or* elastic, to fly back, to move on springs. — **III** *v/a.* 4. ein Bett 2 to fill a tick with feathers, to make a feather-bed. — 5. *hunt.* einen Vogel 2 (anschießen)

[Federnelke] — 360 — [fehlgebären]

(slightly) to graze a bird. — 6. Lynch: e-n teeren u. 2 to tar and feather a p.
Feder-nelke ⚥ (*ᴵᴵ⌣*...) *f* ⑫ feathered (or plumed) pink (*Dianthus pluma'rius*); =**pfriemengras** ⚥ *n* = =gras; =**pfühl** *m* feather-bolster; =**pose** *f* = =kiel; =**reinigungsmaschine** ⊕ *f* feather-cleaner, -beater; =**schloß** *n* spring-bolt, -lock; =**schmuckarbeit** *f* plume-work; =**schmücker(in** *f*) *m* = =arbeiter(in); =**schneider** *m* pen-cutter; =**schraube** *f* spring-vice; =**skizze** *f* pen-and-ink sketch or drawing; =**spalt** *m* slit of a pen or a nib; =**spanner** *m* = =schraube; =**spiel** *n* Falknerei: (s. Zurückrufen der Falken) lure; =**spule** *f* quill; =**stahl** *m* spring-steel; =**stift** *m* e-r Uhr: spring-arbor; =**strich** *m* stroke of the pen; =**tiere** *n/pl. zo.* feathered (⨂ pennigerous) animals *pl.*; =**vieh** *n* poultry, *co.* literary folk(s) *pl.*; =**viehhändler** *m* poulterer; =**wage** *f* spring-balance; =**wagen** *m* spring-carriage; vgl. Feder 3; =**wechsel** *m* = Mauser²; =**weiße(r)** *m* (in voller Gärung befindlicher Weinmost) fermenting new wine in the highest state of effervescence; =**wild** *n*, =**wildbret** *n* wildfowl(s *pl.*), feathered game; =**wisch** *m* pen-wiper; =**wolke** *f* ⚇ cirrus (cloud); ²**wolkig** *a.* ⚇ cirrous; =**zange** *f* spring-tongs *pl.*; =**zeichnung** *f* = =skizze; =**zirkel** *m* spring-callipers or -dividers *pl.*; =**zug** *m* = =strich; (Namenszug) flourish.
Fee (*ᴵ*) [mhd.; fr. *fée*] *f* ⑱ fairy; *poet. auch:* fay; ~ Morga'na *s.* Fa'ta.
feen-artig (*ᴵᴵ*...) *a.* ⑯ fairy-like; =**gestalt** *f* ⑫ fairy-form.
feenhaft (*ᴸ⌣*) *a.* ⑯ fairy-like; weitS. marvellous, prodigious; (prächtig) gorgeous, magnificent, splendid.
Feen-hände (*ᴵᴵ*...) *f/pl.* ⑫ fairy-hands *pl.*; =**könig(in** *f*) *m* f.-king (-queen); =**land** *n* f.-land; =**märchen** *n* f.-tale; =**reich** *n* = =land; =**reigen** *m* fairy-dance; =**ringe** *m/pl.* f.-rings *pl.*; =**schloß** *n* f.-palace; =**stück** *n*, *thea.* pantomime, F show-piece; =**welt** *f* world of fairies.
Feerei, **Feerie** ⓢ (*ᴸ*) [fr.] *f* 1. = Feenwelt. — 2. *thea.* = Feenstück.
Fege-feuer (*ᴵᴵ⌣*...) *n* ⑫ [mhd.] *theol.* purgatory; =**lappen** *m* dish-, dusting-cloth, duster, mop; =**maschine**, =**mühle** ⊕ *f*, *agr.* winnowing-machine, -mill.
fegen (*ᴸ⌣*) [mhd.: fair rein] ⑱ I *v/a.* mit dem Besen: to sweep (auch *fig.*); mit Lappen: to wipe, scour, clean(se); mit Wasser: to wash up; ben Schornstein: to sweep; ein Schwert, Stahl ⁊c.: to polish, to furbish (up); *agr.* das Korn 2 to winnow corn; *fig.* e-m den Beutel (a. e-n) 2 (leeren) to fleece a p., F to clean a p. out; Sprichw. jeder fege vor s-r Tür sweep before your own door, mind your own business. — II *v/n.* (h. u. ſn) vom Winde ⁊c.: durch die Wüste 2 to sweep across the desert; Sturz-seen, die das Deck entlang 2 heavy seas washing the deck; *fig.* (voranstürmen) to rush ahead, to hurry (F scamper) along; to scour the country; to brush past. — III ~ *n* ㉓ sweeping, &c. (f. I); des Hauses: house-cleaning; im Frühling: spring-cleaning.
Feger (*ᴸ⌣*) *m* ㉙, ~**in** *f* ㊵ 1. sweep(er),

scourer, clean(s)er; von Geschirr ⁊c.: washer-up. — 2. *fig.* ein rechter ~ (Sausewind) F a regular harum-scarum or gadabout.
Feg-feuer (*ᴵᴵ⌣*) *n* ⑫ *s.* Fegefeuer.
Fegsel (*ᴸ⌣*) [fegen] *n* ㉒ sweepings *pl.*
Feg-teufel (*ᴵᴵ*...) *m* ㉖ (Kobold) imp who sweeps the house; (böses Weib) termagant; hag with a broom.
Feh (*ᴵ*) *f* ⑱ ♀ und ⊕ = Fäh.
Fehde (*ᴸ⌣*) [ahd.: feud: Feind] ⓕ ⑱ (Streit) dispute, quarrel; (Feindseligkeiten) feud, (open) warfare; e-m ~ ankündigen, bieten to send a challenge (of defiance) to a p.; mit e-m in ~ liegen to be at (a deadly) war with a p.
Fehde-brief (*ᴵᴵ⌣*...) *m* ⑫ letter of defiance, challenge; =**handschuh** *m* gauntlet; e-m den ~ hinwerfen to fling down the gauntlet to a p.; to hurl defiance at a p.; =**recht** *n* right of feud.
Fehe (*ᴸ⌣*) *f* ⑱ = Fähe.
Fehl (*ᴵ*) [fehlen] I *m* ⓞ*c.* = Fehler. — II **fehl**, fast † *adv.* (fälschlich) wrongly; (ohne Erfolg) amiss, in vain; er geht, tritt, schießt 2, es schlägt 2, vgl. fehlgehen, 2treten, 2schießen, 2schlagen.
fehlbar (*ᴸ⌣*) *a.* ⑯ (ant. unfehlbar) fallible; =**keit** (*ᴸ⌣⌣*) *f* ⑯ fallibility.
Fehl-betrag ⓕ (*ᴵᴵ*...) *m* ⑫ deficit, deficiency, shortage; =**bitte** *f* ungranted petition, vain request; eine ~ tun to meet with a refusal; ²**bitten** *v/n.* (h.) ⑱** to beg (or implore) in vain, to meet with a refusal; =**blatt** *n* Kartenspiel: (nicht Trumpf) inferior (or bad) card; F rubbish; =**bogen** ⊕ *m*, *typ.* imperfect sheet; =**druck** ⊕ *m*, *typ.* misprint, imperfect impression; ²**drucken** ⊕ *v/a.* ⑱** *typ.* to misprint.
fehlen¹ (*ᴸ⌣*) [mhd.: fail; * fr. *faillir*] ⑱ I *v/a.* 1. *hunt.* ⸝ den Hirsch 2 (nicht treffen) to miss the stag; e-n (nicht) Schütze a dead shot. — 2. den Weg (ob. des Weges) 2 (verfehlen) to miss (or mistake) one's way. — II *v/n.* (h.) 3. (irren) to err; to make a mistake or blunder, to blunder; (unrecht handeln) to do wrong; (sündigen) to offend against the law, &c.; to sin; er hat gefehlt (ist im Unrecht) he is in the wrong or at fault; weit gefehlt! you are quite wrong or F in the wrong box! — 4. oft *v/impers.* (nicht vorhanden sein) to be wanting; es 2 viele Bücher (große Summen) many books (large sums) are missing; es fehlt uns an Geld we are in need of (or hard up for) cash, we are (or have run) short of money, we want change; aber: es fehlt uns Geld (das wir vermissen) we are missing some money; an mir soll es nicht 2, daß // it shall not be my fault if //; es an nichts 2 lassen to spare nothing or no pains or no expense; es e-m an nichts 2 l. to let a p. feel no pinch (or not go short) of anything; sich (*dat.*) nichts 2 lassen to deny o.s. nothing, not to stint o.s. in any way; *Biologie* ⁊c.: ²des Glied missing link. — 5. (nicht zugegen sein): in der Schule ⁊c. 2 to be absent from school, &c.; falls er 2 sollte failing him, in (case of) his absence; *jur.*:

auf e-e Vorladung 2 to make default; ❧ diese Waren 2 uns we are out of these goods. — 6. (vom Ziele entfernt sein): es fehlt viel (wenig) daran, daß er seine Absicht ausführt he is (not) far from carrying out his plan; es fehlte wenig, so hätte er es zustande gebracht he very nearly did it; a little more, and he would have done it; es fehlte nur eines Haares Breite, so wäre er gefallen he was within a hair's-breadth of falling; das fehlte (nur) noch!, nie! that crowns it all; what next (will they propose)?; well, I never!; das fehlte mir gerade noch that would just finish me (up) or do for me. — 7. von der Gesundheit: was fehlt Ihnen?, auch: wo fehlt es Ihnen? what is the matter with you?, what ails you?; es fehlt ihm immer et. he is always ailing or indisposed; ihm fehlt nichts there's nothing the matter with him; he is quite well. — 8. (fehlschlagen) to fail, to fall to the ground; es kann mir nicht 2 I cannot fail to succeed or to get on; wenn alles fehlt (schlimmstenfalls) if everything fails, if the worst comes to the worst. — III ~ *n* ㉓ 9. want; (Mangel) defect, deficiency. — IV das ~**de** ⓕ 10. what is missing or lacking, deficit; shortness (of money, &c.).
...**fehlen**² vgl. be², emp².
Fehler (*ᴸ⌣*) [fehlen¹] *m* ㉒ 1. (Mangel) defect; (Makel) blemish, flaw; (Gebrechen) failing, drawback; er (es) hat viele ~, *auch*: he (it) has many shortcomings; *path.* organischer ~ constitutional ailment. — 2. (Versehen) fault; (Schnitzer) blunder; jeder hat seine ~ we all have our faults; no rose without a thorn; ~ gegen die Grammatik, die Syntax grammatical, syntactical mistake or error; ~ gegen die Reinheit der Sprache barbarism; einen ~ begeh(e)n to make a mistake, to (make a) slip, to be at fault; ~ machen to make mistakes, to blunder, to go on the wrong track.
fehler-frei (*ᴵᴵ⌣*...) *a.* ⑯ faultless, correct, flawless, without a flaw; (gesund) sound; =**freiheit** *f* ⑫ faultlessness, correctness; =**grenze** *f*, *math.* approximation; für Maße, Münzen ⁊c.: limit of inaccuracy, maximum (of) deficiency.
fehlerhaft (*ᴸ⌣⌣*) *a.* ⑯ faulty, defective, deficient; (schadhaft) damaged, unsound; (unrichtig) incorrect; ❧ ⊕ ²e Stelle in einem Stoffe ⁊c.: flaw, blemish; Kabel, Telegraphenleitung ⁊c.: fault; ~**igkeit** (*ᴸ⌣⌣⌣*) *f* ⑯ faultiness, unsoundness, incorrectness. [= =frei(heit).
fehler-los (*ᴵᴵ⌣*...) *a.* ⑯, =**losigkeit** *f* ⑯
Fehler-verzeichnis ⓕ (*ᴵᴵ⌣*...) *n* ⑫ *typ.* (list of) errata *pl.*; ²**voll** *a.* ⑯ full of faults or mistakes or blemishes.
fehl-fahren (*ᴵᴵ*...) *v/n.* (ſn) ⑱** to miss (or stray from) one's way or path; weitS. to make a mistake; =**farbe** *f* ⑫ Kartenspiel: (Farbe, die man nicht hat) renounce; =**gang** *m* wrong way or journey; *fig.* useless step, oft *auch*: F goose-chase; ²**gebären** *v/n.* (h.) ⑱f** (zu früh gebären) to have a mis-

Zeichen (f. S. XVII): F familiär; P Volkssprache; ꟼ Gaunersprache; ⸝ selten; † alt (auch gestorben); * neu (auch geboren); ⁺⁺ unrichtig;

[Fehlgeburt] — 361 — [fein]

carriage; =geburt f ⊕ miscarriage; abortion; ≈geh(e)n v/n. (ſn) ⊕** to miss one's way; to go astray or wrong (a. fig.); ⌘ von Briefen ꝛc.: to miscarry; ~ n ⊕ = gang; =greifen v/n. (h.) ⊕b** to miss one's hold, to touch a wrong note; fig. to make a wrong (or bad) choice or a mistake; ~ n, =griff m ⊕ bad choice; mistake; =hieb m cut (or thrust, blow) which misses; F miss; =farte f = =blatt; =kauf ⊕ m bad bargain; ≈kaufen ⊕ v/n. (h.) ⊕** to make a bad bargain; ≈laufen v/n. (ſn) ⊕aſt** to run the wrong way; ≈leiten v/a. ⊕** to lead the wrong way, to mislead; ≈rechnen v/n. (h.) ⊕b** to make a wrong calculation, to miscalculate; ≈ſchießen v/n. (h.) ⊕c(eſ)** to shoot wide of the mark, to miss one's aim or the mark or the bull's-eye; fig. to make a bad hit; =ſchlag m = =hieb; ≈ſchlagen v/n. (h. u. ſn) ⊕b** to miss (in striking) a blow; fig. to fail, to meet with disappointment; die Sache ist fehlgeschlagen the attempt has been unsuccessful or has ended in failure; ~ n ⊕ fig. failure, disappointment, ❡ abortiveness; ≈ſchließen v/n. (h.) ⊕d** to draw a wrong inference or a false conclusion; =ſchluß m false conclusion or inference, ⟨/⟩ paralogism; =ſchuß m shot missing (or wide of) the mark; bad (or stray) shot; vgl. fehlſchießen; =ſprung m leap short of one's aim; =ſtoß m badly aimed blow or thrust or lunge; ≈ſtoßen v/n. (h.) ⊕a** to miss (one's aim) in thrusting or lunging; Billard: to miss the ball; =ſumme ⊕ f = =betrag; ≈treten v/n. (h.) ⊕d** to miss one's footing; to slip, to stumble (a. fig.); =tritt m ⊕ false step, slip (a. fig.); F fig. e-n ~ tun to take a false step, to make a (fr.) faux pas, to get o.s. into trouble; vgl. fehltreten; =wurf m misthrow, F miss; =zug m Schach: bad (or wrong) move.

Fehm=... ꝛc. ſ. Fem-gericht ꝛc.
Fehn (¹) m ⊕c. = Feim(en).
Fehn (¹) m u. n ⊕c. (Sumpf) fen, bog.
Feh=werk (ᴴᵛ) n ⊕ = Fährwerk.
feien (ᴸᵛ) [Feiᵗ = Fee] v/a. ⊕ ſ. e-n ⊕ to endow a p. with magic virtues; ein gefeites Leben a charmed life. — 2. (unverletzbar machen) to make invulnerable; ⊕ gegen to make proof (or safe) against bullets, poison, &c.
Feier (ᴸᵛ) (ahd.: fair; *lt. fē'riae) f ⊕ 1. (Begehung e-s Festes) celebration, solemnization; zur ~ des Tages in honour of the day. — 2. (das Fest ſelbſt) fête, festival; beſ. eccl. feast(day); F fine doings, junketings pl., flare-up; hundertjährige ~ centenary. — 3. (Ruhe von der Arbeit) rest, repose, holiday; (Erholung) recreation, relaxation.
Feier=abend (ᴴᵛ...) m ⊕: a) (heiliger Abend) eve of a festival; b) (Ruhe-ſtunden) cessation from work; weitS. hours pl. of leisure; ~ m., oft: to cease working or from work; =abend-glocke f evening-bell, ehm. curfew-bell; ≈abendlich a. ⊕ (what is done)

in leisure-time, Fabrik ꝛc. auch: in over-time; =gesang m = =klang. [work.]
fei(e)rig (¹(ᵛ)ᵛ) a. ⊕ (arbeitslos) out of Feier=klang (ᴴᵛ...) m ⊕ sacred melody, solemn chant, hymn; =kleid n festive attire or garment, ſ. =tagsanzug.
feierlich (ᴸᵛᵛ) a. ⊕ solemn (silence, &c.), ceremonious (rite, &c.), (würdevoll) grave (air, &c.), dignified (look, &c.); (Achtung einflößend) imposing (ceremony, &c.); ſtärker: awe-inspiring (mien, &c.); bei den Gelegenheiten on state-occasions; ⊕ begeh(e)n to solemnize, to celebrate (with great pomp); ~keit (ᴸᵛᵛ) f ⊕ solemnity, ceremony, ceremoniousness; pomp; (Festfeier) festival.
feiern (ᴸᵛ) [ahd.; * Feier] ⊕a. I v/a. 1. (begehen) to celebrate, solemnize, keep (up) to commemorate an event. — 2. (ehren, preisen) to honour, extol, exalt, praise. — II v/n. (h.) 3. (von der Arbeit ruhen) to (take) rest, to rest from one's labour(s), to cease working; to take (or make) a holiday; (müßig sein) to idle, to lounge about; wir dürfen nicht ⊕ we must not waste (or lose) any time, we must be up and doing. — 4. (die Arbeit einstellen) to leave off (F to stop) work: gemeinſchaftlich: to strike (work), to come (or go) out (on strike); die ~den pl. the strikers pl. — III ~ n ⊕ 5. (ſ. 3) holiday-making; striking, strike. — 6. (ſ. 1) celebration, solemnization; commemoration.
Feier=stunde (ᴴᵛ...) f ⊕ hour of rest or recreation; =tag m day of rest, holiday; eccl. festival, feast-day, beſ. ehm. a. red-letter day; in Schulen: halber ~ half holiday; ~e holidays pl., holiday-time, beſ. Schule u. Gericht: vacation; parl. recess; vergnügte ~e! I wish you pleasant holidays; ≈tägig ⧖, ≈täglich a. ⊕ holiday-like; =tags-anzug m, =tags-kleid n holiday- (or Sunday-)dress or attire; im höheren Stile: festive garb or raiment; ≈tags-mäßig a. festive (joy, &c.).
Feifel (ᴸᵛ) [neu-lt. vi'v(ol)ae] m ⊕, f ⊕ vet. (Mandelentzündung e-s Pferdes) lives pl.
feig¹ (¹), ≈e (ᴸᵛ) [nhd.] I a. ⊕ 1. coward-ly; (furchtsam) timid, nervous, faint-hearted; (kleinmütig) pusillanimous; ⊕e Memme poltroon; ſich ⊕ (adv.) benehmen to behave in a cowardly manner, to show the white feather. — 2. ⚔ (brödelig) crumbling or rotten (stone, rock). — II ~(e)r ⊕ 3. = feige.
Feig²-bohne ⧖ (ᴴᵛ...) [Feige²] f ⊕ lupine (Lupi'nus).
feige¹ (ᴸᵛ) a. ⊕ ſ. feig.
Feige² (ᴸᵛ) [ahd.;* lt. ficus] f ⊕ 1. (Frucht des Feigenbaumes) fig; ⊕ gedörrte~dried fig, eleme. — 2. ⊕ = ~n=baum; gemeine (Eß=)~ common fig-tree (Ficus ca'rica), indische~ =n=faktus. — 3. = Feigwarze.
feigen=ähnlich (ᴸᵛᵛ...) a. fig-like; =apfel m ⊕ fig-apple; ≈artig a. ⊕ path.: ſ. caricous; =baum m ⊕ fig-tree (Ficus); vgl. Feige² 2; =blatt n fig-leaf; ≈förmig a. fig-shaped; =fresser m, orn. (kleiner ital. Wandervogel der Gattung Sy'lvia) beccafico; ≈frucht f (Fleischiger, viele Nüßchen einschließender Fruchtboden) syconium; =kaffee m (Surroga't für Kaffee) fig-coffee; =kaktus ⧖ m (Opu'ntia vulga'ris)

Indian fig(-tree); =korb ⊕ m (v. ca. 34 kg) fig-frail; =mücke f, ent. fig-gnat (Culex fica'rius). — Vgl. auch Feig²...
Feigheit (¹⸗) f ⊕ cowardice; timidity, nervousness, faint-heartedness; pol-troonery; pusillanimity; F funk(iness); eine ~ begeh(e)n to commit a coward-ly act, to act like a coward.
feig¹=herzig (ᴴᵛ⸗) a. ⊕ = feig 1; ~keit (ᴸᵛᵛ) f ⊕ = Feigheit.
Feigling (¹ᵛ) m ⊕d. coward, timid (or nervous) person; poltroon, dastard.
Feig²-warze (ᴴ...) f ⊕ path., fig.: ⚔ sycoma, condyloma; =wurz ❡ f fig-wort (Ranu'nculus fica'ria).
feil¹ (¹) [ahd. käuflich] a. ⊕ 1. (verkäuflich) vendible, (zum Verkauf) to be sold; vgl. feilbieten; ⊕ haben = feilhalten; ⊕ ſein to be for sale; ihm ist alles ⊕ he is ready to sell (or part with) everything (he has); es ist ihm nicht um alles Geld ⊕ he would not sell it for all the money in the world. — 2. fig. merce-nary, venal, (beſtechlich) a. corruptible; ſ. Dirne; Der Mensch hireling. [block.]
Feil²=block (ᴴᵛ) [feilen] m ⊕ filing-
feil¹=bieten (ᴸᵛᵛ) v/a. ⊕a** to offer (or put up) for sale; =bietende(r m) f, =bieter(in f) m seller, vendor; sales-man, auctioneer; =bietung f offering (or putting up) for sale.
Feile (ᴸᵛ) [ahd.: file] f ⊕ file; drei-kantige (vierecktige) ~ three-sided (square) file; mit der ~ glätten to smooth with the file; beſ. fig. die letzte ~ an et. legen to give the finish-ing touch (or the last polish) to a th.; nochmals unter die ~ nehmen to polish again and again.
feilen ⊕ (ᴸᵛ) v/a. ⊕ to file; fig. to polish, to finish (off); gut gefeilt (thoroughly) well finished, highly polished.
Feilen=griff (ᴴᵛ...) m ⊕ file-handle; =halter m file-holder; =hauer m file-cutter; =stiel m = =griff. [for sale.]
feil¹=halten (ᴴᵛᵛ) v/a. ⊕a** to have Feilheit (¹⸗) [feil 2] f ⊕ b.s. mercenari-ness; venality; corruptibility.
Feilicht (¹ᵛ) [feilen] n ⊕d. filings pl., file-dust.
Feil²=kloben ⊕ (ᴴ...) m ⊕ (Handſchraubſtock) hand- (or filing-)vice; =kolben m needle-drill; =kluppe f sloping clamp of a vice; =maschine f shaping-machine.
feilschen (ᴸᵛ) [mhd.;* feil] v/n. (h.) ⊕ um et. ⊕ to bargain for a th., to haggle about a th., to barter (or chaffer) for (or about) a th.; aufs äußerste ⊕ to drive a hard (or close) bargain.
Feilscher (ᴸᵛ) m ⊕, ~in f ⊕ haggler.
Feilsel (¹) n ⊕ = Feilicht.
Feil²=späne (ᴴ...) m/pl. ⊕, =staub m = Feilicht; =stock m filing-vice; =strich stroke of (or cut with) the file.
Feim¹ (¹) [ahd.: foam] m ⊕c. foam, froth. [(Kornſchober) corn-stack.]
Feim² (¹) m ⊕c., ~en (¹ᵛ) [nhd.] fein [mhd.: fine; *fr. fin] I a. ⊕ (ant. grob) 1. (dünn und zart) fine or slender (thread), thin (cloth), delicate (skin), (aus kleinen Teilen bestehend) fine (powder), small (shot); der Regen fine (or drizzling) rain. — 2. (zierlich, ſchön) fine (watch), graceful or beautiful

[Feinbäcker] — 362 — [Felderzahl]

(form), fair (maiden); willst, der Knabe, du mit mir gehn? (g.) my handsome boy, wilt thou come with me?; (vorzüglich) fine, pure, sterling (gold); excellent or splendid (dinner), choice (fruit); F swell (company); der Geschmack refined taste; ein der Herr a fine (or elegant) gentleman; de Sitten, des Wesen elegant manners pl., demeanour; der Tisch excellent (or first-class) table; der Ton aristocratic (or superior) tone; de Welt high life, F fine (or fashionable) people, society-folk; adv. 2 gebildet highly educated, well-bred; 2 geformt well-shaped; highly bred or accomplished; 2 geputzt smartly (or elegantly) dressed; sich 2 machen to adorn o.s., to smarten o.s. up; den ~en spielen to play the fine gentleman, F to do the swell or the grand. — 3. ein der (kluger) Kopf a clever head; eine 2e Bemerkung a subtle (or sharp, shrewd) remark. — 4. ⚔ (gut, sicher) safe, secure; der (ant. fauler) Wechsel ꝛc. good bill, &c.; (sehr) de ob. 2ste (prima) Marke, Sorte prime (or first-rate, first-class, A 1) brand, quality. — 5. ✗ (ant. rauh) (rein von Beimengungen) pure, free from admixtures, refined. — 6. (gut ge=eignet) well adapted; suitable, convenient; (geschmackvoll) tasty; adv. wie 2 er reiten kann how well he can ride; gebt jetzt 2 acht! now pay good (or full) attention! — II ~e(s) n ⊕ 7. etw. ~es s.th. fine, beautiful, &c. (f. I); das ~ste von etwas the pick of the men; the cream of society; the flower of youth.
Fein=bäcker(ei f) (⍺...) m ⊕ fancy-baker(y); =brand m (geläuterter Spiritus) highly rectified spirits pl.; ⍺brennen ⊕ v/a., metall. to refine metals on the hearth; =brenner ⊕ m refiner.
Feind (⍺) [ahd.: fiend Hassender] I m ⊕b., ~in f ⊕ enemy, foe; oft durch anti- zu übersetzen, z.B.: ~(in) der Jesuiten anti-Jesuit; (Gegner) adversary, opponent; ✗ den ~ angreifen, verfolgen to attack, to pursue the enemy; zum ~e übergehen to go over to the enemy (-'s camp); abgesagter, bitter(st)er ~ professed (or inveterate), bitter(est) enemy; vgl. Tod2; der böse ~ the (foul) fiend, the evil one, the devil, F Old Nick; j-s grimmiger ~ sein ... at daggers drawn with a p.; sich e-n zum ~e machen to make an enemy of a p. — II feind a. nur als Prädikat: e-m 2 sein to be hostile (or opposed) to a p., to have a grudge against a p.; e-m 2 werden to fall out with a p.
Feindes=hand (⍺...) f ⊕ hand of an enemy; =land ✗ n hostile country or ground; =liebe f love for (or charity towards) an enemy.
Feindin (⍺) f ⊕ f. Feind.
feindlich (⍺) a. ⊕ hostile to; schwächer: opposed (or unfriendly) to; des Lager hostile camp; der Zusammenstoß hostile encounter; (angreifend) offensive movement; ✗ dem den Feuer ausgesetzt exposed to the enemy's fire, within range of the enemy's guns; adv. 2 gesinnt ill-disposed towards.

Feindschaft (⍺) f ⊕ enmity; stärker: animosity, hostility; (Groll) rancour; grudge (or ill-feeling) against; ill-will towards; in ~ mit e-m steh(e)n ob. leben to be at enmity (or at daggers drawn) with a p.; darum keine ~! no animosity!
feindschaftlich (⍺⍵) a. ⊕ = feindlich.
feindselig (⍺⍵) [nhd. aus † Feindsal u. -ig] a. ⊕ hostile, inimical, (abhold) averse to; (böswillig) ill-inclined, ill-disposed, malevolent; ~keit (⍺⍵-) f ⊕ hostility; ~keiten einstellen to suspend (or stop) hostilities.
Feine (⍺⍵) f ⊕ (o. pl.) = Feinheit; öft. = Feingehalt b. [iron.)
Fein=eisen (⍺⍵...) n ⊕ fine (or refined)
feinen ⊕ (⍺⍵) I v/a. ⊕ to refine. — II ~ n ⊕ refining, refinery.
fein=fadig (⍺...) a. ⊕, ⍺fäd(en)ig ⊕ a. fine-threaded; ⍺fühlig a. sensitive, of delicate (or tender) feeling; =fühligkeit f ⊕ sensitiveness, delicacy (or refinement) of feeling; =gehalt m: a) fineness of gold or silver; b) mint. standard of coinage; ⍺gekerbt ⊕ a.: ⍺ crenulate(d); ⍺gejägt ⊕ a.: ⍺ serrulated; ⍺gesponnen a. fine(ly)-spun; ⍺gezahnt ⊕ a.: ⍺ denticulate(d); =gold ⊕ n fine (or refined) gold.
Feinheit (⍺-) f ⊕ (f. fein) fineness; thinness; slenderness; gracefulness; elegance; refinement, polish.
Fein=herd ⊕ (⍺...) m ⊕ metall. refining-hearth; ⍺hörig a. ⊕ quick (or sharp) of hearing; ⍺körnig a. fine-grained; =kupfer ⊕ n refined copper; =maler(ei) f) mminiature-painter(...ing); =schmecker m gastronome, gastronomist; weitS.: epicure; =schmeckerei f gastronomy; weitS.: epicur(ean)ism; =schmeckerisch a. dainty, epicurean; =schmied ⊕ m, metall. white-smith; =silber ⊕ n fine (or refined) silver.
Feins=liebchen (⍺⍵...) n ⊕ poet. ladylove, sweet-heart; mein ~!, my darling!, my pet!, my love!
Fein=spindelbank ⊕ (⍺...) f ⊕ Spinnerei: fly-roving-frame; =spinnmaschine f, =stuhl m ⊕ spinning-frame, jenny; =stopfer(in f) m finedrawer, renterer; =strahl ✱ m stenactis (Stena′ctis a′nnua); =tischler m cabinet-maker; ⍺wollig ⊕ a. ⊕: ⍺ lanuginous, ...ose; =zinn ⊕ n grain-tin; =zucker ⊕ m refined sugar.
feirig (⍺-) a. ⊕ f. feierig.
feist (⍺) [ahd.: fat] a. ⊕ fat, well-fed; nur von Menschen: stout, corpulent; path. obese; (brall, rund) plump; f. feisten.
Feist (⍺) n ⊕b. hunt. = Fett v. Hirsch u. Reh.
Feiste (⍺) f ⊕ 1. a. Feistheit (⍺-) f ⊕.
Feistigkeit (⍺⍵-) f ⊕ fatness, stoutness; path. obesity. — 2. hunt., auch **Feist=zeit** (⍺⍵...) f ⊕ season when the game is in good (or prime) condition.
feisten (⍺⍵) v/a. ⊕ (feist machen) to fatten a pig; to stuff a goose. [grin.)
feizen (⍺⍵) v/n. (h.) ⊕ (grinsend lachen) to
Felbel ✱ (⍺⍵) [it. felpa Plüsch] m ⊕, f ⊕ (Pelzsamt) feather-shag.
Felber ✱ (⍺⍵) [ahd.] m ⊕ (Silberweide) white willow (Salix alba).
Felch (⍺) m ⊕b., ~e (⍺⍵) f ⊕, ~en m ⊕ whitefish (Core′gonus).

Feld (⍺) [ahd.: field] n ⊕b. 1. (Ackerland) field; auf freiem ~e in the open fields or country; ins ~ hinausgeh(e)n to go into the fields; über ~ geh(e)n to travel (across country); das ~ (be=)bauen to cultivate (or till) the soil or ground; ✗ abgebautes ~ (Gebiet) old workings pl. — 2. fig. e-m freies ~ lassen to give a p. full (or ample) scope or free play; die Elektrizität bietet ein weites ~ zu Entdeckungen electricity offers a large field (or a wide scope) for discovery; das ~ behaupten, räumen to hold, to quit the field or a position (auch ✗); das steht noch weit im ~e ob. im weiten ~e that's looming in the distance; it is still very uncertain; ✗ gegen ein oder et. zu ~e ziehen to oppose a p. or a th.; ✗ das ~ der Ehre the field of honour. — 3. ✗ Truppen ins ~ führen to lead troops into the field; ins ~ rücken ob. ziehen, zu ~e ziehen to take the field (with an army); fig. er hat mich aus dem ~e geschlagen he has outdone (or beaten) me or been too much for me. — 4. Spiel: ~ auf dem Schachbrett ꝛc. square. — 5. ⊕ (elektro)magnetisches ~ (electro)magnetic field; arch., &c.: ~ e-r Decke, Wand ꝛc. panel, compartment. — 6. her. field; quarter. — 7. Rennsport: das ~ (Gesamtheit der Renner) the field.
Feld=ahorn ⍺ (⍺...) m ⊕ common maple (Acer campe′stre); =altar m portable altar; =ameise f, ent. field-ant; =ampfer ⍺ m = Ampfer (kleiner); =apotheke ✗ f field-dispensary; =apotheker m field-apothecary; =arbeit f field-labour, agricultural labour; =arbeiter m agricultural labourer; F field-hand; =armee ✗ f = =heer; =artillerie ✗ f f.-artillery (ant. Fuß-artillerie); =arzt m army-surgeon; ⍺aus (⍺⍵) adv. f. ⍺ein; =ausrüstung ✗ (⍺...) f field-equipment; =bäcker(ei f) ⊕ m army-baker(y); =bau(er) m = Ackerbau, Ackermann; =befestigung ✗ f, frt. für Gefechtszwecke: field-fortification, entrenchment; =beifuß ⍺ m field-southernwood (Artemi′sia campe′stris); =bett n field- (or camp[aign]-) bed; =binde ✗ f (officer's) sash; =blume ⍺ f flower of the field(s), wild flower; =breite f, agr. breadth of a field; =brief ✗ m letter forwarded by field-post; =briefpost f = =post; =brücke ✗ f: a) agr. (Brücke über e-n Graben) bridge across a ditch; b) ✗ pontoon bridge; =chirurg m = =arzt; =diebstahl m theft of crops in the field; =dienst ✗ m service in the field, active service; =dienstordnung ✗ f regulations pl. for the field-service or for active service; =dienst-übung f field-day or practice; military manœuvres pl.; ⍺ein(wärts), auch: ⍺ein und ⍺aus adv. across the fields, weitS. across country; =eisenbahn f light railway; =erbse ⍺ f common pea (Pisum arve′nse).
feldern (⍺⍵) v/n. (h.) ⊕ 2a. von Tauben ꝛc.: to pick up food in the fields.
Felder=wirtschaft (⍺⍵...) f ⊕ agr. farming, husbandry; =zahl f number of fields or squares, &c. (f. Feld).

Signs (see page XVII): F familiar; P vulgar; ℾ flash; ↘ rare; † obsolete (died); * new word (born); ⁺⁺ incorrect; ♪ music;

[**Feldflasche**] **Feld-flasche** ⚔ (ˇ...) f ⊕ soldier's flask or canteen; **=flucht**† ⚔ f desertion (of the colours); **=flüchter** m = =taube; **=flüchtige(r)**† ⚔ m deserter; **=frevel** m, agr., ehm. rural offence or theft, weitS. agrarian crime; **=früchte** f/pl. produce of the field(s); **=geistliche(r)** m = =prediger; **=gepäck** ⚔ n baggage (of troops in the field); **=gerät** n: a) agr. agricultural implements pl.; b) ⚔ equipment for war; **=geschrei** n: a) war-cry; von Wilden auch: war-whoop; b) (Lofung und F.=geschrei) watch-word; **=geschütz** ⚔ n, artill. field-gun or -piece; **=gott** m rustic (or rural) deity; **=gottesdienst** ⚔ m camp-service or =meeting; **=grille** f, ent. field-cricket (Gryllus campe'stris); **=hase** m, zo. (common) field-hare (Lepus ti'midus); **=haubitze** ⚔ f field-howitzer; **=hauptmann** m † ⚔ u. poet. captain of the host; vgl. =herr; **=heer** ⚔ n (total of) military forces pl. in the field; **=herr** ⚔ m commander-in-chief; der größte ~ Frankreichs the greatest general (or military leader) of France; **=herrnkunst** f (good) generalship, (art of) strategy; **=herrn-stab** m (marshal's) baton; **=herrn-würde** f: a) rank of a commander-in-chief; b) dignity of a (supreme) commander; **=hospital** ⚔ n field-hospital; **=huhn** n, orn. = =Rebhuhn; **=hüter** m field-watchman, keeper; **=jäger** m: a) hunt. game-keeper; b) ⚔ royal messenger; **=kalaminthe** ♀ f basil-thyme (Calami'ntha A'cinos); **=kanone** ⚔ f field-gun; **=kaplan** ⚔ m, Cath. eccl. = =prediger; **=kasse** f military chest; **=kessel** ⚔ m field-kettle; **=koch** ⚔ m army-cook; **=kompagnie** ⚔ f company on the march; **=kresse** ♀ f field-cress (Lepi'dium campe'stre); **=krieg** ⚔ m (ant. Festungskrieg) war (conducted) in the open field; **=küche** f field-kitchen; **=kümmel** ♀ m = =Wiesen-k.; **=lager** ⚔ n (military) camp or encampment; field-camp; **=lazarett** ⚔ n field-ambulance or -hospital; fliegendes ~ flying ambulance; **=lerche** f, orn. field-lark (Alau'da arve'nsis); **=mark(ung)** f land-mark; **=marschall** ⚔ m field-marshal; **=marschalleutnant** m öft. lieutenant-general; commander of a division; **=marschall-stab** m = =herrn-stab; **=marschmäßig** ⚔ a. ready (or fit) for active service; **=maus** f, zo. field-mouse (Mus silva'ticus); **=messen** n land-survey; surveying (of land); **=messer** m surveyor; **=mess-kunst** f art of surveying; ⚙ geodesy; **=musik** f military music; **=mütze** ⚔ f foraging-cap; **=obst** n (wildes Obst) fruit growing wild (in the fields); **=paketpost** ⚔ f military parcel-post; **=post** ⚔ f (military) field-post; **=postbrief** m = =brief; **=prediger** m, eccl. army-chaplain; **=propst** m chaplain-general (of the army); **=quendel** ♀ m wild thyme, brother-wort (Thymus Serpy'llum); **=regiment** ⚔ n regiment on the march; **=ruf** ⚔ m = =geschrei; **=salat** ♀ m lamb's-lettuce, corn-valerian, -salad (Valeria'nella olito'ria); **=schaden** m, agr. damage done to the fields; **=schanze** ⚔ f redoubt, entrenchment; field-work; **=scher(er)** ⚔ m, ehm. regimental surgeon; **=scheuche** f scarecrow; **=schlacht** ⚔ f pitched battle; **=schlange** ⚔ f ehm. (Art Geschütz) culverin; **=schmiede** ⚔ f field- (or regimental) forge; **=schnecke** f, zo. common slug (Limax agre'stis); **=schütz(e)** m ⚔ f soldat ⚔ m soldier on the march or in active service; **=spat** m, min. fel(d)spar, feldspath; **=spat-artig** a. ⚙ feldspathic; **=sperling** m, orn. tree-sparrow (Passer monta'nus); **=stecher** m (Fernglas) field-glass; **=stein** m: a) field-stone; coll. =steine pl. auch rubble; b) (Grenzstein) boundary-stone; **=stein-mauer** f, =mauerwerk n rubble-wall, -work; **=stuhl** [corr. aus Falt-st.] m (zf.-legbarer Stuhl) camp-stool, folding-chair; **=taube** f, orn. rock- (or field-) pigeon, blue-rock (Colu'mba li'via); **=telegra'ph(ie)** f m ⚔ field-telegraph(y); **=thy'mian** ♀ m = =quendel; **=truppen** ⚔ f/pl. troops pl. in the field; **=tüchtig** ⚔ a. ready to take the field; **=übung** ⚔ f = =dienstübung; **=ulme** ♀ f common elm (Ulmus campe'stris); **=verpflegung** ⚔ f commissariat; **=vogt** m = =hüter; **=wache** ⚔ f field-watch, outpost, (outlying) picket; **=wächter** m = =hüter; **=wärts** adv. towards the fields; bisw. auch: fieldwards; **=webel** m colour-sergeant, sergeant-major; **=webel-leutnant** m warrant-officer; **=weg** m field-way or -path, country-road; **=wicke** ♀ f = Futter-w.; **=wiese** f, agr. (field turned into) meadow-land; **=wirtschaft** f husbandry, farming; **=zaun** m hedge of a field; **=zeichen** n field-badge; engS. = =Fahne; **=zeug** n army-stores pl.; **=zeugmeister** m a) master of the ordnance; vgl. General=feldzeugmeister; b) öft. infantry general, general of infantry; **=zug** m campaign, (warlike) expedition; e-n ~ mitmachen to take part in a campaign; er hat viele =züge mitgemacht he has seen much active service; **=zulage** ⚔ f field-allowance.

Felge ⊕ (ˇ..) [ahd.: felly] f ⊛ 1. Stellm.: (Rad=) ~ felly, felloe. — 2. agr. (Brachland) fallow (land).

felgen ⊕ (ˇ..) v/a. ⊛ 1. Stellmacherei: das Rad ♀ to provide (or fit) ... with felloes. — 2. agr. Land ♀ (umpflügen) to fallow

Felgen-hauer (ˇ...) m ⊕ (Stellmacher) wheelwright; **=platte** f felly-plate.

Fell (ˇ) [ahd.: fell (film)] lt. pellis] n ⊕b. 1. der Kälber, Ziegen ꝛc.: hide, der Hasen, Katzen ꝛc.: skin, coat, case; path. ~ im Auge film over the eye; auch anat. (innere Haut) membrane; frisches (a. rohes) ~ raw (or green) hide; einem Hasen das ~ abziehen to skin a hare. — 2. fig. e-m das ~ gerben F to give a p. a good hiding or tanning; ein dickes ~ haben to be thick-skinned or callous or indifferent; hüte dich, daß ich dir (nicht) aufs ~ komme F take care, or I shall come down on you or pitch into you; man soll das ~ nicht verkaufen, ehe man den Bären hat oder bevor der Bär erlegt ist catch your bear before you sell his skin, mehr gbr.: do not count your chickens before they are hatched; e-m das ~ über die Ohren ziehen to fleece (or cheat) a p.; er ließ sich das ~ über die Ohren ziehen F he was thoroughly taken in or imposed upon or let in. [currier.) **Fell-bereiter** ⊕ (ˇ...) m ⊛ skin-dresser,/ **Fellchen** ⚔ n ⊛ dim. von Fell.

Fell-eisen† (ˇ...) [mhd. P;*fr. valise] n ⊛ knapsack, portmanteau, carpet-bag; ⚑ mail-bag; **=handel** m trade in skins or hides; fur-trade; **=händler** m skin-merchant, dealer (or trader) in hides, furrier; **=werk** ⚑ n skins, hides, furs pl., peltry; **=wolle** ⚑ f skin-wool; **=zurichter** ⊕ m Gerberei: skin-dresser.

Fels (ˇ) [ahd.: fell] m ⊛ f. Felsen; vom ~ zum Meer from the Alps to the Sea.

Fels-bewohner (ˇ...) m ⊛ = Felsen-b.; **=block** m large piece of rock.

Felsen (ˇ..) [Fels] m ⊛ rock, (Klippe) cliff, crag; künstliche ~ pl. rockwork; sein Haus auf e-n ~ bauen to build ... on a rock.

Felsen-abhang (ˇ...) m ⊛ rocky declivity or slope; **=ader** f vein of a rock; **=artig** a. ⊛ rock-like, rocky, cragged; **=berg** m rocky mountain; **=bewohner(in** f) m crags(wo)man; **=boden** m rocky ground; **=bucht** f bay formed (or enclosed) by rocks; **=burg** f castle built on a rock; **=eck(e** f) n corner of a rock, pointed crag or cliff; **=fest** a. as solid (or firm) as a rock; der Glaube unshaken faith; **=feste** f rocky fortress; **=gebilde** n rocky formation; **=gebirge** ♀ npr/n. Nord-amerika: Rocky Mountains pl.; **=geklüft** n rocky cleft; **=geröll** e n, geol.: ⚙ detritus; **=gestade** n rocky (or rugged) shore; **=gewölbe** n (=gruft f) vault (tomb) cut out of the (living) rock; **=grund** m rocky foundation; **=gruppe** f group (or cluster) of rocks; **=hart** a. as hard as (a) rock; poet. adamantine; **=herz** n heart of stone or flint; **=höhe** f rocky height; **=höhle** f grotto; **=insel** f rock-bound island; **=keller** m cellar cut out of the rock; **=kluft** f cleft (or cave) in a rock; **=kresse** ♀ f rock-pepperwort (Lepi'dium petrae'um); **=masse** f mass of rocks; **=nest** n castle built on a rock; **=pfad** m rocky path; **=platte** f ledge (or shelf) of a rock; **=quelle** f spring flowing from a rock; **=riff** n reef; **=schwalbe** f, orn. rock-swallow or -martin (Co'tyle rupe'stris); **=spitze** f crag; **=stück** n = Felsblock; **=sturz** m fall of rocks; **=tal** n rocky valley; **=wand** f rocky wall; **=weg** m = =pfad.

felsicht ⚑, mft. **felsig** (ˇ..) a. ⊛ rock-like, cliff-like, cragged; consisting (or full) of rocks or crags or cliffs or boulders.

Felsit (⌣¹) [dtsch.-lt.] m ⊛c. min. (Art Feldspat) felsite.

Fels-klippe(ˇ...) f ⊛ rocky ridge, cliff; **=schroffen** m = =klippe; **=sprengung** ⊕ f blasting of rocks; **=stück** n = Felsblock; **=wand** f = Felsen-w. [felucca.) **Feluke** ⚓ (⌣⌣) [fr. *ar.] f ⚔ (Ruderschiff)/ **Feme**¹ (⌣⌣) [mhd.] f ⊛ ehm. (geheime Volksjustiz) vehme; vehmic jurisdiction.

Feme² (⌣⌣) [ndd.] f ⊛ = Eichelmast.

Femel ♀ (⌣⌣) [lt.] m ⊛ = Fimmel¹.

⚔ scientific; ♀ botanical; ⌘ geography; ⊕ machinery; ⛏ mining; ⚔ military; ⚓ marine; ⚑ commercial; ⚑ postal; 🚆 railway.

[**Femgericht**] — 364 — [**Fernsprechkunst**]

Fem-gericht (″...) [Feme¹] n ⑳ vehmic court; **-graf** m judge presiding over a vehmic court.
Femininum (-ᴗᴸᴗ) [lt.] n ⑲ gram. (weibl. Wort, Geschlecht) feminine noun, gender.
Fem-richter (″...) m ⑫ = Femgraf.
Fench ⚹ (ᴸ) (ahd.; *lt. pānĭcum n Hirse) m ⑪b. (Vorstenhirse) bristle-grass (Setaria).
Fenchel ⚹ (ᴸᴗ) [ahd.; *lt. fēnĭcŭlum n] m ㉒ (echter)~ fennel (Foeniculum vulgare).
Fenchel-öl (ᴸᴗ...) n ㉖, **-wasser** n fennel-oil, fennel-water.
Feni-er (ᴸᴗᴗ) m ㉒ (irischer Verschwörer) Fenian; **~tum** (ᴸᴗᴗ—) n ⑳d. Fenianism.
fenisch (ᴸᴗ) [Fenier] a. ⑯ Fenian.
Fenn (ᴸ) [ahd.: fen] m, n ⑪b. fen, bog.
Fennek (ᴸᴗ) (afrik.) m ⑳ zo. (Wüstenfuchs) fennec, fennek, zerda (Canis cerdo).
Fennich ⚹ (ᴸᴗ) = Fench.
Fenster (ᴸᴗ) [ahd.; *lt. fĕnĕstră f] n ㉒ 1. window; mit Flügeln: French window; zum Schieben: (in Engl. gbr.) sash-window; vorspringendes ~ bay-window; (Oberlicht) sky-light; (Laden-)~ shop-window or -front; anat. ㉗ fenestra; hort. ~ e-s Mistbeets glass-frame; das ~ auf- (zu-)machen to open (to shut) the window; aus dem ~ sehen to look out of the window; das ~ geht auf des Nachbars Hof hinaus the window looks down on the neighbour's yard; durch das ~ einsteigen to get in at the window; zum ~ hinein (in) through the window; die ~(scheiben) einwerfen to smash (or break) the window-panes or windows. — 2. fig., bibl.: die ~ (Schleusen) des Himmels the gates pl. of heaven.
fenster-ähnlich (ᴸᴗ...) a. ⑯ window-like, \ windowy; **-austritt** m ⑫ = -vorbau, **-bank** f = -sitz; **-beschläge** m/pl. wi.-fastenings pl.; **-blei** n glazier's (or wi.-)lead; came; **-blende** f wi.-blind, vgl. -vorsetzer; **-bogen** m, arch. wi.-arch; **-brett** n wi.-board, wi.-sill; vgl. Blumenbrett; **-brüstung** f wi.-ledge, parapet; elbow-rest.
Fensterchen (ᴸᴗᴗ) n ㉓ (dim. von Fenster) small (or tiny) window; ⊕ arch. (Oberlicht) skylight.
Fenster-einfassung (ᴸᴗ...) f ⑫ window-case; **-fach, -feld** n wi.-panel; **-flügel** n casement; drehbarer: wi.-valve; am engl. Schiebefenster: sash; **-futter** n wi.-frame; sash-frame; **-gardine** f wi.-blind; vgl. -vorhang; **-geld** n -steuer; **-gitter** n wi.-grate; trellis-work (aus Eisen: grating, iron bars) before a wi.; **-glas** n wi.-glass; **-haspe** f casement-hinge; **-jalousien** f/pl. Venetian blinds pl.; **-kissen** n wi.-cushion; **-kitt** m (glazier's) putty; **-kreuz** n cross-bar of a wi.; **-laden** m (outside, inside) shutter; die ~ vorlegen beim Schließen des Ladens ꝛc.: to put up (or fasten) the shutters; **-lehne** f = -brüstung.
fenstern (ᴸᴗ) v/n. (h.) ㉒a.: ~ geh(e)n (dem Liebchen am Fenster e-n Besuch abstatten) to go courting at one's lady-love's window.
Fenster-nische (ᴸᴗ...) f ⑫ window-bay or -niche; **-öffnung** f, arch. opening (or aperture) for a wi.; **-parade** f parading (or promenading) before a lady's (or one's sweetheart's) window(s); **-pfeiler, -pfosten** m mullion; **-polster**

n = -kissen; **-promenade** f = -parade; **-rahmen** m wi.-frame; **-riegel** m wi.-bolt; **-rose** f, arch. rose-window, rosette; **-scheibe** f wi.-pane; **-schieber** m (sliding) sash of a sash-wi.; **-schirm** m wi.-screen; **-schmiege** f, arch. wi.-splay; **-schweiß** m steam on wi.-panes; **-sitz** m seat by the wi.; **-spiegel** m: a) zwischen zwei Fenstern: pier-glass; b) außen: spy-mirror; **-stab** m, **-stange** f wi.-bar; **-steuer** f ehm. wi.-tax or -duty; **-sturz** m wi.-head, lintel; **-verschluß** m wi.-lock; **-vertiefung** f wi.-recess; embrasure; **-vorbau** m verandah; **-vorhang** m wi.-curtain or -hangings pl.; **-vorsetzer** m wi.-blind, aus feinem Draht: wire blind; **-wand** f wall (provided) with windows; **-werk** n, coll. (all) the windows pl. of a house, &c.; **-wirbel** m window- (or sash-)bolt, sash-fastener.
...fenstrig (...ᴗ) ⑯ zB. drei-≈es Zimmer ... with three windows.
Fenz (ᴸ) [engl.] f ⑯ (Einfriedigung) fence.
Ferch ⚹ (ᴸ) m ⑪b. (böses Wetter) choke-damp. **[Ferdinand.]**
Ferdinand (ᴸᴗᴗ) npr/m. ⑮⑯, ⑮⑯α. (Bn.)
Ferge (ᴸᴗ) [ahd.; * Fähre] m ㊹, oft poet. (Fährmann) ferryman, boatman.
Ferger schwz. (ᴸᴗ) [(Ab)fertiger] m ⑫ (Vermittler, Agent) middleman.
Feri-en (ᴸ(ᴗ)ᴗ) [nhd. 17. sac.; * lt. fēriae] pl., inv. holidays pl.; Schule, Gericht ꝛc. auch: vacation(-time); parl. recess; die großen ~ long vacation.
Ferien-kolonie (″ᴗᴗ...) f ⑫ holiday-camp; **-kursus** m vacation lectures pl.; **-reise** f holiday-trip or -tour; **-zeit** f holiday-time; vacation.
Ferkel (ᴸᴗ) [ahd.: farrow; lt. porcus] n ㉒ young pig; (Span-)~ sucking pig; ein Wurf ~ a litter of pigs.
Ferkelchen (ᴸᴗᴗ) n ㉓ (dim. von Ferkel) sucking pig; co. auch: (little) piggy.
Ferkelei F (ᴸᴗᴸ) f ⑯ piggishness; smut.
Ferkel-kaninchen (ᴸᴗ...) n ㉒ = Aguti; **-kraut** n cat's-ear (Hypochoeris u. Achyrophorus); **-maus** f = Meerschweinchen; **ferkeln** (ᴸᴗ) v/n. (h.) ㉒a. 1. (Ferkel werfen) to farrow, pig. — 2. F (säuisch sein) to be piggish or dirty; in Worten: to be smutty.
Ferkel-ratte (ᴸᴗ...) f ⑯ hog-rat (Capromys); **-stall** m hutch for young pigs; pig-sty.
ferm F (ᴸ) [fr.] a. ⑯: in etwas ≈ (gut bewandert) sein to be well grounded (or to be experienced or versed) in a th.
Ferman (ᴗᴸ) [pers.] m ⑪c. Türkei: (Erlaß des Sultans) firman.
Fermate ♪ (ᴗᴸᴗ) [it.] f ㊽ (Haltezeichen) pause, sign to sustain a note (⌒).
Ferment ᵪ (ᴗᴸ) [lt.] n ⑪b. 1. chm. (Gärungsmittel) ferment, leavening; substance causing fermentation. — 2. P ₊⁺ [: **ferm**] = Bindemittel. **[fermentation.]**
Fermentation (ᴗᴗ—tᵢ(ᴗ)ᴸ) f ⑫ (Gärung)
fermentieren (ᴗᴗᴸᴗ) v/a. ⑬ to ferment.
fern (ᴸ) [ahd.: far] I a. ⑯ u. adv. (ant. nah; comp. f. ferner) 1. far, distant, remote; der ≈e Osten the Far East; in ≈en Landen, Ländern in far-off lands or distant countries; (von) nah und ≈ far and near; von ≈(e) (her) from afar, at a distance; nicht von ≈ not by a long way, not nearly; vgl. da≈, in≈o≈, inwie≈, wo≈. — 2. das sei ≈ (von

mir)! far be it (from my thoughts)!, stärker: Heaven forbid!; vgl. fern-bleiben, -halten, -liegen, -steh(e)n. — II † adv. 3. = fernt.
Fernambuk-holz ⚘ (ᴸᴗ″...) [Pernambuco ⍙ brasil. St.] n ⑳ Brazil-wood (v. Caesalpinia Sappan).
Fern-ansicht (ᴸ...) f ⑫ = -sicht; **-bahn** 🚆 f long-distance (railway-)line, main-line.
fern-bleiben (ᴸᴸᴗ) v/n. (str) ⑪** e-r Sache ≈ to keep (or stand) aloof from ...
Fern-drucker (ᴸ...) m ⑫ (type-) printing telegraph, Morse printer; **-druckerzentrale** f Central News Agency for printed messages or messages received by the printing telegraph.
ferne¹ (ᴸᴗ) adv. = fern.
Ferne² (ᴸᴗ) f ⑱ 1. (~fein) distance, remoteness; aus der ~ from afar, from a distance; aus weiter ~ from a long (or great) distance; aus weiter ~ hergeholt (bibl. fig.) far-fetched; in der ~ a long way off, at a distance; fig. das liegt noch in weiter ~ that is looming in the distance, F it's a long way off (or a long time to come) yet. — 2. paint. (Hintergrund) (distant) background.
Ferner¹ (ᴸᴗ) [Firn²] m ⑫ (Gletscher) glacier.
ferner² (ᴸᴗ) I comp. von fern ⑯ further, ulterior, additional; ≈e Nachrichten further (or later) news. — II als adv. further(more), farther; (außerdem) moreover, besides; also; ≈ hat er Gallien erobert in addition to that, he conquered Gaul; auch ≈ an der Arbeit, im Amte bleiben to continue one's work, in office; ich will ihm ≈ nicht (mehr) schreiben I shall not write to him again or any more.
ferner-hin (ᴸᴗ...) adv. in (or for) the future, henceforth; ≈weit(ig) a. ulterior; adv. further.
Fern-glas (ᴸᴸ) n ⑫ = Fernrohr.
fern-halten (ᴸ...) ⑯a** I v/a. to keep at a distance or out of the way or at arm's length. — II v/refl. sich ≈ von to keep out of the way of, to steer clear of. | adv. to a long distance.
fern-her (ᴸᴸ) adv. from afar; ≈hin (ᴸᴗ) **Fern-hörer** (ᴸ...) m ⑫ (microphone of a) telephonograph; **-kabel** n, elect. teledynamic cable.
fern-liegen (ᴸᴸᴗ) I v/n. (h.) ㉔** das liegt mir fern: a) that's far from my thoughts; b) (das ist nicht mein Fach) F that's out of my line. — II ≈d p.pr. u. a. ⑯ far off, distant, remote.
Fern-malerei (ᴸ...) f ⑫: ㉗ scenography; **-melde-apparat, -melder** m, elect. telegraphic (or telephone) transmitter; **-photograph** m telephotograph; **-rohr** n ⑳ (⑦) d. telescope, fieldglass, F spy-glass; **-schreibe-kunst** \ f telegraphy; **-schreiber** \ m telegraph(ic instrument); **-sicht** f distant view or prospect; perspective (view); ≈sichtig a. ⑯ far- (or long-) sighted; path.: ㉗ presbyopic; **-sprech-amt** n telephone-office, call-room or -office; **-sprech-anschluß** m telephonic (or telephone) connexion; **-sprecher** m telephone; **-sprech-kabel** n telephone cable; **-sprech-kunst** f telephony;

Zeichen (s. S. XVII): F familiär; P Volkssprache; Γ Gaunersprache; \ selten; † alt (auch gestorben); * neu (auch geboren); ₊⁺ unrichtig;

[Fernsprechlinie] — 365 — [Fest

=sprech=linie f telephone-line; =sprech=stelle f = =sprechamt; =sprech=wesen n telephony; =sprech=zelle f call-box; ⊖steh(e)n v/n. (h.) ⊕** to stand (or be) outside, to be a stranger to; er steht uns fern he is a stranger to us; =stehende([r] m) f outsider, onlooker.
fern(t) fast ↑ (↓) adv. (im vorigen Jahre; bei W. u. U.) last year.
Fern-trieb(werk n) m (⁸...) ⊕ mech. long-distance action or working; =verkehr ⊕ m long-distance traffic; =zug ⊕ m main-line train.
Ferri=salze ⊘ (⁸-...) [lt.] n/pl. ⊕ (auch: Ferrid=salze Eisenoxyd...) ferric salts pl.; =zyankalium ⊘ n, chm. (rotes Blutlaugensalz) potassium ferricyanide ($K_3Fe[CN]_6$).
Ferro=salze ⊘ (⁸-...) [lt.] n/pl. ⊕ chm. (Eisenoxydul...) ferrous salts pl.; =zyankalium ⊘ n, chm. (gelbes Blutlaugensalz) potassium ferrocyanide ($K_4Fe[CN]_6$); =zyanwasserstoffsäure f hydroferrocyanic acid ($H_4Fe[CN]_6$).
Ferse (⁸⌣) [ahd.] f ⊕ heel (auch an der Fußbekleidung); fig. e-n auf den ~n haben to have a p. at one's heels; e-m auf den ~n sein oder sitzen to be at a p.'s heels, to pursue (or follow) a p. closely; sich an j-s ~n heften to dog a p.'s footsteps; die ~n zeigen (fliehen) to take to one's heels, to show a good pair of heels, to make tracks.
Fersen=bein (⁸⌣...) n ⊕ anat. heel-bone; =flechse f tendon of Achilles; =geld F n: ~ geben to take to one's heels, biswl.: to give leg-bail; =leder n heel-piece of a boot; =schlag m kick with the heel; =sehne f = =flechse.
fertig (⁸⌣) [ahd.; *Fahrt] a. ⊕ oft verstärkt: fix und ⊖ 1. von Personen: (gerüstet zu et.) ready, prepared; (gewandt, geübt) skilled, accomplished; ein ⊖er Redner, Rechner a fluent speaker, a ready reckoner; sich zur Reise ⊖ halten, machen to get ready (or to prepare) for one's departure or journey; adv. er spricht ⊖ englisch he speaks English fluently or with ease. — 2. von Sachen: (beendet) finished; (vorrätig) ready-made (clothes, &c.); ⊖e Arbeit work done; das Essen ist ⊖ dinner is ready. — 3. mit persönlichem Objekt: mit e-m ⊖ werden to get the better of a p.; to get on (well) with a p.; mit dem will ich bald ⊖ werden I shall soon manage (or settle) him; mit dem Menschen wird man nie ⊖ F there is no (such) getting rid of him, one cannot shake him off; ich kann nicht ohne ihn ⊖ werden I cannot do without him. — 4. mit sächlichem Objekt: mit et. ⊖ (zu Ende) werden, et. ⊖ machen, bekommen, bringen od. schaffen to finish (or terminate) a th.; ⊖ machen Schriftgießerei: to dress; (et. vollenden) to achieve (or accomplish) a th.; F to manœuvre (or manage) a th.; mit et. ⊖ sein to have completed (or finished) a th.; ich bin mit meinem Buche ⊖ I have finished (or done with) ...; er ist mit dem Frühstück ⊖ he has done breakfast; mit e-r Flasche bald ⊖ werden to empty (F to polish off) a bottle very quickly. — 5. Redensarten: ich habe die Hälfte ⊖ I have done half; ich bin ⊖

(mit meiner Rede) I have done; er ist ⊖: a) (betrunken) F he is (dead) drunk; b) (zugrunde gerichtet) he is ruined or F done for; it is all over with him; er muß zusehen, wie er ⊖ wird he must get on as best he can.
fertigen (⁸⌣) v/a. ⊕ = anfertigen I; prov. = ausfertigen 1. [made article.]
Fertig=fabrikat ⊕ (⁸⌣...) n ⊕ ready-)
Fertigkeit (⁸⌣–) f ⊕ (Gewandtheit) skill, dexterity; (Behendigkeit) nimbleness, der Zunge: volubility; (Übung) practice, routine; (leichte Auffassung) facility (in learning); ~en pl. accomplishments pl.; sich ~ in et. aneignen to learn (F to get into) the knack of a th.; ♪ ~ im Spielen execution; eine große ~ im Spiele haben to play with great skill; ~ im Rechnen, im Sprechen readiness in ciphering, fluency in speaking.
Fertig=machen (⁸⌣...) n ⊕ = =stellung; =macher m one who finishes; ⊕ finisher; Schriftgießerei 2c.: dresser; ⊖stellen v/a. ⊕** to complete, finish, get ready; =stellung f completion, achievement, accomplishment; typ., &c. adjuster.
Fes¹ (⁸) n, inv. F flat.
Fes² (⁸) [♀~ (* ar. Fās), Stadt in Marokko] m, inv. u. ⊕ (rote Kappe) fez.
fesch ↑ öft. (⁸) [fash(ionable)] a. ⊕ (D 6): a) = feck; b) (fein, modisch) smart, fashionable, F swell, up to date.
Fessel¹ (⁸⌣) [ahd.: fetter] f ⊕ 1. (Bande) fetters, shackles pl.; (Kette) chain; e-m die ~n abnehmen to unchain (or unfetter, release) a p.; e-m ~n anlegen, e-n in ~n schlagen to put (or lay) a p. in fetters or irons or chains; in ~n schlagen to fetter, to chain (down); die ~n sprengen to break one's bonds; rel. die ~n der Sünde the trammels pl. of sin. — 2. (Spannstrick des Pferdes) tether.
Fessel² (⁸⌣) [Fuß] f ⊕ († m ⊕ ⊕) vet. (Teil der Pferdezehe zw. Huf u. Mittelfußknochen) fetlock, pastern.
Fessel¹=ballon (⁸⌣...) m ⊕ captive balloon; =bein n der Huftiere: pastern; ⊖¹frei a. ⊕ = ⊖los; =²gelenk n pastern-joint; =²haar n fetlock; ⊖¹los a. unfettered, unshackled; free from chains; =¹losigkeit f unfettered condition, perfect freedom.
fesseln (⁸⌣)[mhd.: fetter] I v/a. ⊕ a. 1. Gefangene: to chain, fetter, shackle; to put (or cast) in irons; (binden) to bind (in chains); einem Pferde 2c. die Füße ⊖ to tether a horse, &c.; fig. die Gicht fesselt ihn ans Bett ... confines him to his bed, makes him a prisoner to his couch; ans Bett gefesselt bedridden, laid-up with a cold, &c.; ans Zimmer gefesselt confined to one's room. — 2. fig. die Aufmerksamkeit ⊖ to rivet the attention; die Blicke ⊖ to charm (or arrest) the eye; e-n jungen Mann ⊖ (fangen) to captivate or fascinate ... — II ⊖d p.pr. u. a. ⊕ fascinating. — III ~ ⊖ f. Fesselung (⁸⌣), Feßlung (⁸⌣) f ⊕ 4. ~ von Gefangenen: chaining (up) of captives.
fessel=wund (⁸⌣) a. ⊕ 1. sore from the chains. — 2. sore at the fetlock.
Feßler (⁸⌣) m ⊕ zo. (Geburtshelferkröte) accoucheur toad (A'lytes obstetri'cans).

fest¹ (⁸) [ahd.: fast] a. ⊕(D 6) 1 (ant. flüssig) ⊖es Land dry land, mainland, continent, (lt.) terra firma; phys. ⊖er Körper solid (substance); ⊖ werden to harden, to solidify; das Wasser wird beim Frieren zu einem ⊖en Körper ... becomes solid (or congealed, hard) in freezing. — 2. (ant. weich, locker) ⊖er (Grund und) Boden firm ground or soil, solid earth; fig. ⊖en (sicheren) Boden gewinnen (auch: ⊖en Fuß fassen) to gain a (firm) footing, to take (solid or deep) root; ⊖en Fußes with a firm step; ⊖er (schwerer) Kuchen heavy cake; ⊖er Knoten tight knot; ⊖e Nahrung solid (or substantial) food; ⊖en Schrittes einhergehen to walk along with a firm step, to have a steady gait; ⊖ werden to consolidate; ⌘ ⊖er Wind settled wind; adv. ⊖ im Sattel sitzen to sit firmly in the saddle, to sit a horse well; die Tür ⊖ zumachen to fasten the door (well); immer ⊖ (zu)! go it! — 3. (dauernd, standhaft, unveränderlich) ⊖e Anstellung permanent appointment; ⊖e (unbewegliche) Brücke permanent bridge; ⊖e Freundschaft firm (or lasting, stanch) friendship; ⊖es Gehalt fixed salary; ⊖e Gesundheit robust health; ⊖er Griff firm grasp; ⊖e Masse solid mass; der ⊖en Meinung sein, daß // to be strongly of opinion that //; ⊖er Punkt fixed point; ⊖e Überzeugung settled conviction; ⊖er Wohnsitz settled abode, permanent residence; ⊕: in ⊖en Händen in strong hands; (verkauft) disposed of; placed; ⊖e Kundschaft regular customers pl. or connexion; ⊖er Preis fixed price; adv. ⊖ an et. glauben to believe firmly in a th.; ⊖ auf s-m Entschlusse beharren steadfastly (or unswervingly) to adhere to one's resolution; e-n ⊖ anblicken to look a p. full (or steadily) in the face; steif und ⊖ behaupten to assert (or maintain) positively; ⊖ eingeschlafen fast asleep; ⊖ entschlossen firmly (or fully) resolved; ⊖ schlafen to sleep soundly; ⊖ überzeugt sein to be perfectly convinced; ⊖ versprechen to promise positively or for certain; ich nahm mir('s) fest vor, zu // I thoroughly made up my mind to //; ⊕ die Kurse halten sich ⊖ ... keep firm, ... maintain their level. — 4. in einem Fache, einer Wissenschaft ⊖ (gut bewandert) sein to be well grounded in (or thoroughly conversant with) ..., F to be strong in ... — 5. ⊖ (unverwundbar) sein to be invulnerable; weitS. ⊖ (sicher) sein gegen to be no proof against. — 6. bsd. ⨯ (befestigt) strong, fortified; vgl. Burg 3; ein ⊖er Platz a fortress or stronghold; eine ⊖e (uneinnehmbare) Stellung impregnable position.
Fest² (⁸) [mhd.: feast; *lt.] n ⊕b. 1. allg.: (Freuden⊖) fête; holiday; festivities pl., eccl. (church-)festival, auch: feast(-day); glänzendes ~ brilliant fête, F flare-up, high jinks pl.; eccl. (un-)bewegliches ~ (im)movable feast; ein ~ begeh(e)n to celebrate (or commemorate) a (great) festival or day. — 2. ~ (=mahl n, =schmaus m) feast, ban-

♪ Musik; ⚭ Wissenschaft; ✿ Pflanze; ♀ Geographie; ⊕ Technik; ⚒ Bergbau; ⚔ Militär; ⚓ Marine; ⊕ Handel; ✉ Post; 🚂 Eisenbahn.

[Festabend] — 366 — [Fetischanbeter]

quet; F treat; ein ~ halten to give a (great) banquet.
Fest²-abend (ˈ...) m ⓶ eve of a festival.
fest¹-ankern ⚓ (ˈ...) v/a. ⓶a** to anchor, (vertäuen) to moor (fast).
Fest²-aufzug (ˈ...) m ⓶ = -zug; **=ausschuß** m organizing committee.
fest¹-backen (ˈ...) v/n. (h.) ⓢb** Kochk.: to stick (or grow hard) in baking.
Fest²-ball (ˈ...) m ⓶ dress-ball.
Fest²-ballon (ˈ...) m ⓶ captive balloon; **=bannen** v/a. ⓶** to fix to the spot; wie festgebannt spell-bound; **=begründet** a. ⓶ firmly established, on a solid basis or footing; **=binden** v/a. ⑦** to bind fast, to tie (with cord, &c); **=bleiben** v/n ⓺**; fest bei etwas bleiben to adhere to a th.; v. Preisen: ⓺ to remain firm or steady or unchanged.
Feste (ˈ...) [ahd.] f ⓸ 1. ⚔ = Festung. — 2. bibl. (Himmelszelt) firmament. — 3. 🪨 hard rock. — 4. ♀ hawk's-beard (Crepis). [to fix.]
festen (ˈ...) [ahd.] v/a. ⓺ (seltm.) to fasten,
Fest²-essen (ˈ...) n ⓶ gala dinner, (great public) banquet.
fest¹-fahren (ˈ...) v/a. u. sich ⓺ v/refl. ⓢb** to run aground; sich ⓺, auch: to stick (fast) in the mud, &c.; fig. die Sache ist ⓺gefahren ... is at a deadlock.
Fest²-feier (ˈ...) f ⓶ festival; **=froh** a. ⓶ fond of festivities or of gaiety or of making merry; **=gabe** f festive gift or presentation; **=geber** m founder of the feast, host; **=gebräuche** m/pl. festive customs or rites pl.; **=gelage** n = -essen; **=geläut(e)** n f. peal (or sound) of bells; **=genossen(schaft)** m/pl. fellow-guests, meist -holiday-folk(s) pl.; **=gesang** m festive song or chant.
fest¹-gesetzt (ˈ...) p.p. f. setzen.
Fest²-gewand (ˈ...) n ⓶ festive garment; vgl. **-kleid**; **=halle** f banqueting-hall.
fest¹-halten (ˈ...) ⓺a** I v/a. to hold fast; e-n ⓺ (gefangen halten) to detain a p. (in jail); e-n Dieb ⓺ to stop a thief; Fußballspiel: to collar, festgehalten fairly held. — II v/n. (fn) an seiner Meinung ⓺ to adhere or cling (F to stick) to ...; an der Pflicht ⓺ strictly to fulfil (or do) one's duty; an einer Regel ꝛc. ⓺ (faithfully) to observe a rule. — III sich ⓺ v/refl. sich an etwas, an e-m ⓺ to hold fast (or to cling) to a th., a p. — IV v. ⓶ an e-r: adhesion (or adherence) to s.th.; an der Pflicht: (strict) fulfilment of one's duty.
festigen (ˈ...) v/a. ⓶ 1. = befestigen I, bsp. 5. — 2. ⚔ e-n Wechsel ⓺ to domicil(iat)e ...
Festigkeit (ˈ...) f ⓸ (f. fest) firmness, solidity, solidity; determination; strength of a fortress, &c.; steadiness of character, of prices, &c.; stanchness (or constancy) of a p.'s friendship; fixity of purpose; fixedness of prices; resoluteness of character; soundness or sleep; phys. resistance or strength; mit ~ handeln to act resolutely; **~s-grenze** f ⓶ phys. breaking point. [feit.]
Festivität (ˈ...) [lt.] f ⓸ = Festlich-
Fest²-jungfrau (ˈ...) f ⓶ maiden (dressed in white) who receives the guests.
fest¹-klammern (ˈ...) ⓶a** v/a. to fasten with clamps to; to clinch; sich ⓺ v/refl.

to cling to, F to hook on to; **=kleben** v/n. (h.) ⓶** to adhere (F to stick) to a th.; v/a. to fasten (or stick) with glue or gum or paste.
Fest²-kleid (ˈ²) n ⓶ festive attire or dress or garb; **~er** pl. gala suit or uniform; holiday-clothes pl.
fest¹-knüpfen (ˈ...) v/a. ⓶** to tie fast, to fasten with a knot; **=kommen** ⚓ v/n. (st) ⓶** to run aground, to be stranded; **=land** n ⓶ mainland, continent; **=landreise** f continental tour; **=ländisch** a. ⓶ continental; **=legen**: sich ⓺ ⚓ v/refl. ⓶** (ankern) to (drop the) anchor, to berth; fig. sich für die Zukunft ⓺ to make definite plans (or arrangements) for one's future; et. ⓺ (sichern, klarstellen) to settle a th., to clear up s. th.
festlich (ˈ...) a. ⓶ festive, holiday-like; (feierlich) solemn; (prächtig) splendid, magnificent, glorious; adv. ⓺ begehen to celebrate, solemnize; ⓺ bewirten to fête, to entertain liberally or hospitably; ⓺ gekleidet dressed in festive garb or in holiday-clothes (or arrangements); **~keit** (ˈ...) f ⓸ festivity; solemnity; (Pracht) splendour; (Fest) fête, festival.
Fest²-lied (ˈ²) n ⓶ = -gesang.
fest¹-liegen (ˈ...) v/n. (h.) ⓶** to be fixed to a spot; v. Kranken: to be laid up; to be set fast with rheumatism, &c.
fest¹-machen (ˈ...) (⚓ch) v/a. ⓶** 1. to make fast, to fasten, fix, attach; ⚓ to belay a rope, to clinch a cable; (einrammen) to ram down. — 2. ⚔ eine Stadt ⓺ to fortify ... — 3. einen Flüchtling ⓺ (verhaften) to arrest ...; f. Dingfest. — 4. 🌑 einen Handel ꝛc. ⓺ (abschließen) to conclude a bargain, to settle a business. — 5. =
Fest²-mahl (ˈ²) n ⓶ = -essen. [feien.]
fest¹-mauern (ˈ...) v/a. ⓶a** to build with strong walls; festgemauert in der Erden (SCH.) firmly walled in solid earth; **=meter** n (m) for. ⓶ (abbr. fm) cubic metre; **=nageln** v/a. ⓶a** to nail fast; fig. to clinch, to prove; er will sich nicht darauf ⓺ lassen he won't be bound to it; **=nahme** f ⓸ apprehension, capture, seizure; arrest(ation); **=nehmen** ⚓ v/a. ⓸a** to apprehend (or capture, seize) a thief, to arrest a culprit, &c.; ~ n ⓶ u. **=nehmung** f ⓸ = -nahme. [hänge) festoon.]
Feston (ˈ...) [fr.] n ⓶ (Blumen-, Laub-ge-
festonieren (ˈ...) [fr.] v/a. ⓶ (behängen) to festoon, to deck with festoons.
Fest²-ordner (ˈ...) m ⓶ organizer of a fête; **=ordnung** f program(me) of a fête, order of the day; **=platz** m place where a fête is held; **=prediger** m feast-day preacher; **=predigt** f feast-day sermon; **=rede** f speech of the day; inaugural speech or address; **=redner** m official speaker.
fest¹-schlagen (ˈ...) v/a. ⓢb** to fasten with blows; einen Nagel: to drive in ...
Fest²-schmaus (ˈ...) m⓶; **Fest²-schmuck** m festive adornment or decoration (spl.).
fest¹-schrauben (ˈ...) v/a. ⓶c** to fasten (or fix) with a screw; to screw down or on.
Fest²-schrift (ˈ...) f ⓸ festive publication, paper (or booklet, pamphlet) published in honour of //.

fest¹-setzen (ˈ...) ⓶** I v/a. to establish, settle, arrange; Bedingungen: to lay down, stipulate; e-e Zeit: to fix appoint; den Tag für die Hochzeit ⓺ to name (or fix) the day for the wedding); am festgesetzten Tage on the day appointed or fixed; einee Preis: to fix; jur. (ver-ordnen) to decree; e-n ⓺ to put a p. in jail, F to lay a p. by the heels. — II sich ⓺ v/refl. to establish o.s., to settle (down); v. Gebräuchen auch: to take root. — III ~ n ⓶, **=setzung** f ⓸ establishment, settlement, stipulation; appointment of a day.
fest¹-sitzen (ˈ...) v/n. (h.) ⓶** to sit fast; to be firmly fixed; (nicht weiter können) F to stick fast; ⚓ aground, im Eise: ice-bound or -locked.
Fest²-spiel (ˈ²) n ⓶ festive performance.
fest¹-stampfen (ˈ...) v/a. ⓶** to stamp (or beat, ram) down; **=stehen** v/n. (h.) ⓶** to stand firm or unshaken or unmoved; von Gebäuden ꝛc. oft: to be solidly built or constructed; **=stehend** (unbeweglich) fixed, stationary, constant; von Gebräuchen a. well established; v/impers. fig. es steht fest it is quite certain or sure; **=stellbar** a. ⓶ v. Tatsachen: capable of proof; **=stellen** v/a. ⓶** to establish, to fix; (bestimmen) to determine, to appoint; parl. die Zahl der Anwesenden ⓺ to count (out) the House; man hat festgestellt, daß // it has been ascertained that //; ~ n ⓶, **=stellung** f ⓸ establishment; jur., von Tatsachen: collection of evidence.
Fest²-tag (ˈ...) m ⓶ holiday; vgl. Fest² und Feiertag; **=tägig** a. ⓶ relating to (or connected with) a fête; **=täglich** a. holiday-like, festive; **=tags-ausflug** m holiday-excursion or -outing or -trip.
fest¹-treten (ˈ...) v/a. ⓶d** to fix by treading (down); vgl. ⓺ stampfen.
Festung (ˈ...) [mhd.] f ⓸ fortress, stronghold, strong (or fortified) place; kleinere: fort, citadel; e-e ~ belagern, einschließen, einnehmen, schleifen to besiege, invest, take, raze a fortress.
Festungs-arbeit ⚔ (ˈ...) f ⓶ hard labour in a fortress; **=arrêt** m = **=haft**; **=artillerie** f siege-artillery or -train; **=bau** m building (or construction) of fortresses; **=baukunst** f art of fortification; **=baumeister** m constructor of fortresses; **=graben** m moat of a fortress; **=gürtel** m ring of fortresses; **=haft** f confinement in a fo.; **=kommandant** m commandant of a fo.; **=krieg** m siege operations pl.; **=mauer** f wall of a fortress; battlement; **=netz** n network of fortresses; **=rayon** m rayon of a fortress; **=strafe** f = **=haft**; **=wall** m rampart; **=werk** n fortification; **Fest²-woche** (ˈ...) f ⓶ holiday-week; **=zeit** f festive time or season; holiday-time; **=zug** m festive procession; zu Pferde: cavalcade.
Fete (ˈ²) [fr. fête; Fest] f ⓸ fête.
Fetialen (ˈ²) [lt.] m/pl., inv. Alt.: (röm. Priesterkollegium) Fetiales pl.
fetieren (ˈ²) [fr. fêter] v/a. ⓶ (festlich bewirten) to fête, to entertain.
Fetisch (ˈ²) [port.] m ⓶a. (Götzenbild) fetish; idol; **~=anbeter** m ⓶ fetish-worship-

Signs (see page XVII): F familiar; P vulgar; ꟾ flash; ꞌ rare; † obsolete (died); * new word (born); ⁺⁺ incorrect; ♪ music;

[Fetischanbetung] — 367 — [Feuerfahne]

per; fetishist; idolater; ~anbetung f = ⸗dienst; ~diener m = ⸗anbeter; ~⸗dienst, ~⸗glaube, ⸗ismus m ⓐ fetish- (or idol-)worship; fetishism; idolatry.

fett (ⸯ) [ndd. (= hd. feist): fat] I a. ⓐ (D6) 1. fat, med.: ⚛ adipose; (wohlgenährt) dick und 2 stout, well fed, plump, as fat as butter; vgl. feist; ⚖ m. to fatten; 2 werden to grow (F to get) fat or stout, F to make flesh; chm. 2e (ant. ätherische) Öle fatty oils pl.; typ. 2er Buchstabe fat letter; 2e Linie full-faced rule; 2e Schrift fat-faced (or full-faced) type, fat-face; fig. das macht den Kohl (oder die Suppe) nicht 2 that will not avail (or improve matters) much; adv.: paint. die Farben 2 auftragen to put (or lay) the colours on thick; typ. 2 drucken to print in fat-faced type or bold letters. — 2. fig. (reichlich, einträglich) rich, fat, lucrative; 2er Dienst, 2e Stelle lucrative post; 2e Erbschaft rich (or large) inheritance; 2e Kost, 2e Küche rich (or good) living. — II Fette (ⸯ) n ⓐ fat(ty substance). — III Fett n ⓑ. fat, grease; (Schmalz) lard; (Braten)⸗ dripping; f. abschöpfen 2 ; ~ ansetzen to grow fat or stout; fig. im eigenen ~e braten to stew in one's own grease; er hat sein ~ (seinen Wischer ꝛc.) weg F he got (or caught) it nicely; er wird sein ~ (seine Schelte) schon kriegen he'll catch it (yet or soon).

Fett⸗abfälle (ⸯ...) m/pl. ⓐ fatty offal or refuse sg.; ⸗ablagerung f deposition of fat; med.: ⚛ adiposis; ⸗ammer f, orn. ortolan (Emberi'za hortula'na); ⸗auge n drop of oil (or grease) floating on gravy or broth; ⸗bauch m fat belly, paunch, P fatguts pl.; ⸗bäuchig a. ⓐ paunch-bellied; ⸗bruch m, path.: ⚛ steatocele; liparocele; ⸗darm m, anat. straight gut or intestine; ⸗drüse f, physiol.: ⚛ sebaceous gland. [feit 1.)

Fette¹ (ⸯ) [fett] f ⓐ (o. pl.) = Fettig-)
Fette² (ⸯ) [fr. faîte] f ⓐ = Pfette.
fetten (ⸯ) v/a. ⓐ 1. Kocht.: to cook (or prepare, fry) with dripping, lard or butter. — 2. ⊕ (einschmieren) to oil, grease, lubricate.

Fett⸗federn (ⸯ...) f/pl. ⓐ tail-feathers pl. of a goose; ⸗fleck(en) m spot of grease, grease-spot; ⸗gang m, anat.: ⚛ adipose duct; ⸗gans f, orn. penguin (Apteno'dytes); ⸗geschwulst f, path. fatty swelling, ⚛ lipoma; ⸗gewächs n, path.: wen, ⚛ steatoma; ⸗gewebe n, anat.: ⚛ adipose tissue; ⸗glanz m greasy lustre; ⸗haltig a. fatty, containing fat, ⚛ adipose; ⸗hammel m fat(tened) ram or sheep; ⸗haut f, anat.: ⚛ adipose membrane.

Fett⸗heit (ⸯ-) f ⓐ = Fettigkeit 1.
Fett⸗henne ⚘ (ⸯⸯ) f ⓐ große od. knollige ~ orpine (Sedum ma'ximum od. Tele'phium); sonst = Mauerpfeffer.
(fettig,) fettig (ⸯⸯ) a. ⓐ fatty, like grease; (ölig) oily; (fettbefleckt) greasy.
Fettigkeit (ⸯⸯ-) f ⓐ 1. (Fettsein) fatness, greasiness, ⚛ adiposity; v. Speisen: richness; des Leibes stoutness, a. obesity. — 2. (Fett) fat(ty) matter or substance).

Fettig⸗sein (ⸯⸯ-) n ⓑ = Fettigkeit 1.
Fett⸗klumpen (ⸯ...) m ⓐ lump of fat;

⸗kraut ⚘ n: (blaues) ~ butterwort (Pingui'cula [vulga'ris]); ⸗leber f, path. hypertrophy of the liver; ⚖leibig a. ⓐ corpulent; vgl. ⚖süchtig; ⸗leibigkeit f corpulence, vgl. ⸗sucht; ⸗magen m, zo. (vierter Magen der Wiederkäuer) rennet-bag, ⚛ abomasus; ⸗masse f mass of fat; ⸗pflanze ⚘ f: ⚛ crassula; ⚖sauer a. chm. ⚛ sebacic; ⚖saures Salz sebate; ⸗säure f: ⚛ fatty acid; ⸗schicht f layer of fat; ⸗schwanz m: a) fatty tail of sheep; b) a. ⸗schwanzschaf n, zo. steatopygous sheep (Ovis a'ries steatopy'ga); ⸗sucht f, path. obesity, ⚛ adiposity; ⚖süchtig a. obese. [earth.)
Fetten (ⸯⸯ) [Fett-ton] m ⓐ fuller's)
Fettung (ⸯⸯ) f ⓐ 1. greasing, lubricating.—2. grease, lubricating substance.
Fett⸗vogel (ⸯ...) m ⓐ orn. guacharo, fat- (or oil-)bird (Steato'rnis caripe'nsis); ⸗wachs n, chm. (Leichenfett) ⚛ adipocere; ⸗wanst m = ⸗bauch; ⚖wanstig a. ⓐ fat- (or paunch-)bellied; ⸗wäscher ⊕ m Gerät: greasing-sponge; ⸗werden n growing fat or stout; ⸗wolle f wool in the yolk; ⸗zelle f, physiol.: ⚛ adipose cell or duct.

Fetzen (ⸯⸯ) [mhd.] m ⓑ shred; kleiner ~ scrap; particle; (Lumpen) rag; in ~ in rags (and tatters), ragged; in ~ (Stücke) reißen to tear to pieces; fig. sie lassen keinen guten ~ an ihr they run her down fearfully.
fetzen ⚘ (ⸯⸯ) v/a. ⓐ = zerfetzen.
feucht (ⸯ) [ahd.] a. ⓐ moist; von Häusern, Kleidern ꝛc.: damp; von Kellern ꝛc. auch: dank; ⚛ humid; (sumpfig) boggy; (naß) wet; 2 machen to moisten, to (make) damp; 2 sein (werden) to be(come) moist, to be (to get) damp.
Feucht⸗brett (ⸯⸯ) n ⓑ typ. wetting-board.
Feuchte (ⸯⸯ) f ⓐ = Feuchtigkeit.
feuchten (ⸯⸯ) v/a. ⓐ I v/a. to moisten, damp, wet. — II v/n. (h.) (feucht w.) der Rasen feuchtet schon ... is already getting damp or damping; von Pferden: (schwitzen) to sweat. [drink, F elevated.)
feucht⸗fröhlich (ⸯⸯ) a. ⚖ merry with)
Feuchtigkeit (ⸯⸯ-) f ⓐ (f. feucht) 1. (ant. Dürre) moistness, moisture, dampness, humidity. — 2. (feuchter Körper) moist substance, fluid (body); physiol. kristall(e)ne ~ des Auges ⚛ aqueous humour of the eye.
Feuchtigkeits⸗gehalt (ⸯⸯ-...) m ⓐ ⚖grad m amount, degree of moisture; ⸗messer m, phys.: ⚛ hygrometer; hygrograph; ⸗zeiger m, phys.: ⚛ hygroscope.
feucht⸗kalt (ⸯⸯ) a. ⓐ damp and cold, clammy; vom Wetter auch: raw; ⸗mulde f ⓐ typ. wetting-trough; ⸗sein n dampness; humidity; ⸗werden n growing (F getting) moist or damp.
feudal (ⸯⸯ) [dtsch.-it.] ⓐ I a. (lehnbar) feudal. — II ⸗e(r) m ⓐ upholder of feudal rights; pol. reactionary; aristocrat. [government.)
Feudal⸗herrschaft (-ⸯⸯ...) f ⓑ feudal)
Feudalismus (ⸯⸯⸯ) [feudal] m ⓐ (Lehnssystem) feudalism, weit⸗ reaction.
Feudalist (ⸯⸯⸯ) m ⓐ feudalist; vgl. feudal II; feudalistisch (ⸯⸯⸯ) a. ⓐ feudal, feudalist(ic); reactionary; Feudalität (--ⸯ) f ⓐ feudality.

Feudal⸗recht (-ⸯⸯ...) n ⓑ feudal law; ⸗system n fe. system; ⸗wesen n fe. institutions pl.; ⸗zeit f fe. period.
Feuer (ⸯⸯ) [ahd. -: fire: grch. pyr] n ⓑ 1. fire; helles, schnell aufloderndes ~ blaze; (großer Brand) fire, conflagration; F flare-up; bengalisches ~ Bengal light(s pl.); f. anlegen 1; brennen 1; ~ anmachen od. anzünden to kindle (or light) the fire; ~ ausmachen od. löschen to put out (or extinguish) the fire; bei gelindem ~ braten to roast on a slow fire; ~ fangen to catch (or take) f.; können Sie mir ~ geben? can you give me (or oblige me with) a light?; des ⸯs Herr werden to master the fire, to get the fire under, to subdue the flames; „~!" rufen oder schreien to call (or cry) fire; ~ schlagen to strike a light; ⚔ zwischen zwei ~n between two fires (auch fig.). — 2. ⚔ anhaltendes, heftiges ~ continuous, heavy firing; langsames, lebhaftes ~ slow, brisk firing; wirksames ~ effective fire; wohlgezieltes ~ well directed fire; ~ eröffnen to open fire; ~ geben to fire; das ~ schonen to be sparing of one's ammunition; to reserve one's fire; von Kanonen: ~ speien to belch (forth) fire; im ~ steh(e)n to be under fire; mit ~ und Schwert verwüsten to ravage with fire and sword. — 3. fig. f. brennen 2, 3, 4; er geht für sie durchs ~ he would go through fire and water for them; Öl ins ~ gießen to add fuel to the fire; er gerät gleich in ~ und Flamme he easily blazes up or flies into a passion; his blood (F his monkey) is soon up; vgl. Dach 3; ~ und Flamme sein für etwas to be all fire (or full of enthusiasm) for a th.; ~ u. Flamme speien (sehr aufgebracht sein) to be in a towering rage. — 4. ~ (Glanz) von Edelsteinen: fire, lustre; fig. ~ (Eifer, Lebhaftigkeit) von Personen: fire, ardour, spirit; v. Pferden ꝛc.: mettle; vgl. a. 3.
Feuer⸗alarm(⸗apparat) (-ⸯⸯ...) m ⓐ fire-alarm; ⚖anbetend a. ⓐ fire-worshipping; ⸗anbeter(in f) m fire-worshipper; ⸗anbetung f fire-worship, pyrolatry; ⸗anzünder m one who lights fires, ⊕ contrivance for kindling fires; ⚖artig a. fire-like, ⚛ igneous; ⸗bake ⚓ f beacon; ⸗ball m fire-ball; globe-lightning; ⸗becken n coal-pan, brazier; ⸗bereich ⚔ m fire-zone; ⸗berg m volcano; ⚖beständig a. fire-proof; ⊕ refractory; ⚖beständigkeit f fire-proof nature or virtue, bisw. fireproofness; ⸗bestattung f burning of the dead on the funeral pile; jetzt: cremation; ⸗blick m fiery glance; ⸗bock m andiron; ⸗⚖ f scarlet-runner (Phase'olus multiflo'rus); ⸗brand m fire-stick; firebrand (auch fig.); ⸗brücke ⊕ f im Ofen: fire-stop; ⸗büchse ⊕ f Dampfmaschine: fire-box; ⸗dienst m = ⸗anbetung; ⸗disziplin ⚔ f fire-discipline; ⸗eifer m fiery zeal, hot enthusiasm or passion; ⸗eimer m fire-bucket; ⸗eröffnung ⚔ f opening fire; ⸗esse ⊕ f: a) chimney; b) (Schmiede-)forge; ⸗fahne f, als Zeichen eines Schadenn-

⚛ scientific; ⚘ botanical; ⚖ geography; ⊕ machinery; ⚒ mining; ⚔ military; ⚓ marine; ⚖ commercial; ⚖ postal; 🚂 railway.

[Feuerfalter]

feuers: fire flag; =falter m, ent. small copper (Poly'ommatus); ⚥fangend a. easily catching fire; inflammable, combustible; =farbe f fire- (or fiery) colour; ⚥farben, ⚥farbig a. flame-coloured, of a fiery red; ⚥feſt a. fire-proof; (unverbrennbar) incombustible; ⊕ auch: refractory; ⚥er Geldſchrank safe; ⚥er Ton fire-clay; ⚥e Ziegel m/pl. fire-bricks pl.; =feſtigkeit f fire-proof nature of a substance; ⊕ auch: refractoriness; =fliege f, ent. (Leuchtkäfer) cucujo (Pyro'phorus nocti'lu'cus); weitS. firefly; =freſſer m fire-eater; =funke m spark of fire; =garbe f sheet of fire; auch: fire-sheaf; =gatter n = =gitter; =geben ⚔ n firing, discharge of fire-arms; ⚥gefährlich a. exposed to (or liable to catch) fire; vgl. ⚥fangend; =gefecht ⚔ n der Infanterie: action under fire; der Artillerie: artillery-duel or -fight; =geiſt m fiery (or ardent) spirit; =gerät n: a) contrivance for the extinction of fire; b) am Kamin: (set of) fire-irons; =geſchrei n fire-alarm; =geſchwindigkeit ⚔ f speed of firing; =gewehr n: a) = =rohr; b) = =waffe; =gewölbe n fire-vault; =gitter n hohes, aufrecht ſtehendes: fire-guard; niedriges, flaches: fender; =glanz m brightness (or bright glow) of fire; =glocke f tocsin (=Brandglocke); =gott m god of fire; auch: Vulcan; =hahn ⊕ m an Waſſerleitungsröhren: fire-plug; =haken m fire-hook; =haus n für Feuerlöſchgerätſchaften: engine-house; ⚥hell a. (as) bright as fire; =herd m fire-place, hearth; =himmel m: ⌧ empyrean, empyreal; =holz n fire-wood; =käfer m stag-beetle (Luca'nus cervus); =kana'l ⊕ m fire-tube, flue; =kaſſe f fire- (insurance) office; =kaſten ⊕ m an Dampfkeſſeln: fire-box; =kitt ⊕ m fire-lute; =kopf m hot headed person, hotspur, fiery nature; =krücke f (Schüreiſen) iron rake(r); =kugel f fire-ball, bolide; ast. globe-lightning, (fiery) meteor; =kunſt f pyrotechnics; =künſtler m pyrotechnist; =land ♀ npr/n. Fuegia; =lärm m fire-alarm; ↓ fire-roll; =leiter ⊕ f fire-escape; =leitung ⚔ f directing the musketry or artillery-fire; =leute pl. von mann; =lili-e ♀ f orange-lily (Li'lium cro'ceum); =linie ⚔ f fighting (or front) line (in a pitched battle); ⚥los a. without fire; von Edelſteinen: without lustre; dim, cloudy.

Feuerlöſch=appara't ⊕ (⏑⏑...) m ⚔ = =mittel; =gerätſchaften f/pl. implements pl. for extinguishing fire; fire-appliances pl.; =mannſchaft f fire-brigade; (corps of) firemen; =mittel n fire-extinguisher; =ordnung f = Feuerordnung b; =weſen n organization of fire-brigades; fire-protection.

Feuer=mal (⏑⏑...) n ⚔ burnt mark; scar of a burn; =mann m: a) (Heizer) stoker; engineman, engineer; b) bei der Feuerwehr: fireman; =materia'l n fuel; =mauer f party-wall; =meer n sea (or mass, sheet) of fire or flames, fiery ocean; =melde=appara't m elektriſcher: electric fire-alarm; =melder m ⊕ signal-box; (electric or telephonic)

— 368 —

fire-alarm; (f. =telegraph); =meldeſtelle f fire-station (a. ↓); =meſſer ⊕ m: ⌧ pyrometer; =meſſung f: ⌧ pyrometry. feuern (⏑⏑) I v/n. (h.) ⚔a. 1. to make (or light) a fire; mit Holz, Kohlen ꝛc. 2. to burn wood, coal, &c. — 2. ⚔ (ſchießen) to (give) fire; to discharge fire-arms; to fire at; blind (ſcharf) ⚔ to shoot with blank cartridges (with bullets); blindlings auf e-n ⚔ to take a random (or stray) shot at a p.; drauf los ⚔ to blaze (or fire) away, to waste one's ammunition. — II v/a. 3. = anfeuern 1. — 4. ↘ (anzünden) to kindle, to set fire (or light) to. — 5. F fig. einem eins um die Ohren ⚔ to give a p. a (good) box on the ear; abs. das Pferd feuert hinten tüchtig aus ... kicks out freely (from) behind. — III ~ n ⚔ 6. = Feuerung 1 u. 2.

Feuer=nelke ♀ (⏑⏑...) f ⚔ scarlet lychnis (Lychnis chalcedo'nica); =ofen m fiery furnace; =opa'l m, min. fire-opal; =ordnung f: a) ⚔ order of firing, b) für das Löſchen eines Brandes: fire-regulations pl., rules pl. for extinguishing a fire; =pauſe ⚔ f pause (made) in firing; =pfanne ⚔ f fire-pan; brazier; =pfeil m fire-arrow or -dart; =probe f trial by fire; als Gottesurteil: fire- (or fiery) ordeal; die ~ beſteh(e)n to stand the test, to pass well through a trial; =rad ⊕ n Feuerwerk: pin-wheel, Catherine-wheel; =regen m rain of fire; =rettungsappara't ⊕ m fire-escape; =rohr n: a) ehm.: firelock; b) jetzt: rifle; =roſt ⊕ m fire-grate; ⚥rot a. (as) red as fire, (of a) fiery red; ⚔ werden to turn quite red in the face, to blush; ⚥es Haar F carroty hair; =ruf m fire-alarm; cry of fire; =säule f pillar of fire; column) of fire.

Feuers=brunſt (⏑⏑...) f ⚔ (large) fire.conflagration, angelegte: incendiary fire.

Feuer=ſchaden (⏑⏑...) m ⚔ damage caused by fire; =ſchaufel f fire-shovel; =ſchein m glow (or flare, reflection) of fire; =ſcheu: a) a. afraid (F timid) of fire; b) f dread of fire; ⌧ pyrophobia; =ſchiff ↓ n fire-ship; =ſchirm m (Ofenſchirm) fire-screen; (Raminġitter) fire-guard; =ſchlund m fiery chasm or abyss; fig. der Kanone: the cannon's (fiery) mouth; poet. mouth of hell; =ſchutz m protection against fire; =ſchwaden ⚔ m fire-damp; =ſchwamm m: a) ♀ male agaric (Poly'porus igni-a'rius); b) ⊕ (Zunder) dressed agaric; (German) tinder; touchwood.

Feuers=gefahr (⏑⏑...) f ⚔ danger (arising) from fire, risk of fire; =glut f red glow of fire or flames; blazing fire. feuer=ſicher (⏑⏑...) a. protected from (the) fire, fire-proof; ⚥er (Geld=)Schrank fire-proof safe. [by fire.]

Feuers=not (⏑⏑⏑) f ⚔ distress caused feuer=ſpeiend (⏑⏑⏑) a. ⚔ spitting (or belching) fire, ⌧ ignivomous; ⚥er Berg volcano; =ſpritze ⊕ f ⚔ fire-engine; ⚥ſprühend a. sending forth (or throwing off) sparks (of fire); scintillating; =ſtahl m steel for striking fire; =ſtätte, =ſtelle f: a) scene of a fire or conflagration; b) ⊕ fire-

[Feurung]

place, hearth, grate; =ſtein m fire-stone; (Kieſel) flint; =ſtein=axt f flint hatchet; =ſtein=ſchloß ⚔ n ehm. fire-lock; =werkzeug n flint implement or tool; =ſtoff m, phys. ehm.: igneous principle, jetzt: caloric; =ſtrafe f punishment (or death) by fire; =ſtrahl m stream (or volume) of fire; =taktik ⚔ f firing tactics; =taufe f bſb. ⚔ fire-baptism; die ~ erhalten to be for the first time under fire; F to smell powder for the first time, von Regimentern: to be blooded; =telegra'ph ⊕ m telegraphic fire-alarm; =tod m death by fire; =ton ⊕ m fire-clay; =überlegenheit ⚔ ↓ f in der Schlacht: superior(ity) in) firing.

Feu(e)rung (⏑⏑) f ⚔ 1. making (or lighting) a fire. — 2. ⚔ firing, discharge of fire-arms. — 3. a) (Feuer) fire; b) (Brennmaterial) fuel.

Feu(e)rungs=anlage (⏑...) f ⚔ arrangement (or contrivance) for heating a room, &c.; =bedarf m, =materia'l n fuel.

Feuer=verehrung (⏑⏑...) f ⚔ = =anbetung; ⚥vergoldet ⊕ a. ⚔ fire-gilt; =vergoldung f fire-gilding; =verſicherung f fire-insurance; =verſicherungs=anſtalt, =geſellſchaft f fire-insurance office, company; =verſicherungs=poli'ce f, =ſchein m fire policy; =verſilberung ⊕ f fire-silvering; =wache f fire-station; =wächter m in Fabriken (fire-)watchman; =waffe f (ant. blanke W.) gun; ~n fire-arms pl.; =wahrſagerei f: ⚔ pyromancy; =waſſer n bei den Indianern fire-water; =wehr f fire-brigade; =wehrmann m = =mann b; =werk ⚔ n (display of) fire-works pl.; =werfer m: a) =künſtler: b) ↓ =m ⚔ gunner, artillery-man; =werkerkunſt, =werkskunſt f = =kunſt; =werkerſchule ⚔ f gunnery- (or artillery-)school; =werkskörper m/pl. fireworks pl.; =wirkung ⚔ f effect of (gun-)fire; =wolke f fiery cloud; =wurm m (Glühwurm) glow-worm; =zange f fire-tongs pl.; =zeichen n fire-signal; ↓ beacon (-fire); =zeug n ehm.: flint and steel; jetzt: match-box; =zug m am Ofen: flue.

Feuilleton (fŏi'-j-⏑-tą') [fr.] n ⚔ (belletriſtiſcher Teil e-r Zeitung) feuilleton; ~iſt (fŏi-j-⏑⚔) m ⚔ (auch: ~ſchreiber m ⚔) writer of feuilletons; ⚥iſtiſch (fŏi-j-⏑⚔) f ⚔ etwa: written in a light (or an easy) style or vein; ~ſtil m ⚔ (light and easy) style of a (newspaper) feuilleton.

feurig (⏑⏑) [mhd.] a. ⚔ 1. fiery; burning; bſb. ⌧ igneous; von der Farbe: red as fire; der Himmel iſt ganz ⚔ ... is of a fiery red, ... appears all on fire; (funkelnd, flammend) sparkling, flaming, von Augen ꝛc.: very bright, lustrous; ⚥e Kohle red-hot coal; fig. ⚥e Kohlen auf j-s Haupt ſammeln to heap coals of fire on a p.'s head. — 2. fig. von Menſchen: fiery, ardent, passionate, hot-tempered, hot-headed; (ungeſtüm) impetuous; von Pferden auch: spirited, high-mettled or -bred; vom Wein: heady, strong; von Reden: impassioned, inflammatory, stirring, rousing.

feurio! (⏑⏑⏑) int. fire!

Feurung (⏑⏑) f ⚔ = Feuerung.

Zeichen (ſ. S. XVII): F familiär; P Volksſprache; Γ Gaunerſprache; ↘ ſelten; † alt (auch geſtorben); * neu (auch geboren); ⧓ unrichtig;

Fex (ˊ) *m* ①a. ② s. Berg⁀.
ff. *abbr.* = folgende Seiten, und das Folgende; ✿ sehr fein; **FF** (ˊˊ) *n, inv.*
ff ♪ *abbr.* = fortissimo. [= Effeff.
Fiaker (ˇˊˇ od. ˊˇˇ) [fr.] *m* ② (Mietkutsche) hackney coach, cab, F four-wheeler, P growler; vgl. Droschke.
Fiale (ˇˊˇ; *Hom.* Phiale) [it., *grch.] *f* ④ *arch.* (gotisches Spitztürmchen) Gothic turret.
Fiasko (ˇˊˇ) [it.] *n* ⑤ bsd. *thea.* failure; break-down; ~ machen to prove a (complete) failure *or* fiasco; to break down; F to fall flat.
Fibel (ˊˇ) [ndd.; *Bibel] *f* ④ primer, first spelling-book; ehm. horn-book.
Fiber (ˊˇ; *Hom.* Fieber) [lt.] *f* ④ ⚘, *anat.* (Faser) fibre, (thin) thread, ✍ filament.
Fibrin ✍ (ˇˊ) [neu-lt.] *n* ①c. *chm.* (Faserstoff) fibrin. [fibrous.
fibrös (ˇˊ) *a.* ⑥ *anat., path.,* &c. (faserig)
ficht (ˊ) *pres.* u. *imper.* von fechten.
Fichte ⚘ (ˊˇ) [ahd.] *f* ④ 1. (Rot-tanne) spruce(-fir) (*Pi'cea exce'lsa*). — 2. nordd. P (gem. Kiefer) pine(-tree) (*Pinus silve'stris*).
fichten (ˊˇ) *a.* ⑥ (made) of pine-wood; fichtene Bretter pine boards *pl.*
Fichten-apfel (ˊˇ...) *m* ② = -zapfen; **-baum** ⚘ *m* = Fichte; **-hain** *m* pine-grove; **-harz** *n* (pine-)resin; **-holz** *n* pine-wood; **-kreuzschnabel** *m, orn.* cross-bill *or* -beak (*Lo'xia curviro'stra*); **-nadelbad** *n* pine-needle bath; **-nadelöl** *n* pine-leaf oil; **-spargel** ⚘ *m* pine-sap, yellow bird's-nest (*Mono'tropa Hypo'pitys*); **-spinner** *m, ent.* black arches (*Ocne'ria mo'nacha*); **-stamm** *m* trunk of a pine-tree; **-wald** *m* pine-forest; **-zapfen** *m* pine-cone; **-zweig** *m* pine-branch. [wood.
Fichticht (ˊˇ) *n* ①d. (Fichtengehölz) pine-
Ficke P nordd. (ˊˇ) [ndd.] *f* ④ (Tasche) pocket; einen in die ~ stecken können to be far superior to a p.
Fickfack (ˊˊ) *m* ⑤ (Ausflucht) subterfuge; (Vorwand) pretext.
fickfacken (ˊˊˇ) [ahd.: fickle] *v/n.* (h.) ⑧ to prevaricate, shuffle, intrigue.
Fickfacker (ˊˊˇ) *m* ②, **~in** *f* ④ prevaricator, shuffler, intriguer.
Fickfackerei (ˊˇˇˊ) *f* ⑥ prevarication, shuffling, intriguing.
Fick-mühle (ˊ...) *f* ② = Zwickmühle.
Fide-i-kommiß (ˊˇ-ˇˊ) [lt.] *n* ①a. *jur.* (unveräußerlicher Grundbesitz) entail; property (bsdw. feoffment) in trust.
Fide-i-kommissariat (ˊˇ-ˊˇ-(ˇ)ˊ) *n* ①c. *jur.* entailment.
fidel F (ˇˊ) [nhd., *lt.] *a.* ⑥ bursch.: (lustig) jovial, in high glee; F jolly; ⁀es Haus F jolly fellow; ⁀es Leben merry life; ⁀es Mädchen jolly nice girl.
Fidelität (ˇ-ˇˊ) [nhd., *lt.] *f* ⑥ joviality, F jollity; merry mood; buoyant (*or* high) spirits *pl.* [light, spill.
Fidibus F (ˊˇˇ) [?] *m* ⑪ od. *inv.* pipe-
Fidibus-ständer (ˊ...) *m* ② spill-holder.
Fidschi-archipel ♁ (ˊˇ...) *m* ② Fiji archipelago; **-bewohner(in** *f*) *m* Fiji islander, Fijian; **-inseln** *npr., f/pl.* Australien: Fiji Islands *pl.*
Fiduz (ˇˊ) [lt. *fīdū'ciă f*] *n* ①a., auch *inv.* (Vertrauen) confidence; er zeigt kein ~ (keine Lust) dazu he shows no inclination to do it.

Fiduzit (ˇˊˇ) *n* (*m*) ⑤ und ⁀ *int.* burschikos: (Antwort auf den Trinkgruß: Schmollis) the same to you!, thank you!
Fieber (ˊˇ; *Hom.* Fiber) [ahd.; *lt. *fĕbris f*] *n* ② *path.* fever; gelbes ~ yellow fever, auch: Yellow Jack; (Wechsel-)~ ague; (Sumpf-)~ malaria; schleichendes ~ low fever; vom ~ befallen fever-stricken, F down with fever; ~ haben to be feverish *or* in a (burning) fever.
Fieber-anfall (ˊˇ...) *m* ② *path.* attack of fever; ⁀**artig** *a.* ⑥ fever-like, feverish, ✍ febrile; **-arznei** *f, med.* fever-medicine, ✍ antipyretic drug, febrifuge; **-baum** ⚘ *m* eucalyptus; ⁀**erzeugend** *a.* producing fever, ✍ febrific, febriferous; **-farbe** *f* feverish colour; ⁀**fest** *a.* f.-proof; **-flecken** *m/pl.* f.-spots *pl.*; ⁀**frei** *a.* free from fever; **-frost** *m* feverish chill; ~ haben to be shivering with fever; **-glut** *f* feverish heat.
fieberhaft (ˊˇˇ), *a.* **fieb(e)rig, fieb(e)risch** (ˊ(ˇ)ˇ) *a.* ⑥ feverish, ✍ febrile.
Fieberhaftigkeit (ˊˇˇˇ-), *f* ⑥ feverishness, feverish state.
Fieber-hitze (ˊˇ...) *f* ② feverish heat, ✍ cauma; bis zur ~ to fever-point; **-klee** ⚘ *m* marsh (*or* water-)trefoil, bogbean (*Menya'nthes trifolia'ta*); ⁀**krank** *a.* ⑥ suffering from (*or* F down with) fever; **-kranke(r)** *s.* f.-patient; **-krankheit** *f* illness accompanied with fever; ⁀**los** *a.* feverless; vgl. ⁀frei; **-losigkeit** *f* freedom from (*or* intermission of) fever; **-mittel** *n* = -arznei.
fiebern (ˊˇ) *v/n.* (h.) ⑨a. to be in a (*or* ill of) fever; (phantasieren) to be delirious *or* raving *or* feverish; *fig.* to be intensely agitated.
Fieber-phantasie (ˊˇ...) *f* ② raving; vgl. -traum; **-rinde** *f* = Chinarinde; **-rindenbaum** ⚘ *m* Peruvian bark-tree (*Cincho'na officina'lis*); **-schau(d)er** *m* shivering fit of a fever-patient; vgl. -frost; **-tag** *m* day on which a fever comes on; **-traum** *m* feverish dream, *fig.* fancy of an overwrought brain; ⁀**vertreibend**(es Mittel *n*) *a., med.*: ✍ febrifuge; **-wahn(sinn)** *m, path.*: ✍ delirium; **-zustand** *m* feverishness.
Fiedel F (ˊˇ) [ahd.; mlt. *vi'tula* (it. *vio'la*)] *f* ④ meist *contp.* fiddle; violin.
Fiedel-bogen (ˊˇ...) *m* ② (violin-)bow, *co.* fiddle-stick. [fiddling.
Fiedelei F (-ˇˊ) *f* ⑥ (continuous)
fiedeln F (ˊˇ) *v/n.* (h.) u. *v/a.* ⑨a. 1. to (scrape on the) fiddle. — 2. (rasch hin und her bewegen) to move rapidly up and down.
fieder-artig ⚘ (ˊˇ...) *a.* ⑥: ✍ pinnate(d); **-blättchen** ⚘ *n* ② pinnule, pinnula.
fiedern (ˊˇ) I *v/a.* ⑨a. 1. to provide with feathers. — II **ge-fiedert** *p.p.* u. *a.* ⑥ 2. feathered; die ⁀e Welt the feathered world, (all) winged creation, the world of birds. — 3. ⚘ v. Blättern: pinnate(d).
fieder-spaltig ⚘ (ˊˇ...) *a.* ⑥ v. Blättern: ✍ pinnatifid; **-stiel** *m*: ✍ petiolule; ⁀**teilig** ⚘ *a.*: ✍ pinnatipartite.
Fiedler F (ˊˇ) *m* ② mst *contp.* (wretched *or* vile) fiddler; P gut-scraper.
Fiek (ˊ) [ndd.] *m* ①c. *zo.* (Riemen-, Gürtelwurm) strap-worm (*Li'gula abdomina'lis*).

fiel (ˊ; *Hom.* viel) (u. ⁀e *subj.*) *impf.* v. fallen.
Fi-erant (-ˇˊ) [it.] *m* ② (Meßkrämer) (foreign) trader who attends the fairs (with his goods).
fieren ⚓ (ˊˇ) [ndd.] *v/a.* ⑧: ein Tau ⁀ (ablaufen lassen) to pay out a cable.
Figur (ˇˊ) [lt.] *f* ⑥ 1. (Gestalt) figure, shape; (gute) ~ machen to cut a figure; Bild in ganzer ~ full-length portrait *or* photograph; von guter, schlechter ~ well-made, ill-shaped. — 2. *math.* figure, diagram; eingeschriebene, um(ge)schriebene ~ inscribed, circumscribed figure. — 3. Karten: court- (*or* picture-)card. — 4. Schach: piece, chessman. — 5. (Rede-)~ figure of speech; ✍ metaphor(ical expression).
Figura F (ˇˊˇ) [lt.] *f* ④ wie ~ (der Augenschein) lehrt oder zeigt as is obvious(ly the case), to all appearances.
figural, bsd. ♪ (ˇ-ˊ) [lt.] *a.* ⑥ (mit Tonfiguren verziert) figurate.
Figural-gesang ♪ (ˇ-ˊ...) *m* ②, **-musik** *f* figurate counterpoint.
Figurant (ˇ-ˊ) [lt.] *m* ②, **~in** *f* ④ *thea.* super(numerary); ~in auch: show girl; (aushelfender Schauspieler) utility actor *or* man; weitS. (Nebenperson) (mere) cipher *or* puppet.
Figürchen (ˇˊˇ) *n* ② (*dim.* von Figur) small figure; (Metall- ꝛc.) ~ figurine.
Figuren-fries (ˇˊ...) *m* ② *arch.* sculptured (*or* storied) frieze; ⁀**reich** *a.* ⑥ *paint.* abounding in figures; **-zeichnen** *n* drawing of figures.
figurieren (ˇ-ˊˇ) [lt.] *v/a.* u. *v/n.* (h.) ⑧ (gestalten, darstellen) to shape, (per)form, represent; (auftreten, eine Rolle spielen) to (cut a) figure; als etwas ~ to pose as s.th.; *math.* figurierte Zahl figurate number; ✿ figurierter Stoff fancy material *or* cloth.
figürlich (ˇˊˇ) *a.* ⑥ (bildlich) figurative; *adv.* oder im ⁀en Sinne (speaking) figuratively *or* metaphorically.
Fiktion (ˇtß(ˇ)ˊ) [lt.] *f* ⑥ (Dichtung) fiction, romance.
fiktiv (ˇˊf) [lt.] *a.* ⑥ (erdichtet) fictitious.
Filanda (ˇˊˇ) [it.] *f* ④ (⑤) (Seidenspinnerei) silk-spinning mill.
Filet (ˇle') [fr.] *n* ⑤ 1. weibliche Arbeit: network, netting; in ~ arbeiten, ~ häkeln to net. — 2. Kochkunst: (Lendenstück) fillet of veal. — 3. ⚙ ⑤ Buchbinderei: = Filetstempel.
Filet-arbeit (ˊ...) *f* ② network; **-beefsteak** *n* filleted steak; **-braten** *m* roast fillet; **-handschuhe** *m/pl.* gloves made of netting; **-maschine, -nadel, -schraube** ⚙ *f* netting-machine, -needle, -stretcher *or* -vice; **-stempel** ⚙ *m/pl.* Buchbinderei: back-tools *pl.*; **-stickerei** *f* = -arbeit; **-stock** ⚙ *m* netting-pin.
Filial-anstalt (-(ˇ)ˊ...) *f* ② = Filiale.
Filiale (-(ˇ)ˊˇ) [lt.] *f* ④ (Zweig-anstalt) branch (office *or* establishment); ✉ s. Zweigstelle.
Filial-geschäft (-(ˇ)ˊ...) *n* ② ✿ branch (of a business), branch office; **-kirche** *f, eccl.* chapel of ease.
filieren (ˇˊˇ) [fr.] *v/a.* ⑨: Seide⁀ (zwirnen) to mill (*or* throw) silk.
Filigran ⚙ (-ˇˊ) [it.] *n* ①d. (feine Gold- od. Silberdraht-arbeit) filigree.

Film ⊤ (´) [engl.: Fell] *m u. n* ⓢd.(ⓢ) *phot.*, &c. film.
Filou (ˇlu') [fr. Gauner] *m* ⓢ rogue, sharper, scamp.
filpen (´ˇ) *v/n.* (h.) Ⓑ von Orgelpfeifen: to shrill.
Filter (´ˇ) [fr. *filtre*; *dtsch Filz] *m u.* ⊙ nur *n* ㉒ filter.
filtern (´ˇ) ⓦa. = filtrieren.
Filter=presse (´ˇ...) *f* ⓓ beet-press.
Filtrat (ˇ´) [neu=lt.] *n* ⓦc. filtrate.
Filtration (ˇ-tß(ˇ)´) *f* ⓓ = filtrieren II.
Filtrier=apparat (ˇ´´...) *m* ⓓ *chm.*, &c. filter, percolator; =**bassin** *n* Wasserbau: reservoir for filtering water, filtering-tank, filter-bed; =**beutel** *m* = =sack.
filtrieren (ˇ´ˇ) **I** *v/a.* Ⓑ (durchseihen) to filter, strain, percolate. — **II** ~ *n* ㉓ ⚗ *chm.*, &c. filtration, percolation.
Filtrierer (ˇ´ˇ) *m* ㉒ filterer.
Filtrier=kaffeemaschine(ˇ´...)*f*ⓓ(coffee-) percolator; =**papier** *n* filtering-paper; =**sack** *m* fi.-bag; =**stein** *m* fi.-stone; =**trichter** *m* fi.-funnel; strainer; =**tuch** *n* fi.-cloth, percolator, Müll.: bolting cloth.
Filtrierung (ˇ´ˇ) *f* ⓓ = filtrieren II.
Filtrum (´ˇ) [neu=lt.] *n* ㉘ filter.
Filz (´) [ahd.: felt] *m* ⓤa. **1.** felt; ⚘: ⚗ tomentum; mit ~ bekleiden to (cover with) felt. — **2.** ⊙ *typ.* (-deckel) blanket. — **3.** F (Geizhals) skinflint, miser(ly person), screw; (roher Mensch) ruffian, brutal fellow.
Filz=arbeit (´...) *f* ⓓ felting; ♀**artig** *a.* Ⓐ felt-like.
filzen¹ (´ˇ) Ⓦ **I** *v/a.* **1.** to (cover with) felt. — **2.** F e-n ♀ (schelten) to scold a p., to blow a p. up. — **II** F *v/n.* (h.) **3.** (geizen) to live in a miserly (or mean, niggardly) way, to be stingy. — **III sich** ♀ *v/refl.* **4.** von Wolle, Haar ꝛc.: to cling (or clot) together.
filzen² (´ˇ) *a.* Ⓐ (made) of felt.
Filzer (´ˇ) *m* ㉒ **1.** ⊙ felt-maker or -worker. — **2.** F = Filz 3.
Filz=hut (´...) *m* ⓓ felt hat; harter auch: F bowler; weicher: soft hat, F billycock.
filzicht (´ˇ) *a.* Ⓐ = filzig 1.
filzig (´ˇ) *a.* Ⓐ **1.** (of) felt, felt-like, like felt; ⚘ downy, ⚗ tomentose, tomentous. — **2.** (knauserig) mean, niggardly, close- (or tight-)fisted, stingy.
Filzigkeit (´ˇ-) *f* Ⓑ meanness, niggardliness, stinginess.
Filz=kraut ⚘ (´...) *n* ⓓ cotton-rose (*Fila'go*); =**laus** *f*, *ent.* crab-louse, body-louse (*Pedi'culus pubis*); =**maschine** ⊙ *f* felting-machine; =**mütze** *f* felt cap; =**schuh** *m* felt shoe or slipper; =**sohle** *f* felt sole; =**stiefel** *m* felt boot; =**tuch** ✱ *n* felt -cloth; =**unterlage** ⊙ *f*, *typ.* = Filz²; =**waren** *f/pl.* felt goods or articles *pl.*; =**werk** *n* feltwork.
Fimme (´ˇ) *f* Ⓑ = Feim(en) (Kornschober).
Fimmel¹ ⚘ (´ˇ) [lt. *femella*] *m* ㉒ (P ⁺₊) (männlicher Hanf) fimble-hemp (*Ca'nnabis sati'va*).
Fimmel² ⚒ (´ˇ) *m* ㉒ (Spaltkeil) strong iron wedge.
Finale ♪ (ˇ´ˇ) [lt.] *n* ⓢ finale.
Final=satz (ˇ´´) *m* ⓓ *gram.* (Absichtssatz) (adverbial) clause indicating purpose.
Finanz (ˇ´) [fr. *finance*] *f* Ⓑ meist ~en *pl.* finance(s *pl.*).
Finanz=anschlag (ˇ´...) *m* ⓓ *pol.* estimates *pl.*; =**ausschuß** *m* finance-committee, *pol.* Committee of Ways and Means; =**baron** *m* prince of finance, great financier; =**beamte(r)** *m*, Engl.: clerk of the Treasury; =**bureau** *n* revenue-office; =**frage** *f* financial question.
finanziell (ˇ(ˇ)´) [fr.] *a.* Ⓐ financial.
Finanz=jahr (ˇ´...) *n* ⓓ financial (or fiscal) year; =**kontrolle** *f* financial control; =**mann** *m* financier; =**minister** *m* minister of finance; England: Chancellor of the Exchequer; *Am.* Secretary of the Treasury; =**ministerium** *n* ministry of finance; England: (Board of) Exchequer, Lords of the Treasury; *Am.* Treasury; =**pächter** *m* ehm. farmer of the taxes or of (the) revenue; =**rat** *m* = =beamte(r); =**welt** *f* financial world, (the great) financiers *pl.*, a.: the (fr.) haute finance; =**wesen** *n* financial concerns *pl.*, finance(s *pl.*); =**wissenschaft** *f* science of finance.
findbar (´-) *a.* Ⓐ findable.
Findel=anstalt (´ˇ...) *f* Ⓑ, =**haus** *n* foundling-hospital; =**kind** *n* foundling; =**mutter** *f* (=vater *m*) foster-mother (-father) of a foundling.
finden (´ˇ) [ahd.: find] ⓐ **I** *v/a.* **1.** to find; ich fand es des Nachts sehr kalt I found it very cold in the night; wir finden es sehr freundlich, sehr nett von ihm, daß // we think (or consider) it very kind, very nice of him that //; ich finde (in der Zeitung ꝛc.), daß // I find (or have just read, heard) that //; nirgends zu ♀ nowhere to be found; e-n unerwartet ♀ (treffen) unexpectedly to meet a p.; er hat s-n Mann gefunden he has found his match; er konnte keine Worte ♀ he could not utter a word, he stood speechless; ich fand **an** ihm e-n Freund I found in him a friend. — **2.** Beifall ♀ to meet with (or to reap) applause; et. **an** e-r Sache auszusetzen ♀ to find fault with a th.; Freude am Wohltun ♀ to find (or take) a pleasure in doing good; keinen Glauben ♀ to find no credence, not to be believed; **vor** e-m Gnade ♀ to find favour in a p.'s eyes. — **3.** etwas (für) gut, (für) ratsam ♀ (halten) to find (or think, judge) s.th. right, advisable; wie ♀ Sie die Gegend? how do you like the neighbourhood?; ich finde, daß man hier angenehm lebt I find (or think) life very pleasant here. — **II sich** ♀ *v/refl.* **4.** to find o.s., to be; schöne Seelen ♀ sich (ea.), kindred spirits (are bound to) meet; das wird sich schon ♀ (in Ordnung kommen) that will, no doubt, be arranged or come right; *v/impers.* **es** ♀ sich Menschen, die // there are people who //; es wird sich bald ♀, daß // it will soon be found (or discovered) that //, time will show that //. — **5.** mit *adv.* u. *prp.*: sich **aus** der Sache nicht ♀ können to be unable to see one's way (clearly) out of (or through) a thing; sich **heim** ♀ to find one's way home; sich **in** et. ♀ to put up with a th.; (es begreifen) to understand (or to see through) a th.; er kann sich nicht darein ♀ he cannot reconcile himself to it; sich in die Umstände ♀ to adapt o.s. to circumstances; sich **zu** e-m ♀ (gesellen) to join a p., to associate (o.s.) with a p.; sich **zurecht** ♀ to find one's way about, *fig.* to see one's way clear(ly); ich finde mich im Spanischen nicht mehr zurecht I have forgotten a good deal of my Spanish.
findens=wert (´ˇ...) *a.* Ⓐ worth finding.
Finder (´ˇ) *m* ㉒, ~**in** *f* Ⓑ finder, discoverer; ~=**lohn** *m (n)* finder's reward.
findig (´ˇ) *a.* Ⓐ clever or shrewd (in finding out or discovering); sharp, sagacious; ⚒ einen Gang ♀ machen to discover a lode; ~**keit** (´ˇ-) *f* Ⓑ cleverness, shrewdness.
findlich (´ˇ) *a.* Ⓐ = findbar.
Findling (´ˇ) *m* ⓦd. foundling; ~(s=**block**) *m*, *geol.* erratic block, driftblock.
Finesse (-´ˇ) [nhd. 17. *sae.*, * fr.] *f* Ⓑ finesse, cunning.
fing (´) *ind.*, ♀**e** *subj. impf.* von fangen.
Fingals=höhle ♀ (´ˇ...) *f* Ⓑ auf der Hebrideninsel Staffa: Fingal's Cave.
Finger (´ˇ) [ahd.: finger] *m* ㉒ **1.** finger (auch als Maß); *anat.*: ⚗ digit; *zo. a.* toe; der kleine ~ the little f., bisw. ear-f.; s. Mittel=, Ring=, Zeige=♀; keinen ~ breit not an inch; an den ~n herrechnen to count on one's fingers; sich (*dat.*) in den ~ schneiden to cut one's f.; sich (*dat.*) die ~ verbrennen to burn one's fingers (a. *fig.*); *fig.* lange ~ *pl.* (Diebe) F long-fingered gentry. — **2.** *fig.* mit *v.*: man kann es leicht an den ~n abzählen you can count it on your fingers, it is easily reckoned up or accounted for; er braucht nur die ~ danach auszustrecken he need only stretch out his hand; et. auf die ~ bekommen to get a rap on one's knuckles; gibt man ihm e-n ~, will er die ganze Hand give him an inch, and he'll take an ell; s. geraten 2 am Schluß; mit allen zehn ~n nach etwas greifen to snatch eagerly at a thing; er hat mehr Verstand im kleinen ~ als sie im ganzen Leibe he has more sense in his little finger than she in her whole body; er kann es an den ~n herzählen he has it at his fingers' ends; ihm jucken die ~ danach his fingers itch to have (or to do) it; e-m auf die ~ klopfen to give a p. a rap on the knuckles; was ihm nur unter die ~ kommt whatever falls into his hands; laß deine ~ davon don't meddle with it; er würde sich (*dat.*) die ~ danach lecken ... jump at it; den ~ auf den Mund legen (schweigen) to keep one's lips sealed, F to be mum; lange (oder krumme) ~ machen to be long-fingered or fond of thieving or pilfering; sich (*dat.*) keinen ~ um etwas naß machen not to stir (or lift up) a finger for a th.; sich (*dat.*) et. aus den ~n saugen (aus der Luft greifen) to invent a th., to trump (or hatch) up a story; e-m (scharf) auf die ~ sehen oder passen to keep a strict eye on a p.; e-m durch die ~ sehen (et. hingehen lassen) to wink at a p.'s faults, to make allowance for a p.; mit den ~n auf e-n weisen to point (one's fingers) at a p.; er ist (leicht) um den ~ zu wickeln (nachgiebig) F you can twist him round your little finger, you may do as you like with him; ♪ die ~ (gehörig) setzen to finger (well).

[**Fingerabdruck**] — 371 — [**Fisch**]

Finger=abdruck (⌒ゝ…) m ㉒, als Erkennungszeichen: finger-print; **=ähnlich** a. ⑥⑥ finger-like, ⚛ digital; **=becken** n finger-basin or -bowl; **=bein** n, anat.: ⚛ phalanx, phalange; **=beuger** m, anat.: ⚛ digital flexor (muscle); **=breit** a. a finger's breadth; **=breite** f finger's breadth; **=brett** ♪ n key-board; **=dicke** f finger's thickness; **=entzündung** f (Nagelgeschwür) whitlow, ⚛ panaritium; **=fertig** a. nimblefingered, skilled with one's fingers; **=fertigkeit** f manual skill, dexterity; ♪ rapid (or easy) fingering; **=förmig** a. f.-shaped; ♪: ⚛ digitate, digitiform; **=geschwür** n, path. = **=entzündung**; **=glied** n joint of a finger; **=handschuh** m fingered glove; glove with fingers; **=hirse** ♀ = **Blut-h.**; **=hut** m: a) thimble; b) ♀ fox-glove (Digitalis); gelber ~ yellow fox-glove (D. lutea); roter ~ lady's-glove, dead-men's-bells (D. purpu'rea); **=hut=förmig** a. digitaliform. [ten fingers.| **…fingerig** (…⌒ゝ) i. Zsgn, 3B. zehn**²** with⌟ **Finger=kraut** ♀ (⌒ゝ…) n ㉒ cinquefoil (Potentilla); kriechendes ~ creeping cinquefoil (P. reptans).

Fingerling (⌒ゝ⌒) m ⓓ. zum Schutz eines kranken Fingers: finger-stall, thumb-stall. **fingern** (⌒ゝ) v/n. (h.) u. v/a. ㉒a. to finger, touch; (betasten) to handle; s. gefingert.

Finger=nagel (⌒ゝ…) m ㉒ finger-nail; **=platte** f f.-plate; **=ring** m f.-ring; **=satz** ♪ m fingering; **=schreit(e), =dick(e)** s. =breit(e), =dick(e); **=schlag** m tap(ping) with a finger; **=schnecke** f, zo. spider-shell (Pterocera); **=setzung** ♪ f fingering; **=spitze** f tip of the finger; **=sprache** f finger-language or -talk, ⚛ dactylology; chirology; **=spur** f f.-mark; **=stock** m glove-stick or -stretcher; **=strecker** m: a) **=stock**; b) anat. **=beuger**; **=tier** n, zo. ⚛ chiromys; **=übung** ♪ f fingering-exercise; **=wurm** m, path. = **=entzündung**; **=zahl** f, arith. digit; **=zeig** m indication; (Wink) hint, suggestion, F tip; e-m e-n ~ geben to give a p. the cue or the hint.

fingieren (⌣⌣⌣) I v/a. ㊛ (vorgeben) to feign, pretend, simulate, sham; **fingiert** fictitious, imaginary; ⚙ **fingierter Wechsel** pro-forma (or bogus) bill; **fingierter Wert** nominal value. — II ~ n ㉓ u. **Fingierung** f ㊻ fiction, pretence, sham(ming).

Fink ♪ (⌒) [ahd.: finch] m ㊽, ~e (⌣) m ㊹ 1. orn. finch, ⚛ fringilla; s. Buchfink. — 2. F fig. (liederlicher Hans) loose (or fast) fellow; (lustiger Mensch) jolly fellow, F gay young spark. — 3. univ. (Student, der keiner geschlossenen Verbindung angehört) student who has not joined a students' "corps" or association.

finkeln (⌣⌣) I v/n. (h.) ㉒a* to catch finches, to catch (small) birds. — II ~ n ㉓ bird-catching.

Finken=bauer (⌒ゝ…) m (n) ㊽ cage for finches; **=falk, =habicht** m, orn. = Sperber; **=garn, =netz** n bramble- net; **=herd** m fowling-floor; **=same** ♀ m panicled neslia (Neslia paniculata); **=schlag** m song (or note) of a finch; **=strich** m flight of finches; netting of (a flight of) finches; **=weibchen** n, orn. hen-finch.

Finkler (⌣⌣) m ㉒ = Vogelsteller; fast nur in: Heinrich der ~ (deutscher König, † 936) Henry the Fowler.

Finne¹ (⌣) [ndd.: fin] f ㊽ 1. path., ichth. (Flosse) fin. — 2. ⊕ (schmale Schlagseite des Hammers) hammer-edge, gespaltene: claw of a hammer.

Finne² (⌣) [mhd.] f ㊽ 1. path. (Bläschen, Hautkrankheit im Gesichte) pimple(s pl.), blotch(es pl.), ⚛ acne; durch Trinken erzeugte: F brandy-blossom. — 2. vet. ~n pl. (Aussatz der Schweine) (pig's) measles pl. [Finländer.|

Finne³ (⌣) m ㊹, **Finnin** f ㊼ Volk:⌟ **Finn=fisch** (⌒…) m ㉒ zo. = Finnwal. **finnig** (⌣⌣) [**Finne²**] a. ㊋ pimpled, blotched; vet. von Schweinen: measly. **finnisch** (⌣⌣) [**Finne³**] a. ㊋ Finnish; die Sprache, das ~(e) n ㊱ the Finnish language, Finnish; ♀ =er Meerbusen Gulf of Finland.

Finn=land ♀ (⌒…) [Fenn=] npr/n. ⓓa. (russ. Großfürstentum) Finland. **Finn=länder** (⌒…) I m ㉒, ~in f ㊼ = **Finne³**. — II a. inv., ⚛ **finn=ländisch** (…⌒…) a. ㊋ Finnish, (of) Finland. **Finn=wal** (⌒⌣) m ㉒ zo.: a) finback, fin-fish (Balaenoptera); b) rorqual (Physalus antiquorum).

finster (⌣⌣) [ahd.] I a. ㊋ (D9) 1. (dunkel, trüb) dark, gloomy; es wird schon ² it is already getting dark, night is setting in early; es war eine sehr (a. pech=)²e Nacht … a pitch-dark night. — 2. fig. ²es Aussehen gloomy (or sullen) look; ²e Gedanken sad (or melancholy) thoughts; e-m ² (adv.) ansehen to give a p. black looks. — II **Finst(e)re(s)** n ㊱ 1. darkness, gloom; im ~n (i. b. Dunkelheit) in the dark, in the night, fig. in obscurity; im ²n tappen (wandeln) to grope (to walk) in the dark or in darkness.

Finsterkeit (⌣⌣…) f ㊻ = **Finsternis**. **Finsterling** (⌣⌣…) m ⓓ. 1. one opposed to enlightenment; enemy of progress; obscurantist. — 2. (Nicht-aufgeklärter) ignorant person; F ignoramus.

Finster=mette (⌣⌣…) f ㊽ Cath. eccl. midnight service, (early) matins pl. **Finsternis** (⌣⌣⌣) [ahd.] f ㊸ 1. (Dunkelheit) darkness, gloom, obscurity (oft fig.); in der ~ in the dark; ägyptische ² Egyptian darkness. — 2. bibl. (Trübsal) affliction, adversity; (Sündhaftigkeit) sinful state. — 3. ast. partielle, totale ~ eines Weltkörpers partial, total eclipse; vgl. Mond-, Sonnenfinsternis.

Finte (⌣⌣) [it.] f ㊽ dim. **Fintchen** n ㉓ 1. fenc. (Scheinhieb) feint. — 2. fig. (Kunstgriff) ruse, finesse, dodge, trick, artifice; (Ausflucht, Lüge) hollow (or lame) excuse; ~n=macher (⌣⌣…) m ⊕ (artful) dodger, trickster.

Fips (⌣) m ⓓa. 1. (Nasenstüber) fillip. — 2. F bisw. (leichte, unruhige Person) F fly-away; harum-scarum, gadabout; bsd. Meister ~ (Schneider) F Snip. **fipsen** (⌣⌣) ㊺ I v/a. to fillip. — II v/n. (h.) bsd. ehm. to play with knuckle-bones.

Firlefanz (⌣⌣⌣) [mhd.; fr. virelai u. dtsch. Fant] m ⓓa. 1. (Geck) fop. — 2. (Tand, Narretei) childish play, (tom)foolery, (silly) stuff, F fiddle-faddle.

firlefanzen (⌣⌣⌣⌣) v/n. (h.) ㊼ to play childishly, to act (or talk) in a silly manner; to talk nonsense; **Firlefanzerei** (⌣⌣⌣⌣⌣) f ㊼ = **Firlefanz 2**. **firm** (⌣) [lt.] a. ㊋ (fest) firm. **Firma** ⊕ (⌣⌣) [it.] ㊾ 1. (Geschäftsname) firm; unter der ~ „Walter" Handel treiben to trade under the name of „W."; (für) die ~ zeichnen to sign for the firm. — 2. (Geschäftshaus) (commercial) firm, house of business. **Firmament** (⌣⌣⌣) [lt.] n ⓓb. (Himmelszelt) firmament, sky; poet. canopy of heaven. **Firman** (⌣-, auch ⌣⌣) m = Ferman. **firme(l)n** (⌣⌣) [lt.] I v/a. ㊾ (㉒a.) Cath. eccl. to confirm. — II ~ n ㉓ u. **Firmelung** (⌣⌣⌣) f ㊻ = **Firmung**. **Firmen=buch** ⊕ (⌣⌣…) n ㉒, **=register** n commercial directory or guide, trade-directory. [sign for the firm.| **firmieren** ⊕ (⌣⌣⌣) I v/n. (h.) ㊼ to⌟ **Firmling** (⌣⌣) m ⓓd. Cath. eccl. candidate for confirmation (by the bishop). **Firmung** (⌣⌣) f ㊻ confirmation (by the bishop).

firn¹ (⌣) [= fern] a. ㊋ (ant. heurig) bsd. von Wein und Getreide: last (or the previous) year's produce; weits. (alt) der Wein long old (or well-seasoned) wine. **Firn²** (⌣) schwz. m ㊽ (㉕)b. 1. (vorjähriger Schnee) last year's snow. — 2. peak (or mountain-top) covered with perpetual snow; snow-mountain. **Firner** (⌣⌣) m ㉒ = **Firn²** 2. **Firne=wein** (⌣⌣⌣) m ㉒ well-seasoned wine; der Abt wählt sich den edlen ~ (sch.) the Abbot seizes on the good old wine.

Firnis ⊕ (⌣⌣) [mhd.; *fr. vernis] m ⑫ varnish (a. fig.); **=baum** ♀ m varnish- (or lacquer-)tree (bsd. Rhus vernicifera). **firnissen** ⊕ (⌣⌣⌣) I v/a. ㊺ to varnish (a. fig.); bsd. Töpferei: (glasieren) to ena'mel. — II ~ n ㉓ varnishing, varnish; ena'melling, ena'mel. **Firnisser** ⊕ (⌣⌣⌣) m ㉒ varnisher. **Firn=schnee** (⌒⌣) m ㉒ = **Firn²** 1.

First (⌣) [ahd.] m ⓓa., f ㊻ 1. (Berggipfel) peak, mountain-top; ridge. — 2. ⊕ arch. (oberste Dachkante) ridge of the roof; ~ e-r Mauer coping of a wall. — 3. ⛏, a. ²e f (Decke eines Grubenbaues) roof. **First=balken** ⊕ (⌒…) m ㉒ roof-tree; **=(en=)bau** ⛏ m overhand (or overhead) stoping; **=blech** n ridge-plate; **=blei** n ridge-lead; **=deckung** f Dachdeckerei: ridging; **=pfette** f ridge-pole or -piece or -purlin; **=verzierung** f ridge-ornament; **²(en=)weise** ⛏ adv. on (or near) the surface; **=wulst** m ridge-bead; **=ziegel** m ridge-tile, compass- (or cress-)tile.

Fis ♪ (⌣) n, inv. F sharp; F fig. ins ~ kommen to get into a scrape; **=Dur** F sharp major; **~=Moll** F sharp minor. **Fisch** (⌣) [ahd.: fish: lt. piscis] m ⓓa. 1. fish; s. frisch 5 und fliegen 8; einen Teich mit ~en besetzen to stock a pond (with fish); zu den ~en gehörig: piscine; ~e fangen to (catch) fish; geräucherte ~e cured (or smoked) fish; ~e fressend feeding on fish, ⚛ piscivorous, ichthyophagous; fig. so gesund wie ein ~ im Wasser (as) sound

---

⚛ scientific; ♀ botanical; ♁ geography; ⊕ machinery; ⛏ mining; ⚔ military; ⚓ marine; ⚙ commercial; ✉ postal; 🚆 railway.

[Fischaar] — 372 — [fixieren]

as a roach; weder Fleisch noch ~ neither fish nor flesh, neither (the) one thing nor the other; stumm wie ein ~ (as) mute as a maggot, (as) quiet as a mouse; f. faul 2. — 2. ast. (Sternbild) ~e pl.: ⚹ pisces pl.
Fisch=aar (F...) m ⑫ = =adler; =abdruck m, geol.: ⚹ ichthyolite; =abgang m fish-refuse; =abschupper m (Messer) scaling-knife; =adler m, orn. fishing-eagle, osprey (Pandi'on halia'etus); ²ähnlich a. ⑥⑥ fish-like, piscine; =angel f fish(ing)-hook; ²arm a. containing few fish; ²er Strom river with little (F with poor) fishing; =artig a. ⑥⑥ fish-like, fishy, ⚹ pisciform, ichthyoid; =auge n, min. = Mondstein; =augenstein m, min. = fish-eye stone, ⚹ apophyllite; =bank f fish-stall; =behälter m fish-tank. Kleinerer: fish-can; vgl. =kasten; =bein n whalebone; weißes ~ (innere Schale des Tintenfisches, Se'pia) cuttlebone, cuttle-fish-bone, sepia; ²beinern a. (of) whalebone; =bein=händler m whale-bone-merchant; =bein=reißer m splitter of whalefins; =bein=stäbe m/pl. eines Schnürleibchens whalebones pl. of a corset; =berechtigung f right to fish; =beschreibung f: ⚹ ichthyography; =blase f fish-bladder or -maw, sound, swim; =blut n fishblood; fig. er hat ~ he is extremely cold-blooded; =blütig a. cold-blooded; =brühe f fish-sauce; =brut f fish-fry, spawn. [fish.]
Fischchen (F...) [dim. v. Fisch] n ㉓ small
Fisch=dampfer ⚓ (F...) m ⑫ steam-trawler; =davit ⚓ m (Kran) fishdavit; =egel m, ichth. fish-leech (Pisci'cola geo'metra); =eier n/pl. roe sg.
fischen (F...) I v/a. und v/n. (h.) ⚹ 1. to fish; (angeln) to angle, mit der Rollangel: to troll, mit dem Schleppnetz: to drag; Austern ² to dredge for oysters, Korallen, Perlen etc. to fish for corals, pearls, &c.; ⚓ den Anker ² to drag for (or stow away) the anchor. — 2. fig. nach etwas ² (streben) to fish for a th.; im trüben ² to fish in troubled waters; es ist nichts dabei zu ² there is nothing to be gained by it. — II ~ n ㉓ 3. fishing, angling, mit Netzen: net-fishing, mit Treibnetzen: drift-fishery.
Fischer (F...) m ㉒, =in f ㊵ fisherman, pl. fishermen, fisher-folk, f a. fisherwoman; Frau e-s ~s fisherman's wife.
Fischer=boot (F...) n ⑫ fishing-boat or -smack; =dorf n fishing-village.
Fischerei (F...¹¹) f ㊻ 1. (Fischen) fishing; (Recht des Fischens) fishing-right. — 2. (Fischergewerbe) fisherman's craft or trade, fishery. — 3. (Ort zum Fischen) fishing-ground or -run.
Fischerei=fahrzeug (F...¹...) n ⑫ fishing-vessel; =flottille f flotilla of fishing-vessels; =frevel m infringement of fishing-rights; poaching on a fish-preserve; =gerät n fishing-tackle.
Fischer=fahrzeug (F...) n ⑫ fishing-vessel, -fleet; =gerechtsame f right of fishing, jur. ⚹ piscary; =hütte f fisherman's hut; =innung f Lo.: Fishmongers' Company; =kahn m =boot; =knabe m fisher(man's)-boy;

=meister m master fisher; =ring m des Papstes Fisherman's ring; =stadt f fishing-town. — Vgl. Fisch(erei)=...
Fisch=essen (F...) n ⑫ a) eating fish, fish-diet, ⚹ ichthyophagy; b) Mahlzeit: fish-dinner; =esser m fish-eater, ⚹ ichthyophagist; =fang m catching (of) fish, fishing; =faß n fish-tub; =flosse f fin; ²förmig a. ⑥⑥ ⚹ pisciform; vgl. ²ähnlich, ²artig; =gabel f: a) ⚒ zum Fischen: fishing-fork; vgl. =spieß; b) zum Essen: fish-fork; =garn n fishing-net, (Schleppnetz) drag- (or sweep-)net, (Wurfnetz) net; =gehege n fish-preserve or -park; =gerät ⚒ n fishing-tackle or -gear; =gerechtigkeit f right to fish, jur. piscary; =gericht n dish consisting of fish; =geruch, =geschmack m fishy smell, taste or flavour; =glas n fish-vase; kugelförmiges: fish-globe; =gräte f fish-bone; =grätenstich m Näherei: herring-bone stitch; =gräten=verband ⚒ m Maurerei: herring-bone work; =haken m fish-hook; =hälter m fish-pond; vgl. =behälter; =hamen m (kleines Netz) purse- (or hand-)net; =handel m fish-trade; =händler(in f) m: a) im großen: fish-merchant or salesman; b) im kleinen: fishmonger, f a. fishwoman; =haut f fish-skin; 🐟 shagreen.
fischicht, **fischig** (F...) a. ⑥⑥ of a fishy smell or taste or nature, fishy.
Fisch=kasten (F...) m ⑫ zum Transport: fish-car, -safe, -well, -box; vgl. =behälter; =kelle f fish-slice; =kenner m: ⚹ ichthyologist; =kessel m Kocht. = branchia; =köder m bait (for fish); =konserve(n pl.) f pickled fish; =korb m fish-basket; a. (angler's) creel; =körner ♀ n/pl. (Beeren von Menispe'rmum co'cculus) Indian berries pl., (It.) Cocculus indicus; =kunde f: ⚹ ichthyology; =kundige(r) m = =kenner; =laich m spawn; =lake f fish-brine; =laus f, ent. fish-louse (Cali'gus); =leim m fish-glue, isinglass.
Fischlein (F...) n ㉓ = Fischchen.
Fisch=löffel (F...) m ⑫ fish-ladle; =markt m fish-market; =mehl n (gemahlenes Dorschfleisch) fish-flour or -meal; =messer n fish-knife or -slice or -carver; =milch f milt, soft roe; =netz ⚒ n = =garn; =öl n = =tran; =ordnung f fishing-regulations pl.; =otter m (⚹ a. f) zo. otter (Lutra); =perle f (Art Glasperle) fishpearl; ²reich a. ⑥⑥ abounding in (or well stocked with) fish; =reiher m, orn. common heron (A'rdea cine'rea); =reuse f wear; für Krebse: fish-pot; =rogen m spawn, roe; =säugetiere n/pl., zo. (Wale) ⚹ cetacean mammals, cetacea pl.; =schuppe f fish-scale; =schuppen=ausschlag m, path.: ⚹ ichthyosis; =schwanz m fish-tail; =schwanz=brenner ⚒ m für Gas: fish-tail burner; =speer m fish-spear or -gig; =speise f fish-diet or -food; =spieß ⚒ m harpoon; =stein m, geogn.: ⚹ ichthyolite; =strich m spawning of fish; =tag m Cath. eccl. fish-day; =teich m fish-pond or -pool; =torpedo ⚓ m fish-torpedo, Whitehead torpedo; =tran m fish- (or train-) oil.

Fischung ⚓ (F...) f ⑯ Schiffbau: (Verstärkung auf u. zw. Deckbalken etc.) partners pl.
Fisch=versteinerung (F...) f ⑫ geogn. = =stein; =wehr ⚒ n fish-garth, wear, weir; =weib n fishwoman; =weiher m = =teich; =wirtschaft f management of fisheries; ²= =zucht; =zaun m crawl; =zeit f fishing-season; =zeug n = =gerät; =zuber m fish-tub; =zucht f fish-breeding or -culture or -farming, ⚹ pisciculture; auf die ~ bezüglich: piscicultural; =züchter m fish-breeder or -culturist or -farmer, ⚹ pisciculturist; =züchterei f fish-works pl.; =zucht=verein m: ⚹ piscicultural society; =zug m a) drag-fishing, catch (or haul) of fish; bsd. bibl. draught of fish; b) (Schwarm Fische) shoal of fish.
Fisett=holz (-ʹ...) [fr. fustet] n ⑫ fustet, young fustic.
Fisimatenten F (-᷄᷉ʹ᷉) f/pl., inv. subterfuge(s pl.), idle (or lame) excuses pl.; das sind ~ that's humbug or F rot.
Fiskal † od. bayr. (-ʹ) [lt.] m ⓖ Solicitor to the Treasury; England: (Erster Kronanwalt) Attorney- (or Solicitor-)General; ²isch (-ʹ...) a. ⑥⑥ fiscal; ²ische Prozeß: government proceedings pl.
Fiskus (ʹ...) [lt.] m, inv. od. ㉗ (Staatskasse) exchequer, treasury.
Fist (ʹ) [mhd.] m ⑬ b. foist; vgl. Bofist.
Fistel (ʹ...) [ahd., *lt.] f ⑱ 1. path. fistula, fissure. — 2. ⚹ (Kopfstimme) falsetto, head-voice; durch die ~ singen to sing falsetto or a false treble; ²artig (ʹ...) a. ⑥⑥ path.: ⚹ fistulous; ²artig werden: ⚹ to fistulate; ~=geschwür n, path.: ⚹ fistulous ulcer.
fisteln (ʹ...) v/n. (h.) ⚹ a. vom Singen: to sing falsetto; vom Sprechen: to speak in a thin treble-voice.
Fistel=stimme ♪ (ʹ...) f ⓖ = Fistel 2.
fistulieren (-᷉ʹ) v/n. (h.) ⚹ = fisteln.
Fittich (ʹ...) [ahd.] m ⑭ d. (Flügel) pinion, wing; unter seine ~e nehmen to take under one's wings.
Fitz=band ⚒ (ʹ...) n ⑫ thread made (up) into skeins; =bohne ♀ f = Veits-b.
Fitze ⚒ (ʹ...) [ahd.] f ⑱ (Docke, Strähne) skein of yarn.
fitzen (ʹ...) v/a. ⑨⓪ 1. Garn ² to wind yarn into skeins. — 2. die Stirn ² (falten) to knit one's brow(s). — 3. (züchtigen) to chastise, to punish.
fix (ʹ) [nhd. 17. sae., *lt.] a. ⑥⑥ 1. (fest) fixed, fast, immovable; ²es Gehalt fixed (or regular) salary; ²e Idee (Wahn) fixed idea or notion. — 2. (schnell) prompt; (flint) quick, nimble, alert; F ²er smart fellow; adv. mach' ²! F look sharp!, P buck up! — 3. (fertig) ready, in order; ² und fertig quite ready or complete, all finished; F in apple-pie order; f. fertig.
fixen ⚹ (ʹ...) [fix] v/n. (h.) ⚹ Börsensprache: to operate (or speculate) for a fall, to bear (or sell) stock.
Fix=geschäft ⚹ (ʹ...) n ⑫ transaction (or business) on account; time-bargain.
fixieren (-ʹ) [fr.] I v/a. ⑬ 1. chm., Photographie, Färberei: to fix. — 2. e-n ² (anstieren) to fix one's eyes (or glance) upon a p., to stare at a p. — II ~ n ㉓ 3. = Fixierung.

Fixier-mittel (⌣⌢...) n ⓒ chm., phot., Färb.: fixative, fixing-agent.
Fixierung (⌣⌣́) f ㊻ fixing, fixation.
Fix-punkt (ˊ...) m ⓒ Geodäsie: fixed point; ˌstern m, ast. fixed star.
Fixum (⌣⌣) [lt.] n ㊾ fixed sum; (festes Gehalt) fixed (or regular) salary.
Fjord (ˊ) [dän.] m ⓑ. (felsige Meeresbucht, bjd. in Norwegen) fiord, rocky bay.
fl. abbr. für Florín (j. Gulden).
Flabbe F (⌣⌣) [nbd.] f ㊽ flabby mouth, hanging lip; P (ugly) mug.
flach (ˊᶜʰ) [ahd.] I a. ⓺ (D1) 1. flat; (eben) plain, even; bib. math. plane; (wagerecht) level; ↓ Des Fahrzeug flat-bottomed ship or boat; Des Feld open fields pl., plain; De Hand palm (or flat) of the hand; f. 2; ⚔ mit der Den Klinge schlagen to strike with the flat of the sword; Des Land open country, plain; ↓ De See smooth (or calm) sea; ⊕ 2 machen, schlagen to flatten (or level) down; adv. 2 auf dem Boden liegen to lie flat on the ground. — 2. fig. superficial; das liegt auf der Den Hand that's quite clear or evident, F it's as plain as a pikestaff. — II ~ n ⓓc. 3. flat, flatness; flat ground or stone; (Ebene) plain, level.
Flach-brenner ⊕ (ˊᶜʰ...) m ⓒ flat burner of a lamp; ˌdraht-armatur f, elect. für Kabel: flat wire sheathing.
Fläche (⌣⌣) [mhd.] f ㊽ 1. (Ober=)~ surface, math. superficies; eines Kristalls: face, e-s geschliffenen Steins: facet. — 2. (Ebene) plain, level; sheet of water; expanse of the ocean; in gleicher ~ mit ... (on a) level with ...; phys. math. geneigte (senkrechte) ~ inclined (vertical) plane. — 3. (flacher Teil) flat of a sword; palm of the hand; typ. ~ eines Buchstaben face (or eye) of a type.
Flach-eisen ⊕ (ˊᶜʰ...) n ⓒ (Stabeisen von rechteckigem Querschnitt) flat-iron.
flachen (ˊᶜʰ), **flächen** (⌣⌣) v/a. ⓼⓼ to flatten; (eben machen) to level (down), to smooth.
Flächen-ausdehnung (⌣⌣́...) f ㊽ square dimension(s pl.); ˌinhalt m area, ⌑ superficies; ˌmaß n superficial (or square) measure; ˌmeßkunst, ˌmessung f measurement of areas, engS. plane geometry; ˌraum m = ˌinhalt; ˌwinkel m, geom. dihedral angle, angle formed by two planes; ˌzahl f, geom., cryst. number of faces.
Flach-feld (ˊᶜʰ...) n ⓒ plain, level (country); ˌfeuer ⚔ n horizontal fire; ˌfisch m (Pleurone'ctes) flatfish; ˎgedrückt a. ⓺ flat (tened down), ⚯ depressed ˎgeschliffen a. v. Edelsteinen: tabul; ated; ˌglas n (Tafelglas) plate-glass.
Flachheit (ˊᶜʰ-) f ㊻ 1. flatness. — 2. fig. shallowness of mind; insipidity, platitude, triviality; ˎen pl. trite sayings.
...flächig (..."⌣⌣) ⓺ in Zjsgn, zB.: fünfˎ pentahedral.
Flach-kopf (ˊᶜʰ...) m ⓒ fig. shallow head; (Indianer) F flat head; ˎtöpfig a. ⓺ flat-headed; fig. shallow-headed, superficial; ˌland n = ˌfeld; ˌländer m lowlander; ˌmalerei f flat painting; ˌnase f flat nose; ˎnasig a. flat-nosed; ˌreli-e´f n bas(s)-relief; ˌrennen n Sport: flat race.

Flachs ⚘ (ˊᶜˢ) [ahd.: flax; * flechten] m ⓜa. flax (Linum usitati'ssimum); ~ brechen, hecheln to break, to comb flax.
Flachs-acker (ˊˢ...) m ⓒ flax-field; ˎähnlich a. ⓺, ˎartig a. flax-like, flaxen; ˌbart m flax beard; ˎbärtig a. flaxen-bearded; ˌbau m cultivation (or growing, raising) of flax; ˌbauer m flax-grower or -raiser; ˌbereiter(in f) m = ˌbrecher; ˌbereitung f flax-dressing; ˌbleuel m = ˌschwinge; ˎblond a. with flaxen hair; flaxen-haired; ˌbreche f flax-brake; ˌbrecher(in f) m flax-dresser.
Flach-schlag (ˊᶜʰ...) m ⓒ Tennis: drive; ˌschnäbler m, orn. flat-bill (Platyrhy'nchus); ˎschnäb(e)lig a., orn.: ⌑ pressirostral.
Flachs-darre (ˊˢ...) f ⓒ flax-retting.
flächse(r)n (ˊᶠˢʰ...) a. ⓺ flaxen, of flax.
Flachs-fäden (ˊˢ...) m/pl. ⓒ harl sg.; ˌfarbe f flaxen colour; ˎfarben a. ⓺ flaxen (-coloured); ˌfeld n = ˌacker; ˎgelb a. flaxen; ˌhaar n flaxen hair; ˎhaarig a. = ˎblond; ˌhechel (ˌmaschine) f flax-comb, hatchel.
flachsicht, flächsicht, flachsig, flächsig (ˊᶠˢʰ...) a. ⓺ flaxy, (looking) like flax.
Flachs-kopf (ˊˢ...) m ⓒ flaxen-haired person; ˌmühle f flax-mill; ˌröste, ˌrotte f steep (ing of flax); ˌschwinge f scutcher, swingle; ˌseide ⚘ f dodder (of flax) (Cu'scuta epili'num); ˌspinnerei f = ˌmühle. — Vgl. auch Lein-...
flackerig F (⌣⌣) a. ⓺ flickering; fig. uncertain, unsteady; wavering, vacillating.
flackern (⌣⌣) [: flicker] v/n. (h.) ⓶a. Licht: to flicker, Feuer: to flare, stärker: to blaze (up), Stimme: to shake.
Fladen (⌣⌣) [ahd.] m ⓒ flat cake.
Flader (⌣ˊ) I f ㊽ = Flaser. — II m = Maßholder.
Flagellant (⌣⌣́) [lt.] m ㊷ eccl. ehm. (Geißler) flagellant, scourging friar.
Flageolett ♪ (⌣⌣́) [fr.] n ⓑ. (Instrument u. Tonart) flageolet; ~bläser, ~spieler m ⓒ fl.-player, flageolet.
Flagge ↓ (⌣⌣) [nbd., *stand.] f ㊽ flag; vgl. Fahne; die ~ aufziehen (streichen) to hoist (to strike) the flag or the colours; die britische ~ führen to fly (or carry) the union-jack; die ~ niederholen to haul down the flag or the colours; unter falscher ~ segeln to sail under false colours (auch fig.).
flaggen ↓ (⌣⌣) ⓼ I v/n. (h.) (die Flagge wehen lassen) to display the flag; to show one's colours (a. fig.); die Schiffe haben geflaggt ... have dressed; auf halber Stange (a. halbmasts) 2 to hoist the flag (at) halfmast (high). — II v/a. (mit Flaggen behängen) to dress (with flags), to flag.
Flaggen-knopf ↓ (⌣⌣...) m ⓒ (masthead) truck; ˌsignal n flag-signal(ling); ˌstange f, ˌstock m flag-staff; ˌstoff m, ˎtuch n bunting.
Flagg-leine ↓ (⌣⌣...) f ⓒ flag-line; ˌleutnant m e-s Admirals x. flag-lieutenant; ˌoffizier m (Seeoffizier, der e-e ~ in Rang bezeichnende Flagge führen darf) flag-officer; ˌschiff n flag-ship.

Flakon (⌣ᵗᵍˊ) [fr.] n ⓢ (Fläschchen) small bottle or phial; (Riechfläschchen) scent- or smelling-bottle.
Flamänder (⌣⌣́) m ⓺, ~in f ㊼, **flamändisch** a. ⓺ = Flame, flämisch.
Flamberg (⌣⌣) [fr.] m ⓜd. ehm. (großes Ritterschwert) large battle-sword.
Flame (⌣ˊ) m ㊹, **Flamin** f ㊼ Fleming, Flemish (wo)man, native of Flanders.
Flamingo (⌣⌣́) [port. v. *lt. flamma] m ㊿ orn. flamingo (Phoenico'pterus ro'seus).
flämisch (⌣ˊ) a. ⓺ 1. = fla'm(l)ändisch. — 2. fig. (derb) coarse, boorish; (mürrisch) gruff. — 3. die 2e Sprache, das ~(e) n ⓺⓻ Flemish, the Flemish language.
Flamländer, flamländisch (⌣⌣́) j. Flame, flämisch. [small flame; flamelet.]
Flämmchen (⌣⌣) n ㊸ (dim. v. Flamme)
Flamme (⌣⌣) [ahd.; * lt.] f ㊽ 1. flame (a. fig.); hell lodernde: blaze; in ~n ausbrechen to break out in flames in ~n setzen to set ablaze or alight, to inflame (a. fig.); in (hellen, lichten) ~n stehen to be in flames or all on fire or ablaze. — 2. fig. (Leidenschaft) heat (of passion); j. Feuer 3; e-e alte (Liebe) an old love or sweetheart.
flammen (⌣⌣) ⓸ I v/n. (h.) 1. to be in flames; (lodern) to flare (or blaze) up (blitzen) to flash; 2d flaming, blazing aflame; fig. v. Baustil x. flamboyant. — 2. (leuchten, glänzen) to shine, glare, glitter; (funkeln) to sparkle. — 3. fig.: a) (vor Zorn glühen) to burn (or glow) with anger or rage; b) (Feuer-eifer haben) to be full of fire or zeal. — II v/a. 4. to expose to the flames, to fire; (sengen) to singe. — 5. ⊕ (flammicht aussehen m.) Zeug: to cloud, water, marble, wave; 2des Herz ⚘ (j. Herz).
Flammen-auge (⌣⌣́...) n ㊸ flashing eye; ˌblick m lightning-glance; ˌblume ⚘ f (rispige) phlox (Phlox [panicula'ta]); ˌbogen ⊕ m: elektrischer ~ Voltaic arc; ˌfeuer n blazing fire; ˌglut f (scorching) heat of flames; ˌmeer n sea of flames, fiery ocean, sheet of fire; ˌofen m = Flammofen; ˌpein, ˌqual f torment of flames; ˌsäule f pillar of fire; ˌschrift f letters pl. of fire, fig. indelible writing; ˌschwert n fiery sword; ˎspeiend a. ⓺ belching (forth) flames; ˌstil m, arch. flamboyant style; ˌstrom m torrent of flames; fiery stream; ˌtod m death in the flames; ˌtrieb m: meine ~ pl. (SCH.) my fiery passion; ˌwirbel m volume of flames; ˌzüge m/pl. = ˌschrift.
Flammeri ⟊ (⌣⌣́) [engl., *walij.] m ⓢ flummery; (fr.) blancmange.
Flamm-feuer (ˊ...) m ⓒ = Flammen-f.
flammicht (⌣⌣) a. ⓺ = flammig.
flammier/en (⌣⌣́) (Flamme) I v/a. ⓽⓸ = flammen 5. — II f/ung f ㊻ (buntes Muster) bright-coloured pattern.
flammig (⌣⌣) [Flamme] a. ⓺ 1. like a flame, blazing. — 2. 2e (gewässerte) Stoffe clouded (or waved) goods pl.
Flamm-ofen (ˊ...) m ⓒ metall. flame (or flaming) furnace, reverberatory (furnace); ˌrohr n, ˌröhre f. mach. flame-passage, flue.
Flandern ⚑ (⌣⌣) npr/n. ⓶⓷α. belg.-fr. Landschaft: Flanders; **Flandrer** m ㊷

♪ Musik; ⌑ Wissenschaft; ⚘ Pflanze; ⚑ Geographie; ⊕ Technik; ⚒ Bergbau; ⚔ Militär; ↓ Marine; ● Handel; ✉ Post; 🚂 Eisenbahn

[flandrisch] — 374 — [Flechtenlehre]

Flame; **flandrisch** a. ⓖ Flemish, of Flanders; fig. = flatterhaft. ǀflannel.ǀ
Flanell ⁷ ⓦ (⌣⌣) [engl., *it.] m Ⓤⓓ.
flanellen (⌣⌣⌣) a. ⓖ (D9) (of) flannel.
Flanell-macher (⌣⌣⌣…) m ㉒, **-weber** m flannel-maker or -manufacturer.
Flaneur (⌣nöˈr) [fr.] Ⓜⓓ. (Bummler) lounger, saunterer.
flanieren (⌣⌣́⌣) [fr.] v/n. (h.) ⑬ (bummeln) to lounge (or stroll, saunter) about.
Flanke, meist ⚔ (⌣⌣) [nhd.; fr. *flanc* m; *ahd. v. lenken] f ⑱ flank, Tennis: side; dem Feinde in die ⁓e(n) fallen to take (or press, harass) the enemy's flank, to attack the enemy in the flank.
Flanken-angriff ⚔ (⌣⌣…) m ㉒ flank attack; **-batterie** f, **-feuer** n, **-marsch** m flanking(-)battery, (-)fire, (-)march; **-werk** n flanker.
flankier/en (⌣́⌣) [fr.] ⑬ I v/a. ⚔ frt. (v. der Seite bestreichen) to flank; ⌾des Feuer flank(ing) fire. — II v/n. (h.) = flanieren. — III F/ung (⌣) f flanking.
Flantsch ⁷ (⌣) [engl.] m Ⓜⓐ., mst ⁓e f ⑱ (Verbindungsstück für Röhrenleitungen) flange.
Flaps F (⁷) [nbd.] m Ⓜⓐ. (Bauernlümmel) hobb(!)edehoy, clod-hopper; **flapsig** (⌣⌣) a. ⓖ boorish, uncouth.
Fläschchen (⌣⌣) n ㉓ (dim. von Flasche) small bottle; für Arznei: phial; für Säuglinge: feeding-bottle; für Essig, Öl im Einsatze: cruet.
Flasche (⌣⌣) [ahd.: flask] f ⑱ 1. bottle for wine, water, beer, &c.; große für Säure ꝛc.: carboy; kleinere: flask; geschliffene: decanter; s. Fläschchen; auf ⁓n füllen ob. ziehen to bottle wine, &c.; einem Kinde die ⁓e geben to give a child the (feeding-)bottle; ein Kind mit der ⁓ aufziehen to bring up a child with the bottle or by hand; der ⁓ reichlich zusprechen to drink a great deal, to be (too) fond of the bottle; eine ⁓ Wein trinken to drink (F to crack) a bottle of wine; leere ⁓n empty bottles, F co. dead men pl. — 2. chm. Florentiner ⁓ Florentine receiver; elect. Leidener ⁓ Leyden jar; ⊕ mech. (Rolle des Flaschenzuges) pulley.
flaschen-artig (⌣⌣…) a. ⓖ bottle-shaped; ⚭ lageniform, ampullaceous; **-baum** ⚘ m ⓖ custard- (or sweet-)apple (*Anoˈna squamoˈsa*); **-bier** n (ant. Faßbier) bottled beer or ale; **-bürste** f bottle brush. ǀFlageolett.ǀ
Flaschenett, …inett ♪ (⌣⌣) n Ⓤⓓ.
Flaschen-form (⌣…) ⊕ f ⑱ bottle-mould ⁓**förmig** a. ⓖ = **-artig**; **-füll-apparat** m bottle-charger, bo.-filler, bottling-machine; **-futteral** n bottle-case; **-gestell** n bo.-stand or -rack; (Untersatz) decanter-stand; **-glas** n bo.-glass; **-hals** m neck of a bottle; **-held** m bo.-man, toper; **-kapsel** f (Flaschenverschluß) capsule for bottles; **-keller** m bo.-case or -cellar, wine-cellar; **-korb** m hamper for bottles; **-kühler** m bo.-cooler; für Wein: ice-pail; **-kürbis** ⚘ m bo.-gourd (*Cucuˈrbita lagenaˈria*); **-kürbis-baum** m = Kürbisbaum; **-post** ⚓ f system of communication by means of bottle-papers; **-reif** a. vom Bier ꝛc.: fit (or mature) for bottling; **-reinigungs-** (a. **-spül-)maschine** ⊕ f bottle-washer or

-cleanser; **-ständer** m = **-gestell**; **-stöpsel** m bo.-stopper, cork (of a b.); **-teller, -untersatz** m bo.-stand or -tray; **-verkork-maschine** ⊕ f corking-machine, cork-fastener; **-verschluß** m = **-stöpsel**; **-wein** m bottled wine; **-zange** ⊕ f bo.-pincers pl.; **-zug** ⊕ m, mech. block-and-pulley, block-and-tackle.
Flaschner südb. (⌣⌣) m ㉒ = Klempner.
Flaser f ⑱, auch m ㉒, in Stein, Holz ꝛc.: (Ader) vein, streak; ⁓ig (⌣⌣) a. ⓖ veiny, veined, streaky.
Flatter-binse ⚘ (⌣⌣…) f ⑱ soft rush (*Iuncus effuˈsus*); **-fuß** m, zo. winged foot; **-füße** pl. auch = **-tiere**; **-füßig** a. ⓖ wing-footed, web-winged, ⚭ aliped; **-füßler** m, zo.: ⚭ aliped, vgl. **-tiere**; **-geist** m: a) light-hearted (or fickle, unsteady) person; b) = **-sinn**; **-gras** ⚘ n millet; grass (*Milium effuˈsum*).
flatterhaft (⌣⌣⌣) a. ⓖ changeable, fickle, volatile, inconstant; (leichtsinnig) giddy; ⁓**igkeit** f ⑱ changeableness, fickleness, inconstancy; giddiness.
Flatter-hörnchen (⌣⌣…) n ㉒ zo. flying-squirrel (*Pteˈromys*).
flatt(e)rig ⚔ (⌣⌣) a. ㉒ = **flatterhaft**.
Flatter-katze (⌣⌣…) f ㉒, **-maki** m, zo. flying-lemur (*Galeopitheˈcus volans*); **-mine** ⚔ f, frt. (fr.) fougade, fougasse.
flattern (⌣⌣) [nhd.] I v/n. (h.: bei Ortsveränderung: sn) ⓐ. 1. to flutter; to dangle (to and fro); im Winde auch: to fly, float, wave; ⌾de Fahnen bsd. poet. auch: streaming flags or pennants pl.; ⌾de Haare dishevelled (or loose) hair; von jungen Vögeln ꝛc.: hin und her ⁓ to flutter (or flit) to and fro. — 2. fig. to be fickle or volatile; to flit from one thing to another; (sich ergötzen) to disport o.s. — II ⁓ n ⓑ 3. flutter(ing).
Flatter-scheibe ⚔ (⌣⌣…) f ⑱ Scheibenschießen: moving target; **-sinn** m light-heartedness or -mindedness; fickleness, unsteadiness; volatile mind; **-tiere** n/pl., zo. (Handflügler) ⚭ alipeds, cheiropters pl.
flattieren F (⌣⌣́⌣) [fr.] v/n. (h.) ⑬ e-m ⁓ (schmeicheln) to flatter (or coax) a p.
flattrig (⌣⌣) f. flatterig.
flau (⁷) [nbd.; *fr. *flou*] a. ⓖ 1. (schwach) feeble, faint; (matt) languid (schlaff) lax; (träge) indolent; ich fühle mich ⁓, mir ist ganz ⁓ zumute I feel quite faint (with hunger, &c.); mir wird ⁓ I (begin to) feel queer or faint. — 2. v. Getränken: (schal) stale, flat; v. Gespräch: dull. — 3. ⚘ (schwer zu verkaufen) hanging on hand; Kaffee ist ⁓ (wenig begehrt) … is flat, dull; adv. die Geschäfte geh(e)n ⁓ business is dull or flagging or stagnant or at a standstill; mit seiner Kasse steht es ⁓ F he is short of cash or low in funds; ⌾e Zeit slack time, off-season. — 4. ⚓ vom Winde: ⁓er werden, flauen to calm (or go) down, to drop, slacken.
flauen (⌣⌣) v/n. (h.) ⓖ 1. bsd. ⚓ (s. flau 3) to be flat or dull or lifeless or flagging or depressed. — 2. v. flau 4.
Flauheit (⌣⌣), **Flauigkeit** (⌣⌣…) f ⑱ (s. flau) feebleness, faintness; langour, laxity; ⚘ flatness, dulness, stagnation (of trade); depression (in business).

Flaum¹ (⁷) m Ⓜⓒ. (Tierfett; Bauch- u. Nierenfett des Schweines) fat of animals, lard (from the pig's belly and kidneys).
Flaum² (⁷) [ahd.; *lt. *pluma*] m Ⓜⓒ. down, fluff; am Tuch: nap; ⚘ und zo.: ⚭ pubescence.
Flaum³-bart (⁷…) m ㉒ downy beard, vgl. Milchbart; **-bett** n downy couch; **-(en)feder** f down(-feather), ⚭ plumule; **-enweich** a. ⓖ = flaumweich; **-haar** n: a) = **-bart**; b) ⚘ pubes, pubescence, lanugo; **-haarig** ⚘ a. ⓖ ⚭ pubescent, puberulent.
flaumig (⌣⌣) a. ⓖ downy, fluffy; (as) soft as down; ⚘ u. zo.: ⚭ pubescent.
flaum-weich (⁷⌣⁷) a. ⓖ downy (vgl. flaumig).
Flaus, Flausch [nbd.: Vlies] m Ⓜⓐ. 1. ⁓ (Büschel) Haare ꝛc. tuft of hair, &c. 2. ⚘ und ⊕ Tuchfabr.: (Fries) pilot-cloth, cloth with rough pile.
Flause F (⌣⌣) [nhd.] f ⑱ (mst im pl. ⁓n gbr.) (Ausflüchte) shifts, fibs, dodges pl.; (leeres Geschwätz) F stuff, rubbish; das sind ⁓n! (it's all) humbug!; ⁓**nmacher** m ㉒ fibber, dodger, shuffler; prevaricator; ⁓**n-macherei** f fibbing, dodging, shuffling; prevarication.
Flaus-rock (⁷⌣) m ㉒ frieze (or rough woollen) coat.
Fläz F (⁷) m Ⓜⓐ. (Grobian) coarse (or brutal) fellow; F bully; **fläzen** (⌣⌣) sich ⁓ v/refl. ⑭ to behave (or talk) coarsely or brutally; **fläzig** (⌣⌣) a. ⓖ coarse, brutal, F bullying.
Flebbe (⌣⌣) f ⑱ (Stirnschneppe als Zeichen der Witwentrauer) widow's veil.
Flechse (⁷⌣⌣) [nhd.] f ⑱ anat. (Sehne) sinew, tendon; ⁓**n-ähnlich** (⌣…), ⁓**artig** a. ⓖ sinewy, tendinous; ⁓**n-bänder** n/pl. tendinous ligaments pl.
flechsig (⁷⌣⌣) a. ⓖ sinewy [= sehnicht].
Flecht-arbeit (⁷⌣…) f ⑱ = **-werk**; **-band** n ribbon used in plaiting or braiding.
Flechte (⌣⌣) [nhd.; * flechten] f ⑱ 1. (Geflochtenes): a) (Haar-)⁓ tress, braid, plait(ed hair); b) aus Ruten: wattling; vgl. Flechtwerk b. — 2. ⚘ lichen (Lichen); daher ⁓n: ⁓n pl.; isländische ⁓ Iceland moss (*Cetraˈria islaˈndica*). — 3. path. (Hautausschlag) ⚭ herpes, herpetic eruption, serpigo; - der Kopfhaut: ringworm.
flechten (⁷⌣⌣) [ahd.: lt. *pleˈctere*] ⓑ. I v/a. in ea. ⁓ to intertwine, to interlace, to interweave; (zusammendrehen) to twist; to plait (or braid) hair, &c.; to cane chairs; die Haare in Zöpfen (ob. in Zöpfe) ⁓, a. oft: to wear (one's hair in) tresses; geflocht(e)nes Haar hair in plaits or tresses; einen Korb, einen Kranz ⁓ to make a basket, a wreath; ehm.: Verbrecher aufs Rad ⁓ to break criminals on the wheel; geflocht(e)ner Zaun plashed hedge; ⌾ zwei Tau-enden an-ea. ⁓ to splice. — II sich ⁓ v/refl. to twine (or wind) round a th.
flechten-ähnlich, -artig (⁷⌣…) a. ⓖ: a) ⚘ lichenoid, …ose; b) path.: ⚭ herpetic, serpiginous; ⁓**-ausschlag** m path.: ⚭ herpetic eruption; ⁓**-beschreibung** f: ⚭ lichenography; ⁓**förmig** a.: ⚭ licheniform; ⁓**kranke(r)** path. herpetic patient; ⁓**lehre** f: ⚭ lichenology.

Signs (see page XVII): F familiar; P vulgar; F⸌ flash; ⸜ rare; † obsolete (died); * new word (born); ⁺⁺ incorrect; ♪ music;

[Flechter] — 375 — [fleischfressend]

Flechter (ˇ‿) m ㉒, **~in** f ㊼ plaiter, braider; ~ **von Körben** basket-maker; **~ei** (‿‿ˊ) f ㊻ plaiting, v. **Stühlen**: caning.
Flecht-korb (ˊ...) m ㉒ wicker-basket; **=rohr, =stroh** n plaiting-cane, -straw; **=weide** ⚘ f (Korbweide) osier (*Salix viminaʹlis*); **=werk** ⊕ n: a) plaited work, net-work; b) aus Ruten: wicker- (or hurdle-)work, matwork, wattling, wattlework (auch ⚔ ⚓ *frt.*); c) *arch.* trellis-work; **=zaun** m hurdle.
Fleck (ˊ) [ahd.: fleck] m ⓦb. 1. (Stück Land) piece (or plot) of land; (Stelle) place, spot; **auf dem ~** on the spot; **fünf Stunden auf einem ~ warten** to wait five hours at a stretch; **er kann nicht vom ~ kommen** he cannot get on or along or forward; **nicht vom ~e geh(e)n, sich nicht vom ~e rühren** not to stir (from the spot), not to budge (an inch); **er steht noch auf dem alten** (oder auf demselben) **~e** he is still in the same position or where he was; **den rechten ~ treffen** to hit the right spot or the right nail on the head; **er hat das Herz auf dem rechten ~** his heart is in the right place; **P er hat das Maul auf dem rechten ~** ... a good tongue in his head, ... the gift of the gab. — 2. speck, stain, spot, mark, der Haut a.: blotch, ⚕ macula; *fig.* taint; (Makel) blur, blot, blemish; **e-n ~ bekommen, sich e-n ~ machen** to get stained or marked or blotted; **blauer ~** blue mark; **von ~en reinigen** to take (the) spots (or stains) out of; (Quetschung) bruise; *fig.* **fauler ~** sore point; **j-s Namen e-n ~ (Schande) anhängen** to cast a slur on a p.'s name, to blast a p.'s reputation. — 3. ⊕ ~ **in Diamanten**: cloud; flaw. — 4. (Stück Zeug, Flicken) piece, shred; **zum Kleidungsstück**: patch; ⊕ **Schuhmach.**: (Leder zum Absatz) heel-piece; **einen ~ aufsetzen** to patch (up), to (put in a) piece. — 5. Kocht.: (zerschnittene Kalbaunen) tripes *pl.*
Fleck-aufsetzen ⊕ (ˊ...) n ㉒ Schuhmach.: heeling of boots; **=ausmachen** n taking out stains or spots, cleaning clothes.
Fleckchen (ˇ‿) n ㉒ *dim. v.* Fleck(en); **nicht ein ~ e-r Wolke** not a fleck of a cloud.
flecken[1] (ˇ‿) [Fleck] ㊷ I v/a. 1. (f. Fleck 2) to stain, spot, mark, blot, sully; (sprenkeln) to speck(le). — 2. ⊕ Münze (bem Gelde den richtigen Wert geben) to adjust; Schuhmach.: to heel. — II v/n. (h.) 3. (Flecken machen) to make stains or blots; to stain, to blot; (beschmutzen) to soil. — 4. (leicht Flecken annehmen) to soil easily. — 5. F (vom Flecke kommen) to proceed, to speed; **die Arbeit will nicht** ㊴, v/*impers.* **es fleckt nicht ob. will mit der Arbeit nicht** ㊴ the work is not getting on or forward, we are not making (any) headway; **es fleckt bei ihm nicht** F he is a slow-coach, there is no go in him.
Flecken[2] (ˇ‿) [ahd.: fleck] m ㉓ 1. = Fleck 2 und 3. — 2. *path.* **die ~** *pl.* = Masern. — 3. (großes Dorf) country- or market-town.
flecken-los (ˇ‿...) a. ㊻ stainless, spotless, untainted, taintless, unblemished; vgl. **unbefleckt**; **=losigkeit** f spotless-

ness; **=mal** n = Leberfleck; **=reiniger** ⓞ m, in England: (dyer and) cleaner.
Fleck-fieber (ˊ...) n ㉒ *path.* spotted (⚚ petechial) fever, a. = =typhus.
fleckig (ˇ‿) a. ㊻ (f. flecken 1) stained, spotted, marked, blotted, speckled; **vom Gesicht auch**: freckled; v. Edelsteinen: clouded, flawed; **~keit** f ㊻, **~sein** n ㉓ spottedness, stained (or soiled) condition **~werden** n㉓ v. Zeug: getting soiled, soiling; Obst: showing spots.
Fleck-kugel (ˊ...) f ㊵ ball of cleansing soap; bisw. a. scouring-ball; **=leder** ⓞ n Schuhmach.: heel-leather; **=seife** f (strong) cleansing soap; **=typhus** m spotted typhus, hospital-fever; **=vieh** n, *agr.* spotted (breed of) cattle; **=wasser** n fluid for removing (or taking out) stains or grease; *engS.* benzine; Javelle-water.
fleddern F (ˊ‿) v/a. ㊳a (bestehlen) to rob.
Fleder-hunde (ˊ‿...) *m/pl.* ㊷ *zo.*: pteropidæ; **=maus** f, *zo.* bat (*Vespertilio* u. alle *Chiroptera*), her. a. rearmouse, reremouse; kleine: pipistrel(le)(*Vesperuʹgo pipistrelʹlus*); **=mausartig** a. batty, ⚚ vespertilionine.
fledern (ˊ‿) v/a. ㊳a. 1. to dust with a feather-broom; to whisk off. — 2. F *fig.* e-n ㉒ (hinauswerfen) to turn (F to kick) a p. out; (durchprügeln) F to tan a person's hide, to dust a p.'s jacket.
Fleder-tier (ˊ‿...) n ㉒ *zo.*: ⚚ aliped, cheiropter; **=wisch** m feather-broom, whisk; F (magere Person) lean person, F skin-and-bones; *contp.* = Degen (G.).
Flegel (ˊ‿) [ahd.: flag(eʹllum] m ㉒ 1. *agr.* zum Dreschen: flail; (Klöppel) swip(p)le, swingle. — 2. *fig.* (Grobian) boor, churl(ish fellow), rude man.
Flegelei (‿‿ˊ) f ㊻ boorish (or churlish) conduct; saucy (or impudent, insolent) act or remark; clownishness, coarseness, rudeness, unmannerliness.
flegelhaft, flegelig (ˊ‿‿) a. ㊻ boorish, churlish, saucy, F cheeky; **Flegelhaftigkeit** f ㊻ boorishness, churlishness, sauciness, impudence, F sauce, cheek, unmannerly conduct.
Flegel-jahre (ˊ‿...) *n/pl.* ㉒ years *pl.* between boyhood (girlhood) and (wo)manhood; **noch in den ~n** (still) in one's teens, auch *fig.* unfledged, unpolished, raw.
flegeln (ˊ‿) ㊳a. I v/a. to thrash = dreschen. — II v/n. u. sich ㊴ v/refl. to behave in a rude (or boorish) manner.
flehen (ˊ‿) [ahd.] I v/n. (h.), v/a. ㊳ zu e-m ㊴ to implore (or beseech) a p.; zu Gott ㊴, oft: to pray to God; e-n um Gnade ㊴ f. anflehen I. — II ~ n ㉓ supplication; (humble) petition; prayer. — III **~de(r)** ㊹ suppli(c)ant.
flehentlich (ˊ‿‿) a. ㊻: ⚚e Bitte urgent petition, fervent prayer; *adv.* beseechingly, as suppliant; ㊴ bitten = flehen I.
flei(h)en P nordb. (‿ˊ) v/a. ㊱ (ordnen, putzen) to tidy (up), to smarten (up).
Fleisch (ˊ) [ahd.: flesh] n ⓐa. 1. flesh; f. Fisch 1; **~ ansetzen** to put on flesh; **F vom ~ kommen oder fallen** to lose flesh, to fall away; (ant. Geist) **~ und Bein** the human frame, flesh and bone; **~ und Blut** flesh and blood;

fig. **sich ins ~ schneiden** to injure o. s., or to cut one's own throat; **gegen sein eigenes ~ und Blut wüten** to be cruel to one's own (children or family); vgl. Blut[1] 3, 4 u. 6; *bibl.* **alles ~ ist Heu** (Jes. 40,6) all flesh is grass; **den Weg alles ~es gehen** to go the way of all flesh; **der Augen und des ~es Lust**, oft: carnal lust, sensual pleasures *pl.*; *theol.* **~ werden** to be made (or born in the) flesh. — 2. Schlächterei: (butcher's) meat; **frisch geschlachtetes ~** fresh(-killed) meat; **gepökeltes ~** salt meat, ⚓ salt junk; **~ in Büchsen** tinned (or potted, preserved) meat; **das ~ roh essen** to eat meat raw or uncooked. — 3. *hunt.* **~ von erlegten Tieren** quarry. — 4. *typ.* am Buchstaben beard; *surg., path.*: **wildes** (faules) **~** proud flesh, ⚚ hypersarcoma, ...sis; **~ werden oder ansetzen**: ⚚ to carnify. — 5. ⚘ fleshy part, pulp, ⚚ parenchyma. — 6. *paint.* flesh-colour, carnation.
Fleisch-abfälle (ˊ...) *m/pl.* ㉒ offal (or refuse) of meat; im Schlächterladen: bits *pl.* of meat; für Katzen: cat's meat; **=ähnlich** a. ㊻, **=artig** a. flesh-like, ⚚ sarcoid; **=auswuchs** m fleshy growth or excrescence; *zo.*: ⚚ caruncle; **=bank** f butcher's stall; weitS. shambles *pl.*; **=base** f, *chm.*: ⚚ creatin(e); **=bedarf** m meat-consumption; meat required; **=beil** ⊕ n butcher's chopper or cleaver; **=beschau(er** m) inspection, inspector of butcher's meat; **=bildend** a. flesh-forming; *surg.* sarcogenous, sarcotic; **=bildung** f formation of flesh, *surg.*: ⚚ sarcosis, incarnation; **=bruch** m *path.*: ⚚ sarcocele; **=brühe** f meat-gravy or -broth; von Rindfleisch: beef-tea; bovril; vgl. auch Brühe 1; **=darstellung** f, *paint.*: ⚚ carnation; vgl. Fleisch 6; **=eisen** ⊕ n der Gerber fleshing-knife. [(Hieb) to cut into the flesh.]
fleischen (ˊ‿) v/n. (h.) ㊱ *fenc.* (von e-m)
Fleischer (ˊ‿) m ㉒, **~in** f ㊼ butcher; **~in** (Frau des **~s**) butcher's wife.
Fleischer-bank (ˊ‿...) f ㊵ butcher's bench or stall; **=bursche** m butcher-boy.
Fleischerei-berufsgenossenschaft f ㊷ co-operative association of butchers.
Fleischer-gang (ˊ‿...) m ㉒, *fig.* fool's errand, goose-chase; **=gesell(e** m) butcher's man; **=gewerbe, =handwerk** n butcher's trade, F butchering; **=gilde, =innung** f butchers' guild; **=hund** m butcher's dog; mastiff; **=knecht** m = =gesell; **=laden** m = Fleisch-laden; **=messer** ⊕ n butcher's knife. [Braten: meaty.]
fleischern (ˊ‿) a. ㊻ of flesh, fleshy;]
Fleischer-säge (ˊ‿...) f butcher's meat-saw.
Fleisches-lust (ˊ‿...) f ㊵ carnal desire.
Fleisch-essen (ˊ...) n ㉒ consumption of meat; **=essend** a. ㊻ meat-eating; fond of animal food or diet; **=esser(in** f) m meat-eater; **=extrakt** m, n, *chm.*: ⚚ osmazome; **Liebigsches ~** Liebig's extract of meat; **=farbe** f flesh-colour; **=farben** a., **=farbig** a. flesh-coloured, bisw. auch: incarnate; **=faser** f muscular fibre; **=faß** n salting-tub; **=fliege** f, *ent.* flesh-fly, meat-fly, blow-fly (*Sarcoʹphaga*); **=fressend** a. carnivorous, ⚚ sarcophagous; **~es** (Beutel-

---

⚕ scientific; ⚘ botanical; ⚳ geography; ⊕ machinery; ⚒ mining; ⚔ military; ⚓ marine; ⊛ commercial; ✉ postal; 🚂 railway.

[Fleischfresser] — 376 — [fliegen]

Tier zo.: ⚹ sarcophagan; =fresser m/pl., zo. carnivorous animals, ⚹ carni'vora pl.; =frucht ⚹ f pulpy (or pulpous) fruit; =gabel f meat-fork; =gebung f = darstellung; =genuß m consumption of meat; =geschwulst f, path. wen; =gewächs n fleshy growth, ⚹ sarcoma; ⚹geworden a. theol. incarnate, auch: earth-born; =gift n ⚹ ptomain(e); =hack=maschine f mincing-machine, mincer; meat-chopper; =haken ⊕ m des Schlächters meat-hook; =halle f meat-market; =händler m im großen: meat-salesman, carcass-butcher; =hauer m butcher.

fleischicht, fleischig (⌣⌣) a. ⊛ 1. flesh-like, anat.: ⚹ sarcous; ⚹ pulpy, pulpous. — 2. (beleibt) corpulent, plump, F crumby.

Fleisch=kloß (⌣…) m ⑫ Kocht.: meat-ball; =klumpen m: a) lump of flesh or meat; b) fig. (dicke Person) mountain of flesh; =konser'ven f/pl. preserved (or potted, tinned) meat; =korb m meat-basket; =kost f meat diet, animal food; =laden m butcher's shop; =lake f brine, pickle; =lappen m fleshy appendage, zo.: ⚹ caruncle; =lehre f, anat.: ⚹ sarcology; =leim m: ⚹ sarcocol(la).

fleischlich (⌣⌣) a. ⊛ fleshly; ⚹es Verlangen, ⚹e Lüste pl. carnal desires pl., lust (spl.) of the flesh; (sinnlich) sensual; ⚹er Umgang sexual intercourse; adv. ⚹ gesinnt bibl. fleshly-minded, carnally inclined; ~keit f ⊛ fleshliness; sensuality; bibl. carnal-mindedness.

fleisch=los (⌣ ⌣) a. ⊛ fleshless, (abgemagert) emaciated; =losigkeit f ⑫ fleshlessness; ⚹machend a. — ⚹bildend; =made f maggot, flesh-worm; =markt m meat-market; =mehl n (Dünger) meat-guano; =messer n carving-knife; =mulde ⊕ f meat-trough; =nahrung f = =kost; =paste'te f meat-pie; =räucherer m smoke-drier; =bank=; =schau(er) m = beschau(er); =schneide=maschine f = =hack=m.; =schnittchen n, =schnitte f slice of meat; =seite ⊕ f Gerberei: flesh-side; =speise f dish of meat; vgl. =kost; =spieß m meat-spit; =spind n meat-safe; =steuer f tax on meat or slaughtered cattle; =suppe f Kocht.: meat-soup; vgl. =brühe; =tag m (ant. Fasttag) Cath. eccl. meat-day; =teile m/pl. des Körpers fleshy parts pl.; =ton m, paint. flesh-tint; vgl. =farbe; =topf m meat-pot; bibl. die =töpfe Ägyptens the flesh-pots of Egypt; vgl. =brauch m = =bedarf; =verkäufer m butcher('s salesman), der nicht selbst schlachtet: dead-meat salesman; =wage f meat-scales pl.; =waren f/pl. meat sg.; =waren=händler m provision-dealer or -merchant; =waren=handlung f ham-and-beef shop; =warze f, anat.: ⚹ caruncle; =werdung f, theol. incarnation; =wuchs m = =bildung; =wunde f flesh-wound; =wurst f (German) sausage, saveloy; =zwieback m meat-biscuit.

Fleiß (⌣) [ahd.] m ⑪ a. 1. (rastloses Bemühen) application, assiduity; (Arbeitsamkeit) industry, diligence, sedulousness; (Achtsamkeit) carefulness; painstaking; (Tätigkeit) activity, plodding; ~ anwenden to take pains; ~ auf et. verwenden to apply o.s. to a thing, to bestow care (or pains) on a th.; Sprichw.: ~ bricht Eis diligence conquers all (obstacles); ~ erhält den Preis industry will gain the day; ohn' ~ kein Preis no pains no gains, no sweet without sweat. — 2. mit ~ (absichtlich) on purpose, purposely, intentionally, designedly; ich habe es nicht mit ~ getan I did not do it on purpose, a. I did not mean (to do) it.

fleißig (⌣⌣) a. ⊛ 1. (s. Fleiß 1) assiduous; industrious, diligent, hard-working, sedulous; careful, painstaking; active, busy, plodding, strenuous. — 2. ⚹e (sorgfältige) Arbeit careful work. — 3. ⚹e (häufige) Besuche frequent visits pl.; adv. das Schauspiel ⚹ besuchen to frequent the theatre; ⚹ beten to pray constantly or incessantly; ⚹ über et. nachdenken to give a matter very serious thought or consideration; ⚹ spazieren geh(e)n to take a great deal of (walking) exercise; ⚹ studieren to study hard, to be a hard reader, F to grind at (or pore over) one's books.

flektieren (⌣⌣⌣) [lt.] I v/a. u. sich ⚹ v/refl. ⑬ gram. to inflect = abwandeln 1; ⚹ die Sprachen inflexional languages pl. — II ~ n ㉓ und Flektierung f ㊻ = abwandeln 4.

flennen F (⌣⌣) [ahd.] v/n. (h.) ⑱ to cry, to whine, F to snivel, to blub(ber).

Flenner F (⌣⌣) m ⑫, ~in f ㊼ crying person, F sniveller, blubberer.

Flesche ⚔ (⌣⌣) [fr. flèche; * ndl. Flitz] f ㊺ (Pfeilschanze) redan.

fletschen (⌣⌣) [mhd.] v/a. ⑪ 1. die Zähne ⚹ (blecken) to show one's (white) teeth. — 2. ⊕ to spread out (thin).

fleuch, fleug, fleugt, fleuß 2c. (⌣) †, noch poet. = flich(e), flieg(e), fliegt, fließ(e) 2c.

Flexion (⌣⌣⌣) [lt.] f ⑫ gram. inflexion = abwandeln 4; ⚹s=los (⌣…) a. ⊛ inflexionless, uninflexional.

Flibusti=er (⌣⌣⌣⌣) [fr., * ndl. Freibeuter] m ㉒ filibuster, buccaneer; privateer.

Flicht[1] prov. Rhein ⚓ (⌣) f ㊻ (loses Bodenbrett in einem Boot) cuddy.

Flicht[2] (⌣) imper., ⚹(st) pres. von flechten.

Flick=arbeit (⌣…) f ⑫ patchwork; patching; botching (work).

Flicken[1] (⌣⌣) [ndd.] m ㉓ patch, piece (put on) (= Fleck 4).

flicken[2] (⌣⌣) [Fleck] v/a. ⑱ (heil machen) to mend, repair, patch (up); schlecht: to botch; (zs.-stücken) to piece (or sew) together; Schuhe: to cobble, to vamp; Strümpfe: to darn; vgl. ausbessern I; einen Lappen an (ob. auf) et. ⚹ to put (or sew) a piece (or a patch) on a th.; fig. e-m et. am Zeuge ⚹ to pick a hole in a p.('s coat), to pick a quarrel with a p.

Flicker (⌣⌣) m ⑫, ~in f ㊼ (s. flicken) mender, patcher; botcher; cobbler; darner; s. Kesselflicker; ~ei (⌣⌣⌣) f ㊺ mending, patching, botching; darning; ~lohn m ⑫ fee for (or cost of) mending or patching.

Flick=fleck (⌣…) m ⑫ patch; =gedicht n: ⚹ cento; =lappen m piece (of cloth, &c.) for mending or patching; =reim m inserted (or interpolated) rhyme; =schneider m jobbing tailor, botcher; =schuster m cobbler; =werk n: a) =arbeit; b) = =gedicht; c) von Schriften 2c.: (Zusammengestückeltes) (inferior) compilation; =wort n expletive.

flie (⌣; Hom. flieh) impf. v. fleien.

Flieboot ⚓ (⌣⌣) [ndd.] n ⑫ (Dutch) flight; ~führer m ⑫ = Flibu'stier.

Flieder ⚹ (⌣⌣) f ㊺ (türkischer ob. spanischer) ~ lilac (Syri'nga [vulga'ris]). — 2. = Holunder.

Flieder=baum (⌣…) m ⑫ = Flieder; =blüte f lilac-blossom; =strauch m ⑫ = Flieder.

Fliege (⌣⌣) [ahd.: fly; * fliegen] f ㊺ 1. ent. fly (Musca); ~n pl. flies, ⚹ muscarians, diptera(ns pl.); von ~n beschmißen, beschmutzt fly-blown; spanische ~ Spanish fly, ⚹ cantharis (pl. …ides) (Lytta vesicato'ria); pharm. das daraus bereitete Pflaster: blister; künstliche ~ zum Angeln artificial fly; (das) Angeln mit ~n fly-fishing. — 2. fig. leicht wie eine ~ (as) light as a feather; zwei ~n mit e-r Klappe schlagen to kill two birds with one stone, a. to cut both ways. — 3. F fig. (leichtfertige Person) fast (or loose) p. or girl. — 4. (Bärtchen über dem Kinn) imperial. — 5. ⊕ (Korn am Gewehre) sight of a gun.

fliegen (⌣⌣) [ahd.: fly; lt. plūma] ⑧ast. I v/n. (n, ohne Angabe der Ortsveränderung h.) 1. von Vögeln 2c.: to fly, to be on the wing; hoch ⚹ to soar; s. braten 3; von Fahnen: to fly, wave, stream. — 2. mit ⚹ auf Bäume ⚹ to perch on trees; in die Höhe ⚹ to fly (or soar) up; hin und her ⚹ to fly (or flit) to and fro; hoch in die Lüfte ⚹ to fly (or ascend, mount, soar) high into the air; vorüber ⚹ to fly past; geflogen kommen to come flying along. — 3. fig. to rush (or fly, sweep) along; sie flog an seinen Hals she fell on his neck (to embrace him), she flew (or rushed) into his arms; der Stein flog durch das Fenster … flew through (or smashed) the window; sie flogen von ihren Sitzen they jumped (or flew, rushed) from their seats; von Funken 2c.: nach allen Richtungen ⚹ to fly in all directions; der Ball, der Hut flog unter den Tisch … fell under the table; e-n Drachen, e-e Taube ⚹ lassen to fly a kite, a pigeon; ⚔ die Fahne ⚹ lassen to display the colour(s). — 4. meist ⊕ in die Luft ⚹ (gesprengt werden) to be blown up, to explode; in Stücke ⚹ to burst asunder. — II sich ⚹ v/refl. 5. mit Angabe der Wirkung: sich matt, müde ⚹ to get exhausted, tired with flying. — III ~ n ㉓ 6. flying, flitting, soaring, flight (vgl. Flug). — IV ⚹d p.pr. und a. ⊛ 7. flying, &c. (s. I). — 8. mit ⚹dem Atem with panting breath, panting, F puffed; ⚹de Bahn = Feldeisenbahn; ⚹de Brücke flying-bridge; s. Buchhändler; s. Fahne 1; ⚹de Fähre flying ferry; ⚹der Fisch flying fish (Exocoe'tus); mit ⚹den Haaren with dishevelled hair; ⚹de Hitze bsd. path. sudden flush or heat; ⚹der Holländer (Gespensterschiff) Flying Dutchman; meist ⚔ ⚹de Kolonne, ⚹des Korps flying

Zeichen (s. S. XVII): F familiär; P Volkssprache; ſ Gaunersprache; ⟍ selten; † alt (auch gestorben); * neu (auch geboren); ⁓ unrichtig.

[Fliegenangel] — 377 — [Flockseide]

(or detached) column, corps; ⚔ 2des Lazare'tt ambulance. field-hospital.

Fliegen-angel (″…) f ❂ fly-rod; **=blume** ♀ f a) flower fertilized by flies; b) spinnentragende ~ spider-orchis (*Ophrys aranei'fera*); **=dreck** m fly-dirt; **=falle** ♀ f der Venus Venus's fly-trap (*Dionae'a musci'pula*); **=fänger** m: a) one who catches flies; b) orn. flycatcher (*Musci'capa*); c) ♀ fly-trap (*Apo'cynum androsaemifo'lium*); **=fenster** n von Gaze wire window; **=garn** n = =netz; **=gift** n fly-poison, vgl. =papier; **=gott** m, bibl. fly-god, Beelzebub; **=klappe, =klatsche** f fly-clapper, -flap or -flapper, **=kopf** m: a) fly's head; b) ❂ typ. turned letter; **=kot** m =dreck; **=kraut** ♀ n =orchis; **=netz** n fly-net; an Kronleuchtern: fly-cage; **=orchis** ♀ f fly-orchis (*Ophrys musci'fera*); **=papier** n fly-paper; bisw. auch fly-cemetery; **=pflaster** n blister; **=pilz** ♀ m =schwamm; **=schmiß** m fly-blow; **=schmutz** m fly-speck; vgl. =dreck; **=schnäpper** m, orn. = =fänger b; **=schrank** m meat-safe; **=schwamm** ♀ m fly-agaric (*Aga'ricus musca'rius*); **=schwarm** m swarm of flies; **=stein** m, min. arsenic-powder; **=vogel** m, orn. humming-bird(*Tro'chilus*);**=wanze**f,ent. fly-bug (*Redu'vius persona'tus*); **=wedel** m fly-brush or -whisk, flap for flies.

Flieger (L~) m ❷ 1. (Fliegender; schnelles Pferd, schneller Zug ꝛc.) flier, flyer. — 2. ↓ middle stay-sail; **~rennen** T n Sport: (Rennen auf kurze Distanz) flying race.

flieh (L; *Hom.* flie): a) impf. v. fleihen; b) imper. v. fliehen.

fliehen (L~) [ahd.: flee] ❸b. I v/n. (śn ahd. oft: to fly (nie im impf. flew, stets fled!); to (make one's) escape; schnell 2, bsd. ⚔ to beat a hasty retreat; davon 2, von dannen 2 to run away; von der Zeit: to pass (away), to elapse, fly, slip; zu e-m 2 to take one's refuge with a p.; ⚔ ein 2des Heer a fugitive (or flying) army, an army on its flight; den 2den Feind verfolgen to pursue (or chase) the flying foe or routed enemy; ein ~der ❼ a fugitive. — II v/a. to flee (or slip) from; (meiden) to shun, to avoid. — III ~ n ❸ flight (vgl. Flucht¹).

Flieh-kraft (″…) f ❷ phys. centrifugal force or power.

Fliese ❂ (L~) [ndb., ndl.] f ❹ (Kachel zum Belegen der Wände ꝛc.) glazed (or Dutch) tile; (Steinplatte für Fußböden ꝛc.) flag- (or floor-)stone; mit ~n belegen to flag.

Fließ (L; *Hom.* Vlies) n ❸a. [fließen] (Bächlein) rivulet; im schlammigen ~ (Pfuhl) in the slimy pool.

fließen (L~) [ahd.: fleet] I v/n. (śn u. h.) ❻d. 1. to flow (a. von Gewändern); to run; in Strömen 2 to gush, rush, stream; dick 2 to trickle; sanft dahin 2 to glide along (gently); es wird Blut 2 there will be shedding of blood or bloodshed, blood will be shed; die Ströme 2 durch die Ebene ❼ flow through (or cross, traverse) the plain; die Donau fließt ins Schwarze Meer the Danube flows (or falls, discharges itself) into the Black Sea; der Schweiß floß ihm von der Stirne the perspiration ran (stärker: trickled) from his forehead; die Tränen flossen ihr aus den Augen the tears flowed (or streamed) from her eyes; *fig.* alles, was aus seiner Feder geflossen ist all that has flowed (or proceeded) from his pen, all that his pen has produced; *bibl.* Land, wo Milch und Honig fleußt the land of milk and honey; *fig.* spärlich 2e Quellen, Berichte meagre (or scanty) sources, reports. — 2. das Papier fließt (schlägt durch) … runs. — 3. meist ❂ (flüssig werden) to become fluid or liquid; to liquefy; (schmelzen) to melt away; von der Kerze: to gutter, run. — 4. *fig.* aus et. 2 (hervorgehen) to follow (or ensue) from … — II ~ n ❷❸ 5. flow, flowing, zB. (das) ~ der Rede (the) flow of speech. — III 2d p.pr. u. a. ❻ 6. (f. 1, bsd. am Ende) 2de Gewässer running streams or waters *pl.*; in Krümmungen 2d winding or meandering. — 7. *fig.* 2de Handschrift (good) running (or flowing) hand; 2der Stil fluent (or easy) style; *adv.* 2d schreiben, sprechen to write, speak fluently or with (great) fluency or ease.

Fließ-papier (″…) n ❷ blotting-paper; allg.: unglazed paper.   [lancet.⌉

Fliete (L~) f ❹ vet. (Aderlaß-eisen) fleam,⌊

Flimmer (L~) m ❷ 1. glitter(ing), glimmer, feeble (or wavy, uncertain) light. — 2. zo.: ⚛ flagellum.

Flimmer-härchen (″…) n/pl. ❷ ♀, zo.: ⚛ cilia *pl.*; mit ~ versehen ciliate; Bewegung mittels ~ ⚛ ciliary motion.

flimmern (L~) v/n. (h.) ❷a. 1. (glitzern) to glitter, glimmer, glisten, *poet.* auch: to shimmer; (funkeln) to sparkle; 2de Sterne twinkling stars *pl.* — 2. es flimmert mir vor den Augen it chances (or glitters) before my eyes, my eyes (or senses) are swimming, F I (can) see stars. — 3. (schwirren) to vibrate.

Flimmer-schein (″…) m ❷ faint glimmer, ray of feeble light.

Flinder (L~) m ❷ (flimmerndes Metallblättchen) tinsel; *fig.* (flatterndes Ding) s.th. fluttering or flitting.

flink (L) [ndb.] a. ❻ (behend) agile, nimble, light-footed; (schnell) quick, brisk; (munter) alert; 2e Arbeit quick (or sharp, smart) work; 2 bei der Hand keen and watchful, ever ready; *adv.* (macht) 2! be quick!, look sharp!, F u. P buck up! etwas 2 besorgen to do a th. promptly or smartly or expeditiously; **~heit** (L~) f ❷ agility, nimbleness; quickness, alertness.

Flint (L) [ndb.: Flinz] m ❷b. min. (Feuerstein) flint.

Flinte (L~)[nhd.1630/60,*ndbl.,schwd.*Flint] f ❹ gun (for hunting); für die Bogen-jagd: a) ehm. (Steinschloßgewehr) firelock; b) jetzt: hunt. (glattes Jagdgewehr) *ant.* Büchse) fowling-piece; eine ~ ab-schießen, laden to fire off, to load a gun; *fig.* die ~ ins Korn werfen, etwa: to throw (or give) up the game, to abandon an enterprise.

Flinten-beschlag (″…) m ❷ mounting of a gun; **=futteral** n gun-case; **=kolben** m butt-end of a gun; **=kugel** f gun-ball; **=riemen, =schaft** m, **=schloß** n gun-sling, -stock, -lock; **=schrot** n (small) shot; *bideres*: buckshot; **=schuß** m gunshot, musket-shot; e-n ~ weit bis auf =schußweite within gunshot; **=stein** m (gun-)flint.

Flint-glas (″…) n ❷ flint-glass; **=kon-glomerat** n. *geol.* conglomeratic flint, pudding-stone; **=sand** m flint-sand; **=stein** m flint(stone).

Flinz P (″) m ❶a. min. (Spateisenstein) spathic (or sparry) iron-ore; crystallized carbonate of iron.

flirren (L~) v/n. (h.) ❷ to vibrate, to flit to and fro; weitS. = flimmern.

Flitter (L~) [nhd.] m ❷ 1. (Gold-, Silberdraht zum Sticken ꝛc.) spangle, tinsel; mit ~ besetzt spangled. — 2. *fig.* (Tand) tinsel, frippery, outside show; (Putz) finery, F get-up.

Flitter-glanz (″…) m ❷ false splendour, hollow pomp; tinsel; **=gold** ❂ n, *metall.* Dutch metal, brass-foil, leaf-brass, leaf-gold.

flitterhaft, flitterig (″…) a. ❻ tawdry; weitS. hollow, false; F showy.

Flitter-jahr (″…) n ❷ first year of wedded life; **=kram** m cheap finery or jewellery or trinkets *pl.*; gewgaws *pl.*

flittern (L~) v/n. (h.) ❷a. 1. = flimmern. — 2. (prunken) F to show off one's fine clothes or fine things.

Flitter-sand (″…) m ❷ (glimmerhaltiger Sand) sparkling (or micaceous) sand; **=schein** m = =glanz; **=staat, =tand** m, **=werk** n tawdry dress, fallals *pl.* (vgl. =kram und Flitter 2); **=wochen** [tosen] f/pl. e-s Ehepärchens: honeymoon.

Flitz (″) [ndl.] m ❶a. u. **~bogen** (″…) m ❷ (boy's) crossbow; f. a. Bogen 3.

flitzen F (L~) v/n. (sn) ❾❶ to flit (or shoot) along (rapidly); sie flitzte aus dem Zimmer she flitted (or slipped) out of the room.   [fellow, harum-scarum.⌉

Flitzer (L~) m ❷ thoughtless young⌊

Flitz-pfeil (″…) n ❷ arrow to be used with a crossbow.   [flechten.⌉

flocht (ścht) (flöchte subj.) impf. von⌊

Flocke (L~) [ahd.: flock, flake] f ❹ flake of snow, flock of wool, cotton, &c.; (Werg) hards *pl.*; vom Schnee: in ~n fallen to fall (or come down) in flakes.

flocken (L~) ❸ I v/a. ❂ Wolle ꝛc. 2 to beat … into flocks, to flake … — II v/n. (h., śn) to come down in flakes. — III sich 2 v/refl. (sich zu Flocken ballen) to form (into) flakes or flocks.

flocken-artig (″…) a. ❻ = flockicht; **=bett** n ❷ flock-bed; **=blume** ♀ f centaury (*Centaure'a*), schwarze ~ ball- or crop-, knap-)weed, bull's-head (*C. nigra*); **=erz** n, min. native massicot, ⚛ filamentous arseniate of lead; **=feder** f der Raubvögel flake-feather; **=lesen** n, *path.* der Sterbenden (Zupfen an der Bett-decke): ⚛ floccillation, carphologia, tilmus; **=tuch** ❂ n rough cloth; 2weise *adv.* in flakes.

flockicht, flockig (L~) a. ❻ flaky, like flakes or flocks, fluffy, ⚛ flocculent, *anat.*: ⚛ tomentous, *min.* (faserig): ⚛ filamentous, fibrous.

Flock-papier (″…) n ❷ flock-paper; **=seide** ❷ f sleave- (or floss-)silk,

♪ Musik; ⚛ Wissenschaft; ♀ Pflanze; ⌘ Geographie; ❂ Technik; ⚒ Bergbau; ⚔ Militär; ↓ Marine; ❿ Handel; ❀ Post; ❿ Eisenbahn.

[**Flocktapete**] — 378 — [**Flözsandstein**]

waste-silk; =**tapete** f flock wallpaper; =**wolle** f flock-wool, short wool.
flog (¹) (u. **flöge** subj.) impf. von fliegen.
floh¹ (¹) impf. von fliehen.
Floh² (¹) [ahd.: flea; * fliehen] m ⑦c. flea; Flöhe fangen to catch (or hunt for) fleas; von Flöhen zerstochen fleabitten; fig. e-m einen ~ ins Ohr setzen to put a flea in a p.'s ear; er hört die Flöhe husten he hears the grass grow.
Floh=biß (¹...) m ㉖ flea-bite.
flöhe (¹...) subj. impf. v. fliehen.
flöhen (¹~) v/a., sich ~ v/refl. ⑧⑧ to catch (one's) fleas, to rid (o.s.) of fleas.
Floh=fang (¹...) m ⑨d. ㉖ flea-catching; =**farbe** f: ⚇ puce-colour; ♀**farben** a., ♀**farbig** a. puce-(coloured); =**kraut** ♀ n fleabane (Pulica'ria); gemeines ~ common fleabane (I'nula pulica'ria); =**krebs** m water-flea, fresh-water shrimp (Ga'mmarus pulex); =(**samen**)**wegerich** ♀ m fleaseed or fleawort (Planta'go Psy'llium); =**stich** m = =biß.
Flor¹ (¹) [nhd., *lt.] m ⑨d. 1. (Blüte) bloom, blossom; ② (Blütezeit) flowering (-season or -period). — 2. (blühende Gewächse) blo(ss)oming plants pl.; fig. ein ~ von schönen Mädchen a goodly muster (or F a good show, a bevy) of fair maids. — 3. fig. (Blühen, Gedeihen) flourishing (or prosperous) state; der Handel ist im ~ … is flourishing or F in full swing; in ~ sein to be in vogue or in fashion.
Flor² (¹) [nhd., nbl., *lt.] m ⑨d., auch ⑨d. 1. ⊕: a) (dünnes Gewebe von Seide, Nesselgarn x.) crape, gauze; krauser ~ double crape; einen ~ tragen to wear crape or mourning; b) (Pole des Sammets) pile of velvet. — 2. fig. (Schleier) veil; e-m den ~ von den Augen ziehen to open a p.'s eyes (wide), to undeceive (or disillusion) a p.
Flora (¹~) [lt.] f ㊾ (Gesamtheit der Pflanzen e-s Landes) flora; (Blumenausstellung) flower-show. [crape.)
flor=ähnlich (¹...) a. ㊏ like gauze or]
Florali=en (¹~¹~) [lt.] pl. inv. röm. Alt.: (Fest der Flora, 28. April bis 3. Mai) Floral games pl., (It.) Floralia pl.
flor=artig (¹...) a. ㊏ = =ähnlich; =**band** n ㉖, =**binde** f ribbon, band of crape; am Hute: mourning-hatband. [gauze.)
floren¹ (¹~) [**Flor**²] a. ㊏ of crape or]
Florentia (-⁹ⁱfʸ(~)ᵃ), **Florentine** (~¹~) [lt.] npr/f. ㊽ ⑨ ㊸β. (Bn.) Florence, F dim. Florry.
Florentiner (~¹~) [Florenz] m ㉒, ~**in** f ㊼, **florentinisch** a. ㊏ Florentine; s. Flasche 2. [Florence.)
Florenz ⚥ (-ˢ) npr/n. inv. (it. St.)]
Florett (-ˢ) [fr.] ⑨c., ⑨ I n, fenc. foil. — II m (Seide) floss- (or waste-)silk. =**band** (¹~) n ㉖ ehm. ferret-ribbon; =**fechten** n, fenc. foil-fencing or -practice; =**seide** ♀ f floss-silk.
Flor=fliege (¹...) f, ent. pearl-fly (Heme-ro'bius); =**hut** m craped hat.
florieren (-¹~) [lt.] v/n. (h.) ⑬ (blühen) to flourish, prosper, thrive.
Florin ⚥ (~ʳᵃ) [nhd., *Florenz] m ⑨c. u. ⑫ florin ⓞ Gulden (abbr. fl.).
Florist (-ˢ) [fr., *lt.] m ㊷ (Blumenfreund, =züchter) (amateur) florist.

Flor=schleier m, =**weber**(**in** f) m (¹...) ㉒ gauze- (or crape-) veil, -weaver.
Floskel (¹~) [lt.] f ㊽ (Redeblume) flower of speech. (fine) flourish or phrase.
Floß¹ ⚓ (¹~) [ahd.: float] m u. n ⑦a. (Blockschiff) raft, float.
Floß² ⊕ (¹~) m u. n ⑦a. = Flosse 2.
floß³ (¹~) ²c. impf. von fließen.
flößbar (¹~) a. ㊏ Gewässer: navigable for rafts; Holz: floatable.
Flöß=(bau)holz n, =**baum** m (¹...) ㉒ floated timber, tree.
Floß¹=**beamte(r)** (¹...) m ㉖ inspector of rafts; =**brücke** f floating bridge; raft-bridge.
Flosse (¹~) [ahd.; *fließen] f ㊽ 1. ichth. fin; kleine: ⚇ pinnule. — 2. ⊕ metall. (Roh=eisenstück) iron-pig.
flösse (¹~) subj. impf. von fließen.
Flöße (¹~) f ㊽ 1. floating of timber (down-stream). — 2. (Recht zu flößen) right of floating or of rafting. — 3. ⚓ (Floß) raft, float (auch ⊕ zum Wollwaschen x.). — 4. ⊕ metall. = Flosse 2.
flößen (¹~) [ahd.: float] ⓿ I v/a. 1. = einflößen I. — 2. ⚓ to float (or raft) wood. — II ~ n ㉓ 3. des Holzes floating, rafting.
flossen=artig (¹ˢ...) [Flosse] a. ㊏: ⚇ pinniform; =**füß(l)er** m ⓿ = =füßig; =**grade** (Ruderschnecke): ⚇ pteropod.
Flößer (¹~) m ㉒ raftsman, Am. river-driver; ~**ei** (~¹) f ㊽ floating of wood.
Floß¹=**feder** (ˢ...) [Flosse 1] f ㊽ ichth. fin; mit ~n versehen provided with fins, finned; =¹**führer** m raftsman, =²**füßig** a. ㊏ orn.: ⚇ pinnatiped; =¹**geschäft** (a. **Flöß**=...)n rafting; =**graben** m canal for rafts; =**holz** n floated timber or wood.
flossig (¹~) a. ㊏ ichth. finned, finny.
...**flossig** (...¹~) a. ㊏ in Zssgn, z.B. breit= broad-finned.
Floß¹=**krampe** ⊕ (ˢ...) f ㉖ raft(ing)-dog; =¹**loch** n: ⚓ lock of a river, &c.; =²**loch** ⊕ metall. (Gußrinne) casting-gutter, runner; =¹**meister** m master of a raft, owner (or surveyor) of floated wood; =**ordnung** (a. **Flöß**=...) f bye-laws pl. for the floating of timber; =**platz** m (wood-)yard for floated timber; =**recht** n right of floating wood; =**sack** ⚔ m float (for carrying soldiers) consisting of a large sack filled with straw, hay, &c.; =**wasser** n water on which timber can be floated; =**zeit** f rafting-season.
Flötchen (¹~) ㉓ (dim.: Flöte) little flute; ⚓ bisw.: flageolet; (Vogelpfeife) zuf(f)olo.
Flöte (¹~) [nhd., *fr.] f ㊽ 1. ♪ flute; (die) ~ blasen to blow the flute. — 2. Kartenspiel: (Karten derselben Farbe) flush.
flöten (¹~) [Flöte] v/a. u. v/n. (h.) ⓾ to play (on) the flute; (pfeifen) to whistle; von der Nachtigall x.: e-n in Schlaf ⓿ to warble (or sing) a p. to sleep; e-e ♪de Stimme a flute-like (or silvery) voice; F fig. ⓿ gehen F to go to the dogs or to pot, to be (or get) lost.
flöten=ähnlich ♪ (¹~...) a. ㊏ flute-like; bisw. fluty; =**baß** m ♪ der Orgel recorder; =**begleitung** f flute-accompaniment; =**bläser**(**in** f) m fl.-player, flutist; =**bohrer** ⊕ m, =**macher** m fl.-maker; =**register** n einer Orgel fl.-stop; =**spiel** n fl.-playing; =**spieler**(**in** f) m = =**bläser** (in f: a.) ♪ der Partitu'r:

fl.-part; b) (ähnliche Stimme) sweet or melodious voice; =**stock** m fl.-stick; =**stück** n piece (or music) for the flute; =**ton** m: a) note (or tone) of a flute; b) sweet (or silvery) note; F fig. e-m die (höheren) =**töne** beibringen to put a p. through his paces; =**vogel** m, orn. flute-bird, crow-shrike (Gymno-rhi'na tibi'cen); =**werk** n in Orgeln: flute-(or flue-)work; =**zug** m = =**register**.
Flöter (¹~) m ㉒, **Flötist** (-ˢ) m ㊷ (Flötenbläser) flute-player, flutist.
flott (¹~) [ndd. fließend] I a. ㊏ 1. ⚓ von Schiffen x.: afloat; ⓿ sein (auf dem Wasser schwimmen) to (be a)float; ⓿ machen to float, to get off; wieder ⓿ machen (werden) to set (to get) afloat (again). — 2. fig. (ungebunden) free, unrestrained; (locker) loose; (lustig) gay, merry; burschikos: der Bursche dashing (young) fellow (vgl. fide'l); adv. ⓿ geh(e)n to walk (at) a good (or quick) pace; ⓿ leben: a) (vornehm) to live in fine style; b) (lustig und ungebunden) to live (or lead) a gay and easy life; bei ihnen geht es ⓿ her F they are doing (or going) it fine, they are having a rare old time of it; ⓿ vorankommen to get on swimmingly; ⓿e Geschäfte machen to do a fair (amount of) business, F to drive a rattling (or roaring) trade; s. auch flottweg. — II n (m) ⓿b. 3. floating object; auch = Milchrahm.
Flotte (¹~) [nhd. 17. sae., fr., it., *ndd.] f ㊽ 1. ⚓ von Schiffen: fleet, von Kriegsschiffen: navy; kleine ~ (Flottille) flotilla, (naval) squadron; auf der ~ dienen to serve in the navy. — 2. ⊕ (schwimmendes Gerüst) float(ing stage).
flotten (¹~) ⓿ I v/n. (h.) to (be a)float; alles ⓿ und treiben lassen to let everything drift or go as it may. — II v/a. to set afloat; F to get off.
Flotten=abteilung ⚓ (ˢ...) f ㉖ (detachment of a) squadron; =**base** f naval base; =**führer** m admiral (of a fleet); =**kapitän**, =**offizier** m captain, officer in the navy; =**manöver** n/pl. naval manœuvres pl.; =**schau** f naval review; =**stützpunkt** m naval station or base; =**verein** m Navy League.
Flott=holz (ˢˢ) n ㉖: a) floating wood; b) light wood for making floats.
Flottille ⚓ (~¹l(i)~) [fr.] f ㊽ f. Flotte 1.
Flott=machen ⚓ (ˢ...) n ㉓ eines Schiffes flotation; =**seide** f (gezwirnte Seide) thrown silk.
flott=weg (ˢˢ) adv. smartly, quickly, promptly, briskly, boldly; without ado.
Flöz (¹) [ahd.: flat] n (a. m) ⑨a. geol. (✕ nutzbare) Schicht) (horizontal) layer or stratum or seam; ⚒ fletz; ✕ in ~en in layers or strata; stehendes ~ perpendicular seam.
Flöz=bau ✕ (¹...) m ㉖ working of a seam; =**erz** ✕ n stratified ore; =**formation** f, =**gebirge** n, geol. sedimentary formation or rocks pl., secondary strata pl., old sea-bottom; =**granit** m secondary granite, ♀**leer** ✕ a. devoid of profitable mineral seams; ♀**reich** a. ㊏ rich in workable seams; =**sandstein** m, geol. new red sandstone;

Signs (see page XVII): F familiar; P vulgar; ꟼ flash; ↘ rare; † obsolete (died); * new word (born); ⁺⁺ incorrect; ♪ music;

[Flözschicht] — 379 — [Flugloch]

=ſchicht f (sedimentary) layer; ⚒ weiſe adv. in layers or strata or seams.

Fluch (⌣ᷓ) [ahd.; *fluchen] m ⓓⒸ. 1. (ant. Segen) curse, malediction; (Verwünſchung) imprecation, execration; der Kirche: anathema; j-m zum Fluche gereichen to be (or prove) a curse to a p.; es liegt oder ruht ein ~ auf ihnen a curse rests (or there is a curse) upon them, they are under a. c.; ~ über euch! a curse upon you!; ~ dem Mammon! cursed be Mammon! — 2. (Schwur) oath; e-n gräßlichen ~ ausſtoßen to utter (or use, feierlicher: to pronounce) a terrible oath; (Gottesläſterung) blasphemy.

fluch=beladen (⌣ᷓ...) a. ⑯, ⚒ belaſtet a. (lying) under a curse, accursed.

fluchen (⌣ᷓ⌣) [ahd.] ⑱ I v/n. (h.) to (curse and) swear, to utter (or launch forth) imprecations or oaths; e-m ⚒ to curse a p.; ⚒ wie ein Landsknecht oder Türke to swear like a trooper; **auf** e-n ⚒ (ihn verwünſchen) to execrate a p., to call down curses upon him; eccl. to hurl forth an anathema against a p. — II v/a. ſchwere Flüche ⚒ to swear terribly; vgl. Fluch 2; e-m alles Böſe an den Hals ⚒ to imprecate (or call down) every possible evil upon a p.('s head). — III ~ n ㉓ (cursing and) swearing.

fluch(ens)=wert (⌣ᷓ⌣...) a. ⑯, ⚒ würdig a. execrable, damnable.

Flucher (⌣ᷓ⌣) m ㉒, ~in f ㊼ one who (curses and) swears; (Läſterer) blasphemer.

Flucht[1] (⌣ᷓt) [ahd.: flight, *fliehen] f ⑯ 1. flight; (Entkommen) escape; e-s heftig Verfolgten: race for (dear) life; meiſt ⚔ wilde ~ rout; auf der ~ ſein ... in (or on one's) flight, ... fleeing or flying; in voller ~ in full flight; die ~ ergreifen to take to flight or to one's heels; in die ~ ſchlagen oder treiben to put to flight, ⚔ auch: to rout; ſein Heil in der ~ ſuchen to seek safety in flight, to run for one's life. — 2. fig. der ~ (das Hinſchwinden) der Zeit the (rapid) flight of time. — 3. ⊕ mach. (Spielraum) full play or swing or scope, purchase. — 4. ⊕ arch. (gerade Linie) alinement, straight line, row; vier Häuſer in einer ~ ... in a row; drei Zimmer auf einer ~ (demſelben Stockwert) ... on the same floor.

Flucht[2] (⌣ᷓt) [fliegen] f ㊻ 1. (Haufen fliegender Vögel) flight of pigeons, &c.; covey of partridges, &c.; flock of geese, &c. — 2. ~en pl. (Schwungfedern des Federviehs) pinions pl. of winged game.

Flucht[1]=bau (⌣...) m ㊷ der Füchſe: inmost retreat of a fox's kennel; =ebene f Perspektive: vanishing plane.

flüchten (⌣ᷓ⌣) [erſt nhd. 17 sae.; *ndb.] ⑲ I v/n. (ſn) und ſich ⚒ v/refl. to flee, to take (to) flight; oft auch: to fly; vgl. fliehen I; hinter, unter et. ⚒ to take refuge behind, below a th. — II v/a. einen ⚒ to save a p. by flight. — III ~ n ㉓ flight; escape; vgl. Flucht[1].

flüchtig (⌣⌣) I a. ⑯ 1. (fliehend) fugitive, flying; ⚒ werden, ſich auf den Fuß ſetzen to take (or betake o.s.) to flight, to become a fugitive; (entwiſchen) to (make one's) escape, to abscond, F to make tracks. — 2. (raſch verfliegend) fleeting, transient; (vergänglich) perishable, transitory; (unbeſtändig) fickle; ein ⚒es (flinkes) Pferd a fleet horse; path. eine ⚒e Röte a (sudden) flush; ⚒er Schmerz momentary pain; adv. die Stunden eilen ⚒ dahin ... pass (or slip by) rapidly. — 3. chm., &c. ⚒e (ätheriſche) Öle essential oils pl.; ⚒e Salze volatile salts pl. — 4. (im Fluge gemacht) hasty (glance), passing or desultory (remark); (oberflächlich) casual (notice), superficial (examination), careless (work); der Beſuch flying visit; bei der Durchſicht on a cursory inspection; der (flatterhafter) Menſch careless (or flighty, ſtärker: giddy) person; ⚒e Zeichnung light (or hasty) sketch. — 5. adv. ⚒ hin arbeiten to scamp one's work; ein Buch ⚒ durchleſen, durchblättern to glance at a book, to skim (the contents of) a book; ⚒ erteilen to hurry away in swift flight, to beat a hasty retreat; ⚒ erwähnen to mention by the way. — 6. Kunſt: (in der Luft ſchwebend) flying (or fluttering) robes, drapery, &c. — II ~e([r] m) f ㊼ 7. fugitive (= Flüchtling).

Flüchtigkeit (⌣⌣⌣) f ㊻ (f. flüchtig I) fleetness, transitoriness, rapidity, hastiness, desultoriness, carelessness, cursoriness; flightiness, fig. fugacity; chm. volatility.

Flüchtigkeits=fehler (⌣...) m ㊷ slip (of the pen); oversight.

Flüchtling (⌣⌣) m ⓓd. fugitive; pol. (der in ein anderes Land geflohen iſt) refugee; (Verbannter) exile; (Geächteter) outlaw; ⚔ deserter.

Flucht[1]=linie (⌣cht...) f ㊷, =punkt m Perspektive: vanishing line, point; =röhre f = =bau; =verſuch m attempt to escape.

Fluder (⌣⌣) [ahd.] m (n) ㉒ mill-race.

Flüe ſchwz. (⌣⌣) f ㊻ = Fluh.

Flüe=vogel (⌣ᷓ⌣...) m ㊷ orn. hedgesparrow (Accentor).

Flug (⌣) [ahd.: flight; *fliegen] m ⓓⒸ. 1. flying, flight; orn.: ⚒ vol(it)ation; Möwen verfolgen ihren ⚒ Stunden lang gulls continue (or remain) on the wing for hours; fig. ~ der Zeit flight of time; im ~ e in haste; im ~ e ſchießen to shoot flying or on the wing. — 2. = Flucht[2] 1. — 3. (Flügelweite) width of a bird with outspread wings; her. vol.

Flug=aſche (⌣...) f ㊷ flaky ashes pl.; =bahn f ⚔ und mech. trajectory of a missile; =beutler m, zo. in Neuholland: petaurist (Petaurus); =biene f = Arbeitsbiene; =blatt n fugitive piece, broadsheet, loose leaf; vgl. =ſchrift; =eidechſe f, geol. Foſſil: ⚛ pterosaur.

Flügel (⌣⌣) [mhd.; *Flug] m ㊷ 1. wing (auch eines Gebäudes); (Schwinge) pinion; fig. eines Rockes: flap; mit ~n verſehen, winged, ⚛ alate(d); die ~ hängen (ob. ſinken) laſſen to droop one's wings; fig. to be downcast or despondent or down in the mouth; unter ſeine ~ nehmen to take under one's wings (a. fig.). — 2. fig. e-m die ~ beſchneiden, ſtutzen to clip a p.'s wings; ſich (dat.) die ~ verbrennen (Schaden nehmen) to burn one's fingers; die ~ (Kräfte) wachſen ihm he begins to feel his strength or himself. — 3. ♪ (flügelförmiges Piano) grand (piano). — 4. ⊕ mach. flier; e-r Flügeltür: side (or half) of a folding-door; arch. wing; e-r Windmühle: sail; ⚓ (Anker=)~ fluke; ~ e-r Schiffsſchraube blade of a screw-propeller; ⚔ der linke, rechte ~ the left, right wing of an army. — 5. anat.: ⚛ pinna; ~ der Naſe wing of the nose; (Lappen) lobe of the lungs.

Flügel=adjuta'nt ⚔ (⌣⌣...) m ㊷ aide-de-camp to a royal person, &c.; =ähnlich a. ⑯, =artig a. wing-like, ⚛ aliform, pterotic; =bauer ⊕ m maker of grand pianos; =decke f, ent. der Käfer: wing-case or-sheath, ⚛ tegument; mit ~n verſehen: ⚛ coleopterous; =fell n, anat. am Auge: web-eye, ⚛ pterygium; =fenſter n French (or casement-) window; =förmig a. wing-shaped, ⚛ aliform; =fortſatz m, anat. des Keilbeins: ⚛ pterygoid process or plate; =frucht f winged fruit, wing-seed, ⚛ samara; =haube f woman's cap with lappets; =horn ♪ n bugle(-horn); =hut m, myth. winged hat of Mercury; =kleid n bſd. ehm.: dress trimmed with wing-like frills; =lahm a. lame in one wing or both wings, with drooping wing(s); =los a. wingless, ent.: ⚛ apteran, ...ous; loſe Inſekten n/pl.: ⚛ aptera pl.; =loſigkeit f winglessness; =mauer f, arch. aisle-wall, e-r Brücke: wing-wall; =mann ⚔ m ㆆ fugleman, file-leader; =muskel m, anat.: ⚛ pterygoid (muscle). [II ge-flügelt p.p. ſ. bſd. Art.]

flügeln (⌣⌣) I v/a. ⑳a. to wing. —⎦

Flügel=paar (⌣⌣...) n ㊷ pair of wings; =pferd = =roß n, poet. winged horse, Pegasus; =ſchlag m wing-stroke, flap(ping) of wings; fig. der ~ ſeines Genius the flight (or power) of his genius; =ſchnecke f, zo.: ⚛ stromb(ine), foſſile: strombite; =ſchnell a. with winged speed; =ſchraube ⊕ f winged screw; =ſchüppchen n, ent. der Schmetterlinge: ⚛ pterygode; =ſpitze f wing-tip; =tücher n/pl. e-r Windmühle: sails pl.; =tür(e) f folding-door; =weiſe ⚔ adv. und ⚛⚛ a. in wings; ⚒ Aufſtellung, Gliederung formation in wings; =weite f wing-spread.

flug=fertig (⌣...) a. ⑯ ready to fly; =feuer n ㊷ rapidly spreading fire.

flügge (⌣⌣) [ndd.] a. ⑯ von jungen Vögeln: fledged; noch nicht ⚒ unfledged, (kahl) bare; fig. ⚒ (ſelbſtändig) werden to stand on one's own feet.

Flug=hafer ♃ (⌣...) m ㊷ = Windhafer; =hahn m, ichth. flying-gurnard (Dactylopterus); =haut f der Fledermäuſe: membrane serving as wing, ⚛ patagium; =höhe f (Höhe eines Punktes der Flugbahn) vertical height of a projected body, ordinate of a trajectory; =hörnchen n, zo. flying-squirrel (Pteromys); =huhn n, orn. sand-grouse, rock-pigeon (Pterocles); =hund m, zo. Oſt-J.: fox-bat, kalong (Pteropus); =kraft f flying power, fig. elasticity of the mind, power of imagination; =linie f ⚔, &c. = =bahn; =loch n: a) der Bienen: entrance (or opening) to the hive; b) der Tauben:

⚛ scientific; ♃ botanical; ♁ geography; ⊕ machinery; ⚒ mining; ⚔ military; ⚓ marine; ● commercial; ✉ postal; 🚂 railway.

[**Flugmaschine**] — 380 — [**Flutmühle**]

pigeon-hole; =**maschine** ⊕ f flying machine, aeroplane; =**mehl** n mill-dust.
flugs (¹, F ⁺ₜₛ) [mhd.] adv. (im Fluge) quickly, swiftly, speedily; (sofort) at once, instantly, immediately.
Flug-sand (⁰...) m ⓺² quicksand, shifting sand(s pl.); =**schlag** m Tennis-spiel: volley; =**schrift**(=**schreiber** m) f pamphlet(eer); =**staub** ⊕ m, metall. metallic dust, smoke; =**staub-kammer** ⊕ f, metall. smoke-chamber; =**vermögen** n ⌀ volation; ⁀**weise** adv. in flights; =**zeit** f time of flight.
Fluh schwz. (¹) [ahd. Felswand] f ⓾ (SCH.) steep rocks pl., chasm, precipice, abyss. [fluid.]
Fluidum ⌀ (ᴸ˘˘) [lt.] n ⓾⁹ (Flüssiges)
fluktuieren ⌀ (˘˘ᴸ˘) [lt.] I v/n. (h.) ⓽³ (schwanken) to fluctuate, to vary. — II ~ n ²³ fluctuation, variation.
Flunder (ᴸ˘) [schwd.] m ⓶², f ⓵⁸ ichth. flounder (Pleuroneʹctes ob. Plateʹssa flesus).
Flunkerei (˘ᴸᴵᴵ) f ⓵⁶ fibbing; brag, bounce, swagger.
Flunkerer (ᴸ˘˘) m ²² fibber; braggart, bouncer, swaggerer.
flunkern (ᴸ˘) [ndd.] I v/n. (h.) ⓶ᵃ. 1. = flimmern. — 2. F (lügen) to fib, to draw (or shoot) with the long bow; vgl. aufschneiden 5. — II ~ n ²³ 3. = Flunkerei.
Flun(t)sch Pnordb. (⁵) m ⓶ᵃ., f ⓵⁶ (verzerrtes Maul) F lop-sided mouth, P lopsided (or ugly) mug; einen ~ machen to make a grimace. [nasty face.]
Flun(t)sch-gesicht (ᴸ˘˘...) n ⓺² P ugly mug.
Fluor ⌀ (ᴸ˘) [lt.] n ⓾⁰ chm. fluorine (Fl ober F).
Fluoreszenz ⌀ (˘˘˘ᴸ) [lt.] f ⓵⁶ physiol. phys. (schillernde Färbung, Selbstleuchten) fluorescence. [fluorescent.]
fluoreszierend ⌀ (˘˘˘ᴸ˘) a. ⓾ (schillernd)
Fluor-kalzium ⌀ (˘ᴸ˘˘...) n ⓾ min. = Flußspat; =**wasserstoff**(**säure** f) m, chm. fluorhydric (or hydrofluoric) acid (H Fl).
Flur (¹) f ⓵⁶ [mhd.: floor] I (Feldflur) 1. field, plain, level ground; (Weide) meadow, pasture, lea; engS. (Feldmark) land (or fields pl.) contained in one parish. — II [ndd.] mst m ⓶ᶜ. 2. (Hausflur, Raum im Hauseingange) entrance-hall; größerer: vestibule, (Vorzimmer) lobby; (Gang) hall, passage, corridor; (Treppen=)~ landing (-place) of a staircase. — 3. (Fliese) flagstone, (Stein zum Pflastern) paving-brick or -stone, floor-tile; (Fußboden) floor(ing), gepflasterter: pavement; ↓ (innerer Schiffsboden) floor; ~ einer Scheuer thrashing-floor.
Flur-buch (ᴸ˘...) n ⓺² register of land, jur. terrier; =**decke** f = =**matte**; =**fenster** n corridor- (or hall-)window; =**gang** m: a) im Hause: corridor, hall; b) (feierliche Begehung der Grenzen einer Feldmark) beating the bounds; =**grenze** f landmark, boundary of a parish; =**hüter** m = =**schütz(e)**; =**karte** f map of a district or parish; =**matte** f hall-mat; =**schade(n)** m ⓾ injury done to the fields; =**schütz(e)** m field-constable, rural guard; =**stein** ↓ f floor-ribbon; =**ständer** m für Hüte, Schirme ꝛc.: hall-stand; =**stein** m: a) boundary-stone; b) arch. flag; =**wächter** m = =**schütz(e)**; =**ziegel** m paving-tile.

fluschen F (ᴸ˘) v/n. (h.) ⓽¹ (gelingen) to get on (well), to succeed; das fluscht besser that does (or answers) better, it works more smoothly.
Fluß (⁵) [ahd.] m ⓶ᵃ. 1. (fließendes Wasser) river, running water; kleiner = stream(let), rivulet; ~, in den die Flut dringt tidal river; am Flusse gelegen, liegend by the riverside, (lying or standing) on the river, riverain. — 2. (Fließen) flow(ing), bfd. ⊕ (flüssiger Zustand) flux; fig. ~ der Rede fluency of speech, flow of language, in Versen: lilt; vgl. 5. — 3. ⌀ physiol. monatlicher (Blut)~ = Menstruatioʹn; weißer ~ whites pl.; path. (Erkältung) cold, catarrh. — 4. ⊕ chm., &c. (~mittel, die Schmelzbarkeit erhöhender Zusatz) flux. — 5. ⊕ metall. (Flüssigwerden) liquefaction, (Schmelzen) fusion; Metalle im ~... in fusion, molten ...; in ~ bringen to fuse, to flux, fig. to set the conversation going; in ~ kommen to begin to melt or to liquefy, fig. to get into (full) swing.
fluß-ab(=**wärts**) (ᴸ˘˘) adv. down the river, down-stream.
Fluß-ampfer ♀ (⁵...) m ⓶ water-dock or -sorrel (Rumex Hydrolaʹpathum); =**anwohner(in** f) m person living by the riverside; poet. riparian dweller; =**arm** m branch of a river; ⁀**arm** a. poorly provided with rivers; ⁀**auf**(=**wärts**) (ᴸ˘˘) adv. up the river, upstream; =**bad** n river-bath; =**barke** ↓ f r.-barge; =**barsch** m, ichth. r.-bass (Perca); =**beschreibung** f ⌀ potamography; =**bett** n r.-bed.
Flüßchen (ᴸ˘) n ²³ dim. von Fluß.
Fluß-damm (⁵...) m ⓶, =**deich** m river dam or -wall; quay; =**eisen** ⊕ n, metall. ingot-iron; =**fahrt** f row (or sail or F blow) on a river; =**fahrzeug** ↓ n river-boat, pl. oft: r.-craft; =**fieber** n, path. rheumatic fever (a. = Rheumatismus); =**fischerei** f river-fishing; =**galle** f, vet. wind-gall; =**gebiet** n river-basin; =**geschwelle** n (Flußunterlauf, in dem Ebbe und Flut bemerkbar wird) estuary (of a tidal river); =**gold** n river-gold; =**gott** m, myth. river-god; =**hafen** ↓ m r.-harbour.
flüssig (ᴸ˘) [ahd.: * Fluß] a. ⓾ 1. (ant. fest) (tropfbar-)⁀ liquid, (elastisch-)⁀ fluid; ⁀e Nahrungsmittel pl. liquid food sg., F co. slops pl.; (geschmolzen) melted, auch: molten (gold, &c.); leicht ⁀ fusible; schwer, streng ⁀ refractory; ⁀ machen, werden to melt, ⊕ to liquefy, ⌀ to fluidify. — 2. gram. ⁀e Konsonanten m/pl. (l, m, n, r) liquid consonants pl. — 3. ♀ ⁀e Gelder n/pl. funds pl. in hand, available capital, ready money, cash; sein Vermögen ⁀ machen to turn one's property into cash, to realize it; ⁀ werden to fall due.
Flüssigkeit (ᴸ˘˘) f ⓵⁶ 1. (Flüssigsein) liquid (or fluid) state or condition; ⌀ liquidity, fluidity. — 2. (flüssiger Körper) liquid, fluid (substance), liquor.
Flüssigkeits-maß (ᴸ˘˘) n ⓶ liquid (or fluid) measure; =**wage** f (Senkwage) areometer.
Flüssig-machen (ᴸ˘...) n ⓺², =**machung** f, =**werden** n: a) chm., &c. eines Körpers: liquefaction, bsd. metall. liquation.

b) ♀ e-s Vermögens: realization; =**sein** n = Flüssigkeit 1.
Fluß-insel (⁵...) f ⓵⁶ river-island; =**kahn** ↓ m small r.-boat; =**kanonenboot** ↓ n river-gunboat; =**krebs** m, zo. crawfish (aʹstacus); =**lauf** m river-course; =**mittel** ⊕ n = Fluß 4; =**mündung** f mouth of a river; den Gezeiten unterliegende: estuary; =**muschel** f, zo. river-mussel (Uʹnio); =**netz** n net-work of rivers or watercourses; =**neunauge** n r.-lamprey (Petromyʹzon fluviaʹtilis); =**niederung** f r.-plain; =**nixe**, =**nymphe** f, myth. water-nymph, naiad, bisw. a. undine; =**pferd** n hippopotamus, auch: river-horse (Hippopoʹtamus amphiʹbius); =**quelle** f r.-head; =**räuber** m r.-pirate; =**sand** m r.-sand; ⁀**sauer** a. chm.: ⌀ hydrofluoric; =**säure** f, chm. = Fluorwasserstoff(säure); =**schiff** ↓ n river-boat; =**schiffahrt** ↓ f r.-traffic, r.-navigation; =**schiffer** ↓ m waterman, bargee, master of a r.-boat; =**schlamm** m r.-mud, r.-silt; =**schotter** m rubbish thrown up by the river; =**spat** m, min. calcic fluoride, fluor-spar (CaFl₂); =**spatsäure** f, chm. = Fluorwasserstoff(säure); =**stahl** ⊕ m flowing-steel, easily fusible steel; =**system** n = =**netz**; =**ufer** n bank of a river, riverside; am =**gelegen** riparian, riverain; =**unterlauf** m lower course (or part) of a river; =**verunreinigung** f pollution of rivers; =**wasser** n river-water, weits. fresh water.
Flüsterer (ᴸ˘˘) m ²² whisperer.
flüstern (ᴸ˘) [ndd.] I v/n. (h.) ⓶ᵃ. to (speak in a) whisper, to speak softly or under one's breath; fig. sanft ⁀de Winde soft-whispering breezes. — II ~ n ²³ whisper(ing).
Flut (¹) [ahd.: flood] f ⓵⁶ 1. ↓ (ant. Ebbe) high tide or water; hohe ~ full tide; (auf)steigende ~ rising tide; die ~ kommt, geht the tide is coming in, is going out; es ist ~ the tide is in, it is high tide; die ~ läuft stark the tide is rising fast. — 2. (große Fülle, bfd. von Wasser) flood; (Wogen) waves pl., (Überschwemmung) inundation, stärker: deluge; fig. die ~en der Menschen the (flowing) masses or (thronging) crowds of people; eine ~ von Worten a rich flow (stärker: a torrent) ...
Flut-anker (ᴸ˘...) m ⓵⁶ flood-anchor; =**bett** n (Mühlengerinne) mill-course; =**brecher** ⊕ m (Steindamm) groin, groyne, breakwater; =**deich** ⊕ m mill-dam.
fluten (ᴸ˘) [Flut] I v/n. (abs. h., bei Angabe der Ortsveränderung fn) ⓽⁰ 1. ↓ v/impers. es flutet the tide is rising or coming in, high tide is setting in. — 2. (anschwellen) to swell, to rise, stark ⁀ (strömen) to flow (or roll, rush) along, to surge. — 3. (auf der Flut schwimmen) to float (atop). — II ~ n ²³ (f. 2) 4. swell(ing); fig. beständiges Ebben und ~ constant ebb(ing) and flow(ing), F constant ups and downs pl.
Flut-gerinne (ᴸ˘...) n ⓺², =**graben** m ⊕ bei Wassermühlen waste-pit; =**hafen** m tidal harbour; =**hahn** ↓ m gegen Feuersgefahr: flooding cock; =**karte** f tide-table; =**maschine** f = =**mühle**; =**messer** m tide-gauge; =**mühle** f tide-mill;

Zeichen (s. S. XVII): F familiär; P Volkssprache; ⌐ Gaunersprache; ⋏ selten; † alt (auch gestorben); * neu (auch geboren); ⁺⁺ unrichtig;

[Flutschleuse] — 381 — [Fonds]

=schleuse f, =tor n flood-gate, tide-lock or =gate; =welle f tidal wave; =werk ⚒ n: a) (Hüttenwert) stream-work; b) (naß bereitetes Erz) wash-ore; =zeichen n high-water mark; =zeit f flood-tide.

fm abbr. = Festmeter.

F-Moll ♪ f. F, f ♪.   [board (f. o. b.).]

Fob. ⚓ ↓ abbr. = franko Bord free on

⚓ **Foc....** f. a. Fok...

focht (ǒcht) (föchte subj.) impf. von fechten.

Fock (ǒ) [nbd.] f ⚓: a) (=mast) foremast; b) (=jegel) foresail, foremast sail.

Fock=brasse ↓ (ǒ...) f ⚓ fore-brace; =boleïne f fore-bowline.

Focke ↓ (ǒ⌣) f ⚓ j. Fock.

Fock=mast (ǒ...) m = Fock a; =rahe f foreyard; =segel n = Fock b; =stag n forestay; =want(en pl.) f fore-shroud(s pl.).   [Bündnis] m ⚓ federalism.]

Föderalismus (⌣⌣⌣́) [lt. foedus]

Föderalist (⌣⌣⌣́) m ⚓ federalist; 2ifch (⌣⌣⌣́) a. ⚓ federal.

Föderation (⌣⌣⌣t(y)⁻¹) [lt.] f ⚓ (Staaten=bund) (con)federation, confederacy.

föderativ (⌣⌣⌣́f) [lt.] a. ⚓ federative; ~=staat (⌣́...) m ⚓ federal state, con=federation.

föderieren (⌣⌣⌣́⌣) [lt.] I v/a. und sich 2 v/refl. to confederate. — II föde=riert p.p. u. a. ⚓ (con)federate.

fodern † (⌣́⌣) v/a. ⚓a. = fordern.

Fohe (ǒ⌣) [ahd.] f ⚓ hunt. = Füchsin.

Fohlen (⌣́⌣) [nbd.: foal] n ⚓ (junges Pferd bis 5 Jahre) foal; colt; 2 v/n. (h.) u. v/a. ⚓ to foal.   [Pferde) foal teeth pl.]

Fohlen=zähne m/pl. ⚓ (Milchzähne der)

Föhn schwz. (⌣́) [ahd.; *lt. favo'nius] m ⓜc. south wind, Föhn; (destructive) southerly gale; ~=wind m ⚓ = Föhn.

Föhrde f. Förde.

Föhre ♀ (⌣́) [ahd.: fir] f ⚓ Scotch pine (Pinus silve'stris) (= Kiefer).

Föhren=baum (⌣́...) m ⚓ = Föhre; =holz n fir-wood; =wald m fir-forest.

Föhricht (⌣́⌣) n ⚓d. fir-wood.

Fokus ⊙ (⌣́⌣) [lt.] m, inv., math., ast. und phys. (Brennpunkt) focus.

Fol. abbr. = Folio (Bogengröße).

Folge (ǒ⌣) [folgen] f ⚓ 1. (Aufeinander=folge, Erbfolge) succession; ~ der Jahr=hunderte course of centuries; in einer ~ without a break, F at one stretch or go; (Reihenfolge) series; (Fortsetzung) continuation, sequel; in bunter ~ higgledy-piggledy, pell-mell, pro=miscuously, F anyhow; (Zusammen=gehöriges) set, suit. — 2. (Wirkung) consequence, effect; (Ergebnis) result, fruit; schlimme ~n nach sich ziehen to lead to evil (or serious) consequences; für e-n von (großen) ~ sein to be of (great) importance to a p.; zur ~ haben to result in, to bring about; vgl. (dem)zu2, in(dessen). — 3. für die (Zukunft) for the future, henceforth; in der ~ in course of time, (some day) hereafter, when the time arrives; die ~ wird es lehren the future will show (the truth of) it. — 4. (⌣⌣⌣= folgerung) conclusion, inference. — 5. (Gehorsam) obedience; einem Gesuche ~ geben to comply with a request; e-m ~ leisten to obey a p.; einer Aufforderung, Einladung, Vorladung ~ leisten to

respond to a call, to accept an in=vitation, to answer a summons.

Folge=jahr (⌣́⌣...) n ⚓ ensuing (or subsequent) year; =leistung f com=pliance with, obedience to.

folgen (⌣́⌣) [ahd.: follow] ⚓ I v/n. (in, 2 meist h.) 1. to follow, zB.: e-m (e-m Vorangehenden) 2 to follow (in the footsteps or on the heels of) a p.; e-m auf Schritt und Tritt 2 to dog a p.'s footsteps, bjb. polizeilich: to shadow a p.; es 2 ihm seine Anhänger he is followed (or attended) by his adher=ents; e-r Leiche 2 to attend a funeral; f-m Kopfe 2 to follow out one's (own) ideas; to adhere to one's opinion. — 2. e-m Rate, j-s Rate 2 to follow (or to act upon) a p.'s advice or sug=gestion, to be guided by a p.('s coun=sel); hätte (ob. wäre) man f-m Rate ge=folgt had his advice been followed or taken; e-r inneren Stimme 2 to listen to a voice within; dem Strome 2 to go (or swim) with the stream; 2 Sie mir!, oft: take my advice!, listen to me! — 3. (der Zeit oder dem Range nach) auf et. 2 to follow upon a th. bsd. zeit=lich: to succeed a th.; Sprichw. auf Regen folgt Sonnenschein after rain comes sunshine; aus et. 2 (sich ergeben) to follow (or result, ensue) from a th.; (hervorgehen) to proceed from a th.; das folgt nicht daraus that does not follow; was folgt daraus? what is the result or consequence? — 4. e-m im Amte, in der Regierung 2 to succeed a person in his office, in the govern=ment. — 5. (kommen) das Geld folgt an=bei ... is enclosed (herewith); Fort=setzung folgt to be continued. — II ++ v/a. im p.p. (fr. suivi de) gefolgt von // attended by //. — III 2d p.pr. und a. ⚓(B*) 6. Beb. des inf. — 7. (nach=) 2d oft: subsequent, ensuing; auf ob. nach=einander 2d successive; 2de Seite(n) abbr. f. (ff.) (and the) follow=ing page(s pl.); der 2de Tag the day after; the morrow; ein Brief 2den Inhalts ... worded (or running) as follows, ... couched in the following words. — IV ~de([r] m)f, ~e(s) n ⚓ 8. the following (or next) p., th.; das ~de steht dort geschrieben what is written there is (or runs) as follows; und das ~de (abbr. ff.) and so forth, and so on; 2des sind die Tatsachen the following are the facts, the facts are as follows.

Folgen=..., folgen=... (⌣́⌣...) ⚓ f. Folge=...

folgender=maßen (⌣́⌣...), 2weise adv. in the following way or manner, as follows; seine Rede lautete 2 his words were as follows or to this effect.

folgen=los (⌣́⌣...) a. ⚓ without results; 2reich a. having important consequences or serious results; consequential, portentous; 2schwer a. = 2reich, geh. Spr. momentous, big with fate, grave.

Folger (⌣́⌣) m ⚓, ~in f ⚓ follower.

folge=recht (⌣́⌣...) a. und adv. consist=ent(ly), logical(ly), (triftig) con=clusive(ly); 2richtig a. = 2recht; =richtigkeit f ⚓ consistency, logical accuracy; conclusiveness.

folger/n (⌣́⌣) [folgen] I v/a. und sich 2 v/refl. ⚓a. aus et. 2 to draw a con=clusion (or an inference) from a th.; to conclude (or infer) from a th.; (herleiten) to deduce; aus et. Gesagtem: to gather from s. th. said. — II ~ n ⚓ u. **Folgerung** f ⚓ conclusion, in=ference; deduction; e-e F/ung ziehen = I; f/ungs=weise adv. by way of inference, inferentially.

Folge=satz (⌣́⌣...) m ⚓ conclusion, de=duction; gram. clause denoting a con=sequence; geom. corollary; 2widrig a. inconsistent, illogical; =widrigkeit f inconsistency, illogicalness; =zeiger m, typ. am Schluß der Seite catch-word; =zeit f future (time), time to come; in der ~ in after-days.

folglich (⌣́⌣) adv. u. cj. consequently, in consequence (whereof); (daher) there=fore, hence; (also) thus, so; logisch schließend auch: then.

folgsam (⌣́⌣) a. ⚓ (gehorsam) obedient, submissive, stärker: obsequious; (ge=lehrig) docile, tractable, manageable; (fügsam) pliant; **Folgsamkeit** (⌣́⌣--) f ⚓ obedience, submissiveness; ob=sequiousness; docility; pliancy.

Foliant (⌣⌣́) [lt.] m ⚓ folio(-volume).

Foli-e (⌣́⌣) [lt.] f ⚓ 1. metall. (Metallblatt) foil; (Silber=)~ silver foil; (Spiegel=)~ mercury (foil, tinfoil; e-r Sache zur ~ dienen, auch einer Sache ~ geben to set off a thing, weit⚓. to serve as a foil to (or as a pretext for) a thing. — 2. ⊙ = Folio 2.

Folien=macher (⌣⌣⌣...) m ⚓, =schläger ⊙ m leaf-beater; =zahl f number of folios or pages. — **Fol.** abbr. auch Folio=.

fol-ieren (⌣(⌣)⌣́⌣) [lt.] I v/a. ⚓ 1. ein Buch 2 (mit Seitenzahlen versehen) to page ...; foliiert folioed. — 2. ⊙ e-n Spiegel 2 (mit Folie belegen) to silver, to cover (with tinfoil). — II ~ n ⚓ und **Foli-ierung** f ⚓ 3. (vgl. 1) paging, pagination; ⊙ (j. 2) foliation.

Folio (⌣́(⌣)-) [lt.] n ⚓ ⚓ 1. typ. Buch in (Groß) ⚓ = Folia'nt; groß ⚓ imperial (folio); fig. co. Narr in ~ (Erznarr) thorough fool. — 2. ⚓ (Blattseite) page, folio. [=forma't n folio(size).]

Folio=band (⌣(⌣)⌣́...) m ⚓ folio-volume;

Folter (⌣́⌣) [nbd.] f ⚓ (Marterwerkzeug) rack, instrument of torture; (gerichtliche Peinigung) torture; e-n auf die ~ spannen to put a p. to the rack, to rack (or torment) a p.; ~=bank (⌣́...) f ⚓ rack.

Folterer (⌣́⌣⌣) m ⚓ torturer, tormentor

Folter=gerät (⌣́⌣...) n ⚓, =instrume'nt ⚓ implement (or instrument) of torture or torment; =kammer f chamber of torture, torturing chamber; =knecht m torturer, tormentor.

foltern (⌣́⌣) [mhd.] v/a. ⚓a. to (put to the) rack; to torture, torment; 2de Pein = Folterpein.

Folter=pein (⌣́⌣...) f ⚓, =qual f torture, torment; fig. excruciating pain, agony; =werkzeug n = =gerät.

Fond (fa) [fr.] m ⚓ 1. allg. = Grund. — 2. (Hintersitz) inside seat of a coach. — 3. öft. = Fonds.

Fonds ⚓ (fa) [fr.] m ⚓ 1. (Gelder) funds pl., capital; (pecuniary) means pl.

2. (fundierte Staatspapiere) public funds pl., (consolidated) government-stock. — **3.** fig. (Gehalt) fund or stock of wit, &c.

Fonds-besitzer m ⊕ stock-holder; **=börse** f st.-exchange; **=geschäfte** n/pl. stock-exchange business; **=händler, =makler** m stock-jobber, stockbroker; **=markt** m = =börse; **=spekulation** f st.-exchange speculation or gamble.

Fontäne (fa¹ᵛ) [nhd. 1600, holl., *fr.] f ⊕ (Springbrunnen) (artificial) fountain.

Fontanell n, ~e f (⊍́ᵛ(ᵛ)) [fr. Brünnlein] n ⊕b., † ⊕ **1.** med. bsd. ehm. (künstliches Geschwür) fontanel, issue; einem e-e ~ anlegen to apply a fontanel to a p. — **2.** anat. (offene Stelle am Schädel Neugeborener) fontanel (mould); **~erbse** f ⊕, **~kügelchen** n issue-pea.

foppen (⊍́ᵛ) [nhd. 17. sæ., f 15/16. sae. lügen] v/a. ⊕ bsd. durch Täuschung: to hoax; (necken, höhnen) to tease, to jeer, F to chaff, roast, quiz; to put on toast.

Fopper (⊍́ᵛ) [f 14. sae. simulierender Bettler] m ⊕, **~in** f ⊕ hoaxer; (Necker[in]) teaser; person fond of chaff or chaffing; **~ei** (⊍́ᵛ⁰) f ⊕ hoax(ing); teasing; jeering; chaff, quizzing.

Force (f⊙̃ᵛ) [fr.] f ⊕ **1.** F das ist seine ~ (starke Seite) that's his forte or strong side. — **2.** Spiel, a. **~karte** f ⊕ strong (-est) or (highest) card (of a suit), best trump, F master card.

forcieren (⊍⁻́ᵛ) [fr.] v/a. ⊕ (mit Gewalt nehmen oder durchsetzen) to take (or carry, effect) by force; **forciert** forced, (übertrieben) overdone. [the sea, creek, cove.

Förde ⊥ (⊥́ᵛ) [ndb., nord.] f ⊕ inlet of)

Förder-bahn (⊍́ᵛ...) f ⊕ tramway of a mine or pit or building-yard.

Forderer (⊍́ᵛ) m ⊕ one who demands, &c. (s. fordern); strenger: exactor; als Gläubiger: dun; zum Kampfe: challenger.

Förderer (⊍́ᵛ) m ⊕ = Beförderer.

Förder-göpel (⊍́ᵛ...) m ⊕ = =maschine; **=hund, =karren** m troll(e)y.

förderlich (⊍́ᵛ) a. ⊕ **1.** (fördernd) conducive to a th., promoting a th.; (nützlich) useful, serviceable, profitable; (wirksam) effective; (heilsam) beneficial. — **2.** (schnell) expeditious; bsd. in dem Ausdruck: auf das 2te in the speediest (or promptest) manner (possible).

Förder-maschine (⊍́ᵛ...) f ⊕ gin, whim (-engine), winding-engine.

fordern (⊍́ᵛ) [ahd. *vorder] v/a. ⊕a. **I. 1.** (verlangen) to demand, request, ask (for); et. von e-m ⊋ to demand a th. of a p., to ask a p. for a th.; als Eigentum: to claim; mit Strenge: to exact; zur Rechenschaft ⊋ to call to account; das fordert sein eigenes Gewissen von ihm his own conscience urges (or imposes) that upon him. — **2.** ⊙ als Preis: to charge; ⊋Sie! name your price!, how much do you ask?; zu viel von e-m ⊋ to overcharge a p.; ich habe noch 1000 Mark an ihn zu ⊋ he still owes me fifty pounds; das von ihm Geforderte the sum he asks (for), what he charges, his charges pl. — **3.** viele Opfer ⊋ to kill (or destroy, ruin) many. — **4.** e-n ⊋ (daß er sich stelle) to summon (or send for) a p.; e-n vor Gericht ⊋ F to summons a p.; zum Zweikampfe, bsd. ehm. in England:

to challenge, to call out (for a duel); e-n auf Pistolen ⊋ to challenge a p. to a duel with pistols or a pistol-fight.

fördern (⊍́ᵛ) [ahd.: further] ⊕a. **I** v/a. **1.** (ant. hemmen) auch fig. to further, (help) forward, promote, advance, serve; stärker: to push (or urge) on; (in Gang bringen) to set going; (beschleunigen) to hasten, accelerate, expedite; (ermuntern) to encourage; alles, was die Gesundheit fördert everything that promotes (or benefits or is beneficial to) health; das Volkswohl ⊋d increasing (or adding to, advancing) the welfare of the people. — **2.** ⚒ das Erz (zutage) ⊋ to raise, to haul out, to bring to grass or to the surface; to extract; fig. zutage (ob. ans Licht) ⊋ to bring to light, to unearth a secret, &c. — **II** sich ⊋ v/refl. **3.** ⚒ (sich beeilen) to hurry. — **III** v/n. ⚒) **4.** (vorwärts kommen) to advance, get on; (gelingen) to succeed. — **IV** ~ n ⊕ **5.** = Förderung.

Fördernis (⊍́ᵛ) n ⊕ (f ⊕) = fördern IV.

fördersam (⊍́ᵛ) a. ⊕ = förderlich.

Förder-schacht (⊍́ᵛ...) m ⊕ winding-shaft, whim(sey) shaft.

Forderung (⊍́ᵛ) f ⊕ **1.** demand, request; von seiten einer Behörde: requisition; als Eigentum: claim; übertriebene ~ exaction, ⊕ auch: overcharge. — **2.** ~ vor Gericht summons; zum Duell: challenge. — **3.** ⊕ (Schuld=) (book-debt); er hat viele ~en ausstehen... many outstanding debts.

Förderung (⊍́ᵛ) f ⊕ (zu fördern 1:) furtherance, promotion, advancement; Verein zur ~ von // Society for the promotion of //; ⚒ (zu 2:) haul(ing out), extraction; (Gefördertes) output; **~s-maschine** ⚒(⊍...) f ⊕ gin; **~s-mittel** n means of promotion; encouragement.

Forderungs-recht (⊍́ᵛ...) n ⊕ right of requisition; legitimate claim; **=satz** m, phls. postulate.

Förder-wagen ⚒ (⊍́ᵛ...) m ⊕ tram.

Forelle (-⊍́ᵛ) [nhd.] f ⊕ ichth. trout (Salmo Fa'rio); (Lachs=)~ salmon-trout (Salmo lacu'stris); **~n-bach** m ⊕ trout-stream; **~n-fang** m trout-fishing; **~n-zucht** f breeding of trout, trout-breeding.

forensisch (-⊍́ᵛ) [lt.] a. ⊕ (gerichtlich) forensic.

Forke (⊍́ᵛ) [ahd.] ndb., *lt. furca] f ⊕ agr. (Heugabel) pitchfork.

Form (⊍́) [mhd., *fr.] f ⊕ **I. 1.** (Gestalt) form, shape; durch Umrisse bezeichnet: figure; (Gestaltung, a. des Körpers) conformation, frame; v. Kleidern: fashion, cut, make; e-s Buches: size; in die (gehörige) ~ bringen to shape (properly), to fashion; aus der ~ kommen to get out of shape; ⚒ († Formation) formation; aufgeschlossene ~ close formation. — **2.** (Förmlichkeit, Hergebrachtes) (mere) form, ceremony; usage; gesellschaftliche a.: conventionality; die (~en) beobachten to observe the (proper) forms or formalities; an ~en hängende (ob. klebende) Person stickler for form or etiquette; die äußere ~ wahren to keep up (outside) appearances; in aller ~ (Rechtens) in due (and proper) form; der ~ wegen for form's sake, (lt.) pro forma. — **3.** gr. tätige, leidende

~ active, passive voice. — **4.** ⊕ (Hut=) ~ block; des Schuhmachers: last; metall. (Gieß=)~ mould, cast; typ. form(e), chase; ausgedruckte ~ form(e) worked off; die ~ ausheben, einheben, (auf)schließen to lift out, lift, (un)lock the form(e).

formal ⊘ (⊍́ᵛ) [lt.] a. ⊕ formal, phls. ⊋e (ant. materielle) Ursache outward cause; Pädagogit: ⊋e Bildung, etwa: general education, literary training.

Form-aldehyd (⊍́ᵛ⁻¹) ⊕ m(n)⊕d. chm. formic aldehyde, formaldehyde (CH₂O).

Formali-en (⊍́ᵛ(ᵛ)) [lt.] pl. inv. formalities pl., set (or fixed) rules pl.

Formalismus (⊍́ᵛ⁻) [lt.] m ⊕ (Formenwesen) formalism; **Formalist** (⊍́⁻) m ⊕ (Formenmensch) formalist, pedant.

Formalität (⊍́ᵛ⁻⁻) f ⊕ formality.

Form-arbeit ⊕ (⊍́ᵛ...) f ⊕ Gießerei: cast- (or mould-)work; casting.

Format (⊍́ᵛ) [lt.] n ⊕ c. mst ⊕ typ. (Buchgröße) size (of a book); von großem (kleinem, mittlerem) ~ large- (small-, medium-)sized.

Formation (⊍́⁻tß(ᵛ)⁻¹¹) [lt.] f ⊕ (Gestaltung) formation; geol. auch: system; ⚒ f. Form 1. [mander.)

Form-band (⊍́ᵛ...) n ⊕ Hutmach.: com-)

formbar (⊍́ᵛ) a. ⊕ mouldable, shapable, bsd. ⊕ plastic; (biegsam) bendable; **~keit** f ⊕ mouldability, ⊕ plasticity.

Formel (⊍́ᵛ) [lt.] f ⊕ chm., math., &c. formula (pl. ...as or ...æ), eccl. auch: formulary; (Schema) form, schedule; bloße (ob. leere) ~ mere form or F show.

Formel-buch (⊍́ᵛ...) n ⊕ formulary.

formelhaft (⊍́ᵛ) a. ⊕ formulatory, formal. [formalities pl.)

Formel-kram (⊍́ᵛ¹) m ⊕ contp. (empty))

formell (⊍́ᵛ) [fr.] ⊕ **I** a. formal; adv. formally. — **II** das ~e ⊕ matters pl. of form.

Formel-sammlung (⊍́ᵛ...) f ⊕ = =buch; **=wesen** n formalities pl., ⊕ formulism.

formen (⊍́ᵛ) [lt.] **I** v/a. u. sich ⊋ v/refl. ⊕ **1.** (sich) ⊋ (bilden) to form (o.s.); kunstmäßig: to fashion; schön geformt finely shaped or made or chiselled. — **2.** meist ⊕ nach e-m Modell: to mould, model, cast; Töpferei: to throw; Bäckerei: das Brot ⊋ to shape (or make) the bread; Hutmacherei: den Filz ⊋ to dress the felt; einen Hut ⊋ to block a hat. — **II** ~ n ⊕ **3.** (s. I) formation; fashioning; moulding.

Formen-gießer (⊍́ᵛ...) m ⊕ = Form-g.; **lehre** f: a) gr. accidence; (Wortforschung) etymology; b) math. definitions pl. of figures, &c.; **=mensch** m formalist, pedant, stickler for forms or trifles; ⊋reich a. ⊕ of many forms; **=reinheit** f purity of form; **=reiter** m = =mensch; **=schneider** ⊕ m = Form-s.; **=wesen** n formalism; **=zwang** m conventional restraint, check exercised by (conventional) form(alitie)s.

Former, meist ⊕ (⊍́ᵛ) m ⊕, **~in** f ⊕ (s. formen 2) moulder, modeller; dresser; Töpferei: thrower.

Form-erde (⊍́ᵛ...) f ⊕ Gießerei: moulding- (or modelling-)clay.

Formerei (⊍́ᵛ⁻¹¹) f ⊕ **1.** (Herstellung der Formen für die Gießerei) moulding. — **2.** Ort moulding-house or -shed.

Form=fehler (ˇ...) m ⚙ jur. u. ⊕ informality, (technical) error, flaw; =**flasche** f Gieß.: flask; =**gebend** a. ⚙ formative; =**gebung** f fashioning, shaping, moulding; ⚔**gerecht** a. of regular form, perfect in shape; ⚔**gewandt** a. skilled in matters of form, v. Schriftstellern: perfect in style; =**gießer** m moulder; =**gießerei** f moulding.

formieren (⌣⌢) [lt.] **I** v/a. u. sich ⚓ v/refl. ⚙ to form; sich in Reihen ⚓ (aufstellen) to fall in(to line); ⊕ typ. in Seiten ⚓ to make up into pages. — **II** ~ n ⚓ u. **Formierung** f ⚙ formation; ✕ falling in(to line).

...**förmig** (...ˇ⌣) a. ⚙ z.B. mandel⚓ almond-shaped.

Form=kasten (ˇ...) m ⚙ Gieß.: moulding -box; =**kunst** f (art of) moulding; plastic art; =**lade** f = =**kasten**.

förmlich (⌣⌢) [Form] a. ⚙ (u. adv.) 1.(der Form gemäß) a. jur. formal(ly), in due form, proper(ly). — 2. (feierlich) ceremonious(ly); (aufs äußerste genau) punctilious(ly); ⚓e Erklärung solemn declaration. — 3. F (gehörig) downright; (ausdrücklich) express(ly); es entstand ein ⚓er Aufruhr there was a regular uproar; ein ⚓er Pfeilregen a veritable shower of arrows; ⚓e Schlacht pitched (or real) battle; ein ⚓es Zischen an unmistakable hissing; er raste ⚓ he was fairly raving; er schien ⚓ versessen darauf ... quite (or thoroughly, madly, deeply) in love with it.

Förmlichkeit (⌣⌢-) f ⚙ form(ality); hergebrachte: ceremony; (rule of) etiquette.

form=los (ˇ...) a. ⚙ formless, shapeless; fig. rude, uncouth, unpolished, (mißgestaltet) deformed; ill-fashioned, ill-shaped; =**losigkeit** f ⚙ formlessness, shapelessness; fig. rudeness, uncouthness; (Mißbildung) deformity.

Form=presse (ˇ...) f ⚙ Gieß.: mouldpress; =**rahmen** m Papierfabrikation: mouldingframe; typ. chase; =**sand** m Gießerei: moulding-sand; =**scheibe** f der Töpfer: top of the wheel; =**schneidekunst** f Gießerei: form-cutting; Zeugdruck: printcutting; =**schneider** m Gieß.: form-cutter, moulder; =**stecher** m Gieß.: clearing-iron; =**steg** m, typ. furniture; =**stift** m (Absatzstift) headless nail (for heels).

Formular (⌣⌣ˊ) [lt.] n ⚙c. 1. (vorgeschriebene Weise) prescribed (or set) form; eccl., &c. auch: formulary; jur. auch: precedent. — 2. (Schema) (blank) form; bsd. jur. auch: schedule; ~ für Telegramme telegraph-form; ein ~ ausfüllen to fill up a form.

Formular=buch (⌣⌣ˊ...) n ⚙ jur. precedent-book; =**sammlung** f collection of formulæ; formulary.

formulierbar (⌣⌣ˊ-) a. ⚙ formulable.

formulieren (⌣⌣ˊ⌣) [lt.] **I** v/a. ⚙ to formulate; (deutlich ausdrücken) to express distinctly, to define; (aufsetzen) to draw up. — **II** ~ n ⚓ u. **Formulierung** f ⚙ formulation; definition; (precise) wording.

Formung (⌣⌢) f ⚙ = formen II.

Form=veränderung (ˇ...) f ⚙, =**wechsel** m change of form; ⚔**widrig** a. ⚙ not in the proper form, mst jur. informal.

Formyl (⌣⌣⌢) [lt. formi'ca Ameise] n ⚙c. chm. organisches Radikal: formyl (CHO).

Form=zacken ⊕ (ˇ...) m, metall. twyerplate; =**zwang** m = Formen=z.

forsch F (⌣) [ndb.; *fr. force] a. ⚙ (D6) (stark) strong, robust, vigorous; vgl. flott 2.

Forsch=begier(de) (ˇ...) f ⚙ (great) desire (stärker: thirst) for inquiry or research, weit S. inquisitiveness; ⚔**begierig** a. ⚙ (bent on) inquiring; inquisitive.

Forsche P (⌣⌢) [fr. force] f ⚙ = Nachdruck¹; **forschen** (⌣⌢) [ahd.] **I** v/n. (h.) ⚙ 1. abs. to inquire (or search) into or after; to investigate a th.; to explore, to examine (or dive) into; aus Neugier: to pry into; ⚓e Blicke m/pl. searching (or observing, scrutinizing) glances pl. — 2. mit abhängigem Satze: (nach=)⚓, ob es sich so verhalte to inquire (or make inquiry) whether it is so. — 3. mit prp.: bei e-m (anfragen), ob ... to inquire of a p. whether //, to sound a p. as to //; in et. ⚓ (ob //) to search into a th. (whether //); nach et. ob. e-m ⚓ to inquire after a th., a p.; nach Wahrheit ⚓ to seek after (the) truth; über et. ⚓ (nachfragen) to inquire about (or concerning) a th. — **II** ~ n ⚓ — 4. = Forschung.

Forscher (⌣⌢) m ⚙, ~**in** f ⚓ (s. forschen I) inquirer, seeker after truth; investigator; (Späher) prying p., spy; wissenschaftlicher: scholar (devoted to research), scientific discoverer or explorer or pioneer.

Forscher=blick (⌣⌢...) m ⚙ searching eye (of a scientific inquirer); genius for discovery; =**geist** m spirit of inquiry; =**sinn** m = Forschbegier(de).

Forschung (⌣⌢) f ⚙ (s. forschen I) inquiry; (re)search; investigation; examination; (learned) disquisition.

Forschungs=gebiet (⌣⌢...) n ⚙ (scientific) field of research or investigation; =**reise** f voyage of discovery; =**reisende(r)** m explorer; =**trieb** m love (or taste) for (scientific) research or inquiry, inquiring mind.

Forst (⌣) [ahd.; *fr. it.] 1. m ⚙b. (Wald) forest; Bepflanzung mit ~en afforestation. — 2. f ⚙ (Revier) district.

Forst=akademie (ˇ...) f ⚙, (=**akade'miker** m) school for (student of) forestry; =**amt** n (Board of) Commissioners pl. of Woods and Forests; =**anschlag** m valuation of (the timber of) a forest; =**aufseher** m =hüter; =**bann** m forest; =**beamte(r)** m official in the department of woods and forests; =**betrieb** m management of forests, forestry; =**bezirk** m fo.-district; =**dienst** m fo.-service.

Forstei (⌣ˊ) f ⚙ = Försterei.

Förster (⌣⌢) [mhd.; *Forst] m ⚙ (~**in** f ⚙) bsd. ehm. forester('s wife), jetzt = Forsthüter.

Försterei (⌣⌢ˊ) [mhd.] f ⚙ 1. forester's (or ranger's) district. — 2. forester's (or ranger's) house or residence or lodge.

Förster=haus (⌣⌢...) n ⚙ = Försterei 2.

Forst=ertrag (ˇ...) m ⚙ forest-produce, produce (or yield) of a forest.

Förster=wohnung (⌣⌢...) f ⚙ = Försterei 2.

Forst=fach (ˇ...) n ⚙ forest-department; (science of) forestry; =**frevel** (=**frevler**) m offence (offender) against forest-laws; ⚔**gerecht** a. according to the rules of forestry; v. Wäldern a.: properly managed; in proper condition; =**gerechtigkeit** f ownership of a forest; =**gesetz** n forest-law; =**haus** n = Försterei 2; =**herr** m owner (or proprietor) of a forest; =**hüter** m (forest-)ranger, (game-)keeper; =**inspektor** m inspector of a forest; =**kultur** f = =**wirtschaft**; =**kunde** f = =**wissenschaft**; ⚔**kundig** a. versed in forestry or woodcraft.

forstlich (⌣⌢) a. ⚙ relating to forests.

Forst=mann (ˇ...) m ⚙ forester, one acquainted with forestry; ⚑ sylviculturist; ⚔**mäßig** a. ⚙ = ⚔**gerecht**; =**meister** m, etwa: First Commissioner of Woods and Forests; =**nutzung** f yield of (or profits pl. derived from) a forest; =**ordnung** f fo.-regulations pl.; =**personal** n staff of foresters; =**polizei** f forest-police; =**rat** m, etwa: commissioner of woods and forests; =**recht** n: a) (code of) fo.-laws pl.; b) (Recht, in e-m Forste Holz zu holen) right of free (brush-)wood; ⚔**rechtlich** a. relating to forest-laws; =**regal** n royal (or princely) ownership rights pl. in a forest; =**revier** n = =**bezirk**; =**sache** f forest concern or matter; =**schule** f (=**schüler** m) = =**akademie** (=**akade'miker**); =**schutz** m protection of forests; =**technologie** f forestry technics; =**verbrechen**, =**vergehen** n = =**frevel**; =**vermessung** f survey of (woods and) forests; =**verwalter** m (=**verwaltung** f) administrator (administration) of a forest; =**wächter**, =**wärter** m = =**hüter**; =**wesen** n forestry; fo.-concerns pl.; =**wiese** f forest-glade; =**wirtschaft** f management of forests, forest-culture; ⚑ sylviculture; =**wissenschaft** f (science of) forestry, wood-craft; ⚔**wissenschaftlich** a. relating to forestry; =**zeichen** n an zu fällenden Bäumen blaze; =**zoologie** f sylvatic zoology.

Fort¹ ✕ (⌣) [fr.] n ⚙ (Außenwerk e-r Festung) (detached) fort; kleines: fortlet.

fort² (⌣) [mhd.: forth] adv. 1. (vorwärts) forward, forth, on; es will mit ihm nicht recht ⚓ he does not get on very well; es will mit der Sache nicht ⚓ the matter is at a standstill, there is a hangfire about it. — 2. (ferner, weiter): in einem ⚓, in einem Zuge (F in einer Tour) ⚓ continually, F at a stretch; er schrieb ruhig ⚓ he quietly went on writing; sie schrie in e-m ⚓ she kept on (or continued) screaming; **fort und fort**, auch: immerfort on and on, without cessation or end, for ever, everlastingly; **und so fort** (abbr. **usf.**) and so on, and so forth (vgl. so⚓); weiter ⚓ further on. — 3. nordb. = weg.

fort=..., Fort=... (ˇ...) in Verbind. m. verbs, immer trennbar (**), und in Zusammensetzungen mit verbal nouns und adjectives, bz. oft: a) Vorwärtsbewegung, durch: ... on, ... forward; b) Beharren, durch: to go on or keep on, to continue (mit gerund); c) nordb.: Entfernung (bsf. weg=..., vgl. b5), durch: ... away, ... off.

fort-ab ⚓ (⌣ˊ) = fortan. [ploughing.]

fort=ackern (ˇ...) v/n. (h.) ⚓a** to go on

[fortan] — 384 — [fortreißen]

fort-an (⸝⸝) *adv.* (von jetzt an) henceforth, from this time forward; (künftig) hereafter, in (or for the) future.
☞ **fort-**... im Sinne v. „hinweg" f. weg-...
fort-arbeiten (ˢ...) ⓺** *v/n.* (h.) to continue (or go on) working; *v/a.* = weg=a.; ~ n ㉓ continuation of work; =**bau** m ㉒ continuation of (or addition to) a building; ⸗**bauen** *v/a. u. v/n.* (h.) ⓺** to build on, to go on building, ⚒ to continue working (a mine); ~ n ㉓ going on building; prosecution of building operations; **sich ⸗begeben** *v/refl.* ⓼c*/* = weg=b., ⸗**beißen** *v/a.* ⓺a** = weg=b.; ⸗**bestand** m continuance; ⸗**besteh(e)n** *v/n.* (h.) ⓺*/* to continue (in existence); die Firma besteht noch fort ... is still in existence; ~ n ㉓ continuance; continuity; ⸗**bewegen** *v/a. u. sich ⸗ v/refl.* ⓼*/* (von der Stelle rücken) to move on or forward, to shift; auf Rädern ⸗ to wheel; sich (immer) ⸗ to keep (or go on) moving, F to be for ever on the move; sich langsam, mühsam ⸗ to crawl (or creep) along; ⸗de Kraft locomotive power; ~ n ㉓, ⸗**bewegung** f ⓺ locomotion; progression, vermittels Dampfkraft: propulsion by steam, vermittels Elektrizität: electric propulsion or traction; ⸗**bilden** *v/a. u. sich ⸗ v/refl.* ⓺**: e-n (sich) ⸗ (vervollkommnen) to perfect (o.s.), erziehend: to continue (or finish) a p.'s education; ~ n ㉓, ⸗**bildung** f ⓺ (Unterricht) instruction (of adults); finishing of a p.'s education; ⸗**bildungs-anstalt**, =**schule** f continuation-school or -classes *pl.*; ⸗**bildungs-verein** m, etwa: mechanics' (educational) institute; der engl. Kirche: Young Men's Christian Association; ⸗**blasen** ⓺a** *v/a.* = weg=b.; *v/n.* (h.) to go (or keep) on blowing the flute, &c.; ⸗**bleiben** *v/n.* (ſn) ⓺*** = weg=b.; ⸗**blühen** *v/n.* (h.) ⓺** to continue blo(ss)oming; ⸗**brauchen** *v/a.* ⓺** to go on (or continue) using a medicine, &c.; *v/n.* (h.) = weg=b.; ⸗**bringen** ⓻** *v/a.* und **sich ⸗** *v/refl.*: a) = weg=b.; b) Blumen 2c. ⸗ (zum Gedeihen bringen) to bring ... forward; *fig.* e-n ⸗ (ernähren) to support (or maintain) a p.; **sich mit et.** ⸗ to make a living (or a livelihood) with s.th. or out of a th.; ~ n ㉓, ⸗**bringung** f ⓺ v. Personen: (Ernährung) support, maintenance; ⸗**dauer** f ⓺ continuation, duration, längere: permanency, perpetuity; der Seele nach dem Tode: future existence or state; immortality (of the soul); ⸗**dauern** ⓼a** *v/n.* (h.) to continue, to last; vom Wetter 2c.: to go (F to keep) on freezing, raining, &c.; ~ n ㉓ f. ⸗dauer; ⸗d *p.pr. u. a.* continuous, lasting, permanent; ⸗de Mißbräuche standing abuses *pl.*; ⸗der Regen constant rain; ⸗de Wachsamkeit incessant vigilance; ⸗d (*adv.*) arbeiten, schaffen to work (or labour) assiduously or unremittingly; ⸗**drängen** ⓺** *v/a.* to push (or to drive) on or forward; *fig.* = weg=b.; ⸗**dürfen** *v/n.* (h.) ⓺** = weg=b.
forte ♪ (⸝⸝) [it. stark, laut] *adv.* und **Forte** n ⓺ *forte (abbr. f).*

fort-eilen (ˢ...) *v/n.* (ſn) ⓺** = weg=e.; ⸗**entwickeln** ⓼a** *v/a. u.* (sich) ⸗ to go on developing (o.s.); ~ n ㉓, ⸗**entwick(e)lung** f ⓺ continued (or further, additional) development.
Fortepiano ♪ (⸝⸝⸝⸝) [it.] n ⓹ (Klavier) piano(forte); ~**fabrika'nt** (ˣ...) m ⓺ piano(forte-)maker; ~**spieler(in** f) m (lady) pianist.
fort-erben (ˢ...) *v/n.* (h.): **sich ⸗ v/refl.** ⓺** to descend (by heredity), to be(come) hereditary, to be transmitted by birth; ⸗**erhalten** und **sich ⸗** *v/refl.* ⓺a** to continue in use; ⸗**fahren** ⓺b** *v/n.*: a) (ſn) = weg=f.; b) (h.) (et. weiter fortsetzen, *ant.* abbrechen 6): mit Lesen ⸗ to continue reading; in e-r Erörterung ⸗ to resume one's discussion; er fuhr fort zu heulen he kept on howling; bitte, fahren Sie fort! pray go on!; ⸗**fall** m ⓺ = Wegfall; ⸗**fallen** *v/n.* (ſn) ⓺a** = wegfallen; ⸗**fliegen** *v/n.* ⓺a**: a) (ſn) = weg=f.; b) (h.) to go on flying; ⸗**führen** *v/a.* ⓺**: a) e-n, et. ⸗ = weg=f.; b) et. ⸗ (fortsetzen) to go on with, to continue; ein Gespräch ⸗ to keep up a conversation, ⚒ die Firma ⸗ to carry on the business, to keep up the firm; ~ n ㉓, ⸗**führung** f ⓺ continuation; ⸗**gang** m ⓺ [⸗gehen]: a) = Weg=g.; b) = ⸗führung; die Sache hat (so) ihren ~ ... is going on (somehow); (Fortschritt) advance(ment), progress, improvement; den ~ e-r Sache aufhalten to check the progress of a th.; c) (Erfolg) success; ich wünsche Ihrer Sache guten ~ I wish your cause every success; ⸗**geben** ⓼c** = weg=g.; beim Kartenspiel: to go on dealing; ⸗**geh(e)n** ⓺** *v/n.* (ſn): a) = weg=g.; b) (weitergehen) to go (or walk) on, to continue one's journey; sein Gehalt geht fort (wird ihm nicht abgezogen) ... continues, ... is running on; wenn das nur kurze Zeit noch so ⸗geht if it lasts only a little while longer; unsere Arbeit geht glücklich fort ... is proceeding (or getting forward) well; ⚒ immer denselben Weg ⸗ to pursue the same route; ~ n ㉓ = ⸗gang; ⸗**gesetzt** *p.p.* f. ⸗setzen; ⸗**glimmen** *v/n.* (h.) ⓺a** to glimmer on; unter der Asche: to smoulder under the ashes; ⸗**haben** F *v/a.* ⓾b** = weg=h.; ⸗**halten** *v/a.* ⓺a** a) = weg=h.; b) eine Zeitung ⸗ to keep to (or take in) the same paper; **sich ⸗heben** *v/refl.* ⓲(⓻)b** = (hin)weg=h.; ⸗**helfen** *v/n.* (h.): a) = weg=h.; b) e-m (bisw. *v/a.* e-n) ⸗ (förderlich sein) to further a p.'s interest; **sich** (*dat.*) ⸗ to make a living; **fümmerlich:** to shift for o.s.; ~ n ㉓ assistance (or aid) given a p.; ⸗**hin** (⸝⸝) *adv.* = ⸗**ab**; ⸗**hinken** ⓺***, ⸗**humpeln** ⓺a** *v/n.*: a) (ſn) = weg=h.; b) (h.) to continue limping; ⸗**hüpfen** *v/n.* (ſn) ⓺**; ⸗**huschen** F *v/n.* (ſn) ⓺*** = weg=h.
Fortifikation ⚔ (⸝⸝⸝⸝⸝⸝ˡˡ) [fr.] f ⓺ (Befestigungskunst) (art of) fortification.
fortifikatorisch ⚔ (⸝⸝⸝⸝⸝ˡ) *a.* ⓺ required for (or relating to) fortification.
fortissimo ♪ (⸝⸝⸝⸝) [it. sehr stark] *adv. u.* **Fortissimo** n ⓹ (⓼) *fortissimo* (*abbr. ff*).
fort-jagen (ˢ...) ⓺** *v/a.* = weg=jagen; *v/n.*: a) (h.) to go on hunting; b) (ſn)

to gallop on; ⸗**kommen** *v/n.* (ſn) ⓺**: a) = weg=k.; b) (vorwärtskommen) die Wege sind so schlecht, daß man nicht ⸗kommen od. nicht ⸗ kann ... one cannot get along; von Pflanzen: (gut) ⸗ to do well, to thrive; von Personen: to get on (well), to prosper, to make (or fight) one's way (in the world); sie kam am schlimmsten dabei fort she fared (F got off) the worst; ~ n ㉓ sein glückliches ~ finden to make (or earn) a decent living; e-m zu seinem ~ verhelfen to put a p. in the way of earning a livelihood; ⸗**können** *v/n.* (h.) ⓺**: a) ich kann vor Müdigkeit nicht mehr fort I cannot get (or drag myself) any farther; b) = weg=k.; ⸗**lassen** *v/a.* ⓺a** = weg=l.; ⸗**laufen** ⓺a** *v/n.* (ſn): a) = weg=l.; b) (weiterlaufen) to run on; längs dem Gebirge ⸗ to run along the mountain; der Solb 2c. läuft fort ... continues, ... runs (or goes) on; vgl. ⸗gehen; denselben Weg ⸗ to pursue (or continue) the same route; ⸗d *p. pr. u. a.*: (ununterbrochen) continuous, uninterrupted; ⸗de Erzählung running (in e-r Zeitschrift: serial) story; ⸗de Nummern successive numbers *pl.*; ⸗**leben** *v/n.* (h.) ⓺** to live on, to continue to live; in s-n Kindern, Werken 2c. to survive in ...; f. a. ⸗bestehen; ~ n ㉓ survival; life after death or beyond the grave; ⸗**leiten** ⓺** *v/a.*: a) = weg=l.; b) (weiterleiten) to transmit, to conduct; *v/n.* (h.) to continue guiding; ~ n ㉓, ⸗**leitung** f ⓺ transmission; continued guidance; ⸗**machen** ⓺** *v/n.* (h.): a) to continue with a th.; co so ⸗ to go on in the same way; b) (sich eilen) to hurry (along); **sich ⸗** *v/refl.* = weg=m.; *v/a.*: seine Arbeit ruhig ⸗ to go on quietly with one's work; ⸗**marsch** m ⓺ = Weg=m.; ⸗**marschieren** *v/n.* ⓺*/*: a) (ſn) = weg=m.; b) (h.) to march on, to continue one's march; ⸗**mögen**, ⸗**müssen** *v/n.* (h.) ⓺** = weg=m.; ⸗**nehmen** *v/a.* ⓺a** = weg=n.; **sich ⸗packen** F *v/refl.* ⓺** = sich weg=scheren; ⸗**pflanzen** ⓺** *v/a.* to propagate; *phys., mech., &c.*: to transmit, communicate, conduct; et. auf e-n ⸗ to transmit (or hand down) a th. to a p.; sein Geschlecht ⸗ to propagate one's race; **sich ⸗** *v/refl.* to be propagated, transmitted, &c.; Tiere: to multiply; Krankheiten: to spread; ~ n ㉓ = ⸗pflanzung; ⸗**pflanzer(in** f) m ⓺ propagator; transmitter; ⸗**pflanzung** f ⓺ propagation; transmission, communication, spread of a disease.
Fortpflanzungs-apparat (⸝⸝⸝⸝...) m ⓺ Biologie: ⚤ propagatorium; ⸗**fähig** *a.* ⓺ generative, reproductive; *phys.* transmissible; ⸗**fähigkeit** f generative faculty; reproductiveness; *phys.* transmissibility; ⸗**geschwindigkeit** f des Schalles 2c. velocity of transmission; ⸗**organe** *n/pl.* ♀ und *zo.* reproductive (or generative) organs *pl.*; ⸗**trieb** m bes. der Tiere generative (or propagative) instinct.
fort-raffen, ⸗**räumen** (ˢ...) *v/a.* ⓺** = weg=r.; ⸗**reisen** *v/n.* ⓺**: a) (ſn) = weg=r.; b) (h.) to journey on, to continue one's travels; ⸗**reißen** *v/a.* ⓺a**

Zeichen (f. S. XVII): F familiär; P Volkssprache; ʳ Gaunersprache; ⸶ selten; † alt (auch gestorben); * neu (auch geboren); ⁺⁺ unrichtig;

[fortreiten] — 385 — [Frage]

= weg-r.; b) *fig.* to hurry along; mit sich 2 to carry away with one (a. *fig.*); *thea.*, &c. ⌀ to take the house, &c. by storm; 2reiten *v/n.* (ʃn) ⌾b** =: a) = weg-r.; b) to continue one's journey on horseback; 2rennen *v/n.* (ʃn) ⌾b** = weg-r.; 2rollen ⌾** *v/a.* to roll on or forward; *v/n.* von einer Kugel ꝛc.: a) (ʃn) = weg-r.; b) (h.) to keep on rolling (a. vom Donner); 2rücken ⌾** *v/a.*: a) vorwärts, rückwärts: to push forward, back(-ward); b) = weg-r.; *v/n.* (ʃn): a) = weg-r.; b) *fig.* to make pro′gress, to pro′gress, to advance; 2rudern ⌾a** *v/a.* = weg-r.; *v/n.*: a) (ʃn) = weg-r.; b) (h.) to go on rowing; 2rufen *v/a.* ⌾b** = weg-r.; 2ſatz m ⓬ continuation; *anat.* appendage, …ix; (Knochen)~: ⚛ apophysis; 2ſchaffbar *a.* ⓺ = weg-ſch.; 2ſchaffen *v/a.* ⌾** = weg-ſch.; *v/n.* (h.) = weg-r. etwa: to continue creating; ſich 2ſcheren F *v/refl.* ⌾** = weg-ſch.; 2ſcheuchen *v/a.* ⌾** = weg-ſch.; 2ſchieben ⓻c** *v/a.* = weg-ſch.; *v/n.* to keep on pushing (or playing) skittles, &c.; ≈ſchieb-vorrichtung *f* ⓺ mechanism of propulsion; 2ſchiffen *v/n.* (ʃn) ⌾** to leave by boat; 2ſchleichen *v/n.* (ʃn) und ſich 2 *v/refl.* ⌾aſt** = weg-ſch.; 2ſchlendern *v/n.* ⌾a** : a) (ʃn) to saunter along; b) (h.) to keep loitering about; 2ſchleppen ⌾** *v/a.* to drag (or pull) on; ſich 2 *v/refl.* to drag o.s. along, F to fag on; 2ſchleudern *v/a.* ⌾a**, 2ſchlüpfen *v/n.* (ʃn) ⌾**, 2ſchmeißen *v/a.* ⌾a** = weg-ſch.; 2ſchreiten *v/n.* (ʃn) ⌾b** to stride along or on, to step on or forward; *fig.* to pro′gress, to advance; zu etwas anderem: to proceed to s.th. else; in der Wiſſenſchaft 2 to make progress, *a.* to keep abreast of scientific progress; ~ *n* ⓻ = ≈ſchreitung; 2d *p. pr.* und *a.* progressive, progressional; nicht 2d unprogressive, making no progress; 2de Bewegung locomotion, forward movement; ≈ſchreitung *f* ⓺ progress(iveness), advance(ment); ⚛ und ♃ progression; ≈ſchritt *m* = ≈ſchreitung; (Verbeſſerung) improvement; (Wachstum) growth; von Schülern auch: proficiency; ≈ſchrittler *m* ⓻, ≈ſchrittlich *a.* ⓺ progressive, *pol.* auch: liberal, radical; ♁ die 2ſte der ausgeſtellten Maſchinen the most advanced of the exhibited machines; ≈ſchritts-freund, -mann *m* ⓬ progressive, progressionist, F go-ahead man; ≈ſchritts-partei *f* progressive party, *pol. a.* liberal (or radical) party; 2ſchwemmen *v/a.* ⌾** = weg-ſch.; 2ſchwimmen *v/n.* ⌾a(b)**: a) (ʃn) = weg-ſch.; b) (h.) to go on swimming; 2ſegeln *v/n.* (ʃn) ⌾a** = weg-ſ.; ſich 2ſehnen *v/refl.* ⌾** = weg-ſ.; 2ſein ⌾a** = weg-ſ.; 2ſetzen *v/a.* u. ſich 2 *v/refl.* ⌾**: a) (ſich) 2 to continue; ſeine Geſchäfte wieder 2 to resume (or proceed with) one's business; ſeine Reiſe 2 to proceed on one's journey; das von ihm mit Fleiß 2geſetzte Werk the work diligently carried on (or prosecuted) by him; 2geſetzt (ununterbrochen) continued, continual;

durch 2geſetzte Anſtrengungen by continuous (or unceasing) efforts; b) = wegſetzen; *fig.* ſich über etwas 2ſetzen (es nicht achten) = ſich über etwas hinwegſetzen (ſ. bd.); 2ſetzer(in *f*) *m* ⓬ continuer; successor; ≈ſetzung *f* ⓺ continuation; prosecution of a work, &c.; sequel of a story; ~ folgt to be continued (in our next or in the next number); 2ſollen *v/n.* (h.) ⌾** = weg-ſ.; 2ſpinnen ⌾a** *v/a.* u. ſich 2 *v/refl.* to spin on; *fig.* (hinziehen) to drag on; *v/n.* (h.) to go on spinning; 2ſprengen *v/a.* ⌾**, 2ſpringen *v/n.* (ʃn) ⌾ſ**, 2ſpülen *v/a.* ⌾**, ſich 2ſtehlen *v/refl.* ⌾d**, 2ſtellen *v/a.* ⌾**, 2ſtoßen *v/a.* ⌾a** = weg-ſt.; 2ſtürmen *v/impers.* es ſtürmt noch immer fort it is still stormy, the storm is still raging; b) (ʃn) = weg-ſt.; 2ſtürzen *v/n.* (ʃn) ⌾** = weg-ſt.; 2taumeln *v/n.* (ʃn) ⌾**, 2traben *v/n.* (ʃn) ⌾**, 2tragen *v/a.* ⌾b** = weg-t.; 2treiben ⌾¹** *v/a.*: a) to carry on a business, &c.; es noch immer ſo 2 F to be going on in the same (old) style or way; b) = weg-t.; ~ *n* ⓻, -trieb *m* ⓬ continuation; 2tun *v/a.* ⌾** = weg-t.
Fortuna (⌣⌣) [lt.] *npr/f.* ⓽ *myth.* (goddess of) Fortune.
fort=wagen (⌣…): ſich 2 *v/refl.* ⌾** to venture forth; 2währen *v/n.* (h.) ⌾** to continue (to exist); 2d *p. pr.* u. *a.* ⌾dauernd; *adv.* continually, permanently; (unaufhörlich) incessantly, perpetually, constantly; der Hund bellt 2d the dog keeps (on) barking; 2wälzen *v/a.* ⌾** = weg-w.; 2wandeln *v/n.* (ʃn) ⌾a** to walk on, to go (or pursue) one's way; auf dem Wege der Tugend 2 to keep to the path of virtue; 2wandern *v/n.* (ʃn) ⌾a** = weg-w.; vgl. auswandern 1; 2weiſen *v/a.* ⌾¹** = weg-w.; 2werfen *v/a.* ⌾b** = weg-w.; 2wirken *v/n.* (h.) ⌾** to continue acting or in operation; noch immer 2d still operative; 2wiſchen *v/a.* ⌾¹** = weg-w.; 2wollen *v/n.* (h.) ⌾**: a) = weg-w.; b) ſ. fort² 1; 2wünſchen *v/a.* u. ſich 2 *v/refl.* ⌾¹** = weg-w.; ſich 2 = ſich wegſehnen; 2wurſteln *v/n.* (h.) ⌾a** to go on in one's hum-drum (or bungling) way or in the old groove; 2ziehen ⌾b** = weg-z.; vgl. auswandern 1; ſeines Weges 2 to go on (or pursue) one's way, to march on; ~ *n* ⓻, -zug *m* ⓬ = Wegzug.
Forum (⌣⌣) [lt.] *n* ⓽ u. ⓮ **1.** Alt.: (Marktplatz in Rom) meiſt: Forum. — **2.** jetzt: (Gerichts=hof, -ſtand) forum, tribunal; das gehört nicht vor mein ~ I am not competent to deal with it; it does not come within my province; *fig.* das ~ der Öffentlichkeit the (summary) judgment of public opinion.
foſſil ⚛ (⌣⌣́) [lt.] *geol.* **I** *a.* ⓺ (verſteinert) fossil, petrified; 2 werden to fossilize; 2e Pflanze ⚛ phytolite. — **II** ~ *n* ⓻ fossil; petrifaction.
Foſſili-en=beſchreibung ⚛ (⌣⌣́⌣⌣…) ⓬ biſw. oryctography; =bildung *f* fossilization; =haltig *a.* ⓺ fossiliferous; =kenner, -kundige(r) *m* one who knows fossils, biſw. fossil(og)ist;

=kunde *f*, =lehre *f* knowledge (or study) of fossils, biſw. fossilology; =ſammlung *f* collection of fossils or petrifactions.
Fötus ⚛ (⌣⌣) [lt.] *m*, *inv.* (auch ⓭) *physiol.* (Leibesfrucht) foetus, fetus.
☛ **Fou…, fou…** ſ. Fu…, fu…
Foyer (fṣà-jē) [fr.] *n* (*m*) ⓽ *thea.*, &c. (Vorhalle) lobby, weitS. entrance-hall.
fr. *abbr.* = frei, frankiert (ſ. frankieren I).
Fracht ⓬ u. ♃ (⌣cht)[ndd. (ahd.): freight] *f* ⓺ **1.** (Frachtgebühr) freight(age); charge for carriage, portage, &c.; carriage, cartage. — **2.** (Frachtgut) zu Schiffe: load, cargo, shipment; ein Schiff in ~ nehmen to charter a ship; 🚂 (ant. Eilgut) consignment by goods-train.
Fracht=aufſchlag ⓬ u. ♃ (⌣cht…) *m* ⓬ = =zuſchlag; =aufſeher *m* supercargo.
frachtbar (⌣cht⌣) *a.* ⓺ fit for conveyance.
Fracht=bedingungen ⓬ u. ♃ (⌣cht…) *f/pl.* ⓬ conditions *pl.* of freight or shipment; =beſorger *m* forwarding (or shipping) agent; =brief *m* bill of consignment or lading, way-bill, letter of conveyance; dispatch note; =dampfer ♃ *m* cargo-steamer; =empfänger(in *f*) *m* consignee.
frachten (⌣cht⌣) *v/a.* ⓽ vom Befrachter: to consign, ♃ to ship; vom Fuhrmann oder Schiffseigner: to freight, carry, load.
Frachter (⌣cht⌣) *m* ⓽ freighter, shipper.
fracht=frei ⓬ (⌣cht…) *a.* ⓺ carriage paid; =fuhre *f* ⓬ = =fuhrwerk; =führer *m* carrier; =fuhrmann *m* (*pl.* meiſt: =fuhrleute) carrier, carter; =fuhrwerk *n* goods-wagen; wagon (for heavy goods); =fuhrweſen *n* carriage (or conveyance, removal) of goods; =geld *n* = Fracht 1; =geſchäft *n* carrying-trade; =gut *n* = Fracht 2; =gutſendung *f* consignment by goods-train; =liſte *f* freight-list; =lohn *m* = Fracht 1; =makler *m* ship-broker; =pferd *n* cart-horse; =poſt *f* parcel-post; =preis *m* = Fracht 1; =ſatz *m* rate of shipping, freightage; =ſchein *m* = =brief; =ſchiff ♃ *n* cargo-ship or -steamer; trading-vessel or -boat; =ſchiffer *m* freighter, shipper; =ſtück *n* package, parcel, bale; =verkehr *m* goods-traffic; =verſender *m* consigner, …or; =vertrag *m* charter-party; =wagen *m* = =fuhre; =zettel *m* = =brief; =zuſchlag *m* extra (or additional) freight.
Frack ⓣ (⌣) [nhd. 18. *sae.*; *engl. frock] *m* ⓽ u. ⓛc. dress-coat, F swallow-tail(ed coat); im ~ erſcheinen to appear in a dress-coat or in evening-dress; ~=ſchoß *m* ⓬ tail of a dress-coat; ~=zwang *m* compulsory rule to wear a dress-coat.
Frage (⌣⌣) [ahd.] *f* ⓺ **1.** (ant. Antwort) question, *gram.* u. *rhet.* interrogation; (Erkundigung) inquiry; (Nachforſchung) query; eine ~ aufwerfen (vorlegen) to raise (to propose) a question; eine ~ ſtellen ob. tun to ask (or put) a question; in ~n und Antworten in (the form of) questions and answers. — **2.** (Fragliches, Ungewiſſes) das iſt keine ~ there is no question about it; außer aller ~ ſein to be quite beyond (or out of the) question; in ~ kommen to be in dispute; ſoweit ſein Mut in ~ kommt as far as his courage is concerned; das iſt noch die (oder eine) ~ that's still doubtful, it remains to be seen; der in ~ ſtehende

Punkt the point in question; in ~ stellen to question; ohne ~ unquestionably, undoubtedly; nicht zur ~ (Sache) gehören, nicht bei der ~ stehen to be outside the question; brennende ~ burning (or urgent) question; eine ~ der Zeit a question of time. — 3. ehm. jur. interrogatory; peinliche ~ (Folter) torture. — 4. ⊕ es ist viel ~ nach Zucker, Zucker ist stark in ~ ... is much in demand, ... is in great demand or request.

Frage-bogen (ᴵᴵ‿...) *m* 62 list of queries; jur. schedule, (blank) form; für Prüflinge: (examination-)paper; e-n ~ ausfüllen to fill up a form; alle Prüfungsfragen im ~ beantworten to floor a paper; =buch *n* catechism; =kasten *m* in Zeitschriften: correspondence, queries *pl.*, answers *pl.* to correspondents; =liste *f* = =bogen.

fragen (ᴵ‿) [ahd.: lt. *precāri*] ⑧ (P oft ⁺⁺ §b.) **I** *v/a. u. v/n.* (h.) **1.** to ask a p. (a question), to question a p.; neugierig: to query (F to pump) a p.; ausforschend: to catechize a p.; prüfend: to interrogate a p., Schüler auch: to test, to examine; ich fragte ihn, wieviel Uhr es sei I asked him what time it was; sein Gewissen ⵕ to search one's conscience; e-n **nach** e-r Sache (*dat.*), **um** oder **über** et., **wegen** e-r Sache (*gen.*) ⵕ, **von** e-m et. ⵕ to ask (or to inquire of) a p. about a th.; **nach** e-m ⵕ (ihn zu sprechen wünschen) to inquire (or ask) for a p.; wenn nach mir gefragt wird if I am inquired for, if anybody asks to see me; nach j-s Befinden ⵕ to inquire after a p.'s health; nach dem Preise, dem Wege ⵕ to inquire the price, the way; einen **um Rat** ⵕ to consult a p., to seek a p.'s advice; nicht viel (or lange) ⵕ (entschlossen handeln) not to think long over a th., to be quick about it. — **2. nach** et., **nach** e-m ⵕ (sich darum bekümmern) to care about a th., a p.; er fragt den Henker nach ihm he does not care a straw (or fig, pin, rap) for him; er hat nichts danach zu ⵕ it does not concern (or matter to) him (in the least); F was frag' ich nach ihm? what do I trouble (or care) about him? — **II** sich ⵕ *v/refl.* **3.** mit Angabe der Wirkung: sich heiser ⵕ to make o.s. hoarse with asking (questions). — **III** *v/impers.* **4.** es fragt sich, ob // it is questionable or doubtful (or the question is or arises) whether //. — **IV** ~ *n* ㉓ **5.** asking (questions), &c. (s. I); query; interrogation; interrogatory; inquiry. — **V** ⵕ ⅆ *p.pr.* und *a.* ⒺⒺ **6.** in den Beb. des *inf.*; ⵕe Blicke inquiring glances *pl.*; in ⵕem Tone in an inquiring tone. — **7.** interrogative, interrogatory; *adv.* e-n ⵕ ansehen to cast inquiring (stärker: searching, inquisitive) glances at a p.

Frage-punkt (ᴵᴵ‿...) *m* 62 point in question, doubtful point.

Frager (ᴵ‿) *m* 62, ~in *f* 40 questioner, interrogator, inquirer, biswa.: querist.

Frage-recht (ᴵᴵ‿)*n* 62 jur. right to cross-examine witnesses, &c.

Fragerei (‿‿ᴵ) *f* 40 continuous (or inquisitive, importunate) questioning; mania for asking questions.

Frage-satz (ᴵᴵ‿...) *m* 62 interrogative sentence; =steller(in *f*) *m* interrogator, questioner; =stellung *f*: a) parl. questioning; die ~ machen to put the question; b) *gram.* interrogative form; ~= **und Antwort-spiel** *n* (game of) questions and answers or How, When, and Where; =unterricht *m* Päd.: catechization; =weise *f* method (or mode, way) of questioning; Päd.: catechetical method; ⵕweise *adv.* by way of a question or of inquiry; *gram.* interrogatively; =wort *n*, *gram.* interrogative particle; =zeichen *n*, *gram.* sign (or note) of interrogation, interrogation mark [?].

fraglich (ᴵ‿) *a.* 66 **1.** (in Frage stehend) in question, under discussion; die ⵕen (erwähnten) Dinge the things *pl.* referred to. — **2.** (unentschieden) problematic(al); (zweifelhaft) doubtful, questionable; disputable.

frag-los* (ᴵᴵ) *a.* 66 unquestionable, *adv.* unquestionably.

Fragment (‿ᴵ) [it.] *n* ⑪b. (Bruchstück) fragment; ⵕarisch (‿‿ᴵ‿) *a.* 66 fragmentary; ~ist (‿‿ᴵ) *m* 42 author of fragments.

Fraktion (‿ᴵß(‿)ᴵ) [it.] *f* 40 (Bruch) fraction; bsd. *parl.* (Parteigruppe) parliamentary group or party or faction; ~**s-geist** (ᴵ‿‿) *m* ⓶ party-spirit, b.s. factious spirit.

Fraktur (‿ᴵ) [it.] *f* 40 ⊕ *typ.* (deutsche Schrift; *ant.* Antiqua) Gothic (letters *pl.*), old English, black-letter (or German) type; in ~ schreiben to print.

Frambösie ⑳ (‿‿ᴵ) [fr. *framboise* Himbeere] *f* 48 *path.* (amboinische od. große Pocken) framboesia.

frank¹ (ᴵ) [nhd. 17. *sae.*; fr.; *dtsch* Franke] *a.* 66 meist mit „frei", zB. ich bin ⵕ und frei ... quite free or at liberty; *adv.* ich sage es Ihnen ⵕ und frei (gerade und offen) I tell you plainly or honestly or openly or straight to your face.

Frank² (ᴵ) [fr. 1250] *m* ⑳ 6. (fr. Münze = 80 Pfg., 9·7 pence); zehn ~ ten francs.

Frankatur (‿‿ᴵ) [it.] *f* 40 (pre)payment (or paying) of postage (for letters, &c.).

Franke (ᴵ‿) [ahd. der Freie; *franca* Wurfspieß] *m* 44 (deutscher Volksstamm, heute Bezeichnung der Europäer im Orient), **Fränkin** *f* 40 Frank(ish man, *f* woman).

Franken¹ ⊕ (ᴵ‿) *npr/n.* ㉓α. Franconia.

Franken² (ᴵ‿) *m* 236. = **Frank**².

Franken-land ⊕ (ᴵ‿‿) *n* 62: a) engS. Franconia, b) *poet.* France; =reich *n* = =land b; =sprache *f* im Orient: Frankish language; =stück *n*, *num.* franc-piece; =wald ⊕ *m* Franconian upland(s *pl.*).

Frankfurt (ᴵ‿) *npr/n.* ㉓α. ~ am Main Frankfort-on-the-Main; ~ an der Oder Frankfort-on-the-Oder.

Frankfurter (ᴵ‿‿) **I** *m* 32, ~in *f* 40 inhabitant of Frankfort. — **II** *a.*, *inv.* of (or belonging to) Frankfort; ~ Börse Frankfort exchange.

frankierbar (‿ᴵ‿) [frankieren] *a.* 66 ⵕer Brief letter which can be prepaid.

frankieren (‿ᴵ‿) [it.] **I** *v/a.* ⑬ Briefe 2c. ⵕ (freimachen) to prepay, to pay for, ehm. a. to post-pay, to frank; frankiert (Aufschrift auf Briefen 2c., meist abbr. fr.) ehm. post-paid, (postage) paid (abbr. P.P.); auf Paketen: carriage paid; der Brief war (nicht) frankiert the letter was (not) stamped or prepaid or paid for; nicht genügend frankiert insufficiently stamped. — **II** ~ *n* ㉓ u. **Frankierung** *f* 46 prepayment.

Frankierungs-zwang (‿ᴵᴵ‿...) *m* 62 compulsory prepayment.

fränkisch (ᴵ‿) *a.* 66 Frankish; die ⵕe Sprache, das ~(e) *n* ⑰ Frankish, the Frankish language.

franko (ᴵ‿) [nhd. 17. *sae.*; *it.*] *adv.* 66 frankiert (s. frankieren I), ⊕ ⵕ (bis) Berlin free Berlin (vgl. frei 6).

Frankolin (‿‿ᴵ) *m* ⓓ., ~=huhn *n* 62 *orn.* francolin (partridge).

Frank-reich ⊕ (ᴵᴵ) [Frankenreich] *npr/n.* ㉓α. France; Sprichw. wie Gott (oder der Herrgott) in ~ leben to live like a lord or F like a fighting-cock, to be in clover.

Franje (ᴵ‿) [fr. *frange*] *f* 40 fringe; mit ~n besetzen (a. **fransen** *v/a.* 90) to trim with a fringe (ein Bett: a valance).

Fransen-besatz (ᴵ‿‿...) *m* 62 fringe (edging); =förmig ⯑ *a.* 66 like a fringe, ⯑ laciniate(d); =macher(in *f*) *m* fringe-maker. [fringed, fringe-like.)

fransicht, fransig (ᴵ‿) [Franse] *a.* 66)

Franz (ᴵ) [lt. *Franciscus*; *dtsch* Franke] *npr/m.* ㉕γ. (Bn.) Francis, Frank.

Franz-apfel (ᴵ‿...) [französisch)] *m* ⯑ *hort.* rennet; =band ⊕ *m* Buchbinderei: calf-binding, binding in calf; halber ~ demi-calf (binding; Lederband) book bound in calf, calf-bound volume; =baum *m*, *hort.* dwarf-tree; =branntwein *m* surgical spirit; =brot *n*, =brötchen *n*, etwa: French roll or bread.

Fränzchen (ᴵ‿) *npr/n.* ㉓α.(Bn.): a) (dim. von Franziska) etwa: Fanny; b) (dim. von Franz) kosend: Franky, Frankie.

Franze (ᴵ‿) *m* 44 (Franzose) F Frenchy.

Franziska I (‿ᴵ‿) [it.] *npr/f.* 40 ㉕α. (Bn.) Frances. — **II** (ᴵ‿‿) ehm. ⚔ (fränkische Waffe) francisca.

Franziskaner (‿‿ᴵ‿) [Franz(iskus) (*f.* 1209] *m* 32, ~in *f* 40 *eccl.* Franciscan friar, nun.

Franziskaner-kloster (‿‿ᴵᴵ‿...) *n* 62 Franciscan monastery or convent; =mönch *m*, =nonne *f* = Franziskaner(in); =orden *m* Franciscan order, ehm. auch: order of Grey Friars. [Franz.)

Franziskus (‿ᴵ‿) [it.] *npr/m.* ㉕γ. =)

Franz-mann (ᴵ...) *m* ㉒, ⵕmännisch 66 F = Franzose, französisch.

Franzose (‿ᴵ‿) [a/f. François] *m* 44 Frenchman, F Frenchy; die ~n the French. [French manners or things.)

Französelei (‿‿‿ᴵ) *f* 40 meist b.s. aping)

französeln (‿ᴵ‿) *v/n.* (h.) 92a. meist b.s. to ape French manners or things, to use French words.

franzosen-feindlich (‿ᴵ‿‿...) *a.* 66 anti-French; =holz ⯑ *n* 62 guaiac (wood), (lt.) lignum-vitae (von *Guaia'cum officina'le*); =sucht *f* Gallomania.

Franzosentum (‿‿ᴵ‿) *n* ⓓ. (französisches Volkstum) French nationality.

französieren (‿‿ᴵ‿) **I** *v/a.* 93 to make French, F to Frenchify. — **II** ~ *n* ㉓ u. **Französierung** *f* 46 Frenchification.

Französin (‿ᴵ‿) *f* 40 Frenchwoman.

Signs (see page XVII): F familiar; P vulgar; ⚡ flash; ⧵ rare; † obsolete (died); * new word (born); ++ incorrect; ♪ music;

[französisch] — 387 — [frei]

französisch (⌣‒) **I** a. ⓖ French; ⸜Gallic, Gaulish; nach ꜱer Mode after the French fashion, in the French style; ꜱe Spracheigenheit Gallicism; die ꜱe Sprache, das ~(e) n ⓖ inv. the French language, French; fig. ꜱen Abschied nehmen to take French leave; er spricht gut ~ he speaks good French; **auf** ~, **ins** ~**e** in, into French. — **II** ~ n ⓖ f. **I.**

französisch-deutsch (⌣‒…) a. ⓖ: ꜱer Krieg (1870/71) Franco-German war; ꜱ**englisch** a.: ꜱes Wörterbuch French-English dictionary; ꜱ**russisch** a.: ꜱes Bündnis Franco-Russian alliance.

frappant (⌣‒) [fr.] a. ⓖ (auffallend) striking (likeness, &c.); stärker: astonishing.

frappieren (⌣‒⌣) [fr.] v/a. ⓖ to strike; stärker: to astonish.

Fräse ⊕ (‒⌣) [fr. fraise] f ⓖ **1.** (Schneiderad, Fräsmaschine) (rose-)cutter, cutting-file, fraiser. — **2.** (Halskrause) ruff, ruffle.

fräsen ⊕ (‒⌣) [fr.] v/a. ⓖ Tischlerei: (mit der Fräse schneiden) to fraise, to mill.

Fräser (‒⌣) m ⓖ **1.** one who fraises, &c. **2.** = Fräse 1. [ing-machine, fraiser.⸗]

Fräs-maschine (‒…) f ⓖ Tischlerei: frais-⸗

fraß[1] (‒) impf. von fressen.

Fraß[2] (‒) [ahd. *fressen] m ⓐ a. **1.** (Nahrung der Tiere, contp. von Menschen) (coarse) food, F feed, grub, tuck; ein guter ~ P a good blow-out or belly-ful. — **2.** (Freßlust) voracity, gluttony. — **3.** path. (Knochen-)~: ⚕ caries.

fräße (‒⌣) subj. impf. v. fressen.

fraternisieren (‒⌣⌣‒⌣) [fr.] **I** v/n. (h.) ⓖ (brüderlich verkehren) to fraternize. — **II** ~ n ⓖ fraternization.

Fratz (⌣) [Fratze] m ⓖ a. **1.** (häßliche Person) queer-looking person, F fright; (Narr) fool. — **2.** (böses Kind) naughty child; F brat, young Turk or monkey.

Fratze (⌣⌣) [nhd. 16. sae.; *it. frasche Possen] f ⓖ **1.** (Narretei) tomfoolery, (Posse) buffoonery. — **2.** (Gesichtsverzerrung) grimace, wry (or distorted) face; ~n machen, schneiden to make grimaces, to distort one's face. — **3.** (häßliches Gesicht) ugly face, P mug, phiz(og); arch. gorgon('s head). — **4.** (Zerrbild) caricature.

Fratzen-bild (⌣⌣…) n ⓖ caricature; ⸗**gesicht** n monkey-face.

fratzenhaft (⌣⌣⌣) a. ⓖ wry (face), distorted (features); weitS. grotesque (a. fig.), ridiculous; ~**igkeit** (⌣⌣⌣‒) f ⓖ wryness, distortion; weitS. grotesqueness, ridiculousness.

Fratzen-kopf (⌣⌣…) m ⓖ = Fratze 3; ⸗**macher**(in f) m, ⸗**schneider**(in f) m person who makes grimaces or faces.

Frau (‒) [ahd. Herrin: Fron…] f ⓖ **1.** (weibl. Person) woman, female; lady; (Ehe-)~ wife, spouse, einer Standesperson: consort; junge ~: a) allg.: young woman; b) neu vermählte: newly-married woman, young wife; bsd. während der Flitterwochen auch: bride; alte ~ old (or aged) woman; (worthy) matron; vornehme ~, ~ von Stande lady of rank or position, great (or fine) lady. — **2.** eine ~ nehmen to take a wife, to get married or F co. spliced; er hat eine geborene Müller zur ~ his wife's maiden-name is M.; ein Mädchen zur ~ verlangen to ask a girl in marriage; unter der Herrschaft der ~ stehen co. to be under petticoat-government. — **3.** (Herrin des Hauses) mistress (or lady) of the house. — **4.** als Titel mit npr.: ~ R. Mrs. (= Mistress spricht: mi'z-iz) R.; ohne npr.: gnädige ~ madam; (my) lady; als abliger Titel: your ladyship; (die) Herzogin the (förmlicher: My Lady) Duchess, in der Anrede: Your Grace. — **5.** ~ Dr. Schwarz, ~ Professor Weiß Mrs. S., Mrs. W.; die ~ Oberst the Colonel's wife; nicht übersetzbar in: Ihre ~ Mutter your mother; wie befindet sich Ihre ~ Gemahlin, Herr N.? how is your wife or your good lady or Mrs. N.? — **6.** Cath. eccl. unsere liebe ~ (Jungfrau Maria) Our (blessed) Lady, the holy Virgin, auch: the Madonna.

Frauchen (‒⌣) [dim. v. Frau] n ⓖ little woman or wife; kosend: (dear) wifie.

Frauen-anwalt (⌣‒…) m ⓖ advocate (or partisan) of women's rights, a. feminist; ⸗**arzt** m specialist for women's diseases, ⚕ gynecologist; ⸗**beschäftigung** f employment for women; ⸗**bewegung** f movement for the emancipation of women, or feminist movement; ⸗**bild** n: a) woman's portrait; b) (Frau) woman; ⸗**brust** f woman's breast or bosom; ⸗**diener** m ladies' man, stärker: woman-worshipper; ⸗**fäden** m/pl. gossamer sg.; ⸗**feind** m woman-hater, ⚕ misogynist; ⸗**flachs** ♀ m toad-flax (Linaria vulgaris); ⸗**gemach** n women's apartment, Ostindien: zenana; ⸗**gestalten** Shakespeares ~ (die Frauen aus seinen Werken) Sh.'s female characters pl.; ⸗**glas** n min. Muscovy glass, muscovite; ⸗**gunst** f ladies' favour; ⸗**gut** n woman's property; (Mitgift) dowry; ⸗**haar** n: ♀ maidenhair (Adiantum capillus Veneris).

frauenhaft (‒⌣⌣) a. ⓖ womanlike, womanly; (weiblich) feminine (Ehewelt); wifelike (a. adv.); Dame: ladylike.

Frauen-handschuh (‒⌣…) m ⓖ lady's glove; ⸗**hemd** n chemise; ⸗**herrschaft** f female rule, co. petticoat-government; ⚕ gynarchy; ⸗**hut** m bonnet, lady's hat; ⸗**kleid(ung** f) n woman's gown, robe, anliegendes: dress, fertiges: confection; ⸗**kloster** n convent (for women), nunnery; ⸗**knecht** m = ⸗diener; ⸗**krankheit** f women's disease; ⸗**liebe** f a) woman's love; b) love for women; ⸗**mantel** m lady's cloak; ⸗**minze** f ♀ Marienblatt; ⸗**putz** m women's finery; ⸗**rechtlerin** f defender of women's rights, auch: feminist; ⸗**regiment** n = ⸗herrschaft; ⸗**rock** m woman's (or lady's) gown; ⸗**sattel** m (lady's) side-saddle; ⸗**schmuck** m woman's ornaments pl.; ⸗**schneider** m ladies' tailor; ⸗**schneiderin** f dress-maker; ⸗**schuh** m a) lady's shoe; b) ♀ lady's-slipper (Cypripedium Calceolus).

Frauens-leute P (‒⌣…) pl. ⓖ F womenfolk; ⸗**person** f wench, female.

Frauen-spiegel ♀ (‒⌣…) m ⓖ Venus's looking-glass (Prismatoca'rpus spe'culum); ⸗**stand** m womanhood; engS. state of a wife or a married woman; jur. a.: coverture; ⸗**stift** n = ⸗kloster; ⸗**stimmrecht** n suffrage, f auch: suffragette; ⸗**stuhl** m, eccl. lady's pew; ⸗**tracht** f women's dress or garb, female attire; ⸗**verein** m ladies' association; eccl. auch: ladies' (or women's) working-party; ⸗**volk** n womankind; F womenfolk; ⸗**zimmer** [mhd.] n: a) = ⸗gemach; b) die ~ pl., oft contp. women pl.; c) hb. contp., schwg. g.s. (weibliches Wesen) woman, female, lebiges: spinster; ⸗**zimmerchen** n (dim.) little woman; ⸗**zwinger** m harem.

Fräulein (‒⌣) [mhd.; dim. v. Frau] (abbr. Frl.) n ⓖ (pl. F a. ~s; aber auch als f inv.) miss (auch in der Anrede); weitS. young spinster, single young lady, co. damsel; bin weder ~ weder schön (G., Faust) am neither lady nor fair; die beiden ~ Volz the two Misses V.; das gnädige ~ Marie Lady Mary bleibt unübersetzt in: Ihr ~ Tochter your daughter. [home) for ladies (of rank).⸗

Fräulein-stift (‒⌣…) n ⓖ convent (or

frech (‒) [ahd.] a. ⓖ (D1, 7) (tect) daring, bold, audacious, (unverschämt) impudent, insolent, F saucy, cheeky; von Reden 2c. auch: offensive, loose; mit ꜱer Stirn brazen-faced; ꜱ genug sein, um zu // to have the face (or audacity, F cheek) to //, to make bold to //.

Frechheit (⌣‒) f ⓖ (s. frech) daring, boldness, audacity; impudence, insolence, effrontery, F sauciness, cheek; von Reden 2c. auch: offensiveness, looseness; als Handlung: piece of impudence.

Fregatte (‒⌣‒) [fr., it.] f ⓖ **1.** ⚓ (Art Kriegsschiff) frigate. — **2.** zo. ⸗vogel.

Fregatt(en)-vogel (‒⌣(⌣)…) m ⓖ orn. frigate-bird (Tachy'petes a'quila).

Fregatten-kapitän ⚓ m ⓖ commander.

frei (‒) [ahd.] a. ⓖ (D1,7) **1.** free; at liberty; s. Freie; (umherschweifend) at large; (fesselos) untrammelled, unfettered, unshackled; (unabhängig) free, independent; ꜱ**geben**, auf ꜱen Fuß setzen to set free, to release; ich bin so ꜱ, e-e Frage an Sie zu richten I take the liberty of asking you a question; ich bin so ꜱ, Ihnen meine Dienste anzubieten I venture (or make bold) to offer you my services; darf ich so ꜱ sein, Sie zu begleiten? will you allow me (or may I be allowed) to accompany you? — **2.** ꜱe Ansichten f/pl. liberal opinions pl.; mit ꜱem Anstand with an easy grace; aus ꜱer Hand offhand, out of hand; ꜱe Konkurrenz open competition; ꜱe Künste fine (or polite) arts pl.; e-r Sache ꜱen Lauf lassen to let a th. have (or take) its (free) course; seinen Gefühlen ꜱen Lauf lassen to give (free) vent to one's feelings; ꜱe Rede free (stärker: licentious) speech; ☧ ꜱe Richtung liberal school (of thought), paint., &c. unconventional school, typ. art style; e-m ꜱes Spiel lassen to give a p. full scope or full power or free play; ꜱe Wahl free choice; aus ꜱer Wahl of one's own free ch.; ꜱ von Leidenschaft dispassionate; ꜱ von Sorgen free from cares; ☧ ꜱ weg! forward, march! ꜱ vom Dienst off duty, ꜱ vom Militärdienst free (or

---

⚗ scientific; ♀ botanical; ⚲ geography; ⊕ machinery; ⚒ mining; ⚔ military; ⚓ marine; ⊛ commercial; ✉ postal; 🚆 railway.

exempt) from military service; ⇩ ₂e Schiffahrt free navigation. — 3. (freiwillig) voluntary; aus ₂em (eigenem) Antriebe, aus ₂en Stücken of one's own accord or own free will. — 4. (unbehindert, unbesetzt) keinen ₂en Augenblick haben to have not a moment to spare or to o.s.; ₂e Aussicht über // free view over //; ₂es Feld open country; unter ₂em Himmel in the open air, vgl. Freie 3; ₂er Platz (open) square; ₂er Raum clear space; ₂e Stunde leisure hour; (schul=) ₂er Tag, Nachmittag holiday, half-holiday; von Geschäftsleuten ꝛc.: ₂er Tag off day, day off; ₂e Zeit spare time, leisure (time), spare hours *pl.*; wir haben noch zwei Zimmer ₂ we have two rooms vacant or two spare rooms; vgl. ₂=geben; den Nachmittag ₂h. to have the afternoon free, von Schülern: to have a half-holiday; ⨯ sich (*dat.*) den Rücken vom Feinde ₂ halten to keep one's rear covered. — 5. (ohne Stütze) (aus) ₂er Hand (a. ₂=händig) schießen to shoot without a rest or support; *adv.*: ₂ sprechen to speak extempore or without notes or without preparation; die Kunst, ₂ zu sprechen the art of free delivery or of (making an) impromptu speech; ₂ umhergehen to be at large; ₂ zeichnen to draw free-hand. — 6. (unentgeltlich) gratuitous; ₂ (von Kosten) free of expense, ⊕ all charges (or expenses) paid; (porto=)₂ (pre)paid; alles ₂ everything found; ₂er Eintritt free admission; bei ₂er Station with board and lodging free, (with) everything found; ₂en Tisch und ₂e Wohnung haben to have free board and lodging; ⊕ ₂ ins Haus oder ₂ vor die Tür (delivered) free of charge or free to the door; ⚓ 20 Pfund Gepäck ₂ h. to be allowed twenty pounds of luggage. — 7. *adv.* ₂ heraus (offen) openly, (aufrichtig) candidly, honestly; sincerely, point-blank; sprich ₂ heraus! tell me frankly; be open or candid!; vgl. frank und Freie.

Frei=acker (⁻ʰ...) *m* ⓖ freehold-land; =**antwort** *f*, tel. (pre)paid reply; =**arche** ⊕ *f* Wasserbau (Flutwelle) flood- (or waste-) gate; ₂**bauen** ⚔ *n* covering the expenses (of the mine) by the output; =**bauer** *m* free peasant, peasant proprietor; =**beuter** [ndl.] *m* freebooter, zur See: filibuster, pirate, buccaneer; *fig.* literarischer ~ plagiarist; =**beuterei** *f* freebooting, ...ery; filibustering, piracy; ₂**beuterisch** *a.* ⓖ filibustering, piratical; =**bier** *n* free beer, beer given gratis (F treat of beer) to workmen, &c.; ~ geben (F to treat workmen, &c. to beer; =**bille'tt** *n*, *thea.* (free) pass, order; ⚓ pass (on the line); =**bodenmänner** *m/pl.* Am. free-soilers *pl.*; =**bordhöhe** ⇩ *f* free-board line; =**brief** *m* charter, license, für Waren: permit; für freies Geleit: passport; =**bürger** *m* freeman of a city; free denizen of a republic, &c.; ₂**bürgerlich** *a.* republican; =**denker** T *m*, =**denkerei** *f*, ₂**denkerisch** *a.* f. =**geist** ꝛc.

Freie (⁻ᵘ) ⓖ I *m*, *f* 1. free (wo)man, freeborn citizen (*ant.* Leibeig(e)ner,

Sklave).—II *n* 2. (das Ungezwungene) ease of manner; openness of mind or heart. — 3. (das freie Feld) the open country; ins ~ gehen to go into the open air, to take open-air (or outdoor) exercise; im ~n in the open air or country (*ant.* daheim); Bewegung im ~n outdoor exercise; im ~n schlafen to sleep in the open (air), F to camp out.

frei=eigen (⁻ʰ...) *a.* ⓖ allodial, freehold.

freien (⁻ᵘ) [ndb.] ⓖ **I** *v/n.* (h.), bisw. *v/a.* um ein Mädchen ₂ to court (in geh. Spr.: to woo) ..., to pay one's addresses to ...; — **II** *v/a.* = heiraten; Sprichw.: schnell gefreit, lang bereut marry in haste, repent at leisure; f. jung 2. — **III** ~ *n* ⓖ courtship; geh. Spr.: wooing.

Freie(r)¹ (⁻ᵘ) f. Freie I.
Freier² (⁻ᵘ) [freien] *m* ⓖ wooer, suitor; auf =s=füßen geh(e)n ob. steh(e)n to be bent on marrying; F to be on the look-out for a wife; *co.* to go a-wooing.
Freierei (−⁻ᵘ) *f* ⓖ courtship, wooing.
Freiers=füße (⁻ʰ...) *m/pl.* f. Freier²; =**mann** *m* = Freier².
Frei=exempla'r (⁻ʰ...) *n* ⓖ free (or presentation) copy; des Verfassers: author's copy; =**fang** *m* Fußball: fair-catch; =**frau** *f* baroness; =**fräulein** *n*, etwa: daughter of a lord or peer; spinster lady of title vgl.; Baronesse 2; =**gabe** *f*: a) (f. ₂geben) release; emancipation of slaves, &c.; b) restitution of property; ₂**geben** *v/a.* ⓖ**c.***** to release (or set free) prisoners, &c.; Schule: e-e Woche ₂ to give a week's holiday; der Lehrer gab den Schülern ₂ the Master gave the boys a holiday; ₂**gebig** *a.* (*ant.* karg) open-handed, liberal towards a p.; ₂e Dame, oft: Lady Bountiful; mit et. ₂ sein to be prodigal of (or lavish with) a th.; er ist zu ₂ mit dem Gelde he lavishes (or is too lavish with) his money, he spends it too freely; =**gebigkeit** *f* (*ant.* Kargheit) open-handedness, liberality; ₂**geboren** *a.* free-born, of free birth; =**gebung** *f* =**gabe**; =**geist** *m* free-thinker; *eccl.* latitudinarian; (Zweifler) sceptic; (Gottesleugner) atheist; =**geisterei** *f* free-thinking or -thought; scepticism; atheism; ₂**geisterisch** *a.* free-thinking, sceptical; atheistical; ₂**geistig** *a.* open-minded, unbiassed; ₂es Buch book written by a free-thinker or expressing free-thought; =**gelassene([r]** *m*) *f* ⓖ emancipated (or enfranchised) slave; röm. Alt.: freed(wo)man; =**gepäck** ⚓ *n* (passenger's) free luggage; =**gericht** *n* = Feme; =**gerinne** ⊕ *n* =**arche**; ₂**gesinnt** *a.* liberal-minded; ₂**giebig** ꝛc. = ₂**gebig** ꝛc.; =**glaube** *m*, =**gläubigkeit** *f* rationalism; =**graf** *m* = Femgraf; =**gut** *n*: a) ⊕ goods *pl.* free of duty; b) Lehnswesen: freehold (estate); ehm. allodium; =**gutsbesitzer(in** *f*) *m* freeholder; =**hafen** ⇩ *m* free-port; ₂**halten** *v/a.* ⓖ**a****: e-n ₂ to pay for a p. or a. p.'s expenses, F to treat (or stand treat to) a p.; vgl. a. frei 4; =**halten** *n* paying of another p.'s expenses, F treat(ing); =**handel** (=system *n*) *m* ⓢ (system of) free trade; =**handels=partei** *f* free-

traders *pl.*, auch *pol.*: Cobdenites *pl.*, Manchester School; ₂**händig** *a.* und *adv.* offhand; f. frei 5; =**händler** ⊕ *m* free-trader; ₂**händlerisch** *a.* in conformity with free trade, free-trading; ₂e Gesetzgebung free-trade legislation; =**ha"ndschießen** *n* shooting (-practice) without rest or support; =**ha"ndzeichnen** *n* free-hand drawing; =**haus** *n* house free from certain burdens or taxes.

Freiheit (⁻ᵘ−) [ahd.; *frei] *f* ⓖ **1.** freedom; engS. liberty; bürgerliche: franchise; (Unbeschränktheit) license; (Spielraum) scope; volle ~ h., um et. zu tun to have full power to do a th.; ich nahm mir die ~, an ihn zu schreiben I took the liberty of writing to him; sich (*dat.*) zu viel ~ nehmen ob. zu viele ~en herausnehmen to make too free; in ~ setzen to set free, to liberate; ⨯ auf Ehrenwort in ~ setzen to set free on parole. — **2.** (Befreiung von Lasten) exemption, immunity.

Freiheitler (⁻ᵘ−) *m* ⓖ sham supporter (or friend) of liberty, sham Liberal.
freiheitlich (⁻ᵘ−) *a.* ⓖ concerning liberty or the cause of freedom; engS. *pol.* Liberal.
Freiheits=apostel (⁻ʰ...) *m* ⓖ = =**prediger**; =**baum** *m* tree of liberty; =**raubung** *f* jur. illegal detention; =**beschränkung** *f* restriction of li.; =**drang**, =**durst** *m* desire, thirst for li.; =**kampf**, =**krieg** *m* f. Befreiungskampf; =**liebe** *f* love of liberty; =**mütze** *f* bsd. hist. (fr. Revolution, 1789) red (Phrygian) cap; =**prediger** *m* apostle of liberty; =**regung** *f* Liberal movement; =**sinn** *m* spirit (or love) of freedom; =**strafe** *f* imprisonment.
Frei=herr (⁻ʰ...) *m* ⓖ baron; =**herrin** *f* = =**frau**; ₂**herrlich** *a.* ⓖ baronial, lordly; =**herrn=sitz** *m* baronial manor, lordly estate; =**herrschaft** *f* barony; =**hof** *m*, =**hufe** *f* freehold farm.
Frei=in (⁻ᵘ) *f* ⓖ baroness (= Freifrau).
Frei=jahr (⁻ʰ...) *n* ⓖ year of immunity from taxation, &c.; =**karte** *f* = =**billett**; =**kauf** *m* redemption; =**korps** *n* ⚔ volunteer corps; =**kugel** *f* Volksglaube: bullet which never misses its mark, charmed bullet; =**kuvert** ⚓ *n* stamped envelope; ₂**lassen** *v/a.* ⓖ**a****: to (set) free, to liberate, F to let off; aus dem Kerker, a.: to release, Sklaven: to emancipate, Alt. a. ⚔ to manumit; =**lassung** *f* = =**gabe**, a. jur. gegen Bürgschaft: release (or liberation) on bail; =**lauf** ⊕ *m* Radsport: free wheel; Fahren mit ~ free-wheeling; ₂**legen** *v/a.* ⓖ**a****: to lay open, to free (from obstacles), to clear; =**leh(e)n** *n* freehold (land), jur. auch fee simple.
freilich (⁻ᵘ) [mhd.; *frei] *adv.* **1.** bejahend: certainly, to be sure, quite so, of course; ei ~ why, to be sure; ja ~ yes, indeed; yes, you are right. — **2.** einräumend: ₂ gibt es Dichter, aber (allein, doch) it is, of course, true (or granted) that ..., but (yet); dies ist ₂ nicht so schwer this, I must agree (or confess), is ...
Frei=lichtmaler (⁻ᵍ...) *m* F *paint.* open-airist; =**lichtmalerei** *f* plein-air painting, open-air style (of painting).

Zeichen (f. S. XVII): F familiär; P Volkssprache; Γ Gaunersprache; ⟆ selten; † alt (auch gestorben); * neu (auch geboren); ⁺⁺ unrichtig;

[freimachen] — 389 — [fressen]

frei=machen (ᵘᐟʰᵛ) **I** v/a. ⑱** a) = freilassen; b) to deliver, to liberate; den Weg ⸗ to clear the way; (retten) to rescue; (erlösen) to redeem; sich ⸗ to disengage (Stärker: to disentangle, to clear) o.s. of a th.; den Kopf ⸗ to clear the head; c) Briefe ꝛc.: to prepay, to pay the postage of or for, durch e-e Briefmarke: to stamp; d) ⚔ seine Güter (sich) von Schulden (Verpflichtungen) ⸗ to clear one's estate (o.s.) of debts (obligations); e) ⚔ Soldaten von der Dienstpflicht ⸗ to exempt (or excuse) ... from service. — **II** ~ n ㉓ u. **Freimachung** f ㊻: a) deliverance, liberation; b) von Briefen: (pre)payment.

Frei=mann (ᵘ...) m ㊽ freeman, freeholder; vgl. =bauer; =marke f (postage-)stamp (= Briefmarke); =markt m, etwa: free (or open) market; vgl. =messe; =maurer ⊤ m freemason; =maurerei f freemasonry; =maurerisch a. ㊻ (free-) masonic; =maurer=loge f freemasons' (or masonic) lodge; =maurer=orden m masonic order; =messe f fair with special privileges; =mut m frankness, candour, openness; =mütig a. frank, candid, open; =mütigkeit f = =mut; =paß m free pass, pol. passport; ⸗religiös a. of broad religious principles; ⸗religiöse Gemeinde free community or church; =satz m, =sasse m freeholder, yeoman; =schar ⚔ f band of volunteers or insurgents; =schärler ⚔ m volunteer; insurgent; =schein m license; ⚔ discharge; auch = Freibillett; =schießen n shooting-match (open to all comers); =schule f free (or feeless) school, in England jetzt: (free) elementary school; =schüler(in f) m free scholar, in höheren Schulen auch: exhibitioner, foundation-scholar, bursar; =schütz(e) m marksman shooting with charmed bullets; =schütz(e f) n ㊻ flood-gate; sich ⸗schwimmen v/refl. ⓐ(b)** to do (without artificial aid) one's first long-distance swim; =sinn m: a) enlarged (or enlightened) views pl., liberal-mindedness; b) (freisinnige Partei) the Liberal party, Liberals pl.; ⸗sinnig a. enlightened, liberal(-minded), pol. Liberal; =sinnigkeit f: a) independence of mind; b) pol. und rel. Liberalism; =sitz m = =gut b; =sonntag m Sunday out for servants, &c.; ⸗sprechen v/a. ⓐa** (vgl. frei 5,7) to acquit of a crime, to absolve from an obligation, to clear of suspicion; die Geschworenen haben den Angeklagten ⸗gesprochen the jury brought in a verdict of not-guilty or acquitted the prisoner; für e-n ein ⸗des Urteil auswirken, auch: to obtain a p.'s discharge; ~ n, =sprechung f, =spruch m jur. verdict of not-guilty, acquittal, discharge; vgl. =gabe; =staat m free state, (mit wählbarem Oberhaupt) republic, commonwealth; ⸗staatlich a. republican; =stadt f free city or town; =statt, =stätte f asylum, refuge; im Gotteshause ebm.: sanctuary; bei Spielen: home; ⸗stehen v/n. ⓐ** a) vgl. frei 4; b) fig. es steht Ihnen frei zu geh(e)n oder zu bleiben you are free (or at liberty) either to go or to re-

main; =steh(e)n n ㉓ isolation; ⸗stehend a. isolated; von Häusern oft: detached; mit den Blättern, Blumenblättern: ⚘ eleutherophyllous, eleutheropetalous; =stelle f in Schulen scholarship, exhibition (held at school); ⸗stellen v/a. ⓐ** e-m et. ⸗ to leave a th. to a p.'s discretion or choice, to give a p. the option of doing a th.; =stoß m Fußball: free-kick; =stunde f hour of recreation; in Schulen auch: playtime; =tag m Tag der Freia (sechster Wochentag) Friday; (des) ~s on Fridays; stiller ~ Good F.; ⸗tätig a. self-acting; ⊕ automatic.

Freite provc. (ᴸᵛ) [ndd.: * freien] f ㊻ auf die ~ (Brautschau) geh(e)n to (go to) choose a wife. to go a-wooing.

Frei=tisch (ᵘ...) m ㊽ free board or table; =treppe f flight of steps leading to a house; door-steps pl.; =übung(en) f(pl.) Turnerei: general exercises pl. (without apparatus, drill(ing); =werber(in f) m [freien] suitor's intermediary or proxy, F go-between, match-maker; =werden n e-r Stelle vacancy (arising); chm. von Gasen: disengagement, liberation; ⸗willig a. ㊻ voluntary; (aus eigenem Antriebe) spontaneous; adv. voluntarily, of one's own accord, spontaneously; sich ⸗ erbieten zu ... to volunteer to ...; =willigen=dienst ⚔ m in Deutschland: one year's military service; =willigen=examen (=zeugnis) n examination (certificate) qualifying for one year's service; =willige(r) m ㊻ bsd. ⚔ volunteer; als ~ dienen, in England ꝛc.: to serve as a volunteer; =willigkeit f voluntariness, spontaneousness; =zettel m license; permit; =zügig(keit f) a. privileged (right) to leave (or to settle down in) a place without being taxed; weits. free(dom) to move (about) from place to place.

fremd (ᵞ) [ahd.: from] a. ㊻ 1. strange; f. Feder 1; unter dem Namen reisen to travel under an adopted name, to travel incognito; in e-r Stadt ⸗ sein to be a stranger in ..., not to know ...; er ist mir ⸗ he is a stranger to me; das ist mir ganz ⸗ it is quite foreign (or new) to me; sich ⸗ stellen, ⸗ gegen e-n tun to treat a p. as a stranger, be reserved (or distant) with a p.; Sprichw. ⸗e Länder, ⸗e Sitten other countries, other customs. — 2. (ant. eigen) ⸗es Gut other people's property; durch ⸗e Hand through a third person or party; in den Händen in strange (or other) hands; sich in ⸗e Händel mischen to meddle in other people's concerns; Geiz ist f-m Wesen ⸗ avarice is foreign to his nature. — 3. (ausländisch) foreign, v. Sitten ꝛc. a.: outlandish; ⸗e Länder, Sprachen foreign countries, languages pl. — 4. (seltsam) strange, odd, queer.

fremd=artig (ᵞ...) a. ㊻: a) strange, ⚘ heterogeneous; b) (seltsam) strange, singular, odd; chm. extraneous; ~keit f ㊻: ⚘ heterogeneousness; (Seltsamkeit) strangeness, singularity.

Fremde (ᵟᵛ) s. **I** ~ f ㊻ foreign country or parts pl.; in die ~ gehen to go abroad or on one's travels, to visit foreign

lands; aus der ~ kommen to come from abroad; in der ~ leben to live abroad. — **II** ~([r] m) f ㊻ stranger, (Ausländer) foreigner, nicht naturalisiert: alien; pl. die ~en (Gäste) visitors, guests pl.

Fremden=amt (ᵟ...) n ㊽ intelligence-bureau (or -office) for strangers or visitors, pol. alien-office; =blatt n Visitors' Gazette; =buch n im Gasthofe ꝛc.: visitors' book; hotel register; =bureau n = =amt; ⸗feindlich a. hostile to foreigners; ⸗e Kundgebungen in China demonstrations pl. of hostility to foreigners in China; =führer m guide; in Kunstsammk.: cicerone; als Buchtitel: Visitors' Guide; =legion f Frankreich ꝛc.: foreign legion; =liste f list of visitors or arrivals; =stube f spare room. in geh. Spr.: guest-chamber; in Gasthöfen: general room; =zimmer n = =stube. **fremd=geboren** a. ㊻ alien-born. **Fremdheit** (ᵟ-) f ㊻ 1. (Fremdsein) foreign character. — 2. (etwas Fremdes) strangeness, singularity, oddity, curiosity. **Fremd=herrschaft** (ᵟ...) f ㊻ foreign dominion or yoke; =herrscher m foreign (or alien) ruler; =körper * m foreign substance in the eye, in milk, &c.; ⸗ländisch a. ㊻ foreign, Pflanzen ꝛc. exotic. **Fremdling** (ᵟ-) m ⓓd. stranger, vgl. Fremde **II**; **~s=recht** (ᵟ...) n ㊻ jur. alien-law(s pl.); (Heimfallsrecht) ⚘ escheatage. **fremd=namig** (ᵟ...) a. ㊻ u. adv. under (or bearing) another name; ⸗pseudonymous(ly); =sein n ㊽ = Fremdheit 1; =sprache* f foreign language or tongue; ⸗sprachig a. (eine fremde Sprache redend) speaking a foreign language; ⸗sprachlich a. belonging (or referring) to a foreign language; der Unterricht instruction in a foreign l., linguistic teaching; =sucht f mania for foreign manners or things; =wort n foreign word; =wörterbuch n dictionary of foreign words and expressions.

frequent (ᵟᵟ) [lt.] a. ㊻ (häufig) frequent; (stark besucht) much frequented or patronized, crowded; ⊕ (gangbar) current (article); **=ieren** (ᵞᵛᴸᵛ) v/a. ㊸ (häufig besuchen) to frequent; ⊕ sehr ⸗iertes Geschäft business largely patronized by the public, flourishing shop. **Frequenz** (ᵟᵛ) [lt.] f ㊻ (Gedränge) throng; (Zulauf) attendance (of a school); patronage of a shop; ⚙ traffic on the line. **Freske** (ᵟᵛ) f ㊻, **Fresko** (ᵟᵛ) [lt.] n ㉓ (Wandmalerei auf frischem Kalk) fresco; a(l) fresco malen to paint in fresco. **Fresko=bild** (ᵟ-...) n ㊽, =gemälde n fresco-painting; =maler m fr.-painter; =malerei f painting in fresco. **Freß=begierde** (ᵟ...) f ㊻ = =gier; =beutel m bag for provisions or victuals, provender-bag; der Pferde: nosebag. **Fresse** P (ᵟᵛ) [fressen] f ㊻ (Maul) mouth, P potato-trap, chops pl., mug, snout. **fressen** (ᵟᵛ) [ahd.: fret] **I** v/a., v/n. (h.) und sich ⸗ v/refl.⓯ **1.** vom Vieh: to eat, to feed; vom Menschen: to eat greedily, to devour, F to gobble up, to polish off; Gras, Heu ⸗ to feed on grass, hay; wie ein (Scheunen-)Drescher (oder wie ein Wolf) ⸗ to eat like a wolf or a cormorant; den Kühen zu ⸗ geben

♪ Musik; ⚘ Wissenschaft; ⚘ Pflanze; ⚲ Geographie; ⊕ Technik; ⚒ Bergbau; ⚔ Militär; ⚓ Marine; ⚖ Handel; ✉ Post; 🚂 Eisenbahn.

[Fresser] — 390 — [Freundschaft]

to give the cows (some) food or s. th. to eat, to feed the cows. — 2. mit Angabe der Wirkung: e-n arm 2 to eat a p. poor out of house and home; sich dick, satt, voll 2 to eat (or have) one's fill, to gorge o.s.; die Krippe leer 2 to empty...; das Pferd frißt mehr, als es einbringt the horse is eating its head off. — 3. Sprichw. und *fig.*: er hat den Narren daran gefressen he is infatuated (or in love), with it, F he is mad(ly bent) on it; an e-m e-n (ob. den) Narren gefressen h. to be madly fond of a p., to dote on a p.; seinen Kummer 2c. in sich 2 (nicht äußern) to swallow one's grief, &c.; er denkt, er habe die Weisheit mit Löffeln gefressen he thinks himself a paragon of wisdom; friß Vogel oder stirb! (hier muß man wählen) eat or starve!, sink or swim!, (do) one thing or the other! — 4. (zerstörend wirken) to eat into, to consume; (ätzen) to corrode; *path.* um sich 2 (von Geschwüren 2c.) to spread, to rankle (a. *fig.*). — II ~ n 23 5. eating, &c. (f. I); F das Kind ist zum ~ (allerliebst) one could eat ...; P *fig.* das ist ihm ein gesund(e)nes ~ (et. Erwünschtes) it is water to his mill or F a good find for (or a godsend to) him. — Vgl. a. Futter 1.

Fresser (◡) *m* 23, ~in f 40 large (or greedy, voracious) eater; glutton; F gormandizer, gorger.

Fresserei F (◡◡◡) *f* 46 1. (Fressen) voracious eating, gluttony, gorging, F gormandizing, stuffing. — 2. (Schmaus) F feed, P blow-out.

Freß-fieber (◡...) *n* 22 voracious (or wolfish) appetite; *path.*: ⚕ bulimia, ...y; =gier *f* voracity, gluttony; 2gierig *a.* 46 voracious, gluttonous, ravenous, F co. with a wolf in one's inside; =korb F *m* hamper of eatables or grub; (Brotkorb) bread-basket; =lust *f* f. Fraß 2; vom Vieh: appetite for one's food; die ~ verlieren, oft: F to go off one's feed; =napf m 23, =näpfchen n für Vögel: trough; =sack *m*: a) = beutel; b) (starker Fresser) glutton, great (or voracious) eater; =spitze f, *ent.* labial, maxillary palp; =sucht *f* = =fieber; =trog *m* für Vieh: trough (for food), manger; =wanst F *m* = Fresser; =werkzeuge *n*/*pl. zo.* mouth-organs pl.; *ent.* (a. =zange f): ⚕ trophi.

Frett[1] ⊕ (◡) [ndl. u. engl. fret; * fr. *foret*] *m* (n) ⓌⓑⒹ. gimlet = Frittbohrer.

Frett[2] (◡) [fr. *furet*; it.] *n* ⓌⓑⒹ, mst **Frettchen** (◡◡) *n* 23, ~wiesel (◡◡◡) *n* 22 *zo.* ferret (*Puto'rius furo*); *hunt.* mit Frettchen jagen to ferret (out).

Frette ⊕ (◡) [fr.] *f* 49 (Eisenband, Zwinge) hoop (for binding stakes), ferrule.

Freude (◡◡) [ahd. * freuen] *f* 49 (Frohsein) gladness, joy(fulness), mirth, (Heiterkeit) cheerfulness; hilarity; (Vergnügen) pleasure; (Wonne) delight; ich tue es mit ~n I feel a pleasure in doing it, I do it gladly; es ist eine rechte ~, das zu sehen it is quite a pleasure to see it; sie tanzte, daß es eine (wahre) ~ war it was delightful to see her dance; er hat große ~ am Studieren he takes a great pleasure (or interest) in his studies; sie wird ~ an dem Knaben erleben the boy will be a comfort to her; er findet seine höchste ~ darin, zu // it is his greatest happiness (or joy) to (*inf.*); es wird mir (große) ~ m., zu // I shall be (most) happy to // (*inf.*); herrlich und in ~n leben to live in splendid (or in a sumptuous, luxurious) style; vor ~ außer sich beside o. s. with joy, overjoyed; vor ~ weinen to weep for joy.

freude=bringend (◡◡...) *a.* 40 pleasurable; =bringer *m* 22 bringer of joy; =gefühl *n* feeling of gladness; 2leer, 2los, freudenarm joyless, cheerless, void of mirth.

Freuden-becher (◡◡...) *m* 22 cup of delight or comfort; =bezeigung *f* expression of joy, rejoicing; =botschaft *f* glad tidings pl., good news; vgl. =post; =feier *f*, =fest *n* joyful fête or festivity, (public) rejoicing; =feuer *n* bonfire; =geschrei *n* shouts pl. of joy; (Beifallsruf) cheering; (Zuruf) (loud) acclamation; =kelch *m* cup of joy; =kleid *n* festive garb or garment; =leben *n* life of joy or pleasure; 2leer *a.* 40, 2los *a.* f. freude-leer 2c.; =lied *n* song (or hymn) of rejoicing; =mädchen *n* loose girl, gay woman, prostitute, unfortunate; =mahl *n* feast, festive repast or entertainment; ein =m. geben to give a banquet; =opfer *n* thank-offering; willing sacrifice; =post *f* joyful news; =rausch *m* rapture, exultation; 2reich *a.* full of joy, joyful, rich in happiness; =ruf, =schrei *m* shout of joy; cheer; =schießen *n* festive shooting; joyful booming of guns; =störer *m* spoil-sport, mar-feast, F co. wet blanket; =tag *m* day of rejoicing, festive day; =taumel *m* transport of joy, mad delight; =tränen *pl.* tears pl. of joy; ~ vergießen to cry for joy; =trunk *m* cup of rejoicing.

freude=strahlend (◡◡...) *a.* 40 beaming (or radiant) with joy; 2trunken *a.* brimming over with joy or delight, overjoyed, enraptured; 2voll *a.* joyful, cheerful.

freudig (◡◡) [nhd.] *a.* 40 joyful; gewählter: joyous; (froh) glad; vgl. erfreulich; ~keit *f* 46 joy(fulness); joyousness; gladness; mit Freudigkeit cheerfully, willingly.

freud-leer, 2los, 2voll (◡...) f. freude-...

freuen (◡◡) [ahd.; * froh] 40 I *v*/*a*. — erfreuen I; es freut mich, daß du da bist oder dich hier zu sehen I am glad that you are here or to see you here; es freut mich ungemein, Sie getroffen zu haben I am delighted to have met you. — II sich 2 *v*/*refl.* to be glad or pleased (über et. about a th., at a th.); sich 2 wie ein Kind, a. sich königlich 2, sich 2 wie ein (Schnee=)König to be as happy as a king; sie 2 sich höchlich darüber, daß // they are overjoyed (or greatly delighted) that //; sich e-r Sache (*gen.*) 2 to rejoice at (or in) a th.; sich an et. 2 to take (or find) a pleasure (stärker: to revel) in a th.; sich auf et. 2 to look forward (with pleasure) to a th.; wir 2 uns darauf, ihn zu sehen we are anticipating the pleasure of seeing him.

Freund (¹) [ahd.: friend] *m* Ⓦⓑ., ~in 47 1. (gentleman, lady or male, female) friend; (Bekannte[r]) acquaintance; (Geschäfts=, Handels=) ~ business connexion; correspondent; ~ und Berater friend and guide, a. mentor; alter ~ old friend, F old crony; vertrauter ~ intimate (or bosom-)friend, F (great) chum or P pal; gegen ~ und Feind to (or towards) friend and foe alike; ein (guter) ~ von mir, ihm, uns a (great) friend of mine, his, ours; F sie sind dicke ~e ... hand and glove with each other; F ... as thick as thieves; ~e im Glück fair-weather friends pl.; j-s ~ bleiben oder F ~ bleiben mit e-m to keep friends with a p.; e-m ~ sein to be a friend to a p.; to be a p.'s friend; sie sind wieder gut ~ they are good friends again, they have made it up (between them); ~ erkennen 1. — 2. (Verehrer von et.) ich bin kein ~ von Spielen, von vielen Worten I am no great lover of games, of many words, stärker: I dislike them; er ist ein ~ der Musik he is fond of (or he likes) music; sie ist eine (großmütige) ~in der Kunst she is a (liberal) patroness of art. — 3. *bibl. a.* F (Verwandte[r]) kinsman, *f* kinswoman. — 4. *poet.* ~ Hein (der Tod) Death.

freund-brüderlich (◡...) *a.* 40 like a friend and brother.

Freundes=dienst (◡◡...) *m* 22 friendly service; =gruß *m* friendly greeting; =kreis *m* circle of friends (and acquaintances), s. Freundschaft 3.

freundlich (◡◡) *a.* 40 1. von Personen: (gefällig) friendly, kind, obliging, (liebreich) amiable, (huldreich) gracious, (leutselig) affable, agreeable, (wohlwollend) benevolent; (höflich) courteous; ein ~es Gesicht machen to put on a pleasant face or a smile, to look pleasant; e-m ~e Grüße senden ... one's kind regards to a p.; das ist sehr 2 von Ihnen that is very kind of you; in Büchern oft: Der Leser (Leserin) gentle (fair) reader; sie war so 2, mich einzuführen she was so kind as to introduce me, she very kindly introduced me; *adv.* e-n 2 aufnehmen to give a p. a kind (or hearty) welcome; sagen Sie mir 2st will you kindly tell me //. — 2. von Dingen: 2es Anerbieten kind offer; 2e (heitere) Gegend cheerful (or pleasant) neighbourhood; 2es Gesicht bright (or pleasing, smiling) face; 2es Wetter fair weather, fine (or bright) day.

Freundlichkeit (◡◡◡) *f* 46 (f. freundlich) friendliness, kindness, amiability, affability; courteousness, courtesy; pleasantness of manner; brightness of a scene or face.

freund=los (◡...) *a.* 40 friendless, without friends or a friend, companionless; 2nachbarlich *a.* as a friend and neighbour (and cousin).

Freundschaft (◡◡) *f* 46 1. friendship; (Bekanntschaft) acquaintance; aus ~ for friendship's sake; für e-n ~ hegen to have a friendly feeling towards a p.; in Frieden und ~ leben to live in peace and quietness; mit e-m ~ knüp-

Signs (see page XVII): F familiar; P vulgar; ꟼ flash; ⟍ rare; † obsolete (died); * new word (born); ₊+ incorrect; ♪ music;

[freundschaftlich] — 391 — **[frisch]**

fen, schließen to make friends with a p., auf die Dauer: to form a lasting friendship with a p.; Borgen schadet der ~, Geld kennt keine ~ short reckonings make long friends. — 2. *bibl.* u. F (Verwandtschaft) kinship, relationship. — 3. (Freundeskreis) (circle of) friends or relations or acquaintances *pl.*; family connexion(s *pl.*). — 4. (Freundesdienst) friendly service; e-m eine ~ erweisen to do a p. a good service (or F turn) or a favour.

freundschaftlich (᷄ᷘᷘ) *a.* ⓖ friendly, amicable; *adv.* 2 gegen e-n gesinnt sein ... kindly disposed towards a p.; (*adv.*) et. 2 abmachen to settle a th. amicably; **~keit** f ⓖ friendliness, amicableness, friendly disposition, kind spirit.

Freundschafts=band(e) (᷄ᷘ᷄...) *n* (*pl.*) ⓖ ties *pl.* of friendship; **=beteu(e)rung** f = **=versicherung**; **=bezeigung** f mark of fr.; favour; **=bund** *m*, **=bündnis** *n* friendly alliance; **=dienst** *m*, **=stück** *n* kind service; **=versicherung** f protestation (or profession) of friendship.

Frevel (᷄ᷘ) I [ahd.] *m* ⓖ 1. (sträflicher Leichtsinn) culpable neglect; (Mutwille) wantonness; (Bosheit) wickedness, malice. — 2. (böse Tat) ill (stärker: atrocious) deed, crime, (Vergehen) (punishable) offence, (Übertretung) trespass, contravention; (Eingriff) infringement; (frecher Verstoß) outrage (an et. upon a th.); *rel.* ~ gegen Gott, auch: offence against God('s holy law), (Lästerung) blasphemy, (Entheiligung) sacrilege; der von ihnen verübte ~ the crime (or misdeed) committed (or perpetrated) by them, their misdoing. — II ⌐ frevel *a.* ⓖ 3. = frevelhaft.

frevelhaft (᷄ᷘᷘ) *a.* ⓖ (s. Frevel I) wanton, malicious, wicked, atrocious, criminal, outrageous; sacrilegious; sein 2es Beginnen his evil enterprise, his criminal proceedings *pl.*; **~igkeit** f ⓖ wantonness; malice, wickedness; criminality; outrageousness.

Frevel=mut (᷄ᷘ...) *m* ⓖ = **=sinn**.

freveln (᷄ᷘ) *v./n.* (h.) ⓖa. (s. Frevel I) to commit (or perpetrate) an atrocious deed or a (wanton) crime; an e-m, gegen e-n 2 to wrong (stärker: to injure or outrage) a p.; gegen die Gesetze 2 to transgress (or infringe) the laws, to offend against the law(s).

Frevel=sinn (᷄ᷘ...) *m* ⓖ wanton (or mischievous) disposition; **=tat** f atrocious (or criminal) action; *vgl.* Frevel 2; **=wort** *n* wicked (or insulting) word; *rel.* blasphemy.

freventlich (᷄ᷘᷘ) [nhd.] ⓖ = frevelhaft.

Frevler (᷄ᷘ) *m* ⓖ, **~in** f ⓖ wicked person; evil-doer, transgressor, offender; (Verbrecher) criminal, malefactor; (Schurke) villain; (Gotteslästerer) blasphemer; **2isch** *a.* ⓖ = frevelhaft.

Friaul ⚥ (᷄ᷘ) [it. *Forum Iu'lii*] *npr/n.* ⓖa. it. Landschaft: Friuli.

Frida (᷄ᷘ) *npr/f.* ⓖⓖa. (Vn.) Frederica.

Fridchen (᷄ᷘ) *npr/n.* ⓖa. (Vn.) 1. *dim. v.* (Gottfried) Jeff(ie), little Geoffrey. — 2. *dim. von* Frida.

fried=brüchig (᷄ᷘ...) *a.* ⓖ breaking (or violating) the peace.

Friede (᷄ᷘ) [ahd.] *m* ⓖ 1. peace; (Einklang) harmony; ~ bringend, stiftend pacific; ~ schließen to make peace; laß mich in ~! leave (or let) me alone!; in Krieg und ~ in peace and in war; mit aller Welt in ~ leben to be at peace with everybody; *Sprichw.* ~ ernährt, Unfrieden verzehrt concord nourishes, discord ravishes. — 2. *rel.* zum ewigen ~ eingehen to enter everlasting bliss, to go to one's eternal home; er ruhe in ~! may he rest in peace!, (it.) *requiescat in pace*! — 3. *fig.* dem ~ (der Sache) traue ich nicht I don't trust (it), I don't believe in it.

Friede=fürst (᷄ᷘ...) *m* ⓖ *bibl.* Prince of Peace, the Saviour.

Friedel (᷄ᷘ) *npr/m.* ⓖa. (Vn.); *dim. von* Friedrich) Freddy, little Fred.

friede=los (᷄ᷘ...) *a.* ⓖ without peace; troubled (in one's mind). [= Friede.]

Frieden (᷄ᷘ) [nhd. 18 *sae*.; *Friede] *m* ⓖ **=abschluß** (᷄ᷘ...) *m* ⓖ conclusion of peace; **=antrag** *m* peace-proposal, overtures *pl.* of pe.; **=bedingung** f condition (*pl.* a. terms) of pe.; **=bestand** ⚔ *m* pe.-establishment; **=bote** *m*, **=botschaft** f messenger, message of peace; **=brecher** *m* pe.-breaker; **=bruch** *m* pe.-breaking; breach of the peace. [of peace.] **Friedens=schluß** (᷄ᷘ...) *m* ⓖ conclusion] **Friedens=engel** (᷄ᷘ...) *m* ⓖ angel of peace; **=feier** f, **=fest** *n* peace festivities *pl.*, fête (given) in celebration of peace; **=flagge** f flag of truce; **=fürst** *m* = Friedefürst; **=fuß** ⚔ *m* peace-footing; **=gedanken** *m/pl.* peaceful thoughts *pl.*; peaceable sentiments *pl.*; **=gericht** *n*, etwa: county-court; **=kongreß** *m* peace-congress; **=partei** f pe.-party; **=pfeife** f der Indianer pipe (or calumet) of peace; **=politik** f pacific policy; **=präliminarien** *pl.* preliminaries *pl.* of pe.; **=richter** *m* justice of the peace (*abbr.* J. P.); **=schluß** *m* = Friedenschluß.

Frieden=stifter(in f) *m* (᷄ᷘ...) ⓖ peace-maker; pacifier, mediator; **=stiftung** f pe.-making; pacification, mediation; **=störer(in** f) *m* disturber of (the) peace, peace-breaker; mar-feast.

Friedens=unterhändler (᷄ᷘ...) *m* ⓖ negotiator of a treaty of peace; **=unterhandlungen** f/*pl.* p.-negotiations *pl.*; **=vermittler** *m* mediator; **=vermittlung** f = **=stiftung**; **=vertrag** *m* treaty of p.; **=vorschlag** *m* = **=antrag**; **=zeit** f time(s *pl.*) of p., peaceful period; in ~en in time(s) of peace.

Friederike (᷄ᷘ᷄) [=Friedrich] *npr/f.* ⓖⓖβ. (Vn.) Frederica.

fried=fertig (᷄ᷘ...) *a.* ⓖ peaceable, pacific; *bibl.* die ~en the peace-makers *pl.*; **=fertigkeit** f ⓖ peaceableness; **=hof** [ahd.] *m* (Kirchhof) churchyard; (Begräbnisplatz) cemetery, burial-place.

Fried=länder (᷄ᷘ...) [=Friedland: Stadt in Böhmen mit Wallensteins Schloß (1623)] *npr/m.* ⓖ hist. der ~ (Wallenstein, österreich. Feldherr im dreißigjähr. Kriege) (the) Duke of Friedland.

friedlich (᷄ᷘ) [=Friede] *a.* ⓖ: a) (zum Frieden geneigt) pacific or peaceable (attitude, disposition); 2e Abmachung amicable agreement; b) (Frieden genießend) peaceful or quiet or happy (life); (still) calm.

Friedlichkeit (᷄ᷘ...) f ⓖ pacific character, peaceableness, peacefulness, quietness, happiness; calmness.

fried=liebend (᷄ᷘ...) *a.* ⓖ peace-loving; *vgl.* **=fertig**; **2los** *a.* ⓖ = friedelos.

Friedrich (᷄ᷘ) [bz. Friedefürst] *npr/m.* ⓖⓖα. (Vn.) Frederick, Frederic; s. Friedel; **~s=dor** *m* ⓖd. (ehm. preuß. Goldmünze = 16,829 ℳ) Frederic d'or.

friedsam (᷄ᷘ) [ahd.], **friedselig** (᷄ᷘ) [† Friedsal + -ig] *a.* ⓖ = friedlich.

frieren (᷄ᷘ) [ahd.: freeze] ⓖc. I *v/a. v/impers.* 1. es friert mich, mich friert (mir ist es kalt) I am (stärker: I shiver with) cold, I feel chilled or a chill; es fror ihn an den Händen he had (or complained of, suffered from) cold hands. — 2. es hat Eis gefroren (in der Kälte gebildet) it has been freezing; es friert (Stein und Bein) it is freezing (hard). — II *v/n.* 3. (h.): a) (s. 1) ich friere I am (or feel) cold; b) *v/impers.* (s. 2) es friert it is freezing. — 4. (sn) (erstarren, oft: gefrieren, s. bs) to freeze, to congeal; der Fluß ist gefroren ... is frozen up, ... bears (ice). — III *v/a. v/n.* u. *sich* 2 *v/refl.* mit Angabe der Wirkung: 5. ich habe mir den Arm steif gefroren my arm is numbed (or stiff) with cold; sich zu Tode 2 to be frozen to death. — IV ⌐ *n* ⓖ 6. (Frösteln) chill(ness), shiver(ing). — 7. (Erstarren) freezing, congelation. — 8. F (Fieberfrost) er hat das ~ ... the (cold) shivers.

Fries (᷄) [fr. *frise*] *m* ⓖa. 1. ⓖ Tuchfabr. baize, frieze (s. a. Flaus 2). — 2. *arch.* (Säulengesims) frieze.

Friese¹ (᷄ᷘ) f ⓖ = Fries 2.

Friese² (᷄ᷘ) *m* ⓖ, **Friesin** f ⓖ (Bewohner/in v. Friesland) Frisian, Frieslander.

Friesel (᷄ᷘ) [nbd.; *frieren] *m* und *n* ⓖ, *mst* **~n** *pl.* *path.* purples *pl.*; **~fieber** *n* ⓖ: ☞ miliary fever, miliaria.

friesisch (᷄ᷘ) *a.* ⓖ Friese, Frisian, Friesic, *biswn.*: Friesish; die 2e Sprache, das ~(e) *n* ⓖ Frisian, Friesic.

Friesland ⚥ (᷄ᷘ) *npr/n.* ⓖα. Friesland, Frisia; **Friesländer** *m* ⓖ *m* = Friese²; **friesländisch** *a.* ⓖ = friesisch.

Frikandeau (᷄ᷘ-bō᷄) [fr.] *n* ⓖ Kochkunst: fricandeau, (braised and larded) fillet of veal. [(meat), auch: fricassee.] **Frikassee** (᷄ᷘ᷄) [fr.] *n* ⓖ Kochkunst: mince] **frikassieren** (᷄ᷘ᷄) *v/a.* ⓖ (klein hacken) to chop meat, &c. small, to mince ...

Friktion (᷄ᷘ᷄) [it.] f ⓖ *phys.* u. ⊙ (Reibung) friction.

Friktions=feuerzeug ⊙ (᷄ᷘ᷄...) *n* ⓖ = **=zündhölzchen**; **=getriebe** *n* friction-gear; **=rad** *n*, **=scheibe**, **=walze** f fr.-wheel, -plate, -roller; **=zünder** ⚔ *m*, *artill.* friction-tube; **=zündhölzchen** *n* lucifer(-match).

frisch (᷄) [ahd.: fresh] *a.* ⓖ (D 6) 1. (erquickend) fresh; (kühl) cool; 2e Luft, 2es Wasser fresh air, water; es ist 2 (die air) is fresh or cool; ↓ vom Winde; 2 werden to freshen, to stiffen; *adv.* es weht 2 it blows fresh. — 2. (unverdorben, *ant.* abgestanden, faul) 2e Butter fresh butter; 2 und gesund, 2 wie ein Röschen fresh as a daisy or a rose;

⚛ scientific; ❦ botanical; ⚲ geography; ⊙ machinery; ⚒ mining; ⚔ military; ⚓ marine; ✉ commercial; ✎ postal; 🚂 railway.

[Frischarbeit] — 392 — [fromm]

hale and hearty, safe and sound; eine 2e (gesunde) Gesichtsfarbe a ruddy (or clear, florid) complexion; ⚔ 2e (noch nicht ins Feuer geführte) Truppen f/pl. fresh troops or forces pl. — 3. (neu) new; (kürzlich geschehen oder gemacht) of recent date or make; von älteren Leuten: noch 2 hale, juvenile, robust; 2 machen to freshen up; von Lem afresh, anew; in Lem Andenken behalten to keep fresh in one's memory; Les Brot new bread; Le Eier n/pl. new-laid eggs pl.; ein Les Faß anstechen to tap a fresh (or new) cask; ein Les Grab a new(ly made) grave; ein Les (reines) Hemd anziehen to put on a clean shirt; Len Mut fassen to pluck up (fresh) courage; Le Pferde n/pl. fresh (relay of) horses pl.; auf der Tat ertappen to catch in the very act or deed, von Mördern: to catch red-handed; Le Wäsche clean linen; Le Zufuhr fresh supplies pl.; adv.: 2 (an)gestrichen fresh-painted; 2 gemacht new(ly)made; 2 aus der Küche just up, quite fresh; 2 aus dem Ofen just out of the oven; 2 vom Faß straight from the cask. — 4. (munter) brisk, lively; (wacker) active; (flink) alert, nimble; eine Le (lebhafte) Farbe a bright colour; ein Les Greisenalter a green old age; 2er Mut undaunted courage (vgl. 3); adv. 2 daran!, 2 darauf!, 2 vorwärts! F go it!, look alive!, wire in!, fire away! — 5. Sprichw. Le Fische, gute Fische (handle rasch) delays are dangerous; 2 gewagt ist halb gewonnen well begun is half done; nothing venture nothing have. — 6. ♀ s. Haff, Nehrung.

Frisch=arbeit ⊕ (s...) f ⊛ metall. refining-work, fining-process; 2auf! (L") cheer up!; 2backen (s...) a. ⊛ vom Brote: new(ly) baked); =blei ⊕ n, metall. refined (or pure) lead.

Frische (L") f ⊛ 1. (zu frisch 1:) freshness; coolness of the air, &c. — 2. (zu 4:) briskness, liveliness; v. Farben: brightness; der Gesichtsfarbe: ruddiness. — 3. (Jugend=) vigour (of body and mind). — 4. (Sommer=) holiday- (or health-)resort; in die (Sommer=) gehen to go (on a holiday-trip) into the country. [(or pure) iron.]

Frisch=eisen ⊕ (s...) n ⊛ metall. refined] frischen (L") ⊛ I v/a. und sich 2 v/refl. 1. = erfrischen 1. — 2. hunt. die Hirsche, Hunde 2 (sich) ... are drinking or quenching their thirst. — 3. ⊕ metall. (frisch machen, rein herstellen) to (re)fine; Eisen auch: to puddle; Oxyde: to reduce; die Bleiglätte 2 to reduce (or revive) the litharge. — II v/n. (h.) 4. es frischt (ist frisch) it is (becoming, F getting) fresh or cool; ↓ die Brise frischt (wird stärker) ... freshens, ... is stiffening. — 5. hunt. von der Sau: (Ferkel werfen) to farrow. — III ~ n ⊛ 6. ⊕ (s. 3) (re)fining; puddling, reduction. — 7. ↓ (s. 4) freshening or stiffening of the breeze. [of iron, &c.]

Frischer ⊕ ⚒ (L") m metall. (re)finer]
Frisch=esse (s...) f ⊛ = =herd; =feuer ⊕ n, metall. finery-fire, open fire;

=hammer, =herd m, =hütte f ⊕ metall. (re)fining-forge, finery.

Frischling (L") [ahd.] m ⊕d. hunt. young wild (one-year-old) boar.

Frisch=ofen ⊕ (s...) m ⊛ metall. refining-furnace; =schlacken ⊕ f/pl., metall. finery-cinders pl. or -slag; =sein n freshness; =stahl m rough (or furnace-) steel.

Frischung (L") f ⊛ = frischen III.
Frisch=wasser ↓ (s...) n ⊛ = Süßw.

frisch=weg (L⠀) adv. straight away, straightway, there and then; (auf einmal) at one pull, at a stretch; frisch von der Leber weg (ohne Rückhalt) openly, without mincing the matter, straight (from the heart).

Friseur (=ĭš'r) [fr.] m ⊕d., ~in f ⊛, F a. Friseuse (=ĭš") f ⊛ hairdresser.
Frisier=eisen (="...) ⊕ n ⊛ curling-iron or -tongs pl.
frisieren (="...) [nhd. 1600; (+) fr.] I v/a. u. sich 2 v/refl. 1. (träufeln) to curl; ⊕ Tuchmach.: to frieze. — 2. e-n (sich) 2 (e-m, sich das Haar ordnen) to dress a p.'s (one's) hair. — II ~ n ⊛ 3. (s. 1) curling, &c.; (s. 2) hairdressing.
Frisier=kamm (="...) m ⊛ dressing-comb; =mantel m hairdresser's wrapper; =maschine ⊛ f Tuchfabr.: friezing-machine or -mill; =salon m hair-dressing (or hair-cutting) saloon.

friß (L), frissest (L"), frißt (L; Hom. Frist) imper. u. 2. u. 3. Person sg. pres. v. fressen.

Frist (L; Hom. frißt) [ahd.] f ⊛ 1. space of time; (Zwischenzeit) interval; (Zeitpunkt) point of time; date; (bestimmter Zeitabschnitt) given (or fixed) time; zu jeder, aller ~ at all times, at any time; always; in Jahres=, in the space of a year, within a twelvemonth; in kürzester ~ within a short time, at a very short notice; ⊛ auf kurze ~en ausleihen to loan for short periods. — 2. (gewährter Aufschub) respite; delay; sich eine ~ erbitten to ask for time; e-m eine ~ gewähren to grant a p. a respite; einem zum Tode Verurteilten: to reprieve a p.; ⊛ e-m drei Tage ~ geben to give a p. three days' grace; für eine Tratte noch einen Monat ~ gewähren to extend (or prolong) a draft for another month.

Frist=brief (s...) m ⊛ letter of respite.
fristen (L") ⊛ I v/a. 1. (hinausschieben) to delay, to put off. — 2. e-m das Leben 2 (schenken) to spare a p.'s life; to reprieve a p.; sich (dat.) kümmerlich das Leben 2 to earn a scanty (or bare) livelihood. — II sich 2 v/refl. 3. to keep o.s. alive, to support o.s.

Frist=gesuch (s...) n ⊛ petition for a respite or delay; jur. a.: dilatory plea; =gewährung f grant of a respite; prolongation (of the time allowed); =tag m day of respite or grace.

Fristung (L") f ⊛ delay; ~ des Lebens earning (or making) a living.

Frist=verlängerung (s...) f ⊛ extension of time; (giving or allowing) further grace; 2(en)weise adv. by instalments; =(en)zahlung f payment by instalments.

Frisur (=ĭ") [fr.] f ⊛ 1. (Krause der Haare) curl(iness); (Anordnung der Haare) dressing of the hair; head-dress. — 2. (faltiger Kleiderbesatz) furbelow.

Fritt=bohrer ⊕ (s...) m carp. gimlet.
Fritte ⊕ (L") [it. Gebackenes] f ⊛ Glasfabr. (Glassatz) frit. [masse verglühen) to frit.]
fritten (s") v/a. ⊛ Glasfabr. (die Glas=]
Fritt=gefäß ⊕ (s...) n ⊛ Glasfabr.: frit-basin; =ofen m Glasfabr. frit(ting)-furnace; =röhre* f drahtlose Telegraphie: (Röhrchen mit Metallspänen) coherer.

Fritz (L) ⊛⚒, F ~e (L) npr/m. (Vn.; abbr. v. Friedrich) Fred. [Freddy.]
Fritzchen (L") npr/n. ⊛a. (dim. v. Fritz)]
frivol (-w") [nhd. 17. sae., *fr.] a. ⊛ (leichtfertig) frivolous; von Reden a. flippant, unbecoming; ~ität (-w-") [fr.; it.] f ⊛ frivolity, flippancy.

Frl. abbr. = Fräulein.

froh (L) [ahd.] a. ⊛ 1. (Freude empfindend) joyful, glad; pleased, stärker: delighted; (fröhlich) cheerful; ich war 2, ihn loszuwerden I was thankful (or glad) to get rid of him. — 2. (Freude erregend) joyous, happy; (lustig) merry. — 3. mit gen. des Sieges 2 sein to rejoice in victory; einer Sache (durch Genuß) 2 werden to enjoy a th.; er wird seines Lebens nicht 2 he leads an unenjoyable (or unhappy) life.

Froh=gefühl ("...) n ⊛ joyful (or happy) sensation; 2gelaunt a. ⊛ in a happy humour, in a merry mood.

fröhlich (L") [ahd.; * froh] a. ⊛ 1. (voll Behagen, glücklich) cheerful, joyful, glad, happy, fast poet. blithe(some); vgl. froh=sinnig; 2 machen to cheer, to gladden; 2 und guter Dinge sein to be as merry as a grig or as jolly as a sandboy or as happy as a king; in Ler Laune in good spirits. — 2. (gedeihend) prosperous, thriving, flourishing; ich wünsche Ihnen ein Les Neujahr I wish you a happy (or prosperous, glad) new year.

Fröhlichkeit (L") f ⊛ 1. cheerfulness, joy(fulness), gladness, mirth, fast poet. blithe(some)ness; vgl. Frohsinn. — 2. (Lustbarkeit) rejoicing, merriment, F jolly time; (Fest) fête.

froh=locken ("nd und Ls") [mhd. v. *froh u. locken = lecken³ springen] I v/n. (h.) ⊛ ++ abs. to exult, to shout for joy; über et. 2: a) to rejoice at a th.; b) to triumph over a th.; bibl. frohlocket dem Herrn! rejoice in the Lord! — II ~ n ⊛ exultation, shouts pl. of joy, jubilation; rejoicing; triumph.

Froh=mut ("...) m ⊛ = =sinn; 2mütig a. ⊛ = 2sinnig; =natur f (a.) cheerful disposition; =sinn m cheerful spirit, gaiety (of heart), happy (or bright, merry) disposition or nature, F joviality; 2sinnig a. cheerful, gay, bright, merry; F jovial.

fromm (s) [ahd.] I a. ⊛(D3,7) 1. pious; religious; (gottesfürchtig) godly, bibl. auch: Godfearing; (andächtig) devout; (frömmelnd) bigoted; 2 tun to affect piety, to play the saint or the hypocrite; 2 werden to turn pious, oft auch: to be converted or saved. — 2. Ler (wohlgemeinter) Wunsch (good but) vain desire. — 3. (harmlos) harmless, inoffensive; (sanft) gentle; (sentsam) docile; (unschuldig) innocent; Les Pferd

Zeichen (s. S. XVII): F familiär; P Volkssprache; Γ Gaunersprache; ⚘ selten; † alt (auch gestorben); * neu (auch geboren); ++ unrichtig;

[Fromme] — [fruchtbringend]

quiet (or steady) horse; 2 wie ein (Kirchen=)Lamm gentle as a lamb. — II ~e(r) m, ~e f ⑰ 4. pious (or good) (wo)man; coll. die ~en pl. the pious (folk); (Frömmler) bigoted (or saintly) person, F saint. — 5. hist. Ludwig der ~e (Frankenkönig, 814–840) Louis le Débonnaire, Lewis the Pious.

Fromme † (♪) [frommen] m ㊹, nur in: zu Nutz und ~n von // for the good of //, for the benefit of //.

Frömmelei (♪) f ㊻ affected piety; (Heuchelei) hypocrisy, cant(ing); (frömmelnder Eifer) bigotry; (Scheinheiligkeit) sanctimoniousness.

frömmeln (♪) [nhd. 18. sae.] I v/n. (h.) ㉒a. to affect piety, to play the hypocrite or F the saint. — II ~ n ㉓ = Frömmelei. — III 2d p.pr. und a. ⑯ bigoted, canting; (scheinheilig) sanctimonious; F saintly.

frommen (♪) [ahd.] I v/n. (h.) ㉘: e-m 2 to be useful to a p., to avail (or profit, benefit) a p. — II ~ m = Fromme.

Frömmigkeit (♪) f ㊻ (f. fromm) piety; godliness; devoutness; vgl. Frömmelei.

Frömmler (♪) m ㉒, ~in f ㊴ devotee; (Heuchler) hypocrite, vgl. fromm II.

Fron f [ahd. Herren...] I f ㊻ 1. = Frondienst. — II m ⑭ c. ㊷ 2. = ~arbeiter. — 3. = Büttel.

Fron=acker (″...) m ㊳ hist. land (or field) held in socage; =arbeit f compulsory (or unpaid) labour, (fr.) corvée, weitS. drudgery; =arbeiter(in f) m unpaid labourer or hand; drudge.

fronbar (⌣-) a. ⑯ = fronpflichtig.

Fron=bauer (″...) m ㊷ peasant hist. liable to corvée; =bote m (herrschaftlicher Diener) ehm. usher, jetzt: lackey; =dienst [mhd.] m gratuitous service (to be) rendered to the lord of the manor, compulsory service, statute-labour; vgl. Fronarbeit.

Frone (♪) [mhd.] f ㊻ = Frondienst.

fronen (♪) [mhd. f. Fron] I v/n. (h.) ㉘ 1. ehm. (Frondienste tun) to do compulsory (or statute-)labour, or corvée. — 2. fig. frönen (sklavisch dienen) to serve (slavishly); dem Laster, seiner Leidenschaft 2 to be a slave (or a thrall) to ...; j-s Launen 2 to indulge (or humour) a p.'s whims (and fancies). — II ~ n ㉓ 3. = Frönung.

Fröner (♪) m ㉒, ~in f ㊴ = Fronarbeiter(in).

Fron=feste (″...) f ㊷ hist. (Gefängnis) public jail; =frei a. ⑯ exempt from statute-labour; =freiheit f soke, soc; =fuhre f compulsory carting; =geld n money paid in lieu of corvée; =gut n villain socage; =herr m (land)lord entitled to exact corvée (from his tenants), socage-lord; =hof m, =hufe f farm burdened with corvée; =leichnam † [mhd.] m Cath. eccl. the (holy) body of our Lord; =leichnams=fest n Corpus-Christi day; =leichnams=woche f Trinity-week or ember-week; =pflichtig a. hist. subject to statute-labour; =pflicht(igkeit) f liability to statute-labour.

Front (♪) [fr., *lt.] f ㊻ (Vorderseite) front (auch: arch. und ⚔); face; ⚔: ~ machen to make front; to face up; in der ~ steh(e)n to serve at the front (of an army); to stand in the front ranks.

Fronte (♪) [it.] f ㊻ = Front.

Frontispiz (♪″) [fr.] n ㉑a. arch. (Vordergiebel) frontispiece; ⊕ typ. (Vorderblatt) front page.

Front=marsch ⚔ (♪) m ㊷ front-march.

Fronton (frą̨-tǭ') [fr.] m ㊳ arch. (Ziergiebel) fronton, pediment, fastigium.

Frönung (⌣) [frönen] f ㊻ compulsory labour; vgl. Fron-arbeit, -dienst.

Fron=vogt (″...) m ㊷ hist. task-master; ²weise adv. by way of corvée or statute-labour or forced labour.

fror (⌣) (fröre subj.) impf. von frieren.

Frosch (♪) [ahd.: frog] m ㊆a. 1. zo. frog (Rana); Frösche pl.: ♬ ranidæ; zu den Fröschen gehörig: ♬ ranine, batrachoid. — 2. path. (Geschwulst unter der Zunge): ♬ ranula, vet. (geschwollenes Zahnfleisch der Pferde) carney; lampas. — 3. ⊕ Feuerwerkerei: cracker; mach an Wellen: bracket; am Faß: (chime) bracket; carp. an der Leiter: ladder-peg or -wedge; ♪ (Griffende des Violinbogens) nut, lower end of the bow.

Frosch=ader (♪...) f ㊷ anat.: ♬ ranular vein; =arten f/pl.: ♬ batrachians pl.; ²artig a. ⑯ frog-like, ♬ ranoid, batrachian; =biß ♀ m frog-bit (Hydrocharis morsus ranæ); =blut n fig. cold blood.

Fröschchen (♪) n ㉓ (dim. von Frosch) little frog, froggy.

Frosch=eier (♪...) n/pl. ㊷ = =laich; =esser m frog-eater (auch: Spottname der Franzosen); =fang m frog-catching; =fisch m, ichth.: ♬ batrachid, ...us; =gequalk(e) n croaking of frogs; =geschwulst ♬ path. = Frosch 2; =hüpfen n Knabenspiel: leap-frog; =jagd f = =fang; =keule f = =schenkel; =kraut ♀ n = =löffel; =laich m coll. spawn of frogs; =laich=alge ♀: ♬ batrachospermum (B. monilifo'rme); =laich=pilz ♀ m frog-spawn (Leuconosto'c mesenterio'ides); =löffel ♀ m water-plantain (Ali'sma planta'go); =mäuse=krieg m (komisches griech. Epos aus Homers Zeit) batrachomyomachy, ...ia; =quappe f, zo. tadpole; ²reich a. ⑯ abounding in frogs; =sattel m bursaddle; =schenkel m hindleg of a frog; =teich m pond with many frogs.

Frost (♪) [ahd.: frost: frieren] m ㊆a(b). 1. (strenge Kälte) frost(y weather); severe cold; trockener ~ black frost; durch ~ beschädigt frost-bitten; fig. (Winter) winter(y cold); F co. Jack Frost. — 2. (Empfindung der Kälte) chill; (nipping or numbing cold; ich zittere vor ~ I shiver with cold; (Fieber)~ cold shivers pl., ♬ algor. — 3. (Frost-beulen) chilblains pl.; ~ an den Füßen haben to have (or to suffer from) chilled (or chilblains on one's) feet.

Frost=ballen (♪...) m ㊷, mst =beule f chilblain, ♬ pernio; aufgebrochene ~ broken (or open) ch.; =biß m, hort. frost-bite, mehr gebr.: nipping (or biting) cold.

frösteln (♪) ㉒a. I v/a. to chill, bsd. v/impers. es fröstelt there is a slight frost; mich fröstelt (es) I feel (rather) chilly or a (slight) chill, the cold makes me shiver (a little). — II v/n. (h.) ich fröstle = mich fröstelt (f. I). — III ~ n ㉓ (slight) chill; cold shiver.

frostig (♪) a. ⑯. 1. frosty, stärker: frozen; ²es Wetter frosty weather, nipping cold; die Luft ist sehr 2 there is an Arctic nip in the air; fig. (ohne Wärme) cold, icy, bisw. frigid; (ohne Geist) flat, dull. — 2. (Frost empfindend) sensitive to cold; bsd. von Menschen: chilly.

Fröstler (♪) m ㉒, **Fröstling** (♪) m ⑪d. chilly person or mortal, F cold subject, hothouse plant.

Frost=mittel (♪...) n ㊷ (=pflaster n, =salbe f) remedy (plaster, ointment) for chilblains or frost-bitten limbs; =nacht f frosty night; =schade(n) m injury done by frost; =wetter n frosty weather.

Frottier=bürste (⌣″...) f ㊻ für die Haut: flesh-brush.

frottieren (⌣♪) [fr.] I v/a. ㉑ (reiben) to rub; med. auch: to massage, im römischen Bade: to shampoo. — II ~ n ㉓ (f. I) friction; massage, shampooing.

Frottier=tuch (⌣♪) n ㊷ rough bath-towel; rubber (towel).

Frottierung (⌣♪) f ㊻ = frottieren II.

frotzeln F, wienerisch (♪) v/a. ㉒ a. (necken) to tease, chaff, chip, roast.

Frucht (♪t) [ahd.: *lt. fructus] f ㊱ 1. fruit (a fig.); ~ tragen to bear fruit, fig. to produce (or yield) good results pl.; die Früchte des Feldes the fruits pl. of the earth, the produce of the fields or the land; engS. (Getreide) cereals pl.; corn; die 2 sieht schön the corn is in fine condition. — 2. die ersten Früchte the first fruits pl.; eingemachte Früchte preserve (d fruit); geerntete Früchte, oft: crop, harvest; überzuckerte Früchte candied fruit sg.; fig. verbotene Früchte forbidden fruit sg.

Frucht=abgabe (♪t...) f ㊻ corn-duty; =acker m corn-field; =äther m, chm. ether of a fruity flavour or scent, a. fruit-essence; =auge n fruit-bud; =balg ♀ m = Balgkapsel.

fruchtbar (♪t) a. ⑯ fruitful, fruit-bearing, (viel liefernd) prolific; vom Boden: fertile, productive (beide a. vom Geiste 2c.); ein ²es Jahr a year of plenty, F a bumper year; fig. a. copious, teeming; 2er Schriftsteller voluminous (or prolific) writer; 2 m. to make fertile, to fertilize; (befruchten) to fructify; ~keit f ㊻ fruitfulness; fertility, fecundity, productiveness, copiousness.

Frucht=bau (♪t...) m ㊷ growing (of) corn; =baum m fruit-tree; =behälter m, =behältnis n ♀ (Samengehäuse) capsule, pod; vgl. =hülse; =bildung f fructification; =blatt ♀ n: ♬ carpophyll, zf.=gerolltes: ♬ carpel; =blüte ♀ f female flower; =boden m: a) (Kornboden) corn-loft; b) ♀ (Blütenteil, woraus sich die Frucht bildet): ♬ receptacle, placenta, thalamus, torus; ²bodenständig ♀ a. ♬ epigynous, epiclinal; mit den Blüten: ♬ thalamifloral; =bonbons m/pl. acid (or acidulated) drops pl.; =branntwein m fruit-brandy; ²bringend a. fruit-bearing, ♬ fructiferous; fig. productive, fertile; (vorteilhaft) advantageous.

Früchtchen (⌣‿) n ㉓ (dim. von Frucht) 1. small fruit. — 2. F fig. sauberes ~ (ungeratener Mensch) young scamp, fast (or loose) young fellow, scape-grace, F bad lot, P bad'un, rotter.

fruchten (⌣˙) v/n. (h.) ㊾ to bear fruit (a. fig.); (Nutzen bringen) to have effect, to be of (some) use; nicht(s) ~ to be of no avail or no use.

Frucht-entwick(e)lung ⚥ (˙˙˙) f ㉖ fructification; **=erde** f, agr. mould, top soil; **=ertrag** m crop; yield of fruit; **=essend** a. ㊿ feeding on fruit; ⁊ frugivorous; **=essig** m fruit-vinegar; **=feld** n: a) corn-field; b) productive (or fertile) land; **=fleisch** ⚥ n pulp, ⁊ sarcocarp; **=folge** f, agr. rotation (or succession) of crops; **=fresser** m/pl. zo. (Fledermäuse) ⁊ frugivora; **=garten** m orchard; **=gehänge, =gewinde** n, arch. festoon (of fruit); **=gehäuse** ⚥ n: ⁊ pericarp; **=handel** m: a) corn-trade; b) fruit-trade; **=händler(in** f) m: a) corn-merchant or -dealer; b) (Obsthändler[in]) fruiterer; **=haut** f innere: ⁊ endocarp, mittlere: ⁊ mesocarp; **=holz** ⚥ n (Zweige, woran sich die Früchte bilden) fruit-bearing boughs pl.; **=horn** n horn of abundance, ⁊ cornucopia; **=hülle** ⚥ f: ⁊ pericarp, spermotheca; **=hülse** f shell, husk; (Schote) pod; **=kapsel** f = Balg-kapsel; **=käse** m (getrocknete Obstmarmelade) dried preserve; **=keim** m: a) ⚥ germ; b) physiol.: ⁊ embryo; **=kelch** ⚥ m calyx enveloping the grain; **=kern** m kernel, des Kernobstes: pip, des Steinobstes: stone; **=knoten** ⚥ m: ⁊ ovary; den ~ umgebend: ⁊ perigynous; **=korb** [m fruit-basket; arch. des korinthischen Kapitells: corbel; **=korn** n seed-corn; **=krone** ⚥ f: ⁊ aigret(te); **=kundige(r)** m: ⁊ carpologist; **=lager** ⚥ n Flechten: ⁊ thalamus, apothecium, der Hautpilze: ⁊ hymen(i)ophore; **=land** n corn-land; **=lehre** f: ⁊ carpology.

Früchtlein (⌣‿) n ㉓ = Früchtchen.

Frucht-lese (˙˙˙) f ㉖ gathering (or picking) of fruit; **=los** a. ㊿ without fruit, weitS. unproductive; fig. (auch adv.) fruitless(ly), useless(ly), in-effectual(ly), unsuccessful(ly); adv. (vergebens) in vain; **=losigkeit** f (s. ²los) unproductiveness; fruitlessness, use-lessness; **=mangel** m scarcity of corn or fruit; **=markt** m fruit- (or corn-) market; **=mus** n (fruit-)preserve, jam; **=nießer(in** f) m jur.: ⁊ usufructuary; **=nießung** f: ⁊ usufruct; ²reich a. rich in fruit; fig. fruitful; successful; **=reife** f ripening of fruit; (Jahreszeit) fruit-season ⚥: ⁊ fructescence; **=saft** m juice of fruit; eingekochter: jam, jelly; **=säure** f, chm. acid contained in fruit(s;) **=schale** f: a) fruit-dish, als Tafelschmuck: centre-piece or -dish; b) peel; c) ⚥ (Samenbalg) pod; **=schuppen** ⚥ m/pl. der Koniferen: squamæ pl.; **=speicher** m = boden n; **=staude** f = strauch; **=stein** m = versteinerung; **=stiel** m fruit-stalk, ⁊ podocarp; **=strauch** m fruit-bearing shrub; **=stück** n, paint. fr.-painting or -piece; ²tragend a. = bringend; **=träger** ⚥ m: ⁊ carpophore; **=versteinerung** f: ⁊ carpolite; **=wasser**

n, physiol.: ⁊ amniotic liquor; **=wechsel** m = folge; **=wein** m (Obstwein) wine made of fruit, home-made (or British) wine; **=zins** m rent paid in corn; **=zucker** m fruit- (or grape-) sugar, ⁊ fructose, glucose ($C_6H_{12}O_6$).

frug ⁺⁺, bsd. norbb. (⌣) impf. von fragen.

frugal (‿⌣́) [it.] a. ㊿ (mäßig) frugal; (einfach) plain, simple; s. genügsam.

Frugalität (‿‿⌣́) f ㊻ frugality; plainness, simplicity; s. Genügsamkeit.

früge ⁺⁺, bsd. norbb. (⌣) subj. impf. v. fragen.

früh (⌣) [ahd.: grch. πρωΐ] a. ㊿, bsd. als adv. gbr. 1. early (in the day or the year); in good time; betimes; so ~ wie möglich as early (or as soon as) possible; es ist noch ganz ~ we are in excellent time; er kam ~ an he came (or was) early; gestern ~ yesterday morning; heute ~ early this morning; morgen ~ to-morrow morning; morgens ~ early (F the first thing) in the morning; ~ (um) sechs Uhr at six in the morning; ~ und spät from morning till night; at all hours (of the day). — 2. mit dem ~en Tage abwandern to start in the early morning or betimes; stets ~ aufstehen to be an early riser or F co. an early bird (aber einmal ~ aufstehen to rise [or get up] early; in ²(er)en Zeiten in former times, in times past; formerly. — 3. (vor der rechten Zeit) (over-)hasty, hurried; sich ~ entwickelnd precocious, auf künstlichem Wege: premature; er sank in ein ~es Grab he found an early death, he met with an untimely end.

Früh-apfel (˙˙˙) m ㊻ early (or summer-)apple; **=arbeit** f (early) morning's work; **=auf(steher)** m early riser, F early bird; **=beet** n, hort. hot- (or forcing-)bed; **=birne** f early (or summer-)pear.

Frühe¹ (⌣) f ㊽ (early) morning; (Tagesanbruch) dawn (of day); in aller ~ aufbrechen to start quite early or in the early (or small) hours of the morning or at break of day.

frühe² ⁼ (⌣) a. ㊿ s. früh.

früher (⌣) comp. v. früh 1. (s. früh 1) earlier, sooner; in better time; (vorhergehend) prior (or anterior) to; acht Tage ~ a week before that, a week previously or earlier; in ~ als acht Tagen in less than a week; ich kam ~ als er I was there before him; je ~, desto besser, auch: je ~, je lieber the sooner the better; ~ oder später sooner or later, some day or other. — 2. (ehemals) formerly, in former days or times; wir haben ~ davon gesprochen we have previously (or already) spoken of it; ein ~er Fall a previous case; jur. a precedent; der ~e (verstorbene) Inhaber the late occupier; die ~en (vorigen) Minister the former ministers pl.; ⚤ die ~e Handelsfirma the old firm.

Früh-erbsen (˙˙˙) f/pl. ㊻ early peas pl.; **=ernte** f early harvest; (Vor-ernte) first crop. [riority.|

Früher-sein (˙˙‿‿) n ㉓ priority; anteriority.

früh(e)st (‿) sup. v. früh; er hat die ~en Nachrichten (er weiß es am ersten) he gets the earliest (or first) news; die

~en (ältesten) Zeiten the most distant (or most remote) ages; die ~en Völker the oldest (or most ancient) nations pl.; wer steht am ~en auf? who rises first?, who is the earliest riser? ~ens adv. at the earliest; zum ~en, mit dem ~en at the earliest moment.

Früh-gebet (˙˙˙) n ㊻ early (or morning-)prayer or devotions pl.; **=geburt** f premature birth; (Fehlgeburt) miscarriage, ⁊ abortion; **=gottesdienst** m early service, Cath.eccl.a.: matins pl.; **=jahr** [ndd.] n = Frühling; **=kartoffeln** f/pl. early potatoes pl.; **=kirche** f = gottesdienst; ²klug a. ㊿ precocious or forward (child); **=konzert** n matinée.

Frühling (⌣) [nhd. 15. sæc.] m ⓐd. 1. (Lenz) spring (of the year); ~ des Lebens spring (or prime) of life; auf den ~ bezüglich vernal. — 2. (ant. Spätling) calf, lamb, &c. born early in the year. — 3. (zu früh geborenes Kind) child born before its time, premature birth.

Frühlings-anfang (˙˙˙) m ㊻ (21. März) commencement of spring; **=äquinoctium** n = nachtgleiche; **=bedarf** ⚥ m spring-demand, spring-goods pl.

frühlingshaft (˙˙˙) a. ㊿ spring-like.

Frühlings-hauch (˙˙˙) m ㊻ breath of spring; vernal breeze; **=luft** f vernal air; ²mäßig a. ㊿ vernal; **=morgen** m spring-morning; **=nachtgleiche** f, ast. vernal equinox; **=punkt** m, ast. vernal point; **=saat** f = Frühsaat; **=safran** ⚥ m spring-crocus (Crocus vernus); **=saft** m der Bäume: sap of trees rising in the early spring; **=tag** m sp.-day; **=waren** ⚥ f/pl. spring-goods pl.; **=wetter** n spring-weather; **=zeichen** n/pl., ast. vernal signs pl.; **=zeit** f spring-time.

Früh-messe (˙˙˙) f ㊻ =mette f Cath. eccl. early mass, matins pl.; ²morgendlich ⚐ a. ㊿ ⁊ matutinal; ²morgens adv. early in the (or in the early hours of the) morning, in the early morning; **=obst** n early (or forward) fruit; **=prediger** m, **=predigt** f morning-preacher, -sermon; **=regen** m early shower; ²reif a.: a) early (ripe), premature; b) = klug; **=reife** f precociousness, precocity, forwardness; **=rot** n=Morgenr.; **=saat** f, agr. spring-seed or -sowing; **=schoppen** m morning pint (of ale).

frühstens ⚐ (⌣) f. früh(e)st am Schluß.

Frühstück (˙˙) [nhd.] n ⓑc. breakfast; zweites ~ lunch(eon).

frühstücken (˙˙‿) v/n. (h.) und v/a. ㊾ to (eat one's) breakfast; was haben Sie gefrühstückt? what have you had (or did you have) for breakfast?; man soll gut ~ you should take (or eat) a good breakfast or lay a good foundation.

Frühstücks-tisch (˙˙˙) m ㊻ breakfast-table; **=zeit** f breakfast-time.

Früh-stunde (˙˙˙) f ㊻ early (in geh. Spr.: matutinal) hour; **=tau** m morning-dew; **=trunk** m morning-draught or -potion; ²zeitig a. ㊿ early, adv. a. betimes; (rasch) hasty; (zu früh) untimely; (voreilig) precipitate; **=zeitigkeit** f earliness; hastiness; untimeliness; vgl. =reife; **=zug** m early train.

ft (⌣) int. bei raschem Verschwinden, zB.: ~, weg war er! whisk, and he was gone.

[**Fuchs**] — 395 — [**fühlen**]

Fuchs (⁀ᵗᶻ) [ahd.: fox] m ⓐa. 1. a) fox (*Canis Vulpes*); männlicher ~ he-fox, weiblicher ~, **Füchsin** f she-fox, vixen; junger ~, a. *dim.* **Füchschen, Füchslein** n young fox, fox's cub; den ~ jagen to go fox-hunting; b) = **Fuchspelz**. — 2. *fig.* schlauer ~ (listige Person) sly (or cunning) fox, F artful dodger; Reineke ~ Reynard; Knabenspiel: ~ aus dem Loch hide-fox; bei Pfänderspielen: stirbt der ~, so gilt der Balg Jack's alive; Sprichw. alte Füchse fängt man nicht (leicht) old birds are not caught with chaff. — 3. (Rot-)~ (Pferd) chestnut horse. — 4. (Rothaarige[r]) red-haired (or F carroty) p., F ginger(-pate). — 5. [nhd. 1700] burschikos: (neuer Student) freshman; vgl. Brandfuchs d. — 6. *ent.* (Schmetterling) tortoise-shell (*Vanessa*). — 7. (Goldstück) gold-coin; P yellow boy. — 8. Billard: (zufälliger Treffer) F fluke. — 9. ⊕ *metall.* (Abzugskanal zum Schlot) snorehole (of a furnace).
Fuchs-affe (⁀ᵗᶻ...) m ⓑ *zo.* = Maki; **=angel** f = **=eisen**; **⁀artig** a. ⓖ foxlike, ⁊ vulpine; **=balg** m fox-skin; **=bau** m, *hunt.* fox-earth or -hole; kennel; **=beere** ⁊ f = Einbeere.
Füchschen (⁀ᵗᶻ) n ⓘ f. **Fuchs** 1 a.
Fuchs=eisen (⁀ᵗᶻ...) n ⓑ (Falle) fox-trap.
fuchsen (⁀ᵗᶻ) v/a. u. v/n. (h.) ⓜ meist F *fig.* 1. (ärgern, foppen) to vex, annoy, tease; das fuchst mich it vexes (or provokes) me; F I feel mad about it; sich über et. (arg) ~ to be (greatly) vexed (or annoyed) at a th. — 2. (betrügen) to deceive; (prellen) to cheat, trick, diddle, take in, best. — 3. Billard: einen Ball ~ (durch Zufall machen) to (make a) fluke.
Fuchser, Füchser F (⁀ᵗᶻ...) m ⓑ 1. ● (Börsenmakler) stockbroker, stockjobber. — 2. Billard: (s. fuchsen 3) one who (wins by) flukes; **Fuchserei** (⁀ᵗᶻᵘ) f ⓖ fluking.
Fuchs=falle (⁀ᵗᶻ...) f = **=eisen**; **=fell** n = **=balg**; **=grube** f = **=bau**; **=haar** n: a) fox's hair; b) von Menschen: red (F ginger) hair; **=höhle** f = **=bau**.
Fuchsia ⁊ (⁀ᵗᶻⁱ) [Fuchsia, dtsch. Botaniker, 1501—66] f ⓖ fuchsia.
fuchsicht (⁀ᵗᶻ) a. ⓖ = fuchsig 2.
fuchsig (⁀ᵗᶻ) a. ⓖ 1. fox-like. — 2. (fuchsrot) red as a fox; ⓖ werden (verscheißen) von Samt 2c.: to turn rusty or brown. — 3. F = fuchs(teufels)wild.
Fuchsin ⁊ (⁀ᵗᶻⁱ) [Fuchsia] n ⓒ *chm.* (rote Anilinfarbe) fuchsin(e).
Füchsin (⁀ᵗᶻ) [ahd.: vixen] f ⓖ f. **Fuchs** 1 a.
Fuchs=jagd (⁀ᵗᶻ...) f ⓑ fox-hunt(ing); auf die ~ gehen to go fox-hunting; eine ~ mitmachen to ride to (or follow the) hounds; **=jäger** m fox-hunter.
Füchslein (⁀ᵗᶻ) n ⓘ f. **Fuchs** 1 a.
Fuchs=loch (⁀ᵗᶻ...) n ⓑ = **=bau**; **=major** m burschikos: senior student who supervises the freshmen; **=pelz** m: a) (fur made of) fox-skin; b) coat lined with fox-skin; den ~ anziehen (List gebrauchen) to play the fox, to use cunning; **=prellen** n: a) *hunt.* fox-tossing; b) burschik. auf amerik. Univ.: hazing; **=räude** f, *path.* fox-evil, ⁊ alopecia; **⁀rot** a. ⓖ fox-coloured, F carroty; **=scheck(e)** f m

chestnut-pied horse; **=schrot** m, n, *hunt.* swan-shot; **=schwanz** m: a) foxtail, *hunt.* (fox-)brush; den ~ streichen = **=schwänze(l)n**; b) ⁊ love-lies-bleeding (*Amarantus*); c) ⊕ (Art Säge) pad- (or fox-)saw; **=schwänze(l)n** v/n. (h.) ⓑ (⁀a.).*.*.* (kriechend schmeicheln, schmarotzen) to cajole, fawn, wheedle (round), toady; **=schwänzer(in** ⁊) m cajoler, fawner, wheedler; (Schmarotzer) sycophant, toad-eater, toady; **=schwänzerei** f cajoling; sycophancy, toadyism; **=schwänzerisch** a. cajoling, fawning; toadying; **=schwanz=gras** ⁊ n foxtail (*Alopecurus*); **=stute** f chestnut mare; **⁀(teufels)wild** F a. furious, mad (with anger), in high dudgeon; in a fearful temper, F savage;; **=traube** f Am. fox-grape (*Vitis labrusca* u. *vulpina*).
Fuchtel (⁀ᵗᶻ) [nhd.; * fechten] f ⓖ 1. ⚔ bsd. *ehm.* (Degen zum Flachhauen) flat blade for military punishment; weitS. (Zuchtrute) scourge, rod, ferule; *fig.* e-n unter der ~ (unter scharfer Zucht) halten to keep a p. under an iron rod, to keep a tight (or strict) hand over a p.; unter j-s ~ stehen to be under a p.'s thumb, to be at a p.'s beck and call. — 2. (Degen überhaupt) sword.
fuchteln (⁀ᵗᶻ) v/a. I v/n. (h.) to brandish one's sword; mit den Händen ~ to gesticulate (violently or wildly), to throw one's hands about. — II v/a. einen ~ to strike a p. with the flat blade; weitS. (züchtigen) to chastise, whip, cane, thrash, tan.
Fuchtler (⁀ᵗᶻ) m ⓖ 1. (Fechter) swordsman. — 2. (Raufbold) brawler, bully. — 3. (Prügler), etwa: caner, thrasher.
Fuder (⁀̆ᵘ) [ahd.] n ⓑ 1. (Fuhre) ~ Holz cart- (or waggon-)load of wood. — 2. Flüssigkeitsmaß: ~ Wein, etwa: tun of wine. loads.}
fuder=weise (⁀̆ᵘ⁀̆⁀) *adv.* by tuns or cart-
Fug (⁀) [mhd.; * fügen] m ⓒc. (Erlaubnis) permission; (Recht) right; mit ~ und Recht with full authority or right or license, by right, (lt.) *de jure*.
Fuge¹ (⁀̆ᵘ) [mhd.; * fügen] f ⓖ 1. ⊕ (Gelent) joint, juncture; (Zapfenloch) mortise; (Schlitz) slit, (Kerbe) tally, notch; (Falz) rabbet, groove. — 2. *anat.* (Naht) suture; ⁊ (Verwachsungsstelle der Fruchthälften) commissure. — 3. Redewendungen: aus den ~n bringen to disjoint, to dislocate; *auch fig.* to put out of joint or out of gear; aus den ~n gehn (or), weichen to come apart; *fig.* to go to rack and ruin, to come to grief.
Fuge² (⁀̆ᵘ) [it. *fuga* Flucht] f ⓖ fugue; in Form einer ~ fugued.
Füge=bank (⁀̆ᵘ...) f ⊕ *carp.* jointer; **=hobel** m, *join.* long-plane.
fugen ⊕ (⁀̆ᵘ) v/a. ⓑ 1. Tischlerei 2c.: Bretter an=ea.= od. zs.=⁀ to join (or groove, rabbet) ...; in=ea.=⁀ to fit into each other. — 2. Maurerei Fugen verstreichen) to point, to flush.
fügen (⁀̆ᵘ) [ahd.] ⊕ I v/a. 1. (zusammensetzen) to join (together), to put together; (aufrichten) to erect, to raise; an=ea.=⁀ to put (or arrange) side by side; in=ea.=⁀ to fit together; zu (hinzu=) ⁀ to add. — 2. (passend ordnen) to regulate; *rel.* to dispense; wie Gott es fügt, a. as God wills or ordains. — II sich ⁀ v/refl. 3. sich an oder zu et. ⁀ (daran passen) to fit a th.; sich in=ea.=⁀ to fit into each other; *fig.* oft ⁀ die Dinge sich so, daß // it often happens in such a way that //. — 4. *fig.* (sich bequemen) to accommodate (or reconcile) o.s. to, to yield to, to acquiesce in; sich ins Unabänderliche ⁀ to put up with the inevitable; sich in den Willen Gottes ⁀ to resign o.s. (or to bow) to the will of God; *abs.* sich ⁀ to submit, to give way. — 5. v/impers. es fügt sich (begibt sich) daß // it so happens (or comes to pass) that //; es fügte sich glücklich, daß // by good fortune it chanced (or luck would have it) that //.
fugenhaft ♪ (⁀̆ᵘ⁀) [**Fuge**²] a. ⓖ fugued, like (or in the style of) a fugue.
Fugen=komponist ♪ (⁀̆ᵘ⁀...) m ⓖ fuguist.
Fugen=schnitt ⊕ (⁀̆ᵘ⁀...) m ⓑ Tischlerei 2c.: joint-cut; **=verstreichung** ⊕ f Maurerei: pointing, flushing.
Füge=wort (⁀̆ᵘ⁀) n ⓑ *gr.* conjunction.
fugieren ♪ (⁀⁀̆ᵘ⁀) [**Fuge**²] v/a. ⓖ to compose (or write) in the style of a fugue.
Fug=kelle ⊕ f ⓖ Maurerei: filling-trowel.
füglich (⁀̆ᵘ) [mhd.] a. ⓖ, meist *adv.* (paßlich) convenient(ly), appropriate(ly); (mit Recht) rightly, justly, reasonably; (gelegentlich) opportune(ly); er hätte ⁀ (im Grunde) nachgeben können he might as well have yielded; was nützen ⁀ die paar Groschen? of what use are really the few pence?; er ist ⁀ nur ein Knabe he is, after all, only a boy; **~keit** f (⁀̆ᵘ⁀) ⓖ convenience; reasonableness; opportuneness.
fug=los (⁀) a. ⓖ without reason, unreasonable; (unbefugt) incompetent; unauthorized; **Fug=losigkeit** (⁀̆ᵘ⁀) f ⓖ unreasonableness; incompetence.
fügsam (⁀̆) a. ⓖ accommodating; (lentsam) tractable, docile, manageable; (nachgiebig) yielding, pliant; (folgsam) submissive, meek; **~keit** (⁀̆⁀⁀) f ⓖ tractableness, docility, manageableness; yieldingness, pliancy; submissiveness, meekness.
Fügung (⁀̆ᵘ) f ⓖ 1. (das Fügen und das Gefügte) joining, fitting (together), &c. (s. fügen 1). — 2. *gr.* ~ der Worte arrangement (or order) of words. — 3. ~ in den Willen j-s submission to ... — 4. (Schickung) dispensation (of Providence); durch göttliche ~ by divine ordinance or decree; durch glückliche ~ der Umstände by a happy combination of circumstances, as (good) luck would have it. — 5. (Gliederung) articulation.
fühlbar (⁀̆) a. ⓖ sensible; bsd.: a) körperlich: tangible; (greifbar) palpable; b) geistig: perceptible, noticeable; ⁀e Abnahme marked (or decided) decrease; ⁀er (empfindlicher) Verlust serious (or grievous) loss; der Winter macht sich ⁀ ... makes itself felt; **~keit** (⁀⁀⁀) f ⓖ sensibility; tangibleness; palpableness; perceptibility.
fühlen (⁀̆) [ndd. (ahd.): feel] ⓑ I v/a. 1. to feel; (berühren) to touch; e-m (auch v/n. e-m an) den Puls ⁀ to feel a p.'s pulse (auch *fig.*); et. schmerzhaft (od. emp-

---
⁊ scientific; ⁊ botanical; ⁊ geography; ⊕ machinery; ⁊ mining; ⚔ military; ⚓ marine; ● commercial; ✉ postal; 🚂 railway.

[**Fühler**] — 396 — [**Führung**]

findlich) ~ to smart under a th.; Reue über et. ~ to repent a th.; wir wollen es ihn ~ lassen we'll make him smart for it; ich drücke Ihnen m-n tief gefühlten Dank aus I render you my most heart-felt (or deep-felt, sincerest) thanks. — **II** sich ~ v/refl. **2.** sich glücklich, behaglich ~ to feel happy, comfortable; wir ~ uns fremd we feel strange, we do not feel at home; er fühlt sich nicht ganz wohl he does not feel quite well or quite himself; wie ~ Sie sich heute? how do you feel today?; sich et. ~, abs. sich ~ (das Gefühl seines Wertes haben) to feel o.s. somebody, to be self-conscious. — **3.** sich (tappend) wohin ~ to grope one's way to a place. — **4.** das fühlt sich it can be felt or noticed; it is perceptible or noticeable. — **III** v/n. (h.) **5.** abs. (Gefühl haben) to feel, to be endowed with feeling; sehr fein ~ to have very delicate feeling(s), to be highly sensitive; Sprichw. wer nicht hören will, muß ~ (Strafe leiden), etwa: he who will not be taught must suffer. — **6.** e-m an den Puls ~ f. 1; fig. e-m auf den Zahn ~ to sound a p.('s intentions), F to draw a p. — **IV** ~ n ㉓ **7.** = Fühlung 1.

Fühler (′‿) m ㉒ **1.** (auch: ~**in** f ㊼) feeling person. — **2.** ent., &c. = Fühlfaden, Fühlhorn. — **3.** fig. seine ~ ausstrecken (vorsichtig verfahren) F to send out a feeler; to sound; to feel one's way.

Fühl=faden (″...) m ㉒ ent., &c. feeler, palp, ⚤ tentacle, mit =fäden versehen: ⚤ tentacled, tentaculiferous; =**farn** m sensitive fern (Onocle'a sensi'bilis); =**hebel** m (zum Erkennen sehr kleiner Bewegungen) nipper-lever; =**horn** n antenna, kleines ~: ⚤ antennula; ~**los** a. ㊻ gefühllos.

Fühlung (′‿) f ㊻ **1.** touch. — **2.** contact; ⚔, &c. mit e-m ~ h. to be in touch with a p.; lose, enge ~ gewinnen to get into slight, close contact or touch; fig. ~ nehmen to send out a feeler.

fuhr (′) ind. impf. von fahren.

Fuhre (′‿) [ahd.; *fahren] f ㊸ **1.** (Fahren) carting, carrying, conveyance, carriage, ⚤ vecture. — **2.** (Ladung) cart- (or wagon-)load, cartful. — **3.** ⚙ mit der ~, per ~ senden to send by road or by wheel. — **4.** conveyance, cart. — **5.** = Fuhrlohn.

führe(n¹ pl.) (′‿) subj. impf. v. fahren.

führen² (′‿) [ahd.: fahren] **I** v/a. ㊇ **1.** to lead; e-m Ziele zu: to conduct, to guide; in e-r bestimmten Richtung: to direct; als Lotse: to pilot; ein Kind an der Hand ~ to lead (or take) ... by the hand; f. Eis 1; e-n auf den rechten Weg ~ to direct a p., to put a p. on the right path; auf die Spur ~ to put on the (right) track; irre ~ to misdirect, to misguide, to lead astray; hinters Licht ~ to deceive, F to take in; Gebet: führe uns nicht in Versuchung! lead us not into temptation!; e-m et. zu Gemüte ~ to impress (or urge) a th. on (or to instil a th. into) a p.; das Glas, die Speisen zum Munde ~ to put the food into one's mouth; eine Dame zu Tische ~ to take ... in to dinner; ⚔ das Regiment ~ to command the regiment; Soldaten ins Treffen ~ to lead soldiers into battle or to the charge; 🚂 die Lokomotive ~ to drive the engine; von Dingen: das führt zu nichts that leads to nothing; wohin (a. wozu) soll das ~? what is the purpose (or purport, use) of it?; es würde mich zu weit führen, wenn // it would lead me too far if //. — **2.** (mit sich bringen) sie ~ ihr Handwerkszeug bei sich they carry (or take) their tools with them; sie ~ Geld bei sich they carry (or have) money about them; die Bienen ~ einen Stachel ... are provided (or armed) with stings. — **3.** (tragen) einen Löwen im Wappen ~ to bear (or support) ... in one's coat-of-arms; e-n Namen, Titel ~ to bear a name, title, to go by a (certain) name, title; e-n falschen Namen ~ to go under a false name; ⚓ von Kriegsschiffen: die Flagge eines Admirals ~ to fly the Admiral's flag; fig. et. im Schilde, im Sinne ~ to harbour a design, to have s.th. in view. — **4.** (befördern) aus Spanien wird Wolle nach England geführt England imports wool from Spain. — **5.** ⚙ eine Ware ~ (zum Verkaufe haben) to have goods in stock or for sale; diese Hütte ~ wir nicht we do not keep ... (in stock); mancherlei Ware ~ to stock (or deal in) sundry articles. — **6.** (handhaben) die Feder gut ~ to wield a light (or skilful) pen, to be a clever writer; den Pinsel ~ to handle the brush, to paint (pictures); das Schwert gut ~ to be a fine (or good) swordsman. — **7.** (herstellen, ausführen) einen Damm ~ to construct (or make) a dike; Mauern um die Stadt ~ to build walls round ...; die Mauern höher ~ to raise ...; et. weiter (oder fort) ~ to continue (or to go on with) a th.; e-n Streich ~ to strike a blow. — **8.** (verwalten, in Ordnung oder Gang halten oder bringen) ein Amt ~ to fill a post; die Aufsicht über et. ~ to superintend a th.; den Befehl über Truppen ~ to be in command of troops, &c.; e-n Beweis ~ to furnish a proof; ⚙ Buch ~, die (Handlungs=) Bücher ~ to do the bookkeeping, to keep the books; ein Geschäft, einen Handel ~ to carry on a (house of) business, a trade; ein Gespräch mit e-m ~ to carry on a conversation with a p.; die Haushaltung ~ to keep house; Klage über e-n ~ to lodge a complaint against a p.; das Komman'do ~ to (hold the) command; die Korresponde'nz ~ to act as correspondent; eine Korresponde'nz mit e-m ~ to carry on a correspondence with a p.; Krieg mit einem ~ to wage war with a p.; ein eingezogenes (elendes) Leben ~ to lead a retired life (a miserable existence); ein Protoko'll ~ to take down the minutes; einen Proze'ß ~: a) von Parteien: to carry on a lawsuit; b) von Advokaten: to conduct a case; die Rechnung ~ to keep the accounts; gemeine Reden ~ to use foul language; hochfahrende Reden ~ to talk big; die Regierung, das Regiment ~, fig. das Ruder ~ to hold the reins of government, to steer the helm of state; j-s Sache ~ to plead a p.'s cause; seine Sache selbst ~ to defend one's own case, weit. to manage one's own affairs; eine Untersuchung ~ to hold (or conduct) an inquiry; den Vorsitz ~ to preside, to be in the chair; das Wort ~ to be (head) spokesman; beständig das Wort ~ to lead the conversation; das große Wort im Hause ~ to rule the roost or roast, F to lay down the law. — **9.** mit leblosem Subjekt, z.B.: der Wind führte uns den Staub in die Augen ... sent (or drove) the dust into our eyes; der Fluß führt (enthält) Muscheln ... carries (or contains) mussels; der Kreuzer führt 20 Geschütze the cruiser ships (or mounts) twenty guns. — **II** v/n. (h.) **10.** Sport beim Rennen: Persimmon führte P. was leading or first, P. led the way or the van or the field. — **III** ~ n ㉓ **11.** = Führung 1.

Führer (′‿) m ㉒ **I** von Personen: ~ m, ~**in** f ㊼ **1.** (f. führen 1) leader; conductor, guide, als Buchtitel: Guide; (Haupt, Vorsteher) head, commander, chief; (Leiter) director; ⚙ (Verwalter[in]) manager(ess f); ⚓ steersman; ⚔ ~ (Vordermann) e-r Rotte file-leader; Fußballspiel: captain. — **II** von Sachen: nur m **2.** ♪ theme (or motive, motif) of a fugue. — **3.** ⊕ mach. guide.

Führer=amt (′‿...) n ㉒ office of guide, &c.; leadership, conductorship; ~**los** a. ㊻ without a leader.

Führerschaft (′‿‿) f ㊻ **1.** (f. Führer I) leadership; conductorship, guidance; (Herrschaft) headship, command; (Leitung) direction. — **2.** (sämtliche Führer) all the leaders pl., &c.

Fuhr=frone (″...) f ㊸ hist. corvée labour with cart and horse; =**geld** n = =**lohn**; =**gelegenheit** f means of conveyance; =**herr** m owner of carts or carriages; carrier; (Droschkenbesitzer) cab-owner.

führig (′‿) a. ㊻ hunt. v. Jagdhunden: easily led.

Fuhr=knecht (″...) m ㉒ carter('s man); =**leute** pl. von =mann; =**lohn** m cartage, carriage; charges pl. of conveyance.

Fuhr=mann (″‿) m ㉒ **1.** carter, carman, wagoner; (Kutscher) coachman, driver. — **2.** ast. Wagoner, Auriga.

Fuhrmanns=kittel (″‿...) m ㉒ carter's frock or smock; =**peitsche** f cart (or driving-, driver's) whip; =**pferd** n carthorse; =**wagen** m goods-van, wagon.

Fuhr=park ⚔ (″‿) m ㉒ park.

Führung (′‿) f ㊻ **1.** (f. führen) leading, conduct, guidance; ⊙ der Lokomotive: driving of the engine; ⚙ der Bücher: keeping of books; der Geschäfte: management of affairs; der Feder: wielding of the pen, Fco. quill-driving; ♪ des Bogens: management of the bow; (Leitung) direction; ⚔ (Befehl) command; ⚔ mit der ~ beauftragt holding brevet rank or local rank. — **2.** (Aufführung) behaviour, conduct; gute, schlechte ~ good, bad conduct. — **3.** ⊕ mach. (Vorrichtung, die einem Maschinenteil eine bestimmte Richtung gibt) guide.

Zeichen (f. S. XVII): F familiär; P Volkssprache; ┌ Gaunersprache; ~ selten; † alt (auch gestorben); * neu (auch geboren); ⁙ unrichtig;

[Führungsbuch] — 397 — [fünfstimmig]

Führungs-buch (ᵘ...) n ⓢ = Dienstbuch; ⚔ ~ eines Soldaten soldier's small book or pocket-ledger; **-mannschaft** ⚓ f (boat's crew); **-zeugnis** n certificate of (good) conduct; reference; für Gesinde ꝛc.: character.

Fuhr-unternehmer (ᵘ...) m ⓢ carrier; **-weg** m carriage-road; highway; **-werk** n vehicle, carriage; zweirädriges für Fracht: cart, für Personen: dog-cart, trap, chaise, vgl. Wagen; vierrädriges: wagon, van, dray, für Landpartien ꝛc.: break, char-à-banc, drag; öffentliche ~e public conveyances pl.; zu e-m ~ gehörig vehicular; **⁀werfen** F v/a. v/n. ⓢ*.* to drive about (in a carriage); **-wesen** n carting, carrying (-trade), conveyance; carriage-traffic; coll. carts, carriages pl.; ⚔ wagon-train.

Fulbe (ᵘ) npr/pl. (Volk im Sudan) Fulahs.

Fulgurit ⚛ (ᵘᴸ) [lt.] m ⓒ. min. (Blitzröhre) fulgurite, sand-tube.

Füll-apparat ⚙ (ᵘ...) m ⓒ: a) bsd. mach. feeding-apparatus, feeder; b) für Flaschen: bottle-charger; bottling machine; **-bier** n beer required to fill up the cask; **-brett** n, join. panel (-board).

Fülle (ᵘᴸ) [ahd.: fill; * voll] f ⁴⁸ 1. (reicher Vorrat) plenty, abundance, rich store; übermäßige: profusion, overflow, exuberance; die Hülle und ~ plenty (or enough) and to spare; Geld in Hülle und ~ haben to be rolling in wealth; eine ~ tiefer Gedanken a fund of deep reflection, a mine of thought; aus der ~ seines Herzens sprechen to speak from the depth of one's heart. — 2. (Vollsein) fulness; körperliche ~ stoutness, plumpness, F rotundity; ~ der Sprache, des Ausdrucks copiousness of language, of expression; ~ der Stimme richness of the voice.

füllen¹ (ᵘᴸ) [ahd.: fill, ; * voll] ⓢ I v/a. und sich ⁀ v/refl. 1. to fill (up); wieder ⁀ to replenish; sich ⁀ to fill, to become full; ein Glas bis obenhin ⁀ to fill ... to the brim or to overflowing; e-n Luftballon ⁀ to fill (or inflate) a balloon; seinen Weinkeller ⁀ to stock one's cellar; sich (dat.) den Leib, den Magen ⁀ to eat one's fill, bibl. to fill one's belly; thea. ein wohlgefülltes Haus a well-filled (or a crowded) house. — 2. Kochkunst: eine Kalbsbrust ꝛc. ⁀ to stuff ... — 3. (gießen, schöpfen) Wasser in den Eimer ⁀ to pour water into the pail; Wasser aus der Tonne ⁀ to draw water from the tub; auf (ob. in) Flaschen ⁀ to bottle; in Fässer ⁀ to fill into barrels, to barrel; eine Tonne leer (voll) ⁀ to empty, fill a tub. — 4. hort. gefüllte Blumen double ... — II ~ n ⓢ 5. = Füllung 1.

Füllen² (ᵘᴸ) [ahd.: filly] n ⓢ foal; männliches: colt; weibliches: filly.

füllen³ (ᵘᴸ) v/n. (h.) ⓢ = fohlen.

Füllen-stute (ᵘ...) f ⓒ breeding- (or brood-)mare; **-zahn** m colt's tooth; **-zucht** f breeding of foals, weitS. horse-breeding, rearing of a stud.

Füll-erde (ᵘ...) f ⓒ filling-earth; **-feder(halter** m) f fountain-pen; **-haar** n (hair for) stuffing; **-horn** n horn of plenty, ⚛ cornucopia; **-mauer**

-werk n, arch. = **-werk** a; **-ofen** m magazine-stove, self-filling stove.

Füllsel (ᵘᴸ) [mhd.] n ⓒ 1. Kocht.: stuffing; (Füllfleisch) forcemeat. — 2. = Lückenbüßer.

Füll-steine (ᵘ...) m/pl. ⓒ arch. expletives pl.; vgl. **-werk** a; **-stimme** ♪ f (it.) ripieno.

Füllung (ᵘᴸ) f ⁴⁶ 1. (s. füllen 1) filling; des Luftballons auch: inflation; (s. 2) Kochkunst: stuffing; vgl. Füllsel. — 2. ⚔ (Ladung) charge; ~ der Hohlgeschosse explosive charge. — 3. ⓞ: a) Tischlerei: casing; (einer Tür) panel(ling); b) Maurerei: (einer Mauer) packing.

Füllungs-planken ⚓ (ᵘ...) f/pl. ⓒ filling-in boards pl., planks pl. between the wales.

Füll-wein (ᵘ...) m ⓒ wine required to fill up the cask; **-werk** n: a) arch. filling-in work, rubbie-work; b) Schrifttum: padding; **-wort, -wörtchen** n expletive. [to fumble; to polish.)

fummeln F (ᵘᴸ) v/a. ⓑ a. (tüchtig reiben)

Fund¹ (ᵘᴸ) † u. poet. impf. v. finden.

Fund² (ᵘᴸ) [mhd.; * finden] m ⓒ (†) ⓑ. 1. (das Finden) finding; einen (guten) ~ tun to find s.th. (of value). — 2. (das Gefundene) find, thing found; glücklicher ~ lucky find, F godsend, windfall. — 3. (Erfindung) discovery; invention.

Fundament (ᵘᴸ) [lt.] n ⓑ b. bsd. ⓞ arch. (Grundmauer) foundation; fig. basis; et. aus dem ~ versteh(e)n to know a thing thoroughly.

fundamental (ᵘᴸ) [lt.] a. ⓒ (grundsätzlich, wesentlich) fundamental.

Fundamental-baß ♪ (ᵘᴸ...) m ⓒ fundamental bass; **-satz** m Logik ꝛc. fundamental proposition; **-stern** n, ast. (scharf bestimmter Firstern) clock-star.

fundamentier/en ⓞ (ᵘᴸᴸ) [lt.] arch. I v/a. ⓒ to lay the foundation of. — II ~ n ⓒ und F/ung f ⁴⁶ (laying the) foundation of, founding of.

Fundation (ᵘ-tⁱ(ᵘ)ᴸ) [lt.] f ⁴⁶ (wohltätige ꝛc. Stiftung) foundation.

Fund-bureau (ᵘ...) n ⓒ 🚉, Polizei ꝛc.: lost-property office; **-diebstahl** m jur. illegal detention of s.th. found; **-gebühr** f, **-geld** n = Finderlohn; **-grube** ⚒ f paying mine; fig. mine of wealth, rich source; Dickensche Romane sind eine ~ von Humor ... a storehouse of rich humour.

fundieren (ᵘᴸᴸ) [lt.] v/a. ⓒ (gründen) to found, establish, consolidate; ⊕ fundierte (ant. schwebende) Schuld funded (or consolidated) debt; consols pl.

Fund-ort (ᵘ...) m ⓒ place where s.th. is (or has been) found; ⁀ u. zo.: ⚛ habitat; **-recht** n right of discovery; **-register** n inventory; **-schacht** ⚒ m original shaft of a mine; **-stück** n object (or article) found; **-zettel** m inventory.

fünf (ᵘᴸ) [ahd.: five; lt. quinque: grch. pěmpě] numer. I card. numb. (ohne s. auch: ⁀e) five; es sind unser ⁀(e), wir sind zu ⁀(t), zu ⁀en there are five of us, we are five; ⁀undzwanzig twenty-five; ⁀ Vierteljahre fifteen months; es ist halb ⁀ ... half-past four; ⁀ Prozent oder vom Hundert five per cent.;

fig. er kann nicht (bis) ⁀ zählen he cannot say bo to a goose; ⁀ (eine) gerade (Zahl) sein lassen to be easy-going, not to be over-particular, to overlook things; da muß man seine ⁀ Sinne beisammen haben there you must have all your wits about you. — II (die Zahl) ~ ⓒ, ~e ⓒ f (number) five; auf Würfeln a.: cinque.

Fünf-akter (ᵘ...) m ⓒ thea. five-act play; **⁀aktig** a. ⓒ in five acts; **⁀armig** a. five-armed; **⁀blätt(e)rig** a. ⓒ five-leaved; ⚛ quinquefoliate(d), pentaphyllous; **⁀doppelt** ↘ a. = ⁀fach; **-eck** n, geom. pentagon; **⁀eckig** a. five-cornered; geom. pentagonal.

Fünfer (ᵘᴸ) m ⓒ 1. = fünf II. — 2. (die Ziffer 5, V) (the figure) five. — 3. member of a council (or committee) of five; röm. Alt.: quinquevir. — 4. soldier of the fifth regiment. — 5. anything related to the number five.

fünfer-lei (ᵘᴸ... oder ᵘᴸᴸ) a. inv. of five (different) kinds.

fünf-fach (ᵘ...) a. ⓒ, **-fache(s)** n ⓒ fivefold, quintuple; **⁀fäch(e)rig** ↘ a. five-celled; ⚛ quinquelocular; **⁀fältig** a. = ⁀fach; **⁀fing(e)rig** a. with five fingers, quinquedigitate; **-fingerkraut** ↘ n ⓒ five-finger (grass), cinquefoil (Potentilla reptans); **-flach** n, geom. pentahedron; **-frank(en)stück** n five-franc piece; **⁀füßig** a. with five feet; five-footed; **-füßler** m, pros. (Vers) pentameter; **-häfen** ⚓ m/pl. Cinque Ports pl.; **-herr** m röm. Alt.: quinquevir; **-herrschaft** f pentarchy; **-hundert** a., numer. five hundred; **-hundertste(l)** n five-hundredth (part); **-hundertste(r)** a. u. s. f.-hundredth; **⁀jährig** a. of five years, five years old, quinquennial; **⁀jährlich** a. every (or once in) f. years, quinquennial; **⁀kantig** a. with five edges, **⁀kapselig** ↘ a. ⚛ quinquecapsular; **⁀klappig** ↘ a. ⚛ quinquevalvular, ...; **⁀lappig** a. ⚛ quinquelob(at)ed; **⁀mal** adv. five times; **⁀malig** a. taking place f. times; **⁀männ(er)ig** ↘ a. (mit fünf Staubgefäßen) ⚛ pentandrian; Le Pflanze pentander; **-mark-schein** m, **-stück** ⚒ n, five-shilling note, piece; **-mastschiff** ⚓ n, **-schoner** m five-master; **⁀paarig** ↘ a.: ⚛ quinquejugous; **-paß** m, arch.: ⚛ quinquecusp; **-pfennigstück** n f.-pfennig piece [= about a halfpenny, Am. 1 cent]; **-pfünder** ⚔ m, artill. five-pounder; **⁀pfündig** a. of (or weighing) f. pounds; **⁀prozentig** ⓒ a. at (or bearing) f. per cent.; Le Papiere n/pl. f.-per-cents pl.; **⁀reihig** a. (arranged) in five rows; ⚛ quinqueserial, quinquefarious; **-ruderer** ⚓ m röm. Alt.: quinquereme; **⁀ruderig** a. with five benches of oars; **⁀saitig** ♪ a. with f. strings; **⁀samig** ↘ a. ⚛ pentaspermous; **⁀säulig** a., arch. with five (rows of) columns, ⚛ pentastyle; **Les Gebäude** pentastyle; **⁀schalig** ↘ a. = ⁀klappig; **⁀seitig** a. f.-sided, pentagonal; **⁀silbig** a., gram. of f. syllables, pentasyllabic; **⁀spaltig** a. ⚛ quinquefid; **⁀stellig** a., arith. of five digits; **⁀stimmig** ♪ a. for f. voices; Les Musikstück quin-

♪ Musik; ⚛ Wissenschaft; ↘ Pflanze; ⓠ Geographie; ⓞ Technik; ⚒ Bergbau; ⚔ Militär; ⚓ Marine; ⊕ Handel; ✉ Post; 🚉 Eisenbahn.

[fünfstöckig] — 398 — [Furagierungszug]

tet(to); ²stöckig a. f.-storied; =stromland ♀ n Indien: Punjab; ²stündig a. of (or lasting) five hours; ²stündlich a. occurring once in f. hours; ²tägig a. of five days, f. days old; ²tausend a. numer. f. thousand; =tausendstel, =tausendste(r) a. und s. f.-thousandth.

fünfte (²⌣) ord. numb. ⑩ 1. (the) fifth; das ² Kapitel the fifth chapter, chapter five or the fifth; Heinrich der ~ (gschr.: V.) Henry the Fifth (gschr.: V); Datum: der ~ (am ²n) März (gschr.: 5. März) (on) the fifth of March, March the fifth (gschr.: March 5ᵗʰ, Zeitungen ꝛc.: March 5). — 2. fig. das ² Rad am Wagen sein to be of no consequence or quite superfluous or a mere hanger-on.

fünf(e)halb (²⌣²) a. inv. (4½) four and a half.

fünf-teilig (²...) a. ⑩ in five parts, ⚬ quinquepartite; =teilung f ⑫ division into fifths or five parts.

Fünftel (²⌣) n ⑳ u. ² a. inv. fifth (part); ein ² Kilometer one-fifth (⅕) of a kilometre; drei ~ der Summe three-fifths (⅗) of the sum. [place.]

fünftens (²⌣) adv. fifthly, in the fifth.

fünft-halb (²⌣²) = fünft(e)halb.

fünf=(und)einhalb (²...) a. ⑩ (5½) five and a half; ²undzwanzig (25) twenty-five, or five and twenty.

fünf-weibig ⚥ (²...) a. ⑩ (mit fünf Stempeln) ⚬ pentagynian; ²wink(e)lig a. geom. with five angles, five quinquangular; vgl. ²eckig; ²zackig a. five-pronged; =zahl f number five, ⚬ pentad; ²zähnig a. ⚬ und zo. five-toothed, ⚬ quinquedentate; ²zehig a. five-toed, ⚬ quinquedigitate.

fünfzehn (²⌣) numer. I card. numb. inv. fifteen; Tennis: zu ², ² zu fifteen all; ² (zu) nichts (null) fifteen love. — II (die Zahl) ~ f ⑭ (number) fifteen.

Fünfzehn-eck (²⌣²) n ⑫ geom.: ⚬ quindecagon.

Fünfzehner (²⌣⌣) m ⑳ 1. member of a council (or committee) of fifteen; röm. Alt.: ⚬ quindecemvir. — 2. soldier of the fifteenth regiment.

fünfzehnerlei (²⌣⌣⌣ oder ²⌣⌣||) a. inv. of fifteen (different) kinds.

Fünfzehner-spiel (²⌣⌣²) n ⑫ boss puzzle.

fünfzehn-jährig (²⌣...) a. ⑩: a) of fifteen years, fifteen years old; b) happening every fifteen years.

fünfzehnte (²⌣⌣) ord. numb. ⑩ fifteenth; Ludwig der ~ (gschr.: XV.) Louis the Fifteenth (gschr.: XV); Datum: der (den, am) ~(n) Mai (gschr.: 15. Mai) (on) the fifteenth of May; May the fifteenth (gschr.: May 15ᵗʰ, in Zeitungen ꝛc.: May 15); ²l (⌣⌣) n ⑫ fifteenth (part); zwei ~ (²/₁₅) two fifteenths; in Schulen auch gesprochen: two over (or upon) fifteen; ²ns (²⌣⌣) adv. in the fifteenth (15ᵗʰ) place.

fünf-zeilig (²...) a. ⑩: a) of five lines b) = ²reihig.

fünfzig (²⌣) numer. I card. numb. inv. fifty. — II (die Zahl) ~ f ⑭ (number) fifty [50]; er ist hoch in den ~(en), bisw. a. ~ern he is well on in the fifties, F he is going on for sixty.

Fünfziger (²⌣⌣) I m ⑳ 1. (auch: ~in f ⑭) person fifty (and odd) years old, ⚬ quinquagenarian. — 2. ⊕ (50 Mark) fifty-mark note. — 3. soldier of the fiftieth regiment. — 4. = fünfzig II. — II ² a. inv. 5. die ² Jahre, Zeitrechnung und Lebensalter: the fifties pl. (the years) between fifty and sixty.

Fünfziger=ausschuß (²⌣⌣...) m ⑫ committee of fifty.

fünfziger-lei (²⌣⌣ oder ⌣⌣||) a. inv. of fifty (different) kinds.

fünfzig-jährig (²⌣...) a. ⑩ of fifty years, fifty years old; jemandes ²es Jubiläum feiern to celebrate a p.'s jubilee; =pfe"nnigstück n fifty-pfennig piece, half a mark [50 ₰ = about sixpence, Am. 12 cents].

fünfzigste (²⌣⌣) ord. numb. ⑩ fiftieth; das ² Jahr erreichen to live to the age of fifty; ²ns (²⌣⌣) adv. in the fiftieth (50ᵗʰ) place.

fünf-zöllig (²...) a. ⑩ five-inch, five inches long (wide, high).

fungieren (⌣²⌣) [lt.] v/n. (h.) ⑫ (handeln) to act, to officiate (als ∥ as ∥ or in the capacity of ∥).

Fünkchen (²⌣) n ⑫ small spark, auch: sparklet, fig. particle.

Funke (²⌣) [ahd.] m ⑭⑫ spark; flash, flashing light; ~n sprühen to emit sparks, ⚬ to scintillate; elect. ~n ziehen to draw sparks; elektrischer ~ electric spark; kleiner ~ s. Fünkchen; er hat keinen ~n Verstand he has not a spark (or grain, trace, vestige) of sense (in him); es ist kein ~ Hoffnung (mehr) there is not a gleam (or ray) of hope (left).

funkeln (²⌣) I v/n. (h.) ⑫ a. to sparkle, to flash; ⚬ to scintillate, coruscate, (strahlen) to shine; von Sternen: to twinkle. — II ~ n ⑫ (f. I) sparkling; ⚬ scintillation, coruscation.

funkel(nagel)neu F (²⌣(⌣)²) a. ⑩ quite new, brand-new, just made or bought.

Funken (²⌣) m ⑳ = Funke.

Funken-fänger ⊕ (²⌣...) m einer Dampfmaschine, e-s Schornsteins: spark-arrester or -catcher or -preventer; =leiter ⊕ m, elect. spark-conductor; =sehen n, path.: ⚬ photopsy; =sprühen n flying of sparks, ⚬ scintillation; ²sprühend, ²werfend a. giving off (or emitting) sparks, ⚬ scintillating; =station f, tel. station for wireless telegraphy; =strecke f, tel. wireless telegraph-line; =telegraphen-apparate m/pl. tel. instruments pl. used for wireless telegraphy; =telegraphie f, tel. wireless telegraphy, radio-telegraphy; =zieher m, elect. spark-condenser, -drawer.

Funker * ⚔ (²⌣) m ⑳ tel. (Soldat der Funkenabteilung) soldier belonging to a wireless telegraph corps.

Funk-spruch * (²...) m ⑫ (Depesche der drahtlosen Telegraphie) wireless message, message sent by wireless (or radio-) telegraphy, marconigram; =spruch-station f = Funkenstation.

Funktion (⌣⌣²) [lt.] f ⑭ (Tätigkeit) function; math. algebraische ~ algebraic function; ~är (⌣⌣(⌣)²) m ⑫d. (Beamter) functionary; ²ieren v/n.

(h.) ⑫ = fungieren; ~s-wechsel m ⑫ Biologie ꝛc.: functional change.

für (¹) [ahd.: for] I prp. mit acc. 1. (in exchange) for, in favour of, in lieu of; Bezahlung ² meine Arbeit, Belohnung ² meine Dienste pay (or recompense) for ...; ² den Preis for (or at) that price; das hat viel ² sich that offers great advantages, has much in its favour; F there is something in that; Mädchen ² alles maid of all work; ich habe (esse ꝛc.) es ² mein Leben gern I am exceedingly (or passionately) fond of it; er ist groß ² sein Alter ... tall for his age; das ist kein Betragen ² einen Mann it is conduct (or behaviour) unworthy of a man; ich ² m-e Person as regards myself, speaking for myself, I for my part; alles spricht ² diesen Plan everything speaks in favour of this plan; fürs erste bleiben wir hier for the present ...; ein ² allemal once for all. — 2. aufzählen: fürs erste, zweite first, secondly; Mann ² Mann every man, one and all; sie zogen Mann ² Mann vorüber they marched past one after the other or in single file; er verkauft sie Stück ² Stück eine Mark he sells them a shilling a piece; Schritt ² Schritt step by step; Tag ² Tag day by (or after) day; Wort ² Wort word for word. — 3. nach zahlreichen v. und a., z.B.: sich ² et. interessieren to interest o.s. in a th.; günstig, vorteilhaft ² e-n favourable, advantageous to a p.; bisw. nicht zu übersetzen: ich halte ihn ² e-n Ehrenmann I think him a man of honour. — 4. (beiseite, getrennt) ² sich sein (leben, bleiben) to be (to live, to remain) alone or by o.s.; er lebt nur ² sich ... only for (or quite by) himself; eine Sache ² sich a thing by itself; das ist eine Sache ² sich that's quite a different (or another) matter; er kann ² sich besteh(e)n ... live on his own means; an und für sich (betrachtet) (considered) in itself, apart from the rest. — 5. chm. und bibl., auch poet.: vor, z.B. ² Schrecken bleich pale with fright. — 6. was für ein, pl. was für (welcher) what (kind of); was ² ein Mann ist das? was ist das ² ein Mann? what man is he?; was ² Äpfel sind das? what (kind of) apples are these?; ausrufend: was ² eine Freude! what joy!, what a pleasure!; was ² ein herrlicher See! what a magnificent lake!; was ² Possen! what a farce!; was für Lügen! what lies!; was er immer (oder auch) für Absichten haben mag whatever his intentions may be. — II adv. 7. für und für for ever and ever, on and on, continually. — III Für n, inv. 8. das ~ und Wider the two sides (of the question), oft: the pros and cons pl.

Furage ⚔ (⌣²⌣) [fr. fourrage m; *dtsch. Futter] f ⑭ (Futter) forage, fodder.

furagieren ⚔ (⌣⌣²⌣) [s. Furage] I v/n. (h.) u. v/a. ⑫ to forage, to forage. — II ~ n ⑫ u. Furagierung f ⑭ foraging, forage; Furagierungs-komma'ndo n, =zug m foraging party, expedition.

Signs (see page XVII): F familiar; P vulgar; ⌐ flash; ⚲ rare; † obsolete (died); * new word (born); ⁺⁺ incorrect; ♪ music;

[fürbaß] — 399 — [Fusel]

für=baß (⁻⁻, † ⁻⁻) [mhd.] *adv.* ehm. u. *bibl.*, *poet.* further, forward; 2 ziehen to go (or travel, pass) on.

Für=bitte (⁻⁻⁻) *f* ⊕: a) intercession, mediation, plea; bei e-m ~ einlegen (oder tun) für e-n to intercede (or plead) with a p. for (or on behalf of) a p.; b) *eccl.* (intercessory) prayer (offered up) on behalf of a sinner, a patient, &c.; **=bitter(in** *f*) *m* intercessor, mediator (*f* a. ...ress, ...rix), pleader.

Furche (⁻⁻) [ahd.: furrow] *f* ⊕ 1. (Acker=)~ furrow; *agr.* ~n ziehen to make furrows or ridges; *fig.* eine von ~n (Runzeln) durchzog(e)ne Stirn a wrinkled (or furrowed) forehead or brow. — 2. ⊕ (Rinne an Nadeln und Instrumenten) groove; notch.

furchen (⁻⁻) **I** *v/a.* ⊕ to furrow, to ridge; to trace (or draw) furrows across; die Stirn: to wrinkle; ⚕ gefurcht: ⚗ sulcate(d), *min.*: ⚗ striate(d). — **II** ~ n ⚖ *f.* Furchung.

furchen=artig (⁻⁻⁻) *a.* ⊕ furrowed; wrinkled; ⚗ sulciform; **=förmig** *a.* = **=artig**; **=rain** *m* ⚗ *agr.* furrow-slice; **=schrift** *f* ⚗ boustrophedon; **=wal** *m*, *zo.* fin-fish, finback (*Balaenopera*); **=weise** *adv.* in furrows; **=zieher** *m*, *agr.* furrowing-plough; (Bohr=pflug) drill-plough.

furchig (⁻⁻) *a.* ⊕ furrowed; wrinkled.

Furcht (⁻) [ahd.] *f* ⊕ (o. *pl.*) (Be=forgnis) apprehension of; (Angst) dread of, anxiety (or fright) caused by; (Be=stürzung) alarm caused by; (Schrecken) horror of, e-r Menge: panic; aus ~ vor // for (or from, through) fear of //; durch ~ zu et. bewegen, bringen to frighten into a th.; durch ~ wurden sie angetrieben, sich zu übergeben they were cowed (or awed) into surrender; in ~ geraten to take fright or alarm; e-n in ~ setzen to frighten (or terrify) a p.; von ~ befallen terror- (or panic-)stricken; vor ~ erblassen to turn pale with fear or fright.

furchtbar (⁻⁻) *a.* ⊕ 1. fearful, stärker: frightful, horrible, formidable; eine 2e (gefährliche) Krankheit a terrible (or dreadful) malady, an awful disease. — 2. F *adv.* (in hohem Grade) excessively; F tremendously, awfully.

Furchtbarkeit (⁻⁻⁻) *f* ⊕ (*f.* furchtbar) fearful nature of, terribleness, awfulness; formidableness.

fürchten (⁻⁻) [ahd.] ⊕ **I** *v/a.*, *v/n.* (h.) to fear, to be afraid (or apprehensive) of; to apprehend; (Angst haben vor) to dread, to be in dread (or mortal fear) of; er hat nichts (dabei) zu 2 he runs no risk (by that); für e-n 2 to be anxious about a p.('s welfare); ich fürchte zu fallen oder daß ich falle I fear to fall, I am afraid of falling or lest I may fall; es wird allgemein gefürchtet, daß // it is universally feared that // or lest //; die von ihm gefürchtete Zusammenkunft the interview dreaded by him. — **II** sich 2 *v/refl.* to be afraid or alarmed or apprehensive (vor of); to stand in awe of; fürchte dich (nur) nicht! don't be afraid!; F never (you)

fear!; davor 2 wir uns (noch lange) nicht! F that won't (or it takes s.th. more to) frighten us or alarm us!

fürchterlich (⁻⁻⁻) *a.* ⊕ = furchtbar 1; (erschreckend) terrible; (entsetzlich) dreadful, horrid; (schauderhaft) awful, appalling; (unheimlich) weird; F *fig.* adv. sie ist 2 (ungemein) häßlich F she is fearfully (or awfully) plain or ugly.

Fürchterlichkeit *f* (⁻⁻⁻) ⊕ dreadfulness; awfulness; weirdness.

Furcht=hase (⁻...) *m* ⊕ coward(ly person); **=los** *a.* ⊕ free from fear, fearless; (unerschrocken) intrepid, undaunted; **=losigkeit** *f* ⊕ fearlessness, intrepidity, undauntedness, fortitude.

furchtsam (⁻⁻) *a.* ⊕ timid, timorous; vor drohender Gefahr: apprehensive; (ängstlich) faint-hearted, nervous, P funky; **~keit** (⁻⁻⁻) *f* ⊕ timidity, timorousness; faint-heartedness, nervousness; P funk, funkiness.

Furchung (⁻⁻) *f* ⊕: ⚗ sulcation; Embryologie: ⚗ segmentation.

fürder(hin), fast † (⁻⁻, ⁻⁻⁻ u. ⁻⁻⁻) [ahd.: further] *adv.* örtlich: further; fürder streben to push on(ward); zeitlich: henceforth, henceforward, in the future.

für=einander (⁻⁻⁻) *adv.* for each other, for one another; **2erst** *adv.* for the present or the moment.

Furi=e (⁻⁽⁻⁾⁻) [lt.] *f* ⊕ 1. *myth.* (Rache=göttin) Fury; (grch.) Erin(n)ys. — 2. *fig.* (schreckliches Weib) fury, dragon, F termagant. — 3. (Wut) rage.

furien=artig (⁻⁽⁻⁾⁻...) *a.* ⊕, **=ähnlich** *a.* fury-like; furious.

Furier ⚔ (⁻⁻) [fr. *fourrier*; *dtsch.* Futter] *m* ⊕d. (Quartiermeister) quartermaster; (Unterquartiermeister) quartermaster-sergeant; **~=schütz(e)** *m* ⊕ ehm. officer's man.

Furke(l) (⁻⁻) [lt. *furca*] *f* ⊕ fork.

für=lieb (⁻⁻) *adv.*: mit et. 2 (=)nehmen to content oneself with a th.; mit wenigem: to make shift with little; mit allem: to put up with anything, to be easily satisfied.

für=nehm, fast † (⁻⁻) *a.* ⊕ = vornehm.

Furnier ⊕ (⁻⁻) [furnieren] *n* ⊕d. join. (Auslegestäbchen) ⊤ veneer.

Furnier=blatt (⁻⁻...) *n* ⊕ veneer.

furnieren ⊕ (⁻⁻⁻) [fr. *fournir* mit et. versehen] *v/a.* ⊕ join. ⊤ to veneer, inlay.

Furnierer ⊕ (⁻⁻⁻) *m* ⊕ inlayer.

Furnier=hammer (⁻⁻...) *m* ⊕ veneering- (or inlay-)hammer; **=maschine** *f* veneering-machine, -press.

Furore (⁻⁻⁻) [it.] *n* ⊕, bsp. *thea.* ~ (Aufsehen) machen to make (or create) a sensation, to cause a stir, F to draw (the public), to fill the house.

fürs (⁻) [für das]: 2 erste for the present or the moment.

Für=sorge (⁻...) *f* ⊕ care, stärker: (eifrige) solicitude; ~ treffen für to make provision for; j-s ~ anvertrauen to entrust to a p.('s care); **2sorgend** *a.*, **2sorglich** *a.* careful, thoughtful; **=sorglichkeit** *f* carefulness, thoughtfulness; **=sprache** *f* intercession, vgl. =bitte; auf seine ~ hin on his recommendation; **=sprech** *m* ⊕d. u. ⊕ (Wortführer) spokesman; (Anwalt) advocate;

=sprecher(in *f*) *m* = **=bitter(in)**; (Verteidiger) advocate, apologist.

Fürst (⁻) [ahd. (*sup. v.* für *vorderster*): first erster] *m* ⊕, **~in** *f* ⊕ prince(ss); kleiner ~ (auch ~chen) petty prince, princelet; *bibl.* der ~ dieser Welt (Satan) the Prince of this world or of Darkness.

Fürst=bischof (⁻...) *m* ⊕, ehm. bishop with princely (or sovereign) rank.

Fürstchen (⁻⁻) *dim. von* Fürst (f. ds).

fürsten (⁻⁻) *v/a.* ⊕ 1. to raise a count, &c. to the rank of a prince; gefürsteter Abt abbot with princely power or rank. — 2. to convert a county, &c. into a principality.

Fürsten=bank (⁻⁻...) *f* ⊕, ehm. auf dem deutschen Reichstage: Bench of Princes; **=bund** *m* league of princes; **=diener** *m* attendant of a pr.; (Höfling) courtier; **=geschlecht** *n* princely race or house; **=gunst** *f* favour of a pr. or of princes; **=haus** *n*: a) prince's palace; b) = **=geschlecht**; **=hof** *m* court of a prince; **=hut** *m*, **=krone** *f* princely crown or diadem; **=knecht** *m* prince's flunkey; **=mantel** *m* princely cloak or ermine; **2mäßig** *a.* ⊕ prince-like, princely; **=recht** *n* princely prerogative.

Fürstenschaft (⁻⁻⁻) *f* ⊕ = Fürstenstand, die ganze ~ the whole body of princes.

Fürsten=schule (⁻⁻...) *f* ⊕ (von Fürsten gestiftet) school founded by a sovereign or prince; **=sitz** *m* princely mansion or estate; **=stand** *m* princely rank; bisw. princedom; in den ~ erheben = fürsten 1; **=tag** *m* diet (or congress) of princes; **=titel** *m* princely title.

Fürstentum (⁻⁻⁻) [mhd.] *n* ⊕d. Würde u. Gebiet: principality, Gebiet: dominion of a prince. [dignity.]

Fürsten=würde (⁻⁻...) *f* ⊕ princely]

Fürstin (⁻⁻) *f* ⊕ *f.* Fürst.

fürstlich (⁻⁻) *a.* ⊕ princely, of (or becoming) a prince; *adv.* 2 leben to live in princely style or like a prince; Seine ~e Durchlaucht His Serene Highness.

Fürstlichkeit (⁻⁻⁻) *f* ⊕ 1. princeliness, princely state or splendour or demeanour. — 2. = Fürstliche Durchlaucht (*f.* fürstlich). — 3. ~en *pl.* (fürstliche Personen) princely person(age)s *pl.*, auch: Serene Highnesses.

Furt (⁻ und ⁻) *f* ⊕ (*fahren*) ford: lt. *portus*) *f* ⊕ ford; **furtbar** (⁻ u. ⁻) *a.* ⊕ von Flüssen &c.: fordable.

Furunkel ⚕ (⁻⁻⁻) [it.] *m* ⊕ path. (Blutgeschwür) boil, ⚕ furuncle.

für=wahr (⁻⁻) *adv.* ⊕ a) versichernd: indeed, forsooth, in truth, truly, *bibl.* verily; b) einräumend: certainly; **=witz** (⁻...) † *m* ⊕ = Vorwitz, **2witzig** † *a.* ⊕ = vorwitzig; **=wort** *n*, *gr.* pronoun; **2wörtlich** *a.* pronominal.

Furz P unanst. (⁻) [ahd.] *m* ⊕a. fart; **furzen** (⁻⁻) *v/n.* (h.) ⊕ to fart.

Fuschelei (⁻⁻⁻) *f* ⊕ trickery; underhand dealing or acting.

fuscheln ⊕a., **fuschen** ⊕ (⁻⁻) *v/n.* (h.) 1. (betrügen) to trick, to cheat. — 2. = pfuschen. [2. = Pfuscherei.]

Fuscherei (⁻⁻⁻) *f* ⊕ 1. = Fuschelei.]

Fusel[1] (⁻⁻) [ahd. 18. sae.] *m* ⊕ 1. *chm.* (Fusel=öl) fusel oil, amyl alcohol. —

⚗ scientific; ⚕ botanical; ⚖ geography; ⊕ machinery; ⛏ mining; ⚔ military; ⚓ marine; ⊕ commercial; ✉ postal; 🚂 railway.

[Fusel] — 400 — [Fußpartie]

2. weit S. (Fuselschnaps) spirits *pl.* containing (much) fusel oil, raw (or bad, impure) spirits *pl.* (of wine).
Fusel² F (⏑⏑) *m* ㉖ fuzz, fluff, flue.
fusel¹-frei (⏑⏑…) *a.* ⑥⑥ vom Alkohol: free from fusel (oil); **=geruch** *m* ㉒, **=geschmack** *m* fusel odour, taste; **=haltig** *a.* containing fusel (oil).
Füselier ꝛc. s. Füsilier ꝛc.
fuselicht, fuselig¹ (⏑⏑…) *a.* ⑥⑥ = fuselhaltig.
fuselig² F (⏑⏑) *a.* ⑥⑥ fuzzy, fluffy.
fuseln¹ (⏑⏑) *v/n.* (h.) ⓦa. **1.** (schnapsen) to drink bad spirits. — 2. *prov.* = pfuschen. [to fuzz; to fray (out).]
fuseln² (⏑⏑) *v/n.* (h.) ⓦa. Fäden u. Tuch;
Fusel¹-öl (⏑⏑…) *n* ㉒ *chm.* = Fusel¹ 1;
=schnaps *m* = Fusel¹ 2.
Füsilier ⚔ (⏑⏑') [fr.] *m* ⓘd. (*ant.* Musketier. Grenadier) fusilier, …eer.
füsilieren ⚔ (⏑-⏑') *v/a.* ⑨③ (erschießen) to shoot (by way of military punishment or =execution).
Fusion (-(⏑)') [lt.] *f* ㉒ (Verschmelzung) fusion; **=ist** (-(⏑)-') *m* ㉒, **=istisch** *a.* ⑥⑥ fusionist; **=s-partei** *f* ㉒, etwa: united party.
Fuß (¹) [ahd. foot: lt. ped-; grch. pod-] *m* ⓓa. (doch vgl. 3) **1.** *von Menschen und Tieren:* foot; (*Pfote*) paw; *kleiner ~* (u. *dim.* Füßchen) small foot, Kinderspr. a.: tootsy; ~ e-s Strumpfes = Füßling; ~ e-s Weinglases: stem. — 2. *mit prp.* s. Freier²: **auf die Füße** fallen … on one's feet; (festen) ~ fassen to gain a (firm or solid) footing; **mit Händen und Füßen** arbeiten, sich wehren to struggle with hand and foot; *fig.* to resist with all one's might; mit Füßen (oder unter die Füße) treten (*auch fig.*) to tread under foot, to trample upon; trockenen ~es, mit trockenen Füßen with dry feet, F dry-foot(ed); f. Boden 5; **vom Kopf bis zu den Füßen** from head to foot or to heel, from top to toe; *schmeichelnd:* er läßt sich Ihnen **zu Füßen** legen he sends you his humble(st) respects; zu ~ reisen to travel on foot, to make a pedestrian tour or excursion, F to tramp it. — 3. ⓓa,6 (Längenmaß) foot; einen ~ breit a foot wide; vgl. ~breit; zehn ~ lang ten feet (F foot) long. — **4.** (Maßstab) auf e-m großen ~e leben: a) *co.* (große Füße haben) to have large feet; b) *fig.* to live in great (F grand) style; auf welchem ~e steh(e)n sie zueinander? on what footing (or terms) are they (with each other)?; f. Kriegsfuß. — 5. *pros.* (Versfuß) der Hexameter hat sechs Füße the hexameter consists of six (metrical) feet. — **6.** *fig.* oft: lower (or bottom) part; ~ eines Berges foot …; am ~ des Bettes at the foot (or bottom …; ⏚ ~ e-s Mastes: heel; *arch.* ~ e-r Bildsäule, e-r Säule pedestal of a statue. foot (or base) of a column; *typ.* ~ e-s Buchstabens feet *pl.*…
7. in Verbindung mit *verbs*, ꝛB.: mit dem linken ~ zuerst **aufgestanden** sein (schlechte Laune haben) to be cross(-tempered) or ill-humoured; *vgl.* aufstehen 4; e-m zu Füßen fallen to fall at a p.'s feet; vgl. 2; ~ fassen f. 2; e-m auf dem ~e folgen to follow (close) on a

p.'s heels; zu ~(e) geh(e)n to journey on foot, F to tramp it; die Füße unter j-s Tisch **haben** to board with a p.; die Sache hat Hand und ~ … is cleverly arranged or devised; es hat weder Hand noch ~ it has neither rhyme nor reason; mit e-m auf vertrautem ~e **leben** to live on intimate terms with a p.; sich auf die Füße **machen** to start (on one's journey); F to make off; ⚔ e-m Füße **m.** (*vgl.* Bein 3) to make a p. find his legs, to hurry a p. on; *fig. oc.* die Füße in die Hände **nehmen** to give one's legs free play, to trot along briskly; das **ruht** auf schwachen Füßen that rests on a slender basis, it is feebly supported; gut (schlecht) zu ~e **sein** to be a good (bad) walker or pedestrian; immer auf den Füßen sein to be always on one's feet or legs, to be always stirring, F to be for ever on the move or tramp; e-n auf freien ~ **setzen** to set a p. free or at liberty; auf eigenen Füßen **steh(e)n** to stand on one's own legs or F one's own bottom; auf schwachen Füßen steh(e)n oder ruhen to stand on a weak foundation, F to be in a shaky condition; auf gespanntem ~e mit e-m steh(e)n to have fallen out with a p., to be at variance (or at loggerheads) with a p.; auf gutem (schlechtem) ~e mit e-m steh(e)n to be on good (bad) terms with a p.; auf vertrautem ~e mit e-m stehen to be on intimate terms (or to be hand and glove) with a p.; f. auch 4; **stehenden** ~es (sogleich) on the spot, without delay, at once; soweit die Füße mich **tragen** as far as my legs (will) carry me; mit Füßen **treten** f. 2.
Fuß-abstreicher (⏑"…) *m* ㉒ door-scraper; **=angel** *f*, ⚔ crowfoot; **=artillerie** ⚔ *f* foot-artillery; **=bad** *n* foot-bath; **=ball** *m* football; einfacher ~, ~ ohne Aufnehmen association football or game; gemischter ~, ~ mit Aufnehmen rugby(-football); **=ballen** *m*, *anat.* ball of the foot; **=ballpartie** *f* football-match; **=ballspiel** *n* = **=ball**; **=ballspieler** *m* football-player; **=bänder** *n/pl. anat.* ligaments *pl.* of the foot; **=bank** *f* footstool; foot-rest; gepolstert: hassock; **=becken** *n* basin for washing the feet; *vgl.* **=bad**; **=bekleidung** *f* covering for the feet, *auch:* boots and stockings *pl.*; foot-gear, footwear; **=bett** *n*, *surg.* cushion (or cradle) for an injured leg; **=beuge-, =biege** *f* (Spann) instep; **=binde** *f*, *surg.* bandage for the foot; **=blatt** *n*: a) sole of the foot; b) ♃ duck's-foot, limeplant (*Podophyllum peltatum*); **=block** *m* ehm. (Strafmittel) stocks *pl.*; **=boden** *m* (Diele) floor (-ing), aus Brettern: boarded floor(ing), gepflasterter: paved floor(ing), pavement (vgl. Boden 3); **=breit** *a.* a foot wide; **=breit** *m*: keinen ~ Landes not an inch of land; keinen ~ weichen not to move (F budge) an inch; **=brett** ⚙ *n* am Kutschbock foot-board.
Füßchen (⏑⏑) *dim.* von Fuß (f. ds 1).
Fuß-decke (⏑"…) *f* ㉒ floor-cloth; am Fußende des Bettes: coverlet (am Fuß) vor dem Bette: rug; (Teppich) carpet;

=dick *a.* a (or one) foot thick; **=eisen** *n*: a) (eiserne Fesseln) foot-irons or -chains *pl.*; shackles *pl.* for the feet; b) = **=angel**; c) foot-scraper;
füßeln (⏑⏑) ⓦa. **I** *v/n.* (h.) (mit den Füßen zappeln) to fidget (or kick) about with one's feet. — **II** *v/a.* (einstampfen) to stamp down (with one's feet), to trample down.
fußen (⏑⏑) ⑨⓪ **I** *v/n.* (h.) **1.** auf et. (*dat.* od. *acc.*) ② to set foot upon a th. — 2. *bsd. fig.* auf et. ② (sich auf et. stützen) to rely (or depend) upon a th.; (auf et. bauen) to rest one's hopes upon a th., to count on a th. — **II** *v/a.* u. **sich** ② *v/refl.* **3.** (bauen, gründen) to found, to establish; *fig.* sich ② auf to rest upon.
Fuß-ende ("…) *n* ㉒ des Bettes foot (or foot-end) of the bed. [⚔ octopod.]
…füßler (…"⏑) *m* ㉖ i. Zsfgn. ꝛB. Acht ②]
Fuß-fall ("…) *m* ㉒ prostration; einen ~ vor einem tun to throw o.s. at a p.'s feet, to go down on one's knees before a p.; **=fällig** *a.* ⑥⑥ prostrate; *adv.* on one's knees; **=fäule** *f*, *vet.* foot-rot; **=fehler** *m* Tennis: foot-fault; **=fesseln** *f/pl.* = **=eisen** a; **=fest** *a.* sure-footed; **=förmig** *a.* foot-shaped, ⚔ pediform, ♃ *a.* pedate; **=frei** *a.* ⚑: Der Rock für Frauen: walking-skirt; **=gänger(in** *f*) *m* walker, pedestrian, Sport *auch*: walkist; ⚔ (Infanterist) foot-soldier; **=gänger-sport** *m* pedestrianism; **=garde** ⚔ *f* foot-guards *pl.*; **=gefecht** ⚔ *n* der Kavallerie: engagement of dismounted cavalry, fighting (of horse-soldiers) on foot; **=gelenk** *n* joint of the foot, ankle-joint, ⚔ talus; **=gesims** ⊙ *n*, *arch.* base-moulding; **=gestell** *n*: a) *arch.* e-r Säule: pedestal; b) ⊙ (Bock) trestle; sawframe or -stand; *join.* foot-stool; c) *co.* (Füße) F understandings *pl.*; **=getäfel** ⊙ *n* Tischlerei: inlaid floor; **=gicht** *f*, *path.* gout in the feet, ⚔ podagra; **=hiebe** *m/pl.* Orient: bastinado; **=hoch** *a.* one foot high; der Schnee liegt ② … is a foot deep; ein ②-hoher Strauch a shrub one foot high.
…füßig ("…⏑) *a.* ⑥⑥ in Zsfgn, ꝛB.: rot-② with red feet; f. drei-, vier-= (ꝛc.).
Fuß-kissen ("…) *n* ㉒ foot-cushion; cushion for the feet; hassock; **=klaviatur** ♪ *f* an der Orgel pedal(ling); **=knöchel** *m*, *anat.* ankle(-bone), ⚔ malleolus; **=knochen** *m* bone of the foot; **=kuß** *m* beim Papste kissing the Pope's foot or toe; **=lage** *f* Geburtshilfe: foot-presentation; **=lahm** *a.* with lame feet or a lame foot; **=lang** *a.* a foot long; **=lappen** ⚔ *m* rag (or cloth) for (wrapping round) the foot; **=leidend** *a.* sore-footed, vgl. ②wund; **=leiste** *f*, *arch.* wash-board.
Füßling (⏑⏑) *m* ⓘd. (*ant.* Beinling) foot of a sock or stocking; Strumpf mit einem ~ versehen, einen ~ anstricken to (new-)foot a stocking.
fuß-los ("…) *a.* ⑥⑥ footless, ⚔ apod(al); apodous; ②loses Tier: ⚔ apod; **=maß** *n* ㉒ foot-measure; **=matte** *f* (door- or hall-)mat; **=muskel** *m* muscle of the foot; **=note** *f* footnote; **=partie** *f* walking

[Fußpfad] — 401 — [Gabelantilope]

(or pedestrian) tour, F tramp; =**pfad** m foot-path; =**pfund** n, phys. in Engl. gbr. (Kraft, die ein Pfund einen Fuß hebt) foot-pound, dynam; =**post** f foot-post; =**punkt** m (ant. Scheitelpunkt): a) ast. nadir; b) geom. foot of a perpendicular (line); =**regi'ster** n = »flaviatu'r«; =**reise** f walking-tour, journey on foot, F tramp; =**reisende(r)** m) f pedestrian, wayfarer, wanderer; =**sack** m foot-muff or warmer; =**schellen** f pl. f.-shackles pl.; =**schemel** m = »bank«; =**schwebe** f, med. sling for the foot; =**schweiß** m sweating of the feet; =**sohle** f sole of the foot; ⚕ thenar, planta pedis; =**soldat** ⚔ m foot-soldier, infantryman; =**spange** f Alt.: anklet; =**spitze** f point of the f.; auf den ~n stehen to stand (on) tiptoe; =**spur** f, =**stapfe** f = »tapfe«; =**steig** m foot-path, pathway; =**stock** ⚙ m (Maßstock) f.-rule; =**strick** m (foot-)snare; =**tapfe** f f.-print: track; weitS. trace; in j-s ~n treten to follow in a p.'s footsteps; =**taste** ♪ f der Orgel pedal; =**teppich** m carpet, (Läufer) stair-carpet; =**tour** f =partie; =**tritt** m: a) kick, e-m e-n ~ geben to give a p. a kick, to kick a p.; b) =»spur«; c) ⚙ =»brett«; =**truppen** f pl. =**volk** n ⚔ foot (-soldiers pl.), infantry (troops pl.); =**wand(e)rer** m wayfarer, vgl. »reisende(r)«; =**wand(e)rung** f =»reise«; =**wanne** f foot-bath; =**wärmer** m f.-warmer or -stove; =**waschung** f washing (of) the feet; eccl. am Gründonnerstag: maundy; =**weg** m a) in Städten: (Bürgersteig, Trottoir) pavement; b) =»pfad«; =**werk** n: a) =**bekleidung**; b) F (Füße) the feet pl., F co. the walking appara'tus; ⚕**wund** a. with sore feet, foot-sore; =**wurzel** f, anat.: ⚕ tarsus; =**wurzelgelenk** n: ⚕ tarsal joint; =**wurzelknochen** m, anat. ⚕ tarsal; =**zeh(e)** f) m, anat. toe.

Fust (ˊ) npr/m. ⚙ ⊛ α. (Genosse Gutenbergs, † ca. 1466) John Fust.

Fustage (ˇ¹ᴳˊ) [¨⸱+ fr.] f ⊛ ⚓ barrels, casks pl.; ⊛ package; vgl. Fastage.

Fustik ᵀ ⊛ (ˊ-) m ⊛: a) alter ~ (echtes Gelbholz von Maclu'ra tincto'ria) (old) fustic; b) junger ~ = »Fisetholz«.

futsch P (ˊ) [it. fuggito] int. und prädikatives a. (verloren) lost, g⸗ne, undone; (ausgegeben) spent. [Foochow.]

Futschou ♀ (ˊ-) npr/n. ⊛α. (chin. St.)

Futter¹ (ˊ⌣) [ahd.: fodder] n ⚙ 1. (Nahrung) food, nourishment, nutriment; für das Vieh a.: fodder. forage; grünes ~ green pasture; (Trocken)~ provender; für rastende Pferde auch: bait; dem Vieh, rastenden Pferden ~ geben to feed the cattle, to bait horses; bib. ~ holen, suchen to forage, to go foraging, to fodder. — 2. F für Menschen a.: eating and drinking, provisions, victuals pl., F grub.

Futter² (ˊ⌣) [ahd.] n ⚙ (innere Auskleidung) v. Gewändern, Kisten: (inner) lining; von Fenstern, Türen: casing. case; (Pelz)~ fur. furring; weitS. inner covering.

Futteral (⌣⌣ˊ) [dtsch⸱lt. 15. sae.; * Futter²] n ⊛ d. case, casing, cover(ing); (Scheide) sheath; (Schachtel) box (made of pasteboard); ~**pappe** f cardboard, pasteboard; =**schere** f sheath-scissors pl.

Futter²-a'tlas ⊛ (ˊ⌣...) m ⊛ satin for lining; =¹**bank** f chopping-board; =²**barchent** ⊛ m satin for lining; =¹**bau** m growing (of) forage; =**beutel** m für Pferde nose-bag; =**boden** m hay-loft; =**erbse** f hog-pea; =²**bohlen** ⊙ f pl. inside planking sg.; =²**brett** n, =**diele** f: a) slab; ⚒ carp. einer Treppenstufe: riser; =**flanell** m flannel for lining; =¹**geld** n money paid for the keep of cattle; =**gerste** f: a) two-rowed barley (Ho'rdeum di'stichum); b) barley for cattle; =**gras** n grass for cattle; weitS. green food or fodder; =**hafer** m oats pl. for cattle, feed-oats pl.; =**holen** n. =**holer** m ⚔ foraging, forager; =**holz** ⊙ n inside boarding; =¹**kammer** f forage-loft or -shed; =**kasten** m corn- (or oat-)bin or chest; =²**kattun** ⊛ m calico for lining; =¹**klinge** ⊙ f chopping-blade or -knife; =**knecht** m: a) ostler; b) ⚔ (Soldat, der die Pferde weidet) soldier who grazes the horses; =**koch-apparat** m zum Dämpfen v. Vieh⸗futter: boiler for cattle-food; =**korn** n grain serving as fodder, corn for cattle; =**kräuter** n/pl. feeding herbs pl.; =**krippe** f crib for cattle-food, manger; =²**leinen** ⊛ n linen for lining; =¹**mangel** m scarcity of fodder; =²**mauer** f: a) ⊙ arch. retain- (or revetment-)wall; b) ⚒ sustaining wall.

futtern P (ˊ) v/n. ⚙ a. 1. = »füttern¹ II«. — 2. provc. u. P = schimpfen. fluchen.

füttern¹ (ˊ⌣) [ahd.] ⚙ a. I v/a. 1. ein Tier ⚌ to feed ...., to give ... food, to provide ... with fodder; Kinder, Kranke ꝛc. (durch Zuführung von Speise mit der Hand) ⚌ to feed ... (by hand), to give ... food or s.th. to eat (and drink). — 2. mit dem Futter als obj.: Hafer ⚌ to feed (horses) with oats. — 3. mit Angabe der Wirkung: ein Tier ꝛc. groß ⚌ to raise (or breed, bring up) ...; tot ⚌ to kill by over-feeding. — 4. ⊙ (mit Brennstoff versehen) to feed a furnace. — 5. abs. der Knecht hat die Pferde, das Vieh gefüttert ... has fed the horses, the cattle. — II v/n. (h.) 6. die Pferde haben gefüttert (gefressen) ... have eaten (their food) or fed; F burschikos von Menschen: to dine, F to feed. — III ~ n ⚌ 7. = »Fütterung¹ 1«.

füttern² ⊙ (ˊ⌣) [Futter²] I v/a. ⊛ a. (innen bekleiden) to line (inside), to provide with a(n inside) lining or casing; mit Pelz, Watte ⚌ to fur, to pad; ⊙ mit Blei, Metall, Planken ⚌ to lead, to sheathe, to plank; Tapeziererei: (ausholstern) to stuff. — II ~ n ⚌ = »Fung²«.

Futter¹-netz (ˊ⌣...) n ⚙ agr. feeding-net for cattle; =**not** f = »mangel«; =**pflanzen** f pl. =**kräuter**; =²**rahmen** ⊙ m eines Schiebefensters: (English) casement, sash-frame; =¹**raufe** f in Ställen feedrack; ⚌**reich** a. abounding in forage; =**rübe** f, agr., etwa: mangel-wurzel, swede. vgl. »wurzel«; =**sack** m: a) feedbag; b) = »beutel«; =**schneider** m, agr. fodder-chopper, haycutter; =**schwinge** ⊙ f winnowing basket; =**stätte** f feeding- (für Pferde a. baiting-)place; =²**stoff** ⊛ m lining; =¹**stroh** n, agr. feeding-straw; =**trog** m, agr. feed-trough; manger; =²**tuch** ⊛ n cloth, material for lining.

Fütterung¹ (ˊ⌣) f ⊛ 1. feeding, &c.; (Furagieren) forage. — 2. ⚔ (Futter) fodder, provender. [or casing.]

Fütterung² ⊙ (ˊ⌣) f ⊛ (inside) lining

Futter¹-wagen ⚔ (ˊ⌣...) m ⚙ der Bagage provision-van, wagon with eatables or victuals; =**wicke** ♀ f common vetch (Vi'cia sati'⸗⸗); =**wurzeln** f pl. root-crop sg., vgl. »rübe«; =**zeug** ⊛ = »tuch«.

Futurum (ˇ⸱ˊ⌣) n ⊛ gr. (Zukunft) future (tense); F. exaktum n ⊛ second future.

G

G, g (ˉ) n, inv. Buchstabe G, g.

G, g ♪ n, inv. (Quinte in der C-Durtonleiter) G; G=**Dur** G major, G=**Moll** G minor; G=**Saite** f G string; G=**Schlüssel** m G (or treble) clef.

G ⊛ abbr. auf Kurszetteln: Geld.

g. öft. g abbr. = Gramm.

Gä-a (ˊ⌣) [grch. gaia, gē Erde] npr/f. ⊛ myth. the (goddess) Earth.

gab (ˊ) impf. ind. von geben.

Gabbro (ˊ⌣) [it., *ar.] m ⊛ min. (Gestein) gabbro(nite), diallage-rock.

Gabe (ˊ⌣) [mhd. »geben«] f ⊛ 1. (Geschenk) gift, present; in Geld bestehend a.: größere: donation; b) kleinere: gratuity; (Trinkgeld) tip; milde ~ alms, charity; kleine ~ pittance; (Opfer) offering; um eine milde ~ bitten to beg alms, to ask (for) charity; eine ~ reichen to dispense charity; rel. milde ~n pl. works pl. of charity. — 2. med. (Maßbestimmung) dose. — 3. (Begabung) talent, die ~ zu gefallen the gift (or art) of pleasing; ~ fürs Radfahren ꝛc. knack (or skill) for cycling, &c.; ~ der Rede gift of speech, F gift of the gab.

gäbe (ˊ⌣) I impf. subj. von geben. — II [mhd.] a. (jetzt nur inv.) s. gäng.

Gabel (ˊ⌣) [ahd., *flt.] f ⊛ 1. (Heu⸗, Mist⸗) pitchfork, (Tisch⸗)~ fork; kleine ~ (auch dim. Gäbelchen) small fork, bisw. forket, ♀ = ~ 3; mit der ~ fassen, auf die ~ spießen to (take up with a) fork. — 2. hunt. ~ des Hirschgeweihes forked end of the antlers. — 3. ♀ (Wickelranke) tendril; ~ der Baumzweige crotch. — 4. ⊙ eines Wagens = ~**deichsel**; e-s Scharnierbandes: fork-end. — 5. artill. beim Einschießen: (weite, enge) ~ (long, short) bracket.

Gabel-anker ⚓ (ˊ⌣...) m ⊛ (Bug-anker) (small) bow-anchor; =**antilo'pe** f =

[Gabelarm] — 402 — [Galgenvogel]

=bock a; =arm m eines Wagens shaft, thill; =ast m forked branch; =baum ⊕ m shaft of a thill; =bein n der Vögel: (die beiden verwachsenen Schlüsselbeine) forked bone; ⚕ furcula; =bock m, zo. a) pronghorned antilope, cabrit (Antilo'capra america'na); b) (Rehbock) two-year-old buck, auch = =hirsch.

Gäbelchen (⌣⌣) n ㉓ f. Gabel 1.

Gabel=deichsel ⊕ (⌣⌣...) f ㉖ (pair of) shafts or thills pl. of a carriage.

Gab(e)ler (⌣⌣⌣) m ㉒ = Gabelhirsch.

gabel=förmig (⌣⌣...) a. ㊋ fork-shaped, ⚕ furciform, furcate(d); ⚕⚕ geteilt: ⚕ dichotomous; 2e Teilung =teilung; =frühstück n lunch(eon); ein ~ einnehmen to (take) lunch; =gehörn n, hunt. forked antlers pl. or head; =gemse f. zo. = =antilo'pe; =hirsch m, hunt. (zweijähriger Hirsch) brocket.

gab(e)licht, mst gab(e)lig (⌣⌣⌣) a. ㊋ forked, forky; ⚕ und zo. = gabelförmig.

Gabel=kreuz (⌣...) n ㉓ her. forked cross, pall (Y); =mast ⚓ m forked mast.

gabeln (⌣⌣) ㉒a. I v/a. 1. to fork. — 2. hunt. von Hirschen: (auf die Gabel spießen) to gore. — II v/n. (h.) 3. to eat with the fork; F (zulangen, tüchtig essen) to play a good knife and fork. — III sich ⚕ v/refl. 4. (sich gabelförmig teilen) to fork (off or out), to bifurcate; to branch off. — IV = n ㉓ 5. = G/ung.

Gabel=pferd (⌣...) n ㉓ thill- (or shaft-)horse, thiller; =pflug ⊕ m, agr. forked plough; =punkt m point of bifurcation; =riegel ⊕ m Wagenbau: shaft-bar; =schwanz m, ent. pussmoth (Harpyi'a vi'nula); =spaltung f = =teilung; =stange ⊕ f, mech. forked (or two-pronged) pole; =stiel m handle of a fork, fork-handle; =stück ⊕ n forked piece of wood; =stütze f: a) ⊕ u. ⚔ thill- (or shaft-)prop; b) ehm. ⚔ fork-rest; =teilung f = Gabelung.

Gab(e)lung (⌣⌣⌣) f ㊋ fork(ing); bifurcation, ⚕ dichotomy.

Gabel=wagen ⊕ (⌣⌣...) m ㉒ thill-cart; =weih(e) f m, orn. glede, (fork-tailed) kite (Milvus rega'lis); =zacke(n m) f, =zinke(n m) f prong of a fork.

Gabler (⌣⌣) m ㉒ = Gabelhirsch.

gablicht, gablig f. gabelicht, gabelig.

Gabri-el (⌣⌣⌣) [hebr. Gottes Held] npr/m. ㉝ ㊌ α. (auch Bn.) Gabriel; ~e (⌣⌣⌣) npr/f. ㉝ ㊌ β. (Bn.) Gabriella.

gack(s) (⌣) int., ~ n, inv. Stimmen von Hühnern ꝛc. nachahmend: cluck! cluck!

gacke(l)n ㉘ (㉒a.), gackern ㉒a., gacksen ㉚ [ahd. lautm.] (⌣⌣) I v/n. (h.) v. der Henne: to cluck, von Gänsen ꝛc. (auch contp. von Menschen): to gaggle, cackle, fig. (schwatzen) to chatter, jabber; Sprichw. Hühner, die viel ⚕ legen wenig Eier, etwa: people who talk most do least; great boast small roast. — II ~ n ㉓ cackling; fig. chattering, F gab.

Gademer (⌣⌣⌣) [Gaden] m ㉒ = Häusler.

Gaden südd. (⌣⌣) [ahd.] m (h) ㉓ (Hütte mit 1 Gemach) cottage (or hut) consisting of one room.

gadhelisch (⌣⌣⌣) [gäl.] a. ㊋ (die schott. Gälen betr.) Gadhelic.

Gaffel¹ obb. (⌣⌣) [it.* dtsch. (Ab)gabe] f ㊽ (Zunft, Innung) corporation, guild.

Gaffel² (⌣⌣) [ndd. = Gabel] f ㊽ 1. fork. — 2. ⚓ (Segelstange) gaff; eine ~ toppen to peak a gaff; ~=fall n ㊿ gaff-fall; ~=klaue f jaw (of a gaff); ~=(topp)=segel n gaff-(top)sail.

gaffen (⌣⌣) [md.: gape] ㊿ I v/n. (h.) 1. to gape, to stand gaping or agape, to gape in the air. — 2. fast †: (gähnen) to yawn. — 3. (stieren) to stare, gaze. — II sich ⚕ v/refl. 4. mit Angabe der Wirkung: sich blind ⚕ to stare one's eyes out. — III ~ n ㉓ 5. gaping, &c. (f. I).

Gaffer (⌣⌣) m ㉒. ~in f ㊼ gaper; ~ei (⌣⌣⌣) f ㊾ = gaffen III.

Gagat ⚕ (⌣⌣) [grch. Gagá ⚕ St. i. Lyzien; vgl. Jett] n (m) ㊿e. min. jet; pitch-coal.

Gage (⌣⌣⌣) [nhd. 17. sae.; fr. gage m; *dtsch. Wette] f ㊿ (Gehalt) von Beamten, Schauspielern ꝛc.: salary, pay; von Offizieren: pay; von Dienern: wages pl.

Gagel ⚕ (⌣⌣) m ㉖ (sweet) gale, Dutch myrtle (Myri'ca gale).

gäh ⚓ (⌣) a. ㊋ = jäh.

gähnen (⌣⌣) [ahd.: yawn] I v/n. (h.) ㊿ to yawn, ⚕ to oscitate; Oder (klaffender) Schlund yawning (or open) chasm. — II ~ n ㉓ yawning, ⚕ oscitation; das ~ steckt an yawning is catching or infectious.

Gähner (⌣⌣) m ㉒, ~in f ㊼ yawner.

Gahnit ⚕ (⌣⌣⌣) [J. G. Gahn, schwed. Chemiker] m, min. gahnite ($Zn Al_2 O_4$).

Gähn=krämpfe ("...) m/pl. ㊿ convulsive yawning sg.; =laut m, gr.: ⚕ hiatus; =sucht f yawning fit, ⚕ oscitancy.

Gaikawar Ost-J. (⌣⌣⌣) m ㉕ (Fürst v. Baroda) Gaekwar, Guicowar.

Gala (⌣⌣⌣) [nhd. 17. sae.; *span.] f ㊽ 1. (Hoftracht) gala, pomp, state; in großer ~ in full dress, F in full rig. — 2. (Hoffest) drawing-room (or great reception) at which court-dress is worn.

Gala=anzug (⌣⌣...) m ㊿ dress- (or gala-)suit; court-dress; =degen ⚔ m dress-sword; =kleid n = =anzug.

Galan (⌣⌣) [span.] m ㊵d. co. (Liebhaber) galla'nt, lover, paramour, sweetheart; ihr ~ her young man.

Galander (⌣⌣⌣) m ㉒ 1. [mhd.,* grch.] orn. (Haubenlerche) crested lark. — 2. [fr. calandre] ent. (Kornwurm) corn-weevil.

galant (⌣⌣) [nhd. 1670;*fr.] a. ㊋ galla'nt; (höflich) courteous, polite (to the ladies); 2es Abenteuer love-affair, (amorous) intrigue. [manner(s pl.); courtesy.]

Galanterie (⌣⌣⌣⌣) [fr.] f ㊾ galla'nt]

Galanterie=arbeit ⚔ (⌣⌣⌣...) f ㊽ cheap (or imitation) jewellery or ornaments pl.; =arbeiten pl. = =waren a; =arbeiter m maker of fancy-goods; working jeweller; =arti'kel m fancy-article; =degen m dress-sword; =handel m jewellery trade; trade in fancy-goods; =händler m (cheap) jeweller; dealer in f.-goods; =waren f/pl.: a) f.-goods pl., f.-stationery or =wares pl.; b) (cheap or imitation) jewellery; =waren=händler m: a) dealer in fancy-goods, f.-stationer; b) = =händler; =waren=handlung f f.-business.

Gala=tag (⌣⌣...) m ㊿ gala-day.

Galater (⌣⌣⌣) [Kelten] m ㉒, ~in (⌣⌣⌣) f ㊼ Alt.: Galatian; bibl. der Brief Pauli an die ~ Paul's Epistle to the Galatians.

Galati-en ⚕ (⌣⌣(⌣)⌣) npr/n. ㉝α. (alte Landschaft in Klein-asien) Galatia.

Gala=Uniform (⌣⌣...) f ㊵ dress-uniform; =vorstellung f, thea. dress-performance.

Galban (⌣⌣) n ⚕ d. u. ㊵, ~harz n ㊿, ~um (⌣⌣) n ⚕ f. * hebr.] pharm. (Harz von Fe'rula galbani'flua) galbanum.

Gäle (⌣⌣) npr.m. ㊸ f. Gälen.

Galeasse ⚓ (⌣⌣⌣⌣) [it.] f ㊽ ehm. (großes, armiertes Ruderschiff) galeas, galliass.

Galeere ⚓ (⌣⌣⌣) [nhd., fr., span.,* grch.] f ㊽ ehm. ⚓ (gr. Ruderschiff) galley; zu den ~n verurteilen, ehm.: to send to the galleys, jetzt: to penal servitude; =arbeit f ㊽ (forced) labour at the galleys; jetzt: penal servitude; =ofen ⊕ m, metall. galley-furnace; =sklave m galley-slave; wie ein ~ arbeiten F to work like a nigger or a slave; =strafe f = =arbeit; =sträfling m = =sklave; =volk n crew of a galley.

Gälen (⌣⌣) m/pl. ⊕ (keltischer Volksstamm) Gaelic people, Gaels pl.; vgl. gälisch.

galenisch (⌣⌣⌣) [Gale'nos, ...us, griech. Arzt (131–201) Galen(us)] a. ㊋ med. Galenic(al); Galenist (⌣⌣⌣) m ㊵ ehm. Galenist, follower of Galenus.

Galeone ⚓ (⌣⌣⌣⌣) [span.] f ㊽ (ehm. span. Kriegsschiff) galleon.

Galeote ⚓ (⌣⌣⌣⌣) [span., it.] f ㊽ (ehm. kleines Ruderschiff) galliot, galiot(t).

Galerie (⌣⌣⌣) [nhd. 17. sae.; it. v. * Galilää] f ㊽ 1. gallery; f. Bilder=2, Gemälde=2. — 2. thea.: a) (oberster Teil des Hauses) gallery; co. the gods pl.; b) (freier Raum, wo die Zuschauer sich ergehen können) lobby. — 3. ⚔ frt. (bedeckter Gang) gallery, covered passage. — 4. ⚓ (Heck=)~ (stern) gallery.

Galgant ⚕ (⌣⌣) [mhd.,* ar., pers.] m ㊵d. (Alpi'nia oder Mara'nta gala'nga); ~=harz n ㊿. ~=wurzel f galanga (gum, root).

Galgen (⌣⌣) [ahd.: gallows] m ㉓ 1. gallows, gibbet; an den ~ bringen, schicken to hang, to send to the gallows; an den ~ kommen to come to the gallows, to be hanged, F to swing; es steht ~ und Rad darauf it is a capital offence, F it is a hanging matter; er sieht aus, wie vom ~ gefallen F he has a hang-dog look about him; er verdient den ~ he deserves to be hanged. — 2. ⊕ (Querholz) cross-beam or -timber; (der Baum für den Schwengel des Schöpfbrunnens) post (or tree) for the swipe (of a well). — 3. ⚓ (Gerüst auf dem Oberdeck zum Auflegen von Rundhölzern) gallows(-bitts pl.).

Galgen=frist (⌣⌣...) f ㊿ reprieve; weil S. short grace; e-m eine ~ gewähren to grant a p. a short respite; =gesicht F n gallows-face, hang-dog look; =holz n gallows-tree; =ig wie ~ thoroughly false; =humo'r m grim (or sorry) humour, reckless merriment; =kanda're f, man. port-mouthed bit; =männchen n männlein n = Alraun 2; =mäßig a. ㊋ fit for the gallows; bisw.: ⚕ patibulary; =physiognomie f = =gesicht; =schelm m, =schwengel m, co. gallows-bird, hang-dog, ehm. auch: Tyburn-blossom; =strick m, =vogel m

good-for-nothing, ne'er-do-well, young scamp.
Galici-en ♀ (⏑–(⏑)⏑) *npr/n.* Ba. (spanische Provinz) Galicia; vgl. Galizien.
Galiläa ♀ (⏑⏑–⏑) [hebr. Kreis] *npr/n.* Ba. Alt.: (nördl. Teil v. Palästi'na) Galilee.
Galiläer (⏑⏑–⏑) *m* (22) *fig.* = Christus, † = Christ, **~in** *f* (47), **galiläisch** *a.* (22) Galilean; Galiläisches Meer (See Genezareth) Galilean Lake, Sea of Galilee, Sea of Genesaret.
Galimathias öst. = Gallimathias.
☞ **Galio…** s. Galeo… und Galjo…
gälisch (–⏑) *a.* (66) (hochschottisch [u. irisch]), die Le Sprache, das ~(e) (67) Gaelic
Galitzen-stein (⏑⏑–) *m* (62) = Zinkvitriol.
Galizien ♀ (⏑–⏑⏑) [slaw. *Halicz*] *npr/n.* Ba. (öst. Kronland) Galicia.
Galizier (⏑–⏑⏑) *m* (23), **~in** *f* (47), **galizisch** (⏑–⏑) *a.* (66) Galician.
Galjaß ⚓ (⏑–) *f* (47) = Galeasse.
Galjon ⚓ (⏑–) [span.] *n* ⓓ. (51) (Schiffsschnabel) head, prow; auch = Galjonsbild.
Galjons-bild ⚓ (⏑–…) *n* (62), **-figu'r** *f* (geschnitztes Bild am Bug des Schiffes) figure-head of a ship.
Galjot ⚓ (⏑–) *f* (46) = Galeote.
Gall-apfel ⚘ (–⏑⏑) [nhd.] *m* (62) gallnut, gall(-apple), oak-apple or -ball.
Gallapfel-aufguß (–⏑⏑…) *m* (62), **-extra'kt** *m* infusion, extract of gallnuts; **-eiche** ⚘ *f* = Galleiche; **-gerbsäure** *f*, *chm.* gallotannic acid; **Lsauer** *a.*, 2c. = gallus-sauer 2c.
Galle[1] (–⏑) [ahd.: gall: grch. *chŏlē'*] *f* (48) **1.** *physiol.* gall, bile (a. *fig.* = Zorn, Groll); *fig.* auch: bitterness, venom; ~ abführend(es Mittel) ⚗ cholagogic; ~ enthaltend, ~ führend bilious, ⚗ biliary; *fig.* a. choleric. — **2.** *fig.* s-e ~ ausschütten to vent one's spite or rage or anger; e-m die ~ erregen, ins Blut treiben to stir up a p.'s bile or spleen; er schreibt mit Gift und ~ his pen is dipped in gall; Gift und ~ speien to fret and fume, to be in a towering rage; die ~ läuft ihm über his blood is boiling, F his monkey is up; s. Honig.
Galle[2] (–⏑) [mhd., *span., it.] *f* (48) **1.** *vet.* = Geschwulst. — **2.** ⚙ Gießerei: (Blase in Gußstücken) flaw, honeycomb; Glasmacherei: (oben schwimmende schaumige Masse) glass-gall. — **3.** *agr.* (nasse Stelle) water- (or weather-)gall. [*cus infecto'ria*).
Gall-eiche ⚘ (–…) *f* (62) gall-oak (*Quer-*
gallen (–⏑) *v/a.* (88) **1.** ⚙ Färberei: = gallieren. — **2.** Kochk.: e-n Fisch L (ausnehmen) to take the gall-bag out of a fish.
Gallen-ader (–⏑…) *f* (62) *anat.*: ⚗ cystic vein; **-behältnis** *n*, *anat.* = -blase; **Lbitter** *a.* (66) (as) bitter as gall; **-blase** *f*, *anat.* gall-bladder, ⚗ vesicle of the gall; **-blasen-blut-ader** *f* = -ader; **-blasen-gang** *m*, *anat.* = Gallengang; **-blasen-stein** *m*, *path.*: ⚗ cystic calculus; **-brechen** *n*, *path.* bilious sickness or vomiting, ⚗ cholemesia; **-ergießung** *f*, *path.* overflow(ing) of the bile; **-fett** *n*, *chm.*: ⚗ cholesterin(e)($C_{27}H_{45}$.OH); **-fieber** † *n*, *path.* bilious fever; **-gang** *m*, *anat.* gall- (or bile-, cystic) duct; **-gefäße** *n/pl.* *anat.* biliary vessels *pl.*; **-kolik** *f*, *path.* bilious (or biliary) colic; **-krankheit** *f*, *path.* bilious attack or complaint; **-lehre** *f*: ⚗ cholology; **-leiden** *n* affection of the gall-bladder; **-säure** *f*, *chm.*: ⚗ (Cholsäure) cholic acid ($C_{24}H_{40}O_5$); **-stein** *m*, *path.* gallstone, ⚗ biliary calculus.
Gallert (–⏑) *n* ⓓ. [Gelee], mst **~e** (⏑–⏑) *f* (48) [mhd.] **1.** jelly, gelatine, aus Tierknochen: glue; (sich) in ~ verwandeln to turn to jelly, ⚗ to gelatinize. — **2.** *pharm.* (Brei) pulp. — **3.** ⚘ = ~pilz, ~schwamm.
gallert-ähnlich (–⏑…) *a.* (66), **Lartig** *a.* jelly-like, gelatinous; **-masse** *f* (62) jelly-like (or gelatinous) substance; **-pilz** *m*: ⚗ tremella (*Treme'lla*); **-säure** *f*, *chm.*: ⚗ pectic acid; **-schwamm** ⚘ *m* slimesponge (*Myxospo'ngia*).
gallicht (–⏑) *a.* (66) = gallig.
Galli-en ♀ (–(⏑)⏑) [lt.] *npr/n.* Ba. (das alte Frankreich) Gaul, land of the Gauls.
Galli-er (–(⏑)⏑) *m* (22), **~in** *f* (47) Gaul.
gallieren ⚙ (⏑–⏑) [dtsch-lt.] *v/a.* (93) Färberei: (mit Gall-äpfeln färben) to (dye with) gall.
gallig (–⏑) *a.* (66) full of bile, bilious; *physiol.* (Galle führend, aus Galle entstehend): ⚗ biliary; *fig.* rancorous, choleric; (jähzornig) irascible; **~keit** (–⏑–) *f* (46) biliousness; *fig.* irascibility.
gallikanisch (⏑⏑–⏑) [lt.] *a.* (66) (französisch-katholisch) Gallican (church, rites, &c.).
Gallimathias (⏑⏑–⏑⏑, ↘ ⏑⏑–⏑⏑) [fr. *galimatias*, ſt. **gallus Matthiae*] *m* (*n*) *inv.* (sinnloses Zeug) nonsense.
☞ **Gallio-…** s. Galeo-… u. Galjo-…
gallisch (–⏑) *a.* (66) Gallic, Gaulish.
gallisieren (⏑⏑–⏑) *v/a.* (93) **1.** (französisch machen) to Frenchify. — **2.** [L. Gall, 1852] to improve wine by Gall's treatment, to gall(is)ize.
Gallitzen-stein (⏑–⏑…) *m* (62) = Zinkvitriol.
Gallizismus (⏑⏑–⏑) [lt.] *m* (27) (französische Spracheigentümlichkeit) Gallicism.
Gall-milbe (–…) *f* (62) *ent.* gall-mite (*Phyto'ptus*); **-mücke** *f*, *ent.* gall-gnat (*Cecidomy'ia*).
Gallo-grieche (–⏑…) *m* (62), **-griechin** *f*, **Lgriechisch** *a.* (66) Gallo-Greek; **-mani'e** *f* (48) (Franzosenliebe) gallomania.
Gallon (⏑–) [engl., *lt. (s. Gelte)] *n* (51), **~e** *f* (48) (engl. Hohlmaß = 4,54 Liter) gallon.
Gallo-romane (–⏑…) *m* (62), **-romanin** *f* od. **-römer(in** *f*) *m* Gallo-Roman.
Gall-stoff (–…) *m* (62) *chm.*: ⚗ bilin(e); **-sucht** *f*: a) *path.* = Gelbsucht; b) *fig.* choleric temperament; **Lsüchtig** *a.* (66): a) *path.* = gelbsüchtig; b) *fig.* choleric; sour-tempered.
gallus-sauer ⚗ (–⏑…) *a.* (66) gallic; **L-saures** Salz gallate; **-säure** *f* (62) gallic acid ($C_7H_6O_5$); **-tinte** *f* gallnut ink.
Gall-wespe (–…) *f* (62) *ent.* (Insekt, dessen Stich die Gall-äpfel hervorruft) gall-fly or -insect (*Cynips tincto'ria*).
Galmei ⚒ (⏑–) [nhd.; fr. *calamine*; *grch. *kadmei'a*] *m* ⓒ. *min.* (Zinkerz) calamin(e), cadmia, galmey; edler ~ zinc-spar; **~blumen** *f/pl.* (unreines Zinkoxyd) tutty. [(Litze) galloon.]
Galon (⏑–') [it., fr.] *m* (51), **~e** (⏑–⏑) *f* (48)
galonieren (⏑⏑–⏑) [fr. *galonner*] *v/a.* (93) Uniformen 2c.: to (trim with) galloon, to edge with gold- (or silver-) lace.
Galopp (⏑–) [nhd. 1600; fr.; * dtsch gallischer od. Ge(h)lauf] *m* ⓓ. gallop (a. Tanz u. Musik dazu); *man.* im ~ at a gallop; im kurzen ~ at an easy canter; im vollen ~ at full gallop, at full tilt; F at a tearing pace; im gestreckten ~ voranjagen to gallop ahead at full speed or in hot haste; ⚔ sie brachten zwei Kanonen im ~ ins Treffen they galloped two guns into action; *fig.* es geht mit ihm im ~ (sehr rasch) zu Ende his end is fast approaching, he is rapidly sinking.
Galoppade (⏑⏑–⏑) [fr.] *f* (48) *man.* (gehobener Bahngalopp) und Tanz: gallopade.
galoppieren (⏑⏑–⏑) [fr.] **I** *v/n.* (h.) (93) *man.* (Galopp reiten) to gallop, to (ride at a) canter; Tanzkunst: to (dance a) gallop; *path.* Lde Schwindsucht galloping (or rapid) consumption. — **II** ~ *n* (23) gallop(ing), gallopade.
Galosche (⏑–⏑) [nhd. 16. sae.; * fr. *galoche* aus mlt. *gallica socca*] *f* (48) (überschuh) mst *pl.* ~n galoshes, goloshes *pl.*
galt (–) (gälte ↘ *subj.*) *impf.* von gelten.
galvanisch (⏑–⏑) [Galva'ni, it. Naturforscher, 1737—1798] *a.* (66) (u. *adv.*) *phys.*: ⚗ galvanic(ally); s. Batterie 2; *typ.* Le Matrize electrotyped matrix; Le Säule *phys.* galvanic (or voltaic) pile; Ler Strom galvanic current; ⚙ Le Vergoldung, Versilberung electro-gilding, -plating; Ler Vergolder, Versilberer electro-gilder, -plater; L (*adv.*) verkupfertes Eisen electro-copper.
galvanisieren (⏑⏑⏑–⏑) **I** *v/a.* (93) *phys.*: ⚗ to galvanize; ⚙ to electroplate. — **II** ~ *n* (23) u. **Galvanisierung** *f* (46) galvanization; ⚙ electroplating.
Galvanismus (⏑⏑–⏑) [neu-lt.] *m* (27) *phys.*: ⚗ galvanism; galvanic (or voltaic) electricity.
Galvano (⏑–⏑) *n* (51) *typ.* (Kupferklischee) electrotype (plate); **~graphie** (⏑–⏑…") *f* (48) galvanography; electrography; **Lgra'phisch** *a.* (66) galvanographic; **~kaustik** *f* (46) galvano-cautery; **~meter** *n* (*m*) (22) *phys.* ⚙ galvanometer; **~plastik** (1836) *f* (46) galvanoplastic art, electrometallurgy, electrotyping; **~pla'stiker** *m* (22) electro-metallurgist, electrotyper; **Lplastisch** *a.* galvanoplastic, electro-metallurgic; Lplastischer Abdruck electrotype; **~skop** ⚗ *n* ⓓ. *phys.* (Messer kleiner Elektrizitätsmengen) galvanoscope; **~typie** *f* (48) galvanotypy.
Gamander ⚘ (⏑–⏑) [lt. (*grch.) *chamae'drys*] *m* (22) (echter) ~ germander (*Teu'crium* [*Chamaedrys*]).
Gamander-ehrenpreis (⏑–⏑…) *m* (62) germander-speedwell (*Vero'nica chamae'drys*).
Gamasche (⏑–⏑) [fr. *gamache*] *f* (48) **1.** mst *pl.* ~n gaiters *pl.*; kurze ~ spats *pl.*; lederne ~n leggings, uppers *pl.* — **2.** F *fig.* (Angst) er hat höllische ~n davor he is in awful dread (or terribly afraid) of it, F he's very funky about it.
Gamaschen-dienst (⏑–⏑…) *m* (62) (soldatisches Wesen) military pedantry, F pipe-clay; **-held** *m* pipe-clay (soldier); (strenger Offizier) F martinet; **-knopf** *m* gaiter-button.
Gambe ♪ (–⏑) [it.] *f* (48) ehm. bass-viol.
Gambit (⏑–) [it.] *n* (51) Schachspiel: gambit; abgelehntes ~ gambit refused.

[Gambohanf] — 404 — [Gänsehaut]

Gambo-hanf ● (⌣⌣) m ⓢ brown hemp, fibre of the roselle, Ambaree fibre, Deccan hemp (v. *Hibi'scus canna'binus*).

Gams provc. (⌣) f ⓢ = Gemse.

Ganasche (⌣⌣) [fr. *ganache*] f ⓢ vet. (part of) a horse's lower jaw.

Gan-erbe (″...) [ahd. Miterbe] m ⓢ ehm. jur. joint heir, coheir, ⁊ coparcener; **-erbschaft** f (gemeinsames Erbrecht): ⁊ coparcen(ar)y.

ganfen (⌣) [hebr.] v/a. ⓢ (stehlen) to steal, ℱ u. P to gonof, pinch, nick.

Gang (⌣) [ahd.: gang; *gehen] m Ⓓb. 1. (Art des Gehens) walk; nur v. Menschen: gait; (Schritt) step, pace; einen aufrechten ~ haben to have an upright gait, to walk upright; e-n lahmen, hinkenden ~ haben to walk lame, to limp; e-s Pferdes: action, carriage, bearing; vgl. ~art; (Tennis) rally, rest; der ~ (Lauf) des Flusses, der Gestirne the course of the river, of the stars; fig. der ~ der Ereignisse the march of events; ~ e-s Gespräches drift of a conversation; das ist einmal der ~ der Welt that is the way of the world; ⊕ mech. (Betrieb) work(ing); metall. des Ofens: working condition of the furnace. — 2. (das Gehen zum Vergnügen od. in Geschäften) walk(ing); einen ~ um die Stadt machen to (take a) walk (or stroll) round the town; j-s Gänge belauern, bewachen to watch a p.'s movements; wir haben mehrere Gänge zu besorgen ... to go to (or to call at) several places; Gänge gehen, machen to run (or go) errands, to do commissions; den ~ kann er sich sparen he may save himself the trouble of going; einen vergeblichen ~ tun to go on a fruitless errand or journey; eines Arztes: visit; ~ eines Briefträgers rc.: round; der ~ zum Eisenhammer (SCH.) the errand (or message) to the forge. — 3. (Weg) er weiß alle Gänge und Schliche he knows every move (on the board), he is wide-awake. — 4. (Tätigkeit, Lauf) ~ einer Maschine movement, motion, action, play of a machine; ~ e-s Schiffes course, headway, rate of going; im ~ bleiben to keep in motion or ℱ on the move; e-e Maschine in ~ bringen to set ... going or in motion; eine Mode rc.: to bring ... into vogue; to introduce (or start, set up, bring about) ...; ein Unternehmen rc.: to set on foot, to put life into; aus dem richtigen ~e bringen to throw out of gear, weits. a. to disarrange; et. in ~ erhalten to keep a th. going or alive; e-n ~ erhalten to keep a p. going or on the move or trot; das Recht muß seinen ~ geh(e)n justice must take (or have) its course; es geht alles seinen gewohnten ~ things are going on as usual or moving in the old groove; in ~ kommen to come into action or operation or play; ich kann damit nicht in ~ kommen I cannot get on with it; einer Sache ihren ~ lassen to let a th. take its course; e-n (un-) günstigen ~ nehmen to take a(n un-) favourable turn; im ~e sein to be in operation or in progress; in vollem ~e in full working order, in full swing; diese Münze ist nicht mehr im ~e ... is no longer in circulation or currency; außer ~ setzen ⊕ to throw out of gear, to put out of action. — 5. ♪ (Lauf) passage. — 6. fenc. pass, bout; Bogen: round; fig. e-n ~ mit e-m wagen to try a fall with a person. — 7. (langer, schmaler, eingeschlossener Verbindungsweg): a) passage; (Flur) auch: corridor; (Vorhalle) hall; unterirdischer, geheimer ~ subterraneous, private passage; ⚒ frt. bedeckter ~ gallery; ⚓ gangway; (Planken-)~ strake; b) anat. passage, canal, duct; im Ohr: ⁊ meatus. — 8. hort. (Weg zwischen den Beeten) path, zwischen Baumreihen: avenue. — 9. Kochkunst: (zusammen Aufgetragenes) course; letzter ~ last course, dessert. — 10. ⚒, geol. (Erz-)~ lode, vein, streak; gallery; ausgebauter ~ exhausted seam; seigerer, söhliger ~ vertical, horizontal lode; tauber ~ dead (or poor) lode; nach Gängen schürfen to search (or prospect) for lodes. — 11. ⊕ (Schrauben-, Gewinde-)~ groove, toter ~ slip of a screw; ~ (Windung) eines Taues um die Welle coil; ~ (Triebwerk) einer Maschine running; einer Mühle mill-work, run.

gäng (gäng) (⌣) [ahd.: gehen] a. inv., fast nur in: das ist ⁊ und gäbe that is the general custom or ℱ the usual thing.

Gang-art (⌣⌣) f ⓢ: a) walk; e-s Menschen auch: gait, e-s Pferdes (Schritt, Trab, Galopp): pace; Pferd von guter ~ good goer or stepper; b) ⚒ (taubes Gestein) dead rock, gangue.

gangbar (⌣-) a. ⓢ 1. (zum Gehen geeignet) passable, practicable; Wege ⁊ erhalten to keep ... in good condition or repair. — 2. von Münzen: current; von Arzneiwaren: officinal; ⁊e Ware saleable (or marketable) goods pl.; ⁊e Marken, Preise favourite (or popular) brands, prices pl.; nicht mehr ⁊ no longer in demand, out of fashion, unsaleable. — 3. ⁊er (viel befahrener) Weg much-frequented road.

Gangbarkeit (⌣--) f ⓢ passableness (or condition) of a road; currency of a coin; ⊕ saleableness (or marketableness) of goods; ⊕ good working of a machine.

Gangbar-machung (⌣-...) f ⓢ e-s Weges putting a road into good condition or repair, repairing a road.

Gang-bildung ⚒ (⌣-...) f ⓢ formation of gangues; **-bord** ⚓ m gangway.

Gängel (⌣) [Gehender] m ⓢ: ~ (Läufer) einer Wiege rocker of a cradle.

Gängel-band (⌣-) n ⓢ, womit man Kinder gehen lehrt: leading-strings pl.; fig. er wird von s-r Mutter am ~ geführt he is tied to his mother's apron-strings; sie führen ihn am ~e ℱ they lead him by the nose.

gängeln (⌣-) a. I v/n. (fn) 1. to doddle like a little child. — II v/a. 2. to lead a child by strings, mehr poet.: to teach a child to walk; fig. to keep a baby in leading-strings. — 3. die Wiege ⁊ to rock the cradle.

Gängel-wagen (⌣-...) m ⓢ für Kinder: children's go- (or mail-)cart.

Gänger (⌣-) m ⓢ walker; bsd. in Zssgn, z.B.: Fuß-⁊ pedestrian.

Gang-erz ⚒ n ⓢ gangue-ore.

Ganges-delphin (⌣-...) m ⓢ zo. platanist, Ost-J.: susu (Platani'sta gange'tica); **-gavial** m, **-krokodil** n, zo. gavial, nakoo (Gavia'lis gange'ticus).

Gang-gebirge ⚒ (⌣-...) n ⓢ (rock with) streaky formation of ore; **-gestein** ⚒ n = Gangart b.

ganghaft (⌣-) a. ⓢ = gangbar 2.

Gang-häuer ⚒ (⌣-...) m ⓢ lodesman.

gängig (⌣-) a. ⓢ: hunt. ⁊er Hund quick-footed dog, fleet hound; schwz. ⁊e Beine nimble legs pl.; ⊕ (vgl. ab2) ⁊e Ware saleable (or marketable) goods pl.

Gang-kreuz ⚒ (⌣-...) n ⓢ crossing (or intersection) of two lodes.

Gangli-en-system ⁊ (⌣⌣-...) [grch.] n ⓢ anat., physiol. ganglious system.

Ganglion ⁊ (⌣⌣-) [grch.] n ⓢ physiol. (Nervenknoten) ganglion.

Gang-masse ⚒ (⌣-...) f ⓢ = Gangart b.

Gangräne (⌣⌣) [grch.] f ⓢ path. (feuchter Brand) gangrene; **gangränös** (⌣-⌣) a. ⓢ (D10) (brandig) gangrenous.

Gang-spill ⚓ (⌣-...) n ⓢ (senkrechte Ankerwinde) capstan; **-spill-achse** f spindle of the capstan; **-stück** ⚒ n cutting; **-trum** ⚒ m thin (or poor) lode; **-weise** adv.: a) e-n ⁊ bezahlen to pay a p. for each commission (singly); b) ⚒ in lodes or streaks; **-werk** n: a) e-r Mühle: driving-gear or -machinery; b) e-r Uhr: works pl.; **-woche** f Cath.eccl. (Himmelfahrtswoche) Rogation week.

Ganner (⌣-) [: Gans] m ⓢ orn. merganser, goosander (Mergus merga'nser).

Gans (⌣) [ahd.: goose: lt. anser] f ⓢ 1. orn. goose (Anser); junge ~ (a. Gänschen, Gänslein n) little goose, gosling; gebrat(e)ne ~ roast goose. — 2. fig. dumme ~ (auch dummes Gänschen) silly (or simple-minded) woman or girl, ℱ silly goose. — 3. ⊕ ⁊ = Ganz.

gans-ähnlich (⌣...) a. ⓢ, **⁊artig** a. goose-like, ⁊ anserine; **⁊braten** m ⓢ = Gänse-... [bd 1 u. 2).]

Gänschen (⌣-) n ⓢ dim. von Gans (s. 1).

gänse-artig (⌣-...) a. ⓢ resembling geese, ⁊ anserine; **-blümchen** ♀ n ⓢ daisy (Bellis peren'nis); **-blume** ♀ f: a) = -blümchen; b) = Maßlieb; **-braten** m roast goose; **-brust** f a) breast of a goose; b) fig. bei Menschen: narrow chest; **-distel** ♀ f sow-thistle (Sonchus), gemeine ~ milkweed (S. olera'ceus); **-feder** f goose-feather or -quill; s. a. Feder 2; **-fett** n g.-dripping; **-fingerkraut** ♀ n g.-grass, silver-weed (Potenti'lla anseri'na); **-fuß** m goose's foot; -foot (Chenopo'dium); stinkender ~ stinking blite or goosefoot (Ch. vulva'ria); weißer ~ lamb's-quarters pl. (Ch. album); ⊕ typ. **-füße** pl. (auch **-füßchen** n/pl.) (Anführungszeichen, dtsch.: „", „", engl.: " ", ' ') inverted commas, quotation-marks pl.; **-gekröse** n = -klein; **-geschnatter** n cackling of geese.

gänsehaft (⌣⌣-) a. ⓢ after the manner of a goose; fig. (einfältig) silly, stupid.

Gänse-haut (⌣-...) f ⓢ goose-skin or -flesh; ich bekam eine ~ (mich schauderte) my flesh began to creep, it made my

flesh creep; =**hirt**(**in** *f*) *m*, =**junge** *m* goose-herd; g.-boy (-girl); =**kiel** *m* g.-quill; =**klein** *n* Kochk.: g.-giblets *pl.*; =**kraut** ⚘ *n*: a) = =kresse; b) = =finger=kraut; =**kresse** ⚘ *f* wall-cress (*A'rabis* [*hirsu'ta*]); =**küchlein, kü(c)ken** *n* gosling; =**leber=pastete** *f* goose-liver pie, Straßburger: Strassburg pie; =**mädchen** *n* goose-girl; =**marsch** *m* g.-step, single file; im ~ (hinter=ea.) antreten to walk (in) single file; =**pfeffer** *m*, =**ragout** *n* = =klein.

Gänserich¹ (ˊ◡◡) [nhd. 16. *sae.*] *m* [D]d. (Männchen der Gans) gander.

Gänserich² ⚘ (‿) [nhd. (P : Gänserich¹) *Grensing] *m* [D]d. = Gänsefingerkraut.

Ganser(t) *provc.* (ˊ◡) *m* [22] = Gänserich¹.

Gänse=schmalz (ˊ◡...) *n* [62] = =fett; =**schwarz**(=**sauer**) *n* Kochk.: goose-giblets *pl.* served up in g.-blood; =**seuche** *f*, *vet.* gargil; =**stall** *m*, =**steige** *f* g.-shed or -coop; =**trift** *f* pasture for geese; village-green; =**wein** *m* (Wasser) Adam's ale; =**zucht** *f* breeding of geese. [bs 1).

Gänslein (ˊ-) *n* [23] *dim.* von Gans (s.

Gant $ obd. (ˊ) [nhd.; *fr. *encan*; *lt. *in quantum*? wie teuer?] *f* [46] 1. = Auktio'n. — 2. (Konkurs) bankruptcy, failure (in business); die ~ verhängen über to declare *a. p.* bankrupt.

ganten $ südd. (ˊ◡) *v/n.* (h.) [88] to order the sale of a bankrupt stock.

Ganter ⚙ (ˊ◡) [fr. *chantier*] *m* [22] (Unterlage für Bierfässer) scantling, gantry.

Ganymed (◡◡ˊ) [grch.] [33][37]α. ~**es** (◡◡ˊ◡) [16]γ *npr/m*, *myth.* (Mundschenk der Götter, Liebling des Zeus) Ganymede(s).

ganz (ˊ) [ahd.] **I** *a.* [66] (bei Städte= u. sächlichen Ländernamen ohne *art.* und *inv.*, zB. ~ Rom, ~ Italien) **1.** (ungeteilt) whole, entire; undivided, all; ~ Europa all (or the whole of) Europe; ⚒ ~es Gestein solid rock; ich wünsche es von ~em Herzen ... with all my heart; ein ~es Jahr a whole year; Krieg durchtobte das ~e Land the war raged throughout the whole (length and breadth of) the country; die ~e Leitung des Geschäfts the entire management ...; er ist ein ~er Mann he is every inch a man, he is quite a man; ein ~er Redner quite an orator; die ~e Welt the whole world (all the world: meist = jedermann); in der ~en Welt all the world over; eine ~e Zahl *arith.* a whole number, ⚗ an integer; die ~e Zeit hindurch during the whole (of the) time, all the time. — **2.** (vollständig) complete, total; ~ machen to complete; to make whole, (flicken) to mend; der ~e Betrag the total amount, the sum total; eine ~e Stunde a full hour; ♪ ~e Note semibreve; *paint.* Bild in ~er Figur life-size portrait. — **II** *adv.* **3.** (s. I) wholly, entirely; all; thoroughly, quite, completely, totally, altogether; fully; nicht ~ achtzig Jahre alt not quite (or something less than) eighty years old; et. ~ anderes (a. ~ (et)was anderes) quite a different thing or F another story; vgl. Bauer² 1 am Ende; ~ durchlesen to read right through; ~ ebenso gut quite as good; ~ nackt stark naked; ~ naß wet through; ~ still=steh(e)n to make a dead stop; ~ unrichtig altogether wrong; ~ verkehrt entirely wrong, quite perverse; ~ wohl quite well. — **4.** verstärkt durch **gar**: ~ und gar nicht not at all, not in the least, not a bit of it, by no means; ~ und gar falsch absolutely false. — **5.** mit *adv.* (in hohem Grade): ~ besonders more especially; ~ gewiß most certainly or assuredly; der Brief ist ~ hübsch geschrieben ... very nicely written. — **6.** mit *s.*: es hat ~ das Aussehen, als ob // it has every appearance as if //; sie war ~ Ohr she was all ear; er ist ~ der Mann dazu ... quite the man for it. — **III** ~**e(s)** (ˊ◡) *n* [67] **7.** (the) whole; (Gesamtbetrag) (the) total number or sum; (Gesamtheit) totality, bulk; das große ~e the (sum) total; ein ~es bildend forming a complete set or body; *math.* in ~en ausgedrückt expressed in integers; **im** ~en (sc. =gerechnet) taken altogether or in the bulk; (in Bausch u. Bogen) $ in the lump; wholesale; im ~en genommen (übrigens) taking everything into consideration, when all is said, upon the whole, roughly speaking; im großen (und) ~en on the whole, in the bulk.

Ganz, Gänz ⚒ (ˊ) *f* [10], [18] (Roheisenbarren) (mst. *pl.* Gänze) pig of iron. [band.

Ganz=franzband ⚙ (ˊ...) *m* [62] = =leder=

Ganzheit (ˊ-) *f* [46] (vgl. ganz, Ganzes) entireness, entirety, completeness; unbrokenness; (Gesamtheit) totality; (one and) all.

Ganz=holländer ⚙ (ˊ...) *m* [62] Papierfabr.: pulp-engine, -grinder, -machine, -mill, beating-engine; ~**hufig** *a.* [66] *zo.* whole-hoofed, ⚗ solidungular; =**lederband** ⚙ *m* Buchbind.: calf-binding, calf-bound volume, (full) calf.

gänzlich (ˊ◡) **I** *a.* [66] = ganz I; in ~er Unwissenheit in entire (or total, utter, complete, thorough, absolute) ignorance. — **II** *adv.* = ganz II; ~ verdorben entirely (or totally, utterly, completely, thoroughly) spoilt.

ganz=randig ⚘ (ˊ...) *a.* [66] v. Blättern: entire; =**schluß** ♪ *m* [62] perfect cadence; ~**wollen** *a.* all wool; =**zeug** ⚙ *n* Papierfabr.: (paper-)pulp; =**zeug=holländer** ⚙ *m* = =holländer; =**zeugkasten** ⚙ *m* Papierfabr.: stuff-chest.

gar (ˊ) [ahd.: yare] **I** *a.* [66] **1.** (fertig zubereitet) ready; bsd. von Speisen: done; well (or thoroughly) cooked; nicht ganz ~ underdone; mehr als ~ overdone. — **2.** ⚙ Gerberei: das Leder ~ machen to dress ...; *metall.* (*ant.* roh) den Stahl ~ machen to (re)fine ... — **II** *adv.* **3.** verstärkend mit *a.* und *adv.*, nicht *verbs*: entirely, fully, quite, very; vgl. ganz, bsd. 4; ~ bald very soon; ~ nicht not at all, not in the least; ~ nichts nothing at all; Sprichw. besser spät als ~ nicht better late than never; ~ keine Sorge no care whatever; eine ~ liebliche Gegend a most charming neighbourhood; ~ mancher Ritter a great many knights, *poet.* full many a knight; ~ oft very often, many a time; ~ **zu** (auch: ~ **so**) too (much); ~ zu viel (wenig) far too much (little); ~ zu sehr overmuch; ~ zu selten extremely (or exceedingly) rare, *adv.* very rarely; ~ zu vorsichtig overcautious. — **4.** steigernd: = sogar (s. bs.) even; nun will sie ~ auf Bälle gehen now she even wants to go to balls; nun verlangt er ~ noch // nay, he goes so far as to demand //; und nun ~ noch ein Gewitter and now, to crown all, a storm; vielleicht ist er im Dorfe oder ~ in diesem Hause ... or in this very house; warum nicht ~!, ich dächte ~! why, indeed!, I should think so, indeed!, you don't say so or mean it!

Garage* (◡ˊ◡) [fr. *garage m*] *f* [48] (Automobilschuppen) garage, coach-house (or shed) for motor cars. [guarantor.

Garant $ (◡ˊ) [fr.] *m* [42] (Bürge)

Garantie (◡◡ˊ) [nhd. 17. *sae.*; fr.; *dtsch. (Ge)währ] *f* [48] guarantee, (Bürgschaft) security; ~=**fonds** *m* [62] guarantee-fund.

garantieren (◡◡ˊ◡) [fr.] *v/a.* [8] to warrant = verbürgen. [tificate of warranty.

Garantie=schein ⚙ (◡◡ˊ...) *m* [62] cer-

Garanzin (◡◡ˊ) [fr. *garance* Krapp] *n* [D]*d. chm.* garancin(e).

Gar=arbeit ⚙ (ˊ...) *f* [62] *metall.* (re-)fining (work), refinement; =**arbeiter** *m* (re)finer.

Gar=aus (ˊ- und -ˊ) [gar aus] *m* (*n*) *inv.* finishing-stroke; e-m den ~ machen to undo (or ruin) a. p.; (ihn vollends töten) to put an end to a p., to do for a. p., P to settle his hash, to put out his light.

Garbe¹ (ˊ◡) [ahd.] *f* [48] *agr.* sheaf; in ~n binden to bind into sheaves.

Garbe² ⚘ (ˊ◡) [ahd.: yarrow] *f* [48] milfoil, yarrow; s. Schafgarbe.

gärben ⚙ (ˊ◡) [= gerben] *v/n.* [8] *metall.* (schweißen) to weld.

Garben=band (ˊ◡...) [Garbe¹] *n* [62] *agr.* wisp of straw for tying sheaves; =**binde=maschine** ⚙ *f* sheaving-machine; =**binder** ⚙ *m* Werkzeug: sheaf-binder; ~**förmig** *a.* [66] in (form of) sheaves; sheaf-like, sheafy; =**halter** *m*, *agr.* e-r Mähmaschine: packer; =**haufe(n)** *m* pile of sheaves; =**schichter** *m* one who piles up sheaves; =**schober** *m* shock (of sheaves).

Gär=bottich ⚙ (ˊ...) *m* [62] für Bier, Wein ꝛc.: fermenting-tub or -vat.

Garçon (◡ˊ) [fr.] *m* [51] **1.** ↘ (Kellner) waiter. — **2.** (Junggeselle) bachelor.

Garde ⚔ (ˊ◡) [nhd. 16. *sae.*; fr. *garde*; *dtsch. Warte] *f* [48] guard(s *pl.*); in Engl.: Guards *pl.*, Household Brigade.

Garde=infanterie (ˊ◡...) *f* [62], etwa: foot-guards *pl.*; Engl.: the Brigade of Guards (4 Regimenter), Grenadier (Coldstream, &c.) Guards *pl.*; =**kavallerie** *f* Engl.: (the) Horse Guards *pl.* (1 Regiment) u. Life Guards *pl.* (2 Regimenter); =**offizier** *m* officer in the Guards.

Garderobe (◡◡ˊ◡) [fr.] *f* [48] (Kleiderkammer, =vorrat) wardrobe; stock of dresses or clothes; clothing; (Kleiderablage) cloak-room.

Garderoben=aufseher(**in** *f*) *m* (◡◡ˊ◡...) [62] keeper of the wardrobe; am engl. Hofe auch: Groom *m* of the Stole, Mistress *f* of the Robes; =**geld**(**er** *pl.*) *n thea.* allowance to actors and actresses

[Garderobenmeister] — 406 — [Gartensalbei]

for dress; =meister m, thea. (Requisitenmeister) property-master; =raum m = =zimmer a; =zimmer n: a) dressing-room (a. thea.); b) (Ab-ort für Damen) ladies' cloak-room.
Garderobier (⌣⌣-bie´) m ⑳, -e (⌣⌣-biä´⌣) [+,+fr.] f ㊽ = Garderoben-aufseher(in).
Gardine (⌣Ĺ⌣) [nhd. 16. sae.; ndl.; *(+,+) fr. courtine; it. cortina] f ㊽ (Vorhang) curtain; schmale oben das untere Fenster: (short) blind; schmale oben am Betthimmel: valance.
Gardinen=arm (⌣⌣"…) m ㉒ curtain-arm or -band or -clasp; =franſen f/pl. cu.-fringes pl.; =haken m = =arm; =halter m cu.-peg; =predigt f cu.-lecture; =ring m cu.-ring; =rolle f cu.-pulley; =ſchraube f cu.-pin; ~ſpinnerei f cu.-works pl.; =ſtange f cu.-pole. [man.
Gardiſt ⚔ (⌣´) [+,+fr.] m ㊷ guards-
Gare (Ĺ⌣) [gar] f ㊽ 1. (das Garſein) readiness, well-cooked state; (Reife) ripeness. — 2. Gerberei: a) dressing of the leather; b) (Ballen von gar zu machenden Häuten) parcel (or batch) of (twentyfour)hides to be dressed; agr. (Düngung) Dünger) manuring; manure.
Gäre (Ĺ⌣) = Gärung (s=mittel).
Gar=eiſen (″…) n ㉒ metall. iron-rod for testing smelted copper.
garen ⊕ (Ĺ⌣) I v/a. ⑧⑧ = gar machen (ſ. gar 2). — II ~ n ㉓ = Garmachen.
gären (Ĺ⌣) [mhd. (ahd.): yeast; *gar]㋰ ⑱ I v/n (h.) 1. to ferment; (aufſchäumen) to effervesce, to bubble up; v. Wein u. Bier auch: to work; 2 laſſen to (let) ferment; der Teig fängt an zu 2, oft: … is beginning to rise. — 2. v/impers. fig. es gärt in den Köpfen, Gemütern the heads, minds (of the people) are in a ferment or in an excited state. — II ſich 2 v/refl. und 2 v/n. (in) 3. der Wein hat ſich klar gegoren … has become clear (or sparkling) through fermentation. — III ~ n ㉓ 4. = Gärung.
Gar=erz (″…) n ㉒ roasted ore; =faß n Gerberei: dressing-tub or -vat; =feuer n roasting-fire; =gekrätz n = =ſchlacke; =herd m refining-hearth.
Gär=kammer (″…) f ㊽ fermenting-house or -chamber.
Gar=koch (″…) m ㊷, =köchin f keeper of a cook-shop or an eating-house; =küche f a; (öffentliche Küche) soup-kitchen (for the poor); b) (Speiſewirtſchaft) cook-shop, eating-house; =kupfer n refined (or pure) copper; =kupfer-abgang m waste (incidental to the refinement) of copper; =leder n Gerberei: dressed hides pl.; =machen n: a) refining of copper, &c.; b) Gerberei: dressing of hides; =macher m = =arbeiter.
Gär=mittel ⊕ (″…) n ㉒ ferment.
Garmond ſübd., öſt. (Ĺ mg) [Garamond, fr. Graveur 1500–61] f ㊽ typ = Korpus.
Garn n [ahd.: yarn] n ⓑ. 1. ⊕ (geſponnener Faden) thread; yarn; gezwirntes: twine, doubled yarn; wollenes: worsted (yarn); baumwollenes: cotton (yarn); zweibrüdiges: two-cord yarn; ~ zum Zeichen der Wäſche markingthread. — 2. hunt., Fiſcherei: (Netz) net; (Schleppnetz) trammel; fig. toils pl.; das ~aufſtellen (auswerfen) to spread

(to cast) the net; in das ~ geh(e)n to fall into the snare or trap; fig. auch: to become entangled; ins ~ locken to ensnare, decoy, trap (auch fig.); in ſein ~ ziehen to draw into one's meshes or toils. — 3. F fig. ~ ſpinnen (erzählen) to spin yarns.
Garnale (⌣Ĺ⌣) f ㊽ = Garnele.
Garn=baum ⊕ (″…) m ㉒ am Webſtuhl thread- or yarn-beam, yarn-roll; =druck-maſchine f yarn-printer.
Garnele (⌣Ĺ⌣) [ndl.] f ㊽ zo. (kleiner Seekrebs) shrimp (Crangon vulga´ris).
Garnelen=fang (⌣″…) m ㉒ shrimp-catching, shrimping.
garnen (Ĺ⌣) a. ⑥⑥ (of) thread or yarn.
Garn=ende (″…) n ㉓ thrum; =fabrikant m yarn-spinner; =färber m dyer of yarn; =geſchäft n, =handel m y.-trade; =händler m dealer in yarn or cotton; =haſpel f y.-reel, y.-winder.
garnieren (⌣Ĺ⌣) [fr., *dtſch.] I v/a. ⑨⑨ (einfaſſen) to trim, edge, border; Kochkunſt: to garnish. — II ~ n ㉓ und Garnierung f ㊽ trimming, &c. (ſ. I); Kochkunſt: garnish(ing).
Garniſon ⚔ (⌣Ĺ⌣) [nhd. 1600,*fr.,dtſch.] f ㊽, ⚔ f (jetzt: Standort) garrison; ~=dienſt m ㉒ garrison-duty.
garniſonieren ⚔ (⌣⌣-Ĺ⌣) v/n. (h.) ⑧⑧ (ſtehen) to lie in garrison, to be stationed or garrisoned; ⓩ garrisoned.
Garniſons=lazarett (⌣⌣″…) n ㉒, etwa: military hospital.
Garniſons ⚔ (⌣-″…) ㊷ = Garniſon-…; z.B.: =leben n garrison-life. [town.
Garniſon=ſtadt (⌣Ĺ″…) f ㊽ garrison-
Garnitur (⌣Ĺ⌣) [fr.] f ㊽ 1. (Beſatz) trimming; (Ausſtattung) fittings, mountings pl. — 2. (Zſ.-ſtellung) ~ von Schmuckſachen, Werkzeugen ꝛc. set of ornaments, tools, &c.; typ. (Schrift-)~ series.
Garn=knäuel (″…) n(m) ㉒ ball of thread; =meiſter m master fisherman; =preſſe ⊕ f Spinnerei: bundle-press, bundling-machine; =prüfer ⊕ m (Vorrichtung) yarn-tester; =röllchen n bobbin, reel; vgl. =ſpule; =ſpule f spool, twill; =ſträhne f skein of yarn; =weber m yarn-weaver =weberei ⊕ f yarn-weaving factory; =wickel m thread-paper; =winde ⊕ f Spinnerei: yarn-windle, twine-reel, cop; =winder m yarn-winder, reeler; =zug m Fiſcherei: draught (of fishes).
Gar=ofen (″…)m ㉒, =pfanne f, metall. refining-furnace, -pan; =probe f assay (-ing) of copper-ore. [menting-pipe.]
Gär=röhre ⊕ (″…) f ㊽ für Bier: fer-
Garrotte (⌣Ĺ⌣) [fr., *ſpan.] f ㊽ (Halseiſen zum Erdroſſeln; Hinrichtung damit) garrotte.
garrottier/en (⌣⌣-Ĺ⌣) I v/a. ⑨⑨ to garrotte. — II ~ n ㉓ u. G/ung f ㊽ garrotting.
Gar=ſchaum (″…) m ㉒ metall. kish; =ſcheibe f plate of refined copper, rose-copper disk; =ſchlacke f sinter-slag, refinery-slag; =ſein n = Gare 1.
garſtig (Ĺ⌣) [nhd.: It. ho´rridus] 1. (ekeln, widerlich) nasty, unpleasant, objectionable, ſtärker: loathsome; (ſchmutzig) filthy, dirty; (gemein) mean; (unſittlich) offensive, immoral, indecent; (häßlich) plain (-looking), ſtärker: ugly; 2e Redensarten f/pl. nasty expressions pl., ſtärker: foul language sg; 2es Wetter bad (or

foul, dirty) weather. — 2. adv. F fig. (in unangenehmer Weiſe) unpleasantly; er iſt 2 angeführt worden F he has been badly (or fearfully) taken in.
Garſtigkeit (Ĺ⌣-) f ㊽ (ſ. garſtig) nastiness; meanness; ugliness; foulness.
Gär=ſtoff ⊕ (″…) m ㊷ = =mittel.
Gar=ſtück ⊕ (″…) n ㉒ Saline: lump of refined salt.
Gärtchen (Ĺ⌣) n ㉓ (dim. von Garten) small (or pretty little) garden.
Garten (Ĺ⌣) [ahd.: yard (garden * fr.): It. hŏrtus, grch. chŏ´rtos]-m ⑳ garden; botaniſcher, zoologiſcher ~ botanical, zoological gardens pl.
Garten=ammer (Ĺ⌣…) f ㊽ orn. ortolan (Emberi´za hortula´na); =ampfer ♀ m garden-sorrel, patience (Rumex patie´ntia); =anlage f: a) (Anlegen e-s Gartens) laying out a garden; b) pleasure-grounds pl.; =arbeit f gardening; =arbeiter m (jobbing or working) gardener; =aſter ♀ f china aster (Aster chine´nsis); =bank f garden-seat or -bench; =bau m gardening, ⚘ horticulture; (Handelsgärtnerei) market-gardening; =aus-ſtellung f horticultural show; =beet n garden-bed, mit Blumen verziert: flower-bed; =biberne´lle ♀ f = Becherblume; =blume f gardenflower; =buch n gardening-book; =erdbeere ♀ f (Frucht) garden-strawberry, (Pflanze) cultivated strawberry-plant (Fraga´ria vesca culta); =erde f garden-mould; =feld n enclosed ground; =feſt n garden-party; open-air fête; =freund m amateur gardener, ⚘ horticulturist; =frucht f fruit grown in gardens; =gemüſe n greens, garden-vegetables pl.; =gerät n, =gerätſchaften f/pl. garden(ing)-tools pl.; =gewächſe ♀ n/pl. garden-stuff or -produce; =grasmücke f, orn. ga.-warbler (Sy´lvia horte´nsis); =haus, =häuschen n summer-house; =kelle f gardener's trowel; =kerbel ♀ m garden-chervil (Scandix cerefo´lium); =kohl m garden-cabbage (Bra´ssica olera´cea); =kräuter n/pl. Kochkunſt: pot-herbs pl.; vgl. =gewächſe; =kreſſe ♀ f garden- (or pepper-) cress (Lepi´dium sati´vum); =kunſt f gardening, ⚘ horticulture; =künſtler m: ⚘ horticulturist; =kürbis ♀ m pumpkin (Cucu´rbita cepo); =lattich ♀ m cultivated lettuce (Lactu´ca sati´va); =laube f arbour, bower, summer-house; =lauch ♀ m common garlic (A´llium sati´vum); =lokal n public (or tea-) garden; =mauer f garden-wall; =melde ♀ f mountain-spinach (A´triplex horte´nse); =meliſſe ♀ f lemon-balm (Meli´ssa officina´lis); =meſſer n pruning-knife; =minze ♀ f garden-mint (Mentha sati´va); =mohn ♀ m garden- (or opium-)poppy (Papa´ver somni´ferum); =nelke ♀ f clove-carnation or -pink or -gillyflower (Dia´nthus caryophy´llus); =pflanze ♀ f garden-plant; =pumpe f garden-pump; =raute ♀ f herb (-of) -grace, common rue (Ruta grave´olens); =rhabarber ♀ m English (or rhapontic rhubarb (Rheum Rhapo´nticum); =ringelblume ♀ f common marigold (Cale´ndula officina´lis); =ſaal m large room in a summer-house; hall (built) in a garden; =ſäge f pruning-saw; =ſalbei

Signs (see page XVII): F familiar; P vulgar; ſ flash; ⚹ rare; † obsolete (died); * new word (born); +,+ incorrect; ♪ music;

[Gartensänger] — 407 — [Gastpredigt]

♃ m, f garden-sage (Sa'lvia officina'lis); =sänger m, orn. bastard-nightingale (Hippola'is); =schaufel f garden-shovel; =schere f garden-shears pl.; =schläfer m, zo. garden-dormouse (Eli'omys nite'la); =schnecke f, zo. ga. snail (Helix horte'nsis); =schwertel ♃ m gladiolus (Gladi'olus commu'nis); =spritze f garden-syringe or -squirt or -engine; =stuhl, =tisch m garden-chair, -table; =tor n, =tür f garden-gate, -door; =tulpe ♃ f common garden-tulip (Tu'lipa Gesneria'na); =vergnügen n garden-entertainment or -amusement; =walze f garden-roller; =wesen n gardening, =horticulture; =wirtschaft f: a) =wesen; b) =lokal; =zaun m garden-fence.

Gärtlein (⏑–) n 23 = Gärtchen.

Gärtner (⏑⏑) m 22, ~in f 40 gardener (f gardener's wife); (Freund der Gärtnerei): ⚘ horticulturist; (Handels-)~ market-gardener; nursery-man or -gardener; s. Bock¹ 1; ~bursche m 62 gardener's boy; under-gardener.

Gärtnerei (⏑⏑⏑) f 46 1. (Kunst des Gärtners) (art of) gardening. ⚘ horticulture; ~ treiben to do gardening. — 2. (Anwesen e-s Gärtners) (market-) gardener's nursery-grounds pl. or establishment.

gärtnerisch (⏑⏑⏑) a. 66: ⚘ horticultural.

Gärtner-kunst (⏑⏑...) f 62 = Gärtnerei 1.

gärtnern F (⏑⏑) v/n. (h.) 92 a. to do gardening; F to potter about the garden.

Gärung (⏑⏑) f 46 (s. gären) fermentation, effervescence; fig. ebullition, commotion, tumult; F ferment; ~ der Gemüter effervescent or tumultuous, turbulent) state of the (people's) minds.

gärungs-fähig (⏑⏑...) a. 66 capable of fermentation, fermentable; =küpe ⊕ f 62 Färb.: steeping-trough; =lehre f: ⚘ zymology; =messer m: ⚘ zymo(si)-meter; =mittel n ferment; =pilz ♃ m yeast-plant (Saccharomy'ces cerevi'siae); =prozeß m, =verfahren n process, method of fermentation.

Gas (˘, ⁀ ⌣) [van Helmont, † 1644] n 🜨 a. phys., chm. gas(eous body); (Leuchtgas) (lighting-)gas; natürliches ~ natural gas; das ~ abschneiden (die Gasleitung unterbrechen) to cut off the gas; das ~ anzünden, ausdrehen to light, to turn off (or out) the gas; mit ~ beleuchtet lighted (up) with gas, auch: gas-lit; das ~ höher (niedriger) drehen to turn the gas higher (lower) or on (down); 🚂 e-n Zug mit ~ versehen to gas a train.

Gas-anlage ⊕ (⏑...) f 62 gas-plant; =anstalt f gas-works pl.; =anstecker, =anzünder m gas-lighter; =arm m gas-bracket; =armleuchter m gaselier, a. gas-chandelier; =art f kind of gas; gaseous substance; =artig a. 66 gaseous, gasiform; =äther m = Gasolin; =ausströmung f leakage of gas, vgl. =entweichung; =behälter m gasometer; =beleuchtung f gas-light(ing), illumination with gas; =bereitung f manufacture (or making) of gas; ⁹bildend(er Körper) a.: ⚘ gazolyte; =bildung f = =erzeugung; =brenner m gasburner; s. a. Brenner 3.

gäschen (⏑⏑) [s. Gäscht] v/n. (h.) 90 (aufschäumen) to foam.

Gäscht (´) [: yeast] m 🜨 a. (Hefe) yeast.

Gascogne (⏑⏔´) [fr.; *Vasco'nia, Basken) npr/f. 48 Gascony. ~r(in f 47) m 22, gascognisch a. 66 Gascon.

Gas-direktor (´...) m 62 director of a gas-company; =druckmesser ⊕ m gas-indicator; =dynamo m gas-dynamo; =einrichtung f gas-fittings pl.; =entbindungs-rohr ⊕ n gas-delivery tube; =entweichung f escape of gas, gas-escape, vgl. =ausströmung; =entwickelung f production of gas; ⁹erzeugend a. 66 giving forth gas, gas-producing; =erzeugung f: ⚘ gasification; =fabrik f gas-works pl.; =feuerung f heating by (means of) gas; =flamme f gas-light or -jet; ⁹förmig a. = ⁹artig; =förmigkeit f gaseousness, gaseity; =gebläse n gas-blowpipe; =gesellschaft f gas-company; =glühlicht n incandescent gas; ⁹haltig a. containing gas, gaseous; =heizung f heating by | gasig (´⌣) a. 66 (gasartig) gaseous. [gas.

Gas-kalk ⊕ (´...) m gas-lime; =kocher m gas-cooker; =kohle f (Retortenkohle) gas-coal.

Gaskonade (⏑⏑´⏑) [fr.; *Gascogne) f 48 (Prahlerei) boasting, bragging.

Gas-kraftmaschine ⊕ (´...) f 62 gas-engine; =lampe f, =laterne f gas-lamp; =leiter m gas-pipe; =leitung f gas-supply; =leitungsröhre f = =leiter; =licht n gas-light; =maschine f = =kraftmaschine; =messer m gas-meter; =motor m gas-engine; =ofen m gas-stove.

Gasolin (⏑⏑´) [Gas + lt. ol(eum) Öl + -in] n ⚬ chm. gasolene, gasoline; ~automobil (⏑´...) n 62 gasolene motor.

Gasometer ⊕ (⏑⏑´⏑) m (n) 22 gas-meter (= Gasmesser).

Gas-quelle (´...) f gas-spring, source of (natural) gas; =retorte ⊕ f gas-retort; =röhre f gas-pipe; =röhren-leger m gas-fitter.

Gäßchen (⏑⏑) n 23 dim. von Gasse (s. ds 1).

Gasse (⏑⏑) f [ahd.: gate] f 49 1. in Norddeutschland: narrow street; südd. u. md. = Straße; enge (od. schmale) ~ (a. Gäßchen n) narrow lane, alley; coll. Gäßchen pl. (Armenviertel) oft: slums pl.; auf der ~ in the street; auf der ~ herumlaufen to run about the street(s); (immer) auf der ~ liegen to walk the streets, to be on the street; er ist Hans in allen ~n he is a busybody, he is everywhere, F all over the shop; fig. das findet man nicht auf der ~ that's not to be picked up in the street or on hedges, that's most uncommon. — 2. hohle ~ (Schlucht) hollow, gorge, ravine. — 3. fig. von Menschen: eine ~ (zwei Reihen) bilden to make a lane; sich (dat.) eine ~ machen to push (or work) one's way through the crowd. — 4. ⊕ typ. (Raum zwischen den Regalen) alley, row.

Gassen-bettelei (⏑⏑...) f 62, =bettler(in f) m street-begging, -beggar; =bube m = =junge; =dirne F st.-walker; =hauer [nhd. 16/7. sae.] m street-ballad, popular song or ditty; =junge m st.-boy, bsd. Lo.: st.-Arab; =jungen-streich m mischievous (boy's) trick; =kehrer(in f) m scavenger, Lo. als Bettler(in): crossing-sweeper; =kot m street-mud; =laufen n ehm. ⚔ running the gauntlet;

=lied n = =hauer; =pöbel m rabble; =sänger(in f) m st.-singer; =treter m tramp, vagabond, loafer; =troß m rabble; =witz m low humour; vulgar jest(ing). — Vgl. auch Straßen-...

Gast (´) [ahd.: guest: lt. hostis Fremdling] m ⑦ b., † ~in (´⌣) f 40 1. stranger; mit Rücksicht auf den Wirt, auch im Gasthofe: guest; (Besucher) visitor; Gäste empfangen to receive guests or company, to do the honours of the house; Gäste (Besuch) haben to have (or entertain) company; e-n zu ~ bitten to ask (or invite) a. p. to dinner or to supper; wollen Sie (zu Mittag) mein ~ sein? will you dine with me?; bei e-m zu ~e sein to be staying (or on a visit) with a p.; ungebet(e)ner ~ unbidden (or uninvited) guest, intruder, interloper; Sie sind mir ein willkommener ~ you are very welcome. — 2. thea. (fremder Künstler v. Ruf) star (ring actor or singer). — 3. (Kunde) customer; im Kaffee- oder Wirtshause: frequenter, regular guest or customer; gelegentlicher ~ chance customer. — 4. fig. grober ~ (Kerl) rude (or rough) customer; schlauer (schlimmer) ~ sly (or bad, wicked) fellow, ugly customer. — 5. ⚓ Sb. = Matrose (meist mit bestimmter Verrichtung, vgl. Backsgasten); die ~en the ship's ratings pl. or company.

Gast-becher (´...) m 62 cup to drink the health of a guest (with), goblet for pledging guests; =bett n visitors' (or spare) bed; =bitter(in f) m person inviting the guests; Wirt[in] host(ess).

Gasterei (⏑⏑´) f 46 = Gastmahl.

gast-frei (´...) a. 66 hospitable; =freiheit f 62 hospitality; =freund m (gastlich Empfangende[r], Empfangend[er]) one showing, receiving hospitality; Alt.: person connected with another by ties of old friendship and hospitality; ⁹freundlich a. hospitable; ⁹ aufnehmen to receive hospitably; =freundschaft f hospitality; ⁹freundschaftlich a. = ⁹freundlich; =geber(in f) m host(-ess); founder (f foundress) of the feast; =gebot n = =mahl; =gemach n Fremdenstube; =geschenk n present given (or received) by a guest; =haus n inn, tavern; =hof m hotel, bsd. ehm. hostelry; =hofs-besitzer(in f) m ehm. host(ess) of an inn; jetzt: hotel-keeper proprietor (f ...tress) of a hotel; vgl. =wirt(in); =hofs-küche f hotel-fare.

gastieren (⏑⏑´) [dtsch-lt.] 93 I v/a. 1. (als Gast bewirten) to entertain (as a guest or hospitably). — II v/n. (h.) 2. = schmausen. — 3. thea. (Gastrollen geben) to give a few performances; to star. — III ~ n 23 u. **Gastierung** f 46 4. entertainment of guests. — 5. thea. short (or starring-)engagement.

gastlich (´⌣) a. 66 hospitable; ~keit f 46 hospitableness, hospitality.

Gast-mahl (´...) n 62 feast, banquet; =mutter f im Hospitale: matron; im Kloster: sister who receives strangers; =ordnung f regulations pl.: a) for guests or visitors; b) for hotel-keepers; =predigt f sermon by a strange preacher; zur Probe: proba-

---

⚛ scientific; ♃ botanical; ⚲ geography; ⊕ machinery; ⚒ mining; ⚔ military; ⚓ marine; ⦿ commercial; ✉ postal; 🚂 railway.

[Gastrecht] — 408 — [Geadelte]

tionary sermon; =**recht** *n* right of hospitality; =**reise** *f*, *thea*. starring-tour.
gastrisch (ˇˇ) [grch. *gastē'r* Magen] *a*. ⑥⑥ gastric; ˇes Fieber gastric fever.
Gast=rolle (ˇ...) *f* ⑫ *thea*. part played by a starring actor or singer; ~n geben to make a starring-tour, to have a starring-engagement.
Gastronom (ˇˇˇ) [grch.] *m* ㊷ (Feinschmecker) gastronomer, ...ist, ~**ie** (ˇˇˇˇ) *f* ㊽ ...y; **Lisch** (ˇˇˇˇ) *a*. ⑥⑥ gastronomical.
Gast=spiel (ˇ...) *n* ⑫ *thea*. starring(-performance); =**stube** *f* in Privathäusern: spare bedroom (for guests); in Gasthöfen: general (or coffee-) room; =**tafel** *f*, =**tisch** *m* ordinary; (fr.) table d'hôte; ˇ**weise** *adv*. as (or like) a guest; =**wirt**(**in** *f*) *m* landlord (*f* landlady), innkeeper; vgl. Hofs=besitzer(in); =**wirtschaft** *f*: a) hotel-keeping; ~ betreiben to keep a hotel or an inn; b) (Anwesen eines =wirts) hotel; inn; =**zimmer** *n* = Fremdenzimmer.
Gas=uhr (ˇ...) *f* ⑫ gas-meter; =**wandleuchter** *m* gas-bracket (= =arm); =**wasser** *n* (Ammoniakwasser) gas-liquor or -water, ammoniacal liquor.
Gat ↓ (ˇ) *n* = Gatt. ☛ **Gät**=... f. Gät...
gätlich ↑ (ˇ) [nbd.] *a*. ⑥⑥ (passend, angenehm) (G.) suitable, pleasant.
Gatt ↓ (ˇ) [nbd.] *n* ㉕b. u. ㉔ (Loch) hole.
Gatte (ˇˇ) [mhd.] *m* gather, together/ *m* ⑩, **Gattin** *f* ㊵ = Ehe=gatte, =gattin; Ihre Gattin your wife, oft a.: Mrs. (mit dem Namen des Mannes) ...
gatten (ˇˇ) ㊶ I *v*/*a*. 1. (paaren) to couple, pair, match; *fig*. (vereinigen) to join. — II sich ² *v*/*refl*. 2. allg.: to copulate. — 3. *fig*. to be(come) united; to join (in marriage); to wed, to marry.
Gatten=glück (ˇˇ...) *n* ㊶, =**liebe** *f* conjugal happiness, love; ˇ**los** *a*. ⑥⑥ without a spouse; unmated.
Gatter (ˇˇ) [ahd.] *n* ㉒ 1. railing, grating; aus Holz: lattice (or trellis)-work; vgl. Gitter. — 2. ◎ einer Sägemühle: saw-gate; ✻ eines Pochwerkes: grate.
gattern¹ (ˇˇ) [: gather] *v*/*a*. ㉒a. = erˇ².
gattern² schwz. (ˇˇ) [Gatter] *v*/*n*. (h.) ㉒a. (klaffen wie e. Gatter) to show wide gaps.
Gatter=tor (ˇˇ...) *n* ㉒ barrier; (fivebarred) gate; =**werk** *n* = Gatter 1.
gattieren schwz. ✻ (ˇˇˇˇ) [dtsch.=it.; *gatten] *v* /*a*. ㉓ die Erze ² (mengen) to mix the [ores.
Gattin (ˇˇ) ㊵ f. Gatte.
gättlich (ˇˇ) *a*. ⑥⑥ = gätlich.
Gattung (ˇˇ) *f* ㊽ kind, sort; bsd. ♀, *zo*. species; (Geschlecht) genus (*pl*. genera); (Familie) family; (Rasse) race; von Tieren auch: breed; Leute, Häuser von jeder ~ ... of every description; all kinds (or sorts) of ...
Gattungs=begriff (ˇˇˇ...) *m* ㊷, =**character** *m* specific (or generic) notion, character; =**name** *m*, *gr*. generic name, appellative (name or noun); =**wort** *m* = =name.
Gau (ˇ) [md. (ahd.)] *m* († *n*) ⑪⑫㉕c., obb. **Gäu** *n* ⑨c. (Bezirk) district, canton; (flaches Hochland) plateau.
Gauch (ˇch) [ahd.: gawk] *m* ⑫⑦c. F (Hahnrei) cuckold; weitS. (Laffe) gawk, simpleton, P mug; (Geck) fop; fool; armer ~ (Tropf) poor devil (of a fellow).

Gauch=blume ♀ (ˇch...) *f* ⑫ cuckoo-flower = Wiesenkresse; =**heil** *n* (*m*) (corn-)pimpernel (*Anagallis*).
Gau=dieb (ˇ...) [nbd. gau = gäh, jäh] *m* ⑫ rogue, vagabond.
Gau=ding (ˇ...) [Gau] *n* ㉓ = =gericht.
Gaudium F (ˇˇˇ) [lt.] *n* ⑬ = Freude.
gaufrieren ◉ (goˇˇˇ) [fr.; *dtsch. Waffel] *v*/*a*. ㉓ (kräuseln) to goffer.
Gaufrier=maschine ◉ (goˇˇ...) *f* ㊽ goffering-machine.
Gau=gericht (ˇ...) *n* ㉓ *hist*. cantonal (in Engl.: county-, ehm. shire-)court; petty sessions *pl*.; =**graf** *m*, *hist*. etwa: justiciary of a canton, ? gaugraf; =**grafschaft** *f* jurisdiction of a gaugraf.
Gaukel=bild (ˇˇ...) *n* ⑫ phantasmagory, phantasm, (alluring) vision; (fr.) mirage, (Blendwerk) (optical) delusion; =**bude** *f* juggler's booth.
Gaukelei (ˇˇˇˇˇ) *f* ㊽ juggling, jugglery, conjuring, legerdemain, sleight-of-hand, bisw.: prestidigitation; (Täuschung) deception, delusion, hocus-pocus, trickery, tricks *pl*.; (Betrug) fraud.
gaukelhaft, gaukelig (ˇˇˇˇ) *a*. ⑥⑥ juggling; delusive; (trügerisch) deceptive.
Gaukel=kunst (ˇˇ...) *f* ⑫ juggler's art, juggling; vgl. Gaukelei.
gaukeln (ˇˇ) [ahd.: juggle; *lt. *iocula'ri*] ㉒a. I *v*/*n*. (h.) 1. (bei Ortsveränderung it.: (hin und her flattern) to flutter (or flit) about; (rasch vorbeihuschen) to pass by rapidly, to flit by. — 2. (die Sinne täuschen) to delude the senses; (Taschenspielerei treiben) to practise sleight-of-hand or legerdemain; to juggle; F to do tricks; (Possenspiel treiben) to play the buffoon or clown. — II *v*/*a*. 3. (2b hervorbringen) to produce by magic or jugglery (to conjure up or forth). — III sich ² *v*/*refl*. 4. (sich hin und her wiegen) to rock to and fro. — IV ~ *n* ㉓ 5. = Gaukelei.
Gaukel=posse(**n** *pl*.) (ˇˇ...) *f* ⑫ juggler's tricks *pl*., F conjuring; =**spiegel** *m* magic mirror; =**spiel** *n*, =**spielerei** *f* = Gaukelei; =**tasche** *f* juggler's bag, conjuring case; =**werk** *n* = Gaukelei.
Gaukler (ˇˇ) [ahd. f. gaukeln] *m* ㊷, ~**in** *f* ㊵ 1. (Zauberkünstler) conjurer, juggler, magician; a. legerdemainist, illusionist, prestidigitator; (Spaßmacher) buffoon, clown; (Marktschreier) Cheap Jack; mountebank. — 2. *fig*. eine bezaubernde ~**in** a bewitching sorceress.
Gaukler=bande (ˇˇ...) *f* ⑫, etwa: travelling performers *pl*.; =**blume** ♀ *f* monkey-flower (*Mi'mulus lu'teus*).
Gauklerei (ˇˇˇˇˇ) *f* ㊽ juggler's trade, conjuring (tricks *pl*.); vgl. Gaukelei.
gauklerhaft, gauklerisch (ˇˇˇ) *a*. ⑥⑥ delusive (= gaukelhaft).
Gaul (ˇ) [mhd.] *m* ⑦⑩c. horse (of inferior breed), nag; alter, schlechter ~ worn-out jade, F old crock; Sprichw. e-m geschenkten ~ sieht man nicht ins Maul never look a gift horse in the mouth.
Gaumen (ˇˇ) [ahd.: gum] *m* ㉓ *anat*. palate, roof of the mouth; am ~ (an)kleben to cleave to the roof of the mouth; zum ~ gehörig palatal.
Gaumen=bein (ˇˇ...) *n* ㉓ *anat*.: ⚛ palatine (bone); =**buchstabe** *m*, *gr*. (k, g)

palatal letter or consonant; =**kitzel** *m* fondness for delicacies; =**knochen** *m* = =bein; =**laut** *m* palatal (sound); =**naht** *f*, *surg*.: ⚛ palatorrhaphy; =**segel** *n* soft palate; =**spalte** *f*, *path*. fissure of the palate.
Gauner (ˇˇ) [nhd. 18. sae. (F 16. sae.); *hebr. *janā* betrügen] *m* ㉓, ~**in** *f* ㊵ rogue, swindler, sharper, blackleg, cheat; feingekleideter ~ swell mobsman; ~**bande** *f* ⑫ gang of swindlers, set of sharpers, feinere: swell mob.
Gaunerei (ˇˇˇˇ) *f* ㊽ swindling, cheating; als Handlung: piece of roguery.
gaunerhaft (ˇˇˇ) *a*. ⑥⑥ roguish.
Gauner=herberge (ˇˇ...) *f* ⑫ thieves' lodging-house; ˑ flash ken.
gaunerisch (ˇˇˇ) *a*. ⑥⑥ = gaunerhaft.
Gauner=leben (ˇˇ...) *n* ㉓ rogue's life.
gaunern (ˇˇ) I *v*/*n*. (h.) ㉒a. to swindle, to cheat. — II ~ *n* ㉓ = Gaunerei.
Gauner=sprache (ˇˇ...) *f* ⑫ thieves' cant or Latin; =**streich** *m*, =**stück** *n* roguish trick, swindle, F take-in.
Gaunertum (ˇˇˇ) *n* ⓪d., **Gauner=welt** (ˇˇˇ) *f* criminal world or classes *pl*.
Gauß ⚛ (ˇ) [F. K. F. Gauß, dtsch. Mathematiker, 1777—1855] *n*, *inv*. (Einheit der Polstärke) gauss, unit magnetic pole.
Gautsch=brett ◎ (ˇ...) *n* ⑫ Papierfabr.: pressing-board.
gautschen ? ◎ (ˇˇ) [engl.] Papierfabr.: ⑩ 1. *v*/*a*. to couch. — 2. *v*/*n*. (h.) to lay the sheets on the pressing-board.
Gautscher ◎ (ˇˇˇ) *m* ㊷ Papierfabr.: coucher.
Gautsch=presse, =**walze** ◎ *f* couch-roll.
Gau=verband (ˇˇ...) *m* ㊸ Turnerei ꝛc.: cantonal association, in Engl.: county-club or -association.
Gavial (ˇwˇˇ) [fft.] *m* ⓪d. *zo*. (Rüssel=Ganges=Crokodil) gavial (*Gavia'lis*).
Gavotte (ˇwˇˇ) [fr.] *f* ⑫ (Tanz) gavotte.
Gaze ◎ ☀ (ˇˇ) [fr.; (*Gaza, St.)] *f* ㊽ Weberei: gauze; sehr feine: gossamer.
gaze=artig ◎ u. ☀ (ˇˇ...) *a*. ⑥⑥ gauzy; =**artigkeit** *f* ⑫ gauziness; =**band** *n* gauze-ribbon.
Gazelle (ˇtˇˇ) [fr., *ar.] *f* ⑫ *zo*. gazelle (*Anti'lope* oder *Gaze'lla dorcas*); ~**n=auge** (ˇ...) *n* ⑫ eye of a gazelle, hazel-eye.
Gaze=stuhl (ˇˇ...) *m* ⑫ Weberei: gauze-loom; =**weber**(**in** *f*) *m* gauze-weaver.
gbr. *abbr*. für gebräuchlich, gebraucht.
G=Dur ♪ (ˇ) *n*, *inv*. f. G ♪.
Ge=.... **ge=**... (ˇˇ...) [ahd.] Vorsilbe, dient zur Bildung 1. vieler Wiederholungswörter, alle *n*, aus *verbs*, zB. Ge=ächze [ächzen] (incessant) groaning, moaning. — 2. vieler Sammelwörter, alle *n*, aus *nouns*, zB. Ge=bein [Bein] *coll*. bones *pl*. — 3. von *adjectives* aus *nouns*, um ein Vorhandensein zu bezeichnen, zB. ge=armt [Arm] (provided) with arms. — 4. von *verbs* aus *verbs*, zB. ge=fallen [fallen] to please. — 5. des *p.p.*, zB. ge=achtet [achten] esteemed; in der Dichtkunst und Volkssprache oft weggelassen, zB. kommen statt ge=kommen.
Ge=ächtete(**r** *m*) *f* (ˇˇˇˇ) ㊿ outlaw(ed person); (Verwiesene[r]) exile.
Ge=ächze (ˇˇˇ) *n* ㉓ f. Ge=... 1.
Ge=adelte(**r** *m*) *f* (ˇˇˇˇ) ㊿ one (recently) raised to the nobility or peerage, newly created peer.

Zeichen (f. S. XVII): F familiär; P Volkssprache; ˑ Gaunersprache; ◌ selten; † alt (auch gestorben); * neu (auch geboren); ↯↯ unrichtig.

[Geäder] — 409 — [geben]

Ge-äder (⌣⌣) n ⓶ 1. ⚚ anat. blood-vessels pl., veins and arteries pl. — 2. (aderförmige Verzierungen) veins pl.
ge-ädert (⌣⌣) a. ⓺ veined, veiny; (marmoriert) marbled. [claws pl.]
Ge-äfter (⌣⌣) n ⓶ zo. (Afterklauen) dew-
ge-armt (⌣⌣) a. ⓺ f. ge= 3.
ge-artet (⌣⌣) p.p. f. arten III.
Ge-äse (⌣⌣) n ⓶, **Ge-äß** (⌣⌣) n ⓵a. hunt. 1. = Äsung. — 2. (Maul des Wildes) mouth.
Ge-äst(e) (⌣⌣)(⌣)[Äst] n ⓵b.(⓶) branches pl.
ge-äugt (⌣⌣) a. ⓺ = äugig.
geb. abbr. für geboren (a.: *) (f. ge=bären III) u. gebunden.
Ge-bäck (⌣⌣) n ⓵c. 1. (Backware) baker's (or baked) ware or goods pl.; feines: fancy-bread; (Kuchenwerk) pastry, confectionery. — 2. (mit einem Male Gebackenes) batch, backing.
ge-backen (⌣⌣) p.p. von backen; **Ge-back(e)ne(s)** (⌣⌣) n ⓺ = Gebäck 1.
Ge-balge (⌣⌣) n ⓶ = balgen 5.
Ge-balk ⊕ (⌣⌣) n ⓵b. carp. timber- (or frame-)work; joists, beams pl.; ~ für Dielen floor-timber; arch. ~ für Säulen: ⚚ entablature; ~=träger m, arch. atlas.
ge-ballt (⌣⌣) a. ⓺ her. fessed.
ge-ballt (⌣⌣) p.p. u. a. ⓺ 1. Bed. des inf. ballen. — 2. ⚕, anat.: ⚚ conglobate(d).
Ge-bammel (⌣⌣) n ⓶ s.th. dangling.
Ge-bände (⌣⌣) n ⓶ (Bandschmuck) ornamental ribbons pl.
ge-bar (⌣⌣) impf. von gebären.
Ge-bär-anstalt (⌣⌣⌣) f ⓺ med. lying-in hospital.
Ge-bärde (⌣⌣) [ahd.] f ⓺ 1. (Aussehen) appearance, look; (Gesichts-ausdruck) air, mien, countenance; (Auftreten) carriage, deportment; (Benehmen) demeanour; (Haltung) attitude. — 2. (Bewegung des Körpers, bsd. der Hand) gesture; heftige: gesticulation; stumme ~n dumb show sg.; ~ n m. gesticulate.
ge-bärden (⌣⌣) I sich 2 v/refl. ⓺ to carry (or deport) o.s.; ich weiß nicht, wie ich mich gebärdete... how I looked, F what (kind of a) figure I cut; sich ernst 2 to put on a serious (or grave) countenance; sich närrisch 2 to behave foolishly, to make a fool of o.s.; sie gebärdet sich, als ob // she puts on an air (or she behaves) as if //. — II ~ n ⓶ =
Ge-bärden-kunst (⌣⌣⌣...) f ⓺ mimic art; =spiel n gestures pl.; mimic action; play of features or the facial muscles; thea. posture, pose, action; stummes: pantomime, dumb show; =spieler(in f) m, thea. mimic, mime; =sprache f language of signs and gestures; thea. mimicry.
Ge-bärdung (⌣⌣) f ⓺ 1. = Gebärde 1. — 2. gesticulation. [impf. v. gebären.]
ge-bäre (⌣⌣) ind. pres. u. subj. pres. u.]
ge-baren (⌣⌣) [mhd.] ⓺* I ⚚ v/n. (h.) to appear. — II sich 2 v/refl. ⓺ to put on a certain air or look; (sich benehmen) to deport (or conduct) o.s., to behave. — III ~ n ⓶ (f. I u. II) appearance; air, look; deportment, behaviour.
ge-bären (⌣⌣) [ahd.: bear] V v/a. ⓺f* 1. to bear, to bring forth; to give birth to a child, to bring a child into the world; vor der Zeit: to miscarry;

2d in labour, ⚚ parturient; von Tieren: to drop, to bring forth, to have young; physiol. lebendige Junge 2d: ⚚ viviparous. — 2. sie hat ihm drei Söhne geboren she bore (or gave) him ...; geboren werden to be born; rel. wiedergeboren werden to be born again (in the spirit). — 3. fig. (hervorbringen) to produce; (erzeugen) to beget, to breed. — II ~ n ⓶ 4. (child-)bearing, birth; ⚚ parturition, parturiency; (Niederkunft) child-bed, confinement, delivery. — III **geboren** p.p. u. a. ⓺(D 9) 5. born; adlig 2 born of noble blood or stock; blind 2 born blind; neu 2 new-born; vgl. neu-2; tot 2 still-born. — 6. Der Engländer Englishman by birth, (natural-)born Englishman, auch: true-born Briton; sie ist eine 2e Jones her maiden name is J.; Frau S., geborene T. Mrs. S., maiden name T. (or F Miss T. that was formerly Miss T.). — 7. fig. er ist ein 2er Herrscher, zum Herrscher 2... a born ruler, ... born in the purple; nicht für die Arbeit 2 not cut out for (or intended to) work.
Ge-bärerin (⌣⌣⌣) f ⓸ woman in labour or childbed, woman giving birth to a child.
Ge-bär-haus (⌣⌣...) n ⓺ = =anstalt; =mutter f, anat. womb, ⚚ uterus; die ~ betreffend: ⚚ uterine; =stuhl m chair of delivery, obstetric chair.
Ge-barung (⌣⌣) f ⓺ = gebaren III.
Ge-bärung (⌣⌣) f ⓺ = gebären II.
Ge-bär-zeit (⌣⌣...) f ⓺ time of delivery, (date) of confinement.
Ge-bäude (⌣⌣) [bauen] n ⓶ 1. allg.: building, structure; größeres: edifice; stattliches: noble pile, in geh. Spr.: great (or monumental) fabric; aufgesetztes: ~ superstructure. — 2. (Wohnung) dwelling(-house), premises pl.; tenement; großes, prächtiges: mansion; abgesondertes: detached residence. ~=steuer f ⓺ inhabited-house duty.
Ge-baue (⌣⌣) n ⓶ building mania.
Ge-baumel (⌣⌣) n ⓶ s.th. dangling.
Gebe-apparat (⌣⌣...) m ⓺ tel. transmitter; =fall m, gram. dative.
Ge-bein (⌣⌣) n ⓵c. 1. coll. bones pl. (of the human body), bony structure of an animal('s body), skeleton; mir flog es durch alle ~e I trembled in every limb. — 2. ~e pl. (sterbliche Hülle) mortal remains pl.; corpse.
Ge-belfer (⌣⌣) [ndd.] n ⓶, **Ge-bell(e)** (⌣⌣)(⌣) n ⓵b.(⓶) barking, yelping, yapping; von Menschen: bawling, (hooting and) howling, (Schelten) scolding.
geben (⌣⌣) [ahd.: give] ⓶c. I v/a. 1. e-m et. geben to give a p. s.th.; (schenken) to present a p. with s.th.; (verleihen) to bestow (or confer) s.th. upon a p.; zurück=2 to give back, to return. — 2. Redensarten mit s..: f. Abschied 3; f. acht=2; e-m ein Almosen 2 to give alms (or to dole out charity) to a p.; Antwort 2 to (give an) answer, to (make) reply; e-m Aufklärung über etwas 2 to enlighten a p. on a th.; den Ausschlag 2 to turn the scales; f. Blöße 2; ich werde mir die Ehre 2,

sie zu besuchen I shall give myself the pleasure of calling (up)on you; f. Fersengeld; ⚔ Feuer geben to (give) fire; f. Finger 2, Frist 2 ⊕; e-m Gehör 2 to give (or grant, vouchsafe) a p. a hearing; e-r Sache gern Gehör 2 to lend a willing ear to a th.; Karten 2 to deal (the cards); er muß (Karten) 2 it is his deal; Kredit 2 to (give) credit; das wird einen Lärm (et. Schönes) 2 there will be a great stir or F row (a fine piece of work); sich (dat.) Mühe 2 to take pains; Rabatt 2 to grant (or allow, take off) (a) discount; Rechenschaft (Zeugnis) von etwas 2 to give an account of a th.; e-m recht 2 to agree with a p., to acknowledge that a p. is (in the) right; thea. eine Rolle 2 to fill (or take) a part; e-m einen Verweis 2 to reprimand a p.; was wird das noch 2? what will be the end (or upshot) of it all?; ein Wort gab das andere one word led to another; Zeugnis 2 to bear witness, to give evidence; Sprichw. jeder gibt, was er kann, F ein Schuft gibt mehr, als er hat every one gives according to his means(, but you can't give more than you have). — 3. (hervorbringen) der Acker gibt gutes Korn ... yields good corn; die Bäume 2 viel Obst ... bear much fruit. — 4. (zeigen) das gibt schon der Augenschein it is seen at a glance. — 5. von Gott: alle Tage, die Gott gibt ... which Heaven grants us; der Himmel gab (fügte) es, daß // ...ordained (or willed) that //; als Wunsch: Gott geb's, daß //! may it please God that //! — 6. (hinzutun) to add; (hinzugießen) to pour into; fig. seinen Senf dazu 2 to add a few words, to put in one's spoke. — 7. (mit Worten ausdrücken) to render, express, interpret; gut gegeben! well done! — 8. mit a., f. die betreffenden a., zB. bloß 2 frei= 2, kund= 2 ꝛc.; et. verloren 2 to give a thing up for lost. — 9. mit prp.: an: sein Leben an et. (a. daran=)2 (setzen) to stake (or risk) one's life for a th.; d(a)ran= 2 (fahren lassen) to give up, to abandon; f. a. Hand 4; auf: auf die Post 2 to (put in the) post ...; f. Borg¹; sein Geld auf Zinsen 2 to put out ... at interest, to invest ...; sie 2 wenig darauf they lay little store by (or attach little value to) it; in: in Druck 2 to have printed, to publish (in print); in Kost 2 to put out to board with a p.; seinen Sohn in Pension 2 to place ... at a boarding-school; in Verwahrung 2 to deposit with a p.; von: sie will ihre Kinder nicht von sich 2 she does not want to part with her children; keinen Laut von sich 2 not to utter a sound; F er kann es nicht von sich 2 he does not know how to express himself; Speise wieder von sich 2 to bring up one's food; phys. von sich 2 to emit, to radiate; zu mit dem Inf.: wir 2 Ihnen zu bedenken, daß // we would have you consider that //, we would remind you that //; e-m zu essen und zu trinken 2 to give a p.

♪ Musik; ⚚ Wissenschaft; ⚘ Pflanze; 🜨 Geographie; ⊕ Technik; ⚒ Bergbau; ⚔ Militär; ⚓ Marine; ⬤ Handel; ✉ Post; 🚂 Eisenbahn.

s.th. to eat and to drink, to provide a p. with food and drink. — **II ſich** ⌒ v/refl. 10. to give in, to yield; f. bloß ⌒, preis ⌒ — 11. ſich gefangen ⌒ (erklären) to declare o.s. a prisoner; ſich verloren ⌒ to give o.s. up for lost; ſich zufrieden ⌒ to content o.s., to acquiesce; er gibt ſich für etwas anderes, als er iſt he pretends to be s.th. different from what he (really) is. — 12. ſich zu erkennen ⌒ to make o.s. known. — 13. ſich in etwas ⌒ (ergeben) to resign o.s. to a th. — 14. (nachlaſſen) der Schmerz wird ſich bald ⌒ ... will soon abate; F er wird ſich ſchon ⌒ (nachgeben) he will soon give in or be more yielding or F come down a peg or two; es wird ſich ſchon ⌒ it will come right in the end. — 15. unperſönlich: es gibt ſich nicht gut, wenn // one cannot easily give when //; wie es ſich gerade gibt just as it may happen. — **III es gibt ꝛc.** v/impers. 16. there is, there are; was gibt es (oder gibt's) Neues? what is the (latest) news?; F es wird etwas ⌒ F there will be a row; kann es etwas Schöneres ⌒? can there be anything more beautiful? — 17. ſ. 15. — **IV** ~ n ⊕ 18. giving; das ~ hat bei ihr kein Ende she is for ever giving; Kartenſpiel: am ~ ſein to (have the) deal. — **V ge-geben** p.p. u. a. ⊕(D♂) 19. (ſ. I) im 2n Falle in a given case, vgl. gegebenenfalls; das ~e ⊕ the thing given or supposed or agreed upon.

Geber¹ (⌣⌣) m ⊕ (auch **~in** f ⊕) **1.** giver; (Schenker) donor; (Austeiler) dispenser; jur. (ſ. der ein Recht überträgt) transferor; ♃ ~ und Nehmer pl. sellers and buyers pl. — **2.** tel. (Übertragungs-apparat) transmitter.

Geber² (⌣⌣) [perſ. gäbr Giaur] m ⊕ (Feuer-verehrer, Parſe) Gueber, Guebre.

Ge-bet (⌣⌣) [ahd: bead] n ⊕c. **1.** prayer; (beten) praying; einſames ~ private devotions pl.; ~ des Herrn (Vater-unſer) the Lord's Prayer; ſein ~ verrichten to say one's prayers. — **2.** F fig. e-n ins ~ nehmen (ſtreng verhören) to question (or examine) a p. closely, to take a p. severely to task.

Ge-bet=buch (⌣⌣...) n ⊕ prayer-book.

ge-beten (⌣⌣) p.p. von bitten.

Ge-bet(s)=formel (⌣⌣...) n f ⊕ form of prayer; **=maſchine** f der Buddhiſten: praying-machine or -wheel; **=riemen** m. =ſchnur f der Juden: phylactery; **=ſtimmung** f devotional (or prayerful) frame (or attitude) of mind.

Ge-bett(e) (⌣⌣)(⌣) n ⊕b(⊕) (Bettwerk) (set of) bedding.

Ge-bettel (⌣⌣) [betteln] n ⊕ importunate (or incessant) begging.

Ge-bet-teppich (⌣⌣...) m ⊕ ſ. Bettteppich¹; **=zeit** f prayer-time.

ge-beut (⌣⌣) poet. 3. Perſon sg. pres. von gebieten. [bären.]

ge-bier imper., 2ſt, 2t (⌣⌣) pres. v. ge-]

Ge-biet (⌣⌣) [mhd.] n ⊕c. **1.** territory; eines Fürſten auch: dominion; (Krongut) domain; auf deutſchem ~e on German soil; ſtädtiſches ~ township, purlieus pl. of a town, municipal area; ~ e-s Fluſſes = Flußgebiet. — **2.** fig. (Bereich) sphere, range of science, literature, &c.; domain (or province) of arts, &c.; line of business; ein weites ~ a vast field.

ge-bieten (⌣⌣) [ahd.] v/a. u. v/n. (h.) ⊕a* **1.** (befehlen) einem et. ⌒ to order (or to tell, ſtärker: to command) a p. to do a th.; (heiſchen) to bid a p. do a th.; Achtung, Ehrfurcht ⌒ to command respect; Stillſchweigen ⌒ to impose silence; was uns die Pflicht gebietet (poet. gebeut) what duty dictates or enjoins upon us; gram. 2e Form imperative (mood). — **2.** (herrſchen) to be a ruler over; über ein Volk ⌒ to rule over (or to sway) a nation; fig. über ſeine Leidenſchaften ⌒, ſ-n Leidenſchaften ⌒ to govern (or control, check) one's passions, to restrain one's passions.

Ge-bietende(r) (⌣⌣⌣) ⊕ = Gebieter(in).

Ge-bieter (⌣⌣) m ⊕, **~in** f ⊕ commander, ruler, governor; (Herr) master (f mistress); Herr und ~ lord and master; ~in des Hauſes mistress (or lady) of the house; unumſchränkter ~ autocrat; Rom, ehemals die ~in der Welt Rome, once the mistress of the world.

ge-bieteriſch (⌣⌣⌣) a. ⊕ commanding, ſtärker: imperious, domineering; (herriſch) despotic; 2er Ton categoric (or peremptory) tone; fig. 2e Macht der Verhältniſſe irresistible force of circumstances.

Ge-biets=abtretung (⌣⌣...) f ⊕ cession of territory; **=erweiterung** f extension of territory.

Ge-bilde (⌣⌣) n ⊕ **1.** creation; (Erzeugnis) product; (Geſtaltung) form(ation) (a. geol.); (Bild) image, likeness; die ~ eines erregten Menſchengehirns the visions pl. of an excited human brain. — **2.** Weberei: (Drillichmuſter) diaper.

ge-bildet (⌣⌣), **Ge-bildete(r)** ſ. bilden IV.

Ge-bimmel (⌣⌣) n ⊕ = bimmeln III.

Ge-binde (⌣⌣) n ⊕ **1.** bundle (or packet) of things tied together. — **2.** ⊕ agr. sheaf of corn; Böttcherei: barrel; carp. ~ e-s Dachſtuhls truss of a roof; Spinnerei: ~ Garn skein (or hank) of yarn.

Ge-bind=ſparren (⌣⌣) (⌣⌣...) m ⊕ carp. &c. tie-beam.

Ge-birge (⌣⌣) [ahd.; *Berg] n ⊕ **1.** ♀ mountain-chain or -range; weitS. mountainous region; oft a. highlands pl. — **2.** ⚒ (Geſtein) rock(y country); (taubes Geſtein) gang(ue); feſtes ~ bed-rock; gutes ~ workable ground; lockeres ~ loose formation.

ge-birgig (⌣⌣) a. ⊕ mountainous.

Ge-birgs=abhang (⌣⌣...) m ⊕ mountain-side. mo.-slope; **=art** ⚒ f = Gebirge 2; **=artillerie** ⚔ f mo.-artillery; **=aſt** m, **=ausläufer** m spur (or branch) of a mo.-range; **=bahn** ⊕ f = =eiſenbahn; **=beſchreibung** f: ⚒ orography; **=bewohner(in** f) m mo.-dweller, mehr gbr.: mountaineer, high-lander; **=bildung** f formation of mountains, mountainous formation; **=eiſenbahn** ⊕ f mo.-railway; **=fluß** m = =ſtrom; **=gegend** f mountainous region; **=grat**, **=kamm** m mountain-ridge, crest of a mo.; **=karte** f: ⚒ orographical map; **=keſſel** m hollow (between mountains), deep basin-like valley; **=kette** f mo.-chain chain (or range) of mountains; **=krieg** ⚔ m mountain-warfare; **=kunde** ⚒ f orology, geognosy; **=kundige(r)** m: ⚒ orologist, geognost; **=land** n mountainous country, highland(s pl.); **=lehre** f = =kunde; **=luft** f mo.-air; **=paß** m mo.-pass; ⚔ defile; vgl. =ſchlucht; **=pflanze** f mo.-herb; **=reiſe** f mo.-tour; **=rücken** m = =grat; **=ſchlucht** f mo.-gorge, ravine; (enges Tal) glen; **=ſtrom** m mo.-stream, torrent; **=tal** n mo.-valley; **=tor** n gap in a mountain-range; **=volk** n mo.-tribe; **=wand** f rocky shelf; **=zug** m = =kette; **=zweig** m = =aſt.

Ge-biß (⌣⌣) [ahd.; *beißen] n ⊕a. **1.** set of teeth (auch von falſchen Zähnen); (beide Zahnreihen) double row of teeth; ein gutes ~ a good set (F good mouthful) of teeth; ſein ~ geb. Spr. u. co. a. the fence of his teeth. — **2.** man. (eiſernes Mundſtück am Pferdezaum) (bridle) bit; mit Kinnkettenſtange: curb-bit; am ~ kauen to champ the bit.

ge-biſſen (⌣⌣) p.p. von beißen.

Ge-blaffe (⌣⌣) n ⊕ (Bellen) barking.

Ge-blaſe (⌣⌣) n ⊕ = blaſen II.

Ge-bläſe ⊕ (⌣⌣) [blaſen] n ⊕ **1.** blast-engine, ⚒ blower; (die Bälge) the forge-bellows pl. — **2.** metall. (~luft) blast; das ~ abſtellen to shut off the blast; das ~ anlaſſen to turn on the blast, to set the bellows going.

Ge-bläſe=luft ⊕ (⌣⌣...) f ⊕ metall. blast(-air); **=maſchine** f blowing-engine or -machine; vgl. Gebläſe 1.

ge-blaſen (⌣⌣) p.p. von blaſen.

Ge-bläſe=ofen (⌣⌣...) m ⊕ blast- (or blowing-)furnace; **=vorrichtung** f blast- (or blowing-)apparatus.

ge-blichen ⌣ (⌣⌣) p.p. von bleichen I.

ge-blieben (⌣⌣) p.p. von bleiben.

Ge-blök(e) (⌣⌣) [blöken] n ⊕c.(⊕) von Rindvieh: (bel)lowing; v. Schafen: bleating.

ge-blümt (⌣⌣) [p. p. von blümen] a. ⊕ flowered, flowery; ♃ figured; ⊕ Weberei auch: diapered.

Ge-blüt (⌣⌣) [Blut] n ⊕c. **1.** (the) blood in a living body. — **2.** (Stamm, Geſchlecht) descent, lineage, line, stock, race; (Geburt) birth; Prinz von ~ (königlichem) ~ ... of the blood (royal); es ſteckt im ~ it runs in the blood or in the family; das ~ verleugnet ſich nicht, etwa: blood will show (itself), v. Verwandten: blood is thicker than water.

ge-bogen (⌣⌣) p.p. v. biegen; vgl. krumm; **~heit** (⌣⌣⌣) f ⊕ = Biegung.

Ge-bohre (⌣⌣) n ⊕ continued boring.

ge-boren (⌣⌣) ſ. gebären III. [ing.]

Ge-borge (⌣⌣) n ⊕ incessant borrow-]

ge-borgen (⌣⌣) p.p. v. bergen; **~heit** (⌣⌣⌣) f ⊕ safety, security.

ge-borſten (⌣⌣) p.p. von berſten.

Ge-bot¹ (⌣⌣) [ahd.: bode; *gebieten] n ⊕c. **1.** (Befehl) order, ſtärker: command; ausdrückliches: (strict) injunction; (Erlaß) decree; (Geſetz) law, (Vorſchrift) precept; rel. die zehn ~e the Ten Commandments pl., the decalogue sg.; Sprichw. Not kennt kein ~ necessity has (or knows) no law. — **2.** e-m zu ~(e) ſtehen or ſein to be at a p.'s command or a p.'s beck and call; ſowie

Signs (see page XVII): F familiar; P vulgar; ♭ flash; ⌣ rare; † obsolete (died); * new word (born); ⁒ incorrect; ♪ music;

[gebot] — 411 — [Gedächtnis]

Geld steht mir nicht zu~ ... is not within my reach or at my disposal. — 3. = Aufgebot 1 u. 2. — 4. (der gebotene Preis) offer, bsd. bei Versteigerungen: bid(ding); höheres ~ als // advance on //; ein ~ tun to make an offer or a bid; das erste ~ machen to start a price.

ge-bot² (ʌʹ) ind., **ge-böte** (ʌʹʋ) subj. impf., **ge-boten** (ʌʹʋ) p.p. von (ge)bieten.

gebr. abbr. = gebräuchlich, gebraucht.

Ge-bräch (ʋʹ) n ⓐc. hunt. = Gebrech(e) 2.

ge-bracht (ʋʹ) p.p. von bringen.

Ge-bräme (ʋʹ) n ㉒ border, edging of cloth, &c., an Kleidern auch: furbelow.

ge-brannt (ʋʹ) p.p. von brennen.

ge-braten (ʋʹʋ) p.p. von braten.

Ge-bratene(s) (ʋʹʋ) n ⑰ f. braten III.

Ge-bräu (ʋʹ) [brauen] n ⓐc. 1. = Brau 2. — 2. (Mischung) mixture; (Trank) draught.

Ge-brauch (ʋʹʋ) m ⓐc. 1. use; z.B. ~ von et. machen to make use of a th.; in ~ kommen, nehmen to come, take into use; außer ~ (ob. aus dem ~e) kommen to go (or grow) out of use, to fall into disuse; (Anwendung) employment; ~ der Waffen 2c. auch: practice. — 2. (Herkommen) usage; (Sitte) custom; (Gepflogenheit) observance, (Gewohnheit) habit; (Weise) mode; festlicher: ceremony (a. rel.), bei Hofe 2c.: etiquette; heilige Gebräuche pl. sacred rites pl.; durch langen ~ vorgeschrieben prescriptive; es war damals (der) ~, zu // it was customary (or the custom) at that time to //.

ge-brauchen (ʋʹʋ) v/a. ⑧* 1. (anwenden; dafür oft: brauchen 1, f. ds) ich kann es nicht ② I cannot make use of it, it is useless (or of no use) to me; sich ② lassen zu // to lend o.s. to //; etwas ② (handhaben) to handle a th. — 2. ⧖ ob. P (nötig haben) = brauchen 2.

ge-bräuchlich (ʋʹʋ) a. ⓖ in use or usage; v. Wörtern 2c. a. current, commonly used; (gewöhnlich) ordinary, common; (herkömmlich) customary, usual, wonted; nicht mehr ② (gone) out of use or fashion; obsolete, antiquated, out of date. [commonness; customariness.]

Ge-bräuchlichkeit (ʋʹʋ-) f ⓖ currency;]

Ge-brauchs-anweisung (ʋʹʋ...) f ⓖ = ~vorschrift; muster ⚓ n traveller's sample; ~vorschrift f. med. directions pl. for use; ~zettel m label attached to medicines or drugs.

ge-braucht (ʋʹʋ) [p.p. v. gebrauchen 1] a. ⓖ used; ②e Kleider clothes that have been worn, worn clothes pl.

Ge-bräude (ʋʹʋ) n ㉒ = Gebräu.

Ge-braus (ʋʹ) n ⓐa., **Ge-brause** (ʋʹʋ) n ㉒ = brausen III.

ge-brech ⚔ (ʋʹ) a. ⓖ (zerbrechlich) brittle, fragile; (weich) soft, crumbling.

Ge-brech(e) (ʋʹʋ) [brechen] n ⓐc.(㉒) 1. continued vomiting. — 2. hunt.: a) (Rüssel des Wildschweins) boar's snout; b) (Stelle zum Wühlen) rooting place. — 3. ⚔ coll. soft stone, crumbling rock.

ge-brechen (ʋʹʋ) I v/n. (h.) ⓑa* 1. mir gebricht Geld, mehr gbr. v/impers. es gebricht mir an Geld I am in need (or want, lack) of money, F I am short of money or hard up; es gebricht ihnen an allem they are quite destitute, es soll ihm an nichts ② he shall not want

for anything. — II ~ n ㉓ 2. (das Fehlen) need, want. — 3. sehr gbr. mit pl. (körperlicher Fehler) physical (or bodily) defect or imperfection; affliction, infirmity.

ge-brechlich (ʋʹʋ) a. ⓖ 1. allg. (schwach) weak, feeble; (leicht brechend) fragile, brittle; von Möbeln 2c.: rickety. — 2. bsd. von Personen: infirm, physically afflicted, suffering from (some) infirmity; (hinfällig) frail, delicate; (trübselhaft) crippled; (abgelebt) decrepit.

Ge-brechlichkeit (ʋʹʋ) f ⓖ (f. gebrechlich) weakness, feebleness; ricketiness; infirmity; frailty; decrepitude.

ge-brecht (ʋʹ) p.p. von brechen 6.

Ge-breit (ʋʹ) n ⓐc., ~e † f ㊽ (Acker, Feld) (G.) field; broad acres pl.

Ge-breste(n) (ʋʹʋ) n ㉒(㉓) (Gebrechen) infirmity; (Krankheit) complaint, malady.

ge-brochen (ʋʹʋ) p.p. von (ge)brechen (f. bsd. brechen I); ②e Ziffer typ. (type for) fractions pl.; **~heit** (ʋʹʋ-) f ⓖ brokenness, broken(-down) condition; der Stimme: broken voice.

Ge-bröckel (ʋʹʋ) n ㉒ crumbling substance; coll. crumb(ling)s; fragments

Ge-brodel (ʋʹʋ) n ㉒ = brodeln II. [pl.]

Ge-brüder (ʋʹʋ) m/pl. ㉒: die ~ Grimm the brothers G.; ⚘ ~ Wolfram Wolfram Brothers.

Ge-brüll (ʋʹ) n ⓑb. = brüllen III.

Ge-brumm(e) (ʋʹʋ)(~) n ⓑb(㉒) growling, growls pl. (= brummen II.

Ge-bühr (ʋʹ) [ahd.] f ㊻ 1. (Verpflichtung) duty, obligation; über die ~ to excess, excessively, immoderately. — 2. (das e-m Zukommende) a p.'s due; nach ~ according to a p.'s desert, deservedly; über die ~ beyond (all) measure; more than is due; wider alle ~ (Schicklichkeit) contrary to (the rules of) propriety or decency, quite improper. — 3. bsd. ~en pl. (Zahlung) fee(s pl.), charges, dues pl.; (Honorar) honorarium, für Advokaten: fee; (Abgaben) duty, taxes pl.; ⚘ (Provision) commission.

ge-bühren (ʋʹʋ) [ahd.] v/n. (h.) u. sich ② v/refl. ⑧* 1. einem ② (zukommen) to be due to a p., to belong (by rights) to a p.; gebt ihm, was ihm gebührt ... his due; unser Dank gebührt ihm he is entitled to our gratitude, to him our thanks are due; Sprichw. Ehre, dem Ehre gebührt honour to whom honour is due. — 2. a. dat.: sich ② (geziemen) to be proper or seemly or befitting; v/impers. es gebührt sich, daß // it is meet (or proper) that //; wie es sich für seinen Stand gebührt in accordance with his rank. — II ②d p.pr. u. a. ⓖ 3. (f. 1) due; adv. duly. — 4. (f. 2) proper, seemly, befitting, meet; adv. properly. in a seemly (or befitting, becoming) manner.

ge-bührender-maßen, ②weise (ʋʹʋ-ʋʹʋ) adv. duly, properly, deservedly; in a seemly manner, becomingly.

Ge-bühren-erlaß (ʋʹʋ...) m ㉒ remission of fees, &c.; ②frei a. exempt from duty or taxes; **~nachlaß** m = ~erlaß.

ge-bührlich (ʋʹʋ) a. ⓖ = gebühren II; **~keit** (ʋʹʋ-) f ㊻ propriety. seemliness.

Ge-bührnis ⚔ (ʋʹʋ) n ⑰, mst pl. ...nisse soldier's pay and dues.

Ge-bund (ʋʹ) n ⓑb. = Bund² u. Bündel 1; ~ Schlüssel bunch of keys.

ge-bunden (ʋʹʋ) bount, f. binden V; **~heit** (ʋʹʋ-) f ㊻ constraint, restraint; (Unterwerfung) subjection.

Ge-bürste f (ʋʹʋ-) n ㉒ much brushing.

Ge-burt (ʋʹ) [ahd.: birth; *gebären] f ㊻ 1. = gebären II; leichte ~ easy confinement; zu frühe ~ f. Frühgeburt; auf die ~ bezüglich natal. — 2. birth; bei j-r ~ at his birth, when he was born; ein Ire von ~ an Irishman born or by birth; vor Christi ~ before Christ (abbr. B.C.); nach Christi ~ after Christ (abbr. A.D., f. ds); von hoher (niedriger) ~ (Herkunft) of high (low) extraction or birth. — 3. fig. (Entstehung) rise; in der ~ ersticken to nip in the bud. — 4. (Frucht) offspring; (Erzeugnis) production.

ge-bürtig (ʋʹʋ) [nhd.] a. ⓖ: aus Berlin ② a native of...; aus Frankreich ② (herstammend) of French extraction or descent.

Ge-burts-adel (ʋʹ...) m ㉒ nobility by birth, inherited title or rank; **~anzeige** f notification of b.; eine ~ machen to give notice of a b., to register (the b. of) a child; **~arbeit** f (child-)labour; **~attest** n = ~schein; **~fehler** m natural (⚕ congenital) defect, inborn blemish; **~feier, ~fest** n birthday-celebration or -fête; **~helfer(in** f) m accoucheur m (accoucheuse, midwife f), ⚕ obstetrician; **~helferkröte** f f. Fessler; **~hilfe** f midwifery, assistance at a confinement, ⚕ obstetrics; ②hilflich a. ⓖ relating to confinements, ⚕ obstetric (-al); **~jahr** n year of birth; **~land** n native land or country, land of one's b.; **~liste** f register of births; **~mal** n b.-mark, mole; **~ort** m birth- (or native) place; **~recht** n b.-right; **~register** n = ~liste; **~schein** m certificate of birth; **~schmerzen** m/pl. = ~wehen; **~stadt** f native town; **~stern** m, astrol. natal star; **~stolz** m pride of b.; **~stunde** f hour of birth, natal hour; **~tag** m birthday, natal day; **~tags-** = ~tags-geschenk n birthday-poem, -present; **~tags-kind** n person celebrating his (or her) birthday; **~teile** m/pl., anat.: ⚕ genital organs, genitals pl.; **~wehen** f/pl. labour-pains pl., ehm. a.: travail; **~zange** f, surg.: ⚕ obstetric(al) instrument or forceps; **~zeit** f time of confinement or delivery, date of birth.

Ge-büsch (ʋʹ) n ⓐa. bushes pl.; (Dickicht) thicket; (Gehölz) copse, underwood.

Geck (ʹ) [ndd.] m ㉒ 1. fool, idiot, simpleton, F ninny, P mug. — 2. (Zierbengel) fop, dandy, F masher, swell; bsd. ehm. coxcomb; alter ~ old beau; junger ~ young spark; den ~(en) mit et. treiben to fool about with a th.

geckenhaft (ʹʋ-) a. ⓖ (f. Geck 2) foppish, dandyish, F dandified; bisw.: coxcombical; **~igkeit** (ʹʋʋ-) f ㊻ foppishness, dandyism, F masherdom.

Gecko ⚕ (ʹ-) m ㊺, a. ⓖ (pl. Gecko'nen) zo. (wall-)gecko, gecco, fanfoot (Platyda'ctylus mura'lis).

ge-dacht (ʋʹ) p.p. von (ge)denken (f. bsd. denken III.); ②e (ʋʹʋ) impf. von gedenken.

Ge-dächtnis (ʋʹʋ) [mhd.; *(ge)denken] n ⑰ recollection, (Erinnerung) remem-

⚕ scientific; ⚘ botanical; ⚲ geography; ⚙ machinery; ⚔ mining; ⚓ military; ⚓ marine; ⚘ commercial; ⚘ postal; ⚒ railway.

[Gedächtnisbuch] — 412 — [gediegen]

brance; aus dem ~ from memory, by heart; zum ~ in remembrance (or commemoration) of; in ~ bewahren to treasure (or store up) in one's memory, to bear in mind; ein starkes (schwaches) ~ haben to have a retentive (weak) memory; wenn mich mein ~ nicht trügt if my memory serves me, if I recollect (or remember) rightly; e-m et. ins ~ zurückrufen to call a th. back to a p.'s memory, to remind a p. of a th. **Ge-dächtnis-buch** (`⌣⌣…`) n ⑫ memorandum-book; **=fehler** m slip of the memory; **=feier** f, **=fest** n commemoration(-day); (Jahresfeier) anniversary; **=kirche** f memorial church; **=kraft** f power (or retentiveness) of (the) memory; **=kram** m (mere) matter of memory, facts pl. stored (up) in the memory, vgl. **=werk**; **=kunst** f: ⚔ mnemonic art, mnemo(tech)nics; **=künstler** m: ⚔ mnemonician; **=münze** f commemorative medal; **=predigt** f, **=rede** f commemorative sermon, speech or address; **=schwäche** f weakness (or defect, shortness) of (the) memory; **=stein** m memorial stone; **=tafel** f commemorative tablet; **=tag** m commemoration-day, anniversary (day); **=übung** f mnemonic exercise; **=werk** n knowledge acquired with the aid of the memory, things pl. learnt by rote, vgl. **=kram**.
ge-dackt ☉ (`⌣⌣`) a. ⓖ von Orgelpfeifen: stopped with a lid.
Ge-dämpfte(s) (`⌣⌣`) [dämpfen 4] n ⑰ Kochkunst: s.th. stewed, stew.
Ge-danke (`⌣⌣⌣`) [abd.; *denken] m ⑳, a. **~n** ㉓ 1. thought; (Vorstellung) conception, idea; (Begriff) notion; Sprichw. ~n sind zollfrei thoughts are free; das war ein guter ~ (Einfall) … a bright idea, … a happy inspiration; der ~ **an** die Zukunft the thought of the future; der bloße ~ daran the mere thought of it; seine ~n beisammen haben (halten) to have (or keep) one's wits about one; es fallen mir allerlei ~n ein many thoughts (or things) pass through my mind; seinen ~n nachhängen to be lost (or deeply absorbed) in thoughts. — 2. Nebensarten: e-n **auf** andere ~n bringen to divert a p.'s thoughts, to make a p. change his ideas; e-n auf den ~n bringen to put a notion into a p.'s head; das hat mich auf den ~n gebracht that first suggested the idea (or it) to me; ich kam auf den ~n the thought occurred to me, the idea struck me, vgl. 6; auf andere ~n kommen to change one's mind; in ihren ~n ist sie schon Gräfin in her fancy (or imagination) she is already a countess; ich bin in ~n bei euch I am present with you in spirit or in mind; er griff in ~n nach seinem Stock in his distraction (or absence of mind) he seized his stick; in ~n (versunken) sein to be absorbed (or lost) in thought or brooding or F woolgathering; in ~n (zerstreut) sein, seine ~n nicht beisammen haben to be absent-minded; Sie sind ja ganz in ~n why, you are deep in thoughts, F co.

a penny for your thoughts; wo waren Sie mit Ihren ~n? what were you thinking of?; sich ~n **über** et. machen to alarm (or disquiet) o.s. about a th. — 3. (Wunsch, Vorhaben) seine ~n geh(e)n zu hoch he has too high notions or F too big ideas; er geht mit dem ~n um zu reisen he is thinking of travelling, he contemplates travelling. — 4. (Ansicht) opinion; auf j-s ~n eingeh(e)n to enter into a p.'s ideas or views. — 5. (Erinnerung) recollection; sie kommt mir nicht aus den ~n she is never out of (or absent from) my mind or thoughts. — 6. (Vermutung) supposition; das brachte mich auf den ~ that led me to suppose; wie kamen Sie auf den ~? how came you to think it?, what made you suspect such a thing? — 7. (Hoffnung) hope; sich ~n auf et. machen to buoy o.s. up with the hope (or to entertain hopes) of gaining s.th. — 8. (Spur, Kleinigkeit) kein ~ daran not a trace (or vestige) of it; einen ~n dünner a trifle (or F a shade) thinner.
ge-danken-arm (`⌣⌣⌣…`) a. ⓖ lacking ideas; **=armut** f ⓯ lack (or poverty) of ideas; barrenness of (the) mind; **=flug**, **=fluß** m flight, flow of thoughts; **=folge** f = **=gang**; **=freiheit** f freedom of thought; **=fülle** f abundance of ideas, fertility of (the) mind; depth of thought; **=gang**, **=kreis** m train, circle of thought(s); order, range of ideas; **=leer(e** f) a. = **=arm(ut)**; **=leser** n, **=leser(in** f) m thought-reading, -reader; **=los** a. thoughtless, void of ideas, vacant; unthinking; (leichtsinnig) lighthearted; adv. without thinking, unthinkingly; ⚲ dahinleben to give no thought to the future, to live in a fool's paradise; **=losigkeit** f thoughtlessness, vacancy (of mind); lightheartedness; ⚲**reich** a. rich in ideas; of deep meaning; **=reichtum** m = **=fülle**; ⚲**schnell** a. (as) quick as thought; ⚲**schwer** a. = ⚲**reich**; **=späne** m/pl. disconnected thoughts, aphorisms, scraps pl.; **=strich** m dash break; typ. metal rule (—); **=übertragung** f transmission of thought(s); (mental) suggestion; ⚲**voll** a.: a) full of (or deep in) thought; thoughtful, contemplative, pensive; vgl. ⚲**reich**; b) (sorgenvoll) full of care; **=vorbehalt** m mental reservation; **=welt** f world of ideas, weitS. ideal (or intellectual) world; **=wesen** n creature of fancy, (mere) abstraction.
ge-danklich (`⌣⌣⌣`) a. ⓖ relating to thought(s), intellectual.
Ge-därm(e) (`⌣⌣(⌣)`) [abd.; *Darm] n ⑪b. (㉒) entrails, bowels pl.; ⚔ intestines pl., F guts pl.; Kochk.: tripe.
Ge-deck (`⌣⌣`) n ⑪c. 1. covering; Dachdeckerei auch: roof; (Pferdedecken) horse-rugs pl. — 2. (Tischzeug) table-linen; einzelnes ~ cover. — 3. ♪ der Orgel: register of covered organ-pipes.
ge-deckt (`⌣⌣`) p.p. s. decken, bsd. 1.
ge-deihen (`⌣⌣⌣`) [abd.; *dich] I v/n. (sn) ⑪ (\ ⑱)* 1. (guten Fortgang haben, wachsen) to prosper, thrive, grow, in-

crease; (blühen) to flourish; (gelingen) to succeed, to get on (well); Sprichw. unrecht Gut gedeiht nicht ill got ill spent. — 2. ohne Rücksicht auf den Vorteil **zu** etwas ⚲ (gereichen) to turn out well, ill, to grow into s.th. — 3. (kommen, geraten) die Sache ist dahin (ob. so weit) gediehen, daß // the matter has now so far developed that //, b.s. matters have reached such a pitch (or have come to such a pass) as to //. — **II ~** n ㉓ 4. (s. I) prosperity, growth, increase; success; development; Gott gebe sein ~ dazu! may God give it his blessing or bestow his blessing upon it!, rel. auch: may the Lord prosper (or bless) it!
ge-deihlich (`⌣⌣⌣`) a. ⓖ 1. (gedeihend) prosperous, thriving, flourishing; successful. — 2. (heilsam) beneficial; wholesome; **~keit** f ㊽ wholesomeness.
Ge-denk-blatt (`⌣⌣…`) n ⑫ commemorative leaf; **=buch** n memorandum-book; bsd. chm. (Stammbuch) album, jetzt: birthday-book.
ge-denken (`⌣⌣⌣`) I v/a. und v/n. (h.) ⓦ* 1. e-m et. ⚲ (nicht verzeihen) to bear a grudge (or spite) against a p. about (or for) s.th.; F to bottle it up; ich werde es ihm ⚲ he shall remember it, F I'll make him pay for it; vgl. denken 2. — 2. j-s, e-r Sache ⚲ (eingedenk sein) to bear … in mind, to remember (or recollect) …, to be mindful of …; gedenke mein! remember me!, think of me!; wir werden seiner stets dankbar, liebevoll ⚲ we shall always bear him in grateful, affectionate remembrance; er gedachte meiner mit keiner Silbe he did not mention a syllable about me, he did not make the slightest allusion to me; dessen nicht zu gedenken, daß // without mentioning that //, setting aside that //; vgl. denken 1. — 3. ⚲ zu … (inf.) (vorhaben) to think of (or to intend, purpose, contemplate) doing a th.; vgl. denken 3, bsd. b. — **II ~** n ㉓ 4. = Gedächtnis; seit Manns-, Menschen-⚲ within the memory of man, weitS. for ages, from time immemorial.
Ge-denk-feier (`⌣⌣…`) f ⑫ commemoration; **=spruch** m motto; (Wahlspruch) device; **=stein** m commemorative (or memorial) stone; **=tafel** f (memorial or commemorative, mural) tablet.
ge-deucht (`⌣⌣`) p.p. von dünken.
Ge-deute(l) (`⌣⌣⌣`) n ㉒ = Deutelei.
Ge-dicht (`⌣⌣`) n ⑪b. poem, piece of poetry, verse(s pl.); ein ~ hersagen to recite a poem; ~e machen to compose (or write) poems or poetry, to make verse, to versify; **~-form** (`⌣…`) f ⑫ poetic (or metrical) form; **~-sammlung** f collection (or selection) of poems; (Blütenlese) anthology.
ge-diegen (`⌣⌣⌣`) [abd. p.p. v.*gedeihen] a. ⓖ (D9) 1. (derb, dicht) solid, compact; (handfest) robust. — 2. ⚔ min. (rein unvermischt) pure, unalloyed, unmixed; ⚲es Eisen native iron; aus ⚲em Golde (made) of pure (or solid, sterling) gold. — 3. fig. (echt, lauter) genuine, sterling; of intrinsic value; ⚲e Arbeit solid work

Zeichen (s. S. XVII): F familiär; P Volkssprache; Γ Gaunersprache; ⟍ selten; † alt (auch gestorben); * neu (auch geboren); ⁂ unrichtig;

[Gediegenheit] — 413 — [gefallen]

(manship); ~e Kenntnisse *f. pl.* sound knowledge, ripe scholarship *sg.*

Ge-diegenheit (‿‿‿) *f* ⑯ (f. gediegen) solidity; pureness; genuineness; sterling quality; intrinsic value; soundness.

ge-dieh (‿¹) *ind.*, ~e *subj. impf.*, ~en (‿‿) *p.p.* von gedeihen.

Ge-dinge (‿‿) *n* ㉒ 1. (Feilschen) bargain(ing), haggling. — 2. agreement about pay(ment); bsd. ⚒ (Stücklohn) payment by the job; (Erzantheil des Bergmanns) tribute; im ~ arbeiten to work by contract or by the job; ~arbeit (‿‿‿) *f* ⑫ job-work, piece-work.

Ge-donner (‿‿) *n* ㉓ constant thundering or rumbling or claps of thunder; thunder-like (F thundering) noise.

ge-doppelt (‿‿) *a.* ⑯ double.

Ge-dränge (‿‿) *n* ㉒ 1. = Drang 1; Fußball: scrimmage, scrummage. — 2. *fig.* (Not) trouble, embarrassment, F straits *pl.*, fix; ins ~ geraten, kommen to be landed in (or to get into) a great difficulty or a tight place, F to be pushed into a corner.

ge-drängt (‿‿) *p.p. u. a.* ⑯ f. drängen V; ~heit (‿‿‿) *f* ⑯ closeness, compactness; der Ereignisse: rapid succession of events; der Schreibweise: conciseness (or terseness) of style, ⚕ syntomia.

ge-dreht (‿¹) *a.* ⑯ und *p.p.* von drehen; bsd. ⚘: ~e Blumenkrone: ⚕ contorted corolla; spiralig ~: ⚕ tortile.

ge-dritt (‿¹) *a.* ⑯: ⚕ ternary, ternate; trinal; *astrol.* (Aspect) ~er Schein, auch: **Ge-dritt-schein** *m* ⑪d. (Abstand zweier Planeten um 120 Grad): trigon, trine.

ge-droschen (‿‿) *p.p.* von dreschen.

ge-drückt (‿‿) *a.* ⑯ u. *p.p.* (f. drücken V).

Ge-druckte(s) (‿¹-) *f* printed matter.

Ge-drückt-heit (‿¹-) *f* ⑯ depression, depressed (or dejected) condition (a. 😊).

ge-drungen (‿‿) *a.* ⑯ (D9) und *p.p.* von dringen (f. ds III); ~heit *f* ⑯ (Dichtigkeit) closeness, compactness; des Körperbaues: F stout (or square) build, squattiness.

Ge-dudel F (‿¹‿) *n* ㉒ = Dudelei.

Ge-duld (‿¹) [ahd.; *dulden] *f, inv.* patience; (Nachsicht) forbearance, indulgence; (Ausdauer) endurance, perseverance; sich in ~ fassen to take patience; mit e-m ~ haben to have patience (or to bear, to be forbearing) with a p.; hab' ~! be patient!; mir riß (oder ich verlor) die ~ I lost patience, my patience gave way; ~ überwindet alles patience overcomes all things, patience is a plaster for all sores; Sprichw.: mit ~ und Zeit kommt man weit, etwa: patience and time make all things chime; co. mit ~ und Spucke fängt man manche Mucke, etwa: patience and a snare catch many a hare.

ge-dulden (‿‿) sich ~ *v/refl.* ⑨* to have patience, to wait patiently; Sie müssen sich ein wenig ~ you must have a little patience or consideration.

ge-duldig (‿‿) *a.* ⑯ patient; (nachsichtig) forbearing, indulgent; Sprichw. das Papier ist ~ one can put anything on paper, paper won't blush; *adv.* ~ warten to wait patiently.

Ge-duld(s)-faden (‿⁸...) *m* ⑫: der ~ reißt mir my patience is at an end, I'm losing (all) patience; ~probe *f* trial of patience; ~spiel *n* (Chinese) puzzle; exercise of patience.

ge-dungen (‿‿) *p.p.* von dingen.

ge-dunsen (‿‿) [*p. p.* v. dunsen] *a.* ⑯ (D9) puffed up, bloated, turgid; ~heit (‿‿-) *f* ⑯ bloatedness, turgidness.

ge-durft (‿⁸) *p.p.* von dürfen.

ge-eckt (‿⁸) *a.* ⑯ = eckig.

Ge-ehrte(s) 🙏 (‿¹‿) *n* ⑰: Ihr ~ vom // your favour (or esteemed letter) of //.

ge-eignet (‿¹‿) *a.* ⑯ und *p.p.* von eignen (f. II); zB. die Sache war kaum ~ (fähig), ihn zu fesseln the matter was little calculated (or scarcely such as, hardly adapted) to attract him; er ist dafür nicht ~ he is not cut out (or fitted) for it; der ~e Zeitpunkt the favourable moment.

Geer(de) ⚓ (¹(‿) [= Gehre] *f* ㊾ (㊽): ~ (Gilling) eines Segels: vang.

Geer(d)-läufer (‿¹...) *m* ⑫, ~schenkel *m* pendant of a vang.

Geescha (‿¹) *f* ㊻ (jap. Teemädchen) geisha.

Geest (‿¹) [ndd.: güst] *f* ㊻, ~land (‿¹...) *n* ⑭ *pl.*) (ant. Marsch²) high and dry land or ground.

gef. *abbr.* = gefälligst.

Ge-fabel (‿¹‿) *n* ㉒ fabulous tales *pl.*

Ge-fächel (‿¹‿) *n* ㉒ constant fanning.

Ge-fahr (‿¹) [ndd.: fear: lt. *pēr-icul-*] *f* ㊻ danger, (Gefährdung) endangerment; sehr nahe, persönliche: peril; (Wagnis) risk, hazard, venture, jeopardy; es hat keine ~ there is no danger; der ~ aussetzen, in ~ bringen to expose to danger; to risk, hazard, jeopardize; in ~ kommen to run (or get) into danger; (große) ~ laufen to run a (great) risk; ~ laufen to run the risk of losing s.th., &c.; in ~ setzen to endanger, imperil; wir sind noch nicht außer ~ we are not yet out of danger or F out of the wood; auf seine ~ at his risk or peril; mit ~ m-s Lebens at the risk (or hazard) of my life; Sprichw. wer sich in ~ begibt, kommt darin um he that courts (or runs into) danger must expect to perish therein; vgl. Verzug.

gefahr-bringend (‿¹‿...) *a.* ⑯ leading into (or causing) danger, dangerous, menacing; vgl. ⚕voll.

Ge-fährde (‿¹‿) *f* ㊽ 1. = Gefahr. — 2. (Arglist) cunning, deceit, deceitfulness; (Betrug) fraud, deception.

ge-fährden (‿¹‿) *v/a.* ⑨* to endanger, to imperil; to expose to danger or peril; (aufs Spiel setzen) to risk, hazard, jeopardize; (schädigen) to prejudice, to hurt; j-s Gesundheit, Kredit ~ to shatter (or injure, undermine) a p.'s health, credit; seine Ehre ist gefährdet his honour is compromised.

ge-fahr-drohend (‿¹‿...) *a.* ⑯ = ⚕bringend.

Ge-fahre (‿¹‿) *n* ㉒ constant driving (or running, movement, din, rattling) of vehicles or carriages.

ge-fahren (‿¹‿) *p.p.* von fahren.

Ge-fahren-klasse (‿¹...) *f* ⑫ Versicherungswesen: (class of insured belonging to the) accident-branch.

ge-fährlich (‿¹‿) *a.* ⑯ 1. (f. Gefahr) dangerous, perilous; risky, hazardous, venturesome; (ernst, schlimm) grave, critical. — 2. *fig.* (bedeutend) important, considerable; sehr ~ m. (übertreiben) to exaggerate; das ist nicht so ~ that's of no great consequence, there is not much to fear.

Ge-fährlichkeit (‿¹‿-) *f* ⑯ (f. gefährlich 1) danger(ousness), peril(ousness); riskiness. gravity of a situation.

ge-fahr-los (‿¹...) *a.* ⑯ without danger or risk, bisw. dangerless; (sicher) safe; ~losigkeit *f* ⑯ absence of danger; (Sicherheit) safety, (perfect) security.

Ge-fährte(¹) (‿¹‿) [ahd.] *n* ⑩c. (㉒) (Fuhrwerk) vehicle; vierspänniges ~ carriage and four.

Ge-fährte² (‿¹‿) [ahd.] *m* ㊹, **Ge-fährtin** *f* ㊼ (male, female) companion, associate, auf lange Zeit: mate, partner, auf e-r Reise: fellow-traveller, (Kamerad) comrade, F pal, chum.

ge-fahr-voll (‿¹‿) *a.* ⑯ full of danger; risky, hazardous, venturesome, fraught with peril.

Ge-fäll..e (‿¹‿) [Fall] *n* ⑩b., ㉒ 1. e-s Flusses: fall; e-s Daches, Weges: incline, slope, descent; 🚂 (falling) gradient; F co. er hat ein gutes ~ he can drink like a fish, F he has a good swallow. — 2. ~e *pl.* (Grundlasten) expenses (or outgoings) *pl.* of an estate.

Ge-falle, ~n¹ (‿¹‿) *m* ⑳, ㉓ (Gefälligkeit, Liebesdienst) kind service, favour, kindness; e-m zu ~n leben to live for (or to devote o.s.) to a p.; e-m zu ~n reden to agree (in every word) with a p.; es geschieht mir ein ~n damit I consider it (F it will be doing me) a favour; e-m e-n ~n tun (ob. erweisen, erzeigen) to do a p. a favour or a good service; e-m et. zu ~n tun to do a th. to please (or oblige) a p.; tun Sie mir doch den ~n zu kommen do me the favour to come, (you will) oblige me by coming; vgl. gefallen² II.

ge-fallen² (‿‿) [ahd.] **I** *v/n.* (h.) ⑨a* 1. to please; er gefällt mir I like (the look of) him; das Buch will mir nicht ~ ... is not to my taste, I do not like (or fancy) ...; *v/impers.* es gefällt mir in dieser Stadt I like (staying in) this town; er tut, was ihm gefällt he does as he pleases. — 2. sich (*dat.*) in et. ~ (daran Freude finden) to find a pleasure in a th.; er gefiel sich in dem Gedanken, daß // he was pleased with the idea that //. — 3. sich (*dat.*) etwas ~ lassen: a) (es gutheißen) to agree with (or to approve of) a th.; lassen Sie es sich bei uns ~ make yourself at home with us; sich ~ lassen, daß etwas geschieht to consent to s.th. being done; das lasse ich mir ~, das kann man sich noch ~ lassen that's what I like, F that's proper or something like it; b) (sich in et. fügen) to yield (or submit) to a th.; es läßt sich ohne Scherz ~ he knows how to take a joke; das muß sich jeder ~ lassen everybody has to put up with that; so et. lasse ich mir nicht ~ I won't pocket (or swallow) that or such an insult; er

♪ Musik; ⚕ Wissenschaft; ⚘ Pflanze; 🌍 Geographie; ⊙ Technik; ⚒ Bergbau; ⚔ Militär; ⚓ Marine; 🏛 Handel; ✉ Post; 🚂 Eisenbahn.

[gefallen] — 414 — [geflissentlich]

läßt sich nicht viel 2 he would not stand much. — II ~ n²³ 4. pleasure; ~ an et. finden to be pleased (stärker: charmed, delighted) with a th., to take a pleasure (stärker: a delight) in a th.; Ihnen zu ~ (in order) to please (or oblige) you, for your pleasure; e-m zu ~ sein to be at a p.'s beck and call. — 5. (Willen) will, wish; handeln Sie ganz nach Ihrem ~ you must act according to your own discretion or ideas, kürzer: (you must entirely) please yourself; nach ~ (soviel man will) arbeiten to work as much or as little as one likes; vgl. Gefallen(n).

ge-fallen³ (⌣⌣) p.p. von fallen u. a. 66 fallen (a. fig.); fig. degraded, F low (in the world); ~e([r] m) f (⌣⌣⌣) 67 one who has fallen, fallen one (a. fig.); ~e ruined girl, unfortunate; ⚔ die ~en m/pl. the killed or fallen or dead pl.

ge-fällig (⌣⌣) I a. 66 1. (gütig) kind; (angenehm) pleasant, agreeable; (dienstfertig) obliging, ready to serve; (zuvorkommend) accommodating, bisw. auch: complaisant; (höflich) courteous; um Ihnen 2 zu sein (in order) to oblige (or please) you; wollen Sie so 2 sein, mir zu sagen will you be so kind (or so good) as to tell me. — 2. (genehm) ist es Ihnen jetzt 2 zu unterschreiben? are you now agreeable to sign?; was ist (Ihnen) 2? what is it you wish for?; im Laden: what can I get you or do for you?; wenn j. nicht verstanden hat: I beg your pardon!; klingeln Sie, wenn es Ihnen 2 ist! ring, if you please!; (will you) kindly ring!; vgl. gefälligst. — 3. er hat ein 2es (angenehmes) Äußere he has a pleasing appearance; die Musik ist leicht und 2 the music is light and pleasing; 🖉 Ihr 2es Schreiben von unserm letzten Zeilen pl.; Ihrer 2en Antwort entgegensehend awaiting the favour of your reply. — II das ~e n 67 4. pleasantness (or pleasing, agreeable character) of a p. or a th.; stärker: the charm of a p. or a th.

Ge-fälligkeit (⌣⌣-) f 46 1. (das Gefälligsein) kindness; pleasantness; obligingness, readiness to serve; (Höflichkeit) courteousness. — 2. (freundlicher Dienst) kind service or act; ich danke Ihnen für alle mir erwiesenen ~en ... for every favour (that you have) shown me or for all your good offices; Sprichw. eine ~ ist der andern wert one good turn deserves another.

Ge-fälligkeits-akzept (⌣⌣-...) n 62, =wechsel m 🟦 accommodation-bill.

ge-fälligst (⌣⌣) adv. in Höflichkeitswendungen: nehmen Sie 2 Platz please (or pray) be seated; sit down, if you please; wollen Sie mir 2 das Salz reichen I shall thank you for the salt, please pass me the salt.

Ge-fall-sucht (⌣⌣-⌣) f 46 (excessive) desire to please or to attract notice or to be admired; love of admiration; weibliche: coquetry, coquettishness.

ge-fall-süchtig (⌣⌣-⌣) a. 66 desirous of pleasing, eager (or anxious) to please or to be admired; coquettish; ~e f 67 coquette; flirt.

ge-falten (⌣⌣) p.p. von falten.
ge-fangen (⌣⌣) I p.p. von fangen in allen Bedeutungen. — II a. 66 (D9) (in fremder Haft) captive, (detained or locked up) in prison or in jail; ⚔ sich 2 geben to give o.s. up as a prisoner (of war); von Truppen: to lay down arms, to surrender; e-n 2 halten to detain a p. in prison or as prisoner; 2 sein, 2 sitzen to be (or sit) in jail, geh. Spr. to linger in durance vile.

Ge-fangen-anstalt (⌣⌣-...) f 62 =haus, =aufseher m inspector of a prison.

Ge-fang(e)ne (⌣⌣(⌣)⌣) m, f 67 captive; prisoner, F jail-bird; ⚔ ~ auswechseln to exchange prisoners (of war); e-n zum ~n machen to take a p. prisoner.

Ge-fangen-haltung (⌣⌣-...) f 62 imprisonment, detention; =haus n house of detention; vgl. Gefängnis 1; =nahme f = =nehmung; =nehmen v/a. 🖱a. ***: e-n 2 to apprehend (or arrest) a p.; ⚔ to take a p. prisoner; ⚔=genommene Soldaten prisoners pl. of war; =nehmung f capture; apprehension; (Verhaftung) arrest.

Ge-fangenschaft (⌣⌣⌣) f 46 captivity; (Haft) imprisonment, detention (in jail); (Gewahrsam) custody; aus der ~ befreien to free from captivity; (loskaufen) to ransom; in ~ geraten to be taken captive or prisoner (auch ⚔).

ge-fangen-setzen (⌣⌣⌣-) v.a. 🟦***: e-n 2 to put a p. in prison; =setzung f 62 imprisonment; =wärter m jailer, keeper (of a prison); (Schließer) turnkey.

ge-fänglich (⌣⌣) a. 66 captive, imprisoned; 2e Haft detention in prison, imprisonment, adv. e-n 2 einziehen to arrest (or imprison) a p., to put a p. in prison or in jail.

Ge-fängnis (⌣⌣) [mhd.] n 13 († f 46) 1. prison, jail, P quod, F choker; (Kerker) dungeon; (Polizei-)~ lock-up; im ~ (confined) in prison, (kept) under lock and key, F u. P in quod, euph. in trouble; aus dem ~ ausbrechen to break out of prison, ins ~ setzen (ab. sperren) lassen to put (or cast, throw) into (or to commit to) prison, to take into custody, F to put in quod. — 2. (Strafe) drei Tage ~ three days' imprisonment or ⚔ cell; zu zwei Jahren ~ verurteilt w. to be sent two years to prison, to be sentenced to two years' imprisonment, F to get two years.

Ge-fängnis-arbeit (⌣⌣-...) f 62 prison-labour; =direktor m governor of a prison; =haft f detention; =hof m pr.-yard; =strafe f = Gefängnis 2; entehrende ~ geh. Spr. a. durance vile; =wagen m prison-van, F Black Maria; =wärter m jailer, turnkey; =wesen n, =zucht f pr.-system, -discipline.

Ge-fasel (⌣⌣) n 22 (seichtes Gerede) drivel (-ling talk), trash, (silly) twaddle.

Ge-fäß (⌣) [ahd.; * fassen n 🟦a. 1. (Behältnis) vessel, receptacle (auch fig.); irdenes ~ earthen vessel or jar; rel. auserlesenes ~ des Herrn (von Gott Auserwählter) chosen vessel of the Lord; anat. ~e (Kanäle u. Röhren) vessels (for the circulation of blood and lymph), ducts, canals pl.; Beschreibung der ~e

⚕ angiography; auf ~e bezüglich: ⚕ vascular; f. leer 2. — 2. (Griff am Degen) hilt (of a sword).

Ge-fäß-barome'ter (⌣⌣...) n 62 phys.: ⚕ cistern-barometer; =beschreibung f: ⚕ angiography; =bildung f vascular formation; ⚕ vascularization; =erweiterung f dilation of the vessels; =förmig a. 66: ⚕ vasculiform; =lehre f ⚕ angiology; =nerv m, anat.: ⚕ vascular nerve; =pflanze ⚘ f: ⚕ vascular (or vasculiferous) plant; =sporenpflanzen ⚘ f/pl. (Farnpflanzen) vascular cryptogams pl.; =syste'm n vascular system. [~heit (⌣⌣-) f 46 = Fassung 3.]

ge-faßt (⌣) p.p. u. a. 66 f. fassen V.

Ge-fecht ⚔ (⌣) I n 🟦b. fight, combat; (Treffen) action, engagement; (Handgemenge) (af)fray; (Scharmützel) skirmish; unvermutetes: encounter; in der Hitze des ~s in the heat (or fury, turmoil) of battle, außer ~ setzen to put out of action; Truppen ins ~ ziehen to engage troops (in battle), to lead soldiers into action; ⚓ ein Schiff zum ~ klar m. to clear for action, to clear the decks. — II auch: ~e n 22 constant fighting or skirmishing.

Ge-fechts-bereich ⚔ (⌣⌣-) m, n 62 fighting-zone; =bereitschaft ⚔ f readiness for action; =bericht ⚔ m report of an engagement; =form(ation) f battle-formation, order of battle; =klar a. 66 clear for action; =lehre f (military) tactics; =linie ⚔ f fighting line; 2mäßig a. 66 battle-like; =mast ⚓ ⚔ m (mit Schnelladekanonen) fighting-mast; =ordnung f battle-array; =übung f manœuvre, sham fight.

Ge-fege (⌣⌣) n 22 constant sweeping.

Ge-feierte(r) (⌣⌣) s. 67 = Jubila'r.

ge-feit (⌣) p.p. u. a. 66 f. feien.

Ge-fertigte(r) öft. (⌣⌣-) s. 67 (Unterzeichnete[r]) undersigned.

Ge-fieder (⌣⌣) [ahd.; * Feder] n 23 1. e-s Vogels plumage, feathers pl. — 2. (gefiedertes Geschöpf) bird, F one of the feathered tribe.

ge-fiedert (⌣⌣) p.p. u. a. 66 f. fiedern II.

ge-fiel (⌣) (2e subj.) impf. v. gefallen.

Ge-fild ⚘ (⌣) n 🟦b., mst ~e (⌣⌣) [ahd.; *Feld] n 22 fields pl.; open (tract of) country. [digitate.]

ge-fingert (⌣⌣) a. 66 fingered, zo., ⚘: ⚕]

Ge-flacker, Ge-flatter (⌣⌣) n 22 constant flickering, fluttering. [clouded.]

ge-flammt (⌣) p.p. u. a. 66 Marmor ꝛc.]

Ge-flecht (⌣) n 🟦b. 1. plaited (or braided) work; aus Holz: hurdle- or wicker-)work. — 2. (Gewebe) texture, anat.: ⚕ plexus, rete, reticulum.

ge-fleckt (⌣) a. 66 spotted (leopard); speckled or freckled (face), stained (glass); (befleckt) blotted, blotched; 2e Katze F tabby (cat).

Ge-flenne F, Ge-flicke, Ge-flimmer (⌣⌣) n 22 (constant or endless) crying, mending, glittering.

ge-flissen (⌣⌣) a. 66 studious, diligent.

Ge-flissenheit (⌣⌣-) f 46 application; studiousness, diligence, zeal.

ge-flissentlich (⌣⌣⌣) a. 66 assiduous, (absichtlich) intentional, wilful; adv. a.: purposely, on purpose, designedly.

Signs (see page XVII): F familiar; P vulgar; ꜰ flash; ⟍ rare; † obsolete (died); * new word (born); ⧺ incorrect; ♪ music;

[geflochten] — 415 — [Gegend]

Ge-flochten (⌣ʹ⌣ʹ), **-flogen, -flohen** (⌣ʹ⌣ʹ), **-flossen** (⌣ʹ⌣ʹ) p.p. von flechten, fliegen, fliehen, fließen. [foul cursing.)
Ge-fluche (⌣ʹ⌣ʹ) n ㉒ constant swearing.
Ge-fluder ⊕ (⌣ʹ⌣ʹ) n ㉒ ⚔ metall. (Wasserrinne) gutter, water kennel.
Ge-flügel (⌣ʹ⌣ʹ) n ㉒ (Federvieh) birds pl., poultry; weitS. (geflügelte Wesen) winged creatures pl.; F the feathered tribe; **~ausstellung** f ㊻ poultry-show; **~händler** m poulterer; **~haus** n, **~markt** m poultry-house, -market.
ge-flügelt (⌣ʹ⌣ʹ) a. ㊻ winged (a. fig.); orn. ⚛ pinnate(d); ♀ ⚛ alate(d); fig. ⚛ Worte n/pl. household-words, familiar quotations or sayings pl.
Ge-flügel-zucht (ʺ⌣...) f ㊻ breeding (or rearing) of poultry, poultry-farming.
Ge-flunker (⌣ʹ⌣ʹ) n ㉒ 1. (Schimmer) gleam. — 2. (Aufschneiderei) brag, bounce.
Ge-flüster (⌣ʹ⌣ʹ) n ㉒ whispering.
ge-fochten (⌣ʹ⌣ʹ) p.p. von fechten.
Ge-folge (⌣ʹ⌣ʹ) [ahd.] n ㉒ 1. suite, retinue, train; attendants, followers pl., ehm.: retainers pl.; ohne ⚛ unattended; (Bedeckung) escort. — 2. fig. (Begleitung) accompaniment; etwas Schlimmes im ~ (besser: zur Folge) haben to have evil consequences, to lead to (or be attended with) serious results.
Ge-folgschaft (⌣ʹ⌣ʹ) f ㊻ bsd. ehm. (body of) retainers or vassals pl.; train of servants. [Fürsten: follower, retainer.)
Ge-folgs-mann (⌣ʹ⌣⌣ʹ) m ㊷ ehm. der dtsch.)
Ge-frage (⌣ʹ⌣ʹ) n ㉒ constant (cross-) questioning; searching interrogation; cross-examination; F pumping.
ge-fragt (⌣ʹ⌣ʹ) p.p. von fragen u. a. ㊻ inquired after, in demand, in (great) request; wenig ⚛ neglected, not much inquired for or sought after.
ge-franst (⌣ʹ⌣ʹ) p.p. von fransen u. a. ㊻ fringed, ♀: ⚛ fimbriate(d).
ge-fräßig (⌣ʹ⌣ʹ) a. ㊻ voracious, ravenous, gluttonous, greedy; wolfish; Der Mensch glutton, F gormand(izer); **~keit** (⌣ʹ) f ㊻ voracity, voraciousness, ravenousness, gluttony, greediness.
Ge-freite(r) ⚔ (⌣ʹ⌣ʹ) m ㊿ lance-corporal, acting corporal.
ge-fressen (⌣ʹ⌣ʹ) p.p. von fressen.
Ge-frier-apparat ⊕ (⌣ʹ⌣⌣ʹ...) m ㊷ freezing(-)apparatus, freezer.
ge-frierbar (⌣ʹ⌣ʹ) a. ㊻ freezable, ⚛ congealable; **~keit** f ㊻: ⚛ congealableness.
ge-frieren (⌣ʹ⌣ʹ) I v/n. (fn) ㊼* f. frieren 4. — II ~ n ⓑ.(㉒) freezing (up); congealing, phys.: ⚛ congelation.
Ge-frier-punkt (⌣ʺ...) m ㊷ phys. freezing(-)point, Thermometer: auf dem ~ stehen to be at zero.
ge-froren (⌣ʹ⌣ʹ) I p.p. v. (ge)frieren. — II **Ge-fror(e)ne(s)** n ㊷ ice, ice-cream.
Ge-füge (⌣ʹ⌣ʹ) n ㉒ 1. (die Fugen) the joints pl. — 2. (Zf.-fügung) joining (together), (Bau) structure, texture, construction, frame; e-s Körpers: articulation, geol.: ⚛ stratification.
ge-fügig (⌣ʹ⌣ʹ) a. ㊻ (geschmeidig) pliable, supple; (biegsam) flexible; (willfährig) pliant, tractable, accommodating.
Ge-fügigkeit (⌣ʹ⌣ʹ⌣) f ㊻ pliability, suppleness; flexibility; pliancy, tractableness, accommodating nature.

Ge-fühl (⌣ʹ) [nhd. 17. sae.] n ⓒ c. 1. feeling; sentiment; (Regung) emotion, (Einsicht) sense; ein feines ~ haben to be delicate of feeling; kein ~ (Mitleid) haben to be unfeeling or hard-hearted, to have no compassion or sympathy; mit ~ singen ... with feeling or expression. — 2. als Sinn: touch; zB. durch das ~ erkennen to know by the touch; als Wahrnehmung: sensation; zB. ~ der Wärme sensation of warmth.
ge-fühl-los (⌣ʺ...) a. ㊻ unfeeling, insensible, apathetic; (hartherzig) callous, hard(-hearted); adv. ⚛ mit e-m verfahren to act harshly (or cruelly) towards a p.; **-losigkeit** f ㊻ unfeelingness, insensibility; apathy; callousness; hard-heartedness.
Ge-fühls-art (⌣ʺ...) f ㊷ (natural) disposition; **-austausch** m interchange of sentiments; **-duselei** f sentimentalism, F gush, sentimental bosh; **-mensch** m person with a warm (or affectionate, feeling) nature, contp. sentimentalist, F gushing person; **-organ** n, **-sinn** m organ of feeling, sense of feeling or touch.
gefühl-voll (⌣ʺ) a. ㊻ full of feeling or sentiment or warmth; (empfindsam) of delicate feeling, sensitive; (liebevoll) affectionate, (zärtlich) tender; (rührselig) sentimental; adv. a. feelingly, with feeling or expression.
ge-funden (⌣ʹ⌣ʹ) p.p. von finden.
ge-fünft (⌣ʹ⌣ʹ) I a. ㊻ (aus fünf Teilen bestehend); ⚛ quinary, astrol.: Der Schein (a.: **Ge-fünft-schein** m ⓓ.): ⚛ quintile. — II ~(e) n ⓑ.(㉒) arch., hort., &c. (Kreuzstellung :·:): ⚛ quincunx.
Ge-funkel (⌣ʹ⌣ʹ) n ㉒ sparkling.
ge-fürstet (⌣ʹ⌣ʹ) a. ㊻ f. fürsten 1.
Ge-gacker (⌣ʹ⌣ʹ) n ㉒ endless cackling.
ge-gangen (⌣ʹ⌣ʹ) p.p. von gehen.
ge-geben (⌣ʹ⌣ʹ) p.p. u. a. f. geben V.
ge-gebenen-falls (⌣ʹ⌣⌣ʺ) adv. in a given case; should the opportunity arise or an occasion present itself.
gegen (⌣ʹ) [ahd.: (a)gain] I prp. mit acc. 1. örtlich: towards; ⚛ Süden towards (or to the) south, southward; Schulter ⚛ Schulter shoulder to shoulder; zeitlich: ⚛ 11 Uhr about eleven (o'clock); ⚛ Ende der Woche towards the end ...; ⚛s (⚛ das) Licht halten to hold against the light; persönlich: dankbar, grausam, gütig ⚛ // grateful, cruel, kind to //; seine Nachsicht ⚛ uns his indulgence to (or towards) us. — 2. widerstrebend: against; jur. auch: ⚛ versus; Krieg führen ⚛ to make war upon; ⚛ den Strich against the grain; ⚛ die Vernunft contrary to reason; drei ⚛ eins wetten to bet three to one; ⚛ seinen Wunsch contrary (or in opposition to) his wish(es); ⚓ ⚛ den Wind in the teeth of the gale. — 3. bestimmend: ⚛ zwanzig Jahre alt about (or nearly) twenty years old. — 4. tauschend: (in exchange) for //; ⚛ Bezahlung von // on payment of //; ⚛ Bürgschaft on bail, on security; ⚛ ⚛ bar for cash, for ready money; ⚛ Quittung on receipt. — 5. vergleichend: in comparison (or compared) with or to. — II **Gegen** n, inv. 6. f. für III.

Gegen-..., **gegen-...** (ʺ...) Vorsilbe in Zssgn bezeichnet: 1. feindliche Beziehung, zB. **~papst** m antipope, Widerstand, zB. **~anspruch** m counter-claim. — 2. Widerspiel, zB. **~meinung** m contrary opinion. — 3. Erwiderung, Wechselseitigkeit, zB. **~liebe** f mutual love; **~schuld** f reciprocal debt.
Gegen-abdruck ⊕ (ʺ...), **-abzug** m ⓓd. Kupferstecher ꝛc.: counter-proof, **-absicht** f ㊻ contrary (or opposite) intention, cross-purpose; **-anerbieten** n ㉓ counter- (or return-)offer; **-angriff** ⚔ m ㊷ counter- (or mutual) attack; **-anklage** f ㊽ jur. counter-accusation, countercharge; eine ~ erheben to make a countercharge; **-anschlag** m ⓓd. counter-project, counterplot; **-anspruch** m ⓓd. counter-claim; **-anstalt** f ㊻: ~en machen to make counterefforts; **-antrag** m ⓓd. counter-proposal; parl. counter-motion; **-antwort** f ㊻ reply, rejoinder; jur. replication; (treffende Entgegnung) repartee; **-arz(e)nei** f ㊻ med. counteracting medicine; antidote; **-auftrag** m ⓓd. counter-order; einen ~ geben to countermand an order; **-aussage** f ㊽ jur. contradictory deposition, counter-evidence; **-batterie** ⚔ f ㊽ counter-battery, opposite battery; **-bedingung**. meist ⚛ f ㊻ counter-stipulation. wir machen es zur ~, daß // we stipulate on our part that //; **-befehl** m ⓓd. counter-order, countermand, countermandate; **-bemerkung** f ㊻ retort, rejoinder; (Entgegnung) reply; **-bericht** m ⓓc. counter-statement, contradictory report; **-beschuldigung** f ㊽ jur. countercharge, bisw. auch: recrimination; **-besuch** m ⓓd. return-visit or -call; e-m e-n ~ m. to return a p.'s call; **-bewegung** f ㊻ counter-move(ment); reaction; ⚔ c.-manœuvre; **-beweis** m ⓓa. counter-evidence; einen ~ führen to traverse (or upset) an indictment; **-bild** n ⓓc. (Gegenstück) companion picture; counterpart; (Vor- od. Nach-bild) (anti)type, original; copy; (Gegensatz) contrast; **-bitte** f ㊽ counter-request or -petition; eine ~ stellen to (present a) counter-petition; ich habe eine ~ an Sie I would ask you a favour in return; **-böschung** f ㊻ bsd. ⚔ frt. (innere Böschung) counterslope; ⚛ **brassen** ⚓ v/a. ㊿** nur im inf. (gegen den Mast brassen) to brace aback; **-buch** n ⓓd. customer's book; für Kunden e-r Bank: pass-book; **-bürge** m ㊹, **-bürgschaft** f ㊻ ⚛ counter-security or -surety.
Gegend (⌣ʹ) [mhd. (fr. contrée)] f ㊻ 1. (Landschaft) country, region; Malerei: scenery, landscape; (Himmelsstrich) climate; aus welcher ~ stammen Sie? where do you come from?; P iro. auch eine schöne ~! F a nice place to be in! — 2. umliegende ~ surroundings, environs pl.; in unserer ~ in our neighbourhood; in jener ~ in those parts; in welcher ~? where about(s)? — 3. anat. (Stelle am Körper) ~ des Herzens cardiac region; ~ des Unterleibs abdominal region or parts

---

⚛ scientific; ♀ botanical; ♁ geography; ⊕ machinery; ⚒ mining; ⚔ military; ⚓ marine; ● commercial; ✉ postal; 🚆 railway.

[Gegendampf] — 416 — [gegenüber]

pl. — 4. ♀ (Himmels=)~ quarter (of the globe); aus welcher ~ bläst der Wind? from which quarter does the wind blow?. in what qu. is the wind? **Gegen=dampf** ⊙ (ᴵᵘ...) m ⓣc. counter-steam; =**dienst** m ⓑc. counter-service, service rendered in return; similar favour; (lt.) quid pro quo; e-m einen ~ leisten to reciprocate (or return) a p.'s favour, to make a return for a p.'s services; =**druck** m ⓣc. mech. counter-pressure, reaction; ⚹ renitence.

gegen-ein-ander (ᴵᵘ‿ᵇᵘ) adv. against (or towards, to, opposite) one another or each other; (gegenseitig) reciprocally, mutually; et. ℒ **haben** to be at variance or F at loggerheads; ℒ **halten** (vergleichen) to put side by side, to compare; ~**halten** (ℒ...) n ⓑ, =**haltung** f juxtaposition; (Vergleichung) comparison; ℒ **stellen** to put face to face, to confront witnesses; =**stellung** f jur. confrontation.

Gegen=erbieten (ᴵᵘ...) n ⓔ counter-offer; =**erklärung** f ⓯ (gegenseitige Erklärung) mutual declaration; (entgegengesetzte Erklärung) counter-declaration, protest; (Ableugnung) denial, dissent; =**flut** f ⓯ counter-tide; =**forderung** f ⓯ counter-claim or -demand; ⚹ set-off, offset; =**form** ⊙ ⓯ Guß: counter-mould; Weberei: co.-plate; =**frage** f ⓯ counter-question; =**füßler** m/pl. ⓔ: ⚹ antipodes, antiscii, antiscians pl.; =**gabe** f ⓯ =geschenk; =**gang** ⚹ m ⓣc. counter-lode; =**gefälligkeit** f ⓯ =dienst; auch: reciprocated favour; =**gesang** m ⓣc. eccl. anthem; =**geschenk** n ⓑc. return present, gift presented in return; ein ~ m. to make a return (in shape of a present); =**gesuch** m ⓑd. counter-petition, requesting a favour in return; =**gewicht** n ⓑc. counter-weight, counterpoise; e-m, einer Sache das ~ halten to counterbalance a p., a th.; =**gift** n ⓑc. antidote; bisw.: counterpoison; als ~ dienend antidotal; =**grund** m ⓣc. counter-argument; contrary reason, opposite motive; =**gruß** m ⓣa. return-bow; responsive greeting; ↓ return-salute; =**hall** m ⓑc. = Widerhall; =**halt** m ⓑc. (Widerstand) resistance; (Stütze) support, s. th. to lean against, prop, rest; fig. auch: backing; ℒ**halten** ⓯ a ** v/a. = gegeneinander (s. bs) halten; (auch abs.) Spiel: to back a card against a p.; v/n. (h.) to resist, to offer resistance; (dauern) to last, to endure; (stützen) to support, to uphold; =**hieb** m ⓑd. counter-stroke or -cut; fenc. home-thrust; =**intrige** f ⓯ counter-plot; =**kaiser** m ⓑ im alten Deutschen Reiche: anti-emperor, rival emperor, imperial rival; =**keil** ⊙ m ⓑd. mech. tightening-key; =**klage** f ⓯ counter-plea or -charge; =**kläger**(in f ⓰) m ⓔ counter-pleader; =**kompliment** n ⓑc.: e-m ein ~ machen to return a p.'s compliment; =**könig** m ⓑd. anti-king, rival king; =**kraft** f ⓲ phys. counter- (or opposing) force; =**kritik** f ⓯ counter-criticism or -critique; =**laufgraben** ⚹ m ⓴ counter-approach or -trench;

=**leistung** f ⓯ return service, equivalent (for a service rendered); ⚹ u. jur. consideration; (lt.) quid pro quo; unter der Bedingung einer ~ on reciprocal terms; =**licht** n ⓓc. paint. (falsches Licht) wrong light, counter-light; =**liebe** f ⓯ responsive love; mutual affection; er fand keine ~ his love met with no response or was not reciprocated, he was disappointed in love; =**list** f ⓯ counter-stratagem or -practice, countermine, counterplot; =**macht** f ⓾ opposing (or hostile) power or force; =**marke** f ⓯ counter-ticket, check; =**marsch** m ⓣa. ⚹ u. Tanzkunst: countermarch; =**maßregel** f ⓯ prevent(at)ive measure; =**mauer** ⚹ f ⓯ frt. counter-mure; =**meinung** f ⓯ opposite (or contrary, conflicting) opinion; =**mine** ⚹ f ⓯ counter-mine; ℒ**minieren** ⚹ v/n. (h.) ⓯** to counter-mine; =**mittel** n ⓔ remedy (against), remedial measure, cure (for); vgl. =gift; =**ort** ⚹ m ⓑc. ob. ⓣc. counter-excavation; =**papst** m ⓣc. antipope; =**part** ⓑc.: a) n — Gegenteil; b) m (Gegner) opponent, adversary, antagonist; (Mitteilhaber) partner; =**partei** f ⓯ opposite (or hostile) party; jur. opponent; =**pfahl** m ⓑd. her.: mit =pfählen versehen counterpaled; =**pfand** n ⓑc. counterpledge; =**pfeiler** m ⓔ Wasserbau: ~ eines Deiches counter-fort, e-r Brücke: corner-arch; =**plan** m ⓑd. counter-project; =**posten** ⚹ m ⓔ counter-post or -item; set-off; =**prall** m ⓑc. rebound; ℒ**prallen** v/n. (sn) ⓯** to rebound; =**probe** f ⓯ counter-proof; =**protest** m ⓑc. counter-protest; =**rechnung** f ⓯ balancing of accounts, (=forderung) counter-reckoning, contra-account; set-off; durch ~ ausgleichen to counterbalance, to offset; =**rede** f ⓯ reply; rejoinder, contradiction; (Einwand) objection, jur. counter-plea; ℒ**reden** v/n. (h.) ⓯** to reply, raise objections, contradict; =**reformation** f ⓯ eccl. hist. counter-reformation; =**reiz** m ⓣa. med. counter-irritant; =**revolution** f ⓯ counter-revolution, anti-revolution; =**rimesse** ⚹ f ⓯ counter-remittance; =**ronde**, =**runde** ⚹ f ⓯ counter-round.

gegens (ᴵᵘ) zsgs. aus gegen das.

Gegen=satz (ᴵᵘ...) m ⓣa. (Entgegengesetztes) contrast; (the) contrary, (the) opposite; log., &c.: ⚹ antithesis; (Unvereinbarkeit) antagonism; im ~ zu as contrasted with, in contradistinction (or opposition) to; in ~ zu einem stehen (stellen) to be (to set up) in opposition to a p.; ⚹ (Gegenwert) equivalent; als ~ per contra; als ~ für // in return (or payment) for //; ℒ**sätz-lich** a. ⓯ contrary, opposite; antagonistic; gr., log. disjunctive; adv. in opposition to; ℒ**schattig** ⚹ a. ⓯: ℒe Völker n/pl.: ⚹ antiscii, antiscians, antoeci pl. = =füßler; =**schein** m ⓑd. phys. reflection; ast. (Stand eines Planeten in gerader Linie mit Erde und Sonne) opposition; ⚹ counter-bill, jur. co.-deed; =**schenkung** f ⓯ (making a) return present; =**schiene** ⚲ f ⓯ guard-

rail; =**schlag** m ⓣd. counter-blow or -stroke, reaction, phys. percussion; =**schraffierung** f ⓯ cross-hatching; =**schreiber**(in f ⓰) m ⓔ controller, checking clerk; =**schrift** f ⓯ written reply; (Widerlegung) refutation; jur. defence; =**schritt** m ⓑc. counter-step; ~e tun to take counter-measures; =**schuld** ⚹ f ⓯ mutual (or reciprocal) debt or indebtedness; =**seite** f ⓯ opposite side, einer Münze: reverse; fig. contrary view; ℒ**seitig** a. ⓯: a) ⚹ (entgegengesetzt) opposite, contrary; b) (wechselseitig) mutual, reciprocal; ⚹ ℒen Forderungen ausgleichen to balance (or settle) accounts; c) sich ℒ ... in Verbindung mit v., z.B. sich ℒ loben to praise one another; phls., &c. sich ℒ beziehend correlative; =**seitigkeit** f ⓯ mutuality, reciprocity, reciprocalness; =**seitigkeitsgesellschaft** f ⓯ co-operative association or union; =**seitigkeits-prinzip** n co-operative principle; =**sicherheit** f counter-security; =**siegel** n ⓔ counter-seal; =**sinn** m ⓑc. contrary sense; (falscher Sinn) wrong sense; (falsche Deutung) misconstruction; ℒ**sinnig** a. ⓯ contrary, (mißverstanden) misconstrued; (unsinnig) preposterous; =**sonne** f ⚹ ast.: ⚹ anthelion, parhelion, F mock-sun; =**spiel** n ⓑc. playing against a p., F opponent's game; weitS. opposition; (Gegenteil) reverse; e-m das ~ halten to hold one's own against a p.; =**spieler** m ⓔ opponent in playing; =**sprecher** m ⓔ, =**sprech-telegraph** m ⓵ tel. duplex telegraph; =**stand** m ⓣc.: a) object; (behandelter oder zu behandelnder Stoff) subject, theme; ~ des Gelächters laughing-stock; ~ e-s Streites bone of contention; von dem ~e abschweifen to digress (from the subject under discussion); ich betrachte den ~ (die Angelegenheit) als erledigt I consider the affair (or matter) as settled; b) das ist kein ~ (nicht viel) that is not worth mentioning, F that's (a mere) nothing; co. so ein ~ von (so etwa) zehn Faß F something like ...; ℒ**ständig** ⚹ a. ⓯ opposite; ℒ**ständlich** a. ⓯ objective; ℒ**ständlichkeit** f ⓯ objectivity, objectiveness; ℒ**standslos** a. ⓯ without object; (zwecklos) to no purpose, fruitless; ...**es** Gerede empty talk, twaddle; =**steigerung** f ⓯ rhet.: ⚹ anticlimax; =**stimme** f ⓲ counter-part; bei Wahlen ⚹: adverse vote; =**stoß** m ⓣa. push-back, fenc. counter-thrust; phys. rebound; =**strom** m ⓣd., =**strömung** f ⓯ counter- (or opposing) current, cross-current; =**strophe** f ⓯ pros.: ⚹ antistrophe; =**stück** n ⓑc. f. =bild; =**tausch** m ⓣa. exchange; =**teil** n ⓑd. contrary, reverse; im ~ on the contrary; das ~ behaupten to maintain the contrary; er tat (gerade) das ~ ... (just) the reverse; ℒ**teilig** a. ⓯ opposite; to the contrary; nichts ~es nothing to the contrary.

gegen-über (ᴵᵘ‿ᴸ) I adv., prp. mit dat. oder von. **1.** opposite (to); facing, fronting, in front of; F over against; over the way; solchen Tatsachen ℒ in the face of such facts; nur von Personen:

Zeichen (f. S. XVII): F familiär; P Volkssprache; Γ Gaunersprache; ⚹ selten; † alt (auch gestorben); * neu (auch geboren); ┼ unrichtig;

[gegenüberliegen] — 417 — [geheimhalten]

ea. 2 face to face. — II ~ n ⑳ person (or object) facing another; bfb. (2 =ſitzende, ⸗wohnende Perſon) p. (sitting, living) opposite; opposite neighbour; (fr.) *vis-à-vis*; er hatte zum ~ eine junge Dame he had a young lady opposite (or in front of) him.
gegenüber=liegen (⸗⸗⸗...) v/n. (h.) ⑭** to lie opposite..., to face...; 2d opposite; *geom.* e-m Winkel 2de Seite line subtending an angle; ⸗**ſetzen** v/a. ⑨⁰**: ſetzen Sie ſich mir gegenüber! sit opposite me!; ⸗**ſteh(e)n** v/n. ⑨⁴** to stand opposite (or in front of) a p. or a th.; kampfgerüſtet: to face (or to be pitted against) an adversary; 2d *p.pr.* oppositiſte; ⸗ mit 2den Blättern: ⚘ oppositifolious; ⸗**ſtellen** v/a. ⑧⁸** to oppose, als Paar: to match; bfb. jur. to confront (with each other); *fig.* to contrast; ⸗**ſtellung** f ㊻ opposition; confrontation; contrast(ing); ⸗**treten** v/n. ⑥d**: a) to step in front of b) *fig.* e-r Anlage 2 to face...

Gegen=umwälzung (⸗⸗...) f ㊻ counter-revolution; ⸗**unterſchrift** f ㊻ countersignature; ⸗**unterſuchung** f ㊻ jur. counter-inquiry or -investigation; ⸗**verpflichtung** f ㊻ counter-obligation, mutual duty; ⸗**verſchanzung** ⚔ f ㊻ der Belagerer: contravallation, counterfort; ⸗**verſchreibung** f ㊻: a) ❀ counter-bond; b) jur. counter-deed; ⸗**verſicherung** f ㊻: a) (entgegengeſetzte Verſicherung) conflicting (or contradictory) statement; b) ❀ mutual assurance (vgl. Rückverſicherung); ⸗**verſprechen** n ㉓, ⸗**verſprechung** f (⸗⸗⸗) mutual promise; ⸗**vormund** m ①d. u. 2d. co-guardian; ⸗**vorſchlag** m ⑩d. counter-proposal; ⸗**vorſtellung** f ㊻ remonstrance; e-m ~en m. e. to remonstrate with a p.; ⸗**wall** ⚔ m ⑦c. *frt.* counter-scarp; ⸗**wart** [abh.] f, *inv.*: a) presence; in meiner ~ in my presence; von Reden: to my face, in my hearing; v. Handlungen: before my eyes, in my sight, F under my (very) nose; b) (Jetztzeit) present (time); *gr.* present (tense); Ideen der ~ ideas pl. of our time or of the present day; in der ~ at the present time, in these days (of ours); 2**wärtig** [abh.] a. ⑥: a) (*ant.* abweſend) present; bei einer Feier 2 ſein to be present at (or to attend)...; ❀ die 2en Preiſe the actual (or current, ruling) prices; 2es Schreiben (a. ~es n) dient, Ihnen zu melden by the present (or by these lines or herewith) we wish to inform you; b) 2e Zeit present (time); *adv.* at (or for the) present, nowadays, now; ⸗**wechſel** ❀ m ㉒ counter-bill, bill given in return; ⸗**wehr** f ㊻ self-defence; ſich zur ~ ſetzen to offer resistance; ⸗**wert** m ⑦c. equivalent; ⸗**wind** ⚓ m ⑩c. contrary wind; ⸗**winkel** m ㉒ *math.* opposite angle; A und C ſind ~ A and C are exterior and interior opposite angles; 2**wirken** v/n. (h.) ⑧** to counteract; to react; ⸗**wirken** n ㉓ u. ⸗**wirkung** f ㊻ counter-action, reaction; ⸗**wirkungs=rad** n (Waſſerrad) reaction-wheel; ⸗**wohner**

m ㉒ antipode; ⸗**zeichen** n ㉓: a) ⚓ u. ⚔ countersign(al); b) ❀ (counter)mark; 2**zeichnen** v/n. (h.) ⑨²b** to countersign; ⸗**zeichnung** f ㊻ counter-signature; ⸗**zeuge** m ㊹ hostile witness, witness for the other side or for the defence; ⸗**zug** m ⑩d. counter-move.
ge=geſſen (⸗⸗) *p.p.* von eſſen.
Ge=girre (⸗⸗) n ㉒ cooing of doves.
ge=glichen, ge=gliſſen, ge=glitten, ge=glommen (⸗⸗⸗) *p.p.* von gleichen, gleißen, gleiten, glimmen.
Gegner (⸗⸗) m ㊵, ⸗**in** f ㊼ opponent; (Widerſacher) adversary, antagonist; (Feind) foe; (Angreifer) assailant; (Nebenbuhler) rival, competitor; ~ der Revolution antirevolutionist; 2**iſch** (⸗⸗) a. ㊺ opposed, of the opposite party; adverse, antagonistic; (feindlich) hostile; ~**ſchaft** f ㊻: a) *coll.* opponents pl.; b) opposition, antagonism; rivalry, competition; hostility.
ge=golten (⸗⸗⸗), **ge=goren** (⸗⸗⸗), **ge=goſſen** (⸗⸗⸗), **ge=graben** (⸗⸗⸗), **ge=griffen** (⸗⸗⸗) *p.p. v.* gelten, gären, gießen, graben, greifen. [ceſſant) grunting.|
Ge=grunze (⸗⸗⸗) n ㉒ constant (or in-ƒ **geh.** *abbr.* = geheftet.
ge=haben (⸗⸗⸗) [abh.]: ſich 2 v/refl. ⑧* 1. = benehmen 3, er gehabt ſich als reicher Herr he plays the rich gentleman. — 2. (ſich befinden) gehab(e) dich wohl! farewell!, good bye!
Ge=halt (⸗⸗) m ⑩b. 1. (Beſtandteile) constituents, ingredients pl.; (Inhalt) contents pl.; (Feingehalt von Münzen) standard; Gold, Silber von geringem ~e ... of base alloy; *chm.* ~ an Stickſtoff proportion (or admixture, percentage) of nitrogen. — 2. *fig.* (weſentlicher Inhalt) substance; quality; (innerer Wert) intrinsic value or worth; von Flüſſigkeiten: strength, body; von Schriften 2c.: merit, power; ⚒ von Erzen: yield; von geringem ~ of small (or inferior) value. — 3. (Geräumigkeit eines Gefäßes) solid capacity, weitS. (interior) space. — 4. mſt n ⑩b. b. (Amtseinkünfte) salary, (fixed) stipend; emoluments pl.; (Sold) pay; ~ beziehen to draw one's salary or pay; in feſtem ~ ſtehend having (or drawing) a fixed salary, salaried.
ge=halten (⸗⸗) *p.p.* von halten.
ge=halt=leer (⸗⸗) a. ㊺, 2**los** a. von Schriften uſw.: without value, worthless, empty, shallow; without grit or backbone, F flabby, flimsy, trashy; ⸗**loſigkeit** f ㊻ worthlessness, emptiness; flabbiness, flimsiness; 2**reich** a. of intrinsic value, of great worth or merit, substantial, solid; von Büchern a. F weighty; v. d. Nahrung: rich, nourishing, nutritious.
Ge=halt(s)=abzug (⸗⸗...) m ㊷ deduction from the (or reduction of) salary; ⸗**aufbeſſerung**, ⸗**erhöhung**, ⸗**vermehrung**, ⸗**zulage** f increase (or raising) of a p.'s salary, additional (or better) pay; ⸗**ſätze** m/pl. scale of salaries.
ge=halt=voll (⸗⸗) a. ㊺ = 2**reich**.
Ge=hämmer (⸗⸗) n ㉒ constant hammering, ♪ strumming, pounding.
Ge=hänge (⸗⸗) n ㉒ 1. (Abhang v. Bergen) slope, declivity, incline; (hangende

Blumen, Trauben 2c.) garland, festoon. — 2. *hunt.* ~ (lange Ohren) des Hundes long (flabby) ears pl. of a dog. — 3. (Ohr-) ear-drops, pendants pl. — 4. ⚔ ~ des Degens sword-belt, ehm.: hanger.
ge=hangen (⸗⸗) *p.p.* von hangen.
ge=harniſcht (⸗⸗) a. ㊺ f. harniſchen.
ge=häſſig (⸗⸗) a. ㊺ 1. (Haß hegend) full of hatred; spiteful, malicious (attack, &c.), ill-natured (remark, &c.); e-m 2 ſein to have a spite against a. p., to bear a p. a grudge. — 2. (Haß erregend) odious, hateful; (anſtößig) obnoxious; das ~e an der Sache iſt // the hateful part of it is //.
Ge=häſſigkeit (⸗⸗⸗) f ㊻ 1. (f. gehäſſig 1) hatred; spite, animosity. — 2. (f. gehäſſig 2) odiousness, hatefulness.
Ge=hau (⸗⸗) n ⓐa. 1. (ohne pl.) repeated blows pl. — 2. (mit pl.) *for.* (Revier für die Holzung) timber-tract or -wood, in England auch: coppice, Am. clearing.
ge=hauen (⸗⸗) *p.p.* von hauen.
Ge=häuſe (⸗⸗) [nhd.: * Haus] n ㉒ 1. (Kaſten) box; (Behältnis) box, receptacle; (Futteral) case, casing; (Kapſel) capsule; ⊕ e-s Flaſchenzuges: shell; e-r Windmühle 2c.: cage; ⚓ des Kompaſſes: binnacle; mit e-m ~ umgeben to (enclose in a) case, to encase. — 2. ⚘ ~ eines Apfels 2c.: core; *zo.* e-r Schnecke: shell; für die Puppe einer Seidenraupe: cocoon.
gehbar (⸗⸗) a. ㊺ = gangbar 1.
Ge=heck(e) (⸗⸗) n ⓒc. (㉒) 1. = hecken II. — 2. *hunt.* (Raubtierbrut) hatch, brood.
Ge=hege (⸗⸗) [nhd.: * Hag] n ㉒ 1. (Einfriedigung) enclosure, fence; (Hürde) hurdle(s pl.). — 2. (eingefriedigter Bezirk) enclosure, close, park; *for.* (Schonung) nursery (for young trees); *hunt.* preserve, für Kaninchen: warren, für Faſanen: walk; *fig.* e-m ins ~ kommen (ob. gehen, treten) to encroach (or trespass) upon a p.'s (private) preserve; to put a spoke in a p.'s wheel; F to put a p.'s nose out of joint.
Ge=hege=aufſeher (⸗⸗⸗...) m ㉒, ⸗**bereiter** m keeper, ranger.
ge=heiligt (⸗⸗) *p.p.* zu heiligen u. a. ㊺ sacred, sanctified, hallowed.
ge=heim (⸗⸗) [nhd.: * Heim] a. ㊺ 1. secret; im 2en, ins2 secretly, in secret, clandestinely, by stealth; unbeknown to a p.; (ohne Zeugen) privately. — 2. (verborgen) hidden, concealed; (unbekannt) unknown, (geheimnisvoll) mysterious; *phls.*: ⚘ esoteric; 2es Einverſtändnis secret (or private) agreement; 2es Fach secret drawer; 2er Leiter *pol.*, &c. wire-puller; 2e Polizei secret police, detective force; 2e Tinte sympathetic ink; 2e Wiſſenſchaft occult science. — 3. in Titeln: 2er Rat: a) f. ~rat; b) (ſämtliche Räte) Privy Council; (Miniſterium) Cabinet (Council).
Ge=heim=bote (⸗⸗⸗...) m ㉒ confidential messenger; Diplomatie: (secret) emissary; ⸗**brief** m (des Königs) ehm. in England: (royal) warrant or writ, Frankr.: *lettre de cachet*; ⸗**buch** ❀ n private journal; ⸗**bund** m secret alliance or league; ⸗**fonds** m secret funds pl.; et. 2**halten** v/a. ⑧⁶a.** to

♪ Muſik; ⚘ Wiſſenſchaft; ⚘ Pflanze; ♀ Geographie; ⊕ Technik; ⚒ Bergbau; ⚔ Militär; ⚓ Marine; ❀ Handel; ✉ Poſt; 🚂 Eiſenbahn.

[**Geheimhaltung**] keep a th. dark or F snug; seine Gesinnung vor e-m 2 to keep ... from a p., to keep a p. in the dark about ...; =**haltung** f keeping (of a) secret; die ~ der Sache wird schwer sein it will be difficult to keep it dark or F snug; =**lehre** f, phls.: ⚹ esoteric doctrine or teaching; =**mittel** n patent (or quack-)medicine; nostrum, arcanum.

Ge‑heimnis (⌣́⌣) n ⓱ secret; (Verborgenes) mystery; ein ~ aus et. machen to conceal a th.; er macht kein ~ daraus he makes no secret (or mystery) of it; ein ~ ausplaudern to let the cat out of the bag, F to give the game away; e-n in das ~einweihen to let a p. into the secret, to initiate a. p.; e-m ein ~ entlocken to draw a p.'s secret from him, to worm a th. out of a p.; ein ~ vor e-m h. to conceal (or keep) a th. from a p.; das ist ein ~ für ihn it is a mystery (auch: a sealed book) to him; ein tiefes ~ a deep mystery, a dead secret.

Ge‑heimnis‑krämer(in f) m F (⌣́⌣...) ⓯ mysterious person; ⚹ mystagogue; =**krämerei** F f (affected) mysteriousness, mysterious conduct; 2**voll** a. mysterious; mystic (writing, &c.); (verborgen) hidden, dark; (verschwiegen) discreet; (zugeknöpft) reserved, close; in ein 2es Dunkel gehüllt wrapt in mystery.

Ge‑heim‑polizist (⌣́⌣...) m ⓬ detective, F Pinkerton, P tec(k); =**rat** m Privy Councillor (in Engl. mit dem Titel: Right Honourable); vgl. geheim 3; =**rätin** f wife of a Privy Councillor (in Engl. nur als Mrs. mit dem Namen des Mannes angeredet); =**schreibekunst** f cipher-writing; ⚹ cryptography, steganography; =**schreiber** m private secretary, confidential clerk; =**schrift** f secret writing or character, cipher, code; ⚹ cryptograph; Telegramm in ~ code-message or -telegram; ~en pl. f. Apokryphen; =**sekretär** m = =**schreiber**; =**siegel-bewahrer** m Lord Privy Seal; =**sinn** m hidden sense; =**sprache** f secret language, ⚹ cryptology; 2**tun** v/n.(h.) ⓰** to act the mysterious, to affect to know secrets; =**tuerei** f, =**tun** n affected) mysteriousness; =**vorbehalt** m mental reservation; =**zeichen** n secret sign; =**zimmer** n (private) cabinet.

Ge‑heiß (⌣́⌣) [heißen I] n ⓰a. order, command; injunction; auf sein ~ by his orders, at his bidding.

ge‑heißen (⌣́⌣) p.p. von heißen.

geh)**e**)**n** (́⌣) [ahd.: go] I v/n. (sn), bisw. v/a., a. v/impers. ⓮ **1.** allg. to go, z. B. e-m entgegen 2 to go to meet a. p.; laßt uns (weg) 2! let us go or F be off; hinaus 2 to go (or walk) out; er ist gegangen (weg) he is gone, he has left; wir sehen ihn lieber 2 als kommen we like his room better than his company; gehend going, walking; gemächlich: ambling, ambulant; eilig: walking quickly, going fast, running. — **2.** (ant. kriechen, springen, laufen) to walk; (ant. reiten, fahren) to walk on foot, F to tramp it; man hat drei Stunden zu 2 it is a three hours' walk; dort kommt er gegangen there he comes (walking along). — **3.** von leblosen Dingen: a) mech.: 2 (im Gange sein) to work, to act, stärker: to be in full swing; die Maschine geht ... is going or running or at work; meine Uhr geht nicht ... is not going, ... has stopped; b) die Post ꝛc. geht (fährt) um 6 Uhr (ab) ... leaves (or starts) at six (o'clock); c) der Teig fängt an zu 2 ... begins to work or to rise; das Eis fängt an zu 2 ... is beginning to break up or to move; d) es 2 allerlei Gerüchte all sorts of rumours are afloat or are being circulated; es geht die Rede, daß // people say that //, there is a rumour that //; e) es geht ein starker Wind there is a strong wind blowing; f) ⓯ die Geschäfte 2 gut there is plenty of business (doing), trade is good; die Geschäfte 2 schlecht business is slack. — **4.** das geht nicht (läßt sich nicht m.) it cannot be done; versuche nur, es wird schon 2 ... you will do it (yet); es wird ja schon 2 it will come right in time; es geht durchaus nicht it is impracticable or not feasible; das geht denn doch nicht that won't do, what are you thinking of?; wie es (eben) geht just as it may happen. — **5.** mit **lassen**: e-n 2 lassen: a) (fortlassen) to let a p. go or leave; b) to let a p. pursue his way; c) (in Ruhe lassen) to leave a p. at rest; d) F to let (or leave) a p. alone; sich 2 l. (ohne sich zu zügeln) to go ahead, to indulge one's inclination(s), to launch out (freely); es sich gut 2 l. to take good care of (or to look well after) o.s.; ⓯ eine Ware nicht unter dem Preise 2 l. not to reduce (or lower) one's price; etwas durch verschiedene Hände 2 l. to pass a th. through several hands. — **6.** der imper. als int. der Aufforderung oder Zurückweisung: geh, tu mir den Gefallen! come, do me the pleasure or favour!; 2 Sie doch! süddeutsch: ach gehn's! ach gängen's! come now!, you don't say so or mean it!, I never (heard of such a thing)! — **7.** in Verbindung mit v. (Absftr.) in den Wald 2, (um) Bäume zu fällen to go to the wood to fell trees; 2, um e-n zu treffen to go to meet a p.; ohne zu: früh **schlafen** 2 to go to early to bed; **spazieren** 2 to go (or to take) a walk. — **8.** mit unabhängigem Kasus: a) mit acc. des Maßes: zwei Meilen 2 to walk two (German or nine English) miles; drei Stunden 2; b) mit acc. der Bestimmung: das Pferd geht einen ruhigen Gang ... has a steady pace; still seinen Gang 2 to go quietly about one's business or on one's way; f. Krebsgang; denselben Weg 2 to go the same way, to take the same route; seinen geraden Weg 2 (ehrlich handeln) to be straightforward; c) mit gen.: seines Weges 2 to pursue one's course; geh deiner Wege! go along!, be gone!, F be off!; d) v/a. und **sich** 2 v/refl. mit Angabe der Wirkung: sich (dat.) die Absätze schief 2 to walk the heels (of one's boots) down on one side; er hat sich Blasen unter die Füße (die Füße wund) gegangen he blistered his feet (made his feet sore) with walking; sich (acc.) müde 2 to tire o.s. (out) with walking; e) v/impers. refl.: es geht sich schlecht, es läßt sich schlecht 2 it is bad walking here. — **9.** mit adv.: a) des Ortes: **abwärts** 2 to go down(wards) or down-hill, to descend; f. abwärts 1, bergab, **auf und ab** 2 to walk (or pace) up and down; **aus und ein** 2 to go in and out; meine Ansicht geht dahin, daß // my opinion is that //, I consider that //; f. daran 5, darauf 7, darüber 2 (drunter und drüber), entgegen III, heim 2; **hinab**= 2 to go down, to descend; **hinauf**= 2 to walk (or go) up, to mount; **hin und her** 2 to go (or walk) to and fro; das geht mir **nahe** (zu Herzen) it grieves me to the heart or core; **rückwärts** 2 to go backward; längs des Ufers **stromaufwärts** 2 to walk up-stream; **von hinnen** 2 to go hence, to depart; **voran** 2 to walk in front or in advance; to take the lead; 2 Sie voran! after you!; **weit** 2 to go (or walk) far; weit in s-n Ansprüchen 2 to make large pretensions; zu weit 2, daß // to go so far as to // (inf.); zu weit (über die Schicklichkeit hinaus) 2 to go too far, to overstep the mark or the bounds; das geht zu weit, schweigen Sie! that's enough ...! **wohin** 2 Sie? where are you going (to)?; viel wohin 2 to frequent a place; b) der Art und Weise: es ging **anders** things took a different turn; das geht nicht anders it can't be done any (or there is no) other way; f. auswärts 1, **barfuß**, ohne Schuhe 2 to walk (or go) barefooted; **bunt** 2 to wear colours; Ihre Uhr geht **falsch** ... is wrong; sie geht zu schnell ob. geht **vor** (geht zu langsam ob. geht **nach**) it is fast (slow), it gains (loses); sie geht 10 Minuten vor, nach it is ten minutes fast, slow; F es geht **faul** things are in a queer way; **fehl**= oder irre= 2 to lose (or miss) one's way; es geht ihm **gut**: a) (er ist gesund) he is well; von einem Kranken: he is doing well; b) (er gedeiht) he gets on well; (er ist wohlhabend) he is well-off; ich machte es, so gut es 2 wollte I did my best; ⓯ die Ware geht gut ... is selling (F going off) well; die See geht (die Wellen 2) **hoch**, **hohl** the sea runs (the waves run) high, the sea is rough or stormy; **irre**= 2 f. o.: fehl= 2; **müßig** 2 to be idle, to lead an easy (or a lazy) life; **nach**= 2 f. o.: falsch= 2; das Kartengeben geht **reihum** the deal goes the round or by turns; die Sache geht (ob. es geht mit der Sache) **schief** the affair is going wrong; es geht ihm **schlecht** he gets on (or is doing) badly, F things go hard with him; es geht sich hier sehr **schlüpfrig** it is very slippery here; sehr **schnell** 2 to go (or walk) very fast, to hurry (or F trot) along; **schwanger** 2 to be with child or in the family-way; fig. mit großen Entwürfen schwanger 2 to be full of vast schemes; **schwarz** 2 to wear black or mourning; **sicher** 2 to be sure-

[gehen] footed, bſd. *fig.* to walk warily, to take every precaution; um ſicher zu ☬ to make sure, to be on safe ground; ſo geht es, wenn man // that is what usually happens, if one //; ſo geht es gewöhnlich that's usually the case; ſo geht es mir auch, it is the same with me; ſo geht es in der Welt that is the way of the world, such is life; es geht ihm ſo ſo F he is rubbing along somehow; Sprichw.: wie man's treibt, ſo geht's as you make your bed so you must lie on it; ↓ ſehr **tief** ☬ to have deep draught, to draw much water; **verloren** ☬ to get lost, ſ. verluſtig; **vor**=☬ o..: falſch ☬; **wie** geht es mit Ihrer Geſundheit? wie geht es Ihnen? how are you?, how are you getting on?; wie ☬ die Geſchäfte? how is business?; wie geht's? how do you do?; wie geht's damit? how are things (or how is it) getting on?; wie ich gehe und ſtehe just as I am; (ohne mich umzukleiden) in the clothes in which I stand; es mag ☬ wie es will whatever may happen or come to pass; wie wird es mir ☬? what will become of me?; es geht ihm ganz **wohl** he is quite well; wacker **zu**=☬ to walk (at) a good pace. — **10.** mit abhängigen *prp.:* **an:** bis an et. ☬ (reichen) to go (or reach) as far as, to extend to; *jur.* an das Berufungsgericht ☬ to appeal to a higher court, to go to a court of appeal; ⚔ heiß ging es an den Feind we engaged the enemy in a hot fight, F we went at them tooth and nail; das geht ihm an den Geldbeutel that touches his purse; e-m an die (ob. zur) Hand ☬ to lend a p. a (helping) hand; e-m mit Rat an die Hand ☬ to advise a p.; es geht ihm an den Kragen it may cost him his life; an Krücken ☬ to walk with (or to go on) crutches; ↓ an(s) Land ☬ to go on shore, to land, to disembark; ſobald er kam, ging es an ein Tanzen … they started dancing; das Waſſer ging ihm bis an die Bruſt the water came up (or rose) right to his chest; **auf:** aufs Dorf ☬ to go (in)to the village; ſ. Freier 2; mein Fenſter geht auf den Garten … faces (or looks out on) the garden; e-r Sache auf den Grund ☬ to go to the bottom of …, to sift … thoroughly; der Mantel geht ihm bis auf die Hacken … goes (or reaches) down to his heels; ſ. Jagd 1; aufs Land ☬ to go into the country; es geht auf Leben und Tod it is a matter of life and death; auf den Leim ☬ to fall into the snare; auf die Neige ☬ to be running short or drawing to an end; das Faß geht auf die Neige … is just upon empty; es ☬ hundert Pfennig(e) auf eine Mark a hundred pfennig(e) make (or go to) one mark; das geht nicht auf dieſes Papier there is no room for it on …; auf Reiſen ☬ to go on a tour, to set out on one's travels; auf die andere Seite ☬ to pass (over) to the opposite side; das geht auf dich ſo gut wie auf ihn it touches (or is meant for) you as much as (for) him; auf Stelzen ☬ to walk on stilts; die Uhr (od. es) geht auf zehn it is going on for ten; auf Urlaub ☬ to take one's holiday, ⚔ ↓ to go on furlough; **aus:** ☬ Sie mir aus den Augen! go out of my sight!; aus e-m Orte ☬ to leave a place; aus dem Dienſte ☬ to leave (or quit) service; auseinander ☬ to separate, to part (company); von einer Verſammlung: to disperse, to dissolve; ⊖ aus den Fugen ☬ to come apart or undone, to fall (or go) to pieces; aus e-r Hand in die andere ☬ to pass from hand to hand, to change hands; aus Rand u. Band ☬ to get out of order or beyond control; aus dem Wege ☬ to move (or step) aside; einem aus dem Wege ☬ to make room for a p., (ihn vermeiden) to shun a p., to give a p. a wide berth; ♪ das Stück geht aus G … is in G; **durch:** durch ein Land ☬ to pass through (or to traverse) a country; ſ. dick 7, Feuer 2; *fig.* das ging mir (ſchneidend) durch das Herz, durch Mark und Bein it cut me to the quick, it went right home; durch dies Zeug geht kein Waſſer … is water-proof; **gegen:** das geht gegen mein Gewiſſen my conscience rebels against it; es geht gegen den Winter winter is at hand or approaching; **hinter:** einer hinter dem andern ☬ to go in single file; hinter e-m her ☬ to follow a p.; das Geſchäft geht hinter ſich (rückwärts) … is going down; hinter die Schule ☬ to play (the) truant; **in:** die Tür geht in Angeln … moves on hinges; F das geht ins Aſchgraue, in die Puppen! that beats everything or the record!; ins Bad ☬ to go bathing, to take a bath; in Dienſt ☬ to go into (or to enter) service; ins einzelne ☬ to go (or enter) into particulars or detail; in Erfüllung ☬ to come to pass; in die Falle ☬ to go (or fall) into the trap; der Wagen geht in Federn … moves (or hangs) on springs; in die Höhe ☬ to go up, to rise; er geht in ſein elftes Jahr he is entering (or in) his eleventh year; mit in den Kauf ☬ to go into the bargain; es ☬ hundert Perſonen in den Saal the hall holds (or accommodates) a hundred people; ↓ in See ☬ to put to sea; *rel.* in ſich ☬ to commune with o.s.; (Reue fühlen) to repent; in Stücke ☬ to go to pieces or F to smash; das geht nicht in meine Taſche F it won't go into …; das geht in die Tauſende it runs into thousands; die Erbſchaft geht in gleiche Teile … is equally divided; in Trümmer ☬ to crumble (or fall) to pieces, to go to rack and ruin; ins unglaubliche ☬ to be (almost) incredible; das Wort geht nicht in den Vers … does not fit (into) the metre; wie oft geht fünf in zehn? how many times does five go into ten?, how many fives make ten?; **mit:** mit e-m ☬ to accompany a p.; der Fluß geht mit Eis … carries (floating) ice; mit einem Kinde (ſchwanger) ☬ to be with child; F et. mit ſich ☬ heißen (entwenden) to run away with a th., to steal (P to nick, pinch) a th.; geht mit euern Poſſen! stop your pranks!, leave off your tomfoolery!; *v/impers.* es geht ſchlecht mit et. it is going wrong, F it is in a bad way; wie geht es mit dem Prozeß? how is the lawsuit getting (or going) on?; **nach:** nach Italien, nach Rom ☬ to go to Italy, to Rome; Sprichw. die Kunſt geht nach Brot, etwa: art goes a-begging; nach Hauſe ☬ to go home; nach e-r Regel ☬ to follow a rule; alles geht nach Wunſch all goes well, everything is as it should be; wenn es nach ihm, nach ſ-m Sinne ginge if it rested with him, if he had his (own) way; **neben:** neben einem ☬ to walk by a p.'s side; nebeneea. ☬ to walk side by side; ſ. daneben; **über:** über e-n Berg ☬ to cross a mountain; der Brief geht über Berlin … goes via Berlin; das geht über alle Begriffe, F über die Bäume, die Hutſchnur that beats (or tops) everything, it exceeds all bounds; über Feld ☬ to go across country; es geht nichts über den Frieden there is nothing like peace; e-m über ſein Geld ☬ (ihm davon nehmen) to rob a p. of some money; das geht über meine Kräfte it is beyond my strength; das geht ihm über alles, es geht ihm nichts darüber he prizes it above everything; das geht über m-n Verſtand that passes my comprehension; vgl. Verſtand 2; Sprichw. Zufriedenheit geht über Reichtum contentment is above wealth; et. über ſich ☬ laſſen ſ. ergehen 4; **um:** um die Stadt ꝛc. ☬ to walk round the town, &c.; ſ. Bart 4, Brei 3; beim Spiel: es geht um Geld we are playing for money; es geht um euer Vermögen your fortune is at stake; **unter:** unter (die) Leute ☬ to go into society, to mix with (the) people; unter die Soldaten ☬ to become a soldier, to enlist; **von:** von e-m (weg) ☬ to leave a p. (in the lurch); ſ. dannen 1 u. davon II; vom Flecke, vonſtatten ☬ to go on swimmingly, to get on, advance, progress; es geht ihm von der Hand he is quick (or smart) at his work; von Hand zu Hand ☬ to pass from hand to hand; es geht ihm von Herzen it comes from his heart; einem nicht von der Seite (F nicht vom Halſe) ☬ never to budge from a p.'s side, to cling to a p. (like a leech); von Tür zu Tür ☬ to go (begging) from door to door; **vor:** vors Tor ☬ to walk outside the gate; ſ. Gewalt 3; wir ☬ vor (haben den Vorzug) we come first; we have the precedence or first claim; die Sache wird heute vor ſich ☬ … will take place to-day; ↓ ſ. Anker 1; **wider:** es geht mir wider den Sinn, F wider den Strich it goes against the grain (with me); **zu:** zu e-m ☬ to go (up) to a p.; ins Haus: to call upon a p.; zum Abendmahl ☬ to take the sacrament or the Lord's supper; ſ. Beichte, Bett 1; zu Ende ☬ to come to an end, to draw to a close; zu Fuß(e) ☬ to go on foot, to walk, F to tramp it; zugrunde ☬: a) ↓ to go down or to the bottom; b) *fig.* to perish; e-m zur Hand ☬ ſ. 10 an; ſein Schmerz geht mir ſehr zu Herzen [gehen]

⚗ scientific; ⚘ botanical; ⚱ geography; ⊖ machinery; ⚒ mining; ⚔ military; ↓ marine; ⚭ commercial; ✉ postal; 🚂 railway.

[Gehenk] — 420 — [Gehrung]

greatly afflicts (or grieves) me; zur Kirche 2c. 2 to go to church; e-m (hart) zu Leibe 2 to press a p. hard; zur Linken (Rechten) e-r Person 2 to walk on the left (right) hand of a p.; F geh zum Kuckuck, zum Teufel! F go and be hanged!, stärker: go to hell!; zur Neige 2 to be drawing to an end, to be nearly empty; mit e-m zu Rate 2 to consult a p.; f. Rüste; zur Schule 2 to go to school; e-m zur Seite 2 to walk by a p.'s side; zu Tische 2 to sit down to dinner or supper; behutsam zu Werke 2 to go (or set) cautiously to work. — II ~ n ㉓ 11. = Gang 1. — 12. das ~ wird ihm sauer walking is (becoming) a trouble to him; des ~s müde tired of walking; sein ~ und Kommen his coming and going; aufs ~ bezüglich ambulatory.
Ge-henk ⚔ (⌣⌣) n ⓑb. sword-belt.
Ge-henkte(r) (⌣⌣) f. henken II.
ge-heuer (⌣⌣) [mhd.] a. ⓖⓞ nur gbr. mit neg.: die Gegend ist (ob. es ist hier) nicht recht 2 it is not quite safe (or all is not right) here; (es spukt) the place is haunted; ihm war nicht recht 2 zumute he did not feel quite at (his) ease.
Ge-heul (⌣⌣) n ⓒc. constant howling or hooting or yelling or bawling; des Sturmes, der Wellen: howling, roaring.
ge-hießen *prov.* (⌣⌣) p.p. von heißen.
Ge-hilfe (⌣⌣) [ahd.; *helfen] m ⓖ, **Gehilfin** f ㊼ assistant (auch e-s Dozenten); weitS. colleague, helpmate, (Handlungs-)diener) clerk; weitS. employee, (fr.) employé(e f); ~ eines Apothekers chemist's assistant; angehender ~ improver; bei Handwerkern: (journey)man, mate.
Ge-hirn (⌣⌣) [mhd.] n ⓑb. anat.: (the whole) brain; das kleine ~: ♋ the cerebellum; auf das ~ bezüglich cerebral; auf ~ und Rückenmark bezüglich cerebrospinal; fig. (Verstand) sense, intellect; (Denkvermögen) brain(s pl.), brainpower; er hat kein ~ im Kopfe he is empty-headed or co. addle-brained.
Ge-hirn-abszeß (⌣⌣…) m ⓛ path. abscess on the brain; =behälter m, anat. brain-pan, ♋ cranium; =bruch m. path.: ♋ encephalocele; =entzündung f, path. brain-fever, ♋ encephalitis; =erschütterung f concussion of the b.; =erweichung f softening of the b., ♋ encephalomalacia; =fett n, physiol.: ♋ cerebrin(e), cerebrot(e); =haut f, anat.: ♋ cerebral membrane; =hautentzündung f, path.: ♋ meningitis; =höhle, =kammer f, anat. ventricle of the brain, cerebral cavity or ventricle; =kasten F m brain-pan, skull; =krankheit f disorder of the brain, mental disease; ♋ cerebropathy; =lappen m, anat. lobe of the brain; =los a. brainless, ♋ anencephalic; =mark n, =masse f, anat. (medullary) substance of the brain, ♋ (lt.) medulla cerebri; =schlag m, path. apoplexy of the brain; =schwund m, path. softening (or shrivelling) of the brain, ♋ anencephalotrophia; =tätigkeit f, physiol. cerebral activity, cerebration; =wassersucht f, path. water on the brain, ♋ hydrocephalus; vgl. Hirn-…

☞ **gehn** (⌣) f. gehen.
ge-hoben (⌣⌣) p.p. von heben.
Ge-höft (⌣⌣) n ⓑb. (Bauernhof) farm (buildings pl.), farmyard, farmstead; (Heimstätte) homestead.
ge-holfen (⌣⌣) p.p. von helfen.
Ge-hölz (⌣⌣) n ⓑa. 1. coppice, copse, thicket, weitS. grove, wood. — 2. (Holzwert) wood-work.
Ge-hör (⌣⌣) n ⓑc. 1. (Sinn des Hörens) hearing; gutes, scharfes ~ quick ear, good hearing; ein feines ~ haben to be quick of hearing; das ~ verlieren to lose one's hearing, to become (or grow) deaf; auf das ~ bezüglich phys.: ♋ acoustic; anat.: ♋ auditory. — 2. musikalisches ~ musical ear, good ear (for music); er hat eine gute Stimme, aber kein ~ … but no ear; nach dem ~ spielen to play by ear. — 3. (Anhören) tel. nach dem ~ aufnehmen to take down a message by ear; ~ finden to obtain a hearing; er fand bei ihnen ein williges (aufmerksames) ~ they readily (attentively) listened to him; ein ~ geben ob. schenken to lend one's ear (or to give audience or ear, to listen) to a p.; er gab mir kein ~ he would not listen (or attend) to me; fig. der Vernunft ~ geben to listen (or yield) to reason.
ge-horchen (⌣⌣) I v/n. (h.) ⓖ*: e-m 2 to obey a person; willig 2 to yield ready obedience; dem Könige muß man 2 the king must be obeyed; e-m nicht 2 to disobey a p. — II ~ n ㉓ obedience.
ge-hören (⌣⌣) [ahd.] ⓖ* I v/n. (h.) 1. to belong to, to be owned by; meist fig. to appertain to; wem gehört der Hut? to whom does the hat belong?, whose hat is it?; dem Arbeiter gehört (gebührt) sein Lohn the worker deserves (or is entitled to) his wage; dem elektrotechnischen Erfinder gehört die Zukunft the electrical inventor has a great future (lying) before him. — 2. das gehört nicht auf die Rechnung that has nothing to do with (or that should not be upon) the bill; Sprichw. auf e-n groben Klotz gehört ein grober Keil, etwa: hard logs need hard tools; das Wort gehört hier nicht her … is out of place here; das gehört nicht hierher that's beside the purpose (or the question) in view; Sie 2 nicht hierher this is not your place; wo gehört dies hin? where does this belong (or go) to?; die Bücher 2 in die Bibliothek … belong to (or go into) the library; in die Suppe gehört Salz the soup requires salt; sie 2 unter die (ober zu den) größten Männern(n) der Zeit they may be counted (or reckoned) among the greatest men of the age; die Sache gehört vor das Gericht … should be brought before (or taken to) a court of (law); diese Gebühren 2 zu meinen Einkünften these fees form (a) part of my income or emoluments; das gehört nicht zur Sache it is beside (or lies outside) the question; wir 2 zu seinen besten Freunden we are among his …; dazu gehört (braucht man) viel Geld, Zeit it requires (or needs, wants, takes) much money, time; alles, was zu e-m bequemen Leben gehört all that

contributes (or adds) to a comfortable life. — II v/refl. impers. 3. es gehört (gebührt) sich so it (or that) is proper, right, becoming; so gehört es sich (von Rechts wegen) (by rights) it should be so; wie es sich (oder sich's) gehört properly, duly, becomingly, (tüchtig) thoroughly (well).
Ge-hör-fehler (⌣⌣…) m ⓛ defect of the ear, vgl. =mangel; =gang m, anat.: ♋ auditory canal or passage, acoustic duct.
ge-hörig (⌣⌣)[ahd.]a.ⓖⓛ 1. e-m ㉓ (angehörend) belonging to, owned by, (zu et. gehörend) forming part of, appertaining to. — 2. (wohin gehörend) referring to; nicht zu et. 2 foreign (or not pertinent) to s.th.; alle zur Sache (nicht) 2en Bemerkungen all remarks having (no) reference to the subject; jur. vor ein Gericht 2 cognizable before a court of law. — 3. (wie sich's gehört) proper, appropriate, fit; right, becoming, due, just; (e-m zustehend) competent; f-e 2 Wirkung tun to have the proper effect; zu 2er Zeit in due time; das ~e the required (or needful) thing. — 4. (tüchtig) good; F tremendous; 2er Hieb violent (or fearful) blow; adv.: iro. er hat es 2 bekommen he was well served, F he got all that he deserved.
Ge-hörigkeit (⌣⌣…) f ㊻ 1. (das Passende) propriety, appropriateness, fitness, becomingness. — 2. (Rechtszuständigkeit) competence, competency.
Ge-hör-krankheit (⌣⌣…) f ⓛ path. disease of the ear; =lehre f, phys.: ♋ acoustics; 2los a. ⓖⓞ deaf; =mangel m imperfect (or defective) hearing.
Ge-hörn (⌣⌣) [mhd.; *Horn] n ⓑb. 1. e-s Rindes 2c.: horns pl. — 2. hunt. des Hochwildes: antlers pl. [auditory nerve.]
Ge-hör-nerv (⌣⌣…) m anat.: ♋
ge-hörnt (⌣⌣) p.p. u. a. ⓖⓞ f. hörnen IV.
Ge-hör-organ (⌣⌣…) n ⓛ: ♋ auditory organ; =rohr m = =trichter.
ge-horsam (⌣⌣-) [ahd.; *hören] I a. ⓖⓞ obedient; (folgsam) tractable, docile, submissive; (pflichtgetreu) dutiful; in Briefschlüssen: Ihr 2(st)er Diener Your (very) obedient servant; Yours (most) obediently; iro. 2er Diener! No, thank you!, not I! — II ~ m ⓑd. obedience, (Folgsamkeit) tractableness; submissiveness, dutifulness; gegen den Landesherrn: allegiance; e-m ~ leisten to render a p. obedience; e-m den ~ aufkündigen, verweigern to renounce one's allegiance to a p., to refuse to obey him; zum ~ bringen to reduce to obedience.
ge-horsamen (⌣⌣-⌣) v/n. (h.) = gehorchen.
Ge-hör-schnecke (⌣⌣…) f ⓛ: ♋ cochlea; =sinn m (sense of) hearing; =trichter m ear-trumpet; =rohr m, anat. vestibule of the ear; =werkzeug n = =organ.
Gehre(n m ㉓) f ⓛ (⌣) [:gore] (et. schräg Zulaufendes) 1. agr. wedge-shaped field. — 2. Näherei: (Zwickel) gusset; gore; (Falte) pleat; (Schoß) skirt. — 3. carp. (schräge Richtung) bevel, slope, incline; vgl. Gehrung.
Geh-rock (⌣⌣) [aus Gehr-rock; *Gehre(n)] m ⓑc. frock-coat; (überzieher) overcoat.
Gehrung ⓧ (⌣) vgl. Gärung) f ㊻ meist carp. bevel; typ. mitre; auf ~ verbinden

Zeichen (f. S. XVII): F familiär; P Volkssprache; ⌐ Gaunersprache; ⋰ selten; † alt (auch gestorben); * neu (auch geboren); ⸚ unrichtig;

[Gehrungenschneidemaschine] — 421 — [Geistesrichtung]

to mitre; ~en=schneidemaschine f, typ. mitring machine; ~&=linie f mitre-line; ~&=stoßlade f mitre-block.
ge-huft (⌣⌢) [huf] a. ⓞ hoofed.
Geh-werk (⌣⌢) n ⓶ a) F (die Füße) feet, F co. trotters pl.; b) Uhrm.: works (or movements) pl. of a clock.
geien ↓ (⌣⌢) v/a. ⓞ (zi=schnüren) to brail (or clew, haul) up sails.
Geier (⌣⌢) [ahd.; *Gier] m ⓶ 1. zo. vulture (Vultur). — 2. fig. (für Teufel) hole ihn der ~!, daß er beim ~ wäre! the deuce take him!, I wish him at Jericho (and a thousand miles beyond)!
Geier=adler ⌣ m ⓶ = Bartgeier; 2artig a. ⓞ: ⚡ vulturine; 2es Wesen (Gefräßigkeit) vulturism; =falk(e) [corr. aus Gierfalke] m ⚡ gerfalcon (Poly'borus); =klauen f/pl. (a) vulture's talons pl.
Geifer (⌣⌢) [mhd.] m ⓶ 1. von Kindern ꝛc.: drivel, slaver; von Fallsüchtigen u. Tieren: foam, froth. — 2. fig. (Ärger, Groll) spleen, anger, rancour; seinen ~ wider e-n auslassen to vent one's spleen (or displeasure) on a p.
Geiferer (⌣⌢⌢) m ⓶ 1. driveller, slaverer. — 2. (giftiger Mensch) rancorous p.
Geifer=läppchen (⌣⌢...)=lätzchen n für Kinder: slavering- (or slobbering) bib.
geifern (⌣⌢) v/n. (h.) ⓶a. 1. to drivel; to slaver; vor Wut 2 to foam with rage. — 2. fig. (i-n Zorn äußern) to vent one's anger (or passion, wrath) on a p.
Geifer-tuch, =tüchlein n ⓶ = =lätzchen.
Geige ♪ (⌣⌢) [mhd.; *gagen] f ⓶ violin, F fiddle; (auf der) ~ spielen to play (on) the violin; (die) erste ~ spielen to play the first violin or fig. first fiddle; fig. der Himmel hängt ihm voll(er) ~n he is brimful of (or swimming in) delight, he sees everything (fr.) couleur de rose or from the rosy side.
geigen ♪ (⌣⌢) [mhd.] v/n. (h.) u. v/a. ⓞ 1. to play (on) the violin, F to (play the) fiddle; e-e Sonate ~ to play a sonata on the violin. — 2. fig. ich werde dir etwas ~ (das will ich wohl bleiben lassen) I won't do it, F you won't catch me (doing it), you may whistle for it; e-m derb die Wahrheit ~ to give a p. a piece of one's mind.
geigen=artig ♪ (⌣⌢...) a. ⓞ violin-shaped; =bogen m ⓶ violin-bow, fiddle-stick; =bohrer ⊕ m = Drillbohrer; 2förmig a. vi.-shaped; =futteral n vi.-case; =harz n colophony, mehr gbr.: rosin; =holz n vi.-wood; =macher m violin-maker; =saite f violin-string; =schlüssel m treble clef; =spiel n playing (on) the violin; =spieler(in f) m = Geiger(in); =steg m bridge of a violin; =stück n (piece of) music for the violin; =ton m sound (or note) of a violin; =werk n, =zug m der Orgel vi.-stop; =wirbel m vi.-peg.
Geiger ♪ (⌣⌢) m ⓶ ⓞ violin-player, F fiddler; v. besonderem Talente: (clever) violinist; ~ei (⌣⌢⌣) f ⓞ constant fiddling.
geil (⌣) [ahd.] a. ⓞ 1. (üppig) rank, luxurious, luxuriant; (wuchernd) exuberant; 2 Boden rich (or fat) soil; 2es Fett rank fat or grease; path. 2es Fleisch proud flesh. — 2. (munter) gay; (übermütig) wanton; (begierig) covetous. — 3. (wollüstig) lascivious, lewd, lecherous, goatish, voluptuous; beschönigend: passionate, hot, P warm (customer); von Tieren: ruttish.
Geile (⌣⌢) f ⓞ 1. ohne pl. = Geilheit. — 2. mit pl. (Hoden) testicle.
geilen (⌣⌢) v/n. (h.) ⓞ 1. (munter springen) to frolic, skip, caper. — 2. (geil sein) to be lascivious or lewd or lecherous; von Tieren: to rut.
Geilheit (⌣⌢) f ⓞ 1. (s. geil 1) rankness, luxuriance, exuberance; ~ des Bodens richness of the soil. — 2. (s. geil 3) lasciviousness, lewdness, lechery, goatishness; von Tieren: ruttishness.
Geilung (⌣⌢) f ⓞ agr. (Übergüngung) over-manuring.
Geisel ⚔ (⌣⌢) [ahd.] m ⓶, f ⓞ (Leibbürge) hostage, z.B. ~n geben (stellen) to give (or furnish) hostages; vgl. Geißel.
Geiser (⌣⌢) [isl.] m ⓶ (isländischer heißer Quellsprudel) geyser.
Geiß (⌣) [ahd.: goat: lt. haedus] f ⓞ (she-)goat (= Ziege); (Weibchen [v. Gemse, Reh u. Damwild]) doe.
Geiß-baum ⚑ (⌣⌢) m ⓶ = Esche; =blatt ⚑ n woodbine (Loni'cera pericly'menum); durchwachsenes ~ honeysuckle (Caprifo'lium perfolia'tum); =bock m he-goat, F billy goat.
Geißel (⌣⌢) [ahd.: goad] f ⓞ 1. (Peitsche) whip, zur Kasteiung: scourge; fig. die ~ der Kritik the lash of criticism; die ~ der Kritik über e-n schwingen (severely) to criticize a p., F to slate (or to pitch into) a p. — 2. weitS. (Plage) scourge, F pest (auch von einer Person).
Geißel-bruder (⌣⌢...) m ⓶ eccl. Mittelalter: flagellant; =hieb m lash with a scourge.
geißeln (⌣⌢) I v/a. u. sich 2 v/refl. ⓶a. 1. (sich) 2 to scourge (o.s.), ehm. a. eccl.: to flagellate; (auspeitschen) to whip, to lash. — 2. fig. (züchtigen) to chastise; (heftig tadeln) to censure, to criticize severely, F to run down, to slate. — II ~ n ⓷ 3. = Geißelung.
Geißel-rute (⌣⌢...) f ⓞ scourge; =tierchen n/pl. (Infusorien) mastigopods pl.
Geißelung (⌣⌢⌢) f ⓞ (s. geißeln I) scourging, flagellation, whipping; chastisement; censure, criticism.
Geiß-fell (⌣⌢...) n ⓞ goat's skin; =fuß m: a) goat's foot; b) ⚑ ash-weed, goutwort, goutweed (Egopo'dium podagra'ria); ⊕ carp. socket-chisel; =hirt(e) m goatherd; =klee ⚑ m: a) laburnum (Cy'tisus labu'rnum); b) hagweed (C. scopa'rius).
Geißlein (⌣⌢) n ⓷ (dim. von Geiß) kid.
Geißler (⌣⌢) [mhd.; *geißeln] m ⓶, ~in f ⓞ eccl. ehm.: scourging friar (f nun); vgl. Geißelbruder.
Geiß-raute ⚑ (⌣⌢) f ⓞ goat's-rue (Gale'ga officina'lis).
Geist (⌣) [ahd.: ghost] m ⓷b. (doch f. 2) 1. ghost; spirit; (Lebensodem) breath; ein heller ~ (Verstand) a clear mind, a bright intellect; den (ober seinen) ~ aufgeben (sterben) to give up the ghost, to breathe one's last; den ~ ausbilden to cultivate the mind; das zeigt, wes ~es Kind er ist ... what kind of person (or F genius) he is, ... what his disposition is; im ~e war ich bei euch I was with you in the spirit; ich kann sie im ~e sehen she is in my mind's eye; ein Mann von ~ a clever (or ingenious, witty) man; ein Mann von hohem ~e a (man of) great genius or wit, a master mind; rel. die Armen im ~e the poor in spirit; der Heilige ~ the Holy Ghost. — 2. ⚗. chm., &c., fast † spirit, essence. — 3. ~ des Christentums spirit of Christianity; ~ der Sprache genius of the language. — 4. (unkörperliches Wesen; ant. Fleisch und Bein) ghost, spectre; (Erscheinung) apparition, phantom; ein guter ~ a (kind) genius (Fauch: genii sg. u. pl.); böser ~ evil spirit, demon; vgl. Gespenst.
geist-anstrengend (⌣⌢...) a. ⓞ fatiguing (or taxing, F fagging) the mind or the brain; =bildend a. improving the mind, instructive, educational.
Geistchen (⌣⌢) n ⓷ ent. = Federmotte.
geister=ähnlich (⌣⌢...) a. ⓞ ghostlike, spectral; =banner m ⓶, =beschwörer m: a) (der Geister ruft) necromancer; b) (der Geister austreibt) exorcizer, exorcist; =bannung, =beschwörung f necromancy; exorcism; =bild n phantom; 2bleich a. (as) pale as a ghost, F ghastly pale; =erscheinung f (ghostly) apparition or vision, phantasm; =furcht f fear of ghosts or spirits; =geschichte f ghost-story; =glaube m belief in spirits; spirit(ual)ism.
geisterhaft (⌣⌢⌢) a. ⓞ ghostlike, spectral; weitS. supernatural; ghastly.
Geister=hand (⌣⌢...) f ⓞ ghostly hand, hand of a spectre; =klopfen n, =klopfer m spirit-rapping, -rapper; =lehre f mst co. ghostlore, ⚡ pneumatology.
geist-erquickend (⌣⌢...) a. ⓞ refreshing (to) the mind.
Geister=reich (⌣⌢...) n ⓶ spirit-world; =schar f host of spirits; =schrift f Geisterglaube: spirit-writing, ⚡ psychography; =seherei f seeing ghosts, second sight, weitS. spirit(ual)ism; =seher(in f) m ghost-seer; fig. visionary; =stunde f ghostly hour; poet. a. witching midnight-hour; =welt f spirit-world, dominion of spirits.
geistes=abwesend (⌣⌢...) a. ⓞ absent-minded; distracted; =abwesenheit f ⓞ absent-mindedness; distraction; =arbeit f mental occupation; brain- (or head-)work; =armut f poverty of mind, poorness of intellect; =bildung f mental culture; =fähigkeit f capacity of the mind, intellectual power; =flug m =schwung, =freiheit f intellectual freedom, liberty of the mind; =friede m peace of mind; =frische f freshness of mind; =funke m thought flashing through the mind, sparkling (or brilliant) idea; =gabe f intellectual gift; vgl. =fähigkeit; =gegenwart f presence of mind; =größe f greatness of mind; =(hochherzigkeit) magnanimity; =kraft f mental power or vigour; 2krank a. mentally diseased or deranged, insane; F co. off one's chump; =krankheit f mental disease or disorder; insanity; =nacht f mental darkness; =nahrung f intellectual food or nourishment; =richtung f intellectual

♪ Musik; ⚡ Wissenschaft; ⚑ Pflanze; ⚐ Geographie; ⊕ Technik; ⚒ Bergbau; ⚔ Militär; ⚓ Marine; ⚖ Handel; ✉ Post; 🚂 Eisenbahn.

tendency; =ruhe f ⑫ peace of mind; equanimity; ⸗schwach a. ⑯ weak-minded, feeble-minded; (beschränkt) narrow-minded; (blödsinnig) idiotic, imbecile; =schwäche f feeble-(or narrow-)mindedness; idiocy, imbecility; =schwung m soaring (or elevation) of the mind; (Begeisterung) enthusiasm; =spannung f mental strain; =stärke f mental vigour; =störung f mental derangement or disorder, insanity, ⚚ psychopathy; =stumpfheit f mental torpor; dulness; ⸗träge a. mentally indolent; ⸗trägheit f mental indolence; =verfassung f frame of mind; ⸗verwandt a. of congenial (or kindred) mind; =verwandtschaft f congeniality (or kinship) of mind; =verwirrung, =zerrüttung f derangement (or alienation) of the mind, F brain-storm; =werke n/pl. fruits pl. of the intellect; (Schriftwerke) literary productions pl.; =zustand m state of (the) mind, mental condition; =zwang m mental compulsion or restraint.

geistig (⸗⸗) a. ⑯ 1. (unkörperlich) spiritual; incorporeal, immaterial; ⸗e Beschaffenheit, oft: spirituality. — 2. (die Denkkraft betreffend) intellectual; mental; ⸗e Anlage mental capacity or ability, ⸗e Armut poorness of intellect; ⸗es Auge mind's eye, mental vision; ⸗es Eigentum literary property; ⸗e Kraft mental force; ⸗e Liebe Platonic love; adv. ⸗ beschränkt narrow-minded. — 3. (spiritushaltig) spirituous; alcoholic; ⸗e Getränke n/pl. (Spirituosen) alcoholic liquor (s pl.), (ardent) spirits pl.

Geistigkeit (⸗⸗-) f ㊻ (f. geistig) 1. spirituality; incorpore(al)ity; weitS. immateriality. — 2. intellectuality. — 3. spirituous (or alcoholic) nature (or strength) of a liquid; bisw.: spirituosity.

geistlich (⸗⸗) a. ⑯ 1. (auf Gottesverehrung bezüglich) spiritual; ⸗es Konzert, ⸗es Lied, ⸗e Musik sacred concert, song, music; adv.: bibl. selig sind, die da ⸗ arm sind blessed are the poor in spirit. — 2. (auf Geistliche bezüglich) clerical; (kirchlich) ecclesiastical; ⸗er Berater spiritual adviser; ⸗e Güter n/pl. estates pl. of the church; ⸗er Orden religious order; ⸗es Recht canonical law; ⸗er Stand ecclesiastical order, clergy; in den ⸗en Stand treten, als Anglikaner: to enter the church, to take holy orders; als Dissenter: to enter the ministry; die ⸗e Weihe empfangen to be ordained, to receive holy orders.

Geistliche(r) (⸗⸗⸗) m ㊼: a) Anglikaner: clergyman or churchman, ecclesiastic; hoher: church-dignitary; (Pfarrer) parson, vicar; b) Dissenter: minister; c) (Priester) priest; d) coll. Geistliche pl., a. Geistlichkeit f ㊻ clergy; (body of) ministers pl.

geist=los (⸗...) a. ⑯ (ohne Kraft, Leben) spiritless, lifeless; dead, torpid; (langweilig) dull; (fade) insipid, stale, senseless; =losigkeit f ㊻ spiritlessness, lifelessness, deadness; dulness; ⸗reich a. full of life and wit, witty; (sinnreich) ingenious, clever; F smart, piquant, racy; ⸗tötend a. impoverish-

ing the mind, stupefying; (eintönig) monotonous; ⸗voll a. spirited; full of wit, (highly) intelligent; vgl. ⸗reich.

Gei=tau ↓ (⸗⸗) [geien] n ⑫ leech-line.

Geiz (¹)[uhd.; *geizen] m ⑫a. 1. avarice; (Gier) greed, avidity, bsd. bibl. covetousness; (Knauserei) stinginess, niggardliness, meanness. — 2. ⚘ agr. (Kurztrieb) shoot; sucker.

geizen (⸗⸗) [mhd.] ⑩ I v/n. (h.) 1. to be avaricious or greedy or stingy. — 2. mit et. ⸗ (sparsam umgehen) to make spare of a th., to economize a th.; mit s-n Mitteln, der Zeit ⸗ to husband one's resources, one's time. — 3. nach et. ⸗ (verlangen) to desire a th., to aspire to a th., bsd. bibl. to covet a th. — II v/a. 4. ⚘ agr. (den Geiz ausbrechen) to clip (or clear) off the shoots or suckers, to prune the trees, &c.

Geiz=hals (⸗...) m ⑫, =hammel m miser, skinflint; stingy (or mean, niggardly, close-fisted) fellow.

geizig (⸗⸗) ⑯ I a. avaricious, greedy (of gain), bsd. bibl. covetous; (knickerig) stingy, niggardly; schmutzig (oder F stinkend) ⸗ sordid, miserly; F (as) mean as the grave. — II ⸗e([r] m) f ㊼, Geiz=kragen m = Geizhals.

Ge=jage (⸗⸗⸗) n ⑫ continual chase or galloping; constant rushing and running. [tation, incessant wailing.]

Ge=jammer (⸗⸗⸗) n ⑫ endless lamen-⌋

Ge=jauchze, Ge=jodel, Ge=jubel (⸗⸗⸗) n ⑫ great jubilation, loud cheering.

Ge=johle (⸗⸗⸗) n ⑫ howling, hooting.

ge=kannt (⸗⸗) p.p. von kennen.

Ge=feife (⸗⸗⸗) n ⑫ constant sparring or squabbling or jarring or F nagging.

ge=kelcht ⚘ (⸗⸗⸗) a. ⑯: ⚚ caliculate(d).

ge=kerbt (⸗⸗) a. ⑯ 1. ⊕ (gezackt) indented, notched, jagged. — 2. ⚘: ⚚ crenate(d); fein ⸗: ⚚ crenulate(d).

Ge=kicher (⸗⸗⸗) n ⑫ constant tittering.

ge=kielt ⚘ (⸗⸗) a. ⑯: ⚚ carinated.

Ge=kitzel (⸗⸗⸗) n ⑫, Ge=kläff(e) (⸗⸗⸗) n ⑫b. continued tickling, yelping.

Ge=klage (⸗⸗⸗), Ge=klapper (⸗⸗⸗) n ⑫ constant complaining, rattling.

Ge=klatsch(e) (⸗⸗⸗) n ⑫a. (⑫) 1. (long-)continued clapping (of hands). — 2. (Schwatzen) gossip(ing), prattle, tittle-tattle; F mag, magging.

Ge=kleckse (⸗⸗⸗) n ⑫ wretched scrawl or scrawling; paint. daub(ing).

Ge=klimper (⸗⸗⸗) n ⑫ (constant) jingling, mit dem Gelde: chinking; auf dem Klavier: F strumming.

Ge=klinge(l) (⸗⸗⸗) n ⑫ tinkling of bells.

Ge=klirr(e) (⸗⸗⸗) n ⑫ (⑫) clanking;

ge=kloben (⸗⸗⸗) p.p. v. klieben. [clashing.]

ge=klommen (⸗⸗⸗) p.p. v. klimmen.

Ge=klopfe (⸗⸗⸗) n ⑫ much knocking.

Ge=klüft(e)(⸗⸗⸗) n ⑫b.(⑫) clefts, fissures.

ge=klungen (⸗⸗⸗) p.p. von klingen. [pl.]

Ge=knall (⸗⸗) ⑫b., Ge=knatter (⸗⸗⸗) n ⑫ constant banging, rattling of musketry.

ge=knäuelt (⸗⸗⸗) a. ⑯: ⚚ glomerate(d); (knotig) ⚚ nodose.

ge=kniet ⚘ (⸗⸗) a. ⑯: ⚚ geniculate(d).

ge=kniffen (⸗⸗⸗) p.p. von kneifen.

Ge=knirsche (⸗⸗⸗) n ⑫ crunching; gnashing (of teeth);

Ge=knister (⸗⸗⸗) n ⑫ des Feuers ꝛc.: crackling, ⚚ crepitation; e-s Kleides: rustling. [or growling or murmuring.]

Ge=knurre (⸗⸗⸗) n ⑫ constant snarling⌋

ge=kommen (⸗⸗⸗) p.p. v. kommen.

ge=konnt (⸗⸗) p.p. von können.

ge=köpert ⊕ (⸗⸗⸗) a. ⑯ twilled (cloth).

ge=koren (⸗⸗⸗) p.p. v. kiesen. [granulated.]

ge=körnt (⸗⸗) p.p. u. a. ⑯ min. grained,⌋

Ge=kose (⸗⸗⸗) n ⑫ caressing, love-making; (Geplauder) chatting.

Ge=krach (⸗⸗⸗) n ⑫c. crash(ing), cracking; des Donners: peals pl. of thunder; der Gewehre: banging, rattling.

Ge=krächze (⸗⸗⸗) n ⑫ croaking. [refuse.]

Ge=krätz(e) ⊕ (⸗⸗⸗) n ⑫a. (⑫) metall.⌋

Ge=kräusel(⸗⸗⸗) n ⑫ des Haares: crimping, curling; der Wellen: rippling, ripple.

Ge=kreisch(e) (⸗⸗⸗) n ⑫a. (⑫) (constant) screaming or shrieking or screeching.

ge=krischen (⸗⸗⸗) p.p. v. kreischen.

Ge=kritzel (⸗⸗⸗) n ⑫ scribbling, scrawl, scrawling.

ge=krochen (⸗⸗⸗) p.p. von kriechen.

Ge=kröse (⸗⸗⸗) [mhd.] n ⑫ 1. (Krause) ruffle, frill. — 2. anat. (Bauchfellfalten): a) Dünndarmbekleidung: ⚚ mesentery; b) Dickdarm⸗: ⚚ mesocolon; c) Mastdarm⸗: ⚚ mesorectum. — 3. Koch.: (Kalbs⸗) pluck.

ge=krumpen (⸗⸗⸗) p.p. von krumpen.

ge=künstelt (⸗⸗⸗) I p.p. von künsteln. — II a. ⑯ (künstlich) artificial; (geziert) affected, finical, prim.

Ge=küsse (⸗⸗⸗) n ⑫ repeated kissing.

Ge=lache (⸗⸗⸗) n ⑫ continual laughing; bursts (or peals) pl. of laughter.

Ge=lächter (⸗⸗⸗) [lachen] n ⑫ 1. loud laughing; schallendes ⸗ roars (or peals) pl. of laughter; in ein lautes ⸗ ausbrechen, in lautes ⸗ erheben to burst out laughing, to break out into a fit of laughter. — 2. (Gegenstand des Lachens) zum ⸗ w. to make o. s. ridiculous, to become the laughing-stock of people; e-n, et. zum ⸗ machen to turn ... into ridicule, to make sport of ...

ge=laden (⸗⸗⸗) p.p. von laden.

Ge=lag(e) (⸗⸗⸗) [uhd.; *legen] n ⑫c. (⑫) 1. feast, banquet; von Zechern: drinking-bout, carousal; wildes ⸗ orgy. — 2. fig. ins Gelag hinein (wild darauf los) helter-skelter, at random.

ge=lähmt (⸗⸗) p.p. von lähmen und a. ⑯ lame(d), paralysed.

ge=lahrt (⸗⸗), Ge=lahrtheit (⸗⸗⸗) [mhd.] altfränkisch für gelehrt, Gelehrtheit.

Ge=lände (⸗⸗⸗) [ahd.] n ⑫ 1. poet. ob. obb. country-side, tract of land, open fields pl. — 2. ⚔ (Terrain) ground, territory.

Ge=lände=falte f ⊕ undulating ground.

Ge=länder (⸗⸗⸗) [mhd.; *Lander] n ⑫ rail(ing); an den Seiten eines Abhanges auch: hand-rail; (Docken⸗) ⸗ balustrade; an Treppen: banister; (Spalier) trellis (-work); mit e-m ⸗ einschließen, absondern to rail in, off.

Ge=länder=docke (⸗...) f ⑫, =säule f ⊕, arch., &c. baluster, rail-column, rail(ing)-post; =riegel ⊕ hand-rail; =stab m railing; =stange f hand-rail.

ge=lang (⸗⸗) impf. von gelingen.

ge=langen (⸗⸗⸗) I v/n. (in) ⑱* 1. to arrive at (or to go to) a place, mit Anstrengung: to reach one's destination; auf

---

Signs (see page XVII): F familiar; P vulgar; P flash; ❦ rare; † obsolete (died); * new word (born); ⁺⁺ incorrect; ♪ music;

[gelappt] — 423 — [Geldmensch]

die Nachwelt ⁓ to come (or to be handed) down to posterity; **in** andere Hände ⁓ to pass into other (or to change) hands; **zu** Ansehen ⁓ to gain respect, to acquire influence; **zur** Ausfuhr ⁓ to be exported; **zu** Reichtum ⁓ to make a fortune; zu einem Schlusse ⁓ to arrive at a conclusion; zum Ziele, Zwecke ⁓ to attain one's end or object. — 2. et. an e-n ⁓ lassen to forward (or remit, dispatch) a th. to a p. — II ⁓ *n* ㉓ 3. arrival; (Erlangung) attainment.

ge-lappt (⌣⌣) *a.* ㊋ ⛞lobate(d). [noise.|
Ge-lärm(e) (⌣⌣) *n* ⑪ b.(㉒) never-ending|
Ge-laß (⌣⌣) [mhd.: *lassen] *n* (*m*) ⓦa. (Räumlichkeit) space, room, für Gäste: accommodation, eng S. = Kammer; s. a. Behältnis 1; das Haus hat viel ⁓ ... is very spacious or F roomy.

ge-lassen (⌣⌣) **I** *p.p.* von lassen. — **II** *a.* ㊋ (D 9) calm, collected; (leidenschaftslos) even-tempered, unruffled; (unerschütterlich) imperturbable, (gemäßigt) moderate; ⁓ bleiben to remain cool, to keep one's temper; *adv.* ⁓ handeln to act with composure or moderation; du sprichst ein großes Wort ⁓ aus (G.) you utter a great word with unconcern.

Ge-lassenheit (⌣⌣⌣) *f* ㊺ calm, calmness, collectedness; even temper; coolness, composure; unconcern.

Gelatine ⊕ (g⌣⌣) [fr.] *f* ㊽ (Gallert) gelatine; ⁓**blättchen** *n* gelatine disk.

Ge-läuf (⌣⌣) *n* ⓦc. 1. *hunt.* (Spuren des Federwildes) track of wild fowl. — 2. Rennsport: (die zu durchlaufende Bahn) course, distance to be run.

Ge-laufe (⌣⌣) *n* ⓦc. (constant) running to and fro, gadding about.

ge-laufen (⌣⌣) *p.p.* von laufen. ⁓ kommen to come running along.

ge-läufig (⌣⌣) *a.* ㊋ fluent, ready, easy; ein ⁓es Mundwerk oder eine ⁓e Zunge haben ... a voluble (or glib) tongue or great fluency of speech; das Fach ist ihm ⁓ (bekannt) the subject is familiar to him, he is well acquainted with the subject; *adv.* er spricht ⁓ französisch he speaks French fluently or with (great) ease.

Ge-läufigkeit (⌣⌣⌣) *f* ㊺ fluency, readiness, facility; volubility; familiarity, thorough acquaintance with; ease.

ge-launt (⌣⌣) *a.* ㊋ gut (schlecht) ⁓ in good (bad) humour, good- (ill-)humoured.

Ge-läut(e) (⌣⌣(⌣)) [mhd.] *n* ⓦc. (㉒) 1. (das Läuten) ringing of bells. — 2. (Ton von Glocken) tinkling of bells, bisw.: tintinnabulation. — 3. (Gesamtheit der Glocken) peal (or set) of bells, chime(s *pl.*); elektrisches ⁓ electric chimes or bells *pl.* — 4. *hunt.* (Gebell der Meute) barking (or speaking) of the hounds.

gelb (⌣) [ahd.: yellow; lt. *helvus*] **I** *a.* ㊋ 1. yellow; ⁓es Fieber ye. fever, ety. jack; *pol.* ⁓e Gefahr yellow peril; ⁓e Gesichtsfarbe sallow complexion; ⁓e Rasse yellow race; ⁓e Rübe carrot (von *Daucus caro'ta*). — 2. es wird mir grün und ⁓ vor den Augen **I** (begin to) feel quite giddy; vgl. blau 2. — **II** (das) ⁓ *n*, ⁓**e(s)** *n* ㉓ 3. yellow, the yellow colour; als Farbstoff auch: yellow dye, yellow colouring substance; Kasseler ⁓ (Malerfarbe) Turner's yellow.

Gelb-beeren ⚘ (⌣⌣⌣) *f/pl.* ㉒ (unreife, getrocknete Beeren verschiedener Rhamnusarten) grains of Avignon, Persian berries *pl.*; ⁓**bleierz** ⛏ *n* yellow lead-ore, wulfenite (P₆M₀O₄); ⁓**braun** *a.* ㊋ yellowish brown; ⁓**buch** *n* in Frankreich: yellow book.

Gelbe (⌣⌣) *f* ⓦ 1. yellow colour, yellowness. — 2. *min.* = Gelberde; (Oder) ochre.

Gelb-eisenstein (⌣⌣⌣) *m* ㊋ yellow iron-ore; ⁓**erde** *f, min.* (Odergelb) yellow earth; ⁓**fieber** *n* yellow jack; ⁓**füßig** *a.* ㊋ *zo.* with y. feet or paws; ⁓**gießer** ⊕ *m* brass-founder; brazier; ⁓**gießerei** ⊕ *f* brass-foundry; ⁓**gießer-ware** ⚘ *f* braziery, brass-ware; ⁓**grau**, ⁓**grün** *a.* ㊋ yellowish grey, green; ⁓**haarig** *a.* with yellow hair.

Gelbheit (⌣⌣) *f* ㊺ = Gelbe 1.

Gelb-holz ⚘ (⌣⌣⌣) *n* ㊋ yellow-wood; echtes ⁓ s. Fustik; ungarisches ⁓ s. Fisettholz; ⁓**kupfer** *n, min.* (Messing) brass.

gelblich (⌣⌣) *a.* ㊋ yellowish.

gelblich-braun (⌣⌣⌣), ⁓**grün** *a.* ㊋ yellowish brown, green; ⁓**weiß** *a.* cream-coloured; ⁓ und *zo.*: ⁓ ochroleucous.

Gelbling (⌣⌣) *m* ⓓ. 1. *orn.* = Goldammer u. Pirol. — 2. *ent.* Art Tagfalter: yellow (Co'leas).

gelb-reif (⌣⌣⌣) *a.* ㊋ *agr.* vom Korn: half ripe; ⁓**rot** *a.* yellowish red; ⁓**schecke(f)** *m* (Pferd) white horse with yellow spots; ⁓**schnabel** *m*: a) (junger Vogel) young bird; b) F *fig.* (junger Fant) greenhorn; (Neuling) newcomer; ⁓**sehen** *n, path.* xanthopsy; kleiner Kinder: yellow-gum; Mittel gegen ⁓: ⚗ icteric; ⁓**süchtig** *a.* jaundiced, ⚗ icteric(al); ⁓**veigelein** ⚘ *n* (U.) = Goldlack; ⁓**wurz** ⚘ *f* = Gilb-w.

Geld (⌣; *Hom.* gelt) [ahd.: guild; *gelten*] *n* ⓓ b., *coll.* ohne *pl.* 1. money; (Münze) coin; kleines ⁓ change, small coin; bares ⁓ ready money, cash, specie; falsches ⁓ base (or counterfeit) coin; ⁓ aufnehmen to raise money or F the wind; in barem ⁓e bezahlen ... (in) ready money or (in) cash; sein ⁓ durchbringen to run through one's money; er läßt es sich viel ⁓ kosten he spends his money lavishly or freely; et. zu ⁓ machen to turn (or convert) a th. into (ready) money; nicht bei ⁓e sein ... out of cash, F ... hard up; ⁓ verdienen to earn (or F make) money (an by); ohne ⁓ impecunious; was für ein Posten ⁓! what an amount (F a heap or lot) of mo.!; ⁓ wie Heu F lots (or heaps) *pl.* of money; für ⁓ und gute Worte for love or mo.; Sprichw. ⁓ macht das Feld money makes the mare go; ⁓ bringt Ansehen, Armut Schande money makes the man, and the want of it the fellow; für ⁓ bekommt man alles mo. buys everything. — 2. (Vermögen, Kapital) viel ⁓ und Gut (a. ⁓ wie Heu) haben to have plenty (of property), to be well off, F to be rolling in wealth or riches; mit fremdem ⁓e handeln to trade with borrowed money or capital; von s-m ⁓e leben to live on one's money or capital; ⁓ in et. stecken to put mo. into a concern; die öffentlichen ⁓er the public funds *pl.* — 3. (Eigentum) er hat kein feines Pfennig ⁓ he has not a farthing (of his own); er ist um all sein ⁓ gekommen he has lost all that he possessed; zu seinem ⁓e kommen to come into one's money or property; Sprichw. ⁓ macht nicht glücklich money does not ensure happiness; wo ⁓ ist, will ⁓ hin money begets money. — 4. 🜨 im Kurszettel: (gesucht, gefragt; *abbr.* G.) wanted, inquired after, buyer.

Geld-adel (⌣⌣⌣) *m* ㊋ plutocracy; bought title (of nobility); ⁓**angelegenheiten** *f/pl.* money (or monetary) affairs or matters *pl.*; ⁓**anlage** *f* investment of capital; ⁓**anleihe** *f* loan (of money); ⁓**anweisung** ✉ *f* money- (or post-office) order; ⁓**aristokratie** *f* plutocracy, *auch.* ㊋ the barons *pl.* of finance; ⁓**arm** *a.* ㊋ without (or pinched for) money, impecunious; ⁓**ausgabe** *f* expenditure, disbursement; ⁓**ausleiher** *m* moneylender; ⁓**bedarf** *m*: a) (Mangel) want (or lack) of mo.; b) (so viel j. braucht) sum required by a p.; ⁓**beitrag** *m* contribution in mo. or cash; (Unterstützung) *auch.* subscription to a charity, &c.; ⁓**belohnung** *f* pecuniary reward, remuneration; ⁓**beutel** *m*: a) = Sack; b) = Börse 1; ⁓**bewilligung** *f* money-grant; *parl.* supply; ⁓**brief** ✉ *m* letter containing money, mo.-letter; vgl. ⁓anweisung; ⁓**büchse** *f* mo.-box; ⁓**buße** *f* = Strafe; ⁓**durst** *m* thirst after (or for) mo.; ⁓**einlage** *f* enclosure of mo.; ⁓**einnahme** *f* receipt of mo.; receipts *pl.*; ⁓**einnehmer** *m* receiver of money; ⁓**entschädigung** *f* indemnity, reimbursement, compensation.

Gelder-land ♀ (⌣⌣⌣) *n* ㉒, **Geldern** ♀ (⌣⌣) *n* ㉓α. (nbl. Provinz) Guelderland.

Geld-erwerb (⌣⌣⌣) *m* ㊋ earning (of) money, mo.-making.

Geldes-wert (⌣⌣⌣) *m* ㊋ money's worth; 🜨 (Attiva) assets *pl.*; Geld und ⁓ money and valuables *pl.*

Geld-forderung (⌣⌣⌣) *f* ㊋ money owing to a p., mo. due; (Mahnung) dunning; ⁓**fürst** *m* prince (or king) of finance; ⁓**geschäft** *n* money-transaction; größeres: financial enterprise or venture; ⁓**geschenk** *n* gratuity; größeres: donation; (Trinkgeld) tip; ⁓**gier**(ig *a.* ㊋) greed(y) after money; ⁓**handel** *m* bullion-trade, exchange; banking; ⁓**händler** *m* mo.-changer; banker; ⁓**heirat** *f* marriage for mo.; ⁓**herrschaft** *f* plutocracy; ⁓**jude** *m* usurer; ⁓**kasse** *f* (iron) safe; im Laden: till; ⁓**kasten** *m* money- (or cash-)box, strong box; ⁓**katze** *f* mo.-pouch, mo.-belt; ⁓**kiste** *f* strong box; ⁓**klemme** *f* scarcity of mo.; pecuniary embarrassment or difficulty; sich in einer ⁓ befinden to be in (great) straits (for money); ⁓**krise**, ⁓**krisis** *f* monetary crisis; ⁓**kurs** *m* rate of exchange; ⁓**kurszettel** *m* exchange-list, market-quotation of the (daily) rates of exchange; ⁓**leute** *pl.* moneyed people, financiers *pl.*; ⁓**makler** *m* mo.-broker; ⁓**mangel** *m* lack (or want) of mo.; ⁓**mann** *m* moneyed man, financier, F goldbug; ⁓**markt** *m* mo.-market; ⁓**mensch** *m* F mo.-grubber;

⚚ scientific; ⚘ botanical; ♀ geography; ⊕ machinery; ⛏ mining; ⚔ military; ⚓ marine; 🜨 commercial; ✉ postal; 🚂 railway.

[Geldmittel] — 424 — [Gelenkentzündung]

vgl. =mann; =mittel n/pl. means pl.; pecuniary resources pl.; =muschel f cowrie (Cyprae'a mone'ta); =not f pecuniary embarrassment; = tightness of money; =posten m sum of money; =preis m rate of exchange; =protz F m purse-proud man, rich upstart; =quelle f source of income; =sache f = angelegenheiten; Sprichw. in ~n hört die Gemütlichkeit auf business is business, a bargain is a bargain; =sack m ohne den Inhalt: mo.-bag; mit dem Inhalt: bag of mo.; fig. person rolling in wealth; =sammlung f collecting money; raising a subscription; =schatz m hoards pl. of mo.; =schinder, =schneider m usurer, extortioner; =schneiderei f usury, extortion; =schrank m money-chest; (iron) safe; =schuld f (pecuniary) debt; =sendung f remittance (of money), cash-remittance; =sorte f sort of coin; =spende f money-gift, contribution; =spind n (m) = =schrank; =stolz a. proud of one's money, purse-proud; =stolz m rich man's pride; =strafe f fine; mit e-r ~ belegen to fine, to mulct; f. a. Buße 2; =stück n piece of mo., coin; =sucht f avarice; =süchtig a. avaricious; =summe f sum of mo.; =tasche f leather purse; =tisch m counter; =umlauf m circulation of mo.; =umsatz, =verkehr m turnover; volume of business; =verlegenheit f pecuniary embarrassment; shortness of (F pinch for) money; =verlust m pecuniary loss; =vorschuß m advance of mo.; mo. paid in advance; =wage f mo.-scales pl., -balance; =währung f standard, currency; =wechsel m mo.-changing, exchange of money; =wechsel-geschäft n money-changer's business; =wechsler m mo.-changer; =wechsler-geschäft n, =laden m mo.-changer's trade, business; =wert m value of mo.; =wesen n money-affairs, monetary concerns pl.; financial business; =wucher m usury; =wucherer m usurer; =zins m interest on money.
Ge-lecke F (ᵕ⌣) n ㉒ much licking or kissing or F slobbering.
Gelee (Gᵕ⌣) [fr. gelée f] n ㉖ u. ㊿ (Gallert) jelly; ~form f ㊻ jelly-mould.
Ge-lege (ᵕ⌣ᵕ) n ㉒ (Eierlegen) laying (eggs); (gelegte Eier) number of eggs laid (by one hen).
ge-legen (ᵕ⌣ᵕ) [ahd.] I 1. p.p. von liegen. (bsd. österr.) ² sein, oft: = liegen. — II a. ㊽ (D9) 2. örtlich: lying, situated, located. — 3. örtlich und zeitlich: (passend) convenient, appropriate; e-n ²en Ort wählen to choose a suitable place; das kommt mir recht ² it comes just at the right time or F very handy; er kommt mir sehr ² he comes in the (very) nick of time, he is just the man I want; zur ²en Zeit at a (most) suitable moment or time; opportunely, in season. — 4. mir ist daran ² (mir liegt daran), daß ich ihn spreche it is urgent for me (or I am anxious) to speak to him; es mir nichts daran ², ob // it does not (much) matter (auch: it is of little consequence or of no importance) to me whether //.

Ge-legenheit (ᵕ⌣ᵕ-) [mhd.] f ㊻ 1. (Anlaß) occasion; bei allen ~en on every occasion; günstige ~ favourable opportunity; bei erster ~ at the first opportunity; bei vorkommender ~ when (-ever) the opportunity offers or presents itself; e-e gute ~ a good (or lucky) chance; er benutzt jede ~, um Englisch zu sprechen he avails himself of every opportunity for speaking English; er hatte eine treffliche ~, zu steigen he had a splendid chance of rising; bei der ~ will ich bemerken I may remark by the way or in passing; Sprichw. ~ macht Diebe opportunity makes the thief. — 2. ⚙ ~ zum Senden (means of) conveyance. — 3. (Beschaffenheit) nach ~ der Umstände according to circumstances. — 4. (Örtlichkeit) alle ~en e-s Hauses kennen to know every nook and corner (or the whereabouts) ...
Ge-legenheits-arbeiter (ᵕ⌣ᵕ-...) m ㊷ jobbing man, jobber; =dichter m writer of occasional poetry; impromptu poet; =gedicht n poem written for a special occasion, occasional poem; thea. topical verse; =gesellschaft f syndicate formed for a special venture or enterprise; =kauf m chance (or occasional) purchase; ⚙ auch F job-lot; =macher(in f) m go-between; =schrift f pamphlet.
ge-legentlich (ᵕ⌣ᵕᵕ) a. ㊻ occasional, incidental; (zufällig) accidental; ²er Kunde stray (or chance) customer; adv. und prp. mit gen. occasionally, on certain occasions; on the first opportunity, when there is an opportunity or a chance; (zufällig) accidentally, by chance; (nebenbei) by the way; (zuweilen) now and again; ² bemerken to mention incidentally.
ge-lehrig (ᵕ⌣ᵕ) [lehren] a. ㊻ docile, teachable; (lenksam) tractable, gentle, manageable; amenable to discipline; ~keit f ㊻ docility; tractableness.
ge-lehrsam (ᵕ⌣-) a. ㊻ = gelehrig; ~keit (ᵕ⌣--) f ㊻ learning; (deep) reading; (vast) scholarship; bsd. in alter Literatur: erudition; (ausgebreitetes Wissen) extensive knowledge; f. Aufwand.
ge-lehrt (ᵕ⌣) [mhd.] I a. ㊻ 1. learned; well (or deeply) read, scholarly, F bookish; bsd. in alter Literatur: erudite; ²e Frau, oft: blue-stocking; ²e Gegenstände m/pl. learned (or scientific) subjects pl.; ²e Gesellschaft learned (or literary) society; ²e Welt republic of letters; scientific world; F fig. ein ²es Haus, a regular pundit; Sprichw. je ²er, desto verkehrter the more learned the less wise; adv. ² sprechen to speak in a learned (or pedantic) way or tone. — 2. (in et. geschult) well instructed (or trained, schooled, versed) in a th. — II ~e(r) (ᵕ⌣ᵕ) s. ㊶ 3. learned (or well-read, F bookish) (wo)man, (great) scholar, auch: savant, man of letters; in mathematisch-technischen Dingen: scientific man or discoverer; pl. die ~en the learned; Sprichw. es ist noch kein ~er vom Himmel gefallen no man is born a scholar; ~en ist gut predigen a word to the wise (is enough).

Ge-lehrten-lexikon (ᵕ⌣ᵕ-...) n ㊷ biographical dictionary of 'Men of Letters'; =republik f republic of letters; =schule f school with a classical curriculum, Latin grammar-school; =stand m: a) vocation of a man of letters; b) learned profession(s pl.); =stolz m learned pride; =verein m learned (or literary) society; =welt f world of science and literature; =wesen n science and literature; =zunft f body of literary and scientific men. | keit.
Ge-lehrt-heit (ᵕ⌣-) f ㊻ = Gelehrsam-
Ge-leier (ᵕ⌣ᵕ) n ㉒ constant playing (or grinding) of a barrel-organ; F fig. (eintöniger Vortrag) humdrum music or speech; immer das alte ~ the same old tune or song, the same thing over and over (again).
Ge-leise (ᵕ⌣ᵕ) n ㉒ [mhd. (ahd. leisa: It. lira] 1. rut; track. — 2. ☉, ⛟ (Fahrbahn) permanent way; (Schienen) rails pl.; einfaches, doppeltes ~ single, double line or track. — 3. fig. (vorgezeichnete Bahn) im (alten) ~ bleiben to keep to the same groove, to follow the same track; wieder ins ~ bringen to put right (F to rights) again; aus dem ~ kommen: a) = entgleisen; b) fig. to quit the old routine or ways, to get off the old beaten track, to get out of one's groove.
Ge-leit(e) (ᵕ⌣(ᵕ)) [mhd.; *leiten] n ⑪ c.(㉒) 1. (das Geleiten) accompaniment; e-m (fortgehendem Besuch) das ~ geben to see a p. to the door; F nehmen Sie das ~ mit! pray excuse me not seeing you to the door!; (Trauer-)~ funeral procession. — 2. (Bedeckung) ⚔ ⚓ escort, convoy; freies (oder sicheres) ~ safe-conduct; e-m das ~ geben to escort a p.
ge-leiten (ᵕ⌣ᵕ) [ahd.] I v/a. ㊾ (f. Geleit) to accompany, an die Tür: to see to the door; an den Bahnhof 2c.: to see off; ⚔ ⚓ to convoy; rel. Gott geleite ihn! God speed him (well)! — II ~ n ㉓ f. Geleit 1.
Ge-leiter (ᵕ⌣ᵕ) m ㉒, ~in f ㊸ conductor; attendant; e-r Dame a.: chaperon.
Ge-leit(s)-brief (ᵕ⌣...) m ㉒: a) (letter of) safe-conduct; b) ⚙ letter of consignment; =mann m = Geleiter; =schein m = =brief; =schiff ⚓ n convoy(-ship); =stern m, ast. satellite.
Ge-lenk¹ (ᵕ⌣) [mhd.: link; *lenken] n ⑪ b. 1. anat. joint; ⚕ articulation; (Hand-)~ wrist; die ~e (Knöchel) der Finger the knuckles pl.; sich (dat.) den Arm aus dem ~ fallen to dislocate one's arm by falling, to put it out of joint; fig. ⚲ prov. ~e h. to be very clumsy or awkward (in one's movements). — 2. ♃ joint, knot. — 3. ⚙ mech. (bewegliches Stück) joint; ~ (Glied) e-r Kette: link; (Gewinde) turning-joint; mit ~en versehen jointed, articulate, linked.
ge-lenk² (ᵕ⌣) [mhd.] a. ㊻ f. gelenkig 2.
Ge-lenk-band (ᵕ⌣...) n ⑫: a) ligament of a joint, articular ligament; b) ⊕ Schlosser: turning-joint, joint-frame or -hinge; =bruch m, surg. fracture of a joint; =drüsen f/pl.; ⚕ synovial glands pl.; =entzündung f, path. in-

[Gelenkfortsatz] — 425 — [Gelüste]

flammation of a joint, ⚕ arthritis, arthrosis; =fortsatz m der unteren Kinnlade; ⚕ condyloid process; =fügung f: ⚕ articulation; =höhle f: ⚕ cotyle. ge-lenkig (⌣⌣) a. ⓐ 1. jointed, articulate(d), & a. knotty. — 2. loose-jointed; (biegsam) flexible, pliable; (geschmeidig) supple, nimble, agile, active. Ge-lenkigkeit (⌣⌣-) f ⓐ (vgl. gelenkig) flexibility, pliability; suppleness, nimbleness, agility. Ge-lenk=lehre (⌣⌣...) f ⓐ: ⚕ arthrology; =neurose f, path.: ⚕ arthroneuralgia; =pfanne f socket of a joint, articular cavity, vgl. =höhle; =puppe f swivel-doll; =rheumati'smus m, path. rheumatism in the joints, articular rheumatism; =ring ⓜ m swivel; =schmerz m, path. pain in the joints, ⚕ arthralgia; =schmiere f joint-oil, ⚕ synovia, =steifigkeit, =verwachsung f, path. stiffness (or stiffening, hardening, ossification) of a joint, ⚕ anchylosis; =wassersucht f, path. dropsy in the joints, ⚕ hydrarthrosis.
ge-lernt (⌣⌣) f. lernen III.
Ge-lese (⌣⌣) n ⓐ much reading.
ge-lesen (⌣⌣) p.p. von lesen.
Ge-leuchte ⚒ (⌣⌣) n ⓐ des Bergmanns i. d. Grube: miner's lamps and lights pl.
gelfe(r)n (⌣⌣) [: yelp] v/n. ⓐ (ⓐa.) to yelp, yap, bark.
Ge-lichter (⌣⌣) [ahd. lëhtar Mutterleib] n ⓐ gang, set, tribe, F lot; (Art, Schlag) species, stamp; ich kenne das ~ I know that class (or sort) of people.
Ge-liebte (⌣⌣) [p.p.v.lieben] ~r m, ~f ⓐ 1. beloved one, sweetheart, F darling; b.s. paramour; eine alte ~ an old flame. — 2. (Bewerber, Freier) wooer, lover; seine ~, auch: F his lady-love, b.s. his mistress; vgl. Liebhaber.
ge-liehen (⌣⌣) p.p. von leihen.
ge-lind, 2e (⌣⌣(⌣) [lind] a. ⓐ soft (air); gentle (rain); mild (weather); slight (pain); bei einem 2en Feuer braten ... on a slow fire; 2es Fieber mild attack of fever; 2e Kälte moderate cold; 2ere Saiten aufziehen to moderate one's tone, to come down a peg (or two); vgl. aufziehen 5; bei 2erem Wetter in more genial weather; um das 2este Wort, den 2esten Ausdruck zu gebrauchen, 2estens (adv.) gesagt to put it (very) mildly; adv. e-n 2 behandeln, mit e-m 2 verfahren to deal gently (or leniently) with a p.; to indulge (or spare) a p.
Ge-lindheit (⌣⌣), Ge-lindigkeit (⌣⌣-) f ⓐ (vgl. gelind[e]) softness; gentleness, mildness, moderation; leniency, indulgence.
ge-lingen (⌣⌣) [ahd.] I v/n. (su) ⓐft* 1. to succeed, to be successful, to turn out well; sein Vorhaben ist ihm nicht gelungen he failed in his design, his scheme failed; v/impers. es gelingt mir (dir 2c.), er tun I (you, &c.) succeed in doing it; es ist ihm noch gerade gelungen zu entkommen he just managed (or contrived) to escape. — II ~ n ⓐ 2. success. — III ge-lungen p.p. u. a. ⓐ (D 9) 3. Bed. des inf. — 4. F (vortrefflich) excellent,

F famous; ein 2er Mensch an amusing fellow; e-e 2e Geschichte a capital story, a good joke. fine fun; das 2ste an der Sache ist, daß // F the funniest part of it is that //.
Ge-lispel (⌣⌣) n ⓐ continual lisping; (Geflüster) (soft) whispering.
ge-litten (⌣⌣) p.p. von leiden.
gellen (⌣⌣) [ahd.: yell] I v/n. (h.) ⓐ to yell, to utter shrill (or piercing) sounds; es gellt mir in den Ohren my ears are tingling. — II 2d p.pr. u. a. ⓐ yelling. shrill, piercing.
ge-loben (⌣⌣) [ahd.] I v/a. ⓐ* to promise solemnly; eidlich 2 to vow with an oath; mit Hand und Mund 2. c. zu tun to pledge o.s. to do a th.; e-m (ewige) Treue 2 to promise to be (ever) faithful to a p.; er hat Gehorsam und Selbstverleugnung gelobt he is pledged to obedience and self-denial; bibl. das Gelobte Land the Land of Promise, the Holy Land. — II ~ n ⓐ = Gelöbnis.
Ge-löbnis (⌣⌣) n ⓐ solemn promise or vow or pledge; ein ~ tun to vow.
Ge-lock(e)[1] (⌣⌣) [Locke] n ⓐ.(ⓐ) 1. (Lockigmachen) curling (the hair). — 2. (Lockenhaar) curled hair; (mass of) curls or ringlets or locks pl.
Ge-lock(e)[2] (⌣⌣) [locken[2]] n ⓐ.c.(ⓐ) bfd. hunt. decoying; weits. allurement, enticement, charm.
ge-lockt (⌣⌣) [Locke] a. ⓐ curly, with curly hair, curly-haired.
ge-logen (⌣⌣) p.p. von lügen.
ge-loschen (⌣⌣) p.p. von löschen.
Gelse öft. (⌣⌣) f ⓐ (Mücke, Schnake) gnat.
gelt[1] obd. (⌣; Hom. Geld) [verkürzte 3. Prs. sg. pres. subj. v. gelten] int. nach einer Frage: F eh?, is it not so?, is it not true?; P now, ain't it?; im Anfang des Satzes: surely, to be sure.
gelt[2] (⌣) [ahd.: geld] a. ⓐ agr. von Tieren (unfruchtbar) barren; (ohne Milch) giving no milk.
Gelte provc. od. † (⌣⌣) [ahd.; *lt. gal(l)e'ta] f ⓐ (Gefäß) pail, bucket. tub.
gelten (⌣⌣) [ahd.: yield] ⓐe. (impf. subj. a. gälte) I v/n. (h.) 1. to be of (or to have a certain) value; die Sache gilt mir viel ... is of great importance (or consequence) to me; es gilt mir wenig it matters little to me; das Getreide gilt jetzt viel grain has (or commands, fetches) a good (or high) price now; mir gilt Ehre mehr als das Leben I esteem (or prize) honour more highly than life; was gilt die Wette? how much will you bet?; das gilt mir (alles) gleich it is (all) the same to me. — 2. (gültig sein) von Gesetzen, Regeln 2c.: to be in force or in operation, to obtain, to be valid; hier gilt kein Zaudern there is no time to be lost, there must be no delay; die Münze gilt hier nicht ... is of no value (or has no currency) here; Spiel 2c.: das gilt nicht that is against the rules, it is not fair; im Kriege 2 alle Vorteile everything is fair in war; etwas 2 lassen to approve of a th.; schwächer: to let a th. pass; beifällig: das laß ich 2! well

done!, bravo! — 3. (Ansehen, Bedeutung haben): (viel) 2 to be held in great respect or esteem; viel bei e-m 2 to have great influence (or weight) with a p., to be in high favour with a p.; fie 2 viel bei Hofe they enjoy great credit at court; bibl. bei Gott gilt kein Ansehen der Person God is no respecter of persons; der Prophet gilt nicht(s) in s-m Vaterlande a prophet hath no honour in his own country. — 4. für oder als etwas 2 (gehalten werden) to pass for ..., to be considered as ...; für e-n klugen Mann 2 to be looked upon as (or to have the reputation of) a shrewd man; er möchte für e-n Märtyrer 2 he would like to pose as a martyr. — 5. von e-m, einer Sache 2 (mit Recht behauptet werden) to be valid or true; was von dir gilt, gilt auch von mir what (or the same that) applies to you, applies to me likewise; dasselbe gilt von den andern the same holds good with (regard to) the others. — 6. diese Bemerkung gilt dir (ist auf dich abgesehen) ... is intended (or meant) for you. — II v/impers. es gilt: 7. alleinstehend: a) es (das Spiel, die Wette) gilt! agreed!, right!; jetzt gilt es (ist es Ernst) now we come to the point!; now is the time!; was gilt es? what will you bet?; vgl. gelt[1]; b) ⚒ (es kann so geschehen) let it be so! — 8. es gilt (ist nötig) zu handeln there is (urgent) need of acting; hier gilt es Mut this wants (or requires) courage; es gilt einen Versuch an attempt must be made. — 9. es gilt Ihr (od. Ihnen) das Leben your life is at stake or in jeopardy; es gilt unser alles we risk our all. — 10. (vgl. 6) gilt's mir? is it meant for me? — III ~ n ⓐ. 11. f. Geltung. — IV 2d p.pr. u. a. ⓐ. 12. in den Bed. des inf. — 13. valid (vgl. gültig); s-n Einfluß bei e-m 2d machen to use one's influence with a p.; jur. Verjährung 2d machen to plead prescription; sich 2d machen to assert o.s., to make one's influence felt.
Geltend-machung (⌣⌣...) f ⓐ assertion of one's rights; vgl. gelten 12.
Geltung (⌣⌣) f ⓐ 1. (f. gelten 1 und 2) (Wert) worth, value; (Bedeutung) importance; currency of a coin; acceptation of a word. — 2. etwas in (od. zur) ~ bringen to make a th. valid, to enforce the law, to assert one's authority, to show off one's knowledge; zur ~ kommen, sich (dat.) ~ verschaffen to become important, to gain prevalence or authority. — Vgl. auch Gültigkeit.
Ge-lübde (⌣⌣) [ahd.: *geloben] n ⓐ 1. = Gelöbnis. — 2. rel. vow; ein ~ ablegen oder tun, ein ~ auf sich nehmen to make (or take) a vow; ein ~ brechen to break a vow; ein ~ erfüllen to keep (or perform, fulfil) a vow.
ge-lungen (⌣⌣) f. gelingen III.
Ge-lüst(e) (⌣⌣) [ahd.: *Lust] n ⓐb.(ⓐ) desire or longing (nach et. for a th., after a th.); (starkes Verlangen) hankering after; rel. fleischliches ~ carnal appetite, lust; nach e-r Sache ein ~

[gelüsten] — 426 — [gemeinschaftlich]

haben to long for (or to covet) a th., to have set one's mind upon it.

ge-lüsten (⌣´⌣) [ahd.: list] **I** v/impers.. v/n. (h.) ⑨* es gelüstet mich (oder mir) et. oder eines Gegenstandes nach et., persönlich: ich gelüste (oder ich lasse mich ⚑) nach et. I feel a great (or burning) desire for a th., I long to do (or have) a th.; geh. Spr.: I lust after a th. — **II** ~ n ㉓ = Gelüst(e).

gelzen (⌣´) v/a. ⑨⓪ (verschneiden) to castrate.

ge-mach¹ (⌣´ch) [ahd.] **I** a. ⑥⑥ (meist adv.) slow(ly), (sanft) gentle (gently), soft(ly), (ruhig) quiet(ly), calm(ly); (nur) ⚑! (nicht so hitzig) (do it) gently! keep cool!, F don't flurry yourself; Sprichw. ⚑ geht auch weit slow and steady wins the race; soft and fair goes far.

Ge-mach² [ahd.] n ⓶c., poet. ⓶c. (Stube) room, apartment, kleines: cabinet, closet; (Ankleidezimmer) boudoir; heimliches ~ (Abtritt) privy, water-closet (W. C.)

ge-mächlich (⌣´⌣) [ahd.] a. ⑥⑥ **1.** = gemach¹. — **2.** (Ruhe genießend) easy, at one's ease. — **3.** (Ruhe gewährend) comfortable, convenient, snug; er führt ein ⚑es Leben he leads an easy life, he jogs along comfortably. — **4.** adv. (behaglich) ⚑ an die Arbeit gehen to go leisurely (or slowly, lazily, F lackadaisically) to work.

Ge-mächlichkeit (⌣´⌣⌣) f ㊻ (f. gemächlich) ease; comfort(ableness), convenience; leisure, slowness.

Ge-mächt(e) (⌣´(⌣)) [mhd., ahd.] n ⓶b. ㉒ **1.** F = Genitalien. — **2.** Kocht.: (Fett u. a. Zutaten) dripping (or goodness) for cooking. — **3.** (Vermächtnis) legacy, bequest.

Ge-mahl (⌣´-) [ahd.] m u. (geh. Spr. bes. für ~ in f) n ⓶c, ~in f⁺ feierlich: consort; sonst: spouse, husband, f wife; Ihr Herr ~, Ihre Frau ~in Mr. N., Mrs. N., vertraulich: your husband, wife; your good gentleman, lady.

ge-mahlen (⌣´⌣) p.p. von mahlen.

ge-mahnen (⌣´⌣) [ahd.] v/a. ⑨⑧* mst mit sächlichem Subjekt in geh. Spr.: e-n an et. ⚑ to remind a p. of a th.

Ge-mälde (⌣´-) [ahd.; * malen] n ㉒ painting; picture (auch fig.); (Öl-)~ oil-painting; fig. (Beschreibung) (graphic) description.

Ge-mälde-ausstellung (⌣´⌣⌣⌣) f ㉖ exhibition of paintings; =galerie f picture-gallery; =händler m picture-dealer; =sammlung f collection of paintings or pictures.

Ge-mansche F (⌣´⌣) n ㉒ F mess(ing).

Ge-markung (⌣´⌣) f ㊻ (Grenze) boundary; (Feldmark) landmark.

ge-mäß¹ (⌣-´) [ahd.; * Maß] a. ⑥⑥, meist adv. ob. prp. mit dat. conformable (or agreeable) to; in agreement with; (zufolge) in consequence (or pursuance) of; der Natur ⚑ according to nature; der Vernunft ⚑ handeln to follow the dictates of reason, to act reasonably; der Wahrheit ⚑ truthful(ly); ⚑ Ihren Aufträgen ⚑ in conformity (or compliance) with your orders; vgl. dem⚑, zeit⚑.

Ge-mäß² (⌣-´) n ⓶a. measure(ment).

Ge-mäßheit (⌣-´⌣) f ㊻ conformity; in ⚑ der Sachlage in accordance with the situation, F according as matters stand.

ge-mäßigt (⌣-´⌣) **I** p.p. und a. ⑥⑥ **1.** in den Bed. des inf. mäßigen. — **2.** a. moderate; adv. with moderation; ⚑ ⚑e Zone temperate zone. — **II** ~e(r) m/ f ⑥ ⑦. **3.** mst pl. die ~en the moderates.

Ge-mäuer (⌣-´⌣) n ㉒ **1.** (Mauerwert) masonry. — **2.** altes oder verfallenes ~ old ruins, mouldering (or crumbling, dilapidated) walls pl.

Ge-mecker (⌣´⌣) n ㉒ bleating of goats.

ge-mein (⌣-´) [ahd.: mean: lt. com-mu'nis] **I** a. ⑥⑥ **1.** common, z.B. das ⚑e Recht common law; mit e-m eine ⚑e Sache haben (machen) to make common cause with a p.; der ⚑e Verstand common sense; etwas mit e-m ⚑ haben to have a th. in common with a p.; der Tod ist allen ⚑ death is common to all. — **2.** (allgemein, gewöhnlich) ⚑ ⚑e Ausgaben ordinary expenses pl.; das ⚑e Beste the public weal or welfare; ⚑er Bruch vulgar fraction; ⚑e (ant. heilige) Geschichte profane history; ⚑es Jahr (ant. Schaltjahr) ordinary year; ⚑e Lasten common burdens pl.; im ⚑en Leben in the ordinary course of life, in every-day life, generally; Ausdruck des ⚑en Lebens familiar expression; der ⚑e Mann, das ⚑e Volk the common people or folk, the man in the street; parl. the commonalty; ⚑es Meta'll common (or base) metal; ⚑es Recht common law; ⚑ der ⚑e Soldat, ein ~e(r) m the private soldier, a private; ins⚑ ordinarily, usually, as a rule. — **3.** (niedrig) mean, low, base, F low-class; (pöbelhaft) vulgar, (roh) coarse; von ⚑er Herkunft of low (or humble) origin; ⚑er Kerl, oft: blackguard, ruffian; ⚑es Pack rabble, (vulgar) mob; roughs, hooligans pl. — **4.** ⚑ machen to vulgarize, b.s. to degrade; sich (mit e-m) ⚑ machen (mit ⚑en Leuten umgehen) to keep company with a low set (of people), F to make o.s. (too) common or too cheap. — **II** der ~e(r) m ⑦. **5.** f. 2 ⚑; parl. die ~en pl. Commoners pl.; Engl.: Haus der ⚑en House of Commons. — **III** ~e(s) n ⑥⑦. **6.** (f.3) meanness, lowness; er hat etwas ~es an sich he has s.th. low (or vulgar, common) about him, F he's a low-bred fellow..

Ge-mein-besitz (⌣´⌣⌣) m ㉒ common.

Gemeinde (⌣´⌣) [ahd.] f ㊽ (Genossenschaft) community; bsd. pol. commonalty; Land-, Stadt-~ country-, town-district; parish; in Frankreich etc. commune; städtische ~ municipality, municipal corporation, borough; eccl. congregation, als Bezirk: parish; Mitglied der (Kirchen-)~ member of the congregation, parishioner; der ~ zur Last fallen to come upon the parish.

Gemeinde-acker (⌣´⌣⌣) m ㉒ parish plot or field; municipal plot; =angelegenheit f pa. affair or concern; =anger m common (pasture-land); =auflagen f/pl. local rates pl.; =beamte(r) m pa. officer; =bezirk m parish; municipal district or borough; =glied n member of a community; engS. parishioner; =haus n town-hall; (Armenhaus) parish workhouse; =land n common; =mit-

glied n = ⚑glied; =ordnung f parish (or municipal) by-laws pl.; =rat m: a) parish (or town) councillor; b) coll. parish (or town) council; ebm. vestry; =schreiber m pa. clerk; =schule f parish (or elementary) school; =stier m pa. bull; =unterstützung f pa. relief; =vertreter m representative of a parish; =vertretung f parish board; eccl. vestry; =verwaltung f local administration or board; =vorstand m local board; vgl. =rat b; =vorsteher m chairman of a parish council; vgl. =rat a; =wahlen f/pl. municipal elections pl.; =weg m parish road; =weide, =wiese f village common. [Gemeinde-...]

Ge-meinds-... (⌣´⌣...) ⑥⑥ bsd. schwz. =⚑

Ge-meine¹ (⌣´⌣) f ㊻ eccl. = Gemeinde.

Ge-meine²(r) m, **Ge-meine(s)** (⌣´⌣) n ⑦ f. gemein II und III.

ge-mein-faßlich (⌣-´⌣) a. ⑥⑥ intelligible to all; popular; ⚑gefährlich a. dangerous to the commonwealth; =gefühl n ㉒ =sinn; =geist m public spirit, engS. (fr.) esprit de corps; =gläubiger ⚑ m/pl. creditors pl. of a bankrupt (estate); ⚑gültig a. universally (or generally) accepted; =gut n common estate, public property; das Wissen zum ~ machen to popularize ...

Ge-meinheit (⌣-´⌣) f ㊻ meanness, lowness; baseness; vulgarity; coarseness; stärker: blackguardism; als einzelne Handlung: mean, &c. act; F dirty trick.

ge-mein-hin (⌣-´⌣) adv. commonly, ordinarily, generally (speaking).

ge-meiniglich (⌣-´⌣⌣) adv. commonly, usually, vgl. gemeinhin.

ge-mein-nützig (⌣-´⌣...) a. ⑥⑥ of general utility or use; beneficial to all; =nützigkeit f ㊻, =nützlichkeit f public utility, general usefulness; =platz (T) [nhd. (W.1770)] m commonplace (expression); truism, platitude; ⚑rechtlich a. based upon common law.

ge-meinsam (⌣-´⌣) a. ⑥⑥ joint; ⚑e Sache machen mit // to make common cause with //, to act conjointly with //, to throw in one's lot with //; ⚑e Verpflichtung joint liability; ~keit f ㊻ joint (or united) action; vgl. Gemeinschaft.

ge-mein-schädlich (⌣-´⌣...) a. ⑥⑥ injurious to the commonwealth; prejudicial to all or to the public welfare.

Ge-meinschaft (⌣-´⌣) [ahd.] f ㊻ **1.** der Güter, Interessen etc.: community of property, interests, &c.; brüderliche ~ confraternity; ~ der Gefühle congeniality, harmony; eccl. ~ der Gläubigen communion (or congregation) of the faithful; ~ der Heiligen communion of saints. — **2.** (Verbindung, Verkehr) connexion; intercourse, companionship, (good) fellowship; commerce; mit e-m ~ haben to be in communication (or F touch) with a p.; zu ~ be connected with a p.; in ~ mit // jointly (or together, in common) with //.

ge-meinschaftlich (⌣-´⌣⌣) a. ⑥⑥ common, joint; adv. in common (or jointly, conjointly, in company, in concert) with; ⚑er Besitz joint property; auf ⚑e Kosten, für ⚑e Rechnung for joint account; ⚑er Freund mutual friend; ⚑e

Signs (see page XVII): F familiar; P vulgar; ⚑ flash; ⚑ rare; † obsolete (died); * new word (born); ⚑ incorrect; ♪ music;

[Gemeinschuld] — 427 — [genau]

Sache common cause; f. gemeinsam; adv. sich 2 in et. teilen to share equally or alike; et. 2 tun to do a th. jointly or by combined efforts.

Ge-mein=schuld ⊕ (⌣⌣...) f ⑫ bankrupt('s) estate; =**schuldner** ⊕ m bankrupt; =**sinn** m: a) =**geist**; b) (gesunder Menschenverstand) common sense; 2**verständlich** a. intelligible to the common folk; popular (lecture &c.); =**wesen** n commonwealth, the community (at large); =**wohl** n common (or public) weal or good.

Ge-menge (⌣⌣) n ⑫ 1. (das Mengen) mixing, mingling; ✕ (Hand=)~ hand-to-hand fight, affray, fray of battle. — 2. (Gemengtes) mixture (a. chm. Glasm. frit; vgl. Gemengsel. [seed(ing).)

Ge-meng=saat (⌣⌣⌣) f ⓐ agr. mixed

Ge-mengsel (⌣⌣) n ⑫ (strange) medley of colours, &c.; odd mixture, hodge-podge; (Durcheinander) heap of confusion.

ge-messen (⌣⌣) p.p u. a. ⑥ (D 9) 1. in den Bed. des inf. messen. — 2. (genau bestimmt) strict (injunction), express (order), measured (step), slow (pace); thoughtful (speech), grave (dignity); 2es (feierliches) Wesen formal (or reserved) manner, stately demeanour or deportment; mit 2en Worten in dignified words.

Ge-messenheit (⌣⌣⌣) f ⓐ (f. gemessen) strictness, precision, gravity; (Feierlichkeit) formality, reservedness, stateliness, dignified manner.

Ge-metzel (⌣⌣) n ⑫ carnage; (Abschlachten, bsd. von Wehrlosen) butchery, slaughter; (Blutbad) massacre.

ge-mieden (⌣⌣) p.p. von meiden.

Ge-misch (⌣⌣) n ⓐ a. (Mischen u. Gemischtes) mixture; chm. und mint. von Metallen: ⚗ alligation. — Vgl. Gemenge.

ge-mischt (⌣⌣) p.p. u. a. ⑥ f. mischen III; 2=**linig** a. geom.: ⚗ mixtilineal, mixtilinear (figure). [stein) gem.

Gemme (⌣⌣) [It.] f ⓐ (geschnittener Edel-

Gemmen-abdruck (⌣⌣...) m ⑫, =**abguß** m paste; =**beschreibung** f: ⚗ glyptography, dactyliography; =**funde** f: ⚗ dactyliology; =**kundige(r)**, =**liebhaber** m connoisseur of gems, lapidary, lapidarist; ⚗ dactyliographer.

ge-mocht (⌣⌣) p.p. von mögen.

ge-molken (⌣⌣) p.p. von melken.

Ge-morde (⌣⌣) n ⑫ wholesale murder, continued butchery or slaughter.

Gems=ballen (⌣...) m ⑫ German bezoar; =**bart** m chamois-beard; =**blume** ⚘ f = Wohlverleih; =**bock** m ch.-buck, ⚥ gems-bock. [alpine goat (Rupi'capra tragus).

Gemse (⌣⌣) [ahd.] f ⑱ zo. chamois,

Gemsen=jäger (⌣⌣...) m ⑫, =**steiger** m chamois-hunter.

Gems=haut (⌣...) f ⑫ =**leber**; =**horn** n chamois-horn; =**jagd** f ch.-hunting; =**jäger** m ch.-hunter; =**leber** n ch.-leather or -skin; ⊕ auch: shammy; =**ziege** f doe of the chamois.

Ge-müll (⌣⌣) n ⓐ b. rubbish, refuse.

Ge-munkel (⌣⌣) n ⑫ (dark) whispering pl., mysterious rumour or report.

Ge-murmel (⌣⌣) n ⑫ murmur(ing), muttering, buzz(ing) of voices.

Ge-murre (⌣⌣) n ⑫ muttering, (loud) grumbling, murmurs pl., Fgrowling.

Ge-müse (⌣⌣) [mhd.; * Mus] n ⑫ vegetables, greens pl., F green stuff; (Suppenkräuter) pot-herbs pl.

Ge-müse=bau (⌣⌣...) m ⑫ growing (or cultivation) of vegetables, ⚗ olericulture; (Handelsgärtnerei) market-gardening; =**beet** n vegetable-bed; =**gänsedistel** ⚘ f milk-weed (Sonchus olera'ceus); =**garten** m kitchen-garden; =**gärtner** m market-gardener; =**händler(in** f) m green-grocer; als Straßenhändler: costermonger; =**pflanzen** ⚘ f/pl. vegetables, ⚗ oleraceous plants pl.; =**schüssel** f vegetable-dish; =**suppe** f Kochkunst: vegetable- (or spring-) soup, (soup à la) julienne.

ge-müßigt (⌣⌣) [p.p. von müßigen] compelled; sich 2 sehen, et. zu tun to see o.s. obliged to do a th., to find o.s. under the necessity of doing a th.

ge-mußt (⌣⌣) p.p. von müssen.

Ge-mut (⌣⌣) [mhd.] a. ⑥ f. wohl2.

Ge-müt (⌣⌣) [ahd.; * Mut m] n ④c. 1. (Gefühl; Seele) feeling; soul; (Herz) heart; gut von ~ sein, ein gutes ~ haben to be good-natured or kind-hearted; er ist ganz ~ he is full of feeling or all sentiment; Mensch ohne ~ person without (any) feeling; Mensch von ~ person with (kindly) feeling; vgl. Gemütsmensch; sein ~ erleichtern to ease (or disburden) one's mind. — 2. (Sinnesart) disposition, turn of mind; heiteres (finsteres) Gemüt bright (gloomy) disposition; liebreiches ~ lovable nature; von sanftem ~ of gentle disposition, mild-tempered. — 3. die Gemüter pl. (Menschen) the minds of men. — 4. e-m etwas zu ~e führen (ans Herz legen) to bring a th. home to a p., to urge a th. (strongly) upon a p.('s consideration), to impress a th. on a p.; sich (dat.) et. zu ~e führen ob. ziehen: a) (es beherzigen) to take a th. to heart; stärker: to sink it deep into one's soul; b) F co. (es sich aneignen, verzehren) to appropriate (F to grab) a th.; to devour (F to gobble up) a th.; sich eine Flasche Wein zu ~e führen to empty (F to discuss, to negotiate) a bottle of wine.

ge-mütlich (⌣⌣) (als echt deutsches Wort nur annähernd übersetzbar) I a. ⑥ 1. von Orten u. Dingen: (behaglich) comfortable; cozy, snug; (heimlich) homely; (angenehm) pleasant; ein 2es Eckchen F a snuggery; in der Kneipe war es recht 2 F... it was very jolly; es war mir dort nicht recht 2 I did not feel quite at my ease (or at home) there; bei einer 2en Tasse Kaffee over a cozy (or quiet) cup of coffee. — 2. von Personen: agreeable, easy-going, sociable, jovial, kindly disposed; 2e Menschen homely people, good-natured folk pl.; ein 2er Kerl F a jolly good fellow; F (nur) immer 2! don't lose your temper!, don't get angry!, be gentle! — 3. (voll Gemüt) full of (kind) feeling; (gedankenvoll) full of (deep) thought; 2e Dichtung sentimental poetry. — II ~e[r] m f ⑰ 4. sociable (or jovial) person; vgl. 2.

Ge-mütlichkeit (⌣⌣⌣) f ⓐ (f. gemütlich 1 und 2) comfort; coziness, snugness;

homeliness; ease, sociability, joviality, kind disposition, good nature.

ge-müt=los (⌣⌣) a. ⑥ unfeeling, devoid of feeling or sentiment; =**losigkeit** f ⓐ unfeelingness, want of feeling or sentiment, insensibility.

ge-müts=arm (⌣⌣) a. ⑥ lacking (or devoid of) feeling or heart; =**art** f ⑫, =**beschaffenheit** f mental constitution, disposition; (Stimmung) temper; vgl. Gemüt 2; =**bewegung** f, stärker: (Affekt) excitement; 2**krank** a. diseased in mind; (schwermütig) melancholy; (wahnsinnig) insane; =**krankheit** f mental disorder; (Schwermut) melancholy; (Geistesstörung) insanity; =**lage** f frame of mind; =**leben** n inner life; =**mensch** m person of deep feeling or thought; =**neigung** f natural inclination; =**regung** f = =**bewegung**; =**ruhe** f calmness, evenness of temper, peace of mind, serenity; =**stimmung**, =**verfassung** f condition (or frame) of mind; mood, humour; sentiment; =**unruhe** f disturbed state of mind, uneasiness, anxiety; =**zustand** m state of mind, mental condition, disposition.

ge-müt=voll (⌣⌣) a. ⑥ full of feeling or sentiment; tender-hearted.

gen † (⌣) [mhd. zsgs. aus gegen] prp. mit acc., oft poet. ob. bibl., in hochd. Prosa nur mit s. ohne art., z.B. 2 Himmel to(wards) heaven, heavenward.

Ge-nage (⌣⌣) n ⑫ constant gnawing.

Ge-nähe (⌣⌣) n ⑫ endless sewing.

ge-nannt (⌣⌣) p.p. von nennen.

genant (q⌣⌣) [fr. gênant] a. ⑥ (genierlich) inconvenient, troublesome, awkward.

ge-nas (⌣⌣) ind. impf. v. genesen.

ge-näschig (⌣⌣) a. ⑥ fond of dainties.

ge-näse (⌣⌣) subj. impf. v. genesen.

ge-nau (⌣⌣) [mhd.; * Not] a. ⑥ 1. exact. accurate, (pünktlich) precise, punctual; (streng) strict, rigorous, (sorgfältig) careful; 2 bewachen to look well (or sharp) after; er ist ängstlich (ober peinlich) 2, er nimmt es sehr 2 he is very (or exceedingly) particular or scrupulous, he is painfully exact; wir sind 2e Bekannte, ich kenne ihn 2 we are intimate friends, I know him intimately or very well; 2e Nachsuchung close search; 2este(r) Preis lowest price; nach 2er Überlegung after mature (or careful) consideration; 2e Unterscheidung nice distinction; 2e Zeichnung accurate drawing; adv.: 2 dasselbe just the same, the very same thing; 2 so viel als // just as much as //; etwas 2 berechnen to make a close calculation of a th.; er nimmt es nicht 2 he is not very particular or exact(ing), he is easy-going or lenient or lax; 2 genommen strictly speaking, et. 2 kennen to know a th. thoroughly; 2 mit dem Glockenschlage at the (very) stroke of the clock; 2 um vier Uhr at four o'clock precisely, F at four sharp. — 2. (ins einzelne gehend) minute, in detail; ein 2er Bericht a detailed (or circumstantial) account; ich habe ihm alles ganz 2 (adv.) erzählt I told him everything minutely, I gave him full particulars; et. aufs 2este untersuchen to investigate a th. most minutely or

---

⚗ scientific; ⚘ botanical; ⚱ geography; ⊕ machinery; ⚒ mining; ⚔ military; ⚓ marine; ● commercial; ✉ postal; 🚂 railway.

[Genauigkeit] — 428 — [Geniesoldat]

closely, to go to the (very) root (or foundation) of a th. — 3. (sich eng anschließend) closely fitting; adv. zu 2 anliegen to fit (too) tightly. — 4. (knapp) barely sufficient; mit der Not with great difficulty, barely, F by the skin of one's teeth; mit der Not entkommen to have a hairbreadth (or narrow) escape. — 5. (sparsam) economical, sparing, stärker: parsimonious; (geizig) niggardly, mean, close-fisted, near. — II adv. 6. f. 1, 2, 3.

Ge-nauigkeit (⌣⌣⌣-) f ⓥ (f. genau) exactness, accuracy; precision, punctuality, strictness, rigour; nicety; (Sparsamkeit) economy, parsimony.

Gendarm (Gₐ-bä'rm) [fr.] m ⓥ police-soldier; (fr.) gendarme; **~erie** (Gₐ⌣⌣) f ⓥ military police-force; (fr.) gendarmery.

Genealog, **~e** ⌐ (⌣⌣⌣(⌣) [grch.] m ⓥ, ⓥ (Stammbaumkenner) genealogist; **~ie** (⌣⌣⌣⌣) f ⓥ (Geschlechtskunde) genealogy; **Lisch** (⌣⌣⌣⌣) a. ⓥ genealogic(al).

Ge-necke (⌣⌣⌣) [necken] n ⓥ (constant) teasing or chaffing.

ge-nehm (⌣⌣) [ahd.:* nehmen] a. ⓥ agreeable; (willkommen) welcome; (passend) fitting, suitable; ihm ist alles 2 he agrees with (or to) everything; wenn es Ihnen 2 ist if such be your pleasure, if (it be) convenient (or agreeable) to you.

ge-nehmigen (⌣⌣⌣⌣) I v/a. ⓥ* 1. et. Angebotenes: to agree (or assent) to, to approve of, to allow. — 2. eine Bitte: to accede to, to grant; einen Vorschlag: to accept; to sanction; einen Vertrag ꝛc. 2 (bestätigen und vollziehen) to ratify … — II ~ n ⓥ und **Ge-nehmigung** f ⓥ 3. agreement, assent, approval; accession to; acceptance of; ratification; acknowledgment; mit (ohne) ~ ihrer Eltern with (without) the consent (or permission) of her parents; in ~ Ihres Abschiedsgesuches // in accepting your resignation //.

ge-neigt (⌣⌣) p.p. und a. ⓥ 1. in den Bedeut. des inf. neigen. — 2. (abschüssig) inclined, sloping, on the incline. — 3. fig. (wohlwollend) well disposed (or favourably inclined) towards; (huldvoll) gracious; um Les Gehör bitten to ask for a patient hearing; e-m Les Gehör schenken to lend a willing ear to a p. — 4. zu et. 2 subject (or liable, prone) to do a th.; b.s. addicted (or given) to drinking, &c.; er ist 2 nachzugeben he feels inclined (or is willing) to give way.

Ge-neigt-heit (⌣⌣-) f ⓥ (zu geneigt 2:) incline, slope; (zu 3:) kind disposition (or inclination) towards; favour; willingness; (zu 4:) proneness, b.s. addictedness, propensity; vgl. Hang.

General (⌣⌣⌣) [nhd. 16. sae., * fr.] m ⓥ⑦d., **~in** f ⓥ general (a. Oberhaupt e-s religiösen Ordens); Kommandierender ~ general in command (or at the head) of a force; **~in** f general's wife.

General-adjuta'nt (⌣⌣⌣…) ⱴ m ⓥ adjutant-general; **agent** magent-general (auch Titel des Vertreters e-r englischen Kolonie in London); **=arzt** ⱴ m surgeon-general.

Generalat ⱴ (⌣⌣⌣-) [it.] n ⓥc. (Würde, Rang) generalship; (Bezirk) a general's district of inspection.

General-baß (⌣⌣⌣…) m ⓥ thorough-bass; **=befehl** ⱴ m general order; **=beichte** f eccl. general confession; **=bevollmächtigte(r)** m chief representative or delegate; **=bila'nz** ⓥ f annual balance; **=direktor** m chief (or head) manager; ⓥ general manager; **=feldmarschall** ⱴ m field-marshal-general; **=feldzeug-meister** ⱴ m in England seit 1904: Master-General of the Ordnance; **=fiska'l** m attorney-gen.; **=gouverneu'r** m governor-general (a. Titel eines engl. Vizekönigs, abbr.: Gov. Gen.).

Generalin (⌣⌣⌣) f. General am Schluß.

General-inspekteur ⱴ (⌣⌣⌣…) m ⓥ inspector-general; **=intenda'nt** m: a) thea. head (or chief) manager; b) ⱴ head of the commissariat; commissary-general.

generalisieren (⌣⌣⌣⌣⌣⌣) [fr.] v/a., v/n. (h.) ⓥ (allgemeine Schlüsse ziehen) to generalize.

Generalissimus ⱴ (⌣⌣⌣⌣⌣) [it.] m ⓥ⑪ od. ⓥ Commander-in-Chief, ehm. a. Generalissimo.

Generalität (⌣⌣⌣⌣) [it.] f ⓥ 1. (Allgemeinheit) generality. — 2. ⱴ (Gesamtheit der Generale) body (or staff) of generals.

General-karte (⌣⌣⌣…) f ⓥ general map; **=kommando** ⱴ n chief command; **=konsul** m consul-gen.; **=kriegs-zahlmeister** m paymaster-gen.; **=leutnant** ⱴ m lieutenant-gen.; **=majo'r** ⱴ m major-gen.; **=marsch** ⱴ m: ~ schlagen (Alarm) to beat the general; **=nenner** m arith. least common denominator (abbr. L. C. D.); Brüche unter den ~ bringen to bring (or reduce) fractions to the L. C. D.; **=pardo'n** m general amnesty or pardon; **=probe** f, thea. dress-rehearsal; **=quartiermeister** m (österr.) quartermaster-general.

Generalschaft ⱴ (⌣⌣⌣⌣) f ⓥ 1. generalship. — 2. = Generalität 2.

Generals-rang (⌣⌣⌣…) m rank, dignity of a general; generalship.

General-staaten (⌣⌣⌣…) m/pl. ehm. (Niederlande) States-General; **=stab** ⱴ m (general) staff; **=stabs-arzt** m in England director-general of the medical department; **=stabs-karte** f ordnance-map; **=stabs-offizier** m staff-officer; **=stabs-werk** n work composed by a general staff; **=superintendent** m, eccl. superintendent general.

Generals-würde ⱴ (⌣⌣⌣…) f ⓥ = =rang.

General-truppen-inspektor ⱴ öft. (⌣⌣…) m ⓥ in Engl.: Inspector General (of the Army); **=versammlung** f gen. assembly; **=vollmacht** f jur. gen. power of attorney.

Generation (⌣⌣-tʃ(⌣)ɪ) [it.] f ⓥ (Geschlecht (folge), Menschenalter) generation; **~s-wechsel** m, zo.: ⌐ metagenesis.

generell (⌣⌣⌣) [it.] a. ⓥ (allg..) general; (ausnahmslos) universal.

generisch ⌐ (⌣⌣⌣) [it.] a. ⓥ (zu einer Art gehörig, dieselbe betreffend) generic.

generös (⌣⌣⌣) [fr.] a. ⓥ (freigebig, großmütig) generous; **Generosität** (⌣⌣⌣⌣) [fr. u. lt.] f ⓥ generosity.

ge-nesen (⌣⌣) [ahd.] I v/n. (fn.) ⓥ b.* (p.p. 2) 1. von e-r Krankheit 2 to recover from an illness, to regain one's health (and strength), to be restored (to health), to get better; er fängt an zu 2 he is beginning to mend or on the road to convalescence. — 2. eines Kindes 2 to be delivered of (or to give birth to) a child. — II. ~ n ⓥ 3. = Genesung. — III 2d p.pr. u. a. ⓥ, **~de(r)** m f ⓥ 4. convalescent.

Genesis ⌐ (⌣⌣⌣) [grch.] f (sg. inv., pl. …ses) (Entstehungsgeschichte) genesis; (bibl.: 1. Buch Mosis, Geschichte der Schöpfung) (Book of) Genesis.

Ge-nesung (⌣⌣⌣) f ⓥ recovery, restoration to health; langsame ~ convalescence; auf dem Wege der ~ on the (or in a fair) way of recovery; **~s-haus**, **=heim** (⌣…) n ⓥ convalescent home.

genetisch ⌐ (⌣⌣⌣) [grch.] a. ⓥ (zur Zeugung gehörig) genetic, adv. genetically.

Genetiv (⌣⌣-) [it.] ⓥd. = Genitiv.

Genette (Gⱴ⌣⌣) [fr., * ar.], a. **Genett-katze** (Gⱴ⌣⌣⌣) f ⓥ zo. genet (Vive'rra gene'tta).

ge-neu(e)s)t † (⌣⌣) pres. v. geniesen.

Genever (Gⱴ⌣w) [ndl.; *fr. genièvre (lt. juni'perus)] m ⓥ (Wacholderbranntwein) gin, feiner, holl.: ⓥ hollands.

Genezareth ⓥ (⌣⌣⌣⌣) [hebr.] npr/n ⓥa. bibl. See ~ Lake of Gennesaret, Sea of Galilee.

Genf ⓥ (⌣) npr/n. ⓥa. (Stadt und Kanton in der Schweiz) Geneva.

Genfer (⌣⌣) I m ⓥ, **~in** f ⓥ Genevese, inhabitant of Geneva. — II a. inv. (auch **Lisch** ⓥ) Genevese, (of) Geneva; ~ See Lake of Geneva, auch: Lake Leman; ~ Konferenz, Konvention f Geneva Conference, Convention.

genial (⌣(⌣)ɪ) [fr.], fast † **Lisch** a. ⓥ full of genius, gifted, ingenious.

Genialität (⌣(⌣)⌣⌣) [fr.-lt.] f ⓥ genius, giftedness; geniality.

Ge-nick (⌣⌣) [mhd.; * nicken, Nacken] n ⓥc. nape, back (F scruff) of the neck; (Hals) neck; (sich dat.) das ~ brechen to break one's neck.

Ge-nick-brechen (⌣⌣…) n ⓥ breaking one's neck; **=drüse** f cervical gland.

Ge-nicke (⌣⌣) n ⓥ (wiederholtes Nicken) repeated (or frequent) nodding.

Ge-nick-fang (⌣⌣…) m ⓥ hunt. stab in the neck (with a hunting-knife); **=fänger** m (Sagdmesser) hunting-knife, hanger; **=schmerz** m pain in the nape or neck; **=starre** f, path. cerebrospinal meningitis.

Genie (Gⱴ⌣) [fr. génie] n ⓥ 1. genius (pl. …es); Mann von ~ man of genius, F a perfect genius; was für ein ~ (Mensch) ist er denn? F what kind of a genius is he really?; b.s. liederliches, sonderbares ~ fast, queer fellow. — 2. ⱴ (Ingenieurkorps) the engineers pl.

Genie-korps ⱴ (Gⱴ⌣…) n ⓥ corps (or regiment) of engineers.

Geni-en (⌣⌣⌣) pl. von Genius.

genieren (ⱴGⱴ⌣) [fr. gêner] v/a. u. sich 2 v/refl. ⓥ (belästigen) to molest, trouble, inconvenience, incommode, bother; sich nicht 2 (nicht Anstand nehmen), et. zu tun not to mind (F to make no bones about) doing a th.; er geniert sich, sie anzureden he is too timid (F doesn't like) to speak to her; 2 Sie sich nicht! don't stand on ceremony!, make yourself (wenn mehrere: yourselves) at home!, F co. don't be bashful!

Genie-soldat ⱴ (Gⱴ⌣…) m ⓥ engineer.

[Genieß] — 429 — [Georgel]

Ge-nieß† (⌣⌣́) [mhd.] m ①a. = Genuß.
ge-nießbar (⌣⌣́⌣) a. ⑥⑥ enjoyable; relishable, palatable, savoury; (erträglich) tolerable; (lesbar) readable; (eßbar, trinkbar) eatable, drinkable; das Fleisch ist nicht mehr 2 the meat is uneatable or no longer fit to eat; **~keit** (⌣⌣⌣́) f ⑥⑥ enjoyable nature of a th.; relish, palatableness, savouriness; bisw.: eatableness.
ge-nießen (⌣⌣́⌣) [ahd.; *Nutz(en)] v/a. ⑤d* 1. to enjoy; von et. 2 to taste a th.; langsam, recht 2 to relish; Speise und Trank 2 (zu sich nehmen) to eat and drink, to partake of some refreshment or of food; nicht zu 2(d) unpalatable, unsavoury; (unerträglich) intolerable. — 2. er hat eine gute Erziehung genossen he has received (F had) a good education; 🟡 guten Kredit 2 to enjoy (or have) a good credit.
ge-nießlich (⌣⌣́⌣) a. ⑥⑥ enjoyable.
Ge-nießling (⌣⌣́⌣) m ①d. sensualist.
Genie-streich (ɢⱼ⌢⌣...) m ⑥⑥ stroke of genius; iro. stupid (or ridiculous, foolish) act(ion). F silly thing to do; **-truppe** ⚔ f (military) engineers pl.; **-wesen** ⚔ n military engineering.
Ge-nippe¹ (⌣⌣́) n ㉒ = nippen II.
Ge-nist(e) (⌣⌣́(⌣)) [mhd.; *Nest] n ①b. (㉒) 1. ohne pl. nest-building; hatching. — 2. mit pl. (Gestrüpp) brushwood, underwood; (Zweige) twigs, boughs pl.; (Abfall von Stroh ꝛc.) sweepings, straws pl., refuse.
Genitali-en (⌣⌣⌣́(⌣)⌣) [lt.] pl. inv. (Geschlechtsteile) genital organs or parts, genitals pl.
Genitiv (⌣́⌣⌣) [lt. geněti'vus] m ①d., auch: **~us** (⌣⌣́⌣⌣) m ⑬ gr. (Besitzfall, Wesfall) genitive, possessive case.
Genius (⌣́⌣⌣) [lt.] m ㉗ myth. genius (pl. genii); in Märchen auch: sg. genii; guter **~** tutelary deity; vgl. Schutzengel.
ge-nommen (⌣⌣́⌣) p.p. von nehmen.
Ge-noß¹ (⌣⌣́) impf. v. genießen.
Ge-noß² (⌣⌣́) [ahd. Mitgenießender] m ㊷, **Ge-nosse** (⌣⌣́⌣) m ㊹, **Ge-nossin** f ㊼ (male, female) companion, associate, mate, comrade; Sozialismus: member of a socialist union or club; (Amts=) ~ colleague; (Partei=) ~ partisan; (Spießgeselle) confederate; (Helfershelfer) accomplice; abettor; 🟡 die Herren Armstrong ꝛc. Genossen Messrs. A., W., & Co. (= Company); (Geschäfts=) partner; * co. die Genossen the Socialists pl. **I** (⌣⌣⌣) p.p. von genießen.
ge-nösse¹ (⌣⌣́⌣) subj. impf., **ge-nossen**
Ge-nossenschaft (⌣⌣́⌣⌣) f ㊻ company, association; fellowship; party; confederacy; engl. S.: co-operative society; 🟡 (Handels=) ~ partnership; syndicate, F ring; stille ~ sleeping partnership; eingetrag(e)ne ~ registered association or company; **~er** m ㉒ partner.
ge-nossenschaftlich (⌣⌣́⌣⌣⌣) a. ⑥⑥ referring (or belonging) to an association.
Ge-nossenschafts-bank (⌣⌣́⌣⌣...) f ... joint-stock bank; **-gesellschaft** f co-operative society; **-register** n register of public companies; **-vertrag** m partnership deed; **-wesen** n co-operative trading- system. [Geneviève.|
Genoveva (⌣⌣⌣́f⌣) npr/f. ㊻ ⑤①α. ㊴ ㊾ß.]

Genre (ɢₐ'r) [fr.] n ㊿: **~bild** (⌣́...) n ⑥② picture representing every-day life or family-scenes, von leblosen Gegenständen auch: still-life; **~maler(in** f) m (**~malerei** f), etwa: painter (painting) of family-life; a. genre-painter (painting). [Stadt in Belgien] Ghent.)
Gent ♀ (⌣́) npr/n. ⑤α. (alte flämische
Genua ♀ (⌣́⌣⌣) [it.] npr/n. ⑤α. (alte it. Hafenstadt) Genoa; **Genu-eser(in** f) m ㉒ u. **genu-esisch** a. ⑥⑥ Genoese.
ge-nug (⌣́, ⌣́) [ahd.: enough] adv. 1. enough; 2 Gutes, Gutes 2 plenty of enough good things or deeds pl.; Wein 2, 2 Wein, des Weines 2 wine enough, sufficient (or plenty of) wine; ist nicht Manns 2 dafür? is he not man enough to do it?; das war ihm nicht 2 that did not satisfy him; 2 der Tränen! no more tears!; an einem ist schon 2 one is quite enough. — 2. Redewendungen: wir haben daran 2 we want no more of it; 2 davon! let it suffice!, no more of this!, F that will do!; ich habe 2 davon (bin es müde) I have enough (or am tired) of it; der hat 2 he has his full share or as much as he can carry or bear; wir haben 2 zu leben ... enough (F plenty) to live upon; es ist nicht 2, daß man ehrlich handelt it is not sufficient to act honestly; laß dir das 2 sein! let this be enough!; lasset 2 sein des grausamen Spieles let this cruel sport now end!; Sprichw. 2 ist besser als viel enough is as good as a feast. — 3. nicht 2, daß er sie lobte, sondern // not only did he praise her, but // ; man kann es nicht 2 bewundern it cannot be too much admired. — 4. f. genugtun. — 5. als int.: 2! enough!, stop!; 2, ich kann nicht! suffice it to say (or in short), I cannot (do it)!
Ge-nüge (⌣⌣́⌣) [ahd.; *genug] f ㊽ (auch n ㉒) (ohne pl.) 1. sufficiency; zur ~ sufficiently, enough, F a. plenty; er hat es zur ~ erfahren daß // he has richly (or fully, abundantly) experienced that //; e-n, et. zur ~ kennen to know a p., a th. well. — 2. Sie sollen Ihr ~ haben (befriedigt werden)! you shall be satisfied or have your full share!; e-m ~ tun to do a p. justice, to give a p. satisfaction; den gestellten Anforderungen ~ leisten to come up to the mark, to have the necessary qualifications; dem Gesetze ꝛc. ~ tun od. leisten to comply with ...
ge-nügen (⌣⌣́⌣) [ahd.; *genug] ⑧* **I** v/n. (h.) 1. (genug sein) to suffice; das genügt that's enough. — 2. das wird ihm 2 (ihn befriedigen) that will satisfy him. — 3. ich lasse mir et. (od. an et.) 2 (begnüge mich damit) I content myself (or rest content) with a th. — **II ~** n ㉓ 4. = Genüge. — **III** 2d p.pr. und a. ⑥⑥ 5. (befriedigend) satisfactory; als Zensur der Schüler, etwa: fair; ein 2des Auskommen (an income) sufficient to live upon, a competency.
ge-nüglich (⌣⌣́⌣) n. ⑥⑥ sufficient; vgl. genügsam; **~keit** (⌣⌣⌣́) f ⑥⑥ sufficiency; vgl. Genügsamkeit.

ge-nugsam (⌣⌣́⌣) [genug] a. ⑥⑥ sufficient, sufficing; als adv. = genug 1.
ge-nügsam (⌣⌣́⌣) [genügen] a. ⑥⑥ content, easily satisfied or pleased; (mäßig) sober, frugal, temperate; (gemäßigt) moderate; er ist sehr 2 (in seinen Ansprüchen) he is very unpretentious; **~keit** (⌣⌣⌣́) f ⑥⑥ contentment; sobriety, frugality, temperance; moderation; Sprichw. ~keit geht über Reichtum contentment is better than riches.
ge-nug-tun (⌣⌣́...) v/n. ⑨⑤**: e-m 2 to give (e-m Beleidigten: to render) a p. satisfaction; **2tuend** a. ⑥⑥ satisfactory, giving satisfaction; **-tuung** (⌣⌣⌣́) f ㊻ satisfaction; für eine Beleidigung: reparation; (Sühne) atonement; ~ fordern to demand reparation; e-m ~ geben to make a p. reparation (für et. for s.th.); e-m zur ~ gereichen to give a p. satisfaction or pleasure; sich (dat.) von e-m ~ verschaffen to obtain one's rights from a p., to set o.s. right with a p.
Genus (⌣́⌣) [lt. Geschlecht] n (sg. inv., pl. Ge'nera) bsd. gram. gender.
Ge-nuß (⌣⌣́) [erst mhd. 18 sae. für † Genieß] m ⑧a. 1. enjoyment; der Sinne: gratification, indulgence; hoher ~ delight, F (a rare) treat; Genüsse des Lebens pleasures pl. of life; ~der politischen Rechte enjoyment (or possession) of political rights; mit ~ essen, trinken, sehen ꝛc. to enjoy. — 2. ~ von Speisen (eccl. des Abendmahls) ꝛc. partaking of food (of the Lord's Supper), &c.
genuß-fähig (⌣⌣́...) a. ⑥⑥ capable of enjoyment; **-mensch** m ㊷ man of pleasure, sensualist, epicure(an); F fast liver; **-mittel** n means of enjoyment, pl. auch: luxuries (of life); **2reich** a. full of e., enjoyable; **-sucht** f (inordinate) love of (or desire for) enjoyment or pleasure, sensuality; **2süchtig** a. fond of (or eager after) enjoyment, pleasure-seeking, sensual; **-süchtige(r)** man, woman (fond) of pleasure, epicurean, sensualist.
Geo-däsie ⚓ (-⌣-⌣́) [grch.] f ㊽ (Erdmessung) geodesy; **geo-dätisch** (-⌣⌣́⌣) a. ⑥⑥ geodetic, geodetical.
Geo-gnosie ⚓ (-⌣-⌣́) [grch.] f ㊽ (Gesteinkunde) geognosy.
Geo-gnost ⚓ (-⌣⌣́) m ㊷ geognost; 2isch a. ⑥⑥ geognostic(al).
Geo-graph (-⌣⌣́f) m ㊷ geographer; **~ie** (-⌣⌣⌣́) f ㊽ (Erdbeschreibung) geography; **2isch** a. (-⌣⌣́⌣) ⑥⑥ geographical.
ge-ohrt, ge-öhrt (⌣⌣́) a. ⑥⑥ provided with ears, eared; ♀ ⚓ auriculate(d).
Geo-log ⚓ **~e** (-⌣⌣́) [grch.] m ㊷, ㊹ geologist; **~ie** (-⌣⌣⌣́) f ㊽ (Lehre von der Erdbildung) geology; **2isch** (-⌣⌣́⌣) a. ⑥⑥ geological.
Geo-mant ⚓ (-⌣⌣́) [grch.] m ㊷ geomancer; **~ie** (-⌣⌣⌣́) f ㊽ (Punktierkunst) geomancy; **2isch** (-⌣⌣́⌣) a. ⑥⑥ geomantic(al).
Geo-meter (-⌣⌣́⌣) m ㊷ geometrician; (Feldmesser) surveyor; **-metrie** (-⌣⌣⌣́) f ㊽ (Raumlehre) geometry, als Schulfach a. Euclid; **geo-metrisch** (-⌣⌣́⌣) a. ⑥⑥ geometrical; 2es Zeichen geometrical drawing. [(Vn.) George.]
Georg (-⌣́) [grch. Landmann] npr/m. ⑬ ⑯α.]
Ge-orgel (⌣⌣́⌣) n ㉒ = Orgelei.

♪ Musik; ⚛ Wissenschaft; ⚘ Pflanze; ♀ Geographie; ⊙ Technik; ⚒ Bergbau; ⚔ Militär; ⚓ Marine; 🟡 Handel; ✉ Post; 🚂 Eisenbahn.

[Georgien] — 430 — [geraten]

Georgi-en ♀ (-⌣⌣⌣) [pers. (P: Georg, Schutzheiliger)] npr/n. ㉓α. (russ. Gouvernement) Georgia; **Georgi-er(in** f ㊼) m ㉒ (-⌣(⌣)⌣) Georgian, Grusian.
Georgine¹ (-⌣⌣⌣) [Georg] npr/f. ㊷ ẞ. (Bn.) Georgi(a)na.
Georgine² ♀ (-⌣⌣⌣) [Georgi, Prof. in Petersburg] f ㊸ dahlia, georgine (*Da'hlia* ob. *Georgi'na varia'bilis*).
ge-paart (⌣⌣) p.p. v. paaren; (arranged) in pairs, paired, ♀: ♋ geminate; **~heit** f ㊻ arrangement in pairs.
Ge-päck (⌣⌣) n ⓑc. luggage, ⚔ baggage; mit sämtlichem ~ with bag and baggage.
Ge-päck-abfertigung (⌣⌣...) f ㉒ dispatch of luggage; **=annahme, =aufnahme** f luggage- (or parcel-) office; **=ausgabe, =auslieferung, =expeditio'n** f parcel-delivery; luggage-office; **=droschke** f, etwa: cab which takes luggage; **=revision** f examination of luggage; **=schein** m luggage-ticket; **=träger** m (luggage-) porter; railway-porter; **=wagen** m luggage-van; **=zettel** m = =schein; **=zimmer** n cloak-room.
Gepard (⌣⌣) [fr.: *dtsch. Geb-hart] m ⓑd., a. **=katze** (⌣⌣⌣⌣) f ㊷ zo. cheetah, hunting-leopard (*Cynailu'rus iuba'tus*).
Ge-pfeife (⌣⌣⌣) [pfeifen] n ㉒ constant (or persistent) whistling.
ge-pfiffen (⌣⌣) p.p. von pfeifen.
ge-pflogen (⌣⌣) p.p. von pflegen; **~heit** (⌣⌣⌣) f ㊻ — Gewohnheit.
Ge-piepe (⌣⌣⌣) n ㉒ whining, puling.
Ge-pinsel (⌣⌣) n ㉗ daubing.
Ge-plack(e) (⌣⌣) n ⓑc. (㉒) drudgery, F fagging, slaving, sweating (work).
Ge-plänkel ⚔ (⌣⌣⌣) n ㉒ skirmishing.
Ge-plapper (⌣⌣) n ㉒ (useless) babble or babbling; F clack, gab, mag.
Ge-plärr (⌣⌣) n ⓑb. bawling, crying.
Ge-plätscher (⌣⌣) n ㉒ constant splashing, ripple (or purling) of a stream.
Ge-plauder (⌣⌣⌣) n ㉒ chatting, chit-chat, prattling, F confab; small talk, tittle-tattle.
Ge-poche (⌣⌣⌣) n ㉒ continual knocking or hammering or pounding, des Herzens: beating, palpitation.
Ge-polter (⌣⌣⌣) n ㉒ 1. loud rumbling, din, crash, banging, uproar. — 2. (Geisterspuk) noisy visit of hobgoblins, ghostly visitation.
Ge-präge (⌣⌣⌣) n ㉒ 1. = prägen II. — 2. (Bild)(im)print, impression; (Stempel auf Münzen) coinage. — 3. fig. (Merkmal) stamp, cast, feature; das edle ~ seines Wesens the noble bend of his nature; das ~ tiefer Forschung tragen to bear the stamp (or mark) of deep research.
Ge-prahle (⌣⌣⌣) n ㉒ idle boasting.
Ge-pränge (⌣⌣⌣) n ㉒ = Prunk.
Ge-prassel (⌣⌣) n ㉒ constant crackling or rustling; vom Gewehrfeuer: rattle.
Ge-prickel (⌣⌣) n ㉒ = prickeln II.
ge-priesen (⌣⌣) p.p. von preisen.
Ge-quake (⌣⌣⌣) n ㉒ constant croaking of frogs or quacking of ducks.
Ge-quäle (⌣⌣⌣) n ㉒ endless torment or trouble or vexation; (lästiges Bitten) importunate begging; worrying.
Ge-quieke (⌣⌣⌣) n ㉒ constant squeaking or squealing; piping of a voice.
ge-quollen (⌣⌣⌣) p.p. von quellen.

Ger (⌣) [ahd.] m ⓑc. nur noch Turnerei: wooden spear, long pole (for leaping).
ge-rade¹ (⌣⌣⌣) [ahd.: rath(e)r] rasch] I *a*. ⓑ u. *adv*. 1. (*ant*. frumm) straight; von der Haltung auch: upright, erect; v. Wege auch: direct; in 2r Linie in a straight line, auch: in a bee-line, as the crow flies; seine 2n Glieder haben to have straight (or shapely) limbs or (all) one's limbs straight; sich 2 (adv.) halten to hold o.s. upright; ⚔ die Schultern 2 halten to square up one's sh ulders; 2 machen to make straight, to straighten; fig. auch: to set right, to (put) right; — 2. fig. (unumwunden) straight, straight-forward; (aufrichtig) plain, sincere; (bieder) blunt. — 3. (*ant*. schräg) direct; 2r Lichtstrahl direct ray of light; ea. 2 gegenüberstehend just opposite (math., &c. diametrically opposed to) each other; in 2m Widerspruche quite contradictory, in direct opposition. — 4. (et. scharf hervorhebend, meist adv.) just, exact(ly); 2 um fünf Uhr precisely at five o'clock, F at five sharp; 2 (genau) ein Jahr a year to the very day; 2 an dem Tage on that very day; ich war 2 dabei zu schreiben I was just writing or going to write; das 2 Gegenteil, 2 das Gegenteil just (or quite) the contrary, the very opposite; sie ist nicht 2 schön she is not exactly a (or no particular) beauty; nun sollst du es 2 nicht haben now you shall not have it on any account; er hat 2 noch das Leben gerettet he barely saved his life; das kam 2 recht it came in the (very) nick of time; F der kommt mir 2 recht he may wait a while; so ist's 2 recht that's just the (very) thing; 2 so gut just (or quite) as good or as well; wie es 2 kommt just as it comes, F anyhow; 2 als wenn oder ob just as if or as though; das kommt mir 2 so vor, wie // it seems to me the same as if //; 2 darum, weil // for the very reason that //, just because //; 2 deshalb kam er that's just why he came. — 5. s. nachgerade. — II ~ ⓕ 6. = Geradheit. — 7. *math*. straight line.
gerade² (⌣⌣⌣) [ahd. gezählt] *a*. ⓑ (*ant*. un2) (durch 2 ohne Rest teilbar) 2 Zahl even number; 2 ob. ungerade even or odd; ♪ 2r Takt binary measure; fünf 2 sein lassen s. fünf I.
Ge-rade³ † (⌣⌣⌣) [Gerät] f ㊸ (fahrende Habe) goods and chattels pl.
ge-rade-aus (⌣⌣⌣⌣) *adv*. straight ahead, in a straight line; 2 gehend walking straight on (or along); fig. (ohne Falsch) straightforward; **=halter** (⌣⌣...) m orthopædic instrument; back-board; phot. head-support; **2heraus** (⌣⌣⌣⌣) *adv*. mit der Sprache 2 gehen to speak out plainly or F plump and plain; sagen wir es 2! let us not mince the matter!; **2hin** (⌣⌣⌣) *adv*.: a) straight away; b) fig. (rückhaltlos) straight to a p.'s face, point-blank; **2legen** (⌣⌣⌣...) v/a. ⓑ** to put a th. straight; **2sitzen** to sit upright; **2so** wie just like, exactly as if.
ge-rades-wegs (⌣⌣⌣⌣) straightforward (-ly), directly; (unmittelbar) straightway.

ge-rade-über *adv*. (just) opposite; **2weg** *adv*. straight (to the point), straightforwardly; **2zu** *adv*.: a) straightway(s), immediately; ich nenne das 2 Betrug I call it a downright fraud; er hat sich 2 geweigert he positively (or absolutely) refused; b) fig. (unumwunden) without (much) ceremony or ado, candidly, frankly, bluntly, in plain English or words; vgl. 2hin b.
ge-rad-flüg(e)lig (⌣⌣...) *a*. ⓑ (=flügler m ㉒) ent. (insect) with straight wings, ♋ orthopterous (orthopteran); **=führung** f, mach. slide-guide.
Ge-radheit (⌣⌣) f ㊻ 1. einer Linie 2c.: straightness; einer Zahl: evenness. — 2. fig. straightforwardness, uprightness, rectitude; (Offenheit) openness, outspokenness, frankness.
Ge-rad-lauf (⌣⌣...) m ㊷ straight (or direct) course; **2läufig** *a*. ⓑ by a straight (or direct) course, direct; ⚓ orthodromic (course, route); **=linig** *a*. in a straight line, ♋ rectilinear, ...; **=linigkeit** f; ♋ rectilinearity; **=sinn** m (Geradheit) straightforwardness; (Offenheit) openness; **2sinnig** *a*. straightforward, upright; open, outspoken.
Geranium ♀ (⌣⌣⌣⌣) [lt.] n ㉓ geranium.
ge-rannt (⌣⌣) p.p. von rennen.
Gerant (⌣⌣, G⁓ra') [fr.] m ⓜ, ㊿ (Geschäftsführer) manager.
Ge-rassel (⌣⌣) n ㉒ von Ketten, Waffen: clanking, clashing; v. Wagen: rattling.
Ge-rät¹ (⌣⌣) [ahd.: *Rat] n ⓑc. (Werkzeug) tools, implements, utensils *pl*.; zum Fischen: tackle; (Einrichtung) e-s Ladens 2c.: fittings *pl*.; ein. Fabrik 2c.: plant; (Haus-)geschirr) dishes and plates *pl*., crockery, china; (Turn-)~ gymnastic apparatus, ⚔ (Kriegs-)~ military stores *pl*.
ge-rät² (⌣⌣) 3. pers. sg. pres. von geraten.
ge-raten¹ (⌣⌣⌣) [ahd.: *raten] I v/n. (ſn) ⓑa.* 1. an, auf, in 2c. to come by chance into (or upon) a th., to get into the wrong groove, to fall into an ambush, to hit upon a lucky idea. — 2. mit *prp*. oft statt kommen: an eine falsche Adresse 2 to go to the wrong address; an e-n 2 to fall in with a p.; sie sind an ea. 2 (handgemein geworden) they came to blows; ⚔ im Gefechte 2 to come to close quarters; an den Rechten, Unrechten 2 to come to the right, wrong person; auf e-n Abweg (ober falschen Weg) 2 to get on the wrong track, to go astray or wrong; er geriet auf den Einfall, Gedanken an idea (or it) occurred to him, the thought (or an idea) struck him; ⚓ auf den Grund, den Sand 2 to run aground; aus der Bahn, den Schienen 2 to get off the track, the rails, v. e-m Zuge: to derail; außer sich 2: a) F to go off one's head; b) vor Ärger 2c.: to be beside o.s. with vexation, &c., vor Freude, Entzücken: to be overjoyed, enraptured; gegen et. 2 to knock (or strike) against a th.; in Angst 2 to be seized with anxiety; in Brand 2 to catch fire; in Gefahr 2 to run into danger; in Gefangenschaft 2 to fall into captivity; sich (dat.) in die Haare 2 to come to

Signs (see page XVII): F̄ familiar; P vulgar; F flash; ⚊ rare; † obsolete (died): * new word (born): ⁺⁺ incorrect; ♪ music;

[geraten] high words or to blows, to fall out; in Harnisch 2 to become indignant; in Hitze 2 to fire up; f. Lage 1 am Ende; in der Leute Mund 2 to become the talk of the town, F to get into people's mouths, F to run into debt; in Schweiß 2 to break out in a perspiration; ins Stocken 2 to come to a standstill; in Streit 2 to set about quarrelling; in (den) Verdacht 2, et. getan zu haben to incur the suspicion of having done s. th.; in Verfall 2 to (fall into) decay; in Verwirrung 2 to become confused (auch von Personen); in Wut, Zorn 2 to fly into a rage, a passion; **nach**: das Schiff geriet durch den Sturm nach Irland the ship was cast (or driven) by the storm to Ireland; **über**: wenn er über die Bücher gerät when once he gets to (or among) his books; **unter** Diebe 2 to fall among thieves; e-m unter die Finger 2 to fall into a p.'s hands or clutches — 3. mit adv. der Art: (gelingen) to have (good, ill) success; die Arbeit ist ihm gut 2 his work has turned out well; schlecht 2 to prove a failure; to fail; die Erbsen sind gut (schlecht) 2 there has been a good (bad) crop of peas; wohl 2e Kinder well-bred ...; abs. = gut 2, z.B. alles (nichts) gerät ihm he succeeds (fails) in everything. — II p.p. u. a. (D9) 4. Beb. des inf. 2 u. raten. — 5. (ratsam) advisable; (vorteilhaft) advantageous; das 2te wäre // the best (or most advisable, most commendable) thing (or course) would be //. [f. bs II.]

ge-raten² (⌣⌣) p.p. v. raten (u. geraten¹

Ge-rate=wohl (⌣⌣⌣) [imper. v. geraten] n, nur gen: in aufs 2 at random, (at) haphazard, at all risks; on speculation; Schuß aufs ~ random (or chance) shot, auch: snap-shot.

Ge-rät=kammer (⌣⌣...) f (Rumpelkammer) lumber- (or store-)room; =**kasten** m tool-box or -chest.

Ge-rätschaft (⌣⌣) f = Gerät.

Ge-rät=turnen (⌣⌣...) n, =**übungen** f/pl. Turnerei: gymnastic (bar-, pole-, &c.) exercises pl.

Ge-raufe (⌣⌣) n = Rauferei.

ge-raum (⌣) [mhd.; *Raum] a. ample, 2e (ausgedehnte) Zeit considerable space of time; seit 2er Zeit for a long time.

Ge-räumde (⌣⌣) n for. (abgeholzter Waldplatz) clearing; (ausgehauener Richtweg) forest-path.

geräumig (⌣⌣) a. spacious, roomy, capacious; (völlig ausreichend) ample, (weit ausgedehnt) vast, wide, extensive, very large; **~keit** (⌣⌣) f spaciousness, roominess; ampleness, vastness, vast extent, width.

Ge-räusch (⌣) [mhd.; *rauschen] n. 1. noise; din; (Geschrei) shouting, clamour, (Getriebe) bustle, (Gelirr) clash(ing); (Geraffel) rattling; (Plätschern des Wassers) ripple, murmuring; beim leisesten ~ at the slightest (or faintest) noise; viel ~ machen to make a great noise, fig. to make a great stir or sensation. — 2. hunt. heart, lungs, and liver of game.

ge-räusch=los (⌣⌣...) a. noiseless (carriage, &c.), quiet (dwelling, &c.) (ohne Aufregung) calm; **=losigkeit** f noiselessness, quietness; calmness; **=voll** a. noisy, boisterous; stärker: tumultuous, uproarious; (Aufsehen erregend) loud, sensational.

Ge-räusper (⌣⌣) n clearing of throats; suppressed coughing.

Gerb(e)=bank (⌣(⌣)...) f bench for (pre)paring hides on, (tanner's) paring-bench; **=brühe** f tanning-liquor, tan-ooze; **=hobel** m smoothing-plane; **=mühle** f husking-mill.

gerben (⌣⌣) [ahd. *gar m.] I v/a. 1. (Häute zu Leder zubereiten) to dress hides, to curry; rot 2to tan; sämisch 2 to shamoy, to do chamois-dressing; gegerbte Haut dressed (or tanned) skin; fig. e-m den Buckel (oder F das Fell, die Haut) 2, e-n 2 (durchprügeln) to give a p. a sound beating or F a good hiding or tanning or thrashing. — 2. metall. Stahl 2 (raffinieren) to (re)fine steel. — 3. Metall 2 (polieren) to polish (or burnish) metal. — II v/n. ~ n 4. dressing hides, tanning, &c. (f. I); vgl. Gerberei 1.

Gerber (⌣⌣) m leather-dresser, currier; Loh=, Rot= ~ tanner; Sämisch=, chamoiser, chamois-dresser; Weiß=~ tawer. [sumac(h) (Rus coria'ria).)

Gerber=baum (⌣⌣...) m (tanner's))

Gerberei (⌣⌣⌣) f 1. (Gerben) leather-dressing; (Sämisch-)~ chamoising. — 2. (Gerberwerkstatt) tannery, tan-yard or -house, tanner's yard or shed.

Gerberei=betrieb (⌣⌣⌣...) m, **=geschäft** n tanner's business or trade.

Gerber=fett (⌣...) n = Degras; **=gesell(e)** m tanner's (journey) man; **=grube** f tan-pit; **=handwerk** n currier's (or tanner's) trade; **=hof** m tan-yard; **=kalk** m slaked lime; **=lohe** f tan(ner's bark), oak-bark; **=meister** m master tanner; **=messer** n fleshing-knife; **=mühle** f oak-bark mill; **=sumach** m = =baum; **=werkstatt** f = Gerberei 2.

Gerbe=stahl (⌣...) m = Gerb-st.

Gerb=haus (⌣...) n tan-house or -shed, tannery; **=materialien** n/pl. =stoff; 2**saure** a. chm.: tannic; 2**saures tannate**; **=säure** f tannic acid, tannin ($C_{14}H_{10}O_9$); **=stahl** m: a) (raffinierter Stahl) refined steel; b) (Werkzeug zum Polieren) polishing-steel, burnisher; **=stoff** m, chm.: a) substance used for tanning; b) = =säure; **=stube** f room for aluming hides.

Gerbung (⌣⌣) f = gerben II.

ge-recht (⌣⌣) [ahd. *recht] I a. 1. just, righteous; (der Billigkeit entsprechend) fair, equitable; 2er Richter fair-minded or impartial judge; 2e Sache right (or righteous) cause; 2er (rechtmäßiger) Anspruch legitimate (or well-established, well-founded) claim; 2e (verdiente) Strafe für // just (or condign, well-deserved) punishment for //. — 2. in allen Sätteln 2 sein to know s.th. of everything, to be fit for anything, F to be a jack of all trades; e-m 2 werden to do (or mete out) justice to a p., to give a p. his due; einer Sache 2 werden to put a th. to good account. — 3. **~** = genehm. — 4. hunt. = jagd=. — II **~e([r]** m) f 5. just (wo)man, fair-thinking p.; rel. die ~en pl. the just, the righteous pl.

Ge-rechtigkeit (⌣⌣⌣) f 1. (f. gerecht 1) justice, righteousness; fairness, equitableness, fair-mindedness, impartiality; legitimacy; e-m, e-r Sache ~ widerfahren l. to do justice to a p., a th. — 2. personifiziert: (even-handed) Justice; poet. Themis; e-n der ~ (den Gerichten) überliefern to deliver a p. up to justice, to hand a p. over to the tender mercies of the law. — 3. rel. ~ des Wandels righteousness; ~ (Rechtfertigung) durch den Glauben justification by faith. — 4. (Berechtigung) right; (Vorrecht) privilege, prerogative; (Freiheit von Abgaben 2c.) immunity, exemption; oft in Zssgn, z.B. Druck=2 printing license.

Ge-rechtigkeits=liebe (⌣⌣⌣=...) f love of justice, fair-mindedness; **2liebend** a. fair(-minded), equitable; **=pflege** f administration of justice.

Ge-rechtsame (⌣⌣⌣) f right; (Vorrecht) privilege, prerogative; e-r Stadt 2c. auch: franchise, freedom.

Ge-rede (⌣⌣) n 1. talk(ing); (Klatscherei) (idle) gossip, scandal; vgl. Geschwätz; es geht das ~ (Gerücht), daß // there is a rumour (or report) that //, it is noised abroad that //. — 2. sich (e-n) ins ~ bringen to make o.s. (a p.) the talk of the town; ins ~ kommen, oft: to get talked about; ich kümmere mich nicht um das ~ der Leute I do not care what the world says, I don't trouble about people's gossip or talk.

Ge-reibe (⌣⌣) n continued rubbing.

ge-reichen (⌣⌣) v/n. (h.) zu et. 2 to cause a th.; (beitragen) to contribute (or conduce) to a th.; (ausschlagen) to turn out (or to prove) to be s.th.; to redound to a p.'s honour, &c.; das wird ihm zur Ehre (zum Verderben) 2 it will be a credit to him (be his ruin); vgl. Ehre 2; das wird ihm nicht zum Nutzen (Vorteil) 2 that will not be to his interest (advantage), he will derive no benefit (profit) from it; e-m zur Schande 2 to bring a p. into discredit or disgrace or disrepute; es gereicht mir zum Vergnügen, daß // it affords (or gives) me pleasure that //, I am pleased that //.

Ge-reime, Ge-reimsel (⌣⌣) n rhyming, (writing) silly poetry = Reimerei.

Ge-reiße (⌣⌣) n (pulling and) tearing; scramble; es ist ~ um diese Ware there is a great demand (F quite a scramble) for ...; es ist ein förmliches ~ um ihn, oft: he is very much courted or sought after. [irritation.)

ge-reizt (⌣) p.p. v. reizen; **~heit** (⌣⌣) f)

ge-reuen (⌣⌣) [mhd.] v/impers. es gereut ihn, daß er es gesagt hat he repents (or is sorry for) having said it; sich et. 2 lassen to regret (or rue) a th.; er läßt sich keine Mühe 2 he spares (or grudges) no trouble.

Gerhard (⌣⌣) [Sper=hart] npr/m. (Bn.) Gerard.

🔬 scientific; 🌿 botanical; 🜨 geography; ⊕ machinery; ✕ mining; ⚔ military; ⚓ marine; ● commercial; ✉ postal; 🚂 railway.

[Gericht] — 432 — [Gerinne]

Ge-richt (⌣ˊ) [ahd.] n ⓶b. 1. (die Richter) court (of justice), tribunal; the bench, the judges pl.; vor ~ in court, before the judge(s), geh. Spr.: at the bar of justice; sich auf ein höheres ~ berufen to appeal to a higher court (of justice); eine Sache vor ~ bringen to go to law about a th.; e-n vor ~ fordern, laden to summons (or sue) a p.; eine Sache vor ~ führen to defend a case; sich vor ~ stellen to appear in court; to take one's trial; e-n beim ~e verklagen to take legal proceedings (or to enter an action) against a p.; adv. von ~s wegen by decree of the court. — 2. (Gebäude) law-court, eines niederen Gerichtshofs: county-court, session-house; des Lo. Justizpalastes in Fleet-Street: (the) Law Courts pl. — 3. (Gerichtsverhandlung) sitting of the court; (quarter-)session; ~ halten ob. zu ~(e) sitzen über e-m ob. e-n to sit in judgment upon a p., to try a p.('s case). — 4. rel. mit e-m ins ~ geh(e)n to judge a p.; fig. mit e-m scharf ins ~ geh(e)n to take a p. severely to task; bibl. jüngstes ~ (last) day of judgment, doomsday. — 5. (Rechtsprechung) jurisdiction. — 6. (Speise; Schüssel) dish; bibl. ein ~ Linsen a mess of pottage; (Gang) course; ein ~ auftragen to serve up a dish.

ge-richtlich (⌣⌣ˊ) a. ⓶ judicial; (richterlich) a. judiciary; (vor Gericht dienlich) forensic (eloquence, &c.); der Rechtsform gemäß ⚡ juridical; (gesetzlich) legal; lawful; ⚡e Medizin forensic medicine; ⚡e Schritte tun to take (or resort to) legal measures; ⚡es Verfahren legal proceedings pl.; adv. e-n ⚡ belangen oder verfolgen to proceed against a p., to bring a p. to justice; vgl. belangen I; ⚡ bestellt appointed by a court of law, judicially ordered; Zeugen ⚡ vorladen to subpœna witnesses.

Ge-richts-akten (⌣ˊ⌣...) pl. ⓶ legal records pl., rolls pl. (of the court); =aktuar m registrar (of the court); =amt n f. Amt 4; =bank f bench (of judges). **Ge-richts-barkeit** (⌣ˊ⌣--) f ⓶ jur. (Recht u. Pflicht, Gericht zu halten) jurisdiction; cognizance of a court; als Bezirk: jurisdiction; venue of a judge.

Ge-richts-beamte(r) (⌣ˊ⌣...) m ⓶ allg. magistrate; (Richter) member of the bench; ehm. justiciary; =befehl m (judge's) warrant, writ of the court; =behörde f court; =beisitzer m assistant judge; =bezirk m jurisdiction (of a court), (judge's) circuit or venue; =bote m messenger of the court; vgl. =diener; =brauch m = =gebrauch; =buch n register (or rolls pl.) of a court; =diener m usher of the court; der vorlädt: process-server; der ein Urteil vollstreckt: bailiff; =direktor m senior judge, president of the lowest; =ferien pl. recess, vacation(s pl.); =gang m judicial (or legal) procedure; =gebäude n = Gericht 2; =gebrauch m usage of a court; legal practice; =gebühren f/pl. court-fees pl.; =halle f judgment-hall; =halter m (officiating) judge or magistrate; =halter m = =herr; =handel m lawsuit, legal action; =haus n = Gericht 2; =herr m, bso. ehm.: justiciary; =herrschaft f jurisdiction, (right of) judicature; =hof m court (of law), court of justice, tribunal; (die Richter) the bench; vgl. Gericht 2; höherer ~ superior court, high court of justice; höchster ~ supreme court of appeal, in Engl.: Privy Council (für Indien u. die Kolonien); House of Lords; =kanzlei f record-office; =kosten pl. law-costs, legal charges or expenses pl.; =laube f judgment-hall; =lokal n = Gericht 2; =offizier ⚔ m officer acting as prosecutor at a court-martial; =ordnung f rules pl. of a court; =person f = =beamte(r); =pflege f administration of justice; =präsident m presiding judge; =rat m (Advokat) King's Counsel; (Richter) (junior) judge; =saal m session-hall, court; feierlich: judgment-hall; =sache f = =handel; =schöppe m assistant judge; =schranke f bar; =schreiber m clerk of the court; =siegel n seal of a court; =sitzung f sitting (or session) of a court; =sporteln f/pl. = =gebühren; =sprache f = =stil; =sprengel m = =bezirk; =stand m competency of a court; =stätte f etwa: place of judgment; vgl. =saal; =stil m legal language or style, law terms pl.; =stube f = =saal; =stuhl m judge's seat or chair, feierlich: judgment-seat; =tag m court-day; =termin m day of hearing, day on which a case is to be heard or tried; =verfahren n = =gang; =verfassung f constitution of law-courts; =verhandlung f legal (or judicial) proceedings pl., trial; pleading (of counsel); =verwalter m = =herr; =verwaltung f = =verweser m administration, administrator of justice; =vollzieher m (court-)bailiff; =wesen n judicial affairs pl.; =zeit f term, session (of a court); =zwang m jurisdiction.

ge-rieben (⌣⌣ˊ) p.p. von reiben; auch F a. ⓶ (D9) cunning (= durchtrieben); ~heit f ⓶ = Durchtriebenheit.

gerieren (⌣⌣ˊ) [it., fr.] ⓶ I v a. (führen) to manage. — II sich ⚡ v/refl. (sich benehmen) to conduct (or behave) o.s.

Ge-riesel (⌣⌣ˊ) n ⓶ ripple; purling; (Geräusch rieselnden Wassers) soft murmur of the brook, &c.; des Regens: drizzling.

ge-riet(e subj.) (⌣⌣ˊ) impf. v. geraten.

ge-ring (⌣⌣ˊ) [ahd.] I a. ⓶ 1. (unbedeutend) slight, trifling, unimportant, inconsiderable; (geringfügig) insignificant; (klein) small, slender; (beschränkt) limited; mit den Ausnahmen with but few exceptions; ⚡en Eindruck machen to make very little (or a slight) impression; sein ⚡es Einkommen his modest stipend, his moderate income; ⚡tes Gebot lowest bid; er besitzt ⚡e Kenntnisse he has but a small modicum of knowledge, F he's a poor scholar; mit den Mitteln with limited means; um einen ⚡en Preis kaufen to buy at a low price or for a trifling sum; mein ⚡es Verdienst my humble desert, what little merit I have; ich kam in nicht ⚡e Verlegenheit I was not a little embarrassed, I felt more than a little puzzled; er kam nicht in die ⚡ste Verlegenheit he was not in the least (or not at all) perplexed. — 2. (ohne inneren Wert) without (intrinsic) value; (schlecht) bad; indifferent; (gemein) common, ordinary; ⚡es Gold, ⚡er Wein inferior gold, wine; Mensch von ⚡er Herkunft ... of low (or mean) extraction; ⚡e Leute the lower class(es pl.), people in modest (or humble) circumstances. — 3. im comp.: less; der Schaden ist ⚡er, als ich dachte the loss is smaller (or less heavy) than I thought; ⚡er dem Stande, Werte, Gehalte nach: inferior (als j., et. to a p., a th.); ⚡er m. to lessen, diminish, reduce; ⚡er w. to decrease, diminish, fall off. — 4. im sup.: least; er erwacht beim ⚡sten Geräusche ... at the slightest noise; ohne den ⚡sten Zweifel without the least (or a shadow of) doubt; nicht im ⚡sten not in the least; F not a bit (of it), not a jot; vgl. 1 am Schluß. — 5. in Verbindung mit verbs: et ⚡ achten to think little of a th.; e-n ⚡(er) achten to have little (less) regard for a p.; von e-m ⚡ denken to have no good (or high) opinion of a p.; etwas ⚡(=)schätzen to attach little value to a th., (verachten) to despise a th. — II ~e([r] m) f, ~e(s) n ⓶ 6. die ~en wie die Großen the lowly (or humble) as well as the great; der ~ste auf Erden the humblest person on earth. — 7. um ein ~es for a trifle or a (mere) bagatelle; er bildet sich nichts ~es ein he has no mean opinion (F he thinks no small beer) of himself; es ist nichts ~es it is no trifling (or insignificant) matter; kein ~erer als no less a p. than; das ~ste the slightest (or least) thing; es fehlt nicht das ~ste: a) (gar nichts) there is not the least thing missing; b) (das Bedeutendste) the most important thing is wanting; er ist auch im ~sten treu he is loyal even in mere trifles; vgl. 4.

Ge-ring-achtung (⌣ˊ⌣...) f ⓶ = =schätzung; =fügig a. ⓶ trifling, insignificant, unimportant; trivial, petty, little; (armselig) paltry, mean, miserable; =fügigkeit f ⓶ insignificance; triviality, pettiness, littleness; paltriness; ⚡haltig a. of low (or inferior) value; von Münzen 2c.: of low (or base) standard; ⚡es Silber ... of base (or inferior) alloy.

Ge-ringheit (⌣ˊ⌣...) f ⓶ littleness, smallness, dwarfishness.

ge-ring-schätzig (⌣ˊ⌣...) a. ⓶ disdainful, derogatory, disregardful; adv. ⚡ behandeln to treat with contempt or disdain, to slight; ⚡ beurteilen to underrate, to disparage; =schätzigkeit f ⓶, =schätzung f disdain, disregard; contempt, disparagement.

ge-rinnbar (⌣ˊ⌣) a. ⓶; ⚡ coagulable, congealable; ~keit f ⓶; ⚡ coagulability, congealableness.

Ge-rinne (⌣⌣ˊ) [rinnen] n ⓶ 1. ohne pl. perpetual running or flowing or stream(ing). — 2. mit pl.: a) (rinnendes

Zeichen (f. S. XVII): F familiär; P Volkssprache; ℱ Gaunersprache; ⚡ selten; † alt (auch gestorben); * neu (auch geboren); ⚡+ unrichtig;

[gerinnen] — 433 — [gesamt]

Waſſer) running water, water-course; ⊕ einer Mühle: mill-tail; b) ⊕ (Rinne für fließendes Waſſer) (conduit-)pipe; channel; mill-trough or -race or -spout; ~ (Goſſe) einer Straße gutter.

ge-rinn/en (‿‿) **I** v/n. (ſn) ⑳b(a)* von Milch ꝛc.: to curdle, to turn (to curds); ⚔ to coagulate; durch Kälte: to congeal; vom Blute: to clot; 2 machen oder laſſen to curdle, ⚔ to coagulate, to congeal; geronnene Milch curdled milk, curds pl. — **II** ~ n ㉓ = Ⓖ/ung.

Ge-rinnſel (‿‿) n ㉒ (geronnene Flüſſigkeit) coagulated (or clotted) mass.

ge-rinnt ‿ (‿‿) a. ⓺ canaliculate(d).

Ge-rinnung (‿‿) f ㊻ curdling, &c. (ſ. gerinnen I), ⚔ coagulation, congelation; ~s-mittel n ㉒: ⚔ coagulator.

Ge-rippe (‿‿) [nhd. 17. sae.] n ㉒ 1. (tieriſches Knochengerüſt) bony structure or frame, skeleton. — 2. ⚓ ~ e-s neuen Schiffes auf Stapel: carcass, framework. — 3. Zeichnen: rough outline.

ge-rippt (‿‿) [Rippe] a. ⓺ ribbed (auch ⊕ von Papier); ⚓ u. zo.: ⚔ costate(d); ⊕ von Zeug: corded. [reiten.]

ge-riſſen, ge-ritten (‿‿) p.p. von reißen,]

Germane (‿⊥‿) [flt.] m ㊹, **Germanin** f ㊼ Germanic, pl. a. oft: Germani.

Germanen-tum (‿⊥‿-) n ⓶d.: a) Germanic (or German) life or manners pl.; b) Germanic people pl.

Germania ♀ (‿⊥(‿)/) [lt.] f ㊶α., **Germani-en** (‿⊥‿) n ㉓α. npr.(Land der alten Deutſchen) Germania, ancient Germany.

Germanikus (‿⊥‿‿) [lt.] npr/m. ⑯γ († 19 n. Chr.) Germanicus.

Germanin (‿⊥‿) f ㊼ ſ. Germane.

germaniſch (‿) a.⓺Germanic, Teutonic; 2e Sprachen Germanic languages pl.

germaniſier/en (‿‿⊥‿) **I** v/a. ㊽ (germaniſch ob. deutſch machen) to Germanize. — **II** ~ n ㉓, Ⓖ/ung f ㊻ Germanization.

Germanismus (‿‿‿) m ㉗ gram. (deutſche Redewendung) Germanism.

Germaniſt (‿‿‿) m ㊸ (Kenner deutſcher Dinge) Germanic scholar, one versed in Germanic lore or languages; 2iſch a. ⓺ Germanistic, referring to Germanic law or philology.

Germer ♀ (‿‿) [ahd.] m ㊷: weißer ~ white hellebore (Vera'trum album).

gern, auch **2e** (‿/‿) [ahd.: yearn; *(be-) gehren] adv. (comp. mſt lieber) 1. gladly, with pleasure, cheerfully; (bereitwillig) readily, willingly, with a will; (aus freien Stücken) freely, of one's own accord; ich tat es herzlich 2 ... with the greatest pleasure, with all my heart; 2 oder ungern, ich muß I must whether I like it or not. — 2. das glaube ich 2 I quite believe it; er iſt überall 2 geſehen ... welcome everywhere; ich würde es (nicht) 2 ſehen, wenn Sie // I should (dis)like it if you //; dafür kann j. gut und 2 zehn Mark geben it is well worth ten shillings (of anybody's money). — 3. et. 2 tun (mögen) to be fond of (doing) a th.; etwas 2 eſſen, trinken to be fond of (or to like) a th.; 2 gut eſſen und trinken to be fond of good eating and drinking or of a good table; er iſt Fleiſch lieber als Obſt he

likes meat better than fruit, he prefers meat to fruit; e-n 2 haben ob. mögen to be fond of (ſtärker: in love with) a p.; ich möchte 2 wiſſen, ob // I should like to (biswl. auch I would fain) know whether //; mit neg.: er möchte 2 keinen beleidigen he would like to offend nobody; er möchte keinen 2 beleidigen he would be sorry to offend anybody; er geht, tanzt ꝛc. nicht 2 he is averse to (ſtärker: he hates) walking, dancing, &c.; et. nicht 2 eſſen not to relish a th.; et. (nicht) 2 h. (not) to fancy a th. — 4. fig. bei Lebloſem: der Baum wächſt 2 in feuchtem Boden ... likes (or prefers) a damp soil.

gern(e)-geſehen (‿(‿)‿...) a. ⓺ welcome; -groß a. u. s. would-be-great; -mögen n liking (or appetite) for, affection for.

Ge-röchel (‿‿) n ㉒ rattling (in the throat). [b) poet. ob. F co. od rächen.]

ge-rochen (‿‿⚔) p.p.: a) von riechen;]

Gerold (⊥‿) [Speer=walt] npr/m. ⑮⑯α. (Vn.) Gerald. [rumbling (noise).]

Ge-rolle (‿‿) n ㉒ constant rolling or]

Ge-röll(e) (‿‿) n ⑳b.㉒) 1. allg.: rolling stones, &c.; (Geſtein an Flußbetten und Felſgebirgen) kleineres: rubble(-stones pl.), größeres: boulders pl. — 2. (Schutt) wreckage; ruins, debris pl.

ge-ronnen (‿‿) p.p. von gerinnen.

Gerſte (‿‿) [ahd.: lt. ho'rdeum] f ㊾ u. agr. barley (Ho'rdeum); zweizeilige ~ two-rowed b. (H. di'stichum); ſechszeilige ~ six-rowed b. (H. hexa'stichum); vierzeilige (ober gemeine) ~ spring b. (H. vulga're); gerſten [ahd.] a. ⓺ (of) barley.

Gerſten-acker (‿‿...) m ㉒ barley-field; -ähre f ear of barley; -bier n beer brewed with b.-malt; -brot n b.-bread or -loaf; -ernte f b.-crop; -feld n b.-field; -graupen f/pl. peeled b.; -grütze f b.-groats pl.; -kaffee m roasted b.; -kleie f b.-bran; -korn n: a) b.-corn (auch als kleines Gewicht); b) path. (Geſchwulſt am Augenlid) sty, ⚔ hordeolum; -kuchen m bibl. (Heſ. 4, 12) barley-cake; -malz m ⚔ Brauerei: barley-malt; -mehl n barley-meal or -flour; -ſaft m: a) = Waſſer; b)(Bier) biswl.: b.-broth or -wine; -ſchleim m = trank; -ſchrot n bruised (coarsely) barley; -ſtroh n b.-straw; -ſuppe f b.-soup; -trank m, -waſſer n b.-water, pharm.: ⚔ ptisan; -zucker m b.-sugar; pharm.: weißer: ⚔ alphenic.

Gertchen (‿‿) n ㉓ dim. von Gerte.

Gerte (‿‿) [ahd.: yard: lt. hasta] f ㊽ rod; (Weidenrute) osier twig; (Stab) wand; kleine ~ (Gertchen) little switch.

Gerten-hieb (‿‿...) m ㉒ cut (or stroke) with a switch. [Gertrude.]

Gertr(a)ud (‿-) ㊴ ㊻β. npr/f. (Vn.)]

Ge-ruch (‿‿ch) [mhd.;* riechen] m ⑦c. (pl. nur in 2). (Sinn) sense of smelling, ⚔ olfaction; einen feinen ~ haben to have a keen scent or a fine nose. — 2. (was man riecht) smell, odour; guter, angenehmer ~ perfume, fragrance, scent; übler ~ unpleasant (or offensive) smell; ~ von Speiſen, auch: fumes pl.; ~ verbreitend odoriferous, fragrant; ohne ~ without odour or smell or scent, inodorous; von Gerüchen befreien to deodorize; von ekelhaftem ~ malodorous,

fetid; von lieblichem ~ sweet-scented. — 3. fig. (Ruf) reputation, repute; in gutem ~ bei e-m ſtehen to be in good odour with a p.; im ~e der Heiligkeit ſtehen to bear a saintly character; in üblem ~ ſtehend (held) in evil repute, ill-famed, notorious.

ge-ruch-los (‿‿ch...) a. ⓺ scentless, inodorous; =loſigkeit f ㊷ scentlessness, inodorousness; =reich a. (strongly) scented or perfumed, odoriferous; =ſinn m = Geruch 1.

Ge-ruchs-nerv (‿‿ch...) m ㊷: ⚔ olfactory nerve; -vermögen n power (or faculty) of smelling; -werkzeug n organ of smell, ⚔ olfactory organ; nose.

Ge-rücht (‿‿) [nbd.: ruchbar, Ruf] n ⑳b. 1. rumour, report; hearsay; es geht (ob. läuft) das ~ (ob. das ~ iſt im Umlaufe), daß // a rumour (or report) is spreading (or afloat) that //, it is rumoured (or reported) that //; e-n in ein böſes ~ bringen to bring a p. into ill repute; ein ~ unter die Leute bringen to spread (or circulate) a rumour. — 2. perſoniſiziert: (Fama) Fame.

Ge-rücht-weiſe (‿‿⊥‿) adv. according to rumour; ich habe es 2 erfahren I heard it by the way; 2 verlautet the story goes, it is noised abroad or rumoured.

Ge-rufe (‿⊥‿) n ㉒ frequent calling.

ge-rufen (‿⊥‿) p.p. von rufen.

ge-ruhen (‿⊥‿) [ahd.: reck] v/n. (h.) ⑧* to deign (or condescend) to; 2 Eure Majeſtät may it please your Majesty.

ge-ruhig (‿⊥‿) [mhd.] a. ⓺ = ruhig.

Geröll(e) (‿‿) n ⑳b. (㉒) (Durcheinandergeworfenes) (heap of) rubbish.

Ge-rumpel (‿‿) n ㉒ constant (or continued) rumbling, e-s Wagens: jolting.

Ge-rümpel (‿‿) n ㉒ (altes Zeug) lumber, rubbish; old (broken) furniture; ~-kammer f ㉒ lumber (or store-)room.

Gerundium (‿⊥(‿)) [lt.] n ㉘ gr. (als Hauptwort gebrauchtes Zeitwort) gerund;

gerundiviſch (‿⊥‿w) a. ⓺ gerundial.

ge-rungen (‿⊥‿) p.p. von ringen.

Ge-runzel (‿‿) n ㉒ constant frowning.

Ge-rüſt, ~e (‿‿) n ⑳b., ㉒ für Bau-arbeiter: scaffold(ing), für Schauſtellungen: stage, platform, für Hinrichtungen: scaffold; ⊕ arch. (Geſtell) trestle; ſchwimmendes ~ floating stage; ein ~ aufſchlagen (abbrechen) to put up (to take down) a scaffold(ing).

Ge-rüſt-brücke (‿‿...) f ㉒ trestle-work bridge; -ſtange f ㊷ scaffolding-pole.

Ge-rüttel (‿‿) n ㉒ continual (or unpleasant) shaking; e-s Wagens: jolting.

Ger-werfen (⊥‿) n ㉓ throwing of the spear, spear-exercise or practice.

Ges ♪ (⊥) n, inv. G flat; ~=Dur G flat major; ~=Moll G flat minor.

ge-jägt ♀ (‿‿) a. ⓺ serrate(d).

Ge-ſalbte(r) (‿‿) s. ⓺ anointed.

ge-ſalzen (‿‿) **I** p.p. ⓺ von ſalzen. — **II** ~e(s) n ⓺ salt provision.

Ge-ſäme (‿⊥‿) n ㉒ seeds pl.

ge-ſamt (‿‿) [ahd.;* ſammeln] **I** a. ⓺ mit art. vor e-m Kollektiv: the whole or entire; die 2e Menſchheit all mankind. the whole human race; das 2e Volk the whole (or entire) nation, all the people pl.; alle 2 all jointly; (taken

♪ Muſik; ⚔ Wiſſenſchaft; ♀ Pflanze; ♀ Geographie; ⊕ Technik; ⚒ Bergbau; ⚔ Militär; ⚓ Marine; ● Handel; ✉ Poſt; 🚆 Eiſenbahn.

[Gesamtabsatz] — 434 — [Geschäftssprache]

collectively or together. — II ~e(s) n ⓺ the whole, the (sum) total.
Ge͞samt-absatz ⚜ (⌣ˊ…) m ⓶ total (amount of) sale; **=ausfuhr** ⚜ f total export; **=ausgabe** f complete edition; **=begriff** m general idea; comprehensive term; **=betrag** m sum total. total (or aggregate) amount; **=bild** n entire picture or scenery; **=eigentum** n total (or collective) property; **=eindruck** m general impression; **=einfuhr** ⚜ f total import; **=einnahme** f the whole of the receipts; **=erbe** m (**=erbin** f) sole heir (heiress); **=ertrag** m entire proceeds pl. or produce; ⚔ total output; **=forderung** ⚜ f total charges pl. or claim; **=gläubiger** m general creditor; **=gut** n (der Eheleute) joint property or estate; **=haftung** f jur. joint liability.
Ge͞samtheit (⌣ˊ…) f ⓵ (ant. Einzelheit) total(ity), the whole of the troops, &c.; entire number; (Summe) sum total.
Ge͞samt-kassenumsatz (⌣ˊ…) m ⓶ total turnover; ehm. **=leh(e)n** n fief held by several in common; **=macht** f united forces pl., combined power; **=masse** ⚜ f total estate; **=ministe'rium** n all the cabinet(-ministers); **=petitio'n** f joint petition; **=produktio'n** f = ertrag; **=regierung** f joint (or central) government.
Ge͞samtschaft † (⌣ˊ…) f ⓵ = Gesamtheit.
Ge͞samt-schuldner (⌣ˊ…) m ⓶ general debtor; **=staat** m united state or country; **=summe** f (sum) total, total amount; **=übersicht** f general survey; comprehensive view; **=verbindlichkeit** f joint responsibility; solidarity; **=vermögen** n entire fortune, the whole of a p.'s property; **=wert** m aggregate (or total) value; **=wohl** n public (or common) weal; **=zahl** f total number.
ge-sa͞ndt (⌣ˊ) p.p. v. senden; **~e(r) m)** f ⓺, f a.: **Gesandtin** ⚜ allg.: messenger; (Botschafter) ambassador (f a.'s wife; ambassadress); außerordentlicher ~ und bevollmächtigter Minister am russischen Hofe envoy extraordinary and minister plenipotentiary at the Russian Court; päpstlicher ~ nuncio; vgl. Botschafter, Geschäftsträger.
Ge-sa͞ndtschaft (⌣ˊ…) f ⓵ (Gesandter und sein Personal) embassy, legation.
ge-sa͞ndtschaftlich (⌣ˊ⌣…) a. ⓺ ambassadorial; Ler Auftrag diplomatic mission.
Ge-sa͞ndtschafts-attaché (⌣ˊ⌣…) m ⓶ attaché (to an embassy); **=hotel** n embassy; **=personal** n legation; **=posten** m ambassador's (or ambassadorial) post or position; **=prediger**, **=sekretär** m chaplain, secretary to an embassy.
Ge-sa͞ng (⌣ˊ) [ahd.; *singen] m ⓵ b. 1. (Singen) singing, ♪ vocal music; der Vögel auch: warbling; (Zwitschern) chirping. — 2. (Lied) song, ditty; (Melodie) air, tune, melody; zweistimmiger: duet; mehrstimmiger: part-song, glee; (Kirchen)~ hymn, rezitativer: chant. — 3. (Gedicht) poem; (Teil e-r Dichtung) canto.
Ge-sa͞ng-buch (⌣ˊ…) n ⓶ book of songs; eccl. hymn-book; **=fest** n singing-festival, in Wales: eisteddfod; **=lehre** f choral art; **=lehrer(in** f) m singing-master (-mistress). [vocal (effect, &c.)]
ge-sa͞nglich (⌣ˊ⌣) a. ⓺ of singing, auch

ge-sa͞ng-reich (⌣ˊ…) a. ⓺ rich in song; melodious; **=schule** f ⓶ singing-school, singing-classes pl.
Ge-sa͞ngs-einlage (⌣ˊ…) f ⓶ f. Einlage 2; **=kundig** a. ⓺ versed in singing; **=kunst** f art of singing.
Ge-sa͞ng-stimme (⌣ˊ…) f ⓶ vocal part; **=stunde** f singing-lesson; **=unterricht** m instruction in singing; **=verein** m choral society; **=weise** f melody, tune; ₂weise adv. in the manner of a song; by (way of) singing.
Ge-säß (⌣ˊ) [mhd.; *sitzen] n ⓶ a. seat, fundament, F bottom, backside, behind, posterior; anat.: ♂ anus; **~-arte'rien** f pl. ⓶, **~-muskeln** m/pl.: ♂ gluteal arteries, muscles pl.; **~-schwiele** f: ♂ gluteal callosity.
Ge-sa͞ufe (⌣ˊ⌣) n ⓶ immoderate (or hard) drinking; F boozing, swilling.
Ge-sa͞use (⌣ˊ⌣) n ⓶ des Windes: whistling; der Wogen: hissing; der Ohren: buzzing, singing (in the ears).
Ge-sä̆usel (⌣ˊ⌣) n ⓶ soft murmurs pl.; (gentle) rustling; bisw. ♂ susurration.
ge-scha͞cht (⌣ˊt) a. ⓺ her. chequered.
ge-scha͞ffen (⌣ˊ⌣) p.p. von schaffen.
Ge-schä̆ft (⌣ˊ) [mhd.; *schaffen] n ⓶ b. 1. business; (Unternehmung) transaction; (Angelegenheit) affair; glänzende ~e machen to do a roaring (or rattling good) business or trade; ein gutes ~ machen to do a good stroke of business, to make a good bargain; in ~en reisen to travel on business; mit e-m ~e h. to have (business-) dealings with a p.; von ~en reden to speak of bu., F to talk shop; wie geh(e)n die ~e? how is business? — 2. (Handel) commerce; das ~ (oder die ~e) mit dem Auslande (im Inlande) foreign (home) trade; ⚜ ~ in Wolle dealing (or transaction) in wool; wenig ~e in Reis little doing in rice. — 3. (Gewerbe, Stand) trade; was für ein ~ betreibt er? what is his trade or occupation?, F what line of business is he in? — 4. ⚜ (Handelshaus) commercial house or firm; großes ~ large house or firm; ~(e) im großen wholesale trade; er hat ein kleines ~ he has a small business; ~(e) im kleinen retail trade; ein ~ anlegen, kaufen, führen to set up, to buy, to carry on a business; sein ~ verkaufen to dispose of one's business. — 5. ein natürliches ~ (seine Notdurft) verrichten to relieve o.s., to ease nature.
Ge-schä̆ftchen (⌣ˊ⌣) n ⓷ (dim. v. Geschäft) small business or transaction.
ge-schä̆ftig (⌣ˊ⌣) a. ⓺ busy, active, at work; (arbeitsam) hard-working; (betriebsam) industrious; (rührig) pushing, energetic; (eifrig) officious, b.s. fussy, interfering; immer sehr ~ sein to be always doing or bustling about or F on the go; anscheinend ₂e Person busybody; **~keit** (⌣ˊ⌣-) f ⓵ activity, hard work, industry; push, energy, F go; officiousness, b.s. fussiness.
ge-schä̆ftlich (⌣ˊ⌣) a. ⓺ relating to business; ⚜ commercial; adv. ₂ betrachtet from a business (or commercial) point of view.

ge-schä̆ft-los (⌣ˊ…) a. ⓺ f. geschäftslos.
Ge-schä̆fts-adresse mst. ⚜ (⌣ˊ…) f ⓶ business-address; **=karte** f bu.-card; **=angelegenheit** f bu.-matter, commercial transaction; **=anteil** m share in a bu.; **=aufgabe** f closing of a (or giving up) bu.; **=auftrag** m commission; **=bericht** m trade-report; **=betrieb** m management of a bu.; **=branche** f branch of a (a) bu.; **=briefe** m pl. commercial (or business-) letters pl.; **=buch** n commercial book; account-book; **=bücher** pl. (the) books pl. (of a firm); **=drang** m pressure of bu.; **=eifer** m = fleiß; ₂erfahren a. experienced in bu.; **=erfahrenheit**, **=erfahrung** f experience in bu.; **=fach** n bu.-department; ₂fähig a. capable of doing (or managing) a business; jur. responsible, competent; **=fertigkeit** f bu.-routine; **=fleiß** m application to bu.; ₂frei a. free from bu.; ₂e Stunde leisure-hour; **=freund** m bu.-connexion; correspondent; ₂führend a.: Ler Ausschuß managing committee; **=führer** m manager of a bu., F managing clerk or man; einer Fabrik auch: superintendent, overseer; **=führung** f management of a bu.; **=gang** m: a) daily routine (or round) of a bu.; b) (Gang in Geschäften) walk for business purposes; errand; **=gebrauch** m commercial (or trade-) custom; **=gegend** f business-quarter, neighbourhood rich in shops; **=geheimnis** n business-secret; **=geist** m commercial spirit; **=genoß** m partner in bu.; **=gewandtheit** f commercial skill; **=haus** n house of bu., commercial firm; **=herr**, **=inhaber** m owner of a bu., principal; **=kenntnis** f knowledge of bu.; **=kniff** m commercial trick; **=kreis** m sphere of activity; **=kunde** f skill in bu.; ₂kundig a. = Lerfahren; **=lage** f state of the market; **=leben** n bu.-life; (Handel und Wandel) trade; mercantile affairs pl.; ₂leitend a. = ₂führend; **=lokal** n bu.-premises pl.; (Bureau) office, counting-house; (Laden) shop; ₂los a. without a business or trade; vom Markte: no business done; stagnant, dead, lifeless, dull; **=losigkeit** f unemployment, inactivity, des Marktes: stagnation, lifelessness, dulness of trade; **=mann** m (pl. **=leute**) bu.-man (pl. bu.-men), man (pl. men) of bu., tradesman (pl. tradesmen); ₂männisch. ₂mäßig a. und adv. businesslike; **=neid** m jealousy of competitors; **=ordnung** f bu.-rules pl.; parl. standing orders pl.; **=papiere** ⚜ n/pl. commercial papers pl.; **=personal** n employees pl. of a firm, persons pl. employed in a house of bu.; staff; **=raum** m = Llokal; **=regel** f rule in bu.; **=reise** f, lange: bu.-tour; kurze: journey on bu.; **=reisende(r)** m commercial traveller; **=routi'ne** f = Lgang a; **=sache** f bu.-transaction, commercial affair; **=schluß** m close of (the day's) business; Börse: beim ~ at the close of the day, when the market closed; **=sprache** f commercial language, mercantile terms pl.;

Signs (see page XVII): F familiar; P vulgar; ſ flash; ↘ rare; † obsolete (died); * new word (born); ⧺ incorrect; ♪ music;

[Geschäftsstelle] | [Geschirrschnalle]

=stelle* f e-r Zeitung ꝛc. office; **=stil** m commercial style; **=stille, =stockung** f stagnation of business, dulness of trade; **=stube** f office, counting-house; **=stunden** f pl. business- (or office-) hours pl.; **=tätigkeit** f activity in bu.; **=teilhaber** m partner; **=träger** m: a) e-s Handlungshauses: agent, representative; b) e-s Staates: (fr.) chargé d'affaires; **=übernahme** f, **=übertragung** f transfer of a bu.; **=unternehmung** f commercial enterprise or venture; **=verbindung** f bu.-relations pl.; in ~ mit e-m stehen (treten), oft: to be in (to enter into) correspondence with a p.; **=verhältnisse** n/pl. condition (s pl.) of trade vgl. =lage; **=verkehr** m commercial intercourse. bu.-dealings pl.; **=verlegung** f removal of a bu.; **=verwalter** m = führer; **=viertel** n e-r Stadt business quarter; **=zimmer** ⚓ n office, bureau; **=zweig** m branch (or department) of a bu.; besonderer ~ speciality, F special line.

Ge-schäker (◡´◡) n ⏺ jesting, joking, banter; play, playing; F larking.

Ge-scharre (◡´◡) n ⏺ (much) scraping, von Pferden auch: pawing (the ground).

Ge-schaukel (◡´◡) n ⏺ swinging (up and down), see-saw; e-r Wiege ꝛc.: rocking.

ge-scheckt (◡´) a. ⏺ piebald.

ge-schehen (◡´◡) [ahd.: scihen] I v/n. (ſn), meiſt impers. ⏺ a* **1.** to happen, to chance; (ſich zutragen) to occur, to come to pass; (ſtattfinden) to take place; was auch ⏺ mag whatever may happen, come what may; es iſt ein Unglück ⏺ there has been an accident. — **2.** als pass. von „machen": Dein Wille geschehe! Thy will be done!; es geschieht viel für die Armen much is (being) done for the poor, the poor are well looked after; es geschehe! be it so!; es iſt gern ⏺! don't mention it!; es iſt ſo gut als ⏺ it is as good as done; **ſo geschieht das** that is the way to do it; was ſoll damit ⏺? what is to be done with it? — **3.** ⏺ **laſſen** (nicht hindern) to allow, suffer, tolerate; nicht ⏺ laſſen to prevent, stop, check. — **4.** (zugefügt werden) mit dat. der Perſon: es geschieht ihm Abbruch he is suffering (an) injury; es geschieht mir ein großer Dienst damit that is doing me a real service or kindness; es wird dir nichts zuleide (ob. kein Leid) ⏺ no harm will come to you; es geschieht dir schon ganz recht, daß du // it serves you quite right that you //, you quite deserve to have to // (inf.); ich weiß nicht, wie mir geschieht I feel I don't know how; I don't know what can be the matter with me; es iſt ihm zu viel ⏺ he has been harshly dealt with or F put upon. — **5.** es iſt um mich ⏺ (ich bin verloren) I am done for or lost; it is all over with me. — **II** p.p. u. a. ⏺ **6.** Bed. des inf. — **7.** (fertig, vollendet) done, finished; Sprichw. Le Dinge ſind nicht zu ändern what's done can't be undone; vgl. ändern 2. — **8.** Kanzleiſtil: ſo ⏺ (ausgefertigt) zu Paris, den 1. März 1898 decreed ..., so done ...

Ge-schehene(s) (◡´◡◡) n ⏺ what is done, accomplished facts, by-gones pl.

Ge-schehen-laſſen (◡´◡◡) n ㉓ letting things go, oft auch: (fr.) laissez-aller.

Ge-schehnis (◡´◡) n ⏺ occurrence.

Ge-scheide (◡´◡) n ㉒ hunt. (Magen u. Gedärme e-s Wildes) (n)umbles pl.

Ge-schein(e) ⚓ (◡´(◡)) n ⓒ (㉒) (Weinblüten) first bud of a vine.

ge-scheit (◡´) [mhd.: *ſcheiden] a. ⏺ (flug) shrewd; (einſichtsvoll) intelligent; (vernünftig) sensible; (ſcharfſinnig) sagacious, keen, smart; der Kopf clever head; ſei doch ⏺! be reasonable!, listen to reason!. F don't be a fool!; er iſt nicht recht ⏺ he is not in his right senses or F not quite right (in the upper story); F ich kann aus der Sache nicht ⏺ w. I cannot make head or tail of it; adv. et. ⏺ anfangen to do (or manage) a th. cleverly; Sprichw. vgl. flug; **~heit** (◡´◡) f ⏺ shrewdness, intelligence, good sense; sagacity, keen insight, smartness; cleverness.

Ge-schelte (◡´◡) n ㉒ constant scolding.

Ge-schenk (◡´) n ⓑ. present; (Gabe) gift; für e-n Dienſt: acknowledgment, gratification; kleines ~, bſd. von Geld: gratuity, F tip; großes: donation, largess(e); e-m ein ~ mit et. machen to make a p. a present of a th.; ſie hat es zum ~ bekommen she had it given her (for a present); **~fuß** F m: mit e-m auf dem ~e ſtehen (to be on such a footing as to) exchange presents with a p.; **~geber(in** f) m donor, giver; **~nehmer(in** f) m recipient (of a present), auch: donee.

Ge-scherze (◡´◡) n ㉒ great joking.

ge-scheut[1] (◡´) a. ㉒ ✝ für geſcheit.

ge-scheut[2] (◡´) p.p. von ſcheuen.

ge-schicht ⚓ (◡´) P u. poet. = geſchieht.

Ge-schichtchen (◡´◡◡) n ㉓ (dim. v. Geſchichte) short tale or story; anecdote.

Ge-schichte (◡´◡) [ahd.: *geſchehen] f ㊽ **1.** story, tale; (Erzählung) narrative, narration; e-e ~ erzählen to tell a tale; davon läßt ſich eine lange ~ erzählen there is a long history attached to that, thereby hangs a tale; iro. das iſt e-e ſchöne ~! a nice thing, indeed! here's a pretty business!; das wäre e-e ſchöne ~! if there would be a fine kettle of fish!, we should be in a fine pickle!; e-e alte ~ an old story or tale; die ganze ~ the whole concern or business. — **2.** alte, mittlere, neuere ~ ancient, medieval, modern history; bibliſche (heilige) ~ Scripture (sacred) history.

ge-schichten-artig (◡´◡...) a. ⏺ storylike; anecdot(ic)al; **=buch** n ㉓ storybook; **=erzähler(in** f) m story-teller.

ge-schichtlich (◡´◡) a. ⏺ historical.

Ge-schichts=buch (◡´◡...) n ㉒ historical book or work.

Ge-schichts=schreiber (◡´◡...) m ㉒ historian, historical writer, ⚆ historiographer; **=schreibung** f historical writing; als Amt: ⚆ historiography.

Ge-schichts=erzählung (◡´◡...) f ㉒ historical account or narrative; **=forſcher** m historian; **=forſchung** f historical research, study of history;

=gemälde n = malerei; **=kalender** m historical almanac; **=kenntnis, =kunde** f hist. knowledge, science; **⚛kundig** a. ⏺ versed (or deeply read) in history; **=maler(in** f) m historical painter; **=malerei** f hist. painting; painting of hist. subjects; **⚛mäßig** a. historical; **=tabellen, =tafeln** f/pl. historical tables pl.; **=unterricht** m teaching of history; **=urkunde** f hist. record; **=werk** n hist.

Ge-schick (◡´) [mhd.: *ſchicken] n ⓒ. **1.** v. Sachen: (rechte, gehörige Art) right shape, fitness; der Rock hat kein ~ the coat does not fit, F there is no fit (or shape) about it, it is a bad fit; etwas ins ~ bringen to set (or put) a thing right. — **2.** von Perſonen: (Befähigung) aptitude, ability; (Gewandtheit) skill; bſd. körperliche: dexterity, geiſtige: cleverness, adroitness, ingenuity; er hat kein ~ F he has no knack about him; er hat ſehr wenig ~ dafür he has very little aptitude for it, F he is a very bad (or poor) hand at it. — **3.** (Verhängnis) destiny, fate (myth. als Gottheit: Fate); unvermeidliches: fatality, (Los) lot, (Zufall) chance. — **4.** ⚒ pl. ~e (zu gewinnende Erzarten) paying ore, mineral lode sg.

Ge-schicke (◡´◡) n ㉒ frequent (sending of) messages, many errands pl.

Ge-schicklichkeit (◡´◡◡) f = Geſchick 2.

ge-schickt (◡´) [mhd.] p.p. und a. ⏺ **1.** Bed. des inf. ſchicken. — **2.** (ſ. Geſchick 2) apt, skilled, dexterous; clever, adroit, ingenious; bſd. mit den Händen: F handy; (erfahren) expert (in et. at a th., in (doing) a th.); adv. ⏺ ausgedacht ingeniously (or cleverly) contrived. — **3.** e-n zu et. ⏺ (tauglich) machen to enable a p. to do a th., to fit a p. for a th.; zu et. ⏺ ſein to be fit(ted) for a th.

Ge-schiebe (◡´◡) n ㉒ **1.** continuous pushing. — **2.** ⚒, geol. erratic blocks or boulders pl., shifting rocks pl.; **~lehm** m ⏺ geol. boulder-clay.

ge-schieden (◡´◡) p.p. von ſcheiden.

ge-schieht (◡´) 3. Prſ. sg. præs. v. geſchehen.

ge-schienen (◡´◡) p.p. von ſcheinen.

Ge-schieße (◡´◡) n ㉒ much shooting.

Ge-schimpfe (◡´◡) n ㉒ volley of abuse, abusive language; invective(s pl.).

Ge-schirr (◡´) [ahd.: ſchirren] n ⓑ. **1.** = Gerät. — **2.** (Gefäß) vessel; coll.: irdenes ~ earthenware, pottery; (Küchen=)~ pots and pans pl., crockery; eiſernes: iron saucepans pl.; (Silber=)~ plate. — **3.** ✠ ~ für Zugtiere: harness, trappings pl.; von Pferden: ſie legen ſich (ober gehen) ins ~ (ziehen eifrig) they are pulling hard, F fig. von Menſchen: (ſtrengen ſich an) they are working with a will or F with a vengeance, they are putting their shoulders to the wheel. — **4.** (Wagen u. Geſpann) horse and carriage; eines Fuhrmanns: cart (or van, wagon) and horses.

Ge-schirr=bürſte ⊕ (◡´◡...) f ㉒ harnessbrush; **=druck** m, **=fach** n ⏺ m Weberei: leaf; **=kammer** f harness-room; **=laden** m china-shop; **=leder** n ha. leather; **=meister** m: a) ha.-keeper; b) ⚓ guard of the mail; **=schnalle** f ha.-buckle.

⚛ scientific; ⚘ botanical; ⚲ geography; ⊕ machinery; ⚒ mining; ⚔ military; ⚓ marine; ⚛ commercial; ⚭ postal; 🚆 railway.

[Geschlabber] — 436 — [Geschreibe]

Ge-schlabber P (⌣‿⌣) [nbb.] n 22 (Schlürfen) lapping; (Geifern) slavering; (Geschwätz) babble, idle talk or talking.

ge-schlafen (⌣‿⌣) p.p. von schlafen.

ge-schlagen (⌣‿⌣) p.p. von schlagen.

Ge-schlecht (⌣‿) [ahd.; * schlagen] n ⓑb., poet. ⓑb. 1. (Art) kind, species. — 2. das männliche (weibliche) ~ von Tieren, Pflanzen male (female) sex; das schöne (schwache, starke) ~ the fair (gentle[r], strong) sex; ⚥ mit getrennten ~ern: ⚥ diclinous. — 3. gr. das männliche, weibliche, sächliche ~ the masculine, feminine, neuter gender. — 4. (Abstammung) race, stock, origin; (Familie) family; von altem ~ of ancient lineage or descent; ein edles ~ a noble house. — 5. (Menschen-alter) das gegenwärtige ~ the present (or rising) generation; künftige ~er future generations or ages pl.

Ge-schlechter-kunde (⌣‿⌣…) f 62 genealogy; **=kundige(r)** m genealogist.

…geschlechtig (…⌣‿) 66 i. Zssgn., z.B. getrennt~ ⚥: ⚥ diclinous.

ge-schlechtlich (⌣‿⌣) a. 66 1. sexual; Der Umgang sexual intercourse. — 2.(einer Gattung angehörig) generic(al).

Ge-schlechts-adel (⌣‿…) m 62 hereditary nobility; **=alter** n generation, age; **=art** f generic type; **=baum** m genealogical tree, pedigree; **=eigentümlichkeit** f sexual characteristic; **=endung** f, gr. termination marking the gender; **=fall** m, gr. genitive (case); **=folge** f lineage, descent; successive generations pl.; **=forscher** m genealogist; **=glied** n, physiol. sexual organ; **=glieder** genitals pl.; **=krankheit** f sexual disease or malady; **=kunde** ꝛc. = Geschlechterkunde ꝛc.; **=leben** n, **=liebe** f sexual life, love; **=linie** f line of descent.

ge-schlecht(s)-los (⌣‿…) a. 66 without (distinction of) sex or gender; ⚥: ⚥ agamic, agamous; zo. ⚥lose Zeugung: ⚥ agamogenesis; **=losigkeit** f 62 absence of sex or gender.

Ge-schlechts-name (⌣‿…) m 62: a) family name, surname; b) ⚥, zo. generic name; **=organ** n = =glied; **=register** n genealogical table; vgl. =baum; **=reife** f puberty; **=tafel** f genealogical table; **=teile** m/pl. genital (or privy) parts, genitals pl., ⚥ genitalia pl., ⚥: ⚥ stamina (or stamens) and pistils pl.; **=trieb** m sexual instinct or desire; **=unterschied** m difference of sex or gender; **=urkunde** f documentary pedigree; **=verschiedenheit** f = =unterschied; **=wahl** f sexual selection; **=wappen** n family crest or arms pl.; **=wissenschaft** f genealogy; **=wort** n, gr. article; **=zeichen** n/pl. = =teile.

Ge-schleife (⌣‿⌣) n 22 hunt. entrance to a badger's kennel.

Ge-schleppe (⌣‿⌣) n 22 1. = schleppen IV. — 2. (Schleppe am Kleide) train. — 3. hunt. (Witterung für Fuchshunde) drag.

ge-schlichen (⌣‿⌣) p.p. von schleichen.

ge-schliffen (⌣‿⌣) p.p. von schleifen; **~heit** f 46 e-s Edelsteins: polish; fig. des Stils, auch: elegance, ease. [gluttony.]

Ge-schlinge¹ (⌣‿⌣) n 22 (v. pl.) (Fressen)

Ge-schlinge² (⌣‿⌣) [Schlund] n 22 (mit pl.) interlacing parts pl., bsd. hunt. u. Schlächterei: pluck (or liver, heart, and lights) of game or beast; giblets pl. of a goose. &c.

ge-schliffen, **ge-schloffen**, **ge-schlossen** (⌣‿⌣) p.p. von schließen, schleifen, schließen.

Ge-schluchze (⌣‿⌣) n 22 great sobbing.

ge-schlungen (⌣‿⌣) p.p. von schlingen.

Ge-schmack (⌣‿) [ahd.; * schmecken] m ⓣc. (pl. F co. auch ⓒc.) 1. taste, von Speisen a. flavour. angenehmer: relish. scharfer: piquant flavour, piquancy; einen bittern ~ im Munde h. to have a bitter taste in one's mouth; ohne ~ flavourless, insipid. — 2. fig. taste (or liking) for; ~ an et. finden to take (a) delight in a th., to fancy (or relish) a th.; sie kann der Sache keinen ~ abgewinnen she does not take to it; e-m den ~ an et. verderben to set a p. against a th.; ein Mädchen ganz nach seinem ~ a girl quite to his taste or after his own heart.

Ge-schmack-los (⌣‿…) a. 66 tasteless (unschmackhaft) unsavoury (schal) stale, insipid, flat; fig. (ohne Sinn für das Schöne) without taste; (abgeschmackt) in bad taste; **=losigkeit** f 46 tastelessness, unsavouriness, staleness; fig. want of taste, bad taste. [taste.]

Ge-schmack-sache (⌣‿…) f 62 matter of

Ge-schmacks-empfindung (⌣‿…) f 62 sensation of taste; ⚥frei a. 66 tasteless; **=lehre** f: ⚥ aesthetics; **=nerv** m, anat.: ⚥ gustatory nerve; **=organ** n organ of taste; **=richtung** f taste, ⚥ aesthetical tendency; **=sache** f = Geschmack-s.; **=sinn** m taste, ⚥ gustation; path. Mangel des ~s: ⚥ ageusia, ageusis; **=verirrung** f aberration (or perverseness) of taste; **=werkzeuge** n/pl. anat.: ⚥ gustatory organs pl.; ⚥widrig a. contrary to (good) taste, in bad taste; **=widrigkeit** f bad taste.

ge-schmack-voll (⌣‿…) a. 66 (schmackhaft) savoury, appetizing; fig. tasteful, F tasty; (anmutig) graceful, elegant; ein ⚥(adv.) eingerichtetes Haus an elegantly furnished house; ⚥widrig s. geschmacks-…

Ge-schmause (⌣‿⌣) n 22 long (or continued) feasting or banqueting.

Ge-schmeichel (⌣‿⌣) n 22 = Schmeichelei.

Ge-schmeide (⌣‿⌣) [ahd. * schmieden] n 22 jewellery, jewels pl.; (Schmuck) ornaments, trinkets pl.; **~handel** m trade in jewellery; **~händler(in** f) m dealer in jewels, jeweller; **~kästchen** n jewel-case or -box.

ge-schmeidig (⌣‿⌣) [mhd. * schmieden] a. 66 supple (a. fig.); (biegsam) bendable, flexible, pliant; (gewandt) versatile; (glatt) smooth; De Zunge glib (or voluble) tongue; von Metallen: (hämmerbar) malleable, (dehnbar) ductile, (weich) soft; fig. (folgsam) docile; (nachgiebig) yielding; **~keit** f 46 suppleness, flexibility, pliancy; versatility; smoothness; malleability, ductility, softness; fig. docility; yieldingness.

Ge-schmeiß (⌣‿) [mhd. * schmeißen] n ⓐa. 1. excrements pl., dung; von Fliegen: fly-dirt(s pl.) or -blows pl. — 2. (ekles Gewürm) vermin; fig. von Menschen:

dregs pl. of humanity, outcasts pl. of society, scum (of the earth). rabble.

Ge-schmetter (⌣‿⌣) n 22 loud blare. shrill sounds pl.; flourish of trumpets.

Ge-schmier(e) (⌣‿) n ⓒc. (22) 1. paint, daub, daubing. — 2. (Gekritzel) scrawl, scrawling, scribbling. — 3. von Weinen: adulteration.

ge-schmissen (⌣‿⌣) p.p. von schmeißen.

ge-schmolzen (⌣‿⌣) p.p. von schmelzen.

Ge-schmunzel (⌣‿⌣) n 22 smirking (and smiling).

Ge-schmus (⌣‿), **…se** (⌣‿) [hebr.] n ⓐa., 22 (Geschwätz) talk, prattle.

Ge-schnäbel (⌣‿⌣) n 22 billing (and cooing); vgl. Geküsse.

ge-schnäbelt (⌣‿⌣) a. 66 beaked, ⚥: ⚥ rostrate(d). [tinued) snoring.]

Ge-schnarche (⌣‿⌣) n 22 (loud or con-

Ge-schnatter (⌣‿⌣) n 22 cackling; fig. (Geplapper) gabbling, chattering, F mag, magging, jabbering.

Ge-schnaufe (⌣‿⌣) n 22 puffing (and blowing, panting).

ge-schniegelt (⌣‿⌣) p.p. u. a. f. schniegeln.

ge-schnitten (⌣‿⌣) p.p. von schneiden.

ge-schnoben (⌣‿⌣) p.p. von schnauben.

Ge-schnörkel (⌣‿⌣) n 22 scrolls pl.; Kunst: fanciful carved work; Schrift: flourishes pl.

Ge-schnüffel (⌣‿⌣) n 22 sniffing.

Ge-schnurre (⌣‿⌣) n 22 whiz(zing), buzz(ing); v. Rädern: rattle; v. Katzen: purr(ing). [von schieben, schelten.]

ge-schoben (⌣‿⌣), **ge-scholten** (⌣‿⌣) p.p.

Ge-schöpf (⌣‿) [vgl. Schöpfer] n ⓑb. creature, weit. production; armes ~ poor creature or F thing!; jämmerliches ~ miserable wretch.

ge-schoren (⌣‿⌣) p.p. von scheren.

Ge-schoß (⌣‿) [ahd. * schießen] n ⓐa. 1. (geschossener oder geschleuderter Körper) projectile, missile, dart; ⚥ artill. Geschosse pl., auch: shot and shell. — 2. (Schuß an Pflanzen) shoot. — 3. (Stockwerk) story, floor; flat.

Ge-schoß-bahn (⌣‿…) f 62 path of a projectile, (Flugbahn) trajectory.

ge-schossen (⌣‿⌣) p.p. von schießen.

Ge-schoß-garbe ⚥ (⌣‿…) f cone of dispersion; **=geschwindigkeit** f speed of a projectile; **=kern**, **=mantel** m body, coating of a projectile; **=wirkung** f effect of a shot, execution (wrought by artillery).

ge-schraubt (⌣‿) a. 66 fig. affected; **~heit** f 46 affectation, stilted manner, mannerism.

Ge-schrei (⌣‿) n ⓐa. 1. cry(ing), shriek, shrieking, scream(ing); lautes ~ shouting, vociferation, F bawling; von Tieren: (Esel) braying, (Hahn) crowing, (Eule) screeching, (Katze) mewing, caterwauling; großes ~ erheben, machen to set up a great shout or a loud cry, to clamour aloud. — 2. fig. (übertreibendes Gerede) great noise or stir or F fuss; viel ~ [wahrscheinlich aus Ge-scheererei] und wenig Wolle (auch: um nichts) much ado about nothing; great boast, little roast. — 3. (übles Gerücht) evil report; e-n ins ~ bringen to bring a p. into disrepute or discredit.

Ge-schreibe (⌣‿⌣) n 22 much writing.

Zeichen (s. S. XVII): F familiär; P Volkssprache; Ρ Gaunersprache; ⸜ selten; † alt (auch gestorben); * neu (auch geboren); +† unrichtig;

[Geschreibsel] — 437 — [Gesellschaft]

Ge-schreibsel (⌣́⌣) n ㉒ (Geschriebenes) writing; (Gekritzel) scrawl, scribbling.
ge-schrieben (⌣⌣́), **ge-schrien** (⌣́) p.p. von schreiben, schreien.
ge-schritten (⌣⌣́) p.p. v. schreiten.
ge-schroben (⌣⌣́) p.p. von schrauben.
ge-schroten (⌣⌣́) p.p. von schroten.
ge-schuht (⌣́) a. ⓖ shod, with shoes.
ge-schunden (⌣⌣́) p.p. v. schinden.
ge-schuppt (⌣́) p.p. von schuppen und a. ⓖ scaled, scaly; ♃ und zo.: ⚕ imbricate(d); her. (e)scalloped. [shaking.]
Ge-schüttel (⌣⌣́) n ㉒ continuous
Ge-schütz ⚔ ⚓ (⌣́) [mhd.: *schießen] n ⑪a. artill. cannon, (big) gun; coll. ordnance; das grobe ~ big guns pl., heavy artillery or pieces pl. of ordnance, fig. weighty arguments pl.; bespanntes ~ mounted gun; gezogenes, glattes ~ rifled, smooth-bored cannon; die ~e auffahren to place the guns (in position); e. ~ bedienen, richten, abfeuern, entladen to serve, lay, fire, unshot a gun.
Ge-schütz-aufstellung ⚔⚓(⌣⌣́...) f ㊻ putting the guns in position; **=bank** f barbette; **=bedienung** f = Bedienung(s-mannschaft); **=bohrerei** ⊙ f boring of guns; **=bronze** f gun-bronze; **=donner** m roar (or booming) of the guns; **=einschnitt** m emplacement; **=feuer** n fire (or practice) of the guns; **=führer** m leading gunner; **=gießerei** ⊙ f gun-factory; **=kugel** f cannon-ball; **=kunst** f gunnery; **=metall** n gun-metal; **=park** m park (or train) of artillery; **=pforte** ⚓ f porthole; **=probe** f testing of ordnance; **=protze** f carriage of a gun; **=rohr** n barrel of a gun; Seele eines ~s bore of a gun; **=salve** f charge (or volley) of artillery; ⚓ broadside; **=stand** m ground for the gun; **=wagen** m gun-carriage, limber; **=weite** f bore (of a cannon); **=wesen** n gunnery, artillery; **=zubehör** n gun-gear, gunner's requisites pl.; **=zug** m = park.
Ge-schwader ⚓ (⌣⌣́) [nhd. 16. sac.; *it. squadra f] n ㉒ (Flottenabteilung) squadron; **~chef** m ㊷ commodore.
...geschwänzt (...⌣⌣́) i. Zsfgn., z.B. lang-~ long-tailed.
Ge-schwätz (⌣́) n ⑪a. idle (or empty) talk, babble, chit-chat, (silly) prattle, gabble; (Klatscherei) gossip, tittle-tattle; endloses ~ long rigmarole; poet. ripple of the waves, murmur of the brook.
ge-schwätzig (⌣⌣́) a. ⓖ talkative, loquacious, stärker: garrulous, (wortreich) verbose, full of talk; **~keit** (⌣⌣⌣́-) f ㊻ talkativeness, loquacity, loquaciousness, garrulity; verbosity.
ge-schweift (⌣́) p.p. und a. ⓖ curved.
ge-schweige (⌣⌣́) [nhd.] adv. u. cj. (e-e Behauptung steigernd), z.B. ich täte es nicht für mich, ~ (viel weniger) denn für ihn ... much less for him; noch nicht ein Viertel, ~ denn die Hälfte not as much as a quarter, let alone one half.
ge-schweigen (⌣⌣́) [ahd.] v/n. ~ (nur inf. u. 1. Person pres. gbr.) 1. dessen zu ~, was er getan hat omitting or not to mention or to say nothing of ... 2. parenthetisch: ~ (um) zu ~ = geschweige.
Ge-schwelge (⌣⌣́) n ㉒ revelry.

Ge-schwemm(e) (⌣⌣́(⌣)) n ⑪b. ㉒ 1. continual floating. — 2. (Flut) flood.
ge-schwiegen (⌣⌣́) p.p. von schweigen.
ge-schwind a. **=e** (⌣́(⌣)) [mhd.: gesund] a. ⓖ quick; (flink) swift, fleet, nimble; (rasch arbeitend) prompt, expeditious, smart; (schleunig) rapid, speedy; Se Reise fast (or quick) journey; adv. ~ reisen, sprechen to travel, to speak fast or quickly; ~er gehen to walk (or go) faster, to quicken (or mend) one's pace; er wußte nicht, was er ~ (in der Eile) tun sollte he did not know at (or for) the moment (or at once) what to do; (mach') ~! make haste!, look sharp!
Ge-schwindigkeit (⌣⌣⌣́-) f ㊻ (s. geschwind) quickness, swiftness; speed (s. affenartig), celerity; mech. auch: velocity, der Zunge: volubility; e-s Schiffes: headway; im Handeln, Fördern: promptness, expedition, dispatch; mech. gleich-mäßige (beschleunigte, verzögerte) ~ uniform (accelerated, retarded) velocity; reißende ~ rapidity; in der ~ in a hurry, hurriedly; on the spur of the moment; Sprichw. ~ ist keine Hexerei conjuring (or legerdemain) requires no magic or sorcery.
Ge-schwindigkeits-messer (⌣⌣⌣́-⌣⌣) m ㉒: a) ⊙ mach.: speed-indicator, tachymeter; b) ⚓: ⚕ sillometer; **=meß-kunst** f: ⚕ tachymetry; **=übersetzung** f ⊙ in Automobilen: speed-gear.
Ge-schwind-marsch ⚔ (⌣⌣́...) m ㊷ quick (or rapid) march; im ~ in (or by) forced marches; **=schreibe-kunst** f shorthand (-writing), ⚕ stenography, tachygraphy; **=schreiber(in** f) m short-hand-writer; **=schrift** f shorthand (system); **=schritt** ⚔ m double-quick step, quick march; im ~ at the double.
Ge-schwirr (⌣́) n ⑪b. whizzing, buzz.
Ge-schwister (⌣⌣́) [mhd.: *Schwester] n ㉒ (jetzt meist pl.): sie sind wie ~ they are like brother and sister; alle meine ~ all my brothers and sisters.
Ge-schwister-kind (⌣⌣́...) n ㊷: wir sind ~er, ich bin ~ mit ihm (ihr) I am his (her) first cousin, we are first cousins; sie ist ~ mit mir she is a first cousin of mine.
ge-schwisterlich (⌣⌣⌣́) a. ⓖ of brother and sister; brotherly, fraternal, sisterly.
Ge-schwister-liebe (⌣⌣́...) f ㊷ brotherly (or sisterly) love or affection; **=paar** n brother and sister.
ge-schwollen, ge-schwommen (⌣⌣́) p.p. von schwellen, schwimmen.
ge-schworen¹ (⌣⌣́) p.p. von schwären.
ge-schworen² (⌣⌣́) ⓖ (D 9) I p.p. von schwören und a. 1. in den Bed. des inf. — 2. (durch einen Eid gebunden) sworn (in); Ser (abgesagter) Feind sworn (or mortal) enemy; Ser Freund friend for life. — II **~e(r)** m ㊸ 3. (Mitglied des Schwurgerichts) juryman; Gesamtheit der ~en the jury; m-e Herren ~en! gentlemen of the jury!; e-n vor die ~en stellen to send a p.'s case before a jury, to commit a p. for trial. — 4. (vereidigter Beamter) sworn-in officer.
Ge-schwor(e)nen-gericht(s-hof m) n (⌣⌣́⌣⌣) ㊷ court of assizes; **=liste** f

jury-list, panel; auf die ~ setzen to empanel; **=obmann** m foreman of the jury.
Ge-schwulst (⌣́) [ahd.; *schwellen] f ⑩ mst path. swelling; ⚕ inflation.
ge-schwunden, ge-schwungen (⌣⌣́) p.p. von schwinden, schwingen.
Ge-schwür (⌣́) [ahd.; *schwären] n ⑪c. meist path. boil; (Eiter-ansammlung) ulcer, abscess, ⚕ aposteme; krebsartiges: tumour, cancer; (offene, unheilbare Wunde) running sore; eiterndes ~ gathering; ein ~ aufstechen to lance an ulcer or abscess; mit ~en bedeckt ulcerous.
Ge-schwür-bildung (⌣́...) f ㊷ ulceration; **=erzeugend** a. ⓖ producing ulcers; ⚕ exulceratory. [ated.]
ge-schwürig (⌣⌣́) a. ⓖ path. ulcer-]
Ge-schwür-öffnung (⌣́...) f ㊷, **=schnitt** m, surg. cutting open an abscess.
ge-sechst (⌣́st) a. ⓖ astrol. Ser Schein (a.: **~schein** m ㊷): ⚕ sextile aspect.
ge-segnen, fast † (⌣⌣́) [ahd.] v/a. ㊴b* = segnen, z.B. Gott gesegne es ihm! God bless him for it!
ge-sehen (⌣⌣́) p.p. von sehen.
Ge-selchte(s) südb. (⌣⌣́) n ㊶ (Rauchfleisch) smoked meat.
Ge-sell, ~e (⌣́(⌣)) [ahd.; *Saal] m ㊵, ㊹, **~in** f ㊷ 1. companion, (Kamerad) comrade, mate, F pal; fauler ~ idle fellow or vagabond; langweiliger ~ dull companion, slow fellow; lustiger ~ merry boon-companion, jolly fellow or F chap. — 2. Handwerk: (ausgedienter Lehrling) journeyman, z.B. Sattler-Lehrling journeyman saddler; a. oft: ~meister.
ge-sellen (⌣⌣́) [ahd.] I v/a. und sich ~ v/refl. ⑧⁂: sich ~ zu to strike up a companionship with; to associate with, to join; sich zu-ea. ~ to flock together; durch die Ehe ~ ~ to ally (o.s.), to unite in wedlock, &c.; Sprichw. s. gleich 7. — II ~ n ㉓ = Gesellung.
Ge-sellen-bildungsverein (⌣⌣⌣́...) m ㊷ working men's institute; **=herberge** f etwa: journeymen's lodging-house; **=jahre** n/pl., **=leben** n, **=lohn** m journey-man's years of service, life, wages pl.
Ge-sellenschaft (⌣⌣⌣́) f ㊷ 1. condition (or status) of a journeyman. — 2. coll. body (or union) of journeymen.
Ge-sellen-stand (⌣⌣́...) m ㊷, **=verein** m journeymen's condition or status, association or union; **=zeit** f = ~jahre.
ge-sellig (⌣⌣́) [mhd.] a. ⓖ companionable, sociable, convivial; von Tieren (auch fig. von Menschen): gregarious; Ses Leben social life; Ser Verein club (for sociable purposes); Se Zs.=kunft convivial (or sociable) gathering.
Ge-selligkeit (⌣⌣⌣́) f ㊷ companionableness, sociability, conviviality; gregariousness; sociality; **~s-trieb** (⌣⌣⌣...) m ㊷ sociable instinct.
Ge-sellschaft (⌣⌣́) f ㊷ 1. society; (Genossenschaft) companionship; bürgerliche ~ civil community; aus der menschlichen ~ ausgestoßen outside the pale of human society; in seiner ~ in his company or presence. — 2. feine(re) ~ high life, society, aristocratic circles pl.; flotte ~ gay (or smart) set; geschlossene ~ club; lockere ~ loose company, fast set; iro. e-e saubere ~

♪ Musik; ⚕ Wissenschaft; ♣ Pflanze; ♀ Geographie; ⊙ Technik; ⚒ Bergbau; ⚔ Militär; ⚓ Marine; ⚖ Handel; ✉ Post; 🚆 Eisenbahn.

[Gesellschafter] — 438 — [Gesichtslähmung]

a nice set; in ~ gehen to go into (or mix in) society; e-m ~ leisten to keep a p. company; sich in guter ~ bewegen to move in good society or circles. — 3. geladene ~ invited company, guests pl.; kleine ~ small party; große ~ large party, a.: crush; (Abend=)~ (fr.) soirée; (Tanz=)~ dancing-party; ~en geben to give parties, to receive company, weitS. to keep open house; wir hatten ~ we had (asked) a few friends. — 4. (Künstler=)~ (travelling) company; ♣ (Handels=)~ company; ~ mit beschränkter Haftung (abbr. G. m. b. H.) limited (liability) company; mit e-m in ~ (Kompanie) treten to enter (or go) into partnership with a p.
Ge-sellschafter (~~~) m ㉒, **~in** f ㊼ 1. companion; associate; guter (schlechter) ~ good (bad) company. — 2. ~in einer alten Dame ꝛc. lady companion. — 3. ♣ (Handlungs=)~ partner; stiller (tätiger) ~ sleeping (acting) partner.
ge-sellschaftlich (~~~) a. ⓖ social (intercourse, position, &c.); (gesellig) sociable (talents, &c.); ℒe (feine) Bildung good breeding; ℒe Manieren society manners pl.; aus ℒen Rücksichten from social considerations; seine ℒe Stellung verlieren to lose caste or one's social position; ℒer Verkehr social intercourse; **~keit** f ㊻ social life or intercourse; sociality; vgl. Geselligkeit.
Ge-sellschafts-anzug (~~~) m ㊅㉒ evening (or full) dress; **=bank** ♣ f joint-stock bank; **=dame** f lady companion; **=firma** f firm of partners; **=fonds** ♣ m funds pl. of a company; **=glied** n member of a society; **=handlung** ♣ f commercial company; **=haus** n club-house; in engl. Bädern oft: assembly-rooms pl.; **=inseln** ♀ npr. f/pl. (in der Südsee, französischer Besitz) Society Islands pl.; **=kapital** ♣ n capital of a company; **=kreis** m social circle; **=mitglied** n = =glied; **=name** ♣ m name of a firm (of partners); **=ordnung** f social contract; **=rechnung** f, arith. rule of partnership; **=reise** f tour organized by a company, Cook's &c. tour; **=spiel** n society game, Karten: round game; ~e pl. für das Haus (im Freien) indoor (outdoor) games or sports pl.; **=sprache** f language of polite society; **=stück** n, paint. scene from high life; **=tänzchen** n private dance; **=theater** n amateur theatre, private theatricals pl.; **=ton** m tone (prevailing in good society); **=trieb** m sociable (or gregarious) instinct; **=vermögen** n = =kapital; **=vertrag** m: a) = =ordnung; b) ♣ agreement (or deed) of partnership; **=wagen** m omnibus, break, wagonette; **=widrig** a. ⓖ contrary to the rules of (good) society; antisocial; **=wissenschaft** f sociology; **=zimmer** n reception-room. [alliance.]
Ge-sellung (~~) f ㊻ association;
Ge-senk (~~) n ⑩b. 1. (Senkung) cavity, hollow; (Grube) pit; (Schlucht) ravine, ⚒ (Vertiefung) socket; deep level; (Boden eines Schachtes) bottom of a pit. — 2. Fischerei: sinking-weight for dragnets; Messerschmiede: (vertiefte Form) swage.

Gesenke ♀ (~~~) [(P) tschech. Eichengebirge] npr. n ⑫α. das Mährische ~ the Moravian Mountains pl.
ge-sessen (~~~) p.p. von sitzen.
Ge-setz (~~) [mhd.; *setzen] n ⑩a. law, geschriebenes: statute; bibl. das ~ (5 Bücher Mosis) u. die Propheten the law and the prophets; ein ~ einbringen, durchbringen to bring in, to pass a bill; ~e geben to legislate; sich et. zum ~e machen to make a rule of s.th.; zum ~ werden to pass into law; nach dem Buchstaben des ~es according to the letter of the law, in the literal acception (or by a strict interpretation) of the law.
Ge-setz-antrag (~~~...) m ㊅㉒ bill; einen ~ stellen, durchbringen to move, to carry a bill; **=ausleger** m expounder of the law, bsd. röm. Altertum: jurisconsult; **=buch** n statute-book; code; **=entwurf** m legislative project, (draft of a) bill; dem Parlament einen ~ vorlegen to submit (the draft of) a bill to (or to introduce a bill in) parliament.
Ge-setzes-auslegung (~~~...) f ㊅㉒ interpretation of the law; **=bruch** m infraction (or infringement) of the law; **=kraft** f legal power or force; ~ erhalten, erlangen to pass into law, to be enacted; **=übertreter** m law-breaker.
ge-setz-gebend (~~...) a. ⓖ legislative (assembly, body, &c.); ℒer Körper m legislature; **=geber** m law-giver, legislator; ♁ nomothete; **=geberisch** a. legislative; **=gebung** f legislation; **=gebungs-gewalt** f legislative power; **=kräftig** a. legal(ly valid); **=kunde** f knowledge of the law, legal knowledge; **=kundige(r)** m lawyer; ♁ jurist.
ge-setzlich (~~~) a. ⓖ = gesetzmäßig; ℒes Datum date fixed (or appointed) by law; **~keit** f ㊻ = Gesetzmäßigkeit.
ge-setz-los (~~...) a. ⓖ lawless, without law(s); (ohne Oberhaupt) anarchical; **=losigkeit** f lawlessness, anarchy; **=mäßig** a. lawful (remedy), legitimate (heir, claim), legal (force), constitutional (rule, right); adv. ℒ bestimmt determined by law; **=mäßigkeit** f lawfulness; legitimacy; legality; **=rolle** f bsd. ehemals: scroll containing laws; **=sammlung** f body (or code) of laws.
ge-setzt (~~) p.p. u. a. ⓖ 1. in den Bed. des inf. setzen. — 2. (ruhig, maßvoll) quiet, sedate, calm; (gefaßt) composed; (ernst) grave, serious; (nüchtern) sober, staid, steady; (bescheiden) modest; von ℒem Alter of mature age, middle-aged; ℒes Wesen staid (or dignified) demeanour. — 3. ℒer Fall supposition; ℒen Fall, ℒenfalls // (let us) suppose that /; ℒ, daß es so wäre, ℒ, et (od. dem) wäre so provided such was the case.
Ge-setz-tafeln (~~...) f/pl. ㊅㉒ bei den Juden: Decalogue; bei den Römern: Twelve-Table Law(s pl.).
Ge-setzt-heit (~~) f ㊻ (s. gesetzt 2) quiet manner, sedateness; gravity; staidness, steadiness.
Gesetz-übertretung (~~~) f ㊅㉒, **=umgehung** f transgression, evasion of the law; **=vollstreckung** f execution (or administration) of the law; **=vor-**

=schlag m legislative proposal, vgl. =antrag; **=widrig** a. ⓖ contrary to law, unlawful, illegal; **=widrigkeit** f unlawfulness, illegality.
Ge-seufze (~~~) n ㉒ endless sighing.
Ge-sicht (~~) [ahd.; *sehen] n ④b. (~ 4: ⑩b.) 1. (Sehvermögen) (eye-)sight, (range of) vision; (Augen) eyes pl.; ein kurzes ~ haben to be short- (or near-)sighted; aus dem ~e verlieren to lose out of sight, to lose sight of; ↓ das Land aus dem ~ verlieren to lay the land; etwas ins ~ fassen to face a th.; fig. etwas im ~ behalten to keep a th. in view; et. zu ~e bekommen to notice (or see) a th., F to catch sight of a th.; ↓ Land zu ~ bekommen to sight land. — 2. (Angesicht, Antlitz) face, countenance, poet. visage; (Miene) mien, physiognomy, Pphiz; das ~ betr. facial; auf sein ehrliches ~ hin for the sake of his honest face or look; er ist seinem Vater aus dem ~e geschnitten he is the very image (or F spit) of his father; F fig. ein anderes ~ aufsetzen to change one's countenance, F to pull quite a different face; den Hut ins ~ drücken to pull one's hat over one's eyes; die Sonne im ~ haben to have ... in one's face; e-m ins ~ lachen to laugh in a p.'s face; e-m ein böses (freundliches) ~ machen to frown (to smile) at a p.; ~ to look angrily (pleasantly) at a p.; ein langes (saures) ~ m. to make a long (a sour) face; ich werde es ihm ins ~ sagen I will tell him so to his face; j-m ins ~ schlagen to strike a p. in the (or to slap a p.'s face; fig. aller guten Sitte ins ~ schlagen to act in defiance of all rules of decency; e-m (gerade) ins ~ sehen to look a p. (straight or full) in the face; er lacht übers ganze ~ he laughs all over his face. — 3. ~er (Grimassen) machen, schneiden to make grimaces or F faces at a p.; e-m schiefe ~er m. F to make mouths at a p.; sie macht ein ~ wie die Katze, wenn es donnert she makes a face (or she looks) as black as thunder. — 4. (pl. ~e) (übernatürliche Erscheinung) vision, apparition; (Sinnestäuschung) hallucination; das zweite (oder doppelte) ~ (prophetische Gabe) second sight. — 5. ⚔ = Visier 2.
Ge-sichtchen (~~~) n ㉔ (dim. von Gesicht), small face; hübsches ~ pretty face.
Ge-sichter-schneiden (~~~...) n ㊅ making grimaces; **=schneider(in** f) m one who makes grimaces.
Ge-sichts-achse (~~~...) f ㊅㉒ visual axis; **=ausdruck** m expression of the face; features pl., countenance, mien; **=bildung** f conformation (or shape) of the face, physiognomy; **=deuter(in** f) m; ♁ physiognomist; **=deutung** f: physiognomy; **=farbe** f complexion; **=feld** n: a) range of vision (fig. of ideas); b) ⚔ fire-zone; **=form** f = =bildung; **=krampf** m = =lähmung; **=kreis** m horizon (a. fig.); im =kreise within sight; vgl. =feld; j-m ~ erweitern to extend one's (intellectual) horizon, to expend one's views; einen beschränkten ~ haben to have narrow views, to be narrow-minded; **=lähmung** f, path.

Signs (see page XVII): F familiar; P vulgar; ↯ flash; ↘ rare; † obsolete (died); * new word (born); ⁺⁺ incorrect; ♪ music.

[Gesichtslänge] — 439 — [gesprächsweise]

(facial) neuralgia; paralysis of the face; =länge f length of face; =linie f: a) outline of the face, feature; b) opt. visual line; =muskel m, anat. facial muscle; =nerv m, anat.: a) facial nerve; b) (Sehnerv) optic nerve; =punkt m point of view (a. fig.); unter verschiedenen ~en, a. from different sides or aspects; =rose f, path.: ⚕ erysipelas; =schmerz m, path. face-ache, neuralgia in the face; =schnitt m cast (F cut) of the face; =schwäche f weak(ness of) sight; =sinn m (eye-)sight, ⚕ visual faculty; =strahl m, opt.: ⚕ visual ray; =täuschung f optical delusion; hallucination; =verzerrung f distortion of the face, grimace; =weite f range of sight, eye-shot; =winkel m: a) anat. facial angle; b) opt.: ⚕ visual angle; =zug m lineament; =züge features.

ge-siebent (‿‿)[7] p.p. u. a. 66 septenary.

Ge-sims ⊕ (‿‿) [mhd.;* Sims] n ⑳a. arch. moulding; (Kranz=)~ cornice; (Kamin=)~ mantel-piece or -board or -shelf; (Getäfel) wainscot(ting); ~hobel m ⑫ join. moulding-(or cornice-)plane.

Ge-sinde (‿‿) [ahd.; *senden] n ㉒ (establishment of) servants pl.; vgl. Dienerschaft;~ =amt, =bureau n registry-office for servants; =kammer, =kost f servants' room, board.

Ge-sindel (‿‿) [nhd. dim. von Gesinde] n ㉒ rabble, mob; herrenloses ~ unruly (gang of) vagabonds or tramps pl.

Ge-sinde-lohn (‿‿ ...) m ㉒ servants' wages pl.; =ordnung f regulations pl. for servants; =stube, =tisch m servants' hall, table; =zeugnis-buch n = Dienstbuch.

Ge-singe (‿‿) n ㉒ (indifferent) singing, sing-song, humdrum tune.

ge-sinnt (‿‿) [Sinn] a. 66 1. anders⁓ of different views, of a different opinion. edel ⁓ noble- (or high-)minded; feindlich ⁓ hostile; gut (übel) ⁓ well (ill) disposed or affected; er ist liberal ⁓ he is a Liberal (in his politics), he holds (or sides) with the Liberals; die vaterländisch ~en people who are patriotically inclined, the patriotically minded; wie ist er ⁓? what opinions does he hold?; in der Politik: to what party does he belong? — 2. = gesonnen.

Ge-sinnung (‿‿) f ㊻ disposition, mind, way of thinking; feeling, sentiment; character; (Überzeugung) conviction; (Meinung) opinion, view; edle ~ noble-mindedness; treue ~ loyal attachment, loyalty; wohlwollende ~ kind(ly) disposition; seine ~ ändern to change one's mind, pol. to change sides.

Ge-sinnungs=genosse (‿‿ ...) m ⑫ one who holds the same opinion or views; (political) partisan or adherent; ⁓los a. 66 unprincipled; without a settled opinion; =losigkeit f lack of principle; ⁓treu a. loyal; =treue f loyalty; ⁓tüchtig a. of sound views, stanch, true (to the colours); =tüchtigkeit f (political) soundness, stanchness; =wechsel m change of opinion or views.

Ge-sippe (‿‿) n ㉒ kith and kind.

ge-sippt (‿‿) a. 66 akin (f. verwandt).

ge-sittet (‿‿) [Sitte] a. 66 1. mit Angabe des Wie: fein, gut ⁓ well-bred, of good breeding or behaviour or manners. — 2. abs. (fein⁓) well-mannered or -behaved; (gebildet) (highly) educated, polished; (höflich) courteous, (anständig) decent; hoch ⁓, a. of high moral principles; ein ⁓es Volk a (highly) civilized nation; ⁓ machen to civilize, polish.

Ge-sittung (‿‿) f ㊻ (f. gesittet) good breeding or manners pl.; civilization.

Ge-söff P (‿‿) n ⑳b. inferior beverage, bad drink, F slops pl.; (Saufen) F boozing.

ge-soffen (‿‿), ge-sogen (‿‿), ge-sonnen, ge-sotten, ge-spalten (‿‿) p.p. von saufen, saugen, sinnen, sieden, spalten.

Ge-span¹ (‿‿) [mag. ispan;* slaw. zupan] m ⑩c. (ungarischer Graf) lieutenant (or governor) of a county or district.

Ge-span² fast † (‿‿) [mhd.; *spannen] m ⑩c. u. ㊷ (Genosse), bsd. typ. bei Schriftsetzern: (Gassen=)~ companion.

Ge-spann (‿‿) [spannen] n ⑳b. 1. Zugtiere: yoke of bullocks; team of horses, oxen, &c., set of carriage-horses; feines ~ von Wagen u. Pferden F smart turn-out. — 2. fig. v. Personen u. Sachen: couple, pair.

Ge-spanschaft (‿‿) f ㊻ in Ungarn, etwa: county, administrative district.

ge-spannt (‿‿) p.p. u. a. 66 1. in den Bed. des inf. spannen. — 2. (straff) tight(ly stretched), tense, ↓ taut; fig. intense; path. (over-) excited, nervous; hoch ⁓e Erwartungen high expectations pl. — 3. fig.: a) ⁓e (angestrengte) Aufmerksamkeit close (or eager) attention; in der ⁓esten Erwartung on the tiptoe of expectation, in the most anxious suspense, on tenter-hooks; ich bin sehr auf den Ausgang ⁓ I am very anxious (or curious) to see the end of it, I am anxiously awaiting the upshot of it; ich bin ⁓, ob er es wirklich tut I wonder whether he will really do it; b) ⁓e (getrübte) Beziehungen, Verhältnisse zw. Freunden strained relations pl., coolness; in der Politik ꝛc. auch: tension; f. Fuß 7.

Ge-spannt-heit (‿‿) f ㊻ (f. gespannt) 1. eines Seiles ꝛc.: tightness, tension; path. (over-)excitement, nervousness. — 2. fig. ~ der Beziehungen strained relations pl. between friends, countries, &c.

Ge-sparr(e) ⊕ (‿‿) [Sparren] n ⑳b. (⑫) carp. rafters pl.

Ge-spaße (‿‿), südd. Ge-spaße (‿‿) n ㉒ jesting, joking, fun.

Ge-spenst (‿‿) [ahd. Lockung] n ⑳a. (Trugbild) phantom, spectre, ghost; (spukhafte Erscheinung) (ghostly) apparition; (Poltergeist) hobgoblin; es geht dort ein ~ um the place is haunted (by a ghost); fig. das ~ im Hause the skeleton in the cupboard.

ge-spenster=artig (‿‿ ...) a. 66 phantom-like, spectral; =erscheinung f (ghostly) apparition; =furcht f fear of ghosts; =geschichte f ghost-story; =glaube m belief in ghosts.

ge-spensterhaft (‿‿ ...) = gespenstisch.

Ge-spenster=reich (‿‿ ...) n ㉒ world (or realm) of spirits or spectres; =schiff n phantom-ship, Flying Dutchman; =spuk m ghostly visit(s pl.), hubbub caused by ghosts or goblins, F spook; =stunde f ghostly hour, poet. witching midnight-hour.

Ge-spenst=(heu)schrecke (‿‿...) f ⑫ ent. spectre (Phasma); =motte f Federmotte.

gespenstisch (‿‿) a. 66 phantom-, ghost-like, spectral, ghostly; F spookish; (sehr bleich) ghastly.

Ge-sperr (‿‿) n ⑳b. hunt. (die mit den Alten zs. haltenden Hühner) brood, covey (= Kette, Volk).

Ge-sperre (‿‿) n ⑫ 1. o. pl.: a) (Sperren) shutting (off); b) (Sichsperren) resistance; c) (Versperrung) stoppage, obstruction, block. — 2. mit pl. ⊕: a) = Gesparr; b) Uhrm. (Sperrad) ratchet with catch; Schlosserei: (Haken zum Verschluß) catch; ✠ an Fördermaschinen: safety-catch.

Ge-spiele (‿‿) [mhd.; *spielen] I n ㉒ endless play(ing). — II ~ m ㊷, Ge-spielin f ㊻ play-mate or -fellow.

ge-spien (‿‿) p.p. von speien.

Ge-spinne (‿‿) n ㉒ (much) spinning.

Ge-spinst ⊕ (‿‿) [mhd.; * spinnen] n ⑩a. (Gesponnenes) spinning, spun yarn or goods pl.; (Gewebe) woof, textile fabric. Ge-spinst=faser (‿‿ ...) f ⑫ textile fibre; =pflanze ⚘ f textile plant.

ge-splissen, ge-sponnen (‿‿) p.p. von spleißen, spinnen.

Ge-sponst (‿‿) [lt. sponsus, sponsa] m u. n ⑩a. fast †, jetzt nur F co. = Bräutigam, Braut und (bsd. n) Gemahl.

Ge-spött (‿‿) [spotten] n ⑳b. 1. mocking, mockery, scoffing, derision; sein ~ mit e-m, et. treiben to mock (or scoff, deride) a p., a th. — 2. (Gegenstand des Spottes) laughing-stock; sich zum ~ machen to expose o.s. to ridicule, to make o.s ridiculous.

Ge-spotte, Ge-spöttel (‿‿) n ㉒ (incessant) mocking or jeering; raillery.

Ge-spräch (‿ᷤ) [ahd.; * sprechen] n ⑳c. 1. (Austausch der Gedanken) talk; in geh. Spr.: colloquy; (Unterhaltung) conversation; thea., &c. (Zwie=⁓) dialogue; gelehrtes ~ learned discourse; polemisches, öffentliches: discussion, debate, conference; Plato(n)s ~e Plato's Dialogues pl.; ein ~ abbrechen to break off a conversation; ein ~ mit e-m anknüpfen, sich in ein ~ mit e-m einlassen to enter into (F to start) a conversation with a p.; das ~ auf et. bringen to bring a th. on the carpet, to broach a subject; ein ~ mit e-m führen to carry on a conversation with a p.; das ~ im Gang erhalten to keep the conversation going or the ball rolling. — 2. (allg. Besprochenes) (general) topic of conversation; er ist das ~ der (ganzen) Stadt ... the talk of the town, ... in everybody's mouth.

ge-sprächig (‿ᷤ) a. 66 talkative, fond of talking; (mitteilsam) communicative, (leutselig) affable; der Wein machte ihn ⁓ ...made him communicative, ...loosened his tongue; ~keit f ㊻ talkativeness, communicativeness, affability.

Ge-sprächs=buch (‿ᷤ ...) n ㉒ book of dialogues; =form f colloquial form; in ~, a. in (the) form of a dialogue; =gegenstand, =stoff m topic of conversation; =ton m colloquial (or conversational) tone; ⁓weise adv. colloquially; by way (or in the course) of conversation; in form of a dialogue.

⚕ scientific; ⚘ botanical; ⊕ geography; ⊖ machinery; ✠ mining; ⚔ military; ⚓ marine; ⚖ commercial; ✉ postal; 🚂 railway.

ge-spreizt (⌣́⌣) *p.p. v.* spreizen *u. a.* ⑥⑥ stilted, affected; **~heit** (⌣́⌣) *f* ④⑥ stiltedness, affectation, F (putting on)side; in der Kunst: mannerism.

ge-sprenkelt (⌣⌣́⌣) *p.p. von* sprenkeln *und a.* ⑥⑥ speckled, splashed, flecked.

Ge-springe (⌣⌣́⌣) *n* ㉒ constant jumping or springing or leaping.

ge-sprochen (⌣⌣́⌣), **ge-sprossen** (⌣⌣́⌣) *p.p.* von sprechen, sprießen.

Ge-sprudel (⌣⌣́⌣) *n* ㉒ 1. *o. pl.*: (perpetual) bubbling or spouting or sputter(ing); (Geplätscher) ripple. — 2. mit pl.: (das sprudelnde Meer) foaming (or seething) sea, surf.

ge-sprungen (⌣⌣́⌣) *p.p. v.* springen.

Ge-spuke (⌣⌣́⌣) *n* ㉒ ghostly apparitions *pl.*; *vgl.* Gespensterspuk.

gest. (a. †) *abbr.* für gestorben (f. sterben).

Ge-stade (⌣⌣́⌣) [mhd.;* Staden] *n* ㉒ allg.: bank, waterside; des Meeres: shore, coast; flaches ~ beach, foreshore.

Gestalt¹ (⌣́) [mhd.; *stellen] *f* ④⑥ 1. form(ation); durch die Umrisse bedingt: shape, figure; configuration; des Körpers auch: frame; (Wuchs, Statur) build, stature; (Größe) size, bulk; (Miene) mien, look; eine hohe, majestätische ~ a tall, majestic form or figure; der Ritter von der traurigen ~ (Don Quixote) the knight of the rueful countenance; von vielerlei ~ multiform. — 2. *ecol.* das Abendmahl in beiderlei ~ communion in both kinds, bread and wine; Arznei in ~ von Pulver nehmen to take medicine in the (form of powder); eine andere ~ annehmen, gewinnen to assume another (or to change in) form, to be(come) transformed; nach der ~ (Lage der Dinge) according to circumstances, F as things may go or be; sich in s-r wahren ~ zeigen to show o.s. in one's true colours or character. — 3. *adv.* im gen., mst zu einem Worte verbunden: der- (ob. dieser-), gleicher-⌣ in that manner or way or measure or fashion; *vgl.* derart; folgender-⌣ in the following way; gleicher-⌣ in like manner; solcher-⌣, sotaner-⌣ in such a manner or way.

...gestalt² ⤫ (⌣́) [ahd.] *a.* ⑥⑥ f. miß-, un-⌣, wohl-⌣. [(f. gestalten III).]

ge-stalt³ ⤫ (⌣́) (nur attributiv) = gestaltet)

ge-stalten (⌣⌣́⌣) [Gestalt] ⑥⑨* *I v/a.* h. ⑥⑥ to form, shape, fashion; Bildhauerei *2c.*: to model, to mould; ⌣d creative; plastic. — **II sich** ⌣ *v/refl.* 2. to assume (or take) a form or shape; sich anders ⌣ to take a different turn, to assume a new aspect; es gestaltete sich zu seinem Besten it turned to (or it proved) his advantage. — **III gestaltet** *p.p. u. a.* ⑥⑥. 3. in den Bed. des *inf.* 4. wohlgestalteter Mensch well- (or finely) made (or shaped) man. — 5. bei so gestalt(et)en Umständen under these circumstances, such being the case. — **IV** ~ *n* ㉒ 5. = Gestaltung 1.

ge-stalten-reich (⌣⌣́⌣...) *a.* ⑥⑥ presenting many forms or aspects, rich in form(s).

...gestaltig (...⌣⌣́⌣) in Zssgn, zB. viel-⌣ of many shapes or forms, multiform.

ge-stalt-los (⌣́⌣) *a.* ⑥⑥ shapeless, without (distinct) shape or form, ⌣

amorphous; (körperlos) immaterial; **=losigkeit** *f* ④⑥ shapelessness, ⌣ amorphism; immateriality.

Ge-staltung (⌣⌣́⌣) *f* ④⑥ 1. formation, shaping, &c. (f. gestalten I). — 2. (das Gestaltete) conformation, configuration; (Zuschnitt) fashion, style; (Zustand) state of affairs, condition; (Stufe) stage; (Lage) situation, position.

Ge-staltungs-fähigkeit (⌣⌣́⌣...) *f* ④⑥ plastic faculty, plasticity; **=lehre** ⚕ *u. zo.*: ⌣ morphology; **=talent** *n* organizing talent, creative genius.

Ge-stammel (⌣⌣́⌣) *n* ㉒ stammering (speech), stuttering; mumbling.

Ge-stampfe (⌣⌣́⌣) *n* ㉒ continued stamping or trampling or pattering (of feet).

ge-stand (⌣⌣́) *ind.*, **ge-stände** (⌣⌣́⌣) *subj. impf.* von gestehen.

ge-standen (⌣⌣́⌣) *p.p. v.* stehen *u.* gestehen.

ge-ständig (⌣⌣́⌣) [gestehen] *a.* ⑥⑥ confessing (or admitting) one's guilt; ⌣ sein, oft: to plead guilty of an offence, to own up; er ist es (*gen.*) ⌣: a) he avows (or owns, acknowledges) it; b) (er räumt es ein) he grants (or admits) it.

Ge-ständnis (⌣⌣́⌣) [gestehen] *n* ⑰ confession, admission, avowal, acknowledgment; ein ~ von etwas ablegen to confess a th., stärker: to make a clean breast of it; e-n zum Geständnisse von etwas bringen to make a p. avow (or confess, admit, F own up) a th.

Ge-stänge (⌣⌣́⌣) [Stange] *n* ㉒ 1. *agr.* (Stangenzaun) fence formed of stakes or poles; railing. — 2. *hunt.* (Geweih mit vielen Enden) ramified antlers *pl.* — 3. ⊕ *u.* ⚒ (Fahr=) (Geleise) rails *pl.*; *mach.* balancing (or guiding) rods *pl.*

Ge-stank (⌣⌣́) *m* ⑦b. stench, bad (or offensive, unpleasant) smell; weniger anständig: F stink; e-n fürchterlichen ~ von sich geben to emit a pestilential (or fetid) smell or odour; **Ge-stänker** F (⌣⌣́⌣) *n* ㉒ *fig.* (Gezänke) squabbling.

ge-statten (⌣⌣́⌣) [ahd.; *Statt] *I v/a.* ⑥⑨* etwas ⌣ to allow (or permit) a th. (to take place); (einwilligen) to consent to a th., to grant (leave for) a th.; wir ⌣ (erlauben) uns, Ihnen mitzuteilen we beg (leave) to inform you. — **II** ~ *n* ㉒ *u.* **Ge-stattung** *f* ④⑥ (f. I) permission; consent; leave.

Geste (⌣́⌣) [lt.] *f* ④⑥ (Gebärde) gesture.

ge-steh(e)n (⌣́⌣) [ahd.] ⑥④* *I v/a.* to confess a sin, to admit an error, to avow one's faith, to acknowledge the truth, to own a deed; die Wahrheit zu ⌣, offen gestanden to tell (you) the truth; F verwundernd: das muß ich ⌣! indeed!, well, I never (heard the like)!, you don't say so!, fancy (that)! — **II** ~ *n* ㉓ = Geständnis.

Ge-stein (⌣́) *n* ⑩c. large blocks *pl.* of stone, rock(y boulders *pl.*); *min.* mineral (ore); plutonisches ~ Plutonic rocks *pl.*; ⚒ taubes ~ dead rock, F deads *pl.*, attle.

Ge-stein(s)-art (⌣́...) *f* ⑥② kind of mineral; **=bohrmaschine** *f* perforating-machine; **=gang** ⚒ *m* streak, lode; **=kunde** ⌣ petrology, mineralogy; geognosy; **=kundige(r)** *m*: ⌣ petrologist, mineralogist; geognost; **=lehre**

f = **=kunde**; **=schicht** *f* layer of rocks.

Ge-stell (⌣́) [mhd.; * stellen] *n* ⑪b. 1. stand; (Bock) trestle, horse, jack; für e-e Bildsäule: pedestal; für Bücher: shelf, book-stand; für Essig und Öl: cruet-stand; für Handtücher: towel-horse; ⊕ e-s Hochofens: hearth-casing; e-s Regenschirms, e-r Säge *2c.*: frame; für Regenschirme: umbrella - stand; eines Wagens (überhaupt größerer Dinge): framework. — 2. F *fig.* ein schnurriges ~ a queer body, F a rum fellow.

Ge-stelle (⌣⌣́⌣) *n* ㉒ *for.* (Schneise) lane (or path) through the forest.

Ge-stell-säge ⊕ (⌣́...) *f* ⑥② frame-saw; **=stein** *m* des Ofens: stone serving for the construction of the hearth.

Ge-stellung ⚔ (⌣⌣́⌣) *f* ④⑥ presentation, appearance; **~s-befehl** *m* order for conscripts or recruits to present themselves; **⌣s-pflichtig** *a.* ⑥⑥ bound to appear at a muster.

gestern (⌣́⌣) [ahd.: yester] **I** *adv.* yesterday; ⌣ morgen yesterday morning; ⌣ abend last evening; ⌣ nachmittag yesterday afternoon; ⌣ nacht last night; ⌣ vor acht (vierzehn) Tagen yest. week (fortnight); *fig.* ich bin auch nicht von ⌣ I was not born yesterday. — **II** ~ *n*, *inv.* the (immediate) past; f. vor⌣, ehe⌣.

ge-sternt (⌣́) *a.* ⑥⑥ starry, starred.

ge-stiefelt (⌣⌣́⌣) *p.p. u. a.* ⑥⑥ booted; weit-⌣. shod; der ⌣e Kater puss in boots.

ge-stiegen (⌣⌣́⌣) *p.p. von* steigen.

ge-stielt (⌣́) *a.* ⑥⑥: a) ⌣ von Messern *2c.*: with a handle; von Werkzeugen: helved; b) ⚘: ⌣ petiolate(d), pedunculate(d).

Gestikulation (⌣⌣⌣⌣-tsi̯ón) [lt.] *f* ④⑥ gesticulation; *thea., &c. auch:* action.

gestikulieren (⌣⌣⌣⌣) [lt.] **I** *v/n.* (h.) ⌣ (Gebärden machen) to gesticulate. — **II** ~ *n* ㉓ gesticulation; übertriebenes ~, *oft:* theatrical action(s *pl.*).

Ge-stirn (⌣́) [ahd.; * Stern] *n* ⑪b. (all) the stars or celestial bodies *pl.*; (Sternbild) constellation; (Stern) star of the first or second magnitude.

ge-stirnt (⌣́) [Stern] *a.* ⑥⑥ starry, covered with stars.

ge-stoben (⌣⌣́⌣) *p.p. von* stieben.

Ge-stöber (⌣⌣́⌣) [nhd.] *n* ㉒ drift; (Schnee=)~ snow-drift or -storm.

ge-stochen (⌣⌣́⌣), **ge-stohlen** (⌣⌣́⌣) *p.p.* von stechen, stehlen.

Ge-stolper (⌣⌣́⌣) *n* ㉒ stumbling.

ge-storben (⌣⌣́⌣) *p.p. von* sterben.

ge-stoßen (⌣⌣́⌣) *p.p. von* stoßen.

Ge-stotter (⌣⌣́⌣) *n* ㉒ = Gestammel.

Ge-strampel (⌣⌣́⌣) *n* ㉒ kicking (out), wriggling (or fidgeting) with one's legs.

Ge-sträuch (⌣́) [nhd.] *n* ⑪c. (Sträuche) shrubs, bushes *pl.*; (Buschwerk) shrubbery; (Unterholz) copse.

ge-streift (⌣́) *p.p. u. a.* ⑥⑥ 1. in den Bed. des *inf.* streifen. — 2. (mit Streifen versehen) striped, streaky; ⌣ striate(d).

ge-streng (⌣́) [mhd.], ⤫ ⌣e (⌣⌣́) *a.* ⑥⑥ 1. fast † = streng(e). — 2. (ehm. Titel des niederen Adels) ⌣er Herr, ⌣e Frau, Ew. ~en, etwa: Gracious Sir, Madam. — 3. die ⌣en Herren (11., 12., 13. Mai), etwa: the three severe days in May.

Zeichen (f. S. XVII): F familiär; P Volkssprache; Γ Gaunersprache; ⤫ selten; † alt (auch gestorben); * neu (auch geboren); ⁺⁺ unrichtig;

[gestrichelt] — 441 — [getrenntblumig]

ge-strichelt ♃ (⌣⌣⌣) a. ⓖ: ⚹ striate(d), striose, lineate(d).
ge-strichen (⌣⌣) p.p. von streichen; typ. Des Papier coated paper. [knitting.]
Ge-strick (⌣⌣) n ⓒc. (Stricken, Strickzeug)
gestrig (⌣⌣) [gestern] a. ⓖ yesterday's, of yesterday; am Den Tage yesterday; am Den Abend last night; mit der Den Post by yesterday's mail; ☙ mit Be- zug auf unser ~es referring (or with reference) to our lines of yesterday; untern ~en of yesterday('s date), dated yesterday.
ge-stritten (⌣⌣) p.p. von streiten.
Ge-strüpp (⌣⌣) [nhd.; * struppig] n ⓒb. brambles, briers, thorns pl.; brush- wood, underwood, copse.
Ge-stüb(b)e ⊕ (⌣⌣⌣) [stieben] n ② metall. (Kohlenstaub) coal-dust; (Kohlenstaub und Lehm) brasque; dust-cement.
Ge-stühl(e) (⌣⌣(⌣)) n ⓒc. (②) chairs, seats pl.; der Kirche: pews, sittings pl.
Ge-stümper (⌣⌣⌣) n ② = Stümperei.
ge-stunken (⌣⌣) p.p. von stinken.
Gestus (⌣⌣) [lt.] m ㉗ = Geste.
Ge-stüt (⌣⌣) [nhd.; * Stute] n ⓒc. stud; breeding-farm for horses; ~garten (⌣⌣) m ② stud; ~hengst m stud- horse, stallion; ~meister (Oberstallknecht) stud-groom; ~stute f brood-mare; ~verwalter m manager of a stud.
Ge-such (⌣⌣) [suchen] n ⓒc. request, demand; schriftliches: petition, suit, memorial; untertäniges: supplication, flehentliches: entreaty; ein ~ gewähren, abschlagen to grant, to refuse a re- quest or petition; was ist sein ~? what does he want or ask for?
ge-sucht (⌣⌣cht) p.p. u. a. ⓖ 1. in den Bed. des inf. suchen. — 2. (much) sought after; (umworben) (greatly) courted; (aus-erlesen) choice; ~ sein to be in (great) demand or request or favour; sehr ~ much inquired after or for, at a (high) premium; Wolle ist wenig (minder) ~ there is little (less) de- mand (or call, inquiry) for wool. — 3. (geziert) affected, studied, F put on; (gekünstelt) artificial, laboured; (weit hergeholt) far-fetched; sie hat et. ~es in ihrem Wesen she is somewhat affected, she is rather finical in her ways.
Ge-suchtheit (⌣⌣cht-) f ⓖ choiceness; affectation, studied manner; manner- ism, F side (put on).
Ge-sudel (⌣⌣⌣) n ② daub; scrawl.
Ge-summ(e) (⌣⌣(⌣)) n ⓒb.(②) (continual) hum(ming) or buzz(ing) or whiz(zing).
ge-sund (⌣⌣) [ahd.: sound: lt. sānus] ⓖ (D3) I a. 1. healthy, in good health, well; durch und durch ~ in the pink of health, sound to the core; frisch und ~ hale and hearty, safe and sound, F (very) fit; s. Fisch I; De Gesichtsfarbe ruddy complexion; ~ an Körper und Geist sound in body and mind; e-n (wieder) ~ machen to restore a p.'s health; wieder ~ werden to recover one's health, to get well again. — 2. (der Gesundheit förderlich) conducive to health, wholesome, sa- lubrious; (heilsam) salutary; Des Klima healthy climate; De Nahrung whole- some food; Der Schlaf sound sleep;

die Lektion ist ihm (ganz) ~ ... does him (a world of) good; iro. das ist ihm ganz ~ it serves him right. — 3. Der Geist sane (or rational, sound) mind; Der Menschenverstand common sense. — II ~e([r] m) f ⓖ7 4. person in good health; die ~en pl. the healthy (people).
Ge-sund-bad (⌣⌣...) n ⓖ2 watering- place, spa; **-beten** n curative prayer, healing by means of prayer, Christian science; **-brunnen** m mineral (or med- icated) spring or well.
ge-sunden (⌣⌣) v/n. (sn) ⓖ* to regain one's health, to recover.
Ge-sundheit (⌣⌣-) f ⓖ 1. health(iness); healthy (or sound) state or condition; F fitness; von Tieren und Dingen: soundness (auch fig. von Ansichten rc.); des Geistes: saneness; von zarter ~ in delicate (or in a delicate state of) health; wie geht es mit seiner ~? how is his health?; how is he?; auf j-s ~ trinken to drink a p.'s health; j-s ~ ausbringen to propose a p.'s health, to toast to a p. — 2. (Heilsamkeit) wholesomeness; salu- tariness; e-s Klimas: healthiness.
ge-sundheitlich (⌣⌣-) a. ⓖ referring (or relating) to health; sanitary, hygienic.
Ge-sundheits-amt (⌣⌣-...) n ⓖ2 board of health, sanitary board or com- mission; **-beamte(r)** n officer of h.; **-bericht** m san. report; **-flanell** ☙ m sanitary flannel (s pl.) or underwear; **-förderlich** a. ⓖ salubrious, conducive to health; **-geschirr** in Töpferei: sanitary crockery or ware; **-göttin** f, myth. (goddess of) Health; Hygiea; **-halber** adv. for health's sake, for reasons of health; **-kommission** f = -amt; **-kordon** m san. cordon; **-kunde**, **-lehre** f science of health, ⚹ hygiene, hygienics; **-paß** m = -schein; **-pflege** f cultivating (or taking care of) one's health, ⚹ dietetics; öffentliche ~ public hygiene, sanitation; **-polizei** f sani- tary police, in England: san. inspectors pl.; **-probe** ↓ f quarantine; **-rat** m board of health; **-regel** f rule of diet, regimen; **-rücksichten** f pl.: aus ~ from considerations of health; **-schädlich** a. injurious to h., unhealthy, unwhole- some; **-schein** m certificate of h., (clean) bill of h.; **-vorschriften** f/pl. sanitary regulations pl.; **-widrig** a. unwhole- some, vgl. -schädlich; **-zeugnis** n = -schein; **-zustand** m e-r Person: state of a p.'s health, einer Gegend rc.: sanitary (or hygienic) condition(s pl.).
Ge-sundheit-trinken (⌣⌣-...) n ⓖ2 drink- ing a p.'s health.
Ge-sund-machen (⌣⌣...) n ⓖ2, **-machung** f restoration (to health), cure. [singen.]
ge-sungen, ge-sunken (⌣⌣⌣) p.p. v.
Ge-tadel (⌣⌣⌣) n ② fault-finding, (in- cessant) grumbling or criticism.
Ge-täfel ⊕ (⌣⌣⌣) [Tafel] n ② (Holzbeklei- dung) wainscot(ing), panelling; des Fußbodens: inlaid wooden floor.
ge-tan (⌣⌣) p.p. von tun.
Ge-tändel (⌣⌣⌣) n ② dallying, toying.
Geten (⌣⌣) m/pl. ㊹ hist. Alt.: (thrakische Völkerschaft) Getae pl. [beasts pl.)
Ge-tier (⌣⌣) [Tier] n ⓒc. animals,
ge-tigert (⌣⌣⌣) a. ⓖ spotted, striped.

Ge-tobe (⌣⌣⌣) n ② (frantic) raving or raging; fretting and fuming.
Ge-tön(e) (⌣⌣(⌣)) n ⓒc. (②) (musical) sounds pl.; strumming on the piano, tinkling of bells; (Lärm) din.
Ge-tose, Ge-töse (⌣⌣⌣) n ② loud noises pl. or clashing, crash(ing), bang(ing), turmoil; der Elemente: (violent) uproar; (furious) storming; howling of the wind; roaring of the waves.
Ge-trabe (⌣⌣⌣) n ② trotting.
ge-tragen (⌣⌣⌣) p.p. von tragen.
Ge-trampel (⌣⌣⌣) n ② trampling.
Ge-tränk (⌣⌣) [nhd.; *trinken] n ⓒb. drink, beverage; med.: ⚹ potion, de- coction; ~e pl. auch: drinkables pl.; be- rauschende ~e pl. intoxicating drink(s pl.), intoxicants pl.; gegorenes ~ fer- mented liquor; geistige ~e pl. alcoholic liquor(s pl.), spirits pl.; ~(e)-steuer f ⓖ duty on alcohol(ic liquor), F spirit-tax.
Ge-trappel (⌣⌣⌣) n ② pattering of feet.
Ge-tratsch(e), Ge-trätsch(e) (⌣⌣⌣) n ⓐa. (②) idle gossip, twaddle.
ge-trauen (⌣⌣⌣) [ahd.] v/a. und sich ~ v/refl. ⓖ*: ich getraue mich dessen, ge- traue es mir I make bold (wage es: venture) to do it; sie ~ es sich nicht they dare not do it, they won't risk it; sich wohin ~ to venture (to go) to a place; sie ~ sich nicht (da)hin F they won't venture (to go) there.
Ge-treibe (⌣⌣⌣) n ② 1. constant urging. — 2. agitation; (reges Leben) bustle, ac- tivity, stir, life; (Menge) crowd, throng.
Ge-treide (⌣⌣⌣) [ahd.; *tragen] n ② grain, corn; cereals, cerealia pl.; ~ auf dem Halm standing crop; das ~ steht gut (schlecht) the crops are in good (poor or bad) condition.
Ge-treide-acker (⌣⌣⌣...) m corn-field; plough-land; **-art** f species of grain; ~en pl.: ⚹ cereals, cerealia; **-ausfuhr** f exportation of grain; **-bau** m corn- growing, cultivation of grain, cereal culture; **-boden** m: a) soil adapted for corn(-growing), corn-land; b) (Scheune) granary, corn-loft; **-börse** ☙ f corn-exchange; **-brand** ⚹ m, agr. smut (Ustila'go carbo); **-einfuhr** ☙ f importation of grain; **-feld** n corn- field; **-geschäft** n corn-business or trade; **-grube** f, agr. silo; **-halm** m corn-stalk; **-handel** m = -geschäft; **-händler** m corn-chandler or -dealer or -merchant; **-haufen** m heap of corn; **-kasten** m corn-chest; **-korn** n grain; **-land** n: a) = -boden a; b) corn- growing country; **-mäh(e)maschine** ⊕ f machine for cutting corn, reaping- machine; **-markt** m, **-maß** n, **-mühle** f corn-market, -measure, -mill; **-preis** m price of grain or corn; **-reinigungs- maschine** f, agr. corn-sifting machine; **-rost** ♃ m rust, ⚹ puccinia (Pucci'nia gra'minis); **-sack** m corn-sack; **-schwinge** ⊕ f winnow(ing-machine); **-sendung** f shipment of grain; **-speicher** m gra- nary; **-sperre** f embargo on the export of grain; **-vorrat** m stock (or supply) of grain; **-wagen** m corn-wagon; **-zoll** m duty on (imported) grain.
ge-trennt-blumig ♃ (⌣⌣...) [trennen p.p.] a. ⓖ (zweihäusig): ⚹ diœcian,

♪ Musik; ⚹ Wissenschaft; ♃ Pflanze; ♀ Geographie; ⊕ Technik; ⚒ Bergbau; ⚔ Militär; ↓ Marine; ☙ Handel; ✉ Post; 🚂 Eisenbahn.

[getrenntgeschlechtig] — 442 — [Gewalt]

diœcious (= diözisch); ⚥geschlechtig ⚥: ♂ diclinous (= diklinisch).
Ge-trennt-heit (⌣́-) f ㊻, Ge-trennt-sein (⌣́-,¹) n ㉓ separation, separate state, separateness, detachment.
ge-treten (⌣́⌣) p.p. von treten.
ge-treu (⌣́) [ahd.] I a. ㊿ = treu, ʒB. Ser Diener faithful servant. — II ~e(r) s. ㊼ im Mittelalter: (Vasallen in der Anrede des Landesherrn) unseren lieben ~en to our trusty and well-beloved (lieges); seine ~en his (faithful) followers.
ge-treulich (⌣́⌣) [mhd.] a. ㊿ bes. adv. = treu, treulich.
Ge-triebe (⌣́⌣) [Trieb] n ㉒ 1. ⊙ mech. (Rad, das ein anderes Rad 2c. treibt) driving-gear or -wheel, driver; (kleines Rad zwischen zwei größeren) pinion; (Drehling) trundle, lantern; Uhrm.: (Zahnräder) wheel-work, mechanism (F works pl.) of the watch; ein Rad aus dem ~e bringen to disengage (or uncouple) a wheel. — 2. fig. (political) machinery; inner working; (Beweggründe) motives pl.; ~ des Lebens bustle of life.
ge-trieben (⌣́⌣) p.p. von treiben.
Getrieb(e)-, Getriebs-scheibe⊙(⌣́⌣(⌣)...) f ㊽ face of the pinion, pinion-plate; -zirkel m pinion-compass.
Ge-trippel (⌣́⌣) n ㉒ 1. tripping (or pitapat) of little feet. — 2. F fine (or drizzling) rain, drizzle.
ge-troffen (⌣́⌣) p.p.: a) v. treffen; b) ⚲ v. triefen; ge-trogen (⌣́⌣) p.p. v. trügen.
ge-trost (⌣́) [ahd.] a. ㊿ 1. (voll Zuversicht) confident, of good cheer, hopeful; (keck) plucky, daring; adv. auch: cheerfully; ich will es ² wagen I will boldly face it; seid ²(en Mutes)! be of good cheer!, summon (F sum) up courage! — 2. prove. er ist nicht recht ² (bei Troste) he is not in his right mind or senses.
ge-trösten (⌣́⌣)u. sich ² v/refl. ㊽*: sich e-r Sache (gen.) ² to be confident of a th., to expect a th. confidently, to rest one's hope and confidence upon it.
ge-trunken (⌣́⌣) p.p. von trinken.
Getto (⌣́-) [it.] m u. n ㊾ Ghetto.
Ge-tue (⌣́⌣) [: ado] n ㉒ (idle) doings pl.; nutzloses ~ F useless pottering.
Ge-tümmel (⌣́⌣) [tümmeln] n ㉒ violent exercise or motion; tumult, stir.
Ge-tümmel (⌣́⌣) [mhd. Lärm] n ㉒ 1. (bewegte Menge)crowd. — 2.(Getöse)turmoil, tumult; loud (or noisy) bustle.
ge-tüpfelt ⚲ (⌣́⌣), ge-tupft (⌣́) a. ㊿ spotted, sprinkled, ♂ guttate(d).
Ge-tute (⌣́⌣) n ㉒ tooting.
ge-übt (⌣́) p.p. u.s.a. ㊿ f. üben III; Ge-übtheit f ㊻ practice; expertness.
Geuse (⌣́⌣) [ndl.; *fr. gueux Bettler] m ㊾ hist. (League of the) Gueux (1566).
geuß, ʒest, ʒt(⌣) †, noch poet., imper. und pres. von gießen.
Ge-vatter (⌣́⌣) [ahd.; * Vater (nach lt. computer)] m ㉚, ~in f ㊼ 1. (Taufzeuge) godfather, f godmother; sponsor; e-n zu ~ bitten to ask a p. to stand (or be) godfather (godmother) to a child; bei einem Kinde (zu) ~ steh(e)n to stand (or be) godfather (godmother) to a child. — 2. fig. ~(in) (guter Freund, gute Freundin) ehm.: gossip; jetzt: (great)

friend; F pal, chum, (old) crony; ~ Schneider und Handschuhmacher (set of) small shopkeepers or tradespeople pl.; the lower middle class; F co. von Sachen: seine Uhr steht ~ (ist versetzt) ... is pledged or in pawn or F up the spout or at his uncle's.
Ge-vatter-brief (⌣́⌣...) m ㉖ letter asking (or inviting) a p. to stand (or be) godfather (godmoth.) to a child.
Ge-vatterschaft (⌣́⌣...) f ㊻ 1. godfathership, godmothership; sponsorship; das ist meine erste ~ it is the first time that I have stood godfather (godmother), I never stood godfather (godmother) before. — 2. coll. (sämtliche Gevattern) = Gevatters-leute.
Ge-vatter-schmaus (⌣́⌣...) m ㉖ (in England selten), etwa: christening dinner or party or feast.
Ge-vatters-leute (⌣́⌣...) pl. ㉖ godfather(s pl.) and godmother(s pl.); sponsors pl.; weitS.(great) friends pl.; family connexions pl.; F pals, chums, (old) cronies pl.; -mann = Gevatter.
ge-viert (⌣́) [vier] I a. ㊿ 1. (quadratisch) square(d), quadrate, …ic. — 2. (in vier Teile geteilt) divided in(to) four parts, quadrated; (aus vieren bestehend) quaternary; arith. Ze (mit sich selbst multiplizierte) Zahl square (number); her. quartered; ast(rol) Zer Schein = Geviertschein. — II ~(e) n ⑪b. (⚷) square(ness); ast.: ♂ quadrate, astrol.: ♂ tetragon; ⊙ typ.: em (quadrat); ins ~ bringen to (raise to a) square.
Ge-viert-maß (⌣́...) n ㉒ square measure; -meile f square mile; -schein m, ast.: ♂ quadrate; astrol.: ♂ quartile, tetragon.
Ge-wächs (⌣́⌣ts) [wachsen] n ⑪a. 1. ⚷ anything that grows (from the earth); vegetable (growth), (Pflanze) plant. — 2. (Gezogenes) produce; unser eigenes ~: a) (Wein) vintage, wine of our own growth, our home produce; b) (Zuchtvieh) our own breeding. — 3. fig. (Sprößling) offspring, descendant. — 4. (Auswuchs) growth; anat. auch: protuberance; path. auch: excrescence; (Beule) tumour.
ge-wachsen (⌣́⌣ts) p.p. v. wachsen.
Ge-wächs-erde (⌣́⌣ts...) f ㉘ (rich) garden-mould; -haus n conservatory, greenhouse, glass-house; (Treibhaus) hothouse; -kunde, -lehre f botany; (Pflanzenbeschreibung): ♂ phytography; -kundige(r) m botanist; -reich: n vegetable kingdom; ²reich a. rich in plants.
Ge-wackel (⌣́⌣) n ㉒ (constant) shaking or jostling; engS. tottering (or unstable) gait; wabbling, waddling.
Ge-wählte(r) (⌣́⌣) [p.p. v. wählen] s. ㊼ chosen one; (s)elected candidate.
ge-wahr (⌣́) [ahd.: aware] a. nur gbr. in: ² werden (gen. od. acc.) to become aware of a th., to notice (or discover, perceive, remark, see) a th.
Ge-währ¹ (⌣́) [mhd.] f ㊻ guarantee; (Bürgschaft) surety, security; für e-n leisten to become (or give) security for a p., to stand bail for a p.; ⚯ ohne ~ without prejudice.
Ge-währ² (⌣́) = Gewehr.

ge-wahren (⌣́⌣) [mhd.; *gewahr] I v/a. ㊽* et. od. e-r Sache (gen.) ² = gewahr (s. ds) werden. — II ~ n ㉓ = Gewahrung.
ge-währen¹ (⌣́⌣) [ahd.: warrant] I v/a. ㊽* 1. e-m eine Bitte ² to grant a p.'s petition or request; (einräumen) to accord, vouchsafe, concede; (gestatten) to allow. — 2. a. mit sachlichem Subjekt: (geben)to give satisfaction, &c.; (darbieten) to afford pleasure, &c.; (verschaffen) to procure (or furnish) means, &c.; (verschaffen) to confer a benefit, &c.; Vorteil ² to offer an advantage, to yield a profit. — II ~ n ㉓ 3. = Gewährung.
ge-währen² (⌣́⌣) [mhd.; *wahr] v/n. (h.) ㊽*: et. (fort) ² (bestehen) lassen to let a th. go on (its way); e-n ² (frei schalten) lassen to give a p. full play or power; to let a p. do as (s)he likes; laß ihn ²! let (or leave) him alone!
Ge-währ-fehler (⌣́...) m ㊵ = -mangel; ²leisten v/a. u. v/n. (h.) ㊽** für et. ² to warrant (or guarantee) a th.; er leistet dafür Gewähr he guarantees it, he vouches for it; -leister(in f) m ㊷ guarantor; bes. für Geldzahlungen: security, surety; bail; -leistung f guarantee; vgl. Gewähr¹ I; -mangel m defect in a horse, &c., for which the seller is (held) liable to the purchaser.
Ge-wahrsam (⌣́-) m u. n ⑪c., f ㊻ 1. et. in sein(en) ~ nehmen to take charge of a th.; in ~ halten to keep in (one's) custody. — 2. (Haft) detention, imprisonment; (Gefängnis) prison, jail, lock-up; in sicherem ~ in safe keeping or custody; in (engen) ~ bringen, nehmen to commit to close custody, put into jail. [certificate, bond.]
Ge-währ-schein (⌣́...) m ㉖ warrant;
Ge-währs-mann (⌣́⌣) m ㉖: a) = Gewährleister; b) (j. auf den man sich beruft) authority (adduced or quoted).
Ge-wahrung (⌣́⌣) f ㊻ discovery, sight.
Ge-währung (⌣́⌣) f ㊻ granting, &c. (s. gewähren¹); concession; er hat die ~ seiner Bitte erlangt he attained the object of his suit.
Ge-walt (⌣́) [ahd.; *walten] f ㊻ 1.(Macht) power, might; amtliche: authority; höchste: supreme power, sovereignty; unumschränkte: absolutism, dictatorship, despotism, autocracy; (Einfluß) influence; (Herrschaft) dominion, sway, rule; die bürgerlichen ~en the civil authorities pl.; vollziehende ~ executive. — 2. in seine ~ bekommen to gain the mastery of; in j-s ~ geraten to fall into a p.'s hands; e-n, et. in j-r ~ haben, ~ über e-n, et. haben to have full power (or sway) over a p., a th.; to have a p., a th. in one's grip or grasp or F clutches; s-e Leidenschaften (a. sich) in der ~ haben to keep one's passions (oneself) under control or in check; eine Sprache in j-r H. to have (complete) mastery of (or a ready command over or of) ... — 3. (zwingende Macht) force; (Zwang) restraint; (Gewalttätigkeit) violence; e-m, einer Sache ~ antun to force a p., a th.; j-n Gefühlen ~ antun to do violence to (or to restrain) one's feelings; sich (dat.) ~ antun to restrain o.s.; dem Sinne

Signs (see page XVII): F familiar; P vulgar; ⚐ flash; ⚲ rare; † obsolete (died); * new word (born); ⨦ incorrect; ♪ music;

[Gewaltanmaßung] — 443 — [Gewerbszweig]

einer Stelle ~ antun to strain (or stretch, wrench) the meaning of a passage; ~ anwenden, gebrauchen to employ force, to use violence; Sprichw. ~ geht vor Recht might (is) above right. — 4. adv. aus aller ~ (Leibeskräften) schreien to shout with all one's might; mit ~ forcibly, perforce; mit aller ~ with might and main, by main force; es regnet mit aller ~ it is pouring as fast as it can, it's raining cats and dogs; er will mit aller ~ (durchaus) reisen he is bent upon travelling or determined to travel.
Ge-walt=anmaßung (‿‿…) f ⓺ usurpation of power; =anwendung f employment of force; =haber m (Machthaber) person in power or authority; (absolute) master, dictator, despot, autocrat; ⁀haberisch a. ⓺ despotic; =handlung f deed of violence; =herrschaft f despotism, tyranny; =herr(scher) m despot, tyrant.
ge-waltig (‿‿) I a. ⓺ 1. (Macht habend) powerful, mighty; (stark) strong; (heftig) vehement. — 2. (sehr groß) very great or large; immense, F tremendous; ein ⁀er Geist a lofty mind; von ⁀er Höhe of enormous (or stupendous) height, of gigantic stature; das ist ein ⁀er Unterschied that is a vast difference; adv. ⁀ (sich) immensely; er irrt sich ⁀ he is mightily (or very much) mistaken; ⁀ lärmen to make a deafening noise; ⁀ schreien to scream lustily. — II ~e(r) m ⓶: 3. die ~en auf Erden the mighty (or the rulers) of this earth.
ge-wältigen ⚒ (‿‿‿) v/a. ⓺*: Grubenwasser ⁀ to keep water under control).
Ge-walt=marsch (‿‿…) m ⓶ forced march; =maßregel f violent (or drastic) measure; =raub m robbery with violence, pol. usurpation.
ge-walt=sam (‿‿-) a. ⓺ violent; ⁀e Schritte high-handed (or strong) measures pl.; ⁀er Tod violent death; adv. ⁀ handeln to use force; ~keit (‿‿--) f ⓺ violence, force.
Ge-walt=schritt (‿‿…) m ⓶ violent (or illegal) proceeding, forcible measure or step; =streich m arbitrary act, bold stroke; =tat f act (or deed) of violence, outrage(ous act); ⁀tätig a. violent, outrageous; (roh) brutal; =tätigkeit f violence, outrage; brutality; rowdyism, hooliganism.
Ge-wand (‿‿) [ahd.; *winden²] n ⓶ (poet. ⓶)b. garment, gown; (Kleid, Kleidung) dress, attire; habiliment; feierlich: vestment, bibl. raiment; paint. (Darstellung der) Gewänder drapery.
Ge-wände (‿‿) n ⓶ (Seitenwand e-r Tür, e-s Fensters) jamb, (door-, window-) casing, mould-stone.
Ge-wand=haus (‿‿…) n ⓶ ehm. clothworkers' hall; =maler m painter of drapery; =malerei f drapery-painting; =schneider † m merchant tailor.
ge-wandt (‿‿) [mhd.] I p.p. in den Bed. des inf. wenden. — II a. ⓺ (flink) agile, nimble, active; (geschmeidig) supple, (geschickt) skilled, F handy, geistig: adroit, versatile; in et. ⁀ sein to be clever (or apt, F good) at a th.; eine ⁀e Feder führen to wield a skilful (or facile) pen; ⁀er Redner ready (or fluent) speaker; ⁀er Stil clever (F smart) style; ~heit (‿‿-) f ⓺ agility, nimbleness; suppleness, skill, adroitness, versatility; readiness (or fluency) of speech; cleverness (F smartness) of style; ⬥ business capacity.
Ge-wandung (‿‿‿) f ⓺ Kunst: drapery.
ge-wann¹ (‿‿) impf. v. gewinnen.
Ge-wann² (‿‿) n ⓶b. agr. (Flur in der Dorfgemarkung) tilled (or ploughed) land.
ge-warten † (‿‿‿) [ahd.] ⓶* = gewärtigen.
ge-wärtig (‿‿‿) [mhd.; *warten] a. (nur als Prädikat) 1. e-m ⁀ sein to be ready to serve a p. — 2. einer Sache (gen.) ⁀ sein = gewarten: ⬥ Ihrer Aufträge ⁀ awaiting your orders.
ge-wärtigen (‿‿‿‿) v/a., v n.(h.) ⓶* et. od. e-r Sache (gen.) ⁀, mst. im inf. gbr. to expect a th.; er hat nichts Gutes zu ⁀ he has nothing good to look forward to; he has no (good) prospects.
Ge-wäsch(e) (‿‿) [waschen] n ⓶a.(⁀) idle talk; chit-chat, F mag(ging).
ge-waschen (‿‿‿) p.p. v. waschen.
Ge-wässer (‿‿) [mhd.; *Wasser] n ⓶ expanse (or piece) of water; im chinesischen ~ in Chinese waters or seas.
ge-wässert (‿‿‿) p.p. von wässern u. a. ⓺ ⊙ von Stoffen: watered, cloudy.
Ge-webe (‿‿) [ahd.; *web; *weben] n ⓶ tissue (a. fig.); web, weft, woof (a. ⊙); texture (a. anat.); ⊙ textile fabric; ~lehre f ⓺: ⚗ histology.
ge-weckt (‿‿) I p.p. in den Bed. des inf. wecken. — II a. ⓺ alert, wide-awake, quick-witted; (lebendig) lively, F alive; (munter) bright, brisk; ~heit (‿‿-) f ⓺ alertness; liveliness; briskness.
Ge-wehr (‿‿) [ahd.; *wehren] n ⓶c. 1. († jede Wehr u. Waffen, a. blanke Seitenwaffen) weapon, coll. arms pl. — 2. ⚔ bsd. (Feuer-)~ ehm. musket, mit Luntenschloß: matchlock; jetzt: gun; pl. auch: firearms; gezogenes ~ rifle; (Seiten-)~ sword, der Seeleute: hanger. — 3. ~e in die Hand nehmen to pile arms!; präsentiert das ~! present arms!; ein ~ in Ruh' setzen to put a gun at half-cock, to half-cock a gun; jetzt die ~e zusammen! pile arms!; das ~ strecken to lay down arms; an die ~e! stand to your arms!, to arms!; ins ~! to arms!; ins ~ treten to get under arms; mit ~ bei Fuß steh(e)n to be at the order; unter dem ~e stehen to be under arms; unter ~ treten to take up one's arms; Kommandorufe: ~ ab! order arms!; ~ auf! advance arms!; ~ über! slope arms! — 4. hunt. (Hauzahn) tusk.
Ge-wehr=fabrik ⚔ (‿‿‿…) f ⓶ (manu-) factory of (small) arms; =feuer n musketry-fire; =händler m gun-smith, gun-maker; =kammer f armoury; =kasten m gun-case or -chest; =kolben m butt-end of a gun or musket; =kugel f rifle-ball; =lauf m barrel of a gun; =magazin n armoury; =mitte f stand for piling arms; =pfropf m gun-wad(ding); =probe f testing of guns; =pulver n gun- (or musket-) powder; =pyramide f pile of arms; =riemen m rifle-strap, sling; =salve f volley of musketry; =schaft m musket-stock; =schloß n gun-lock, ehm. firelock; =schmied m gunsmith; =schrank m armoury; =stand m stand of arms.
Ge-weih (‿‿) [mhd. „Kampf"wertzeug] n ⓶c. hunt. horns pl., F head; bsd. die Enden des ~s: antlers, branches pl.; attires pl. (auch her.).
Ge-weine (‿‿‿) n ⓶ endless crying or weeping or F blubbering, whining.
Ge-wende (‿‿) [mhd.] n ⓶ 1. turning; bsd. agr. (mit dem Pfluge) ein ~ machen to take one turn with the plough; als Feldstück: field which can be ploughed without turning of the plough. — 2. (et. zum Umwechseln) ein ~ Kleider a change of clothes.
Ge-werbe (‿‿) [mhd.; *werben] n ⓶ 1. (Auftrag) commission, errand. — 2. (Erwerb) trade; (Beruf) profession, vocation; (Industriezweig) branch of industry, F line of business; er ist seines ~s ein Bäcker he is a baker by trade; sich (dat.) ein ~ aus et. machen to make a business of s.th.; ein ~ treiben to follow (or pursue, carry on) a trade. — 3. (Gesamtheit gewerblicher Berufsarten) oft: the trade.
Ge-werbe=ausstellung ⬥ (‿‿‿…) f ⓶ industrial exhibition; =ausübung f pursuit (or exercise) of a trade; =betrieb m industrial activity; =freiheit f freedom of trade; =gericht n, etwa: arbitration-court for trade-disputes; =gesetzgebung f industrial legislation; =halle f pantechnicon; =krankenkasse f sick-fund of a trade(s-union); =krankheit f disease peculiar to a trade; =museum n industrial museum, museum for industrial products; =ordnung f industrial system; =schein m = Gewerbschein; =schule f technical school or college, polytechnic, trade-school, school for artisans; =schüler m pupil of a technical school; technical student; =steuer f trade-license; =steuergesetz n law relating to trade-licenses; ⁀steuerpflichtig a. ⓺ bound to take out a (trade-)license; =verein m = Gewerb-
Ge-werb=fleiß (‿‿‿…) m ⓶ industry, industrial activity or operations pl.; ⁀fleißig a. ⓺ industrious; =kunde f technology; ⁀kundig a. knowing a trade, acquainted with industrial arts or life; technological; =kundige(r) m technologist; =leben n industrial life, industrialism.
ge-werblich (‿‿‿) a. ⓺ industrial; ⁀e Arbeiter industrial workers or employees pl.; ⁀e Fachschule trade-school.
ge-werb=los (‿‿…) a. ⓺ without (a) trade; =losigkeit f ⓺ lack of (a) trade; ⁀reich a. industrious.
ge-werbsam (‿‿‿) a. ⓺ industrious; ~keit (‿‿--) f ⓺ industry.
Ge-werbs=anstalt ⬥ (‿‿…) f ⓶ industrial establishment.
Ge-werb=schein (‿‿…) m ⓶ trade-license; license for carrying on a trade.
Ge-werbs=mann (‿‿…) m ⓶, pl. =leute tradesman, pl. tradesmen, tradespeople; ⁀mäßig a. ⓺ (u. adv.) professional(ly); =zweig m branch of industry or trade, industrial branch.

⚗ scientific; ♃ botanical; ♀ geography; ⊙ machinery; ⚒ mining; ⚔ military; ⚓ marine; ⬥ commercial; ✉ postal; 🚂 railway.

[gewerbtätig] — 444 — [gewinnsüchtig]

ge-werb-tätig (⌣ˊ…) a. ⓰ industrious; **-tätigkeit** f ⓬ industry; **⸗treibend** a. industrial, carrying on a trade; **~e(r)** m tradesman; **⸗verein** m tradesmen's club or union; (Gewerkverein) trade(s)-union; **⸗verständige(r)** m expert on industrial matters.

Ge-were (⌣ˊ⌣) [ahd.: wear tragen] f ehm. jur. (rechtlicher Besitz) lawful possession.

Ge-werk (⌣ˊ) n ⓝb.1. (Triebwerk) works pl. of a clock; machinery; (Erzeugnis) produce, manufacture. — 2. (Genossenschaft) corporation, guild, company; (the) trade.

Ge-werke (⌣ˊ⌣) m ⓭ 1. † [bsd. Bau-] Handwerker) mechanic (in the building trade). — 2. ⚒ (Grubenarbeiter) miner, pitman.

Ge-werkschaft (⌣ˊ⌣) f ⓮: a) (Gewerkverein) trade(s)-union; b) ⚒ mining company (vgl. Knappschaft); **~ler(in** f ⓭) m ⓬ trade-unionist; **⸗lich** (⌣ˊ⌣) a. ⓰ relating to trade(s)-unions or ⚒ to mining companies.

Ge-werk(s)-genossenschaft (⌣ˊ…) f ⓬ trade(s)-union; **⸗meister** m industrial employer; **⸗schule** f trade-school; **⸗verein** m trade union, trade(s)-union; **⸗vereinswesen** n trade-unionism.

ge-wesen (⌣ˊ⌣), **ge-wichen** (⌣ˊ⌣) p.p. v. sein, weichen.

Ge-wicht (⌣ˊ) [mhd.: weight; *wiegen¹] n ⓝb. weight; phys. spezifisches ~ specific gravity; gutes ~ geben to give good (or full) weight; zu leichtes ~ short (or light) weight, underweight; nach dem ~e verkaufen to sell by the weight; die Kiste hat zwei Kilogramm an ~ the case weighs two kilograms; schwer ins ~ fallen to weigh heavily, fig. to be of great weight or importance or consequence; fig. ~ auf et. legen to lay great stress upon (or to attach great weight to) a th.

Ge-wicht-abnahme (⌣ˊ…) f ⓬ decrease (or shrinkage) of weight; **⸗ausschlag** m excess of weight, overweight.

ge-wichtig (⌣ˊ⌣) a. ⓰ 1. von Münzen 2c.: of full weight, (schwer) weighty, heavy, ponderous; phys.: ⚛ ponderable. — 2. fig. weighty, of great weight or moment; (wichtig) important, consequential, momentous, (einflußreich) influential, powerful; (überwiegend) predominant; **~keit** f ⓮ weight(iness); importance, consequence, momentousness; influence, power(fulness); predominance.

ge-wicht-los (⌣ˊ⌣) a. ⓰ weightless, phys.: ⚛ imponderable; fig. without weight, unimportant; **⸗losigkeit** f ⓮ weightlessness, ⚛ imponderability; fig. unimportance.

Ge-wichts-abgang ☉ (⌣ˊ…) m ⓬ deficiency in weight, short(ness) of weight, underweight.

Ge-wicht-schnur ☉ (⌣ˊ…) f ⓬ an Fallfenstern: sash-line. [ness of weight.]

Gewichts-manko ☉ (⌣ˊ…) n ⓬ short-

Ge-wicht-stange (⌣ˊ…) f ⓬ (ropedancer's) balancing-pole; **⸗stein** m stone (serving as) weight.

Ge-wichts-uhr ☉ (⌣ˊ…) f ⓬ clock with weights; **⸗verlust** ☉ m loss of (or deficiency in) weight, underweight; **⸗voll** a. = gewichtig 2.

ge-wiegt (⌣ˊ) [: weighed] I p.p. v. wiegen². — II a. ⓰ (erfahren) expert, experienced, (schlau) shrewd, artful, F smart, deep.

Ge-wieher (⌣ˊ⌣) n ⓬ neighing.

ge-wiesen (⌣ˊ⌣) p.p. von weisen.

ge-willt (⌣ˊ) [mhd.: *Wille] a. ⓰ willing, inclined, disposed, ready; ich bin ~, es zu tun, auch: I have a good (or great) mind to do it.

Ge-wimmel (⌣ˊ⌣) n ⓬ swarming; (Menge) swarm, crowd, crush, throng, teeming multitude.

Ge-wimmer (⌣ˊ⌣) n ⓬ whining, whimpering; (muffled) sobs pl.; (Jammern) wailing, lamentation.

Ge-winde (⌣ˊ⌣) n ⓬ 1. o. pl.: (Winden) winding, twisting; (Sichwinden) contortion. — 2. mit pl.: twist, coil; eines Weges: winding path; von Blumen 2c.: garland, festoon; von Garn: skein of thread; e-r Muschel: whirl; anat. im Ohre: ⚕ labyrinth; einer Schraube: thread, worm; eine Schraube mit ~ versehen to thread a screw. — 3. ☉ ~ pl. an Fenstern und Türbändern hinges pl.

Ge-winde-bohrer ☉ (⌣ˊ…) m ⓬ screw-tap; **⸗fenster** n window on hinges; **⸗gang** m thread (or worm) of a screw.

Ge-winn (⌣ˊ) [ahd., † gewinnen] m ⓝb. 1. (Gewinnen) winning a battle, &c.; gaining time, &c.; earning money, &c. — 2. (Gewonnenes) gain, b.s. lucre; Spiel 2c.: winnings pl.; (Verdienst) earnings pl.; in der Lotterie: prize, winning number, F lucky draw; (Nutzen) benefit; (Vorteil) profit, advantage; unverhoffter: windfall, godsend; ~ bringen to be profitable or advantageous; mit ~ verkaufen to sell with a profit or to advantage; ~ aus et. ziehen to turn a th. to account, F to make a good thing of s.th.; ⚫ auf gemeinschaftlichen ~ und Verlust for common profit and loss. — 3. (Erwerb) proceeds pl.; ⓔ return(s pl.); reiner ~ net gain, clear profit(s pl.); (großen) ~ abwerfen to leave a (handsome) margin or profit; to pay (well).

Ge-winn-anteil (⌣ˊ…) m ⓬ share of the profits, percentage; dividend; thea. des Verfassers: royalty; ⚫ mit ~ arbeiten to work on commission; **⸗anteilschein** ⚫ m dividend-warrant; **⸗beteiligung** ⚫ f profit-sharing; **⸗bringend** a. ⓰ profitable, lucrative.

ge-winnen (⌣ˊ⌣) [ahd.: win] ⓝa(b)* I v/a. 1. durch Arbeit: to gain a livelihood, to earn money; to win a race; to carry off a prize; (erlangen) to obtain; die Oberhand (einen Vorteil) über e-n ~ to get the better of a p., to gain an advantage over a p.; e-n Prozeß ~ to win a lawsuit, to gain the day; s. Spiel; einen Vorsprung vor e-m ~ to get the start of a p., to steal a march upon a p. (auch fig.); dadurch wird wenig gewonnen there is little (to be) gained by it; damit ist viel gewonnen that helps a great deal, it's a great step forward; ~ (für sich) ~ to win a p. over, to bring a p. to one's (own) side; e-n für et. ~ to interest a p. (or to enlist a p.'s

interest) in a th.; (zu etwas bekehren) to convert a p. to a th.; e-n für sich zu ~ suchen to court a p.('s favour), to curry favour with a p.; Sprichw. gut begonnen (auch: frisch gewagt) ist halb gewonnen a good beginning makes a good ending; wer nicht wagt, (der) nicht gewinnt nothing venture nothing have; wie gewonnen, so zerronnen lightly come lightly gone. — 2. ☉ agr. viel Heu, viel Obst 2 to reap much …; Weizen wird durch Samen gewonnen … is raised from seed; Zucker wird aus Runkelrüben gewonnen sugar is extracted from (or made of) beet(root)s; ⚒ Erz ~ to raise (or extract) ore. — 3. e-e Strecke Weges ~ (zurücklegen) to cover a long distance, F to do many miles; ⚓ die hohe See ~ (erreichen) to reach the main, to get out to sea; die offene See ~ to make the offing. — 4. e-n, et. zu et. ~ (machen), z.B. e-n zum Freunde ~ to make a friend of a p. — 5. meist fig.: Ansehen ~ to acquire influence, to gain credit; e-e Ansicht, Überzeugung ~ to gain a conviction, to become convinced; Geschmack, Lust, Neigung zu et., ~ to acquire a taste (or to get a liking) for a th., to take to a th.; eine feste Gestalt ~ to assume a solid shape; die Nachricht gewinnt Glauben … is credited; j-s Teilnahme ~ to enlist a p.'s sympathy; neue Kraft ~ to gain new strength; seinen Lebensunterhalt ~ to make a living, to earn one's livelihood; Zeit ~ to gain time; es über e-n ~ to prevail upon a p.; es über sich ~ to bring o.s. to do a th.; to brace o.s. up for a th.; v impers.: es gewinnt den Anschein, als ob ∥ it appears as though ∥. — 6. von Bäumen 2c.: Augen 2c. ~ (treiben) to put on (or send forth) buds, &c. — 7. e-n, et. lieb ~ to become fond of (or attached to) a p., a th., to take a liking to a p., a th. — II v/n. (h.) 8. mit leicht ergänzbarem Objekte: wir haben gewonnen (die Schlacht 2c.) we have won, we are the winners, we have carried the day; im Wettrennen: mit Leichtigkeit ~ to win in a canter; to have a walk-over; an Kraft ~ to gain (in) strength; von et. ~ to profit by a th. — 9. abs.: a) (sich zum Vorteile verändern) to change for the better; er hat sehr gewonnen he has (or is) greatly improved; b) sie hat ein ~des Wesen … winning ways, … engaging manners pl.; c) Sport: ~des Pferd winner. — III n ⓬ 10. = Gewinn 1.

Gewinner (⌣ˊ⌣) m ⓬, **~in** f ⓭ winner; ~ e-s Preises prize-winner, prizeman.

Ge-winn-liste (⌣ˊ…) f ⓬ list of prizes or drawn numbers; **⸗los** a. ⓰ unprofitable, unremunerative; **⸗los** n winning number; **⸗rechnung** ⚫ f profit-account; **⸗reich** a. profitable, lucrative; **⸗sucht** f greed (or love) of gain, passion (or thirst) for lucre, bib. bibl. covetousness; bisw.: worship of the golden calf; **⸗süchtig** a. greedy of gain, thirsting after lucre; covetous;

Zeichen (s. S. XVII): F familiär; P Volkssprache; ⌐ Gaunersprache; ↘ selten; † alt (auch gestorben); * neu (auch geboren); ₊₊ unrichtig;

[Gewinnüberschuß] — 445 — [gewöhnlich]

=überschuß m surplus profits or earnings pl.; = und Verlustkonto n profit-and-loss account.
Ge-winnung (⌣⌣) f ⓴ 1. f. Gewinn 1. — 2. ⊕ ~ der Erze, des Zuckers ꝛc. extraction, production.
Ge-winsel (⌣⌣) n ㉒ = Gewimmer.
Ge-winst (⌣⌣) [nhd.] m (n) ⓫ b. = Gewinn.
Ge-wirbel (⌣⌣) n ㉒ whirling; whirligig; einer Trommel: roll of a drum.
Ge-wirk (⌣⌣) n ⓫ b. texture; woof, weft.
Ge-wirr(e) (⌣⌣) n ⓫ b.(㉒) entanglement, confusion, tangled (or confused) mass, huddled heap, nur fig. imbroglio, intricacy, whirl, whirligig; maze of lanes or alleys.
ge-wiß (⌣⌣) [ahd.; *wissen] I a. ⓰ A3† (D 10) 1. certain, (sicher) sure, 3B. es ist ganz ⌣, daß //, objektiv: it is quite certain that //; subjektiv: I am quite sure (or certain) that //; f-e Stimme ist mir ⌣ I am sure (or certain) of his vote; ich bin gewiß, daß // I am positive (auch: certain) that //, I can positively assert that; typ. gewisses Geld establishment-wages pl.; in gewissem Gelde (stehend) permanently engaged, on the staff; adv. certainly, surely; stärker: (most) assuredly; ei ⌣, ja! why, to be sure!; ei ⌣ nicht! no, certainly not!; of course, not!; er wird ⌣ kommen he will come without fail, he is sure to come; sie tut es ⌣ nicht she is not likely (stärker: most unlikely) to do it; Sie werden doch ⌣ nicht glauben, daß //? you will surely not believe that //?; ich weiß ⌣, daß // I know for certain (or for a certainty) that //. — 2. (nicht näher bestimmt) meist unbetont: in gewissen Fällen in certain (or some) cases; ein gewisser Herr N. a certain Mr. N., oft nicht übersetzt: ein gewisses Etwas a something (indescribable); adv. Sie werden ⌣ (ohne Zweifel) glauben, daß // you will, no doubt, believe that //. — II ge-wisse(r), ge-wisse(s) s. ⓰ ⌣ 3. ein gewisser a certain person, a somebody. — 4. et. Gewisses (Geld) a certain sum (of money); et. Gewisses (feste Einkünfte) haben ob. beziehen to have a fixed income or a regular salary; nichts Gewisses nothing certain or settled.
Ge-wissen (⌣⌣) [ahd. *It. conscie'ntia] n ㉓ conscience; rel. auch: (the) inner voice; (the) better self; ein böses (gutes) ~ an evil or a bad (an easy or a good) conscience; mit gutem ~ with a light c.; auf Pflicht und ~ in obedience to one's c.; nach bestem (Wissen und) ~ most conscientiously; um des ~s willen for conscience' sake; wider besseres Wissen und ~ contrary to the behests of one's conscience; sich mit f-m ~ abfinden, sein ~ beruhigen to quiet (or silence) one's c.; er macht sich ein ~ daraus, es zu tun he feels it his duty to do it; er macht sich kein ~ daraus zu lügen he has no scruple about telling lies. Sprichw.: ein gutes ~ ist ein sanftes Ruhekissen a clear conscience makes a soft pillow.
ge-wissenhaft (⌣⌣⌣) a. ⓰ conscientious; (ehrenhaft) high- principled; (ängstlich)

scrupulous; adv. a. strictly, religiously; ~igkeit f ⓵ conscientiousness; scrupulousness.
ge-wissen=los (⌣⌣...) a. ⓰ unscrupulous; (unredlich) dishonest, dishonourable; =losigkeit f ⓵ unscrupulousness; want of principle; dishonesty.
Ge-wissens=angst (⌣⌣...) f ⓶ pangs pl. of conscience; =bedenken n conscientious scruple; =biß m remorse, compunction; =fall m, =frage f question of c.; vgl. =sache; =freiheit f freedom of c.; rel. religious liberty; =pein f = =qual; =punkt m = =sache; =qual f qualms pl. of (a troubled) conscience, vgl. =angst; =rat, =richter m keeper of a. p.'s conscience, spiritual director; (Beichtvater) confessor; =ruhe f easiness (or ease) of a p.'s c.; peace of mind; =sache f matter of c.; =skrupel m conscientious scruple; =wurm m remorse; =zwang m moral compulsion; rel. religious intolerance; =zweifel m scruple, pl. auch: qualms of c.
ge-wisser-maßen (⌣⌣⌣⌣) adv. to a certain degree, in a certain measure or manner, to some extent, F in a way; so to speak, as it were.
Ge-wißheit (⌣⌣) f ⓵ certainty, surety, assurance; augenscheinliche ~ evidence; verbürgte ~ authenticity; mit voller ~ most assuredly or positively, for a (dead) certainty; ich werde mir ~ darüber verschaffen I will clear up the matter or ascertain the truth of it or F get to the bottom of it.
ge-wißlich (⌣⌣) adv. = gewiß 1.
Ge-witter (⌣⌣) [ahd.; * Wetter¹] n ㉒ (thunder)storm, electric storm; es ist ein schweres ~ im Anzuge there is a heavy storm brewing or gathering; das ~ brach los the storm broke forth.
ge-witterhaft (⌣⌣⌣) a. ⓰ stormy (a. fig.); boding a storm; vgl. gewitterschwanger.
Ge-witter-himmel (⌣⌣...) m ㉒ stormy sky; =kunde, =lehre f: ⚡ brontology; =luft f sultry (or oppressive) air previous to a thunderstorm.
ge-wittern (⌣⌣) v/n. (h.) ㉒ a* bsd. v/impers. es gewittert there is a storm (brewing); (es donnert) it thunders.
Ge-witter-nacht (⌣⌣...) f ⓶ stormy night; =regen, =schauer m heavy shower (with thunder and lightning); ⌣schwanger, ⌣schwer, ⌣schwül a. ⓰ v. d. Luft: sultry, oppressive; charged with electricity; die Luft ist ⌣ there is thunder in the air; =schwüle f sultriness of the air before a storm; =wolke f thunder-cloud, storm-cloud.
Ge-witzel (⌣⌣) n ㉒ joking, jesting, poor (or bad) jokes pl., silly fun.
ge-witz(ig)t (⌣⌣) [Witz] a. ⓰ (klug gemacht) made wise (or taught) by experience; (klug) shrewd, sharp, wide-awake.
ge-woben ⚡ (⌣⌣) p.p. von weben.
Ge-woge (⌣⌣) n ㉒ 1. waving, fluctuation; rolling of the sea; v. Menschen: throng; vgl. Geschaukel. — 2. (die Wogen) the waves pl., the rolling sea.
ge-wogen¹ (⌣⌣) p.p. von wägen, wiegen.¹
ge-wogen² (⌣⌣) [nhd.] a. ⓰ (D 9) kindly (or well-) disposed towards; (geneigt) favourably inclined to(wards); friendly

(stärker: attached) to; bleiben Sie mir ⌣! (pray) continue your good-will towards me!; F iro. don't worry me!, let me alone!, be off!; sich (dat.) e-n ⌣ m. to gain (or win) a. p.'s favour, to ingratiate o.s. with a p.; e-m ⌣ sein to show partiality (or a liking) for a p., to be partial to a p.; ~heit f ⓵ favour; friendliness, attachment, good-will; partiality; h. Sie die ~heit, mich anzuhören do me the favour (or have the kindness) to listen to me.
ge-wöhnen (⌣⌣) [ahd.] v/a. und sich ⌣ v/refl.: e-n an et. ⌣ to accustom (bisw. habituate) a p. to a th.; (vertraut machen mit) to familiarize with; an Hitze, Kälte: to inure to; (abrichten) to break a horse in for riding, &c.; Tiere an das Haus ⌣ to domesticate ...; sich an et. ⌣ to get accustomed (or used) to a th.; sich an ein Klima ⌣ to get acclimatized to a country; sich ans Rauchen ⌣ to contract the habit of smoking; er ist nicht an Damengesellschaft gewöhnt he is unused (or not used) to ladies' society. — II ~ n ㉓ = Gewöhnung.
Ge-wohnheit (⌣⌣) f ⓵ wont, (Herkommen) custom, (alter Gebrauch) usage; (Mode) fashion; ~ e-s einzelnen: habit, mode of life; es war seine ~ den ganzen Tag zu rauchen it was his practice or his wont ...; Sitten und ~en manners and customs pl.; aus (reiner) ~ from (sheer) habit; eine ~ annehmen to contract a habit; das ist so seine ~ that is a habit with him or his usual way (of doing things); aus der ~ kommen to go out of use or fashion; zur ~ werden to grow into a custom or habit; ~ wird zur zweiten Natur habit becomes a second nature or grows upon one.
ge-wohnheits-mäßig (⌣⌣⌣...) a. ⓰ customary; usual; adv. in the accustomed way; a. mechanically; =mensch m ㉒ creature (or slave) of habit; =recht n right founded upon custom, prescriptive law or right; =säufer(in f) m habitual drunkard, old toper or tippler; =sünde f habitual (or besetting) sin; =tier F n = =mensch.
ge-wöhnlich (⌣⌣) [a. ⓰ wonted, (herkömmlich) customary, (gebräuchlich) usual, in use; (alltäglich) ordinary, general, (alltäglich) commonplace, (gemein) common, stärker: vulgar, low; ⌣ w. to grow common or vulgar; ⌣es Gericht standing dish; die ⌣e Kost the ordinary (or customary) fare; seine ⌣e Mäßigkeit his wonted (or usual) moderation; ein ⌣er Privatmann an ordinary private citizen; ⌣e Redensart common saying; Menschen vom ⌣en Schlage the common run of people, the million; unter ⌣en Verhältnissen under ordinary circumstances; adv. ich gehe ⌣ I walk as a rule, I generally walk; so geschieht es ⌣ it usually (or commonly) happens like that; sie radelte ⌣ she used to cycle; er tut das ⌣ he makes a rule (or practice) of that; wie ⌣ as usual. — II ~e(s) n ㉗ the usual (way), the ordinary (thing); das ist das ~ste that's the most usual thing.

♪ Musik; ⚘ Wissenschaft; ⚘ Pflanze; ⚲ Geographie; ⊕ Technik; ⚒ Bergbau; ⚔ Militär; ⚓ Marine; ⚫ Handel; ✉ Post; 🚂 Eisenbah-

[**Gewöhnlichkeit**] — 446 — [**Gichtpulver**]

Ge-wöhnlichkeit (⌣⌣́⌣-) f (f. gewöhnlich) customariness, usualness; commonplace character, commonness.

ge-wohnt (⌣́) [adj.: wont] a. a) prädikativ: einer Sache (gen.) od. et. (auch: an et.) ℒ sein to be accustomed (or used) to a th., to be in the habit of doing a th.; schwere Arbeit ℒ accustomed to hard work; ich bin ℒ früh aufzustehen I am accustomed to rise early; an ein hartes Leben ℒ inured to a hard life; et. ℒ werden to get accustomed (or used) to a th.; Sprichw. jung ℒ, alt getan as the twig is bent the tree's inclined; the child is father to the man; b) attributiv: die ℒe Formel the accustomed (or traditional, customary) form; er tat's mit dem ℒen Eifer he did it with his usual (or wonted) zeal.

Ge-wohnt-sein (⌣́-⌣́) n wontedness, habit, custom, use.

Ge-wöhnung (⌣⌣́) f accustoming, &c. (f. gewöhnen I); habit, familiarity, use; domestication of animals.

Ge-wölbe (⌣⌣́) [wölben] n 1. arch. vault; feuerfestes ~ fire-proof vault or depository; (Bogen) arch; (Gruft) family-vault; verkehrtes ~ counter-vault; ⊕ f. Arbeits-ℒ; fig. ~ des Himmels canopy (or dome, vaulted arch) of heaven. — 2. ☩ † = Kramladen.

Ge-wölbe-bogen (⌣⌣⌣́...) m arch. arch (of a vault); **-pfeiler** m buttress of an arch; **-(schluß)stein** m keystone; **-stütze** f (Schwebebogen) arched (or flying) buttress.

Ge-wölf (⌣⌣́) [Wölfe] n (gathering) clouds pl., group (or body, masses pl.) of clouds; bisw. auch: cloudland.

ge-wönne (⌣⌣́) subj. impf. v. gewinnen.

ge-wonnen, ge-worben, ge-worden, ge-worfen, ge-wrungen (⌣⌣́) p.p. von gewinnen, werben, werden, werfen, wringen.

Ge-wühl (⌣́) n 1. (öfteres Wühlen) frequent burrowing; pol. agitation. — 2. das ~ (Durcheinander) der Menschen the tumult (or bustle) of the crowd; (gedrängte Menge) dense crowd or throng, great concourse; im dichten ~ der Schlacht in the thickest of the fight.

ge-wunden (⌣⌣́) I p.p. in den Bed. des inf. winden. — II a. (D 9) winding, sinuous, spiral; bsd. fig. tortuous; arch. ℒe Säule twisted column.

ge-würfelt (⌣⌣́) I p.p. in den Bed. des inf. würfeln. — II a. (tariert) chequered, checked; ℒer Fußboden tessellated floor.

Ge-würm (⌣́) [mhd.: *Wurm*] n (all sorts of) worms or creeping things or reptiles pl.; (Ungeziefer, auch fig. von Menschen) vermin.

Ge-würz (⌣́) [Wurz] n spice, spicery; (würzende Zutat) seasoning, condiment; (wohlriechende Pflanzenstoffe) aromatic drugs, aromatics, scented herbs pl.; ~ an die Speisen tun to spice (or season) …

ge-würz-artig (⌣⌣́...) a. aromatic, spicy; **-büchse** f spice-box; **-essig** m aromatic vinegar; **-extrakt** m (n) aromatic essence or extract.

Ge-würz-handel (⌣⌣́...) m spice-trade; (Spezereigeschäft) grocery business; **-händler** m trader in spice (s pl.); grocer.

ge-würzig (⌣⌣́) a. = gewürzhaft.

Ge-würz-inseln (⌣⌣́...) npr. f. pl. im Malaiischen Archipel: the Moluccas pl.; **-kram** m: a) grocer's shop, b) = **-handel**; **-krämer(in** f) m (retail or small) grocer; **-laden** m = **-kram** a; **-myrte** f allspice-tree. pimenta (Myrtus pimeʹnta); **-nägelein** n/pl., **-nelken** f pl. cloves pl.; **-nelkenbaum** m clove-tree (Caryophylʹlus aromaʹticus); **-nelken-öl** n (essential) oil of cloves; **-pflanze** f aromatic herb, ℒreich a. rich in spice(s), spicy; aromatic, scented; **-stoffe** m/pl. spices pl.; **-strauch** m Carolina allspice (Calycaʹnthus floʹridus); **-waren** f/pl. spices, groceries pl.; **-wein** m spiced wine.

ge-wußt (⌣⌣́) p.p. von wissen.

gez. abbr. = gezeichnet (signed).

ge-zackt (⌣⌣́) p.p. u. a. f. zacken III.

Gezäh(e) ⚒ (⌣́(⌣)) n (Arbeitsgerät der Bergleute) miner's tools pl.

ge-zähnelt (⌣⌣́) a. dentate(d), denticulate(d). [zahnen.]

ge-zahnt, ge-zähnt (⌣́) p.p. u. a. f.

Ge-zänk (⌣́) n (⌣), **Ge-zanke** (⌣⌣́) frequent quarrelling, incessant squabbling or disputing or wrangling.

Ge-zappel (⌣⌣́) n kicking, sprawling, fidgeting; von Kindern auch: restless (or fidgety) ways or habits pl.

Ge-zeche (⌣⌣́) n copious draughts pl.; drinking, carousing, F boozing.

ge-zehnt (⌣́) [zehn] a. math. denary; decimal; astrol. ℒer Schein (auch **=schein** m ⓓ.) ehm. decil(=) aspect.

Ge-zeit (⌣́) f = Zeit; meist pl. **-en** ↧ tide; den ~en unterworfen tidal; **-en-strömung** f tidal current, race.

Ge-zelt (⌣́) n bsd. poet. tent; pavilion: anat.: 🜨 tentorium.

Ge-zerr(e) (⌣⌣́(⌣)) n constant pulling or dragging.

Ge-zeter (⌣⌣́) n loud scolding.

Ge-zeug ⊕ (⌣́) n (set of) tools pl.

Ge-ziefer fast † (⌣⌣́) n = Ungeziefer.

ge-ziehen (⌣⌣́) p.p. von zeihen.

ge-ziemen (⌣⌣́) n [ziemen] I v/n. und v/impers. (h.), sich ℒ v/refl. * to be becoming or meet or seemly or fit; es geziemt e-m Mädchen zu // (inf.) it becomes a girl to //; so geziemt es sich that is as it should be, F that's the thing; es geziemt (sich) (nicht) für uns, zu //it behoves(it is not becoming for) us to, F it is (not) good form for us to //; wie es sich geziemt as is fit or proper; as it should be; wie es seinem Stande geziemt in accordance with (or suitably to) his rank. — II ℒd p.pr. u. a. (a. **ge-ziemlich** a.) becoming, meet, seemly, fit; (anständig) decent, decorous, adv. a. with propriety, in a becoming manner; mit ℒder Ehrfurcht with due (or proper) respect; ℒderweise becomingly.

Ge-ziere (⌣⌣́) n affectation.

ge-ziert (⌣́) I p.p. von zieren. — II a. affected; von Mädchen auch: F namby-pamby(ish); (gesucht) studied, laboured;

(steif) stiff, prim; (geckenhaft) foppish, dandyish, F putting on side; adv. auch: with affectation; in a studied manner; **~heit** (⌣⌣́) f affectation, stiffness, primness; foppishness, studied manner, mannerism.

Ge-zimmer (⌣⌣́) n 1. carpenter's work. — 2. framework, timber-work.

Ge-zirpe (⌣⌣́) n (much) chirping.

Ge-zisch(e) (⌣⌣́) n ⓐ. hissing.

Ge-zischel (⌣⌣́) n (low) whispering, hushed speech.

ge-zogen (⌣⌣́) p.p. von ziehen.

Ge-zücht (⌣́) [mhd.; *Zucht] n ⓑ. (low) breed; (numerous) offspring; F contp. brood, tribe, gang.

ge-züngelt (⌣⌣́) a. lambent (flames, &c.).

Ge-zweig(e) (⌣́) n ⓒ. branches, boughs pl.; **ge-zweigt** (⌣⌣́) a. branched.

ge-zweit (⌣́) a. (aus zwei bestehend) in twos, ℒ binary.

Ge-zwerg (⌣́) [mhd.] n ⓑ. 1. = Zwerg. — 2. coll. race of dwarfs. [ter(ing).]

Ge-zwitscher (⌣⌣́) n chirping, twit-

ge-zwungen (⌣⌣́) I p.p. in den Bed. des inf. zwingen. — II a. (D 9) 1. (auf Zwang beruhend) forced, compulsory, et. ℒerweise tun to do a th. under compulsion. — 2. (affettiert) affected, (steif, abgemessen) stiff, starched, formal, constrained; **~heit** f affectation, stiffness, formality, constraint.

☞ **Gh** … vgl. G…   [giaour.]

Giaur (⌣⌣́) [türk.] m (Nichtmohammedaner)

gib (⌣́) imper., ℒst 2., ℒt 3. Person sg. pres. ind. von geben.

Gicht¹ (⌣́) [mhd.; *gehen] f (pl. ⟋) path. gout(iness), gouty complaint, 🜨 arthritis; an ~ leidend gouty, suffering from gout; gegen ~ wirkend, die ~ heilend curing the gout, 🜨 antarthritic; mit der ~ behaftet troubled with the gout; ~er pl. path. (Krampfanfall v. Kindern) 🜨 eclampsia of children.

Gicht² ⚒ (⌣́) [geben] f metall. (Schachtofenmündung) throat (or mouth) of a furnace, tunnel-hole.

Gicht¹-anfall (⌣́...) m attack of (the) gout; ℒartig a. gouty, 🜨 arthritic; **-²aufzug** ⊕ m, metall. furnace-hoist, lift of the furnace; ℒ¹brüchig a. bibl. paralytic, palsied; **-brüchige(r)** m bsd. bibl. paralytic, person afflicted with palsy; **-brüchigkeit** f bsd. bibl. paralysis, palsy; **-²brücke** ⊕ f, metall. bridge leading to the mouth of the furnace; **-¹fieber** n: 🜨 arthritic fever; **-²flamme** ⊕ f, metall. top-flame; **-galerie** f top-gallery; **-gas** n waste gas of the furnace top-gallery; ℒ¹heilend a.: 🜨 antarthritic.

gichtisch (⌣⌣́) [Gicht¹] a. gouty, afflicted with gout, 🜨 arthritic(al).

Gicht¹-knoten (⌣́...) m gouty concretion or knot or node, gout-stone; ℒkrank a. suffering from (or ill of) the gout; gouty; bettlägerig: laid up with gout; **-kranke(r)** s. gouty patient, F co. goutee; **-krankheit** f, **-leiden** n gouty disease, affection; vgl. Gicht¹; **-²mantel** ⊕ m, metall. wind-wall of a blast-furnace; **-¹mittel** n remedy for gout, 🜨 antarthritic; **-papier, -pflaster, -pulver** n antarthritic paper, plaster,

Signs (see page XVII): F familiar; P vulgar; ⌐ flash; ↘ rare; † obsolete (died); * new word (born); +⁺ incorrect; ♪ music;

[Gichtrauch] — 447 — [Gilde]

powder; =**rauch** m = Hütten-r.; =¹**rose** ⚚ f peony (*Paeo'nia*); =**schmerzen** m/pl. gouty pains pl., twitches pl. of the gout; =²**stoff** ⚒ m, metall. tutty, (furnace-) cadmia or calamine; =¹**stoff** m gouty matter; =**watte**, =**wolle** f gout-padding. [cock-a-doodle-doo.]

Gickel (⌣) m ㉒ Kinderspr. (Hahn) rooster.
Gick-gack F (⌣⌣) m ㉒ cackling of geese; fig. (dummer Mensch) stupid (fellow).
gicksen (⌣⌣) [ahd.: kick] ⑩ = ficksen.
gieb (´) ꝛc. s. gib ꝛc.
Giebel¹ (´⌣) [ahd.] m ㉒ 1. (Gipfel) top; pinnacle. — 2. ⊕ arch.: a) (First eines Hauses) house-top, gable(-end); b) (dreieckige Wand zw. e-m Satteldach) gable-wall.
Giebel² (´⌣) [ahd.; * lt. *gobio*] m ㉒, f ⓫ ichth. (Steinkarausche) gibel (*Gibe'lio*).
Giebel¹=**ähre** (″...) f ㊅ gable-ear; =**balken** m top-joist; =**bruch** m = Gipfel-b.; =**dach** n gabled roof; =**feld** n tympan, pediment; =**fenster** f gable-window; (Dachfenster) attic window; =**förmig** a. ㊅ gable-shaped; =**haus** n house with a g.-roof; =**mauer** f gable-wall; vgl. Giebel¹ 2b; =**seite** f gable-side, frontispiece; =**spieß** m, =**spitze** f top of a gable(-end); =**stube** f garret, attic; =**verzierung** f top- (or gable-) mouldings pl.; =**wand** f gable(-end); =**zinne** f: ⚹ acroterion (pl. ...ia).
Giek=**baum** ⚓ (″⌣) m ㉒ (unteres Rundholz für Gaffelsegel) spanker-, main-, mizzen-boom. [tackle; purchase.]
Gien ⚓ (´) n ⓒc. (Flaschenzug) winding
Gien=**muschel** (″...) [nhd.; * gähnen] f ㉒ zo.: ⚹ chama.
giepen ⚓ (´) v/n. (h.) ⑩ to gybe.
Gier¹ (´) [ahd.: * gern] f ㊇ greed(iness), eagerness, avidity; ~ nach Reichtum eager (or keen) desire for wealth, thirst(ing) for (or hankering after) riches. [swing-bridge.]
Gier=**brücke** ⊕ (″...) [gieren²] f ㊇
Gierde (´⌣) [ahd.] f ㊈ = Gier.
gieren¹ (´⌣) [Gier] v/n. (h.) ㊇ nach et. ≗ to long eagerly (or to yearn) for a th.
gieren² ⚓ (´⌣) [ndd.] v/n(h)㊇ (hin und her schwanken) to yaw; to fall away (or to drift) from the (right) course.
Gieren=**ziegel** (″...) m ㉒ Dachdeck.: triangular (or three-cornered) tile.
Gier=**falke** (″⌣⌣) [nhd.] m ㉒ orn. gerfalcon (*Falco gyrfa'lco*).
gierig (´⌣) [ahd.] a. ㊅ greedy after or of, covetous of; auf Geld ≗ money-grubbing; ≗ essen to eat greedily or voraciously, to gormandize; ≗ verschlingen to gulp down, to bolt; ~**keit** (´⌣) f ㊇ greed(iness), covetousness.
Gier=**ponte** (″...) f ㊇ = Gierbrücke.
Giersch (´) m ⓐa. goat's-foot, goutweed (*Ægopo'dium Podagra'ria*).
Gieß=**bach** (″...) m ㉒ (mountain-)torrent; =**bad** n shower-bath, douche; =**buckel** m casting-cone.
gießen (´⌣) [ahd.: gush] v/a. u. v/n. (h.) ⓓd. 1. to pour (out); Öl auf die Lampe ≗ to put oil into the lamp; Wasser durch einen Trichter ≗ to pour (in) water through a funnel; Öl ins Feuer ≗ to pour oil into the flame, fig. to add fuel to the fire. — 2. (verschütten) to spill; die Brühe auf das

Tischtuch, über sein Kleid ≗ to spill the gravy on the table-cloth, over one's dress. — 3. metonymisch für „begießen": die Blumen ≗ to water the flowers; abs. ist heute schon gegossen? have the flowers, &c. been watered to-day? — 4. den Becher voll ≗ to fill the cup (to the brim). — 5. fig. (ausströmen lassen) to shed forth upon a th. — 6. ⊕ Gießerei: e-e Glocke, e-e Statue ≗ to found, to (cast in a) mould; Kugeln ꝛc. ≗ to cast bullets, &c.; gegossene Arbeit cast (metal) work; gegossene Lichte n/pl. mould-candles pl.; Roheisen in Gangstücken ≗ to cast pigs; fig. von Kleidern: wie gegossen sitzen to fit like a glove. — 7. der Himmel gießt, mehr gebr. es gießt (regnet heftig) it is pouring (with rain). F it's raining cats and dogs.
Gießer ⊕ (´⌣) m ㉒ **1.**~(**in** f ㊇) m founder, moulder; caster; auch = Schriftgießer. — 2. sachlich = Gießkanne a.
Gieß=**erde** (″...) f ㊇ mould.
Gießerei ⊕ (-⌣´) f ㊇ 1. founder's art. — 2. = Schriftgießerei. — 3. (Gießhaus) casting-house or -shed, foundry.
Gieß=**erz** (″...) n ㊇ cast bronze; =**form** f Gießerei: casting- (or ingot-)mould; s. a. Form 4; =**haus** n, =**hütte** f Gießerei: casting-house or -room, foundry; =**kanne** f: a) zum Begießen der Hände water-jug; ewer; b) der Blumen: watering-can; =**kelle** f casting- (or foundry-)ladle, founder's scoop; =**kunst** f art of casting (in moulds), founder's art; =**loch** n Gießerei: für das ab- und einfließende Erz: funnel of the furnace; casting-gutter or -hole; =**mutter** f, typ. =**matrix**; =**ofen** m founding-furnace; =**rinne** f: a) in Küchen ꝛc.: sink; b) Gießerei: = =**loch**; =**sand** m founder's sand; =**tafel** f casting-plate; =**tiegel** m zum Gießen der Lichte: crucible for moulding; =**zange** f zum Gießen des Metalls: founder's tongs pl.; =**zapfen** m Gießerei: runner. — Vgl. a. Guß-...
Gift (´) [ahd.: gift Gabe; *geben] n ⓑb. 1. allg. poison, von Tieren auch: venom, zB. ~ von Schlangen ꝛc.: poison (or venom) of snakes, &c.; schleichendes ~ slow poison; fig. darauf kannst du ~ nehmen you may rest assured of it or take my word for it. — 2. (Ansteckungsstoff) virus; contagious matter, germs pl. of infection. — 3. fig. (Wut, Bosheit) venom; rage, fury, malice; ~ und Galle, ~ und Geifer speien to vent one's anger (or spleen) upon a p.; ~ break forth in a fury against a p.
gift=**abtöfend** (⌣⌣...) a. ㊅ Leş Mittel med.: ⚹ alexipharmic (⌣...) ; =**artig** a. poison-like, poisonous; =**baum** ⚘ m ㉒: a) upas (-tree) (*Anti'aris toxica'ria*); b) = =**sumach**; =**becher** m cup of poison, poisoned (or poison-)cup; =**beere** f poisonous berry; ≗**bereitend** a. ㊅ u. zo.: ⚹ venenifluous; =**beschreibung** f: ⚹ toxicography; =**bissen** m poisoned morsel or dish; =**blase** f, =**bläschen** n der Schlangen poison-gland or -bag, venom-sac; fig. sie ist eine kleine ~ she is a little sneak or wretch; =**drüse** f einer Schlange venom-gland; =**dunst** ⊕ m poisonous fumes pl.; =**erz** n, min. arsenic-ore;

frei a. = Gloş; =**geschwollen** a. swollen with poison or venom; =**gewächs** ⚘ n poisonous plant or shrub; =**hahnenfuß** ⚘ m marsh-crowfoot (*Ranun'culus scelera'tus*); ≗**haltig** a. containing poison; =**handel** m trade in (or sale of) poisons; =**hauch** m poisonous breath, blight; =**hütte** ⚒ f arsenic-works pl.
giftig (´⌣) a. ㊅ **1.** (s. Gift 1 u. 2) poisonous, venomous, virulent, contagious; ⚹ toxic, toxical, toxicant; (vergiftet) poisoned. — 2. fig. (s. Gift 3) malignant; full of venom or malice; (ergrimmt) enraged, furious; (verderblich) pernicious; ℓer Mensch spiteful person; auf e-n ≗ sein to be angry (F cross) with a p.; F e-n ≗ machen to make a p. angry with a p., to incite (or set) a p. against a p.
Giftigkeit (´⌣⌣) f ㊇ (s.giftig 1) poisonousness, venomousness, poisonous (or venomous) nature of a plant, a snake, &c.; virulence of a disease; fig. (s. giftig 2) malignity, malice; rage, fury.
Gift=**kies** ⚒ (´...) m ㉒ arsenical pyrites; =**kraut** ⚘ n poisonous herb, a. = Tabak; =**kunde**, =**lehre** f: ⚹ toxicology; =**kundige(r)** m: ⚹ toxicologist; =**lattich** ⚘ m strong-scented lettuce (*Lactu'ca viro'sa*); pharm. Milchsaft des ~s: ⚹ thridace; =**los** a. ㊅ free from poison, poisonless; non-poisonous; =**mehl** n arsenic-powder, white arsenic (As_2O_3); =**mischen** n = =**mischerei**; =**mischer(in** f) (woman or lady f) poisoner; =**mischerei** f (murder by) poisoning; =**mittel** n (Gegengift) antidote; =**mord** m (murder by) poisoning; =**mörder(in** f) m = =**mischer(in**); =**pflanze** f poisonous plant; =**pille** f poisoned pill; =**pilz** ⚘ m = =**schwamm**; ≗**reich** a. abounding in (or full of) poison; =**schlange** f, zo. venomous (or poisonous) snake or serpent, ⚹ thanatophidian; =**schnecke** f, zo. toxoglossate; =**schwamm** ⚘ m poisonous mushroom or toadstool; =**stoff** m poisonous substance or matter, med. virus; =**sumach** ⚘ m poison-ivy or -oak (*Rhus toxicode'ndron*); =**tier** n, zo. venomous (or poisonous) animal; =**trank** m poisoned draught or potion; =**zahn** m der Schlangen venom-tooth, poison-fang; =**zunge** f, fig. venomous (or envenomed, malicious) tongue.
Gigant (-´) [grch.] m ㊷ myth. giant; ≗**enhaft** (-⌣´⌣), ≗**isch** (-⌣´) a. ㊅ (riesig) gigantic, colossal, enormous.
Gigerl(⌣⌣) [öst. v. *Gickel(hahn), vgl. fokett] m u. n ㉒, ⓓd. (Modegeck) fop, dandy, swell, beau, F masher, Am. dude.
gilb (´) ꝛc. s. gelb. [ochre.
Gilbe (´⌣) [nhd.] f ㊈ min. yellow iron-**Gilb**=**kraut** ⚘ (″...) n ㉒ dyer's-weed (*Rese'da luteo'la*); =**vogel** m, orn. (Pirol) oriole; =**weiderich** ⚘ m loosestrife (*Lysima'chia vulga'ris*); =**wurz** ⚘ f (root of) curcuma (*Cu'rcuma longa*).
Gilde (´⌣) [nhd.: Gülte, gelten] f ㊈ **1.** (geschlossene Gesellschaft) exclusive company. — 2. (Innung, Zunft) guild, corporation; die Londoner ~ der Handschuhmacher, Seidenhändler ꝛc. the (worshipful) Company of Glovers, Mercers, &c. —

⚹ scientific; ⚘ botanical; ⓖ geography; ⊕ machinery; ⚒ mining; ⚔ military; ⚓ marine; ⓒ commercial; ⓟ postal; 🚆 railway.

[Gildebrief] — 448 — [glänzen]

3. meeting (or banquet) of (the members of) a corporation.
Gilde-brief (ˬ...) m ㉒, **-bruder** m charter, member of a corporation; **-herr**, **-meister**, **-vorsteher** m master of a guild, chairman of a corporation.
Gilling, Gillung ↓ (ˬ) f ㊻ (Krümmung, Wölbung d. Hinterschiffs) counter; ~ (bogenförmiger Ausschnitt) eines Segels: roach, gore. [gültig ꝛc.]
giltig ⁺⁺ (ˬ) [gelten, gilt] a. ㊺ ꝛc. =
gilt(ſt) (ˢ) (2.) 3. Perſon *pres.* von gelten.
Gimpe ☉ ♨ (ˬ) [ndd.; *(⁺⁺) fr. *guimpe*.] f ㊽ gimping, gimp-lace.
Gimpel (ˬ) [mhd.] m ㉒ 1. *orn.* bullfinch (*Pyrrhula vulgaris*). — 2. *fig.* (leicht zu Berückender) simpleton, F jay; (Dummkopf) blockhead, dunce, dummy.
Gimpelei (ˬˬ) f ㊻ foolishness.
gimpelhaft (ˬˬ) a. ㊺ foolish.
Ginever (ˬˬ), **Ginevra** (ˬˬ) ㊴ ㊸. ㊺ ㊶ *a. npr. f.* (König Arturs Gemahlin) Guenever, Guinevere.
ging (ˢ) (꞉ɇ *subj.*) *impf.* von gehen.
Gingang ☀ (ˬ) [fr. *guingamp*.] m ㊵ (im Garn gefärbtes Zeug) gingham.
Ginster ♀ (ˬ) [lt. *genista* f] m ㉒ broom (*Genista*); deutscher ~ German broom (*G. germanica*); englischer ~ English broom (*G. anglica*).
Gipfel (ˬ) [mhd. 15. sae. dim. v. Kuppe, Kopf] m ㉒ (höchster Punkt) summit; top of a tree, &c.; peak of a mountain; pinnacle of a temple, gable of a house; *fig.* climax, meridian; ~ e-r Laufbahn ꝛc. culminating point, acme; er stand auf dem ~ seiner Macht he was at the zenith (or had attained the meridian) of his power.
Gipfel-bruch (ˬˬ...) m ㉒ *for.* breaking of tree-tops under the weight of snow and ice; **ˀförmig** ♀ a.: ꜛ fastigiate(d).
gipf(e)lig (ˬ(ˬ)ˬ) a. ㊺ ending in a point or top; conical; meist in Zssgn, z.B. drei-ꝛ with three summits or peaks.
gipfeln (ˬˬ) ☁a. I v/a. to crown with a summit, to (provide with a) top. — II v/n. (h.) u. **sich ꝛ** v/refl. to culminate, to attain one's acme or culminating point or zenith; (fich erheben) to tower, to rise (to a lofty height).
Gipfel-punkt (ˬˬ...) m ㉒ highest (*fig.* auch: culminating) point; ꝛreich a. ㊺ with many summits or peaks; ꝛständig ♀ a.: ꜛ apical, bisw.: apicular; terminal.
gipflig (ˬˬ) s. gipf(e)lig.
Gips (ˢ) [ahd., *grch.] m ㉒ a. gypsum, plaster of Paris; *chm.* (hydrated) sulphate of calcium or lime (CaSO₄); gebrannter ~ burnt (or calcined) gypsum; (grob) gemahlener ~ ground gy.
Gips-abdruck ☉ (ˢ...) m ㉒, **-abguß** m plaster cast, gypsoplast; **-arbeit** f plaster- (or stucco-)work; **-arbeiter** m plasterer, stucco-worker; **ꝛartig** a. ㊺ like plaster (of Paris), gypseous; **-bewurf** m plastering (or coating) of a wall; **-bild** n plaster of Paris figure, plaster image; **-brei** m plaster (or gypsum) paste; paste of gypsum; **-brenner** m plasterer; **-brennerei** f: a) gypsum-calcination; b) (Ort dazu) gypsum-kiln; **-bruch** m: a)

quarry; **-büste** f plaster-bust; **-decke** f plaster ceiling; **-druse** f, *min.* crystallized gypsum.
gipsen¹ ☉ (ˬˢ) [Gips] v/a. ㊐ to plaster; *agr.* (mit Gips düngen) to manure (or fertilize) with gypsum; **Gipser** m ㉒ plasterer, plaster- (or stucco-)worker; *vgl.* Gipsfigurengießer.
gipsen², **gipsern** (ˬˢ) a ㊺ (made) of gypsum or plaster (of Paris).
Gips-erde (ˢ...) f ㊸: a) *agr.* gypseous soil; b) *min.* earthy gypsum or sulphate of lime; **-estrich** m plaster floor; **-figur** f = -bild; **-figuren-gießer**, **-händler**, **-macher**, F **-mann** m maker of plaster of Paris figures, plaster-image maker, (Italian) image-seller or -boy; **-form** f Gießerei: plaster mould; **-grube** f gypsum-pit; **-guß** m plaster cast(ing); **ˀhaltig** a. gypseous, ꜛ gypsiferous; **-kalk** m plaster-lime; **-malerei** f fresco-painting; **-marmor** m imitation marble, stucco; **-mehl** n plaster-powder; **-mergel** m, *min.* gypseous marl; **-mörtel** m plaster; auch = **-stuck**; **-mühle** f gypsum- (or plaster-) mill; **-ofen** m gypsum-kiln; **-sand** m, *min.* gypseous sand, spar; **-spat** m, *min.* gypseous spar; **-statue** f plaster statue; **-stein** m, *min.*: a) gypseous stone; b) plaster-stone; **-stuck** m stucco; **-verband** m, *surg.* plaster of Paris (or gypsoplastic) dressing; für den Oberkörper: plaster-jacket; einen ~ anlegen to dress (or put) a broken limb, &c. in plaster of Paris; **-wand** f plastered wall.
Gipüre ☉ ♨ (ˬˣˬ) [fr. *guipure*] f ㊸ (Gimpengeflecht) guipure.
Gipür-spitzen (ˬˣ...) f/pl. ㊶ (mit gedrehter Seide überſponnen) guipure-lace *sg.*
Giraffe (ˬˬˬ) [fr., span., *ar.] f ㊸ *zo.* giraffe (*Camelopardalis giraffa*).
Girandole (ɢ-ˬˬˬ) [it.] f ㊸ (Feuerwerk) girandole.
Girant ♨ (ɢ-ˢ) [it.] m ㊷ endorser; **Girat** (ɢ-ˢ) m ㊷ endorsee; **girierbar** (ɢ-ˢ-) a. ㊺ endorsable; **girieren** (ɢ-ˢˬ) [it.] v/a. ㊛ (in Umlauf setzen) to put in(to) circulation; e-n Wechsel ꝛ to endorse a bill (auf, an e-n upon a p.).
Girlande (ˬˬ) [fr. *guirlande*; *dtsch] f ㊸ (Laubgewinde) garland, festoon, wreath.
Girlitz (ˬˬ) m ㉑a. *orn.* (Art Fink) serin (-finch) (*Serinus hortulanus*).
Giro (ɢˢ-) [it. 17. sae., it.] m u. n ㊴ (㊸) (Aufschrift auf der Rückseite e-s Wechsels ꝛc.) endorsement; einem Wechsel sein(en) ~ geben to endorse a bill; ~ in blanco blank endorsement; **~-bank** f (deposit-) bank; **~-geschäft** n, etwa: billbroker's business; **-verkehr** m clearing-house business. [Tauben: to coo.]
girren (ˬˬ) [mhd.] v/n. (h.) ㊶ bfd. von
Gis ♪ (ˢ) *n, inv.* G sharp; **~-Dur** G sharp major; **~-Moll** G sharp minor.
gischen (ˬˢ) v/n. (h.) ㊑ to foam.
Gischt (ˢ) [: yeast] m ㉑a. foam, froth.
gissen ↑ ♨ (ˬˢ) [*guess*] v/a. (h.) ㊐ to make a rough calculation of; gegißte Besteckrechnung dead reckoning.
Gissung ↓ (ˬˢ) f ㊻ rough calculation (by the log-book), ship's account, way-reckoning; Besteck durch ~position by dead reckoning.

Gitarre ♪ (ˬˢˬ) [nhd. 18. sae.; ꞉fr. *guitare*] f ㊸ guitar; **~(n)-saite** f㊻ guitar-string; **~(n)-spieler** m ㉒ gu.-player.
Gitter (ˬˬ) [mhd.: Gatter] n ㉒ 1. lattice- (or trellis-)work; *arch.* screen; (Geländer) rail(ing); (Zaun) fence. — 2. (Querstangen) iron bars *pl.* or grating (a. am Kerker); ꜛ aus Draht zum Schutze von Pflanzen ꝛc.: wire netting; vor e-m Kamine: fender, guard. — 3. Zeichnen: durch das ~ verkleinern to reduce by squares.
gitter-artig (ˬˬ...) a. ㊺ = **ˀförmig**; **-bett** n ㊸ railed cot; **-brücke** ☉ f lattice-bridge; **-fenster** n lattice-window; mit Eisenstangen: window with cross-bars, barred window; **ˀförmig** a. lattice-like, latticed, trellised, ꜛ cancellate(d); **-gang** m trellised walk; wire enclosure.
gitterig (ˬˬ) a. ㊺ = gitterförmig.
Gitter-laden (ˬˬ...) m ㉒ Venetian blind; **-laube** f arbour (made) of trellis-work.
gittern (ˬˬ) v/a. ㊑a. to lattice; gegittert, a.: barred; railed (enclosed), (gewürfelt) chequered, ꜛ cancellate(d).
Gitter-schrank (ˬˬ...) m ㉒ für Fleisch ꝛc. wire safe for meat, &c.; **-spektrum** n, *phys.* grate-spectrum; **-tor** n, **-tür** n: F = Gatter-tor; **-werk** n: a) = Gitter 1; b) *arch.* im Kirchenchor ꝛc.: ꜛ cancelli *pl.*; **-zaun** m fence of trellis-work or wire netting.
Glacé F (ˬˢˬ) ㊴ = Glacéhandschuh.
Glacé-handschuh (ˢ...) m ㉒ kid-glove; **-(leder)schuhe** m/pl. kid-boots *pl.*
glacieren (ˬˢˬ) [fr.] v/a. ㊓: a) (gefrieren m.) to freeze, to congeal; b) (glänzend m.) to make glossy; *vgl.* glasieren.
Glacis ⚔ (ˬˢˢ) [fr.] n ㊵ *frt.* (Feldabdachung) glacis; **~-abhang** m, **~-böschung** f ㊷ slope (or scarp) of the glacis.
Gladiator (ˬˬˬˢˬ) [it.] m ㉑ röm. Alt. (Schaufechter) gladiator; **ꝛenhaft** (ˬ(ˬ)-ˬˬ) a. ㊺ = ꝛisch; **~en-spiele** n/pl. ㊶ gladiatorial games *pl.*; **ꝛisch** (ˬ(ˬ)-ˢˬ) a. ㊺ gladiatorial.
Glanz (ˢ) [mhd.] m ㊆(㉒)a. (*pl.* ꝛⁱ) 1. blendender: brightness, stärker: glare, leuchtender: brilliancy, resplendence, refulgence, strahlender: radiancy; (blanke Politur) lustre of a diamond, &c. (auch *fig.*), polish of furniture, &c.; ~ ausstrahlend, verbreitend shedding (or spreading) a lustre (around), lustrous; den ~ verlieren, bfd. von Metallen: to tarnish. — 2. *fig.* ~ der Gesundheit, Jugend ꝛc. bloom; (Herrlichkeit) splendour; (Gepränge) pomp, show; eine Prüfung mit ~ bestehen to pass an examination with distinction or honours; *vgl.* glänzen IV. — 3. ☉ gloss(iness) of satin, &c.; (Glätte) smoothness; polish.
Glanz-bürste (ˢ...) f ㊻ polishing- (or lustring-)brush.
glänzen (ˬˬ) [ahd.: glint, *vgl.* Glast] ㊐ I v/n. (h.) 1. to be bright or brilliant; (strahlen) to radiate, to beam; (schimmern) to shine, (funkeln) to sparkle, to flash, (glitzern) to glitter; seine Augen ꝛ vor Freude his eyes sparkle with joy or delight; er glänzt im Reiche der Dichtkunst he is a shining star in the realm of poetry; sie glänzt als Schriftstellerin she is a

[Glänzer] — 449 — [Glasschrank]

brilliant authoress;• durch seine Abwesenheit ≗ to be conspicuous by one's absence; Sprichw. es ist nicht alles Gold, was glänzt all is not gold that glitters; in Jugend und Schönheit ≗d (strahlend) resplendent with youth and beauty. — 2. ⊙ von Stoffen ꝛc.: to have (or show) a lustre or gloss, to be lustrous or glossy. — II v/a. 3. ⊙ (durch Glätten Glanz geben) to polish; F to shine up; Metall auch: to burnish; Leder: to lacquer, Papier: to glaze. — III ~ n ⓘ 4. (s. I) brightness, brilliancy; radiance, glitter(ing), lustre, resplendence. — IV ≗d 5. p.pr. u. a. ⑥ Bed. des inf. — 6. bright, brilliant; (strahlend) radiant, resplendent; ⊙ von Zeugen ꝛc.: lustrous, lustred, glossy. — 7. (prachtvoll) splendid, magnificent; fig. ≗de Tat glorious deed, brilliant feat; er hat das Examen ≗d bestanden he has passed a brilliant examination, he gained high honours.

Glänzer ⊙ (♪) m ⓘ (s. glänzen II) polisher; burnisher; (Lackierer) lacquerer.

Glanz-farbe ⊙ (ᵍ...) f ⓘ brilliant (or bright) colour; =firnis ⊙ m glazing- (or polishing-)varnish; =geber ⊙ m = Glänzer; =gold n Dutch gold, imitation gold-leaf; =gras ♀ n various-leaved canary-grass (Pha'laris arundina'cea).

Glanz-hammer m ⓘ polishing-hammer.

Glanz-kattun ⊙ (ᵍ...) m ⓘ glazed calico; =kobalt m, min. tin-white cobalt; =kohle f, min. glance-coal, anthracite; =leder ⊙ n patent-leather; =lederschuhe m/pl. patent-(leather) boots or shoes pl.; =leinwand ⓘ f glazed lining for dresses, &c.; =leistung f brilliant feat, splendid achievement; ≗los a. without lustre, lustreless; dull, dim, von Edelsteinen auch: cloudy; fig. without splendour; =losigkeit f lack of lustre, dulness; =papier ⊙ n glazed paper; =pappe f (glazed) pasteboard, typ. pressing-board; =periode f brightest (or most brilliant) period, glorious (or palmy) days pl.; =presse f für Tuch: glazing-calender; =punkt m, fig. culminating (or highest) point, climax, acme; ≗reich a. of a rich lustre; very bright or lustrous or glorious; =seide ⓘ f = taffet.

Glänz-stahl (ᵍ...) m ⓘ burnisher, polishing-iron or -steel or -tool.

Glanz-stärke (ᵍ...) f ⓘ glazed starch; =taf(fe)t ⓘ m (silk-) lustring; =tapeten f/pl. satined wall-papers pl.

Glänzung ⊙ (ᵍ...) f ⓘ polishing, &c. (s. glänzen II); von Hüten ꝛc. a. lustring.

glanz-voll (ᵍ...) a. ⓘ full of splendour, splendid, brilliant, resplendent; vgl. ≗reich; =wichse ⊙ ⓘ polishing-paste, paste for patent leather; =zwirn ⊙ m glacé thread; patent bobbin.

Glas (nbb.◡, obb. ⌣) [ahd.: glas (urspr. = Kristall, Bernstein; später auf ↯ übertragen)] n ⓘa. (vgl. 2 u. 3) 1. glass; (matt ge)schliffenes ~ cut (ground) glass; schlechtes grünes ~ bottle-glass; f. Spiegel-⌇; phys. in ~ verwandeln, zu ~ werden: ↯ to vitrify; Sprichw. Glück und ~ wie leicht bricht das, etwa: glass and luck, brittle muck. — 2. (gläsernes Trinkgefäß, als Maß ⓓs.) glass; ohne Fuß für Wasser od. Bier, auch: tumbler; volles ~ bumper; zwei ~ Wein two glasses of wine; ein englisches ~ Bier half a pint of ale; gern ins ~ gucken to be fond of one's glass or F of a drop; ein Gläschen über den Durst trinken, zu tief ins ~ gucken to drink too much, F to have (or take) a drop too much; mit den Gläsern anstoßen (in England nicht üblich) to touch glasses. — 3. ⚓ Sa. (½ Stunde) bell.

glas-ähnlich (ᵍ...) a. ⓖ glasslike, vitreous; =arbeit f ⓘ: a) glass-work; b) ♞ = waren; =arbeiter m glass-worker; ≗artig a. glassy, vitreous; ↯ hyalescent; =artigkeit f glassiness, vitreousness; hyalescence; =ätzkunst, =ätzung f: ↯ hyalography; =auge n: a) glass eye; b) fig. (Auge mit starrem Blick) glassy eye; c) vet. (mit glasigem Ring um den Stern) wall-eye; d) co. ~n pl. (Brille) glasses pl., F goggle-eyes, goggles pl.; ≗äugig a.: a) with a glass eye; b) vet. walleyed; =ballo'n m für Säuren ꝛc. glass balloon, carboy; =bereitung f glass-making, ↯ hyalurgy; =bild n glass negative; crystallotype; =blaselampe f gl.-blower's (or enamelling-) lamp; =blasen n gl.-blowing; vor der Lampe: enamelling; =bläser m gl.-blower; =bläse-tisch m enamelling-table; =bohren n gl.-drilling; =brocken m/pl., =bruch m Glasfabr.: cullet; =bürste f bottle-brush; =chemie f: ↯ hyalurgy. [bes. 2).]

Gläschen (ᴸ◡) n ⓘ dim. von Glas (s. bs.)

Glas-dach (ᵍ...) n ⓘ glass-roof, skylight; =deckel m gl. cover or lid; =diama'nt m strass; ≗elektrisch a. ⓖ: ↯ vitreo-electric; =elektrizitä't f, phys. vitreous (or positive) electricity.

Glaser (ᴸ◡) m ⓘ. ~in f ⓘ 1. glazier('s wife f). — 2. (a. Gläser) = Glasbläser.

Glaser-arbeit (ᴸ◡...) f ⓘ, =handwerk n glazier's work, trade; =blei n = Fensterblei; =diama'nt m glazier's diamond, diamond(pencil) for cutting glass.

Glaserei (~◡ᴸ) f ⓘ glazier's business or workshop or premises pl. [putty.]

Glaser-kitt (ᴸ◡...) m ⓘ (Fensterkitt) glazier's

Gläser-klang (⌣◡...) m ⓘ jingling (sound) of glasses; =korb m basket for tumblers or glass ware.

Glaser-meister (ᴸ◡...) m ⓘ master glazier. [work.]

gläsern[1] (ᴸ◡) v/n. (h.) ⓘa. to do glazier's (gläsern, sübb. **glasern**[2] (ᴸ◡) a. ⓘ (of) glass, glassy, vitreous; vom Auge, Blick: glassy (eye), fixed (glance); ≗e Augen n/pl., a. F goggle-eyes pl.; ≗e Flasche glass bottle.

Glas-erz ⚒ (ᵍ...) n ⓘ silver-glance or ore; =fabrik f glass-works pl. or -factory; =fabrikation f manufacture of glass, gl.-making; =fäden pl. spun glass; =färben n gl.-staining; ≗farbig a.: ↯ hyaloid; =fenster n gl. window; =flasche f gl. bottle, geschliffene: decanter; =flügler m, ent. clearwing (Se'sia); =fluß ⊙ m glassy flux, vitreous paste; =fritte f = =satz; =galle f Glasfabrikation: (Schaum, der sich beim Schmelzen bildet) glass-gall, sandiver; =gehäuse n gl. case; =gemälde n painting on glass; =geschirr n gl. ware or vessel(s pl.); =glocke f für Uhren, Vasen ꝛc.: glass shade, für Butter ꝛc.: gl. cover, für Lampen: globe, für Pflanzen ꝛc.: gl. bell; chm. gl. jar; =griff m gl. handle; Glasfabr.: (Eisenstab zum Ausheben der =masse ꝛc.) bisw.: ferret; ≗grün a. bottle-green; =hafen ⊙ m: a) glass jar; b) = tiegel; =handel ⓘ m gl.-trade; =händler(in f) m dealer in glass, a. F gl.-man; beim ~ at a glass- and china-shop; =harmo'nika ♪ f musical glasses pl.; glass-chord; ≗hart a. (as) hard as glass or flint; =haus n glass house; phot. studio; =haus-pflanze f, hort. hothouse-plant; =haut f. anat. des Auges: ↯ hyaloid membrane, hyaline; ≗hell a. transparent as glass. ↯ hyaline; =hütte f = fabrik.

glasicht (ᴸ◡) a. ⓖ glassy, glasslike.

glasieren ⊙ (~◡ᴸ) [(P: Glas) fr. glacer] v a. ⓖ to glaze (auch von Töpferei ꝛc.); Eisenwaren ꝛc.: to ena'mel; Leder, Gemälde ꝛc.: to varnish; mit Zuckerguß glasierter Kuchen iced (or frosted) cake.

glasig (ᴸ◡) a. ⓖ 1. mixed with glass, full of (broken) glass. — 2. = glasicht.

Glas-industrie (ᵍ...) ⓘ f glass-industry, manufacture of glass; =infrustation ⊙ f incrusted glass; =kasten m glass case; =kitt m diamond- (or giant-)cement; =kolben m, chm. flask, =kopf m, min. (Rot-eisen-erz): ↯ hematite; =koralle f glass bead or bugle; =korb m: a) (Lattenkiste) crate; b) (gläserner Korb) glass basket; =körper m vitreous humour of the eye; =kram ⓘ m = =laden; =krämer(in f) m = händler(in); =kraut ♀ n: a) wall-pellitory (Parieta'ria); b) = Queller; =krug m, =kruke f gl. jug or mug; =kugel f gl. globe or sphere, einer Lampe: globe; =laden ⓘ m glass- (and china-)shop; =laterne f gl. lantern; =lava f, min.: hyalite; =linse f, phys. gl. lens; =macher m gl.-maker; =macherseife ⚒ f (Braunstein) gl.-maker's soap, manganese; =maler m gl.-painter = -stainer, painter on gl.; =malerei f gl.-painting or -staining; =masse f: a) =satz; b) flüssige ~ gl.-metal; =ofen m gl.-oven or -furnace; =palast m Lo. Crystal Palace; =papier n gl.-paper; =perle f gl. bead; =photographie f =bild; =platte f gl. plate; =porzellan n vitreous porcelain; =preß-form f gl. mould; =rahmen m, hort. gl.-frame; =raute f lozenge-shaped pane, bsd. ehm.: quarrel, quarry; =röhre f gl. tube; =sand m, min. vitreous sand; =satz ⊙ m frit; =scheibe f pane of glass; =scherbe f piece of broken gl.; =schleiche f: amerikanische ~ glass-snake (Ophiosau'rus ventra'lis); =schleifen ⊙ n gl.-cutting or grinding; =schleifer m gl.-cutter or -grinder; =schmalz ♀ n = Queller; =schmelzer m gl.-founder; =schmelzhafen ⊙ m Glasfabr.: gl.-pot; =schmelzofen m gl.-furnace; =schnecke f, zo. gl.-snail (Vitri'na); =schneider m = =schleifer; =schrank m: a) gl.-cupboard;

♪ Musik; ↯ Wissenschaft; ♀ Pflanze; ⚘ Geographie; ⊙ Technik; ⚒ Bergbau; ✕ Militär; ⚓ Marine; ⓘ Handel; ✉ Post; 🚂 Eisenbahn.

[Glasschwamm] — 450 — [glauben]

b) wardrobe with mirrors; =ſchwamm m, zo. gl.-rope (Hyalone'ma); =ſpiel ♪ n = harmo'nifa; =ſpinnerei f gl.-spinning works pl.; =ſplitter m splinter of glass; vgl. =ſcherbe; =ſtein m paste, imitation (or artificial) jewel or gem; =ſtürze f glass shade.

Glaſt ↘ (ˈ) [mhd.: gloss] m⊕b. mit poet. (Glanz) lustre, brilliancy.

Glas-tafel (ˈ...) f ⑫ glass plate; =tiegel m glass-melting pot, crucible for melting glass; =träne f, phys. (plötzlich abgekühlter Glastropfen) glass tear or drop, detonating bulb; =trichter m gl. funnel; =tropfen m/pl. gl. drops or tears pl.; =tür(e) f gl. door.

Glaſur ⊙ (ˈ) [+ fr.; vgl. glaſieren] f ⑯ Töpferei ꝛc.: (potter's) glazing; (Schmelz) ena'mel, für Backwerk: icing, für Stoffe ꝛc.: glaze, varnish; dem Geſchirr ~ geben to glaze pottery; mit ~ beſprengen to spattle; =erz n ⑫ min. (Bleiglanz) potter's ore, alquifou; =ofen m glazing-kiln or -furnace.

Glas-vergoldung (ˈ...) f⑫ glass-gilding; =verſchlag m, =wand f gl.-partition; =vorſatz m gl. screen; =waren ⑫ f/pl. gl. goods or articles pl. or ware; ⚹ vitrics pl.; =werk n: a) =arbeit c; b) ⚹ =waren; =zange f gl.-tongs pl., stretching-pincers pl.; =zeolith m, min. vitreous zeolite; =ziegel ⊙ m glass brick; =zylinder m chimney of a lamp.

glatt (ˈ) [ahd.] a. ⑯ (D3) 1. (ant. rauh) smooth, sleek; (eben) even; (⊙ und glänzend) glossy; (poliert) polished, glazed; es iſt ſehr ⊙ auf der Straße it is very slippery outside; ⊙es Geſicht smooth (or girlish) face; ⊙e Haut soft skin; ⊙er Stoff, ⊙es Zeug plain cloth; ⊙e Zunge ⚹ (F slippery) tongue; ↓ ⊙es Deck flush deck; ⚹ mit ⊙em (nicht gezogenem) Laufe smooth-bored (gun); typ. ⊙er Satz common (or ordinary) matter; ⊙ bürſten to smooth (or polish) by brushing; ⊙ feilen to make smooth by filing; ⊙ ſtreichen to smooth down; ⊙ durchſchlagen von Kugeln ꝛc.: to go clean through; adv. ⊙ raſiertes Geſicht clean-shaved (or -shaven) face. — 2. (unbehaart) hairless; ⚹ u. zo.: ⚹ glabrous; vom Kinn: beardless. — 3. (wohlgenährt) well-fed; sleek; (in jugendlicher Friſche) in the bloom of youth; (ſchmuck) good-looking (youth, girl); buxom (lass). — 4. fig. (ohne Anſtoß) plain, straightforward; eine Sache ⊙ machen to settle a matter; adv. (ohne weiteres) without ado; (ganz) thoroughly; es ging alles ⊙ ab all went off smoothly or without a hitch; ⊙ herausſagen to tell frankly or bluntly. — 5. (einſchmeichelnd) insinuating, bland; ⊙e Reden flattering speeches, fair words pl.; mit ⊙en Worten locken to entice with honeyed (or sugared) words, to talk (F to butter) over; ſ. eingehen 4.

Glätt-bank ⊙ (ˈ...) f ⑫ polishing-bench or -table.

glättbar (ˈ-) a. ⑯ polishable. [chin.]

glatt-bärtig (ˈˈ...) a. ⑯ with beardless

Glätt-bein (ˈ-) = =holz.

Glatt-butt (ˈ...) m ⑫ ichth. ſ. Butt 1; =deck ↓ n flush deck; =decks-fregatte f flush-decked frigate.

Glätte (ˈ) f ⑭ 1. (ſ. glatt 1) smoothness, sleekness; evenness; gloss (-iness), polish, glaze; ~ der Straßen slipperiness (or slippery state) of the streets; die ~ iſt ſehr ſtark it is exceedingly slippery. — 2. ⚒ (beim Treiben ablaufendes Blei-oxyd) litharge.

Glatt-eis (ˈˈ) n ⑫ smooth (or slippery) ice: es iſt draußen ~ the roads are like (or as slippery as) glass; fig. e-n aufs ~ führen to get a p. into trouble or F into a scrape, to lead him away.

glatt-eiſen (ˈˈ...) v/n. impers. (h.) ⊛⚹⚹ es glatteiſt the streets are slippery with ice, vgl. Glatteis.

Glätt-eis (ˈˈ...) n ⑫ = =ſtahl.

glätten (ˈˈ) [glatt] v/a. u. ſich ⊙ v/refl. ⊛ (ſich) ⊙ to (grow or get) smooth or sleek; typ. (preſſen) to press; ⊙ (eben m.) to plane, (glänzend m.) to polish, glaze, finish, Klingen: to burnish, Tuch: to calender, Kunſtwerke ꝛc. to touch up, to polish, Geſchriebenes auch: to file; Falten ⊙ to take out creases or pleats.

Glätter ⊙ (ˈ...) m ⑫, ~in f ⑭ 1. (ſ. glätten) smoother; polisher, finisher, burnisher. — 2. = Glättholz.

Glätt=, Glätt-feile ⊙ (ˈˈ...) f ⑭ Schloſſer ꝛc. smoothing-file.

glatt-flächig (ˈˈ...) ⊙ a. ⑯: ⊙e Feile smooth-faced file. [glass.]

Glätt-glas (ˈˈ)n⑫ Tuchfabr.: sleeking-f

glatt-haarig (ˈˈ...) a. ⑯ smooth- (or sleek-)haired; =hai m ⑫ ichth. smooth dog-fish, musteline (Muste'la laevis).

Glätt-hammer (ˈˈ) m ⑫ sleeking-hammer.

glatt-häutig (ˈˈ...) a. ⑯ soft-skinned.

Glatt-heit (ˈ-) f ⑯ = Glätte 1.

Glätt-hobel ⊙ (ˈ...) m ⑫ = Glätthobel.

Glatt-hobel (ˈˈ...) m ⑫ smoothing-plane; =holz n polishing- (or sleeking-)stick, polisher; =horn n der Sattler: smoothing-horn; =keule f = =holz; =kolben m Buchbind. planisher. [headed.]

glatt-köpfig (ˈˈ...) a. ⑯ smooth-, sleek-f

Glätt-maſchi'ne (ˈˈ...) f ⑭ smoothing- (or sleeking-) machine; =platte f: a) Papier: calender; b) Gießerei: sleeker; =preſſe f, typ. standing press.

glatt-randig ⚹ (ˈˈ...) a. ⑯ entire; ⊙rindig, ⊙ſchuppig a. smooth-rinded, -scaled.

Glätt-ſcheibe (ˈˈ...) f ⑫ sleeking-board; =ſtab m Web.: sleeking-tool; =ſtahl m burnishing-, sleeking-steel, burnisher; =ſtein m Papier: sleeking-stone.

glatt-weg (ˈˈ) adv. plainly, flatly.

Glätt-werkzeug ⊙ (ˈˈ...) n ⑫ smoothing-tool; =zahn m polisher, burnisher.

glatt-züngig (ˈˈ...) a. ⑯ smooth-(or honey-)tongued, smug, mealy-mouthed; ~keit f smoothness of tongue, smugness.

Glatze (ˈ...) [mhd.;* glatt] f ⑭ 1. (Kahlheit) baldness of the head; (kahle Stelle) bald place; er bekommt eine ~ he is growing bald, his hair is falling off. — 2. (geſcherene Platte der katholiſchen Geiſtlichen) tonsure. — 3. (kahler Kopf) bald head or F pate, F co. moonshine.

glatzig (ˈˈ) a. ⑯ bald(-headed), F bald-pated. [son]; ⊙köpfig a. ⑯ bald.

Glatz-kopf (ˈˈ...) m ⑫ bald-head(ed per-f

glau (ˈ) [ahd.] a. ⑯ (hell) Luft: bright, clear; Augen: bright, sparkling; (ſcharfſichtig) keen-eyed, clear-sighted; ⊙äugig a. ⑯ bright- (or keen-)eyed.

Glaube. ~n¹ (ˈˈ) [ahd. ſ. glauben] m ⑰, ⑬ 1. (Fürwahrhalten) belief in; (vertrauensvolles Feſthalten) faith in; (Zutrauen) confidence, trust; blinder ~ implicit faith; feſter ~ firm belief; ~ an Gott belief (or faith) in God; e-r Sache ~n beimeſſen (od. ſchenken) to put faith in a th., to give credence to it, to credit it; das findet nirgends ~n that finds no belief (mehr gbr.: it is not believed or credited) anywhere, a. that is universally discredited; dazu gehört ein ſtarker ~ that is hard to believe; er hat keinen ~n an die Heilkraft von ∥ he has no faith in the healing power of ⁁; er lebt des ſicheren ~ns, daß ∥ he firmly believes (or is fully confident) that ∥; auf Treu und ~n in good faith, on trust; auf Treu und ~n (auch: in gutem ~n) annehmen, handeln to accept, to act in good faith or with full confidence. — 2. rel. (religious) faith or profession, creed; religion; der chriſtliche ~ the Christian faith; er iſt ſeines ~ns ein Kalviniſt he is a Calvinist by faith, he is of the Calvinist faith or denomination, he professes himself a Calvinist; einen ~ annehmen to accept (or embrace, adopt) a creed or religion; e-n ~ bekennen to profess a religion; bibl. der ~ macht ſelig he that believeth shall be saved.

glauben² (ˈˈ) [ahd.:believe;*(er)lauben, loben] ⑱ I v/a. 1. to believe in the truth of s.th.; etwas Gehörtes, Mitgeteiltes: to credit (or to give credence to) a report, &c.; nicht ⊙ to disbelieve; das glaube ich gern I willingly (ſchwächer: quite) believe it; iro. jawohl, wer's glaubt! don't come with such tales!, tell that to the marines!; ich glaube es Ihnen I (quite) believe you; wir ⊙ (es) ihm aufs Wort we believe every word (that) he says; er lebt noch, ⊙ Sie (es) mir!, ... you may be sure or take my word for it!; ich glaube, daß ich recht habe od. recht zu haben I believe I am (in the) right; es iſt kaum zu ⊙, daß ∥ it is hardly credible that ∥; das iſt nicht zu ⊙, das kann man nicht ⊙ that's incredible, one cannot believe (or credit) it; hätte man es ⊙ ſollen? who would have believed (or credited, thought) it? — 2. (für et. halten) e-n (ſich) reich ⊙ to consider a p. (o.s.) rich; e-n im Rechte ⊙ to hold that a p. is (in the) right, ſchwächer: to think (or fancy) a p. (in the) right. — 3. (annehmen, meinen) to accept as (or to take for) true; beſtätigend: das glaube ich, will ich ſchon ⊙ I should think so (indeed)!; er glaubte, ich ſei fort he thought (or fancied) I had gone; wir ⊙, daß es eine Fabel iſt we take it for a (mere) legend; man ſollte ⊙, daß ∥ one would suppose (or think) that ∥; wie ich glaube, irrt er ſich in my opinion he is mistaken; man glaubt, er ſei tot it

Signs (see page XVII): F familiar; P vulgar; Ƒ flash; ↘ rare; † obsolete (died); * new word (born); ⁓ incorrect; ♪ music

[glaubenlos] — 451 — [gleichen]

is thought that he is dead, he is believed to be dead. — **II** v/n. (h.) **4.** to believe, to have faith (an ... in ...); (vertrauen) to put one's faith (or confidence, trust) in; an Gespenster 2 to believe in (the existence of) ghosts; sie 2 fest daran they swear to it, they take it for gospel (truth); wenn man ihm 2 soll if one may believe (or trust) him, to hear him (speak); man glaubt ihm nicht mehr nobody believes him any longer or puts any faith in him now. — **5.** daran 2 müssen (i-m Geschick verfallen) to succumb (or resign o.s.) to one's fate; er hat daran 2 (ben Tod leiden) müssen he paid the last penalty, he suffered death. — **III** sich 2 v/refl. **6.** s. 2. — **IV** ~ n 23 u. m 23 **7.** = Glaube. [unbelieving.] **glauben-los** (ᴜᴸ) a. ᴳ without faith, **Glaubens-abfall** (ᴜ...) m ᴳ: 𝛁 apostasy; =abtrünnige(r) s. renegade, apostate; =änderung f change of faith or religion; =angelegenheit f, =artikel m matter, article of faith; =bekenntnis n profession of faith, creed; politisches ~ political creed, F platform; Christen von verschiedenem ~ ... of different creeds or denominations; =bote m apostle, evangelist, missionary; =bruder m brother in the faith (von Christen a. in Christ); weit S. co-religionist; =eifer m religious zeal; fanaticism, zealotism; =eiferer m fanatic, zealot; 2eifrig a. ᴳ zealous in the faith; 2fest a. firm (or stanch, steadfast) in one's faith; =festigkeit f stanchness (or steadfastness) in one's faith; =formel f creed; =freiheit f religious liberty or freedom; =genoß oder =genosse m, =genossin f fellow-believer, co-religionist; Christ: fellow-Christian; =genossenschaft f community of believers or faith; =gericht n Mittelalter: (court of) inquisition; =heilung f faith-cure, Christian science; =held(in f) m champion of the faith, religious martyr; =heuchler(in f) m (canting) hypocrite; =kampf, =krieg m religious strife, war; =lehre f: a) einzelne: dogma; b) coll. dogmatic teaching, religious doctrine(s pl.), 𝛁 dogmatics; =lehrer m dogmatist; apostle; =meinung f rel. opinion; =neuerer m rel. innovator; =partei f rel. sect or denomination; =punkt m point of doctrine, doctrinal point or question; =regel f rule of faith; =richter m bsd. ehm.: inquisitor; =sache f matter of faith; =satz m article of faith, dogma; =schwärmer m rel. enthusiast, vgl. =eiferer; =schwärmerei f rel. enthusiasm, vgl. =eifer; =spaltung f schism; 2stark a. strong in faith; =streit(igkeit f) m rel. dispute or controversy or argument; =streiter(in f) m rel. champion or controversialist; vgl. =held(in); =verbesserung f doctrinal reform; (rel.) reformation =verleugner m renegade, apostate; 2voll a. full of faith; =vorschrift f doctrinal precept; =wahrheit f doctrinal truth; =wechsel m = =änderung; =wut f rel. frenzy; =zeuge m witness of the faith, martyr; =zunft f rel. sect; =zwang m compul-

sion in matters of faith; rel. intolerance; =zweifel (=zweifler) m scruple (sceptic) in matters of faith; =zwist m religious squabble; dissent. **Glauber-salz** (ᴜ‿ᴗ) [Glauber, btsch. Arzt, 1604–1668] n ᴳ pharm. Glauber's salt; chm. sulphate of soda, sodium sulphate. [~igkeit f ᴳ = Glaubwürdigkeit.] **glaubhaft** (ᴸ) a. ᴳ = glaubwürdig. **gläubig** (ᴸ‿) [ahd.] **I** a. ᴳ rel. believing, faithful; streng 2 orthodox; (fromm) pious. — **II** ~e([rᴵ] m) f ᴳ (true) believer or follower; die ~en, a. the faithful pl. **Gläubiger**[2] (ᴸ‿‿) m ᴳ, ~in f ᴳ (ant. Schuldner) creditor (f bisw.: ...tress); ~schaft f ᴳ all the creditors pl.; =versammlung f meeting of creditors. **Gläubigkeit** (ᴸ‿‿) f ᴳ full belief or confidence; rel. faith; strenge 2 orthodoxy. **glaublich** (ᴸ‿) [ahd.] a. ᴳ credible, believable; (wahrscheinlich) likely, probable; nicht 2 incredible; unlikely; ~keit f ᴳ credibility; likelihood. **glaub-würdig** (ᴸ‿‿‿) a. ᴳ worthy of belief or confidence; von Nachrichten: credible; (verbürgt) authentic; aus 2er Quelle from a reliable source; on good authority; ~keit f ᴳ credibility; authenticity. **glauch** (ᴸ‿) a. ᴳ **1.** [mhd.] (bläulichweiß) glaucous, sea-green. — **2.** [ndd.] = glau. **Glauch-herd** ⚒ (ᴜ‿...) m ᴳ nicking-buddle. [Star) glaucoma.] **Glaukom** 𝛁 (-ᴸ) [grch.] n ᴳ d. path. (grüner **Glb.** abbr. = Ganzlederband. **gleich** (ᴸ) [ahd.: like; *Leiche*] **I** a. ᴳ u. adv. **1.** (a) like; (eins) identical, (the) same; (2 an Bedeutung) equal (a. math.); on the same footing or level; Tennis: deuce; geom. 2 und ähnlich equal in all respects; e-m an Kräften 𝑒. 2 kommen to be a match for a p.; dem Boden (oder der Erde) 2 even (or level) with the ground; 2 en Anteil haben to have equal shares, to go halves; auf 2 e Art und Weise in like manner; im 2 en Augenblicke, zu 2 er Zeit at (one and) the same moment or time, simultaneously; auf 2 er Höhe on the same level; auf 2 er Höhe mit dem Erdboden level with the ground; in 2 er Entfernung equidistant; mit 2 er Münze in the same coin; zu 2 en Teilen equally; 2 breit, 2 lang of the same width, length; 2 schwer of like weight, equally heavy; von 2 em Umfange of like volume, 𝛁 co-extensive; von 2 em Werte equivalent; viermal drei ist (2) zwölf four times three are twelve; mir ist alles 2 it is all one to me; es ist mir ganz 2 it is all the same (or it makes no difference) to me; (es ist) 2 viel, wer kommt it is quite indifferent who comes; vgl. 2 viel; an Wert 2 sein, oft: to be equivalent (or tantamount) to; vgl. 2 bleiben, 2 kommen, 2 machen, 2 tun. — **2.** (höchst ähnlich) very similar, of striking resemblance; sich so 2 sehen wie ein Blatt (Ei, Wassertropfen) dem andern to be like two peas in a pod; das sieht ihm nicht 2 that is not like him. — **3.** (gerade) straight, uniform; die Häuser stehen nicht 2 ... are not in a

line; (flach) plain, level. — **II** 2 e(r) m, 2 e f, 2 e(s) n ᴳ **4.** der, die, das 2 e (derselbe 𝑒.) the same; vgl. ‿‿gleichen. — **5.** ~e(s) n ᴳ the same thing; ~es mit ~em vergelten to render like for like, to give tit for tat, to pay back in the same coin; ~es von ~em bleibt ~es if equals be taken from equals the remainders are equal; ins (2e) ~e bringen, setzen, stellen to set things in order, to put things straight or right; es kommt aufs 2 e (dasselbe) hinaus it comes to the same thing (in the end), F it's much of a muchness; ein ~es tun to give (or contribute) the same (amount), to do as much (as he, &c.). — **6.** ohne art. u. Endung: Sprichw. 2 und 2 gesell sich gern birds of a feather flock together, like will to like. — **III** nur adv. **7.** (auf der Stelle) on the spot; (sogleich) instantly, at once, directly; als Antwort auf einen Ruf: 2! I am coming!; es wird 2 regnen it will soon be raining, it will rain before (or ere) long; es ist 2 fünf (Uhr) it is nearly (or close upon) five; das ist 2 geschehen it is quickly (or soon) done; 2 anfangs, 2 von Anfang an from the very commencement, from the first; 2 bei seiner Geburt at his very birth; 2 nach der Schlacht immediately after ... ; 2 zur Hand ready at hand. — **8.** verstärkend: wie heißt er doch 2?, wie ist doch 2 der Name? what ever (or now what) is his name?, I can't remember his name for the moment; das dacht' ich (doch) 2 I thought something of the kind or as much. — **9.** bedingt einräumend: ist er 2 nicht reich, wenn (oder ob) er 2 nicht reich ist though he may not be rich. — **10.** in Vergleichungen: s. gleichwie. **gleich-abständig** (ᴸ...) a. ᴳ, 2 abstehend a. = 2 weit; 2 achsig a. cryst. equiaxe(d); 2 alt(e)rig a. of the same age, 𝛁 coeval; 2 armig a. with like (or equal) arms; 2 artig a. of the same kind, 𝛁 congenerous, homogeneous; von 2 em Wesen congenial; chm. 2 zs.-gesetzt 𝛁 isomeric(al); =artigkeit f ᴳ: 𝛁 homogeneousness; des Geistes, Wesens: congeniality; chm.: 𝛁 isomerism; 2 bedeutend a. equally significant with, equivalent to; gr. synonymous with, math., chm. homologous; (vertauschbar) convertible (term); 2 berechtigt a. having (or enjoying) the same rights or privileges; =berechtigung f ᴳ equality of rights; sich (dat.) 2 bleiben v/refl. ᴳ** to remain the same or unchanged; to be always the same; das bleibt sich gleich that's all the same (to me); 2 bleibend a.: sich (dat.) 2 always the same; (unveränderlich) invariable, unchangeable; (beständig) constant, (konsequent) consistent; 2 denkend a. of the same mind or opinion; congenial. **Gleiche** (ᴸ‿) [mhd.] f ᴳ (Ebenheit) evenness, smoothness; s. a. gleich II. **gleich-empfindend** (ᴸ...) a. ᴳ sympathetic, sympathizing. **gleichen** (ᴸ‿) ᴳast († ᴳ) **I** v/a. u. sich 2 v/refl. **1.** (gleichmachen) to (make) equal to, to equalize; (eben machen) to make even, to level; ⊕ Gewichte 𝑒. 2

[...gleichen] — 452 — [Gleis]

(e-m Maßstabe gleichmachen) to adjust ... (f. eichen³); fig. (bibl.) ihr sollt euch ihnen nicht ≈ you shall not do like (unto) them. — II v/n. (h.) 2. e-m, einer Sache ≈ (ähnlich sein) to be like (or to resemble) a p., a th.; (entsprechen) to correspond to a th.; sie ≈ sich ob. ea. nicht (sehr) there is no (a strong) likeness between them; er gleicht seiner Mutter he takes after (auch F: he favours) his mother. — III ~ n ⊕ 3. (f. I) equalization; levelling; ⊕ adjustment. — 4. (f. II) likeness, resemblance.

...gleichen (..."L~) [gleich 4] in Zssgn.: meines≈, seines≈ my, his equals pl., people like me, him; F the like(s) of me, of him; er hat nicht seines≈ there is no one like (or to match) him, he is matchless or peerless or unrivalled; wie mit seines≈ on terms of equality; ohne= (oder sonder=)≈ without an equal, unmatched; (einzig) unique; f. der=, des=≈.

gleich=entfernt (ʺ...) a. ⊕ = ≈weit.

Gleicher (L~) m ⊕ 1. ⊕ (Äquator) equator. — 2. ⊕ = Eicher, Justierer.

gleicher=gestalt (L~...), ≈maßen, ≈weise adv. in like manner, in (just) the same way, likewise, equally.

gleich=falls (ʺ...) adv. = ebenfalls; ≈farbig a. ⊕ of like colour, ⊄ isochromatic; ≈flüg(e)lig a. ent.: ⊄ isopterous, homopterous; ≈flügler m/pl. ⊕ ent.: ⊄ isoptera, homopter(ans) pl.; ≈förmig a. of like form, uniform; adv. conformably with a th.; (in gleichem Schritt) even, equable, (eintönig) monotonous; =förmigkeit f uniformity; conformity, evenness, monotony, sameness; ≈fühlend a.=≈empfindend; ≈geartet a. =≈artig; ≈geltend a. equivalent, equipollent; ≈geschlecht= lich a.: of the same sex; ≈gesinnt a. like-minded; die ihm (politisch ꝛc.) ~en his (political, &c.) sympathizers or partisans pl.; ≈gestaltet, ≈gestaltig a. of like shape; chm., cryst., &c.: ⊄ isomorphous, ...ic; ≈gestellt a. co- ordinate; gesellschaftlich: on the same level, equal (in rank); ≈gestimmt a.: a) ♪ von Klavieren ꝛc.: tuned to the same pitch; b) fig. in accord; =gewicht n equilibrium, equipoise; politisches ~ balance of power, relative strength of (great) states; ins ~ bringen to equilibrate, equipoise; im ~ erhalten to balance (equally); e-r Sache das ~ halten to counterpoise a th.; =gewichts-lehre f: ⊄ statics; =gewichts-punkt m point of equi- librium; =gewichts-stange f balancing- pole; ≈gradig a. equally graduated, of the same degree; on the same scale; ≈gültig a. indifferent, v. Per- sonen a. unconcerned (or listless) about; (gefühllos) callous, unfeeling, (stumpf) apathetic; =gültigkeit f indifference, unconcern, callousness, apathy.

Gleichheit (L~) f ⊕ equality, von Dingen derselben Art: ⊄ parity; (Einerleiheit) identity, sameness; (Gleichförmigkeit) conformity, uniformity; (Gleich-artig- keit): ⊄ homogeneousness; (Ähnlichkeit) likeness, resemblance, similarity; bei Spielen, Rennen, Wahlen: ~ der Points,

der Stimmen tie; ~s-apostel m apostle of equality, leveller; ~zeichen n, math. sign of equality (=), typ. equal mark.

gleich=jährig (ʺ...) a. ⊕ = ≈alterig; =klang m ⊕: a) ♪ accord, unison (auch fig.); (Harmonie) consonance; b) gr.: ⊄ homonymy; v. stammverwandten Wörtern: ⊄ isonymy; von Vokalen: as- sonance; ≈klappig a. v. Muscheln: equivalve(d); e-m, einer Sache ≈kommen v/n. (fn) ⊕** to come up to (the level of) a p., a th.; nicht ≈ to be no match for, to fall short of; ≈lastig ↓ a. on an even keel; =lauf m, geom. parallelism; ≈laufen v/n. (fn) Daft** to run parallel with; ≈laufend p. pr. u. a. parallel; =laut m = =klang; ≈lautend p. pr. u. a. conso- nant; gr.: ⊄ homonymous; ≈ (u. stamm- verwandt) ⊄ isonymic; ≈ sein to tally, to correspond; ≈e Abschrift duplicate, (exact or true or conform) copy; ≈ gr. ≈es (stammverwandtes) Wort ⊄ homo- nym, isonym; adv. ⊕ conformably; ≈machen v/a. ⊕** to make equal to, to equalize, to (make) level with; Städte der Erde ≈ to raze ... to the ground; der Tod, der alles gleich- macht death, the great leveller; =macher m equalizer, pol. leveller; =macherei f pol. levelling (mania); =machung f: a) des Bodens, fig. der Stände ꝛc.: levelling; b) (gleiche Ver- teilung) equalization, even distribu- tion; ≈männig ♀ a.: ⊄ isandrous; =maß n = Ebenmaß, ≈mäßig a. equable; ≈ (adv.) beschleunigt mech. uniformly accelerated; ≈e Bewegung uniform motion; ≈ ≈ (adv.) gefiedert ⊄ paripinnate; vgl. ebenmäßig; =mäßigkeit f equableness, evenness, uniformity of motion, re- gularity of action; vgl. Ebenmaß; ≈messend a.: ⊄ isometric; =messer ⚲ ♀ ast. equator; =mut m equanimity, evenness of temper; (Gelassenheit) calmness, serenity; (Standhaftigkeit) stoicism, imperturbability; (Er- gebung) resignation; vgl. ≈gültigkeit; ≈mütig a. (f. =mut) even-tempered; bisw.: equanimous; (gelassen) calm, (un- erschütterlich) imperturbable; vgl. ≈gültig; =mütigkeit f = =mut; ≈namig a. ⊕ of the same name; ⊄ homonymous, geom. homologous; math. von Brüchen: hav- ing the same denominator; phys. ≈e Elektrizität same (kind of) electricity; ≈namige Pole like poles pl.; =namig- keit f sameness (or identity) of name, ⊄ homonymy; =namig-machen n von Brüchen: reduction to the same de- nominator.

Gleichnis (L~) [ahd.] n ⊕ 1. (Bild) image, rhet. simile. — 2. (bildliche Erzählung) allegory, bibl. parable; (bildlicher Ausdruck) figure of speech, metaphor; (Vergleich) comparison; in Gleichnissen sprechen to speak alle- gorically or in parables.

Gleichnis-rede (ʺ...) f ⊕ figurative spech, allegory, simiele; vgl. Gleichnis 2; ≈weise adv. allegorically, para- bolically, figuratively; by way of com-

parison; =wort n figurative (or meta- phorical) expression or word or term.

Gleich-richter ⊕ (ʺ...) m ⊕ elect. rectifier.

gleichsam (L~) adv. so to speak or to say, as it were, F in some way (or other); (gewissermaßen) to some extent, to a certain degree, F in a way.

gleich=schalig (ʺ...) a. ⊕ = ≈klappig; ≈schenk(e)lig a. geom. von Dreiecken (mit zwei gleichen Seiten) isosceles; ≈sehen v/n. ⊕a **: e-m ≈ (ähnlich sein) to resemble a p., to look (or be) like a p.; ≈seitig a. geom., ⊕ (mit gleichen Seiten) equilateral; =seitigkeit f equality of the sides; ≈setzen v/a. ⊕** (auf gleiche Art be- denken, beschenken) to treat alike; ≈silbig a. gr.: ⊄ parisyllabic(al); =sinn in sympathy; ≈sporig ♀ a.: ⊄ isosporous; =stand m Tennis: deuce; ≈steh(e)n v/n. (h.) ⊕** (≈stellen v/a. ⊕**) to stand (to put) on a par (or on an equality) with; sich e-m ≈stellen to put o.s. on a level (or on an equal footing) with a p.; ≈stehend (e[r m] f) a. on an equality with; =stellung f equalization; ≈stimmig a. ♪ und fig. unisonous, harmonious; vgl. ≈ stimmt; =stimmigkeit f unison, har- mony, accord; =strom m, elect. (nach gleicher Richtung fließender Strom) direct (or continuous) current; =strom- dynamo-maschine f continuous-cur- rent dynamo; ≈teilig a. in (or with) equal parts; =teiligkeit f: ⊄ isomeria; =tritt m measured step; es e-m ≈tun v/a. ⊕** to compete with a p., to equal (or match) a p.; er tut es ihm gleich he rivals (or comes up to) him.

Gleichung (L~) f ⊕ 1. = gleichen III. — 2. ⊕ ast. (Zeit)~ (Unterschied zw. wahrer und mittlerer Sonnenzeit) equation of time; math. equation; einfache, quadratische, kubische ~ (a. ~ des ersten, zweiten, dritten Grades) simple, quadratic, cubic(al) equation; eine ~ mit einer Unbekannten lösen to solve an eq. with one unknown; ~ mit mehreren Unbekannten simultaneous eq.; chemische ~ chemical equation.

gleich=viel (ʺ...) cj. just as much, in the same degree; ≈ ob // no matter if //; vgl. gleich 1 am Ende; ≈weit a. ⊕ at the same distance, equidistant; ≈wertig a. ⊕ equivalent, of the same value; ≈e Ausdrücke convertible terms pl.; =wertigkeit f ⊕ equivalence, ...cy; convertibleness of terms; ≈wie adv. just as; ≈wink(e)lig a.. math. equi- angular, ⊄ isogonous; ≈wohl adv. u. cj. = dennoch; ≈zeitig a. simultaneous, synchronous; adv. auch: at the same time; ≈ geschehend coincident; (gleich lange dauernd) ⊄ isochronal, ...ic; (zeitgenössig) contemporaneous, ...ary (mit with); ≈es Bestehen, Dasein co- existence; ≈ vorhanden sein to co- exist; eccl. Der Besitz mehrerer Pfründen plurality (of benefices); =zeitigkeit f simultaneousness, syn- chronism, coincidence; (gleiche Dauer) ⊄ isochronism; (Zeitgenossenschaft) con- temporaneousness, contemporary existence; co-existence.

Gleis (L) n ⊕a. = Geleise.

Zeichen (f. S. XVII): F familiär; P Volkssprache; Γ Gaunersprache; ⚲ selten; † alt (auch gestorben); * neu (auch geboren); ⁺⁺ unrichtig;

[Gleiseck] — 453 — [Glockengehäuse]

Gleise* (´‿) f ⑱ math. parallel (line). **Gleis=eck*** (´‿) n ⑫ math. parallelogram. **Gleisel*** (´‿) m ⑫ parallelepiped. ...**gleisig** (...´‿) ⑥ z.B. ein≗ single-railed. **Gleis=kreuzung** 🚃 (´‿...) f ⑫ (level) crossing. **Gleisner** (´‿) [mhd. v. † gleisen; *gleich] m ⑫, ~**in** f ㊼ hypocrite, dissembler, double-faced person; als m auch: pharisee; ~**ei** (‿‿´) f㊻ hypocrisy, dissimulation, double-facedness; **=isch** (´‿‿) a. ⑥ hypocritical, dissembling, double-faced, pharisaical. **Gleiß** ⚘ (´) m ⑫a., a. **Gleiße** (´‿) f ⑱ fool's-parsley (*Æthu'sa cyna'pium*). **gleißen** ⚘ (´‿) v/n. (h.) ⑥a. u. ⑨ **1.** [ahd. glisten] to glisten, to glitter. — **2.** †⁅ gleisen (sich verstellen) s. Gleisner. **Gleiß=käfer** (´‿...) m⑫ ent. golden beetle. **Gleit=bahn** (´‿...) f ⑫: a) auf dem Eise: slide, place for sliding; b) ⚙ Dampfmasch.: slideway; c) (schräge Bahn) (toboggan-)shoot; **=block** m: a) ⚙ slider; b) ⚙ Dampfmasch.: slide-guide. **gleiten** (´‿) [ahd.: glide] v/n. (in der Bedeutung „schlittern": h.) ⑥b.(⑧⑨) to glide, to slip (along); to slide; sanft über et. hin≗ (fließen) to flow (or move) gently over (or across, along) s.th.; ⚙ ⓒ de Skala sliding scale. **Gleiter** (´‿) m ⑫, ~**in** f ㊼ auf dem Eise: slider, one who slides. **Gleit=fläche** ⚘ (´‿...) f cryst. gliding plane; **=schiene** f, mach. slide-bar or -guide or -rail. [glacier (= Ferner¹).) **Gletscher** (´‿) [mhd.; *fr. glacier*] m ⑫) **Gletscher=beifuß** ⚘ (´‿...) m ⑫ = Silberraute; **=bildung** f formation of glaciers, ⚙ glacial form. **gletscherhaft** (´‿...) a. ⑥: ⚙ glacial. **Gletscher=lehre** (´‿...) f ⑫: ⚙ glaciology; **=moräne** f moraine; **=schliff** m rock polished by a moving glacier; **=schutt** m glacier-drift, moraine; **=spalte** f crevasse; **=tisch** m: ⚙ glacier-table; **=tor** n, geol.: ⚙ glacier-mouth. **glich** (´) (⒧e subj.) impf. von gleichen. **Glied** (´) [ahd.] n ⒋c. **1.** limb, (Körperteil) member (or part) of the body; (Gelenk) joint (auch ⚘ u. anat.); männliches ~ (It.) penis, membrum virile; das geht mir durch alle ~er I feel it in every limb; der Prozeß liegt ihm schwer in den ~ern the lawsuit greatly troubles him or is a great burden on his mind; er kann kein ~ rühren he cannot move (a limb), he is set fast with rheumatism, &c.; ich fühle Schmerzen in allen ~ern I ache in every joint. — **2.** ⚙ u. fig. ~ e-r Kette link of a chain. — **3.** bibl. bis ins dritte und vierte ~ (Geschlecht) unto the third and fourth generation. — **4.** ⚔ (Tiefstellung von Soldaten) file; hinteres, vorderes ~ rear, front rank; in zwei ~ern in two ranks; in Reih' und ~ in rank and file; Truppen in Reih' und ~ aufstellen to draw up ...; die ~er schließen to close the ranks; aus dem ~e treten to quit the ranks; Kommando: bleibt in Reih' und ~! keep your ranks!; in ~ern links (rechts)! left

(right) file! — **5.** math. (Ausdruck) term; äußere und innere ~er einer Proportion extremes and means pl. **Glieder=abstand** ⚔ (´‿...) m⑫ space (or interval) between the ranks; **=band** n, anat.: ⚙ ligament; **=bau** m structure of the limbs, ⚙ articulation; F build; von starkem ~ strong-limbed, F of stout build; gr. ~ einer Periode construction, structure; **=fuge** f: ⚙ articulation; **=geschwulst** f swelling of the limbs; **=gicht** f, path. gout in the joints, ⚙ arthritis. **glied(e)rig** (´(‿)‿) a. ⑥ **1.** = gliedern II. — **2.** (...~) in Zssgn., z.B. fein≗ with delicate limbs. **Glieder=krankheit** (´‿...) f ⑫ path.: ⚙ articular disease; **=lahm** a. ⑥ path. paralysed, paralytic; **=lähmung** f, path. paralysis; **=mann** m, paint. lay-figure, manikin. **gliedern** (´‿) I v/a. ⑫a. **1.** to divide into articulated parts; to arrange the parts; ⚔ to draw up in files; logisch ⒧ to arrange in logical (or systematical) order or sequence; (einrichten) to organize. — II **gegliedert** p.p. u. a. ⑫ **2.** in den Beb. des inf. — **3.** vom Gliederbau, nur mit adv.: gut ⒧ with good limbs, F well-built; well set up (in the limbs). — **4.** ⚘: ⚙ articulate, geniculate(d). — III ~ n ⓘ⓼ **5.** s. Gliederung. **Glieder=puppe** (´‿...) f ⑫ joint- (or swivel-)doll, automaton, (Marionette) puppet; **=reißen** n, **=schmerz** m, path. (neuralgic or shooting) pain(s pl.) in the joints, ⚙ articular rheumatism; **=salbe** f, pharm. liniment for sprained limbs; **=spinnen** f/pl. ent.: ⚙ arthrogastra pl.; **=tier** n: ⚙ articulate animal; ~e pl. auch: ⚙ articulata pl. **Gliederung** (´‿‿) f ㊻ arrangement of the parts; logical (or systematical) order; organization; gr. ~ einer Periode construction, structure; ~ (Modulation) der Stimme: ⚙ articulation. **Glieder=weh** (´‿...) n ⑫ = **=reißen**; **=weise** adv.: a) limb by limb, link by link; b) ⚔ in files; **=zucken** n, **=zuckung** f, path.: ⚙ articular spasms pl. **Glied=kraut** ⚘ (´‿) n ⑫ iron-wort (*Sideri'tis*); **=los** a. ⑥ without limbs, ⚙ anarthrous; **=maß(e** f) n [mhd.] (⚘ im sg.) limb; von gesunden ~en sound in body and limb. ...**gliedrig** (...´‿) in Zssgn. s. glied(e)rig. **Glied=wasser** (´‿...) n ⑫ anat. (Gelenkschmiere): ⚙ synovia(l fluid); **=wassersucht** f = Gelenkwassersucht; **⒧weise** adv. = gliederweise. **glimmen** (´‿) [ahd.: glim(mer), gleam] I v/n. (h.) ⑨a., ⑧ to burn faintly, to spread a faint light, to glimmer; das Feuer glimmt unter der Asche the fire is smouldering (or alive) beneath (or under) the ashes; das Licht glimmt nur noch there is only a glimmer of light to be seen; ⒧der Docht faintly burning wick, smoking wick. — II ~ n ⓘ⓼ faint light or glow, glimmer. **Glimmer** (´‿) [mhd.] m ⑫ **1.** faint light, glimmer. — **2.** min. (Katzensilber, -gold): ⚙ mica.

glimmer=artig (´‿...) a. ⑥ micaceous; **=erde** f ⑫ mica(ceous earth); **=gesteine** n/pl. micaceous rocks pl., lime; **⒧haltig** a. micaceous; **=kalk** m micaceous lime. **glimmern** (´‿) v/n. (h.) ⑫a. to glimmer, glint; (funkelnd schimmern) to sparkle. **Glimmer=schiefer** (´‿...) m ⑫ min. micaschist or -slate; ⚘ u. **kalk=haltig** a. geol. micaceo-calcareous. [weed, cig.) **Glimm=stengel** F (´‿...) m ⑫ cigar, F) **Glimpf** (´) [ahd.] m ⑫ ⚘ b. **1.** ⚘ (Billigkeit) fairness, (Mäßigkeit) moderation, (Schonung) indulgence, (Zurückhaltung) discretion. — **2.** fast †: honour; sich mit ~ (Ehre) aus e-r Sache ziehen to get creditably out of an affair. **glimpflich** (´‿) [mhd.] a. ⑥ (s. Glimpf) fair; moderate, indulgent; adv. oft: gently; ⒧ davonkommen to get (or come) off unhurt or unscathed or with a small (or trifling) loss. [gleißen.) **gliß** (´) ind. u. **glisse** (´‿) subj. impf. v.) **Glitsch=bahn** (´‿) f ⑫ slide (= Gleitbahn). **Glitsche** F (´‿) f ⑱ slide; **glitschen** v/n. (in n. h.); vgl. gleiten) ⑨ to glide, to slide; **glitsch(e)rig** F (´‿(‿)‿) (glatt) a. ⑥ slippery; **Glitsch(e)rigkeit** F f ㊻ slipperiness. **glitschig** (´‿) a. ⑥ = glitsch(e)rig. **glitt** (´) ind. u. ⒧e (´‿) subj. impf. v. gleiten. **glitzern** F (´‿) [mhd.: glitter; *gleißen] v/n. (h.) ⑫a. to glitter; (funkeln) to sparkle, (von Sternen) to twinkle. **Globus** (´‿) [lt. glo'bus Kugel] m ⑫, ⑰, inv. (Erdkugel) globe. **Glöckchen** (´‿) n ⑬ (dim. v. Glocke) (Klingel, Schelle) small bell, hand-bell. **Glocke** (´‿) [ahd.; *clocc, *flt.] f ⑱ **1.** bell; (Glas-)~ (bell-shaped) glass-shade; auf e-r Lampe: globe; phys e-r Luftpumpe: recipient; ⚘ (Blumenkelch) bell-shaped calyx; vgl. ~n=blume: die ~n läuten a) v/n. (h.) the bells are ringing or tolling; b) v/a. to ring the bells; Schillers Lied von der ~ Lay of the Bell. — **2.** fig. etwas an die große ~ hängen, bringen, binden (ausschreien) to spread a thing abroad, to trumpet it forth, to make a great noise (or fuss) about it; er hat läuten hören, weiß aber nicht, wo die ~n hängen he has heard something, but is (made) no wiser through it. — **3.** (an Schlag=uhren) strike; weit S. Uhr, z.B. die ~ hat zehn geschlagen the clock (or it) has struck ten; F Glock' (Schlag) elf Uhr at (or upon) the stroke of eleven, F at eleven sharp: fig. ich will ihm sagen, was die ~ geschlagen hat (Bescheid sagen) I will tell him what I mean. — **4.** Rapier: guard. **glocken=ähnlich** (´‿...) a. ⑥ = ⒧förmig; **=apparat** m ⑫ electric bell; **=balke** m bell-beam; **=blume** f: a) allg. bell-flower; b) bib. Canterbury bell, campanula (*Campa'nula*); rundblättrig ~bl. blue (or hare-)bell (*C. rotundifo'lia*) zu den ~n gehörig: ⚙ campanulaceous; **⒧blumig**, **⒧blütig** a. ⑥ ⚙ campan form (plants); **=bronze** f, **=erz** n bell metal; **=form** f bell-mould; **⒧förmig** a. bell-shaped, ⚙ campaniform; **⒧förmiges Zelt** bell-tent; **=gehäuse**

♪ Musik; ⚙ Wissenschaft; ⚘ Pflanze; ⚘ Geographie; ⚙ Technik; ⛏ Bergbau; ⚔ Militär; ⚓ Marine; 🜚 Handel; ✉ Post; 🚃 Eisenbahn.

[Glockengeläute] — 454 — [Glückswurf]

= =haus; =geläut(e) n = Geläute; =gelenk-kurbel f bell-crank; =gerüst n = =stuhl; =giebel m bell-gable; =gießer(ei f) m bell-founder (-foundry); =guß m bell-casting or -founding; =gut n = =bronze; =hammer n = =klöppel; =haus n belfry; ⁰hell a. (as) clear as a bell; =klang m sound of bells; =klöppel m bell-clapper; =läuten n = Geläute; =läuter m = Glöckner; =mantel m cope of a bell-mould; =metall n = =bronze; =register ♪ n e-r Orgel bell-stop; =ring m ring of the clapper; =ruf m call (or summons) of the bell; =schlag m stroke of a clock; auf den ~, mit dem ~e at (or on) the stroke of the clock, at the exact time; =schnur f bell-rope; =schwengel m: a) = =klöppel; b) bell-crank; =seil n rope of a church-bell; =speise f = =bronze; =spiel n chime, (set of musical bells pl.; =spieler m chimer; =stimme f voice as clear as a bell; =strang m = =seil; =stube f bell-loft; vgl. =haus; =stuhl m bell-cage; =stunde f: alles mit der ~ machen to go by the clock, to do everything at the exact hour; eine ~ (volle Stunde) warten to wait a full hour; =tierchen n/pl. zo.: ⚹ campanularia pl.; =ton m sound (or tone) of a bell; =tönig a. poet. ringing out like a bell; vgl. ⁰hell; =turm m, arch. bell-tower, einer Kirche oft: steeple; =zug m: a) bell-pull; b) ♪ der Orgel: bell-stop.

...glockig (♪~) a. ⑥, in Zssgn, bsd. ♣, z.B. viel-⁰ with many bells.

Glöcklein (♪~) n ㉓ = Glöckchen.

Glöckner (♪~) m ㉒ bell-ringer, sexton.

glomm (♪) ind., **glömme** (♪~) subj. impf. von glimmen.

Glori-e (L~) [lt.] f ㊽ glory.

Glori-en-schein (L...) m ㉒ fig.: ⚹ halo; paint. aureola.

glorifizieren (~♪L~) v/a. ㉝ to glorify.

glor-reich (ᴴ,⸱), ⁰würdig (ᴴ,♪~) a. ⑥ glorious, illustrious, renowned; palmy.

Glossar ⚹ (♪~) [grch.-lt.] n ㉑c und ㉙ (erklärendes Wörterbuch) glossary.

Glossator ⚹ (♪L~) m ㉑ bsd. des Korpus juris: ⚹ glosser, glossarist, glossator.

Glosse [grch.] f ㊽ (Randbemerkung) marginal note, ⚹ gloss; fig. zu allem seine ~n (Bemerkungen) machen to comment (b.s. to pass sneering remarks) upon everything.

Glossen-macher (♪~...) m ㉒ = Glossator; =sammlung f glossary.

glossieren (~L~) [Glosse] v/a. ㉝ to gloss (or comment) upon; fig. to censure.

Glotz-auge (♪~...) n ㉕ goggle-eye; =äugig a. ⑥ goggle-eyed.

glotzen (♪~) [mhd: gloat] v/n. (h.) ⑨⓪ to stare, to open one's eyes (wide) with astonishment. [goggled.]

glotzig (♪~) a. ⑥ von Augen: staring,

gluchsen... =en (Lfg.) v/n. ⑨⓪ = gluckern 1.

gluck! (♪) Geräusch beim Ausgießen aus der Flasche: cluck!

Glück (♪) [mhd.: luck] n ⓪b. (pl. ♣, mehr gbr.-⁰s-fälle,-⁰s-umstände) **1.** äußeres ~: (good) fortune, (good)⁽ᶠ⁾ luck, lucky chance, (Wohlergehen) prosperity; (Erfolg) success; zum größten ~ war nie- mand dort very fortunately (or very luckily) nobody was there; zu meinem ~ luckily for me; Wünsche: ~ auf!, ~ auf!, ~ zu!, viel ~! good luck to you!, good speed!, a God-speed to you!, F co. more power to your elbow!; viel ~ auf den Weg! may your journey be a successful one!, I wish you a pleasant journey!; viel ~ zum Geburtstage! (I wish you) many happy returns (of your birthday or of the day)!; viel ~ zum neuen Jahre! (I wish you) a very happy new year! — **2.** Redensarten zu 1: das wird dir ~ bringen it will bring you luck; Freunde im ~ fair-weather friends pl.; ein Günstling des ~es one of fortune's favourites or minions; er hat in allem ~, immer ~ he succeeds in everything, is always lucky; auch: all his cards are trumps; Spiel: ~ haben, im ~ sitzen to be winning or on the winning side; mehr ~ als Verstand haben to be more fortunate than wise, to get more by hit than by wit; F damit werden Sie (wohl) kein ~ haben you won't gain (or benefit) much by that; sein ~ m. to make one's fortune; sein ~ zu machen suchen to hunt after fortune; das hat mein ~ gemacht that was the making of me; er kann von großem ~ sagen, daß er noch lebt he may think himself very lucky that he is alive; F he may thank his lucky stars that he is alive; im ~ sitzen to be in affluence or in clover; sein ~ versuchen to try one's luck; das ~ ist ihm hold, will ihm wohl fortune smiles upon him or favours him; es ist ein (sein) ~, daß // it is fortunate (for him) that //; e-m zu seinem ~ verhelfen to put a p. in the way of making his fortune, to give a p. a lift in life; Sprichw. sieh Braut 2; Glas 1; wo das ~ kommt, kommt's im Haufen it never rains, but it pours; ~ in der Liebe, Unglück im Spiel lucky in love, unlucky at cards. — **3.** (Gefühl von ~) happiness, stärker: bliss, felicity. — **4.** (Geschick) fate, lot; (Zufall) chance, hazard; sein ~ versuchen to make a bid for fortune; Sprichw. jeder ist s-s ~es Schmied every man is the architect (or founder) of his (own) fortune.

Glück-auf (♪~ᴴ) n ⓪ f. Glück 1; ⁰begünstigt (♪) a. ⑥ favoured by fortune, ⁰bringend a. bringing (good) luck, lucky, auspicious. [Gluckhenne.]

Glucke¹ (♪~) [mhd: glucken] f ㊽ =]

Glucke² (♪~) f ㊽ ent. lappet-moth (Gastro'pacha).

glucken (♪~) [: cluck lautm.] v/n. (h.) ㊽ **1.** wie Hennen: to cluck, to chuck. — **2.** F wie Wasser aus e-r Flasche: to gurgle.

glücken (♪~) v/n. u. v/imp. (sn u. h.) ㊽ = gelingen I, z.B. alles ist ihm geglückt he has succeeded (or been lucky) in everything, he has never failed or known what failure is.

gluckern F (♪~) v/n. (h.) ㉕a. = glucken 2.

Gluck-henne (♪~,♪~) f ㊽ clucking (or brood-)hen.

glücklich (♪~) I a. ⑥ (f. Glück 1 und 3) fortunate, lucky, prosperous, successful; happy, blessed; (günstig) favourable; (vorteilhaft) advantageous; ein ⁰er Gedanke a happy thought or hit; ich schätze mich ⁰, arbeiten zu können I esteem myself very fortunate (auch: I am greatly pleased, F I thank my lucky stars) that I can work; ich schätze mich glücklich, Ihre Bekanntschaft zu machen I am delighted to make your acquaintance; e-m eine ⁰e Reise wünschen to wish a p. a safe (or pleasant) journey; adv. ⁰ ankommen to arrive safely; ⚹ von Waren a. in good condition; ⁰ davonkommen to escape unhurt; ein ⁰ gewählter Ausdruck a felicitous expression. — **II** ⁰e(r m) f ⑯ fortunate (or happy) one; Sie ⁰er! you (are a) lucky fellow!

glücklicher-weise (♪~~,♪L~) adv. luckily, fortunately, happily, by a lucky chance, as luck would have it.

Glücks-bahn (♪~...) f ㊽ (high) road to fortune; =ball m, fig., etwa: toy of fortune; =bote m bearer of glad tidings or good news; =botschaft f glad tidings; =bude f auf Jahrmärkten: booth with a wheel of fortune; raffling-shop.

glückselig (♪~) [† Glückjal + -ig] a. ⑥ blessed, blissful; (strahlend) radiant or overflowing with happiness or joy.

Glückseligkeit (♪L~) f ㊽ bliss, supreme (or perfect) happiness or joy; felicity.

Glückseligkeits-lehre (♪...) f ㊽ phls.: ⚹ eudæmonism.

glucksen (♪~) v/n. (h.) ⑨⓪ = glucken 1.

Glücks-fall (♪~...) m ㉒ (f. Glück Zeile 2) piece of good luck, lucky incident, stroke of good fortune; =göttin f goddess of fortune, als npr.: Fortune; =gut n: a) worldly possession; b) güter pl. (Reichtum etc.) riches pl; mit=gütern gesegnet blest (or blessed) with the good things of this world, rolling in wealth; =hafen m safe harbour or port (meist fig.); =haube f, anat. caul; =jäger m = =ritter; =jägerei f fortune-hunting; =karte f beim Spiel: lucky card; =kauf m lucky bargain; =kind n fortune's favourite or minion, p. blessed with (good) fortune, F lucky chap or dog; vgl. =pilz; =pilz m lucky fellow, one born under a lucky star; vgl. =kind; =rad n wheel of fortune (auch zum Spielen); =ritter m fortune-hunter; (Abenteurer) adventurer; =sache f matter of chance or good luck; lottery; =sohn m = =kind; =spiel n game of hazard or chance; =spinne f, ent. money-spider (Epible'mum sce'nicum); =stern m lucky star; =stunde f, =tag m happy (or lucky, propitious) hour. day.

Glück-stifter (♪~...) m ㉒. ~in f ㊼ founder (or promoter) of happiness.

Glücks-topf (♪~...) m ㉒ fortune's urn; in den ~ greifen to dip into the lucky bag, to have a stroke of good fortune.

glück-strahlend (♪~...) a. ⑥ beaming with happiness or joy; vgl. glückselig.

Glücks-umstände (♪~...) m/pl. ㉒ (f. Glück Zeile 2) fortunate (Wohlstand: easy) circumstances pl.; =wahn m imaginary blessing or happiness; =wechsel m change of fortune, vicissitudes pl. of life; (Unglück) reverse; =wurf m

---

Signs (see page XVII): F familiar; P vulgar; Ϝ flash; ⚹ rare; † obsolete (died); * new word (born); ⧺ incorrect; ♪ music;

[Glückszufall] — 455 — [Gobelintapete]

lucky hit, stroke of fortune; =zufall m lucky chance.
glück=verheißend (³…) a. ⊛ of happy (or good) augury, auspicious, propitious; =wunsch m ⊛ congratulation, good wishes pl.; geh. Sprache: felicitation; e-m seinen ~ abstatten to offer a p. one's congratulations to a th., to congratulate a p. on a th.; wunsch= schreiben n letter of congratulation.
Glüh=asche (″…) f ⊛ embers pl.; =eisen n red-hot iron.
glühen (⌣̄) [ahd.: glow] ⊛ I v/n. (h.) 1. to be red-hot or aglow, to glow; (weißglühend sein) to be white-hot or incandescent. — 2. fig. der Himmel glüht the sky is (all) aglow or (all) on fire; mein Kopf glüht my head burns or is (all) on fire; nach etwas (leidenschaftlich verlangen) to have a burning desire for a th., to be ardently (or fervidly) longing for (or after) a th.; vor Lust, Wonne to be aglow (or transported) with joy, delight; vor Wut to be heated (or fired) with rage. — II v/a. 3. ⊙ to make red-hot; (abkühlen) to anneal glass, &c. — 4. (lebhaft bezeugen) to utter passionately; Rache to breathe vengeance. — III ~ n ⊛ 5. = Glut. — IV ⊇ p.pr. u. a. ⊛ 6. Bed. des inf. — 7. red-hot; e Kohlen red-hot (or live) coals pl.; fig. wie auf en Kohlen sitzen to be on thorns or on tenter-hooks; fig. ardent, fervid; e Sprache fiery (or passionate) language; mit en Worten in glowing terms.
Glüh=farbe (″…) f ⊛ colour of fire; flame-colour; =feuer n slow-burning (or smouldering) fire; live coal(s pl.); =hitze f intense heat; rote, weiße ~ red, white heat; =körper m =strumpf; =lampe f, elect. glow-lamp; =licht n incandescent light; =ofen m: a) (Kühl=ofen) annealing-furnace; b) (Röst=ofen) calcining-furnace; =span ⊙ m forge-scale, hammer-slag; =strumpf m, elect. incandescent mantle; =wachs ⊙ n gilder's (or gilding-) wax; =wein n mulled wine, negus; =wurm m, =würmchen n, ent. glow-worm (Lampy'ris noctilu'ca).
glupen P (⌣̄) v/n. (h.) ⊛ to look sullen.
glup(i)sch prov. (⌣̄) a. ⊛ (heimtückisch) underhand; (boshaft) malicious, ill-tempered or -natured.
Glut (⌣̄) [ahd.: * glühen] f ⊛ 1. glow, des Feuers red-heat, slow(-burning) fire; ~ der tropischen Sonne (blazing) heat of the tropical sun; die ~ der brennenden Stadt the flames pl. of the burning town; die ~ schüren to stir the fire. — 2. fig. ardour, fervour, glow, fire, passion; die ~ ihres Hasses the intensity of their hate; in ~ geraten to fire (or blaze) up. [gluten.]
Glutin (-⌣̄) [lt.] n ⊛c. (Knochenleim)
Glut=meer (″…) n ⊛ ocean (or sea) of fire, fiery ocean; =messer ⊙ m, phys.: pyrometer; =pfanne ⊙ f brazier; rot a. ⊛ (as) red as fire, of a fiery red.
Glykochol=säure (⌣⌣̄̄…) [grch.] f ⊛ chm. (Gallensäure) glycocholic acid ($C_{26}H_{43}NO_6$).

Glykogen (⌣⌣̄) [grch.] n ⊛c. chm. (Leberstärke) glycogen.
Glykokoll (⌣⌣̄) [grch.] n ⊛b. chm. („Leimsüß" zucker) glycocol, glycocine ($C_2H_5NO_2$). [glucose.)
Glykose (⌣̄⌣) [grch.] f⊛(Traubenzucker)
Glykosid (⌣⌣̄) [grch.] n ⊛c. chm. glucoside, glycoside.
Glyptik (⌣̄) [grch.] f ⊛ (Steinschneide=kunst) glyptic art, glyptics.
Glyptothek (⌣⌣̄) f ⊛ (Gemmensammlung) glyptotheca; (Skulpturen) collection of works of sculpture.
Glyzerin (⌣⌣̄) [lt.; *grch. glyky's süß] n ⊛c. chm. (Süß) glycerine ($C_3H_8O_3$); mit ~ behandeln to glycerize.
Glyzerin=säure (″…) f ⊛ glyceric acid ($C_3H_6O_4$); =seife ⊛ f glycerine-soap.
G. m. b. H. abbr. = Gesellschaft mit beschränkter Haftpflicht limited liability
G=Moll ♪ (⌣̄) n ⊛ f. G ♪. [company.)
Gnade (⌣̄) [ahd.] f ⊛ 1. grace; Wir …, von Gottes ~n König ꝛc. We, by the grace of God, King …; durch die ~ Gottes by the grace of God; by divine mercy or dispensation; j-s ~ besitzen, bei e-m in ~n steh(e)n to be in a p.'s good graces, to enjoy a p.'s favour; zu ~ kommen to find favour with a p. — 2. (Milde) clemency, leniency; (Barmherzigkeit) mercy; (Mitleid) pity; (Gunst) favour; (Schonung) quarter; e-m ~ angedeihen lassen to grant a p. a pardon, to have mercy upon a p.; sich (dat.) eine ~ ausbitten to beg for a favour; ~ für Recht ergehen lassen to temper justice with mercy; sich auf ~ u. Ungnade ergeben to surrender at discretion, to make an unconditional surrender; in ~n bewilligt graciously granted; e-n in ~n entlassen to dismiss a p. graciously, to bid a p. a gracious farewell; ohne ~ without mercy; ohne ~ u. Barmherzigkeit without the slightest commiseration; um ~ bitten (einen um ~ flehen) to ask (to sue a p.) for mercy; von j-s ~ abhängen to be at a p.'s mercy, to be dependent on a p.'s good graces; vor j-s Augen ~ finden to find favour in a p.'s eyes; † halten zu ~n! no offence intended!, pray excuse me, sir or madam!, may it please your Lordship or Ladyship! — 3. Titel: Euer (Ew.) ~n Your Grace (in England Titel von Herzögen nicht königlichen Geblüts u. von Erzbischöfen); in Österreich allgemeiner: wie befinden sich Ew. ~n? how do you do, sir or madam?
gnaden (⌣̄) v/n. (h.) ⊛ to be gracious or merciful; gnade uns Gott! God (or the Lord) have mercy upon us!
Gnaden=akt (″…) m ⊛ act of grace, gracious act; =bewilligung f, Cath. eccl. indult; =bezeigung f favour (shown a p.); vgl. =zeichen; =bild n, Cath. eccl. miraculous (or miracle-working) image; =brief m (written) pardon, weitS. diploma; =brot n scanty living; das ~ bei einem essen to live on a p.'s charity; e-m das ~ geben to make an old servant, &c. a small allowance; =bund m, theol. covenant of grace; =frist f reprieve, respite; =gabe f:

a) charitable gift; b) theol. gift of grace; =gehalt, =geld n pension, yearly allowance; =geschenk n gratification; donation; =gesuch n petition for pardon; =jahr n year of grace or of our Lord; im bsd. (Gehalt e-s Beamten, das der Witwe ein Jahr lang nach s-m Tode gezahlt wird) widow's bounty; =kraut n water-hyssop (Grati'ola officina'lis); =lohn m gratuity; =mittel n, theol. means of grace; =ort m, Cath. eccl. place containing a miraculous image; holy shrine; =pforte f gate of mercy; =reich a. gracious, merciful; (mildtätig) charitable; =sache f affair (or matter) of grace; =sold m = =gehalt; =stoß m death-blow, finishing stroke, (fr.) coup de grâce; =stuhl m, bibl. mercy-seat, throne of mercy; =tage m/pl. days pl. of grace; =thron m Gottes: throne of grace, mercy-seat; =verheißung f, theol. promise of grace; =wahl f, theol. predestination; =weg m: auf dem ~e by special grace, by an act of pardon; im ~e by way of grace; =werk n, theol. work of grace; =zeichen n mark (or token) of favour bestowed on a p.
gnädig (⌣̄) a. ⊛ (f. Gnade) 1. gracious; geh. Sprache: propitious; (nachsichtig) lenient, merciful; (gunstvoll) favourable, (huldvoll) affable, (wohlwollend) kind, indulgent; adv. a.: with kindness or indulgence; er ist noch ~ davongekommen he has had a narrow escape or F squeeze, F he got off pretty well; machen Sie es ! don't be too hard (on me, him, &c.)!, F draw it mild!; der Fürst hat st eingewilligt, zu // (inf.) … has most graciously consented to //. — 2. als Titel (vgl. Gnade 3): unser ster Herrscher our most gracious sovereign; ja, meine (st)e Frau, auch s. meine e yes, madam or mylady!; wie die e Frau befehlen as your Ladyship wishes.
gnädiglich (⌣⌣̄) adv. = gnädig.
Gneis (⌣̄) m ⊛a. min. (granit=artiges Gestein) † gneiss. [gnome, goblin.)
Gnom (⌣̄) [fr. *grch.] m ⊛ (Erdgeist)
Gnome (⌣̄) [grch.] f ⊛ (Sinnspruch) apophthegm, maxim, gnome.
Gnomen=dichtung (″…) f ⊛ gnomic (or sententious) poetry.
gnomenhaft (⌣⌣̄) a. ⊛ like a gnome or goblin. [(or sententious) writer.)
Gnomiker (⌣⌣̄) [grch.] m ⊛ gnomic
gnomisch (⌣̄) a. ⊛ gnomic, sententious.
Gnomon (⌣̄) [grch.] m ⊛ ast. (Sonnen=zeiger) gnomon; pointer (or hand) of a sun-dial.
Gnomonik (-⌣̄) f ⊛ gnomonics.
Gnostiker (⌣⌣̄) [grch.] m ⊛ gnostisch (⌣̄) a. ⊛ theol. (2. sae.) Gnostic.
Gnostiker=kreuz (⌣⌣̄) n ⊛ fylfot (卐).
Gnostizismus (⌣⌣⌣̄) [grch. gnosis Erkenntnis] m ⊛ eccl. (Erforschung Gottes) gnosticism.
Gnu (⌣̄) [hottentott.] n ⊛ (⊛c.) zo. Süd=Afrika: gnu (Cato'blepas gnu).
Gobelin (⌣⌣̄́) [fr. *npr. 15. sae.] m ⊛ (pl. auch ~e ⌣⌣̄⌣) (Wirkbild) Gobelin, worked tapestry; ~tapete (″…) f ⊛ = Gobelin.

⁇ scientific; ⚘ botanical; ⌘ geography; ⊛ machinery; ⚒ mining; ⚔ military; ⚓ marine; ⊛ commercial; ✉ postal; ⛕ railway.

[Gockelhahn] — 456 — [Golgatha]

Gockel=hahn m rooster, *poet.* chanticleer.
Godegisel [Gottesgeißel] *npr/m.* (Attila) Scourge of God.
Go-i [hebr. Fremdling] m (*pl.* Gojim) (Christ) Christian.
Gold [ahd.: gold] n 1. gold; *chm.* aurum (Au); achtzehn=karätiges ~ eighteen-carat gold; feines ~ fine gold; gediegenes, gemünztes ~ native, coined gold; ungeprägtes ~ gold in bars or ingots; in ~ gefaßt set in gold; tausend Mark in ~ £50 (= fifty pounds) in gold. — 2. et. mit ~ aufwiegen to pay for a th. its weight in gold; das ist nicht mit ~ zu bezahlen that is worth more than all the gold in the world, it is priceless; f. glänzen 1 und Morgenstunde.
Gold=abfluß m a) drain (or efflux) of gold; =ader f: a) streak or vein of g.; b) *path.* (bleeding) piles *pl.*; hemorrhoids *pl.*; =adler m, *orn.* golden eagle (*A'quila chrysa'etus*); =ammer f, *orn.* yellow-hammer or -bunting (*Emberi'za citrine'lla*); =ampfer m golden dock (*Rumex mari'timus*); =amsel f, *orn.* oriole; =anstrich m gold-paint; =apfel m: a) (Apfelsorte) golden pippin; b) = Liebesapfel; =arbeit f goldsmith's work; =arbeiter m goldsmith; =artig a. like gold, resembling gold, aureous; =auflösung f solution (or tincture) of g.; =ausbeute f der Bergwerke: outgut of gold; =ausgang m gold withdrawal; =barre(n m) f metall. bar (or ingot) of g.; =bergwerk n gold-mine; =beryll m, min. chrysoberyl; =blättchen n gold-leaf or -foil, leaf-gold; =blatt-elektroskop n, *phys.* g.-leaf electroscope; =blech n g.-foil; Zahnheilkunde ꝛc.: plate of g.; =blume f corn-marigold (*Chrysa'nthemum corona'rium*); =borte f g.-lace; =braun a. auburn, chestnut; =brokat m goldbrocade; =bronze f gold- (or gilt-) bronze; =buchstabe m gold (or gilt) letter; =butt(e f) m, *ichth.* plaice (*Pleurone'ctes plate'ssa*); =chlorid n, *chm.* auric chloride (AuCl₃); =chlorür n, *chm.* aurous chloride (AuCl); =distel f golden thistle (*Sco'lymus hispa'nicus*); =draht m gold wire; =druck m Buchbinderei: gold-printing; =durchwirkt a. interwoven with gold (threads), goldbrocaded; =durst m thirst after g.; immoderate desire for gold.
golden [ahd.] a. (D 9) 1. gold(en), of gold; Se Uhr gold watch; ~e Bulle golden bull; *bibl.* das Se Kalb the golden calf; das Se Kalb (den Mammon) anbeten to worship the golden calf; *myth.* das ~e Vlies the golden fleece. — 2. *fig.* golden, precious, (prächtig) magnificent; er ist noch 2 gegen sie f he is gold (or an angel) by the side of (or compared with) her; e-m Se Berge versprechen to make extravagant promises to a p., to promise a p. mountains of gold or F heaps of money; *path.* Se Ader f. Goldader b; Se Hochzeit golden wedding; *arith.* Se Regel rule of three; Se Worte n/pl. golden words pl.; *ast.* Se Zahl (für Berechnung der Osterzeit) golden number.

Gold=erde f auriferous earth; ~erz n gold-ore; =faden m gold thread; =farbe f gold-colour; =farben a., =farbig a. gold-coloured, golden, aureous; =fasan m, *orn.* golden pheasant (*Phasia'nus pictus*); =finger m ring-finger; =fink m goldfinch (= Distelfink); =firnis m gold-varnish; =fisch m: a) *ichth.* goldfish (*Cara'ssius aura'tus*); b) F *fig.* (reiche Erbin) rich heiress; =flimmer, =flitter m g.-spangle; =forelle f, *ichth.* = Forelle; =fuchs m: a) (Pferd) light chestnut horse; b) F (Goldstück) gold coin, F yellow boy; =führend a. gold-bearing; auriferous; Se Erde pay-dirt; =gefäße n/pl. golden vessels pl.; gold plate; =gehalt m percentage of g. contained in ore, coins, &c.; =gelb a. golden-yellow; aureate; =geld n gold coinage; =gelockt a. with golden locks or curls or ringlets; =geschirr n =gefäße; =geschmeide n gold ornaments pl.; =gespinst n golden weft; spun gold; =gestickt a. embroidered with gold; =gewicht n gold- (in Engl. auch: troy-)weight; =gier f greed after gold, *vgl.* =durst; =glanz m lustre of g., golden splendour; =glänzend a. of golden lustre, shining like gold; =glätte f, min. gold-litharge; =glimmer m, min. yellow mica, gold-glimmer; cat-gold, ammochryse; =gräber m g.-digger; =gras n = Ruch=g.; =grube f gold-diggings pl.; *fig.* eine wahre ~ quite a gold-mine or a mine of wealth; =grund m: a) Vergoldung: gold-size; b) von Stoffen: g.-ground or -foundation; =gulden m g.-florin; =haar n: a) golden hair; b) golden maidenhair (*Chryso'coma*); =haarig a. with golden hair, golden-haired; =hafer m yellow oats (*Trise'tum flave'scens*); =hähnchen n, *orn.* golden-crested wren, goldcrest (*Re'gulus*); =haltig a. containing gold; auriferous, aurous; =handel m gold-trade; =haufen m heap of gold; =hell a. (as) bright as gold; *vgl.* Se glänzend.

goldig a. = golden 1.
Gold=junge F m = =sohn; =käfer m: a) *ent.* (Rosenkäfer) rose-chafer (*Ceto'nia aura'ta*); b) F *fig.* = =fisch b; =käferschuhe m/pl. bronze-coloured shoes or boots pl.; =kalk m, *chm.* calcined gold; =kies m, min. auriferous pyrites; =kind n charming (or darling) child, pet; =klumpen m lump (Nugget) of gold; =könig m, *chm.*: regulus of g.; =körnchen n (small) grain of g.; =kräße f (Abschabsel) gold sweepings pl.; =krone f golden crown; =kupfer n copper with an admixture of gold, pinchbeck; =küste f (West-afrika) Gold Coast; =lack m: a) gold-coloured varnish; b) wallflower (*Cheira'nthus Cheiri*); =lahn m flattened gold wire; =lahn-schläger m flatt(en)er of gold wire; =land n gold-(bearing) country; =legierung f alloy of g.; =leiste f gilt moulding or cornice; =lockig a. = =haarig; =macher m chm. alchemist; =macherei, =macherkunst f alchemy; =mann m tosend: darling man or husband; =masse f mass- (or

lump) of gold; =mensch m wealthy man, rich financier, F gold-bug; =milzkraut n golden saxifrage (*Chrysosple'nium alternifo'lium*); =mine f g.-mine; =münze f gold coin, piece of gold; =münzfuß m, =münzsystem n = =währung; =nessel f yellow dead-nettle (*Galeo'bdolon lu'teum*); =niederschlag m precipitate of gold; =onkel F m rich uncle; =oxyd n, *chm.* auric o'xide (Au₂O₃); =oxydul n, *chm.* aurous oxide (Au₂O); =papier n gold-paper, gilt paper; =pepin(g) m = =apfel a.; =platte f plate of gold; =plattierung f gold-plating; =probe f assay of g.; =pulver n gold-powder or -dust; =purpur m (rote Farbe für Glasmalerei ꝛc.) powder of Cassius; =quarz m auriferous quartz; =regen m: a) *myth.* shower of gold; b) laburnum (*Cy'tisus labu'rnum*); =regenpfeifer m, *orn.* golden-plover (*Chara'drius pluvia'lis*); =reich a. rich in gold; =reif, =ring m gold(en) ring; =renette f (Apfel) bsd. spine.-golding; =rute f gold(en)-rod (*Solida'go*); =sachen f/pl. gold ornaments pl.; =salz n, *chm.* aurate; =sand m gold-(bearing) sand; auriferous sand; =säure f, *chm.* auric acid (H₃AuO₃); =schale f gold(en) cup; =schaum m g.-leaf, leaf-gold; (Flitter) tinsel; =scheider m g.-refiner; =schläger=form, =haut f, =häutchen n) m gold-beater('s skin); =schlägerei f gold-beating; =schmied=arbeit f) m goldsmith('s work); =schmiedekunst f goldsmith's art; =schnitt m Buchbinderei: gilt edge; mit ~ gilt-edged; =schnur f gold lace; =sohn m, =söhnchen n F excellent son, darling (or pet) boy; *iro.* spoilt boy, young hopeful or rascal; =spinner m spinner of gold thread; =staub m g.-dust; =sticken n = =stickerei; =sticker(in f) m embroiderer in gold; =stickerei f embroidery in g.; =stoff m g.-cloth or -brocade; =stück n gold coin or piece; =stufe f sample of g.-ore; =tinktur f tincture of g.; =tochter f, =töchterchen n F darling (or pet) daughter; =tresse f g.-lace; =überzug m coating of gold; =wage f gold-scales pl. or -balance, scales for weighing gold; *fig.* jedes Wort auf die ~ legen to weigh every word, to pick and choose one's words, to use very choice language; =währung f gold-standard; =ware f jewellery; =waren=handel m jeweller's trade or business; =wäsche(rei) f: a) washing of auriferous ore or of g.-bearing sand; b) (Ort) g.-washing(s pl.); =wäscher m g.-washer; =weide f = Dotter-w.; =wert m value (or equivalent) in gold; =wespe f, *ent.* goldwasp, golden fly (*Chrysis*); =wirker m gold-weaver; =wirkerei, =wirkerkunst f gold-weaving; =wolf m. zo. jackal (*Canis au'reus*); =zieher m = gold-wire drawer; =zyanür n, *chm.* aurous cyanide (Au Cy).
Golf (F) [mhd.: gulf;* fr. golfe] m b. (Meerbusen) gulf.
Golf=strom m (warme Meeresströmung aus d. Golf v. Mexiko) GulfStream.
Golgatha [grch.;* hebr. „Schädelstätte"] *npr/n.* a. *bibl.* Golgotha.

Zeichen (f. S. XVII): F familiär; P Volkssprache; ☠ Gaunersprache; ✳ selten; † alt (auch gestorben); * neu (auch geboren); ‡ unrichtig;

[Goliath] — 457 — [Gottesglaube]

Goliath (ˈ(ˇ)ˇ) [hebr. Ozean] npr/m. ⑨⑨a. bibl. (Samuel 1, 17) Goliath.
gölte (ˇˇ) impf. subj. von gelten.
Gomorr(h)a (ˇˇ) (ˊˇ) [hebr. überflutung] npr/n. ⑨a. bibl. Gomorrha; **gomorr(h)isch** a. ⑥⑥ of Gomorrha.
Gondel (ˇˇ) [it.] f ㊽ **1.** ⚓ venetianische ~ gondola; (kleines Boot) small (pleasure-)boat. — **2.** ~ am Luftschiffe: car.
gondel-ähnlich (ˇˇ…) a. ⑥⑥, -artig a. gondola-like; **-fahrer** m ㊁, **-führer** m, **-schiffer** m = Gondelier; **-fahrt** f trip (or excursion) in a gondola; **-(führer)lied** n (Venetian) barcarolle.
Gondelier, Gondolier (ˇˇㄴ) m ①d. (Venetian) gondolier; waterman, bargee.
gondeln (ˇˇ) ⊕a. **I** v/n. (h.) to go boating or rowing. — **II** v/a. to row (or to take about) in a gondola or boat.
Goniometrie ↗ (ˇ(ˇ)ˇˇㄴ) [grch.] f ⑲ math. (Winkelmessung) goniometry.
gönnen (ˇˇ) [ahd.: own] v/a. ㊹ not to (be)grudge (or envy) a p. a th.; wir ⓁⓁ es ihm von Herzen we wish him every joy to (or with) it; er gönnt sich (dat.) das liebe Brot nicht he denies (or grudges) himself the very bread; er gönnt sich keine Ruhe he does not give (or allow) himself any rest; wir ⓁⓁ ihm einige Tage Ruhe we grant him a few days' rest.
Gönner (ˇˇ) m ㊁, ~**in** f ㊼ well-wisher, patron (f…ess), protector (f…tress); (Wohltäter[in]) benefactor (f…tress).
gönnerhaft (ˇˇˇ) a. ⑥⑥ patron-like, (herablassend) patronizing. [air or look.]
Gönner-miene (ˇˇ…) m ㊁ patronizing⌐
Gönnerschaft (ˇˇˇ) f ㊻ (s. Gönner) **1.** patronage, protection. — **2.** coll. patrons, promoters pl.
Göpel ⊕ (ˊˇ) m ㊁ (liegende Winde) (machine-)whim, (horse-)capstan; ~**kette** (ㄴˇ…) f ㊽ whim-chain; ~**pferd** n capstan-horse; ~**werk** n horse-gear.
gor (ˊ) impf. von gären.
Gör F (ˊ, nbb. jˊ) [: girl] n ㉙c. (Kind) child.
Gording ⚓ (ˇˇ) f ⑱ (Tau zum Festmachen e-s Raßsegels) buntline.
gordisch (ˇˇ) [Gordius, Kg. v. Phrygien] a. ⑥⑥: Der Knoten Gordian knot; den Len Knoten zerhauen to cut the Gord-⌐
Göre¹ (ˊ) f ㊻ = Gör. [ian knot.]
göre² (ˊ) subj. impf. v. gären.
Gorgo (ˊˇ) [grch.] npr/f. ㊿ myth. Gorgon.
gorgonen-artig (ˇㄴˇˇ…) a. ⑥⑥, -**haft** a. poet. (schrecklich) ↗ Gorgonean,…esque; -**haupt** n ㉗ myth. auf dem Schilde der Athene: Gorgon's head, ↗ gorgoneion.
Gorilla (ˇㄴˇ) [afr.] m ⑤ zo. gorilla.
Gösch ⚓ (ˊ) m ①a., a. f ⑱ (Bugspriet- flagge) jack, (G. für England :) Union Jack.
Gosen (ˊˇ) [äg.] npr/n. ⑨a. bibl. das Land ~ the land of Goshen (1.Mos.45,10).
goß (ˊ) impf. von gießen.
Göttchen (ˇˇ) n ⑳ dim. v. Gosse.
Gosse (ˇˇ) [nhd.: gut; *gießen] f ㊻ auf den Straßen: gutter, drain; in Küchen: (a. ~**n-stein** m ㊁) sink.
Got(e)¹ (ˊ(ˇ)) [ahd.] m ㊷(㊹) godfather, **Gote** (ˊˇ) ⊕ godmother.
Gote² (ˊˇ) m ⑰, **Gotin** f ㊼ Goth.
goethesch, goethisch (ˊˇ) [Joh. Wolfg. v. Goethe, dtsch. Dichter, 1749—1832] a. ⑥⑥ of Goethe, Goethian.

Gotik (ˊˇ) [dtsch=grch.] f ㊻ arch. Gothic (or pointed) style.
Gotin (ˊˇ) f ㊼ f. Gote.
gotisch (ˊˇ) a. ⑥⑥ Gothic; ~ f, inv., ℒe Schrift typ. **Gothic** letters pl.; **black-letter, Gothic**.
Gott (ˊ) [ahd.: god] m ⓶b. **1.** God; (das höchste Wesen) the Supreme Being, the Holy One; ~ der Herr our Lord God, our Heavenly Father; ~es Sohn the Son of God; das Wort ~es the word(s pl.) of God; er ist beim lieben ~ (gestorben) he is with God or with his Heavenly Father; mit ~es Hilfe können wir es tun God willing we can do it; um ~es Lohn for the love of God, for charity's sake; von ~es und Rechts wegen by rights; es war ~es Wille it was God's will, God willed it so; f. Gnade 1. — **2.** fig. ~ (auch: unsern Herrgott) e-n guten Mann sein l. (sich um nichts kümmern) to let things take their course or shift for themselves, not to trouble (about anything); wie ihn ~ erschaffen hat (nackt) in nature's (or in his natural) garb, in a state of nudity; er weiß von ~ u. der Welt nichts … absolutely nothing; co. ~es Wort vom Lande country parson; f. Frankreich. — **3.** in Ausrufen: ach ~!, großer (auch gerechter, guter) ~! good (or great) Heavens!, good Lord!, dear me!; leider ~es! alas!; der alte ~ lebt noch! God is (ever) with us!; ~ befohlen! adieu!, farewell!, feierlicher: may Heaven preserve you!, God be with you!, God speed you!; ~ behüte!, ~ bewahre!, da sei ~ vor!, das wolle ~ nicht! God (or Heaven) forbid!; f. erbarmen I; sie sieht aus, daß ~ erbarm' od. ~ soll sich erbarmen! she looks a pitiful object or a picture of misery; ~ gebe es!, wollte ~, daß es geschähe! would to God it were so!, may it please God to grant it!; ~ grüße dich, euch!, grüß ~! good day (or morning) to you; f. gottlob; ~ lohn' es!, ~ vergelt' es! God bless you for it!, Heaven may reward you!; in ~es Namen! for heaven's sake!, feierlicher: in God's holy name!; (meinetwegen) be it so!, F for all I care!; ~ sei bei uns! God be with us!; f. Gottseibeiuns!; ~ sei Dank! thank God!, F thank goodness!; ~ steh mir bei! the Lord have mercy upon me!, God be merciful (unto me)!; ~ weiß es!, weiß ~! Goodness knows!, feierlicher: God (or Heaven) knows!; das weiß der liebe ~! oder F das wissen die Götter! who knows?, Heaven knows!; beteuernd: ~ weiß, so wahr ein ~ lebt! by Heaven!, by Jove!, feierlich: as true as there is a living God!; so ~ will! (if it) please God, in Briefen oft: D.V. = lt. deo volente!; um ~es willen! for goodness' (or mercy's) sake!, feierlich: for God's (or Heaven's) sake!; tue es um ~es willen nicht I beg of you don't do it, don't do it on any account; wie ~ will! as it may please God, auch: as God wills or pleases!; bsd. in Flüchen: (dafür oft Potz, Kotz) ~es Donnerwetter! Hang it all!, Oh

botheration! — **4.** Sprichw. an ~es Segen ist alles gelegen! God's blessing is needed for everything; ~ gibt's den Seinen im Schlafe good fortune comes over night; bei ~ ist kein Ding unmöglich with God all things are possible; was ~ tut, das ist wohlgetan God does everything for the best; hilf dir selbst, so hilft dir ~ God helps them that help themselves; f. Not 4. — **5.** (Gottheit, Götze) god, deity; die (alten) heidnischen Götter the (old) pagan gods; fig. Geld ist sein ~ … is his god or his idol; er singt wie ein junger ~ he has a heavenly voice, he is a wonderful (or splendid, fine) singer.
gott-ähnlich (ˊˇ…) a. ⑥⑥ resembling God; godlike; **ähnlichkeit** f ㊻ resemblance to God; godlikeness; ℒ**be-geistert** a. inspired by God, filled with the divine spirit; ℒ**begnadet**, ℒ**begnadigt** a. endowed with divine grace; von Dichtern rc.: highly gifted, heaven-inspired.
Götter-baum ♀ (ˊˇ…) m ⓶ = Ailantus; -**berg** m Alt., myth. Olympus; -**bild** n image of a god, idol; -**bote** m, -**botin** f, myth. messenger of the gods; grch. m Hermes, f Iris; -**brot** n ambrosia; -**dämmerung** f twilight of the gods; -**funke(n)** m: Freude, schöner ~ (SCH.) oh Joy, thou purest spark divine.
gott-ergeben (ˊˇ…) a. ⑥⑥ submitting (or resigned, bowing) to the will of God; devout; -**ergebenheit** f ㊽ acquiescence in the will of God; pious devotion.
Götter-geschlecht (ˊˇ…) n ㊁ race of gods; -**gestalt** f divine figure or form; ℒ**gleich** a. ⑥⑥ like (the) gods.
götterhaft (ˊˇˇ) a. ⑥⑥ = göttergleich.
Götter-hain (ˊˇ…) m ㊁ sacred grove; -**himmel** m der Griechen rc.: Olympus, der Germanen: Walhalla; -**kunde**, -**lehre** f mythology; -**leben** n life (like that) of the gods; delightful life; -**mahl** n banquet of the gods; -**sage** f myth (-ical account); -**sitz** m habitation (or seat) of the gods; -**speise** f: a) myth. ambrosia; b) delicious food; -**spruch** m oracle; -**trank** m nectar; -**verehrung** f worship of (the) gods; paganism; -**versammlung** f assembly of the gods; -**welt** f the gods pl. (of Olympus).
gott-erzeugt (ˊˇ…) a. ⑥⑥ descended from God or a god.
Gottes-acker (ˊˇ…) m ㊁ cemetery; -**anbeter(in** f) m: a) worshipper of God; b) -**anbeterin** f, ent. (Fangheuschrecke) praying-cricket (Mantis religiosa); -**dienst** m divine service; den ~ abhalten, dem ~ beiwohnen to officiate at, to attend div. serv.; ℒ**dienst-lich** a. ⑥⑥ relating to divine service; -**erde** f = -welt; -**friede** m: a) ehm. truce of God, cessation of hostilities; b) divine peace; -**furcht** f fear of God, (Frömmigkeit) piety; ℒ**fürchtig** a. fearing God, God-fearing; (fromm) pious; -**gabe** f gift of God; unerwartete: godsend; -**geißel** m f. Godegisel; -**gelahrtheit** fast = f theology, divinity; -**geld** n (Draufgeld) earnest (-money); -**gelehrte(r)** m theologian, divine; -**gelehrtheit** f = -gelahrtheit; -**gericht** n = -urteil; -**glaube**

m belief in God, weitS. religion; =**gnade** *f*: es ist eine ~, daß // it is a (heavenly) mercy that //; =**gnadentum** *n* divine right (of kings); =**haus** *n* house of God, place of worship; church, chapel; =**fasten** *m*, *eccl.* poor- (or collection-)box, *bibl.* treasury of (the temple); =**kinder** *n/pl.* children *pl.* of God; =**kindschaft** *f* adoption by God; =**küchen** *n*, *ent.* lady-bird or -cow (*Coccine᾽lla*); =**lamm** *n, eccl.* lamb of God, Jesus Christ; =**lästerer** *m*, =**läst(r)erin** *f* blasphemer; **lästerlich** *a.* blaspheming, sacrilegious; =**lästerung** *f* blasphemy, sacrilege; =**lehre** *f*: a) religion; b) theology; =**leugner(in** *f)* *m* atheist; **leugnerisch** *a.* atheistic; =**leugnung** *f* atheism; =**lohn** *m* heavenly reward; habt ~ dafür! God bless you for it!; an e-m einen ~ verdienen to do a charity to a p.; =**reich** *n* kingdom of God; =**sohn** *m* Son of God; =**tisch** *m* (holy) communion-table; =**urteil** *n* (durch Kampf, Feuerprobe ꝛc.) *ehm. jur.* ordeal; =**verachten** *m*, =**verachtung** *f* despiser, contempt of God; =**verehrung** *f* worship of God; =**vergeß** ? *n* = Taubnessel; =**vergessen(heit** *f) a.* = gottlos, Gottlosigkeit; =**weisheit** *f*: 𝔄 theosophy; =**welt** *f* world, universe; auf der ~ nichts haben to have nothing (of one's own) in God's wide world, not to have a penny to bless o.s. with; =**wort** *n* word of God, Scripture, Holy Writ.

Gottfried (𝔍-) ⑮⑯α. I *npr/m.* (Vn.) Godfrey, Ge(o)ffrey. — II *m* F (alter Hausrock) old easy coat or dressing-gown.

gott-gefällig (𝔊-...) *a.* ⑥ pleasing (or agreeable to) God; ein ~es Leben a pious life, *rel. a.* a life devoted (or agreeable) to the Lord; =**gesandt** *a.* sent by God; der ~e the Saviour, the Messiah; =**geweiht** *a.* consecrated to God.

Gott-hard (𝔊-) *npr/m.* ⑮⑯α. (Vn.) bisw.: Goddard; ♀ (Sankt-)~ (Berg und Paß in der Schweiz) St. Gothard.

Gott-heil ? (𝔊ᵗ) *n* ⓓ. = Brunelle.

Gott-heit (𝔍-) [mhd.] *f* ⑯ divinity; godhead; (Gott, Göttin) (male, female) deity, god, goddess.

Göttin (𝔍ᵥ) *f* ⑯ *myth.* goddess (*a. fig.*).

göttlich (𝔍ᵥ) I *a.* ⑥ 1. divine; godlike. — 2. F *fig.* (ergötzlich) droll, funny. — II **~e**(s), das ~e *n* ⓜ 3. (a, the) divine attribute; F das ~ste an der Sache the funniest part of the matter.

Göttlich-keit (𝔍ᵥ-) *f* ⑯ divinity; godship. **gott-lob!** (𝔊²) *int.* thank God!, F thank goodness!, feierlich: Heaven be praised!; =**los** (𝔊-...) *a.* ⑥ godless, ungodly, (Gott leugnend) atheistic(al); (sündhaft) impious, sinful, (ruchlos) wicked, depraved; (leichtfertig) frivolous, (mutwillig) wanton, mischievous; =**lose(r)** *m f* ⑰ Sie ~! you wicked one!; die =**losen** the godless, the wicked; =**losigkeit** *f* godlessness, ungodliness, atheism; impiety; wickedness, depravity; =**mensch** *m*, *rel.* God incarnate, =**sei-bei-uns** F *m* (Teufel) the Evil one, F Old Nick, Old Harry; =**selig** (𝔊-) *a.* godly; (fromm) pious, devout; Der Tod passing away in the Lord; peaceful death; =**seligkeit** *f* godliness, piety, devotion.

gotts-erbärmlich F (𝔊-...) *a.* ⑥ pitiful, pitiable; =**jämmerlich** F *a.* pitiable, piteous.

Gott-Vater (𝔊ᴵᴵᵥ) *m* ⑫ God the Father; =**verflucht** (𝔊-...) *a.* ⑥ accursed (in the eyes of God); =**vergessen**(=**heit** *f) a.* = -los, -losigkeit; =**verhaßt, =verlassen** *a.* hated, forsaken by God; =**vertrauen** *n* trust in God; =**voll** *a.*: a) filled with the divine spirit; b) F (köstlich) delightful, most amusing, exceedingly funny.

Götze (𝔍ᵥ) [mhd.; *Gott od. (ge)goss(enes Bild)] *m* ⑭ (Abgott) idol, heathen(ish) god or deity; ~**n** (falschen Göttern) dienen to practise idolatry, to worship idols.

Götzen-bild (𝔊ᵥ...) *n* ⑫ idol; =**diener(in** *f) m* idol-worshipper, idolater (*f* ...tress); =**dienerisch** *a.* ⑥ idolatrous; =**dienst** *m* idol-worship, idolatry; *fig.* mit e-m, et. ~ treiben to idolize a p., a th.; =**hain** *m* grove consecrated to a pagan deity; =**priester**, =**tempel** *m* priest, temple of an idol.

Götzentum (𝔊ᵥ-) *n* ⓓ. = Götzendienst.

Gourmand (gur-ma᾽) [(⁺₊) fr. Vielfraß] *m* ⑭ gourmand; (Fresser) gormandizer, gorger; (Prasser) epicure.

Gouvernante (gu-w-𝔍ᵥ) [(⁺₊) fr. (fr. *institutrice)] *f* ⑯ (Erzieherin) governess (*a.* Lehrerin e-r Schule); ~**n-heim** (″...) *n* ⑯ home for governesses.

Gouvernement (gu-w-ma᾽) [fr.] *n* ⑳ (Regierung) government; **~al** (gu-w-ᵥᵥᵥ᾽l) *a.* ⑥ governmental; ministerial.

Gouverneur (gu-w-nö᾽r) [fr.] *m* ⑭d. (⑮) (Statthalter) governor.

Grab¹ (¹, *a.* 𝔍) [ahd.: grave; *graben] *n* ②c. 1. zur Beerdigung: grave; aus Mauerwerk: tomb; das Heilige ~ Christi in Jerusalem: the Holy Sepulchre; *bibl.* übertünchte Gräber whitened sepulchres *pl.*; e-n zu ~e geleiten to attend a p.'s funeral; e-n ins ~ legen, senken, zu ~e tragen to lay a p. in the grave, to inter (or bury) a p. — 2. *fig.* bis ins ~ unto (or till) death; er fand ein nasses ~, ein ~ in den Wellen he sank into a watery grave; er würde sich im ~e herumdrehen he would turn in his grave; mit e-m Fuße schon im ~e steh(e)n, am Rande des ~es steh(e)n to have one foot in the grave, to be on the brink of the grave; verschwiegen wie das ~ (as) silent as the grave, very close.

Grab²-... (ᵘ...) [graben] f. Grabmeißel ꝛc.

grab¹-ähnlich (𝔤-...) *a.* ⑥ sepulchral.

grabbeln F (𝔍ᵥ) [ndd.] *v/n.* (h.) ⓶a. (tasten) to fumble about; (kitzeln) to tickle.

Grab¹-denkmal (𝔤ᵛ...) *n* ⑫ = -mal.

Grabe-land (ᴵᴵᵥ...) [graben] *n* ⑫ spadeland or -soil.

Graben¹ (ᴸᵥ) [ahd.] *m* ㉑ ditch; f. Abzugs-, Lauf-, Schützen-ꝛc.; Gräben ziehen, machen to cut ditches, to ditch; F *fig.* er ist noch nicht über den ~ he is not out of the wood (yet), he is not quite out of danger.

graben² (ᴸᵥ) [ahd.: grave, grub] ⓑb. I *v/n.* (h.) 1. to dig with a spade, &c.; immerfort ~ to be digging and delving; (Gräben ziehen) to cut ditches or trenches. — 2. ☉ mit dem Grabstichel in Metall ~ to engrave on metal. — II *v/a.* 3. e-n Brunnen, ein Grab, ein Loch ꝛc. ~ to dig a well, a grave, a hole, &c.; (aushöhlen) to hollow out; ein Fundament, einen Grund zu einem Gebäude ~ to dig out (or excavate) the foundations; Sprichw. f. Grube. — 4. ☉ (mit dem Grabstichel eingraben) to engrave (*a. fig.*); to cut into metal, &c.; gegrab(e)ne Arbeit chisel-work, engraving. — 5. e-m den Dolch ins Herz ~ (bohren) to plunge the dagger into a p.'s heart. — 6. (herausfördern) Kohlen, Torf ꝛc. ~ to dig (or extract) coal, peat, &c.; Schätze ~ to dig (or search) for treasures. *hunt.* einen Fuchs ꝛc. ~ to dig out (or unearth) a fox, &c. — 7. et. in den Boden ~ to dig up a th., to hide a th. in (a hole dug in) the ground. — 8. *agr.* das Land (um-)~ (bearbeiten) to dig the land (over), to turn the ground over with the spade. — III sich ~ *v/refl.* 9. mit Angabe der Wirkung: sich müde ~ to tire o.s. out with digging. — 10. die Kaninchen ~ sich in die Erde rabbits burrow (holes) in the ground or go to warren. — 11. *fig.* ein Bild gräbt sich ins Gedächtnis ... sinks deep into the memory, ... deeply impresses (or imprints) itself on the mind; das ist mir ins Herz gegraben that is inscribed (*poet.* [en]graven) on my heart. — IV ~ *n* ㉓ 12. digging, &c.; (f. 3) excavation of foundations; (f. 6) extraction of coal, &c.; (f. 8) *agr.* spading (work).

Graben¹-böschung 𝔍 (ᴵᴵᵥ...) *f* ⓕ counterscarp; =**damm** *m* (raised) bank of a ditch; ⚔ (Kastenbamm) coffer-dam; =**pflug** ☉ *m*, *agr.* ditching- (or furrowing-)plough; =**sohle** *f* bottom of a ditch or (⚔ *frt.*) trench; =**ziehen** *n*, =**zug** *m* ditching; draining.

Gräber¹ (ᴸᵥ) *pl.* von Grab und Gräber².

Gräber² (ᴸᵥ) [graben] *m* ㉒ 1. digger; (f. der Gräber macht) ditcher; ⚔ *frt.* trencher (f. Toten-~ ꝛc.). — 2. *zo.* ~ *pl.* (grabende Tiere) burrowing animals, burrowers *pl.*

Gräber¹-fund (ᴵᴵᵥ...) *m* ⑫ object(s *pl.*) found in a tomb; =**geruch** *m* sepulchral (or mouldy) smell; =**schmuck** *m* decoration(s *pl.*) of a grave.

Grabes-dunkel (ᴵᴵᵥ...) *n* ⑫ darkness (or gloom) of the grave; =**kirche** *f* in Jerusalem church of the Holy Sepulchre; =**moder** *m* mouldy smell of a grave; =**nacht** *f* = -dunkel; =**rand** *m* brink of the grave; *fig.* am ~e on the verge of the gr.; =**ruhe** *f*, =**stille** *f* peace of the gr., weitS. deathlike silence.

Grab¹-fund (-...) *m* ⑫ = Gräberfund; =**geläut(e)** *n* tolling of bells at a funeral; geh. Sprache: death-knell; =**gerüst** *n* catafalque; =**gesang** *m* = -lied; =**gewölbe** *n* tomb, sepulchral vault, auch. family-vault; =**hügel** *m* barrow, schott. cairn; 𝔄 tumulus (*pl.* ...i); =**legung** *f* interment, burial, sepulture; =**lied** *n* funeral chant or song or dirge; =**mal** *n* tomb, sepulchre;

[Grabmeißel] — 459 — [Granitgebirge]

=²meißel m = =stichel; =¹platte f: a) aus Marmor: marble slab (on a grave); b) aus Bronze: bronze tablet, poet. monumental brass or bronze; =rede f funeral sermon; =²schaufel f gardener's shovel; =scheit n spade, (square) shovel; digger; =¹schrift f epitaph; =stätte f place of burial, tomb; unterirdische ~n pl. in Rom ꝛc. catacombs pl.; =stein m tombstone, headstone (of a grave); =²stichel ⊙ m Kupferstecherei ꝛc.: graving-tool or -chisel, graver's chisel, graver; burin, pointrel.
Grabung (᷄) f ⊕ = graben² IV.
Grab=²weipe (ⁿ...) f ⊕ ent.: sand-wasp (Ammo'phila); digger-wasp (Sphex); ~n pl.: ⚵ fossores, crabronidæ pl.
Gracht (ᵡᵗ) [ndl.] f ⊕ (Stadtgraben) canal (through a town).
Grad (᷄; Hom. Grat) [ahd.; *lt. grădus] m⊕c,6 **1.** degree (a. phys., math.., ♀); der Verwandtschaft: degree, remove; phys. rate of speed, &c.; 15 ~ Wärme (Kälte) fifteen degrees above (below) zero or the freezing point [in Engl. wird im allgemeinen die Fahrenheitsche, nur für wissenschaftliche Zwecke die Celsiussche Skala gebraucht]; im Sommer steht der Thermometer oft 80 ~ (Fahrenheit) im Schatten in the summer the thermometer often stands at (or registers) eighty degrees in the shade; in ~e teilen to graduate; bei Null ~ at zero; ⚔ ~ der Bereitschaft degree of readiness. — **2.** mit a. in gewissem ~e to a certain degree or extent, in some measure; hoher ~ intensity, in hohem ~e in a high degree, in a great measure, greatly, highly; der höchste ~ the highest degree or pitch; im höchsten ~e in the highest degree, extremely, exceedingly; supremely (happy). — **3.** univ. (academical) degree; ⚔, &c.: grade, rank. — **4.** path. stage of a disease.
Grad=abteilung (ⁿ...) f ⊕ division into degrees, scale, ⚵ graduation; ast.: graduction; =abzeichen ⚔ n stripe, epaulette, &c. showing the rank of a soldier, an officer, &c.
Gradation ⚵ (᷄-tᶻ(᷄)᷄) [lt.] f ⊕ bsb. rhet. (Abstufung) gradation; (Steigerung) climax.
Grad=bogen (ⁿ...) m ⊕ graduated arc; zum Zeichnen ꝛc.: protractor; =einteilung f = =abteilung.
gradieren ⊙ (ᵛ᷄) [Grad] **I** v/a. ⊛ Saline: die Sole ⚵ to graduate (or refine) the brine. — **II** ~ n ⊛ = Gradierung.
Gradier=haus ⊙ (ᵛⁿ...) n ⊛ Saline: graduation-house; =herd, =ofen m hearth, furnace (or oven) for graduation; graduator.   [duation.|
Gradierung ⊙ (ᵛ᷄) f ⊛ der Sole: gra-|
Gradier=wage ⊙ (ᵛ᷄) f ⊕ (Senkwage zur Prüfung der Sole) areometer; =wasser n graduated water; =werk n graduation-works pl.
...gradig (᷄) a. ⊛ in Zssgn mit a., z.B.: viel=⚵ of many degrees; hundert=⚵ vom Celsiusschen Thermometer: centigrade.
Grad=leiter (ⁿ...) f ⊕, =messer m. phys. graduated scale; ⚵ graduator; =messung f measurement of degrees; =sterne ⚔ m/pl. der Offiziere: stars pl.

showing the rank of a German officer; =teilung f ⸳ =abteilung.
Gradual(e) (᷄ᵛ(᷄)) [lt.] n ⊕d. (29) Cath. eccl. (Stufengesang u. Buch dafür) gradual.
gradu=ell (᷄ᵛ᷄) [fr.] a. ⊛ gradual.
gradu=ier/en (᷄ᵛ᷄) [lt.] **I** v/a. ⊛ (abstufen) to graduate; univ. (einen akademischen Grad erteilen) to bestow a degree upon a p. — **II G/te(r)** s. ⊕ graduate of a university. — **III** ~ n ⊛ und G/ung f ⊕ (Abstufung; Erwerbung eines akademischen Grades) graduation.
Grad=wage (ⁿ...) f ⊕ (Federwage) spring-steel yard; ⚵weise adv. u. F a. gradual(ly), successive(ly); adv. a. by degrees, (lt.) gradatim.
Graf (᷄) [ahd.] m ⊕, (Titel ⊕ ⊕). **Gräfin** f ⊕, dim. Gräfchen (᷄ᵛ), Gräflein (᷄ᵛ) n ⊛ englischer: earl, nichtenglischer: count (f beide: countess).
Grafen=bank (ⁿ...) f ⊕ der alten deutschen Reichsversammlung Counts' bench; =krone f earl's (or count's) coronet; =sitz m earl's seat or manor or estate; =stand m englischer: earldom, nichtenglischer: rank (or dignity) of a count; =titel m title of an earl or a count.
Grafentum (᷄...) n ⊕d. = Grafschaft.
Gräfin f ⊕ u. **Gräflein** dim. s. Graf.
gräflich (᷄ᵛ) a. ⊛ belonging to (or like) an earl, a count or a countess.
Grafschaft (᷄ᵛ) f ⊕ **1.** engl. Würde: earldom. — **2.** Gebiet: county, shire; ~s=gericht n England: county-court.
Gräkomanie (᷄ᵛ᷄) f ⊕ Græcomania.
Gral (᷄) [fr.; *span.] m ⊕c.: der Heilige ~ (sagenhafter Kelch mit Blut des Heilands) the Holy Graal or Grail.
Gram (᷄) [mhd.; *⊙ II vgl. Gries=⊙] **I** m ⊕c. grief, sorrow; (Betrübnis) affliction, sadness; voll ~ sein to have great trouble, to be full of trouble or greatly troubled. — **II gram** [ahd.; *grimm] a. ⊛ meist prädikativ: averse; e-m ⚵ sein to bear a p. a grudge, to be ill-disposed towards a p.; e-m ⚵ werden to take a dislike to a p.
Grämelei ⚴ (᷄ᵛ) [Gram] f ⊛ useless worry(ing) or fretting; brooding over one's trouble.
grämeln (᷄ᵛ) [Gram] v/n. (h.) ⊕a. to worry over things; (übellaunig sein) to be ill-humoured or fretful or irritable.
grämen (᷄ᵛ) [ahd.; * gram] v/a. u. sich ⚵ v/refl. ⊕ to grieve (a.refl.); to afflict a p.; sich ⚵, auch ⚵ to feel grieved or downhearted at (or about) a th.; to sorrow (or fret, worry) about (or over) a th.; sich um et. ⚵ to take a th. to heart; ⚵ Sie sich nicht so! don't fret (or F take on) so!, don't be so downhearted; sich zu Tode ⚵ to pine (or F take on) so!, to pine away; das soll mich wenig ⚵ (bekümmern) that will not (F won't) trouble (or worry) me much; a. v/impers. es grämt mich, daß // I feel grieved (or truly sorry) that //, it grieves me that //.
gram=erfüllt (ⁿ...) a. ⊛ = ⚵voll; =gebeugt a. bowed down with grief.
Gramineen ⚵ ⚵ (᷄ᵛ(᷄)) [lt.] f/pl. ⊕ (Gräser) gramineæ, graminaceæ pl.
Grämler (᷄ᵛ) m ⊛ bisw. a. ~in f ⊕ morose, (or peevish, sullen) person.

grämlich (᷄ᵛ) a. ⊛ morose, peevish, sullen; sour-tempered; ~keit f ⊛ moroseness, peevishness, sullenness.
Grämling (᷄ᵛ) m ⊕d. = Grämler.
Gramm (᷄) [fr.; *grch.] n ⊕e, 6., (abbr. **g**, öft. **g**) gramme; zwei ~ schwer weighing two grammes.
Grammatik (᷄ᵛ᷄) [grch.] f ⊛ (Sprachlehre) grammar; gegen die ~ verstoßen to offend against grammar, to make a grammatical mistake.
grammatikalisch (᷄ᵛᵛ᷄) a. ⊛ relating to grammar, grammatical; ⚵er Fehler grammatical mistake or blunder.
Grammatiker (᷄ᵛ᷄) m ⊛ grammarian.
grammatisch (᷄ᵛ᷄) a. ⊛ according to grammar, grammatical; adv. ⚵ falsch grammatically wrong.   [weight.|
Grammen=gewicht (᷄ᵛ...) n gram(me)-|
Grammophon (᷄ᵛ᷄) [grch.] n ⊕d. (Geschützte Marke) eine Sprechmaschine gramophone: Langenscheidtsche Grammophonplatten für den Sprachunterricht Langenscheidt's gramophone records for language-teaching; ~platte (᷄...) ⊕ f gramophone record.
gram=versunken (ⁿ...) a. ⊛ steeped in grief; geh. Sprache: woe-begone; ⚵voll a. sorrowful, full of affliction, deeply afflicted or grieved.
Gran (᷄) [it. Korn] n (m), für Juwelen: **Grän** [fr., *lt.] n ⊕d, 6. grain.
Granadill=holz f. Grenadillholz.
Granat (᷄ᵛ) [mhd.; *lt. getörnt] m ⊕c. ⚵c. **1.** (dunkelroter Edelstein) (precious or oriental) garnet; grüner ⚵ grossular; gelber ⚵ succinite. — **2.** ⚵c. = Garnele.
Granat=apfel (ⁿ...) ⚵ m pomegranate; =(apfel)baum ⚵ m pomegranate-tree (Pu'nica grana'tum); =apfelblüte, =schale f pomegranate-blossom, -peel; ⚵artig a. ⊛ garnet-like.
Granate (᷄ᵛ᷄) f ⊕ **1.** ⚵ = Grana't. — **2.** ⚵ = Grana't=apfel(=baum). — **3.** [mhd. 16. sae.; *it.] ⚔ artill. shell, grenade; mit ~n beschießen, bestreichen, bewerfen to shell; ~n werfen to throw shells; Schießen n mit ~n shell-practice, shelling a position, &c.
granat=farbig (ᵛⁿ...) a. ⊛ coloured like garnet; =fels ⊕ min. garnet-rock; =feuer ⚔ n, artill. shell-fire; =hagel ⚔ m shower of shells; =kartätsche, öft. =kugel ⚔ f shrapnel-shell; =schmuck m garnet ornament(s pl.); =splitter m, =stück n ⚔ min. splinter, piece of a shell or grenade; =stein m, min.: a) = Granat; b) rock containing garnets.
Grand (᷄) [ndd.: grind] m ⊕b. (Kies) coarse sand, gravel.
Grande (᷄ᵛ) [span.] m ⊕ grandee (auch fig. = vornehme Person); **Grandezza** (᷄ᵛᵖᵛ) f ⊕ grandeeship; weitS. grandeur.
grandicht, grandig (᷄ᵛ) a. ⊛ gravelly.
grandios (᷄ᵛ(᷄)ᵛ) [it.] a. ⊛ (D 10) (großartig) grand, (prächtig) magnificent.
Granit (᷄ᵛ) [mhd.; *it. getörnter Stein] m ⊕c. min. granite.
granit=ähnlich (᷄ᵛⁿ...) a. ⊛, ⚵artig a. granitelike, ⚵ granitic, ...oid, ...iform; =bildung f ⊕: ⚵ granitification.
graniten (᷄ᵛ᷄) a. ⊛ (D 9) of granite.
Granit=felsen (᷄ᵛ...) m ⊕, =gebirge n granite- (or granitic) rock, mountains

⚵ scientific; ⚵ botanical; ⚵ geography; ⊙ machinery; ⚒ mining; ⚔ military; ⚓ marine; ⚵ commercial; ⚵ postal; ⚞ railway.

[granithaltig] — 460 — [grau]

pl.; ⁀haltig *a.* ⓖ granitic; ⁀pflaster *n* granite pavement; ⁀porphyr *m, min.* granite-porphyry; ⁀sand *m* granitic sand; ⁀tapete *f* jasped paper.

Granne (⌣⌣) [ahd.] *f* ⓐ **1.** ⁀ (Achel am Getreide ꝛc.) awn, beard, ⚹ arista; kleine ~ beardlet; mit ~n versehen bearded; mit kurzer ~: ⚹ aristulate. — **2.** (Borste) bristle.

grannen-artig ⁀ (⌣⌣...) *a.* ⓖ beardlike; ⁀los *a.* awnless, beardless.

grannig ⁀ (⌣⌣) [Granne] *a.* ⓖ awned.

grantig F *prov.* (⌣⌣) *a.* ⓖ ill-humoured.

Granulation ⚹ (⌣⌣-tß(⌣)ᴸ) [lt.] *f* ⓐ granulation; ~s-gewebe *n* ⓐ *surg. v.* Heilflächen: granulation-tissue.

Granulier-appara't ⊙ (⌣⌣"...) *m* ⓐ *metall.* granulating machine, auch: granulator.

granulieren (⌣⌣ᴸ⌣) [lt.] ⓐ **1** *v/a.* ⊙ Metalle ꝛc. (körnen) to granulate. — **II** *v/n.* (h.) *surg.* von einer Wundfläche (Körnchen bilden): ⚹ to granulate. — **III** ~ *n* ⓐ ⊙ u. ⚹ granulation.

Granulit ⚹ (⌣⌣ᴸ) *m* ⓐⒸ *min.* (Art weißer Granit) granulite; ⁀isch *a.* granulitic. [granulous, granular.)

granulös ⚹ (⌣⌣ᴸ) [lt.] *a.* ⓖ (D 10) (körnig))

Granulose ⚹ (⌣⌣ᴸ) [lt.] *f* ⓐ *chm.* (Bestandteil der Stärkekörner) granulose.

Graphik ⚹ (⌣ᴸ⌣) [grch. Schreiben] *f* ⓐ (darstellende Kunst) graphic art(s *pl.*); writing and designing.

graphisch (⌣ᴸ⌣) *a.* ⓖ graphic.

Graphit (⌣ᴸ) [grch.] *m* ⓐⒸ *min.* (Art Kohle) graphite, plumbago; (Reißblei) black-lead.

graphit-ähnlich (⌣ᴸ"...) *a.* ⓖ, ⁀haltig *a., min.*: ⚹ graphitoid, graphitic.

graphitisch (⌣ᴸ⌣) *a.* ⓖ *min.* graphitic.

Graphit-stift (⌣ᴸ"...) *m* ⓐ black-lead pencil, black crayon.

Grapholog ⚹ ⓐ, ~e ⚹ (⌣ᴸ⌣(⌣) [grch.] *m* (Handschriftkundiger) graphologist, expert in handwriting.

grapsen F (⌣⌣) [nhd.: grasp] *v/a.* u. *v/n.* (h.) ⓐ **1.** (gierig fassen) to seize eagerly, to snatch (up), F to grab. — **2.** (stehlen) F u. P to pinch, to nick.

Gras (nhd. ⚹, bb. ᴸ) [ahd.: grass] *n* ⓐ *a.* **1.** grass; ⁀ Gräser *pl.* grasses, ⚹ gramineal (or gramin(ac)eous) plants, gramin(ac)eæ *pl.* — **2.** F *fig.* ins ~ beißen to die, F to bite the dust, to kick the bucket, to hop the twig; wo er hinschlägt, da wächst kein ~ (mehr) what he hits he smashes to atoms, his fist is like a sledge-hammer; es ist (viel) ~ darüber gewachsen it has (long) been forgotten, it is ancient history or a thing of the past; er kann das ~ wachsen hören he can hear the grass grow, he thinks (or fancies) himself a very clever fellow.

Gras-affe (⚹...) *m* ⓐ *contp.* young fool; ⁀ähnlich *a.* ⓖ grass-like, grassy ⚹: ⚹ gramineal, gramin(ac)eous; ⁀ährchen *n*, ⁀ähre *f* ⚹ spikelet, spike; ⁀anger *m* green; *vgl.* ⁀and; ⁀art *f* species (or kind) of grass; ⚹ ~arten *pl.*: ⚹ gramin(ac)eæ *pl.*; ⁀artig *a.* — ⁀ähnlich; ⁀bank *f* grassy bank; in Flüssen ꝛc.: grass-bar; ⁀bewachsen *a.* gr.-grown; *vgl.* ⁀reich; ⁀blätt(e)rig *a.*: ⚹ gra-

minifolious; ⁀blume ⚹ *f* = ⁀nelke; ⁀boden *m* grassy soil; ⁀büschel *m* tuft of grass; tussock; ⁀butter *f* (*ant.* Stoppelbutter) butter from the milk of grazing cows. *a.* grass-butter.

Gräschen (⌣ᴸ) *n* ⓐ (*dim. von* Gras) blade of grass. [prairie(-land).)

Gras-ebene (⚹...) *f* ⓐ grassy plain.)

grasen (⌣ᴸ) [ahd.: graze; *Gras] ⓐ **I** *v/n.* (h.) **1.** vom Vieh: to graze, to go grazing; ⚹ lassen to turn out (or put) to grass. — **2.** (Gras mähen) to cut (or mow) the grass. — **3.** *fig.* auf eines anderen Wiese ⚹ (e-m ins Gehege kommen) to trespass on another p.'s property, to encroach, F to get in another p.'s way. — **4.** von Kugeln: (den Boden berühren u. abprallen) to (touch the ground and) ricochet. — **II** ~ *n* ⓐ **5.** (f. 1) grazing, pasturage; (f. 2) cutting (or mowing) of grass.

Graser (⌣ᴸ) *m* ⓐ, ~in *f* ⓐ mower of grass, grass-cutter. [of grass.)

Gräserei (⌣⌣ᴸ) *f* ⓐ cutting (or mowing))

Gras-eule (⚹...) *f* ⓐ *ent.* antler-moth (*No'ctua gra'minis*); ⁀fleck *m:* a) grass-plot; b) auf Kleidern: green stain; ⁀fressend *a.* ⓖ grass-eating, ⚹ graminivorous; ⁀fresser *m/pl.,* zo.: ⚹ graminivora *pl.*; ⁀futter *n* grass-fodder, green food; ⁀fütterung *f* feeding on grass; ⁀geschmack *m* grassy taste; ⁀grün *a.* (as) green as grass; grass-green; ⁀halm *m* blade of grass, gr.-blade; ⚹: ⚹ culm; ⁀hecht *m:* a) *ichth.* small pike; b) F nbb. *fig.* tall and lean young fellow; ⁀hopser, ⁀hüpfer *m, prov.* grasshopper (*Locu'sta*); ⁀hügel *m* grass-grown hill.

grasicht, grasig (⌣ᴸ) [ahd.] *a.* ⓖ **1.** = grasähnlich. — **2.** (mit Gras bewachsen) covered with grass, (over)grown with grass, grassy; *poet.* auch: herbaged.

Gras-land (⚹...) *n* ⓐ grass-land; (Weide) pasture- (or meadow-)land; ⁀lauch ⚹ *m* Spanish garlic, rocambole (*Al'lium Scorodo'prasum*).

Gräslein (⌣ᴸ) *n* ⓐ (*dim. zu* Gras) little blade of grass.

Gras-leinen ⚹ (⚹...) *n* ⓐ grass-cloth or -linen (v. *Boehme'ria ni'vea*); ⁀lilie ⚹ *f:* große ~ lily-spiderwort (*Anthe'ricum Lilia'go*); ⁀mäher *m* grass-cutter or -mower; ⁀mücke *f, orn.* garden-warbler, white-throat (Arten von *Sy'lvia*); zu den ~n gehörig: ⚹ sylvian; ⁀nelke ⚹ *f:* echte ~ cushion pink, lady's-cushion, sea-cushion (*Arme'ria vulga'ris*); ⁀pferd(chen) *n* = ⁀hopser; ⁀platz *m* = ⁀anger; (Rasen) lawn; ⚹reich *a.* grass-covered, rich in grass, grassy.

graß (⚹) [ahd.] *a.* ⓖ (D 10) horrible; (grausig) horrid, awful; *vgl.* gräßlich.

Gras-same(n) (⚹...) *m* ⓐ grass-seed; ⁀sense *f*, ⁀sichel *f* scythe, sickle for cutting grass.

grassieren (⌣⌣ᴸ) [lt. einhergehn] *v/n.* (h.) ⓑ *med.* to rage, spread, prevail.

gräßlich (⌣ᴸ) [nhd.: grisly; *graß] *a.* ⓖ terrible; (schauderhaft) horrible, awful, *geh. Spr.:* dire; (entsetzlich) frightful, dreadful, (scheußlich) hideous, (gespenstisch) ghastly; (grausam) atrocious; ⚹e Hitze fearful (or intolerable) heat; ⚹e Kälte

intense (or biting, bitter) cold; ⚹ (*adv.*) leiden to suffer agony or a martyrdom; ~keit (⌣⌣) *f* ⓐ horribleness, awfulness, direness; hideousness, ghastliness, atrociousness; als Tat: atrocity.

Gras-steppe (⚹...) *f* ⓐ grassy steppe; ⁀stoppel *f* stubble of grass; ⁀stück *n* = ⁀anger; ⁀teppich *m* carpet-like (or velvety) lawn.

Grasung (⌣ᴸ) *f* ⓐ = grasen II.

Gras-wachsen (⚹...) *n* ⓐ growing (of) grass; ⁀weide *f* pasturage, pasture-land; ⁀wuchs *m* growth of grass.

Grat (⌣ᴸ; *Hom.* Grad) [mhd.] *m* ⓑ *c.* **1.** (scharfe Kante) (sharp) edge, an Messern auch: wire-edge; (Leisten) rabbet; (Bergrücken) ridge, crest. — **2.** ⊙ *arch.* (scharfe Kante) arris; vorspringender: groin(ing); (~sparren) hip; *typ.:* ~ am Buchstaben bur. — **3.** *anat.* = Rückgrat. [groining.)

Grat-bogen (⌣ᴸ...) *m* ⓐ groined arch;)

Gräte (⌣ᴸ) [mhd.; *Grat] *f* ⓐ fish-bone, bone of a fish; *fig.* er hat eine ~ (Schwierigkeit) darin gefunden it has given him (unexpected) trouble, F he did not find it all honey.

gräten-artig (⌣"...) *a.* ⓖ like fish-bone; ⁀fisch *m* ⓐ *ichth.* bony fish; ⁀los *a.* ⓖ Fischen: without bones; ⁀reich *a.* von Fischen: full of bones; ⁀stich *m* Näherei: herring-bone stitch. [plane.)

Grat-hobel ⊙ (⌣"...) *m* ⓐ dovetail-)

Gratial(e) (-tß(⌣)ᴸ(⌣) [lt.] *n* ⓑⒸ.(29) (Ehrengeschenk) presentation, (Belohnung) gratuity.

Gratias (⌣ᴸ⌣) [lt.] *n. inv.:* das ~ (Dankgebet nach Tische) sprechen to return thanks, to say grace after dinner.

Gratifikation (-⌣⌣-tß(⌣)ᴸ) [lt.] *f* ⓐ gratuity; (Zulage) extra pay; für Überstunden: overtime. [angry, vexed.)

grätig (⌣ᴸ) *a.* ⓖ a) = grätenreich; b) *fig.*)

gratis (⌣ᴸ) [lt. *gratiis* (abl. *pl.*) aus Gefälligkeit] *adv.* gratis, free of charge, for nothing, without payment.

Gratis-beilage (⌣"...) *f* ⓐ von Zeitungen ꝛc. (free) supplement; ⁀exempla'r *n* ⓐ presentation-copy.

grätsch-beinig (⌣"...) *a.* ⓖ (sperrbeinig) with straddled legs, straddling.

Grätsche (⌣ᴸ) *f* ⓐ = Grätschstellung.

grätschen (⌣ᴸ) *v/n.* (h.) ⓑ Turnerei: to straddle (one's legs), to do the splits.

Grätsch-stellung (⌣"...) *f* ⓐ Turnerei: straddling (of the legs), splits.

Grat-sparren (⌣"...) *m* ⓐ *arch.* hip-, arris-rafter; ⁀tier *n* (Gemse) chamois.

Gratulant (⌣⌣ᴸ) [lt.] *m* ⓐ person who congratulates, auch: congratulator.

Gratulation (⌣⌣⌣-tß(⌣)ᴸ) [lt.] *f* ⓐ (Glückwunsch) congratulation, felicitation; ~s-besuch (⚹...) *m* ⓐ, ~s-schreiben *n* ⓐ congratulatory visit, letter.

gratulieren (⌣⌣ᴸ⌣) [lt.] *v/n.* (h.) ⓑ (Glück wünschen) e-m zu et. ⚹ to congratulate (or felicitate) a p. on a th.; e-m zum Geburtstage ⚹ to wish a p. many happy returns (of the day).

Grat-ziegel (⌣"...) *m* ⓐ hip-tile.

grau (ᴸ) [ahd.: grey] **I** *a.* ⓖ **1.** grey, gray; etwas ⚹ greyish; vom Haar ꝛc. auch: grizzled, grizzly; geh. Sprache: hoary; ⚹ werden to grow (or turn)

Zeichen (s. S. XVII): F familiär; P Volkssprache; ⌐ Gaunersprache; ⚹ selten; † alt (auch gestorben); * neu (auch geboren); ₊₊ unrichtig.

[grauäugig] — 461 — [greifen]

grey or white; seine 2en Haare his grey hair; zo. 2er Bär grizzly bear (Ursus horri'bilis); ⚔ im Dienste 2 w. (er2en) to grow grey (or old) in the service; co. das 2e Elend (Katzenjammer) the blues pl.; path. 2er Star grey cataract; fig. sich über (ob. um et.) 2e (seine 2en) Haare wachsen lassen to worry (not to trouble one's head) about a th. — 2. (ant. lebensfrisch) aging. aged. decaying; ancient; (tebtos) lifeless, (matt) languishing; (düster) gloomy; 2 ist alle Theorie, etwa: all theory is stale; von der Zeit: 2es Altertum hoary (or remote) antiquity; vor 2en Jahren in times of old or of yore or out of mind; aus, seit 2er Vorzeit from times immemorial, since the dawn of history. — II ~(e) n 🏛 3. grey (colour); ins ~e spielen to have a greyish tint or shade; in ~ gekleidet dressed in grey; paint. ~ in ~ grey in grey, camaieu. — 4. das ~ des Morgens the dawn of day, the grey (light) of the morning. — III ~e(r) s. 🏛 5. grey-headed person, greybeard; (Greis, Greisin) greyhead. — 6. der ~e (Esel) donkey, bisw. F neddy, P moke, Jerusalem pony.
grau-äugig (⁻ᴜ...) a. 🏛 grey-eyed; ⹂bart m greybeard; ⹂bärtig a. grey-bearded; ⹂blau a. greyish blue; ⹂braun a. dun (-coloured, a. fuscous).
Grau-bünden ♀ (-ᴗ⁻) npr. n. 🏛 a. (Schweizer Kanton) Grisons pl.
Grau-bündner (-ᴗ⁻) I m 🏛, ~in f 🏛 Grison. — II a. inv. (a. grau-bündnerisch a. 🏛) Grison.
Grauchen (⁻ᴗ) n 🏛 = grau 6.
Grau-drossel (⁻...) f 🏛 orn. thrush, provc. grey-bird (Turdus mu'sicus).
Gräu-el (⁻ᴗ) 2c. f. Greuel 2c.
grau-eln (⁻ᴗ) 🏛 a. = graulen.
grau-en[1] (⁻ᴗ) [ahd.; *grau] I v/n. (h.) 🏛 (grau w.) to turn grey; der Tag (ob. Morgen, Himmel, a. v/impers. es) graut the day begins to dawn or is breaking, it dawns, it (or the day) is dawning. — II ~ n 🏛 (s. I) beim ~ des Tages at the dawn (or break) of day, at day-break.
grau-en[2] (⁻ᴗ) [mhd. (ahd.); *Graus] I v/n. (h.) und sich 2 v/refl., v/impers. 🏛 (stärker als „graulen" und schwächer als „grausen") to be afraid (or frightened of a th.; (schaudern) to shiver (or shudder) at a th.; es graut mir vor ihm (davor) I fear (or dread) him (it); the thought of him (of it) makes me shudder; mir graut's vor dir (G.) I shudder at your sight. — II ~ n 🏛 horror; fear, dread; es wandelte ihn ~ an a shudder crept (or came) over him, he was seized (or stricken) with horror or fear or dismay; von ~ ergriffen horrorstruck or -stricken, horrified.
grau-en-erregend (⁻ᴗ...) a. = ⹂voll.
grau-en-haft (⁻ᴜᴗ) a. 🏛 = grauen-erregend; weitS. (unheimlich) dismal, sinister.
grau-en-voll (⁻ᴜᴗ) a. 🏛 horrid, horrible, ghastly, appalling, full of horror, dire.
grau-farbig (⁻ᴗᴗ) a. 🏛 of a grey(ish) colour, grey(-coloured).

Grau-fink (⁻...) m 🏛 orn. ring- (or rock-) sparrow (Fringil'la petro'nia); ⹂grün a. 🏛 sea-green, glaucous; ⹂haarig a. grey-haired; ⹂kehlchen n 🏛 hedge-sparrow (Acce'ntor modula'ris); ⹂kopf m greyhead. grey-headed person; ⹂köpfig a. grey-headed.
graulen (⁻ᴗ) v/n. (h.), provc. sich 2 v refl. 🏛 to be afraid (or frightened) of ghosts or spectres; v imp. es grault mir, a. ich graule mich I feel nervous.
graulich[1] (⁻ᴗ) [grauen[2] a. 🏛: a) grauen-erregend; b) passivisch: ich bin 2 (habe Angst) I am afraid or frightened.
graulich[2], **gräulich** (⁻ᴗ; Hom. greulich) [grau] a. 🏛 greyish; grizzly; bisw. fig. (düster) gloomy. [white.
gräulich-weiß (⁻ᴜ⁻) a. 🏛 greyish⟩
Grau-malerei (⁻...) f 🏛 paint. camaieu(-painting). painting grey in grey; ⹂meise f, orn. grey titmouse (Parus palu'stris).
Graupe (⁻ᴗ) [nhd. 15. sae.; *slaw.] f 🏛 1. (Gersten) ~n pl. hulled (or peeled) barley, barley-groats pl. — 2. F (Schnee-) ~n = Graupeln.
Graupeln[1] (⁻ᴗ) f pl. inv. sleet.
graupeln[2] (⁻ᴗ) v/n. u. imp. 🏛 to sleet; es graupelt sleet is falling, there is sleet falling or in the air.
Graupel-wetter n 🏛 sleety weather.
Graupen-grütze (⁻ᴗ...) f 🏛 barley-groats pl.; ⹂mühle f barley- (or hulling-, peeling-)mill; ⹂schleim m gruel, barley-water; ⹂suppe f barley-broth.
grau-rot (⁻...) a. 🏛, ⹂rötlich a. reddish-grey; roan.
Graus[1] (⁻) [mhd.: Grieß, Grus] m 🏛 a. (ohne pl.) (Steinschutt) rubble.
Graus[2] (⁻) [mhd.] I m 🏛 a. (ohne pl.) (starkes Grauen) horror, terror, dread, fright, great fear or alarm; das war mir ein ~ it made me shudder, it gave me a shock. — II graus a. 🏛 (D 10) horrible, horrid, terrible, dreadful, frightful, awful.
grausam (⁻ᴗ) [mhd.; *grauen[2]] I a. 🏛 1. cruel (gegen e-n to a p.); (hart) hard, (unmenschlich) inhuman, barbarous, (erbarmungslos) pitiless, unmerciful, merciless; (grimmig) fierce; (blutdürstig) bloodthirsty, truculent (tyrant, &c.); 2es Herz heart of stone or flint or steel; 2e Qual agonizing pain or torment. — 2. F = greulich 2. — II ~e(r) m f 🏛 3. cruel (or inhuman, &c.) one or person.
Grausamkeit (⁻⁻⁻) f 🏛 (vgl. grausam) cruelty; inhumanity, pitilessness; fierceness; bloodthirstiness, truculency; wilde ~ a. savagery, alsTat: savage (or ferocious) act or deed; atrocity.
grau-scheckig (⁻...) a. 🏛 mottled grey, grey-chequered; ⹂schimmel m 🏛 grey horse; ⹂schwarz a. greyish black.
grausen (⁻ᴗ) [ahd.] I v/n. (h.), v/impers. 🏛 ich grause, bss.: mir graust I shudder at a th., I dread a th. — II ~ n 🏛 = Graus[2] I.
grausen-erregend (⁻ᴗ...), **grausen-haft** (⁻ᴜᴗ), **grausig**, **grauslich** (⁻ᴗ) a. 🏛 horrid, dreadful, frightful, awful.
Grau-specht (⁻...) m 🏛 orn. grey woodpecker (Picus canus).
Grauß (⁻) = Graus[1].

Grau-stein (⁻...) m 🏛 geol. greystone; ⹂tier F n (Esel) donkey; vgl. grau 6; ⹂wacke f, geol. 🏛 greywacke; ⹂werden n turning grey; ⹂werk 🏛 n Kürschnerei: (Fell des sibirischen Eichhörnchens) calabar (-skins), squirrel-skins pl., miniver.
Graveur 🏛 (⁻ᴗᴗ⁻) [fr.] m 🏛 d. (Stempel-, Stein-schneider) engraver.
Gravier-anstalt 🏛 (⁻ᴗⁱ⁻ʳ...) f 🏛 engraver's studio or establishment or business (premises pl.); ⹂arbeit f engraver's work, engraving.
gravieren[1] 🏛 (⁻ᴗⁱ⁻) [fr.; *dtsch. graben] v a. 🏛 mit dem Grabstichel: to engrave.
gravieren[2] (⁻ᴗⁱ⁻) [lt.] (beschweren) to weigh down; jur. sich stark 2 deeply to involve o.s., to make o.s. very (or highly) suspicious; 2d (belastend) 2de Umstände aggravating circumstances.
Gravier-kunst 🏛 (⁻ᴗⁱ⁻...) f 🏛 art of engraving, engraver's art, celature; ⹂meißel m graver('s chisel); ⹂raum m engraver's workshop.
Gravierung (⁻ᴗⁱᴗ) f 🏛 (s. gravieren[1]) engraving; (s. gravieren[2]) charge; (Erschwerung der Schuld) aggravation.
Gravier-zeug (⁻ᴗⁱ⁻...) n 🏛 coll. engraving-tools or -implements pl.
Gravis (⁻ᴗ) [lt.ᴗ] m, inv. (pl. bisw. lt. Form: Graves) gr. grave accent.
Gravität (⁻ᴗᴗ⁻) [lt.] f 🏛 (würdiges Auftreten) gravity, grave (or solemn) look or air; F bumptiousness, pomposity.
Gravitation ⹉ (⁻ᴗᴗ⁻tsi(ᴗ)⁻) [lt.] f 🏛 phys. (Schwerkraft) gravitation, gravity; ~s-gesetz (⁻...) n, ⹂kraft f 🏛 law, force of gravity.
gravitätisch (⁻ᴗᴗ⁻ᴗ) [lt.] a. 🏛 grave, solemn; F bumptious, pompous.
gravitieren ⹉ (⁻ᴗᴗ⁻⁻)[lt.]v/n. (h.) phys. (dem Schwerpunkte zustreben) to gravitate.
Gravüre (⁻ᴗᴗ⁻) [fr.] f 🏛 ([Kupfer-]Stich) engraving.
Grazi-e (⁻ᵗsi(ᴗ)⁻) [lt. grātia] f 🏛 1. myth. die (drei) ~n the (three) Graces. — 2. grace (= Anmut).
graziös (-tsi⁻ᴗ) [fr.] a. 🏛 (D 10) graceful.
gräzisieren (-ᴜ⁻ᴗ) v/a. 🏛 (griechisch machen); ⹉ to Græcize, to Hellenize; **Gräzismus** (-ᴗᴗ) m 🏛, **Gräzität** (-ᴗ⁻) f 🏛 (grch. Sprach-eigentümlichkeit) peculiarity of the Greek (language); Greek idiom, ⹉ Græcism.
Gregor (⁻ᴗ, -⁻) 🏛 🏛 🏛 🏛 🏛 🏛 a.. ~ius (⁻ᴗ(ᴗ)⁻) 🏛 y. Gregory; Lianisch (⁻-(⁻)...) a. 🏛 Gregorian; Lianischer Kalender [Papst ~ XIII. 1582] Gregorian Calendar.
Greif (⁻) [ahd.; grch.] m 🏛 c. ob. 🏛 1. Fabel u. her.: griffin. — 2. orn. (Kammgeier) condor (Sarcorha'mphus condor);
greif-bar (⁻ᴗ⁻) a. 🏛 seizable, ⹉ prehensible; fig. (faßbar) tangible, palpable; nicht 2 impalpable, unsubstantial; 2 m. to materialize, substantiate.
greifen (⁻ᴗ) [ahd.] 🏛 b. I v/a. 1. to seize = ergreifen I. — 2. einen Ton, eine Seite auf e-m Instrumente 2 (angeben) to strike a note, to touch a chord. fig. to take a false step. — 3. fig. die Nachricht ist aus der Luft gegriffen ... is a mere fabrication; es ist mit Händen zu 2 it is quite palpable or obvious or evident; die Zahl ist zu hoch gegriffen (angegeben) the figure (or

🎵 Musik; ⹉ Wissenschaft; 🌱 Pflanze; ♁ Geographie; ⊙ Technik; ⚒ Bergbau; ⚔ Militär; ⚓ Marine; ⚖ Handel; ✉ Post; 🚂 Eisenbahn.

[Greifer] — 462 — [Grenzzollamt]

amount) is (put or fixed) too high. — **4. Platz** ⁑ (eine feste Stelle gewinnen) to gain ground or a footing; to become settled. — II v/n. (h.) 5. to hold out one's hand. — 6. mit prp.: **an** den Hut ⁑ to touch one's hat; einem Kranken an den Puls ⁑ to feel a patient's pulse; fig. das greift an den Beutel that drains one's purse, that touches one's pocket. F it runs into money; e-m an die Ehre ⁑ to touch a p.'s honour; der Künstler muß **aus** dem Leben ⁑ ... must draw from (or delineate) life; **in** et. (hinein) ⁑ to thrust one's hand into a th.; in-s Beutel ⁑ to dip into a p.'s pocket or purse; in die Saiten ⁑ to touch (or to run one's fingers over) the strings; er muß oft in die Tasche ⁑ he has often to put his hand(s) in(to) his pocket; von Maschinenteilen: in- ea.⁑ to fit (or catch, lock) into each other; e-m in die Haare ⁑ to pull a p. by the hair; e-m Pferde in die Zügel ⁑ to seize (or take) a horse by the bridle; fig. in seinen eigenen Busen ⁑ to dive into (or to search) one's own heart, to commune with o.s.; **nach** et. ⁑ to stretch out one's hand after a th., to clutch at a th.; to catch (hold of) a th.; fig. nach jedem Mittel ⁑ to snatch at every straw; **um** sich ⁑ to put one's hands about one; fig. (sich verbreiten) to spread, propagate, gain ground; e-m **unter** das Kinn ⁑ to touch (P to chuck) a p. under the chin; fig. e-m unter die Arme ⁑ to give a p.'s aid or support or F a lift; **zu** et. ⁑ to take (hold of) a thing, wählend: to select a th.; zum Äußersten ⁑ to go to extremes, to proceed (or run) to extremities; zu gelinden Maßregeln ⁑ to adopt gentle measures; zu einem Mittel ⁑ to have recourse (or to resort) to ...; zu den Waffen ⁑ to take up arms; zum Schwerte ⁑ to draw the sword. — **7.** (einwirken) to have effect, F to take; ⊙ von Schrauben ꝛc.: to bite, vom Anker auch: to grip. — III sich ⁑ v/recip. 8. to try to catch one another. — IV ~ n ⊛ 9. (f. I und II) catching, capture; seizure; touch(ing). — 10. ~ Kinderspiel: playing (or game) at catch(ing).

Greifer (⸍⸌) m ⊛ 1. (auch: ~**in** f ⊛) p. who seizes (or snatches) a th.; F (Polizist) copper. — 2. Nähmaschine ꝛc.: (Sperrvorrichtung) catcher; typ. gripper.

Greif=fuß (⸍ ...) [greifen] m ⊛ der Krustentiere: ⸗ prehensile foot; **=klaue** f, orn. der Raubvögel: claw, talon; **=schwanz** m, zo.: ~ der Affen: ⸗ prehensile tail; **=zirkel** ⊙ m (side-)cal(l)ipers, cal(l)iper-compasses pl.

greinen (⸍⸌) [ahd.: groan] v/n. (h.) ⊛ 1. to whine, to whimper, to (set up a) cry, F to blubber. — 2. F nordb. (gute Miene zum bösen Spiel m.) to grin and bear it, F to laugh on the wrong side of one's face or mouth.

Greiner (⸍⸌) m ⊛, ~**in** f ⊛ whining person, F blubberer.

Greis[1] (⸍) [(mhd.) ndd.] m ⊛ a. (⊛), **Greisin** f ⊛ aged (wo)man; (wo)man advanced in years.

greis[2] [mhd.: grizzle] a. ⊛ (D10) (grau, bsd. Haare) grey, stärker: hoary; fig. (alt) aged, senile: im greisen Alter at an advanced age.

Greisen=alter (⸌⸍ ...) n ⊛ advanced (or old) age, ⁊ senility.

greisenhaft (⸌⸍⸌) a. ⊛ senile (auch ⁊ path.), aged; ~**igkeit** f ⊛ senility.

Greisin (⸍⸌) f ⊛ f. Greis[1].

Greisler, Greißler provc. (⸍⸌) [Grieß] m ⊛ retail dealer, (small) grocer.

grell (⸍) [mhd.] a. ⊛ von Tönen: (durchdringend) shrill, harsh; piercing, yelling: (sehr hell) dazzling, bright; ⁊e (sehr lebhafte) Augen n/pl. very lively (or sparkling) eyes pl.; ⁊e (schreiende) Farben f/pl. glaring (or gaudy) colours pl.; mit ⁊en Farben schildern to depict in glowing (or flaming) colours ꝛc.; (scharf abstechend) prominent; der Unterschied striking difference; adv. ⁊ gegen et. abstechen to form a sharp contrast to (or with) a th.; v. Farben ꝛc.: to jar; to blend (or harmonize) with; **~heit** (⸍⸌) f ⊛ shrillness, harshness; des Lichtes: dazzling brightness, von Farben: glaringness, gaudiness; fig. einer Schilderung: exaggeration.

Grempel=markt provc. (⸍⸌⸌) [it. compra Kauf] m ⊛ (Trödelmarkt) old-clothes market; **Grempler** (⸍⸌) [mhd. f. o.] m ⊛ old-clothesman.

Grenadier ⚔ (⸌⸌⸍) [fr. Hand-„granaten-"werfer] m ⊛d. (Infanterist, wie Füsilier u. Musketier) grenadier; **~regime'nt** (⸌⸍) n ⊛ grenadier-regiment; (in Engl. bsd. das Erste Garderegiment zu Fuß) Grenadier Guards pl.

Grenadill(holz)=baum ♃ (-⸌⸍...) m ⊛ granadilla tree (v. Brya E'benus).

Grendel, Grengel (⸍⸌) [ahd.] m ⊛ (Pflugbaum) plough-beam or -tree.

Grensing ♃ (⸍⸌) [ahd.; *Grans] m ⊛ d. = Gänserich[2], Gänsefingerkraut.

Grenz=acker (⸍...) m ⊛ boundary-field; **=aufseher** m, **=aufsichtsbeamte(r)** m custom-house officer or official; **=bach** m stream forming a boundary-line or frontier; **=baum** m: a) tree marking a boundary, b) = **=pfahl**; **=befestigung** ⚔ f fortification of the frontier; **=bereiter** m mounted custom-house officer; **=berichtigung** f rectification (or delimitation) of the frontier; **=besichtigung** f inspection of landmarks; **=bevölkerung** f, **=bewohner** m/pl. people living on the frontier; bsd. zw. England u. Schottland: borderers pl.; **=bezeichnung** f demarcation; **=bezirk** m frontier-district; borders pl.; ehm. auch: (Mark) marches pl.; **=dorf** n border-village.

Grenze (⸍⸌) [mhd.; *poln.] f ⊛ limit (auch math.); (Scheidelinie) boundary (-line); von Ländern: frontier, borders pl.; (Saum) edge, verge; (äußerstes Ende) extremity; (Grenzgebiet) confines pl.; die ~n des Kirchspiels bezeichnen to beat the bounds; der Ural bildet die ~ zwischen Europa und Asien the Ural forms (or marks) the boundary between Europe and Asia; alles hat seine ~n there is a limit to every-

thing; die ~ eines Landes überschreiten to cross the frontier; fig. ~n der Bescheidenheit überschreiten to exceed the bounds of modesty; das geht über alle ~n that is beyond all bounds; gewisse ~n halten to keep within certain bounds; eine scharfe ~ ziehen zwischen ǁ to draw a sharp line between ǁ.

grenzen (⸍⸌) v n. (h.) ⊛ **1. an** (oder mit) etwas ⁑ to border on a th., to touch a th.; to be contiguous (or adjacent) to a th.; Frankreich grenzt im Norden an Belgien France is bounded on the north by Belgium; seine Felder ⁑ an die meinen his fields adjoin (or are next) to mine. — **2.** fig. das grenzt an Narrheit it verges (or borders, trenches) on folly; das grenzt ans Unmögliche it is well-nigh (or next to) impossible.

grenzen=los (⸍⸌⸌) a. ⊛ boundless, without limit(s); (unbegrenzt) unlimited, illimitable, (un-endlich) infinite, (ermeßlich) immense, immeasurable; (ungeheuer) enormous; (maßlos) excessive, unbounded; endless; **=losigkeit** (⸍⸌⸌⸍) f ⊛ boundlessness, infinitude; immensity, immeasurableness.

Grenzer (⸍⸌) m ⊛, ~**in** f ⊛ person living on the frontier; bsd. zwischen England und Schottland: borderer; **~=leben** (⸍⸌...) n ⊛ border-life.

Grenz=festung ⚔ (⸍...) f ⊛ frontier-fortress; **=fluß** m, **=gebirge** n river, mountains pl. forming a boundary or frontier; **=gebiet** n confines pl., vgl. **=land**; **=gemeinschaft** f contiguity; **=gott** m röm. myth. Terminus; **=graben** m boundary-ditch; **=jäger** m = **=aufseher**; **=kette** f, **=kordon** n military cordon; **=land** n border-land or -territory, frontier-country, vgl. **=gebiet**; **=linie** f boundary-line, line of demarcation; **=mal** n boundary-mark, landmark; **=mark** f = **=land**; **=mauer** f b.-wall, zwischen Häusern: partition- (or party-)wall; **=nachbar** m next-door (or near) neighbour; **=nachbarschaft** f close proximity; **=ort** m frontier-place; **=pfahl** m boundary-post; **=punkt** m fig. extreme point; **=regulierung** f = **=berichtigung**; **=säule** f pillar marking the frontier; vgl. **=stein**; **=scheide, =scheidung** f marking (off) the boundary, delimitation; **=schloß** n frontier-castle; **=soldat** m soldier serving on the fr.; **=sperre** f embargo on fr.-trade; prohibition of fr.-traffic; **=stadt** f fr.-town; **=stein** m boundary- (or border-)stone, landmark; **=streit(igkeit** f) m dispute about boundaries, frontier-dispute; **=strich** m frontier-zone; **=verkehr** m trading (or traffic) across the frontier; **=vertrag** m agreement about boundaries, boundary-convention; **=wache** ⚔ f frontier-guard, weit S. military cordon; **=wächter** m: a) fr.-guard; b) = **=aufseher**; **=wall** m rampart along (or marking) the boundary; **=wehr** f barrier; **=wert** m, math. limit, maximum (or minimum) value; **=winkel** m, opt.: ~ der Brechung critical angle; **=zaun** m boundary-fence; **=zoll** m custom; **=zollamt** n custom-

---

Signs (see page XVII): F familiar; P vulgar; ꟊ flash; ⸍ rare; † obsolete (died); * new word (born); ✢ incorrect; ♪ music.

[Grenzzollbehörde] — 463 — [grinsen]

house; =zollbehörde f custom-house authorities pl.

Gretchen (⌣⌣) [dim. von Grete] npr/n. (Vn.) Ba. etwa: Maggie, Meg, Margery; Peg(gy); ~tasche f ⊕ ehm.: chatelaine.

Grete (⌣) [abbr. aus Margarete] ⊕ß. Marguerite; vgl. Gretchen; Hans und ~ Jack and (his) Jill or Jenny.

Gretel(ein) (⌣⌣(-) [dim. von Grete] npr/n. (Vn.) Ba. kosend: = Gretchen.

Greu-el (⌣⌣) [mhd.] m ⊕ 1. (Schaudern) horror; (Abscheu) abomination, detestation; es ist mir zum ~ I detest (or loathe) it. — 2. (et. das Grauen erregt) object of a p.'s horror; (-tat) horrible (or atrocious, infamous, nefarious) deed, atrocity; er ist mir ein ~ I detest (or abhor) him; F he is my abomination; die ~ des Krieges the horrors pl. of war.

Greu-el-tat (⌣⌣-) f ⊕ deed of horror.

greulich (⌣⌣) [mhd.: *Greuel] a. ⊕ 1. = gräßlich u. grauenerregend. — 2. F (ungeheuer) enormous, excessive; ⊇e Menge immense quantity; F awful lot.

Griebe (⌣⌣) [ahd.: gr(e)aves] f ⊕ (Speck=)~n gr(e)aves pl.

Griebs ♀ (⌣) m ⊕a. (Kerngehäuse im Obste) core of an apple, &c.

Grieche (⌣⌣) m ⊕, **Griechin** f ⊕ 1. Greek; (Alt=)~, auch: ⟨? Hellene; rel. member of the Greek church; der König der ~n (von Griechenland) the King of the Greeks (of Greece). — 2. (Kenner des Griechischen) Greek scholar, ⟨? Hellenist.

Griechen-freund(in f) (⌣⌣-...) m ⊕: ⟨? philhellene.

Griechenland ♀ (⌣⌣,⌣) npr/n. ⊕α. Greece; (Alt=)~ ancient Greece, ⟨? Hellas; vgl. Grieche 1.

Griechentum (⌣⌣-) n ⊕d. Greek ways and manners pl.; ⟨? Hellenism.

Griechen-volk (⌣⌣,⌣) n ⊕ Greek nation.

griechisch (⌣⌣) a. ⊕ Greek, geh. Sprache: Grecian; die ⊇e Sprache, das ~(e) ⊕ the Greek language, Greek; (alt=)⊇, a. ⟨? Hellenic; ⊇es Feuer Greek fire; ⊇er Jude Greek Jew, eccl. Hellenist; das ⊇e Kaisertum the Byzantine empire; Kenner der ⊇en Sprache Hellenist, Grecian; f. gräzifieren.

griechisch-katholisch (⌣⌣-...) a. ⊕ rel. belonging to the Greek church; ⊇lateinisch(es Wörterbuch) a. Greek-Latin (dictionary); ⊇römisch a. Græco-Roman; ⊇türkisch(er Krieg) a. Græco-Turkish (war).

Gries (⌣) rc. f. Grieß rc. [bear.]

Griesel-bär ⟨? (⌣-) m ⊕ zo. grizzly]

Griesgram (⌣⌣) [mhd.] m ⊕d. 1. (mürrische Stimmung) sullen humour, peevishness; F grumbling mood. — 2. (Person) grumbler, F growler.

gries-grämig, ⊇grämisch, ⊇grämlich(⌣-⌣) a. ⊕ sullen, peevish, morose.

griesicht, griesig¹ (⌣⌣) a. ⊕ agr. u. path. gravelly, gritty, ⟨? sabulous.

Griesig² (⌣⌣) n ⊕ dirt of bees.

Grieß(⌣)[ahd.: grit] m ⊕a. 1. grit, coarse sand, gravel. — 2. ⚒ (Kohlenklein) dusty coal. — 3. path. (Nieren=, Blasen=) gravel, ⟨? arena. — 4. (grob geschrotetes Getreide) grits, (fine) groats pl.; (Reis=) ground rice, (Grießmehl) semolina.

Gries-säule (⌣-...) f ⊕ agr. am Pfluge: piece connecting the plough-beam and the slade.

Grieß-brei (⌣-...) m ⊕ Kocht. gruel, semolina (milk-)pudding; =kloß m dumpling made of ground rice; =mehl ⚘ n semolina, ground rice, meal groats pl.; =suppe f semolina soup; =wart, =wärtel [Grieß = Arena] m ehm. herald, king-at-arms; steward (or marshal) at a tournament.

griff¹ (⌣) impf. von greifen.

Griff² (⌣) [ahd.: grip; *greifen] m ⊕b. 1. (Greifen) seizing, seizure; catching, capture; beim Ringen: grapple, close, hug; (Handschlag) grip (or grasp) of the hand; e-n ~ nach et. tun to snatch (or clutch) at a th.; e-n guten (glücklichen) ~ tun to make a good (lucky) hit; e-n falschen ~ tun to make a mistake, to blunder; einen ~ in die Tasche tun to dive into one's pocket; von Turnern: ~ wechseln to change hands. — 2. (Art des Greifens) manner of grasping (or handling) a th.; er hat den richtigen ~ heraus he has the knack (of doing it), he knows how to do (or to work) it; et. am (ob. im) ~e haben to know how to handle (or to manage) a th.; F to be a good hand (or a dab) at a th. — 3. ⚔ ~ (auch: ~e-machen n) handling (of) arms, manual exercise or drill. — 4. ♪ (Spiel) touch; von Geigenspielern: e-n sicheren ~ haben to play very correctly; e-n falschen ~ tun to strike a false note. — 5. fig. ~e (Ränke, Schliche) intrigues pl., trickery. — 6. ⊕ (Stiel) handle, des Beils, Messers rc.: handle, haft, des Degens: hilt, einer Schrotsäge: tiller, einer Schublade: knob, einer Tür: knob, pull; ↓ ~ e-s Riemens handle of an oar; ⊕ = Griffbrett; typ. ~ am Preßbengel rounce-handle. — 7. als Maß: (Handvoll) handful; (Fingerspitze voll) pinch. — 8. hunt. (Klaue der Raubvögel) clutch, claw, talon.

Griff-brett ♪ (⌣-...) n ⊕ einer Geige rc.: fret-board; eines Klaviers rc.: finger-(or key-)board.

Griffel (⌣⌣) [ahd. (P: *Griff)] m ⊕ 1. Alt. (Schreibstift) style, ⟨? graphium, stylus; fig. (Schreibfeder) pen. — 2. jetzt meist: (Schieferstift) slate-pencil. — 3. ⊕ Kupferstechkunst: = Grabstichel. — 4. ♀ (des Fruchtknotens) ⟨? pistil, style, stylus.

griffel-ähnlich(⌣-...)a.⊕⟨?stylar,...oid, ...iform; anat. ⊇er Fortsatz styloid apophysis; ⊇förmig a. = ähnlich.

...griff(e)lig (..."⌣(⌣)⌣) a. ⊕ zB. viel⊇ ⟨? stylous, polygynian.

griffel-los ♀ (⌣⌣...) a. ⊕ without pistil(s), ⟨? acephalous; =schiefer m ⊕ min. grapholite; =spitzer m pencil-sharpener. [(the) shape of a handle.]

griff-förmig (⌣-...) [griff-förmig] a. ⊕ in]

Grille (⌣⌣) [ahd.; *grell] f ⊕ 1. ent.: a) cricket (Gryllus); b) bisw. = Heuschrecke u. Heimchen. — 2. [nhd.] fig. (wunderlicherEinfall) freak,whim,fancy;(Schrulle) crotchet, fad; ~n pl. (imaginary) cares, anxious thoughts pl.; F fit of the blues; ~n fangen, sich mit ~n plagen to brood over one's troubles, to conjure up sad thoughts, to be in a brown study; to (be full of) worry, to be low-spirited; e-m ~n in den Kopf setzen to turn a p.'s head or brain.

Grillen=fänger(in f) (⌣⌣-...) m ⊕ whimsical (or capricious, crotchety) person, F faddist; =fängerei f whimsicalness, fancifulness, crotchetiness; whims and fancies pl.; ⊇fängerisch a. ⊕ whimsical, capricious, fanciful, crotchety; festful, maggoty, faddy.

grillenhaft (⌣⌣⌣) a. ⊕ (voller Launen) capricious, changeable; (wunderlich) eccentric, queer (vgl. grillenfängerisch).

Grillenhaftigkeit (⌣⌣⌣-) f ⊕ capriciousness, changeableness, eccentricity (vgl. Grillenfängerei).

grillen-krank (⌣⌣-...) a. ⊕: ⟨? hypochondriac(al); =krankheit f ⊕: ⟨? hypochondria(sis).

grillig (⌣⌣) a. ⊕ = grillenhaft

Grimasse (⌣⌣⌣) [nhd. 1700; fr. grimace; *ahd. grima Maske] f ⊕ (Fratze) grimace; e-m ~n machen oder schneiden to make grimaces or (wry) faces at a p.

grimassen-artig(⌣⌣⌣-...)a.⊕, **grimassen-haft** (⌣⌣⌣) a. grimacing, grinning.

Grimassen-schneider (⌣⌣⌣-...) m ⊕ one who makes grimaces. [badger.]

Grimbart (⌣⌣) m ⊕d. Tierfabel: (Dachs)]

grimm¹ (⌣) [ahd.: grim] a. ⊕ very angry or cross (vgl. grimmig).

Grimm² (⌣) [nhd.; *⊇¹] m ⊕ (violent) anger, wrath, stärker: fury; (Wut) rage, (Erbitterung) exasperation; in ~ geraten to get into a rage or a temper, to fly into a passion, to grow angry.

Grimm-darm (⌣⌣-) m ⊕ anat.: ⟨? colon; =darm-entzündung f,path.: ⟨?colonitis; =darm-gekröse n, anat.: ⟨? mesocolon.

grimmen (⌣⌣) [ahd.] I v/a. ⊕ 1. to cause great pain; v/impers. es grimmt mich (ob. mir) im Bauche I have the gripes. — 2. fig. das grimmt (verdrießt) mich it vexes (or annoys) me. — II ~ n ⊕ 3. = Bauchgrimmen; path. auch: colic.

grimm-erfüllt (⌣⌣-) a. ⊕ full of anger or wrath, wrathful, furious, F in a rage.

grimmig (⌣⌣) [ahd.] a. ⊕ (f. Grimm) full of anger or wrath; furious, enraged, exasperated, fierce; ⊇es Tier ferocious (or savage) beast; er hat ein ⊇es Aussehen ... a grim look (about him); F fig. (schrecklich) terrible; (übermäßig) excessive; mit ⊇em Blick with a face (or look) as black as thunder; adv. es ist ⊇ kalt it is bitterly (or intensely, F icy) cold.

Grimmigkeit (⌣⌣-) f ⊕ fierceness; ferocity; grimness.

Grind (⌣) [ahd.: Grand] m ⊕b. path. scab, scurf, scald; chronischer: ⟨? impetigo; (Schorf, Krustenbildung) ⟨? eschar; (Räude der Haustiere) mange; Bildung e-s ~es: ⟨? incrustation.

Grind-ampfer ♀ (⌣-...) m ⊕ bitter dock (Rumex obtusifo'lius); ⊇artig a. ⊕ path.: ⟨? scabious.]

Grindel — Grendel. [⟨? scabious.]

grindicht, grindig (⌣⌣) a. ⊕ scabbed, scabby, ⟨?impetiginous;(räudig)mangy.

Grind-kopf (⌣-...) m ⊕ P scald-head; ⊇köpfig a. ⊕ P scald-headed; =kraut ♀ n = Skabiose.

grinsen (⌣⌣) [nhd.: grin; *greinen] I v/n. (h.) ⊕ to grin; ⊇b grinning;

⟨? scientific; ♀ botanical; ♀ geography; ⊕ machinery; ⚒ mining; ⚔ military; ↓ marine; ⊛ commercial; ⊷ postal; 🚂 railway.

simpering, smirking and smiling. — II ~ n Ⓔ (broad) grin.

Grippe (ˇ) [fr.]; *ndd. greifen] f ⓼ 1. *path.* influenza, grip. — 2. (Rieselrinne) irrigation-canal.

Grips F (ˇ) [greifen] m Ⓐa. (power of) comprehension, brain(s *pl.*); er hat wenig ~ F... little (or no) gumption.

Griseldis (ˇˇ) [it.] *npr f. inv.* Griselda.

Grisette (ˇˇ) [fr.] f ⓼ grisette.

Grison (ˇˇ) m Ⓓ *zo.* grison (*Galictis*).

gr.-kath. *abbr.* = griechisch-katholisch.

grob (ˇ, flektiert: ˇˇ) [ahd.: gruff] **I** *a.* ⓺(D 2,7) 1. (*ant.* fein, höflich) rude, uncivil, impolite; (roh) coarse, uncouth, brutal; (ungeschliffen) rough, unpolished, ill-bred, churlish; s. Bohnenstroh; der Flegel insolent (or impertinent) fellow; der Kerl oder Mensch = Grobian; *Sprichw.* auf e-n groben Klotz gehört ein der Keil, *etwa*: a rough customer needs rough handling, diamond cut(s) diamond. — 2. (stark, dick) coarse, stout, *z.B.* des Brot, Tuch *2c.* coarse bread, cloth, &c.; die Arbeit rough work; der Betrug, Fehler gross imposition, error; des Geschütz great (or heavy) guns *pl.* or ordnance; der Lügner impudent liar; die Münze large coin; die Stimme rough voice; die Unwahrheit great untruth, big lie; s. Unfug, des Vergehen grievous offence; des Versehen serious oversight or blunder; die Züge coarse features *pl.*; *adv.* e-n Ⓔ anfahren to snub a p., F to give a p. the rough side of one's tongue. — **II** ~e(s) n Ⓔ 3. coarse part or quality; aus dem Ⓔ (gröbsten) arbeiten to work in the rough, to rough-hew; *fig.* to pave the way. — **III** ~ n Ⓓ 4. = Kroppzeug.

Grob-blech Ⓞ (ˇ...) m ⓺ strong tinned iron; =**draht** m (Drähtig *a.* ⓺) coarse-thread(ed); =**fadig**, =**fäd(en)ig** ⓺ *a.* coarse-threaded; =**faserig** *a.* coarse-fibred; =**feile** ⓼ f rasp, rough file; =**garn** ⓼ n coarse-spun; =**gewicht** ⓼ n gross-weight; Ⓓglied(e)rig *a.* large-limbed; stoutly built; Ⓓhaarig, Ⓓhäutig *a.* coarse-haired, -skinned.

Grobheit (ˇˇ) f ⓺ 1. (grobes Benehmen) rude, &c. (s. grob 1) conduct; rudeness; coarseness, uncouthness; roughness; insolence. — 2. (grobe Rede, Handlung) incivility; insolence, impertinence; einem ~en sagen oder F an den Hals werfen to talk coarsely (or roughly) to a p., stärker: to shower abuse on (or to abuse) a p.

Grobian (ˇ(ˇ)-) [dtsch-lt.] m Ⓓd. rude (or coarse, ill-bred, &c.) fellow; s. grob 1; boor, churl; stärker: bully, brute, bear.
[stone.⌉

Grob-kalk (ˇ...) m ⓺ *geol.* coarse lime-⌋ **grob-körnig** (ˇ...) *a.* ⓺ coarse-grained.

gröblich (ˇ) [mhd.] *a.* ⓺ 1. *von Zerkleinertem*; somewhat coarse. — 2. *adv.* (stark) sich Ⓔ irren to be grossly (or greatly) mistaken.

Grob-mörtel (ˇ...) m ⓺ = Beton.

Gröbs (ˇ) [mhd.] m Ⓐa. 1. ♀ = Griebs. — 2. *anat.* = Kehl(n)opf.

Grob-sack P (ˇ...) m ⓺ = Grobian; =**schmied** m blacksmith, farrier; =**schmiedearbeit** f blacksmith's (or farrier's) work; =**sinnlich** *a.* ⓺ grossly sensual; =**zeug** F n = Kroppzeug; =**zwilch**, =**zwillich** ⓼ m (made) of coarse twill.

Groden (ˇ) [ndd.; *grün] m Ⓔ pastureland formed by alluvial soil.

Groenhart-holz (grü"nˇ...) [ndl.] n ⓺ greenheart- (or bebeeru-) wood (von *Nectandra Rodiaei*).

Grog ⚓ (ˇ) [engl.] m Ⓓ grog.

grölen, *a.* **gröhlen** P (ˇ) [ndd.; *grell] *v/n.* (h.) und *v/a.* ⓼ to squall, bawl (out), scream; **Gröler(in** f ⓺) m ⓺ squaller, bawler, F grizzle-pot.

Groll (ˇ) [mhd. 14. *sae.*] m Ⓓb. resentment, rancour; malice, grudge; (eingewurzelter Haß) inveterate hatred, animosity; e-n ~ gegen e-n haben to have a spite (or grudge) against a p.

grollen (ˇˇ) [mhd.: growl] *v/n.* (h.), *bisw.* *a. v.a.* ⓼ 1. vom Donner: to roll, peal, rumble; oder Donner, *auch*: claps (or peals) *pl.* of thunder. — 2. (Groll hegen) einem Ⓔ to have a spite (or grudge) against a p.; Ⓔd resentful, spiteful; **Groller(in** f ⓺) m ⓺ rancorous (or spiteful) person. [⓺α. Greenland.⌉

Grönland ♀ (ˇˇ) [isld. Grünland] *npr/n.*⌋ **Grönländer** (ˇˇ) **I** m ⓺, ~**in** f ⓺ Greenlander. — **II** *a. inv.* (*a.* **grönländisch** *a.* ⓺) Greenland(ish).

Grönland-fahrer ⚓ (ˇˇ...) m ⓺ Greenlandman, whalefisher, whaler.

Gros[1] (größ) [fr. *grosse* f: 12 Dtzd.] n Ⓔ6. gross; 5 ~ Stahlfedern 5 gross of nibs. **Gros**[2] (grō) [fr.] Ⓔ **I** n (Haupttheer) ⚔ das ~ der Armee the main body (or the bulk) of the army. — **II** ⚓ m (schwerer Seidenstoff) ~ de Naples *a., inv.* gros(-) de(-)Naples. — **III** s. en gros.

Groschen (ˇˇ) [mhd.; *lt. *grossus*] m Ⓔ 1. (ehm. [Silber-] ~ von 12 Pfennigen, jetzt F Zehnpfennigstück) *etwa*: penny. — 2. *meton.* (Geld) er hat keinen ~ he hasn't a farthing (to bless himself with); je-paar ~ his few pence, the little money (that) he has; einen schönen ~ verdienen to earn good money, to make a fine⌉

Groß[1] (ˇ) n Ⓐa. = Gros[1]. [income.⌉ **groß**[2] (ˇ) [ahd.: great] **I** *a.* ⓺ (D 10) 1. great; (dick) big, stout; (umfangreich) large, bulky, voluminous, F sizable; (geräumig) spacious, ample, stärker: vast; (ungeheuer) huge, immense, enormous; der (langer) Mensch tall man; der (bedeutender) Mann great (or eminent) man; er ist Ⓔ für sein Alter he is tall for his age; Ⓔ, größer m. to make great, to enlarge, *fig.* to aggrandize; Ⓔ, größer werden to grow large(r) or big(ger) or tall(er), to increase (in size or bulk); eine größere (ziemlich große) Zahl a pretty large number. — 2. sich (*dat.*) ein Ⓔs Ansehen geben, eine Ⓔ Miene annehmen to assume (or give o.s.) great airs; Ⓔ Augen machen to open one's eyes wide; Ⓔ Ausgaben machen to spend a great deal of money, to have large (or great) expenses; sein Ⓔr (erwachsener) Bruder his grown-up (or big) brother; der Buchstabe capital letter; auf dem Fuße leben to live in grand (or fine) style; den Dank! great (or many) thanks!; eine Ⓔ Dummheit a very silly thing, a most foolish act; Ⓔ Geschäfte important business (transactions *pl.*); die größere Hälfte the greater half, vom Gewinn: the lion's share; ⓼ Ⓔs Handlungshaus great (or large) firm; der Ⓔ Haufe, die Ⓔ Masse des Volkes the great multitude, the common herd, F the million; ein Ⓔs Haus m. to keep up a fine establishment; den Ⓔn Herrn spielen to play the fine gentleman, F to do the swell; Ⓔ Kinder grown-up children; das Ⓔ Los the first prize in a lottery; im Ⓔn Maßstabe on a large scale; ♀ der ~e Ozean the Pacific (Ocean); mit um so größerem Rechte with all the more reason; der größere Teil the larger (or better) half; der größte Teil the greatest part or portion; F *co.* ein Ⓔs Tier a great gun or swell; ein der Umweg a long way round; die Ⓔ Welt: a) the world in general; b) the fashionable world, society (people); die Ⓔ Zehe big toe; ⚓ der Mast, Ⓔs Segel *2c.* = Groß-mast, =segel *2c.*; ♪ die Terz, Quint *2c.* major third, fifth, &c. — 3. zur Maßbestimmung mit *acc.*: ein sechs Fuß Ⓔer Soldat a soldier six feet high; gleich Ⓔ of the same size; von einer Person: of the same height or stature; so Ⓔ wie eine Erbse as big (or large) as a pea; ich bin um e-n Kopf größer als er I am (by) a head taller than he (is); wie Ⓔ ist der Baum? (of) what size (or height) is the tree?; wie Ⓔ ist er, sie? what is his, her height?; wie Ⓔ war seine Freude! how great was his joy!; der Rock ist zu Ⓔ für mich the coat is too large (or big) for me. — 4. *adv.* einen Ⓔ achten to have a high (or great) opinion of a p.; einen Ⓔ anblicken to stare at a p., to look in blank amazement at a p.; sich nicht Ⓔ um et. bekümmern not to trouble (o.s.) much about a th.; Ⓔ denken to think nobly; Ⓔ von einem denken to think highly of a p.; bei ihnen geht's Ⓔ her they live in splendid (or F grand) style, F they are going it; Ⓔ handeln to act magnanimously or nobly; sich mit et. Ⓔ machen to (make great) boast of a th.; et. nicht Ⓔ nötig haben to have no great need of a th.; Ⓔ sprechen to talk big; Ⓔ tun *s. bsd. Art.* — **II** ~**e(r)** m, ~**e(s)** n Ⓔ 5. die ~en *pl.*: a) (Erwachsene) grown-up people, adults *pl.*; b) (Vornehme) the great (of this world), F grandees, big folks *pl.*; die ~en und Geringen high and low; ~e u. Kleine, Ⓔ und klein great and small, old and young. — 6. Friedrich der ~e Frederick the Great; Karl der ~e Charlemagne. — 7. das ~e an ... what(ever) is great in ...; et. ~es something great or big; im Ⓔn (und ganzen) on the whole; on an average; ⚓ nur im Ⓔn verkaufen to sell only wholesale; er (be)treibt sein Geschäft im Ⓔn he does business wholesale or on a large scale or in a large way; es ist et. ~es im Werke there is some great (or important) scheme on foot; im ~en wie im Kleinen treu sein to be faithful both in great things and in small.

Zeichen (s. S. XVII): F familiär; P Volkssprache; F Gaunersprache; ~ selten; † alt (auch gestorben); * neu (auch geboren); +* unrichtig;

[Großadmiral] — 465 — [Grube]

Groß=admira'l ↓ (″…) m ⊕ Lord High Admiral, in Engl.: Admiral of the Fleet; =almosenier m Grand Almoner; ⚥artig a. ⊕ grand, imposing; (erhaben) lofty, sublime; ℓes Denkmal noble monument; ℓe Entwürfe vast schemes pl.; F iro. das ist 2! that's too much (of a good thing)!; =artigkeit f grandeur, loftiness; vastness; ⚥äugig a. large-eyed; =aventurhandel ❀ m gross adventure, large speculation; =bauer m yeoman, F large farmer; ⚥beerig ⚘ a. big-berried; =betrieb m wholesale trade or manufacture; ⚥blätt(e)rig ⚘ a. large-leaved; ⚥blumig ⚘ a. with large flowers; =brita″nnien ⚥ n (Engl. u. Schottland) Great Britain; =brita″nnisch a. of Great Britain, British; ⚥deutsch a. belonging to Greater Germany, Pan-Germanic; =dutzend n = ⊕.

Größe (⌣) [ahd.] f ⊕ 1. (s. groß 1) greatness; (Dicke) bigness, stoutness; von Früchten, Steinen 2c.: size, v. Personen: tallness, height, stature; (Ausdehnung) dimension(s pl.); (Geräumigkeit) width, spaciousness, ⚘ amplitude, stärker: vastness; (Raum=inhalt) volume, bulk, e=s Gefäßes: cubical contents pl.; ~ e=s Vergehens grievousness (stärker: enormity) of an offence; Dichter erster~ first-rate poet; ast. Stern erster, zweiter ~ star of the first, second magnitude. — 2. math. (un)bekannte, gegebene ~ (un)known, given quantity or value. — 3. (berühmte Person) eminent person, notability, in der Kunst 2c.: star; neue ~ rising star; unbekannte ~ fig. unknown magnitude.

groß=elterlich (″…) a. ⊕ of (or belonging to) the grandparents; =elter=mutter f ⊕ great grandmother; =eltern pl. grandparents pl.; =elter=vater m great grandfather; =enkel(in f) m great grandson (f great granddaughter).

Größen=lehre (⌣″…) f ⊕ math. geometry, weitS. mathematics; =reihe f, math. series of values or quantities; progression.

großen=teils (⌣⌢″) adv. to a large extent, in a great measure; mostly.

Größen=verhältnis (″⌣…) n ⊕ proportion in size or magnitude; =wahn (=sinn) m mad (or morbid) ambition, ⚘ megalomania.

Größer=werden (⌣⌣⌣⌣) n ⊕ increase of size or bulk or height, growth.

Groß=falter (″…) m/pl. ⊕ ent.: macrolepidoptera pl.; =flügler m, ent. megaloptera pl.; =fürst(in f) m grand-duke (f -duchess); ⚥fürstlich a. ⊕ gr.-ducal; ⚥gemustert ❀ a. of a large pattern; ⚥gesinnt a. high-minded; =gewerbe ❀ n wholesale industry or manufacture; =gewicht ❀ n gross weight; ⚥glied(e)rig a. large-limbed, athletic; =griechenland ⚥ n (Alt.: das griechische Unteritalien) Greater Greece; =gru″ndbesitz m large estates pl., great landed property; =gru″nd=besitzer(in f) m great land-owner; =handel ❀ m wholesale trade; ~ treiben to do (or carry on) business (or to trade) wholesale; =händler(in f) m wholesale dealer or trader; (whole-sale) merchant; ⚥händlerisch a. wholesale; =handlung(=shaus n) f ❀ wholesale firm or house or business.

Großheit (⌣⌣) f ⊕ fig. greatness, loftiness of mind.

Groß=herr (″…) m ⊕: a) suzerain (lord); b) bsd. ehm. Titel des Sultans: Grand S(e)ignior; ⚥herrlich a. ⊕ lordly; ⚥herzig a. of the Grand S(e)ignior; ⚥herzig a. magnanimous, (edelmütig) noble-minded, generous; =herzigkeit f magnanimity, noble-mindedness, generosity; =herzog(in f) m grand-duke (f -duchess); ⚥herzoglich a. grand-ducal; =herzogtum n grand-duchy or -dukedom; =hirn n, anat.: ⚘ cerebrum; =hundert n (120 Stück) long (or great) hundred, hundred and twenty.

Grossierer ❀ (⌣⌣⌣) [fr. † grossier] m ⊕ = Großhändler.

Groß=industrie (″…) f ⊕ wholesale manufacture or industry; =industrielle(r) m head of a large industrial concern or establishment, F large manufacturer or mill-owner; =inquisitor m ehm. grand-inquisitor.

Großist (⌣⌣) [it.] m ⊕ = Großhändler.

groß=jährig (″…) a. ⊕ of (full) age; =jährigkeit f ⊕ majority; =kämmerer, =kammerherr m Lord Chamberlain; =kanzler m (High) Chancellor; =kapitalist m great (or large) capitalist; =kind n grandchild; =knecht m headman (or upper man-servant) on a farm; ⚥knochig a. large-boned; =kopf m, ent. (Schwammspinner) gipsy-moth (Ocne′ria dispar); ⚥köpfig a. large- (or big-) headed, ⚘ macrocephalous; =kordon m (breites Ordensband zum Großkreuz) grand-cordon; ⚥körnig a. large-grained; =kreuz n eines Ordens: grand-cross (a. Inhaber e=s solchen); =macht f (great (or first-rate) power; die=mächte the great powers pl.; ⚥mächtig a. high and mighty //; als Titel: ~fier // great and mighty //; =macht=kitzel m eagerness to become a great power; =macht=stellung f position as (or of) a great power; =magd f upper maid-servant on a farm; =mama′ F f grandmamma; =mannssucht f = Größenwahn; ⚥maschig a. with large (or wide) meshes; =mast ↓ m mainmast; =maul n large and wide mouth; fig. boaster; vgl. =sprecher; ⚥mäulig a. large-mouthed; fig. big in one's talk, boastful; =mäuligkeit F f boastfulness; =meister m eines Ritterordens 2c. grand-master, a. GrandMaster; =meisterschaft f, =meistertum n, =meister=würde f grand-mastership; ⚥mögend a. = ⚥mächtig; =mo′gul m in Indien Great Mogul; =muhme f = =tante; =mut [Mut m] f generosity; vgl. ⚥herzig; ⚥mütig, ⚥mut(s)voll a. generous (-hearted), large-minded; =mütigkeit f = =mut; =mutter f grandmother; vgl. =mama; =mütterchen N f granny; ⚥mütterlich a. grandmotherly, …like; ⚥näsig a. big-nosed; =neffe m, =nichte f grandnephew m, grandniece f; bisw. great-nephew m, -niece f; =oheim, =onkel m granduncle, great-uncle; =Okta′v n: a) ❀ large octavo; b) ♪ (Hauptregister einer Orgel) great (or full) organ; =papa′ F m grandpapa′; =prahler(ei f) m = =sprecher(ei); ⚥prahlerisch, F ⚥pratschig a. = ⚥sprecherisch; =prior m grand-prior; =Qua′rt ⚥ n large quarto; =regal(papier) ❀ n imperial; =schiffahrts=kanal, =weg m grand canal, canal for sea-going vessels; =siegel=bewahrer m Keeper of the Great Seal, Lord Keeper; =sinn m loftiness of mind; ⚥sinnig a. lofty-minded; =sohn m grandson; =sprecher (in f) m great boaster, braggart, F braggadocio, one who talks big, windbag; =sprecherei f big (or vain-glorious) talk, boasting and bragging, F gas(ing); ⚥sprecherisch a. boastful, F full of brag, talking big; ⚥spurig = breitspurig; =staat m powerful state; vgl. =macht; =stadt f large (or big) town, (populous) city, ⚘ metropolis; =städter(in f) m inhabitant of a large town or city; ⚥städtisch a. (characteristic) of a large town or city, ⚘ metropolitan; =sulta′n m = =herr b; =tante f grandaunt, great-aunt; =tat f great (or noble) deed or exploit; =tausend n (1200 Stück) twelve hundred.

größten=teils (⌣⌣″⌣) adv. for the most part, mostly, chiefly, generally; in a great measure, to a large extent.

größt=möglich (″⌣⌣) (bff.: möglichst groß) greatest possible, as large as possible.

Groß=tuer(in f) m (″…) swaggerer, vgl. =sprecher(in); =tuerei f swagger (-ing), vgl. =sprecherei; ⚥tuerisch a. swaggering, boastful; ⚥tun v/n. (h.) ⊕⚘⚘ to give o.s. great airs, to talk big, to swagger; mit et. 2 to boast (or brag) of a th.; =türke m Grand Turk; =vater m grandfather, geh. Spr.: grand-sire; ⚥väterlich a. grandfatherly, …like; =vater=stuhl m easy- or arm-chair, F soft: grandfather's chair; =verkehr ❀ m wholesale trade; =vieh n large cattle; =vika′r m, Cath. eccl. apostolic vicar; =weidwerk n, hunt. shooting (or hunting for) big game; =wesir m grandvizier; =würden=träger(in f) m high dignitary (or office-bearer) of the crown; ⚥ziehen v/a. ⊕⚘⚘ to rear; =ziehen n, agr. breeding (or rearing) of cattle; ⚥zügig a. on a large (or grand) scale.

Grot (⌣) m ⊕ c.6. (ehm. norbb., bsd. bremische u. hamburgische Scheidemünze) groat.

grotesk (⌣⌣) [it. nach Art der „Grotten"-gemälde] a. ⊕, ~ f ⊕ typ. (Steinschrift) grotesque; ~e ⊕ Kunst: grotesque (-ness); ~(en)=maler(ei f) m grotesque-painter(-painting). [grotto.]

Grotte (⌣⌣) [it.; * grch. Krypta] f ⊕

Grotten=arbeit (⌣⌣…) f ⊕ = =werk; =arbeiter, =macher m rock-work maker; =tempel m temple in rock-work; =verzierung f, =werk n grotto-, rock-work.

grub (⌣) impf. von graben.

Grübchen (⌣⌣) n ⊕ (dim.: Grube) dimple; ~=spiel n ⊕ cherry-pit, mit Münzen: pitch-and-toss, mit Knöpfen: pitch-button.

Grube (⌣⌣) [ahd. ⌣, grove, *graben] f ⊕ pit, ⚒ a. mine, (Vertiefung) pit; (Höhlung) hollow, hole, cavity, excavation; anat., zo. ⚘: ⚘ fovea; (Pocken)~ pockmark; Sprichw. wer andern eine ~ gräbt, fällt selbst hinein he who digs a pit for

[grübe] — 466 — [gründen]

others (often) falls in himself; harm watch, harm catch; a. the engineer hoist with his own petar(d) (SH.); fig. e-n in die ~ bringen to cause a p.'s death; bibl. in die ~ fahren to go down into the grave or pit.

grübe (⌣́) subj. impf. v. graben.

Grübelei (‿⌣́) f ⑯ close search, minute investigation (tiefes Sinnen) brooding, pondering, reverie, (deep) meditation, rumination, speculation; musing, F brown study; (Spitzfindigkeit) subtlety, hair-splitting.

grübeln (⌣́‿) (ahd.: *graben) I v/n. (h.) ⑫a. 1. to make minute investigations about; (tief nachsinnen) to brood (or ponder, ruminate) on or over; to puzzle (or rack) one's brains about. — 2. (in etwas herumgraben) to stir a th. up. — II ~ n ⑳ 3. (f. 1) = Grübelei. — 4. (f. 2) stir.

Gruben=anteil ⚒ (⌣́‿...) m ⚒ = Kux; =**arbeit** f (ant. Tagarbeit) work(ing) in the mine, a.: underground-work; =**arbeiter** m miner, pitman; =**bau**, =**betrieb** m mining (work), underground working; =**blende** f miner's lantern; =**brand** m underground fire (in a coal-pit); =**explosion** f colliery explosion; =**fahren** n going down (or descent) into a mine or shaft; =**feld** n: a) field containing a mine, Am. u. Australien oft: (mining) claim; b) mining district; =**förderung** f output of a mine; =**gas** n: a) (schlagende Wetter) fire- (or choke-)damp; b) chm. = Sumpfgas; =**gebäude** n underground-workings pl.; =**gericht** n court of miners; =**gezähe** n, coll. mining (or miner's) tools pl.; =**grund** m bottom of a mine; =**junge** m miner's boy; =**kittel** m miner's frock or dress; =**kohle** f Kohlenbrennerei: small coal; =**kompaß** m miner's compass; =**licht** n miner's (or Davy-)lamp, oft: davy; =**mütze** f miner's cap; =**sand** m pit-sand; =**sohle** f level of a mine; =**steiger** m overseer of a mine; =**unfall** m, =**unglück** n accident in a mine; =**wasser** n water in a mine; =**werk** n pit-work; vgl. =**arbeit**; =**wetter** n = =**gas** a; =**zimmerung** f timbering of a mine.

grubig (⌣́‿) a. ⑯ full of pits or holes or cavities; (mit Grübchen) pitted.

Grübler (⌣́‿) m ⑱, ~**in** f ⑰ (f. grübeln) ponderer, brooding (or ruminating, pensive, meditative) person; (Träumer) dreamer, (idle) speculator; ⌣isch a. ⑯ pensive, meditative; dreamy.

Grübling (⌣́‿) m ⑱d. = Kartoffel.

Grude (⌣́‿) (nhd.) f ⑱: a) (heiße Asche) hot ashes or cinders pl.; b) (Herd mit heißer Asche) hearth (heated) with hot ashes; c) ~**herde**, ~**ofen** oven (or hearth) heated with small coke.

Gruft (⌣́) (ahd.) f ⑩ 1. (Grabgewölbe) tomb, (family-)vault, fürstliche a.: mausoleum. — 2. (Grube) pit, (Höhle) cave(rn).

Gruft=begräbnis (⌣́...) n ⑫, =**gewölbe** n = Gruft 1; =**kirche** f crypt.

Grum(me)t prov. (⌣́‿, ⌣́) (mhd. Grünmahd) n ⑱(d). agr. (Heu zweiter Schnitt) second hay-crop, aftermath.

grum(me)ten (⌣́‿)(⌣́‿) v/n. (h.) ⑫ agr. to get in the second hay-crop, to gather (in) the aftermath.

Grum(me)t=ernte (⌣́‿...) f ⑫ second (or after-)crop of hay; =**heu** n = Grum(me)t; =**mahd** f = =**ernte**.

grün (⌣́) [ahd.: green] I a. ⑯ 1. green, her. vert; (grünend) verdant, ☞ virescent; (knospend) budding, growing, shooting; ♃e Saat green (or fresh) crop; (wieder) ♃ w. to grow green (again), von der Natur auch: to put on (fresh or new) verdure; ♀ die ~e Insel (Irland) Emerald Isle; ~es Vorgebirge Cape Verde. — 2. (unreif) green or unripe (fruit, &c.); ♃e Bohnen French beans, scarlet runners pl.; ♃e Häute raw hides pl.; fig. von Personen: new, inexperienced; ♂er Junge greenhorn, raw youth; (Flegel) saucy (or F cheeky) fellow. — 3. fig. er kommt auf keinen ♃en Zweig he does not thrive or prosper or get on (in the world); F sich an j-s ♃e (Herzens-)Seite setzen to sit (or move up) close to a p.('s side); sich ♃ und gelb ärgern to turn green with (or to be full of) vexation; s. blau 2 u. gelb 2; F e-m ♃ (gewogen) sein to be partial to a person; deutsche Spielkarten: der ♃e König the king of spades; ♂er Tisch für Sitzungen green table or board or cloth, official board; (Spieltisch) gam(bl)ing- (or card-) table. — II s. ⑰ 4. ~ n green (colour); anything green; der Natur a.: verdure; P bei Mutter ~ (im Freien) schlafen ob. kampieren to sleep in the open (air) or under the green trees, F to camp out. — 5. ~**e(s)** n ⑰ (Gemüse, Kräuter ꝛc.) vegetables pl., F greens pl., green food. — 6. ~**e(r)** m/f person dressed in green; (unerfahrene Person) greenhorn, fresh comer, new hand, novice.

grün=äugig (⌣́...) a. ⑯ green-eyed; ♃**belaubt** a. clad (or clothed) in green foliage; verdant; ♃**bewachsen** a. covered with (fresh) verdure; ♃**blau** a. greenish blue, bsd. poet. glaucous.

Grund (⌣́) [ahd.: ground] m ⑩b. 1. ground; agr. (Erdboden) soil; (Vertiefung) low ground, dale, (Schlucht) gorge, glen; (Tiefe des Meeres ꝛc.) bottom; ~ haben to be within one's depth, ↓ von Schiffen: to be in (or on) soundings; mit dem Senklote keinen ~ mehr finden to be off (or out of) soundings. — 2. ein Glas bis auf den ~ austrinken to empty ... to the last drop; e-r Sache (dat.) auf den ~ geh(e)n to go to the root of a th.; bis auf den ~ geh(e)n to go right to the bottom (or depth) of a th.; ↓ auf den ~ geraten to be (or run) aground; ↓ auf den ~ stoßen to strike ground, to touch bottom; ct. aus dem ~ (ob. von ~ aus) verstehen to understand a th. thoroughly, to have thoroughly mastered a subject; im ~e at bottom, fundamentally; fig. really, in truth; im ~e genommen after all, when all is said; e-n **in** ~ und Boden schmettern to stun (or dumb-found) a p., to give a p. a crushing blow; vgl. bohren 1; **von** ~ **aus** from the very bottom, completely, right through; radically; von ~ aus ein schlechter Mensch a thorough-paced scoundrel, a villain of the deepest dye; von ~ aus zerstören to pull down to the ground, to destroy root and branch; vgl. zugrunde geh(e)n, richten. — 3. paint., &c. (Hintergrund) background; ⊕ Weberei ꝛc.: back, main warp. — 4. ~ und Boden (als Besitztum) s. Boden 2; liegende Gründe (landed) estate, (Boden, auf dem gebaut wird) piece of ground for building, building-plot. — 5. = Bodensatz. — 6. (Fundament) foundation; den ~ zu einem Gebäude ꝛc. legen to lay the foundation to (or of) a building, &c.; vgl. zugrunde legen, liegen; fig. auf ~ seiner Macht in virtue of his authority. — 7. fig. (Beweis=)~ reason, argument; (Beweg=)~ motive; (Ursache) cause, (Veranlassung) occasion; keinen ~ zur Klage h. to have no reason for complaining; man hat ~ anzunehmen there is reason to believe; **auf** ~ seiner Aussage on the strength of his evidence; auf ~ von dem, was ich gehört habe (to judge) from what I have heard, **aus** welchem ~e? for what reason?, from what cause?, wherefore?; aus diesem ~e for this reason; aus guten Gründen for good reasons; **mit** um so besserem ~e with all the more reason, **ohne** ~ without cause; ohne vernünftigen ~ without rhyme or reason.

Grund=abgabe (⌣́...) f ⑫ = =**steuer**; =**adel** m landed aristocracy; =**akko'rd** ♪ m fundamental chord; =**angel** f = =**leine**; =**angeln** n ground-angling, bottom-fishing; =**artikel** m fundamental article (of faith, &c.); =**ball** m Tennis: base-ball; =**baß** ♪ m fundamental bass; =**bau** ⊕ m, arch. foundation (-beam), substructure; =**bedeutung** f primary (or original) meaning; =**bedingung** f main (or fundamental, principal) condition; =**begriff** m fundamental notion or idea; =**besitz(er)** m = =**eigentum** ꝛc.; =**bestand** m original stock; =**bestandteil** m primary component or constituent or ingredient; element(ary principle); =**birne** ♀ f = Kartoffel; =**blei** ↓ n sounding-lead, plummet; =**bohrer** ⊕ m auger, terrier; ♃**böse**, ♃**bra"v** a. thoroughly wicked, good or honest; =**buch** n register of land(ed property); engl. hist. (von Wilhelm dem Eroberer verfaßt) Doomsday-book; =**buch(s)=amt** n, in Engl. unbekannt, etwa: registration-office (or registry) for land; =**charakter** m original character; ♃**deutsch** a. thoroughly German; ♃**e"hrlich** a. downright (or thoroughly) honest, honest to the backbone or as the day; =**eigentum** n landed (or real) property, jur. auch: immovables pl.; =**eigentümer** m landed proprietor, land-owner; =**einkommen** n income derived from land; =**eis** n ground-ice; der Fluß geht mit ~ the river is full of drift-ice.

Grundel, **Gründel** (⌣́‿) [Grund] f ⑯ ichth. (Meer=) ~ black goby, rock-fish (Go'bius niger).

gründen (⌣́‿) [Grund] ⑯ I v/a. 1. to found, to lay the foundation of; (ein-

[Gründer] — 467 — [Gründungsschwindel]

richten) to establish, (einsetzen) to institute, (schaffen) to create; einen Hausstand ⁓ to set up housekeeping; fest gegründet firmly (or well) established, fig. deeply rooted; ⬛ e-e Aktienbank ⁓ to float (or promote, F get up) a joint-stock bank; ein Geschäft ⁓ to start (or open) a business. — 2. = ergründen 1. — 3. ⊕ (Gemälde ꝛc. mit einem Hintergrunde ausstatten) paint. die Leinwand ⁓ to ground (or prime) the canvas. — 4. ⬛ meist b.s. to set up (or start, float) a bubble (or bogus) company; eine bestehende Fabrik ⁓ to change (or transform) ... into a company of shareholders. — II v/n. (h.) 5. ⬛ to promote (or float) companies; b.s. to float bogus concerns, to ensnare the public by delusive prospectuses. — 6. ⊥ to feel bottom. — III sich ⁓ v/refl. 7. sich auf et. (acc.) ⁓ to rest (or to be founded or based) on a th.. — IV ~ n ㉓ 8. = Gründung.

Gründer (⁓) m ㉒, ~in f ⬛ founder (f foundress); (Schöpfer) creator, ⬛ e-r Gesellschaft: promoter; b.s. company-promoter, city-shark, swindler who lives on company-promoting.

Gründer=jahr (⁓...) n ㉒, =periode f ⬛ year, period of bubble companies; =schwindel m bogus-company swindle, engl. 18. sac.: South Sea Bubble.

Grund=ertrag (⁓...) m ㉒ revenue (derived) from land; vgl. =rente.

Gründertum (⁓...) n ⓪d. bubble-company mania or fever; company-promoting.

Gründer=welt (⁓...) f ㉒ coll. company-promoters pl.; =wesen n = Gründertum.

grund=falsch (⁓...) a. ⓪ fundamentally (or radically, quite) wrong, thoroughly false; =farbe (⁓...) f ㉒: a) paint. ground- (or prime-) colour, grounding; b) phys. elementary (or simple) colour; ²faul a. very lazy, F bone-lazy; ²fest a. very solid; ²es Eigentum = =eigentum; =feste f foundation; das Haus in seinen ⁓n erschüttern to shake ... to its very foundation(s); =firnis m priming-varnish; =fischerei f = =angeln; =fläche f basis, base (a. geom.); =form f primitive (or primary) form or type, chm., &c. auch: radical; =gebäude n = =bau; =gebirge n, geol. primitive rock(s pl.); =gedanke m fundamental (or original) idea, (Hauptgedanke) leading idea; ²gei"zig, ²gele"hrt a. most (or exceedingly) avaricious, learned; =gerechtigkeit, =gerechtsame f prerogative (or rights pl.) attaching to land; ²gesche"i"t a. exceedingly clever or F smart; =gesetz n fundamental law, einer Gesellschaft: organic statute; ²gesetzlich a. jur. statutory; =graben ⊕ m Bauwesen: foundation-trench; ²gu"t, ²gü"tig a. very (or extremely) kind or good-hearted, thoroughly good; ²hä"ßlich a. very ugly or F plain, as ugly as sin; =herr m landlord, lord of the manor, land-owner; ²herr(schaft)lich a. territorial; =herrlichkeit f territorial rights pl.; =herrschaft f: a) lordly (or baronial) rule; b) lord (f lady) of the manor; =hold(e) m ⓪c. ㉔ (㉔) (Höriger) serf tied to the soil.

Grundier=anstrich ⊕ (⁓...) m ㉒ ground- (or priming-)colour.

grundier/en ⊕ (⁓⁄⁓) [Grund] I v/a. ㉓ = gründen 3. — II ~ n ㉓ s. G/ung.

Grundierer ⊕ (⁓⁄⁓) m ㉒ primer; Keramik: ground-layer.

Grundier=maschine ⊕ (⁓...) f ㉒ paper-staining machine; =schicht f Stubenmalerei: first coat(ing) or colouring. [Keramik: ground-laying.]

Grundierung (⁓⁄⁓) f ㊻ priming; bsd.)

grundig (⁓⁄⁓) a. ⓪ muddy, turbid; in Zssgn. ("⁄⁄⁓) ₃B. hell⁓ with a light background.

Grund=irrtum (⁷...) m ㉒ fundamental error; =kapital ㉒ n original stock (of a company); =kette f Web.: main- (or ground-)warp; =kraft f primary (or primitive) force; =lage f groundwork, foundation, e-r Wissenschaft a. elements, rudiments pl.; (Fußgestell) foot, bottom, pedestal; =lasten f/pl. burdens pl. on the land; ²legend a. ⓪ fundamental; =legung f (laying of a) foundation; weit S. establishment; =lehre f fund. doctrine; ~n pl. einer Wissenschaft: elementary principles, rudiments pl.; =leine f ⊥ u. Fischerei: ground-line.

gründlich (⁓⁄⁓) [mhd.: *Grund] a. ⓪ 1. (ant. oberflächlich) solid (work); (tief) profound (study), deep (scholar); (v. Grund aus) thorough (change), radical (reform): ⁓e Kenntnisse in et. haben to be well-grounded (or thoroughly versed) in a th. — 2. F ein ⁓er (starker) Regen a heavy shower; adv. er hat uns ⁓ (tüchtig) angeführt F he has done us (or taken us in) nicely; ⁓ untersuchen to examine thoroughly, to sift to the bottom.

Gründlichkeit (⁓⁄⁓) f ㊻ (s. gründlich 1) solidity; profoundness; thoroughness.

Gründling (⁓⁄⁓) m ⓪d. ichth.: a) groundling; b) (Flußgründling) (common) gudgeon (Go'bio vulga'ris).

Grund=linie (⁷...) f ㉒: a) geom., &c.: base (auch ⚔); Zeichnen: ground- (or base-)line, Tennis: (Spiel an der) ~ base-line (game); b) ~n pl. (erster Entwurf) rough (or first) draft or outline; ²los a. ⓪: a) (unergründlich) bottomless, unfathomable; b) (unbegründet) groundless, unfounded, baseless; =losigkeit f: a) bottomlessness; b) groundlessness, baselessness; =mauer(werk n) f ⊕ arch. foundation-wall(ing), substructure.

Grün=donnerstag (¹⁓⁓⁓) m ㉒ Maundy- (or Cath. eccl. Holy) Thursday.

Grund=ordnung (⁷...) f ㉒ Statut; =peilung ⊥ f sounding; =pfahl m foundation-pile; =pfeiler m pillar, weit S. strong support; =quell(e f) m original fountain or source; =rechnungs=arten f/pl. arith.: die vier ~ the first four rules pl. of arithmetic; =recht n: a) landlord's (or proprietary) right(s pl.); b) pol. ~e des Volkes: constitutional rights, fundamental laws pl.; ²rechtlich a.: a) (forming part) of a landlord's rights; b) constitutional; =regel f fundamental rule; axiom, (first) principle; =rente f ground-rent; =riß m: a) arch. (Zeichnung e-r Grundfläche) ground-plan (of a building); b) fig. (gedrängte Skizze, bsd. Lehrbuch) short sketch, outline; compendium, primer; (Anfangsgründe) rudiments pl.; =satz m fundamental truth, principle; (als unbestreitbar angenommene Wahrheit) axiom, phls., rel. dogma; (Lebensregel) maxim; ein Mensch von guten (schlechten) ⁓sätzen a person of sound (unsound) principles, a well- (ill-)principled person; er hat es sich zum ~e gemacht zu // he has made it a (fixed) rule to // (inf.); s-n ⁓sätzen untreu werden to forsake (or to act contrary to) one's principles; ²sätzlich a. founded on (certain) principles, systematic; adv. er tut es ⁓ he does it on principle; ²satzlos a. without principle(s), b.s. unprincipled; =satzlosigkeit f lack of principle(s); =säule f foundation-pillar, pillar of support (a. fig.); ²schle"cht a. wretchedly bad, execrable, thoroughly wicked; =schoß m land-tax; =schuld f debt (resting) on landed property, mortgage; =schwelle f: a) ⊕ arch. ground-sill, groundsel, foundation-timber; b) ⊞ sleeper; =see ⊥ f ground-swell; =silbe f, gr. radical syllable; =sprache f: a) (Stammsprache) original language; b) des Urtextes: language of the original text; ²ständig ⁓ a. v. Blättern: ⚚ basilar; =stein ⊕ m, arch. foundation-stone; first stone; den ~ legen to lay the foundation-stone of a building; =stein=legung f laying (of) the found.-st.; =steuer f tax on land; vgl. =rente; =stimme ♪ f fundamental bass; =stoff m: a) chm., phys. element(ary substance), radical; b) ⊕ (Rohstoff) raw material; =strecke ⚔ f level gangway; =strich m: a) (ant. Haarstrich) in der Schrift: down-stroke, typ. body-stroke, stem; b) paint. first coating of an oil-painting; =stück n: a) plot of land, (Landgut) (landed) estate; b) chief piece or part; =stütze f main support or prop; =suppe F f (Bodensatz) grounds pl., sediment; ⊥ fig. bilge-water; =teilchen n: ⚚ atom; =text m original text; =thema ♪ n leading air or melody, oft auch: (btsch) leit-motif; =ton m: a) paint. fundamental tone; b) ♪ keynote; c) ⬛ Börse: der ~ der Börse war fester the prevailing tone (or undertone) of the market was more settled; =trieb m natural impulse or instinct; =tugend f cardinal virtue; =übel n original evil or drawback.

Gründung (⁓⁄⁓) f ㊻ 1. foundation, establishment, institution; (Schöpfung) creation. — 2. ⬛ b.s. (s. gründen 4) promotion of bubble companies, auch: (company-)promoting.

Grün=dünger (¹¹...) m ㉒ agr. vegetable manure or fertilizer.

Gründungs=gesetz (⁵⁓...) n ㉒ organic law; =jahr n year of foundation; =kosten pl. expense of founding a th.; =plan m plan (or scheme) of foundation; =schwindel m = Gründerschwindel.

⚚ scientific; ♀ botanical; ⚲ geography; ⊕ machinery; ⚒ mining; ⚔ military; ⊥ marine; ⬛ commercial; ✉ postal; ⊞ railway.

Grund=unterschied (⁓...) m ⓶ = =verschiedenheit; =ursache f: a) primary (or original) cause; b) für das Handeln: main (or chief) reason; =verfassung f fundamental constitution; ⁓verke"hrt a. altogether wrong, most perverse; =vermögen n: a) capital, principal; b) landed property; =verpfändung f mortgaging of land; ⁓verschie"den a. entirely different, utterly opposed; =verschiedenheit f fundamental (or radical) difference; =wahrheit f fundamental truth; =wasser(=stand n (level of the) underground- (or sub-soil-)water; =werk n groundwork; =wesen n inner (or true) nature, (quint-) essence; =wissenschaft f fundamental knowledge or science; =wort n, gr. primary word; (Wurzel) root; =zahl f, math.: a) (Zahl, die e-m System zugrunde liegt) radix of a numerical (or base of a logarithmic) system; b) (auch =zahl-wort n) cardinal number; =zehnte m tithe (payable) on land; =zins(pflich-tig a.) m (liable to pay) ground-rent; =zug m (characteristic) feature, mark of distinction; den =zügen nach gleich substantially alike.

Grüne (⁓⁓) f ⓸ 1. greenness, green colour, der Natur: verdure. — 2. (grüner Rasenplatz) green lawn; (Wiese) green field, meadow. [iron-ore.}

Grün=eisenstein (¹⁸⁰¹) m ⓸ min. green

grüneln ⟨, **grüneln** ⟨ (⁓⁓) v/n. ⓶a. to grow green, von der Natur: to don a fresh garb of verdure or foliage.

grünen (⁓⁓) I v/n. (h.) ⓼ 1. (grün sein) to be green or verdant. — 2. a.: sich ⁓ v/refl. (grün werden) to grow green or verdant; von Bäumen: to burst into leaf, to put forth leaves; fig. ⁓ und blühen (gedeihen) to be in a flourishing (or prosperous) condition. — II ⁓ n ⓸ 3. ⁓ der Bäume verdure (or green foliage) of the trees.

Grün=erde (⁓...) f ⓸ min. green earth; =fink m, orn. greenfinch (Fringi'lla chloris); =futter n, agr. green food or fodder; =gelb a. ⓺ greenish yellow; =grau a. greenish grey; =holz n = Groenhart.

Grünitz (⁓⁰) [: Krinitz, *poln.] m ⓶a. orn. (Kreuzschnabel) cross-beak, cross-bill.

Grün=kern=suppe (f) m (⁓...) ⓸ (soup made of green rye; =kohl ⁀ m (green) kale; =kram m greengrocery, F greens pl., green stuff; =kram=handel ⁀ m trade in vegetables or F in green stuff, greengrocery business; =kram=händler (=in f) m greengrocer; =kraut n green (or pot-)herbs pl.; vgl. =kram.

grünlich (⁓⁰) a. ⓺ greenish; ⁓blau a. greenish blue, bsd. poet. glaucous; ⁓gelb a. greenish yellow.

Grünling (⁓⁰) m ⓶d. 1. ⁺ green agaric (Aga'ricus furca'tus). — 2. orn. = Grünfink. — 3. contp. greenhorn.

Grün=mahd (⁓...) f ⓸ = Grummet; =markt m vegetable-market; =rock m, co. = Jäger; =rost m verd-antique; =schnabel ⁀ m = Gelbschnabel ⁀; =schwarz a. greenish black; =span [mhd.] m ⓶d. chm. &c. verdigris; ⁊ ærugo. subacetate of copper; vgl. =rost; mit ⁓beschlagen covered with verd., verdi-

grised; =span=ähnlich a.: ⁊ æruginous; =specht m, orn.: a) popinjay (Picus vi'ridis); b) fig. = Gelbschnabel b; =stein m. min. greenstone, ⁊ diorite; =werden n der Bäume bursting into leaf; =wurzel f = Erdrauch.

grunzen (⁓⁰) [ahd.: grunt] I v. a. ⓽ vom Schweine: to grunt (a. F fig. von murrenden Menschen). — II ⁓ n ⓶ grunt(ing).

Grün=zeug (⁽⁵⁾) n ⓸ =fram u. =kraut.

Grunz=ochs (⁓...) m ⓶ zo. grunting-ox, ⁊ yak (Bos od. Poe'phagus gru'nniens).

Gruppe (⁓⁰) [fr. groupe n] f ⓸ group; v. Bäumen ⁊c. auch: clump, cluster; ⁕ syndicate (or F ring) of financiers.

Gruppen=anordnung (⁓...) f ⓸, grouping; =bild n, phot. picture of a group, persons pl. taken in a group; =bildung f = =anordnung; =führer ⁀ m, etwa: leader of a squad; =verteilung f = =anordnung; ⁓weise adv. (F a. a.) (arranged) in groups.

gruppieren (⁓⁰) [fr.] I v/a., v/n. (h.) u. sich ⁓ v/refl. ⓾ to form groups, nur v/a. to group (together). — II ⁓ n ⓸ und **Gruppierung** f ⓶ grouping.

Grus (⁻; Hom. Gruß) [mhd.] m ⓶a. 1. = Graus¹. — 2. ⁊ ⁓(=kohle f) small coal, coal-dust, coal-slack, smudge (-coal). [shivers pl.; vgl. Graus².}

Grusel F (⁻⁰) m ⓶ shudder(ing),}

gruselig (⁓⁰⁰) a. ⓺ shuddering, shivering; meton.: Le Geschichte ghastly tale, ghost-story (which makes one's flesh creep).

gruseln F (⁻⁰) [mhd.: *grausen] v/n. (h.) u. sich ⁓ v/refl. ⓶a.: ich grusele (mich), mir gruselt's I shudder, I am shivering (with fear), my flesh creeps.

grusicht, grusig(⁓⁰) [Grus] a. ⓺ v. Kohle ⁊c. dusty, smudgy.

Gruß (⁻; Hom. Grus) [ahd.: greet] m ⓶a. 1. (Grüßen) salutation, vertraulicher: greeting; (Verbeugung) bow, (Abnehmen der Mütze) capping; ⚔ militärischer ⁓ salute; eccl. englischer ⁓ = Engelsgruß. — 2. (oft pl. Grüße) compliments, regards, respects, greetings pl.; vertraulich: love; vgl. bestellen 4; (bestelle ihm) e-n schönen ⁓ (oder schöne Grüße) von mir! give him my kind(est) regards (förmlicher: my best respects, vertraulich: my love!; remember me to him!; in Briefen: freundlichen ⁓!, herzliche Grüße! many kind regards or hearty greetings!; mit freundlichem ⁓e Ihr... with best (or kindest) compliments (vertraulich: best love) Your(s) ... — 3. (Willkomm) welcome.

grüßbar (⁻⁰) [grüßen] a. ⓺ etwa: on bowing terms; ⚔ &c. to be saluted.

grüßen (⁻⁰) [ahd.: greet] I v/a. ⓽ (f. Gruß) to salute, to greet; to bow to durch Abnehmen der Mütze ⁊c.: to (doff one's) cap, durch Nicken: to nod to, durch Handbewegung: to wave one's hand to: feierlich: to hail, to welcome; ⁓ Sie ihn (von mir)! give (or make) my kindest regards (or respects, bei Freunden und Verwandten: my love) to him!; er läßt Sie freundlichst ⁓ he sends you his best respects or compliments or (vertraulich) his love; he wishes to be kindly remembered to you; wieder ⁓

to return a p.'s bow, ⚔ to return a p.'s salute, to resalute. — II ⁓ n ⓶ = Gruß 1. [or hailing or ⚔ salutation.}

Gruß=formel (⁽"⁾...) f ⓸ form of greeting}

Gruß=fuß (⁻...) m ⓶: mit e-m auf dem ⁓e (steh)en to be on bowing terms with (or a bowing acquaintance of) a p.

grütz=artig(⁓...) a. ⓺ gruelly; =beutel m ⓶ path. uft an der Kopfhaut: ⁊ atheroma.

Grütze (⁻⁰) [ahd.: grit, groats] f ⓸ 1. groats, grits pl.; weit ⓶. = Grütz=suppe. — 2. F fig. (Verstand) F gumption; er hat keine ⁓ im Kopf his head is empty.

Grütz=handel (⁻...) m ⓶, =händler(in f) m trade, dealer in grits; =kopf m (=töpfig a.) blockhead(ed), F fat-head(ed); =macher m = =müller; =mühle f mill for grinding grits; =müller m maker of groats or grits; =suppe f (oatmeal-)porridge.

Guacharo (⁓⁰⁻⁰⁻⁰) [span.] m ⓶ orn. gua-charo, oil-bird (Steato'rnis caripe'nsis).

Guajak (⁻⁻⁰) [span.] m ⓺ gu(a)iac(um) (Guaia'cum officina'le); ⁓holz n pock-wood, ⁊ guaiacum, lignum vitae; ⁓säure f, chm.: ⁊ guaiacic acid.

Guano ⁕ (⁻⁰) [peru.] m (u) ⓺ (südamerikanischer Vogeldünger) guano.

Guardian (⁓⁻⁽⁾⁻, engl. : gā'⁻dɪən) [it.] m ⓶c. ⚔ (Vater) ⁓ (Kloster) ⁀ abbot, prior.

Guasch (⁻⁰) [fr. gouache] ⁊ paint. (Deckfarbe mit wässerigem Bindemittel) gouache (-colour), (it.) guazzo; ⁓malerei (⁓⁰...) f ⓸ gouache-painting.

Gub F (⁻⁰) m ⓶c. = Blick.

Guck=auge (⁻...) n ⓸, =äugelchen, =äuglein n little eye, F peeper.

Gückel (⁻⁰) m ⓶ = Gockel(hahn).

gucken (⁻⁰) [mhd. 13. sæc.] I v/n. (h.) to look (furtively or inquisitively) at; nach, auf et. ⁓ to peep at a th.; (hinschielen) F to squint at a thing; gern tief ins Glas ⁓ to be fond of a drop; nach den Sternen ⁓ to gaze at the stars; von Sachen ⁓ (hervorsehen) aus to peep out from; die Einfalt guckt ihr aus dem Gesicht she looks a simple girl, her simple mind is written on her face. — II v/a. und sich ⁓ v/refl. mit Angabe der Wirkung: sich (dat.) die Augen aus dem Kopfe ⁓, sich (acc.) blind ⁓ to gaze (or stare) o.s. blind.

Gucker (⁻⁰) m ⓶, ⁓in f ⓸ 1. one who peeps or spies, peeper (Neugierige[r]) inquisitive person, F quiz. — 2. nur m: a) =Augenglas; b) =Guck=fenster, =loch.

Guck=fenster (⁻...) n ⓸ peep-hole or -window, zum Ausspähen: look-out; =glas n spy-glass; =in=die=welt m (n) ⓺ (junge unerfahrene Person) young novice or beginner, youngster, greenhorn; =kasten m (peep-)show, panorama; =kastenmann, =kästner m showman; =loch n look-hole (auch ⁕), peep- (or spy-)hole.

Gudscharat ⁕ (⁻⁰) npr/n. ⓺a. Ost=J.: Guzerat.

Guer(r)illa (gĕ⁻ɪl'⁻jä) [span.] f ⓺ ⓸ (a.: ⁓krieg m) (Kleinkrieg) guerrilla (-warfare); pl. ⁓s = Streifscharen; ⁓bande f, ⁓häuptling m guerrilla-band, -captain.

Guffer=linie schwz. (⁻⁰) (⁻...) f ⓸ geol. medial moraine. [cowl. monk's hood.}

Gugel (⁻⁰) [lt. cucullus] f ⓸ (Mönchskappe)}

[Guhr] — 469 — [Gürtel]

Guhr ⚒ (¹) f ⊕ f. Gur.
Guido (gi'-) [it.; *dtsch. Wido] npr/m. ⊕ ⊠ α. (Bn.) Guy.
guillochier/en (gi(l)-ĭ-ſchī'-r'n) [fr.] I v/a. ⊕ to guilloche(e). — II G/ung f ⊕ (Schlangenverzierung) guilloche.
Guillotine (gil-ĭ-tī'-nĕ) [Guillotin, fr. Arzt 1792] f ⊕ (Fallbeil) guillotine;
guillotinieren (gil-ĭ-tī-nī'-r'n) v/a. ⊕ to (execute with a) guillotine.
Guinea (gī-ne'-ā) npr/n. ⊠ α. (West-afrika) Guinea; f. Neuguinea.
Guinea=fahrer ⚓ (⌐...) m ⊕ bsd. ehm.: Guineaman; =gras ⚘ n Guinea-grass (Pani'cum ma'ximum); =körner m/pl. ⊕ grains of Guinea or of paradise (v. Amo'mum granum paradi'si); =pfeffer ⚘ m guinea-pepper (von Ca'psicum und andern Gewürzpflanzen); =wurm m, ent. guinea-worm, tank-worm (Fila'ria medine'nsis).
Guinee ⑂ ⊛ (gī-ne'(-ĕ)) [(aus) Guinea(gold)] f ⊕ (ehm. engl. Goldmünze, jetzt nur Rechenmünze = 21 M.) guinea. [f. Gi...]
☛ **Guipure, Guirlande, Guitarre**]
Gulasch (⌐ᴗ) [mag.] n ⊠α. Kochkunst: stew of minced meat with bacon, onions, pepper, &c.
Gulden [mhd.: *gülden] m ⊕ (abbr. fl.; Nennwert = 2 M.) florin; holländischer ~ Dutch guilder or florin (= 1.69 Mark = 1s. 8d.). [golden.]
gülden [mhd.] a. ⊕ (D 9) chm. =]
Gülle (⌐ᴗ) f ⊕ (Jauche) liquid manure.
Gült, ~e¹ obb. (⌐ᴗ) [mhd.: guilt; *gelten] f ⊕, ⊠: a) (jährl. Ertrag eines Gutes) revenue of an estate; b) (Grundzins) ground-rent; =buch n ⊕ rent-roll.
gülte² † (⌐ᴗ) subj. impf. v. gelten.
gültig (⌐ᴗ) [Gült(e)] a. ⊕ valid, von Münzen: current, good, passable; (zulässig) admissible, (gesetzlich) legal(ly binding), legitimate, lawful, (beglaubigt) authentic, in due form; kirchlich ≙ canonical; ⎈, &c. von Fahrkarten: available (for eight, &c. days); wie lange ist meine Fahrkarte ≙? for what period is my ticket available?, (for) how long does my ticket run?; (für) ≙ erklären, ≙ machen to make valid; to legalize, legitimate, legitimate; ≙ sein für to hold good for, to be applicable to, to apply to; **~keit** (⌐ᴗ) f ⊕ validity, currency; legality, lawfulness; ⎈, &c. availability.
Gültigkeits=dauer (⌐ᴗ...) f ⊕ jur. (period of) validity; ⎈, &c. e-r Fahrkarte: availability, (full) run; **=erklärung** f validation, legalization.
Gültig=machen (⌐ᴗ...) n ⊕, **=machung** f jur. validation, legitim(iz)ation.
Gummi (⌐ᴗ-) [lt.; grch.] n u. (Radier≙) m ⊕ gum; harz=artiges auch: rosin, resin.
Gummi=arabikum (⌐ᴗ...) n ⊕ gum-arabic; **≙artig** (⌐ᴗ...) a. ⊕ gummy, gummous; **=artigkeit** f gumminess; **=artikel** ⚒ m india-rubber article, vgl. =waren; **=ball** m india-rubber ball; **=band** n elastic (band); **=baum** ⚘ m: a) allg.: gum-yielding tree. bsd.: b) india-rubber tree (Ficus ela'stica); c) neuholländischer ~ gumtop-tree, eucalyptus (Eucaly'ptus).
gummicht (⌐ᴗ...) a. ⊕ = gummi-artig.
Gummi-ela"stikum n india-rubber.

gummieren ⊕ (⌐ᴗ) v/a. ⊕ to (stick or stiffen with) gum; **gummierter Zettel** gummed (or adhesive) label; **Gummierer** m ⊕ gummer.
Gummier=maschine ⊕ (⌐ᴗ...) f ⊕, **=wachs** n gum-machine, -wax.
Gummi=erz ⛏ n ⊕ min. (Uran-oxyd) gummite; **=fluß** m der Steinobstbäume: gumming, ⚕ gummosis; **=gebend** a. ⊕, **=haltig** a. gum-yielding or -producing, gummy, ⚕ gummiferous.
Gummigutt ⚘ (⌐ᴗ) n ⊕b. (o. pl.) gamboge, gum guttæ; **~=baum** ⚘ m ⊕ gamboge-tree (Garci'nia); **≙haltig** a. ⊕ gambogian, ...ic.
Gummi=harz (⌐ᴗ...) (=harzig a. ⊕) n ⊕ chm.: ⚕ gum-resin(ous); **=kordel** ⚒ f (eingewebtes Gummi) shirr; **=kugel** f zum Ausradieren rubber-ball; **=lack** ⚒ m gum-lac; **=reifen** ⚒ m für Zweiräder, Droschken ꝛc.: india-rubber tire; **=rock** m india-rubber coat, waterproof, mackintosh; **=schlauch** m india-r. tubing; **=schnur** f elastic string; **=schuhe** m/pl. india-rubber shoes, galoshes pl.; **=stoff** ⚒ m waterproof cloth; **=überschuhe** m/pl. = =schuhe; **=waren** f/pl. india-r. goods pl. or ware; **=wäsche** f india-rubber collars and cuffs pl.; **=wasser** n gum-water; **=zug=stiefel** m/pl. m elastic(-boots pl.).
Gundel=rebe ⚘ (⌐ᴗ...) [mhd.] f ⊕, **Gunder=mann** m ⊕c. (o. pl.) ground-ivy (Glecho'ma hedera'cea).
Günsel ⚘ (⌐ᴗ) [nhd.*lt. conso'lida f] m ⊕ (Aiu'ga): kriechender ~ bugle (A. reptans); gelber ~ ground-pine (A. chamae'pitys).
Gunst [mhd.: *gönnen] f ⊕ († ob. adv.; vgl. zu≙en) ⊕ **1.** favour; kindness (shown to a p.); (Wohlwollen) goodwill; (parteiische Vorliebe) favouritism, partiality; bei e-m in ~ steh(e)n, sich der ~ j-s erfreuen to be in favour with a p., to be in a p.'s good graces or ⸕ good books; sich bei e-m in ~ setzen to ingratiate o.s. with a p.; bei e-m wieder in ~ kommen, sich bei e-m wieder in ~ setzen to be reinstated in (or to regain) a p.'s favour, to reingratiate o.s. with a p.; beim Volke in großer ~ steh(e)n to be very popular with the people; es geht hier alles nach ~ everything here goes by favour; sich um j-s ~ bemühen, bewerben to court a p.'s favour, F to curry favour with a p.; j-n um eine ~ bitten to beg (or ask) a favour of a p.; zu ≙en j-s (zu-m Besten) in favour (or for the benefit) of a p.; alles spricht zu meinen (meines Freundes, j-s) ~en everything tells in my (my friend's, somebody's) favour; zu unser(e)n ~en in our favour, ⚒ to our credit. — **2. mit ~(en)** (bsd. zur Entschuldigung) with your (kind) leave or permission.
Gunst=bemühung (⌐ᴗ...) f ⊕, **=bewerbung** f efforts (made) to obtain a p.'s favour, currying favour with a p.; **=beweis** m mark of favour; **=bezeigung** f = Gunst 1.
günstig (⌐ᴗ) [Gunst] a. ⊕ favourable, propitious, (gütig) kind(ly inclined), (zugetan) affectionate (vorteilhaft) advantageous,(bequem gelegen)convenient,

conveniently situated;(Gutes verheißend) auspicious; das Glück war uns ≙ luck was in our favour, fortune smiled upon us; den ≙en Augenblick abwarten to wait for a favourable moment, to watch one's opportunity; im günstigsten Falle at (the) best, under the most favourable circumstances; bei ≙em Wetter if the weather permits, weather permitting.
Günstling (⌐ᴗ)[nhd.:*Gunst]m⊕d., **~in** f ⊕ favourite, (Liebling) pet, darling, contp. minion; **~=regierung** f, **=unfug** m, **=wirtschaft** f (mischievous) influence of favourites, favouritism.
Gur ⚒ (¹) [gären] f ⊕ (aufgelöste Mineralien im Gestein; ⚕ ⚕ guhr.
Gurgel (⌐ᴗ) [ahd.; *lt. gurgu'lio m] f ⊕ (vorderer Teil des Halses) throat; anat.: ⚕ jugulum; (Schlund) gullet; vgl. Kehle; alles durch die ~ jagen to waste (or spend) everything on drink; e-m an die ~ springen to fly at a p.'s throat.
Gurgel=abschneider (⌐ᴗ...) m ⊕ = Kehlabschneider; **=ader** f, anat. ⚕ jugular vein; **=geräusch** n gurgling (or rattling) in the throat.
gurgeln (⌐ᴗ) [: gargle, gurgle] I v/n. (h.), v/a. u. sich ≙ v/refl. ⊕a. 1. ≙, (sich) den Hals ≙, sich ≙ to gargle (one's throat). — 2. (Gurgeltöne ausstoßen) to gurgle, to utter guttural sounds. — **II ~** n ⊕ **3.** (f. 1) gargling (one's throat), gargarization; (f. 2) guttural sound or speech.
Gurgel=schnitt (⌐ᴗ...) m ⊕ surg.: ⚕ bronchotomy; **=ton** m guttural sound, gurgling in the throat; **=wasser** n, med. gargle, medicine for gargling, ⚕ gargarism, F co. = Branntwein.
Gurke (⌐ᴗ) [ndd.: *slaw.] f ⊕ ⚘ **1.** (echte, gewöhnliche) ~ cucumber (Cu'cumis sati'vus); Pfeffer≙ gherkin [dtsch]; saure ~n pickled cucumbers pl.; ein Gesicht machen wie saure ~n to make a face (or to look) as sour as vinegar; Zeit der sauren ~n = Sauregurkenzeit. — **2.** fig. (große, dicke Nase) bottle-nose.
gurken=artig (⌐ᴗ...) a. ⊕, **=förmig** a. cucumber-shaped, ⚕ cucumiform; **=käfer** m, ent. cu.-beetle; **=kern** m cu.-seed; **=kraut** ⚘ n borage (Bora'go); **=mistbeet** n cu.-frame; **=salat** m (sliced) cucumber dressed as salad.
Gurre F (⌐ᴗ) [mhd.] f ⊕ (schlechtes Pferd) old knacker or hack or jade.
gurren (⌐ᴗ) [mhd.: girren, lautm.] v/n. (h.) ⊕ von Tauben: to coo.
Gurt [mhd.: gürten; *gürten] m ⊕b., fast † (⌐ᴗ-(e) f ⊕(⊠) **1.** aus Leder ꝛc.: belt, als Schmuck ꝛc. a. girdle, e-s Pferdes: girth; an der Schulmappe: strap; (Leibbinde, Schärpe) sash. scarf; (Spannstab) am Bett ꝛc.: stretcher. — **2.** arch.: a) ~ um Säulen plinth; b) bei Gewölben, ein die Fächer verbindender Bogen: binding-vault, archivolt. — **Gurt-band** ⚒ (⌐ᴗ...) n ⊕: a) waistband, Weberei: elastic tape, webbing; b) arch. (innerer Sockel) tablet, table; **=bett** n folding-bed (stead); **=bogen** m, arch. = Gurt 2b.
Gürtel (⌐ᴗ) [ahd.: girdle] m ⊕ **1.** (f. Gurt1) belt, girdle; von Damen getragen auch: waist-belt, zo.: cingulum; an Unter-

[**Gürtelassel**] — 470 — [**gut**]

Kleidern: waistband; body-belt; ela'stischer ~ elastic belt; geweihter ~ (Leibstrick) gewisser Orden: cordon; ⚔ von Festungswerken: ring (or circle) of forts; mit e-m ~ versehen, e-n ~ tragend belted, cinctured. — 2. als Zeichen der Jungfräulichkeit oft: virgin-knot. — 3. ⚓ ast., geogr., math.: zone.
Gürtel-assel (⚓...) f ⑫ ent. armadillo; **=ausschlag** m = **=rose**; **=bahn** f circle-railway; **=flechte** f = **=rose**; ⚥förmig a. ⑥ belt- (or girdle-)like; **=kette** f chatelaine; **=los** a. without a belt or girdle; **=rose** f, path. shingles pl., ⚓ (herpes) zoster; **=schloß** n clasp of a belt; **=schnalle** f = Gurtschnalle; **=tier** n, zo. armadillo, dasypodine (*Da'sypus*).
gürten (⚓) [ahd.: gird] v/a. und sich ⚓ v/refl. ⑨ 1. (sich) to gird (o.s.), (e-n Gürtel anlegen) to put on a girdle; das Schwert um den Leib ⚓, sich mit dem Schwerte ⚓ to gird on one's sword. — 2. fig. sich ⚓ (rüsten) to prepare o.s. (for travelling or fighting), to get (or make o.s.) ready; to set to, F to buckle to; bibl. seine Lenden ⚓ to gird up one's loins.
Gurt=gehenk (⚓...) n ⑫ sword-belt; **=(ge)sims** n, arch. string-course; **=gewölbe** n rib-vault(ing); **=haken** m girth-hook.
Gürtler (⚓) [Gürtel] m ⑫ 1. ehm. belt-maker, girdler. — 2. jetzt = Gelbgießer.
Gurt=riem(en)(⚓...) m ⑫ Sattlerei: girth-leather (or -strap); **=schnalle** f buckle of a belt or girdle.
Guß (⚓) [ahd.;* gießen] m ⑧ a. 1. (Gießen) pouring, spilling, fig. effusion. — 2. (auf- oder ein=gegossene Flüssigkeit) poured-out fluid. — 3. (heftiger Regen) (pelting or heavy) shower, torrent of rain. — 4. beim Backwerk: icing; mit ~ iced. — 5. ⊕ Gießerei: founding, casting, wie aus einem Gusse (gemacht) from the same mould; fig. (in sich vollendet) of a piece, highly finished. — 6. = Gußeisen. — 7. (Öffnung zum Ausgießen) = Gußrinne, -loch.
Guß=abdruck ⊕ (⚓...) m ⑫ typ. cliché, stereotype (plate); **=arbeit** f: a) casting, moulding; b) cast-work, castings pl.; **=eisen** n (ant. Schmiede=eisen) cast-iron; auch: raw (or pig-) iron; **=eisenwaren** f/pl. cast-iron goods or articles pl.; ⚓**eisern** a. ⑥ (made of) cast-iron; **=fehler** m flaw in the casting; **=form** f (casting-)mould; **=kasten** m casting-box; **=loch** n Gießerei: funnel of a furnace; **=modell** n casting-pattern; **=mutter** f matrix; **=naht** f einer Kugel: casting-mark, joint; **=regen** m (heavy) shower of rain, torrential shower; F pouring rain, downpour; **=rinne** ⊕ f: a) am Hochofen: casting-gutter, -runner; b) = **=stein**; **=schale** f mould; **=stahl** m cast-steel; **=stahlwerk** n cast-steel works pl.; **=stein** m sink; drain, sewer, gutter; **=stück** n cast article; **=waren** f/pl. cast goods, castings, foundry-goods pl.; ⚓**weise** adv.: es regnet ⚓ it is pouring (or the rain is falling) in torrents; **=werk** n: a) (gegossene Ware) cast goods, castings pl.; b) (Hüttenwert) foundry; **=zwieback** m iced (or sugared) biscuits pl.
güst prov. (⚓) a. ⑥ (unfruchtbar) barren (= gelt²).

Gustav (⚓f) [schwd. = Gunt-(Kampf)stab] npr/m. ⑮⑯α. (Vn.) Gustavus, dim. Guss(ie).
Gustchen (⚓) n ㉓α., **Guste** f ⑭⑧., **Gustel** f ⑱⑧., **Gustelchen** n(⚓⚓)㉓α. npr. (Vn., dim. v. Auguste) Gussie, Gussy.
gut (¹) [ahd.: good] I a. ⑥ (comp. besser, sup. best, f. bsd. Artikel; co. bisw. gutester) (ant. böse, schlecht) 1. good, adv. meist well; (fördernd) conducive, (heilsam) beneficial, (vorteilhaft) advantageous, (nützlich) useful, serviceable; Grußformeln: Den Morgen!, good morning!, Den Tag! je nach der Tageszeit: good morning, g. afternoon, bsd. beim Abschied: good day!; Den Abend!, Le Nacht! good evening!; bsd. beim Abschied v. Bekannten: good night!; e-m e-n Den Tag wünschen to bid a p. the time of (the) day; Tennis: ⚓! in-play!, right!, up!; ~ Heil! Turnergruß: etwa: well met!, hail! — 2. auch adv.: sein Des Auskommen haben to have a good (or comfortable, F nice) income; f. ausnehmen 5, ausgehen 4; ich wünsche Ihnen ⚓e Besserung I hope you may soon be better; f. Einvernehmen, Fuß 7; Des Gedächtnis good (or tenacious) memory; es geht ihm ⚓ he is getting on well or comfortably or F nicely; es geht sich heute ⚓ it is good (or capital, admirable, fair) walking to-day; in Dem Glauben in good faith; er tat's auf ⚓ Glück he chanced (or risked) it; es ⚓ haben to be well off; er hat es ⚓ bei s-m Herrn he has a kind master; et. für ⚓ halten to consider a th. right, to approve a th.; sich ⚓ halten: a) to keep o.s. upright; b) to keep (or to preserve o.s.) well; F De (alte) Haut dear good fellow, good-natured person; f. Hoffnung 2; De Karten bekommen to get good (or splendid) cards; e-n ⚓ kennen to know a p. (thoroughly) well or intimately; vgl. Letzt; das hat er sehr ⚓ gemacht he has done that very well, he did it capitally or F first-rate; vgl. Dmachen; De Manieren f/pl. polite manners pl.; oft iro. wißt Ihr auch, Der Mann, daß //? do you know, my dear fellow, that //?; De Person good (a. oft iro. silly) person; ich weiß es aus Der Quelle I have it on excellent authority, I heard it from a good (or reliable) source; ⚓ riechen to have a nice (or pleasant) smell; ⚓ sein für od. zu // to be good (or fit, suitable, appropriate) for //; es ist ⚓ (abgemacht)! all right!, settled!; es ist schon ⚓! that will do!; ich weiß besser, was dir ⚓ ist I know better what is good for you; so weit ist alles ⚓ all's well so far; für diesmal mag es ⚓ sein it may pass this time; lassen Sie das (oder Sie's) ⚓ sein!: a) well, let it be (so) or pass!; b) (seien Sie überzeugt) believe me!; c) (keine Komplimente) no compliments!; d) (lassen Sie das sein) leave it alone!; lassen wir das ⚓ sein (brechen wir davon ab)! let us change the subject!; wie geht es Ihnen? es muß halt (ob. schon) ⚓ sein; ... pretty (or tolerably) well! I must be satisfied!; es wäre vielleicht ⚓, zu // it might be as

well (or not be amiss) to // (inf.); iro. da sind wir ⚓ dran! now we are in a fine pickle!; seien Sie so ⚓ u. nehmen Sie das mit will you be so kind as to take (or would you mind taking) that with you; seien Sie so ⚓, mir das Brot zu reichen kindly pass me ..., I will thank you for ...; etwas so ⚓ als (bff.: wie) möglich tun to do a th. in the best manner possible or in the best possible way or as well as could be; das geht so ⚓ als möglich one could not wish it (to go) better; es ist so ⚓, als besäß' ich's schon it is as good as if it were mine already; so ⚓ wie: er muß so ⚓ warten wie ich he must wait as well as I; hundert Pfennig sind so ⚓ wie eine Mark ... are equivalent to ...; ich bin so ⚓ wie er I am as good as he (is); sie ist so ⚓ schuld daran wie ich it is her fault as much as mine; eins ist so ⚓ wie das (oder wie's) andere they are equally good or F much of a muchness; der Prozeß ist so ⚓ wie gewonnen ... is as good as won; das ist ein Der Spaß it is good (or capital, F jolly) fun; von e-m ⚓ sprechen to speak well (or highly) of a p.; vgl. Dsagen; der Weizen steht ⚓ ... is in good (or fair) condition; vgl. Dsagen; De Stube (Putzstube) bestroom, drawing-room; zu Der Stunde at the right hour, in the nick of time; De Tage (oder es ⚓) haben to lead a pleasant (or an easy) life, F to have a good time of it; vgl. Dtun; ⚓ und wohlbehalten safe and sound; es hat De Wege damit, das hat De Wege (macht keine Beschwerde) there is no difficulty (or anxiety, trouble) about that; Der Wind fair wind; wir wissen sehr ⚓ (adv.), daß // we know very well that //; sich (dat.) De Zeit, einen Den Tag machen to spend a happy time, day; F to make a day of it; er hat e-n Den Zug am Leibe he drinks like a fish. he is a very thirsty soul, f. 5 am Schluß. — 3. gegen e-n ⚓ (freundlich) sein to be kind to a p.; sie ist ihm ⚓ (hold) she has a liking for him, she is fond of him einem De Worte geben to speak a p. fair, F to talk softly to a p.; einem ⚓ werden to take a liking to a p., to become fond of a p.; wieder ⚓(Freund) werden to become reconciled; ⚓ werden (heilen) to get well, to heal, to mend; ⚔ Wer da? ⚓ Freund! who goes there? a friend. — 4. fig. Redensarten und Sprichw.: halb ⚓, halb schlecht neither good nor bad, indifferent(ly well); kurz und ⚓! in short!, to cut it short!; schon ⚓! never mind!; aus fremdem Leder ist ⚓ Riemen schneiden, etwa: it is easy to be generous (or liberal) with other people's money; f. Ende 1, Gelehrte(r), Gewissen; (nicht) für Geld und De Worte (not) for love or money; man muß De Miene zum bösen Spiel machen one must grin and bear it; ein Des Wort findet e-e De Statt oder Stelle kind words go a long way. — 5. ⚓ (volle) dreißig Jahre good (or quite) thirty years; eine De Stunde dauern to last a good (or

Signs (see page XVII): F familiar; P vulgar; ⚡ flash; ⚓ rare; † obsolete (died); * new word (born); ++ incorrect; ♪ music;

[gut] — 471 — [gutsagen]

full) hour; es sind 2(e) drei Stunden it is good three (or three good) hours; mehr als 2 more than enough; 2 und gern fully, quite; easily; er hat 2 und gern zehntausend Mark ... fully (or at least) five hundred pounds (£ 500); eine 2e Weile a good while, a long time; das hat 2e Weile there is no hurry about it; bei 2er Zeit in good time, pretty early; ein 2er Zug a deep draught, f. 2 am Schluß. — 6. (leicht, bequem) easy, convenient; Sie haben 2 (oder klug) reden, Sie sind reich it is all very well for you (to say so), you are rich; davon verschieden: Sie haben 2 reden (Sie reden umsonst) you speak in vain or to no purpose. — 7. pleonastisch bei Zeitbestimmungen, wie „schön": eines 2en Morgens // one fine morning //. — 8. ♥ vgl. gutschreiben; ich habe noch 200 Mark bei ihm (zu) 2 he still owes me (or is indebted to me for) ten pounds. — 9. in Verbindung mit verbs (meist in einem Worte): gutheißen 2c. — II Gute(r) m, Gute f, Gute(s) n ⓖ 10. der ~e the good man; die ~en pl. the good (people), good folk(s) pl.; ein ~er a good man. — 11. das ~e the good (part); ~es und Böses the good and the bad; er hat ~es und Böses im Leben erfahren he has seen good days and bad, he has had his ups and downs (in life); ~es genug enough (or sufficient) good; alles ~e und Schöne all that is (or everything) good and beautiful; das ~e bei (od. an) der Sache ist // the (one) good part of (or point in) it is //; alles hat sein ~es there is some good in everything, a. sprichw.: there is a silver lining to every cloud; iro. Sie haben da etwas ~es angerichtet you have made a nice mess of it; was bringst du ~es? what is the best news?, what brings you here?; nichts ~es gegen e-n im Sinne haben to have no good intentions towards (F to mean no good to) a p.; des ~en zu viel tun to do too much of a good th.; (zu viel essen) to overeat o.s.; zum 2en lenken ob. wenden to turn for the best; die Sache wendet sich zum 2en things are taking a good (or favourable) turn; Sprichw. man muß des ~en nicht zu viel tun there can be too much of a good thing. — 12. im 2en: (ohne Streit) in a friendly (or an amicable) way; (freiwillig) willingly, of one's own accord; e-m etwas im 2en (in 2em) sagen ... in kind words, in a friendly tone; e-m zum 2en reden to advise a p. for the best, vgl. zugut(e). — III Gut n ⓒc. 13. the good (things); das höchste ~ (lt. summum bonum) the greatest good. — 14. (Besitztum) f. Blut¹ 3; fahrendes ~ movable property, goods and chattels pl.; Hab und ~ verlieren to lose all one's belongings; sich bei ~ und Leben verpflichten to pledge one's life and property; Güter (Vermögensstücke) effects, jur. assets pl.; anvertrautes ~ deposit; zeitliche Güter temporal possessions pl.; Sprichw. f. gedeihen 1. — 15. (ländliches Grundstück) (landed) estate; liegende Güter pl. landed property; auf seine Güter reisen to go to one's estate(s). — 16. ⓖ Güter pl. (Ware) goods pl., merchandise; ⓖ u. ↓ (Fracht) freight, consignment. — 17. a) das liebe ~ (Brot) the daily bread; b) Cath. eccl. das hochwürdige ~ (die geweihte Hostie) the holy wafer, the Host. — 18. ⊕ Gießerei: (Speise) metal bronze; Töpferei: irdenes ~ (Geschirr) earthenware, pottery, common china.

Gut-achten ("...) n ⓖ (professional or expert) opinion; von Rechtsgelehrten: counsel's opinion; ein ~ abgeben to give one's decision or verdict; ein ~ einholen to take expert (or counsel's) opinion; ein ~ bei e-m einholen to consult a p. on a question; 2achtlich a. ⓖ by way (or in form) of an (expert's) opinion; adv. sich 2 dahin äußern, daß // to state authoritatively that //; 2artig a.: a) good-natured, good-tempered; b) path. von Krankheiten: benignant, mild (fever, &c.); -artigkeit f good nature, path. mildness; -befinden n: a) = -dünken; b) satisfactory state; 2besetzt a.: a) allg.: well supplied; b) thea.: well filled; von Rollen: well cast.

Gütchen (ⓛ⌴) n 1. ⓖ (dim. von Gut) f. gut III) small estate or property. — 2. ⓖ (dim. v. Güte) sich ein ~ tun to have a good time of it. [inclined.]

gut-denkend ("...) a. ⓖ kindly (or well)

Gut-dünken ("...) n ⓖ judgment; nach meinem ~ in my opinion; Sie dürfen nach eigenem ~ handeln you may use your own discretion or do as you like.

Güte (ⓛ⌴) f ⓖ 1. v. Personen: kindness; von Dingen u. Personen: goodness, intrinsic worth, virtue, excellency; haben Sie die ~ zu warten (will you) be so kind as to wait, pray oblige me by waiting. — 2. mit ~, in aller ~ (f. gut 12) amicably; by fair means, by friendly arrangement; eine Sache in ~ abmachen to settle a matter amicably. — 3. (Beschaffenheit) quality; von hoher, geringer ~ superior, inferior; ⓖ Waren von erster ~ first-class (or first-rate) goods pl.; von mittlerer ~ middling. — 4. bei Bestellungen: durch ~! by favour of //.

Gut-edel ⓥ (ⓛ⌴) m ⓖ (weiße süße Traubenart) chasselas. [cellency quality.]

Güte-grad ("⌴...) m ⓖ degree of ex-

Güter-abfertigung ⓡ, &c. ("⌴...) f ⓖ dispatch (or consignment) of goods, goods-department, goods-office; -abtretung ⓖ f surrender (or assignment) of a bankrupt('s) estate; -agent(ur f) m estate-agent (-agency); -annahme f = -abfertigung; -anschlag m valuation of an estate or of goods; -bahnhof ⓡ m goods-station; -ballen ⓖ m bale of goods; -beförderung f forwarding (of) goods; vgl. -abfertigung; -bestätiger m, -bestätter m, -besteller m forwarding agent, carrier; -dienst ⓡ m goods-service; -expedition ⓡ f = -abfertigung; -gemeinschaft f bsd. unter Ehegatten joint property; weit2. common (or community of) ownership, communism; -halle f, -hof m ⓡ goods-platform, goods-yard; -handel m real estate agency or business; -kauf m purchase (or buying) of estates; -makler m estate-agent, land-agent; -masse ⓖ f bankrupt('s) estate; -schlächter F m = -makler; -schuppen, -speicher ⓡ m goods-shed, -loft; -stück n parcel, lot; -tarif m ⓡ goods-tariff; -transport m carriage of goods, goods-traffic; -verkehr m goods-traffic; -verlader ⓖ m lader (or loader) of goods, ↓ shipping-agent; -verladung f loading (of) goods, ↓ shipment; -versicherung f insurance of goods; -verwalter m manager of estates; -verwaltung f: a) management of estates; b) ⓖ goods-office; -vorsteher m manager of the goods-traffic; -wage f scales pl. for weighing goods; -wagen ⓡ m goods- (or luggage-)van; offener: lowry, truck; -wagenvoll m truck-load; -zug ⓡ m goods-train, slow train, mit Personenbeförderung: mixed train; -zug-lokomotive f goods-engine or -locomotive.

gut-geartet ("...) a. ⓖ well-mannered; 2gelaunt a. in good humour, good-humoured; 2gemeint a. well-meant; 2gesinnt a. well-disposed or -meaning; -gesinntheit f ⓖ kind disposition; -gewicht ⓥ n overweight; -haben ⓥ n outstanding debt; sein ganzes ~ the whole sum due to him; 2heißen v/a. ⓖd** (billigen) to approve, to sanction; (bestätigen) to confirm; -heißung f approbation; confirmation.

Gut-heit ⌴ (ⓛ⌴) [mhd.] f ⓖ goodness.

gut-herzig ("...) a. ⓖ good- (or kind-)hearted, kind; (mildtätig) charitable, liberal; ~keit f ⓖ kind-heartedness, kindness; charitableness, liberality.

gütig (ⓛ⌴) [gut] a. ⓖ good(-natured), kind(-hearted); (freundlich) friendly, affable, (nachsichtig) indulgent, (mild, wohltätig) benevolent, charitable; mit Ihrer 2en Erlaubnis with your kind permission; Sie sind sehr 2 you are very kind; seien Sie so 2, es ihm zu geben (oder F und geben es ihm) (will you) kindly give it him, be so kind as to give it him; wollen Sie mir 2st gestatten will you kindly allow me; erlauben Sie 2st please allow me; ⓖ Ihr 2es Schreiben ist soeben eingelaufen your favour has just come to hand; ~keit (ⓛ⌴) f ⓖ goodness, kindness; affability, benevolence.

gut-launig ("...) a. ⓖ good-tempered.

Gut-leut-haus (ⓛⓛⓛ) n ⓖa. ([Aussatz-]Hospital) hospital (for lepers).

gütlich (ⓛ⌴) a. ⓖ, mst. adv. 1. = mit Güte (f. das 2); — 2. sich 2 tun to enjoy (or regale) o.s. [manner or way.]

Gütlichkeit (ⓛ⌴-) f ⓖ (gütliche Weise)

gut-machen ("...) v/a. ⓖ** etwas wieder 2 (ersetzen) to make a thing good, to make amends (or reparation) for a th.; einen Fehler wieder 2 to repair a mistake; ein Unrecht wieder 2 to make restitution for a wrong; nicht wieder gutzumachen(d) irreparable, irretrievable; ~ n, -machung f reparation; -mütig(keit f) = -herzig(keit); für e-n, et. 2sagen v/n. (h.) ⓖ** (bürgen) to make o.s. (or to be) answerable for

---
ⓥ scientific; ⓟ botanical; ⓒ geography; ⊕ machinery; ⚔ mining; ⚔ military; ↓ marine; ⓖ commercial; ⓟ postal; ⓡ railway.

[Gutsagung] — 472 — [Haareisen]

a p., a th.; ~ n, =ſagung f (standing) security, (giving) bail.
Guts=beſitzer(in f) m ("..) ⑫ owner of an estate, landowner, gentleman-farmer.
gut=ſchreiben ("..) v/a. ⑳**: e-m ct. 2 (anrechnen) to credit a th. to a p.; e-m einen Betrag 2 to credit a sum to a p., to pass it to a p.'s credit; ~ ⦿ n ㉓ crediting a sum to a person, putting a sum to a p.'s credit; =ſein n ㉓ goodness.
Guts=frau ("..) f ⑫ (lady) proprietress, lady of the manor; squire's wife; =herr m landed proprietor, lord of the manor; squire; 2herr(ſchaft)lich a. manorial; =herrſchaft f: a) ownership of an estate; b) lord and lady of the manor; c) bisw. co. squirearchy; =kauf m purchase of an estate; =pachter, =pächter m tenant (of an estate or a farm). (tenant-)farmer.
gut=ſprechen ("..) v/n. (h.) ⦿a., 2ſteh(e)n v/n. (h.) ⑳*** = gutſagen.
Guts=verkauf ("..) m ⑫ sale of an estate; =verwalter m steward (or manager, bailiff) of an estate; =verwaltung f stewardship (or management) of an estate.
Guttapercha (⌣⌣⌣) [engl.; *malaiiſch] f ㊶, n ㊾ gutta-percha; ~baum ⚲ m gutta-percha tree (Isonandra gutta).
Gut=tat ⚲ (").. f ㊻ ꝛc. = Wohltat ꝛc.
gut=tun ("..) v/a. u. v/n. (h.) ⑳*** (wirken) to take effect, to operate; (ſ-e Pflicht tun) to do one's duty; e-m ct. 2 (vergüten) to indemnify (or compensate) a p. for a th.
guttural (⌣⌣⌣) [lt.] a. ⑯ guttural; ~laut m, ~is (⌣⌣⌣⌣⌣) f ㊾ (pl. a. ꝏeʃ) (Kehllaut) guttural sound.
gut=willig ("..) a. ⑯; (von gutem Willen beſeelt) willing, well-intentioned, ready (to serve), (gefällig) obliging; adv. etwas 2 tun to do a th. voluntarily or of one's own free will; =keit f ㊻ willingness, readiness (to serve); obligingness, complaisance.
Gymnaſial=abituri=ent (⌣⌣(⌣)"..) m ⑫ Deutſchland ꝛc.: (leaving) student from a classical state-school; =bildung f classical teaching; literary culture; =direktor m headmaster of a classical state-school or a grammar-school; =klaſſen f pl. e-r engl. Schule classical side; =lehrer, =ſchüler m master, scholar of a grammar-school; =unterricht m classical instruction or teaching.
Gymnaſiaſt (⌣⌣(⌣)⌣) [grch.] m ⑫ scholar of a grammar-school or a classical side; (German) grammar-school boy.
Gymnaſium (⌣⌣(⌣)⌣) [lt.. *grch.] n ⑳ Deutſchland ꝛc.: classical state-school, in England: classical side of a public school; grammar-school; ein ~ beſuchen to go to a public school.
Gymnaſt (⌣⌣) [grch.] m ⑫ (Turner) gymnast; ~ik (⌣⌣⌣) f ㊻ gymnastics; ~iker m ⑫ gymnast, athlete; 2iſch a. ⑯ gymnastic, gymnastical.
Gynäkolog ⚲ ⚹, ~e ⚳ (---⌣′(⌣) [grch.] m (Frauenarzt) specialist for women's diseases, gynæcologist; 2iſch a. ⑯ gynæcologic(al).
Gyps ꝛc. ſ. Gips ꝛc.

H

H, h (′) n, inv. (Buchſtabe) H, h; aſpiriertes (d. h. geſprochenes) H H aspirate; ſtummes (d. h. nicht geſprochenes) H H mute.
H, h ♪ n, inv. (ſiebenter Ton der diatoniſchen C-Dur-Tonleiter) B natural; H-Dur B major; H-Moll B minor.
H ⦿ abbr. = (Gut=)Haben. | ſtoff).
H chm. Symbol für Hydrogen (= Waſſer=ſ h öſt. abbr. = Heller.
H. abbr. = Hoheit.
ha! (′) I int. 1. Ton des Lachens, der Überraſchung: ha(h)!; höhnend: ha!, ha!, etwa: ha(h)! ha(h)!, ho!, Pyah!; tief fühlend: ah! — 2. Ruf für Zugtiere: hoo!, hoy! — II Ha n ㊾ 3. (Ausruf) ha(h).
ha, öſt. ha abbr. = Hektar.
h.a. abbr. = hujus anni [lt. dieſes Jahres] of the present year.
Haag ⚲ (′; Hom. Hag) [= Hag] npr/m. ⑪ a. (Holland) der ~ the Hague; im ~ at the Hague; die ~er Friedenskonferenz (1899) Peace Conference at the Hague; ~er Schiedsgericht International Court of Arbitration at the Hague.
Haar (′) [ahd.: hair] n ⓒc. 1. hair (als Kopfhaar(e) des Menſchen ſtets sg. (the) hair, nie hairs, oft head of hair); ohne ~ hairless; ~e von Tieren, oft coll. coat (of hair); (Flaum) down. — 2. mit a. und v. blonde (dunkle, rote, graue) ~e haben to have fair (dark, red, grey) hair, to be fair (dark, red-haired, grey[-haired]); dichtes, ſtruppiges ~ thick, shaggy (head of) hair, oft: F co. (quite an) umbrella; kurz geſchorenes ~ close crop, auch close shave; wirres ~ matted hair, F mat; ſ. auflöſen 1, dick 5. fliegen 8; ſich (dat.) das ~ kämmen, machen to comb, to dress (F do) one's hair; ich habe mir das ~ ſchneiden laſſen I have had my hair cut; ihr ~ iſt ſilberweiß geworden her hair has turned silvery white; ſ. ausreißen 1, grau 1. — 3. fig. es iſt kein gutes ~ an ihm he has not a redeeming (or a single good) quality; das ~ richtet ſich e-m dabei empor oder ſteht (ſteigt) einem zu Berge, das macht die ~e ſträuben (vor Angſt, Schreck) it makes one's hair stand on end; ~e auf den Zähnen haben to be a man of good sense or great courage; ſich (dat.) in die ~e fahren oder geraten (ſich balgen) to come to blows; ſich (ob. ea.) in den ~en liegen to be at loggerheads or at daggers drawn; ſie liegen ea. immer in den ~en they are for ever quarrelling; ein ~ (= eine Schwierigkeit, ein Nachteil) in et. finden to meet with an obstacle (or to find a flaw) in a th.; ~e laſſen müſſen (Schaden erleiden) to suffer injury, (betrogen werden) to be fleeced; mit Haut und ~(en) (ganz und gar) entirely, completely; von Vergleichungen ꝛc.: mit den ~en herbeigezogen far-fetched, dragged in (by main force). — 4. fig. (kleines, Geringes) man ſoll ihm kein ~ krümmen (Leid zufügen) not a hair of his head shall be touched or hurt; ~e ſpalten ob. klauben (peinlich genau ſein) to split hairs; kein gutes ~ e-m laſſen not to leave a (single) redeeming quality in a p., F to pull a p. (mercilessly) to pieces, to cut him up (nicely); an e-m ~e hängen to hang by a thread; das hat an einem ~e gehangen it was touch and go, F it was a (close) shave; es fehlt nicht ein ~ breit daran there is nothing amiss or not a thing (or pin) awry, F everything is just so; aufs ~, auf ein ~ oder Härchen (ganz genau) to a hair or a nicety, exactly, precisely, F to a T; um ein ~(=breit) oder Härchen within a hair's breadth, very nearly or narrowly; um ein ~ hätte er den Hals gebrochen he was within an ace or a hair's breadth of breaking his neck, he very narrowly escaped breaking his neck; um ein ~ beſſer a trifle better; er iſt um kein ~(=breit) beſſer als die andern he is not one jot (F not any, not a bit) better than the others; nicht um ein ~ breit weichen not to yield (or budge) an inch. — 5. ꝛc.) a) aſt. ſ. Berenike; b) ⚲ ~e Pflanze hair(s pl.), down; feines ~: ⚲ villus; mit feinen ~en bewachſen downy; (haarähnlicher Auswuchs) ⚲ trichome, (Fädchen) filament; (Samentrone) pappus; vgl. Granne. — 6. ⓒ (Faſer) thread; ~ am Tuch: nap, pile; am Plüſch ꝛc.: shag; ~ u. Grund des Tuches both sides of the cloth.
Haar=abſchneiden ("..) n ⑫ hair-cutting; 2ähnlich a. ⑯ hair-like, like a hair, ⚲ capillary, crinite; ⚲ mit den Blättern capillifolious; vgl. ⚲förmig; =arbeit(er) ⓒ f hair-work(er); =aufſatz m head-dress; =ausfallen n fall (or shedding) of the hair, ⚲ alopecia; =balg m, anat.: ⚲ hair-follicle or -sheath; =ballen m im Magen der Haustiere: hairball, ⚲ ægagropila; =band n: a) ribbon to tie the hair, headband, hair-lace or -fillet; b) als Schmuck: bow for the hair; =beſen m hair-broom; =beutel m: a) ehm. hair-bag, als Perücke auch: bag-wig; b) F fig. (leichter Rauſch) e-m einen ~ anhängen to make a p. tipsy, F to lush a p. up; =binde f = =band; =blume ⚲ f snake-gourd (Trichosanthes anguina); =breit a. of a hair's breadth; =breit n hair's breadth; vgl. Haar 4; =breite f hair's breadth. hair-breadth; =bürſte f hairbrush; =buſch m, =büſchel m tuft of hair; als Kopfſchmuck: aigret(te), crest (a. orn.); 2dünn a. = =fein; =eiſen n Barbier ꝛc.: curling-iron(s pl.) or -tongs.

Zeichen (ſ. S. XVII): F familiär; P Volksſprache; Γ Gaunerſprache; ⚲ ſelten; † alt (auch geſtorben); * neu (auch geboren); ‡ unrichtig;

[haaren] — 473 — [haben]

haaren¹ (⌣‿) ⊛ I v/n. (h.) u. sich ² v/refl. v. Tieren: to lose (or shed) one's hair. — II v/a. = abhaaren I.

ha(a)ren² (⌣‿) [nndd.] v/a. ⊛ agr. (dengeln) die Sense ² to sharpen the scythe.

Haar-erz (⌣‿...) n min. capillary native copper; -erzeugungs-mittel n remedy for making the hair grow, hair-restorer.

Haares-breite (⌣‿...) f ⊛ hairbreadth; um ~ by (or within) a hair's breadth.

Haar-färbemittel (⌣‿...) n ⊛, =fär-bungsmittel n hair-dye; =fein a. ⊛ (as) fine (or thin) as a h.; fig. Der Unterschied subtle distinction; =flechte f: a) braid (of hair), tress, plait(ed hair); b) path. hair-lichen; =flechter(in f) m plaiter of (or worker in) hair; =förmig a. hairshaped, capilliform; =förmigkeit f capillary form; =frisur f head-dress; =gefäße n/pl. anat. capillary vessels pl.; =gold n, min. capillary gold; =gras ⅋ n rye-grass (Elymus europaeus); =handel m trade in hair; =händler m dealer in hair.

haaricht (⌣‿) a. ⊛ 1. hair-like, resembling hair, ⊛ capilliform. — 2. = behaart (s. behaaren II).

haarig (⌣‿) a. ⊛ 1. = haaricht. — 2. burschikos: adv. (sehr, ungeheuer) immensely; ² viel Geld plenty (F an awful lot) of ...., F heaps (or lots) of ...

Haar-kamm (⌣‿...) m ⊛ comb for the hair; =klein a. = ²fein; adv. minutely, with full details; e-m et. ² erzählen to give a p. full particulars of a th.; =knoten m top-knot; =krankheit f disease of the hair; =kräusler(in f) m hairdresser; =krone ⅋ f aigret. ⚹ pappus; =künstler m (artistic) hairdresser.

Haarling (⌣‿) m ⊛d. ent.: ⚹ trichodectes.

Haar-locke (⌣‿...) f ⊛ lock, curl, ringlet; ²los a. ⊛ without hair, hairless; (tahl) bald; =losigkeit f hairlessness, baldness; =matratze f h.-mattress; =moos ⅋ n golden maiden-hair (Polytrichum); =mücke f sand-fly (Bibio); =nadel f h.-pin; =nest(el) n weibliche Haartracht: chignon; =netz, =öl n h.-net, -oil; =papille f, anat. papilla of the hair; =pflege f care bestowed on (or culture of) the hair, a. hairdressing; =pfleger* m hairdresser; =pinsel m h.-brush; =puder m hair-powder; =putz m ornament for the hair, hair-dress; =rauch m s. Herauch; =ring m: a) ring (made) of h.; b) ring with a p.'s hair; =röhrchen n, phys., &c. capillary tube; =röhrchen-anziehung, =kraft, =wirkung f capillary attraction, capillarity; =salbe f ointment, pomatum for the hair; =salz n, min.: a) halotrichite; b) (Feder-alaun) hair-salt; ²scharf a.: a) von e-m Messer: very sharp; b) fig. (streng und genau) very exact, overnice, hyper-critical; adv. et. ² beweisen to prove a th. to a nicety; =schärfe f, fig. great exactitude, over-nicety; =scheitel m parting of the hair; =schere f scissors pl. for cutting the hair; =schleife f, =schmuck m bow, jewellery (or ornaments pl.) for the h.; =schneide-kabinett n, =salon m hair-dressing (or -cutting) room or (bsd. Am.) saloon; =schneider

m hair-cutter, mehr gbr. hairdresser; =schnitt m: a) h.-cutting; b) style of head-dress; =schnur f: a) twist of hair; b) surg. = =seil; c) ⊛ Buchbinderei: hair-string; =schopf m = =busch; =schuppen f pl. scurf; =schur f shearing of (the) hair, shaving of the head, &c.; =schweif m e-s Kometen: ⚹ coma; =schwund m loss of hair; =seil n: a) hair-line; b) surg.. ⚹ seton; vet. rowel; =seite ⊛ f Gerberei: hair- (or fur-)side of hides; =sieb n hair-sieve; =sohle f hair-sock to put in shoes; =spalter(in f) m hair-splitter; =spalterei f hair-splitting, subtle argument; =spitze f end of a hair; =stecher ⊛ m an der Büchse h.-trigger; =stern m: a) comet; b) zo. (Strahltier) h.-star, lily-star (Comatula); c) geol.: ⚹ crinite, crinoid; =strang m: a) cord made of hair; b) ⅋ (echter) hog-fennel, sulphur-wort (Peucedanum officinal.); =sträubend a. making the hair stand on end, startling, shocking. =strich m in der Schrift. a. typ. (ant. Grundstrich) hair-line, hair- (or up-)stroke; =tolle f shock (or roll) of hair; =tour f: falsche ~ false front or fringe; =tracht f manner of wearing one's hair, (style of) head-dress; =tuch ⊛ n aus Pferde- oder Kamel-haaren: haircloth; =wachs n cosmetique; =waschmittel n, =wasser n h.-wash; =weh n burisch. co. = Katzen-jammer; =wickel m: a) zum Einwickeln der Haare: curl-paper; b) zum Aufwickeln der Haare: hair-roller; =wild n, hunt. ground-game, furred game; =wuchs m: a) growth of the hair; b) (Hauptbaar) head of h., F thatch; =wulst m shock of hair; twisted (or rolled) hair; =wurzel f: a) anat. root of a hair; b) ⅋ fibrous root; =zange f tweezers pl.; =zeug ⅋ n = =tuch; =zirkel ⊛ m hair-compasses, -dividers pl.; =zopf n von Mädchen: tress, braid of hair; von Männern, Chinesen: pigtail; =zwiebel f, anat. hair-bulb. [Habakkuk.]

Habakuk (⌣‿⌣) npr m. ⊛ x. bibl. (Prophet)

Habe (⌣‿) [ahd.] f ⊛ property, fortune, (one's) belongings ⚹ effects or possessions pl.; jur. bewegliche, fahrende ~ movables pl.; unbewegliche immovables pl.; meine ganze ~ my all, all that I may call my own; als Gepäck: impedimenta pl.; Hab und Gut goods and chattels pl., personal and real estate; vgl. Habseligkeiten.

Habeas-corpus-... (⌣‿⌣‿⌣) [lt. nimm den Körper (des Gefangenen) vor den Richter)] in Zssgn., z.B.: ~akte † f (engl. Staats-grundgesetz z. Schutz d. pers. Freiheit 1679) Habeas Corpus Act. [m ⊛ thanks pl.]

Habe-dank F (⌣‿...) [imper. v. haben]!

haben (⌣‿) [ahd.: have] ⊛b. I v/a. 1. to have (F to have got ist zu vermeiden!), z.B. blaue Augen ² to have blue eyes; bisw. passiv im p.p., z.B.: die gehabte Ehre the honour (which one has) enjoyed; ein Kind auf dem Arme ² to have a child in one's arms; du mußt Geduld ² you must h. patience or be patient; ich hab's (gefunden) I have it; kein Geld ² to h. no (or to be without) money, to be short of cash,

stärker: to be penniless or impecunious or F stumped or P stony-broke; gr. das Wort hat i im Ablativ ... has (or takes) i in the ablative; etwas im Auge ² to have s.th. in one's eye or (fig.) in view; et. im Gange ² to have a th. in full swing; e-n in s-r Gewalt ² to have (or hold) a p. in one's power or clutches, to have the whip-hand of a p.; wir ² nicht weit nach Hause we have but a short way home; wir ² jetzt Sommer we have now (or are now in) summer; et. zu Ende ² to h. finished a th.; zu ² auf allen Post-ämtern to be had (or bought) at all post-offices; ⊛ in allen Buchhand-lungen zu ² sold by (or to be had of) all booksellers; der Artikel ist nirgends zu ² ... not to be had (F got) any-where; das Haus ist noch zu ² ... is still for sale or in the market. — 2. das Kind hat et.. Reizendes an sich there is s.th. charming about ...; die Sache hat wenig auf sich it's (a matter) of small consequence, F there is nothing in it; das hat man davon that's all one gets by it; da ² wir die Bescherung (oder den Braten, die Geschichte, die Pastete ꝛc.)! there we are!; da ² wir's! there's a nice job or a fine state of affairs!; da hast du's (dein Teil ꝛc.)! there you are!, F now, you have (got) it!; da hast du eins (einen Schlag)! there, take that!; Durst, Hunger ² to be thirsty, hungry; es hat viel für (gegen) sich there is much to be said for (against) it; warte, bis ich die Seite herunter (gelesen, geschrieben) habe ... I come to the end of (or I have done) the page; et. los ² (losgemacht h.) to have (got) a th. off; fig. F (gründlich verstehen) to have a th. at one's finger's ends; recht, unrecht ² to be right, wrong; wer hat die Schuld? who is to blame (for it)?, who is at fault?; wir ² Trauer we are in mourning; ich möchte den Rock vom Leibe ² I should like to get my coat off (my back); was hast du (was fehlt dir)? what ails you?, what is the matter with you?; was hat er denn (wandelt ihn an)? what is coming over him?, what is he about? — 3. Sprichw. je mehr man hat, je mehr man will the more one has the more one wants; ein Habich ist besser als ein (oder zehn) Hättich a bird in the hand is worth two in the bush. — 4. mit inf. und zu (nötig haben): to be obliged (or to be in duty bound) to //; das ² wir doch erst ab-zuwarten we must first wait for the result or see how it ends, that re-mains to be seen; s. bedeuten 1b u. c; was hat er uns zu befehlen? what right has he to order us about?; ich habe nur zu bemerken I have only to remark; ich habe (brauche) wohl nicht erst zu bemerken // there is really no need for me to observe //; nie-mand hat danach zu fragen it is nobody's concern or business; das habe ich erst Freitag zu liefern I need not deliver it before Friday; er hat

♪ Musik; ⚹ Wissenschaft; ⅋ Pflanze; ♆ Geographie; ⊛ Technik; ⚒ Bergbau; ⚔ Militär; ⚓ Marine; ⊛ Handel; ⊛ Post; ⊟ Eisenbahn.

[haben] — 474 — [hacken]

nicht mitzureden he has no voice in the matter; er hat sich danach zu richten he is to abide by (or to conform to) it; die Sache hat nicht viel zu sagen (ist unwichtig) ... is of little importance; das hat nichts zu sagen that does not (much) signify, never mind!; was hat er hier zu schaffen? what business has he (to be) here?; du hast dafür zu sorgen (die Obliegenheit), daß es geschieht you have to see that it is done; ich habe viel zu tun I have a great deal to do, I am much engaged; ihm ℨ wir es zu verdanken we are indebted to him for it. — 5. etwas ℨ **wollen** (verlangen) to demand, to ask for, stärker to exact; (wünschen) to wish, to desire; wer will das ℨ (befiehlt es)? who orders it (to be done)?; sie will es nicht ℨ she will not (F she won't) have it, she is dead against it, she forbids it (to be done); ich will ihn damit nicht in Schutz genommen ℨ I don't want to screen him by it. — 6. in bsd. Verbindungen: **Abenteuer** ℨ to meet with adventures; **acht**ℨ to pay attention or heed; abs. to be on one's guard; hunt., &c., hab' acht! mind(, there's s.th. coming)! e-n zum **besten** ℨ f. best 7; e-n, et. **gern** ℨ to be fond of (or to like) a p., a th.; e-n **lieb**ℨ to be (fondly) attached to (or in love with) a p.; lieber ℨ to like better, to prefer; **teil** ℨ f. teilhaben; **Verdacht** auf e-n ℨ to have a suspicion against (or to be suspicious of) a p. — 7. Ausdrücke mit dem unbestimmten Objekte es: es **am** Beine, es **im** Halse ℨ to complain of (or to suffer from) one's leg, throat, F to have a bad leg, throat; **auf** die Uhr hat er's (abgesehen) it's the watch which he wants; es **bequem**, leicht ℨ to have a comfortable (or easy) life; sie ℨ es **eilig** they are in a hurry; er hat es **gut** he is well off, vgl. gut 2; sie ℨ es **leidlich** they are in fairly (or tolerably) good circumstances; es **mit** e-m ℨ: a) to be in league with a p.; b) to have an argument (or a dispute) with a p., to be at variance with a p.; sie hat es dort **schlechter** she is worse off there; es (noch) **weit** ℨ to be a long way off (yet); **wie** hast (hättst) du es damit? what is your idea about it?, what do you think of it? — 8. mit inf. ohne zu: f. gut 6; Sie ℨ leicht fragen it is easy for you to ask (questions); sie ℨ ihren Schmuck in der Schublade liegen they keep their jewellery in the drawer. — 9. mit abhängiger prp.: einen Freund **an** e-m ℨ ob. e-n zum Freunde ℨ to have a friend in a p. or a p. for one's friend; et. am Griffe, am Schnürchen ℨ f. Griff 2; oft mit refl. pron. nach betonter prp.: einen Fehler **an** sich ℨ to have a fault; er hat et. Überspanntes an sich there is s.th. eccentric about him; **auf** alles etwas (zu tadeln) ℨ to have some fault to find with everything; et. auf dem Herzen ℨ to have s.th. on one's mind; das hat nichts auf sich f. auf 9; das hat er **aus** dem Cicero he has borrowed it from Cicero; wir ℨ es aus guter Hand we have (heard) it from a good source; er hat Geld ꝛc. **bei** sich he has ... with him; er hat seine Brüder bei sich he has his brothers with him, zum Besuche: staying with him; etwas bei der Hand ℨ to have a th. (ready) at hand; ich habe nichts **gegen** ihn (dagegen) I have nothing to say against him (it), I have no objection to him (it); das Gepäck, die Mannschaft **unter** sich ℨ to be in charge of the luggage, in command of the men; ell. er hat es **von** ihr: a) (erfahren) he heard it from her; b) (erhalten) he received it from her; c) (geerbt) he has (inherited) it from her; wen glauben Sie denn **vor** sich zu ℨ? what do you take me for? — 10. im imper.: habe (od. ℨ Sie) die Güte, zu // be so kind as to //; habe Dank! my thanks to you!, let me thank you!; in Bedingungssätzen: habe nur Geld, so bist du klug if you have money you will be thought clever. — II v/impers. 11. es hat den Anschein it appears; es hat Eile damit the matter is pressing; es hat keine Not there is nothing to be afraid of; es hat seine Richtigkeit damit it is a fact or quite true; da (= mit) hat es gute Wege, es hat gute Wege damit, es hat gute Weile there is plenty of time (or no hurry) for that, it is looming in the distance. — 12. F v/refl. es hat sich was oder wohl!! (warum nicht gar?) don't tell me (that)!, nonsense!, rubbish!; es hat sich was zu lachen! (es ist nicht zum Lachen) it is no laughing matter. — III ℨ v/refl. 13. f. 12. — 14. F: (wichtig tun) to put on airs; ℨ Sie sich doch nicht so (gefährlich)! F don't put on so!, don't be (so) fussy!; (beruhigen Sie sich) compose yourself!; sich **um** et. ℨ to grieve about a th. — IV als Hilfszeitwort: 15. wir ℨ es gelesen we have read it; sie hatte sich erhoben she had risen; er hat sich gewaschen he has washed (himself); ich habe ihn besucht I have been to see him; hat er Sie besucht? has he called (or did he call) on you?; betont: er **hat** gelebt he has lived; (er ist tot) he is gone; bisw. als imper.: habe nichts gehört! pretend to (or you) have heard nothing! — 16. in Nebensätzen oft wegfallend: glaubst du, daß er sie gesehen (hat)? do you think (that) he saw them? — V ~ n ℨ 17. ℨ (ant. Debet, Soll) (rechte Seite des Hauptbuches) credit (ors pl.); Soll und ~ pl. inv. credit and debit, assets and liabilities pl.

Habe-nichts (ᵘᵛ) m ℨ ob. inv. penniless person; oft: have-not, pauper; co. Baron von ~ (auf Kriegt-auch-nichts) etwa: Lord Stonybroke (Lackland).
Haber¹ obb. (ᴸᵛ) [ahd.] m ℨ = Hafer.
Haber² (ᴸᵛ) [: lt. caper] m ℨ (Bock) he-goat. [ative person, dogmatist.)
Habe-recht (ᵘᵛ)♂m⊕d.(a.)argument-J
Haber¹ **feldtreiben** (ᵘᵛ...) n ℨ lynch-law; **-grütze** f groats pl.; **-stroh** n oat-straw.
Habesch ♀ (ᴸᵛ) npr/n. inv. = Abessinien.

Hab-gier (ᵘ...) f ℨ greed(iness), avarice, covetousness; ℨ**gierig** a. ℨ greedy, avaricious, covetous; grasping; ein ~er ℨ F a grab-all.
habhaft (ᴸᵛ) [haben] a. nur gbr. in: einer (gen.) Sache ℨ werden to seize (or secure) a th., to obtain possession (F to get hold) of a thing.
Hab-ich (ᵘᵛ) n, inv. f. haben 3.
Habicht (ᴸᵛ) [ahd.: hawk] m ℨd. orn. hawk, ℨ accipiter (Falco, Astur); (Hühner-)~ goshawk (Astur palumba'rius).
habichts-artig (ᵘᵛ...) a. ℨ hawk-like, ℨ accipitrine; **-inseln** ℨ npr. f/pl. ℨ = Azoren; **-kraut** n ℨ hawk-weed (Hiera'cium); hohes ~ king-devil (H. praea'ltum); kleines ~ mouse-ear (H. Pilose'lla); **-nase** f aquiline (or hooked) nose.
Habilitation (ᵘᵛ-tß(ᵛ)ᴸ) [lt.] f ℨ habilitation of a university-lecturer, admission of an academical teacher into the faculty.
habilitieren (ᵘᵛᴸᵛ) [lt.] v/refl. ℨ: sich an e-r Hochschule ℨ to take up one's residence as university-lecturer or professor.
Habit F (ᵛᴸ) [fr.] n (m) ℨd. (ℨ) 1. fast † suit (of clothes); garment. — 2. ℨ (Kleidung der Bergleute) miner's dress.
Habitus (ᴸᵛᵛ) [lt.] m, inv. (physical or mental) habits pl., ℨ habitus.
Habsburg ♀ (ᵘᵛ) [Habichtsburg: im Aargau, Schweiz, Stammburg der ~er] I **~er** (in f ℨ) m ℨ one of the Habsburg family or dynasty; die ~er pl. the H. family. — II a. inv., **Lisch** a. ℨ of (the house of) Habsburg.
Habschaft (ᴸᵛ) f ℨ property; bare ~ (ready) cash, money in hand.
Habseligkeit (ᵘᴸᵛ-) f ℨ, mst pl. **~en** all that one has, goods and chattels pl., F (one's) traps or sticks pl.; vgl. Habe.
Hab-sucht (ᵘ...) f ℨ avarice; vgl. -gier; ℨ**süchtig** a. ℨ avaricious; vgl. ℨgierig.
Hack F (ᵛ) n ℨ: ~ und ℨ**mack** (Schund) rubbish; (Pöbel) tag-rag and bobtail; (Gemengsel) medley.
Hack-bank ⊕ (ᵛ...) [hacken] f ℨ chopping-board or bench; **-beil** n chopper, hatchet; **-block** m chopping-block; **-bord** ⊥ n (See) stern; **-brett** n: a) **-bank**; b) ♪ (Zimbel) cymbal, ehm. (16. sae.): dulcimer.
Hacke¹ (ᴸᵛ) [mhd.; *hacken²] f ℨ 1. a) agr. (Karst) hoe (auch ℨ); (Rode-)~ grubbing-axe or -hoe; b) (Haue, Picke) pickaxe, mattock. — 2. agr. (Hacken) hoeing.
Hacke² (ᴸᵛ) [mhd.] f ℨ 1. (Ferse, am Strumpf und Schuh) heel; fig. e-m auf den ~n (nahe) sein oder sitzen to be (close) at (or on) a p.'s heels; F sich auf die ~n machen to take to one's heels, to run away, to bolt; ✕ ~n zusammen! heels closed!, close heels! — 2. ⊥ ~ f einer Stänge heel of a top-gallant mast.
Hack-eisen (ᵛ...) n ℨ chopper.
Hacken¹ (ᴸᵛ) m ℨ = Hacke².
hacken² (ᴸᵛ) [mhd.: hack] ℨ I v/a. und v/n. (h.) 1. von Raubvögeln: (mit Schnabel und Klauen) to pick (or peck, hack, stärker: to tear or pull) to pieces. — 2. mit Angabe der Wirkung: e-m die Augen aus dem Kopfe ℨ to pick a p.'s eyes out (of his head). — 3. F fig. sie ℨ

Signs (see page XVII): F familiar; P vulgar; ⌐ flash; \ rare; † obsolete (died); * new word (born); ⁺⁺ incorrect; ♪ music;

alle auf ihn ein they are all picking holes in him. — 4. ſich 2 v/rpr. to knock (or cut) each other about. — 5. ⊕ to hack, chop, hew; to cut to pieces; klein 2 to mince, Fleiſch a. to hash; Holz 2 to chop (or cut, cleave) ...; ⚔ gehacktes Blei slug. — 6. agr. (mit dem Karſt bearbeiten) to hoe. — II v/n. (h.) 7. (feſt kleben) to stick (fast), to adhere, to cling.

Hacken-leder ⊕ (⸗⸗...) n ㉒ Schuhm.: heel-piece; =ſchuh m high-heeled boot or shoe; =ſtück n = =leder.

Hacker (⸗⸗) m ㉒ 1. agr. one who hoes or grubs; f. Holz2. — 2. ⊕ Spinnerei: (Kamm) comb.

Häckerling (⸗⸗⸗) [nhd.] m ⓓd. 1. ⚹ = Häckſel — 2. F fig. (Wertloſes): ~ (nichts) im Kopfe h. to have an empty (F a poor) head; Sprichw. ſ. aber III.

Hack-fleiſch (⸗⸗...) n minced (or sausage-)meat; =frucht f, agr.: a) allg.: vegetables pl. which require hoeing; b) bſp. potato, turnip and cabbage; =(e=)klotz m = =block; =mack F n ſ. Hack. =maſchine f zum Fleiſchhacken: mincing-machine; agr. (Pferdehacke) chopping-machine; =meſſer n chopping- (or mincing-)knife.

Hackſch prov. (⸗) [: hog; *hecken] m ⓐ a. (Eber) boar-pig.

Häckſel ⊕ (⸗⸗) [nhd.; *hacken] m u. n ㉒ agr. u. ⚔ chopped straw; chaff; ~ ſchneiden to cut chaff.

Häckſel-bank ⊕ (⸗⸗...) f ㉒ bench for cutting straw, straw- (or chaff-)cutter; =maſchine f = =ſchneidemaſchine.

häckſeln ⊕ (⸗⸗) [Häckſel] v/n. (h.) ㉒ a. to cut chaff, to chop (or cut) straw.

Häckſel-ſchneide-maſchine (⸗⸗...) f ㉒ chaff-cutting engine, chaff-cutter.

Hader[1] (⸗⸗) [ahd.: lt.] m ㉖ 1. (Lumpen) rag. — 2. fig. (Lump) ragamuffin; scamp, black-guard, cad.

Hader[2] (⸗⸗) [mhd.] m ㉒ (Streit) dispute, quarrel, squabble; (Händel) brawl(ing), feud; (Zwietracht) dissension.

Had(e)rer (⸗(⸗)⸗) [Hader2] m ㉒ quarreller, squabbler, quarrelsome person.

Hader[1]-lump(en) (⸗⸗...) m ㉒ rag, pl. a. tatters; =mann m rag-and-bone man.

hadern (⸗⸗) [mhd.; Hader2] I v/n.(h.) ㉒ a. 1. (ſtreiten) mit e-m 2 to quarrel (or wrangle, squabble) with a p., to (have a) dispute with a p.; laut 2 to brawl. — 2. bibl. (zürnen) to be angry or wrathful. — II ~ n ㉓ 3. = Hader2.

Hader[2]-ſucht (⸗⸗...) f ㉒ quarrelsomeness, quarrelsome disposition or spirit; =ſüchtig a. ⓖ quarrelsome.

Hades ⚯ (⸗⸗) [grch.] m, inv. myth. ([Gott der] Unterwelt) Hades.

Hadrer (⸗⸗) [hadern] m ㉒ f. Haderer.

Hadſchi (⸗⸗) [ar.] m ⓹⓪ (Pilger) hadjee.

Hafen[1] obb. (⸗⸗) [ahd.] m ⓶⓪ (earthen) pot; (glass) jar or mug.

Hafen[2] ⚓ (⸗⸗) [ndd.: haven] m ⓴ harbour, (sea)port; natürlicher ~ natural harbour; creek; kleiner ~ für Schiffsarbeiten: wet dock; fig. (Ruhe-ort) haven (of rest), safe refuge, (place of) shelter; f. anlaufen 3 u. 8 u. antun 4; in den ~ einlaufen to put into port, to enter a harbour; fig. in den ~ der Ehe einlaufen to enter the conjugal (or matrimonial) state, to get married. — Vgl. Außen-, Binnen-, Kriegs-2.

Hafen[2]-anker ⚓ (⸗⸗...) m ⓶⓶ zum Vertäuen: mooring-anchor; =arbeiten f/pl. harbour-works pl.; =arbeiter m dockyard-labourer; longshoreman / =aufſeher m harbour-master; =bau m construction of a harbour or port; =baum m harbour-boom; =baumeiſter m naval architect; =becken n basin; =damm m jetty, mole, als Promenade bſd. in Seebädern: pier, zum Anlanden: landing-pier or -stage; =damm-aufſeher m piermaster; =dienſt m harbour-duties pl.; =gebühren f/pl., =geld n harbour- (or port-)dues or charges pl., portage; =kapitän m = =aufſeher; =kette f boom-chain; =lotſe, =meiſter m harbour-pilot, -master; =ordnung f harbour-(or port-)regulations pl.; =platz m = =ſtadt; =räumer m dredge, dredging-machine; =ſperre f embargo; im Kriege: blockade; =ſtadt f seaport; =wache f port-watch; =zeit f tide; =zoll m = =gebühren.

Hafer ⚹ (⸗⸗) [ndd. (hd. Haber)] m ㉒ agr. (echter) ~ oats pl. (Avena [sativa]); fig. ihn ſticht der ~ (er wird übermütig) success has spoilt him or made him overbearing; ſ-n wilden ~ ſäen (ſich austoben) to sow one's wild oats.

Hafer-acker (⸗⸗...) m ㉒ = =feld; 2artig ⚹ a. ⓖ: ⚯ avenaceous; =bau m growing of oats; =boden m: a) agr. oat-land; b) loft for (storing) oats; =brei m, =brot n oatmeal-porridge, -bread; =ernte f gathering in the oats; oat-crop; =feld n field of oats, oatfield, oat-ground; =garbe f sheaf of oats; =gries m, =grütze f groats, hulled oats pl.; =kaſten, m, =kiſte f oatbin or -chest; =korn n grain of oats; =kuchen m oatmeal cake; =malz n oatmalt; =mehl n oatmeal; =mehlbrei m porridge; =mühle ⊕ f oat-mill; =mus n oatmeal-porridge; =pflaume ⚹ f bullace; =rohr n (Hirtenpfeife) oaten pipe; =ſack m sack for oats; (Futterbeutel) nose-bag, prov. ⚹ haversack; =ſchlehe ⚹ f bullace; =ſchleim m (water-)gruel; =ſchrot n ground oats pl.; =ſpreu f, =ſtroh n oat-chaff, -straw; =ſtoppel f oat-stubble; =ſuppe f oatmeal soup.

Haff ⚓ (⸗) [ndd.] n ⓓb. (⓾) ⚯ bſd. an der Oſtſee: fresh-water lake adjoining the Baltic, Thaff; ⚯. B. das Friſche (das Kuriſche) ~ the Frische (the Curische) Haff.

Hafner obb. (⸗⸗) [Hafen1] m ㉒ = Töpfer.

...**haft** (...⸗) [haben] Anhängſilbe zur Bildung v. a. u. adv., ...**haftigkeit** (...⸗⸗⸗) zur Bildung von s., bedeutet: a) Vorhandensein oder Beſitz, z.B. mangelhaft a. having faults, faulty, defective, Mangelhaftigkeit f faultiness, defectiveness; b) Neigung, Gewohnheit, z.B. boshaft a. wickedly inclined, malicious, Boshaftigkeit f malice; c) Ähnlichkeit, z.B. fieberhaft a. like fever, feverish, Fieberhaftigkeit f feverishness; d) Erregung, z.B. ekelhaft a. producing nausea, nauseous, Ekelhaftigkeit f nauseousness; e) Wirkung, Ergebnis, z.B. nahrhaft a. nutritious, nourishing, Nahrhaftigkeit f nutritiousness.

Haft (⸗) [ahd.; *haben] I ⓑb. 1. m (n) faſt † (das, was haften macht ob. Halt gibt) binding, fastening, ligament. — 2. m (Haken) hook, (Spange) clasp, (Schnürband) lace. — 3. m (n), chm. phys. (Klebrigkeit) adhesiveness, ⚯ agglutinative property. — 4. m u. n, ent. (Eintagsfliege) ⚯ ephemeral fly. — II f, inv. 5. (Gefangenſein) detention, imprisonment; (close) confinement; geh. Sprache: durance (vile); zur ~ bringen to take into custody, (feſtnehmen) to (put under) arrest; ſeiner ~ entlaſſen to discharge (from jail); in ~ halten to keep in custody, to detain (in prison).

haftbar (⸗⸗) a. ⓖ responsible, liable; ~keit f ⓖ responsibility, liability.

Haft-befehl (⸗...) m ㉒, =brief m warrant for the apprehension of a p., writ of attachment; =dauer f period of detention.

Häftchen (⸗⸗) n ㉓ dim. v. Hafte ſubb. (⸗⸗) f ⓖ = Haft 2.

Haftel (⸗⸗) m u. n ㉒ small hook or clasp.

haften (⸗⸗) [Haft] I v/n. (h.) ⓖ 1. an etwas 2 to cling to a th.; (befeſtigt ſein) to be fixed (or attached) to a th.; (feſtkleben) to adhere (ſtärker: to stick) to a th.; ſeine Blicke auf et. 2 laſſen to fix one's glances (or eyes) upon a th.; es 2 Hypotheken auf dem Gute the property is encumbered (or burdened) with mortgages; es haftet nichts in ſeinem Kopfe ober bei ihm: a) nothing impresses itself on (or F sticks to) his memory, he cannot remember anything; b) (nichts läßt einen Eindruck bei ihm) nothing impresses him; es haftet Verdacht auf ihm suspicion rests upon him; es darf kein Zweifel darauf 2 it must not be left to doubt. — 2. für e-n, etwas 2 = bürgen; ich hafte mit meinem Kopfe dafür I answer with my head for it. — II ~ n ㉓ 3. = Haftung.

Haft-geld (⸗⸗...) n ㉒ = Handgeld; =genoſſe m fellow-prisoner.

...**haftigkeit** (..."⸗⸗) ⓖ f. ...haft.

Häftling (⸗⸗) m ⓓd. prisoner, F jailbird.

Haft-lokal (⸗...) n ㉒ jail; =pflicht f responsibility, liability (vgl. m. b. H.); =pflicht-geſetz n parl. Employers' Liability Act; 2pflichtig a. responsible, liable; =ſtrafe f = Haft II.

Haftung (⸗⸗) f ⓖ (ſ. haften 1) attachment; adhesion; (ſ. 2) = Bürgſchaft 1.

Haft-vollzug (⸗...) m ㉒ imprisonment; =zeher m/pl. zo. (Eidechſen) ⚯ gecoids, ascalabotæ.

Hag (⸗) [mhd.] m ⓜc. 1. (Hecke) (quickset) hedge, (Zaun) fence; (eingefriedigter Raum) enclosure. — 2. (dichtes Geſträuch) (dense) bush, coppice; (Hain) grove; (Wald) wood. — 3. (Wieſe) meadow(-land).

Häge-... (⸗⸗...) ſ. Hege-.

Hage-buche ⚹ (⸗⸗...) f ㉒ (Weißbuche) hornbeam, hardbeam (Carpinus betulus); 2buchen a.: a) of hornbeam; b) [mhd.] P fig. (auch 2büchen) = hahnebüchen; =butte ⚹ f (Frucht der =roſe) hip; =butten-roſe ⚹ f = =roſe; =dorn ⚹ m (Weißdorn) hawthorn, white thorn, als Baum oft: may (-tree) (Cratægus).

⚯ scientific; ⚹ botanical; ⓖ geography; ⊕ machinery; ⚒ mining; ⚔ military; ⚓ marine; ⓖ commercial; ⚯ postal; 🚂 railway.

[Hagel] — 476 — [Haken]

Hagel (⌣́) [ahd.: hail] m 1. (gefrorener Regen) hail; in Flüchen: Blitz, Donner und ~!, damn it!, confounded!, botheration!; alle ~! confound (or hang) it all! — 2. *fig.* ~ von Schlägen blows *pl.* showering down (upon one), sound thrashing or tanning; ~ von Steinen, Geschossen shower of stones, missiles; ~ von Schimpfwörtern volley of abuse. — 3. *path.* ~ (Geschwulst) am Augenlide stye, *⚕* chalazion (vgl. Gerstenkorn). — 4. *hunt.* (Flintenschrot) small shot; *artill.* grape-shot, iron (or lead) fragments *pl.* for charging mortars, &c.

Hagel=ableiter (⌣⌣́...) m phys.: paragrandine; =**dicht** a. (as) thick as hail; =**korn** n: a) hailstone; b) *path.* stye (= Hagel 3).

hageln (⌣́⌣) *v/n.* (h.) ⒶⒶ. (mst *v*/impers.) to hail; es hagelt it hails, hailstones are falling; *fig.* es hagelte Steine auf ihn stones were showered upon him.

Hagel=regen (⌣́⌣...) m hail-storm, downpour of hail; =**schad(en)** m damage done (or loss caused) by hail; =**schauer** m heavy fall of hail, vgl. =**wetter**; =**schlag** m = =schaden, =wetter; =**schloße** f = =korn a; =**schrot** m, n, *hunt.* (Entenschrot) duck-shot; =**sturm** m storm accompanied by hail; a. =**wetter**; =**versicherung(s=gesellschaft)** f insurance (-company) for losses caused by hail; =**wetter** n hail-storm, heavy shower of hail; =**wolke** f hail-cloud.

Hagen (⌣́⌣) [ahd.] m = Hag.
hägen (⌣́⌣) *v/a.* ⒷⒷ *2c.* = hegen *2c.*
hager (⌣́⌣) [nhd.: haggard] a. (D 9) lean (and lanky), thin, (dürr) scraggy, v. der Gestalt auch: slender (form), slim (person), v. den Zügen: haggard (countenance), worn (features); lange 2e Person long and lanky person; ~**keit** f leanness, thinness; slenderness.

Hage=rose ♀ (⌣́⌣...) f dog- (or canker-)rose (*Rosa cani'na*); =**stolz** [Hagebesitzer, jüngerer Sohn] m ⒶⒶ. u. *adj.* a. *adj.* oft *b.s.* (confirmed) old bachelor.

Hagiograph *⚕* (⌣⌣⌣́f), **Hagiolog** (⌣⌣⌣́) [grch.] m (Lebensbeschreiber eines Heiligen) hagiographer, hagiologist.

haha (⌣́⌣) **I** 2! *int.* ha(h) ha(h)! (f. ha). — **II** ~ n ha-ha, haw-haw.
Häher (⌣́⌣) [ahd.] m *orn.* (Eichel2) jay (*Ga'rrulus glanda'rius*).

Hahn (⌣́) [ahd.] m ⒸⒸ. (Ⓑ) 1. a) cock, auch: rooster, in Fabeln *2c.*: chanticleer; junger ~ (auch *dim.* Hähnchen, Hähnlein) young cock, cockerel; kalku'ttischer (oder welscher) ~ turkey-cock; b) allg.: (Männchen des Geflügels und der Singvögel) cock, z.B. cock-pheasant, cock canary, &c. — 2. F *fig.* mutiger ~ (Kämpe) valiant (or plucky) champion or fighter, P fine cock (fighting-)cock; ~ im Korbe: a) (Hauptkerl) cock of the walk, cock on the wall; b) (übermütiger Gesell) saucy (F cheeky) fellow. — 3. *bism. iro.* im Gegensatze zu 2: (gutmütiger Tropf) good-natured fool, simpleton (vgl. Hahnrei). — 4. *fig.* Redens=arten: es kräht kein ~ (oder nicht Huhn oder ~, darans *corr.* nicht Hund

noch ~) danach (es kümmert sich niemand darum) no one troubles about it or pays any heed to it; e-m den roten ~ aufs Dach setzen (das Haus in Brand stecken) to set a p.'s house on fire. — 5. ⚔ ~ am Gewehrschlosse cock; den ~ spannen to cock a gun; mit gespanntem ~ at full cock; den ~ in (die erste oder Vorder=)Ruh setzen ob. abspannen to half-cock a gun; der ~ ist in Ruh the gun is at half-cock; den ~ in Ruh setzen to let down the cock; bei ~ in Ruh losgehen to go off at half-cock (auch *fig.*). — 6. ⊕ ~ am Fasse, für Wasser, Gas *2c.* tap (nicht cock!); den ~ aufdrehen (zudrehen) to turn the tap on (off); den ~ abdrehen to turn off the tap; (Sperr=)~ stop-cock; (Probier=)~ an Dampfkesseln pet-cock.

Hähnchen (⌣́⌣) n f. Hahn 1.
Hahne=... (⌣́⌣...) = Hahn(en)=...
hahne=büchen P (⌣́⌣⌣́) [hagebüchen] a. ⒻⒻ(D 9) coarse, (big and) heavy, clumsy.
Hahnen=balken ⊕ (⌣́⌣...) m *carp.* top-beam, auch: cock-loft; =**bart** m wattle; =**ei** n, *etwa*: pigeon's milk, mare's nest; =**feder** f cock's feather; =**fuß** m: a) cock's foot; b) ♀ crowfoot (*Ranu'nculus*); c) =**füße** *pl.* (Gekritzel) scrawl *sg.*; =**fußgewächse** ♀ *n*/*pl.* ranunculaceæ *pl.*; =**gefecht** n = =kampf; =**kamm** m: a) cock's-comb, ⚕ caruncle; b) ♀ yellow rattle (*Rhina'nthus crista galli*); bsb. großer ~ cock's-comb, cockscomb (*Rhina'nthus ma'ior*); =**kampf** m cock-fight(ing); =**kampfplatz** m cockpit; =**kopf** ♀ m cock's-head, cockshead (*Hedy'sarum*); =**krei** m f. Hahn=...; =**schritt** m strutting (gait) of the cock; =**sporn** m: a) cock's spur, cockspur; b) ♀ (Art Weißdorn) cock's-spur (or cockspur) thorn (*Crataegus Crus galli*); =**tritt** m (Schwebeband b. Dotters) cock('s)-tread(le), ⚕ chalaza. — Vgl. auch Hahn=... [awning.⟩

Hahne=pot ⚓ (⌣́⌣) m ⒸⒸ crowfoot (of an⟩
Hahne=geschrei (⌣́⌣...) n = =schrei.
Hähnlein (⌣́⌣) n f. Hahn 1.
Hahnrei F (⌣́⌣) [nhd.] m ⒷⒷ. (betrogener Ehegatte) cuckold; zum ~ m. to cuckold; ~**feder** f: ~n tragen to be deceived by an unfaithful wife.

Hahnreischaft F (⌣́⌣⌣) f cuckoldom.
Hahn=ruf (⌣́⌣...) m ⒸⒸ, =**fang** m = =schrei; =**schlüssel** m am Fasse key of a tap; =**schrei** m cock-crowing; mit dem ersten ~ at the first crowing (or call) of the cock, in the early dawn. — Vgl. auch Hahnen=...

haho (⌣́⌣) *int. humt.* 2! hey! ho!
Hai (⌣́) [ndl.] m ⒷⒷ. *ichth.* shark (*Squalus*); engS. (Menschen=)~ man-eater, requin (*Carcha'rodon*).

Haide, Haiduk f. Heide, Heiduck.
Hai=fisch (⌣́...) m ⒶⒶ. = Hai.
haifisch=artig (⌣́⌣...) a. ⒸⒸ: ⚕ squaloid, galeoid; =**fang** m catching (or capture of) sharks; =**haut** f shark-skin, shagreen.

Hain (⌣́) [mhd. = Hag(en)] m ⒸⒸ. (Gehölz) wood, coppice; *poet.*: (sacred or hallowed) grove; ~**binse** ♀ f woodrush (*Lu'zula*); ~**buche** ♀ f = Hagebuche; ~**butte** ♀ f = Hagebutte.

Hai=roche(n) (⌣́...) m ⒷⒷ *ichth.* shark-ray (*Rhinoba'tus*); ~**n** betr.: ⚕ rhinobatoid.
Häkchen (⌣́⌣) n (*dim.* von Haken) 1. small hook, hooklet; ⊕ a. crotchet; ⚕ uncinus; *ent.* =**tragend**: ⚕ unciferous. — 2. *gr.*: a) oben rechts v. e-m Buchstaben: apostrophe; b) unter e-m fr. c: cedilla (ç); c) (Anführungszeichen) inverted commas, quotation marks (*abbr.* quotes) *pl.* (dtsch: „ ", engl.: ' ' oder " ..."). — 3. *fig.*: a) ein ~ auf e-n haben (e-m grollen) to have a spite (or grudge) against a p.; b) ein ~ (e-n Sparren) im Kopfe h. to have a screw loose, to be crotchety, to be off one's head or F one's nut; Sprichw. was ein ~ (oder Haken) werden will, krümmt sich bei Zeiten (just) as the twig is bent the tree will grow.

Häkel=arbeit (⌣́⌣...) f crochet-work.
Häkelei (⌣⌣⌣́) f 1. = Häkelarbeit. — 2. F *fig.* (Neckerei) teasing, chaff(ing).
Häkel=garn (⌣́⌣...) n crochet-cotton; =**haken** m crochet-hook.
häk(e)lig (⌣́⌣⌣) [haken] a. ⒸⒸ hooked, ♀ (rauhhaarig): ⚕ hispid(ulous), hamulose; *fig.* (heikel, mißlich) delicate, knotty, nice, intricate, ticklish, trying; von Personen: (empfindlich) touchy, crotchety, sensitive; ~**keit** f ⒸⒸ *fig.* knottiness, intricacy; touchiness, crotchetiness.

Häkel=muster (⌣́⌣...) n crochet-pattern.
häkeln (⌣́⌣) [haken] **I** *v/a.*, *v/n.* (h.) u. sich 2 *v/refl.* ⒶⒶ. 1. (mit der Häkelnadel arbeiten) to (work in) crochet; (tamburieren) to tambour. — 2. (mit Häkchen festmachen) to hook (fast), to fasten (or catch) with small hooks. — 3. *fig.* (sticheln) to tease, to chaff; an etwas 2 to cavil at a th., to find fault with a th. — **II** ~ n ⒸⒸ 4. = Häkelarbeit.

Häkel=nadel (⌣́⌣...) f crochet-needle; zum Tamburieren: tambour-needle; =**seide** f silk for crochet-work; =**stich** m crochet-stitch.

Haken[1] (⌣́⌣) [ahd.: hook] m ⒶⒶ 1. hook, ⚕ uncinus; zum Aufhängen v. Kleidern: peg; ⚓ (Enter=)~ grapple, grappling-iron, an e-r Tafel: tackle-hook; (Schür=)~ crook; (Haspe, Spange) clasp; (Stell=)~ adjusting clasp; (Klampe) clamp; ~ und Öse hook and eye. — 2. *fig.* die Sache hat einen (ob. ihren) ~ (e-e Schwierigkeit, e-n Nachteil) ... has its difficulties, it's not quite easy or as it should be; F there's a flaw (or hitch) somewhere; da ist der ~ that's the difficulty, there is the rub; F Häkchen 3, Sprichw. — 3. ⚔ = Hakenbüchse; ⊕ Schlosserei: = ~**schlüssel**; *agr.* = =**pflug**. — 4. *hunt.* ~ (Wendung) des Hasen doubling (of the hare); einen ~ schlagen to double, to dodge (the hunters, the hounds).

haken[2] (⌣́⌣) [Haken] *v/a.*, *v/n.* (h.) und sich 2 *v/refl.* ⒷⒷ to hook (on); to seize with a hook or a grappling-iron, to fasten with a hook or a clasp; ⚙ Waggons an den Zug 2 to attach or couple ...; *fig.* da ha''tt (hapert) es ob. die Geschichte that's the difficulty or F the pull, F there is a hitch (or flaw) somewhere.

Zeichen (f. S. XVII). F familiär; P Volkssprache; Г Gaunersprache; ⚡ selten; † alt (auch gestorben); * neu (auch geboren); ‡‡ unrichtig;

[hakenähnlich] — 477 — [Halbling]

haken-ähnlich (⌣⌣...) a. ⓖ hook-like, crook-shaped; =**band** ⊕ n ⓖ Schlofferei: plate of a hinge; =**bein** n, anat. der Handwurzel: ☞ unciform (bone); ehm. =**büchse** ⚔ f blunderbuss, arquebuse; ⚬**förmig** a. hook-shaped, hooked, ☞ aduncous, hamose, uncinal, uncinate(d), unci(ni)form; orn. ☞ Schnabel hooked beak, hook-beak; mit ⚬em Schnabel hook-beaked, ☞ uncirostrate, hamirostrate; =**fortſaȥ** m, anat. hooklet, ☞ uncinatum apophysis; =**gimpel** m, orn. pine-grosbeak (Pinicola enuclea'tor); =**nadel** ⚘ f bei Schwämmen: ☞ uncinate; =**nagel** ⊕ m barbed nail, tenter-hook; =**naſe**=**hooked**(or aquiline) nose; =**ſcheibe** ⊕ f hook-plate; =**ſchlag(en** n) m, hunt. (Kreuzſprung des Haſen) double; =**ſchlüſſel** ⊕ m Schlofferei: picklock; =**ſchnabel** m, orn. hook-bill, hooked beak; ⚬**ſchnäb(e)lig** a. orn.: ☞ uncirostrate; ehm. =**ſchüȥ(e)** ⚔ m arquebusier; =**ſpieß** ⚓ m harpoon, harping-iron; =**ſtahl** ⊕ m hooked (or hook-) tool; =**ſteu(e)rung** ⊕ f hook-motion; =**ſtock** m hooked stick; zum Hockenballſpiel: hockey-stick or club; =**zahn** m, zo. corner-tooth.

hakicht, hakig (⌣⌣) a. ⓖ hooked.

Häkler (⌣⌣) 1. m ㉒, ~**in** f ㊼ person who crochets. — 2. nur m, fig. crotchety (or touchy) person.

häklig (⌣⌣) ꝛc. ſ. häkelig ꝛc.

Halali (⌣⌣, ⌣⌣)[fr. ha là lit] n ㊼ hunt.: ~ blaſen to sound the death-halloo, to sound in at the death, ehm. auch: to sound the mort.

halb (⌣) [ahd.: half] I a. ⓖ 1. half; ein ⚬es Pfund half a pound (dagegen: ein Halbpfundgewicht a half-pound); ein ⚬er Groſchen a halfpenny; dreiundein⚬ Prozent, drei und ein ⚬es Prozent three and a half per cent.; ein ⚬es Jahr six months; einundein⚬es Jahr ob. anderthalb Jahr(e) eighteen months pl.; um den ⚬en Preis for half the money or price, at halfprice; ⚬ entzwei brechen to break in two; auf ⚬em Wege entgegenkommen to meet half-way; auf ⚬em Wege ſteh(e)n bleiben to stop (or halt, rest) half-way or midway; um ⚬ elf Uhr, um zehn (und) ein ⚬ Uhr at half-past ten, F a. at ten thirty; die Uhr (ob. es) iſt gerade ⚬ it is just half (past); es ſchlägt ⚬ it (or the clock) is striking the half hour; die Uhr ſchlägt voll und ⚬ ... strikes the (full) hours and (the) half hours; mit ⚬er Stimme in a low (or below one's) voice; ⚬er Vers: ☞ hemistich; vor Ländernamen ohne art. und vor Städtenamen oft inv., zB. das ⚬e (öfter: ~) Frankreich one half of France; ⚬ Paris half (ſtärker betont: one half of) Paris. — 2. (unvollſtändig): a) ⚬ gar, ⚬ gekocht underdone; ⚬ reif half (or not quite) ripe; ⚬e Trauer half-mourning; ♪ ⚬e Note minim; ⚬e Takt-pauſe minim-rest; ⚬er Ton semitone, half-tone; ⚓ auf ⚬er Stange flaggen to fly (or put) the flag at half-mast; b) mit neg. und beſchränkenden Partikeln: nicht ⚬ ſo viel not half as much; ſie iſt nicht ⚬ ſo fleißig wie ihre Schweſter

she is not half (or not nearly) as (or so) industrious as her sister; ſie hat es nur ⚬ fertig gemacht she only half finished it; die Flaſche iſt nur ⚬ voll ... is but half full; er hat den Sinn nur ⚬ verſtanden he did not understand more than half (or a part) of it; c) ⚬ ..., ⚬ ... (einesteils, andernteils): ⚬ zog ſie ihn, ⚬ ſank er hin (G.) partly she drew him in, partly he sank in. — 3. fig. ⚬e Maßregeln f/pl. half-(and -half) measures pl.; er hört nur mit ⚬em Ohre (oder ⚬en Ohren) zu he scarcely listens, he pays no attention; ich bin ⚬ tot ... half dead with fatigue, &c., F ... done up or dead tired; ⚬ unterrichtet partially (or badly) informed; das iſt weder ganz noch ⚬ that's neither one thing nor the other. — 4. **halb und halb** (einigermaßen) by halves, only half, tolerably (well); (beinahe) nearly; ich bin ⚬ und ⚬ fertig I have (or am) just upon finished; nur ⚬ und ⚬ only partially (done), indifferently (finished), incompletely. — 5. (von einer Seite) on one side (only); ⚬e Geſchwiſter ſ. Halbgeſchwiſter. — II ~ s. 6. inv. (one-)half; $1/6$ und $1/3$ iſt zuſammen ein ~ ... make together one-half. — 7. das ~e, ein ~es n ⓖ half, moiety. — 8. ~e(r) m, ~e f ⓖ ell. geben Sie mir e-n ~⚬n (halben Schoppen), eine ~e (halbe Flaſche) ... half a pint, half a bottle; fig. er iſt ein ~er ... neither one nor the other or neither fish nor flesh. — III ...**halb** (...⌣) 9. in Zſſgn, zB. andert⚬ one and a half; außer⚬ outside.

Halb-affe (⌣...) m ⓖ zo. half-ape, ☞ prosimian; ⚬**amtlich** ⚔ ⓖ semi-official, quasi-official; =**ärmel** m half-sleeve; =**atlas** ⚘ m satinet; =**bad** n demi-bath or -bain; =**bataillonskolonnen** ⚔ f/pl. quarter-columns, half-battalions pl.; =**bauer** m: a) (ant. Vollbauer) small farmer; b) tenant who pays half his rent in the shape of produce; =**bier** m small-beer; =**bild** n half-length (or half-size) portrait; ⚬**bildung** f semi-civilization or -culture; =**blut** n, Pferdezucht: half-blood; =**bruder** m half-brother, step-brother; ⚬**bürtig** a. of mixed breed, Oſt-J.: half-caste; ⚬**chor** ♪ m semi-chorus; =**dach** ⚓ n pent-roof; =**damaſt** ⚘ m silk and wool (or silk and cotton) damask; =**deck** ⚓ n quarter-deck; ⚬**dunkel**: a. half-dark; ~ n (dim) twilight, dusk, semi-darkness; im ~ in the dusk, F between the lights; paint. = Helldunkel; ⚬**durchſichtig** a. semi-transparent, ☞ semi-diaphanous; =**duȥend** n : das ~ the half dozen; ein ~ half a dozen.

Halbe (⌣⌣) f ㊼ (Hälfte) half.

Halb-edelſtein (⌣...) m ⓖ half-precious stone; ⚬**eirund** a. ⓖ zo.: ☞ semioval, semiovate.

...halben (...⌣⌣) i. Zſſgn ſ. meinet⚬ ꝛc.

halb-entſchlummert (⌣...) a. ⓖ dozing, ☞ somnolescent.

halber ob. **...halber** (...⌣⌣) in Zſſgn mit f auf -s ſtets zſ.-, ſonſt getrennt oder zſ.-geſchrieben: Geſchäfte ⚬ on account of business, owing to bus. engagements; to travel on business; krankheits⚬ on account of illness, vorſichts⚬ for the sake of precaution; umzugs⚬ owing to removal, ſchulden⚬ on account of debts.

Halb-erbe (⌣...) m ⓖ joint-heir; ⚬**erhaben** ⊕ a. ⓖ demi-relief, (it.) (in) basso-rilievo; ⚬e Arbeit demi-(or bass-)relief, (it.) basso-rilievo; =**eſel** m, zo.: ☞ hemione (Equus hemi'onus); =**fabrikat** ⚘ n semi-manufacture; ⚬**fein** a. semi-genteel; =**fenſter** n half-window; ⚬**flach** a. half flat; =**flügler** m/pl. ent.: ☞ hemiptera; ⚬**flüſſig** a. half liquid, semi-fluid; =**franzband** ⊕ m) n: in ~ binden to bind in half-calf, Buchbind.: half-calf (binding), half-binding; =**frucht** ⚘ f: ☞ hemi-carp; ⚬**gar** a. Kocht.: (only) half done, underdone, fig. underdone, weak; ⚬**gebildet** a. (only) half educated; ⚬**gefiedert** ⚘ a.: ☞ pinnatifid; ⚬**gefüllt** ⚘ a. semi-double; =**gelehrte(r)** m superficial (or unripe) scholar, smatterer, would-be savant; =**geſchoß** n, arch. intermediate story; =**geſchwiſter** pl. half- (or step-)brothers and -sisters; =**gott** m, =**göttin** f demigod(dess f).

Halb-heit (⌣⌣) f ㊼ 1. halfness, incomplete (or imperfect) condition; ~ des Wiſſens ſ. Halbwiſſen. — 2. (et. Halbes) s.th. imperfect; indecisive step; partial remedy.

Halb-hemd (⌣...) n ⓖ chemisette; =**hufner**, =**hüfner** m small farmer or cultivator.

halbierbar (⌣⌣⌣) a. ⓖ divisible into (equal) halves, allowing bisection.

halbier/en (⌣⌣⌣) [mhd.-fr.] I v/a. u. ſich ⚬ v/refl. ⓖ (ſich) to halve (to be halved), to divide (to be divided) into (equal) halves; geom.: ☞ to bisect; ⚬ und zo. halbiert a.: ☞ dimidiate. — II ~ ung f ㊻ halving; geom. bisection. **Halbierungs-ebene** (⌣⌣⌣...) f ㉒, =**fläche** f bisecting plane; =**linie** f bisecting line, ☞ bisector; opt.: ☞ bisectrix.

Halb-inſel (⌣...) f ㊼ peninsula; =**invalide** ⚔ m Preußen: veteran (or old soldier) without pension; =**jahr** n half-year, six months pl.; ⚬**jährig** a. lasting six months, six months old; ⚬**jährlich** a. half-yearly, semi-annual; adv. ⚬ bezahlen to pay every six months or by the half-year or half-yearly; =**kenntnis** f imperfect (or in-accurate) knowledge, (mere) smattering; =**kolonne** ⚔ f half-column; =**kreis** m, geom. semi-circle; ⚬**kreis-förmig** a. semicircular; =**kugel** f: ☞ hemisphere; phys. Guerickeſche (ob. Magdeburger) ~n Magdeburg hemispheres pl.; ⚬**kugel-artig** a.: ☞ hemispheroidal, ⚬er Körper: ☞ hemispheroid; ⚬**kugel-förmig**, ⚬**kug(e)lig** a.: ☞ hemispherical, semi-globular; =**kutſche** f chaise, pony-carriage or -chaise; ⚬**lang** a. of medium length, Lauttehre: half long; ⚬**laut** a. in an undertone; adv. mezzo forte; =**laut(er)** m, gr. semivowel; =**lederband** ⊕ m = =**franzband**; ⚬**leinen** a. half-linen; =**leinen** ⚘ n, a.: =**lein(e)wand** f half-linen cloth, cotton-warp linen; =**leiter** m, phys. imperfect (or weak) conductor.

Halbling, Häbling (⌣⌣) m ⓖ d. a) (Baſtard) mongrel; b) (unentſchloſſene Perſon) shilly-shallying (or vacillating) person.

♪ Muſik; ☞ Wiſſenſchaft; ⚘ Pflanze; ⚕ Geographie; ⊕ Technik; ⚒ Bergbau; ⚔ Militär; ⚓ Marine; ⓖ Handel; ✉ Poſt; 🚂 Eiſenbahn.

[halblinks] — 478 — [Hals]

halb=links ⚔ (⚜) *adv.* half-left.
Halb=mann ↓ (⚜...) *m* ㉒ young (or inexperienced) sailor; **⚓maſt** ↓ *adv.* at half-mast; die Flagge ⚓ hiſſen zum Zeichen der Trauer: to hoist the flag at half-mast (high); **=menſch** *m*: a) demi-man or -mortal; *myth.* centaur; b) *fig.* barbarian; **=meſſer** *m*, *geom.* radius; **=meta'll** *n*, *chm. chm.* semi-metal; **⚓monatlich** *a.* semi-monthly, fortnightly; *adv.* auch: every fortnight, twice a month; **=mond** *m*: a) half-moon; auf Flaggen 2c. bſd. der Türken: crescent; *geom.*: ⚔ lune; b) ⚔ *frt.* (auch: **=mond=ſchanze** *f*) demi-lune; **⚓mond=förmig** *a.* crescent-shaped, ⚔ semi-lunar(y); *anat.*: ⚔ ⚓ sigmoid (-al); **⚓nackt** *a.* half naked, semi-nude; **⚓offen** *a.* half open; die Tür iſt ⚓ ... (or stands) ajar; **⚓offizie'll** *a.* = ⚓amt-lich; **=pacht** *f* renting a farm for half its produce; **=part** *m*: mit e-m ⚓ m. to go halves with a p.; **=pfünder** *m*, *artill.* half-pounder; **=pfund=gewicht** *n* half-pound (weight); **⚓pfündig** *a.* weighing half a pound; **=porzella'n** ⚓ *n* = Steingut; **⚓rechts** ⚔ *adv.* half-right; **=rechts=wendung** ⚓ *f* about-turn; **⚓reif** *a.* half ripe; **⚓roh** *a.* half raw, *fig.* half civilized; **⚓rund** *a.* half-round; *vgl.* ⚓kreisförmig; **=ſam(me)t** *m* terry (or uncut) velvet; **=ſäule** *f*, *arch.* half- (or semi-)column, imbedded column; **=ſchatten** *m* half-shade, *phys.*: ⚔ penumbra; **=ſcheid** (ahd.) *f* half, moiety (= Hälfte); **⚓ſchlächtig** *a.* half-breed, *contp.* mongrel; **=ſchlaf** *m* broken (or disturbed) sleep; **=ſchlummer** *m* light slumber, somnolent (or drowsy) state; **=ſchluß** ⚓ *m* semi-cadence; **=ſchuh** *m* low shoe, (Pantoffel) slipper; **⚓ſchürig** ⚓ *a.*: a) von Wolle: of the second shearing; b) *fig.* inferior; 2e Burſchen half-grown lads, unripe youths *pl.*; **=ſchweſter** *f* half-sister, stepsister; **=ſeide** *f* half-silk, silk mixed with cotton; (Wollſeide) poplin; **⚓ſeiden** *a.* half-silk, half-silk and half-cotton; 2e Stoffe half-silks *pl.*; **⚓ſeitwärts** *adv.* (um 45°) by (or turning) half a right angle; **=ſold** ⚔ *m* half-pay; auf ⚓ ſetzen to put on half-pay; **=ſopra'n** ⚓ *m* mezzo-soprano; **=ſpänner** *m* (Bauer) small farmer; **=ſpieler** *m* Fußball: half-back; **=ſtiefel** *m/pl.* low (laced or buttoned) boots or shoes *pl.*, bisw.: high-lows *pl.*; **⚓ſtocks** ↓ *adv.* = ⚓maſt; **=ſtrumpf** *m* sock; **⚓ſtündig** *a.* lasting half an hour, of half an hour's duration; **⚓ſtündlich** *a.* half-hourly, occurring every half-hour; **⚓tägig** *a.* lasting half a day, half a day's; **⚓täglich** *a.* half-daily, occurring (or repeating) itself twice a day; **=tags=ſchule** *f* morning-school; **=tinte** *f*, *paint.* half-tint; **=ton** *m*: a) ♪ semi-tone; b) *typ.* =töne *pl.* e-s Holzſchnitts 2c. half-tints *pl.*; **⚓tot** (⚓) *a.* half-dead; **=trauer** *f* half-mourning; ⚓ anlegen to put on (or to go into) half-mourning; **=tuch** ⚓ *n* half-cloth, tweed; **=verdeck** ⚓ *n* deck; **=vers** *m, pros.*: ⚔ hemistich; **=vetter** *m* distant cousin; **=voka'l** *m*, *gr.* semivowel; **⚓voll** *a.*

half full; **⚓wach** *a.* half awake, dozing, in a somnolent state; **⚓wachſen** *a.* incomplete; *vgl.* ⚓wüchſig; **=wagen** *m* = Kutſche; **⚓wegs** *adv.* half-way; (einigermaßen) tolerably (well); wenn's nur ⚓ geht if it can possibly be done, if it's at all feasible; **=welt** *f* F shady society, damsels *pl.* of light repute, (fr.) *demi-monde*; **⚓wild** *a.* semi-savage; (ungebildet) uncivilized, unpolished; **=wiſſen** *n* superficial (or imperfect) knowledge, smattering; **=wiſſer** *m* (mere) smatterer, bisw. *a.*: ⚓ sciolist; **=wiſſerei** *f* = wiſſen; **⚓wollen** ⚓ *a.* half-woollen; 2er Stoff linsey-woolsey, 2es Tuch half-woollen (or cotton-warp) cloth; **⚓wüchſig** *a.* half-grown, half-sized; undersized; **=zeit** *f* Fußballſpiel: half-time; **=zug** ⚔ *m* section.
Halde (⚓) [ahd.] *f* ㊽ 1. slope, bank, hillside. — 2. ⚒, ⊙ *metall.* (Haufen taubes Geſtein) heap of dead rock or ore, F deads *pl.*
half (⚓) *impf.* von helfen.
Halfa=gras ⚓ (⚓⚓) [afrik.] *n* ㉒ in Algier u. Tunis = Espartogras.
Halfen (⚓) *m* ⚓ small farmer; **⚓wirtſchaft** *f* ⚓ farming of small holdings.
Halfer ↓ (⚓) *m* ㉒, *mſt pl.*, **Half=leute** men engaged in towing (or hauling) ships up-stream.
Hälfte (⚓) [nbd.: *halb] *f* ⊛ half, moiety; um die ⚓ mehr (teurer) half as much (dear) again; um die ⚓ weniger less by half, only half; m-e beſſere ⚓ (Frau) F my better half; eine gute (volle) ⚓ a good (full) half; Kinder bezahlen die ⚓ children (pay) half-price; Schlächterei: ⚓ eines Rindes, Hammels side of beef, mutton.
hälften (⚓) *v/a.* ⊛ = halbieren.
Halfter[1] (⚓) [ahd.: halter] *f* ⊛, ⚓ *m* u. *n* ㉒ (Zaum) halter.
Halfter[2] (⚓) [nhd.] = Holfter.
Halfter[3] (⚓) = Halter.
Halfter[1]**=geld** (⚓...) *n* ㉒ tip (given to a groom); **=kette** *f* halter-chain; **=leine** *f* = =riemen.
halftern (⚓) *v/a.* ⓶ *a.* to (tie with a) **Halfter**[1]**=riemen** (⚓...) *m* ㉒, **=ſtrick** *m*, **=zügel** *m* halter-rope or -strap.
hälfte=wegs (⚓⚓) *adv.* half-way.
hälftig (⚓) *a.* ⊛ half.
Hall (⚓) [mhd.: * hell] *m* ⓶b. (loud or powerful or clashing) sound, peal, reverberation, clang(ing). [Zoll=amt.)
Hall=amt ſübd. (⚓) *n* ㉒ = Steuer u.)
Halle (F) (⚓) [nhd. 16. sae. (ahd.: hall); *hehlen] *f* ⊛ 1. covered space, (bedeckter Gang) gallery, (äußerer Säulengang) portico, (Kirchen=) ⚓ porch. — 2. (großer, umſchloſſener Raum) hall; *vgl.* Vorhalle. — 3. (Kauf=, Markt=) ⚓ market-hall -house; (großer Laden) stores *pl.*, emporium, baza'r. — 4. ⊙ = Salzkote.
halleluja! (⚓) [hebr.] *int.*, ⚓ *n* (Lobgesang) hallelujah, halleluiah.
hallen (⚓) [hell] *v/n.* (h.) ⊛ to (re)sound.
Hall(enſ)er (⚓, ⚓) [Halle, preuß. Univerſitätsſtadt, Prov. Sachſen] *m* ㉒ (*a.* **=in** *f* ㊼) inhabitant of Halle. [Halle.)
hall(enſ)iſch, **halleſch** (⚓) *a.* ⊛ of)
Hallig (⚓) *f* ㊽ low-lying islet (which becomes) submerged in high tides.

Hall=jahr (⚓...) *n* ㉒ bei den alten Juden jubilee(-year).
hallo (⚓) I *int.* halloo!, hallo!, halloa!, hoy-ho!; *hunt.* (beim Hetzen) tally-ho! II ~ *n* ㊿ bſd. *hunt.* tally-ho; (lauter Ruf) loud shouting or halloing.
Hallore ⊙ (⚓) [dtſch.=lt.] *m* ㊹ workman in a salt-mine (of Halle).
Halluzination (⚓-⚓-tẓ/⚓) [lt. *alucina'tio* Faſelei] *f* ㊻ *physiol.*, *psych.*, *path.* (Sinnestäuſchung) hallucination.
Halm (⚓) [ahd.: halm: grch. *ká'lamos* *m*⓶b. (faſt = ⊛b.) (Stengel des Getreides 2c.) stalk, halm; des Graſes: blade; ⚓: a) culm, (Stroh=) ⚓ straw; die Ernte (oder das Getreide auf dem ⚓ (ver)kaufen to buy (to sell) the standing crop or corn or the corn as it stands.
Hälmchen (⚓) *n* ㉓ (*dim.* von Halm) small stalk or blade; Kinderſpiel: *fig.* ⚓ ziehen to draw lots (consisting of shorter and longer sticks).
Halmen=dach (⚓...) *n* ㉒ thatched roof
Halm=fliege (⚓...) *f* ㉒ *ent.* wheat-fly (*Chlorops*); **=früchte** ⚓ *f/pl.* cereals *pl.*, ⚓ cerealia *pl.*
halmig (⚓) *a.* ⊛ stalked, bladed; ...⚓ (..."⚓) in Zſſgn, zB. kurz=⚓ with a short blade or stem. [knot) of a stalk, node.)
Halm=knoten ⚓ (⚓...) *m* ㉒ joint (or)
Hälmlein (⚓-) *n* ㉓ = Hälmchen.
Halogen ⚔ (-⚓) [grch.] *n* ⓶d. *chm.* (Salzbildner) halogen(ous substance).
Halo=id ⚔ (-⚓) [grch.] *n* ⓶d., ~**=ſalz** (-"⚓) *n* ㉒ *chm.* (Verbindung v. Chlor, Brom, Jod 2c. mit Metallen) haloid(salt).
Hals (⚓) [ahd.: lt. *collum*] *m* ⓶a. 1. *mſt* neck, zB. e-m um den ⚓ fallen to fall on a p.'s neck, to throw one's arms round a p.('s neck); e-n langen ⚓ m. to crane one's neck (forward); (ſich) den ⚓ brechen to break one's neck; *fig.* das wird ihm den ⚓ brechen it will ruin (or F do for) him; einem Hahne den ⚓ umdrehen to wring a rooster's neck mit bloßem Halſe bare-necked; *path.* ſteifer ⚓ stiff neck. — 2. (Kehle, Luftröhre, Speiſeröhre 2c.) throat, windpipe, gullet, &c.; ſich (e-m) den ⚓ abſchneiden to cut one's (a p.'s) throat; der Knochen blieb ihm im Halſe ſtecken ... stuck in his throat; einen ſchlimmen ⚓ haben, Schmerzen (ob. es) im Halſe h. to have a bad (or sore) throat, to suffer from one's throat; es iſt ihm in den unrechten ⚓ (in die Luftröhre) gekommen F it went down the wrong way. — 3. *fig.* ſich (*dat.*) et. an den ⚓ reden to get (o.s.) into trouble by one's (fooliſh) talk; es geht ihm an den ⚓ he is doomed (to die), it may (or will) cost him his life, it will go hard with him; einem alles Üble an den ⚓ wünſchen to wish a p. everything bad; ſ. ärgern 1; bis an den Hals in Geſchäften ſtecken to be up to one's ears in work; bis an den ⚓ ſatt ſein to be right full, to have eaten one's fill; ich habe es bis an den ⚓ ſatt I have had quite enough of it, F u. P I'm fed up with it; bis an den ⚓ in Schulden ſtecken to be over head and ears in debt; et. **auf dem Halſe** h. to have

Signs (see page XVII): F familiar; P vulgar; F' flash; ⚓ rare; † obsolete (died); * new word (born); ++ incorrect; ♪ music;

[Halsabschneider] — 479 — [halten]

a th. on one's shoulders, to be encumbered (or saddled) with a th.; sich (dat.) et. auf den ~ laden to burden o.s. with a th.; sich einen Prozeß auf den ~ laden to become involved in a lawsuit; er liegt mir immer auf dem Halse he is for ever bothering (or molesting, pestering) me; e-m e-n auf den ~ schicken oder hetzen to set some one against a p.; aus vollem Halse lachen, schreien to split (or roar) with laughter, to shout at the top of one's voice; es wächst mir aus dem Halse oder zum Halse heraus I am thoroughly sick of it; das hat er in seinen ~ hineingelogen he has lied in his teeth; e-m über den ~ kommen to take a p. by surprise, to drop in upon a p.; ~ über Kopf (+ über ~ und Kopf) head over heels, headlong, helterskelter; sich um den ~ reden to pay for one's (rash) words with one's life; sich (dat.) et., e-n vom Halse schaffen to get rid (or to rid o.s.) of a th., a p.; f. bleiben 4. — 4. ⚓ (Kragen) collar; Hälschen (Halstuch) neckerchief, muffler. — 5. (hals-ähnlicher Teil) meist ⊕ = neck; ~ einer Flasche neck of a bottle; fig. einer Flasche den ~ brechen F to crack (P to polish off) a bottle; ~ e-r Röhre collar of a pipe; ⚔ artill. ~ des Rohres collar of the muzzle; ~ eines Thermometers 2c. stem; ⚓ = Halse 2.

Hals-abschneider (³...) m ⓶ cut-throat; fig. extortioner; =ader f, anat. ⚊ jugular (vein or artery); =band n: a) ribbon for the neck, neck-band; ~ aus Korallen, Perlen coral, pearl necklace; für Hunde: collar, stachliges für Jagdhunde: pricking collar; b) arch. ⚊ collare, pl. ...ia; =bein n, anat. collar-bone, ⚊ clavicle; =berge f, ehm. ⚔ collaret(te), hauberk; =binde f, lose: tie, bow, fertig gekaufte: made-up tie, steifere: cravat; fig. einen hinter die ~ gießen F to wet one's throat or whistle; =blutader f, anat.: ⚊ jugular blood-vessel; =bräune f, path.: ⚊ angina, mit Entzündung: quinsy, brandige: ⚊ diphtheria, häutige: croup; ⚆brechend ⚆brecherisch a. neck-breaking (stairs), break-neck (affair); dangerous, risky; co. von Geschichten: adventurous, sensational; =bund m am Hembde: neck-band.

Hälschen(³...) n ⓶ dim. v. Hals (f. ds, bsd. 4).
Hals-drüse (³...) f ⓶ anat. tonsil, jugular gland, amygdala.
Halse (³...) [ndd.] f ⓶ 1. hunt. (Halsband) collar. — 2. ⚓ (Hals eines Segels) tack (of a sail), hawser; die ~ aufholen to haul up the tacks. I (Pranger) pillory.
Hals-eisen (³...) n ⓶ iron collar;
halsen (³...) v/a. ⚓ 1. e-n ~ (umhalsen) to embrace a p. — 2. ⚓ to veer (round).
Hals-entzündung (³...) f ⓶ path. inflammation of the (or an inflamed) throat; =flosser m/pl. ichth. (Kehlflosser): ⚊ jugulars pl.; =gericht † n criminal court; =gerichts-ordnung † f criminal code; =geschwulst f (=geschwür n) path. swelling (or tumour, abscess) in the neck or throat; =harnisch m = =stück a.

...halsig (..."³) a. ⓶ in Zsgn, zB. lang= long-necked.
Hals-kappe (³...) f ⓶ cowl, hood; =kette f chain for (or round) the neck, als Damenschmuck: necklet; =koppel ⊕ f Sattlerei: collar of harness, neck-strap; =kragen m collar (auch als Hembkragen); aus Spitzen: lace collar(et), als Schultermantel: cape; =krankheit f, path. throat-disease or -complaint; =krause f ruff or ruffle, frill round (or for) the neck; =kraut ² n throatwort (Campa'nula Trache'lium); =länge f length of a neck; Pferderennen: um eine ~ by a neck.
Hälslein (³...) n ⓶ = Hälschen.
Hals-mandel(³...) f ⓶ =drüse; =muskel m, =nerven m/pl. anat.: ⚊ cervical muscle, nerves pl.; =puls-ader f, anat.: ⚊ carotid (or cervical) artery; =recht † n criminal jurisdiction; =riemen m Sattlerei: neck-strap; =schild m, ent. (erster Brustring): ⚊ prothorax; =schlag-ader f, anat. = =pulsader; =schleife f lady's necklace or necktie; =schlinge f noose; =schmerzen m/pl. =weh; =schmuck m = =gehänge; =schnur f: a) necklet, (pearl) necklace, string of pearls (round the neck); b) = =band b; =schwindsucht f, path.: ⚊ wasting of the larynx, laryngophthisis; ⚆starrig [nhd. 16. sae.] a. headstrong, stubborn, obstinate, refractory, wilful, pigheaded, stiff-necked; =starrigkeit f stubbornness, obstinacy; =stimme f falsetto; =streif m eines Hembes frill; =stück n: a) Schneiderei: part (or piece) round the neck; ehm. ⚔ am Harnisch: neck-piece, gorget; b) ⊕ Schlächterei: ~ eines Rindes, Hammels neck of beef, scrag(-end) of mutton; c) ent. = =schild; =tuch n: a) der Männer: neckcloth; b) der Frauen: neckerchief; =tuch-knoten m knot of a necktie, oft: sailor-knot; ⚆und beinbrechend 2c. = ⚆brechend.
Halsung (³...) f ⓶ hunt. = Halse 1.
Hälsung (³...) f ⓶ shape of a horse's neck.
Hals-wärmer (³...) m ⓶ comforter; =weh n: a) äußerlich: pain in the neck; b) innerlich: sore throat; =weite f eines Hembes 2c. width round the neck; =wirbel(beine n/pl.) m/pl. anat.: ⚊ cervical vertebræ; =wunde f, path. wound at the neck; =zäpflein n, anat.: ⚊ uvula.

Halt¹ (³) [mhd.: *halten] I ~ m ⓶b. 1. (auch ⚊ (Innehalten) halt, stop, pause; ~ machen to (make a) halt, to stop, to pause; Sport: Rennen, bei dem kein ~ gemacht wird non-stop race. — 2. ♪ = Ferma'te. — 3. äußerer ~ (fig.) support, mainstay (auch fig.). — 4. innerer ~ consistency; (Beständigkeit) constancy, stability, steadiness; (Festigkeit) firmness, solidity; einem Dinge ~ geben to steady a thing; ohne ~ unsteady, unsettled; Mensch ohne inneren ~ person without (fixed) principles, F without (any moral) backbone; das Gerücht ist ohne ~ ... without foundation, unfounded; jeden ~ verlieren to lose all balance, to break adrift. — II halt ⁵. int. Stillstand gebietend: ⚊! stop!, halt (auch ⚔)!, pause!, don't go or move!; ⚊ (doch)!

stop (a minute or a moment)!; ⚔ ⚊, wer da? stop, who's there?
halt² (³) [ahd.] adv. südb. methinks; er will ⚊ (mein' ich) nicht kommen he does not want to come, I fancy; es ist ⚊ die alte Geschichte it is the old story, you know or you see.
hält (³) 3. Person sg. pres. v. halten.
haltbar (³-) [halten] a. ⓶ 1. (was sich behaupten läßt) tenable (a. fig.), ⚔ a. defensible; nicht mehr ⚊ untenable, no longer able to hold out. — 2. (standhaft) stable, well balanced; (fest) firm, solid; (dauerhaft) durable, lasting, stärker: imperishable, fixed, v. Farben: fast.
Haltbarkeit (³--) f ⓶ 1. meist ⚔ (s. haltbar 1) tenableness, defensibility (of a fortress, &c.). — 2. (s. haltbar 2) stability; firmness, solidity; durability; ⓶ von Waren: lasting wear, imperishable nature, von Farben: fastness.
Halte-kind (³...) n (=kinder f, =mutter f) ⓶ foster-child (foster-mother).
halten (³ω) [ahd.: hold] ⓶a. I v/a. und sich ⚊ v/refl. 1. (sich) ⚊ to hold (o.s.); to check (o.s.); halt den Dieb! stop thief!; die Zügel kurz (oder straff) ⚊ man. u. fig. to hold (or pull) the reins tightly, to hold in the reins; das Pferd still ⚊ to keep the horse still or well in hand; ich halte mich kaum (ob. ich weiß nicht, was mich hält), daß ich nicht lache I can hardly contain myself (or F keep) from laughing. — 2. mit prp. u. adv.: et. an das Feuer ⚊ to hold a th. to the fire; an der Hand, beim Arme ⚊ to hold (or seize) by the hand, by the arm; er kann sich kaum auf den Füßen ⚊ he is barely able to stand (on his feet); sich für sich ⚊ to keep o.s. to o.s., to lead a retired life; etwas gegen das Licht ⚊ to hold a th. against (or to) the light; die Hand in die Höhe ⚊ to hold up one's hand; es mit e-m, mit j-s Partei ⚊ to hold (or side) with a p., to be on a p.'s side; ich halte es mit Deutschland!, oft: give me Germany!; e-m Kind über die Taufe ⚊ to stand godfather (godmother) to a child; vom Leibe ⚊ to keep off; sich e-n (drei Schritte) vom Leibe ⚊ to keep a p. at arm's length or at a respectable distance; sich vor Lachen nicht ⚊ können to split (or burst) with laughing; sich ein Tuch vors Gesicht ⚊ to cover one's face with a cloth; sich bereit (ob. in Bereitschaft) ⚊ to keep o.s. ready or in readiness; e-n frei ⚊ to treat a p. to a th.; e-n gefangen ⚊ to detain a p. as prisoner or captive, to keep a p. locked up or in jail; den Kopf (ob. sich) gerade ⚊ to hold one's head (o.s.) upright; den Kopf hoch ⚊ to hold up one's head, stärker: to hold one's head high; sich zu e-m ob. zu j-s Fahne ⚊ = es mit e-m ⚊ (s. o.); sich zu seinesgleichen ⚊ to associate with one's equals, to keep to one's own class; viel oder große Stücke (wenig) auf e-n ob. von e-m, auf ob. von et. ⚊ to have a high (no high or F poor) opinion of a p., a thing; to think very highly (very little) of a p., a th.;

⚊ scientific; ⚘ botanical; ⚋ geography; ⊕ machinery; ⚒ mining; ⚔ military; ⚓ marine; ⓶ commercial; ✉ postal; 🚂 railway.

[halten] — 480 — [Haltung]

mehr auf sich als auf andere 2 to esteem o.s. above (or more than) others; viel auf sich 2 to have a good opinion of o.s.; nichts auf et. 2 to set (or lay) no store by a th., to attach no value to a th. — 3. (ansehen, denken, schätzen) **für etwas** 2 to consider (or regard) as; wir 2 ihn für einen ehrlichen Mann we think him (stärker: believe him to be) …; für e-n andern 2 to mistake for somebody else; für eine Ehre 2, zu // to deem it an honour to //; für gut 2 to think proper, to approve (of); mit es, zB. es für gefährlich, nötig ec. 2, zu // (inf.) to consider (eleganter: to deem) it dangerous, necessary, &c. to // (inf.); was 2 Sie **von** ihm? what do you think of him?; ich weiß, was ich davon zu 2 habe I know what to think of it, I have my own opinion about it; e-n hoch, wert, lieb 2 to have a high esteem, a great respect, great affection for a p.; j-s Andenken in Ehren 2 to honour a p.'s memory. — 4. (festhalten, einhalten, bewahren) den Atem **an** sich 2 to hold one's breath; (mit) et. an sich 2 to keep a th. quiet or to o.s.; abs. an sich 2 to contain (or restrain) o.s.; e-n **beim Worte** 2 (ob. nehmen) to keep a p. to (or to take a p. at) his word; etwas **im** Gedächtnisse 2 to store a th. (up) in one's memory, to retain a th.; etwas in Obacht 2 to guard a th.; etwas in Ordnung 2 to keep a th. in (good) order; e-n (seine Begierden, sich) im Zaume 2 to keep a p. (one's passions, o.s.) in check or under control; Freundschaft mit e-m 2 to keep friends with a p.; Frieden und Ruhe 2 to keep peace and quietness; ⚓ den Kurs 2 to keep to one's course; Maß 2 to keep within bounds; fein Maß 2 to exceed the bounds; den Mund (ob. reinen Mund) 2 to hold one's tongue; to keep one's own counsel; Ordnung 2 to keep (or preserve) order; e-n den Rücken, die Stange 2 to back up a p.; (gleichen) Schritt 2 to keep (an even) pace; ⚓ die See 2: a) to keep out at sea; b) to be seaworthy; standʒ 2 to keep one's ground; ♪ Stimmung 2 von Klavieren: to keep well in tune; ♪ Takt 2 to keep time; Wasser 2 to hold water, to be waterproof; sein Wort nicht 2 to break one's word; etwas zu Rate 2 to be sparing with a th.; er wollte **sich nicht** 2 **lassen** nothing could restrain him or hold him in check; F das läßt sich 2, es läßt sich damit noch 2 (es ist nur mittelmäßig) it will just do, F it's not up to much. — 5. (enthalten, fassen) der Garten hält 50 Meter in die Länge 2 is fifty metres (or fifty-five yards) long; der Wagen (das Zimmer) hält 8 Personen the carriage (the room) holds (or accommodates) eight persons; das Schiff hält 800 Tonnen it is an 800 ton ship, the ship's tonnage is eight-hundred. — 6. (behandeln) sein Gesinde gut 2 to treat one's servants well; e-n knapp 2 to keep a p. short (of money); e-n kurz, sehr streng 2 to keep an iron rod (or a strict hand) over a p.; e-n schadlos 2 to guarantee a p. from loss, to indemnify a p. — 7. **sich an et. heran** 2, **sich dazu** 2 (sich damit beeilen) to keep well to a th., to hurry a th. on, F to look sharp. — 8. **es so und so** 2 (einrichten) to act in a certain way; ⚓ Sie es damit wie Sie wollen! you may do as you like about it!; so 2 wir es damit oder so pflegen wir es zu 2 that's our way of doing it, that's what we usually do or are wont to do; wie willst du es damit gehalten haben? how will you have it done?; **sich so und so** 2 (benehmen) to behave in such or such a manner; sich gerade 2 to keep o.s. straight; sich gut 2: a) to be well conducted or behaved; b) to keep well; ⚔ die Festung hat sich gut gehalten … has held out well; sich tapfer 2 to show (great) courage. — 9. (abhalten) s. Abendmahl 2; Abrechnung mit e-m 2 to settle accounts with a p., weitʒ. to come to an agreement with a p., Kartenspiel: Bank 2 to (keep the) bank; ⚔ eine Festung 2 to hold a fortress; Gericht 2 über // to pronounce (or give) a verdict on //; Hochzeit 2 to hold (or celebrate) a wedding; (besorgen, haben) Kostgänger 2 to have boarders; einem Kinde e-n Lehrer 2 to keep a master for a child; eine Lobrede 2 auf e-n to bestow (words of) praise upon; Mahlzeit 2 to (have a) meal; eine gute (schlechte) Mahlzeit 2 to make a good (poor) dinner or supper; Messe 2 to celebrate (the) mass; sein Mittagsschläfchen 2 to have one's siesta, F to take one's forty winks; Musterung 2 to hold a review; Pferde und Wagen 2 to keep horse and carriage; Rast 2 to take rest; e-e Rede 2 to deliver (or make) a speech; Schule 2 to hold (F have) school, (Sieges-)Einzug 2 to make one's (triumphal) entry; eine Stunde, Vorlesung 2 to give a lesson, a lecture; eine Versammlung 2 to hold a meeting; Wache (ob. Wacht) 2 to (be on) watch, ⚔ to mount guard; ⚓ wir 2 diese Ware nicht we do not keep this article; sich (dat.) seine Wäsche selbst 2 to provide o.s. with (or to see to one's own) linen; eine Zeitung 2 to take in a paper. — II e-n (h.) 10. (verweilen) to stop, halt, stay; es hielt ein Wagen vor der Tür a carriage drove up to (or pulled up at) the door; ♪ auf einer Note 2 to rest on … — 11. (Bestand haben) to keep (well), to hold out, to be stable or steady; (dauern) to last, von Kleidern auch: to wear well, badly; der Anker hält ʒ bites; das Eis hält … bears; **an sich** 2 s. 2 4; ⚓ **auf Preis** 2 to hold out for a price; ⚓ dicht **beim Winde** 2 to hug the wind; **hinter dem Berge** 2 to be reserved, to keep one's own counsel. — 12. **auf et. los** (ob. zu) 2 (zusteuern, fließen ec.) to make straight for, to aim (or shoot) at a th. — 13. **auf et.** 2 (achten) to pay heed (or attention) to a th., to take care of a th.; (Wert auf et. legen) to lay great value (or stress) upon a th. — 14. **dafür** 2 to be of opinion. — 15. a) et. hält (fällt) **schwer** a th. gives trouble, presents difficulties; b) v/impers. es hält schwer, zu // it is difficult to // (inf.). — III ~ n ㉓ 16. (f. I) das lange ~ wird mir schwer I am tired from (or with) holding it so long; es war kein ~ (ob. ~s) mehr there was no such stopping (or checking) them; it became impossible to stop us. — 17. das ~ von Dienstboten keeping (of) servants; ~ der Handelsbücher keeping of the books, bookkeeping; ~ e-s Landtages convocation of a diet; das ~ von Reden war verboten it was forbidden to deliver speeches; ~ e-s Versprechens keeping (or fulfilment of) a promise; ~ der Verträge observance of treaties; ~ von Vieh keeping of cattle, cattlebreeding or -rearing; ~ (bsb. von Fuhrwerken) stopping, halt(ing). — Vgl. auch Haltung. — IV **gehalten** p.p. und a. ㊻ (D9) 18. in den Bedeut. des inf. — 19. 2 (verpflichtet) sein, zu // to be obliged (or bound) to // (inf.). — 20. gegen andere sehr 2 (zurückhaltend) sein to be very reserved (or reticent, uncommunicative) with others. — 21. ♪ lang 2e Note drawn-out note. **Halte-platz** (⌣⌣…) m ㉒ halting- (or resting-)place, 🚂 station (at which a train stops), stopping-place; =**punkt** m: a) (Stütze) point of support; ⚔ (Zielpunkt) goal; b) für Wagen: stand. **Halter¹** (⌣⌣) m ⓐ 1. ~ m, ~**in** f ⓕ mst. in Zssgn person who keeps, manages, &c. (f. halten). — 2. Werkzeug: s.th. to hold by; (Feder) penholder; (Stütze) support, hold; (Stiel) handle, (Griff) knob. **halter²** öft. (⌣⌣) = halt². **Hälter** (⌣⌣) [halten] m ㉒ = Behälter. **Halte-stelle** 🚂 (⌣⌣…) f ㊷ (Station) station; =**zeichen** n 🚂 block-signal; ♪ s. Fermate. **haltig**, südd. **hältig** (⌣⌣) a. ⓐ 1. in Zssgn: containing, zB. kohlensäure- containing carbonic acid; mehl- farinaceous. — 2. ⚒ des Erz productive (or paying, rich) ore. **halt-los** (⌣…) a. ⓐ without support, unstable, unsteady; =**losigkeit** f ⓕ lack of support, instability, unsteadiness; 2**machen** v/n. (h.) ⓐ** s. Halt¹ 1; ~ n halt(ing); =**nagel** ⊕ m am Wagenrad: linchpin; =**seil** ⊖ nguy-rope, für Tiere: tether. **hältst** ⌣ 2. Person sg. pres. v. halten. **Haltung** (⌣⌣) f ㊻ 1. = halten III. — 2. (körperlicher Anstand) carriage, bearing, würdige: deportment, port; (Stellung) attitude (a. fig.), theatralische: pose; beim Gehen gait; eine aufrechte ~ h. to keep o.s. upright, to have an erect gait; eine nachlässige, schlechte ~ haben to keep o.s. badly, to have a slovenly gait; würdevolle ~ dignified bearing. — 3. (sittliches Verhalten) conduct, behaviour; herausfordernde ~ defiant attitude; Charakter ohne sittliche ~ without moral principles; politische ~ einer Zeitung ec.: political standpoint or opinion or principles pl. … — 4. paint. (right) proportion of light and shade, tone of the colours: ☛

Zeichen (f. S. XVII): F familiär; P Volkssprache; Γ Gaunersprache; ⚹ selten; † alt (auch gestorben); * neu (auch geboren); ⚦ unrichtig.

[haltungslos] — 481 — [Hand]

der Börse state of the market, tone of the stock-exchange; matte ~ der Preise flatness (or dulness, lifelessness, stagnancy) of prices.
Haltungs=los (‿‿...) a. ⑥ unstable; **=losigkeit** f ⑫ instability; vgl. Halt-...
Halunke (‿‿) [nhd. 16. sae.; *tschech. „Nackter" (Bettler)] m ㊹ rogue (and vagabond), scoundrel, scamp; (roher Geselle) ruffian, blackguard.
Halurgie ⚗ (‿‿‿́) [grch.] f ㊽ chm. (Lehre von der Darstellung des Kochsalzes) halurgy.
Hamadryade ⚗ (‿-‿‿́‿) [grch.] f ㊽ myth. (Baumnymphe) hamadryad.
Hämatin ⚗ (‿‿́) [grch. haima Blut] n ㉔ physiol. (Blutfarbstoff) hæmatin.
Hämatit ⚗ (‿‿‿́) m ⑪c. min. („Blutstein", Roteisenerz) hæmatite. [hæmatogen.]
Hämatogen ⚗ (‿‿‿́) [grch.] n ㉔ chm.)
Hamburg ♀ (‿‿) npr/n. ㊼ a. Hamburg(h); **~er(in** f ㊼) (‿‿‿) m ㉒ inhabitant of Hamburg(h); **~er** a. inv. u. **Lisch** (‿‿) a. ⑥ of Hamburg(h).
Hambutte ♀ (‿‿) f ㊽ = Hagebutte.
Hamen[1] (‿‿) [ahd.] m㉓ (dim. **Hämchen** (‿‿) n ㉓) fishing-hook.
Hamen[2] [ahd.] m㉓ Fischerei: drag-(or purse-)net; hunt. (Kescher) net for bird-catching; (Schlinge) gin.
Hamen[3] provc. (‿‿) m ㉓ = Kum(me)t.
hämisch (‿‿) [nhd.: heimlich, heimtückisch] a. ⑥ malicious, spiteful, rancorous; (hinterlistig) crafty.
Hamit (‿‿́) [Ham, zweiter Sohn Noahs] m ㊷, **~in** f ㊼ (Afrikaner) Hamite.
hamitisch (‿‿‿́) a. ⑥ Hamitic; African.
Hämling (‿‿) [Hammel] m ㉑d. eunuch.
Hammel (‿‿) [ahd.; *hemmen] m ⑱(㉒) (Schöps) wether; ell. = **Hammelbraten**, fig. um wieder auf besagten ~ (unsern Gegenstand) (zurück) zu kommen to return to our mutton or our subject.
Hammel=braten (‿‿‿) m ㊷ roast mutton, **=brühe** f, **=fett** n mutton-broth, -fat; **=fleisch** n mutton; **=keule** f leg of mutton; **=rippchen** n/pl. mutton-cutlets pl., größere: m.-chops pl.
Hammels=... (‿‿‿) = Hammel=...
Hammel=schlegel (‿‿‿) m ⑲ = =keule; **=sprung** m, fig., parl. division (in the lobbies); **=talg** m mutton-suet.
Hammer (‿‿) [ahd.: hammer] m ⑲ 1. hammer (a. am Klavier); hölzerner ~ mallet; schwerer (Schmiede-) ~ sledge-hammer; anat. ~ im Ohr: ⚗ malleus; Behauen mit dem ~ hammer-dressing; fig. unter den ~ kommen, dem ~ verfallen (versteigert werden) to come to (or under) the (auctioneer's) hammer, to be put up for auction or for sale; Sport: den schweren ~ werfen to throw the hammer; Sprichw. f. Amboß. — 2. ~ an der Haustür, in England: (street-door) knocker; ⊕ = Hammerwerk.
Hammer=auge (‿‿‿) n ㊷ eye of the hammer; **=axt** f hammer-axe; **=bahn** f hammer-face.
hämmerbar ⊙ (‿‿‿) a. ⑥ malleable.
Hämmerbarkeit (‿‿‿‿) f ㊻ malleability.
Hammer=beil (‿‿‿) n ㊷ = =axt; **=blech** n hammered sheet-iron; **=block** m anvil-block.
Hämmerchen (‿‿‿) n ㉓ (dim. v. Hammer) little hammer, small mallet.

Hammer=fisch (‿‿...) m ㊷ = =hai; **=förmig** a. ⑥ hammer-shaped, ⚗ malleiform; **=hai** m, ichth. hammer-(or balance-)fish (Zygaena malleus); **=helm** m: a) = =stiel; b) metall. shaft of the hammer; **=herr** m owner of a forge or of iron-works; **=kopf** m hammer-head.
Hämmerlein (‿‿‿) 1. n ㉓ = Hämmerchen. — 2. ~ m ㉓, **Hämmerling** m ㉑d. (der Teufel) Old Nick, the Devil; (Kobold) (hob)goblin; sH.: Puck; Meister ~: a) (der Tod) (King) Death; b) (der Henker) F Jack Ketch.
Hammer=loch (‿‿...) n ㊷ = =auge; **=meister** m forge-master.
hämmern (‿‿) ⓥa. I v/a. ⊙ to hammer, metall. to malleate, (schmieden) to forge; abs. to strike with the hammer; flach (dünn) 2 to flatten (to thin) under the hammer. — II v/n. (h.) (auf etwas los)2 to hammer away at a th., to give hard blows or knocks. — III ~ n ㉓ hammering, metall. malleation; hammering noise.
Hammer=schlacke (‿‿...) f = =schlag b; **=schlag** m: a) stroke (or blow) with a (or of the) hammer; b) (Abgang v. Eisen) hammer-scale, iron-dross; **=schleudern** n Sport: hammer-throwing; **=schmied** m hammersmith; (Grobschmied) blacksmith; **=stiel** m hammer-helm, mehr gbr.: handle of a hammer; **=werk** n hammer-mill, forge, iron-works pl.
Hämoglobin ⚗ (‿‿‿́) n ㉔d. chm. (Blutfarbstoff) hæmoglobin.
Hämorrho=idal=beschwerden ⚗ (‿‿‿‿́...) [grch.] f/pl. hæmorrhoidal complaint, piles pl.; **=blutung** f bleeding piles pl.; **=leiden** n/pl. = =beschwerden.
Hämorrho=idarius F (‿‿‿‿́(‿)) [grch.] m ㊷ path. hæmorrhoidal patient.
Hämorrho=iden ⚗ (‿‿‿‿́) [grch.] f/pl. path. hæmorrhoids, piles pl.
Hampel=mann (‿‿...) [nhd. 17. sae.] m ㊷, **=männchen** n little puppet (which is pulled by a string); **=männisch** a. ⑥ like a puppet.
hampeln (‿‿) v/n. (h.) ⓥa. to dangle.
Hamster (‿‿) [ahd.; *slaw.] m ㉒ (~in f ㊼ nur 3) 1. zo. hamster, German marmot (Cricetus). — 2. = Hamsterfell. — 3. fig.: a) (gieriger Mensch) greedy person, F grabber; b) (j. der eingezogen lebt) person leading a secluded life; recluse, hermit.
Hamster=bau (‿‿...) m ㊷ = hamster's burrow; **=fell** n hamster's skin; **=gräber** m one who digs for hamsters.
Hand (‿) [ahd.: hand] f ⑥c. († ㊺ f. ...händen) 1. hand; f. 5 u. 6; flache ~ palm; hohle ~ hollow of the hand; umgekehrte (ob. verkehrte) ~ back of the hand; Hände weg! hands off!; mit geballter ~ with clenched fist; mit vollen Händen with full hands, fig. profusely, (freigebig) open-handedly; eine ~(=)breit a hand's width, the width of a hand; von Pferden: 15 ~ hoch fifteen hands high; nicht um eine ~=breit not an inch; ⇓ ~ über ~ hand over hand; fig. j-s rechte ~ a p.'s right hand; hist. die tote ~ (der Geistlichen) the dead hand, ⚗ mortmain; Fußballspiel: ~! hands!; ~ auf! touch down!; die ~ auflegen

(anhalten) to touch down. — 2. mit verbs: f. abziehen 4, anlegen 1; et. guten Händen anvertrauen to entrust a th. to (or to put a th. into) safe hands; f. ausstrecken I; e-m die ~ bieten f. bieten 3; zur Versöhnung oft: to make advances (or offers of peace) to a p.; an Händen und Füßen gebunden bound hand and foot; einem die ~ drücken to squeeze a p.'s hand; f. drücken 1; f. falten 2; einem die ~ geben to shake hands with a p.; da haben Sie meine ~! let us shake hands (on the strength of it)!; alle Hände voll zu tun haben to have one's hands full, to be right busy; die ~ bei et. im Spiele haben to have a finger in the pie; freie ~ haben to have one's hands free; to have full scope, to be one's own master; f. Fuß 7; eine offene (freigebige) ~ haben to have an open hand, to be open-handed; e-m freie ~ lassen to give a p. full scope or power, to allow a p. free play; ~ ans Werk legen to put one's shoulder to the wheel; die ~ auf et. legen (et. in Beschlag nehmen) to lay one's hands upon a th., to seize a th.; die ~ aufs Herz legen to lay (or put) one's hand on one's heart; die ~ in den Schoß legen to sit with one's hands before one or in one's lap, to idle away one's time; e-m hilfreiche ~ leisten to lend a helping hand to a p.; weder ~ noch Fuß regen oder rühren not to stir hand or foot, not to move a finger; e-m die ~ reichen to hold out one's hand to a p.; als Gatte: to accept a p. (as husband); sich (dat.), ea. die Hände reichen to join hands; die Hände über=ea. schlagen to fold (or cross) one's hands; e-m die ~ oder Hände schütteln to give a p. a (good) shake of the hand; die Hände sinken lassen to give up all efforts or hope; die Hände in die Taschen stecken to put one's hands in(to) one's pockets; wie man eine ~ umdreht in the turn of a hand, mehr gbr.: in a twinkle or trice or F jiffy, F before one can say Jack Robinson; die ~ nicht umdrehen ob. umkehren to lift (or raise) a finger; ich wasche meine Hände in Unschuld I wash my hands of it; die Hände zs.=schlagen to clap one's hands; die Hände überm Kopf zs.=schlagen to look amazed, to stand aghast. — 3. Sprichw. eine ~ wäscht die andere one good turn deserves another; ehrliche ~ geht durchs ganze Land honesty is the best policy; kalte Hände, warme Liebe cold hands, (a) warm heart; viele Hände machen bald ein Ende many hands make light work. — 4. abhängig von prp.: e-m et. an die ~ geben to put a p. in(to) the way of a thing, to suggest a th. to a p.; e-m an die ~ gehen (ihn unterstützen) to come to a p.'s aid, to give (or lend) a p. one's support; e-n an (ober bei) der ~ haben (oder halten, führen) to lead a p. by the hand; e-n (ob. et.) an (ober bei) der ~ (in der Nähe) haben to have a p. (or a th.) at hand or F handy; e-m et. an die ~ geben to give a p. a rap on the knuckles; das liegt auf

♪ Musik; ⚗ Wissenschaft; ♀ Pflanze; ♁ Geographie; ⊙ Technik; ⚒ Bergbau; ⚔ Militär; ⚓ Marine; ● Handel; ✉ Post; 🚂 Eisenbahn.

[Hand] — 482 — [handeln]

der flachen (oder auf platter) ~ it's self-evident or quite obvious; man muß ihm auf die ~ sehen (aufpassen) he has to be watched very closely, one must have an eye on him; auf (seine) eigene ~ (für sich) et. tun to do s.th. at one's own risk, on one's own responsibility or F hook; einen auf Händen tragen to wait on a p. hand and foot, to show a p. the greatest attention or affection; aus der ~ fressen to eat out of one's hand; etwas aus der ~, aus den Händen geben oder lassen to let a th. go (or slip) out of one's hands; et. aus der ~ legen to put a th. away or aside; aus (oder von) der ~ in den Mund leben to live from hand to mouth; aus freier ~ (ohne Maschine) gemacht hand-worked; aus freier ~ zeichnen to draw without ruler or compasses, to do freehand-drawing; ⊕ f. aus 6; aus freier ~ (ohne Makler) verkaufen ... by hand; e-n bei der ~ fassen to take a p. by the hand, als Gemütsausdruck, oft: to grasp (or grip) a p.'s hand; er ist gleich mit der Antwort bei der ~ he is quick at repartee; alles muß durch seine ~ gehen everything has to pass through his hands; Kartenspiel: hinter der ~ sein oder sitzen to be (or come) last; e-m in die Hände arbeiten to further (or promote) a p.'s cause, to play into a p.'s hands; ⚔ dem Feinde in die ~ fallen to fall into the enemy's hands; einen, et. in der ~ (in Händen) haben to have a p., a thing in one's hands or grasp or power; die Fäden in der ~ haben to pull the wires or the strings; ~ in ~ mit e-m gehen to walk hand in hand with a p.; das geht ~ in ~ damit (the) one thing works into (or helps) the other; es liegt in Ihrer ~ it rests with you; er kam mit e-m Messer in der ~ ... with (or holding) a knife in his hand; in die Hände klatschen to clap (one's hands); co. nehmt die Beine in die ~ (lauft)! put your best leg forward!, F hurry up!; in andere Hände übergeh(e)n to pass into new hands, to change hands; in guten Händen sein to be in good (or safe) hands; mit der ~ gemacht worked with the hand, hand-made; mit der ~ gemalt hand-painted; mit Händen und Füßen arbeiten 2c. ... (with) hand and foot, with might and main; sich mit Händen und Füßen gegen et. stemmen, oft: to resist a thing tooth and nail; mit leeren Händen abziehen to go away empty-handed; das läßt sich mit Händen greifen it is palpable; mit ~ und Mund versprechen to promise solemnly; nach der ~ (auf der Hand die Schwere) abschätzen to weigh (or poise) in one's hand; f. nachder2 = später; vgl. über2; et. unter der ~ (ob. den Händen) haben to have a th. in hand, to be working at (or engaged in) a th.; fig. unterder2 (heimlich) in an underhand way, slily, secretly; unterder2 zu verstehe(e)n geben to suggest (by the way); die Arbeit geht ihm (flink) von der ~ he soon dispatches (F rattles off) his work, he is quick at work; von der ~ in den Mund from hand to mouth, f. oben aus der ~; von langer ~ (her) vorbereiten to prepare long beforehand; von ~ zu ~ from hand to hand; et. von der ~ weisen (zurückweisen) to decline (or reject) a th.; et. vor die ~ nehmen to take a th. in hand; vorder2 (einstweilen) for the present, for the time being, as yet; zu Händen (zu Len) des Herrn N. to be delivered to Mr. N.; e-m zur ~ geh(e)n to lend a p. a hand; et. zur ~ haben to have a th. (ready or near) at hand; zur ~ sein to be (near) at hand. — 5. (Handschrift) hand (writing); eine gute (fließende) ~ a good (a flowing or running) hand; ein Brief von eigener ~ e-s Fürsten 2c.: an autograph letter. — 6. meton. (Person, Seite) aus dritter, vierter ~ from (or through) a third, a fourth party; aus guter ~ from a good authority or source; es fehlt uns an Händen (Arbeitern) we are short of hands or short-handed; es sind zwölf Hände (Matrosen) an Bord there are twelve hands on board; alle Hände auf Deck! all hands aboard!; zur rechten (linken) ~ oder (zu) rechter (linker) ~ on the right (left) hand or side; her. rechte, linke ~ dexter, sinister.

...hand (...⁴) in Zssgn: aller2 all kinds of; vorder2 for the present, &c.

Hand-amboß ⊕ (⁵...) m ⊕ small anvil; =anlegung f: a) seizure, apprehension; b) undertaking; =arbeit f manual labour, handicraft; als Erzeugnis: handiwork, weibliche: needlework, feinere: fancy-work; durch ~ verfertigt hand-made; =arbeiter(in f) m manual labourer, oft: hand; weitS. mechanic, craftsman; (Handlanger) operative; =arbeits-unterricht m instruction in manual trades or arts, für Mädchen: in needlework; =atlas m school-atlas; =aufheben n beim Abstimmung: show of hands; =auflegung f imposition of hands; =ausgabe f e-s Buches pocket- (or handy) edition; =ballen m ball of the thumb, ♁ thenar; =beil ⊕ n hatchet; =betrieb ⊕ m (ant. Dampfbetrieb) manufacture by hand; =beuger m, anat. flexor (muscle) of the hand; =bewegung f movement of the hand, gesticulation; =bibel f small-sized bible; =bibliothek f reference-library, library of select works; =bohrer ⊕ m small gimlet; =breit a. ⊕ of a hand's breadth or width, (as) wide as a hand; =breit f handbreadth, hand's-breadth; =buch n manual, handbook, compendium; weitS. book of reference; politisches ~ statesman's almanac or year-book; =büchse ⚔ f carbine.

Händchen (⁵...) n 23 (dim. v. Hand) small hand, (dear) little hand, F co. little paw, Kindersprache: F handy-pandy.

Hand-decke (⁵...) f ⊕ (small) horse-cloth, rug; =dienst m personal service; =druck m pressure (als Gruß: squeeze, shake) of the hand.

Hände-druck (⁵...) m ⊕, =drücken n grasp (or squeeze, shake) of the hand, F handshake; =geben n joining hands.

Hand-eimer (⁵...) m ⊕ bucket; =eisen n = =fessel; ⎫ of hands.⎬
Hände-klatschen (⁵...) n ⊕ clapping⎭

Handel (⁵...) [mhd.; *handeln] m ⊕ 1. (Vorgang, [schlimme] Geschichte) occurrence, (unpleasant) affair; ein abgekarteter ~ a made-up affair, F a put-up job; ein verdrießlicher ~ a disagreeable business. — 2. (Prozeß) lawsuit; seinen ~ gewinnen to gain (or win) one's action. — 3. Händel pl. (Streit) quarrel, dispute, brawl, (Zank) squabble; sie bekamen Händel im Spiele they quarrelled at cards; Händel mit e-m suchen to pick a quarrel with a p.; sich Händel zuziehen to get (or to be drawn) into a quarrel. — 4. ⊕ (Geschäft) (business) transaction; ein guter ~ a good stroke of business; e-n ~ abschließen, ⅐einig sein to close (or conclude, strike) a bargain; um etwas im ~ steh(e)n to be bargaining (or bartering) about a th.; fig. e-m den ~ auf-kündigen, =sagen to draw back (or to withdraw) from a bargain (or an agreement) with a p. — 5. ⊕ (geschäftlicher Verkehr) trade; mit dem Auslande: foreign trade, commerce; im Inlande: home trade; weitS. traffic; ~ im großen (im kleinen) wholesale (retail) trade or business; ~ mit Zucker, Wolle 2c. sugar-, wool-, &c. trade; unerlaubter ~ illicit trade; einen guten ~ m. to make (or strike) a good bargain; ~ treiben abs. to (carry on) trade, to be engaged in business; mit et. ~ treiben to deal (or trade) in a th.; zum ~ gehörig, oft: commercial; ~ und Gewerbe trade and industry; ~ und Wandel business life, commercial activity; Sprichw. ~ hat Wandel fortune has its reverses, Fortune is fickle; ~ und Wandel kennt keine Freundschaft etwa: business is business; friendship plays no part in commercial life.

Händel-macher(in f) m (⁵...) ⊕ quarrelsome p., quarreller; brawler.

handeln (⁵...) [ahd.: *Hand] 2a. I v/n. 1. to act, (verfahren) to proceed; gut, schlecht an e-m 2 to act well, badly towards a p., to treat (or use) a p. well, ill; er hat als (wie ein) Bruder an mir gehandelt he acted as (he has been) a brother to me; man hat nicht ehrlich an ihm gehandelt he has not been honestly dealt by; er handelt gegen andere, wie sie gegen ihn 2 he does to others as they do to him; seinen Grundsätzen gemäß 2 to act up to one's principles; nach Gutdünken 2 to use one's own discretion, to act as one feels disposed, to do what one thinks right; handle (so schlimm) wie du willst! do as you like!, do your worst!; als es zu 2 galt when it came to the point. — 2. (verhandeln) to negotiate with a p. (um et. about a thing); um den Frieden 2 to negotiate (about) peace; mit e-m um eine Ware 2 (feilschen) to bargain (or barter) with a p. about (or for) ...; er läßt sich nicht (ob. nicht mit sich) 2 he makes no deductions, he has but one price,

Signs (see page XVII): F familiar; P vulgar; ⌐ flash; ⟍ rare; † obsolete (died); * new word (born); ⧺ incorrect; ♪ music;

[Handelsabgabe] — 483 — [handgreiflich]

F he won't be bartered with; (mit) sich ‿ lassen to be ready to (a)bate (from) one's prices, weitS. to be accommodating or an easy person to deal with. — 3. (eingehend sprechen von) to argue on; in diesem Buche handelt Cicero von der Freundschaft ... deals with (or treats, discusses) friendship; wovon handelt die Stelle? what is the passage about? — 4. ❂ (Handel treiben) to (carry on) trade, to traffic; et. herunter ‿ to get the price of a th. reduced; mit e-r Ware ‿ to deal (or trade) in an article; mit Wolle ‿ to deal in wool, to be in the wool-trade; das, womit j. handelt what a p. deals in, a p.'s line of business; mit e-m ‿ to have dealings (or to do business) with a p., nach Indien ‿ to trade (or to do business) with India; nichts zu ‿? (Ruf auf der Straße), etwa: old clothes, rags, and bones! — II sich ‿ v/refl. 5. v/impers. es handelt sich um seine Ehre his honour is involved or at stake or jeopardized; es handelte sich um zwei Stunden it was a matter (or question) of two hours; ich weiß nicht, um was (oder worum) es sich handelt ... what is the matter (or point) in question. — 6. mit Angabe der Wirkung: sich reich (arm) ‿ to enrich (impoverish) o.s. by trade or in business or as a commercial man. — III ~ n ⓔ 7. (f. 1) action (f. Handlung); (f. 4) ❂ trading, trafficking, f. a. Handel 4 und 5. — IV ~de([r] m) f ⓕ 8. p. acting, agent; (Handelsmann) trader, commercial man.

Handels-abgabe ❂ (⌐...) f ⓔ commercial duty; =adreßbuch n commercial (or trade-) directory; =age'nt m com. agent; =akademie f com. academy, a. = =schule; =amt n board of trade; =angelegenheiten pl. matters of (or concerning) trade, business matters pl.; =arti'kel m (marketable) article or commodity; =attaché m commercial attaché; =ausdruck m commercial (or mercantile) term; =ausschuß m committee of com. men; =beflissene(r) m = Handlungsgehilfe; =befugnis, =berechtigung f trading- (or trade-) license; =beschränkungen f/pl. restrictions pl. on trade; =beziehungen f/pl. commercial relationship or connexion; =bila'nz f balance of trade; =blatt n trade-journal, commercial gazette; =brauch m = =gebrauch; =brief m com. letter; =buch n account-book, ledger. **Handelschaft** (⌐...) f ⓔ: a) everything relating to commerce or trade or business, commercial (or trade-) matters; b) body of merchants or traders.

Handels-diener ❂ (⌐...) m ⓔ = Handlungsdiener; ♀einig a. ⓕ, ♀eins a.: ‿ werden to agree about the price, to come to terms; f. Handel 4; =fach n branch of trade, F line of business; =firma f commercial firm; =flagge f merchant-flag; =flotte ⚓ f merchant-fleet, fleet of merchantmen; =frau f woman engaged in trade or business, female trader or F dealer; =freiheit f freedom of trade, weitS. free trade; =freund m business-friend; f. auch Freund 1; =fürst m merchant-prince; =gärtner m market-gardener; f. a. Gärtner; =gärtnerei f: a) market- (or nursery-)gardens pl.; b) market-gardener's trade; =gebrauch m trade-custom, com. usage; =geist m com. (or mercantile) spirit; =genoß m partner (in business); =genossenschaft f partnership; =geographie f commercial geography; =gerechtigkeit, =gerechtsame f = =befugnis; =gericht n commercial court; =geschäft n: a) com. concern or enterprise; b) = =haus a; (Laden) shop; =gesellschaft f (trading) company; sich zu e-r ~ vereinigen to form a company, vgl. =genossenschaft; =gesellschafter m = =genoß; =gesetz(buch) n com. law(-code); =gesetzgebung f com. legislation; =gewicht n England: avoirdupois weight; =gut n marketable (or saleable) goods pl.; =hafen ⚓ m com. (or trading) port; =haus n: a) business-premises pl.; office; b) commercial house or firm, house of business; =herr m (wholesale) merchant; principal (or head) of a firm; =innung f corporation of traders; =interessen n/pl. commercial (or trading) interests pl.; =jude m trading Jew; =kammer f chamber of commerce; =kapital n trading-capital; =kolle'gium n board of trade; =kompanie f = =genossenschaft; ehm. Ostindische ~ East-India Company; =konzessio'n f = =befugnis; =korresponde'nt m, =korrespondenz f com. correspondent, correspondence; =krise, =krisis f com. crisis; =lehrling m merchant's apprentice, appr. in a house of business; =mann m (pl. =leute) trader, commercial man (pl. men); engS. retail dealer, shopkeeper, tradesman (pl. tradespeople); =mari'ne ⚓ f mercantile marine, vgl. =flotte; =mini'ster m minister of commerce, in England: President of the Board of Trade; =ministe'rium n ministry of commerce; in Engl.: Board of Trade; =niederlassung f trading settlement; f. a. Faktorei; =papier n = Aktie; =platz m com. (or trading) town; (Stapelplatz) com. emporium or centre; =politi'k f com. policy; =recht n com. law; =regi'ster n com. register; =reise f journey on business, business-tour or -round; =reisende(r) m = Handlungsreisende(r); =sache f = =angelegenheit; =schiff ⚓ n merchantman (pl. ...men), trading vessel; =schiffahrt f navigation for purposes of trade; engS. (Reederei) carrying-trade; =schule f school of commerce; =sperre f prohibition of (or stop put to) trade; embargo; =sprache f commercial language; =staat m, =stadt f com. state, town; =stand m: a) mercantile (or trading) community, body of traders or merchants; den ~ ergreifen to become a com. man, to go into (a house of) business; b) mercantile avocation or profession; =statistik f commercial statistics; =straße f trade-route, weitS. highway of commerce, outlet for trade; =syste'm n, =tari'f m com. system, tariff.

Händel-stifter (⌐...) m ⓔ; =sucher m = =macher; =sucht f quarrelsomeness; ♀süchtig a. ⓕ quarrelsome, fond of picking quarrels; pugnacious.

Handels-unternehmung (⌐...) f ⓔ commercial enterprise or operation or undertaking or venture; =verband m = =verein; =verbindung f: a) business-connexion; b) = =verein; =verbot n = =sperre; =verein m com. association or confederation; =verkehr m com. intercourse; =vertrag m com. treaty, treaty of commerce; =volk n com. people, nation of traders or contp. of shopkeepers; =vorteile m/pl. com. advantages pl.; =weg m = =straße; =welt f com. world; vgl. =stand a; =wesen n com. affairs pl.; trade, business; =wissenschaft f science of commerce; =zeichen n trade-mark; =zweig m = =fach.

handel-treibend (⌐...) a. ⓕ carrying on (or engaged in) business or trade; trading, commercial; ~e([r] m) f ⓕ trader, commercial man; F dealer.

...handen (...⌐...) i. Zssgn: ab‿, vor‿ absent, present.

Hände-ringen (⌐...) n ⓔ wringing of hands; ♀ringend a. ⓕ wringing one's hands; =waschen n washing one's hands.

Hand-exempla'r (⌐...) n ⓔ copy in (or for one's private) use; =fertigkeit f manual skill, dexterity; =fertigkeits-unterricht m manual instruction; =fesseln f/pl. handcuffs, manacles pl.; e-m ~ anlegen to handcuff (or pinion) a p.; ♀fest a. ⓕ robust, stalwart, stout, sturdy; ↖ ‿ m. to apprehend; =feuerwaffe ⚔ f (ant. Geschütz) portable fire-arm; =fläche f palm (of the hand); =flügler (Flatterer) m, zo.: ⚔ cheiropter; ♀förmig a. hand-shaped, ⚘ palmate(d); =fütterung f Viehzucht: hand-feeding; =galopp m canter; =gebrauch m ordinary (or daily) use; Ausgabe eines Buches zum ~ handy (or portable) edition; =geld n: a) (Draufgabe) earnest (money), ❂ oft: (money paid in) advance, instalment, deposit; b) ⚔ (Werbegeld) England: King's shilling; =gelenk n wrist(-joint); F et. aus dem ~ (leicht) m. to do s. th. with (the greatest) ease; =gelöbnis, =gelübde n solemn promise made by shaking (of) hands; ♀gemein a.: ‿ w. to come to close quarters or to blows; =gemenge ⚔ n hand-to-hand fight, close encounter, affray, fray of battle, (fr.) mêlée; weitS. free fight, scrimmage, scuffle; =gepäck n ⛓, &c. small (or portable) luggage; Am. hand-baggage; ♀gerecht a. ⓕ handy, ready to hand; =geschmeide n bracelet; F co. handcuffs pl.; =gewehr ⚔ n = =(feuer)waffe; =gicht f, path. gout in the hand, ⚘ chiragra; =glocke f hand-bell; =granate ⚔ f, artill. (hand-)grenade; ♀greiflich a. palpable; (in die Augen fallend) obvious, evident, manifest; ‿er Betrug downright fraud; ‿ werden to use one's hands or fists; adv. ‿ be-

---

⚛ scientific; ⚘ botanical; ⚲ geography; ⚙ machinery; ⚒ mining; ⚔ military; ⚓ marine; ❂ commercial; ✉ postal; 🚆 railway.

[Handgreiflichkeit] — 484 — [handwerksmäßig]

weisen, dartun to prove clearly; F 2reden to talk plainly; =greiflichkeit f: a) ohne pl. palpableness, obviousness; b) mit pl. es kam zu ~en they came to blows, it resulted in a (free) fight; griff m: a) grasp, grip (of the hand); (Art des Angreifens) manipulation; (Kunstgriff) knack; die ~e kennen F to know a trick or two; b) ⚔ ~ mit dem Gewehre: manual exercise or drill; c) ⚔ eines Degens ꝛc.: hilt; d) =habe; 2groß a. as big as a hand; =habe f handle of a broom, hatchet, knife, jug, pump, &c., weniger gbr.: haft of an axe, &c.; (Knopf, Knauf) knob; vgl. Griff; mit ~n versehen provided with handles, ⚓ ansatz; 2haben v/a.⊛*⁕* to handle, to manipulate; (verwalten) to manage; (anwenden) to apply; (aufrechthalten) to maintain, to keep; die Rechtspflege 2 to administer justice; schlecht 2 to mismanage; schwer zu 2(d) unwieldy, cumbersome, fig. unmanageable, untractable; ~n 23 u. =habung f ⊛ manipulation; management; application; administration; 2haft a.: auf der (frischer) Tat in the very act, redhanded; =harmonika ♪ f concertina, accordion; 2hoch a. (as) high as (the width of) a hand.

...händig (...'⸗) [Hand] a. ⊛ in Zssgn mit Zahlwörtern und a., z.B. zwei-2 twohanded, ⚓ bimanous; vier-2 spielen to play four-handed(ly); s. ein-2.

Hand-karre(n m) f (⸗⸗) ⊛ truck; bisw. auch: hand-barrow; =kauf m: a) purchase on a rough estimate or in the lump; b) retail business; =klapper f castanets pl.; =koffer m small trunk, hand-bag; =korb m (=körbchen n) (small) hand-basket; lady's (small) work-basket; =krause f frill round the wrist; =kuß m kissing of the hand; zum =kusse bei Hofe zugelassen w. to be admitted to kiss hands; 2lang a as long as a hand, of the length of one's hand; =langer m workman's assistant, handy man, jobbing man; beim Bauen: bricklayer's man), bisw.: hodman; weit⸗S. understrapper, handy man; literarischer ~ b.s. literary hack; =langer-arbeit f mechanical labour; 2lange(r)n v/n. (h.) ⊛ (⊛a.) to act as assistant (to a workman, &c.), to do jobbing work, ⊚ Bausach: to carry bricks and mortar; =laterne f hand-lantern.

Händlein (⸗-) n 23 = Händchen.

Hand-leiter (⸗...) f ⊛ small ladder, short steps pl.; =leitung f guidance of (or for) the hand.

Händler ⊛ (⸗⸗) [handeln] m ⊛, ~in f ⊛ trader, retail dealer; in Zssgn oft: ...monger, z.B. Fisch-2 fishmonger, vgl. Großhändler.

Hand-lesekunst (⸗...) f ⊛ palmistry; =leuchter m short candle-stick.

handlich (⸗⸗) a. ⊛ handy, ready to hand; fig. easy, manageable, tolerable.

Hand-linie (⸗...) f ⊛ line of the hand.

Handlung (⸗⸗) [Hand] f ⊛ 1. action, thea. oft: plot; (Tat) act, deed; solche ~ verdient Strafe such doings deserve punishment. — 2. ⊛ trade, commerce; die ~ lernen to learn a business or trade. — 3. ⊛ (Geschäftshaus) house of business; als Lokal: business-premises pl., shop.

Handlungs-art (⸗⸗...) f ⊛ = weise; =beflissene(r) m = =gehilfe; =buch n ledger; =diener ⊛ m: a) office- (or errand-)boy, messenger; b) = =gehilfe; =firma ⊛ f commercial firm; =gehilfe ⊛ m merchant's (or commercial) clerk; =gesellschafter ⊛ m partner; =haus n = Handelshaus; =herr ⊛ m head of a commercial firm; =kommi's ⊛ = =gehilfe; =lehrling ⊛ m apprentice in a house of business; =personal n (staff of) clerks (or employees) pl. in a house of business; =reisende(r) ⊛ m commercial traveller, F contp. bagman; =weise f manner of acting or proceeding, mode of dealing with a th.; (Verfahren) procedure.

Hand-messer (⸗...) n ⊛ pocket-knife; =mörser m: a) small mortar; b) ⚔ handmortar; =muff(e, f) m, f small muff; =mühle ⊙ f hand-mill, grindingmill; =orgel ♪ f hand- (or portable) organ; (Drehorgel) barrel-organ; =pauke ♪ f tympan; =pferd n: a) (Pferd rechts vom Sattelpferde) off horse, b) (Packpferd) pack- (or baggage-)horse; c) ⚓ becket; =presse ⊛ f bsd. typ. handpress; =pumpe f hand-pump; =ramme ⊙ f paving-ram; =reichung f assistance, aid, ministration; =rücken m back of the hand; =säge ⊙ f hand-saw.

Handschar (⸗⸗) [ar.] m ⊛d. (Krummschwert) handjar.

Hand-schein ⊛ (⸗...) m ⊛ (Verschreibung) note of hand, promissory note; =schelle f = =fessel; =schlag m: a) (Schlag mit der Hand) blow, cuff, stroke with the hand; b) (Einschlagen in j-s Hand) shake (or grip) of the h., F handshake; mit ~ versprechen to promise solemnly (by shaking hands), to pledge one's (word of) honour; =schlitten m hand-sledge; =schmiß, =schmitz F m cut across the (palm of the) hand; =schraubstock ⊙ m handvice; =schreiben n autograph letter; =schrift f: a) (Art der Schrift) handwriting; e-e gute ~, oft: a good hand; kaufmännische ~ business-hand; schlechte ~ scrawl; an der ~ erkennen to know by the (hand)writing; b) ⊛ (Verschreibung) note of hand, bond; c) (geschriebenes Wert) manuscript, alte ~: ⚓ palæograph; =schriften-deutung f: ⚓ graphology; =schriften-kunde f: ⚓ diplomatics; (Kenntnis alter Schriften) palæography; =schriften-kundiger, =leser m: ⚓ graphologist, ⚓ palæographist; =schriften-vervielfältigung f: ⚓ polyautography; 2schriftlich a. written, in writing; in manuscript; ⊛ by note of hand, engS.: ⚓ palæo-graphic(al); adv. bsd. jur.: sich 2 verpflichten to bind o.s. in writing; =schuh [abd.] m ⊛ glove; ⚔ ehm.: eiserner ~ gauntlet; vgl. Fehdehandschuh; mit =en (ohne ~) (un-)gloved; ein Paar weiße ~e tragen to wear a pair of white gloves.

Handschuh-ausweiter (⸗⸗...) m ⊛ glove-stretcher or -stick; =fabrik f gl.-(manu-)factory; =halter ⊙ m glovefastener; =händler m glover (and hosier); =kasten m glove-box; =knöpfer m gl.-buttoner, button-hook; =leder n glove-leather; =macher(in f) m glover.

Hand-schuldschein (⸗...) m ⊛ promissory note; =seife ⊛ f toilet-soap; =seite f (rechte Seite beim Fahren ꝛc.) off side; =siegel n private seal; seal, manual; =spake ⚓ f handspike; =spiegel m h.-mirror; =spritze ⊙ f syringe, hose, der Feuerwehr: small fire-engine; =streich m bsd. ⚔ bold stroke, sudden attack, (fr.) coup de main; =stuhl (=weber) m hand-loom (weaver); =teller m: a) small plate; b) palm (of the hand); =trommel f tamburin(e), tabour(et); =tuch n towel; =tuch-drell ⊛ m towelling; =tuch-gestell n, =halter m, =ständer m towel-horse or -rack; =umdrehen: im ~ in a turn of the hand, mehr gebr.: in a trice or a twinkle or F a jiffy; =verkauf ⊛ m retail (trade); =voll f, inv. handful; eine ~ Leute a handful of people; zwei, einige ~ Erde two, some hands full (a. handfuls) of earth; =waffe ⚔ f portable weapon; =waffen pl. small arms pl.; =wagen ⊛ = =karre(n); =wahrsager(in f) m: ⚓ chiromancer; =wahrsagerei f: ⚓ chiromancy; =walze ⊙ f hand-roller; 2warm a. vom Wasser: = lau(warm); =webstuhl ⊙ m hand-loom; =wechsel ⊛ m note of hand; =weiser m sign-post.

Handwerk (⸗⸗) n ⊛c. 1. (handi)craft: als Geschäft: (mechanical) trade; (Stand) (a)vocation, profession; dem ~e nach ein Schmied a smith by trade; ein ~ betreiben to carry on a (mechanic's) trade; ein ~ lernen to learn a trade; welches ~ treibt er? what is his (or he by) trade?; e-m das ~ legen to forbid a p. the exercise of a craft, fig. to stop a p.'s proceedings; fig. e-m ins ~ pfuschen to encroach upon a p.'s province; Sprichw. s. Boden 5. — 2. coll. body (or guild, corporation) of craftsmen, the craft, the trade; das ~ ansprechen ob. grüßen to call on (bettelnd: to beg alms of) fellow craftsmen.

Handwerker (⸗⸗⸗) m ⊛ craftsman; mehr gbr.: mechanic, artisan; weitS. workman, operative; ~abteilung ⚔ f company of artificers; =bildungsverein m mechanics' institute; =schule f school for mechanics; =verein m artisans' (or workmen's) club; trade(s)-union.

handwerklich (⸗⸗⸗) a. ⊛ relating to a (handi)craft or a trade.

Handwerks-älteste(r) (⸗⸗...) m ⊛ etwa: headspokesman of a craft, master of a guild; =brauch m usage (or custom) of a craft or trade; =bursch(e) m travelling journeyman or artisan; =gesell(e) m = Gesell(e) 2; =gruß m journeyman's greeting or visit or application for relief, vgl. Handwerk 2; =kunde f technology; =lade f chest (or safe) with the documents and money of (a guild of) craftsmen; =mann m (pl. =leute) = Handwerker; 2mäßig a. ⊛ according to trade rules; artisan-like, workmanlike; fig. (mechanisch) mechanical, adv. mechanically, by routine,

[Handwerksmäßigkeit] — 485 — [Hängeweide]

F by rule of thumb; =mäßigkeit f (mechanical) routine; =meister m master craftsman or artisan; =zeug n mechanic's set of tools; =zeug-kasten m chest of tools; =zunft f = Handwerk 2.

Hand-winde (⁂...) ⊙ f ⑫ hand-winch; =wörterbuch n middle-sized dictionary; =wurzel f, anat. wrist, ⚕ carpus; =wurzel-gelenk n, anat.: ⚕ carpal joint; =zeichen n sign manual, F mark serving as signature; =zeichnen n (freehand) drawing; =zeichnung f freehand design, designing, drawing, sketch(ing); =zirkel m small compasses pl.; =zwehle [ahd.] f = =tuch.

Hanf (⁂) [ahd.: hemp; grch. ka'nnabis] m ⓑ b. (pl. ⚕, mst: ~-arten) ⚕ u. ♣ hemp, ehm. oft co.: neck-weed; ⚕ gemeiner ~ common hemp (Ca'nnabis sati'va), ost-indischer ~ Indian hemp (C. i'ndica); männlicher (weiblicher) ~ (fe)male hemp; neuseeländischer ~ flax-bush or -lily (Pho'rmium tenax).

Hanf-acker (⁂...) m ⑫ hemp-field or -plot; =art f species of hemp; pl. ~en f.Hanf; =bau m growing (or cultivation) of hemp; =breche ⊙ f h.-brake or -break; =darre ⊙ f: a) h.-kiln; b) (das Darren) drying (or roasting) of hemp.

hanfen, hänfen (⁂) a. ⑯(D9) hempen.

Hanf-flechte (⁂...) f ⑫ = =zopf; =garn n hemp-yarn; =hechel ⊙ f hemp-comb; =hede f = =werg. [flanze].

Hänfin (⁂) f ④(weibl. Hanfpflanze) female]

Hanf-kamm ⊙ (⁂...) m ⑫ hatchel; vgl. =hechel; =korn n hemp-seed; =leinwand ⊕ f hemp-linen.

Hänfling (⁂) m ⑯ d. orn. linnet (Fringi'lla lino'ta oder Aca'nthis canna'bina).

Hanf-nessel ⚕ (⁂...) f ⑫ hemp-nettle (Galeo'psis te'trahit); =öl ⊙ n hemp-seed oil; =röste ⊙ f: a) retting (or steeping) of hemp; b) Ort: hemp-retting; =saat f, =same(n) m h.-seed; =schwinge ⊙ f Spinnerei: swingler; =seil n, =strick m hemp- (or hempen) rope; =tod ⚕ m branchy broom-rape (Oroba'nche ramo'sa); =werg ⊙ m hemp-hards pl., h.-tow; =zopf ⊙ m, mach. h.-coiling; =zwirn m hempen thread.

Hang (⁂) [mhd.] m ⓑ b. 1. (Abhang) slope, incline. — 2. fig. (Neigung) inclination for a thing, addictedness to a th., zum Bösen: (evil) propensity for a th.; (Richtung) tendency towards a th.; (natürliche Anlage) (natural) disposition (or bent) for a th.; (Vorliebe) predilection (or liking, taste) for a th.; einen leidenschaftlichen ~ zum Spielen 2c. h. to have a passion (stärker: a mania) for gambling, &c.; ~ zur Geselligkeit sociability; s-m natürlichen ~ Folge leisten to follow one's natural propensity or bent. — 3. (o. pl.) = =hangen III; in Zssgn, bsd. Turnerei, zB. Fuß-⁂ hanging (or suspension) by the feet.

Hänge-, ⚕ Hange-backe (⁂...) f ⑫ hanging-down (F baggy) cheek; =bahn 🚋 f (Schwebebahn) suspension-railway; =balken ⊙ m truss-piece; =bauch m paunch, F pot-belly; =boden m, arch. suspension-work, loft; =brücke ⊙ f suspension-bridge, pendent bridge; =dach ⊙ n penthouse; =gerüst ⊙ n hang-ing scaffold, cradle; =kommissio'n f Kunst-ausstellung: hanging-committee; =kompaß ⚓ m hanging (or cabin-)compass; =lampe f hanging- (or swinging-) lamp; =leiter f sloping ladder; =leuchter m chandelier; pendant; =lippe f hanging-down lip.

Hangel-leiter (⁂...) f ⑫ Turnerei: (Reck) horizontal bar.

hangeln (⁂) v/n. (h.) ⓑ a. Turnerei: to move along the horizontal bar by grasping it alternately with the left and right hand.

Hänge-locke (⁂...) f ⑫ bob.

Hangel-tau (⁂...) n ⑫ Turnerei: rope horizontally attached.

Hänge-matte (⁂...) [(P) ndl.; *karib. hamack] f ⑫ hammock; =maul n hanging-down mouth; (Wulstlippe) F blubber-lip.

hangen (⁂) [ahd.: hang] ⓑ b. (das ganze pres. u. der inf. werden oft v. hängen gebildet) I v/n. (h., oft a. s/n) 1. to hang, to be suspended. an e-m Nagel 2c.: on (or by) ...; an der Wand 2c.: against (or on ...); (herab-)⚕ to hang down, to droop, (baumeln) to dangle; von Personen: am Galgen ⚕ oder abs. ⚕ to hang, to be hanged (to be hung jetzt meist von leblosen Dingen), F to swing; fig. das hing an einem Haare, an e-m (seidenen) Faden it hung by a (mere) thread; die Tür hängt in den Angeln the door turns on its hinges; ⚕ und hangen s. bangen 1. — 2. (sich an etwas heften) to hook on to a th.; fig. to cling to a th.; am Gelde ⚕ to be fond of (one's) money, F to be a money-grubber; sie ⚕ sehr an-ea., an ihm they are greatly attached (stärker: devoted) to each other, to him; F und alles, was drum und dran hängt and everything connected with it; burschikos: mit e-m ⚕ to have arranged a duel with a p. — 3. ⚕ (jetzt meist: hängen) bleiben to be caught by, to adhere to; das Kleid blieb an den Dornen ⚕ the dress was caught by (F the dress caught in) the thorns; fig. von seinem Latein ist sehr wenig bei ihm ⚕ geblieben he has forgotten nearly all his Latin, F very little of his Latin has stuck to him; von alten Jungfern: F ⚕ bleiben F to be (put) on the shelf; die Sache blieb lange ⚕ the matter hung fire for a long time or was long pending. — 4. ⚕ (jetzt meist: hängen) lassen, bsd. von Gliedern des Körpers: to drop, to droop; im Gehen die Arme ⚕ l. to swing one's arms in walking; den Kopf, die Ohren ⚕ lassen to hang one's head, ears; fig. die Fittiche (od. Flügel, den Kopf, die Ohren) ⚕ lassen (mutlos sein) to be downcast or dejected; F den Mund (oder P das Maul) ⚕ lassen (maulen) to sulk, F to be in the sulks; Sprichw. wer lang hat, läßt lang ⚕ people with fine clothes like to show them. — 5. (festsitzen) to stop, to be stopped; ⊙ to catch, stick, clog; woran hängt (stößt sich) die Sache oder Sache hängt's? what is amiss (or the matter) with it?; vgl. hapern; die Sache hängt an einer Kleinigkeit there is a slight hitch in the matter; e-n Prozeß ⚕ (jetzt meist: hängen) lassen (aufgeben) to discontinue (or drop) a lawsuit. — 6. fig. an et., e-m ⚕ (davon abhangen) to depend on a th., a p. — 7. von einer Fläche 2c.: (sich neigen) to incline, to slope. — 8. F von et. voll ⚕ (voll sein) to be full (or brimful) of a th.; fig. s. Geige. — II v/a. u. sich ⚕ v/refl. 9. = (sich) hängen. — III ~ n ⚕ 10. (s. 1) suspension, ⚕ pendency; am Galgen: hanging, F swinging; (s. 2 und 3) adhesion; attachment; (s. 5) hitch; (s. 7) incline, slope. — IV ⚕d p.pr. u. a. ⑯ 11. Bed. des inf., auch: suspended, ⚕ pendent; pendulous, pensile; hist. die ⚕den Gärten der Semiramis the hanging gardens of Semiramis. — 12. ⊙ ⚕de Brücke = Hängebrücke. — 13. ⚒ ⚕de Schicht = ~flöz; das ~de (ant. das Liegende) drooping (or sloping) part.

hängen (⁂) [ahd.: hang] I v/a. u. sich ⚕ v/refl. ⓑ (impf. u. p.p. auch ⚕⚕ ⓑ b.) 1. to hang (up), to suspend; vgl. henken (anhaken) to hook on; ein Bild 2c. an die Wand ⚕ to hang a picture, &c. on the wall; etwas an den Nagel ⚕: a) to hang a th. on the nail; b) fig. to give up one's profession, trade, &c.; der Mörder wurde gehängt the murderer was hanged (jur. hung by the neck); Sprichw. s. Dieb 1 ; beteuernd: ich lasse mich ⚕, wenn // I'll be hanged if //; ein Bild höher (niedriger) ⚕ to hang ... higher (lower), to raise (to lower) ... — 2. fig. s. Brotkorb, Glocke 2; sich (dat.) alles an (ob. auf) den Leib ⚕ to spend every farthing on dress, ⚕ to put all one's money on one's back; den Mantel nach dem Winde ⚕ to trim one's sails to the wind, to be a turn-coat or time-server. — 3. et. an e-n Gegenstand ⚕ (heften) to attach (or fasten) a th. to s.th.; fig. sein Herz an et. ⚕ to attach o.s. to a th.; sich an e-n ⚕ to become a p.'s bosom-friend or boon-companion, F to run after a p.; viel Geld an et. ⚕ to lavish (or waste) much money upon a th.; v/n. (h.) s. hangen 1 u. 2; ⚕ bleiben, ⚕ lassen s. hangen 3, 4, 5. — II ~ n ⑲ 24. (s. 1) suspension, e-s Verbrechers: hanging; (s. 3) attachment. — 5. F mit ~ und Würgen (mit Anstrengung) by dint of great efforts, F with a mighty pull.

Hangende ⚒ (⁂...) n ⑰ s. hangen 13.

Hangend-flöz ⚒ (⁂...) n ⑫ (ant. Liegendflöz), =schicht f (ant. Liegendschicht) layer above layer, roof of a seam, hanging wall.

hängens-wert (⁂...) a. ⑯, ⚕würdig a. deserving to be hanged; v. Bildern (bei Ausstellungen 2c.): worth hanging.

Hänge-ohren (⁂...) n/pl. ⑫ lop-ears, long flabby ears pl.

Hanger ⚓ (⁂...) m ⑫ pennant.

Hänger (⁂) m ⑫ a girl's frock without a bodice or girdle.

Hänge-reck (⁂...) n ⑫ Turnerei: trapeze; =säule ⊙ f, carp. truss- (or crown-)post; =schloß n padlock; mit einem =schlosse versehen, verschließen to padlock; =weide f weeping-willow (Salix

♪ Musik; ⚕ Wissenschaft; ♃ Pflanze; ♁ Geographie; ⊙ Technik; ⚒ Bergbau; ⚔ Militär; ⚓ Marine; ⚫ Handel; ⚕ Post; 🚋 Eisenbahn.

[Hängewerk] — 486 — [harmonisch]

babylo'nica); =**werk** ⊕ n (ant. Sprengwerk) trussing, truss-frame.
Hängſel (⏑⏑) n ㉒ s.th. to hang a th. up by; bſd. am Kragen v. Kleidungsſtücken: tab, loop, aus Metall: chain.
Hanke (⏑⏑) [fr. hanche; *dtſch. Anke²] f ㊽ (Hüfte, Hinterſchenkel, bſd. von Pferden) haunch, hind-quarter.
Hanna (⏑⏑) npr/f. ㉞β. ㊺⅝ α. (Vn.) Jane, Joan (= Johanna).
Hannchen (⏑⏑) npr/n. ㉓α. (dim. von Johanna; Vn.) Jenny, Jennet.
Hannover ♀ (⏑⏑⏑) [ndd. (auf dem) hohen Ufer] npr/n. ㊺α. Land u. Stadt: Hanover; ~**er** m ㉒, ~**in** f ㊼ (~a'ner(in) [dtſch/ë]) und ~(**a'n)er** m a. inv., auch: ⸗(a'n)(i)ſch, **hannöver(i)ſch**(⏑⏑⏑⏑)a.㊻ Hanoverian.
Hans (⏑) [Johannes] npr/m. ㉖ẞγ. (Vn.)
1. Jack, John; großer ~: a) big (F strapping or whacking) fellow; b) (beſſer: Groß=²) braggart; F kurioſer ~ queer customer, P rum chap, oft contp. ~ Dampf, etwa F windbag, vgl. Dampf 3; ~ Dumm (a. dummer ~) silly fool or fellow, dunce; ~ in allen (Ecken ob.) Gaſſen Paul Pry, (j: der ſich mit allem befaßt) Jack of all trades; ~ Lieberlich loose (or fast) fellow, debauchee; ~ Ohneſorg careless (F happy-go-lucky) fellow; ~ Tapp (ins Mus) clumsy Jack; ~ und Kunz Jack (mehr gebr.: Dick), Tom, and Harry; ~ und Grete Jack and Gill (or Jill, Jenny); Sprichw. jeder ~ muß ſeine Grete haben every Jack must have his Gill. — 2. ~ heißen to be called Jack; nordd. das Ding heißt ~ (iſt gut) it is all right or alright; ob ich die Sache, oder ich will ~ (a. ein Schelm, Matz ꝛc.) heißen F that's the truth as sure as my name is (not) Jack Robinson.
3. Sprichw. was Hänschen nicht lernt, lernt ~ nimmermehr what Tommy did not learn Tom never will (learn); learn when (you are) young, else you never will; vgl. das engl. Sprichwort: you can't teach an old dog new tricks.
Hanſa (⏑⏑) [ahd. Schar] f ㊾, ~**bund** (⏑⏑...) m ㉒, bſd. Mittelalter: (kaufmänniſcher Bund) Hanse, Hanseatic League or Union; ~**ſtadt** f (bſd. Bremen, Lübeck ꝛc.) Hanseatic (or Hanse-)town.
Hänschen (⏑⏑) npr/n. ㉓α. (dim. v. Hans) Jackie, Jack(e)y, John(n)ie, Johnny; Sprichw. ſ. Hans 3.
Hanſe (⏑⏑) f ㊾ = Hanſa.
Hanſeat (⏑⏑⏑) [dtſch=lt.] m ㊷ Hansard, inhabitant of a (German) Hansetown; **Latiſch** (⏑⏑⏑) a. ㊻ Hanseatic.
Hänſelei (⏑⏑⏑) f ㊽ = hänſeln II.
hänſeln (⏑⏑) [nhd.; *Hans] I v/a. ㉖a. (foppen) to tease, chaff, quiz; to play a trick (or hoax) upon; (necken, lächerlich machen) to make sport (or a laughing-stock) of, to ridicule. — II ~ n ㉓ u. **Hänſelung** f ㊻ teasing, &c. (ſ. I); hoax, practical joke(s pl.); (making) sport; ridicule.
Hanſe=ſtadt (⏑⏑⏑) f ㊺ = Hanſaſtadt.
Hans=narr (⏑⏑) m ㊷, =**närrin** f crazy Jack; (dummer Menſch) blockhead, F mug, juggins; =**wurſt** m ⓪⑦c. buffoon, im Zirkus ꝛc.; clown, auf Jahrmärkten; merry Andrew, bisw. jack-pudding,

auf der Bühne: harlequin, pantaloon; ebm.: pickle-herring; den ~ m. to play the buffoon; ⁀**wurſt=artig**, ⁀**wurſt=mäßig** a. ㊻ buffoonish, clownish, harlequin-like; =**wurſt=komödie** f Punch and Judy; =**wurſt=ſtreich** m, =**wurſterei**, =**wurſtia"de** f buffoonery, clown's business, harlequinade, weitS. tomfoolery, P tommy-rot.
Hantel (⏑⏑) [Hand] m ㉒ (f ㊽) Turnerei: (zwei durch Handhabe verbundene Kugeln) dumb-bell; ⁀**n** v/n. (h.) ⸗a. to practise (with) dumb-bells, to do dumb-bell exercises, to do exercises with the dumb-bells.
hantier/en (⏑⏑⏑) [mhd.: haunt; *fr. hanter oft beſuchen] ⑼⑶ I v/n. (h.) 1. to work with one's hands; (geſchäftig ſein) to be busy or astir. — 2. (ein Gewerbe treiben) to carry on a trade or business; (ſein Weſen treiben) to bustle (or stir) about; (lärmen) to make a noise. — II v/a. 3. (handhaben) to handle, manipulate, operate. — III ~ n ㉓ und **H/ung** f ㊽ 4. (ſ. II) handling, manipulation. — 5. (nur H/ung) = Handwerk.
Hapag ⚓ (⏑⏑⏑) [Hamburg-Amerikaniſche Paketfahrt-Aktiengeſellſchaft] f, inv. Hamburg-American Steamship Line.
haperig F (⏑⏑⏑) a. ㊻ difficult; (verwickelt) knotty; (uneben) rugged, uneven.
hapern (⏑⏑) [ndl. ſtottern] v/n. impers. (h.) ⸗a. to be difficult (to manage), to be hampered, to be at a standstill, F to stick (fast); woran hapert es? what is amiss or in the way?
Häppchen (⏑⏑) n ㉓ (dim. v. Happen) small mouthful, bit, morsel.
happen¹ (⏑⏑) v/n. (h.) ㊽ to snap, to snatch, to seize greedily.
Happen² F(⏑⏑) [: Hippe] m ㉓ mouthful, ein ~ Brot, auch: a hunk of bread.
happig F (⏑⏑) [happen] a. ㊻ snappish, greedy, eager.
Haps F (⏑) [happen] m ⓪a.: mit e-m ~ verſchlingen ... at one gulp; als int. ⸗! bang!, dash!; (flint) F look sharp!
har (⏑) int. Fuhrmannsſprache: (links) hoy!; der eine will hott, der andere ⸗ one pulls to the right, the other to the left.
harangieren (ä-ra-g⏑⏑) [fr.] v/a. (feierlich anreden) to harangue.
Haraß ⚒ (⏑) [fr. harasse f] m ⓪a. (Glaskorb) crate for packing glass in.
Härchen (⏑⏑) [Haar, dim.] n ㉓ little (or tiny) hair; feine ~ pl., oft: down, ♂: ⇛ villi pl.; vgl. Haar, bſd. 4.
Harder (⏑⏑) [ndd.] m ㉒ ichth. grey mullet (Mugil ce'phalus).
Harem (⏑⏑) [ar. Unzugängliches] m ⓾ harem.
hären (⏑⏑) [Haar] I a. ㊻ hairy, (made) of hair; rel. des (Büßer=)Hemd, Gewand hairy (ehm. hairen) gown. — II v/n. (h.) u. ſich ⸗ v/refl. ㊽ = haaren I.
Häreſie (⏑⏑⏑) [grch.] f ㊽ (Ketzerei) heresy; **Häretiker** (⏑⏑⏑⏑) m ㊷ (=⏑⏑⏑⏑) heretic; **häretiſch** (⏑⏑⏑) a. ㊻ heretical.
Harfe ♪ (⏑⏑) [ahd.: harp] f ㊽ harp; (die) ~ ſpielen to play (einmal: on) the harp; ⸗**n** v/n. (h.) ㊽ = ~ ſpielen.
harfen=artig (⏑⏑⏑) a. ㊻ harp-like; =**es Spiel** arpeggio.
Harfenett ♪ (⏑⏑⏑) n ⓪c. small harp.
Harfenist (⏑⏑⏑) m ㊷, ~**in** f ㊼ harpist.

Harfen=klang (⏑⏑...) m ㉒ sound of the harp; unter ~ amid the playing (or sound) of harps; =**mädchen** n girl harpist; =**ſchläger(in** f) m = =**ſpieler(in)**; =**ſpiel** n playing of the harp, harp-playing; =**ſpieler(in** f) m harpist, harper, harp-player; =**ton** m = =**klang**.
Harfner ♪ (⏑⏑) [Harfe] m ㉒, ~**in** f harpist, harper, p. who plays the harp.
härig (⏑⏑) a. ㊻ = haaricht.
Harke ⊕ (⏑⏑) [ndd.: harrow] f ㊽ agr. u. hort. rake (a. der Croupiers); F fig. ich werde ihm zeigen, was e-e ~ iſt (ihm die Wahrheit ſagen) I will show (or tell) him what I mean or F what's what.
harken (⏑⏑) v/a. u. v/n. (h.) ㊽ to rake.
Harker (⏑⏑) m ㉒, ~**in** f ㊼ raker.
Härlein (⏑⏑) n ㉓ dim. v. Haar = Härchen.
Harlekin (⏑⏑⏑) [P.+⁺fr.⁺⁺it.⁺ₜ] [it. arleccki'no] m ⓾d. (㊺) 1. (engl. Pantomime: Geliebter der Kolombi'ne) harlequin; weitS. = Hanswurſt. — 2. ♀ buffoon (or rose) orchis (Orchis mo'rio).
Harlekinade (⏑⏑⏑⏑) f ㊽ harlequinade, buffoonery, clownish tricks pl.
Harlekin(s)=jacke (⏑⏑⏑...) f ㉒, =**kleid** n harlequin's dress; =**poſſe** f, =**ſtreich** m, thea. = Harlekinade; =**pritſche** f h.'s wooden sword; =**tanz** m h.'s dance.
Harm (⏑) [ahd.: harm] m ⓾b. 1. (Kummer) grief, **sorrow**, affliction. — 2. (kränkende Verletzung) harm, wrong; insult; e-m ~ zufügen to do a p. harm or wrong, to wrong (or harm, injure) a p.
Harmel=kraut ♀ (⏑⏑...) [ar.] n ⓪c, =**raute** f, =**ſtaude** f harmel (Pe'ganum ha'rmala).
härmen (⏑⏑) [Harm] ⓼ I ſich ⸗ v/refl. to grieve about (or after) a thing, to be grieved (or to worry, fret) about a th., to take s. th. to heart. — II v/a. e-n ⸗ (betrüben) to grieve (or distress) a p.
harm=los (⏑...) a. ㊻: a) without a care, unconcerned; b) (arglos) harmless, inoffensive, (ohne Bosheit) guileless, (unſchuldig) innocent; nur von Dingen: innocuous; ⸗**loſe Lüge** white lie; =**loſigkeit** f ㊻: a) unconcern; b) harmlessness, inoffensiveness, guilelessness, innocence.
Harmonie (⏑⏑⏑) [grch.] f ㊽ u. fig. (Einklang) harmony, concord, fig. auch: accord; in ~ bringen to harmonize.
Harmonie=geſetze ♪ (⏑⏑⏑⏑...) n/pl. ㉒ rules pl. of harmony, ♂ tonal laws pl.; =**lehre** f (theory of) harmony; =**los** a. ㊻ without harmony; =**muſik** f music of wind-instruments.
harmonieren (⏑⏑⏑⏑) [Harmonie] v/n. (h.) ⑼ ♪ und fig.: ⸗ to harmonize with, weitS. to be in accord (or to agree) with, F to gee in with; v. Perſonen, Farben ꝛc.: mit=ea. ⸗ to harmonize with each other, to agree (or F go) well together.
Harmonik ♪ (⏑⏑⏑) [grch.] f ㊻ = Harmonielehre, a.: (science of) harmonics.
Harmonika ♪ (⏑⏑⏑⏑) [grch.] ㊽, ㊺ (Zieh=) concertina, accordion; vgl. Glas=.
Harmoniker ♪ (⏑⏑⏑⏑) m ㉒ harmonist.
harmoniſch (⏑⏑⏑⏑) [grch.] a. ㊻ (voll Harmonie) harmonious, ♂ concordant; (die Harmonie betreffend) harmonic(al); math. ⸗**e Reihe** harmonical series; ⸗ **machen**, **ſtimmen** (a. **harmoniſieren** v/a. ⑼) ♪ u. fig.: to harmonize, attune.

Signs (see page XVII): F familiar; P vulgar; ⸕ flash; ⸜ rare; † obsolete (died); * new word (born); ⁺⁺ incorrect; ♪ music;

[Harmonium] — 487 — [hartnäckig]

Harmonium ♪ (⌣́⌣⌣) [grch.] n ㉘ u. ⓖ (Art Orgel) harmonium, melodeon.
harm-voll (⌣́⌣) a. ⓖⓖ full of grief.
Harn (⌣́) [ahd.] m ⓐb. urine, F water; den ~ lassen = harnen; f. Uri'n.
Harn-abfluß (⌣́...) m ㉒: unwillkürlicher: ⚕ enuresis, vgl. =fluß; **=absonderung** f passing of urine, path.: ⚕ diuresis; **=artig** a. ⓖⓖ like urine, ⚕ urinous; **=ausscheidend** a.: ⚕ uriniparous; **=beschwerde** f, path. urinary complaint, difficulty in discharging (or passing) urine; vgl. =zwang; **=blase** f, anat. (urinary) bladder, ⚕ urocyst; **=blasenbruch** m, path. rupture of the bladder, ⚕ vesicocele; **=brennen** n burning sensation (in the bladder) during the discharge of urine; **=drang** m, path.: ⚕ micturition.
harnen (⌣́⌣) ⓖⓖ I v/n. (h.) to pass (or discharge) urine, F to make water, to do number one, ⚕ to urinate, P unanst.: to piss, pump-ship. — II v/a. Blut 2c. ⓛ to discharge blood, &c. through the urinary passage. — III ~ n ㉓ discharge of urine, ⚕ urination.
Harn-fluß (⌣́...) m ㉒ discharge (unwillkürlicher: incontinence) of urine; **=gang** m, anat. urinal passage or duct or canal; ⚕ ureter; **=gefäß** n urinary vessel; **=glas** n urinal; **=grieß** m, path. gravel.
Harnisch (⌣́⌣) [mhd., fr. harnais; *flt.] m ⓐa. 1. (gesamte Rüstung) armour, bsd. ehm.: harness; engS. (Brust=)~ cuirass, breast-plate. — 2. fig. e-n in ~ bringen, jagen to put a p. into a passion or F out of temper, to rouse a p.'s anger, to make a p. furious, to enrage (or exasperate) a p.; e-n in ~ bringen gegen // to set a p. against //; in ~ geraten to fly into a passion, to grow warm (with anger).
harnischen (⌣́⌣⌣) I v/a. u. sich ⓛ v/refl. ⓛⓛ: (sich) ⓛ to (lay on one's) armour, ehm.: to harness (o.s.). — II **geharnischt** p.p. ⓖⓖ clad in armour; fig. ⓛe Antwort angry (or sharp, vigorous) retort or reply; ⓛe Worte defiant words pl.
Harnisch-macher (⌣́⌣...) m ㉒ armourer.
Harn-lassen (⌣́...) n ㉒ physiol. passing (of) urine, emission of urine, ⚕ urination; **=leiter** m = =gang; **=röhre** f, anat.: ⚕ urethra; vgl. =gang; **=röhrenentzündung** f, path.: ⚕ urethritis; **=röhren-schnitt** m, surg.: ⚕ urethrotomy; **=röhren-verengerung** f, path.: ⚕ stricture of the urethra; **=ruhr** f, path.: ⚕ diabetes; an der ~ leidend diabetic; **=sand** m = =grieß; **=sauer** a. chm.: ⚕ uric; ⓛsaures Salz: ⓛ urate; **=säure** f uric acid ($C_5H_4N_4O_3$); **=schnur** f = =strang; **=sonde** f, surg. catheter; **=stein** m: ⚕ urinary calculus (pl. ...i); **=stoff** m, chm.: ⚕ urea, carbamide (CH_4N_2O); **=stoff-messer** m: ⚕ ureameter; **=strang** m des Embryos: ⚕ urachus; **=strenge** f: ⚕ dysuria; **=treibend** a. med.: ⚕ (di)uretic(al), ischuretic; ⓛes Mittel: ⚕ diuretic; **=verhaltung** f, path. retention of urine, ⚕ ischuria; **=werkzeuge** n/pl.: ⚕ urinary organs pl.; **=zapfer** m, surg. catheter; **=zwang** m, path. extreme difficulty in passing urine, ⚕ strangury, vesical tenesmus.

Harpune (⌣⌣́⌣) [ndl.; fr.; *Harfe] f ⓖ ↓ u. ⓧ Fischerei: (an e-m Seile befestigter Spieß, bsd. zum Walfischfang) harpoon, harping-iron; eine ~ werfen to (throw a) harpoon; (Fischgabel) fish(ing)-fork; **harpun(ier)en** v/a. ⓖⓖ(⊕) to harpoon a whale, &c.; **Harpunier** (⌣⌣⌣-í'r) m ⓐd., **Harpunierer** (⌣⌣⌣́⌣) m ㉒ harpooner, harpooneer. [harpy (auch fig.).]
Harpyie (⌣⌣́⌣⌣) [grch.] [gr.] npr/f. ⓖ myth.]
harren (⌣́⌣) [ndd.] I v/n. (h.) ⓖⓖ to wait (patiently); to tarry, (ausharren) to persevere; auf et. ⓛ to wait (or stay) for a th., to await (or abide) a th.; bibl. auf Gott ⓛ to (put one's) trust in God. — II ~ n ㉓ waiting; tarrying; perseverance; Sprichw. f. hoffen II.
harsch (⌣́) [ndd.: harsh] a. ⓖⓖ harsh, rough (auch fig.), (spröde) brittle.
harschen (⌣́⌣) (fn und h.) ⓐ to form a scar or crust, ⚕ to cicatrize, von Wunden auch: to close.
Harst prove. (⌣́) [:host] m ⓐb. u. f ⓖⓖ: a) ⚔ (Schar) troop, (Vorhut) vanguard; b) (Heer) host.
hart (⌣́) [ahd.: hard] I a. ⓖⓖ (D 2) 1. (ant. weich) hard, (fest) firm, solid; (so) ⓛ wie Stahl (as) hard as steel, geh. Spr. (like) adamant; so ⓛ wie Stein (as) hard as stone or flint; ⓛes Brot: a) hard bread; b) (altes Brot) stale bread; ⓛe (oder ⓛ gesottene) Eier hard (boiled) eggs pl.; e-n ⓛen Kopf (schwachen Verstand) h. to be slow (or dull) of apprehension, vgl. 2; ⓛe Haut hard skin; ⓛen Leib haben to be costive or constipated; das ist eine ⓛe Nuß (zu knacken) that's a hard nut (to crack) or a difficult thing to do, F it's a puzzler; ⓛes Wasser hard (or chalky, ⚕ calcareous) water; ⓛ machen to harden, ⚕ to solidify; ⓛ werden to grow hard or rigid, to harden, durch Gerinnen: to congeal. — 2. (ant. mild) hard, (barsch) harsh, (streng und rauh) rigid, stern, (gefühllos) unfeeling, pitiless; ⓛer Despo't cruel despot; ⓛe Gesinnung harsh (or rigid, severe) view; einen ⓛen Sinn (oder Kopf, Nacken) haben to have a stubborn head, to be obstinate or inflexible or unbending; e-e ⓛe Stirn (wenig Schamgefühl) h. to be brazen-faced; ⓛer Winter hard (or rigorous, severe, inclement) winter; ⓛe Züge stern features pl.; ⓛ sein gegen die Armen to be hard on (or to grind down) the poor; adv. ⓛ bestraft w. to receive a severe punishment; e-n ⓛ anfahren to talk roughly (or harshly) to a p., to fly (out) at a p.; die Krankheit hat ihn ⓛ mitgenommen ... very much weakened him or pulled him down. — 3. (ant. weichlich) hardy, ⓛ gewöhnt sein to be inured (or accustomed) to great hardship(s). — 4. (ant. leicht) hard, difficult; (mühevoll) troublesome, laborious, (drückend) oppressive; einen ⓛen Stand haben to have a precarious position; ⓛer Verlust heavy loss; es wird ⓛ halten, zu // it will be no easy matter to // (inf.); ⓛ (schwer) hören to be hard of hearing; adv. ⓛ bedrängt hard-beset; es

kommt ihm ⓛ an it comes hard upon him, he finds it hard. — 5. ⓛes Geld (ant. Papiergeld) hard coin, solid cash. — 6. ♪ ⓛe Tonart = Dur. — II nur adv. 7. (dicht, in unmittelbarer Nähe) close (or hard) by; ⓛ an der Kirche close to the church; ⓛ an et. vorbeistreifen to graze a th.; ⓛ an=ea. geraten to come to close quarters or hard blows; e-m ⓛ auf dem Fuße folgen to be at a p.'s heels, to be in close pursuit of a. p., to give stern chase to a p.
Härte (⌣́⌣) [hart] f ⓖ 1. hardness, der Haut: roughness, ⊕ des Stahls auch: temper, path. des Leibes: costiveness. — 2. ~ (Abhärtung) des Körpers hardiness. — 3. ~ des Charakters harshness, sternness, rigour; asperity, unyieldingness, inflexibility; (Grausamkeit) cruelty; f. Hartherzigkeit. — 4. ⊕ metall. hardening(-composition).
Härte-grad (⌣́⌣...) m ⓖ degree of hardness, metall. temper.
härten (⌣́⌣) [hart] ⓖⓖ I v/a. to harden; ⊕ Eisen auch: to temper, durch Einsatz: to case-harden. — II v/n. (h.) u. sich ⓛ v/refl. to harden, to grow hard, (gerinnen) to congeal. — III ~ n ㉓ Härtung.
Härter ⊕ (⌣́⌣) m ㉒ temperer.
Hart-erz (⌣́...) n ⓖ quartzy (or ⚕ quartziferous) copper-ore. [ness.]
Härte-ska'la (⌣́⌣...) f ⓖ scale of hard-]
Hart-flügler (⌣́...) m/pl. ⓖ ent. (Käfer): ⚕ coleopter(an)s, (lt.) coleoptera pl.; **=futter** n (Körnerfutter) mixture of unground oats and barley; **=gesotten** a. ⓖⓖ: a) hard (boiled); b) fig. (verhärtet) hardened; steeped in sin or crime; **=glas** ⊕ ⓛ hardened (or toughened) glass; **=gummi** ⊕ n (m) ebonite, vulcanite, vulcanized india-rubber; **=guß** ⊕ m, metall.: a) das Gießen: case-hardening; b) das Gegossene: case-hardened castings pl.; **=herzig** a. ⓖⓖ hard-hearted, callous; **=herzigkeit** f ⓖⓖ hard-heartedness, callousness; **=heu** ⓛ n (St.) John's-wort (Hype'ricum); durchwachsenes ~ common (St.) John's-wort (H. perfora'tum); vierkantiges ~ hardhay (H. perfora'tum); **=hörig** a. hard (or dull) of hearing, deaf(ish); **=hörigkeit** f bad (or defective) hearing, deaf(ish)ness; **=knochig** a. with hard bones; **=köpfig** a. headstrong; vgl. ⓛnäckig; **=korn** ⓛ n (Gerste, Hafer 2c.) hard grain; **=leibig** a. constipated, costive, F (hard-)bound; **=leibigkeit** f constipation, costiveness.
härtlich (⌣́⌣) a. ⓖⓖ hardish, slightly hard, somewhat hardened or harsh.
Härtling (⌣́⌣) m ⓐd. 1. ⓛ (Holzapfel) crab-apple. — 2. ⊕ metall.(Schlacken) hard slag.
Hart-lot (⌣́...) n ⊕ hard-solder; **=manga'n** n, min. braunite; **=manganerz** n, min. black manganese-ore, psilomelan; **=mäulig** a. ⓖⓖ: a) von Pferden: hard-mouthed; b) fig. unmanageable; **=meißel** ⊕ m cold chisel; **=meta'll** ⊕ n: a) (2 Kupfer, 1 Zinn) hard-metal; b) (4 Zinn, 1 Blei) pewter; **=nackig** a. stiff-necked, stubborn, obstinate, pertinaceous, (verstockt) obdurate; von Krankheiten oft: chronic; ⓛ

⚕ scientific; ⚘ botanical; ⌘ geography; ⊕ machinery; ⚒ mining; ⚔ military; ⚓ marine; ⓖ commercial; ⓟ postal; ⓡ railway.

(adv.) auf et. bestehen strongly to insist upon a th., to be persistent in one's demands; ⸗näckigkeit f stubbornness, obstinacy, pertinicity; obduracy.

Hart-riegel ⚔ (⸗...) m ⓺²: a) (Cornus) roter ~ (bloody) dogwood, dogberry-tree (C. sangui'nea); b) (Ligúster) privet (Ligu'strum vulga're); ⚯rindig a. ⓺⁶ hard-rinded; ⚯schalig a. with a hard shell; zo. hard-shelled, ⚯ testaceous; ⚯schlächtig a. vet. v. Pferden: broken-winded; ⸗schlächtigkeit f, ⸗schlägig-keit f broken-windedness; ⸗sein n hardness, harshness; ⸗traber m von Pferden: high trotter. [tempering.]

Härtung (⸗⸗) f ⓺⁶ hardening; ⊕ ⚯⸗)
Hart-werden (⸗...) n⓺² hardening, ⚯ concretion, congelation; ⸗zinn n = ⸗metall.

Harz (⸗) [ahd.] n ⓺a. resin(ous substance), ⚯ rosin (in Waſſer lösliches: gum; flüſſiges ~ liquid (or terebinthine)resin.

harz-ähnlich (⸗...) a. ⓺⁶, ⚯artig a. resin(ace)ous, like resin; ⸗baum ⚔ m: ⚯ resiniferous tree; ⸗drüſe ⚔ f resingland; ⸗elektrizität f, phys. resinous (or negative) electricity.

harzen (⸗⸗) ⓺⁰ I v/n.(h.) 1. to gather resin. — II v/a. 2. to tap a tree (for resin), to scrape the resin off a tree. — 3. (mit Harz beſtreichen) to resin, ⚯ to rosin.

Harz-fluß (⸗...) ⚔ m ⓺² Krankheit der Nadelbäume: resin-flux; ⚯förmig a. ⓺⁶: ⚯ resiniform; ⸗galle f accumulation of resin (in the wood of pines); ⚯gebend a. yielding resin, ⚯ resiniferous.

harzicht, harzig (⸗⸗) a. ⓺⁶ = harz-ähnlich.
Harz-kana'l (⸗...) m ⓺² resin-passage; ⸗kohle f resinous (or bituminous)coal; ⸗kuchen m cake of resin; ⸗öl n resin-oil; ⸗ſeife f resinous soap, resin-soap; ⸗ſtoffe m/pl. chm.: ⚯ resinoids pl.

Hasard (⸗⸗) [nhd. 17. sae.] n ⓺⁰ (glücklicher Zufall) hazard; ~⸗ſpiel) n game of hazard or chance, gambling.
haſardieren (⸗⸗⸗⸗) v/n. (h.) ⓺⁰ (wagen) to hazard, (ſpielen) to gamble.

haſch (⸗) int. catch!, quick!, look sharp!
Haſchee (⸗⸗) [fr. hachis; *dtſch Hack⸗...] n ⓺⁰ Kochſt.: (Hackfleiſch) hash.

haschen (⸗⸗) [nhd. (md.) LU.] ⓺⁰ I v/a. etwas ⚯ to catch (or seize. snatch) a th. — II v/n. (h.): nach et. ⚯ to try to catch (or seize) a th., to snatch (or clutch) at a th.; (ſich um etwas reißen) to scramble for a th.; fig. eagerly to pursue or to strive for; nach Effekt ⚯ to study effect, thea. to play to the gallery; nach Neuigkeiten ⚯ to hunt for news; nach Volksgunſt ⚯ to court the populace, to strive for popularity; nach Witz ⚯ to try to make jokes, to pose as a wit. — III ſich ⚯ v/refl. Kinderſpiel: to play at catch or touch. — IV ~ n ⓺³ catching, &c. (f. I u. II.)

Häſchen (⸗⸗) [Haſe, dim.] n ⓺³ small (or young) hare, leveret.
Häſcher ehm.(⸗⸗)[haſchen]m⓺²police-spy, informer; detective; (Büttel) bailiff; ehm.: F catchpoll; ~⸗bande f ⓺² gang of police-spies, sheriff's officers pl.

Haſcherei (⸗⸗⸗) f ⓺⁶ foolish pursuit of.
haſchieren (⸗⸗⸗) [fr.; vgl. Haſchee] v/a. ⓺¹ 1. (hacken) to chop, hash, mince. — 2. = ſchraffieren.

Haſchiſch (⸗⸗)[ar.Kraut]n,inv. (Hanfpflanze u. Berauſchungsmittel) hashish, bhang.
Haſe (⸗⸗) [ahd.: hare] m ⓺⁴ 1. zo.: hare (Lepus ti'midus), hunt., co. auch: puss; junger ~ leveret; männlicher ~ male hare, buck-hare; weiblicher ~ ſ. Häſin; fig. ſehen, wie der ~ läuft to see how the cat jumps or the wind blows, auch: to sit on the fence. — 2. fig. von Perſonen: (Feigling) coward, faint- (or pigeon-)hearted (or timid, nervous) person. — 3. Sprichw. da liegt der ~ im Pfeffer (die Schwierigkeit) that's where the difficulty lies, there's the rub; viele Hunde ſind des ~n Tod many hounds soon catch the hare; weit S. the fleetest and strongest must perish at last. [= ~⸗ſtrauch.]

Haſel¹ ⚔ (⸗⸗) [ahd.: hazel] f ⓺⁸ (⚯ m ⓺²)⸗
Haſel², Häſel ⚔ m ⓺ ichth. (Art Weißfiſch) dace (Leuci'scus vulga'ris).
Haſel¹⸗buſch ⚔ (⸗⸗...) m ⓺², ⸗gebüſch n hazel-bush, -wood; ⸗gerte f hazel switch; vgl. ⸗rute; ⸗huhn n, orn. hazel-grouse or -hen (Bona'sia silve'stris).
haſelieren ⚔ (⸗⸗⸗⸗) v/n. (h.) ⓺³ to skip to and fro, to frisk about; (Poſſen treiben) to play tricks, F to lark about.
Haſel¹⸗kätzchen (⸗⸗...) m ⓺² catkin of the hazel; ⸗maus f, zo. common dormouse (Muscardi'nus avella'rius); ⸗nuß f hazel-nut; ⸗nuß⸗bohrer m, ent. nut-weevil, (Bala'ninus nucum); ⸗nuß⸗holz hazel-wood; ⸗nuß⸗öl n hazelnut oil; ⸗rute f hazel rod; vgl. ⸗gerte; ⸗ſtaude f = Haſel¹; ⸗ſtock m hazel stick; ⸗ſtrauch m hazel(nut-tree) (Co'rylus Avella'na); ⸗wurz f hazelwort (A'sarum europae'um).

Haſen⸗art (⸗⸗...) f ⓺²: a) species of hare; b) hare's (timid or faint-hearted) nature; nach ~ in a cowardly way; ⸗auge n, path. zu kurzes Augenlid: ⚯ lagophthalmia; ⸗balg m = ⸗fell; ⸗braten m roast hare; ⸗brot ⚔ n glow-worm grass (Lu'zula campe'stris); ⸗fell n hare's skin; ⸗fuß m: a) hare's foot; b) fig. (Hans) ~ coward, poltroon; timid (or nervous)person, vgl. Haſe 2; ⚯füßig a.: a) hare-footed; b)fig. cowardly; timid, nervous; ⸗gehege n hare-preserve.
haſenhaft (⸗⸗) a. ⓺⁶ 1. like a hare, ⚯ leporine. — 2. fig. (haſenherzig) timid.
Haſen⸗herz (⸗⸗...)n ⓺²: a) hare's heart; b) fig. = ⸗fuß b; ⚯herzig a. ⓺⁶ faint-(or pigeon-)hearted; vgl. ⚯füßig a. ⓺⁶;⸗hetze f = ⸗jagd; ⸗hund m harrier, greyhound; ⸗jagd f hare-hunting or shooting; ⸗klein n Kochkunst: jugged hare; ⸗kopf m: a) hare's head; b) kind of winter-apple; ⸗lager n hare's cover; ⸗lattich ⚔ m hare's lettuce (Prena'nthes purpu'rea); ⸗ohr ⚔ n hare's ear (Bupleu'rum); rundes ~ thorough-wax (B. rotundifo'lium); ⸗panier n: das ~ ergreifen to take to one's heels; ⸗pelz m hare's skin or fur; ⸗pfeffer m = ⸗klein; ⸗pfötchen ⚔ n hare's foot (Trifo'lium arve'nse); ⸗pfote f hare's foot; ⸗ſalat ⚔ m = ⸗lattich; ⸗ſcharte f, path.; surg. harelip, ⚯ lagostoma; mit einer ~ harelipped; ⸗ſchlaf m light sleep with one eye open like a hare; ⸗ſchrot n, hunt. hare-shot; ⸗ſchwanz m: a) hare's tail; b) ⚔ hare's tail (-grass) (Lagu'rus);

⸗ſchwarz n = ⸗klein; ⸗ſprung m hare's leap; ⸗ſpur f, hunt. trace (or scent track, footprints pl.) of a hare.

Häſin (⸗⸗) f ⓺⁸ hare's doe, female hare.
Häslein (⸗⸗) n ⓺³ = Häschen. [rute.]
Haslinger (⸗⸗⸗) [Haſel¹] m ⓺² ⚯ Schloſſerei: ⸗)
Haſpe (⸗⸗:haſp] f ⓺⁶ Schloſſerei: a) (Angel) hinge; (Türband) holdfast; b) (Krampe) hasp, clamp; c) = Haſpel a.
Haſpel ⊕ (⸗⸗)[ahd.] m ⓺², f ⓺⁸: a) (Garnwinde) reel; b) zum Emporwinden: windlass(a. ⚒), winch, ⚓ capstan; c) (Weg⸗) ~ turnstile; ⸗baum m ⓺² roller of a windlass. [f ⓺⁷ reeler, winder]
Haſpeler ⊕ (⸗⸗⸗) [haſpeln] m ⓺², ~in⸗)
Haſpel⸗geſtell (⸗⸗...) n ⓺² = Haſpel; ⸗maſchine f winding-engine.
haſpeln (⸗⸗) [Haſpel] I v/a. u. v/n. (h.) ⓺a. 1. ⊕ Garn: to reel (off), to wind on a reel; (emporwinden)to draw (or pull) up with a windlass; Verwirrtes aus⸗ca. ⚯ to disentangle ... — 2. (eilen) to move quickly; to speed (or rush) along. — II ~ n ⓺³ 3. (f.1) ⊕ reeling, winding.
Haſpler ⊕ (⸗⸗) m ⓺², ~in f ⓺⁷ = Haſpeler.

Haß (⸗) [ahd.: hate; vgl. haſſen] m ⓺⁸a. (o./pl.) (ant. Liebe) hatred, hate; ~ gegen e-n hegen to have a spite (or to harbour a grudge) against a p.; ſich j-s ~ zuziehen to incur a p.'s hatred or dislike.
haſſen(⸗⸗) [ahd.: hate; *hetzen, verfolgen] I v/a. ⓺⁰ to hate, to have a hatred (or grudge) against; (verabſcheuen) to abhor, to detest. — II ~ n ⓺³ = Haß.
haſſens⸗wert (⸗⸗...) a. ⓺⁶, ⚯würdig a. hateful, odious, offensive.
Haſſer (⸗⸗) m ⓺², ~in f ⓺⁷ hater; (Feind) adversary, enemy, foe, opponent.
haß⸗erfüllt(⸗⸗...)a.⓺⁶filled with hatred, full of spite; ⚯erregend a. hateful, odious, invidious.

häßlich (⸗⸗) [mhd.; *Haß] a. ⓺⁶ (ant. ſchön) ugly, unsightly, ſtärker: nasty (-looking), hideous; Geſtalt: deformed; Geſicht: ill-favoured, ſchwächer: plain, plain-looking, F ordinary-looking; Kleider: unbecoming; ⚯ von Charakter ꝛc. wicked, vicious, ſtärker: villainous; ⚯ wie die Nacht as ugly as sin; ⚯er (un-angenehme) Geruch unpleasant (or bad, offensive) smell; adv. ſich ⚯ (ſchlecht) gegen einen benehmen to behave unkindly (or unhandsomely) to a p.; ~keit f ⓺⁶ ugliness, unsightliness.

haſt¹ (⸗) 2. Perſon sg. pres. ind. v. haben.
Haſt² (⸗) [nhd. 17. sae.] f ⓺⁶ hurry, (Eile) haste; in großer ~ in great (or hot) haste.
haſten (⸗⸗) v/n. (h. od. ſn) ⓺⁰ I to hasten, to hurry. — II ſich ⚯ v/refl. to hasten, hurry, rush, Am. ⚯ to hustle.
haſtig (⸗⸗) a. ⓺⁶ 1. hurried, hasty, quick; (überſtürzt) precipitate, rash; adv. a. in a hurry; ⚯ anziehen, anſchnellen to whip on, off; ſie fiel ihm ⚯ (ungeſtüm) in die Rede she suddenly (or sharply) interrupted him; ⚯ hervorſprudeln to splutter forth; ⚯ ſchlucken, trinken to bolt, to gulp down. — 2. (aufbrauſend) quick- (or hot-)tempered, hasty, fiery; (jähzornig) irascible, passionate.
Haſtigkeit (⸗⸗⸗) f ⓺⁶ (ſ. haſtig) hastiness, precipitancy; quick (or hasty, hot) temper; irascibility.
hat¹ (⸗) 3. Perſon sg. pres. ind. von haben.

Hat² ⊕ (ˇ) n ⓶ = Haben.
hätscheln (‿ˇ) I v/a. ⓶a. 1. ein Kind ⓶ (liebkosen) to fondle (or caress) ... — 2. (verzärteln) to pet, to pamper; (verziehen) to spoil. — II ~ n ⓶ u. **Hätschelung** f ⓶ 3. fondling; spoiling.
Hatschier (‿ˇ) [it. *arcie're* Bogenschütze] m ⓪d. 1. ehm.: archer, halberdier. — 2. öst. ⚔ (Leibwächter) imperial (Austrian) life-guardsman. [haben.]
hatte (ˇ) ind., **hätte** subj. impf. von
Hätt-ich (ˇ‿) m, inv. s. haben 3.
Hatz(e) (ˇ) (ˇ) f ⓶ (⓶) hunt(ing) with hounds, chase; run with the hounds.
Hau (ˇ) [mhd.] m ⓪b. 1. fast † = Hieb. — 2. *for.*: a) (Fällen des Holzes) felling of wood or timber; b) (abzuholzender Schlag) timber set apart for felling.
Hau-bajonett ⚔ (‿‿...) n ⓶ rifle-sword.
hau-bar (‿‿) a. ⓶ fit for hewing or cutting, von Bäumen: fellable. [cap.]
Häubchen (‿ˇ) n ⓶ (dim. v. Haube) small
Haube (‿ˇ) [ahd.: Haupt] f ⓶ 1. (woman's or lady's) cap; ehm.: coif; *fig.* ein Mädchen unter die ~ bringen to find a husband, F to get a girl off (one's hands); unter die ~ kommen to get married, to marry, to find a husband. — 2. (Federbusch mancher Vögel) crest, tuft. — 3. Falknerei (Kappe des Falken) falcon's hood. — 4. ⊕ cap, hood; ~ eines Dampfkessels top-vault; ~ e-r Glocke crown; ~ e-s Meilers, Schornsteins 2c.; top; ~ e-r Lokomotive dome. — 5. *zo.* (2. Magen der Wiederkäuer) second stomach of ruminants; ⌇ reticulum.
hauben (‿ˇ) I v/a. ⓶ to provide with a cap. — II **ge-haubt** p.p. u. a. ⓶ with a cap on, *bsd. orn.*: crested, tufted.
Hauben-band (‿ˇ...) n ⓶ *bsd. ehm.*: cap-ribbon; **=ente** f, *orn.* tufted duck (*Fulix ob. Fuli'gula crista'ta*); **=flor** ⊕ m thin crape; **=förmig** a. cap-shaped; **=kopf** m = **=stock**; **=lerche** f, *orn.* crested (or tufted, copped) lark (*Galeri'ta ob. Alau'da crista'ta*); **=macherin** f milliner (= Putzmacherin); **=meise** f, *orn.* crested (or tufted) titmouse (*Lopho'phanes*); **=netz** n Fischerei: drag-net; **=schachtel** f bandbox; **=schleife** f bow for a (lady's) cap; **=stock** m milliner's block; *fig.* (dummer Mensch) blockhead; **=taube** f, *orn.* helmet pigeon, ruff (*Colu'mba galea'ta*); **=taucher** m, *orn.* crested grebe or diver (*Po'diceps crista'tus*). [of howitzers.)
Haubitz-batterie ⚔ (-ˇ‿...) f ⓶ battery
Haubitze ⚔ (-‿ˇ) [nhd. 15/7. sae.: *tschech. Steinschleuder] f ⓶ artill. howitzer.
Haubitz-granate ⚔ (-ˇ‿...) f ⓶ howitzer-
Hau-block (ˇ‿) m ⓶ = *flock. [shell.)
Hauch (ˇ) [nhd.: *hauchen] m ⓪c. 1. breath (a. zur Bezeichnung von Leichtem, Hinschwindendem, engS.: ⌇ exhalation; ~ der Luft (slight) breeze, breath of air, puff of wind; der eisige ~ des Märzwindes the icy (or chilling) blast of the March wind; *fig.* ein ~ antifen Geistes a (slight) touch (or trace) of the antique; leichter ~ e-r Farbe slight tinge (or hue) ... — 2. *gr.*: a) (Hauchen, bsd. eines H) aspiration; mit einem ~ aussprechen to aspirate; b) = ~=laut.
hauchen (ˇch) [mhd.] ⓶ I v/n. (h.) 1. (atmen) to breathe, to exhale. —

2. die Blumen ⓶ (duften) ... spread (or breathe) perfume, send forth (sweet) odour. — II ⓶ 3. mit Angabe der Wirkung: die Finger warm ~ to warm one's fingers by breathing on them. — 4. (aus⓶) to exhale; (ein⓶) to inhale; (weg⓶) to breathe away. — 5. (einen Hauch, Duft über et. verbreiten) to spread a gloss (or haze) over a th.; gehaucht = duftig. — 6. *gr.* to aspirate. — III ~ n ⓶ 7. (s. I u. II) breathing, respiration, exhalation; aspiration.
Hauch=laut (ˇch...) m ⓶ aspirated sound or letter, aspirate; **=zeichen** n aspirate; *grch. gr.* a. spirit (s. *Spi'ritus*).
Hau-degen (ˇ...) m ⓶: a) *fenc.* (ant. Stoßdegen) broadsword, einschneidiger: back-sword; b) *fig.* (s. der den Degen gut führt) expert swordsman; alter ~ (grim) old soldier, *b.s.* swashbuckler.
Hauderer *prove.* (‿ˇ‿) m ⓶: a) hackney-coachman; b) owner of hackney-carriages, carriage-jobber, liveryman.
haudern *prove.* (‿ˇ) v/n. (h.) ⓶a. to let out (or to job) hackney-carriages.
Haue¹ (‿ˇ) [ahd.: hoe] f ⓶ (Hacke) hoe, mattock; pick, pickaxe.
Haue² F (‿ˇ) f ⓶: ~ bekommen to get a (good) beating or whipping or F hiding.
hauen (‿ˇ) [ahd.: hew] ⓪c. (a. ⓶⓶) I v/n. (h.) 1. (schlagen) to strike out (violently); ⓶ und stechen to cut and thrust; nach e-m ⓶ to strike (or slash) at a p.; um sich ⓶ to strike out in all directions, to lay about one; mit der Peitsche auf die Pferde ⓶ to give the horses the whip; *fig.* über die Schnur ⓶ to exceed the bounds. — II v/a. ⓶ 2. einen Hieb ⓶ to strike a blow; e-n ⓶ (schlagen) to strike a p. (mit der Hand with the hand); vgl. durch⓶, bsd. 4.; e-n (mit der Peitsche) ⓶ to whip (or lash) a p.; e-n (ober e-m eins) hinter die Ohren ⓶ to box a p.'s ears; e-n übers Ohr ⓶: a) to box a p.'s ears; b) *fig.* (betrügen) to deceive (or cheat) a p.; drauf!, haut ihn (ober hau ihn, Lukas)! F give it him!, let him have it!; Sprichw. haust du meinen Juden, hau' ich deinen (Juden) as you do to me so I (shall) do to you, tit for tat, measure for measure. — 3. mit e-m Werkzeug zum Schneiden: mit der Art, dem Schwerte 2c. ⓶ to hew, to cut; Bäume im Forste ⓶ (fällen) to cut down, to fell; ⊕ Feilen ⓶ to cut files; Fleisch ⓶ to chop ...; Holz ⓶ to cut (or chop) ...; Steine ⓶ to break ...; (bearbeiten) to dress (or carve) ...; ⚒ Erz ⓶ to pick (or work) ore; *agr.* mit der Sense ⓶ (mähen) to cut (down), to mow; *fig.* das ist nicht gehauen und nicht gestochen, etwa: it is of no use for anything, it's very indifferently done or made. — 4. mit Angabe der Wirkung: e-n frumm und lahm, zum Krüppel ⓶ to break every bone in a p.'s body; klein ⓶, in Stücke ⓶ (hacken) to cut to pieces, to chop into mince-meat; **entzwei**⓶ to break (or cleave, cut, split) in two; sein Schwert entzwei (oder in Stücke) ⓶ to break one's sword in two or to pieces; **von** etwas (**weg**⓶) to knock off, to remove by blows; schartig, stumpf ⓶ to dent, to blunt (in cutting

or fighting); zu Mus ⓶ to beat (or knock) into a jelly; ⊕ glatt ⓶ to smooth (or polish) by beating or cutting; sich matt und müde ⓶ to tire o.s. (out) with beating or hewing or chopping; sich durch die Feinde ⓶ to cut one's way through the enemy('s ranks). — 5. mit Angabe des Wohin: Löcher (oder Wu(h)nen) ins Eis ⓶ to cut holes in the ice; e-m ein Loch in den Kopf ⓶ to knock a hole in (or to break) a p.'s head; die Klauen ins Fleisch ⓶ to fasten one's claws in the flesh; in Stein ⓶ to carve in stone; sich (*acc. ob. dat.*) mit dem Beile in die Hand ⓶ to cut one's hand with the hatchet. — III sich ⓶ v/recip. u. refl. 6. s. 4 u. 5. — 7. sich (selbst) ⓶ to strike (or knock) o.s.; sich (ea.) ⓶ to exchange blows, to (have a) fight, to scuffle. — **IV** ~ **n** ⓶ 8. striking, &c. (s. I u. II); das ~ hilft bei ihm nichts beating (or thrashing) is of no use with him; *agr.* ~ des Korns cutting (or reaping) of corn; ⚒ ~ von Erz extraction of ore.
Hauer (‿ˇ) m ⓶ 1. (hauende Person) hewer, (wood-)cutter, &c. (s. hauen 3). — 2. ~ *pl.* (Hauzähne) fangs (or tusks) of a pig.
Häuer ⚒ (‿ˇ) [hauen] m ⓶ pickman, weitS. pitman, miner.
Hauerei F (-‿ˇ) f ⓶ = Prügelei.
Hauf (ˇ) *inv.* nur gbr. in: zu ~ s. Haufe 5.
Häufchen (‿ˇ) n ⓶ *dim. v.* Haufe 1 am Schluß.
Haufe (‿ˇ) [ahd.: heap] m ⓶ 1. heap, von angesammelten Dingen: accumulation, cluster, group; conglomeration, von bunt durch-ea. gewürfelten Dingen: mass, heap of confusion, von über-ea. geschichteten Dingen: pile (auch von Geld); ~ Holz 2c., auch: stack (a. als Maß); *agr.* ~ Heu haycock; *fig.* ~ Geld pile (F heaps, lots, loads *pl.*) of money, hoards *pl.*; alle auf einem (ob. einen) ~n all of a (or in one) heap; (durch-ea.) pell-mell, higgledy-piggledy; auf einen ~n schichten to heap up in piles, to pile up; in ~n in heaps or clusters or piles; Heu in ~n setzen to stack (or cock) hay; F er sieht aus wie ein ~n (oder *dim.* Häufchen) Unglück he looks the picture of misery. — 2. *fig.* sein Geld auf einen ~n tun to put one's money together or in one's place, weitS. to invest it in one concern, auch: to put one's eggs in(to) one basket; mit einem ~n in one rush; etwas übern (ob. über den, über einen) ~n werfen to knock a th. over or down, to upset (or overthrow) a th.; alle Bedenken über den ~n werfen to put (or throw, cast) aside every consideration or scruple; e-n, et. über den ~n rennen to run over a p., a th.; to knock a p., a th. down in running or driving; e-n, etwas über den ~n schießen to shoot down a p., a th.; to bring a p., a th. down with a shot or a bullet. — 3. (Menge) quantity, (große Anzahl) great number or mass, multitude, F heap(s *pl.*), lot(s *pl.*); (Schar) troop, band, gang; (Schwarm) swarm, crowd, *b.s.* der ~ ob. der große ~ (der Menschen) the great multitude, the (vulgar) mob, F the million,

[häufeln] — 490 — [Hauptstadt]

the common herd; in hellen (ob. dichten) ~n in vast (or dense) multitudes or masses, in one great stream; sich über den gemeinen ~n erheben to rise above the average or the vulgar. — 4. ⚔ ehm. ein ~n, *dim.* ein Häuflein (Soldaten) a detachment, a flying column, *auch*: a handful of men. — 5. ⚓ zu ~n, mehr gbr. zuhauf together, in clusters or groups or crowds, F in a heap.

häufeln (⌣⌣) *v/a.* und *v/n.* (h.) ⓖa. to put in (or to form) heaps or piles; to heap, to pile, Kartoffeln auch: to hill.

Häufel-pflug (⌣⌣...) *m* ⓖ *agr.* ridge- (or ridging-)plough.

Haufen (⌣⌣) *m* ⓖ = Haufe.

häufen (⌣⌣) ⓖ **I** *v/a.* (f. Haufe) to heap (up); to accumulate, amass, pile (up); (vermehren) to multiply, to increase; Geld to hoard (up), to scrape together; Schrecken auf Schrecken 2 to add horror to horror, F to pile up the agony; gehäuft heaped up, conglomerate, aggregate; ein gehäuftes Maß a full (*bibl.* a good) measure. — **II** sich 2 *v/refl.* to accumulate, to amass; (sich vermehren) to multiply, increase, grow. — **III** ~ *n* ⓖ = Häufung.

Haufen-bildung (⌣⌣...) *f* ⓖ formation of heaps or piles or groups, biswl.: ⚯ coacervation; 2förmig *a.* ⓖ like one heap or mass; conglomerate, ⚯ acerval; von Wolken: ⚯ cumulous; 2weise *adv.*, F *a. a.* in heaps, in clusters; (assembled) in crowds or multitudes or great numbers; von Tieren: in flocks, in herds; sich 2 ansammeln, versammeln to flock (or crowd) together; to assemble (in large crowds); **~wolke** *f, phys.*: ⚯ cumulus.

häufig (⌣⌣) [ahd.: *Haufe] *a.* ⓖ (*ant.* selten) frequent, usual, schwächer: repeated; (zahlreich) numerous, stärker: copious, abundant; 2 sein to be plentiful, to abound; 2er werden to increase in number; *adv. auch*: in abundance, (gewöhnlich) commonly, ordinarily; (oft) often; 2 besuchen to frequent; **~keit** (⌣⌣) *f* ⓖ frequency, frequent repetition.

Häuflein (⌣⌣) *n* ⓖ *dim. v.* Haufe (f. ds 4.)

Häufung (⌣⌣) *f* ⓖ accumulation, amassing; increase; conglomeration, aggregation; diese ~ (häufige Wiederholung) von Unfällen ꝛc. this frequent occurrence (or repetition) of ...

Hau-gerechtigkeit (⌣⌣...) *f* ⓖ right to fell timber; **~hechel** ⚷ *f:* ⚯ ononis; dornige ~ thorny rest-harrow (*Ono'nis spino'sa*); gemeine, stinkende ~ cammock, rest-harrow (*O. arve'nsis*); **~holz** *n* timber (or wood) for felling; **~klotz** *m* chopping-block.

Haupt (¹) [ahd.: head: It. *căput*] *n* ⓑ, ⊕, † f.3. **1.** head; bemoostes ~ f. bemoost II; gekrönte Häupter crowned heads *pl.*; das ~ entblößen to uncover one's head; f. bloß 2; *fig.* den Feind aufs ~ schlagen to defeat (or vanquish) the enemy, *bibl.* to smite the enemy hip and thigh; f. feurig 1 (*vgl. auch* Kopf). — **2.** *fig.* (Oberhaupt) head(man), chief, e-s Staates: sovereign; (Häuptling) chieftain, (Führer) leader; (Hauptmann) captain; die Häupter der Stadt the heads of the town, bsd. Lo. the City Fathers *pl.*; Rom war das ~ der Welt Rome was the ruler (or the imperial city) of the world; *eccl.* an ~ und Gliedern (in) root and branch. — **3.** am Bette zu seinen Häupten [ahd.], zu Häupten des Bettes near his pillow, at the head of the bed; uns zu Häupten over (or above) our heads, (just) above us.

Haupt-abschnitt (⌣...) *m* ⓖ principal (or main) section; von der Zeit: most important period; **=absicht** *f* chief intention or design; main drift; **=achse** *f*, *math.* princ. axis; **=ader** *f*, *anat.*: ⚯ cephalic vein; **=agent** *m*, **=agentur** *f* ⚯ principal (or general) agent, agency; **=altar** *m* great (or high) altar; **=anführer** *m* chief leader; **=angelegenheit** *f* princ. concern; **=anstifter** *m* chief instigator, ringleader; **=arbeit** *f* chief (part of the) work; **=armee** ⚔ *f:* a) principal army; b) main body (or the bulk) of the army; **=artikel** *m* chief article, einer Zeitung: leader; **=aufgabe** *f* main task; **=augenmerk** *n:* sein ~ auf et. richten to give one's chief attention to a th.; **=bahn** ⚙ *f* main line, trunk-line; **=bahnhof** *m* chief terminus; **=bank** ⚯ *f* head-bank; **=bastei** ⚔ *f, frt.* princ. bastion; **=begriff** *m* fundamental (or central) notion; **=bestand(teil)** *m* chief ingredient, main constituent; **=betrag** ⚯ *m* chief amount; sum total, total amount; **=beweggrund** *m* leading motive; **=beweis** *m* main proof; **=blatt** *n* einer Zeitung princ. (or first) sheet of a paper; **=buch** *n:* a) principal book; b) ⚯ ledger; **=bureau** *n* head (or central) office; **=eigenschaft** *f* chief property, leading feature; **=einfahrt** *f*, **=eingang** *m* main entrance, gateway; **=erbe** *m*, **=erbin** *f* chief heir(ess *f*); **=erfordernis** *n* principal (or prime) requisite; **=fach** *n:* a) main division; b) princ. subject; das ist sein ~ (was er am besten versteht) that's his speciality; **=farbe** *f* princ. colour; *phys.* ~n *pl.* primary colours *pl.*; **=fehler** *m* principal (or chief) fault or defect; **=fluß** *m* main river; **=frage** *f* main question; **=gebäude** *n* main (part of the) building; **=gedanke** *m* leading idea; **=gewinn**, **=gewinst** *m:* a) first prize in a lottery; b) bulk of the profit; **=grundsatz** *m* leading principle; **=haar** *n* hair of the head; **=hahn** *m:* a) ⚒ für Gas, Wasser ꝛc.: main tap or cock; b) F *fig.* (Hauptkerl) F cock of the walk; **=heer** ⚔ *m* =armee; **=hindernis** *n* principal (or chief) obstacle; **=inhalt** *m* chief contents *pl.*; ⊕ *typ.* summary; (Auszug) abstract, epitome; **=kasse** *f* central pay-office; **=kassier(er)** *m* head cashier; **=kerl** F *m:* a) chief man, F (urspr. *Am.*) boss of the show; b) *fig.* (lustiger Gesell) F jolly (good) fellow; **=kirche** *f* cathedral church; mother-church; **=lehre** *f* main (or cardinal) doctrine; **=lehrer** *m* head teacher, head master; **=leitung** ⊕ *f. tel.* main wire; **=leute** *pl.* f. **=mann**.

Häuptling (⌣⌣) [ahd.] *m* ⓐ*d.* chieftain of a tribe, captain (or leader) of a band;

häuptlings (⌣⌣) *adv.* (kopfüber) head foremost or forward, head over heels.

Häuptlingschaft (⌣⌣⌣) *f* ⓖ chieftainship, leadership.

Haupt-linie (⌣...) *f* ⓖ ⚙ und *tel.* main (or trunk-) line; **=los** *a.* ⓖ: a) headless, ⚯ acephalous; b) *fig.* without a head or leader; **=macht** *f:* a) chief (or central) power; b) ⚔ bulk of the army, main body (of the troops); **=mahlzeit** *f* principal meal (of the day); **=mangel** *m* chief defect; **=mann** *m:* a) (*pl.* meist: =leute) ⚔ captain; b) (*pl.* nur: =männer) chief, leader, leading spirit; *vgl.* Haupt 2; **=markt** *m* chief market; **=masse** *f* bulk; f. *a.* Gros² I; **=mast** ⚓ *m* main-mast; **=merkmal** *n* distinctive (or characteristic) feature; **=mittel** *n* chief means, principal remedy; **=nenner** *m, math.* (least) common denominator; **=niederlage** *f:* a) ⚯ principal store(house) or warehouse; chief emporium or settlement; b) ⚔ crushing defeat, general rout; **=ort** *m* chief place; **=perio'de** *f* chief period; **=perso'n** *f* princ. person; *vgl.* =rolle; ~en *pl.* notabilities *pl.*; **=post** *f*, **=post-amt** *n* general (or chief, central) post-office; **=preis** *m* first prize; **=probe** *f, thea.* general rehearsal; **=produkt** *n* chief (or staple) product (auch ⚯); **=punkt** *m* main (or most essential) point; *vgl.* =sache; **=quartier** ⚔ *n* headquarters *pl.*; das Große ~ the central headquarters (of the staff); **=quelle** *f* main source, fountain-head; **=rechnung** *f* general account; **=rechnungs-arten** *f/pl.* principal rules *pl.* of arithmetic; **=redakteu'r** *m* chief editor; **=regel** *f* princ. rule; **=regi'ster** *n:* a) general table of contents; b) ♪ einer Orgel: main-stop; **=reserve** ⚔ *f* principal reserve; **=rolle** *f, thea.*, &c.: leading (or most prominent) part or character; *fig.* die ~ spielen, oft: to play the first fiddle; **=sache** *f* chief thing or matter; *vgl.* =punkt; (Geld ist für ihn die ~ money is the first consideration (or main thing) with him; in der ~ in the main, generally speaking; der ~ nach in substance; **=sächlich(st)** *a.* principal, main, chief; *adv. auch* especially; das, worauf es 2 ankommt the main concern or point (in question); **=satz** *m, log.* main proposition, *gr.* princ. sentence, ♪ leading theme; **=schiff** *n:* a) ⚓ admiral-ship; b) *arch.* central aisle; **=schlacht** ⚔ *f:* a) most important battle; general engagement; b) (entscheidende Schlacht) decisive battle; **=schlag-ader** *f, anat.*: ⚯ aorta; **=schmuck** *m:* a) adornment for the head; b) princ. ornament; **=schuld** *f:* a) principal debt; b) chief fault; die ~ liegt an ihr the fault lies chiefly with her; **=schuldner** *m* principal debtor; **=schwierigkeit** *f* main difficulty; **=segel** ⚓ *f* mainsail; **=sitz** *m* chief (or central) seat; **=spaß** *m* chief fun; fine (or capital) joke; **=spirale** *f, elect.* primary coil; **=stadt** *f* capital, metropolis; ⚙ Bahn, Zug von der ~ nach der Provinz down-line, down-train; Bahn, Zug von der Provinz nach der ~

Signs (see page XVII): F familiar; P vulgar; ⚡ flash; ⚯ rare; † obsolete (died); * new word (born); ₊₊ incorrect; ♪ music

[Hauptstädter] — 491 — [Hausfreund]

up-line, up-train; =städter(in f) m inhabitant of the capital; =städtisch a. bsd. auf Lo. bezüglich: metropolitan; =stamm m: a) ⚔ main trunk; b) eines Volkes: chief tribe or race, e-r Familie: main stock; =stärke f chief strength; das ist f-e ~ ... his strong(est) point, his forte; =statio'n 🚂 f terminus; =steuer-amt n general inland revenue office; =stimme ♪ f principal voice or part; =straße f princ. street, main road, highway; =streich m masterstroke; (lustiger Streich) capital (or fine) trick; =strom m: a) chief (or main) river; b) ⊕ elect. main current; =stück n: a) princ. piece; e-s Buches ꝛc.: chief passage or section; b) eccl. die ~e des Glaubens the chief articles pl. of faith; =sturm ⚔ m general assault; =stütze f main (or best) support, mainstay; =summe f (sum) total; =täter m chief perpetrator of a crime, &c.; =teil m principal part, e-r Mannschaft: main body; =titel m chief title; ⊕ typ. capital heading; =ton m: a) fundamental tone, keynote; b) gr. chief accent; =treffen ⚔ n: a) bulk (or centre) of the army; b) = =schlacht; =treffer m first prize in a lottery; =treppe f principal staircase; =trumpf m Kartenspiel: highest (or best) trump (-card); =trupp ⚔ m (der Avant-, Arrieregarde; beim Gefecht) main body; =übel n princ. evil; =umstand m chief circumstance, main fact; =unternehmer m Bauwesen ꝛc.: chief contractor; =unterschied m principal difference; =ursache f princ. cause; =verbandplatz ⚔ m central ambulance (for dressing wounds); =verbrechen n capital crime; =verdienst n chief merit; =vergnügen n: a) chief pleasure; b) capital fun or amusement; =vermögen n chief (part of the) property; =versammlung f general meeting; =wache ⚔ f main guard (-station); =waffe f chief weapon; =wall ⚔ m, frt. principal rampart; =weg m = =straße; =werk n princ. work, eines Schriftstellers auch: standard work, masterpiece; =wort n: a) princ. word; b) gr. noun (substantive); =zahl(wort n) f cardinal number; =zeuge m principal (or most important) witness; =zoll-amt n = =steueramt; =zweck m main object.
Haus (´) [ahd.: house] n ③ a. 1. house; zwei-, drei-stöckiges ~ two-, three-storied house; (Wohnung) dwelling, habitation; ärmliche: (mere) hovel, cottage, feinere: mansion, manor; ~ auf dem Lande country-house, ~ in der Stadt town-house; das väterliche ~, geh. Sprache: the paternal roof; ~ und Hof house and home; der Herr (die Frau) vom Hause the master (the mistress) of the house; sein eigenes ~ h. to have a house (or home) of one's own; das ~ hüten to stay in(doors); aus dem Hause jagen, treiben to turn out (of doors); außer dem Hause out of doors; im Hause indoors, within doors; Spiele außer dem, im Hause outdoor, indoor games pl.; in j-s Hause at a p.'s house; nach Hause zurückkehren

(schreiben) to return (to write) home; von ~ aus originally; F to start with; (v. Geburt) by birth; er ist von ~ aus reich he comes from a rich family; von ~ zu ~ from house to house, from door to door; an einem Orte zu Hause sein to be bred and born in (or to be a native of) a place; ich bin hier zu Hause this is my native home; er ist bei uns wie zu Hause he feels at home with us; tun Sie, als wenn Sie hier zu Hause wären make yourself (quite) at home here; er ist nicht zu Hause ... not at home or not within; für niemanden zu Hause out to everybody, not at home to anybody; immer zu Hause hocken to be (or F to stick) for ever at home, to be a home-bird; er ist nirgends zu Hause he has no settled home; wo sind Sie zu Hause? which is your native place?; where do you come from?; s. bestellen 2; ~ an ~ mit e-m wohnen to live next door to a p. — 2. (Familie e-s Fürsten ꝛc.) princely, &c. house; das ~ Habsburg the house of Austria; des Kaisers hohes ~ the Emperor's illustrious dynasty or race. — 3. rel. das ~ Gottes the house of God; thea. das ~ (Theater) war (gedrängt) voll the house was full to overflowing or crowded or F crammed full; das Stück macht ein volles ~ ob. volle Häuser the piece draws full houses or large audiences, it fills the house, it draws (well); s. ausverkaufen 2; parl. ~ der Gemeinen, der Lords House of Commons, of Lords; Lower, Upper Chamber; ein beschlußfähiges ~ bilden to form (or constitute) a quorum; er sprach in e-m vollen Hause ... in a full house or before full benches. — 4. fig. man kann Häuser auf ihn bauen one (or you) can thoroughly rely on him, F he is as solid as a rock; ein großes ~ machen to live in great style, to keep an open house; damit bleib mir zu Hause (komme mir nicht)! leave that alone!; don't bother me with that!; in einem Fache zu Hause sein (Bescheid wissen) to be quite at home in (or intimately acquainted with) a subject; mit seinen Gedanken nicht zu Hause sein to be absent-minded, to pay no attention; mit der Tür ins ~ fallen (plump herausplatzen) to blurt out (or F to come out plump and plain with) a th.; Sprichw. jeder ist Herr in seinem Hause a(n English)man's house is his castle. — 5. (Bau mancher Tiere) ~ des Bibers beaver's lodge; ~ einer Schnecke shell of a snail. — 6. co. bursch.: altes ~, was machst du? how are you, old boy?; fide'les ~ jolly (old) fellow, gay (young) spark.
Haus-altar (´...) m ⑫ domestic altar; =andacht f family-prayer(s pl.), private devotion; =apothe'ke f: a) dispensary; b) medicine-chest; =arbeit f indoor work, housework; domestic duties pl.; =arme(r) s. pauper who receives outdoor relief; =arrest m detention at one's own home; ~ h. to be confined within doors or to one's

room; =arzt m (family-)doctor; ihr ~, oft: their medical man or adviser or attendant; =ausgaben f/pl. household-expenses pl.; =backen a. ⑥⑨ (D9) home-made; fig. (derb) uncouth, (prosaisch) prosy, humdrum; =bau m building (or construction of a house; =bedarf m household requisites pl.; =besitzer (=in f) m house-owner, proprietor (proprietress) of a house, landlord (landlady); =bettel(ei f) m begging from house to house or from door to door; =bewohner(in f) m inmate (or occupant) of a house; (Mieter[in]) tenant, lodger; =bibliothe'k f private library; =boot 🚢 n, bewohnbar: house-boat; =bursche m: a) boy in buttons, errandboy; b) (Stubengenosse) fellow lodger.
Häuschen (´⌣) [dim. von Haus] n ㉔ 1. small house, bisw.: houselet; cottage; am Eingange eines Parkes ob. Gutes: (porter's or keeper's) lodge; für Tiere: hutch, box. — 2. F fig. e-n aus dem ~ (außer sich) bringen to put a p. out of temper, to provoke (or irritate) a p.; er ist leicht aus dem ~ zu bringen he is easily roused or upset, F he soon boils over; aus dem ~ sein to be beside o.s., to be off one's head or F nut.
Haus-dieb(in f) m (´...) ㉓ thievish inmate; =diener m domestic servant, (fr.) valet; =drache F m termagant, vixen, ehm. (a. sh.) shrew, F (regular) tartar; =ehre f: a) honour of the house; b) †, bibl. und co. = Ehefrau; =eigentümer(in f) m = =besitzer(in); =einrichtung f appointments pl. of a house, (Möbel) household furniture.
hausen¹ (´⌣) [ahd.] I v/n. (h.) ⑩ 1. to dwell, reside, live; wo mag er nur ㉒? where may he live or F hang out? — 2. (haushalten) to keep house; to have a household; mit j-m ㉒ to live with a p. — 3. (walten) to manage one's affairs; schlecht mit s-m Vermögen ㉒ to mismanage one's property, to waste (or squander) one's fortune. — 4. (sein Unwesen treiben) to haunt a place; (Verwüstung anrichten) to ravage (or devastate) a place; der Feind, die Seuche hat schlimm (ob. arg) gehaust the enemy, the epidemic has wrought great havoc or destruction; der Sturm hat im Park schlimm gehaust the gale has played great havoc with the park. — II ~ n ㉓ 5. (s. 1) residence, stay. — 6. (s. 4) ravages pl., devastation; havoc (wrought).
Hausen² (´⌣) [ahd.] m ㉓ ichth. (great) sturgeon, isinglass-fish (Acipe'nser huso). [ichthyocol(la).)
Hausen²-blase ⚕ (´...) f ㉒ isinglass,
Haus-ente (´...) f ㉒ orn. domestic duck (Anas dome'stica); =entwässerung f drainage of a house.
Häuser-block (´⌣...) m ⑫ block of houses.
Häuserchen (´⌣⌣) pl. v. Häuschen.
Häuser-kauf m ⑫ purchase of houses.
Haus-er(e)n (´...) m ㉒, =flur m (f) (entrance-) hall, von größerem Umfange: vestibule; =frau f: a) housewife, mehr gbr.: mistress (or lady) of the house; b) (Wirtschafterin) eine gute ~ a good housekeeper; =freund m

---

⚔ scientific; ♦ botanical; 🏆 geography; ⊕ machinery; ⚒ mining; ⚔ military; ⚓ marine; ⑯ commercial; ✉ postal; 🚂 railway.

[Hausfriede] — 492 — [Hauswirt]

friend of the family; =friede m domestic peace; safety of the house; =friedens=bruch m infringement of dom. peace; =gans f, orn. dom. goose (Anser dome'sticus); =gebrauch m dom. (or family-)custom; für den ~ for dom. (or household) use; von Kleidern: noch gut zum ~ good enough to wear in the house; =geflügel n poultry; =geist m familiar spirit; =genosse m person living in the same house or under the same roof, (Mitmieter) fellow lodger; =genossenschaft f (all the) inmates pl. of a house; =gerät n, coll. household utensils pl. or furniture; =gesetz n family-law or =statute; =gesinde n, coll. domestic servants, F domestics pl.; =gespenst n ghost haunting a house; =gespinst ⊙ n homespun; =glocke f house-bell, street-door bell; =götter m/pl. household gods pl., röm. Alt. a. Penates, Lares pl.; =gottesdienst m divine service (held) at home, family-worship or -devotion; =grille f, ent. (Heimchen) house-cricket (Gryllus dome'sticus); =hahn m (house-)cock, feiner: rooster; =halt m household, domestic establishment; e-n ~ anfangen to set up housekeeping; einen gemeinschaftlichen ~ führen to keep house together; ?halten v/n.(h.) ⑧a**: a) to keep house, to carry on a household; mit einem ⌈ to live with a p.; (die Wirtschaft führen) to conduct a household; sie hält ihm haus she keeps house for him; das hilft ⌈ that keeps the home together or going, F it keeps the pot boiling; Sprichw. s. auskommen 6; b) eng s. mit et. ⌈ (sparsam umgehen) to be sparing (or economical) with a th.; mit seinen Mitteln ⌈ to husband one's resources; ~ n ㉓ = =haltung a; =halter, =hälter m manager (or steward) of a house; =hälterin f (lady) house-keeper; ?hälterisch a. economical, thrifty; =haltung f: a) management of a house (-hold), housekeeping; b) =halt, =haltungs=buch n housekeeping-book, book of household accounts; =haltungs=kosten pl. household expenses pl.; =haltungs=schule f etwa: school for domestic economy; =herr(in f) m master (f mistress) of the house; (Wirt[in]) host(ess); für die Dienerschaft: master (mistress); ?hoch a. (a) high as a house; (riesig groß) gigantic, enormous; =hofmeister m steward (of the household), F major-domo (a. oft co.); =huhn n (domestic) fowl (Gallus dome'sticus); =hund m, zo. house-dog (Canis familia'ris).

hausieren ⊕ (-⌣-) [dtsch.=lt.; *Haus] I v/n. (h.) ㉓ mit ⌈ ⌈ geh(e)n to hawk a th. about. — II ~ n ㉓ pedlary, hawking.
Hausierer ⊕ (-⌣-) m ㉒, ~in f ㊼ pedlar(ess f), hawker, itinerant vendor, (Straßenhändler) pavement vendor.
Hausier=(gewerbe=)paß ⊕ (-⌣-) m ㉒, =schein m pedlar's (or hawker's) license; =handel m pedlar's trade, hawking; =wesen n pedlarism.
...häufig (-⌣-) in Zssgn f. ein⌈ 2c.
Haus=industrie (⌣-...) f ㉙ home-industry; =jungfer f housemaid; =ka-

pelle f: a) eccl. private chapel; b) ♪ private band; =kaplan m private chaplain; =katze f domestic (or tame) cat (Felis dome'stica); =kauf m purchase of a house; =kleid n every-day dress, der Frauen oft: morning-dress, deshabille; =knecht m: a) man who does rough dom. work; porter, in Gasthöfen: boots sg.; b) F = =schlüssel; =kollekte f house-to-house collection; =kost f food prepared at home; =kreuz n: a) dom. affliction or trouble; b) = =drache; =laub n, =lauch, =lauf m ⌈ house-leek (Semperviʹvum tecto'rum); =lehrer m private (or family-)tutor; =lehrerin f governess; =lehrer=amt n, =stand m tutor's post, tutorship.
Häuslein (-⌣-) n ㉔ = Häuschen.
Haus=leinwand (⌣...) f ⑫ home-made linen, household linen.
Häusler (-⌣-) [Haus] m ㉓, ~in f ㊼ (Dorfbewohner ohne eigenes Feld) cott(ag)er.
Haus=leute (⌣...) pl. ⑫ von Hausmann.
häuslich (-⌣-) [Haus] a. ㊵ 1. ohne Steigerung (zum Hause gehörig, im Hause stattfindend) domestic; home(-), die den Arbeiten der Schüler the pupils' home(-) lessons pl.; es fehlt ihm an dem Fleiße he does not apply himself to his home(-)work; der Herd dom. hearth; im den Kreise by one's fireside; ein des Leben führen to lead a homely (or family) life; der Mensch, auch oft: Fstay-at-home, home-bird; den Unterricht (ant. Schulunterricht) empfangen to receive home(-)instruction, to have private tuition; die Vergnügungen indoor amusements pl.; adv. sich an e-m Orte ⌈ niederlassen to settle down at a place. — 2. (haushälterisch, sparsam) economical, thrifty. — 3. (gern zu Hause) fond of staying at (stärker: wedded to one's) home; domesticated (person).
Häuslichkeit (-⌣-) f ㊻ 1. (Familienleben) family-life or -circle; meine kleine ~ my little home. — 2. (Liebe zum Hause) domesticity, domesticated spirit or ways pl., love for (or attachment to) one's home. [home-made linen.]
Hausmacher=leinen ⊙ (⌣=⌣-...) n ⑫⌋
Haus=macht (⌣...) f ⑫ private possessions pl. (or power) of a sovereign; =mädchen n: a) general servant, F co. maid of all work; b) (Stubenmädchen) housemaid; =magd f = =mädchen a, =mann m: a) (pl. =leute) = =genosse, (Mietsmann) tenant; =leute pl. = =gesinde; b) (pl. =männer) porter (or door-keeper) at a hotel, &c.; =mannskost f homely (or plain) living or fare; =märchen n, etwa: family-story; =marder m, zo. common (or beech-)marten (Muste'la foi'na); =mast, =mästung f von Schweinen a.: stall-feeding; =meier m, hist. mayor of the palace; vgl. =hofmeister; =meister m housekeeper, auch = =hofmeister; =miete f house-rent; =mittel n household (or familiar) remedy, family-medicine; =mutter f mother of a family, (lt.) materfamilias, weitS. matron; ?mütterlich a. ㊿ motherly; matronly; =nummer f number of a house; =ordnung f rules pl. of a household; in einer Erziehungsanstalt 2c.:

house-regulations pl.; =plage f =kreuz; =posti'lle f: a) collection of sermons for home use; b) co. (talkative) old woman; =rat m = =gerät; =ratte f, zo. common rat (Mus rattus); =recht n: a) (Hausgesetze) domestic regulations pl.; b) (Recht des Herrn) dom. rights pl. or authority; von seinem ⌈ Gebrauch machen to turn an intruder out (of doors); =rock m house-coat, coat (or gown) worn at home, der Frauen: morning-gown, (Schlafrock) dressing-gown; =schatz m domestic treasure (a. fig.); =schlüssel m key of the street-door; latch-key; =schneider m family-tailor; jobbing tailor; =schuhe m/pl. house-shoes, slippers pl.; =schwalbe f, orn. house-martin (Cheli'don u'rbica); =schwamm ⋈ m dry-rot fungus (Meru'lius la'crimans); =schwelle f threshold of a house.
Hausse ⊕ (ho̅-se̅) [fr.] f ⑧ (ant. Baisse) rise of prices or quotations, upward tendency (F bullish tone) of the market.
Haus=segen (⌣...) m ⑧: a) prosperity of the house; b) fig. (Kinder) children, olive-branches pl.
haussen (ho̅-sen) [Hausse] v/n. (h.) ⑨⓪ Kurse zum Steigen bringen) to drive up prices, F to bull (or boom, rig) the market. [adv. out here.)
haußen ⤳ prove. (-⌣-) [mhd. hie(r) außen)⌋
Haussier ⊕ (ho̅-ße̅') [fr.] m ㉚ (Preistreiber) F bull(ish operator).
Haus=speise (⌣...) f ⑫ = =kost; =sperling m, orn. house-sparrow (Passer dome'sticus); =spinne f, ent. house-spider (Tegena'ria dome'stica); =stand m household; e-n eigenen ~ gründen to set up a household of one's own, F to settle down; =stätte f homestead; =steuer f house-tax; =suchung f jur. domiciliary visit; =suchungs=befehl m search-warrant; =taube f, orn. house-pigeon (Colu'mba li'via).
Hau=stein (⌣...) m ⑫ Bauwesen: freestone, ashlar; =stein=werk n freestone work.
Haus=telegraph(ie f) m (⌣...) ⑫ innerhalb des Hauses: telegraph(ing) in a private house; =teufel m = =drache; =tier n domestic animal; =tor n gate; =trauer f family-mourning; =trauung f wedding at a private house; =truppen f/pl. household troops pl.; =tür(e) f street-door; =tür=fenster n fan-light; =tür=glocke f street-door bell; =tür=treppe f door-steps pl.; =tyrann m domestic tyrant; =vater m father of a family, (lt.) paterfamilias, a.: good man of the house; =väterlich a. ⑥⑥ fatherly, like the father of a family; =verschiebung * f removal(or shifting) of a (whole) house (just as it stands); =vertrag m family-compact; =verwalter m steward of a (large) house(hold); =vogt m: a) = =verwalter; b) overseer of a prison or jail; =vogtei f (Gefängnis) prison, jail; =wanze f, ent. bed-bug (Cimex lectula'rius); =wäsche f: a) washing done at home; b) (Weißzeug) house-linen; =wesen n household (affairs pl.); ein ~ anfangen to commence housekeeping; =wirt m: a) = =herr; b) (als Vermieter)

Zeichen (s. S. XVII): F familiär; P Volkssprache; Γ Gaunersprache; ⤳ selten; † alt (auch gestorben); * neu (auch geboren); ⚡ unrichtig;

[Hauswirtin] — 493 — [heben]

landlord; c) ein guter ~ (=halter) sein to be a good manager; =wirtin f: a) =herrin; b) =mutter; =wirtschaft f management of a household; =wurz & f: echte ~ houseleek (Sempervi'vum tecto'rum); =ziege f domestic goat (Capra hircus); =zins m house-rent.

Haut (¹) [ahd.: hide: lt. cŭtis] f ⑩ 1. von Kühen, Ochsen, Pferden (vgl. Fell): skin, hide; hunt. (Fell des Hochwildes) case, coat of deer, chamois, &c.; abgelegte ~ der Schlangen 2c.: slough; ❦ u. zo. auch: covering; anat. tegument, ⚚ derm(a), corium; v. Obst 2c.: peel; dünne ~ (a. dim. Häutchen n): a) ⚚, anat. u. zo.: membrane, ⚚ cuticle, tunic; b) auf Flüssigkeiten: film; obere ~ und anat. ⚚ epiderm(is); (Schalen=) ~ des Embryos: ⚚ chorion; (Frucht=) ~ der Hautpilze: ⚚ hymenium; die ~ betreffend cutaneous, auf die ~ wirkend: ⚚ enderm(at)ic; med. Einspritzung unter die ~: ⚚ hypodermic (or subcutaneous) injection; aufgesprung(e)ne ~ cracked (or chapped) skin; an aufgesprung(e)ner ~ leiden to suffer from chaps, eine leicht heilende ~ haben to have good healing flesh or a healthy skin; ⚘ gegerbte Häute dressed skins pl.; abgezogene grüne (od. rohe) Häute green (or raw, undressed) skins or hides pl.; auf bloßer ~ tragen to wear next to one's skin; durchnäßt bis auf die ~ wet to the skin; er ist nichts als ~ und Knochen he is nothing but skin and bones. — 2. fig. Redensarten: auf der faulen ~ liegen to idle (or lounge) about, F to be bone-lazy; in keiner guten ~ stecken to be in a bad plight or in bad health; ich möchte nicht in deiner ~ stecken I should not like to be in your shoes; mit heiler ~ davonkommen to have a narrow escape, F to escape by the skin of one's teeth, to save one's bacon; s. fahren 1; mit ~ und Haar verschlingen to devour to the (very) last morsel; s. Haar 3; eine (sehr) dünne (empfindliche) ~ haben to be (very) thin-skinned or sensitive; eine (sehr) dicke ~ haben to be (very) thick-skinned or pachydermatous; sich s-r ~ wehren to defend o.s. to the last; e-m die ~ über die Ohren ziehen to skin (or fleece) a p., vgl. Fell 2; e-m die ~ voll schlagen to give a p. a good beating or F hiding, tanning; seine ~ zu Markte tragen to expose one's life, F to take one's life in one's hand; Sprichw. die ~ ist allweg näher als das Hemd near is my shirt, but nearer is my skin; charity begins at home; es ist um aus der ~ zu fahren it is enough to drive one wild. — 3. F (Person, mst g.s.; vgl. Balg 4) eine alte, gute, treue ~ a (dear) good soul, a stanch (or loyal) friend; eine ehrliche ~ an honest (or a) well-meaning person; a good fellow. — 4. ⚓ ~ outside planking; innere ~ inner skin.

Haut-abschürfung (″...) f ⚕ path. excoriation, desquamation; ⚘ ähnlich a. ⚕, ⚘ artig a. skinny, derm(at)oid; =atmung f, =ausdünstung f perspiration; =ausschlag m, path. rash (= Ausschlag 3); =beschreibung f, physiol. ⚚ derm(at)ography, hymenography; =bläschen n pimple; =bräune f, path. croup; =bürste f flesh-brush.

Häutchen (¹⚚) n ㉓ s. Haut 1. [gland.⎞
Haut-drüse (″...) f ⚕ anat.: ⚚ cutaneous⎠
Hautelisse-stuhl (h)ot-li″ß...) [fr.] m ⑫ high-warp loom; =weberei f Weberei: (ant. Basselisse) high warp.

häuten (¹⚚) [mhd.; *Haut] ⑨ I v/a. (strip of one's) skin; to uncase a stag, &c.; (schinden) to flay. — II sich ⚓ v/refl. to cast (or shed) one's skin; v. Schlangen 2c.: to (cast the) slough; durch Krankheit: to peel. — III ~ n ㉓ = Häutung.

Haut-entzündung (″...) f ⚕ path. cutaneous inflammation, ⚚ dermatitis.

Hautevolee (h)ō't-wō-lē″) [fr.] f ⑱ (feine Welt) cream of society, people of high life, a.: upper ten (thousand), (fr.) élite.

Haut-farbe (″...) f ⚕ flesh-colour, colour of the skin, des Gesichts: complexion; helle, dunkle ~ light, dark (stärker: swarthy) complexion; =flügler m/pl. ent.: ⚚ hymenoptera pl.; =gewebe ⚘ n: ⚚ dermatogen.

Hautgout (h)ō-gū') [fr.] m ⑰ (Wildgeschmack) das Rebhuhn hat et. ~ the partridge tastes (or smells, is) rather high or tastes rather strong.

häutig (¹⚚) [Haut] a. ⑥ 1. skinny; s. hautähnlich. — 2. (Häute bildend) ⚚ cuticular, pellicular; ⚘ u. zo.: ⚚ membranous, tunicate(d); path. ⚕ Bräune croup.

Haut-jucken (″...) n ⚕ itching of the skin; =krankheit f skin-disease, cutaneous disease, ⚚ dermat(on)osis; =lehre f, physiol.: ⚚ derm(at)ology, hymenology.

haut-los (″...) a. ⑯ skinless, ⚚ excoriated; =pilze ⚘ m/pl. ⚕: ⚚ hymenomycetes pl.; ⚘ reinigend a. purifying the skin; ⚕es Mittel, oft: cosmetic; ⚘ reizend a. irritating (to) the skin.

Haut-reli-ef (h)ō-⚓(′)⁹) [fr.] n ㉚ (a. ⚒ d.) sculp., &c. (erhabene Arbeit) high relief, (it.) ril-rilievo or -relievo.

Haut-schwiele (″...) f ⚕ hard skin, ⚚ callosity; =talg m. physiol.: ⚚ sebaceous humour, (lt.) sebum cutaneum.

Häutung (¹⚚) f ⚕ skinning, &c. (s. häuten I und II); path.: ⚚ desquamation; s. Haut-abschürfung.

Haut-wassersucht (″...) f ⚕ path. dropsy in the skin, ⚚ anasarca, leucophleg-⎞
Hau-zahn (″,) m ⚕ tusk, fang. ⎣macy.⎠
Havanna ♀ (⚓w⚓-) [span. la Habana] npr/f. (dtsch bff. n) ⚒ α. Stadt auf Kuba) Havana; ~ f ㊻ oder ~ zigarre f ⑫ Havana (cigar).

Havarie (⚓w⚓¹), ⚓ Haverei (⚓f⚓¹) [nhd. 15. sae.; fr. avarie; *ar.] f ⑱ loss (or damage) by sea, average; ~ leiden to suffer damage by sea.

havariert ⚓, ⚓ haveriert (~) a. ⑯ damaged by (the) sea, auch: sea-damaged.

Hawa-i(=Inseln f/pl.) ♀ (⚓⚓-...) npr/n. ⚒ α. inv. Hawaii, ehm. Sandwich-Islands pl.

H. B. öst. abbr. = Helvetisches Bekenntnis Helvetic Confession (1536 u. 1566).

Hbf(r)zbd. abbr. = Halbfranzband.

he! (¹) int. 1. (Ruf) heigh!, I say!, F halloa!; ⚓ da! ho there!, what ho!; stop! — 2. bei Fragen) etwa: eh?; what do you think (of it)?, what do you mean? — 3. (Ausruf der Freude) hurra(h)!; s. juchhe.

Heb-amme (″⚚) [ahd. (P, eigtl. heb(ende) Ahne¹)] f ⑱ midwife, monthly nurse, ⚚ obstetrician.

Hebammen-institut (″⚚...) n ⚒, =kunst f midwifery, ⚚ obstetrics.

Hebe (¹⚚) [grch.] npr/f. ⚒ß. myth. (Göttin der "Jugend") Hebe; fig. (Kellnerin) barmaid, waitress, F co. Hebe.

Hebe-apparat (″⚚...) m ⚒ =maschine; =zeug n, =arm ⊙ m an e-r Maschine (arm of a) lever; =balken, =baum, =bock m crab-bar; heaver; =daumen m bei Pochwerken: lifting-cam, lifter; =eisen n, surg. elevator; =kran m hoisting- (or elevating) crane.

Hebel (¹⚚) [mhd.; *heben] m ⚒ 1. ⊙ mech. lever; einarmiger, zweiarmiger ~ lever of the second kind, of the first kind. — 2. fig. (bewegende Kraft) motor force; alle ~ ansetzen to make every possible effort, to strain every nerve, to do one's (very) utmost.

Hebe-lade ⊙ (″⚚...) f ⚕ hand- (or hoisting-)jack.

Hebel-arm ⊙ (″...) m ⚕ arm of a lever.
Hebe-latte (″...) f bei Pochwerken: stem of a stamping-mill. [purchase.⎞
Hebel-kraft (″...) f ⚕ mech. leverage,⎠
hebeln ⊙ (¹⚚) v/n. (h.) u. v/a. ⚕ a. to use (or apply) levers or leverage; et. ⚓ to set a th. in motion (with the aid of levers).

Hebe-maschine (″⚚...) f ⚕ lifting-engine or -machine; =muskel m, anat.: ⚚ attollent or elevator (muscle).

heben (¹⚚) [ahd.: heave] ⚒(⑦)b. I v/a. u. sich ⚓ v/refl. 1. (sich) ⚓ to lift (o.s.), to raise (o.s.); mit e-m Hebel: to prize (up); der Teig hebt sich the dough is rising; mit Mühe ⚓ to heave; (erhöhen) to elevate (a. fig.); einen Schatz ⚓ (emporfördern) to unearth (or bring up) a treasure; ⊙ Lasten ⚓, auch: to hoist (or draw, heave) up loads, mit dem Kran: to crane up, mit Rollen: to pulley; ⚓ den Anker aus dem Grunde ⚓ to trip the anchor; ein Wrack ⚓ to raise a wreck; fig. e-n bis zum Himmel ⚓ to extol a p., to praise a p. (up) to the skies; sich wieder ⚓ (vom Handel 2c.) to revive. — 2. (beiseite schaffen) to move (or push) aside; alle Schwierigkeiten sind gehoben every difficulty is cleared away or removed; jeden Zweifel ⚓ to set all doubts at rest. — 3. (hebend fortbewegen) e-n aufs Pferd ⚓ to lift a p. into the saddle; eine Dame 2c. aus dem Wagen ⚓ to help a lady, &c. out of a carriage; e-e Tür aus den Angeln ⚓ to unhinge a door, to take it off its hinges; e-n aus dem Sattel ⚓ (beim Turnier 2c.) to unhorse (or dismount) a p.; fig. to discomfit (or supplant) a p., to take a p.'s place; fig. ein Kind aus der Taufe ⚓ to stand godfather (f godmother) to a child; ⊙ typ. die Form aus der Presse ⚓ to take the form out of the press; ein Kind vom Stuhle ⚓ to lift a child off its chair; geh. Spr.: sie huben sich von dannen they took their departure, they betook themselves

[Hebeopfer] — 494 — [heerespflichtig]

elsewhere; hebe dich **weg von mir!** be gone!, get out of my sight!, depart thou hence!; *bibl.* get thee hence, Satan! — 4. *math.* aus einer Gleichung eine Unbekannte ⁐ to eliminate an unknown (quantity) from an equation; einen Bruch ⁐ to simplify (or reduce, cancel) a fraction; dies hebt sich (gegen das andere) these counterbalance each other; 2 von 2 hebt sich two from two leaves nothing; diese Zahlen ⁐ sich (ea.) ... cancel or can be cancelled; p² läßt sich durch p ⁐ (teilen) p² cancels (or divides) by p; *fig.* es hebt sich jetzt! now we are (or that makes us even or quits)! — 5. (schärfer hervortreten lassen) *paint.*, &c.: to put into (bold) relief; to set off. — 6. (begünstigen) to favour, F to push (on); Künste und Wissenschaften ⁐ to encourage (or patronize) arts and sciences. — II *v/impers.* 7. es hebt sich mir alles my heart is heaving. — III sich ⁐ *v/refl.* 8. f. 1, 3 u. 4. — IV ~ *n* ㉓ 9. = Hebung 1; (rhythmisches) ~ und Senken der Stimme cadence. — V ge-hoben *p.p.* u. *a.* ㊿(D 9) 10. in den Bed. des *inf.* — 11. ⁐e Sprache elevated language or style; in ⁐er Stimmung sein, sich ⁐ fühlen to feel elevated, to be in high (or capital) spirits or in a buoyant humour. **Hebe-opfer** (´⁀‿...) *n* ㉓ jüd. Alt.: heave-offering; =pumpe ⊙ *f* lifting-pump; =punkt *m* eines Hebels: fulcrum. **Heber** (´‿) *m* ㉒ 1. (~in *f* ㊼) he (she) who lifts, &c. (f. heben I). — 2. *phys.* (Saug=)~ siphon. — 3. *anat.* = Hebemuskel. — 4. ⊙ *mech.* = Hebewerk; *typ.* (Hebewalze) lifting-roller. **Hebe-rad** ⊙ (´´‿...) *n* ㉓ (Schöpfrad) flush- (or bucket-, scoop-)wheel. **Heber-apparat** (´´‿...) *m* ㉒ Fernspr.: siphon-recorder; =barometer *n* (*m*) siphon-barometer. **Hebe-register** (´´‿...) *n* ㉓ = =rolle a. **heber-förmig** (´´‿...) *a.* ㊿ in the shape of a siphon, ⁂ siphoniform. **Hebe-rolle** (´´‿...) *f* ㊻ a) register of assessment; b) *mech.* pulley. **Heber-pumpe** (´´‿...) *f* ㊻ siphon-pump; =schenkel *m* leg of a siphon. **Hebe-schein** ⦿ (´´‿...) *m* ㉒ coupon; =stange ⊙ *f* lifting-pole or -spike; handspike; =stelle *f* receiver's office; ⁐ und Druckwerk ⦿ lift-and-force pump; =vorrichtung *f*, *mech.* purchase, hydraulische: hydraulic jack; =werk *n*, =winde *f*, *mech.* lifting-jack; elevator; =zeug *n*, *mech.* lifting-gear; ↓ hoisting-gear; Weberei: lifting-bar. **Hebräer** (‿´‿) *m* ㉒, ~in *f* ㊼ Hebrew. **hebräisch** (‿´‿) *a.* ㊿ Hebrew; (jüdisch) Jewish; die ⁐e Sprache, das ⁐(e) ㊼ the Hebrew language, Hebrew; ⁐e Gewohnheit, Sitte Hebraism. **Hebriden** ♀ (‿´‿) [flt.] *npr/f/pl.* ⊛(schott. Inseln) Hebrides, Western Isles *pl.*; **hebridisch** *a.* ㊿ Hebridean. **Hebung** (´‿) *f* ㊻ 1. (zu heben 1:) lifting, elevation, &c.; (zu 2:) removal of difficulties, &c.; (zu 4 *math.*:) elimination of an unknown, cancelling of fractions; (zu 6:) encouragement, patronage; die

~ der Gewerbe begünstigen to favour the improvement (or revival) of trade; ~ des Unterrichtswesens advancement of education. — 2.: a) des Bodens: elevation, swelling; b) *pros.* (ant. Senkung) stress, ⁂ arsis. **Hebungs-versuch** (´´‿...) *m* ㉒ (zB. um ein Schiff zu heben) attempt to raise a ship, &c. **Heb-walze** ⊙ (´´‿...) *f* ㊻ lifting-roller. **Hechel** (´‿) *hbd.*: hatchel] *f* ㊻ Spinn.: hatchel, hackle; f. Flachs=⁐; *fig.* durch die ~ ziehen = durchecheln 2. — 2. ♀ = Granne 1. [bench.) **Hechel-bank** ⊙ (´‿...) *f* ㊻ hackling-) **Hechelei** (‿´‿‿) *f* ㊻ 1. ⊙ continual hackling. — 2. *fig.* severe (or F slashing) criticism, censure, carping, cavilling, F slating. [machine.) **Hechel-maschine** ⊙ (´´‿...) *f* ㊻ hackling-) **hecheln** (´‿) I *v/a.* ㉒a. 1. ⊙ Flachs: to hackle, hatchel, comb. — 2. *fig.* e-n ⁐ to cavil (or gird) at a p.; vgl. durch⁐ 2. — II ~ *v* ㉓ 3. hackling, &c. (f. 1); *fig.* f. durch⁐ II u. Hechelei. **Hechel-stuhl** ⊙ (´‿...) *m* ㉒ hatchel-bench; =zahn *m* tooth of a hatchel. **Hechler** (´‿) *m* ㉒ 1. ⊙ hackler, hatcheller. — 2. *fig.* severe (or carping) critic, caviller. [hough.) **Hechse** (´‿) ♀ *vet.* (Kniebug) hock,) **Hecht¹** (´) [ahd.: hake] *m* ⓑ. 1. *ichth.* pike, jack (*Esox lu'cius*); *fig.* ein ~ im Karpfenteich(e) a pike in a fish-pond, a wolf among the lambs. — 2. F *fig.* (Kerl) das ist ein feiner ~... a fine fellow. **hecht²** ↓ (´) *a.* ㊿ (dicht) tight. **Hecht¹-angel** ⊙ (´´‿...) *f* ㊻ pike-hook, hook for catching pike; =artig *a.* ㊿ like a pike, ⁂ esocid; =barsch *m*, *ichth.* pike-perch (*Luciope'rca*); =blau *a.* (as) blue as a boiled pike; =brut *f* fry of pike; =grau *a.* light grey; bluish grey; =könig *m* (large) old pike; =kopf *m* pike's head; =schimmel *m* light-grey horse; =sprung *m* Schwimmsport: header. **Heck¹** (´) [Hag] *n* ⓑ. 1. (Einfriedigung) fence, (Gattertür) trellis-gate. — 2. ⥀ (hinterster Schiffsteil) stern; ein Schiff mit dem ~ unter Wasser ... with her stern submerged or dipping in water; mit dem ~ zu sternward. **Heck²-...** (´‿...) [hecken] f. =bauer 2c. **Heck¹-balken** ↓ (´´‿...) *m* ㉒ wing-transom; =²bauer *m* (*n*) für Kanarienvögel 2c. breeding-cage; =¹boot ↓ *n* stern-boat. **Hecke¹** (´‿) [ahd.] *f* ㊻ 1. hedge; *Hag* [*f* ㊻ 1. hedge; (Baum=)~ hedge-row; lebendige (grüne) ~ living (or quickset) hedge; mit ~n einzäunen to hedge (or fence) in; vgl. Heck 1. — 2. (dorniges Gebüsch) bramble-bush, thorny shrub, prickly bush, bsd. in Australien: scrub. **Hecke²** (´‿) [nhd.: hatch] *f* ㊻ 1. (Hecken) hatching, breeding; (Zeit des Heckens) hatching- (or breeding-)time. — 2. (Käfig zum Hecken) breeding-cage, mit vielen Vögeln: aviary. — 3. (auf einmal ausgeheckte Vögel) hatch, brood, birds *pl.* hatched in one nest or hatched together. **hecken** (´‿) [nhd.: hatch] I *v/a.* u. *v/n.* (h.) ㊹ 1. bsd. von Vögeln: to hatch, v. Säugetieren u. F v. Frauen: to breed;

engS. (sich stark vermehren) to breed (or multiply) rapidly, F to breed like rabbits; (gebären) to bring forth young. — 2. *fig.* (wuchernd erzeugen) to produce in abundance; (ausfinnen) to contrive, to devise; *b.s.* to concoct (or hatch out, hatch) a plot, &c. — II ~ *n* ㉓ 3. hatching; breeding; (Paarung) mating; *fig.* contrivance; concoction. **Hecken-baum** (´‿...) *m* ㉒ hedge-tree; =beschneider *m* hedge-pruner or -clipper, hedger; =dickicht *n* dense bramble-bush; =gang *m* hedge-row; =hopfen ♀ *m* wild hops *pl.*; =kirsche ♀ *f*: rote ~ fly-honeysuckle (*Loni'cera Xylo'steum*); =knöterich ♀ *m* false buckwheat (*Poly'gonum dumeto'rum*); =macher *m* hedger; =rose ♀ *f* = Hundsrose (*Rosa canina*); =schere *f* hedge-shears *pl.*; =sichel *f* hedge-bill; =winde ♀ *f* bearbind (*Convo'lvulus se'pium*); =zaun *m* = Hecke 1; =zucht [Hecke²] *f* breeding (or hatching) of cage-birds. **Heck¹-feuer** ↓ (´´‿...) *n* ㉓ fire from the stern; =flagge ↓ *f* stern-flag; =galerie ↓ *f*: Galerie 4; =²geld *n* im Volksglauben etwa: penny for luck, lucky sixpence; =¹geschütz *n* ↓ stern-chaser; =²groschen *m* = =geld. **Heckicht¹** (´‿) *n* ⓓ. thicket. **heckicht¹**, heckig (´‿) [Hecke¹] *a.* ㊿ like a hedge, full of hedges or thorny shrubs. **Heck¹-laterne** ↓ (´´‿...) *f* ㊿ poop-lantern; =²pfennig *m*, =taler *m* = =geld; =zeit *f* breeding- (or hatching-)time. **heda** (´‿) *int.* — he!; 2! niemand da? (a)hoy! nobody there?; in Läden: shop! **Hede** nordd. (´‿) [nbd.: hards] *f* ⊛ tow, oakum; hards *pl.*; **heden** *a.* ⊛ (maden) of tow or oakum. **Hederich** ♀ (´‿‿) [mhd.; *lt.* (*Glecoma hedera'cea*) *m* ⓓd. 1. = Gundermann. — 2. hedge-mustard (*Ery'simum*). **Hedschra** (´‿) [ar.] *f, inv.* (Flucht Moham̄eds, 622 nach Chr., Anfang der mohammedanischen Zeitrechnung) Hegira, Hejira. **Hedwig** (´‿) [ahd.] *npr/f.* ♀ ⊛a. (An.) ehm. Edwiga. **Heer** (´; Hom. he(h)r) [ahd.] *n* ⓑc. 1. army; stehendes ~ standing army, vgl. Feld=~; ~, das nur auf dem Papier steht paper army; in das ~ eintreten to go into the army, v. Rekruten: to join the ranks or the regiment; zum ⁐e stoßen to join the army; ein ~ auf den Kriegsfuß stellen to put an army on a war-footing, to mobilize an army. — 2. (große Schar) host, multitude, legion; (Schwarm) swarm; das wilde ~, etwa: the wild hunt or chase. **Heer-bann** ⚔ (´´‿...) [mhd.] *m* ㉒, etwa: militia, reserve; =dienst *m* serving in the army, military service. **Heeres-abteilung** (´´‿...) *f* ㊻ division of an army; =einrichtung *f* army-organization; =ergänzung *f* recruiting (for the army); =flucht *f* desertion; =folge *f* compulsory (military) service; ~ leisten to join the army, to flock to the ranks; die ~ versagen bsd. f. to refuse to obey the call (to the ranks); =kraft *f*, =macht *f* military armament or forces *pl.*, troops *pl.*; =pflichtig *a.* ㊿ liable to (be called out

---

Signs (see page XVII): F familiar; P vulgar; ⚐ flash; ⟍ rare; † obsolete (died); * new word (born); ⁘ incorrect; ♪ music;

[Heeresrat] — 495 — [Heide]

Heer= for) military service; =**rat** m engl.: Army Council; =**teil**(e pl.) m portion(s pl.) of an army; =**verwaltung** f military administration; =**zug** ⚔ m (G.) = Heerzug. **Heer=fahne** ⚔ (ᵘ...) f ⊕ flag, standard, banner; =**fahrt** f campaign, military expedition; =**flucht** ꝛc. = Fahnen ꝛc.; =**flügel** m wing of an army; =**führer** m leader (or commander, geh. Spr.: captain) of an army; =**haufe**(n) m division of an army; =**lager** n (army-) camp; =**meister** m ehm. grand-master of a military order; =**rauch** m f. Herauch; =**raupe** f = =wurm; =**säule** f column of troops; =**schar** f host; bibl. der Herr der ~en the Lord of hosts; die himmlischen ~en the celestial hosts or legions pl.; =**schau** f review (of troops); =**schnepfe** f, orn. common snipe (Sco'lopax galli-na'go); =**straße** f: a) military (or strategic) road or route; b) (common) highway, main road; = **und Wehrordnung** f regulations pl for the defence of the country; =**verpflegung** f commissariat; =**wagen** m baggage-cart or -waggon; =**weg** m = =straße; =**wesen** n (all) military concerns or affairs pl.; =**wurm** m, ent. (Raupe der Baumwollenmotte, Leuca'nia unipu'ncta) army-worm; =**zug** m army on the march, mooving troops pl.

Hefe (ᴸᵛ) [ahd.; *Heben] f ⊕, ⚔ ~n m ㉓ 1. (Gärungsmittel) leaven, yeast, barm. — 2. (Bodensatz e-r Flüssigkeit) dregs, lees, grounds pl.; sediment; fig. den Kelch bis auf die ~ leeren to empty the cup to the very dregs. — 3. fig. ~ des Volkes dregs pl. (or scum) of the people; the lowest strata pl. of society.

Hefen ⚔ (ᴸᵛ) m ㉓ = Hefe.

hefen=ähnlich ⊕ (ᵘ...) [Hefe] a. ⊕, =**artig** a. yeasty, yeast-like; =**brot** n, =**kuchen** m ⊕ leavened bread, cake; =**stück** n, =**teig** m yeast-dough, leavened dough or flour; =**zelle** ♀ f yeast-cell.

Hefe=pilz ♀ (ᵘᵛ) m ⊕ yeast-plant or -fungus, vgl. Bierhefepilz.

heficht, hefig (ᵛ) a. ⊕ = hefen-ähnlich.

Heft (ᵛ) [ahd.: haft] n ⊕b. 1. ⊕ des Messers ꝛc.: handle, seltener: haft; eines Schwertes: hilt; fig. e-m das ~ entwinden to wrest the power from a p.('s hands); das ~ in der Hand (oder in Händen) haben to hold the power (or sway) in one's hands, to be at the helm of affairs. — 2. (Schreibbuch) writing-book; Schule: (für Aufgaben) exercise-book, für Schönschreiben: copy-book; Buchhandel: (geheftetes Büchelchen) stitched (or stitch-)book, (Lieferung) number; in (zwanglosen) ~en erscheinend appearing or issued in (separate) parts or numbers. — 3. ⊕ (Lage von zehn Bogen Papier) ten sheets pl. of paper, auch (fr.) cahier.

Heft=ahle ⊕ (ᵛ...) f ⊕ stitching-awl; =**ausgabe** f Buchhandel: publication in parts or numbers.

Hefte (ᵛ) f ⊕ Weinbau: fastening the tendrils of the vine.

Heft=eisen ⊕ (ᵛ...) n ⊕ Glasfabr.: pointel. **Heftel** ⊕ (ᵛ) m u. n ㉒, f ⊕ (Haken und Öse) hook and eye; (Spange) clasp.

hefteln (ᴶᵛ) v/a. ⊕a. to fasten with hook and eye; to clasp. [Stich) tack.]

Heftel=stich (ᵛᵛ) m ⊕ Näherei: (langer

heften (ᴶᵛ) [ahd. = haften m.] ⊕ I v/a. 1. to attach, to fasten, klebend auch: to stick (an et. to a th.); (festbinden) to tie, (feststecken) to pin; (einhäkeln) to hook, to clasp. — 2. (nähen) a) Näherei: (mit langen Stichen) to tack, to baste; b) ⊕ Buchbinderei: to stitch, to sew; geheftet in sheets, vgl. Heft 2; c) surg. to sew up a wound, &c. — 3. die Augen (oder den Blick) auf e-n, et. ᴸ to fix (or rivet) one's eyes (or glances) upon a p., a th. — II sich ᴸ v/refl. 4. (s. I) to attach o.s., to stick, von Blicken: to be fixed or rivet(t)ed.

Heft=faden ⊕ (ᵛ...) m ⊕ Schneiderei ꝛc.: basting- (or stitching-, sewing-) thread; =**haken** m Buchbinderei: hook of a sewing-press.

heftig (ᴶᵛ) [mhd.; *Haft] a. ⊕ vehement, violent, impetuous; (leicht reizbar) irritable, irascible; (barsch, rauh) rude, rough; (grimmig) fierce, (leidenschaftlich) passionate, (tobend) furious; ᴢ med., phys. intens(iv)e; ᴸes Gemüt, Temperame'nt quick (or hasty) temper; ᴸe Kälte sharp (or severe) cold; ᴸe Sehnsucht intense (or ardent, keen) longing; ᴸer (starker) Windstoß strong gust of wind; ᴸe Worte angry (or high) words pl.; heated dispute or altercation. ᴸ sein to be enraged or out of temper; ᴸ werden to fly into a passion; adv. ᴸ an=ea. geraten to come to close quarters or to blows; ᴸ empfinden to feel keenly; ᴸ lachen to burst out laughing; ᴸ verliebt deeply in love; ᴸ weinen to cry bitterly; ᴸ wirkendes Mittel violent (or strong) remedy; ᴸ wüten to rage fiercely.

Heftigkeit (ᴶᵛ-) f ㊻ (vgl. heftig) vehemence, violence, impetuosity; irritability, rudeness; intensity; hastiness; ardour, keenness.

Heftig=werden (ᴶᵛᴶᵛ) n ㉓ passionate outburst, enragement, violent passion, fit of temper or anger.

Heft=lade ⊕ (ᵛ...) f ⊕ Buchbind.: (binder's) sewing-press; =**nadel** f: a) Buchbinderei: stitching- (or bookbinder's) needle; b) surg. (surgical) needle for sewing wounds, &c., ᴢ fibula; =**pflaster** n, pharm. adhesive (or sticking) plaster, englisches: court-plaster; =**schnur** ⊕ f stitching-thread; ᴸweise adv. (F a.) in numbers; ᴸ erscheinend, auch: serial; vgl. Heft 2; =**zweck**(e f) m drawing-pin; =**zwirn** ⊕ m = =faden.

Hege (ᴸᵛ) [hegen] f ⊕ 1. preservation; ~ und Pflege (great) care and attention, careful nursing. — 2. for. (Schonung) a) für Bäume: nursery (for young trees); b) für das Wild: preserve.

Hege=meister (ᵛᵛ...) m ⊕ for. head game-keeper; vgl. =reiter.

Hegemonie ᴢ (-ᵛᴸ) [grch.] f ⊕ (Führerschaft) hegemony, leadership, headship.

hegen (ᴸᵛ) [ahd.: hug; *Hag] I v/a. ⊕ 1. to enclose with hedges, to fence in. — 2. (schützen) to preserve game, fish, &c. — 3. (auch v/refl.) e-n (sich) ᴸ (sorgfältig pflegen) to bestow care (or attention) upon a p. (o.s.); ᴸ und pflegen to nurse carefully or tenderly, to foster, to cherish, die Künste ꝛc.: to cultivate, patronize, encourage. — 4. (einschließen) to enclose, comprise, contain; mit abstrattem Objekt: Abneigung gegen e-n ᴸ (empfinden) to have an aversion to a p., to dislike (stärker: to detest) a p.; Ehrfurcht vor e-m ᴸ to hold a p. in respect or awe; Groll gegen e-n ᴸ to harbour (or bear) a grudge (or to have a spite) against a p.; Hoffnung ᴸ to entertain (or cherish) a hope; Neid gegen e-n ᴸ to be envious of a p.; Vertrauen ᴸ to have (or feel) confidence; e-n Wunsch nach et. ᴸ to entertain a wish (or to have a desire) for a th.; Zweifel ᴸ to have one's doubts, to be in doubt. — 5. bei sich ᴸ (verbergen) to harbour, to give refuge to. — II ~ n ㉓ 6. (s. I) enclosure; preservation of game, &c.; care bestowed upon.

Heger (ᴸᵛ) [hegen] m ㉒ 1. ~(in f ㊺) m one who nurses, fosters, &c. (s. hegen 3). — 2. = Hegereiter.

Hege=reiter (ᵛᵛ...) m ⊕ for. gamekeeper, warrener, (Titel:) verderer; =**schlag** m, for. = Hege 2; =**wald** m fenced-in forest, preserve; =**wisch** m whisp of hay (on a pole) marking a preserve; =**zeit** f des Wildes: close time (or season) for game, hunt. (de)fence-month.

Hehl (ᴸ) [mhd.; *hehlen] n (m) ⓘc. (Verhehlen) concealment; (Verstellung) dissimulation, (Heimlichkeit) secrecy; kein ~ aus et. (ob. daraus) m. to make no secret of a th.; er hat der Sache (gen.) kein ~, auch: er hat es (gen.) keinen ~ he does not conceal the matter, F he does not keep it dark or snug; et. ohne ~ tun to do a th. openly or without concealment.

hehlen (ᴸᵛ) [ahd.: lt. cela're] I v/a. ⊕ (verheimlichen) to conceal, to keep secret or F dark, durch Verstellung: to disguise the facts, to dissimulate; jur. Gestohlenes ᴸ to receive stolen goods. — II ~ n ㉓ concealment; dissimulation; jur. = Hehlerei.

Hehler (ᴸᵛ) m ㉒, ~**in** f ㊺ one who conceals; jur. accessory after the fact; (Diebs-)~ receiver of stolen goods. F fence, family-man; Sprichw. der ~ ist so gut wie der Stehler the receiver is as bad as the thief.

Hehlerei (-ᴸᴸ) f ㊻ (wrongful) concealment; receiving (of stolen goods.

hehr (ᴸ; Hom. Heer, her) [ahd.] a. ⊕ (erhaben) sublime, augu'st; elevated, high, lofty; (ehrwürdig) venerable, worshipful; (großartig) grand; hoch und ᴸ high and lofty; ~**e** (ᴸᵛ) f ⊕, ~**heit** (ᴸ-) f ㊻ sublimity; loftiness; grandeur.

hei (ᴸ), **heida** (ᴸ-) int. hey!, huzza!, F (how) jolly!; f. heidi 1. **(h)eiapopeia**(-ᵛᴸ) f. eiapopeia.

Heide[1] (ᴸᵛ) [ahd. = heath] f ⊕ (poet. dat. sg. a. ~n) 1. heath, zB. Lüneburger ~ heath of Lüneburg; (unbebautes Weideland) oft: prairie-land, Röslein auf der ~ n (G.) little rose upon the heath. — 2. copse, wood, forest. — 3. ♀ = Heidekraut a.

⚔ scientific; ♀ botanical; ⊕ geography; ⊙ machinery; ⚒ mining; ⚔ military; ⚓ marine; ⊕ commercial; ✉ postal; 🚂 railway.

[Heide] — 496 — [Heiligenschein]

Heide² (⌣́) [ahd.: heathen] m ㊹, **Heidin** f ㊼ **1.** (ehm. in den Kreuzzügen: Sarazene, vgl. ~torn; jetzt: Ungläubiger) heathen; (j. der viele Götter anbetet, zB. Grieche, Römer, Hindu) pagan; (Ungläubiger) infidel; bibl. Juden und ~n Jews and Gentiles pl. — **2.** F fig. (Gewaltiger, vgl. ~n...) stark wie ein ~ (as) strong as a lion or a horse.

Heide¹-bereiter (⌣́...) m ㊷ keeper of the heath or the woodlands; **-besen** m heath - broom; **-biene** heath - bee; **-blume** f flower of the heath; **-boden** m, **-feld** n heathy soil, field; vgl. -land; **-gegend** f heath-land; a. = Heide¹; **-grieß** m, **-grütze** f groats pl. made of buckwheat; **-honig** m honey from the bees of a heath; =²korn [nhd. 15. sae.] & n buckwheat (= Buchweizen); **-¹kraut** & n: a) heather, heath (Eri'ca vulga'ris), allgemein: heath-wort; mit ~ bewachsen heathery, heath-clad; b) (Besenheide) ling (Callu'na vulga'ris); ²kraut-artig a. heathery, & ericaceous; **-land** n heathy ground or land, (moor)land; **-läufer** m nordd. game-keeper.

Heidel-beere & (⌣̆⌣́) f ㊽ bilberry (Vacci'nium [Myrti'llus]).

Heide¹-lerche (⌣́...) f ㊷ orn. woodlark (Ala'uda arbo'rea).

Heiden-angst (⌣́...) [Heide² 1 u. 2 fig.] f ㊷ excessive (or abject) fear; in ~ sein to be in great tremulation, P to be in a blue funk; **-apostel** m: Paulus der ~ Paul the apostle of the Gentiles; **-bekehrer** m missionary. eccl. a. oft: evangelizer, evangelist; **-bekehrung** f conversion of heathens, missionary work in heathen (or pagan) lands; **-bild** n idol; **-christ** m Christian converted from heathenism or paganism. [(Dia'nthus delto'ides).]

Heide¹-nelke & (⌣́⌣) f ㊷ maiden-pink}

Heiden-geld (⌣́...) n ㊷ fig. immense sum (or F a heap, a mint) of money; **-glaube** m pagan belief or faith; **-gott** m pagan god or deity; **-korn** & n = Heidekorn; **-lärm** m, fig. tremendous uproar; vgl. Höllenlärm; **-leben** n heathenish (or pagan) life; **-lehrer** m = -bekehrer; **-mäßig** F a. fig. immense, enormous, tremendous; adv. ⌣́ viel Geld F an awful (stärker : a devilish) lot of money; **-mission** f mission in heathen (or pagan) lands; **-röslein** = Heideröschen.

Heidenschaft (⌣́⌣) f ㊻ = Heidentum.

Heiden-spaß (⌣́...) m ㊷ fig. great (F awful) fun; **-tempel** m pagan temple.

Heidentum (⌣́-) n ㉑d. [Heide²] **1.** (heidnischer Glaube) heathenism, paganism. — **2.** (Gesamtheit der Heiden) heathendom, pagan world.

Heiden-volk (⌣́...) n ㊷ pagan (or heathen) nation; **-welt** f pagan (or heathen) world; **-wetter** F n, fig. miserable (F awful) weather.

Heide¹-rauch (⌣́...) m ㊷ = Herauch; **-reiter** m = -bereiter; **-rose** f, **-röschen** n & heath-rose (Helia'nthemum fuma'na); **-schnecke** f, zo. heath-snail (Helix ericeto'rum); **-schnucke** f, zo. = Heidschnucke; **-torf** m heath-peat.

heidi (⌣́-, -⌣́) int. **1.** (jubelnder Ausruf) hurra(h)!; als Liederrefrain: ⌣́ heida!, ob. ⌣́! didum!, heidideldum!, bsd. ehm.: falderal!, folderol!; tara-boom-de-a! — **2.** F alles ist ⌣́ (= weg)! everything gone!; ⌣́ geh(e)n to vanish.

heidig (⌣́-) [Heide¹] a. ㊺ heathy.

Heidin (⌣́-) f ㊼ s. Heide².

heidnisch (⌣́-) [Heide²] a. ㊺ **1.** heathen, heathenish, pagan; ⌣̆e Götter pl. heathen (or pagan) gods pl.; ⌣̆ machen to paganize. — **2.** weitS. (ungläubig) godless, impious, unbelieving.

Heid-schnucke provc. (⌣̆⌣́⌣) [ndd.] f ㊽ zo. Schaf-art: sheep kept on heaths or downs; ihr Fleisch: heath-mutton; Südengl.: Southdown mutton.

Heiduck (-⌣́) [madj. hajdu(k pl.)] m ㊷ (ungarischer Läufer, Bedienter &c.) Hungarian runner, man-servant, &c.

Heie ⊙ (⌣́-) f ㊽ Böttcherei: mallet.

heikel, heiklig (⌣́-) [nhd.] a. ㊻ **1.** = hät(e)lig fig.; ⌣̆e Angelegenheit delicate (or knotty, ticklish) affair. — **2.** (wählerisch) fastidious, particular, (over-)nice, fussy, difficult to please.

heil¹ (⌣́) [ahd.: whole, hale] a. ㊻ whole, entire; (unbeschädigt) unhurt, intact, unscathed, uninjured; (ganz wohl) safe and sound; (wiederhergestellt) restored, cured; wieder ⌣́ machen to repair, to mend; die Wunde ist ⌣́ ... is healed (up); ⌣́ w. to heal (up), to get well, v. Wunden &c: to close; fig. mit ⌣̆er Haut davonkommen f. Haut 2; F aus ⌣̆er Haut without the least provocation, (ganz plötzlich) quite suddenly.

Heil² (⌣́) [ahd.: hail] n ⓒc. **1.** (Wohlfahrt) welfare, safety, security; theol. das ewige ⌣́ eternal welfare or salvation. — **2.** (Glück ⌣́, zB. sein ~ versuchen to try one's luck or (good) fortune; im Jahre des ⌣̆s 1899 in the year of grace 1899; zu unserm ⌣́ floh der Löwe it was fortunate for us that the lion fled. — **3.** als Anrede ob. feierlicher Glückwunsch: ~ dir! (all) hail!; ~ euch auf eurem Pfade! may good fortune attend you on your way(s)!; ~ dem Könige! God save the King!; Radfahrergruß: All-~!, Turnerruf: Gut-~!, etwa: well met!, good luck (to you)!

Heiland (⌣́-) [ahd. Heilender] m ⓜd., \ **-in** f ㊼ (Befreier) deliverer; bsd. rel. (Christus) the (or our) Saviour or Redeemer (= Messi'as); er hat den ~ gefunden he has found Christ.

Heil¹-anstalt (⌣́...) f ㊷ etwa: health-establishment; weitS. sanatorium, engS. infirmary; **-art** f, med. mode of treatment, cure; **-bad** n: a) medicinal baths pl.; b) mineral waters pl., spa; medicinal well or fountain.

heilbar (⌣́-) a. ㊺ curable, a. healable, & sanable; remediable; **~keit** f ㊻ curableness, & sanability, remediableness.

Heil¹-behandlung (⌣́...) f ㊷ medical treatment, cure; **-bringend** a. ㊺ wholesome, salutary; **-²bringer** m ㊷ rel. = Heiland; **-¹brunnen** m mineral spring; **-butt** (c f) m, ichth. halibut (Hippoglo'ssus vulga'ris).

heilen (⌣́-) [ahd. = heal; *heil¹] ⓖⓔ **I** v/n. (h. u. ſn) von e-r Krankheit: to be cured, von Wunden: to heal (up), to close. — **II** v/a. und sich ⌣́ v/refl.: e-n (sich) von et. ⌣́ (auch fig. von einem Irrtume &c.) to cure a p. (o.s.) of a th.; fig. e-n Fehler ⌣́ (abstellen) to remedy (or mend) a fault or defect. — **III** ~ n ㉓ = Heilung.

Heiler (⌣́-) m ㊷, \ **~in** f ㊼ one who cures or heals or mends, healer.

Heil¹-gehilfe (⌣́...) m ㊷ bsd. ehm.: barber-surgeon; **-gymna'stik** f hygienic gymnastics, & kinesipathy, kinesiatrics.

heilig (⌣́-) [ahd.: holy; *Heil, heil] (mit Ausnahme von 3 meist rel.) **I** a. ㊻ **1.** holy; (dem Dienste e-r Gottheit geweiht) sacred, hallowed; (fromm) saintly (person), godly (life); (frömmelnd) sanctimonious, goody-goody; (unverletzlich) inviolable; (ehrwürdig) venerable; der ⌣̆e Abend (Vor-abend des Weihnachtsfestes) Christmas Eve; das ⌣̆e Abendmahl the Lord's Supper; der ~e Christ Christmas (tide); ⌣̆e Einfalt! oh sweet simplicity; die ⌣̆e Familie the Holy Family; der ~e Geist the Holy Ghost; ⌣̆e (ant. gemeine) Geschichte sacred history; das ~e Grab, Land the Holy Sepulchre, Land; bibl. die ⌣̆en drei Könige the (three) Magi pl.; ⌣̆e Pflicht solemn duty; die ~e Schrift Holy Writ, the (Holy) Scriptures pl.; der ~e Stuhl (Sitz des Papstes) the Holy See; der ~e Vater (Papst) the Holy Father; die ~e Woche Passion-Week. — **2.** mit v.: ihm ist nichts ⌣́ nothing is sacred to him; et. ⌣́ halten to keep a thing holy, to hold it sacred; den Sonntag ⌣́ halten to keep (holy) the sabbath(-day), to observe the Lord's day; ⌣́ m. to hallow, to sanctify; schwören bei allem, was ⌣́ ist to swear by all that is holy, to take a solemn oath; adv. ⌣́ versprechen, ⌣́ (und teuer) versichern to promise (or declare) solemnly. — **3.** anat.: das ⌣̆e Bein ⓒ (os) sacrum. — **II** ~ n, inv. **4.** Cath. eccl. (Lobgesang) Sanctus. — **III** ~e(r) m, ~e f ㊷ **5.** saint; (Gott) Holy One; (Frömmler) sanctimonious person, F saint; fig. wunderlicher ~er queer customer, droll fellow. — **IV** das ~e ⓒ **6.** holy (or sacred) things pl.; das ~e an et. the sacred nature (or sacredness) of a th.; unser ~stes our most sacred treasure(s pl.), what is most sacred (or precious) to us.

Heilig-abend (⌣́-⌣́) m ㊷: am ~ on Christmas Eve.

heiligen (⌣́-⌣) [ahd.: hallow] **I** v/a. ㊸ to hallow, to sanctify; Dein Name werde geheiligt hallowed be Thy name; (vergöttern) to deify; (heiligsprechen) to canonize, (seligsprechen) to beatify, (weihen) to consecrate; der Zweck heiligt die Mittel the end justifies the means. — **II** ~ n ㉓ = Heiligung.

Heiligen-bein (⌣́⌣⌣...) n ㊷: a) anat.: & (os) sacrum; vgl. heilig 3; b) bones pl. of a saint; **-bild** n image of a saint; **-dienst** m worship (or adoration) of saints; **-geschichte** f (hi)story of saints; & hagiography, hagiology, bisw.: hagiographa; **-holz** n = Guaja'kholz; **-kalender** m, eccl. & menologium, ...y; **-legende** f = -sage; **-sage** f legend of saints; **-schein** m halo, glory, gloriole, paint. auch: & aureole, ...a; fig. oft: nimbus;

Zeichen (j. S. XVII): F familiär; P Volksjprache; Γ Gaunersprache; \ selten; † alt (auch gestorben); * neu (auch geboren); ⚹ unrichtig;

[Heiligenverehrung] — 497 — [heimlich]

=verehrung f veneration of saints, hagiolatry; vgl. =dienst.
Heiliger (⌣‿) f. heilig III.
Heilig=haltung (⁻‿...) f ⑥ religious (or strict) observance; ~ des Sonntags keeping (or observance) of the Lord's day, strenge: Sabbatarianism.
Heiligkeit (⌣‿) f ⑥ holiness, sanctity, des Lebenswandels: godliness, a. oft iro.: saintliness; (Frömmelei) sanctimoniousness; er (es) stand im Geruche der ~ he (it) had an odour of sanctity about him (it), Cath. eccl. Seine ~ (der Papst) His Holiness.
heilig=machend (⁻‿...) a. ⑥ hallowing, sanctifying; =macher m ⑫ sanctifier; ⁰sprechen v/a. ⑥a⁎⁎ to canonize; =sprechung f ⑯ canonization.
Heiligtum (⌣‿) (ahd.) n ⓓd. 1. (heiliger Ort) sanctuary, (holy) shrine, temple, poet. fane; a. (lt.) sanctum (a. co.). — 2. (Heiliges) holy (or sacred) object; von Heiligem herrührend und fig. (sacred) relic; wie ein ~ verwahren to preserve like a most precious relic.
Heiligtums=entweiher (⁻‿‿...) m ⑫, =schänder m profaner of holy places or things, bisw.: sacrilegist; =entweihung f, =raub m, =schändung f sacrilege; =räuber m sacrilegious robber; ⁰schänderisch a. ⑥ sacrilegious.
Heiligung (⌣‿) f ⑥ hallowing, sanctification, (Vergötterung) deification.
Heil=kraft (⁻‿...) f ⑫ healing (or curative, ⚕ sanative) power; ⁰kräftig a. ⑥ healing, curative, ⚕ sanative; =kraut ⚘ n medicinal (pharm. officinal) herb; =kunde f medical science, ⚕ therapeutics; ⁰kundig a. skilled in (the art of) medicine; =kundige(r) m (erfahrener Arzt) practician, physician; =kunst f healing art, medical art; =künstler m (Arzt) physician; mst iro. empiric, medical quack; ⁰los a.: a) (unheilbar) incurable, past remedy, (verzweifelt) desperate; (beklagenswert) deplorable; nur v. Sachen: (unheilvoll) fatal, disastrous; b) (gottlos) godless, impious; (böse) wicked, vicious, malicious; c) F (in hohem Grade) awful, dreadful; ⁰lose Unordnung terrible (or frightful) disorder; ⁰ (adv.) hungrig, müde terribly (or awfully) dreadfully) hungry, tired; =losigkeit f incurable, desperate, &c. state (f. ⁰los a); godlessness, wickedness (f. ⁰los b); =methode f = =art; =mittel n, med.: ~ (gegen ...) remedy (against ...), weitS. medic(in)al drug, ⚕ curative; =mittel=lehre f ⚕ pharmacy, pharmacology; vgl. =kunde; =pflanze f medicinal herb; =pflaster n healing plaster; =prozeß m healing process, cure; =quell(e f) m mineral springs pl., vgl. =bad b; =salbe f healing ointment or salve.
heilsam (⌣‿) (ahd.) a. ⑥ wholesome, salutary; (förderlich) beneficial, useful, advantageous, good; für die Gesundheit: healthy (exercise), salubrious (climate), (heilend) curative, sanative, medicinal; ~keit f ⑯ wholesomeness, salutariness; healthiness, salubrity.

Heils=armee (⁻‿...) f ⑫ salvation army, salvationists pl.; =botschaft f, bibl. good tidings of great joy, evangel.
Heil¹=serum (⁻‿...) n ⑫ med. antitoxic serum, antitoxin.
Heils=lehre (⁻‿...) f ⑫, =mittel n, theol. doctrine, means of salvation or grace; =ordnung f, etwa: road to salvation; göttliche ~ divine dispensation.
heil¹ u.²=spendend (⁻‿...) a. ⑥ conferring health and happiness; weitS. beneficent, salutary; =stätte f ⑫ health-resort.
Heils=wahrheit (⁻‿...) f ⑫ gospel-truth, [true word of God.]
Heil¹=trank (⁻‿...) m ⑫ medicinal draught or potion; =trunk m toast.
Heiltum (⁻‿) n ⓓd. holy place.
Heilung (⌣‿) f ⑯ aktiv u. passiv: cure, healing, mending, aktiv auch: (curative) treatment.
Heilungs=prozeß (⁻‿‿...) m ⑫ healing process, cure, (Genesung) recovery.
Heil¹=verfahren (⁻‿‿...) n ⑫ medical (⚕ therapeutic) treatment; ⁰voll a. ⑥ salutary, fortunate; =¹wissenschaft f medical (⚕ therapeutic) science.
Heim¹ (⌣) [ahd.: home] n ⓒc. home; (Wohnsitz) dwelling (place).
heim² [ahd.: home (acc. v. ~)] adv. (nach Hause) home, to one's house or home; (in die Heimat) homeward.
...heim ⚕ (...¹) [: ...ham] in Zsgn, zB. Oppenheim. [worker, outworker.]
Heim¹=arbeit(er) (⁻‿...) m ⑫ home-]
Heimat (⌣‿) [ahd.; *Heim¹] f ⑯ native place or country or soil, engS. home; jur. domicile; (Vaterhaus) paternal roof or hearth; von Pflanzen &c.: ⚕ habitat; in meiner ~ in my country or home, where I come from; seine zweite ~, oft: his adopted country, the land (or country) of his adoption; in die ~ zurückkehren to return home.
heimat=berechtigt (⁻‿...) a. ⑥, etwa: native to the soil; settled (in a place); =berechtigung f ⑫ claim to citizenship or to naturalization; =gesetzgebung f legislation respecting (the conditions of) citizenship; =kunde f knowledge of one's (native) country; =land n native land or country, mother-country, auch: home.
heimatlich (⌣‿) a. ⑥ native, of (or relating to) one's (native) country; meine ⁰en Berge my native mountains.
heimat=los (⁻‿...) a. ⑥ (D 10) homeless, without a home or a settled (place of) abode; =lose(r) m f ⑥ oft: outcast, ⚕ expatriate; =schein m ⑫ certificate of naturalization or citizenship; (Paß) passport.
Heimats=kunde (⁻‿...) f ⑫ f. Heimat=...; =ort m native place; =recht n rights (or privileges) pl. of domicile or citizenship; denizenship.
Heimat=staat (⁻‿...) m ⑫ native country; =verband m einer Gemeinde body of citizens in a parish; ⁰zuständig a. ⑥: nach e-m Orte ⁰ sein to be a native of a place, to belong to a parish.
heim²=begeben (⁻‿...) v/refl. ⓒc⁎/⁎ to go (or make for) home, to wend one's way homeward; ⁰begleiten v/a. ⑥⁎/⁎ to see (or accompany) home; ⁰bezahl-

len v/a. ⑥⁎/⁎ f. ⁰zahlen; ⁰bringen v/a. ⑨⁎⁎ to bring home.
Heimchen (⌣‿) [mhd., dim. v. †(ahd.)Heime] n ㉓ (house-)cricket (Gryllus domesticus); fig. ein rechtes ~ (winziges Persönchen) a little dot (of a man, &c.). [home(ward).]
heim²=eilen (⁻‿...) v/n. (sn) ⑧⁎⁎ to hasten]
heimelig (⌣‿) a. ⑥ südd. = heimlich 3.
heim²=fahren (⁻‿...) v/n. (sn) ⑧b⁎⁎ to drive (or ride) home in a carriage; to cycle (or motor) h.; =fahrt f ⑫ home-return, homeward journey or voyage; auf der ~, auch: on the return-journey; vgl. =reise; =fall m jur. devolution, mehr gbr.: reversion, ehm.: escheat; ⁰fallen v/n. (sn) ⑥a⁎⁎ jur. (an den ursprünglichen Besitzer zurückfallen) to revert to; =fallen n = =fall; ⁰fällig a. ⑥ revertible, reversionable; =falls=recht n reversionary right; ehm.: escheatage, (fr.) droit d'aubaine; ⁰finden v/n. (h. u. sn) u. sich ⁰ v/refl. ⑪⁎⁎ to find one's way home; ⁰führen v/a. ⑧⁎⁎ to take (or lead) h.; fig. e-e Braut ⁰ to take home one's bride; Sprichw. f. Braut 2; =führung f taking home (the bride); =gang m ⁰gehen]: a) going home, home journey; b) fig. (Tod) death, a. going to one's everlasting (or F long) home; ⁰gefallensein n = =fall; =gegang(e)ne(r m) f ⓓ departed one, deceased; ⁰geh(e)n v/n. (sn) ⑭⁎⁎: a) to go (or return) h.; b) fig. to die, auch: to go to one's everlasting (or F long) home, to depart this life; ⁰holen v/a. ⑧⁎⁎ to fetch home.
heimisch (⌣‿) [mhd.] a. ⑥ (eingeboren) native, indigenous, F to the manner born; (zum Heim gehörig) domestic; (vaterländisch) national, v. der Sprache: vernacular; ⚕ unsere ⁰en Fabrikate our home manufactures pl.; hier fühle ich mich ⁰ (südd. a. heimelich, f. 5S 3) here I feel at home or comfortable; ⁰ m. to acclimatize; an e-m Orte ⁰ sein: a) to live (or to be domiciled ...); b) to be at home ...; c) v. Pflanzen: to be indigenous ..., to grow ...; in einer Wissenschaft ⁰ sein to be versed in ..., to be familiar (or conversant) with ...
Heim²=kehr (⁻‿...) f ⑫, =kehren n return home, auch: home-return; vgl. =gang; ⁰kehren v/n. (sn) ⑧⁎⁎ to return home; ⁰kommen v/n. (sn) ⑭⁎⁎ to come (or return) h.; das wird dir ⁰ (vergolten w.) that will come (or be paid) home to you; =kunft f = =kehr; ⁰leuchten v/n. (h.) ⑧⁎⁎: e-m ⁰: a) bisw.: to light a p. home; b) F fig. to give a p. a rough welcome, to send a p. about his business, F to send a p. home with a flea in his ear.
heimlich (⌣‿) [mhd.; *Heim¹] a. ⑥ 1. (geheim) secret, concealed, b.s. clandestine; ⁰es Gemach: a) private cabinet; b) privy, water-closet (W.C.); ⁰es Gericht = Feme; auf ⁰e Weise in an underhand way; adv. secretly, clandestinely, stealthily, by stealth, furtively, F on the sly; ⁰ lachen to laugh in one's sleeve; sich ⁰ aus dem Staube m. to run away, F to make tracks; to bolt; bei Nacht und Nebel auch: F to shoot the moon. — 2. v. Personen: (verschlossen) close; ⁰er Mensch reticent

[**Heimlichhaltung**] — 498 — [**heißen**]

(or reserved) person; ⸺ halten to conceal, to keep close or F snug or in the dark; ⸺ sein to be secretive; ⸺ tun (als ob man Geheimnisse hätte) to assume (or affect, F put on) a mysterious air. — 3. südd. (traulich) snug, comfortable; (heimisch) familiar, intimate; (anheimelnd) homely; (friedlich) peaceful.

Heimlich-haltung (″-...) f ⸺ keeping a th. secret or F snug, concealment.

Heimlichkeit (⸗⸗) f ⸺ (s. heimlich) 1. (Heimlichsein) secrecy; (Verschwiegenheit) closeness, reticence, secretiveness; weitS. mysteriousness. — 2. (heimliche Sache) secret, mystery; ~en pl. (heimliche Anschläge) deep (or dark) plots, deep-laid schemes pl.

Heimlich-sein (″-...) n ⸺ s. Heimlichkeit 1; ⸗tuerei f, ⸗tun n (s. heimlich 2) mysterious air or behaviour.

heim¹**-los**(″-...)a.⸺ homeless; ⸗²**reise** f ⸺ homeward journey, ⚓ home-voyage; auf der ~ auch: on the journey home, ⚓ (when) homeward bound; vgl.⸗fahrt; ⸗²**reisen** v/n. (sn) ⸺** to journey (or return) home; ⸗²**reiten** v/n. (sn) ⸺b** to ride h., to return h. on horseback; ⸗**ritt** m ride h.; ⸗²**schicken** v/a. ⸺**: a) to send h.; b) fig. e-n gehörig (od. mit langer Nase) ⸺ to give a p. a rebuff, vgl. ⸗leuchten b; **sich ⸗²sehnen** v/refl. ⸺** to long for home, to feel home-sick; ⸗¹**stätte** f homestead; ⸗²**suchen** v/a. ⸺**: a) e-n Ort ⸺ to go to (see) a place, bsd. b.s. to infest (or haunt) a place; von Mäusen ⸺gesucht infested (or overrun) with mice; b) rel. von Gott ꝛc.: to visit; die Prüfungen, mit denen uns Gott heimsucht the trials with which God visits (or afflicts) us; c) e-n für et. ⸺ (strafen) to punish a p. for a thing; rel. to visit the sins of the fathers upon the children, &c.; ⸗**suchung** f ⸺: a) visitation; Cath. eccl. ~ Mariä (2. Juli) Visitation of the Virgin or our Lady; b) ~en pl. (Mißgeschick) trials, afflictions, tribulations pl.; ⸗**tragen** v/a. ⸺b** to carry h.; ⸗**treiben** v/a. ⸺**** to drive home; ⸗**tücke** [nhd.] f: a) astuteness, stärker: (secret) malice or spite(fulness); (Verräterei) treachery; v. Krankheiten ꝛc. oft: insidiousness; b) = tückischer Streich; ⸗**tückisch** a. astute, stärker: malicious, spiteful; treacherous; von Krankheiten ꝛc. oft: insidious; Ler Streich, oft: underhand (or F nasty) trick; ⸗**wärts** adv. homeward; ⸺ ziehen to strike out (or set out, make) for home; ⸗**weg** m way home; sich auf den ⸺ machen to set out for h.; ⸗**weh** n home-sickness, ⚕ nostalgia; das ~ haben to be homesick; ⸗**wesen** n small estate or habitation; ⸗**wollen** v/n. (h.) ⸺**** to be desirous of getting home, to wish o.s. home; ⸗**zahlen** v/a. ⸺** to pay home, to pay a p. home or in his own coin, to retaliate upon a p.; ⸗**zahlung**/reimbursement;⸗**ziehen** v/n. (sn) ⸺ b** to return home, to journey (or march) homeward; ⸗**zug** m = ⸗fahr.

Hein (¹) [ndd.; abbr. v. Heinrich] m ⸺c. Freund ⸺ poet. (King) Death; auch: F co. Grand Old Leveller.

Heinrich (¹⸗) [ahd. Heimfürst] I npr/m. ⸺α. (Vn.) Henry, Harry; ~ I. von England Henry the First, auch: Henry Beauclerc; F sanfter ~, etwa: good-natured fool, F soft one, juggins. — II ⸗ m ⸺d. guter ~ good (King) Henry (Chenopo'dium bonus Henri'cus).

Heinz (¹) [Kf. v. Heinrich] m I npr. ⸺γ. F Hal, Harry. — II m ⸺a., ⚒ &c. (Eimerwerk) paternoster-pump.

Heinzel-männchen (″-...) [ndd.] n ⸺ gnome, (hob)goblin, schott.: brownie.

Heirat (¹⸗) [ahd. Hei(m-be)rat(ung) „Hausbesorgung"] f ⸺ marriage; eine gute (schlecht passende) ~ (Partie) a good (an ill-assorted) match; ~ aus Liebe love-match; auf die ~ (freien) gehen to go wooing or courting, to look out for a wife; eine ~ schließen, F tun to marry, to get married or F co. spliced; in höheren Kreisen: to form (or contract) a matrimonial alliance; eine reiche ~ machen to marry a fortune.

heiraten (¹⸗⸗) ⸺ I v/a. e-n ⸺ to marry (or wed) a p., geh. Spr.: to espouse a p.; vom Manne auch: to take (or choose) as wife, von der Frau: to accept as husband. — II v/n. (h.) to get married or F co. spliced; to contract a marriage; vom Manne auch: to take a wife to o.s. or to one's bosom; von der Frau: to change one's name; unter s-m Stande ⸺ to marry below one's station. — III ⸗ n ⸺ marriage, matrimony, matrimonial union; Erlaubnis zum ~ marriage-license; er denkt nicht ans ~ he does not think of marrying, auch F: he's not a marrying man.

Heirats-antrag (″-...) m ⸺ marriage-proposal; einer Dame einen ~ machen to propose to a lady, F to pop the question to her; ⸗**anzeige** f notification (or notice) of marriage; ⸗**bureau** n matrimonial agency or office; ⸗**fähig** a. ⸺ marriageable; ⸗**fähigkeit** f marriageableness, marriageable state; ⸗**gedanke** m: sich mit ~u tragen to be thinking of marrying; ⸗**gesetze** n/pl. marriage-laws pl.; ⸗**gesuch** n matrimonial suit; ⸗**gut** n dowry, marriage-portion; ⸗**kandidat** m suitor, wooer; ⸗**kontra'kt** m ⸺vertrag; ⸗**lustig** a. desirous of (stärker: bent on) marrying; ⸗**register** n marriage-register; ⸗**schein** m marriage-license; (Trauschein) marriage-certificate; ⸗**stifter(in** f) m match-maker; ⸗**vermittler(in** f) m match-maker, go-between, als Geschäft: matrimonial agent; ⸗**versprechen** n promise of marriage; ⸗**vertrag** m marriage-contract or -settlement.

heisa (¹⸗) int. = hei.

heischen (¹⸗) [ahd.: ask] I v/a. ⸺ (fordern) to ask, demand, request; ⚕ to postulate. — II ~ n ⸺ Heischung.

Heische-satz (″-...) m ⸺ phys., math.: ⚕ postulate. (lt.) postulatum; gr. imperative sentence.

Heischung (¹⸗) f ⸺ demand, request.

heiser (¹⸗) [ahd.: hoarse] a. ⸺(D 9) hoarse, raucous, (belegt) husky; sich ⸺ reden, schreien to talk, shout o.s. hoarse; ⸺ zu werden to grow (F to get) hoarse; **Heiserkeit** f ⸺ hoarseness, huskiness.

heiß (¹) [ahd.: hot] a. ⸺(D 10) (ant. kalt) 1. hot; brennend ⸺ burning (hot), scorching; glühend ⸺ red-hot; kochend (siedend) ⸺ boiling (scalding) hot; F piping hot; fig. v. Leidenschaften: burning, fiery, ardent; (heftig) vehement, violent, (inbrünstig) fervent; ⸺e Tränen vergießen to shed bitter tears; es ist sehr ⸺ (es Wetter) it is intensely hot (weather); sein Lester Wunsch his most ardent desire; ⸺e Zone torrid zone; mir ist ⸺ I feel (or am) hot; mir wird ⸺ I begin to grow (or get) hot; ⸺ **machen** to make hot, to heat; fig. e-m die Hölle ⸺ machen to make a p. shake in his shoes, to frighten a p. out of his wits, P to put a p. in a blue funk; e-m den Kopf ⸺ m. to make a p.'s head burn or whirl. — 2. fig. Les Blut h. to be passionate or hot-blooded or hot-tempered; es ist hier ein Les Pflaster (teures Leben) it is very expensive living here; Sprichw. was ich nicht weiß, macht mich nicht ⸺ what the eye does not see the heart does not grieve for, vgl. ein 8; adv. dort ging es ⸺ her it was a hot encounter or a stubborn fight.

heißa (¹⸗) int. = hei.

heiß-blütig (″...) a. ⸺ warm- (stärker: hot-)blooded; zo.: ⚕ hæma(to)thermal; fig. hot-tempered, passionate, fiery.

heißen¹ (¹⸗) [ahd.: hight] ⸺d. I v/a. 1. (befehlen) e-n et. tun ⸺, bisw. auch: e-m et. (zu) tun ⸺ to bid a p. do a th., to order (or command) a p. to do a th. — 2. Redewendungen: wer hat dir das geheißen? who told (or desired) you to do that?; er hat ihn schweigen ⸺ (geheißen) he told him to be quiet, he enjoined silence upon him; tut, was euch geheißen wird! do as you are bid!; et. mitgehen (mitnehmen) ⸺ to help o.s. to a th., co. to take care of a th.; wer heißt ihn, sich um die Sache kümmern? who told him to trouble about such things?; wer hat Sie denn rauchen ꝛc. ⸺? what made you smoke, &c.?, what business (or need) had you to smoke, &c.?; wer hieß mich auch alles wagen? how could I be so foolish (or mad) as to risk all? — 3. (benennen) to call, to name; (bezeichnen) to designate; e-n „du" ⸺ to call a p. "thou"; ehm. to "thou" (or "thee") a p.; gut⸺, et. etwas geschieht to approve of a thing being done; e-n willkommen ⸺ to welcome a p., to make a p. welcome; prägnant: das heiße ich e-n Ehrenmann that I would call ... — II v/n. (h.) 4. (e-n Namen führen) to be called or named, to go by the name of; er heißt ebenso wie ich he has (auch: bears) the same name as I or my name; wie heißt er? what's his name?; vgl. Haus 2. — 5. (bedeuten) to signify; z.B. opus heißt auf deutsch // opus signifies (or means) in German //; wie heißt das auf französisch? how is that expressed (or what is it) in French?; what is the French for it?; das heißt auf lateinisch // the Latin name (or word, expression) for it is //, F it is in Latin //; streben heißt arbeiten striving means

Signs (see page XVII): F familiar; P vulgar; ⸗ flash; ⚬ rare; † obsolete (died), * new word (born); ⚬ incorrect; ♪ music.

[heißen] — 499 — [helfen]

(or is equivalent to) working; das will (et)was 2 that means a good deal; das will nichts 2 it signifies nothing; was 2 hundert Seiten? what are a hundred pages?; da sieht man, was es heißt, reich (zu) sein that shows what it is to be rich; staunend, tadelnd: was soll das 2? what does all that mean?, what is the meaning of it all?; was heißt das anders als //? what does it mean but //? — **6. das heißt** (abbr. **d. h.**) that is (to say), to wit, (lt.) *id est* (abbr. **i. e.**) beschränkend: er wird stets für dich sorgen, das heißt, solange du fleißig bleibst ... that is (to say), as long as you remain studious; betonend: das heißt denn doch des Guten zu viel! I call that (or that is) too much of a good thing (, indeed)!; das heißt mir gleich viel that is all the same (or that makes no difference) to me; das heißt soviel als wenn // that is the same (thing) as if //; das hieße ebensoviel wie // that would be equivalent (or tantamount) to //; das heißt geschlafen ob. ein fester Schlaf I call that (or that's what I call) a sound sleep; s. Hans 2. — **III** v/impers. **7. es heißt** (wird gesagt) they (or people) say, it is (being) said or reported or rumoured, the rumour (or story) goes; es hieß ausdrücklich it was positively asserted; der Fürst ist hier, wenigstens heißt es so ... at least, so (or that's what) they say; es heißt in der Bibel it says (or tells us) in the Bible; wie es bei Schiller heißt as Sch. has (or expresses, puts) it; damit es nicht heiße // lest it should be said //; da hieß es: Aufgepaßt! then I (we, &c.) had to be careful; hier heißt es „entweder — oder" (here) it must be either (the) one thing or the other; now take your choice.

heißen² (⌣́) [nhd.] ⑩ ⇟ = hissen.

heiß-erfleht (⌣́...) a. ⑥ devoutly implored, eagerly desired; **≈geliebt** a. fondly (or dearly, stärker: ardently) loved, von vielen: greatly beloved; **≈hunger** m ⑫ voracious (or ravenous, wolfish) appetite; path.: ⚕ bulimy, bulimia, limosis; fig. keen (or eager) desire after or for a th.; **≈hungrig** a. voracious, ravenous(ly hungry), with a greedily appetite; fig. nach et. 2 sein to be extremely eager after (or very covetous of) a th.; **≈luft-bad** n hot-air bath; **≈luft-maschine** ⊙ f caloric engine; **≈sporn** (T) m, fig. hotspur (SH. H. IVa).

Heister ⚘ provc. (⌣́) [nhd.] m ⑫ (f ⑬) for. (junger Baum) young tree, sapling; provc. (junge Buche) young beech.

...heit (...́-) [ahd. ... hood] f ⑭ Anhängesilbe (suffix), dient zur Bildung: **1.** von abstrakten s/f. aus s. und a., z. B. falsch a. false, Falschheit f falsehood. — **2.** von coll. z. B. Christ m Christian, Christenheit f Christendom.

heiter (⌣́) [ahd.] **I** a. ⑥ (D9) **1.** (ant. ernst) serene; (flar) clear, bright; das Wetter wird 2 the weather (or sky) is clearing or brightening, it is getting brighter; fig. ein Blitz aus 2em Himmel F a bolt from the blue. — **2.** (fröh-

lich) cheerful, in high glee, in a good humour.; (munter) gay, bright, merry, in high spirits, F jolly, in geh. Spr.: hilarious; (frohstimmend) cheering; 2 machen to cheer (up), to brighten (up); 2 werden to cheer up, to unbend; iro. das wird 2 F there will be a fine bother or row. — **II** ~ n ⑳ (o. pl.).

Heit(e)re ⚘ f ⑱ 3. ~e des Himmels clear (or serene, unclouded) sky.

Heiterkeit (⌣́-) f ⑯ (s. heiter) serenity of the sky, the countenance, &c.; clearness, brightness; cheerfulness; merriness, mirth, F jollity; geh. Spr.: hilarity.

Heiz-apparat ⊙ (⌣́...) m ⑫ heating-apparatus; heater, radiator; arch. (unter dem Fußboden): ⚕ hypocaust.

heizbar (⌣́-) a. ⑥ easily heated; v. Zimmern: containing a fire-place or stove.

heizen (⌣́) [ahd.: heat; *heiß] **I** v/a. u. v/n. (h.) ⑩ to heat (auch ⊙) to light a fire in a stove, in a room; mit Gas 2 to heat (or warm) with gas; Steinkohle heizt besser als Holz coal gives off (or throws out) more heat than wood; v/refl. das Zimmer heizt sich gut ... is easily warmed, ... has a good fire-place, ... soon gets warm. — **II** ~ n ㉓ = Heizung.

Heizer (⌣́-) m ⑫ p. who lights fires; ⊙ mach. stoker (a. 🚂); auch: fireman.

Heiz-fläche (⌣́...) f ⑭ mach. heating- (or generating-)surface; **≈körper** m body radiating (or throwing out) heat; **≈kraft** f heating-power; **≈loch** n, metall. stoke-hole; **≈material** n fuel; **≈raum** m fire-place; mach. am Dampfkessel: firebox; **≈rohr** n firetube; **≈stoff** m fuel; **≈tür** f, am Dampfkessel: door of the firebox.

Heizung (⌣́-) f ⑭ heating, firing; warming; lighting a fire in a room, &c.

Heiz-vorrichtung (⌣́...) f ⑫ contrivance (or apparatus) for heating.

Hekate (⌣́-) [grch.] npr/f. ⑨ ⑬. ⑭ d. myth. (Wegegöttin, Here) Hecate.

Hekatombe (⌣⌣́⌣) [grch.] ⑫ Opfer v. 100 Stieren] f ⑬ hecatomb; fig. (großes Opfer) great sacrifice.

Hektar (⌣́) [fr.; *grch. hek(a)t- (100) und Ar] n (m) ⑬ c. 6. (100 Ar = 2·47 acres; abbr. **ha**, öft. *ha*) hectare.

Hektik ⚕ (⌣́) [grch.] f ⑭ path. (Schwindsucht) hectic state, consumption; **~er** (⌣⌣́) m ⑫ hectic person; **hektisch** (⌣́) a. ⑥ hectic; 2es Fieber hectic fever.

Hekto-gramm (⌣⌣́) [fr., *grch.] n ⑮ b, 6. (100 Gramm = 1543·23 grains) hectogram (abbr. **hg**, öft. *ha*); **≈graph** ⊙ (⌣⌣́) [grch.] m ⑫ (Vervielfältiger) hectograph, copying-press; **≈graphieren** (⌣⌣́⌣́) v/a. ⑬ to hectograph; **≈liter** (⌣⌣́) [fr., *grch.] n (m) ⑯. (100 Liter = 22 gallons; abbr. **hl**, öft. *hl*) hectolitre; **≈meter** (⌣⌣́) n (m) ⑫. (100 Meter = 328 feet; abbr. **hm**, öft. *hm*) hectometre.

Held (⌣́) [ahd.] m ⑫, **~in** f ⑭ hero(ine f); (Vorkämpfer) champion of a cause; alte (mittelalterliche) ~en pl. ancient (medieval) worthies pl.; den ~en spielen to play the hero or a heroic part; fig. ~ des Tages lion of the day; ~ im Saufen mighty toper; er ist kein ~ im Latein(ischen), im Rechnen he is not much of a Latin scholar, of an arithmetician.

Helden-alter (⌣́...) n ⑫ heroic age or time; **≈bahn** f heroic career; **≈buch** n (Sammlung deutscher Gedichte, 13. sae.) etwa: book of worthies or heroes; **≈dichter** m epic poet; **≈dichtung** f, **≈gedicht** n epic (or heroic) poem; scherzhaftes ~ heroicomical poem; **≈geist** m heroic spirit; **≈gesang** m = ≈lied.

heldenhaft (⌣́⌣) a. ⑥ heroic, adv. heroically, like a hero.

Helden-jüngling (⌣́...) m ⑫ heroic youth, youthful (or young) hero; **≈kaiser** m (Wilhelm I., Deutscher Kaiser), etwa: Hero-Emperor; **≈kühn** a. ⑥ (as) bold (or brave) as a hero; **≈lied** n song in praise of heroes, epic (song); **≈mädchen** n heroic maiden, young heroine; **≈mäßig** a. = ≈mütig; **≈mut** m h. valour or courage, heroism; **≈mütig** a. heroic, hero-like; adv. heroically, with heroic courage; **≈rolle** f, thea. part (or rôle) of a hero; **≈ruhm** m heroic fame; **≈sage** f (ancient) legend of a hero, epic tale; **≈schar** f band of heroes; **≈sinn** m heroic mind, heroism; **≈tat** f heroic deed or exploit, act of heroism; **≈tod** m death of a hero; den ~ sterben to die as a hero. [spirit.]

Heldentum (⌣́⌣) n ② d. heroism, heroic]

Helden-weib (⌣́...) n ⑫ heroic woman, heroine; **≈zeit** f = ≈alter.

Helder ⚘ [nhd.] m, ⑫ (noch nicht eingedeichtes Marschland, ant. Polder) marshy country unprotected by dams or dikes.

Helene (⌣⌣́) npr/f. ⑨ ⑬ß. (Wn.) Helen(a).

helfen (⌣́) [ahd.: help] ⓑ. **I** v/n. (h.) **1.** to help; (fördern) to aid, promote, advance; (unterstützen) to assist, to support; (behilflich sein) to lend a hand to, to minister to (a p.'s wants); (aus der Not befreien) to relieve, succour, save; er hat sich (dabei) 2 lassen he has had help or assistance (for it); Gott helfe euch! God bless you!, rel. the Lord be with you!; Gott helfe mir! God be merciful unto me!; Beteuerung: so wahr mir Gott helfe! so help me God!; drohend: wart', Schlingel, ich werde dir 2! wait, rascal, I shall be (or come) after you!; Sprichw. hilf dir selbst, so wird dir Gott ~ God helps those who help themselves; wem nicht zu raten ist, dem ist nicht zu 2 he who cannot be advised cannot be saved; where counsel fails no cure prevails, vgl. raten 1. — **2.** mit inf.: e-m et. tun 2 to assist a p. (or to lend a p. a hand) in doing a th., to help a p. to do a th.; er hat ihn tragen 2 (geholfen) he helped to carry him. — **3.** mit prp.: e-m **auf die Beine** 2 to set a p. on his legs, to pick a p. up; e-m **auf die Sprünge** (oder auf die Spur, F e-m darauf) 2 to put a p. on the (right) scent, to put a p. in the way of (F to put a p. up to) a th.; to assist a p.'s memory; e-m **aus der Not** 2 to save a p. from distress, to relieve a p.; e-m **aus der Patsche**, der Verlegenheit 2 to help a p. out of a difficulty; F to get a p. out of a scrape; e-m **aus dem Wagen** 2 to assist a p. out of a carriage; e-m **bei der Arbeit** 2 to aid a p. in his work; e-m **durch** den Sumpf, über den Berg

---

⚕ scientific; ⚘ botanical; 🌐 geography; ⊙ machinery; ⚒ mining; ⚔ military; ⚓ marine; ⊕ commercial; ✉ postal; 🚂 railway.

2 to help a p. through the bog, across (or in crossing) the mountain, *fig.* to help a p. over a difficulty; e-m **hinter** die Geheimnisse 2 to reveal secrets to a p., to unfathom (or discover, ferret out) secrets for a p.; e-m **in** der Not 2 to assist a p. in his distress; e-m in den Überzieher 2 to help a p. on with his overcoat; e-m **von** et. 2 to rid a p. of a th.; e-m vom Brote 2 to take the bread out of a p.'s mouth; e-m **zu** et. 2 to aid a p. in obtaining a th., to help a p. to get a th.; e-m zu e-m Amte 2 to procure a p. an appointment; e-m zu f-m Rechte 2 to see that a p. obtains (or gets) his rights; er hat sehr dazu geholfen (beigetragen) he has done (or contributed) much towards it. — 4. mit *adv.* der Richtung: e-m **davon** 2 to assist a p. in (making) his escape; to help a p. off with a th.; e-m **fort** 2 to help a p. over a difficulty; e-m **herauf** 2, **hinauf** 2 to aid a person in mounting or rising; e-m **hinab** 2, **hinaus** (ob. **heraus**) 2, **hinein** (ob. **herein**) 2, **hinüber** 2 ꝛc. to aid a p. in getting (or to help a p. to get) down, out, in, over (or across), &c; e-m **weg**2 to aid a p. in getting (or to help a p. to get) away. — 5. **sich** (*dat.*) 2 to find a way (or to get) out of a difficulty, to extricate o.s. (from a precarious position); to shift for (or manage by) o.s., to make shift; sich vorwärts 2 to push (or fight) one's way through difficulties, to make one's way in the world; er weiß sich zu 2 he knows how to set to work, F he knows a trick or two; sich immer zu 2 (und zu wenden) wissen to be full of resource(s) or fertile in expedients or F up to every dodge; sich nicht (mehr) zu 2 und zu raten wissen to be put to one's last shifts, not to know what to do or which way to turn; wir wissen uns nicht anders zu 2 we have no other alternative or expedient; man muß sich nur zu 2 wissen one must know how to manage things or to help o.s.; Arzt, hilf dir selber! physician, heal thyself! — 6. ich kann mir nicht 2: a) (weiß keinen Rat) I am at my wits' end or at a loss what to do; b) (kann nicht umhin) I cannot help it; ich konnte mir nicht 2, ich mußte hinein I walked in against my will or involuntarily, I could not (do otherwise) but go in; das ist erlogen, ich kann mir nicht 2 it's a falsehood, I cannot help (or forbear) saying so. — 7. (abhelfen) da ist nicht zu 2 there is no help for it; hier ist nicht (mehr) zu 2 there is no remedy against this, it cannot be helped or remedied. — 8. (dienen) to serve for a purpose, &c.; (nützen) to be useful for or of use to; die Bäder haben ihm geholfen the baths have benefited him or done him good; das hilft gegen Zahnschmerzen that's a good remedy (or F it's good) for the toothache; nichts wollte 2 nothing would avail; ihm ist nicht zu 2 he is beyond help or past all remedy or cure (auch

von einem Kranken); es hilft (gar) nichts it is (quite) useless or of no avail (whatever), F it's no (earthly) good; wozu kann das 2? what is the use of that?, of what use can that be?; was hilft es ihm, daß er läuft? of what avail is (or F what's the good of) his running?; da hilft nichts vor (L.) it cannot be helped or avoided; *bibl.* dein Glaube hat dir geholfen thy faith has made thee whole; *iro.* das wird ihm auch recht was 2 he will not profit much by that, F *iro.* much good may it do him! — II ~ 2 9. help(ing), aid(ing) = Hilfe.

Helfer (⏑⏑) m 22, **~in** f 47 he (she) who helps, aids, assists; helper (f oft: lady helper), aider; (Adjunkt) coadjutor, (Stellvertreter) assistant; (Pfarr-) ~curate; ~ in der Not rescuer, saviour (oft *rel.* Saviour = Heiland), vgl. Helfershelfer.

Helfer=amt (⏑⏑...) n 62 office of coadjutor or assistant or a helper; **=hand** f helping hand.

Helfers-helfer (⏑⏑⏑⏑) m 22 accomplice, (aider and)abettor, *jur. auch:* accessory; (Anhänger) supporter.

Helge ↓ (⏑⏑) [ndd.] f 48, **~n** m 23 = Helling. [land.]

Helgoland ♀ (⏑⏑⏑) *npr./n.* 16α. Heligo-

Helgoländer (⏑⏑⏑⏑) I m 22, **~in** f 47 inhabitant of Heligoland. — II *a. inv.* a. **helgoländisch** *a.* 66 of Heligoland.

helikonisch (⏑⏑⏑) [grch. He'likon ♀ m, Berg, Musensitz] *a.* 66 Heliconian.

heliochromisch ⌀ (⏑⏑⏑⏑) [grch.] *a.* 66 *phot.* heliochromic.

Heliographie ⌀ ⊕ (⏑⏑⏑f) [grch.] f 48: a) (Herstellung v. Lichtbildern) heliography; bisw.: sun-painting; b) (Signalisieren mit Spiegeltelegraph) heliography, ...ing; **heliographisch** (⏑⏑⏑fv) *a.* 66 ...ic(al).

Helio-gravüre ⌀ ⊕ (⏑⏑⏑⏑) [grch.-fr.] f 48 (Kupferlichtdruck) heliogravure; **=meter** (⏑⏑⏑⏑) n (m) 22 heliometer; **=plastik** (⏑⏑⏑⏑) [grch.] f 46 phototypography, phototypy.

Helios (⏑⏑⏑) [grch.] *npr./m.* 16γ., *myth.* (Sonnengott) Helios, Phœbus (Apollo).

Helioskop ⌀ (⏑⏑⏑⏑) [grch.] n ⓪d. *ast., phys.* (Sonnenfernrohr) helioscope; 2isch (⏑⏑⏑⏑) *a.* 66 helioscopic.

Heliostat ⌀ (⏑⏑⏑⏑) [grch.] m ⓪c. (+ 42) *ast., phys.* (Art Sonnenspiegel) heliostat.

Heliotrop ⌀ (⏑⏑⏑⏑) [grch. Sonnenwende] n ⓪d.: a) ♀ heliotrope (auch lila-rötliche Farbe), turnsol(e) (*Heliotro'pium peruvia'num*); b) (a. m) min. (grüne Quarzart mit roten Flecken) heliotrope, bloodstone; c) *ast.* (Sonnenspiegel) heliotrope.

heliozentrisch ⌀ (⏑⏑⏑⏑) [grch.] *a.* 66 *ast.* (mit der Sonne als Mittelpunkt) heliocentric, heliocentrical.

hell[1] ↓ (⏑) [ahd. *hallen] I *a.* 66 1. vom Klange: clear (voice), sonorous (organ); (schmetternd) blaring (trumpet), ringing (cheer); (gellend) shrill (note); 2es Gelächter loud (or hearty) laugh, F horse-laugh. — 2. (*ant.* dunkel) Licht: clear, bright, (leuchtend) luminous, (strahlend) brilliant, shining; (durchsichtig) transparent, (a) diaphanous; *fig.* (erleuchtet) enlightened; (scharfsinnig) sagacious, clear-sighted; 2e

Augenblicke eines Irrsinnigen lucid intervals *pl.*; 2e Farben f/pl. light colours *pl.*, 2es Haar light (or fair) hair; ein 2er Kopf a clear-headed person, a bright, intelligent p.; ein 2er Tag a bright day; es ist heute ein 2er Tag it is a fine day (to-day); es ist schon 2er Tag, die Sonne scheint schon 2 (*adv.*) it is quite light, the sun is already shining or up; am 2en (lichten) Tage in broad daylight; bis in den 2en Tag hinein schlafen to sleep till late in the day; die 2e Wahrheit the plain truth; ein 2es Zimmer a light (or bright) room; es bleibt lange 2 it remains light a long time; es wird 2 it is getting light, it begins to dawn; 2 m. to make bright, to brighten (or polish) up; *adv.* 2 glänzen to shine brightly; 2 lodernde Flamme blaze, blazing (or flaring) fire. — 3. in 2en Haufen in dense throngs, in large numbers; die 2en Tränen stehen ihr im Auge her eyes are filled (or wet) with (large) tears or *poet* with 'dewy pearls. — II ~ n we. (o. *pl.*), ~e(s) n 67 4. clearness, brightness; (Licht) light.

Hell[2] ↓ (⏑) [Hölle] n ⓪b. (Behältnis für Tauwerk ꝛc.) boatswain's store-room.

Hellas ♀ (⏑⏑) [grch.] *npr.n.* inv. Alt. (das eigentliche Griechenland) Hellas, Greece.

hell[1]**-auf** (⏑⏓) *adv.* 2 lachen to laugh out aloud, to burst out laughing; **=äugig** (⏑⏑...) *a.* 66, **=blickend** *a.* bright- (or clear-)eyed, *bsb. fig.* keen-sighted; **=blau** *a.* light blue; **=blond** *a.* very fair; **=braun** *a.* light brown, von Pferden: light bay; **=denkend** *a.* clear-thinking or -headed, (klug) shrewd; **=dunkel** a. u. n = halbdunkel ꝛc.

Helle[1] (⏑⏑) f 48 (f. hell[1]) clearness, brightness; luminousness, brilliancy; transparency; vgl. Hellsehen.

Helle[2] ⌀ (⏑⏑) = hell[1] n f. hell[1] II.

Hellebarde ⚔ (⏑⏑⏑) [mhd.; fr. *Helm[2] barte „Stielart"] *f* 48 ehm.: halberd, partisan; **Hellebardier** (⏑⏑⏑⏑) m ⓪d. halberdier, billman.

Helle-gatt ↓ (⏑⏑⏑) n 62 (Aufbewahrungsraum) store-room. [= aufhellen I.]

hellen (⏑⏑) [mhd.] v/a. u. sich 2 v/refl. 68

Hellene (⏑⏑⏑) [mhd.] m 44 (Grieche) Hellene, Greek; **~ntum** (⏑⏑⏑) n ⓪d. Hellenic (or Greek) world; **~n=volk** n 62 Hellenic nation, Greek people, Greeks *pl.*

hellenisch (⏑⏑⏑) [grch.] *a.* 66 Hellenic, Greek, Grecian; **hellenisieren** (⏑⏑⏑⏑) v/a. 93 to Hellenize; **Hellenismus** (⏑⏑⏑⏑) m 27 (griechisches Wesen) Hellenism, Grecism; **Hellenist** (⏑⏑⏑) m 42 (Kenner des Altertums) hellenist; **hellenistisch** (⏑⏑⏑⏑) *a.* 66 hellenistic.

Heller (⏑⏑) [mhd. *Häller *a.* (aus Schwäbisch-Hall ♀)] m 22 etwa: half a farthing, (öst. *abbr.* h); *bibl.* mite; er hat keinen (roten) ~ he has not a farthing (or penny-piece) to bless himself with; ich gäbe keinen ~ dafür I would not give half a farthing for it; das ist keinen ~ wert that's not worth a farthing or a rap; auf ~ und Pfennig Rechnung ablegen to give a very exact (or accurate) account; bei ~ und Pfennig

[helleuchtend] — 501 — [Henne]

bezahlen to pay to the last (*bill.* to the uttermost) farthing; Sprichw. wer den ~ nicht ehrt, ist des Talers nicht wert take care of the pence, and the pounds will take care of themselves. [brilliant, luminous.}
helleuchtend (⸗ᴗ) [hell-leuchtend] *a.* ⓖⓡ
hell¹-farbig (⸗...) *a.* ⓖⓡ light-coloured, v. Personen: fair; ⸗**gelb** *a.* light yellow, *a.* straw- (or cream-)coloured; ⸗**glänzend** *a.* of a bright lustre; ⸗**grau**, ⸗**grün** *a.* light grey, green; ⸗**haarig** *a.* light-haired, fair; ⸗**hörig** *a.* quick of hearing. [broad daylight.}
hellicht (⸗ᴗ) [hell-licht] *a.* ⓖⓡ Der Tag
Helligkeit (ᴗ⸗) *f* ⓕⓖ = Helle¹; ⸗**grad** *m* ⓖⓡ, mst *ast.* degree of brightness.
Helling ⚓ ⊙ (⸗ᴗ) [ndd.] *m* ⓜⓑ, *a.* ⓕ: a) (schiefe Schiffbauunterlage) slip; b) (Schiffbauplatz) ship-building yard.
Hell-kammer (⸗...) *f* ⓖⓡ *phot.* camera lucida; ⸗**klingen** *n* sonorousness; ⸗**klingend** *a.* ⓖⓡ sonorous; **hellodernd** (⸗ᴗ) [hell-lodernd] *a.* ⓖⓡ blazing (up); **hell-rot** *a.* light red, bsd. *poet.* damask.
Hell-sehen *n* (⸗...) ⓖⓡ, ⸗**seherei** *f* clear-sightedness; der Mesmerisierten: (fr.) clairvoyance; ⸗**sehend** *a.* ⓖⓡ: a) clear-sighted, shrewd; b) (fr.) clairvoyant; ⸗**seher**(**in** *f*) *m* (fr.) clairvoyant(e*f*); ⸗**sichtig** *a.* = ⸗**sehend**; ⸗**sichtigkeit** *f* clear-sightedness; ⸗**stimmig** *a.* clear-voiced; ⸗**strahlend** *a.* brilliant.

Helm¹ (⸗) [ahd.: helmet; *hehlen] *m* ⓜⓑ. 1. ⚔ helmet (auch ♞); (Sturmhaube) bsd. ehm.: casque (auch ♀ helmförmige Oberlippe der Lippenblütler); leichter offener ~, chemals: casquet. — 2. ⊙ *arch.* (rundes Dach von Türmen) dome, cupola; *chm.* e-r Destillierblase: head, cap.
Helm² (⸗) [ndd.: helm] *m* und *n* ⓜⓑ. 1. † (Stiel) helve, haft, handle. — 2. ⚓ (Ruderpinne) helm, rudder.
Helm¹-binde (⸗...) *f* ⓖⓡ band of a helmet; ⸗**busch** ⚔ *m* plume (or crest) of a helmet; ⸗**dach** ⊙ *n, arch.* spire; vgl. **Helm¹** 2 *arch.*
helmen (⸗ᴗ) [Helm¹] *v/a.* ⓖⓡ to provide (or protect, adorn) with a helmet.
Helm¹-feder (⸗...) *f* ⓖⓡ feather on (or of) a helmet; ⸗**förmig** *a.* ⓖⓡ helmet-shaped, ♀: ⸗ galeate(d); ⸗**gewölbe** *n, arch.* domed (or spherical) vault; ⸗**gitter** *n* visor; ⸗**kleinod** *n* = ⸗**schmuck**; ⸗**schmuck** *m* ornament of a helmet; ⸗**sturz** *m* = ⸗**gitter**; ⸗**überzug** *m* beim Manöver: helmet-cover(ing); ⸗**visier** *n* = ⸗**gitter**; ⸗**zeichen** *n* badge on a helmet; ⸗**zierat** *m*, ⸗**zier**(**de**) *f* = ⸗**schmuck**.
Helote (ᴗ⸗ᴗ) [grch.] *m* ⓖⓡ Alt.: (spartanischer Staatssklave) helot (auch *fig.*).
Helotentum (ᴗ⸗ᴗ) *n* ⓖⓓ. helotism, helotry; weitS. serfdom, slavery.
helotisch (ᴗ⸗ᴗ) *a.* ⓖⓡ like (or of) a helot, weitS. slave-like. [Elsinore.}
Helsingör ♀ (⸗ᴗ⸗) *n* ⓖⓓ. (dän. Stadt)
Helvetia ♀ (⸗ᴗ⸗ᴗ) *n* [lt., *flt.] npr/n. ⓖⓓ *a.* Alt.: Helvetia; jetzt: Switzerland.
Helveti-er (ᴗ⸗ᴗ) *m* ⓖⓡ, ~**in** *f* ⓖⓡ Helvetian; jetzt: Swiss.
helvetisch (ᴗ⸗ᴗ) *a.* ⓖⓡ Helvetic, Helvetian; jetzt: Swiss, vgl. H. B.
h(**e**)**m** (⸗) *int.* hem!, hum!

Hemd(**e**) (⸗(ᴗ)) [ahd.] *n* ⓖⓔ(ⓖⓕ) 1. für Männer: shirt; für Frauen: chemise, ehm. shift; das ~ ablegen to take off one's shirt or chemise; rel. härenes (Büßer-) ~ f. hären I; ⓒ (leinene Verpackung) canvas wrapping or packing-cloth. — 2. *fig.* e-n bis aufs ~ ausziehen to fleece a p., F to clean a p. out; Sprichw. das ~ ist mir näher als der Rock near is (or close sits) my shirt, but nearer is (or closer still) my skin.
Hemd-ärmel (⸗...) *m* ⓖⓡ shirt- (am Frauenhemd: chemise-)sleeve; ⸗**ärmelig** *a.* ⓖⓡ in one's shirt-sleeves.
Hemdchen (⸗ᴗ) *n* ⓖⓓ (*dim. v.* Hemd) little shirt; (Vorhemdchen) chemisette.
Hemd(**en**)**-einsatz** (⸗(ᴗ)...) *m* ⓖⓕ shirt-front; ⸗**fabrikant**(**in** *f*) *m*, ⸗**händler**(**in** *f*) *m* shirt-maker; ⸗**knopf** *m* shirt-button; zum Herausnehmen: stud; (Doppelknopf) sleeve-link; ⸗**kragen** *m* shirt-collar; ⸗**krause** *f* shirt-frill; ⸗**leinwand** *f* shirting; ⸗**matz** F *m* baby with nothing but a shirt on; ⸗**nadel** *f* shirt-pin; ⸗**schnitt** *m* cut of a shirt or chemise.
Hemds-ärmel *2c.* f. **Hemd-ärmel** *2c.*
☞ **Hemi**... ⓖⓡ [grch. halb] f. Zssgn.
Hemisphäre ⓖⓡ (ᴗ⸗(ᴗ)) *f* ⓖⓕ (Halbkugel, ♀ Erdhälfte) hemisphere.
hemisphärisch (ᴗ⸗) *a.* ⓖⓡ hemispherical.
hemmen (⸗ᴗ) [ahd.: hamper] I *v/a.* und sich ⌐ *v/recip.* ⓖⓡ 1. (zurückhalten; *ant.* fördern) to stop, check, arrest, ⊙ *a.*: to deaden; sich (ea.) ⌐ (behindern) to obstruct or incommode or inconvenience (one another); (verhindern) to hinder, hamper, impede; (verzögern) to retard, to slacken; (aussetzen) to suspend; einen Strom, den Atem ⌐ to intercept ...; die Wirkung e-s Stoßes ⌐ to deaden the effect of a shock; ein Rad, e-n Wagen ⌐ to lock (or skid) ..., to put the brake on ... (auch 🚂); ⚓ ein Schiff: to ease her, to slacken her (speed). — 2. *fig.* Leidenschaften *2c.* ⌐ (zügeln) to curb, check, restrain; (fesseln) to fetter; (unterdrücken) to repress, to suppress. — II ~ *n* ⓖⓒ 3. = Hemmung.
Hemm-kette ⊙ (⸗...) *f* am Wagen: drag- (or lock-)chain, brake, skid; *mech.* stop-chain; ⸗**klotz** *m* am Wagen: locking-pole, brake-shoe.
Hemmnis (⸗ᴗ) *n* ⓖⓡ check, obstruction; (Hindernis) hindrance, impediment.
Hemm-rad ⊙ (⸗...) *n* Uhrmacherei: stop- (or locking-)wheel; ⸗**schraube** *f* stop-screw; ⸗**schuh** *m* Fuhrwesen: brake, drag, skid-pan; den ~ anlegen to put on the brake or the drag; ⸗**stange** *f* am Wagen: stopper; ⸗**tau** *n* rope-drag.
Hemmung (⸗ᴗ) *f* ⓕⓖ (f. hemmen I) 1. stopping, stoppage, check(ing), arrest; hindrance; retardation; interception; repression, suppression. — 2. ⊙ (etwas Hemmendes) am Schießgewehr: escapement; Uhrm.: ruhende ~ dead-beat; *mach.* selbsttätige ~ safety-stop; (Sperrhaken) detent-pin, lock-hook; zurückspringende ~ recoil-escapement.
Hemmungs-rad ⊙ (⸗ᴗ...) *n* Uhrmach.: escapement-wheel.
Hemm-vorrichtung ⊙ (⸗ᴗ...) *f* ⓖⓕ *mech.* brake (a. 🚂), spoke, stop; Bohrer mit ~ stop-drill; ⸗**zeug** *n* (wheel-)drag.

Henequen ♀ u. ⓒ (⸗ᴗ⸗) [span.; *indian.] *m* ⓖⓓ (Art Aloefaser) henequen.
Hengst (⸗) [ahd.] *m* ⓜⓐ. stallion; arabischer ~ Arab steed; *a.* vom Esel, Zebra, Kamel: male ass, zebra, camel.
Hengst-fohlen (⸗...) *n* ⓖⓕ, ⸗**füllen** *n* colt.
Henkel (⸗ᴗ) [nhd.; *henken] *m* ⓖⓕ handle; an Töpfen auch: ear; ~ einer Glocke ear (or cannon) of a bell.
Henkel-glas (⸗ᴗ...) *n* ⓖⓡ mug.
henkelicht (⸗ᴗᴗ) *a.* ⓖⓡ (provided) with a handle or with handles.
...**henk**(**e**)**lig** (...⸗(ᴗ)ᴗ) in Zssgn, zB.: **zwei**⸗, **two-handled**. [handle; ⸗**krug** *m* jug.}
Henkel-korb (⸗ᴗ...) *m* ⓖⓡ basket with a
henkeln (⸗ᴗ) *v/a.* ⓖⓡ to put a handle to; gehenkelt with a handle (to it), ⚘ ansate.
Henkel-töpfchen (⸗ᴗ...) *n* ⓖⓡ small pot with a handle; *fig.* das ~ machen (die Arme einstemmen) F to put (or to stand with) one's arms a-kimbo.
henken (⸗ᴗ) [ahd.: hang] I *v/a.* ⓖⓡ: e-n ⌐ to hang a p., ⚘ to gibbet a p.; ehm. hängen 1. — II Ge-**henkte**(**r**) *m* *f* ⓖⓡ person hanged (on a gallows), ehm. *jur. sus*(*pensus*) *per coll*(*um*).
henkens-wert (⸗ᴗ...) *a.* ⓖⓡ deserving to be hanged.
Henker (⸗ᴗ) [mhd.; *henken] *m* ⓖⓡ hangman; weitS. executioner, F *co.* Jack Ketch, in Verwünschungen *2c.*: hol' dich der ~!, scher' dich zum ~!, daß dich der ~! (you may) go to hell or to the devil or to old Nick!, schwächer: go to Bath!; hol' ihn der ~! I'll see him at Jericho first!, stärker: damn the fellow!, the deuce take him!; abs. den ~ auch!, zum ~ damit!, hol's der ~! (what) the deuce!, damn it!, hang it all!; ich frage den ~ danach! I don't care a fig or a button or a straw or F a hang!; das daut' ihm der ~! it's (no more than) his duty!; nun hat's der ~ that's too bad, things have come to an awful pass; das taugt den ~ nichts! it's good for nothing, F it's (all) rotten!; daraus werde der ~ klug! I cannot make head or tail of it, F that would puzzle old Nick himself!
Henker-beil (⸗ᴗ...) *n* ⓖⓡ, ⸗**block** *m*, ⸗**dienst** *m* f. Henkers⸗...
henker-mäßig (⸗ᴗ...) *a.* ⓖⓡ hangman-like; savage, truculent.
Henkers-beil (⸗ᴗ...) *n* ⓖⓡ, ⸗**block** *m* executioner's axe, block. [sword.}
Henker-schwert (⸗ᴗ...) *n* ⓖⓡ executioner's
Henkers-dienst (⸗ᴗ...) *m* ⓖⓡ executioner's services *pl.* or office; ⸗**hand** *f*: durch ~ sterben to die by the hand of the executioner; ⸗**knecht** *m* in Engl.: hangman's assistant; weitS. (Peiniger) tormentor, torturer; ⸗**mahl**(**zeit** *f*) *n* last meal of a p. awaiting execution; F *co.* farewell-repast.
Henker-strick (⸗ᴗ...) *m* ⓖⓡ hangman's rope, rope for hanging.
...**henkerig** (...⸗ᴗᴗ) f. ...henkelig.
Henna ♀ (⸗ᴗ) [ar.] *f* ⓖⓡ (auch ~**strauch** *m*) henna (*Lawsonia iner'mis*); ⸗**pulver** *n* ⓖⓡ zum Haarfärben henna.
Hennchen (⸗ᴗ) *dim. von* Henne (f. das 1).
Henne (⸗ᴗ) [ahd.: hen; *Hahn] *f* ⓕⓖ 1. hen, fowl, kleine (ob. junge) ~ (auch

[Hennegatt] — 502 — [Herabnehmung]

dim. Hennchen, Hennlein) (young) pullet, weitS. (little) chicken; Fkosend: mein Hennchen! little duck(ie) or darling!; f. Ei 2 Sprichw.; eine blinde ~ findet auch wohl ein Korn a blind man may perchance hit the mark. — 2. weitS. (Weibchen von Vogel-arten) hen, zB. kalkuttische ~ turkey-hen. — 3. ♀ F fette ~ f. Fetthenne.

Hennegatt ↓ (⌣⌣) [ndd.] *n* ㊃c., ⓜ (Öffnung für den Ruderhals) helm-port.

Hennegau ♀ (⌣⌣|) *npr/m.* ㊃α. (belgische Provinz) Hainau(l)t.

hennegauisch (⌣⌣⌣⌣) *a.* ㊅ of Hainau(l)t.

Henning (⌣⌣) [Hahn] *npr/m.* ㊃α. (in der Tierfabel) etwa: chanticleer, cockalorum; rooster. [(f. d. 1).]

Hennlein (⌣-) *n* ㊄ *dim.* von Henne}

Henoch (⌣⌣) *npr/m.* ㊃α. *bibl.* Enoch.

Henriette (⌣⌣⌣), bisw. a. **Henrike** (⌣⌣) *npr/f.* ㊃㊄. (Vn.) Harriet, a. Henrietta.

Hephthemimeris ⌣ (⌣|t—||⌣) [grch.] *f* (*sg. inv., pl. ...res*) pros. (Zäsur des Hexameters nach der 1. Silbe des 4. Fußes) hephthemimeral cæsura; vgl. Penthemimeris.

Heptachord ♪ (⌣⌣⌣) [grch.] *m* ㊃c. Alt.: heptachord. [(Sieben-eck) heptagon.]

Heptagon ⌣ (⌣|⌣||) [grch.] *n* ㊃d. *math.*}

Heptandria ♀ ⌣ (⌣⌣⌣) [grch.] *f* ㊾ (siebente Klasse nach Linné) heptandria.

heptandrisch (⌣⌣⌣) *a.* ㊅ (siebenmännig: mit sieben Staubgefäßen) heptandrian.

Heptarchie ⌣ (⌣⌣⌣) [grch.] *f* ㊾ (Siebenherrschaft, bsd. *hist.* die sieben angelsächsischen Reiche in England) (the) Heptarchy.

her (⌣, in Zssgn mit nachfolgendem *adv.* oder *prp.* ⌣) [ahd.: here hier] *adv.* **1.** (Bewegung in der Richtung auf den Sprechenden andeutend; *ant.* hin) hither(ward), in der Umgangssprache oft: here; oft verbunden mit der *prp.* zu, zB.: das Kind ging zu ihm hin und kam dann wieder zu mir ℒ ... returned to me; kommt ℒ come here (to me). — 2. *ell.* mit Auslassung des *verb* in lebhafter Rede: sobald er mich sieht, er ℒ zu mir ... he at once came to(wards) me, F auch: he up to meet me; bsd. als *imper.* nur immer ℒ! come (or hand it) to me directly!; ℒ damit! give it (up) to me!, hand it over!; F out with it!; (rasch) ℒ zu mir! come here or to me (at once)!, F hurry up!; ℒ mit dem Geld! out with the money!, F pay up! — 3. mit Nennung des „von wo?", meist nicht übersetzbar, zB. aus der Tiefe ℒ from the depth (below); von da (od. dort) ℒ from that place, (from) thence; von außen (innen) ℒ from without (within); von hinten ℒ from behind; von oben (unten) ℒ from above, below; wo kommt er ℒ? (= woher kommt er?) whence does he come?, where does he come from?; wo ist er ℒ? what countryman is he?; wo hat er das ℒ? where did he get it (from)?, *contp.* where did he pick it up?; wo in aller Welt kommt ihr ℒ? where on earth do you come (or spring) from?; **nicht weit ℒ sein**: a) to live near by; b) meist *fig.* (nicht viel bedeuten) to be of small importance; es ist nicht weit ℒ mit ihm (damit) F he (it) is not up to much; oft ohne „von" und mit dem Worte verschmelzend: dorther (from) thence,

himmelher (down) from heaven. — 4. (mit Angabe des erfüllten oder durchlaufenen Raumes) ihr Jubel erscholl (über) die Tafel ℒ their cheers re-echoed across the festive board. — 5. nach dem von e-r *prp.* regierten *s.*, nicht immer übersetzbar: **an** (oder **neben**) et. ℒ beside (or by the side of) a th.; an der Mauer, Küste ℒ fahren to drive along the wall, to sail along the coast; **hinter** e-m ℒ geh(e)n to walk in a p.'s footsteps or behind him; hinter e-m ℒ sein (verfolgend) to be at a p.'s heels, F to be after a p.; F hinter e-r Sache ℒ sein to be keenly bent upon a th., F to be after a th.; **über** et. ℒ sein to be busily engaged in (doing) a th.; **um mich ℒ** around me; *fig.* um e-n ℒ sein to throng (or crowd) around a p., to pay great attention to a p.; **vor** e-m ℒ geh(e)n to walk in front of a p. — 6. verbunden mit **hin**: a) örtlich: drei Stunden hin und drei (Stunden) ℒ three hours there and three back, three hours each way; b) **hin und ℒ** to and fro, hither and thither; (schwankend) now this way, now that; hin und ℒ geh(e)n to go and return or come back; c) *fig.* er weiß nicht (oder weder) hin, noch ℒ (nicht aus, nicht ein) he does not know which way to turn, he is perplexed or F flummuxed; das ist nicht hin, nicht ℒ (ohne entschiedene Richtung) that's neither one thing nor the other, it's a half-and-half (or a half-hearted) affair; ein paar Groschen hin oder ℒ (mehr oder minder) a few pence more or less, up or down; et. hin und ℒ bedenken, überlegen to consider a th. from every point of view, to turn a th. well over (or to revolve a th.) in one's mind; Worte hin, Worte ℒ! what are (or never mind) a few words!; d) als *s.*: das Hin und Her the going and returning, (the journey) there and back; *fig.* wavering, shilly-shallying; e) **hin und ℒ** ... in Zssgn mit *v.* und *s.* f. bsd. Art. (nach hinüberziehen). — 7. zeitlich: **bis jetzt ℒ** up to the present, until now; von alters ℒ from the remotest times, for many ages (past); (ehemals) (in days) of old; von je ℒ at all times, stärker: ever since the world began, since Adam; es ist schon ein Jahr ℒ, daß // it is now a year ago (or past) since //; wie lange ist es ℒ? how long is it ago?

☞ **her-...**, **Her-...** (″...) in Verbindung mit *verbs*, immer trennbar (**), u. in Zssgn mit *verbal nouns* und *adjectives*: a) um die Richtung zum Sprechenden zu bezeichnen, oft: hither, (as far as) here, this way, to this place, towards me (or us), near, &c. nach dem *verb*; b) für gedankenloses Aufsagen ꝛc., oft: off ob. over ob. forth ob. by rote nach dem *verb*; c) um den Ursprung anzudeuten, oft die *prp.* from nach dem *verb*. **her-ab** (⌣⌣) *adv.* down (this way), weitS. downwards; die Treppe ℒ down the stairs (towards me), downstairs; von oben ℒ from above; vom Himmel: from on high; von oben ℒ ansehen to view from above, verächtlich: to look down upon a p.; den Strom ℒ downstream.

her-ab-..., **Her-ab-...** (⌣⌣...) in Verbindung mit *verbs*, immer trennbar (**), u. in Zssgn mit *verbal nouns* und *adjectives*, die Richtung von oben nach unten zu dem Sprechenden hin bezeichnend, oft: down here, down to(wards) me or us, down this way nach dem *verb*: ℒbaumeln *v/n.* (h.) ㊃a** to dangle; sich ℒbegeben *v/refl.* ㊃c*/* to come down (to us); ℒbemühen *v/a.* (*v/refl.*) ㊃*/*: einen (sich) ℒ to trouble a p. (o.s.) to come down (here); ℒbeugen ㊃** = ℒbiegen; ℒbewegen *v/a.* u. sich ℒ *v/refl.* ㊃*/* to move down(wards); ℒbiegen *v/a.* u. sich ℒ *v/refl.* ㊃aft** to bend down(wards); ⌣ to deflect; ℒblicken *v/n.* (h.) ㊃** to look down (at us); ℒblinken *v/n.* (h.) ㊃** to shed a feeble light (von Sternen: to twinkle) at us below; ℒbringen *v/a.* ㊆**: a) to bring (or carry) down; b) *fig.* to bring down in the world, to reduce in circumstances; sich ℒbücken *v/refl.* ㊃** to stoop down; ℒdrücken *v/a.* ㊃**: a) to press down; b) ⓜ to depress the market, to force down prices; ℒeilen *v/n.* (fn) ㊃** to hurry down here; ℒfahren ㊆b**: *v/n.* (fn) to come down (to us) in a carriage or boat, &c., to drive (or sledge, cycle, motor, &c.) down here; *v/a.* to convey down here (in a carriage, boat, &c.); ℒflehen *v/a.* ㊃**: Gottes Segen auf e-n, etwas ℒ to call down (or invoke) God's blessing upon a p., a th.; ℒfliegen *v/n.* (fn) ㊄a** to come flying down (here); von Kugeln: to fall (or pour) down; die Treppe ℒ to fly (or rush) downstairs; ℒgeh(e)n ㊃**: *v/n.* (fn) to walk down here; b) ⓜ von den Preisen u. Kursen: to go down, to (have a) fall, to drop, give way, recede, ease off; =geh(e)n *n* ㊄ descent on foot; ⓜ fall (or drop) of prices, stärker: collapse of the market; ℒgekommen *a.* ㊅ decayed, von Personen: down in the world; =gekommenheit *f* ㊶ decay; ℒgleiten *v/n.* (fn) ㊃b** to glide down (here); ℒhangen, ℒhängen *v/n.* (h.) ㊄b** to hang down (this way), to droop, vom Haar: to hang down loose); ℒhängen ㊃** to hang lower down; ℒhängend *a.* ㊅ pendulous, pendent; über et.: impending over; ℒholen *v/a.* ㊃** to fetch down here; ℒkommen *v/n.* (fn) ㊄a** to come down, to descend; ℒlangen *v/n.* (h.) ㊃** to extend down to us; ℒlassen ㊄a** *v/a.*: a) to let down; b) (niedriger machen) to (put) lower; sich ℒ *v/refl.*: a) to descend; b) *fig.* sich zu j-s Standpunkte ℒ to put o.s. on a level with a p.; *abs.*, auch *iro.* to be condescending or patronizing; c) sich zu etwas ℒ to stoop (or condescend) to do a th.; ℒlassend *a.* ㊅ (leutselig) affable; =lassung *f* ㊶: a) descent; b) *fig.* condescension, (Leutseligkeit) affability; ℒlaufen *v/n.* (fn) ㊄aft** to run down, von Flüssigkeiten auch: to flow (or trickle) down; ℒlaufend *a.* ㊅ running down; ℒ: ⌣ decurrent; ℒmüssen *v/n.* (h.) ㊃** to be obliged to come down, to have to dismount; ℒnehmen *v/a.* ㊃a** to take down, to lower; =nehmung *f* ㊶: *rel.* ~ Christi vom Kreuze descent from

the cross; ⸺schießen Ⓜ︎c(e)ft**: v/a. to bring down with a shot or a bullet; Strahlen ꝛc. ⸺ to send down (or dart) rays, &c.; v/n.: a) (h.) to shoot down (here) with a gun, &c.; b) (ſn) to rush down (here); ⸺sehen v/n. (h.) Ⓐa**: a) auf et. ⸺ to look (or glance) down at a th.; b) fig. auf einen ⸺ to look down upon (or contemptuously at) a p.; =sehen n ㉓ glance from above; fig. disdainful glance; ⸺senden v/a. Ⓖa** to send down to us; uns die Sonne: glühende Strahlen auf uns ⸺ to dart down fiery rays upon us; ⸺setzen Ⓜ︎** v/a.: a) to (put) lower; fig. to degrade, to debase; b) ⚭ to reduce (or abate, lower) a price, the rate of interest; von Waren: to reduce goods in price, to sell them at a discount; Löhne ⸺ to cut down (or lower, reduce) wages; c) fig. e-n durch unſer Urteil ꝛc. ⸺ to depreciate, (beschimpfen) to disparage, F to run down; (geringſchätzen) to disdain, to underrate; ⸺setzend p.pr. und a. Ⓖ in den Bed. des inf.; bjd. zu c fig.: degrading, depreciatory; disdainful; =setzung f ㊻ (ſ. ⸺setzen): a) lowering, fig. auch: debasement; b) ⚭ reduction of prices, &c.; discount on goods; c) fig. depreciation, disparagement; disdain; ⸺sinken v/n. (ſn) Ⓣft**: a) to sink (down) in a fluid, in the air, &c.; b) fig. to be(come) degraded, to fall from a higher position; c) ⚭ to sink (or fall) in price; ⸺steigen v/n. (ſn) Ⓔ**: a) to dismount from one's horse, &c.; to descend from a hill, &c.; b) fig. zu e-m ⸺ = ſich laſſen b; ⸺stimmen **: v/a.: a) ♪ ein Klavier ꝛc. ⸺ to lower the pitch of a piano, &c.; b) fig. (mäßigen) to moderate; ſ-e Ansprüche ⸺ to abate one's claims or pretensions; in ſ-r Zuverſicht ſehr ⸺gestimmt with one's confidence greatly shattered; ſich ⸺ v/refl. to relax; =stimmen n ㉓ und =stimmung f ㊻ (ſ. ⸺stimmen a und b) fig. moderation, abatement; relaxation; ⸺stürzen Ⓜ︎** v/a. (und ſich ⸺ v/refl.) to throw (o.s.) down headlong; v/n. (ſn) to fall (or rush) down headlong; ⸺wärts adv. downward(s); ⸺wünschen Ⓤ**: den Segen des Himmels auf e-n ⸺ to call down a heavenly blessing upon a p.; ⸺würdigen v/a. (und ſich ⸺ v/refl.) Ⓖ** to degrade (o.s.), to debase (o.s.), to disgrace (o.s.), to demean (o.s.); zum Tiere ⸺ to bring down to the level of a brute, to brutalize; =würdigung f ㊻ degradation, abasement; ⸺ziehen Ⓣb** v/a.: a) to draw (or drag, pull) down; b) fig. e-n zu ſich ⸺ to drag a p. down to one's own level or standard or (miserable) position; v/n. (ſn) to move (or come) down (to us). — Vgl. auch ab=..., herunter=...

herakle-iſch (‿‿⸗‿) a. ㊷ Heracle(i)an.

Herakles (⸗‿‿) [grch.] npr/m. ①γ. Heracles (= He'rkules).

Heraklide(-‿‿‿) m ④ (Abkömmling des He'rakles) Heracleid, pl. oft: Heraclidæ.

Heraklit (‿‿⸗) npr/m. ⑤ⓡα. (grch. Philoſoph um 500 v. Chr.) Heraclitus; ⸺iſch a. ㊻ Heraclitean.

Heraldik (‿⸗‿) [fr.] f ㊺ (Wappenkunde) heraldry, heraldic art, armory; ⸺er m ㉒ one versed in heraldry, blazoner·

heraldiſch a. ㊻ heraldic, armorial.

her-an (‿⸗) adv. (up) this way; near to this place; kommt ⸺!, ell. nur ⸺!, immer ⸺! (abbr. F immer ran) come on!, come along this way! dicht ans Ufer ⸺ right up to the bank, close to the shore. — Vgl. auch herbei.

her-an=..., Her-an=... (‿⸗‿...) in Verbindung mit verbs, immer trennbar (**), u. in Zſſgn mit verbal nouns und adjectives, die Bewegung nach einem zu erreichenden Gegenſtande bezeichnend, oft: up (to), near (to), along nach dem v.; ⸺bilden Ⓖ** v/a. to train (up), to educate; ſich ⸺ v/refl. to educate o.s., to be trained or educated; ⸺blühen v/n. (ſn) Ⓖ** to (develop into full) blossom or bloom, fig. to grow up; ⸺bringen v/a. Ⓖ** to bring near; (auflegen) to apply; ſich ⸺drängen v/refl. Ⓖ** to press near; ⸺geh(e)n v/n. (ſn) Ⓖ** to go (or walk) up to; an etwas ⸺ to take a th. in hand; an die Arbeit ⸺ to set to work; ⸺holen v/a. Ⓖ** to fetch here, to bring near; (anſpannen, anſtrengen) to put to hard work; die jungen Leute müſſen herangeholt werden the young men must be put to serious tasks; ⸺kommen v/n. (ſn) Ⓖ** to come this way, to come along or near; von der Zeit ꝛc. auch: to draw near, to approach; F (einkehren) to call at a place; =kommen n ㉓ = =kunft; ⸺kriegen F v/a. Ⓖ** fig. (zu et. überreden) to talk into a th.; =kunft f ⑩ approach, arrival; ſich ⸺machen v/refl. Ⓖ**: ſich an et. ⸺ to set to work at a th.; ſich an e-n ⸺ to sidle up to a p.; ⸺nahen v/n. (ſn) Ⓖ** to approach; von der Zeit ꝛc.: to draw near, v. drohenden Gefahren: to be imminent; =nahen n ㉓, =nahung f ㊻ approach; imminence; ⸺reichen v/n. (h.) Ⓖ**: an et. ⸺ to reach up to a th.; ⸺reifen v/n. (ſn) Ⓖ** to grow to maturity; zum Manne (Weibe) ⸺ to grow up to be a (wo)man or to (wo)man's estate; to attain (wo)manhood; ⸺rücken Ⓖ** v/a.: den Tiſch ꝛc. ⸺ to move (or push) ... near; v/n. (ſn) to advance (towards us), to approach, to come on; von der Zeit ꝛc.: to draw near, to be at hand; =rücken n ㉓ advance, approach; ſich ⸺schlängeln v/refl. Ⓖa**: ſich an e-n ⸺ to sidle (or creep) up to a p., fig. to curry favour with a p.; ⸺schleichen v/n. (ſn) Ⓖaſt** to sneak up to, to steal near; ⸺treten v/n. (ſn) Ⓖd ** to step up to; ⸺wachsen v/n. (ſn) Ⓖb** to grow up or into (wo)manhood, vgl. ⸺reifen; ⸺d a. growing, von Perſonen auch: ⚭ adolescent; das ⸺de Geſchlecht the rising generation; ⸺gewachsen a. von Perſonen: grown-up, adult; =wachsen n ㉓ growth, ⚭ adolescence; ſich ⸺wagen v/refl. Ⓖ**: ſich an e-n, et. ⸺ to venture to approach a p., a task; ⸺ziehen Ⓣb** v/a.: a) to draw a p. near to one, (anziehen) to attract a p.; b) fig. to interest a p. in a th.; ⚭ zum Kriegsdienſte ⸺ to call to the ranks or the colours, to compel to serve in the army; v/n. (ſn) to approach, to come up or near; vgl. ⸺rücken. — Vgl. auch die Zſſgn mit auf=...

He-rauch (‿⸗‐ch) [nbd. hei trocken] m Ⓓd. (misty) fog, haze; peat-smoke.

her-auf (‿⸗) (ant.: hinauf; herab, herunter) adv. up here, up to(wards) us; upwards; den Fluß ⸺ up the river, up stream; die Treppe ⸺ upstairs; (von) unten ⸺ from below; in rising; (von) dort ⸺ (from) up there; ell. ⸺! come up (to us)!; ⸺ und herab ob. hinab (going) up and down, in ascending and descending; upstairs and downstairs.

her-auf=..., Her-auf=... (‿‿⸗‿...) in Verbindung mit verbs, immer trennbar (**), und in Zſſgn mit verbal nouns und adjectives, die Richtung von unten nach oben zu dem Sprechenden hin bezeichnend, oft: up (here), up to me or to us; uphill, upstream, upstairs; ⸺beschwören v/a. Ⓣb/** to conjure up, to call from below, evoke, raise; weitS. to conjure up (or bring on) a war, &c.; ⸺bringen v/a. Ⓖ**: a) to bring (or take) up a th., a. p.; b) mit Mühe: to get a th., a p. up a hill, the stairs, &c.; ⸺fahren v/n. (ſn) Ⓢb** to come up (to us) in a carriage, &c., to drive (or cycle, motor, sail, &c.) up here; v/a. to convey up here (in a carriage, &c.; ⸺führen v/a. Ⓖ** to lead up a street, a hill, &c.; to show upstairs; ⸺kommen v/n. (ſn) Ⓖ** to come up here, to step (or walk) up; engS. (emporkommen) to get up, to get a rise, to be moved up (a. in der Schulklaſſe); er ließ mich ⸺ he sent for me (ſtärker: he ordered me) to come up; ⸺steigen v/n. (ſn) Ⓖ** to mount up here; von einem Gewitter: to gather, to be brewing; ⸺ziehen Ⓣb**: v/a. to draw (or pull) up here; (aufſchürzen) to tuck (or hitch) up; fig. zu ſich ⸺ to raise to one's own level or standard; v/n. (ſn): a) = ⸺steigen; b) to move into an upper story of a house. — Vgl. auch die Zſſgn mit auf=...

her-aus (‿⸗) adv. **1.** out (here); aus et. ⸺, zu et. ⸺ out of a th.; aus dem Hauſe, zum Fenster ⸺ sehen to look out of the window; nach vorn ⸺ wohnen to live in the front or in a front room, to occupy the front part of a house; von innen ⸺ from within (to without); med. von innen ⸺ heilen to cure internally or radically; die Maſern ꝛc. ſind ⸺ the measles, &c. have come out. — **2.** mit Ortsadverbien: da ⸺: a) out there; b) imperativiſch: (get) out there!; c) fragend: da ⸺? is that the way out?; hier ⸺ out here; oben ⸺, unten ⸺ out above, below. — **3.** ell. mit fehlendem verb: ⸺! (F a. abbr. raus!) come out!; engS. come along!; (geh[t] weg) be off! ⚔ (Herausrufen des Poſtens) turn out!, to arms!; ⚔ Brust ⸺! chest(s) out!; ⸺ mit dem Briefe! out with (or let me have or see) the letter!; ⸺ mit dem Degen! draw your sword(s)!; raus mit ihm! turn (or kick) him out!; ⸺ damit!, ⸺ mit der Sprache! speak up!, tell us plainly

[heraus=...] — 504 — [herausmustern]

or the plain truth!; frei (ober gerade, offen, rund) 2 frankly, openly, plainly; nun ist's 2: a) now the truth has come (or leaked) out or is out, now we have found it out; b) (nun ist's gesagt) now it's off my mind or F off my chest; 2 und herein in and out; 2 oder herein!! (you must) either come in or go out! **her-aus=...**, **Her-aus=...** (⌣...) in Verbindung mit *verbs*, immer trennbar(**), u. in Zssgn mit *verbal nouns* und *adjectives*, Ausgang von e-m Orte mit der Richtung zum Sprechenden hin bezeichnend, oft: out (here), out to(wards) me or us, out of, outside, forth (bei Zeitwörtern des Gehens ꝛc. auch): up, back) nach dem v.; auch: e(x)..., de...; re... (als Präfix) vor dem v.; **²arbeiten** ⑧** v/a: a) to work out; aus dem groben 2 to rough-work, Holz ꝛc.: to rough-hew; (feiner bearbeiten) to work into shipshape; b) (hervortreten l.) to put in (bold) relief, to emboss; sich 2 v/refl. to work one's way out (of); fig. to free (or extricate) o.s. from a th. by dint of (hard) work or by strenuous efforts; **²beißen** ⑧a** v/a. to pull (or drive) out by biting; F den seinen Herrn 2 to put on the airs of a gentleman, F to be doing the swell; sich 2 v/refl. to bite one's way out; F fig. = sich ²arbeiten; **²bekommen** v/a. ⑧*/*: a) einen Nagel ꝛc.: to get (mit Mühe: to succeed in getting) out; ein Geheimnis: to worm (or ferret, find) out; ein Geständnis: to draw forth, to elicit; ein Rätsel ꝛc.: to puzzle (or work) out, to solve; den Sinn e-r Stelle ꝛc.: to make out, to decipher; *arith.* was (ob. welches Fa'zit) hast du 2?; what (answer) did you get (out)?; ⊕ sein Geld wieder 2 to get back (or recover) one's money; to recoup o.s.; b) et. (Geld) 2 to get some change back; Sie bekommen zwei Mark wieder heraus your change comes to two shillings; ich habe nichts 2 I had no change given me, I received no change; **²brechen** ⑧a** v/a.: a) e-n Zahn ꝛc.: to take out, to extract; b) to vomit (forth); v/n. (fn) to rush out, to sally forth; **²bringen** v/a. ⑧**: a) to bring out; die Brust 2 to put (or throw) out one's chest; b) mit Mühe: to succeed in taking (or getting) out a stain or in extracting a tooth, &c. or in turning out a troublesome person; *fig.* s-e Kosten 2 to cover one's expenses; es läßt sich nichts aus ihm 2 one can draw (or elicit) nothing from him; kein Wort 2 (können) to be unable to utter a word; vgl. c; c) fig. (erraten, entziffern) to guess, decipher, make out; den Sinn e-r Stelle 2 to make (or find) out the meaning of a passage; vgl. ²bekommen a; kein Wort in e-m Briefe ꝛc. 2 not to understand a single word; **²fahren** ⑧b** v/n. (fn): a) to drive out in a carriage, &c.; b) mit heftiger Eile: to burst (or rush) forth, to start (suddenly or rapidly); vom Blitz: (aus den Wolken) 2 to flash (out of the clouds), von Gefühlen: to find vent, von Worten: (entfahren) to slip

(out); er hat so eine Art 2zufahren he has a peculiar way of relieving his feelings or of blurting out, F he goes off; v/a. to take out in a carriage, &c.; **²fersen** v/a. ⑩** Fußballspiel: to heel out; **²finden** ⑩** v/a. to find out, unter vielen: to discover; sich 2 v/refl. to find one's way out, to extricate o.s.; fig. (sich zurechtfinden) to see one's way out of a difficulty; =forderer m ② challenger; **²fordern** v/a. ⑧a**: a) to ask for the return of; b) zum Kampfe: (auch: v/recip. sich oder ea. 2) to challenge (one another) to mortal combat, to call (each other) out; weitS. (Trotz bieten) to defy, to provoke; zum Wettstreite, zur Kritik 2 to invite competition, criticism; 2d p.pr. und a. ⑥ provoking (words), defiant (attitude); (lockend) inviting; ~ n u. =forderung f ⑥ (s. ²fordern v/a. b) challenge, provocation; weitS. open defiance; **²fressen** ⑧** v/a.: die Ratte hat (ein Stück) aus dem Käse 2gefressen the rat has eaten (or nibbled) a hole into (or a piece out of) the cheese; sich 2 v/refl.: a) von Würmern ꝛc.: to eat one's way out (of); b) F to feed well, to grow fat by good eating and drinking; **²fühlen** v/a. ⑧** to discover (or find out) by touching or (the sense of) feeling, to feel (through); to notice; =gabe f ⑥ giving up, restitution; **²geben:** v/a. ⑧c**: a) to give (or deliver) up, to hand over; aus der Speisekammer: to give out; b) (zurück-erstatten) to give back, to restore; (das Kleingeld, den Überschuß) 2 to give (the) change, the balance; auf ein Zwanzigmarkstück 2 to give (or to hand over the) change for a sovereign; c) Bücher, Zeitschriften ꝛc. 2 to publish (or to bring out) ..., nur vom Verfasser: to edit ...; eine Serie ꝛc.: to issue; d) F das (oder es) gibt et. heraus it brings in something; (es ist ein Überschuß da) there is s.th. (or a balance) over; ~ n = =gabe; =geber m eines Buches ꝛc. (s. ²geben c) publisher; editor (= Redakteu'r); **²geh(e)n** v/n. (fn) ⑧**: a) aus der Tür 2 to come out of a door; fig. aus sich 2 to become more communicative or genial, F to come out of one's shell; b) das Zimmer geht auf die Straße heraus ... faces the street; c) (vorstehen) to stand out, to project; d) der Fleck wird nicht 2 the stain will not come out; e) fig. mit der Sprache 2 (offen sprechen) to speak out or up or freely; to speak one's mind; ~ n: beim ~ aus dem Theater in coming out of (or on leaving) the theatre; **²greifen** v/n. ⑧b** to pick (or single) out; **²gucken** F v/n. (h.) ⑧** to look out; **²haben** v/a. ⑩b**: a) to have a th. out; b) fig. to have discovered or solved; ich hab's heraus! I have (found) it!; c) etwas 2 (gut verstehen) to know (or understand) a th. thoroughly, to have at one's fingers' ends; **²hauen** ⑧c** v/a.: a) to hew (or cut) out; b) ⚔ ein Bataillon 2 to rescue a battalion by cutting (a lane) through the enemy; sich 2 v/refl. to cut (or fight) one's way through (the enemy); **²heben** v/a.

²(⑦)b** to lift (or take) out, to raise from a depth; e-n aus dem Wagen 2 to hand (or help) a p. out of a carriage; (hervorheben) to set off, to bring into relief; **²helfen** v/n. (h.) ⑧b**: e-m aus einer Grube 2 to help (or get) a p. out of a pit; abs. e-m (aus der Not) 2 to relieve a p. in his distress; **²klopfen** v/a. ⑧** to knock out; e-n aus dem Schlafe 2 to rouse a p. (from sleep) by knocking; **²kommen** v/n. (fn) ⑧**: a) aus dem Hause ꝛc. 2 to come out of ...; kommen Sie zu uns heraus (aufs Land) (will you) come and join us out here; ⚔ aus einem Engpasse ꝛc. 2 to debouch ...; aus der Verwunderung gar nicht 2 to be lost in amazement; sie mögen sehen, wie sie da 2 it's their own look-out how to extricate (or clear) themselves; b) sein Los (oder er) ist mit einem Gewinne 2gekommen he has drawn a prize; c) von Büchern: (erscheinen) to appear, to come out, to be published or brought out, in Lieferungen: to be issued; soeben 2gekommen just out (of the press); d) (ruchbar w.) to become known, to spread (abroad), to transpire; e) mit etwas (redend) 2 to ventilate a subject; f) es kommt (gerade) 2 heraus (klingt so), als ob ich unrecht hätte it sounds as if (or one would think that) I was in the wrong; g) (ein Ergebnis liefern) to give a (certain) result; auf eins (oder dasselbe) 2 to come to the same thing, F to be all the same; die Rechnung kommt (richtig) heraus the sum comes (or works) out (correctly); mein Exempel kommt anders heraus my example works out differently, I get a different result or answer; es kommt nichts dabei heraus there is nothing (to be) gained by it, F no good will come of it; das kommt dabei heraus, wenn man lügt that is the fruit of (or what results from) telling lies; was kam dabei heraus? what did it lead to?, what was the upshot of it (all)?; **²können** v/n. (h.) ⑧** to be able to go (or F get) out; **²kriegen** F v/a. ⑧** to get out; **²lassen** v/a. ⑧a** to let out, to allow to go out, einen Gefangenen: to release; **²legen** v/a. ⑧** to lay (or put) out or outside; **²lesen** v/a. ⑫a**: a) = auslesen 1; b) etwas aus einem Buche 2 to read a th. out of (or in) ..., to gather (or learn) from ...; **²locken** v/a. ⑧**: a) to entice outside; b) ein Geheimnis aus e-m 2 to draw (or worm) a secret out of a p.; F to pump a th. out of a p.; Geld aus e-m 2 to squeeze money out of a p.; **²lügen** v/a. (und sich 2 v/refl.) ⑩d** to save (o.s.) by telling lies; **²machen** F v/a. ⑧** to get (or take) out; sich 2 v/refl.: a) (abreisen) to leave; (aufs Land kommen) to go into the country; b) (vorwärts kommen) to get on, to make progress, to prosper, to rise (in the world); c) = sich ²arbeiten; **²müssen** v/n. (h.) ⑧**: a) to be obliged to go out; b) es muß heraus, was ich auf dem Herzen habe I must make a clean breast of it or get it off my heart; sich **²mustern** F v/refl. ⑫a** =

Zeichen (s. S. XVII): F familiär; P Volkssprache; ⚡ Gaunersprache; ⟋ selten; † alt (auch gestorben); * neu (auch geboren); ⚍ unrichtig;

[herausnehmen] — 505 — [herbemühen]

sich 2machen b, sich 2fressen b; 2nehmen v/a. ⓐa**: a) to take out of the oven, the river, &c., to remove from; e-n Zahn 2 to pull out (or extract) ...; typ. die Form 2 to lift out the form; hort. Pflanzen aus den Töpfen 2 to unpot ...; b) ⚔ die Brust 2 to put (or throw) out one's chest; c) fig. sich (dat.) et. 2 (anmaßen) to presume too much, to make too bold; ein Recht: to usurp; sich Freiheiten 2 to take liberties; 2platzen v/n. (fn) ⓜ**: a) to burst (forth); b) fig. 2 mit to utter suddenly; mit einem gräßlichen Fluch 2 to rap out a terrible oath; mit Vertrauensfachen 2 to blurt (or let) out confidential matters; 2poltern v/n. (fn) ⓜa**: a) to come blundering out; b) fig. mit et. 2 F to blab out a th.; vgl. 2platzen b; 2pressen v/a. ⓜ** to press out; 2putzen v/a. (und sich 2 v/refl.) ⓜ** to adorn (o.s.), to trick (o.s.) up, to deck (o.s.) out, F to tog (o.s.) up; to dress (o.s.) up; fein gepuzt finely dressed or F got up; 2ragen v/n. (h.) ⓜ** = 2stehen; 2reden ⓜ** v/n. (h.): frei 2 to speak out or up; v/a. und sich 2 v/refl. to extricate o.s. by one's talk, to get off by fine excuses or subterfuges; er weiß sich stets 2zureden he always knows how to make his story good, he always has an excuse at the tip of his tongue; 2reißen v/a. ⓜa**: a) to tear (or pull) out; Unkraut: to pull up weeds, to weed out; b) fig. (auch: sich 2 v/refl.) to extricate (o.s.) from a difficult position; 2rücken ⓜ** v/a.: a) to push a th. out (here); aus der Reihe 2 to move s.th. over (or across) the line; b) F Geld 2 (hergeben) to pay up, to loosen one's purse-strings, F to come down with the ready (cash), to shell out or up; v/n. (fn): a) ⚔ aus dem Lager 2 to move (or march) out of the camp; b) mit etwas 2 to come out with a th.; mit der Sprache 2 to speak one's mind freely; 2rufen v/a. ⓑ**: e-n 2 to call a p. out (of a house or a room) or forth; thea. to call actors before the curtain, to give actors a call; ⚔ die Wache 2 to turn out the (men on) guard; 2sagen v/a. ⓜ** to declare (or utter) freely, to tell frankly; fagen wir es (nur) gleich heraus! let us say so at once, let us be quite candid!; (eingestehen) to admit; es frei 2 to speak plainly or openly; 2schaffen v/a. ⓜ**: a) to convey (or F lug) out(side); (verschwinden machen) to get out of the way; b) ⚒ aus der Grube 2 to extract; ~ n ㉓ conveyance of goods; ⚒ extraction (or output) of ore; 2schinden P v/a. ⓻** to squeeze out money; 2schlagen ⓜb** v/a.: a) einem den Degen aus der Hand 2 to knock ... out of a p.'s hand; b) fig. Geld aus et. 2 (gewinnen) to make money by (or a profit out of) a th., to turn s.th. into money; seine Kosten 2 to (re)cover (or pay) one's expenses; mühsam 2 to squeeze out; v/n. (h.) die Flamme schlägt zum Dache heraus ... leaps up to (or bursts through) the roof; sich 2schleichen v/refl. ⓜaft** to sneak (or slink) out or forth; 2fein ⓜa** ell.: a) 2(gekommen) sein to have come (or got) out; to be out (a. v. Büchern); v. Geheimnissen: to have leaked out or transpired; b) 2 (=gezogen) sein: der Zahn ist heraus ... has been pulled out, ... is out; c) F er ist schön (a. fein) heraus (=gekommen) he has come off well, he is well (or comfortably) off or in clover; 2sollen v/n. (h.) ⓜ**: er soll heraus he has (or is) to come out (here), he shall go out; 2staffieren P v/a. (u. sich 2 v/refl.) ⓜ*/* = 2putzen; 2stecken v/a. ⓜ** to put (or F stick) up outside; eine Fahne 2 to put up a flag; 2steh(e)n v/n. (h.) ⓜ** to stand (or stick) out, to project; 2stellen ⓜ** v/a. to put (or place) out(side); sich 2 v/refl. to prove (to be), to show o.s.; er stellte sich als ein (oder einen) Betrüger heraus, v/impers. es stellte sich heraus, daß er ein B. war he proved (or turned out) to be an impostor; die Sache stellt sich ganz anders heraus the matter appears in quite a different light; seine Unschuld wird sich bald 2 his innocence will soon be proved or come to light; 2stoßen v/a. ⓜa**: Worte mühsam 2 to force out one's words, to bring one's words by a great exertion; 2strecken v/a. ⓜ**: die Zunge 2 to put out one's tongue (e-m at a p.); 2streichen ⓜaft** v/a.: a) to strike out a passage, &c.; b) fig. (sehr loben) und sich 2 v/refl. und v/recip.: e-n (sich, ea.) 2 to praise (o.s., one another) to the skies, F to sound a p.'s (one's own, one another's) trumpet; 2stürzen ⓜ** v/a. (und sich 2 v/refl.) &c. to throw (o.s.) out of a window, &c.; v/n. (fn) aus dem Wagen 2c. 2 to fall (or rush) out of the coach, &c.; 2tragen ⓜb**, 2treiben ⓜ** v/a. to carry, drive (out)side; 2treten v/n (fn) ⓜd**: a) to step out (to me or us), to come forth; b) mit et. (vor die Welt) 2 to come forward with s.th., to put a th. before the public; abs. 2 (bekannt werden) to rise into fame, to emerge from obscurity; c) path. von Eingeweiden 2c.: to protrude; ~ n stepping out or forth; path. protrusion of the bowels, &c.; 2tun v/a. ⓜ** to put out (or outside); 2wachsen v/n. (fn) ⓜb**: a) von Pflanzen: to sprout (or shoot) out of the ground, &c.; b) surg. aus e-r Wunde 2c. 2 to grow out of ...; F fig. das wächst mir zum Halse heraus I am (growing) sick and tired of it; c) er ist aus seinen Kleidern 2gewachsen he has outgrown his clothes; sich 2wagen v/refl. ⓜ** to venture (to come) forth; fig. sich mit der Sprache 2 to make bold to speak; 2wickeln ⓜa**, 2winden ⓜ** v/a. (u. sich 2 v/refl.) to free (o.s.) from a snare or net; fig. to extricate (o.s.) from a difficulty; v/refl. a. to wriggle out of a th. (a. fig.); 2wollen v/n. (h.) ⓜ**: a) ell. 2(gehen) wollen to be desirous of going out or wanting to go out; b) fig. nicht mit der Sprache 2 to show o.s. disinclined (or unwilling) to speak; er will mit der Wahrheit nicht heraus he is shy of telling the truth, F he won't come out with it; 2zahlen v/a. ⓜ**: a) to pay up; noch 2 müssen to have to pay in return or as (a) balance; b) = auszahlen I; 2zerren v/a. ⓜ** to lug out; 2ziehen ⓜb** v/a. to pull (or draw, mit Mühe: to drag) out; mit der Wurzel 2 to pull up by the root, to uproot; v/n. (fn) to move (or march) out here; sich 2 v/refl. (aus e-r mißlichen Lage) to extricate o.s. from a difficulty; F to draw (or back, get) out of a th.

herb (ͮ) [ahd.; *Harm] I a. ⓰ harsh; (scharf v. Geschmack) sharp, acrid, ↘ acerb, (zj.-ziehend) tart, astringent; (sauer) sour, acid, Wein: dry; Worte: bitter; 2es Obst sour (or unripe, green) fruit; 2e Rede severe (or harsh) language; 2er Spott bitter mockery, biting sarcasm. — II ~e(s) n ⓰ harshness; sharp, &c. (s. f.) taste; vgl. Herbe.
Herbarium ꜛ (ͮ(ͮ)ͮ) [lt.] n ㉘ (Pflanzensammlung) herbarium, (botanist's) collection of (dried specimens of) plants.
Herbe (ͮͮ) f ⓰ (s. herb) harshness; sharpness, acridity, acerbity; tartness, astringency, von Wein: dryness, von Worten: bitterness, offensiveness.
her-begeben (ͮ...): sich 2 v/refl. ⓜc*/* to proceed hither, to come here.
her-bei (ͮͮ) adv. here, hither, this way; near to me or us; ell. 2! come here (to me)!, come on!
her-bei-..., Her-bei-... (ͮͮ...) in Verbindung mit verbs, immer trennbar (**), und in Zssgn mit verbal nouns, die Bewegung nach dem Sprechenden hin in dessen Nähe bezeichnend = heran-...: 2bringen v/a. ⓜ**: a) to bring on here; b) (beibringen) to produce; 2führen ⓜ** to lead to(wards) me or us; fig. to bring on or about; (nach sich ziehen) to involve, to entail; eine Entscheidung rasch 2 to precipitate matters, to bring matters quickly to a crisis; 2holen v/a. ⓜ** to fetch here, to go for; 2kommen v/n. (fn) ⓜ*** to come along here; 2lassen ⓜa** v/a. to allow to come here, to admit; sich 2 v/refl.: sich zu et. 2 (verstehen) to condescend or consent, agree) to do a th.; 2locken v/a. ⓜ** to allure, decoy, entice; 2rufen v/a. ⓜb** to call here or in; 2schaffen v/a. ⓜ** to convey to this spot; (verschaffen) to procure, produce, furnish; (zj.-bringen) to collect; Geld: to raise, F to find; 2wünschen v/a. ⓜ**: e-n et. 2 to wish for a p., a th. (to come here, to appear on the scene); 2ziehen ⓜb** v/a. to draw (or pull) to(wards) us; fig. bei den Haaren 2gezogen dragged in (by main force), farfetched; v/n. (fn) to move nearer.
her-bekommen (ͮ...) v/a. ⓜ*/* to procure; wo soll ich es denn 2? where am I to get it from?; 2bemühen v/a. (v/refl.) ⓜ*/*: e-n (sich) 2 to trouble a p. (o.s.) to come here.

♪ Musik; ꜛ Wissenschaft; ⚘ Pflanze; ⏳ Geographie; ⚙ Technik; ⚒ Bergbau; ⚔ Militär; ⚓ Marine; ☙ Handel; ✉ Post; 🚂 Eisenbahn.

[Herberge] — 506 — [hereinziehen]

Herberge (ᵍᵛ⁓) [ahd. Heer=bergende] f ⁴⁸ 1. (Obdach) (place of) shelter, rest for travellers; lodging; harbouring place, harbourage; (Wirtshaus) (roadside) inn; (Nachtlager) night-shelter; (common) lodging-house; (Zuflucht) place of refuge; ~ der Heilsarmee salvation-army shelter. — 2. (Versammlungs=ort eines Gewerks, in England unbekannt), etwa: (journeymen's) house of call or meeting-place.

herbergen (ᵍᵛ⁓) v/n. (h.) ⁶⁸: bei e-m ⁀ to lodge with a p., to stay at a p.'s house, to find shelter under a p.'s roof.

Herbergs=mutter (ᵍᵛ...) f ⁶², =**vater** (auch =**wirt**) m hostess, host of a (common) lodging-house, innkeeper.

her=bestellen (ᵘ...) v/a. ⁶⁸*/*: a) to send for a p.; to ask for a p. to come; b) zu e-r Zs.=kunft: to make an appointment with a p.; c) (gerichtlich vorladen) to summons a p.; ⁀**beten** v/a. ⁶⁸** to say (off) mechanically, F to rattle (or gabble) off; ein Vaterunser ⁀ to say the Lord's prayer (over). [Herbe.

Herbheit (ᵍ⁻), **Herbigkeit** (ᵍ⁻⁻) f ⁴⁶ =]

her=bitten (ᵘ...) v/a. ⁶⁴** to ask a p. to come here, to invite a p.; ich habe ihn hergebeten I have invited (or asked) him (to come here).

herblich (ᵍᵛ⁻) a. ⁶⁶ somewhat harsh or tart or astringent or bitter.

her=bringen (ᵘ...) v/a. ⁶⁷** to bring here or in or up; f. hergebracht.

Herbst (ᵍ) [ahd.: harvest Ernte] m ⓐa. 1. autumn; im ~e in the autumn, auch: at the fall (poet. in the sear) of the leaf. — 2. (Ernte=zeit) harvest(-time); (Weinlese) vintage.

Herbst=abend (ᵍ...) m ⁶² autumnal evening; =**anfang** m (23. Sept.) beginning of autumn; =**äquinoktium** n, ast. autumnal equinox; =**bedarf** m autumn-demand or -goods pl.; =**blume** f autumnal flower.

herbsten (ᵍᵛ⁻) ⁶⁶ I v/impers. (Herbst werden) es herbstet, etwa: we are nearing (or F getting into) autumn, autumn is (drawing) near, it (or the air) is (getting) autumnal. — II v/a. u. v/n. (h.) (ernten) to (gather in the) harvest, to get in the crops; to pick the grapes, the fruit, &c. — III v/n ⁀ n ²³ = Herbstung. [days pl. or vacation.]

Herbst=ferien (ᵍ⁻) pl. ⁶² autumn-holi=]

herbsthaft (ᵍᵛ⁻) a. ⁶⁶ 1. = herbstlich 2.

herbstlich (ᵍᵛ⁻) a. ⁶⁶ 1. (zum Herbste gehörig) autumnal, of autumn. — 2. (dem Herbste ähnlich) autumnal, resembling (or like) autumn; es wird ⁀ it (or the air) is (becoming) autumnal.

Herbstling (ᵍᵛ⁻) m ⓐd. ⁂ autumnal fruit; Vieh: young (calf, &c.) born in autumn.

Herbst=luft (ᵍ...) f ⁶² autumnal air; ⁀**mäßig** a. ⁶⁶ autumnal; =**monat** m autumn-month; engl. September; =**morchel** f yellowish turban-top (Helvella leucophae'a); =**nachtgleiche** f = äquinoktium; =**nebel** m, =**obst** n autumnal fog, fruit; =**punkt** m autumnal point; =**reise** f autumn-tour; =**rose** ⁂ f = Stockrose; =**saat** f sowing in autumn; =**stürme** m/pl. autumnal (or equinoctial) gales pl.; =**tag** m autumnal day.

Herbstung (ᵍᵛ⁻) f ⁴⁶ harvest(ing); harvest-operations pl.

Herbst=wetter (ᵍ...) n ⁶² autumnal weather; =**zeichen** n/pl. ast. autumnal signs pl. (of the zodiac); =**zeit** f autumn (-time or -months pl.), harvest-time; =**zeit=lose** ⁂ f ⁶⁷ meadow-saffron (Co'lchicum autumna'le).

her=buchstabieren (ᵘ...) v/a. ⁶³*/* to spell a word over or off.

Herd[¹] (¹) [ahd.: hearth] m ⓐb. 1. hearth, fireplace; ⊙ (Treib=)~ cupelling-furnace; metall. eines Treib=ofens: sole, eines Gebläse=ofens: (inner) crucible, (Heizraum einer Dampfmaschine) body; Gießerei: ~ in der Formerei open sand (for moulding). — 2. seinen eigenen ~ haben (gründen) to have (to set up) a home of one's own; gastlicher ~, oft: hospitable roof; am häuslichen ~e by (or at) one's fireside, within the (narrow) family-circle; weder Haus noch ~ haben to have neither hearth nor home; fig. ~ (Mittelpunkt) einer Verschwörung ꝛc. centre (or focus, central seat) of a rebellion, &c.; Sprichw. f. eigen 1. — 3. hunt. (zum Vogelfange mit Lockvögeln besetzter und mit Garnen umlegter Platz) fowling-floor, decoy.

Herd[²]... (ᵘ...) [Herde] f. Zssgn.

Herd[¹]=**asche** ⊙ (ᵘ...) f ⊙ hearth-(or furnace-)ashes pl.; =**besen** m hearth-broom or -brush; =²**buchgesellschaft** (ᵘ...) f (Viehzuchtverein) Association of (German) cattle-breeders.

Herde (ᵍᵛ⁻) [ahd.: herd] f ⁴⁸ 1. herd of cattle or swine, flock of sheep; (Trift) drove of cattle, &c. — 2. fig. (Schar) troop, multitude; in ~n lebend living in herds, gregarious, herding (or flocking) together.

Herden=glocke (ᵘ⁻...) f ⁶² herd-bell; =**hammel** m bell-wether; =**mensch*** m gregariously inclined person, one who goes with the multitude or the common herd, F one of the million; ⁀**reich** a. ⁶⁶ abounding in herds or flocks; =**tier** n: a) gregarious animal; b) *contp.* = =**mensch**; =**vieh** n cattle in herds, drove cattle; =**weise** adv. (F a.) (living) in herds or flocks or troops; gregariously.

Herd[¹]=**feuer** (ᵘ...) n ⁶² fire on a(n open) hearth; =**formerei** ⊙ Gießerei: open-sand moulding; =**frischen** ⊙ n, metall. finery-process; =**guß** ⊙ m Gießerei: casting in open sand-moulds, open-sand casting; =**haken** m pot-hook or -hanger; =**platte** ⊙ f iron (or steel) plate covering the hearth, hearth-plate. [press (or push) this way.]

her=dringen (ᵘ...) v/n. (fn) ⓓf** to]

Herd[¹]=**rost** (ᵘ...) m ⁶² fire-grate.

her=dürfen (ᵘ...) v/n. (h.) ⁶⁸** to be allowed (or at liberty) to come here.

her=eilen (ᵘ...) v/n. (fn) ⁶⁸** to hasten (or hurry) hither, to rush (up) here.

her=ein (⌣ᵘ) adv. 1. in, in here, into this place; von (dr)außen ⁀ from outside or without. — 2. ell. (immer) ⁀! walk in, please!; ich rief ⁀! I called out "come in!"; als Tür=aufschrift: ⁀, ohne anzuklopfen (please) open without knocking; hier ⁀! (please) step in this way!; den Bauch ⁀! put in your stomach!, bellies in!; f. heraus 3.

her=ein=..., **Her=ein=...** (⌣ᵘ...) in Verbindung mit verbs, immer trennbar (**), und in Zssgn mit verbal nouns, das Einbringen in etwas nach dem Sprechenden hin bezeichnend, oft: in(to), in here, into this place or one's house: **sich ⁀bemühen** v/refl. ⁶⁸*/* to trouble o.s. to come in; ⁀**bitten** v/a. ⁶⁴** to invite to come in, to ask a p. in(to one's house); ⁀**brechen** v/n. (fn) ⓐa** = einbrechen II; das Unglück, das über sie ⁀gebrochen ist ... which has befallen (or overtaken) them; ⁀**bringen** v/a. ⁶⁷**: a) to bring in (here), mit Mühe: to get (or lug) in; b) südd. (bes. öst.) = einbringen; ⁀**dringen** v/n. (fn) ⓓf** to enter forcibly; ⁀**dürfen** v/n. (h.) ⁶⁸** to be allowed to come in; ⁀**eilen** v/n. (fn) ⁶⁸** to hurry in (here); =**fall** m ⁶² (F **Reinfall**) trap, F take-in; ⁀**fallen** v/n. (fn) ⁶⁰a**: a) to tumble into ...; fig. mit der Tür ins Haus ⁀ to blurt out a th.; b) F mst: **reinfallen** (angeführt werden) to be cheated or F diddled or taken in; e-n reinfallen lassen to cheat (F to diddle) a p., F to take a p. in; ⁀**führen** v/a. ⁶⁸** to show (or usher) in(to this room); ⁀**geh(e)n** v/n. (fn) ⓐ4**: a) to enter (here), to walk (or step) in (here); b) (Platz finden) to go (or fit) in(to a place); ⁀**holen** v/a. ⁶⁸** to fetch in (here); ⁀**kommen** v/n. (fn) ⓐ4** to come in (here), unerwartet: to drop in; ⁀**können** v/n. (h.) ⓐ4** to be able to go (or step) in; ⁀**lassen** v/a. ⁶⁰a** to let in, to give access to, to admit; ⁀**legen** ⁶⁸** : a) v/a. ⁀ in to put (or lay) a th. in here; F (pressen) to take in; b) sich ⁀ v/refl. to lie down (to sleep) in a bed, &c.; ⁀**müssen** v/n. (h.) ⓐ4** to be obliged to enter (here); die Stühle müssen herein ... must be brought in; ⁀**nehmen** v/a. ⓐa** to take in (here); ⁀ Börse: to carry over; ⁀**nötigen** v/a. ⁶⁸** to force (durch Zureden: to press) a p. to come in; ⁀**reichen** v/a. ⁶⁸** to hand a th. in to me; ⁀**reiten** ⓐb** v/n. (fn) to come in (here) on horseback; F sich ⁀ (F **reinreiten**) v/refl. to get o.s. into trouble; ⁀**scheinen** v/n. (h.) ⓐ1**: a) to shine into (the room, &c.); b) to shed (or cast) light into (this place); ⁀**schießen** v/n. (h.) ⓐc(e)ft** to fire into; ⁀**schlagen** v/a. ⓐb**=einschlagen 1 u. 2; F Speisen ⁀ to bolt one's food; sich ⁀**schleichen** v/refl. ⓐft** to sneak in (here); ⁀**schneien** v/n. (h.) ⓐ3**: a) v/impers. es schneit herein it is snowing in(to the room, &c.); b) F fig. (plötzlich erscheinen) to appear suddenly on the scene; ⁀**stürzen** v/n. (fn) ⓐ4**: a) in e-n Graben ꝛc. ⁀ to tumble into a ditch, &c.; b) to rush in(to); unvermutet bei e-m ⁀gestürzt kommen to take a p. by storm, F to rush (upon) a p.; c) von Unglücksfällen: über e-n ⁀ to overwhelm a p.; ⁀**treten** v/n. (fn) ⓐd** to step in (here); ⁀**ziehen** ⁶⁸** v/a. to draw (or pull) in(to); v/n. (fn) to move in(to a house, the town, &c.); sich ⁀ v/refl. der Geruch zieht sich herein in das Zimmer ... is

Signs (see page XVII): F familiar; P vulgar; ⌐ flash; ⧵ rare; † obsolete (died); * new word (born); ⁺⁺ incorrect; ♪ music;

[hererzählen] — 507 — [hermetisch]

coming (or penetrating, spreading) into the room. — Vgl. a. die Zssgn mit ein=... **her-erzählen** (⹁...) v/a. ⊛*/* to relate (or tell) from beginning to end; ~ n, =**erzählung** f ⊛ complete (or detailed, accurate) account; ⁜**fahren** ⊛b** v/n. (jn): a) to arrive or come (in a carriage or sledge or motor-car, by railway or boat or omnibus, on a cycle, &c.); ⚓ neben dem Ufer ⁜ to (sail along the) coast; bisw. engS. to return; vor e-m ⁜ to move (or drive, sail, cycle, motor, ride, &c.) in front of a p.; b) to approach swiftly; hier ist die Kugel ⁜gefahren here the bullet touched ground or hit its mark; über etwas ⁜ = ⁜fallen; v/a. eine Person, Steine zc. ⁜ to convey ... in a carriage, a cart, &c.; =**fahrt** f⊛ arrival; journey hither; =**fallen** v/n. (jn) ⊛a**: über e-n, et. ⁜ to pounce upon (or rush in upon) a p., a th.; über e-n ⁜, a.: to fall upon (stärker: to make a dead set at) a p.; engS.: a) to attack (or assail) a p., to fall foul of a p.; b) mit Vorwürfen: to come down upon a p., to inveigh against a p., to load a p. with abuse; über et. (e-e Mahlzeit, Arbeit zc.) ⁜ to fall (or set) to; **sich ⁜finden** v/refl. ⊛** to find one's way here; ⁜**fließen** v/n. (jn) ⊛d**: a) to flow this way; vom Gebirge ⁜ to flow (or spring) from the mountains; neben et. ⁜ to flow (or glide) along (or beside) a th.; b) fig. (sich ableiten aus) to emanate (or originate from); ⁜**fordern** v/a. ⊛a** to summon (here), gerichtlich: to summons; =**fracht** ⚓ f ⊛ home (or inward) freight; **sich ⁜fragen** v/refl. ⊛ (⹂+ ⊛b)** to inquire one's way here; ⁜**für** (⹂⹂) † od. poet. = ⁜vor; ⁜**führen** (⹁...) v/a. ⊛** to conduct here, to guide hither; was führt Sie her? what brings you here?, höflicher: what is your pleasure?; =**gabe** f ⊛: ~ des Geldes handing over (or returning) the money; ~ des Namens allowing one's name to be used; =**gang** m ⊙c.: a) walk back, return-journey; b) (Art, wie et. zugegangen ist) course of events, proceedings pl.; (Vorfall) occurrence; das ist der ganze ~ that is how it all happened, F that's the whole story; ⁜**geben** ⊛c** v/a. to give (or deliver) up, to hand over; (liefern) to furnish a proof, evidence, &c.; seinen Namen zu etwas ⁜ to lend one's name to a th., to allow one's name to be used for a th.; **sich ⁜** v/refl.: sich zu et. ⁜ to lend o.s. to a th.; ⁜**gebracht** a.: a) p.p. v. ⁜**bringen** (s. ds) b) (auf uns überkommen) handed down (or transmitted) to us, traditional; weitS. (allgemein eingeführt) (well-) established; (üblich) customary, usual, conventional; ⁜e Redensart stereotyped phrase; ⁜**er-ma"ßen** adv. according to established custom, traditionally; ~**e(s)** n ⊙ (established) custom, usage; ⁜**geh(e)n** ⊛** v/n. (jn): to walk here; to approach; dicht hinter e-m ⁜ to follow close upon a p.'s heels; neben=ea. ⁜ to march side by side; zwei Diener gingen vor ihm her ... walked in front of him, he was pre-

ceded by ...; v/impers.: a) es geht über et., e-n her a th., a p. is being assailed or attacked; es wird über Sie ⁜ they will be hard down upon you, they will pitch into you; b) (sich zutragen) (so oder so) ⁜ to happen (in such or such a manner); so geht es in der Welt her that is how the world goes or the way of the world; hier geht es hoch her there are grand goings-on here, F we are having a fine time or high jinks (here); bei ihnen geht es knapp her they are very hard up, they live on short commons; es ging bei der Schlacht scharf her there was some hot fighting in that battle; es geht hier schlimm her F things here look bad; ⁜**gehören** v/n. (h.) ⊛*/* to belong to the place, to be to the purpose; nicht ⁜ to be out of place; das gehört hier nicht her that has nothing to do with it, that lies (or is) outside the question; ⁜**gehörig** a. ⊛ to the purpose, pertinent; ⁜**gelaufen** p.p. f. ⁜**laufen**; ⁜**geraten** v/n. (jn) ⊛a*/* to get accidentally to a place; ⁜**haben** v/a. ⊛b**: wo hast du das her? where did you get that from?; ⁜**halten** v/a. ⊛a** to hold out; to tender; die Hand ⁜ to stretch out one's hand; abs. ob. v/n. (leiden) to suffer; to submit to; als Gegenstand des Spottes: to be made the target of people's fun or jokes; er muß immer ⁜ (bezahlen) he has always to pay (the piper) or F to stand (treat); ⁜**holen** v/a. ⊛** to fetch here; bsd. fig. weit ⁜ to fetch from afar; to drag in; weit ⁜geholt far-fetched (reasons, &c.).

Hering (⹁⹂) [ndd. (ahd.).] : herring; *Heer] m ⹁d. ichth. herring (Clu'pea hare'ngus); frischer (a. grüner) ~ fresh herring; geräucherter ~ smoked herring, bloater; gedörrter ~ kipper(ed herring); gesalz(e)ner (oder saurer) ~ pickled h.; fig. er ist ein wahrer ~ ... as thin as a lark, ⚓ ... as thin as a shotten h.; ... quite a skeleton; wie ~e zs.=gepackt jammed (or packed) like sardines in a box, close together. **Herings-büse** (⹁⹁...) ⚓ f ⊛ (Boot der Heringsfischer) herring-buss; =**fang** m he.-fishing; =**fänger**, =**fischer** m: a) he.-fisher, herringer; b) ⚓ (Art Boot) he.-smack; =**fischerei** ⁜=**fang**; =**könig** m, ichth. (John) Dory (Zeus faber); falscher ~ herring-king (Rega'lecus glesne); =**lake** f brine for herrings; =**milch** f soft roe of a herring; =**sala't** m (in England unbekannt) salad (mixed) with pickled herring; =**seele** f: a) (Blase im Innern eines Herings) bladder of a herring; b) fig. contp. (niedriger Mensch) low fellow; =**tonne** f herring-keg. **her-kommen** (⹁...) v/n. (jn) ⊛**: a) to come hither or here, to approach; vom Essen ⁜ to come (straight) from dinner; b) (abstammen) to descend from, to originate with or in or from; to be caused by; (sich ableiten) to be derived from; wo kommt das Wort, die Sprache her? what is the derivation, the origin of the word, the language? ~ n: a) =**kunft**; b) (alter

Gebrauch) old custom or usage; gesellschaftliches: conventionality; b.s. (Schlendrian) (mechanical) routine; ⁜**kömmlich** a. ⊛ conventional; =**kömmlichkeit** f ⊛ conventionality; ⁜**können** v/n. (h.) ⊛** to be able to come here.

Herkules (⹂⹂⹂) npr/m. ⊙γ myth. (grch. Halbgott, Sohn des Zeus und der Alkme'ne) Hercules, a. Alcides.

Herkules-arbeit (⹁⹁...) f ⊛: die (12) ~en the (twelve) labours (or tasks) of H.; fig. ~ herculean task, gigantic (piece of) work; =**käfer** m, ent. Hercules-beetle (Dyna'stes He'rcules); =**säulen** f/pl. (Berge zu beiden Seiten der Straße von Gibraltar) Pillars of Hercules.

herkulisch (⹁⹂⹂) [it.] a. ⊛ Herculean. **Her-kunft** (⹁...) f ⊚: a) arrival; b) (Herstammen) descent, origin, derivation; von niederer ~ of low birth or extraction, low-born; ⁜**laden** v/a. ⊛, ⊛b** to invite here, to summon; ⁜**lallen** v/a. ⊛** to mumble, to stutter forth; ⁜**langen** ⊛** v/a. einen Teller zc.: to hand, to pass (on); v/n. (h.) to extend as far as here; er kann nicht ⁜ he cannot reach as far as here; ⁜**lassen** v/a. ⊛a** to allow to come here; ⁜**laufen** ⊛**f** v/n. (jn) to run hither; hinter e-m ⁜ to run after a p.; ⁜**gelaufen** p.p. und a. strange, alien; ⁜**gelaufener** Mensch adventurer, new comer, outsider, intruder; ⁜**legen** v/a. ⊛** to lay down here; ⁜**leiern** v/a. ⊛a** to drawl out, F to rattle (or reel) off; ⁜**leiten** v/a. ⊛**: a) to lead (or conduct) hither; b) = ableiten 3.

Herling ⚘ (⹁⹂) [Herbling] m ⹁d. sour unripe grape.

her-locken (⹁...) v/a. ⊛** to entice (here); **sich ⁜machen** v/refl. ⊛**: sich über e-n ⁜ to fall (or pounce) upon a th., a p., to tackle a th., a p.

Hermann (⹂⹂) [ahd.] npr/m. ⊙ ⊛α. (Vn.) Herman(n); hist. ~ der Cheruskerfürst (deutscher Heerführer) Arminius.

Herm-aphrodit (⹁⹁⹂") [grch.] ⊛ I npr/m. myth. (mit der Nymphe Sa'lmakis zu einem Körper verbunden) Hermaphroditus. — II ⚥ m (Zwitter) hermaphrodite; ⁜**isch** a. ⊛ hermaphroditic(al); ⚘ ⁜e Blume hermaphrodite flower.

Her-marsch (⹁...) m ⊛ march(ing) hither. **Herme** (⹂⹂) [grch.] f ⊛ arch. statue of Hermes or Mercury; hermes-column; herma, hermes (pl. hermæ).

Hermelin (⹁⹂⹂) [dim. v. † Harm Wiesel] ⹁d.: a) n, zo. ermine, stoat (Muste'la ob. Puto'rius ermi'neus); b) m = ⁜**pelz**; mit ~ besetzt ermined; ~**kragen** m ermine cape; ~**mantel** m cloak lined with ermine, als Abzeichen richterlicher zc. Würde; ermine; ~**muff(e)** m, f ermine muff; ~**pelz** m ermine (fur).

Hermeneutik ⚥ (⹁⹂⹂") [grch.] f ⊛ (Auslegekunst) hermeneutics, art of interpretation.

Hermen-säule (⹂⹂...) f ⊛ = Herme. **Hermes** (⹂⹂) [grch.] npr/m. ⊙γ myth. (grch. Gott der Kaufleute, Götterbote) Hermes, bei den Römern Mercury; ~**säule** f = Herme.

hermetisch (⹁⹂⹂) [grch.] a. ⊛ (luftdicht) hermetic(al), air-tight; adv. ⁜ verschlossen hermetically sealed.

⚓ scientific; ⚘ botanical; ⚥ geography; ⊙ machinery; ⚒ mining; ⚔ military; ⚓ marine; ⊛ commercial; ✉ postal; 🚂 railway.

her=murmeln (⁀...) v/a. ☉a** to mutter (forth or over); ☉**müssen** v/n. (h.) ☉** to be obliged to come (here); ☉**nach** (⌣‿ch) adv. after(wards), after that, thereafter; subsequently; den Tag ☉ the day after, on the following day; ☉**nehmen** (⁀...) v/a. ☉a**: a) to take (or draw from; wo das Geld ☉ und nicht stehlen? where am I to get the money from without stealing it?; den Beweis von et. ☉ (entlehnen) to deduce (or draw) one's proof from a th.; b) F (schelten) to take to task, to abuse, F to blow up; e-n arg ☉ to be hard down on a p., to pitch into a p., ☉**nieder** (⌣‿) adv. feiner als herunter (s. ds), ☉**nötigen** (⁀...) v/a. ☉** to force (or importune) a p. to come here.

Herodes (-⌣‿) [hebr.] npr/m. ☉γ. bibl. Herod (auch fig. = Wüterich, Tyrann).

herodisch (-⌣‿) [Herodes] a. ☉ bibl. Herodian, of Herod.

Herodot (-⌣‿) ☉☉a., ~os, ~us (-⌣‿) ☉γ. npr/m. (grch. Geschichtschreiber, etwa 484—425 v. Chr.) Herodotus; ☉**e-isch** (-⌣‿⌣) a. ☉ Herodotean, of Herodotus.

Hero-en-alter (-⁀...) [Hero'en, pl. v. Heros] ☉ heroic age or period; ☉**haft** a. ☉ = hero'isch; **=kultus** m hero-worship.

Hero-en-tum (-⌣‿) [grch.] n ☉d., etwa: glory (or exploits pl.) of ancient heroes; age of heroism.

Hero-en=zeit(alter n) f(-⁀...) ☉ = =alter.

Hero-ide (-⌣‿) f ☉, **Hero-in** (-⌣‿) f ☉, **Hero-ine** (-⌣‿⌣) [grch.] f ☉ myth. demigoddess; thea. (Heldin) heroine.

hero-isch (-⌣‿) [grch.] a. ☉ (helden-artig) heroic, heroical. — II ~e(s) n ☉ heroic deed(s pl.), heroism. [comical.]

hero-isch-komisch (-⁀...) a. ☉ heroi-)

Hero-ismus (-⁀...) [grch.] m ☉ heroism.

Herold (⌣‿, poet. a.-⌣‿) [mhd. 14. sae.; fr.; *dtsch Heer-walt] m ☉c., bisw. a.: ~in f ☉ herald; weitS. (Verkünder) harbinger, (town-)crier; public messenger.

Herolds=amt (-⌣‿...) n ☉: a) herald's office; a.: heraldship, heraldry; b) coll. heraldic college or chapter; **=kunst** f heraldic art, heraldry.

Herold=stab (-⌣‿) m ☉ herald's wand or rod; caduceus, caduce.

Herons=ball, **=brunnen** (-⁀...) [Heron, grch. Mathematiker, 2. sae. v. Chr.] m ☉ phys. Hero's fountain.

Heros (⌣‿) [grch.] m ☉ (pl. Hero'en) myth. demigod; (Held) hero.

her-plappern (-⁀...) v/a. ☉a** to repeat mechanically, F to rattle (or gabble) off.

Herr(s)[ahd.comp.v.*hehr] m ☉, ☉6, ~in f ☉ 1. (Gebieter[in]) master, f mistress; ein strenger ~, oft: a taskmaster; ~(in) im höheren Sinne: lord (f lady) of the manor, &c.; ~ eines Landes ruler (or sovereign) of a country; (Besitzer[in]) owner, proprietor (f...tress); (Brot-)~ employer; im kaufmännischen Geschäft: principal, chief, F governor; zu Dienstboten: ist der ~ zu Hause? is your master within?; bibl. niemand kann zween ~en dienen no man can serve two masters. — 2. rel. der ~, a. als Ausruf oft: ~e(Gott)! the Lord, God Almighty; als Ausruf: O Lord!, O God!; Jesus Christus, unser ~ our Lord Jesus Christ; als Ausruf: ~ Jesus!, ~ du meine Güte! Good Lord!, Good Gracious!. Goodness alive!, feierlich: Good God!, Good Heavens!; der ~ der Heerscharen the (mighty) Lord of hosts; das Haus des ~n (die Kirche) the House of the Lord or of God; der Tag des ~n (Sonntag) the Lord's Day; der Tisch des ~n (das Abendmahl) the Lord's Table, the communion-table; im ~n wandeln to walk with (or in the ways of) the Lord; Geliebte im ~n! my beloved brethren. — 3. ehm. reichsunmittelbarer Adliger, jetzt noch von (meist bürgerlichen) Rittergutsbesitzern, z.B.: ~ Oliver, etwa: Sir Oliver; f. 4; gnädiger ~!, gestrenger ~! your worship!; in der Anrede an Richter des ersten Ranges 2c.: my Lord!, your Lordship!; an Richter des zweiten Ranges 2c.: your Honour!; f. gestreng 3. — 4. jetzt allgemein als Titel: mein ~! (Anrede) sir! (für engl. Baronets mit dem Vornamen, z.B.: Sir Andrew!; f. 3); ~ Spring Mr. (abbr. für mister) Spring; ja,~ Spring!, einfach: yes, sir!; Ihr ~ Vater your Father; ~ Hauptmann!, ~ General! Captain!, General!; der ~ Hauptmann, der ~ General the Captain, the General, der geistliche ~ the Reverend Gentleman, the Reverend Mr. N.; Allergnädigster ~ und König Most Gracious Sovereign; in Briefen: geehrter ~ Professor N.! dear Sir, vertraulicher: dear Professor N.; hochgeschätzter ~ (B.)! dear Sir, vertraulicher: dear Mr. B. (Sir allein wird in Briefen jetzt meist nur als fast feierliche od. als herausfordernde Anrede gebraucht!); ~ Präsident!, in Versammlungen, stets: Mr. Chairman!. (im House of Commons: Mr. Speaker!); dagegen: der ~ Präsident the Chairman; geehrte ~en!, in Briefen: Gentlemen; meine (Damen und) ~en! (Ladies and) Gentlemen!; ☉ die ~en Brown und Smith Messrs. (abbr. für Messieurs) B. and S. — 5. (Mann aus den höheren Ständen) gentleman; bei Studenten: alter ~ old member of a students' club; alte ~en, oft: middle-aged (für: elderly) gentlemen; in Fabeln: ~ Fuchs master Fox; ein großer ~ a great person, a lord, F a great swell or gun; iro. ein sauberer ~ a good-for-nothing fellow, iro. a fine bird; Eisenbahn 2c.: „Für ~en!" "(For) Gentlemen!"; der Schneider arbeitet nur für ~en ... for (gentle)men only. — 6. Redensarten: den ~n spielen: a) to play the (part of the) master; b) to play (or F do) the (fine) gentleman, F auch: to cut a dash; er will den großen ~n spielen he wants to lord it or F to do the swell; als großer ~ leben to live in grand (or fine) style, F to do it fine or fat; sein eigener ~ sein to be one's own master; ~ über Leben und Tod sein to have power over life and death; ~ sein über seine Leidenschaften, ein Volk 2c. to rule over ...; ~ über sich sein to have (or possess) self-command; des Feuers ~ werden to subdue (or master) the fire, F to get the fire under (control); Sprichw. wie der ~, so der Knecht like master like man; mit großen ~en ist nicht gut Kirschen essen he that sups with the devil must have a long spoon.

Herrchen (⌣‿) n ☉ (dim. von Herr) little (or young) gentleman; als Titel im Hause: the young master; (Stutzer) co. young spark; dandy, fop, F masher.

Herre (⌣‿) m ☉ F u. bibl. f. Herr, bsp. 2.

her=rechnen (⁀...) v/a. ☉b** to reckon (or cast) up, to enumerate; ☉**reichen** v/a. u. v/n. (h.) ☉** to pass on; **=reise** f ☉ (ant. Hinreise) journey here or hither, home- (or return-)journey or voyage; ☉**reisen** v/n. (sn) ☉** to journey hither, to travel as far as here; ☉**reiten** v/n. (sn) ☉b** to ride (or come) on horseback as far as here; to ride back.

Herren=anzug (⌣‿...) m ☉ gentleman's dress or suit; **=arbeit** f: a) ehm. (Fronarbeit) compulsory service, (fr.) corvée; b) jetzt, von Schneidern 2c.: (nur) ~ machen to work for gentlemen (only); **=artikel** ☉ m/pl. gentlemen's hosiery or wearing-apparel or goods pl.; **=bank** f ehm. auf Reichstagen 2c.: lords' bench; **=brot** n: a) fine white bread; b) bread earned in service; ~ essen to serve under a master; **=diener** m gentleman's man-servant or valet; contp. lackey, flunkey; **=dienst** m service rendered to one's master or lord; (Frondienst) corvée; Sprichw. ~ geht vor Gottesdienst, etwa: man (has to be) served before God; the earthly lord is more exacting than the Lord in Heaven; **=essen** n: a) (leckeres Essen) fine dinner; b) gentlemen's dinner-party; **=fahrer** m Radsport: gentleman rider; **=gesellschaft** f = =essen b; **=gunst** f favour of a master, lordly favour; **=haus** n: a) lordly manor or mansion, hall; b) (Erste Kammer in Preußen 2c.)Upper House or Chamber; **=haus-mitglied** n member of the Upper House; Engl.: member of the House of Lords, peer; **=hof** m lordly estate, manor-house; **=hut** m, **=kleider** n/pl. gentleman's hat, clothes pl. or clothing; **=leben** n gentleman's life; ein ~ führen, oft: to live like a lord; **=los** a. ☉: a) (ohne Dienstherrn) out of service; b) (ohne Besitzer) without a master, ownerless, unclaimed; ☉loser Hund stray dog; ☉loses Gut unclaimed property, jur. derelict, waif; **=losigkeit** f: a) being out of service; b) being unclaimed; **=mode(n** pl.) f gentlemen's fashions pl.; **=recht** n lordly privilege, seignorial right; **=reiten** n Sport: gentlemen's race; **=reiter** m Rennsport: gentleman rider; **=sitz** m = **=hof**; **=stand** m: a) lordly rank, gentleman's estate; b) coll. gentry and nobility; **=stiefel** m/pl. gentleman's (in Läden: [gentle]men's) boots pl.; **=stube** f: a) in Gasthöfen 2c.: gentlemen's room, private bar; b) (Ratsstube) council-chamber; **=tafel** f, **=tisch** m gentlemen's table, vornehm: family-table; **=toilette** f gentlemen's lavatory.

Herr=gott F (⌣‿) m ☉c. 1. ohne pl.: the Lord (our) God, God our Lord; er lebt wie (unser) ~ in Frankreich he lives on the fat of the land or like a

[**Herrgottshändler**] — 509 — [**hertreiben**]

fighting-cock; *fig.* unseren ~ einen guten Mann sein lassen, s. Gott 2. — 2. mit *pl.*: image of our Lord or our Saviour; crucifix.

Herrgotts-händler(in *f*) *m* dealer in crucifixes; **=käferchen** *n*, **=kühlein** *n*, *ent.* (Marienkäfer) lady-bird (*Coccine'lla puncta'ta*); **=schnitzer** *m* südd. carver of crucifixes.

her-richten (″...) *v/a.* : a) to set in order; to fit (or fix) up, to arrange, to prepare; Wäsche: to do up; *vgl.* **=stellen** b; **=rieseln** *v/n.* (in) to trickle down (this way).

Herrin (ᴗ⌣) *f* s. Herr.

herrisch (ᴗ⌣) [mhd.] *a.* lordly; (gebieterisch) imperious, dictatorial, commanding, masterful, domineering; (hochmütig) haughty; (barsch) severe, harsh, F bullying; *adv.* 2 verfahren to carry things with a high hand, to act arbitrarily, F to lord it (over people).

Her-ritt (″ᴗ) *m* ⑪c. ride back or home.

herrje(mine) (ᴗ⌣ᴗ) [s. jemine], **herrje-rum** (-ᴗ⌣), **herrje(se)s** (ᴗ⌣(ᴗ) F *int.* [*corr.* aus „Herr Jesus"] goodness (me)!, gracious alive!, oh my (eye)!, F lor' (, bless me)!

Herrlein (ᴗ⌣) *n* = Herrchen.

herrlich (ᴗ⌣) [mhd.] *a.* magnificent; (köstlich) delicious; (reizend) delightful, glorious, charming; (glänzend) brilliant, splendid; (vortrefflich) excellent, exquisite; (prunkvoll) sumptuous, grand; (lustig) capital, F jolly; 2es Denkmal noble monument; 2er Einfall brilliant idea; 2er Spaß fine (or capital) fun; 2e Tage glorious days *pl.*

Herrlichkeit (ᴗ⌣) [mhd.] *f* 1. (s. herrlich) magnificence; brilliancy, splendour; grandeur; (Glanz) (shining) lustre; die ~ Gottes the glory (or majesty) of God. — 2. (et. Herrliches) *s.*th. magnificent or delightful; (Wonne) delight; F das ist die ganze ~! that is all!, P that's the (blessed) lot!; die ~ (Freude) wird nicht lange dauern F it won't last long; bald war es mit seiner ~ zu Ende soon his glory (or pleasure, joy) came to an end. — 3. (Oberherrschaft) sovereignty; suzerainty; (Gerichtsbarkeit) jurisdiction. — 4. Titel: Ew. (Euer) ~ Your (Serene) Highness.

Herrnhuter (ᴗ⌣ᴗ) [Herrnhut, Stammsitz h. v. Graf. Zinzendorf († 1760) i. b. sächs. Oberlausitz gegründeten Brüdergemein(d)e] *m* , ~in *f* Herrnhuter, Moravian; in *Engl.*: one of the Plymouth Brethren.

her-rollen (″...) *v/a.* to roll this way or down here.

Herrschaft (ᴗ⌣) [ahd.] *f* 1. dominion, sway, mastery, persönliche: rule, unbestrittene: empire; (Regierung) government, eines Fürsten: reign; (Gewalt) power; auf sittliche Kräfte gestützt: authority; (höchste Macht) supreme command or control, im Staate: sovereignty; die ~ führen über // to rule (or govern) //, to exercise full authority over //; die ~ zur See haben to have command of the sea; unter seine ~ bringen to bring under one's rule or dominion or control, to subdue. — 2. *coll.* (herrschende Personen) master and mistress; weitS. employers *pl.*; er (sie) hat eine gute ~ ... a good master or mistress; die ~, bei der ich diene oder bin, jetzt oft: the family (or the people) with whom I live or am; meine ~en! ladies and gentlemen!; hohe ~en people of high rank, illustrious persons *pl.*; fürstliche ~en princely personages *pl.*; königliche ~en Royalties *pl.*, Royalty *sg.* — 3. (Länderei) domain, (Gebiet) dominion, territory; (Grund-) (manorial) estate.

herrschaftlich (ᴗ⌣ᴗ) *a.* belonging to or referring to a master or lord or high personage; lordly (estate), territorial (rights); (grundherrlich) manorial; 2er Wagen (gentleman's or lady's) private carriage; 2e Wohnung elegant (or high-class, first-class, in Zeitungen auch: most eligible) family-residence.

Herrschafts-recht (ᴗ⌣ᴗ) *n* sovereign (or territorial) rights *pl.*; **=wohnung** *f* owner's mansion or residence.

Herrsch=(be)gier(de) (ᴗ⌣...) *f* lust of power; *vgl.* =sucht; **=(be)gierig** *a.* greedy of power; *vgl.* =süchtig.

herrschen (ᴗ⌣) [ahd.; *hehr* (P: *Herr*)] I *v/n.* (h.) 1. to rule, to be in power, to have supreme command, als Fürst: to reign, als Minister *2c.*: to govern. — 2. (vorwalten) to prevail, to predominate; (im Schwange sein) to be in vogue; es 2 dort schlimme Krankheiten *2c.*: ... are raging (or prevalent) there; es herrscht große Tätigkeit auf den Werften great activity is being displayed in the dockyards. — 3. örtlich = beherrschen 3. — 4. (herrisch gebieten) sprach, herrschte er, etwa: come, thundered he in a commanding tone. — II ~ *n* 5. = Herrschaft 1. — III 2d *p.p.* und *a.* 6. in den Bed. des *inf.*; z.B. die 2e Partei the ruling (or dominant) party.

Herrscher (ᴗ⌣) [ahd.] *m* , ~in *f* (s. herrschen) ruler, sovereign, governor; (Fürst[in]) prince(ss); unumschränkter ~ absolute monarch, autocrat; zum ~ geboren born to rule or to be a ruler.

Herrscher=blick (ᴗ⌣...) *m* commanding glance; **=familie** *f* (reigning) dynasty; **=gabe** *f*, **=geist** *m* talent, spirit of a commander or ruler; **=geschlecht** *n* dynasty; **=gewalt** *f* sovereign power; **=haus** *n* = =familie; **=macht** *f* = =gewalt; **=miene** *f* commanding air; **=sitz** *m* residence of a sovereign; **=stab** *m* sceptre; **=stuhl** *m* throne; **=ton** *m* commanding tone; **=wille** *m* sovereign will; **=willkür** *f* despotism; **=wort** *n* word of command; **=würde** *f* sovereign rank; **=zeichen** *n/pl.* insignia *pl.* of sovereignty, emblems *pl.* of power.

Herrsch=geist (ᴗ⌣...) *m* , **=sucht** *f* craving for (or after) power, inordinate ambition; **=süchtig** *a.* striving after power, fond (or desirous) of ruling; very ambitious, overbearing, imperious.

her-rücken (″...) *v/a. u. v/n.* (in) to move this way, to draw near; **2rufen** *v/a.* to call (up) here; **2rühren** *v/n.* (h.) : a) to proceed (or arise, originate, result) from; b) von et. 2 (verursacht sein) to be due (or owing, attributable) to); von den Voreltern 2d ancestral; *bsd.* aus Deutschland 2d of German origin or make, oft F *u. co.* made in Germany, Germanmade; **2sagen** *v/a.* Auswendiggelerntes: to recite a poem, to say one's lesson, to repeat a prayer, to tell one's beads; *vgl.* 2beten u. 2plappern; er kann es am Schnürchen 2 he knows it by rote, he has it at his fingers' ends; wieder 2 to say over again; ~ *n* recitation; **2schaffen** *v/a.* to convey here (auch), to bring (or take, carry) to the spot; wo wird er die Mittel 2? where will he get the means from?; **2schauen** *v/n.* (h.) to look this way; **sich 2scheren** F *v/refl.* to come here, F to toddle this way; **2schicken** *v/a.* to send here; **2schieben** *v/a.* 2c to push this way; **2schießen** 2(e)ß *v/a., a. v/n.* (h.) to shoot this way; *v/n.* (in) (auch: 2geschossen kommen) to come rushing along; **2schleichen** *v/a.* (in) aft to sneak this way, to come creeping along; hinter e-m 2 to sneak (or slink) at the back of a p., to dog a p.'s footsteps; **2schleppen** *v/a.* to drag here; **2schreiben** *v/a.*: a) er hat 2geschrieben he has written to us; b) s-n Namen 2 to affix one's signature; sich 2 *v/refl.* = 2rühren; **2sehen** *v/n.* (h.) to look this way; **sich 2sehnen** *v/refl.* to long to come here; **2sein** *v/n.* a f. her 3, 5, 7; **2senden** *v/a.* to send here; **2setzen** *v/a. u. sich 2 v/refl.* to seat (o.s.) here, to place (o.s.) near; **2singen** *v/a.* it to sing off (by rote), to recite (in a mechanical way); **2sollen** *v/n.* (h.) : er soll her(kommen) he is to come here; **2springen** *v/n.* (in) it to leap this way; 2gesprungen kommen to come jumping along; **2stammeln** *v/a.* to stutter (or stammer) forth; **=stammen** *v/n.* (h.) to descend (or come) from a good stock, &c.; to date from a former period; *gr. v.* Wörtern: to be derived from; **=stammung** *f* descent, origin, *gr.* derivation; **2stellbar** *a.* (s. 2stellen): a) feasible; b) (wieder) 2 mendable, *med.* curable; **2stellen** *v/a.* : a) to place here or near; b) (wieder) 2 to restore, *med. a.* to cure; Beschädigtes: to mend, to repair, F to put to rights; Abgeschafftes: to re-establish; (wieder neu m.) to renew, renovate; c) (machen) to make, manufacture, (hervorbringen) to produce; **=steller**(in *f*) *m* restorer; maker, producer; **=stellung** *f* restoration, repair(ing); re-establishment; renovation; manufacture, production; ~ von Tuch cloth-manufacture; **=stellungs-arbeiten** *f/pl.* restorative work *sg.*; **=stellungs-kosten** *pl.* cost of production, prime-cost; **2stottern** *v/a.* = 2stammeln; **2strecken** *v/a.* to pass on; **2strömen** *v/n.* (in) to stream towards us; **2stürzen** *v/n.* (h.) to rush (headlong) our way; sich 2 *v/refl.*: sich über e-n, et. 2 to rush (or fall) upon a p., a th.; **2tragen** *v/a.* b to carry hither, to bring here or to us; **2treiben** *v/a.* ** to drive this way; vor sich 2 to

[hertreten] — 510 — [herumspazieren]

chase before one; ˢtreten v/n. (ſn) ⓢd** to step this way.

her-über (⌣⌣) adv. over (here), across this way or my way or to our side; ˢ! come over (or across) here!; ˢ und hinüber this way and that, hither and thither.

her-über-...(⌣⌣⌣...) in Verbindung mit verbs, immer trennbar (**), eine Annäherung an den Sprechenden über et. hinweg bezeichnend, oft: over here, across to(wards) me or us, across this way; ſich ˢbemühen v/refl. ⓢ*/* to take the trouble (or to trouble o.s.) to come over here; ˢbringen v/a. ⓜ** to bring across to(wards) me or us; ˢgeben v/a. ⓢc** to hand over (here); ˢhelfen v/n. (h.) ⓜb**: e-m ˢ to help a p. to come over here; ˢholen v/a. ⓢ** to fetch over; ˢreichen ⓢ** v/a. = ˢgeben; v/n. (ſn) to extend over here or across this way.

her-um (⌣⌣) adv. 1. um et. ˢ (a)round a th., z.B. um den Tiſch ˢſitzen to sit round the table; rund (ob. rings) ˢ round about; er wohnt gleich um die Ecke ˢ he lives just round the corner; die Reihe ˢ (each one) in turn; fig. fortwährend um e-n ˢ ſein to be constantly about (or in attendance on) a p.; mit Orts-adverbien: dort ˢ, hier ˢ thereabout(s), hereabout(s); rund ˢ, rings ˢ round about, all around. — 2. (um die eigene Achſe) turning (or spinning) round. — 3. (bald hier, bald da) here and there, everywhere, anywhere; das Gerücht iſt ſchon in der ganzen Stadt ˢ ... has spread all over the town. — 4. bei Zahlangaben: (ungefähr) so um hundert Mark ˢ about (or F somewhere near) five pounds.

her-um-..., Her-um-... (⌣⌣...) in Verbindung mit verbs, immer trennbar (**), und in Zſſgn mit verbal nouns und adjectives, a) eine Bewegung wie im Kreisbogen oder um die eigene Achſe bezeichnend, oft: (a)round, about nach dem v.; b) fig. Überrebung bezeichnend, oft: over nach dem v.; c) ein zielloſes Irren oder verworrenes Durcheinander andeutend, oft: about, here and there, from place to place, bettelnd auch: from door to door; in all directions, all (a)round, all over, anywhere, anyhow nach dem v.; ſich ˢbalgen v/refl. ⓢ** to (have a) romp or scuffle; ſich ˢbeißen v/refl. u. v/recip. ⓜa** to bite one another; ſie beißen ſich ewig ˢ they are for ever bickering and biting; ˢbekommen v/a. ⓢ*/*: a) to get round; b) to talk over; ˢbetteln v/n. (h.) ⓜa** to go about begging; ˢbringen v/a. ⓜ**: a) to turn (or get) round; b) e-n ˢ (zur eigenen Anſicht) to bring (or win) over (to one's own opinion); (verführen) to seduce, to tempt away; c) Nachrichten ꝛc. ˢ to spread (or circulate) news, &c.; ˢdrehen v/a. u. ſich ˢ v/refl. ⓢ** to turn round (about); ſich ſchnell ˢ to twirl (or spin) round; alles dreht ſich mit mir herum everything is swimming before my eyes, mehr gebr.: my head swims, I feel giddy; fig. er dreht mir die Worte im Munde herum he misconstrues (or twists and turns) every word I say; ſich ˢdrücken F v/refl. ⓢ** to crouch first in one corner, then in another; to sneak (or slink) from place to place; ˢfahren ⓢb** v/n. (ſn): a) um die Stadt ˢ to drive (or cycle, motor) round the town; ⚓ um ein Kap ˢ to (sail) round ..., to double ...; b) um die Ecke ˢ to drive round (or to turn) the corner; c) to drive (or cycle, motor) about here and there; to take a (carriage-)drive or a turn on one's cycle; d) mit den Händen ˢ to gesticulate; v/a. e-n ˢ to drive a p. about, to take a p. for carriage-drives; ˢfechten v/n. (h.) ⓜb** to beg from door to door; ˢfliegen v n. (ſn) ⓜa**: a) to fly about; b) um die Ecke ˢ to fly round the corner; ˢführen v/a. ⓢ**: a) e-n um die Stadt ˢ to take a p. round the town; einen Blinden um die Ecke ˢ to lead (or conduct) a blind man round the corner; b) einen Graben um den Garten ˢ to make a ditch round the garden; c) e-n in der Stadt ˢ (um ihm das Merkwürdige zu zeigen) to show a p. round (or over) the town; d) F e-n bei der Naſe ˢ to lead a p. by the nose; to dupe (or cheat) a p.; ˢgeben v/a. ⓢc** to hand round or about, to circulate; Kartenſpiel: (noch einmal) ˢ to deal round (once more), to have one (more) round; ˢgeh(e)n v/n. (ſn) ⓜ**: a) um die Stadt, Kirche ꝛc. ˢ to walk round ...; fig. e-m um den Bart ˢ to wheedle round a p.; ✕ von der Wache: to make (or go) the round; b) fig. eine Mauer geht um die Stadt herum ... encloses (or encircles, runs round) the town; das Band geht zweimal um den Hut herum the band goes twice round the hat; ein Gericht ꝛc. ˢ l. to hand a dish, &c. round; fig. um den Brei ˢ to beat about the bush; c) = (ſich) ˢdrehen; fig. tauſend Dinge gehen mir im Kopfe herum ... are revolving in my mind; d) das Gerücht geht herum a report is (spreading) about; ſich ˢhauen v/recip. ⓢc** to have a free fight (mit e-m with a p.); ˢholen v/a. ⓢ** aus dem Nachbarhauſe: to fetch (over) from next door; ˢhorchen v/n. (h.) ⓢ**: überall ˢ to go about listening or eavesdropping; ˢirren v/n. (ſn) ⓢ** to wander (or stray) about; ˢd p.pr. vagrant, homeless, stray; ˢkommen v/n. (ſn) ⓢ**: a) um die Ecke ˢ to turn (round) the corner; b) aus dem Nachbarhauſe: to come round or over; c) (reiſen) ˢ to go much about; er iſt weit ˢ gekommen he has seen a great deal (of the world); d) fig. bei den Leuten ˢ to be the talk of the town; von Gerüchten: to (be) spread about, to get wind; ˢkriechen F v/n. (ſn) ⓜdſt** to creep about or around; in allen Winkeln ˢ to furrage about in (or to pry into) every corner; ˢkriegen F v/a. ⓢ** = ˢbringen b; ˢlangen ⓢ** v/n. (h.): das Band langt nicht um den Hut herum the band does not go once round the hat; v/a. et. ˢ to hand a th. round; ˢlaufen v/n. (ſn) ⓜaſt**: a) um et. ˢ to run round a th.; das Rad läuft herum ... is turning (or spinning) round; b) um die Ecke ˢ to run round the corner; c) der Nachbar kam ˢgelaufen ... came running round (to me); d) (ziellos laufen) to run (or roam, ramble) about; müßig ˢ to loaf (or loiter, lounge, F mooch) about; ˢliegen v/n. (h.) ⓢ**: a) um et. ˢ to lie round a th., (es umgeben) to encircle a th.; b) (zerſtreut liegen) to lie (scattered) about; die Soldaten liegen in den Dörfern herum ... are scattered over (or about) the villages; die um den Dom ˢden Straßen the streets in the surroundings (or neighbourhood) of the cathedral; alles (unordentlich) ˢ laſſen to leave everything about; ſich ˢprügeln v/recip. ⓜa** to knock each other about; to have a scuffle or free fight (all round); ˢreichen v/n. (h.) u. v/a. ⓢ** to hand round; ˢreiſen v/n. (h.) ⓜ**: a) um die Erde ˢ to travel round the world, v. Seefahrern: to circumnavigate the globe; b) to travel about, to go touring, F to knock about; in einem Lande ˢ to travel about (or all over) a country; ~ n travelling (about), touring; ˢreiten v/n. (ſn) ⓢb**: a) um et. ˢ to ride round a th.; b) to ride about, to go (horse-)riding, to travel about on horseback; in einem Walde ˢ to ride about (or all over) a wood; c) F fig. auf et. ˢ (es immer im Munde führen) to be for ever harping on a th.; auf e-m ˢ (e-n fortgeſetzt quälen) to be for ever tormenting (F sitting on) a p.; ~ n ⓐ travelling (about) on horseback; ˢſchauen v/n. (h.) ⓢ** = ˢſehen; ˢſchicken v/a. ⓢ**: a) et. ˢ to send a th. round or about; b) e-n ˢ to send a p. (out) on errands or commissions; ˢſchiffen ⚓ v/n. (ſn) ⓢ**: a) um ein Kap ꝛc. ˢ to sail round (or to double) a cape, &c.; b) to sail about; ziellos: to box the compass; ˢſchlagen ⓢb** v/a. to wrap round; ſich ˢ v/recip. = ſich ˢprügeln; ˢſchlendern v/n. (ſn) ⓜa** to stroll (or saunter) about, F to knock about the street(s); ˢſchleppen v/a. ⓢ** to drag (or trail) about; ˢſchnüffeln, ˢſchnuppern v/n. (h.) ⓜa** to go sniffing about, fig. to thrust (or poke) one's nose into (other) people's affairs; ˢſchweifen v/n. (ſn) ⓢ** to wander about, to rove (freely), b.s. to prowl about; er läßt ſeine Gedanken ˢ he lets his thoughts roam freely, his mind is wandering; ˢſchwenken v/n. (ſn) und ſich ˢ v/refl. ⓢ** to wheel (or swing) round; ˢſehen v/n. (h.) ⓜa**: a) to look (or glance) round or back; b) to look about (one); ˢſein v/n. ⓜa**: a) ell. to have completed a turn; um die Ecke ˢ to have turned the corner; b) er iſt weit in der Welt ˢgeweſen he has travelled (or F knocked) about a great deal; c) um einen ˢ to be (busy) about a p.; d) von der Zeit: to have elapsed; die Stunde iſt (ſchon) herum the hour has slipped away; ˢſpazieren ⓢ*/* v/n. (ſn) to walk (leisurely) about; müßig ˢ to stroll

Signs (see page XVII): F familiar; P vulgar; ꟼ flash; ⸲ rare; † obsolete (died); * new word (born); ᛭ incorrect; ♪ music;

[herumspringen] — 511 — [hervorheben]

about; ~ n ⓘ easy (or leisurely) walking or strolling; ⚬springen v/n. (ſn) ⓐſt**: a) to skip (or leap) about, mutwillig: to frolic about; b) schnell zu Nachbarn ⚬ to run round to one's neighbours; c) der Wind springt herum ... is shifting (or veering, chopping) round; ⚬ſtch(e)n v/n. (h.) ⓐ**: a) to stand around a th.; b) to stand about idly (auch von Menschen); ⚬ſtöbern v/n. (h.) ⓐa** to furrage (or poke, rummage) about in a th., ⚬ſtören v/n. (h.) ⓑ** = ⚬ſtöbern; ⚬ſtreichen ⓐaſt** v/a.: Öl um et. ⚬ to oil a th. all round; v/n. (ſn) to ramble (or loaf, F gad) about; vgl. ⚬ſchweifen; ⓑ d p. pr. roaming, roving, vagrant, on the tramp; =ſtreicher(in f ㊷) m ㉒ loafer, F gad-about; tramp; ⚬ſtreifen v/n. (ſn) ⓑ** to tramp about; ſich ⚬ſtreiten v/recip. ⓑb** to wrangle (or quarrel) persistently; ~ n ⓘ (persistent) wrangling; altercation; ⚬ſuchen v/n. (h.) ⓑ** to seek all around, to search in all directions; ⚬tappen v/n. (ſn) ⓑ** to grope (or F fumble) about; ⚬tragen v/a. ⓑb**: a) to carry round; b) to carry about (the neighbourhood); Nachrichten: to spread (or retail) about (the town), Waren: to hawk about; c) fig. et. im Kopfe ⚬ to carry about (or harbour) in one's mind; ſ-n Kummer mit ſich ⚬ to nurse one's grief; ~ n ⓘ hawking (about); ⚬treiben ⓐ** v/a. to drive cattle round a corner; v/n. (h.) auf dem Waſſer ⚬ to float about the water; ſich ⚬ v/refl. to loaf (or F gad, knock) about; ſich betteln ⚬ to go about begging; =treiber(in f ㊷) m ㉒ = =ſtreicher(in); ⚬trinken v/n. (h.) ⓐſt** to have a drink round, to pass the cup (or bottle) round; ⚬tummeln ⓐa** v/a. man. ein Pferd ⚬ to exercise (or work) a horse well; fig. ſeine Leute ⚬ to drive one's people; ſich ⚬ v/refl. to take good exercise, to bustle about; ⚬wandern v/n. (ſn) ⓐa** to wander about, to lead a roving life; ⚬werfen ⓐb** v/a. to throw about, F v/n. (h.) im Reden mit etwas ⚬ (ſich brüſten), etwa: to make great boast of a th.; ſich ⚬ v/refl. to turn sharply round; ⚬wühlen v/n. (h.) ⓑ** to wallow about in a th.; vgl. ⚬ſtöbern; ſich ⚬zanken v/recip. ⓑ** to squabble (with one another); ⚬zauſen ⓐ***, ⚬zerren ⓐ** v/a. (u. ſich ⚬ v/recip.) to haul (each other) about, to pull (each other) about; ⚬ziehen ⓑb** v/a.: a) to draw (or pull) round a th., einen Graben um ein Feld ⚬ to cut (or dig) a ditch round ...; b) fig. e-n mit ſchönen Verſprechungen ⚬ to put a p. off with fair promises; v/n. (ſn): a) to wander about; um die Stadt ⚬ to march round (or about) the town; b) er iſt zu mir ⚬gezogen he has moved near me or round to me; c) oft die Wohnung wechſeln) to chop and change about; ~ n ⓘ frequent removal; nomadic habits pl., vagrant life, vagrancy; ⓑ d p.pr. u. a. strolling (player), itinerant (vendor), nomadic (tribe), wandering (gipsy).

her-unter (⏑⏑) adv. (ant. herauf) 1. meiſt = herab. — 2. mit Ortsadverbien, z.B.: da ⚬, hier ⚬ down there, down (here); gerade ⚬ straight (ſenkrecht: vertically) down; von oben ⚬ down from on high, from above; ell. ⚬ (mſt F runter)! down!; die Hüte ⚬! hats off!; ⚬ mit ihm! down with him!, pull him down! — 3. fig. er iſt an Kräften, Vermögen ꝛc. ⚬ he is (low) down (in the world) or reduced to a low ebb, F he's on his last legs.

her-unter=..., Her-unter=... (⏑⏑...) in Verbindung mit verbs, immer trennbar (**), und in Zſſgn mit verbal nouns und adjectives: ⚬fallen v/n. (ſn) ⓐ** to fall (or tumble) down; ⚬geh(e)n v/n. (ſn) ⓐ** = herabgehen; ⚬ mit dem Preiſe ⚬ to reduce (or abate) one's price, F to come down with one's price; ⚬gießen v/a. ⓑd** to pour down; F ein Glas Wein ⚬, auch: to gulp down, to drink at one draught; ⚬handeln v/a. ⓐa**: etwas vom Preiſe ⚬ F to knock s.th. off the price by bargaining; ⚬hauen v/a. ⓑc** to hew down; e-m eins ⚬ to give a p. a whipping or a good box on the ear; ⚬klappen v/a. ⓑ**: ſeinen Rockkragen ⚬ to turn down the collar of one's coat; einen Tiſch: to let down (the leaves of) a table; ⚬kommen v/n. (ſn) ⓐ**: a) to come (or go) down; b) to decline, decay, sink, fall off; von Perſonen: ⚬gekommen ſein to be (low) down (in the world) or in reduced circumstances or ruined; ⚬laſſen v/a. ⓑa** to let down; ⚬ ich kann nichts vom Preiſe ⚬ I cannot take anything off (the price) or make any reduction or go down any lower; thea. den Vorhang ⚬ to drop (or let down) ...; ⚬leiern v/a. ⓐa** to rattle off, to gabble; ⚬machen v/a. ⓑ**: a) to lower, den Kragen: to turn down; b) fig. e-n ⚬ (ſchelten) to reprimand (or scold, F blow up) a p.; c) ein Werk: to depreciate, F to run down, cut up, slate; ⚬nehmen v/a. ⓐa** to take down from a shelf, the wall, &c.; von e-m Haken auch: to unhook; ⚬purzeln F v/n. (ſn) ⓐa**: die Treppe ⚬ to tumble down the stairs or downstairs; ⚬reißen v/a. ⓑa**: ein Haus: to pull (or take) down; fig. (a. ſich, ea. ⚬ v/recip.) F to pick holes in (each other), to pull (one another) to pieces; ⚬ſchlagen v/a. ⓑb**: a) Apfel ꝛc. ⚬ to knock down ...; b) die Klappe des Wagens ⚬ to let down the carriage-top; ⚬ſchrauben v/a. ⓑc**: die Lampe ⚬ to turn down ...; ⚬ſetzen v/a. ⓑ** = herabſetzen; ⚬werfen v/a. ⓑb** to throw (or cast) down (here); ⚬ziehen ⓑb** v/a. to draw (or drag) down; v/n. (ſn): a) to come (or march) down; b) to move lower down. — vgl. herab=...

her-verſetzen (⸗⏑...) v/a. ⓐ**/**: von Beamten ꝛc. to transfer (to our town, &c.); ſich im Geiſte ⚬ mentally to transpose o.s. (to this place).

her-vor (⏑⸗) adv. forth, forward; aus et. ⚬ out of a th.; ⚬ mit euch! come out!, come to the front!, show yourselves!; hinter dem Baume ⚬ from behind the tree; unter dem Schrank ⚬ from under (or beneath) the cupboard.

hervor=..., Hervor=... (⏑⸗...) in Verbindung mit verbs, immer trennbar (**), u. in Zſſgn mit verbal nouns und adjectives, das Heraustreten aus einem inneren Raume bezeichnend, oft: forth, forward, up; to the surface, to light, to the world, to the front; out of, from behind, from below nach dem v.; pro..., de..., e(x)... (als Präfixe) vor dem v.: ⚬arbeiten ⓐ** v/a. to bring (or get) to the surface, aus der Erde auch: to unearth; (freimachen) to (set) free; (ans Licht fördern) to bring to light; ſich ⚬ v/refl. to work one's way out, to extricate o.s., to disengage o.s.; fig. (emporkommen) to work one's way up, to get on (in the world); ⚬blicken v/n. (h.) ⓑ**: a) hinter e-m Baume ꝛc. ⚬ to look (or peep) from behind a tree, &c.; b) (ſich zeigen) to appear; to peep through; ⚬brechen v/n. (ſn) ⓑa** to break (or burst) forth; die Sonne bricht aus dem Gewölke hervor ... is breaking through (or piercing) the clouds; ✕ aus einem Hinterhalte: to sally (or rush) forth (from an ambush); aus e-m Hohlwege: to debouch; ⚬bringen v/a. ⓐ**: a) aus einem Verſteck: to bring forward; (vorzeigen) to show (forth), to produce; b) (ins Daſein rufen) to bring forth, to produce, (erzeugen) to engender, to generate, (ſchaffen) to create; (zur Welt bringen) to bring to the world, to give life to; (bewirken) to effect; wieder ⚬ to reproduce; einen Eindruck ⚬ to make an impression; Früchte ⚬ to bear fruit; nichts ⚬d unproductive; c) er konnte kein Wort ⚬ (herausbringen) he could not utter a word, he stood dumbfounded; ~ n ⓘ u. =bringung f ㊻ production; engenderment, generation, creation; ⚬drängen ⓑ** v/a. to press (or urge) forward; ſich ⚬ v/refl. to force one's way to the front, to make o.s. conspicuous, to obtrude o.s. (on public attention); ⚬dringen v/n. (ſn) ⓐſt**: a) to break forth or through; b) von Flüſſigkeiten: to gush (or rush) forth, to spring up, to ooze out; ⚬geh(e)n v/n. (ſn) ⓐ**: a) to go forth, (ſich erheben) to (a)rise from; b) (entſpringen) to issue (or emerge, spring from; (herrühren) to proceed from, c) aus et. ⚬ (ſich folgern) to result (or follow) from a th.; daraus geht hervor, daß // hence it follows (or may be concluded) that //; d) als Sieger aus einer Sache ⚬ to come off victorious(ly) or (as) victor or with flying colours; ⚬heben ⓑ(ⓕ)b** v/a.: a) to raise (above the surface); b) fig. (bemerkbar m.) to render conspicuous, to bring into prominence, typ. durch den Druck: to display; ein Kleid, welches die Geſtalt ⚬hebt ... which sets (or shows) off the figure (well); ein Wort ⚬ to emphasize (or to lay stress upon) a word; c) ⊕ arch., Bildhauerei ꝛc.: to give relief to; paint., &c.: die Züge ⚬ to mark (out) the features; ſich ⚬ v/refl.: a) to rise (above the surface);

㊼ scientific; ⚘ botanical; ♀ geography; ⊕ machinery; ⚒ mining; ⚔ military; ⚓ marine; ⚫ commercial; ✉ postal; 🜞 railway.

[hervorholen] — 512 — [Herzbeutelentzündung]

b) *fig.* to be(come) conspicuous or prominent; *paint.* sich von dem Hintergrunde 2 to stand out in bold relief; 2holen *v/a.* ⑱** to fetch forth or out; 2keimen *v/n.* (ſn) ⑱** to germ(-inate), to sprout forth; 2kommen *v/n.* (ſn) ⑭** to come forth or forward or to the front; to appear (on the scene); (entstehen) to arise; 2kriechen *v/n.* (ſn) ⑭d ſt** to crawl forth; 2leuchten *v/n.* (h.) ⑱**: a) to shine 'orth or through; b) (ſich auszeichnen) to distinguish o.s., to show brilliant abilities or qualities; c) *v/impers.* es leuchtet (geht) hieraus hervor, daß // this makes it obvious (or clear, evident) that //; 2locken *v/a.* ⑱** to entice (forth), to elicit; ſich 2machen *v/refl.* ⑱** to make one's way (or to skulk) out of a hiding-place, &c., to show o.s.; 2quellen *v/n.* (ſn) ⑭b** to well (or spring) forth; vgl. 2dringen b; 2ragen *v/n.* (h.) ⑱**: a) to jut out, to project, to be prominent, to stand forth or out; über alle(n) 2 to tower above the rest; b) *fig.* to excel (F to top) everybody (else); 2d *p.pr. u. a.* ⑭ salient, projecting, prominent; *fig.* eminent, remarkable, distinguished, conspicuous; ein 2der Kopf a master-mind; 2de Persönlichkeiten notabilities *pl.*; ~ *n* ㉓ *fig.* (pre-)eminence; =ragung *f* ㊻ projection, prominence, *ast.* an der Sonne: solar protuberance; 2rücken ⑱** *v/a.*: den Tiſch ꝛc. 2 to move ... forward; *v/n.* (ſn) to march forward; ⚔ aus einem Engpaſſe ꝛc.: to debouch; 2rufen ⑱b** *v/a.*: a) to call forth, *thea.* einen Schauspieler ꝛc.: to call (for), to encore; b) *fig.* (entstehen m.) to call forth or into existence or into being; to evoke; *phot.* ein Bild: to develop; (bewirken) to bring about, to occasion; Bewunderung 2 to excite admiration; Schweiß 2d sudorific; ~ *n* ㉓ *thea.* call, encore; *phot.* development; 2schauen *v/n.* (h.) ⑱** to look (or peep) out; 2schleichen *v/n.* (ſn) ⑭aſt** to sneak (or come stealing) out of a th.; 2sehen *v/n.* (h.) ⑭a** to glance from behind (or out of) a th.; 2spießen *v/n.* (ſn) ⑭d** = 2keimen; 2springen ⑭ſt** *v/n.* (ſn): a) to leap forward; b) to jut out, to project; 2d *a.* prominent, salient; 2sprossen *v/n.* (ſn) ⑭** = 2keimen; 2sprudeln *v/n.* ⑭a** to bubble forth; 2stammeln *v/a.* ⑭a** to stammer out; 2stechen ⑭a** *v/n.* (h.): to prick (or sting) from beneath or behind; b) to stand forth; 2d *p.pr. u. a.* ⑭ salient, prominent, *fig. a.* conspicuous, striking, von Farben: glaring, F loud; 2steh(e)n *v/a.* ⑭** to stand out (in bold relief); 2stürzen *v/n.* (ſn) ⑭** to rush forward; 2suchen *v/a.* ⑱** to seek (or pick) out; alte Geschichten 2 to rake up old stories; 2tauchen *v/n.* (ſn) ⑱** to emerge from (or to come out of) the water; *fig.* (ſich Bahn brechen) to come to the surface; 2treten *v/n.* (ſn) ⑭d**: a) to step forth or forward; b) *fig.* (ſich abheben) to stand out in bold relief; 2 lassen to throw into relief,

to give prominence to; ſich 2tun *v/refl.* ⑮**: a) (zum Vorſcheine kommen) to come on the scene; b) (ſich auszeichnen) to distinguish o.s.; (emporkommen) to make one's way; 2wachsen *v/n.* (ſn) ⑮b** to grow (or shoot, come) up; aus der Erde 2 to grow out of the ground; (einen Auswuchs bilden) to form a growth or a protuberance; ſich 2wagen *v/refl.* ⑱** to venture forth; 2zaubern *v/a.* ⑱** to conjure up, to produce by magic; 2ziehen *v/a.* ⑭b** to draw forth; aus der Tasche 2 to pull out of one's pocket; *anat.* 2der Muskel ⚚ protractor. — Vgl. *a.* die Zſſgn mit vor-...

her=wagen (ſich) (ꞌ...) *v/refl.* ⑱** to venture to come here or near; 2wärts *adv.* hitherward, this way; =weg *m* ⒟. way here, return (route); auf dem ~e in coming here; 2winken *v/a.* ⑱** to beckon here or hither; 2wünschen *v/a.* ⑪** to wish (to come) here.

Herz (²) [ahd.: heart: lt. *cord*-, grch. *kard*-] *n* ㊲ 1. heart (auch *fig.*); ein gutes ~ haben to have a good heart, to be good-hearted or -natured; ein hartes ~ haben to be hard-hearted; e-m ſein ~ ausſchütten to unburden one's heart (or mind) to a p.; das ~ blutete ihm his heart bled; dies brach ihm das ~ it broke his heart; ihm klopfte das ~, als // he felt his heart beating when //; es tat m-m ~en wohl it did my heart good; mit *prp.*: der Kummer frißt an ſeinem ~en grief is gnawing at (or eating out) his heart; e-n aus ~ drücken to press a p. to one's heart or bosom; die Hand aufs ~ legen to lay one's hand on one's heart; aus tiefſtem ~en from the depth (or bottom) of one's heart; in des ~ens Grunde in one's inmost heart; das war ihm ein Stich ins ~ it cut him to the heart or to the quick; e-n ins ~ ſchließen to have a great affection for a p., F to keep a warm place in one's heart for a p.; mit klopfendem ~en with a throbbing heart; mit schwerem ~en with a heavy (or full) heart; mit dem ~en in der Hand (right) from one's heart; mit ~ und Hand für et. sein to be heart and soul for a th.; mit ~ und Mund with heart and mouth, earnestly, sincerely; ohne ~ heartless; ich kann es nicht über das ~ bringen I have not the (or no) heart to do it, auch: I cannot prevail upon (or bring) myself to do it; ich tue es von ~en gern ... with all my heart, willingly; von ganzem ~en heartily; von ~en kommen to come straight from the heart; zu ~en geh(e)n to go to the heart; ſich (*dat.*) et. zu ~en geh(e)n laſſen, zu ~en nehmen to take a th. to heart; Sprichw. er hat das ~ auf dem rechten Flecke he has his heart in the right place; das ~ auf der Zunge h. to wear one's heart upon one's sleeve; wes das ~ voll ist, des geht der Mund über (*bibl.*) out of the abundance of the heart (kürzer: what the heart thinketh) the mouth speaketh. — 2. (Busen)

bosom; *fig.* (Gemüt, Geist) mind; (Mut) courage, pluck; **a)** Redensarten mit *prp.*: der Knabe ist ihr ans ~ gewachsen ... has endeared himself to her, ... is the apple of her eye; e-m aus ~ legen to urge (or press) a th. on a p.('s attention); to recommend warmly to a p.; das liegt mir am ~en that is nearest to my heart; *fig. auch:* I have it at heart; ſich das ~ aus dem Leibe ärgern to die with vexation; es tut mir im ~en (a. von ~) leid I feel deeply grieved about it; ſich in ſein ~ hinein ſchämen to feel thoroughly ashamed (of o.s.); ein Mann nach meinem ~en a man after my own heart or to my liking; nach ~ens Luſt to one's heart's content; es wird mir leichter ums ~ I feel easier in my mind; ſprechen, wie('s) einem ums ~ iſt to speak as the heart bids one, to speak one's mind (freely); wie iſt dir ums ~? how do you feel?; ein Kind unter dem ~en tragen to be with child or F in the family-way; es ist mir ein Stein vom ~en gefallen a weight has been taken off my mind; ich will es vom ~en haben I want to have it off my mind; e-m von ~en gut ſein to be fondly attached to (or very fond of) a p.; **b)** andere Redensarten: ~, was begehrſt du? dear heart, what do you wish for?; da iſt mir das ~ in die Hoſen gefallen then my heart dropped (or sank) into my boots, mehr gbr.: my heart was in my mouth; ſich (*dat.*) ein ~ faſſen to summon (F to pluck) up courage, geh. Spr.: to take heart of grace; ich kann kein ~ (Vertrauen) zu ihm faſſen I feel no confidence in him; ich habe nicht das ~ zu tun I have not the heart to do it, ſ. hängen 3; ſ-m ~en Luft machen to unburden one's heart or mind; ſolange mir das ~ im Leibe ſchlägt as long as I live; ſie iſt das Weib ſeines ~ens she is the wife of his bosom; ſie ſind e i n ~ und e i n e Seele ob. zwei ~en und e i n Schlag they are hand and glove together or bosom-friends. — 3. Kartenſpiel: ~ iſt Trumpf hearts *pl.* are trumps. — 4. ☉ ~ (innerster Teil) eines Maſtes heart (or centre) of a mast; ~ e-s Kabels, Taues, e-r Schnalle ꝛc.: core (auch ♀ vom Obſt). — 5. ♀ flammendes ~ bleeding-heart (*Dice'ntra specta'bilis*) — 6. 🂡 = ~ſtück. Herz=ader (³...) *f* ⚓ *anat.*: a) great artery; b) (Kranzader) cardiac blood-vessel.

her=zählen (ꞌ/...) *v/a.* ⑱** = 2rechnen; an den Fingern 2 to count by (or on) one's fingers; =zählung *f* enumeration. herz=allerliebſt F (◡◡◡‿) *a.* ⑯: a) dearly beloved; b) charming, F darling; ihr ~er ⑰ her beloved one, her sweetheart; =balſam (³...) *m* ⑫ *pharm.* cordial; =beben *n* palpitation of the heart; 2beklemmend *a.* making one's heart ache, wringing one's heart, distressing; =beklemmung *f* oppression of the heart; 2bekommen *a.* with a heavy (or an anxious) heart, sore at heart; =beſchreibung *f*: ⚚ cardiography; =beutel *m*, *anat.*: ⚚ pericardium; =beutel=entzündung *f*, *path.*: ⚚ peri-

Zeichen (ſ. S. XVII): F familiär; P Volkssprache; ℾ Gaunerſprache; ⦚ ſelten; † alt (auch geſtorben); * neu (auch geboren); ✠ unrichtig;

[Herzbeutelwassersucht] — 513 — [Hesekiel]

carditis; =beutel=wassersucht f: ⚓ hydrocardia; ⚕bewegend a. heart-stirring, (rührend) touching; =blatt n: a) ♀ grass of Parnassus (Parna'ssia palu'stris); (innerstes Blatt) central leaf or leaflet; b) Kartenspiel: a heart; c) F fig. (geliebte Person) darling, pet; =blättchen n = blatt a. u. c; =blut n heart's blood; fig. mein ~ (Leben) my (very) life; ⚕brechend a. heart-breaking.

Herzchen (♃~) n ㉓ (dim. von Herz) little heart, bisw.: heartlet; als Kosewort: love, darling, sweet one, F duckie.

Herz=dame (♃...) f ㉖ bsd. Kartenspiel: queen of hearts.

Herze ↘ (♃) n ㉗ s. Herz.

Herze=leid (♃...) n ①d. soreness of heart, bitter grief, deep affliction or sorrow; great trouble or worry or distress; e-m ein ~ antun to wound (stärker: to break) a p.'s heart; Sprichw. das schönste Kleid ist oft gefüttert mit ~ the finest dress often hides a heart's distress.

Herz(e)lein (♃(~) n ㉓ = Herzchen.

herzen (♃) v/a. ⑳ to press to one's heart, to fondle, embrace, caress, hug; sie 2 und küssen sich they are billing and cooing.

Herzens=adel (♃...) m ㉖ nobleness of heart; =angelegenheit f love-affair; amour, intrigue; =angst f great anxiety, anguish of heart; =bruder m beloved brother; bosom-friend, F great chum or pal; =dieb m vanquisher of hearts; =einfalt f simplicity (or singleness) of heart, simple-mindedness; =ergießung f, =erguß m outpouring of the heart, effusion, F contp. gush; =freude f joyfulness of h., heart's delight; =freund(in f) m bosom- (or beloved, intimate) friend; ⚕froh a. ⑯ rejoicing with(in) one's heart, exceedingly glad or pleased; =geheimnis n inmost secret; =glaube m inmost belief, true faith; ⚕gut a. kind- (or good-)hearted; er ist ein 2er Mensch he is a dear good fellow; =güte f kindness of heart, kind-heartedness; =härte, =härtigkeit f hard-heartedness, hardness of heart; =jammer m wretchedness of h.; =junge n, =kind n darling (or beloved) boy, child; dear good boy, child; =königin f lady-love; =kummer m deep-felt grief, great worry; =kündiger m, bibl. (Gott) Searcher of hearts; =lust f =freude; nach ~ (soviel man will) to one's heart's content; =mann m, =männchen n darling (F love of a) man; als Zärtlichkeitsausdruck für den Gatten: mein ~!, oft: dear (or darling) hubbie; =meinung f true (or real) opinion; =not f = =angst; =qual f anguish of mind, worry; =reinheit f purity of heart; =ruhe f calmness (or peace) of mind; =sache f = =angelegenheit; =sprache f language of the heart; =wunsch m heart's (or most ardent) desire, fondest wish.

herz=entzückend (♃...) a. ⑯ most delightful; =entzündung f ㉒ path. inflammation of the heart, ⚓ carditis.

herz=erfreuend (♃...) a. ⑯, ⚕erfreulich a. gladdening the heart, most cheering;

⚕ergreifend a. heart-moving, affecting (sight); ⚕erhebend a. elevating, edifying, poet. heart-expanding; ⚕erleichternd, ⚕erquickend a. easing, refreshing (to) one's mind or heart; ⚕erschütternd a. heart-rending, appalling; =erweiterung f ㉒: dilatation of the heart, ⚓ cardiectasis; =fehler m, path. defect (or weakness) of the h.; =fell n, anat. = =beutel; =fieber n, path. cardiac fever; =finger m, poet. ring-finger; =form f shape of a heart; ⚕förmig a. heart-shaped; ⚓ cordiform; ♀: ⚓ cordate(d); umgekehrt 2: ⚓ obcordate; =gegend f, anat. cardiac region; =geliebte(r) s. well-beloved one, darling; =geräusch n, physiol. cardiac sounds or murmurs pl.; =gespiel n sweetheart; ⚕gewinnend a. h.-winning, winning people's affections; =grube f, anat. pit of the stomach, ⚓ procardium.

herzhaft (♃) [mhd.] a. ⑯ 1. (mutig) stout-hearted, courageous, valiant, brave; (tek) bold, audacious. — 2. (entschieden) resolute, determined; (tüchtig) strenuous, vigorous; 2e Mahlzeit hearty meal; adv. 2 lachen to laugh heartily, to have a hearty laugh.

Herzhaftigkeit (♃~) f ㉖ (s. herzhaft) 1. stout-heartedness, courage(ousness), valour, bravery. — 2. resolution, resoluteness, determination; vigour; heartiness.

Herz=höhlung (♃...) f ㉒ anat. cavity of the heart, cardiac cavity.

her=ziehen (♃...) ⑥b** I v/a. to draw here, to pull this way. — II v/n.(h.): a) to come to live here; b) 2, hergezogen kommen to draw near(er), to come moving (or marching) along; c) fig. über einen, et. 2 (losziehen) to run a p. down. — III v/impers. es zieht von dort her there is a draught from over there.

herzig (♃~) a. ⑯ 1. = herzlich 1. — 2. lovable; (lieb und traut) dear(ly beloved); (allerliebst) charming, sweet, lovely. — 3. von Bäumen: (mit Kernholz) with a heart. — 4. in Zssgn, zB. hart2 hard-hearted.

herz=innig (♃...) a. ⑯ hearty, heart-felt, cordial; adv. from the bottom (or depth) of one's heart; =kammer f ㉒: ⚓ ventricle of the heart; =kirsche f white-heart(cherry), bigaroon; =klappe f valve of the heart ⚓ cardiac valve; =klappenfehler m, path.: ⚓ mitral disease; =klopfen n beating (or palpitation) of the heart; =kohl ♀ m = Wirsingkohl; =krank a. suffering from the h., fig. sick at h.; ⚕kränkend a. (deeply) mortifying, h.-grieving; =krankheit f h.-disease, ⚓ cardiopathy; =kränkung f (intense) mortification, sore grief; =lähmung f, path.: ⚓ paralysis of the heart; =leiden n heart-complaint.

herzlich (♃~) [mhd.] a. ⑯ 1. cordial; (innig empfunden) coming from the heart, heart-felt; (aufrichtig) sincere, true, loyal; adv. a. with all one's heart; ich lachte 2 darüber I laughed heartily at it; aufs. auf das 2ste most heartily, most cordially. — 2. (liebevoll) affectionate, loving; 2 (adv.) an j-s

Schmerz teilnehmen // truly to sympathize with a p., to show (or feel) sincere sympathy for a p.'s grief; er läßt Sie 2st, aufs 2ste grüßen he sends you his kindest regards or (vertraulich!) his best love. — 3. als adv. auch: (gehörig, sehr) exceedingly, extremely, very; ich tue es 2 gern ... with great pleasure; wir sind es 2 satt we are heartily (or thoroughly) sick of it; es ward mir 2 sauer it came uncommonly hard to me; 2 schlecht wretchedly (or thoroughly) bad.

Herzlichkeit (♃~) f ㉖ cordiality; heartiness; sincerity; (real) affection.

herz=lieb (♃...) a. ⑯ dearly(-)beloved, darling; =liebchen n ㉓, =liebste([r]m) f = Herzchen; ⚕los a.: a) zo. without a heart (auch fig.); ⚓ acardiac; b) fig. (ohne Gefühl) heartless, unfeeling, unsympathetic; =losigkeit f ㉖: a) zo.: ⚓ acardia; b) fig. heartlessness, unfeelingness, lack of sympathy; =muschel f, zo. cockle (Ca'rdium).

Herzog (♃~,-) [ahd. Heer u. zog: lt. dux] ⑪d, als Titel ⑭⑮, vor flektierten npr. oft inv., ~in f ㊴ duke, f duchess; in England höchster Adelstitel, zB. Duke (f Duchess) of Westminster, und Bezeichnung der jüngeren Söhne rc. (royal dukes) des Souveräns, zB. Duke (f Duchess) of Connaught.

herzoglich, als Titel: ~ (♃~, ♃~) a. ⑯ ducal, a duke's, of a duke, like a duke. [m ducal coronet, title.]

Herzogs=krone (♃~..., ♃~,) f ㉖, =titel

Herzogtum (♃--, ♃~) n ①d. (Gebiet) duchy; (Würde) dukedom; ~ Koburg duchy of Coburg.

Herz=ohr (♃...) n ㉒ anat.: ⚓ auricle of the heart; =pochen n = =klopfen; =sack m = =beutel; =schlächtig(keit f) a., vet. broken-winded(ness); =schlag m: a) palpitation (or throbbing) of the heart; bis zu meinem letzten ~e to the last moment of my life; b) path.: ⚓ apoplexy of the heart; ⚕stärkend a. ⑯ cordial; ein 2er Trank, oft: F s.th. that warms (or goes to) the cockles of one's heart; =stärkung f cordial, restorative, F co. creature comfort; =stoß m: a) pulsation of the heart, ⚓ ictus cordis; b) fig. (Gnadenstoß) finishing (or death-)blow, P settler; =stück n 🚂 (Schienenkreuzung) crossing, railway-frog; =tätigkeit f action (or function) of the heart; Aufhören der ~ stoppage of the heart, ⚓ asystole; =töne m/pl. ⚓ cardiac sounds pl.

her=zu (♃...) (♃~, ♃~...) = herbei(=...) und heran(=...).

Her=zug (♃...) m ㉒ moving (or marching) this way or back, return.

Herz=verfettung (♃...) f ㉒, =vergrößerung, =verknöcherung f: ⚓ obesity, hypertrophy, ossification of the heart; =wassersucht f, path. dropsy of the h.; =weh n: a) heart-ache, ⚓ cardialgia; b) fig. heart-felt grief; =wurm m, ent. larva of the cabbage-moth; =zergliederung f: ⚓ cardiotomy; ⚕zerreißend a. ⑯, ⚕zerschneidend a. heart-rending.

Heseki=el (♃~) npr/m. ⑭ a. bibl. Prophet: Ezekiel, Jehezekel.

Hesiod (–⌣) ⓓ α., **Hesiodos** (–⌣⌣) ⓑ γ. npr/m. Alt.: (lehrhafter griechischer Dichter um 770 v. Chr.) Hesiod.

Hesperiden (⌣–⌣⌣) [Hesper] npr., f/pl. ⓑ myth. (Töchter des Atlas) Hesperides pl.

Hesperiden-garten (ᴸ...) m ⓑ myth. (mit goldenen Äpfeln) garden of (the) Hesperides, Hesperidian garden.

Hesperi-en ♀ (⌣ᴸ(⌣)⌣) [grch. „Abend"land] npr/n. ⓑ α. Alt.: (Abendland: Italien, Spanien) Hesperia.

hesperisch (⌣ᴸ⌣) a. ⓒ Hesperian.

Hesperus (ᴸ⌣⌣) npr/m. ⓑ γ. myth. Hesperus, evening-star (poet. = Abendstern).

Hesse (ᴸ⌣) m ⓐ, **Hessin** f ⓓ Hessian.

Hessen-fliege (ᴸ⌣...) f ⓑ ent. Hessian fly (Cecidomy'ia destru'ctor).

Hestia (ᴸ⌣⌣) npr/f. ⓑⓑ α. = Vesta.

Hetäre ♀ (⌣ᴸ⌣) [grch. Freundin] f ⓓ (Buhlerin) courtesan, F lady of easy virtue. [schaft] hetæria.]

Hetärie ♀ (⌣–ᴸ) [grch.] f ⓓ (Kampfbrüder-)

heterodox ♀ (⌣⌣⌣ᴸ) [grch. anders-, irrgläubig] a. ⓒ heterodox.

Heterodoxie ♀ (⌣⌣⌣⌣ᴸ) [grch. Irrlehre] f ⓓ heterodoxy.

heterogen ♀ (⌣⌣⌣ᴸ) [grch. fremdartig] a. ⓒ heterogeneous.

Heterogen(e)ität ♀ (⌣⌣⌣⌣⌣(–)⌣ⁿ) f ⓓ heterogeneousness, heterogeneity.

hetz (⌣) [zu hetzen] int., hunt. 2! 2! Ruf für Jagdhunde, wenn das Wild in Sicht ist: tally-ho!, at him!

Hetz-bahn (⌣...) f ⓑ hunt. (hunting-) course; **-blatt** n paper (or journal) devoted to (violent) agitation, mischief-making paper.

Hetze (ᴸ⌣) [nhd. 16. sae.; *hetzen] f ⓓ 1. hunt, hunting, run with the hounds, bait(ing), coursing; fig. (wilde Verfolgung) headlong (or hot) pursuit; (wildes Rennen) wild race; (Eile) hurry. — 2. (Ort des Hetzens) hunt, course, chase. — 3. (Koppel Hetzhunde) pack of hounds; fig. (Menge) multitude.

hetzen (ᴸ⌣) [ahd.] ⓚ I v/a. 1. die Hunde auf e-n Ochsen, hinter e-m her ⚶ to set the dogs at a bull, at a p.; hunt. die Hunde auf den Hirsch ⚶ to start the stag; fig. to hound (or egg) on; Leute an- (gegen- ob. wider-) ea. ⚶ to set people together by the ears, to make mischief between people. — 2. mit Angabe der Wirkung: die Hunde matt ⚶ to weary (or F to fag) the hounds with coursing; fig. er hetzt seine Diener halb tot he drives his domestics, he worries them (almost) to death. — 3. metonymisch mit dem Verfolgten als Objekt: a) e-n Hasen rc. ⚶ to hunt (or course) ...; einen Fuchs rc. ⚶ Tode ⚶ to run ... down or to ground; fast zu Tode gehetzt almost harassed (or worried) to death, spent; fig. (hitzig verfolgen) to pursue eagerly, to chase; b) fig. eine Redens-art, ein Bild rc. zu Tode ⚶, oft: to flog a dead horse; mit allen Hunden gehetzt (sehr durchtrieben) sein to be up to every dodge or trick, to be very cunning or artful, F to know a thing or two. — II v/n. (h.) 4. (jagen) to hunt, mit der Meute ⚶ to run with the hounds; fig. (auf ein Ziel losstürmen) to rush for //, to hurry towards //. —

III sich ⚶ v/refl. 5. mit Angabe der Wirkung: sich matt ⚶ und abs. sich ⚶ to wear o.s. out (with running and racing); sich müde ⚶ to tire o.s. with running and racing, F to fag o.s. out. — IV ~ n ⓑ 6. = Hetze 1 u. 2.

Hetzer (ᴸ⌣) m ⓑ 1. hunt. baiter; whipper-in. — 2. fig. (Feindschaftstifter) instigator, mischief-maker; (Wühler) agitator.

Hetzerei (⌣⌣ᴸ) f ⓓ 1. continual harassing or rushing. — 2. fig. system of instigation or incitement or baiting or mischief-making; agitation.

Hetz-hund (⌣...) m ⓑ hound, stag-hound; **-jagd** f hunting of foxes and other wild animals; eine ~ mitmachen to go hunting or coursing; **-peitsche** f hunting-whip; mit der ~ hinter e-m her sein to spur (or egg) on a p.; **-presse** f press carrying on an agitation or stirring up the passions, auch: sensational (Am. yellow) press; **-zeit** f hunting-season. — Vgl. a. Parforce-...

Heu (¹) [ahd.: hay; *hauen] n ⓑ b. hay; ~ machen to make hay, to be hay-making; das ~ wenden to toss the hay; fig. Geld wie ~ haben to have plenty (or F piles, heaps, lots, tons) of money, to be rolling in wealth.

Heu-baum (ᴸ...) m ⓑ hay-pole, hay-tree; **-bazillus** ⚶ m hay-bacillus; **-binder(in** f) m binder (or trusser) of hay; **-boden** m, **-bühne** f hay-loft; **-bund** m, **-bündel** n truss (or bottle) of hay. [ance.]

Heuchel-busse (ᴸ⌣...) f ⓑ sham repent-]

Heuchelei (⌣⌣ᴸ) f ⓓ hypocrisy; (Verstellung) dissimulation, sham(ming), imposture, deceit, F put-on; (Falschheit) falsehood, false pretence; (Gleisnerei) bigotry, sanctimoniousness.

Heuchel-glaube (ᴸ⌣...) m ⓑ hypocritical (or sham) faith.

heucheln (ᴸ⌣) [nhd.] ⓚ a. I v/n. (h.) to play the hypocrite; to feign, dissemble, sham; to put on an air of piety or righteousness. — II v/a. = erheucheln 2; e-m Liebe ⚶ to feign (or affect) love for a p., to pretend to love a p. — III ~ n ⓑ = Heuchelei.

Heuchel-rede (ᴸ⌣...) f ⓑ hypocritical (or dissembling) speech; **-schein** m sham appearance, false pretence; **-träne** f crocodile-tear; **-wort** n deceitful word or speech.

Heuchler (ᴸ⌣) m ⓑ, **~in** f ⓓ hypocrite; dissembler, impostor, F sham(mer).

heuchlerisch (ᴸ⌣⌣) a. ⓒ hypocritical, feigning, dissembling, sham(ming), deceitful; adv. auch: like a hypocrite; in a dissembling tone.

heuen (ᴸ⌣) [Heu] agr. I v/n. (h.) to make hay. — II ~ n ⓑ haymaking.

Heuer¹ (ᴸ⌣; Hom. Häuer) [Heu] m ⓑ, **~in** f ⓓ hay-maker.

heuer² ⚶ ob. sübd. (ᴸ⌣) [ahd. hie-Jahr] adv. this year, in the present year.

Heuer³ ⚶ (ᴸ⌣) [ndd.: hire] f ⓓ wages.

Heuer³-bas ⚶ (ᴸ...) m ⓑ shipping-master; b.s. (Matrosenmakler) crimp.

Heuerling (ᴸ⌣) m ⓓ d. hireling.

heuern (ᴸ⌣) [ndd.: hire] v/a. to hire, ein Gut: to rent; ⚶ ein Schiff: to charter, Matrosen: to engage, to ship; sich ⚶ lassen to sign on.

Heu-ernte (ᴸ...) f ⓑ hay-harvest, haymaking season.

Heuer³-vertrag ⚶ (ᴸ⌣...) m ⓑ articles pl. (to be signed by a seaman on being engaged).

Heu-fieber (ᴸ...) n ⓑ path. hay-fever; **-gabel** f hay-fork, pitchfork; **-haufen** m haycock, load of hay; vgl. -schober.

Heul-bruder (ᴸ...) m ⓑ blubberer, whiner, F grizzle-pot; (Griesgram) Peter Grievous.

heulen (ᴸ⌣) [ahd.: howl] I v/n. (h.) ⓒ to (set up a) howl; vom Winde auch: to roar; von Eulen: to hoot; von Hunden: to yelp; (laut schreien) to cry aloud, to scream, to shriek, von Kindern auch: to squall; (plärren) to blubber, (weinen) to cry (laut stöhnen) to wail, to moan (a. vom Winde); vor Wut ⚶ to howl with rage; Sprichw. s. Wolf. — II ~ n ⓑ howling, &c. (s. I); bibl. ~ und Zähneklappen weeping and gnashing of teeth.

Heuler (ᴸ⌣) m ⓑ, **~in** f ⓓ (s. heulen) one who howls, roars, &c. (howler, F jetzt meist ⚶ = et. Gewaltiges); Schreier [-in] screamer; (Plärrer[in]) blubberer.

Heulerei (⌣⌣ᴸ) f ⓓ (endless) howling, whining, roaring, screaming, &c.

Heul-michel (ᴸ...) m ⓑ = **-bruder**; **-pfeife** ⚶ f siren.

Heu-machen (ᴸ...) n ⓑ haymaking; **-macher(in** f) m haymaker; **-magazin** n storehouse for hay; **-mahd** f: a) (Wiese) hayfield; b) = **-machen**; **-mähen** n = **-machen**; **-mäher(in** f) m = **-macher(in)**; **-markt** m hay-market; **-maschine** f haymaking machine; **-miete** f = **-schober**; **-monat**, **-mond** m hay-month, July.

Heune (ᴸ⌣) m ⓓ = Hüne.

Heu-ochs (ᴸ...) m ⓑ, **-ochse** m full-grown ox; **-pferd** n, ent. large green grasshopper (Locu'sta viridi'ssima); **-presse**, **-raufe** f, **-rechen** m hay-press, -rack, -rake.

Heureka (mft –ᴸ⌣) [grch. ᴸ⌣ ich habe (es) gefunden! (dem Mathematiker Archimedes beigelegter Ausruf)] int. eureka (auch a.).

Heurer ⚶ (ᴸ⌣) [heuern] m ⓑ freighter.

heurig (ᴸ⌣) [ahd.; *heuer²] a. ⓒ (ant. firn) this year's; **~e(r)** (ᴸ⌣⌣) m ⓒ (Wein vom letzten Jahr) wine of the last (or of this year's) vintage; (junger Wein) this year's wine or vintage.

Heu-same (ᴸ...) m ⓑ hay-seed; **-scheuer**, **-scheune** f barn for (keeping) hay; vgl. -schuppen; **-schneide-maschine** ⊙ f hay-cutter; **-schober** m hayrick, haystack; **-schrecke** [ahd.] f ⓑ ent. grasshopper (Ortho'ptera saltato'ria); vgl. Heupferd, Wander-.

heuschrecken-artig (ᴸ⌣...) a. ⓒ locust-like; ent. des Insekt: ♀ locustarian; **-baum** ⚶ m ⓑ West-indien: locust(-tree), courbaril (Hymenae'a Cou'rbarii); **-krebs** m, zo. locust-shrimp, sea-mantis (Squilla mantis); **-schwarm** m swarm of locusts.

Heu-schuppen (ᴸ...) m ⓑ shed for storing hay; **-seil** n hay-band; **-speicher** m = **-boden**; **-stadel** m barn for hay.

heut(e) (ᴸ⌣) [ahd. hie-Tag] I adv. 1. to-day, this day; ⚶ oder morgen either to-day or to-morrow; ⚶ über acht

Signs (see page XVII): F familiar; P vulgar; Γ flash; ⟍ rare; † obsolete (died); * new word (born); ⧺ incorrect; ♪ music;

[heutig] — 515 — [hieratisch]

(vierzehn) Tage to-day (or this day) week (fortnight); 2 über ein Vierteljahr (ein Jahr) three months (a year) hence or from to-day, this day three months (twelvemonth); noch 2 this very day; bis 2 up to this day; *fig.* er ist nicht von 2 (oder von gestern) he was not born yesterday; Sprichw. 2 reich, morgen arm a man one day, a mouse the next; 2 rot, morgen tot, *etwa*: here to-day, gone to-morrow; 2 mir, morgen dir to-day me, to-morrow thee; every dog has his day. — 2. 2 abend, 2 morgen to-night, this morning; 2 nachmittag this afternoon; 2 den ganzen Tag the whole of to-day, all this day; von 2 auf morgen between this and to-morrow; 2 vor acht Tagen a week ago to-day; f. heutzutage. — II das ~ n, *inv.* 3. to-day, this day, the present time.

heutig (⌣́⌣) [ahd.] *a.* ⓖ to-day's, of this day or date; (gegenwärtig) present; (tatsächlich) actual; die 2e Zeitung to-day's paper; die 2en Entdeckungen the discoveries of our age or time; bis zum 2en Tage up to this day or our days; mit 2er Post by to-day's (or to-night's) mail; unser ~es n ⓜ ⓐ our (or my) letter of this day, höflicher: our respects *pl.* of to-day; am ~en, unter ~em this day (to-day).

heutigen=, bef. **heutiges=tags** (⌣́⌣⌣́), **heutzutage** (⌣́⌣⌣́) *adv.* nowadays, in our days or time or age, at the present day or time, F at this time of day.

Heu=wagen (⌣́...) *m* ⓖ hay-cart or -wagon; **=wiese** *f* hayfield; **=zeit** *f* haymaking time.

Hexa=eder ⊿ (⌣́⌣⌣) [grch.] *n* ⓖ geom. (Würfel) hexahedron; **hexa=edrisch** *a.* ⓖ (tubisch) hexahedral.

Hexameter ⊿ (⌣́⌣⌣) [grch.] *m* ⓖ *pros.* (6füßiger Vers) hexameter; **hexametrisch** (⌣́⌣⌣) *a.* ⓖ hexametric, hexametrical.

hexandrisch ⊿ (⌣́⌣) [grch.] *a.* ⓖ (sechsmännig: mit 6 Staubgefäßen) hexandrian.

Hexe (⌣́; *Hom.* Hechse) [ahd.: hag] *f* ⓐ, *dim.* Hexchen, Hexlein *n* witch, sorceress; *bewundernd*: enchantress; F charmer; *schimpfend*: die alte ~ the old hag or vixen; *milder*: die kleine ~ the little witch or huzzie, the artful minx; *mitleidig*: die arme ~ the poor creature, the poor thing.

hexen (⌣́⌣) I *v/n.* (h.) to practise witchcraft or sorcery or magic; durch Zaubersprüche: to work a charm; man müßte 2 können, um es zu tun it cannot be done except by magic; wie gehext as if bewitched; (rasch, flott) rapidly, at a marvellous pace or speed; es geht wie gehext it goes like steam or as if by magic. — II *v/a.* to do a th. by magic; vgl. anhexen.

hexen=artig (⌣́⌣...) *a.* ⓖ like a witch; bewitched; **=besen** *m* ⓖ (Zweigbüschel an Birken 2c.) witches' besom or broom; **=brut** *f* brood (or set) of witches; **=ei** *n* egg without a yolk; **=fahrt** *f* witches' ride (through the air); **=fest** *n* witches' revels *pl.* or festive meeting; *a.* Witches' Sabbath; **=geschichte** *f* witch-story; **=glaube** *m* belief in witches.

hexenhaft (⌣́⌣⌣) *a.* ⓖ = hexenartig.

Hexen=kessel (⌣́⌣...) *m* ⓖ witches' kettle; *fig.* (Gelärm) hurly-burly, hubbub; **=kraut** ⓔ *n*: a) enchanter's nightshade (*Circaea*); b) = Alraun 2; **=kreis** *m* magic circle, witches' (or fairy-)ring; **=kunst** *f* witchcraft, sorcery, magic (art); **=männchen** ⓔ *n* (Alraun) mandrake; **=mehl** *n* (Bärlappsamen) lycopodium powder, witch-meal; **=meister** *m* wizard, sorcerer, magician; ich bin kein ~ I cannot do things by magic; er ist kein großer ~ he is no shining light; **=probe** *f* witches' ordeal or trial; **=prozeß** *m* trial for witchcraft, witches' trial; **=ring** *m* = =kreis; **=ritt** *m* = =fahrt; **=sabbat** *m* Witches' Sabbath; **=schuß** *m*, *path.* lumbago, ⊿ lumbar rheumatism; **=segen**, **=spruch** *m* magic formula; **=stich** *m*, *path.* Näherei: herring-bone stitch; **=tanz** *m* = =fest; **=werk** *n* work of witches, witchery, magic doing; **=zunft** *f* witches' tribe.

Hexer (⌣́⌣) *m* ⓖ = Hexenmeister.

Hexerei (⌣⌣́) *f* ⓐ witchcraft, witchery, sorcery, magic, black art; (Kunst der Gaukler) jugglery; das ist keine ~ there is no great art (or nothing wonderful) in that; das muß mit ~ zugehen there must be some hocus-pocus (or magic, trickery, devilry) in that; Sprichw. f. Geschwindigkeit.

Hexerich (⌣́⌣⌣) *m* ⓜ. = Hexenmeister.

Hf. *abbr.* = Halbfranzband.

HGB. *abbr.* = Handelsgesetzbuch.

hi (́) *vgl.* hihi.

Hiatus ⊿ (⌣́⌣) [lt. Gähnen] *m, inv. gr.* (Zf.=treffen zweier Vokale) hiatus.

Hiberni=en ♀ (⌣⌣́(⌣)⌣) *npr/n.* ⓑ (Irland) Hibernia, Ireland; **hibernisch** *a.* ⓖ Hibernian, Irish. [= Eibisch.)

Hibiskus ♀ (⌣⌣́⌣) [lt., *grch.*] *m, inv.*

Hibride ⊿ 2c. f. Hybride 2c.

hie (́) [ahd.] *adv.* † und *poet.* = hier; 2 Welf!, 2 Waiblingen!, *etwa*: here Guelphs!, there Ghibellines!

hieb[1] (́) *impf.* von hauen.

Hieb[2] (́) [uhd.; * hieb] *m* ⓜ c. 1. stroke, blow, (Knuff, Puff) thwack, cuff, thump, mit der flachen Hand: smack; mit *schneidender Waffe*: cut. stärker: slash; ⚔ *fenc.* ~ mit der Rückschneide cut with the back edge of the sword; auf ~ und Stoß fechten oder gehen to cut and thrust; e-n ~ führen auf (a) (deal a) cut at; der ~ sitzt, *etwa*: (it is) a good cut or hit; F es hat ~e gesetzt there has been (some) sharp fighting; wuchtiger, zu Boden schmetternder ~ (Schlag) smashing blow, F floorer; ~e (Schläge) austeilen (bekommen) to deal out (to receive) blows, to administer (to get) a drubbing; zehn ~ mit der Rute ten strokes (or stripes) with the birch(-rod); Sprichw. auf einen (od. den ersten) ~ fällt kein Baum Rome was not built in a (or one) day. — 2. (Wundenmal) scar (of a wound); er hat viele ~e im Gesicht he has many gashes in his face. — 3. *fig.* (anzüglicher Bemerkung) hit (or cut, F dig) at a p., sarcasm intended for a p., invective against a p.; das war ein ~ auf mich that was meant for me or a hit

at me. — 4. P einen ~ (Schluck) nehmen to take a draught (or F a drop) of something; einen ~ haben F to have (taken) a drop too much, to be half seas over or well on.

Hieber (⌣́⌣) *m* ⓖ = Hiebwaffe; bsd. = Haudegen a; (Schläger) rapier; (zweischneidiger Pallasch) two-edged sword.

Hieb=fechten (⌣́...) *n* ⓖ broadsword exercise; **2fest** *a.* ⓖ proof against swords, weit S. invulnerable; **~= und Stoß=waffen** *f/pl.* ⓐ arms for cut-and-thrust; **=waffe** *f* weapon (or sword) for cutting; broadsword; **=wunde** *f* sword-cut, wound from a cut, wound caused by a broadsword.

hie=durch † (⌣́⌣), **hie=für** † (⌣́⌣), **hie=gegen** † (⌣́⌣), **hie=her** † (⌣́⌣) = hierdurch 2c.

hielt([e]st) (́(⌣)) *impf. von* halten.

hie=mit (⌣́⌣), **hie=nach** † (⌣́⌣), **hie=neben** † (⌣́⌣) = hiermit 2c.

hie=nieden (⌣́⌣⌣) *adv.* here below, on (this) earth, in this life (of ours).

hier (́) [ahd.: here] *adv.* 1. here; 2 die Stelle here is the place; 2 bin ich here I am; 2 sind wir here we are; 2 kommt er there he comes, 2 draußen (drinnen) out (in) here; 2 herum about here, hereabouts; er ist von 2 he was born here, he is a native of this place; er ist fort von 2 he has gone away (from here) or left the town; ⚭ Wechsel auf 2 bills *pl.* on this place or town; auf 2 verladen, für 2 bestimmt shipped, bound for this place. — 2. 2 auf Erden = hienieden; 2 beigefügt (herewith) enclosed, annexed; (in der Anlage) in the enclosure; 2 folgend hereafter; **hie(r) und da** here and there; (zerstreut) scattered (about), sporadically; zeitlich: now and then, at times; 2 und dort here and there (or yonder); in this place and in that; f. hierzulande. — 3. auf Brief=adressen: Herrn N. 2 ob. hie(r)selbst Mr. N. of this town (auf Briefen, die mit der Post gehen, meist rechts Name der Stadt, links: Local). — 4. Frau Gräfin 2, Frau Gräfin da (endloses Komplimentieren) *etwa*: (nothing but) Countess this and Countess that, C. here and C. there. — 5. (in diesem Falle) in that case, (diesmal) this time; (bei diesen Worten) at these words; 2 (da, dann) stand er auf (her or that, upon that, thereupon) he rose, he then rose. — 6. zeitlich: now; von 2 an henceforth, from this day (forth); from that time (forth).

hier=amts (⌣́...) *adv.* at the bailiff's office, at this office.

hier=an (⌣́⌣, *nachdrücklich*: ⌣⌣́) *adv.* 1. (an diesen Ort) to(wards) this place or town. — 2. (an bfr Sache) at that, of (or to) that (= daran 1); hereat, hereon; 2 kehre ich mich nicht I don't trouble about that, I pay no heed to that; 2 sieht man one may see by that.

Hi=erarch (⌣⌣́) [grch.] *m* ⓔ *eccl.* hierarch; **~ie** (⌣⌣⌣́) *f* ⓕ (Kirchenverfassung) hierarchy; **Lisch** *a.* ⓖ hierarchical.

hi=eratisch (⌣⌣́⌣) *a.* (grch., priesterlich) ⓖ hieratic(al); 2e Schrift (alt=ägypt. Priester=schrift) hierogram.

⊿ scientific; ♀ botanical; ♀ geography; ⓖ machinery; ⚒ mining; ⚔ military; ⚓ marine; ⓐ commercial; ⓟ postal; 🚂 railway.

hier-auf (-ˊ, nachdrücklich: ˊ-) *adv.* hereupon. upon this; ≗**hin** *adv.* upon the strength (or in consequence) of this.

hier-aus (-ˊ, nachdrücklich: ˊ-) *adv.* from (or out of) this; hence.

hier-bei (-ˊ, nachdrücklich: ˊ-) *adv.* 1. hereby, hereat, herewith. — 2. (beigeschlossen) (herewith) enclosed or appended or annexed; ≗ senden wir // we enclose //.

hier=bleiben (ˊˊ...) *v/n.* (sn) [81]** to stay here; ~ *n* [23] stay here; während seines ~s while he is staying here; ≗**durch** (-ˊ, nachdrücklich: ˊᵕ) *adv.* örtlich: through here, this way; ursächlich: by this (means); by so doing or acting; thereby; jur. (kraft dieses) by these presents; ≗**ein** *adv.* herein; ≗**für** *adv.* for this; ≗**gegen** *adv.* against this; ≗**her** *adv.* örtlich: hither (as far as) here; zeitlich: bis ≗ hitherto, (up) to this day; ≗**herum** *adv.* hereabout, hereabouts, near this place; ≗**herwärts** *adv.* this way; ≗**hin** *adv.* ✣ = hierher (*ant.* dahin); ≗ und dorthin here and there; ≗**in** *adv.* in(side) this, in(side) it; vgl. darin 1 und 2; ≗**ländisch** *a.* [66] customary (in this country); native, indigenous; ≗**lands** *adv.* = ≗zulande; ≗**mit** *adv.* herewith, with this or it; (bei diesen Worten) at (or with) these words, in saying this; ≗**nach** *adv.* hereafter, after this or that or it; ≗**nächst** *adv.* örtlich: close by, next door; zeitlich etc. a) (nächst diesem) next to this; b) (außerdem) besides; ≗**neben** (-ˊᵕ) *adv.* next to this; ≗**nieden** (-ˊᵕ) *adv.* = hienieden.

Hi-eroglyphe (ᵕᵕᵕˊfᵕ) *f* [48] [grch.] (bildliches Schriftzeichen) hieroglyph; **~n=schrift** *f* (a. **Hi-eroglyphik** *f* [46]) hieroglyphics *pl.* (*ant.* Buchstabenschrift);
hi-eroglyphisch *a.* [66] hieroglyphical.

Hi-eronymos, ...us (ᵕᵕˊᵕᵕ) [grch.] *npr/m.* [16]γ. (auch Vn.) Hieronymus, Jerome.

Hi-erophant (ᵕᵕᵕfˊ) [grch.] *m* [42], bisw. **~in** *f* [47] (Priester) hierophant; ≗**isch** *a.* [66] hierophantic.

hier=orts (ˊˊ...) = ≗zulande; **=sein** *n* [23] being here, presence here; ≗**selbst** *adv.* here; a. in this town; s. hier 3; ≗**über** (-ˊᵕ, nachdrücklich: ˊ-ᵕ) *adv.* over (or about) this; ≗**um** *adv.* around this; ≗**unter** *adv.* beneath (or underneath) this or it; among these; ≗**von** (ˊfᵕ) *adv.* hereof, herefrom; genug ≗ enough of this; ≗**vor** *adv.* before (or in front of) this; ≗**wider** *adv.* against (or contrary to) this; ≗**zu** *adv.* hereto, (in addition) to this; ≗**zulande** *adv.* in this country (of ours); ≗**zwischen** (-ˊᵕ) *adv.* between these.

hie-selbst (ˊᵕ) *adv.* = hierselbst.

hiesig (ˊᵕ) [nhd. 17. *sae.*;* hie] *a.* [66] (*ant.* dortig, dasig) of (or in) this place or town; ≗e Verhältnisse *n/pl.* (our) local (or parochial) affairs *pl.*; ✱ die ≗e Industrie our local (or home) industry; auf ≗em Platze in this (or our) town or city; ≗es Vieh our home-bred cattle.

hieß (ˊ) *ind.*, ≗**e** (ˊᵕ) *subj. impf.* v. heißen.

hieven ⚓ (ˊwᵕ) [ndd.] *v/a.* [88] (mit dem Spill heben) to heave.

hie-von † (ˊfᵕ), **hie-vor** †, **hie-wider** †, **hie-zu** † (ˊˊ) = hiervon etc.

Hift (ˊ) [Hief Hornsignal] *m* [11]b. *hunt.* bugle-sound; **~=horn** *n* [62] (huntsman's) bugle or horn; hunting-horn.

hihi (-ˊ) *int.* (das Lachen nachahmend) bisw: ha ha ha!, gröber: haw-haw!

Hilarius (ᵕˊ(ᵕ)ᵕ) [lt.] *npr/m.* [16]γ. Hilary.

hilf (ˊ) *imper.* von helfen.

Hilfe (ˊᵕ) [ahd.: help; *helfen] *f* [48] 1. help; (Beistand) assistance, aid, (Rettung) succour, (Unterstützung) support, von Armen auch: relief to the poor; (Abhilfe) redress of an evil, (Heilmittel) remedy for a complaint, relief to a patient; schnelle, schleunige ~ prompt assistance; ~ (Heilung) finden in // to be relieved by //, to derive benefit from //; mit ~ von with the aid (or assistance) of; mit ~ der Nacht under cover of night or darkness; e-m ~ leisten to render a p. assistance or aid, to assist (or aid, succour) a p.; e-n um ~ bitten, zu ~ rufen, bei e-m ~ suchen to call in a p.'s aid or assistance; *abs.* (um) ~ rufen to call (or cry) for help; e-m zu ~ kommen (eilen) to come (to hasten or fly) to a p.'s assistance or aid; ~ nötig haben to be in need of assistance or in trouble; e-n, et. zu ~ nehmen to use (or avail o.s. of) a p., a th; (zu) ~! help! help!; zur ~ dienend auxiliary. — 2. ⚔ = Hilfs=heer, =truppen.

hilfe=bittend (ˊᵕ...) *a.* [66], ≗**flehend** *a.* imploring (for) help or aid, suppliant; **=leistung** *f* [62] (rendering) assistance or aid; succour(ing); ⚓ salvage; **=ruf** *m*, **=rufen** *n* calling (or cry) for help or assistance; ≗**suchend** *a.* seeking (for) help.

Hilf=leistung (ˊ...) *f* [62] = Hilfe=l.

hilf=los (ˊ...) *a.* [66] helpless, defenceless; (im Stiche gelassen) deserted, forlorn, abandoned; (in großer Not) in (great) distress, destitute, necessitous; betrunken und ≗ drunk and incapable, F incapably drunk; **=losigkeit** *f* [46] helplessness; distress, destitution; ≗**reich** *a.* helpful; (mildtätig) charitable, benevolent.

Hilfs=amt (ˊ...) *n* [62] assistant's office or post; **=arbeiter(in** *f*) *m* additional worker, help(er), assistant; (überzähliger Beamter) supernumerary; **=armee** ⚔ *f* = =heer; ≗**bedürftig** *a.* [66] requiring help, needing assistance, stärker: indigent; vgl. hilflos; **=bedürftige(r)** *s.* one in great need or distress; (Armer) pauper; **=bedürftigkeit** *f* need, distress; destitution, indigence, pauperism; ≗**bereit** *a.* ready to assist or to (give) help; **=bischof** *m* suffragan; **=buch** *n*: a) additional (or subsidiary) book; b) work of reference; c) manual of instruction; a. help, guide; **=gelder** *n/pl.* subsidies *pl.*; an eine Dampferlinie etc. ~ zahlen to subsidize a line of steamers, &c.; **=handbuch** *n* book of reference; **=heer** ⚔ *n*: a) auxiliary army or force(s *pl.*); reinforcements, supports *pl.*; b) (Entsatz) relief(-column or -force); **=kasse** *f* relief-fund, provident (or charitable) fund; **=kirche** *f* chapel (of ease); **=lehrer** *m* assistant master or teacher; **=lehrerin** *f* governess; **=leistung** *f* s. Hilfe=l.; **=linie** *f* subsidiary line; **=macht** *f*: a) allied power; b) = =heer; **=maschine** ⚙ *f* assistant- (or pilot-)engine; **=mittel** *n* remedy, help, resource; (Auskunftsmittel) expedient, shift; auf seine eigenen ~ angewiesen depending (or being thrown back) on one's own resources, having to shift for o.s.; zum letzten ~ greifen to try one's last resource; **=prediger** *m* e-s anglikanischen Pfarrers curate; **=quelle** *f* resource; **=satz** *m*, *math.*, *phls.*: ✎ corollary.

hilfst (ˊ) 2. Pers. *sing. pres. ind.* v. helfen.

Hilfs=truppen ⚔ (ˊ...) *f/pl.* [62] auxiliary troops, auxiliaries *pl.*; vgl. =heer; **=verb** *n* = =zeitwort; **=verein** *m* relief-society, charitable (or benevolent) society or institution; ~ der englischen Volksklassen friendly society (die engl. Friendly Societies haben zahlreiche Verzweigungen, wie: Odd Fellows, Foresters, &c.); vgl. =kasse; **=vertrag** *m*: a) subsidiary treaty; b) treaty of alliance; **=völker** ⚔ *n pl.* = =truppen; **=vorrichtungen** *f/pl.* e-r Maschine etc.: accessory pieces or parts *pl.*; **=wissenschaft** *f* subsidiary (or auxiliary) science or branch of knowledge; **=wort** *n*, *gr.* (das den Sinn ergänzt) expletive; weitS. auxiliary word; **=wörterbuch** *n* vocabulary (or glossary) appended to a work, special dictionary; **=zeitwort** *n*, *gr.* auxiliary verb; **=zug** 🚂 *m* relief-train, extra train.

hilft (ˊ) 3. Pers. *sing. pres. ind.* v. helfen.

Himalaja ♀ (ᵕˊᵕᵕ) [skt. Stätte des Schnees] *npr/m.* [51]α.: der ~, auch: das **~=gebirge** the Himalaya (Mountains *pl.*).

Himbeere ⚘ (ˊˊᵕ) [ahd. Hindinbeere] *f* [48] 1. raspberry. — 2. = Himbeerstrauch.

Himbeer=eis (ˊˊ...) *n* [62] raspberry-ice; **=essig** *m* r.-vinegar; **=saft** *m* r.-juice; **=strauch** *m* r.-bush (*Rubus Idae'us*); **=wein** *m* r.-wine.

Himmel (ˊᵕ) [ahd.: heaven; *Hemd Decke] *m* [22] 1. heaven; *eccl.* (a. ~=reich *n*) Heaven(s *pl.*), (Heavenly) Paradise, Abode of Bliss; (Seligkeit) Eternal Bliss or Glory; *bibl.* ~ aller ~ heaven of heavens; dein Wille geschehe auf Erden wie im ~ Thy will be done in Earth as it is in Heaven; du lieber ~!, gerechter ~! Good Heavens!, Good Lord!, F Good Gracious!; dem ~ sei Dank! Thank Heaven!, Heaven be praised!; in den Himmel kommen to go to heaven; um(s) ~s willen, tun Sie das nicht! for goodness' (feierlich: for Heaven's) sake, don't do that!; *fig.* aus allen seinen ~n gefallen (enttäuscht) sein to be stripped of all illusions; im siebenten (dritten) ~ (entzückt) sein to be in the seventh (third) heaven (of delight) or in ecstasy or supremely happy; er war wie im ~ ... as in heaven or thoroughly happy; ~ u. Erde in Bewegung setzen to move heaven and earth; Sprichw. s. blau 4, Ehe, fallen 4. — 2. (Himmelsgewölbe) sky, skies *pl.*; firmament; am westlichen ~ in the western sky; bis in den ~ erheben to praise (or extol) to the skies; bis in den ~ hineinragend towering to the skies, von Gebäuden F *co.* sky-scraping; unter freiem ~ schlafen to sleep in the open air or under

[**himmelab**] — 517 — [**hinabwärts**]

the open sky; vom ~ herab (down) from the heavens or from on high; wie ein Blitzstrahl aus heiterem ~ like a bolt from the blue; *fig.* (wie) vom ~ fallen (plötzlich kommen) to drop from the sky, to come unexpectedly; vgl. fallen 4; das Blaue vom ~ herunterschwatzen to talk a donkey's hindlegs off; Sprichw. f. Dudelsack; der ~ hängt ihm (oder er malt sich den ~) voller (Baß-)Geigen f. Geige. — 3. = ~s-strich. — 4. = Bett-♀; ~ (Verdeck) e-s Wagens 2c. top (or outside) of a carriage, &c.
himmel=ab (♂...) *adv.* (down) from heaven; ♀**an** *adv.* (up) to heaven or to the skies, heavenward(s); ♀**angst** F *a.*, ~ f ♀: mir ward ♀, ich hatte eine ~ I was in mortal fear or terribly frightened or greatly alarmed; ♀**auf** = ♀an; bfd. ehm. =**bett** *n* tester- (or canopy-)bed; mit Vorhängen: fourpost-bedstead; ♀**blau** *a.* u. ~ *n* sky-blue, azure, *poet.*: cerulean; =**brot** *n* bibl. (heavenly) manna; =**fahrt** *f, rel.*: a) Christi ~ Ascension of Christ or of the Lord; b) Mari'ä ~ Assumption of the Virgin (Mary); =**fahrts=fest** *n*, =**tag** *m* (f. =fahrt): a) Ascension-day; b) (Feast of the) Assumption; =**fahrts=woche** *f* Rogation week; ♀**her** *adv.* = ♀ab; ♀**hoch** *a.*: a) sky-high, towering (to the sky); b) *fig.* e-n ♀ bitten to beg and implore a p.; ♀ jauchzend (*G.*) shouting with great joy, intensely jubilant.
himmeln (♂~) v/n. (h.) ♀ *a.* 1. to fly in the air. — 2. (frömmeln) to play the saint.
Himmel=reich (♂~) *n* ♀ *rel.* kingdom of heaven; vgl. Himmel 1; Sprichw. des Menschen Wille ist sein ~ man's sweetest of dishes is that which he wishes; =**saal** *m* f. Himmels=.
Himmels=achse (♂...) *f* ♀ *ast.* axis of the heavens; =**bahn** *f* celestial space; =**beschreibung** *f* description of the celestial world, ⟨✦⟩ uranography; =**bewohner** *m* = =bürger; =**bläue** *f* sky-blue, azure; =**bogen** *m* celestial vault; =**bote** *m* messenger from heaven; =**braut** *f, eccl.* bride of Heaven, nun; =**burg** *f* celestial abode; =**bürger** *m* inhabitant of heaven, celestial being; *pl.* auch: celestials.
Himmel=schlüssel (♂...) f. Himmels=...; ♀**schreiend** *a.* ♀ crying to heaven; (schändlich) shameful, revolting, atrocious; ♀e Sünde, oft: infamous shame.
Himmels=erscheinung (♂...) *f* ♀ *phys.* meteor; =**feste** *f* firmament; =**feuer** *n*: a) fire of (or from) heaven; (Blitz) lightning; b) *fig.* heavenly fire, heaven-inspired ardour; =**gabe** *f* gift from heaven, heavenly gift; =**gegend** *f*: a) ♀ quarter (of the heavens); die vier ~en the four quarters of the globe, the four chief points of the compass; b) =strich; =**gewölbe** *n* canopy of heaven, celestial vault; vgl. =zelt; =**globus** *m*, =**karte** ♀ celestial globe, chart; =**königin** *f* heavenly queen; *myth.* Juno; *Cath. eccl.* the Blessed Virgin; =**körper** *m* celestial body; =**kost** *f* ambrosia; vgl. =speise; =**kratzer** *m* bfd. *Am.* (hochstöckiges Haus) sky-scraper; =**kreis** *m* celestial

sphere; =**kugel** *f* celestial globe; =**kunde** *f*: a) = =lehre; b) (Sternkunde); ⟨✦⟩ astronomy; =**lehre** *f*: ⟨✦⟩ uranology; =**leiter** ♀ *f* blue Jacob's-ladder (*Polemo'nium caeruleum*); =**licht** *n* heavenly light; ~er *pl.* (Gestirne) celestial luminaries *pl.*; =**luft** *f* (fluid) ether; =**pforte** *f* gate of heaven; =**punkt** *m, ast.*: a) (Scheitelpunkt) vertical point, zenith; b) (Fußpunkt) nadir; =**rand** *m* horizon; =**raum** *m* celestial space; *poet.* die ~räume ethereal regions *pl.*; =**richtung** *f* = =gegend; in welcher ~ ist der Wald gelegen? in what direction does the forest lie?; =**saal** *m, rel.* Heavenly Abode; =**schlüssel** *m*: a) key of heaven; b) ♀ primrose (*Pri'mula*); =**speise** *f* food for celestials; vgl. =kost; =**strich** *m* zone, clim(at)e; (Gegend) region; =**stürmer** *m* f. Himmel=st...; =**tau** *m* dew from heaven; *bibl. u. fig.* manna; =**trank** *m* nectar; =**tür** (e) *f, rel.* door of Heaven.
himmel=stürmend (♂...) *a.* ♀ Titanic; *poet.* heaven-assailing; =**stürmer** *m* ♀ *myth.* Titan; *iro.* firebrand.
Himmels=wagen (♂...) *m, ast.* the Great Bear, Charles's Wain; =**weg** *m, rel.* way to Heaven; =**wonne** *f* heavenly delight; =**zeichen** *n* celestial sign; des Tierkreises: sign of the zodiac; =**zelt** *n, poet.* vault of heaven, celestial vault or dome, (azure) sky, firmament.
himmel=wärts (♂...) *adv.* heavenward(s); ♀**weit** *a.* ♀ u. *adv.* eigentlich: (as) distant as heaven from earth; ♀ verschieden diametrically opposed, as different as day and night or as chalk from cheese; ♀ verschieden sein to differ widely; ein ♀er Unterschied an enormous (or a vast) difference.
himmlisch (♂~) I *a.* ♀ 1. heavenly, celestial; (göttlich) divine; (erhaben) sublime, *poet.* ethereal; das ist ♀! that's divine or lovely!; ♀e Fügung divine ordination, will of Heaven; die ♀en Mächte the heavenly powers *pl.*, the powers above; ♀ das ~e Reich (China) the Celestial Empire; *rel.* unser ♀er Vater Our Father in Heaven. — 2. (auf das Jenseits gerichtet) spiritual, zB. ♀e Sehnsucht spiritual longings *pl.*; *Cath. eccl.* ♀er Gruß = Ave. — II *s.* ♀ 3. der (die) ~e celestial (or divine) being; *myth.* (Olympian) god, deity; die ~en the celestials *pl.*; (Selige) the blessed *pl.* — 4. das ~e heavenly (or divine) matters or things *pl.*
hin (♂) [ahd.] *adv.* 1. örtlich: a) Bewegung vom Orte des Sprechenden weg, nach e-m Ziele zu (*ant.* her): thither, there; b) in Verbindung mit e-r adverbialen Bestimmung des Zieles, meist nicht zu übersetzen, zB. auf den Berg ♀, nach dem Berge ♀ to(wards) the mountain; c) mit örtlichen *adv.*, oft zu einem Worte verschmolzen, meist nicht zu übersetzen: f. da=, dort=hin, ferner=hin, weit=hin; überall ♀ in all directions; d) (Ausdehnung) **an** der Grenze, dem Ufer ♀ (entlang) along...; über die ganze Welt ♀ all over the world. — 2. zeitlich: (Dauer): a) vom Morgen bis zum Abend ♀ from morning till night; spät in die Nacht ♀ till far into the night, till late at night; es ist noch lange ♀ it is a long time yet (to come); b) die Sache

dehnt (oder schleppt, zieht) sich (endlos) ♀ ... drags on (a long time). — 3. allgemein: (Verschwinden): (weg) gone, lost; (zugrunde gegangen), F smashed up; (verflossen, vergangen) past; meine Ruh' ist ♀ (*G.*) my peace is gone; sie ist ganz ♀ (erschöpft) she is quite exhausted or spent or done up; ich weiß nicht, wo mein Tuch ♀ ist ... what has become of my handkerchief; Sprichw. ♀ ist ♀, verloren ist verloren (what is) spent is spent, (what is) lost is lost, F what's gone is gone. — 4. (Grund) auf ... ♀ (infolge von, auf Grund von) in consequence (or on the strength) of; in conformity with; auf die Gefahr ♀, alles zu verlieren at the risk of losing everything; auf sein Versprechen ♀ relying (or in reliance) on his promise; aufs ungewisse ♀ at hazard, at all hazards, at random; ich wage es **darauf** ♀ I consequently venture. — 5. Bfd. Ausdrücke: ♀ **und her** f. her 6; in Zssgn f. S. 523; das ist ♀ wie her (F Jacke wie Hose) (ganz gleich) one is as good as the other; F it's much of a muchness; das ist nicht ♀ noch her it is neither one thing nor the other; ♀ **und wieder** here and there; zeitlich: now and then, at times; ♀ **und zurück** there and back, going and coming; ♀ outward and inward (goods); ⚓ (voyage) out and home; 🚂 **Fahrschein** für ♀ und zurück return-ticket.
hin=..., Hin=... (♂...) in Verbindung mit *verbs*, immer trennbar (**), u. in Zssgn mit *verbal nouns* u. *adjectives*, bz.: a) Bewegung von dem Sprechenden weg nach e-m Ziele zu; mit *verbs* der Bewegung ot thither, there; somewhere; to(wards) the place, to his (or its) destination; out, forth; along; b) oberflächliches Tun, oft: carelessly, heedlessly, thoughtlessly, at random; c) langsames Vergehen ob. Zerfallen, oft: on, away, out.
hin=ab (♂) *adv.* down there, downward(s); going (or coming) down the hill, &c. (*ant.* hinauf; vgl. herab; ♀! *ell.* down (with you)! den Fluß ♀ down the river, down stream; hinauf und ♀ (going) up and (coming) down; die Treppe hinauf und ♀ up and down the stairs, upstairs and downstairs.
hin=ab=..., Hin=ab=... (♂...) in Verbindung mit *verbs*, immer trennbar (**), und in Zssgn mit *verbal nouns* u. *adjectives*, die Richtung von oben nach unten, von dem Sprechenden weg, bezeichnend: ♀**bringen** v/a. ♀** to bring (or take) down; ♀**fahren** v/n. (sn) ♀b** to drive or cycle, motor, ride) down the hill; to go (or sail) down the river; =**fahrt** *f* ♀ driving, &c. down; weit♀. descent; ♀**geh(e)n** v/n. (sn) ♀** to go down; ♀**lassen** v/a. ♀a** to let down, to lower (down); sich ♀**schlängeln** v/refl. ♀a** to wind down the hill, &c.; ♀**steigen** v/n. (sn) ♀**: e-n Berg ♀ to descend (or climb down) a mountain; ♀**stürzen** v/n. (sn) ♀** to tumble down; to fall into (or down) a pit, a chasm, &c., to fall over the edge of a precipice.
hin=ab=wärts (♂,♂) *adv.* downward(s).

[hinaltern] — 518 — [hinderlich]

hin-altern (˘…) v/n. (ſn) ⓐa** to grow old or aged, to get on in years.

hin-an (˘⸗) adv. **1.** up (there); den Felſen ⸗ up the rock; zu den Sternen ⸗ up to the stars. — **2.** (hoch) ⸗ up (on) high. — **3.** ell. friſch ⸗! at it!, F go it, (boys)!, look alive!, look sharp!

hin-an-…, Hin-an⸗… (˘⸗…) in Verbindung (ſeltener als heran) mit verbs, immer trennbar (**), u. in Zſſgn mit verbal nouns, eine Bewegung vom Sprechenden zu einer höhern hin bezeichnend, oft: near (to); up: ⸗geh(e)n v/n. (ſn) ⓜ** to go near (an et. to a th.); den Berg ⸗ to go up the mountain; ⸗kommen v/n. (ſn) ⓜ** to come (or get) up; ⸗steigen v/n. (ſn) ⓜ** to mount a hill, to ascend a mountain; ~ n e-s Berges ꝛc. ascent …

hin-arbeiten (˘…) v/n. (h.) ⓜ**: auf et. ⸗ to aim at a th., to work (or direct one's efforts) towards a th.; ſich ⸗ v/refl.: a) ſich nach et. ⸗ to work (or struggle) towards a th.; b) abs. to wear o.s. out with (excessive) work, to work o.s. to death.

hin-auf (˘ˊ) adv. (ant.: a) herauf, b) hin-ab, hinunter) up (there), in an upward direction; (bis) zum Himmel ⸗ up to the sky, up to heaven; (bis) ganz ⸗ right to the top or the summit; den Fluß ⸗ up the river, upstream; die Treppe ⸗ upstairs.

hin-auf-…, Hin-auf⸗… (˘ˊ…) in Verbindung mit verbs, immer trennbar (**), und in Zſſgn mit verbal nouns und adjectives, eine Bewegung vom Sprechenden weg nach e-m höheren Orte hin bezeichnend: up, up to or into; (up) to the top, upstairs; up the river, upstream; ſich ⸗arbeiten v/refl. ⓜ** to toil up a steep slope, &c.; to rise (or mount) by dint of great efforts; fig. ſich ⸗ to work one's way up (in the world); ⸗blicken v/n. (h.) ⓜ** to look (or glance) up; ⸗bringen v/a. ⓜ** to bring (or carry, take) up; ⸗geh(e)n v/n. (ſn) ⓜ** abs. to go (or mount) up, to walk up, to go upstairs; (bitte,) geh(e)n Sie hinauf! (please) step up there!; mit der Stimme ⸗ to raise the pitch of one's voice; ⸗laſſen v/a. ⓜa** to allow to go (or come) up; ⸗laufen v/n. (ſn) ⓜaſt** : den Berg ⸗ to run up …; ⸗schrauben v/a. ⓜⓒc** to screw up, e-e Lampe ꝛc. to turn on; Steuern ⸗ to pile up taxes; ⸗steigen v/n. (ſn) ⓜ** abs. to mount (up), to step (or climb) up; to ascend a ladder, a mountain, &c.; ~ n ⓑ ascent; beim ~ in mounting or ascending; ⸗tragen v/a. ⓜb** to carry (or take) up; ⸗treiben v/a. ⓜ** to drive (or push) up, ⚘ Preiſe, Aktien ꝛc. ⸗ to run (or send, mark) up prices, &c., F to boom (or bull) a stock, &c.; ſich ⸗wagen v/refl. ⓜ** to venture up; ⸗wärts (˘ˊ˘) adv. upward(s); ⸗ziehen ⓜb** v/a. to draw (or pull) up; v/n. (ſn) to move (higher) up.

hin-aus (˘ˊ) adv. **1.** (ant. hinein, vgl. heraus) out (there); oben ⸗ out (from) above; nach vorn ⸗ wohnen to live in the front, to occupy a front room; zum Fenſter, zur Tür ⸗ out of the window, out through the door. — **2.** ell. (für: ⸗gehen) ⸗ mit euch! out you go!, be off!, get out!; ⸗ mit ihm! turn him out!; ⸗ müſſen to be obliged to go out; er weiß nicht (mehr) wo ⸗ he does not know which way to turn, he is at his wits' end; wo ſoll das ⸗? where is that to end?, what will it lead to? — **3.** über etwas ⸗ over (or across, fig. beyond) a th.; über die Kinderjahre ⸗ past (one's) childhood, no longer a child; über die Fünfzig ⸗ on the shady side of fifty.

hin-aus-…, Hin-aus⸗… (˘ˊˊ…) in Verbindung mit verbs, immer trennbar (**), u. in Zſſgn mit verbal nouns und adjectives; Ausgang von einem Orte mit der Richtung von dem Sprechenden weg bezeichnend; wenn die Richtung von dem Sprechenden nicht hervortritt, ſo iſt die Überſetzung oft dieſelbe wie die von „heraus-…" (ſ. d$), ſonſt oft: out (there or yonder); outside, out of doors nach dem v., auch: e(x) (als Präfix) vor dem v.: ⸗begleiten v/a. ⓜ*/* to see a p. out or to the door; ⸗bringen v/a. ⓜ** to bring (or take) out(side); e-n ⸗ (aus dem Zimmer treiben) to turn a p. out (of doors); ⸗drängen v/a. ⓜ** to push (or crowd) out; ⸗fahren v/n. (ſn) u. v/a. ⓜb**: a) to drive out in a carriage, motor-car, &c., to ride (or cycle) out, to sail out; b) über et. ⸗ to drive over (or beyond) a th.; to pass a th. in a carriage, &c.; ⸗führen v/a. ⓜ** to lead forth, to take out; ⸗geh(e)n v/n. (ſn) ⓜ**: a) to go (or walk) out (there); das Zimmer geht auf den Hof hinaus … looks upon (or faces) the yard; b) auf et. ⸗ (endigen) to end (or result, terminate) in a th.; c) über et. ⸗ to go (or pass) beyond a th.; fig. to surpass (or exceed) a th.; ⸗graulen v/a. ⓜ** to frighten away; ⸗laufen v/n. (ſn) ⓜaſt**: a) to come running out; b) fig. (enden) to result in; auf eins ⸗ to be the same (thing) or an (exact) equivalent; es läuft auf daſſelbe hinaus it comes (or amounts) to the same thing (in the end); auf nichts ⸗ to lead to nothing; ⸗legen v/a. ⓜ** to put out; ſich zum Fenſter ⸗ to lean out of the window; ſich ⸗machen, F ſich ⸗packen v/refl. ⓜ** to get out(side), F to take (or pack) o.s. off; ⸗ragen v/n. (h.) ⓜ** to project beyond; (hoch) über et. ⸗ to tower (high) above a th.; ⸗rücken v/a. u. v/n. (ſn) ⓜ** to move out; ~ n ⓑ removal; zeitlich: postponement; ⸗schaffen v/a. ⓜ** to get out (-side); ⸗schieben v/a. ⓜc**: a) to push (or F shove out); b) fig. (aufſchieben) to postpone, to put off; ⸗schießen v/n. (h.) ⓜc(e)ſt**: über et. ⸗ to shoot (or dart) beyond a th.; fig. über das Ziel ⸗ to overstep (or overshoot) the mark; ⸗schmeißen v/a. ⓜa** = ⸗werfen; ⸗sein v/n. (ſn) ⓜa** to be out(side); über et. ⸗ to be past (or beyond) a th.; ſie ſind über alle Gefahr hinaus they are out off all danger; über ſolche Kleinigkeiten iſt er hinaus he is above such trifles; ⸗setzen ⓜ** v/a. to put out or outside; ſich ⸗ v/refl. to sit down outside; ⸗stoßen v/a. ⓜa** to push (or thrust) out, to eject; fig. to cast off or adrift; ⸗stürzen v/n. (ſn) ⓜ** to rush (or bolt) out (of doors); ⸗treiben v/a. ⓜ** to drive out, to expel; es treibt ihn in die Welt hinaus an irresistible desire drives (or impels) him to see the world; ⸗weiſen v/a. ⓜ** to show out; vgl. ⸗werfen; ⸗werfen v/a. ⓜb** to throw out of the window, &c.; (zur Türe) ⸗ to turn out (of doors), to expel, to eject; er wirft ſein Geld zum Fenſter hinaus he throws (F fribbles) away (or squanders) his money; ⸗wollen v/n. (h.) ⓜ**: a) ell. to be wanting to get out; b) fig. (bezwecken) to aim at; wo will das hinaus? what is the purport of it?; hoch (oder oben) ⸗ to aim high, to have lofty aspirations; zu hoch (oder über ſeinen Stand) ⸗ to soar (or aspire) too high; ⸗ziehen ⓜb** v/a.: a) to draw (or drag) out or outside; b) (in die Länge ziehen) to protract; v/n. (ſn): a) to march out; b) aufs Land ⸗ to move out (or to remove) into the country, F to go into the country to live; ſich ⸗ (in die Länge ziehen) v/refl. to drag on, to hang fire; to be (much) delayed.

hin-befördern (˘…) v/a. ⓐa** to convey (or carry) there; ſich ⸗begeben v/refl. ⓐc*/* to proceed (or repair, go) there; ⸗begleiten v/a. ⓐ*/* to accompany there or to a place; ⸗bekommen v/a. ⓐ*/* to succeed in conveying to a place, F to get a th. there; ⸗bestellen v/a. ⓐ*/*: zu e-m, nach einem Orte ⸗ to bid a p. go (or proceed) to a p., a place; ⸗blick m ⓜc.: a) glance at a th.; b) fig. (Rückſicht) regard, consideration; im ~ auf in consideration of, with a view to; ⸗blicken v/n. (h.) ⓜ** to look (or glance) at or towards; ⸗bringen v/a. ⓜ*: a) an einen Ort, zu e-m ⸗ to take or bring (eine Perſon auch: to conduct) to a place, a p.; b) die Zeit ⸗ to spend (or beguile, pass away) - ſein Leben kümmerlich ⸗ to eke out a bare existence, to lead a wretched life; die Stunden müßig ⸗ to idle away the hours; c) ſein Vermögen ⸗ (verſchwenden) to dissipate (F to run through) one's fortune; ⸗brüten v/n. (h.) ⓜ** to sit brooding, to brood away one's time; ~ n ⓑ brooding; gloomy meditation; ⸗dämmern v/n. (h.) ⓐa** to continue (or be) in a somnolent state, to doze (on).

hin-bann(en) † (˘ˊ(˘)) [mhd.] adv. hintan.

Hinde † (˘˘) [ahd.: hind] f ⓐ = Hindin.

hin-denken (˘…) ⓜ** v/n. (h.) to think of (a distant place); wo denkſt du hin? what are you thinking about or of?; ſich an einen Ort ⸗ v/refl. to imagine o.s. in a place, to wander (or roam) in one's thoughts to a place.

hinderlich (˘˘˘) [hindern] a. ⓑ impeding the traffic, &c., obstructive to trade, &c.; (beſchwerlich) troublesome, F in the way, (unbequem) inconvenient; e-m ⸗ ſein to be in a p.'s way; e-m in ſ-m Erfolg, Glück ſein to stand in a p.'s light or way.

Signs (see page XVII): F familiar; P vulgar; ⸗ flash; ⸗ rare; † obsolete (died); * new word (born); +⸗ incorrect; ♪ music;

[**Hinderlichkeit**] — 519 — [**hingeben**]

Hinderlichkeit f ⚛ obstructiveness; inconvenience.
hindern (⌣⌣) [ahd.: hinder; *hinter]
I v/a. ⚔a. (unmöglich machen) to prevent; (aufhalten) to hinder, to stop; (hemmen) to impede, hamper, check, arrest; (versperren) to obstruct; (durchkreuzen) to thwart; (stören) to upset; e-n am Schreiben (ver=)⚬ to prevent a p. from writing; was könnte ihn ⚬, sie zu heiraten? what could stop his (mehr gbr.: him from) marrying her? — **II** ~ ⚙ hindering, &c. (f. I); prevention.
Hindernis (⌣⌣⌣) n ⚙ hindrance; (Hemmnis) impediment, check; tie; äußerliches: obstacle; (Schwierigkeit) difficulty; (Widerwärtigkeit) reverse; drawback; alle Hindernisse aus dem Wege räumen to remove all obstacles; e-m ein ⚬ (oder Hindernisse) in den Weg legen to put (or throw) obstacles in a p.'s way; frei von Hindernissen, auch: untrammelled, unfettered.
Hindernis=mittel ⚔ (⌣⌣⌣...) n/pl. ⚙ frt. entanglement, obstacle, wire fence; **=rennen** n steeplechase, hurdle-race.
Hinderung (⌣⌣⌣) f ⚛ = hindern II.
hin=deuten (⚬...) v/n. (h.) ⚙** auf et. ⚬ to point (or hint) at a th.; fig. to indicate (or intimate) a th.; **=deutung** f ⚛ hint, hinting at a th.; indication (or intimation) of a th. [tuh) hind.]
Hindin (⌣⌣) [Hinde] f ⚙ zo. u. hunt. (Hirsch=)
Hin=draht ⊕ (⚬...) m ⚙ tel. outward wire; **=drängen** ⚙** v/a. to push to or towards ...; sich ⚬ v/refl. to crowd (or throng) to(wards) ||, path. vom Blute: to congest; **=dringen** v/n. (fn) ⚙st** to press (or crowd) to(wards) ||.
hin=durch (⌣⚬) adv. **1.** through(out), across; ganz ⚬ right through; oft verbunden mit „durch": ein Schuß durch die Lungen ⚬ a shot right through the lungs; hier ⚬, dort ⚬ through here, through there; mitten ⚬ right (or straight) through. — **2.** zeitlich: during; through(out); die ganze Nacht ⚬ all through the night, all night long; das ganze Jahr ⚬ all the year round, throughout the year; sein ganzes Leben ⚬ all through his life, throughout (the whole course of) his life; die ganze Zeit ⚬ all the time, all along, F right through.
hin=durch=..., Hin=durch=... (⌣⚬...) in Verbindung mit verbs, immer trennbar (**), und in Zssgn mit verbal nouns = durch=... I (f. ds).
hin=dürfen (⚬...) v/n. (h.) ⚙** ell. to be allowed to go there; **=eilen** v/n. (fn) ⚙** to hurry (or hasten) there.
hin=ein (⌣⚬) adv. (ant. hinaus) **1.** in(to a place); in ... ⚬ into, in(side); da ⚬, hier ⚬ in there, in here; bis tief in die Erde ⚬ deep (down) into the (bowels of the) earth; bis ins Herz ⚬ into the very heart; bis in Tibet ⚬ right into the interior (or heart) of Tibet; zur Tür ⚬ in at (or by) the door; mitten ⚬ (in ||) right into the middle or midst of (||). — **2.** ell. nur ⚬! (please) walk (or step) in!; ⚬ und hinaus in and out. — **3.** in den Tag ⚬ s. Tag; s. auch blau 4, Gelag(e) 2.

hin=ein=..., Hin=ein=... (⚬"...) in Verbindung mit verbs, immer trennbar (**), und in Zssgn mit verbal nouns und adjectives, eine Bewegung in das Innere eines Raumes von dem Sprechenden weg bezeichnend: in, into, inside nach dem v.; auch: in... (als Präfix vor dem v.). Wenn die Richtung von dem Sprechenden weg nicht hervortritt, so ist die Übersetzung oft dieselbe wie die von „herein=..." und „ein=..." (f. dfe): **=arbeiten** v/a. to work (or fit) into; e-e Öffnung ꝛc. ⚬ in || to effect an opening, &c. into ||; sich ⚬ v/refl. to work one's way into; fig. to make o.s. acquainted (or conversant) with a th., to familiarize o.s. with a subject; sich **=begeben** v/refl. ⚙c*/* to go in(to); **=bekommen** v/a. ⚙*/* : (nicht) ⚬ (not) to get (in)to; **=bringen** v/a. ⚙**: a) to take (or carry) in(to), mühsam: to lug in(to); b) fig. e-n ⚬ (in die Patsche) to get a p. into trouble or into a scrape; sich **=denken** v/refl. ⚙**: sich in et. ⚬: a) to go deeply into a th., to dive into a subject; b) sich in j-s Lage ⚬ to (try to) realize (or understand) a p.'s position, to put o.s. in a p.'s place; **=dringen** v/n. (fn) ⚙st** to penetrate (or pierce) into; **=fallen** v/n. (fn) ⚙a** to fall (or tumble) in(to); F fig. to be taken in; iro. da bin ich schön ⚬ gefallen! I am nicely sold!; ⚬ I. to take a p. in; sich **=finden** v/refl. ⚙**: sich in et. ⚬ to accommodate (or reconcile, resign) o.s. to a th.; to familiarize o.s. with a th.; **=geh(e)n** v/n. (fn) ⚙**: a) to go in(to), to enter; bis in (oder zu) et. ⚬ to penetrate (right) into a th.; b) in den Saal geh(e)n zehn Betten hinein the room accommodates (or holds) ...; **=geraten** v/n. (fn) ⚙a*/* accidentally to get (or find one's way) into; **=leben** ⚙** v/n. (h.): in den Tag ⚬ to give no thought to the morrow, to take things easily or as they come; sich ⚬ v/refl. = sich **=finden**; **=lesen** v/refl. ⚙a** to read well into ||; vgl. einlesen II; **=mischen** v/a. und sich ⚬ v/refl. ⚙**, ~ n ⚙ = einmengen; **=müssen** v/n. (h.) ⚙** to be obliged to go in; **=ragen** v/n. (h.) ⚙**: in die Straße ⚬ to project (or jut out) into the street; **=reden** ⚙** v/n. (h.): in e-n ⚬ to give a p. a good talking to; ins Blaue ⚬ to talk at random; sich ⚬ v/refl.: sich in Zorn ⚬ to talk o.s. into a (fit of) passion, to grow angry in talking; sich in Unsinn ⚬ to end up with nonsense; **=reiten** ⚙b** v/n. (fn) to ride (on horseback) into; F v/a. u. sich ⚬ v/refl.: e-n (sich) schön in et. ⚬ to get a p. (o.s.) into a nice pickle or mess; Sie haben mich schön ⚬ geritten you have dragged (or let) me in nicely; **=schaffen** v/a. ⚙** to get (or take) in(to); **=schieben** v/a. ⚙c** to push (or F shove) into; to pass one's finger, &c. into a wound, &c.; **=stecken** v/a. ⚙** to put in(to); ⚙ sein Vermögen in et. ⚬ to put one's money into (or to invest it in) s.th.; **=stoßen** v/a. ⚙a** to push (or thrust) in(to); **=treten** v/n. (fn) ⚙d** to step in(to), to put one's foot inside; **=tun** v/a.

⚙** to put in(to); einen Blick ⚬ to peep (or gaze) into; sich **=wagen** v/refl. ⚙** to venture (to go) in(side); **=wärts** adv. inward(s); **=werfen** v/a. ⚙b** to throw in(to); **=wollen** v/n. (h.) ⚙** to want to go in; das will mir nicht in den Kopf hinein I cannot realize (or understand) that; **=ziehen** ⚙b** v/a.: a) to pull (or draw) in(to); b) fig. e-n in et. ⚬ (verwickeln) to implicate (or involve) a p. in s.th.; v/n. (fn) to move in(to); **=zwängen** ⚙** to force (or squeeze) into.

hin=fahren (⚬...) v/n. (fn) ⚙b**: a) to drive (or go) in a carriage, &c. to a place; b) an et. ⚬ (entlang) to drive along a place, ⚓ to sail along the coast; c) über et. ⚬ to pass (or skim) over a th.; d) fig. (fortgehen) to go away; fahre hin! farewell!, good bye!; e) (sterben) to pass away; v/a. to carry (or take) in a carriage, &c. to a place; mein Kutscher soll Sie ⚬ ... shall drive you there; **=fahrt** f ⚙ driving (or drive) there, 🚂, &c. journey out or there, single journey, ⚓ voyage out or there; fig. (Tod) decease, demise, death; Hin= und Rückfahrt journey there and back, double journey, ⚓ voyage out and home; **=fall** m: a) fall(ing down); b) 🜛 med. prostration; **=fallen** v/n. (fn) ⚙a** to fall (or tumble) down; der Länge nach: to fall down full length; **=fällig** a. ⚛ decaying, declining; (gebrechlich) frail, fragile, vor Alter: decrepit; (schwach) weak, feeble, infirm; (Einsturz drohend) tumble-down; fig. (vergänglich) transient, perishable; von Gründen: (unhaltbar) untenable, shaky; **=fälligkeit** f ⚛ frailty, decrepitude; weakness, feebleness, infirmity; perishableness; **=finden** v/n. (h.) ⚙** und sich ⚬ v/refl. to find one's way to a place; sich **=fläzen** P ⚙**, sich **=flegeln** F ⚙a** v/refl. to sprawl (o.s.) down; **=fliegen** v/n. (fn) ⚙af**: a) to fly there; b) (fortfliegen) to fly away; c) an der Erde ⚬ to skim the ground; **=fliehen** v/n. (fn) ⚙b** to flee (or fly) to a place; die Zeit flieht hin time flies or passes away rapidly; **=fließen** v/n. (fn) ⚙d** to flow towards a place; fig. von der Zeit: to pass away.
hin=fort (⌣⚬) adv. henceforth, for (or in) the future, from this day (forth).
Hin=fracht ⚙ (⚬...) f ⚙ outward freight; Hin= u. Her=fracht freight out and home.
hin=fristen (⚬...) v/a. ⚙** to pass, to spend one's time; **=führen** v/a. und v/n. (h.) ⚙** to lead there, to conduct to a place.
hin=für(o) † (⌣⚬...) = hinfort.
hing (⚬) ind., **=e** (⌣⌣) subj. impf. v. hangen.
Hin=gabe (⚬...) f ⚙ surrender, abandonment; (Ergebenheit) devotion, devotedness, resignation; **=gang** m: a) going to a place; beim ~e in going there; b) (Tod) decease; vgl. =tritt; **=geben** ⚙c** v/a.: a) e-m et. ⚬ (reichen) to pass a th. (on) to a p.; b) (überlassen) to give (or deliver) up, to surrender; (fahren lassen) to abandon; (opfern) to sacrifice; sein Leben ⚬ to lay down

─────────
⚛ scientific; ❀ botanical; ♀ geography; ⊕ machinery; ⚒ mining; ⚔ military; ⚓ marine; ⚙ commercial; ✉ postal; 🚂 railway.

one's life for a p. or a th.; ſich ⌾ v/refl.: a) ſich e-m, einer Sache ⌾ to give o.s. up (or to devote o.s.) to a p., a cause; b) ſich düſteren Gedanken ⌾ to give way to gloomy thoughts, to fall into a reverie; ſich einem wüſten Leben ⌾ to abandon o.s. to (or to pursue) a profligate life; rel. ſich der Sünde, dem Böſen ⌾ to fall into sin, into evil ways; ⌾d p.pr. u. a. ⊕ devoted, self-denying, self-sacrificing; ~n ⌾ u. =gebung f: a) =gabe; b) (Selbſtverleugnung) self-denial, (Ergebung) resignation.

hin-gegen (⌣⌢) adv. (im Gegenteil) on the contrary; (anderſeits) on the other hand; (zum Erſatze) in return.

hin-gegoſſen (⌣...), ⌾gehaucht p.p. u. a. ⊕ ſ. ⌾gießen, ⌾hauchen; ⌾geh(e)n v/n. (ſn) ⊕**: a) to go there, to proceed (or repair) to a place; F da geht er hin und ſingt nicht mehr!, etwa: there, he has had enough (of it)!; it is all up with him; b) an et. ⌾ to go along a th.; über et. ⌾ to pass over a th., to skim (or graze) the surface of a th.; c) fig. leicht über et. ⌾ to pass lightly over a th., F to treat it offhandishly; d) wo geht (führt) dieſer Weg hin? where does this (road) lead to?; wo geht die Fahrt (ob. Reiſe) hin? where are you going to or bound for?, geh. Spr.: whither are you (v. e-m Schiffe: is she) bound?; e) (vergehen) to pass away, to elapse; f) ſo vor ſich ⌾ to saunter along carelessly; ſo ⌾ (erträglich ſein) to be passable; es geht ſo hin it may pass, it will (just) do; g) et. (ungeſtraft) ⌾ laſſen to pass a thing over, to overlook a th., to let it go unpunished; das ſoll dir nicht ungeſtraft ⌾!, oft: F you shall pay for it!; ⌾gehören v/n. (h.) ⊕**/*: wo gehört das hin? where does that go (or belong) to?; es gehört dahin it goes there; da gehört er nicht hin that's not his (proper) place; ⌾gelangen v/n. (ſn) ⊕**/* to arrive at (or to get to) a place, to reach one's destination, fig. to attain one's end; ⌾geraten v/n. (ſn) ⊕a*/* to come (or get) to a place by chance or accident; wo bin ich ⌾? where have I got to?; ⌾geriſſen p.p. v. ⌾reißen; =geſchiedene(r) s. ſ. ⌾ſcheiden; ⌾gießen ⊕d** v/a. to pour out or forth; ⌾gegoſſen p.p. und a.: a) poured out; b) poet. (anmutig liegend) in a charming (or picturesque) attitude, gracefully (or negligently) reclining; ⌾gleiten v/n. (ſn) ⊕b** to glide along; über etwas ⌾ to glide over a th.; ⌾halten v/a. ⊕a**: a) to hold out, to present; b) fig. (vertröſten, warten laſſen) to put off, to keep in suspense; e-n mit der Bezahlung ⌾ to make a p. wait for his money; e-n mit Hoffnungen ⌾ to buoy a p. up (with vain hopes); =haltung f keeping in suspense; ⌾hängen v/a. ⊕** to hang up (there); ⌾hauchen v/a. ⊕** to breathe (lightly) on ...; fig. wie ⌾gehaucht light and graceful; paint. put on with a light (or delicate) touch; ⌾helfen v/n. (h.) ⊕b**: e-n oder e-m ⌾ to aid a p. in reaching

(or getting to) a place; ⌾holen v/a. ⊕** to fetch to a place; ⌾horchen, ⌾hören v/n. (h.) ⊕** to listen for a th.

Hinke-bein (⌣⌣) n ⊕, =fuß m limping person, F dot-and-go-one.

Hinkel prov. (⌣⌣) n ⊕ = Hünkel.

hinken (⌣⌢) [ahd.] I v/n. (h.; bei Ortsveränderungen ſn) 1. to limp, to halt, to go lame, F to hobble (along); auf einem Fuße ⌾ to be lame on one foot; ſie hinkt ein wenig she has a slight limp. — 2. (auf e-m Fuße hüpfen) to hop along on one foot. — 3. fig. (ſich langſam fortbewegen) to drag o.s. (wearily) along; jedes Gleichnis hinkt all comparisons are imperfect; die Sache hinkt, es hinkt damit the matter is hanging fire, there is a hitch (or a screw loose) somewhere; ſeine Verſe ⌾ there is verse lacks rhythm, his lines are clumsy. — II ~ n ⌾ 4. limp(ing), lameness. — III ⌾d p.pr. und a. ⊕ 5. limping, lame, F hobbling (along). — IV ~de([r] m) f ⊕ 6. limping (or lame) person. ⌾de(r) (ſ. hinken IV.).

Hinker(in) ⌣(⌣⌣v)m ⊕ (f ⊕) = Hinfenſ

Hinke-teufel (⌣⌣...) m ⊕ devil on two sticks; =vers m, pros.: ⌣ choliamb(us).

hin-knien v/n. ⊕** to kneel down; ⌾kommen v/n. (ſn) ⊕**: a) to come (or get) to a place; ich komme nirgends hin I go nowhere, I don't go out (or visit) much; b) = ⌾geraten; wo ist meine Uhr ⌾gekommen? what has become of my watch?; ⌾können v/n. (h.) ⊕** to be able to go (or get) there; ⌾fränfeln v/n. (h.) ⌾a** to pine away (or ⌾; ⌾kriechen v/n. (ſn) ⊕dſ** to crawl there, to creep along; ⌾kritzeln v/a. ⌾a** to scribble down (at random).

Hink-ſtand (⌣...) m ⊕ Turnerei: standing (or posture, position) on one foot.

Hin-kunft (⌣⌣) f ⊕ arrival (bſſ. Anfunft).

Hink-vers (⌣⌣) m ⊕ = Hinfevers.

hin-langen (⌣...) ⊕** v/a. to hand over, to pass on; v/n. (h.): a) ⌾ nach et. to reach for a th.; b) ⌾ (bis) zu ... to extend as far as ...; ⌾länglich a. ⊕ sufficient, adequate, (völlig genügend) ample; nicht ⌾ insufficient; adv. a. enough; =länglichkeit f ⊕ sufficiency, adequacy, ⌾laſſen v/a. ⊕a** ell. to allow to go there; ⌾läſſig † a. = nachläſſig; ⌾laufen v/n. (ſn) ⊕aſt**: a) to run there; wo iſt er ⌾gelaufen? where has he gone to?; b) von Sachen: to extend; längs (ob. neben) et. ⌾ to run alongside a th.; ⌾leben v/n. (h.) ⊕** to live (thoughtlessly) on; ſtill für ſich ⌾ to live in quiet seclusion; ⌾legen ⊕** v/a. to lay (or put) down in a place; ſich ⌾ v/refl. to lie down; F ſich ⌾ und ſterben to lie down to die; ⌾leiten ⊕**, ⌾lenken ⊕** v/a. to lead (or conduct) to a place; j-s Aufmerkſamkeit auf et. ⌾lenfen to direct a p.'s attention to a th.; ⌾locken v/a. ⊕** to entice (or allure) there; ⌾machen ⊕** v/a.: et. ſo ⌾ to make a th. in a careless way; ſich ⌾ v/refl. to proceed (or betake o.s.) to a place; =marſch m march there or out; auf dem ~e in marching there; ⌾marſchie

ren v/n. (ſn) ⊕*/* to march there; ⌾müſſen v/n. (h.) ⊕** to be obliged to go there, to be bound to proceed to a place; =nahme f ⊕ acceptance, unterwürfige: submission to; ⌾nehmen v/a. ⊕a**: a) to take; auf Treu und Glauben ⌾ to accept with the fullest confidence, to take upon trust; b) (ſich gefallen laſſen) to put up with, to submit to, F to swallow an insult; c) e-n mit ⌾ to take a p. to a place; ⌾neigen ⊕** v/a. u. ſich ⌾ v/refl. to incline to(wards) //; v/n. (h.): zu et. ⌾ (Hang haben) to have a propensity for, to lean to, to be inclined (or prone) to; ~ n u. =neigung f ⊕ inclination, leaning, propensity.

hinnen (⌣⌣) [ahd.: hence] adv.: (von) ⌾ (from) hence; von ⌾ geh(e)n to go away, F to be off; fig. von ⌾ ſcheiden (ſterben) to die, to pass away, rel. to depart this life.

hin-opfern (⌣...) v/a. ⌾a** (u. ſich ⌾ v/refl.) to sacrifice (o.s.); geh. Spr.: to immolate; ~ n ⌾ u. =opferung f ⊕ immolation; ⌾paſſen v/n. (h.) ⊕** u. ſich ⌾ v/refl. to fit in(to) a place, to be suitable for //; er paßt nicht hin he is out of place there, he is not adapted for that place; ⌾pflanzen v/a. (u. ſich ⌾ v/refl.) ⊕** to plant (o.s.) there, weitS. to place (o.s.) there; ⌾plappern F v/a. ⌾a** to mumble (indistinctly); ⌾purzeln F v/n. (ſn) ⌾a** to tumble down; ⌾raffen ⊕** to carry (or take) off or away; ⌾reden v/a. ⊕**: et. nur ſo (ob. ohne Nachdenken) ⌾ to say (or utter) without thinking; ⌾reichen ⊕** v/a.: die Hand ⌾ to stretch out one's hand; v/n. (h.) (ausreichen, genügen) to suffice, to be sufficient; ⌾reichend a. ⊕ = ⌾länglich; =reiſe f ⊕ (ant. Herreiſe) journey there or out, ⌾ voyage out, outward passage; auf der ~ on the way (or journey) there; ⌾reiſen v/n. (ſn) ⊕** to (make a) journey there, to travel to a place; ⌾reißen ⊕** v/a. to carry off forcibly; fig. zur Bewunderung ⌾ to enrapture, to enchant; ſich vom Zorn ⌾ laſſen to be carried away by (or to give way to) one's passion; von Wonne ⌾geriſſen transported with joy; ⌾reißend p.pr. u. a. ⊕ rapturous, enchanting, charming; ⌾reiten v/n. (ſn) ⊕b** to go (or ride) there on horseback; ⌾richten ⊕** v/a.: a) auf et. ⌾ to direct to (-wards) a th.; b) (zugrunde richten) to ruin; c) (aus dem Leben ſchaffen) to execute, to put to death, mit dem Schwerte: to decapitate, to behead, durch den Strang: to hang; ſ. Beil 1; er ließ die Räuber ⌾ he had the robbers put to death; ⌾gerichtet w. to be executed, to suffer the extreme penalty of the law, Hingerichtete(r) s. ⊕ executed criminal; p. who has suffered capital punishment; =richtung f ⊕ execution, capital punishment, mit dem Schwerte: decapitation, =ritt m @c. ride out or there; ⌾rücken ⊕** v/a. to (re)move there; v/n. (ſn) to march there; ⌾ſagen v/a. ⊕** = ⌾ſprechen; ⌾ſchaffen v/a. ⊕** to convey (or carry) there; =ſchaffung f ⊕ conveyance, carriage;

Zeichen (ſ. S. XVII): F familiär; P Volksſprache; ſ Gaunerſprache; ⌾ ſelten; † alt (auch geſtorben); * neu (auch geboren); +* unrichtig;

₂ſchauen v/n. (h.) ⓖ** = ₂ſehen; ₂ſcheiden v/n. (ſn) ⓔ** to pass away (peacefully), to die, to depart this life; =geſchiedene(r) ⓖ (the) deceased; rel. oft: (the) departed; ~ ↘ n ㉓ decease, demise; ſich ₂ſcheren F v/refl. ⓖ***, etwa: to go off there; ₂ſchicken v/a. ⓖ*** to send there; ₂ſchießen ⓖc(e)n** v/a. u. v/n. (h.) to shoot (or fire) at a th.; v/n. (ſn) to shoot (or rush, dart) along; ₂ſchiffen ⓖ** v/n. (ſn) to steer one's course towards (or to make for) a place; längs (od. an) der Küſte ₂ to hug (or keep close to) the shore or the land; v/a. to ship (or to send by water) to a place; ₂ſchlachten v/a.ⓖ*** to slaughter (cruelly), to butcher, to massacre; ₂ſchlagen ⓖb** v/n.: a) (h.) to strike down on; b) F (ſn) (heftig ſfallen) to fall down heavily, Reitſport: F to go (or come) a cropper; der Länge nach ₂ to fall (or go) down full length; v/a. e-m den Ball ₂ to send a p. the ball with a racket, a cricket-bat, &c.; ſich ₂ſchlängeln v/refl. ⓖa** to wind along, to meander (along); ₂ſchleichen v/n. (ſn) u. ſich ₂ v/refl. ⓖaſt**: a) to sneak to a place; b) von der Zeit: to creep on, to hang on hand; vom Fluſſe: to creep wearily (or steadily) along; ₂ſchlendern v/n. (ſn) ⓖa** to saunter (or jog) along; ₂ſchleppen v/a. (u. ſich ₂ v/refl.) ⓖ** to drag (o.s.) along; ₂ſchleudern v/a. ⓖa** to fling (or hurl) there; ₂ſchlüpfen v/n. (ſn) ⓖ** to slip there; über et. ₂ to pass (or skim) lightly over (or across) a th.; ₂ſchmachten v/n. (ſn) ⓖ** to pine (or waste) away, to languish; ₂ſchmelzen v/n. (ſn) ⓖb(e)ſt** to melt away; ₂ſchmieren v/a. ⓖ** malend: to daub, ſchreibend: to scribble, to scrawl; ₂ſchreiben v/a. ⓖ** to write down, to pen; flüchtig ₂ to jot down, to dash off; vgl. ₂ſchmieren; ₂ſchütten v/a. ⓖ** to pour down or out, (verſchütten) to spill; ₂ſchwimmen v/n. (ſn) ⓖa(b)** to swim to(wards) a place; da ſchwimmt er hin there he is swimming (along); ₂ſchwinden v/n. (ſn) ⓔ** to pass (or dwindle, fade) away, to vanish; ₂d a. ⓖ evanescent; ₂ſegeln v/n. (ſn) ⓖa** to sail along or to a place; vgl. ₂ſchiffen; ₂ſehen v/n. (h.) ⓖa** to glance towards a place; ſehen Sie hin! look there!; ohne ₂zuſehen without looking; feſt auf et. ₂ſehen to fix one's eyes on a th.; ſich ₂ſehnen v/refl. ⓖ**: ſich nach der Heimat ₂ to long for one's home; ₂ſein v/n. ⓖa** ſ. hin 3; ₂ſenden v/a. ⓖa** = ₂ſchicken; ₂ſetzen v/a. (u. ſich ₂ v/refl.) ⓖ** to set (to sit) down; to (take a) seat; =ſicht f ⓖ regard, (Erwägung) consideration, (Beziehung) reference; in dieſer ~ in this respect; in ~ auf ſeine Verdienſte 2c. in consideration of …, on the strength of …; ₂ſichtlich, ₂ſichts prp. mit gen. with regard (or reference) to, in respect of; regarding, respecting, concerning; as regards, as to; about; ₂ſiechen v/n. (ſn) to waste away (through sickness), to be (slowly) dying; ₂ſingen v/n.

(h.) ⓖſt**: leiſe (od. halblaut) vor ſich ₂ to hum to o.s.; ₂ſinken v/n. (ſn) ⓔſt**: a) to sink down; tot ₂ to drop down dead; vor Schwäche ₂ to collapse, to break down; b) (ſ.-ſtürzen) to crumble away, to fall to the ground or to ruins; ₂ſollen v/n. (h.) ⓖ** ell. to have to go there; wo ſoll es hin?: a) where is it to go?; b) where are we bound for?; ₂ſprechen v/a. ⓖa**: (nur ſo) ₂ to talk lightly or inconsiderately; vor ſich ₂ to talk to o.s.; es war das ſo ₂geſprochen worden it had been uttered in an offhandish way; ₂ſpringen v/n. (ſn) ⓔſt** to jump (or leap) down; ₂ſtellen v/a. (u. ſich ₂ v/refl.) ⓖ**: a) to place (o.s.) somewhere; b) fig. e-n als Muſter ₂ to put a p. up as a pattern or model; als zweifelhaft ₂ to declare doubtful; ſich ₂ als et. to represent o.s. as s.th., fälſchlich: to pose as s.th.; ₂ſterben v/n. (ſn) ⓔb** to die (or have) a slow (or lingering) death; to vanish, to drop off, von der Stimme: to die away; ~ n ㉓ lingering death; ₂ſtolpern v/n. (ſn) ⓔa** to stumble and fall; ₂ſtreben v/n. (h.) ⓖ**: nach et. ₂ to strive for a th.; phys. to tend (or gravitate) towards //; ₂ſtrecken ⓖ** v/a.: a) die Hand ₂ to stretch out one's hand; b) e-n ₂ to fell (or knock) a p. to the ground, to lay a p. low; ₂geſtreckt liegen to lie prostrate; ſich ₂ v/refl. to stretch o.s. (down) on the grass, &c.; ₂ſtreichen v/n. (ſn) ⓖaſt**: a) von der Zeit: to slip by; b) an et. ₂ to graze a th.; ₂ſtreuen v/a. ⓖ** to strew (or scatter, sprinkle) about; ₂ſtürzen v/n. (ſn): a) = ₂ſchlagen b; b) nach e-m Orte ₂ to rush to a place; v/a. to bring to the ground; ₂ſudeln v/a. ⓖa** = ₂ſchmieren.

hint-an (ⓤ) [umgedeutet aus hindann] adv. (beiſeite, weg) aside, out of the way; (hinten andern) behind, in the rear.

hint-an=…, Hint-an=… (ⓤ…) in Verbindung mit verbs, immer trennbar (**), u. in Zſſgn mit verbal nouns Beſeitigung, Zurückſetzung bezeichnend: aside, behind, back; with disdain nach dem v.

hin=tändeln (ⓤ…) v/a. ⓖa** to trifle away one's time.

hint-an=halten ↘ (ⓤ…) v/a. ⓖa** to stop, to check; ₂ſetzen v/a. ⓖ** to set aside, to put in the background; (vernachläſſigen) to slight, neglect, disregard; (für nichts erachten) to set at naught; ~ n u.=ſetzung f ⓖ slight(ing), neglect, disregard; mit ~ aller Rückſichten setting (or casting) all considerations aside; ~ der Pflicht dereliction of (one's) duty; ₂ſteh(e)n v/n. (h.) ⓔ** to be left behind; ₂ müſſen to be obliged to stand back; ₂ſtellen v/a. ⓖ** to (treat with) disdain, to leave in the cold; vgl. ₂ſetzen.

hin-tappen (ⓤ…) v/n. (ſn) u. ſich ₂ v/refl. ⓖ** to grope to a place; ₂taumeln v/n. (ſn) ⓖa** to stagger (or totter) along, to reel forward.

hinten (ⓤ) [ahd.: (be)hind] adv. (ant. vorn) behind; (im Hintergrunde) in the rear, at the back, in the back-ground;

(ganz am Ende) quite at the end; ↓ aft; nach ₂ gelegenes Zimmer back-room; ₂ hin to the rear, ↓ sternward(s); ₂ hinaus at the back (of the house); nach ₂ (heraus) wohnen to live at the back of the house, to live in a back room; von ₂ from behind, from the back, ⚔, ↓ from the rear; ₂ anfügen an e-n Brief 2c. to add (or append) to …; von ₂ angreifen to attack in the rear; ſich ₂ anſchließen to bring up the rear; ₂ ausſchlagen to kick from behind, to kick up one's heels (a. fig.); ₂ bleiben to stay (or linger, lag) behind; ₂ weit in der Türkei, etwa: in the far East, in far-away Turkey: fig. Peter ₂, Peter vorn (beſtändiges Scherwenzeln) (nothing but) Peter this and Peter that; Peter here, there, and everywhere.

hinten-an (ⓤ…) adv. behind, in the rear, at the back; ₂an=ſetzen v/a. ⓖ** to set back; vgl. hintanſetzen; ₂drein = ₂an; zeitlich: afterwards, after the event, after the fair; ₂hin to(wards) the back; ₂nach = ₂an; ₂über upside down, backwards.

hinter (ⓤ) [ahd.] prp. (mit dat. auf die Frage wo?, mit acc. auf die Frage wohin?; bisw. auch verſchmelzend mit def. art.: ₂m = ₂ dem, ₂n = ₂ den, ₂s = ₂ das) 1. behind; ₂ der Tür ſteh(e)n, ₂ die Tür ſtellen to stand behind the door; ₂ e-m geh(e)n to walk at the back of a p.; vgl. Leinander. — 2. ſ. Binde 4, bringen 8; ₂ e-m her ſein, ₂ einer Sache her ſein to be after a p., a matter; ſ. hetzen 1; ſich ₂ die Arbeit (her)machen to set (vigorously) to work, to put one's shoulders to the wheel; fig. e-n ₂s Licht führen to deceive (or gull) a p.; e-m ₂ die Ohren ſchlagen to box a p.'s ears; fig. er hat's (dich) ₂ den Ohren he is very sly or cunning or artful, F he knows a thing or two; ich werde es mir ₂ die Ohren ſchreiben I will remember it or bear it in mind; e-n ₂ Schloß und Riegel bringen to put a p. under lock and key or in(to) jail or in(to) prison, to lock a p. up; die Tür ₂ ſich zumachen to close … after one; ſ. Berg 2, Hand 4; ₂ die Sache, ₂ j-s Schliche kommen to get to the bottom of a matter, to find out (or detect) a p.'s trickery; ₂ die Schule gehen to play (the) truant; e-n ₂ ſich laſſen to outrun (or distance, outstrip) a p.; weit ₂ andern zurück ſein to be far behind others in knowledge, &c.; ₂ der Zeit zurück ſein to be behind the times or the age; er ſteckt ₂ der Sache he is at the bottom of it (all); es ſteckt nicht viel ₂ ihm there is not much (sense) in him, F he's not up to much; unmittelbar ₂ immediately after, auch: in the wake of.

hinter=…, Hinter=… (ⓤ…) I in Zſſgn mit s., a. und v. I in Zſſgn mit s. (ⓤ…) bz., daß et. hinten gelegen iſt (ant. Vor(der)=…), zB. ~fuß, ~haupt.

II in Zſſgn mit verbs (ⓤ…), immer trennbar (**), in den „nach hinten hin" und wird meiſt durch Orts-adverbien oder adverbiale Redens-arten gegeben, zB.

[Hinterachse] — 522 — [hinterschlucken]

₂gehen v/n. — III in sogenannten echten Bssen mit v. („..." unbetont), immer untrennbar(*), hat verschiedene uneigentliche Bed., zB. ₂gehen v/a.

Hinter=achse ☉ (ˊ‿...) f ⊕ mach. hind axle-tree, e-r Lokomotive: trailing-axle; =**ansicht** f, arch., Zeichenkunst: back-view; =**backe** f buttock, Schlächterei auch: hind-piece; =**bein** n hind-leg; sich auf die ~e setzen ob. stellen: a) von Tieren: to rear up (behind); b) fig. (sich zur Wehre setzen) to put o.s. in a state of defence, to defend o.s. (stubbornly); to show one's teeth, F to show fight; v. Hunden: sich auf die ~e setzen to sit up (and beg); her. auf den ~en stehend rampant; ₂**bleiben** (ˊ‿‚L‿) v/n. (sn) ⊕¹** to remain (or stay) behind; (ˊ‿‚‿ˊ) v/n. (sn) ⊕¹**: vier Söhne sind geblieben (s)he left ... behind; =**bliebene**[r] m f ⊕ survivor; jur. relict; bsd. pl. die ~en the mourning survivors, the mourners pl.; ₂**bringen** v/a. (ˊ‿‚‿) ⊕¹** to take to the back; (essen) to eat, F to pack away; (ˊ‿‚‿‚) ⊕¹**: e-m et. ₂ to give a p. (secret) information of a th., (secretly) to inform a p. of a th.; (angeben) to denounce, in Schulen: F to sneak; ~ n ⊕ u. =**bringung** f ⊕ (secret) information; denunciation, F sneaking; =**bringer(in** f ⊕) m ⊕ informer; (police-)spy; weitS. tell-tale, F sneak; =**bug** (ˊ‿...) m ⊕ vet., zo. ham; =**deck** ⊥ n quarter-deck, poop; ₂**drein** (ˊ‿‚‿ˊ) adv. afterwards, subsequently; vgl. hintendrein; ₂**drücken** (ˊ‿‚‿ˊ) v/a. ⊕¹** to push back.

hintere (ˊ‿‿) I a. ⊕ (D9) (ant. vordere, mittlere) 1. (of) behind; in the rear, at the back; ↔ posterior (a. ♀, anat., &c.). — II s. ⊕ 2. der (die, das) ~ the one (who is) behind or in the rear, that which is hindmost or at the back. — 3. der ~e m, Hinterer posterior, weniger anständig: F bottom, backside, behind, P bum.

hinter-einander (ˊ‿‚‿‚ˊ‿): ₂ weg without a pause, F at a stretch; ₂ geh(e)n to walk single file or in a line; sie kommen ₂ ... one after another; drei Tage ₂ ... in succession, ... running, F ... at a stretch, seltener: ... successively or consecutively; ₂ geschaltet elect. von Zellen: in series; ~**schaltung** f ⊕ elect. series arrangement or connexion; ₂ weg without a pause, F at a stretch.

Hinter=eisen ☉ (ˊ‿...) n ⊕: a) = Pflugschar; b) Hufschmiede: hind-shoe; =**fuß** m hind-foot; rechter ~ eines Pferdes spearfoot; ₂**füßig** a. ⊕ orn.: ↔ pygopodous; =**galerie** ⊥ f stern-gallery; ₂**gangen** (ˊ‿‚‿‚) p.p. v. hintergehen; =**gang(e)ne**[r] m f ⊕ dupe, F jay; =**gäßchen** (ˊ‿...) n slum, alley; =**gasse** f back-street; =**gebäude** n back-premises pl., building at the back; =**gedanke** m mental reservation, deep (or crooked) design, (fr.) arrière-pensée; ₂**geh(e)n** (ˊ‿‚‿‚) v/n. (sn) ⊕¹** to walk behind; (ˊ‿‚‿‚ˊ) v/a. ⊕* (täuschen) to deceive, dupe, beguile, circumvent, hoodwink, impose upon; F to take in, to diddle; beim Spiele ₂ (betrügen) to cheat, weitS. to trick; ~ n ⊕ und

=**gehung** f ⊕ deception, imposition; F take in, sell; =**geschirr** ☉ (ˊ‿...) n Sattlerei: crupper; des Wagenpferdes: breeching; =**gestell** ☉ n: ~ eines vierrädrigen Fuhrwerks: back part of a coach or carriage, am Pfluge: hind-carriage; =**glied** n (im pl. a. =**gliedmaßen** inv.): posterior limb or part; math. ~ eines Verhältnisses: ↔ consequent; ✕ rearrank, rear-file; =**grund** m e-s Gemäldes ıc.: background; fig. im ~e steh(e)n to be (put) in the background; in den ~ treten to recede into the background, to stand back; =**haar** n back-hair; =**halt** m: a) meist ✕ ambush, ambuscade; in e-n ~ fallen, geraten to fall into an ambush or a trap; e-n (sich) in e-n ~ legen to form an ambush; im ~e liegen to lie in ambush; b) (Nachstellung, Fallstrick) insidious attack, snare; e-m e-n ~ legen to lay (or set) a trap for a p.; c) fig. = =**gedanke**, zB. ohne ~ without reserve, unreservedly; d) ✕ (Reservemannschaft) reserve; weitS. support, mainstay; e-n starken ~ h. to have strong support or supporters, to be backed up well; ₂**haltig** a. ⊕ (verschwiegen) reserved, close; =**hand** f: a) ~ des Affen ıc. = =**fuß**; b) man. (hintere Hälfte des Pferdes) hind-hand; hind-quarter (of a horse); c) Spiel: die ~ h., in der ~ (hinter dem Ausspielenden) sein, sitzen to come (or play) last, to have the last hand; =**haupt** n back (part) of the head, hind part of the head, bisw. hindhead, anat.: ↔ occiput; =**haupt**(ˊ‿...)=**bein** n, =**knochen** m: ↔ occipital bone; =**haus** n back-part of the house; back-premises pl.; ₂**her** (ˊ‿‚ˊ) adv. a) örtlich: behind, in the rear, at the tail-end; ₂ laufen to run behind; F sehr ₂ (hinter et. her) sein eagerly to pursue a th., F to be (working) hard at a th.; b) zeitlich: afterwards, when it is (or was) too late; Sprichw. ₂ ist man am klügsten (it's) easy to prophesy after the event; =**hof** (ˊ‿...) m ⊕ back-yard, back-garden, (Hühnerhof) poultry-yard; =**indien** ☉ npr/n. ⊕ a. Further India, weitS. Indo-China; ₂**indisch** a. ⊕ of (or relating to) Further India, Indo-Chinese; =**kammer** f (small) back-room, back-chamber; =**kastell** ⊥ n quarter-deck; =**keule** f leg of mutton, veal, &c.; =**kiemer** m, zo. (Schnecken) ↔ opisthobranch(iate); =**kopf** m = =**haupt**; =**laden** m: a) shop at the back; back-part of the shop; b) (hinterer Fensterladen) back-shutter; =**lader** ✕ m (ant. Vorder-l.) breech-loading rifle, breech-loader; =**lage** f a) deposit; b) ⊕ für Bilder, Spiegel ıc.: scale-board; =**land** n: a) interior of a country or continent; far-away land; (Absatzgebiet) outlet; b) ⚥ in Afrika ıc.: ⸀ hinter-land; ₂**lassen** (ˊ‿‚‿‚) v/a. ⊕ a** to let a p. go to the back; (ˊ‿‚‿‚ˊ) v/a. ⊕ a*: e-m ein Andenken ıc. ₂ to leave a p. a souvenir, &c. (behind); (sterbend zurücklassen) to leave (at one's death); e-m et. (letztwillig) ₂ to leave a p. s.th. in one's will, to bequeath a p. s.th.; ₂e Werke von // posthumous works pl. of //; eine Botschaft, Nach-

richt ₂ to leave a message, to leave word; die ~en the survivors (or mourners) pl. of a p.; ~ n ⊕ = =**lassung**; =**lassenschaft** (ˊ‿‚‿‚ˊ) f ⊕ property left, estate; =**lassung** f ⊕ leaving, &c.; e-r Erbschaft: bequest to a p., legacy left to a p.; =**last** ⊥ (ˊ‿...) f stern-freight; ₂**lastig** ⊥ a. ⊕: das Schiff ist ₂ the ship is overloaded at (or she is too much by) the stern; =**lauf** m, hunt. hind-leg; =**leder** n: a) Schuhmacherei: quarter(s pl.) of a shoe or boot; b) ✕ = Arsch-l.; ₂**legen** ⊕ (ˊ‿‚‿ˊ) v/a. ⊕* to deposit; ~ n ⊕ = =**legung**; =**leger**(in f ⊕) m ⊕ depositor; =**legung** f deposit; (Teilbedung) margin; gegen ~ von // on depositing; =**legungs-stelle** f office for (receiving) deposits; =**leib** (ˊ‿...) m ⊕ hind-quarter of an animal; zo. back- (↔ posterior) part of the body, bei Fischen, Insekten, Reptilien, Vögeln: ↔ abdomen; Schneiderei: back of a dress; =**list** f: a) artifice, (Tücke) cunning, (Betrug) fraud, cheating, deception, (Verrat) treachery; b) (Falschheit) falseness, perfidiousness, deceit(fulness), F depth; ₂**listig** a. artful, cunning, crafty, fraudulent; treacherous, false, perfidious, deceitful, F deep, (ränkevoll) designing; =**listigkeit** f ⊕ = =**list** b.

hinterm (ˊ‿) = hinter dem (s. hinter). **Hinter=mann** (ˊ‿...) m ⊕: a) one who is (or marches) behind; ✕ rear-rank man; ⊥ next astern, pl. rear-ships; b) ⊕ ~ auf Wechseln: later (or next, subsequent) endorser of a bill; c) Spiel: wer ist mein ~? who comes (or plays) after me?, who comes next?; d) (Anstifter) wirepuller, instigator, (Stützender) backer; =**maschine** f ⊕ mach. operator; elect. electromotor (for conversion of electrical into mechanical force); =**mast** ⊥ m (Besanmast) mizzen-mast; =**mauerung** f, arch. spandrel.

hintern (ˊ‿) = hinter den (s. hinter).

Hinter=pferd (ˊ‿...) n ⊕ shaft-horse; =**pförtchen** n (dim. von =**pforte**) back-door (a. fig.); =**pforte** f: a) back-gate, postern; b) ⊥ stern- (chase) port; =**pfote** f hind-paw or -foot; =**quartier** n apartments (or lodgings) pl. at the back (or rear) of a house, back-room; auch ⸀ hintere 3; =**rad** ☉ n back-wheel, hind-wheel, mach. e-r Lokomotive: trailingwheel; =**rast** ☉ f beim Gewehre: top-bent, full-cock notch; =**raum** m (space at the back) back-room; ⊥ after-hold; =**reihe** ✕ f rear-file; ₂**rücks** adv. from behind, from the back; fig. behind one's back, perfidiously, in an underhand way.

hinters (ˊ‿) = hinter das (s. hinter). **Hinter=satz** (ˊ‿...), =**sasse** m ⊕: a) (Nachkomme) descendant; b) Lehnswesen: copyholder; c) (Pächter) tenant-farmer, under-tenant; =**satz** m: a) log. conclusion; b) gr. (Nachsatz) ↔ apodosis; =**schanze** ⊥ f poop; =**schenkel** m: a) back(-part) of the thigh, b) hind-leg; =**schiff** ⊥ n stern, (ship's) steerage, after-body; ₂**schlingen** ⊕¹**, ₂**schlucken** ⊕¹** F v/a. to swallow down (greedily), to bolt; bsd. Flüssiges-

---

Signs (see page XVII): F familiar; P vulgar; ʃ flash; ⸙ rare; † obsolete (died); * new word (born); ⁺⁺ incorrect; ♪ music;

[Hintersegel] — 523 — [hinunterwerfen]

to gulp (down), F to swill (down); =segel ↓ n after-sail; =seite f hindpart, back, rear (nicht: backside!; f. hintere 3); (Rückseite) reverse (side) of a medal, &c.; =sitz m back-seat; =spieler m Fußball: back(s), three-quarter-back.

hinterst (ˇ…) sup. v. hinter(e) ⊕ u. =e([r] m) f ⑰ hindmost, (letzt) last; ↓ sternmost; adv. zu² hindmost, last (of all); ↓ sternmost, aftmost.

Hinter=steven ↓ (ˇ…) m ⑫ stern-post, main-post; =stich ⊕ m Näherei: back-stitch; =stube f back-room; =stück n hind-piece; Braten aus dem ~ (des Rindes) topside of the round (of beef); =teil m, n hind- (or back-)part, back, rear of a house, &c.; hind-quarter of an ox, &c.; eines Hemdes ꝛc.: seat, tail, eines Kiraffes: back-plate, eines Schiffes: after-body, quarter, (Heck) stern; e-s Wagens: back; =treffen ⚔ n rear-guard of an army; ins ~ kommen, geraten to fight a rear-guard action, fig. to bring up the rear; =treiben v/a. (ˇ…ˇ…) ⑪** to drive (to the) back; (ˇ…ˇ…) ⑪*: et. ² to prevent (or hinder, stop) a th.; (einen Querstrich durch et. machen) to thwart a p.('s designs), (vereiteln) to frustrate, durch Gegenlist: to counteract; ~n ㉓, =treibung f ⑯ prevention, hindrance, frustration, counteraction; =treppe (ˇ…) f back-stairs pl., auch: servants' staircase; =treppen=politik f backstair (or under-hand) policy; =treppen=roman m cheap novel, F shilling-shocker, penny-dreadful; =trinken v/a. ⑪* to drink (greedily), to gulp down; =tür(e) f back-door; postern(-door); fig. (Schlupftür) loop-hole, escape, outlet, hole to creep out of; sich (dat.) eine ~ offen halten to keep (o.s.) a back-door open (where to slip out at), to keep o.s. a loop-hole; =verdeck ↓ n quarter-deck; =viertel n bsd. vom Schlachtvieh: hind-quarter, loin of beef, &c.; =wagen ⊕ m = =gestell; =wäldler (T) m back-woodsman, Am. u. Austr. auch: squatter; =wand f: a) back-wall; b) thea. back-scene(ry); =wärts adv.: a) to(wards) the back or the rear; bisw. hindward, ↓ aft; (rückwärts) backwards, (v. hinten) from behind; b) = zurück; =zacken ⊕ m, metall. des Frischherdes: back-plate, ash-plate; =zeug n = =geschirr; =ziehen (ˇ…ˇ…) ⑪b* v/a. to drag (to the) back; v/n. (n) to move to the back; (ˇ…ˇ…) v/a. ⑪b* (unterschlagen) to embezzle, to defalcate; Steuern ² to defraud the revenue; ~ n ㉓ u. =ziehung f ⑯ embezzlement, defalcation; =zimmer (ˇ…) n back-room.

hin=traben (ˇ…) v/n. (n) ⑪** to trot along; =tragen v/a. ⑪b** to carry to a place; =treiben ⑪* v/a. to drive to a place; v/n. (n) ↓ to drift to(wards) a place; =treten v/n. (n) ⑪d** vor ² to step (or alight) somewhere; vor e-n ² to (take one's) stand before a p.; =tritt m (Tod) decease, demise, death, rel. oft: last journey; =tun v/a. ⑪** to put somewhere; ich weiß nicht, wo ich ihn ² soll I know his face, but I can't remember his name.

hin-über (ˇ…) I adv. over (there); to the other side, across; oft mit über, z.B.: über die Berge ² beyond (or over) the mountains; fig. wir sind noch nicht über den Berg ² we are not out of the wood yet; er ist ² : a) he has crossed; b) fig. (ist tot) he has passed away, poet. he has crossed the bar. — II ~ n ⑫: ~ u. Herüber (passage) across and back.

hin-über=..., Hin-über=... (ˇ…) in Verbindung mit verbs, immer trennbar (**), und in Zssgn mit verbal nouns, Entfernung v. Sprechenden über et. hinweg bezeichnend: over, across, to the other side; beyond nach dem v.; auch: trans-... (als Präfix) vor dem v.; =beförderung f ⑯ ferrying over; sich ²begeben v/refl. ⑨c** to cross (over); ²blicken v/n. (h.) ⑱** to look (or glance) across a river, &c.; zu e-m ² to glance towards a p.; ²bringen v/a. ⑰** to take (or carry, get) over or across, to convey across; math. auf die andere Seite einer Gleichung ² to transpose; ~ n ㉓ carriage (or conveyance) across; math. transposition; ²eilen v/n. (n) ⑱** to hasten (or hurry) across; ²fahren ⑥b** v/n. (n) to pass to the other side, to cross the river, &c.; v/a. to convey across, to take over; ²fliegen ⑥** , ²fließen ⑥b** v/n. (n) to fly, flow across; ²führen v/a. ⑱** to conduct (or lead) across; ²geh(e)n v/n. (n) ⑭**: a) to walk across; über die Alpen ² to cross the Alps; b) fig. (sanft sterben) to pass gently away; ²greifen v/n. (h.) ⑥bf**: in et. ² to encroach (or infringe) upon s.th. (a. fig.); to dovetail into s.th.; ²helfen v/n. (h.) ⑥b** to help a p. across the stream, &c. or over a difficulty, &c.; ²kommen v/n. (n) ⑭** to come (or get) across, to cross over; ²können v/n. (h.) ⑱** to be able to cross or to get across; ²lassen v/a. ⑥a** to allow to cross (over); ²laufen v/n. (n) ⑥af** to run across; ²müssen v/n. (h.) ⑱** ell. to be obliged to cross; Schule: er muß mit hinüber (in die höhere Klasse) he has to be moved up (or promoted) with the others; ²reichen ⑱** v/n. (h.) to reach (or extend) across; v/a. über den Tisch ² to pass (or hand) across the table; ²schaffen v/a. ⑱** = ²bringen; ²schießen ⑥(e)ft** v/a. to shoot (or fire) across; v/n. (n) to shoot (or dart) across; ²schwimmen v/n. (n) ⑥a(b)** to swim across; ²sein v/n. ⑥a** f. hinüber I; ²setzen ⑩** v/a. to ferry over, to take across; v/n. (n) to ferry over, to cross a river, &c.; ²spielen v/n. (h.) ⑱**: ins Blaue ² to have a tinge of blue or a bluish tint; ²springen v/n. (n) ⑪ft** to jump (or leap) over (or across) a ditch, &c.; schnell zu e-m (oder von einem Orte zum andern) ² to run over to a p., a place; ²steigen v/n. (n) ⑪** to mount over a th.; ²tragen v/a. ⑪b** to carry over or across; ²wollen v/n. (h.) ⑱** to have a wish (or a mind) to cross or get across; ²ziehen ⑪b** v/a. to

drag (or pull) across; v/n. (n) to move across; sich ² v/refl. to extend (or reach, stretch) beyond.

hin und her ... (ˇ…ˇ…) in v. u. Zssgn mit v. u. Hin= und Her=... ⑫ in Zssgn mit s.: ² bedenken v/a. to turn over (or to revolve) in one's mind, to consider carefully; ² bewegen v/a. to move to and fro, to set in motion; sich ² v/refl. to move to and fro; (nicht stillstehen) to keep moving or F on the move; (Schwingungen machen) to swing to and fro, to oscillate; =bewegung f motion to and fro; swing of the pendulum, oscillation; ² fahren v/n. (n) to drive to and fro (in a carriage, &c.); weitS. to run here and there or backwards and forwards; ↓ to ply (or sail) between two ports, &c.; =fahrkarte ⍟ f return-ticket; =fahrt f drive (or journey) there and back, double journey (auch ⍟); ² geh(e)n v/n. (n) to go (or pass) to and fro; =geh(e)n n auf der Straße: (street-)traffic; nach vielem ~ after much running to and fro, after many (useless) journeys; =gerede n much (useless) debating or F palavering; ² laufen v/n. (n) to run to and fro or backward(s) and forward(s); =laufen n much (useless) running about; ² rennen v/n. (n) = ² laufen; ² schicken v/a. to send hither and thither or here and there or to and fro; ² schwanken v/n. (n) to sway to and fro, (taumeln) to totter; fig. (unschlüssig sein) to vacillate, to waver; =schwanken n, fig. vacillation; ² streiten v/n. (h.) to dispute, to argue, to bandy words; =streiten n (long) disputation or argument; ² wogen v/n. (h.) to flow to and fro.

Hin= und Rück=fahrt, =reise (ˇ…ˇ…) f journey (↓ voyage) there (or out) and back, double journey (auch ⍟).

hin-unter (ˇ…) adv. (ant. hinauf) down (there), downward(s): den Hügel ² down the hill, downhill; die Treppe ² down the stairs, downstairs; er hat eine Gräte verschluckt? ist sie ²? ... has it gone down?; ² mit ihm! down with him!; push (or throw) him down!; mit Ortsadverbien: da ², dort ² down there, down that way.

hin-unter=..., Hin-unter=... (ˇ…) in Verbindung mit verbs, immer trennbar (**), und in Zssgn mit verbal nouns und adjectives, = hinab=..., die Richtung vom Sprechenden hinweg bezeichnend; ²bringen v/a. ⑰** to take (or get) down; ²essen v/a. ⑱** to eat greedily, F to stuff down; ²fallen v/n. (n) ⑥a** to fall (or tumble) down; ²geh(e)n v/n. (n) ⑭** to go down the steps, &c.; ²gießen F v/a. ⑪d** to pour down (quickly), e-n Schnaps ꝛc.: F to toss off; ²schlucken v/a. ⑱** to swallow down; ²sinken v/n. (n) ⑪ft** to sink (or drop) down; ²spülen v/a. ⑱** to wash down; ²stürzen ⑪** v/a. = ²gießen; v/n. (n) to fall down (heavily); ²tragen v/a. ⑪b** to carry (or take) down; ²wagen v/refl. ⑱** to venture down; ²werfen v/a. ⑥b** to throw (or fling, hurl, cast)

⚛ scientific; ♣ botanical; ⊕ geography; ⊖ machinery; ⚒ mining; ⚔ military; ↓ marine; ● commercial; ✉ postal; ⍟ railway.

[hinunterwürgen] — 524 — [Hirn]

down; würgen v/a. ⓫** to cram (or worry) down (one's throat).
hin-wagen (ᵍ...): ſich v/refl. ⓫** ell. to venture to (go to) a place; wandern v/n. (ſn) ⓬a** to walk (or journey on foot) to a place; wanken v/n. (ſn) ⓫** to totter along or to a place; wärts adv. on the way thither or there; weg¹ m ⓬ journey to a place; auf dem ~e on the way there or out, a. in going (there).
hin¹-weg² (⌣̆) [mhd. (P) in den Weg] adv. away, off; ich will I want to get away or to be off; !, mit euch! get away!, be off!, F out you go!; geh. Spr.: begone!, avaunt!
hin-weg-..., Hin-weg-... (⌣̆...) in Ver= bindung mit verbs, immer trennbar (**), und in Zſſgn mit verbal nouns, = =weg= (f. dſ) fig. auch ein Unbeachtet= laſſen bezeichnend, wird dann oft durch over nach dem v. oder over... (als Präfix) vor dem v. ausgedrückt: eilen v/n. (ſn) ⓫** to hurry away; über et. to pass a th. hurriedly over, to skip a th.; geh(e)n v/n. (ſn) ⓬**: a) to go away; b) über etwas to touch lightly on (or to overlook) a th.; mit paß (lachend) über etwas to pooh-pooh (to laugh off) a th.; ſich heben v/refl. ⓭(⓱)b** to withdraw, to move away; hebe dich hinweg von mir! get out of my sight!, geh. Spr.: avaunt!; kommen v/n. (ſn) ⓫**: über e-e Schwierigkeit to get over or overcome a difficulty; raffen v/a. ⓫** to snatch away; die Krankheit hat ihn gerafft ... has cut him off in the prime of life; räumen v/a. ⓫** to remove; ſehen v/n. (h.) ⓬a**: a) to look over a th.; b) fig. über et. to overlook a th., to shut one's eyes to a th.; ſein v/n. (ſn) ⓰a**: über et. to be beyond (or past) a th.; er iſt über ſolche Vorurteile hinweg (erhaben) ... above such prejudices; ſetzen ⓫** v/a. to put away; ſich v/refl.: ſich über et. to make light of a th., to disregard a th., to pay no heed (or regard) to a th.; ſpringen v/n. (ſn) ⓫** to skip over; ſpülen v/a. ⓫** to wash away; tun v/a. ⓯** to put away; ziehen v/a. ⓭b** to pull away.
Hin-weis (ᵍ...) m ⓬a. hint at, indica= tion of; (Verweiſung) reference to; unter ~ auf // referring to //; weiſen v/a.: e-n auf den rechten Weg to show a p. the right way; v/n. (h.): auf et. to point towards a th.; to indicate (or hint at) a th.; (verweiſen) to refer to a th.; weiſend p.pr. u. a. ⓰, gram. demonstrative; =weiſung f ⓮ = =weis; mit (a. unter) ~ auf // in referring to //; welken v/n. (ſn) ⓫** to fade away; weitS. to sicken, to waste away; wenden v/a. u. ſich v/refl. ⓰a** zu ob. nach // to turn towards //; wer= fen ⓭b** v/a.: a) to cast (or fling, throw) there; b) to throw down; er warf die Karten hin he flung down the cards, fig. he threw up the game; c) fig. auf das Papier to sketch out (or jot down) on paper, F to dash off an essay; d) geworfene Bemerkung

casual (or stray) remark; geworfene Skizze sketch hastily drawn, rough sketch; geworfenes Wort word care= lessly dropt (by the way); ſich v/refl. to throw o.s. down; ſich vor e-m to throw o.s. at a p.'s feet, to prostrate o.s. before a p.; wieder(um) (⌣⌣⌣) adv.: a) in return; b) (zeitlich) again, once more; wirken (ᵍ...) v/n. (h.) ⓫** to tend to produce a result or an effect; wollen v/n. (h.) ⓫** ell. to be desirous of (ſtärker: to be bent on) going there; fig. ich weiß, wo Sie (worauf Sie zielen) I know what you are driving (or aiming) at; Sprichw. wo Geld iſt, will Geld hin money begets money; wünſchen ⓫** v/a.: ich wünſchte ihn hin, wo der Pfeffer wächſt I wished him at Jericho; ſich v/refl. to wish o.s. to a place.
Hinz (ˆ) ⓰⑤α, ~e (⌣̆) ⓴ npr/m. 1. Harry, Hal; ~ und Kunz Smith and Jones; (der große Haufe) Dick, Tom, and Harry. — 2. (auch: ~e ⓮) (Kater im „Reineke Fuchs") Grimalkin; tom-cat, Tom(my).
hin-zahlen (ᵍ...), zählen v/a. ⓫** to pay, to count down; zaubern v/a. ⓬a** to effect by magic, to conjure up; zeigen ⓫** v/a. to point at; weitS. weiſen v/n. (h.) wo zeigt der Wegweiſer hin? which way does the sign-post point?; ziehen ⓭b** v/a.: a) to draw (or pull) to(wards) //; am Boden to trail along the ground; b) eine Sache to draw out (or drag on) an affair, to delay (or protract, put off) a matter; c) e-n = halten b; d) fig. (an ſich ziehen) to draw, to at= tract; ſich zu einem gezogen fühlen to feel o.s. attracted (or magnetized) by a p.; v/n. (ſn): a) nach et. to move (or march) towards a th.; rel. zieh(e)t hin in Frieden! depart in peace!; b) nach Berlin to move to ...; ſich v/refl.: a) (zeitlich) ſich lange to drag on a long time; b) (räumlich) to extend (or spread) towards a place; ~ n u. =ziehung f ⓮ delay(ing), protraction; zielen v/n. (h.) ⓫** to aim at a th., fig. auch: to have a th. in view; die Worte zielten auf uns hin ... were aimed (or levelled) at us or intended for us.
hin-zu (⌣́) adv. 1. to the spot, near (the place); there. — 2. (außerdem) besides, moreover, into the bargain, in addition, with it.
hin-zu-..., Hin-zu-... (⌣⌣...) in Verbindung mit verbs, immer trennbar (**), und in Zſ.=ſetzungen mit verbal nouns u. adjec= tives, a) vom Sprechenden entferntere Be= wegung nach einem Orte zu bezeichnend, oft ausgedrückt durch: to(wards), near, close (to), up, to the place, b) Vermehrung, Zuſatz bezeichnend, oft gegeben durch: in (or as an addition, besides, addition= ally nach dem v., auch: ad..., super... (als Präfix) vor dem v.: bekommen v/a. ⓫*/* to receive besides or addition= ally; denken v/a. ⓬**: to add in one's thoughts or one's mind; dichten v/a. ⓫** to invent besides, to add to a poem or a romance; ſich drängen v/refl. ⓫** to press near or close (to), to flock (or crowd) to a place; fügen

v/a. ⓫** to add (or append, annex) to a th.; die gefügten Bemerkungen the notes added (thereto), the additional remarks pl.; ~ n ⓳ und =fügung f ⓮ ad= dition; geh(e)n v/n. (ſn) ⓫** to go near, to approach; ſich geſellen v/refl. ⓫*/* to join, to associate o.s. with; kommen v/n. (ſn) ⓫**: a) to come up (to), unvermutet: to come unawares, to drop in; b) noch (neu) to be (super)added (to), to come in as an addition, to super= vene; es kommt noch hinzu, daß it must be added that //; d additional, zufällig: accessory; laſſen v/a. ⓬a** to admit; legen v/a. ⓫** = fügen; rechnen v/a. ⓬b** to add, to include (in a sum), to throw in; =rechnung f ⓮ addition (to a number or sum); unter ~ von // adding (or including) //; ſetzen v/a. ⓫** = fügen; ſetzung f ⓮ addition; treten v/n. (ſn) ⓫**d**: a) to step near (to); b) (friſch) to be added to ..., (ſich anſchließen) to join; es trat noch eine andere Krankheit hinzu another illness supervened; =tritt m ⓪ c.: a) approach; b) accession; =tun v/a. ⓯** to add; ~ n ⓳ addition; ohne j-s ~ without anybody's inter= vention; =wahl f ⓮ co-optation; wählen v/a. ⓫** to elect in addition, to co-opt; werfen v/a. ⓭b** to throw in with a heap; zählen v/a. ⓫** to reckon (or count) in with; vgl. rech= nen; ziehen v/a. ⓭b**: a) to add; b) e-n zu et. (e-r Geſellſchaft) to draw a p. into a society, party, &c.; einen zweiten Arzt to fetch (or consult) a second physician; ~ n ⓳ u. =ziehung f ⓮ addition; mit ~ der Koſten ex= penses included, adding all charges; ~ eines zweiten Arztes consultation of a second physician. [bibl. Job.]
Hiob (ᒪᵘ) [hebr. der Verfolgte] ⓰⓸⑤α.)
Hiobs-bote (ᴵᴵ...) m ⓰ fig. bearer of ill tidings or bad news; =poſt f bad (or shocking, alarming) news.
Hippe¹ (⌣̆) [ahd. *LU., *md., ndd.] f ⓮ 1. ⓰ (Gärtnermeſſer mit gebogener Klinge) bill-hook, hedging-bill, hedging-knife, pruning-knife; agr. sickle. — 2. (Senſe, bſd. des Todes ꝛc.) scythe.
Hippe² prov. (⌣̆) f ⓮ = Ziege.
Hippe³ (⌣̆) [mhd.] f ⓮ (oblatendünner Kuchen) wafer.
Hippodrom (⌣⌣́ˊ) [grch.] m ⓰d. (Rennbahn) hippodrome, circus, ring, F the tan.
Hippogryph (⌣⌣́f) [it.] m ⓰d. u. ⓬ myth. (Flügelroß, Pegaſus) hippogriff, winged steed.
Hippokras (⌣⌣́) [t.+ grch.; r-r Hypokras] m, inv. (Würzwein) spiced (or medicated, drugged) wine.
hippokratiſch (⌣⌣ᒪ⌣) [Hippo'krates grch. Arzt 460—359 ob. 377 vor Chr.] a. ⓰ Hippocratic; med. Ges Geſicht eines Sterbenden: Hippocratic face.
Hippokrene (⌣⌣ᒪ⌣) [grch.] f ⓮ Alt.: (Muſen= quelle am Helikon) Hippocrene.
hippur-ſauer ☌ (⌣ᒪ...) [grch.] a. ⓰ chm. hippuric; ſaures Salz hippurate; =ſäure f ⓬ im Pferdeharn: hippuric acid $(C_9H_{10}NO_3)$.
Hirn (ᵍ) [ahd.] n ⓪b. 1. anat. u. fig. brain = Gehirn; zum ~ gehörig cere-

bral. — 2. ⚙ Holz-arbeit: (Ebene im Holze, die mit den Fasern e-n rechten Winkel macht) cross-cut or -section; über ~ sägen to cut crosswise or across the grain.

Hirn-gespinst (ˊˊ…) *n* [62] fancy, chimera, phantasm(agoria); (Traumgesicht) vision; **-holz** *n* (*ant.* Aderholz) cross-grain wood; **⁀krank** *a.* [66] suffering from the brain; **-schädel** *m*, **-schale** *f* brain-pan, skull, ⚗ cranium; **-seite** ⚙ *f* des Holzes: cross-grain or -way; **⁀verbrannt**, **⁀verrückt** *a.* hare-brained, crazy, mad, F wrong in the head, cracked; **-windung** *f* convolution of the brain; **-wut** *f* frenzy; ⚗ encephalitis; **⁀wütig** *a.* frantic; raving (mad); *anat.* vgl. Gehirn-…

Hirs-brei (ˊˊˊ) *m* [62] = Hirse(n)brei.

Hirsch (ˊ) [ahd.: hart] *m* [11]a. **1.** *zo.* stag (*Cervus e'laphus*); *hunt.* (bsd. der mehr als fünfjährige) hart; weitS. (red) deer; Rudel ~e herd of stags; ~ von zwölf Enden stag of twelve points; der ~ schreit oder röhrt the stag bells or roars or troats, the deer whistles; e-n ~ betreffend: ⚗ cervine. — 2. *ent.* fliegender ~ = Hirschkäfer.

Hirsch-antilope (ˊˊ…) *f* [62] *zo.* cervine antelope (*Anti'lope bu'balus*); **⁀artig** *a.* [66] stag-like, ⚗ cervine; **-bock** *m* stag, (male) hart, s. Hirsch 1; **⁀braun** *a.* = ⁀farben; **-dorn** ⚘ *m* = Kreuzdorn (echter); **-eber** *m*, *zo.* horned hog, babiroussa (*Porcus babyru'ssa*); **-fährte** *f*, *hunt.* (foot-)scent of a stag, slot; **-fänger** *m* (Weidmesser) hunting-knife, hanger, cutlas(s), bsd. ⚔ rifle-sword; schott. dirk; **-farbe** *f* fawn (colour); **⁀farben**, **⁀farbig** *a.* fawn-coloured, fallow, buff; **-garten** *m* deer-park; **-gelös** *n* = -losung; **⁀gerecht** *a.* [66] *hunt.* in accordance with the rules of deer-stalking; **-geschrei** *n* belling (or troat, whistling) of a stag; **-geweih** *n* antlers (or horns, bsd. *her.* attires) *pl.* of a stag; **-geweih-sprosse** *f* point, branch; **-hals** *m* des Pferdes: ewe-neck; **-hatz** *f* = -jagd; **-haut** *f* deerskin; **-horn** *n* stag-horn, stag's horn; ☿ hartshorn; **-horn-salz** *n*, *chm.* (kohlensaures Ammoniak) bsd. ehm.: volatile salt of hartshorn, jetzt: carbonate of ammonia; **-hund** *m*, *hunt.* staghound; **-jagd** *f* stag-hunting, weitS. deer-stalking; **-käfer** *m*, *ent.* stag-beetle (*Luca'nus cervus*); **-kalb** *n* fawn, young deer; **-keule** *f* haunch of venison; **-kuh** *f* hind, female hart; **-lager** *n* lodge (or lair) of a stag; **-lauf** *m* foot of a stag or deer; **-leder** ☿ *n* deerskin, buckskin; **⁀ledern** *a.* (of) buckskin; **-losung** *f*, *hunt.* fumets *pl.*; **-park** *m* = -garten; **-ruf** *m* = -geschrei; **-schröter** *m*, *ent.* = -käfer; **-talg** *m* suet of deer; **-trüffel** ⚘ *f* hart's-truffles *pl.* (*Elapho-my'ces granula'tus*); **-wurm** *m*, *ent.* stag-worm (*Oestrus*); **-ziemer** *m* saddle of venison; **-zunge** ⚘ *f* (Zungenfarn) hart's-tongue (*Scolope'ndrium officina'rum*).

Hirse ⚘ (ˊ⏑) [ahd. nur *m*] *f* [48]: a) echte ~ millet, panic(-grass) (*Pani'cum milia'ceum*); b) indische ~ = Mohrenhirse.

Hirse(n)-brei (ˊ⏑…) *m* [62] millet-gruel; **-fieber** *n*, *path.*: ⚗ miliaria; **⁀förmig** *a.* [66] miliary; **-gras** ⚘ *n* = Flattergras; **-korn** *n* millet-grain or -seed.

Hirt (ˊ) [ahd.: herd; *Herde] *m* [42], **~e** [44] herdsman; *Am.* Prairie⁀: cow-boy; (Schäfer[in]) **shepherd;** vgl. Gänsehirt; *fig.* u. *poet.* **swain;** *rel.* der Gute ~ (der Heiland) the Good Shepherd; (Seelen-) ~ pastor, parson, shepherd of a flock.

Hirten-amt (ˊ⏑…) *n* [62] shepherd's duties *pl.* or calling; *eccl.* pastoral office, pastorate, clerical living; **⁀artig** *a.* [66] shepherd-like, pastoral; **-brief** *m*, *eccl.* pastoral letter or address; **-flöte** *f* shepherd's flute or pipe, ⚗ syrinx; **-gedicht** *n* pastoral (or bucolic) poem, ⚗ eclogue; weitS. idyl; **-gott** *m*, *myth.* god of shepherds; Pan.

hirtenhaft (ˊ⏑⏑) *a.* [66] pastoral.

Hirten-haus (ˊ⏑…) *n* [62] shepherd's hut; **-hund** *m* sh.'s dog; **-knabe** *m* shepherd-boy; **-leben** *n* sh.'s (or pastoral, nomadic) life; **-lied** *n* sh.'s (or pastoral) song; **⁀los** *a.* [66] without a shepherd; *eccl.* without a pastor or clergyman; **-mädchen** *n* sh.-girl, shepherdess; **⁀mäßig** *a.* shepherdlike, bucolic, pastoral; **-pfeife** *f*, **-rohr** *n* sh.'s (or rustic) pipe; (Schalmei) shawm, shalm; vgl. -flöte.

Hirtenschaft (ˊ⏑⏑) *f* [46] **1.** shepherd's calling. — 2. body of shepherds or herdsmen.

Hirten-spiel (ˊ⏑…) *n* [62] pastoral game; **-stab** *m* shepherd's crook or staff; *eccl.* (bishop's) crosier; **-tasche** ⚘ *f*: gemeine ~ shepherd's-purse or -pouch (*Capse'lla bursa pasto'ris*); **-volk** *n* pastoral (or nomadic) tribe or nation.

Hirtin (ˊ⏑) *f* [47] shepherdess.

hirtlich (ˊ⏑) *a.* [66] pastoral, weitS. rustic.

His ♪ (ˊ) *n*, *inv.* (einen halben Ton höher als H) B sharp (B ♯).

Hiskia(s) (⏑ˊ⏑) [hebr.] *npr/m.* [51]α([16]γ.) *bibl.* (König von Juda, 727–698 v. Chr.) Hezekiah.

hiß (ˊ) *int.* (Zuruf an Hunde) go!

Hisse ⚓ (ˊ⏑) [ndd.] *f* [48] pulley, tackle.

hissen ⚓ (ˊ⏑) [ndd.] *v/a.* [90] to hoist, to pull up; vgl. heißen².

hist (ˊ) *int.* (Fuhrmannssprache: nach links; *ant.* hott; vgl. a. har) to the left!; nicht ⁀ noch hott wissen not to know which way to turn.

Histolog, ~e ⚗ (⏑⏑ˊ(⏑) [grch.] *m* [42], [44] *anat.* (Gewebekundiger) histologist; **~ie** (⏑⏑⏑ˊ) *f* [48] (Gewebelehre) histology; **⁀isch** (⏑⏑ˊ⏑) *a.* [66] histologic(al).

Histörchen (⏑ˊ⏑) *n* [23] (*dim.* v. Histo'rie) short (or nice) tale or story, anecdote.

Histori-e (⏑ˊ(⏑)⏑) [mhd., *lt.] *f* [48] (hi)story.

Histori-en-maler (⏑ˊˊ(⏑)⏑…) *m* [62] (Geschichts…) historical painter.

Historik (⏑ˊ⏑) [grch.] *f* [46] art of writing history.

Historiker (⏑ˊ⏑⏑) [grch.] *m* [22] (Geschichtsforscher) historian, historical student or authority or writer.

Historiograph (⏑-(⏑)⏑ˊf) [grch.] *m* [42] (Geschichtschreiber) historian, …ographer.

historisch (⏑ˊ⏑) [grch.] *a.* [66] (geschichtlich) historical.

Hitz-blase P (ˊˊ…) *f* [62], **-blatter(n** *pl.*) *f* (heat-)pimple, pustule; ⚗ vesicle, eczema; **⁀blatterich** *a.* [66]: ⚗ eczematous.

Hitze (ˊ⏑) [ahd.: heat; *heiß] *f* [48] **1.** heat, bisw. hotness of the blood, &c.; *path.* fliegende ~ hot fit; *chm.* fließende ~ temperature of fusion; starke ~, stechende ~ (Glut) intense (or burning, oppressive) heat of summer, &c.; diese Kohlen erzeugen große ~ … throw out great heat; es herrscht e-e unausstehliche ~ it (or the weather) is intolerably hot; dem Braten zu große ~ geben to put the joint in(to) too hot an oven; in der ~ trinken to drink when (one is) heated; vor ~ fast vergehen to be sweltering (or broiling) in the heat; der Wein, das Gewürz hat zu viel ~ … is too heating. — 2. *fig.* warmth, ardour, fervidness, fervour; (Aufregung) excitement, fluster; (zornige Aufwallung) fit of anger; jugendliche ~ youthful ardour; in der ersten ~ in the heat (or excitement) of the moment, in the first flush (of passion); in der ~ des Gefechts in the heat of (the) battle; e-n in ~ bringen to put a p. into a passion or F a temper; in ~ geraten to fire up, to fly into a passion, F to get one's monkey up; Sprichw. die erste ~ erkaltet the novelty soon wears off. — **3.** 🔨 (Anstrengung) heating work, violent effort; *bibl.* des Tages Last und ~ the burden and heat of the day.

Hitze-grad (ˊˊ⏑…) *m* [62] degree of heat; **-(grad)messer** *m*, *phys.*: ⚗ pyrometer; **-(grad)messung** *f*: ⚗ pyrometry.

hitzen (ˊ⏑) [ahd.] *v/a.* [90] to heat; vgl. heizen.

hitzig (ˊ⏑) [mhd.] *a.* [66] **1.** (heiß) (burning) hot; ⁀e Krankheit acute complaint or malady. — 2. *fig.* (leidenschaftlich) hot-blooded or -headed or -tempered, passionate, hasty; (feurig, ungestüm) fiery, impetuous, lively; v. Pferden a.: high-mettled; (heftig) violent, vehement, peppery; (jähzornig) irascible, choleric; er ist sehr ⁀ he has a hot temper; ⁀ hinter etwas her sein to be keen(ly bent) on a th.; (nur) nicht so ⁀! don't put yourself out!, (take it) gently!; ⁀ werden, oft: to fire up, to lose one's temper.

Hitzigkeit (ˊ⏑-) *f* [46] hotness; *fig.* auch: hot-bloodedness, hot temper; fiery spirit.

Hitz-kopf (ˊˊ…) *m* [62] hot-headed (or passionate, violent) person, hotspur; **⁀köpfig** *a.* [66] hot-headed, passionate; **-pickel** *m/pl.*, **-pocken** *f/pl.* *path.* heat- (or spring-)rash, F heat-bumps *pl.*; vgl. -blase; **-schlag** *m* heat-stroke, heat-apoplexy, sunstroke.

hl, öft. ***hl*** *abbr.* = Hektoliter.

Hl. *abbr.* = Halblederband.

hl. *abbr.* = heilig.

hm (ˊ) *int.* (a)hem!

h. m. *abbr.* = hujus mensis [lt. dieses Monats] inst. (*abbr.* v. instant).

ho (ˊ) *int.* ho (there)!; vgl. hoho.

hob (ˊ), (**höbe** *subj.*) *impf.* v. heben.

Hobel ⚙ (ˊ⏑) [mhd. (ndd.): howel] *m* [22] plane; Böttcherei, Tischlerei: (Schlicht-) ~ jointer; Buchbinderei: = Beschneide-⁀.

Hobel-bank ⚙ (ˊˊ⏑…) *f* [62] planing-bench, carpenter's bench or lathe; **-eisen** *n* plane-iron; **-maschine** *f* planing- (or surface-)machine.

hobeln ⚙ (ˊ⏑) [Hobel] *v/a.* [92]a. to plane; aus dem groben: to rough-plane, to jack (down); glatt⁀ to cut even, to smooth, to dress wood; F er ist noch

[Hobelspäne] — 526 — [hoch]

nicht recht gehobelt he is not sufficiently polished or refined; vgl. abhobeln I. [chippings pl.]
Hobel-späne (˝‿...) m/pl. ⊕ shavings.
Hobler ⊙ (‒‿) m ⊕ planer.
Hobo-e ♪ (‒‿) [it. *o'boe m*; *fr. *hautbois m*] f ⊕ hautbois, hautboy, oboe; **~bläser** m ⊕, a. **Hobo-ist** (‒‒‿́) m ⊕ hautboy(-player), hautboyist, oboist.
hoch (‒́ch) [ahd.: high] **I** a. ⊕ (vor e wird das ch zu h, zB. hohe(r), hohes; *comp.* höher, *sup.* höchst) **1.** high, zB. hoher Berg high mountain, tall, zB. ein Mann, ein Baum von hohem Wuchs a man, a tree of tall growth, a tall man, tree; elevated, zB. in hoher Lage in an elevated position; lofty, zB. ein hohes Zimmer a lofty room; *fig.* ein hoher Sinn a lofty mind; hohe Flut high tide or water, auch: flood-tide; *hunt.* mit hohem Geweih high-palmed; er hat eine hohe Schulter he is high-shouldered; hohe Temperatur high (or great) temperature; der Fluß ist (od. geht) ⚹ the river is high or (very much) swoln; die Mauer ist 3 Meter ⚹ the wall is ten feet high or in height; der Schnee ist (einen halben Fuß) ⚹ the snow is (half a foot) deep; das Wasser ist um einen Fuß höher the water is a foot higher or has risen one foot; ein 10000 Fuß hoher Berg a mountain ten thousand feet high or in height; *adv.* ⚹ emporragend towering; ⚹ erhaben über // looking down upon //; der Vogel fliegt ⚹, höher ... flies high, higher; ⚓ Riemen ⚹! oars up!
— **2.** *fig.* der hohe (vornehme) Adel the (old) nobility, the highest aristocracy, the best blood of the land, in Engl.: the peerage; hohes Alter great (or advanced) age; das hohe Altertum remote antiquity; hohes Amt high (or important) office or post; in hohem Ansehen stehen to enjoy high esteem; höhere(r) Beamte(r) high official; auf Hohen oder (Aller-)Höchsten Befehl in Engl.: by Royal command; höherer Blödsinn, Ulk utter rubbish, great nonsense or F bosh; hohe Blüte full bloom; in hoher Blüte stehen to enjoy great prosperity, to be very prosperous; nach hohen Dingen trachten to aspire to great things, to have a lofty ambition; an hohen Feiertagen od. Festen on high-days and holidays; hohe Finanzwelt great financiers pl., (fr.) *haute finance*; ein höheres Gebot tun to make a higher offer or bid; der höchste Genuß the greatest enjoyment; hohes Gericht superior court; höchster Gerichtshof supreme court (of judicature or of appeal); höhere Gewalt superior force, (fr.) *force majeure*; hoher Gewinn in der Lotterie big prize: gr. höher (höchster) Grad comparative (superlative); das höchste Gut the greatest good, the highest possession; das Leben ist der Güter höchstes nicht (SCH.) life is not the richest of our treasures; hohe (vornehme) Häuser great (or noble, princely) houses pl.; von hoher Herkunft of high descent or degree, of exalted birth; hohe(r) Herr gentleman of high position; distinguished gentleman; der Hohe Herr, etwa: His Lordship, His Eminence; hohe Herrschaften f/pl. people of high (or noble) rank, lords, exalted personage(s) pl.; in höchster Höhe at the greatest (or highest) elevation; f. Kante 1; die höheren Kreise the higher (or better) circles (of society); f. Hohelied; höhere Lehranstalt secondary school; hohes Lob high praise; höchste Lust greatest of pleasures, F top of delight; höhere Mathematik higher mathematics; im hohen Norden in the extreme north; hohe Nummer high number; eine hohe Nummer bei e-m haben, etwa: to be in great favour with a p., to be in a p.'s good graces; mit Erlaubnis der hohen Obrigkeit with the permission of the authorities; höherer Offizier superior officer; höher(e)n Ort(e)s (bei einer höheren vorgesetzten Behörde) with the (higher) authorities; hohe Person eminent person; oft *iro.*(er) in hoher Person (he)himself, he in person, auch: his noble self; sich aufs hohe Pferd setzen to ride the high horse; f. Pforte 1; der höchste Preis the highest prize; höchster Punkt highest (or most elevated) point, *fig.* culminating point, ⚹ acme; der Hohe Rat the Great Council; *Engl.*: the Privy Council; die Hohe Regierung His Majesty's Government; ⚹ zu Roß (mounted) on horseback; Hohe Schule: a) = Gymnasium; b) = Hochschule; *fig.* er hat die Hohe Schule durchgemacht he has been through a good (or long) school (a. *iro.*); ⚓ hohe See (offene See) open sea, main, offing; auf hoher See in mid-ocean; in the offing; fürwahr, der Graf trug hohen Sinn (BÜRGER) ... was high-minded or noble-hearted; in höherem Sinne in a higher sense; der hohe Sommer the hottest part (or the height) of summer; hohes Spiel high stakes pl.; die höheren Stände the higher classes pl.; hohe Strafe heavy fine; bei hoher Strafe under a heavy penalty; es ist hoher Tag it is broad day-light; Höhere Töchterschule High School for Girls, young ladies' school; hoher Ton high tone (auch ♪); höchster Ton highest note; in hohem Tone reden to speak in a high (or lofty) strain; ⊙ Fahrrad mit hoher Übersetzung high-geared cycle or machine; höherer Unterricht higher teaching, advanced instruction; *eccl.* höhere Weihen holy orders pl.; das Höchste Wesen (Gott) the supreme Being; von der höchsten Wichtigkeit of the outmost importance; ⚹ Feuern n in hohem Winkel (Steilfeuer) high-angle fire; es ist hohe Zeit it is high time. — **3.** ⊕ die Kurse sind (od. stehen) ⚹ the prices are up or better or have advanced; ich finde den Preis zu ⚹ ... too high or too dear; wie ⚹ stehen Italiener? how are Italians (quoted)?, F how much (or at what figure) are Italians?; hohe Zinsen tragen to bear large (or heavy) interest. — **4.** ♪ hoher Ton high tone or note; *fig.* e-n hohen Ton anschlagen oder annehmen to assume a lofty tone or manner, F to talk big; das Klavier ist zu ⚹ gestimmt the piano is tuned (or pitched) too high. — **5.** *comp.* höher, oft: superior; höher gelegen als ... overlooking ...; *sup.* höchst highest, uppermost, topmost; (hervorragend, erhaben) eminent, sublime; der höchste Teil (Gipfel) the top (part); die höchsten Ehren erlangen to attain the highest honours, F to get to the top of the tree or the ladder; in höchster Not in the utmost (or greatest) distress, in the last extremity; außerordentlich ⚹ vom Preise: exorbitant, excessive(ly high); *abs.* höchste(r) (über den nichts hinausgeht) supreme, paramount, (unübertrefflich) unsurpassable, peerless, incomparable, above everything, F A 1 or A. 1 or A one; höchste Vollkommenheit pink of perfection; höchste Narrheit height of folly, ⊕ der höchste Betrag, Preis the maximum amount, price. — **6.** als *adv.* in Verbindung mit *verbs*: (in hohem Grade) in a high degree, highly; (sehr) (very) much, largely, *a.* extremely, excessively; bei e-m ⚹ angeschrieben sein to be in a p.'s good books, to be in great favour with a p.; f. anrechnen 2, aufhorchen, aufnehmen 8; ⚹ aufspringen to jump (up) high, to take a high leap; f. belaufen II; ⚹ bieten auf eine Ware to make a high bid (or to offer a large sum) for ...; f. bringen 7; ⚹ ehren to honour highly, to keep in high esteem; ⚹(=)entzückt highly delighted, exceedingly charmed; ⚹(=)erfreut sein to be greatly (or highly) pleased; ⚹ geh(e)n to rise high; die See ging ⚹ the sea was high or rough; ⊕ die Ware geht ⚹ ... runs up high; wie ⚹ möchten Sie gehen? to what price would you like to go?; da geht es ⚹(lustig)her they are making very merry, F they are having a high old time; ⚹ und heilig, ⚹ und teuer geloben to promise solemnly, to make a solemn vow; den Kopf ⚹ halten to hold one's head up (high); to cherish a p.'s memory, &c.; ⚹ hängen to hang up high; f. Brotkorb; die Trauben hingen dem Fuchse zu ⚹ ... were too high (up) for the fox; ⚹ heben to lift up (high); (aufschürzen) to turn (or tuck) up; *fig.* to exalt; ich kann nicht so ⚹ (steigend, singend) kommen I cannot pitch so high a note; die Ware kommt uns sehr ⚹ (zu stehen) we have to pay very dearly for ...; wenn's ⚹ kommt: a) if it comes (or mounts, rises) high; b) (höchstens) at the most; das wird ihm ⚹ (od. teuer) zu stehen kommen it will cost him a great deal (of money), it will be an expensive matter to him; höher können to be able to rise higher; e-n ⚹ leben lassen to drink a p.'s health, to toast a p., to give three cheers for a p.; er lebe ⚹! long may he live!; meist mit dem Namen oder Titel der Person, zB.: ⚹ lebe der König! long live the King!; der Schnee liegt sehr ⚹ ... is (or

Signs (see page XVII): F familiar; P vulgar; ⚡ flash; ⚲ rare; † obsolete (died); * new word (born); ⧺ incorrect; ♪ music;

[hochachtbar] — 527 — [hochhalten]

lies) very deep; höher machen: a) to make higher; b) to raise (up); das Kleid 2 nehmen to take up one's dress; wie 2 rechnen Sie das Pfund Sterling? at how much do you value (or what do you charge) for a sovereign?; wenn man's 2 rechnet, etwa: at the (very) highest or most; die Lampe höher schrauben to turn up …; 2 und teuer schwören to swear (or take) a solemn oath; 2 sein: das ist mir zu 2 that is beyond my reach or means; die sind zu 2 (vornehm) für ihn they are too high up (or F too high and mighty) for him; s. Brett 7; die Saiten 2 spannen to tighten the strings, fig. to aim (too) high; 2 spielen to play for high stakes; 2 über den anderen steh(e)n to be far above the others; ✱ 2 im Preise steh(e)n to be dear or expensive, to stand at a high figure, vgl. oben 3; die Papiere steh(e)n 2 the stocks are high or up, vgl. 3; 2 steigen to rise to a great (or considerable) height; sehr 2 (im Leben) steigen, oft: to reach the top (rung) of the ladder; höher steigen to mount (v. Vögeln auch: to soar) higher; immer höher steigen to rise higher and higher; höher stellen to put in a higher place; fig. (befördern) to promote; 2 streben to aim higher, engS. to be very ambitious; 2 tönende Phrasen high-sounding phrases pl.; den Kopf, die Nase 2 tragen F to stick up one's nose (in the air), to be stuck-up; 2 treiben to make (or cause to) rise; ✱ die Preise höher treiben to send up (or lift) the prices; e-n 2 verehren to hold a p. in high (or great) esteem; vgl. 2verehrt; 2 und teuer versichern (versprechen) to give a solemn assurance (promise); höher werden (von Bäumen ꝛc.) to grow in height; 2 wohnen to live in a top story or room; zwei Treppen 2 wohnen to live on the second floor; er wohnt einen Stock höher als wir he lives on the floor above us. — 7. (hinter-ea. aufgestellt, tief) ✕ zwei Mann 2 two (men) deep; sie kamen acht Mann 2 zu mir eight of them came to (see) me, they called on me eight in number. — 8. math. 4 2 5 (geschrieben: 4⁵) four to the fifth (power). — II höchst: 9. a. s. I, bsd. 5. — 10. adv. (nur vor a.) very, exceedingly, extremely; most; ein höchst furchtsamer Mensch a most timid person; höchst lächerlich most (or exceedingly) ridiculous. — 11. sein Ruhm war aufs höchste gestiegen he had reached the pinnacle (or summit) of his fame; ich bin Ihnen aufs höchste verbunden … extremely obliged (or deeply indebted) to you; als die Not aufs höchste gestiegen war when things were at their worst or at their lowest ebb; adv. aufs, auf das höchste, zum höchsten in the highest degree, very highly, exceedingly. — III höchstens: 12. adv. (im höchsten Falle) at the highest or most, in the highest case, at best. — IV s. ⓘ 13. der, die Hohe the great (or mighty)

one; hoch und niedrig, Hohe und Niedrige high and low. — 14. der Höchste (Gott), etwa: the (Lord) Almighty. — 15. das Hohe, etwa: high and lofty matters pl.; fig. the sublime; das Hohe an … the high (or exalted) part (or nature) of … — 16. das Höchste the highest (or most sublime, exalted) things pl.; fig. the culminating point, F the tip-top; sein Sinn ist auf das Höchste gerichtet his mind aims at the highest objects. — V Hoch n 17. inv. s. 13. — 18. ⓘ (a. inv., pl. bff. ~rufe) ein Hoch a cheer; (Toast) a toast; ein Hoch auf e-n ausbringen to cheer (or toast) a p.

hoch-achtbar (²ch…) a. ⓘ highly (or most) estimable or respectable; 2achten v/a. ⓘ** to esteem highly, to respect greatly or very much; =achtung f ⓘ (high) esteem, (deep) respect, high(est) regard; in Briefen: mit der größten (ob. mit vorzüglicher) ~ verbleibe ich Ihr …, einfach: I remain, with best respects or compliments Yours …; 2achtungsvoll(st) a. ⓘ (most) respectful, adv. auch: with the greatest (or profoundest) respect; Briefschluß: wir verbleiben 2 Ihr // we remain Yours respectfully //; -acker m, myth. field with traces of ancient cultivation; 2ad(e)lig a. ⓘ belonging to the (old) nobility or the peerage, F of blue blood; =alpen ♀ pl. High Alps pl.; =altar m, eccl. high altar; =amt n high mass; 2ansehnlich a. highly respectable or respected, eminent; =asien ♀ f Plateau of (Central) Asia; =ätzung ⊙ f (Hochlithographie) acrography; =auf-(=an-)schlag m (mit Drehball) Tennisspiel: overhand-(twist-)service; =bahn 🚂 f high-level railway, overhead (or elevated) railway or line; elektrische ~ overhead electric railway; =bau m, bsd. 🚂 overground workings pl., structure above ground; superstructure; 2bedeutsam a. highly important or significant; 2begabt a. highly gifted or talented; 2beglückt a. most fortunate, auch: thrice-blessed; 2beinig a. high-legged; 2bejahrt a. advanced (or well on) in years; 2berühmt a. greatly (or highly) renowned, bar-famed, (most) illustrious; die 2en Männer eines Landes, Zeitraumes, a. the most eminent men …, the shining stars …; 2besteuert a. heavily taxed; 2betagt a. of a great age, (very) aged; vgl. 2bejahrt; 2blau a. of a bright blue, azure; =bord ⚓ m high-deck; =bordschiff ⚓ n vessel with a high freeboard, high-built ship; 2brüstig a.: a) high-breasted; b) fig. (stolz) proud, haughty; 2busig a. high-bosomed; =dero(selbe), =derselbe, fast † — dero; 2deutsch a. (jetzt bsd. von der Sprache; ant. plattdeutsch) High German, weitS. refined (or pure) German; ~(e) n ⓘ High German; =druck ⊙ m: a) mach. high pressure; fig. mit ~ at high (or full) pressure; b) typ. relief-printing; =druck-dampf(=maschine f) m ⊙ mach. high-pressure steam(-engine); =ebene

f elevated plain, plateau, tableland; 2edel a. most (or right) noble; =edelgeboren †, a., eigentlich: of right noble birth, nach dem Namen etwa: Esq. (= Esquire); =ehrwürden, Titel v. ev. Geistlichen, geringer als =würden (s. ds). Ew. ~ Reverend Sir, ob. einfach: (Dear) Sir; =ehrwürdig a. worshipful; als Titel von Geistlichen: the (Very) Reverend N., auf Briefen: To the (Very) Rev. N.; 2elegant a. highly elegant, most stylish; 2entzückt, 2erfreut a. highly delighted, overjoyed; 2erhaben a.: a) ⊙ Bildhauerei: Le Arbeit s. relief; b) fig. exalted, very lofty, sublime; 2fahrend a. haughty, (stolz) proud, (übermütig) overbearing, high-handed, arrogant; (gebieterisch) imperious; 2des Wesen, oft: overbearing nature, arrogance; 2farbig a. highly coloured, of high colour; 2fein a. superfine, exquisite, ✱ auch: very choice, first-rate, of the finest quality, A 1; =fläche f = =ebene; 2fliegend a. soaring (high); fig. lofty, aiming high, ambitious; =flut f high tide or water, stärker: full tide, fig. auch: great prosperity, ✱ boom; 2fürstlich a. = fürstlich; 2geachtet a. highly esteemed, 2gebenedei(e)t a. v. d. heiligen Jungfrau: most blessed; =gebietend a. High and Mighty (Lord); 2gebildet a. highly cultured or educated, most accomplished; =gebirge n high mountainchain; Alps pl.; =gebirgs-welt f alpine world; =geboren a. high-born, illustrious; ~ als Titel des engl. Adels (mit Ausnahme der Herzöge) und der Privy Councillors: Right Honourable; vgl. 2wohlgeboren; 2geehrt a. highly honoured; in Briefen: Ler Herr, nur: (Dear) Sir; =gefühl n exalted feeling, rapture; overflow of joy; im ~ des Sieges in the flush of victory; =gehen ✱ n der Preise: rise; 2gehend a. (von der See) running high. heavy; overgrown; 2gelb a. of a bright yellow; golden; 2gelegen a. lying high, elevated; 2gelehrt a. deeply (or very) learned, erudite; 2gelobt a. (most) blessed; 2gemut a. in good cheer or spirits; 2geneigt(est) adv. (most) graciously; =genuß m great (or thorough) enjoyment; ein wahrer ~ F a real treat; 2gepriesen a. highly praised, exalted; =gericht n supreme criminal court; 2gerötet a. (highly) flushed, ruddy; =gesang m anthem, ode; 2gesinnt a. high-minded, (edel) noble-hearted; 2gespannt a. von Dämpfen: of high tension, fig. oft: high-strung; Le Erwartungen high (or overgreat, exaggerated) expectations pl.; Le Hoffnung anxious hope; 2gestellt a. in high position or office; 2gestimmt a. v. Instrumenten: tuned to a high pitch; 2gewachsen a. of high growth, tall; 2gewölbt a. arch. with high arches; 2gieb(e)lig a. with a high gable; =glut f intense heat; 2gradig a. of a high degree or grade; path. u. fig. oft: intense; =gradigkeit f intensity; 2grün a. (of a bright) green; 2halten v/a. ⓘa** to esteem

⚛ scientific; ♣ botanical; ♀ geography; ⊙ machinery; ✕ mining; ✠ military; ⚓ marine; ✱ commercial; ✉ postal; 🚂 railway.

(or value) highly; j-s Andenken 2 to cherish the memory of a p.; ?heilig a. very (or most) holy; =heimer [Hoch= heim ⚥ a. Main (Rheingau)] m ㉒: = (Wein) ⚥ hock; ?herzig a. high-minded or souled, magnanimous; =herzigkeit f magnanimity; ?inter= essant a. highly interesting; =kant m, =kante f ⊕ eines Brettes edge of a shelf; =kirche f England: High Church, weitS. Church of England; =kirchliche(r) m (High-)churchman; =klingend a. high-sounding, bombastic, =konser= vativ a. ultra-conservative, strongly conservative; =land: a) n mountainous country; upland; b) ⚥ npr/n.: Schotti= sches ~ Scotch Highlands pl.; =länder (=in f) m Scotch Highlander; ?ländisch a.: Se Tracht Highland costume.

höchlich (↙) adv. (weniger stark als „hoch") vor a.: very, exceedingly, F rather, awfully; vor a. u. v.: highly, greatly, eminently.

hoch=löblich (↙ch...) a. ㊅ worshipful (als Titel der Behörden nicht zu übersetzen); =meister m ㉒ grand-master; =meister= tum n grand-master's office or dignity; =messe f, Cath. eccl. = amt; ?mode'rn a. quite modern, up to date; =mögend a. =gebietend; =mut m haughtiness, (great) pride, (An= maßung) arrogance, (Aufgeblasenheit) pomposity, bumptiousness, gelehrter ~ priggishness; Sprichw. s. Fall¹¹; ?mütig a. (s. =mut) haughty, (very) proud, arrogant, pompous, bump= tious; priggish; =muts=teufel m (demon of) pride; der ~ ist in ihn ge= fahren he is eaten up with pride; ?nasig, ?näsig F a. supercilious, F stuck-up; =näsigkeit f superciliousness; ?notpeinlich † a. penal; =ofen ⊙ m, metall. (blast-)furnace; =ofen=gase n/pl. furnace-gases pl.; =parterre n raised ground-floor; =plateau n high plateau; ?poe'tisch a. highly poetical or romantic; ?preisen v/a. ⓟ⁎⁎ to praise to the skies; to extol, to belaud; ?preislich a. very praise-worthy; ?ragend a. very lofty. rising high, towering, =reli=ef ⊙ n Bild= hauerei ꝛc.: high relief; vgl. Hautrelief; ?rot a. of a bright (or deep) red; vom Gesichte oft: F co. (as) red as a turkey-cock, (highly) inflamed; =rund a. convex; =saison f height of the season; ?schäftig a.: a) Se Stiefel high boots pl.; b) ⊕ Weberei: Ꝛ (gewebt) with a high warp; Se Tapete high-warp tapestry; ?schätzbar a. highly estim= able; ?schätzen v/a. ⓟ⁎⁎ =achten; =schätzung f = =achtung; =schlag m Tennisspiel: lob; =schule f academy, university; technische = technical col-lege or university; central engineer-ing-school; =schüler m academician, university student; collegian; ?schul= t(e)rig a. high-shouldered; =schuß m bullet aimed too high; ?schwanger a. in an advanced state of pregnancy, mehr gbr.: very near her confinement or her time; =see=fischerei f deep-sea fishery; =see=(torpedo)boot ↓ n deep-sea torpedo; ?selig a. late (lamented)

of blessed memory; Ihr Ler Vater your late (lamented) Father; der Le König His late Majesty; ?sinnig a. = ?gesinnt; =sommer m midsummer; im ~ in the height of summer; =spannung f, elect. high tension or voltage; =spannungs=anlage f, elect. high-tension plant; =spannungs= leitung f, elect. high-tension conduit; =spannungs=strom m, elect. high-ten-sion (or high-voltage) current; =sprung m Turnerei: high jump.

höchst (↙) sup. von hoch (f. ds I, bsd. 5); als adv. f. hoch II; als s. f. hoch 14 u. 16.

Hoch=stamm (↙ch...) m ㉒ high trunk, tall (or full-grown) tree; ?stämmig a. ㊅ von Bäumen und fig. von Menschen: of tall growth; =stapelei f high-class swindling or robbery; ?stapeln ↘ v/n. (h.) ⓦa⁎;⁎ to live by one's wits or by swindling (the public), F to be on the high-fly or on the make; =stapler m fashionably dressed swindler, F swell-mobsman; pl. a. F swell mob, F high mob, blades pl. on the high-fly.

höchst=besteuert (↙...) a. ㊅ most highly assessed or rated or taxed; die ~en the highest ratepayers, those who are (the) most highly taxed; =betrag m ㊇ maximum (amount); =bietende(r) m ㊆ highest bidder; =dero, Titel: ~ Sohn Your Son; the Son of Your (Royal) Highness or of Your Majesty; =derselbe, =dieselben You(r Highness); Your (or His) Majesty.

hoch=stehend (↙ch...) a. ㊅ standing high; vgl. ?gestellt; ♀ hoch stehende Aktien high-priced shares pl.

höchst=eigenhändig (↙...) a. ㊅ with His (f Her) own hand; autograph (letter. &c.).

höchstens (↙) adv. f. hoch III.

Höchst=gebot (↙...) n ㊆ bei Versteigerungen: highest bid or offer; =geschwindigkeit f maximum speed; =grenze f m. limit.

Hoch=stift (↙ch...) n ㊆ (grand) chapter of a cathedral; =stifts=kirche f cathedral-church.

Höchst=kommandierende(r) ⚔ (↙...) m ㊆ generalissimo, Engl.: Commander-in-Chief; =leistung ⊙ f, mach., &c. maxi-mum (amount of) work; ?möglich a. ㊅ as great (or high) as possible.

Hoch=straße (↙ch...) f ㊆ highway; ?strebend a. ㊅ aiming (or aspiring) high, von Plänen: high-flying, lofty.

Höchst=selbe (↙...) m ㊅ His (f Her) Ma-jesty; =stand ⚥ m ㊇ der Preise: highest level of prices; ?wahrscheinlich a. ㊅ most probable or likely; adv. most probably, in all likelihood.

Hoch=ton (↙ch...) m ㊇ pros. chief accent or stress; ?tönend a. ㊅, ?tönig a. = ?trabend b; ?tonig high-toned; =tory m(true)Tory, advanced Conservative, true blue; ?trabend a.: a) von Pferden: high-stepping, Les Pferd high-step-per; b) fig. of proud (or haughty) bearing; (sich überhebend) self-assuming; von Reden: high-sounding (phrases), grandiloquent (speeches), F tall (talk); (schwülstig) bombastic, pompous, F big, grand; adv. sich Ꝛ gebaren F to do the grand, to cut a dash; =trabenheit f haughty (or haughtiness of) bearing;

=traber m, man. high-stepper; ?tragisch a. highly tragical; ?verdient a. very deserving; um das Vaterland Ler Mann one who has well deserved of his country; ?verehrt a. highly respected or esteemed; =verrat m high treason; =verräter m one guilty of high treason; ?verräterisch a. highly treasonable; =wald(ung f) m (extensive or fine old) timber-forest; =wasser n: a) e-s Flusses: high water, swol(le)n state of the river; b) der See: high tide or water; =wasser=marke f, =stand(s)= zeichen n high-water mark; ?weise a. most wise, oft iro. sapient, too clever; (schulmeisterlich) pedantic; als Titel von Magistraten ꝛc. nicht zu übersetzen; ?wichtig a. highly important, v. wich-tigen Fragen: of great consequence; =wild n, hunt. coll. big game; ?will= kommen a. most welcome; ?winden ⊙ v/a. ⓟ⁎⁎ (ant. abwinden 2) to raise (by means of a windlass); =wohl= geboren a. als Titel von höher gestellten Bürgerlichen nicht oder durch Esq. (= vgl. =geboren; als Titel von Edelleuten (in Engl. vom Baron aufwärts bis zum Duke, vgl. Herzog, etwa: His (in der Anrede: Your) Lordship, vollständiger: (To the) Right Honourable Lord; =würden Titel von hohen Geistlichen (vgl. ehrwürden), etwa: Your (His) Reverence, als Titel von engl. Archidiakonen: the Venerable Arch-deacon; Ew. ~, oft: Right Reverend Sir; vgl. Bischof; ?würdig a.: a) most venerable, als Titel hoher Geistlichen: Right Reverend; b) Cath. eccl. das ~ste ausstellen to elevate the Host.

Hoch=zeit (↙ch=) [mhd.] f ㊅ 1. (Vermählung) wedding, nuptials pl.; bsd. bibl. bridal feast; (Trauung) marriage; den Tag für die ~ bestimmen to fix the day for the wedding, vgl. Hochzeitstag; wann machen Sie ~? when is the wedding to be or to come off?; ~ machen to celebrate one's wedding, to give a wedding-party; s. diamanten 2, gol-den 2 und silbern. — 2. typ. (doppelt gesetztes Wort) double.

Hoch=zeiter (↙ch=~) m ㉒, ~in f ㊵ bridegroom, bride.

hoch=zeitlich (↙ch=~) a. ㊅ nuptial, bridal.

Hoch=zeit(s)=anzug (↙ch=...) m ㊆ des Bräutigams: wedding-suit; der Braut: w.-dress; =bett n nuptial couch, bridal bed; =bitter(in f) m one who invites the wedding-guests; =brief m (letter of) invitation to a wedding; =fackel f nuptial torch, torch of Hymen; =feier(lichkeit f), =fest(lich= keit f) n wedding- (or marriage-)feast; =gast m wedding-guest; =gedicht n nuptial poem; Alt.: ⚥ epithalamium; =geschenk n wedding-gift or -present; =gott m, myth. Hymen; =kleid n wedding-dress, weitS. (a. bibl.) wedding-garb or -garment; =kranz m bridal wreath; =kuchen m w.-cake (wovon in England ein Stückchen an die Freunde gesandt wird); =leute pl. w.-guests pl.; =lied n nuptial song; =mahl n = =schmaus; =mutter f bride's mother; =reise f wedding-trip or -tour; =schmaus m w.-break-

[Hochzeitsstaat] — 529 — [Hofhund]

fast, jetzt in England auch: w.-dinner; weitS. w.-repast or -feast; =**ſtaat** m weddingcostume or -dress; =**tag** m w.-day; den ~ beſtimmen to name the day; =**vater** F m bride's father; =**woche** f first week of the honeymoon or of married life; =**zug** m bridal procession; auch: wedding-party. [to be esteemed.
hoch-zu-ver-ehrend (″ch...) a ⓖ highly
Hocke (⌣) [nhd.] f ⓗ 1. agr. (Haufen Garben) heap (or pile) of sheaves. — 2. Turnerei: sitting (or squatting) posture or position. — 3. — Hucke.
hocken (⌣) [nhd.] ⓗ I v/n. (h.) 1. = aufhocken I. — 2. (auf den Ferſen ſitzen) to squat down (a. Turnerei); auch: v/refl. ſich in e-n Winkel ⟨ to cower down in (or to crouch into) a corner. — 3. F (ſitzend verweilen) to sit long, to stay in the same place; immer zu Hauſe ⟨ to keep indoors, to be a stay-at-home, F to stick (or mope) at home; über den Büchern ⟨ to be poring over one's books. — II v/a. 4. = auf⟨ II.
Hocker (⌣) [hocken] m ⓗ 1. ~ m, ~**in** f ⓗ one who stays much at home, stay-at-home, home-bird, p. fond of his (her) fireside. — 2. (Schemel) stool.
Höcker (⌣) [nhd.] m ⓗ 1. (hügelartige Erhöhung) knoll, elevation; knob, bump, ⟨ protuberance. — 2. (Auswuchs): a) des Kamels, eines Buckligen: hunch(back), hump(back), ⟨ gibbosity; einen ~ haben to be humpbacked or hunchbacked; b) anat.: ⟨ tuberosity (a. path.); kleiner ~ (a. dim. =chen n ⓗ), oft: ⟨ tubercle. — Vgl. auch Buckel¹.
Höcker-grab (⌣⌣) n ⓗ prehistoric grave in which the dead are found in a crouching position.
höckericht, mſt **höckerig** (⌣⌣) a. ⓗ 1. like a hunch or hump. — 2. a) (Höcker habend) full of knobs or humps; (uneben, holperig) uneven, rugged, bumpy; (buckelig) hunchbacked, ⟨ gibbous; b) ⟨: ⟨ (warzig) tuberculate, (knollig) tuberous. — 3. ⓗ (uneben) knobby, rough; (ſchartig) jagged, dented. [testicle, ⟨ orchis.
Hode ⟨ (⌣) [ahd.] f ⓗ, m ⓗ anat.
Hodeget ⟨ (⌣-¹) [grch. Wegweiſer] m ⓗ guide (to knowledge), instructor; ~**ik** f ⓗ (Anweiſung zum wiſſenſchaftlichen Studium) hodegetics.
Hoden (⌣) m ⓗ = Hode.
Hoden-bruch (″...) m ⓗ path.: ⟨ scrotocele, scrotal hernia; orchiocele; ⟨**förmig** a. ⓗ. ⟨ testiculate; =**geſchwulſt** f, path. swelling of the testicles, ⟨ orchidocele; =**ſack** m F purse, anat.: ⟨ scrotum.
hodig (⌣) a. ⓗ having testicles.
Hof (⌣ ob. ⌣) [ahd.] m ⓗ c. 1. yard, court(yard), v. Gebäuden umſchloſſener: quadrangle, in Oxford: quad; auf den ~ geh(e)n to go (in)to the yard; (verſchleiernd) auf den ~ (Abtritt) gehen, auf dem ~ ſein to go to the W. C., to be at the W. C.; vgl. Hühner-⟨, Vieh-⟨. — 2. (ländliche Beſitzung) homestead, tenement, (Meierei) farm; (größeres Beſitztum) estate, (country-)seat; von Haus und ~ treiben to turn out of house and home; (Wohnung des Grundherrn) (lordly) manor or castle. —

3. (anſehnliches Gebäude) mansion; (Gaſt=) ~ hotel, ;B. der Bayriſche ~ Hotel of Bavaria. — 4. (Fürſten=)- (princely) court; (royal) residence; an den ~ geh(e)n to go to court; bei (od. am) ~e at court; bei ~e gern geſehen ſein to be a favourite at court or a court-favourite; (glänzenden) ~ halten to keep (a brilliant) court, to live in great state. — 5. e-m den ~ machen (ſich höflich, dienſtbar erweiſen) to pay one's court to a p., to court (or woo) a p.; e-r Dame a.: to pay one's courtship (or addresses) to a lady, F to step up to a lady; allen Mädchen den ~ machen F to flirt (or spoon) with (or to mash) all the girls. — 6 (Ring um Sonne u. Mond) ⟨ corona, halo, aureola.
Hof-amt (⌣...) n ⓗ appointment (or office) at court or in the Royal Household; =**apotheke** f dispensary attached to the court; =**apotheker** m apothecary (or dispensing chemist) to the court; =**arbeit** f work (done) for the court; =**arzt** m court-physician; =**bäcker** m baker (by appointment) to the court, in Engl.: to the Royal Family; =**ball** m court- (or state-)ball; =**barbier** m hairdresser to the court; =**beamte(r)** m court-official, in Engl.: officer of the Royal Household, =**beſitzer** m owner of a farm or an estate; farmer, yeoman, squire; =**brauch** m usage(s pl.) at court, court-etiquette; =**buchhändler** m bookseller (or publisher) in ordinary to His (Her) Majesty; =**burg** f princely castle or residence; in Wien: Imperial Palace; =**burg-theater** n Theatre attached to the Imperial Palace; =**chargen** pl. ſ. Charge 1; =**dame** f maid of honour, lady of the bedchamber, court-lady, lady at court; dienſttuende ~ lady in waiting; =**dichter** m in England: poet laureate; =**diener** m = =beamte(r); niedrigeren Standes: court-lackey or -servant; =**dienerſchaft** f domestics (or servants) pl. at court; =**dienſt** m: a) attendance at court; b) ehm. auch = Frondienſt; =**fähig** a. ⓗ admissible (or presentable) at court; =**fähigkeit** f right to be presented at court.
Hof-fart (⌣) [mhd. Hoch-fahrt] f ⓗ (o. pl.) (Hochmut) haughtiness, pride, (Übermut) insolence, arrogance, (Prunkſucht) ostentation, pomp(osity), arrogance, (Eitelkeit) vanity, conceit.
hof-färtig (⌣⌣) a. ⓗ haughty, proud, insolent, arrogant, ostentatious, pompous; vain, conceited.
hoffen (⌣) [mhd. (nbd.): hope] I v/a. u. v/n. (h.) ⓗ to hope, (erwarten) to expect, to await; zuverſichtlich: to trust in, to reckon upon, to look for(ward to); (ſich mit et. ſchmeicheln) to buoy o.s. up with a hope; auf beſſere Tage ⟨ to hope for better days; auf das Beſte ⟨ to hope for the best; auf (zu) Gott ⟨ to (put one's) trust in God; das Beſte von e-r Sache ⟨ to set (or rest) one's hope(s) upon..., to be sanguine of ...; ich hoffe, er kommt nicht I hope he won't come; ich hoffe nicht, daß er kommt od. kommen wird I don't expect

he will come; ich will nicht ⟨, daß er es gehört hat I trust he may not have heard it; der gehoffte Erfolg the hoped-for success; die gehoffte Zahlung the anticipated (or expected) payment; die zu ⟨den Vergnügungen prospective pleasures pl., .pleasures in prospect. — II ~ n ⓗ = Hoffnung; Sprichw. ~ und Harren macht manchen zum Narren (bibl.) hope deferred maketh the heart sick.
hoffentlich (⌣⌣) adv. it is to be hoped; er iſt ⟨ geſund I hope (or trust) that (F oft ohne 'that') he is (or may be) well.
Hof-feſt (⌣⌣) n ⓗ court-fête, festivity at court, (great) gala.
höfflich ⚒ (⌣⌣) a. ⓗ promising (good results), opening up well.
Hoffmanns-tropfen (⌣⌣⌣⌣) m pl. ⓗ pharm. (1 Äther, 3 Alkohol) ether drops.
Hoffnung (⌣⌣) [nhd.; *hoffen] f ⓗ 1. hope; (hoffnungsvolle Stimmung) hopefulness; (Erwartung) expectation, anticipation, expectancy; (Zuverſicht) trust, (Ausſicht) prospect; getäuſchte ~ disappointment; wir leben der ~, daß ⟨ we are living in hopes that ⟨; er macht ſich ~, daß ⟨ he is in hopes (ſtärker: he's sanguine) that ⟨; neue ~ ſchöpfen to conceive new hope; guter ~ ſein to be full of hope or of good cheer; vgl. 2; meine ~en waren vernichtet my hopes were dashed to the ground; ſeine ~en auf et. bauen to build (one's) hopes upon a th., to put one's trust in a th.; e-m ~ auf et. machen to hold out hopes (or a hope) to a p., a. fig. to dangle s.th. before a p.'s eyes; ſich (dat.) ~ auf et. m. to entertain the hope of attaining a th., to hope for a th.; ~en in e-m erwecken to raise hopes in a p.; e-n mit leerer ~ abſpeiſen to fill a p. with delusive hopes or expectations; zu ⟨ ſchönen ~en berechtigen to give fair promise (for the future); ⚧ Vorgebirge der guten ~ Cape of Good Hope; Sprichw. ~ läßt nicht zuſchanden werden while there is life there is hope. — 2. fig. guter ~ (ſchwanger) ſein to be in the family-way, feiner: to be in interesting circumstances; ſie iſt guter ~ she is expecting (to be confined).
Hoffnungs-kauf ⚖ (⌣⌣⌣) m ⓗ speculative purchase, F purchase on speculation; =**los** a. ⓗ hopeless, past (all) hope, unpromising; =**loſigkeit** f ⓗ hopelessness; =**reich** a. ⓗ filled with (or full of) hope, sanguine, hopeful; =**ſchimmer** m ⓗ gleam of hope; =**ſtrahl** m ray of hope; =**voll** a. full of hope, a. very promising, bidding fair (for the future).
Hof-fräulein (⌣...) n ⓗ maid of honour; =**furier** m Royal messenger; =**gänger** m (Scharwerker) hired labourer; =**gebrauch** m = brauch; =**geflügel** n poultry of a farmyard, barn-door fowls pl.; =**gericht** n ehm. high court of justice; =**geſinde** n establishment of servants: a) at court, b) at a farm; =**gunſt** f court-favour; =**halt** m = =haltung; ⟨**halten** v/n. (h.) ⓗ to keep (or hold) court, to reside; =**haltung** f princely suite, in England: Royal Household; =**herr** m lord of the manor; =**hund** m house- (or watch-)dog.

[hofieren] — 530 — [Höhenmaß]

hofieren faſt † (⌣⌣´⌣) [mhd.-lt.; *Hof] v/n. (h.) ⊕ **1.** to lead a gay (or jolly) life. — **2.** e-m ⌇ to court a p.

höfiſch (´⌣) [Hof] a. ⊕: a) urſprünglich: courtly; b) jetzt meiſt: courtier-like.

Hof-jäger (²...) m ⊕ royal game-keeper; =**jäger-meiſter** m in England: Master of the Hounds; =**junker** m page; lord-in-waiting; weitS. gentleman at court; =**kabale** f court-intrigue or -cabal; =**kamari'lla** f camarilla, a. = =partei'; =**kammer** f: a) (princely) domain; b) prince's private exchequer; =**kanz-lei** f court-chancery; =**kanzler** m court-chancellor; =**kape'lle** f: a) royal chapel; b) prince's private band; =**kapla'n** m court-chaplain, chaplain in ordinary to the King or Queen; =**kaſſe** f prince's private income or exchequer or funds pl.; =**kavali'er** m courtier; vgl. =junker; =**keller(ei** f) m royal cellars pl.; =**kleid** n court-dress; =**kreiſe** m/pl. court-circles pl.; =**kriegs-rat** m in Wien, etwa: military councillor (or adviser) to the court; =**küche** f kitchen of the palace; =**lager** n (princely) residence; ſein ~ halten to hold (or keep) court; =**lakai'** m royal lackey; =**leben** n life at court; =**leute** pl. von =mann.

höflich (´⌣) [Hof] a. ⊕ (ant. grob) (von äußerem Anſtand) polite, civil, courteous (gegen // to //), (artig) genteel, complimentary, complaisant, gegen Frauen: galla'nt to the ladies; (verbindlich) obliging to(wards) //; ⌇e Redensarten polite phrases pl.; in ⌇er Sprache in civil (or complimentary) terms; e-n auf das ⌇ſte empfangen to receive a p. most courteously or with the greatest politeness or courtesy.

Höflichkeit (´⌣⌣) f ⊕ (ſ. höflich): a) (o. pl.) (das Höflichſein) politeness, civility, courtesy; (feine Lebensart) gentleness, urbanity, polished manner(s pl.); b) mit pl. civil (or kind) act; aus ~ out of politeness, out of compliment; e-n mit ~en überhäufen to shower compliments (or polite phrases) upon a p.; ſ. übertünchen; Sprichw. mit ~ kommt man durch die Welt a little politeness goes a long way.

Höflichkeits-bezeigungen (⌣´⌣...) f/pl. ⊕ marks (or proofs) pl. of civility; attentions, compliments pl.; =**formel** f polite phrase; =**formen** f/pl., =**ge-bräuche** m/pl. forms pl. of politeness, (mere) compliments pl.

Höflich-ſein (´⌣´) n ⊕ = Höflichkeit a.

Hof-liefera'nt (²...) m ⊕ court-purveyor, in Engl.: purveyor (by special appointment) to the Royal Family.

Höfling (´⌣) m ⊕d. courtier; oft b.s. = Hofſchranze; ~s-ſchar (´⌣...) f ⊕ crowd of courtiers.

Hof-luft (²...) f ⊕ air (weitS. surroundings pl.) of the court; =**machen** n courting, love-making; =**macher** m e-r Dame wooer, suitor; =**maler** m court-painter; =**manier** f courtly manner(s pl.); nach ~ court-like; =**mann** m courtier, gentleman attached to the court; ⌇**männiſch** a. ⊕ courtier-like, like a courtier; =**mar'ſchall** m court-marshal;

in Engl.: Lord Chamberlain; ⌇**mäßig** a. courtly, court-like; =**meiſter** m: a) (Verwalter auf Landhöfen) manager, steward, bailiff (of an estate); b) an fürſtlichen Höfen: (Aufſeher über die Dienerſchaft), in England: Controller of the Royal Household; c) (Erzieher vornehmer Kinder) private tutor; (Lehrer) teacher; b.s. den ~ ſpielen to assume a pedantic air, F to act the superior person; =**meiſterei** f pedantry; =**meiſterin** f (ſ. =meiſter) resident governess to a high (or princely) family; ⌇**meiſteriſch**, ⌇**meiſterlich** a. tutor-like, tutorial, b.s. pedantic; ⌇**meiſtern** v/a. u. v/n. (h.) ⌇a *„*: e-n (od. an e-m) ⌇ to play the tutor to a p., weitS. to lead (or guide) a p.; (abkanzeln) to lecture (or sermonize) a p.; =**muſika'nt** m court-musician; =**narr** m court-jester, king's jester; =**partei'** f court-party; =**poe't** m = =dichter; =**prediger** m chaplain in ordinary (to); =**rangordnung** f precedence at court; =**rat** m) a) coll. Aulic Council; in England: Privy Council; b) (Mitglied, auch bloßer Titel) aulic councillor; in England: Privy Councillor; c) F co. = Hahn; =**raum** m courtyard; =**reite** (Wirtſchaftshof, Gut) f farm-yard, estate; =**richter** m judge of a superior court; =**ſchatzmeiſter** m, in England: Treasurer of the Household; =**ſchau-ſpieler(in** f) m actor (actress) attached to a royal theatre; =**ſchneider** m court-tailor; =**ſchranz(e** m u. f) m court-flunkey; =**ſitte** f =brauch; =**ſprache** f language used at court; =**ſtaat** m: a) princely household; b) court-dress; =**ſtatt, ſtätte** f homestead; =**tag** m court-day, in England: Drawing-room (held by ...); =**thea'ter** n court- (or royal) theatre; in Engl.: Theatre Royal; =**tor** n gate leading to the yard; =**tracht** f costume worn (or required) at court; =**trauer** f court-mourning; =**tür(e)** f door of a court-yard; =**welt** f court; society in touch (or connected) with the court; =**weſen** n affairs pl. of the court, court-life; =**zeitung** f court-gazette; =**zeremoniell** n court-ceremonial; =**zirkel** m court-circle; =**zug** m princely (or royal) train; =**zwang** m etiquette (enforced at court).

⌇**hoh...** ſ. hoch.

Höhe (´⌣) f ⊕ (dat. sg. bisw. ~n) **1.** height; math., ast., &c.: ⌇ altitude (of a triangle, of a heavenly body); (Erhebung, Hügel) elevation (of a mountain); die ~ (den Gipfel) erreichen to reach the summit or top; aus der ~ from on high; in der ~ on high; Ehre ſei Gott in der ~! glory be to God on high or (in the heavens) above!; in gleicher ~ mit // on the same (or on a) level with //; ↓ auf der ~ e-s Hafens off a port; ♀ auf der ~ Ortes, Punktes in the same latitude as a place, a point; ⊕ ~ der Preiſe level of prices; die Preiſe können ſich nicht auf dieſer ~ behaupten ... cannot maintain their present (high) level. — **2.** fig. auf der Höhe (dem Gipfel) ſeines Glückes, Ruhmes on the summit (or the highest pitch) of

one's good fortune, on the pinnacle (or in the zenith) of one's fame; auf der ~ der Wiſſenſchaft bleiben to keep in touch with the latest advancement in science or learning; auf der ~ der Zeit of modern type, of the latest shape or fashion, F up to date; auf der ~ ſeiner Zeit ꝛc. ſein to be (well) abreast of one's time, &c.; oft iro. das iſt die rechte ~ (Art) that is the way (to do it). — **3. in die ~** (empor) up(wards); gerade in die ~ straight up; in die ~ bringen to raise (up), ⊕ Preiſe: to run up; in die ~ fahren to start (or jump) up, to leap on one's feet; vor Wut, etwa: to be beside o.s. with rage, to fret and fume; in die ~ geh(e)n (ſteigen) to rise, to go up, ⊕ von Preiſen und Kurſen auch: to improve, go higher, advance, stiffen; ⊕ die Aktien gehen in die ~ the shares are looking up or show an upward tendency or an improvement; in die ~ halten to hold up high; in die ~ heben to lift up; ſein Kleid in die ~ heben to pull up one's dress; in die ~ kommen to rise, to get up (high), fig. to get on, F to get to the top; in die ~ nehmen to hold (↓ to hitch) up; in die ~ ſchießen (auffteigen) (suddenly) to shoot up (a. v. Pflanzen); ſich in die ~ ſchwingen to swing o.s. up, to leap (or bound) up; ⊕ Preiſe in die ~ treiben to run (or force) up prices, v. Spekulanten: to bull (or boom) the market; in die ~ wachſen to grow up; in die ~ werfen to throw up; den Kopf: to toss up; in die ~ winden, ziehen to wind (or twist) up. — **4.** ♪ ~ der Töne pitch; high (F top) notes pl., zB.: die Sängerin hat eine ſchöne ~ ... has very high notes. — **5.** paint. ~ der Farben intensity, brightness. — **6.** ♀ die ~ npr. (Taunus-gebirge in Naſſau) Taunus.

Hoheit (´⌣) [mhd.] f ⊕ **1.** (Erhabenheit) elevation; sublimity, sublimeness; (Groß-artigkeit) grandeur; (Adel) nobility. — **2.** (hoher Rang) high rank; augustness, greatness, eminence. — **3.** (Ober-) bſ. des Landesherrn: sovereignty; (Lehns-) ~ suzerainty. — **4.** (fürſtlicher Titel) Highness; Seine (Ihre) Königliche ~ (abbr. S. (J.) K[gl]. H.) der Großherzog (die Großherzogin) His (Her) Royal Highness the ... (abbr. H. R. H.), öft. S. k. [u. k.] ~: Seine kaiſerliche [u. königliche] ~ His Imperial (and Royal) Highness.

hoheitlich (´⌣⌣) a. ⊕ sovereign (right, &c.).

Hoheits-recht (´⌣...) n ⊕ mſt pl. right(s pl.) or prerogative(s pl.) of a sovereign; eccl. hist. auch: ⌇ regalia pl.; ⌇**voll** a. ⊕ majestic.

Hohe-lied (⌣´⌣) n ⊕ (the) Song of Solomon, (the) Canticles pl.

höhen faſt † (´⌣) [ahd.] v/a. ⊕ = erhöhen.

Höhen-beſchreibung (´⌣⌣...) f ⊕ hypsography; =**inſtrume'nt** n = =meſſer; =**klima** n climate according to altitude or elevation; =**kreiſe** m/pl. ast. circles pl. of altitude, ♀ parallels pl. (of latitude); =**kurort** m health-resort on the hills or mountains; =**linie** ⌇ f, surv. contour(-line); =**maß** n eines

---

Signs (see page XVII): F familiar; P vulgar; ⌐ flash; ⌇ rare; † obsolete (died); * new word (born); ,+, incorrect; ♪ music;

[**Höhenmesser**] Gebäudes ꝛc. measure of elevation; =**messer** m, phys.: ⚗ altimeter; ast.: ⚗ label, astrolabe; surv. theodolite; =**meßkunst**, =**messung** f measurement of elevations or heights, ⚗ hypsometry, altimetry; =**punkt** m f. Höhepunkt; =**rauch** m = Herauch; =**richtung** ⚓ f elevation; =**schicht** f, geol. geological layer (pl. oft: geol. strata); =**unterschied** ♀ m difference of elevation or altitude; =**verhältnisse** n/pl. degree(s pl.) of altitude; =**zug** m range of hills, mountain-chain.

Hohepriester (˘ˉ˘˘) m ⓖ the High Priest; ~**amt** n ⓖ pontificate; ²**lich** a. ⓖ pontifical; ~**tum** n ⓓd. pontificate.

Höhe-punkt (ˉ˘˘) m ⓖ height, altitude, fig. culminating point, acme: ast. und fig. zenith.

höher (ˉ˘) [comp. von hoch, f. d§] higher.

Höhe-rauch (ˉ˘˘) m ⓖ = Herauch.

höher-bewertet (ˉ˘˘...) ⓖ a. ⓖ von Aktien ꝛc.: of higher value, high-priced; =**bieten** n ⓖ, =**gebot** n ⓖ higher bid or offer, (further) advance; =**legung** f raising, elevating; =**liegen** n greater elevation or height.

Hohe-schule (ˉ˘˘˘) f ⓖ = Hochschule; f. a. hoch 2.

hohl (ˉ) [ahd.: hollow] I a. ⓖ hollow, (zellenförmig): ⚗ alveated; (vertieft) concave, (ausgehöhlt) hollowed out; (röhrenförmig): ⚗ fistulous, fistulate, engS. (ausgekehlt) fluted, grooved; (gewölbt) arched; ² machen to hollow (or scoop) out, to excavate; ²e Augen n/pl. hollow (or sunken) eyes pl.; f. Gasse 2; in der ²en Hand in the hollow of one's hand (a. fig.); ²er Kopf empty head, shallow mind; ²er Magen empty stomach; ⚓ ²er Raum zwischen zwei Wellen trough of the sea; ⚓ ²e See heavy swell, rolling waves pl.; die See geht ² the sea runs high or is rolling heavily; ²e Wand vet. dryness of (the) hoofs; ²er Zahn hollow (or carious, decayed) tooth; adv. ² klingen to have a hollow (or dull) sound; ⊕ ² ausarbeiten to hollow out, flute, groove. — II ~ n ꝛc.: a) (hohler Raum) hollow; b) ⚓ (Tiefe des Schiffes) depth of the ship or the hold.

hohl-äugig (ˉˉ...) a. ⓖ hollow-eyed; ²**bäckig** a. hollow-cheeked; =**bauten** ⚔ n/pl. ⓖ frt. casemates, bomb-proof structures pl.; =**bohrer** ⊕ m, join. hollow auger, wimble; mit e-m Zahn: nose-bit; =**botter** ♀ f perfoliated myagrum (Mya'grum perfolia'tum).

Höhle (ˉ˘) [ahd.: hole; *hohl] f ⓖ 1. in der Erde: cave(rn), künstliche: grotto; der wilden Tiere: hole, burrow, kennel, warren, lodge, earth; des Löwen ~ the lion's den; am Eingang e-r ~ at the mouth of a cave; voller ~n cavernous. — 2. (umschlossener leerer Raum) hollow, cavity, ventricle (auch anat.); (Bienenzelle, Zahnhöhle): ⚗ alveolus; (Aushöhlung) excavation; seine Augen traten aus ihren ~n his eyes started from their sockets. — 3. contp. (Wohnung) den of thieves; peasant's hovel.

Hohl-eisen ⊕ (ˉ˘ˉ) n ⓖ hollow iron or chisel, gouge.

höhlen (ˉ˘) v/a. u. sich ² v/refl. ⓖ: (sich) ² to (grow) hollow; (ausgraben) to excavate.

Höhlen-affe (ˉ˘...) m ⓖ zo.: ⚗ troglodyte; ²**artig** a. ⓖ cave-like, cavernous, ⚗ spelæan; vorweltlicher =**bär** m, zo. cave-bear (Ursus spelae'us); =**bewohner(in)** f m cave-dweller, cave-man, ⚗ troglodyte; =**ente** f, zo. sheldrake (Tado'rna vulpa'nser); =**fund** m find made in caves; =**grab** n cave-tomb; =**leben** n cave-life; ⚗ troglodytism; =**mensch** m cave-man; ⚗ troglodyte; =**tempel** m temple carved (or cut) out of the living rock; =**tiere** n/pl. zo. animals pl. living in caves, ⚗ troglodytes; =**tierkreaturen** pl.; =**wohnung** f cave-dwelling.

Höhler (ˉ˘) m ⓖ 1. one who hollows out; excavator. — 2. prov. deep cellar.

hohl-erhaben (ˉˉ...) a. ⓖ phys.: ⚗ concavo-convex; =**fläche** f ⓖ phys. concavity; =**gefäß** n hollow vessel; measure of capacity; =**gehen** ⚓ n der See roll(ing), (heavy) swell; ²**gehend** ⚓ a. running high; ²**geschliffen** a. hollow-ground (razor, &c.); phys. concave (lens); =**geschoß** ⚔ n hollow projectile, shell; =**gießen** n, metall. hollow casting; =**glas** n hollow (or round, concave) glass, h. ware; opt. concave glass; =**guß** m hollow cast(ing).

Hohlheit (ˉ˘) f ⓖ 1. hollowness, (Hohlrundung) concavity. — 2. fig. hollowness, vacuity, emptiness, shallowness; vanity, conceit.

Hohl-hippe (ˉ˘...) f ⓖ Bäckerei: hollow wafer; ²**hörnig** a. ⓖ des Tier zo.: ⚗ cavicorn. [of cavities; cavernous.]

höhlig (ˉ˘) a. ⓖ with hollows or pits, full)

Hohl-kehle (ˉ˘...) f ⓖ = =**rinne**; =**kehlhobel** m hollow (or fluting, round-sole) plane; =**klinge** f hollow(-ground) blade; =**knopf** m shell-button; =**kopf** m empty-headed fellow, F noodle; ²**köpfig** a. ⓖ empty-headed, vacuous, F shallow-pated or -witted; =**kreisel** m humming-top; =**kugel** f hollow sphere or ball, ⚔ hollow projectile, shell; =**leiste** f = =**rinne**; =**linse** f, phys. concave lens; =**maß** n measure of capacity; für Korn ꝛc.: dry measure; =**meißel** m gouge; =**raum** m hollow space; =**rinne** f hollow, groove, channel; an einer Säule ꝛc. a. chamfer; ²**rund** a. concave; =**saum** m Näherei: hemstitch; =**schiene** f hollow rail; =**schliff** ⊕ m hollow grinding; =**spat** m, min. hollow spar; =**spiegel** m, phys. concave mirror.

Höhlung (ˉ˘) f ⓖ 1. = Aushöhlung. — 2. hollow, cavity, (Schlucht) gorge; anat. ~ (Kammer) chamber; path. fistula.

hohl-wangig (ˉˉ...) a. ⓖ = ²bäckig; =**weg** m hollow (way), (Schlucht) ravine, gorge, (Engpaß) narrow pass, bsd. ⚔ defile; =**werden** n der Bäume ꝛc. growing hollow, der Zähne: decay; =**werk** n Maurerei: (mit Hohlziegeln eingelegtes Dach) roof covered with gutter-tiles; =**zahn** ♀ m (Daun) hemp-nettle (Galeo'psis); ²**zellig** a. ♀, zo.: ⚗ alveolate; =**ziegel** m hollow tile or brick; (Dachziegel) tile for roofing; (Kehlziegel) gutter-tile; =**zirkel** m spherical compasses pl.

Hohn (ˉ) [ahd.] m ⓖⓒ. (Geringschätzung) scorn, disdain; (Herausforderung) taunt; (Spott) sarcasm, sneer, jeer, (Verspottung) derision, ridicule, scoff(ing), (bitter) mockery; (beleidigende Prahlerei) bravado; e-m zum ~e (Trotze) in spite (or defiance) of a p.; ein ~ auf die Sittlichkeit an insult to morality; ein Gegenstand des ~es (und Spottes) an object of derision; e-m ~ lachen to laugh a p. to scorn, to sneer at a p., to rail at a p.; e-m ~ sprechen to bid defiance to a p., to challenge (or insult) a p.; der Vernunft ~ sprechen to fly in the face of (sense and) reason.

hohnecken (ˉ˘˘) v/a. ⓖ*,* to jeer at a p., to twit (or banter) a p.; **Hohneckerei** (˘˘˘ˉ) f jeers pl., banter(ing).

höhnen (ˉ˘) [ahd.] v/a. ⓖ to sneer (or jeer) at; vgl. verhöhnen.

Hohn-gelächter (ˉˉ...) n ⓖ mocking (or scornful) laugh; ~ der Hölle fiendish laugh or sneer; mit ~ empfangen to receive with jeers; den Leuten zum ~ w. to become the laughing-stock of (the) people; =**geschrei** n shouts pl. of scorn or defiance.

höhnisch (ˉ˘) a. ⓖ (f. Hohn) scornful, disdainful; sarcastic, sneering, scoffing, mocking, derisive; adv. ² verlachen to mock, to deride.

höhnischer-weise (ˉ˘˘ˉ˘) adv. scornfully, mockingly, with a sneer or a jeer.

Hohn-lächeln (ˉˉ...) v/n. (h.) ⓖ a* to smile disdainfully; ~ n ⓒⓒ disdainful (or mocking) smile; ²**lachen** v/n. (h.) ⓖ*(*) to laugh scornfully, vgl. Hohn; ~ n ⓒⓒ = =**gelächter** f. hohnecken; =**rede** f mockery, words pl. of scorn, scornful (or defiant) speech; ²**sprechen** v/n. (h.) ⓒa**: das spricht allem Rechte hohn (ob. Hohn) that is an open contradiction to all law; er sprach mir hohn (ob. Hohn) he (openly) defied me; vgl. Hohn am Schluß; =**sprecher(in)** f) m mocker, scoffer.

hoho (˘ˉ) int. oho!, oh ho!; pooh!

Hoh-ofen (ˉ˘...) m ⓖ = Hochofen.

hojanen (˘ˉ˘) [ndd. hoch gähnen] v/n. (h.) ⓖ 1. vom Esel: (schreien) to bray. — 2. (laut gähnen) to yawn aloud.

höfen (ˉ˘) [ndd.] v/n. (h.) ⓖ = höfern.

Höfer (ˉ˘) [ndd.: hawker; *hocken] m ⓖ, =**in** f ⓖ hawker, huckster (f a. huckstress), street-vendor, mit Karren: costermonger, (Standkrämer[in]) stallkeeper, (Kleinkrämer[in]) retailer; (Gemüsehändler[in]) greengrocer.

Höferei (˘˘ˉ) f ⓖ hawking, huckstering, costermonger's trade or vocation.

Höfer-frau (ˉ˘...) f ⓖ = =**weib**; =**karren** m coster's truck or barrow; =**kram**, =**laden** m (small) retail-shop; (fruit-)stall; ²**mäßig** a. ⓖ hawker-like; **höfern** (ˉ˘) [ndd.: hawk] v/n. (h.) ⓖ a. to hawk goods about; to trade as a costermonger or street-vendor, to keep a (fruit-)stall.

Höfer-waren (ˉ˘...) f/pl. ⓖ hawker's (or costermonger's) goods pl.; (Gemüse) greengrocery; =**weib** n: a) = Höferin; b) mit Korb, a. basket-woman.

Hokko ⚗ (˘ˉ) m ⓖ orn. (Baumhuhn) hocco, curassow, curaçao-bird (Pauxi u. Crax).

⚗ scientific; ♀ botanical; ⚱ geography; ⊕ machinery; ⚒ mining; ⚔ military; ⚓ marine; ⓖ commercial; ✉ postal; 🚂 railway.

[Hokuspokus] — 532 — [Holz]

Hokus-pokus (⌣–⌢) m. (n) inv. (Gauklerspiel) hocus-pocus, jugglery, (Taschenspielerei) conjuring, sleight-of-hand; fig. (falscher Schein) hollow pretence; sham, humbug; **~macher** (⌣...) m ⓶ juggler; co'njurer; trickster, dodger.

hold (⌣) [ahd. geneigt; *Halde] I a. ⓺⓺ 1. mit dat.: e-m ♀ (zugeneigt) sein to be well-disposed (or favourably inclined) to(wards) a p.; stärker: to be fond of a p.; er ist mir ♀ he likes me, stärker: he is attached to me; das Glück ist ihm ♀ fortune favours (or smiles upon) him; das Glück ist mir nicht ♀ luck is (dead) against me. — 2. (anmutig) graceful, (entzückend) charming, (gefällig) pleasing, (lieblich) lovely, sweet; das ♀e Kind the sweet (or dear) child. — II **~e(r)** s. ⓺ (f auch **Holdin** f ⓺) 3. (Freund[in]) dear (stärker: beloved or sweet) one; mein **~chen**! my love or darling or sweetheart! — 4. (anmutreiche Person) graceful (or charming) person, F charmer, love of a (wo)man; die ~innen (mehr gbr. Huldinnen) the (three) Graces pl.

Holdchen (⌣) n ⓻ s. hold II.
Holder ♀ (⌣) m ⓶ südd. = Holunder.
Holdin f ⓻ s. hold II.
hold-selig (⌣...) a. ⓺: a) (stärker als hold 2) most graceful or charming or pleasing or lovely; enchanting (figure), ravishing (beauty); b) (huldvoll) gracious, kind(ly disposed); **=seligkeit** f ⓺: a) gracefulness, great (or irresistible) charm, loveliness; b) graciousness.

holen (⌣) [ahd.: haul] v/a. ⓺ 1. to (go to) fetch (aus // from //); to come for; ♀ lassen to send for; wo ♀ (kaufen) Sie Ihr Brot ꝛc.? where do you buy ...?; es ist bei ihm nichts zu ♀ (zu finden) there is nothing to be had (or F got) from him; da ist nichts zu ♀ nothing is to be found there, you cannot gain (or get) anything there; hol' ihn der Teufel! let him go to hell (sehr stark: to the devil)!, milder: the deuce take him!; die Braut heim ♀ to fetch home the bride; ⚔ Futter ♀ to go foraging; ⚓ die Waren ♀ (bringen) gute Preise ... fetch (stärker: command) good prices; ⚒ Erz aus der Erde ♀ (gewinnen) to extract ore (from the ground), to produce ore. — 2. Atem ♀ (einziehen) to draw one's (or to take a) breath; sich bei e-m Rat(s) ♀ to seek a p.'s advice, to take counsel with a p., to consult a p. — 3. sich (dat.) et. ♀ (zuziehen) to contract (or catch) a th.; er hat sich e-n Schnupfen geholt he caught (a) cold. — 4. ⚓ (an einem Taue ziehen) to haul (in), to pull; ♀de Part hauling-part.

Holer (⌣) m ⓶ 1. one who fetches. — 2. ⚒ (Fischerei) iron hook; (long) pole.
Holfter (⌣) [mhd.] f ⓺ (Pistolen-♀) holster.
Holk (⌣) [ndd.; *grch. holka's] m u. n ⓷b. (Schiffsrumpf) hulk.
holla (♀ — ob. ⌣) int. holla!, hallo!; um Halt zu gebieten u. damit ♀! stop (there)!, that's enough!, that will do!
Holland ♀ (⌣) [Hohl-land] npr/n. ⓺⓺ (Land und Provinz) Holland; f. Neu-♀; Sprichw. nun ist ~ in Not now we are

in a fine trouble or F pickle; F now we are in for it!, there we are!
Holländer (⌣⌣) 1 m ⓶. **~in** f ⓥ 1. a) (Bewohner[in] Hollands) Dutch(wo)man, a. Hollander. pl. die ~ the Dutch (people); b) Dutch painter; c) ♂ der Fliegende (Geisterschiff), etwa: the Phantom Ship; the Flying Dutchman (a. Name e-s Schnellzuges zw. Lo. u. Bristol; d) ~ Käse (f. 11). — 2. (Milchmeier) dairy-farmer. — 3. ⊙ ~ (Mühle) (Windmühle, bei der nur der obere Teil drehbar ist) smock- (or tower-)mill; Papierfabr. cylinder- (or pulping-, rag-)engine. — 11 a. inv. 4. bff. holländisch (f. ds). **I** dairy-farm(ing); Dutch dairy.
Holländerei (⌣⌣") f ⓥ (Milchwirtschaft)=
holländern (⌣⌣) v n. (h.) ⓥa. 1. ⊙ Papierfabr.: to pulp rags in a rag-engine. — 2. Schlittschuhlaufen: to do the outside (or inside) edge, to cut figures on the ice.
holländisch (⌣⌣) a. ⓺ Dutch; in Titeln, auch: of Holland; ♀er Käse Dutch cheese; die ♀e Sprache, das ~(e) n ⓺⓻ the Dutch language, Dutch.
Holle[1] (⌣) [Holda] npr/f. ⓥⓑ. myth. (altgermanische Göttin): Frau ~ schüttelt ihre Betten aus (es schneit, etwa): Mother Carey is plucking her geese, the angels are shaking their feather-beds.
Holle[2] (⌣⌣) f ⓥ orn. (Federhaube) tuft, crest.
Hölle (⌣) [ahd.: hell; *hehlen u. *Hel Todesgöttin] f ⓥ (dat. bisw. ~n) 1. hell; infernal (or lower) regions pl., bibl. bottomless pit, myth. Hades, poet. (Dante's) inferno, (Fegefeuer) limbo; in die ~ kommen, zur ~ fahren to go to hell; Himmel und ~ aufbieten to move heaven and earth; to set every lever in motion. — 2t e-m die ~ heiß machen (Angst einjagen) to torment a p., to put a p. in mortal fear, to make a place too hot for a p. — 3. fig. (heißer Ort) (place as hot as a) furnace; (schlimmer Ort) F (a) hell of a place. — 4. ⊙ = Schmiede; provc. (Raum hinterm Ofen) chimney-corner, weitS. snug place. — 5. ⚓ = Höll[2].
Höllen-angst (⌣⌣...) f ⓥ mortal fright, P awful funk; **=brand** m: a) hell-fire; b) great conflagration, blazing fire, infernal (or terrible) heat; c) fig. (großer Bösewicht, Teufel) (infernal) villain, (regular) devil; d) F infernal thirst; **=braten** m (Erzschurke) gallows-bird, rake, scamp; **=brut**/hellish imps pl., infernal crew; **=drache** m: a) (Teufel) hellish dragon, Satan; b) P fig. (böse Person) termagant, vixen, dragon; **=fahrt** f descent into hell; **=feuer** n hell-fire, unquenchable flame; weitS. hot blaze; **=fluß** m, grch. myth. Styx, Acheron, Phlegethon, Cocytus; **=fürst** m: a) myth Pluto; b) prince of darkness, Satan; **=gegend** f infernal region; **=gestank** m inf. (or pestilential) smell or stench; ♀**heiß** a. (as) hot as hell; excessively hot, baking (hot); **=hund** m: a) myth. hellhound, Cerberus; b) (Teufel) Satan; **=lärm** m infernal noise, F devilish (or devil of a) row; **=maschine** f (Sprengmaschine) inf. machine; ♀**mäßig** a. infernal; **=pein**, **=qual** f torments pl. of hell; intense

agony; eine ~ ausstehen, oit: to suffer agony or a martyrdom; vgl. =schmerz; **=pforte** f gate of hell; **=pfuhl** m hellish pool, bottomless pit; **=rachen** m =schlund; **=rand** m limbo; **=schlund** m poet. mouth (or jaws pl.) of hell; **=schmerz** m excruciating (or agonizing) pain; vgl. =pein; **=spektakel** =lärm; **=stein**, chm. (salpetersaures Silber in Stangenform) (lunar) caustic, nitrate of silver, med. a. (lt.) lapis infernalis; **=steinlösung** f nitrate of silver solution; **=strafe** f everlasting damnation, eternal punishment; **=trank** m loathsome (or nauseous) beverage, stärker: hell-broth; **=zwang** book for conjuring (or subduing) evil spirits.
höllisch (⌣) a. ⓺⓺ 1. hellish, infernal (a. fig.); (teuflisch) diabolical, fiendish. — 2. F (übermäßig) excessive, immense, enormous; ♀er Durst burning (or unquenchable) thirst; adv. ♀ fluchen, etwa: to swear till all is blue.
Holm[1] (⌣) [ndd.: holm] m ⓺b. 1. nordb. (Erd-erhöhung) elevation, (Hügel) hill, (kleine, hohe Insel) holm, island (high above the water). — 2. ⚓ (Schiffswerft) dry-dock for repairing ships, &c.
Holm[2] ⊙ (⌣) [= Helm[2] m ⓶b. (Querholz) cross-beam, eines Brückenjochs: top- (or head-)beam, am Barren ꝛc.: bar, an e-r Leiter: rung, step.
Holothurie ⚓ (⌣⌣¹(⌣)⌣) [grch.] f ⓺ (Seegurke) sea-cucumber, sea-cactus (Holothu'ria); eßbare ~ trepang (Hol. edu'lis).
Hol-part ⚓ (⌣⌣) m ⓶ (das freie Ende eines befestigten Taues) hauling-part.
holp(e)richt, holp(e)rig (⌣⌣) a. ⓺ rough, uneven, rugged; ♀e Verse unpolished (or clumsy) lines (of poetry); adv. ♀ lesen to stumble (or stutter) in reading; **Holp(e)rigkeit** (⌣(⌣)⌣~) f ⓺ unevenness, ruggedness.
holpern (⌣⌣) [nhd.] v/n. (h.) ⓥa. 1. der Weg holpert ... is rough or uneven. — 2. (sich ungleichmäßig fortbewegen) to jolt (along); to jog along; (stolpern) to stumble; fig. die Sache holpert the matter is at a standstill or hanging fire or proceeding with difficulty.
holter, diepolter (⌣⌣~⌣) helter-skelter.
hol=über! (⌣⌣⌣) int. (Ruf für den Fährmann) come over!, ferry me over!
Holunder ♀ (⌣⌣) [ahd.; *hohl] m ⓶ 1. elder (Sambu'cus) = Flieder; roter ~ clustered elder-tree (S. racemo'sa); schwarzer ~ common elder (S. ni'gra). — 2. spanischer ~ lilac (Syri'nga vulga'ris); **~baum** ♀ (⌣⌣...) m ⓶ = ~; **=beere**, **=blüte** f elder-berry, -blossom; **=mark** n elder-pith; **=staude** f, **=strauch** m = ~ 1.
Holz (⌣) [ahd.: holt] n ⓺a. 1. wood, ⚔ lignum; (Bau-♀) timber; f. Brenn-♀, Nutz-♀; versteinertes ~ petrified wood, ♀ lignite; (Gehölz) wood, grove; ~ hacken to chop wood; ~ (Bäume) fällen to fell (or hew) timber; ein Stück ~ sägen to saw a piece of wood, fig. (schnarchen) to snore; bibl. am grünen ~ in the green tree; fig. Männer aus (ob. von) anderem ~e (Schlage) men of a different stamp or race. — 2. (Billard und Kegelspiel) wieviel ~ (ist noch)? how many points have we made?, how is the game

Zeichen (f. S. XVII): F familiär; P Volkssprache; Γ Gaunersprache; ⚘ selten; † alt (auch gestorben); * neu (auch geboren); ⁺⁺ unrichtig;

[Holzabfall] — 533 — [Holzweg]

going on? — 3. P das ist viel ~ (Geld) that's a great deal (of money) or F a big sum. — 4. ⊙ s. berinden II.
Holz-abfall (⁂...) m ⑫ (Späne) chips pl. of wood, waste of a timber-yard; =acker m woodland; **ähnlich** a. ⑥ woodlike, ⚗ xyloid; vgl. **artig**; =anlage f plantation of wood or timber; =apfel(=baum) ⚘ m crab-apple (tree) (*Pirus malus silve'stris*); =arbeiten ⚒ f pl. = waren; =arbeiter m worker in wood, woodworker; =arm a. lacking (in) wood(s), scantily wooded; =art f species (or kind) of wood; =artig a. woodlike, resembling wood. woody, ⚗ ligneous, ligniform; vgl. ähnlich; =asche f wood-ashes pl.; =ast m (Hauptast) chief branch of a tree; =auktion ⚒ f public sale of timber; =axt ⊙ f wood(s)man's axe; kleinere: chopper, cleaver; =bahn ⊙ f wood(en) pavement; railway with wooden rails.
holzbar (⁂...) a. ⑯ for. (ready) to be felled.
Holz-bau (⁂...) m ⑫ wooden structure; =bedarf m (amount of) wood required, supply of wood; =beize ⊙ f stain for wood; =bekleidung f wooden lining, wainscot(ting); =bestand m stock of wood or timber; =biene ⚘, ent. carpenter-bee (*Xylo'copa*); =bildhauer m carver in wood, wood-carver; =bildhauerei f = =schnitzerei; =birne f: a) wild pear; b) ⚘ (Baum) wild pear-tree (*Pirus commu'nis*); =block m wood-block, log (of wood); =bock m: a) (Sägebock) sawing-jack, sawhorse; b) ⊙ = Feuerbock; c) F fig. (plumper Mensch) clumsy fellow; d) ent. (Zecke) tick (*Ixo'des*); (Bockkäfer) capricorn beetle (*Cera'mbyx*); =boden m: a) soil adapted for (growing) timber; b) wood-loft or -shed; c) wooden floor(ing); =bohrer m: a) ⊙ auger (for boring wood); b) ent. (Insekt, das sich ins Holz einbohrt) wood-beetle or -borer or -fretter, ⚗ xylophagan (bes. Gattung *Lymno'ria*); vgl. Bohrkäfer; =bohrwurm m, ent.: a) teredine (*Tere'do*); b)= =bohrer b; =brücke f wooden bridge; =bündel n bundle of wood, faggot.
Hölzchen (⁂...) n ㉓ (dim. v. Holz) 1. small piece (or little bit) of wood. — 2. (Wäldchen) small wood, grove.
Holz-diebstahl (⁂...) m theft (or stealing) of wood; =draht ⊙ m match-wood; =drechsler m turner in wood; =druck m print(ing) on blocks, ⚗ xylographic impression; =druck-kunst f block-printing, ⚗ xylography.
holzen[1] (⁂...) ⑯ I v/n. (h.) 1. to cut (or fell) wood (or timber) in the forest; (Holz sammeln) to gather wood; (Reisholz binden) to make faggots. — II v/a. 2. to supply (or furnish) with wood; ⚒ (durch Holzwände verkleiden) to timber the shaft of a mine. — 3. F burschikos: (prügeln) to cudgel, F to drub; **sich** ⚒ v recip. to have a (free) fight with sticks. — III ~ ⑬ 4. = Holzung.
holzen[2] (⁂...) [ahd.] a. ⑯ in Zssgn, z.B. ebenes (made) of ebony(-wood).
Holz-erde (⁂...) f ⑫ soil mixed with decayed wood, ligneous earth or mould.
Holzerei F (⁂...) [holzen[1] 3] f ⑯ fight (-ing) with sticks; weitS. vulgar row.

hölzern (⁂...) [Holz] a. ⑯ 1. wooden, (of) wood; Le Brücke, Schiene timber-bridge, -rail; Ler Teller = Holzteller. — 2. fig. (ohne Leben) dead-alive; (steif) wooden, clumsy. stiff; (linkisch) awkward; das ~e ⑯ the clumsiness.
Holz-ertrag (⁂...) m ⑫ yield of wood; =essig m wood-vinegar, wood-acid, chm.: ⚗ pyroligneous (or ...ic) acid; =essig-geist m, chm.: ⚗ pyroligneous (or pyroxylic) spirit; =fackel f wooden torch; =fällen n felling of timber; wood-cutting; =fäller m vgl. =hacker; =farbe f colour of wood, wood-colour; =faser f: a) ⚘ woody (or ligneous) fibre; b) chm.: ⚗ lignine, cellulose; =fäule f (dry-)rot; =feu(e)rung f firing (or heating) with wood; =firnis m varnish for wood; =floß n, =flöße f; wooden raft, float of wood; =flößen n rafting, floating (of) rafts; =flößer m raftsman; =frei a. von Papier: without (or free from) cellulose; =fressend a. zo. wood-eating, ⚗ lignivorous, xylophagous; =frevel (=frevler) m offence (offender) against forest laws; =fuhre f cart-load of wood; =geist m, chm. wood-spirit, w.-alcohol, ⚗ pyroxylic spirit, methylic alcohol, methal (CH_3OH); =gerät n = =ware; =gerechtigkeit f: a) free supply of wood, jur. fire-bote; b) ownership of a wood; =gewebe n wood-tissue; ⚘: ⚗ xylem; =gitter n wooden railing; =gleite ⊙ f slide for timber; =hacken n wood-cutting; =hacker m wood-cutter or -cleaver, im Walde: wood(s)man, Am. lumberman, lumberer; =häher m, orn. jay (*Ga'rrulus glanda'rius*); =handel ⚒ m wood- (or timber-)trade; =händler ⚒ m dealer in wood, timber-merchant, Am. lumberman; =hauer m = =hacker; =haufen m pile of wood, wood-stack; =hof m wood- (or timber-)yard, Am. lumber-yard.
holzicht, **holzig** (⁂...) a. ⑯ woodlike, ⚗ ligneous, xyloid; v. Obst xc.: (as) tough as wood; ⚘ Le Frucht: ⚗ xylocarp.
Holz-imprägnierung (⁂...) f ⑫ ⊙ wood-preserving; =käfer m, ent. wood-beetle, im faulen Holz: xylophilan; vgl. =bohrer b; =kammer f cupboard (or place) for wood; =kasten m a) wooden box; b) wood-box; vgl. =kiste f =kauf m purchase of wood; =kiste f: a) wooden box or chest; b) box for (fire-) wood; =klammer f für Wäsche: clothes-peg; =klotz m: a) block of wood; vgl. =block; b) F fig. = =kohle c: =kohle f charcoal; min. xylanthrax; =kohlen=meiler ⚒ m charcoal-pile or -stack; =korb m wood-basket; =krähe f (Schwarzspecht) black woodpecker; =lack m: a) (Stocklack) stick-lac; b) (zum Lackieren) lacquer for (varnishing) wood; =lager n: a) =hof; b) wooden support or bed; =laus f, ent. wood-louse (*Psocus*); =malerei f painting on wood; panel-painting; =mangel m scarcity of wood; =markt ⚒ m: a) timber-market; b) timber-trade; =maß n (=messer m) wood-measure(r); =mast f der Schweine in Wäldern: acorn-mast; =mehl n wood-dust, dust of worm-eaten wood; =meise f, orn.

cole-mouse (*Parus ater*); =milbe f, ent. wood-mite; =mosaik f inlaid woodwork, marquetry; =nagel ⊙ m wooden peg, dowel; =öl n (aus *Chloro'xylon Swiete'nia*) wood-oil; =opal m. min. wood-opal, ligneous opal; =papier n wood-paper; =pflaster(ung f) n w.-pavement; =pflock m plug; vgl. =nagel; =platte ⊙ f, worauf der Holzschnitt gestochen wird: wood-cut-block; =platz m place for stacking wood; vgl. =hof; =pritsche f plank-bed; =puppe f wooden doll; =raspel ⊙ f wood-rasp; =raum m = =platz; ⚘ =reich a. abounding in wood, (waldreich) well wooded or timbered; =röhre f wooden tube; =säge f wood-saw; =schachtel f (small) wooden box; =scheit n piece (or log) of wood; =schicht f layer of wood; =schiene f wooden rail, timber-rail; =schiff ⚓ n a) wooden vessel or craft; b) ship carrying wood or timber, timber-ship; =schlag m: a) = =fällen; b) for. (Revier zum Holzen) clearing (in a forest); =schlegel m (hölzerner Hammer) mallet; =schneide-kunst f wood-carving, (art of) engraving on wood, ⚗ xylography; =schneider m: a) engraver in wood, w.-engraver, ⚗ xylographer; b) = =hacker; =schnitt m a) (Schneiden von Bildern in Holzplatten) wood-engraving; b) (in Holz geschnittenes Bild) w.-cut or -engraving, ⚗ xylograph; =schnitzer m = =bildhauer; =schnitzerei f a) w.-carving, b) ⚗ xylography; =schober m wood-stack; vgl. =schuppen; =schraube ⊙ f: a) (Metallschraube für Holz) wood-screw; b) (hölzerne Schraube) wooden screw; =schrift f, typ. wooden type; =schuh m wooden shoe, (fr.) sabot, mit Oberleder: clog; =schuh-tanz m clog-dance or -dancing; =schuppen m shed for storing wood or timber, woodshed; =span m (Splitter) chip of wood; =späne pl. vom Hobeln w.-shavings pl.; =splitter m splinter of wood; =stab ⊙ m: dünner ~ für die Fensterjalousien slat; =stall m = =schuppen; =stand m stock of timber; =stengel ⚘ m ligneous stem; =stich m = =schnitt; =stift m für Schuhsohlen: peg; =stock m: a) wooden stick; b) = =platte; ⊙ m ⊙ Papierfabr.: wood-pulp; b) chm.: ⚗ cellulose, lignine, xylogen; =stoff-fabrik ⊙ f cellulose-works pl.; =stoß m stack (or pile) of wood; (Scheiterhaufen) stake; =taube f, orn.: a) große ~ wood-pigeon, ring-dove (*Palu'mbus torqua'tus*); b) w.- (or stock-)dove (*Colu'mba oenas*); =teer ⚒ m wood-tar, vegetable tar; =teller m trencher, platter; =torf m wood-peat.
Holzung f ⑯ (s. holzen[1] 1) 1. cutting (or gathering) wood. — 2. (Gehölz) copse; ~s-recht (⁂...) n ⑫ = Holzgerechtigkeit.
Holz-verbrauch (⁂...) m ⑫ consumption of wood; =verkauf m sale of wood or timber; =verschlag m: a) wooden cupboard; b) = =wand; =verwalter ⚓ m inspector of timber-yards; =wagen m timber-cart or -wagon; =wand f wooden partition; =ware ⚒ f wooden ware; =weg m path (or cart-road) through a wood or forest; fig. auf dem ~ (Irrwege) sein to be on the wrong scent or out of one's reckoning, to

[Holzwerk] — 534 — [Horchrohr]

be mistaken; =**werk** n wood-work; ⊕ (Zimmerwert) timber-work, (Getäfel) wainscotting, (Gestell) frame; ↓ eines Schiffes: carcass; =**wespe** f, ent. wood-wasp, horntail (Sirex oder Uro'cerus); =**wolle** ⊕ f wood-wool, fine wood-shavings pl.; =**wurm** m, ent.: a) allg. wood-worm; im bsd. = =**bock** d u. =**käfer**; b) an Schiffen: bore-worm (Tore'do); c) (Totenuhr) death-watch (Ano'bium pe'rtinax); =**zapfen** m wooden pin or plug; =**zaun** m wooden fence or paling; =**zucht** f growing of forests; =**züchter** ⊕ m, carp. dresser of timber.

homerisch (⌣⌣́⌣) [Home'r, grch. Dichter, 850–800 vor Chr.] a. ⓖ Homeric, of Homer; die ~en Gedichte (Ilias u. Odyssee) Homer's epics pl.; Les (schallendes) Gelächter (nach Art der olympischen Götter) Homeric (or loud) laugh(ter), roar of laughter.

Homiletik ⌒ (⌣⌣́⌣) [grch.] f ⓖ theol. (Kanzelberedsamkeit) homiletics; **homiletisch** a. ⓖ homiletic, homiletical.

Homilie ⌒ (⌣⌣́) [grch.] f ⓖ (Predigt-art, Kanzelvortrag) homily; ~**n-sammlung** (⌣...) f ⓖ collection of homilies, homiliary; ~**n-schreiber** m writer (or author) of homilies, homilist.

homogen ⌒ (⌣⌣́) [grch.] a. ⓖ (gleichartig) homogeneous; ~(**e-**)**ität** (⌣⌣(-)⌣́) f ⓖ homogeneousness, homogeneity.

homolog ⌒ (⌣⌣́) [grch.] a. ⓖ (übereinstimmend) homologous, homological.

Homonym ⌒ (⌣⌣́) [grch.] n ⓓ d. gr. homonym; ⇌(isch) (⌣⌣́(⌣)) a. ⓖ homonymous.

Homöopath ⌒ (⌣-⌣́) [grch. (Hahnemann 1796)] m ⓐ (ant. Allopath) homœopath(ist); ~**ie** (⌣-⌣́) f ⓖ homœopathy; **-isch** a. ⓖ homœopathic; Lische Dosis homœopathic (or minute) dose; adv. Lisch behandeln to treat homœopathically.

honett (⌣́) [fr. honnête] a. ⓖ (ehrenhaft) honourable, honest; (anständig) respectable; Le Behandlung fair treatment; ~**ität** (⌣⌣́) f ⓖ honourableness, honesty.

honicht (⌣́⌣) a. ⓖ honied, sweet as honey.

Honig (⌣́⌣) [ahd.: honey] m ⓓ d. honey; den ~ aus den Waben ausnehmen to drain the honeycombs; mit ~ bedeckt, so süß wie ~ honeyed (a. fig.); von ~ fließend mellifluent; fig. e-m ~ ums Maul schmieren ob. um den Bart streichen to wheedle round a p., F to give a p. butter; sie ist der reine ~ she is a sweet girl, F she's real jam or a nice bit; Sprichw. ~ im Munde, Galle im Herzen honeyed tongue, heart of gall; freier: soft of speech, hard of heart.

Honig-anzeiger (⌣́⌣...) m ⓐ orn. = =**kuckuck**; =**apfel** m, hort. honey-apple; =**artig** a. ⓖ honey-like, ⇌ melligenous; =**bär** m, zo. common (or brown) bear (Ursus arctos); =**bau** m culture of honey; vgl. Bienenzucht; =**behälter** m, =**behältnis** n receptacle for honey, ⇌: ⇌ nectary, nectarotheca; =**bereitend** a. producing honey, ⇌ mellific, melliferous; =**bereitung** f production of honey, ⇌ mellification; =**biene** f, ent. honey-bee (Apis melli'fica); =**birne** f, hort. honey-pear; =**blase** f (im Leibe der Bienen) honey-bag, honey-stomach;

=**blume** ⇌ f: a) allgemein: honey- (or melliferous) flower; b) honey-flower (Melia'nthus); =**dachs** m, zo. h.-badger (Melli'vora); =**drüse** ⇌ f nectar-gland; =**ernte** f honey-harvest, cutting (of) the honey-combs; =**erzeugend** ⇌ a.: ⇌ melliferous; =**erzeugung** f = =**bereitung**; =**essend** a. = =**fressend**; =**essig** m, pharm.: ⇌ oxymel; =**farbe** f colour of honey; =**farben**, =**farbig** a. honey-coloured; =**fließend** a. = =**mellifluous** (a. fig.); =**fressend** a. zo.: = mellivorous; =**fresser** m/pl. orn. honey-sucker (Familie Melipha'gidae); =**gefäß** ⇌ n honey-cup; =**geschmack** m taste of honey; =**gras** ⇌ n (Holcus): weiches ~ creeping soft grass (H. mollis), wolliges ~ broomgrass, woolly soft grass, velvet-grass (H. lana'tus); =**klee** ⇌ m melilot (Melilo'tus); =**kuchen** m ginger-bread; =**kuckuck** m honey-guide (Cu'culus indica'tor); =**lese** f = =**ernte**; =**monat**, =**mond** m (Flitterwochen) honeymoon; =**mund** m honeyed tongue, mellifluous speech; =**reich** a. abounding in honey; =**saft** ⇌ m einer Blüte nectar; =**saugend** a. zo.: mellisugent; =**sauger** m/pl. orn.: nectarineidæ; =**scheibe** f honey-comb; =**seim** m liquid honey; =**stein** m, min. h.-stone, mellite; =**süß** a. (as) sweet as honey; =**tau** ⇌ m (klebriger Saft auf Blättern) honey-dew, ⇌ melligo; =**topf** m: a) (für Honig) honey-pot; b) (voll Honig) pot of honey; =**wabe** f honey-comb; =**wasser** n, pharm.: ⇌ hydromel; =**worte** n/pl. honeyed words pl.; =**zelle** f cell in a honeycomb, ⇌ alveolus.

Honneur (∼õ'r) [fr. Ehre] n ⓑ **1.** Kartenspiel: court-card; vier ~s haben to have four by honours. — **2.** ☿ † = **Ehrenbezeugung.** — **3.** fig. die ~s machen to receive the guests, to play the host or the master of ceremonies, auch: to do the honours.

Honorant ⇌ (⌣⌣́) [lt.] m ⓐ acceptor (of a bill in favour of another person).

Honorar (⌣⌣́) [lt.] n ⓓ d. (Belohnung) gratification; ~ e-s Arztes, Advokaten ꝛc. physician's, counsel's, &c. fee.

Honorar-professor (⌣⌣́...) m ⓐ (Professor dem Titel nach) professor by title (only).

Honoratioren (⌣⌣-iſch(⌣)⌣́) [lt.] pl. inv. people of distinction or rank, notabilities pl.

honorieren (⌣⌣⌣́) [lt.] **I** v/a. ⓖ 1. = ehren. — 2. (gebührend belohnen) to fee, to pay a fee to. — 3. ⇌ e-n Wechsel ⇌ (zahlen) to honour (or to give due protection to) a bill; nicht ⇌ to dishonour (or to refuse payment of) a bill. — **II** ~ n ⓑ und **Honorierung** f ⓖ 4. (s. 1) honour bestowed on a p.; (s. 2) payment of a fee; (s. 3) due honour paid to (or acceptance of) a bill.

honorig F (⌣⌣́) [lt.] a. ⓖ = anständig 1.

hop (⌣́) int. = hopp.

Hopfen (⌣́⌣) [mhd.: hop] m ⓐ ⇌ (die Pflanze) hop(-plant) (Hu'mulus Lu'pulus); Brauerei: (die Blüten) hops pl.; fig. da ist ~ und Malz verloren there is no cure (or remedy) for that, it's a hopeless case; an dem ist ~ u. Malz verloren he is past mending or all cure, he is incurable, F it's all thrown away on him.

hopfen (⌣́⌣) v/a. ⓐ: Bier ⇌ to hop ...

Hopfen-acker (⌣́⌣...) m ⓐ = =**feld**; =**ähnlich** a. ⇌ lupuline; =**bau** m hop-culture or -raising; =**bauer** m = =**züchter**; =**bier** n hopped beer; =**bitter** n hop-bitter(s pl.), ⇌ lupulin, ...ite; =**buche** f hop-hornbeam (O'strya virgi'nica, carpinifo'lia. &c.); =**darre** ⊕ f hop-kiln or drier; =**ernte** f hop-picking; =**feld** n hopfield; =**garten** m hop-garden; =**handel** m hop-trade; =**händler** m hop-merchant; =**klee** ⇌ m hop-medick (Medica'go lupuli'na); =**öl** n hop-oil; =**ranke** ⇌ f hop-vine or -bine; =**seiher** ⊕ m Brauerei: hop-back; =**spalier** n hop-frame; =**spinner** m ghost-moth (Hepi'alus hu'muli); =**stange** f: a) hop-pole; b) F fig. long and lanky person, F lamp-post; =**züchter** m hop-grower.

Höpfner (⌣́⌣) m ⓐ grower of hops.

Hoplit ⇌ (⌣⌣́) [grch.] m ⓐ grch. Alt.: (Schwerbewaffneter) hoplite.

hopp (⌣́) int. (spring!) hop!, jump!, go!

hoppeln (⌣́⌣) v/n. (h.) ⓐ = hopsen.

Hoppel-poppel (⌣́⌣,⌣́⌣) n ⓐ (Eiergrog aus Eigelb, Zucker u. Rum) etwa: egg-flip.

hoppla (⌣́⌣) int. go it, away!, look alive!; now be off!; im Zirkus: hoopla!; vgl. hopp.

Hops (⌣́) **I** m ⓐ a. hop. — **II** **hops**, auch: **hopsa** (⌣́⌣) int. = hopp. [jump.

hopsen F (⌣́⌣) v/n. (h.) ⓐ to hop, skip,]

Hopser (⌣́⌣) m ⓐ 1. F hopping (or skipping) person, jumper; nimble (little) fellow. — 2. (Art Walzer) hop-waltz.

Hora (⌣́⌣) [it., *grch.] f ⓖ 1. Stunde, Zeitpunkt: hour. — 2. die Horen ober ⇌ (lt. acc. pl., Stundengebete in Klöstern) singen to chant the horary prayers. — 3. myth. die Horen (Zeitgöttinnen) Horae pl.; goddesses of the seasons.

Hör-apparat ⊕ (⌣́...) m ⓐ Fernspr.: (Ende der Leitung, das man ans Ohr hält) receiver.

Horatier (⌣⌣́iſch(⌣)⌣) [lt.] m/pl. ⓐ röm. Alt.: die (drei) ~ the (three) Horatii pl.

Horatius (⌣⌣́iſch(⌣)⌣) npr/m. ⇌, **Horaz** (⌣⌣́) ⓖ 65 γ. Alt.: (röm. Dichter, 65–8 v. Chr.) Horace; **horazisch** (-⌣́) a. ⓖ of (or by) Horace, Horatian; die ~en Oden Horace's odes pl.

hörbar (⌣́-) a. ⓖ audible, within earshot or reach of the ear; (verständlich) intelligible; nicht ⇌ inaudible.

Hörbarkeit (⌣́--) f ⓖ audibility.

Horche (⌣́⌣) f ⓐ: sich auf die ~ stellen to stand listening, to go eavesdropping.

horchen (⌣́⌣) [ahd.: hark, hearken; *hören] **I** v/n. ⓐ 1. to listen (attentively), to hearken, to prick up one's ears, als Spion: to spy; horch, es klopft! hark, there is a knock!; er will nicht auf uns ⇌ (achten) he pays no heed (or no attention) to us. — **II** ~ n ⓑ listening, &c. (s. I); b.s. = **Horcherei**.

Horcher (⌣́⌣) m ⓐ, ~**in** f ⓖ listener, b.s. eavesdropper, spy; Sprichw. der ~ an der Wand hört seine eigne Schand listeners never hear any good of themselves. [spying.

Horcherei (⌣⌣́⌣) f ⓖ eavesdropping,]

Horch-gang ⚔ (⌣́...) m ⓐ = einer Mine: listening-gallery; =**rohr** n, phys.: ⇌ acoustic tube; med. (zur Auskultation der Brust) ⇌ stethoscope.

Signs (see page IX): F familiar; P vulgar; ⌐ flash; ⇍ rare; † obsolete (died); * new word (born); ⇎ incorrect; ♪ music;

[horchsam] — 535 — [Hornkraut]

horchsam (⌣⌣) a. 🕮 (zu horchen geneigt) attentive(ly) listening.
Horch-winkel (⌣...) m 🕮 secret nook where a listener may hide, bisw. auch: listening-corner.
Horde (⌣⌣) [russ.; * pers. *ordu* Heer] f 🕮 horde, nomadic (or wandering) tribe; weitS. band, troop, gang.
horden-weise (⌣⌣...) adv. in hordes or bands or troops or gangs.
Hören (-⌣) pl. v. Hora.
hören (⌣⌣) [ahd.: hear] 🕮 I v/a. u. v/n. (h.) 1. to hear; gut, scharf, fein ≳ to hear well, to have good hearing; schwer ≳ to be hard (or dull) of hearing; man konnte das leiseste Geräusch ≳ one might have heard a pin drop; an dem Gepolter hörte er, daß // he knew by the rumbling (noise) that //; ich habe es **von** ihm gehört I heard it from him, stärker: I have it from his own lips; man hört ja schöne Sachen von ihm one hears strange (*iro.* fine) things about him; so ≳ Sie denn, es ist // let me tell you that //; ich muß doch ≳, was es gibt I must go and hear (or see) what is the matter; ich habe (für sicher) gehört, daß // I have been told (for certain) that //; wer hat je so et. gehört? who ever heard of such a thing?; man muß beide Seiten ≳ you must hear both sides or versions; wenn man ihn hört, sollte man glauben // to hear him, one would think //; mit *inf.*: ich hörte ihn rufen I heard him call; ich habe ihn sagen ≳ (st. *p.p.* gehört) // I have heard him say //. — 2. e-m etwas **zu** ≳ **geben** to give a p. s.th. to understand; nichts von sich ≳ **lassen** to send no news, to be silent, to live in seclusion; er hat schon lange nichts von sich ≳ lassen he has not been heard of (or has not written) for a long time; ≳**sagen** (durch andere erfahren) to be told, to know from hearsay; (von) et. **nicht(s)** ≳ **wollen** to shut one's ears (or to refuse to listen) to a th.; Sprichw. s. fühlen 5; Kinder ≳ alles little pitchers have large (or long) ears. — 3. (aufmerksam lauschen) to hearken; to listen to; auf einen, et. ≳ to pay attention to a p., a th.; to follow (or heed) a p.'s advice; hört nicht auf sein Geschwätz don't (or you must not) mind his twaddle; auf s-n Namen ≳ to answer to a name; hör, was ist das? hark, what is that?; ≳ Sie doch! I say!; now, listen to me!; *bibl.* wer Ohren hat zu ≳, der höre! he that hath ears to hear let him hear! — 4. ein (theologisches ꝛc.) Kolleg ≳ to attend a course of (divinity, &c.) lectures; bei e-m Professor ≳ to attend a professor's lectures, geh. Spr.: to sit at the feet of a great teacher; die Messe ≳ to hear (or attend) mass. — 5. *gram.* von Buchstaben: gehört werden (lauten) to sound. — II sich ≳ v/refl. 6. er hört sich (selbst) gern he likes to hear himself talk; er hört sich gern loben he likes to be (or is fond of being) praised. — 7. das hört sich gut (an) (klingt gut) that sounds well. —

8. sich ≳ **lassen** to make o.s. heard; sich vor e-m (redend, singend ꝛc.) ≳ lassen to speak, sing, &c. before a p.; als Künstler auch: to give a performance (or recitation) before a p.; das läßt sich ≳: a) (klingt gut) that sounds well or plausible; b) (verdient Beachtung) there is something in that, F that's the thing; diese Gründe lassen sich ≳ these are plausible reasons. — III ~ n 🕮 9. hearing, bisw. 🞛 audition; es verging ihm ~ und Sehen his senses left him, he became quite unconscious.
Hören-sagen (⌣⌣⌣) n 🕮: et. nur von ~ wissen to know a th. only from hearsay; e-n nur von ~ kennen to know a p. only by reputation.
Hörer (⌣⌣) m 🕮, ~**in** f 🕮 1. hearer; *coll.* die ~ *pl.* the audience. — 2. *univ.* = Student. — 3. am Fernsprecher: = Hörapparat. [or listeners *pl.*, audience.]
Hörerschaft (⌣⌣⌣) f 🕮 (body of hearers)
Hör-fehler (⌣...) m 🕮 = Gehörfehler.
hörig (⌣⌣) [hören] I a. 🕮 (living) in bondage, serving (as a slave or thrall). —~II e([r] m) f 🕮 bond(s)man (f bond(s)woman), bondslave, serf, unter den Normannen: villein.
Hörigkeit (⌣⌣⌣) f 🕮 bondage, bond-service, serfdom, ehm.: villeinage.
Horizont (⌣⌣⌣) [grch.] m 🕮c. = Gesichtskreis; *fig.* das geht über meinen ~ that is beyond me or out of my ken, it passes my comprehension.
horizontal (⌣⌣⌣⌣) I a. 🕮 (wagerecht) horizontal, perfectly level; ≳ machen to (make) level; 🜨 ≳es Wasserrad turbine. — II ~**e** f 🕮 *math.* (Schichtlinie) horizontal line.
Horizontal-linie (⌣⌣⌣⌣...) f 🕮 horizontal line; *surv.* auch: datum-line; **=projektion** f horizontal projection; **=schuß** m, *artill.* (Kernschuß) point-blank (shot); **=wage** f spirit- (or water-)level.
Hör-maschine (⌣...) f 🕮 = ≳rohr.
Horn¹ (⌣) [ahd.: horn: lt. *cornu*] n 🕮. (f. 2) 1. horn of a cow, &c.; Tier mit langen Hörnern longhorn; auf die Hörner spießen to gore; Hörner tragend horned, 🜁 cornigerous, *fig.* sich die (tollen) Hörner ablaufen, abstoßen to sow one's wild oats; e-m Hörner aufsetzen to cuckold a p.; das ~ des Überflusses the horn of plenty, 🜁 cornucopia; s. einzelnen 1 u. Fühlhorn. — 2. als Stoff ohne *pl.* ("Horn-arten": 🕮 *pl.* ≳e) horn(y substance); (hornige Haut) horn(y skin). — 3. ♪ (Blasinstrument) (French) horn; a. (it.) *corno*; englisches ~ (Art Oboe) English horn, (it.) corno inglese; (Jagd-)~ bugle; auf dem ≳e blasen, ins ~ stoßen to blow (or wind) one's horn, to sound the horn; *fig.* mit e-m in ein (on. in dasselbe) ~ blasen to act in concert (or to pull the same way, to be hand and glove) with a p.; *b.s.* to collude with a p. — 4. ♭ a) (Landspitze) tongue of land; b) (Bergspitze) peak.
Horn² † md. (⌣) m 🕮b.: großer ~ = Januar, kleiner ~ (Hornung) = Februar.
horn¹-ähnlich (⌣...) a. 🕮 like horn, 🜁 corneous, 🜁 ≳**artig**; **=arbeiter** m worker in horn, vgl. **=bereiter**; ≳**artig**

a. hornlike, horny; (as) hard as horn; vgl. ≳**ähnlich**; **=baum** ♀ m = Hagebuche; **=bereiter** m horn-dresser; **=bläser** ♪ m horn-blower, bugler; **=blei** n, *min.* h.-lead; **=blende** f, *min.*: 🜁 ⧸ hornblende, amphibole; 🜁**blendeartig** a.: 🜁 hornblendic; **=blendefels** schistous amphibolite; **=blendeschiefer** m, *min.* horn-slate; **=brille** f spectacles *pl.* (made) of horn; **=buche** ♀ f = Hagebuche.
Hörnchen (⌣⌣) n 🕮 (*dim. von* Horn) small horn, hornlet, 🜁 cornicle.
Horn-drechsler (⌣...) m 🕮, **=dreher** m turner in horn, bone-turner.
hornen (⌣⌣) v/n. (h.) ⚤ (auf dem Horn blasen) to blow (on) the horn.
hörnen¹ (⌣⌣) 🕮 I v/a. 1. to provide with horns, to put horns on. — 2. (hornig machen) to make horny, to hornify. — II sich ≳ v/refl. 3. *hunt.* (das Gehörn abwerfen) to cast one's horns or antlers. — III v/n. (h.) 4. (mit den Hörnern stoßen) to butt. — IV **ge-hörnt** *p.p.* u. a. 🕮 5. horny, 🜁 cornigerous, corniculate; der ≳e Siegfried horny Siegfried.
hörnen² (⌣⌣) [ahd.] a. 🕮 = hörnern.
hörner-artig (⌣⌣...) a. 🕮 like horns; **=klang** m 🕮 sound of horns or bugles.
hörnern (⌣⌣) [nhd.] a. 🕮 horny, of horn.
Hörner-schall (⌣⌣...) m 🕮 = ≳klang; **=schluß** m, *log.* horns *pl.* of a dilemma; **=tragend** a. 🕮 having horns, horned, 🜁 cornigerous; **=träger** m horned beast.
Hör-nerv m 🕮 *physiol.* auditory nerve.
Horn-erz (⌣...) n 🕮 *min.* horn-silver (ore); *chm.* chloride of silver; **=eule** f, *orn.* horned owl (*Bubo ma'ximus*); **=fäule** f, *vet.* des Hornviehs horn-distemper; **=fisch** m, *ichth.* trigger-fish (*Bali'stes*); ≳**förmig** a. 🕮 horn-shaped, 🜁 corniform, cornute(d); **=frosch** m, zo. horned frog (*Cerato'phrys cornu'ta*); ≳**hart** a. (as) hard as horn, horny; **=haut** f: a) (an Händen und Füßen) horn(y skin), 🜁 callosity; b) *anat.* ~ des Auges horny coat (of the eye), 🜁 corneous tunic, cornea; **=haut-entzündung** f, *path.* inflammation of the cornea, 🜁 ceratitis; **=hautfleck** m, *path.* speck of the cornea or on the eye; ≳**häutig** a. horny, 🜁 callous; **=hecht** m, *ichth.* horn-fish, gar(fish) (*Be'lone vulga'ris*).
hornicht, hornig (⌣⌣) a. 🕮 1. = hornartig. — 2. gehörnt (s. hörnen¹ IV).
...**hörnig** (...⌣) [Horn] in Zssg., zB. lang≳ with long horns. [= Hornisse.]
Hornis (⌣⌣) [ahd.: hornet] f 🕮 (m 🕮)
hornisieren (⌣⌣⌣) v/a. 🕮 = hörnen¹ 2; Kautschuk ≳ to vulcanize caoutchouc.
Horniße (⌣⌣) [s. Hornis] f 🕮 *ent.* hornet (*Vespa crabro*). [nest.]
Hornißen-nest (⌣⌣...) n 🕮 hornets']
Hornist ♪ (⌣⌣) [dtsch.-it.; *Horn] m 🕮 hornist; ⚔ bugle-man, bugler.
Horn-käfer (⌣...) m 🕮 *ent.* = Hirschkäfer; **=kamm** m horn comb; **=klee** ♀ m bird's-foot (*Lotus cornicula'tus*); **=kluft** f, *vet.* cleft in a hoof; ≳**klüftig** a. *vet.* with a cloven hoof; **=knopf** m horn button; **=köpfchen** ♀ n ceratocephalus (*Ceratoce'phalus falca'tus*); **=koralle** f, zo. sea-whip (*Anti'pathes*); **=kraut** ♀ n mouse-ear chickweed (*Cera'stium*).

⚛ scientific; ♀ botanical; ♁ geography; 🜨 machinery; ⚒ mining; ⚔ military; ⚓ marine; 🕮 commercial; 📯 postal; 🚂 railway.

[Hörnlein] — 536 — [hübsch]

Hörnlein (⌣-) n = Hörnchen.
horn-los (⌣̄...) a. ⑥ hornless; **-losigkeit** f ㊻ hornlessness; **-löffel** m ㊷ horn-spoon; **-mohn** ⚥ m horned arvense (or seaside) poppy (Glau'cium lu'teum); **-musik** ♪ f horn-music; **-ochse** m, fig. = vieh b: **-platte**, **-presse**, **-raspel** ⊕ f horn-plate, -press, -rasp; **-quecksilber** n, min. horn-quicksilver or -mercury; **-rabe** m, orn. hornbill (Buco'rvus); **-ruf** m = signal; **-schabsel** ⊕ n horn-shavings pl.; **-schlange** f = -viper; **-signal** n ⚔ u. hunt. bugle-call or -signal; **-silber** n = erz; **-späne** ⊕ m/pl. horn-shavings or -raspings pl.; **-spitze** f horn tip; **-stein** m, min. horn-stone; **-stoß** m bugle-call; **-substanz** f horny substance; **-tiere** n/pl. zo. cornigerous animals pl.

Hornung (⌣⌣) [ahd.; *Horn² m ⓐd. jetzt meist poet. (month of) February.

Horn-vieh (⌣̄...) n ㊷: a) horned cattle, ⚔ cornigerous animals pl.; b) fig. (Dummkopf) blockhead; **-viper** f, zo.: a) hornsman (Clotho cornu'ta); b) ägyptische ~ horned serpent or snake (Cera'stes aegypti'acus oder cornu'tus); **-waren** ⊕ f/pl. = werk a; **-werk** n: a) 🛡 articles pl. in horn; b) ⚔ frt. (hornförmiges Außenwerk) horn-work.

Horoskop ⚔ (-⌣́) [grch. Stundenschauer] n ⓐd. astrol. horoscope; e-m das ~ stellen to cast (or calculate) a p.'s nativity, weits. to forecast a p.'s fate or future.

horrend (⌣́⌣) [lt.] a. ⑥ horrid, awful; (sehr groß) enormous, F tremendous.

Horrido (⌣⌣́⌣) [ho! Rüd', ho!] n ㊿ hunt. (Jagdruf) tally-ho.

Hör-rohr (⌣̄...) n ㊷ für Taube: eartrumpet, hearing-trumpet or -tube; ⚔ acoustic tube; **-saal** m für Vorlesungen: lecture-hall, auditorium.

Hörsamkeit * (⌣́⌣-) f ㊻ = Akustik.

Horsd'œuvre (h)ôr-bö̂'wr) [fr.] n ㊿ (a. inv.) made-up dish, French dish.

Horst (⌣́) [ahd.] m ⓐa(b). 1. (Gesträuch) bush; (Gehölz) wood, thicket. — 2. (hochragendes Nest, bfd. der Raubvögel) eyrie, aerie; (Wohnung) dwelling, F den.

Hör-stein (⌣́⌣) n anat. in der Flüssigkeit der Hörzellen: ⚔ otolith, otolite.

horsten (⌣́⌣) v/n. (h.) ㊾ von Adlern etc.: to build an eyrie, to (make one's) nest in a lofty place; weits. (sich aufhalten) to live (in a top room).

Hort (⌣́) [ahd.: hoard] m ⓐb. 1. treasure; ~ der Nibelungen the Nibelungen hoard. — 2. (sicherer Ort) safe retreat; (Zufluchtsort) place of refuge, shelter. — 3. (et. Schutz Gewährendes) support, protection; (Schild) shield.

Hortensi-e (⌣⌣(⌣)⌣) [lt.] I npr/f. ⓐß. (Bn.) Hortensia. — II ⚥ [Hortense Barré: Geliebte von Commerçon, der die Pflanze 1767 in China entdeckte] f ㊻ hydrangea (Hydra'ngea horte'nsis).

Hortikultur ⚔ (⌣⌣⌣⌣̄) [lt.] f ㊻ (Gartenbau) horticulture; gardening.

Hör-trichter (⌣̄...) m ⚙ = -rohr; **-weite** f, etwa: earshot; range of the voice or the ear; außer ~ out of hearing, beyond reach of the voice; in ~ within hearing or hail; **-werkzeug** n: ⚔ acoustic instrument.

hosanna (-⌣́-) [hebr.] int. und ~ n ㊿ = hosia'nna.

Hosche (⌣́⌣) f ㊺ (Gleitebahn) slide.

Höschen (⌣́⌣) dim. v. Hose (f. ds, bf. 3).

Hose (⌣́⌣) [ahd.: hose] f ㊺ 1. (kurze) ~, meist pl. ~n ob. ein Paar ~n (pair of) breeches, knickerbockers, bisw. (meist co.) auch: small clothes pl.; lange ~n (pair of) trousers or F togs pl.; weite ~n, a. F bags pl.; oben weite, unten enge: F peg-tops pl.; in Damengesellschaft und co. heißen ~n auch: unmentionables, inexpressibles pl.; die ~n anziehen, ausziehen to put on, to take off one's trousers or F breeches; e-m Knaben lange ~n anziehen (in England im 11. bis 12. Lebensjahre) to put a boy in(to) trousers; lange ~n bekommen to go into trousers. — 2. fig. sie hat die ~n an (die Herrschaft im Hause) she wears the breeches, auch: she is master; das Herz fiel ihm in die ~n his heart was in his boots or in his mouth. — 3. von Tieren: a) (Unterschenkel) (lower) thigh; beim Federvieh: feathered legs or trousers pl.; b) auch dim. **Höschen** (⌣́⌣) n ㉓ (bei Bienen der Blumenstaub an den Beinen) covering (or coating) of pollen on a bee's legs. — 4. ⚔ (Gehäuse) casing, case, box, covering. — 5. = Wasserhose.

hosen (⌣́⌣)[Hose] v/a. ㊾ (mit Hosen versehen) to put in(to) breeches or trousers.

Hosen-band (⌣́⌣...) n ㉒ ehm.: kneeband, (Strumpfband) garter; **-band-orden** m (England) Order of the Garter; Ritter vom ~: Knight of the Garter (abbr. K. G.); **-bein** n leg of a pair of trousers; **-biene** f bee with pollen-covered legs; **-boden** m seat of a pair of trousers; **-bund** m waistband of trousers; **-flicker** m mender of breeches, botching tailor; **-klappe** f = -latz; **-knopf** m trousers- (or breeches-) button; **-latz** m fly; ehm. (noch jetzt bei Arbeitern etc.): flap (of the trousers); **-los** a. without breeches or trousers; **-matz** F m (Knabe, der die ersten Hosen trägt) boy in his first pair of trousers; **-rolle** f, thea. co. gentleman's part (filled by an actress); **-schlitz** m slit (or opening) of trousers; auch = -latz; **-schnalle** f buckle for (or on) tr.; **-schneider** m maker of tr.; **-stoff** m = -zeug; **-strecker** m stretcher for tr.; **-tasche** f breeches-pocket, a. trouserspocket; in meiner ~ in the pocket of my tr.; **-träger** m (a. m/pl.) (pair of) braces pl.; **-zeug** n material for trousers, trousering.

hosianna (-(⌣)⌣-) [hebr.] int. u. ~ n ㊿ (a. inv.) hosanna.

Höslein (⌣́-) = Höschen.

Hospital (⌣⌣⌣́) [ahd.; *Hospital²] n ⓐⓑd. für Kranke: hospital, infirmary; für Altersschwache, Genesende etc.: home; **~arzt** (⌣́...) m ㊷ physician to a hospital, hospital-doctor; **~brand** m, path. hospital(-)gangrene.

Hospitaliter (⌣⌣⌣⌣̄) [lt.] m ㊷, **~in** f ㊽ bfd. ehm.: Hospitaller (of St. John of Jerusalem).

Hospital-krankenpflegerin (⌣⌣⌣⌣̄...) f ㊽ hospital-nurse; **-schiff** ⚓ n hospital-ship, floating hospital.

Hospitant (⌣⌣⌣́) [lt. hospes Gast] m ㊷ univ. one who attends lectures as an outsider. [lectures as an outsider.)

hospitieren (⌣⌣⌣⌣̄) v/n. (h.) ㊾ to attend)

Hospiz (⌣⌣́) [lt.] n ⓐa. place of refuge, asylum; (place of) shelter, home.

Hospodar (⌣⌣⌣̄) [slaw.] m ⓐd. u. ㊷ (ehm. Titel des Fürsten der Moldau u. Walachei) hospodar.

Hosti-e (⌣́(⌣)⌣) [lt.] f ㊺ eccl. host; geweihte ~ the holy (or consecrated) wafer.

Hosti-en-erhebung (⌣́(⌣)⌣...) f raising of the host; **-gefäß** n: ⚔ pyx, ciborium; **-häuslein** n tabernacle; **-teller** m paten.

Hotel (⌣⌣́) [fr. ㊿⑤ garni⑥](Gasthof)hotel; **~garni**' (pl. ~s garnis) private hotel, boarding-house; **~besitzer(in** f) m, **~ier** (-⌣́ε') m ㊿ hotel-keeper or -proprietor, landlord (of a hotel); **~wagen** m carriage belonging to a hotel; **~waggon** 🚂 m bsd. Am. hotel-car, Pullman (car), restaurant-car.

hott (⌣́) [mhd. 16. sae.] int. Fuhrmannsruf: a) (nach rechts; ant. hist) to the right; Sprichw. f. har; b) zum Antreiben des Pferdes überhaupt: gee ho!, gee up!, hoy!

Hotte (⌣́⌣) f ㊺ (kleines Faß) tub.

hotten F (⌣́⌣) [hott] v/n. (h.) ㊾ to drive a carriage; vorbei ⚔ to drive past.

Hottentott (⌣⌣⌣́) [ndl. Stotterer] m ㊷, **~e** (⌣⌣⌣́⌣) m ㊸, **~in** f ㊽(Eingeborene[r] v. Südafrika) Hottentot; f auch: Hottentot woman, girl; **Lisch** a. ⑥ Hottentot, Hottentotic.

hotto! (⌣́-) int. = hott.

Hotto (⌣́⌣) [mhd. 16. sae.] n ㉛, auch: **~gaul** m, **~pferd** n Kindersprache: gee-gee.

hotto-hü (⌣⌣⌣́) int. = hott b.

hr (⌣́) int. = hurr.

hu! (⌣́) int. schaudernd: ugh!, hugh!

hü! (⌣́) int. Zuruf an die Pferde: a) = hist (links); b) (vorwärts) go on!

hub¹ (⌣́) † u. poet. impf. ind. v. heben.

Hub² (⌣́) m ⓐc. 1. (das Heben) heaving, lifting, raising; elevation; ⚓ ~ der Gezeiten range of the tides; ⊕ ~ des Kolbens stroke of the piston. — 2. (das Gehobene) quantity lifted or raised (by one pull or stroke).

Hube obb. (⌣⌣́) [ahd.] f ㊺ = Hufe.

hübe (⌣́) † u. poet. impf. subj. v. heben.

Hübel provc. (⌣́⌣) m ㊷ small hill, hillock.

hüben (⌣́⌣) adv. (ant. drüben) on this side, on our side.

Hub-länge ⊕ (⌣̄...) f ㊺ Dampfmaschine: length of the stroke; **-pumpe** ⚒ f lifting-pump.

hübsch (⌣́) [mhd. höfisch] a. ⑥ 1. (von gefälligem Äußern) pretty, comely; nice-looking, good-looking; (allerliebst) charming, delightful; (anziehend) attractive; eins der Hübschesten Mädchen one of the prettiest (F nicest-looking) girls. — 2. (fein, artig) polite, agreeable; es ist 2 von Ihnen, daß Sie mich besuchen it is nice (or kind) of you (auch: you are a dear good person) to come and see me; iro. das ist 2 von dir, mich so anzuführen you are a nice fellow so to mislead me; eine 2e Gelegenheit a fine opportunity; das wird eine 2e Geschichte w. there will be a fine bother(ation) or F rumpus. — 3. (gehörig, gut) suitable,

Zeichen (s. 'S. XVII): F familiär; P Volkssprache; Γ Gaunersprache; ⚔ selten; † alt (auch gestorben); * neu (auch geboren); ⁂ unrichtig;

[Huchen] — 537 — [Huker]

fit; eine 2e Gelegenheit a nice (or good) opportunity; oft faſt pleonaſtiſch: ſei 2 artig! (try to) be good!, do behave yourself!; das werde ich 2 bleiben laſſen I shall take (good) care to leave it alone. — 4. (bedeutend) conſiderable; ein 2es Stück Geld a nice round sum; ein 2es Stück Geld verdienen to earn a good income, F to make a good deal of money; ein 2es Vermögen a handsome (or large) fortune. [lachs] huck (*Salmo hucho*).

Huch(en) (^⌣) *m* ⓤc.(㉓) *ichth*. (Donau-ſ

Hucke (^⌣) *f* ㊽ **1.** ↗ *agr.* = Hocke. — **2.** *provc.* P = Rücken; e-m die ~ voll lügen to tell a p. a pack of lies.

Hucke-bein (⌣-⌣) *m* ⓤd.: Hans ~, der Unglücksrabe etwa: Jim Crow, the unfortunate raven.

hucken (^⌣) Ⓢ **I** *v/n.* (h.) = hocken. — **II** *v/a.* to carry on one's back.

hucke-pack (⌣-⌣) [hucken und Pack] *adv.*: e-n 2 tragen to carry a p. (auch: to give a p.) pickaback. [flock.ſ

Hude *provc.* (^⌣) [nbd.: hüten] *f* ㊽ (Herde)ſ

Hudel- *provc.* (^⌣) [: Hader] *m* ㉒㊽ **1.** (Lumpen) rag. — **2.** *fig.* (Lump) ragamuffin, scamp.

Hudelei F (⌣-⌣^) *f* ㊻ **1.** (liederliche Arbeit) careless (or scamped, hurried) work, botching. — **2.** (Plackerei) trouble, troublesome task; F slaving, fagging; (Ärger) vexation.

Hud(e)ler F ↗ (^(⌣)⌣) *m* ㉒, ~in *f* ㊵ **1.** (Pfuſcher) careless worker, botcher. — **2.** (j. der andere plackt) taskmaster, F slave- (or nigger-)driver; (Quäler) tormentor, worrier, teaser.

hud(e)lig F ↗ (^(⌣)⌣) *a.* ㊻ botched, badly done, bungled.

hudeln F (^⌣) [: huddle] ⓑa. **I** *v/n.* (h.) **1.** (faulenzen) to idle, (nachläſſig ſein) to work carelessly, to scamp (or botch) one's work. — **II** *v/a.* **2.** Arbeit 2 (liederlich betreiben) to do … carelessly, to scamp (or botch) …; (verderben) to spoil. — **3.** e-n 2 to harass (*Am.* to hustle) a p.; (quälen, plagen) to torment (or vex, worry, annoy, tease) a p.

hudern (^⌣) *v/n.* (h.) ⓑa. v. Hühnern: (im Sande baden) to take a sand-bath.

Hudler, hudlig (^⌣) ſ. Hudeler, hudelig.

Huf (^) [ahd.: hoof] *m* ⓤ(† ⑦)c. hoof, v. Pferden ꝛc.: mit dem ~ ſchlagen to kick (out); mit geſpaltenem ~ with a cloven hoof, cloven-footed or hoofed.

huf-artig (^…) *a.* ㊻ like a hoof, ungual; **=bein** *n* ㉖ *vet.* coffin-bone; **=beſchlag** *m* shoeing of horses, horseshoeing.

Hufe (^⌣) [nbd.] *f* ㊽ *agr.* (ehm. Stück Land von verſchiedener Größe) hide (of land).

Huf-eiſen (^…) *n* ㉖: a) Huffſchmiede: horseshoe; e-m Pferde die ~ auflegen (abreißen) to (un)shoe a horse; b) am Stiefel: (iron) tip. [of a horseshoe.ſ

hufeiſen-förmig (⌣…) *a.* ㊻ in the shapeſ

Hufeiſen-klee ⚘ (⌣…) *m* ㉒ horseshoevetch (*Hippocre'pis como'sa*); **=magnet** *m, phys.* horseshoe-magnet; **=ſpitz-bogen** *m, arch.* pointed horseshoe (or Moorish) arch.

Hufen-gut (⌣…) *n* ㉒ field of one hide.

huf-förmig (^…) *a.* ㊻ hoof-shaped, ungulate; **=gänger** *m/pl.* ㉒ *zo.*: ꝛ ungulata, unguligrades *pl.*; **=gelenk** *n, vet.* coffin-joint; **=kiſſen** *n* horse's hoof-pad or -cushion; **=lattich** ⚘ *m* colt's-foot (*Tussila'go fa'rfara*); **=meſſer** *m, vet.* horseshoe-gauge; **=nagel** [: hobnail] *m* horseshoe-nail.

Hüfner (^⌣) [Hufe] *m* ㉒ owner of one hide (of land); small farmer.

Huf-räumer (^…) *m* ㉒ hoof-pi ꝛ. **=ſchlag** *m*: a) (Tritt des Pferdehufes) kick from a (horse's) hoof, horse's kick; b) tread of a horse, a. hoof-beat; tramp of a horse's feet or of horses; **=ſchmied** ⊕ *m*: a) farrier, shoeing-smith; b) *fig.* (plumper Arbeitender) clumsy workman; **=ſchmiede** *f* farrier's workshop or smithy, farriery; **=ſpur** *f* track of a horse's hoofs, hoof-mark.

Hüft-ader (^…) *f* ㊻: ꝛ sciatic (or ischiatic) blood-vessel; **=bein** *n, anat.* hip-bone, ꝛ coxa.

Hüfte (^⌣) [ahd.: hip; *Haufe] *f* ㊽ hip, haunch, ꝛ ischion, coxa.

hüften-lahm (^⌣…) *a.* ㊻ = hüftlahm.

Hüft-gelenk (^…) *n* ㉖ hip-joint, ꝛ coxofemoral articulation; **=gelenk-entzündung** *f, path.* inflammation of the hip-joint, ꝛ coxitis; **=horn** *n* = Hiftthorn. [*pl.*: ꝛ ungulata *pl.*ſ

Huf-tier (^⌣) *n* ㉖ *zo.* hoofed animal;ſ

Hüft-knochen (^…) *m* ㉒ = **=bein**; **=lahm** *a.* ㊻ v. Menſchen und Pferden: lame in the hip, biſw.: hip-shot; **=lahmheit** *f* lameness in the hip; **=nerv** *m* sciatic nerve; **=pfanne** *f* socket of the hip-joint, an der Bruſt e-s Inſekts: ꝛ cotyloid; **=ſchmerz** *m* = **=weh**; **=weh** *n, path.* sciatic pain, sciatica, ꝛ coxalgia, coxagra. — Vgl. auch Lenden-…

Huf-zeug (^…) *n* ㉖ shoeing-tools *pl.*; **=zwang** *m, vet.* contraction of the hoof; **=zwangig, =zwängig** *a.* ㊻ hoofbound, narrow-heeled.

Hügel (^⌣) [nbd.; *hoch] *m* ㉒ **1.** hill, kleinerer: hillock, knoll; *hyperl.* ꝛ tor; weitS. (Erhöhung) elevation, eminence, height; swelling (of the ground); (Abhang) declivity; (Erdhaufen) mound, (Hünengrab) barrow; (Sand-) ꝛ (bſ. in Süd-england) downs. — **2.** ↗ ꝛ *anat.* tubercle, prominence, excrescence.

hügel-ab (^…) (2an, 2auf) *adv.* downhill (uphill), down (up) the hill; **=abhang** *m* hillside; **=artig** *a.* ㊻ = hüg(e)licht 1.

Hügelchen (^⌣⌣) *n* ㉓ (*dim. von* Hügel) hillock, mound; rundes ꝛ knoll.

hügel-förmig (^⌣…) *a.* ㊻ = hügelicht; **hüg(e)licht, hüg(e)lig** (^(⌣)⌣) *a.* ㊻ **1.** (hügelartig) (shaped) like a hill. — **2.** (mit Hügeln bedeckt) hilly, mountainous.

Hügel-kette (^⌣…) *f* ㊽ = **=reihe**; **=land** *n* hill-country; **=reich** *a.* ㊻ hilly, covered with hills; **=reihe** *f* chain (or range) of hills.

Hugenotte (⌣-⌣⌣) [fr.; *dtſch. Eidgenoſſe] *m* (fr. Proteſtant) (16. sae.) Huguenot.

hüglicht (^⌣) ꝛc. ſ. hügelicht ꝛc.

Hugo (^-) *npr/m.* ⓢ㉔a. (Vn.) Hugh.

huh, hüh (^) *int.* = hu, hü.

Huhn (^) [ahd.; *Hahn] *n* ⓒc. **1.** hen, junges ~ chicken, pullet; *coll.* Hühner *pl.* poultry; *fig. co.* ein verrücktes ~ a madcap, a crazy person. — **2.** (ohne Rückſicht auf das Geſchlecht) fowl. — **3.** *orn.* türkiſches, kalkuttiſches ~ (Puter) turkey (-hen); *hunt. a.* = Rebhuhn. — **4.** Kochkunſt: gebratenes ~ roast chicken.

Hühnchen (^⌣) *n* ㉔ (*dim. v.* Huhn) **1.** (young) chicken or pullet; F *fig.* liebkoſend: mein ~ (my) duckie!, auch: my (little) chick! — **2.** *fig. id.* ich habe noch ein ~ mit ihm zu pflücken od. zu rupfen (et. mit ihm zu ſchlichten) I have a bone (or a crow) to pick (or s.th. to settle) with him.

Hühner-aar (^…) *m* ㉒: **=adler** *m, orn.* kite (*Milvus rega'lis*); **=ähnlich** *a.* ㊻, **=artig** *a.*: ꝛ gallinaceous; **=auge** *n*: a) eye of a chicken; b) [hürnen Auge] corn; meine ~n ſchmerzen, tun mir weh my corns are shooting or painful; **=augen-operateur, =ſchneider** *m* corn-cutter, ꝛ chiro'podist; **=augen-pflaſter, =pfläſterchen** *n* corn-plaster; **=augen-ring** *m* corn-ring; **=biß** ⚘ *m* campion (*Cuccu'balus ba'ccifer*); **=blindheit** *f, path.* night-blindness, ꝛ hemeralopia; **=braten** *m* roast fowl or chicken; **=bruſt** *f* breast of a fowl or a chicken; *path.* pigeon-breasted; **=darm** *m*: a) entrails *pl.* of a fowl; b) ⚘ chickweed (*Stella'ria me'dia*); **=dieb** *m* stealer of poultry, auch: roost-robber; **=ei** *n*: a) egg of a fowl, hen's egg; b) *zo.* (Muſchel) china-shell (*O'vulum o'vum*); **=falke** *m* = **=habicht**; **=fang** *m, hunt.* etwa: partridge-catching, vgl. =jagd; **=fleiſch** *n* flesh (or meat) of a fowl; **=frikaſſee** *n* Kochkunſt: stewed chicken, chicken-fricassee; **=geier** *m* = **=aar**; **=habicht** *m, orn.* hen-hawk, goshawk (*Astur palumba'rius*); **=händler(in** *f*) *m* ♥ poulterer; **=haus** *n* hen-house, vgl. =ſtall; **=hof** *m* poultry-yard; **=hund** *m, hunt.* pointer, setter; **=jagd** *f* partridge-shooting; **=korb** *m*: a) (für Hühner) hen-coop; b) (Hühner enthaltend) coop (or basket) full of chickens; **=latte** *f* hen-roost; **=leiter** *f* chicken-ladder; *fig.* breakneck stairs *pl.*; **=paſtete** f Kochkunſt: chicken-pie; **=ruf** *m* partridge-call; **=ſchrot** *n, hunt.* partridge-shot; **=ſtall** *m* fowl-house, chicken-roost; **=ſtange** *f* perch for fowls, roosting-place; vgl. =latte; **=ſteige, =ſtiege** *f* = =leiter; **=ſuppe** *f* chicken-broth; **=vögel** *m/pl. orn.*: ꝛ gallinaceous birds *pl.*; **=volk** *n, co.* poultry, the fowls *pl.*; **=weih(e** *f*) *m* = =aar; **=zucht** *f* rearing (or breeding, keeping) of poultry.

Hühnlein (^-) *n* ㉔ = Hühnchen.

hui (^⌣) **I** *int.* **1.** swish; (im Nu) und 2 war er fort! and away he went like steam! — **2.** freudig: 2, das ſchmeckt! oh, it is good!; vorne 2, hinten pfui nothing but outside show. — **3.** verächtlich: ho!, bah! — **II** ~ *m. inv.* **4.** in einem ~ in a trice, in a jiffy, in (less than) no time.

hujus (^⌣) [lt. diejes (*gen.*)] *dem. pron.* of this month; den fünften 2 (on) the fifth instant. [hookah.ſ

Huka (^⌣) [perſ.] *f* ㊺ (㊵) (Waſſerpfeife)ſ

Huker ↓ (^⌣) *m* ㉒ (Fiſcherboot) hooker.

♪ Muſik; ꝛ Wiſſenſchaft; ⚘ Pflanze; ♀ Geographie; ⊕ Technik; ⚔ Bergbau; ⚔ Militär; ⚓ Marine; ♥ Handel; ✉ Poſt; 🚂 Eiſenbahn.

Huld(⌄) [ahd.; *hold] f ⓰ (wohlwollende Geneigtheit) graciousness, good graces pl., (Gunst) favour, (Zuneigung) affection; (Güte) benevolence, kindness; (Milde) clemency, gentleness.

huld=erfüllt (⌄...) a. ⓰ full of graciousness; benevolent (or kindly) inclined; **=göttin(nen** pl.) f ⓲ myth. (the three) Grace(s pl).

huldig|en (⌄⌣⌣) I v/n. (h.) ⓼⓼ 1. to do (or pay, render) homage to a prince, to swear (the oath of) allegiance to one's sovereign; sich (dat.) von e-m 2 l. to receive a p.'s homage or oath of allegiance. — 2. fig. e-m 2 (Verehrung bezeigen) to pay one's respects to a p.; e-r Dame 2 to pay one's attentions (or courtship) to a lady; e-r Ansicht 2 to profess (or embrace) an opinion; dem Fortschritte 2 to be a friend (or on the side of) ...; to favour ... — II ~ n ㉓ u. **H/ung** f ⓰ 3. (doing) homage, (taking the) oath of allegiance; die ~ leisten to do (or render) homage. — 4. respects pl. paid to a p.

Huldigungs=eid (⌄⌣⌣...) m ㉒ oath of allegiance; **=feier** f, **=fest** n, **=tag** m day on which homage is rendered or on which the oath of allegiance is taken, für Beamte: swearing-in day.

Huldin ⸺ (⌄⌣) f ⓱ = Huldgöttin.

huld=reich (⌄...) a. ⓰ gracious; affable, benevolent, kind; **=reiz** m ⓶ gracefulness, attractiveness, fascinating charm; **=voll** a. = **=reich**.

hülfe[1] (⌄⌣) impf. subj. von helfen.
▪=Hülfe[2] (⌄⌣) ꝛc. s. Hilfe ꝛc.
Hulk ⇩ (⌄) = Holk.
Hüll=blatt ⚘ (⌄...) n ㉒ ⚘ involucre, involucral leaf; **mit =blättern umgeben** involucrate(d); **=blättchen** n der Korbblütler: ⚘ phyllary.

Hüllchen (⌄⌣) n ㉓ small cover, coverlet; ⚘: ⚘ involucel, involucret.

Hülle (⌄⌣) [ahd.: hull; *hehlen] f ⓲
1. wrap(per), cover(ing), envelope; ⊕ case, casing, jacket; anat., zo., &c.: ⚘ (in-)tegument, ⚘ a.: ⚘ involucre. sackartige: pocket, ⚘ sac; (abgestreifte) ~ e-r Schlange ꝛc. slough. — 2. fig. irdische (oder sterbliche) ~ des Menschen mortal frame, poet. tenement of clay; die sterbliche ~ ablegen, oft: to shuffle off this mortal coil (sh.); (Überreste der Toten) earthly remains pl.; (Leiche) corpse, lifeless body or frame. — 3. (Schleier) veil; (Maske) mask; (Deckmantel) cloak; ~ für die Augen bandage; fig. mir fällt eine ~ von den Augen a veil is taken from my eyes, I begin to see clearly; mit einer ~ vor den Augen with a mist (or a haze) before one's eyes, befogged. — 4. (Gewand) garment, geh. Spr.: vestment, bibl. raiment; (Gewandung) drapery. — 5. die ~ und Fülle s. Fülle 1; in ~ und Fülle in abundance, abundantly, plentifully, profusely, vgl. Fülle 1.

hüllen (⌄⌣) [ahd. f. Hülle] I v/a. u. sich 2 v/refl. 1. (sich) 2 to wrap (o.s.) up, to cover (o.s.); in Flammen gehüllt enveloped in flames. — 2. fig. sich in Schweigen 2 to be wrapped (or wrapt) in silence, to seal one's lips, F to be mum; in Dunkel(heit) gehüllt veiled (or shrouded) in darkness or obscurity; in Nebel gehüllt enveloped (or hidden) in fog. — 3. aus et. 2 (herausnehmen) to unwrap. — II ~ n ㉓ 4. wrapping; envelopment.

Hüllen=... (⌄⌣...) in Zssgn = Hüll=...
hüll=früchtig (⌄...) a. ⓰: ⚘ angiocarpous, **=früchtler** m ㉒: ⚘ angiocarpian; **=kelch** m: ⚘ periclinium; **=samer** ⚘ ⚘ m/pl. angiospermatous plants, angiosperms pl.; **=schuppig** a. imbricate(d).

Hülschen (⌄⌣) n ㉓ (dim. v. Hülse) small husk or shell or pod or case.

Hülse[1] (⌄⌣) [ahd.; *hüllen] f ⓲ 1. (häutige Schale) hull, husk (a. v. Korn), (Schale) shell; (Schote, ⚘ Kapselfrucht der Schmetterlingsblüten) pod, auch: cod, ⚘ legume(n), (Kapsel) capsule, (Balg) glume. — 2. ⊕ case, casing, jacket, ⚔ des Bajonetts: socket, für Patronen: cartridge-case, für Raketen: rocket-case; mach. (Muff) coupling box; ~ eines Schraubstocks box of a vice.

Hülse[2] ⚘ (⌄⌣) f ⓲ = Hulst (Stechpalme).

hülsen (⌄⌣) ⓼⓪ I v/a. 1. = aushülsen. — II. sich 2 v/refl. 2. (sich von den Hülsen absondern) to separate from the husks or shells, to come off. — 3. ⚘ (Schoten bekommen) to pod.

Hülsen=frucht (⌄⌣...) f ⓶ (ant. Ährenfrucht); **=legume(n)**; **=früchtig=artig** ⚘ a. ⓰: ⚘ leguminous, **=frucht=förmig** a.: ⚘ leguminiform; **=gewächs** n, **=pflanze** f: ⚘ leguminous plant; **=tragend** a. bearing pods, ⚘ leguminous.

hülsicht (⌄⌣) a. ⓰ 1. husked, husky, ⚘ like pods, ⚘ leguminous. — 2. (auch **hülsig**) ⚘ v. Schmetterlingsblüttern: podded, bearing (or producing) pods.

Hulst, Hülst ⚘ (⌄) [ahd.; *hüllen] m ⓶a(b). (Stechpalme) holly.

hum (⌄) int. (auch: hm) h(e)m!, humph!
human (-⌄) [lt.] a. ⓰ (menschlich) human; (menschenfreundlich) humane, (sanft) gentle; **~iora** ⚘ (--⌣⌣) pl. inv. (klassische Gelehrsamkeit) humanities pl., classical learning; **=isieren** (--⌣⌣) v/a. ⓼⓼ to humanize, to civilize; **~ismus** (--⌣⌣) m ㉗ humanism, classical education; **~ist** (--⌣) m ㊷ humanist, classical student; **=istisch** (--⌣) a. ⓰ humanistic; civilizing; **~itär** (--⌣⌣) [fr.] a. ⓰ humanitarian. — **Humanität** (--⌣⌣) [lt.] f ⓰ (Menschlichkeit) humanity, (Menschenfreundlichkeit) humaneness; **~s=bestrebungen** (⌞...) f/pl. humanitarian efforts or tendencies pl.; **~s=studien** n/pl. classical studies pl. or research.

Humbug (⌄⌣) ꝉ F [engl.] m ⓶ humbug, swindle; der reine ~ a regular h.

Humerale (-⌣⌣⌣) [lt.] n ㉙ (pl. a. Humeralia) (bsd. Schultertuch der kath. Geistlichen) cape, ⚚ humeral, amice.

Hummel[1] (⌄⌣) [ahd.: humble] f ⓲ 1. ent. humble= (or bumble=)bee (Bombus). — 2. fig. (wilde) ~ (wilde Person) gad=about, harum=scarum, romp; von Mädchen auch: tomboy. — 3. ♪ sort of bagpipe. [bull for breeding.) **Hummel**[2] provc. (⌄⌣) m ⓶ (Zuchtstier)} **hummen** F (⌄⌣) v/n. (h.) ⓼⓼ to hum.

Hummer (⌄⌣) [ndd.; *skand.] m ㉒ (obb. ㉙) zo. lobster (Ho'marus vulga'ris); **~be=hälter** (⌄⌣...) m ㉒ lobster=car; **=falle** f lobster=pot; **=fang** m lobstering; **=fänger** m lobsterman; **=salat** m lobster=salad; **=schere** f claw of a lobster.

Humor [lt.] I ⚘ (⌣⌞) m ㉑ (pl. Humo= res) 1. (Saft des Körpers) humour. — II (⌣⌞) m ⓪d. 2. (Laune, Stimmung) frame of mind, mood; guter (schlechter) ~ good (ill or bad) humour; verstohlener ~ sly humour. — 3. (heitere Welt=anschauung) humour, a. humorous vein. F squib.

Humoreske (⌣⌣⌣) f ⓲ humorous sketch or tale, **Humorist** (⌣⌣⌞) [Humo'r II] m ㊷ humorist, humorous person or writer; **=isch** a. ⓰ humorous; (scherzhaft) facetious; **~ika** pl. humorous (or facetious) writings pl.

Hump(e)ler (⌄⌣)(⌣) m ㉒ one who hobbles (or limps) along; **hump(e)lig** a. ⓰ hobbling, limping.

humpeln (⌄⌣) [ndb.] v/n. (h.) ⓼⓼ a. to hobble (or limp) along.

Humpen (⌄⌣) [ndb.] m ㉓ bumper, goblet, beaker, tankard, large drinking=vessel or =cup; ein voller ~ a bumper.

Humpes ꝛc. s. Humpeler ꝛc.

Humus (⌞⌣) [lt.] m, inv., agr., geol. (Pflanzen=erde) mould, vegetable earth, ⚘ humus; chm. auch: ulmous substance; **~boden** m ⓶ vegetable soil; **~pflanzen** ⚘ f/pl. humus=plants pl.; **=reich** a. rich (or abounding) in humus, with rich mould; **=sauer** a. chm.: ⚘ humic, ulmic; **=saures Salz** humate, ulmate; **~säure** f humic (or ulmic) acid.

Hund (⌄) [ahd.]: hound: lt. cănis: grch. ky'ōn] m ⓶b. 1. dog (a. als Schimpfwort u. ☆ Förderung=wagen); (Jagd=) ~ hound (a. Schimpfwort); kleiner (junger) ~ (auch dim. **Hündchen**) little (puppy=)dog, F doggie; elender ~ cur (a. Schimpfwort); müde wie ein ~ thoroughly tired out or fagged; vgl. hundsmüde. — 2. fig. wie ~ und Katze leben to lead a cat=and=dog life; F e=n auf den ~ (ins Elend) bringen to drag a p. down, to ruin a p.; F auf den ~ kommen to come down in the world, F to go to the dogs or to pot; F auf dem ~ sein to be down on one's luck, to be in reduced circumstances, P to be stone=broke; er geht vor die ~ e (zugrunde) he is going to rack and ruin or F to go to the dogs; s. bekannt 4. Hahn 4, hetzen 2, begraben 2; der Knüppel liegt beim ~ e, vergleiche unter Knüppel 1; damit lockt man keinen ~ vom Ofen that is of no use whatever, F it's no go, it won't draw; es nimmt fein ~ ein Stück Brot von ihm no one will have anything to do with him. — 3. Sprichw. ein blöder ~ wird selten fett faint heart never won fair lady; kommt man über den ~, so kommt man auch über den Schwanz when the chief (or main) part is done the rest is a mere trifle; den Letzten beißen die ~ e the devil take the hindmost!; begossene ~ e fürchten das Wasser a burnt child dreads the fire; bellende ~ e beißen nicht barking dogs seldom bite; ein toter ~ beißt nicht dead men tell

---
Signs (see page XVII): F familiar; P vulgar; F̶ flash; ⸺ rare; † obsolete (died); * new word (born); ⁺⁺ incorrect; ♪ music;

[**Hündchen**] — 539 — [hungerig]

no tales. — 4. ⚒ (Förderwagen) miner's truck or trolly, vgl. 1.
Hündchen (⌣‿) [Hund, *dim.*] *n* little (or tiny) dog, puppy, f. Hund 1.
Hunde-arbeit *f* (⌣‿...) *f* hard (or fagging) work, drudgery; =**art** *f*: a) species (or breed) of dogs; b) nach ~ after the manner of dogs, *contp.* like a (contemptible) cur; ⚏**artig** *a.* ⚏: a) *zo.* like dogs, dog-like, ⚋ canine; b) *contp.* currish, mean, low; =**ausstellung** *f* dog-show; =**tuchen**, =**dieb** *m* dog-stealer; =**fell** *n* dog's skin; =**fraß** *m* (a. *fig.*), =**fressen** *n* dog's food, vgl. =futter; =**führer** *m* bei der Hetzjagd: whipper-in; =**futter** *n*: a) food for dogs (auch *fig.*); b) *fig.* miserable dinner, wretched fare; =**gebell** *n* dog's bark (-ing); =**geld** *n* paltry sum of money; für ein ~ dirt-cheap; =**geschlecht** *n* canine race; =**haar** *n* unter der Schafwolle: dog-hair; =**halsband** *n* dog-collar; =**händler** *m* dog-fancier; =**haus** *n*. =**hütte** *f* dog-kennel or -hutch; =**junge** *m*: a) boy who feeds the dogs or the hounds; b) *fig.* (elender Mensch) good-for-nothing, (young) scamp; =**kälte** *f*: es ist eine ~ the cold is biting, it's bitterly cold; =**kette** *f* dog's chain; =**kopf** *m* dog's head; =**krankheit** *f* distemper (of dogs); =**kuchen** *m* (= Spratt's patent) dog-biscuit; =**laus** *f* dog-louse (*Trichode'ctes canis*); =**leben** *n* dog's life (a. *fig.*); miserable (or wretched) existence; =**leder** *n* dog's leather; vgl. =fell; =**liebhaber** *m* lover of dogs; =**loch** *n*: a) dog-kennel; b) *fig.* wretched hole; *fig.* dungeon; =**marke** *f* dog-license; =**mäßig** *a.* dog-like; miserable, wretched; =**müde** *a.* = hunds-m.; =**nase** *f* dog's nose; =**peitsche** *f* dog- (or horse-)whip; =**pfeife** *f* dog-whistle.
hundert (⌣‿) [ahd.: hund(red = Zahl): It. *cent(um)*] *numer.* I *card. numb.* hundred; (an die) ⚏ Menschen, ⚏ Jahre a (or one) hundred people, years; (etwa) ⚏ Stück Nägel (about) a (or one) hundred nails; ⚏ Jahre alt a hundred years old, auch: centenary, ...ian; ⚏ gegen eins wetten to lay a hundred to one; viel ⚏, viele ~ (Personen) many hundreds *pl.* (of people); einige ⚏ Bäume some hundreds of trees; zu ⚏en by hundreds. — II ~ *n* ⚏d. (nach Zahlen *pl.* ⚏ *inv.*) hundred; 🟰 *cent*; fünf vom ~ (für das Jahr) five per cent.; a shilling in the pound; hundert vom ~ cent. per cent.; (ganze) ~e von Menschen hundreds of people.
hundert-armig (⌣‿...) *a.* ⚏ with a hundred arms; ⚏**blätt(e)rig** ⚘ *a.*: centifolious; ⚏**ein(s)** hundred and one.
Hunderter (⌣‿‿) *m* 1. *arith.* (a) hundred. — 2. (die Ziffer 100, C) (number) hundred.
hunderter-lei (⌣‿‿‿) *adv.* of a hundred (different) kinds or sorts.
hundert-fach (⌣‿...) *a.* ⚏: a) *a.* ⚏**fältig** *a.* hundredfold, centuple; ⚏ vermehren (or centuple); b) das ~e einer Zahl hundred times a number; ⚏**füßig** *a.* with a hundred feet, ⚋ centipedal; ⚏**gradig** *a. phys.* centigrade; ⚏**jährig** *a.* of a hundred years, a hundred years old, centenary, ...ian; der ⚏e Krieg zwischen Frankreich und England (14. u. 15. *sae.*) the hundred years' war; ⚏e Feier hundredth anniversary, centennial celebration, centenary; b) der, die ~e *s.* ⚏ centenarian; ⚏**jährlich** *a.* occurring once every (or in a) hundred years, coming once in a century, centennial; ⚏**köpfig** *a.* hundred-headed, bisw.: ⚋ centicipitous; ⚏**mal** *adv.* a hundred times; ⚏**malig** *a.* done (or repeated) a hundred times (over); ⚏**pfünder** ⚒ *m* ⚏ hundred-pounder; ⚏**pfündig** *a.* weighing a hundred pounds.
hundertst (⌣‿) *ord. numb.* ⚏ hundredth, *fig.* vom ~en ins Tausendste kommen to ramble from one subject to another; das weiß der ~e nicht not one in a hundred (or a thousand) knows it; ~**el** (⌣‿‿) *a.*, *n* ⚏ hundredth (part); ⚏**ens** (⌣‿‿) *adv.* in the hundredth place.
hundert-tägig (⌣‿...) *a.* ⚏ lasting (or of) a hundred days; ⚏**tausend**: a) *numer. a.* a hundred thousand; b) ~e *n/pl.* von Exemplaren hundreds of thousands of copies; ⚏**teilig** *a.*: a) divided in(to) a hundred parts, centesimal; b) = ⚏**gradig**; ⚏**torig** *a.* with a hundred gates; das ⚏e Theben hundred-gated Thebes; ⚏**weise** *adv.* by (or in) hundreds; ⚏ verkaufen to sell by the hundred or by hundreds.
Hunde-schlag (⌣‿...) *m* ⚏ breed of dogs; ⚏**schlecht** *a.* ⚏: es ist mir ⚏ I feel as sick as a horse; =**sperre** *f* muzzling-order; =**stall** *m* dog-kennel; =**staupe** *f, vet.* (dog's) distemper; =**steuer** *f* dog's license; =**töle** P *f* cur; =**trab** *m, man.* jog-trot, slow trot; =**wache** ⚓ *f* (von Mitternacht bis 4 Uhr morgens) midnight watch; =**wagen** *m* (in England unbekannt) cart drawn by dogs; =**wärter** *m* dog-keeper, feeder of dogs, Sport: kennel-man; =**wetter** *n* wretched weather; es ist ein ~, auch: it is not fit to turn a dog out, F it's a beastly day; =**zecke** *f. ent.* (Holzbock) (dog-) tick (*Ixo'des cani'nus*); =**zucht** *f* breeding of dogs; =**züchter** *m* breeder of dogs, dog-fancier. — Vgl. a. Hunds-.
Hündin (⌣‿) [Hund] *f* ⚏ bitch (a. Schimpfwort = gemeines Weib); F *co.* lady-dog.
hündisch (⌣‿) [Hund] *a.* ⚏ doggish, currish, ⚋ canine; *fig.* (kriechend) crouching, fawning, F carneying; (schamlos) shameless, stärker: cynical, (unzüchtig) smutty, dirty.
Hündlein (⌣‿) *n* ⚏ = Hündchen.
Hunds-affe (⌣‿‿) *m* ⚏ *zo.* cynopithecus, ⚋ coid (*Cynopithe'cus*); schwarzer ~ black ape (*C. niger*); ⚏**äugig** *a.* ⚏ with dog's eyes; =**beere** ⚘ *f* dogberry (Frucht von *Cornus sangui'nea*); =**dill** ⚘ *f* = =famille ⚘; =**fisch** *m, ichth.* mud-fish or -minnow (*Umbra*); =**fliege** *f, ent.* dog-fly (*Musca canicula'ris*); =**fott** *m* ⚏c.: a) F u. P (Schuft) scoundrel, rogue, scamp, cur; (feiger Kerl) coward; Sprichw. ein ~ gibt mehr, als er kann you cannot give more than you have; b) ⚓ becket; =**fötterei** F u. P *f* ⚏ scoundrelism, roguery; =**föttisch** F u. P *a.* roguish, stärker: base, infamous; ⚏**gemein** *a.* very low or vulgar or common or mean; villainous; =**gemeinheit** *f* low(est) depth of vulgarity; villainy; ⚏**hai** *m, zo.* hound (-fish), hound-shark (*Ga'leus canis*); =**familie** ⚘ *f*: a) several kinds of Anthemis; b) bsd. stinkende ~ stinking camomile (*A'nthemis co'tula*); =**kerbel** *m* common rough chervil (*Anthri'scus vulga'ris*); =**kopf** *m*: a) dog's head; b) *zo.* (Fledermaus) bat; ⚏**köpfig** *a.* with a dog's head, ⚋ cynocephalic; ⚏**ledern** *a.* made of dog's skin; ⚏**loden** *pl. provc.* (Vorwürfe) reproaches *pl.*, F blowing-up *sg.*; ⚏**mäßig** F *a.* like a dog, weitS. = hündisch, bsd. *fig.*; =**maul** *n* dog's snout; ⚏**müde** F *a.* dead tired, F dead beat; =**petersi'lie** ⚘ *f* fool's parsley (*Aethu'sa cyna'pium*); =**pint** *m*, =**pünte** ⚓ *f* e-s Taues: point of a rope; =**quecke** ⚘ *f* dog-wheat (*Tri'ticum cani'num*); =**raute** ⚘ *f* bastard-rocket (*Eruca'strum Polli'chii*); =**rose** ⚘ *f* dog-rose (*Rosa cani'na*); =**schierling** ⚘ *m* = =petersi'lie; ⚏**schlecht** *a.* execrable, wretched(ly bad); =**stern** *m, ast.* dog-star; ⚋ Sirius, Canicula; =**tage** *m/pl.* (²³/₇.—²³/₈.) dog-days, canicular days *pl.*; =**tags-ferien** *pl.* summer holidays *pl.* or vacation; =**veilchen** *n*, =**vio'le** ⚘ *f* dog-violet (*Vi'ola cani'na*); =**wut** *f, path:* ⚋ hydrophobia, rabies; ⚏**wütig** *a.* suffering from hydrophobia or rabies; =**zahn** *m*: a) dog's tooth; b) *anat.* (Spitzzahn des Menschen neben den Schneidezähnen) canine (or eye-)tooth; =**zunge** *f*: a) dog's tongue; b) ⚘ dog's- (or hound's-) tongue (*Cynoglo'ssum*); echte ~ rib (*C. officina'le*); c) *ichth.* burbot.
Hüne (⌣‿) [udd.] *m* ⚏, **Hünin** (⌣‿) *f* fabulous giant(ess *f*); (wo)man of gigantic stature.
Hünen-gestalt (⌣‿...) *f* ⚏ gigantic figure or stature; =**grab** *n* barrow, cairn; ⚏**haft** *a.* ⚏, ⚏**mäßig** *a.*: a) von Gestalt: gigantic; b) an Kraft: of a giant's strength, of powerful stature; ⚏**stark** *a.* (as) strong as a giant, of gigantic strength; =**weib** *n* giantess, powerful woman.
Hunger (⌣‿) [ahd.: hunger] *m* ⚏ 1. hunger (a. *fig.*), nach et. after (or for) a th.); ~ haben, leiden to be hungry or ravenous, to be (kept) on short commons; der ~ sieht ihm aus den Augen he looks half starved; (des) ~s sterben to die of hunger or starvation, to starve, to be starved (to death); Sprichw. ~ ist der beste Koch hunger is the best sauce. — 2. (~snot) famine, starvation.
Hunger-blümchen ⚘ (⌣‿...) *n* ⚏ whitlow-grass (*Ero'phila verna*); =**brunnen** *m* = =quelle.
Hung(e)rer (⌣(‿)‿) *m* ⚏ starving (or hungry) person (= Hungerleider).
hunger-erregend (⌣‿...) *a.* ⚏ giving a p. an appetite, making a p. hungry; =**folter** *f* ⚏ torture by starvation or hunger; =**gestalt** *f*: a) famished shape or figure; b) body emaciated by starvation, (mere) skeleton.
hung(e)rig (⌣(‿)‿) *a.* ⚏ 1. hungry, stärker: ravenous; (ausgehungert) starving, famished; ich bin sehr ⚏ I am very hungry,

---

⚋ scientific; ⚘ botanical; 🜨 geography; ⊕ machinery; ⚒ mining; ⚔ military; ⚓ marine; ● commercial; ✉ postal; 🚂 railway.

[Hungerigkeit] — 540 — [Huster]

I am ravenous or starving; ich fühle mich ⚬ I feel hungry or F peckish; ⚬ wie ein Wolf (as) hungry as a hunter, ravenous(ly hungry); Sprichw. e-m leeren Magen ist schlecht predigen a hungry belly has no ears. — 2. fig. ⚬ (begierig) nach // greedy after //. — 3. (kümmerlich, armselig) poor, wretched, miserable, auch: starved (concern, &c.).

Hung(e)rigkeit (ˊ(ˇ)ˇ-) f ㊻ hungriness, hunger, starvation; fig. greediness.

Hunger=jahr (ˊˇ...) n ㊷ year of famine; =künstler m (professional) starving man; =kur f, med. low(er)ing diet, starving- (or fasting-)cure or system; eine ~ durchmachen to be put (or to put o.s.) on a low diet, stärker: to starve o.s.; =leider m starving person, starveling; =leiderei f starvation, pinching poverty; =lohn m, etwa: starvation-wage(s pl.); =mahlzeit f scanty meal, meagre repast.

hungern (ˊˇ) ⓐ. I v/impers. es hungert mich, mich hungert (sehr) I am (very) hungry, stärker: I feel ravenous or famished. — II v/n.(h.): ⚬ wie ein Wolf to be as hungry as a hunter, F co. to have a wolf in one's inside; (Hunger leiden) to suffer (from) hunger, to starve, freiwillig: to starve (or pinch) o.s., (fasten) to fast; aus Gesundheitsrücksichten: to diet o.s.; fig. auf et. ⚬ to hunger after a th., to be very greedy after (or desirous of) a th.; ⚬de Menschen, ~de pl. hungry (or starving) people, starvelings pl. — III sich ⚬ v/refl. mit Angabe der Wirkung, z.B.: sich tot (ob. zu Tode) ⚬ to starve o.s. to death, to die from starvation.

Hunger=pfote (ˊˇ...) f ㊷ nur in: ~n saugen = am =tuche nagen (s. =tuch); =quelle f nur in nassen Jahren fließend: stream which flows only in wet seasons, intermittent spring.

Hungers=not (ˊˇ,ˊ) f ㊷ (Mangel an Lebensmitteln) famine, (Teuerung) dearth; von ~ heimgesuchter Ort famine-stricken place, F co. starvation camp.

Hunger=stein (ˊˇ...) m ㊷ (Pfannenstein) scales pl. in the salt-pan; =stelle f poor(ly paid) situation; =tod m (death from) starvation; =tuch (urspr. schwarzes Altartuch für die Fastenzeit) nur fig. gebr.: am ~(e) nagen to be starving or famishing or on the point of starvation; =typhus m. path. hunger-typhus.

Hungrer (ˊˇ) m ㊷ s. Hungerer.
hungrig (ˊˇ) ꝛc. s. hungerig ꝛc.
Hünkel prove. (ˊˇ) [Huhn, dim.] n㊷ chicken.
Hunne (ˊˇ) m ㊶, Hunnin f ㊷ Hun.
Hunnen=könig (ˊˇ...) m ㊷, =reich n king. kingdom of the Huns.
hunnisch (ˊˇ) a. ㊺ Hun. Hunnic.
hunzen (ˊˇ) [uhd.*Hund] v/a.㊹ (schimpfen) to scold, reprimand; (abweisen) to snub.

Hupe ♪ (ˊˇ) [udd.] f ㊷ 1. (Baßpfeifchen) whistle made of bark. — 2. Blasinstrument mit nur einem Ton: horn with only one note: (Tute am Automobil) siren.

Hupf (ˊˇ) m ㊹ b. jump; (Sprung) leap.
hupfen (ˊˇ) [ahd.] v/n. (h.) ⓖ: fig. das ist gehupft wie gesprungen that's the same either way, it's much of a muchness, there is not much to choose between.

hüpfen (ˊˇ) [mhd.: hop] I v/n. (h., bei Ortsveränderung sn) ⑧ to hop, skip, jump; freudig: to frisk (about); to jump for joy; gaukelnd: geschäftig: to flit about; ihm hüpfte das Herz vor Freude his heart leapt for (or with) joy. — II ~ n ㉓ hopping, &c. (s. 1); (Freudensprünge) gambols pl.

Hüpfer (ˊˇ) m ㊷ 1. ~, auch ~in f ㊼ one who hops or skips or jumps; auch: hopper, skipper, jumper. — 2. co. = Floh ꝛc.

Hüpferling (ˊˇ) m ㊷ d zo. water-flea (Cyclops).

Hüpf=maus (ˊˇ...) f ㊷ zo. deer-mouse (Zapus hudsonius); =spiel n hopping game, auch: hop-scotch.

hup(p), hups (ˊ) int. ⚬ hopp.
Huppe ♪ (ˊˇ) f ㊷ = Hupe.

Hürde (ˊˇ) [ahd.: hurdle] f ㊸ 1. hurdle, wickerwork, wattle. — 2. agr. (Pferch für Schafe) auch: fold, pen.

hürden (ˊˇ) v/a. ㊹ agr. (pferchen) to pen (up), to put in a fold, to hurdle; ge=hürdetes Land land manured by sheep.

Hürden=geflecht (ˊˇ...) n㉒ wicker-work, hurdle-work; =rennen n hurdle-race; =schlag m pen(ning), fold; hurdling; =wand f = =geflecht.

Hure (ˊˇ) [ahd.: whore] f ㊸ whore, harlot (a. bibl.), strumpet; weniger anstößig: (common) prostitute, F street-walker, bad woman or wench. a. (an) unfortunate (pl.unfortunates), lady of easy virtue, anonyma, P bad 'un (= one); sie ist eine (gemeine) ~ F she walks (or parades or is on) the streets.

huren (ˊˇ) [ahd.] I v/n. (h.) ⑧ to whore, to lead the life of a whore(-monger m), to fornicate, to lead a lecherous life; nur von Weibern: to be (or live as) a prostitute, to prostitute o.s.; mit e-m ⚬ to have illicit (sexual) intercourse with a p. — II ~ n ㉓ = Hurerei.

Hurer (ˊˇ) m ㊷ whoremonger, debauchee; bibl. fornicator.

Hurerei (-ˊˇ) f ㊻ whore(monger)'s life. harlotry; prostitution, social evil; bibl. fornication.

Huri (ˊˇ) [ar.] f ㊹ (Schöne in Mohammeds [Paradies) houri.
hürnen (ˊˇ) [Horn] a. ㊺: ~ Siegfried s. hörnen 5.

hurr (ˊ) von et. Schwirrendem: [whiz!
hurra (ˊ- u. -ˊ) [mhd.*hurr(e) hunt.] int. u. ~ n ㉑ Ruf der Freude: (hip, hip,) hurra(h)!, huzza!; mit ~ begrüßen to receive with (loud) cheers; ⚬en (-ˊˇ) v/n. (h.) ⑧ to (shout) hurra(h). to (give a) cheer; to raise shouts of joy.

Hurra=geschrei (ˊˇ...) n ㉒, =ruf m shouts pl. of (or shouting) hurra(h).

hurten (ˊˇ) (: hurtig) v/a. ㊹ Turnerei: to run and push.

hurtig (ˊˇ) [mhd.] a. ㊺ brisk, swift; (schnell bei der Arbeit) quick at work, smart, (munter) alert, (flink u. gewandt) nimble, agile; adv. oft: with dispatch, expeditiously, speedily; ♪ presto; mach' ⚬! be quick, look sharp!; ~keit f ㊻ briskness, swiftness; quickness, smartness, alertness, nimbleness, agility; speed, speediness.

Husar ⚔ (-ˊ) [mhd. 16. sae.; *madj.] m ㊷ hussar; fig.⚔ (starkes Weib) oft: dragoon, virago, F bouncer.

husarenhaft (-ˊˇˇ), husarisch (-ˊˇ) a. ㊺ (dressed or accoutred) like a hussar.

Husaren=jacke (-ˊˇ...) f ㊷ dolman; ⚘=mäßig a. ㊺ like a hussar; = (pelz)mütze f busby; =säbel m cavalry-sabre or -sword; =tasche f sabretache.

husch (ˊ) [mhd.] I int. 1. (rasch!) quick!, go!, als Scheuchruf: shoo! — 2. (still!) hush!, 'sh! — 3. (hu, wie kalt!) ugh!, how cold! — II ~ m ⓐ a. 4. sudden movement; touch-and-go; auf den ~, unterm ~ in a moment, in passing, without stopping. — 5. (kurzer Regenschauer) passing (or light) shower. — 6. (Ohrfeige) box on the ear.

Husche (ˊˇ) f ㊸ = husch 5 u. 6.
husch(el)ig (ˊˇ) a. ㊺ hasty; (oberflächlich) (highty-)flighty; (zappelig) fidgety.

huscheln (ˊˇ) [huschen] v/n. (h.) a. sich ⚬ v/refl. ⓐa. to whiz (or whisk, flit) along, to rustle; (zappeln) to fidget about; sie huschelte sich unter die Decken she slipped between the blankets.

huschen (ˊˇ) ⓐ I v/a. 1. F e-n ⚬ to box a p.'s ears; v/recip. sich mit e-m herum~ ⚬ to have a (stand-up) fight (or a tussle) with a p. — 2. (rasch fortnehmen) to snatch (or F whip) away. — II v/n. (in) 3. to glide swiftly (über et. across a th.); to whisk (or flit) away; fig. über et. (flüchtig) hin (ob. fort) ⚬ to skim (or to pass lightly over) a th.

Husch=kopf F (ˊˇ,ˊ) m ㊷ (Kopf mit ungekämmten Haaren) head with unkempt (or dishevelled) hair, a. shock-head.
husch(l)ig (ˊˇ) a. ㊺ s. huschelig.

Hüsing ⚓ (ˊˇ) [ndd.] f ⑱ (Taubewicklung) housing, house-line.

hussa (ˊˇ-) int. huzza!
Hussit (-ˊ) [Hus, † 1415] m ㊷ eccl. Hussite; ~en-krieg m 1419 ff. Böhmen: Hussite war.
hussitisch (-ˊˇ) a. ㊺ Hussite.

hüsteln (ˊˇ) [husten] v/n. (h.) ⚬a. to have a slight (or F a little) cough.

husten¹ (ˊˇ) [ahd.: wheeze] I v/n. (h.) 1. to (have a) cough, F co. to bark; fig. die Flöhe ⚬ hören to hear the grass grow; auf (ob. in) etwas ⚬ (nichtachten) not to care a straw (or a rap) for a th., to snap one's fingers at a th. — II v/a. 2. = aus=⚬. — 3. mit Angabe der Wirkung: e-m die Ohren voll ⚬ to worry a p. with one's cough (-ing). — 4. fig. ich werde dir (et)was ⚬ (du kannst lange warten) you may whistle for it! — III sich ⚬ v/refl. mit Angabe der Wirkung: 5. sich halbtot ⚬ to cough o.s. almost (or nearly) to death.

Husten² (ˊˇ) [ahd. *⚬¹] m ㉓ path. cough (-ing). F co. bark(ing); ein kurzer ~ a hacking cough; den ~ haben to have a cough; Lakritze löst den (hartnäckigsten) ~ liquorice loosens a (the most obstinate) cough; ~anfall m ㊷ fit of coughing, coughing fit; =bonbons m/pl. cough-drops or -lozenges pl.; =fieber n feverish (symptoms accompanying a) cough; =krampf m convulsive cough; =mittel n remedy for (or against) a cough or for coughs; vgl. Brustmittel; =stillend a. ㊺ stilling (or quieting) a cough, pectoral.

Huster (ˊˇ) m ㊷, ~in f ㊼ one who coughs, auch: cougher.

Zeichen (s. S. XVII): F familiär; P Volkssprache; Γ Gaunersprache; ⚘ selten; † alt (auch gestorben); * neu (auch geboren); ⚈ unrichtig;

[Hut]

Hut¹ (¹) (ahd.: hood) m ⓞc. 1. hat; niedriger (Filz-)~: a) weicher: wide-awake, Am. crush-hat; b) steifer: F bowler, ehm. billycock; (Schlapp-~) slouch-hat; dreieckiger ~ three-cornered hat; ~ mit breiter, schmaler Krempe broad-brimmed, narrow-brimmed hat; s. Damenhut; ~ ab! hat(s) off!, off with your hat(s)!; den ~ aufbehalten to remain covered; den ~ vor e-m ab-nehmen ob. ziehen to take off (or F to doff) one's hat to a p.; den ~ auf haben to have one's hat on, to be covered; den ~ auf's Ohr setzen to put one's hat on one side (of the head); den ~ ins Gesicht drücken to pull one's hat over one's eyes; e-n mit der Hand am ~e grüßen to touch one's hat to a p.; fig. viele Köpfe unter einen ~ bringen to reconcile conflicting opinions or spirits, to harmonize many (dissentient) voices, auch: to gather many adherents around one flag; Sprichw. mit dem ~e in der Hand kommt man durch das ganze Land, etwa: hat in hand you may pass through all the land. — 2. fig. bisw. = (Herr) gentleman. — 3. ~ (Brot) Zucker loaf of sugar; ~ der Pilze cap (or top) of mushrooms.

Hut² (¹) [ahd.: heed] f ⓥ 1. (Aufsicht, Schutz) guard(ianship); in Gottes ~ in God's keeping; es wurde in seine ~ gegeben it was entrusted (or confided) to his care; et. in seine ~ nehmen to take a th. under one's care or protection or into one's charge; in j-s ~ sein to be in a p.'s (safe) keeping or custody. — 2. (Wache, Wachtposten) guard, watch, lookout; auf s-r (ob. der) ~ (vorsichtig) sein to be on one's guard, to be careful; F to mind one's P's and Q's; sei auf deiner ~! take care!, beware! — 3. (Recht, das Vieh zu weiden; Weide) right of pasturage; pasture, pasture-land.

Hut¹-abnehmen (¹...) n ⓥ, -abziehen n taking off (or F doffing) one's hat; -band n hat-band, am Frauenhute: bow (or ribbon) to a hat; -besatz m trimming of (or to) a hat or bonnet; -borte f binding of a hat; -bürste f hat-brush. [hat or bonnet.)

Hütchen (¹~) n ⓥ [dim. zu Hut¹] small)
hüten (¹~) [ahd.: heed; *Hut²] ⓥ I v/a. 1. to guard, keep, take care of, look after; (bewachen) to watch (over); das Vieh 2 to tend the cattle; fig. das Bett, Zimmer 2 to keep one's bed, room. — 2. e-n vor et. 2 to protect a p. against (or from) a th., vgl. be2 2. — 3. abs. F Gott soll 2! God forbid! — II sich 2 v/refl. 4. (sich in acht nehmen) to be on one's guard; sich vor et. 2 to guard against a th., to keep clear of a th.; 2 Sie sich vor ihm! beware of him!; ich werde mich 2 das zu tun ob. F und das tun I shall take good care not to do it, I'll have nothing to do with it, F iro. (you won't) catch me doing such a thing!; er mag (ob. soll) sich 2! let him beware (of me)! — 5. sich selbst 2 to take care of o.s. —

III-~n ⓥ 6. guard, guarding; protection; preservation; des Viehs: tending, pasturage.

Hüter (¹~) m ⓥ, **~in** f ⓥ guardian, keeper, custodian; (wo)man on watch; (Vieh-)~ herdsman (s. Hirt); (Wächter) bsd. ehm.: warden; e-s Turmes 2c. auch: lookout man; (Aufseher)superintendent, F co. ~ der Ordnung (Schutzmann) etwa: representative of the law, guardian of the peace; bibl. soll ich m-s Bruders ~ sein am I my brother's keeper?
Hüterschaft (¹~) f ⓥ guardianship.
Hut¹-fabrik (¹...) f ⓥ hat-manufactory; -fabrikant m = -macher; -feder f plume, feather on a hat or bonnet; -filz m felt for hats; -form f: a) shape of a hat; b) hatter's form or block; ²förmig a. ⓥ hat-shaped, ²: -futter n lining of a hat; -futteral n (Schutzkasten); ²geld n fee (paid) for pasturage; -¹geschäft, -gewerbe n hatter's business or trade; -gestell n e-s Frauen-hutes shape of a bonnet or hat; -handel m = -geschäft; -händler m hatter; ²haus n miner's tool-house; -¹kopf m, -krempe f crown, (b)rim of a hat; ²los a. hatless; uncovered, bareheaded; neue Sitte (seit 1905) der losen hatless craze; ²²los a. unguarded, untended; -¹macher m hat-maker; -macherei f, -macher-handwerk n hat-maker's (or hatter's) trade; -nadel f hat-pin; -putz m = -besatz; -schnur f hat- (or bonnet-) box, auch: band-box.
Hutsche, Hütsche md. (¹~) f ⓥ = Hitsche.
Hut¹-schleife (¹...) f ⓥ cockade; -schnalle f = -spange; -schnur f: a) hat-band (or -string); b) F fig. das geht über die ~ (über alles Maß) it exceeds all bounds, that beats all or everything; -schwenken n waving of hats; -spange f buckle for the hat-band; -ständer m hat- (or hall-)stand.
Hüttchen (¹~) n ⓥ (dim. von Hütte) small hut or cottage, hutch.
Hütte (¹) [ahd.] f ⓥ 1. (schlichtes Häuschen) cot(tage), cabin, Onkel Toms ~ (amerit. Roman v. Harriet Beecher Stowe, 1812—96) Uncle Tom's Cabin; (~ der Wilden, bloßes Schutzdach) hut, hovel; shelter; (Bretterbude) booth; nur bibl.: tabernacle; hier laßt uns ~n bauen let us build here a Tabernacle, one for Thee, one for Moses, one for Elias. — 2. ⓞ metall. (Gieß- ob. Schmelz-)~ smelting-works pl. or -house, foundry; (Puddel-, Blech-, Zinn- 2c.)~ forge; (Walz-werk) rolling-mill. — 3. ⚓ (Mittelaufbau des Schiffes, Kampanje) companion.
Hütten-amt ⚒ (¹~...) n ⓥ managing (or managerial) board of a foundry; -arbeit f smelting operations pl., work done in a foundry; -arbeiter m smelter, founder workman (employed) in a foundry; -bau m: a) building (of) huts or cottages; b) construction of forges or foundries; vgl. -arbeit; -beamte(r) m official of a foundry; -besitzer m = -herr; -bewohner(in f) m cottager, occupant of a cottage, p. dwelling in a hut; -deck ⚓ n e-s Kriegs-schiffes poop-deck, upper poop; -glas n (in der Masse gefärbtes Glas) pot-metal; -herr m owner (or proprietor) of a foundry; -kunde f metallurgy; -kun-

[Hydrolog]

-dige(r) m metallurgist; -lager ⚒ n barrack-camp, camp (consisting) of huts; -mann m, pl. -leute: a) = -bewohner; b) = -arbeiter; -herr; ²män-nisch a. metallurgic(al); -meister m head manager (or overseer) of a foundry; -rauch m: a) metallic fume, furnace-smoke; b) chm. arsenical fumes pl., white arsenic; -reise ⚒ f working-season of a blast-furnace; -schreiber, -steiger m manager, overseer of a foundry; -werk n smelting-house; vgl. Hütte 2; -wesen n smelting business, concerns pl. of a foundry; vgl. -kunde; -zinn n grain-tin.
Hüttlein (¹~) n ⓥ = Hüttchen.
Hüttner (¹~) [Hütte] m ⓥ (kleiner Landwirt) small farmer, cottager.
Hut¹-tresse (¹...) f ⓥ gold lace (worn) round (or on) a hat.
Hutung (¹~) f ⓥ agr. pastur(ag)e.
Hütung (¹~) f ⓥ = hüten III.
Hutzel prov. (¹~) [mhd.] f ⓥ (dürres Obst) dried apple or pear.
Hut¹-zucker ⓞ (¹...) m ⓥ loaf-sugar, sugar in loaves.
Hyalit ⓟ (¹~¹) [grch.] m ⓞc. min. (Glasopal) hyalite.
Hyalo-graphie ⓟ (¹~~¹) [grch.] f ⓥ (Kunst auf Glas zu ätzen) hyalography.
Hyäne (¹~¹) [grch.] f ⓥ zo. hyena (Hyae'na); ⚔ ~n des Schlachtfeldes (Leichenräuber) camp-followers pl. who rob the dead bodies, a. death-hunters pl.; ²n-artig a.: ⓟ hyenic, hyeniform; ~n-hund m ⓥ zo. hyena-dog (Canis pictus). [(roter Zirkon) hyacinth.]
Hyazinth (¹~¹) [lt., *grch.] m ⓞc. min.
Hyazinthe ⓟ (¹~¹~) [lt., *grch.] f ⓥ hyacinth (Hyaci'nthus).
Hybride ⓟ (¹~¹) [lt., *grch.] f ⓥ, bsd. ⓟ (Mischling) hybrid; **hybrid(isch)** (¹~(¹~) a. ⓥ hybrid; **Hybridität** (¹~~¹) f ⓥ (Bastardschaft) hybridity, hybridism.
Hyder (¹~) [grch.] f ⓥ = Hydra.
Hydra (¹~) [grch.] f ⓥ 1. zo. (Wasserschlange) hydra. — 2. myth. lernä'ische ~ (neunköpfige Schlange) Lernæan hydra.
Hydrant ⓞ (¹~¹) [grch.] m ⓥ (Wasserschlauch) hydrant, hose for flushing the streets, &c., zum Löschen: fireman's hose.
Hydrat ⓟ (¹~¹) [grch.] n ⓞc. chm. (Verbindung mit Wasser) hydrate; ~wasser n ⓥ water (contained) in a hydrate.
Hydraulik ⓟ (¹~¹~) [grch.] f ⓥ phys. (Mechanik der flüssigen Körper) hydraulics.
hydraulisch ⓞ (¹~¹~) a. ⓥ hydraulic; ²er Aufzug hydraulic lift; ²e Presse hydraulic (or Bramah's) press.
Hydrochinon ⓟ (¹~¹~) n ⓞd. chm. hydroquinone ($C_6H_4(OH)_2$).
Hydro-dynamik ⓟ (¹~¹~) f ⓥ phys. (Wasserkraftlehre) hydrodynamics; **hy-dro-dynamisch** a. ⓥ hydrodynamical.
Hydrogen ⓟ (¹~¹~) n ⓞd. chm. (Wasserstoff) hydrogen (H).
Hydro-graph ⓟ (¹~¹f) m ⓥ hydrographer; ~ie (¹~¹~¹) f ⓥ (Beschreibung der Gewässer) hydrography; ²isch (¹~¹~) a. ⓥ hydrographic, hydrographical.
Hydrolog ⓟ (¹~¹) [grch.] m ⓥ, ~e (Wasserkundiger) hydrologist; ~ie (¹~¹~¹) f ⓥ (Wasserkunde) hydrology; ²isch (¹~¹~) a. ⓥ hydrological.

♪ Musik; ⓟ Wissenschaft; ⚘ Pflanze; ⓥ Geographie; ⓞ Technik; ⚒ Bergbau; ⚔ Militär; ⚓ Marine; ⚖ Handel; ✉ Post; 🚂 Eisenbahn.

[Hydrolyse] — 542 — [Ichthyolith]

Hydro-lyse ⚬ (⏑⌣⌣⌣) [grch.] f ⚭ chm. (Zersetzung durch Entziehen v. Wasser) hydrolysis. [draulik.
Hydro-mechanik ⚬ (⏑⌣⌣⌣) f ⚭ = Hy-
Hydro-meter ⚬ (⏑⌣⌣⌣) n (m) ⚭ phys. (Instrument zum Messen der Geschwindigkeit des fließenden Wassers) hydrometer; **hy-drometrisch** a. ⚭ hydrometric(al).
Hydro-oxygen(=gas) ⚬ (⏑⌣⌣⌣⌣⌣) [grch.] n ⚭d. = Knallgas.
Hydro-path ⚬ (⏑⌣⌣) m ⚭ med. hydropathist; ~**ie** (⏑⌣⌣⌣) f ⚭ (Wasserkur) hydropathy; **Lisch** (⏑⌣⌣) a. ⚭ hydropathic (treatment, establishment, &c.).
Hydro-phobie ⚬ (⏑⌣⌣⌣⌣) [grch.] f ⚭ path. (Tollwut) hydrophobia.
Hydro-statik ⚬ (⏑⌣⌣⌣) f ⚭ (Lehre vom Gleichgewichte der Flüssigkeiten) hydrostatics; **hydro-statisch** a. ⚭ hydrostatic(al).
Hydro-technik (⏑⌣⌣⌣) f ⚭ hydrotechnics.
Hydro-therapie ⚬ (⏑⌣⌣⌣⌣) f ⚭ (Wasserheilkunde) hydrotherapeutics.
Hydroxyd ⚬ (⏑⌣⌣) n ⚭c. chm. (wasserhaltiges Oxyd) hydroxide.
Hydroxylamin ⚬ (⏑⌣⌣⌣⌣) [grch.] n ⚭d. chm. hydroxylamine (NH_3O).
Hyeto-meter ⚬ (⏑⌣⌣⌣) [grch.] n (m) ⚭ (Regenmesser) hyetometer.
Hygie(i)a (⏑⌣⌣⌣) [grch.] npr/f. ⚭ ⚭ myth. (Göttin der Gesundheit) Hygeia.
Hygi-ene (⏑⌣⌣) [fr. hygiène; *grch. hygieina' pl.] f ⚭, **Hygi-enik** (⏑⌣⌣⌣) f ⚭ ⚬ (Gesundheitspflege) hygienics, hygiene.
Hygi-eniker ⚬ (⏑⌣⌣⌣⌣) m ⚭ hyg(i)eist, hygienist.
hygi-enisch a. (⏑⌣⌣⌣) [grch.] a. ⚭ (gesundheitlich) hygienic.
Hygro-meter ⚬ (⏑⌣⌣⌣) [grch.] n (m) ⚭ (Feuchtigkeitsmesser) hygrometer; **hygro-metrisch** a. ⚭ hygrometric(al).
Hygro-skop ⚬ (⏑⌣⌣) [grch.] n ⚭c. phys. (Feuchtigkeits-anzeiger) hygroscope; **Lisch** (⏑⌣⌣) a. ⚭ hygroscopic(al).
Hymen (⏑⌣) [grch.] **I** npr/m. ⚭α. myth. (Gott der Ehe) Hymen. — **II** ⚬ n ⚭ anat. (Jungfernhäutchen) hymen.

Hymne (⏑⌣) [f. Hymnus] f ⚭ 1. eccl. (geistliches Lied) hymn. — 2. (Lobgesang, bsd. im Alt.) hymn, song of praise; (Kriegsgesang) (war-)chant.
hymnen-artig (⏑⌣...) a. ⚭ : hymnal; **-buch** n ⚭ hymn-book; **-dichter** m writer of hymns, hymnographer, hymnodist; **-dichtung** f hymnography; **-sammlung** f collection of hymns, hymnody; **-singen** n singing (or chanting) of hymns, hymnody.
hymnisch (⏑⌣) [grch.] a. ⚭ hymnic.
Hymnus (⏑⌣) [lt., *grch.] m ⚭ = Hymne 2.
Hyoszyamin ⚬ (-⌣⌣⌣) [grch.] n ⚭d. chm. hyoscyamine ($C_{17}H_{23}NO_3$).
Hyper-ämie ⚬ (⏑⌣⌣⌣) [grch.] f ⚭ path. (Blutüberfüllung) hyperæmia.
Hyper-ästhesie ⚬ (⏑⌣⌣--⌣) f⚭physiol.(starke Reizbarkeit e-s Gefühlssinns) hyperæsthesia.
Hyperbel (⏑⌣⌣) [grch.] f ⚭ 1. rhet. (Übertreibung) hyperbole; in ~n sprechen, schreiben to exaggerate, to hyperbolize. — 2. math. (Doppelkegelschnitt) hyperbola. [boliform.
hyperbel-förmig (⏑⌣⌣...) a. ⚭ hyper-
hyperbelhaft (⏑⌣⌣⌣), **hyper-bolisch** (⏑⌣⌣⌣) a. ⚭ rhet., math. hyperbolic(al).
Hyper-boreer ⚬ (⏑⌣⌣⌣⌣) m/pl. ⚭ Alt.: (Völker im fernen Norden) Hyperboreans; **hyper-bore-isch** (⏑⌣⌣⌣) a. ⚭ Hyperborean.
hyper-kritisch (⏑⌣⌣⌣) a. ⚭ hypercritical.
Hypersthen ⚬ (⏑⌣⌣) m ⚭d. min. hypersthene, Labrador hornblende.
Hyper-trophie ⚬ (⏑⌣⌣⌣) f ⚭ path. (zu starke Ernährung e-s Organs) hypertrophy; **hyper-trophisch** a. (⏑⌣⌣⌣) a. ⚭ path. (über(er)nährt) hypertrophic(al).
Hypnose ⚬ (⏑⌣⌣) [grch. hy'pnos Schlaf] f ⚭ (Erzeugung von Schlaf) hypnosis.
hypnotisch (⏑⌣⌣) a. ⚭ (schlaf-erzeugend; den magnetischen Schlaf betr.) hypnotic.
Hypnotiseur (⏑⌣⌣ö'r) [fr., *gr.] m ⚭d. hypnotizer.
hypnotisieren (⏑-⌣⌣⌣) v/a. ⚭ (in magnetischen Schlaf versetzen) to hypnotize.
Hypnotismus (⏑⌣⌣⌣) m ⚭ hypnotism.

Hypochonder ⚬ (⏑⌣⌣⌣) [grch.] m ⚭ path. (Milzsüchtige[r]) hypochondriac, splenetic person; **Hypochondrie** (⏑⌣⌣⌣) f ⚭ hypochondria, spleen; **hypochondrisch** a. ⚭ hypochondriac(al), splenetic; **Hypochondrist** (⏑⌣⌣⌣) m ⚭ = Hypochonder.
Hypotenuse ⚬ (⏑⌣⌣⌣) [grch.] f ⚭ geom. (größte Seite e-s rechtwinkligen Dreiecks) hypotenuse.
Hypothek (⏑⌣⌣) [grch. Unterpfand] f ⚭ jur. mortgage; erste, zweite ~ first, second mortgage; ein Gut mit ~en belasten to burden (or encumber) an estate with mortgages, to mortgage it.
Hypothekar (⏑⌣⌣⌣) m ⚭d. jur. = Hypothekengläubiger; **Lisch** a. ⚭ as (or in the shape of) a mortgage, hypothecary; **Lischer Gläubiger** mortgagee; **Lische Sicherheit** security by mortgage; adv. Geld Lisch aufnehmen to raise ... by (or on a) mo.; ~**schuld** f ⚭ debt secured by a mo., hypothecary debt; ~**schuldner(in** f**)** m mortgager.
Hypotheken-bank ⚭ (⏑⌣⌣⌣...) f ⚭ mortgage-bank; **-brief** m mortgage, **-buch** n official register of mortgages; **-gläubiger** m mortgagee; **-register** = mortgage-register; **-urkunde** f mortgage-deed; **-wesen** n all that concerns mortgages.
Hypothese ⚬ (⏑⌣⌣⌣) [grch.] f ⚭ (Voraussetzung) hypothesis, (mere) supposition; **hypothetisch** a. ⚭ hypothetic(al), suppositional.
Hypsometer ⚬ (⏑⌣⌣⌣)[grch.]n(m)⚭phys. (Instrument zur Höhenmessung) hypsometer.
Hypsometrie (⏑⌣⌣⌣) [grch.] f ⚭ phys. (Höhenmessung durch den Siedepunkt des Wassers) hypsometry.
Hysterie ⚬ (⏑⌣⌣) [grch.] f ⚭ path. (Nervenkrankheit bei Frauen) hysterics, hysteria, F co. (the) strikes.
hysterisch (⏑⌣⌣) a. ⚭ hysterical; der Anfall fit of hysterics; einen den Anfall bekommen to go into hysterics.

J

J, i (⌣) **I** n, inv. (Buchstabe) I, i (vowel); i mit Trennungszeichen i with diæresis; der Punkt, das Tüpfchen auf dem i the dot on the i; fig. das Tüpfchen auf dem i (das Winzigste) nicht vergessen (not to forget) to dot one's i's, to be very exact or punctilious. — **II** i int. F = ei; i freilich! why, of course!; i sehen Sie mal! do (or come and) look! i warum nicht gar! P i wo! what next!, nothing of the kind!, what are you talking about!
i. A. abbr. = im Auftrage.
i-ah! (-⌣) int. [lautm. vom Eselschrei] heehaw. [heehaw.
i-ahen (-⌣⌣) v/n. (h.) ⚭ to bray;
Jambe ⚬ (⏑⌣) m ⚭ = Jambus.
Jamben-dichter (⏑⌣⌣...) m ⚭ writer of iambics, ⚬ iambographer; **-dichtung** f iambic poetry or verse.
iambisch (⏑⌣) [grch.] a. ⚭ pros. Der Vers iambic (verse).

Jambus ⚬ (⏑⌣, oft ⊹+ jäm...) [grch.] m ⚭ pros. iambus, iambic foot (⌣⌣).
Iberer (⏑⌣) (Ebro) m/pl. ⚭ hist. Alt.: (= Basken) Iberians pl.; **Iberi-en** ♀ (⏑⌣(⌣)) npr/n. ⚭α. (a. poet. = Spanien) Iberia; **iberisch** a. ⚭ Iberian.
Ibis (⏑⌣) [ägypt.] m ⚭ orn. ibis (Ibis).
Ibisch-strauch ♀ (⏑⌣⌣ch) [lt.=gr. hibiscus] m ⚭ = Eibisch.
ich (⌣) [ahd.: **I**: lt. grch. ego] **I** personal pron. der ersten Person ⚭ A1 (3t). **1.** I; ich selbst I myself, my own self or person; hier bin ich! here I am!; ich bin's! it is I, F it is me; ich bin selbst dort gewesen I have been there myself; bist du bereit? ja, ich bin es are you ready? yes! I am; vor dem Vokativ: ich Armer! poor me! (fast nie: poor I!). — 2. nicht zu übersetzen nach e-m personal pron.: ich, der ich sie liebte I who loved her. — **II** Ich n ⚭ (a. inv.) **3.** (the) 1, a. (lt.) ego; (my)self; sein früheres Ich his former self; mein ganzes Ich my whole being or self; das liebe Ich one's own dear self, F co. number one; er liebt sein Ich zu sehr he is too fond of self, he is too selfish or egotistic; mein and(e)res (ob. zweites) Ich my other (or second) self, oft a. (lt.) alter ego. [Ich-roman.
Ich-form * (⌣⌣) f ⚭ : Roman in der ~ =
Ichheit (⌣-) f ⚭ phls. etwa: my own individuality or self, ⚬ egoity.
Ichneumon ⚬ (⏑⌣⌣) [grch. Nachspürer] m u. n ⚭d. zo.: (Pharaonsratte) ichneumon (Herpestes Ichneu'mon).
Ich-roman * (⌣...) m ⚭ novel in which the hero tells his own tale.
Ich-sucht (⌣⌣cht) f ⚭ egotism.
Ichthyographie ⚬ (⏑⌣⌣⌣fī) f ⚭ (Abhandlung über Fische) ichthyography.
Ichthyol (⏑⌣⌣)[grch.=lt. Fischöl]n ⚭d. med. ichthyol.[ichthyolite, fossilized fish.]
Ichthyo-lith ⚬ (⏑⌣⌣⌣) [grch.] m ⚭c., ⚭

Signs (see page XVII): F familiar; P vulgar; F flash; ⚬ rare; † obsolete (died); * new word (born); ⊹+ incorrect; ♪ music;

Ichthyolog ⚯ (‵⌣⌣‶) m ㊷, ~e ㊹ (Fischkenner) ichthyologist; ~ie (‵⌣⌣‶) f ㊸ (Fischkunde) ichthyology.

Ichthyophag(e) ⚯ (‵⌣⌣″⌣) m ㊷ (㊹) (Fisch=esser) ichthyophagist.

Ichthyosaurus ⚯ (‵⌣⌣″⌣) m ㊅㊷ zo. (fossile Fisch=eidechse) ichthyosaur.

ideal¹ (-‵⌣′) [spät=lt.] **I** a. ㊻ (vorbildlich) ideal, (begrifflich) notional, (eingebildet) imaginary, visionary. — **II** das ~e n ㊆ the ideal character (an et. of a th.).

Ideal² (-‵⌣′) n ⑪d. (Musterbild) ideal, (Vorbild) auch: model, pattern; ein ~ von Schönheit an ideal beauty; das ~ eines Redners a model speaker, a. oft: the (fr.) beau-ideal of a speaker.

idealisch (-‵⌣′) a. ㊻ ideal.

idealisieren (-⌣-‵⌣′) **I** v/a. ㊺ (vorbildlich gestalten) to idealize. — **II** ~ n ㉓ u. **Idealisierung** f ㊻ idealization.

Idealismus ⚯ (-⌣-‵⌣′) m ㉗ phls. (ideale Lebensauffassung) idealism.

Idealist ⚯ (-⌣-‵) m ㊷ phls. idealist; ⚲isch a. ㊻ idealistic.

Idealität (-⌣-‵⌣′) f ㊻ ideality.

Ideal-konkurrenz (-⌣″⌣⌣) [grch.=lt.] f ㊶ jur. ideal concurrence of crime.

Idee (-‵) [grch.] f ㊸ (Gedanke) idea; nach seiner ~ in his idea, (according) to his way of thinking; fixe ~ fixed idea or notion, F crotchet; an einer fixen ~ leiden to suffer from monomania; eine gute ~ a happy thought; man kann sich keine ~ davon machen it is impossible to form an idea of it, one cannot realize it; F ohne die ~ (Spur) von Scham without the least notion (or idea, trace, vestige) of ...

ide-ell (-⌣‵) [fr.] a. ㊻ (auf der Vorstellung beruhend) ideal; imaginary, fanciful.

Ideen-folge (-″⌣..) f ㊶, **=gang** m order (or sequence) of ideas, train of thought; **=kreis** m circle of ideas; seinen ~ erweitern to enlarge (or extend) one's horizon or ideas; **=lehre** f, phls.: ⚯ ideology; ⚲los a. without ideas; ⚲reich a. rich in (or brimming full of) ideas, resourceful, inventive; **=verbindung** f association of ideas; in ~ stehende Begriffe notions pl. intimately associated with each other; **=welt** f ideal world, world of ideas.

Iden (‵⌣) [lt.] f/pl. ㊸ Alt., röm. Kalender, bsd. die ~ des März (15. März) the Ides of March.

identifizieren (-⌣⌣‶⌣) [lt.] **I** v/a. und **sich ~** v/refl. ㊹: (sich) mit et. ~ (eins machen) to identify (o.s.) with a th., v. Schauspielern a. thoroughly to enter into a part. — **II** ~ n ㉓ u. **Identifizierung** f ㊻ identification.

identisch (-‵⌣) [lt.] a. ㊻ (eins, gleich) identical (mit with); (self)same; ~**sein** n ㉓, **Identität** (-‵⌣″) f ㊻ identity; sameness; perfect equality or harmony; **Identitäts=nachweis** m Zollwesen: certificate of origin.

Ideolog, ~e (-⌣⌣‵⌣) [grch.] m ㊷, ㊹ fig. (Schwärmer, Utopist) ideologist, visionary; ⚲isch a. (⌣⌣″⌣) ㊻ ideologic(al).

Idio-latrie ⚯ (⌣(⌣)‵) [grch.] f ㊸ (Selbstanbetung) idolatry.

Idiom ⚯ (⌣‵) [grch.] n ⑪d. gr.: a) (Sprach=eigenheit) idiom; b) (Mund=art) dialect; **Latisch** a. ㊻: a) idiomatic, idiomatical; b) dialectal.

Idiosynkrasie ⚯ (⌣(⌣)⌣‵) [grch.] f ㊸ (persönliche [Ab]=Neigung idiosyncrasy.

Idiot (⌣‵) [grch.] m ㊷ (Blödsinniger) idiot, half-witted person; **~en=anstalt** f ㊶ asylum (or home) for idiots, idiot-asylum; **~ie** (⌣(⌣)-‵) f ㊸ (angeborener Blödsinn) idiocy.

idiotisch (⌣(⌣)‵⌣) a. ㊻ idiotic.

Idiotismus ⚯ (⌣(⌣)-⌣) m ㉗: a) Spracheigenheit) idiom(atic expression); b) = Idiotie. [idocrase, volcanic schorl.]

Idokras ⚯ (-⌣‵) [grch.] m ⑪a. min.

Idol ⚯ (-‵) [grch.] n ⑪d. (Götzenbild) idol.

Ido(lo)latrie ⚯ (-‵⌣⌣..., ‵⌣⌣‵) [grch.] f ㊸ (Götzendienst) idolatry.

Idyll (-‵) [grch. Bildchen] n ⑪d., ~e f ㊸ poet., paint. idyl, pastoral poem; **~en=dichter** m ㊷ writer of idyls, pastoral (or bucolic) poet.

idyllisch (-‵⌣) [grch.] a. ㊻ (ländlich [schön], einfach) idyllic, pastoral, bucolic; primitive, unsophisticated.

Igel (‵⌣) [ahd.] m ㊷ **1.** zo. hedgehog, bisw.: urchin (Erina'ceus); gemeiner ~ European hedgehog (Er. europae'us). — **2.** ⊕ Spinnerei: (Läufer) urchin; agr. (Furchen=egge) drill-harrow.

igel-artig (‵⌣″⌣..) a. ㊻ hedgehog- (or urchin-)like, ⚯ erinaceous; **=fisch** m ㊷ ichth. hedgehog(-fish) (Di'odon).

Ignorant (-‶-‵) [lt.] m ㊷ (Unwissender) ignorant person, Fignoramus; **Ignoranz** f ㊻ (Unwissenheit) ignorance.

ignorieren (-⌣‵⌣) [lt.] **I** v/a. ㊹ **1.** (nicht wissen) to be ignorant of, not to know. — **2.** (unbeachtet lassen) to ignore, to take no notice of, to pass over, to disregard; e-n ~ (nicht kennen wollen), auch: to pretend not to know a p., stärker: F to cut a p. — **II** ~ n ㉓ u. **Ignorierung** f ㊻ **3.** ignoring, &c. (f. 2); unter (voller) ~ von etwas taking no notice (whatever) of a th.

ihm (‵) [ahd.] dat. von er und es ㊻A1.: **1.** a) (to) him; von Dingen: (to) it; ich habe es ~ gegeben I gave it (to) him; reich es ~!, sag es ~ nicht! pass it to him!, do not tell him!; wir sind ~ sehr verpflichtet we are greatly obliged to him; v. Dingen: ~ (dem Rock) neue Knöpfe annähen to put new buttons to (or on) it, to give it new buttons; b) alleinstehend in Antworten: (to) him; wem klagt sie? ~ to whom does she complain? to him; wem gehorcht sie? ~ whom does she obey? him. — **2.** nach prp.: him, zB. von ~ (or from, &c.) him; wir sind von ~ abhängig we are dependent on him. — **3.** bisw. durch possessive pron.: ich habe ~ die Hand gedrückt I pressed his hand; der Mann hat ~ ins Gesicht geschlagen ... struck him in the face; dagegen: der Stein hat ~ das Gesicht verletzt ... struck (or injured) his face. — **4.** bsd. ehm. = als erniedrigende Anrede (vgl. er 2) (to) you, zB. ich schenke ~ das I give it (to) you.

ihn (‵) [ahd.] acc. von er ㊻A1. **1.** him, von Dingen: it; ich sehe ~ I see him; wir sahen ~ selbst we saw him himself; ich ließ ~ (den Hut) bügeln I had it ironed. — **2.** bsd. ehm. als Anrede:

~ (vgl. ihm 4) you, zB. ich werde ~ wegschicken I shall send you away.

ihnen (‵⌣) [ahd.] dat. pl. von er, sie, es ㊻A1. **1.** (to) them; ich habe es ~ gegeben, gesagt I gave it (to) them, I told them; das ist ~ (für sie) ein Leichtes it is an easy thing for (or to) them. — **2.** nach prp.: them; mit, von ~ with, of (or from) them; bei ~ with them, at their house; das Haus gehört ~ the house belongs to them, the h. is theirs. — **3.** ~ (dat. von Sie) zu Personen die man siezt: (to) you; ich verdanke ~ mein Glück, ~ verdanke ich mein Glück I owe you my good fortune, I owe my good fortune to you, seltener: to you I owe my good fortune; das Buch gehört ~ the book belongs to you, the book is yours.

ihr (‵) **1** pers. pron. **1.** [ahd.] dat. v. sie ㊻A1., entsprechend dem m ihm: (to) her, v. Dingen: (to) it; ich versprach ihr das Buch, ich versprach es ihr I promised her the book, I promised it to her; sie sind ihr (der Tugend) ergeben they are devoted to it. — **2.** [ahd.] pl. von du ㊻A1: you (bibl. u. poet. auch ye); ~ selbst yourselves; was wollt ihr (oder Ihr)? what do you want?; ihr schöne Damen you (poet. a. ye) fair ladies; nicht zu übersetzen nach dem relative pron.: ihr, die ihr das sagt you who say that. — **II** [mhd.] a. u. poss. pron.: m ihr, f ihre, n ihr ㊻A2, C1. **3.** von einer Besitzerin: her, von Dingen: its; ihr Bruder her brother; einer ihrer Brüder a brother of hers; mein und ihr Bruder my brother and hers; von Dingen: die Rose und ihre Bewunderer the rose and its admirers. — **4.** von mehreren Besitzern: their; meine Eltern, Freundinnen 2c. haben ihr Haus (oder Häuser) verkauft ... have sold their house(s). — **5. Ihr** zu Personen, die man siezt: your; haben Sie Ihr Geld erhalten? ... your money? — **III 6.** a) **ihrer, ihre, ihres** ㊻; b) mit dem def. art. der (die, das) **ihre** oder **ihrige** hers, theirs, in höflicher Anrede: yours; als s.: sie und die ~(ig)en (they) and hers (theirs); Sie und die Ihr(ig)en you and yours; ich bin ganz der Ihr(ig)e, etwa: I am Yours very truly; sie tut (tun) das Ihr(ig)e she does (they do) her (their) best; tun Sie das Ihr(ig)e: a) do what you can; b) do your best or your utmost.

ihrer (‵⌣) [ahd.] ㊻A1.: a) gen. sg. v. sie: of her; b) gen. pl. von sie: of them; es waren 2 zehn there were ten of them; c) **Ihrer** gen. von Sie, in höflicher Anrede: of you; er gedenkt Ihrer noch he still remembers (or thinks of) you.

ihrer=seits, ~ (″⌣.‵) adv. in her, their, your turn; on her, their, your part.

ihres=gleichen, ~ (″⌣.‵⌣) inv. the like(s) of her, them, you; her, their, your kind or equals pl.; sie hat nicht ~ there is no one (in the world) like her or to match her, she has not her equal.

ihres=teils (″⌣.‵) adv. on her, their part.

ihret=halben (″⌣.‵⌣), (um) **~wegen** (″⌣.‵⌣) ob. **~willen** (″⌣.‵⌣) adv. on her, their account; for her sake, their sakes.

⚯ scientific; ⚘ botanical; ⚱ geography; ⊕ machinery; ⚒ mining; ⚔ military; ⚓ marine; ⊛ commercial; ✉ postal; 🚂 railway.

[ihrig] — 544 — [Imperial]

ihrig (⌣́⌣) s. ihr III.
Ihro, fast † (⌣́⌣) Kurialstil: His (Your).
ihrzen (⌣́⌣) [Ihr (5.)] v/a. ⑳ (vgl. duzen) to call a p. (one another) „Ihr".
i. J. abbr. = im Jahre.
Ikonographie ⤳ (⌣⌣́⌣ǐ⌣) [grch.] f ㊽ (Bilderbeschreibung) iconography.
Ikonoklast ⤳ (⌣⌣⌣́) [grch.] m ㊷ (Bilderstürmer) iconoclast.
Ikonolatrie ⤳ (⌣⌣⌣⌣́) [grch.] f ㊽ (Bilderanbetung) iconolatry.
Ikosa-eder (⌣⌣⌣́⌣) [grch.] n ㉒ math. (Zwanzigflach) icosahedron.
Iktus ⤳ (⌣⌣) [lt.] m, inv. pros. metrical accent. [sound. the vowel) i.]
I-Laut (⌣́⌣) m ⑰ the letter (or the
Ile ⊙ (⌣́) f ㊽ scraper for horn or ivory.
ilen ⊙ (⌣́⌣) v/a. (h.) Kammacherei: to scrape horn or ivory.
Ilex ⤳ (⌣́) [lt.] f ⑱ ilex = Stechpalme; **~säure** f ㊻ chm.: ⤳ ilicic acid.
Iliade (⌣(⌣)⌣́⌣) f ㊽, **Ilias** (⌣́(⌣)⌣) [grch. v. l'Ilion] f, inv. Homerisches Epos: Iliad.
Ilion (⌣́⌣) [grch.], **Ilium** [lt.] npr/n. ㊳α., ⤳ **Ilios** (⌣́(⌣)⌣) f, inv. Alt. (Troja) Ilium, Troy.
ill. abbr. = illustriert (s. illustrieren).
illegal (⌣̆⌣́) [lt.] a. ⑥⑥ (ungesetzlich) illegal; **~ität** (⌣̆⌣⌣́) f ㊻ illegality.
illegitim (⌣̆⌣⌣́) [lt.] a. ⑥⑥ (außer-ehelich) illegitimate (offspring, child); **~ität** (⌣̆⌣⌣⌣́) f ㊻ illegitimacy.
illiberal (⌣̆⌣⌣́) [lt.] a. ⑥⑥ (nicht freigebig) illiberal; bsd. pol. (nicht freisinnig) not liberal; **~ität** (⌣̆⌣⌣⌣́) f ㊻ illiberality.
illoyal (⌣̆la̅-i̯⌣́) [fr.] a. ⑥⑥ (untreu) disloyal, not loyal.
Illuminat (⌣⌣⌣́) [lt.] m ㊷ eccl. one of the Illuminati. **~en-orden** m ㊶ (1776 in Ingolstadt) Order of the Illuminati.
Illumination (⌣⌣⌣⌣-tsi̯⌣́) [lt.] f ㊽ (Festbeleuchtung) illumination.
illuminier/en (⌣⌣⌣́⌣) [lt.] ⓘ v/a. 1. (erleuchten) to light up, festlich: to illuminate (a. abs.). — 2. paint. (ausmalen) to illuminate, colour. — **~ung** f ㊻ lighting up; illumination.
Illusion (⌣⌣⌣́) [lt.] f ㊽ (Wahn) illusion, (Einbildung) imagination, fancy; sich **~en** machen über // to have illusions (or to be deluded) as regards //.
illusorisch (⌣⌣⌣́⌣) a. ⑥⑥ illusory, delusive.
Illustration (⌣⌣⌣-tsi̯⌣́) [lt.] f ㊽ (Abbildung) illustration (a. fig.). **~s-druck** ⊙ m ㊷ typ. impression of illustrations.
Illustrator (⌣⌣⌣́⌣) [lt.] m ㊷ illustrator.
illustrieren (⌣⌣⌣́⌣) [lt.] v/a. ㉝ (mit Bildern schmücken) to illustrate (auch fig.); illustrierte Zeitung illustrated (newspaper); Illustrierer m = Illustrator.
Illyri-en ♀ (⌣́⌣⌣) npr/n. ㉓α. Illyria; **Illyri-er**(in f ㊵) m ㉒, **illyrisch** (⌣⌣́⌣) a. ⑥⑥ Illyrian.
Ilme prov. ♀ (⌣́⌣)[ahd.: elm = lt. ulmus].
Ilse¹ (⌣́⌣) f ㊽ ichth. = Alse. [Lizzie.]
Ilse² (⌣́⌣) (Eli'sabeth) npr/f. ㊵㉓.(Bn.)
Iltis (⌣́⌣) [ahd.] m ⑰ zo. polecat, fitchew, fitchet [Puto'rius fe'tidus]; **~fell** n ㉒, **~pelz** m ㊷ polecat-skin.
im (⌣́) [in dem]: in the; ⸗ Augenblick in a moment; ⸗ Jahre 1815 in (the year) 1815.
imaginär (⌣⌣G̯⌣, ⌣⌣⌣́) [fr.] a. ⑥⑥ (eingebildet) imaginary; math. ⸗e Größe im. value.

Imbiß (⌣́⌣) [ahd.] m ㉔a. light meal or repast, cold collation; zwischen Frühstück und Mittag: lunch(eon); e-n kleinen ~ nehmen to make (or to partake of) a light meal, auch oft: to have a snack, to eat a little something.
Imitation (⌣⌣⌣-tsi̯⌣́) [lt.] f ㊽ (Nachahmung) imitation; **imitieren** (⌣⌣⌣́⌣) v/a. ㉝ (nachahmen) to imitate.
Imker (⌣́⌣) [ndd.; *Imme] m ㉒ und **~ei** (⌣⌣́) f ㊻ = Bienen-züchter, -bau.
immanent (⌣⌣⌣́) [lt.] a. ⑥⑥ (einwohnend) inherent; auch: indwelling; **Immanenz** (⌣⌣⌣́) f ㊻ immanence.
Immanuel (⌣⌣⌣́⌣) [hebr. Gott mit uns] npr/m. ⑮ ⑯α. (mst Bn.) Emmanuel.
immateriell (⌣⌣⌣-(⌣)⌣́) [fr.] a. ⑥⑥ (stofflos) immaterial.
Immatrikulation (⌣⌣⌣⌣⌣-tsi̯⌣́) [lt.] f ㊽ matriculation of students, enrolment;
immatrikulierbar (⌣⌣⌣⌣⌣́⌣) a. ⑥⑥ qualified for matriculation; **immatrikulieren** (⌣⌣⌣⌣⌣́⌣) v/a. ㉝ (in ein Register eintragen) to (enter in a) register; Studenten ⸗ (einschreiben) to matriculate (or enrol) students.
Imme prov. (⌣́⌣) [ahd.] f ㊽ = Biene.
Immediat-eingabe (⌣⌣⌣⌣́⌣⌣) [lt. unmittelbar] f ㊽, **⸗gesuch** n, **⸗vorstellung** f personal petition (presented) to the sovereign; **⸗vortrag** m personal report (made) to the sovereign.
immens (⌣⌣́) [lt.] a. ⑥⑥(D10.) (riesig) immense; adv. ⸗ reich immensely wealthy.
immer (⌣́⌣) [ahd. je mehr] adv. 1. always; (fortwährend) continually, incessantly, perpetually, (beständig) constantly; (den ganzen Tag) all day (long); er liest ⸗ Romane he is for ever reading novels, he does nothing but read novels; ⸗ und ewig for ever and ever; **auf** (⸗ für) ⸗ for ever; **noch** ⸗ still, even now; noch ⸗ nicht not yet, not even now; **wie** ⸗ as usual; er tat es ⸗ wieder he kept on (or never ceased) doing it; ⸗ und ⸗ wieder over and over again; nur ⸗ zu! keep it going! keep the game alive!, F keep the pot boiling! — 2. fig. vor comp. (dauernde Steigerung) ⸗ mehr (vgl. ⸗ ...) more and more; er wird ⸗ reicher he grows richer and richer; sie ängstigen sich ⸗ mehr they are growing more and more anxious; iro. das wird ja ⸗ schlimmer (oft iro. besser) things are going from bad to worse; das Feuer wird ⸗ größer the fire goes on (or continues) increasing; ⸗ weiter further and further. — 3. (jedenfalls) under any circumstances; wir wollen uns jetzt nur ⸗ ausruhen well, let us rest a while (in any case); es ist doch ⸗ gewagt it is certainly (or undoubtedly) risky; du mußt gehorchen, er ist doch ⸗ dein Vater ..., for he is your father after all. — 4. bei Zahlwörtern = je, z.B. ⸗ vier zu vier (always) four at a time; ⸗ den dritten Tag every third day. — 5. beim imper. fast pleonastisch (=doch): fang nur ⸗ an do make a beginning; wo mag er nur ⸗ sein? where on earth can he be? — 6. verallgemeinernd: ... ever, z.B. **sobald** es nur ⸗ möglich ist as soon as in any way possible, as soon as ever

feasible; **wann auch** ⸗ whenever; **was auch** ⸗ what(so)ever; was er auch ⸗ für Gründe haben mag whatever reasons he may have; was er auch (nur) ⸗ sagen mag whatever he may say; **wen auch** ⸗ whom(so)ever; **wenn auch** ⸗ der Satz an und für sich richtig ist (al)though the sentence itself may be correct; **wer auch** ⸗ who(so)ever; **wie auch** ⸗ (a. so wie nur ⸗) in whatever manner (it may be); how(so)ever; **wo auch** ⸗ where(so)ever, in whatever place (it may be); wo ich ihn auch ⸗ treffen mag wherever I may meet him; **wohin auch** ⸗ wherever, bibl., &c. whithersoever; in Fragesätzen mit „doch": wo er doch ⸗ bleiben mag? wherever can he be?
immer-dar (⌣́⌣...) adv. for ever; **⸗fort** adv. continually, constantly, without ceasing, on and on, geh. Spr.: evermore; es regnete ⸗ it kept on raining; **⸗grün** a. ⑥⑥ evergreen; ⸗e Stein-eiche evergreen oak (Quercus ilex); ⸗ ~ n periwinkle (Vinca); **⸗hin** adv.: a) zeitlich: for ever, constantly; b) einräumend: for all that, still, nevertheless, (meinetwegen) for aught I care; er mag ⸗ kommen (still) he may come if he likes; Sie mögen es ⸗ haben you are welcome to it all the same; **⸗mehr** adv. fast † for ever and ever, poet. evermore; **⸗während** a. u. adv. = beständig 2; **⸗zu** adv.: fahre nur ⸗! (immer weiter) go on!, never mind! [real estate.]
Immobiliar-vermögen (⌣⌣-⌣(⌣́)⌣...) n ㊷
Immobili-en (⌣⌣́(⌣)⌣) [lt.] pl. inv. (Grundstücke, ant. Mobilien) real estate; jur. auch: immovables pl.; ⑱ (totes Inventar) dead stock; **~-konto** ⊙ n ㊷ deadstock account.
Immoralität (⌣⌣⌣⌣́) [fr.⸗lt.] f ㊻ (Unsittlichkeit) immorality, immoral conduct.
Immortelle ♀ (⌣⌣⌣́⌣) [fr.] ㊽ (Strohblume) everlasting flower (Helichry'sum); **~kranz** m wreath of everlasting flowers.
immun (⌣⌣́) [lt.] a. ⑥⑥ (seuchenfrei) immune. [(or render) immune.]
immunisieren (⌣⌣⌣́⌣) v/a. ㉝ to make
Immunität (⌣⌣⌣́) [lt.] f ㊻ (Freiheit von Lasten ꝛc.) immunity from disease, taxes, &c.; exemption from a duty, &c.; (Vorrecht) privilege.
Imperativ ⤳ (⌣́⌣⌣f) [lt.] m ⑳c.: a) gr. (Befehlsform) imperative (mood); b) phls. Kants katego'rischer ~ Kant's categorical imperative.
imperativisch (⌣⌣⌣-í⌣⌣)[lt.]a. ⑥⑥ (befehlend) imperative; adv. gr. ⸗ (gebraucht) (used) imperatively or in the imperative (mood).
Imperator (⌣⌣⌣́⌣) [lt.] m ㉛ röm. Alt.: (Feldherr) (chief) general, als Titel: imperator; (Kaiser) emperor **⸗isch** (⌣⌣⌣́⌣) a. ⑥⑥ of a general or imperator; (kaiserlich) imperial.
imperfekt (⌣⌣⌣́) [lt.] ⓘ a. ⑥⑥ (unvollkommen) impe'rfect. — ⓘⓘ **~(um)** (⌣, ⌣⌣⌣́) n ㊷d.(㊳) gr. impe'rfect (tense), auch: past tense.
Imperial (⌣-(⌣)⌣́) [fr.] 1. m ㉓ mint. (russ. Goldmünze v. 15 Rubel) imperial. — 2. ⑱ **~(⸗papier)** n v. ca. 56×81 cm.

Zeichen (s. S. XVII): F familiär; P Volkssprache; ⌐ Gaunersprache; ⸜ selten; † alt (auch gestorben); * neu (auch geboren); ⁺⁺ unrichtig;

[**Imperiale**] imperial (paper). — 3. ⊙ *typ.* ~(-schrift) *f* nine-line pica.
Imperiale(-) [fr.] *f* ⊕ (Wagenverdeck mit Sitzen) top (or outside) of a tram-car, omnibus, &c. with seats.
Imperialismus [lt.] *m* (Kaiserherrschaft; Weltmachtssucht) imperialism.
Imperialist *m* imperialist; ~isch *a.* (kaiserlich) imperialistic.
impertinent [lt.] *a.* (unverschämt) impertinent; F *co.* (*adv.*) blond red-haired; **Impertinenz** *f* impertinence.
Impf-anstalt *f* vaccinating-office, central place for vaccination of children; =**arzt** *m* vaccinating physician or surgeon.
impfbar *a.* med. vaccinable.
impfen [? ahd., med. nhd.] **I** *v/a.* 1. fast † *hort.* (propfen) to inoculate, (en)graft. — 2. med. e-m Kinde die Blattern, (Kuh=)Pocken, metron.: ein Kind to vaccinate a child with the lymph of cows (i. einimpfen I); wieder to re-vaccinate. — 3. *fig.* die Tugend in das Herz e-s Kindes to engraft (or implant) virtue in a child's heart. — **II** ~ *n* 4. f. Impfung.
Impfer *m* 1. fast † *hort.* inoculator, grafter. — 2. med. vaccinator.
Impf-gegner *m* antivaccinationist; =**gesetz** *n* vaccination-act.
Impfling *m/d.* child to be vaccinated; candidate for vaccination.
Impf-lymphe *f* vaccine (lymph); =**nadel** *f* vaccinating-needle; ⊙pflichtig *a.* liable to (or bound to undergo) vaccination; =**reis** *n*, fast † *hort.* (Pfropfreis) graft(-twig); =**schein** *m* certificate of vaccination; =**stoff** *m* = =lymphe.
Impfung *f* 1. fast † (zu impfen 1:) inoculation, (en)grafting. — 2. (zu 2:) vaccination, zweite ~ re-vaccination; die ~ war erfolglos the vaccine did not take. [vaccination.]
Impf-zwang *m* compulsory]
Impi-etät [lt.] *f* (Unfrömmigkeit, Ehrfurchtlosigkeit) impiety.
implizieren [lt.] *v/a.* (mit verwickeln, hineinziehen) to implicate.
implizite [lt.] *adv.* (ausdrücklich) implicitly, expressly.
Imponderabile [lt.] *n* mst *pl.* ...bi'lien (unwägbare Stoffe) imponderable substances, imponderables *pl.*
imponieren [lt.] *v/n.* (h.) e-m (Achtung, Bewunderung einflößen) strongly (or powerfully) to impress a p., *auch:* to strike a p.; ~d imposing (scene, &c.), majestic (air, &c.)
Import [neu-lt.] *m* (Einfuhr) importation; ~en *pl.* (Eingeführtes) import (article), imported goods *pl.*
Import=... (..(")..) = Einfuhr-. [cigar.]
Importe *f* imported Havana]
Importeur [fr.] *m/d.* importer.
importieren *v/a.* to import.
imposant [fr.] *a.* (Achtung einflößend) imposing.
Impost [lt.] *m* b. 1. = (Waren=)Steuer. — 2. arch. (Kämpfergesims): impost.
impotent [lt.] *a.* physiol., path. (unfähig) impotent; **Impotenz** *f* impotence, weitS. incapacity.

Imprägnation (v--tẹ(ʼ)) [lt.] *f* physiol. (Schwängerung), chm. (Tränkung) impregnation; **imprägnieren** (v--ʼ) v/a. to impregnate; ⊙ mit Kreosot to creosote; mit Kupferlösung to copperize.
impraktikabel [lt.] *a.* (untunlich) impracticable, unfeasible.
Impresario [it.] *m* (a. (Unternehmer von Theater-ꝛc. Vorstellungen) (head) manager, impresario; e-s Künstlers *auch:* business-man or -manager, financial agent.
Impressionismus [neu-lt., fr.] *m* paint. (den ersten Eindruck wiedergebende Malerei) impressionism.
Imprimatur [lt. es werde gedruckt] *n* printing-license, *a.* imprimatur; auf Korrekturbogen: press; das ~ erteilen to sign for press, vom Zensor: to allow a book, &c. to be printed or published.
Improvisation [it.] *f* (Stegreifdichtung) extempore poetry, *auch*: improvisation.
Improvisator *m* ⨀, ~in *f* improvisator, extempore poet(ess *f*); **improvisieren** v/a. u. v/n. (h.) to improvise, to make extempore poetry or speeches.
Impuls [lt.] *m* a. (Antrieb) impulse; **impulsiv** *a.* (dem inneren Antrieb rasch folgend) impulsive.
Imse *prov.* [ahd.] *f* ⨀ = Ameise.
im-stande [in dem Stande] prädikatives *a.*: sein to be able; er ist nicht aufzustehen he cannot get up; sie ist nicht mehr das Haus zu führen she is no longer able (or fit. strong enough) to manage the house.
Im-stiche-lassen *n* leaving a p. in the lurch, abandonment of a p.
in [ahd.: in: lt. *in*: grch. *en*] *prp.* mit dem dat. auf die Frage: wo?, zeitlich: wann?, mit dem acc. auf die Frage: wohin? Mit dem dat. des Artikels „dem" oft zf.-gezogen in „im", mit dem acc. „das" in „ins": **1.** räumlich (ant. aus) a) (Frage: wo?) in, at; (Frage: wohin?) (in)to; in der Fremde in foreign lands, abroad; in die Fremde to foreign lands, abroad; in dem (a. im) Gefängnisse in jail, in prison; in unserem (unsern) Garten in(to) our garden; im Hause in(side) the house, indoors; ins Haus gehen ... into the house or indoors; in die Höhe steigen to ascend; in der Stadt in the town (in London oft: in town); im ersten Stocke on the first floor; in jenem Orte at (genauer: in) that place; in der Kirche (Schule) sein ... at church (school); in die Kirche (Schule) gehen ... to church (school); im Bette liegen to lie in bed *or* (P u. †) abed; ins Bett schlüpfen to slip into bed; im Theater at the theatre, ins Th. to the theatre; b) vor den Namen der Länder, Inseln ꝛc.: in Preußen in Prussia; in der Türkei in Turkey; in West-Indien in the West Indies; in Sizilien in Sicily; im Amazongebiete in the basin of the Amazon; im südlichen Frankreich in the south of France; in ganz Deutschland in the whole of Germany, throughout G.; in die

Schweiz reisen to go to Switzerland; in Zentral-Afrika eindringen to penetrate into central Africa; c) vor Städtenamen meist: at, um das Innere der Stadt zu bezeichnen, *auch*: in, zB. in Köln at Cologne, genauer: in Cologne (itself); vor den Namen großer Hauptstädte meist: in; in London in (nie.: at) London; in Paris in (weniger genau: at) Paris; in der Stadt Lyon in the city of Lyons; Herr Professor N. in (od. an der Universität) Bonn Professor N. of Bonn (University); d) vor Schriftstellernamen u. Werken: in; im Milton in Milton, im ganzen Shakespeare in the whole of Sh.('s works); es kommt im Faust vor it occurs in Faust; e) nach einem Superlativ: der reichste Kaufmann in der Stadt, im Lande the richest merchant in the town, in the land; f) auf die Frage: wie lang?, wie breit? ꝛc., zB. zehn Fuß in die (od. der) Länge, Breite ꝛc. ten feet in length, width. &c. — **2.** zeitlich: a) Dauer (= binnen während): in drei Tagen vollenden to complete (with)in three days; in m-r Jugend in my youth or young days, when I was young; im vorigen Jahre in the past year; last year; in diesem Jahre in the present year; this year; in dieser (späten) Stunde at this (late) hour; b) Termin (= nach Verlauf von): wir reisen in acht Tagen we shall leave in a week('s time) or within a week or a week hence; heute in vierzehn Tagen this day fortnight; c) vor Jahreszahlen, Monatsnamen ꝛc.: im Jahre 1899 in (the year) 1899; im (Monat) Februar in (the month of) February; im Frühling, Herbst in (the) spring, in (the) autumn; in der Fastenzeit in (or during) Lent; in den frühen Morgenstunden in the early (or small) hours of the morning, *auch*: at dawn; in der Nacht in the night, at night(-time). — **3.** Art und Weise: in großer Eile in great haste; im Frieden leben mit // to live at peace with //; in Gala, im Gesellschafts-anzuge in full dress; ich habe es ihm ins Gesicht gesagt I told him to his face; in gewisser Hinsicht in some respects; im Kreise in a circle; in kurzen Worten in short, briefly; in voller Trauer in full mourning. — **4.** äußere Verhältnisse, Lebensstellung ꝛc.: in Armut (Reichtum) in poverty (wealth), in poor (good) circumstances; ein Mann in seinen Jahren (seiner Stellung) a man of his years (in his position); Kassierer in einem Bankhause cashier in (or at) a bank; Offizier in der Garde officer in the Guards. — **5.** Einteilung, Verwandlung: in drei Teile (ein)teilen to divide in(to) three parts; in ein Tier verwandeln to change (or transform) into an animal. — **6.** Redens-arten: in der besten Absicht with the best intention; in Geschäften ausgehen to go out on business; in ärmlicher Kleidung with scanty clothing; so et. habe ich in meinem ganzen Leben nicht gesehen I have never seen the like; in Schutz nehmen to take under one's

protection; in See stechen to put to sea; in unseren Tagen in our days, nowadays; ich habe ihn in (seit) vierzehn Tagen nicht gesehen I have not seen him for a fortnight; er war in Verlegenheit ... puzzled, ... at a loss what to do or to say; sich in Wein betrinken to get drunk (F boozed) on wine; es ist et. Anziehendes in seinen Zügen there is something attractive in (or about) his features; in (langen) Zwischenräumen at (long) intervals.

In¹... (ᵛ...) in Zssgn mst durch das gerund der verbs übersetzt, zB.: In-die-handnehmen n taking in hand.

in²... (ᵛ...) [It.] als negatives Präfix vor (it.) a. u. s. (= un...), zB.: **in-adäquat** (ᵛᵛ‿ᴸ) ☞ a. ⑯ (unzureichend) inadequate.

in-akkurat (ᵛᵛ‿‿) [It.] a. ⑯ (ungenau) inaccurate; not quite exact.

in-aktiv ⚹ (ᵛᵛ‿) [fr.] a. ⑯ (untätig) inactive; **In-aktivität** (ᵛᵛ‿ᵛᵛ‿) f ㊻ inactivity; (Muße) leisure.

In-angriff-nahme (ᵛ‿ᵛᵛ‿ᴸᵛ) f ㊽ (first) start (or beginning) made with a th., setting-about a th.; 🚂 a. cutting (or breaking the ground for) a railway; weitS. operations pl. preliminary (or introductory) to a larger enterprise.

In-anklage-stand-(ver)setzung (ᵛ‿ᵛᵛ‿ᴸᵛ) f ㊽ jur. putting a p. on his defence; prosecution of a p.

In-anspruch-nahme (ᵛ‿ᵛᵛ‿ᵛᴸᵛ) f ㊽ laying claim to, ⚹ requisition; ~ seiner Zeit taking up his (or one's) time; völlige ~ engrossment, complete absorption. [sprochen) inarticulate.]

in-artikuliert (ᵛᵛ‿ᵛ‿ᴸ) a. ⑯ (undeutlich ge-

In-aufnahme-kommen (ᵛ‿ᴸᵛ‿ᵛᵛ) n ㊽ coming into vogue or favour or fashion.

In-augural-rede (ᵛ‿ᵛ‿ᴸ‿‿) [It.] f ㊷ inaugural speech or address.

in-augurieren (ᵛ‿ᵛᴸᵛ‿) [It.] I v/a. (eröffnen, einweihen) to inaugurate. — II ~ n ㊽ u. **-ung** f ㊻ inauguration.

In-aussicht-stellung (ᵛ‿ᴸᵛ‿ᵛᵛ) f ㊻ opening up a prospect, holding out hopes; die ~ der Bezahlung prospect of (or prospective, promised) payment.

In-begriff¹ (ᵛᵛ‿) m ⓜc. 1. mit ~ aller Einzelheiten including (or inclusive of) all particulars; ⚫ mit ~ der Spesen all charges included. — 2. (alles zfgefaßt) sum, total, totality, aggregate, (fr.) *tout ensemble*; (Wesen) substance; (Auszug) epitome; kurzer ~ summary (of contents), brief extract, abridgment.

inbegriff² sein f. Begriff. [begreifen II.)
in-begriffen ⚹ (ᵛᵛᵛ) a. u. adv. = ein-)
In-betracht-nahme (ᵛ‿ᵛ‿ᵉᵈᵗ‿ᴸᵛ) f ㊽ taking into consideration.

In-betrieb-setzung, -stellung (ᵛ‿ᵛ‿ᴸᵛ‿) f ㊻ setting in(to) working order; ~ einer Eisenbahn, Straßenbahn 2c. opening of a railway, a tramline, &c.

In-brunst (ᴸᵛ) [Brunst] f ⑩ fervour, devoutness, ardour; mit ~ fervently, ardently; **in-brünstig** (ᴸᵛᵛ) a. fervent, devout, ardent.

Inchoativ(um) ☞ (ᵛ‿ᴸf, ᵛᵛ‿ᴸ) [It. inc(h)ōhātus (nur) angefangen] n ⓜd. gr. (Übergangszeitwort) inchoative (verb).

in-deklinabel (ᵛ‿ᵛ‿ᴸᵛ) [It.] a. ⑯(D9) gr. (unbeflektierbar) indeclinable (noun).

in-dem (ᵛ‿ᴸ) I adv. 1. at that moment; weitS. = indes I. — II cj. 2. Gleichzeitigkeit: whilst, while; mit verschiedenem Subjekt in beiden Sätzen: bibl. 2 er säete, fiel etliches an den Weg (Luther) when he sowed some seeds fell by the wayside; jetzt mst mit gleichem Subjekt in beiden Sätzen, oft durch das *p.pr.* übersetzt, zB.: 2 er sprach, sah er whilst speaking he saw; die Deutschen eroberten, 2 sie bekehrten (Ranke) the Germans conquered while (they were) converting. — 3. ⚹ Grund: since, as, because. — 4. Mittel: meist by mit *p.pr.*, zB. er gewann, 2 er einen kühnen Zug tat ... by making a bold move.

Indemnität (ᵛᵛ‿ᵛᴸ) [It.] f ㊽ (Straflosigkeit) indemnity.

In-den-Wind-schlagen (ᵛ‿ᴸ‿ᴸᵛ) n ㊽ casting to the winds, paying no heed (or attention) to.

independent (ᵛ‿ᵛᴸᵛ) [fr.] a. ⑯ u. ~ m ㊷ (unabhängig) independent, *eccl.* auch congregationalist.

Inder (ᴸᵛ) [It.; grch.; *Hindu] m ㉒, ~in f ㊵ Indian, Hindoo (woman f).

in-des (ᵛᴸ) [in des], **in-dessen** (ᵛᴸᵛ) I adv. 1. during that time, (mittlerweile) meanwhile, in the meantime. — II cj. 2. mit dem v. am Satzende: indem 2. — 3. mit dem v. vor dem Subjekt: (dennoch) nevertheless, for all that; (dessen-ungeachtet) despite (of) all that; (immerhin) yet, still; however.

Index (ᴸᵛ) [It.] m ⓜa.㊺ (Verzeichnis, Zeiger an Werkzeugen, Zeigefinger, *eccl.* Verzeichnis der verbotenen Bücher) index; *Cath. eccl.* Bücher auf den ~ setzen to put ... on the index or the expurgatory.

in-dezent (ᵛᵛᴸ) [It.] a. ⑯ (unanständig) indecent; **Indezenz** f ㊽ indecency.

India-faser (ᴸᵛ(ᵛ)‿ᵛ) f ㊹ = Agavefaser.

Indianer (ᵛ‿(ᵛ)ᴸᵛ) [span. ⁓ Kolumbus hielt Amerika für Indien] m ㉒, ~in f ㊵ (Ureinwohner[in] von Amerika) Red Indian; pl. auch: red-skins pl.

Indianer-geschichte(n pl.) f (ᴸ...) ㊵ Red Indian tale(s pl.); **-häuptling** m ㉒ Red Indian chief; **-sommer** m, Am. (Spätsommer) Indian summer; **-stamm** m Red Indian tribe; **-territorium** ⚥ n Indian Territory; **-weib** n Red Indian woman, Am. squaw.

indianisch (ᵛ‿(ᵛ)ᴸᵛ) a. ⑯ (den Indianern eigen) (Red) Indian, of the red man.

Indices = Indizes.

In-die-Hände-klatschen (ᵛ‿ᴸᵛ‿ᴸᵛ‿) n ㊽ clapping of hands, applause.

Indien ⚥ (ᴸᵛ(ᵛ)) [It. *I'ndia*] *npr* n ㉓α. (East) India, *poet.*, &c. auch: the (East) Indies pl.; vgl. Hindustan; das englische ~ British India; Ministerium für ~ India Office; bfd. ehm. **~fahrer** ⚹ m ㉒ (Schiff) Indiaman.

In-dienst-stellung (ᵛ‿ᴸ‿ᴸᵛ‿) f ㊻: a) ⚹ call(ing in) of troops; b) ⚓ e-s Kriegsschiffes commissioning of a man-of-war.

Indier ⚥ (ᴸᵛ(ᵛ)) m ㉒, **~in** f ㊵ = Inder.

indifferent ☞ (ᴸ‿ᵛᵛᴸ) [It.] a. ⑯ (gleichgültig) indifferent (a. *chm.*); **Indifferentismus** (ᵛᵛᵛᵛᵛ) m ㉗ *phls., rel.* indifferentism; **Indifferenz** (ᵛᵛᵛᴸ) f ㊽ indifference (a. *phys., chm.*); **Indifferenz-punkt** m ㉒ *phls.* point of indifference, neutral line.

indig-blau (ᴸᵛ...) ⚹ a. ⑯ u. ~ n ㉒. *chm.* indigo blue, ☞ indigotin ($C_{16}H_{10}N_2O_2$); **-blau-schwefelsäure** f, *chm.* ☞ sulphindigotic acid; vgl. Indigo...

Indigenat (ᵛᵛᵛᴸ) [neu-lt.] n ⓜc. (Heimatsrecht) denizenship; (Rechte e-s Eingeborenen) native (or indigenous) rights pl., rights pl. of natives or aborigines.

indigniert (ᵛᵛᴸ) [It.] a. ⑯ (voll) of indignation or wrath.

Indigo (ᴸᵛᵛ) [span. indischer...] m ⓙ 1. ♀: a) gemeiner ~ Indian indigo (*Indigo'fera tincto'ria*); b) wilder ~ wild indigo, indigo-broom (*Bapti'sia tincto'ria*); c) deutscher ~ = Färberwaid. — 2. 🗲 (blauer Farbstoff) indigo; roter ~ cudbear.

Indigo-(auf)lösung 🗲 u. ⓧ (ᴸᵛᵛ‿ᵛ‿) f ㉒ indigo solution; **-bau** m, **-bereitung** f culture, preparation (or manufacture) of ind.; **-braun** n ind. brown; **-ernte** f ind. crop; **-fabrik** f ind. works pl.; **-farbe** f indigo(-dye); **-haltig** a.: ~ indigotic; **-karmin** m indigo carmine, soluble ind.; **-küpe** f ind.-vat; **-lösung** f = **-auflösung**; **-pflanze** ♀ f ind. plant; vgl. Indigo 1.; **-sauer** a. *chm.*: ~ indigotic, **-saures** Salz indigotate; **-säure** f indigotic acid; **-tinktur** f indigo-tincture or -composition; **-weiß** n indigo white, ☞ indigogen; vgl. auch Indig-...

Indikativ (ᴸᵛᵛ‿f ob. ᵛᵛ‿ᴸf) [It.] m ⓜd. *gr.* (Wirklichkeitsform) indicative (mood); **Lisch** (ᵛᵛᵛᴸᵛ) a. ⑯ *gr.* indicative, adv. a. in the indicative; **~konstrukti'on** f ㉒ construction with the indicative.

indirekt (ᴸᵛᴸ) [It.] a. ⑯ (mittelbar) indirect, *jur. 2c.* oft: collateral; ⚹ 2es Feuer indirect (or high-angle) fire; 2e Frage indirect question; *pol.* 2es Wahlrecht, oft: class franchise.

indisch (ᴸᵛ) [Indien] a. ⑯ Indian, Hindoo; ♀ ~er Ozean Indian Ocean.

indiskret (ᵛᵛᴸ) [It.] a. ⑯ (unbesonnen) indiscreet; **~ion** (ᵛᵛ‿tz(ᵛ)ᴸ) f ㊽ indiscretion, ill-considered action.

in-disponiert (ᵛᵛᵛ‿ᴸ) [It.] a. ⑯ (nicht aufgelegt) indisposed.

Indium ☞ (ᴸᵛ(ᵛ)) [neu-lt.] n ㉓ (o. pl.) *chm.* (seltenes Metall) Indium.

individualisieren (ᵛᵛᵛ‿ᵛ‿ᵛᴸᵛ‿) [fr.] I v/a. ㉙ (einzeln behandeln) to individualize. — II ~ n ㉓ u. **Individualisierung** f ㊻ individualization.

Individualismus (ᵛᵛᵛ‿ᵛᵛᴸᵛ) m ㉗ (Stellung des einzelnen) individualism.

Individualität (ᵛᵛᵛ‿ᵛᵛᴸ) [fr.-lt.] f ㊽ *phls.* (Eigenart) individuality.

individuell (ᵛᵛᵛ‿ᵛᴸ) [fr.] a. ⑯ (eigentümlich, persönlich) individual.

Individuum (ᵛᵛᴸᵛᵛ) [It.] n ㉘ (Einzelwesen) individual (being or person).

Indiz (ᵛᴸ) [It. *indi'cium*] n ㉙ *jur.* circumstantial evidence.

Indizes (ᴸᵛᵛ) *pl. v.* Index.

Indizi-en-beweis (ᵛᴸ(ᵛ)ᵛ...) m ㉒ proof by means of circumstantial evidence.

indizieren ☞ (ᵛᵛᴸᵛ‿) [It.] v/a. ㉙ (anzeigen) to indicate; *mech.* indizierter Druck indicated pressure.

Indizium (ᵛᴸᵛ(ᵛ)) [It.] n ㉘ = Indiz.

Signs (see page XVII): F familiar; P vulgar; F̄ flash; ⚹ rare; † obsolete (died); * new word (born); ⁺⁺ incorrect; ♪ music;

[Indochina] — 547 — [inhalieren]

Indo-china ♀ (⸗-...) n ⑫ Indo-China; **⸗europäisch** a. ㊻; **⸗germane** m Indo-European, Aryan; **⸗germanisch** a. Indo-Germanic.

Indossament ⊛ [it. f. Indosso], **Indossement** [fr.] (⌣⌣⸗) n ⑪b. endorsement; **Indossant, Indossent** (⌣⌣⸗) m ㊷ endorser; **Indossat** (⌣⌣⸗) m ㊷ endorsee; **indossieren** (⌣⌣⸗⌣) v/a. ㊺ (auf der Rückseite quittieren) to endorse a bill.

Indosso ⊛ (⌣⸗-) [it. *in dosso* auf dem Rücken (unterzeichnet)] n ⑪ ㊽ endorsement.

Induktion ⚗ (⌣⌣tẓ(⌣)⸗) [lt.] f ㊻ (phls. Schluß vom Besonderen zum Allgemeinen, ant. Deduktio'n; elect. Erregung e-s Nebenstromes) induction.

Induktions-apparat (⸗...) m ㊷ elect. inductive machine, induction-coil; **⸗beweis** m inductive proof; **⸗elektrizität** f inductive electricity; **⸗rolle, ⸗spule** f induction-coil; **⸗strom** m inductive (or induction-)current; **⸗wage** f von Hughes: induction-balance.

induktiv ⚗ (⌣⌣f) [lt.] a. ㊻ phls., elect. (ant. deduktiv) inductive. [ductor.)

Induktor (⌣⌣⸗) [lt.] m ㉛ elect. in-)

Indult (⌣⸗) [lt. Nachsicht] m ⑪b. Cath. eccl. (päpstlicher Erlaubnisbrief) indulgence, indult; ⊛ (Stundung) grace.

Industrie (⌣⸗⌣⸗) [lt.] f ㊻ (Gewerbfleiß) industry, industrialism, manufactures pl.; weitS. trade.

Industrie-akti-en ⊛ (⌣⸗⌣⸗⸗⸗) f/pl. ㊷ industrial shares pl. or stock(s pl.); **⸗ausstellung** f industrial exhibition; **⸗erzeugnis** n industrial product, produce of manufactures.

industriell (⌣⸗⌣⸗)[fr.] I a. ㊻ (gewerbfleißig) industrial. — II ⁓e(r) m ㊸ (large) manufacturer, industrial producer.

Industrie-papiere ⊛ (⌣⸗⌣⸗...) n/pl. ㊷ shares pl. of industrial concerns; vgl. ⸗aktien; **⸗pflanze** f (Flachs, Runkelrübe ⁊c.) plant used for industrial purposes; **⸗ritter** m high-class (or elegant) swindler or sharper, one who lives by his wits, F swell-mobsman, pl. F swell mob; **⸗zweig** m branch of industry or trade, manufacturing branch, line of business.

induzieren ⚗ (⌣⸗⌣⸗) [lt.] I v/a. ㊺ phys. elektrizit. ob. magnetiSch ⁓ (beeinflussen) to induce; ⁓ ⸗ der Strom induction-current; induzierter Strom induced current. — II ⁓ n ㉓ = Induktio'n.

in-ein-ander(⸗-⸗⸗) adv. into one another, into ach other, one into the other.

in-ein-ander⸗..., In-ein-ander⸗... (⸗-⸗⸗...) in Verbindung mit verbs (immer trennbar) und in Zssgn mit verbal nouns und adjectives, zB.: ⁓ **bringen** v/a. ⑰** to put into each other; **⸗flechten** v/a. ⑪b** to interlace, intertwine, intertwist; ⁓n interlacement; **⸗fließen** v/n. (jn) ⑭d** to flow (or merge) into each other, v. Farben: to run into one another; **⸗fügen** v/a. ⑬** to fit into each other, to encase⁁; ⁓ n ㉓, **⸗fügung** f ㊻ encasement⁁; **⸗greifen** v/n. (h.) ⑭bf** to be linked together; mach. to gear (or work) into each other, to interlock; fig. to work (harmoniously) together; ⁓ n ㉓ der Ereignisse ⁊c. concatenation (or sequence, series,

chain) of events, &c.; ⁓münden anat. v/n. (h.) ⑨** von Gefäßen: ⚗ to inosculate, to anastomose; ⁓ ㉓ ⚗ inosculation, anastomosis; **⸗schieben** ⊛ v/a. ⑭c** to telescope; **⸗übergeh(e)n** n ㉓ transition (from one to the other), zo., &c.: ⚗ interosculation; **⸗weben** ⚗ v/a. ⑭b(⑱)** to interweave; **⸗winden** v/a. ⑰** to intertwine; **⸗wirken** n ㉓ working into each other's hands, co-operation.

In-empfang-nahme(⸗-⸗⸗⸗⸗-) f ㊻ e-r Sendung ⁊c.: receipt; e-r Person: reception.

infallibel (⌣⌣⸗⌣) [neu-lt.] a. ㊻ (unfehlbar) infallible. [Papstes: infallibility.)

Infallibilität (⌣⌣⸗⌣⸗⸗) f bſd. des)

infam (⌣⸗) [lt.] a. ㊻ 1. (ehrlos) infamous; eine ⁓e (schändliche) Geschichte a disgraceful affair. — 2. F das ärgert mich ⁓ (sehr) it vexes me very much or F awfully. [disgrace.)

Infamie (⌣⌣⸗) f ㊻ (Schande) infamy,)

Infant (⌣⸗) [span. Kind] m ㊷, **⁓in** f ㊼ (Prinz[essin] von königlichem Geblüt) (Spanish) infante, f infanta.

Infanterie ⚔ (⌣⌣⌣⸗, F ⌣(⌣)⸗) [nhd. 17. sae.; fr.; *span. Infantengarde] f ㊻ (Fußvolk) infantry, foot-soldiers pl.; ⁓ und Kavallerie, auch: foot and horse pl.

Infanterie-gewehr ⚔ (⌣⌣⌣⸗⸗⌣⸗) n ⑪ infantry gun; **⸗offizier** m infantry officer, officer serving in a foot-regiment; **⸗regime'nt** n infantry (or foot-) regiment.

Infanterist ⚔ (⌣⌣⌣⸗ ob. ⌣(⌣)⸗) m ㊷ foot-soldier, soldier serving on foot or in a foot-regiment, infantryman.

Infektion (⌣⌣tẓ(⌣)⸗) [lt.] f ㊻ (Ansteckung) infection; **⁓s-krankheit** (⸗...) f ㊻ infectious disease.

Infel (⸗⌣) [lt. *infula*] f ㊻ eccl. (Bischofsmütze) (bishop's) mitre.

Inferiorität (⌣⌣(⌣)-⌣⸗) [lt.] f ㊻ (Minderwert) inferiority.

infernal(isch) (⌣⌣⸗(⌣)) [lt.] a. ㊻ (höllisch) infernal, of hell.

infiltrieren (⌣⌣⸗⌣) v/a. u. v/n. (h.) ㊺ (durchseihen, eindringen) to infiltrate.

Infinitesimal-rechnung ⚗ (⌣-⌣-⌣⸗...) [neu-lt. unendlich klein] f ㊻ math. infinitesimal (or differential) calculus.

Infinitiv ⚗ (⸗⌣⸗f) [lt.] m ⑪d. gram. infinitive (mood); **⁓isch** (⸗⌣-⸗⌣) [lt.] a. ㊻ infinitival; adv. oft: in the infinitive; **⁓satz** m ㊷ infinitival (or noun-)clause or sentence.

infizierbar (⌣⸗⌣⸗) [lt.] a. ㊻ infectible.

infizieren (⌣⸗⌣⸗) [lt.] I v/a. ㊺ (anstecken) to infect. — II ⁓ n ㉓ und **Infizierung** f ㊻ infection.

in flagranti (⸗⌣⸗⌣) [lt.] red-handed.

Inflexion (⌣⌣(⌣)⸗) [lt.] f ㊻ gr., &c. inflexion. [influenza, F co. a. influ.)

Influenza (⌣⌣⸗⌣) [it.] f ㊻ path. (Grippe)

influieren (⌣⌣⸗⌣) [lt.] v/a. und v/n. (h.) ㊺ (Einfluß ausüben) to influence a p., to exert (or have) influence over a p.

In-fluß-bringen (⸗-⸗⸗⌣) n ㉓ bſd. ⊛: fusion, liquation, liquefaction; fig. setting a th. afloat or going, auch: flotation of companies, &c.

in-folge (⸗⸗⌣) prp. mit gen.: ⁓ Ihres Anerbietens in consequence of (or owing to, on the strength of) your

offer; **⁓dessen** (⸗⸗⌣) adv. consequently, owing to this or to which.

Information (⸗⌣⸗tẓ(⌣)⸗) [lt. *informā'tiō*] f ㊻ 1. (Mitteilung) information; behufs ⁓ for the purpose of inquiry. — 2. (Lehren) instruction.

informieren (⌣⌣⸗⌣) v/a. u. sich ⁓ v/refl. ㊺ 1. (in Kenntnis setzen) to inform; sich ⁓ to seek (or gather) information, to make inquiry. — 2. (lehren) to instruct.

In-frage-stellung (⸗-⸗⸗⌣⸗) f ㊻ questioning a th.; casting doubts upon a th.

Inful (⸗⌣) [lt.] f ㊻ f. Infel; **infulieren** (⌣⌣⸗⌣) v/a. ㊺ to (invest with a) mitre; infulierter Abt mitred abbot.

Infusion (⌣-(⌣)⸗) [lt.] f ㊻ (Aufguß) infusion; **⁓s-tierchen** n (pl.), **Infusori-en** (⌣-⸗(⌣)⸗) n/pl. ㉘ infusoria(ns), animalcules, (it.) animalculæ pl.

In-gang-setzung ⊛ (⸗-⸗⸗⌣⸗) f ㊻: ⁓ e-r Maschine setting a machine going, gearing an engine.

Ingenieur (⸗G⁀ni̇ȷ̈⸗r) [fr.] m ⑪d. engineer; **⁓-korps** ⚔ (⸗⸗...) n ⑫ corps of engineers, engineer-corps; **⁓-kunst** f (science of) engineering; **⁓-offizier** ⚔ m officer of engineers.

Inger (⸗⌣) m ㉒ ichth. (Bauchkiemer) hag(-fish), myxine (*Myxi'ne glutino'sa*).

Ingermanland ♀ (⸗⌣⌣) npr/n. ⑨ a. Ingria; **ingermanländisch** a. ㊻ Ingrian.

In-gesinde (⸗⸗⌣⌣) n ㉓ poet. = Gesinde.

in-gleichen ⚗ (⸗⸗⌣) adv. likewise, in the same way; (ferner) moreover, besides.

Ingredi-ens (⸗⌣⸗⌣) n ㉚, **Ingredienz** (⸗-(⌣)⸗) [lt.] f ㊻ (Zutat) ingredient, component.

In-grimm (⸗⌣) m ⑪c. concealed rage or anger, inward (or secret) wrath, spite; **in-grimmig** (⸗⌣⌣) a. ㊻ deeply enraged, very angry, full of (secret) wrath or spite.

ingrossieren (⌣⌣⸗⌣) [neu-lt.] v/a. ㊺ jur. Urkunden ⁓ (ins reine schreiben) to engross ...; **Ingrossist** (⌣⌣⸗) m ㊷ engrosser.

Ingwer ♀ (⸗⌣) [mhd., grch., *ind.] m ㊷ ginger (Wurzelknollen von *Zi'ngiber officina'le*); **⁓-artig** a. ㊻: ⚗ zingiberaceous; **⁓-bier** n ㉓, **⁓-limona'de** f ginger-beer or -ale, F gi.-pop; **⁓-eingemachte(s)** n preserved gi.; **⁓-pulver** ⊛ n powdered gi.; **⁓-wein** m gi.-wine; **⁓-wurzel** ♀ f whole ginger(-root).

In-haber (⸗⌣⌣) m ㊷, **⁓in** f ㊼ holder, person in possession, e-s Hauses ⁊c.: occupier, occupant, tenant, (Eigentümer) owner, proprietor, e-s Geschäfts: head (of the firm), principal; univ. ⁓ e-s akademischen Grades graduate (of a university); eccl. ⁓ e-r Pfründe incumbent; ⚔ ⁓ e-s Regiments honorary colonel ...; ⊛ ⁓ e-s Patents patentee; e-s Wechsels: bearer; auf den ⁓ lautend (payable) to bearer; auf den ⁓ lautender Zahlschein cheque to bearer; **⁓-papier** ⊛ n ㉓ scrip (or bond) payable to bearer.

inhaftieren (⌣⌣⸗⌣) [dtsch-lt. *Haft] I v/a. ㊺ = verhaften. — II ⁓ n ㉓ u. **Inhaftierung** f ㊻ imprisonment.

Inhalation ⚗ (⌣⌣-tẓ(⌣)⸗) f ㊻ physiol. (Einatmung) inhalation, weitS. breathing; **⁓s-apparat** m inhaler; **inhalieren**(⌣-⌣⸗⌣) v/a. ㊺ (einatmen) to inhale, breathe.

⚗ scientific; ♀ botanical; ♀ geography; ⊛ machinery; ⚒ mining; ⚔ military; ⚓ marine; ⊛ commercial; ✉ postal; 🚂 railway.

[Inhalt] — 548 — [inner]

In-halt (⌣‒) m ⓐc. 1. e-s Gefäßes: contents pl. of a jar, &c.; matter contained in a box, &c.; e-s hohlen Raumes: capacity; körperlicher ~ einer räumlichen Figur volume of a solid body, solid or cubic(al) contents pl.; ~ e-r Fläche area of a surface. — 2. ~ (Stoff) e-s Gespräches ꝛc. tenor (or purport, subject-matter) ...; wesentlicher ~ main substance or purport, gist; Brief ꝛc. des folgenden ~s ... running as follows, ... to the following effect.

in-haltlich (⌣⌣) adv. as (or with regard) to the contents or purport of a letter, &c.; as far as the matter (or substance) is concerned.

inhalts ⊕ (⌣‒) (nach Inhalt) Kanzleistil: ♀ dieses by virtue of these presents.

In-halts-angabe (⌣‒...) f ⑫ statement of contents; vgl. =verzeichnis; =anzeige f = =verzeichnis; =bestimmung f, math. measurement of a square surface or a solid, ⊕ e-s Fasses ꝛc.: gauging; ♀gleich a. ⓖ math. of equal (or like) volume.

in-halt(s)-leer (⌣⌣...) a. ⓖ, ♀los a. empty; (de)void of substance; ♀reich, ♀schwer a. full of meaning or matter; (wesentlich) essential; most important; (bedeutsam) significant, momentous, weighty.

In-halts-verzeichnis (⌣‒...) n ⑫ list (v. Büchern): table of contents, summary, am Schlusse e-s Buches: index; ♀voll a. ⓖ full of significance; (reich) copious, (umfangreich) comprehensive; vgl. inhaltreich; =wert ⊕ m value of (the) contents; =zeichen n, =zettel m label, ticket.

Inhärenz ⃞ (⌣‒⌣) [lt.] f ⓖ (Anhaften) inherence, inherency.

inhärieren (⌣⌣‒⌣) v/n. (h.) ⓖ: e-r Sache (dat.) ♀ to be inherent in a th.; ♀d inherent.

inhibieren (⌣⌣‒⌣) [lt.] I v/a. ⓖ (verbieten) to prohibit, jur. a. to inhibit; (einhalten) to stay (or stop) proceedings or a suit. — II ~ n ⓑ u. **Inhibierung** (⌣‒⌣) f ⓖ prohibition, inhibition; jur. a. estoppel.

inhuman (⌣‒) [lt.] a. ⓖ (unmenschlich) inhuman; ~ität (⌣‒‒⌣) f ⓖ inhumanity.

Initial-buchstab(e) (⌣⌣(⌣)‒‒(⌣) m ⑫, **Initiale** (⌣-tß(⌣)‒) f ⓖ typ. (Anfangsbuchstabe) initial (letter).

Initiative (⌣⌣tß(⌣)-‒⌣⌣) f ⓖ = Anregung; die ~ ergreifen to take the initiative or the lead, to make the first move; aus eigener ~, auch: of one's own accord; keine ~ h. to be lacking initiative or independence of action.

Injektion (⌣tß(⌣)‒) [lt.] f ⓖ (Einspritzung) injection; ~s-spritze ("...) f ⓖ syringe for injection.

Injektor ⊕ (⌣⌣⌣) [lt.] m ⑪ (Einspritzer) injector, steam-blower. **[to inject.)**

injizieren ⃞ (⌣‒⌣) v/a. ⓖ (einspritzen)ʃ

Injuri-e (⌣‒(⌣)) [lt.] f ⓖ defamation, libel, insult, tätliche: assault.

Inka (‒⌣) [peruanisch] m ⓑ (ehm. herrschende Kaste in Peru) Inca.

inkarnat¹ ⃞ (⌣⌣‒) [lt.] a. ⓖ (fleischfarben) flesh-coloured; pink.

Inkarnat² (⌣‒) [lt.] n ⓐc. flesh-colour, paint. auch: flesh-tints pl.

Inkarnation (⌣⌣tß(⌣)‒) [lt.] f ⓖ bsd. rel. (Fleischwerdung) incarnation.

Inkarnat-klee ♣ (⌣⌣‒...) m ⑫ flesh-coloured trefoil (Trifo′lium incarna′tum).

inkarniert (⌣⌣‒) [lt.] a. ⓖ (fleischgeworden) made flesh, incarnate.

Inkasso ⊕ (⌣‒⌣) [lt.] n ⓓ (⑱) (Einziehung von Geldern) encashment; zum ~ einsenden to send bills for encashment or to be (en)cashed; e-n Wechsel zum ~ erhalten to undertake the cashing (or collecting) of a bill.

Inkasso-spesen (⌣⌣⌣...) f/pl. ⓖ charges for cashing or recovery.

inkl. abbr. = **inklusive** (einschließlich).

Inklination (⌣⌣‒tß(⌣)‒) [lt.] f ⓖ, bsd. phys. (Abweichung von der Horizontalen) inclination; ~s-nadel f ⓖ dipping-needle, inclination compass.

inklinieren (⌣⌣‒⌣) v/n. (h.) ⓖ: zu et. ♀ (hinneigen) to incline to(wards) a th.

inklusive (⌣⌣‒⌣) [lt.] adv. (einschließlich) inclusively, with inclusion of; ⊕ ♀ Sack sack included.

inkognito¹ (⌣‒⌣⌣) [lt.] adv. (unter fremdem Namen) incognito, F incog.

Inkognito² (⌣‒⌣⌣) n ⓓ incognito; das ~ wahren to preserve one's incognito.

inkommensurabel (⌣⌣⌣‒⌣⌣) [lt.] a. ⓖ math. (ohne gemeinschaftliches Maß) incommensurable.

inkommodieren (⌣⌣⌣‒⌣) [lt.] v/a. ⓖ (belästigen) to incommode, inconvenience.

inkompetent (⌣⌣⌣⌣) [lt.] a. ⓖ (unzuständig) incompetent; (unfähig) unfit. [fitness.)

Inkompetenz (⌣) f ⓖ incompetence; unʃ

in-komplett (⌣⌣⌣) [lt.] a. ⓖ (unvollständig) incomplete. [sistent.)

inkonsequent (⌣⌣⌣⌣) [lt.] a. ⓖ inconʃ

Inkonsequenz (⌣⌣⌣⌣) f ⓖ inconsistency.

Inkorporation (⌣⌣⌣-tß(⌣)‒) [lt.] f ⓖ (Einverleibung) incorporation.

inkorporieren (⌣⌣⌣‒⌣) v/a. ⓖ to incorporate, to embody; inkorporiert incorporate. [correct.)

inkorrekt (⌣⌣⌣) [lt.] a. ⓖ (ungenau) inʃ

Inkorrektheit (⌣⌣‒⌣) f ⓖ incorrectness.

In-kraft-treten (⌣.‒.‒⌣) n ⓑ coming into force, e-r Verordnung: passing into law.

inkriminieren ⃞ (⌣⌣⌣‒⌣) [neu-lt.] v/a. ⓖ jur. (anklagen) to incriminate, to charge.

Inkrustation ⃞ (⌣⌣-tß(⌣)‒) [lt.] f ⓖ (das Verkrusten) incrustation.

inkrustier/en ⃞ (⌣⌣‒⌣) [lt.] I v/a. und sich ♀ v/refl. ⓖ to incrust(ate); sich ♀ to get incrusted or covered with a crust. — II ~ n ⓑ, ♀ung f ⓖ incrustation.

Inkubations-zeit ⃞ (⌣⌣-tß(⌣)‒...) f ⓖ (Brütezeit) time (or period) of incubation.

Inkubus ⃞ (⌣‒⌣) [lt.] m ⓟ path. = Alp¹ 2.

Inkulpat (⌣⌣‒) [lt.] m ⓐ = Beschuldigter.

Inkunabel(n pl.) ⃞ (⌣-‒⌣) [lt.] f ⓖ (Erstlingsdruck(e)) incunabula pl.

inkurabel (⌣‒‒⌣) [neu-lt.] a. ⓖ (D9) (unheilbar) incurable, beyond (all) remedy.

In-lage (⌣‒⌣) f ⓖ = Einlage.

In-land (⌣‒) [mhd.: inland] n ⓐc. (pl. ⧹) (ant. Ausland) home (or native) country; (Innere des Landes) interior of the country; im In- und Auslande at home and abroad; ⊕ fürs ~ arbeiten ⓖ to work for home consumption or for the home market; im ~e angefertigt, hergestellt home-made; im ~e gelegen (lying) inland.

In-land-anleihe ⊕ (⌣‒...) f ⓖ internal loan. [(of the country).)

In-länder (⌣‒⌣) m ⓐ, ~in f ⓖ nativeʃ

inländisch (⌣‒⌣⌣) a. ⓖ native, home-born, indigenous, ⊕ home-made (goods), inland (trade), internal (traffic).

In-lands-absatz ⊕ (⌣‒...) m ⓖ home-consumption; =paß m passport for the home country. [central letter.)

In-laut (⌣‒) m ⓐc. gram. medial sound,ʃ

inlautend (⌣‒⌣) a. ⓖ medial, central.

Inlet(t) (⌣‒) [ndd. Einlaß] n ⓐc. (Überzug für Federbetten) bed-tick.

in-liegend (⌣‒⌣) a. ⓖ enclosed, adv. as (an) enclosure; ~e(s) n ⓖ the enclosed

in-mitten prp. mit gen. in the midst (or middle, centre) of //; die Zunge der Wage steht ♀ the scales are evenly balanced. [niffen) in kind.)

in natura (⌣‒⌣‒⌣) [lt.] (in Naturerzeug-ʃ

inne (⌣⌣) [ahd.] adv. I (in Besitz) in one's possession; in Verbindung mit verbs (immer trennbar) und in Sssgn mit verbal nouns: **inne-behalten**: a) v/a. ⓐa*/* to retain; jur. (vorenthalten) to detain; b) ~ n ⓑ retention; detention; ♀haben: a) v/a. ⓑb** to hold, have, possess; eine Stadt ꝛc.: to occupy; eine Sprache: to be master of; eine Stelle to fill; oft ⧺ ♀de Stelle (statt: Stelle, die j. hat) situation held by a p.; b) ~ n ⓑ possession, occupancy, occupation; ♀halten ⓐa**: a) v/a. die richtige Entfernung ♀ to observe the right distance; die Zeit ♀ to keep to the time, to be punctual; b) v/n. (h.) ♀ to stop, (eine Pause machen) to (make a) pause (a. ♪); mit der Arbeit ♀ to suspend work, to cease (or leave off) working; c) ~ n ⓑ, =haltung f ⓖ: zu a: observation; zu b: pause; suspension. — II within; (im Hause) indoors; mittendrinne just in the middle, right in the centre; in Verbindung mit verbs (meist zu einem Worte vereinigt, immer trennbar): **inne-lassen** v/a. ⓐa** to leave at home.

innen (⌣‒) adv. (ant. außen) within, (on the) inside, internally, (im Hause) indoors; Straßenbahn ꝛc.: ♀ alles besetzt full (or no room) inside; ♀ und außen within and without, inside and out(side), nach ♀ zu inwards, towards the interior or centre; ⊕ auch: home; von ♀ (heraus) from within.

Innen-bekleidung (⌣‒...) f ⓖ, =belag ⚓ ⊥ interior (or inside) planking; ♀bords ⚓ adv. inboard; =fläche f interior (or inner, inside) surface; =front ⚓, arch. e-r Mauer inner side (or surface) of a wall; =haut f: a) anat. inner skin, internal membrane; b) ⚓ der Fruchthülle ⃞ endocarp; =leben n internal life; =raum m interior (space); =seite f = =fläche; =wache ⚓ ⊥ im Biwak: inner guard; =weite f eines Zimmers ꝛc. internal dimensions pl.; =welt f internal (or intellectual) world, auch: realm of thought, ⃞ microcosm; =winkel m, math. internal angle. — Vgl. a. Binnen=...

inner (⌣‒) [ahd.: inner] ⓖ(D9) I a. = Position nur Attribut, als Prädikat dafür „innerlich", comp. fehlt, sup. innerst) 1. interior; (tiefer im Innern liegend) inner, central; (verborgen) inward, internal (part, disease, &c.), hidden (recess)

Zeichen (s. S. XVII): F familiär; P Volkssprache; F Gaunersprache; ⧹ selten; † alt (auch gestorben); * neu (auch geboren); ⁺+ unrichtig.

[Innerafrika] — 549 — [inspizieren]

(wesentlich) intrinsic (value, virtue, &c.); (das eigene Haus ob. Land betr.) domestic, home, v. Streitigkeiten 2c. auch: intestine; die 2en Angelegenheiten domestic (or home) affairs, pol. home department; aus dem Antrieb spontaneously, of one's own free will; 2e Einrichtung internal arrangement(s pl.); ⚔ 2e Linie inner line; eccl. 2e Mission home mission; 2e Stimme inner voice; was die 2e Stimme spricht (SCH.) what the voice within us tells. — 2. 2ft sup. in(ner)most; die 2ften Gedanken the most intimate (or most secret) thoughts. — II ~e(s) n ⓖ 3. interior, inside; heart of a country or town; (Mitte) midst; im ~n der Erde in the bowels (or within the womb) of the earth; pol. Minister des ~n minister for home affairs, in England: Home Secretary; Ministerium des ~n Home Office. — 4. im sup. das ~ste @ the innermost (or most central) part; (Mittelpunkt) centre; im ~sten treffen, verletzen to strike home; sein ~stes his inmost soul, a. rel. the most secret folds of his heart; bis ins ~ste to the (very) core or heart, to the in(ner)most depth.

Inner-a'frika ♀ (⌣⌢…) n ⓖ interior (or central regions pl.) of Africa; **afrika'nisch** a. ⓖ in the interior of Africa.

inner-halb (⌣⌢⌣) I adv. within, (on the) inside; inwardly. — II prp. örtlich mit gen., zeitlich mit gen. od., wenn der gen. inv., mit dat.): 2 eines Jahres, zweier Jahre within one year, two years; aber: 2 vier Jahren within (or before the end of), bsd. Am. inside of) four years.

innerlich (⌣⌣⌣) a. (ant. äußerlich) = inner 1; (herzlich) heartfelt, cordial, vgl. innig; 2er Beruf inner vocation; adv. inwardly, internally, within; (geistig) mentally, at heart, rel. spiritually; pharm. Aufschrift: 2 anzuwenden for internal use.

Innerlichkeit (⌣⌣⌣⌢) f ⓖ inwardness, internal nature; (Herzlichkeit) cordiality.

inner-politisch (⌣⌣…) a. ⓖ: 2e Fragen questions pl. of home politics or internal policy.

innerst, Innerst (⌣⌣) (sup. von inner) adv. u. s. f. inner 2 u. 4.

inne-werden (⌣⌣…) v/n. (in) ⓒ**: e-r Sache (gen.) ob. etwas 2 to perceive (or become aware of) a th., (erfahren) to learn a th.; 2wohnen v/n. (h.) ⓒ** to dwell within, to be inherent.

innig (⌣⌣) [mhd.] a. ⓖ intimate (friendship), close (attachment), fond (love); (aus der Seele kommend) fervent, devout; (tief empfunden) heart-felt, profound, (herzlich) cordial, (zärtlich) tender; adv. e-n aufs 2ste bemitleiden to pity a p. most sincerely or from the bottom of one's heart; sich 2 freuen to rejoice heartily, to be heartily glad.

Innigkeit (⌣⌣⌣) f ⓖ intimacy, closeness; fervour, devoutness, cordiality, tenderness; (Aufrichtigkeit) sincerity.

inniglich ↘ (⌣⌣⌣) [ahd.] adv. = innig.

Innung (⌣⌣) [mhd.] f ⓖ guild, corporation; (Zunft, Gewerk) craft, company, in Lo. a. livery; weitS. corporate body.

inoffiziös (⌣⌣⌣(⌣)⌢) [lt.] a. ⓖ (D 10) (nichtamtlich) unofficial.

inokulieren ⚘ (⌣⌣⌣⌢⌣) [lt.] v/a. ⓖ med.) [= einimpfen.]

inopportun (⌣⌣⌣⌢) [lt.] a. ⓖ (unzweckmäßig) inopportune, untimely, out of place, out of season.

Inosin-säure ⚘ (⌣⌣⌢…) [grch. ís, in-Sehne] f ⓖ chm. inosic acid ($C_{10}H_{14}N_4O_{11}$).

Inosit (⌣⌢) [grch.] m ⓒ. (Fleischzucker) inosite, muscle-sugar ($C_6H_6(OH)_6$).

in petto (⌢ ⌢⌣) [it. in der Brust]: etwas 2 haben to have s.th. on one's mind.

Inquirent (⌣⌣⌢) [lt.] m ⓖ jur. (Untersuchungsführer) examining magistrate.

inquirieren (⌣⌣⌢⌣) [lt.] v/a. ⓖ to examine.

Inquisit † (⌣⌣⌢) m ⓖ = Angeklagte(r).

Inquisition (⌣⌣⌣-tsi(o)⌢n) [lt.] f ⓖ 1. jur. examination. — 2. Cath.eccl. (Ketzergericht) inquisition. [inquisition.]

Inquisitions-gericht (⌣…) n ⓖ court of)

Inquisitor (⌣⌣⌢⌣) [lt.] m ⓖ 1. = Inquire'nt. = 2. Cath.eccl. inquisitor. [torial.]

inquisitorisch (⌣⌣⌣⌢⌣) [lt.] a. ⓖ inquisi-)

In-ruhe-setzen (⌣⌢…⌢⌣) n ⓖ allowing (or giving) rest to; ⚔ ~ des Flintenhahnes putting a gun at half-cock.

ins (⌢) [zsgz. in das (↘ in des)] into the.

In-saß (⌣⌢) ⓖ, **In-sasse** (⌣⌣⌣) ⓖ [sitzen] m, **In-sassin** f ⓖ inmate, occupier, occupant, tenant, e-r Stadt 2c.: inhabitant.

In-sassenschaft (⌣⌣⌣⌣) f ⓖ body of inmates or inhabitants.

ins-besondere (⌣⌢⌣⌣⌣) adv. in particular, particularly, (e)specially.

In-schrift (⌣⌢) [mhd.; *lt.] f ⓖ auf Denkmälern 2c. inscription, ⚘ epigraph.

In-schriften-kenner (⌣⌢…) m ⓖ: ⚘ epigraphist, epigrapher; **kunde** f: ⚘ epigraphics, epigraphy.

in-schriftlich (⌣⌢⌣⌣) a. ⓖ inscriptive, serving as inscription; (Inschriften betr.) inscriptional, ⚘ epigraphic(al).

Insekt (⌣⌢) [lt. eingeschnitten] n ⓒb. (Kerbtier) vollkommen entwickeltes ~ perfect insect, ⚘ imago; geol. versteinertes ~: ⚘ entomolite.

insekten-ähnlich (⌣⌢⌣…) a. ⓖ, **artig** a. insect-like, like an insect, ⚘ insectile, insectiform, entomoid; **beschreibung** f ⓖ: ⚘ entomography; **fressend** a.: ⚘ insectivorous; **fresser** m/pl.: ⚘ insectivora, entomophagans pl.; **kenner** m ⓖ: **kunde** f, **lehre** f entomology; **nadeln** ⊕ f/pl. pins pl. for mounting insects, entomological pins; **pulver** ⚘ n insect-powder or -destroyer, insecticide; **puppe** f chrysalis, pupa; **sammler** m collector of insects; **sammlung** f collection of insects, entomological collection; **vertilgend** a. insecticidal; **zergliederung** f: ⚘ entomotomy.

Insel ♀ (⌣⌢) [mhd.; *lt.] f ⓖ island, isle; die ~ Malta the island of Malta; die Grüne ~ (Irland) ⓖ the Emerald Isle.

insel-artig (⌣⌢⌣⌣) a. ⓖ insular; **bewohner(in** f) m ⓖ islander.

Inselchen (⌣⌣⌣) n ⓖ (dim. von Insel) islet. [cluster) of islands.]

Insel-gruppe (⌣⌢…) f ⓖ group (or)

inselhaft (⌣⌢⌣) a. ⓖ insular.

Insel-land ♀ (⌣⌢…) n ⓖ country consisting of islands, insular country; **meer** n archipelago; **perron** m auf belebten Plätzen island; **reich** a. rich in (or studded with) islands; ~ n insular country; **staat** m = reich; **volk** n insular nation; **welt** f archipelago.

Inserat (⌣⌣⌢) [+lt.] n ⓒc. (Anzeige) advertisement, inserted announcement or paragraph; **en-teil** (⌣⌣…) m ⓖ e-r Zeitung advertisement-columns pl.

Inserent (⌣⌣⌢) [lt.] m ⓖ advertiser.

inserieren (⌣⌣⌢⌣) [lt.] I v/a. ⓖ (einrücken) to insert, to advertise. — II ~ n ⓖ u. **Inserierung** f ⓖ insertion.

Insertion (⌣⌣⌢-tsi(o)⌢n) [lt.] f ⓖ insertion; **~s-gebühren**, **kosten** f/pl. ⓖ charges pl. for advertising or advertisements, cost of advertising an article, a book, &c.

ins-geheim (⌣⌢⌣…) adv. in secret, secretly; **~gemein** adv. in general, ordinarily, usually; **~gesamt** adv. in a body or F a lump, altogether.

In-sich-geh(e)n (⌣⌣⌣⌢(⌣)) n ⓖ bsd. rel. self-communion or -examination, heart-searching.

In-sich-versunken-sein (⌣⌣⌣⌣⌢) n ⓖ deep absorption, being lost to the outer world, brooding (state).

In-siegel (⌣⌢⌣) [ahd.; *mlt. insi'gnia] n ⓖ von Behörden, Beamten: official seal.

In-signi-en (⌣⌣⌢⌣) [lt.] pl. (Abzeichen des Amtes) insignia pl., badges pl. of office.

Insinuation (⌣⌣⌣-tsi(o)⌢n) [lt.] f ⓖ 1. (Einflüsterung) insinuation, prompting, suggestion; (Einschmeichelung) wheedling, coaxing. — 2. jur. (Einhändigung, Zustellung) serving a summons upon a p.

insinuieren (⌣⌣⌢⌣) [lt.] I v/a.: e-m etwas 2 to insinuate (or prompt, suggest) a th. to a p. — II sich 2 v/refl. (einschmeicheln) to ingratiate o.s. (bei e-m with a p.). — III ~ n ⓖ u. **Insinuierung** f ⓖ insinuation.

ins-künftige (⌣⌢⌣⌣) adv. in (or for) the future, henceforth.

Ins-leben-treten (⌣⌣⌣⌢⌣) n ⓖ coming into life, beginning, rise.

in-sofern adv. 1. (⌣⌢⌣) 2 (soweit) hast du recht so far you are right. — 2. (⌣⌣⌢) (in) so far as, in as much as.

Insolation ⚘ (⌣⌣⌢-tsi(o)⌢n) [lt.] f ⓖ phys. (Bestrahlung) insolation, solarization.

insolvent ⓖ (⌣⌣⌢w⌣) [lt.] a. ⓖ jur. (zahlungs-unfähig) insolvent; 2 w. auch: to stop payment; **Insolvenz** f ⓖ (Zahlungs-unfähigkeit) insolvency.

in-sonderheit ↘ (⌣⌣⌣), **in-sonders** † (⌣⌣⌣) adv. in particular, particularly.

in-soweit (⌣⌣⌢ u. ⌣⌢⌣⌢) adv. = insofern.

Inspektion (⌣⌣⌢-tsi(o)⌢n) [lt.] f ⓖ (Besichtigung) inspection; (Beaufsichtigung) supervision; **~s-dienst** (⌣…) m ⓖ inspection duty; **~s-offizier** ⚔ m inspecting officer; **~s-reise** f tour of inspection.

Inspektor (⌣⌣⌢⌣) [lt.] m ⓖ (Aufseher) inspector, overseer, e-s Gutes: steward; 🚂 station-master; **~-amt** n ⓖ, **~at** (⌣⌣⌢) n ⓒc. inspector's post, inspectorship, stewardship; **~bezirk** m inspector's district or round; **~stelle** f = amt.

Inspiration (⌣⌣⌢-tsi(o)⌢n) [lt.] f ⓖ (Begeisterung) inspiration; f ⓖ to inspire.

inspirieren (⌣⌣⌢⌣) [lt.] v/a. ⓖ (begeistern)

Inspizi-ent (⌣⌣⌢⌣) [lt.] m ⓖ inspector.

inspizier/en (⌣⌣⌢⌣) [lt.] I v/a. ⓖ (besichtigen) to inspect; (beaufsichtigen) to

[installieren] — 550 — [Internum]

superintend. — II ~ n ㉓ u. З/ung f ㊻ inspection; superintendence.
installier/en (⌣⌣⌣́⌣) [dtsch=lt.] ⑱ **I.** v/a. (bestallen) to install. — **II sich** (selbst) v/refl. to undertake one's post. — **III** ~ n ㉓, З/ung f ㊻ installation.
in-stand (⌣⌣́...) [in Stand]: halten to keep in good repair or order; setzen v/a. to put in(to) good repair, to do up; wieder setzen to restore.
In=stand=haltung (⌣́⌣.⌣́.⌣́) f ㊻ keeping in good repair or order; maintenance.
in=ständig (⌣́⌣⌣) [ahd.] a. ㊻ urgent, pressing, earnest; auf sein es Bitten at his urgent request; e-n auf das ste bitten to beg very hard of a p., to implore (or beseech) a p.; **~keit** f ㊻ urgency, earnestness.
In=stand=setzung (⌣́.⌣.⌣́.⌣) f ㊻ repairing, (doing) repairs pl.; restoration.
Instanz (⌣⌣́) [lt.] f ㊻ jur. (Gerichtshof) court (of justice); untere, höhere ~ lower, higher court; höchste ~ (in England für Zivilsachen das Richterkollegium im House of Lords) supreme court of appeal; letzte ~ last resort; in der letzten ~ sprechen to give (or pronounce) the final judgment (from which there is no appeal).
Instanzen=gang (⌣⌣́⌣...) m ㉒ jur. = =weg; =verweigerung f nonsuit.
Instanzen=weg, =zug (⌣⌣́...) m ㉒ (successive) stages pl. of appeal; den ~ durchmachen to appeal from court to court; sich auf dem ~ beschweren to complain to one's immediate superior.
instanz-mäßig (⌣⌣́...) a. ㊻ in conformity with the rules of appeal.
Inste (⌣́⌣) [ndd. Insasse] m ㊹ = **Insaß**, Einlieger 1. [~e(s) n ㊷ contents pl.)
in-stehend (⌣́⌣⌣) a. ㊻ herein contained.)
Inster (⌣́⌣) m u. n ㉒ nordd. = **Geträse**.
Instinkt (⌣⌣́) [lt.] m ⓑ. (natürlicher Trieb) instinct; aus ~ by instinct, instinctively; =artig a. ㊻ = =mäßig.
instinktiv (⌣⌣⌣́f) [lt.] a. ㊻ instinctive.
instinktmäßig (⌣⌣́...) a. ㊻ instinctive; **~keit** f instinctiveness.
Institut (⌣⌣⌣́) [lt.] n ⓑc.: a) (Einrichtung) institution; (Anstalt) establishment; b) (Erziehungs-anstalt) (boarding-)school, college; c) ● (Finanz)~ financial institution.
Institution (⌣⌣=tз(⌣)⌣́) [lt.] f ㊻ institution; die =en Justinian's (Teil des *Corpus juris*) Justinian's Institutes pl.
Inst=mann (⌣́...) m, pl. =leute (Häusler, Gutstagelöhner) agricultural labourer attached to the estate.
instruieren (⌣⌣⌣́⌣) [lt.] v/a. to instruct; jur. e-n Prozeß (vorbereiten) to prepare a case. — **II sich** v/refl. to inform o.s. about a th., to inquire into a th.
Instruktion (⌣⌣=tз(⌣)⌣́) f ㊻ (Anweisung) instruction, 🞝 und ⚔ auch: orders, regulations, directions pl.
Instruktions=buch ⚔ (⌣́...) n ㊷ der Soldaten (jetzt: Vorschriften) service-regulations pl.; =mäßig a. ㊻ und adv. according to instructions or regulations; =richter m jur. examining magistrate; =stunde ⚔ f hour of instruction; lesson; =widrig a. u. adv. contrary to instructions.

instruktiv (⌣⌣⌣́f) [lt.] a. ㊻ (belehrend) instructive.
Instrument (⌣⌣⌣́) [lt.] n ⓑb. **1.** (Werkzeug, Gerät) instrument (a. ♪), tool. — **2.** jur. (Urkunde) legal instrument, deed.
instrumental ♪ (⌣⌣⌣́) [lt.] a. ㊻ instrumental; **~begleitung** ♪ (⌣⌣⌣́...) f ㊷ accompaniment on a musical instrument; =musik f instrumental music; =verein m orchestral society.
Instrumenten=fabrikant (⌣⌣⌣́...) m ㊷ musical instrument maker; =handlung f musical instrument business, music-shop; =kasten m, surg. case of instruments; =macher m = =fabrikant.
instrumentier/en ♪ (⌣⌣⌣́⌣) **I** v/a. ⑱ to arrange the instrumental parts of a composition, bisw.: to instrument a score. — **II** ~ n ㉓ und З/ung f ㊻ instrumentation, orchestration.
Insubordination (⌣⌣⌣=tз(⌣)⌣́) [lt.] f ㊻ (Unbotmäßigkeit) insubordination, disobedience; **~s=vergehen** (⌣́...) n ㊷ act of insubordination.
Insulaner (⌣⌣⌣́⌣) [lt.] m ㉒, **~in** f ㊷ (Inselbewohner[in]) islander, inhabitant (or native) of an island.
insultier/en (⌣⌣⌣́⌣) [lt.] **I** v/a. ⑱ (beleidigen) to insult. — **II** ~ n ㉓ u. З/ung f ㊻ (j-s) insult(s pl.) (offered to a p.).
Insurgent (⌣⌣⌣́) [lt.] m ㊷ (Aufständischer) insurgent; **~en=heer** n ㊷ insurgent army. [(stand) insurrection, rebellion.)
Insurrektion (⌣⌣⌣⌣tз(⌣)⌣́) [lt.] f ㊻ (Aufs)
Ins=werk=setzen (⌣́.⌣.⌣́⌣) n ㉓ setting in operation or into working-order.
In=szene=setzen (⌣.⌣́⌣.⌣́⌣) n ㉓ = **In=szenierung**.
inszenier/en (⌣⌣⌣́⌣) [lt.] **I** v/a. ⑱ thea. to (put on the) stage, to get up; herrlich inszeniert splendidly got up, with gorgeous scenery. — **II** ~ n ㉓ u. Inszenierung f ㊻ putting on the stage, get(ting)-up of a play, auch (fr.): *mise en scène*. [unhurt.)
intakt (⌣⌣́) [lt.] a. ㊻ (unversehrt) intact.)
Intarsi=en=malerei (⌣⌣́(⌣)⌣...) [lt.] f ㊻ (Holzmosaik) tarsia style of painting.
integral ⁓ (⌣⌣⌣́) [lt.] **I** a. ㊻ (ganz) integral, whole. — **II** ~ n ⓑd., **~e** f ㊷ math. integral (value), integer; **Integral=rechnung** (⌣⌣⌣́...) f ㊻ math. integral calculus.
integrierend (⌣⌣⌣́⌣) a. ㊻ (wesentlich): e Teile integrant (or component) parts pl.
Intellekt (⌣⌣⌣́) [lt.] m ⓑb. intellect; **~ualismus** (⌣⌣⌣⌣⌣⌣́) m ㊲ intellectualism; Quell (⌣⌣⌣⌣́) [fr.] a. ㊻ intellectual, mental. [intelligent, F sharp.]
intelligent (⌣⌣⌣́) [lt.] a. ㊻ (einsichtig))
Intelligenz (⌣⌣⌣́) f ㊷ intelligence; F sharpness; **~blatt** n ㊷ (kleines Annoncenblatt), etwa: intelligencer, advertising medium; **~bureau**, **~kontor** n inquiry-office, information-bureau.
Intendant (⌣⌣⌣́) [neu=lt.] m ㊷, **~in** f ㊷ superintendent, thea. stage-manager, ⚔ commissariat-officer; **~en=bezirk** m, =stelle f superintendent's district, post.
Intendantur (⌣⌣⌣́) [neu=lt.] f ㊻ superintendent's office; board of management; ⚔ commissariat.
Intendantur=rat ⚔ (⌣⌣⌣́⌣...) m ㊷ official in the commissariat department; =wesen n managerial concerns pl.; ⚔ commissariat (affairs pl.).
Intendanz (⌣⌣⌣́) f ㊻ thea. board of management.
Intensität ⁓ (⌣⌣⌣́) [lt.] f ㊻ phys., &c. (innere Kraft, Spannung) intensity, intensiveness; **intensiv(isch)** (⌣⌣⌣́f, ⌣⌣⌣⌣) a. ㊻ intens(iv)e. [intention.)
Intention (⌣⌣⌣tз(⌣)⌣́) [fr., *lt.] f ㊻ (Absicht))
Interdikt (⌣⌣⌣́) [lt.] n ⓑb. **1.** (Verbot) prohibition. — **2.** eccl. (Kirchenbann) interdict; e-n mit dem ~ belegen to lay a p. under an interdict.
interessant (⌣⌣⌣́) [fr.] a. ㊻ (anziehend) interesting, attractive.
Interesse (⌣⌣⌣́) [lt.] n ㊷ (Teilnahme) interest; Einheit des s unity of action; es liegt in seinem (eigenen) Interesse zu // it is to his own interest to //; er nimmt an nichts ~ (Anteil) he takes no interest (or does not interest himself) in anything; =los a. ㊻ taking no interest (in anything), uninterested; **⊛~n** pl.(Zinsen)interest; **~n=rechnung** f㊻(Zinsrechnung) interest-account or -sum; **~n=sphäre** f, pol. sphere of influence.
Interessent (⌣⌣⌣́) [neu=lt.] m ㊷, **~in** f ㊷ (Beteiligte[r]) interested person or party.
interessieren (⌣⌣⌣⌣́⌣) [fr.] ⑱ **I.** v/a. to interest; e-n für (oder bei) et. to interest a p. in a th. — **II** v/refl. **sich** für e-n to interest o.s. (or to take an interest) in a p., to have a p.'s interest at heart. — **III interessiert** p.p. u. a. ㊻ interested; vgl. eigennützig.
Interim (⌣́⌣⌣) [lt. mittlerweile] n ㊾ interim, meanwhile; **~istikum** (⌣⌣⌣́⌣) n ㉘ interim state, provisional arrangement; istisch (⌣⌣⌣́⌣) a. ㊻ (zeitweilig) interimistic, provisional.
Interims=bescheid (⌣́⌣⌣...) m ㊷ jur. provisional sentence; =jacke f, =rock m ⚔ fatigue-jacket; =regierung f provisional government; =quittung f, =schein m ● für Staatspapiere 𝔠. (interim) receipt, scrip; =uniform ⚔ f undress uniform or clothes pl. or suit; in ~ in undress.
Interjektion (⌣⌣⌣tз(⌣)⌣́) [lt.] f ㊻ gr. (Ausrufungswort) interjection.
Interlinear=übersetzung (⌣⌣⌣⌣⌣...) [lt. zwischen den Zeilen] f ㊻, =version f interlinear translation.
Intermezzo (⌣⌣⌣́df-) [it.] n ㊾ (㊽) thea. (Zwischenspiel) intermezzo, interlude.
intermittierend ⁓ (⌣⌣⌣⌣́⌣) a. ㊻ (aussetzend) intermittent.
intern (⌣⌣́) [lt.] **I** a. ㊻ = innerlich. — **II ~e([r]m)** f ㊷ (Schüler[in] einer Kostschule) boarder. — **III ~a** n/pl. s. **Internum**.
Internat (⌣⌣⌣́) [lt.] n ⓑc. (Kostschule) boarding-school or -establishment.
international (⌣⌣⌣⌣tз(⌣)⌣́) [fr.] a. ㊻ (völkerrechtlich) international; **~e** (⌣⌣⌣⌣́⌣) f ㊸ (europäische Arbeiterverbindung, 1864) International (Association).
internieren (⌣⌣⌣́⌣) [lt.] **I** v/a. ⑱ (gefangen halten) to keep in confinement, to confine (with)in a fortress, &c. — **II Internierte([r]** m/f) ⑲ (political, &c.) prisoner, p. confined in a fortress, &c.
Internum (⌣⌣́⌣) [lt.] n ㊾. mst pl. **Interna** (innere Angelegenheiten) internal affairs pl.

Signs (see page XVII): F familiar; P vulgar; ⸸ flash; ⟋ rare; † obsolete (died); * new word (born); ⁺⁺ incorrect; ♪ music;

[Interpellant] — 551 — [irgend]

Interpellant (⌣⌣⌣́) [lt.] m ⓐ parl. interrogator, one who puts a question (to a minister); **Interpellation** (⌣⌣́-tß(⌣)ʰ) f ⓑ (Anfrage) interpellation; **interpellieren** (⌣⌣⌣́⌣) v/a. ⓑ (befragen) to interrogate, to address a question (to a minister).

interpolier/en ⚹ (⌣⌣⌣́⌣) [lt.] I v/a. ⓑ (fälschlich einschieben) to interpolate. — II ~ n ⓒ u. **Jung** f ⓑ interpolation. **Interpolierer** (⌣⌣⌣́⌣) [lt.] m ⓐ (Fälscher v. Schriften) interpolator.

Interpret (⌣⌣́) [lt.] m ⓐ (Dolmetscher, Erklärer) interpreter, expounder; **Lierbar** (⌣⌣⌣́⌣) a. ⓑ interpretable.

interpretier/en (⌣⌣⌣́⌣) [lt.] I v/a. ⓑ (erklären) to interpret (a. ♪ u. thea.), to expound. — II ~ n ⓒ u. **Jung** f ⓑ interpretation of a passage, &c.

interpungier/en, interpunktieren (⌣⌣⌣⌣́⌣) I v/a. ⓑ gr. to punctuate. -- II ~ n ⓒ und **Jung**, **Interpunktion** (⌣⌣⌣-tß(⌣)ʰ) f ⓑ ([Setzung von] Satzzeichen) punctuation, putting in the stops; ~-z- stop.

Interregnum (⌣⌣́⌣) [lt.] n ⓑ (Zwischenherrschaft) interregnum, interval between two reigns; weitS. unstable (or disorderly) government.

Interrogativ (⌣⌣⌣-́⌣) [lt. fragend] n ⓑd. ~um; **-partikel** (⌣⌣...) f ⓑ, **-pronomen** n interrogative particle, pronoun; ~-satz m interrogative sentence; ~um (⌣⌣-́⌣) [lt.] n ⓑ gr. interrogative pronoun.

Intervall (⌣⌣⌣́) [lt.] n ⓑd. (Zwischenraum, -zeit) interval (auch ♪, ⚔), intervening space or time.

intervenieren (⌣⌣⌣⌣́) [lt.] meist jur.: I v/n. (h.) ⓑ (sich ins Mittel legen) to intervene, to interpose. — II ~ n ⓒ u. **Intervenierung**, a. **Intervention** (⌣⌣⌣-(⌣)ʰ) f ⓑ intervention, interposition; jur. auch: ⚹ estoppage.

interviewen ꜛ (⌣⌣ji·́n) [englt.] v/a. ⓑ Zeitungswesen: (sich mit e-m unterreden) to interview a p., to have (or arrange) an interview with a p.

Intestat-erbe (⌣⌣́...) [ft. o. Testament] ⓐ m, **-erbin** f jur. abintestate heir(ess).

Inthronifation (⌣⌣⌣-tß(⌣)ʰ) f ⓑ eccl. (Thronerhebung) enthronement.

intim (⌣́) [lt.] a. ⓑ (vertraut) intimate; sein **Ler Freund**, auch: his bosom-friend, F his (great) pal; **Intimität** (⌣⌣⌣́) f ⓑ intimacy; **Intimus** (⌣́⌣⌣) m ⓐ intimate friend, a. F chum.

intolerant (⌣⌣⌣́) [lt.] a. ⓑ (unduldsam) intolerant; **Intoleranz** f ⓑ intolerance.

intonier/en ♪ (⌣⌣⌣́) [neu-lt.] I v/a. ⓑ to intone (s. anstimmen 2). — II ~ n ⓒ u. **Jung** f ⓑ intonation. [innerhalb.)

☞ **intra...** ⚹ (⌣⌣...) [lt.] intra... (=)

Intrade (⌣⌣́) [it.] f ⓑ 1. ♪: a) (Einleitung) prelude; b) ♪ (Trompetentusch) flourish of trumpets. — 2. ~n pl. (Einkünfte v. Grundvermögen) revenue.

Intransigent (⌣⌣⌣⌣́) [lt.] m ⓐ pol. (Unversöhnlicher) intransigent. **intransigent.** irreconcilable.

intransitiv ⚹ (⌣⌣⌣⌣́) [lt.] a. ⓑ gr. (zielloß) intransitive; ~(um) (⌣, ⌣⌣⌣́⌣) n ⓑd. ⓑ intransitive verb, verb neuter.

intrigant (⌣⌣⌣́) [fr.] I a. ⓑ (ränkevoll) intriguing, scheming, plotting, designing. — II ⚹ m ⓐ, **~in** ⓑ intriguer,

schemer, plotter; thea. villain (of the piece), f designing woman or witch, dragon. [trigue, scheme, plot.)

Intrige (⌣⌣́) [fr.] f ⓑ (Ränkespiel) in-ʃ

intrigieren (⌣⌣⌣́⌣) [fr.] v/a. u. v/n. (h.) ⓑ to (form an) intrigue, to (plot and) scheme, to hatch plots.

Introduktion (⌣⌣⌣-tß(⌣)ʰ) [lt.] f ⓑ (Einleitung) introduction; **introduzieren** (⌣⌣⌣-́) v/a. ⓑ (einleiten) to introduce.

Intuition (⌣⌣⌣-(⌣)ʰ) [lt.] f ⓑ phls. (Anschauung) intuition; **intuitiv** (⌣⌣⌣-́f) a. ⓑ (anschaulich) intuitive.

Inulin ⚹ (⌣⌣-́) [lt.] n ⓑd. chm. (♀) (Stärkemehl der Alantwurzel) inulin(e) (C₆H₁₀O₅).

In-umlauf-fetzen ⚹ (⌣,⌣-,-́⌣⌣) n ⓒ von Wertpapieren: emission, circulation.

invalid (⌣w⌣́) [lt.] I a. ⓑ (entkräftet, altersschwach) invalid, disabled; ⚓ u. ⚔ als ⌣ nach der Heimat beurlaubt w. to be invalided home. — II ~e(r) m ⓑ disabled soldier or sailor.

Invaliden-dank (⌣⌣w-́⌣...) m ⓐ (Berlin 1872) home for invalided soldiers; **-haus** n hospital for disabled soldiers, in Lo. Chelsea Hospital; **-pension, -rente** ⓑ f old-age pension.

Invalidität (⌣⌣w-́⌣) [lt.] f ⓑ (Dienstunfähigkeit) disablement, incapacity for work or service; invalid(ed) state; **-s-versicherung** (⌣...) f ⓑ insurance.

Invektive (⌣⌣w-́⌣w) [lt.] f ⓑ (Schmähung) invective; strong censure or criticism.

Inventar (⌣⌣w-́) [lt.] n ⓑd., **~ium** (⌣⌣w-́(⌣)⌣) n ⓑ 1. jur.: a) = **Inventur**; b) (Vorrat von Waren &c.) (articles pl. mentioned in an) inventory, catalogued goods pl. — 2. F fig. altes ~(ium) old furniture.

Inventar(ien)-stück (⌣⌣w-́(⌣)⌣...) n ⓒ part of an inventory, piece of (household-)furniture, im Laden: fixture.

inventarisieren (⌣⌣w-́⌣) [lt.] I v/a. to (put down in an) inventory; to catalogue. — II v/n. (h.) to make an inventory, ⓑ auch: to take stock.

inventar-mäßig (⌣⌣w-́⌣) a. ⓑ (u. adv.) inventorial(ly).

Inventur ⚹ (⌣⌣w-́) [lt.] f ⓑ (Inventarverzeichnis) inventory, bei Versteigerungen auch: catalogue; (die) ~ aufnehmen to draw up an inventory; **~-aufnahme** f ⓑ making (or taking) an inventory, ⓑ auch: stock-taking.

Inversion (⌣⌣⌣-(⌣)ʰ) [lt.] f ⓑ gr., math., &c. (Umkehrung) inversion; **invertieren** (⌣⌣w-́) v/a. ⓑ (umkehren) to invert, to put in inverted order.

Invert-zucker (⌣⌣w-́⌣) [lt.] m ⓐ (Gemisch v. Trauben- u. Fruchtzucker) invert-sugar.

investier/en (⌣⌣w-́) [lt.] bsd. Cath. eccl. I v/a. ⓑ: e-n mit e. ⌣ (bekleiden, belehnen) to invest a p. with a th.; (e)teß (angelegtes) Kapital invested capital. — II ~ n ⓒ u. **Jung** = **Investitur**.

Investitur (⌣⌣w-́⌣) [lt.] f ⓑ investiture of bishops, &c.; **~-streit** m ⓑ hist. question of or dispute about) investiture.

invitieren (⌣⌣w-́) [lt.] ⓑ (einladen) to invite, to ask (a. Kartenspiel).

Invokavit (⌣⌣w-́⌣w) [lt. (Pf. 91, 15] m, inv. (1. Fastensonntag) first Sunday in Lent.

involvieren (⌣⌣w-́) [lt.] ⓑ (in sich begreifen) to involve, comprise, imply.

in-wärts (⌣-́) adv. = inwendig.

in-wendig (⌣⌣⌣́) (ant. auswendig) I a. ⓑ inward, internal, interior; vgl. inner 1; adv. auch: within, inside; ich weiß, wie das Haus ⌣ aussieht I know how the inside of the house looks; et. in- und auswendig kennen to know the ins and outs of a th. — II ~e(s) n ⓑ = inner II.

in-wiefern (⌣-́), **in-wieweit** (⌣-́) adv. (in) how far, to what extent; fragend ⌣? how far?, in what way?, how so?

in-wohnend (⌣́⌣⌣) a. ⓑ dwelling within, ⚹ inherent, immanent; **In-wohner(schaft)** ⓑ m/pl. ⓑ = **Einwohner** pl.

In-zicht ⚹ (⌣́⌣) [ahd.; *zeihen] f ⓑ jur. 1. (Beschuldigung) accusation, charge. — 2. (internal) evidence, proof.

Inzidenz (⌣⌣⌣́) [lt.] f ⓑ 1. phys., bsd. opt. (Auffallen der Strahlen &c.) incidence of rays, &c. — 2. fig. (Zwischenfall) incident, incidental point.

In-zucht (⌣-́⌣) f ⓑ agr., &c. inbreeding.

in-zwischen (⌣⌣⌣́) [ahd.] adv. = indessen.

Jon ⚹ (⌣́) [grch.] n ⓑ (pl. ɪ-ɪ ~ten) elect., chm. (elektrochemischer Urbestandteil des Stoffes) ion; **~en-theorie** f ⓑ ionic theory.

Joni-en ⚹ (⌣́⌣(⌣)) [grch.] npr/n. ⓑa. Alt. Ionia; **Jonier(in** f ⓑ) m ⓐ Ionian; **ionisch** (⌣⌣-́) [grch.] a. ⓑ Ionian; ♀ die ~en Inseln the Ionian Islands; **Le Schule** Ionic School; arch. **Le Säulen-ordnung** Ionic order; **Ler Vers** Ionic verse or line (-⌣⌣⌣ ob. ⌣⌣--). [(eigenheit) Ionism.)

Jonismus ⚹ (⌣-́⌣) m ⓐ (ionische Spracht)

Jota (⌣́) [grch.] n ⓑ iota; **nicht ein ~** (gar nichts) not the least bit, bibl. not a jot or a tittle (f. **Jot**); **~zismus** m ⓐ (Aussprache von η = i) iotacism.

Jpekakuanha(-wurzel f) (-⌣⌣-́⌣) [mex.] f ⓑ u. pharm. (Brechwurz) ipecacuanha (von Cephaëlis Ipecacuanha).

Jper ♀ (⌣́) [Ypern ♀ in Flandern] f ⓑ (Ulmenart) common elm (-tree) (Ulmus campestris).

Iphigeni-e (-f⌣-́(⌣)) [grch.] npr/f. ⓑa. ⚗. myth. u. ast. Iphigenia.

J-Punkt (⌣,-́) m ⓐ dot over the i.

Jrade (-⌣-́) [türk.; *ar. Wille] m u. n ⓑ (Verordnung des Sultans) irade.

Jran ♀ (-⌣-́) npr/n. ⓑa. (Neuperfien) Iran; **~-ier(in** f ⓑ) m ⓐ, **Lisch** a. ⓑ Iranian.

irden (⌣́⌣) [ahd.; *Erde] a. ⓑ (Dg) earthen; **Les Geschirr, Le Waren** earthen vessels or pots pl., earthenware, crockery.

irdisch (⌣́⌣) [ahd.; *Erde] I a. ⓑ earthly, terrestrial, (zeitlich) temporal, (weltlich) worldly, (menschlich) human; die **Len Dinge**, oft: things pl. on (or of) this earth or here below, sublunary affairs pl. — II ~e(r) m, ~e f, ~e(s) n ⓑ der ~e earthly being, mortal man; das ~e earthly things or concerns pl.; (the things of) this world.

Jre (⌣́) m ⓐ, **Jrin** f ⓑ Irishman, Irishwoman, pl. die **Jren** auch: the Irish; feiner: Hibernian, spöttisch nur m: F Pad(dy), Pat, Son of Erin.

irgend (⌣́⌣) [ahd.] verallgemeinerndes adv. 1. mit indef. art. u. pron. und mit adv., oft zu einem Worte zs.-geschrieben: ⌣(=)**ein**, pl. ⌣(=)**welche** some (one), allg.: any (one), pl. some, any; ⌣(=)**ein Buch** some book

⚹ scientific; ♀ botanical; ♂ geography; ⊙ machinery; ⚒ mining; ⚔ military; ⚓ marine; ⓑ commercial; ✉ postal; ⛕ railway.

[irgendeiner] — 552 — [irrlichterieren]

(or other), any book; 2 ein anderer some one else, anybody else; negativ stets: any, zB. ohne 2(=)welche Kosten without any expense (whatever); 2(=)einer, 2(=)jemand, 2 wer somebody, some one, allgemein oder negativ: anybody, any one; 2 j. hat gesagt // somebody (or other) has said //; wenn 2 j. es wüßte if any person (stärker: anybody in the world) knew it; 2 einmal (at) some time or other, allg.: at any time; 2 etwas, 2 ein Gegenstand something, allgemein oder negativ: anything, stärker: F any mortal thing; gibt es 2 etwas Schöneres? can there be anything more beautiful?; 2s ~ (~) adv. somewhere; 2wann, zu 2(=) einer Zeit at some time or other, allg.: at any time; 2(=)was any mortal thing, something or other; 2(=)welcher somebody; hat er 2(=)welche Absichten? has he any intentions at all?; 2wie, auf 2(=)e-e Art somehow, in some way (or other), allgemein: anyhow; stärker: by hook or by crook; wer 2(wie) kann anybody who possibly can or who is at all able to; 2wo somewhere, in some place (or other), allg.: anywhere; 2wo anders somewhere else; 2woher from some place (or other), allg.: from anywhere; 2wohin to some place (or other), allg.: to any place (whatsoever), seltener: whithersoever (it may be). — 2. im Anschluß an *relative pron.* u. *cj.*: wann (wo) es 2 geht whenever (wherever) it may be possible; was man 2 finden kann whatever (or anything) one can find; wenn 2 daran gedacht werden kann if the matter can be at all thought of; wer (nur) 2 anständig ist any respectable person, anybody (who is) commonly (or at all) decent; so rasch wie 2 möglich as soon as ever possible.

iridisieren = (~v~v) = irisieren.
Iridium = (~v(v)v) [lt., *grch.] n (o. pl.) chm. seltenes Platinmetall: iridium (Ir); mit ~ bedecken to iridize; ~oxyd n iridium (or iridic) oxide (Ir O).
Irin (Lv) f s. Ire.
Iris (Lv) [grch.] f, inv. 1. npr. myth. (Götterbotin, Regenbogen) Iris (a. ast.). — 2. anat. (Regenbogenhaut) iris. — 3. ♀ (Schwertlilie) iris (Iris).
Iris-bogen (Lv...) m rainbow.
irisch (Lv) a. 1. Irish, feiner: Hibernian; 2e Sprach-eigentümlichkeit Irishism, Hibernicism; 2e Mund-art Irish brogue; ♀ ~es Meer Irish Sea; 2e Sümpfe Irish bogs pl.; 2er (dummer) Witz Irish bull.
Iris-druck ⊙ (Lv...) m Zeug- u. Papierdruck: iris(at)ed print; =farbe f iridescent colour; =glas n iridescent glass.
irisieren (~v~v) [Iris] I ⊙ v/a. durch galvanischen Prozeß ꝛc.: to iris(at)e. — II = v/n. (h.) (schillern) to iridesce; 2e Wolken iridescent clouds pl. — III ~ n (f. II) iridescence, rainbow-hues pl.
Irland (Lv) [gälisch E(i)rin West-insel] npr. n. ♀ a. Ireland, auch: Hibernia, Erin, Emerald Isle, spöttisch: Patland.
Irländer(in f) m = Ire, Irin;
irländisch a. = irisch; 2'sches Moos ♀ carrageen (-moss) (*Chondrus crispus*).

Irokese (~v~v) m , Irokesin f (Indianer[in], irokesisch a. Iroquois.
Ironie (~~~) [grch.] f (verhüllter Spott) irony; ironisch (~Lv) a. ironical; ironisieren (~~vLv) v/a. (h.) to treat [with irony.
irr (v) a. = irre.
irrational (vvtʒ(v)vL) [lt.] a. math. (nicht genau berechenbar) irrational.
irrationell (vvtʒ(v)vʒ) [fr.] a. (vernunftwidrig) unreasonable, irrational.
irre (vv) [ahd.] I a. u. adv. 1. astray, off the right way, on the wrong track (a. fig.), lost; fig. moving, (unstet) wavering, (verwirrt) perplexed, confused, (wirr, geistes-abwesend) mentally deranged, out of one's mind or wits, jur. non compos (mentis); vgl. 2=sein. — 2. mit verbs: vgl. 2=führen, 2=gehen, 2=leiten, irr(e) sein s. irresein; 2 werden v/n. (sn) to grow (or get) confused or puzzled or delirious. — II ~ f 3. (Irr(e)sein) erring (a. fig.); (Irrtum) error, mistake; in die ~ führen to mislead, fig. to lead astray; in der, die ~ gehen to go astray. — 4. (sich vielfach windender Weg) entangled path, intricate way; labyrinth, maze. — III Irre[r] m f 5. insane (or delirious) person, stärker: madman, f mad woman; lunatic; ♀ psychopath(ic).
Irrede (Lv) [Irr-rede] f senseless talk, mad speech; vgl. irrereden.
irre-führen (Lv...) v/a. to mislead, misguide, misdirect, mst fig. to lead astray, to put on the wrong scent; (täuschen) to deceive; sich durch et. 2 l. to be misled or F taken in, a. oft: to be caught napping; ~n misguidance; 2geh(e)n v/n. (sn) to go astray, to stray (from the right path), to lose one's way. v. Briefen oft: to miscarry; ~n going astray, wandering, von Briefen: miscarriage.
irregulär (v~vL) [lt.] a. (unregelmäßig) irregular; ⚔ 2e Truppen, ~e(n) m/pl. oft: irregulars pl.; Irregularität (v~v~vLʒ) f (Unregelmäßigkeit) irregularity.
irre-leiten (Lv...) v/a. = 2=führen.
irrelevant (v~vvv) [lt.] a. (unerheblich) irrelevant, trifling.
irreligiös (vvʒʒ(v)L) [lt.] a. (D 10) irreligious, without a religion; Irreligiosität (vvʒ(v)vvLʒ) f irreligiousness, irreligion, lack of religion.
irre=machen (Lvvʒv) v/a. (verwirren) to bewilder; (außer Fassung bringen) to disconcert, confuse, perplex; es läßt sich durch nichts 2 nothing could put him out or divert him from his purpose (vgl. irren 6).
irren (Lv) [ahd.] v/refl. *fr.*: It. erra're. I v/n. (h., bei Ortsveränderung sn) 1. förperlich: to err, to go astray, to miss (or lose) one's way; to be off the right path, (umherschweifen) to rove, ramble, stray; 2der Ritter knight-errant. — 2. geistig: to commit a mistake or an error, to be mistaken or wrong or in error or F beside the mark; (sich Täuschungen hingeben) to be deluded, to suffer from delusions or illusions; wenn ich nicht irre if I am not (or unless I be) mistaken. — 3. *rel.* (milder als: fehlen, sündigen) to stray from

the right path, *bibl.* to offend against the law; Sprichw. wir 2 alle we are all liable to err(or). — II fast † v a. 4. = irreführen, weit s. — irremachen (verwirren) to confuse, (stören) to disturb, trouble, upset; (erschüttern) to shake. — III sich 2 v/refl. 5. to make a mistake, vgl. 2; sich beim Schreiben 2 to make a slip (in writing); sich im Datum 2 to be mistaken in the (or to put the wrong) date; wir haben uns in (ob. an) ihm geirrt we have been mistaken in him; sich in s-r Rechnung (stark) 2 to be (far) out in one's calculation or reckoning; ich müßte mich sehr 2, wenn // I must be very much mistaken if //. — 6. er läßt sich 2 (irremachen) he is not easily put out, it is difficult to talk him out of (or into) a thing. — IV ~ n 7. = Irrfahrt, Irrtum, Irrung; Sprichw. ~ ist menschlich to err is human.
Irren-anstalt (Lvvʒv) f lunatic asylum, madhouse, in England auch oft: Bedlam; =arzt m specialist for mental diseases, F co. mad-doctor, ⚕ psychopathist; =haus n, =heil-anstalt f =anstalt; =häusler m lunatic, madman, a. oft: Bedlamite; vgl. irre 5; =heil-kunde f: ⚕ psychotherapeutics, psychotherapy.
irre=reden (Lv...) v/n. (h.) ✱✱ to talk incoherently or irrationally, to rave; vgl. irre sein; ~n incoherent (or irrational) talk; vgl. Irrede.
irre(=)sein v/n. (sn) ⊙ a ✱✱ to be bewildered or confused or puzzled; (verrückt sein) to be crazy or delirious, F co. to be off one's chump; da sind Sie sehr irre (im Irrtum) there you are quite mistaken or wrong; ich bin irre an ihm I don't know what to think (or to make) of him; ~ n perplexity, bewilderment, distraction, confused (stärker: delirious) state, mental alienation.
Irr-fahrt (Lv...) f wandering, pl. a.: erratic movements, vagaries; ~en pl. des Odysseus wanderings (or travels) pl. of Ulysses; =gang m: a) erratic or round-about journey; b) (labyrinthischer Weg) labyrinth, maze; =garten m, =gebäude n, =gebüsch n = =gang b; =glaube m erroneous belief, (Ketzerei) heresy; =gläubig a. heterodox, (ketzerisch) here'tical; =gläubige(r) m f he'retic; =gläubigkeit f heresy.
irrig (Lv) a. 1. erroneous; (ungenau) inexact, incorrect, (falsch) wrong, false, (erdichtet) fictitious; 2erweise adv. erroneously, by (a) mistake, through an error, wrongly. — 2. v. Personen: (sich täuschend) mistaken, (in the) wrong; misled.
Irrigkeit (Lv~) f (i. irrig) erroneousness; inexactness, incorrectness, falseness, fictitiousness; mistaken view.
irritieren (v~vL) [lt.] v/a. 1. (reizen) to irritate. — 2. P ++ = irremachen.
Irr-lehre (Lv...) f false doctrine, heterodoxy, (Ketzerei) heresy; =lehrer m heterodox (or here'tical) teacher; =licht n: a) Will-o'-the-wisp, Jack-o'-lantern (a. fig.), (lt.) ignis fatuus; b) fig. delusive light; 2lichtelieren, 2lichterieren v/n. (h.) ✱✱ to move

[Irrpfad] — 553 — [ja]

erratically (like a Will-o'-the-wisp); *fig.* to act without purpose, to commit vagaries; ⹁pfad *m* = ⹁weg; ⹁rede *f* s. Irrede, irrereden.

Irrſal(⸗⸗)[ahd.]*n*(*m*)ⓓd. going astray, wandering; vgl. Irr⹁fahrt, ⹁gang.

irr⹁ſein *v/n.* u. **Irr⹁ſein** *n* s. irresein ⲥc.

Irr⹁ſinn(⸗...) *m* ⓶ mental derangement or alienation, insanity, distraction; ⹁ſinnig *a.* ⓺ mentally deranged, insane; ⹁ſtern *m, ast.* comet.

Irrtum(⸗⸗)[irre]*m* ⓓd. error, mistake; (Versehen) oversight, beim Reden: slip of the tongue, in der Zeitrechnung: anachronism; (Mißverständnis) misunderstanding; da ſind Sie (gewaltig) im ⁓e there you are (quite) mistaken or wrong, F you're (far) out in your reckoning; in einen ⁓ verfallen to fall into an error; ⬤ Irrtümer (und Auslaſſungen) vorbehalten errors (and omissions) excepted, mſt abbr. E. (& O.) E.

irrtümlich(⸗⸗) *a.* ⓺ erroneous; **Ler⹁weiſe** *adv.* by mistake.

Irrung(⸗⸗)[irren] *f* ⓰ 1. = Irrtum. — 2. (Zerwürfnis) difference, dispute; (Abweichung) deviation, divergence.

Irr⹁wahn(⸗...) *m* ⓶ mistaken idea, delusion; (Vorurteil) prejudice, (Aberglaube) superstition; ⹁weg *m* wrong way or path; auf ⁓e geraten to lose (or miss) one's way, to go astray, F to get on the wrong track (a. *fig.*); ⹁wiſch *m*: a) = ⹁licht; b) (tückiſcher Kobold) (mischievous or malicious) imp.

Irvingianer(⸗⸗)*m* ⓶, ⁓in *f* ⓱, **irvingianiſch** *a.* ⓺ [Irving, Stifter der Sekte, † 1834 in Glasgow] *eccl.* Irvingite.

Iſabelle (⸗⸗)[ſpan. = Eliſabeth] I *npr/f.* ⓶β. od. **Iſabella** ⓶α. (Vn.) Isabel(la). — II [⁓ v. Spanien] *f* ⓰ cream-coloured horse.

Iſabell⹁farbe(⸗⸗...) *f* ⓰ cream-colour, auch: isabel; **⹁farben** *a.* ⓺ isabel(le)-yellow, cream-coloured.

Iſchariot(⸗⸗)[hebr. Mann aus Kariot] *m* ⓶α. *bibl.* Judas ⁓ (Apoſtel u. Verräter Jeſu) Judas Iscariot.

Iſchias ⚕ (⸗⸗) *f, inv. path.* (Hüftweh) sciatica, ⚕ ischiagra.

Iſegrim(⸗⸗)[ndd. (ahd.) Eiſenhelm] *m* ⓓd. 1. (Wolf in der Tierfabel) Isengrim. — 2. *fig.* (Griesgram) grumbler, F bear.

Iſidor(us)(⸗⸗⸗)[grch. Iſis⹁geſchenk] *npr/m.* ⓶α(γ). (a. Vn.) Isidore. [Isis.

Iſis(⸗⸗) [äg.] *npr/f. inv. myth., ast.*]

Iſlam(⸗⸗) [ar. Ergebung] *m* ⓓd. (a. *inv.*), **⁓ismus**(⸗⸗) *m* ⓲ (mohammedaniſche Religion) Islam(ism); **Iſieren**(⸗⸗⸗) *v/a.* ⓳ (zum ⁓ bekehren) to Islamize; **Iſiſch**(⸗⸗⸗) *a.* ⓺ (mohammedaniſch) Islamic, Islamitic.

Island(⸗⸗) [Eisland] *npr/n.* ⓶α. Iceland; **Isländer(in** *f* ⓱) *m* ⓶ Icelander; **isländiſch** *a.* ⓺ Icelandic; *min.* Ler Doppelſpat Iceland spar; ⚕ Les Moos Iceland moss (*Cetrária islá ndica*).

Isma⹁el(⸗⸗) [hebr.] *npr/m.* ⓶α. *bibl.* Ishmael; **⁓it**(⸗⸗⸗) *m* ⓶ Ishmaelite.

iſochron ⚗ (⸗⸗⸗) [grch.] *a.* ⓺ *phys.* (gleich lange Zeit während) isochronic, isochronous; of equal duration.

Iſolator ⚡ ⊙ (⸗⸗⸗) [it.] *m* ⓵ *phys.* (Nichtleiter) insulator, insulating-stool.

iſolierbar(⸗⸗⸗⸗) *a.* ⓺ isolable.

iſolieren(⸗⸗⸗⸗) [fr.; *it. *isola* Inſel] I *v/a.* u. ſich ⸗ *v/refl.* ⓰ 1. (ſich) ⸗ (vereinſamen) to isolate (o.s.). — 2. *elect.* (durch Nichtleiter abſondern) ⚡ to insulate. — II ⁓ *n* ⓶ 3. = Iſolierung.

Iſolier⹁haft(⸗⸗⸗) *f* ⓰ solitary confinement; **⹁maſſe** *f* insulating substance; **⹁ſchemel, ⹁ſtuhl** *m* ⓶ Iſola'tor; **⹁ſchicht** *f* insulating layer.

Iſoliert⹁heit(⸗⸗⸗⸗) *f* ⓰ (ſ. iſolieren) 1. isolation. — 2. *phys.* insulation.

Iſolierung(⸗⸗⸗⸗) *f* ⓰ (zu iſolieren 1:) isolation, (zu 2:) insulation.

Iſolier⹁zelle(⸗⸗⸗...) *f* ⓰ cell for solitary (or single) confinement.

iſomer ⚗ (⸗⸗⸗) [grch.] *a.* ⓺ *chm.* (von gleicher Iſ.⹁ſetzung) isomeric.

iſometriſch(⸗⸗⸗⸗) [grch.] *a.* ⓺ (gleichmeſſend) isometrical.

Iſothere ⚗ (⸗⸗⸗) [grch.] *f* ⓲ (Linie gleicher, mittlerer Sonnenwärme) isothere.

Iſotherme ⚗ (⸗⸗⸗⸗) [grch.] *f* ⓲ (Linie gleicher, mittlerer Jahreswärme) isotherm(al line); **iſothermiſch** ⚗ (⸗⸗⸗⸗) *a.* ⓺ isothermal.

Iſra⹁el(⸗⸗ od. ⸗⸗⸗) [hebr. Streiter Gottes] *npr/m.* (Perſon u. Vn.) u. ⚕ *n* (Volt) ⓶α. Israel; **⁓it(in** *f* ⓱) *m* ⓶ Israelite, Jew, auch: Hebrew; **Litiſch**(⸗⸗⸗⸗) *a.* ⓺ Israelite, ...ic, Jewish; auch: Hebrew.

iß(⸗) *imper.*, **iſſeſt**(⸗⸗), **iſt**(⸗; *Hom.* iſt) 2. u. 3. Perſon *sg. pres. ind. von* eſſen.

iſt(⸗; *Hom.* ißt) 3. Perſon *sg. pres. ind. v.* ſein.

Iſt⹁Ausgabe ⚖ (⸗⸗...) *f* ⓰ actual issue; **⹁Beſtand**(*ant.* Soll⸗...) *m* actual (or real) amount or stock or quantity; **⹁Einnahme** *f* net receipts (or F takings) *pl.*

iſthmiſch (⸗⸗) [grch.] *a.* ⓺ Isthmian (games, &c.); **Iſthmus** ⚑ *m* ⓲ (Landenge, bſd. von Korinth) isthmus.

Iſtri⹁en(⸗⸗⸗) [lat.] *npr/n.* ⓶α. (öſterreichiſches Kronland) Istria; **Iſtri⹁er(in** *f* ⓱) *m* ⓶, **iſtriſch**(⸗⸗) *a.* ⓺ Istrian.

Iſt⹁Stärke(⸗...) *f* ⓰ = Iſt⹁Beſtand.

Italer(⸗⸗) [lat.] *m* ⓶ Alt.: Italian, *pl.* oft: (It.) Itali, vgl. Italiker.

Itali⹁en ⚑ (⸗⸗(⸗)⸗) [phöniz. Langeland] *npr/n.* ⓶α. Italy; ſ. Ober⸗, Unter⸗; **Itali⹁ener(in** *f* ⓱) *m* ⓶ (⸗⸗(⸗)⸗⸗⸗) Italian; **itali⹁eniſch**(⸗⸗(⸗)⸗⸗) *a.* ⓺ Italian; Le Oper Italian opera; **italieniſieren**(⸗⸗(⸗)⸗⸗⸗⸗) *v/a.* ⓰ to Italianize.

Italiker(⸗⸗⸗⸗) [lt.] *m* ⓶ ancient inhabitant of Italy; **ita'liſch** *a.* ⓺ Italic.

item(⸗⸗) [lt.] *adv.* 1. (ferner) also moreover, besides. — 2. (desgleichen) likewise.

iterativ(⸗⸗⸗⸗f) [lt.] *a.* ⓺ *gr.* (wiederholend) iterative; **⁓um**(⸗⸗⸗) *n* ⓓd. *gram.* iterative verb.

Ithaka ⚑ (⸗⸗⸗) *npr/n.* ⓶α. grch. Alt.: (Inſel und Reich des Odyſſeus) Ithaca; **Ithak(eſi)er(in** *f* ⓱) *m* ⓶ (⸗⸗(⸗)⸗(⸗), ⸗⸗⸗ithakiſch(⸗⸗⸗⸗) *a.* ⓺ Ithacan.

Itinerar(ium) ⚗ (⸗⸗⸗⸗(⸗)) [lt.] *n* ⓓd. (⓶[⓱]) Wegweiſer, Reiſeführer: itinerary, (traveller's) guide.

J⹁Tüpfel(⸗...) *m, n* ⓶ dot over the i. ⁓⁓... ſ. jetz...

i. V. *abbr.* = in Vertretung. [ⓓα.Ivan.

Iwan (⸗⸗) [Johann] *npr/m.* (ruſſ. Vn.)]

Z

Z, j (jot) *n, inv.* (Buchstabe) J, j; vgl. a.

J. *abbr.* = Jahr year. [Jot.]

J *chm.* Symbol für Jod.

ja (⸗, bisw. ⸗) [ahd.: yea (yes)] I *adv.* 1. (*ant.* nein) yes, bisw.: aye, feierlich: yea; zu allem ja ſagen to say yes (or to consent) to everything; ich kann weder ja noch nein ſagen I cannot say whether or no; er will weder ja noch nein ſagen he does not want to commit himself (either way), he is wavering; **ja doch** surely; **ja freilich** in truth, of course; **ja gewiß** certainly, feierlich: forsooth; **jawohl** yes, indeed; *iro.* ja, es hat ſich wohl!, ja, großen Dank!, ja, proſ(i)t Neujahr!, P ja Kuchen! I (should) think so, indeed!, thank you, indeed!; *bibl.* eure Rede ſei ja, ja, nein, nein! let your communication be yea, yea; nay, nay! — 2. nach einer *neg.* (= doch, allerdings) yes, of course; haſt du es nicht gehört? ja, doch! did you not hear it? of course, I did! or I did hear it! — 3. (⸗) interjektions⹁artig (= nun, unter dieſen Umſtänden): ja, da fällt mir noch ein, daß // there now, it strikes me that //; ja, da haben Sie auch recht! I think there you are right!; ja, wiſſen Sie // why, you know //. — 4. (ſogar, ſelbſt) ja, der König ſelbſt nay, (even) the king himself; Hunderte, ja Tauſende // hundreds, nay thousands //; er iſt arm, ja bettelarm he is poor or, what is more, a pauper. — 5. auf Bekanntes hinweiſend, oft nicht zu überſetzen: das iſt ja gar nicht ſchwer it is not at all difficult; das iſt ja rein zum Davonlaufen, Verrücktwerden that's enough, I am sure, to make one run to the ends of the earth, to drive one mad; es ſchadet ja gar nichts you know (or you see) it does not matter; da ſind Sie ja! there you are (at last)!; ich habe es dir ja geſagt didn't I tell you?, you know (that) I told you; ja, was ich ſagen wollte oh, by the by or by the way! — 6. in Bedingungsſätzen (= überhaupt): er kommt wohl ſpät! wenn er ja kommt ... if he comes at all; wenn es ja durchaus ſein muß if, indeed, it must be (so); if it really has to be (so). — 7. mit lang gedehntem Vokale, Wichtiges hervorhebend: ja, mit ſeinem Reichtum // yes, with such wealth as his, indeed //;

[Jabruder] — 554 — [Jäger]

mit dem Imperativ: schreiben Sie ja recht bald be sure and write soon; kaufen Sie es ja nicht do not buy it on any account; er soll ja im Bett bleiben let him stay in bed by all means or under any circumstances. — **II Ja** n ⓝ ob. inv. yes; parl. aye; mit e-m lauten Ja with a loud yes; eine Frage mit Ja beantworten to answer ... in the affirmative; er bleibt bei Ja und Nein he says only yes and no, he does not open his mouth (much); ich gebe mein Ja nicht dazu I do not (give my) consent to it; ihre Tante ist ihr Ja und Amen she swears by ..., ... is everything and everybody; er bleibt bei (dem) Ja und Nein he adheres to what he said (before), F he sticks to his word; parl. die mit Ja Stimmenden haben die Mehrheit, die Mehrheit stimmt mit Ja the ayes have it.
Ja-bruder (″...) m ⓑ p. who always says yes or who has no will of his own.
jach (ʲᵃ) [mhd.] a. ⓑ = jäh.
Jacht ↓ (ʲᵃcht) [*ndl. = Jagd] f ⓑ yacht.
Jacht-taufe (ᶜʰ...) f ⓑ = Nottaufe.
Jacht-klub ↓ (ʲᵃcht...) m ⓑ yachting club; **-schiff** n = Jacht; **wettfahrt** f yachting race.
Jack-baum ♀ (ʲᵃ...) m ⓑ jack(-tree) (Artoca'rpus integrifo'lia).
Jäckchen (ʲᵃ) n ⓑ (dim. v. Jacke) short (or small) jacket.
Jacke (ʲᵃ) [fr. † jaque] f ⓑ **1.** jacket; ehm. (Roller) jerkin; kurze ~ für Männer pea-jacket; wollene: jersey (auch Tracht der „Heils-armee"); (Unter-)~ (under-) vest, guernsey. — **2.** F fig.: e-m die ~ voll hauen to give a p. a sound drubbing or thrashing; e-m die ~ voll lügen to cram a p. (or to stuff a p. up) with lies; das ist eine alte ~ (Geschichte) that's an old story; das ist ~ wie Hose that's as long as it's broad, it's all the same.
Jackett (ɡᵃ) [fr. jaquette f] n ⓑc.(ⓢ): a) (kurzer Herrenrock) short (or morning-)coat; b) (Jacke für Kinder c.) jacket, frock.
...jackig (ʲᵃ) [Jacke] a. ⓑ mst in Zssgn, z.B.: schwarz-² dressed in a black jacket.
Jacquard (ɡᵃ-tᵃ'r) [fr. Mechaniker in Lyon, 1752–1834]: **~maschine** ⊕ f ⓑ, **-stuhl** m (mechanischer Webstuhl) Jacquard loom.
Jagd (ʲᵃ, bisw. ⁺) [mhd.: *jagen] f ⓑ **1.** hunt, hunting; (Verfolgung) chase, pursuit; mit der Flinte: shooting, im Dickicht: cover-shooting; ~ auf Motten, Schmetterlinge catching moths, butterflies, auch: mothing, butterflying; ~ auf Walfische whaling; auf die ~ geh(e)n (auf der ~ sein) to go (to be) out hunting or shooting; ~ auf etwas m. to hunt after a th., to chase (or pursue) a th., ↓ a. to give chase to a ship, a whale, &c. — **2.** (Weidmannskunst) art of hunting, huntsman's craft or pursuit, huntsmanship. — **3.** coll. (Jäger, Hunde, Pferde) the field, the hunt, the meet. — **4.** = ~bezirk.
Jagd-anzug (ʲᵃ...) m ⓑ hunting-suit, huntsman's dress or apparel; **-aufseher** m game-keeper; **-ausbeute** f = -beute; **-ausdruck** m hunting-term or -expression.

jagdbar (ʲᵃ-) a. ⓑ hunt. fit for hunting; wenn Birkhühner ⚥ sind auch: when grouse are fair game; **~keit** f ⓑ fitness for hunting.
Jagd-berechtigung (ʲᵃ...) f ⓑ right to shoot over a district, engS. shooting-license; **-beute** f booty, fig. (huntsman's) bag, für die Hunde: quarry; eine gute ~ m. to make a good bag, to bag plenty of game; **-bezirk** m hunting-ground or -field, preserve; **-büchse** f sporting-rifle; **-eifer** m zeal for hunting; **-eröffnung** f opening (or beginning) of the shooting-season; **-falke** m, orn. common-falcon (Falco gyrofa'lco); **-flinte** f gun (für hunting), für Vögel: fowling-piece; **-freund** m lover of the chase, weitS. sportsman; **-frevel** m poaching; **-frevler** m poacher; **-garn** n = -netz; **-gebiet** n = -bezirk; **-gehege** n preserve; **-gelegenheit** f (facilities pl. for) hunting or shooting; **-gerät** n huntsman's equipment; ⚥**gerecht** a.: a) skilled in huntsmanship; b) huntsmanlike; **-gerechtigkeit** f = -recht; **-geschichte** f hunting-story, huntsman's (or sportsman's) yarn; **-geschütz** ↓ n = -stück c.; **-gesellschaft** f hunting-party or -field; hunt, chase; **-gefilde** n/pl.: die seligen ~ der Indianer the happy hunting-grounds pl.; **-gesetze** n/pl. game-laws pl.; **-göttin** f goddess of the chase, Diana; **-gründe** m/pl. = -gefilde; **-haus**, **-häuschen** n hunting-box; vgl. -schloß; **-hieb** m lash with a horsewhip, auch = Ohrfeige; **-horn** n hunting-horn, bugle; **-hund** m hound, sporting-dog; f. Bracke¹ und Hühnerhund; **-hüter** m game-keeper; **-joppe** f shooting-jacket; **-kalender** m sporting-almanac; **-kleid** n hunting-dress or -garb; ⚥**kundig** a. = ⚥gerecht a.; **-kunst** f huntsmanship; **-leiter** m master of the hounds; **-leopard** m, zo. = Ge'pard; **-liebhaber** m = -freund; ein (leidenschaftlicher) ~ sein to be (passionately) fond of hunting; **-lust** f pleasure of the chase, (huntsman's) sport; **-machen** ↓ n chase; ⚥**machendes** Schiff chaser; **-messer** n hunting-knife, hanger; **-mütze** f hunting-cap; **-netz** n hunter's (or hunting-)net; **-ordnung** f rules pl. of the chase, regulations pl. for huntsmen; **-partie** f hunting-party, shooting-expedition; **-peitsche** f hunting-whip; **-pferd** n hunter; **-recht** n: a) right of shooting, hunting-license; vgl. -berechtigung; b) game-laws pl.; ⚥**rechtlich** a. in conformity with the rules of the chase; **-reiten** n Sport: hunt-race; **-revier** n = -bezirk; **-rock** n huntsman's coat, shooting-jacket, für die Fuchsjagd: pink hunting-coat; **-ruf** m hunting-call, sounds pl. of the chase, tally-ho; **-schein** m shooting-(or game-)license; **-schlitten** m hunting-sledge; **-schloß** n hunting-lodge or -seat; **-spieß** m hunting-spear; **-stück** n: a) (Gemälde) picture representing the hunting-field; b) etwa: melody (or air) imitating the (sounds

of the) chase; c) ↓ (Kanone zunächst dem Vorbersteven) (bow-)chaser; **-tasche** f hunting-(or game-)bag, sportsman's bag; **-trophäen** f/pl. huntsman's trophies pl., spoils pl. of the chase; **-uhr** f hunting-watch, a. hunter; **-vergnügen** n pleasures pl. of the chase; **-wagen** m, etwa: dog-cart, light carriage or trap; **-wesen** n hunting affairs pl., concerns pl. of the chase; **-zeit** f hunting-(or shooting-)season; **-zeug** n: a) = -anzug; b) = -gerät; **-zug** m: a) hunting-expedition; b) (die zur Jagd Ausziehenden) hunting train, hunt, shooting party; c) (Viergespann) carriage and four, four-in-hand; d) 🚂 (Eilzug) fast (or express) train, F flier, flyer.
jagen (ʲᵃ)[ahd.] ⓑ **I** v/a. **1.** to hunt, (treiben) to drive; (verfolgen) to chase, pursue, ehm. auch: to prick a hare; (hetzen) to run (to death or to earth or to ground), mit Hunden auch: to course; (schießen) to shoot, (beschleichen) to stalk a deer. — **2.** e-n aus dem Dienste ⚥ to send a p. away, F to sack a p., to give a p. the sack; aus dem Hause ⚥ to turn (P to kick) out (of doors); aus-⚥ to scatter, to disperse; f. Bocks-horn; in die Flucht ⚥ to put to flight, to rout; von Haus und Hof ⚥ to turn out of house and home, jur. to evict; zum Teufel (Henker ob. Kuckuck) ⚥ F to send to the devil. — **3.** fig. e-m den Degen durch den Leib ⚥ to run one's sword through a p.'s body, to run a p. through with one's sword; sein Gut (ob. Vermögen) durch die Gurgel (ob. Kehle) ⚥ to spend one's fortune in drink; e-m e-e Kugel durch den Kopf ⚥ to send a bullet through a p.'s head, to blow out a p.'s brains; ein Witz jagte den andern, etwa: the jokes came in rapid succession or as fast as bullets. — **4.** mit Angabe der Wirkung: müde ⚥ to tire out with galloping; ein Pferd zu Tode ⚥ to ride ... to death. — **II** v/n. (h., bei Ortsveränderung sn) **5.** (sich rasch vorwärts bewegen) to rush or dash, drive, ride, gallop ahead or along, to move (or run) with great (or at a furious) speed, F to pelt along; das Automobil jagte über die Brücke the motor darted (or flew, raced) across the bridge; fig. er jagte durch das Buch he raced through the book. — **6.** nach etwas (es als Ziel verfolgen) to hunt (or run) after a th., to pursue one's aim. — **7.** hunt. to go (out) hunting or shooting, to (take part in a) hunt. — **III sich ⚥** v/refl. sich (herum)⚥ to rush about, to dash (madly) along. — **IV ~** n ⓑ (f. I, II) hunt(ing), mit der Flinte: shooting; chase, pursuit; run, course; rush, gallop; sein tolles ~ (Fahren) his reckless (or furious) driving, his mad career; das wilde ~ nach Reichtum the mad pursuit of (or race after) wealth.
Jäger (ʲᵃ) [ahd.] m ⓑ, **~in** f ⓑ **1.** hunter, f huntress; huntsman, sportsman; (Wildhüter) game-keeper,

Signs (see page XVII): F familiar; P vulgar; ꞉ flash; ↘ rare; † obsolete (died); * new word (born); ⁺⁺ incorrect; ♪ music;

[**Jägerbataillon**] — 555 — [**Jakob**]

(Förster) ranger; der Wilde ~, etwa: the wild huntsman; vgl. Jagdfreund. — 2. ⚔ rifleman, sharpshooter; hundert ~, auch: a hundred rifles; ⚔ ~ pl. zu Pferde mounted riflemen pl.

Jäger=bataillo'n ⚔ (⁻◡...) n ⑫ battalion of riflemen or sharpshooters; **=büchse** f ⚔ sharpshooter's rifle; **=bursche** m huntsman's boy, game-keeper's assistant.

Jägerei (⁻◡⁻) f ㊻ **1.** = Jägerkunst; weitS. hunt(ing), chase. — **2.** = Jägerhaus; pl. ~en (Jagdbezirke) hunting-grounds pl.

Jäger=garn (⁻⁻...) n ⑫ hunter's net; **=haus** n, **=hof** m gamekeeper's (or ranger's) house or lodge; **=horn** n hunting-horn, bugle; **=kleid** n huntsman's dress or garb; **=kleidung** (G. Jäger, geb. 1832) f Jaeger clothing; **=kunst** f huntsmanship; **=latein** n: a) sportsman's slang; b) (erlogene Jagdgeschichten) huntsman's tough yarns or F tall stories pl., **=lehrling** m = **=bursche**; **=mäßig** a. like a hunter, sportsmanlike; **=meister** m master of the hunt(smen); vgl. Jagdleiter; **=mütze** f: a) huntsman's cap; b) ♀ side-saddle flower (Sarrace'nia purpu'rea); **=recht** n: a) huntsman's right or fee; b) (Anteil vom Wilde) share of the booty, an die Hunde: quarry.

Jägers=mann (⁻◡⁻)m(pl.=leute) = Jäger 1.

Jäger=sprache (⁻⁻...) f ⑫ hunter's (or sportsman's) language, hunting-terms pl.; vgl. =latein a.

Jaguar (⁻◡⁻) [brasil.] m ⑫d. zo. jaguar, American tiger (Felis onca).

jäh, ㅤe¹ (⁻◡) [ahd.] a. ㉞ **1.** sudden, hasty, (ungestüm) impetuous, (stürzend) precipitous; ㅤe Flucht headlong flight; ㅤer Schrecken sudden fright, v. vielen: panic; ㅤer Tod sudden death. — **2.** als präd. a.: (vorschnell) rash, (aufbrausend) hasty, (kurz angebunden) abrupt; (unbesonnen) thoughtless; sei nicht so ㅤ! don't be so impetuous! — **3.** (abschüssig) steep, precipitous; ㅤer Abhang declivity, stärker: precipice; die ㅤ (adv.) vor uns aufsteigenden Felsen the sheer cliffs before us, the rocks rising sheer in front of us. — Vgl. auch jählings.

Jähe² (⁻◡) f ㊻ (zu jäh 1:) suddenness, haste, precipitancy; (zu 2:) rashness, hastiness; (zu 3:) steepness, precipitousness; declivity, (Abgrund) precipice.

Jä=herr (⁻⁻) ㉚ = Jabruder.

Jäh=hunger (⁻⁻...) m ⑫ ravenous (or voracious) appetite, fierce hunger.

jählings (⁻◡) adv. (f. jäh) (all) of a sudden, precipitously; abruptly; ㅤ voranstürzen to rush on headlong.

Jahr (⁻) [ahd.: year] n ⑫c,6. **1.** year, (volle zwölf Monate) (a) twelvemonth; astronomisches, bürgerliches = astronomical, civil year; ein ganzes ~ a whole year, a (whole) twelvemonth; ein viertel ~ three months; ein halbes ~ half a year, mehr gebr.: six months; dreiviertel ~ nine months; anderthalb ~ eighteen months pl. — **2.** vor Jahres-zahlen: im ~e 1899 in (the year) 1899; im ~e des Heils 1870 in the year of grace 1870, mehr gbr.: A.D. = lt. anno domini; 1870; im ~e 30 vor Christi Geburt in the year 30 B. C. (= before

Christ); in den achtziger ~en in the eighties. — **3.** als zeitliche Bestimmung: alle ~e every year; alle zehn ~e einmal once every ten years; in diesem ~e this (or in the present) year; im nächsten (vorigen) ~e next (last) year; heute in einem ~e f. übers Jahr; es geht schon ins zehnte ~, daß // it is now more than nine years since //; **nach** ~en after (many) years; **seit** einigen ~en for some years past; seit ~ und Tag for many years, for many a long day; über ~ und Tag in years to come, (many) years hence; übers ~ this day (or to-day) twelvemonth, a year hence; ein ~ ums andere every year; heute vor e-m ~e a year (ago) to-day, just a twelvemonth ago; vor (vielen) ~en (many) years ago; **während** einiger ~e during (or for) several years; ein ~ wie das andere oder wie alle ~e (immer gleich) every year the same. — **4.** als Maß des Lebensalters: er ist zwölf ~e alt, er zählt zwölf ~e he is twelve years old, a. kurz: F he is twelve; er geht in sein neuntes ~ he is in his ninth year; er ist in den dreißiger ~en ... over thirty or between thirty and forty; über fünfzig ~e alt sein to be turned fifty or on the wrong side of fifty; vgl. Fünfziger 5; schon bei ~en sein to be advanced (or well on) in years; in den besten ~en sein to be in one's best years or in the prime of life; das wird sich mit den ~en verlieren it will go (or pass) away as (s)he grows older; vor seinen ~en (in der Kindheit) sterben to die before one's time; zu ~en kommen to get on (or advance) in years; Sprichw. mit den ~en kommt der Verstand wisdom comes with age. — **5.** ⚔ sein ~ (seine zwei ~e) dienen to serve one's year (one's two years) in the ranks or the army.

Jahr=acker (⁻⁻...) m ⑫ field that is ploughed every year; **jahr=aus** (⁻⁻) ⒛, ~ ein year after year, from one year's end to another.

Jahr=buch (⁻⁻ch) n ⑫ yearbook, almanac, calendar; **=bücher** pl. annals pl.; **=buchschreiber** m annalist, chronicler.

Jährchen (⁻◡) [Jahr, dim.] n ㉓ short year; ein ~ barely a twelvemonth.

jahre=lang (⁻◡⁻) a. ㊻ lasting (or continuing) for years; adv. for (whole) years; viele Jahre lang for many years (in succession).

jähren (⁻◡): sich ㅤ v/refl. ⑱: es jährt sich heute, daß // it is a year (or a twelve-month) to-day (or ago) since //.

Jahres=abschluß (⁻⁻...) m f. **=schluß**; **=anfang** m beginning (or commencement) of the year; **=ausgaben** f/pl. annual expenses pl.; **=ausweis** ☸ m annual return or statement; **=bericht** m annual report; **=einkommen** n, **=einkünfte** f/pl. yearly income; **=einnahme** f (annual) revenue, income; **=feier** f, **=fest** n annual fête or celebration, anniversary; **=folge** f succession of years; nach der ~ erzählen to relate in chronological order; **=frist** f space of a year; nach ~ within (or after) a twelvemonth; **=gedächtnis** n annual commemoration; vgl. **=feier**; **=kontinge'nt**

⚔ n von Rekruten annual levy; **=kursus** m, **=pensum** n einer Schule scholastic year, annual course; **=rapport** m = **=bericht**; **=rate** f yearly instalment, als Rente: annuity; **=rechnung** ☸ f annual account or balance; **=ring** m im Holze annual ring; **=schluß** m: a) close (or end, last day) of the year; b) ☸ year's (or yearly, annual) balance or balancing; **=tag** m = **=gedächtnis**; **=trieb** ♀ m year's growth; **=verbrauch** m yearly consumption; **=versammlung** f annual meeting; **=viertel** n quarter; **=wechsel** m (coming of the) new year; **=wende** f: bei der ~ at the turn of the year; **=wuchs** = **=trieb**; **=zahl** f (number indicating the) year; date; **=zeit** f season; der ~ angemessen seasonable; außer (je nach) der ~ out of (according to the) season: **=ziel** ☸ n lapse of a year, year's time; **=zinsen** pl. annual interest.

Jahr=fünft (⁻⁻) n ⑫c. space of five years; **=gang** (⁻⁻...) m ⑫: a) agr. year's growth or vintage; b) Buchhandel: annual publication; der ganze ~ e-r Zeitschrift ꝛc. the whole year's numbers pl. ...; **=gehalt, =geld** n yearly (or annual) salary or stipend or allowance; **=hundert** (⁻⁻⁻) n century; viele ~e lang (lasting) for (many) centuries or ages; noch nach ~en in centuries to come, in future ages.

jährig (⁻◡) a. ㊻ **1.** in Zsfgn mit Zahlen, 3B.: zwölf=ㅤ of (or lasting) twelve years, twelve years old. — **2.** (1 Jahr dauernd) lasting a year. — **3.** (1 Jahr her) es ist nun ㅤ, daß // it is now a year since //; der hundertjährige Gedenktag the hundredth anniversary, the centenary. — **4.** = großjährig.

jährlich (⁻◡) [Jahr] a. ㊻ (jedes Jahr wiederkehrend ob. zahlbar) yearly, annual: er hat ein ~es Einkommen von 6000 Mark he has (an income of) three hundred (pounds) a year; adv. auch: every year, ☸ a. (It.) per annum.

Jährling (⁻◡) [Jahr] m ⑫d. (bes. Schaf, Wildschwein) yearling.

Jahr=markt (⁻⁻...) m ⑫ fair; **=markts-geschenk** n present (or trinket) bought at a fair; **=pacht** f yearly tenancy (or tenure) of land; **=ring** ♀ m f. Jahres-r.; **=schuß** ♀ m annual shoot or growth; **=tausend** (⁻⁻⁻) n a thousand years, millennium; **=weise** (⁻⁻) ~ adv. by the year, yearly, annually; **=wuchs** m yearly growth or crop; **=zahl** f = Jahres-z.; **=zehnt** (⁻⁻) n space of ten years, decade. — [**Jehova**] Jah(veh).

Jahve (⁻◡⁻) [hebr.] npr/m. ⑫㉘ a. (r-r für) **Jäh=zorn** (⁻⁻) m ⑫c. sudden anger or wrath, violent fit of temper or passion; als Eigenschaft: passionateness, hot temper, irascibility; **jäh=zornig** (⁻⁻◡) a. ㊻ passionate, hot-tempered, irascible; (wütend) furious.

Jak (⁻) [tibet.] m ㊿ zo. = Jak=ochse.

Jakaranda=holz (⁻ ◡⁻⁻...) n [brasil.] f. jacaranda-wood, rose-wood.

Jak=baum ꝛc. f. Jack...

Jako (⁻⁻) [afrik.] m ㊾, orn. (Papagei) jaco (Psi'ttacus eri'thacus).

Jakob (⁻◡) [hebr.] npr/m. ⑫㉘ a. **I** (jüdischer Patriarch) Jacob. — **II** (Bn.) Ja-

[**Jaköbchen**] — 556 — [**jauchzen**]

cob, James; F der wahre ~ the real Simon (Pure); das ist der wahre ~! that's the man or the right sort!

Jaköbchen (⌣⌣⌣) npr/n. ⓑα. (dim. von Jakob) etwa: (little) Jim, Jemmy.

Jakobi (⌣́⌣) gen. v. Jakobus: zu ~ (am Jakobstage, 25. Juli) on St. James'(s) day; ~kirche f St. James'(s) Church.

Jakobine (⌣⌣́⌣) npr/f. ⓑⓑ. (Bn.) Jacobine, Jemima, bisw.: Jamesina.

Jakobiner (⌣⌣́⌣) m ⓑ, ~in f ⓑ 1. Cath. eccl. ~(=mönch, =nonne) Dominican (monk, nun). — 2. fr. hist. (Mitglied des ~klubs, 1790/4) Jacobin; ~klub m ⓑ (tagte im =kloster in Paris) Jacobin club; ~mütze f red (Phrygian) cap (of the Jacobins). [ic(al).)

jakobinisch (⌣⌣́⌣) [fr.] a. ⓑ Jacobin-J

Jakobit (⌣⌣́) m ⓑ engl. hist. (Anhänger der Stuarts, seit Jakob II. 1689) Jacobite.

Jakobs=(kreuz)kraut ♀ (⌣́...) n ⓑ staggerwort (Sene'cio Jacobae'a); =leiter f: a) bibl. Jacob's ladder; b) ⚓ = Himmels=l.; =stab m Jacob's staff ⊕ ⚒ Fuß e-r Feldmesserboussole); =tag m = Jakobi.

Jakobus (⌣́⌣) ⓖγ. I npr/m. (Bn.) Jacob(us). — II m, mint. (alte engl. Goldmünze = 25 Mark) jacobus. [yak.)

Jak=ochs (⌣́...) [s. Jak] m ⓑ (Grunzochs))

Jakonett (⌣⌣́) [engl., *fr.] m ⓑc. (feiner Baumwollstoff, Musselin) jaconet.

Jakute (⌣́⌣) m ⓑ, **Jakutin** f ⓑ (ostsibir. Volk) Yakut, Yakoot.

Jalappa ♀ (⌣́⌣) [~, mex. St.] f ⓑ: echte ~ = Jalappentrichterwinde; falsche ~ beauty-of-the-night (Mira'bilis Ja'lapa).

Jalappen=trichterwinde ♀ (⌣⌣́⌣) f ⓑ jalap-plant (Ipomoe'a od. Exogo'nium Purga); =wurzel f, pharm. (Abführmittel) jalap(-root) (von Ipomoe'a Purga).

Jalousie (Gä-lu-fi') [fr. Eifersucht] f ⓑ (Rolladen) Venetian blind; (Wettervorhang) awning; ~zug m ⓑ blind-lift, pull (or cord) of a Venetian blind.

Jam f (s) m ⓑ = Jampflanze.

Jama=ika ♀ (⌣⌣́⌣) [indian. Quelleninsel] npr/n. ⓑα. (e-e der Großen Antillen) Jamaica; ~holz ♀ n ⓑ Jamaica-wood.

jama=ikanisch (⌣⌣⌣́⌣) a. ⓑ Jamaican.

Jamaika=pfeffer ♀ und ♀ (⌣⌣́⌣...) pharm. Jamaica-pepper, allspice (Semen amo'mi); =Rum m Jamaica rum.

Jambe 2c. f. Jambe 2c.

Jambuse ♀ (⌣́⌣) [ost=indisch] f ⓑ, ~n=baum m ⓑ jambu (Jambo'sa).

Ja=mensch (⌣́.⌣) m ⓑ = Jabruder.

Jammer (⌣́⌣) [ahd. ⌣́⌣] m ⓑ 1. (tiefes Elend) extreme misery or distress, (Drangsal) calamity; (Herzeleid) affliction, (Verzweiflung) despair; (Mitgefühl) compassion; ein Bild des ~s darbieten to look a picture of misery or wretchedness. — 2. (Wehklagen) lamentation, wailing, (Ächzen) moaning, groans pl. — 3. ~ (schmerzliches Sehnen) nach // deep longing for //. — 4. F ~ und Schade ist's, auch: es ist Jschade! it is a great pity or a thousand pities!; verächtlich: es ist ein ~! it is a wretched affair! — 5. F burschikos = Katzen=J.

Jammer=anblick (⌣́...) m ⓑ deplorable (or woeful) sight; =bild n picture of misery, =erregend a. ⓑ piteous, pitiable, =geschrei n cry (or cries pl.) of distress, lamentation; =gesicht n sorrowful (or woeful) countenance; =gestalt f woebegone figure.

jammerhaft (⌣́⌣⌣) a. ⓑ = jammervoll.

Jammer=leben (⌣́⌣...) n ⓑ wretched life, life of misery or wretchedness, miserable (or pitiable) existence.

jämmerlich (⌣́⌣⌣) a. ⓑ 1. pitiable (vgl. jammervoll), woeful; es ist 2 anzusehen it is a pitiful (or deplorable) sight; der Anblick sad (or sorry) sight or spectacle; 2 aussehen to present a piteous spectacle, to look wretched; e-n fgotts=2 prügeln to beat a p. unmercifully. — 2. (armselig) miserable, wretched. — **Jämmerlichkeit** (⌣́⌣⌣) f ⓑ (s. jämmerlich) pitiableness, woefulness; (Elend) misery, wretchedness.

Jämmerling (⌣́⌣) m ⓑd. poor wretch.

jammern (⌣́⌣) [ahd.] ⓑα. I v/n. (h.) to lament, (ächzen, wimmern) to wail, moan, groan; (verzweifeln) to despair; nach et. Verlorenem 2 to grieve sorely over s.th. lost, to bewail (or mourn) the loss of a th. — II v/a. (a. v/impers.) e-n 2 to rouse (or move) a p.'s pity or compassion; der Mensch jammert mich, bisw. es jammert mich des Menschen I pity (or feel sorry for) the poor fellow. — III ~n ⓑ = Jammer 2.

Jammer=ruf (⌣́⌣...) m ⓑ = =geschrei; **Jschade**. =tal n: (irdisches) ~, oft: vale of woe, BUNYAN: Slough of Despond; =ton m doleful tone, sound of distress or woe; =voll a. wretched, full of misery or wretchedness, (herzzerreißend) heart-rending, (Mitleid erregend) lamentable, piteous, pitiable, deplorable.

Jam=pflanze ♀ (⌣́...) [afrik. inja'me] f ⓑ, =wurzel f yam (Dioscore'a).

Jangtsekiang ♀ (⌣⌣́) [chines.] npr/m. ⓑα. (Fl.) Yangtze-kiang, Yantsekiang.

Jan=hagel (⌣́.⌣) [ndd., ndl.] m ⓑ (o. pl.) vulgar mob, rabble, riff-raff, tag-rag and bob-tail; the low class(es pl.), the common herd, the scum of the cities.

Janitschar ⚔ (⌣⌣́) türk. neue Truppe] m ⓑ ehm.: (Soldat der 1826 aufgelösten türkischen Garde) janizary; =en=musik f ⓑ janizary (or Turkish) music.

Jänner †, poet. u. provz. (⌣́⌣) [mhd., *It.] m ⓑ u. inv. = Januar.

Jansenismus (⌣⌣́⌣) [holl. kath. Bischof Jansen(ius), 1585—1638] m ⓑ eccl. (Lehre v. d. Gnade u. Prädestination) Jansenism; **Jansenist** (⌣⌣́) m ⓑ Jansenist.

Januar (⌣́⌣=) [lt.] m ⓑ (month of) January; der erste ~ the first of January, auch: New Year's Day.

Janus (⌣́⌣) [lt.] npr/m. ⓑγ. (röm. Gott mit zwei Gesichtern) Janus; **Jköpfig** a. ⓑ =tempel m ⓑ in Friedenszeiten geschlossen: temple of Janus.

Japan ♀ (⌣́⌣, a. dG⌣́=) npr/m. ⓑα. (ostasiatisches Inselreich) Japan.

Japaner (⌣⌣́⌣) m ⓑ, ~in f ⓑ, weniger gut **Japanese** (⌣⌣́⌣) m ⓑ, **Japanesin** f ⓑ Japanese, F Jap; **japanesisch** a. ⓑ = japanisch.

japanieren ⊕ (⌣⌣́⌣) [Japan] v/a. Porzellanfabrikation 2c.: to japan.

japanisch (⌣⌣́⌣) a. ⓑ of Japan, Japanese, F Jap; de Sprache, das ~(e) n ⓑ the Japanese language, Japanese; der Brauch Japanism; ⚒ ~e Erde Japan earth, catechu; zo. der Hirsch Japanese deer (Cervus sica); ⚒ de Lackwaren japanned goods or wares pl.; ~es Meer m Japan Sea, Sea of Japan.

Japhet (⌣́=) [hebr.] npr/m. ⓑⓑα. bibl. (dritter Sohn Noahs) Japheth.

Japhetiden (=⌣⌣́⌣) m/pl. ⓑ (Arier) descendants of Japheth, Aryans, bisw. a. ⚒ Japetidæ pl.

japhetisch (=⌣⌣́⌣) a. ⓑ Japhetic, Japhetian.

jappen ⓑ, **japsen** ⓑ (⌣́⌣) [ndb. = gaffen] v/n. (h.) to gasp, (keuchen) to pant.

Jardini=ere (G⌣⌣(⌣)⌣́=) [fr. Gärtnerin] f ⓑ (Blumentischchen) ornamental flowerstand, (fr.) jardinière.

Jargon (Gär-ga̍') [fr. eigtl. Geschnatter] m ⓑ vulgar speech, (fr.) jargon; slang, thieves' cant; F St. Giles'(s) Greek, lingo, co. double Dutch.

Ja=sager (⌣́⌣⌣) m ⓑ = Jabruder.

Jasmin ♀ (⌣́⌣, ofr. G⌣́) [pers. Duft] m ⓑd. jessamine, jasmine (Jasmi'num); gelber ~ Cape-jasmine (Garde'nia flo'rida); wilder (oder gemeiner) ~ white syringa (Philade'lphus corona'rius).

Jasmin=baum ♀ (⌣́...) m ⓑ red jasmine (Plume'ria rubra); =blatt n, =blüte f jessamine leaf, blossom; =laube f jessamine arbour.

Jasp=achat ⚒ (⌣⌣́) m ⓑc. = Jaspisacha't.

jaspieren ⊕ (⌣⌣́⌣) [Jaspis] v/a. (in Kieselerde verwandeln) to jasperize; Töpferei: jaspiert (gesprenkelt) jasped, (fr.) jaspé.

Jaspis (⌣́⌣) [mhd., grch., *hebr.] m ⓑ oder inv. min. (Art Kiesel) jasper.

Jaspis=achat (⌣́...) m ⓑ jaspagate; =aderung f jaspure; Jartig a. ⓑ like jasper, ⚒ jaspidean, jaspideous, jaspoid; Jhaltig a. jasperated, jaspery; =opal m jasp(er)-opal; =porzellan n jasper- (or Wedgwood) ware.

Jatagan (⌣⌣́) [türk. — ⌣́ Verteidiger] m ⓑd. ⚔ (gekrümmter, langer Dolch) yataghan.

jäten (⌣́⌣) [ahd.] v/a. u. v/n. (h.) ⓑ agr., hort. to weed, to clear of weeds.

Jäter (⌣́⌣) m ⓑ, ~in f ⓑ weeder, person pulling (or grubbing) up weeds.

Jät=gabel (⌣́...) f ⓑ weeding-fork or -iron; =hacke, =haue ⊕ f hoe for weeding, weeding-hoe or -hook; =grubbing-axe; =maschine ⊕ f weeder, aberuncator, averruncator; =zange f weeding-forceps or =pincers or -tongs pl.; =zeit f weeding-time.

Jauche (⌣́⌣) [ndd., *poln.] f ⓑ 1. stale water; bsd. (=Mist) ~ liquid manure or dung; fig. (schlechtes Bier) stale beer, inferior ale, F slops pl., hogwash. — 2. path. (zersetzter Eiter) putrid pus, ⚒ ichor, sanies.

Jauche(n)=behälter (⌣́⌣...) [Jauche 1] m ⓑ, =grube f pit for liquid manure.

Jauchert (⌣́⌣) s. Juchart.

jauchhaft, jauchicht, jauchig (⌣́⌣⌣) a. ⓑ (faulig) putrid; path.: ⚒ ichorous, sanious; jauchige Blutvergiftung: ⚒ ichor(r)hæmia.

Jauch=höhle (⌣́...) [Jauche 2] f ⓑ path. suppurating cavity, abscess.

jauchzen (⌣́⌣) [ahd. lautm.] ⓑ I v/n. (h.) to jubilate, to exult, to shout (or yell) exultingly or triumphantly; ihm jauch=

Zeichen (s. S. XVII): F familiär; P Volkssprache; Γ Gaunersprache; ⟨ selten; † alt (ausgestorben); * neu (auch geboren); ‡ unrichtig;

[Jauchzer] — 557 — [jener]

zet das Volk the people acclaim (or applaud) him or lustily cheer him. — II v/a. (2d äußern) to shout forth, to express by (sounds of) jubilation; e-m Beifall 2 to receive a p. with loud applause or cheers. — III ~ n ⓝ jubilation, exultation, exultant (or jubilant) shouts or yells pl.; (lusty) cheers pl.
Jauchzer (´-ɥ) m ⓜ 1. jubilant (or exultant) person. — 2. = jauchzen III.
jaulen (´ɥ) [: yawl, yowl] v/n. (h.) ⓑ to whine, to howl, to yowl.
Java-kaffee ⊕ (´ɥɥ...) m ⓜ Java (coffee).
javanisch (ɥ´ɥ) [♀ Java im Indischen Ozean] a. ⓑ Javanese.
ja-wohl (ɥ´) adv. s. ja 1.
Ja-wort (´-) n ⓝ yes, yea; (word of consent); e-m Freier das ~ geben to accept a suitor, to plight one's troth.
je[1] (´) int. 1. **Je** [Je(sus)] Herr Je! (a. Je'mer, Je'mine, Je'mini, Je'rum, Je're(m), Jes) good gracious!, good heavens!, oh Lord!, goodness alive!, dear me!, P jemini! — 2. je, da kommt er! lo (or why), there he comes!; je nun? now then?, what do you want or mean?; je nun, das Klagen hilft nichts well now, it's no use lamenting; vgl. ja 3 u. ei.
je[2] (´) [ahd.: i(mmer)] adv. u. cj. 1. **von je(her)** at all times, from times immemorial, stärker: from all eternity. — 2. **je und je**: a) on and on, always; b) (von Zeit zu Zeit) from time to time, bisw.: sometimes, at times, occasionally. — 3. in fragenden, verneinenden, bedingenden und Relativsätzen, auch bei „als" nach comp. = zu irgendeiner Zeit: ever, at any time; ohne ihn je gesehen zu haben without ever (or once) having seen him; er war reicher, als er sich je hätte träumen l. he was rich beyond the dreams of avarice. — 4. distributiv bei Haupt- und Ordnungszahlen: je (immer) zwei und zwei two at a time, two by (or and) two, by twos; er gab den drei Knaben je eine Mark he gave each of the three boys a shilling; je einer nach dem anderen oder um den anderen each one in his turn; nach je drei Jahren (after) every three years; tel. für je zehn Wörter for every ten words. — 5. vor „nach" zur Bezeichnung von Maß und Verhältnis: **je nach** ihrem Fleiße können sie zehn bis zwölf Mark verdienen according to (their) industry they can earn from ten to twelve shillings; **je nachdem** die Umstände es erfordern according as circumstances may require it; je nachdem die Preise steigen oder fallen according (or just) as the prices may rise or fall, in accordance with the rise or fall of prices; s. nachdem. — 6. in Nebensätzen mit e-m comp., Übereinstimmung bezeichnend: **je mehr** man hat, **je** (oder **desto, um so**) mehr man will the more we have, the more we want; je weniger ihrer sind the fewer there are of them; je bescheidener du bist, desto zufriedener werde ich sein in proportion as you are modest I shall be content; je eher, je lieber the sooner the better; je länger, je lieber the longer the better; je weiter wir kamen the further we proceeded, as we advanced. — 7. je mehr und mehr (immer mehr) more and more; es wird mit ihm je länger, je schlimmer the longer it lasts, the worse he gets.
jeden-falls (´ɥ..., ´ɥ...˝) adv. in any case, under any circumstances, at any rate, by all means, at all events; (in der einen ob. anderen Weise) somehow or other; (was auch geschehen mag) whatever may happen; er ist 2 arm he is certainly (or undoubtedly) poor; ♀ orts adv. everywhere.
jeder (´ɥ) [ahd.: either] m indefinite pronoun, jede f, jedes n ⓝ A 2, B* (wie def. art.) 1. adjektivisch, individualisierend: each; verallgemeinernd: every, any; von zweien auch: either; 2 Schüler muß sein Buch mitbringen each pupil must bring his book; 2 Schüler muß Aufgaben machen every pupil must do lessons; 2 Zehnte every tenth man, one out of (every) ten; jedes kleinste Versehen even the slightest error, any mistake be it ever so trivial; er wird mit jedem Tage dreister he grows bolder every day or from day to day; ohne jeden Zweifel without any (or the slightest) doubt; (zu) 2 Zeit (von größerem Nachdruck als 2zeit) at any given time; unter 2 Bedingung upon any terms, whatever the conditions may be; zu 2 Stunde at any (given) hour. — 2. substantivisch: each (or every) one, each (or every) (wo)man; each thing, everything; ein jedes (alle Leute) everybody, all (the) people; 2 von den beiden either of them; 2 dieser Männer hat sein Verdienst, seltener: diese Männer haben 2 ihr Verdienst each (or every) one of these men has his (special) merit; 2 meiner Gedanken my every thought; 2 seiner Wünsche ist erfüllt worden his every wish has been fulfilled; nicht 2 kann Gutes tun not all are (or not everybody is) able to do good; **all und 2** each and all, all and sundry; Sprichw. 2 für sich und Gott für uns alle every one for himself and God for us all; 2 hat s-e Fehler we all have our faults; 2 ist sich selbst der nächste charity begins at home; 2 nach seiner Art every one after his own fashion, each (one) in his own way; ein kehre 2 vor der eigenen Tür let each attend to (or mind) his own business.
jeder-lei (´ɥ-, -´ɥ) a. inv. = allerhand.
jeder-mann (´ɥ-´) indef. pron. m everybody, any one, each (or every) one, co. all the world and his wife; das ist nicht 2s Sache that's not a thing that everybody would care about (doing), it's not every one's taste; ~s-freund m ⓜ everybody's friend; F co. hail-fellow-well-met.
jeder-zeit (´ɥ´) adv. at any time, at all times, always; for ever.
jedes-mal (´ɥ-) adv. each (or every) time; 2 wenn whenever, as often as.
jedes-malig (´ɥ-ɥ) a. ⓑ in (or for) each case; die 2e Beschaffenheit der Dinge the actual state of affairs; bei 2er Sendung with each consignment; wie es die 2en Zustände erheischen as the circumstances may require it, according to the exigencies of the case.
jedoch (ɥ´ɥ) adv. however, still, yet; (nichtsdestoweniger) nevertheless, for all that.
jedweder m, **jedwede** f, **jedwedes** n (-´ɥ ɥɥ) [ahd.: jeder von beiden], a. **jeglich** (´ɥ) [ahd.: each] indef. pron. ⓑ = jeder; ein jeglicher, jegliches each (or every) one, all.
je-her (-´ u. ´-) adv.: von 2 s. je[2] 1.
Jehova (--ɥ´ u. -´-ɥ) [s. Jahve] npr/m. ⓑ α. rel. (Name Gottes) Jehovah.
Jehovist (--ɥ´) m ⓜ (Jehova-anbeter) Jehovist.
jehovistisch (--ɥ´ɥ) a. ⓑ Jehovistic.
Je-länger-je-lieber ♀ (´ɥ´ɥ´ɥ) m, n ⓝ honeysuckle (Loni'cera caprifo'lium).
je-mals (´-) adv. ever; s. je[2] 3.
je-mand (´-) [ahd.: *je u. Mann] indef. pron. m ① (dat. und acc. besser inv.) 1. somebody, some one; fragend od. verneinend, oft: anybody, any one; es kommt 2 there is somebody coming; es ist 2 bei ihm there is some one with him, auch oft: he has company; hat 2 geschellt? did anybody ring (the bell)?; habe ich 2 schellen hören? did I hear somebody ring?; **irgend** 2 anybody; 2 **anders** some (or any) other person or F body; kann sonst 2 es getan haben? can any one (or somebody) else have done it?; als ob 2 sagen wollte // as if some one would say //, as who should say //. — 2. (bestimmte, doch nicht näher bezeichnete Person) ich kenne einen (gewissen) ~, der // I know a (certain) person who //, I know somebody who //; dieser 2 this individual. — 3. adjektivisch vor substantivisch gebrauchten a.: 2 Hohes some great (or exalted, high) person(age), somebody important, F some (great) swell.
Jemen ♀ (´ɥ) [ar. rechts, d. i. südlich] npr/n. ⓑ α. (Küstenstrich Arabiens) Yemen.
jemer (´ɥ), **jemine**. ...i (´ɥ-) [Je(su do'-)mine!] int. s. je[2]!; vgl. o2!, herr2!
jener (´ɥ) [ahd.: yon(d[er])] m demonstrative pronoun, jene f, jenes n ⓝ A 2, B* (wie def. art.) 1. adjektivisch: that, pl. those; in geh. Spr. u. P. auch: yon(der); jene guten Leute those good people pl.; 2 selbe Weg that same road; 2 Verwandte von mir that relative of mine; jenes Ufer yonder (or the opposite) bank; von fernen Dingen: in jenem Leben in the life to come, in yonder (or in the other) world; in jenen Tagen: a) Vergangenheit: in those days (of the past), auch: in days of yore; b) Zukunft: in future days; in jener Welt in the other world, in the world beyond (the grave). — 2. substantivisch: that one, pl. those ones; hat M. recht ob. N.? dieser sagt weiß, jener schwarz ... the former says black, the latter white; bald dieser, bald jener now (this) one, now the other; von diesem und jenem sprechen to speak of one thing and another; wie jener (das Sprichwort) sagt as the (old) adage says; milder Fluch: das soll dieser und 2 holen! the deuce take it!

♪ Musik; ⚙ Wissenschaft; ♀ Pflanze; ⏚ Geographie; ⊕ Technik; ⚒ Bergbau; ⚔ Militär; ⚓ Marine; ● Handel; ✉ Post; 🚂 Eisenbahn.

[Jennymaschine] — 558 — [Jodür]

Jenny=maschine ⚆ ⊕ (G⁀ᵉⁿⁱ...) [engl.] f ⓶ Spinnerei: (spinning) jenny.
jen-seit (⸝⁄) prp. s. jenseits.
jen-seitig (⸝⁄⸍) a. ⓺ 1. (situated) on the other (or on yonder, F on the off) side; lying beyond, further; das ⸿e Ufer the opposite bank. — 2. (der anderen Partei angehörig) der ⸿e Advokat counsel for the other (or the opposite side).
jen-seits (⸝⁄) I prp. mit gen. 1. on the other (or on yonder, on the further) side; ⸿ der Alpen (gelegen) beyond the Alps, transalpine; ⸿ des Atlantischen Meeres across the Atlantic, transatlantic; ⸿ der Brücke transpontine (bfd. von Süd=London); ⸿ des Grabes beyond the grave, auch: in the world to come, hereafter; ⸿ des Meeres across the sea, transoceanic, (fr.) d'outre mer (bfd. von Frankreich). — 2. adv. on the other side, yonder; further on. — II ~ n, inv. 3. the other (or the next) world, the life to come; ein besseres ~ a brighter and a better world, a life of bliss; ins ~ befördern to launch (or hurl) into eternity, vgl. befördern 6.
Jeremia, ~s (--⸝⁄) npr/m. ⓺ γ. (gen. bibl. --miä) (jüd. Prophet 626 v. Chr.) Jeremiah, F Jeremy; Klagelieder Jeremiä Lamentations pl. of Jeremiah.
Jeremiade (--⸝⁄⸍) [fr.] f ⓶ jeremiad, woeful tale, lamentation, doleful story.
Jerez=wein (ch⸍⸿s⸍) [span.] m ⓶ sherry.
Jericho ♀ (⸝⁄⸍, r-r ⸍⸝) npr/n. ⓶α. bibl. (Stadt in Palästina) Jericho.
jerichonisch (--⸝⁄⸍) a. ⓺ of Jericho.
Jericho=rose ♀ (⸝⁄⸍...) f ⓶ rose of Jericho (Anastatica hierochuntica).
Jerobeam (--⸝⁄⸍) [hebr. Ja'robam] npr/m. ⓶α. bibl. (König von Israel) Jeroboam.
jerum F (⸝⁄) [corr. Jesus] int. o ~! oh, dear me!
Jerusalem ♀ (-⸍⸿⸍) [hebr. Wohnung des Friedens] npr/n. ⓶α. (Hauptstadt von Palästina) Jerusalem; rel. das neue, himmlische ~ (Wohnort der Seligen) New Jerusalem, celestial abode.
Jerusalems=blume ♀ (⸍...) f ⓶ = Feuernelke; =gerste ♀ f = Davidsgerste.
Jes F (⸝⁄) int. s. je¹ 1.
Jesabel (⸝⁄⸍, --⸝⁄) npr/f. ⓶ bibl. Jezabel, Jezebel (auch fig. = böses Weib).
Jesa-ias, Jesaja (-⸝⁄⸍(⸍)) [hebr.] npr/m. ⓺ γ. bibl. (Prophet 740—700 v. Chr.) Isaiah.
Jesuit (--⸝⁄) [Jesus] m ⓶, ~in (-⸝⁄⸍) f ⓶ Jesuit (Orden 1540).
Jesuiten=general (⸿⸍⸝⸍⸍...) m ⓶ general of the Jesuits; =orden m Jesuit order, Society of Jesus; =pulver [von den Jesuiten im 17. sae. nach Spanien gebracht] n, pharm. (gepulverte Chinarinde) ehm.: Jesuits' powder, jetzt: (powdered) Peruvian bark; =schule f Jesuit college.
Jesuitentum (--⸝⁄⸍) n ⓶d. Jesuitism.
Jesuiter F (--⸝⁄) m ⓶ contp. = Jesuit.
Jesuiterei F (--⸝⁄⸿⸍) f ⓶ = Jesuitentum.
Jesuiter=nuß ♀ (--⸝⁄⸍) f ⓶ (Frucht von Trapa natans) Jesuits' nut.
jesuitisch (--⸝⁄⸍) a. ⓺ Jesuitic(al).
Jesuitismus (--⸿⸍⸝⸍⸍) m ⓶ Jesuitism.
Jesulein (⸝⁄⸍-⸍) n ⓶ = Jesuskindlein.
Jesus (⸝⁄⸿) [grch.; *hebr. Josua Gott hilft] npr/m. ⓶ 1. Jesus; ~ Christus Jesus Christ, Christ Jesus; eccl. Gesellschaft

Jesu = Jesuitenorden; im Namen Jesu in the name of Jesus; der Herr ~ the Lord Jesus, our Lord; oft als Ausruf: ~ (Maria Joseph)!, etwa: good Lord! — 2. bibl. das Buch ~ Sirach Ecclesiasticus. [(or infant) Jesus]
Jesus=kind(lein) (⸝⁄⸍...) n ⓶ the child
Jett ⚆ (G⸍) [engl., fr. (*Gagat)] n ⓶c. min. = Gagat; imitiertes ~ artificial jet.
Jettchen (⸝⁄) [(Henri)ette] npr/n. ⓶α.,
Jette F (⸝⁄) npr/f. ⓶β. (Vn.) Henrietta, Harriet, Netta.
jetzig (⸝⁄⸍) a. ⓺ of the present time or age; (gegenwärtig) actual; die ⸿e Herzogin von York the now (or the present) Duchess of York; in der ⸿en Zeit in our days or times, nowadays; das ⸿e Zeit=alter our own time, this present age; die ⸿en Zustände the prevailing condition of affairs; ⓶ ⸿e Preise current prices or rates pl.
jetzo † (⸝⁄⸍) = jetzt.
jetzt (⸝⁄) [mhd.] I adv. 1. now, at present, at the present time or day, in our days; (in Wirklichkeit) actually; eben ⸿ just now; erst ⸿ only now, but now; gleich ⸿ at once, instantly; noch ⸿ even now, to this (very) day; ⸿ und allezeit od. immerfort now and for ever, eccl. now and evermore; ⸿ sind es fünf Jahre her it is now five years ago; ⸿ oder nie galt es ist was a case of now or never; wie die Sachen ⸿ stehen as things now are; phot. ⸿! now steady! — 2. bei lebhafter Erzählung = da, z.B. ⸿ erhob er sich then (or with that) he rose. — 3. nach prp. bis ⸿ until now, so far, as yet, hitherto; für ⸿ for the present (moment); von ⸿ ab oder an henceforth, from this time (or day) forward; von ⸿ bis dahin between now and then; zwischen ⸿ und Ostern between this and Easter. — 4. ⸿ dieser, ⸿ (oder bald, nun, dann) jener now this one, now that (one); auch: first one, then the other. — II ~ n, inv. auch: ~=welt (⸿⸍⸍), ~=zeit (⸿⸿⸍) f ⓺ (schlecht, ft. Neuzeit, Gegenwart) the present time or day or world; modern times pl., these days pl. of ours. [jetzt.]
jetzund(er) (⸍⸝⁄(⸍)) [mhd.] fast † adv. =
je-weilen adv., **jeweilig** (-⸝⁄⸍ u. -⸝⁄) a. ⓺, **je-weils** (⸝⁄) adv. at times; (gelegentlich) occasional(ly).
jo (⸝⁄) int. lauter Ruf: ho!, I say! [(Könige).]
Joas (⸝⁄) npr/m. ⓺ γ. bibl. Joash
Jobber ⚆ (⸝⁄) [engl.] m ⓶ u. ⓶ (stock-)jobber; ~ei (⸍⸍⸝⁄) f ⓶ stock-jobbing.
jobbern (⸝⁄) v/n. (h.) ⓶α. to act (or operate, deal) as a (stock-)jobber.
Jobst (⸝⁄) npr/m. ⓶ ⓶α. Jodocus.
Joch (⸝⁄) [ahd.: yoke: lt. iŭg-um] n ⓶c, 6. 1. (Zuggeschirr) (neck-) yoke; e-m Ochsen das ~ abnehmen to unyoke an ox; ins ~ spannen to (put to the) yoke; fig. das ~ abschütteln oder abwerfen to shake off one's yoke; e-m ein ~ auf(er)legen, e-n unter sein ~ bringen to impose a yoke on a p.('s neck), to bring a p. under one's yoke, weits. to reduce a p. to submission or obedience, to subdue a p. — 2. ein ~ (Paar) Ochsen a yoke (or

pair, couple) of oxen. — 3. agr. (chm. Feldmaß) 9 ~ Acker(s) nine yoke of land. — 4. (Trag- oder Schulter=)~ yoke for carrying pails. — 5. ⚧, a. ⓶c. (Bergrücken, der zwei Gipfel verbindet) (intermediate) mountain-ridge. — 6. ♀ (Blättchenpaar am Hauptstiele) pair of opposite leaflets. — 7. ⊕ arch. (Bindebalken) transom, tie-beam, girder, cross-beam; vgl. Brückenjoch. — 8. ⚓ ~ (kurze Querstange) des Steuers yoke of the rudder.
Joch=bein (⸝⁄ch...) n ⓶ anat. cheek- (or yoke-)bone; ⚯ zygoma(tic bone); =blätterig a. ⓺: ⚯ zygophyllaceous; =bogen m, anat.: ⚯ zygomatic arch; =brücke ♀ f, arch. pile-bridge.
jochen (⸝⁄ch⸍) [Joch] v/a. ⓺ = anjochen.
Joch=feld ⊕ (⸝⁄ch...) n ⓶ Brückenbau: bridge-bay, bay of a bridge; =hölzer ⊕ n/pl. e-r Brücke cross-beams, sleepers pl.; =muskel m; ⚯ zygomatic muscle, zygomaticus; =nagel ⚓ m yoke-pin; =ochs m yoked ox; =pfahl ⊕ m pile of a bridge; =spannung f ⊕ Brückenbau: span of a bridge-bay, =träger ⊕ m, carp. top piece, capping beam; =weite ⊕ f Brückenbau: width of the bays; =welle ⚙ f, mach. yoke-arbour.
Jockei ⚆ (G⸝⁄) [engl.] m ⓶ (gewerbsmäßiger Rennreiter) jockey; ~klub m ⓶ für Rennsport: Jockey Club; ~rennen n race for jockeys or professionals.
Jod ⚗ (⸝⁄) [grch. io'des „veilchen"farben verdampfend] n ⓶c. chm. Metalloid: iodine (J); mit ~ behandeln, präparieren to treat with iodine, ⚯ to iodize.
Jodat ⚗ (-⸝⁄) [neu=lt.] n ⓶c. chm. = Jodsäuresalz.
Jod-äthyl (⸍...) n ⓶ chm. (Äthyljodid) ethyl iodide, iodide of ethyl (C_2H_5J); =blei n lead iodide; =dämpfe m/pl. iodide fumes pl. [⓶a. to yodle, to yodel.]
jodeln (⸝⁄⸍) [jo schreien] v/n. (h.) und v/a.
Jod=grün ⸝⁄ (⸍...) n ⓶ iodine-green; =haltig a. ⓺ iodiferous.
Jodid ⚗ (-⸝⁄) n ⓶c. chm. (Jodverbindung) (higher) iodide; Quecksilber=⸿ = Jodquecksilber b; **jodieren** (-⸝⁄⸍) v/a. ⓶ phot. 2c.: (mit Jod behandeln) to iodize.
jodig (⸝⁄⸍) [Jod] a. ⓺ chm. iodous.
Jod=kalium (⸝⁄...) n ⓶ chm. (Kaliumjodid) potassium iodide, iodide of potassium (KJ); =kalzium n calcium (or calcic) iodide (CaJ_2); =krankheit f, path.: ⚯ iodism.
Jodler (⸝⁄⸍) m ⓶ 1. ⚆ yod(el)ling, Tyrolese song. — 2. (auch: ~in f ⓶) ⚆ yod(el)ler. [=metall n metallic oxide.]
Jod=messung (⸍...) f ⓶ iodometry;
Jodoform ⚗ (-⸍⸝⁄) [grch.=lt.] n ⓶d. chm. iodoform (= iodide of formyl) (CHJ_3).
Jodokus (⸝⁄⸍) npr/m. ⓺ γ. (Vn.) Jodocus.
Jod=quecksilber (⸍...) n ⓶: a) (Quecksilberjodür) mercurous iodide (Hg_2J_2); b) rotes: (Quecksilberjodid) mercuric iodide (HgJ_2); =sauer a. ⓺ iodic; ⸿es Salz iodate; =säure f iodic acid ($H_2J_2O_6$); =säure=salz n iodate; =silber n silver iodide, iodide of silver (AgJ); =stärke(=mehl n) f amylum iodide; =stickstoff m nitrogen iodide; =tinktur f, med. tincture of iodine.
Jodür ⚗ (-⸝⁄) n ⓶c. chm. (lower) iodide.

Signs (see page XVII): F familiar; P vulgar; ⸿ flash; ⸍ rare; † obsolete (died); * new word (born); ‡ incorrect; ♪ music.

[Jodvergiftung]   — 559 —   [Jüdin]

Jod-vergiftung (⸗...) f ⓶ path. iodism; **⸗wasser-stoff** m, chm. hydrogen iodide, hydriodic acid (HJ).
Johann (‿˘) [~es] npr/m. ⓐⓐα. (Vn.) John; ~ ohne Land (engl. König, † 1216) John Lackland. — Vgl. auch Hans.
Johanna ⓐⓐα., **Johanne** ⓐⓐβ. (‿˘‿) npr/f. (Vn.) Joan, Jane, bisw. = Johanna.   [Johannine.
johanne-isch (‿‿‿) a. ⓐ Johannean,
Johannes (‿˘‿) [grch.; *hebr. Gottesgabe] npr/m. ⓐγ. (gen. oft: ...nis, dat. ...ni) (a. Vn.) John, bisw. ~ Johannes; der Evangelist ~ Saint John the Evangelist; ~ der Täufer (Saint) John the Baptist.
Johanni(s) (‿˘) [gen. von Johannes] inv. (24. Juni, a. engl. Quarta'lstag) Midsummer (Day); nächsten ~ next Midsummer.
Johannis-apfel (‿˘‿...) m ⓶ chm.: apple-john; **⸗beer-blattwespe** f, ent. currant-worm (Ne'matus ribis); **⸗beere** ⚘ f: rote, schwarze ~ red, black currant (Ribes au'reum, nigrum); **⸗beer-saft** m currant-juice; **⸗beer-strauch** ⚘ m currant-bush or -tree (Ribes); **⸗beer-wein** m currant-wine; **⸗blume** ⚘ f = Maßlieb; **⸗brot** ⚘ n St. John's-bread, carob (-bean); **⸗brot-baum** ⚘ m carob- (or locust-)tree (Cerato'nia si'liqua); **⸗fest** n = Johanni(s); **⸗feuer** n = Sonnwendfeuer S. John's fire; **⸗jünger** m disciple of John the Baptist; **⸗käfer** m: a) = Brachkäfer; b) **⸗würmchen**; **⸗kraut** ⚘ n John's-wort, hardhay (Hyperi'cum); **⸗tag** m = Johanni(s); **⸗trieb** m etwa: amourous promptings (or desires) pl. of an elderly bachelor; **⸗würmchen** n, ent. glow-worm (Lampy'ris noctilu'ca).
Johanniter (‿‿‿) [1070 zu Jerusalem] m ⓶ knight of St. John, white-cross knight, Hospitaller, auch Johannite; **~orden** m ⓶ order of St. John or of Malta; **~ritter** m = Johanni'ter.
johlen F (‿‿) [jo schreien] v/n. (h.) ⓐ to howl, yell, yowl, bawl; **Johler(in** f) m ⓶ howling (or yelling) p., howler.
Jojakim (‿‿) npr/m. ⓐⓐα. bibl. Jehoiakim (2. Könige 23, 24 ꝛc.).
Jokohama ⚘ (‿‿‿) [jap. Querstrand] npr/n. ⓐα. (japan. St.) Yokohama.
Jokus (‿‿) [lt.] m, inv. (Scherz) joke, ▶ **Jol...** f. **Johl...**   [(Kurzwort) fun.⌋
Jolle ⚓ (‿‿) [ndd.] f ⓶ jolly-boat, wherry; (Fähre) ferry; **Jollen-führer** m ⓶ wherry-man, bargee; ferryman.
Jonas (‿‿) [hebr.] npr/m. ⓐγ. bibl. (Prophet) Jonah; **~fisch**, **~hai** = Hai; **~kürbis** ⚘ m = Flaschenkürbis.
Jonathan (‿˘˘) [hebr.] npr/m. ⓐⓐα. (a. Vn.): a) bibl. Jonathan; b) fig. David und (sein) ~ (treue Freunde) two bosom-friends; c) Bruder ~ (co. = U.S.-bürger) Brother Jonathan.
Jongleur (Qg-glö'r) [fr.; *lt. ioculator] m ⓐd. (ⓐ) (Gaukler, Taschenkünstler) juggler, conjurer; **jonglieren** (Qg...) v/a. u. v/n. (h.) ⓐ to juggle, conjure.
Jonquille (Qg-tl'j-ĕ) [fr.; *lt. iuncus] I f ⚘ jonquil(le) (Narci'ssus jonqui'lla). — II ⚘ a. inv. (hochgelb) jonquil.
Joppe (‿‿) [mhd., it. *ar.] f ⓶ shooting-jacket, light short coat.
Jordan ⚓ (‿‿)[hebr.] npr/m. ⓐα. & bibl. (Fluß in Palästina) Jordan.

Jörg (‿) npr/m. ⓐⓐα. (dim. von Georg) Georgie, little George.
Josaphat ⚓ (‿˘‿, oft: ‿‿‿) [hebr. Gott richtete] npr/m. ⓐα. bibl.: das Tal ~ bei Jerusalem (moham.: Ort des Weltgerichts) the valley of Jehoshaphat.
Josef ꝛc. öft. = Joseph ꝛc.
Joseph (‿‿) [hebr. Gott vermehre!] npr/m. ⓐⓐα. (Vn.) Joseph, F Joe; oft iro. keuscher ~ bashful Joe; **Josepha** (‿‿‿) f ⓐⓐα., **Josephine** (‿‿‿‿) f ⓐⓐβ. npr. (Vn.) Josepha, Josephine.
Josias (‿‿‿) [hebr.] npr/m. ⓐγ. (Kg. v. Juda, 640—09) Josiah.
Jost (‿) npr/m. ⓐⓐα.=Jobst. [Joshuah.⌋
Josua (‿‿) [vgl. Jesus] npr/m. ⓐα. bibl.
Jot (‿) [grch. io'ta] n, inv. (a. ⓐ) 1. name of the letter J. — 2. fig. kein ~ not a jot, not a wee bit, F not a trace or dust.
Jota (‿‿) n ⓐ f. Jota; kein ~ not a jot.
Joule ⚡ (bGaul, ‿, engl. Physiker 1818—89) n ⓐ. elect. (Einheit der elektr. Arbeit) joule, volt-coulomb.
Journal (Qu‿‿) [fr.] n ⓐd. (Zeitschrift, Tagebuch) journal; ⓐ = eintragen (a. **journalisieren** v/a. ⓐ) to enter (or post) in the journal or day-book or diary, to journalize.
Journalismus (Qu‿‿‿) m ⓶ (Zeitungs- und Zeitschriften-wesen) journalism.
Journalist (Qu‿‿) [fr.] m ⓶ (Zeitungs-schreiber) journalist, pressman, writer for the press or the newspapers; (Berichterstatter) reporter, correspondent; **~en-tag** m ⓶ congress of journalists; **~en-tribüne** f reporters' gallery, platform for the reporters or the press; **~ik** (‿‿‿) f ⓐ journalism, weitS. the (newspaper-)press; **Lisch** a. ⓐ journalistic, of journalists.
Journal-mappe (Qu‿...) f ⓶ portfolio for newspapers; **⸗nummer** f copy of a newspaper; **⸗posten** ⚫ m entry (or item) in the journal.
jovial (‿w(v)‿) [spät=lt.] a. ⓐ (urspr.: den Planeten Jupiter betr., dann: gutge-launt) jovial, cheerful, F jolly; **~ität** (‿w(v)-‿‿) f ⓐ joviality, jovialness, cheerfulness, F jollity.
Juan (ⓗu‿) [span. = Johann] npr/m. ⓐα. (Vn.) Don ~ (oft: dᵨ Güu-' od. dᵨ' Gü-än) fig. favourite (or lover) of the fair sex, (gay) Lothario, auch Don Juan; vgl. Damenheld.
Jubää ⚘ (‿‿) [lt.] f ⓐ coquito (Jubae'a).
Jubel (‿‿) [nbd.; *jubilieren] m ⓶ jubilation, exultation, shouts pl. of joy, noisy (or loud) merriment, merry-making; allgemeiner ~ universal rejoicing(s pl.) or joy.
Jubel-braut (‿‿...) f ⓶ (**⸗bräutigam** m), etwa: jubilee bride(groom); **⸗feier** f, **⸗fest** n nach 25 od. 50 (60) Jahren: jubilee, nach 100 Jahren: centenary (celebration or fete); **⸗gesang** m: a) song of joy, b) jubilee song or chant or hymn; **⸗geschrei** n loud acclamation, merry (or exultant) shouts, vociferous cheers pl.; **⸗greis** m = Jubilar; **⸗hochzeit** f silver (or golden, diamond) wedding, auch: jubilee nuptials pl.; **⸗jahr** n jubilee year; et. alle ~e einmal tun to do a th. only once in a way or F in a moonshine; **⸗lied** n = Gesang.

jubeln (‿‿) I v/n. (h.) u. v/a. ⓐa. 1. to jubilate, to shout lustily or merrily, to rejoice; ⓑ jubilant; vgl. jauchzen I. — 2. (lustig leben) to lead a merry (or gay, jolly) life. — II ~ n ⓶ = Jubel.
Jubel-paar (‿‿...) n ⓶ (old) married couple celebrating their silver (or golden) wedding; **⸗ruf** m loud acclamations pl.
Jubilar (‿‿‿) [lt.] m ⓐd. man in ripe years (or official of many years' service) celebrating his jubilee.
Jubilate (‿‿‿) [lt.: jauchzet! Psalm 66] m eccl. (Sonntag) ~ (3. Sonntag nach Ostern) Jubilate.
Jubilä-um (‿‿‿) [lt., *hebr.] n ⓐ (Gedenkfeier) jubilee, (fiftieth, &c.) anniversary; ein ~ feiern to celebrate a jubilee.   [(h.) ⓐ = jubeln.⌋
jubilieren (‿‿‿‿) [mhd., lt., *hebr.] v/n.
jubilo (‿‿‿) [lt.] m ⓐ: in dulci ⓐ leben to lead a life of pleasure, to live (or have) a gay (or merry) life.
juch (‿ⱨ), **Jhe**, **Jhei** (‿‿), **Jheidideldum** (‿‿‿‿), **Jheiraffafsa** (‿‿‿‿), **Jheifsa** (‿‿‿), **Jheißa** (‿‿‿) int. hurra(h)!, huzza!, hey-day!, F oh, jolly!   [etwa: acre.⌋
Juchart (‿ⱨ) [ahd.; *Joch] m ⓐd, 6.
juchen F (‿ⱨ‿) [Luth.] v/n. (h.) ⓐ to shout hurra(h), to fill the air with merriment, geh. Spr.: to make the welkin ring.
Juchert = Juchart.
juchhe(i) (‿ⱨ‿‿) int., auch: **Jdideldum**, **Jßa** ꝛc. f. juch. — II ~ F m, n, inv. thea. (höchster u. wohlfeilster Platz) F the gods pl.
juchhei-en (‿ⱨ‿‿‿) v/n. (v/a.) ⓐ = juchen.
Jucht(en) ⓐ u. ⓐ (‿ⱨ‿) [nhd. 17. sae.= *russ. juftu Paar] m ⓐd.(ⓐ) Russia(n) (or Muscovy) leather or hides pl.; **juchten** a. ⓐ (made) of Russian leather.
Juchten-band ⓐ (‿ⱨ‿‿...) m ⓶ Buchbinderei: Russia(n)-leather binding; **⸗leder** n = Juchten; **⸗stiefel** m/pl. boots pl. made of Russian leather.   [juchen.⌋
juchzen F (‿ⱨ‿ⱨ) v/n. (h.) ⓐ = jauchzen,
jucken (‿‿) [ahd.: itch] ⓐ I v/n. (h.) und v/a. 1. to itch; ⓐ path.: ⚕ pruriginous; fig. prurient; Frostbeulen ⓐ gewaltig chilblains itch frightfully; ihm ⓐ die Finger danach his fingers itch to take (or to do) it; ⓐ itching, itchy, ⚕ prurient. — 2. a. impers. mich juckt's am ganzen Leibe I feel itching (or I itch) all over my body; Sprichw. wen's juckt, der kratze sich let those whom the cap fits wear it. — II v/a. (und sich ⓐ v/refl.) 3. to scratch (o.s.). — III ~ n ⓐ 4. itching, path.: ⚕ prurigo; fig. pruriency.
Juda (‿‿) [hebr.] npr/m. ⓐα. (4. Sohn Jakobs) u. ⚘ npr/n. (Reich) ⓐⓐα. ⓐ Judah; das Reich ~ the kingdom of Judah.
Judäa ⚘ (‿‿‿) npr/n. ⓐα. Judea.
juda-isieren (‿‿‿‿‿) I v/n. (h.) ⓐ (jüdisch leben) to Judaize. — II ~ n ⓐ und
Judaisierung f ⓐ Judaization.
Juda-ismus (--‿‿) m ⓐ Judaism.
Judas (‿‿) [hebr.] npr/m. ⓐγ. Judas; ⓐ **Jscha'riot** Judas Iscariot, fig. (Verräter) a Judas; **⸗baum** ⚘ m Judas-tree (Cercis siliqua'strum); **~kuß** m traitor's kiss.
Jüdchen (‿‿) n ⓐ dim. v. Jude.
Jude (‿‿) [ahd., lt., *hebr.] m ⓐⓐ, **Jüdin** f ⓐⓐ 1. als Volksname: Jew(ess f); P biß.

⚡ scientific; ⚘ botanical; ⚘ geography; ⓐ machinery; ⚒ mining; ⚔ military; ⚓ marine; ⓐ commercial; ⓐ postal; 🚂 railway.

[**Jüdelei**] — 560 — [**Jüngelchen**]

im Ost-ende v. London: ꝉ Yid(disher); der Ewige ~ the Wandering Jew. — 2. *fig.* (Wucherer) Jew, usurer; ein echter ~ a thorough (F a regular) Jew; Sprichw. f. hauen 2.

Jüdelei (-´-) *f* ㊻ Jewish ways or business methods *pl.* or speech.

jüdeln (´ᴗ) [Jude] *v/n.* (h.) ㉒*a.* 1. to live like a Jew, to Judaize; (jüdisch feilschen) to bargain like a Jew, F to jew other people. — 2. (wie ein Jude sprechen) to talk like a Jew, (jüdisch-deutsch sprechen) to speak Yiddish.

Juden-art (´ᴗ...) *f* ㉒ Jewish ways *pl.*, Jewishness; =bart *m:* a) Jewish (or goat's) beard; b) ⚥ wandering Jew, sailor-plant (*Saxifraga sarmento'sa*); =bekehrung *f* conversion of (the) Jews; =busch ⚥ *m* F jew-bush (*Pedila'nthus*); =christ(in *f*) *m* converted Jew(ess *f*); =deutsch *n* Jewish German, Lo. Yiddish; (Kauderwelsch) gibberish; =dorn ⚥ *m* jujube (*Zi'zyphus juju'ba, vulga'ris,* &c.); =eid *m* Jewish oath; =englisch *n* Jewish English; ⚥feindlich *a.* anti-Jewish, anti-Semitic; =frage *f* Jewish question; =frau *f* Jewess; =gasse *f* Jews' street, ehm.: jewry; =genoß *m*, =genossin *f* person converted to Judaism; =gesicht *n* Jewish face or physiognomy; =harz *n* = =pech; =hetze *f* Jew-baiting; =hetzer *m* Jew-baiter; =junge *m* Jewish (F Jew) boy, F Ikey; =kirsche ⚥ *f* winter-cherry, alkekengi (*Physalis Alkeke'ngi*); =leim *n, min.* = =pech; =mädchen *n* Jewish girl; =pech *n, min.* asphalt(e), bitumen.

Judenschaft (´ᴗᴗ) *f* ㊻ (body of) Jewish inhabitants *pl.*; Jewry, Jewdom.

Juden-schule (´ᴗ...) *f* ㉒: a) Jewish school; b) (Tempel) synagogue; ein Lärm wie in der ~ F a (regular) hubbub or babel, an (awful) uproar; =stadt *f* Jewish quarter or neighbourhood, ehm.: ghetto; ehm.: =steuer *f* Jews' tax, tax imposed on Jews; =tempel *m* synagogue.

Judentum (´ᴗ-) *n* ㉘d. Judaism.

Juden-viertel (´ᴗ...) *n* ㉒ = =stadt; =weihrauch ⚥ *m* storax.

Judika (´ᴗᴗ) [lt. richte! (Psalm 43,1)] *m, inv. eccl.* (Sonntag) ~ (2. Sonntag vor)

Jüdin (´ᴗ) *f* ㊶ f. Jude. [Ostern) Judica.]

jüdisch (´ᴗ) I *a.* ㊻ Jewish; Judaic; P Lo. Yiddish; *adv.* like a Jew. — II das ~e ㊺ the Jewish character or look; Jewishness.

Juft(en), juften f. Juchten, juchten.

Jugend (´ᴗ) [ahd.: youth] *f* ㊻ 1. (days *pl.* of) youth, early years *pl.* or life, vgl. ~zeit; in der Fülle der ~ in the bloom (or flush, prime) of youth; in früher ~ in early childhood; von ~ auf from a child, from a boy (*f* girl). — 2. *coll.* die ~ young people or folk(s) *pl.*, the rising generation; die deutsche ~ young Germany; die studierende ~ academical youths, students pl.; Sprichw. ~ hat keine Tugend boys will be boys; you cannot put old heads on young shoulders; ~ muß (sich) austoben youth must (or will) have its fling.

Jugend-alter (´ᴗ...) *n* ㉘ youth(ful age); =arbeit *f* early work, juvenile attempt; =blüte *f* flower of youth;

=erinnerung *f* recollection from (one's) youth or childhood, *pl.* auch: early (or juvenile) reminiscences *pl.*; =feuer *n*, =freude *f* fire (or ardour, heat), joy (or pleasure) of youth; =freund(in *f*) *m:* a) (Freund[in] der Jugend) friend (or lover) of the young; b) (Freund[in] aus der Jugendzeit) friend from childhood, early friend, (old) school-fellow; =frische *f* youthful freshness, youthfulness; f. a. Frische 3; vgl. =kraft; =fülle *f* vigour of youth; in ~ prangen to be in the bloom (or flush) of youth; =gefährte, =genosse, =gespiele *m* companion of one's youth or childhood, (old) playfellow; =göttin *f, myth.* goddess of youth, Hebe; =jahre *n/pl.* early years, youthful days *pl.*; *v. Hunden a.* puppyhood; sie ist über die ~ hinaus she is no child or F no chicken, she has reached the years of discretion; =kraft *f* youthful strength or vigour; ⚥kräftig *a.* ㊻ vigorous.

jugendlich (´ᴗᴗ) *a.* ㊻: a) (der Jugend gleich) youthful; ein ~er Greis a hale and hearty old man; fast tadelnd.: juvenile; (kindlich) childlike, (knabenhaft) boyish; b) * ++ = jung; ~keit *f* ㉒ youthfulness.

Jugend-liebe (´ᴗ...) *f* ㉒ early love-affair or attachment; (geliebte Person) old sweetheart or F flame; =mut *m* youthful courage; =schriften *f/pl.*, =schriftsteller *m* writings *pl.*, writer for the young; =spiele *n/pl.* children's games; =stil *m* moderne Kunstrichtung in Dtschld.: modern style in German art; =streich *m* youthful (or boyish) trick or folly; =sünde *f* sin of one's youth, youthful offence; =traum *m* youthful dream, dream of (one's) youth; =wehr(en *pl.*) *f* lads' brigade(s); =welt *f* young people, *pl.* juvenile world; =zeit *f* (days *pl.* of) youth, youthful days *pl.*; in m-r ~ in my young days.

Jukka ⚥ ⚲ (´ᴗ) [span.] *f* ㊺ (Palmlilie) yucca. [Juliet, Julietta.)

Julchen (´ᴗ) *npr/n.* ㉓*a.* (*dim. v.* Julie))

Juli (´-) [lt. *Iulius* (Caesar)] *m* ㊱ (month of) July.

Julia ㊺ⓐ*a.*, **Juli-e** ㊹ⓑβ. (´(ᴗ)ᴗ) [lt.] *npr/f.* (Bn.) Julia; „Ro'meo und ~" (Trauerspiel *v. SH.*) "Romeo and Juliet".

Julian (-(´)ᴗ´ *u.* ´(ᴗ)-) [lt.] *npr/m.* ㊵ⓐ*α.* (*a.* Bn.) Julian. [Juliana.)

Juliane (-(ᴗ)´ᴗ) *npr/f.* ㊹β. (Bn.)

julianisch (-(´)ᴗ´ᴗ) *a.* ㊻ Julian: ℒer (von Julius Cäsar eingeführter) Kalender Julian Calendar (vgl. *a.* St.).

Juli-e (´(ᴗ)ᴗ) f. Julia.

Juli-er (´(ᴗ)ᴗ) *npr/m* ㊵ 1. *pl.* = julisches Haus. — 2. *sg.* ⚥ (schwz. Paß) Julier.

Juli-hitze (´ᴗ...) *f* ㉒ heat of July.

julisch (´(ᴗ)ᴗ) *a.* ㊻ 1. ℒes Haus Julian house, imperial dynasty of Julius Cæsar. — 2. ⚲ ~e Alpen Julian Alps *pl.*

Julius (´(ᴗ)ᴗ) [lt.] *npr/m.* ㊵γ. (Bn.) [Julius.)

jun. *abbr.* = junior.

jung (´) [ahd.: young] *a.* ㊻ (D 2,7) (*ant.* alt) 1. young, youthful, juvenile; von ~ auf from early days; ℒ und frisch young and fresh, in the freshness of youth; ℒ und alt, ~e und Alte

young and old; der Jüngere (*abbr. d.* J.) junior (*abbr.* jun.) the younger (one), die Jüngeren the younger ones, the juniors *pl.*; er ist 5 Jahre jünger als du he is five years younger than you (are), he is five years your junior; sie sieht jünger aus, als sie ist she does not look her age; sie ist nicht mehr ℒ she is no chicken; mein jüngerer, jüngster Bruder my younger, youngest brother; ℒer Greis one grown old before his time, *auch:* young old man; die jüngeren Schüler the junior boys or scholars *pl.*; wieder ℒ w. to grow young again. — 2. ℒe Beine h. to be light of foot, to have nimble legs; ℒes (noch gärendes) Bier (*a.* Jungbier) fresh (or new) ale; f. Blut 7, Bursche 1; ℒe Eheleute *pl.* young (or newly-married) couple; ℒe Frau young wife, bride; ℒes Gemüse young vegetables *pl.*; sich ℒ kleiden to dress young or in juvenile fashion; jüngstes Kind baby; ℒe Leute, die ℒe Mannschaft young people, youths *pl.*; jüngster Leutnant junior lieutenant; ℒer Wein new wine; ℒe Zweige *m/pl.* young branches *pl.*; Sprichw. ℒ gefreit hat nimmer gereut happy's the wooing that is not long doing; ℒ gewohnt, alt getan the child is the father of the man (vgl. alt 2 am Schlusse). — 3. der ℒe (frühe) Morgen ob. Tag the early morning; das ℒe Jahr the early part of the year; in seinen ℒen Jahren in his early youth or days; ℒ heiraten to marry young or early in life. — 4. (vor kurzem geschehen, letzt) *im comp. u. sup.*: recent, late; in den jüngsten Jahren of late years; Ihr jüngstes Schreiben your last letter; in der jüngsten Zeit (*a. adv.* jüngst) lately, latterly, quite recently, (only) the other day. — 5. (zukünftig) das Jüngste Gericht, der Jüngste Tag the last (day of) judgment; doomsday (*a. co.*).

Jung-bier (´...) *n* ㉒ f. jung 2; =brunnen *m* fountain of youth; =deutschland *n* young Germany.

Junge (´ᴗ) I substantiviertes *a.* ㊷: die ~n und die Alten young and old; Sprichw. f. Alte 1. — II *m* ㊹ (F *pl. a.* ~ns) (young) boy, F youngster, P nipper; et. älter: lad, stripling; dann: youth, young man; (*ant.* Mädchen) *auch:* male child; meine ~ns! my (dear) boys!, ⚓ my hearties!; dummer ~ stupid fellow; f. aufbrummen II; geriebener ~ sharp (or smart) boy, knowing fellow; f. grün 2; kleiner ~ little boy, vgl. Jüngelchen; ungezogener ~ rude boy, F young rip or Turk; (Lehr-)~ apprentice; ⚓ (Schiffs-)~ cabin-boy. — III ~(s) *n* ㊲ (das ~, ein ~s) von Tieren: young one, von Hunden: puppy, von Raubtieren: cub, e-s Elefanten: calf, *a. co.* baby elephant; ~ werfen ob. setzen to bring forth (or to bear) young (ones), *v. Hunden*: to pup, *von wilden Tieren:* to cub; vgl. jungen.

Jüngelchen F (´ᴗᴗ) *n* ㉓ [*dim. von* Junge II] little boy or F nipper, young lad(die), F *co.* tommy.

Zeichen (f. S. XVII): F familiär; P Volkssprache; ſ‾ Gaunersprache; ⸜ selten; † alt (auch gestorben); * neu (auch geboren); ++ unrichtig;

jungen (⌁) *v/n.* (h.) ⊕ meist von Haustieren: to get (or have) young (ones).
Jungen-arbeit (⌁...) *f* ⊕ boy's (or boys') work, work done by boys or apprentices.
jungenhaft (⌁) *a.* ⊕ boyish, boylike.
Jungen-jahre (⌁...) *n/pl.* ⊕ years *pl.* of boyhood or apprenticeship; **=streich** *m* boyish trick.
Jünger (⌁) [ahd.] **I** *m* ⊕ disciple (a. *bibl.*), follower; (Anhänger) adherent; ~ der Wissenschaft votary of science, scientist. — **II** ⌁ *comp.* von jung.
Jüngerschaft (⌁) *f* ⊕ **1.** discipleship. — **2.** *coll.* body of disciples or followers.
Jungfer (⌁) [mhd. Jungfrau] *f* ⊕ **1.** F = Jungfrau a, bsd. v. Mädchen niederen Standes, zB.: ~ Karoline Miss Caroline; a. als spöttischer Titel: ~ Naseweis, Neugier Miss Pert, Miss Curiosity; alte ~ old maid, elderly spinster, F co. unappropriated blessing, ehm. a.: ape-leader, alte ~ bleiben to remain an old maid, F co. to be put (or to remain) on the shelf. — **2.** F = Jungfrau b; sie (er) ist noch ~ she (he) is a virgin. — **3.** = Kammer-, Laden-, Zimmer-jungfer. — **4.** *co.* (verweichlichter Mann) effeminate man, F (old) coddle (Wärmflasche) warming-pan or -bottle. — **5.** ⊕ ~ im Grünen od. in Haaren, im Netz ragged-lady (*Nigella damasce'na*). — **6.** *ent.* (Libelle) dragon-fly. — **7.** ⊕ (Ramme) paving-ram, pavier's beetle. — **8.** ⚓ = Jungfernblock.
Jungfer-... (⌁...) s. Jungfern-...
Jüngferchen (⌁), **Jüngferlein** (⌁) *n* ⊕ (*dim.*: Jungfer) little maid or miss.
jüngferlich, jungfer(n)haft (⌁) *a.* ⊕ maidenish, maidenlike, maidenly; spinster-like; (zurückhaltend) coy, demure, prim, shy, reserved; **Jüngferlichkeit** *f* ⊕ maidenish conduct; coyness, demureness, primness.
Jungfern-block ⚓ (⌁...) *m* ⊕ dead-eye; **=erde** *f* virgin earth; **=glas** *n*, *min.* mica; **=gold** ⊕ *n* native gold.
jungfernhaft s. jüngferlich.
Jungfern-häutchen (⌁...) *n* ⊕ *anat.*: ⚕ hymen; **=honig** *m* virgin honey; **=kamm**, *zo.* (Muschel) virgin-cockle (*Arca antiqua'ta*); **=kind** *n* natural (or illegitimate) child; **=kloster** *n* nunnery; **=knecht** *m* ladies' man, adorer of the (fair) sex; **=kranz** *m* bridal wreath; **=milch** *f*, *pharm.* milky fluid formed by dripping benzoin(e) tincture in(to) water; **=öl** ⊕ *n* virgin oil; **=pergame'nt** ⊕ *n* virgin parchment, vellum; **=raub** *m* rape (of maidens), ravishment; **=räuber** *m* ravisher (of maidens); **=rede** *f* maiden speech.
Jungfernschaft (⌁) *f* ⊕ virginity, maidenhood, purity; (*sH*) virgin-knot.
Jungfern-schänder (⌁) *m* ⊕ = **=räuber**; **=schwefel** *m*, *min.* native sulphur; **=stand** *m* spinsterhood, maidenhood; **=wachs** ⊕ *n* virgin wax.
Jung-frau (⌁) *f* ⊕: a) (Mädchen, ledige Person) spinster (lady), maid(en); zur ~ herangewachsen ripened into womanhood (vgl. Jungfer); b) (Mädchen von makelloser Keuschheit) virgin (auch *fig.* von reinen Junggesellen und von Festungen, die

sich noch keinem ergeben haben); die ~ von Orleans the maid of Orleans; die heilige ~ the Holy Virgin, bsd. ehm. auch: Our Lady; *bibl.* die törichten ~en the foolish virgins *pl.*; c) *ast.* Virgo; **=frauenhaft** *a.* ⊕ maidenlike, maidenly, demure; **=fräulich** *a.* ⊕: a) = **=frauenhaft**; b) (unbefleckt) virginal, immaculate; *fig.* der Boden virgin soil; *ent.* des Insekt: ⚕ virgin; **=fräulichkeit** *f* virginity, maidenhood, maidenly modesty, demureness, vgl. Jungfernschaft; **=frauschaft** *f* = Jungfernschaft; **=gesell(e)** *m*: a) bachelor, single (or unmarried) man; (eingefleischter) alter ~ (confirmed, F regular) old bachelor; b) bei Handwerkern: youngest journeyman; **=gesellen-leben** *n*, **=stand** *m* bachelor's life, bachelorhood, a. *co.* single blessedness; **=gesellen-wirtschaft** *f* bachelor's household or domestic arrangements *pl.*; **=gesellen-wohnung** *f* bachelor's chambers *pl.*
Jüngling (⌁) [ahd.] *m* ⊕ d. youth, young man; (junger Bursche) (growing) lad, young fellow or F chap; schöner ~ handsome youth, F Adonis; **=haft** *a.* ⊕ like a youth.
Jünglings-alter (⌁...) *n* ⊕ youth(ful age), early manhood, ⚕ adolescence; **=bund** *m* = **=verein**; **=jahre** *n/pl.* years *pl.* of early manhood; **=liebe** *f* young man's love(-affair); **=mäßig** *a.* ⊕ like a youth or a young man; **=verein** *m* young men's club; christlicher ~ Young Men's Christian Association (*abbr.* Y. M. C. A.).
Jung-sein (⌁) *n* ⊕ youth(ful state), youthfulness, freshness of youth.
jüngst (⌁) *sup.* von jung (s. ds, bsd. 4 u. 5, als *adv.* 4 zu Ende); **=ens**, **=hin** *adv.* a short time ago; newly (bought, &c.), (quite) recently, lately; **=geboren** (⌁...) *a.* ⊕ youngest born, last born.
Jung-tier (⌁...) *n* ⊕ *hunt.* young doe; **=vieh** *n* young cattle.
Juni (⌁) [lt.] *m* ⊕ (month of) June; **~käfer** *m* ⊕ *ent.* June-bug (mehrere Käfer: *Lachnoste'rna*, *Allorhi'na*, *Rhizo'trogus*).
junior (⌁(⌁)) [lt. jünger] *a. inv.* (*abbr.* jun.; *ant.* se'nior): Herr Lux ⊕ Mr. L. junior; vgl. d. F.
Junius (⌁(⌁)) [lt.] *m*, *inv.* = Juni.
Junker (⌁) [mhd. Jungherr] *m* ⊕ young nobleman, ⚔ F = Fahnen⌁; vgl. Kraut⌁.
junkerhaft (⌁) *a.* ⊕ squire-like, like a haughty nobleman or aristocrat, *adv.* auch: cavalierly.
Junker-herrschaft (⌁...) *f* ⊕ rule of the landed aristocracy, a. squirarchy.
junkerlich (⌁) *a.* ⊕, **junker-mäßig** *a.* = junkerhaft. [country-squires.]
Junker-partei (⌁) *f* ⊕ party of the **Junkerschaft** (⌁) *f* ⊕ *coll.* (all the) squires *pl.*, landed aristocracy.
Junkertum (⌁) *n* ⊕ d. **1.** country-squire's ways *pl.* — **2.** = Junkerschaft.
Juno (⌁) [lt.] *npr/f.* ⊕ ⊕ *a.* (*pl.* auch Junonen) *myth.* (Gemahlin Jupiters) Juno (a. *ast.*); **junonisch** (⌁⌁) *a.* ⊕ Junonian, (tall and) majestic. [lung) junta.]
Junta (⌁) [span.] *f* ⊕ (Ratsversamm-)
Jupiter (⌁) [lt.] *npr/m.* ⊕ (*gen.* ⊕ Jovis) *myth.* (Göttertönig) Jupiter (a. *ast.*), Jove;

~ Pluvius (Regenspender) etwa: rain-dispensing Jove, the weeping heavens *pl.*
Jupiter(s)-bart ⚘ (⌁...) *m* ⊕ Jupiter's-beard (*Anthy'llis barba Iovis*); **=ferne**, **=nähe** *f*, *ast.* der =monde: ⚓ apojove, perijove; **=monde**, **=trabanten** *m/pl.* *ast.* (four) satellites of (the planet) Jupiter.
Juppe (⌁) *f* ⊕ = Joppe, Jacke 1.
Jura[1] (⌁) [klt.] *npr/m.* ⊕ *a.* der ~ the Jura Mountains *pl.* = Schwäbische(r) ~ Suabian Alps *pl.*
Jura[2] (⌁) [lt., *pl.* von iūs] *n/pl. inv.* ~ (die Rechte) studieren to study (for) the law, to read (or prepare) for the bar.
Jura-bewohner(in *f*) (⌁...) *m* ⊕ inhabitant of the Jura-mountains; **=bildung**, **=formation** *f*, *geol.* Jurassic (or oolitic) formation or system; **=gebirge** ⚘ *npr/n.* = Jura[1]; **=kalk** *m*, *geol.* Jura limestone; **=kalk-haltig** *a.* ⚘ Jurassic; **=schichten** *f/pl. geol.*: ⚓ Jurassic strata *pl.*
jurassisch (⌁⌁) [Jura[1]] *a.* ⊕ of the Jura Mountains, ⚓ Jurassic.
juridisch (⌁⌁) [lt.] *a.* ⊕ (rechtlich) legal, ⚓ juridical; **Jurisdiktion** (⌁⌁⌁⌁) *f* ⊕ (Gerichtsbarkeit) jurisdiction; **Jurisprudenz** (⌁⌁⌁) *f* ⊕ (Rechtsgelehrsamkeit) jurisprudence.
Jurist (⌁) [lt.] *m* ⊕ lawyer, ⚓ jurist; (Rechtsgelehrter) jurisconsult; (Studierender der Rechte) law-student; er will ~ werden he is intended to be a lawyer, he is studying for the law; **~erei** F (⌁⌁⌁) *f* ⊕ jurisprudence, *b.s.* lawyer's trickery or sharp practice; **juristisch** (⌁⌁) *a.* ⊕ relating to the law, of the law, legal, ⚓ juridical; *adv.* auch: in law; ⌁ische Fakultät faculty of law; die ⌁e Laufbahn verfolgen to follow the law, to practise at the bar or as a barrister; ⌁e Redensart law-term.
Jurte (⌁) [russ.] *f* ⊕ (Nomadenhütte) yourta.
Jury ⚓ (bgl.⌁ u. ⌁) [engl.] *f* ⊕ (*pl.* auch Juries) (Geschwornen- u. Preis-gericht) jury.
Jus[1] (⌁) [lt.] (⌁ *n* (*sg. inv.*, *pl.* Jura), vgl. Dr. jur. [ronnene Bratenbrühe) gravy.]
Jus[2] (Gü) [fr. *m*] *f*, *inv.* (Gallerte, ge-)
just F (⌁) [fr.; *lt.*] *adv.* **1.** just, even now; sie ist ⌁ keine Schönheit … not exactly a beauty; er ist ⌁ kein Narr … not quite (or altogether) a fool. — **2.** (eben erst) only just (now).
justament F (⌁⌁) *adv.* just (now).
Justier-block (⌁⌁) *m* ⊕ adjusting-block.
justier/en (⌁) [lt.] **I** *v/a.* ⊕ (abrichten) to adjust, Münzen auch: to size, to standard; *typ.* die Mater ⊕ to fit up the matrix. — **II** ~ *n* ⊕ = ⌁ung.
Justierer (⌁⌁) [lt.] *m* ⊕ adjuster, justifier (s. justieren).
Justier-feile (⌁⌁) *f* ⊕ adjusting-file; **=maschine** *f*, *typ.* justifier.
Justierung (⌁⌁) *f* ⊕ (s. justieren) adjustment, justification.
Justier-wage (⌁⌁) *f* ⊕ adjusting balance or scales *pl.*
justifizieren (⌁⌁⌁) [lt.] **I** *v/a.* ⊕ **1.** (rechtfertigen) to justify. — **2.** ⊕ (berichtigen) to check an account. — **II** ~ *n* ⊕ **3.** justification; ⊕ checking accounts.
Justinus (⌁⌁) [lt.] *npr/m.* Justin.
Justitiar (⌁⌁⌁(⌁)) [lt.] *m* ⊕ d. ehm. auch = Gerichtshalter.

Juſtiz (⌣˘) [lt.] f ⓐ (Rechtspflege) justice. **Juſtiz=beamte(r)** (⌣˘ᵘ...) m ⓑ law-officer; **=behörde** f legal authority; **=kanzlei** f, etwa: Registrar's office or court; **=kolle'gium** n judges pl. constituting a court; **=mini'ſter** m minister of justice, in England etwa: Lord Chancellor; **=miniſterium** n ministry of justice (in Engl. gibt es kein ~!); **=mord** m judicial murder; **=palaſt** m in Engl.: Law Courts pl. (in Fleet Street, Lo.); **=pflege** f (administration of) justice; **=rat** m in England: King's Counsel (abbr. K.C.); **=ſache** f judicial (or law) matter; **=verwaltung** f = **=pflege**; **=weſen** n judicial (or law) affairs pl., judicature, auch oft: the law.

Jute ⟂ ⊕ ⓑ (⌣˘, oft: ᵇǴū'-tˢ) [bengal.] f ⓑ, **~hanf** (ʰ...) m ⓑ (Baſtfaſer v. *Co'rchorus*) jute, pat.

Jüten (⌣˘) [Goten] m/pl. ⓐ (Bewohner Jütlands) Jutes pl. (ſ. Jütländer); **jütiſch** ⌣˘ ⓑ = jütländiſch.

Jütland ♀ (⌣˘) npr/n. ⓑα. (dän. Halbinſel) Jutland.

Jütländer (⌣˘˘) m ⓑ, **~in** f ⓑ Jutlander, f a.: Jutland woman; ſ. Jüten.

jütländiſch (⌣˘˘) a. ⓑ Jut(land)ish.

Jutta (˘˘) npr/f. ⓑⓐα. (Bn.) Joan, Jane.

Juwel (˘⌣) [fr. *jouer* ſpielen] n ⓑd. (m ⓑc.) jewel, gem (a. fig.); **~en** pl. jewellery, (Edelſteine) precious stones pl.

juwelen (˘⌣˘) a. ⓑ (made) of jewels.

Juwelen=arbeit (˘⌣ᵘ...) f ⓑ jewellery; **=artig** a. ⓑ jewel-like; **=diebſtahl** m jewel-robbery; **=faſſung** f setting of jewels; **=handel** ⓑ m jeweller's trade; **=händler(in** f) m jeweller; **=käſtchen** n jewel-case, casket; **=laden** m jeweller's shop; **=ſchmuck** m set of jewels, jewel ornaments pl.; **=uhr** f watch set with precious stones, jewelled watch. — Vgl. a. Juwelier=...

Juwelier ⊕ (-⌣ˈ) m ⓑd. jeweller.

Juwelier=arbeit (-⌣ᵘ...) f ⓑ jeweller's work, jewellery; **=geſchäft** n, **=laden** m jeweller's business or shop; **=wage** ⊕ f jeweller's scales pl.; **=waren** f/pl. jewellery, jeweller's goods pl.

Jux P (⌣ˈ) [lt. *iocus*] m ⓑa. 1. great fun, frolic, F lark; ſich einen ~ machen to have good fun, F to go on the spree, to have a good (old) time. — 2. e-n (auch Juxen) machen (betrügen) to cheat. — 3. (wertloſes Zeug) rubbish, trash, useless stuff.

juxen P (⌣˘) I v/n. (h.) to have good fun. — II v/a. to make fun of.

Juxerei P (⌣˘ᵘ) f ⓑ frolicking.

juzig (⌣˘) a. ⓑ frolicsome, F larky.

K, k (ˈ) n, inv. (Buchstabe) K, k.
K öſt. abbr. = Krone (Münze).
K chm. Symbo'l für Kalium.
k. öſt. abbr. = kaiſerlich, königlich.

Kaaba (⌣˘˘) [ar. Kubus] f ⓑ (Heiligtum der Mohammedaner in Mekka) Caaba.

kaaken (⌣˘) [ndl.] v/a. ⓑ: Heringe ⟂ to gut and salt (and barrel) herrings.

Kabache (˘⌣˘) [ndb., *ruſſ.] f ⓑ 1. (elendes Wirtshaus) low beer-shop or pothouse. — 2. (elende Wohnung) miserable dwelling or hut, P (mere) hole.

Kabale (˘⌣˘) [fr.; *Kabbala] f ⓑ cabal, plot, intrigue, ʒB. „~ und Liebe" (SCH.) "Intrigue and Love"; ~ ſchmieden to hatch (out) plots, to intrigue; **~n=macher, ~n=ſchmied(er)** m ⓑ caballer, mehr gbr.: plotter, intriguer.

kabalieren (˘⌣⌣˘) [fr.] v/n. (h.) ⓑ to cabal, plot, intrigue, scheme.

Kabbala (˘˘˘) [hebr. überlieferung] f ⓑ (jüdiſche Geheimlehre) cabbala; **Kabbaliſt** (˘˘ˈ) m ⓑ cabbalist; **Kabbaliſterei** (˘˘⌣ˈ) f ⓑ cabbalistic art; **kabbaliſtiſch** (˘˘ˈ˘) a. ⓑ cabbalistic, cabbalistical.

Kabbelei F (˘⌣ᵘ) f ⓑ squabbling.

kabbeln (˘˘) [ndb.] I v/n. (h.) ⓑa. 1. Würfelſpiel: to decide the game by a last throw of the dice. — 2. ⟂ die See kabbelt (die Wellen laufen bei umſpringendem Winde gegen=ea.) the waves are struck (or lashed) by a contrary wind, the sea is choppy. — II ſich ⟂ v/refl. 3. F to square, to quarrel.

Kabbel=ſee (˘ˈ˘ˈ) f ⓑ high-running waves pl., choppy sea.

Kabel¹ (⌣˘) [mhd.; *fr. *câble*] n ⓑ ⟂ u. tel. (telegraphic) cable; unterirdiſches, unterſeeiſches ~ underground, submarine cable; ein ~ abrollen to pay out a cable; ein ~ legen to lay a cable; mittels ~s telegraphieren to cable.

Kabel² (⌣˘) [ndl.] f ⓑ (Anteil) lot, share.
Kabelar ⟂ (⌣˘ˈ) m ⓑd., **~ing** (⌣˘ˈ) f ⓑ (Kette) messenger.

Kabel¹=bahn ⊕ (⌣˘ᵘ...) f ⓑ cable-tramway = Seilbahn; **=behälter** m cable-tank; **=bericht** m, tel. cable-message, cablegram, F cable; **=boje** f cable-buoy; **=garn** n cable-yarn, rope-yarn; **=gatt** n cable-room or -stage; **=gramm** n, tel. cablegram, cable-message.

Kabeljau (⌣˘ˈ) [ndb., ndl.] m ⓑb., ichth. cod(fish) (*Gadus mo'rrhua*); junger ~ codling, vgl. Laberdan.

Kabel¹=kern (⌣ᵘ...) m ⓑ tel. cable-core; **=länge** f cable('s) length; **=legung** f laying of a cable or of cables; **=meſſer** f; **=prüfer** m cable-tester.

kabeln (⌣˘) [Kabel¹] v/a. u. v/n. (h.) ⓑa. (mittels Kabels telegraphieren) to cable; to send a cable-message or a cablegram.

Kabel¹=ſchiff (⌣˘ᵘ...) n ⓑ cable-ship, vessel for laying cables; **=ſchlag** m cable-laid rope; **=ſeil, =tau** n cable, hawser; **=verbindung** f cable-communication.

Kabine mſt ⟂ (˘⌣˘) [fr., *Klt.] f ⓑ cabin.

Kabinett (˘˘ˈ) [fr., *Klt.] n ⓑc.: a) Gemach) cabinet (a. kleiner Schrank); small room, closet; b) (geheimer Rat, Miniſterium) cabinet, cabinet ministers pl., government, vgl. ~s=ſitzung.

Kabinett=ausgabe (˘˘ˈ...) f v. Büchern: cabinet edition; **=bild** n, phot. cabinet (photograph or portrait); **=format** n cabinet size; **=photographie** f = =bild.

Kabinetts=ausleſe ⊕ (˘˘ˈ...) f ⓑ cabinet wine; **=befehl** m, pol. order in council; **=frage** f cabinet question; wcht. question of vital importance; **=juſti'z** f arbitrary (or high-handed) administration of justice; **=kri'ſis** f cabinet (or ministerial) crisis; **=mini'ſter** m cabinet minister; **=order** f = =befehl; **=rat** m: a) coll. = =ſitzung, b) (Person) Geheimer ~ Privy Councillor; **=ſiegel** n privy seal; **=ſitzung** f cabinet council, meeting of the cabinet.

Kabinett=ſtück (˘˘ˈ...) n paint. cabinet picture; ⓑ curio(sity).

Kabriolett (˘˘⌣ˈ) [fr.] n ⓑc. (einſpänniger Wagen) light trap, gig, ehm. cabriolet, vgl. Tab.

Kabuſe (˘⌣˘) [ndb., ndl.] f. ⓑ 1. = Kabache 2. — 2. ⟂ (Schiffsküche) caboose.

Kabyle (˘⌣ˈ) [fr. *kabyle*; *ar. Stamm] m ⓐ, **Kabylin** f ⓑ (Bewohner[in] Nord-afrikas), **kabyliſch** a. ⓑ Kabyle.

kacheltiſch ⌣ (⌣⌣ˈ) [grch.] a. ⓑ path. (kränklich) sickly, ⌣ cachectic(al).

Kachel ⊕ (⌣˘) [ahd.] f ⓑ (glaſierter Ziegel) Dutch (or glazed) tile.

kacheln (⌣˘) v/n. (h.) ⓑa. = einkacheln.

Kachel=ofen (⌣˘ˈ...) m ⓑ stove made of Dutch tiles.

kachern (⌣˘) (laut lachen) v/n. (h.) ⓑa.: kichern und ⟂ to laugh and giggle.

kacken P (⌣˘) [ndb., *lt.] v/n. ⓑ to relieve o.s., to ease nature, P to cack, von Kindern: to have a motion.

Kadaver (˘⌣˘˘) [lt. n] m (a ⟂ n) ⓑ (Leiche) corpse, dead body, (As) carcass.

Kadenz ♪ (˘⌣ˈ) [it.] f ⓑ (Schlußfall) cadence; **=ieren** (˘⌣⌣˘) v/a. ⓑ to cadence.

Kader¹ ✠ (⌣ˈ) [fr. *cadre*] m ⓑ (Stamm, Rahmen) regimental staff of officers, ✠ (fr.) *cadre*.

Kader² *prov.* (⌣˘) m ⓑ double chin.

Kadett ✠ (˘⌣ˈ) [fr. *cadet* jüngſter] m ⓑ ✠ (Offiziersſchüler) cadet; ⟂ ſ. See².

Kadetten=anſtalt ✠ (˘˘ˈ...) f, **=haus** military school or academy; **=korps** n corps of cadets; **=ſchiff** ⟂ n training-ship (for the navy), (Schulſchiff) schoolship; **=ſchule** f = =anſtalt.

Kadi (⌣ˈ) [ar.] m ⓑ (Richter) cadi.

Kadiz ♀ (⌣ˈ) [phön.] npr/n. inv. (alte span. Hafenſtadt) Cadiz.

Kadmium ⌣ (⌣˘˘) [lt., *grch.] n ⓑ chm. Metall) cadmium (Cd); **~gelb** n ⓑ (Malerfarbe) cadmium-yellow, sulphide of cadmium; **~oxyd** n, chm. cadmic oxide.

Käfer (⌣ˈ) [ahd.] m ⓑ: chafer; *Kiefer] m ⓑ 1. beetle, chafer, ⌣ coleopter. — 2. F fig. einen ~ haben: a) to be ill-humoured; b) F to have had a drop too much; c) to have a bee in one's bonnet, to be wrong in the head.

Käfer=art (⌣ᵘ...) f ⓑ ent.: ⌣ species of coleopters; **=artig** a. ⓑ ent. beetle-like, ⌣ coleopteral, ...ous.

Käferchen (⌣⌣˘) n ⓑ (dim. von Käfer) small beetle or ⌣ coleopter.

Signs (see page XVII): F familiar; P vulgar; Ϝ flash; ⟍ rare; † obsolete (died); * new word (born); ⁺⁺ incorrect; ♪ music.

Käfer-kenner(ᵘ⁄...) m ⚇: ⚇ coleopterist; =kunde f: ⚇ coleopterology; =sammlung f collection of beetles or ⚇ of coleopters.

Kaff (ᵛ) [ndb.: chaff] n ⓑb. **1.** agr. (Spreu) chaff (a. fig.). — **2.** fig. (wertloses Zeug) rubbish, lumber.

Kaffee (ᵛ⁻) [nhd. 17. sae., *ar.] m ⓑ: **a)** coffee; gemahlener, gebrannter ~ ground, roasted coffee; s. Mokka-₂; als Getränk: e-e Tasse ~ a cup of coffee; ~ trinken to drink (or take) coffee; ~ mit Milch coffee with milk; schwarzer Kaffee black coffee; **b)** (~-gesellschaft): einen ~ geben to give a coffee-party; **c)** ⚘ = ~baum.

kaffee-ähnlich (ᵛ⁻...) a. ⚇ coffee-like; =ballen ⚇ m ⚇ bale of coffee; =bau m cultivation of coffee, coffee-growing; =baum ⚘ m coffee-tree (Co'ffea ara'bica); =beere ⚘ f c.-berry; =beutel m c.-strainer; =bitter c. = Kaffein; =bohne [ar.bunn(e)] f c.-bean; =bohnen pl. auch: ungrounded coffee sg.; =brand ⚘ m c.-blight; =braun a. (as) brown as coffee; c.-coloured; =brenner m c.-roaster (a. ⚇ = =trommel); =brennerei f establishment for roasting coffee; =brett n tea-tray, waiter; =bruch ⚇ m broken coffee; =bude f auf der Straße c.-stand; =farbe f c.-colour; =garten m coffee-garden; =gebäck n fancy bread for c.; in Engl.: tea-cake; =gerät, =geschirr n c.-service or -set or -things pl.; =gesellschaft f = Kaffee ⓑ; =grund m =satz; =haus n coffee-house or shop, feineres: café; =kanne f coffee-pot; =klappe P f low-class c.-house; =klatsch m gossip (or scandal) at a c.-party; =kocher m = =maschine; =kuchen m = =gebäck; =laus f, ent. coffee-bug (Leca'nium co'ffeae); =löffel m tea-spoon; =lokal n coffee-room, feineres: café, restaurant, im Hotel: coffee-room; =maschine f c.-machine; =mühle f c.-mill or -grinder; =pest f = =brand; =pflanzer m c.-planter; =pflanzung f c.-plantation; =sack m c.-bag, c.-sack; =satz m grounds pl. of coffee; =säure f, chm.: ⚇ caffeic acid; =schale f c.-cup; =schwester f person (who is) fond of coffee; weitS. gossip, scandalmonger; =sorten ⚘ f/pl. coffees pl.; =surrogat n substitute for coffee; =tasse f coffee-cup; =topf m c.-pot; =trichter m c.-strainer; =trommel ⚘ f c.-roaster or -drum; =vergiftung f, path.: ⚇ caffe(in)ism; =visite f, etwa: social cup of coffee; =wicke ⚘ f (Art Bocksdorn) species of milk-vetch (Astra'galus bae'ticus); =wirt(in f) m keeper of a coffee-house or a café; =wirtschaft f = =lokal, =klappe.

Kaffe-in ⚇ (ᵛ⁻ᵘ) n ⓑd. chm. (Alkaloid der Kaffeebohne) caffeine ($C_8H_{10}N_4O_2$).

Kaffer¹ (ᵛ⁻) [ar. = Kaffir] m ⚇ Südafrika: Kafir, a. Kaffir, Caffre.

Kaffer² F (ᵛ⁻) [nhd. *? hebr. Dörfler] m ⚇ contp. clod-hopper, (Flegel) boor, (Dummkopf) blockhead, duffer.

kaff(e)risch¹ (ᵛ(ᵛ)⁻) [Kaffer¹] a. ⚇ Kafir, Caffre. [ish; dull.]

kaff(e)risch² (ᵛ(ᵛ)⁻) [Kaffer²] a. ⚇ boor-}

Kaffer(n)-korn ⚘ (ᵛ⁻ᵘ⁻) n = Mohrenhirse; =land ⚘ n Caffre-land, Caffraria; =sprache f Kafir (language).

kaffrisch (ᵛ⁻) a. ⚇ = kafferisch.

Käfig (ᵛ⁻) [ahd.; *lt. ca'vea f] m (⚘ n) ⓓd. cage; in einen ~ sperren to put into a) cage.

Käfig-vogel (ᵘ⁻...) m ⚇ cage-bird.

Kafiller (ᵛ⁻ᵛ⁻) [? hebr.] m ⚇ = Abdecker.

Kafir (ᵛ⁻) [hebr.] m ⚇ = Giaur.

Kaftan (ᵛ⁻, poet. ᵛ⁻) [türk.,*ar.] m ⓓd. (⚇) (langer Tuchrock) caftan; mit einem ~ bekleidet wearing a caftan, caftaned.

kahl (ᵛ) [ahd.: callow; *lt. calvus] a. ⚇ (D1) **1.** allg.: bare, (entblößt) denuded; von Bäumen auch: stripped of leaves or flowers or branches; von Kleiderstoffen: threadbare, shiny; von Wänden: blank, von e-r Landschaft: barren, bare, bleak. — **2.** von Personen und Tieren: (geschoren) shorn, short-clipped; (rasiert) shaved; (ohne Haare am Kopfe) bald(-headed); ⚘ wie eine Ratte, wie ein Rattenschwanz (as) bald as a badger; Karl der ~e Charles the Bald. — **3.** fig. (ärmlich) poor, paltry; (leer) empty; ein 2er Stil a bald (or plain) style.

kahl-geschoren (ᵘ⁻...) a. ⚇ closely shorn, close-cropped.

Kahlheit (ᵛ⁻) f ⚇ (zu kahl 1:) bareness, denuded state; blankness, barrenness; (zu 2:) baldness, baldheadedness.

Kahl-kinn (ᵘ⁻...) n ⚇ man with a smooth (or shaven) chin; =kopf m: **a)** bald head; **b)** bald(-headed) person; ⚘köpfig a. ⚇ bald-headed or -pated; =köpfigkeit f baldheadedness, baldness.

Kahm (ᵛ) [ahd.: coom] m ⓓc. mould forming on beer, wine, &c., ⚇ mycoderm.

kahmen (ᵛ⁻) v/n. (h. u. sn) ⚇ to mould, to grow (or turn, F go) mouldy.

kahmicht, kahmig (ᵛ⁻) a. ⚇ mouldy, musty, fusty, ⚇ mycodermic.

Kahm(icht)-pilz ⚘ (ᵘ(ᵛ)...) m ⚇ mycoderm (Saccharomy'ces Mycode'rma); =werden n ⚇ growing (or turning, F going) mouldy.

Kahn¹ (ᵛ) m ⓓc. = Kahm.

Kahn² ⚓ (ᵛ) [ndb.] m ⓓc. (small) boat, skiff; (Baum-)~ canoe; (flaches Boot) punt; (Lichterschiff) lighter; (Brücken-)~ pontoon.

kahnbar (ᵛ⁻) a. ⚇ navigable for (small) boats or small craft; boatable.

Kahn-bein (ᵘ⁻...) n anat.: ⚇ scaphoid bone; =brücke f boat-(or pontoon-)bridge.

Kähnchen (ᵛ⁻) n ⚇ dim. von Kahn.

kahnen¹ ⚓ (ᵛ⁻) v/n. (h. und sn) ⚇ to go boating, to row (or take) a row.

kahnen² (ᵛ⁻) v/n. (h.) ⚇ = kahmen.

kahn-fahren ⚓ (ᵘ⁻...) v/n. (sn) ⚇b** = kahnen¹; F to take a turn on the river; ~ ⚇ boating, rowing, (Wassersport) aquatics; =fahrer m ⚇ one who rows (or F handles) a boat; vgl. =führer; =fahrt f ⚇ = =fahren, a.: trip (or F turn, blow) on the river, lake, &c.; ⚘förmig a. ⚇ boat-shaped, anat.: ⚇ scaphoid, ⚘ ⚇ cymbi form, ...ate; =führer m ⚇ boatman, ferry-man, bargee; vgl. =fahrer; =ladung f boatful; =schnabel m, orn. boatbill, crab-catcher (Cancro'ma cochlea'ria); =schnecke f, zo. boatshell (Cy'mbium); fossile ~: ⚇ scaphite.

Kai (ᵛ) [ndl.] m ⚇ (ⓑb.) (Uferdamm) quay, wharf; weitS. landing-place, jetty.

kai-en ⚓ (ᵛ⁻) [ndl.] v/a. ⚇: die Rahen ⚘ to brace the yards lengthwise.

Kai-gebühren (ᵘ⁻...) f/pl. ⚇, =geld n ⚇ (charges pl. for) quayage, wharfage.

Kaiman (ᵛ⁻) [brasil.] m ⓓd. (⚇) zo. cayman, alligator (Alliga'tor).

Kai-meister ⚓ (ᵘ⁻...) m ⚇ wharfinger.

Ka-in (ᵛ⁻) [hebr.] npr/m. ⚇⚇α. bibl. (Bruder u. Mörder Abels) Cain.

Kainit ⚇ u. ⊕ (ᵛ⁻) [grch. kaino's neu...] m ⓓc. min., agr., chm. kainite.

Ka-ins-mal (ᵘ⁻...) n ⚇, =stempel m, =zeichen n (1. Mos. 4,15) mark (or brand) of Cain; weitS. (Schandfleck) stigma; =opfer n Cain's offering.

Ka-iphas (ᵛ⁻ᵛ⁻) [hebr.] npr/m. ⚇γ. (Hoherpriester zur Zeit Jesu) Caiaphas.

Kairo ⚘ (ᵛ⁻) [ar. die Siegreiche] npr/n. ⓓα. (Hauptstadt Ägyptens) Cairo.

Kais. abbr. = Kaiserlich.

Kaiser (ᵛ⁻) [ahd.; *lt. Caesar] m ⚇ (vor Eigennamen, wenn ohne Art., oft ohne Flexionszeichen), ~in f ⚇ **1.** emperor, f empress; der Deutsche ~ the German Emperor, auch oft: the Kaiser; ~ Wilhelm (the) Emperor William. — **2.** fig. sich um des ~s Bart streiten to quarrel (or squabble) about nothing; to split hairs; Sprichw. wo nichts ist, hat der ~ sein Recht verloren, etwa: where nought's to be got, kings lose their scot, vgl. das engl. Sprichw.: you cannot get blood out of a stone; s. Katze 2.

Kaiser-adler (ᵘ⁻...) m ⚇ imperial eagle; orn. vgl. Königsadler; =burg f imp. palace; =fisch m, ichth. emperor-fish (Holaca'nthus impera'tor); =garde f imperial guard; =haus n imp. house.

Kaiserin (ᵛᵛᵛ) f ⚇ s. Kaiser; ~mutter f (the) Emperor's Mother, als ~witwe auch: (the) Empress Dowager.

Kaiser-krone (ᵘ⁻...) f ⚇: **a)** imperial crown; **b)** ⚘ crown imperial, fritillary (Fritilla'ria imperia'lis).

kaiserlich (ᵛᵛᵛ) a. ⚇ imperial; röm. Alt. auch: Cæsarean; adv. meist as (or like an) emperor; in an imperial manner or tone; Titel: Seine ~e Majestät His Imperial Majesty; Se. ~ Königliche (K. K.) Hoheit, Se. ~e [und Königliche (abbr. S. k.[u. k.]) Hoheit His Imperial and Royal Highness; die ~en m/pl.: **a)** ⚔ the Imperial army or troops pl.; **b)** pol. the (party of) imperialists pl.

Kaiserling (ᵛ⁻ᵛ) m ⓓd.: **a)** pol. imperialist; **b)** ⚘ (Pilz) golden agaric (Aga'ricus caesa'rius).

kaiser-los (ᵘ⁻...) a. ⚇ without an emperor; =mantel m ⚇: **a)** imperial cloak; **b)** ent. (Perlmutterfalter) fritillary (Ar'gy'nnis); =reich n empire; =saal m imp. hall, hall of the Emperors; =schlange f, zo. (Riesenschlange) boa-constrictor; =schnitt m, surg. Cæsarian (Cæsarean) operation or section, ⚇ hysterotomy; =specht m, orn. ivory-billed woodpecker; =stadt f imperial city; =tee m imp. tea; =titel m imp. title.

Kaisertum (ᵛ⁻ᵛ) n ⓓd. empire.

Kaiser-wahl (ᵘ⁻...) f ⚇ election of an emperor; =wetter n, etwa: King's weather; =Wilhelms-Kanal ⚘ m (Nordostseekanal) Baltic Canal; =wort n imperial promise; =würde f imperial rank or dignity or position.

Kai-spesen (ᵘ⁻...) pl. ⚇, =zoll m = Kaigeld

[Kajak] — 564 — [Kaliumchlorid]

Kajak ↓ (⌣⌣) m, n ⑪d. ⑳ (grönländisches Boot) kayak.
Kajeputt=baum ⑫ ⚥ (⌣⌣́...) [malai.] m ⑪c. u. ⑳ cajuput(-tree) (Melaleu'ca).
kajolieren F (⌣⌣⌣́⌣) [fr.] v/a. u. v/n. (h.) ⑬ (liebkosen) to cajole.
Kajüte ↓ (⌣⌣́⌣) [nhd., ndl.; *Koje] f ㊽ (Zimmer auf dem Hinterteile des Schiffes) cabin; auf Passagierschiffen: Erste ~ saloon; Große ~ state-room.
Kajüten=, Kajüts=junge ↓ (⌣⌣́⌣(⌣)...) m ㊷ cabin-boy; =kappe f (überbau) companion; =passagier m cabin-(or saloon-) passenger; =treppe f companion-ladder or -way or -stairs pl.
Kakadu (⌣⌣⌣́) [ndl., *malai.] m ⑪e. u. ⑳ orn. cockatoo (Plisso'lophus).
Kakao (⌣⌣́⌣) [span., *mex.] m ⑳(⑬) cocoa, med. auch: cacao.
Kakao=baum ⚥ (⌣⌣́⌣...) m ㊷ cocoa-tree (Theobro'ma); =bohne f c.-bean; =butter f c.-butter or -fat; =masse f c.-paste; =pflanzung f c.-plantation; =pulver n c.-powder; =(schalen)tee m c.-tea.
Kake ⚓ (tēt) [engl.] m ㊽ = Reef.
kakeln F (⌣́⌣) v/n. (h.) ㉒a. to cackle (= gackeln, auch fig.).
Kakerlak (⌣⌣́⌣) [ndl., *ind.] m ㊵d. 1. ent. (Schabe) cockroach, F black beetle (Blatta orienta'lis). — 2. (Albino) albino.
Kakophonie (⌣⌣⌣́) [grch.] f ㊽ (Mißklang) cacophony. [cactaceæ.
Kakte=en ⚥ (⌣́⌣(⌣) [Kaktus] f/pl. ⑬: ⌕
Kaktus ⚥ (⌣́⌣) [grch.] m ㊷ (pl. Kakteen) u. inv., a. ⑰ cactus(-plant) (Cactus).
Kaktus=artig (⌣́⌣...) a. ㊺: ⌕ cactaceous; =gewächs n ⑫: ⌕ cactaceous plant, F a. hedgehog-thistle; =schild=laus f, ent. cochineal (Coccus cacti); =zaun=könig m, orn. cactus-wren (Campylorhy'nchus).
Kalabasse ⚥ (⌣⌣́⌣) = Kalebasse.
Kalabreser (⌣⌣⌣́⌣) [Kalabrien] m ㉒ (Art Schlapphut) broad-brimmed hat.
Kalabri=en ⚥ (⌣́⌣⌣) npr/n. ㉓α. (Land in Unter-Italien) Calabria.
Kalaminthe ⚥ (⌣⌣⌣́) [grch.] f ㊽ field-balm (Meli'ssa calami'ntha).
Kalamität (⌣⌣⌣́) [lt.] f ㊻ (Mißstand) calamity, mishap, misfortune.
Kalander ⚓ (⌣⌣́⌣) [nhd., ndl., *fr.] m ㉒: a) (Zylinder-, Walzen=mange) calender, typ. rolling-machine; b) = Galander.
kalandern, kalandrieren (⌣⌣́⌣, ⌣⌣⌣́) v/a. ㉒a., ⑬ (satinieren, glätten) to calender, (walzen) to roll.
Kalands=bruder (⌣́⌣⌣) [lt. calendae] m ㉒ 1. eccl. one of the brethren (or brotherhood) of the Calends. — 2. F (Lebemann) gay (or fast) fellow.
Kalasche ndd. (⌣⌣́⌣) [russ.] f ㊽ (Tracht Prügel) drubbing, sound beating.
Kalauer (⌣́⌣⌣) [P⌣⌣: Kalau, Calembour] m ㉒ (Wortspiel) pun; (alter Witz) old (or stale) joke, oft auch: Joe Miller.
kalauern (⌣́⌣⌣) v/n. (h.) ㉒a. to pun, to make puns, to crack bad jokes.
Kalb (⌣) [ahd.: calf] n ㉓b. 1. calf: vom Rotwilde: fawn; ein ~ abbinden, absetzen to wean a calf; bibl. das goldene ~ anbeten to worship the golden calf (oft fig.); mit fremdem ~e pflügen to plough with another man's heifer, fig. to reap the fruit of other people's work; ein gemästet ~ schlachten to kill the fatted calf. — 2. fig. (ausgelassener Bursche) gay (or merry) young fellow; schimpfend: großes ~ F great fool or ass.

Kälbchen (⌣́⌣) n ㉔ (dim. v. Kalb) little (or young) calf.
Kalbe (⌣́⌣) f ㊽ (junge Kuh) heifer.
kalben (⌣́⌣) v/n. (h.) ㉔ v. Kühen: to calve.
Kälberei F (⌣⌣́) f ㊻ tomfoolery, wanton sport, practical joking, F larking.
Kälber=gekröse (⌣⌣́⌣...) n ㉔ calf's pluck.
kälberhaft, kälberig (⌣⌣́⌣) a. ㊺ like a (great) calf, fig. foolish, wanton, playful.
Kälber=kropf ⚥ (⌣⌣́⌣...) m ㊷ chervil (Chaerophy'llum); knolliger ~ parsnip-chervil (Ch. bulbo'sum); =lab n, =magen m calf's rennet.
kalbern F (⌣́⌣) = kälbern 3.
kälbern (⌣́⌣) I v/n. (h.) ㉒a. 1. = kalben. — 2. F (sich erbrechen) to vomit, to bring up one's food. — 3. F (sich ausgelassen benehmen) to frolic, romp, dally, F to lark (or gad) about. — II subb. a. ㊺ 4. (made of) calf, (of) veal.
Kälber=zahn (⌣́⌣...) m ㉔: a) calf's tooth; b) ⊙ arch. dentil, denticle.
Kalb=fell (⌣́...) n ㉓: a) calf's skin, calf(skin), pl. ⚥ auch: calves; b) ⚔ co. drum; er muß auf das ~ schwören to must serve (in the army); =fleisch n veal; =fleisch=pastete f veal(-)pie; =leder n calf(-leather); in ~ gebunden bound in calf; =leder=band ⊙ m Buchbinderei: calf-binding, volume (bound) in calf; ⁀ledern a. ㊺ of calf(-leather).
kalbs=artig (⌣́⌣...) a. ㊺ calf-like, ⌕ vituline; =auge n ㉔ calf's eye, weitS. large goggle-eye; =braten m (joint of) roast veal; =bregen m calf's-brains pl.; =bröschen n, =drüse f sweetbread; =fuß m calf's-foot (a. Kochkunst); =fuß=sülze f calf's-foot jelly; =gekröse, =geschlinge n = Kälbergekröse; =keule f leg of veal; =kopf m: a) calf's head; b) fig. F (Dummkopf) blockhead, dunce; =kotelett n veal cutlet; =leber f calf's liver; =milch f = =bröschen; =nieren=braten m loin of veal; =rippchen n veal cutlet; =schlegel m = =keule; =schnitte f, =schnitzel n veal cutlet; =viertel n quarter of veal.
Kaldaune(n pl.) (⌣⌣́⌣) [nhd.; *mlt. caldu'men] f ㊽ bowels, F guts pl., als Speise: tripe; F sich die ~n vollschlagen to fill one's belly, to gorge (or stuff) o.s.
Kalebasse ⚥ (⌣⌣́⌣) [ar. trockner Kürbis] f ㊽ calabash (= Flaschenkürbis).
Kaledoni=en ⚥ (⌣⌣́⌣) npr/n. ㉓α. († u. poet.) = Schottland) Caledonia.
kaledonisch (⌣⌣́⌣) a. ㊺ Caledonian.
Kaleidoskop ⌕ (⌣⌣́) [grch.] n ⑪d. (optisches Instrument) kaleidoscope; ⁀isch (⌣⌣⌣́) a. ㊺ kaleidoscopic.
kalekut(t)isch (⌣⌣́⌣) a. ㊺ = kalkuttisch.
Kalendarium (⌣⌣⌣́⌣) [lt.] n ㉓ (astronomische Zeittafel) calendar, almanac.
Kalende(n pl.) (⌣⌣́⌣) [lt.] f ㊽ altröm. Kalender: (1. Tag des Monats) calends pl.
Kalender (⌣⌣́⌣) [nhd. 15. sae.; *lt. calenda'rium n] m ㉒ calendar, mit astronomischen ꝛc. Angaben: almanac, bisw. almanack; julia'nischer, gregoria'nischer ~ Julian, Gregorian Calendar; hundertjähriger ~ perpetual almanac; fig. das steht nicht in unserem ~ we know nothing about it; wir müssen e-n roten Strich im ~ machen (wie bei einem großen Ereignis) we must chalk it up (as something wonderful).
Kalender=berechnung (⌣⌣́⌣...) f ㊷ computation of the almanac; =macher m almanac-maker; F fig. (Grillenfänger) crotchety p.; =macherei f almanac-making; =monat m calendar-month.
Kalesche (⌣⌣́⌣) [nhd. 17. sae.; *serb.] f ㊽ light carriage; fly; ehm.: calash.
Kalfakter ㉒, Kalfaktor ㉛ (⌣⌣́⌣) [lt.] m, ~in f ㊼ fire-lighter; weitS. domestic, attendant; b.s. eye-servant, toady, spy; (Anschwärzer) backbiter.
Kalfaterer ↓ (⌣⌣́⌣⌣) m ㉒ caulker.
kalfatern (⌣⌣́⌣) [ndl., *ar.] v/a. und v/n. (h.) ㉒a.: ein Schiff ⌕ (ausdichten) to caulk a ship.
Kalfat=hammer ↓ (⌣⌣́...) m ㉒ caulking mallet; =werg n oakum.
Kali ⌕ (⌣́) [ar.] n ⑪⑬ (o. pl.) chm. (anhydrous) potash; chlorsaures ~ potassium (or potassic) chlorate ($KClO_3$); essigsaures ~ acetate of potassium or potash, potassium acetate; hypermangansaures ~ hypermanganate of potash; (saures) kohlensaures ~ (bi-)carbonate of potash or potassium; salpetersaures ~ (Kalisalpeter) potassium nitrate, (common) saltpetre (KNO_3).
Kali=alaun (⌣́...) m ㉒ chm. (common) alum ($AlK(SO_4)_2 \cdot 12H_2O$).
Kaliber (⌣⌣́⌣) [fr., * ar.?] n (⚓ m) ㉒ 1. (Durchmesser eines Zylinders, ⚔ Geschütz=weite) (Walzen=)~ groove; calibre; ⚔ Geschütz von kleinem ~ gun of small bore. — 2. fig. (Sorte) sort; von demselben ~ of the same calibre, fig. of the same capacity, on a level.
Kaliber=bohrer ⊙ (⌣⌣́⌣...) m ㉒ für Geschützrohre: gun-borer; =maß n calibre-gauge; =(maß)stab m calibre-rule or -scale; =zirkel m callipers pl.
kalibrier=en ⊙ (⌣⌣́) [Kaliber] I v/a. ⑬ to calibrate, gauge, size. — II n ㉓ u. K/ung f ㊻ calibration.
...kalibrig (⌣⌣́...) in Zssgn mit a., zB.: groß-2 of large bore.
Kalif (⌣́) [ar. chalife Nachfolger (Mohammeds)] m ㉒ caliph; ~en=würde f ㊽ (a. Kalifat (⌣⌣́) n ⑪c.) caliphate.
Kaliforni=en (⌣⌣⌣́⌣) npr/n. ㉓α. California; Kaliforni=er(in f ㊼) m ㉒, kalifornisch (⌣⌣́⌣) a. ㊺ Californian.
kali=haltig (⌣́...) a. ㊺: ⌕ potassic; =hydra't n ⑪ (⌕ Ätzkali) potassium hydrate, caustic potash (KHO).
Kaliko ⌕ ㊽ (⌣́⌣) [Calicut ⚥ oftind. St.] m ⑳ (unbedruckter Kattun) calico.
kalikut(t)isch (⌣⌣́⌣) a. ㊺ = kalfuttisch.
Kali=lauge (⌣́...) f ㊷ solution of caustic potash; =metall n = Kalium; =salpe'ter m (common) nitre, nitrate of potash (KNO_3), vgl. Kali am Schluß; =salz n potassium salt; =seife f potash-soap, soft soap; =syndikat ⊙ n Potash Combine.
Kalium (⌣́⌣) [neu-lt., *Kali] n ⑬ (Leichtmetall, Davy 1807) potassium (K).
Kalium=chlori'd ⌕ (⌣́(⌣)⌣...) n ⑬ chm. (Chlorkalium) potassium (or potassic)

[Kaliumeisenzyanid] — 565 — [Kaltherzigkeit]

chloride(KCl); =eisen=zyanid (=zyanür)n potassium ferricyanide(ferrocyanide); =hydroxyd n potassium hydroxide, caustic potash (KHO); =jodi'd n = Jodkalium; =(mon)oxy'd n potassium monoxide (K_2O); =salz n potassic salt; =silizium=fluori'd n = Kieselfluorkalium; =superoxy'd n potassium tetroxide (K_2O_4); =zyanid (Zyankalium) potassium cyanide (KCN).

Kali=werk ⊕ (⁻...) n ㉒ potash works pl.

Kalk (J) [ahd.; *lt. calc-] m ⊕b. lime, chalk; gebrannter ~ burnt lime; gelöschter ~ slaked lime; ungelöschter (gebrannter) ~ quicklime (s. Atzkalk); chm. kieselsaurer, kohlensaurer, phosphorsaurer ~ silicate, carbonate, phosphate of lime; ⊕ Bauwesen: mit ~ bewerfen, bestreichen to rough-cast, plaster, parget; mit ~ tünchen to whitewash, to lime-wash.

Kalk=ablagerung (J...) f ㊵ min., &c. limestone-deposit, chalky sediment; =anstrich ⊕ m whitewash.

Kalkant (J) [lt.] m ㉒ 1. bellows-blower. — 2. thea. = Orchesterdiener.

Kalk=anwurf (J...) m ⊕ plaster; =artig a. ㊺ lime-like, chalky, ⚗ calcareous; =äscher ⊕ m Gerberei: lime-pit; =beule f, path. chalky swelling; =bewurf ⊕ m Bauwesen: coat of plaster, plastering; parget of lime; =bildung ⚗ f calcification; =brennen n, =brenner m ⊕ limeburning, -burner; =bruch ⊕ m limestone quarry or pit; =brühe ⊕ f lime-water, whitewash; =eisenstein m, min. ferruginous limestone.

kalken (J) [Kalk] v/a. ㊺ to mix with lime; to soak in lime(-water); auch v/n. (h.) to slake (or temper) lime.

Kalk=erde (J...) f ㊺ calcareous earth; =faß ⊕ n lime-tub; =fels m calcareous rock; °frei a. ㊺ free from lime; °führend a.: ⚗ calcariferous; =gebirge n chalky (or calcareous) mountain; =grube ⊕ f lime-pit; °haltig a. min.: ⚗ calcareous, calciferous; der Boden chalky soil; =hütte ⊕ f = ofen; =hydra't n: ⚗ hydrate of lime (CaH_2O_2).

kalkicht (J) = kalkig.

kalkieren (J) [fr. calquer] v/a. ㊺ (durchzeichnen) to calk, mehr gbr.: to trace.

kalkig (J) a. ㊺ of lime, chalky, rich in chalk, ⚗ calcareous, calciferous.

Kalk=kelle ⊕ (J...) f ㊺ Bauwesen: trowel; =lauge f = =milch; =licht n lime- (or oxyhydrogen) light; =loch ⊕ n = =grube; =löschen ⊕ n slaking of lime; =malerei f fresco- (or wall-)painting; =mehl ⊕ n Maurerei: powdered (quick-)lime; =mergel m chalky marl; =meta'll m = Ka'lzium; =milch f (fluid) slaked lime, chm. auch: milk of lime, ⊕ Zuckerfabr.: temper; =mörtel ⊕ m (lime-)mortar, mit feinem Sande: bastard stucco; =ofen ⊕ m lime-kiln; =salz n, chm. calcium (or calcic) salt; =sand, =schiefer, =sinter, =spat m, min. chalky (or calcareous) sand, slate, sinter, spar; =stein m, min. limestone, chalky (or calcareous) stone; =stein=bruch m limestone-quarry; =superphospha't n superphosphate of lime; =teilchen n calcareous particle; =tuff m, min. tufaceous limestone, calcareous tuff; =tünche f Bauwesen: lime-wash.

Kalkül (⁻tū'l u. J) [fr.; *lt. calculus, dim. v. calx] m ⊕d. (Berechnung) calculation, computation; ~ation (⌣⌣ -tş(⌣)ł) [lt.] f ㊵ calculation.

Kalkulator (⌣⌣⌣⌣) [lt.] m ㉑ (Rechner) calculator, (ready) reckoner; als Beamter: controller; Lisch (⌣⌣⌣⌣) a. ㊺ (rechnungsmäßig) calculating; Kalkulatur (⌣⌣⌣⌣) f ㊵ calculation, controller's office; kalkulieren (⌣⌣⌣⌣) v/a. u. v/n. (h.) (=berechnen) to calculate, compute, reckon.

Kalk=uranglimmer (J...) m ㉒, =uranit m, min. calcareous uranite.

Kalkutta ♀ (⌣⌣) npr/n. ㊵α. (Hauptstadt von Bengalen, Ost-indien) Calcutta; kalkuttisch a. ㊺: der Hahn turkey cock.

Kalk=wasser (J...) n ㉒ chm., &c. (Lösung von Atzkalk) lime-water; =wurf ⊕ m = =bewurf; =zuschlag ⊕ m zum Schmelzen der Eisen-erze c. limestone flux.

Kalle F (J⌣) [jüd.] f ㊺ sweetheart.

Kalligraph (⌣⌣f) [grch.] m ㉒ (Schönschreiber) calligrapher, ...ist; ~ie (⌣⌣fl) f ㊺ calligraphy; elegant (or fine) writing, penmanship; Lisch (⌣⌣fl) a. ㊺ calligraphic, calligraphical.

Kalmank (⌣⌣) [grch.] m ⊕d. (mit Atlas geköperter Wollstoff) calamanco.

Kalmäuser F (⌣⌣⌣) [nhd. 16./17. sae. = jüd. bursch. *ca'lamus Federfuchser] m ㉒: a) (Kopfhänger)(idle)dreamer, one given to musing or moping; b) (Geizhals) mean (or niggardly) fellow, miser; ~ei (⌣⌣⌣ll) f ㊺: a) musing, moping, F brown study; b) mean (or niggardly) spirit, miser's life; 2n v/n. (h.) ㉒a.: a) to muse, to mope, to lead a lonely life; b) to live in a mean way.

Kalme(n¹ pl.) ↓ (J⌣) [ndb., *fr.] f ㊺ calm region(s) or latitude(s pl.).

kalmen² ↓ (J) [fr.] v/n. (h.) ⊕ v. Winde, Meere: to be(come) calm or still, F to settle down (into a dead calm).

Kalmen¹=zone (J⌣...) f ㊺ calm zone.

kalmieren (⌣⌣⌣) [fr.] v/a. ㊺ (beruhigen) to calm, quiet, still, appease.

Kalmuck (⌣⌣) m ⊕c.㊿ 1. ⊛ Zeug: kalmuck. — 2. = Kalmück.

Kalmück (⌣⌣f) [tatar. Abtrünniger] m ㊷, ~in f ㊸ (Westmongole) Kalmuck (woman f); Lisch (⌣⌣f) a. ㊺ Kalmuck.

Kalmus ♀ (J⌣) [lt. ca'lamus Halm] m ⊕㉑ 1. (echter od. gemeiner) ~ sweet calamus or cane, sweet-flag, sweet-rush (A'corus ca'lamus). — 2. unechter ~ sword-flag (Iris pseuda'corus).

Kalomel ⚗ (⌣⌣ł) [grch.] n ㊶ pharm. (Quecksilberchlorür als stark abführendes weißes Pulver) calomel.

Kalorie ⚗ (⌣⌣l) [fr.] f ㊺ phys. (Wärme, die 1 kg Wasser um 1 Grad C. wärmer macht) heat unit, caloric unit, calory.

Kalorik ⚗ (⌣⌣l) f ㊺ (Wärmelehre) calorics.

Kalori=meter ⚗ (⌣⌣⌣l) n (m) ㉒ (Wärmemesser) calorimeter; =metrie (⌣⌣⌣⌣ł) f ㊺ calorimetry; °metrisch (⌣⌣⌣l) a. ㊺ calorimetric(al); =motor m ㉒ (galvanischer Wärme-erzeuger) calorimotor.

kalorisch (⌣⌣l) a. ㊺ caloric; 2e (Heißluft-)Maschine caloric engine.

Kalotte ⚗ (⌣⌣) [fr.] f ㊺ math. (Kugel-abschnitt) calotte.

Kalpak ⚔ (⌣⌣)[madj.,*türk.] (Tuchzipfel der Husarenmütze) m ⊕d.(㊿) kalpac(k), busby.

kalt (J) [ahd.: cold: lt. ge'lidus] I a. ㊻ (D2) 1. (ant. warm, heiß) cold; frigid (zone); chilly (air, room, &c.); (kühl) cool; (frostig) frosty, icy (cold); 2 und naß raw; 2 und öde bleak; es ist 2 (es Wetter) it is cold, a cold (or bleak) day; mir ist 2 I feel cold; 2 machen (abkühlen) to cool down, to chill, ⚗ to refrigerate; F fig. (morden) to murder a p., F to do for a p.; 2 stellen to put in a cool place, to cool (down), in Eis: to ice; F fig. to send to Coventry, to boycott; es überläuft mich 2 I am coming over (quite) cold, F I have (a fit of) the shivers; 2 werden to grow (F to get) cold, (sich abkühlen) to cool down; mir wird 2 I am getting cold; Sprichw. 2e Hände, warme Liebe cold hands, a warm heart. — 2. Redewendungen: s. Aufschnitt 2; mit 2em Blute with cool blood, cool-bloodedly; 2e Küche cold meal or lunch; s. blasen 1; ⊕ einen Ofen 2 legen (niederblasen) to blow out a furnace; 2er (nicht zündender Blitz-)Schlag harmless flash; mit 2em Verstande with an unimpassioned mind. — 3. fig. cold, cool (and collected); (gleichgültig) indifferent, callous; 2 bleiben to keep cool, to keep one's temper, F to take it coolly; er empfing sie sehr 2 he gave them a cool reception; das läßt ihn 2 it leaves him unmoved, it does not affect him; 2 sein für // to be indifferent to //; kälter werden to cool down (in one's ardour), to flag in one's zeal. — II ~es n ㊹ s. th. cold, cold things pl.

Kalt=baden (J...) n ㉒ cold bathing; =blüter m, zo. cold-blooded animal; °blütig a. ㊺ cold-blooded, with cool blood (auch zo. von Fischen rc.); fig. cold, cool-headed, (gleichgültig) indifferent, (phlegmatisch) phlegmatic; adv. oft: in cold blood, deliberately; =blütigkeit f cold-bloodedness, cold blood (a. fig.); (Gleichgültigkeit) indifference (Gleichmut) equanimity, composure; 2brüchig ⊕ a. metall. cold-short.

Kälte (J⌣) f ㊺ (s. kalt) cold(ness), ⚗ frigidity; (Kühle) chill(iness), frostige: frostiness; vor ~ erstarrt numb(ed) with cold; vor ~ zittern to shiver with cold; Thermometer: fünf Grad ~ five degrees below zero; fig. coldness, coolness, indifference, callousness; e-n mit ~ behandeln to give a p. the cold shoulder, to snub a. p.

Kälte=erzeuger (J...) m ㉒, =erzeugungs=maschine f, phys. refrigerating-machine, ⚗ cryogen; =grad m degree of cold or below zero; =mischung f, phys. freezing-mixture.

kalten (J) v/n. (fn) ㊺ (kalt w.) = er2.

kälten (J⌣) (kalt m.) v/a. ㊺ to chill, ⚗ to refrigerate, mit Eis: to (cool with) ice.

kalt=feucht (J...) a. ㊺ cold and damp, beim Anfassen: clammy; =hämmern ⊕ n ㉓ cold-hammering; =haus n, hort. green-house, glass-house without heating-apparatus; =herzig(keit f) a.

♪ Musik; ⚗ Wissenschaft; ♀ Pflanze; ♁ Geographie; ⊕ Technik; ⚒ Bergbau; ⚔ Militär; ↓ Marine; ⊛ Handel; ✉ Post; 🚂 Eisenbahn.

[kalthöflich] — 566 — [Kammbürste]

fig. cold-hearted(ness); 2höflich *a.* studiedly (or frigidly) polite.

kältlich (⌣⌣) *a.* ⓖ (etwas kalt) coldish, chilly, chilled; (kühl) cool, F coolish.

kalt-machend (⌣'...) *a.* ⓖ chilling, ⚙ refrigerating; =schale *f* ⓖ Kocht.: cold beer- (or wine-)soup; =schmied ⊕ *m* brazier (who works without fire); =sinn *m* coldness, frigidity; unconcern, callousness; 2sinnig *a.* cold, frigid; unconcerned, callous; =wasser-arzt *m*: ⚙ hydropath(ist); =wasser-bad *n* cold-water bath; =wasser-heil-anstalt *f*: ⚙ hydropathic establishment; =wasser-heilkunde *f* cold-water treatment, ⚙ hydropathy, hydrotherapeutics; =wasser-kur *f* cold-water cure, ⚙ hydropathic treatment; =wasser-umschlag *m* cold-water bandage or compress or dressing; =werden *n* turning (or growing) cold, cooling down, ⚙ refrigeration.

Kalvari-en-berg (⌣⌣''...) [lt.; *hebr. Golgatha] *m* ⓖ bibl. (Mount) calvary.

Kalville ♀ (⌣⌣⌣) [fr. *m, f*] *f* ⓖ (*m* ⓖ) (Apfelsorte) bisw. calville.

kalvinisch (⌣⌣'⌣) *a.* ⓖ = kalvinistisch.

Kalvinismus (⌣⌣⌣) *m* ⓖ eccl. Calvinism; Engl.: Puritanism, Dissent.

Kalvinist (⌣⌣⌣') *m* ⓖ, ~in *f* ⓖ Calvinist; England: Puritan, Nonconformist, Dissenter; ~en-kirche *f* ⓖ oft: dissenting chapel.

kalvinistisch (⌣⌣⌣'⌣) *a.* ⓖ Calvinist, Calvinistic; Engl.: puritan, puritanic, nonconformist, dissenting.

kalzinierbar (⌣⌣⌣'⌣) *a.* [lt.=dtsch.] ⓖ *chm. u.* ⊕ *metall.* calcinable.

kalzinieren (⌣⌣'⌣) [lt.] *chm.,* ⊕ *metall.* I *v/a.* ⓖ (glühen, rösten) to calcine. — II ~ *n* ⓖ = Kalzinierung.

Kalzinier=herd (⌣⌣''...) *m* ⓖ calcining hearth; =ofen *m* calcar, calciner; =topf *m* calcining crucible.

Kalzinierung (⌣⌣'⌣) *f* ⓖ calcining, calcination. [calcite.]

Kalzit ⚙ (⌣') [lt.] *m* ⓖ *min.* (Kalkspat)

Kalzium ⚙ (⌣'⌣⌣) [lt.] *n* ⓖ *chm.* calcium (Ca); 2artig *a.* ⓖ calcium-like, weitS. calcareous; =chlorid ⓝ *n* calcium chloride (CaCl₂); =hydroxyd *n* (gelöschter Kalk) hydrate of calcium; =karbid *n* calcium carbide (CaC₂); =karbonat *n* calcium (or calcic) carbonate (CaCO₃); =oxyd *n* calcium (or calcic) oxide (CaO).

kam (⌣) *ind. impf.* von kommen.

Kamaldulenser (⌣⌣⌣⌣) [Cama'doli, it. Benediktinerkloster in den Apenninen] *m* ⓖ, ~in *f* ⓖ, kamaldulensisch *a.* ⓖ rel. Camaldolite. [ⓖ (Hofpartei) camarilla.)

Kamarilla (⌣⌣⌣'⌣, F oft: ⌣⌣⌣') [span.] *f*

☞ Kamasche öft. = Gamasche.

Kambodscha (⌣⌣'⌣) *npr/n.* ⓖⓐ. (fr. Schutzstaat in Hinter=indien) Cambodia;
kambodschisch *a.* ⓖ Cambodian.

Kambri=er (⌣'⌣) *m* ⓖ, ~in *f* ⓖ (Bewohner[in]) Cambrian, Welsh(wo)man.

Kambrik ♀ ⓖ (⌣'⌣) [Cambrai ♀ *fr. Stadt*] *m* ⓖ (feine Leinwand) cambric.

kambrisch (⌣'⌣) [kelt.] *a.* ⓖ (walisisch) Cambrian, Welsh; *geol.* 2e (silu'rische) Formation, Gruppe ⚙ Cambrian formation, group.

Kambüse ⚓ (⌣⌣) [fr., ndl.] *f* ⓖ (Kabuse) caboose.

käme (⌣') *subj. impf. v.* kommen.

Kamee (=⌣'⌣) [nhd. 16./18. sae., fr. camée *m*; *it.] *f* ⓖ (geschnittener Edelstein) cameo.

Kamel (⌣') [mhd., lt. *m, *ar.] *n* ⓒ. 1. *zo.* camel, bisw. ~in *f* ⓖ female camel; zweihöckeriges ~ (Bactrian) camel (Came'lus bactria'nus); einhöckeriges ~ dromedary (C. droma'rius); *bibl.* Mücken seihen und ~ verschlucken to strain at a gnat, and swallow the camel. — 2. ⚓ (Maschine, Schiffe zu heben) camel. — 3. burschikos: (philiströser Mensch) Philister; (Student, der keiner Verbindung angehört) student not attached to a club; P schimpfend: great donkey.

kamel=artig (⌣''...) *a.* ⓖ: ~ cameline. Des Tier: ~ camelid; ~=fleisch *n* ⓖ camel's flesh; =führer *m* camel-driver; =füllen *n* young camel; =garn *n* = Kämel-garn. [Angora-yarn.)

Kämel-garn ⓖ (⌣''...) *n* ⓖ mohair;

Kamel=haar (⌣''...) *n* ⓖ: a) camel's hair; b) = Kämelgarn; =haar-pinsel *m* camel's hair brush; =hals-fliege *f, ent.* camel-necked fly (Raphi'dia); 2hären *a.* ⓖ (of) camel-hair; =hengst *m* male camel; =heu ⓖ *n* camel-grass (Andropo'gon).

Kameli=e (⌣⌣(⌣)⌣) [Ka'mel, mähr. Jesuit, 17. sae.] *f* ⓖ came(l)lia (Came'llia).

Kamel=korps ⚔ (⌣''...) *n* ⓖ im Sudan ꝛc.: camel-corps; =kuh *f* female camel; =last *f* camel's load; =milch *f* c.'s milk.

Kamelopard (⌣⌣⌣') [grch.] *m* ⓖⓐ. ⓖ *zo.* bsd. ehm. camelopard (= Gira'ffe).

Kamelott (⌣⌣') [fr., *ar.] *m* ⓒ. (Stoff) camlet; ~=anzug *m* ⓖ camlet suit.

kamelotten ⓖ (⌣⌣'⌣) *a.* ⓖ (D9) (of) camlet.

Kamelott=fabrikant(in *f*) *m* ⓖ (⌣⌣'⌣) ⓖ camlet-maker; =kleid *n* = =anzug; =stoff *m* camleting.

Kamels=... (⌣''...) in Zssgn = Kamel;
Kamel=stute (⌣''...) *f* ⓖ female camel; =tier *n* = Kamel 1; =treiber *m* camel-driver, cameleer; =wolle *f* camel's wool; =ziege *f, zo.*: a) Angora-goat (Capra hircus angore'nsis); b) = Lama; c) alpaca (Anche'nia pacos).

Kamera (⌣'⌣⌣) [lt.] *f* ⓖ *phot.* = camera.

Kamerad (⌣⌣⌣') [nhd. 17. sae.; *fr.] *m* ⓖ, ~in *f* ⓖ comrade, (Genosse, Geselle) companion, mate, F pal, chum; (Schul=)~ school-fellow; ⚔ fellow soldier, unter Offizieren: brother officer; *iro.* du bist ein netter ~ you're a pretty (or fine) fellow; 2lich *a.* ⓖ as a comrade.

Kamerad=schaft (⌣⌣⌣') *f* ⓖ 1. comradeship, ⚔ auch: esprit de corps; weitS. companionship, good fellowship. — 2. *coll.* all the comrades *pl.,* F *iro.* the whole clique or gang or set.

kameradschaftlich (⌣⌣⌣'⌣) *a.* ⓖ like a comrade, companionable, F chummy.

Kamerali-en (⌣⌣⌣'⌣) [lt.] *n/pl. inv.* (Staatswissenschaft) fiscal science(s *pl.*), cameralistics; weitS. (science of) finance, political economy.

Kameralist ⚙ (⌣⌣⌣') *m* ⓖ student of fiscal questions, ⚙ cameralist; weitS. financier; ~ik *f* ⓖ: ⚙ cameralistics; 2isch *a.* ⚙ fiscal, cameralistic.

Kameral=wesen ⚙ (⌣⌣''...) *n* ⓖ fiscal affairs *pl.,* weitS. department of finance;

=wissenschaft *f* fiscal science, weitS. political economy; *pl.* = Kamera'lien.

Kamerun (⌣⌣⌣') [port. camarões Krabben(=Fl.)] *npr/n.* ⓖⓐ. (seit 1884 deutsche Kolonie in West=afrika) Kamerun, the Cameroons *pl.,* Cameroon; ~er *m* ⓖ native (or inhabitant) of Kamerun.

Kamille ♀ (⌣⌣) [mhd., *grch.] *f* ⓖ: a) echte ~ German camomile (Matrica'ria chamomi'lla) b) römische ~ (large) camomile (A'nthemis no'bilis); c) (Hunds=)~ dog's (or stinking) camomile (A'nthemis co'tula); ~n=blüten *f/pl.* ⓖ camomiles *pl.*; ~n=öl *n* (essential) oil of camomile; ~n=tee *m* camomile tea.

Kamin (⌣') [mhd., lt., *grch.] *m, n* ⓓ. 1. a) (Schornstein) chimney(-pot); b) (Herd im Zimmer) fireplace, fireside. — 2. mst *n* (in den Alpen) Öffnung e=r Schlucht) mouth of a ravine.

Kamin=aufsatz (⌣''...) *m* ⓖ mantelpiece ornament; =besen *m* chimney-brush, kleiner für den Herd: hearth-broom; =einsatz *m* hob; =feger *m* chimney-sweep(er); =gerät *n* = =zubehör; =gesims *n* mantelpiece, mantel-board or -shelf; =gitter *n* (fire-)guard, niedriges: fender; =mantel *m* = =gesims; =ofen *m* (German) stove; =rohr *n* flue; =schirm *m* fire-screen; =sims *n* = =gesims; =teppich *m* hearth-rug; =vorsetzer *m* fender; =zange *f* fire-tongs *pl.*; =zubehör *n* (set of) fire-irons *pl.*

Kamisol (⌣⌣⌣') [fr., it.] *n* ⓓ. ehm. doublet; vgl. Jacke 1.

Kamm (⌣') [ahd.; comb] *m* ⓑ. 1. comb; enger ~ small-tooth(ed) comb; weiter ~ large-toothed comb; ~ aus Schildpatt (Elfenbein) tortoise-shell (ivory) comb; *fig.* alle(s) über einen ~ scheren (gleich behandeln) to treat everybody (everything) alike; sie sind alle über einen ~ geschoren ... all tarred with the same brush. — 2. (langgedehnte Erhöhung e=s Gebirges, e=r Düne, e=s Festungswerkes, einer Welle): crest, ridge. — 3. *anat.* und *zo.* (kamm=ähnlicher Teil) cock's comb, crest; *fig.* ihm schwillt (ob. wächst) der ~ (er wird übermütig) he is growing arrogant or haughty, (gerät in Zorn) his blood is up, he is getting angry. — 4. an Pferden ꝛc.: (der mit der Mähne bekleidete Rand des Halses) edge of the neck under the mane. — 5. ⊕: a) *mach.* (Radzahn) cog of a wheel; b) *mech.* (Hebebaumen) cam, tappet; c) Weberei: slay, reed; d) der Krempelmaschine: comber.

Kammacher (⌣'⌣) *m* ⓖ [Kamm=macher] ⓖ comb-maker or -cutter; ~ei *f* ⓖ comb-making or -cutting.

kamm=ähnlich (⌣'...) *a.* ⓖ, 2artig *a.* ⓖ comb-like, ⚙ pectinate(d).

Kamm=maschine ⊕ (⌣'...) [Kamm=maschine] *f* ⓖ comb-making machine;

Kämm=maschine ⊕ (⌣'⌣⌣) [Kämm=maschine] *f* ⓖ combing-machine.

Kamm=baumwolle ⊕ (⌣''...) *f* ⓖ carded cotton; =blase *f, zo.* der Rippenquallen: ⚙ ctenocyst; =blatt *n*: a) ⊕ Spinnerei: ~ der Kratzmaschine comb-blade; b) ⚙ ⚙ ctenophyllum; =blume *f* = Kamille *a* und *b*; =bürste *f* brush for cleaning combs, comb-brush.

Signs (see page IX): F familiar; P vulgar; ⚡ flash; ⟍ rare; † obsolete (died); * new word (born); +⁺ incorrect; ♪ music;

[Kämmchen] — 567 — [kampfbereit]

Kämmchen (⌣⌣) n ☉ (dim. von Kamm) little (or tiny) comb.
Kamm=eidechse (⌣...) f ☉ zo. iguana.
Kämmel=garn (⌣⌣⌣) n ☉ = Kämelgarn.
kämmeln ⊕ (⌣⌣) v/a. ⓐa.: Wolle ⓠ to comb (or card) wool.
kämmen (⌣⌣) [ahd.; *Kamm] v/a. u. v/n. (h.) ⓐ **1.** to comb, auch v/refl. sich ⓠ to comb one's hair or o.s. — **2.** ⊕ Spinnerei: to comb (or card) wool. — **3.** ⚔ = bestreichen **4.** — **4.** von den Wellen: to (swell and) break, to form breakers.
Kammer (⌣⌣) [ahd.; *lt. că'mĕră] f ☉ **1.** chamber (a. anat., zo. u. ⊕ = abgeschlossener Raum); (Stube) apartment, (small) room, kleinere: closet, f. Schlaf=; phys. f. Camera; anat. f. Herz=. — **2.** parl. Erste ~ upper (or hereditary) chamber, England: Upper House, House of Lords; Zweite ~ lower (or elective) chamber, Frankreich 2c.: Chamber of Deputies, England: Lower House, House of Commons; die ~n einberufen (auflösen) to convoke (to dissolve) parliament; (Finanz=)~ Board of Revenue; vgl. Handels=. — **3.** ⚔ ⊕ ~ e-r Kanone, e-s Gewehrs: chamber; (Abteilung) compartment. — **4.** ⚔ (erzhaltiger Gang) lode. — **5.** ⚔ regimental depot. — **6.** ⚓ (Verschlag) room, cabin, berth.
Kämmer ⊕ (⌣⌣) [kämmen] m ☉, ~in f ☉ comber, carder (of wool, &c.).
Kammer=amt (⌣...) n ☉: a) pol. board of finance or revenue; b) in Städten: municipal board or offices pl.; **=auflösung** f dissolution of parliament.
Kämmerchen (⌣⌣⌣) [Kammer dim.] n ☉ small chamber or closet, ⚘ chamberlet; ♀ (kleines Fach): ⚡ locule; ♀ u. anat.: mit ~ versehen: ⚡ loculose; Kinderspiel: ~ vermieten puss-in-the-corner.
Kammer=dame (⌣⌣...) f ☉ = =fräulein; **=diener** m valet, des Königs a.: groom of the chamber; **=dienerschaft** f a sovereign's household (servants pl.).
Kämmerei[1] (⌣⌣⌣⌣) [Kämmer] f ☉ a) staatliche od. städtische Behörde: board of finance, in England: Exchequer, (Board of) Treasury; vgl. Kammer=amt b; b) (Sitzungssaal, Bureau) office(s pl.) of the board of finance, England: (offices pl. of the) Exchequer or Treasury.
Kämmerei[2] ⊕ (~) [kämmen] f ☉ (Woll=)~ combing, carding.
Kämmerei[1]**=gut** (⌣⌣...) n ☉ land belonging to a town(ship) or a parish; **=kasse** f municipal exchequer or treasury; **=verwaltung** f municipal administration of finance.
Kämmerer (⌣⌣⌣) m ☉ **1.** keeper (or custodian) of a museum, &c. — **2.** Hofwürde: chamberlain; vgl. Kämmerherr. — **3.** (städtischer Finanzbeamter) treasurer of a town.
Kammer=frau (⌣⌣...) f ☉ chambermaid, lady's maid; auch: waiting-woman or =maid; **=fräulein** n lady of the bedchamber, maid of honour; **=gericht** n, etwa: superior court of justice; highest court of appeal; **=gerichtspräsident** m president of a superior court; **=gut** n crown-land, (royal) domain; **=herr** m chamberlain, Gentleman of the Bedchamber, lord-in-waiting; **=herrnschlüssel** m chamberlain's golden key; **=herrnwürde** f chamberlain's rank, chamberlainship; **=jäger** m vermin-destroyer, (Rattenfänger) rat-catcher; **=jungfer** f = =frau; **=junker** m Gentleman (or Groom) of the Bedchamber; **=kapelle** f a sovereign's (or prince's) private band; **=katze** f f, **=kätzchen** [ndl.] n = =zofe, co.: abigail; **=kollegium** n Chamber of Accounts; **=konzert** ♪ n chamber-concert; **=lakai** m prince's private attendant or footman.
Kämmerlein (⌣⌣⌣) n ☉ = Kämmerchen.
Kämmerling (⌣⌣⌣) m ☉d. chamberlain.
Kammer=mädchen (⌣⌣...) n ☉, bisw. a. **=magd** f chambermaid; **=musik** ♪ f: a) (ant. Opernmusik) chamber-music; b) = =kapelle; **=musikus** m musician belonging to a (prince's) private band; **=präsident** m, parl. Frankreich 2c.: President of the Chamber of Deputies, England: Speaker of the House of Commons; **=rat** m, etwa: councillor of the board of finance, England: permanent official of the Treasury; **=sänger** ♪ m singer at concerts; **=schlüssel** m key of a chamber or room; **=stenograph** m parliamentary reporter, shorthand writer (employed) in parliament; **=stück** ♪ n piece adapted for chamber-music; **=ton** ♪ m concert-pitch; **=tuch** ✿ n = Ka'mbrif; **=tür** f door of a chamber or room; **=unteroffizier** m non-commissioned officer in charge of a military depot; **=verhandlung** f parliamentary debate; **=wesen** n finance(s pl.) of a state or country; **=wissenschaft** f = Kamera'lwissenschaft; **=zofe** f chambermaid.
Kamm=fett (⌣...) n ☉ horse-oil; **=förmig** a. ⊕ in shape of a comb or a crest, ⚡ ctenoid; vgl. Zähnlich; **=futteral** n comb-case; **=garn** ⊕ n worsted (yarn); **=garn=spinner(ei** f) m worsted-spinner (-spinning); **=gras** ♀ n dog's-tail grass (Cynosu'rus crista'tus); **=grind** m, vet. mange in horse's mane; **=haar** n: a) (Mähne des Pferdes) horse's mane; b) (Haare, die beim Kämmen ausgehen) combings pl.; **=kieme** f, zo.: ⚡ ctenidium; **=kiemer** m/pl. zo.: ⚡ pectinibranch(ian)s, ⚡ ctenidiobranchia(ta) pl.; **=kiemig** a. zo.: ⚡ ctenidiobranchiate.
Kämmling ⊕ (⌣⌣) m ☉d. mst pl.: **=e** combings pl.; **=s=seide** (⌣⌣...) f ☉ (Florettseide) floss-silk.
Kamm=lippfisch (⌣...) m ☉ ichth. ctenolabrus, ...oid; **=los** a. ☉ combless, crestless; ⊕ carp., join. out of joint; **=macher** 2c. f. Kammacher; **=maschine** f. Kammaschine.
Kämm=maschine ⊕ (⌣...) f. Kämmaschine.
Kamm=molch (⌣...), **=muschel**, **=muskel** f. Kammolch, Kammuschel, Kammuskel.
Kammolch (⌣⌣) [Kamm=molch] m ☉c. zo. iguana (= Kammeidechse).
Kamm=rad ⊕ (⌣...) n ☉ mech. cogged (or cog=)wheel; **=ratte** f, zo. (Gundi) comb-rat; ⚡ ctenomys (Ctenoda'ctylus); **=reinigungs=bürste** f = =bürste; **=schneidemaschine** ⊕ f comb-cutting machine;

=schupper m, ichth.: ⚡ ctenoidean, ...ian; **=schuppig** a. ichth.: ⚡ ctenoid; **=setzer** ⊕ m Weberei: carder; **=spinne** f, ent. ctenophora; **=stein** m, min.: ⚡ pectolite; **=tragend** a. crested, ent.: ⚡ ctenophor.
Kammuschel (⌣⌣⌣) [Kamm=muschel] f ☉ zo. scallop (Pecten); **=artig**, **=förmig** a.: ⚡ pectinaceous, pectiniform; **~tier** n ☉: ⚡ pectinacean; **~versteinerung** f: ⚡ pectinite.
Kammuskel (⌣⌣⌣) [Kamm=muskel] m ☉ anat. des Herzens: ⚡ pectinate muscle.
Kamm=walze ⊕ (⌣...) f ☉ doffer, doffing-cylinder; **~n e-s Walzwerks** cogged wheels pl. of a rolling-mill; **=wolle** f worsted (wool), carded wool; **=wollen=garn** n worsted yarn; **=wollen=zeuge** n/pl. worsted fabrics or goods or articles pl.; **=woll=spinnerei** ⊕ f worsted-manufacture; **=zahn** m tooth of a comb; **=zähnig** a. ichth.: ⚡ ctenodont; **=zug** ⊕ m Spinnerei: sliver.
Kamöne (⌣⌣⌣) [lt. Că'mē'nă] f ☉ röm. myth. Muse.
Kamp (⌣) [lt.] m ☉b. bsd. nordd. (Einzäunung) enclosed field, enclosure.
Kampagne (käm-, t̑a-pä'n-j) [fr.] f ☉ **1.** ⚔ (Feldzug) campaign. — **2.** ⊕ ☉ (Betriebsdauer e-r Fabrikation 2c.) bsd. metall. (Hütten=, Ofen=reise) campaign, working-season; agr. season for the manufacture of beet(-root) sugar. — **3.** ⚓ = Kampanje. [war-horse, charger.]
Kampagne=pferd (⌣...) n ☉ (Schlachtroß)
Kampaner=blut (⌣⌣⌣) ...) n ☉ (römischer Wein) wine of Campania.
Kampani=en ♀ (⌣⌣(⌣)) [lt.] npr/n. ☉a. (Landschaft in Süd=italien) Campania.
Kampani=er (⌣⌣(⌣)) [lt.] m ☉, ~in f ☉, **kampanisch** (⌣⌣) a. ☉ Campanian.
Kampanje ⚓ (⌣⌣⌣) [ndl.] f ☉ (Schiffshinterteil) poop; **~deck** n ☉ poop-deck.
Kämpe (⌣⌣) [nhd.; f. Kampf] m ☉ (Vorkämpfer) champion of liberty, &c.; (Gegenbrecher) tilter, im Turnier a. jouster.
kämpeln (⌣⌣⌣), **sich** ⓠ v/refl. ⓐa. to quarrel, to brawl, to be at loggerheads with.
Kampesche=baum ♀ (⌣⌣⌣...) [Campeche (⌣⌣tʃe) ♀, mex. Staat] m ☉ logwood (Haemato'xylon Campechia'num); **=holz** n = Blauholz.
Kampf (⌣) [ahd.; *lt. Campus (Martius)] m ☉b. combat; (Gefecht) action, engagement, F brush (with the enemy); (feindlicher Zusammenstoß) encounter; (Ringen) wrestling, (Schlägerei) fight, fisticuffs pl.; (Kampfführung) contention, wiederstrebender Kräfte: conflict; (Bewerbung) contest; ⚔ den ~ beginnen, eröffnen to open hostilities; et. in ehrlichem ~e davontragen to carry (or conquer) a th. in open warfare; sich zum ~e rüsten to prepare for the fight; im Gewühl des ~es in the fray of the battle; ~ auf Leben und Tod fight to the death, desperate battle; ~ Mann gegen Mann hand-to-hand fight; ~ ums Dasein struggle for existence, battle of life.
Kampf=begier(de) (⌣...) f ☉ eagerness to fight; **=begierig** a. ☉ eager to fight or for battle, combative, pugnacious; **=bereit** ⚔ a. ready for battle,

---

⚡ scientific; ♀ botanical; ♀ geography; ⊕ machinery; ⚔ mining; ⚔ military; ⚓ marine; ☉ commercial; ✉ postal; 🚂 railway.

[Kampfbereitschaft] — 568 — [Kännchen]

↓ v. Schiffen: cleared for action; =bereitschaft ⚔ f readiness for battle, (state of) mobilization; in ~ in (good) fighting-trim; =brüderschaft f brother-hood (or companionship) in arms; =einheit f ↓, ⚔ fighting unit.
kämpfen (ᴗ–) [ahd.] ⊛ I v/n. (h.) 1. to fight, in e-r Schlacht: to (engage in) battle, in Scharmützeln: to skirmish, ringend: to struggle, to wrestle, sich balgend: to scuffle; geh. Spr.: to combat, to contend against great odds; mit den Fluten ⚔ to buffet (with) the waves; mit Nahrungssorgen ⚔ to fight for one's existence; mit dem Schicksal ⚔, oft: to have an uphill fight; sie hatten mit großen Schwierigkeiten zu ⚔ they had great difficulties to contend (or grapple) with or to overcome; vgl. Dummheit. — II v/a. 2. poet. einen Kampf ⚔ to fight a battle. — 3. mit Angabe der Wirkung, auch v/refl.: e-n zu Boden (od. nieder=)⚔ to lay a p. low, to floor a p.; sich müde ⚔ to tire o.s. with fighting. — III ~ n ⓶ 4. fight, battle, struggle; combat, contention.
Kampfer (ᴗ–) [mhd.,*ind.] m ⓶ (flüchtige aromatische Droge) camphor ($C_{10}H_{16}O$).
Kämpfer¹ (ᴗ–) [kämpfen] m ⓶ fighter, wrestler; ⚔ combatant, warrior; (Faust=)~ pugilist, prize-fighter; ~ für Frauenrechte champion (or advocate) of women's rights, feminist; ~ für das Frauenstimmrecht (woman-)suffragist; vgl. Kämpe.
Kämpfer² ⊕ (ᴗ–) [ahd.; *lt. (fr. chevron)] m ⓶ arch. (Strebepfeiler) (a)butment; (Widerlager) springing-stone.
kampfer=artig (ᴗ–...) a. ⊛: ᴣ camphor(ace)ous; =baum ⚕ m ⓶ camphor-tree (Cinnamo'mum ca'mphora); =essig m, pharm. camphorated vinegar; =geist m = =spiritus.
Kämpfer²=gesims ⊕ (ᴗ–...) n ⓶ arch. impost(-moulding). [phoric.
kampfer=haltig (ᴗ–...) a. ⊛: ᴣ cam-
Kämpfer²=linie ⊕ (ᴗ–...) f ⓶ arch. e-s Bogens: springing-line.
Kampfer=öl ⊕ (ᴗ–...) n ⓶ camphor-oil; =sauer a. ⊛ chm.: ᴣ camphoric; =saures Salz ᴣ camphorate; =säure f camphoric acid ($C_{10}H_{16}O_4$).
Kämpfer²=schicht ⊕ (ᴗ–...) f ⓶ arch. springing-course.
Kampfer=spiritus (ᴗ–...) m ⓶ pharm. camphorated spirits pl. (of wine).
Kampfes=luft ꝛc. (ᴗ–...) f ⓶ = Kampf=...
kampf=fähig (ᴗ–...) a. ⊛ able to fight, ⚔ effective; =fertig a. = =bereit;
=freudig, =froh a. rejoicing in battle, warlike; =gefährte ⚔ m ⓶ companion (or brother) in arms, fellow combatant; =gefilde n field of battle; =genoß m = =gefährte; =gerüstet a. armed for battle; =gespan m = =gefährte; =gewohnt a. accustomed to fight, trained in war; =gewühl n turmoil of battle; im ~ in the thick of the fight; =hahn m: a) fighting- (or game-)cock; b) fig. (Zänker) squabbler, quarrelsome fellow, (Raufbold) brawler; c) orn. (Art Strandläufer) ruff f reeve, combatant (Mache'tes pugnax); =handschuh m gauntlet, boxing-glove; =läufer m, orn. =

=hahn c; =lust f love of fighting or of combat, warlike ardour; =lustig, =mutig a. bellicose, courageous; vgl. =begierig; =platz m scene of action, battle-field, in Kampfspielen: (the) lists pl.; den ~ betreten to enter the lists, weitS. arena, ring; =preis m prize (of battle); =recht n: a) right to fight; b) laws pl. of combat; =richter m umpire; =roß n war-horse, charger; =schnepfe f = =hahn c; =spiel n combat, (Turnier) joust, tilting, (Boxerei) prize-fight; röm. Alt.: gladiatorial games pl.; ⚔unfähig a. disabled, ⚔ invalided, ⚔ machen to disable, ↓ ein Schiff: to put out of action, to cripple; =welle ⊕ f Mühlenbau: axle, carp. impost; =zeuge m second.
Kamphu (ᴗf–) [chin.] m ⓹⓪ (Tee) campoi.
kampieren (ᴗ–′) [fr.] v/n. (h.) ⓭ (lagern) to camp, to be encamped (bsd. ⚔).
Kamtschadale (ᴗᴗ–ᴗ) m ⓬, ...lin f⓭ Kamchadale; Kamtschatka (ᴗᴗ–ᴗ) npr/n. ⓹⓪ α. (russ. Halbinsel in Ostasien) Kamchatka.
Kana ⚥ (–ᴗ) npr/n. ⓹⓪ α. bibl. (Flecken in Galiläa) Cana.
Kana-an ⚥ (–ᴗ–) [hebr. Niederland] npr/n. ⓹⓪ α. (bibl.) (the land of) Canaan, a land of promise; ~iter(in f ⓮⓱) m ⓬, =itisch a. ⓺⓺ Canaanite.
Kanada ⚥ (–ᴗᴗ) [indian. Stadt] npr/n. ⓹⓪ α. (britische Kolonie in Nord-amerika) (Dominion of) Canada; Kanadi=er(in f ⓮⓱) m ⓬ (ᴗ–′(ᴗ)ᴗ), kanadisch (ᴗ–ᴗ) a. ⓺⓺ Canadian, Am. Canack.
Kanake (ᴗ–ᴗ) m ⓭ (Hawaier) Kanaka.
Kanal (ᴗ–′) [lt.] m ⓮ d. 1. natürlicher: channel, künstlicher: canal; (Abzugs=)~ drain, sewer, (Röhrenleitung) conduit, (Gosse) gutter; einen ~ anlegen to make (or build, dig, excavate) a canal; anat. u. ⚥ (Röhre) canal, duct, tube. — 2. ⚥ Britischer ~ (Ärmelmeer) British Channel, auch: the Channel.
Kanal-anlage ⊕ (ᴗ–′...) f ⓮⓱ Wasserbau: canal-making; =arbeiter m navvy, excavator; sewerman; =bau m canal-building, canalization; drainage; =boot ↓ n canal-boat, auch: canaller; =eisenbahn ⚔ f proposed submarine railway between Calais and Dover; =fracht ⚔ f (freight for) carriage by canal; =inseln ⚥ f/pl. Channel Islands.
Kanalisation ⊕ (ᴗᴗᴗ–ᴗ′) [lt.] f ⓮⓱ Wasserbau: canalization.
kanalisierbar ⊕ (ᴗᴗ–ᴗ–) a. ⓺⓺ drainable.
kanalisier=en ⊕ (ᴗᴗ–ᴗ′ᴗ) [Kanal] I v/a. ⓺⓺ to canalize, to drain. — II ~ ⊕ u. K/ung f ⓮⓱ canalization, drainage.
Kanal-netz (ᴗ–′...) n ⓮⓱ system of canals; =schiffahrt f canal-navigation, traffic by (or on) canals; =schleuse f canal-lock; =system n system of canalization or drainage, drain-(or sewer-)pipes pl.
Kanapee (ᴗᴗ–) [uhd.18.sae.; *fr. canapé m] n (m) ⓮⓱ couch, sofa, settee; vgl. Sofa.
Kanari=en=gras ⚥ (ᴗ–′ᴗ′ᴗ...) [s. kanarisch] n ⓮⓱ canary-grass (Pha'laris canarie'nsis); =(gras=)same m canary-seed; =holz n (v. Apollo'nia canarie'nsis) canary-wood; chm. =sekt m canary-(wine); =vogel m canary, canary-bird or -finch (Seri'nus cana'rius); =wein m = =sekt.

kanarisch (ᴗ–′ᴗ) [lt.] a. ⓺⓺ Canarian; ⚥ ~e Inseln Canary Islands pl.
Kanaster (ᴗ–′ᴗ) [span.] m ⓭ = Knaster¹.
Kandare (ᴗ–′ᴗ) [mag.] f ⓮⓱ man. (ant. Trense) curb, bridle-bit; englische ~ port-mouth(ed) bit; ⚔n v/a. ⓺⓺ to put the curb on; ~n=zügel m bridle-rein.
Kandelaber (ᴗᴗ–′ᴗ) [lt.] m ⓮⓱ (Kronleuchter) chandelier with two or more brackets.
Kandel=zucker (ᴗᴗ–...) m ⓮⓱ = Kandis.
Kandidat (ᴗᴗ–′) [lt.] m ⓮⓱ (Amtsbewerber) candidate (or applicant) for a post; für ein Predigeramt ꝛc.: probationer; bei Wahlen: aufgestellter ~ nominee; parl. als ~ auftreten to come forward (or put up) as a candidate, to contest a seat in parliament; ~en=liste f ⓮⓱ list of candidates; ~en=rede f: a) eines Theologen: probation-sermon; b) eines Abgeordneten ꝛc.: electioneering speech.
Kandidatur (ᴗᴗᴗ–′) [lt.] f ⓮⓱ candidature; kandidieren (ᴗᴗ–′ᴗ) v/n.(h.) ⓺⓺ to be (or to come forward as, put up as) a candidate for ..., pol. to contest a seat in Parliament.
kandieren (ᴗ–′ᴗ) [fr.; *Kandis] I v/a. und sich ⚥ v/refl. ⓺⓺ (überzuckern) to candy, kandiert candied (fruit). — II ~ ⓶ candying. [(⚥–ᴗ) m ⓶ sugar-candy.
Kandis ⊕ (–′ᴗ) [sft.] m, inv., ~=zucker
Kaneel ⚥ (ᴗ–′) [mhd., it., fr. canelle f (Zimt=)Röhrchen] m ⓶ d. cinnamon; ~=baum ⚥ m ⓶ white (or wild) cinnamon (-tree) (Cane'lla alba); ⚥=baum=artig a. ⓺⓺ F: ᴣ cancellaceous; ~=stein m, min. cinnamon-stone, ᴣ essonite.
Kanephora (ᴗ–′ᴗᴗ) [grch.] f ⓹⓪ arch. (korb-tragende Bildsäule): ᴣ canephorus.
Kanevas ⊕ (–′ᴗᴗwäß) [fr.] m, inv. ⑰ (Segeltuch, starke Leinwand, Stramin) canvas; kanevassen a. ⓺⓺(⓴) (of) canvas.
Känguruh (–ᴗ–) [austral.] n ⓶d. u. ⓹⓪ zo. kangaroo (Ma'cropus giganti'eus); kleineres ~ rock-kangaroo, wallaby (Petro'gale); ~=maus ⚥ n ⓶ ka.-mouse (Perogna'thus); ~=ratte f ka.-rat (Hypsipry'mnus).
Kanin ⚥ ⊕ (ᴗ–′) [ndl.; fr. †connin] ⓶d. Kürschnerei: (Kaninchenfell) rabbit-skin.
Kaninchen (ᴗ–′ᴗ) [dim. v. Kanin] n ⓶ zo. cony, mehr gbr.: rabbit; wildes ~ wild rabbit (Lepus cuni'culus); zahmes ~ tame rabbit (Lepus dome'sticus).
Kaninchen=bau (ᴗ–″...) m ⓶ rabbit-warren, cony-burrow; =behältnis n rabbit-hutch; =berg m = =bau; =fell n rabbit-skin; =frikassee n stewed rabbit; =gehege n rabbit-warren; vgl. =bau; =haare ⚔ n/pl. rabbit-flue.
kaninchenhaft (ᴗ–″ᴗ) a. ⓺⓺ like rabbits, bsd. fig. (fruchtbar) prolific.
Kaninchen=haus (ᴗ–″...) n ⓶ rabbit-house; =hecke f rabbit's nest; =jagd f rabbit-shooting; =wärter m rabbit-keeper, warrener.
Kanker¹ (ᴗ–′) [mhd.] m ⓶ ent. daddy-long-legs (= Weberknecht).
Kanker² (ᴗ–′) [lt. cancer] m ⓶ hort. (Krebs) etwa: spreading disease.
Kankro-id ᴣ (ᴗ–′) [grch.] m ⓮c. path. (Hautkrebs) cancroid.
kann (ᴗ–) 1. und 3. Person des pres. ind. von können.
Kännchen (ᴗ–) n ⓶ (dim. von Kanne) small can or jug, a. cannikin.

Kanne (ᴗ⌣) [ahd.: can] *f* ⑱ can, pot; (Krug) jug, als Trinkgefäß: tankard, als Maß: litre; ~ Bier pint (or pot) of beer; es gießt wie mit Kannen it's coming down in torrents, F it's pouring cats and dogs.

Kanne-gießer (ᴗ⌣ᴗ) *m* ㉒ **1.** ⊙ = Kannengießer. — **2.** F *fig.* (politischer) ~ pothouse politician, one who dabbles in politics, auch: stump-orator; (lit.) quidnunc; **~ei** (ᴗ⌣ᴗ⌣́) *f* ㊻ pothouse (or amateur) politics; a.: stump-oratory; **⚥n** *v/n.* (h.) ㉗a.*⁕* to rant (or drivel) about politics.

Kannel (ᴗ⌣) [: Kanal] *f* ㊽ (Rinne) gutter.

kannelier/en (ᴗᴗ⌣́) [fr.] **I** *v/a.* ⑱ to channel, flute, groove. — **II** ~ *n* ㉓ u. **K/ung** *f* ㊻ chanelling, fluting; (Hohlrinne) groove, chamfer.

Kannen-bürste (⌣ᴗ⌣...) *f* ⑱ bottle-brush; **-deckel** *m* lid of a can or a jug; **⚥för-mig** *a.* ⑯ in shape of a can or jug, pitcher-shaped, anat.: 🜛 arytenoid; **-gießer** ⊙ *m* pewterer; *fig.* = Kannegießer 2; **-kraut** ⚥ *n* shave-grass (Equise'tum arve'nse); **-strauch** ⚥ *m*: 🜛 nepenthes; **⚥weise** *adv.* by pots or pints; **⚥zinn** ⊙ *n* pewter.

Kannibale (ᴗᴗ⌣́ᴗ) [span. *Kar(a)ibe] *m* ㊹ **1.** (Bewohner der Kari'bischen Inseln) Carib(bean). — **2.** (Menschenfresser) cannibal, *pl.* auch: 🜛 anthropophagi. — **3.** *fig.* (wilder grausamer Mensch) ferocious (or savage) fellow. ⎰balismus.⎱

Kannibalentum (ᴗᴗ⌣́ᴗ-) *n* ⓪d. = Kanni

kannibalisch (ᴗᴗ⌣́ᴗ) *a.* ⑯ like a cannibal, man-eating, 🜛 anthropophagous, *fig.* cruel, ferocious, savage; F als *adv.* (in hohem Grade, sehr) extremely, F awfully, deucedly; **⚥ voll** F beastly (or dead, helplessly, blind) drunk.

Kannibalismus (ᴗᴗᴗ⌣́) *m* ㉒ cannibalism, 🜛 anthropophagy, ...ism.

kannst(ˢ) 2. Person *sg. pres. ind.* v. **können**.

kannte(st) (ᴗ⌣) *impf. ind.* von **kennen**.

Kanon (⌣́ᴗ) [grch.] **I** *m* ㊾ (*pl.* a. Ka'nones) **1.** (Maßstab, Richtschnur; Verzeichnis klassischer Schriften, eccl. Verzeichnis biblischer Bücher, sowie der Heiligen; Vorschrift, Gebetsformel; ♪ fortlaufende Fuge) canon. — **2.** *jur.* (Erb=ob. Grund=zins) ground-rent. — **II** *f* ㊿ **3.** ⊙ *typ.* (Schriftgattung): grobe ~ double paragon; kleine ~ two-line great primer; englische ~ = Missal.

Kanonade ⚔ (ᴗ-ᴗ⌣́ᴗ) [it.] *f* ㊽ cannonade, artillery-fire, roar of guns.

Kanone (ᴗ⌣́ᴗ) [it. großes Rohr] *f* ㊽ **1.** ⚔ *artill.* cannon (*pl.* a. cannon), piece of ordnance, (great or big) gun; gezogene ~ rifled gun; ~ mit Hinterladung, mit Vorderladung breech-loading, muzzle-loading gun; s. bedienen 2; mit ~ beschießen to cannonade; eine ~ vernageln to spike a cannon, F unter der ~ below contempt, execrable. — **2.** ⊙ ~ eines Uhrschlüssels cannon. — **3.** ~*n* *pl.* [ursprünglich Stiefel der Kano'niter] top-boots *pl.*

Kanonen-boot ⚓ (ᴗ⌣́ᴗ...) *n* ㉒ gunboat; **-donner** *m* roar(ing) (or booming) of cannon; **⚥fest** *a.* ⓐ cannon-proof; **-fieber** *n* (Angst vor Feuer u. Pulver) dread of powder and shot, bisw.: bullet-fever; **-futter** [*vgl.* food for powder (SH. H. IV. I, IV₂)] *n*, *fig.* von Soldaten: gut genug als ~ good enough to stop a bullet; **=gießer(ei** *f*) *m* gun-founder (-foundry); **=gut** *n* (Kupfer u. Zinn gemischt) gun-metal; **-kugel** *f* cannon-ball, round shot; **-ofen** *m* cylindrical iron stove; **-pulver** *n* cannon-powder; **-schlag** *m* Feuerwerferei: explosive (or booming) charge; **-schuß** *m* c.-shot; **-schußweite** *f* range of big guns, (within) reach of the guns; **⚥sicher** *a.* cannon-proof; **=stiefel** *m/pl.* = Kanone 3; **-visier** *n* cannon-sight, sight of a gun; **⚥voll** F *a.* burschikos: (as) drunk as a fiddler or a lord, gloriously drunk; **-wischer** *m* gunner's sponge or swab.

Kanonier ⚔ (ᴗᴗ⌣́) [fr.] *m* ⓐd. *artill.* ehm. cannoneer, bombardier, jetzt: gunner, artilleryman; **~boot** ⚓ *n* ㉒ gunboat; **~dienst** *m* gunner's duties *pl.* or work or employment, artillery-service.

kanonieren ⚔ (ᴗᴗ⌣́ᴗ) [fr.] **I** *v/a.* u. *v/n.* (h.) ⑬ to cannonade, to fire (with) cannon; den ganzen Tag ⚥, auch: to blaze (or boom) away all day. — **II** ~ *n* ㉓ cannonade; boom(ing) of guns.

Kanonier-kammer ⚓ *f* gun-room.

Kanonikat (ᴗᴗᴗ⌣́) [it.] *n* ⓐc. *eccl.* (Dompfründe) canonry, canonship; **Kanonikus** (ᴗ⌣́ᴗᴗ) *m* ㉓, **Kanonikus** [nach dem Kanon Lebender] *m* ⑤ (Domherr) canon, prebendary; **kanonisch** (ᴗ⌣́ᴗ) *a.* ⑯ (kirchlich gültig) canonical; ƺes Recht canon-law, canonical law.

kanonisier/en (ᴗᴗᴗ⌣́ᴗ) [it.; * Kanon 1] **I** *v/a.* ⑬ *eccl.* (heiligsprechen) to canonize. — **II** ~ *n* ㉓ u. **K/ung** *f* ㊻, **Kanonisation** (ᴗᴗᴗ-tsi⌣́ᴗ) *f* ㊻ canonization.

Kanonissin (ᴗᴗ⌣́ᴗ) [it.] *f* ㊺ canoness.

Kanonist ⚔ (ᴗᴗ⌣́) [grch.] *m* ㉒ (Kirchenrechtslehrer) canonist.

Kanonizität (ᴗᴗᴗᴗ⌣́) [it.] *f* ㊻ (kirchliche Gültigkeit, Vorschriftsmäßigkeit) canonicity.

Kantabri-en (ᴗ⌣́ᴗᴗ) *npr/n.* ㉗a. (ehm. span. Landschaft, jetzt Bista'ya) Cantabria; **kantabrisch** (ᴗ⌣́ᴗ) *a.* ⑯ Cantabrian.

Kantate¹ (ᴗ⌣́ᴗ) [it.] *f* ㊽ (feierliches Singstück mit Instrumentalbegleitung) cantata.

Kantate² (ᴗ⌣́ᴗ) [lt. singet] *n* ⑯ *eccl.* chant commencing with "Cantate"; engs. the 98th psalm; (Sonntag) ~ *m* fourth Sunday after Easter.

Kant-beitel ⊙ (⌣́...) *m* ㉒ cant-chisel, wheeler's chisel.

Kante (⌣́ᴗ) [ndd.: cant; *grch.] *f* ⑱ **1.** (Durchschnittslinie je zweier an-ea.-stoßender Flächen) edge, (Ecke) corner; (Rand) border, margin, e-s Abgrundes: brink, e-s Gefäßes: brim; (Leiste) (narrow) ledge, strip; ~ des Trottoirs kerbstone; ⊙ (Seite des Holzes ⁊c.) face; abgestoßene ~ broken-off edge or corner; abgestumpfte ~ truncated edge, *carp.* chamfer; stumpfe ~ rounded edge; vorspringende ~ ledge; auf die (hohe) ~ stellen to put up edgeways, to tilt up; F *fig.* Geld auf die hohe ~ legen to put money by, to save money; an allen Ecken und ~n (a. Enden) in every corner, on all sides. — **2.** ⊙ (Leiste des Tuches) selvedge(-list), fag-end. — **3.** ⊙ geklöppelte ~*n pl.* (Spitzen) lace, point(-lace); gewebte ~*n* woven lace *sg.* — **4.** *hort.* (schmales Beet) narrow side-bed.

Kantel (⌣́ᴗ) [Kante] *n* (*m*) ㉒ (vierkantiges Linea'l) square rule(r); **⚥n** *v/a.* ㉗a. to rule paper; s. **kanten¹** 3.

kanten¹ (⌣́ᴗ) [Kante] *v/a.* ⑱ **1.** (kantig m.) Steine ⁊c.: to square. — **2.** (mit e-m Rande versehen) to edge, to border. — **3.** ⊙. auch **kanteln** *v/a.* ㉗a. (auf die Kante stellen) to set (up) on edge, to put up edgeways.

Kanten² (⌣́ᴗ) [ndd.] *m* ㉓ des Brotes: top and bottom crust of a (German) loaf.

Kanten-abnahme (⌣́ᴗ...) *f* ⑫ *min.* narrowing of the edges; **=kleid** *n* dress trimmed with lace; **=schiene** 🜛 *f* edged rail; **=tuch** *n* lace-trimmed neckerchief, handkerchief edged with lace; **=winkel** *m* angle formed by two planes; **=zwirn** *m* fine thread or cotton.

Kanter¹ (⌣́ᴗ) [fr., * lt.] *m* ㉒ = Ganter.

Kanter² ♞ (kä́ntər) *m* ㉒ (Handgalopp) canter.

Kant-haken ⚓ (⌣́ᴗ...) *m* (⊙...) ⑯ cant-hook, grappling-iron; F *fig.* e-n beim ~ fassen to collar (or seize) a p.

Kantharide 🜛 (ᴗᴗ⌣́ᴗ) [grch.] *f* ⑱ ent., *mit med.* (spanische Fliege) Spanish fly, blister-fly or -beetle, cantharis (Lytta oder Ca'ntharis vesicato'ria); **~n-pflaster** (⌣́...) *n* ⑱ *med.* blister; ~ **n-tinktu'r** *f* tincture of cantharides.

Kant-holz ⊙ (⌣́...) *n* ㉒: a) ⊙ squared (or dressed) timber; b) = Kantel.

Kantianer (ᴗᴗ⌣́ᴗ) [Kant, dtsch. Philosoph 1724–1804] *m* ㉒ *phls.* disciple of Kant, Kantian, Kantist.

kantig (⌣́ᴗ) [Kante] *a.* ⑯ edged, with (sharp) edges, angular; ⊙ ⚥ (*adv.*) behauen *p.p.* squared.

Kantilene ♪ (ᴗᴗ⌣́ᴗ) [it.] *f* ㊽ cantilena.

Kantille (ᴗ⌣́ᴗ|-j-) [fr. *cannetille*] *f* ㊽ (spiralförmig gewundener Gold- und Silberdraht) purl; ⚔ = Raupen.

Kantine (ᴗ⌣́ᴗ) [it.] *f* ㊽ (Schenke in Kasernen, Fabriken ⁊c.) canteen, (soldiers') bar; **~n-wirt** *m* canteen-keeper, (*fr.*) *cantinier*.

kantisch (⌣́ᴗ) *a.* ⑯ *phls.* of Kant, Kantian.

Kanton (ᴗ⌣́, fr. tą') [fr., it., *flt.] *m* ⓐd. (*fr.* ⑳) (Gau, bsd. Einzelstaat der Schweiz) canton.

kantonal (ᴗᴗ⌣́) [Kanton] *a.* ⑯ cantonal.

kantonier/en ⚔ (ᴗᴗ⌣́ᴗ) [fr.] **I** *v/a.* ⑬ to canton. — **II** ~ *n* ㉓ u. **K/ung** *f* ㊻ cantonment.

Kantonist ⚔ (ᴗᴗ⌣́) [fr.] *m* ㉒ man who is called to the colours; F *fig.* das ist ein unsicherer ~ (Mensch) he is unreliable, he's not to be trusted.

Kantonnement ⚔ (ᴗᴗ⌣́(⌣)mą') [fr.] *n* ㊿ (Orts-unterkunft) cantonment; ~s beziehen (lassen) to canton.

Kanton-regierung (ᴗ⌣́..., *tą*́...) *f* ⑫ cantonal government; **=wesen** *n* cantonal (or local) affairs *pl.*

Kantor (⌣́ᴗ) [lt.] *m* ㉑ (Vorsänger) precentor, leader of a choir; (Dorfschrer) parish schoolmaster; **~at** (ᴗᴗ⌣́) *n* ⓐc., **~ei** *f* ㊻ precentorship; precentor's (or schoolmaster's) house.

Kant-ring ⊙ (⌣́...) *m* ⑫ *carp.* cant-hoop.

Kantschu (⌣́-) [slaw., *türk.] *m* ⓐd. ㊿ kind of knot, cat-o'-nine-tails.

Kanu ⚓ (⌣́-) [engl., *karib.] *f* ㊿ canoe.

Kanüle (ᴗ⌣́ᴗ) [fr.] *f* ㊽ *surg.* (Wundröhrchen) can(n)ula, tubule.

[Kanzel] — 570 — [kapitulieren]

Kanzel (ᷟ)[ahd.: chancel; * lt. *cance'lli* Gitter]/⊕ pulpit; von der ~ herab from the pu.; die ~ besteigen to mount the pu. **Kanzel=beredsamkeit** (ᷟ...) f ⊕ pulpit-eloquence or oratory; **=brüstung** f pu.-rail; **=dach** n, **=deckel** m sound-board; **=kissen** n cushion on the pulpit.
Kanzelle ☉ (ᴗᴗ) [lt.] f ⊕ arch. screen; (Gitter vor dem Chor) choir-screen.
Kanzel=lied (ᷟ...) n ⊕ hymn before (or after) the sermon; **⚥mäßig** a. ⊕ suitable for the pulpit.
kanzeln (ᷟ) [lt.] v/n. (h.) u. v/a. ⚥a. 1. to speak like a preacher. — 2. fig. c-n ⚥ (abkanzeln) to sermonize a p.
Kanzel=pult (ᷟ...) n ⊕ pulpit-desk; **=rede** f sermon (f. Predigt); **=redner** m pulpit-orator; **=stil** m pu.-style; **=ton** m preaching-tone; er spricht immer im ~ F he is for ever sermonizing; **=vortrag** m address from the pulpit.
Kanzlei (ᴗ́) [mlt.] f/⊕ chancellery, chancery, weitS. government-office; a. *coll.* staff of a ministerial department.
Kanzlei=amt (ᴗᵘ...) n ⊕ chancery-office; **=beamte(r)**, **=bote** m, **=diener** m official, messenger of a chancery, a. tipstaff; **=gericht(shof** m) m court of ch.; Mündel des gerichts ward in chancery; **=herrschaft**/bureaucracy; **⚥mäßig** a. ⊕ after the manner of a ch., weitS. in lawyer fashion; **=papier** n foolscap (paper); **=rat** m, *etwa:* councillor of a chancery; **=schreiber** m clerk (or copyist) employed in a chancery; **=schrift** f engrossing (or civil-service) hand; **=sprache** f, **=stil** m legal (or official) language or style; **=vorsteher** m head clerk (or chief official) of a chancery.
Kanzler (ᷟ) [mlt.] m ⊕, **~in** f ⊕ chancellor's wife f); **~amt** n ⊕: a) chancellor's office, chancellorship; b) = Kanzlei = amt; **~stelle**, **~würde** f chancellor's position or dignity.
Kanzlist (ᴗ́) [Kanzlei] m ⊕ clerk of a chancery(-court), chancery-clerk.
Kanzone ♪ (ᴗᴗ́) [it.] f ⊕ canzone; **Kanzonette** (ᴗᴗ́ᴗ) f ⊕ (Liedchen) ditty.
Kaolin ᾱ (-ᴗ́) [chin. *Kao-ling* ♀ „hohes Gebirge"] n ⊕d. min. (Porzellan-erde) kaolin, porcelain-earth.
kaolinisier/en (-ᴗᴗ́ᴗ) [Kaoli'n] I v/a. ⊕ (in Kaolin verwandeln) to kaolinize. — II ~ n **K/ung** f ⊕ kaolinization.
Kaolin=porzella'n ☉ u. ⊕ (-ᴗᵘ...) n ⊕ kaolinic porcelain.
Kap (ᵃ) [nhd. 17. sae.; * lt. *caput*] n ⊕d. ⊕ 1. (Vorgebirge) cape, promontory; (Landzunge) tongue of land, headland, a. naze, head, foreland, &c.; ♀ = der guten Hoffnung (an der Südspitze von Afrika) Cape of Good Hope. — 2. = **Kap.** abbr. = Kapitel. [Kapkolonie.f
kapabel (ᴗᴗ́) [lt.] a. ⊕ (fähig) capable.
Kapaun (ᴗ́) [mhd.,*grch.] m ⊕d. capon; **⚥en** (ᴗ́ᴗ) v/a. ⊕ (verschneiden) to capon, to castrate; **⚥enhaft** a. ⊕ capon-like.
Kapazität (ᴗᴗᴗ́) [lt.] f ⊕ 1. (Fähigkeit) capacity; a. *elect., physiol.* ~ für Magnetismus, Wärme ꝛc. capacity for magnetism, heat, &c.; (Geräumigkeit) capaciousness. — 2. fig. (begabter Mensch, Fachgröße) man of great ability, eminent specialist.

Kapell= ♪ (ᴗᷟ...) in Zssgn = Kape'llen=...
Kapellan ↘ öft. = Kaplan.
Kapellchen (ᴗᴗ́ᴗ) n ⊕ 1. *eccl.* (dim. von Kape'lle 1) small chapel. — 2. ♪ (dim. von Kape'lle 2) small band.
Kapelle[1] (ᴗ́ᴗ) [ahd.; *fr.] f ⊕ 1. *eccl.* chapel; königliche ~ chapel royal. — 2. [it.] ♪ (Musikbande) musical band.
Kapelle[2] ♀ (ᴗ́ᴗ) [++ aus fr. *coupelle*] f ⊕ *chm., metall.* (Treibscherben) cupel, test.
Kapellen=ofen (ᴗ́ᴗ...) [Kapelle[2]] m ⊕ *chm., metall.* cupelling-furnace; **=probe** f cupel-assay, cupellation-test; **=zange** f cupel-tongs pl.
kapellieren (ᴗᴗ́ᴗ) [Kapelle[2]] I v/a. ⊕ *chm., metall.* (abtreiben) to cupel, to refine. — II ~ n ⊕ cupellation.
Kapell=meister ♪ (ᴗ́ᷟ...) m ⊕ band-master, conductor of a band or an orchestra.
Kaper[1] ↓ (ᴗ́ᴗ) [ndl.] m ⊕ 1. (Freibeuter) freebooter, privateer; corsair, pirate. — 2. = Kaperschiff.
Kaper[2] ♀ (ᴗ́ᴗ) [uhd., lt., *grch.] f ⊕ (unentfaltete Blüte des Kapernstrauches) caper.
Kaper[1]**=brief** ↓ (ᴗ́ᵘ...) m ⊕ (Erlaubnis zur Freibeuterei) letters pl. of marque.
Kaperei (-ᴗᴗ́) [Kaper[1]] f ⊕ privateering; auf ~ ausgehen, ausgehen to go privateering, to practise piracy.
Kaper[1]**=gasten** ↓ (ᴗ́ᵘ...) m/pl. ⊕ crew of a privateer or pirate.
kapern (ᴗ́ᴗ) [Kaper[1]] ⊕a. I v/n. (h.) to carry on piracy. — II v/a. (als Beute nehmen) to capture, to carry off; gekapertes Schiff prize; fig. e-n, et. ⚥ to collar (or seize) a p., a th. — III ~ n ⊕ (f. I) piracy, privateering (vgl. Kaperei); (f. II) capture.
Kaperna-um ♀ (-ᴗ́ᴗ ob. -ᴗᴗ́) npr/n. ⊕α. (Stadt in Palästina) Capernaum.
Kapern=brühe (ᴗ́ᵘ...) [Kaper[2]] f ⊕ **=sauce**; **=gewächse** ♀ n/pl. ⊕ capparidaceæ pl.; **=sauce** ♀ Kochkunst: caper-sauce; **=strauch** ♀ m caper-bush (Ca'pparis spino'sa).
Kaper[1]**=schiff** ↓ (ᴗ́ᵘ...) n ⊕ privateer, pirate (ship), corsair; **=zug** m privateering (expedition).
Kapetinger (ᴗᴗᴗ́ᴗ) [Hugo Kapet, †996] m/pl. ⊕ (fr. Königshaus) Capet(ian) dynasty.
Käpfer (ᷟ) [lt.] m ⊕ arch. = Kämpfer[2].
Kap=holländer (ᵃ...) m ⊕ (native) Dutchman in Cape Colony.
kapieren F (ᴗᴗ́) [lt., it.] v/a. ⊕ (begreifen) to understand, to grasp, F to take in.
kapillar (ᴗᴗᴗ́) [lt.] a. ⊕ (Haar-...) capillary.
Kapillar=attraktio'n ᾱ (ᴗᴗᵘ...) f ⊕ *phys.* capillary attraction; **=elektrometer** n (m), *elect.* capillary electrometer.
Kapillaren ᾱ (ᴗᴗᴗ́ᴗ) [lt.] f/pl. ⊕ *anat. zo.* (Haargefäße) capillaries pl.
Kapillar=gefäß ᾱ (ᴗᴗᵘ...) n ⊕ *anat.* capillary vessel.
Kapillarität ᾱ (ᴗᴗᴗᴗ́) [lt.] f ⊕ *phys.* capillarity, capillary attraction.
kapisch (ᴗ́ᴗ) [Kap] a. ⊕ of the Cape.
Kapital (ᴗᴗ́) [lt.] I n ⊕d. ⊕ 1. ♀ (pl. mst Kapita'lien ᵉ⁹): a) allg. (Geldsumme) capital; b) (ant. Zinsen) principal; eisernes, festgelegtes ~ invested capital, money sunk; flüssiges (ob. verfügbares) ~ available funds pl., money in hand; fig. ~ aus et. schlagen to make capital out of a th., to benefit

by a th. — 2. ⊕ Buchb.: headband. — II 2.*a.* ⊕ 3.(hauptsächlich) chief, principal; F (vorzüglich) capital, excellent; ein 2er Hirsch a capital (or first-rate, very fine) stag; vgl. Kapitalhirsch.
Kapital (ᴗᴗ́) n ⊕d. u. ⊕ = Kapitell.
Kapital=anlage (ᴗᴗ́ᴗ...) ♀ f ⊕ investment (of capital or money); **=besitz** m: a) capitalism; b) cash property; **=buchstabe** m, *typ.* capital (letter).
Kapitälchen ⊕ (ᴗᴗ́ᴗ) n ⊕ (dim. von Kapita'l) 1. ♀ small capital. — 2. ☉: a) = Kapita'l 2; b) *typ.* small capital (letter).
Kapital=hirsch (ᴗᴗ́ᵘ...) m ⊕ royal stag.
kapitalisierbar ♀ (ᴗᴗᴗ́ᴗ) [Kapita'l 1] *a.* ⊕ realizable, weit S. available.
kapitalisier/en ♀ (ᴗᴗᴗ́ᴗ) [Kapita'l 1] I v/a. ⊕: a) (mit Kapital versehen) to capitalize, to finance; b) (in Geld umwandeln) to convert into capital, to turn into money, to realize (in the market). — II ~ n ⊕ u. K/ung f ⊕ capitalization, realization.
Kapitalismus ♀ (ᴗᴗᴗ́ᴗ) m ⊕ (neult.) ⊕ (Macht, Herrschaft des Kapitals) capitalism.
Kapitalist ♀ (ᴗᴗᴗ́) [fr.] m ⊕, **~in** f ⊕ capitalist, financier, F moneyed man.
Kapital=junge (ᴗᴗ́ᴗ...) m ⊕ capital (or F brick of a) boy; **=konto** ♀ n capital account; **⚥kräftig** ♀ *a.* ⊕ well provided with capital.
Kapitals=... (ᴗᴗᵘ...) ♀ = f. Kapita'l=...
Kapital=verbrechen (ᴗᴗᵘ...) n ⊕ (schweres Verbrechen) capital crime; **=vermögen** n funded property, entire capital.
Kapitän (ᴗᴗ́) [fr. „Haupt"mann] m ⊕d. ↓ captain; auf Flußschiffen ꝛc. auch: skipper, auf Handelsschiffen: master(-mariner); ⚔ Kriegsflotte: ~ zur See captain R. N. (= of the Royal Navy); **~leutnant** (ᵘ...) m ⊕ senior lieutenant.
Kapitel (ᴗᴗ́) [mlt. *capi'tulum*] n ⊕ 1. Abschnitt e-s Buches: chapter; das fünfte ~ the fifth chapter, ch. the fifth; fig. e-m ein (ob. das) ~ lesen (e-n Verweis geben) to reprimand (or F lecture) a p. — 2. = Domkapitel.
Kapitel=beschluß (ᴗᴗ́ᷟ...) m ⊕ resolution of the (canons in) chapter; **=einteilung** f division into (or of the) chapters; **⚥fest** *a.* ⊕ well-read in the scriptures; vgl. bibelfest; weit S. in et. ⚥ sein F to be well up in a th.
Kapitell (ᴗᴗ́) [lt. *capite'llum*] n ⊕d. *arch.* (Säulenknauf) capital; korinthisches (ionisches)~ Corinthian (Ionic) capital.
kapiteln (ᴗᴗ́) v/a. ⊕a. 1. to divide into chapters. — 2. fig. e-n ⚥ (schelten) to scold (or F lecture, sermonize) a p.
Kapitol (ᴗᴗ́) [lt.] n ⊕d. Alt.: (Hügel Roms mit Zupitertempel) Capitol; **kapitolinisch** (ᴗᴗᴗ́ᴗ) *a.* ⊕ Capitoline.
Kapitulant (ᴗᴗᴗ́) m ⊕ (weiterdienender Soldat) soldier who re-enlists or serves beyond his time, re-enlisted soldier.   [member of a chapter.]
Kapitular (ᴗᴗᴗ́) [Kapitel 2] m ⊕ (⊕d.)f.
Kapitulation ⚔ (ᴗᴗᴗᴗ́) [lt.] f ⊕ 1. (übergabe e-r Festung ꝛc.) capitulation. — 2. (Weiterdienen) re-enlistment.
kapitulieren ⚔ (ᴗᴗᴗ́ᴗ) [lt.] I v/n. (h.) ⊕ 1. v. Belagerten: to capitulate, surrender. — 2. v. Soldaten: to re-enlist in the army. — II ~ n ⊕. 3. = Kapitulation.

Signs (see page XVII): F familiar; P vulgar; ⸂ flash; ↘ rare; † obsolete (died); * new word (born); ++ incorrect; ♪ music;

[Kapkolonie] — 571 — [Karbonat]

Kap=kolonie ♀ (ˊ...) f ⊕ Südafrika: Cape Colony, a. the Cape.
Kaplan (‿ˊ) [mhd., mlt.; *Kapelle] m ⊙d. [P] =Kapau'n. [rot=⚹ with a red hood.) chaplain; **~ei** (‿ˊ‿) f ⓕ (Pfründe und Wohnung eines Kaplans) chaplaincy.
Kap=land ♀ (ˊ‿) n ⊙a. = Kapkolonie.
Kaponni-ere ⚔ (‿‿ˊ‿) [fr.] f ⓕ frt. (bedeckter Gang) caponier(e).
kapores F (‿ˊ‿) [hebr. Sühnopfer] a. ⓕ: ⚹ geh(e)n = kaput't gehen.
Kapotte (‿ˊ‿) [fr.] f ⓕ (Regenmantel mit Kapuze) hooded cloak, auch: capote.
Käppchen (ˊ‿) n ㉓ (dim. von Kappe) small cap, für Herren: smoking-cap, bsd. ehm. auch: skullcap; für Priester: calotte; (kleine Kapuze) small hood.
Kappe (ˊ‿) [ahd. *cap, cope; *mlt. cappa Mantel] f ⓕ **1.** (Mütze) cap (a. = Haube), mit Schirm: cap with a peak; vgl. Bare'tt; (Kapuze) hood, der Mönche a. cowl; (Mantel mit Kapuze) hooded cloak or mantle. — **2.** fig. e-m eine (ob. et. auf die) ~ geben to give a p. a box on the ear or a slap in the face; et. auf seine ~ (seine Schultern) nehmen to take a th. on one's (own) shoulders, to make o.s. responsible for a th.; Sprichw. gleiche Brüder, gleiche ~n birds of a feather flock together; vgl. Bruder 4; jedem Narren gefällt seine ~ every fool likes his own bauble (or hobby) best. — **3.** ♀ (kegelförmiges Hütchen an den Moosen): ⚤ calyptra. — **4.** ⊕ (et. kappen-artig Deckendes) casing; top piece or part; oft: calotte (vgl. Haube); Glasfabr.: vault, bsd. arch. böhmische ~ coved vault; (Mauer=) coping; (Gewölbe=) vaulted cell, sectroid; e-s Schornsteins: chimney top; Wasserbau: ~ eines Dammes top of a dike; ~ des Pfeilerhauptes capping of the cut-water; Schneiderei: patch, piece for strengthening weak parts of a garment; Schuhmacherei: (Lederbesatz an der Fußspitze) toe-piece, tip; Strickerei: ~ an den Fersen der Strümpfe heel-piece. — **5.** ⚓ Kajüts=⚹, Luken=⚹ companion hood, hood over the hatchway of the cabin. — **6.** ⚔ (auf 2 Türstöcken aufliegendes Querholz) cap, lid; ~ e-s Türgerüstes lintel, cap-sill.
kappen[1] (ˊ‿) [Kappe] v/a. ⓑ **1.** (mit e-r Kappe versehen) to cap; Strümpfe ⚹ to heel stockings; Stiefel ⚹ to tip boots. — **2.** F fig. e-n ⚹ (abfahren lassen) to snub a p.; er hat ihn gehörig gekappt he gave him a sharp rebuff.
kappen[2] (ˊ‿) [ndd., ndl.: chop] v/a. ⓑ (die Spitze, den Wipfel abschneiden) die Krone e-s Baumes, einen Baum ⚹ to lop (or poll, top) a tree; ⚓ den Mast ⚹. ⚹ to cut ~
kappen[3] (ˊ‿) [Kapaun] v/a. ⓑ Hähne ~ (verschneiden) to capon (or F to doctor)...
Kappen=fläche ⊕ (ˊ‿...) f ⓕ surface of a sectroid; =**förmig** a. ⓕ bsd. cowled, hooded, ⚤ cucullate(d), cuculliform; =**gebiß** ⊕ n scatch; =**gewölbe** n, arch. Welsh vault; =**macher(in** f) m cap-maker; =**mantel** m hooded cloak; =**mundstück** n =gebiß; =**robbe** f, zo. hooded seal (Phoca crista'ta); =**zeug** ⊕ n Weberei: (strong) cloth for caps.
Kappes ♀ (ˊ‿) [ahd.; *lt. caput] m, inv. (Kopfstoß) common white cabbage.

Kapp=fenster (ˊ...) n ⓑ arch. small dormer- (or attic-)window; =**hahn** m [P] =Kapau'n. [rot=⚹ with a red hood.)
Kapp=laken ⚓ (ˊ...)[ndl.] n ⓑ primage, captain's percentage of the freight; =**loch** n =fenster; =**naht** f flat seam; =**rock** m child's hooded dress.
Kapp=zaum (ˊ‿) [P; *it. cavezzone] m ⓕ man. cave(s)son; fig. check, curb.
Kapriccio ♪ (kä-pri't-scho) [it.] n ⓑ ob. ⓕ (leichte phantastische Tondichtung) capriccio.
Kaprice (‿ˊ‿) [fr.] f ⓕ (Laune) caprice, (passing) humour, freak, whim, fancy.
Kapriole (‿‿ˊ‿) [it.; *lt. capra Ziege] f ⓕ Reitkunst ꝛc.: (Bocksprung) capriole, mehr gbr.: caper; ~n m. to caper; fig. (toller Streich) mad trick; ~n=**macher** m ⓕ caperer; trickster.
kapriolieren (‿‿‿ˊ‿) [it.] v/n. (h.) ⓑ to cut capers, to caper (about).
kapriz(ion)ieren (‿‿ˊ‿, ‿‿(‿)ˊ‿)[fr.]; sich ⚹ v/refl. ⓑ: sich auf et. ⚹ to fancy a th., to take a th. into one's head.
kapriziös (‿‿(‿)ˊ) [fr.] a. ⓕ (D 10) (launisch) capricious, whimsical.
Kapsel (ˊ‿) [lt.] f ⓕ **1.** anat. u. ♀ capsule; ♀ ~ der Moose urn, ⚤ pyxis, theca. — **2.** case, casing (a. zum Schutz e-r Uhr ꝛc.); Zündhütchen: percussion-cap, Töpferei: (Brenn=)~ saggar, sagger; metall. (guß-eiserne Schale) chill; chm. (Abdampfschale) evaporator.
kapsel=artig (ˊ‿...) a. ⓕ, =**förmig** a. like a capsule, ⚤ capsular, capsuliform; =**frucht** ♀ f ⓕ: ⚤ capsular fruit, capsule.
...**kapselig** (...ˊ‿‿) a. ⓕ in Zssgn mit Zahlen: ⚤ ..capsular, ꝛc. zwei=⚹ bicapsular.
Kapsel=stoß ⊕ (ˊ‿...) m Töpferei: bung; =**ton** ⊕ m saggar-clay; ⚹=**tragend** ♀ a. ⓕ: ⚤ capsuliferous; =**uhr** f watch in a case.
Kap=stadt ♀ (ˊ‿) f ⓕ Süd-afr. Cape Town.
kaptivier/en (‿‿‿ˊ) [lt.] **I** v/a. ⓑ (für sich einnehmen) to captivate. — **II** ~n ㉓ u. K/ung f ⓕ captivation.
kaputt (‿ˊ) [fr. capot] a. ⓕ (mst präbitativ) (zugrunde gerichtet) ruined, F u. P smashed, up a tree; ⚹ geh(e)n: a) von Sachen: to get broken, (verderben) to spoil; b) v. Tieren: to perish, to die; ⚹ machen to ruin, F to smash (up).
Kapuze (‿ˊ‿) [it.] f ⓕ hood, d. Mönche: cowl; (Mäntelchen) cape; vgl. Kappe 1.
Kapuzinade (‿‿ˊ‿) [fr.] f ⓕ capuchin's sermon, F long lecture, sermonizing.
Kapuziner (‿‿ˊ‿) [it. 1525; *Kapuze] m ⓕ **1.** ~, ~**in** f ⓕ eccl. capuchin (monk or friar, f nun). — **2.** orn. Süd-amerika. capuchin (Gymnoce'phalus calvus).
Kapuziner=affe (‿‿ˊ‿...) m ⓕ capuchin (-monkey); ⚤ capucine (Cebus capuci'nus).
kapuzinerhaft (‿‿‿ˊ‿) a. ⓕ like a capuchin, weits. monkish, monastic.
Kapuziner=kloster (‿‿ˊ‿...) n ⓕ capuchin convent; =**kresse** ♀ f Indian cress, ⚤ nasturtium (Tropae'olum maius); =**kutte** f capuchin's cowl or hood; =**mönch** m, =**nonne** f = Kapuziner 1; =**orden** m capuchin order; =**predigt** f = Kapuzina'de; =**vogel** m = Kapuziner 2.
kapverdisch ♀ (‿ˊ‿) [port. Cabo Verde: „Grünes Vorgebirge"] a. ⓕ: ~e Inseln in West=afrika: Cape Verd(e) Islands pl.

Kap=wein ⓒ (ˊ‿) m ⓕ (südafrik. Wein) Cape wine, wine from the Cape.
Kar öft. (ˊ) n ⓒc. (Kessel, Gebirgsschlucht) gorge, ravine, hollow.
Karabiner (‿‿ˊ‿) [fr. *Kalabrier] m ⓕ: a) ⚔ (Stutzbüchse) carbine; b) ⊕ ~ an der Uhr — ~=**haken**.
Karabiner=futteral (‿‿ˊ‿...) n ⓕ carbine-thimble; =**haken** ⊕ m Uhrmacherei: spring-hook; =**riemen** m carbine-strap.
Karabinier ⚔ (‿‿‿ˊ) [fr.] m ⓕ carbineer, soldier armed with a carbine.
Karaffe (‿ˊ‿) [fr., *pers.] f ⓕ (Flasche für Wasser: water-bottle, für Wein ꝛc.: decanter; ~**n=schildchen** n ⓕ decanter-label; =**n=untersatz** m ⓕ decanter-stand.
Karaffine (‿‿ˊ‿) [Karaffe] f ⓕ (kleine Karaffe) small decanter.
Kara-ibe (‿‿ˊ‿) = Karibe.
Karakal (ˊ‿‿)[türk. ⚤] m ⓕ (Wüstenluchs) ⚤ caracal (Lynx caraca'l).
Karambolage (‿‿‿ˊ‿) [fr.] f ⓕ Billard. (Anstoßen zweier Bälle durch den Spielball) cannon; **Karambole** (‿‿ˊ‿) f ⓕ (roter Ball) red ball; **karambolieren** (‿‿‿ˊ‿) v/n. (h.) ⓑ to (make a) cannon, F fig. mit e-m ⚹ (zs.=stoßen) to run (or dash) against (or into) a p.
Karamel (‿‿ˊ) [fr.] m ⓑ, ~**le** (‿‿ˊ‿) f ⓕ (gebrannter Zucker) caramel.
Karat ⊕ (‿ˊ) [mhd., fr., ar., *grch.] n ⓒc. carat; =**gewicht** (‿ˊ...) n ⓕ (Gold- und Silber-gewicht) troy weight.
karatieren (‿‿ˊ‿) [Kara't] v/a. ⓑ: das Gold ⚹ to alloy gold with other metals.
...**karätig** ⊕ (...ˊ‿‿) [Karat'] a. ⓕ in Zssgn: achtzehn=⚹es Gold eighteen carat gold (gold containing eighteen parts of pure gold and six of alloy); vier=und=zwanzig=⚹es Gold pure (or fine) gold.
Karatschi ♀ (‿ˊ‿) npr/n. ⊙a. (Hafenstadt in Ost=indien) Kurrachee.
Karausche ♀ (‿ˊ‿) [mhd., *poln., *grch.] f ⓕ ichth. crucian (Cara'ssius vulga'ris).
Karavelle ⚓ (‿‿ˊ‿) [span.] f ⓕ (leichtes Segelschiff) caravel; light sailing-ship.
Karawane (‿‿ˊ‿) [it., *pers.] f ⓕ (Handelszug im Orient) caravan.
Karawanen=führer (‿‿ˊ‿...) m ⓕ leader of a caravan; =**handel** ⓒ m caravan-trade; =**herberge** f = Karawanserei; =**straße** f caravan-route or -road; =**tee** ⓒ m caravan-tea.
Karawanserei (‿‿‿‿ˊ), (öst. r-r ..**rai** ...‿) [Karawa'ne und Serail] f ⓕ caravanserai, oriental inn.
Karbatsche (‿ˊ‿) [slaw., *türk.] f ⓕ koorbash, leatherscourge, (Reitpeitsche) horsewhip; ⚹n v/a. ⓑ to scourge, horsewhip.
Karbe ♀ (ˊ‿) [mhd., *ar.] f ⓕ (Kümmel) common caraway (Carum carvi); ~**n=distel** (ˊ‿‿‿) ♀ = Kardobenediktenkraut.
Karbol (‿ˊ) [neu=lt.] n ⓒd. P = ~=säure; ⚹**sauer** a. ⓕ chm. carbolic; ~**es Salz** carbolate; ~**säure** f ⓕ (des=infizierende Flüssigkeit) carbolic (or phen[yl]ic) acid, ⚤ phenol (C_6H_5OH); mit ~f. getränkt ⚤ carbolated, carbolized; ~**seife** ⓒ f carbolic soap; ~**watte** f, surg. carbolized cotton-wool.
Karbonade (‿‿ˊ‿) [fr., it.] f ⓕ Kocht.: (Rippchen) mutton, pork chop, veal cutlet.
Karbonat ⚤ (‿‿ˊ) [lt.] n ⓒc. chm. (kohlensaures Salz) carbonate; vgl. Bi⚹.

⚤ scientific; ♀ botanical; ♀ geography; ⊕ machinery; ⚔ mining; ⚔ military; ⚓ marine; ⓒ commercial; ✉ postal; 🚂 railway.

[**Karbonisation**] — 572 — [**Karragheenmoos**]

Karbonisation ⚗ (‿‿‿-tz(‿)ˊ) [lt.] f ㊻ (Verflüchung) carbonization; **karbonisieren** (‿‿‿ˊ‿) [lt.] v/a. ⑬ (verkohlen) to carbonize, to turn into coal.

Karbunkel (‿‿‿) [lt.] m ㉒ 1. path. carbuncle, ⚗ anthrax, (Blutgeschwür) furuncle. — 2. min. = Karfunkel.

Karburation ⚗ (‿‿‿-(‿)ˊ) [lt.] f ㊻ chm. (Mischen des Leuchtgases mit Benzin) carbonization; **karburieren** (‿‿ˊ‿) v/a. ⑬ (mit Kohlenwasserstoff verbinden) to carburize, to carbonize. [mann) carter.]

Kärcher (ˊ‿‿)[† Karch m ⓓb.] m ㉒ (Fuhr-

Kardamom (‿‿ˊ) m u. n ⓓd. (grch.) cardamom (Same von *Amoˊmum cardamoˊmum, Elettaˊria* und anderen Amoˊmen).

kardanisch (‿ˊ‿) [*Cardano*, it. Mathematiker, 1501—1576] a. ㊿ ℒe Formel (zur Lösung kubischer Gleichungen) Cardan's rule.

Kardätsche (‿ˊ‿) f ㊻ 1. ① (Wollkratze) card. — 2. (Striegel) curry-comb, horse-brush. — 3. ⚔ ✚ = Kartäˊtsche.

kardätschen (‿ˊ‿) v/a. ⑬ 1. ④ Spinnerei: to card, to tease. — 2. Pferde ⚘ (striegeln) to curry, to brush. — 3. ⚔ ✚ = kartäˊtschen.

Kardätschen-draht ④ (‿ˊ‿...) m ㊺ wire for (making) cards; **‿macher** m cardmaker; **‿tisch** m ④ Spinnerei: carding- (or combing-)table.

Kardätscher ④ (‿ˊ‿‿) m ㉒, **‿in** f ㊽ Spinnerei: carder (of wool), teaseler.

Karde (ˊ‿) [ahd., *lt.*] f ㊸ a.: ♀ teasel (*Dipsacus*); b) ♀ Tuchfabr.: (Fruchtknopf der Kardendistel) teasel, thistle-head.

karden ④ (ˊ‿) v/a. ㊾ = kardätschen 1.

Karden-ausstecher ④ (ˊ‿‿...) m ㊺ preen; **‿distel** ♀ f = Karde a; **‿gewächse** ♀ n/pl.: ⚗ dipsaceæ; **‿kreuzholz** ④ n cardingframe; **‿rahmen** ④ m teasel-frame; **‿saal** ④ m card-room.

kardieren ④ (‿ˊ‿) v/a. ⑬ Spinnerei: (kardätschen) to card.

Kardinal (‿‿ˊ) [lt. *cardo* Angel] m ⓓd. 1. *Cath. eccl.* Würde: cardinal. — 2. *orn.* cardinal (-bird) (*Cardinaˊlis virginiaˊnus*). — 3. (Getränk aus Wein, Zucker und Pomeraˊnzen) cardinal.

Kardinal-bischof (‿‿ˊ‿...) m ㊺ *Cath. eccl.* cardinal bishop; **‿punkt** m (Hauptpunkt) cardinal or chief point.

Kardinals-hut (‿‿ˊ‿...) m ㊺ cardinal's (red or scarlet) hat; **‿kollegium** n college of cardinals, sacred college; **‿rock** m cardinal's gown; **‿würde** f cardinal's rank or dignity, cardinalate, cardinalship.

Kardinal-tugend (‿‿ˊ‿...) f ㊶ *rel.* cardinal virtue; **‿zahl** f (zB. 5; 100) cardinal number. [turve) cardioid.]

Kardio-ide ⚗ (‿‿‿ˊ) f ㊻ *math.* (Herz-

Kardobenedikten-kraut ♀ (‿‿‿‿‿ˊ...) [lt. *Carˊduus benedicˊtus*] n ㊺ pharm., auch: holy thistle (*Cnicus benedicˊtus* ob. *Centaureˊa benedicˊta*).

Kardone ♀ (‿ˊ‿) f ㊸, **‿n-artischocke** f ㊸ (Golddistel) cardoon (*Cyˊnara carduˊnculus*).

Karenz-jahr (‿ˊ...) [lt. *carens* entbehrend] n ㊺, **‿zeit** f year, time during which the emoluments of a living (or an office) are stopped or held back.

Karer ♀ (ˊ‿) m ㉒, **‿in** f ㊼ Carian.

karessieren (‿‿‿ˊ‿) [fr.] v/a. ⑬ (liebkosen) to caress, hug, fondle, F to cuddle.

Karette (‿ˊ‿) [fr.] f ㊸, **Karett-schildkröte** (‿ˊ‿ˊ‿‿) f ㊸ zo. hawk's-bill, hawk-billed turtle (*Cheloˊne imbricaˊta*).

Karfiol ♀ obb. (‿ˊ) [nhd.; *it. cavolo fiore* Blumenkohl] m ⓓd. cauliflower.

Kar-freitag (ˊ‿‿ˊ) [ahd.: *care* : karg] m ㉒ Good Friday.

Karfunkel (‿ˊ‿) [mhd. (P: funkeln) *Karbunkel*] m ㉒ *min., path.* carbuncle.

karfunkeln (‿ˊ‿‿) v/n. (h.) ㉒a. to shine (or sparkle) like a carbuncle. [nose.]

Karfunkel-nase (‿ˊ‿...) f ㊸ brandy-

karg (ˊ) [mhd.: *chary*] a. ㊿ (D 5) 1. (ant. freigebig) (sparsam) economical, parsimonious; (tnickerig) mean, niggardly, stingy, close-fisted, spare; 2 mit Worten sparing of one's words. — 2. Gabe: (ärmlich) scanty, stärker: poor, paltry.

Kargadeur ♪ (‿‿‿ˊr) [fr.] m ㉒, **Kargador** (‿‿ˊ) [span.] m ⑬ ⓓ. (Aufseher über die Ladung von Handelsschiffen) supercargo, cargador.

kargen (ˊ‿) v/n. (h.) ⑱ (f. karg) to be very economical or parsimonious or mean or spare.

Kargheit (ˊ-) f ㊻ (ant. Freigebigkeit) economy, parsimony, meanness.

kärglich (ˊ‿) [karg] a. ㊿ sparing(ly meted out), (dürftig) scanty, (armselig) piteous, paltry; ℒe Mittel slender (or limited) means *pl.*; *adv.* die Natur hat ihn 2 bedacht nature has not lavished her gifts upon him; **Kärglichkeit** f ㊻ scantiness.

Kargo ♪ (ˊ-) [span. *Last*] m (n) ⑤ (Ladung) cargo; goods pl. carried on board.

Karibe (‿ˊ‿) m ㉕, **Karibin** f ㊼ Carib, Caribbean; **karibisch** a. ㊿ Caribbean; ♀ Karibische Inseln (Kleine Antillen) Caribbean (or Caribbee) Islands pl.

Kari-en ♀ (ˊ(‿)‿) npr/n. ㉓a. Alt. (Landschaft in Klein-asien): Caria.

karieren ④ [fr. *carrer* quadrieren] I v/a. ⑬ (mit Würfelzeichnung mustern) to chequer. — II **kariert** (‿ˊ) p.p. u. a. ㊿ (mit Kaˊros gemustert, gewürfelt) checked, chequered; ℒe Artikel, Stoffe, auch: checks *pl.* (Knochenfraß) caries.

Kari-es ⚗ (ˊ(‿)‿) [lt. *cäˊries*] f, inv. *path.*

Karikatur (‿‿‿ˊ) [it.] f ㊻ (Zerrbild) caricature, politische Auch: cartoon; **‿en-maler, ‿zeichner** m caricaturist.

karifieren (‿‿ˊ‿) [it. *caricare* überladen] v/n. ⑬ ℒ, karifiert zeichnen to caricature, to make a caricature of.

kariös ⚗ (‿ˊ‿) [lt.] a. ㊿ *kariöse* (angefaulte) Zähne carious (or decayed) teeth.

karisch (ˊ‿) a. ㊿ 1. [Karien] Carian. — 2. ℒes Meer, Nutzland: Sea of Kara.

Karkasse ⚔ (‿ˊ‿) [fr.] f ㊸ artill. (Brandgranate) carcass.

Karl (ˊ) [= Kerl] npr/m. ㊿ ㉔a. (a. Vn.) Charles; ~ der Dicke, der Einfältige, der Kühne Charles the Fat, the Simple, the Bold (vgl. kahl 2); ~ I. (König von England, 1625—49) Charles I; ~ V. (Kaiser von Deutschland, 1519—56) Charles V; ~ der Große (768—814) Charlemagne.

Karlchen (ˊ‿) npr/n. ㉓a. (dim. v. Karl) Charley, Charlie.

Karlismus (‿ˊ‿) [Kronbewerber Karl in Spanien, 19. Jahrh.] m ㊲ Carlism; **Karlist** (‿ˊ) m ㉒, **karlistisch** a. ㊿ Carlist.

Karlmann (ˊ‿) npr/m. ㊿ ㉔a. Carloman.

Karls-distel ♀ (ˊ‿...) f ㉖ (Eberwurz) carline thistle, stemless carline (*Carliˊna acauˊlis*).

Karmel ♀ (ˊ‿) [hebr. Baumgarten] npr/m. ㊿a. *bibl.* Berg ~ Mount Carmel.

Karmeliter (‿‿ˊ‿) m ㉒, **‿in** f ㊼ *Cath. eccl.* Carmelite (friar or monk, f nun), auch: white friar; **‿kloster** (ˊ‿...) m ㊺ Carmelite convent; **‿mönch** m, **‿nonne** f (Karmeliter[in]) Carmelite friar, nun.

karmesin (‿‿ˊ) [it., span.; *Kermes*] a. ㊿, **~ n** ⓓd. crimson; **‿farbe** f, **‿farbig, ‿rot** a. ㊿ crimson; **‿schildlaus** f, ent. kermes (*Coccus iˊlicis*); **‿zeug** ⚛ n crimson cloth or material.

Karmin (‿ˊ) [zsgz. aus karmesin] m ⓓd. (das ‿rot) carmine (auch *chm.* roter Färbstoff); **‿farben, ‿rot** a. ㊿ carmine, crimson-hued; **‿lak** ✪ m cochineal lake; **‿rot**: a) a. f. ‿farben; b) n = Karmin; **‿säure** f, *chm.*: ⚗ carminic acid ($C_{17}H_{17}O_9HO$); **‿spat** m, min.: ⚗ carmine spar, carminite. [farmeſiˊn.]

Karmoisin (‿ma͂ˊ) [fr. *cramoisi*] a. ㊿ =

Karneol ⚗ (‿‿ˊ) [it.] m ⓓd. *min.* Halbedelstein: carnelian, red chalcedony.

Karneval (ˊ‿‿‿) [nhd.; *it.*] m (n) ⓓd. ㊿ (Carnival) carnival; **~like** ~. = Fastnacht...

Karnickel F (‿ˊ‿‿) n (P m) ㉒ = Kaninchen, der ~ (niemand) hat angefangen F Mr. Nobody (or the cat) has done it.

Karnies ⚗ (‿ˊ) [fr. *corniche* f] n ⓓa. *arch. u. join.* cornice, cyma; **‿steigendes ~** reversed ogee; **‿bogen** m ㊺ reversed ogee-arch; **‿gesims** n cornice-architrave; **‿hobel** m, *carp.* cornice- (or ogee-)plane; **‿stahl** m ogee-tool, chisel for turning cymas.

karnisch ♀ (ˊ‿) [Karner, flt. Volk] a. ㊿: ‿e Alpen zw. Tirol u. Italien: Carnic Alps pl.

Kärnten ♀ (ˊ‿) [ft. *karnisch*] npr/n. öft. Kronland: Carinthia; **Kärntner**(in f ㊼) m ㉒, **kärnt(ner)isch** a. ㊿ Carinthian.

Karo (ˊ‿) [fr. *carreau*] n ⑪: a) (Viereck eines Zeugmusters) check; b) Kartenspiel: diamond(s pl.); **‿könig** (ˊ‿...) m ㊺ king of diamonds.

Karoline (‿‿ˊ‿) npr/f. ㊾ ㊿z.: a) (Vn.) Caroline; b) ♀ die **‿n**(-inseln) im Großen Ozean: the Caroline Islands pl.

Karolinger (‿‿ˊ‿) [mlt.] m ㉒ *hist.* (Nachfolger Karls des Großen in Deutschland, 814—911), **karolingisch** a. ㊿ Carolingian, Carlovingian. [Caroline.]

karolinisch (‿‿ˊ‿) [mlt.; *Karl*] a. ㊿ =

Karosse (‿ˊ‿) [fr., *it.*] f ㊸ elegant carriage, fine coach, state-coach.

Karosserie ④ (‿‿‿ˊ) [fr.] f ㊸ am Automobil: upholstery of a motor-car.

Karotte ♀ (‿ˊ‿) [fr.] f ㊸: a) *hort.* (Mohrrübe) carrot; b) (Tabaksrolle) carrot.

Karpat(h)en ♀ (‿ˊ‿) npr/f/pl. inv. auch: **‿gebirge** ♀ (zwischen Ungarn u. Galizien) Carpathians, Carpathian Mountains pl.; **karpat(h)isch** a. ㊿ Carpathian.

Karpenter-bremse ⚙ (‿ˊ‿...)[Carpenter, Erfinder] f ㊸ Carpenter brake.

Karpfen (ˊ‿) [ahd.] m ㉒ *ichth.* carp (*Cypriˊnus caˊrpio*); **‿ähnlich** (ˊ‿...) a. ㊿, **‿artig** a.: ⚗ cypriniform, cyprinoid; **‿brut** f ㊸ fry of carp; **‿fischerei** f carp-fishing; **‿teich** m carp-pond (f. Hecht 1).

Karragheen-moos ♀ (‿ˊ‿‿) n ㊺ [Carrageen ♀, ir. Ort] n ㊺ (a. *pharm.*:

[**karrarisch**] Brusttee) carrag(h)een moss, Irish moss (*Chondrus crispus*).
karrarisch (⌣⌣⌢) [Carrara ♀, it. St.] a. ⑥: Der Marmor Carrara marble.
Kärrchen (⌣⌣) n ㉓ (*dim. v.* Karren) small cart or barrow; für Kinder: (child's) little go-cart, mail-cart.
Karre (⌣⌣) [ahd., mlt., *flt.] f ㊽ cart; (Hand-)~ wheelbarrow; eine ~ schieben to drive (or push) a (wheel)barrow.
Karree (⌣⌢) [fr.] n ㉛ (Viereck) square; im Tanz: set (vgl. Quadrille); ein ~ sprengen to break through (F to rush) a square; ~**formierung** ⚔ f ㊷ square formation, forming (a) square.
Karren (⌣⌣) [f. Karre] m ㊷ 1. (Schub-)~ wheelbarrow; ein ~ voll, a. a barrowful; vgl. Karre; einen ~ schieben to push a wheelbarrow. — 2. (zweirädriges Fuhrwerk) cart; starker niedriger ~ dray (-cart); (Höker-)~ coster's barrow or truck; (Schutt-)~ tumbrel (a. ehm. Verbrecher-~); ein ~ voll a cart- (or truck-)load; vgl. 1; mit einem Karren fortschaffen to cart away. — 3. *fig.* der ~ hat sich festgefahren we (they, &c.) are stuck in the mud, things have come to a standstill; den ~ in den Kot (oder Dreck) schieben to muddle up (or entangle) matters, F to make a mess of it all; mit einem an e-m ~ ziehen to work hand in hand with a p., to row in the same boat with a p.
karren (⌣⌣) [Karre] v/a. u. v/n. (h.) ㊽ 1. Erde ꝛc. ⚒ to remove … on a wheelbarrow or a truck or a cart; *abs.* to wheel (or push) a barrow. — 2. F (langsam fahren) to drive slowly. — 3. mit Angabe der Wirkung: e-n über den Haufen ⚒ to run (or knock) a p. down with a wheelbarrow or a cart; v/refl. sich müde ⚒ to tire o.s. with wheeling (or pushing) a barrow.
Karren-fahrer (⌣⌣…) m ㊷ = Kärrner; =**feld** n = Karst²; =**führer** = Kärrner; =**gabel** ⊚ f shaft (or thill) of a cart; =**gaul** m cart- (or dray-)horse, jade; *fig.* ein guter ~ (beschränkter, aber fleißiger Arbeiter) a plodding, hard-working fellow; =**gefangene(r)** m convict (working with the wheelbarrow); =**geleise** n cart-rut; =**gestell** n, =**kasten** m ⊚ body of the cart; =**ladung** f cart-load; barrowful; =**rad** n cart-wheel; =**schieber** m one who pushes a wheelbarrow or a truck, barrowman; =**seil** n cart-rope; =**spur** f rut of a cart, cart-rut; =**strafe** f criminal's wheelbarrow labour, weitS. penal servitude; =**tuch** n cart-tilt; =**weg** m (narrow) cart-road.
Karrete F (⌣⌢) [span.: *Karre*] f ㊽ rough (or clumsy) cart; wretched conveyance.
Karri-ere (⌣(⌣)⌣) [fr.; *Karre*] f ㊽ 1. (Laufbahn) career, eine gute ~ m. to have a good career, to work one's way up. — 2. *man.* (in) ~ reiten to ride (or go) at full gallop.
karriert 3ft. (⌣⌢) a. ⑥ = kariert.
Karriol F (⌣(⌣)⌢) [fr., it.; *Karre*] n ㊱, ~e f ㊽ (Jagdwagen) gig, dog-cart; =en v/n. (h. u. sn) ㊾ to drive along (at a quick pace), to race along; ~**post** f ㊷ (light) mail-coach (for letters).

Kärrner (⌣⌣) [Karren] m ㉒ carter, carman, drayman; ⊛ (Fuhrmann, der Waren befördert) carrier.
Karrosse = Karosse.
Kar-samstag (⌢⌣…) m ㉒ Saturday before Easter.
Karst¹ ⊚ (⌢) [ahd.] m ⓵(⑦)a. *agr.* mattock; (zweizinkige Hacke) prong-hoe.
Karst² (⌢) [it. *Carso*] m ⓵a. bare and rocky Alpine tract or region.
karsten ⊚ (⌢⌣) [Karst¹] v/a. ㊾ *agr.* to (work with the) mattock, to hoe.
kart. *abbr. v.* kartoniert (f. kartonieren).
Kartätsche (⌣⌢⌣) [nhd., *flt. (*Karte)] f ㊽ 1. ⚔ canister-shot, grape-shot; ehm. (Büchsen-)~ case-shot; mit ~n zusammenschießen to shoot down (or ply) with canister- (or grape-)shot. — 2. ✳ = Kardätsche.
kartätschen (⌣⌢⌣) v/a. u. v/n. (h.) ㊼ 1. to shoot (or fire) with canister- (or case-,grape-)shot. — 2. ✳ = kardätschen.
Kartätschen-feuer ⚔ (⌣⌢…) n ㉚ grape-shot fire; =**kasten** m case for grape-shot; =**kugel** f bullet for canister- (or grape-)shot; =**schuß** m (discharge of) canister-shot.
Kartätsch-grana'te ⚔ (⌣⌢⌣…) f ㊽ shrapnel(-shell); =**rakete** f case-rocket.
Kartaune ⚔ (⌣⌢⌣) [nhd. 17. *sae.*; *it.] f ㊽ ehm. *artill.* cannon-royal.
Kartause (⌣⌢⌣) [nhd.; *mlt.* = Chartreuse] f ㊽ *eccl.* Carthusian convent or monastery, ehm. a. charterhouse.
Kartäuser (⌣⌢⌣) [~] m ㉒, ~**in** f ㊵ Carthusian (monk, / nun); ~**kloster** n ㉚ = Kartause; ~**likör** m chartreuse (liqueur); ~**mönch** m Carthusian friar, (fr.) chartreux; ~**nelke** ♀ f (Karthäuser, *bsch.* Naturforscher, 18. *sae.*] Carthusian pink (*Dianthus carthusiano'rum*).
Karte (⌣⌣) [fr., it.] f ㊽, *dim.* Kärtchen (⌣⌣) n 1. (Spiel-)~ card; ein Spiel ~n a pack of cards; (die) ~ abheben to cut (the cards); abgehob(e)ne ~ turn-up card; eine hohe (niedrige) ~ ausspielen to play a high (low) card; gute, schlechte ~n bekommen (haben) to get (to have) good, bad cards or a good, bad hand; (die) ~n geben to deal the cards, to (have the) deal; wer gibt (die) ~n? whose deal is it?; e-m die ~n legen to tell a p.'s fortunes from cards; die ~n mischen to shuffle (F to make) the cards; e-m in die ~n sehen to look at a p.'s cards, *fig.* to discover a p.'s plans, to spy out a p.'s secrets; ~n spielen to play cards; die ~n vergeben to misdeal; *fig.* eine abgeredete ~ (Sache) a preconcerted plant, F a put-up job; die ~n durchschauen (etwas klar durchblicken) to see clearly through a th.; alles auf eine ~ setzen to stake all (in one venture), to have all one's eggs in one basket. — 2. (Land-)~ (geographical) map; (See-, Stern-ꝛc.)~ chart. — 3. (Billett, Fahr-)~ ticket; (Eintritts-)~ card of admission. — 4. auf Bällen: (Verzeichnis der Tänze) programme of the dances; a. card. — 5. = Speise-~, Visiten-~. — 6. (Verfassungs-urkunde) charter.
Kartell (⌣⌢) [fr., it.; *Karte] n (m) ⓪d.(㊶): a) (Herausforderung zum Duell) challenge; ~ tragen to bear (or deliver) a challenge; b) (Übereinkunft zwischen verschiedenen Parteien, Studentenverbindungen ꝛc.) agreement, convention, *auch:* cartel; vgl. ~**vertrag**.
Kartell-bruder (⌣⌢…) m ㉒ bei der Studentenschaft member of one of the confederate "Corps" or associations; =**schiff** ⚓ n (Parlamentärschiff) cartelship; =**träger** m Studentenmensur ꝛc.: second who acts as intermediate between the two principals or duellists; =**verband** m federation of students' associations; =**vertrag** ⚔ m wegen Auswechslung von Kriegsgefangenen cartel.
Karten-auswerfer ⊚ (⌣⌣…) m ⊛ *typ.* an Tiegeldruckpressen: card-dropper; =**bild** n picture on a card; =**blatt** n (single) card; =**brief** ⊛ m letter-card; =**fabrik(ation)** f manufactory (manufacturing or making) of cards; =**fabrikant** m =**macher**; =**geben** n dealing of cards; =**geber(in)** f) m dealer; =**geld** n card-money; =**gesellschaft** f card-party; =**haus** n house of cards, *fig.* castle in the air, fragile affair; =**königin** f queen (at cards); =**künstler** m one who knows card-tricks, conjurer, juggler; =**kunststück** n card-trick; =**macher** m: a) card-manufacturer; b) designer of maps, map-maker, ⚓ cartographer; =**maler** m card-painter; =**mischen** n shuffling of cards, =**netz** n outline-(or skeleton-)map; =**papier** n thin cardboard; =**pappe** f cardboard; =**presse** f card-press; =**sammlung** f collection of maps or charts, als Buch: atlas; =**schlag** m: a) card-player's trick; b) fortune-telling; =**schläger(in)** s. fortune-teller; =**schlägerei** f fortune-telling; =**spiel** n card-playing, game of cards; =**spieler** m card-player; =**stamm** m (Geld, um das gespielt wird) pool; =**stecher** ⊚ m engraver of maps and charts; =**stempel** m stamp (or duty) on cards, card-stamp; =**werk** n atlas; =**zeichnen** n: ⚓ cartography; =**zeichner** m: ⚓ cartographer.
kartesianisch, kartesisch ⚓ (⌣-(⌣)⌢⌣, ⌣⌢⌣) [It. *Cartesius*, *fr. René Descartes*, Philosoph u. Mathematiker 1596 bis 1650] a. ⑥ Cartesian; Der Teufel ob. Taucher Cartesian devil or diver, *auch:* bottle-imp.
Karthag(inien)er(in f ⓸) m (⌣⌢(⌣), ---(⌣)⌢⌣), **karthag(inien)isch** a. ⑥ röm. Alt.: Carthaginian, Punic.
Karthago ♀ (⌣⌢⌣) [phön. *Neustadt*] *npr/n.* ⓷a. römisches Alt.: (phönizische Stadt in Nord-afrika) Carthage.
kartieren (⌣⌢⌣) [Karte] v/a. ㊾ to trace (out), to enter (or mark) on a map.
Kartoffel (⌣⌢⌣) [nhd. 17/8. *sae.*, *corr.* aus *it. tartu'folo (bianco)* m (weiße) Trüffel] f ㊽ 1. potato; (geschälte und) gesottene ~n boiled potatoes pl.; ~n in der Schale potatoes in the(ir) skins or with their jackets on; ~n pflanzen, ausmachen to sow, to lift potatoes; ~n schälen to peel potatoes. — 2. ♀ potato-plant (*Sola'num tubero'sum*). — 3. F *fig.* (dicke Uhr) big and clumsy watch, F turnip, ehm.: Nuremberg egg.
Kartoffel-aushebepflug ⊚ (⌣⌢…) m ⊛ potato-digger; =**bau** m, *agr.* cultivation

♪ Musik; ⚛ Wissenschaft; ♀ Pflanze; ⊕ Geographie; ⊚ Technik; ⚒ Bergbau; ⚔ Militär; ⚓ Marine; ⊛ Handel; ⧈ Post; 🚂 Eisenbahn.

[Kartoffelbranntwein] — 574 — [Kassendiebstahl]

(or growing, planting) of potatoes; =branntwein m potato spirit(s pl.); =brei m Kocht. mashed potatoes pl.; =ernte f pot.-crop; =feld n pot.-field; =käfer m, ent. Colorado beetle (Chrysome'la decemlinea'ta); =kloß m pot.-dumpling; =krankheit f pot.-disease or -rot or -blight; =krankheits-pilz ♀ m potato-fungus; =mehl n pot.-flour; =mus n = =brei; =pflug ⊕ m (Schollenbrecher) tormentor; =puffer, =salat m, =suppe f Kocht. potato-pancake, -salad, -soup; =stärke ♀ f potato-starch.

Kartograph ⊙ (‿‿⸝) [grch.] m ㊷: (Kartenzeichner) cartographer; =ie (‿‿⸝⸝) f ㊸ cartography; ℒisch (‿‿⸝⸝) a. ㊻ cartographic, cartographical.

Karton ⊙ (‿⸝⸝) [fr.; *Karte] m ⑪e ㊶: a) (Pappe) cardboard, pasteboard; b) (Pappschachtel) card-board box, hand-box; c) (große Mappe) portfolio; d) (Entwurf e-s Gemäldes) cartoon.

Kartonage ⊙ (‿‿⸝G‿) [fr.] f ㊸, ~=arbeit (ℤ...) f ㊷ pasteboard work.

kartonieren (‿‿⸝‿) v/a. ㊹ Buchbinderei: (steif broschieren) to put in boards; kartoniert (bound) in boards.

Kartonierer ⊙ (‿‿⸝‿) m ㊷, ~=in f ㊺ pasteboard worker.

Karton=papier ♀ (‿ta"...) n ㊷ fine card-board; =schere ⊕ (f strong) scissors pl. for (cutting) cardboard. [bag.)

Kartusch=beutel ⚔ (‿‿⸝...) m ㊷ cartridge-

Kartusche ⊙ (‿‿‿) [fr., it.] f ㊸ 1. a) (Patrone) cartridge; b) (Patronentasche) cartridge-box, bism. cartouch(e). — 2. arch., paint. (Zierrahmen, verzierte Einfassung) ⚓ cartouch(e).

Kartusch=nadel ⚔ (‿‿⸝...) f ㊷ vent-pricker; =papier n cartridge-paper; =trage ↓ f cartridge-box or -case.

Karu ♀ (‿⸝) f ㊺ Süd-afrika: kar(r)oo.

Karussell (‿‿⸝) [fr. carrousel] n ⑪d. (㊶) =reiten v/i. ㊹ going (or F turn, twist) on a roundabout.

Karutsche (‿⸝‿) = Karausche.

Kar=woche (⸝"‿⸝‿) f ㊷ Passion-week.

Karyatide (‿‿‿⸝‿) [grch.] f ㊸ arch. (Gebälkträgerin) caryatid; ~n=ordnung f ㊷ order of caryatid(e)s.

Karzer (‿⸝‿) [lt. carcer Kerker] m, n ㉒ (Schulstrafe) detention (out of school-hours); (Stube) lockup (room).

Karzinom ⊙ (‿‿⸝) [lt., *grch.] n ⑪d. path. (Krebsgeschwür) carcinoma.

Käsch (⸝) [chines.] n ⑪a, 6. num. cash.

Kaschelott (‿‿⸝) m ⑪d. zo. (Pottwal) cachalot, sperm-whale (Ca'todon ob. Physe'ter).

Kaschemme ⎡ (‿‿‿) f ㊸ (Diebskneipe) thieves' lodging-house or den.

Kaschmir (⸝⸝) ㊺a. I ♀ npr/n. Reich in Nord-indien: Kashmer, Cashmer. — II ♀ m ⑪d. (feiner Wollstoff) cashmere.

Kaschmir=schal ♀ ("...) m ㊷ cash-mere shawl; =strümpfe m/pl. cashmere stockings pl.; =wolle f (downy) cashmere wool; =ziege f, zo. Kashmer goat (Capra hircus la'niger).

Käse (⸝‿) [abd., *it.] m ㉒ 1. cheese (Sahnen=)~ cream-cheese; holländischer, Schweizer ~ Dutch, Swiss cheese; f. Chester=~; gerösteter ~ toasted cheese, a. Welsh rabbit (r-r-

rarebit). — 2. F fig. v. kleinen Leuten: drei ~ hoch F not bigger than two twopenny loaves; puny, tiny, diminutive, under-sized. — 3. (geronnene Milch) curds pl.

käse=artig (‿⸝...) a. ㊻ cheese-like, cheesy, ⚓ caseous. caseiform; =bereiter m ㊷ cheese-maker; =bereitung f ch.-making; =blatt, =blättchen F n, iro. (kleine Zeitung) F trumpery little paper; =bohrer m ch.-scoop or -taster; =fabrik f cheesery; =faß n cheese-vat; =fliege f, ent. ch.-fly (Pio'phila ca'sei); =form f ch.-mould; =glocke f cheese-plate cover; ♀haltig a. ⚓ caseous; =händler(in f) m ♀ cheesemonger; =haus n = =hütte; =hürde f cheese-crate; =hütte f ch.-dairy.

Käse=in ⊙ (‿‿⸝) [lt.] n ⑪d. = Käsestoff.

Käse=kammer (⸝‿...) f ㊷ cheese-room; vgl. =hütte; =krämer m 2c. = =händler; =kuchen m cheese-cake. [chasuble.)

Kasel (⸝‿) [lt.] f ㊸ eccl. (Meßgewand)

Käse=lab (⸝...) n ㊷ rennet; =leim m cheese-glue; =macher(in f) m ch.-maker; =made f, ent. (Larve der Käsefliege) cheese-maggot or -hopper.

Kasematte ⚔ (‿‿⸝‿) [fr., *it.] f ㊸ frt. casemate; ~n=batteri'e f ㊷ casemate battery. [Festung: to casemate.)

kasemattieren ⚔ (‿‿‿⸝‿) v/a. ㊹ fig. von)

Käse=messer (⸝⸝...) n ㊷: a) cheese-knife; b) ⚔ F iro. (Degen, Seitengewehr) ch.-toaster; =milbe f, ent. cheese-mite (Tyro'glyphus siro).

käsen (⸝‿) ⚕ I v/n. (h. u. ſn) to curd, to curdle, ⚓ to coagulate; die Milch käst the milk curdles. — II v/a. die Milch 2: to turn milk into cheese. — III ~ n ⚕ curdling, ⚓ coagulation; cheese-making.

Käse=napf (⸝"...) m ㊷ cheese-bowl; =papier n waste paper; =pappel ♀ f mallow (Malva negle'cta); =presse ⊕ f cheese-press.

Käserei (‿‿⸝) f ㊶ cheese-dairy.

Käse=reich (⸝"...) a. ㊻ caseous; =rinde f ㊷ rind of cheese, a. ch.-paring.

Kaserne ⚔ (‿⸝‿) [it. Waffenhaus] f ㊸ barracks pl., auch: barrack.

Kasernen=arre'st ⚔ (‿‿‿⸝...) m ㊷ detention in barracks; ♀artig a. ㊻ barrack-like; =dienst m barrack-duty; =hof m barrack-yard; =hof=blüte f fig., etwa: drill-sergeant's joke, jest in the style of Tommy Atkins; =inspe'ktor m barrack-master; =schiff ⚓ ↓ n receiving-ship; =stube f barrack-room; =wärter m doorkeeper at barracks.

kasernieren ⚔ (‿‿⸝‿) [fr.] v/a. ㊹ to put into (or to house in) barracks.

Käse=röster ⊕ (⸝"...) m ㊷ cheese-toaster; ♀sauer a. ⚓ chm.: ⚓ caseic; ♀saures Salz caseate; =säure f caseic acid; =stecher m = =bohrer; =stoff m, chm.: ⚓ casein(e); =teller m cheese-plate; ♀weich a. (as) soft as butter; ♀weiß a. (as) white as a ghost or a sheet, deadly white; =wirtschaft f cheese-dairy.

käsicht, käsig (⸝‿) a. ㊻ 1. cheese-like, cheesy, ⚓ caseous. — 2. F = käseweiß.

Kasino (‿⸝‿) [it. Häuschen] n ⑨ clubhouse, casino, in engl. Bädern: assembly-rooms pl.

Kaskade (‿⸝‿) [fr., it.] f ㊸ (kleiner, oft künstlicher Wasserfall) cascade; ~n=bach m ㊷ stream forming a waterfall; ~n=ladung f, elect. mehrerer Leidener Flaschen: charge by cascade.

Kaskarilla ⚓ (‿‿⸝ja) [span. cascara Rinde] f ㊹ pharm., Kaskarill=rinde f ㊷ (v. Croton eleuthe'ria) cascarilla (bark).

Kaskett (⸝⸝) [fr.] n ⑪c (㊶) 1. (Helm) helmet. — 2. (Mütze) cap.

Kaspar (⸝‿) [perf. Schatzmeister] npr/m. ⓈⓈa. (Bn.) Jasper.

Kasperl(e) (⸝‿(‿)) m ㊷ Punch; ~=theater n ㊷ Punch-and-Judy (show).

Kasperliade (‿‿‿⸝‿) f ㊸ buffoonery, clownish trick or fun.

kaspisch ♀ (⸝‿) [lt.] a. ㊻: ~es Meer, Kaspi=see (⸝‿,⸝) npr/m. ⑨ (ruff. Binnenmeer nördl. von Persien) Caspian Sea.

Kassa ♀ (⸝‿) [it.] f ㊹ = Kasse; per ~ bezahlen to pay in cash.

Kassa=buch (⸝‿...) n ㊷ cash-book; =geschäft n cash-(or ready-money) business; =konto n cash-account; =preis m cash-price.

Kassation (‿‿⸝‿) [lt.] f ㊸ (f. kassieren) 1. jur. (Aufhebung eines Urteils) cassation, quashing, rescinding, setting aside. — 2. (Dienst-entlassung) eines Beamten: dismissal, discharge; ⚔ († Entfernung aus dem Heere) cashiering.

Kassations=gesuch (‿‿⸝(‿)"...) n ㊷ jur. notice (or petition) of appeal; =hof m jur. court of cassation, in England: (highest) court of appeal.

Kassawa (‿⸝‿) f ㊹,㊺ [brasil.] 1. ♀ cassava, manioc (Ia'tropha ma'nihot). — 2. ~ (mehl n) pharm. (Mehl und Brotkuchen aus der Wurzel dieser Pflanze) cassava.

Kasse (⸝‿) [nhd., *it.] f ㊸ 1. (Geldkasten) cash-(or money-)box, (money-)chest, in Läden: till; (Geldschrank) (money-)safe. — 2. (Geldannahmestelle) pay-office, 🕮, &c. an der ~ at the booking-(or ticket-)office, thea. auch: at the box-office, in Läden: at the desk, in Banken: over the counter. — 3. Redens-arten: bei ~ sein to be in funds; gut bei ~ flush of money, in affluence; knapp bei ~, nicht bei ~ without funds, out of cash, short of money, F stumped, hard up, P broke(n); wie ist er bei ~? how is he off for cash or for money?; die ~ führen to act as cashier, to keep the cash, to handle the money; gemeinschaftliche ♀ ~ common purse or exchequer; ♀ ~ machen to make (or balance) up the (cash-)accounts; thea. volle ~ m. to sell every seat in (F to sell out) the house, to draw a full house, to fill the house.

Kassen=abschluß ♀ (⸝‿...) m ㊷ closing (or balancing) of (cash-)accounts; =anweisung f: a) (Schatzschein) treasury-bill; b) (Papiergeld) banknote; =beamte(r) m cashier; =bestand m cash (or balance) in hand, cash balance; =betrug m = =diebstahl b; =bote m messenger of a bank (or a house of business) who collects bills; =bureau n, etwa: money-office; =defe'kt m deficit (or deficiency) of money, vgl. =dieb-stahl b; =dieb m embezzler; =diebstahl m: a) theft from a cash-box or safe;

Signs (see page XVII): F familiar; P vulgar; ⎡ flash; ⚓ rare; † obsolete (died); * new word (born); ⁺⁺ incorrect; ♪ music;

[**Kasseneinnehmer**] — 575 — [**katechetisch**]

b) embezzlement (or defalcation, peculation) of money entrusted to a p.; **=einnehmer** m receiver, collector, (Kassierer) cashier; **=ertrag** m cash proceeds pl.; **=führer(in** f) m cashier, treasurer, weitS. financial manager; **=markt** m Börse: money-market; **=revision** f = Sturz; **=revisor** m official(ly appointed) auditor; **=saldo** m cash balance; **=schein** m = Anweisung; **=schlüssel** m key to the cash-box; **=schrank** m (money-)safe; **=stück** n, thea. piece which draws, F financial success, money-making piece; **=sturz** m audit of the (cash-)accounts; **=übersicht** f balance-sheet, **=verwalter(in** f) m = Führer(in); **=wart** m cashier; **=wesen** n matters pl. relating to the accounts; **=zimmer** n: a) strong-room; b) counting-house. — Vgl. auch Kassa-...

Kasserolle (⏑⏓⏑) [fr.] f ⊕ (Kochpfanne) iron saucepan; flache und weite auch: preserving- (or stew-, stewing-)pan.

Kassette (⏑⏓) [fr.] f ⊕ 1. cash-box. — 2. arch. coffer of a ceiling.

Kassetten-decke (⏑⏓⏑...) f ⊕ coffer-work ceiling, ceiling with bays.

kassettieren ⊕ (⏑⏑⏓⏑) v/a. ⊕ arch. to coffer; kassettierte Decke coffered ceiling (= Kassettendecke).

Kassia(=baum m ⊕) (⏓(⏑)⏑...) [grch.] f ⊕: a) ✱ cassia (Ca'ssia); b) ⊕ (Rinde) cassia-bark; **=blüten=öl** n cassia-oil.

Kassiber (⏑⏓⏑) [jüd. Schreiben] m ⊕ clandestine communication between prisoners, F stiff; einen ~ absenden, befördern F to fly a stiff.

Kassi-e (⏓(⏑)(⏑)) f ⊕ = Kassia.

Kassi-en=rohr ♀ (⏓(⏑)⏑)... n ⊕ cassia-stick; **=zim(me)t** ⊕ m canella.

Kassier (⏑⏓) [it.] m ⊕ d. = Kassierer.

kassieren (⏑⏓⏑) [nhd.; *Kasse] I v/a. ⊕ 1. jur.: ein Urteil ꝛc. ♀ (für ungültig erklären) to quash, to rescind, to set aside; (aufheben) to annul, to invalidate. — 2. e-n Beamten ♀ (entsetzen) to dismiss ..., to discharge ..., Offiziere auch: to cashier. — II ~ n ⊕ 3. = Kassation.

Kassierer (⏑⏓⏑) [fr.] m ⊕, ~**in** f ⊕ cashier; (Schatzmeister) treasurer; 🚂 (Schalterbeamter) booking-clerk.

Kassierung (⏑⏓⏑) f ⊕ = Kassation.

Kassiopeia (⏑(⏑)⏓⏑) [grch.] npr/f. ⊕ ⊕ ⊕. myth.(Mutter der Andro'meda)u. ast.(Sternbild am nördlichen Himmel) Cassiope(i)a.

Kassiteriden ♀ (⏑⏑⏓⏑) [grch., *phön.] npr/f/pl. inv. (Zinn-inseln der Phönizier ꝛc.) Cassiterides, jetzt Scilly Isles pl.

Kassonade (⏑⏑⏓) [fr.] f ⊕ = Farin.

Kastagnette (⏑⏑nj⏓) [span. *Kastanie] f ⊕ castanet, pl. a. F bones; **=n spielen** to play the castanets or bones.

Kastani-e (⏑⏓⏑) [nhd. 15. sae.; *grch.] f ⊕ 1. chestnut; (zahme, große, bsd. it.) ~ edible (or sweet) chestnut, maroon; (unechte od. wilde) ~ horse-chestnut; fig. die ~n für e-n aus dem Feuer holen to pull the chestnuts out of the fire for a p., F to do a p.'s dirty work (for him). — 2. ♀ = Kastanienbaum.

Kastani-en=allee (⏑⏓⏑(⏑)...) f ⊕ avenue of chestnut-trees; **=baum** m a:(echter) Spanish (or sweet) chestnut(-tree) (Casta'nea sati'va); b) (wilder) common (or horse) chestnut-tree (Ae'sculus hippoca'stanum); **=braun**: a) a. chestnut (-coloured), maroon; **=s Haar** chestnut (or auburn) hair; b) n chestnut (colour); **=pflanzung** f chestnut-plot; **=schale** f (outer) skin of a chestnut; **=wald** m, **=wäldchen** n chestnut-grove.

Kästchen (⏓⏑) n ⊕ (dim. v. Kasten) small box or case, für Juwelen: casket.

Kaste (⏓⏑) [nhd., fr., *port.] f ⊕ caste; a. close corporation.

kastei-en (⏑⏓⏑) [ahd.; *lt. castiga're] I v/a. u. sich ♀ v/refl. ⊕: rel. seinen Leib ♀, sich ♀ durch Selbstverleugnung: to keep one's body in subjection, stärker: to mortify (or crucify) one's flesh; durch peinigende Übungen: to practise self-castigation (vgl. geißeln 1). — II ~ n ⊕ = Kasteiung.

Kastei-er (⏑⏓⏑) m ⊕ monk (or person) who mortifies his flesh; vgl. Geißelbruder.

Kasteiung (⏑⏓⏑) f ⊕ mortification of one's flesh; self-castigation, ehm. auch: flagellation.

Kastell (⏑⏓) [it.] n ⊕ d. 1. strong castle, stronghold, citadel, fort. — 2. ⚓ (ehm. erhöhtes Stockwerk großer Schiffe) nur in: a) Vor(der)kastell forecastle; b) Hinterkastell aftcastle, quarter-deck.

Kastellan (⏑⏑⏓) [Kaste'll] m ⊕ d., ~**in** f ⊕ 1. (Burgvogt) castellan, f chatelaine. — 2. (Hausmeister) steward; majordomo.

Kasten (⏓⏑) [ahd.] m ⊕ ⊕(⊕) 1. chest, (Kiste) box, (Koffer) trunk; (Brief=, Post=) ~ letter-box; (Geld=)~ strong-box; e-n Brief in den ~ (Schalter) werfen to post a letter; fig. er hat Kisten, ~ u. Keller voll he has more than he knows what to do with. — 2. F contp.(elende Baracke) wretched hovel; a. = Klavier, Kutsche, Schiff; bibl. der ~ (die Arche) Noahs Noah's Ark. — 3. (Geld=)~ money-box, coffer, safe; (öffentliche Kasse) (public) treasury; ~ für die Armen poor-box. — 4. ♪ ~ der Saiteninstrumente resonance-box; ~ an der Orgel organ-case or -chamber. — 5. opt. o'ptischer ~ = Guckkasten. — 6. ⊕ ~ eines Brunnens water-cistern, shaft; ~ eines Klaviers frame-work (or case) of a piano(forte); ~ e-r Kutsche boot of a coach; Juwelier-kunst: (Ring=)~ zur Fassung eines Steines: bezel, collet; typ. (Setz=, Schrift=) (letter-)case. — 7. ⚒ (Ausstimmerung) timbering. — 8. ⚔ F = Arre'st ♀.

Kasten=balken ⚓ (⏓⏑...) m ⊕ an eisernen Schiffen box-beam; **=damm** m cofferdam; **=deckel** m lid of a box; **=geist** [Kaste] m caste-feeling, exclusiveness; **=hänge** f. hinge of a chest; **=herr** m, eccl. churchwarden; **=herrschaft** [Kaste] f rule of a caste; **=macher** m box-maker; **=mäßig** [[Kaste] a. ⊕ like a caste or a close corporation; **=regal** n, typ.: a) geschlossenes: cabinet; b) mit Setzpult: frame-rack; c) ohne Setzpult: case-rack; **=schloß** n: a) box-lock; b) lock of a box; **=wagen** m (Rollwagen) trolly, dray, lowry; **=werk** n, arch. ehm. coffer-work.

Kastilianer (⏑⏑(⏑)⏓⏑) m ⊕, ~**in** f ⊕, **kastilianisch** a. ⊕ Castilian.

Kastili-en ♀ (⏑⏓(⏑)) [Kastelle] npr/n. ⊕ a. span. Landschaft: Castile.

Kastili-er (⏑⏓(⏑)⏑) m ⊕ = Kastilia'ner.

Kastor[1] (⏓⏑) [lt.] npr/m. ⊕: ~ **u. Pollux**: a) myth. (Brüder der He'lena) Castor and Pollux; b) phys. ⚡ = Elmsfeuer; c) ast. (Sternbild) Gemini pl.

Kastor[2] (⏓⏑) [lt.] m ⊕ e ⊕ = Biber.

Kastor[2]=**hut** (⏓⏑...) m ⊕ beaver hat; **=öl** n, bsd. med. (Ricinus-öl) castor-oil.

Kastrat (⏑⏓) [lt.] m ⊕ (Entmannter) eunuch.

kastrieren (⏑⏓⏑) v/a. ⊕ to castrate.

Kasuali-en 🜚 (⏑⏓(⏑)) [lt.] pl. ⊕ 1. extra(ordinary) duties or functions pl. — 2. evangel. Prediger: casual fees pl.

Kasuar (⏑⏓) [austral.] m ⊕ d. (⊕) orn. (straußähnl. Vogel) cassowary (Casua'rius).

Kasuist (⏑⏓) [lt.] m ⊕ (Gewissensrat, spitzfindiger Klügler) casuist; ~**ik** (⏑⏓⏑⏑) f ⊕, **=isch** a. ⊕ casuistic(al).

Kasus (⏓⏑) [lt.] m, inv. (Fall) case (auch gram.); der ~ Genitivus the genitive case; obliquer(abhängiger) ~ oblique case.

Kasus=endung (⏓⏑...) f ⊕ case-termination; **=regeln** f/pl. rules pl. about (the) cases. [catafalque.]

Katafalk (⏑⏓) [it. Schaugerüst] m ⊕d.)

Katakomben ⊕ (⏑⏓⏑) [mlt., *grch.] f/pl. ⊕ catacombs pl.

katalanisch (⏑⏑⏓⏑) a. ⊕ = katalo'nisch.

katalaunisch (⏑⏑⏓⏑) a. ⊕: hist. ~**e Gefilde** Catalaunian Plain.

kataleptisch 🜚 (⏑⏑⏓⏑) [grch.] a. ⊕ pros. von Versen: (unvollständig) catalectic.

Katalog (⏑⏑⏓) [grch.] m ⊕d. (Verzeichnis) catalogue; **=isieren** (⏑⏑⏑⏑⏓⏑) v/a. ⊕ to (put in a or enter in a) catalogue.

Kataloni-en ♀ (⏑⏑⏓(⏑)) npr/n. ⊕α. (nordöstl. Provinz Spaniens) Catalonia; **Kataloni-er(in** f ⊕) m ⊕, **katalonisch** (⏑⏑⏓⏑) a. ⊕ Catalonian, Catalan.

Katapult ⚔ (⏑⏑⏓) [grch.] m ⊕d., ~**e** (⏑⏑⏓⏑) f ⊕ Alt.: (Wurfmaschine) catapult.

Katarakt (⏑⏑⏓) [grch.] m ⊕c.: a) (Wasserfall), b) ⊕ mach. (Steuervorrichtung) cataract; c) ~**a** ⊕, ~**e** ⊕ f, path. (grauer Star) cataract.

Katarrh (⏑⏓) [grch.] m ⊕d. path. (Entzündung einer Schleimhaut) catarrh; (Schnupfen) cold (in the head); **=al=fieber** (⏑⏓⏑...) n ⊕ path. fever accompanying a cold, 🜚 catarrhal fever.

katarrhalisch (⏑⏑⏓⏑) a. ⊕ path. catarrhal.

Kataster (⏑⏓⏑) [it., fr. "Kopf"steuer f] m u. n ⊕ (Steuerregister) register of assessment; (Grundbuch, in England seit dem Doomsday Book Wilhelms des Eroberers unbekannt) land-register, cadastre.

Kataster=auszug (⏑⏓⏑...) m ⊕ extract from a land-register; **=beamte(r), =kontroleur** m, etwa: government surveyor, commissioner of assessment.

katastrieren (⏑⏑⏓⏑) ⊕ I v/n. (h.) (zum Kataster aufnehmen) to make an assessment, to register landed property. — II v/a. Steuern ♀ to assess taxes. — III ~ n ⊕ u. **Katastrierung** f ⊕ registration, assessment.

Katastrophe (⏑⏑⏓⏑) [grch.] f ⊕ (Verhängnis, Unfall) catastrophe (a. im Drama).

Kate provc. (⏓⏑) f ⊕ farmer's cottage.

Katechese 🜚 (⏑⏑⏓⏑) [grch.] f ⊕ teaching by way of questions and answers, catechizing, catechesis.

Katechet 🜚 (⏑⏑⏓) m ⊕ catechist; weitS. (religious) teacher; ~**ik** (⏑⏑⏓⏑) f ⊕, **=isch** a. ⊕ catechetic(al).

⚛ scientific; ♀ botanical; ♀ geography; ⊕ machinery; ⚒ mining; ⚔ military; ⚓ marine; ⊕ commercial; ✉ postal; 🚂 railway.

[Katechisation] — 576 — [Katzensilber]

Katechisation ⚇ (⌣⌣--tẑ(⌣)¹) f ㊻ (Frage-unterricht, bsd. *rel.*) catechization.
katechisieren (⌣⌣-⌣⌣¹) v/a. ㊳ to catechize; (ausfragen) to question. [catechism.]
Katechismus (⌣⌣⌣⌣) m ㉗ meist *eccl.*
katechismus-artig (⌣⌣⌣⌣...) a. ㊻ mst. *eccl.* catechistic(al); **-lehre** (**-moral**) f ㊷ (moral) teaching of the catechism; **-schüler(in)** f m pupil who is taught the catechism; (Konfirmand[in]) candidate for confirmation, ehm.: **catechumen**; **-stunde** f lesson on the catechism.
Katechu (⌣⌣ʃ⌣¹) [ost=ind. *kātschu*] n ㊵ *pharm.* catechu, (lt.) terra Japonica.
Katechu-gerbsäure ⚇ (⌣...) f ㊷ *chm.* catechutannic acid ($C_{19}H_{18}O_8$).
Katechumen(e) (⌣⌣-⌣¹) [grch.] m ㊷(㊹) catechumen (= Katechismusschüler).
Katechu-palme ♀ (⌣⌣ʃ⌣''...) f ㊷ areca (*Are'ca ca'techu*); **-pille** f cachou, cashew; **-säure** f = Catechin; **-tinktu'r** f, *pharm.* tincture of catechu.
Kategorie (⌣-⌣¹) [grch. Aussage] f ㊸ (Begriffsfach, Klasse) category.
kategorisch (⌣¹⌣) a. ㊻ (entschieden) categoric(al) (f. Imperativ).
Kater (¹⌣) [ahd., f. Katze] m ㉒ **1.** male cat, tomcat; der Gestiefelte Kater (im Märchen) Puss in boots. — **2.** (mürrischer Mensch) morose fellow, (growling) bear, grumbler. — **3.** *co.* burschikos wortspielend: a) = Kata'rrh; b) = Katzenjammer.
Katharine (⌣⌣¹⌣) [grch. die Reine] npr/f. ㊹㊸. (Bn.) Catherine, Katherine, Catharine, Catharina; **~n-rad** (⁂...) n ㊷ *arch.* (Fensterrose) Catharine-wheel.
Käthchen (¹⌣) npr/n. ㉒a., **Kathe**, **Käthe** f ㊺㊸. (*dim. v.* Katharine) Kate, Kitty.
Katheder (⌣¹⌣) [grch.] m, n ㉒ professor's chair (a. *fig.* =Professur); (Pult) lecturing-desk; vom ~ (herab), oft: (lt.) ex cathedra.
Katheder-blüte (⌣¹⌣⌣) f ㊷ professor's (stale) joke; **-held** m learned disputant or combatant; **-sozialismus** m professorial (or doctrinaire) socialism; **-sozialist** m socialist(ic) doctrinaire; **-weisheit** f professorial wisdom.
Kathedrale (⌣⌣¹⌣) [lt.] f ㊸, **Kathedral-kirche** (⌣⌣¹¹⌣⌣) f ㊷ cathedral (church); Stadt mit ~ cathedral city.
Kathete (⌣¹⌣) [grch. „herabgelassenes" Lot] f ㊸ *geom.* one of the (two) sides of a right-angled triangle which contain the right angle. [röhrenfonde) catheter.]
Katheter ⚇ (⌣¹⌣) [grch.] m ㉒ *surg.* (Harn-
katheterisieren ⚇ (⌣⌣⌣⌣¹) f, **katheteren** (⌣¹⌣) ㊳ a. v/a. *surg.* (einen Katheter einführen) to catheterize.
Kathode ⚇ (⌣¹⌣) [grch. Rückkehr] f ㊸ *elect.* (*ant.* Anode) cathode.
Katholik (⌣⌣¹) [grch. *katholiko's* für die ganze Welt] m ㊷, **~in** f ㊷, **katholisch** (⌣¹⌣) a. ㊻ *eccl.* (Roman) Catholic.
katholisieren (⌣⌣⌣¹⌣) v/n. (h.) ㊳ *eccl.* (katholisch machen, werden) to catholicize.
Katholizismus (⌣⌣⌣⌣) m ㉗ *eccl.* (Roman) Catholicism; auch: *contp.* Popery, Popish religion.
Kathrine F (⌣¹⌣) f ㊸㊸. ㊳ = Katharine; schnelle ~ (Durchfall) looseness of the bowels, diarrhœa, P jerry-go-nimble.
Katilinarisch (⌣⌣¹⌣) a. ㊻ Catilinarian; Ciceros 2e (ben Aufwiegler Catilina anklagende) Rede Cicero's Catiline speech; 2e Existen'zen (pl.) restless (or revolutionary) individual(s pl.).
Kätner (¹⌣) [Kate] m ㉒ (humble) cottager.
katonisch (⌣¹⌣) [lt.=dtsch.; * Cato] a. ㊻ Catonian (auch *fig.* streng tugendhaft).
Katoptrik ⚇ (⌣¹⌣) [grch.] f ㊻ *opt.* (Lehre v. der Spiegelung der Strahlen) catoptrics;
katoptrisch (⌣¹⌣) a. ㊻ catoptric(al).
Kattafel ↓ (ᴱ¹⌣) [Ratt-tafel] n ㉒ cat-tackle. [ſ↓ to cat the anchor.]
katten¹ ↓ (¹⌣) [hdd.] v/a. ㊳ den Anker
Katte² pl.) (⌣) [lt. C(h)atti; *Hesse(n)] m ㊹ *hist.* Catti pl.
Katt-fall (ᴱ¹...) n ㉒, **-läufer** m cat-rope or -fall; **-haken** m cat-hook; **-schiff** n mit schmalem Spiegel: cat(-ship); **-stopper** m cat-stopper; **-tafel** n f. Kattafel.
Kattun ⚇ (⌣¹) [mhd. 14. sae.; ndl.; ar. Baumwolle] m ㊸d. calico, weiß. cotton fabric or goods pl.; (Möbel-)~ chintz, cotton damask; bedruckter ~ für Kleider ꝛc. print; karierter ~ cotton check.
Kattun-druck (⌣¹...) m ㉒, **-druckmaschine** f ㊷ = **-drucker**ei ꝛc.; **-drucker** m calico-printer; **-druckerei** f: a) calico-printing; b) print(ing)-works; **-druckpresse** f calico-printing machine.
kattunen ⚇ (⌣¹⌣) a. ㊻ (of) calico, (of) cotton, (of) chintz.
Kattun-fabrik ⚇ (⌣¹¹...) f ㊷ calico-factory or works pl.; **-färber** m cotton-dyer; **-kleid** n print(-dress), weiß. cotton gown; **-leinwand** f linen with a cotton weft, union; **-papier** n chintz-paper; **-presse** f calico-press; **-weber** m calico-weaver; **-weberei** f calico-manufacture.
katz-balgen F (ᴱ⌣) [mhd. 16. sae.] sich ⚇ v/refl. ㊳*⁎* to scuffle, spielend: to romp.
Katz-balgerei (⌣⌣⌣¹¹) f ㊻ scuffling, scuffle, tussling, tussle, romp(ing).
Kätzchen (¹⌣) n ㉓ (*dim. von* Katze) **1.** (little or young) kitten, F little pussy, schmeichelnd: mein ~! little duckie! — **2.** ♀ Blütenstand: catkin, gosling, ♀ amentum, ament.
Katze (¹⌣) [ahd. : cat] f ㊸ **1.** *zo.* cat, *poet.* ꝛc. auch: grimalkin; zahme ~ domestic cat (*Felis dome'stica*); wilde ~ wild cat (*Felis catus*); männliche ~ f. Kater; weibliche ~ tib-cat, F tibby, *co.* lady-cat; bunte (ob. getigerte) ~ tabby-cat; *fig.* so naß wie eine ~ (as) wet as a drowned rat; f. Hund 2. — **2.** *fig.* Redensarten: f. anhängen 1, Brei 3; es war keine ~ (niemand) da there wasn't a soul in the place; das ist für die ~! that's of no (earthly) use!, F u. P that's no good (to any one)!; die ~ im Sack kaufen to buy a pig in a poke; sieht doch die ~ den Kaiser an a cat may look at a queen; die ~ trägt es auf dem Schwanze weg it is as light as a feather or a mere nothing; ein Gesicht machen wie die ~, wenn's donnert to make a face as sour as vinegar. — **3.** Sprichw. die ~ läßt das Mausen nicht; was von der ~ ist, fängt Mäuse what's bred in the bone will come out in the flesh; auch: cat will after kind; bei Nacht sind alle ~n grau, etwa: by night all witches are fair as day; hüte dich vor den ~n, die vorne lecken und hinten kratzen, etwa: beware of fawning creatures and their treacherous ways, vgl. lecken² 3; wenn die ~ nicht zu Hause ist, tanzen die Mäuse auf Tisch und Bänken when the cat's away the mice will play. — **4.** *fig.* von Personen: (Schmeichler[in]) cajoler, F carneying p.; (falscher Mensch) treacherous (or false) p.; bsd. v. Weibern: (spiteful or nasty) cat. **5.** = Geld=2. — **6.** ↓ neunschwänzige ~ (Tau zum Prügeln) cat-o'-nine-tails.
Katzen-art (¹⌣...) f ㊷: a) *zo.* feline species; b) nach ~ after the manner of cats; ♀**artig** a. ㊻: a) *zo.* of the feline species; b) cat-like, feline, treacherous; *adv.* like a cat; **-auge** n: a) ~n haben to have eyes like a cat; b) *min.* (Art Quarz) cat's-eye; ♀**äugig** a. with eyes like a cat; **-bart** m cat's whiskers pl.; **-buckel** m cat's (arched) back; e-n ~ machen: a) von Katzen und Menschen: to put up one's back; b) *fig.* (sich demütig verbeugen) to bow (or stoop) very low; im demselben Sinne: ♀**buckeln** v/n. (h.) ㉒a *⁎*⁎* to crouch (or cringe) before a p., to eat humble pie; **-eichhorn** n, *zo. Am.* cat-squirrel (*Sciu'rus cine'reus*); **-fell** n cat's skin, catskin; ♀**freundlich** a. u. *adv.*, etwa: with malice in one's heart, but a smile on one's face; (heuchlerisch) dissembling; 2e Manieren und Redensarten, oft: feline amenities pl.; **-gamander** ♀ m = **-kraut**; **-ge-schlecht** n family of cats, feline kind or tribe; **-geschrei** n mewing (or howling) of cats, caterwauling; **-glimmer** m, *min.* specular gypsum, gypsum spar; **-gold** n, *min.* cat-gold, yellow mica; ♀**grau** a. grey like a cat.
katzenhaft (¹⌣⌣) a. ㊻ = katzenartig.
Katzen-hai (¹⌣...) m ㉒ *ichth.* cat-shark (*Tri'acis semifascia'tus*); **-jammer** F m (a sick) headache on the morrow of a carousal, seediness following debauchery or hard drinking; ~ haben to feel seedy; moralischer ~ auch: (moral) depression, penitent (or dejected) frame of mind, low spirits pl.; ♀**jämmerlich** F a. ㊻ seedy, down in the dumps; mir ist ganz 2, auch: I feel very low-spirited; **-kopf** m: a) cat's head (a. Name v. Äpfeln); b) (einfältiger Mensch) silly person, blockhead, dunce; c) F (Ohrfeige) box on the ear; **-kraut** n cat-thyme (*Teu'crium marum*); **-leben** n (zähes Leben) cat's (or tough) life, great vitality; **-liebe** f, *fig.* false love; **-minze** ♀ f cat-mint, cat-nip, field-balm (*Ne'peta Cata'ria*); **-musik** f caterwauling, rough music, bisw. cat-music; (verhöhnendes Ständchen) tin-kettle serenade or concert; *co.* infernal row, hell let loose; e-m eine ~ bringen to hoot and howl before a p.'s house; ~ machen *co.* to make night hideous with discordant sounds; **-natur** f: eine ~ haben to have as many lives as a cat; **-pfötchen** n: a) cat's paw; b) ♀ cat's-foot (*Gnapha'lium dioi'cum*); **-pfote** f cat's paw; **-rücken** m = **-buckel**; **-schnurren** n cat's purr; **-schwanz** m: a) cat's tail; *fig.* feinen ~ (eine Kleinigkeit) a mere trifle; b) ♀ (Schachtelhalm) cat's-tail (*Equise'tum*); **-silber** n, *min.*: ⚇ argentine mica;

[Katzensprung] — 577 — [Kaupfeffer]

=sprung m: a) cat's leap; b) F fig. (kurze Strecke) es ist nur ein ~ bis dahin it is only a stone's throw; =steig m narrow stile or path; =teller m small plate; =tiger m, zo. tiger-cat (Felis tigri'na); =tisch(chen n) m F = Trompetertisch; =tritt m (schleichender Tritt) cat's gentle pace or gait or step; =volk n the cats pl., the feline tribe; =wäsche f cat's lick; =wels m, ichth.: nordamerikanischer ~ cat-fish, horn-pout (Pimelo'des catus).

Kätzlein (⸗⸗) n ㉓ = Kätzchen.

kaudern (⸗⸗) [lautm.] v/n. (h.) ⓐ. 1. (schreien wie ein Truthahn) to gobble. — 2. = kauderwelschen.

Kauder-welsch (⸗⸗⸗) [nhd. 16. sae., mhd.: (P: kaudern) *Chur-welsch] n ㉔ⓐ. u. ⓐ. ⓖ: ~, ⁊es Geschwätz gibberish, pedlars' cant. St. Giles's Greek, F double Dutch; (Zigeunerisch) Romany; ⁊en (⸗⸗⸗⸗) v/n. (h.) u. v/a. ⑪ *** to talk gibberish or F double Dutch, to jabber; ~er m ㉒ jabberer.

kaudinisch (⸗⸗⸗) [lt.] a. ⓐ röm. Alt.: das ~e (fig. ⁊e) Joch the Caudine Forks pl.

Kaue ✕ (⸗⸗) [mhd.; *lt. ca'vea Höhle] f ⓐ hut at the pit's mouth.

kauen (⸗⸗) [ahd. = chaw, chew] I v/a. u. v/n. (h.) ⑪ 1. to chew, to masticate, schmatzend: to munch, knirschend: (zer⸗)⁊ to crunch; an den Nägeln, den Fingern ⁊ to bite one's nails; v. Pferden: aufs Gebiß ⁊ to champ the bit. — 2. fig. an etwas ⁊ (emsig arbeiten) to plod(away) at a th., to pore over one's books or lessons; e-m et. zu ⁊ geben to give a p. a hard nut to crack; die Worte, Silben ⁊ (gedehnt sprechen) to drawl out one's words. — II ~ n ㉓ 3. physiol. chewing, ⚬ mastication.

Kauer (⸗⸗) m ㉒, ~in f ㊼ (s. kauen) chewing (or munching) person.

kauern (⸗⸗)[nhd.: cower] v/n. (sn) u. sich ⁊ v/refl. ⓐ. to cower (or squat) down; ⁊d, a.: crouching down, huddled up.

Kauf (⸗) [ahd.: ch(e)ap, chaffer] m ⓒc. 1. (Kaufen; ant. Verkauf) buying, purchasing, purchase, im großen: buying up (whole-sale); (Handeln) bargain (-ing); einen ~ abschließen to close (or strike) a bargain; et. zum ~ anbieten to offer a th. for sale; ⓢ 20 Mark auf den ~ (als Handgeld) geben to pay a sovereign as (a) deposit or on account; Sprichw. ~ ist ~ a bargain is a bargain. — 2. (Gekauftes) purchase, bargain, (Erworbenes) acquisition; et. mit in den ~ geben to give s.th.into (or to include s. th. in) the bargain, F to throw s.th. in; et. mit in den ~ nehmen to take s.th. into the bargain, mehr gebr. to allow s.th. to be included in a bargain, fig. to (have to) put up with a th., to (have to) make the best of a bad bargain. — 3. et. guten(ob. billigen, wohlfeilen) ~s geben to give a th. cheaply, ⓢ to let it go at a moderate price; fig. ich bin noch billigen (ob. leichten) ~s davon gekommen I got off cheaply or fairly well or easily, I came off with (but) a small loss.

Kauf-abschluß ⓢ (⸗⸗⸗) m ⓒ completion of a purchase; =anschlag m: a) valuation of s. th. to be sold; b) announcement of a sale.

kaufbar (⸗⸗) a. ⓐⓐ purchasable.

Kauf-bedingungen ⓢ (⸗⸗⸗⸗) f/pl. ⓒ conditions pl. of purchase; ⁊begierig a. ⓐⓐ eager (or anxious) to buy; =brief m purchase-deed, agreement between seller and buyer; (Besitzerklärung) title-deed.

kaufen (⸗⸗) [ahd. s. Kauf] I v/a., v/n. (h.) u. sich ⁊ v/refl. ⑨ 1. et. von e-m ⁊ to buy (or purchase) a th. of (bisw. a.: from) a p.; aus erster (zweiter) Hand ⁊ to buy at first (second) hand; wieder (ob. von neuem) ⁊ to repurchase; wollen Sie viel auf dem Markte ⁊? do you intend making large purchases in the market?; bei wem ⁊ Sie gewöhnlich? where (or from whom) do you generally get your supply?, what firm(s) do you mostly patronize?; jur. an sich ⁊ to acquire by purchase. — 2. mit Angabe der Wirkung: sich von et. frei ⁊ to free (or exempt) o.s. from a th. by payment. — 3. F u. P was ich mir dafür kaufe! (darauf gebe ich nichts) what is the use of that?, F that's all bosh or rubbish!; den werd' ich mir ⁊! I will give him a sharp talking to!, F I'll let him have it! — 4. fig. = er⁊ ⁊. — 5. Kartenspiel: Karten ⁊ (vom Talo'n so viel Karten nehmen, als man wegwirft) to buy cards. — II ~ n ㉓ 6. = Kauf; eccl. von Pfründen: simony.

Käufer (⸗⸗) [ahd.] m ㉒, ~in f ㊼ buyer, purchaser; jur. auch: vendee; (Kunde) customer; wenn ich e-n ~ finden kann if I can meet with a purchaser; ⓢ ohne ~ no buyers, not saleable, no sale for it, F hanging on hand.

Kauf-fahrer ⚓ (⸗⸗⸗) m ㉒: a) owner of a merchant-vessel; b) (Handelsschiff) merchant- (or trading-)vessel, merchantman; =fahrtei f ㊻ maritime trade; merchant-service, navigation for purposes of trade or commerce; =fahrtei-flotte f merchant-fleet, mercantile fleet; =fahrtei-schiff n merchant-vessel, merchantman; =fartei ⁊c. = =fahrtei ⁊c.; =frau f: a) merchant's wife; b) woman (or female) dealer or trader; =geld n purchase-money; =gericht n, in Engl.: court of arbitration; =geschäft n mercantile transaction; =gesuch n offer to buy; in Anzeigen oft: Required (to buy) //, Wanted //; =gut n merchandise; =halle f market-hall or -house, salesroom, exchange; =handel m (ant. Tauschhandel) commerce, trade; =haus n: a) = Handelshaus; b) (Haus mit Kaufläden) premises pl. containing (many) shops; c) (Lagerhaus) warehouse, storehouse, stock-rooms pl.; =herr m = Handelsherr; =karten f/pl. Kartenspiel: cards pl. which can be bought; =kontrakt m contract of purchase, vgl. =brief; =kraft f purchasing power; ⁊kräftig a. ⓐⓐ; ⁊es Publikum people able to buy; =laden m (grocer's) shop, store, größeren Stils: stores pl., emporium; =leute pl. v. =mann, s. bsb. Art.

Käuflich (⸗⸗) [ahd.; *Kauf] I a. ⓐⓐ purchasable; for (or on) sale, to be sold; F to be had (or got) for money; ⓢ ⁊e Ware marketable goods pl.; b.s. von Personen: (bestechlich) venal, corruptible, mercenary. — II adv. by purchase; ⁊ an sich bringen (ob. erwerben) to acquire by purchase; ⁊ überlassen to sell, to transfer by sale.

Käuflichkeit (⸗⸗⸗) f ㊻ being purchasable or for sale; (Bestechlichkeit) venality, corruptibility.

Kauf-liebhaber(in f) m (⸗⸗⸗⸗) ⓒ = =lustige(r); =lust f wish (or inclination) to buy; ⁊lustig a. ⓐⓐ desirous of buying; =lustige(r)s. intending purchaser.

Kaufmann (⸗⸗) [mhd.: chapman] m ⓒc. (pl. meist Kaufleute): a) trader, (retail) dealer, commercial man, (small) shopkeeper, tradesman; b) (Großhändler) wholesale dealer, merchant; c) engS. grocer, druggist; ~ werden to go into (or learn a) business, to become a business-man or commercial man.

kaufmännisch (⸗⸗⸗) a. ⓐⓐ commercial, mercantile; ⁊e Beziehungen f/pl. business-connexions pl.; ⁊e Handschrift commercial (or business-) hand; ⁊es Haus commercial firm, house of business; adv. ⁊ geschult commercially trained, brought up in business.

Kaufmanns-brauch ⓢ (⸗⸗⸗) m ⓒ commercial (or mercantile) usage.

Kaufmannschaft (⸗⸗⸗) f ㊻ coll. (body of) merchants or commercial men pl.

Kaufmanns-diener ⓢ (⸗⸗⸗) m ㉒: a)commercial (or merchant's) clerk; b) = =junge; =gilde f corporation (or company) of traders; =hand f business-hand; =junge m messenger in a house of business, office-boy; =stand m mercantile calling; coll. commercial men pl.; =ware f merchandise, commercial wares or goods pl.

Kauf-preis ⓢ (⸗⸗⸗) m ⓒ = =geld; =recht n right of purchase, right to buy; =schilling m sum paid on account, earnest(money); weitS. = =geld; =summe f = =geld; =vertrag m contract of sale; vgl. =brief; ⁊weise adv. by (way of) purchase; =wert m value of a th. to the purchaser, auch: marketable value; =zettel m note of purchase.

Kau-gummi (⸗⸗⸗)n(m)ⓒ chewing-gum.

Kaukasien ⓠ (-⸗(⸗)⸗) npr/n. ⓐ. (russ. Provinz) Caucasia; Kaukasier(in f) m ㉒, kaukasisch (-⸗⸗) a. ⓐⓐ Caucasian; Kaukasus ⓠ (⸗⸗⸗) npr/m. inv. (Gebirge) Caucasus (Mountains pl.).

Kaul-barsch (⸗⸗⸗) [mhd. (mhd.) Kaule Kugel] m ⓒ ichth. blacktail, ruff(e)(Aceri'na ce'rnua); =frosch m = =quappe; =kopf m, ichth. miller's-thumb (Cottus go'bio); =quappe f, zo. tadpole.

kaum (⸗) [ahd. „fläglich"] adv. scarcely, hardly, (nur gerade) barely; ⁊ je hardly ever; er war ⁊ ins Haus getreten, als // he had only just stepped inside when //; ⁊ hatte er sich erhoben, als // no sooner had he risen than //; das ist ⁊ zu begreifen it is difficult (or hard) to conceive.

Kau-magen (⸗⸗⸗) m ⓒ ent. gizzard, ⚬ gigerium; =mittel n, med. u. pharm. ⚬ masticatory; =muskel m, anat.: ⚬ masticatory muscle, masseter; =pfeffer ⓢ m betel.

Kauri (⌣́) m ⑭, f ⑯ zo. ⊕ cowrie(-shell) (Cypraeʹa moneʹta).
Kausal (⌣́) [lt.] a. ⑯ (ursächlich) causal; **~ität** (⌣⌣⌣́) [lt.] f ⑯ causality.
Kausalneʹxus (⌣⌣́...) m ⑫, interdependency of cause and effect; **-partiʹkel** f, gr. causative particle; **-satz** m adverbial clause denoting cause; **-zusammenhang** m = nexus.
kausativ (⌣⌣́f) [lt.] a. ⑯ gr. causative.
Kausch(e) ⚓ (⌣́) [ndl.; dän.; *fr. cosse Schote] f ⑯ (⑭) (Segelring) (iron) thimble, traveller, bull's-eye.
Kaustik (⌣́) [grch.] f ⑯ art of etching.
kaustisch (⌣́) [grch.] a. ⑯ (ätzend) caustic; fig. Le Bemerkung cutting remark; **Kaustizität** (⌣⌣⌣́) f ⑯ causticity.
Kau-tabak (⌣́...) m ⑫ chewing-tobacco.
Kautel (⌣́) [lt.] f ⑯ jur. precaution.
kauterisier/en (⌣⌣⌣́⌣) [grch.] surg. I v/a. ⑱ (ätzen) to cauterize. — II ~ n ㉓ u. **K/ung** f ⑯ cauterization.
Kaution (-tz(v)́) [lt.] f ⑯ (Sicherheit) security; ⑭ (Bürgschaft vor Gericht im Strafverfahren) bail; ~ stellen to give bail.
Kautions-bestellung ⊕ (-tz(v)́...) f ⑯ giving (or providing) security; **-fähig**, **-pflichtig** a. ⑯ able, liable to give security or bail.
Kautschuk ⊕ (⌣́) [fr.; *brasil.] m u. n ⑭d. caoutchouc, india-rubber (getrockneter Saft v. Siphoʹnia, Castilloʹa, Ficus elasʹtica u. a. ⚑ **-baum** ⚘ m ⑫ = Federharzbaum; **-waren** ⊕ f/pl. india-rubber goods pl.
Kau-werkzeuge (⌣́...) n/pl. ⊕ anat.: ⚐ masticatory organs, masticators pl.
Kauz (⌣́) [mhd.] m ⑤a. orn.: 1. a) (Wald)~ brown (or tawny) owl, wood-owl (Syrʹnium aluʹco); b) (Stein)~ little owl (Atheʹne nocʹtua). — 2. F fig. (G. a. ⑫) (wunderliche Person) queer (or strange, F rum) fellow or customer; es muß auch solche Käuze geben (G.) there must be some of all sorts; weitS. = Kerl, zB.: alter ~ F old fogey, codger; reicher ~ rich fellow, moneyed man, F gold-bug.
Käuzchen (⌣́) n ㉓ (dim. v. Kauz) little owl, owlet; fig. funny little man.
Kavalier (⌣⌣⌣́) [fr., it.] m ⑫d. 1. a) (Herr, im Gegensatz zu e-r Dame) gentleman; (Beschützer e-r Dame) cavalier; b) (Edelmann) nobleman, (Ritter) knight, cavalier. — 2. (Springer im Schachspiel) knight.
kavalier-mäßig (⌣⌣⌣́...) a. ⑯ like a cavalier, gentlemanly.
Kavalkade (⌣⌣⌣́) [fr.] f ⑯ (Reiterzug) cavalcade, mounted procession.
Kavallerie ⚔ (⌣⌣(⌣)⌣́) [fr., it.; *ar. khayal pl.] f ⑯ (Reiterei) cavalry, horsemen pl., horse coll.; **~angriff** m ⑫ cavalry attack; **-gefecht** n cavalry engagement or fight; **-offizier** m cav. officer, officer of horse; **-posten** m mounted sentinel, horse-guard; **-regiment** n cav. regiment, regiment of horse; **-relais** n relay of cav. horses.
Kavallerist (⌣⌣(⌣)⌣́) [fr.] m ⑫ cavalry-(or horse-)soldier, trooper, cavalry-man.
Kavatine ♪ (⌣⌣⌣́) [it.] f ⑯ (kurze Arie ohne Wiederholung) cavatina.
Kavent (⌣⌣́) [lt.] m ⑫ = Bürge.
Kaviar (⌣́w(⌣)) [it.; *Kaffa ⚘ St.] m ⑭d. (gesalzener Rogen v. Acipeʹnser huso) caviare (-brötchen n ⑫ caviare sandwich).

kavieren (⌣⌣⌣́) [lt.] v/n. (h.) ⑱ = bürgen (vgl. Kavent).
Kawaß (⌣⌣́), **Kawasse** (⌣⌣⌣́) [türk., *ar.] m ⑫, ⑭ (türk. Polizist) kavass, cavass.
Kayenne-pfeffer (⌣⌣(⌣́⌣...) [Kayenne fr. Kolonie in Süd-amerika] m ⑫ Cayenne pepper, cayenne.
Kazike (⌣⌣́) [span.] m ⑭ Mexiko 2c. (ehm. Häuptling, jetzt Bürgermeister) cacique.
Kebse (⌣́) [ahd.] f ⑯ = Kebsweib.
Kebs-ehe (⌣́...) f ⑯ concubinage; **-frau** f = -weib; **-kind** n natural (or illegitimate) child, bastard; **-weib** n concubine, F kept woman.
keck (⌣́) [mhd.: quick: lt. vivʹ-] a. ⑯ bold, audacious; (herzhaft) plucky, (verwegen) daring, (frech) pert, impudent, F cheeky, saucy; **Keckheit** f ⑯ boldness, audacity; pluck; daring, pertness, impudence, F cheek; **kecklich** (⌣⌣́) adv. boldly, pluckily.
Keck T (⌣́) m ⑳ Gebäck: cake, biscuit.
Kefir (⌣́) [tatar., *türk.] m ⑭d. (gegorene Kuhmilch) kephir.
Kegel¹ (⌣́) [ahd.: kayle] m ⑫ 1. zum Spiele: skittle, (nine)pin; ein Spiel ~ a set of ninepins; die = aufsetzen to put (or set) up the skittles; ~ schieben = kegelschieben. — 2. (kurze, kleine Person) squat (or dumpy) little person. — 3. ⚱ conical (mountain-)peak; math. cone; abgestumpfter ~ conical frustum, truncated (or ⚐ frustum of a) cone; kleiner ~, auch: conicle. — 4. ⊕ typ. Schriftgießerei: (Stärke des Buchstabens) body (or thickness, depth) of type of a letter. — 5. ⊕, ⚔ (Zünd-)~ am Perkussionsgewehre cone of the percussion-cock.
Kegel² F (⌣́) [mhd. un-eheliches Kind] m ⑫: Kind und ~ the whole family or tribe, F the whole kit (of them); er hat nicht Kind noch ~ he has neither chick nor child, he has no kith nor kin; mit Kind und ~ with all one's belongings, with bag and baggage.
Kegel¹-achse (⌣⌣́...) f ⑯ math. axis of a cone; **-ähnlich** a. ⑯, **-artig** a. = **-förmig**; **-aufsetzer** m = -junge; **-bahn** f skittle- (or bowling-)alley, skittle-ground; **-brett** n sk.-board; **-fläche** f, math. conical surface; **-förmig** a. conical, coniform; tapering, like a sugar-loaf; **-früchtig** ⚘ a.: ⚐ conocarpous; **-geld** n fee for the use of a skittle-ground.
keg(e)lig (⌣́(⌣)) a. ⑯ = kegelförmig; **-spitz** a. ⊕ vom Schnabel: ⚐ conic-acute.
Kegel¹-junge (⌣⌣́...) m ⑫ skittle-boy, boy who sets up the ninepins; **-kugel** f sk.-ball; **-mantel** m, math. (outer) surface of a cone.
kegeln (⌣́) [nhd.] v/n. (h.), v/a. u. sich ⚐ v/refl. ⑫a. to play (at) skittles or ninepins; weitS. to bowl, to throw.
Kegel¹-partie (⌣⌣́...) f ⑯ game at skittles or at ninepins; **-punkt** m, geom. einer Fläche conical point; **-quadrille** f quadrille with four couples encircling one gentleman; **-rad** n, mach. conical wheel; **-rad-getriebe** n bevel-pinion; **-schieben** v/n. (h.) to play (at) skittles or ninepins; **-schieben** n playing (at) skittles or ninepins; **-schieber** m one who plays (at) skittles or ninepins;

-schnäbler m/pl. orn.: ⚐ conirosters, ...tres; **-schnecke** f, zo.: ⚐ cone (Conus); **-schnitt** m, math. conic section; Lehre von den ~en conic sections, a. conics pl.; **-spieler** m = -schieber; **-stein** m, geol. conical echinite; **-stumpf** m, math.: ⚐ frustum of a cone; **-ventil** ⊕ n, mach. conical valve, spindle (or mitre-plug) valve; **-wurf** m throw at ninepins.
Kegler (⌣́) m ⑫ = Kegelschieber.
Kehl-abschneider (⌣́...) m ⑫ cut-throat; **-ader** f, anat. jugular vein or artery; **-balken** ⊕ m, arch. valley-beam; **-blech** ⊕ n für Dachkehlen: gutter-lead, flashing; **-bohrer** ⊕ m moulding-bit; **-brett** ⊕ n, join. valley-board; **-deckel** m, anat. throat-flap, ⚐ epiglot(tis); **-drüse** f, anat. jugular gland.
Kehle (⌣́) [ahd.: lt. gulaʹ] f ⑯ 1. anat. throat, (Schlund) gullet, F swallow, ⚐ guttur; eine verschleimte ~ h. to have phlegm (F co. a bone) in one's throat; sich die ~ ausspülen, schmieren (trinkend netzen) to rinse (or moisten) one's throat, F to wet one's whistle; mir war die ~ wie zugeschnürt I felt choking, F I felt a lump in my throat; an der ~ packen to seize by the throat; e-m das Messer an die ~ setzen to put the knife to a p.'s throat, fig. to put extreme pressure upon a p.; aus voller ~ lachen to laugh heartily, to burst out laughing; to shout with laughter; sein Vermögen durch die ~ jagen to spend one's fortune in drink; wenn et. in die unrechte ~ (die Luftröhre) kommt if anything goes down the windpipe or F the wrong throat; mit der ~ singen to sing from the throat. — 2. ⊕ arch. chamfer, channel, flute.
kehlen ⊕ (⌣́) I v/a. ⑱ 1. arch. = auskehlen I. — 2. Fischerei: Heringe ⚐ (aufschneiden) to gut. — II ~ n ㉓ 3. = Auskehlung.
Kehl-flosser (⌣́...) m/pl. ⊕ ichth. jugulars pl. (Juguluʹres); **-füß(l)er** m/pl. zo. (Flohkrebse): ⚐ læmodipod(an)s pl. (Læmodiʹpoda); **-hobel** ⊕ m, join. moulding-plane. [fluted.]
kehlig (⌣́) ⊕ arch. channelled, **...kehlig** in Zssn (mit Kehlen versehen) zB. tausend-⚐ with a thousand throats.
Kehl-kopf (⌣́...) m ⊕ anat.: ⚐ larynx; **-kopf-bänder** n/pl. anat.: ⚐ laryngeal ligaments pl.; **-kopf-entzündung** f, path. inflammation of the larynx, ⚐ laryngitis; **-kopf-katarrh** m cold in the larynx, ⚐ laryngeal catarrh; **-kopf-knorpel** m, anat. Adam's apple (Pomum Adaʹmi); **-kopf-krampf** m, path.: ⚐ laryngospasm, laryngismus; **-kopf-nerven** m/pl. anat. laryngeal nerves; **-kopf-schnitt** m, surg. laryngotomy; **-kopf-schwindsucht** f, path.: ⚐ laryngophthisis; **-kopf-spiegel** m, med. laryngoscope; **-kopf-stimme** f, med.: ⚐ laryngophony; **-lappen** m/pl. eines Hahns: gills pl.; **-laut** m guttural sound; **-leiste** f = -stoß; **-linie** ⚔ f, frt.: halbe ~ demi-gorge; **-stoß** ⊕ m, arch. talon, gula; **-stück** ⚔ n eines Harnisches: throat-piece, gorget; **-ton** m guttural sound.
Kehlung (⌣́) f ⑯ 1. = Auskehlung. — 2. ⊕ join. moulding.

[Kehl=ziegel] — 579 — [keinerseits]

Kehl=ziegel ⊕ (ʺ...) m ② arch. gutter-tile, hollow tile.
Kehr¹=aus (ʺ...) [kehren¹] m, inv. bei Bällen: last (or break-up) dance; weitS. close, end; **=besen** m ② broom (for sweeping), besom; **=bürste** f whisk, crumb-brush.
Kehre (ᴗ́) [kehren²] f ❽ 1. (Wendung) turn (-ing). — 2. obb. (Reihe, die e-n trifft) er hatte die ~ it was (or it came to) his turn.
kehren¹ (ᴗ́) [ahd.] v/a., v/n. (h.) ⑱ to sweep; (stäuben) to dust; fig. jeder kehr' vor seiner Tür! mind (or attend to) your own business!; vgl. fegen I u. Besen 1.
kehren² (ᴗ́) [ahd.] v/a., v/n. (ʃn) u. ſich ᴗ v/refl. 1. (wenden) to turn (over); e-m den Rücken ᴗ to turn one's back upon a p.; ſich ᴗ (umwenden) to turn round (on one's heels); ⚔ (abſchwenken) to wheel aside or about; (rechts um) kehrt! (right) about face! — 2. (zum Ausgangspunkte zurückgehen, mehr gbr. in Zssn: heim=, wieder=, zurück=) ᴗ to return, to turn (or come) back; nach Hauſe, in die Heimat ᴗ to return (to one's) home. — 3. das Innerſte nach außen ᴗ to turn (a th.) inside out; das Oberſte zu unterſt ᴗ to turn (everything) upside down; fig. die beſte Seite nach außen ᴗ to show o.s. (or a th.) to the best advantage; die rauhe Seite heraus (oder nach außen) ᴗ to show a p. one's rough side, to be rude to a p., F to cut up rough. — 4. mit prp.: ſich an e-n, et. ᴗ (auf e-n, et. achten) to heed (or mind) a p., a th.; ſich an nichts ᴗ to pay no regard (or heed) to anything; ſich gegen e-n ᴗ to turn against (F to round upon) a p.; den Blick der Seele in ſich ſelbſt ᴗ to commune with o.s., to turn one's glances inwardly; in ſich gekehrt ſein to be wrapt (or lost) in meditation or thought; alles zum beſten ᴗ to turn everything to account or to advantage, to put a good face upon everything.
Kehrer (ᴗ́) [kehren¹] m ㉒, **~in** f ㊵ person who sweeps or handles the broom, sweep(er); weitS. cleaner; (Straßenkreuzungs-)~crossing-sweeper.
Kehr²=eule (ʺ...) f ㉓ (tugelförmiger Besen) Turk's-head, mop; vgl. Eule 4; **=frau** f woman who sweeps, charwoman; **=haufen, =kaſten** m, **=loch** n = Kehrichthaufen, =faß, =loch; **=herd** ⊕ m, metall. sweep(ing)-table.
Kehricht (ᴗ́) m u. n ⑳d. sweepings pl., weitS. dust, dirt, rubbish, F muck.
Kehricht=abfuhr (ʺ...) f ㉓ removal of rubbish (by the dustmen); **=eimer** m, **=faß** n, **=kaſten** m dust-bin; **=haufe(n)** m dust-heap, heap of rubbish, F muckheap; **=loch** n dust-hole; **=ſchaufel** f dustman's shovel, kleinere: dust-pan.
Kehr²=reim ♪ (ʺ...) [kehren²] m ㉒ burden of a song; **=ſcheibe** f revolving target; **=ſeite** f other (or wrong) side, reverse; Sprichw. jedes Ding hat ſeine ~ there is a black side to everything, auch: no rose without a thorn.
Kehrt (ᴗ́) [kehren²] n, inv.: ᴗ=machen ⚔ to face about (vgl. kehren² 1 ⚔); (zurückkehren) to turn back, to return.
Kehr²=tunnel 🚂 (ʺ...) m ㉒ helicoid tunnel, loop-tunnel; **=um** m: a) (Sack-

gaſſe) blind alley; b) = =reim; c) im ~ (im Handumdrehen) in the turn of a hand, F in a jiffy; **=um** adv. (abwechselnd) alternately, in turns; **=wieder** m u. n (Sackgaſſe) blind alley; **=¹wiſch** m duster, rubber.
keifen (ᴗ́) [ndd.] v/n. (h.) ⑱ († ⑳b.) to scold, ⚲ chide; (ſich zanken) to squabble, brawl, jangle; to abuse one another, to spar; ſie ᴗ den ganzen Tag they are bickering and biting all day.
Keifer (ᴗ́) m ㉒, **~in** f ㊵ squabbler, brawler, abusive person; f auch: scold.
Keil (ᴗ́) [ahd.: key] m ⓧc. 1. ⊕ wedge, typ. quoin; mech. (Bolzen), arch. (Schluß-ſtein) key; mach. ~ und Löſe=ᴗ gib and key, gib and cotter; Näherei: piece let in, (Zwickel) gore; ⚔ artill. (Verſchluß-) ~ coin; F ~ Brot hunk of bread; das ſchmälere Ende des ~s the thin end of the wedge (auch oft fig.). — 2. Sprichw. ein ~ treibt den andern one nail drives another; ſ. grob 1. — 3. F burſchikos: ~e pl. = Prügel; ~e kriegen to get a good beating or drubbing.
keil=ähnlich ⊕ (ʺ...) a. ㊺, **=artig** a. wedge-like, vgl. ⚯förmig; **=ärmel** m ㉒ der Damen: leg-of-mutton sleeve; **=bein** n, anat. wedge-bone, des Hinterhauptes: ⚘ sphenoid bone; **=beinflügel=knochen** m, anat.: ⚘ pterygoid (bone); **=bein-naht** f: ⚘ sphenoid suture; **=bohrer** ⊕ m wedge-terrier; **=ein=ſchlagen, =ein-treiben** n driving in wedges, wedging; **=eiſen** n Walzwerk: wedge-iron.
keilen (ᴗ́) I v/a. ⑱ 1. to (cleave with a) wedge; in etwas ᴗ to wedge into a th.; (mit Keilen befeſtigen) to fasten with wedges. — 2. [nhd. 18. sae.] F, bſb. burſchikos: a) = prügeln; b) für et. ᴗ (werben) to canvass for a th. — II ~ n ㉓ 3. (ſ. 1) wedging. — 4. (ſ. 2): a) = Prügelei; b) canvassing.
Keiler¹ ⊕ (ᴗ́) [keilen] m ㉒ one who wedges, wedger. [hunt. wild boar.]
Keiler² (ᴗ́) [nhd. 17. sae., *lit.] m ㉒ zo.,]
Keilerei F (ᴗ́) f ㊵ (Prügelei) fight.
Keil=fäuſtel ⚒ (ʺ...) n ㉓ (Hammer) wedge-driver; **=förmig** a. ㊶ wedge-shaped, wedged, cuneiform, ⚘ cuneate(d), anat.: ⚘ sphenoid(al); **=hacke, =haue** ⚒ f (miner's) pick, pickaxe, mattock; **=inſchrift** f: ⚘ cuneiform inscription; **=joch** ⚒ n wedging-crib or -curb; **=kiſſen** n wedge-shaped bolster; **=kranz** m wedging-crib; **=preſſe** ⊕ f Ölfabr.: wedge-press; **=rahmen** m, typ. quoin-chase; **=ſchlegel** m = =treiber; **=ſchnäbler** m/pl. orn.: ⚘ cuneirostres pl.; **=ſchrift** f der Aſſyrier cuneiform (or arrow-head) writing, wedge-character(s pl.); **=ſchriftkunde** f: ⚘ sphenography, ⚯ſchwänzig a. orn. wedge-tailed; **=ſteg** m, typ. inclined quoin; **=ſtein** m Maurerei: quoin; **=ſtück** n wedge-shaped piece; (Zwickel) gore; **=treiber** ⊕ m wedge-driver; **=ziegel** m wedge-shaped brick or tile; **=zieher** m, typ. shooting-stick.
Keim (ᴗ́) [ahd.] m ⓧc. ⚘, zo. 1. germ, seed-bud; physiol.: ⚘ ovum, ovule; befruchteter ~ embryo; ~ des Malzes sprout; ~e treiben to germinate, ſ. keimen 1. — 2. fig. im ~e in the bud,

a. in posse; ~ e-r Krankheit germs pl. of a disease, seeds pl. of a malady; ſ. erſticken 3.
keimbar (ᴗ́) a. ㊺ = keimfähig.
Keim=bläschen (ʺ...) n ㉓: ⚘ germinal vesicle, blastocyst; **=blatt** n ⚘ cotyledon; **=blätterig** a. ㊺ cotyledonous; **=drüſe** f ⚘, zo. germ-gland.
keimen (ᴗ́) [ahd.] ⑱ I v/n. (h.), bei Veränderung des Zustandes oder Ortes a. ſn) 1. ⚘, zo. to germ(inate) (auch fig.); (hervorkommen) to come up, vom Barte: to grow, to show (itself); (treiben) to shoot (up), to sprout, to spring up; (entſtehen) to arise, to spring forth (a. fig.), (knoſpen) to bud; ⚮ germinating, ⚮ germinant, (entſtehend) nascent; ⚮e Leidenſchaft rising (or growing) passion. — II v/a. 2. (ᴗ machen) to bring to germination; (als Keim hervortreiben) to send (or sprout) forth. — 3. ⊕ Brauerei: die Gerſte wird gekeimt (gequellt)... is being soaked. — III ~ n ㉓ 4. germination; rise; budding.
Keim=faden ⚘ (ʺ...) m e-r Spore germ-tube; **=fähig** a. ㊺ capable of germinating; **=fähigkeit** f germinative (or reproductive) faculty; **=fleck** m germinal dot or spot; chalaza; **=frucht** f der Kryptogamen: ⚘ sporocarp; **=haut** f germ-membrane, blastoderm; **=hülle** f perisperm; **=kern** m germinal nucleus; **=knoſpe** f germ-bud; **=korn** n der Kryptogamen spore; **=plasma** n germplasma; **=ſack** m embryo-sac; **=ſcheibe** f germ-disk; **=ſtoff** m des Eies: ⚘ blastema; **=tötend** a.: ⚘ germicidal.
Keimung (ᴗ́) f ㊵ ⚘, zo. germination; (Wachstum) growth; (Entſtehung) rise; **~s=reife** f ㉓: ⚘ mature germination.
Keim=wall (ʺ...) m ㉒, **=wulſt** m, f ⚘, zo.: ⚘ germinal swelling; **=würzelchen** n radicle; **=zeit** f (period of) germination; **=zelle** f germ-cell; **=züchtung** f culture of germs, ⚮ germiculture.
kein [nhd.] indef. pron. 1. als a. kein m, keine f, kein n ⑯ (C.) no, not any; er ſchuldete mir ᴗ Geld he owed me no money, he did not owe me any money; ᴗe Menſchenſeele not a soul; es ſind (noch) ᴗe vier Wochen her it is not (quite) four weeks ago; es gibt ᴗe Feen mehr there are no more fairies now, ſ. have ceased to exist; ſ. Kind 1 u. 2; er hat gar (ob. durchaus) ᴗ Vertrauen he has no confidence whatever or not the least confidence; ᴗe Silbe weiter not another syllable. — 2. als s. ᴗer m, ᴗe f, ᴗ(e)s n ⑯ keine(r) s. none, not (any) one, no one, nobody, not ... anybody; ᴗ(e)s not one, nothing, not ... anything; ᴗer (ᴗ(e)s) von beiden neither (of the two), neither one nor the other; ᴗer von ihnen not a (single) one of them; ᴗ and(e)rer als Gott none other but God; er iſt ᴗer der Klügſten he is not one of the most prudent (ones).
keinen=falls = keinesfalls.
keiner=lei (ᴗʺ=ᴗ́) [nhd.] a. inv. not of any sort or kind; auf ᴗ Weiſe in no wise or manner or way.
keiner=ſeits (ᴗʺ=ᴗ́) adv. on neither side, in neither quarter or direction.

⚮ scientific; ⚘ botanical; ⚱ geography; ⊕ machinery; ⚒ mining; ⚔ military; ⚓ marine; ⊛ commercial; ✉ postal; 🚂 railway.

[keinesfalls] — 580 — [Kenter]

keines-falls (⁻ᵘ⁻´) adv. not in any case, on no account, on no condition.
keines-wegs (⁻ᵘ⁻´) adv. in no way or wise, by no means, not in the least.
kein-mal (⁻´⁻´) adv. not a single time, not (or never) once; Sprichw. f. einmal 1.
...keit (...'-) [mhd. aus ...heit nach c, f, ch, g] f ⑩ an Abjektive auf =ig, -lich, -bar, -jam angehängt.
Kelch (⁻´) [ahd.; lt. cǎlic-] m ⑪b. 1. cup, goblet, mit Henkel: mug; eccl. chalice, communion-cup; fig. der (bittere) ~ der Leiden the (bitter) cup of sorrow or grief. — 2. (Blumen=)~: ⚹ ♀ calyx; zo. ~ eines Korallenpolypen: ⚹ calice.
kelch-ähnlich (⁻´...) a. ⑥, ⚹artig a. like a cup or calyx, ⚹ calycine, calycoid; =blatt ♀ n ⑫: ⚹ sepal; mit vielen =blättern: ⚹ polysepalous; =blume ♀ f: a) ⚹ calycinal flower; b) ⚹ calycanthus; =blüter ♀ m/pl.: ⚹ calyciflorae; ⚹blütig a.: ⚹ calycifloral; =deckel m, Cath. eccl. patin(e), paten; ♀förmig a. in shape of a cup, ♀: ⚹ calyciform; ♀las n glass in shape of a cup; =hülle ♀ f: ⚹ calycle; ♀los a. without a calyx, ⚹ acalycinous; =narbe ♀ f ⑫ an Früchten: umbril; =schüsselchen n = =deckel; ♀ständig a.: ⚹ calycinal; =streit m, eccl. hist. dispute about the use of the chalice by laymen; =tellerchen n = =deckel; ♀tragend a.: ⚹ calyciferous; =tuch n, Cath. eccl. corporal, purificatory.
Kelle (⁻´) [ahd.] f ⑭, dim. Kellchen (⁻´) n ㉓ 1. (Schöpf=)~ scoop, für Suppe: (soup-)ladle, (Fisch-)~ fish-slice; ⊕ (Gieß-)~ (founder's) ladle; (Maurer=)~ trowel. — 2. F essen was die ~ gibt to take pot-luck.
Keller (⁻´) [ahd.; *lt. cella'rium n] m ㉒ cellar, für Kohlen: coal-cellar; (unterirdisches Gewölbe) (subterraneous) vault, (Vorratsgewölbe) warehouse; (unterirdische Wohnung) underground habitation or room(s pl.), basement.
Keller-assel (⁻´...) f ⑬ zo. wood-louse, sow-bug (Oni'scus ase'llus); =aufzug m lift from a cellar or underground floor, cellar-lift. [small cellar.
Kellerchen (⁻´...) n ㉓ (dim. v. Keller)
Kellerei (⁻´⁻´) [mhd.] f ⑭ cellarage, large cellar; (Wein=)~ wine-cellar; (Brauerei) brewery
Keller-fenster (⁻´...) n ㉓ cellar-window or -skylight; =geschoß n underground floor, auch (fr.) souterrain; =gewölbe n (underground) vault; =hals m: a) mouth (or opening) of a cellar; b) ♀ (Seibelbaft) daphne; echter ~ mezereum (Daphne meze'reum); gelber ~ copse-laureal (D. Laure'ola); =laden m shop in a basement, underground shop or store; =loch n air-(or vent-) hole of a cellar; =lokal n. =wirtschaft; =luft f (damp or fusty) air of a cellar; =luke f = =loch; =magd f cellar-maid; =meister m butler; =miete f rent of a cellar, cellarage; =raum m: a) space in a cellar; b) = Keller; =schlüssel m key of a cellar; =spinne f, zo. cave-spider (Sege'stria cella'ris); =wechsel ⊛ m accommodation-bill; =wirt(in) f m keeper of an under-

ground bar or beer-shop; =wirtschaft f underground bar or restaurant; =wohnung f underground dwelling.
Kellner (⁻´) [mhd.; *Keller] m ㉒, ~in f ⑭ 1. (Kellermeister) butler. — 2. (Aufwartende[r] in Cafés ꝛc.) waiter (f waitress), in Bierlokalen: barman (f barmaid), auch: tapster, F pot-boy (f bisw. auch: pot-girl); fig. f. Koch.
Kelte (⁻´) m ⑭, **Keltin** f ⑭ Celt, ⟵ Kelt.
Kelten-stamm (⁻´...) m ⑫ Celtic (auch: Keltic) nation or tribe.
Kelter ⊕ (⁻´) [ahd.; *lt. calcatu'ra v. calca're treten] f ⑱ (m ㉒) wine-press; ~baum m ⑫ beam of a wine-press; ~bütte f press-vat or -tub.
Kelterer ⊕ (⁻´⁻´) m ㉒ = Kelterknecht.
Kelter-haus (⁻´...) n ⑫ press-shed; =knecht m man who attends to the wine-press; =lohn m fee for use of a w.-press.
keltern ⊕ (⁻´) v/a. ⓐa.: die Trauben ② to press (the juice from the) grapes.
Kelter-schraube ⊕ (⁻´...) f ⑫ (large) screw of a wine-press; =wein m wine from the juice of pressed grapes.
Kelt-iberer (⁻´⁻ᵘ⁻´) m ㉒, ~in f ⑭, Alt.: Celtiberian; **Kelt-iberi-en** ♀ (⁻´⁻ᵘ⁻´) npr/n. ⓐa. (Landstrich im alten Spanien) Celtiberia; **Kelt-iberisch** (⁻´⁻ᵘ⁻´) a. ⑥. Celtiberian.
Keltin f ⑭ f. Kelte. [Celtiberian.
keltisch (⁻´)[Kelte] a. ⑥ Celtic (⟵ Keltic).
Kem(e)nate (⁻´ᵘ´⁻) [ahd.; *lt. Kamin; f ⑱: a) room with a chimney or stove; b) women's apartment or abode, poet. ladies' bower.
kennbar (⁻´-) a. ⑥ knowable, (erkennbar) recognizable; (unterscheidbar) discernible, distinct; **Kennbarkeit** f ⑯ discernibility, distinctness. [letter.
Kenn-buchstabe (⁻´...) m ⑫ characteristic
Kennel-kohle (⁻´ᵘ⁻´) [engl.] f ⑫ (wasserstoffreiche, matte Kohle) cannel-coal.
kennen (⁻´) [ahd.: con, ken; *können] I v/a. u. sich ② v/refl. ⑯b. to know by name, &c.; (bekannt sein mit) to be acquainted with; (verstehen) to understand; et. durch und durch ② to know a th. thoroughly, to know the ins and outs of a th., to have a thorough knowledge of it; gründlich ② to be conversant with or versed in or F well up in; er kennt seinen Plato gründlich he is quite at home in his Plato; das ② wir!, das kennt man schon! we know (all about) that!, those are well-known (or old) tricks!; sie kannten kein Erbarmen they knew (or had) no mercy; wir ② ea. vom Theater we know each other from (or became acquainted at) the theatre; er kennt sich vor Hochmut nicht mehr pride has turned his head, his pride has become unbearable; er ist gar nicht wieder zu ② one would not know him again, you would not recognize him; et. ② lernen to become acquainted with a th.; e-n ② lernen to make a p.'s acquaintance; ein Geschäft ② lernen to learn a business; wir ② seine Absicht nicht we are not acquainted with (or cognizant of) his intention; Sprichw. f. Gebot 1. — II ~ n ㉓ knowing, &c. (f. I); vgl. Kenntnis, bsf. Artikel.

kennens-wert (⁻´...) a. ⑥ worth knowing or learning.
Kenner (⁻´) m ㉒, ~in f ⑭ one who knows, connoisseur, (good) judge, (Fachmann) expert, specialist; (Eingeweihte[r]) adept; er ist ein ~ von Sprachen he is a linguist, F he is a dabster at languages; ~ des Lateinischen, Griechischen Latin, Greek scholar; ~auge (⁻´...) n ⑫, =blick m, =miene f eye, glance, air of a connoisseur or judge; F knowing look.
Kennerschaft (⁻´...) f ⑯ 1. connoisseurship; thorough (or intimate) knowledge, expertness. — 2. coll. (all) connoisseurs pl.
kenn(e)te (⁻´(ᵘ)⁻´) impf. subj. von kennen.
kenntlich (⁻´) [kennen] a. ⑥ knowable, distinguishable, easy to recognize; (bemerklich) conspicuous, durch Zeichen: marked (vgl. kennbar); (sich) ② machen to make (o.s.) known; ~keit (⁻´-) f ⑯ conspicuousness.
Kenntlich-machung (⁻´ᵘ⁻´ᵘ) f ⑯ designation, bes. Eigentums oft: ear-marking; durch aufgeklebte Zettel: labelling.
Kenntnis (⁻´) [kennen] f ⑯ 1. knowledge; (Kunde) information, (Auskunft) intelligence; et. zu j-s ~ bringen, e-n von et. in ~ setzen to inform (or apprise) a p. of a th., to make a th. known (or to intimate a th.) to a p.; es ist zu m-r ~ gelangt, daß // it has come to my knowledge (or I have been informed) that //; ~ von et. nehmen to take not(ic)e (or cognizance) of a th.; sich ~ von et. verschaffen to obtain information about a th., to post o.s. up in a th. 2. Kenntnisse pl. (Wissen) knowledge, information, (Bildung) culture, education; (Fertigkeiten) acquirements, attainments pl.; gute Kenntnisse in seinem Fach besitzen to have a good knowledge of (or a thorough acquaintance with) one's department; sich gründliche Kenntnisse erwerben to acquire (a stock of) solid learning, to make o.s. a thorough scholar; ein Mann von umfangreichen Kenntnissen a man with a large range of knowledge or a vast store of information.
kenntnis-arm (⁻´...) a. ⑥, ♀los a. deficient (or lacking) in knowledge, (unwissend) ignorant; =nahme f ⑱ notice, cognizance; zur (geneigten) ~ for your (better) information or instruction; bei näherer ~ on further investigation or examination; ♀reich a. rich in knowledge, full of information.
Kennung (⁻´) f ⑯ 1. = Kennzeichen. — 2. vet. (Kunde) eye. — 3. ⚓ (Land=)~ landmark.
Kenn-wort (⁻´...) n ⑫ = Motto; =zeichen n mark of distinction, sign, token, des Eigentums: ear-mark; einer Krankheit: symptom; dazu: ♀zeichnen v/a. ⑯b*, * to characterize; to earmark (a. fig.); (stempeln) to stamp (a. fig.); sich ② v/refl. to distinguish o.s.; =ziffer f, math.: ~ (ganze Zahl) eines Logari'thmus: characteristic.
Kenotaphion (⁻´ᵘf(ᵘ)⁻) [grch.] n ㉓ (leeres Ehrengrab) cenotaph.
Kentaur ꝛc. f. Zentaur ꝛc. [(wo)man.
Kenter[1] (⁻´) m ㉒, ~in f ⑭ Kentish

Zeichen (f. S. XVII): F familiär, P Volkssprache, Γ Gaunersprache, ⟵ selten; † alt (auch gestorben); * neu (auch geboren); ⁺⁺ unrichtig;

Kenter²-haken ↓ (ᵛ...) [fentern] *m* ⓶ grappling-iron, *Am.* cant-hook.
fentern (ᵛ) [nbb.; *Kante] ⓶a. **I** *v/a.* 1. ⊕ = fanten¹ 3. — 2. ↓ e-n Kahn ⚓ to upset (or overturn) a boat. — **II** ↓ *v/n.* (sn) 3. vom Schiffe: (umschlagen) to capsize; *fig.* v. e-m Schirm: to be turned inside out.
Keramik (ᵛ᪾) [grch.] *f* ⓯ (Töpferkunst) ceramic (or potter's) art or department, ceramics.
keramisch (ᵛ᪾) [grch.] *a.* ⓯ ⓸amic.
Keratin (ᵛ᪾) [grch.] *n* ⓶d. (Hornstoff) ceratin(e).[(in)dent,(Sägeschnitt)a.kerf.
Kerbe ⊕ (ᵛ) [:kerf; *ferben] *f* ⓷ notch,
Kerbel (ᵛ) [ahd. lt., *grch.] *m* ⓶ (*Chaerophy'llum, Anthri'scus, Myrrhis*): betäubender ~ rough chervil (*Chaerophy'llum te'mulum*); echter ~ (true) chervil (*Anthri'scus cerefo'lium*); spanischer ~ sweet chervil (*Myrrhis odora'ta*).
ferben (ᵛ) [mhd.: carve] **I** *v/a.* ⓷ 1. to notch, to (in)dent; Nadeln: to channel. — 2. (ausz.acken) ⚘ to cren(ul)ate; Münzen ⅔. ⚓ (ränbeln) to gnarl, to mill; ⚘ gekerbt: ⚘ crenate(d); fein gekerbt: ⚘ crenulate(d). — **II** ~ *n* ⓶ 3. = Kerbung 1.
Kerb-holz (ᵛ᪾) *n* ⓶ tally, notched stick, score; Kerben aufs ~ schneiden to tally, to score; *fig.* aufs ~ setzen to book (down), F to chalk up; bei e-m auf dem ~ stehen to be on a p.'s books, to be in debt with a p.
Kerb-messer ⊕ (ᵛ...) *n* ⓶ (cooper's) notching-knife; **=schnitt** *m* scallop; **=schnitzerei** *f* chip-carving; **=stock** *m* =holz; **=tier** *n*, *zo.* insect.
Kerbung (ᵛ) *f* ⓯ (f. ferben I) 1. notching, indentation. — 2. ⅔: ⚘ crenature.
Kerb-zahn ⚘ (ᵛ...) *m* ⓶: ⚘ crenature; ⚘**zähnig** ⚘ *a.* ⓯: ⚘ crenato-dentate, crenate(d). [(= Kerbtier, Insekt).]
Kerf (ᵛ) [nbb. Kerb...] *m* ⓶b. insect]
Kerker (ᵛ) [ahd.; *lt. *carcer*] *m* ⓶ jail, prison, (Berlies) dungeon; in den ~ werfen to put into jail.
kerker-artig (ᵛ...) *a.* ⓯ dungeon-like; **=fieber** *n* ⓶ jail-fever; **=haft** *f* incarceration, imprisonment; **=meister** (in *f*) *m* jailer, turnkey; **=pforte** *f* prison-gate; **=strafe** *f* = =haft; ~ leiden to be incarcerated, to suffer imprisonment, to sit in jail; **=turm** *m* keep. — Vgl. auch Gefängnis...
Kerl (ᵛ) [ahd.: churl] *m* ⓶c. (P ⓷) fellow, F chap, P bloke; weitS. individual; bisw. (Bedienter) man-servant, F flunkey; armer ~ poor fellow, F poor chap or devil; durchtriebener ~ F artful dodger or blade; ehrlicher ~ honest fellow; elender ~ wretch, villain; ein ganzer ~ a splendid (or fine) fellow, F a brick (of a fellow), a trump; gemeiner ~ common (or low) fellow, blackguard; geriebener ~ smart (or cunning) fellow; grober ~ rude (or rough) fellow, churl; guter ~ good(-natured) fellow, er ist ein guter ~, a. oft: F he is a good (or the right) sort; langer ~, lang aufgeschossener, schmächtiger ~ long, lanky fellow, F lamp-post; liederlicher ~ fast (or gay) fellow, rake; lustiger ~ jolly fellow, F merry sort; oft *iro.* du bist (mir) ein netter ~ you are a nice fellow or F a nice sort or a beauty; schlechter ~ scoundrel, rogue, scamp.

Kerlchen (ᵛ) *n* ⓷ (*dim.* von Kerl) little fellow or F chap, F *co.* whippersnapper, hop-o'-my-thumb; das ist ein tapferes (schmuckes) ~ he is a brave (dapper) little man.
Kermes (ᵛ) [ar. pers.; *sft.] *m*, *inv.* ent. kermes(-grains *pl.*).
Kermes-baum ⚘ (ᵛ...) *m* ⓶ = =eiche; **=beere** ⚘ *f* foxglove, pigeon-berry (*Phytola'cca deca'ndra*); **=eiche** ⚘ *f* kermesoak (*Quercus cocci'fera*); **=törner** ⊕ *n/pl.* = =Kermes; **=rot** *a.* ⓯ u. *n* cochineal; **=schildlaus** *f*, *ent.* kermes(-insect) (*Loca'nium i'licis*).
Kern (ᵛ) [ahd.: kern(el); *Korn] *m* ⓶b. 1. kernel, ⚘ nucleus (a. *ast.* von Kometen); ~ im Griebs von Äpfeln u. Birnen, in Apfelsinen, Weinbeeren: pip, ⚘ pyrene; von Steinobst: stone, einer Haselnuß ꝛc.: kernel, von Getreide: grain. — 2. ~ (Mark) von Bäumen: pith; ~ (Herz) von Salat ꝛc.: heart; ~ (Seele) e-r Kanone: bore, e-s Taues core; *fig.* der ~ (das Innerste) einer Sache the pith (or gist) of a matter; (das Wichtigste) the quintessence, the most essential (or vital) point, the main issue; ~ (Auswahl) der Gesellschaft, des Heeres élite (or cream) of society, flower of the army; bis in den ~ von etwas dringen to get to the very core (or bottom) of a th.; das also war des Pudels ~! (*G.*) this then was the poodle's purport!, weitS. that's what it meant; hierzu F des Pudels ~ the gist of the matter, the main substance or thing.
Kern-apfel (ᵛ) *m* ⓶ calville; **⚘artig** *a.* ⓯ kernel-like, ⚘ nucleoid; vgl. ⚘**förmig**; **=ausdruck** *m* pithy (or vigorous, strong) expression; vgl. =wort; **=beißer** *m*, *orn.* gros(s)beak (*Cocco-thrau'stes*); gemeiner ~ cherry-finch, hawfinch (*C. vulga'ris*); großer ~ silverbill, waxbill (*Pini'cola enuclea'tor*); ⚘**brav** *a.* honest to the backbone, thoroughly good; **=büchse** ⊕ *f* Gießerei: core-box; ⚘**deutsch** *a.* German to the core; **=drehbank** ⊕ *f* core-frame.
fernen¹ (ᵛ) *v/a.* ⓯ = auskernen I.
fernen² nordb. (ᵛ) [nbb...] *v/a.* ⓯ (buttern) to churn.
kern-faul (ᵛ...) *a.* ⓯ rotten at (or to) the core; ⚘**fest** *a.* very solid, (as) firm as a rock; **=feuer** ⚘ *n* ⓶ central fire; **=fleisch** *n*: a) prime cut, solid meat; b) = Brustkern; ⚘**förmig** *a.* in shape of a kernel or pip, ⚘ pyrenoid; ⚘**frisch** *a.* quite fresh; **=frucht** *f* stone-fruit, ⚘ pyrenocarp; **=gehäuse** *n* einer Frucht core; ⚘**gesund** *a.* thoroughly healthy, (as) sound as a roach; **=guß** ⊕ *m* Gießerei: casting upon a core, cored work; ⚘**gut** *a.* thoroughly good, of sterling quality.
fernhaft (ᵛ...) *a.* ⓯ = kernig 2 (mst *fig.*); **~igkeit** (ᵛ...) *f* ⓯ = Kernigkeit.
Kern-haus ⚘ (ᵛ...) *n* = =gehäuse; **=holz** *n* heart of (the trunk of) a tree, heartwood, ⚘ duramen.
fernicht (ᵛ...) *a.* ⓯ 1. like a kernel or pip or grain. — 2. = kernig 1.

kernig (ᵛ...) *a.* ⓯ **1.** full of pips or grains, ⚘ acinose. — **2.** *fig.* (martig) pithy; (derb) solid, v. Worten: forcible; (fest) firm; (start) strong, robust, vigorous, (gesund) sound, healthy.
Kernigkeit (ᵛ...) *f* ⓯ (f. kernig 2) pithiness; solidity, forcibleness; strength.
Kern-lied (ᵛ...) *n* ⓶ select song or hymn, popular air; ⚘**los** *a.* ⓯ without kernel or core, coreless, ⚘ enucleate(d), *fig.* without strength or a backbone; **=mensch** *m* ⓶ genuine person; **=obst** ⚘ *n* (Äpfel, Birne ꝛc.) fruit with pips, kernel-fruit; **=punkt** *m* essential point; den ~ treffen to hit the main point or the mark; **=saft** *m*, *physiol.*: ⚘ enchylema, nucleoplasm; **=schatten** *m* deepest (or darkest) shadow, *ast.*: ⚘ umbra; **=schuß** *m* point-blank (shot); einen ~ tun to make a bull's-eye; **=schußweite** *f* point-blank range; **=seife** *f* grained soap; first-class soap; **=spindel** ⊕ *f* Gießerei: core-spindle; **=sprache** *f* vigorous (or terse, pithy, forcible) language; **=spruch** *m* pithy (or expressive) saying; **=stahl** *m* solid (or first-rate) steel; **=truppen** *f/pl.* picked troops *pl.*; **=ware** ⚘ *f* first-class (or choice, select) goods *pl.*; **=wolle** ⚘ *f* prime wool or locks *pl.*; **=wort** *n* expressive term, word of deep (or full) meaning.
Kersey ᵀ (tö-r-f°) [nbb.; ⚘ ~ engl. Dorf] *m* (*n*) ⓸ (grober Wollstoff) kersey.
Kerze (ᵛ) [ahd.; *f* ⓷, *dim.* Kerzchen (ᵛ) *n* ⓷ candle; (Wachslicht) wax candle, (Wachsstock) taper; (Talglicht) tallow (or dip-)candle. (Binsenlicht) rush-light.
Kerzen-anzünder (ᵛ...) *m* ⓶ (Gerät u. Person) candle-lighter; **=beere** ⚘ *f* (Frucht von *Aleuri'tes tri'loba*) candleberry; **=docht** *m* wick of candle; ⚘**gerade** *a.* ⓯ (as) straight as a die or an arrow, erect as a dart; er hält sich ~ he walks very (or bolt-)upright; **=gießer** ⊕ *m*=**gießmaschine** ⊕ *f* candle-maker, chandler; candle-moulding machine; ⚘**glühend** *n* incandescent candle-light; **=halter** ⚘ *m* candle-holder; **=händler** ⚘ *m* chandler; ⚘**hell(er Saal)** *a.* (room) lit up with candles; **=leuchter** *m* candle-stick; ⚘**licht** *n*, **=schein** *m* candle-light; beim ⚘**lichte** by candle-light; **=stärke** *f*, *phys.*, &c. (Lichtstärke einer Kerze) candle-power; *elect.* Lampe von 8 ~n eight-candle-power lamp; **=träger(in** *f*) *m* taper-bearer; **=weihe** *f*, *Cath. eccl.* blessing of candles; biS. (Lichtmeß) Candlemas; **=ziehmaschine** ⊕ *f* candle-dipper.
Kescher (ᵛ...) [lit.] *m* ⓶ (Netz zum Schmetterlingsfange) butterfly-net, auch: ring- (or gauze-)net; (kleines Fischnetz) landing- (or spoon-)net; ⚘**n** *v/a.* ⓷a. to catch with a ring-net, weitS. F to net.
Kessel (ᵛ) [ahd.: kettle] *m* ⓶ 1. kettle, ehm. auch caldron; ein ~ voll a kettleful; ~ am Herde, der Dampfmasch. ꝛc.: boiler; großer ~ für Wäsche ꝛc.: copper; (Tee-) ~ tea-kettle; *Cath. eccl.* ~ für das Weihwasser: holy-water pot or font; verzinnter ~ tinned kettle or copper; den ~ ans Feuer setzen to put the kettle on; ~ flicken to mend kettles or

[Kesselarbeit] — 582 — [kichern]

pots and pans; *fig.* alles in e-n ~ werfen to treat all alike. — 2. (kesselförmige Vertiefung) deep hollow, ⚒ excavation, (Wasserbecken) basin; ⚓ Wasserbau: (Schleusenkammer) sluice-chamber; ⚘ (von Bergen umschlossene Gegend) basin-shaped valley or gorge; die Stadt liegt (wie) in e-m ~ ... lies buried in a valley, ... is encircled by mountains; ~ e-s Vulka'ns crater. — 3. ⚒ ~ eines Mörsers ꝛc.: bell-muzzle. — 4. *hunt.* kennel of a badger, &c., couch of a boar; (Platz, in den das Wild eingestellt wird) enclosure. — 5. ⚓ (Krümmung am Ufer) curved (or winding, sinuous) bank or shore, trend.
Kessel-arbeit (ˢ◡...) ⊕ *f* ⚙ bsd. Dampfm.: boiler-work; **-batterie** *f*: a) ⚒ mortar-battery; b) ⚙ battery of boilers; **-bekleidung** *f* = -wandung; **-blau** *n* furnace-blue; **-blech** ⊕ *n* boiler-plate; **-bombe** ⚒ *f* mortar-bomb; **-braun** *n* furnace-brown; **-brunnen** *m* fountain flowing into a basin; **-feuerung** ⊕ *f* furnace of a boiler; **-flicker** *m* tinker; **-förmig** *a.* in shape of a kettle or caldron, *v.* Tälern: basin-like; **-gestell** *n* kettle-stand or -rest; **-gewölbe** *n, arch.* cupola; **-haken** *m* pot-hanger; **-jagd** *f, jagen n, hunt.* wholesale slaughter of game which is gradually driven into an enclosure, auch: battue(-shooting); **-lager** ⊕ *n* bedding of a boiler, boiler-bearer; **-pauke** ♪ *f* kettledrum, tymbal; **-probe** *f*, **-revision** ⊕ *f* boiler-test(ing); **-schläger** *m*, **-schmied** ⊕ *m* brazier, coppersmith; **-schmiede** ⊕ *f* brazier's forge; **-stein** ⊕ *m* fur (collected) in boilers; **-steuern** ⊕ *f/pl.* stays *pl.* of a boiler; **-tal** *n* ⚘ deep basin-shaped valley; **-treiben** *n* = -jagd; **-tuch** ⊕ *n* cloth dyed in the piece; **-wandung** ⊕ *f* shell of a boiler; **-waren** ⊕ *f/pl.* iron cooking- (or kitchen-) utensils, (iron) pots and pans *pl.*
Keßler ⊕ (ˢ◡) *m* ⚙ 1. = Kesselschmied. — 2. = Kesselflicker.   [work.]
Keßler-arbeit ⊕ (ˢ◡...) *f* ⚙ brazier's
Keßlerei ⊕ (ˢ◡ˡˡ) *f* ⚙ = Kesselschmiede.
Keßler-waren ⊕ (ˢ◡...) *f/pl.* ⚙ = Kesselwaren.
Kettchen (ˢ◡) *n* ⚙ (*dim. von* Kette) little chain, chainlet.
Kette¹ (ˢ◡) [ahd.: chain; * It. *catĕnă*] *f* ⚙ 1. chain, kleine ~, a. chainlet (vgl. Kettchen); ⚘ (Uhr-)~ watch-chain; *mech.* endlose, geschlossene ~ endless chain; *phys.* galvanische ~ (Verbindung) galvanic circuit or connexion; die ~ bilden, in die ~ treten to form a chain, an die ~ legen to fasten to a chain, to chain up; in ~n legen (werfen) to put (to cast) into chains or fetters; von der ~ losmachen to unchain; und wär' er in ~n geboren (SCH.) had he born in bondage; *fig.* ~ der Ereignisse, der Tatsachen series of events, concatenation of facts. — 2. ⊕ ~ ohne Ende endless chain; Weberei: warp; ~ und Einschlag warp and woof. — 3. ⚒ (Posten-)~ chain of posts, a. (fr.) cordon. — 4. ⚘ (Berg-)~ range of mountains, mountain-chain. — 5. (Längenmaß von 10 Metern) decametre (annähernd: 10 yards 2 feet 10³⁄₄ inches).

Kette² (ˢ◡) [ahd.] *f* ⚙ *hunt.* ~ Rebhühner covey of partridges.
Kettel (ˢ◡) [Kette] *m* ⚙, *f* ⚙ = Kettchen.
ketteln (ˢ◡) *v/a.* ⚒a. 1. to attach (or fasten) with a small chain. — 2. Näherei: (am Stickrahmen sticken) to tambour.
ketten (ˢ◡) *v/a. u.* sich² *v/refl.* ⚙: (sich) ² to tie (o.s.) with a chain, to chain (o.s.).
Ketten-anker ⚓ (ˢ◡...) *m* ⚙ chain-moorings *pl.*; **-anscheren** *n* Weberei: warping; **-anscherer** *m* Weberei: warper; **-baum** *m* am Webstuhl: warp-beam; **-bruch** *m, math.* continued fraction; **-brücke** *f* chain- (or suspension-)bridge; **-dampf-schiffahrt** *f* = -schlepp-schiffahrt; **-druck** ⊕ *m* Zeugdruckerei: printing of the warp; **-faden** ⊕ *m* Weberei: warp-thread; **-fähre** *f* chain-ferry; **-feier** *f, Cath. eccl.*: Petri ~ (1. Aug.) Lammas(-day); **-förmig** *a.* (shaped) like a chain, ⚘ catenary; **-garn** *n* Weberei: warp(-thread); **-gebläse** *n* chain-blowing apparatus, **-geklirr** *n* clanking of chains; **-gelenk** *n* link of a ch.; ch.-loop; **-gerassel** *n* rattling of chains; **-getriebe** *n, mach.* ch.-gear; **-hund** *m* chained-up watch-dog; **-kasten** ⚓ *m* chain-locker; **-kupplung** ⊕ *f* ch.-coupling; **-länge** ⚓ *f* ch.-length; **-linie** *f, math.*: catenary curve; **-naht** *f* chain-stitch seam; **-nietungsstoß** ⚓ *m* ch.-riveted butt; *ehm.* **-panzer** ⚒ *m* ch.-mail; **-rechnung** *f*, **-regel** *f ehm.*: chain-rule, *jetzt*: compound (or double) rule of three; **-ring** *m* = -gelenk; **-scheren** *n* Weberei: warping; **-scherer** *m* warper; **-schlepp-schiffahrt** ⚓ *f* chain-towing; **-schluß** *m, phls.* ch.-syllogism, ⚘ sorites; **-schmied** *m* smith who forges chains, ch.-maker; **-schuß** *m ehm.* ⚒ ch.-shot; **-seide** ⚘ *f* organzine; **-spul-maschine** ⊕ *f* Weberei: winding-frame or -engine; **-stange** *f* Weberei: warp-rod; **-stich** *m* Näherei: chain- (or tambour-, warp-) stitch; **-stift** *m* ch.-pin; **-strafe** *f* (sträfling *m*) confinement (convict) in chains or irons; **-stropp** ⚓ *m* ch.-sling; **-stuhl** *m* Weberei: warp-loom; **-tau** ⚓ *n* chain-cable; **-trieb-rad** ⊕ *n* chain-pulley; **-werk** *n* ch.-work; **-winde** ⚓ *f* ch.-jack; **-wirbel** ⚓ *m* ch.-swivel.
...kettig ⊕ (...ˢ◡) *a.* ⚙ in Zssgn, Weberei, zB. hoch- (ob. senkrecht-)² with a high warp.
Kettler ⊕ (ˢ◡) *m* ⚙ chain-maker.
Ketzer (ˢ◡) [mhd.; * grch. *kátharo's*] *m* ⚙ 1. (auch **-in** *f* ⚙) *eccl.* (Andersgläubige(r)) heretic (auch *fig.* von Andersgesinnten). — 2. ⊕ = Kötzer.   [heterodoxy.]
Ketzerei (◡ˢ◡ˡ) *f* ⚙ *eccl.*, &c. heresy,
Ketzer-gericht (ˢ◡...) *n hist.* (court of) inquisition; **-geschichte** *f* history of heresy, ⚘ heresiography; **-haupt** *n*: ² heresiarch.
ketzerisch (ˢ◡) *a.* ⚙ heretical; heterodox.
Ketzer-richter (ˢ◡...) *m* ⚙ inquisitor; **-riecher** *m, hist.* heretic-hunter; **-verbrennung** *f*, **-verfolgung** *f* burning, persecution of heretics.
keuchen (¹◡) [mhd.: cough] **I** *v/n.* (h.) ⚙ 1. to pant, to gasp, to breathe with difficulty, to wheeze, von Pferden: (pfeifen) to roar; ²d und schnaufend ² puffing and blowing. — 2. (engbrüstig sein) to be short-winded or asthmatical, von Pferden a. to be broken-winded. — **II** ~ *n* ⚙ 3. panting, &c. (f. I); (Engbrüstigkeit) short- (or broken-) windedness, asthma.
Keucher (¹◡) *m* ⚙, **~in** *f* ⚙ one who pants or gasps, weitS. asthmatical person; von Pferden: roarer.
Keuch-husten (¹¹◡) *m* ⚙ *path.* whooping-cough, ⚘ *tussis convulsiva.*
Keule (¹◡) [mhd.] *f* ⚙ 1. a) als Waffe (a. von Geistlichen im Mittelalter) und als Turngerät: club; (Knüttel) cudgel, bludgeon; mit der ~ (erschlagen to club (to death); b) *ent.* ~ am Fühler der Käfer: *clavola*, ...*et*. — 2. ⚘ ~ des Mörsers pestle of a mortar. — 3. Schlächterei, Kocht. (Oberschenkel v. Tieren) leg of mutton, of a goose, &c.; (Vorderbug von Schlachtvieh) shoulder of mutton, &c.
Keulen-ärmel (¹◡...) *m* ⚙ leg-of-mutton sleeve; **-förmig** *a.* ⚙ club-shaped, clubbed, ⚘ claviform, clavate(d), corynidan, *ent.* v. Käfern: mit den Fühlern, Tastern: clavicorn, clavipalp; **-früchtig** ♃ *a.* von Moosen: ⚘ cladocarpous; **-granne** ♃ *f*: corynephorus; **-käfer** *m, ent.*: ⚘ corynodes; **-polyp** *m, zo.*: ⚘ corynid; **-schlag** *m* blow (or stroke) with a club; **-schmiele** ♃ *f* = -granne; **-schwamm** ♃ *m* club-top, goat's-beard (*Clava'ria*); **-schwinger** *m* one who brandishes a club; **-träger** *m* clubman, man bearing a club; **-wurm** *m, zo.*: geschwänzter ~ tailed worm (*Pria'pulus*).
Keuler (¹◡) *m* ⚙ = Keiler².
keulig (¹◡) *a.* ⚙ club-shaped.
Keuper ⚘ (¹◡) *m* ⚙ *geol.* (obere Trias-schicht) † keuper, red marl.
keusch (¹) [ahd.] *a.* ⚙ chaste; (rein, unbefleckt) pure, innocent, untainted, immaculate; ein ²es Mädchen, a. oft: a modest (or respectable, virtuous) girl.
Keusch-baum ♃ (¹¹...) *m* ⚙, **-lamm(-strauch** *m*) *n* (weidenähnlicher Baum) *n* chaste-tree, agnus castus (*Vitex agnus castus*).
Keuschheit (¹◡) *f* ⚙ (f. keusch) chastity; purity, innocence; modesty, virtue; Gelübde der ~ vow of chastity.
Keusch-kraut ♃ (¹¹◡) *n* ⚙ = Sinnpflanze.
kg, öft. *kg abbr.* = Kilogramm.
Kgl., **Kgr.** *abbr.* = königlich, Königreich.
k. H. *abbr.* = kurzerhand.
Khaki (¹◡) [pers. *Kaki*] *n* (Farbe), *m* (Stoff) khaki; ²**farben** (¹¹◡...) *a.* ⚙ khaki(-coloured); **~uniform** ⚒ *f* ⚙ khaki uniform.
Khan (t¹, r-r ◡) [türk, *ar.*] *m* ⚙d. (⚙): a) (tatar. Fürst) khan; b) ² Han (Herberge); **~at** (...¹) [lt.] *n* ⚙c. (Herrschaft, Würde e-s ~s) khanate.
Khedive (t-¹◡, r-r ◡...) [türk. *pers.*] *m* ⚙ (Vizekg. v. Ägypten) khedive.
Kiautscho-u ⚘ (tj◡¹◡...) [chin. Lehmstadt] *npr. n* ⚙α. (dtsch. Pachtgebiet seit 1897) Kiouchou.
Kibitka ⚒, ...**ke** (◡¹◡) [russ.] *f* ⚙ (rundes Kirgisenzelt u. russisches Fuhrwerk) kibitka.
Kicher(-erbse ♃) (¹◡) *m* Ab.; * It. *ci'cer n* ⚙ chick-pea (*Cicer arieti'num*); (Platterbse) vetchling (*La'thyrus*).
kichern (ˢ◡) [ahd.] **I** *v/n.* (h.) ⚒a. to giggle, titter, chuckle, F to snigger. — **II** ~ *n* ⚙ = Gekicher.

[kichersauer] — 583 — [Kilowatt]

kicher=sauer (⁵⌣...) a. ⚛ chm.: ⚗ ciceric; =säure f ⚗ ciceric acid.
kicken ĭ (ᴵ⌣) [engl.] v/a. ⚽ Sport: to kick.
Kicks (ᴵ) [lautm.] m ①a. Billard: miss, F boss; einen ~ m. = kicksen; **kicksen** (ᴵ⌣) v/n. (h.) ⚽ to miss (the ball).
Kiebitz (ᴵ⌣)[mhd. lautm.] m ①a. orn. lapwing, peewit, plover (*Vanellus cristatus*); ~ei n: a) lapwing's egg; b) ♀ guineahen (flower) (*Fritillaria meleagris*).
Kiefer¹ (ᴵ⌣) [mhd.: Käfer] m ② 1. anat. u. zo. jaw(-bone), ⚗ maxilla; bef. v. Tieren auch: chop; Ober= (Unter=)2 upper (lower) jaw. — 2. zo. bef. ~ der Insekten: ⚗ mandible.
Kiefer² ♀ (ᴵ⌣) [nhd. *Kienföhre] f ⚛ pine, bef. gemeine ~ Scotch pine (*Pinus silvestris*).
kiefer¹-**förmig** (ᴵᴵ⌣...) a. ⚛: ⚗ maxilliform, mandibuliform.
Kiefericht¹ (ᴵ⌣⌣) n ①d. pine-wood.
kiefericht² (ᴵ⌣⌣) a. ⚛ (of) pine; (harzig) resinous.
kieferig (ᴵ⌣⌣) [Kiefer¹] a. ⚛ 1. provided with jaws or mandibles, ⚗ mandibulate(d). — 2. in Zssgn, z.B. groß=2 with large jaws or jaw-bones.
Kiefer¹-**klemme** (ᴵᴵ⌣...) f ⚛ med. lockjaw; =los a. ⚛ without a jaw or mandible; =muskel m, anat.: ⚗ maxillary (muscle).
kiefern (ᴵ⌣) [Kiefer²] a. ⚛ (of) pine.
Kiefer(n)²-**blattwespe** (ᴵᴵ⌣...) f ⚛ pineworm (*Lophyrus*); =bohle f pine plank, deal board; =gehölz n pine-wood; =holz n pine-timber; =kreuzschnabel m, orn. parrot-crossbill (*Loxia pityopsittacus*); =schwärmer m, ent. pine-hawkmoth (*Sphinx pinastri*); =¹taster m der Insekten: maxillary palp; =²wald m pine-wood; =zapfen m pine-cone; =¹zungenmuskel m, anat. ⚗ genioglossus.
Kieke prove. (ᴵ⌣) [ndb.] f ⚛ (Fußwärmer) warming-pan, foot-warmer.
kieken F prove. (ᴵ⌣) [ndb. = gucken] v/n. (h.) ⚽ (gucken) to peep; **Kieker** m ⚛ = Fernrohr, Lorgnette, Lupe; **Kiek-in-die-welt** (ᴵ⌣⌣⌣⌣) m ⚽ (Neuling) greenhorn.
Kiel¹ (ᴵ) [mhd.: quill] m ①c. 1. quill of a pen; (die ganze Feber) (quill-)pen. — 2. (enge Röhre) narrow tube; ~ an der Angel float of a fishing-line. — 3. hort. (Zwiebel) bulb.
Kiel² (ᴵ) [ndb. = keel] m ①c. 1. ⚓ (Grundbalken des Schiffes) keel; vom ~ bis zum Flaggenknopf from keel to truck. — 2. a) orn. (Kamm des Brustbeins), b) ♀ (Schifchen v. Schmetterlingsblüten): ⚗ carina.
Kiel³ (ᴵ) [ahd.] m ①c. poet. = Schiff.
Kiel¹-**bett** (ᴵᴵ...) n ⚛ feather-bed; =²blätter ♀ n/pl. der Schmetterlingsblüter: keel-petals pl.; =block ⚓ m keel-block; =bogen ⚛ m, arch. keel-arch; =boot ⚓ n keel-boat.
kielen¹ (ᴵ⌣) [Kiel¹] ⚽ I v/n. 1. (zu von Federn: (sprossen) to grow (to full size); die Federn sind dem Vogel gekielt the bird's feathers are fully grown. — 2. (h.) (Kiele bekommen) die Gans hat gekielt ... is fledged. — II v/a. 3. ein Klavier 2 to quill a piano.
kielen² ⚓ (ᴵ⌣) [Kiel²] v/a. ⚽ 1. ein Schiff 2 (mit einem Kiel versehen) to furnish ... with a keel. — 2. = kielholen.

Kiel¹-**feder** (ᴵᴵ...) f ⚛ quill-pen; =¹förmig a. ⚛ quill-shaped; =²förmig a. ⚛ keel-shaped, keeled, ⚗ carinate(d); =fuge f Schiffbau: rabbet; =gang ⚓ m garboard-strake or -streak; =geld ⚓ n keelage; 2holen ⚓ v/a. ⚛*,* ein Schiff 2 (auf die Seite legen) to careen ..., to heave down ...; e-n Matrosen 2 (ehm. zur Strafe unterm Schiff durchziehen) to keelhaul ...; ~ n ⚛, =holung f ⚛ careening, careenage; keelhauling; =laschung ⚓ f keelscarf; =lichter ⚓ m f. Bullen; 2los a. ♀ u. zo. keelless; =¹pinsel m paint-brush made of a quill; =²planke ⚓ f garboard-plank; =platz m f. =werft; =raum ⚓ m ship's hold; =schwein, =schwinn ⚓ n keelson; =sims ⚛ m, arch. keel-moulding; =wasser ⚓ n wake (of the ship), dead-water; =werft f careening-beach, -wharf.

Kieme (ᴵ⌣) [ndb. = Kiefer¹] f ⚛ ichth., &c.: ~n pl. (Atmungsorgane der Fische u. niederen Wassertiere) gills, ⚗ branchiæ pl.
Kiemen=atmer (ᴵᴵ⌣...) m ⚛ ichth., &c. gill-breather; =atmung f gill-breathing; =bogen ⚛ m, arch. gill-arch; =deckel m, ichth., &c. gill-cover or flap, ⚗ opercle, operculum; =faser f gillfilament; 2förmig a. ⚛: ⚗ branchiform; =fuß m ⚛ branchireme; =füß(l)er m/pl. water-fleas, ⚗ branchiopods pl.; =haut f gill-flap, ⚗ branchiostegite; =hautfisch m ⚗ branchiostegan; =höhle f gill-cavity, -chamber, -sac; =öffnung f gill-opening; =schwänze m/pl. (Krebstiere) branchiura pl.; =spalte ⚛ m gill-cleft, -slit; =tiere n/pl.: ⚗ ichthyoids pl.; 2tragend a.: ⚗ branchiferous.
Kiemer (ᴵ⌣) m ⚛ in Zssgn. ichth., &c., meist: ⚗ ...branchiate, z.B. Büschel=2 m: ⚗ lophobranchiate.

Kien (ᴵ) [ahd.] m ⚛c. resinous (pine) wood; ~apfel m ⚛ pine-(or fir-)cone; ~baum m pine-tree; ~bohrer m, ent. pine-weevil (*Pissodes strobi*).
kienen (ᴵ⌣) [Kien] a. ⚛ (made) of resinous (pine)wood.
Kien=föhre ♀ (ᴵᴵ...) f ⚛ f. Kiefer²; =harz n resin of pine-trees; =holz n resinous (pine)wood.
kienicht, kienig (ᴵ⌣) a. ⚛ resinous.
Kien-öl ♀ (ᴵᴵ...) n ⚛ pine-oil; =ruß m pine-soot; =span m zum Leuchten burning chip (or splinter) of pinewood.
Kiepe (ᴵ⌣) [ndb.: coop] f ⚛ 1. back-basket, dosser; (Korb mit Deckel) wicker-basket (closed) with a lid. — 2. (tiefenförmiger Stroh- ob. Basthut) bef. ehm. poke-bonnet.
Kieper (ᴵ⌣) m ⚛ 1. = Köper. — 2. = Küfer.
Kies (ᴵ) [mhd.] m ⚛a. 1. ~(=sand) gravel (ly sand); grober ~ am Meeresstrande 2c. shingle. — 2. ⚒ u. min. (Erz, worin nichtmetallische Stoffe vorherrschen): ⚗ pyrites.
Kies=ader ⚒ (ᴵᴵ...) f ⚛ streak of pyrites; 2ähnlich a. ⚛, 2artig a. gravelly, shingly; ⚒ u. min.: pyritous; =bach m stream which carries gravel or shingle; =boden m gravelly soil; =brenner ⚒ m pyriteskiln or -burner.
Kiesel (ᴵ⌣) [ahd.: *Kies] m ⚛ pebble, flint, ⚗ silex, prove. ~ Hagel.
Kiesel=ader ⚒ (ᴵᴵ⌣...) f ⚛ im Schiefer: vein of flint; 2artig a. ⚛ flinty, ⚗ silicious; =erde f flinty (or siliceous) soil or earth; chm. silica (SiO_2); 2erdehaltig a.: ⚗ siliciferous; =fels m flinty rock; =fluor-kalium n, chm. potassium silico-fluoride (K_2SiF_6); =fluorwasserstoff-säure, =flußsäure f, chm. silicofluoric (or hydro-fluosilicic) acid (H_2SiF_6); =gebirge n, geol. silicious rocks pl.; =glas ⚛ n flint-glass; =grund m pebbly soil; =gur f, geol., min. infusorial silica, fossil dust, silicious marl.
kiesel=haltig (ᴵᴵ⌣...) a. ⚛ flinty, ⚗ siliciferous; 2hart a. (as) hard as flint; =härte f ⚛ hardness of flint, extreme hardness; =herz n, fig. heart of flint.
kieselig (ᴵ⌣⌣) a. ⚛ = kiesel-artig, 2haltig.
Kiesel-kalk (ᴵᴵ⌣...) m ⚛ geol. und min. silicious limestone; 2kalk-haltig a. ⚛ silicocalcareous; =kristall m pebble-crystal; =kupfer n silicated copper; =mangan m silicious manganese, rhodonite; =mehl n pulverized flint; =meta'll n, chm. (metallic) silicid; =pflaster n flint pavement; 2reich a. flinty, pebbly; =sand m pebbly sand; 2sauer a., chm. silicic, ⚗ saures Salz silicate; =säure f silicic acid (H_4SiO_4); =säure-anhydrid n, chm. (Kiesel-erbe) silicic anhydride (SiO_2); =schiefer m silicious schist, flinty slate; =sinter m silicious sinter; =stein m pebble-flint or -stone; =stoff m, chm. silicium (Si); =wasserstoff m, chm. siliciuretted hydrogen (SiH_4); =zuschlag ⚒ m, metall. silicious flux. [with) gravel.
kiesen¹ (ᴵ⌣) [Kies] v/a. ⚛ to (cover)
kiesen² (ᴵ⌣) [ahd.: choose = küren] v/a. ⚛ (a. impf. kor, p.p. gekoren) to choose.
kies-etig P [kiesend im Essen] a. ⚛ nordd. dainty, fastidious.
Kies-grube (ᴵᴵ...) f ⚛ gravel-pit; =grund m gravelly ground.
kiesicht, kiesig (ᴵ⌣) a. ⚛ = kies-ähnlich.
Kies=sand (ᴵᴵ...) m ⚛ gravelly sand; =schicht f, arch. layer (or bed) of gravel; =schüttung ⚛ f ballasting of the roads, gravelling of a path; =straße f, =weg m gravelled (or gravel-)walk.
Kieze (ᴵ⌣) [ndb.: kit] f ⚛ (Korb) basket.
kiff(e) † (ᴵ⌣) impf. ind. (subj.) v. keifen.
Kifel-kafel (ᴵᴵ⌣ᴵ⌣) [lautnachahmend] m u. n ⚛ chit-chat, tittle-tattle, F gab, mag.
kikeriki (⌣⌣ᴵ) [lautm.] I ⚛ int. ⚽ (Krähen des Hahns) cock-a-doodle-doo. — II ~ m ⚛ = Hahn.
kikeriki-en (⌣⌣ᴵ⌣) v/n. (h.) ⚽ vom Hahne: to crow, biew.: to cock-a-doodle-doo.
Kill(e) ⚓ (ᴵ⌣) f ⚛(⚓) narrow channel.
killen ⚓ (ᴵ⌣) v/n. (h.) ⚽ (hin u. her schlagen, von Segeln) to flap, to shiver.
Kilo F (ᴵ⌣) [grch. 1000] n ⚛ = Kilogramm.
Kilo=gramm (ᴵᴵ⌣...) n ⚛ (abbr. kg, öft. **kg**) (1000 g = 2'205 lbs avoirdupois) kilogram(me); =liter n (m) (abbr. kl, öft. **kl**) (1000 Liter = 220 gallons) kilolitre; =meter n (m) (abbr. km, öft. **km**, 1000 m = 1093'637 yards or ⁵⁄₈ mile) kilometre; =meterfresser m F co. (rasch Fahrender) milemonger, F scorcher, als Automobilist: road-hog; =ster n (m) (1 Kubikmeter = 35317 cubic feet or 1308 cubic yards) kilostere; =watt n, mech. (Einheit der Arbeitskraft = 1000 Watts) kilowatt.

⚗ scientific; ♀ botanical; ⚛ geography; ⚙ machinery; ⚒ mining; ⚔ military; ⚓ marine; ⚛ commercial; ✉ postal; 🚂 railway.

[Kimbern] — 584 — [Kinkhorn]

Kimbern (⌣⌣) [ahd.] *npr/m/pl.* f. Cimbern.
Kimm ↓ (ˊ) [ndd. Rand] *m* ⓦb.: a) (flacher Boden in der Mitte des Schiffes) bilge; b) (Seehorizont) visual horizon.
Kimme (ˊ⌣) [ndd.] *f* ④ 1. (Vertiefung) dip, notch, vgl. Visier-2; (Hervorragung) projection; (Rand) edge, border. — 2. ⊕ Böttcherei: (Vorsprung der Dauben über den Boden) chime. — 3. ↓ = Kimm a.
kimmen ⊕ (ˊ⌣) *v/a.* ⓦ Böttcherei: die Fässer 2 to chime …
Kimmung ↓ (ˊ⌣) [Kimm(e)] *f* ④: a) = Kimm a; b) (Luftspiegelung) mirage.
Kimm=wäger (ˊ...) *m* ② bilge-plank.
Kind (ˊ) [ahd.: kin(d): lt. *gent*-] *n* ⓦb., *poet.* a. ⓦb. 1. child, bſd. ſchott. bairn, weitS. offspring, issue; (Balg) brat; ihre ~er her children, a.: her family or progeny; kleines ~ baby, babe; kleine ~er, oft: little ones, F *co.* little steps, P kids *pl.*; totgeborenes ~ still-born child, ungeborenes ~ unborn child, in der ersten Entwickelung: ⚇ embryo, fetus, unmündiges ~ infant; verlassene ~er deserted children, waifs and strays *pl.* (of society); ~er bekommen to get (or have) children or a family; ſ. genesen 2; kein ~ mehr sein to be no longer a child, to be past childhood; an ~es Statt annehmen to adopt; von ~ auf from (one's) infancy, from (early) childhood, from a child; ſ. Kegel². — 2. *fig.* ſ. ausschütten 1, freuen II; ein ~ des Glücks a minion of fortune, F a lucky dog; ein ~ des Todes a dead (or lost) man; ein echtes Pariser (Londoner) ~ a true Parisian (Londoner, F cockney); ich weiß nicht, wes Geistes ~ er ist … what kind of person (or F of genius) he may be; sich bei e-m lieb(es) ~ machen to ingratiate o.s. with a p.; das ~ beim rechten Namen nennen to call a spade a spade; sei doch kein ~! F don't be so silly!; er stellt sich wie ein ~ he behaves in a childish (or silly) way; unschuldig wie ein neugeborenes ~ (as) innocent as a new-born baby or a babe unborn; das weiß ja jedes ~ a(ny) child (or fool) knows that. — 3. *Sprichw.* aus ~ern werden Leute, etwa: the boy is the father of the man; ſ. brennen 3; ~er sind ~er, etwa: one cannot put old heads on young shoulders; ~er und Narren sprechen die Wahrheit children and fools speak the truth.
Kind=bett (ˊ...) *n* ② childbed; im ~e liegen to be in childbed, to be lying(-)in; =betterin *f* woman in childbed; =bett=fieber *n*, *path.* puerperal fever; =bett=zeit *f* lying-in time.
Kindchen (ˊ⌣) *n* ② (*dim. von* Kind) little child, baby, infant (ſ. Kindlein).
Kindel=bier *provc.* (ˊ⌣...) *n* ② christening (feast); =mutter *f* = Hebamme; =vater *m* father of the christened child or of the infant to be christened.
Kinder=amme (ˊ⌣...) *f* ② (children's) nurse; =art *f* children's manner or way; =ball *m* children's ball, juvenile dancing party; =bett *n* (child's) cot or crib; =bewahr=anstalt *f* infant-(or minding-)school, unentgeltliche (fr.)

crèche; =bräune *f*, *path.* croup; =brei *m* (baby's) pap; =brut *f* (troublesome) brats *pl.*; =buch *n* child's book, book for children.
Kinderchen F (ˊ⌣⌣) *inv., pl. zu* Kindchen.
Kinderei (⌣⌣ˊ) *f* ④ childish nonsense or trifling or ways *pl.*; childishness.
Kinder=frau (ˊ⌣...) *f* ②: a) = Wärterin; b) = Hebamme; =fräulein *n* = Gouvernante; =fresser *m* ogre, (Schreckgespenst) F bogie; =freund(in *f*) *m* friend of children, als Buchtitel etwa: children's annual, child's own book; =garten *m*: (Fröbelscher) ~ ↑ kindergarten; =gärtnerin *f* kindergarten teacher; =geschichten *f/pl.* stories *pl.* for children, nursery-tales *pl.*; vgl. =märchen; =geschrei *n* crying (or screaming) of children; =gesellschaft *f* children's (or juvenile) party; =jahre *n/pl.* infancy, (years *pl.* of) childhood; =klapper *f* (Spielzeug) baby's rattle; =kleid *n* child's frock or dress; =krankheit *f* children's complaint, disease of children; =lehre *f* (instruction in the) catechism; =lehrer *m*: a) teacher of children; b) catechist; =leicht *a.* extremely easy, as easy as ABC; =liebe *f*: a) der Kinder zu den Eltern: children's love, filial affection; b) der Eltern für die Kinder: love for one's children, parental affection; =lieder *n/pl.* songs for children, nursery-songs *pl.*; =literatur *f* juvenile literature; =los *a.* childless, without (a) family; =losigkeit *f* childlessness; =mädchen *n*, =magd *f* nurse(ry)-maid, nurse-girl, als Erzieherin: nursery-governess; =märchen *n/pl.* children's fairy-tales *pl.*; vgl. =geschichten; =mord *m* murder of children (vgl. Kindesmord), ⚇ infanticide; =narr *m* great lover of children; =närrin *f* one who dotes on children; =papp *m* baby's pap; =pistole *f* toy pistol; =possen *f/pl.* childish tricks or pranks *pl.*; =pulver *n*, *med.* (soothing)powder for children; =puppe *f* child's doll; =reich *a.* prolific, blessed with a large offspring; =schriften *f/pl.* books (or publications) *pl.* for the young, juvenile literature; =schriftsteller(in *f*) *m* author(ess) who writes for the young; =schuhe *m/pl.* children's shoes *pl.*; *fig.* er hat die ~ aus- ob. ab=getreten he is no longer a child or a boy; (er ist über die 19) he is out of his teens; =schule *f* infant-school; =schürze *f* child's (or baby's) pinafore; =spiel *n* children's play (-ing) or game; *fig.* das ist für ihn nur ein ~ it is mere child's play (or but a trifling matter) to him; =spielwerk, =spielzeug *n* children's toys or playthings *pl.*; =sport *m* sport for children; =sprache *f* infant's language, child(ren)'s prattle; =stimme *f* child's (or childish) voice; =streich *m* child's trick; =stube *f* nursery; =stuhl *m* child's (or baby's) chair; =taufe *f* infant-baptism; =uhr *f* (child's) penny-watch; =volk *n* =welt; =wagen *m* für kleine Kinder: bassinet, perambulator; für größere: go-(or mail-)cart,

von Ziegen gezogener: goat-chaise; =wärterin *f* children's nurse; vgl. =mädchen; =welt *f* children, young people, the young *pl.*, juvenile world; =zeit *f* infancy, babyhood, childhood; =zeug *n* baby-linen; =zucht *f* bringing up (or management, training) of children, ⚇ pedagogic art.
Kindes=alter (ˊ⌣...) *n* ② tender (or early) age, babyhood; vgl. Kinderzeit; =aussetzung *f* exposure of infants; =beine *n/pl.*: von ~n an from the earliest childhood; =kind *n* grandchild; weitS. ~finder great-grandchildren, descendants *pl.*; =liebe *f* child's love, filial affection; =mord *m* child-murder; vgl. Kindermord; =mörder(in *f*) *m* murderer of a child, ⚇ infanticide; =not *f*, =nöte *pl.* labour preceding a confinement, bſd. *bibl.* travail; in ~nöten sein to labour with child, to be in labour; =statt *f*: bff. Kindes Statt (ſ. Kind); =teil *m u. n. jur.* child's portion; =unschuld *n* childlike innocence.
Kindheit (ˊ-) *f* ④ childhood, infancy; von ~ an from childhood, from a child, from an early age, from the cradle; seit ihrer ersten ~ since (or from) her earliest days or youth.
kindisch (ˊ⌣) *a.* ⓦ nur *b.s.* (*ant.* kindlich): childish, babyish, F babified; der Greis childish old man, old dotard.
Kindisch=werden (ˊ⌣ˊ⌣) *n* ② dotage, (entering one's) second childhood.
Kindlein (ˊ-) *n* ② (*dim. von* Kind) = Kindchen; unschuldige ~ *pl.*, oft: innocent babes, guileless infants *pl.*
kindlich (ˊ⌣) *a.* ⓦ nur *g.s.* (*b.s.* ſ. kindisch): a) (e-m Kinde gemäß) childlike, like a child; b) (auf die Eltern bezüglich) filial; c) (unbefangen) simple (-minded) as a child; =keit *f* ④ childlike nature or simplicity, simple mindedness.
Kinds=... (ˊ...) in Zssgn = Kindes=...
Kindschaft (ˊ⌣) *f* ④: a) (Verhältnis des Kindes zu den Eltern) relationship of a child to its parents, bisw.: ⚇ filiation; b) *theol.* (Verhältnis zu Gott) filial relationship to God.
Kind=taufe (ˊ...) *f* ② christening (of a child); =tauf=schmaus *m* christening (feast or party).
Kinematik ⚇ (⌣⌣ˊ⌣) [grch.] *f* ④ (Bewegungslehre) kinematics.
Kinemato=gramm (⌣⌣⌣ˊ) [grch.] *n* ⓦd., =graph (...ˊ) *m* ② (zum Aufnehmen und Vorführen sich bewegender Bilder) cinematograph, kinematograph, biograph.
Kineto=graph (⌣⌣ˊ) [grch.] *m* ② zur Aufnahme von Momentphotographien: biograph, kinetograph; =skop (...ˊ) *n* ⓦd. zum Vorführen von Momentphotographien: bioscope.
Kink¹ (ˊ) ↓ [ndd.] *f* ④ u. *m* ⓦb. (Schleife im Tau) kink; ~en bekommen to kink.
Kink² (ˊ) *m* ⓦb. *min.* slaty (or blue) clay.
Kinkaju (ˊ⌣⌣) [Südamer.] *m* ⓦ *zo.* (Wickelbär) kinkajou (*Cercole'ptes caudivo'lvulus*).
Kinkerlitzchen (ˊ⌣⌣⌣) [fr. *quincaillerie*] *n/pl.* ② trifles, F fallals *pl.*; (Nippsachen) knickknacks *pl.*
Kink=horn (ˊ...) *n* ② 1. ♪ bugle(-horn). — 2. *zo.* (Schnecke) whelk, ⚇ buccinum (*Bu'ccinum*); versteinertes ~: ⚇ buccinite.

Zeichen (ſ. S. XVII): F familiär; P Volkssprache; Γ Gaunersprache; ✴ selten; † alt (auch gestorben); * neu (auch geboren); ⧺ unrichtig;

[Kinn] — 585 — [kirchlich]

Kinn (ˇ) [ahd.: chin] n ①b. 1. chin; (untere Kinnlade) lower (or nether-)jaw. ⚔ inferior maxilla, zo.: ⚔ mandible; doppeltes ~ double chin. — 2. arch. (ausgekehlter Teil e-r Kranzleiste) groove of a cornice. — 3. ↓ (auch ~back m ㊷) fore-foot of the keel.

Kinn-backe(n m) f (ˇ...): a) anat. jaw, jaw-bone, zo.: ⚔ mandible; b) ↓ = Kinn 3; **-backen-drüse** f, anat.: ⚔ maxillary gland; **-backen-krampf** m, path. lock-jaw, locked jaw, ⚔ trismus; **-band** n am Helme: helmet-strap; **-bart** m imperial; tuft on the chin, chin-tuft; **-grübchen** n dimple in the chin; **-kette** ⊙ f, man. curb (-chain); e-m Pferde die ~ anlegen to curb a horse; **-ketten-haken** m curb-hook; **-ketten-stange** f cheek of the bit, curb-bit; **-lade** f, anat. = backen a, Kiefer; ⚲**laden-förmig** a.: ⚔ mandibuliform; **-riemen** m am Helm: cheek-strap; man. am Geschirr: chin-strap.

Kino (ˇ-) m, n ⑩ pharm. und ⊙ Färberei (eingetrockneter Saft tropischer Bäume, bsd. v. *Pterocarpus Marsu'pium*) kino.

Kiosk (ˇˇ) [türk., *pers.] m ⑪a. (Gartenhäuschen, Verkaufsbude) kiosk.

Kipfel (ˇˇ) [mhd.] n ㉒ (Gebäck) (French) roll; small loaf.

Kippe (ˇˇ) [ndd.] f ㊽ 1. tilt; auf der ~ stehen (umzustürzen drohen) to be on the tilt, F to stand atilt; fig. to be in imminent danger or on the brink of ruin; auf die ~ stellen to tilt up. — 2. ~ und Wippe = Kipperei. — 3. (Schaukelbrett) seesaw.

kipp(e)lig P (ˇ(ˇ)ˇ) a. ⑥ = wack(e)lig.

kippeln P (ˇˇ) v/n. (h. u. ſn) to be on the tilt or F on the seesaw.

kippen¹ (ˇˇ) [Kippe] ㊽ I v/n. (h. u. ſn) 1. (h.) (das Gleichgewicht verlieren) to lose one's balance; (ſchaukeln) to seesaw. — 2. (ſn) (umfallen) to tip (or topple) over; mit dem Stuhle 2 to balance o.s. on a chair. — II v/a. 3. ein Faß 2c. 2 to tilt ..., e-n Stein 2c.: to tilt up ..., mit e-m Hebel: to prise up; F fig. einen Krug 2c. 2 (leeren) to drain ...

kippen² (ˇˇ) [mb.] I v/a. u. v/n. (h.) ㊽ 1. (tappen) to lop; Münzen 2 (beschneiden) to clip money. — 2. 2 und wippen (schlechtes Geld in Umlauf bringen) to circulate counterfeit (or base) coin. — II ~ n ㉓ 3. lopping, &c. (ſ. 1); ~ und Wippen circulation of counterfeit coin.

Kipper (ˇˇ) m ㊷ clipper of money; ~ und Wipper counterfeiter of coin.

Kipperei (ˇˇˇ) f ㊻ 1. clipping of money; ~ und Wipperei circulation of counterfeit coin. — 2. (Wucherhandel) usurious trade or dealing.

Kipper-geld (ˇˇˇ) n ㊽ counterfeit coin.

kippern (ˇˇ) v/n. (h.) ㉒a. to forge coin; (wuchern) to carry on a usurious trade.

Kipp-geld (ˇ...) n ㊽ clipped money; **-karren** m tilting- (or tipping-)cart, tumbrel, 🚆 trolley.

kipplig P (ˇˇ) a. ⑥ = wack(e)lig.

Kipp-pfanne (ˇˇ...) f ㊷ Zuckerfabrik: seesaw (or swing-)pan; **-regel** f, surv.: ⚔ telescopic graphometer; **-vorrichtung** ⊙ f tipper; **-wagen** 🚆 m tipcar, tipping-wagon.

Kirch-dach (ˇ...) n ㊷ roof of a church, ch.-roof; **-dorf** n village with a ch.

Kirche (ˇˇ) [ahd.. church (kirk);*grch. *kyriakó'n* (Haus) des Herrn] f ㊵ 1. church, für Diſſidenten: chapel; weitS. House of God, the Lord's House; in die ~ geh(e)n to go to (regelmäßig: to attend) church (vgl. englisch²). — 2. (Gottesdienst) divine service; ~ halten to hold the service; als die ~ aus war, nach der ~ when the service was over, after church or the service.

Kirchen-age'nde (ˇˇ...) f ㊷ form of public worship; vgl. Handbuch; **-älteste(r)** m churchwarden, in engl. Diſſenterkirchen auch pl. elders; **-amt** n ecclesiastical function or duties pl., bei Diſſenters mſt: ministerial office, ministry; ⚲**amtlich** a. ⑥ relating to an eccl. (or ministerial) office; ⚲**artig** a. church-like, ecclesiastical; **-bann** m gegen einzelne: excommunication, gegen ganze Länder 2c.: interdict; vgl. Bann 3; **-bau** m building (or erection) of a church; **-bau-kaſſe** f funds pl. for building (or repairing) a church; **-beamte(r)** m church-officer; **-beſuch** m attendance at church; der ~ war leidlich gut the church was fairly well attended; **-buch** n parochial (or parish-)register; **-buße** f penance imposed by the church; **-chor** m (church-)choir; **-diener** m verger; (Küſter) sexton; (Schreiber) (parish-)clerk; **-dienſt** m: a) divine service, church-service; vgl. Handbuch; b) = -amt; ⚲**dienſtlich** a. relating to divine service, ministerial; **-entweiher(in** f) m profaner of a church; **-entweihung** f profanation of a ch., sacrilege; **-fahne** f: a) ch.-banner; b) auf der Spitze des Kirchturms: vane of a church; **-fenſter** n ch.-window; **-feſt** n ch.-festival; **-frevel** m sacrilege; **-fürſt** m prince (or dignitary) of the church, prelate; **-gänger(in** f) m ch.-goer, regular attendant at (a) church; **-gebet** n: a) engl. Kirche: prayer prescribed by (or read in) the ch.; b) Diſſenters: prayer offered up by the minister; **-gebet-buch** n der engl. Staatskirche: Book of Common Prayer (nicht in Diſſenterkirchen gebraucht); **-gebrauch** m ecclesiastical rite or observance; **-gefäße** n/pl. church-plate; **-gehen** n attendance at church; **-gemeinde** f parish; **-gemeinſchaft** f eccl. community, a. oft: band of the faithful; **-gerät** n ch.-furniture; **-gesang** m: a) (Lied) chant, (Lobgesang) (church-)hymn; b) (Singen der Gemeinde) congregational singing; **-geschichte** f ecclesiastical (or church) history; **-geſetz** n canonical law, canon-law; ⚲**geſetzlich** a. canonical; **-glocke** f church-bell; ⚲**gotisch** n, typ. Ecclesiastic; **-gut** n church-lands pl., patrimony; **-halle** f porch; **-hand-buch** n church-service ritual, liturgy; **-jahr** n ecclesiastical year; **-kalender** m church-almanac; im engl. Gebetbuche: ch.-calendar containing the lessons for every Sunday; **-kaſſe** f funds pl. of a church; **-kolle'kte** f: a) collection (made) for ch.-purposes; b) (Gebet) collect; **-konze'rt** n

ch.-concert; **-land** n ch.-land; **-lehre** f ch.-doctrine, teaching of the ch.; **-lehrer** m teacher of the ch., engS. = -vater; **-licht** b; **-licht** n: a) ⑥ b. church-illumination; b) ④b. (großer -lehrer) luminary (or shining light) of the church; **-lied** n chant, hymn; (Pſalm) psalm; **-maus** f: ſo arm wie eine ~ (as) poor as a church-mouse or as Job; **-muſik** f sacred music; **-ordnung** f: a) rules pl. of the church; b) liturgy; **-parade** ⚔ f ch.-parade; **-patron** m: a) patron of a church; b) (patron) saint of a ch.; **-pfründe** f church-living or -preferment; **-politik** f ecclesiastical policy; **-rat** m: a) coll. church-committee; vgl. -vorſtand; b) Perſon: churchwarden; **-raub** m spoliation of a church, sacrilege; **-räuber** m spoliator of a ch., bisw.: sacrilegist; **-recht** n canonical law; ⚲**rechtlich** a. canonical; **-rechts-lehrer** m professor of the canonical law, auch: canonist; **-reform** f ch.-reform; **-regime'nt** n church-government, hierarchy; **-regiſter** n = -buch; **-ſache** f ecclesiastical affair; **-ſänger** m member of a choir, chorister; **-ſatzungen** f/pl. ordinances (or rules) pl. of the church; **-ſchein** m certificate extracted from the ch.-register; **-ſchiff** n, arch. nave; **-ſchmuck** m decoration of a church; **-ſpaltung** f schism within a ch.; **-ſprengel** m diocese; **-ſtaat** m ehm. ⚓ Pontifical State; **-ſtreit** m ecclesiastical controversy or dissension or dispute; **-ſtuhl** m pew; **-tag** m synod.

Kirchentum (ˇˇ-) n ②d. everything relating to the church, church-doctrine; (die Kirche ſelbſt) the Church; churchism; weitS. = Kirchlichkeit.

Kirchen-vater (ˇˇ...) m ㊷ Father of the Church; die -väter, a. patristic writers pl.; **-verbeſſerer** m (church-)reformer; **-verbeſſerung** f (church-)reformation; **-verfaſſung** f constitution of the ch., hierarchy; **-vermögen** n = -gut; **-verſammlung** f: a) ch.-meeting; eccl. hist. council; b) weitS. synod; **-verwaltung** f administration of a church or of ch.-property; **-viſitatio'n** f parochial visit(ation); **-vorſtand** m church-wardens pl.; ehm.: vestry; **-vorſteher** m churchwarden; vgl. -älteſte(r); **-weſen** n church-matters or -affairs pl.; **-zeitung** f ecclesiastical journal, engS. ch.-magazine; **-zettel** m ch.-notice announcing the services of the week; **-zucht** f church-discipline.

Kirch-gang (ˇ...) m ㊷ going to church; vgl. Kirchenbesuch; erſter ~ einer Wöchnerin churching of a woman after her confinement; **-gänger(in** f) m church-goer, one who attends church; **-gemeinde** f = -ſpiel; **-genoſſ** m parishioner; **-hof** m: a) cemetery (vgl. Friedhof); b) an der Kirche: churchyard.

Kirchlein (ˇˇ) n ㉓ small church or chapel.

kirchlich (ˇˇ) [Kirche] a. ⑥ of the church, ecclesiastical, (gottesdienſtlich) ritual; (geiſtlich) spiritual; (kirchenrechtlich) canonical; (Geiſtliche betreffend) clerical; ſtreng 2er od. 2 geſinnter Mann strict

♪ Muſik; ⚔ Wiſſenſchaft; ❀ Pflanze; ♁ Geographie; ⊙ Technik; ⚒ Bergbau; ⚔ Militär; ↓ Marine; 🏛 Handel; ✉ Post; 🚆 Eiſenbahn.

[Kirchmesse] — 586 — [flagbar]

churchman, faithful son of the Church; ~keit f ⑯ loyalty (or attachment) to the church.
Kirch=messe ⌇ (ˊ...) f ⑫ = Kirmes.
Kirchner (ˊ◡) m ㉒ verger, sexton; ~ei (◡◡¹) f ⑯ verger's (or sexton's) post.
Kirch=schwalbe (ˊ...) f⑫=Hausschwalbe; =spiel n parish; zum ~ gehörig parochial; =spiel=abgabe f parish-rate; =spiel=eingesessene(r) s. parishioner; =spiel=versammlung f meeting of parishioners; =sprengel m diocese; =stuhl m pew; =turm m, spitzer steeple, spire; ohne Spitze: tower of a church, church-tower; =turm=interessen n/pl. parochial concerns pl.; =turm=patriotismus m local patriotism; =turm=rennen n steeple-chase; =turm=spitze f highest point of a steeple or a spire; =turms=politik f local politics; =weg m way to church; =weih(e) f: a) consecration of a church; b) (Fest) parish fair, annual fête, country-wake; =weih=fest n (=weih=e) b; =zeit f churchtime, hour of (divine) service.
Kirgise (◡ˊ◡) [türk. Räuber], Kirgis=kaisake (◡ˊ‒◡) m ㊹ (Nomade im Südwesten von Sibirien), kirgisisch (◡ˊ◡) a. ⑯ Kirgheez, Kirghiz.
Kirke (ˊ◡) npr/f. ⑨ß. = Circe.
Kirmes (ˊ◡) [mhd.] = Kirchmesse] f ⑮, pl. a. Kirmse(n) = Kirchweih(e) b, auch: country-fair, ⚔ kermess, kermis.
kirre (ˊ◡) [mhd.] a. ⑯ (zahm) tame(d down); (vertraulich) familiar; weit S. (sich fügend) docile, tractable; (untertänig) submissive, humble; e-n kirre machen to tame a p. down.
kirren (ˊ◡) I v/a. ⑱ 1. hunt. (ködern) to bait, decoy, allure. — 2. (zahm, gefügig m.) to tame (down), to render tractable, to force into submission. — II ~ n ㉓. = Kirrung 1.
Kirrung (ˊ◡) f ⑯ 1. baiting, allurement. — 2. (Köder, Lockspeise) bait.
Kirsch (ˊ◡) m ⓐ, ɢ. = Kirschbranntwein.
Kirsch=baum ⚲ (ˊ...) m ⑰ cherry-tree (Prunus ce'rasus); =blüte f ch.-blossom; =branntwein m ch.-brandy.
Kirsche (ˊ◡) [ahd.: cherry; mlt. cere'sia] f ⑪ (die Frucht) cherry; saure ~ morel(lo); weiße (Herz=)~ white-heart (cherry), a. bigaroon; fig. mit großen Herren ist nicht gut ~n essen, etwa: great lords deal harshly with small folks; mit ihm ist nicht gut ~n essen he is not a nice (or pleasant) customer to deal with. — 2. ⚲ = Kirschbaum.
Kirsch=eis (ˊ.¹) n ⑫ cherry-ice.
kirschen (ˊ◡) a. ⑯ of cherry-wood.
Kirschen=... (ˊ◡...) ⑫ = Kirsch=...
Kirsch=gummi (ˊ...) n ⑫ cherry-gum; =kern m ch.-stone; =kuchen m ch.-cake; =lorbeer ⚲ m bay-cherry or -laurel (Prunus laurocerasus); ⁰rot a. ⑯ cherrycoloured, auch: (fr.) cerise; =rotglut f cherry-red heat; =stein m = =kern; =stiel m ch.-stalk; =wasser n = =branntwein; =zeit f cherry-season.
Kißchen (ˊ◡) n ㉓ (dim. v. Kissen) small cushion or pillow or pad.
Kissen (ˊ◡) n ㉓ cushion; *fr. coussin] n ㉓ 1. cushion; (Kopf=)~ pillow; (Polster unterm Kopf=Ω) bolster; (Luft=)~ für Kranke:

air-cushion; (Watttierung) pad(ding); phys. (Reib=)~ der Elektrisiermaschine: rubber; med. (Kräuter=)~ pulvinar. — 2. ⚛ arch. (Ruhestein) (fr.) coussinet.
kissen=artig (ˊ◡...) a. ⑯ cushion-like, ɑ pulvinar, zo. pulvinate(d); arch.: ⚛ aufgebauscht pulvinated; =bezug m ⑫=überzug; =förmig a. cushion-shaped, ɑ pulviniform; =riemen ⊕ m am Kummet top-strap; =überzug m pillow- (or bolster-)case or -slip.
Kistchen (ˊ◡) n ㉓ (dim. von Kiste) small box or chest or case.
Kiste (ˊ◡) [ahd.: chest; *grch.] f ⑪ box (a. = Koffer), für Waren: chest, case, zum Einpacken: packing-case (a. grch. Alt. zo.: ɑ cist, (Truhe) coffer; starke ~ für lange Reisen overland box; beschlagene: ⚛ ironbound chest or case; ⚛ eine ~ Zigarren a box of (100) cigars; ⚔ ~ für den Abhub limp; f. Kasten 1.
Kisten=deckel (ˊ◡...) m ⑫ lid of a box or case; =holz n wood for boxes (boxwood = Buchsbaumholz); =macher m box- (or trunk-)maker or manufacturer.
Kithäron ⚲ (◡ˊ◡) [grch.] npr/m. ⑫ₐ. (Gebirge an der Grenze v. Böotien) Cithæron.
Kitt (ˊ) [ahd.: lt. bitu'men] m ⑫b. cement (a. fig.), bsd. chm. zur Verdichtung von Gefäßen: lute; (Glaser=)~ putty; mit ~ bestreichen to putty.
Kittel (ˊ◡) [mhd.] m ⑫ smock, (loose) frock; (überwurf) overall; beim ~ kriegen to (seize by the) collar, to pull by the sleeve.
kitten (ˊ◡) v/a. ⑱ (f. Kitt) to cement, chm. auch: to lute; Glaserei: to putty; weit S. to glue (or stick, piece) together. [pozz(u)olana.]
Kitt¹=erde (ˊ◡...) f ⑯ cement-clay, auch:
Kitt²=fuchs ⚲ (ˊ◡=f◡ʃ) [engl.=dtsch] m ⑫ zo. (Präriefuchs) kit-fox (Vulpes velox).
kitt=los (ˊ...) a. ⑯ without cement; =messer n ⑫ der Glaser: putty-knife; =schläger m cementer; =spalte f, arch. (fr.) abreuvoir; =verglasung f puttyglazing.
Kitz (ˊ) n ⑫ₐ. (junges Reh im ersten Jahre) fawn in its first year.
Kitze (ˊ◡) f ⑪ 1. [: kitten; *Katze] female cat. — 2. [ahd.: kid; *Geiß] (Junges von gewissen Tieren, bsd. Zicklein, kid, hunt. (Rehkalb) fawn.
Kitzel (ˊ◡) [mhd.; *Kitzeln] m ⑫ 1. tickle, tickling, ɑ titillation; (Jucken) itching; fig. auch: pleasant sensation, gratification (of the senses). — 2. fig. (sinnliches Verlangen) sensual appetite or desire, ɑ pruriency. [cough.]
Kitzel=husten (ˊ◡...) m ⑫ path. tickling]
kitz(e)lig (ˊ(◡)◡) a. ⑯ ticklish; (empfindlich) sensitive, delicate, eine ²e (schwer zu behandelnde) Sache a ticklish (or delicate, difficult, nice) matter.
Kitz(e)ligkeit (ˊ(◡)◡‒) f ⑯ ticklishness.
kitzeln (ˊ◡) [ahd.: kittle] ⑫a. I v/a. und v/impers. 1. to tickle, ɑ to titillate; es kitzelt mich s.th. tickles me, I feel a tickling in my throat, &c.; (es juckt mich) I itch. — 2. fig. to cause a pleasant sensation, to gratify the senses, F to tickle a p.'s fancy; es kitzelt ihn nach Ruhm und Ehren he itches (or has an itching) for fame and honours. —

II sich ² v/refl. 3. to tickle o.s.; fig. sich an (oder mit, über) et. ² (heimlich freuen) to take a secret delight in a th., to gloat over a th. — III ~ n ㉓ 4. tickle, ɑ titillation; vgl. Kitzel.
Kitzler (ˊ◡) [kitzeln] m ⑫ 1. (a. ~in f ⑯) tickler. — 2. anat.: ɑ clitoris.
kitzlig (ˊ◡) f. kitz(e)lig.
Kiwi (ˊ‒) [austral.] m ⑩ orn. kiwi, ɑ apteryx (A'pteryx austra'lis).
Kix (ˊ), kixen, f. Kicks, kicksen. [year.
k. J. abbr. = künftigen Jahres of next]
k. k. öst. abbr. = kaiserlich=königlich (für alle öst. Behörden; vgl. k. u. k.).
kl, öst. kl abbr. = Kiloliter.
Kl. abbr. = Klasse.
klabastern F nordd. (◡ˊ◡) v/n. (sn) ⓐₐ. to trot (or toddle, potter) about.
Klabauter=mann ⚓ (◡ˊ◡‒) m ⑨c. (Kobold) hobgoblin, bogy man.
klack int. (auch ²₈) (slap-)bang!; ², da liegt es! bang, there it goes!; f. flick. [⓮ₐ. = Klecks.]
Klacks ⓧ I int. f. klack. — II F ~ m]
Kladde (ˊ◡) [ndb., ndl.] f ⑯ (Entwurf) first (or rough) draft; ⓮ ~(n=buch n) waste- (or day-)book.
Kladderadatsch (◡◡◡ˊ◡◡) [lautnachahmend] I F int. 1. ²! (slap-)bang!, there (it goes)! — II ~ m ⓐₐ. (sg. auch inv.) 2. great noise or F row. — 3. (Berliner Witzblatt seit 1848, ähnlich dem Londoner 'Punch') Kladderadatsch.
klaffen (ˊ◡) [ahd.] I v/n. (h. und sn) ⓮ (aus=ea.=stehen) to form a chink, to gape, to stand apart, auch: to yawn; (halb offen sein) to be half open, Tür: to be ajar; (nicht gut anschließen) to fit loosely; ²d gaping, yawning, a. (wide) apart, ♃: ɑ dehiscent; ²de Wunde gaping wound, gash. — II ~ n ㉓ gaping, &c. (f. I); loose fit; ♃: ɑ dehiscence.
kläffen (ˊ◡) [mhd.] v/n. (h.) ⓮: a) von jungen Hunden: to yelp, yap, bark, von Jagdhunden bisw.: to open; b) fig. von Personen: to clamour, to brawl.
Kläffer (ˊ◡) m ⑫ 1. yelping (or barking) dog or cur. — 2. (auch Kläfferin f ⑯) von Personen: brawler, f auch: scold, F nagging woman, bsd. ehm.: shrew.
Klafter (ˊ◡) [ahd.] f ⑯, a. m und n ⑫ 1. Längenmaß etwa: fathom (a. ⚓). — 2. (ehm. Brennholzmaß) = 3⅓ cbm) cord (or line) of wood. [stacked) wood.]
Klafter=holz (ˊ◡...) n ⑫ corded (or]
klafterig (ˊ◡‒) a. ⑯ one fathom long, measuring one cord; oft in Zssgn mit Zahlen, zB. drei² three fathom long.
Klafter=maß (ˊ◡...) n ⑫ cord-measure.
klaftern (ˊ◡) I v/a. u. v/n. (h.) ⓐₐ. to (measure by the) fathom; Holz ² to cord (up) ... — II ~ n ㉓ cordage of wood.
Klafter=setzer (ˊ◡...) m ⑫ one who cords (or stacks) wood; =stock m = =maß; ²tief a. ⑯ one fathom deep. [plaint.]
Klag=artikel (ˊ‒...) m ⑫ jur. grievance,]
klagbar (ˊ‒) a. ⑯ jur. actionable, von Schulden: recoverable by (process of) law, von Unzuträglichkeiten: indictable (nuisances, &c.); et. ² machen to bring a matter into court; ² werden gegen einen to institute proceedings (or to proceed) against a p., to bring (or enter) an action against a p.

Signs (see page XVII): F familiar; P vulgar; ⸘ flash; ⌇ rare; † obsolete (died); * new word (born); ⁺⁺ incorrect; ♪ music;

[Klage] — 587 — [klappen]

Klage (⌣́) [ahd.] f ⓐ 1. complaint; (jammern) wailing, lamentation, (ächzen) moaning; laute ~n erheben to make loud complaints; über et. ~ führen to complain of a th. — 2. jur. (Beschwerde) grievance, matter of complaint; charge; ~(=schrift) plaint; eine ~ gegen einen anstellen ob. anhängig machen to bring an action for damages, &c. against a p., to sue a p., kriminell: to prosecute a p.; mit seiner ~ abgewiesen werden to be nonsuited.

Klage-beantwortung (⌣́⌣…) f ⓐ answer to (or refutation of) a charge; =frau f röm. Alt. ꝛc.: woman hired to lament over a dead person; =gedicht n elegy, elegiac poem; =gesang m = =gedicht u. =lied; =geschrei n = Klaggeschrei; =grund m cause of complaint, grievance; =laut m plaintive sound or note; vgl. =ruf; =lied n plaintive (or funeral, mournful) song, dirge; ein lautes ~ anstimmen to raise (or set up) a great lamentation, vgl. klagen 1 u. Jeremia; ²lustig a. ⓐ fond of complaining; vgl. klagesüchtig.

klagen (⌣́) [ahd.] ⓐ I v/n. (h.) 1. to complain, to utter complaints; (jammern) to wail, to lament, (ächzen) to moan; laut über et. ² to utter loud lamentations about a th.; worüber klagt sie? what does she complain of?, what ails her?; um etwas ² to mourn (over) a th.; jur. to go to law about a th.; s. Schaden=ersatz. — II v/a. 2. e-m et. ² to complain to a p. about a th.; einem sein Leid ² to pour out one's trouble(s) (or complaints, grief) to a p. — 3. bibl., &c. die Toten ² (beklagen) to mourn the dead. — 4. mit Angabe der Wirkung: e-m die Ohren voll ² to pour one's tale of distress into a p.'s ears. — III sich ² v/refl. 5. mit Angabe der Wirkung: sich heiser ² to make o.s. hoarse with wailing or lamenting. — IV ~ n ⓐ 6. complaining, &c. (s. I); vgl. Klage. — V ²d p.pr. u. a. ⓐ 7. Beb. des inf. — 8. plaintive; jur.: der ²de Teil the plaintiff.

klagen=reich (⌣́⌣…) a. ⓐ full of complaints, plaintive. [deplorable.]
klagens=wert (⌣́⌣…) a. ⓐ lamentable,]
Klage=punkt (⌣́⌣…) m ⓐ matter complained of, jur. a count of an indictment.
Klager (⌣́⌣) m ⓐ, ~in f ⓐ one who complains, querulous person, F croaker.
Kläger (⌣́⌣) m ⓐ, ~in f ⓐ jur., im Zivilprozesse: (f female) plaintiff or complainant, in einer Kriminal'sche: prosecutor (f …trix); (Staats=anwalt) public prosecutor; vgl. Ankläger u. auftreten 3; sich zum ~ aufwerfen to appear as plaintiff or accuser.
Klagerei (–⌣́) f ⓐ = Geklage.
Klag=erhebung (⌣́…) f ⓐ lodging a plaint, making a charge.
klägerisch (⌣́⌣⌣) a. ⓐ jur. referring to the plaintiff or accuser; der ²e Anwalt plaintiff's counsel, counsel for the plaintiff. [part of the plaintiff.]
klägerischer=seits (⌣́⌣⌣⌣) adv. on the]
Klage=ruf (⌣́⌣…) m ⓐ plaintive cry, call of distress; vgl. =laut; =sache f jur. legal action, lawsuit; =schrift f jur. plaint, writ; =sucht f litigiousness, querulousness; ²süchtig a. ⓐ litigious, querulous; =ton m plaintive tone, doleful sound; =weib n = =frau.

Klag=geschrei (⌣́…) n ⓐ plaintive cry, wailing, (loud) lamentation.

kläglich (⌣́⌣) [Klage] a. ⓐ 1. (klagend) plaintive (voice). — 2. (beklagenswert) lamentable, deplorable; (betrübend) distressing, sorrowful. — 3. (erbärmlich) piteous, doleful, woeful, wretched.

Kläglichkeit (⌣́⌣⌣) f ⓐ (zu kläglich 1:) plaintiveness of a voice; (zu 2:) lamentableness, sorrowfulness; (zu 3:) piteousness, dolefulness, wretchedness.

klag=los (⌣́…) a. ⓐ without complaint; jur.: ² stellen (befriedigen) to satisfy.

Klamei=eisen ⚓ (⌣́⌣…) n ⓐ (Dichteisen) caulking- (or horsing-)iron.

klameien ⚓ (⌣́⌣⌣) v/a. ein Schiff ² to caulk a ship with a horsing-iron.

klamm (⌣́) [mhd.; *klemmen] I a. ⓐ 1. (beengt) tight, close(ly packed). — 2. (nbd.) (erstarrt) numb(ed), (feuchtkalt) clammy. — 3. (knapp) spare, scarce; wir sind ² our funds are low, F we are hard up or short of cash, P we're stone-broke. — 4. ⚔ (gediegen) solid; pure. — II ~(e) f ⓐ (⓪), oberb. (⌣́) f ⓐ (⓪) 5. gorge forming the bed of a torrent, in Kalifornien: cañon.

Klammer (⌣́) [mhd.; *klemmen] f ⓐ 1. ⚙ cramp-iron (a. typ.), clamp, clasp, bracket, Bauwesen: brace; (Nagel zum Vernieten) clinching-iron, clincher, arch. brace; hölzerne ~ zum Feststecken der Wäsche auf der Zugleine: wooden peg, clothes-peg. — 2. gram., typ. meist: parenthesis; math., typ. bracket; runde ~n ( ) round brackets, parentheses pl.; eckige ~n [ ] square brackets pl., crotch sg., crotchets pl.; typ. zusammenfassende ~n { } brace sg; eine Bemerkung in ~n einschließen, setzen to enclose a remark in parenthesis or …es, to add a note by way of parenthesis; math. die ~n fortschaffen (lösen) to remove (to solve) the brackets; in ~n setzen to put (or enclose) in brackets, to bracket.

Klammer=affe (⌣́…) m ⓐ zo. sapajou, coaita (A'teles pani'scus); =band n, arch. tie-piece, brace; =beutel m bag with clothes-pegs; =eisen ⚙ n grappling-iron; =gesims ⚙ n, arch. brace-mould; =loch n Maurerei: cramp-hole.

klammern (⌣́⌣) v: clamber] ⓐ a. I ⚙ v/a. to cramp, clasp, brace, clinch. — II sich ² v/refl.: sich ² an … to cling (or to fasten o.s.) to …

Klamotte(n pl.) ⚙ (–⌣́) f ⓐ [Ziegelsteinstück(e)] broken (auch: half-)bricks pl.

Klampe (⌣́) [nbd.: clamp] f ⓐ = Klammer 1; ⚓ cleat; vgl. Belegklampe.

klang (⌣́) impf. ind. von klingen.

Klang (⌣́) m ⓐ b. clank (lautm.; *klingen) I m ⓪b. sound; ringing (or tinkling), chiming of bells, chinking (or ring) of money, tone of the voice; (Widerhall) resonance; liebliche Klänge (Musik) sweet chords or notes pl., soft strains pl. of music; mit Sang und ~ with flourish of trumpets or ringing of bells; with loud rejoicing(s); ohne Sang und ~ abziehen to leave unceremoniously, to depart silently or secretly; ohne Sang und ~ begraben to bury without military honours; fig. sein Name hat guten ~ (Ruf) his name is in good repute, he is held in high esteem; das gibt keinen guten ~ that does not sound well or blend well or go well together. — II ² int. kling, ²! von Glocken: ding-dong!

Klang=boden ♪ (⌣́…) m ⓐ einer Geige ꝛc. sounding-board.

klänge (⌣́) impf. subj. von klingen.

Klang=farbe (⌣́…) f ⓐ: a) tonality; b) phys. (fr.) timbre; =figur f, phys. Chladni's acoustic figure; ²gebend a. ⓐ sonorous; ²e Eigenschaft sonorousness; =lehre f, phys. (theory of) sound, acoustics; ²los a. toneless, without (a) sound; (stumm) mute; ²lose Stimme hollow voice; fig. (ohne Festlichkeit) unceremonious; =losigkeit f tonelessness, absence of sound; =messer m, phys.: ⚙ phonometer; =nach=ahmend a. imitating a sound, gr.: ⚙ onomatopoetic; =nach=ahmung f imitation of a sound, gram.: ⚙ onomatopœia; ²reich a. of rich tone, fullsounding, sonorous; =stufe f (musical) interval; ²voll a. = ²reich; =welle f, phys. sound-wave; =wirkung f effect of sound; =wort n sonorous word.

klapp! (⌣́) ²! (²!) bang! crash!, flop!; vgl. klipp ²!

Klapp=bettstelle ⚙ (⌣́…) f ⓐ folding-bedstead; =boot ⚓ n folding-boat; =brett n an der Wand: slab; =brücke f lever-drawbridge.

Klappe (⌣́) [nbd.] f ⓐ 1. (Fliegen-)~ flap for killing flies; fig. zwei Fliegen mit einer ~ schlagen to kill two birds with one stone; (Scheu-)~n pl. der Pferde blinkers pl. — 2. an e-r Seite befestigter, beweglicher Teil: ⚙ (Falltür) flap- (or trap-)door, mit einer Feder: spring-door, am Taubenschlage: trap; ~ e-s Tisches flap of a table; Fernspr.: ~ am ~schrant annunciator; mach. (Ventil) valve; am Back=ofen ꝛc.: damper, e-r Pumpe ꝛc.: clack; Schneiderei: flap, (Hosenlatz) fly; ♪ ~ der Blasinstr.: key, stop, piston, an Orgelpfeifen: stopple, ♪, anat., ꝛc.: ⚙ valve, valvule. — 3. fig. die ~ zumachen (mit et. aufhören) to stop (a th.), F to shut up shop, F halten Sie die ~ (den Mund)! stop your jaw! — 4. F (Bett) bed; sich in die ~ legen to lie down (to rest), F to turn in between the sheets.

klappen (⌣́) [nbd.: clap] ⓐ I v/n. (h.) 1. (geräuschvoll an=ea. schlagen) to clap, clack, click, clink, clash, clatter, flap, vgl. klappern 1. — 2. F (gehörig in=ea. greifen) to fit properly, to work well (together), to tally, F to gee in; es klappt alles (sehr gut) all is going (off) well, all is right, F it's O.K. (= all correct); es klappt nicht there is s.th. wrong or some hitch in the matter. — II sich ² v/refl. u. v/n. (h.) 3. (wie eine Klappe bewegen) (sich) in die Höhe to start (or spring, jerk) up. — III ~ n ⓐ 4. clapping, &c. (s. I); fig. wenn es

⚙ scientific; ♀ botanical; ♁ geography; ⓐ machinery; ⚔ mining; ⚔ military; ⚓ marine; ⓐ commercial; ⓐ postal; ⓐ railway.

[Klappenartig] — 588 — [Klassenzimmer]

zum ~ kommt when it comes to the point or to business or F to the push. **Klappen-artig** (⸗...) a. ⊕ like a valve, ⚕ valvar, valvate, valviform; =**feder** f ⚕ Orgel: stop-spring; =**fehler** m, path. valvular defect; 2**förmig** a. = 2artig; =**horn** ♪ n key-bugle; =**instrument** n keyed instrument; =**loch** n e-s Blasebalges vent; =**schrank** m Fernsprechwesen: switch-board; =**signalhorn** ♪ n =horn; =**system** n Fernsprechw.: annunciator, switch-system; 2**tragend** a.: ⚕ valviferous; =**ventil** n, mach. clack- (or flap-, clapper-)valve; =**wirbel** m, mach. valve-stem.

Klapper (⸗...) f ⊕ als Vogelscheuche, Kinderspielzeug: rattle; ⊕ ~ einer Mühle clap.

Klapper-apfel (⸗...) m ⚕ calville; =**bein** n (living or walking) skeleton, F rattle-bones; Freund ~ auch: F co. death; 2**dünn**, 2**dürr** a. (as) thin as a lark, (as) lean as a rake.

Klapperei (⸗⸗ⁱⁱ) f ⊕ = Geklapper.

Klapper-hülse ⚕ (⸗...) f ⚕ rattlebox (Crotala'ria).

Klapp(e)rig (⸗⸗⸗) a. ⊕ 1. rattling; clattering. — 2. F fig. (hinfällig, gebrechlich) F shaky.

Klapper-kasten F (⸗...) m ⚕: a) (schlechtes) Klavier) tin-kettle; auf dem ~ pauken to strum on the (old) piano; b) (altes Fuhrwerk) rattletrap; =**mann** m man with a rattle; auch: = bein; =**maul** n (Plappermaul) chatterbox; =**mühle** f: a) mill with a clap; b) fig. ihre Zunge geht wie eine ~ her tongue goes nineteen to the dozen, F she has an interminable clack.

Klappern (⸗⸗) [mhd.] ⊕ a. I v/n. (h.) 1. to rattle; vom Storche: mit dem Schnabel 2 to clatter, bisw.: to clapper; mit den Zähnen 2 to chatter (with) one's teeth; mit den Füßen 2 to patter; (klimpern) to clink, mit dem Gelde 2 to chink one's money; vgl. klappen 1. — 2. (schwatzen) to chat(ter), to prattle; vgl. plappern. — 3. (Reklame machen) F to puff one's trade, to sound one's trumpet, to beat the big drum. — II v/a. 4. mit Angabe der Wirkung: e-n aus dem Schlafe 2 to rouse a p. from his sleep. — III ~ n ⚕ 5. rattling (noise), clattering, &c. (f. I); Sprichw. ~ gehört zum Handwerk puffing (or advertising) is part of the trade.

Klapper-rose ⚕ (⸗...) f ⚕ = Klatschmohn; =**schlange** f, zo. rattlesnake (Crotalus); =**schlangen-wurzel** ⚕ f snakeroot (Poly'gala se'nega); =**schote** f = hülse; =**stein** n, min. eagle-stone, ⚕ aetites; =**stock** m der Mühle clack; =**storch** m (common white) stork; der ~ hat das Kindchen gebracht the stork (or doctor) has brought the baby; =**topf** m yellow-rattle (Rhina'nthus crista galli); vgl. Hahnenkamm b.

Klapp-fächer (⸗...) m ⚕ folding-fan; =**fenster** n trap-window; =**horn** ♪ n key(ed)-bugle, cornopean, auch (fr.) cornet-à-piston; =**horn-bläser** m cornet (-player); =**horn-vers** m limerick; =**hut** m opera- (or crush-)hat.

Klappig ⚕ (⸗...) a. ⊕; ⚕ valvar, valvate; in 2ffn ...valve, z.B. zwei2 bivalve.

Klapp-kragen (⸗...) m ⚕ lay- (or turn-) down collar; =**laden** m Bauw.: folding-shutter; =**leiter** f folding-ladder, jointed ladder; =**messer** n spring- (or jack-)knife; =**muschel** f, zo. spring-oyster, water-clam (Spo'ndylus).

klapprig (⸗...) f. klapp(e)rig.

Klapp-sessel (⸗...) m ⚕ = Klappstuhl; =**sitz** m folding- (or flap-)seat; =**stiefel** ⚘ m/pl. (Stulpstiefel) top-boots pl.; =**stuhl** m folding-chair, camp-stool, reclining-chair, a. American chair; =**tisch** m folding-table; =**trompete** ♪ f key-trumpet; =**tür** f trap-door; =**ventil** n clack- (or trap-)valve; =**visier** ⚔ n in Feuerwaffen: folding-sight.

Klaps (⸗) [ndd.; *klapp!] I m ⚕⊕⚘ a., dim. Kläpschen (⸗⸗) n ⚕ tap, slap, knock. — II ⚘! (slap-)bang!, crash!, click!, flop!, F there goes!

klapsen (⸗) I v/n. ⚕ bisw. = klappen 1. — II v/a. to tap, slap, smack.

klar (⁻) [mhd.: clear; *lt. clārus] I a. ⊕(D1) 1. clear (a. fig.; f. 4) F 2 wie Kloßbrühe (as) clear as day(-light) or noonday, as plain as a pikestaff. — 2. (hell) bright (auch vom Himmel), in geh. Spr.: serene. — 3. (durchsichtig) transparent, a. limpid; (rein) pure; 2en Wein einschenken to tell a p. the plain (or unvarnished) truth. — 4. fig. (deutlich) distinct; (verständlich) intelligible, vom Stil: lucid; (bündig) plain; (offenbar) evident, manifest; 2 und deutlich clear and distinct; 2 (adv.) denken to have a clear understanding; es ist ja 2, daß // it stands to reason that //; das ist ganz 2! that's quite plain or certain!; et. 2 (adv.) sehen to see one's way clear; bald wird es Ihnen 2 sein you will soon understand it or see (the drift of) it; über et. 2 werden to grasp (or comprehend) a th.; sich (dat.) 2 werden to make up one's mind. — 5. agr. den Boden 2 machen to clear the ground; ⊕ Glasfabrikation: Spiegelglas 2 schleifen to smooth plate-glass, to grind it for the second time. — 6. ↓ von Tauen ⚓.: (ungehindert) clear; 2e Kette clear hawse; 2e Küste clear coast; 2 zum Gefecht, zur Abfahrt clear (or ready) for action, for sailing; 2 zum Wenden! ready about!, ready all!, about ship!; 2 machen to clear; die Riemen 2 machen to ship the oars; ein Takel 2 scheren to underrun a tackle. — II s. 7. das ~e: a) vom Ei: the white of the egg; b) fig. (Klarheit) what is clear or evident; et. ins 2e bringen od. setzen to clear a matter up, to arrange (or settle) a th.; mit et. ins 2e kommen to make up one's mind about a th.; über et. im 2en sein to be fully enlightened about a th., to see (or understand) it clearly.

Klara (⁻) [lt.] npr/f. (Vn.) ⚕⚕⚕⚘, dim. **Klärchen** n ⚕α. Clara, Clare. [house.]

Klär-anstalt ⊕(⁻...) f ⚕ Zuckerfabr.: curing-; **klär-äugig** (⁻...) a. ⊕ bright-eyed.

Klär-bassin (⁻...) n ⚕ = becken n: a) bei der Kochsalzfabrikation: clearer; b) Wasserwerk: setting-pond or -reservoir.

klar-blickend (⁻...) a. ⊕ clear-sighted, discerning, sagacious.

Kläre (⁻) [mhd.] f ⚕ (Klarheit) clearness.

klaren ↓ (⁻⁻) v/a. ⊕ (klar m.) to clear; die Flagge ⚓. 2 to clear the flag, &c.

klären (⁻⁻) [klar] I v/a. ⊕ to clear (up); ⊕ (läutern) to clarify, (reinigen) to purify, (durchseihen) to percolate; geistige Getränke 2 (schönen) to fine (down) ... — II ⚕ 2 v/refl. to become clear, von trüben Flüssigkeiten a. to settle. — III ~ n ⚕ clearing, purification, fining.

Klär-faß (⁻...) n ⚕ settler; =**gefäß** n für Zucker: clarifier, clearing-pan.

Klarheit (⁻) f ⚕ 1. (f. klar) clearness (a. fig.); brightness, serenity; transparency; fig. distinctness, plainness, des Stils: lucidity; ~ in eine Sache bringen to shed light on a question. — 2. (Hellleuchtendes) shining (or bright, brilliant) light.

klarieren ↓ (⁻⁻⁻) [neu-lt.] I v/a. ⚕: ein Schiff 2 to clear a ship at the custom-house. — II ~ n ⚕ u. **Klarierung** f ⚕ clearance, clearage.

Klarierungs-brief (⁻⁻...) m ⚕, =**schein** m (bill of) clearance; =**spesen** pl. charges pl. for clearance.

Klarinette ♪ (⁻⁻⁻) [fr.] f ⚕ clarinet, a. clarionet. [player.]

Klarinettist ♪ (⁻⁻⁻) m ⚕ clari(o)net-

Klarissa (⁻⁻) ⚕⚕α., **Klarisse** ⚕⚕⚘ npr/f. (Vn.) Clarissa; **Klarissin(nen** pl.) (⁻⁻⁻) f ⚕ (Nonnen-orden) nun(s pl.) of St. Clare, auch (Poor) Clare(s pl.).

Klär-kessel (⁻...) m ⚕ = gefäß.

klar-legen (⁻...) v/a. ⊕** to clear up; 2**machen** v/a. ⊕**: et. 2 to make a th. clear, to explain a th.; f. a. klarlegen.

Klär-mittel (⁻...) n ⚕ clarifier; =**pfanne** f = Klärgefäß.

Klar-schleifen ⊕ (⁻...) n ⚕ von Spiegelglas: smoothing (or second grinding) of plate-glass.

Klärsel ⊕ (⁻⁻) n ⚕ Zuckersiederei: clear liquor, golden syrup, clarified sugar.

klar-stellen (⁻...) v/a. ⊕** = klarlegen; =**stellung** f ⚕ clearing up (of) a matter; explanation, elucidation.

Klasse (⁻⁻) [mhd. 16. sac.; *lt. classis] f ⚕ class, division; nach ~n einteilen to classify; in der ersten, zweiten ~ sitzen to be in the first, second class, eine ~ überspringen to skip a form; oberste ~ e-r Schule: head form, einer engl. Gelehrtenschule: sixth form; die höheren und niederen ~n der Gesellschaft the higher and the lower classes or ranks or grades pl. (of society), auch: the classes and the masses pl.; Fahrschein erster (zweiter) ~ first-class (second-class) ticket.

Klassen-älteste(r) (⁻⁻...) s. ⚕, =**aufseher** m e-r engl. Schule: monitor; =**buch** n list of absence; roll; =**einteilung** f classification; =**erste(r)** s. pupil (or boy, f girl) at the head of a class or form; auch: first in the class; =**geist** m caste-feeling; =**haß** m class-hatred; =**herrschaft** f rule of the upper classes; =**lehrer** m class-teacher, master of a form; =**lotterie** f lottery with several drawings; =**steuer** f graduated income-tax; =**system** n system of classes or classification; =**zimmer** n class- (or school-)room.

Zeichen (f. S. XVII): F familiär; P Volkssprache; ⸕ Gaunersprache; ⚘ selten; † alt (auch gestorben); * neu (auch geboren); ⚘⸕ unrichtig;

[Klassifikation] — 589 — [kleben]

Klassifikation (⌣⌣–tz(⌣)¹) [lt.] f ⊕ classification; **klassifizieren** (⌣⌣–⌣¹) v/a. ⑬ (in Klassen einteilen) to classify.

...klassig (...⌣) a. ⊕ in Zsfgn. z.B. fünf-2 of (or with) five classes.

Klassiker (⌣⌣⌣) [lt.] ⑫ m classic, classical writer or work, standard author; ~-ausgabe f ⑫ edition of classics or standard authors.

klassisch (⌣⌣) [lt.] a. ⊕ 1. (mustergültig) classical; 2er Stil classicism. — 2. fig. das ist 2 (erstaunlich)! it's wonderful!, that beats all!

Klassizismus (⌣⌣⌣⌣) [lt.] m ㉗ classicism; **Klassizist** (⌣⌣⌣) m ㉒ classicist, student of the classics; **Klassizität** (⌣⌣–¹) f ⊕ weitS. high standard, excellency.

Klater (¹⌣) [ndd.] m ㉒ sloven(ly woman), slut; **klat(e)rig** (¹(⌣)⌣) (G., W.) (schmutzig, faul) slovenly.

klatsch! (⸗) [nhd. lautnachahmend] I int. 1. flitsch-2! flip-flap!, smack!, pop! — II ~ m ⑪ a. 2. = Klaps 1; (Peitschenknall) cracking (or smacking, smack) of a whip. — 3. (Basengeschwätz) gossip, tittle-tattle.

Klatsch-base (⸗...) f ⊕ woman fond of gossiping; vgl. -gevatterin; **=bruder** m gossip, scandal-monger; **=blatt** F n newspaper full of gossip, society-paper; **=büchse** f = Ballerbüchse.

Klatsche (⌣⌣) f ㊽ 1. flap for (killing) flies; vgl. Klappe 1. — 2. F = Klatsch-base, -bruder. — 3. Schule: (Angeber) F sneak.

klatschen (⌣⌣) [nhd. lautm. v. *klatsch!] ⑩ I v/n. (h.) 1. to smack, to pop; der Regen klatscht herab oder zu Boden, v/impers. (es regnet, daß) es klatscht the rain comes pattering down, F it's pouring (cats and dogs); die Wogen klatschten übers Verdeck the billows washed overboard or struck the deck. — 2. mit den Händen (oder in die Hände) 2 to clap one's hands, als Beifallszeichen: to applaud; e-m 2, als v/a. e-m Beifall 2 to applaud (F to clap) a p. — 3. F fig. (plaudern) to gossip, to chat; (übles nachreden) to talk scandal, F to scandalize; e-m einen Prozeß an den Hals 2 to involve a p. by one's gossip in a lawsuit. — II v/a. 4. f. 2 u. 3. — 5. (klatschend schlagen) to slap, to smack; fig. er ist geklatscht he is done for. — III ~ n ㉓ 6. (f. 1) smacking, &c.; (f. 2) clapping (one's hands), applause; (f. 3) gossip, scandal.

Klatscher (⌣⌣) m ㉒, ~in f ㊼ person who claps or applauds, auch: clapper.

Klätscher (⌣⌣) m ㉒, ~in f ㊼ (person fond of) gossip, tell-tale, chatterbox, prattler, b.s. scandal-monger; (Angeber[in]) informer, F sneak.

Klatscherei, Klätscherei (⌣⌣⌣") f ⊕ (idle) gossip, (women's) prattle or talk or F gab, b.s. malicious tales pl.; scandal; (Verlästerung) slander, backbiting; ~en machen = klatschen 3.

Klatsch-geschichte (⸗...) f ⊕ idle tale, malicious gossip, (piece of) scandal; **=gesellschaft** f company of gossips, b.s. set of scandalmongers; **=gevatterin** f, **=liese** f prattling (or cackling) woman, gossip, chatterbox;

klatschhaft, klatschig (⌣⌣) a. ⊕ fond of gossip or tittle-tattle or scandal, talkative, chatty; (nicht verschwiegen) indiscreet; **Klatschhaftigkeit** (⌣⌣–) f ⊕ propensity for gossip or tittle-tattle, talkativeness.

Klatsch-maul F (⸗...) n ㉒ prattling (or cackling) woman, gossip, chatterbox; **=mohn** ⚘ m red (or corn-)poppy (Papaver Rhoeas); **=naß** F a. ⊕ wet (or soaked) to the skin; **=nest** n, (small) town abounding in gossip(s) or in scandal; **=rose** ⚘ f = -mohn; **=schwester** F f, **=weib** F n (idle) gossip, b.s. scandal-monger, slanderer.

klauben (¹⌣) [ahd.: cleave; *klieben] v/a. u. v/n. (h.) ⑱ to pick (to pieces), to cull, weitS. to take great pains with a th.; fig. (tritteln) to cavil at a th.; (nachdenken) to ponder (or brood) over things.

Klauber (¹⌣) m ㉒, ~in f ⊕ picker; fig. caviller; **~ei** (–⌣¹) f ⊕ picking, culling; fig. cavilling, hair-splitting.

Klaue (¹⌣) [ahd.: claw] f ⊕, dim. **Kläuchen** (¹⌣) n ⊕ 1. (Zehe ob. Fuß mit Krallen) der Raubtiere: claw; der Raubvögel, auch: fang, talon, pounce, anderer Tiere: paw, der Füchse, Wölfe ꝛc.: foot; mit den ~n packen to claw. — 2. F fig. e-n in den ~n h. to have a p. in one's grip; e-n in seine ~n bekommen to get a p. into one's clutches; eine ~ (schlechte Handschrift) a bad handwriting or F fist, an awful scrawl; Sprichw. an den ~n erkennt man den Löwen you know the lion by his claws, (lt.) ex ungue leonem. — 3. (Huf) cloven foot, hoof cloven (auch myth. von Waldgöttern, vom Teufel ꝛc.) mit gespaltenen ~n cloven-footed, ⚚ bisulcate, bisulcous.

klauen (¹⌣) v/a. ⊕ 1. to claw, (kratzen) to scratch. — 2. (mit Klauen versehen) nur als p.p. geklauet = klauig. — 3. P im Schmutze 2 to wade (or splash) through the mud. — 4. F (klemmen, stibitzen) to nick, prig, pilfer.

Klauen-fett (¹⌣...) n ⊕ neat's-foot oil; **=förmig** a. ⊕ shaped like a claw, ⚚ unguiform; **=füßig** a. claw-footed; **=hammer** ⊕ m claw-hammer; **=los** a. clawless; **=seuche** f, vet. claw-sickness, foot-rot, von Schafen auch: foot-and-mouth disease; **=wild** n cloven-footed animals pl. or game.

klauig (¹⌣) a. ⊕ having claws or fangs, clawed, fanged, ⚚ unguiculate; auch in Zsfgn. z.B.: rot-2 with red fangs.

Klaus (¹) [(Ni)k(o)laus] npr/m. ⊕ γ. (auch Bn.) Nicholas (selten Nick, das meist den Teufel bz.); **Kläuschen** (¹⌣) npr/n. ⊕ α. (dim. v. Klaus) little Nicholas.

Klause (¹⌣) [ahd.: close; *mlt.] f ⊕ 1. (Felsenspalte) cleft (or crack) in a rock; (Gebirgspaß) mountain-pass, defile; (enge, abgeschiedene Wohnung) small secluded dwelling; (Mönchszelle) cell, (Einsiedelei) hermitage; fig. er kommt nie aus seiner ~ F he never leaves his den or hole, he lives like a hermit. — 2. ⊕ metall. sink, wastewater flume.

Klausel (¹⌣) [nhd.; *lt.] f ⊕ jur. clause (auch parl.), proviso, stipulation.

Klausner (¹⌣) [Klause] m ㉒, ~in f ㊼ hermit (f bisw. ...ess), recluse, anchorite; **~leben** n ㉒ hermit's life, solitary existence.

Klausur (–¹) [lt.] f ⊕ Prüfungs-arbeiten in der ~, unter ~ (unter Aufsicht) machen to work examination-papers (under supervision).

Klausur-arbeit (–¹...) f ⊕ (in England die allg. vorherrschende Prüfungsmethode) examination-paper (worked under supervision).

Klaviatur ♪ (–w(⌣)–¹) [lt.] f ⊕ keyboard, keys pl.; stumme ~ (zum Üben der Finger:) ⊕ chirogymnast; **~schrank** m ⊕ bei Orgeln key-desk.

Klavi-chord ♪ (–w–r–) [lt.-gch.] n ⊕ c. (alte Art Klavier, 18. sae.) clavichord.

Klavier ♪ (⸗w–¹) [(⸗⸗) fr. clavier] n ⊕ d. pianoforte, piano; (Flügel) Flügel 3 und Pianino; ~ spielen (Klavierspieler[in] sein) to play the piano, einmal: to play (stümperhaft: to strum) on the piano, zur Übung: to practise the piano; meisterhaft ~ spielen to be a first-class (or a brilliant) pianist, to excel (F to shine) on the piano; ~ spielen lernen to learn (or to take lessons on) the piano.

Klavier-auszug ♪ (⸗w–"...) m ⊕ music (or score) arranged for the piano; **=kasten** m case of a piano(forte); **=lehrer(in f)** m piano-teacher; **=macher** m piano(forte)-maker; **=mechanik** f, **=mechanismus** ⊕ m piano-action or -movement; **=schule** f (Werk) exercises pl. (or manual) for the piano, auch: pi.-school; (Lehranstalt) school for music, piano-classes pl.; **=spiel** n piano-playing; **=spieler(in f)** m pianist, piano-player; **=stimmer** m piano(forte-)tuner; **=stück** n piece of music (arranged) for the piano; **=stuhl** m music-stool; **=stunde** f (=unterricht m) lesson (instruction) on the piano.

Klavi-zimbel ♪ (–w–"⌣) n ㉒ (Art Klavier 15/8. sae.) manichord; vgl. Klavichord.

Klebe-blatt (¹⌣...) n ⊕ posted-up bill, poster; **=kraut** n catch-weed, goosegrass, hairif(f), cleavers pl. (Galium aparine); **=mittel** n: ⚚ agglutinant.

kleben (¹⌣) [ahd.: cleave] ⑨ I v/n. (h.) 1. an et. (fest) 2 to adhere (or stick, cling, cleave) to a th.; das klebt wie Pech it sticks like glue or wax (auch fig.); Kletten 2 an den Kleidern burs stick (or attach themselves) to the clothes; 2 bleiben to stick fast. — 2. fig.: a) Blut klebt an seinen Händen his hands are stained (or soiled) with blood; diese Schande wird ewig an ihm 2 (bleiben) that disgrace will attach (or F stick) to him for ever; die Zunge klebt mir (vor Trockenheit) am Gaumen my tongue (is so parched that it) sticks (or cleaves) to the roof of my mouth; F die Hände (oder et. an den Fingern) 2 lassen (entwenden) to pilfer, F to have long fingers; es bleibt nichts an ihm 2 nothing adheres (or sticks) to his memory or to him; b) am Buchstaben 2 to adhere to the letter, to take a th. literally; am Irdischen 2 (hangen) to cling to earthly things, to have a worldly

♪ Musik; ⚚ Wissenschaft; ⚘ Pflanze; ⊕ Geographie; ⊕ Technik; ⚒ Bergbau; ⚔ Militär; ⚓ Marine; ⊛ Handel; ✉ Post; ⊞ Eisenbahn.

[**Klebenelke**] — 590 — [**klein**]

mind. — **II** v/a. **3.** to glue, paste, stick (fast), mit Gummi: to gum (down or fast); weitS. (anheften) to attach, to fasten; ○b: ☞ agglutinant. — **III** ~ n ⓢ **4.** (f. I) adhesion; attachment.
Klebe-nelke ♀ (ᴸ‿…) f ㊵ = Pech ㊂; =**pflaster** n adhesive (or sticking-)plaster.
Kleber (ᴸ‿) m ㉒ **1.** ~(in f ㊵) one who glues or pastes, &c. (f. kleben II), sticker of bills, &c.; F *fig.* (lästige Person) F sticker-on, bore. — **2.** ☞ chm. (Pflanzenleim): ☞ gluten. — **3.** ○ und *orn.* = Kleiber.
kleb(e)richt ↘, mſt **kleb(e)rig** (ᴸ‿‿) a. ㊶ adhesive, F sticky, ↘ gluey, ☞ viscous, viscid, glutinous; (feucht) clammy.
Klebe-stoff (ᴸ‿…) m ㉒ = Klebstoff; =**taf(fe)t** m (englisches Pflaster) courtplaster; =**zettel** m adhesive label.
Kleb-kraut ♀ (ᴸ‿…) n ㉓ = Klebekraut.
Klebrigkeit (ᴸ‿‿) f ㊶ (f. kleberig) adhesiveness, F stickiness, ☞ viscosity, viscidness, clamminess.
Kleb-stoff (ᴸ‿…) m ㉒ adhesive substance, ☞ gluten; =**zettel** m = Klebezettel.
Kleck (◡) m ⓐb. = Klecks.
klecken[1] (◡‿) [ahd.]: es will nicht ㊈ (vonstatten gehen) that won't do.
klecken[2] (◡‿) [mhd.: clatch] v/a. u. v/n. (h.) ⓼ = klecksen.
Klecker (◡‿) m ㉒ **1.** = Kleckser. — **2.** F (f. kleckern) bſb. in ~fritze m, ~liese f F dirty little muck, auch: mud-lark.
kleckern F (◡‿) v/n. (h.) ⓼a. to eat in a dirty (or nasty) manner; to slobber; v/refl. ſich voll ㊈ F to mess o.s. all over (or to beslobber o.s.) in eating.
Klecks (◡) [nhd. 18. sae.; *flecken] m ⓐa., *dim.* ~chen n ㉓ ink-blot, blotch; Klecke auf Papier m. to blot …
klecksen (◡‿) v/a. und v/n. (h.) ⓽ to blot (with ink), to make (ink-)blots; die Feder klecksſt … (makes) blots or splashes; weitS. (schlecht schreiben) to scrawl, to scribble; (schlecht malen) to daub.
Kleckser (◡‿) m ㉒ (f. der schlecht schreibt) scrawler, scribbler, F ink-spiller, ink-slinger; (schlechter Maler) dauber.
Kleckserei (◡‿ᴸ) f ㊵ (f. klecksen) constant blotting, F ink-spilling, weitS. scrawling, daubing, daub.
klecksig (◡‿) a. ㊶ blotted, full of blots.
Klee (ᴸ) ♀ [ahd.: clover] m ⓔe. **1.** clover, trefoil, in Irland: shamrock (*Trifo′lium*); fleischroter ~ carnation clover (*T. incarna′tum*); roter englischer ~ (common) purple clover or trefoil (*T. prate′nse*); weißer ~ white (or Dutch) clover (*T. repens*); *fig.* F et. über den grünen ~ loben to praise a th. to the skies. — **2.** (von klee-artigen Pflanzen), zB. ewiger ~ lucerne (*Medica′go sati′va*).
Klee-acker (ᴸ‿…) m ㉒ clover-field; ♂**artig** *a.* ㊶ like clover or trefoil; =**bau** m ㉒ cultivation of clover; =**blatt** n trefoil-leaf, als irisches Nationalzeichen: shamrock; *fig.* (Gesamtheit von dreien) triplets *pl., co.* trio; ein sauberes ~ F three of a kidney, weitS. a pack of rogues, *iro.* a nice set (of fellows); =**blattbogen** ○ m, *arch.* trefoil-arch; ♂**förmig** *a.* formed like a trefoil-leaf; =**blüte** f bloom (or blossom) of clover; =**feld** n field of clover; =**futter** n clover as fodder for

cattle; =**saat** f sowing of clover, cloverseed; =**salz** n, *chm.* salt of sorrel, ☞ potassium oxalate ($C_2K_2O_4$); =**same(n)** m clover-seed; ♂**sauer** *a. chm.*: ☞ oxalic, ♂**saures Salz**: ☞ oxalate; =**säure** f: ☞ oxalic acid ($C_2H_2O_4$).
Klei (ᴸ) [ndd.: clay] m ⓔb. clay, marl; ~ =**acker** m ㉒ clay field.
kleiben ○ (ᴸ‿) [ahd.] **I** v/a. = kleben II; Maurerei: e-e Wand ㊈ to make (or to put up, to build) a mud-wall, to clay (or loam) a wall. — **II** † v/n. (kleben bleiben) to adhere, to stick (fast).
Kleiber (ᴸ‿) m ㉒ **1.** ○ (Maurer, der Wände kleibt) one who makes mud-walls. — **2.** *orn.* nuthatch (*Sitta*, bſb. *cae′sia*).
Klei-boden (ᴸ…) m ㉒ clay(ey) soil.
Kleid (ᴸ) [mhd. 12. sae.: cloth] n ⓒ. **1.** garment, garb, weitS. article of dress, in geh. Spr.: vestment; langes ~ der Frauen, Kinder dress, loses: gown (a. der Orientalen, englischer Magistratsperſonen ꝛc.), (Reit)~ riding-gown, habit; ~er clothes *pl.*, (Anzug) apparel, attire, vgl. Gewand u. Kleidung 2; f.aufſchürzen, ausſchneiden 2; anſteigendes, hohes ~ dress made high at the neck, highneck dress; Sprichw. ~er machen Leute fine feathers make fine birds. — **2.** *fig.* das ~ (der äußere Schein) der Tugend the garb (or cloak) of virtue, &c.; das ~ des Elends the (ragged) garb of misery.
Kleidchen (ᴸ‿) n ㉔ (dim. von Kleid) little dress or gown or smock.
kleiden (ᴸ‿) [mhd.: clothe] ⓼ **I** v/a. u. sich ㊈ v/refl. **1.** (sich) ㊈ to clothe (o.s.), to dress (o.s.); sich gut (schlecht) ㊈ to dress well (badly); sie ㊈ sich in die reichſten Gewänder they attire themselves in the costliest apparel, they put on the costliest garments; sie ㊈ sich schwarz, bunt they dress (or go) in black, in colours; sich selbſt (auf eigene Koſten) ㊈ to pay for (F to find) one's own clothes; anſtändig gekleidet respectably dressed, in decent clothes. — **2.** e-n Altar ꝛc. ㊈ (bedecken) to dress an altar, &c. — **3.** *fig.* in Worte ㊈ to clothe (or express) in words; in anmutige Formen ㊈ to cast (or shape) in(to) graceful forms. — **II** v/a. u. v/n. (h.) **4.** e-n (P a. e-m) ㊈ (e-m anſtehen) to suit (or become) a p.; das Kleid ㊈ Sie vorzüglich that suits you admirably, it fits you like a glove; *abs.* das kleidet (gut) that's most becoming. — **III** ~ n ㉓ **5.** clothing, &c. (f. I).
Kleider-ablage (ᴸ‿…) f ㊷ = Garderobe; =**aufwand** m expensive (or sumptuous, costly, lavishing) style of dress(ing); =**besen** m, etwa: carpet-broom, whisk; =**bock** m = =gestell; =**bürste** f clothesbrush; =**büste** f ○ (Gliederpuppe in Läden) clothes-dummy; =**geld** n allowance for dressing; =**geschäft** ● n clothing establishment, warehouse for readymade clothes or gentlemen's outfit; vgl. =handel; =**gestell** n clothes-horse or rack, im Hausgange: hall-stand; =**haken** m zum Aufhängen von Kleidern: clothes-peg or rack; =**halter** m = Aufschürzer; =**handel** ● m dealing (or trade) in old or second-hand clothes; =**händler(in** f) m: a dealer in (old)

clothes, second-hand clothes-dealer, (Trödler) old-clothes man; b) (Schneider) merchant-tailor, outfitter; =**handlung** f = =laden; =**kammer** f wardrobe; =**kasten**, =**koffer** m clothes-box; =**laden** m clothes-shop; =**laus** f, *zo.* bodylouse (*Pedi′culus vestime′nti*); =**macher** m (ladies') tailor; =**macherin** f dressmaker; =**magazin** n = =geschäft; =**markt** ● m old-clothes market, *co.* auch: ragfair; =**motte** f, *ent.* (clothes-)moth (*Ti′nea pellione′lla*); =**narr** m, **närrin** f person overfond (or madly fond) of dress or finery; =**ordnung** f regulations *pl.* regarding dress (Aufwandsgesetze) sumptuary laws *pl.*; =**pracht** f luxuriousness in dress(ing); =**rechen**, =**riegel** m peg-board, clothes-rail or -rack; =**schmuck** m finery, gorgeous attire, F adornments *pl.*; =**schrank** m, =**spind** n cupboard for clothes, clothespress, wardrobe; =**ständer** m = =gestell; =**stoff** m clothing- (für Frauen auch) dress-) material, tailor's cloth; =**tasche** f pocket; =**tracht** f costume, fashion (in dress); =**trödler(in** f) m = =händler(in) a; =**verleiher(in** f) m person who lets out clothes, *thea.* costumier; =**verwahrer(in** f) m wardrobe-keeper; =**vorrat** m stock of clothes, wardrobe.
Kleid-keule ○ (ᴸ‿…) f, =**kiel** m (hölzerner Hammer) serving-mallet.
kleidsam (ᴸ‿) *a.* ㊶ becoming, fitting well; nicht ㊈ unbecoming; ~**keit** f ㊶ becomingness, mehr gbr.: becoming (or suitable) style of dress.
Kleidung (ᴸ‿) [mhd.] f ㊶ **1.** (das Kleiden) clothing, dressing; weitS. rigging (out). — **2.** (Gewandung, Tracht) clothing, clothes *pl.*, dress, (wearing-)apparel, habiliment, costume, F toggery, togs *pl., bibl.* &c. raiment; ⚔ auch: accoutrement, equipment, Kunst: drapery; bürgerliche ~ plain (or civilian's) clothes *pl.* or dress; farbige (schwarze, weiße) ~ tragen to be dressed (or to dress) in colours (in black, in white).
Kleidungs-stoff (ᴸ‿…) m ㉒ material for (gentlemen's) clothes; =**stück** n article of clothing or dress, ~e *pl.* wearing-apparel, F togs, ↘ slops *pl.*
Kleie (ᴸ‿) [ahd.] f ㊷ Müllerei: bran, pollard, grit, ☞ furfur.
kleien (ᴸ‿) [Kleie] *a.* ㊶ (of) bran.
kleien-artig (ᴸ‿…) *a.* ㊶ branny, *path.* ☞ farinaceous, furfuraceous, pityroid; =**bad** n ○ vor dem Färben oder Gerben branning; =**beize** f der Gerber: a) branmaceration; b) = =wasser; =**brot** n bran-bread; =**flechte** f, =**grind** m, *path.* ☞ pityriasis; =**kasten** m Müllerei: branchest; =**mehl** n pollard, grit; =**wasser** n bran and water.
klei-icht, klei-ig[1] (ᴸ‿) [Klei] *a.* ㊶ clayey.
klei-icht, klei-ig[2] (ᴸ‿) [Kleie] *a.* ㊶ branny, ☞ furfuraceous.
klein (ᴸ) [ahd.: clean rein] (ant. groß) **I** *a.* ㊶ (D1) **1.** little, small, *comp.* u. *sup.:* smaller, smallest, nur abstrakt: less(er), least; (winzig) minute, tiny, von Gestalt: diminutive; (unbedeutend) trifling, petty, insignificant, exiguous; (zwerghaft) dwarfish, pigmean, Lilliputian; ㊈ und dick dumpy

Signs (see page XVII): F familiar; P vulgar; ℱ flash; ↘ rare; † obsolete (died); * new word (born); ‡ incorrect; ♪ music.

[Klein] — 591 — [Klempnerhandwerk]

F podgy; bisw. zur Verstärkung: ein ≈es, ≈es Körnchen a tiny little grain; ein ≈ bißchen oder wenig a wee (little) bit. — 2. mit v.: sich ≈ machen to make o.s. small, fig. to humble o.s.; ≈ schneiden, hacken to chop small, v. Fleisch zc.: to mince; ≈er werden to grow less, to shrink, to decrease; ≈er m. to shorten, to reduce in size; kurz und ≈ schlagen to knock to pieces or F to smithereens. — 3. mit s.: ≈es Alphabet, ≈er Buchstabe, ≈er Druck small alphabet, letter, print; ≈(er)er, ≈ster Bruder younger, youngest brother; ≈er Diebstahl jur. petty larceny; ≈er Geist small (or narrow) mind; ≈es Geld small coin, change; ≈es Holz small (pieces pl. of) wood, fire-wood; ein ≈er Kerl a little fellow or F chap; ein ≈es Kind allg.: a little child, ≈ für sein Alter: a small child; ≈e Kinder little children or folk(s), F small fry; der ≈e Krieg ✕ f. Kleinkrieg, ≈e Leute small people (auch fig.); ein ≈er Mann a short man; ein ganz ≈es Männchen quite a little man or F dot; ohne die ≈ste (geringste) Mühe without the least (or slightest) trouble; ≈e Okta've minor octave; bibl. ≈e Propheten minor prophets pl.; ≈es Schläfchen short nap, F forty winks pl.; ≈e Schulden petty debts pl.; ≈ste Verzögerung shortest (or least) delay; ≈es Wildbret small game. — 4. adv. er hat ≈ angefangen he began in a small way; f. beigeben 2; ≈ denken to have narrow views; es geht bei ihnen ≈ her they live in a small (or poor, F trumpery) way; F fig. ich kann es nicht ≈ kriegen I cannot make it out. — II ≈(r) m, ≈e f, ≈e(s) n ⓶ (oft klein gschr.) 5. der ≈e the little boy, die ≈e the little girl; die ≈en the little ones pl. — 6. ≈ inv.: von ≈ ab (an oder auf) from an early age, from a (little) child; groß und ≈, ≈e und Große (both) great and small, (both) old and young. — 7. sachlich: et. ≈es a small thing; es ist nichts ≈es it is no trifle or joke; das wäre ihm ein ≈es it would be (a) child's play to him; Sprichw. wer das ≈e nicht ehrt, ist des Großen nicht wert, etwa: take care of the pence, and the pounds will take care of themselves; auch das ≈ste kann schaden even the smallest thing can do harm. — 8. mit prp. im ≈en on a small scale, in detail; paint., &c. in miniature; im ≈en wie im Großen both in great and small things; im ≈en verkaufen to sell (by) retail, ● to retail; eine Sache bis ins ≈ste untersuchen od. beraten to go (or enter) into full particulars; bis ins ≈ste prüfen ... most minutely or closely; Sprichw. mit ≈em fängt man an, mit Großem hört man auf, etwa: small beginnings, great endings; everything comes to him who can wait; über ein ≈es (Weilchen) in a short time, after a little while; um ein ≈es by a little, very nearly; um ein ≈es dicker a trifle (F a bit) stouter; um ein ≈es (in kurzem) after a little (or short) while.
Klein (¹) n ⓒ c. f. Gänse≈, Kohlen≈.

Klein-asien ♀ (ʺ...) n ⓶ Asia Minor, auch: Lesser Asia; ≈äugig a. ⓺ small-eyed, ⚇ microphthalmic; ≈bahn ⇌ f branch-line, light railway; ≈bauer m small farmer, crofter; ≈betrieb ● m establishment on a small scale, sm. concern; ≈blätt(e)rig ♀ a. sm.-leaved; ≈blumig, ≈blütig ♀ a. with small flowers or blossom(s); ≈bürger m humble citizen, small man; ≈bürgerlich a. plebeian. [baby.)
Kleinchen F (¹˅) n ⓶ (kleines Kind) (little))
klein-denkend (ʺ...) a. ⓺ narrow-minded.
Kleine (¹˅) f ⓺ f. klein 5.
kleiner(e)n-teils (ʺ˅(˅)¹) adv. to a smaller extent.
Kleiner-werden (ʺ˅⤴˅) n ⓶ growing less, shrinkage, decrease, diminution.
klein-füßig (ʺ...) a. ⓺ small-footed; ≈geisterei f ⓶ narrowness of mind, mean spirit; ≈geistig a. of a narrow mind or a mean spirit; ≈geld n small coin, change; ≈geschäft ● n = ≈handel; ≈gewehr ✕ n sm. arms pl., musketry; ≈gewehr-feuer ✕ n musketry-fire; ≈gewerbe(≈betrieb m) n ● sm. industry; ≈gläubig a. of little faith, lacking in faith or confidence; vgl. ≈mütig; ≈gläubigkeit f lack of faith or confidence; ≈handel ● m retail business, small trade; ≈händler(in f) m ● retail dealer, small trader.
Kleinheit (¹) f ⓺ (f. klein) littleness, smallness; (Winzigkeit) minuteness, diminutiveness, tininess.
klein-herzig (ʺ...) a. ⓺ = ≈mütig.
Kleinigkeit (¹˅) f ⓺ small (or light) thing or matter, trifle; (Unbedeutendes) petty (or insignificant) matter (elender Kram) paltry concern; ≈en pl. small (or minor) details, petty matters, auch (it.) nugæ pl.; (Spielzeug) toys pl.; für eine ≈ kaufen to buy for a mere song; ≈s-krämer(in f) m (ʺ˅-...) ⓶ pedant(ic fellow), punctilious (or fussy) person; ≈krämerei f pedantry, fuss(iness).
klein-kalibrig ✕ (ʺ...) a. ⓺ (of) small bore; ≈kinder-bewahr-anstalt f ⓶ day-nursery, unentgeltliche: (fr.) crèche; ≈kinder-schule f infant-school; ≈kopf ichth. morris (Leptoce'phalus); ≈köpfig a. small-headed, ⚇ microcephalous; ≈körnig a. small-grained; ≈kram ● m small shop; ≈krieg ✕ m guerrilla (or irregular) warfare; ≈laut a. fig. downcast, dejected, F down in the mouth; e-n ≈ m. to put a p. down, F to take a p. down a peg (or two); ≈ werden to assume a (more) modest tone, F to sing small, to draw in one's horns; ≈leben n simple (or humble) life.
kleinlich (¹˅) a. ⓺ petty, paltry; (beschränkt, von Anstichten) narrow-minded (sehr genau) punctilious, fussy; (gemein) mean, shabby (a. von Sachen = armselig; ≈keit f ⓺ petty spirit, paltriness; punctiliousness; meanness, shabbiness; narrow-mindedness.
Klein-malerei f (ʺ...) ⓶ miniature-painting; ≈meister m small craftsman; ≈meisterei f business (or vocation) of a sma'l craftsman; ≈mut m pusillanimity, despondency, faint-heartedness; ≈mütig a. pusillanimous,

despondent, faint-hearted; ≈ werden to lose heart; ≈mütigkeit f = ≈mut.
Kleinod (¹-) [mhd.] n ⓒ c. (pl. auch Kleino'dien ⓶) jewel, gem, trinket; (Schatz) treasure; königliche ≈ien emblems pl. of royalty, regalia, crown-jewels pl.; fig. die Gesundheit ist das köstlichste ≈ health is the most precious of (earthly) possessions.
Klein-Okta'v (ʺ...), ≈Quart n ⓶ Buchh., small octavo, quarto; ≈russe m, russin f Little Russian; ≈rußland ♀ npr/n. Little Russia; ≈schlächter m retail (or small) butcher; ≈schmied m toolmaker; ≈schmiede-arbeit, ≈schmiederei f tool-making; ≈staat m small (or minor, second-rate) state; ≈staaterei f system of small states; ≈staatlich a. belonging to a small state; ≈städter(in f) m inhabitant of a sm. (or provincial, country-)town; ≈städtisch a. (characteristic) of a sm. town, provincial, F countrified; ≈verkauf, ≈verkäufer ● m = ≈handel, ≈händler; ≈vieh n small cattle; ≈zähnig a., zo. u. anat. small-toothed, ⚇ microdont.
Kleio (¹˅) = Klio. [size.)
Kleister (¹˅) [mhd.] m ⓶ (starch-)paste,)
Kleister-aal (ʺ...) m ⓶, ≈älchen n, zo. paste-eel (Angui'llula glutino'sa).
Kleisterei (-˅¹) f ⓺ (much) pasting.
Kleister-eimer (ʺ...) m ⓶ paste pail.
kleist(e)rig (¹(˅)¹) a. ⓺ like paste, pasty, weitS. sticky, adhesive; vom Brot: slack-(or half-)baked. [paste or size.)
kleistern (¹˅) v/a. ⓶ a. to (stick with))
Kleister-pinsel (ʺ...) m ⓶ paste-brush; ≈tiegel, ≈topf m paste-pot.
Klemens (¹˅) npr/m. ⓓ γ. Clement.
Klemme (¹˅) [mhd.] f ⓺ 1. implement for squeezing or pressing, holdfast, clamp; (Schraubstock) (screw-)vice. — 2. fig. (Enge) tigh corner, pinch; (Verlegenheit) dilemma; F scrape; in der ≈ sein (sich befinden oder sitzen, stecken) to be in great straits or distress, to be hard pressed (for money), F to be in a fix or corner.
Klemm-eisen ⊕ (ʺ...) n ⓶ vice-cheek or -chop, Schlosserei: horse-bit.
klemmen (¹˅) [ahd.] I v/a. 1. to squeeze, pinch, press (tightly); (quetschen) to jam; fig. zwischen Zweifel und Angst geklemmt kept in suspense between doubt and fear. — 2. F etwas ≈ (mitnehmen) to filch, to pilfer, F to nick, prig, pinch. — II sich ≈ v/refl. 3. von Türen zc.: to catch (auch mach.); die Räder e-r Maschine ≈ sich (die Maschine klemmt sich) the wheels of a machine get (or the machine gets) jammed. — III ~ n ⓶ 4. (f. 1) squeeze, pinch, (tight) pressure; (f. 2) filching, &c.
Klemmer (¹˅) m ⓶ 1. = Klemme 1. — 2. = Kneifer 2. — 3. F (f. klemmen 2) pilferer, F prig, pincher.
Klempner ⊕ (¹˅) [nhd.; *Klampe] m ⓶ tinsmith, tinman, tinker, (Kupfer-, Messer-schmied) brazier, (Blei-arbeiter) plumber; ~arbeit f tinsmith's work.
Klempnerei ⊕ (-˅¹¹) f ⓺ tinsmith's trade r ware or workshop.
Klempner-handwerk (˅...) n ⓶ tinsmith's trade or craft.

⚇ scientific; ♀ botanical; ♀ geography; ⊕ machinery; ✕ mining; ✕ military; ⚓ marine; ● commercial; ✉ postal; ⇌ railway.

[Klempnern] — 592 — [Klinkhaken]

Klempnern (⏑⏑) v/n. (h.) ⓐa. to work as a tinsmith or a tinker.
Klempner=ware (⏑⏑…) f ⓔ tinware.
Klepper (⏑⏑) [ndd.; * klappen] m ㉒ 1. † fleet horse; (Reitpferd) saddle-horse. — 2. jetzt contp. hack, jade.
Klepsydra ⏑ (⏑⏑) [grch.] f ㊽ (Wasseruhr der Alten) clepsydra.
klerikal (–⏑–́) [grch. klēros Los] a. ⓖ clerical; ~e([r) m) f ㊼ clerical partisan, churchman; ~ismus (–⏑–⏑) m ㉗ clericalism.
Kleriker (–́⏑⏑) m ㉒ clerk in holy orders, clergyman, F cleric.
Klerisei (–⏑–́) f ㊻ clergy (ant. laity), als Partei: clerical party; weit S. (Sippschaft) clique, band, set, F tribe, gang.
Klerus (–́⏑) [grch.=lt.] m ㉘ (o. pl.) (Geistlichkeit) clergy, F clerical tribe.
Klette (⏑⏑) [ahd.] f ㉑ 1. (Blütenkelch von A'rctium) bur. — 2. ♀ (die Pflanze) burdock (A'rctium), bsd. gemeine ~ common bur(dock) (A'rctium Lappa). — 3. fig. fest hängen ob. kleben, sitzen wie eine ~ to stick like a bur or like a leech; er ist (wie) eine ~ (nicht loszuwerden) F he is a sticker-on or a bore; sich wie eine ~ an e-n hängen to hang to a p.'s coat-tails or skirts, F to stick like glue to a p.
Kletten ⊕ (⏑⏑) [Klette] v/a. ⓩ Tuchm.: die Wolle ㉒ to cull (or card) the wool.
kletten=artig (⏑⏑…) a. ⓖ burry; =distel ♀ f ㉒ bur-thistle (Ca'rduus persona'ta); =walze ⊕ f Spinnerei: burring-engine; ㉒weise adv. like a bur; =wurzel f burdock-root.
Kletterei (⏑⏑–́) f ㊻ frequent climbing.
Kletter=eisen (⏑⏑…) n/pl. ⓔ climbing-irons, prickers pl.
Kletterer (⏑⏑⏑) m ㉒ climber.
Kletter=farn (⏑⏑…) m ㉒ climbing-fern (Lygo'dium palma'tum); =fisch m, ichth. climbing-perch, tree-climber (A'nabas scandens); =fuß m, orn.: scansorial foot; ⓔfüßig a. ⓖ orn.: yoke-footed or -toed, ⏑ zygodactylous, …ic; =mast m = =stange.
klettern (⏑⏑) [nhd.; * Klette] I v/n. (h., bei Ortsveränderung sn) ㉒a. to climb; auf einen Baum ㉒ to climb (or to swarm up) a tree; auf einen Berggipfel ㉒ to mount (up) a peak; mit Mühe: to clamber (or scramble) up. — II ~ n ㉓ climbing, &c. (s. I). — III ⓓ p.pr.: u. a. ⓖ, bsd. ♀ creeping, twining, orn.: ⏑ scansorious, …ial.
Kletter=pflanze ♀ (⏑⏑…) f ㉑ climbing plant, creeper; =stange f auf Turnplätzen rc.: climbing-pole, bei Volksfesten: greasy pole; =vögel m/pl. orn. climbers, ⏑ scansores pl.
Klick (⏑) int. click!; ㉒flack! flipflap!
Klicker (⏑⏑) m Kinderspiel: marble, taw; ㉒n v/n. (h.) ㉒a. to play marbles.
Kli=ent (–⏑) [lt. Höriger] m ㉒, ~in f ㊷ röm. Alt. und jur. (vom Anwalte Vertretene[r]) client; ~el (–⏑–́), =schaft (⏑–) f ㊻ clientship, (fr.) clientele. (Kundschaft) customers pl., connexion.
Klima (–́⏑) [grch.] n (sg. ⓓ, pl. ~te) (a. ⓢ, ⓖ) ♁, phys. (Himmelsstrich) climate (sich) an das ~ gewöhnen to acclimatize (o.s.).

klimakterisch ⏑ (–⏑–́⏑) [grch.] a. ⓖ med. (auf die Lebensstufen bezüglich) climacteric(al); ㉒e Jahre, ㉒e Zeit change of life, climacteric period.
klimatisch (–⏑–́) [Klima] a. ⓖ climatic; ㉒e Veränderung change of climate or of air; ㉒e (Witterungs=) Verhältnisse climatic conditions pl.
Klimatologie ⏑ (–⏑⏑–́) [grch.] f ㊽ (Lehre vom Klima) climatology. [climate.]
Klima=wechsel (–́⏑…) m ㉒ change of
Klimax ⏑ (–́⏑) [grch. f Leiter] f ⑬, oft m ⑪ ⓖa. rhet. (Steigerung) climax.
Klimbim P (⏑–́) m, n ㉟ humbug, tricks pl. (of the trade), trickery; viel ~ (Reklame) für et. machen to make a great fuss about a th., to puff a th., to blazon it forth.
klimmen (⏑⏑) [ahd.: climb] v/n. (h. u. sn) ㉒a. (auch ⓢ) to climb (up), fig. to strive for; er ist bis zum Gipfel des Ruhmes geklommen he rose (or ascended) to the pinnacle of fame.
Klimperei (⏑⏑–́) f ㊻ = Geklimper.
Klimperer (⏑⏑⏑) m ㉒, **Klimp(r)erin** f ㊷ p. who strums on the piano or jingles on the guitar, &c.; indifferent (or clumsy) musician.
Klimper=kasten (⏑⏑…) m ㉒ = Klapperkasten; =lied n jingling (burden of a) song, humdrum tune.
klimpern (⏑⏑) [nhd. lautm.] I v/n. (h.) u. v/a. ㉒a. 1. to jingle, to tinkle, mit dem Gelde: to chink one's money. — 2. (meist schlecht spielen) auf dem Klavier ㉒ to strum on the piano, auf der Gitarre ㉒ to play (indifferently) on the guitar, F to twang on the guitar. — II ~ n ㉓ 3. = Geklimper.
Kling! (⏑) [schallnachahmend] I int. ㉒ ㉒! a. klingling(ling)!, ㉒klang! tinkle, tinkle!; von Glocken: ding-dong! — II ~ m, inv. mit ~ und Klang with beating of drums, amid ringing of bells or strains of music.
Klinge¹ (⏑⏑) [nhd.] f ㊽ 1. blade of a knife, a sword, &c.; weit S. (Schwert) sword; fenc. die ~n kreuzen to cross (the) swords; Hiebe mit flacher ~ blows with the flat of the sword; vor die ~ fordern to challenge (to a duel with swords); er schlägt e-e gute ~: a) fenc. he is a good swordsman; b) beim Essen: he plays a good knife and fork; ⚔ die Garnison über die ~ springen l. to put the garrison to the (edge of the) sword; fig. bei der ~ (Sache) bleiben to keep to one's subject or to the point. — 2. ⊕ join.: e-s Hobels plane-iron.
Klinge² (⏑⏑) [ahd.] f ㊽ (Gießbachschlucht) bed of a torrent, ravine.
Klinge=beutel (⏑⏑…) m ㉒=Klingelbeutel.
Klingel (⏑⏑) f ㉑ (small) bell, hand-bell.
Klingel=beutel (⏑⏑…) m ㉒ in der Kirche: bag for collecting the offertory, bsd. ehm. a. bell-purse; =draht m bell-wire; =feder f bell-spring.
klingeln (⏑⏑) [nhd.; * klingen] ㉒a. I v/n. (h.): a) v. Personen: to ring (the bell), to pull (or touch) the bell; e-m ㉒ to ring for a p.; ist (nach) dem Mädchen geklingelt worden!? has the servant been rung for?; b) v. Glocken rc.: to

tinkle, ⏑ to tintinnabulate; v/impers. es klingelt there is a ring (of the bell), the bell rings. — II v/a. e-n aus dem Schlafe ㉒ to waken a p. by ringing, to ring a p. up. — III ~ n ㉓ (s. I) ringing (of) the bell, ⏑ tintinnabulation; von Dienstboten: auf das ~ hören ob. achten to answer (or attend to) the bell.
Klingel=schnur (⏑⏑…) f ㉒ bell-cord or -rope; =wecker m electric alarum; =zug m pull of a bell, bell-pull; =zugwinkel ⊕ m Schlosserei: bell-wire lever.
klingen (⏑⏑) [ahd.: clink lautm.] ⓞft I v/n. 1. (h.) to sound, (erklingen) to resound; die Glocken ㉒ the bells are ringing or chiming or tinkling; das klingt sonderbar, wie ein Märchen it sounds (or seems) strange, like a fairy-tale; mir ㉒ die Ohren my ears are tingling, I have a singing in the ears; ㉒ lassen to chink, tinkle, ring; schön ㉒de Worte words of a pleasant sound; ㉒e Münze ready money, hard cash, specie; ✕ mit ㉒dem Spiele with drums beating, with fifes and drums, with full band. — 2. mst ⓖ: mit den Gläsern ㉒ (in Engl. nicht üblich) to touch glasses; auf j-s Wohl ㉒ to touch glasses in toasting a p. — 3. (sn) (sich ausbreiten) sein Ruf ist bis in ferne Länder geklungen (gedrungen) his fame has spread to distant lands. — II ~ n ㉓ 4. sounding, &c. (s. I); ~ in den Ohren singing (or humming) in the ears.
Klingen=probe ⊕ (⏑⏑…) f ㉒ testing (or assay) of sword-blades; =schmied m sword-cutler or -maker.
Klinger (⏑⏑) m ㉒ gr. (Selbstlaut) vowel.
Kling=fähigkeit ♪ (⏑…) f ㉒ quality of tone; =klang m: a) jingling (a. v. Gläsern), tinkling, bibl.~: jingle-jangle, ting-ting; fig. sonorous (or high-sounding) phrases pl.; b) int. s. kling I.
klingklang, klingling (⏑–́), **klinglingling** (⏑⏑–́) int. s. kling I.
Kling=stein (⏑–́) m ㉒ min. clinkstone, ⏑ phonolite.
Klinik (–́⏑) [grch. kli'nē Bett] f ㉒ med. treatment of patients at an infirmary; (Krankenhaus) infirmary, hospital; (Armen=apotheke) dispensary; ~er m ㉒ physician (or student) at an infirmary; ~um n ㉘ course of hospital (or clinical) lectures.
klinisch (–́⏑) [grch.] a. ⓖ clinical.
Klinke ⊕ (⏑⏑) [md.; * klingen] f Schlosserei: latch (= Drücker 2), catch of a door; (Rutschhaken) door-handle.
klinken (⏑⏑) v/n. (h.) u. v/a. ⓖ: am Schlosse, an der Tür(e), am Drücker ㉒ to put up (or put down) the latch; schließend: to latch the door, öffnend: to unlatch it.
Klinken=blech (⏑⏑…) n ㉒ latch-plate; =schloß n trunk-lock, lock opening with a latch-key.
Klinker (⏑⏑) [ndd.; * klingen] m ㉒ (hartgebrannter Ziegel) (Dutch) clinker, hard-baked tile; ㉒weise adv. ↓ ㉒weise gebaut clincher-built; ⊕ ㉒weise gefügt clinchered; ~werk n ㉒ (schindelartige Beplankung) clincher-work.
Klink=haken ⊕ (⏑…) m ㉒ catch of a lock, staple of a latch.

[Klio] — 593 — [Klosterzwang]

Klio (´-) [grch.] *npr f.* 💫. *myth.* (Muse der Geschichte) Clio.
klipp (´) [lautm.] **I** *int.* ~!, **klapp**! ~ und **klapp**! flip-flap!, click-clack!, mit v. Füßen: pit-a-pat! — **II** *adv.* ~ und **klar** clear as day-light, quite evident; ich sagte ihm ~ und klar, daß // I told him straight to his face that //.
Klipp-dachs (´...) *m* 🐾 zo. rock-badger or -rabbit (*Hyrax*).
Klippe (´∪) [ndd.: cliff] *f* 🌊 cliff, niedrige: reef, spitze: crag; (Fels) rock; blinde (oder verborgene) ~ hidden (or sunken) rock; (Sandbank) shelf.
klippen (´∪) *s.* klippern.
Klippen-dachs (´...) *m* 🐾 zo. = Klippdachs; **-fisch** *m*: a) *ichth.* clippfish (*Chaetodon*); b) 🐟 *m* dry (or dried, cured) cod, bisw. a. haberdine; **-küste** ↓ *f* craggy (or rocky) coast; ~los *a.* 🌊 reefless; 2reich, 2voll *a.* full of cliffs or reefs, craggy, rocky.
Klipper ↓ (´∪) [ndl.] *m* 🚢 (scharfgebauter Schnellsegler) clipper.
klippe(r)n (´∪) [klipp] *v/n.* (h.) 🔔 (🗣) to clip, to click.
Klipp-fisch (´...) *m f* 🐟 = Klippenfisch.
klippig (´∪) [Klippe] *a.* 🌊 craggy, rocky.
Klipp-klapp (´...) *n* ⚙ einer Mühle: click-clack; **-kram** *m* small wares, toys, cheap trinkets *pl.*; **-schenke** *f* wretched inn, small beer-shop, bsd. ehm. **-schule** *f* dame-school, (Armenschule) ragged-school; **-schüler** *m* abecedarian, elementary scholar; **-werk** *n* = -kram.
klirr (´) [lautm.] *int.* etwa: cräsh!, smash!
klirren (´∪) [nhd. lautm.] **I** *v/n.* (h., bei Ortsveränderung *s/n*) 🔔 to clash, to clatter; bsd. v. Ketten, Waffen, Sporen, Fenstern: to clank, clink, rattle, v. Gläsern ꝛc.: to jingle; sie ~ mit den Ketten they clank their chains; sie ~ mit den Schwertern they clash their swords (together); 2des Geräusch clash(ing sound). — **II** ~ *n* 🔔 clashing, &c. (s. I); clanking of chains, clash(ing) of arms, rattling or shaking of windows, jingling of glasses.
Klischee ⊙ (∪´) [fr. *cliché m*] *n* 🖨 *typ.* stereotype-plate, abgekürzt: stereo, (fr.) cliché; **klischieren** (∪´) [fr.] *v/a.* 🖨 to dab; **Klischier-maschine** ⊙ (∪´...) *f* 🖨 dabbing machine.
Klistier (∪´) [grch. *klystē'r*] *n* ⚕ *med.* injection, enema; ein ~ geben, setzen to administer an enema.
klistieren (∪´∪) *v/a.* ⚕ e-m 2 to apply (or administer) an enema to a person.
Klistier-geben (´∪...) *n* ⚕ *med.*, &c. (making or giving) injection, administering an enema; **-pumpe** *f* enema, bsd. ehm.: clyster-pump; **-schlauch** *m* india-rubber tube of an enema; **-spritze** *f* syringe, enema, ehm.: clyster-pipe.
Klitoris (∪´∪) [grch.] *f, inv.* (*pl.* auch Klito'rides) *anat.* clitoris.
klitsch! (´) [lautm.] 2(=)**klatsch**! *s.* klatsch...
Klitsche *prov.* (´∪) 🏠 (kleines Gut) small estate. [slack-baked bread.]
klitschig (´∪ u. ´) [ndd.] *a.* 🍞 2es Brot]
Kloake (∪´∪) [lt. *cloā'cā*] *f* sewer, drain, cesspool, röm. Alt. u. zo.: 🔲 cloaca; **~n-öffnung** *f* outlet of a sewer, opening of a drain; **~n-tier** *n*: 🐾 monotreme.

klob (´) (**klöbe** ∪´ *subj.*) *impf. v.* klieben.
Klobe (´∪) *f* 🌳 = Kloben 1.
Klöb-eisen ⊙ (´...) *n* ⚙ Böttcherei: (Spaltmesser) riving-knife, cleaver.
Kloben (´∪) [ahd. *klieben*] *m* 🌳 **1.** (Stück Holz) log (of wood). — **2.** *hunt.* ~ des Vogelstellers perch (or trap) of the bird-catcher. — **3.** *fig.* = Klotz 2. — **4.** *agr.* (Gebinde v. Flachs ꝛc.) bottle. — **5.** ⊙ *mach.* ~ (Scherwange) der Wage cheek of the balance; weitS. (Gegenstand, woran et. klemmend befestigt ist) pivot; *mech.* pulley, block; feststehender ~ fixed (or immovable) pulley.
Kloben-deichsel (´∪...) *f* 🪵 = Gabeldeichsel; **-holz** *n* wood in logs.
klobig (´∪) *a.* ⊙ coarse, rude, rough (and ready), boorish, clumsy, heavy.
klöhnen P (´∪) [ndd.] *v/n.* (h.) to be gasing, to spin yarns.
klomm (´), **klömme** (´∪) *impf. ind.* und *subj.* von klimmen.
klonisch (´∪) [grch.] *a.* 🏥 *path.* 2er (vom Willen unabhängiger) Krampf clonic spasm; 2er Zustand clonicity.
Klopf-deich ⊙ (´...) *m* 🌊 Wasserbau: beaten dike. [hiding.]
Klopfe (´∪) *f* 🥊 (Prügel) beating, f]
Klöpfel (´∪) [klopfen] *m* ⚒ = Klüpfel.
klöpfeln (´∪) [klopfen] *v/n.* (h.) und *v/a.* ⚒ a. to tap (or rap, knock) gently.
klopfen (´∪) [ahd.] ⚒ **I** *v/n.* (h.) **1.** to knock, rap, tap, strike; an die Tür 2 to rap (or knock) at the door; in Busch 2; e-m auf die Finger 2 to give a p. a rap on the knuckles (a. *fig.*); e-m sanft auf die Schulter 2 to tap a p. on the shoulder; e-m auf die Wange ~ to pat a p. on the cheek; F *fig.* Geld auf den Schwanz 2 (streuen) to spend money lavishly; das Herz klopft mir (auch *v/impers.*) es klopft mir im Busen) my heart is beating or throbbing. — **2.** ⊙ 2 (auslochen) to punch. — **II** *v/a.* **3.** Fleisch mürbe 2 to make meat tender by beating it; *typ.* die Form 2 to plane down...; e-n Nagel in die Wand 2 to knock (or drive) a nail into the wall; den Staub aus den Kleidern 2 to beat the dust out of the clothes; mit Angabe der Wirkung: e-n aus dem Schlafe 2 to rouse a p. from sleep by rapping or knocking; Steine 2 to break stones. — **III** ~ *n* 🔔 **4.** knocking, &c. (s. I); ich hörte ein leises ~ I heard a gentle tap(ping) or knock. — **5.** *physiol., med.* ~ des Herzens palpitation, throbbing; ~ des Pulses pulsation; zur ärztlichen Untersuchung: 🩺 percussion.
Klopfer (´∪) *m* ⚙ **1.** (s. klopfen) ~ (in *f* 🙂) person who knocks or taps; *hunt.* (Treiber) beater. — **2.** ⊙ (Schlegel) beetle, *tel.* sounder.
Klopf-fechter (´...) *m* 🥊 swash-buckler, prize-fighter, pugilist, bully; *fig.* (streitsüchtiger Schriftsteller) polemical writer; **-fechterei** *f* prize-fighting, pugilism; *fig.* polemical writing; **-fechterisch** *a.* 🥊 pugilistic; **-garn** *n* yarn for wicks; **-geist** *m* noisy ghost or goblin; **-hengst** *m* castrated stallion, gelding; **-käfer** *m, ent.* deathtick or -watch (*Ano'bium*).

Klöppel (´∪) [ndd.] *m* ⚒ **1.** ⊙ (Klopfholz) beetle. — **2.** ~ einer Glocke clapper. — **3.** (Knüppel) cudgel. — **4.** (hölzerne Nadel zum Spitzenklöppeln) lace-bobbin.
Klöppel-arbeit ⊙ (´∪...) *f* bsd. ehm.: bobbin-work; **-arbeiter(in** *f*) *m* lace-maker; **-garn** 🌸 *n* yarn (or thread) for making lace; **-kissen** *n* cushion for bone-lace weaving, lace-pillow; **-mädchen** *n* girl engaged in lace-making; **-maschine** *f* bobbin-machine; **-muster** *n* pattern for lace.
klöppeln ⊙ (´∪) *v/a.* 🌸 *a.* to make (or weave) bone- (or fuseau-) lace.
Klöppel-nadel (´∪...) *f* ⊙ needle for working lace; **-seide** 🐛 *f* lace-silk; **-spitzen** *f pl.* bone- (or fuseau-) lace, weitS. real lace; **-zwirn** *m* = -garn.
Klöppler (´∪) *m* ⚒, ~**in** *f* 🌸 lace-maker.
Klops (´) [ndd.: collop] *m* 🍲 *a.* Kocht. (Art Fleischkloß) German mince-meat ball.
Klosett ᵀ (∪´) [engl.] *n* 🏠. (water-) closet (*abbr.* W.C.).
Kloß (´) [ahd.] *m* 🍲 *a.* **1.** lump, soft (or doughy) ball; (Erdscholle) clod. — **2.** Kocht.: dumpling, mit Fleisch: meat-ball; (Kartoffel)~ potato-ball; ~ mit großen Rosinen, in Eng.: sultana pudding.
kloß-artig (´´...) *a.* 🍲 like a dumpling; **-brühe** *f* gravy with force-meatballs.
Klößchen (´∪) *n* 🍲 (*dim. von* Kloß) Kochkunst: small dumpling; (Fleisch-)~ force-meat ball (*vgl.* Kloß 2).
Kloster (´∪) [ahd.: cloister; *mlt.*] *n* 🏛 allg.: (abgeschiedener Ort) cloister, bsd. für Mönche: monastery, bsd. für Nonnen: convent, nur für Nonnen: nunnery; ins ~ gehen to enter (or go into) a monastery or convent, von Mönchen a. to turn monk, v. Nonnen a. to take the veil; ins ~ stecken ob. sperren to shut up (or put away) in a convent.
Kloster-brauch (´∪...) *m* monastic rule or custom; **-bruder** *m* friar, (Laienbruder) lay brother; **-frau** *f*, **-fräulein** *n* nun; **-gang** *m* cloister; **-garten** *m* convent-garden; **-geistliche(r)** *m* monk, friar; **-gelehrsamkeit** *f* monastic (or monkish) learning; **-gelübde** *n* mon. vow; **-gewand** *n* mon. garb; **-gewölbe** *n* cross-arched vault; **-gut** *n* property of (or lands *pl.* belonging to) a monastery or convent; **-kirche** *f* conventual church, church belonging to a mon.; **-leben** *n* life in a monastery or convent, monastic life; **-leute** *pl.* friars and nuns *pl.*, bisw. a. conventuals *pl.*
klösterlich (´∪∪) *a.* 🏛 (dem Kloster angehörend) conventual; (Mönche betr.) monastic; (abgeschieden, einsam) cloistered, claustral, cloistral, secluded; **~keit** *f* 🏛 monasticism; (cloistered) seclusion.
Kloster-mauer (´∪...) *f* 🏛 convent-wall; **-ordnung** *f* regulations *pl.* of a monastery or convent; *vgl.* -brauch u. -zucht; **-pforte** *f* gate of a monastery; **-regel** *f* monastic rule; **-schule** *f* convent-school; **-schwester** *f* nun, (Laienschwester) lay sister; **-wesen** *n* monastic affairs *pl.*, monasticism; **-zelle** *f* monk's (or nun's) cell; **-zucht** *f* mon. discipline; **-zwang** *m* confinement in a convent, bisw. claustration.

[Klotho]

Klotho (́-) [grch.] *npr/f.* ⑤ ⓈⓂ. *myth.* (Parze, die den Lebensfaden spinnt) Clotho.
Klotz (́) [mhd.: clot] *m* ⓉⓐⒶ. 1. (wooden) block or log, schwerer clog; (knorriges Holz) knotted wood; (Baumstamm) trunk (of a tree), (Baumstumpf) stump (of a tree), ⚔ (Lafetten=)~ carriage-block; *fig.* taub wie ein ~ (as) deaf as a post; Sprichw. f. grob 1. — 2. *fig.* (ungehobelter Mensch) clumsy (or coarse, unpolished) fellow, clod-hopper, F hobb(l)edehoy.
klotzen F (́) [Klotz] *v/n.* (h.) ⑳ 1. to behave like a clod-hopper. — 2. er hat tüchtig 2 (bezahlen) müssen he has had to pay through the nose or to stump up heavily. — **klotzig** F (́) *a.* ⑥ 1. (f. Klotz 2) clumsy, coarse, unpolished; (schwerfällig) heavy, F lumpy. — 2. (gewaltig) mighty, enormous.
Klotz=kopf (́...) *m* ⑥ *fig.* blockhead; **=maschine** ⊕ *f* Kattundruck: padding-machine; **=schuh** *m* wooden shoe, mit Oberleder: clog; **=wagen** ⊕ *m* drag.
Klub ⁊ (́) [engl.] *m* ⑳ (Verein) club, weitS. association, society, union.
Klubbist (́̆) *m* ⑳ = Klubmitglied.
Klub=hütte (́...) *f* ⑳ Alpen: chalet built by the Alpine Club; **=leben** *n* club-life; *vgl.* **=wesen**; **=lokal** *n* club-house, (premises *pl.* of a) club; **=mitglied** *n* member of a club, a. clubman, clubbist, clubster; **=wesen** *n* clubdom, clubbism, life in clubs.
▶ **kluch..., klüch...** f. gluch..., glüch...
Kluft¹ (́) [ahd.: cleft; *klieben] *f* ⑩ 1. (Spalt) gap, crevice, crack, bsd. in einem Berge, Felsen: cleft, hollow, cave, (grundlose Tiefe) chasm, gulf, abyss (a. *fig.*); es trennt sie eine breite ~ there is a wide gulf between them. — 2. ⚔ fissure, cleavage, cleft; *vgl.* Fall¹ 8. — 3. ⊕ (Zange) tongs *pl.*
Kluft² P (́) [f jüd.] *f* ⑯ bursch. u. co. (Kleidung) clothes, garments, F togs *pl.*
klüften (́) [Kluft¹] *v/a.* ⑳ to cleave.
Kluft=holz (́..) *n* ⑳ logs *pl.* of wood.
kluftig, klüftig (́) [Kluft¹] *a.* ⑥ cleft, split, cracked; (voll Spalten) full of crevices or cracks.
klug (́) [mhd., ndd.] I *a.* ⑥ (D 2,7) 1. (verständig) sensible, judicious, intelligent; (vorsichtig) prudent, cautious, (weise) wise; (scharf unterscheidend) shrewd, discerning, F sharp, (scharfsinnig) sagacious; (fähig) able, (geschickt) clever, ingenious, skilled, F smart; (schlau) sly, cunning, artful, F deep; ein 2er Einfall, Gedanke, oft: a happy thought; du bist ein 2er Mensch you are a wise man, *iro.* you are very knowing; *bibl.* 2 wie die Schlangen und ohne Falsch wie die Tauben wise as serpents and harmless as doves. — 2. jetzt bin ich noch gerade so 2 wie vorher now I know as much as (I did) before, I am none the wiser (for it); er ist nicht recht 2 he is not in his right senses, F he is cracked; 2 (*adv.*) handeln to act prudently or discreetly; 2 reden, schwatzen, sprechen, F schnacken to think o.s. wonderfully clever or smart, to talk very conceitedly; Sie reden sehr 2, a. Sie haben 2 reden it is easy for you to talk (like that); ich kann nicht 2 aus

ihm werden I cannot fathom him, he is a puzzle (or mystery) to me; ich kann nicht 2 daraus werden I cannot make head or tail of it, F I can't make it out, it is beyond me; durch Schaden 2 w. to learn (or be taught) by experience; Sprichw. durch Schaden wird man 2 experience bought is better than experience taught; a. live and learn; f. Gi 2. — II der, die, das **=e**(Klügste) ⓉⒶ 3. the (most) prudent person, thing; der Kluge (a. Klügste) gibt nach the wiser head gives in; das klügste wäre (a. es wäre das klügste ob. am klügsten) zu zahlen the most prudent (or sensible, advisable) course would be to pay.
Klügelei (-́) [klug] *f* ⑯ sham wisdom, subtle tomfoolery, sophistry.
klügeln (́)*v/n.*(h.)Ⓑa. to affect wisdom, to indulge in subtle arguments; (brüten) to ponder over things.
Klugheit (́) *f* ⑯ (f. klug) good sense, judiciousness; prudence, caution; wisdom; shrewdness, discernment, sagacity; cleverness; slyness, cunning, aus Rücksichten der ~ from prudential considerations; **~s=lehre**, **=regel** *f* ⑫ rule of wisdom, maxim of prudence.
Klügler (́) *m* ⑳, **~in** *f* ⑯ = Klügling.
klüglich (́) *adv.* (f. klug) judiciously; prudently, wisely; cleverly; cunningly.
Klügling (́) *m* ⑳ d. conceited person, prig; wiseacre, sham philosopher.
Klug=schmuser, **=schnacker**, **=schwätzer**, **=sprecher** (II...) *m* ⑳ conceited talker or fool, self-opinionated p.; *vgl.* klug 2.
Klump (́) [ndd.] *m* ⓉⒷ. = Klumpen.
Klümpchen (́) *n* ⑫ (*dim. v.* Klumpen) little lump or clod, small particle, (Kügelchen) globule; ~ Butter dab of butter; ~ Gold nugget of gold.
Klumpen (́)[ndd.: clump]*m* ⑫ 1. lump of sugar, of lead, &c., (solid) mass; ~ Blut (Blutkuchen) clot of blood, *physiol.:* ↠ crassamentum; ~ Butter pat of butter; ~ Erde clod of earth; gegossener ~: a) Gold ꝛc.: ingot, bar; bsd. in der Erde gefundener ~ Gold nugget of gold; b) Eisen, Blei, Zinn ꝛc.: pig. — 2. (Haufen) heap, bulk, ↠ conglomeration; alles auf einen ~ werfen to heap (or lump) things together; in einem ~ all of a heap or a lump.
klumpen (́) *v/n.* (h.) u. **sich** 2 *v/refl.* ⑳ to clot (together), to form lumps.
Klumpen=gold (́..) *n* ⑫ gold in ingots or bars or nuggets; **=weise** *adv.* (F a. a.) in lumps or clods.
klump(e)rig (́(̌)) *a.* ⑥ cloddy, clotted.
Klump=fuß (́..) *m* club-(or clump-)foot, *anat.:* talipes; **=füßig(keit** *f) a.* club-footed(ness); **=hand** *f* club-hand.
klumpicht ↘, mst **klumpig** (́) *a.* ⑥ lumpy, massive, ↠ agglomerate.
Klüngel (́) [ahd. Knäuel] *m* (*n*) ⑳ (Parteigetriebe) cliquism.
Klunker P (́) *f* ⑯, *m* ⑳ 1. allg.: s.th. hanging (down) or dangling, appendage. — 2. (Quast) tassel, bob. — 3. (Rotsklümpchen) lump (or clod) of mud or dirt or F muck.
klunk(e)rig *provc.* (́(̌)) *a.* ⑥ (unordentlich) bedraggled; **klunkern** (́) [mhd.

[Knackwurst]

baumeln] *v/n.* (h.) Ⓑa. to hang down (or dangle) like a tassel or bob.
Klunker=wolle ⊕ (́...) *f* ⑫ breechings *pl.*, clotted wool, *provc.* dag-wool.
Klunse *provc.* (́̌) *f* ⑬ = Riß, Spalte.
Kluppe ⊖ (́) [*klieben*] *f* ⑬: a) (Werkzeug zum Schneiden der Schrauben) screw-cutting tool; b) (Beißzange) pincers *pl.*; F *fig.* in (ob. unter) die ~ bekommen (ob. F kriegen) to get into one's clutches.
kluppen (́) *v/a.* ⑳ to clutch, seize.
Klus (́) *f* ⑯, **Kluse** (́̌) *f* ⑬ = Klause.
Klüse ⚓ (́̌) [ndd.] *f* ⑬ (Öffnung für die Ankertaue in der Bordwand) hawse.
Klutter (́̌) *f* ⑬ (Lockpfeife) decoy-whistle.
Klüver ⚓ (́̌̆) [ndd.] *m* ⑫ (vorderstes Stagsegel) jib; **~baum** *m* ⑫ jib-boom; **~fall** *n* jib-halliard; **~kopf** *m* jib-head.
▶ **Klystier** ꝛc. f. Klistier ꝛc.
km, öft. *km* abbr. = Kilometer.
km², **km³** öft. = Quadrat-, Kubik-kilometer. [month, *prox.* (= *proximo*).]
k. M. abbr. = künftigen Monats of next
knabbern (́) [ndd.] *v/n.* (h.) u. *v/a.* Ⓑa. to nibble, to gnaw (an et. at a th.); an knuspriger Gebäck 2 to crackle ...
Knäbchen (́) *n* ⑬ little (kleineres: baby) boy, young lad, F nipper.
Knabe (́) [ahd.: knave] *m* ⑭ (männliches Kind) male child; (young) boy, F youngster, nipper, etwa v. 13. Jahre ab a. lad, stripling, (Jüngling) youth; F *iro.* ein alter ~ an old boy.
Knaben=alter (́́...) *n* ⑫ (years *pl.* of) boyhood, boyish age.
knabenhaft (́́̆) *a.* ⑥ boyish, boylike, *b.s.* puerile; **~igkeit** (́́̆́) *f* ⑯ boyishness, *b.s.* puerility.
Knaben=kraut ♀ (II...) *n* ⑫ orchis (*Orchis*); **geflecktes** ~ spotted orchis (*O. maculata*); **2mäßig** *a.* ⑥ boylike; **=schänder** *m* sodomite; **=schänderei** *f* sodomy; **=schule** *f* boys' school; **=spiel** *n* boys' game, game for boys; **=streich** *m* boy's (or boyish) trick; **=wurz** *f* = **=kraut**; **=zeit** *f* (time of) boyhood.
Knäblein (́-) *n* ⑬ = Knäbchen.
knack (́) [*lautm.*] I Ⓞ! *int.* crack!, snap!, bang! — II ~ *m* ⑫ = Knacks.
Knack(el)beere ♀ (́(̌)...) *f* ⑫ wild (or (wood-)strawberry (*Fragaria viridis*).
knacken (́̌) [: knock] ⑧ I *v/n.* (h.) to crack(le), von einem Gewehrhahn, Schloß ꝛc.: to click; (mit scharfem Tone brechen) to snap. — II *v/a.* to crack (open); *fig.* wir haben noch eine Nuß mit=ea. zu 2 I have a bone to pick with him (you. &c.), we have s.th. (yet) to settle; e-m eine harte Nuß zu 2 geben to give a person a hard nut to crack.
Knacker (́̌) *m* ⑫ cracker.
Knack=laut (́̆..) *m* ⓉⒶ Phonetik: glottal stop; **=mandel** *f* shell-almond.
knacks (́) [*lautm.*] I *int.* = knack. — II **Knacks** *m* ⓉⒶ. (́) (Springen v. Glas ꝛc.) crack(ing); das Glas hat einen ~ bekommen ... has cracked; *fig.* er hat einen ~ (Schaden) wegbekommen he had to suffer (with the others), F he came in for (some of) it, he caught it.
Knack=stiefel (́..) *m* ⑫ alter ~ old grumbler, old fogey; **=wurst** *f* saveloy, smoked sausage.

Signs (see page XVII): F familiar; P vulgar; ⌐ flash; ↘ rare; † obsolete (died); * new word (born); ✧ incorrect; ♪ music.

[Knagge] — 595 — [Knebler]

Knagge (⌣) [ndb.: knag] f ⊕ 1. (Knorren im Holze) knot, knag. — 2. ⊕ join. (Fußgestell) trestle; mach. = Knaggen 2.
Knaggen (⌣) m ⊕ 1. = Knagge 1. — 2. ⊕ mach. tappet, cam, zur Steuerung der Dampfmaschine: tappet for distributing.
Knäk-ente (⌣⌣) f ⊕ orn. garganey, summer-teal (Anas querquedula).
Knall (⌣) [nhd.: knell] I m ⊕(⑦)b. 1. clap of thunder, crack of a whip, (loud) report of a gun, crash of falling houses; chm. detonation, F pop; mit lautem ~ zerplatzen to burst with a loud explosion. — 2. e-n ~ und Fall erschießen to shoot a p. (down) on the spot or there and then; f.j. ~ u. Fall (plötzlich) all of a sudden, without much ado. — II ≈! int. 3. (Schuß) bang! — III ≈ a. ⊕ 4. v. Farben: (schreiend) glaring, loud.
Knall-blei (⌣...) n ⊕ chm. fulminating lead; **=bonbon** m, n cracker; **=büchse** f pop-gun; **=effekt** m, fig. stage-effect, sensation, claptrap.
knallen (⌣) ⊕ I v/n. (h.) 1. (f. Knall 1) v. Sachen: to clap, to crack, to give a (loud) report, to crash; to explode, chm. to detonate, to fulminate, F to pop; v/impers. es knallte zweimal there were two loud reports; v. Farben: ⊕d (schreiend) glaring. — 2. von Personen: mit dem Gewehr ≈ to shoot off a gun; mit der Peitsche ≈ to crack (or smack) one's whip; e-n Pfropfen ≈ l. to let off a cork. — 3. (in) (zerspringen, in die Luft fahren) der Pulverturm knallte in die Luft … exploded or was blown up or blew up (with a terrific crash). — II v/a. 4. mit Angabe der Wirkung: et. in die Luft ≈ to blow up a th. — 5. e-m ein(e) Pistol(e) vor den Kopf ≈ to shoot off a pistol close to a p.'s head; e-m die Peitsche um die Ohren ≈ to crack one's whip close to a p.'s ears. — III ~ n ⊕ 6. = Knall 1.
Knall-erbse (⌣...) f ⊕ toy-torpedo; **=gas** n, chm.: a) explosive gas; b) oxyhydrogen gas; **=gas-gebläse** n oxyhydrogen blowpipe; **=gas-licht** n oxyhydrogen- (or calcium-)light; **=glas** ⊕ n candle-bomb, anaclastic glass; **=gold** n fulminating gold; **=pulver** n fulminating powder or compound, friction-powder; **=quecksilber** n fulminate of (or fulminating) mercury; **≈rot** F a. ⊕ of a glaring red (colour); **≈sauer** a.: ⊘ fulminic; **≈saures Salz** fulminate; **=säure** f fulminic acid (CN. OH); **=signal** ⊕ n (detonating) fog-signal; **=silber** n fulminating silver (CNOAg).
knapp (⌣) [ndb.] a. ⊕ 1. (eng) v. Kleidungsstücken: tight, fitting tightly, close (to the body); nett und ≈ (adv.) angezogen neatly and smartly dressed; fig. ein ≈er Stil a concise (or terse) style. — 2. (nur eben ausreichend) barely sufficient, scanty (meal), narrow (space); sein ≈es Auskommen haben to have barely (or just) enough to live upon; ≈e Kost, oft: short commons pl.; die Zeiten sind ≈ these are hard times; mit ≈er Not with great difficulty, only just, by a hair's breadth or a hairbreadth, by the skin of one's teeth. — 3. (kärglich, ärmlich) mean,

shabby; (dürftig) meagre, poor; adv. es geht ≈ bei ihnen zu they are in straitened circumstances, oft a. they (have to) pinch and screw; seine Leute sehr ≈ halten to treat one's people very meanly, to keep them very short, to stint them; ≈ messen to give short measure. — 4. (in geringer Menge vorhanden) scarce; das Geld ist (bei) ihm sehr ≈ he is very short of cash, F his funds are very low; das Geld wurde (bei) ihm sehr ≈ he ran very short of money, F he was stumped.
Knappe¹ (⌣) [ahd.: *Knabe] m ⊕ 1. ehm. (Edelknecht) page, (Schildträger) shield-bearer, squire; (Lehrling im Rittertum) esquire, candidate for knighthood. — 2. jetzt ⊕ (Lehrling, Gesell, bsd. bei Müllern ꝛc.) miller's, &c. apprentice or journeyman; ⚒ = Bergknappe.
Knappe² (⌣) [knapp, schallnachahmend] ⊕ (Schmitze der Peitsche) lash of a whip.
knappen¹ (⌣) [knapp] v/a. u. v/n. (h.) ⊕ (knapp halten) to keep short of money, &c.; (knausern) to stint, to live meanly.
knappen² (⌣) [Knappe²] v/n. (h.) ⊕ Peitsche ꝛc.: (knallen) to crack, smack; obb. vom Feuer: (knistern) to crackle.
Knappen³ (⌣) m ⊕ = Knappe¹.
knappern (⌣) v/n. = knabbern.
Knapp-hans ⚒ P (⌣,⌣) m ⊕ keeper of a canteen, canteen-keeper.
Knappheit (⌣-) f ⊕ (f. knapp) tightness (or tight fit) of clothes; conciseness (or terseness) of style; scantiness of food, &c.; hardness of times; meagre-ness of supply; scarcity (or shortness, lowness) of funds. [wallet.]
Knapp-sack (⌣) [ndl.] m ⊕ knapsack,
Knappschaft (⌣) [Knappe¹] f ⊕ 1. ehm. novitiate of a knight. — 2. jetzt ⊕ coll. (Genossenschaft der Knappen) (body of) millers', &c. journeymen; bsd. ⚒ = Berg-≈ (vgl. Gewerkschaft b); **~s-kasse** ⚒ f miners' provident fund; **~s-verband** ⚒ m miners' association or union.
knaps (⌣) [schallnachahmend] int. = knack I.
knapsen (⌣) [ndb.: *knapp] v/n. (h.) ⊕ (abwacken) to pinch off.
Knarre (⌣) f ⊕ der Nachtwächter: rattle; ⚒ P = Gewehr; Sprichw. f. Pfarre.
knarren (⌣) [nhd.: lautm.] I v/n. (h.) ⊕ 1. von Sachen: to creak (a. von Türangeln und Schuhen), to squeak; das Ohr verletzend: to grate on the ear; von Fenstern ꝛc.: to rattle; von brennendem Holz ꝛc.: (knistern) to crackle; von Fahrzeugen ꝛc. unter einer Last: to groan; ⊕des Geräusch jarring sound. — 2. von Personen: mit etwas ≈ to rattle a th.; abs. (mit der Knarre) ≈ bsd von der engl. Polizei: to spring a policeman's rattle. — II ~ n ⊕ 3. (f. 1) creaking, &c. (noise); (f. 2) rattling. [von der Stimme: grating.]
knarrig (⌣) a. ⊕ creaky, squeaking,
Knast (⌣) [ndb.: Knust] m ⊕b. knot in the wood; ⊕ (Eichklotz) log of oak-wood.
Knaster¹ (⌣) [ndl. f. Kanaster] m ⊕ (Art Rauchtabak) bsd. ehm.: canister-tobacco; weitS. (bad or inferior) tobacco.
Knaster², **~er** F (⌣⌣) m ⊕ (grämlicher Mensch) grumbler; alter ~: a) fast † (alter Schulschriftsteller) F old stager or fogey;

b) F co. (alter zäher Mann) tough old fellow; **~bart** m ⊕ old grumbler, sour-tempered fellow, gruffold man.
knastern (⌣) [lautm.] v/n. (h.) ⊕a. to crackle (vgl. knistern).
knattern (⌣) [lautm.] I v/n. (h.) ⊕a. to rattle (auch vom Gewehrfeuer); von brennendem Stroh ꝛc.: to crackle. — II ~ n ⊕ rattling; ~ der Gewehre rattle of musketry.
Knäuel (⌣⌣) [nhd.] n (m) ⊕ 1. ball of thread, bsd. als engl. Maß für Garn: clue; in (oder auf) ein ~ wickeln to wind (or make up) into a ball. — 2. fig. (Verschlungenes) entanglement, tangle; maze of streets, throng of people, confused heap of objects, train of thought; (Haufen) heap, pile, ⊘ agglomeration, aggregation; ein ~ bilden to (form a) cluster, to agglomerate. — 3. ♀ German knot-grass (Scleranthus).
Knäuel-binse ♀ (⌣⌣...) f ⊕ common rush (Iuncus conglomeratus); **≈förmig** a. ⊕ shaped like a ball (of thread), ⊘ globular; **≈n** = Knäulgras.
knäueln (⌣⌣) v/a. ⊕a. 1. to wind (into balls); (verwirren) to entangle. — 2. (auch sich ≈ v/refl.) bisw.: to coil (up), ⊘ to agglomerate, to conglob(at)e.
Knäuel-wickel-maschine ⊕ (⌣⌣...) f ⊕ ball-winding (or balling-)machine, (ball-)winder.
Knauer ⚒ (⌣⌣) m ⊕ min. (linsenförmiges Aggregat in Gesteinen) lenticular conglomerate in rocks.
Knauf (⌣) [mhd.: knob] m ⊕c. 1. knob, am Schwerte: pommel of the hilt. — 2. arch. ~ einer Säule capital of a column (= Kapitell).
Knäulchen (⌣⌣) n ⊕ (dim. Knäuel) small ball of thread, pellet of paper, &c.
Knaul-gras (⌣⌣) [mbd.] n ⊕ cock's-foot grass (Dactylis glomerata).
knaupeln prov. (⌣⌣) v/n. = knabbern.
Knauser (⌣⌣) [nhd.] m ⊕, **~in** f ⊕ niggardly (or mean, stingy) person, miser, skinflint; **~ei** (⌣⌣⌣) f ⊕ niggardliness, meanness, stinginess.
knauserig (⌣⌣⌣) a. ⊕ niggardly, mean, stingy, sordid; **knausern** v/n. (h.) ⊕a. to save, to pinch and screw; to live in a niggardly (or mean, stingy) way.
knautschen F (⌣⌣) v/a. ⊕ (zf.-drücken) to crumple, to crease; **knautschig** a. ⊕ crumpled, creased; ruffled.
Knebel (⌣⌣) [ahd.] m ⊕ 1. (Knüttel) cudgel, short stick. — 2. (kurzes, dickes Querholz): a) zum Packen: packing-stick; b) ⚓ toggle, ~ zum Schnüren woolder; c) (Mund=)~ gag; d) ~ am Halse der Hunde: clog; e) (Koppelungs=)~ für Pferde packing-stick. — 3. = ~=bart. — 4. orn. ~ zw. Augen u. Schnabelwurzel: ⊘ mastax. [up moustache(s pl.).]
Knebel-bart (⌣⌣) [ndb.] m ⊕ (turned-)
knebeln (⌣⌣) I v/a. ⊕a. 1. (mit e-m Knebel festschnüren) to tie up (or fasten) with a short stick; (binden) Garben ≈ to bind sheaves. — 2. e-n ≈ (durch einen Knebel am Schreien hindern) to gag (or garrotte) a p.; fig. die Presse ≈ to muzzle the press. — II ~ n ⊕ 3. (f. 2) gagging.
Knebel-trense ⊕ (⌣⌣...) f ⊕ man. snaffle.
Knebler (⌣⌣) m ⊕ gagger, garrotter.

⊘ scientific; ♀ botanical; ♁ geography; ⊕ machinery; ⚒ mining; ⚔ military; ⚓ marine; ⊕ commercial; ⊙ postal; 🚂 railway.

[**Knecht**] — 596 — [**Kniehang**]

Knecht (´) [ahd.: knight] *m* ⓑb. **1.** man serving (or working) on a farm-yard, farm-labourer, plough-boy; weitS. menial servant, drudge; im Hotel: boots; (Stall=)~ stable-man or boy; f. Ruprecht; Sprichw. f. Herr 6. — **2.** (Unfreier) slave, thrall, (Leibeigener) serf, bond(s)man, ehm. in Engl. auch: villein. — **3.** *fig.* von Sachen: (Gestell) trestle, jack; fauler ~ (r-r. ~ der Faulen) ready reckoner. — **4.** ↓ (Masten=)~ knight.

knechten (´) ⓢ **I** *v/n.* (h.) : e-m ~ to serve a person (in a menial capacity). — **II** *v/a.* : einen ~ (zum Knechte machen) to make a drudge (or a slave) of a p., to enslave a p., geh. Spr. : to enthral, to cast into bondage; (unterjochen) to subdue; (herrisch behandeln) to tyrannize (over), to oppress. — **III** ~ *n* ⓔ = Knechtung.

Knechtes-sinn (´·´) f. Knechts-...
knechtisch (´·) *a.* ⓖ like a servant, menial; slavish, servile, submissive; (triechend) cringing, grovelling.
Knechts-arbeit (´...) *f* ⓖ servant's work, drudgery, F slaving.
Knechtschaft (´·) *f* ⓖ slavery, servitude, bondage, geh. Spr. : thraldom.
Knechts-dienst (´...) *m* ⓖ menial service; **=gestalt** *f*, *bibl.* : Er (Jesus Christus) nahm ~ an He took upon Himself the form of a servant.
Knecht(s)-sinn (´...) *m* ⓖ servile spirit; **=stand** *m* menial capacity.
Knechtung (´·) *f* ⓖ (f. knechten) enslavement, subjugation; tyrannization, oppression; während ihrer ~ during their servitude; vgl. Knechtschaft.

Kneif (´) [ndd.: knife] *m* ⓒc. (Einschlagemesser) clasp-knife; *hort.* hedgingbill; (Schustermesser) paring-knife.
kneifen (´) [ndb.; *kneipen] ⓑb. **I** *v/a.* **1.** *v/a.* to pinch, nip, gripe; gekniffen pinched; mit gekniffenen (blinzelnden) Augen with blinking eyes; die Gekniffenen (schlau Durchtriebenen) the artful (or crafty) ones *pl.* — **2.** ↓ den Wind ~ to keep close to (or to hug) the wind; v. Tauen: ↓d running foul. — **II** *v/n.* **3.** *fenc.* F (furchtsam hinter die Mensur zurückgehen) to draw back beyond the chalk-line.
Kneifer (´·) *m* ⓖ **1.** ~(**in** *f* ㊻) *m* person who pinches, &c. (f. kneifen 1), pincher. — **2.** (Augenglas) (double) eye-glasses *pl.* (Klemmer).
Kneif-küßchen (´...) *n* ⓖ pinching and kissing a baby's cheek; **=mal** *n* (blue) mark of a pinch; **=zange** *f* (pair of) pincers or nippers, kleine: tweezers *pl.*
Kneip¹ *provc.* (´) *m* ⓒc. = Kneif.
Kneip²-abend (´...) [kneipen²] *m* ⓖ evening spent in drinking, students' carousal or drinking-bout; **=bruder** *m* toper, tippler, *co.* thirsty soul, F (old) boozer; lustiger ~ jolly boon-companion.
Kneipe (´·) [nhd.; *ndl.] *f* ㊻ **1.** pincers *pl.* — **2.** (Schenke) ale-(or beer-)house, beer-shop, mehr gbr. : public-(house), F pub, pot-house, außerhalb der Stadt: halfway house, country-inn; (Studenten=)~ students' club. — **3.** burfch.: (Wohnung) lodgings, F diggings *pl.*

kneipen¹ (´·) [ndb.] *v/a.* ⓖ (faft † ⓖbft) **1.** = kneifen 1. — **2.** die Schuhe ~ mich ... are pinching me; mit glühenden Zangen ~ to pinch with red-hot tongs; oft *impers.* es kneipt mich im Magen I feel gripes (or twitches) in the stomach. — **II** ~ *n* ⓔ **3.** pinching; (Leibschmerzen) gripes *pl.*
kneipen² (´·) [Kneipe] **I** *v/n.* (h.) u. *v/a.* ⓖ burschikos: (zechen) to drink beer, tipple, carouse, F to booze; to go to (or sit in) the beer-house, to frequent the pub(lic house); Bier ~ to drink (or tipple) beer; Luft, Natur ~ to take fresh air. — **II** ~ *n* ⓔ drinking (-bout), tippling (beer); **Kneipen-leben** *n* life (spent) in ale-houses or F pubs.
Kneiperei F (-´·´) *f* ㊻ hard drinking, tippling, F boozing, lushing-up; (Zechgelage) carousal, drinking-bout, pot-house revelry.
Kneip²-genie *n* = Kneipbruder.
Kneipier (-jē´) [dtsch-fr.] *m* ⓖ **1.** = **2.** = Kneipbruder.
Kneip²-lied (´´...) *m* ⓖ drinking-song; **=name** *m* nickname by which a student is known at his club.
Kneipp-kur (´´·´) [Pfarrer Kneipp in Wörishofen, 1821–97] *f* ㊻ (Wasserkur) (Father) Kneipp's (water-)cure.
Kneip²-tag (´´...) *m* ㊷ (appointed) day on which students meet at their club; **=wart** *m* student who looks after the supply of beer, &c.; **=wirt(in** *f*) *m* host of a public house, ale-house keeper, publican, F mine host; **=¹zange** ⊕ *f* = Kneipzange.
kneißen ⊕ (´·) *v/a.* ⓖ Gerberei: to strip off the hair. [paring-knife.]
Kneiß-messer ⊕ (´´...) [kneißen] *n* ⓖ]
Kneller (´·) [knallen] *m* ㊷ inferior tobacco. [to smell bad.]
knellern (´·) *v/n.* (h.) ⓖ*a.* vom Tabak]
kneten (´·) [ahd.: knead] **I** *v/a.* ⓖ **1.** to knead (or work) the dough; mit den Füßen: to tread, to stamp; den Lehm mischen und ~ to temper the loam or clay; Wachs ~ to mould wax. — **2.** *med.* den Körper ~ to massage ..., im Dampfbade: to shampoo ... — **II** ~ *n* ⓔ **3.** (f. 1) kneading, &c.; (f. 2) massage, shampoo(ing).
Kneter ⊕ (´·) *m* ㊷, **=in** *f* ㊻ kneader.
Knet-kur (´´...) *f* ⓖ massage; **=maschine** *f* kneading-machine or -mill; **=trog** *m* Bäckerei: kneading-trough.
Knick¹ (´) [lautnachahmend] *int.* click!
Knick² (´) *m* ⓑb. **1.** (Sprung) crack, ⊕ (Bruch) flaw, damaged part, bruise; *fig.* von Menschen: F e-n ~ bekommen to break down. — **2.** (gebrochene Linie) break, bend, ↓ angle. — **3.** nordb. (lebendige Hecke) quickset hedge with interlacing boughs.
Knicke-bein (´´...): a) *n* weak-jointed leg, *m* weak-(or knock-)kneed person; b) *n*, *m* liqueur with the yolk of an egg beaten into it; **=beinig** *a.* ⓖ weak-(or knock-)kneed. [damaged) egg.]
Knick-ei ⊕ (´·´) *n* ⓖ cracked (or]
knicken ⓖ [ndd.] ⓖ **I** *v/n.* (h. u. ſn) **1.** to crack, (zerbrechen) to break; (Riſſe bekommen) to split, burst, get flawed. — **2.** er knickt beim Geh(e)n he bends his knees in walking, his legs (or knees) give way under him. — **II** *v/a.* **3.** (ſ. 1) to crack, to break; to split, burst, flaw; e-n Halm ꝛc. ~ to break ... in bending; (zerdrüden) to crush; und durften ſie (die Flöhe) nicht ~ (J., Fauſt) and durst not crack them; *fig.* ich bin ganz geknickt F I am quite down (in the mouth) or done for or broken (down); ein geknicktes Daſein, Leben a blighted existence, a blasted life; ſ-e geknickte Gestalt his bent form; geknickter Greis broken down old man.
Knicker (´·) [nhd.: knicker] *m* ㊷ **1.** = Knauſer. — **2.** bjd. med.: (einzuknickender Sonnenſchirm) sunshade with folding-stick. — **3.** (Klicker) marble.
Knickerei (´··´) *f* ㊻ = Knauſerei;
knick(e)rig (´·(·)·) *a.* ⓖ = knauſerig;
knickern (´·) *v/n.* (h.) ⓖ*a.* = knauſern.
Knick-holz (´´...) *n* ⓖ (niedriges Buſchholz) underwood, brushwood.
knicks! (´) [ndd.] **I** *int.* **1.** = knick¹. — **II** ~ ⓖ*a.* **2.** = Knick² 1. — **3.** ~, *dim.* **=chen** *n* ⓔ (Verbeugung mit Einknicken der Beine) curtsy; einen ~ machen to make (or drop) a curtsy; (Kniebeugung, bſd. *eccl.*) genuflexion.
knicksen (´·) [knicken] *v/n.* ㊿ **I** *v/a.* **1.** = knicken **II**. — **II** *v/n.* **2.** (h.) to drop (or make) a curtsy, to curtsy. — **3.** (ſn) (ſich ~d fortbewegen) : ſie ~ von dannen they retire curtsying, they curtsy (or bow) themselves out.
Knick-ſtag ↓ (´´...) *n* ⓖ (federnde Stütze) spring-stay, top-stay; **=ſtütz** *m* Turnerei: bent-arm rest.
Knie (´) [ahd.: knee] *n* ⓖ (ⓒc.) **1.** (auch bei Tieren) : auf den ~n on one's (bended) knees; auf den ~n liegen to be on one's knees, to kneel (down); auf die ~! to your knees!; auf die ~ fallen to fall (or go down) on one's knees; das ~ vor e-m beugen to bend one's knee(s) before a p. — **2.** *fig.* etwas übers ~ brechen (ſchnell abmachen) to hurry (F to rush) a matter, to make short work of a th. — **3.** ~ (**Knid**) e-s Weges, Fluſſes ꝛc. : bend; ⊕ ~ eines Maſchinenſtückes, einer Waſſerleitung ꝛc. : joint; ~ einer Kurbel, zB. am Zweirad: crank; vgl. **=rohr**; ↓ angle.
Knie-band (´´...) *n* ⓖ : a) (Strumpfband) garter; b) *anat.* ligament of the knee; **=beuge** *f* Turnen: knee-crooking; **=beugung** *f* bending of the knee(s); genuflexion; **=biege** *f* = **=kehle**; **=biegung** *f* = **=beugung; =decke** *f* am Wagen (coach-)
knieen (´·) ſ. knien. [man's) apron.]
Knie-fall (´´...) *m* ㊷ going down on one's knees before a p., prostration; **=fällig** *adv.* : e-n ~ bitten to implore a p. on one's (bended) knees; **=flechſe** *f*, *anat.* knee-string, bſd. *vet.* hamstring; mit zerſchnittener ~ Menſchen und Tieren: hamstrung; **=förmig** *a.* formed (or jointed) like a knee; ⊕ : ⚹ geniculate(d); **=galgen** *m* gallows with cross-beam, **=geige** *f* *m.* : a) (Gambe) bass-viol; b) (Cello) violoncello; **=gelenk** *n* knee-joint, ⚹ poples; **=gelenk-entzündung** *f*, *path.* gon(arthr)itis; **=gicht** *f*, *path.* gout in the knees, ⚹ gonagra; **=hang** *m* Turnerei:

Zeichen (ſ. S. XVII): F familiär; P Volksſprache; Γ Gaunerſprache; ⚹ ſelten; † alt (auch geſtorben); * neu (auch geboren); +⁺ unrichtig;

suspension by the knees; =hebel ☉ m bent lever; ²hoch a. up to the knees, vgl. ²tief; =holz n: a) ↓ knee-timber; b) ♀ knee-pine (Pinus pumi'lio); =hosen f/pl. knee-breeches, für Knaben: knickers, knickerbockers pl.; =kehle f hollow of the knee, ham, vet. a. hough, hock; =kehlen-muskel m: ⚒ poplitic muscle, vgl. =flechse; =kissen n für Betende hassock; für Kricketspieler ꝛc.: pad(ding) for the knee, legging; =leder n: a) knee-strap, der Dachdecker auch: knee-pad, der Schuhmacher ehm: stirrup; b) = =decke. [a kneeling attitude.]
knielings (⌣⌣) adv. on one's knees, in knien (⌣́) ☉ I v/n.: a) (h.) to kneel, to be on one's knees; b) (ſn) to kneel down, to go down on one's knees or P marrow-bones, eccl to genuflect, ♀d p.pr. kneeling. — II ſich ² v/refl. mit Angabe der Wirkung: ſich wund (oder die Knie wund) ² to make one's knees sore with kneeling. — III ~ n ㉓ kneeling (attitude or position), bſd. eccl.: ⚒ genuflexion
Knie-polſter (⌣́...) n ㊷ = =kiſſen; =riem m: F Meiſter~ Master Cobbler; =riemen m shoemaker's stirrup; =rohr n ☉ einer Leitung: piece of pipe (or tube) bent at right angles, elbow(-pipe); =ſcheibe f, anat. knee-cap, -pan, ⚒ patella; =ſchiene ♀ f am Harniſch: knee-piece, greaves pl., =ſchmerz m, path. pain in the knee, ⚒ gon(y)-algia, =ſchnalle f buckle to the garters; ²ſchüſſig a. ⚒ knock-kneed; =ſchwamm m, path., vet. white swelling; =ſparren ☉ m knee-rafter; =ſtück n: a) paint., &c. half-length portrait; b) ☉ = =rohr; ²tief a. knee-deep; vgl. ²hoch; =welle f Turnerei: knee- (or leg-)grinder.
Kniff¹ (⌣́) impf. ind. von kneifen.
Kniff² (⌣́) [kniff¹] m ⓐb. 1. (ſ. kneifen 1) pinch(ing). — 2. (Fleck vom Kneifen) mark caused by a pinch. — 3. (Falte) fold, crease. — 4. F fig. (Kunſtgriff) trick, knack, dodge, artifice, device, (Anſchlag) stratagem; ſchlaue ~e sly manœuvres or intrigues, artful dodges pl., underhand work.
Kniffelei F (⌣⌣́) [Kniff² 4] f ㊻ trickery.
kniff(e)lig (⌣́⌣) a. ㊺ 1. = kniffig. — 2. (verzwickt) affected.
kniffeln (⌣́⌣) v/n. (h.) ㊺a. to intrigue, to manœuvre.
kniffen (⌣́) [Kniff² 3] v/a. ㊺ to fold, to make creases in, e. Buch. to dog's-ear; er kniffte den Brief (zi) he crunched the letter (between his fingers).
kniffig F (⌣́) [Kniff² 4] a. ㊺ tricky, wily, artful, full of tricks; ~keit f ㊻ trickiness, wiliness, artfulness.
Kniffler F (⌣́) [Kniff² 4] m ⓐ, ~in f ㊼ trickster, dodger
knifflig (⌣́⌣) ſ. kniffelig.
knipp¹ (⌣́) co. impf. ind. von kneipen.
knipp² (⌣́) [lautm.] I ♩! int. click!, snap! — II ~ m ⓐb., dim. =chen (⌣́) n ㉓ snap of one's fingers; (Naſenſtüber) fillip.
knippen (⌣́) v/n. (h.) ㊺ = knipſen I.
Knipp-käulchen n ㊵. =kugel f = Klicker.
knipps! (⌣́) [knipp²] I ♩. knaps! int. — II ~ I. — II ~ m ⓐa., dim. Knips-

chen (⌣́) n ㉓ snap of one's fingers, rap on the knuckles; (Schneller) jerk.
knipſen (⌣́) v/n. (h.) ㊿ I v/n. to snap one's fingers. — II v/a. (ab-², ein-²) to clip (or punch) a ticket; *F = kodaken; Knipſer *F (⌣́) m ㉒ = Kodaker. [scissors pl.]
Knipſ-ſchere (⌣́..) f ㊷ short pointed
Knirps F (⌣́) m ⓐa. little man, pigmy, hop-o-my-thumb, whipper-snapper, F shrimp, little dot, (Junge) F nipper; dickbäuchiger ~, oft: tub, Punch.
knirpſig (⌣́) a. ㊺ undersized, dwarfish, diminutive, of small stature.
knirren (⌣́) [mhd.] v/n. (h.) ㊺ = knarren.
knirſchen (⌣́) [mhd.] ☉ I v/n. (h.) ㊺ 1. to creak (auch vom Schnee), to grate. — 2. mit den Zähnen ² to gnash one's teeth; vor Wut ² to foam with rage. — II v/a. ³ (quetſchen) to crunch; (zermalmen) to crush, squash, mash.
Kniſter-gold (⌣́⌣) n ㊷ = Rauſchgold.
kniſt(e)rig (⌣́⌣⌣) a. ㊺ crackling, creaking, rustling, ⚒ crepitant.
kniſtern (⌣́⌣) [ndb. lautm.] I v/n. (h.) ㊺a. vom Feuer. to crackle, vom Schnee ꝛc.: to creak, von Kleidern: to rustle; chm., min. vom Kochſalz ꝛc.: ⚒ to crepitate. — II ~ n ㉓ (ſ. I) crackling, &c., ⚒ crepitation.
Kniſter-raſſeln (⌣́⌣⌣) n ㊷ path. tranſer Lungen- ⚒ crepitation, crepitus.
Knittel (⌣́) ſ. Knüttel. [Rauſchgold.]
Knitter (⌣́) m ⓐ crease; ~=gold n = knitt(e)rig (⌣́⌣⌣) a. ㊺ 1. = kniſt(e)rig. — 2. (zerknittert) crumpled, creased, ruffled. — 3. (reizbar) irritable, F waxy.
knittern (⌣́⌣) [lautm.] ㊺a. I v/n. (h.) = kniſtern I. — II v/a. to crumple, crease, ruffle. — III ~ n ㉓ (zu I·) = kniſtern II; (zu II:) crumpling, &c.
Knix, knixen ſ. knicks II, knickſen.
Knöbel (⌣́) [mhd. lautm.] ſ. Knöchel 1a.
Knöbel-becher (⌣́⌣..) m ⓐ (Würfelbecher) dice-box. [würfeln.]
knobeln F (⌣́) [mhd.] v/n. (h.) ㊺a. =
Knoblauch ♀ (⌣́-) [ahd. (ge)klob(ener) Lauch] m ⓐd. garlic (A'llium sati'vum)
Knoblauch(s)-artig (⌣́⌣...) a. ㊺ like garlic, garlicky, ⚒ alliaceous; =brühe f ㊷ garlic-sauce; =geruch m, smell of garlic; =hederich m, =rauke ♀ f garlic-mustard, hedge-garlic, Jack-by-the hedge (Allia'ria officina'lis); =ſtrauch ♀ m g.-shrub (Adenocaly'mna allia'cea), =zehe ♀ f clove of garlic
Knöchel (⌣́) [mhd.: knuckle; * dim. v. Knochen] m ⓐ 1. anat. a) am Fingergelenk: knuckle; b) am Fußgelenk: ankle, ⚒ malleolus; c) am Ellbogen: knuckle of the elbow. — 2. pl. zum Spielen: bones pl.; (Würfel) dice. [ſelar.]
Knöchel-artig (⌣́⌣...) a. ㊺ anat.: ⚒ mal-
Knöchelchen (⌣́⌣⌣) n ㉓ (dim. v. Knochen u. Knöchel) small bone or ankle, ⚒ osselet, ossicle. [orn. heel-joint.]
Knöchel-gelenk (⌣́⌣..) n ㊷ ankle-joint,
knöcheln (⌣́⌣) [Knöchel 2] v/n. (h.) ㊺a. 1. = fipſen II. — 2. to play (at) dice.
Knöchel-ſpiel (⌣́⌣.) n ㊷ (game of) knuckle-bones pl.
Knochen (⌣́) [mhd., vgl. Knöchel] m ⓐ bone; ſ. Haut 1 am Ende; ohne ~ boneless; ſtarke ~ haben to have strong bones, to be very bony; e-m Hunde einen

hinwerfen to throw a bone to a dog; e-m alle ~ im Leibe zerſchlagen to break every bone (or rib) in a p.'s body; zu ~ werden to ossify; fig. bis auf die ~ (durch und durch) thoroughly, (right) to the core.
Knochen=ähnlich (⌣́⌣...) a. ㊹ bone-like, bony, ⚒ osseous, ossiform, osteal; =arbeit(en pl.) ☉ f ㊷ bone-work; ²artig a. = ²ähnlich; =aſche f bone-ash(es pl.), chm. phosphate of lime; =auswuchs m, path. bony growth, ⚒ exostosis, =bau m bony frame, ⚒ osseous structure; =beſchreibung f: ⚒ osteography; ²bildend a.: ⚒ osteo-blastic, osteoplastic; =bildung f ossification; =brand m, path. ⚒ (osteo-)necrosis; =bruch m, surg. fracture of a bone, ⚒ osteoclasis, osteocele; =brüchigkeit f brittleness of the bone(s); =drechſler m bone-turner; =dünger m bone-manure; ²dürr a. all skin and bones, very thin or lean; =einrichter m bone-setter; =entzündung f, path. ⚒ ost(e)itis; =erde f, chm. bone-earth; =erweichung f, path. softening of the bone, ⚒ osteomalacia; =fortſatz m, anat.: ⚒ apophysis; =fraß m, path.: ⚒ caries, cariousness; =fügung f articulation of a bone, ⚒ symphysis; =gerüſt n (osseous) frame (or structure) of the body, skeleton; =geſchwulſt f, path.. ⚒ osteoma; =gewebe n bone-tissue; ²hart a. (as) hard as bone; =hauer m (Schlächter) butcher; =haus n charnel-house; =haut f, anat.: ⚒ periosteum, =haut-entzündung f, path.: ⚒ periostitis; =hecht m, ichth. bill-fish (Lepi-doʹsteus); =höhle f, geol. bone-cave; =kohle f bone-black; =konglomerat n, geol.: ⚒ bone-breccia; =lehre f: ⚒ osteology; =leim m bone-glue or -binder, ⚒ osteocolla; ²los a. boneless; =mann m a) skeleton; b) F (Tod) Death; =mark f marrow of a bone, ⚒ osteomyelon; =mehl n bone-meal or -dust, ground (or powdered) bones pl.; =mühle f bone-mill; =naht f, anat. suture; =pfanne f articular cavity; =ſäge f b.-saw, surg.: ⚒ osteotome; =ſchmerz m, path. pain in a bone, ⚒ osteocope; =ſchwarz n = =kohle; =ſplitter m splinter of a bone; =ſyſtem n, anat. osseous system; =tier n, zo.: ⚒ osteozoan; =wuchs m: a) = =bildung; b) = =gerüſt; =zange f, surg. bone-nippers pl.; =zelle f, anat. b.-cell.
knöcherigt, mſt knöcherig (⌣́⌣⌣) a. ㊹ bony, fleshless.
knöchern (⌣́⌣) a. ㊹ (of) bone, ⚒ osseous.
knochicht ⚒ mſt knochig (⌣́⌣) a. ㊹ 1. bony, ⚒ osseous. — 2. (derb, ſtark) ² of a strong frame. — 3. in Zſſgn, zB. fein-² with thin (or delicate) bones.
Knödel (⌣́) [mhd.: *Knoten dim.] m ㉒ Kochkunſt: dumpling; vgl. Kloß 2.
Knöllchen (⌣́) n ㉓ dim. v. Knolle(n).
Knolle (⌣́) f ㊷ = Knollen 2.
Knollen (⌣́) [mhd.: knoll] m ㉓ 1. lump, clod; roundish mass. — 2. = Knorren 2; ♀ und anat. auch: ⚒ tubercle; hort. (Zwiebel) bulb; (kugelförmiger Stempelteil der Kartoffel ꝛc.) tuber.

[knollenförmig] — 598 — [Knüppelbrücke]

knollen=förmig (⸚...) a. ⊕: ⚹ bulbous, tuberous, tuberiform, bsd. anat. tubercular; =gewächs ⚹ n ⓶: ⚹ tuberous (or bulbiferous) plant; =kümmel ⚹ m earth- (or ground-)nut, hawknut, pignut (Carum Bulboca'stanum); ⚶tragend a.: ⚹ bulbiferous; =wicke ⚹ f Indian potato, groundnut (A'pios tubero'sa); =wurzel ⚹ f: ⚹ bulbous root; =zwiebel ⚹ f: ⚹ bulbo-tuber, corm.

Knoll=fink(e) F (⸚...) m = Klotz 2.

knollicht ⸝, mst knollig (⸚⸌) a. ⊕ ⚹ 1. lumpy, like a clod; bsd. von Pflanzenwurzeln: ⚹ bulbous, tubered, tuberous. — 2. F fig. = klotzig.

Knopf (⸌) [ahd.: knob] m ⑦ b. 1. button; Weste ⚹c. mit zwei Reihen Knöpfen double-breasted waistcoat, &c.; Manschetten=)⁓ stud, doppelter: link; ~ am Bettpfosten, an e-m Stocke ⚹c.: knob, einer Turmspitze auch: ball, am Degengefäße: pommel, an der Florettspitze: button, e-r Stecknadel: head; ⚓ (Knoten) knot in the log-line; ⊕ (Druck)⁓: a) einer elektrischen Klingel: bell-button; b) eines Weckers: bell-push; auf den elektrischen ⁓ drücken to press the button or knob; ⚔ F die Knöpfe bekommen to be promoted lance-corporal. — 2. ⚹ (Knospe) bud; ~ (Knäuel) einer Blüte: ⚹ glomerule. — 3. F fig. mit den Knöpfen (dem Gelde) herausrücken to pay (or F dub) up, F to fork out (the ready or the shiners or the chink); bisw. g.s. F das ist ein (ganz) guter ~ he is a capital fellow or F a nice chap.   [(Iuncus conglomera'tus).|

Knopf=binse ⚹ (⸌⸚) f ⚹ common rush;

Knöpfchen (⸚⸌) n ⓶ (dim. von Knopf) small button or knob or ball; ~ zum Durchstecken in Manschetten ⚹c. a. stud.

Knopf=draht (⸚⸌) m ⓶ ⚹ zu Nadelköpfen button- (or head-)wire.

knöpfeln (⸚⸌) v/a. ⓶a. to knot.

knöpfen (⸚⸌) [Knopf] v/a. to button.

Knopf=fabrik ⊕ (⸚⸌) f ⓶, =fabrikant m button-manufactory, -manufacturer; =form f button-mould; ⚶förmig a. ⊕ in the shape of a button; =gabel f bu.-cleaner; =gießer m bu.-founder; =handel m bu.-trade; =klette f bu.-bur (Xa'nthium struma'rium); =loch n bu.-hole (auch = =loch=sträußchen n); =lochmacher (in f) m button-hole maker, bu.-holer; =macher m bu.-maker; =macherware f bu.-ware; =öhr n, =öse f bu.-shank.

Knöpf=schuhe (⸌⸚) m/pl. ⚹ button-boots, buttoned boots or shoes pl.

Knopf=seide (⸌⸚) f ⚹ silk for buttons; =überzug m covering of a button; =zieher m button-hook.

Knopper ⚹ u. ⚹ (⸚⸌) [ndd.: *Knopf] f ⚹ (Gall-auswuchs an Eichelkelchen) kind of gall formed on young acorns of the ægilops, drillet, valonia; ~=eiche ⚹ (⸚⸌) f ⚹ ægilops, valonia (Quercus Ae'gilops).

Knorpel (⸚⸌) [mhd.] m ⓶ anat. und ⊕ cartilage, Schlächterei ⚹c.: gristle; ⚹ chondrus; netzförmiger ~ ⚹ fibrocartilage; ⚶ähnlich (⸚⸌...)a. ⊕, ⚶artig a. cartilaginous, gristly, ⚹ chondroid; ~fische m/pl. ichth. cartilaginous fishes pl. (Chondropte'rygii); ~flosser m/pl. ichth.: ⚹ chondropterygians pl.; ~geschwulst f, path.: ⚹ (ec)chondroma.

knorpelhaft (⸚⸌), knorp(e)licht ⸝, mst knorp(e)lig (⸚⸌⸝) a. ⊕ cartilaginous, ⚹ cartilaginiform.

Knorpel=haut (⸚⸌...) f ⓶ anat.: ⚹ perichondrium; =kirsche f = Herzkirsche; =leim m, chm.: ⚹ chondrin(e); =tang m carrageen.

Knorren (⸚⸌) [mhd.: gnarl] m ⓶ 1. knot in wood, gnarl(ed branch). — 2. (Auswuchs) hard excrescence or protuberance or hump; ⚹ u. anat.: ⚹ exostosis, tuberosity; (Verhärtung) concretion.

knorricht, mst knorrig (⸚⸌) [Knorren] a. ⊕ knotted, gnarled, knobby, knaggy.

Knöspchen (⸚⸌) n ⓶ (dim. von Knospe) small (or tiny) bud, ⚹: ⚹ gemmule, der keimenden Pflanze: ⚹ plumule.

Knospe (⸚⸌) [mhd.] f ⓶ 1. ⚹ bud; (Blüten=)⁓ flower-bud; (Blatt=)⁓ leafbud, ⚹ gemmule; (erster Aufang der ~, Auge) eye, ⚹ gemma; ~n ansetzen treiben to show buds, to bud, vgl. knospen; sich durch ~n vermehrend: ⚹ gemmiferous. — 2. fig. (unentwickeltes Wesen) tender shoot or offspring.

knospen (⸚⸌) I v/n. (h.) ⚹ (s. Knospe) 1. ⚹ to bud, to put forth buds; weitS. to sprout (forth), to shoot; ⚹ b to bud, ⚹ proliferous. — 2. fig. (sich entfalten) to burst into leaf or blossom, to unfold. — II ~ n ⓶ 3. budding, &c. (s. I), ⚹ gemmation.

knospen=ähnlich ⚹ (⸚⸌...) a. ⊕, ⚶artig a. bud-like, ⚹ gemmaceous; =bildung f ⓶: ⚹ gemm(ul)ation, ⚶förmig a. in (the) form of a bud, ⚹ gemmiform; =häutchen n, =hülle f ⚹ cap, ⚹ hymen, perule; =lage f der Blätter: ⚹ vernation; ⚶tragend a. full of buds, ⚹ gemmiferous; =zeit f budding-season or -time, ⚹ gemmation.

knospig (⸚⸌) ⸝, mst knospig (⸚⸌) a. ⊕ ⚹ 1. = knospen=ähnlich. — 2. covered with buds, full of buds.

Knospung (⸚⸌) f ⚹ = knospen II.

Knötchen (⸚⸌) n ⓶ (dim. von Knoten) small knot, ⚹ nodule, ⚹ u. med. a. tubercle.

knötchen=ähnlich (⸚⸌...) a. ⊕, ⚶förmig a. like a small knot, ⚹ nodular, noduliform; med. tuberculiform; ⚶reich ⚹ a.: ⚹ nodulose, ...ous; =stich ⚹ m ⚹ knot-stitch; ⚶tragend a.: ⚹ noduliferous.

Knote (⸚⸌) [ndd. Genosse] m ⓸ burschikos, b.s. (Handwerksgeselle) journeyman, weitS. (gemeiner Mensch) low(-bred) fellow, cad; (ordinärer Philister) townsman.

knoten, knöteln (⸚⸌) v/n. (h.) u. v/a. ⓶a. to make (or put in) knots, to knot.

Knoten¹ (⸚⸌) [ahd.: knot] m ⓶ 1. knot, ⚹ joint; der gordische ~ the Gordian knot; einen ~ knüpfen ob. schürzen (auflösen) to tie (to undo) a knot (a. fig.); fig. ~ eines Dramas ⚹c. plot, intrigue, entanglement; der ~ löst sich (verschlingt sich) the plot is unravelling (thickening); Schürzung des ~s: ⚹ epitasis, vgl. Knäuel 2. — 2. fig. (Schwierigkeit) difficulty, knotty point or problem; die Sache hat einen ~ there's a hitch somewhere; einen ~ lösen to solve a difficulty; vgl. Haken 2. — 3. = Knorren 2. — 4. ⚓ (= 1852 Meter) knot; zwölf ~ die Stunde twelve knots an hour. — 5. ast. (Durchschnittspunkt der Himmelsbahnen): (auf=, nieder=steigender) ~ (ascending, descending) node.

Knoten² (⸚⸌) v/a. u. v/n. (h.) ⚹ to (tie a) knot, to make knots in a rope, &c.

knoten¹=artig (⸚⸌...) a. ⊕ knotty; vgl. knotig¹ 2; =bildung f ⓶: ⚹ nodulation, path. tuberculization; =fänger ⊕ m Papierfabr.: (Art Sieb) knotter, pulp-strainer; ⚶förmig a. in the shape of a knot, ⚹ nodiform.

knotenhaft (⸚⸌...) a. ⊕ = knotig¹ u. ².

Knoten¹=holz (⸚⸌...) n ⓶ knotted (or gnarled) wood; ⚶los a. ⊕ without knots, knotless; ⚹ jointless; =lösung f im Drama unravelling (of) the plot, tragische: catastrophe; =punkt m, math. point of junction, ⚹ node; ⏚ junction, central station, railway centre; ⚶reich a. full of knots, knotty; =schürzung f im Drama working up (or entangling) the plot, ⚹ epitasis; =stich ⊕ m Näherei: knot-stitch; =stock m knotty stick; =tau n knotted rope.

Knöterich ⚹ (⸚⸌) [Knoten] m ⓶ d. knotgrass, knotweed (Poly'gonum); gemeiner ~ spotted persicaria (P. persica'ria); scharfer ~ biting persicaria (P. hydro'piper).

knotig¹ (⸚⸌) [Knoten] a. ⊕ 1. = knorricht. — 2. a) (mit Knötchen versehen): ⚹ nodular, path. tubercular, tuberculous; b) ⚹ (knotenreich): ⚹ nodose, nodulated; articulate; path. tubercular.

knotig² (⸚⸌) [Knote] a. ⊕ low(-bred), vulgar, F caddish.

Knotigkeit¹ (⸚⸌⸝) f ⚹: ⚹ nodosity.

Knotigkeit² (⸚⸌⸝) f ⚹ lowness (of breeding), F caddishness.

Knubbe F (⸌⸚) f ⚹, Knubbel m ⓶, Knubben m ⓷ [ndd.: Knopf] knob, knot.

Knuff F (⸌) m ⑦ b. blow (with the fist), cuff, thump.

knuffen (⸚⸌) [ahd.] v/a. ⚹ to cuff, thump, pommel.

knuffig F (⸚⸌) a. ⊕ (roh) rude, coarse; fig. (ungeheuer) immense, F tremendous.

knüll(e) provv. F (⸌⸝) a. ⊕ drunk, tipsy, F boozy, well on.

knüllen (⸚⸌) v/a. ⚹ to crumple, crease, ruffle; (bauschig machen) to pucker.

knüpfen (⸚⸌) [ahd.; *Knopf] v/a. u. sich ⚹ v/refl. ⚹ 1. (zs.-, zu=) to tie, to knot, to join (closely), to knit (together); e-n Knoten, fig. ein Bündnis ⚹ to tie a knot, to form an alliance; Knoten aus=ea. ⚹ to undo ...; e-n an den Galgen ⚹ to attach a p. to the gallows, to hang a p., F to string a p. up. — 2. fig. Bande enger oder fester ⚹ to tighten the bonds of friendship, &c.; an diese Frage ⚹ sich große Interessen large interests are tied up with (or involved in) this question.

Knüppel (⸚⸌) [ndd.] m ⓶ 1. cudgel, club, (short) stick; hard log (of wood); eichener ~ der Iren shillelagh; ~ für Hunde clog; fig. e-m ~ in die Räder stecken to put obstacles in a p.'s way; Sprichw. ~ liegt beim Hunde there is no (F it's Hobson's) choice; either do or die; we must do as we can. — 2. F (Brötchen) French roll.

Knüppel=band ⊕ (⸚⸌...) n ⓶ Seilerei: winch-handle rope; =brücke f log-bridge, bridge made of logs.

Signs (see page XVII): F familiar; P vulgar; ⸝ flash; ⸜ rare; † obsolete (died); * new word (born); ⁺⁺ incorrect; ♪ music;

[Knüppelchen] — 599 — [Kogel]

Knüppelchen (⌣⌣⌣) n ㉓: a) small cudgel or stick or log; b) = Knüppel 2.
Knüppel=damm (⌣⌣⌣) m ㉒ fascine road, road paved with logs (or blocks) of wood, Am. corduroy road.
knüppelhaft, knüppelicht (⌣⌣⌣) a. ㊌ like a cudgel, &c. (f. Knüppel); fig. clumsy. [wood in logs, fagots pl.]
Knüppel-holz (⌣⌣⌣) n ㉒ knotty wood,
knuppern (⌣⌣) = knabbern.
Knurps F (⌣) = Knirps.
knurpsen F (⌣⌣) v/n. (h.) ㊌ = knabbern.
knurren (⌣⌣) [lautmalend] I v/n. (h.) ㊌ von Hunden, Bären: to growl, snarl, gnarl; von Personen auch: to grumble; von Katzen: (fauchen) to spit; von leeren Gedärmen: to rumble. — II ~ n ㉓ growling, &c. (f. I); rumbling (noise) in the bowels, ⚕ bombus, borborygmus.
Knurr=hahn (⌣⌣) m ㉒: a) orn. Birkhahn; b) ichth. gurnard, ehm. gurnet, tub-fish (Trigla).
knurrig (⌣⌣) a. ㊌ growling, snarling; von Personen: grumbling.
Knurr=kater (⌣⌣⌣) m ㉒: a) growling tom-cat; b) fig. (auch =kopf, =peter m) grumbler, growler.
Knusperchen * (⌣⌣⌣) n ㉓ = Reef.
knusp(e)rig (⌣(⌣)⌣) a. ㊌ crisp, F short.
knuspern (⌣⌣⌣) v/n. (h.) und v/a. ㉒ a. to nibble, to crunch; vgl. knabbern.
Knust (⌣) [ndd.] m ①①b. = Kanten 2.
Knute (⌣⌣) [ruff.; *ifand. Knoten=] f ⓮ knout; die ~ bekommen to be knouted;
knuten (⌣⌣) v/a. ㉒ to give the knout to, to knout. [crummy.]
knutsch(e)lig F (⌣(⌣)⌣) a. ㊌ plump,
knutschen F prov. (⌣⌣) ㉒ (drücken) to squeeze, cuddle; (herzen) to fondle.
Knüttel (⌣⌣) [ahd.; * Knoten] m ㉒ = Knüppel; ~vers (⌣⌣⌣) [nhd. 16. sae.] m ㉒ pros. (holperiger Vers) doggerel rhyme or verse or line.
knütten F prov. (⌣⌣) v/a. ㊌ to knit.
Ko. ⚕ abbr. = Kompanie. [coadjutor.]
Koadjutor (⌣⌣⌣⌣) [it. Mithelfer] m ㉚]
koalisieren (⌣⌣⌣⌣⌣) v/refl. ㉒ (fich verbünden) to form a coalition.
Koalition (⌣⌣⌣⌣) f ㊻ pol. (Bündnis) coalition, combination, alliance; ~s-recht (⌣⌣⌣) n ㉒ right of combining.
Kobalt ⚕ (⌣⌣) [Kobold] m, (chm. u. ⊙:) n ①d. (schweres Metall) cobalt (Co).
Kobalt=beschlag ⚕ (⌣⌣⌣) m ㉒ cobalt-crust; =blau n smalt; =blüte f cobalt-bloom; =chlorid n cobaltic chloride (Co_2Cl_6); =chlorür n cobaltous chloride ($CoCl_2$); =glanz m cobalt-glance, co-baltin(e) ($CoAsS$); =glas n (blue) cobalt-glass; =grün n c.-green, green smalt; =haltig a. ㊌ cobaltiferous; =oxyd n cobaltic sesquioxide (Co_2O_3); =oxydul n cobaltous oxide (CoO); =speise f arseniuret of cobalt ($CoAs_2$); =cyanür n cobaltous cyanide $CO(CN)_2$.
Kobel (⌣⌣) [Koben, dim.] m ㉒ (Hütte, Verschlag) hud, shed; ~ente (⌣⌣⌣) f ⚕ garrot (Fuligula cla'ngula).
Koben (⌣⌣) [mhd.] m ㉒ 1. (Schweinestall) pig-sty. — 2. fig. hovel.
Kober (⌣⌣) [nhd. 15. sae.] m ㉒ (Korb) basket, hamper; vgl. Kiepe 1.
Kobold (⌣⌣) [Koben-walt] m ①d. imp, goblin, hobgoblin, familiar spirit,

ehm. a. puck; 2artig (⌣⌣⌣) a. ㊌ like a hobgoblin, impish; ~spuk m ㉒ apparition of hobgoblins; ~streich m impish (or mischievous) trick.
Kobolz F (⌣) [fr. culbute f] m ①a.: ~ schießen, auch: kobolzen (⌣⌣) v/n. (h.) ㊌ to somersault, to cut (or throw, turn) a somersault. [(=de-capello).]
Kobra (⌣⌣) [port.] f ㊻ Schlange: cobra
Koch (⌣⌣) [ahd.: cook; *lt. coquus] m ①c., Köchin f ⓮ cook (m. or f.: man- or male) cook); fig. man weiß nicht, wer ~ oder Kellner ist it is difficult to say who is master and who is man; Sprichw. f. Brei 3 am Schluß u. Hunger 1.
Koch=birne (⌣⌣⌣) [kochen] f ㉒ cooking- (or stewing-)pear; =buch n cookery-book; =butter f cooking-butter, butter for cooking, clarified butter.
kochen (⌣⌣) [ahd.: cook; *lt. co'quere] I v/n. (h.) 1. von Speisen: to be cooking, gelinde: to simmer, von Wasser, Milch: to boil; nahezu 2 F to be near the boil; stark 2 (sieden) to wallop, (aufwallen) to bubble up. — 2. fig. das Blut kocht ihm in den Adern his blood is boiling or up; er kocht vor Wut, als v/impers.: es kocht in ihm he is boiling (or mad) with rage; die See kocht the sea is seething or rough or boisterous. — II v/a. 3. Gemüse, Fleisch ꝛc. 2 to cook or boil ...; Wasser 2 to boil ...; Kaffee, Schokolade ꝛc. 2 to make ...; ⊙ Leim 2 to heat the glue; Seife 2 to boil soap; gekochtes Hammelfleisch, Rindfleisch boiled mutton, beef. — 4. ohne Objekt: to cook, to do (or attend to) the cooking; dort wird gut gekocht the cooking there is good; Sprichw. es wird überall mit Wasser gekocht, etwa: the people are much the same everywhere, human nature is much the same all the world over. — III sich 2 v/refl. 5. (mit Angabe der Wirkung) sich mürbe 2 to become tender (or soft) in cooking or boiling; Kartoffeln ꝛc., die sich gut 2 (lassen), oft: F good cookers pl. — IV ~ n ㉓ 6. (f. I u. II) cooking, cookery, boiling; das ~ versteh(e)n to understand cookery or the culinary art, to be a professed cook.
Kocher (⌣⌣) m ㉒ 1. ⚕ one who cooks, bsd. in Zssgn, z.B. Kaffee-2 one who makes the coffee. — 2. (Gefäß zum Kochen) cooking-vessel, cooker, boiler; auch = Kochmaschine.
...kocher (...⌣⌣) [kochen] m ㉒ in Zssgn, z.B. Eier-2 egg-boiler.
Köcher (⌣⌣) [ahd.] m ㉒ quiver.
Köcherei (⌣⌣⌣) f ㊻ (inferior) cooking.
Köcher=fliege (⌣⌣⌣) f ㊻, =jungfer f. ent. caddis-fly, spring-fly, water-moth (Phryga'nea); Larve der ~ caddis; =voll m quiverful; =wurm, zo.: 2 amphitrite.
Koch=feuer (⌣⌣⌣) n ㉒ fire for cooking or boiling; =gerät, =geschirr n cooking- (or kitchen-)utensils or F things pl.; =herd m cooking-stove, kitchen-range.
Köchin (⌣⌣) f ⓮ f. Koch.
Koch=kelle (⌣⌣⌣) f ㉒ basting (or kitchen-)ladle; =kessel m kleinerer: kettle, größerer: copper; ⊕ Papierfabr.: pulp-digester; =kiste f (Selbstkocher) self-cooker; =kunst f art of cooking,

culinary art; =künstler(in f) m clever cook; =loch ⚔ n im Biwat: hole for cooking; =löffel m = kelle; =maschine f, =ofen m cooking-apparatus or -stove, kitchener; =pfanne f (sauce-)pan; =salz n common (or rock-, kitchen-)salt, chm. sodium chloride ($NaCl$); =stück n Schlächter: piece of meat for boiling; =topf m pot for cooking, cooker, boiler, weitS. saucepan; =zeug n cooking-implements pl.; =zucker n powdered sugar, in England: brown (or moist) sugar.
Kockels-körner ⚕ (⌣⌣⌣) [lt. co'cculus] n/pl. ㊸ pharm. Hopfensurrogat: Indian berries pl.; =körner-baum ⚕, =strauch m moon-seed, cocculus (Menispe'rmum co'cculus); =säure f, chm. ⚕ menispermic acid.
Koda ♪ (⌣⌣) [it.] f ㊻ (pl. auch Kode) (Schlußsatz) coda.
Köder (⌣⌣) [ahd.] m ㉒ 1. Fischerei, hunt.: bait, lure; weitS. enticement; in den ~ beißen to take the bait, to have a bite. — 2. Schuhmacherei: (Leder-streifen an der Kappe, woran der Absatz befestigt ist) leather to which the heel is attached.
Köder=fisch ⚕ (⌣⌣⌣) m ㉒ Fischerei: live bait.
ködern (⌣⌣) v/a. ㉒ a.: eine Angel 2 to bait a fishing-line; fig. (locken) to allure, entice, decoy.
Köder=sandwurm (⌣⌣⌣) m zo. worm for baiting; auch = Sandwurm.
Kodex ⚕ (⌣⌣) [lt. codex, bff. caudex] m ①a., ㊸ 1. old manuscript. — 2. (Gesetz-buch) code. — 3. tel. (Kurzschrift, Sammlung von vereinbarten Kürzungen) code.
Kodex=telegramm ⊙ (⌣⌣⌣) n ㉒ code telegram or wire.
Kodifikation ⚕ (⌣⌣⌣⌣) [it.] f ㊻ (Zusammenstellen von Gesetzen ꝛc.) codification.
kodifizier=en ⚕ (⌣⌣⌣⌣) [it.] I v/a. ㉒ (Gesetze 2 sammeln) to codify. — II ~ n ㉓ und K=ung f ㊻ codification.
Kodizill ⚕ (⌣⌣) [lt.] n ①d. jur. (Anhang zum Testament) codicil.
kodizillarisch ⚕ (⌣⌣⌣⌣) a. ㊌ codicillary.
Ko=effizient ⚕ (⌣⌣⌣⌣) [it.] m ㉒ math., phys. (Vervielfachungszahl, z.B. 7 in 7x) coefficient.
Kofen (⌣⌣) [ndd.] m ㉓ = Koben.
Kofent (⌣⌣) [Konve'nt] m ⓰b. weak beer.
Koffe-in (⌣⌣⌣) n ①c. chm. = Kaffein.
Koffer (⌣⌣) [(+)fr., *grch.] m(n) ㉒ 1. (Reise-)2 (travelling-)box, aus Blech: tin box; aus Leder: leather trunk, kleinerer: portmanteau; seine(n) ~ packen to pack up (one's box(es) or one's things) — 2. ⚔ frt. (Graben-)~ caponier.
Köfferchen (⌣⌣⌣) n ㉓ (dim. von Koffer) small box, aus Leder: portmanteau.
Koffer=deckel (⌣⌣⌣) m ㉒ lid of a box; =fisch m, ichth. coffer- (or trunk-)fish (Ostra'cion); =garn n Fischerei: sweep-net; =macher ⊕ m trunk-maker; =nagel ⊕ m trunk-nail; =riemen m, =schloß n strap, padlock to a trunk; =träger m (railway-, &c.) porter.
Kog prov. (⌣) [ndd.] n ㉒ (durch Ein-deichen gewonnenes Land) reclaimed land.
Kogel prov. (⌣⌣) m ㉒, f ⓮ (Bergkuppe) domeshaped mountain-top.

⚕ scientific; ⚘ botanical; ⚔ geography; ⊙ machinery; ⚒ mining; ⚔ military; ⚓ marine; ⚖ commercial; ✉ postal; 🚂 railway.

[Kognak] — 600 — [Kolben]

Kognak ♃ (tŏ'n-jät) [Cognac, fr. St.] m ⑪d.⑭ (feiner Franzbranntwein) (superior) French brandy; cognac.

Ko-gnat (⌣⌣́) [lt.] m ㊷ (Blutsverwandte[r] mütterlicherseits; ant. Agnat) relative on the mother's side.

Ko-härenz ⌣ (--⌣́) [lt.] f ㊻ phys. (das Zſ.hängen) coherence. [coherer.]

Kohärer* ♃ (-⌣́-) m ㉒ elect. (Fritröhre)

ko-härieren ⌣ (--⌣́-) v/n. (h.) ⑬ phys. (zusammenhängen) to cohere. [herence.]

Ko-häſion ⌣ (--⌣)́ f ㊻ cohesion, co-

Kohl¹ (⌣́) [ahd.: cole, kale; *lt. *caulis*] m ⑪c. 1. cabbage (*Bra'ssica*), (Kraus)~ kale. — 2. *fig.* aufgewärmter ~ (alte Geſchichte) old (or raked-up) story; das macht den ~ nicht fett that won't help much or make much difference; mach' keinen langen ~ (ein langes Geſchwätz)! I don't draw it out too long!

Kohl²-amſel (⌣́...) [Kohle] f ㉒ orn. = Amſel; -**arten** ❦ f/pl.: ⌣ brassicaceous plants pl.; -**artig** a. ㊶ like cabbage, ⌣ brassicaceous; -**blatt** n cabbage-leaf.

Kohle (⌣́) [ahd.: coal] f ㊽ (mineral) coal (meiſt = Steinkohle); (Holz-)~ charcoal; ~ zum Zeichnen, für elektriſches Licht ꝛc.; ausgeglühte ~n cinders pl., glühende ~n red-hot (or live) coal(s pl.), glimmende ~n embers pl.; ~n (Holz zu ~n) brennen to make charcoal (vgl. brennen 7); ~n hauen to pick (or break down) coal(s) (from the seam); in ~ verwandeln to char, to carbonize; zu ~ werden to turn to coal, to be (or become) carbonized; mit ~ flüchtig zeichnen to sketch with carbon; ⌣ ~n einnehmen to (take in) coal; *fig.* auf glühenden ~n ſitzen oder ſtehen oder liegen oder ſein to be on thorns or tenter-hooks; ſ. feurig 1.

Kohle-druck ⊙ (⌣́...) m ㉒ phot. (Pigmentdruck) pigment-printing; -**lichtdruck** m carbon-print.

kohlen¹ (⌣́) I v/a. u. v/n. (h.) ⑬ 1. von einem Dochte: to burn with a sooty flame. — 2. Holz ⌣ (zu Kohle machen) to char or carbonize ... — 3. (mit Kohle zeichnen) to draw (or sketch) with carbon. — II ~ n ⑪c. 4. (ſ. 2) charring, ⌣ carbonization, carburization.

kohlen² P (⌣́) [Kohl¹ 2] v/n. (h.) ㊹ F to talk bosh or rubbish.

Kohlen-bau (⌣́...) m ㊷ coal-mining or -digging, working of a coal-mine; -**ähnlich** a. ㊶, -**artig** a. like coal, carbon-like; -**arbeiter** m coal-miner, a. oft: pitman; -**becken** n: a) coal-pan, brazier; b) ⚒ coal-bed or -field; -**behälter** m c.-hole, -bin; -**bergwerk** n c.-mine, colliery; -**bezirk** m c.-district; -**bildung** f formation of coal; -**blende** f, min. (schistous) anthracite; -**börſe** f c.-exchange; -**brenner** m charcoal-burner; -**brennerei** f: a) charcoal-burning; b) (Ort) charcoal-kiln; -**bunker** ⌣ m (coal-)bunker; -**dampf** m = ; -**dämpfer** m c.-extinguisher; -**diſtrikt** m c.-district; -**dunſt** m smoke of (burning) coal; -**eiſen** n. chm. carburet of iron; -**feld** n c.-field; -**feuer** n c.-fire; -**feu(e)rung** f heating with coal; ⊙ combustion of coal; -**flöz** n, geol. layer (or bed) of coal, coal-seam or

-measure; -**förderung** f output (or extraction) of coal; -**gas** n coal-gas; -**gebirge** n carboniferous mountains pl.; -**gefäß** n coal-scuttle; -**gelaß** n c.-bin; -**geſtübe** n c.-dust or -breeze; -**glut** f heat of burning coal; -**gräber** m collier; -**grube** f c.-pit; -**grus** m ſ. Grus 2; -**haltig** a. containing coal, carboniferous; -**handel** m coal-trade; -**händler** ♃ m coal-merchant, im kleinen: coal-man; -**handlung** f c.-merchant's business; -**kalk** m, -**kalkſtein** m, min. carboniferous limestone; -**kammer** f c.-cellar; -**kaſten** m c.-box, vgl. -gefäß; -**klein** n small coal, coal-dust, slack; -**lager** n: a) ⌣ c.-depot or stores pl.; b) geol. c.-bed or -seam; -**lichter** ⌣ n c.-lighter; -**magnat** m wealthy owner of c.-mines; -**makler** ♃ m coal-broker, -factor, -agent; -**maß** n c.-measure; -**meiler** m charcoal-pile; -**meſſer** m coal-meter; -**niederlage** f = -lager; -**oxyd** n, chm. carbonic oxide, oxide of carbon (CO); -**pfanne** ⌣ = -becken; -**raum** ⌣ m bunker; -**ſack** m c.-sack; -**ſauer** a., chm. carbonic; ²**ſaurer Kalk** carbonate of lime, calcic carbonate ($CaCO_3$); ²**ſaures**, baſiſch ²ſaures, doppelt ²ſaures Salz carbonate, subcarbonate, bicarbonate; ²**ſaures Kali** potassium carbonate (K_2CO_3); ²**ſaures Waſſer** carbonic (or aerated) water; -**ſäure** f carbonic acid (H_2CO_3); -**ſäure-hydrid** n carbonic anhydride (CO_2); -**ſäure-brot** n aerated bread; -**ſäure-haltig** a. carbonic, aerated; -**ſäure-meſſer** m (Gerät) ⌣ carbonometer, anthracometer; -**ſäure-ſalz** n, chm. carbonate; -**ſchacht** m coal-pit; -**ſchaufel** f c.-shovel; -**ſchiff** ⌣ n c.-barge, collier; -**ſchlacke** f coal-cinder; -**ſchuppen** m c.-shed; -**ſieb** n c.-screen; -**ſpitze** f, elect. carbon-point; -**ſplitter** ſ, elect. für Fernſprecher: granulated carbon; -**ſtation** ⌣ und 🚂 f coaling-station; -**ſtaub** m coal-dust; -**ſtoff** m, chm. carbon (C); -**ſtoffhaltig** a. carbon(ifer)ous; -**ſtoff-verbindung** f carburet; -**tiegel** m carbon crucible; -**träger** m coal-heaver or -porter, -**trichter** ⌣ m coal-shoot; -**verſchlag** m = -behälter; -**wagen** m c.-cart or -truck or -wagon; -**waſſerſtoff-gas** n) m ⌣ chm. carburetted hydrogen, carbohydrate; leichtes ~ (Sumpfgas) marsh-gas, ⌣ methane (CH_4); ſchweres (ölbildendes) ~ olefiant gas, ⌣ ethylene (C_2H_4); ²**waſſerſtoff-haltig** a.: ⌣ hydrocarbonaceous; -**zeche** f coal-pit; colliery.

Köhler (⌣́) [mhd.; *Kohle] m ㉒ 1. charcoal-burner or -man. — 2. ichth. coal-fish (*Gadus carbona'rius*).

Köhlerei (-⌣́-) f ㊻ charcoal-works pl., charcoal-burner's business.

Köhler-glaube(n) (⌣́-...) m ㉒ simple (or blind, implicit) faith; -**hütte** f, etwa: plain cottage.

Kohl¹-**eule** (⌣́...) f ㉒ ent. cabbage-moth (*Mame'stra brassicae*); -**fliege** f, ent. ca.-fly (*Anthomy'ia brassicae*); -**floh** m, ent. ca.-flea (*Ha'ltica consobri'na*); -**garten** m c.-field; -**gärtner** m one who grows cabbages; -**gemüſe** n cabbage; -**käfer**

m. ent. ca.-beetle (*Phyllotre'ta vitta'ta*); -**kopf** m (head of) cabbage; -**lauch** ❦ m cabbage-garlic (*A'llium olera'ceum*); -**markt** m vegetable-market; -²**meiſe** [: coal-mouse] f, orn. (big) oxeye, great titmouse (*Parus maior*); -¹**palme** ❦ f cabbage-palm (*Are'ca olera'cea*); -²**pechraben-ſchwarz** F a. = ²ſchwarz; -¹**pflanze** ❦ f: a) young ca.-plant grown from seed; b) ~n pl. = -arten; -²**rabe** m, orn. common raven (*Corvus corax*); -**raben-ſchwarz** F a. = ²ſchwarz; -¹**rabi** (⌣́⌣̀) [it.] m ⑩ ob. inv. turnip-cabbage, -tops pl., ⌣ kohlrabi (*Brassica olera'cea*); -**raupe** f, ent. v. weißling ca.-caterpillar or -worm; -**rübe** f, ⌣ turnip-rooted cabbage (*Brassica Napobra'ssica*); b) = -ra'bi; -**ſaat** ❦ f ⌣ colza, cole- (or rape-) seed (*Brassica campe'stris*); -²**ſchwarz** a. (as) black as a coal or as ink, jet-black; -¹**ſproſſen** m/pl. agr. (Brussels) sprouts pl.; -**ſtengel** m, -**ſtiel**, -**ſtrunk** m cabbage-stalk.

Kohlung (⌣́) f ㊻ = kohlen¹ II.

Kohl¹-**wanze** (⌣́...) f ㊷ ent. cabbage-bug (*Murga'ntia histrio'nica*); -**weißling** m, ent. cabbage-butterfly (*Pi'eris rapae*).

Kohorte ⚔ (-⌣́-) [lt.] f ㊺ röm. Alt.: (300 bis 600 Mann Fußvolk) cohort.

Ko-itus (⌣́⌣) [lt.] m, inv. coition, copulation, (Beiſchlaf) cohabitation.

Koje ⌣ (⌣́) [ndl.; *lt. *ca'vea*] f ㊻ (kleine Kajüte) berth, (small) cabin.

Koka ⌣ (⌣́) [braſil.] f ㊶ coca (*Erythro'xylon coca*); **Koka-in** ⌣ (-⌣́) n ⑪d. chm. (Alkaloid der Koka) cocaine ($C_{17}H_{21}NO_4$); ~**vergiftung** f ㊷: ⌣ cocainism.

Kokarde (-⌣́-) [fr.] f ㊺ cockade.

Koker (⌣́) [ndd. Köcher] m ㉒ 1. ⊙ Töpferei: (Brennkapſel) saggar. — 2. ⌣ (Pumpenkaſten) trunk of a pump; ⌣ (Öffnung zur Aufnahme des Maſtes) case for a mast.

kokett (⌣́) [fr.] ㊶ I a. (gefallſüchtig) coquettish. — II ~**e** f ㊶ coquette, flirt.

Koketterie (⌣⌣⌣́) [fr.] f ㊻ (Gefallſucht) coquetry, flirtation.

kokettieren (⌣⌣́) [fr.] v/n. (h.) ㊹ to coquet (or flirt) with a p.; weitS. to put on affected airs or fine graces.

Kokon (⌣ta') [fr.] m (n) ㊿ Naturgeſchichte: (Puppe, bſd. der Seidenraupe, auch Gespinſt für die Eier mancher Spinnen und Fiſche) cocoon; einen ~ machen (ſich einſpinnen) to cocoon, to spin (or make) a cocoon.

Kokos ❦ (⌣́) [span., port., grch.] f, inv. ~**baum** ❦ m ㊶ coco(a)-nut tree (*Cocos*); ~**faſer** f = -nußbaſt; -**läufer** m strip of coco(a)-nut matting; ~**nuß** f coco(a)-nut; ~**nuß-baſt** m, -**faſer** f coco(a)-nut fibre, coir (auch Tau aus -nußfaſern); ~**nuß-öl** n coco(a)nut oil; ~**palme** f = -baum; ~**ſtearin-ſäure** f, chm. ⌣ cocinic acid, cocinin ($C_{13}H_{26}O_2$).

Koks ⌦ (⌣́) [engl. *coaks] m ⑪a., mſt pl. coke; ~**brennofen** m (⌣́...) m ㊷ coke-oven; ~**gichten** ⊙ f/pl. metall. coke-charges pl.

Kokytos (-⌣́-) [grch.] = Kozytus.

Kola-nuß ❦ (⌣́⌣) f (⌣́⌣) ㊷ cola-nut.

Kölbchen (⌣́) n ㉓ (dim. von Kolben) small club, ❦ spikelet.

Kolben¹ (⌣́) [ahd.] m ㉓ 1. allg.: (thick) end of a cylinder; bſd. (Keule) club, mace; ~ e-s Gewehres butt-end of a

Zeichen (ſ. S. XVII): F familiär; P Volksſprache; F Gaunerſprache; ⌣ ſelten; † alt (auch geſtorben); * neu (auch geboren); ⌣ unrichtig;

[Kolben] — 601 — [Kolophonium]

gun; ⚔ mit dem ~ dreinschlagen to (deal blows with the) butt-end. — **2.** (große Flasche) large flask; (Korbflasche) carboy, demijohn; *chm.* = Destillierhelm. — **3.** ♀ (walzenförmiger Blütenstand) von Mais ꝛc.: spike, ⚔ spadix. — **4.** Klempnerei ꝛc. (Löt-)~ soldering-iron; Buchbinderei ꝛc.: (Glätt-)~ polishing-tool, -stick; in Pumpen: piston; (Dampf-)~ piston of a steam-engine; durchbroch(e)ner ~ perforated piston, valve-piston; massiver ~ solid piston, plunger.

kolben² (⌣ˊ) ⊕ **I** v/n. (h.) **1.** ♀ (Kolben bekommen) der Mais kolbt... is putting on its spikes. — **2.** (mit Kolben spielen) to play with clubs. — **II** v/a. **3.** ⊕ ein Gewehr ⚔ to put (or fix, attach) the butt-end to a gun.

kolben=ähnlich (ˊ⌣⌣...) a. ⊕ club-shaped, ♀: ⚔ spadiceous; **=ansatz** ⊕ m ⓺₂ *mach.* up-stroke of the piston; **⚯artig** a. = ⚯ähnlich; **=deckel** ⊕ m, *mach.* piston-cover; **=gebläse** ⊕ n, *mach.* piston blowing-machine; **=geschwindigkeit** ⊕ f, *mach.* piston speed; **=hebel** ⊕ m, *mach.* beam-lever; **=hirse** ♀ f Italian millet (*Seta'ria ita'lica*); **=hub** ⊕ m stroke of the piston; **=liderung** ⊕ f packing of the piston; **=molch** m, *zo.* Mexiko: axolotl (*Stego'porus mexica'nus*); **=moos** ♀ n club-moss (*Lycopo'dium*); **=niedergang** ⊕ m, *mach.* down-stroke of the piston; **=platte** ⊕ f e-r Uhr: upper plate; **=pumpe** ⊕ f piston-pump; **=scheibe** ⊕ f, *mach.* piston-head; **=schlag** ⚔ m blow (or stroke, knock) with the butt-end of a gun; **=spiel** ⊕ n, *mach.* play of the piston, up-and-down stroke; **=stange** ⊕ f piston-rod; **=stoß** ⚔ m thrust with the butt-end of the gun; **⚯tragend** ♀ a.: ⚔ spadiceous; **=ventil** ⊕ n, *mach.* piston-valve; **=zahn** ⊕ m e-s Rades: club-tooth.

kolbig (⌣ˊ) a. ⊕ club-like, knobby.

Kolder=gatt ⚓ (ˊ⌣...) n ⓺₂ whip-staff hole; **=stock** m whip-staff.

Koleo=pter(n pl.) ⚯ (⌣⌣⌣ˊ⌣) [grch. Scheideflügler, Käfer] f ⚯ *ent.* coleopter(a).

Kolibri (ˊ⌣⌣) [amerikanisch] m ⓾ *orn.* humming-bird (*Tro'chilus*).

Kolik (⌣ˊ, r-r.: ˊ⌣) [grch. a. zu Kolon 3] f ⓺ *path.* colic, gripes pl.; f. Bleifolik; **=anfall** ("...) m ⓺ attack of colic.

Kolk (ˊ) [ndb.] m ⊕⑦b. **1.** (tiefes Wasserloch) (deep) pool or pond. — **2.** ~ (Wirbel) in einem Flusse whirlpool, eddy.

kolken F (ˊ) v/n. (h.) ⓺ = quatschen.

Kolkothar ⚯ (⌣ˊ) [mlt.] m (n) ⓺₁ d. colcothar (= Caput mortuum).

Kolk=rabe (ˊ⌣⌣) [nhd. *provc.* *folken* lautm.] m ⓺ *orn.* common raven (*Corvus corax*).

Kollaborator (⌣⌣⌣ˊ⌣) [lt.] m ⓺ (Mitarbeiter) collaborator, fellow-worker, auch = Hilfslehrer; **Kollaboratur** (⌣⌣⌣⌣ˊ) f ⓺ collaborator's post.

kollaborieren (⌣⌣⌣ˊ⌣) v/n. (h.) ⓺ (mitarbeiten) to collaborate.

kollateral (⌣⌣⌣ˊ) [lt. Seiten...] a. ⓺ collateral; **~erbschaft** ("...) f ⓺ collateral succession; **~verwandte(r** m) f collateral relation.

kollationieren (⌣⌣⌣tś(ⱼ)ˊ⌣) [lt.] **I** v/a. ⓺ *typ.* ꝛc.: ein Werk ⚔ (mit dem Original vergleichen, die Reihenfolge der Bogen prüfen ꝛc.) to collate (or check)... — **II** ~ n ⓺ collation.

Kolleg (⌣ˊ) [lt.] n ⓺ **1.** ~ = Kollegium. — **2.** bsd. (akademische Vorlesung) ein ~ belegen (besuchen, hören) to enter one's name for (to attend) a **course** of university-lectures; ins ~ geh(e)n to go to the lecture-room; ein ~ (über Logik) halten to deliver a course of lectures or to lecture (on logic).

Kollege (⌣ˊ⌣) [lt.] m ⓺ (Amtsbruder) colleague; (Fachgenosse) one of the same profession or craft, (fr.) confrère, unter Arbeitern ꝛc.: F chum, mate, pal.

kollegial, -isch (⌣⌣ˊ⌣(⌣)ˊ) [lt.] a. ⓺ **1.** as (or like) a colleague; ⚯ (adv.) handeln to act as a good colleague. — **2.** (vom Kolle'gium ausgehend) ⚯e Ansicht opinion of the council. — **Kollegialität** (⌣⌣⌣(⌣)ˊ) [lt.] f ⓺ good feeling (or fellowship) between colleagues.

Kollegi=en=gelder (⌣⌣ˊ(⌣)⌣...) n/pl. ⓺ der Professoren: amount of students' fees; **=heft** n student's note-book.

Kollegin (⌣ˊ⌣) f ⓺ lady colleague, woman of the same trade.

Kollegium (⌣ˊ(⌣)⌣) [lt.] n ⓺ (Behörde) municipal, &c. council, board of supervision, executive committee, staff of professors; vgl. College of Physicians, of Surgeons, of Preceptors, &c.

Kolleκtane=en (⌣⌣ˊ⌣⌣) [lt. Gesammeltes] pl. inv. literary extracts or gleanings pl., cuttings. (from periodicals, &c.) pl.; **~buch** n ⓺ common-place-book.

Kollektant (⌣⌣ˊ) [lt.] m ⓺ collector.

Kollekte (⌣ˊ⌣) f ⓺ ([Geld-]Sammlung) collection; *eccl.* (Gebet) collect.

Kollekteur (⌣⌣täˊr) [fr.] m ⓺ d. (Sammler) collector.

kollektieren (⌣⌣ˊ⌣) (Kollekte) v/a. u. v/n. (h.) ⓺ ([Geld]) sammeln) to collect (money), F to hand round the bag or the hat, to raise funds.

kollektiv (⌣⌣ˊf) [lt.] **I** a. ⓺ collective. — **II** ~ n ⓺ d., auch ~**um** (⌣ˊ⌣m) n ⓺ *gr.* (Sammelname) collective noun.

Kollektiv=begriff (⌣⌣ˊf...) [lt. Gesamt-] m ⓺ *gr.* collective; **=gesellschaft** ♂ f ⓺ joint-stock company; **=note** f collective note. [*elect.* commutator.]

Kollektor ⊕ (⌣ˊ⌣) [lt. Sammler] m ⓺₁

Koller¹ [mhd.: *fr. collier* m] n (m) ⓺₂ collar, cape; (Wams) pea-jacket; studentisch: ~ und Kanonen leather breeches and top-boots pl.

Koller² (ˊ⌣) [ahd.: choler; *gr. Galligkeit] m ⓺ **1.** vet. (Dummr²) staggers pl., weit⚯: giddiness. — **2.** F *fig.* von Personen: fury, rage, frenzy, choler; den ~ bekommen to fly into a (violent) passion, F to have a mad fit.

kollerig (ˊ⌣⌣) a. ⓺ (f. Koller²) staggering, giddy; *fig.* raving, in a temper.

kollern¹ (ˊ⌣) v/n. (h.) ⓺a. **1.** bsd. von der Stimme e-s Puters: to gobble, von Tauben: to coo, von den Gedärmen: to rumble, to gurgle. — **2.** a. v/a. Steine vom Berge herab⚯ to roll (or push)... down the mountain-side.

kollern² (ˊ⌣) (Koller²) v/n. (h.) ⓺a. *vet.* have the staggers, *fig.* v. Personen: to rave, to be in a great passion.

Kollett (⌣ˊ) [fr.] n ⓺ c. ⓺ (Wams) collar.

Kolli ♂ (⌣ˊ) *pl.* v. Kollo.

kollidieren (⌣⌣ˊ⌣) [lt.] **I** v/n. (h.) ⓺ (widerstreiten) to collide, to clash. — **II** ~ n ⓺ collision, vgl. Kollision.

Kollimation ⚯ (⌣⌣⌣(⌣)ˊ)[lt.] f ⚯ *ast., opt.* (Berichtigung der Sehtiefe) collimation.

Kollision (⌣⌣ⁱˊ⌣) [lt.] f ⓺ (Widerstreit) collision, clashing, conflict.

Kollo ♂ (⌣ˊ) [lt.] n ⓺ ⓺ single parcel or bale or packet (jetzt Frachtstück).

Kollodium ⚯ (⌣ˊ(⌣)⌣) [grch.=lt. Klebäther] n ⓺ *surg., chm., phot.*: (Auflösung von Schießbaumwolle in Äther) collodion; **~bild** n ⓺ *phot.*: collodiotype; **~häutchen** n (das nach Verdampfen des Äthers verbleibt) collodion film; **~platte** f wet plate; **~verfahren** n (Überziehen des Negativs mit ~) collodion process.

Kolloquium (⌣ˊ(⌣)⌣) [lt. ⌣ˊ⌣⌣] n ⓺ (Gespräch) colloquy, colloquial examination.

Köln ♀ (ˊ) [lt. *Kolonie*] npr/n. ⓺α. (Stadt a. Rhein) Cologne (on the Rhine).

Kölner ♀ **I** m ⓺, ~**in** f ⓺ inhabitant of Cologne. — **II** a. inv. = kölnisch; der ~ Dom the Cologne Cathedral.

kölnisch (ˊ⌣) a. ⓺ (of) Cologne; ⚯e Erde (braune Farbe) Cologne earth; ⚯es Wasser (Riechwasser) eau-de-Cologne; ~e Zeitung Cologne Gazette.

Kolombine (⌣⌣ˊ⌣) [it.] npr/f. ⓺ ⚯β. bsd. *thea.* (Geliebte Harlekins) Columbine.

Kolon (ˊ⌣) [grch.] n ⓺ **1.** *gr.* (Doppelpunkt) colon, two dots (a. ⊕ *typ.*). — **2.** *rhet.* (Abteilung e-s Satzes) colon. — **3.** *anat.* (Grimmdarm) colon.

Kolone (⌣ˊ⌣) [lt.] m ⓺ *röm. Alt. ꝛc.*: (Bauer, Ansiedler) peasant, colonist.

Kolonel (⌣⌣ˊ) [fr.] f ⓺ *typ.* minion type.

kolonial (⌣⌣⌣ˊ⌣) [lt.] a. ⓺ colonial.

Kolonial=geschäft (⌣⌣⌣ˊ⌣...) n ⓺ **=handel** m colonial business, trade; dealings pl. (or trade) with the colonies; **=minister** m colonial minister, in England: Secretary for the Colonies; **=ministerium** n colonial ministry, in Engl.: Colonial Office; **=politik** f col. policy; **=rat** m Behörde: etwa: colonial board; **=system** n col. system; **=waren** f/pl. col. goods pl. or produce; engS. groceries pl.; **=waren=geschäft** n col. business, grocery-business; **=waren=handel** m col. trade; grocer's trade; **=waren=händler** m col. dealer; grocer.

Kolonie (⌣⌣ˊ) [lt. *colo'nia*] f ⓺ (Ansiedlung) colony, settlement; ~n gründen to found colonies, to make settlements.

kolonisatorisch (⌣⌣⌣⌣ˊ⌣) a. ⓺ colonizing.

kolonisieren (⌣⌣⌣ˊ⌣) [Kolonie] **I** v/a. ⓺ (besiedeln) to colonize. — **II** ~ n ⓺ und **K=ung** f ⓺ colonization.

Kolonist (⌣⌣ˊ) m ⓺ (Ansiedler) colonist, settler; (Pflanzer) planter, owner or proprietor of a plantation. [colonnade.]

Kolonnade (⌣⌣ˊ⌣) [fr.] f ⓺ (Säulengang)

Kolonne (⌣ˊ⌣) [fr. Säule] f ⓺ (⚔ Abteilung, *typ.* Spalte) column; ♀ fliegende ~ flying column; in geschlossenen ~n in close columns or files; **~n=angriff** ⚔ m attack, march in columns or files; ⚯n=marsch ⚔ m attack, march in columns or files; ⚯n=weise adv. ⚔ u. *typ.* in columns, ⚔ auch: in files.

Kolophonium ⚯ (⌣⌣ˊ(⌣)⌣) [lt.; * grch. * **Kolophon** ♀ St.] n ⓺ (Geigenharz) colophony, mehr gbr.: rosin.

♪ Musik; ⚯ Wissenschaft; ♀ Pflanze; ♀ Geographie; ⊕ Technik; ⚒ Bergbau; ⚔ Militär; ⚓ Marine; ♂ Handel; ✉ Post; 🚂 Eisenbahn.

[Koloquinte] — 602 — [kommen]

Koloquinte ♀ (⌣⌣⌣) [fr., *grch.] f ⊕ (Purgiergurke) colocynth, bitter-apple (*Citrullus colocynthis*).

Kolorado-Käfer (⌣⌣"...) [Kolorado ♀, amer. Staat] m ⊕ ent. (Kartoffelkäfer) Colorado beetle (*Chrysomela decemlineata*).

Koloratur (⌣⌣⌣́) [it.] f ⊕ 1. = Farbengebung. — 2. ♪ (Verzierung) coloratura, flourish, (Triller, Läufer) trill, shake, quaver. — **~sängerin** (⌣...) f ⊕ lady singer (or primadonna) who sings with flourishes or shakes.

kolorier/en (⌣⌣⌣́) [it.] v/a. ⊕ 1. (färben) to colour, to illuminate; *paint*. to touch in. — 2. ♪ to ornament with flourishes. — 3. **~** n ⊕, **K/ung** f ⊕ colouring, coloration, illumination.

Kolori-meter ⌐ (⌣⌣⌣"́) [it.-grch.] n (m) ⊕ phys. colorimeter.

Kolorist (⌣⌣⌣́) [it.] m ⊕, **~in** f ⊕ Kunst: (j. der koloriert oder sich aufs Kolorit versteht) colourist; **Kolorit** (⌣⌣⌣́) [it.] n ⊕c. colour(ing), hue, shade.

Koloß (⌣⌣́) [grch. Riesenstatue (zu Rhodos)] m ⊕a. colossus; **~ mit tönernen Füßen** colossus with feet of clay.

kolossal,²isch (⌣⌣⌣́)[Koloß]a.⊕(sehr groß) colossal, gigantic, enormous, huge; **~sta'tue** f ⊕ colossal (or giant) statue.

Kolosser (⌣⌣́) [Kolossä, ehm. Stadt in Phrygien] m ⊕, **~in** f ⊕ bibl. Brief an die **~, ~brief** m ⊕ Paul's Epistle to the Colossians.

Kolosse-um (⌣⌣⌣́) [it.] n ⊕ Colosseum.

Kolpak (⌣⌣́)[mag.*türk.]m⊕d.⊕ — Kalpak.

Kolportage (⌣⌣⌣́á) [fr.] f ⊕ hawking of books, &c. by itinerant vendors.

Kolportage-artikel (⌣⌣⌣"⌣́...) m ⊕ article for street-vendors; **=(buch)handlung** f itinerant bookseller's business; **=roman** m, etwa: cheap (sensational) novel, penny-novel, *co.* pennyshocker; **=verlag** m publication of cheap literature (hawked about by street-vendors).

Kolporteur (⌣⌣⌣ö"́r) [fr.] m ⊕d. ⊕ (hausierender [Buch-]Händler) itinerant bookseller; hawker, street-vendor.

kolportieren (⌣⌣⌣́) [fr.] v/a. ⊕ to hawk about, to sell in the streets; *fig.* Nachrichten **~** to circulate (or report, disseminate, spread about)...

Kol-schwein (⌣⌣), **Kol-schwinn** (⌣⌣), **Kolsem** (⌣⌣) n ⊕d. = Kielschwein.

Kolter¹ (⌣⌣́) [mhd.; *it. *coltra*] m ⊕ (f ⊕) quilt, (cloth) coverlet. [of a plough.]

Kolter² (⌣⌣́) [it. *culter*] n ⊕ *agr.* coulter]

Kolumbarium (⌣⌣⌣⌣́) [it. Taubenhaus] n ⊕ röm. Alt. (Begräbniskammer mit Nischen für die Aschenkrüge) columbarium.

kolumbisch (⌣⌣⌣́) *a.* ⊕ *U.S.* Columbian; Süd-amerika: Colombian.

Kolumbus (⌣⌣́) *npr m.* ⊕γ. (Genueser, der 1492 mit spanischen Schiffen West-indien entdeckte; 1436—1506) Christopher Columbus.

Kolumne ⊕ (⌣⌣́) [it.] f ⊕ *typ.* ⊕ (Spalte) column; (Druckseite) page, **~n-maß** n ⊕ page-gauge, rule; **~n-schnur** f pagecord; **~n-titel** m headline, running title; **2n-weise** adv. (arranged) in columns; **~n-ziffer** f folio.

Kolur ⌐ (⌣⌣́) [grch.] m ⊕ *ast.* (Meridian, der durch die Äquinoktialpunkte oder die Wendepunkte der Sonnenbahn geht) colure.

Kombattant ⚔ (⌣⌣⌣́) [fr.] m ⊕ (Kriegsteilnehmer) combatant.

Kombination (⌣⌣⌣—tẓ⌣")[neu=lt.] f ⊕ (Zusammenstellung) combination; **~s-gabe** f ⊕ gift of combination, constructive talent; **~s-lehre** f, *math.*, *phls.*, &c. theory of combination(s); **~s-schloß** ⊕ n Schlosserei: combination-lock.

kombinatorisch ⌐ (⌣—⌣⌣"́) [neu-lt.] *a.* ⊕ (clever in) combining.

kombinieren (⌣—⌣́⌣) [neu=lt.] v/a. ⊕ (zf.-stellen) to combine, to put one thing with another.

Kombüse ♭ (⌣⌣⌣́) f ⊕ = Kambüse.

Komet ⌐ (⌣⌣⌣́) [grch.Haarstern]m⊕*ast.*comet, in Butler's Hudibras: hairy meteor.

kometen-artig (⌣⌣"...) *a.* ⊕ *ast.* like a comet; *adv. a.* comet-wise; **=bahn** f ⊕ path of a comet; **=kern** n nucleus of a comet; **=lehre** f: ⌐ cometology; **=maschine** f: ⌐ cometarium; **=schweif** m tail of a comet; **=sucher** ⊕ m Art Fernrohr: comet-finder; **=system** n cometary system.

Komfort ⌐ (⌣⌣́, *a.* tẓ-fö'r) [engl.] m ⊕c. u. ⊕ (Behaglichkeit) comfort, ease; **komfortabel** (⌣⌣⌣"́) *a.* ⊕ (behaglich) comfortable, easy, snug, cosy.

Komik (⌣⌣́) [grch.] f ⊕ comical things *pl.*, comicality, fun, (low) humour, *engs.* humorous poetry; **~er** (⌣⌣́) m ⊕ comic actor or author, *thea.* auch: (low) comedian.

komisch (⌣⌣́) [grch.] *a.* ⊕ (spaßhaft) comical, (launig) comic, z.B. ein **2er** Kerl a comical (or droll, queer) fellow, **2e** Dichtkunst, Oper comic poetry, opera; eine **2e** (seltsame) Geschichte a strange (or curious) story; er ist sehr **2** he is very peculiar.

Komitat (⌣⌣⌣́) [it.] n ⊕c. 1. (Gefolge) suite. — 2. ♀ (ungarische Gespanschaft) comitat, (Hungarian) county.

Komitee (⌣⌣⌣́) [fr. *comité* m] n ⊕ (Ausschuß) committee; **~mitglied** n ⊕ member of a committee, auch: committee-man.

Komitial=verhandlungen (⌣⌣tẓ(⌣)"...) [it. Volksversammlungs=, Wahl=...] f/pl. ⊕ röm. Alt.: debates *pl.* of the comitia.

Komiti-en (⌣⌣tẓ⌣⌣) n/pl. inv. röm. Alt.: (Volksversammlungen) comitia.

Komma (⌣⌣́) [grch.] n ⊕ 1. *gr.* (Beistrich) comma; *arith.* = Dezimalbrüchen: decimal point or dot; z.B. 6,4 (sechs **~** vier) 6'4 (six decimal four). — 2. *gr.* (Satzabschnitt), ♪ (Intervall) comma. — 3. *ent.* comma (butterfly) (*Papilio Comma*).

Komma=bazillus ⌐ (⌣⌣⌣...) m ⊕ *path.* u. *zo.* comma bacillus.

Kommandant ⚔ (⌣⌣⌣́) [fr.] m ⊕ commander, commandant; governor; **~ur** (⌣⌣⌣́) f ⊕ commander's (or governor's) appointment or residence.

Kommandeur (⌣⌣⌣ö"́r) [(+) fr.] m ⊕d. ⊕ (⚔ Ritter der obersten Klasse eines Ordens) commander; **kommandieren** [fr.] v/a. u. v/n. (ḥ.) ⊕ (bfh. ⚔) (befehlen) to command troops, &c., to be in command of ...; to give a p. orders, F to order people about; e-n zu et. **2** to command (or order) a p. to do a th.; sie wurden zum Vorpostendienst kommandiert they were told off (or detailed) for picketing (duty).

Kommanditär ⊕ (⌣⌣⌣́) [fr.] m ⊕d. ⊕ shareholder of a limited (liability) company; (stiller Teilnehmer) sleeping partner; **Kommandite** (⌣⌣⌣́) f ⊕ (Zweiggeschäft) branch of a commercial firm, branch business or establishment; *a.* = Kommanditgesellschaft; **Kommanditist** (⌣⌣⌣—́) m ⊕ = Kommanditär.

Kommandit= (und Aktien=)gesellschaft ⊕ (⌣⌣⌣"́...) f ⊕ company (of shareholders) with limited liability, *a.* limited (liability) company.

Kommando ⚔ (⌣⌣⌣́) [mlt., it.] n ⊕ 1. (Befehl[swort]) (word of) command, order; auf **~** by command; das **~** zum Feuern the order to fire; das **~** führen to be in command; das **~** in der Schlacht führen to command in the battle; das **~** übernehmen to take the command. — 2. (Abteilung Soldaten) detachment.

Kommando-brücke ♭ (⌣⌣"́...) f ⊕ conning-bridge, pilot-bridge; **=flagge** ⚔ f commander's flag; **=pfeife** ♭ f boatswain's whistle; **=ruf** m = **=wort**; **=stab** m staff of command, FieldMarshal's baton; **=wechsel** ⚔ ♭ m change of command(ers); **=wort** ⚔ ♭ n word of command.

kommen (⌣⌣́) [ahd.: *come*] **I** v/n. (ḥ.) ⊕ (*p.p. poet. a.* 2) 1. to come, wieder **2** to come back, to return; oft wohin **2** to frequent (or haunt) a place; als ich (frisch) dahin kam when I (first) arrived there; da kommt er! there he comes!; man kommt! somebody is (or they are) coming or approaching!; er wird bald **2** he will soon be here, F he won't be long; es dauert lange, bis sie **2** they are a long time coming; **2** Sie mit? will you come with me or us?; Sie **2** wie gerufen you (have) come in the nick of time or most opportunely; sie **2** denselben Weg (od. desselben Weges) they are coming the same way or our (their, &c.) way; wenn Weihnachten kommt // when Christmas comes //, F u. P come Christmas //; wie komme ich nach Bonn? how can I get to ..?; ich werde morgen zu ihm **2** I shall come to (or F and) see him to-morrow; eine Reihenfolge bezeichnend: erst kommt ein Dorf, dann eine Wiese first comes ..., then ..., die Jahre **2** und geh(e)n the years come and go; spät kommt Ihr, doch Ihr kommt (*SCH*) Sprichw. better late than never; wer zuerst kommt, mahlt zuerst first come first served; kommst du nicht heut, so kommst du morgen (s)he won't be hurried, (s)he just dawdles along (in an easy-going style). — 2. (hingehören) die Brille kommt ins Futteral the spectacles (have to) go into the case; das kommt auf die Rechnung that shall go (or be put) on the bill. — 3. *v/impers.* es **2** viele Leute (her) there are many people coming (this way); es kam mir in den Sinn it occurred to me, it struck me; es kommt ein Gewitter there is a storm brewing or threatening; es mag **2** (geschehen) was (da) will come what may; **woher** (oder **wie**) kommt es, daß // ? what is the reason (or how is it) that //?, geh. Spr.: how

Signs (see page XVII): F familiar; P vulgar; ſ flash; ↘ rare; † obsolete (died); * new word (born); ↔ incorrect; ♪ music;

[**kommen**] — **603** — [**kommen**]

comes it that ...?; es kommt bisweilen so things sometimes happen like that or that way; wie kam es, daß sie hier war? how came she to be here?; Sprichw. kommt Zeit, kommt Rat oder über Nacht kommt guter Rat, etwa: time smoothes (the way for) all things. — **4.** mit *p.p.*: ≳ gefahren, gelaufen 2c. ≳ to come riding, driving, running, &c. along; da kommt er geradelt there he comes (spinning along) on his bicycle. — **5.** a) mit *inf.* der Absicht: er kam uns zu sagen he came to tell us; ≳ (um) et. zu holen to come to fetch a th.; b) mit folgendem, fast pleonastischem „und": er kam und setzte sich zu uns he came and sat (or to sit) with us; einen Zufall bezeichnend: er kam oben zu liegen he happened to lie on top. — **6.** ≳ **lassen**: den Arzt ≳ (holen) l. to send for the doctor; dahin dürfen Sie es nicht ≳ l. you must not let things get (or go, drift) so far; drohend: laß ihn nur ≳! let him come! ⚭ Muster, Waren ≳ l. to order samples, goods. — **7. so weit** ≳, **daß** //: er ist (ob. es ist mit ihm) so weit gekommen, daß er nichts essen kann he has got so far (or so low down) as to be unable to eat anything; es wird noch so weit (ob. dahin) ≳, daß er betteln muß we shall see him begging yet, the day will come when he will have to beg. — **8.** mit persönlichem *dat.*: das kommt mir erwünscht ob. gerade recht that suits me admirably or F to a T; e-m grob ≳ to be rude to a p.; wenn Sie mir so ≳ if you talk to (or deal with) me like that; so mußt du mir nicht ≳! you need not try that (or those tricks) on me!; Sprichw. kommst du mir so, so komm' ich dir so, etwa: tit for tat; drohend: der soll mir nur wieder ≳! (just) let him come again!; er soll mir zuerst ≳ (entgegenkommen) he shall make the first advance or move; ⚭ mir ≳ (gebühren) nach der Abrechnung noch 120 Mark when all is settled, there will be £ 6 owing (or due) to me. — **9.** mit *adv.* in eigentümlichen Wendungen: f. **abhanden**; nächstes Jahr wird es noch ganz **anders** ≳ next year things will be even much worse; es konnte nicht anders ≳ it was bound to come to that; das kommt bloß **daher**, daß er so faul ist that is entirely due to his being so lazy, it all arises from his great idleness; f. **dahin** 3, **daran**5, **davon**II, **dazu**2, **dazwischen**II, **fort**..., **heim**..., **her**..., **herab**..., **heran**..., **herauf**..., **heraus**..., **herbei**..., **herein**..., **herum**..., **herunter**..., **hervor**...; *zB.* dahin ≳ zu ... to get so far as to // (*inf.*): muß es dahin ≳? must it come to this? **frei** (ob. **los**) ≳ to become free, F to get off, f. **gleich**2; **hierzu** kommt noch, daß // it must be added that //; f. **hoch** 6; es kommt mir selbst höher oder teurer (zu stehen) I have to pay more (or a higher price) myself; **nahe**≳ to draw near, to approach; der Wahrheit nahe ≳ to come near(er) the truth; was wird nun (noch) ≳? what will be the next thing or move?, what next?; so kommt's immer it's always like that, that's generally the case; **spät** ≳ to be late or behind time; allmählich **vorwärts** ≳ to advance by degrees; mit dem Gelde wird er nicht **weit** ≳ he won't get far with ...; wie weit sind Sie in der Mathematik gekommen? how far did you advance (F get) in your mathematics?; weiter ≳ to advance, to get on, to (make) progress; es ist weit gekommen things have come to a fine pass; ist es so weit mit ihm gekommen? has he come to that? wie es auch ≳ mag oder komme es, wie es wolle come what may (Tennyson, Maud): let come what come may), whatever may happen; wie es gerade kommt according to circumstances, as the case may be; mit et. **zurecht**≳ to succeed in a th.; Sprichw. erst komme ich und dann komme ich noch einmal charity begins at home. — **10.** mit *prp.*: **an**: a) örtlich: an einen Fluß ≳ to come to (the banks of) a river; ans Land ≳ to land, an Ort und Stelle ≳ to arrive at one's destination; b) *fig.* an e-n ≳ (fallen) to pass into a p.'s hands; sie können nicht an ihn ≳ (ihm nicht schaden) they cannot get at him or touch him; lassen Sie es (ruhig) an sich ≳! take it easy!, don't hurry yourself!; f. **Bettelstab**; an den Galgen ≳ to (come to) be hanged; ans Licht, an den Tag ≳ to come (or to be brought) to light; es ist an den rechten Mann gekommen it has fallen into good hands; an die Reihe ≳ to have one's turn; die Reihe kommt an mich it is my turn; scharf (ober hart) an≋ea. ≳ to have a fierce (or sharp) encounter, (handgemein w.) to come to blows; **auf**: auf einen Berg ≳ to get to (or to reach) the top of a mountain; wenn es aufs Äußerste kommt if the worst comes to the worst; wie sind Sie darauf gekommen? what put that idea into your head?, how came you to think of it?; ich kam auf den Einfall the idea struck me, it occurred to me; im Fallen wieder auf die Füße ≳ to fall (or light) on one's feet (a. *fig.*); wieder auf die Beine ≳ to recover one's feet or legs, to pick o.s. up; im Gespräche auf et., e-n ≳ to touch a th., a p. in conversation; auf dem Fahrrade ≳ to come (or arrive) on one's cycle or wheel, to come cycling; f. **Hund** 2; es kommt so viel auf jeden each person's share amounts to so much; auf seine Kosten ≳ to cover one's expenses; auf die Nachwelt ≳ to be handed down to posterity; ich kann nicht wieder auf den Namen ≳ (mich besinnen) I cannot recollect the name; auf die Schule kommen to be sent to school; wieder auf die alten Sprünge ≳ to fall into the old (bad) ways or habits; e-r Sache auf die Spur ≳ to get to the bottom of a th.; e-m auf die Spur ≳ to get on a p.'s track, to track a p.; wieder auf den Weg ≳ to find one's way (back) again; auf die Welt ≳ to be born, F to be ushered into this world; et. nicht auf sich ≳ l. (stoutly) to deny a charge; auf e-n nichts ≳ l. to take a p.'s part in everything, to see no fault in a p.; **aus**: aus der Fassung ≳ to lose one's self-command, friedlich aus≋ea. ≳ to part peaceably; er kommt nie aus dem Hause he never stirs (or goes) out; nicht aus den Kleidern ≳ to keep on (or not to take off) one's clothes; aus der Mode ≳ to go (or get, grow) out of fashion; f. **Regen**; das ist mir aus dem Sinn gekommen it has slipped (from) my memory; ♪ aus dem Takte ≳ not to keep time; **außer**: f. das ≳ u. Atem; **durch**: durch eine Stadt ≳ to pass through ...; **hinter**: hinter j-s Schliche ≳ to find out a p.'s pranks; hinter die Wahrheit ≳ to discover the truth; **in**: in Anschlag ≳ to be taken into account; f. **Betracht**; wenn sie ins Erzählen ≳, sitzen sie die ganze Nacht (when) once they start telling tales or commence spinning yarns ...; das Regiment ist nicht ins Feuer gekommen ... did not come under fire; f. **Gang** 4; in Gefahr ≳ to run into danger; f. **Gehege** 2; ins Gerede ≳ to get talked about; in andere Hände ≳ to pass into other hands; in den Himmel ≳ to get to (or enter) heaven; über et. ins klare ≳ to (begin to) see through a th.; in einer Kutsche ≳ to come in a coach; in die Lehre ≳ to enter one's apprenticeship, to be apprenticed; es ist mir nicht in den Sinn gekommen it never entered my head; in Schweiß ≳ to break out in(to) a perspiration; in Verlegenheit ≳ to get embarrassed; e-m in den Weg, in die Quere, in den Wurf ≳ to come across a p., to fall in with a p., F to run against a p.; **mit**: mit der Eisenbahn, dem Schiffe, der Straßenbahn, dem Zuge ≳ to come by rail(way), by boat, by tram, by train; immer mit den alten Geschichten ≳ to tell the old tales over and over again; mit Gewehren 2c. ≳ to come armed with guns, &c.; e-m ewig mit Klagen ≳ to be for ever complaining to a p.; komm mir nicht mit deinen Witzen! leave your jokes (aside)!; **nach**: nach Hause ≳ to come (or return) home; ≳ Sie gut nach Hause! I trust you may reach home safely!; F take care of yourself!; es kommt nichts (kein Erfolg) danach nothing comes of it; **über**: über e-n ≳ to fall upon a p.; über j-s Schwelle ≳ to cross a p.'s threshold; Furcht kam über ihn he was seized with fear; keine Klage kommt über seine Lippen no (word of) complaint escapes (or comes from, falls from) his lips; ein tiefer Schlaf kam über ihn he fell into a profound sleep; es ist Unglück über sie gekommen misfortune has befallen them; **um**: um et. ≳: a) (das man besitzt) to lose (or to be done out of) a th.; b) (das man erwartet) to be disappointed of a th.; ums Brot ≳ to be thrown out of employment; ums Leben ≳ to lose one's life, to perish; **unter**: e-m nie wieder unter die Augen ≳ f. weiter unten „vor"; e-m unter die Hände ≳ to fall into a p.'s

---

⚛ scientific; ✿ botanical; ⚲ geography; ⊕ machinery; ⚒ mining; ⚔ military; ⚓ marine; ⚭ commercial; ✉ postal; 🚂 railway.

[Kommende] — 604 — [komödiantisch]

hands; unter Leute 2 to mix with other people, von Neuigkeiten: unter die Leute 2 to spread (or get) abroad, to become known; **von**: von e-m 2 to come from a p.'s house); vom Dienste, von f-r Stelle 2 to lose one's place or berth or post; vom Flecke, von der Stelle 2 to make headway; die Sache kommt nicht vom Fleck the matter is at a standstill; das kommt von guter Hand it comes from a good source; von Kräften 2 to lose one's strength; der Rock kam mir nicht vom Leibe my coat never came off my back, I never took my coat off; er kommt mir nicht von der Seite he never leaves me, he sticks to me like glue or like a leech; F so was kommt von so was that's what happens when you //, serves you right if you //; et. von weitem 2 sehen to see a th. (coming) a long way, a. fig. to smell a th. from afar; ↓ der Wind kommt von Westen ... is in the west(erly quarter); das kommt davon, wenn man raucht 2c. that comes (or results) from smoking, &c.; **vor**: e-m nicht wieder vor Augen 2 never to come into a p.'s presence again; er soll mir nicht wieder vor die Augen 2! I will never see him again! vor den Richter 2 to appear before ...; der Braten kam vor der Suppe the joint was served before the soup; **zu**: wieder zu sich 2 to recover one's senses; er ist zu der Ansicht gekommen, daß // he has taken it into his head that //; zu Atem 2 to recover (one's) breath; zur Besinnung 2 to regain (one's) consciousness; wenn's zum Bezahlen kommt when it comes to paying; ich bin noch nicht zum Essen gekommen I have not found time for (my) dinner; f. Fall¹ 1; es kam zum Kampfe it came to fighting; wenn es zum Klappen kommt when it comes to the point; wieder zu Kräften 2 to recover one's strength; zu nichts 2 to come (or lead) to nothing; als mir die Sache zu Ohren kam when I (first) heard (or was told) of it; zu Pferde kommen to come (or approach) on horseback; 2 wir gleich zur Sache! let us go straight to the point!; zu Schaden 2 to come to grief, to suffer harm; es kam zu Schlägen it (or they) came to blows; mit etwas zustande od. zu Ende 2 to accomplish a th.; e-m zustatten, zugute 2 to benefit (or profit) a p.; feine Unschuld ist zutage gekommen ... has come to light; zum Vorschein 2 to appear, to make one's appearance; er konnte nicht zu Worte 2 he could not get a word in edgeways; e-n zu Worte 2 l. to let a p. speak; fie ließen ihn nicht zu Worte 2 they would not give him a hearing; zum Ziele 2 to attain one's object or end; wie 2 Sie auch dazu, das zu sagen? how come you to say that?; ♪ der Sänger kommt bis zum hohen C ... can pitch the high C. — **II** v/a. **11.** F e-m et. 2 to stand a p. a drink. — **III** ~ n ㉓ **12.** coming, arrival; das (beim) ~ und Gehen the (in) coming and going. — **IV** 2 d p. pr. u. a. ㊏ **13.** coming, approaching; 2des Jahr

next year; 2de Zeiten future ages pl.; **~de([r] m)** f ㊆ die Gehenden und die ~den the people going and coming, a. comers and goers pl.

Kommende (~ʊ~) [mlt.] f ㊽ (Ordenspfründe) prebend, ohne Seelsorge: sinecure.

kommensurabel ⚯ (~ʊ~ʊ) [lt.] a. ㊏ (D9) math. (meßbar) commensurable; **Kommensurabilität** (~ʊ~ - ~ʊ~) f ㊻ (Meßbarkeit) commensurableness.

Komment (~ma') [fr.] m ㊿ burschikos: regulations pl. (or convivial style) prevailing (or in vogue) among students.

Kommentar ⚯ (~ʊ~) [lt.] m ⑪d. ㉙ (Erläuterung) commentary; **Kommentator** (~ʊ~) m ㉛ commentator, annotator.

kommentieren (~ʊ~) v/a. ㊚ (erläutern) to comment upon, to annotate.

komment=mäßig (2widrig) (~ma" ...) a. ㊏ burschikos: according (contrary) to academical custom.

Kommers (~ʊ) [lt.] m ⑪a. burschikos: students' revelry or drinking-bout; **~=buch** n ㊵ book of drinking-songs; **kommersieren** (~ʊ~) v/n. (h.) ㊚ to hold a drinking-bout.

Kommerz ⊛ (~ʊ) [lt.] m ⑪a. (Handel) commerce; **2i=ell** (~ʊ~ʊ) a. ㊏ commercial; **~i=en=rat** m ㊷ ㊵ (dtsch. Titel) etwa: Councillor of Commerce.

Kommilitone (~ʊ~ʊ) [lt.] m ㊹ (Studiengenosse) fellow-student.

Kommis (ko-mi') [fr.] m ㉟ (commercial) clerk, counting-house clerk.

Kommiß ⚔ (~ʊ) [lt.] m (n) ⑪a. = **~=anzug**; beim ~ dienen to serve in the army or ranks; als a. 2 in undress.

Kommiß=anzug ⚔ (~ʊ ...) m ㊷ (ant. eigener Anzug) undress; (Arbeits=anzug) fatigue-dress or -uniform or -suit.

Kommissar, ...är (~ʊ~) [lt.] m ⑪d. (Vertreter) commissioner, weniger gbr.: commissary; ⚔ auch: commissariat officer; Polizei: inspector (or commissioner) of police; **Kommissariat** (~ʊ~(~)ʊ) n ⑪c. commissionership; ⚔ commissariat; **kommissarisch** (~ʊ~) a. ㊏ (u. bes. adv.) provisional(ly); **Kommissarius** (~ʊ~(~)ʊ) m ㉗ = Kommissar.

Kommiß=bäcker ⚔ (~ʊ ...) m ㊷ military baker; **=brot** n ammunition-bread; **=flinte** f service rifle; **=gegenstände** m/pl. ammunition, commissariat; **=gewehr** n regulation gun.

Kommission (~ʊ~(~)ʊ) [fr.] f ㊻: a) = Ausschuß 4; parl. ~ des Abgeordnetenhauses parliamentary commission; b) (Auftrag) commission, order; ⊛ in ~ in consignment, in trust; on commission; e-e Nachricht in ~ nehmen to spread (about) a report; **~är** (~ʊ~(~)~ʊ) m ⑪d.: a) commissioner; b) ⊛ commission-agent; c) (Dienstmann) commissionaire, (Packträger) porter.

Kommissions=artikel (~ʊ~(~)ʊ ...) m/pl. goods pl. in consignment or on commission; **=beratung** f, parl. committee-stage of a bill; **=bericht** m, parl. report of a committee or a commission; **=buch** n order-book; **=bureau** n (commission-)agent's office, agency; **=gebühr** f commission-agent's charge or percentage; **=geschäft** n firm of commission-agents, commission-agency;

=handel m agency (or agent's) business; **2weise** adv. by way of commission, ⊛ on commission.

kommiß=mäßig ⚔ (~ʊ ...) a. ㊏ military, F co. pipe-clay; **=mütze** f ㊷ fatigue-cap.

Kommissorium (~ʊ~(~)~ʊ) [lt.] n ㉘ (Auftrag) commission, order.

Kommiß=stiefel ⚔ (~ʊ ...) m/pl. ㊷ ammunition- (or regulation) boots pl.; **=vermögen** n F regular portion (required to get a marriage-license).

Kommittent ⊛ (~ʊ~) [lt.] m ㉗ (Auftraggeber) one who orders (goods, &c.); (Empfänger) consignee; **kommittieren** (~ʊ~) v/a. ㊚ to commission (zu etwas to do a th.). [handiness.]

Kommlichkeit (~ʊ~) f ㊻ suitableness,]

kommod (~ʊ) [(~.+.)fr.] a. ㊏ = bequem.

Kommode (~ʊ~) [fr.] f ㊻ (Möbel mit Schubladen) chest of drawers.

Kommodität (~ʊ~ʊ) [lt.] f ㊻ = Bequemlichkeit; a. = Abtritt 2.

Kommodore ⚓ ↓ (~ʊ~(~)~) [engl.] m ㉖ ⊛ (Geschwaderführer) commodore; **~=ständer** m ㊷ Commodore's broad pennant.

kommst (kömmst) 2., kommt (kömmt) (⚯) 3. Person pres. ind. von kommen.

kommun (~ʊ) [lt.] a. ㊏ (gemein) common, vulgar, low, (roh) coarse, rough.

kommunal (~ʊ~ʊ) [lt.] a. ㊏ (die Gemeinde betreffend) communal, parochial; (städtisch) municipal, urban.

Kommunal=beamte(r) (~ʊ~ʊ ...) m ㊷ parish official, municipal officer; **=garde** ⚔ † f local militia; **=gardist** ⚔ † m militia-man; **=schule** f parish school; **=steuern** f/pl. parish rates pl.; **=weg** m parish road.

Kommune (~ʊ~ʊ) [fr., *lt.] f ㊻ (Gemeinde) parish, (local) community, municipality; (Schreckensherrschaft in Paris 1871) Commune; **~aufstand** m ㉗ revolution(ary establishment) of the C.

Kommunikant (~ʊ~ʊ~) [lt.] m ㊷, **~in** f ㊴ (Abendmahlsgänger[in]) communicant.

Kommunikation (~ʊ~~~ʊ~) [lt.] f ㊻ (Verbindung) communication; **~s=galerie** (~...) f ㊻ passage of communication; **~s=gräben** ⚔ m/pl. approaches pl.; **~s=linie** f line of communication.

Kommunion (~ʊ~(~)~ʊ) [lt.] f ㊻ bes. eccl. (Abendmahl) (Holy) Communion, Lord's Supper; an der ~ teilnehmen to partake of the Lord's Supper, vgl. kommunizieren II; **~s=kelch** m ㊷ communion-cup; **~s=tisch** m communion-table.

Kommunismus (~ʊ~ʊ~) [fr., *lt.] m ㉗ (Gütergemeinschaft) communism.

Kommunist (~ʊ~ʊ~) m ㊷ communist; **~erei** (~ʊ~~~ʊ) f ㊻ communistic ideas pl.; **2isch** a. ㊏ communistic, socialistic.

kommunizieren (~ʊ~ʊ~) [lt.] ⓘ v/a. ([schriftlich] mitteilen) to communicate. — II v/n. (h.) eccl. = das Abendmahl empfangen.—III 2d p.pr. u. a. ㊏ phys.: 2de Gefäße communicating vessels.

Kommutator ⊚ (~ʊ~ʊ) [lt.] m ㉛ elect. (Umschalter) commutator; **~=hebel** m ㊷ commutator-arm.

Komödiant (⚯~(~)~)[grch.=it.] m㊷, **~in** f ㊴ mit contp. comedian; actor (f actress), (theatrical) performer, player, pl. oft: professionals pl.; **2enhaft** (~ʊ~ʊ~) a., **2isch** a. ㊏ theatrical, a. pro-

Zeichen (s. S. XVII): F familiär; P Volkssprache; ⚐ Gaunersprache; ⚲ selten; † alt (auch gestorben); * neu (auch geboren); ⁺⁺ unrichtig;

[Komödiantentum] — 605 — [Konditor]

fessional; ~entum (⸺(⌣)⸌⸻) n ②d. life (or ways pl.) of actors and actresses.
Komödi-e (⸺¹(⌣)⌣) [grch. Komosfang] f ㊽ (Luftspiel) comedy; play; fig. es ist die reine ~ it's a mere farce, it's quite a pantomime; ~spielen (schauspielern) to act (off the stage), to dissemble, to sham.
komödi-enhaft (⸺¹(⌣)⌣⌣) a. ㊻ (f. Komödie) like a comedy or a play; theatrical, stagy; fig. farcical.
Komödi-en-haus (⸺¹¹(⌣)⌣…) n ㊷ play-house; =schreiber m comedy-writer, weitS. playwright; =spiel n (theatrical) play; =zettel m play-bill.
Kompagnie (⌣vá-ni') [fr.] f ㊽ 1. ⚔ company. — 2. ✱ f. Kompanie.
Kompagnie-chef ⚔ (⸏…) m ㊽ leader of a company, captain (in the army); =exerzieren n company drill; =feldwebel m colour-sergeant; =front f: in ~en vorbeimarschieren to file past in companies; =führer m = =chef; ²weise adv. in companies.
Kompagnon (⌣vǎn-jǫ̆') [(+) fr.] m ㊿ 1. ✱ (Handelsgesellschafter) partner (in business). — 2. (Mitarbeiter) collaborator.
kompakt (⌣⸌) [lt.] a. ㊻ compact; phys. solid; ~heit f ㊽ compactness, solidity.
Kompanie ✱ (⸌⸻ᴴ)[fr.]/㊽, abbr. Ko(mp).; das Haus S. u. ~ the firm S. and Company (meist abbr.: & Co.); ~geschäft n ㊷, =handlung f ㊽ firm of partners.
Komparation (⸺⸻tf(⌣)⸌) [lt.] f ㊽ bſd. gram. (Vergleichung) comparison; ~=grade m/pl.㊷degreespl.of comparison.
Komparativ (⸌⸻ᴴ) [lt.] I m ②d. gram. comparative (degree) of adjectives, adverbs, &c. — II ²(iſch) (⸌⸻ⱽ⸻ᴴ⌣⌣) a. ㊻ (vergleichend) comparative.
Komparent (⸌⸺⸌) [lt. Erſcheinende(r)] m ㊽, ~in f ㊽ jur. one who gives (legal) evidence, ⚖ declarant.
Komparse (⌣⸌⌣) [it.] m ㊹ thea. super.
Kompaß ↓ (⌣⸌) [(+) it. Zirkel] m ㊵a. (mariner's) compass.
Kompaß-büchſe ↓ (⌣⸌…) f ㊽ compass-box; =häuschen n binnacle; =kurs m: verbesserter ~ true course; =nadel f c.-needle, auch magnetic needle; =peilung f c.-bearing; =pflanze ♀ ⚥ c.-plant (Silphium lacinia'tum); =roſe, =ſcheibe f c.-card; =strich m point of the c.
kompendiarisch (⸌⸺(⌣)⸻ᴴ), kompendiös (⸌(⌣)ᴴ) [lt.] a. ㊻ (kurz zſ.-gedrängt) compendious, epitomized, succinct.
Kompendium (⌣⸌(⌣)⌣) [lt.] n ㉘ (Handbuch) manual, short (or abridged) treatise; (Auszug) abstract, auch: compendium.
Kompenſation (⸌⸻tf(⌣)⸌) [lt.] f ㊽ (Erſatz) compensation; ~s-methode f compensation-method; ~s-pendel n (m) mech. Uhrmach.: compensation-(or gridiron) pendulum; ~s-unruhe ⊙ f comp.-balance.
kompenſier/en (⸌⸻ᴴ) [lt.] I v/a. ㊼ (ausgleichen) to compensate, counterbalance; to make good a loss. — II ~ n ㉓ und K/ung f ㊽ compensation.
kompetent (⸌⸌) [lt.] I a. ㊻ ✝ jur. (zuſtändig) competent, cognizant. — II ~ m ㊵ (Mitbewerber) competitor.
Kompetenz (⸌⸌) [lt.] f ㊽ 1. ✝ jur. (Zuſtändigkeit) competence, cognizance, jurisdiction. — 2. (Einkünfte) competency, income; ⚔ ✝ = Gebührnis. — 3. (Mitbewerbung) competition.
Kompetenz-konflikt (⸌⸻⸌…) m ㊷, =ſtreit m dispute about competence or jurisdiction.
Kompilation (⸌⸻tf(⌣)⸌) [lt. -pīl-] f ㊽ (Zſ.-tragung) compilation; Kompilator (⸌⸻ᴴ) m ㊵ compiler; kompilieren v/a. ㊼ to compile (a dictionary, &c.)
Komplement (⸌⸌⸌) [lt. -plē-] n ⑪b. math. (Ergänzungswinkel zu 90 Grad) complement of an angle or arc; gram. (Ziel des Zeitworts) object.
Komplementär-farben (⸌⸻ⱽ⸻ᴴ…) f pl. ㊽ phys. (die zſ. Weiß bilden) complementary colours pl. [plete, entire.]
komplett (⌣⸌) [lt.] a. ㊻ (vollſtändig) com-⎦
komplettieren (⸌⸻ᴴ) v/a. ㊼ to (make) complete, to (bring to a full) complement, to raise to the full number.
Komplex (⌣⸌) [lt.] I m ⑪a. 1. whole; (Grundſtück) plot of land. — II ²⸺ a. ㊻ 2. math. complex. — 3. (verwickelt) complicated. [accomplice.]
Komplice (⌣⸌⸻) [fr.] m ㊹ (Mitſchuldiger)⎦
Komplikation (⸌⸻tf(⌣)⸌) [lt.] f ㊽ (Verwickelung) complication.
Kompliment (⸌⸌⸌) [fr.] n ⑪c. 1. in Worten: compliment; den Damen ~e (Artigkeiten) machen od. F reißen, ſchneiden to compliment ..., to pay compliments to ...; ich mache Ihnen mein ~ darüber, dazu I compliment (or congratulate) you on it; er (fie) macht feine ~e (s)he is not a (wo)man of many compliments, (s)he makes (very) little ceremony or fuss. — 2. [+ fr.] Verbeugung) bow, (Knicks) curtsy.
Komplimente(n)-macher(in f) m (⸌⸻ⱽ⸺…) ㊵, =ſchneider(in f) m one who pays (many) compliments, flatterer.
Komplimentier-buch (⸌⸻ⱽ⸻ᴴ…) n ㊷ book on (rules of) courtesy; ehm. a. bſd. als Buchtitel: glass of fashion.
komplimentieren (⸌⸻ᴴ) [fr.] v/a. to compliment (or flatter) a p.
komplizieren (⸌⸻ᴴ) [lt.] v/a. ㊼ (verwickeln) to complicate; kompliziert complicated, intricate.
Kompliziertheit (⸌⸻ᴴ…) f ㊽ complicacy, mehr gbr.: intricacy.
Komplott (⌣⸌) [fr.] n ⑪c. plot, conspiracy; ein ~ anzetteln od. ſchmieden (auch: ſieren) v/n. (h.) ㊼ to (lay a) plot, to conspire (together).
komponieren ♪ (⸌⸻ᴴ) [lt.] v/a. u. v/n. (h.) ㊼ to compose, to set to music;
Komponier-kunst ♪ (⸌⸻ᴴ…) f ㊽ art of composing or composition, composer's art.
Komponiſt ♪ (⸌⸌) [lt.] m ㊷ (Tonſetzer) composer (of music, of operas, &c.).
Kompoſite(n pl.) ⚥ ♀ (⸌⸻ᴴ) [lt.] f ㊽ (Korbblütler) composite flower(s pl.), ⚥ compositæ pl.
Kompoſition (⸌⸻tf(⌣)⸌) [lt.] f ㊽ 1. ♪, Kunſt ꝛc.: (Abfassung, Dichtung ꝛc., a. das Kunſtwerk) composition, composing, e-s Liedes a.: setting. — 2. ⊙ (Miſchung von Metallen ꝛc.) compo(sition). [mony.]
Kompoſitions-lehre ♪ (⸻…) f ㊽ har-⎦
Kompoſitum (⸌⸻ᴴ) [lt. -pōs-] n ㉘⁵⁹ gr. (zſ.-geſetztes Wort) compound (word).
Kompoſt (⌣⸌, ⸌⌣) [mhd. * fr., it.] m ⑪b. agr. (Miſchdünger) compost.

Kompott (⌣⸌) [nhd. 16. sæc.; * fr. compote f] n ⑪c. ⑯ Koch.: (Eingemachtes) stewed (or preserved) fruit. zu Mus gekocht: jam, preserve; ~ſchale f ㊽ dish for preserve, preserve-dish.
kompreß (⌣⸌) [lt.] a. ㊻ (D10) close, compact; ⊙ typ. kompreſſer (enger) Satz solid (or close) matter.
Kompreſſe (⌣⸌⸻) [lt.] f surg. (Bauſche) bandage, auch: compress.
Kompreſſions-pumpe (⸌⸻ⱽ⸻ᴴ…)f㊽phys. force- (or forcing-, condensing-) pump.
Kompreſſor (⌣⸌⸻) m ㊵ compressing air-pump, compressor.
komprimieren (⸌⸻ᴴ)[lt.]v/a.㊼(zſ.-preſſen) to compress; Gaſe ꝛc.: to condense.
Kompromiß (⸌⸻⸌) [lt.] m u. n ⑪a. (Ausgleich) compromise; ein(en) ~ ſchließen to (make a) compromise, a. to come to an agreement; ~ rad 🚲 n ㊷ (Ausgleichsrad) compromise-wheel.
kompromittieren (⸌⸻ⱽ⸻ᴴ) [lt.] v/a. (und ſich ² v/refl.) ㊼ (bloßſtellen) to expose (o.s.). [Tochter e-s Grafen) countess.]
Komteſſe (⌣⸌⸻) [fr.] f ㊽ (Frau ob. bſd.⎦
Komtur (⌣⸌) [mhd.; * fr.] m ⑪d. commander of an order.
Komturei (⸌⸻ᴴ) f ㊽ commandery (a. Gebäude, Pfründe der Ordensritter).
Konchy-ide ⚥ (⸌⸻ᴴ) [grch.] f ㊽ math. (Muſchellinie) conchoid.
Konchyli-e(n pl.) ⚥ (⌣⸌(⌣)ᴴ) [grch.] f ㊽ zo. (Schaltiere, Muſcheln) shell-fish, shell(s), ⚥ conchylia pl. ²artig a. like shells, ⚥ conchyliaceous; Konchyliologie (⸌⸻(⌣)⸻ⱽ⸻ᴴ) f ㊽ (Muſchelkunde) conchology.
Kondenſation (⸌⸻tf(⌣)⸌) [lt.] f ㊽ phys., chm. (Verdichtung) condensation; ~s-apparat ⊙ m ㊽ mach. condenser; ~s-kammer f ㊽ condensing-chamber; ~s-röhre f, chm., metall. adapter; ~s-waſſer n condensing- (or waste-) water.
Kondenſator ⊙ (⸌⸻ᴴ) [lt.] m ㊵ Dampfm., electr., &c.: condenser; ~(-dampf)maſchine f condensing engine.
kondenſierbar (⸌⸻ᴴ) a. ㊻ phys. condensable, capable of condensation.
kondenſier/en (⸌⸻ᴴ) [lt.] I v/a. ㊼ phys., ⊙ (verdichten) to condense, durch Abdampfen: to boil down; f/te (jetzt bff.: eingedickte) Milch condensed milk. — II ~ n ㉓, K/ung f ㊽ condensation.
Kondition (⸌⸻tf(⌣)⸌)[lt.=fr.](Beſchaffenheit) condition; (Dienst) service; (Stelle) situation; in ~ geh(e)n, ſteh(e)n to enter (to be in) service or a situation.
konditional (⸌⸻tf(⌣)⸌) [lt.] a. ㊻ (bedingt) conditional.
Konditionalis ⚥ (⸌⸻tf(⌣)⸻ᴴ⸻) m (sg. inv., pl. …les) gr. conditional (mood).
Konditional-ſatz (⸌⸻tf(⌣)⸌…) m ㊷ gr. conditional clause. [tional.]
konditionell (⸌⸻tf(⌣)⸌) [fr.] a. ㊻ condi-⎦
konditionieren (⸌⸻tf(⌣)⸻ᴴ) [(+) fr.] ㊼ I v/n. (h.) to be in a situation, von Dienſtboten auch: to be in service, von Ladendienern: to serve behind the counter, to be in employment. — II ⊙ v/a. Seide ꝛc. (auf den Grad ihrer Feuchtigkeit prüfen) to condition ..., to test ... by drying and then weighing it.
Konditor (⌣⸺, a. ⸌⌣) [lt.] m ㊵ (Zuckerbäcker) confectioner; (Kuchenbäcker) pastry-cook; (Verfertiger v. Eis) ice-cream man.

♪ Muſik; ⚥ Wiſſenſchaft; ♀ Pflanze; ⚥ Geographie; ⊙ Technik; ⚒ Bergbau; ⚔ Militär; ⚓ Marine; ✱ Handel; ✉ Post; 🚂 Eiſenbahn.

Konditorei (ˊ◡◡ˊˊ) f ⓖ (Zuckerbäckerei) confectioner's (or pastry-cook's) shop; ~ feinerer Art (Italian or Swiss) café.
Konditor-laden (ˊ◡ˊ...) m ⓑ confectioner's shop, F a. sweetshop; **waren** f/pl. confectionery, pastry; (Zuckerzeug) sweetmeats, F sweets pl.
Kondolenz (ˊ◡ˊ)[lt.-döl-] f ⓖ = Beileid; ~... in Zssgn = Beileids-; **kondolieren** (ˊ◡ˊˊ) v/n.(h.) ⓒ (Beileid bezeigen): e-m 2 to condole with a p. [(Rammkeule) condor.
Kondor m [span.: *peru.] m ⓔ.(ⓢ)
Konduite (vˊdüˊ) [fr. conduite Aufführung] f ⓔ conduct; **~n-liste** (ˊ...) f ⓑ secret record on the conduct of government officials.
Kondukt (ˊ◡ˊ) [lt.] m ⓑ.b. (train of) mourners pl., funeral procession.
Kondukteur (ˊ◡ˊtöˊr) [fr.-Geleiter] m ⓑ.d.(ⓖ) 🚂 guard; auf Omnibussen rc.: conductor.
Konduktor ⓐ (ˊ◡ˊ) [lt.] m ⓐ phys. (Leiter) conductor of electricity, heat, sound, &c.
Konfekt (◡ˊ) [lt.] n ⓑ.b. (Zuckerwerk) confectionery, sweetmeats (mehr gleh. F sweets) pl.; **~büchse** f box of sweets.
Konfektion (ˊ◡ˊ(v)ˊˊ) [lt. Anfertigung] f ⓖ trade in ready-made clothing or clothes; **~är** (ˊ◡ˊˊ)m ⓑ.d. dealer in ready-made clothes; **~euse** (ˊ◡ˊ(v)ˊnöˊ) [fr.] f ⓑ = Probiermamsell.
Konfektions-artikel (ˊ◡ˊtz(v)ˊˊ...) m/pl. ⓖ, **=gegenstände** m/pl. ready-made (articles pl. of) clothing; **=geschäft** n establishment (or warehouse) for all articles of wear or clothing.
Konferenz (ˊ◡ˊ)[lt.] f ⓖ(Besprechung) conference, weitS. (Versammlung) meeting; eine ~ halten to hold a co. or meeting.
Konferenz=saal (ˊ◡ˊ...) m ⓑ, **=zimmer** n conference-(or meeting-)room, in engl. Schulen: masters' room.
konferieren (ˊ◡ˊˊ) [lt.] v/n. (h.) ⓖ (sich beraten) to confer (or consult) together, to deliberate (über et. (up)on a th.).
Konferve (ˊ◡ˊv) [lt.] f ⓔ (Wasserfaden) conferva, pl. ...væ (Conferˊva).
Konfession (ˊ◡ˊ(v)ˊˊ) [lt.] f ⓖ: a) (religiöses Bekenntnis) confession, (religious) creed; Augsburger ~ (1530) Augsburg Confession; katholische, evangelische ~ Catholic, Protestant faith or religion; b) (kirchliche Gemeinschaft) (religious) denomination. [ational.
konfessionell (ˊ◡ˊ(v)◡ˊˊ) a. ⓖ denomin-
Konfessions=los (ˊ◡ˊ(v)ˊˊ...) a. ⓖ undenominational or unsectarian school, &c.; **=losigkeit** f ⓖ undenominationalism; **=schule** f ⓑ sectarian (in Engl.: voluntary) school, engS. church-school; **=wechsel** m change of creed or faith, bisw.: conversion.
konfidentiell (ˊ◡ˊtz(◡)ˊˊ) [lt.] a. ⓖ (vertraulich) confidential.
Konfirmand (ˊ◡ˊ) [lt.] m ⓑ, **~in** f ⓑ eccl. candidate for confirmation, a. confirmation(-)candidate; boy (f girl) to be confirmed; **=en-unterricht** m ⓑ instruction given to candidates for confirmation, a. confirmation(-)classes pl.
Konfirmation (ˊ◡ˊtz(v)ˊˊ) [lt.] f ⓖ bsd. eccl. (Einsegnung) confirmation; **~s-schein** m ⓑ certificate of confirmation.
konfirmieren (ˊ◡ˊ) [lt.-firm-] v/a. ⓖ bsd. eccl. (einsegnen) to confirm; konfirmiert

w., auch: to receive the first communion; der (die) Konfirmierte ⓖ the person confirmed, ↘ the confirmee.
Konfiskation (ˊ◡ˊ-tz(v)ˊˊ) [lt.: *Fiskus] f ⓖ (Einziehung) confiscation.
konfiszierbar (ˊ◡ˊˊ) [lt.] a. ⓖ confiscable, liable to confiscation or seizure.
konfiszieren (ˊ◡ˊˊ) [lt.] I v/a. ⓖ (beschlagnahmen) to confiscate, to seize; F fig. ein konfisziertes (verdächtig aussehendes) Gesicht a suspicious-looking (a. hang-dog) face. — II ~ n ⓑ u.
Konfiszierung f ⓖ confiscation.
Konfitüre(n pl.) (ˊ◡ˊˊ) [fr.] f ⓔ (Zuckerfrüchte) candied fruit; weitS. = Konfekˊt.
Konflikt (ˊ◡ˊ) [lt.] m ⓑ (Zwist) conflict; in ~ geraten to enter into (or engage in) a' conflict with; F to get into hot water.
Konföderation (ˊ◡ˊ-◡ˊˊ) [lt.] f ⓖ (Bund) confederation, confederacy.
konföderieren (ˊ◡ˊˊ) [lt.] I sich 2 v/refl. ⓖ to form (or to enter into) a confederacy. — II **Konföderierte**([r] m) f ⓖ confederate; (Verbündete[r]) ally.
konform (◡ˊ) [lt.] a. ⓖ (übereinstimmend) conformable to, in conformity with.
Konformer ↑ (◡ˊˊ) [engl.] m ⓖ eccl. conformist.
Konformität (ˊ◡ˊˊ) [lt.] f ⓖ (Übereinstimmung) conformity.
Konfrontation (ˊ◡ˊ◡ˊˊ) [lt.] f ⓖ (Gegenüberstellung) confrontation.
konfrontieren (ˊ◡ˊˊ) [lt.] v/a. (h.) ⓖ (gegenüberstellen) to confront (or to put face, to face) with.
konfus (◡ˊ) [lt.] a. ⓖ(D 10) (verwirrt) confused, in (a) confusion, F muddled, mixed, in a muddle; nur von Personen: perplexed, F flummuxed, flabbergasted, taken aback; **konfuser Mensch** muddle-headed fellow.
Konfusion (ˊ-(v)ˊˊ) f ⓖ confusion, F muddle, (Verlegenheit) perplexity; **~arius** F (ˊ-(v)ˊ(v)ˊˊ) m ⓑ, a. **~s-rat** m ⓑ muddle-head(ed fellow), muddler, unmethodical person.
Konfutse (ˊ◡ˊ) (chin.) npr/m. (Stifter der chin. Religion, 551–478 v. Chr.) Confucius.
konfuzisch (◡ˊ◡ˊ) a. ⓖ of Confucius, Confucian.
Konfuzius (◡ˊ(ˊ)◡) [lt.] ⓖγ. = Konfutse.
Kongestion (ˊ◡ˊ(v)ˊˊ) [lt.] f ⓖ (Blutandrang) congestion (of the blood to the head).
Konglomerat ⓐ (ˊ◡ˊˊ) [lt. -glóm-] n ⓑ.c. geol., min. (Trümmergestein, Gemenge) conglomerate, conglomeratic rock.
Kongo ⓕ (◡ˊ) npr. ⓓa. 1. n (St. u. Land in West-afrika) Congo; Neger der ~rasse Congo. — 2. m der ~ (Fl.) the Congo; **~staat** m ⓑ (1885) Congo (Free) State.
Kongregation (ˊ◡ˊ-(v)ˊˊ) [lt. -grégˊ-] f ⓖ (freie Gemeinde) congregation; **~alist** (ˊ◡ˊ-(v)ˊˊˊ) m ⓑ (Mitglied e-r ~) congregationalist.
Kongreß (◡ˊ) [lt.] m ⓑa. (Zusammenkunft) congress; **~mitglied** n ⓑ member of a congress; U.S. member of Congress.
Kongreve-druck ↑ (töˊnˊs-griw...) [Congreve, Erfinder] ⓖ m ⓑ typ. in mehreren Farben zugleich: Congreve impression.
kongru-ent ⓐ (ˊ◡ˊ◡ˊˊ)[lt. -grüˊ-] a. ⓖ geom. (gleich u. ähnlich) equal in all respects, equal and similar, bisw. a. congruent;

Kongru-enz (ˊ◡ˊ◡ˊˊ) [lt. -grüˊ-] f ⓖ perfect equality, bisw. congruence.
kongruieren ⓐ (ˊ◡ˊ◡ˊˊ) [lt.] v/n. (h.) ⓖ geom. to be equal in all respects, to be equal and similar.
Konifere(n pl.) ⓐ (-(v◡ˊ◡)) [grch.=lt. Zapfenträger] f ⓖ (Nadelholzbaum) coniferous tree, pl. a.: ⓐ coniferæ.
König (ˊv) [ahd.: king] m ⓑ.d. (Titel ⓑⓔ) (f f. Königin) 1. king, z.B. ~ von Spanien king of Spain; (der) ~ Karl King Charles; der ~ und seine Gemahlin the King and his Queen; kleiner ~ kinglet; als ~ einsetzen, zum ~ m. to make (a) king, to invest with royal dignity, to raise to the throne; er ward zum ~e gewählt, ausgerufen he was elected (or created) king, he was proclaimed king. — 2. fig. der ~ der ~e (Gott) the King of Kings; bibl. die heiligen drei ~e the three Magi; das Erste (Zweite) Buch der ~e the First (Second) Book of Kings. — 3. Kartenspiel: der ~ und die Dame (the) king and (the) queen; Herz=(rc.)2 king of hearts, &c. — 4. ⓖ metall. (geschmolzenes reines Metall): ⓐ regulus.
Königin (ˊ◡ˊ) [ahd.] f ⓑ 1. queen; **~mutter** (=witwe) queen mother (dowager). — 2. Schachspiel: queen; sich eine ~ holen (für e-n Bauer eintauschen) to get a (or to go to) queen, to queen a pawn. — 3. ⓐ ~ der Nacht queen of the night (Ceˊreus ob. Cactus grandifloˊrus).
Königlein (ˊ◡ˊ) n ⓑ (dim. von König) contp. kinglet, small (or petty) king.
königlich, als Titel: **Königlich** (ˊ◡ˊ) [ahd.] a. ⓖ royal (dignity, power), kinglike or queenlike, kingly or queenly (manner), regal (insignia); adv. sich 2 freuen to feel as happy as a king, F to be as pleased as Punch.
König=reich (ˊˊ) [ahd.] n ⓑ.d. kingdom of ..., realm (a. fig.); fig. nicht für ein ~ not for the world, F not for a pension.
Königs=adler (ˊ◡ˊ...) m ⓑ orn. golden eagle (Aˊquila imperiaˊlis); **=apfel** ⓕ m: a) pomeroy; b) = Aˊnanas; **=banner** n royal banner; **=blau** n royal blue; **=blume** ⓕ f = Päonie; **=burg** f royal castle; **=freund** m royalist; **=geier** m, orn. king-vulture (Sarcorhaˊmphus papa); **=kerze** ⓕ f: große ~ high taper, mullein (Verbaˊscum thapsus); **=krone** f: a) king's (or royal) crown; b) ⓕ fritillary (Fritillaˊria imperiaˊlis); **=lilie** f Turk's-cap (Liˊlium maˊrtagon); **=macher** m engl. hist. (Bn. v. Richard Nevil, Earl of Warwick, † 1471) Kingmaker; **=mantel** m royal mantle; **=mord**, **=mörder** m regicide; **2mörderisch** a. ⓖ regicidal; **=rose** f = Päonie; **=schießen** n, etwa: final ties pl. in a rifle-match; **=schloß** n royal castle; **=schuß** m (durch den j. Schützenkönig wird) best (or final) shot; **=sitz** m: a) throne; b) king's residence; **=sohn** m king's son, royal prince; **=stadt** f royal city or residence; **=tag** m = Dreikönigstag; **=thron** m royal throne; **=tiger**, zo. Bengal (royal) tiger (Felis tigris ob. Tigris regaˊlis); **=titel** m royal title; **=tochter** f king's daughter, royal princess; **=wahl** f election of a king; **=wasser** n, chm.

[Königswürde] — 607 — [Konsistenz]

(Salpetersalzsäure) aqua regia, nitrohydrochloric acid; =würde f royal dignity; =zeit f regal period or time.
Königtum (⌣–⌣) [w. 1792] n ②d. royalty (von Gottes Gnaden by Divine Grace), kingship, bsd. ehm. auch: kingcraft, weitS. kingly (or monarchical) rule or sway or power.
konisch (⌣–) [Konus] a. ⑥ (kegelförmig) conic(al); ⊕ ⸗es Räder= (ob. Trieb=)werk bevel-gear(ing), bevelled gear; ⸗e Scheibe conical (speed-) pulley.
Konjektur (⌣⌣–) [lt.] f ⑯ (Vermutung) conjecture; ~al=kritik, =politik (⌣⌣–...) f ⑫ conjectural criticism, politics pl.
konjizieren (⌣⌣–) [lt. cŏnĭ'cere] v/a. u. v/n. (h.) ⑬ (vermuten) to conjecture, to make conjectures.
Konjugation (⌣⌣–tß(⌣)") [lt. -iŭg-] f ⑯ gr., Biologie u. ♀ conjugation.
Conjugations=kern ♀ (⌣...) m ⑫ Biologie: conjugation-nucleus; =tabelle f, gr. table of conjugation.
konjugierbar (⌣⌣–⌣) a. ⑥ conjugable.
konjugieren (⌣⌣–) [lt.] v/a. ⑬ gr. to conjugate ...; chm., med., phys., &c. konjugiert: ♀ conjugate.
Konjunktion (⌣⌣–tß(⌣)") [lt.] f ⑯ gr. (Bindewort), ast. (ℬ=treffen zweier Planeten) conjunction; ⸗al (⌣⌣–tß(⌣)"), ⸗ell (...⁵) a. ⑥ conjunctional.
Konjunktiv (⌣⌣–f) [lt.] m ⑭d. gr. subjunctive (mood), (in.) conjunctivus; ⸗isch (⌣⌣–⌣) a. ⑥ in the (or as) subjunctive; ~satz m ⑫ clause (with verb) in the subjunctive mood.
Konjunktur (⌣⌣–) [lt.] f ⑯ (Geschäftsverhältnis) juncture (of affairs), ♣ tide (or turn) of the market; günstige ~ good (or favourable) opportunity or chance, propitious moment.
konkav (–⌣f) [lt.] a. ⑥ (ant. konve'x) (ausgehöhlt) concave. [mirror.]
Konkav=spiegel (–...) m ⑫ concave
Konklave (–⌣w) [lt.] n ⑳ (geheimes Gemach, geheime Versammlung) conclave.
konklusiv (⌣–⌣f) [lt.] a. ⑥ (endgültig) conclusive, final.
Konkordanz (⌣⌣–⁵) [lt. übereinstimmung] f ⑯ Wörter= u. Redensarten=verzeichnis: biblische ~ concordance to the Bible.
Konkordat (⌣⌣–) [lt.] n ⑪c. Cath. eccl. (Vertrag zw. Staat und Kirche) concordate.
Konkordia (⌣–⌣(⌣)) [lt.] npr/f.⑲ℬ.⑯⍺. (Göttin der Eintracht) Concord(ia).
Konkordi=en=buch (⌣–⌣(⌣)...) n ⑳ ev.eccl. (Sammlung der symbolischen Bücher der lutherischen Kirche, 1580) Book of Concord; =formel f (1577) Formula of Concord.
konkret ♀ (⌣–) [lt. zs.=gewachsen] a. ⑥ gr., phls. (greifbar; ant. abstra'tt begrifflich) concrete; das ~e ⑰ the concrete.
Konkretion ♀ (⌣–tß(⌣)") [lt.] f ⑯ min. (Schwiele) concretion. [crete noun.]
Konkretum ♀ (⌣–⌣) [lt.] n ⑳ gr. con-
Konkubinat (⌣⌣–) [lt.] m, n ⑪c. concubinage (= Kebsehe); Konkubine (⌣⌣–⌣) f ⑯ concubine (= Kebsweib).
Konkurrent (⌣⌣–) [lt.] m ⑫ competitor.
Konkurrenz (⌣⌣–⁵) [lt.] f ⑯ (Mitbewerb) competition; e-m ~ machen to enter into competition (or to compete) with a p.; eine ~ ausschreiben to offer a contract (or job) for open compe-

tition; ⸗fähig a. ⑥ able to compete; ~geschäft ♣ n ⑫ rival business or firm; ein ~ gründen to set up (or start) a competition; ~prüfung f ⑫ competitive examination.
konkurrieren (⌣⌣–⌣) [lt.] v/n. (h.) ⑬: um den Preis ♀ to compete for the prize.
Konkurs (⌣–⁵) [lt.] I m ⑪a. 1. ♣ (Bankbruch) bankruptcy, insolvency, failure; in ~ geraten to become a bankrupt, to become (or to declare o.s.) insolvent, to fail (in business), F to be sold up. — 2. (das Konkurrieren) competition. — II ♀ a. nur als Prädikat 3. ♣ sich ♀ erklären to declare o.s. insolvent, jur. to file a bill in bankruptcy.
Konkurs=erklärung ♣ (⌣⁵...) f ⑫ declaration of insolvency; =eröffnung f opening of bankruptcy proceedings, preliminary steps pl. in (a case of) bankruptcy; =gläubiger m creditor of a bankrupt('s) estate; =masse f bankrupt('s) estate; =(massen=)verwalter m (official) liquidator, trustee in bankruptcy; =ordnung f legislation on bankruptcy; =verfahren n bankruptcy proceedings pl.
können (⌣–) [ahd.: can] v/a. u. Hilfszeitwort ⑬ I Hilfszeitwort mit danebenstehendem oder zu ergänzendem inf. 1. a) to be able to do a th., to be capable of doing a th.; nicht ♀ to be unable; ich kann I can; das kann er (gar) nicht tun he cannot (possibly) do it, that's (far) beyond him; das kann sein that may be; das kann nicht sein it cannot be; er kann gut schwimmen he can swim well, auch: he swims well; kann sie es erraten haben? can (or may) she have guessed it? has she been able to guess it?; er hätte nicht laufen ♀ (st. gekonnt) he could not have run, he would have been unable to run; sie ♀ nicht mehr arbeiten they cannot work any longer, they are no longer able to work, they are incapacitated from work; b) mit weggelassenem inf., der im Englischen oft gegeben werden muß, zB.: ich weiß, was ihr könnt I know what you can do; er kann nicht auf(=stehen) he is not able to get up; wir ♀ nicht weg (hinein) we cannot get away (get in); laufe was du (laufen) kannst run as fast as you can; ich kann nicht mehr I am done (or knocked) up; wie kann? how can I (do it)? —
2. Bes. Redensarten: er schrie was er konnte he screamed with all his might; er macht es so gut wie (ob. er tut was) er kann he does his best or the best he can; er lief was er konnte (aus Leibeskräften) he ran with all his might, he tore along as fast as he could, F he ran his hardest; er hat damit nicht fertig werden ♀ he did not accomplish his object or purpose; das ♀ Sie leicht sagen it is easy for you to say so; man kann nicht sagen, nicht wissen there is no telling, no knowing; ich kann nichts dafür it is not my fault, it's no fault of mine; Sie ♀ es glauben (you may) believe me; ich kann nicht anders I cannot do otherwise, I have no choice left, I cannot help it. — 3. er kann (darf) es

nicht (tun) he may (or dare) not do it; vgl. 1.; du kannst hingehen you may go there. — II v/a. 4. et. ♀ (gelernt h.) to know how to make use of a th.; s. auswendig 2; Französisch ♀ to know (or to be acquainted with) French; das Gekonnte wieder vergessen to forget what one knew; er kann nichts he knows (or has learnt) nothing. — III ~ n ⑫ 5. (s. I) ability, power, faculty; (s. II) knowledge.
Konnetabel (⌣⌣–⌣) [fr.] m ⑫ (Kronfeldherr, auch Ehrentitel) high constable.
Konnex (⌣–⁵) [lt.] m ⑫a. (Zusammenhang) connexion; ♂ nexus.
Konnexion (⌣⌣–) [lt.] f ⑯ 1. = Konner. — 2. ~en pl. (einflußreiche Bekanntschaften) influential connexions or friends pl.
Konnivenz (⌣–w⁵) [lt.] f ⑯ (Nachsicht) connivance; konnivieren (⌣–w–) v/n. (h.) ⑬ to connive at a th.
Konnossement ♣ ⚓ (⌣⌣–) [it.] n ⑪c. (Seefrachtbrief) bill of lading.
Konrad (⌣⌣) npr/m. ⑲ℬ⍺. (Bn.) Conrad; ~s=kraut ♀ n ⑫ Hartheu (vierkantiges).
Konrektor (⌣–⌣) [lt.] m ⑫ vice-principal, vice-master, auch: second master.
Konsekration (⌣⌣–tß(⌣)") [lt. -sēcr-] f ⑯ eccl. (Weihe) consecration.
konsekrieren (⌣⌣–⌣) [lt.] eccl. I v/a. (weihen) to consecrate. — II ~ n ⑫ consecration. [consent.]
Konsens (⌣–⁵) [lt.] m ⑫a. (Genehmigung)
konsequent (⌣⌣–) [lt.] a. ⑥ (folgerichtig) consistent; ♀ sein, oft: to act consistently, to act up to one's principles.
Konsequenz (⌣⌣–⁵) [lt.] f ⑯ 1. (Folgerichtigkeit) consistency. — 2. (Folgerung) consequence; logical conclusion.
Konsequenzen=macher(in f) m (⌣⌣–...) ⑫, =zieher(in f) m person who draws conclusions, b.s. one who twists other people's words or remarks.
konservativ (⌣⌣–w⌣f) [lt.] I a. ⑥ pol., &c. Conservative. — II ~e(r) m ⑰ Conservative; ein echter ~er, ein Hoch=⸗er, auch: a true(-blue) Tory.
Konservator (⌣⌣–⌣) [lt.] m ⑫ (Erhalter) conservator, keeper of a museum, &c.; ~ium (⌣⌣–w–(⌣)⌣) n ⑳ (Musikschule) (fr.) conservatoire, school o music.
Konserve (⌣–⌣w) [fr.] f ⑯ (Dauerspeise in Büchsen) preserve; ~n=fabrik(ant m) f ⑫ factory (maker) of preserves.
konservier/en (⌣⌣–w–) [lt.] I v/a. u. sich ♀ v/refl. ⑬ to preserve, to keep; sie hat sich gut k/t she carries her age well, she keeps up her good looks. — II ~ n ⑫, ⸗ung f ⑯ preservation.
Konsignant ♣ (⌣⌣–) [lt. -sign-] m ⑫ (Verfrachter) consignor, ...er; Konsignatar (⌣⌣–⌣) m ⑫e. (Empfänger) consignee; Konsignation (⌣⌣–tß(⌣)") f ⑯ (Warensendung) consignment.
konsignieren (⌣⌣–⌣) [lt.] v/a. ⑬ 1. (verfrachten) to consign. — 2. ⚔ (Soldaten in die Kaserne weisen) to consign.
konsiliieren (⌣⌣–(⌣)⌣) [s. Consilium abeundi] v/a. ⑬ to rusticate a student.
Konsilium (⌣⌣–(⌣)⌣) [lt.] n ⑳ (Beratung) council; vgl. Consilium abeundi.
konsistent (⌣⌣–) [lt.] a. ⑥ (haltbar) consistent; solid; Konsistenz f ⑯ (Bestand) consistency; solidity.

⚛ scientific; ♀ botanical; ⚱ geography; ⊕ machinery; ⚒ mining; ⚔ military; ⚓ marine; ● commercial; ✉ postal; ⛙ railway.

[Konsistorialgericht] — 608 — [Kontrapunktist]

Konsistorial=gericht (⌣⌣‒(⌣)ᴵᴵ…) [lt.] *n* ⓖ₂ ecclesiastical (or spiritual) court, in Engl. auch: Court of Arches; =**rat** *m* (als Titel unübersetzbar) etwa: Ecclesiastical Councillor or Commissioner.

Konsistorium (⌣ᴵᴵ(⌣)⌣) [lt.] *n* ⓖ₈ eccl. (geistliche Behörde) consistory(-court).

konskribier/en ⚔ (⌣‒ᴵᴵ) [lt.] **I** *v/a.* ⓖ₃ (ausheben) to raise (or levy, enrol) troops. — **II** Ḵ/**te(r)** *m* ⓖ₇ conscript.

Konskription ⚔ (⌣‒tḫ(⌣)ᴵᴵ) [lt.] *f* ⓖ₆ (Aushebung) conscription, enrolment of soldiers; =**s=frei** *a.* ⓖ₆ exempt from conscription; =**s=liste** *f* ⓖ₂ list of conscripts; =**s=pflichtig** *a.* subject to conscription, liable to serve in the army.

Konsole (⌣ᴸ‒) [fr.] *f* ⓖ₈: a) *arch.* (Kragstein) console; b) (Wandbrett) bracket; c) (Konsol-, Pfeiler-, Spiegel=tisch) pier-(table)glass.

konsolidier/en (⌣‒ᴵᴵ) [lt.] **I** *v/a. u. sich* ⌣ *v/refl.* ⓖ₃ (befestigen) to consolidate; sich ⌣ *a.* to grow firm; konsolidierte Staatspapiere (a. **Konsols**, f. ds) consolidated funds or stocks, a. consols *pl.* — **II** ∼*n* ⓖ₃ u. Ḵ/**ung** *f* ⓖ₆ consolidation. [sols *pl.* (f. konsolidieren).]

Konsols ⊤ ⊛ (⌣‒) [engl.] *pl. inv.* con-

Konsonant (⌣‒⨯) [lt.] *m* ⓖ₂ *gr.* (Mitlaut(er); *ant.* Vokal) consonant; stimmhafter, stimmloser ∼ voiced, voiceless cons.; ∼**en=verbindung** *f* ⓖ₂ combination of consonants. [consonantal.)

konsonantisch (⌣‒ᴵᴵ) *a.* ⓖ₆ (*ant.* voka´lisch)

Konsonanz ⚔ (⌣‒ᵛ) [lt.] *f* ⓖ₆ (Übereinstimmung) consonance, concord, agreement.

Konsorte (⌣ᴸ⌣) [lt.] *m* ⓖ₄ *jur. u. oft b.s.*: N. und ∼*n* N. and his associates or his set or his gang, F auch: N. and Co.

Konsortium (⌣‒tḫ(⌣)⌣) [lt.] *n* ⓖ₈ association, ⊛ syndicate, F ring, gang.

konspirieren (⌣‒ᴵᴵ) [lt.] *v/n.* (h.) ⓖ₃ (sich verschwören) to conspire, to plot (together).

Konstabler ⊤ (⌣ᴸ‒) [engl.] *m* ⓖ₂ (Schutzmann) (police) constable, policeman.

konstant ⚔ (⌣ᴸ) [lt.] *a.* ⓖ₆ (stetig) constant; *elect.* Ξer Strom constant current; ∼**e** (⌣ᴸ‒) *f* ⓖ₆ *math.* constant (value).

Konstantin (⌣‒) *npr/m.* ⓑⓖ₆ *α.* Constantine; ∼**opel** ♀ (⌣‒ᴵᴵ) [∼ b. Gr. 330] *npr/n.* ⓖ *α.* (Hauptstadt der Türkei, f. Byzanz) Constantinople; =**opeler** *m* ⓖ₂ u. *a. inv.* Constantinopolitan.

Konstanz (⌣ᴸ) **I** ♀ *npr/n. inv.* (St. am Bodensee) Constance. — **II** *npr/m.* ⓖⓖ *γ.*, ∼**e** (⌣ᴸ‒) ♂ ⓖⓖ *β.* (Vn.) Constance *m, f.*

konstatier/en (⌣‒ᴵᴵ) [lt.] **I** *v/a.* ⓖ₃ (behaupten) to state, (feststellen) to verify, ascertain; (wahrnehmen) to notice, observe. — **II** ∼*n* ⓖ₃ u. Ḵ/**ung** *f* ⓖ₆ statement; verification.

Konstellation (⌣‒tḫ(⌣)ᴵᴵ) [lt.] *f* ⓖ₆ (Stand, Lage) constellation; position (of affairs).

konsternieren (⌣‒ᴵᴵ) [lt.] *v/a.* ⓖ₃ (verblüffen) to consternate; konsterniert, auch: F flabbergasted, taken aback.

Konstituante (⌣‒ᴸ‒⌣) [fr.] *f* ⓖ₈ (konstituierende Versammlung, bsd. in Frankr. 1789 bis 91) Constituent Assembly.

konstituieren (⌣‒ᴵᴵ) [lt.] *v/a., sich* ⌣ *v/refl.* ⓖ₃: (sich) ⌣ (einsetzen) to constitute (o.s.), to form (a. *refl.*); Ξ**d**, *oft.* constituent.

Konstitution (⌣‒tḫ(⌣)ᴵᴵ) [lt.] *f* ⓖ₆ *pol., med., &c.* (Verfassung) constitution; er hat eine starke ∼ he has a strong const.,

he is strongly constituted; ∼**alismus** (⌣‒-lḫ(⌣)ᴵᴵ) *m* ⓖ₇ constitutionalism; **Ξell** (⌣‒tḫ(⌣)ᴸ) [fr.] *a.* ⓖ₆ constitutional; =**s=widrig** *a.* ⓖ₆ *pol.* unconstitutional, hostile to the constitution.

konstruierbar ⚔ (⌣‒ᴵᴵ‒) *a.* ⓖ₆ constructible; **konstruieren** (⌣‒ᴵᴵ) *v/a.* ⓖ₃ *gr., math., &c.* (errichten, zs.-fügen) to construct, klassische Schriften *2c.*: to construe…: falsch ⌣ to misconstruct, eine Schrift: to misconstrue; **Konstruktion** (⌣‒tḫ(⌣)ᴵᴵ) *f* ⓖ₆ *gr., &c.* construction; ∼**s=aufgabe** *f*, *geom.* geometrical construction or problem; ∼**s=fehler** *m* constructional (or structural) fault or flaw.

konstruktiv (⌣‒ᴵᴵf) [lt.] *a.* ⓖ₆ constructive.

Konsul (⌣‒) [lt.] *m* ⓖ₂ₔ (röm. Alt.: höchster Magistrat, jetzt: Handels-⌣) consul.

Konsular=agent (⌣‒ᴵᴵ…) *m* ⓖ₂ consular agent; =**gericht(sbarkeit** *f*) *n* consular jurisdiction.

konsularisch (⌣‒ᴵᴵ) [lt.] *a.* ⓖ₆ consular.

Konsulat (⌣‒ᴵᴵ) [lt.] *n* ⓖ₈ c. consulate; bsd. römisches Alt.: consulship; ∼**s=dienst** *m* ⓖ₂ für Vertretung von Handels-interessen im Auslande consular service or duties *pl.* or office; ∼**s=verweser** *m* acting consul.

Konsulent (⌣‒ᴸ) [lt.] *m* ⓖ₂ *jur.* counsel retained by a litigant, weitS. barrister.

Konsultation (⌣‒tḫ(⌣)ᴵᴵ) [lt.] *f* ⓖ₆ (Befragung, bsd. e-s Arztes; a. Beratung) consultation; **konsultierbar** (⌣‒ᴵᴵ‒) *a.* ⓖ₆ consultable; **konsultieren** (⌣‒ᴵᴵ) *v/a.* ⓖ₃ (befragen) to consult; to ask a p.'s advice.

Konsum (⌣ᴸ) [lt.] *m* ⓖd. (Bedarf) consumption; ∼**ent(in** *f*) (⌣‒) *m* ⓖ₂ (*ant.* Produzent) consumer; **Ξieren** (⌣‒ᴵᴵ) *v/a.* ⓖ₃ (aufbrauchen) to consume (auch ⊛).

Konsumtion (⌣‒tḫ(⌣)ᴵᴵ) *f* ⓖ₆ consumption (auch ⊛ of eatables, of fuel, &c.).

Konsum=verein (⌣ᴸ‒ ⌣ᴸ) *m* ⓖ₂ co-operative society; **Warenlager e-s ∼s** co-operative stores *pl.*, engS. Army(-)and(-)Navy (or Civil-Service) Stores *pl.*

kontagiös ⚔ (⌣‒(⌣)ᴸ) [lt.] *a.* ⓖ₈ (D 10) *path.* (ansteckend) contagious; **Kontagium** ⚔ (⌣ᴸ(⌣)⌣) *n* ⓖ₈ contagion.

Kontakt (⌣ᴸ) [lt.] *m* ⓖb. (Berührung) contact (a. *phys., &c.*); ∼**draht** *m* ⓖ₂ *elect.* Straßenbahn: contact wire, trolley wire; ∼**hebel** ⊝ *m* contact lever; ∼**lager** ⊛ *n* contact-deposit; ∼**ring** *m, elect.*: ∼ des Kommutators contact disc of the commutator; ∼**rolle** *f, elect.* Straßenbahn: trolley; ∼**winkel** *m, math.* angle of contact; ∼**wirkung** *f, phys. u. chm.* contact action; ∼**zone** zone of contact.

kontant ⊛ (⌣ᴸ) [it.] **I** *a.* ⓖ₆ von Personen: (zahlungsfähig) solvent; vom Gelde: (bar) in cash, F in (hard) coin. — **II** ∼**en** *pl.* (bares Geld) specie.

Kontant=geschäft ⊛ (⌣ᴸ…) *n* ⓖ₂ cash transaction or business.

kontemplativ (⌣‒ᴵᴵf) [lt.] *a.* ⓖ₆ (beschaulich) contemplative, meditative.

Konter=admiral ⚓ (⌣‒…) *m* ⓖ₂ Rear-Admiral; =**bande** [fr.] *f* ⓖ₈ bsd. ⚔ (geschmuggelte Ware) contraband (of war).

Konterfei ⚔ [: counterfeit; *fr. contrefait* nachgebildet] *n* ⓖe. image, likeness, portrait; **Ξen** (⌣‒ᴸ) *v/a.* ⓖ₃ to portray.

Konter=marke (⌣‒ᴵᴵ…) *f* ⓖ₂ pass-ticket, check; =**mine** ⚔ *f* countermine; Börse: die ∼ bauen the bears *pl.*; =**order** ⚔ *f* =

Gegenbefehl; =**tanz** *m* square dance, engS. quadrille.

Kontext (⌣ᴸ) [lt.] *m* ⓖa. (Zf.-hang) context; aus dem ∼ (der Fassung) bringen to put out (of countenance); to confuse.

Kontinent (⌣‒ᴸ) [lt.] *m* ⓖc. (Festland) continent, auch: (it.) terra firma.

Kontinental=handel (⌣‒ᴸ‒…) *m* ⓖ₂ continental trade; =**sperre** *f*, =**system** *n, hist.* gegen englische Waren (unter Napoleon I., 1806 *2c.*) Continental System.

Kontingent (⌣‒ᴸ) [neu-lt.] *n* (m) ⓖb. (⚔ Beitrag an Mannschaft, Geld *2c.*) contingent, contribution, quota; **Ξieren** (⌣‒ᴵᴵ) *v/a.* ⓖ₃ *2c.* to fix the contingent(s), &c.; ⊛ (Gewinn *2c.* teilen) to pool.

kontinuieren (⌣‒ᴵᴵ) *v/a.* ⓖ₃ to continue.

kontinuierlich (⌣‒ᴵᴵ) [lt.] *a.* ⓖ₆ (fortdauernd, ununterbrochen) continuous;

Kontinuität ⚔ (⌣‒ᴸ) [lt.] *f* ⓖ₆ continuity.

Konto ⊛ (⌣‒) [nhd.; *it.*] *n* ⓖ₈ u. ⓖ₀ (Rechnung) account, F score; ein ∼ eröffnen to open an account with a p.; auf ∼ nehmen to take on credit or F on tick.

Konto=buch ⊛ (⌣‒…) *n* ⓖ₂ account-book; =**inhaber** *m* customer of a bank; =**korrent** *n* account-current.

Kontor ⊛ ((⌣ᴸ) [nhd., *it.*] *n* ⓖe. (Geschäftszimmer) (merchant's) office, counting-house; ∼**bote**, ∼**diener** *m* ⓖ₂ office-messenger; ∼**bursche** *m* office-boy or -lad. — **Kontorist** (⌣‒ᴸ) *m* ⓖ₂ clerk in an office, counting-house clerk; vgl. **Kommis**. — **Kontor=personal** (⌣ᴸ‒…) *n* ⓖ₂ (clerical) staff of an office; =**stuhl** *m* office-stool.

kontra (⌣ᴸ) [lt. gegen, wider] **I** *adv.* against (jur. versus); ⊛ per ⌣ against which, per con(tra). — **II** ∼ (⌣ᴸ) *n, inv.*: das Pro und ∼ the pro and contra, F the pro(s) and con(s).

Kontra=alt ♪ (⌣ᴸ…) *m* ⓖ₂ (contr)alto; =**altist(in** *f*) *m* (contr)alto (singer); =**baß** ♪ *m* contrabass, double bass; =**buch** ⊛ *n* customer's book.

kontradiktorisch (⌣‒ᴵᴵ) [lt.] *a.* ⓖ₆ (widersprechend) contradictory.

Kontrahent (⌣‒ᴸ) [lt.] *m* ⓖ₂ (Vertragschließender) contracting party.

kontrahieren (⌣‒ᴵᴵ) [lt. zf.-ziehen, abschließen] ⊛ **I** *v/n.* (h.) **1.** to make a contract. — **II** *v/a.* **2.** eine Anleihe ⌣ to contract a loan. — **3.** burfch.: ein Due´ll ⌣, *aber abs.* ⌣ to engage in a duel.

Kontrakt (⌣ᴸ) [lt.] **I** *m* ⓖb. (Vertrag) contract (auch Bauwesen, jur. *2c.*), agreement; stillschweigender ∼ tacit agreement or understanding; einen ∼ abschließen to enter into a contract, ⊛ auch: to close a bargain. — **II** ⌣ *a.* ⓖ₆ ⚔ *path.* (zf.-gezogen) contracted (muscle); (gelähmt) lame, paralysed.

Kontrakt=bruch (⌣ᴸ…) *m* ⓖ₂ breach of contract; =**brüchig** *a.* ⓖ₆: ⌣ werden to break (or infringe) a contract.

kontraktlich (⌣ᴸ…) [lt.] *a.* ⓖ₆ (stipulated or fixed) by contract; *adv.* ⌣ bei e-m in die Lehre geben to article with a p.

kontrakt=mäßig (⌣ᴸ…) *a.* ⓖ₆ = kontra´ktlich.

Kontrakt(s)=verhältnis (⌣ᴸ…) *n* ⓖ₂: in einem ∼ zu e-m steh(e)n to be bound by contract (or agreement) to a p.

Kontra=punkt ♪ (⌣‒ᴸ…) *m* ⓖ₂ counterpoint; =**punktist** *m* contrapuntist.

Zeichen (s. S. IX): F familiär; P Volkssprache; ⸗ Gaunersprache; ⟍ selten; † alt (auch gestorben); * neu (auch geboren); ⁑ unrichtig;

[konträr] — 609 — [kopernikanisch]

konträr (⌣́) [fr.] *a.* ⓖ: a) (entgegengesetzt) contrary; b) F (schwer zu lenken) hard to manage. [zeichnen] to countersign.)
kontrasignieren (⌣⌣⌣́⌣) *v/a.* ⓖ (gegen-
Kontrast (⌣́) [it.] *m* ⓑ. (Abstechen) contrast; F set-off; **-ieren** (⌣⌣́⌣) *v/n.* (h.) ⓖ to (form a) contrast with.
Kontraveni-ent (⌣⌣⌣́⌣) [it.] *m* ㊷, ~**in** *f* ㊸ contravener of a legal precept, offender against a law; *auch:* trespasser.
kontravenieren (⌣⌣⌣⌣́⌣) *v/n.* (h.) ⓖ (entgegenhandeln) to contravene (or infringe) a rule, &c.; (ein Gesetz überschreiten) to trespass, transgress; **Kontravention** (⌣⌣⌣⌣⌣́⌣) *f* ㊻ contravention.
Kontra-zettel ● (⌣⌣́⌣) ... *m* ㊷ voucher.
☞ **Kontre-**... in Jfgn f. Konter...
Kontribuent (⌣⌣⌣́) [it.] *m* ㊷ contributor; **kontribuieren** (⌣⌣⌣⌣́⌣) *v/a.* ⓖ (besteuern) to contribute; **Kontribution** ✕ † (⌣⌣-tß(⌣)⌣́) *f* ㊻ (Beitreibung) contribution.
Kontroll-amt (⌣́ ...) *n* ㊷ office of supervision or control; **-apparat** *m* controlling-apparatus, check; **-beamte(r)** *m* controller; **-buch** 🕮 *n* ㊷ check-book.
Kontrolle (⌣́⌣) [fr. *contrôle m* „Gegenrolle"] *f* ㊽ (Aufsicht) control, supervision; checking (or overhauling, auditing) of accounts, &c.
Kontroller (⌣́⌣) *m* ㊷ elect. (Stromregler) controlling magnet.
Kontrolleur (⌣⌣ß⌣́r) [fr.] *m* ⓓ., ~**in** *f* ㊸ controller; auditor of accounts; Straßenbahn 2c., für die Fahrzeiten: timekeeper.
kontrollierbar (⌣⌣⌣́⌣) *a.* ⓖ controllable.
kontrollieren (⌣⌣⌣́⌣) [fr. *contrôler*] *v/a.* ⓖ (beaufsichtigen) to control, check.
Kontroll-manometer ⊖ (⌣́ ...) *n* ㊷ control-steam-gauge; **-versammlung** ✕ *f* muster of reserve-men; **-zeichen** *n*, **-zettel** *m* check. [controversial.]
kontrovers (⌣⌣́⌣ß) [it.] *a.* ⓖ (D10)(streitig)
Kontroverse (⌣⌣⌣́⌣) [it.] *f* ㊽ (wissenschaftl. Erörterung, Glaubensstreit 2c.) controversy.
Kontrovers-prediger (⌣⌣⌣́⌣...) *m* ㊷ controversialist, militant preacher; **-predigt** *f* controversial sermon; **-punkt** *m* controversial point.
Kontumaz (⌣⌣́) [it.] *f* ㊻ jur. (sträfliches Nichterscheinen) contumacy, contempt of court, default (of appearance); in ~ (it. *in contumaciam*) verurteilen, **-ieren** (⌣⌣-⌣́⌣) *v/a.* ⓖ jur. to punish (or fine) for contempt of court, to sentence by default; ~**urteil** *n* ㊷ judgment (which goes) by default.
Kontur (⌣́) [fr. *contour m*] *f* ㊻, ~ *m* ⓓ. (Umriß) outline, a. (fr.) contour; ~**schrift** *f*, *typ.* contour- (or outline) face.
Kontusion (⌣-(⌣)́⌣) [it.] *f* ㊻ path., *surg.* (Quetschung) contusion.
Konveni-enz (⌣⌣⌣(⌣́)ß) [it.] *f* ㊻ (Bequemlichkeit) convenience; (Füglichkeit) suitableness; ~**ehe**, ~**heirat** (✕...) *f* ㊷ conventional marriage.
konvenieren (⌣⌣⌣́⌣) [it.] *v/n.* (h.) ⓖ to be convenient to a p.; *vgl.* anstehen 7.
Konvent (⌣⌣́) [it.] *m* ⓑ. **1.** (Versammlung) convention, assembly.— **2.** *hist.* fr.(National')~(1792—95): National Convention. — **3.** oft *n* (Kloster) convent.
Konventikel (⌣⌣⌣́⌣) [it.] *n* ㉘ *bsd. hist.* (Gottesdienst der Puritaner) conventicle;

Konventikel-wesen (⌣⌣⌣⌣́⌣...) *n* ㉒ (secret) doings (or services) *pl.* of conventiclers, *weit S.* puritanism.
Konvention (⌣⌣-tß(⌣)́⌣) [it.] *f* ㊻ (Vertrag) convention, agreement; *pol. a.* treaty.
Konventional-strafe (⌣⌣⌣-tß(⌣)⌣⌣́...) *f* ㊷ (Vertrags-...) *jur.* penalty (or fine) for non-fulfilment of a contract.
konventionell (⌣⌣-tß(⌣)⌣́) [fr.] *a.* ⓖ (herkömmlich) conventional.
Konventions-münze (⌣⌣-tß(⌣)́⌣...) *f* ㊷ *num.* Deutschl.: convention-coin.
Konventual ⊕, *bsf.* ~**e** ㊷ *m*, ~**in** *f* ㊸ (⌣⌣⌣⌣(⌣)́) [it.: *Konvent*] (Kloster-bruder, -schwester) conventual.
Konvergenz ⚛ (⌣⌣⌣́) [it.] *f* ㊻ *math.*, *phys.* (Zs.-laufen in e-m Punkte) convergence, ...cy; **konvergieren** (⌣⌣⌣⌣́⌣) *v/n.* (h.) ⓖ to converge, to run to a point; 2d converging, convergent.
Konversation (⌣⌣⌣-tß(⌣)́⌣) [fr.] *f* ㊻ (Unterhaltung) conversation, a. chat, light talk; ~**s-lexikon** *n* ㊷ (en)cyclopædia; ~**s-sprache** *f* colloquial language or speech; ~**s-stück** *n*, *thea.* light and humourous piece; ~**s-stunde** *f* lesson in conversation, conversational lesson.
konversieren (⌣⌣⌣́⌣) [it.] *v/n.* (h.) ⓖ: mit e-m 2 (sich unterhalten) to converse with a p.
konvertierbar ⚛ (⌣⌣⌣⌣́⌣) *a.* ⓖ (umsetzbar) convertible, capable of conversion.
konvertier-en (⌣⌣⌣́⌣) [it. umwandeln] I *v/a.* ⓖ Zinsfuß 2c.: to convert ... — II ~ *n* ㉓ u. **K/ung** *f* ㊻ conversion.
Konvertit (⌣⌣⌣́) [it.] *m* ㊷, ~**in** *f* ㊸ *eccl. und theol.* (Bekehrte[r]) convert.
konvex ⚛ (⌣⌣́) [it.] *a.* ⓖ (*ant.* konka'v) (rund-erhaben) convex; ~**ität** (⌣⌣⌣́) *f* ㊻ convexity, convexness.
Konvikt (⌣⌣́) [it.] *n* (m) ⓑ. auf Hochschulen: **1.** *bsd. ehm.:* (free) commons *pl.*, free board. — **2.** *ietzt:* dining-hall of foundationers or sizars, refectory.
Konviktuale (⌣⌣⌣⌣́⌣) [it.] *m* ㊹ *ehm.:* student who eats at commons, sizar; *jetzt:* exhibitioner.
Konvivium (⌣⌣́⌣⌣⌣) [it.] *n* ㉘ (Gelage) convivial gathering, banquet.
Konvolut (⌣⌣⌣́) [it. Zs.-gerolltes] *n* ⓒ. roll (or bundle, scroll) of paper(s), &c.
Konvulsion (⌣⌣⌣́⌣) [it.] *f* ㊻ (Zuckung) convulsion, spasm.
konvulsivisch (⌣⌣⌣⌣́⌣) [it.] *a.* ⓖ (krampfhaft) convulsive, spasmodic.
Konzentration (⌣⌣⌣-tß(⌣)́⌣) [it.] *f* ㊻ (Zs.-ziehung nach einem Punkte hin) concentration.
konzentrier-en (⌣⌣⌣́⌣) [neu-lt. um einen Punkt zs.-drängen] I *v/a.* u. sich ~ *v/refl.* ⓖ *phys., chm.*, 2c.: to concentrate; sich 2, *auch:* to become concentrated; seine Gedanken auf et. 2 to concentrate (or centre) ... upon a th.; *chm.* f/t (unverdünnt) concentrated (acid). — II ~ *n* ㉓ u. **K/ung** *f* ㊻ concentration.
konzentrisch (⌣⌣́⌣) [nlt.] *a.* ⓖ: ✕ 2es Feuer concentric fire, (Kreuzfeuer) cross-fire; *math.* concentric.
Konzept (⌣⌣́) [it.] *n* ⓑ. (Entwurf) first (or rough) draft or copy; minute, *fig.* aus dem ~(e) kommen to lose the thread, to grow confused, to break down in a speech, &c.; e-m das ~ verderben oder verwirren to put a p. out.

Konzept-buch (⌣⌣́...) *n* ㊷ scribbling-(or draft-) book; **-papier** ● *n* scribbling- (or common writing-)paper.
Konzert ♪ (⌣⌣́) [it.] *n* ⓑ. concert (*auch fig.*); ~, in dem das Rauchen gestattet ist smoking-concert; in ein ~ gehen to go to a concert; ~ veranstalten to give a c.; ~**besucher(in** *f*) *m* ㊷ concert-goer; ~**flügel** *m* concert-grand; ~**geber** *m* person who gives (or organizes) a concert; ~**haus** *n* concert-hall.
konzertieren (⌣⌣⌣́⌣) *v/n.* (h.) ⓖ to play in (or to give) concerts or a concert.
Konzert-meister (⌣⌣́...) *m* ㊷ conductor of a band (*vgl.* Kapellmeister); ~**sänger(in** *f*) *m* concert-singer; ~**stück** *n* concerto.
Konzession (⌣⌣(⌣)́⌣) [it.] *f* ㊻ (Einräumung) concession; (Privile'g) patent, (Verkaufsrecht) license; ~**är** (⌣⌣(⌣)⌣́) *m* ⓓ. — ~**s-inhaber**, **-ieren** (⌣⌣(⌣)⌣́⌣) *v/a.* ⓖ: e-n 2 to grant a p. a concession or a license, to license a p.; f/ter Gastwirt licensed victualler or hotel-keeper.
Konzessions-inhaber(in *f*) *m* (⌣⌣(⌣)́⌣...) ㊷: a) (Besitzer[in] eines Privilegs) concession(n)aire; patentee; b) (Besitzer[in] eines Verkaufsrechts) licensee.
konzessiv (⌣⌣⌣́) *a.* ⓖ (einräumend) concessive; ~**satz** *m* ㊷ *gr.* concessive clause.
Konzil ✝ (⌣⌣́) [it. *conci'lium*] *n* ⓓ. *eccl.* (Kirchenversammlung) council; ein ~ berufen to call a council.
Konzipi-ent (⌣⌣⌣́) [it.] *m* ㊷ (Entwerfer e-r Schrift 2c.) draftsman; **konzipieren** (⌣⌣⌣́⌣) *v/a.* ⓖ (entwerfen) to draft, to jot down, F to put roughly on paper.
konzis (⌣́) [it.] *a.* ⓖ (D 10) (kurz, gedrängt) concise. [operation.]
Ko-operation ⊖ (-⌣⌣-tß(⌣)́) [it.] *f* ㊻ co-
Ko-operativ-genossenschaft (-⌣⌣́f ...) *f* ㊷ co-operative association or union.
ko-operieren (-⌣⌣⌣́) [it.] *v/n.* (h.) ⓖ (zs.-wirken) to co-operate.
Ko-optation (-⌣-tß(⌣)́) [it.] *f* ㊻ co-optation (= Hinzuwahl). [to co-opt.]
ko-optieren (-⌣⌣́)[it.] *v/a.* ⓖ (hinzuwählen)
Ko-ordinate ⚛ (-⌣⌣́) [it.] *f* ㊷ *math.* co-ordinate; ~**n-achse** *f* ㊷ axis of coordinates. [ordination.]
Ko-ordination (-⌣⌣-tß(⌣)́) [it.] *f* ㊻ co-
ko-ordinier-en (-⌣⌣⌣́) [it.] I *v/a.* ⓖ (neben-ordnen) to co-ordinate (a. *gr.*). — II ~ *n* ㉓ u. **K/ung** *f* ㊻ co-ordination.
Kopa-iv(a)-balsam (-⌣⌣́f..., -⌣⌣́⌣...) [brasil.] *m* ㊷ *pharm.* (balsam of) copaiva or copaiba (*von Copai'fera officina'lis*).
Kopal ● (-́) [merifk.] *m* ⓓ. ein Harz: copal; ~**baum** ♀ *m* ㊷ copal-tree (*Vate'ria i'ndica*); ~**firnis**, ~**lack** *m* copal-varnish; ~**gummi** *n* (*m*) (Harz *v. Hymenae'a cou'rbarii*) copal-gum.
Kopeke (⌣́⌣) [russ. von *kopje* Lanze] *f* ㊸ *num.* (2 Pf., 1/100 Rubel) copeck, kopeck, Russian halfpenny.
Kopenhagen (⌣⌣́⌣) [= Kaufhafen] *npr/n.* ㊷ α. (dänische Hauptstadt) Copenhagen; ~**er(in** *f*) ㊷ *m* ㊷ (inhabitant) of Cop.
Köper u. ⊕ (⌣́) [ndl.] *m* ㊷ Weberei: twill; **köpern** *v/a.* ⓖ 2α. to twill; ge**köperte Stoffe** *m/pl.* twilled cloths *pl.*
kopernikanisch (⌣⌣⌣́⌣) [Kope'rnikus, bsch. Astronom, 1473—1543] *a.* ⓖ Copernican: 2es (Welt-)System (planetary) system of Copernicus.

♪ Musik; ⚛ Wissenschaft; ♀ Pflanze; ⚲ Geographie; ⊖ Technik; ⚒ Bergbau; ✕ Militär; ⚓ Marine; ● Handel; ✉ Post; 🚂 Eisenbahn.

Kopf (⁵) [ahd.: co(o)p, cup; *lt. cupa f* Gefäß] *m* ⑦b. **1.** head; den ~ betr.: ☞ cephalic; (Schädel) skull, brain-pan, P noddle, pate, knowledge-box, (cocoa-)nut; vom ~ bis zu den Zehen from head to foot, from top to toe; kahler ~ F bald pate; Kocht.: (Kalbs-, Lachs-)jowl; f. Kohl-2; ☉ head of a nail, pin, screw, beam, sail, &c.; am ~e des Bettes at the head of the bed; ~ oder Schrift (a. Rücken) e-r Münze: head(s) or tail(s); *typ.* (Titel-)~ heading; ~ e-r Seite top of a page. — **2.** mit *verbs*: er kann mir den ~ nicht abbeißen he cannot bite my head off (f. abbeißen 2); e-m den ~ abschlagen to behead a p., F to chop a p.'s head off; f-n aufsetzen to insist on a th.; den ~ (oben) behalten to keep one's head (up), to bear up against trouble; f. brummen 1, eingenommen 3, einnehmen 7, faul 2; einen guten ~ haben to have a good head or a good brain or good brains; den ~ hängen I. to hang one's head (down), F to be down in the mouth; er lernt Latein, daß ihm der ~ raucht F he is grinding (or sweating) away at Latin; der ~ saust mir noch von dem Lärm, etwa: I have not yet recovered from …; den ~ schütteln to shake one's head; der ~ schwindelt e-m davon it makes one's head whirl or swim; er weiß nicht, wo ihm der ~ steht … which way to turn or what to do (first); vgl. kopfste(e)n; mir tut der ~ weh my head aches; e-m den ~ verdrehen to turn a p.'s head; den ~ verlieren to lose one's head or presence of mind; den ~ voll h. to have one's head full (of serious matter) or one's mind fully (pre)occupied; e-m den ~ waschen (oder zurecht-rücken oder -stutzen) to reprimand a p. (severely), to take a p. to task, F to comb a p.'s hair, to give a p. a rub-down; sich den ~ zerbrechen to rack (or tax, cudgel) one's brain. — **3.** (Leben) es gilt den ~, es geht an ~ und Kragen (a. darauf steht der ~) it is a capital crime or offence, it's a hanging matter; vgl. kosten³ am Schluß; den ~ zum Pfande (oder aufs Spiel) setzen to stake one's head or life; f-n ~ auf (die Erreichung von) et. setzen to risk one's head for a th.; to carry (out) one's proposal by hook or by crook. — **4.** (Sinn, Verstand, Urteil) sense, understanding, judgment, F brain(s *pl.*); (Gedächtnis) memory; vgl. 8. — **5.** (Willen) f-n ~ durchsetzen to carry one's point, F to get one's way; seinem eigenen ~e folgen to follow one's own bent; einen eigenen (oder seinen) ~ h., f-n für sich h. to have a head (or a mind) of one's own, to be self-willed or stubborn. — **6.** (Mensch [von geistiger Fähigkeit]) oft: (good or fine) head, (able) thinker, person of (sound) judgment; beobachtender (offener) ~ observing (open) mind; beschränkter ~ narrow mind; erfinderischer ~ inventive genius, ingenious person; hohler (a. leerer) ~ empty head, emptyheaded fellow. — **7.** (einzelne Person): es kamen 100 Mark auf den ~ each p.'s portion was £5, each received (or had to pay) £5; ☉ 10 Mark pro ~ ten shillings a head or a piece; Sprichw. viel(e) Köpfe, viel(e) Sinne many men, many minds. — **8.** mit *prp.*: **an:** f. fahren 1; sich e-m an den ~ werfen (aufdrängen) to thrust o.s. upon a p.; er ist nicht **auf** den ~ gefallen he is no fool or F no stupid; es macht 3 Mark auf den ~ it makes three shillings a head; ich nehme die Verantwortlichkeit auf meinen ~ I take all responsibility on my own shoulders; e-m et. auf den ~ (zu)sagen to tell a p. a th. to his face; e-n Preis auf f-s ~ setzen to set a price on a p.'s head; auf dem ~e steh(e)n to stand on one's head; *fig.* auf f-m ~e (be)stehen to insist on one's wish(es); alles auf den ~ stellen to put everything topsy-turvy, to turn everything upside down; und wenn sie sich auf den ~ stellen in spite of anything (that) they may do, if they try ever so hard; **aus** dem ~e by rote, by heart; e-m et. aus dem ~e bringen to put (or F get, knock) a th. out of a p.'s head or mind; et. aus dem ~e (Gedächtnisse) hersagen (diktieren) to recite (to dictate) a th. from memory; er kann es aus dem ~e wiederholen he knows it by rote; sich (*dat.*) et. aus dem ~e schlagen to banish a th. from one's mind, F to get a th. out of one's head; sie mögen sich (*dat.*) die Augen aus dem ~e sehen they may look till they are blind; das will mir nicht aus dem ~e I cannot banish it from my thoughts or F get it out of my head; den ~ aus der Schlinge ziehen to slip (one's head out of) the (hangman's) noose; e-n **bei** dem (ob. beim) ~e nehmen to seize a p. by the collar; **durch:** f. fahren 1; sich (*dat.*) e-e Kugel durch den ~ jagen to blow out one's brains, to shoot o.s.; et. **für** seinen ~ (auf eigene Faust) tun to do a th. on one's own responsibility; **in:** et. im ~ behalten to keep a th. (fresh) in one's memory, to retain a th.; ich weiß nicht, was ihm in den ~ gefahren ist … what (idea) can have entered his head or taken possession of him or possessed him; es geht ihm et. im ~e herum there is s.th. revolving in his mind; et. im ~e haben: a) Verstand: to know s.th., F to have s.th. in one's head; b) Gedanken: to be full of thought(s); was man nicht im ~e hat, muß man in den Beinen haben, etwa: a weak memory makes work for the legs; c) Sorge: to have cares, to brood over one's trouble(s); d) e-n Rausch: to have (taken) a drop too much; große Dinge im ~ h. to have great schemes; im ~e rechnen to compute mentally, F to reckon (or do) in one's head; er ist im ~e nicht richtig he is not in his right senses, F he's off his chump or his nut; sich (e-m) et. in den ~ setzen to get (to put) an idea into one's (a p.'s) head; die Sache will mir nicht in den ~ I do not see (any reason for) it; Sprichw. das Herz läuft mit dem ~e davon, etwa: the heart prevails over (or gets the better of) the head; mit dem ~e gegen die Wand laufen, rennen to run one's head against the wall (auch *fig.*); er handelt nur nach f-m ~e he follows nobody's advice but his own; Blutandrang nach dem ~e congestion of the brain; es ist ganz nach meinem ~e it is quite to my liking or just what I wished; **über:** f. Hals 3; e-m das Haus über dem ~e anstecken to set a p.'s house on fire; bis über den ~ in Schulden stecken to be head over (bisw. head and) ears in debt; e-m über den ~ wachsen to outgrow a p.; das Geschäft ist ihm über den ~ gewachsen the business has become too great an undertaking for him or has grown too large (or too much) for him; die Hände über dem ~e zf.-schlagen (vor Verwunderung) to be taken aback; **um** einen ~ größer sein to be a head taller or taller by a head; nicht **von** seinem ~e abgehen not to give way, F to stick to one's guns; ein Brett **vor** dem ~e h. to be blockheaded, to be devoid of sense; e-m den ~ vor die Füße legen to have a p. beheaded or a p.'s head cut off; e-n vor den ~ stoßen to give offence (or umbrage) to a p.; starker Wein steigt **zu** ~e … flies to the head.

Kopf-abschlagen (⁵…) n ②, **-abschneiden** n beheading, decapitation, ☞ decollation; **-arbeit** f mental (or head-, brain-)work; **-ausschlag** m, *path.* eruption on the head; **-balken** m, *carp.* head-beam, e-r Brücke: top-beam; **-band** n: a) head-band(age) b) ☉ = Tragband b; **-bedeckung** f covering for the head, head-gear; **-bekleidung** f e-r Mauer: top-facing; **-binde** f = Hauptband a; **-blüten** ♀ f/pl.: ☞ aggregate flowers pl.; **-blut-geschwulst** f, *path.*: ☞ cephalhæmatoma; **-blütig** ♀ a. aggregate; **-bohrer** m, *surg.* trepan, perforator; **-bolzen** ☉ m head-bolt; **-brechen** n 2c. = zerbrechen 2c.; **-brett** n e-r Bettstelle: head-board; **-brummen** F n noises pl. in the head; **-brust-stück** n, *ent.*: ☞ cephalothorax; **-bürste** f head- (or hair-)brush.

Köpfchen (⁵…) n ㉓ (dim. v. Kopf) small head, bisw.: headlet; ♀ cluster, ☞ capitulum. [cell.

Köpfchen-zelle ♀ (⁵…) f ⑫ einer Röhren-

Kopf-decke (⁵…) f ⑫ für Pferde: blanket for (covering) the head, head-cloth.

köpfen (⁵…) ⑧ I v/a. **1.** = enthaupten I. — **2.** Bäume, bsd. Weiden ② to poll (or top, lop) … — **3.** Nadlerei: (antöpfen?) to head. — II v/n. (h.) **4.** (Köpfe bekommen) von Salat, Kohl: to put on hearts or heads. — III ~ n ㉓ **5.** = Enthauptung.

Kopf-ende (⁵…) n ⑫ des Bettes: head of the bed; **-förmig** a. ⑯ in the shape of a head, ☞ capitate, cephaloid, …ic; **-fuge** ☉ f, *arch.* heading-joint; **-füß(l)er** m/pl., *zo.* cephalopods pl.; **-geschirr** n, *man.* head-harness; **-gicht** f, *path.* gout in the head, ☞ cephalagra; **-grind** m, *path.* scald-head, ☞ porrigo; **-haar** n hair of the head; **-halter** ☉ m des Photographen: head-rest, bei Opera-

---

Signs (see page XVII): F familiar; P vulgar; ꟿ flash; ◣ rare; † obsolete (died); * new word (born); ⁎⁺ incorrect; ♪ music.

tionen: cephalostat; =hänger(in f) m = Duckmäuser(in); =hängerei f = Duckmäuserei; ₴hängerisch a. moping, (scheinheilig) sanctimonious, F saintly; =haube f, orn. crest; =haut f scalp; =hülle f, ent. head-case.

köpfig (⸗ᷨ) a. ⊕ 1. (eigensinnig) headstrong. — 2. in Bfgn, zB. blond⸗? fairheaded; zwei⸗? two-headed, ⚕ bicephalous; anat. zwei⸗ler Muskel: ⚕ biceps, drei⸗ler Muskel: ⚕ triceps (muscle). [in the head, crazy.]

..köpfisch (...ᷨ) in Bfgn: rappel⸗? wrong⸗

Kopf=jagd (ᷡ...) f ⊕ wilder Völker: headhunting; =keilbein n, anat.: ⚕ sphenoid bone; =kissen n pillow (vgl. =pfühl); =kissen-überzug m pillow-case; =kohl m common white cabbage (Brassica oleracea capitata); =länge f Rennsport: head; =laterne f einer Locomotive head-light; =laus f, ent. head-louse (Pediculus capitis).

Köpflein (⸗ᷨ) n ⊕ = Köpfchen.

Kopf=leiste (ᷡ...) f ⊕ typ. head-piece.

köpflings (⸗ᷨ) adv. head foremost.

kopf=los (ᷡ...) a. ⊕ headless, zo.: ⚕ acephalous; fig. brainless, (unbesonnen) giddy; =losigkeit f ⊕ headlessness, ⚕ acephalia; fig. giddiness.

Köpf=maschine (⸗ᷨᷨ) f ⊕ guillotine.

Kopf=messer (ᷡ...) n ⊕ Gerät: ⚕ cephalometer; =messung f: ⚕ cephalometry; =naht f, anat. suture of the head; =nicken n nod(ding) of the head; =nicker m, anat. annuent muscle; =nuß f: a) ♀ (Mandel-ahorn): ⚕ caryocar; b) blow (or F clump, clout) on the head; =pfühl m (n) bolster; =putz m head-dress; =rechnen n mental arithmetic; =rose f, path.: ⚕ erysipelas; =salat m ♀ common (or round-headed garden) lettuce, cabbage-lettuce (Lactuca sativa capitata); =scheibe f ⚔ head-target; ₴scheu a. ⊕ von Pferden: restive, skittish, fig. von Personen: shy, reserved; e-n ~ machen to alarm a p.; =schlag-ader f, anat.: ⚕ cephalic artery; =schleife f topknot; =schmerz m, path. headache; ~en haben to have a headache; heftige ~en violent (or splitting) headache; =schuppen f/pl. scurf, dandruff; =schütteln n shaking (or shake) of the head; =schwelle 🚂 buffer-bar or -beam; =sprung m header; einen ~ ins Wasser machen to take a header, to dive; =station ⚓ terminus; =steg m, typ. head-stick; ♀steh(e)n v/n. (h.) ⚕** to stand on one's head; =stein ⊕ m, arch. headstone, header; ehm. =steuer f poll-tax; =stimme ♪ falsetto (voice); =stück n: a) head-piece, des Pferdes auch: head-stall; b) einer Querflöte mouthpiece; c) F co. = nuß b; =tuch n head-cloth, kerchief; ₴über adv. head foremost, head over heels; ⸘, ₴unter adv. pell-mell, head-long.

Köpfung (⸗ᷨ) f ⊕ f. Enthauptung. [über.]

kopf-unter (ᷨᷨ) adv. head down; vgl.

Kopf-wäsche (ᷡ...) f ⊕ shampooing; =wassersucht f, path. water on the brain, ⚕ hydrocephalus; =weh n = =schmerz; =wunde f wound in the head; =zahl f number of persons; =zerbrechen n racking (F cudgelling) of the brain, severe mental effort; e-m viel ~(s)

machen to give a p. much to think about; ₴zerbrechend a. ⊕ very trying to the brain; ₴e Arbeit severe brain-work.

Kopiali-en (⸗ᷡ(⸣)⸢) [lt.] pl. inv. (Schreibgebühren) copying-fee, fee for copying.

Kopie (⸗ᷡ) [lt.] f ⊕ 1. (Abschrift) copy, duplicate. — 2. Kunst: (Nachbildung eines Originals) copy, ⚕ replica, replication; (Nachahmung) imitation.

Kopier=block ⊕ (⸗ᷡ...) m ⊕ copyingblock; =buch n ⊕ copying-book.

kopieren (⸗ᷡ) [lt.] v/a. ⊕ to copy.

Kopier=farbe ⊕ (⸗ᷡ...) f ⊕ copying-ink; =maschine, =presse f c.-press; =stift m c.-pencil; =telegraph ⚓ m copyingtelegraph; =tinte f = =farbe. [copying-clerk; f. Ab-]

Kopist (⸗ᷡ) m ⊕ copying-clerk; f. Ab-

Koppe (⸗ᷡ) [= Kuppe] f ⊕ dome-shaped peak (f. Schneekoppe).

Koppel (⸗ᷡ) [mhd.; *lt. copula f Band] I f ⊕, ⚔ mst n ⊕ 1. (Band) coupling, hunt. für Jagdhunde: leash, ⚔ (Wehrgehenk, Säbelkoppel) sword-belt. — II f ⊕ 2. hunt. e-e ~ (b.h.3) Hunde leash (weitS. pack) of hounds; auf Märkten: ~ (zs.-gebundene) Pferde train (or set, string) of horses. — 3. (Besitztum von mehreren) (plot of) land belonging jointly to several persons, common pasturage or hunting-ground or (right of) fishing. — 4. agr. (Einfriedigung) enclosure.

Koppel=fischerei (ᷡ...) f ⊕ common (right of) fishing; =gerechtigkeit f, agr. intercommonage, (joint) right of using a common; =hund m, hunt. leashed hound; =hut f pasture belonging to several persons; jur. common of pasture; =jagd f common hunting-ground, shooting (rights) belonging to several persons; =leine f, hunt. für die Meute: leash.

koppeln (⸗ᷡ) v/a. ⊕ a. 1. hunt. Hunde (an-ea.) ⊕ to leash hounds. — 2. Pferde ⊕ to tie (or string) ... together. — 3. (verbinden) ♪ Orgelbau: die Griffbretter ⊕ to join the keyboards (together). — 4. agr. ein Feld ⊕ (einfriedigen) to enclose (or fence in).

Koppel=recht (ᷡ...) n ⊕ right of (using a) common; =riemen m, =seil n, hunt. leash; die Jagdhunde vom ~ loslassen to slip the hounds; =trift f = =weide.

Koppelung (⸗ᷡ) f ⊕ leashing, &c. (f. koppeln); ~s-knebel m ⊕ f. Knebel 2 e.

Koppel=weide (ᷡ...) f ⊕ agr.: a) = =hut; b) enclosed pasture-land; =wirtschaft f, agr. rotation of crops.

koppen (⸗ᷡ) I v/a. ⊕ 1. = kappen². — 2. Müllerei: Korn ⊕ to prepare ... — II v/n. (h.) ⚕ vet. v. Pferden: (rülpsen) to belch.

Kopra (⸗ᷡ) ⚕ (⸗ᷡ) [ind.] f ⊕ (getrockneter Kokostern) copra.

Koprolith ⚕ (⸗ᷡᷡ) [grch.] m ⊕c. ⊕ geol. (fossiler Kot) coprolite.

Kopte (⸗ᷡ) [(ᷡ)gypter] m ⊕, Koptin f ⊕ Copt; koptisch (⸗ᷡ) a. ⊕ Coptic.

Kopula (⸗ᷡ) [lt.] f ⊕ gram. und log. (Satzband) copula.

Kopulation (⸗ᷡᷡᷡ) [lt.] f ⊕ (kirchliche Trauung) marriage-ceremony, auch: nuptial blessing.

kopulieren (⸗ᷡᷡ) [lt.] v/a. ⊕ 1. to unite, to pair, durch das Eheband: to join in marriage, to marry. — 2. hort. to graft.

Kopulier=reis (⸗ᷡᷡ...) n ⊕ hort. grafting-twig. [von Kiesen².]

kor (¹) f. Hom. Chor, Korps] impf. ind.

Korah (¹⸗) [hebr.] npr/m. inv.: die Rotte ~ bibl. the company of Korah, weitS. gang (or band, set) of rogues, ruffians.

Koralle (⸗ᷡ) [mhd.; *grch.] f ⊕ zo., ⊕ coral; fossile ~: ⚕ coral(in)ite.

korallen (⸗ᷡ) a. ⊕ zo., ⊕ (made of, consisting of) coral.

Korallen=achat (⸗ᷡᷡ...) m ⊕ min. coral agate; =ähnlich a. ⊕, =artig a. ⊕ zo. coral-like, coralline, coralloid; =ast m coral-branch; =baum ♀ m coral-tree (Erythrina Crista galli); =fang m c.-fishing or -fishery; ₴farbig a. ⊕ zo. coralline; =fischer m coral-fisher or -diver; =fischerei f = =fang; ₴förmig ♀ zo. coral-shaped, ⚕ coralliform; =garn n = =netz; ₴haltig a. coralled; =holz ⊕ n coral-wood; =insel f coral-island; =kalk(stein) m, geol. coral-rag; =moos ♀ n coral-moss (Corallina); =netz n c.-net; =perle f c.(-)bead; ₴artig a. c.-plant (Jatropha multifida); =polyp m = Korallpolyp; =riff n coral-reef; =schnur f coral(-)necklace; =tang ♀ m = Koralline; =tier n = Korallpolyp.

Koralline ⚕ (⸗ᷡᷡ) f ⊕, zo. (Seeschwamm) coral-moss, coralline (Corallina).

Korall=polyp (ᷡ...) m ⊕ zo. coral-insect, coralline; pl. auch: ⚕ corralligena pl.

koram F (¹⸗) [lt. coram angesicht] adv. burfch.: einen ⊕ nehmen, auch Lieren F (⸗ᷡᷡ) v/a. ⊕ to take a p. to task.

Koran (¹⸗, ar. ⸗¹) [ar. Vorgelesenes] m ⊕d. (moham. Bibel) Koran; vgl. Alkoran.

koranzen P (⸗ᷡ) = kuranzen.

Korb (ᷡ) [ahd.: corf; *lt. corbis f (m)] m ⊕b,6. 1. basket (mit einem Henkel, zwei Henkeln with one handle, two handles, für Cheeren: hamper, für Fische: creel, für Porzellan: crate, für Wäsche: washingbasket; (Binsen)~ für Feigen 2c. frail; ~ zum Tragen von Kranken 2c. stretcher; (Trag-)~ für Saumtiere: pannier; (Bett-)~ cradle-basket; ⚔ (Förder-)~ basket, corb, drum; ⚔ (Schanz-)~ gabion. — 2. fig. f. Hahn 2; e-m (bsd. einem Freier) e-n ~ (abschlägigen Bescheid) geben to give a p. a refusal or a denial or a rebuff; einen ~ bekommen to be refused, to get a rebuff. — 3. ⚔ (Säbelkorb) basket-hilt.

Korb=arbeit ⊕ (ᷡ...) f ⊕ basket-work, -making; =arbeiter m b.-maker; =ball m b.-ball; =binse f ♀ u. ⊕ frail; ₴blütig ♀ a. ⊕ ⚕ synantherous; =blütler m/pl. composite flowers, (lt.) compositae pl.

Körbchen (⸗ᷡ) n ⊕ (dim. von Korb) small basket or hamper; arch. corbe(i)l; ♀ (Blüten-)~: ⚕ calathidium, calathium.

Korb=degen (ᷡ...) m ⊕ basket-sword; =eidechse f, zo. b.-lizard (Gerrhosaurus); =flasche f ♀ wicker- (or osier-)bottle, größere: demijohn, für Säuren: carboy; =flechter m = =macher; =flechter-arbeit ⊕ f = =arbeit; ₴förmig a. ⊕ basket-shaped, ⚕ calathiform; =gefäß n eines Schwertes b.-hilt; =geflecht n wickerwork; =gitter n basket-grate; =handel ⊕ m b.-trade; =henkel m b.-handle; =macher m b.-maker; =muschel f, zo.: ⚕ corbis, corbuloid; =rapier n,

[Korbschläger] — 612 — [Kornmähmaschine]

=schläger m b.-hilted rapier; =fessel m -stuhl; =stich m, =stickerei f ⊙ basket-couching; =stuhl m b.-chair; =träger m basket-carrier; =voll m basketful; =wagen m basket-carriage or -chaise; =ware ⚙ f basket-ware; =weide ⚘ f osier (Salix vimina'lis); =wiege f wicker cradle; bassinet.

Korde ⊙ (⌣ˡ) [fr. cord] m ⑪b. (starker gerippter baumwollener Stoff) corduroy (bes. für Hosen der Arbeiter).

Korde ⊙ (⌣ˡ; Hom. Chorde) [fr.] f ㊽ Weberei c. cord.   [string, cord.]
Kordel (⌣ˡ) [nhd.,* fr.] ㊽ bes. rhein.
Kordelia† (⌣ˡ(⌣)⌣)npr/f.㊾㊽⑯⑤㊱(Vn.; bei SH. König Lears jüngste Tochter) Cordelia.

kordelieren ⊙ (⌣⌣ˡ) [it.] v/a. ㉝ to cord; (mit Schnur einfassen) to braid.
kordial (⌣ˡ(⌣)ˡˡ [it.] a. ㊱ (herzlich) cordial.
Kordialität (⌣ˡ(⌣)⌣ˡˡ) f ㊻ cordiality.
Kordilleren ⊙ (⌣ˡ(⌣)ˡˡ) [span. „Ketten"- gebirge] npr/f/pl. ㊽ amer. Gebirge: Cor- dilleras (de los Andes).   [cordite.]
Kordit ⚔ T (⌣ˡ) m ⑪c.(rauchschwaches Pulver)
Kordon (⌣a') [fr. Schnur] m ⑪ (Postenkette) cordon, ⚙a. line of posts; e-n ~ ziehen um to post (or draw) a cordon (a)round.
Korduan ⊙ (⌣ˡ⌣ˡ) [Ko'rdova, spanische Stadt] m ⑪d. (a. ~leder n) Spanish leather, cordwain, cordovan; ~arbeiter, =ger- ber, =macher m ⚖ cordwainer.
töre (⌣⌣) subj. impf. v. tiesen.
Korea ⚘ (⌣ˡ⌣) npr/n. ⑳a. (Reich in Hinter- asien) Corea, bss. Korea.
Koreaner (⌣ˡ⌣ˡ) m ㊺, ~in f ㊺, ko- re(an)isch a. ㊱ Corean, bss. Korean.
Korfiot ⊙ (⌣(⌣)ˡˡ) [Korfu] m ㊺, ~in f ㊺ inhabitant of Corfu, Corfiote.
Koriander ⚘ (⌣ˡ⌣)[grch. Wanzensame] m ㉒ (a. pharm.) coriander (Coria'ndrum sati'vum).   [grch. Stadt] Corinth.]
Korinth ⚙ (⌣ˡ) npr/n. ⑳a. (sehr alte)
Korinthe ⚘ (⌣ˡ⌣) [nhd. 15. sac.; *fr. (v. Korinth)] f ㊽ currant.   [currants.]
Korinthen=ernte ("...) f ㊷ crop of
Korinther (⌣ˡ⌣) m㊺,~in f㊺, korinthisch a. ㊱ Corinthian; arch. ㊷(Säulen-)Ord- nung Corinthian order (of columns).
Koriolanus (⌣ˡ⌣⌣ˡ⌣) [aus Cori'oli, ⚘ ehm. Volksstadt] npr/m. ⑯γ. (röm. Feld- herr, 490 v. Chr.) Coriolanus.
Kork ⚙ [nhd.⊙ cork; *span. (v. lt. cortex Rinde)] m⑪(⑦, P oft ㉕)b. cork, ⚙ suber; zum Angeln: float; (Flaschenpfropfen) stopper (or cork) of a bottle; nach dem ~ schmeckend tasting of the cork, corky; den ~ ziehen to draw the cork.

kork=ähnlich (ˡ...) a. ㊱, =artig a. cork- like, corky, ⚙ suberose, suber(e)ous; =asbest m ⊙ min. cork-fossil; =baum m =eiche; =bildner(ei f) m ⚖ carver (carving) in cork; =boje ⚓ f cork(-) buoy; =eiche ⚘ f cork(-tree), cork-oak, ⚙ suber (Quercus suber).
korken¹ (⌣ˡ) [Kork] a. ㊱ (of) cork.
korken² (⌣) v/a. ㊳: Flaschen ⚙ to cork …, to put corks on …
kork=erzeugend (ˡ...) a. ㊱ producing cork, ⚙ phellogenetic; =flossen f/pl. ⚙ corks pl. of a fishing-net; =holz n (Holz west-indischer Bäume) cork-wood; =jacke f als Rettungsmittel: cork jacket; =kohle f charred (or burnt) cork; =leder n cork-leather; =maschine f c.-

fastener, corking-machine; =pappe f c.-board; =platte f c.(-)leaf or -sheet; =presse f für Stöpsel cork-press(er) or -squeezer; ⚗saure a. chm.: ⚙ suberic; =saures Salz suberate; =säure f suberic acid($C_8H_{14}O_4$); =schicht ⚘ f: ⚙periderm; =schneide=maschine f cork-machine; =schneider m (Arbeiter) cork-cutter; =schnitzerei f c.-carving or -sculpture, ⚙ phelloplastics; =schwamm m, zo.: ⚙ alcyonium; =sohle f c.(-)sole; =stoff m, chm. suberin(e); =stöpsel m cork stopper; =teppich m c. carpet, linoleum; =weste f cork waistcoat; =zieher m corkscrew; =zieher(=locke f) m cork- screw curl.

Kormoran (⌣⌣ˡ)[fr.; *It. corvus Rabe u. flt. mor Meer: Seerabe] m ⑪d. orn. cormorant (Phalacro'corax); ~scharbe f ㊷ common cormorant (Ph. Carbo).

Korn [ahd. ⊙ corn: lt. grān-um] n ②b. u. (pl. ~e = ~arten)⑪d. 1. grain (auch coll.); (Samen=)~ (grain of) seed; Körner tragend: ⚙ graniferous; viele Körner sand Pulver ꝛc. many grains of sand, powder, &c.; coll. (Getreide) cereals pl., corn; (Roggen) rye; wel- ches ~ maize; der Acker gibt (oder trägt) das zehnte ~ the field bears tenfold; das ~ steht schön the corn is in fair (or good) condition; fig. fein ~ ohne Spreu no wheat without chaff; das ist so gut wie ~ auf dem Boden it is as safe as a house; s. Flinte. — 2. Münze: (Gehalt an feinem Golde oder Silber) standard, (sterling) value; von richtigem (oder gutem) Schrot und ~ of due weight and value; fig. von altem (oder echtem) Schrot und ~ of the good old sort, of the right stamp. — 3. bes. ⚔ (Richt- oder Visier-)⚔ auf Schußwaffen (fore- or front- sight of a gun; fein (voll) ~ fine (full) sight, e-n et. aufs ~ nehmen to (take) aim at a p., a th.; e-n auf dem ~e h. (scharf beobachten) to keep a sharp eye upon a p., b.s. to have designs upon a p. — 4. (Narbenseite des Leders) grain; von Steinen ein feines, rauhes ~ a fine, rough grain or grit. — 5. ⚙ Uhrmacherei: pivot-hole, stay- hole. — 6. ⚙b, 6 = ~branntwein.

Korn=acker (ˡ...) m ㊷ field of corn; ⚗ähnlich a. ㊱ like a grain, ⚙ grani- form; =ähre f ear of corn; =ast.: ⚙ Spica (Virginis).   [führer.]
Kornak (⌣ˡ) [ind.] m ⑪ = Elefanten-
korn=artig (ˡ...) a. ㊱ like corn, ⚙ frumentaceous; (gekörnt) granulated; =ätzung f typ. process block in half-tones; =aufkäufer ⚙ m fore- staller of corn; =aufzug=maschine ⊙ f corn-elevator or -lift; =ausfuhr ⚙ f exportation of corn or grain; =bau m, agr. growing (or cultivation) of corn; =bauer m c.-grower; =becher=pilz ⚘ m c.-bells (Cy'athus vernico'sus); =blume f allg.: corn-flower, bes. blue-bottle (Centaure'a cy'anus); =blumen=blau a.: ⚙ cyaneous, cyanean; =boden m: a) soil suitable for corn(-growing); b) corn-loft; granary; =börse ⚙ f c.- exchange; =brand ⚘ m blight (or rust) in corn, smut; =branntwein m

corn- (or malt-)spirit(s pl.), whisky.
Körn=büchse ⊙ (ˡ...) f ㊷ Pulverfabrika- tion ꝛc. granulating-box.
Körnchen n ㉔ (dim. v. Korn) little grain, ⚙ granule; fig. ein ~ Wahr- heit a grain of truth; nicht ein ~ not an atom or a trace; ~=bildung f surg.: ⚙ granulation.
Korn=dieb (ˡ...) m ㊷ orn. corn-thief (Sturnus praedato'rius).   [kirsche.]
Kornel=baum ⚘ (⌣ˡˡ⌣) m ㊷ = Kornel=
Korneli-a, ...-e (⌣ˡ⌣) [lt.] npr/f.㊾㊽β. ㊱ ⚙ α. (Vn.) Cornelia.   [Cornelius.]
Kornelius (⌣ˡ(⌣)⌣) [lt.] npr/m. ⑯γ.
Kornel=kirsche ⚘ (⌣ˡˡ...) f ㊷ a) Baum: cor- nel-tree (Cornus ma'scula); b) Frucht: cor- nel-cherry or -berry.   [=kornelkirsche.]
Kornelle(⌣⌣ˡ)[ahd.: *mlt. co'rnulus] f ㊷
tornen (⌣ˡ) [Korn] I v/n. (h.) 1. vom Getreide: to form the grain, to run to seed. — 2. auch: sich ⚙ v/refl. v. Salze, Zucker ꝛc.: to granulate. — II v/a. 3. ⊙ metall. to reduce to grains, to corn, granulate; Schießpulver: to grain, granulate. — 4. ⊙ Leder ⚙ (zu Chagri'n verarbeiten) to grain (or shagreen) … — III ~ n ㉓ 5. = Körnung. IV gekörnt p.p. und a. ㊱: 6. in den Bed. des inf. — 7. = körnig 2.
Körner n ㊺ centre-punch.
körner=fressend (ˡ...) [Körner, pl. v. Korn] a. ㊱ zo.: ⚙ granivorous; =früchte f/pl. ㊷ (Weizen ꝛc.) grain sg.; =lack ⚙ m seed-lac.
Korn=ernte (ˡ...) f ㊷ agr. crop of corn, harvest of grain.
körner=reich (ˡ...) a. ㊱ full of grains, grainy; =tragend ⚘ a. grain-bearing, ⚙ graniferous.
Kornett (⌣ˡ) [fr., *span.] ⑪c. u. ㊵ I ⚔ m ehm. (Fahnenjunker) cornet. — II [fr., it.] ♪ n cornet(-à-pistons); ~bläser m ㊺, auch **Kornettist** (⌣ˡ⌣) m ㊺ cornet (-player), one who plays the cornet.
Korn=fege(=maschine) (ˡ...) f ㊷ agr. winnowing-machine; =feld n corn- field; =fliege f, ent. ⚙ c.-fly (Chlorops); ⚗förmig a. ㊱: ⚙ granular, …ated; =früchte f/pl. cereals pl., grain sg., breadstuffs pl.; =garbe f sheaf of corn; =gesetz n c.-law; =grube f, agr. silo; =handel m corn-trade; =händler m c.-merchant or -chandler; =haus n c.-magazine, granary.
Körn=haus ⊙ (⌣ˡˡ) n ㊷ für Pulver ꝛc. granulating-house or -mill.
körnig (⌣ˡ⌣) a. ㊱ 1. = kernig 1. — 2. (gekörnt) granular, …ate(d), …ous, grainy; fig. körniger (kräftiger) Stil vigorous (or racy, terse) style. — 3. in Zssgn: fein-⚙, grob-⚙ fine-, coarse-grained.
kornisch (⌣ˡ⌣) [Cornwall] a. ㊱ Cornish, of (or relating to) Cornwall.
Korn=jahr (ˡ...) n ㊷ year with a good harvest of corn; =jude m Jewish dealer (or speculator) in grain; =kam- mer f granary; =kappe f foresight- cap or -cover; =kasten m corn-bin; =keller m ⊙ hopper; =keller m, agr. silo; =land n grain-producing (or corn- growing) country.   [Körnchen.]
Körnlein (ˡ⌣) n ㉓ (dim. von Korn) =
korn=los (ˡ...) a. ㊱ cornless, without grain; =mäh=maschine ⊙ f ㊷ corn-

Zeichen (s. S. XVII): F familiär; P Volkssprache; ⁓ Gaunersprache; ⚐ selten; † alt (auch gestorben); * neu (auch geboren); ⁒ unrichtig,

[Kornmakler] — [korybantisch]

harvester; **=makler** m corn-broker or -factor; **=markt** m c.-market.
Körn=maschine ⊕ (⌢...) f ⊕ für Pulver 2c.: granulating-machine.
Korn=maß ⊕ (⌢...) n ⊕ corn-measure; **=messer** ⊕ m (Person) corn-measurer.
Körn=platte ⊕ (⌢...) f ⊕ für Leder: graining-plate.
Korn=rade ♀ (⌢...) f ⊕ corn-campion, cockle (*Agroste'mma githa'go*); ♀**reich** a. ⊕ rich (or abounding) in grain; **=reinigungsmaschine** ⊕ f, agr. corn-cleaner, c.-dressing machine, winnowing-mill; **=schaufel** f c.-shovel; **=schober** m c.-stack; **=schrot=maschine** ⊕ f grain-bruiser; **=schwinge** f, **=sieb** n corn-fan, winnowing-sieve.
Körn=sieb ⊕ (⌢...) n ⊕ für Pulver 2c.: corning-sieve, granulator.
Korn=speicher (⌢...) m ⊕ corn-loft; **=sperre** f prohibition to export grain; **=steuer** f = **=zoll**; **=trocken=apparat** ⊕ m grain-drier.
Körnung (⌢⌣) f ⊕ (zu körnen 2 u. 3:) granulation; (zu 4:) graining
Kornut (⌣⌣́) [lt. Gehörnter] m ⊕ typ. (junger Gehilfe) F printer's devil.
Korn=wage (⌢...) f ⊕ scales pl. for weighing corn, selbsttätige: grain-scale.
Körn=walze ⊕ f ⊕ granulating-roller.
Korn=weih (e m, f) m (⌢...) ⊕ orn. hen-harrier or -harm, ring-tail (*Stri'giceps cya'neus*); **=wiebel** m = **=wurm**; **wucher**(er) m usurious dealing (dealer) in corn; **=wurm** m, ent.: a) brauner od. schwarzer ~ corn-weevil (*Cala'ndra grana'ria*); b) weißer ~ grain-moth (*Ti'nea grane'lla*); **=zange** ⊕ f corn-tongs pl.; **=zinn** ⚔ n grain-tin; **=zoll** m ⊕ corn-tax, duty (levied or put) on grain.
Korollar(ium) ⌢ (⌣⌣́I(⌣)⌢) [It.] n ⊕ phls. u. math. (Folgesatz) corollary.
Korona (⌣⌣́) [lt. Kranz] f ⊕: a) ast. corona; b) (Zuhörerkreis) audience, crowd (or circle) of listeners.
Körper (⌢⌣) [mhd.; *lt. corpor-n] m ⊕ body (auch fig. v. Wein 2c.); fester, flüssiger, luftförmiger ~ solid, liquid, gaseous body or substance.
Körper=anlage (⌢⌣...) f ⊕ mit Bezug auf: a) Gesundheit 2c.: constitution, b) Gemütsbeschaffenheit: temperament; **=bau** m structure of the body, F build; von schönem ~ of handsome figure or shape, finely shaped; vgl. **=wuchs**; **=bemalung** f tattooing; **=beschaffenheit** f condition of the body, physique; **=bildung** f formation of the body; schöne ~, oft: fine (or handsome) appearance.
Körperchen (⌢⌣) n ⊕ (dim. von Körper) small body, particle, ⌢ corpuscle.
Körper=fülle (⌢⌣...) f ⊕ corpulence; **=größe** f size (or height) of the body, stature.
körperhaft (⌢⌣) a. ⊕ = körperlich 1.
Körper=haltung (⌢⌣...) f ⊕ deportment, bearing, carriage; **=inhalt** m, math. solid contents pl.; **=kraft** f physical strength; **=lehre** f = ⌢: a) somatology; b) math. solid geometry.
körperlich (⌢⌣) a. ⊕ 1. endowed with (or formed like) a body; (in der Weise e-s Körpers) bodily (strength, &c.); (stofflich) corporeal, substantial, material,

phys., &c. a.: ⌢ corpuscular; math. Der Inhalt solid contents pl., volume; Der Winkel solid angle. — 2. (leiblich) of the body, corporal (punishment, &c.), physical (defect, &c.); ⌢ somatic (idea, &c.).
Körperlichkeit (⌣⌣⌢) f ⊕ (s. körperlich) corpore(al)ity, substantiality, solidity, materiality, ⌢ somatism.
körper=los (⌢⌣...) a. ⊕ without (a) body, bodiless, incorporeal; **=losigkeit** f ⊕ incorporeal (or immaterial) state; **=maß** n ⊕ cubic measure, measure of capacity; **=messung** f, math. mensuration of solids.
Körperschaft (⌢⌣) f ⊕ corporation, (corporate) body; **2lich** a. ⊕ (u. adv.) corporate(ly), weitS. collective(ly).
Körper=schwäche (⌢⌣...) f ⊕ bodily weakness; **=stellung** f attitude; **=strafe** f corporal punishment; **=teil** m part (or member) of the body; **=übung** f physical exercise, gymnastics; **=verletzung** f bodily injury; **=wärme** f warmth of the body; **=welt** f material world; **=winkel** m, math. solid angle; **=wuchs** m stature, F build.
Korporal ⚔ (⌣⌣́) [nhd.; *fr. (it.) caporal(e)] m ⊕d. in Deutschl. nur noch F = Unteroffizier, in Engl. noch jetzt: corporal; **~schaft** f ⊕ corporalship, squad; **~schafts=führer** m leader of a squad.
Korporation (⌣⌣⌢-tß(⌣)⌢) [It.] f ⊕ = Körperschaft; **~s=recht** n ‡ (Rechtsfähigkeit) corporate right.
korporativ (⌣⌣⌢-f) [It.] a. ⊕ corporate.
Korps (kör; Hom. Chor, kor) [fr.] n ⊕ 1. bes. ⚔ corps, body of troops; fliegendes ~ flying column. — 2. auf dtsch. Universitäten: "Corps" (Students' Club or Association, with distinctive colours and emblems, such as caps and ribbons); vgl. Burschenschaft u. Couleur.
Korps=bruder (kör⌣...) m ⊕, **=bursche** m member of a "Corps"; f. Korps 2; **=geist** m (fr.) esprit de corps, pol. party-spirit; **=manöver** ⚔ n/pl. manœuvres pl. of an army-corps; **=student** m student belonging to a "Corps".
korpulent (⌣⌣⌢) [It.] a. ⊕ (beleibt) corpulent, stout, ⚖ obese; **Korpulenz** f ⊕ corpulency, stoutness, ⚖ obesity.
Korpus (⌢⌣) [It.] inv. I n, F m = Körper; jur. **Korpusdelikti** n ⊕ (Beweisstück), etwa: convicting object, (tangible proof for the) evidence; **Korpus juris**, inv. law-code. — II typ. ~(=schrift) f, etwa: long primer.
Korreferent (⌣⌣⌣⌢) [It. Mitberichtender] m assistant (or junior) reporter or referee. [**=heit** f ⊕ correctness.]
korrekt (⌣⌢) [It.] a. ⊕ (richtig) correct;|
Korrektion (⌣⌢-tß(⌣)⌢) f ⊕ = Besserung.
Korrektiv (⌣⌣⌢f) [It.] n ⊕d. corrective.
Korrektor (⌣⌢) [It.] m ⊕ meist ⊕ typ. printer's (or press-)reader, a.: corrector of (or reader for) the press; **~stelle** f ⊕ readership.
Korrektur (⌣⌣⌢) f ⊕ 1. (Verbesserung) correction. — 2. ⊕ typ. = ~abzug; ~(en) lesen to read (or correct) the proofs, to see a book, &c. through the press.
Korrektur=abzug (⌣⌣⌢...) m ⊕, **=bogen** m proof(-sheet); in zweiter Korrektur: re-

vise; **=lesen** n reading of proof-sheets, weitS. reading for the press; **=zeichen** n (press-)reader's mark; correction.
Korrelat (⌣⌣⌢) [It.] n ⊕c. additional report or reference; (Wechselbegriff) correlate; **~ion** (⌣⌣⌢-tß(⌣)⌢) f ⊕ correlation; **2iv** (⌣⌣-⌢f) ⊕ (in Wechselbeziehung zu-ea. stehend) correlative.
Korrespondent (⌣⌣⌣⌢) [fr.] m ⊕ (Briefschreiber) correspondent, ⊕ business-friend or -connexion; **~reeder** ⚓ m ⊕ ship's husband.
Korrespondenz (⌣⌣⌣⌢) f ⊕ (Briefwechsel, Briefschaften) correspondence; s-e ~ besorgen to write one's letters, to attend to one's correspondence, auch: to dispatch the mail; f. führen 8; **~gegenstand** m ⊕ subject of (a) correspondence; **~karte** f chm. = Postkarte.
korrespondieren (⌣⌣⌣⌢) [neu-lt.] v/n. (h.) ⊕ 1. mit e-m ⊕ (Briefe wechseln) to correspond (or to be in correspondence) with a p.; mit-ea. ⊕ to exchange letters, to write to each other; ⊕des Mitglied corresponding member. — 2. mit et. ⊕ (übereinstimmen) to correspond to (or to agree with) a th.
Korridor (⌢⌣) [fr., it.] m ⊕d. (Zwischengang) corridor, passage, hall.
Korrigenda (⌣⌣⌢) [It.] pl. inv. misprints, printer's mistakes, (it.) errata pl.
korrigieren (⌣⌣⌢) [It.] I v/a. ⊕ (bessern) to correct, (a)mend; ⊕ typ. to read (or look over) the proofs, zum zweiten Male: to revise. — II ~ n ⊕ (s. I) correction; ⊕ typ. revision, F revise.
Korroborri (⌣⌣⌣⌢) [ngl.] f ⊕ (Fest- u. Kriegstanz der Australneger) corroboree.
korrosiv (⌣⌣⌢f) [It.] a. ⊕ (ätzend) corrosive.
korrumpier=en (⌣⌣⌣⌢) [It.] v/a. ⊕ (verderben) to corrupt; f/te Stellen corrupt (or spurious) passages pl.; (bestechen) to bribe. [wicked, bad.]
korrupt (⌣⌢) a. ⊕ corrupt(ed), weitS.|
Korruption (⌣⌣⌢-tß(⌣)⌢) f ⊕ corruption; (Bestechung) bribery.
Korsak (⌢⌣) m ⊕ zo. (sibirischer Steppenfuchs) corsac, adive (*Vulpes corsac*).
Korsar (⌣⌢) [It., span.] m ⊕ 1. ⚓ (See-räuber) corsair, buccaneer, pirate. — 2. ichth. corsair (*Sebasti'chthys rosa'ceus*).
Korsaren=schiff (⌣⌣⌢...) n ⊕ pirate vessel.
Korse (⌢⌣) m ⊕, **Korsin** f ⊕ Corsican.
Korsett (⌣⌢) [nhd. 18. sae.; *fr. Leibchen] n ⊕b. (lederlinnen) corset(s pl.); leichteres: stay, mehr gbr.: (pair of) stays pl.; **~macher**(in f) m ⊕ corset-maker; **~stange** f (corset-)busk.
Korsika ♀ (⌣⌣) [gr.] npr/n. ⊕α. Corsica; **~ner**(in f ⊕) m ⊕, **korf**(ikan)isch (⌣(⌣⌣́)⌢) a. ⊕ Corsican.
Korso (⌢-) [it.] m ⊕ (a. inv.) carriage-drive, course for carriages, Lo. Rotten Row; **~fahrt** f ⊕ driving (-sport).
Korund ⌢ (-⌢) [indisch] m ⊕c. min. (Demantspat) corundum; **~feile** ⊕ f ⊕ corundum-file; **~spitze** f am Drillbohrer der Zahn-ärzte: cor.-point.
Korvette ⚓ (⌣v⌢) [fr.; *It.] f ⊕ corvette; **~n=kapitän** m ⊕ ehm. captain of a corv.; jetzt Titel: commander.
Korybant (⌣⌣⌢) [grch.] m ⊕ grch. Alt. (Priester der Cybele) corybant; **2isch** a. ⊕ corybantic (a. fig. = rasend).

[Koryphäe] — 614 — [Kotau]

Koryphäe (⌣⌣ˊ⌣) [grch.] *m* ㊽ 1. Alt.: leader of the chorus. — 2. jetzt: master-mind, intellectual leader.

Korzyra ♀ (⌣ˊ⌣) *npr/n.* ⑨ *a.* grch. Alt.: (jetzt Korfu) Corcyra.

Kos ♀ (ˊ) *npr/n. inv.* (türk. Insel) C(e)os.

Kosak (⌣ˊ) [russ. *käsa'k*] *m* ㊽ Cossack; Ҷisch (⌣⌣ˊ) *a.* ㊻ Cossack, of Cossacks.

Koschenille (⌣⌣ˊⅰ⌣) [span.] *f* ㊽ und ⊕ (scharlachrote Farbe) cochineal. **Koschenille(n)=baum** ♀ (Ҷ...) *m* ㊷, **=fackel-distel** *f* nopal, Indian (or cochineal) fig (*Opu'ntia coccinilli'fera*); **=farb(e)=stoff** *m*, **=rot** *n* cochineal (dye), vermilion; **=schild=laus** *f*, ent. cochineal (insect) (*Coccus cacti*).

koscher (ˊ⌣) [jüd.=chald.] *a.* ㊻ (D9) bei den Juden: kosher, pure, clean; ⸺n *v/a.* ⑨ *a.* to make kosher or clean.

Kose=form (ˊ⌣˘ˊ) *f* ㊷ = **=wort**

Ko-sekante ⸺ (ˊ⌣⌣˘) [neu=lt.] *f* ㊽ math. (Sekante des Komplements eines Winkels) cosecant (*abbr.* cosec.) of an angle.

kosen (ˊ⌣) [ahd.] I *v/n.* (h.) u. *v/a.* ⑨ (zärtliche Liebe zeigen) to caress, fondle, to whisper to one's sweetheart, F to talk soft nonsense, to spoon. — II ~ *n* ㉓ = Gekose.

Kose=name(n) (ˊ⌣...) *m* ㊷ pet name; **=wort** *n* term of endearment.

kosig (ˊ⌣) *a.* ㊻ caressing, (traulich) cosy.

Ko-sinus ⸺ (ˊ⌣⌣) [neu=lt.] *m*, *inv. math.* (Sinus des Komplements e-s Winkels) cosine (*abbr.* cos.) of an angle.

Kosmetik (⌣ˊ⌣) [grch.] *f* ㊽ cosmetics. **kosmetisch** (⌣ˊ⌣) [grch. *kosmei'n* schmücken] *a.* ㊻ cosme'tic; Ҷes Mittel cosme'tic, mehr gebr.: cosmetique.

kosmisch ⸺ (ˊ⌣) [grch. *kosmos* Weltall] *a.* ㊻ (das Weltall betr.) cosmic; Ҷer Staub cosmic dust, meteor-dust.

Kosmogonie (ˊ⌣⌣ˊ) [grch.] *f* ㊽ (Weltentstehung) cosmogony. [gonic(al).) **kosmogonisch** ⸺ (ˊ⌣⌣ˊ⌣) *a.* ㊻ cosmo-ʃ **Kosmograph** ⸺ (ˊ⌣⌣ˊ) *m* ㊷ (Weltbeschreiber) cosmographer; **~ie** (ˊ⌣⌣ˊⅰ) *f* ㊽ (Weltbeschreibung) cosmography; Ҷisch (ˊ⌣⌣ˊ⌣) *a.* ㊻ (weltbeschreibend) cosmographical.

Kosmopolit ⸺ (ˊ⌣⌣⌣ⁿ) *m* ㊷ (Weltbürger) cosmopolite, ...tan; Ҷisch *a.* ㊻ cosmopolitan; **~is'mus** *m* ㊧ cosmopolitism.

Koso ♀ (ˊ⌣) [abess.] *m* ㊷, **~strauch** *m* ㊷ cusso, kousso (*Hage'nia abyssi'nica* ob. *Bray'ea anthelmi'ntica*).

Kossat (⌣ˊ), **Kossäte** (⌣ˊ⌣) [ndd. = Kotsasse] *m* ㊷, ㊹ small farmer, peasant proprietor, cottager, cotter, crofter.

Kost (ˊ) [mhd.] *f* ㊽ food; (Lebensmittel) victuals *pl.*; ein Liebhaber guter ~ sein to be fond of good eating and drinking; magere (ob. kärgliche) ~ meagre (or slender) fare, poor living, *med.* low diet; auf knappe ~ setzen to put on short commons; kräftige (ob. reichliche) ~ rich (or good, high) living; freie ~ Wohnung free board and residence (or lodging); in die ~ geben to put out to board; sich in die ~ geben to board out, to go into a boarding-house; e-m ~ und Logis geben to board and lodge a p.; in ~ nehmen to take as a boarder.

kostbar (ˊ⌣) *a.* ㊻ (wertvoll) precious, valuable, weitS. (vortrefflich) excellent,

(herrlich) splendid; das ist doch wirklich ⸺ (ergötzlich)! that's very amusing or funny! — **Kostbarkeit** (ˊ⌣⌣) *f* ㊽ 1. (o. *pl.*) preciousness, valuableness. — 2. (mit *pl.*) (Wertvolles) precious thing or object, *pl.* oft: valuables.

kosten¹ (ˊ⌣) [ahd.: lt. *gusta're*] I *v/n.* (h.) ⑨ 1. to taste of a dish, &c., F to get a taster of a th., schlürfend: to sip. — 2. von Genüssen im allg.: to get a taste of; to try, experience. — II ~ *n* ㉓ 3. tasting, ⸺ gustation, weitS. trial.

Kosten² (ˊ⌣) [ahd.: costs; *mlt.] pl. inv.* cost(s *pl.*), expense(s *pl.*), charges *pl.*; f. Abzug 3); große, schwere ~ heavy expenses *pl.*; wie hoch belaufen sich die ~? what do the expenses amount (or F run) to?; die Hälfte der ~ wurde von der Stadt bestritten one half of the cost was borne by the town; seine ~ herausschlagen to pay (or cover) one's expenses; e-m große ~ m. to put a p. to (F to run a p. into) great expense; er scheut keine ~ he spares no expense; die ~ tragen to bear the expense; auf meine ~ at my expense; *fig.* ich habe es auf meine ~ erfahren I know it to my cost; auf ~ f-s Lebens at the cost of his life; sich in ~ stürzen to go to (or incur) great expense; *jur.* in alle (ob. zu den) ~ verurteilt condemned to pay all costs; mit großen ~ at great expense.

kosten³ (ˊ⌣) [mhd.; *Kosten²] v/n.* (h.) ⑨ to cost; es koste, was es wolle! a. koste es, was es koste! cost what it may, whatever it may cost!; das kostet ihn (ob. ihm) viel it costs him a great deal, it comes expensive to him; was kostet der Ring? im Laden: what is the price of (F what is, how much is) ...?; zu e-m Bekannten nach dem Kauf: how much (or what) did you pay for ...?; er hat es sich viel Geld 2 lassen he spent a great deal of money on (or over) it; *fig.* das Buch hat mich (ob. mir) viel Schweiß gekostet I have spent much labour on ...; es wird dich (ob. dir) ja den Kopf nicht 2 it won't cost your life; der Marsch kostete uns zwei Tage ... took us two days.

Kosten²=ansatz (ˊ⌣...) *m* ㊷ bsd. der Sportein: taxing of costs; **=anschlag** *m* estimate; **=aufwand** *m* expenditure; **=ersatz** *m*, **=erstattung** *f* compensation for out-of-pocket expenses or outlay incurred, indemnification; **=ersparnis** *f* saving of expense; der ~ halber (in order) to save expense, for economy's sake; ⸺**fällig** *a.* ㊻ obliged (or condemned) to pay the costs; ⸺**frei** *a.* free of cost, ㊼ clear of (all) charges; e-n 2 halten to pay for a p., to treat a p.; ⸺**los** *a.* u. *adv.* free (of cost), without any expense, for nothing; **=preis** ㊼ *m* cost-price, prime cost; unter dem ~preise below cost-price, at a (dead) loss; **=punkt** *m* (matter of) expense(s *pl.*); **=rechnung** *f* bill of costs (defrayed); **=vorschuß** *m* advance on the costs. [taster.)

Koster (ˊ⌣) [kosten¹] *m* ㊷ tea-, wine-, &c.ʃ **Kost=frau** (ˊ...) *f* ㊷ woman who keeps (or proprietress of) a boarding-house;

⸺**frei** *a.* having free board; e-n 2 halten to board a p. for nothing, to keep a p. in board; **=gänger(in** *f*) *m* boarder; =gänger h. to take in boarders, to keep a boarding-house; **=geber** *m* keeper of a boarding-house, vgl. Gastwirt; **=geld** *n*: a) (cost of) board, F keep, *jur.* alimony; b) *v.* Dienstboten: allowance (or sum allowed) for board; ~ erhalten to receive (or to be on) board-wages; c) ㊼ = Prolongatio'ns=gebühr; **=geschäft** *n* contango-business; **=halter(in** *f*) *m* keeper of a boarding-house; **=häppchen** F *n* ober **=happen** *m* daintylittle morsel or bit, *a.*(fr.) bonne-bouche; **=haus** *n* boarding-house; **=kind** *n* (Ziehkind) foster-child.

köstlich (ˊ⌣) [kosten¹] *a.* ㊻ 1. (wohlschmeckend) delicious, savoury, delicate, dainty. — 2. (wertvoll) precious, valuable. — 3. (reizend) charming, delightful. **Köstlichkeit** (ˊ⌣⌣) *f* ㊽ (f. köstlich) 1. (o. *pl.*) deliciousness, savouriness, daintiness; preciousness. — 2. (mit *pl.*) **=en** *pl.* delicacies *pl.*; valuables *pl.*

Kost=nehmer ㊼ (ˊ...) *m* ㊷ Börse: p. who takes up stock; **=schule** *f* boarding-school; **=schüler(in** *f*) *m* boarder (in a school), boy (*f* girl) placed at a boarding-school.

Kost=spielig (ˊ⌣ˊ⌣) [*provc.* Spiel = Menge] *a.* ㊻ expensive, costly, dear, durch Aufwand: sumptuous; **~keit** *f* ㊽ expensiveness, costliness, dearness, sumptuousness.

Kostüm (⌣ˊ) [fr.] *n* ⑨d. (Tracht) costume, dress; **~=ball** *m* ㊷ fancy-dress ball. **kostümieren** (⌣⌣ˊ⌣) [fr.] *v/a.* (u. sich 2 *v/refl.*) ⑨ to dress (o.s.) up; sich 2, auch: to put on a fancy-dress. **Kostüm=kunde** (⌣ˊ...) *f* ㊽ (historical) study of costumes.

Kost=verächter(in *f*) *m* (ˊ...) ㊷ dainty (or fastidious) p.; **=wurz** ♀ *f*: a) costus (*Costus ara'bica*) b) putchock (*Auckla'ndia costus*); **=wurzel** *f* costus-root.

Kot¹ (ˊ) [ahd. übles] *m* ⑨c. (o. *pl.*) 1. (schmutzige Masse) mud, mire, muck, (Dreck) dirt, filth; (morastiger Grund) marshy soil, bog; flüssiger ~, oft: F slush; mit ~ bespritzen to splash (or bespatter) with mud; durch den ~ ziehen to bedraggle; im ~e stecken bleiben to stick in the mud; sich im ~e wälzen to wallow in the mire; *physiol.* von ~ lebend: ⸺ coprophagous. — 2. (entleerter Darminhalt) excrements *pl.*, *med.* discharge of the bowels, ⸺ fæces *pl.*; *v.* Tieren oft: droppings, F dirt(s *pl.*), *hunt.* ehm.: fumet(s *pl.*), fiants *pl.*; (Dünger) dung.

Kot² (ˊ) [ndd. = cot(e)] *n* ⑨c. 1. humble cot(tage) (= Kate). — 2. ㊼ Saline: (Anteil an einem Salzwert) salt-cote.

Kot¹**=abfuhr** (ˊ...) *f* ㊷ removal of dung, emptying of sewers.

Ko-tangente ⸺ (ˊ⌣⌣⌣) [lt.] *f* ㊽ math. (Tangente des Komplements eines Winkels) cotangent (*abbr.* cot.) ⸺ an angle.

kot¹**=artig** (ˊ...) *a.* ㊻ muddy, ⸺ stercoraceous, fæcal(oid).

Kotau (⌣ˊ) [chin.] *m* ㊷ (Berühren des Bodens mit der Stirn als chin. Ehrenbezeigung) kotow; ~ machen to kotow.

Kot[1]=blech (″…) *n* [62] am Wagen, Fahrrad ꝛc. mud-guard; **=brechen** *n*, *path.*: ⚗ stercoraceous vomiting; **=deckel** *m* = =blech.

Kote *provc.* (′⏑) *f* [48] = Kate.

Köte (′⏑) [ndd.] *f* [48] *vet.* (Fessel[gelenk]) pastern(-joint) of a horse.

Kötel (′⏑) [Kot[1] *dim.*] *m* [22] dung (or dirts *pl.*) of sheep, goats, mice.

Kotelett (⏓⏑′) [fr. *côtelette f* Rippchen] *n* [11]c., **~e** *f* [48] **1.** veal, lamb cutlet; pork, mutton chop. — **2. ~en** *pl.* (Art Backenbart) Piccadilly weepers *pl.*

Köten=gelenk (″⏑…) *vet.* *n* [62] = Köte; **=haar** *n* fetlock.

Köter (′⏑) [ndd.] *m* [22] **1.** large watch-dog. — **2.** *contp.* cur (a. *fig.*).

Koterie (′⏑″) [fr. Bund] *f* [48] clique.

Kot[1]=fliege (″…) *f* [62] *ent.* dung-fly (*Scato'phaga*); ≗**fressend** *a. zo.*: ⚗ coprophagous; **=grube** *f* open sewer.

Kothurn (⏑′) [lt., *grch.] *m* [11]d. *thea.* buskin, ⚗ cothurnus; *fig.* auf hohem ~ in a tragic (or pompous) style; ≗**=artig**, ≗**haft** *a.* [66] pompous, lofty.

kotig (′⏑) *a.* [66] (s. Kot[1]) muddy; mucky; dirty, filthy; marshy, boggy; F slushy; bsd. *med.*: ⚗ stercoraceous, fæcaloid.

Kotillon (′⏑ljõ) [fr.] *m* [51] cotillion 𝄞.

Kot[1]=klümpchen (″…) *n* [62] s. Klunker 3; **=[2]knecht** ⚙ *m* Saline: salt-boiler; **=[1]lache** *f* pool of mud, dirty puddle; **=leder** *n* an Wagen: mud-protector; vgl. =blech.

Kötner (′⏑) [ndd.; *Kot[2](e)] *m* [22] = Kossat.

Kot[2]=saß (″…) *m* [62], **=sasse** *m* = Kossat.

Kotschinchina=huhn (′⏑″⏑…) *n* [62] *orn.* Cochin-China fowl, auch: cochin.

Kot[1]=schützer (″…) *m* [62] = =blech; **=stein** *m* = Koprolith.

kottisch ♁ (′⏑) *a.* [66]: ~e Alpen (fr. Grenzgebirge) Cottian Alps *pl.*

Kotyledone(n *pl.*) ⚘ (⏑⏑⏑′⏑) [grch.] *f* [48] (Samenlappen) cotyledon(s *pl.*).

kotz P (′) [Gott's] *int.* etwa: by Jove!

Kotze (′⏑) [ahd.] *f* [48] (wollene Decke) woollen cloth, blanket.

kotzen P (′⏑) [nhd.] *v/n.* (h.) [90] to vomit, to bring up one's food.

Kötzer ⚙ (′⏑) *m* [22] (Garnwinde) cop.

Kozytus (-′⏑) [lt.; *grch.] *npr/m.* [16]γ (Fluß der Unterwelt) Cocytus.

kr öst. *abbr.* = Kreuzer.

Krabbe (′⏑) [ndd.: crab; vgl. Krebs] *f* [48] **1.** *zo.* (kl. Taschenkrebs) (common) crab (*Ca'rcinus maenas*). — **2.** F (kleine) ~ little dot; *contp.* brat, urchin; die süße ~! (Kleine) the sweet little thing or pet!

Krabbelei (′⏑″) *f* [46] crawling, sprawling.

krabbeln (′⏑) [ndd.] [92]a. **I** *v/n.* (h. u. sn) **1.** (h.) (zappeln) to wriggle, jerk. — **2.** (sn) u. **sich** ≗ *v/refl.* (vorankriechen) to crawl along. — **II** *v/a.*, *v/n.* (h.) u. *v/imp.* (jucken, prickeln) **3.** to cause (or have) a crawling (or creeping) sensation; beim Rheumatismus ꝛc.: to have pins and needles; es krabbelt mir im Halse I feel a slight creeping (or tickling) in the throat. — **III ~** *n* [23] **4.** wriggling, &c. (s. I). — **5.** crawling (or creeping) sensation, F crawl, creeps *pl.*

krabben=artig (″⏑…) *a.* [66] *zo.* crab-like, ⚗ cancriform, carcinoid; **=beutler** *m* [62] *zo.* crab-dog (*Dide'lphys cancri'vora*); **=fang** *m* crab-catching; **=fänger** *m* (Gerät und Person) crab-catcher; ≗**förmig** *a.* = ≗artig; **=spinne** *f*, *zo.* crab-spider (*Thomi'sus*); **=taucher** *m*, *orn.* alle (*Me'rgulus Alle*).

krach[1] (′ch) [lautm.: crack] *int.* bang!, crash!, smash!, crack!

Krach[2] (′ch) [ahd.: crack] *m* [11]c. **1.** crash; ~ e-s Gewehrs ꝛc. (loud) report …; mit Ach und ~ only just (in time), vgl. ach II. — **2.** ● commercial crisis, (general) crash or breakdown or F smash; **~=zeit** ● *f*, etwa: time of panic, period of general collapse.

krachen (′ch⏑) [ahd.: crack] **I** *v/n.* (h. u. sn) [88] **1.** (h.) to crash, crack, fulminate, stärker: to burst (with a loud explosion), vom Donner: to roar, vom Feuer: to crackle. — **2.** (sn) (mit Geräusch brechen, niederstürzen) die Eiche krachte entzwei … fell (or split) with a thundering noise. — **3.** ● to crash, to collapse. — **II ~** *n* [23] **4.** crash(ing), &c. (s. 1); ~ der Gewehre rattle of musketry; ~ des Donners peals *pl.* (or roar) of thunder.

krächzen (′⏑) [nhd.: croak; *krachen] *v/n.* (h.) [90] **1.** to caw; to croak (a. *fig.* v. Personen); er singt nicht, er krächzt nur … he is only screaming. — **2.** (ächzen, stöhnen) to groan, to moan, F to croak.

krack (′) *int.* = krach[1].

Kracke P (′⏑) [ndl., fr.] *f* [48] (schlechtes Pferd) wretched jade, F old crock.

Kraft[1] (′) [ahd.: craft List] *f* [10] **1.** strength, F backbone, (Macht) power; heilende ~ healing power, virtue; (Wirksamkeit) efficacy; (Rüstigkeit) vigour, F stamina; Kräfte der Natur ꝛc.: forces *pl.* of nature, &c.; *mech.* bewegende, treibende ~ moving, propelling force, auch: prime motor; ⚔ zerstreute Kräfte scattered forces *pl.*; geistige ~ (Fähigkeit) ability; (Schwung) (poetic) fire. — **2.** s. anstrengen 1 u. aufbieten 3; aus allen Kräften with all one's might; in ~ allein des Ringes (*L.*) solely by means (or by the sole power) of the ring; nach besten Kräften to the best of one's ability; das geht über meine Kräfte that is beyond me or my strength; wieder zu Kräften kommen to regain (or recover) one's strength; was (nur) in meinen Kräften steht my utmost. — **3.** (Gültigkeit) von Gesetzen ꝛc.: aus ~ des // = kraft[2], s. ds.; in ~ sein to be in (full) force; in ~ setzen to put into operation; in ~ treten to come into force, to take effect; außer ~ setzen to make (or declare) invalid, to invalidate.

kraft[2] (′) [mhd., *dat. sg.* v. Kraft[1]] *prp.* (vermöge, mittels): ≗ meines Amtes by virtue of my office; ≗ s-r Autorität on the strength of his authority.

Kraft=anstrengung (″…) *f* [62] exertion (of power); **=aufwand** *m* expenditure of power or energy or force, effort; **=ausdruck** *m* vigorous (or pithy, racy) expression; **=äußerung** *f* demonstration (or manifestation) of force; **=bedarf** ⚙ *m* e-r Maschine: requisite power; **=brühe** *f* Kochk.: strong gravy or broth; **=einheit** *f*, *mech.*, *phys.* unit of force, ⚗ dynamical unit; vgl. Dyne.

Kräfte=messer (″⏑…) *m* [62] = Kraftmesser; **=paar** ⚙ *n*, *mech.* couple (of forces).

kraft=erfüllt (″…) *a.* [66] full of strength, vigorous; **=fuhrwerk** *n* [62] motor, self-propelled carriage; vgl. =wagen; **=fülle** *f* fulness (or plenitude) of power, full vigour; **=gefühl** *n* feeling of strength; **=genie** *n* mighty (or powerful) genius; **=gesang** *m* impressive song.

kräftig (′⏑) [ahd.] *a.* [66] **1.** (voll Kraft) strong, vigorous, (handfest) robust; (tat=)≗ energetic; (mächtig) powerful; (gesund) healthy; (wirksam) efficacious, effective; (nahrhaft) nourishing; ≗er Verweis severe reprimand; ≗en Widerstand leisten to offer stout resistance. — **2.** (rechts=)≗ valid, in force.

kräftigen (′⏑⏑) [88] **I** *v/a.* to strengthen, to invigorate; (stählen) to harden, steel, fortify; (erquicken) to refresh, to restore; neu ≗ (beleben) to put new life into, to set up afresh, to revive. — **II sich** ≗ *v/refl.* to gain strength. — **III ~** *n* [23] = Kräftigung.

Kräftigkeit (′⏑-) *f* [66] (s. kräftig) **1.** vigour, robustness; energy; efficaciousness. — **2.** validity; (full) force.

Kräftigung (′⏑⏑) *f* [46] strengthening, invigoration; restoration.

Kraft=lehre (″…) *f* [62]: ⚗ dynamics; **=leistung** *f*: a) feat of strength, athletic feat; b) ⚙ v. Maschinen: effective work; **=linien=streuung** ⚙ *f* der Dynamomaschinen: leakage; ≗**los** *a.* [66] without strength or vigour; (schwach) feeble, weak, impotent, (entkräftet) enfeebled, *med.*: ⚗ atonic; (matt) languishing, languid; (ungültig) invalid, (null and) void; für ≗ erklären to invalidate, to annu'l; **=los=erklärung** *f* jur. (Mortifikation) invalidation, annu'lment; **=losigkeit** *f* lack of strength or vigour; feebleness, impotence; *med.* debility, ⚗ atony; **=maschine** ⚙ *f*, etwa: motor, receiver; **=mehl** *n* (Stärke[mehl]) amylum, weitS. starch; **=mensch** *m* powerful man, person endowed with great strength, a. athlete; **=messer** *m*: ⚗ dynamometer; **=mittel** *n* powerful remedy, efficacious means; **=quelle** *f*, *mech.* source of power; **=sammler** ⚙ *m* accumulator; **=spender** *m*, *mech.* power-producer; **=sprache** *f* vigorous (or energetic, pithy) language; **=stuhl** ⚙ *m* Weberei: power-loom; **=suppe** *f* = =brühe; **=übertragung** *f* transmission of power or force(s); **= und Licht=station** *f*, *elect.* power-and-light station, vgl. =werk; ≗**voll** *a.* full of strength, vigorous, (tatkräftig) energetic; **=wagen** *m* (Automobil, bsd. für Lasten) motor-car, motor, automobile; **=werk** *n*, *elect.* power-station; **=wirkung** *f*, *mech.*: ⚗ dynamical effect; **=wort** *n* strong word, forcible term; vgl. =ausdruck; **=zentrale** *f*, *elect.* (central) power-station.

Krägelchen (′⏑⏑) *n* [23] (*dim.* v. Kragen) small collar; für Damen, aus Spitzen, Pelz ꝛc.: collaret, collarette.

Kragen (′⏑) [ahd.] *m* [23] ([20]) **1.** am Rocke ꝛc.: collar, s. fassen 1, gehen 10; ~ am Hemde shirt-collar; leinener ~ zum Anknöpfen linen (a. white) collar; *fig.* mit Kopf und ~ neck and crop. — **2.** zum Umhängen für Damen ꝛc.: cape (a. Halsstück des Mantels); (Pelz=)~ tippet, fur cape.

⚗ scientific; ⚘ botanical; ♁ geography; ⚙ machinery; ⚒ mining; ⚔ military; ⚓ marine; ● commercial; ✉ postal; 🚂 railway.

[Kragenbolzen] — 616 — [krank]

Kragen=bolzen ⊕ (⏑⏑...) m Schmiede: collar-bolt; =**eidechse** f frill-lizard (Chlamydosau'rus); =**mantel** ⚹ mantle with cape; =**schoner** m collar-protector; =**zelle** f, zo. collar-cell.
Krag=stein ⊕ (⏑́⏑) [mhd.; *Kragen] m ⓰ arch. console, corbel-head; auf ~en ruhend corbelled.
Krähe (⏑́⏑) [ahd.: crow] f ⓲ orn. crow (Corvus); graue~ hooded crow (C. ornix); (Saat=)⚹ rook (C. frugi'legus); Sprichw. eine ~ hackt der andern die Augen nicht aus there's honour among thieves, F rogues don't split on each other.
krähen (⏑́⏑) [ahd.: crow] I v/n. (h.), bisw. v/a. u. sich ⚹ v/refl. ⊛ mit Angabe der Wirkung: 1. vom Hahne: to crow; fig. f. Hahn 4; e-n aus dem Schlafe ⚹ to waken (or rouse) a p. by crowing; sich heiser ⚹ to crow o.s. hoarse; fig. v. Pers.: zu früh ⚹ to crow (or boast) too soon. — 2. F fig. (gellend schreien) to scream forth, to screech. — II ~ n ⓳ 3. crowing.
krähen=artig (⏑́⏑...) [*Krähe] a. ⊛ like a crow, ⚹ corvine; =**auge** n ⓲: a) crow's eye; b) ♀ poison- (or vomic) nut, mehr gbr.: (lt.) nux vo'mica; c) path. = Elster= auge; =**beere** ♀ f crakeberry, crowberry (E'mpetrum); =**feder** f feather (or quill) of a crow; ⚹**förmig** a. orn.: ⚹ corviform; =**fuß** m crow's-foot; fig. =**füße** pl.: a) (unförmliche Buchstaben) (illegible or bad) scrawl; b) (Runzeln in den Augenwinkeln) F crow's-feet pl.; =**horst** m rookery; =**hütte** f, hunt. hut from which rooks (and other birds) may be shot; =**indianer** m/pl. Crows pl.; =**nest** n: a) rookery, crow's nest; b) ↓ (Mastkorb) crow's-, bird's-nest. [rake.]
Krahl (⏑́; Hom. Kral) m ⓳c. (Feuerschaufel)/
Krähwinkel (⏑́⏑⏑) [erdichtete Kleinstadt in Kotzebues Lustspiel „Die deutschen Kleinstädter"] npr/n. ⓳α. etwa: Gotham; ~**ei** (⏑⏑́⏑⏑) f ⊛ parochial politics;
Krähwinkler(in f ⓲) m ⓳ wise (wo)man of Gotham, Gothamist, ...ite, stupid p. from a (small) countrytown, narrow-minded provincial.
Krain ♀ (⏑́) npr/n. ⓳α. (slaw.) (öft. Kronland) Carniola; ~**er(in** f ⓲) m ⓳ Carniolan, inhabitant of Carniola.
Krakau ♀ (⏑́⏑) [Krakus oder Krok, myth. poln. Fürst] npr/n. ⓳α. (galizische Stadt) Cracow; ~**er(in** f ⓲) m ⓳, **=isch** a. ⓳ Cracovian. [Kraken.]
Krake (⏑́⏑) [norw.] m ⓯ (See=ungeheuer)/
Krakeel F (⏑⏑́) [ndl. P; *fr. querelle] m ⓳d. squabble, quarrel, F row; ⚹**en** (⏑⏑́⏑) v/n. (h.) ⓳ (sich zanken) to squabble, to quarrel, stärker: to brawl, F to (have a) row; (schimpfen) to use abusive language; ~**er(in** f ⓲) m ⓳ squabbler, quarrelsome (or F litigating) person, stärker: brawler, rowdy; ⚹**erisch** F (⏑⏑́⏑), a. ⚹**ig** (⏑⏑́⏑) a. ⓳ squabblesome, quarrelsome, a.: F litigating, fond of a row.
Krakel=beine F (⏑́⏑...) n/pl. ⓳ ob. =**füße** m/pl. (schlechte Schrift) scrawl.
krakeln (⏑́⏑) = kritzeln.
Kraken (⏑́⏑) = Krake.
Krakowiak (⏑⏑́⏑⏑) m ⓳ = Cracovienne.
Kral (⏑́; Hom. Krahl) [port. curral Schafhürde] m u. n ⓳c. (Hottentottendorf) kraal.

Kralle (⏑́⏑) [nhd.] f ⓳ 1. (gekrümmter Nagel an der Klaue e-s Raubtieres) (sharp) claw, ⚹ ungula. — 2. (Klaue mit solchen Nägeln) claw; bsd. von Vögeln: pounce, talon; weitS. (auch von der Hand) clutch.
krallen (⏑́⏑) [nhd.] ⓳ I v/n. (h.) to show (or use) one's claws, to scratch with one's claws or talons. — II v/a. to (seize with a) claw; weitS. (packen) to clutch (hold of).
krallen=artig (⏑́⏑...) a. ⓳, ⚹**förmig** a. claw-shaped, ⚹ unguiform, ungual; =**hieb** m ⓲ stroke with a claw; =**zahl** f number of claws.
krallicht (⏑́⏑) a. ⓳ like a claw.
krallig (⏑́⏑) a. ⓳ (mit Krallen versehen) provided with claws or talons, clawed; oft in Zssgn, z.B.: lang=⚹ with long claws.
Kram (⏑́) [mhd.] m ⓳c. 1. ♀ retail (trade), keeping a shop. — 2. (Laden) small (or retail) shop; (Bude) booth, stall, stand, F pitch; einen ~ anfangen to open (or set up) a (small) shop. — 3. (Ware) (retail)goods, commodities, small articles or wares pl.; (Schnittwaren) haberdashery; (Spezerei= waren) grocery; (Metallsachen) ironmongery, hardware; (allerlei Zeug) stuff, lumber, odds and ends pl. (of things); elender ~ rubbish, lumber, trash. — 4. fig. da liegt der ~! F there goes the lot or the whole concern!; das paßt gerade in meinen ~, mir in den ~ it serves my purpose admirably, F that suits me to a T; das taugt nicht in meinen ~ that's not what I want, F that won't do for me; seinen ganzen ~ bei sich tragen to carry one's goods and chattels about or on one's back; seinen ~ (seine Fähigkeiten) preisen, etwa: to advertise o.s., to puff one's trade; den ganzen ~ verderben to spoil the whole business.
Krambambuli F (⏑⏑́⏑⏑) [Kram(me)t u. slaw. buli Wacholderschnaps] m ⓳ ob. inv. Art Likör: kind of liqueur, pick-me-up, bursch. (Getränk allg.) drink, tipple.
Kram=bude ♀ (⏑́...) f ⓲ f. Bude.
kramen (⏑́⏑) v/n. (h.) ⓳ 1. in (ob. unter) et. ⚹ (durchsuchen) to rummage in s.th.; man hat immer et. zu ⚹ there is always s.th. to (be) put in order. — 2. ♀ to carry on a small business or a (retail)shop. — 3. mit et. ⚹ (prunken) to put a th. for show.
Kramer, **Krämer** (⏑́⏑) [mhd.; *Kram] m ⓳, ~**in** f ⓲ (small) shopkeeper, general dealer, retail trader, retailer, auch: (small) tradesman.
Kramerei (⏑⏑́) [kramen] f ⓲ rummaging, putting things in order, clearing up.
Krämerei (⏑⏑́) [Krämer] f ⓲ shopkeeping, retail trading, weitS. trade.
Krämer=geist (⏑́⏑...) m ⓲ commercial (or mercenary)spirit,shoppiness,narrow-mindedness (of a small trader); ⚹**haft** (⏑́⏑⏑) a. ⓳ like a shopkeeper; commercial, mercenary, shoppy; **Krämer=herrschaft** (⏑́⏑...) f ⓲ co. shopocracy; =**innung** f guild of traders, engS. in Engl.: Haberdashers' (or Mercers', Grocers') Company, ⚹**mäßig** a. ⓳ = krämerhaft; =**seele** f sordid (or narrow) mind, vgl. =**geist**; =**volk** n (wie Napoleon I.

verächtlich die Engländer nannte) nation of shop-keepers; =**ware** f = Kram 3.
Kram=handel (⏑́...) m ⓲ = Kram 1; =**haus** n = Kaufhaus, =**laden** m general store(s pl.), (haberdasher's) shop, vgl. Kram 2.
Kram(me)ts=vogel (⏑́⏑)...) [mhd. Kran(ich)wiede = Wacholder] m ⓲ orn. fieldfare (Turdus pila'ris).
Krampe ⊕ (⏑́⏑) [ndd.] f ⓳ carp. cramp (-iron), clamp; (Balkenband) beam-tie.
Krampf (⏑́) [ahd.: cramp] m ⓴b. path. cramp, spasm, stärker: convulsion; Krämpfe haben, in Krämpfe (ver)fallen to go (off) into convulsions, to have (an attack of) spasms; epileptische Krämpfe, oft: epileptic fit(s); Mittel gegen Krämpfe: ⚹ antispasmodic; Krämpfen unterworfen, zu Krämpfen neigend liable to spasms, ↘ convulsible.
Krampf=ader (⏑́...) f ⓲ path. varicose vein, ⚹ varix; =**ader=bruch** m: ⚹ varicocele; ⚹**ader=förmig** a.: ⚹ variciform; ⚹**artig** a. like cramp, spasmodic.
krampfen (⏑́⏑) ⓳ I v/a. u. sich ⚹ v/refl.: (sich) ⚹ to contract(o.s.) convulsively; da krampften sich ihm die Hände (zs.) then his hands were tightly clenched. — II v/n. (h.) to have the cramp, to suffer from spasms or convulsions.
krampfhaft (⏑́⏑) a. ⓳ 1. path. spasmodic, convulsive; (zuckend)convulsed, ⚹ clonic; ⚹es Lachen (Schluchzen) convulsive laughing (sobbing), oft a.: laughing-(crying-)fit. — 2. (a. adv.) fig. bisw.: (sehr) F immensely, awfully.
Krampf=husten (⏑́...) m ⓲ path. convulsive cough; vgl. Keuchhusten; =**mittel** n, med.: ⚹ antispasmodic (remedy); ⚹**stillend** a. calming, ⚹ antispasmodic.
Kramts... f. Krammets=...
Kram=waren (⏑́...) f/pl. ⓲ = Kram 3.
Kran ⊕ (⏑́) [= Kranich] m ⓳c.⓶ 1. (Windemaschine) crane; mit ~e heben to (raise by a) crane; mit dem ~ emporwinden to hoist up with a cr., to crane up. — 2. (Zapfen) tap, (stop-)cock.
Kränchen (⏑́⏑) n ⓳ dim. v. Kran.
Kran(en)=arbeiter (⏑́⏑...) m ⓲ man working (at) a crane; =**arm** m cranebeam; =**balken** ↓ m cat-head; =**baum** m crane-post; =**geld** ♀ n (fee for) cranage.
krängen ↓ (⏑́⏑) v/n. (h.) ⓳ (sich nach einer Seite hinüberlegen) to heel over, to list.
Kranich (⏑́⏑) [ahd.: crane; grch. ge'ranos] m ⓳d. orn. crane (Grus cine'rea); ⚹**artig** a. ⓳ orn. like a crane, ⚹ gruiform; ~**jagd** f ⓲ crane-shooting; ~**schar** f flock of cranes; =**schnabel** m: a) crane's beak; b) ♀ stork's-bill (Pelargo'nium); ~**schnabel=zange** f, surg. crane's-bill; ~**vögel** m/pl. orn.: ⚹ gruidæ pl.
Kraniologie ⚹ (-(⏑)⏑⏑́) f ⓲ (Schädellunde) craniology. [craniometry.]
Kraniometrie ⚹ (~) f ⓲ (Schädelmessung)/
krank (⏑́) [mhd.: crank] a. ⓳ (D 2,7) (ant. gesund) 1. ill (im Sinne von ⚹ nur prädikativ); (siech) sick of the palsy, &c., sickly, stärker: diseased (oft v. einzelnen Körperteilen), (leidend) afflicted, suffering, ailing, in ill (or bad, weak) health, i'nvalid, F poorly out of sorts, P off colour; (schwach) infirm, broken-down, feeble, fig. von Schiffen zc. **crazy**,

Zeichen (s. S. XVII): F familiär; P Volkssprache; ſ Gaunersprache; ↘ selten; † alt (auch gestorben); * neu (auch geboren); ⧺ unrichtig;

[Kränke] — 617 — [Krätze]

crank(y); *poet.* (matt) languid; sich 2 fühlen to feel ill [nicht: sick!] or F queer; 2 w. to fall (or be taken) ill; to sicken of scarlet-fever, &c.; wieder 2 w. to have a relapse. — 2. Redensarten: 2 an allen Nerven to be unstrung (in one's nerves); am Fieber 2 sein to be down with a fever; an der Gicht 2 sein to be afflicted with (or suffering from) (the) gout; 2 an Leib und Seele diseased in mind and body; *fig.* 2 am Beutel impecunious, short of money, F low (in funds); 2 vor Ärger, Kummer ill with (or through) grief; sich 2 essen to make o.s. ill with eating (too much), to overeat o.s.; sich, 2 lachen (wollen) to split (one's sides) with laughing; er stellt sich 2 he shams (or feigns) illness, he pretends to be ill, ⚔ meist he malingers; *pol.* der 2e Mann (Sultan) the Sick Man. — II ~e([r] m) f ⑥⑦ 3. sick(ly) person, i'nvalid, afflicted person, vom Arzte behandelte(r): patient.
Kränke (⌣) [krank] f ㊵ 1. ⤳ *path.* = Fallsucht. — 2. P das ist um die ⌣ zu kriegen! it's enough to kill one!; daß dich die ~! the plague (or the deuce) take you!
Kränkelei (⌣⌣) f ㊶ = kränkeln II.
kränkeln (⌣⌣) [krank] I *v/n.* (h.) ⑫a. to be sickly or suffering or F poorly; to be in bad (or F poor) health; to sicken (a. von Tieren und Pflanzen); sie fing an zu 2 her health began to fail her or to decline or to give way. — II ~ n ㉓ sickly state, sickliness, F poorliness; durch sein ~, oft: owing to his failing health.
kranken (⌣⌣) *v/n.* (h.) ⑥⑧ to be (for ever) ailing, to be diseased; an et. 2 to be afflicted with a th., to suffer from a th.
kränken (⌣⌣) [mhd.] ⑥⑧ I *v/a.* 1. (verletzen) to injure, (beleidigen) to offend; (demütigen) to humble; e-n an der Ehre 2 to injure a p.'s honour, to blast a p.'s reputation; j-s Rechte 2, an seinen Rechten 2 (schädigen) to infringe (or to encroach upon) a p.'s rights; das hat ihn tief (sehr) gekränkt it deeply (sorely) grieved him, it cut him to the quick; ohne Objekt: das kränkt it hurts; *v/impers.* es kränkt mich, daß // it mortifies (or annoys) me that //. — 2. e-n um et. 2 to despoil (or deprive) a p. of a th. — II sich 2 *v/refl.* 3. to feel hurt or grieved or annoyed; sich zu Tode 2 to die with grief. — III ~ n ㉓ 4. = Kränkung.
Kranken-abteilung (⌣⌣) f ㉒ sickward; =anstalt f infirmary; vgl. =haus; =bericht m bulletin; hospitalreport, ⚔ sick-report; =besuch m visit to a patient, call on an i'nvalid (friend); des Arztes: attendance, visit, des Geistlichen: visitation of the sick; =bett n sick-bed; ans ~ gefesselt confined to one's bed, bedridden; vom (=e) aufsteh(e)n to rise from a sick-bed, to recover from an illness; =diät f = =kost; =haus n hospital, infirmary; =kasse f sick-fund; =korb m ⚓ = =trage; =kost f patient's diet(ary) = =lager n = =bett; =liste f sick-list; =pflege f nursing (the sick), attendance on a patient, care of an i'nvalid;

=pfleger(in f) m = =wärter(in); =saal m sick-room, hospital-ward; =sänfte f = =trage; =schein m doctor's certificate; =schiff ⚓ n hospital-ship; =stube f sickroom; =stuhl m i'nvalid-chair; =stuhlwagen m Bath- (or i'nvalid-)chair; =trage f stretcher (or litter) for the conveyance of patients, ⚔ ambulance; =träger ⚔ m ambulance-man; =transp'ort ⚔ m ambulance-service; =verein m sick-club; =verschlag ⚓ m sick-bay; =wagen m i'nvalid-carriage, ⚔ ambulance-cart or -wagon; =wärter(in f) m person nursing a patient or attending on an i'nvalid; f in Hospitälern: hospital-nurse; =zelt ⚔ n hospital tent; =zimmer n = =stube. — Vgl. Krankheits-...
krankhaft (⌣⌣) *a.* ⑥⑥ diseased, *path.* morbid (symptom), abnormal (colour, &c.); ~igkeit (⌣⌣⌣) f ㊶ diseased (or morbid, suffering) state, morbidness.
Krankheit (⌣⌣) f ㊶ illness, sickness, malady, dauernde: disease; (Leiden) complaint; (Unwohlsein) indisposition, disorder, (Unpäßlichkeit) ailment; *vet.* v. Hunden ⚛: distemper; heftige, schwere ~ severe illness, serious (or malignant) complaint; e-e ~ bekommen to be taken ill, durch Ansteckung: to catch an illness; an e-r ~ sterben to die of an illness or a disease; sich (*dat.*) e-e ~ zuziehen to contract a disease; *path.* s. englisch² I.
Krankheits-anfall (⌣⌣-...) m ⑥² *med., path.* attack of illness, fit; =bericht m doctor's report, bulletin; =beschreibung f: ⤳ pathography; =entscheidung f crisis; =erreger m: ⤳ morbific agent; =erscheinung f (pathological) symptom; =fall m case of illness; =geschichte f history (or course) of an illness; ²halber *adv.* through (or owing to, on account of) illness; =herd m: ⤳ nidus; =lehre f: ⤳ pathology; =lehrer m: ⤳ pathologist; =stoff m contagious matter; =übertragung f infection; =verlauf m progress of an illness; = in symptom (of disease); =zustand m diseased or morbid state. — Vgl. Kranken...
Krank-lachen (⌣-...) n ⑥²: zum (Sich=)~ (enough) to make a cat laugh.
kränklich (⌣⌣) [krank] *a.* ⑥⑥ sickly, of weak health, delicate, v. Kindern: peaky; 2er Mensch, oft: valetudinarian; ~keit f ㊶ sickliness, weak (or bad) state of health.
Kränkung (⌣⌣) f ㊶ (das Kränken u. etwas Kränkendes) offence, mortification, vexation, annoyance; eine schwere ~ a grievous wrong; e-m eine ~ zufügen to offend (or wrong) a p.
Kran-schnabel ⚓ (⌣⌣...) m cat-head of a crane; =schreiber ⚙ m clerk of the crane; =wärter ⚒ m crane-man.
Kranz (⌣) [ahd.] m ①a. 1. wreath, garland, chaplet; zo.: ⚓ coronal, *ent.*: ~ von Haaren coronet; ♀ ⚓ der Randblüten: ⤳ corona, s. Braut-²; einen ~ winden, flechten to wind (or make) a wreath. — 2. *arch.* festoon (cornice a. ⚙). — 3. *poet.* ein ~ von holden Damen a circle of fair ladies, a galaxy of beauty.

Kranz-ader (⌣-...) f ⑥² = Herz-ader b; =binder(in f) m = flechter(in); =blume ♀ f garland-flower (*Hedy'chium*).
Kränzchen (⌣⌣) n ㉓ (*dim. von* Kranz) 1. small wreath or garland. — 2. (geschlossene Gesellschaft) party of friends who periodically meet; club, private circle, Am. auch: bee.
kränzen (⌣⌣) *v/a.* ⑨⑨ = befränzen.
Kranz-flechter(in f) m (⌣⌣-...) f ⑥² winder (or maker) of wreaths; =förmig *a.* ⑥⑥ formed like a wreath, ⤳ coroniform, ...ary; ²geschmückt *a.* wearing a wreath, adorned with garlands; =gesims ⚙ n, *arch.* cornice, ⤳ corona; =jungfer f (Brautführerin) bridesmaid.
Kränzlein (⌣⌣) n ㉓ = Kränzchen 1.
Kranz-leiste ⚙ (⌣-...) f ⚙ a. drip-stone; vgl. =gesims; ²los *a.* ⑥⑥ without a wreath; =naht f, *anat.*: ⤳ coronal.
Krapfen, mst nordd. (⌣⌣) [ahd. Hafen] m ㉓ Kochkunst: apple-fritter.
Krapp¹ ♀ ⚙ (⌣) [ndl.] m ⓐb. (Färberröte) (dyer's) madder (*Ru'bia tincto'rum*).
krapp² ⚓ (⌣) *a.* ⑥⑥: ²e See (kurzer Seegang mit steilen Wellen) choppy sea.
Krapp¹-bau ⚙ (⌣-...) ⚙ m cultivation of madder; =druck m madder-style; =farbe f: a) dye prepared from madder; b) m.-colour; =färben n m.-dyeing; =farben-druck m = =druck; =farbstoff m: ⤳ alizarin, garancin(e); ²gelb *a.* ⑥⑥: ⤳ xanthine; =karmin m madder-carmine; =lack m m.-lake, rubric lake; =mühle f m.-mill; =orange n m.-orange; =pflanze f = Krapp¹; ²rot *a.* madder-coloured; =rot n: ⤳ alizarin, ⚗ alizari; =wurzel ♀ f: a) (die Wurzel) madder-root; b) = Krapp¹.
Krasis ⚕ (⌣) [grch. Mischung] f, *inv. gram.* (Zi.-ziehung zweier Silben) crasis.
kraß (⌣) [nhd. 18. *sae.*: crass; *lt.] *a.* ⑥⑥ (D 6, 10) 1. (stark hervortretend) crass, gross, strong(ly marked), F unmitigated, awful; krasse Unwissenheit crass (or gross) ignorance. — 2. burschikos: (plump) clumsy, (roh) unpolished.
Krater (⌣) [grch.] m ⑥² (Alt.: Mischkrug; jetzt: Schlund e-s Vulkans) crater; *geol.* kleiner, auch: ⤳ craterlet; ²-artig (⌣...) *a.* ⑥⑥, ²-förmig *a.* crater-shaped, crateriform; ~-bildung f ⑥² *geol.* formation of craters.
Kratz F (⌣) [mhd.] m ⓐa. scratch.
krätz-artig (⌣-...) *a.* ⑥⑥ resembling the itch, ⤳ scabious, psoroid.
Kratz-bohne ♀ (⌣-...) f cowh(h)age (*Mucu'na pru'riens*); =bürste f: a) ⚙ (hard, scrubbing-brush; b) F *fig.* (widerhaarige Person) bad- (or ill-)tempered (or cross, irascible) person, F Tartar, P wax-pot; ²bürstig *a.* ⑥⑥ bad-tempered, cross, peevish; =distel ♀ f: a) horse-thistle (*Ci'rsium arve'nse*); b) (krause Distel) curled thistle (*Ca'rduus crispus*).
Krätze ⚕ (⌣⌣) [mhd.: *kratzen*] f ⑥⑦ 1. *path.* itch, ⤳ scabies, psora, psoriasis, prurigo; mit der ~ behaftet itchy, ⤳ psoric, vgl. krätzig. — 2. ⚙ (Abfälle der Metalle) waste metal, metal waste or scrapings or sweepings *pl.*

♪ Musik; ⤳ Wissenschaft; ♀ Pflanze; ♁ Geographie; ⊙ Technik; ⚒ Bergbau; ⚔ Militär; ⚓ Marine; ⚙ Handel; ⚛ Post; 🚂 Eisenbahn.

[Kratzeisen] — 618 — [Kreatin]

Kratz-eisen (⸚) n ㉓ zum Reinigen der Schuhe: scraping-iron, scraper (auch ⊕ Klinge zum Schaben).
kratzen (⸚) [ahd.] ⑳ **I** v/a., v/n. (h.) u. sich ⸚ v/refl. 1. to scratch (o.s.); die Feder kratzt scratches; sich am Kopfe ⸚ to scratch one's head; sich wund ⸚ to make o.s. sore with scratching; Sprichw. s. jucken 2. — 2. et. aufs Papier ⸚ (schlecht schreiben) to scrawl (or scribble) s.th. on paper; F auf der Geige ⸚ (schlecht spielen) to play upon the violin, F to scrape on the fiddle; der Wein kratzt (schmeckt sauer) ... has a tart (or harsh) taste. — 3. der Rauch kratzt mich (oder mir) im Halse ... irritates my throat; v/impers. es kratzt mich im Halse I feel a scratching in my throat. — 4. auf einen Haufen ⸚ (scharren) to scrape into a heap. — 5. ⊕ mit der Kratzbürste ⸚ to scrub; Spinnerei: to card, to tease. — **II** F v/n. (fn) 6. von der Stelle ⸚ to get away, F to slope off, to hook it.
Kratzen=beschlag ⊕ (⸚...) m ⊕ Spinn.: plant (of machinery) for carding, card-clothing; **=rahmen** n Web.: card-frame.
Kratzer (⸚) m ㉒ scratcher (Schaber) scraper, ⊕ scraping-iron or -tool.
Krätzer (⸚) [kratzen] m ㉒ 1. (im Halse kratzender Wein) tart (or sourish) wine. — 2. ⊕ (Kratzer) scraping-iron, (Scharre) rake(r). — 3. ⚒ bei Vorderladern: (Schußzieher) wad-hook, worm.
Kratz-fuß F (⸚...) m ㉒ (awkward) curtsy or bow; einen ~ machen to curtsy, F to scrape a leg; **=füßer(in** f) m person who curtsies (or who is scraping and bowing) to people.
krätzig (⸚) [Krätze 1] ⑥⑥ path. **I** a. itchy, ⚕ scabious, psoric, psorous, psoroid, pruriginous. — **II** ~e([r] m) f itchy person, ⚕ patient infected with (or suffering from) scabies.
Krätz=kranke([r] m) f (⸚...) ⑫ path. p. suffering from the itch; **=kupfer** ⊕ n, metall. copper obtained from the tailings or from waste copper-ore.
Kratz=maschine ⊕ (⸚...) f ㉒ Spinnerei: carding-machine.
Krätz=milbe (⸚...) f ㉒ ent. itch-mite (Sarcoptes scabie'i); **=mittel** n remedy for the itch, ⚕ psoric; **=salbe** f, pharm. ointment (or salve) against (or for) the itch, ⚕ antipsoric (ointment).
Kräuel fast † (⸚) [ahd.] m ㉒ (f ⑭) nur bibl., Kochkunst: fork with bent prongs.
krauen (⸚) [ahd.] v/a. ⑭ (⑫a.) (sanft jucken) to scratch softly or gently; (streicheln) to stroke; fig. e-m die Ohren ⸚ (schmeicheln) to wheedle round a p.
kraus (⸚) [mhd.] a. ⑥⑥(D6,10) 1. meist vom Haare: (lockig) curly, curled, frizzled, wavy, (gekräuselt) crisp, ⚕: ⚕ crisp (-ated); (gerunzelt) wrinkled (forehead), (gefältelt) ruffled (sleeve, &c.); ⸚ machen, ⸚ werden to curl, frizzle, crisp; das Gesicht (oder die Stirn) ⸚ ziehen to knit one's brow. — 2. F fig. = bunt 4, ⸚⸚: es zu ⸚ machen to go (or to carry matters) too far.
Krause¹ (⸚) [kraus] f ⑭ 1. curliness, waviness, crispness. — 2. (kraus Gefälteltes) ruff(le), frill.

Krause² (⸚) [mhd.: cruse] f ⑭ = Krug.
Kräusel (⸚) [kraus] m (n) ㉒ (dim. von Krause) small ruff(le) or frill.
Kräusel=eisen ⊕ (⸚...) n ⑫ für das Haar: curling- (or frizzling-)iron, curling-tongs pl.; **=holz** n curling-tool; **=maschine** f: a) Tuchfabr. ⚒.: crimping- (or friezing-)machine, crimper, goffering-press; b) Münze: = =werf; **=mühle** f Tuchfabr.: friezing-mill.
kräuseln (⸚) [kraus] **I** v/a. und sich ⸚ v/refl. ⑳a.: (sich) ⸚ to curl, frizzle, crinkle, crisp, crimp; Vorhembchen ⚒. ⸚ (fälteln) to frill shirt-fronts, &c.; (rundfälteln) to goffer; Münzen: to mill; Tuch ⚒.: to crimp, to frieze; sich ⸚: a) von Stoffen: to pucker (up), to bunch; b) vom Wasser: to ripple, ruffle, be ruffled; c) vom Rauche: to wreathe, curl up. — **II** ~ n ㉓ u. **Kräuselung** f ⑭⑥ curling, &c. (s. I); vom Meere: rippling, ripple.
Kräusel=werk ⊕: (⸚...) ⑫ ⚒ mint. milling-machine. [*(Mentha crispa)*.]
Kraus=minze ⚕ (⸚...) f ⑭⑥ curly-mint}
krausen (⸚) ⑳ **I** v/n. (h.) to curl, frizzle, crisp; to pucker up. — **II** v/a. = kräuseln I.
Kraus=flor ⚒ (⸚...) m ⑫ crisped crape; **=haar** n curly hair; ⸚**haarig** a. ⑥⑥ curly-haired or -headed, with frizzled ⚕ ulotrichan, ⚕...ous.
Krausheit (⸚) f ⑭⑥ = Krause¹ 1.
Kraus=kohl ⚕ (⸚...) m ⑫ = Wirsingkohl; **=kopf** m curly head, curly-headed person; ⸚**köpfig** a. ⑥⑥ curly-headed.
Kräusler (⸚) m ㉒, ~in f ⑭⑥ one who curls, &c. (s. kräuseln I), auch: frizzler, weitS. hairdresser; ⊕ (Tuch=)~ friezer.
Kraus=machen (⸚...) n ⑫ crisping, ruffling; **=salat** ⚕ m crisped lettuce (*Lactu'ca sati'va crispa*); **=sein** = Krause¹ 1; **=tabak** ⚒ m shag (tobacco).
Kraut (⸚) [ahd.] n ⑫c.1. herb; (Arznei)~ medicinal herb, bsd. ehm.: simple; (Pflanze) plant, (bsd. Gemüse) vegetable, (Unkraut) weed, weitS. wild-growing plant; bei Rüben ⚒.: top(spl.), ⚒. ~ der weißen Rübe turnip-tops pl.; ⚕ grünes ~ = Grünkohl; ⊕ Gerberei: (Sumach) sumach, zo. Kräuter fressend: ⚕ herbivorous; pharm. Kräuter sammeln to herborize. — 2. von Pflanzen: ins ~ schießen ob. wachsen: to run into leaves or foliage. — 3. fig. wie ~ und Rüben (durch=ea.) higgledy-piggledy, in (a heap of) confusion, F in a mess, anyhow; Sprichw. Muß ist ein bitter ~ 'must' is a bitter word, need will have its course, necessity is a cruel master; für den Tod ist kein ~ gewachsen there is no remedy against death. — 4. iro. creature, (Taugenichts) good-for-nothing; ein sauberes ~ a scamp. — 5. am Rheine ⚒. (eingemachtes Obst) jam, preserve of plums, pears, &c. — 6. ehm. ⚒ = Zündkraut.
Kraut=acker (⸚...) m ⑫ cabbage-field; vgl. =feld; ⸚**ähnlich** ⚕ a. ⑥, ⸚**artig** a. ⑥ herblike, ⚕ herbaceous, herbescent, oleraceous; **=beet** n vegetable-bed.
Kräutchen (⸚) n ㉔ (dim. von Kraut) little herb or plant, small vegetable or weed; auch: herblet. [to weed.]
krauten (⸚) v/a. ⑭ hort. to hoe; (gäten)}
Kräuter=absud (⸚...) m ⑫ decoction of herbs; **=arznei** f herb-medicine;

=aufguß m = =tee; **=auszug** m extract of herbs; **=bad** n, med. herb-lotion, medicated bath; **=boden** m loft for drying herbs; **=brühe** f Kochkunst: vegetable-soup; vgl. =suppe; **=buch** n herbal (-ist's book); **=doktor** m herb-doctor, **=frau** f herb-woman; ⸚**fressend** a. ⑥⑥ feeding on vegetables, ⚕ herbivorous; **=garten** m vegetable- (or kitchen-) garden; **=händler(in** f) m herbalist.
kräuterig (⸚) [Kraut] a. ⑥⑥ covered with herbs, ⚕ herbose, herbous.
Kräuter=kammer (⸚...) f ⑫ pharm. room for drying (or storing) herbs; **=käse** m green cheese; **=kenner(in** f) m herbalist, botanist; **=kenntnis** f knowledge of herbs, weitS. botanical knowledge; **=kissen** n herb-cushion, medicated cushion; **=kunde** f, **=lehre** f botany; vgl. =kenntnis; **=kur** f cure by means of herbs; **=laden** m herb-shop; **=mann** ⚕ m herbalist, gatherer of herbs; **=markt** m market for herbs; bisw. vegetable-market; ⸚**reich** a. ⑥⑥ rich (or abounding) in herbs; vgl. kräuterig; **=säckchen** n = =kissen; **=saft** m juice of herbs, herbal syrup or decoction; **=sala't** m salad made up of herbs; **=salbe** f ointment prepared from herbs, herbal salve; **=sammler (=in** f) m = =mann, =frau; **=sammlung** f: ⚕ herbarium; **=suppe** f Kochkunst: (fr.) julienne; vgl. =brühe; **=tee** m infusion of herbs; **=trank** m herbal draught; **=wein** m, pharm. medicated wine; **=zucker** m, pharm. conserve.
Kraut=esel F (⸚...) m ⑫ jackass; **=feld** n field planted with vegetables, cabbage-field; ⸚**förmig** a. ⑥⑥ formed like a plant, ⚕ herbiform; **=garten** m, **=gärtner** m vegetable-garden, -gardener; **=hacke** f hoe; **=haupt** n = Kohlkopf; **=hobel** ⊕ m cabbage-slicer; **=junker** F m country-squire, contp. country-bumpkin; **=junkertum** n (manners pl. of) country-squires pl.
Kräuticht, Kräutig (⸚) n ⑪d. herbage.
krautig a. ⑥⑥ herbaceous.
Kraut=kopf (⸚...) m ⑫ = Kohlkopf.
Kräutlein (⸚) n ㉔ f. Kräutchen.
Kraut=markt (⸚...) m ⑫ = Kräutermarkt.
Krawall F (⸚) m ⑫d. noisy gathering, uproar(ious meeting), riot, row.
Krawaller (⸚) m ㉒ rioter, brawler.
krawall(ier)en (⸚⸚) v/n. (h.) ⑳ to create a disturbance, to riot, brawl.
Krawatte (⸚) [mhd.; fr.; *Kroate] f ⑭⑥ cravat, neck-tie; f. Halsbinde.
Krawatten=einlage (⸚⸚...) f ⑫ stiffening of a cravat or neck-tie; **=fabrikant**, **=macher** m ⑲ maker of cravats or neck-ties; **=tuch** n neck-cloth.
kraweel ⚓ (⸚) [Karavelle, † Schiff] a. ⑥⑥: ⸚ gebaut carvel-built; ~**bau** m ⑫ carvel-work. [strap or knot.]
Kraxe obb. (⸚) f ⑭⑥ (Traggestell) porter's}
kraxeln F (⸚) ⑳a. **I** v/a. (auf dem Rücken tragen) to carry on one's back. — **II** v/n. (fn) (mühsam steigen) to climb (or clamber) up with difficulty.
Kreas(leinen (⸚) ⑭ (⸚(⸚⸚) [fr., span.] n (m), inv. (Lederleinwand) creas.
Kreatin (⸚⸚) [grch.] n ⑪d. chm. (Alkaloid der Muskelfaser) creatin(e) ($C_4H_9N_3O_2$).

Signs (see page XVII): F familiar; P vulgar; ⚡ flash; ⚒ rare; † obsolete (died); * new word (born); ⚕ incorrect; ♪ music;

Kreatinin ~ n⊕d.chm. creatinin(e) (C₄H₇N₃O).

Kreatur ~ [It.] f ⊕ (Geschöpf) creature; contp. = Weibsbild; fig. (Werkzeug) tool.

Krebs (¹) [ahd.: Krabbe] m ⓐa. 1. zo. crayfish, prov. u. Am. crawfish (A'stacus fluvia'tilis). — 2. ast.: ~ im Tierkreise: ⚹ Cancer, f. Wendekreis. — 3. path. (bösartiges Geschwür): ⚹ cancer. — 4. ⊕ Buchhandel: (unverkauft zurückgehendes Buch) unsold copy, pl. Krebse auch: dead stock, stock on hand. — 5. [nhd. 15/6. sae.; *~ 1] ehm. ⚔ (Panzer), nur noch fig., bibl. ~ des Glaubens breast plate of faith.

krebs=artig (ᵘ...) a. ⊕: a) zo. like a crayfish, ⚹ astacine, ...oid; b) path. like cancer, ⚹ cancerous, cancroid, carcinoid; =artigkeit f ⊕ path.: ⚹ cancerousness; =bildung f, path.: ⚹ canceration; =brühe f = =suppe; =distel ♀ f cotton-thistle (Onopo'rdon aca'nthium).

krebsen (ᴸ~) [Krebs] v/n. ⊕ 1. (h.) to catch crayfish or crabs. — 2. F (h. u. sn) to be astir, F to keep on the move.

Krebs=fang (ᵘ...) m ⊕ catching of crayfish; ⊆förmig a. ⊕: a) zo.: ⚹ cancriform, cancrine; vgl. ⊇artig, b) path.: ⚹ cancerous; =gang m sidling walk of a crab or crayfish; (Rückgang) going backward, ⚹ retrogradation; (Untergang) decline, decay; den ~ geh(e)n to go back(ward), ⚹ to retrograde, decline, decay; =geschwür n, path.: ⚹ cancerous ulcer(ation).

krebshaft, krebsig (ᴸ~) a. ⊕ = krebs=artig.

Krebs=kranke([r] m) f (ᵘ...) ⊕ path. p. suffering from cancer, cancer-patient; =krankheit f cancerous disease or malady; =nase Kochkunst: shell of crayfish dressed with stuffing; =reuse ⊕ f bow-net; ⊇rot a. ⊕ (as) red as a turkey-cock or a lobster; =schäden m: a) path.: ⚹ cancerous affection or sore; b) fig. deep-seated evil, poet. auch: canker; =schale f = =schere; =schere f: a) shell, claw of a crayfish; b) ♀ water-aloe, crab's-claw (Stratio'tes aloi'des); =suppe f Kochkunst: crayfish-soup; =tiere n/pl. zo.: ⚹ crustacea pl.; =topf m Fischerei: crab-pot; =zucht f crab-farming.

Kredenz (~ˇ) [it.] f ⊕ = Kredenztisch.

kredenzen (~ˇ~) [nhd.-; *it. beglaubigen (durch Borkosten)] v/a. ⊕ to taste the wine; (den Becher darreichen) to present the cup after tasting its contents.

Kredenzer (~ˇ~) m ⊕ taster, cup-bearer.

Kredenz=teller (~ˇ...) m = salver; =tisch m sideboard, auch (fr.) buffet; eccl. zum Abendmahl: ⚹ (table of) prothesis.

Kredit¹ (~ˇ) [nhd. 17. sae.; *fr., it.] m ⊕ c. credit; auf ~ on credit, F on tick; er hat guten ~ his credit is good; weitS. (Ansehen) repute, reputation.

Kredit² (~ˇ) [It. er leiht] n ⊕ (Haben) ant. De'bet, Soll) credit; im ~ steh(e)n to be on the credit(or)-side.

Kredit=anstalt f, =bank (~ˇ...) f ⊕ loan-bank; =brief m: a) letter of credit; b) = Krediti'v; =eröffnung f opening a credit with; ⊇fähig a. ⊕ trustworthy; =fähigkeit f trustworthiness; =genossenschaft f, etwa: mutual loan society.

kreditieren ⊕ (~ᵘᴸ) [fr.; *Kredit¹] v/a. u. v/n. (h.) ⊕: e-m et. ⊇: a) (stunden) to give a p. s.th. on credit; b) (gutschreiben) to put (or place) s.th. to a p.'s credit, to credit s.th. to a p.

Krediti'v (~ᵘf) [It.] n⊕d.:~ (Beglaubigungsschreiben) e-s Gesandten credentials pl.

kredit=los (~ˇ~ᴸ) a. ⊕ without credit, discredited. [creditor.]

Kreditor ⊕ (ᴸ~~) [it.] m ⊕ (Gläubiger)]

Kredit=posten ⊕ (~ˇ...) m ⊕ entry on the credit-side; =seite f im Hauptbuche: credit-(or creditor-)side; ⊇würdig a. ⊕ deserving (of) credit.

Kredo (ᴸ~) [It. ich glaube] n ⊕ Cath. eccl. credo; weitS. (Glaubensbekenntnis) creed.

kregel (ᴸ~) [ndd.: Krieg] a. ⊕(D9) (munter, lebhaft) lively, brisk.

Kreide (ᴸ~) [ahd.-; *It. cre'ta] f ⊕ 1. chalk, paint. crayon; rote ~ = Rötel; spanische ~ French (or Spanish) chalk; mit ~ behandeln, entwerfen, schreiben to chalk; mit ~ skizzieren, zeichnen to chalk, to crayon. — 2. chm. (kohlensaurer Kalt) carbonate of lime. — 3. F fig. mit doppelter ~ (zu viel) anschreiben to overcharge, F to pile it on; bei e-m in die ~ geraten to run up an account with a p., to get into a p.'s debt; weitS. (Borg, Schuld) indebtedness; mit 40 Mark auf (oder in) der ~ steh(e)n to owe (a debt of) two pounds; tief in der ~ sitzen to be deeply in debt.

kreide=ähnlich, (ᵘ~...) a. ⊕ like chalk; ⊇artig a. chalky, ⚹ cretaceous; =bildung f ⊕ chalk-(or chalky) formation; ⊇blaß a. = ⊇weiß; =erde f chalky soil; =fels m chalkcliff; =formation, =gruppe f, geol.: ⚹ cretaceous formation, group; =grube ⊕ f chalk-pit; =grund m chalk bottom, chalky soil; ⊇haltig a. ⊕: ⚹ cretaceous; =lager n chalk-bed; =mergel m, geol. chalk-marl.

kreiden (ᴸ~) v/a. ⊕ to (write with) chalk, to mark with chalk.

Kreide=schiefer (ᵘ~...) m ⊕ geol. chalk-slate; =stift m chalk (pencil), crayon; farbiger ~ coloured chalk; =strich m chalk line or mark; ⊇weiß a. ⊕ (as) white as chalk or as a sheet, a deadly pale; =zeichnung f chalk- (or crayon-) drawing or sketch. [cretaceous.]

kreidicht, kreidig (ᴸ~) a. ⊕ chalky, ⚹]

kre-ier/en (~ᵘᴸ~) [It.] I v/a. ⊕ (schaffen) to create; (ernennen) to appoint, to make. — II ~ n ⊕ u. K/ung f ⊕ creation.

Kreis (¹) [ahd.] m ⓐa. 1. math., &c. circle; f. beschreiben 3, bewegen 2; größter ~ einer Kugel, der Erde 2c. great circle ...; ast. Kreise (Bahnen) der Planeten orbits pl.; im Kreise herum (moving) in a circle, round about; sich in e-m Kreise aufstellen to form a circle or a ring; sich im Kreise (herum) drehen to revolve (in a circle), to spin (or whirl, twirl) round, to rotate; Wort des Archimedes: störe meine Kreise nicht! mind my circles!, weitS. do not disturb my meditations! — 2. e-n blauen ~ um die Augen haben to have dark rings round the (or one's) eyes; einen ~ um et. schließen to encircle or enclose; hem in) a th.; es geht alles mit mir im Kreise herum my head is swimming,

I feel dizzy. — 3. fig. (Gebiet) district, sphere; (Amtsbezirk) circuit; das liegt außer meinem Kreise that is beyond (or outside) my province or department; ~ von Freunden circle of friends; im Kreise seiner Familie in the bosom (or midst) of one's family; in allen Kreisen des Lebens in every walk of life; die höchsten Kreise, oft: the upper ten (thousand), the aristocracy.

Kreis=abschnitt (ᵘ...) m ⊕ math. segment; =amtmann m, etwa: district-bailiff; =arzt m medical officer of a district; F parish doctor; =ausschnitt m, math. sector; =bahn f: a) circular path, ast. orbit; b) circular railway; =beamte(r) m district-officer; =behörde f, etwa: central authority of a district; =bewegung f circular motion, revolution; =bogen m, math. arc of a circle, arch. circular arch.

kreischen (ᴸ~) ⊕ (fast † ⊕a(e)st) I v/n. (h.) 1. to scream, shriek; yell; von Kindern auch: to squall, v. Eulen 2c.: to screech, von der Butter in der Pfanne: to hiss, von e-r Feile, Säge: to grate (on the ear), von der Türangel: to creak; ⊇de Stimme, a. shrill voice. — 2. fig. von zu grellen Farben: to offend the eye; ⊇de Farben glaring (or loud, gaudy) colours pl. — II ~ n ⊕ 3. scream(ing), shriek(ing), yell(ing); squall(ing), &c. (f. I).

Kreischer (ᴸ~) m ⊕ screamer, shrieking person; screecher (a. v. Vögeln).

Kreis=drehung (ᵘ...) f ⊕ rotation; =einteilung f, a. math. division of the circle; b) division into districts.

Kreisel (ᴸ~) [eigtl. Kräusel, P: Kreis] m ⊕ (Spielzeug) top, bsd. ehm. auch: whirligig, zum Peitschen: whipping- (or peg-)top; (Brummer)~ humming-top; f. drehen 5; einen ~ geh(e)n lassen (treiben) to spin (to whip) a top.

Kreisel=bewegung (ᵘ...) f ⊕ mech. gyration; ⊇förmig a. ⊕ like a top, ⚹ turbiniform, turbinoid, geol. auch: strombuliform; mech. ⊆e Bewegung gyration, ⚹ turbination.

kreiseln (ᴸ~) ⊕a. I v/n. (h. u. sn) u. sich ⊇ v/refl. to whirl round (auch von einem Strudel), to twirl (or twist) round, mech. to gyrate. — II v/n. (h.) (mit dem Kreisel spielen) to whip (or to play with) a top, to spin a top.

Kreisel=peitsche (ᵘ...) f ⊕ whip for whipping a top; =rad ⊕ n turbine; =schnecke f, zo. top-shell (Turbo); geol. fossile ~: ⚹ turbinite; ⊇schneckenartig a. ⊕: ⚹ trochoid; =spiel n playing with tops, whipping (or spinning) a top. — Vgl. auch Dreh...

kreisen (ᴸ~) [mhd.; *Kreis] ⊕ I v/n. (h., bei Ortsveränderung sn), a. sich ⊆ v/refl. 1. to turn round (or move) in a circle, to circle (or go, spin) round, to revolve, rotate; von Raubvögeln: to hover round. — 2. (e-n Kreis bilden) to form a circle; ⊇der Gang circular course. — 3. = kreißen. — II v/a. 4. (im Kreise drehen) to turn round (in a circle). — III ~ n ⊕ 5. circular movement, rotation, der Gestirne: revolution.

Kreiser (ᴸ~) m ⊕ (Feldhüter, Forstläufer) etwa: keeper, ranger.

[Kreisersatzkommission] — 620 — [kreuzen]

Kreis=ersatzkommission ⚥ (″...) f ㊷ recruiting commission of a district; =fläche f circular surface, *math.* area of a circle; =form f circular form; =förmig(keit f) *a.* circular (form); =gang *m:* a) labyrinth, maze; b) = bewegung; =gericht *n* district- (in England county-)court; =gestalt f = =form; =hauptmann *m, etwa:* prefect of a district, in England: Lord Lieutenant of a county; =lauf *m* circular course, revolution, *mech.* gyration; ~ von Pflichten ꝛc. round of duties, &c.; =linie f circular line, *math.* circumference; =messung f, *math.* mensuration of the circle, ⚥ cyclometry, engS. measurement of the circumference; =ordnung f bye-laws of a district; =peripherie f = =umfang; =physikus *m* † = =arzt; =richter *m* district- (in Engl.: county-court) judge; =ritt *m, man.* riding in a circle, volt; ◌rund *a.* (as) round as a circle, circular, ⚥ orbicular; =säge f circular saw, rotary cutter; ◌schattig *a.*: ⚥ periscian; =schnitt *m* circular incision; =schul=inspektor *m* inspector of schools in a district.

kreißen (L~) [mhd. kreischen] **I** *v/n.* (h.) ㊾ to be in (child-)labour, to have labour-pains, bsd. bibl. to (be in) travail; *med.* 2d, auch: ⚥ parturient; *fig.* Der Berg mountain in labour. — **II** ~ *n* ㉓ child-labour, labour-pains *pl.*, ⚥ parturiency.

Kreißerin (L~v) f ㊷ woman in labour. **Kreis=stadt** (″...) f ㉘ chief town of a district, in England: county-town; =stände *m/pl.* in Deutschland ꝛc.: (members *pl.* of a) provincial diet; =ständig ̌a. ㊺ cyclic(al); =steuer f district-rate; =strom ⊕ *m, elect.,* &c. circular current; =synode f district-synod; =tag *m* provincial diet or assembly; =truppen f/pl. troops pl. located (or garrisoned) in a district; =umfang *m, math.* circumference of a circle, periphery; =versammlung f = =tag; =viereck *n, math.* quadrilateral (or four-sided figure) inscribed in a circle; =viertel *n, math.* quadrant; =vierung f, *math.* quadrature of the circle; =wund=arzt *m* district-surgeon.

Krematorium (⌣~L~(⌣)⌣) [it.] *n* ㉘ (Feuerbestattungsanstalt) crematorium.

Kreml(in) (⌣(″)) [russ.] *m* ㊿ (Zarenpalast in Moskau) Kremlin.

Kremor=tartari (L~⌣⌣L~) [it.] *m* ㊿ *pharm.* (gereinigter Weinstein) cream of tartar.

Krempe (̂~) [ndd.: crimp =Krampe] f ㊽ edge, border, e-s Hutes: brim; Hut mit breiter ~ broad-brimmed hat, broadbrim; Hut mit herabhängender ~ slouched hat.

Krempel¹ F (̂~) [it.] *m* ㉒ = Trödel, Trödelkram.

Krempel² ⊕ f (̂~) [(mhd.) ndd.; *Krampe] f ㊽ (Wollkamm) card(ing-comb).

Krempel²=kamm (″...) *m* ㊷ carding-comb; =maschine f carding-machine.

krempeln ⊕ (̂~) *v/a.* u. *v/n.* (h.) ⊕a. Spinnerei: Wolle ꝛc. 2 to card or comb...

Krempel²=stube ⊕ (̂~...) f ㊷ Spinnerei: card(ing)-room.

krempen (̂~) *v/a.* ㊸ e-n Hut ꝛc.: to turn up, to bend at the edge; machen, daß et. krimpt to bend a th. up at the edge.

Kremser¹ (̂~) [~ in Berlin, 1825, Erfinder] *m* ㉒ (vielsitziger Wagen zu Ausflügen): break, pleasure-van, char-à-banc.

Kremser²=weiß ⊕ (̂~L) [Krems, österr. St.] *n* ㊷ (feines Bleiweiß) krems, Kremnitz white, silver-white.

krenelieren ⚥ (~⌣~L) [fr.] *v/a.* ㊹ *frt.* (mit Zinnen versehen) to crenel(l)ate.

Kreole (⌣L~) [fr., span.] *m* ㊹, **Kreolin** f ㊼ in den amerikanischen Kolonien: (Abkömmling v. Europäern) Creole; **kreolisch** *a.* ㊺ Creole(an). [creosol ($C_8H_{10}O_2$).)

Kreosot ⚕ (~~L) [grch. -it.] *n* ⑭d. *chm.*)

Kreosot ⚕ (~~L) [grch.] *n* ⑭c. (schwere ölartige, aus Holzteer bereitete fäulniswidrige Flüssigkeit) *chm.* creosote, creasote; =ieren ⚥ (~~L) *v/a.* ㊸ (mit ~ durchtränken) to creosote, to creasote.

krepieren (⌣~L) [nhd., *it.] ㊸ **I** *v/n.* (ſn) 1. v. Tieren: (verenden) to die, fall, perish; P contp. v. Menschen auch: F to peg out, to kick the bucket, to hop the twig. — 2. ⚥ v. Geschossen: (platzen) to burst. — **II** *v/a.* 3. F das krepiert (ärgert) mich that vexes (or annoys) me.

Krepp ⊕, (̂~) [fr. *crépe*] *m* ㊿ (⊕b.) (Seidengewebe) crape; vgl. Flor² 1.

Krepp=flor (̂~...) *m* ㊷ crisped (or double) crape; =maschine ⊕ f ㊷ craping-machine; =tuch *n* crape-cloth, crape.

Kresol ⚥ (~L) *n* ⑭d. *chm.* cresol, cresylic alcohol (C_7H_8O).

Kresse ♃ (̂~) [ahd.: cress] f ㊸ cress, peppergrass (*Lepi'dium*); vgl. Bitter=, Brunnen=, Garten=, Kapuziner=2.

Kreßling ♃ (̂~) *m* ⑭d. (ein eßbarer Schwamm) kind of mushroom.

Kreta ♁ (L~) npr/n. ⑭a. (Insel im Mittelmeere) Crete, jetzt auch: Candia.

Kret(ens)er(in *f* ㊼) *m* (L~(⌣) -̂~) Cretan, inhabitant of Crete, auch Cretian, **kret(ens)isch** (L~) (-̂~) *a.* ㊺ Cretan, of Crete, *a.* Cretian.

Krethi und Plethi (L~ ♃ ″...) [hebr. Kreter und Philister] meist *m/sg. inv.* 1. *bibl.* (Davids Leibwache, 2. Sam. 8, 18) Cherethites and Pelethites *pl.* — 2. F *fig.* (Gesindel) tagrag und bobtail, riffraff; (allerlei Volk) Dick, Tom, and Harry; F a mixed lot.

Kretin, ~**e** (-t̂ä', -L~) [fr.] *m* ㊿, ㊹ (Blödsinniger) underwitted (or half-witted) p., idiot, *path. a.* cretin; ~**bildung** f ㊻ *path.*: ⚥ cretinism.

Kretinen=anstalt (~L~...) f ㊸ idiot-asylum, home for idiots.

kretinenhaft (~L~⌣) *a.* ㊺ (blödsinnig) underwitted, half-witted, idiotic.

Kretinismus ⚥ (~~L⌣) *m* ㊲ *path.* (Blödsinn) cretinism, idiocy.

kretisch (L~) [Kreta] *a.* ㊺ Cret(i)an.

kreucht (L~) †, noch *poet.* = kriecht.

Kreuz (L) [ahd.; *lt. *cruc-(crux* f)] *n* ⑭(④)a. 1. cross; an=~=heften, schlagen to fasten (or fix, nail) to the cross, to crucify; ins ~ (ob. über(s) ~) legen to lay crosswise or cross-ways; die Arme über(s) ~ falten to fold one's arms crosswise, to cross one's arms; *her.* einfaches ~ mit abgerundeten Ecken cross-pommel; ⚥ Eisernes ~ als

Auszeichnung: iron cross; *her.* liegendes ~ (×) saltier; ⚥ rotes ~ der Krankenträger red cross; Verein vom Roten ~ Red-Cross Society; das ~ nehmen, als Kreuzfahrer: to take (up) the cross; das ~ predigen to preach the cross. — 2. mst *fig.* das ~ schlagen to make the sign of the cross, to cross o.s.; das ~ vor e-m machen oder schlagen to detest a p., to hold a p. in abhorrence; das ~ über et. m. (es verloren geben) to give a th. up as lost; zu ~e kriechen (sich bemütigen) humbly to submit, to humble o.s., F to eat humble-pie, to knuckle under or down. — 3. *fig.* (Leid) cross, affliction, tribulation; sein ~ auf sich nehmen to take up the cross, to bear up against adversity or with one's afflictions; Sprichw.: jeder hat sein ~ zu tragen every one has his cross to bear, we all have our trouble(s *pl.*). — 4. in Flüchen: ~ Donnerwetter!, ~ sackerlot!, ~ (schock)schwerenot!, F confound (or damn) it!, hang it all!, the deuce! — 5. in die ~ und Quere, *adv.* kreuz und quer this way and that, bisw. auch: criss-cross; weits. in all directions. — 6. (allg. für Rückgrat, insbesondere dessen unteres Ende), von Pferden: croup, crupper, vom Rindvieh: chine, von Menschen: small of the back; mir tut das ~ weh my back aches, my loins ache; sich (*dat.*) das ~ brechen to break one's back. — 7. Kartenspiel, bsd. bei franz. Karten: clubs *pl.* (= Treff²). — 8. ♪ (#, Zeichen, daß eine Note um ½ Ton erhöht werden soll, und: ,,b") sharp, diesis; mit einem ~e bezeichnen to (mark with a) sharp. — 9. ☉ *typ.* = Aufhängekreuz; als Zeichen (†): dagger, obelisk. — 10. ♃ (Anker-)~ crown (or cross) of an anchor.

Kreuz=abnahme, =abnehmung (″...) f ㊷ *rel.* descent from the cross; =band *n:* a) *carp.* cross-bar, cr.-stay; b) ⊚ wrapper, paper cover; unter ~ under wrapper or cover, by book-post; *anat.* cross-ligament; =band=sendung ⊚ f sending (or s.th. sent) by book-post; =batterie ⚥ f cross-battery; =bau *m, arch.* transept; =beere ̌f (vom =dorn) buckthorn-berry; =bein *n, anat.* rump-bone, ⚥ (os) sacrum; vgl. Kreuz 6; =berg *m, rel.* (Mount) Calvary; =bild *n, rel.* crucifix; =bindel ̌n crossseizing; =blume f: a) ♃ cr.-flower, milkwort (*Poly'gala vulga'ris*); b) *arch.* finial, panache; =blütig ♃ *a.* ㊺ cruciferous; =blütler ̌a *m/pl.* crucifers, ⚥ *cruciferæ pl.*; =bogen ⊕ *m, arch.* = Gratbogen; =bramrahe ⚓ f mizzentopgallant yard; =bramsegel ⚓ *n* mizzen-topgallant sail; =brassen ⚓ f/pl. mizzen-top braces *pl.*; ̌brav (L~L) *a.* honest to the backbone.

Kreuzchen (L~) *n* ㉓ (*dim.* v. Kreuz) small cross, auch: crosslet.

Kreuz=donnerwetter (″...) P *n u. int.*, s. Kreuz 4; =dorn ̌ *m* (echter) purging buckthorn (*Rhamnus [catha'rtica]*).

kreuzen (L~) **I** *v/a., v/n.* (h.) u. sich ⚥ *v/refl.* ㊿ 1. to (mark with a) cross; die Arme ⚥ to cross (or fold) one's arms; die Schwerter ⚥ to cross (or

---

Zeichen (s. S. XVII): F familiär; P Volkssprache; Γ Gaunersprache; ⟍ selten; † alt (auch gestorben); * neu (auch geboren); ⁺⁺ unrichtig;

[Kreuzer] — 621 — [Kriechtier]

measure) swords; eine Straße ⚓ to cross (or traverse) a road; sich ⚓ (bekreuzen) to cross o.s.; sich ⚓ und segnen to make the sign of the cross; ihre Briefe ⚓ sich their letters cross; zwei Linien ⚓ sich ... cut each other, ... intersect; fig. j-s Pläne ⚓ (vereiteln) to thwart (or traverse) a p.'s plans. — 2. ⚓ (hin u. her fahren) to cruise (about), (lavieren) to tack. — 3. Viehzucht, zo., &c.: Rassen ⚓ to cross breeds, to interbreed. — II ~ n ㉓ (f. I) 4. crossing of roads, of swords, of letters, &c.; intersection of lines; ⚓ cruising, cruise; vgl. Kreuzung. — III ge-kreuzt p.p. und a. ㊻ 5. in den Bed. des inf.; ⚓ Weben mit ²er Kette cross-weaving. — 6. ♀: ⚓ decussate, cruciate (vgl. kreuz-förmig u. -ständig).

Kreuzer (⌣⌢) m ㉒ 1. [mhd. 13. sae.; *Kreuz öft. († südd.): kreu(t)zer (= nearly a farthing); das ist keinen ~ wert that's not worth a farthing. — 2. [kreuzen 2] ⚓ cruiser; kleiner geschützter ~ small protected cruiser, auch: scout. Kreuzer=flotte ⚓ (⌣⌣⌢...) f ㊻, =geschwader n fleet, squadron of cruisers.

Kreuz(es)=erfindung (⌣(⌣)⌢...) f ㊻ eccl. (3. Mai) Invention of the Cross; =erhöhung f (14. Sept.) Exaltation of the Cross. — Kreuzes=stamm (⌣⌣⌢...) m ㊻ tree of the cross, † Holy Rood; =tod m death on the cross, crucifixion; =zeichen n sign of the cross.

Kreuz=fahne (⌢⌣...) f ㊻ banner (or standard) of the cross; =fahrer m, hist. crusader; =fahrt f: a) ⚓ =zug; b) ⚓ cruise; =feuer ⚔ n cross-fire or -firing; ins ~ nehmen to take between two fires; ²fide'l F a. ㊻ (as) merry as a sandboy grig or a cricket; ein ²er Bursche a very jolly fellow; ²förmig a. cross-shaped, ⚓ cruciform; =frage f cross-questioning; =fuchs m, zo. crossfox (Vulpes cruci'gera); =gang m: a) procession led by a cross; b) ⚓ =weg; c) in Klöstern cloister; d) ⚒ cr.-cutting or -gallery; =gewölbe ㊻ n, arch. crossarched vault, cr.-vaulting; =gurt ㊻ m: a) Sattlerei: cross-girth; b) arch. = Gratbogen; =haspel ㊻ f, mech. windlass; =heer n, hist. army of crusaders; =hieb m, fenc. cross-cut; =hieb=feile f) m ㊻ cross-cut (file); =holz ♀ n = Mistel, auch = Wegedorn.

kreuzig/en (⌣⌣) [ahd.] I v/a. ㊻ 1. to crucify, to fix (or fasten, nail) to the cross. — 2. fig. sein Fleisch ~ (martern) to mortify one's flesh. — 3. = IV. — III K/er (⌣⌣) m ㉒ 4. one who crucifies the Saviour, &c., weitS. executioner. — IV K/ung f ㊻ 5. (f. I) crucifying, crucifixion (Gemälde: Crucifixion); fig. mortification of the flesh.

Kreuz=kirche (⌢⌢...) f ㊻: a) church built in the form of a cross; b) Church of the Holy Cross; =knoten ⚓ m sailor's knot; =kopf ㊻ m Dampfm.: Querhaupt) cross-head; =kraut ♀ n groundsel (Sene'cio); =kröte f, zo. natterjack (toad), rush-toad (Bufo calami'ta); =labkraut n cross-wort, mug-weed (Ga'lium crucia'tum); =lahm a. lame in the hip or back, broken-backed; e-n ⚓ schlagen

to beat a p. till he is lame; =mars ⚓ m mizzen-top; =maß ㊻ n, surv. surveyor's rule or square; =mast ⚓ m mizzen-mast; =naht f cross(-stitched) seam; =orden m order of the Cross; =otter f, zo. common adder or viper (Pe'lias berus); =peilung ⚓ f cross-bearing; =predigt f, hist. sermon in favour of a crusade; eine ~ halten to preach a crusade; =punkt m: a) math. point of intersection; b) 🚆 crossing; =rahe ⚓ f mizzen-top-yard; =riemen m, man. loin-strap, crupper; =ritter m, hist. crusading knight, vgl. =fahrer; knight of the Cross; =sackerlot P n u. int. f. Kreuz 4; =schiff n, arch. er-Kirche: transept; =schlag m Tennis: cross-drive; =schmerzen m/pl. pains pl. in the loins, back-ache, rheumatische: =schnabel m, orn. cross-beak or -bill, sheldapple (Lo'xia curviro'stra); ²schnäb(e)lig a. orn.: ⚓ curvirostral; =schnäbler m/pl. orn.: ⚓ curvirostra pl.; =schnitt m, surg. crucial incision; (schoch=schwerenot P f u. int. f. Kreuz 4; =schraffierung f Zeichenkunst: cross-hatching; =schwelle 🚆 f crosssill, cr.-sleeper; =segel ⚓ n mizzentop sail; =spinne f, zo. cross-(or garden-) spider (Epei'ra diade'ma); =sprung m Tanz: cross-caper; vgl. Entrechat; hunt. v. Hasen: =sprünge m. to double; =stab ㊻ m cross-staff; ²ständig ♀ a.: ⚓ decussate(d), cruciate, cruciform; =ständigkeit ♀ f decussation; =stange ㊻ f: a) Sattlerei: cross-rod; b) 🚆 cr.-head; =steg ㊻ m, typ. cross, head-stick; ²steif a. stiff in the loins or the back; =stelle 🚆 f crossing; =stellung f position in form of a cross; ♀: ⚓ decussation; =stenge ⚓ f mizzen-top mast; =stich m cross-stitch; =strebe f, arch. cross-stay; ²tragend a. cross-bearing, ⚓ crucigerous; =träger m bearer of the cross, cr.-bearer, weitS. (patient) sufferer; =tragung f carrying the cross (a. paint.); = und Querzüge m/pl. cross-country travels or rambles.

Kreuzung (⌣⌢) f ㊻ (f. kreuzen 1): ~ von Linien, Wegen 2c. intersection; 🚆, &c. crossing of the line; (f. 3) crossing of breeds, interbreeding, ⚓ hybridization; (Mischraffe) cross-breed. Kreuzungs=ader ⚒ (⌣⌢...) f ㊻ crosslode; =punkt m, =stelle f 🚆 (level-) crossing; (Knotenpunkt) junction.

Kreuz=verband ㊻ (⌢⌢) m ㉒ der Maurer: cross-bond; =verhör n jur. cross-examination; ein ~ mit e-m anstellen to cross-examine (or cross-question) a p.; =weg m cross-road or -way, crossing; =weh n = =schmerzen; ²weise adv. crosswise, crossways, across; her. saltierwise; ² legen, setzen, stellen to cross, to lay (or put) crosswise; (sich) ⚓ (durch=schneiden) to intersect; als a.: ⚓ Stellung = =stellung; =woche f, eccl. (Himmelfahrtswoche) Rogation week; weitS. Holy War; zum ~ auffordern to preach a crusade or the) kribb(e)lig (⌣⌢) a. ㊻ fretful. [Cross.⎦ Kribbel=kopf (⌣⌢...) m ㉒ hot-headed (or short-tempered, irritable) person (vgl. Hitzkopf); ²köpfig a. ㊻ hot-

headed, short-tempered, irritable; =krankheit f = Kriebelkrankheit. kribbeln (⌣⌣) ㉒a. I v/n. (h.) 1. (trabbeln) to crawl, creep; (wimmeln) to swarm like ants. — 2. (prickeln) to prickle, tingle, tickle. — II v/a. 3. das kribbelt (ärgert) ihn that vexes (or irritates) him. — III ~ n ㉓ 4. swarming, &c. (f. I); ich fühle ein ~ in den Fingern I have pins and needles in my fingers.

kribblig (⌣⌣) a. ㊻ f. kribbelig.
Kribs=krabs F (⌣⌢) [mhd.] m, n, inv. nonsense. [cric(k)-crac(k)!⎦
krick (⌢) [lautm.] int. ♀! crack!, ♀-krac(k)!⎦
Krickelei (⌣⌣⌢) f ㊻ 1. (Gekritzel) illegible scrawl, auch: F crincum-crancum. — 2. (Verdrießlichkeit) annoyance. ~ (Quengelei) über Kleinigkeiten F fuss(iness). Krickel=krakel F (⌣⌣⌢) m und n ㉒ = Krickelei 1. [to scribble, to scrawl.⎦ krickeln F (⌣⌣⌢) v/a. ㉒a. (schlecht schreiben))
Krick=ente (⌢...) f ⚓ = Kriek=ente. Kricket ? (⌣⌢) [engl.: *fr. criquet] n ㊻ cricket; ~ spielen to play cricket, to have a game of cricket; Partie (Wettkampf im) ~ cricket-match, game of cricket; ~spiel n ㊻ = Kricket; ~spieler m cricket-player, cricketer; auch: F (Angreifer) bowler, (Verteidiger) batsman, (Ballfänger) fielder.

krick=krack int. f. krick. [schuldner) bankrupt.⎦
Kridar ⚒ (⌣⌢) [mlt.] m ㉒d. (Gemein=
Kriebel=krankheit (⌣⌣⌢...) f ㊻ path. (Vergiftung mit Mutterkorn) ergotism.
Kriech=bohne ♀ (⌣⌢...) f ㊻ dwarf-bean (Phase'olus nanus).
Krieche (⌣⌢) [ahd.] f ㊻ = ~pflaume. kriechen (⌣⌣) [ahd.] I (ant. geh(e)n) v/n. (h., bei Ortsveränderung ſu) ㉖ft. 1. to creep, langsam: to crawl, mühsam: to drag o.s. along, wie ein Wurm: to worm (one's way); auf allen vieren ⚓ to crawl on all fours; durch enge Löcher ⚓ to squeeze through ...; wie eine Schnecke ⚓ to crawl along like a snail, to walk at a snail's pace. — 2. die Hühnchen ⚓ aus dem Ei the little chicks come out of the eggs or are hatched; die Kröte kriecht aus ihrem Loche the toad comes (crawling) out of its hole; in alle Winkel ⚓ (um et. zu suchen) to hunt in every corner; F er möchte vor Angst in ein Mauseloch ⚓ he is terribly frightened, F he is in a blue funk; F vor e-m ⚓ to cringe (or grovel) before a p. — II ~ n ㉓ 3. creeping, &c. (f. I); fig. = Kriecherei. — III ²d p.p. und a. ㊻ 4. in den Bed. des inf. — 5. ♀: ⚓ humifuse; zo. ²des Tier reptile.
Kriechen=pflaume ♀ (⌣⌣⌢...) f ㊻ bullace (-plum) (Prunus insiti'tia).
Kriech=ente (⌢⌢...) f ㊻ = Kriek=ente. Kriecher (⌣⌢) m ㉒, ~in ㊻ cringing (or grovelling, F carneying) person, cringer, toady, F crawler, sneak; ~ei (⌣⌣⌢) f ㊻ cringing, grovelling, F sneaking; ²isch a. ㊻ cringing, grovelling, servile.
Kriech=pflanze ♀ (⌣⌣⌢...) f ㊻ creeping (or trailing) plant, creeper; =sucht f (bsd. fig.) grovelling spirit, toadyism; =tier n, zo. (Reptil) reptile.

♪ Musik; ⚓ Wissenschaft; ♀ Pflanze; ⚱ Geographie; ㊻ Technik; ⚒ Bergbau; ⚔ Militär; ⚓ Marine; ⚕ Handel; ✉ Post; 🚆 Eisenbahn.

[**Krieg**] (¹) [mhd. (ahd.)] *m* ⑭c. (*ant.* Friede) war(fare), (Fehde) feud; (Streit) quarrel; f. Bürger=2; ~ auf Leben und Tod, ~ bis aufs Messer war to the knife; e-m ob. an e-n (den) ~ erklären to declare war against a p.; ~ führen gegen e-n ob. mit e-m to wage (or to carry on) war against (or with) a p., to make war upon a p.; im ~e sein mit to be at war with; ein Land mit ~ überziehen to invade (or overrun) a country; den ~ wieder anfangen to resume hostilities; in den ~ ziehen to go to war, to take the field.

kriegen (¹⌣) [mhd.; *Krieg] ⊗ **I** *v/n*. (h.) 1. geh. Spr. to wage (or carry on) war, to (go to) war. — **II** *v/a*. u. sich ⚔ *v/recipr*. 2. (ergreifen) to seize, to catch hold of; sie 2 sich an den Haaren they pull each other by the hair. — 3. = bekommen I u. III. — 4. mit *adv*. oft = bringen 7.

Krieger (¹⌣) *m* ㉒, **~in** *f* ㊵ warrior (*f* female warrior, auch: Amazon); (Kämpfer) fighter, combatant, *poet*. son of Mars. — Vgl. auch Soldat.

Krieger=bund (¹¹⌣...) *m* ㉒ = =verein.

kriegerisch (¹⌣⌣) *a*. ⑥⑥ (den Krieg liebend) warlike, bellicose, fond of fighting; (zum Kriege gehörig) martial, (Soldaten, das Heer betr.) military, soldier-like.

Krieger=kaste (¹¹⌣...) *f* ㉒ caste of warriors, military caste; =**leben** *n* warrior's life; =**stand** *m* military profession, *coll*. military men *pl*.; =**verein** *m* association (or club) of veterans.

krieg=fertig (¹¹...) *a*. ⑥⑥ ready (prepared) for war, mobilized; 2**führend** *a*. engaged in war, belligerent; 2e Mächte belligerents *pl*.; =**führung** *f* ㉒ warfare, belligerence.

Kriegs=adel ⚔ (¹¹...) *m* ㉒ military nobility; =**akademie** *f* mil. academy, in England auch: Woolwich Academy; =**angelegenheit** *f* mil. concern; =**artikel** *m/pl*. martial law; =**ausrüstung** *f* armament, mobilization; =**bataillo'n** *n* battalion on war-footing or on active service; =**bau-kunst** *f* military engineering, (art of) fortification; =**baumeister** *m* mil. engineer; =**bedarf** *m*, =**bedürfnisse** *n/pl*. requisites *pl*. of war, mil. stores *pl*.; =**behörde** *f* mil. authorities *pl*., in Engl.: War Office; 2**bereit** *a*. ⑥⑥ ready for war; =**bereitschaft** *f* readiness for war, (state of) mobilization; in ~ setzen to mobilize; vgl. =fuß; =**brauch** *m* custom in war; =**budget** *n* military (or army-)budget; =**denkmünze** *f* war-medal; =**dienst** *m* mil. service, service in the army; ~e nehmen to enlist (in time of war); =**drommete** *f* war-trumpet; =**eifer** *m* mil. zeal or ardour; =**entschädigung** *f* war-indemnity; 2**erfahren** *a*. experienced in war; =**erfahrung** *f* mil. experience; =**erklärung** *f* declaration of war; =**eröffnung** *f* opening (or commencement) of hostilities; =**fach** *n* mil. profession or science; =**fackel** *f* torch of war; =**fahne** *f* mil. standard, in Engl.: colour(s *pl*.); =**fall** *m* [lt.] casus belli; im ~e in case of war; =**flotte** ⚓ *f* navy, naval squadron or force, fleet of battle-ships; in Dienst gestellte ~ fleet in commission; =**fuhrwerk** *n* conveyance used in war; =**fuß** *m* war-footing; auf (den) ~ setzen to put (or place) on a war-footing; Truppen auf ~ mobilized troops *pl*., troops equipped for war; vgl. =bereitschaft; =**gebrauch** *m* usage of war; =**gefahr** *f* danger (or risk) of war; =**gefährte** *m* companion in arms; =**gefangene**([r]m) *f* prisoner of war, captive; =**gefangenschaft** *f* captivity; 2**gemäß** *a*. in warlike manner; =**gerät**(schaften *f/pl*.) *n* implements *pl*. of war, baggage; vgl. =vorrat; =**gericht** *n* court-martial; vor ein ~ stellen to court-martial; ~ über e-n halten to try a p. by court-martial, to court-martial a p.; 2**gerichtlich** *a*. by court-martial; =**gerichtsrat** *m* († Auditeur) Judge-Advocate; =**gerücht** *n* rumour of war, warlike rumour; =**geschichte** *f*: a) mil. history; b) war story or tale; =**geschrei** *n* war-cry, von Wilden: war-whoop; (Feldgeschrei) watchword; =**geschwader** ⚓ *n* (naval) squadron equipped for war, fleet of warships; =**gesetz** *n* mil. (or martial) law; =**getöse**, =**getümmel** *n* din of battle, tumult of war; 2**geübt** *a*. practised in (or inured to) war; =**gliederung** *f* order of battle, battle-array; =**glück** *n* fortune (or chance) of war; =**gott** *m*, *myth*. god of war, Mars; =**göttin** *f*, *myth*. goddess of war, Bellona; =**hafen** ⚓ *m* naval port; =**handwerk** *n* mil. profession; =**heer** *n* army (in the field), military force(s *pl*.); =**held** *m* warrior-hero, hero of war; =**herr** *m* supreme commander (or chief) of an army, *bibl*., &c. auch: lord of hosts; =**jahr** *n* year of war; =**kamerad** *m* =**gefährte**; =**kanzlei** *f* war(-)office; =**karte** *f* war-map, mil. map; =**kasse** *f* war-chest; =**kassierer** *m* paymaster (general); =**knecht** *m* (simple) soldier or trooper; =**kommissaria't** *n* commissariat; =**kommissa'r**(ius) *m* ↿ commissariat-officer; =**konterbande** *f* contraband of war; =**kosten** *pl*. war-expenses *pl*., cost of war; 2**kundig** *a*. skilled in war; =**kundige**(r) *m* tactician, strategist; =**kunst** *f* art of war(fare); tactics, strategy; =**lärm** *m* warlike reports *pl*.; vgl. =getöse; =**lazare'tt** *n* military hospital; =**leben** *n* mil. life, life in war; =**leute** *pl*. warriors, fighting men. fighters *pl*.; =**lied** *n* war-song; =**list** *f* stratagem, ruse adopted in war; =**lust**(ig *a*.) *f* eagerness (eager) for war, love for (fond of) fighting; =**macht** *f*: a) military force(s *pl*.); b) (kriegführende Macht) belligerent power; =**mann** *m*: a) allg.: warrior; b) (tüchtiger Streiter) good fighter, champion; =**mannschaft** *f* troops *pl*. (in active service); =**mantel** *m* mil. cloak; =**marine** ⚓ *f* a country's navy; vgl. =flotte; =**maschine** *f* engine of war; =**mini'ster** *m* minister of war, in Engl.: Secretary for (*Am*. of) War; =**ministe'rium** *n* ministry of war, in Engl.: War Office, *Am*. War Board; 2**müde** *a*. weary (or tired) of war; =**not** *f* stress of war; =**partei** *f* war-party; =**pflicht** *f*: a) obligation (or liability) to serve (in the army); b) mil. duty; 2**pflichtig** *a*. liable to military service; =**pflichtigkeit** *f* = =pflicht a; =**rat** *m*: a) council of war; b) (Beamter) clerk in the War Office; =**recht** *n*: a) usage of war; b) martial law; =**rese'rve** *f* reserve(-force); =**reservi'st** *m* reserve-man, soldier belonging to the reserve; =**roß** *n* war-steed, charger; =**ruf** *m* cry of war; warlike appeal or summons; =**ruhm** *m* mil. glory; =**rüstung** *f*: a) e-s einzelnen: mil. equipment or accoutrement; b) ~en *pl*. warlike preparations *pl*.; =**schade**(n) *m* damage (or loss) inflicted by war; =**schatz** *m* military chest; =**schatzung** *f* war-contribution; =**schauplatz** *m* seat (or theatre) of war; =**schiff** ⚓ *n* man-of-war, war-ship or -vessel; (Schlachtschiff) battle-ship; weit S. armed vessel; ein ~ in Dienst stellen to commission a man-of-war; =**schuld** *f* war-debt, debt incurred by war; =**schule** *f* mil. school; vgl. =akademie; =**spiel** *n*: a) game of war; b) (Spiel) war-game, ↿ kriegspiel; =**sprache** *f* military language; =**stand** *m*, =**stärke** *f* war-footing; =**steuer** *f*: a) (Brandschatzung) contribution exacted from the enemy; b) war-tax; =**strafe** *f* mil. punishment; =**straße** *f* mil. road or route; =**tagebuch** *n* war-diary; =**tanz** *m* war-dance; =**tat** *f* warlike deed, mil. exploit; =**telegra'ph** *m* telegraph (used) for mil. purposes; =**tracht** *f*: a) der Wilden *ac*. war-attire or -paint; b) = =rüstung a; =**tüchtig**(keit *f*) *a*. fit(ness) for war, efficient (mil. efficiency); =**übung** *f* mil. manœuvre; =**verpflegung** *f* provisioning of an army in the field; =**verpflegungs=amt** *n* (army) commissariat; =**volk** *n* troops, mil. forces *pl*.; =**vorrat** *m*, =**vorräte** *m/pl*. mil. stores *pl*.; ammunition; =**werft** ⚓ *f* navy-dockyard, arsenal; =**wesen** *n* mil. affairs or concerns *pl*.; =**wissenschaft** *f* mil. (or strategical) science; =**wut** *f* warlike fury; =**zahl=amt** *n* army pay-office; =**zahlmeister** *m* paymaster in the army; =**zeit** *f* time of war; in ~en in times of war, during a war; =**zucht** *f* mil. discipline; =**zug** *m* mil. expedition, campaign; =**zulage** *f* allowance for service in the field; =**zustand** *m* state of war, war-footing; =**zweck** *m*: für ~e for purposes of war, for warlike purposes.

Kriek=ente (¹¹⌣⌣) *f* ㊵ *orn*. creek-duck, teal (*Anas crecca*).

Krim ♀ (¹) *npr/f*. ㊾a.: die ~ (russ. Halbinsel am Schwarzen Meere) the Crimea.

kriminal (⌣⌣¹) [lt.] *a*. ⑥⑥ *jur*. (strafrechtlich) criminal (*ant*. zivil, bürgerlich 2).

Kriminal=abteilung (⌣⌣¹¹...) *f* ㉒ *jur*. criminal department, Lo.: Criminal Office; =**anklage** *f/cr*. charge; =**beamte**(r) *m* officer of the cr. department; =**gericht** *n* cr. court, Lo.: (Central)Criminal Court, Old (jetzt: New) Bailey; =**gerichtlich** *a*. criminal, penal; =**gerichtsbarkeit** *f* cr. jurisdiction; =**gerichts=ordnung** *f* cr. procedure; =**gesetzbuch** *n* cr. (or penal) code.

Signs (see page XVII): F familiar; P vulgar; F flash; ⚡ rare; † obsolete (died); * new word (born); ++ incorrect; ♪ music;

[Kriminalist] — 623 — [Krone]

Kriminalist (-ˌ-ˈ-) m ⊕ jur. (Lehrer des Strafrechts; ant. Zivilist) criminalist.
Kriminalität (-ˌ-ˌˈ-) f ⊕ (Straffälligkeit) criminality.
Kriminal-klage (-ˌ-ˈˌ...) f ⊕ jur. criminal charge; **=prozeß** m cr. case; **=psychologie** f psychology of crime; **=recht** n penal law; **=richter** m judge sitting upon criminal cases; Lo. a. judge of the (Central) Criminal Court or the Old Bailey; **=statistik** f criminal statistics; **=verfahren** n criminal proceeding.
kriminell (-ˌˈ-) a. ⊕ criminal.
krim(i)sch (ˈ-) [Krim] a. ⊕ Crimean.
Krim-krieg ⚔ (ˈ-ˌ-) m ⊕ hist. (1853—1856) Crimean war. [Crimean lambskin.]
Krimmer ⊕ (ˈ-) m ⊕ Kürschnerei.]
Krimpe ⊕ (ˈ-) f ⊕ Tuchm.: (Dekatieren) sponging of cloth; in die ~ geh(e)n to be sponged, fig. to shrink.
krimpen ⊕ (ˈ-) [ndd.] ⊕ (p.p. a. gekrumpen) I v/n. (fn) und sich ⊵ v/refl. von genetztem Tuche: to shrink. — II v/a. Tuch ⊵ to sponge, to shrink.
krimp-frei ⊕ (ˈ-ˌ-) a. ⊕ vom Tuche: not liable to shrink, thoroughly shrunk.
Krimskrams (ˈ-ˌ-) m ⓐ a. ⓐ (Plunder) lumber, trash, rubbish.
Krim-stecher (ˈ-ˌ-) m ⊕ opt. field-glass.
Kringel (ˈ-) [mhd. dim. v. Kring] m ⊕ = Brezel. [crinoline, hoop-petticoat.)
Krinoline (-ˌ-ˈ-) [fr.] f ⊕ ehm. (Reifrock)]
Krippe (ˈ-) [ahd.: crib] f ⊕ für das Vieh: crib, manger.
Krippen-beißen (ˈ-ˌ-) n ⊕ von Pferden: crib-biting; **=beißer** m crib-biter; weitS. (wretched) jade; **=damm** ⊕ m aus Holzblöcken u. Erde: crib-dam; **=reiter** m poor farmer, (Schmarotzer) sponger; **=setzen** n, **=setzer** m — **=beißen, =beißer**.
Krips F (ˈ) m ⊕ a.: beim ~ (Kragen) nehmen to (take by) the collar.
Kris (ˈ) m ⓐ a. (malaiischer Dolch) creese.
krisch(e) (ˈ(-)) impf. (subj.) v. kreischen.
Krise (ˈ-) f ⊕, **Krisis** f ⊕ [grch.] (Wendepunkt) crisis; eine Krisis durchmachen to pass through a crisis; **kriseln** (ˈ-) v/n. (h.) ⓐ. bsd. pol.: es kriselt (im Ministerium) there is a crisis (in the ministry), (ministerial) affairs are coming to a crisis or a head.
Krispin (-ˈ-) [lt.] npr/m. ⓐⓐα. (Schutzheiliger der Schuster) Crispin(us).
Kristall (-ˈ-) [ahd., *grch.] ⓐd. 1. m, chm., min., &c. crystal (a. ⊕ Glasfabr.); ~e bilden, in ~en anschießen to form crystals, to crystallize. — 2. n (feine Glasware) crystal goods pl. or ware.
kristall-ähnlich (-ˈˌ...) a. ⊕ like crystal, ⊕ crystalline, ...oid; **=anschuß** m ⊕ crop of crystals; **=bildung** f formation of crystals, crystallization; **=druse** f, min. cluster (or bunch) of crystals.
Kristallehre (-ˈˌ-) [Kristall=lehre] f ⊕: ⊕ crystallology. [crystal.)
kristallen (-ˈ-) a. ⊕ (D 9) (as clear as)]
Kristall-fabrik (-ˈˌ-) f ⊕ ⊕ crystal-works pl.; **=fabrikation** ⊕ f manufacture of crystal; **=feuchtigkeit** f, anat. des Auges; ⊕ crystalline (or vitreous) humour; **=fläche** f, min. facet; **=flasche** f decanter; **=form** f; ⊕ crystalline form; **=formenbeschreiber** m: ⊕ crystallo-

grapher; **=formenbeschreibung** f: ⊕ crystallography; **=glas** ⊕ ⊕ n crystal; **=haltig** a. min.: ⊕ crystalliferous; **=hell** a. (as clear as) crystal, ⊕ crystalline, weitS. transparent, translucid; **=himmel** m crystal sky.
kristallig (-ˈ-) a. ⊕ like crystal.
kristallinisch (-ˌˈ-) ⊕: ⊕ crystalline; ~werden (-ˌ-ˈˌ-) n ⊕ = Kristallisation.
Kristallinse (-ˈˌ-) [Kristall=linse] f ⊕ des Auges; ⊕ crystal (or hyaline) lens.
Kristallisation (-ˌˌ-ˈˌ-) f ⊕, ⊕ crystallization; **~s-gefäß** n ⊕, **=kasten** m, chm. crystallizing-pan, crystallizer.
kristallisierbar (-ˌˌ-ˈ-) a. ⊕: ⊕ crystallizable; **=keit** f ⊕ crystallizability.
kristallisieren (-ˌˌ-ˈ-) I v/a., v/n. (fn) u. sich ⊵ v/refl. ⊕ to crystallize. — II ~ n ⊕ u. K/ung f ⊕ crystallization.
Kristall-kiesel (-ˈ...) m ⊕ crystal pebble; **=klar** a. ⊕ = **=hell**; **=kunde, =lehre** f. Kristallehre; **=linie** f. Kristallinse.
Kristallographie ⊕ (-ˌˌ-ˌˈ-) [grch.] f ⊕ crystallography — Kristallkunde.
Kristall-palast (-ˈˌ...) m ⊕ zu Sydenham, Lo. Crystal Palace; **=sachen** f/pl. = **=waren; =schleifer, =schneider** ⊕ m polisher, cutter of crystal; **=system** n, min., &c.: ⊕ crystalline system; **=waren** f/pl. crystal goods pl. or ware; **=wasser** n, chm.: ⊕ water of crystallization.
Kriterium (-ˈ-(-)) [grch.] n ⊕ phls. (Merkmal) criterion, (Probe) test.
Kritik (-ˈ-) [grch.] f ⊕ (Beurteilungs[gabe]) criticism; (wissenschaftliche ⓐ Besprechung) criti'que, review; in e-r ~ besprechen, e-r ~ unterziehen to criticize, von Büchern: to review; tadelnde ~, auch: stricture (passed upon), censure, F unter aller ~ below contempt, wretchedly bad, execrable.
Kritikaster F (-ˌ-ˈ-) m ⊕ wretched cri'tic, blundering reviewer.
Kritiker (ˈ-) [grch.] m ⊕ critic, von Büchern ⓐ auch: reviewer.
kritik-los (ˈ-) a. ⊕ without critical faculty, undiscriminating; **=losigkeit** f ⊕ lack of discrimination.
kritisch (ˈ-) [grch.] a. ⊕ (kunstrichterlich) critical, (fein urteilend) judicious, keen(ly judging); (bedenklich, mißlich) precarious; im Len Augenblick at the critical moment, in the nick of time; Ler (bedeutender) Zeitpunkt critical moment, important juncture; Ler Kopf fine (or subtle) mind or head; sich in Len (schlimmen) Umständen, Verhältnissen befinden to be very awkwardly situated.
kritisieren (-ˌ-ˈ-) [grch.] v/a. u. v/n. (h.) ⊕: ein Werk ⊵ to criticize..., to judge keenly, ein Buch auch: to review; milde: to comment upon, tadelnd: to pass strictures upon, F to pitch into, to run down, to handle roughly. [cism.)
Kritizismus (-ˌ-ˈ-) [grch.=lt.] m ⊕ criti-]
Krittelei (-ˌ-ˈ-) [kritteln] f ⊕ carping (or captious) criticism, fault-finding.
Kritt(e)ler(in f ⊕) (ˈ-) m ⊕ (ˈ(-)(-)) carping (or censorious) critic.
kritt(e)lig (ˈ(-)(-)) a. ⊕ 1. fault-finding, censorious, captious. — 2. (leicht ärgerlich) irritable, peevish, (ränke-

süchtig) scheming. — 3. Le (mühsame) Arbeit close (or trying) work.
kritteln (ˈ-) v/n. (h.) ⓐa.: über et. ⊵ to make critical comments (or adverse remarks) upon a th.; vgl. bekritteln.
Krittler(in), krittlig f. Kritt(e)ler ⓐc.
Kritzelei (-ˌ-ˈ-) [kritzeln] f ⊕ = Gekritzel.
kritz(e)licht, kritz(e)lig (ˈ(-)(-)) a. ⊕ Handschrift: fine and close, (unleserlich) illegible.
kritzeln (ˈ-) [nhd., ahd.] I v/n. (h.) u. v/a. ⓐa. 1. (traßen) to scratch; meine Feder kritzelt und spritzt beim Schreiben ... scratches and splashes ... — 2. (schlecht schreiben) to scribble, to scrawl. — II ~ n ⊕ 3. (f. 1) scratching; (f. 2) scribbling, scribble, scrawl.
Kritzler (ˈ-) m ⊕, **~in** f ⊕ scribbler.
Kroate (-ˈ-) m ⊕, **Kroatin** f ⊕ Croat; **Kroati-en** ⊕ (-ˈ-ˌ(-)) npr/n. ⓐα. Österreich: Croatia; **kroatisch** (-ˈ-) a. ⊕ Croatian. [von kriechen.)
kroch (ˈ-), **kröche** (ˈ-) impf. ind. u. subj.]
Krocket ⊺ (ˈ-) n ⓔ, **~spiel** n ⊕ croquet; ~ spielen to play croquet, to croquet; **=hammer** m ⊕ (croquet) mallet.
krockieren (-ˌ-ˈ-) v/a. ⊕ Krocketspiel: to croquet.
Kroki ⚔ (ˈ-) [fr.] n ⊕ surv. sketch.
krokieren (-ˌ-ˈ-) [fr. croquer] v/a. ⊕ (stizieren) to sketch, to make a sketch of.
Krokodil (-ˌ-ˈ-) [grch.] n ⓐd. zo. crocodile (Crocodi'lus); amerikanisches ~ alligator, cayman; **⊵artig** (ˈ-ˌ...) a. ⊕ crocodilian; **~eidechse** f ⊕ f. Dragoneer; **~eier** n/pl. crocodile's eggs pl.; **~s-tränen** f/pl. fig. crocodile (or sham, false) tears pl.; **~wächter** m, orn. crocodile-bird (Curso'rius aegy'ptius).
krokon-sauer (-ˌ-ˈ-) a. ⊕ chm. croconic; **⊵saures Salz** croconate; **=säure** f ⊕ croconic acid. [(Safran) crocus (Crocus).)
Krokus ⚘ (ˈ-) [grch.] m, inv. ob. ⓐ]
krollen, kröllen (ˈ-) v/a. u. sich ⊵ v/refl. ⊕ to curl (up); (krausen) to crisp, frizzle; (sich rund rollen) to coil (o.s.) up.
Kroll-erbsen (ˈ-ˌ...) f/pl. Kocht.: boiled peas pl. served up whole; **=haar** n frizzled hair; **=hecht** m pike served up whole with its tail stuck in its mouth; **=kopf** m curly head; **=tabak** m shag.
Kromlech (ˈ-) [gäl.] m ⓐd. ⊕ cromlech.
Kron-amt (ˈ-ˌ...) n ⊕ office under the crown; **=anwalt** m attorney-general; solicitor for the crown; **=beamte(r)** m officer of the crown; **=bein** n, anat. des Pferdefußes; ⊕ coronal bone; **=bewerber** m pretender to the crown; **=bewerbung** f pretendership.
Krönchen (ˈ-) n ⊕ little crown, coronet; ⚘ (Samen=)~: a coronule.
Krone (ˈ-) [ahd.: crown; *lt. cŏrōna] f ⊕ 1. crown; päpstliche (dreifache) ~ triple crown, tiara; (Adels-)~ coronet; (Stirnband) diadem; e-m Könige die ~ aufsetzen to place the crown on a king's head, to crown a king. — 2. (das Höchste, Vollendetste) acme, (pink of) perfection, die ~ aller Frauen the pearl (or paragon) of womanhood; Sprichw. dem Verdienste s-e ~! honour to whom honour is due! f. aufsetzen 2. — 3. (Kranz) (floral) crown, garland, wreath; ⚘ (Blumen=)~: ⚘ corolla; ~ e-s Baumes top (or crown) of a tree. — 4. ⊕ (Kronleuchter) chandelier; ~ e-r

---

⚛ scientific; ⚘ botanical; ⚲ geography; ⊕ machinery; ⚒ mining; ⚔ military; ⚓ marine; ⊕ commercial; ✉ postal; 🚂 railway.

Mauer, ⚔ Kamm e-s Festungswerkes *xc.*: crest; *typ.* ~ der Presse cap of a press. — 5. (Gipfel des Nadelholzes) top shoots *pl.*; *hunt.* (die obersten Ecken des Geweihes) crown-antlers *pl.* — 6. ❀ (Zehnmarkstück) ten-mark piece, half a sovereign; öst. (*abbr.* K) Austrian crown, half a sovereign (a crown ist in England gleich five shillings). — 7. F (Kopf) es ist mit ihm nicht ganz richtig unter der ~ F he is not quite right in the upper story; et. in der ~ h. (angetrunken sein) F to have had a drop too much; was ist ihm in die ~ gefahren? what has befallen him or made him cross? [the crown.]

Kron=einkünfte (⁻…) *pl.* ⑫ revenue of

krönen (⁻ᵕ) [mhd.; *Krone] **I** *v/a.* u. **sich** ∼ *v/refl.* ⑱: (sich) ∼ to crown (o.s.); e-n (sich) ∼ auch: to put or place the crown on a p.'s (on one's own) head; zum Könige ∼ to crown as (a) king; preisgekrönter Aufsatz prize-essay; gekrönter Dichter poet-laureate; *fig.* (vollenden) to crown, finish, cap, top; s. Erfolg am Schlusse. — **II** ~ *n* ㉓ s. Krönung.

kronen=artig (⁻ᵕ…) *a.* ⑯ like a crown, ♀ coron*al*, …ary; **=blatt** ⚘ *n* ⑫: ♀ petal; ∼**blatt=ähnlich**, ∼**blatt=förmig** ⚘ *a.*: ♀ petaloid, petaliform; ∼**blatt=ständig** *a.*: ♀ petaline; **=brenner** ⊙ *m* für Gas: rose-burner; **=fortsatz** *m*, *anat.* des Unterkiefers: ♀ coronoid process; **=gehörn** *n* = Krong.; **=gold** *n* eighteen-carat gold; ∼**los** *a.* crownless, ⚘: ♀ apetalous; **=orden** *m* Preußen: Order of the Crown; **=papier** ⊙ *n* crown-paper; **=rad** ⊙ *n* Uhrmacher: canting-wheel; ∼**ständig** ⚘ *a.*: ♀ epipetalous; **=taler** *m* (= 6 Frank) French crown-piece; **=taube** *f*, *orn.* crown-pigeon (*Megape'lia, Goura*); **=träger(in** *f*) *m* crowned head, sovereign.

Kron=erbe (⁻…) *m* ⑫ (**=erbin** *f*) heir (heiress) to the throne; vgl. =prinz; **=erbse** ⚘ *f* crown-pea (*Pisum sati'vum umbella'tum*); ∼**förmig** *a.* ⑯ crown-shaped, ♀ coroniform; **=gehörn**, **=geweih** *n*, *hunt.* crown of a stag's head; **=glas** *n* Optik: crown-glass; **=gut** *n* crown-land or -demesne; estate of the crown; **=hirsch** *m*, *hunt.* stag with crown-antlers. [son of Kronos.]

Kronide (ᵕ⁻ᵕ) [grch.] *m* ㊹ *myth.* (Zeus)

Kron=insigni-en (⁻…) *f/pl.* ⑫ insignia *pl.* of the crown; **=juwelen** *n/pl.* crown-jewels *pl.*; **=kolonie** *f* crown-colony; **=land** *n*: a) = =gut; b) ♀ (öst. Provinz) crown-land; bsd. ehm. **=leh(e)n** *n* fief of the crown; **=lehn=inhaber** *m* tenant in chief or *in capite*; **=leuchter** *m* chandelier; **=prinz** *m* (ältester Sohn e-s Königs) Crown Prince, Prince Royal, in Engl.: Prince of Wales, e-s Kaisers: Prince Imperial, e-s andern regierenden Fürsten: hereditary prince; allg.: heir apparent, heir to the throne; **=prinzessin** *f* (Gemahlin e-s =prinzen) Crown Princess, in Engl.: Princess of Wales; (älteste Tochter e-s Königs von England *xc.*) Princess Royal; allg.: hereditary princess, heiress to the throne; ∼**prinzlich** *a.* relating to the Crown Prince; **=rad** ⊙ *n*, *mach.* crown-wheel; **=rat** *m* in England: Privy Council; **=räuber** *m* usurper of the crown; **=richter** *m* für die Totenschau: coroner; **=säge** ⊙ *f* crown- (or drum-)saw. [= Preiselbeere.]

Krons=beere ⚘ *prov.* (⁻…) [Kran(ich)s=] *f*

Kron=stahl ⊙ (⁻…) *m* ⑫ crown-steel.

Krönung (⁻ᵕ) *f* ⑯ crowning, coronation.

Krönungs=eid (⁻ᵕ…) *m* ⑫ coronation-oath; **=feierlichkeit** *f* cor.-festivities *pl.*; **=mahl** *n* cor.-banquet; **=münze** *f* medal (or coin) struck in honour of a coronation; **=saal** *m* cor.-hall; **=sessel** *m* cor.-chair; **=tag** *m* cor.-day.

Kron=werk (⁻…) *n* ⑫ *frt.* crown-work; **=wicke** ⚘ *f* sickle-wort (*Coroni'lla*); **=zeuge** *m* crown-witness, witness of the crown, gegen Mitschuldige: King's evidence.

Kropf (⁻) [ahd.: crop] *m* ⑦b. 1. *orn.* (Vormagen) crop, maw, gizzard. — 2. *path* (Geschwulst vorn am Halse, Anschwellung der Schilddrüse) wen, *a.* (fr.) goitre, ♀ bronchocele, tracheocele. — 3. (Anschwellung bei Tieren) (dropsical) swelling. — 4. ⚘ excrescence. — 5. ⊙ Papiermühle: ~ e-s Holländers breasting of a rag-engine.

kropf=artig (⁻…) *a.* ⑯ *path.* wenny, goitrous, ♀ strumous, strumose.

kröpfen (⁻ᵕ) [Kropf] ⑱ **I** *v/n.* (h.) 1. *hunt.* v. Raubvögeln: to gorge (o.s.). — **II** *v/a.* 2. Gänse *xc.* ∼ (stopfen) to cram (or stuff) … — 3. *for.* Bäume ∼ = kappen². — 4. ⊙ (rechtwinklig biegen) to bend at right angles. — **III** ~ *n* ㉓ 5. s. Kröpfung.

Kröpfer (⁻ᵕ) *m* ㉒ *orn.* = Kropftaube.

Kropf=gans (⁻…) *f* ⑫ *orn.* white pelican (*Peleca'nus onocro'talus*); **=geschwulst** *f* = Kropf 2.

kropficht, kropfig, kröpfig (⁻ᵕ) [Kropf] *a.* ⑯ *path.* goitrous, afflicted with a wen, ♀ strumous, strumose.

Kropf=kranke(r) (⁻…) *s.* ⑫ *path.* p. afflicted with a wen, goitrous patient; **=rad** ⊙ *n* Müllerei: breast-wheel; **=taube** *f orn.* pouter, cropper (*Colu'mba gutturo'sa*).

Kröpfung (⁻ᵕ) *f* 1. cramming, &c. (s. kröpfen II). — 2. ⊙ *arch.* (vorstehender Teil) breast-work, breasting, (round) moulding.

Krop(p)=zeug F (⁻⁻) [ndd.] *n* ⑫ (Gesindel) ragamuffins *pl.*; das kleine ~ the young fry or brats *pl.*

kröschen (⁻ᵕ) *v/a.* ⑪ Kochk.: to fry in butter or dripping or lard.

kröseln ⊙ (⁻ᵕ) [fraus] *v/a.* ⑫a. to rabbet; Böttcherei: to groove. [reicher Mann).]

Krösus (⁻ᵕ) *npr m.* ⑱γ. Crœsus (*fig.* =

Kröte (⁻ᵕ) [ahd.] *f* ㊸ 1. *zo.* toad (*Bufo*), bisw. *a.* paddock; kleine ~ (*a. dim.* Krötchen *n* ㉓) little toad, *a.* toadlet, toadling. — 2. P (boshafte Person) ill-natured person, F snake in the grass; ekelhafte, giftige ~ nasty, spiteful creature. — 3. F *g.s.* (kleines Wesen) little creature, F (dear) little thing or tot. — 4. P ein paar ~n (Groschen) in der Tasche haben to have a few pence (F coppers) in one's pocket.

kröten=artig (⁻ᵕ…) *a.* ⑯ *zo.* toad-like, toadish; **=binse** ⚘ *f* ⑫ toad-rush (*Juncus bufo'nius*); **=eidechse** *f* horned frog or toad (*Phrynoso'ma*); **=gift** *n* toad's venom; **=loch** *n* toad's hole; **=stein** *m* toad-stone; *geol.* fossiler ~: ♀ bufonite, batrachite; **=weibchen** *n* female toad.

krötig, krötisch (⁻ᵕ) *a.* ⑯ 1. of (or like) a toad. — 2. *fig.* full of venom or malice.

Kroton ⚘ (⁻ᵕ, F ⁻ᵕ) [grch.] *m* ㉛ croton (*Croton*); s. bsd. Purgier∼.

Kroton=öl (⁻…) *n* ⑫ aus dem Samen v. Purgierkroton: croton-oil, ♀ (lt.) oleum tiglii; ∼**sauer** *a.* ⑯ *chm.*: ♀ crotonic; ∼saures Salz crotonate; **=säure** *f* crotonic acid ($C_4H_6O_2$).

Krücke (⁻ᵕ) [ahd.: crutch, crook] *f* ㊸ 1. crutch; ~ eines Stocks: crook; an ~n gehen to go (or walk) on (or with) crutches. — 2. ♪ peg of a violin, &c. — 3. ⊙ forked stick or hook; T-(or Y-)shaped tool; rake of a croupier; bridge of a billiard-table; handle of a scythe; ~ zum Rühren des Kalks: beater Salzfabrik: (Salz=)~ scraper; Färberei: (Rühr=)~ stirrer; *metall.* ~ zum Puddeln des Eisens: crutch, rake, rabble.

krücken=förmig (⁻ᵕ…) *a.* ⑯ in (the) shape of a crutch or a T; **=kreuz** *n*, *her.* potent, (Zeichen des Deutschordens) Teutonic cross, potence(-cross) (T).

Krück=stock (⁻…) *m* ⑫ stick with a crook (to it), crutch-stick.

Krug¹ (⁻) [ahd.; *Kkt.] *m* ⑦c, 6 1. jug, größerer für Wasser: pitcher, ohne Griff u. Schnauze: jar; (Henkelglas) mug; ~ zum Trinken (*a.* aus Metall) tankard; Sprichw. der ~ geht so lange zu Wasser, bis er bricht the pitcher goes so often to the well, that it comes home broken at last. — 2. (Topf, *a.* Maß) pot; bsd. Alt.: (Aschen=)~ (cinerary) urn.

Krug² norbd. (⁻) [ndd. 13/15. *sae.*] *m* ⑦c. (Schenke) (village-)inn, (old-fashioned) tavern, ale-house, pot-house.

Krügelchen (⁻ᵕᵕ), **Krüglein** (⁻ᵕ) *n* ㉓ (*dim.* von Krug¹) small jug, mug.

Krüger (⁻ᵕ) [Krug²] *m* ㉒, **~in** *f* ㊸ innkeeper, ale-house keeper, publican.

krug¹=förmig (⁻…) *a.* ⑯ in the shape of a jug or a pitcher, ♀ urceolar.

Krug²=gerechtigkeit *f* ⑯ license for keeping an ale-house, publican's license.

Krüglein (⁻ᵕ) *n* ㉓ small jug or pitcher.

krug¹=weise (⁻…) *adv.* in jugs (full).

Krug²=wirt (⁻…) *m* ⑫ = Krüger; **=wirtschaft** *f* = Krug².

Kruke (⁻ᵕ) [ndd. = Krug] *f* ㊸ 1. stone jug or bottle or jar. — 2. P *fig.* putzige ~ (schnurrige Person) F queer fish.

krüllen (⁻ᵕ) = krollen.

Krull=farn ⚘ (⁻,⁻) *m* ⑫ = Frauenhaar.

Krümchen (⁻ᵕ) *n* ㉓ [*dim.* von Krume] 1. = Brosam. — 2. *fig.* (ein bißchen, ein wenig) a wee (little) bit, a mere crumb.

Krume (⁻ᵕ) [ndd.: crumb] *f* ㊸ 1. (Brot=) ~ crumb (of bread) (*ant.* Rinde). — 2. **~n** *pl.* (bei Tische abfallende Brosamen) crumbs *pl.* [Krume) = Krümchen.]

Krümel(chen) (⁻ᵕ(ᵕ)) *n* ㉒(㉓) (*dim.* von

krüm(e)lig (⁻(ᵕ)ᵕ) *a.* ⑯ crumbling, crumbly, in crumbs.

Krümel=kohle ⚒ (⁻ᵕ…) *f* ⑫ small coal.

krümeln (⁻ᵕ) ⑫a. **I** *v/n.* (h.) u. **sich** ∼ *v/refl.* to crumble (away). — **II** *v/a.* to crumble.

Krümel=zucker (⁻ᵕ…) *m* ⑫ moist sugar, aus Süd-amerika: Demarara (sugar).

krümlig (⁻ᵕ) *a.* s. krüm(e)lig.

krumm (⁻) [ahd.] *a.* ⑯ (D 3,7) (*ant.* gerade) 1. (gebogen) crooked, bent;

[krummästig] — 625 — [Küche]

(hakenförmig) hooked, ⌒ aduncous; (bogenförmig) arched, (geschweift) curved, ⌒ sinuous; (gewunden): a) regelmäßig: winding, meandering; b) unregelmäßig: tortuous, ⌒ anfractuous; (verbogen) twisted, (verdreht) (a)wry, out of shape; adv. e-n ~ anblicken to look askance (or awry) at a p. (a. fig.) — 2. ℒe Beine crooked (F bow-) legs pl.; ℒe Beine haben, a. F to be bandy-legged; s. Buckel² 4; ℒe Finger machen to steal, to pilfer, F to pinch, crib, nick; ℒe Nase hooked nose, F co. beak; fig. e-n Len Rücken m. to stoop. — 3. mit verbs: ℒ biegen to bend, to curve, mit Gewalt: to twist; vgl. krümmen; ℒ geh(e)n to stoop in walking; fig. es geht ℒ mit ihm things go wrong with him; sich ℒ halten to stoop, to hold o.s. badly; sich ℒ lachen to split (one's sides) with laughing; ℒ liegen: a) to lie in a bent position; b) fig. to pinch and screw; vgl. ℒnehmen; e-n ℒ und lahm schlagen to beat a p. most unmercifully or within an inch of his life, F co. to pound a p. into a jelly; e-n ℒ schließen to tie a p. hand and foot, to put a p. in chains; Sie schreiben ℒ und schief you write up and down the line, you do not write straight; ℒ sein to be curved or crooked, (fehlerhaft geneigt) to be warped, von Personen: to stoop, to bend; ℒ sitzen to sit with a crooked back; sich ℒ sitzen to grow crooked with sitting; ℒ wachsen to grow up crooked or deformed; ℒ werden to bend, to curve, durch Alterschwäche: to be bowed down with age. — 4. fig. (unredlich) crooked, dishonest; ℒe Wege geh(e)n to pursue crooked (or tortuous) ways; das Gerade ℒ und das ~ gerade m., etwa: to twist the truth, to call black white and white black.

krumm=ästig (ˢ...) a. ⊛ with crooked (or gnarled) branches.
krümmbar (ˢ...) a. ⊛ bendable.
Krumm=bein (ˢ...) n ⊛ F bandy- (or bow-)legged person; ℒbeinig a. ⊛ bandy- (or bow-)legged, (kniescheifig) knock-kneed; =biegen n bending, ⌒ incurvation; ℒblätt(e)rig a.: ⌒curvifoliate; =buckel m (p. with a) crooked (or humped) back; =darm m, anat.: ⌒ ileum; =darm=gicht f, path.: ⌒ ileus.
Krümme (ˢ...) [ahd.] 1. (Krummsein, Krummes) crookedness, bend; curvature, winding, ⌒sinuosity; vgl. Krümmung 2. — 2. fig. crookedness, dishonesty, tortuosity; crooked (or tortuous) ways pl.
krümmen (ˢ...) [ahd.] I v/a. u. sich ℒ v/refl. ⊛ 1. (sich) ℒ to crook, bend, curve, twist; to wind (round); sich ℒ, a. to form a bend or curve, v. Flüssen: to meander, vom Wurme: to turn. — 2. sich ℒ und winden to wriggle (about); sich vor Schmerzen ℒ to be writhing (or F bent double) with pain; Sprichw. der getretene Wurm krümmt sich even a worm will turn when it is trodden on. — 3. fig. sich vor e-m ℒ to stoop before a p.; fig. ich werde ihm (or F co.) kein Härchen ~ not a hair of his head shall be touched, I shan't lift (or raise) a finger (for that); s. Haar 4. — II ~ n ⊛ 4. = Krümmung 1.

krumm=flächig (ˢ...) a. ⊛ with curved surface; =hals m ⊛ wry neck, path.: ⌒ torticollis; ℒhalsig a. with a wry neck, path.: ⌒ torticollar; =holz ⊥ n crooks pl., compass-timber, knee-piece; =holz=kiefer ⊛ ⚥ knee-pine (Pinus pumi'lio); =holz=öl n templin-oil; =horn n: a) twisted (or crumpled) horn; b) beast with twisted horns; c) ♪ crooked horn; (Pfeife und Register der Orgel) cromorna; ℒhörnig a. with twisted horns.
Krümmling ⊛ (ˢ...) m ⊛d. arch. curved joist or beam.
Krumm=linie (ˢ...) f ⊛ math.: ⌒ curve; ℒlinig a.⊛ math.:⌒curvilinear; =linigkeit f: ⌒ curvilinearity; ℒmäulig a. with a mouth all on one side; ℒnasig a. hook-nosed; ℒnehmen v/a. ⊛a**: F fig. (einem) et. ℒ to take a th. amiss (of a p.); =säbel ⚔ m orientalischer: scimitar; =schnabel m: a) crooked beak; b) orn. = Kreuzschnabel; ℒschult(e)rig a. round-shouldered, ⌒ Krümme 1; =stab m crook, e-s Bischofs: crozier; fig. episcopal rule; =stroh n finely chopped straw, litter.
Krümmung (ˢ...) f ⊛ 1. crooking, &c. (s. krümmen I). — 2. (Krümmen) curve; (gekrümmte Stelle) bend, curvature; ~en eines Baches ꝛc.: turns, windings pl.; path. krampfhafte ~ contortion; ~ des Rückgrats curvature of the spine; math. ~ e-r Kurve: ⌒flexure of a curve.
Krümmungs=halbmesser (ˢ...) m ⊛ math.: ⌒ radius of curvature.
Krumm=werden (ˢ...) n ⊛ growing crooked, crooked growth; =zapfen ⊛m, mach. crank; =zirkel ⊛ m cal(l)ipers pl.
krumpeln, krümpeln (ˢ...)[ndd.: crumple] v/a. ⊛a. to crumple, to crease, to ruffle, Papier auch: to crinkle; gekrümpelt, auch: puckered (up).
Krümper (ˢ...) m ⊛ 1. Tuchm.: sponger. — 2. ⚔ ehm. (Befreiungskriege, 1808:) halb ausgebildeter Reservist; ~pferd n cast (army-)horse.
Krupp ⚕ (ˢ) m ⊛ path. croup.
Kruppe (ˢ...) [fr. croupe; *dtsch.] f ⊛ (Kreuz) crupper of a horse.
Krüppel (ˢ...) [ndd.: cripple] m ⊛ cripple(d person) (Mißgestalt) stunted person, deformity; milder: afflicted p.; (gebrechliche Person) rickety (or delicate) person; ~ mit e-m Stelzfuße person with a wooden leg, P timber toes; zum ~ m. to cripple; zum ~ w. to be crippled; ~baum m ⊛ stunted tree, tree of stunted growth.
krüppel=haft (ˢ...) a. ⊛ crippled, deformed, milder: (physically) afflicted, rickety, delicate, (verstümmelt) maimed; (nicht voll entwickelt) stunted; ~igkeit (ˢ...) f ⊛ crippled or deformed, maimed) condition, milder: (physical) affliction. [krüppelhaft.]
krüpp(e)licht, krüpp(e)lig (ˢ...) ⚹ =]
Krustace=e ⌒ (ˢ...) [lt.] f ⊛ zo. crustacean (= Krustentier).

Krüstchen (ˢ...) n ⊛ (dim. v. Kruste) small crust of bread.
Kruste (ˢ...) [ahd.; *lt.] f ⊛ des Brotes ꝛc.: crust, des Schweinebratens: crackling; ⊕ mach. in Dampfkesseln: cake; path. (Grind) scab, ⌒ eschar, porrigo, (Schorf) scurf; (sich) mit e-r ~ überziehen to put on a crust, to (en)crust.
krusten=artig (ˢ...) a. ⊛ like a crust, ⌒ crustaceous; =eidechse f zo. heloderm (Helode'rma); =tier n, zo. crustacean, crustaceous animal; Lehre von den ~en: ⌒ crustaceology; ℒtier=artig a. zo. crustacean, ...ceous.
krustig (ˢ...) a. ⊛ crusty, covered with a crust, ⌒ crustaceous; auch in Zssgn, z.B. hart=ℒ covered with a hard crust.
Kruzifere(n pl.) ⚥ (ˢ⌣ˢ⌣) [lt.] f ⊛ (Kreuzblütler) crucifer(s pl.), cruciferæ pl.
Kruzifix (ˢ⌣ˢ⌣) [lt.] n ⊛a. (Kreuz) crucifix.
Kryolith ⌒ (ˢ⌣ˢ⌣) [grch. Eisstein] m ⊛c. ⊛ min. cryolite.
Krypta (ˢ...) f ⊛, Krypte (ˢ...) f ⊛ [grch.] arch. (unterirdische Kirche) crypt.
Krypto=game(n pl.) ⚥ (ˢ⌣ˢ⌣) [grch. Verborgenblütige] f ⊛ (Sporenpflanze) cryptogam(ian plant); ℒgamisch a. ⊛ cryptogamian, ...ic, ...ous; =gramm (ˢ⌣ˢ) n ⊛d. (Geheimschrift) cryptogram.
☞ Krystall... s. Kristall.
k. u. öst. abbr. = königlich ungarisch.

Kuba(=tabak ⊛) ⊛(ᵘ...)[Kuba ⚥, Antillen-insel] m ⊛ Cuba(n) tobacco, auch: Havana; cuartas.
Kubatur ⌒ (-ˣˢ) [lt.] f ⊛ math. (Umwandlung in einen Würfel) cubature.
Kubebe (ˣˢ⌣) [lt., *pers.] f ⊛, ~n=pfeffer m ⊛ pharm. cubeb; ~strauch ⚥ cubeb-shrub (Piper Cube'ba).
Kübel (ˢ⌣) [ahd., * mlt. s. Kufe¹] m (n) ⊛ tub (a. hort. Holzgefäß für große Pflanzen); (Faß) vat, (Eimer) bucket; ⚒ (Förder=) ~ skip; in ~ setzen to tub, to put in(to) tubs; ~=kunst (ˢ...) f ⊛ = Eimerkunst.
kubier=en (ˣˢ⌣) [lt.] math. I v/a. ⊛ (in die dritte Potenz erheben) to (raise to the) cube. — II n ⊛ u. ℒ/ung f ⊛ cubation.
Kubik=berechnung (ˢ⌡...) f ⊛ cubature; =dekameter ⊛ n (m) cubic decametre; =dezimeter n (m) (abbr. cdcm, öft. dm³) cubic decimetre; =inhalt m cubature, ⌒ cubic (or solid) contents pl.; =inhaltsmessung f = =berechnung; =maß n cubic (or solid) measure; =meter n (m) (abbr. cbm, öft. m³) cubic metre; =millimeter ⊛ n (m) (abbr. cmm, öft. mm³) cubic millimetre; =wurzel f, math. cube-root; die ~ ausziehen to extract the cube-root; =zahl f.math. (dritte Potenz) cube; =zentimeter n(m) (ccm, öft. cm³) cubic centimetre.
kubisch ⌒ (ˢ⌣) a. ⊛ math. cubic(al).
Kübler (ˢ⌣)[Kübel] m ⊛(Böttcher) cooper.
Kubus ⌒ (ˢ⌣) [lt., *grch.] m, inv. od. ⊛ math. (Würfel, dritte Potenz: x³) cube; auf den ~ bringen, erheben to cube.

Küche (ˢ⌣) (ahd.: kitchen; *spät-lt. coqui'na) f ⊛ 1. kitchen, cook-house or -room, caboose; (Aufwasch) ~ scullery; bürgerliche ~ (Koch-art) plain cooking or cookery; die ~ besorgen to attend (F see) to the cooking; eine gute ~ führen to keep a good table; in Speisehäusern: frisch aus der ~ (kom-

♪ Musik; ⌒ Wissenschaft; ⚥ Pflanze; ⚱ Geographie; ⊕ Technik; ⚒ Bergbau; ⚔ Militär; ⚓ Marine; ⊛ Handel; ✉ Post; ⛉ Eisenbahn.

mend) just up (from the kitchen); sie versteht die ~ she understands cooking or cookery, she is an expert cook; *fig.* e-n in die rechte ~ weisen to put a p. on the right track; des Teufels ~ hell, P old blazes; in des Teufels (od. Henkers) ~ bringen, kommen to get into a(n awful) scrape or stew or mess; zur ~ gehörig culinary. — 2. kalte ~ (Mahlzeit) cold dinner or lunch(eon) or collation or repast.

Küchel(chen) *n* [22] ([23]) 1. (ˊ◡(◡) [*dim.* v. Kuchen] small cake; vgl. Kuchen 1. — 2. (ˋ◡(◡) [*dim.* v. Küche] small kitchen. — 3. *dim.* = Küchlein³.

Küch(e)ler (ˊ(◡)◡) [Kuchen] *m* [22], **~in** *f* [47] = Kuchenbäcker(in); **küchelu** *provc.* (ˊ◡) *v/n.* (h.) [92]a. to bake cakes.

Kuchen (ˊch◡) [ahd.: cake] *m* [23] 1. cake, (Rosinen=)~: a) kleinerer: Bath bun; b) größerer: plum-cake; (Sandtorte) Madeira cake; kleiner ~, auch: *dim.* Küchel(chen) *n* small cake, little tart, tartlet. — 2. F *iro.* ja, ~! (warum nicht gar!) you don't say so; höhnisch: don't you wish you may get it!, you (they, &c.) may whistle for it!

Küchen=abfälle (ˋ◡...) *m/pl.* [62] kitchen-waste, -refuse; =**amt** *n*: a) k.-office; b) employment in the k., cookery.

Kuchen=backen (ˊˊch◡...) *n* [62] Bäckerei: making cakes or pastry; =**bäcker(in** *f***)** *m* pastry-cook; =**bäckerei** *f* pastry-cook's trade, (Laden) pastry-cook's (shop); =**blech** *n* tin to bake cakes on.

Küchen=brett (ˋ◡...) *n* [62] chopping-board; =**dragoner** F *m* etwa: strong (or powerfully built) kitchen-wench, weitS. horse-godmother; =**einrichtung** *f* appointments *pl.* of a k., k.-furniture; =**fee** *f* F *co.* cook; =**feuer** *n* kitchen-fire.

Kuchen=form (ˊˊch◡...) *f* [62] cake-mould; ≈**förmig** *a.* [66] (shaped) like a cake.

Küchen=garten (ˋ◡...) *m* [62] kitchen- (or vegetable-)garden; =**gerät** *n*, =**geschirr** *n* kitchen-utensils or F -things *pl.*; s. a. Geschirr 2; =**hand=tuch** *n* k.-towel, jack-towel; =**herd** *m* (kitchen-)range, (Sparkoch=ofen) kitchener, (Gaskoch=ofen) gas cooker; =**junge** *m* boy who assists in the kitchen, bsd. ehm.: scullion; =**kräuter** *n/pl.* pot-herbs *pl.*; =**latei'n** F *n* apothecary's (or dog-)Latin; =**magd** *f* kitchen- (or scullery-)maid; =**meister** *m* chef; *fig.* bei ihnen ist Schmalhans ~ they live in a very frugal (or F poor) way, auch: they are on short commons; =**messer** *n* kitchen-knife; =**personal** *n* persons *pl.* employed in the kitchen.

Kuchen=rädchen (ˊˊch◡.ˊ◡) *n* [62] jagging-iron or -wheel.

Küchen=rechnung (ˋ◡...) *f* [62] bill of kitchen-expenses; =**schelle** ⚘ [P] *f* pasque flower ([*Anemo'ne*] *Pulsati'lla*).

Kuchen=schieber (ˊˊch◡.ˊ◡) *m* [62] peel for pastry.

Küchen=schrank (ˋ◡.ˋ) *m* [62] larder, pantry.

Kuchen=teig (ˊˊch◡.ˊ) *m* [62] dough.

Küchen=tisch (ˋ◡.ˋ) *m* [62] kitchen-table, für Schüsseln rc.: dresser.

Kuchen=werk (ˊˊch◡.ˋ) *n* [62] (Backwerk) pastry.

Küchen=wesen (ˋ◡...) *n* [62] culinary matters *pl.*; =**zettel** *m* menu (of a dinner), in Speisehäusern rc.: bill of fare.

Küchlein¹ (ˊ–) *n* [23] (*dim.* v. Kuchen) = Küchel(chen) 1.

Küchlein² (ˋ–) *n* [23] (*dim.* v. Küche) = Küchel(chen) 2.

Küchlein³ (ˊ–) [*dim.* v. ndd. Kü(c)ken] *n* [23] (Junges der Henne) chick(en); vgl. Hähnchen unter Hahn 1 u. Hühnchen 1.

Küchler, Küchner (ˊ◡) *m* [22], **~in** *f* [47] = Kuchenbäcker(in).

☞ **Kuck..., kuck...** [ndd.] s. Guck..., guck...

Kücken (ˋ◡) *n* [23] [ndd.: chicken, *dim.* v. cock, lautm.] (young) chicken.

Kuckuck (ˋ–) [mhd.: cuckoo lautm.] **I** *m* [11]c. 1. *orn.* cuckoo (*Cu'culus cano'rus*). — 2. verwünschend: geh zum ~!, hol' dich der ~!, etwa: go and be hanged!, the deuce take you!; zum ~! confounded!; das weiß der ~ (und sein Küster)! that puzzles (or F beats) me!; ich will des ~s sein, wenn // I'll be hanged if //. — **II** ≈ *int.* 3. (die Stimme des ~s nachahmend) cuckoo; ≈ rufen to cry cuckoo.

kuckucken (ˋ–◡) *v/n.* (h.) [88] to cry (or to imitate a) cuckoo.

Kuckucks=blume ⚘ (ˋ–...) *f* [62]: a) ragged-robin (*Lychnis flos cu'culi*); b): ⚗ orchis; =**ei** *n* egg of a cuckoo; e-m ein ~ ins Nest legen to lay an egg in(to) another bird's nest (auch *fig.*); =**ruf** *m* cuckoo-note; =**schaum=kraut** ⚘ *n* cuckoo-flower (*Cardami'ne prate'nsis*); =**speichel** *m*, *ent.* (schaumartige Absonderung der Schaumzirpe) c.-spit; =**uhr** ⚙ *f* c.-clock; =**vögel** *m/pl.* *orn.*: ⚗ cuculi, cuculidæ *pl.*; =**weibchen** *n*, *orn.* hen of a cuckoo.

Kufe¹ (ˊ◡) [ahd.; *lt. *cūpa*] *f* [48] coop, tub, vat; eine ~ voll a vatful.

Kufe² (ˊ◡) [ahd.] *f* [48] (Schlitten≈) sledge-runner; (Wiegen≈) rocker.

Küf(e)ner ↘ (ˊ(◡)◡) *m* [22] = Küfer.

Küfer ⚙ (ˊ◡) [Kufe¹] *m* [22] cooper, barrel- (or cask-)maker (= Böttcher); (Aufseher des Kellers) cellar-man.

Küferei ⚙ (-◡ˊ) *f* [46] cooper's trade; vgl. Kellerei; **küfern** (ˊ◡) *v/n.* (h.) [92]a. to work as a cooper, to follow the cooper's trade.

kufisch (ˋ◡) *a.* [66] [Kufa ♀ ehm. St. bei Bagdad] Cufic.

Kugel (ˊ◡) [mhd. (*ndd.): coil] *f* [48] 1. ball, globe, *math.*, &c. sphere; hölzerne ~ für Spiele bowl; vgl. Billardball; kleine (Marmor=)~ marble; (Wahl=)~ ballot; *anat.* (Kopf eines Knochens) head of a bone; *phys.* ~ e-s Barometers od. Thermometers bulb; Hasardspiel: die rote und schwarze ~ the red and black ball. — 2. ⚔, *hunt.* (Flinten=)~ bullet; (Kanonen=)~ (cannon-)ball; ~n und Granaten (oder Bomben) shot and shell; matte ~ spent bullet or ball; von ~n bestrichen bullet-swept; von ~n durchlöchert riddled with bullets; sich eine ~ durch den Kopf jagen to blow out one's brains, to shoot o.s.; von einer ~ getroffen hit by a bullet or cannon-ball, shot; ~n wechseln to exchange shots, to fight a duel with pistols; Sprichw. eine jede ~ trifft ja nicht not every bullet hits (home); jede ~ hat ihren Zweck every bullet has its billet.

Kugel=abschnitt (ˊˊ◡...) *m* [62] = =segme'nt; ≈**ähnlich** *a.* [66]: ⚗ spheroidal; vgl. ≈förmig; =**akazie** ⚘ *f*, *hort.* kind of locust-tree (*Robi'nia umbracu'lifera*); ≈**artig** *a.*: ⚗ globular; vgl. ≈förmig; =**ausschnitt** *m* cone with spherical base; =**auszieher** ⚙ *m* (Krätzer) wad- (or worm-)hook; =**bahn** *f*: a) bowling-alley; b) path of a projectile, trajectory; =**bakterien** *f/pl.*: ⚗ sphærobacteria *pl.*; =**becher** *m* Spiel: cup-and-ball; =**bildung** *f*: ⚗ conglobation; =**binse** ⚘ *f* pipewort (*Eriocau'lon*); =**blitz** *m*, *phys.* globular (or globe-)lightning; =**blume** ⚘ *f* globe-daisy, ⚗ globularia (*Globula'ria*); =**büchse** *f* rifle.

Kügelchen (ˊ◡◡) *n* [23] (*dim.* von Kugel) small ball or bullet, von Papier auch: pellet; ⚗ globule, spherule; ~ am Rosenkranze bead; *physiol.* ~ im Blute: ⚗ corpuscle.

Kugel=distel ⚘ (ˊˊ◡...) *f* [62]: kopfige ~ globe-thistle (*Echi'nops sphaeroce'phalus*); =**drei-eck** *n*, *math.* spherical triangle; =**durchmesser** *m*, *math.* diameter of a sphere; =**fang** ⚔ *m* rifle-butt, parapet (or sand-hill) for catching balls, a. *fig.*; ≈**fest** *a.* [66] bullet- (or ball-, shot-)proof; =**fisch** *m*, *ichth.* sea-hedgehog (*Te'trodon hi'spidus*); =**fläche** *f*, *math.* spherical surface; =**form** *f*: a) spherical (or globular) form, sphericalness, ⚗ globosity; b) ⚙ zum Gießen von Kugeln: bullet-mould; ≈**förmig** *a.* in the form of a ball, spherical, globular, ⚗ globose; =**furche** ⚔ *f*, *artill.* groove (or furrow) made by a cannon-ball; =**futter** ⚔ *n* rifle-patch; =**gelenk** *n*, *anat.* socket-joint, cup-and-ball joint, ⚗ arthrodia, aparthrosis; ⚙ *mech.* ball-and-socket joint; =**gestalt** *f*: ⚗ sphericity, globosity; vgl. =form; =**gewölbe** ⚙ *n*, *arch.* spherical vault, cupola; =**haube** *f*, *math.* spherical calotte; =**haufe(n)** ⚔ *m* (pyramidal) pile of balls, shot-pile.

kug(e)licht, kug(e)lig (ˊ(◡)◡) *a.* [66] like a ball, ⚗ conglobate.

Kugel=kalotte (ˊˊ◡...) *f* [62] = =haube; =**leere, lehre¹** *f* ⚔ = =maß; =**lehre²** *f*, *math.* spherics; =**linse** *f*, *opt.* spherical lens, globe-tube; =**loch** *n* Billard: pocket; =**löffel** ⚙ *m* bullet-ladle; =**maß** ⚔ *n* shot-gauge, ball-calibre.

kugeln (ˊ◡) [92]a. **I** *v/a.* u. **sich** ≈ *v/refl.* to roll (like a ball), to make globular; sich ≈, a. to form into a ball, to assume a spherical form, ⚗ to conglobate; sich ≈ vor Lachen to split with laughing. — **II** *v/n.* (h.) to roll (like a ball); in Spielen: to bowl; bei e-r Wahl: to (vote by) ballot. — **III** ~ *n* [23] s. Kugelung.

Kugel=patrone ⚔ (ˊˊ◡...) *f* [62] ball-cartridge; =**pflaster** *n* = =futter; =**regen** ⚔ *m* shower (or hail) of bullets or rifle-shot; =**rolle** ⚙ *f* an Möbeln: ball-caster; ≈**rund** *a.* [66] (as) round as a ball (auch von dicken Leuten), globular; =**schnitt** *m*, *math.* spherical section; =**segme'nt** *n*, *math.* sph. segment; ≈**sicher** ⚔ *a.* = =fest; =**sonde** *f*, *surg.* bullet-probe; =**spiegel** spherical mirror; =**spiel** *n* (game of) bowls; =**spritze** *f* machine-gun, maxim (gun); ehm.: (fr.) *mitrailleuse*; =**streifen** *m*, *math.* spherical zone; =**tee** *m* gunpowder-tea.

Kugelung (ˊ◡◡) *f* [46] rolling, bowling; bei Wahlen: ballot(ing).

Kugel=venti'l ⚙ (ˊˊ◡...) *n* [62] spherical valve, globe-valve; =**wahl** *f* balloting, election by ballot; =**zange** *f*, *surg.* ball-

[**Kugelzieher**] extractor, bullet-forceps; =**zieher** m bullet-hook, *surg.* bullet-drawer; vgl. =**auszieher**; =**zone** f, *math.* spherical zone.
kuglicht, **kuglig** (⌣‿) f. kug(e)licht, tug(e)lig.
Kuguar (⌣‿-) [brasil.] m ⓐd. (⑤) *zo.* coug(o)uar, puma (*Felis co'ncolor*).
Kuh (⌣; *Hom.* Coup) [ahd.: cow] f ⑩
1. cow (*bibl.*, &c. *pl.* a.: kine); junge ~ heifer; e-n anstarren wie die ~ das neue Tor to stare at a p. like mad or like a stuck pig; Sprichw. der eine hat die Kühe, der andere die Mühe, etwa: one has the pains, and the other the gains. — 2. bisw. v. Weibchen der Walfische u. anderer Tiere: cow. — 3. F *fig.* (dumme Person) silly goose. — 4. Spiel: blinde ~ = Blindekuh.
Kuh=**auge** (⌣‿...) n ② eye of a cow; F *fig.* = Glotzauge; =**baum** ⚘ m in Südamerika: cow-tree (*Bro'simum galactode'ndron*); =**blatter** ⚘ = pocke; =**blume** ⚘ f: a) (Dotterblume) marsh-marigold (*Caltha palu'stris*); b) (Löwenzahn) dandelion (*Leo'ntodon Tara'xacum*); =**brücke** ⚓ f orlop-deck; =**dill** ⚘ m = Hundskamille; =**dreck** m cow-droppings *pl.* or =dung.
Küher schwz. (⌣‿) n (m) ② = **Kuhhirt**.
Kuh=**euter** (⌣...) n ② cow's udder; =**fladen** m =**dreck**; =**fleisch** n cow's meat, cow-beef; =**fuß** m: a) foot of a cow; b) ⚙ mech. (Brechstange) crowbar; c) ⚔ *co.* (alte Flinte) old musket, brown Bess; =**futter** n fodder for cows or cattle; =**glocke** f cow's (or cow-)bell; =**haar** n cow-hair; =**handel** m: a) cow-trade; b) *fig. bsp. parl.* bargain; =**haut** f cow's skin, cowhide; *fig.* das läßt sich auf keine ~ schreiben it cannot be put in few words, it's a long story or an endless tale; ⚘**heftig** a. ⑥ =beinig; =**hirt(e)** m cowherd, a. neatherd, *Am.* cowboy; =**horn** n: a) horn of a cow; b) ⚘ cowherd's horn; c) ⚘ =**horn(klee)** fenugreek (*Trigonella Faenum graecum*); =**huf** m hoof of a cow; =**kalb** n cow-calf; =**käse** m cow-cheese.
kühl (⌣) [ahd.: cool, chill] I a. ⑥ 1. cool, fresh, slightly cold; 2 ⑥ coolish, chilly; 2 werden to cool (down); es (das Wetter) wird 2er it is growing (or getting) cooler or fresher. — 2. *fig.* (talt) cold, cool; unfeeling; 2 bis ans Herz hinan (G.) cool to the inmost heart. — II ~ n ⑩, das ~e ⑥ 3. coolness; des Morgens ~ the freshness of the morning; im ~en sitzen to sit in the (cool) shade. — Vgl. a. **Kühle**.
Kühl=**apparat** ⚙ (⌣...) m ② cooling-apparatus, refrigerator; für Getränke auch: ice-pail; =**bottich** m Brauerei: c.-tub or -vat, cooler, refrigerator.
Kühlde ⚓ (⌣‿) f ⑩ (fresh) gale; stehende, steife ~ steady, stiff breeze; heftige ~ (Stoßwind) squall.
Kühle (⌣) [ahd.; *kühl*] f ⑩ coolness (a. *fig.*), freshness, cool hours *pl.* (or part) of the day; in der ~ des Morgens, Abends in the cool (hours) of the morning, evening; *fig.* v. Personen: coldness.
Kühl=**eimer** (⌣‿...) m ② cooling-pail, mit Eis: ice-pail.
kühlen (⌣) I v/a. u. sich 2 v/refl. ⑧ 1. = abkühlen I u. II; in Eis gekühlter Champagner iced champagne; *med.*:

⥰des Mittel: ⚘ refrigerative, ...ant; vgl. Kühlmittel; das Wetter kühlt sich ... is getting cool(er), ... is cooling down. — 2. *fig.* f-n Zorn ② to cool one's anger; f-n Mut (F sein Mütchen) an e-m ② to vent one's anger (or rage) on a p. — II ~ n ③. = Abkühlung.
Kühler (⌣‿) m 1. s.th. cooling or refreshing. — 2. ⚙ (Vorrichtung zum Kühlen) = Kühl=apparat, =bottich, =faß 2c.
Kühl=**faß** (⌣...) n ②, =**gefäß** n cooling-vessel or -cup.
Kühling (⌣‿) m ⓐd. ichth. (Alant) ide.
Kühl=**mittel** (⌣...) n ② *med.* cooling draught, ⚘ refrigerant; =**ofen** ⚙ m Glasfabr. 2c.: cooling-arch or -furnace, annealing-oven; =**pfanne** ⚙ f = =bottich; =**raum** ⚙ m (Eistammer) refrigerating-chamber; =**rohr** ⚙ n der Destillationsblase: worm of a still, condensing-coil; =**salbe** f, *med.* cooling salve; =**schiff** ⚙ n Brauerei: cooling-vat, cooler, =**schlange** ⚙ f = =rohr; =**schwabber** ⚔ m für heiße Kanonen: cooling-swab.
Kühlte ⚓ (⌣‿) f ⑧ = **Kühle**.
Kühl=**trank** (⌣‿) m ② cooling drink.
Kühlung (⌣‿) f ⑥ 1. = **Abkühlung**. — 2. (Kühlendes) cooling draught, shade, &c., ⚘ refrigerant.
Kühl=**wasser** ⚙ (⌣‿...) n ② cooling water.
Kuh=**lymphe** (⌣...) f ② *med.*: bovine lymph, ⚘ vaccine; =**magd** f (servant-)girl attending to the cows, dairy-(or milk-)maid; =**melker(in** f) m cow-milker; =**milch** f cow's milk; frische ~ milk fresh from the cow; =**mist** m = **Kuhdreck**.
kühn (⌣) [ahd.: keen] a. ⑥ bold; (unerschrocken) intrepid, dauntless; (mutig) courageous, brave, valiant; (keck) daring, audacious; (wagehalsig) rash, venturesome, adventurous; (entschlossen) resolute, determined; ich bin so 2 zu // I make bold to //; 2 m. to embolden; 2 w. to grow bold; Karl der ~e von Burgund Charles the Bold of Burgundy; Sprichw. f. mutig.
Kuh=**nelke** ⚘ (⌣‿⌣) f ② cow-herb (*Vacca'ria parifio'ra*).
Kühnheit (⌣‿) f ⑥ boldness; dauntlessness; courage, bravery; daring; rashness, venturesomeness; resoluteness; als Handlung: bold (or daring) deed.
kühnlich (⌣‿) adv. (zu kühn) boldly, &c.
Kuh=**pilz** ⚘ (⌣...) m ② cow-spunk (*Bole'tus bovi'nus*); =**pocke** f, *med.*, *vet.* cow-pox, ⚘ (variolo=) vaccinia; f. einimpfen I; =**pocken**=**gift** n, *med.*: ⚘ vaccine virus; =**pocken**=**impfer** m vaccinator, vaccinist; =**pocken**=**impfung** f vaccination; =**pocken**=**materie** f, =**stoff** m vaccine lymph; =**reigen**, =**reihen** m Alpine cowherd's tune, a. (fr.) *ranz-des-vaches*; =**schaffer** m = =hirt; =**schluck** F m large draught (or F gulp) of beer, &c.; =**schwanz** m cow's tail; =**stall** m cow-shed or -house; =**vogel** m, *orn.* (Kuhstar) cattle-bird (*Mo'lobrus*); =**weide** f pastur(ag)e for cows or cattle; =**weizen** ⚘ m cow-wheat (*Melampy'rum*); =**züchter** m cow-keeper, cattle-breeder.
Kujon P (⌣‿) [fr., *it.*] m ⓐd. scoundrel, infamous fellow; **kujonieren** (⌣‿⌣) v/a. ⑧ to torment, vex, annoy.

k. u. k. öft. *abbr.* = kaiserlich und königlich.
Küken (⌣‿) = Kücken.
kulant ⚏ (‿⌣) [*fr. coulant*] a. ⑥ fair, easy; 2e Bedingungen f/pl. fair (or easy) conditions pl.; 2es Verfahren = **Kulanz**.
Kulanz ⚏ (‿⌣) [‿⌣ fr.] f ⑥ promptness (in business matters); fair dealing.
Kuli (⌣‿) [ind. Volk] m ⓐ (Tagelöhner) coolie; ~=**arbeit** (⌣‿...) f ② coolie labour; ~=**frage** f coolie question.
kulinarisch (‿⌣‿) [lt.] a. ⑥ (auf die Küche bezüglich) culinary (art, &c.).
Kulisse (‿⌣‿) [fr. *coulisse*] f ⑧ 1. thea. wing, mov(e)able scene, side-scene; in die ~n sprechen to speak aside; sl. ~n reißen to play to the gallery. — 2. ⚏ (Nebenräume einer Börse) space (in a stock-exchange) set apart for unofficial business.
Kulissen=**geschwätz** (‿⌣‿...) n ② thea. greenroom talk; =**maler** m scene-painter; =**reißer** m, *sl.* ranter, sensational actor; =**reißerei** f, *sl.* ranting, sensational acting; =**schieber** m scene-shifter; =**tür(e)** f stage-door.
kullern (⌣‿) 2c. f. **kollern** 2c.
Kulm[1] (⌣) [slaw.] m ⓐb. (dome-shaped) mountain-peak.
Kulm[2] ⚒ (⌣) m, n ⓐb. *geol.* culm.
Kulmination ⚘ (‿⌣‿tt(⌣)⌣) [lt.] f ⑥ *ast.* (Höhepunkt) culmination; ~s=**punkt** m ② *ast.* culminating-point, *fig.* acme; **kulminieren** (‿⌣‿‿) v/n. (h.) ⑧ *ast.* (den Höhepunkt erreichen) to culminate.
Kult (⌣) [lt.] m ⓐb. 2c. f. **Kultus** 2c.
kultivierbar (‿⌣‿w‿) a. ⑥ cultivable, capable of (or fit for) cultivation.
kultivieren (‿⌣‿w‿) [lt.] I v/a. ⑧ (anbauen, bearbeiten, bilden) to cultivate; (pflanzen) to grow; j-s Freundschaft ② (pflegen) to cultivate (or keep up) a p.'s acquaintance; kultivierte (gesittete) Menschen cultured (or refined) people, people of culture; hoch kultiviert highly civilized (nation, &c.). — II ~ n ③ u. **Kultivierung** f ⑥ cultivation; der Wissenschaft 2c.: scientific, &c. pursuit.
Kultur (‿⌣) [lt.] f ⑥ (Anbau) cultivation (or tilling, tilth) of the soil; (Züchtung) breeding (or rearing) of cattle; (Anpflanzen) growing of flowers, vegetables, &c.; (Gesittung) (state of) civilization, culture; die ~, die alle Welt beleckt (G., Faust) the gloss of universal polish.
Kultur=**arbeit** (‿⌣...) f ② civilizing work, humanizing efforts pl.; =**aufgabe** f task (or mission) of civilization; =**beförderer** m civilizer; =**bild** n Geschichtschreibung, etwa: history of the civilization of a country or period, survey of human progress.
kulturell (‿⌣‿) a. ⑥ relating to culture or civilization, auch: cultural.
kultur=**fähig** (‿⌣...) a. ⑥ cultivable; ⚘**feindlich** a. hostile to civilization or culture; =**geschichte** f ② history of civilization; ⚘**geschichtlich**, ⚘**historisch** a. relating to the history of civ.; =**kampf** m Deutschland 2c.: struggle between the State and the (Roman Catholic) Church; =**kämpfer** m champion of culture; =**pflanzen** ⚘ f/pl.; cultivated plants or vegetables pl.;

⚘ scientific; ☘ botanical; ⚐ geography; ⚙ machinery; ⚒ mining; ⚔ military; ⚓ marine; ⚏ commercial; ⚘ postal; ⚘ railway.

[**Kulturträger**] =**träger** m supporter (or upholder) of civilization; =**volk** n civilized (stärker: cultured) nation.

Kultus (ˊ⁻) [lt.] m ⑬ (Verehrung) religious, &c. worship; der Künste ꝛc.: cult; ~**miniſter** (ˊ⁻⁻…) m (~**miniſteˊrium** n) ⑥ minister (ministry) of public worship and education.

Kumarin ⚹ (⁻⁻ˊ) [fr.; *guayan.] n ⓪d. chm.(Tonkatampfer)coumarin(e); ~**ſäure** (ˊ⁻…) f ⓬ coumaric acid (C₉H₆O₂).

Kumm (ˊ) [ndd.] m ⓪b. (Rohr, Hülſe) tube.

Kumme (ˊ) [ſ. **Kumpen**] f ⓮ 1. (Schüſſel) basin, bowl. — 2. ↓ basin of a harbour or port.

Kümmel¹ (ˊ)[ahd.: cumin; *lt., grch.] m ㉒ 1. ♀ caraway (*Carum carvi*); römiſcher ~ cumin (*Cuminum cyminum*); vgl. ~=ſame. — 2. F fig. ~ und Salz, auch: ~ und Dill (Miſchfarbe aus Schwarz und Weiß) pepper and salt. — 3. = ~**branntwein**.

Kümmel²=**blättchen** f (ˊ⁻…) [hebr. *gimel* = 3: „Dreiblatt"] n ⓬ threecard trick, kind of game played by sharpers; =¹**branntwein** m cumin-liqueur; =**brot** n bread with caraway-seeds; =**bruder** F m one who is fond of his drops, tippler; =**flaſche** f brandy-bottle; =**körner** n/pl. caraway-seeds pl.

kümmeln (ˊ⁻) ⓶a. I v/a. to flavour with caraway. — II F v/n. (h.) to tipple (cumin-)liqueur, to take one's drops.

Kümmel²=**öl** (ˊ⁻) (ein ätheriſches Öl) cumin-oil, chm. cuminol (C₁₀H₁₂O); =**ſame** m caraway-(or cumin-)seed; =**ſchnaps** m = ~**branntwein**.

Kummer (ˊ⁻) [mhd.: cumber „Schutt"] m ㉒ 1. grief; (Betrübnis) affliction, (Sorge) care, sorrow; (Beſorgnis) solicitude; (Enttäuſchung) disappointment; (Unruhe) trouble, worry; ~ und Sorgen ausſteh(e)n to be full of grief and sorrow, to have a great deal of trouble and anxiety; das iſt mein geringſter ~ that does not trouble me in the least; ſich (dat.) ~ m. über etwas to grieve (or fret, worry) about (or over) a th.; ſich unnötigen ~ machen, a. to distress o.s. about nothing; wir wollen uns darüber keinen ~ m. we won't trouble about it. — 2. (drückender Mangel) (sore) distress, pressing need, destitution, (Elend) misery.

kummer=**frei** (ˊ⁻…) a. ⓰ free from grief or care; =**gefühl** n ⓬ pangs pl. of sorrow or grief.

kümmerlich (ˊ⁻⁻) a. ⓰ 1. grievous, wretched, miserable. — 2. (ärmlich) poor, paltry; (dürftig) needy, indigent, destitute; spare, scanty; (verkümmert) stunted (in its growth), undersized, F underdone; ≗ (adv.) leben to live in a poor way. — 3. adv. (kaum) barely, with great trouble, hardly.

Kümmerling¹ (ˊ⁻⁻) [**Kummer**] m ⓪d. poor (or miserable) creature, undersized child or animal. [⓪d. = Gurke.]

Kümmerling² ♀ (ˊ⁻⁻) [lt. *cu'cumis*] m]

kummer=**los** (ˊ⁻…) a. ⓰ without a (single) care, free from (all) grief.

kümmern (ˊ⁻⁻) [**Kummer**] ⓶a. I v/n. (h. u. ſn) 1. not to thrive or prosper, bſd. von Pflanzen: to be stunted. — II v/a. 2. to grieve, afflict, trouble,

worry, distress. — 3. meiſt neg. ob. interr. das kümmert mich nicht: a) that does not concern me or matter to me; b) it does not grieve me; was kümmert ihn das? what is that to him? — III ſich ≗ v/refl. 4. ſich über et. ≗ to be grieved (or to worry) about a th. — 5. ſich um et. ≗ to attend to (or to mind) a th., to bestow care on s.th.; (ſich einmiſchen) to meddle with a th.; ich kümmere mich nicht darum I pay no heed to it, I don't mind it; er ſoll ſich um ſich (ſelbſt) ≗ let him mind his own business; man muß ſich um das Gerede der Leute nicht ≗ one need not trouble about what people say, a. let people talk; ſ. Ei ≗ 2.

Kümmernis (ˊ⁻⁻) f ⑱ (lasting) grief; (sore) affliction, (great) solicitude, tribulation; (et. das **Kummer** macht)great blow, disappointment.

kummer=**voll** (ˊ⁻,ˊ) a. ⓰ grievous, sorrowful, full of care or trouble or grief, poet. woe-begone.

Kum(me)t ☉ (ˊ⁻) [mhd.; *ſlaw.] n (~ m) ⓒc. Sattlerei: horse-collar hame; ~=**decke** (ˊ⁻…) f ⓬ hame-cover; ~=**geſchirr** n collar-harness; ~=**holz** n hame; ~=**kette** f draught- (or tug-) chain; ~=**macher** m collar-maker, harness-maker; ~=**riemen** m hame-strap; ~=**ſtöcke** m/pl. (pair of) hames.

Kumpan (⁻ˊ) [mhd.;*fr.] m ⓪d. companion, fellow, F mate, beim Zechen: boon-companion; luſtiger ~ jolly fellow.

Kumpen(ˊ⁻)[ndd.]m ㉓, **Kumpf** (ˊ)[ahd.] m ⓪b. basin, bowl, (earthen) pan.

Kumt (ˊ) ꝛc. ſ. **Kummet** ꝛc.

kumulativ ⚹ (⁻⁻⁻ˊ) [lt.] a. ⓰ (anhäufend) cumulative; **kumulieren** (⁻⁻ˊ⁻) v/a. ⓬ bſd. jur. (anhäufen) to accumulate.

Kumys (ˊ⁻) [ruff., *tatar.] m (n) inv. (gegorene Stutenmilch der Tataren) kumiss.

kund (ˊ) [ahd.; *kennen] a. ⓰ (nur prädikativ) 1. well known, ſtärker: notorious; ſ. ≗tun. — 2. ≗ = kundig. [notorious.]

kundbar (ˊ⁻) a. ⓰ known, manifest,]

künd=**bar** (ˊ⁻) a. ⓰: a) ⓜ v. Kapital: at call, liable to be recalled, subject to notice of withdrawal; b) von Hypotheken: liable to be foreclosed.

Kündbarkeit (ˊ⁻⁻) f ⓰ liability to notice or foreclosure.

Kunde (ˊ⁻) [ahd.; *kennen] I m ⓭, ⚥ f ⓲, **Kundin** f ⓮ 1. customer, e-s Arztes: patient, e-s Advokaten: client; ~n anlocken to attract (or tout for) custom(ers); viele ~n haben, oft: to have a good (or large) connexion, v. Ärzten auch: to have an extensive practice. — 2. iro. (Perſon, Schalk) (tricky) fellow; ſchlauer ~ knowing customer, F artful dodger; ſchlimmer ~ dangerous (or F nasty, ugly) customer. — 3. F (reiſender Handwerksburſche) travelling journey-man, (Vagabund) tramp. — II [mhd.] f ⓬ 4. (o. pl.) = **Kenntnis**; e-m ~ von et. geben to inform (or apprise) a p. of a th.; ohne ~ über et. ſein to be without information respecting (or about) a th. — 5. mſt in Zſſgn: (Wiſſenſchaft, Wiſſen) science, scientific knowledge or lore; ſ. Altertums=, Erd=, Heil=, Himmels=, Stern= ꝛc. kunde.

[**künftighin**] **künden** (ˊ⁻) v/a. ⓬ 1. to make known, to announce. — 2. = aufkündigen.

Kunden=**fänger** (ˊ⁻…) =**ſucher** (ˊ⁻…) m tout(er); =**ſprache** f f tramps' language (vgl. **Kunde** 3); =**zahl** f number of customers, connexion, F custom.

kund=**geben** (ˊ⁻…) v/a. ⓬** 1. to notify, to publish; to make a th. known to a p., to give a p. notice of a th.; ſich ≗ to become manifest or known, to show (o.s.); ≗**gebend** a. ⓰ significative; =**gebung** f ⓬ manifestation, political, &c. demonstration.

kundig (ˊ⁻) [mhd.: cunning] I a. ⓰: e-r Sache (gen.) ≗ ſein to have (full) knowledge of a th., to be acquainted (or familiar) with a th., to be experienced (or skilled) in a th.; des Weges ≗ ſein to know the way; ≗er Thebaner iro. learned Theban (SH., King Lear, III, 4). — II ~e([r] m) f ⓰ one who knows, experienced person, F knowing one; (Sachverſtändiger) expert; die ~en those who know, the initiated, F the knowing ones pl.

kündigen (ˊ⁻⁻) [mhd.] ⓬ = aufkündigen.

Kündigung (ˊ⁻⁻) f ⓬ announcement, vorherige: (previous) notice, warning.

Kündigungs=**friſt** (ˊ⁻⁻…) f ⓬ time allowed for (giving) notice; mit halbjähriger ~ subject to (or ⓜ recallable at) six months' notice; =**recht** n right of (giving) notice; =**termin** m = =**friſt**.

Kundin (ˊ⁻) f ⓮ female (or lady) customer, patient, client; ſ. **Kunde** I.

kund=**machen** (ˊ…) v/a. ⓬** = ≗geben; =**machung** f ⓬ notification, publication, e-s Geſetzes: proclamation.

Kundſchaft (ˊ⁻⁻) [ahd.; *Kunde] f ⓬ 1. a) als Verhältnis: custom; (Klientenſchaft) clientship; er braucht unſere ~ nicht he does not want our patronage; b) coll. customers pl., custom, connexion, v. Ärzten: practice; (Klienten) clientele; e-e ~ verkaufen to sell the good-will of a shop, &c. — 2. (Erkundigung) intelligence; ~ einziehen to collect (or obtain) information, ⚔ auf ~ ausgehen (ausſein) to go reconnoitring or scouting; auf ~ ausſchicken to send out as scouts; ≗en (ˊ⁻⁻) v/a. u. v/n. (h.) ⓬ to spy (out), ⚔ to reconnoitre, to do (or go) scouting.

Kundſchafter (ˊ⁻⁻) m ㉒, ~**in** f ⓮ (Ausſpäher) spy, scout (a. ⚔), weit⃝s. explorer; (Geheimbote) emissary; ~**ei** (⁻⁻ˊ) f ⓬ spying, scouting, exploring; ⚔ intelligence department, b.s. (fr.) espionage. [reconnoitring-party.]

kundſchafts=**patrouille** ⚔ (ˊ⁻…) f]

kund=**tun** (ˊ…)v/a.⓬** =**kundgeben**; obrigkeitlich: wir tun kund und zu wiſſen hiermit jedermann know all men by these presents; ≗**werden** v/n. (ſn) ⓒc** to become publicly (or generally) known, to (be)spread about. [ſ. **Abkunft** ꝛc.]

Kunft † (…ˊ) [ahd.; *kommen] f ⓾]

künftig (ˊ⁻) [**Kunft**] a. ⓰** 1. future; ≗es Jahr, die Woche next year, week; in ≗en Zeiten in times to come, in years hereafter; ihr ≗er Gatte her husband that is (or was) to be. — 2. ≗, auch: ≗**hin** adv.: a) (von jetzt ab) henceforth, henceforward, for

the future; b) (ſpäterhin) after that, from that time forth. [Cunegund.\
Kunigunde (-⌣⌣) npr/f. ℬ㊸. (ℬn.)\
Kunkel (⌣⌣) [ahd.; *mlt.] f ㊺: a) (Spinnrocken) distaff; b) (Spinnſtube) room for (or gathering of) spinning women; ~**hof** m ㊷, ~**leh(e)n** n jur. Weiberlehen; ant. Schwertlehen) apron-string hold or tenure. [to scheme, to intrigue.\
kunkeln (⌣⌣) v/n. (h.) ⓦa. (Ränke ſchmieden)\
Kunkel-ſtube (⌣⌣⌣) f ㊷ = Kunkel b.\
Kunktator (⌣⌴⌣) [lat. Zauderer] m, inv., bſd. Fabius ~ (röm. Feldherr u. Gegner Hannibals) Fabius Cunctator.\
Kuno (⌣⌣) npr/m. ℬ㊹a. (ℬn.) Cuno.\
Kunſt (⌣) [ahd.; *können] f ⑩ 1. art; ſ. bilden 6; die ſchönen (ob. freien) Künſte the fine (or liberal, polite) arts pl.; Univerſität: Meiſter der freien Künſte master of arts; ſchwarze ~: a) ehm.: black art, necromancy; b) ⊕ (Kupferſtich in Schabmanier) mezzotint(o); zur ~ gehörig artistic; durch ~ bereitet ob. hergeſtellt artificial(ly prepared); Sprichw. die ~ geht nach Brot, ohne Gunſt iſt alle ~ umſunſt art goes a-begging; the artist cannot live without patronage. — 2. (Geſchicklichkeit) skill, cleverness, ingenuity, cunning; brotloſe ~ unprofitable employment; das iſt keine ~ there is nothing clever in that, a. oft: that's (a mere) nothing; ſeine ~ beweiſen to show what one can do; ſeine ~ an et. verſuchen to try one's skill (or hand) at a th.; ich bin mit meiner ~ zu Ende I am at my wits' end. — 3. (Kunſtgriff) artifice, knack, des Taſchenſpielers: sleight-of-hand; Künſte (Kniffe, Ränke) intrigues, tricks, malpractices, sharp practices pl. — 4. = Kunſtſtück. — 5. ⊕ (künſtliches Waſſerwerk) water-works pl.; ⚒ = Kunſtgezeug.\
Kunſt-akademie (⌣⌣...) f ㊷ academy of arts; =**angelegenheit** f artistic matter or concern; =**anlage** f: a) artistic talent; b) ~n pl. pleasure-gardens or grounds; =**arbeit** f work of art; =**ausdruck** m technical expression or term; =**ausſtellung** f exhibition of works of art, art gallery; ⚹**befliſſen** a. ㊺ devoted to (or skilled in) one's art; =**befliſſene(r)** m) f art-student; =**befliſſenheit** f devotion to art; =**beilage** f pictorial (or artistic) supplement; =**beſtrebungen** f/pl. artistic efforts pl.; =**butter** ⊕ f butterine, margarine; =**denkmal** n (artistic) monument; =**dichter** m learned poet (ant. Volksdichter); =**dichtung** f poetry in conformity with the rules of art (ant. Volksdichtung); =**drechsler** m turner of artistic objects; =**druckpapier** n art paper, enamelled paper; =**dünger** m, agr. artificial manure, fertilizer; =**eifer** m artistic (or artist's) zeal.\
Künſtelei (⌣⌣⌣) f ㊺ artificial work; over-refinement; affectation, affected ways pl.; im Stil: mannerism.\
künſteln (⌣⌣) [Kunſt] ⓦa. I v/n. (h.): an et. ⌣ to take great pains with a th., to bestow great care on a th. — II v/a. to produce with great care or painstaking; (ausklügeln) to puzzle out.

— III ~ n ㉓ = Künſtelei. — IV ge**künſtelt** p.p. u. a. ㊺ highly artistic, refined; (gezwungen) affected, forced, (geſchraubt) stilted, high-flown, (erkünſtelt) artificial, too highly polished; (erdichtet) fictitious; es liegt etwas ~ darin there is s.th. affected in (or about) it; ⚹e Rede over-refined language.\
Kunſt-erfahren(heit f ㊺) a. ㊺ (⌣...) experienced (experience) in art; =**erzeugnis** n production of art; =**färber(ei** f/m ⊕ = Schönfärber(ei); =**fehler** m e-s Arztes: doctor's mistake, wrong medical treatment; ⚹**fertig** a. ㊺ possessing artistic (or technical) skill; =**fertigkeit** f artistic (or technical) skill; =**feuer(werk)** n fireworks pl.; =**feuerwerker** m pyrotechnist; =**feuerwerkerei** f pyrotechnics; =**fleiß** m (artist's) industry; =**freund(in** f) m lover of art, patron(ess f) of art (or artists); ⚹**froh** a. ㊺ fond of art, art-loving; =**gärtner** m florist, nursery-gardener, nursery-man, ⚒ horticulturist; =**gärtnerei** f nursery-gardening, ⚒ horticulture; =**gebiet** n artistic department; =**gebilde** n art. product; =**gefühl** n art. sense; =**gegenſtand** m object of art; bſd. ● article of virtu; ⚹**gemäß** a. ㊺ u. adv. artistic, according to the rules of art; =**genoſſe** m, =**genoſſin** f fellow-artist; =**genoſſenſchaft** f fellowship of artists; =**genuß** m artistic treat; ⚹**gerecht** a. in conformity with the rules of art; =**geſchichte** f (⚹**geſchichtlich** a. relating to the) history of art; =**geſchmack** m artistic taste; =**geſtänge** ⊕ u. ⚒ n beams pl. of water-works; =**getriebe** ⊕ n machinery of water-works); ⚹**geübt** a. practically acquainted with art; =**gewebe** ⊕ n artistic weft; =**gewerbe** n applied art, technical trade or industry; =**gewerbeausſtellung** f, =**museum** n industrial exhibition, museum; =**gewerbe-ſchule** f polytechnic(al) (or trade-)school; =**gezeug** ⚒ n pit-work, water-engine, pumping-engine; =**griff** m artifice, knack, fig. dodge, trick; vgl. Kunſt 3; =**größe** f artistic star, eminent artist; =**halle** f art-museum; =**handel** (=**händler)** m trade (dealer) in works (or objects) of art or in articles of virtu; =**handlung** f fine-art repository; firm dealing in fancy-articles or articles of virtu; vgl. =verlag; =**handwerk** n artistic trade; =**handwerker** m art-worker, craftsman, artisan, mechanic; =**hefe** ⊕ f artificial yeast, hop; =**jünger** m art-student; =**kabinett** n, =**kammer** f cabinet of curios(ities); =**kenner(in** f) m expert (or connoisseur, judge) in matters of art; =**kennerſchaft** f connoisseurship in (matters of) art; =**kniff** m ruse, dodge; vgl. =griff; =**kritik** f art-criticism; =**lehre** f technology, technics.\
Künſtler (⌣⌣) [Kunſt] m ㊷, ~**in** f ⓠ artist; thea., &c. artiſte; performer; auch = Kunſthandwerker.\
Künſtler-druck ⊕ (⌣⌣...) m ㊷ artist's proof; =**geiſt** m artistic mind; =**geſellſchaft** f ſ. Geſellſchaft 4; =**hand** f artist's (cunning) hand.

künſtleriſch (⌣⌣⌣) a. ㊺ artist-like, like an artist; artistic; adv. artistically, as (or like) an artist.\
Künſtler-ruhm (⌣⌣⌣) m ㊷ artist's fame.\
Künſtlerſchaft (⌣⌣⌣) f ㊺ body (or society) of artists.\
Künſtler-werkſtatt (⌣⌣⌣⌣) f ㊷ studio.\
künſtlich (⌣⌣) [mhd.; *Kunſt] a. ㊺ 1. artistic; 2 erſonnen ingenious, clever, cunning(ly devised). — 2. (nachgebildet) artificial, imitated; (unecht) spurious, false; ⚹e Diamanten imitation (or paste-)diamonds pl.; ⚹es Haar false hair; ⚹e Zähne artificial teeth pl.\
Künſtlichkeit (⌣⌣⌣) f ㊺ artificialness.\
Kunſt-liebe (⌣...) f ㊷ love for art; =**liebhaber(in** f) m lover of art, amateur (artist); =**liebhaberei** f artistic taste; =**literatur** f art-literature; ⚹**los** a. artless, devoid of art; weit. natural, simple, primitive, unsophisticated; =**loſigkeit** f ㊺ artlessness; (natural) simplicity, primitiveness; ⚹**mäßig** a. artistic, vgl. ⚹**gemäß**; =**meiſter** ⊕ m einer Waſſerkunſt: manager (or engineer) of water-works; =**mittel** n artificial means or remedy; =**perio'de** f artistic period; =**poeſie** f = =dichtung; =**produkt** n = =erzeugnis; =**rad** n wheel of water-works; =**redner** m rhetorician, orator; ⚹**redneriſch** a. rhetorical, oratorical; =**regel** f rule (or precept) of art; ⚹**reich** a. ingenious; of consummate artistic skill or beauty; =**reiſe** f artist's (or artiste's) professional tour; =**reiter(in** f) m circus-rider, equestrian (f auch: equestrienne); =**reiterei** f circus-riding, equestrianism; =**reiter-geſellſchaft** f equestrian troupe, circus; =**reiter-pferd** n circus-horse; =**reiterſtück** n vaulting; =**reiter-vorſtellung** f equestrian performance; =**richter** m judge in matters of art, art-critic; =**ſache** f artistic matter; =**ſammlung** f art-collection; =**ſchacht** ⊕ m, mach. pump- (or rod-, engine-)shaft; =**ſchatz** m valuable collection of works of art; =**ſchloß** ⊕ n combination-lock; =**ſchreiner** m cabinet-maker; =**ſchule** f: a) school of art, art-school; b) (Künſtler von derſelben Richtung) artistic school; =**ſeide** ⊕ f imitation silk; =**ſinn(ig** a.) m (gifted with) artistic taste or instinct or judgment; =**ſprache** f technical language; terminology; (künſtliche Sprache) artificial language, geheime: cant; =**ſprung** m: =**ſprünge** m. to vault; =**ſtätte** f home of art; =**ſteiger** ⚒ m engineer, surveyor; =**ſtickerei** ⊕ f artistic (or art-)embroidery; =**ſtopfer(in** f) m ⊕ finedrawer; =**ſtopferei** f finedrawing; =**ſtraße** f causeway, turnpike road; =**ſtück** n clever feat, (conjuring-)trick, sleight-of-hand; ~e machen to do (a juggler's) tricks; das iſt (eben) kein ~ there's nothing wonderful, it's no great feat, any one can do that; =**ſtückchen** n/pl.: er kann verſchiedene ~ F he knows a trick or two, he's a cunning fellow; =**tiſchler** m = =ſchreiner; =**tiſchler-arbeit**, =**tiſchlerei** ⊕ f cabinet-making or -work; =**trieb** m artistic (or mechanical)

[Kunstverein] — 630 — [Kur]

instinct; vgl. =ſinn; =verein m art-union; =verfahren n artistic process; =verlag ⊙ m firm of print-publishers, auch: print-(seller's) shop; =verleger m print-publisher; ⚥verſtändig a. expert in (matters of) art; verſtändige(r) s. artistic expert; ⚥voll a. highly artistic; vgl. ⚥reich; =wein m artificial wine; =weiſe f artistic style or manner; =welt f world of art(ists); =werk n: a) work of art; alte =werke antiques pl.; b) = Kunſt 5; ⚥widrig a. contrary to the rules of art; wiſſenſchaft f: ⚯ æsthetical science, æsthetics; ⚥wiſſenſchaftlich a.: ⚯ æsthetical; =wolle f artificial wool, shoddy; =wort n technical term; =zweig m artistic branch or department or line.

kunter-bunt (ᷣ,ᷣ) [nbd.] I a. ⊕ party-coloured, variegated, gaudy; (bunt durch=ea.) in a heap of confusion, higgledy-piggledy. — II n ⊕ heap of confusion, F jumble.

Kunz (ᷣ) [dim. von Konrad] npr/m. (Bn) ⬡⋎γ. Conrad; f. Hinz 1.

Küpe ⊙ (Lᵛ) [nbd.: coop; *It. cūpa] f ⬡ Färberei: copper, boiler, vat.

Kupee * (−Lᴵ) − Coupé.

Kupellation ⊙ (−ᷣ−tß(ᵛ)ⁿ) [fr.] f metall. (Treibprozeß) cupellation; **kupellieren** (−ᵛᴸᵛ) v/a. (abtreiben) to cupel.

Küpen-rahmen (ᷣ...) m ⊕ Färberei: dipping-frame. — **Küper** (Lᵛ) f. Küfer.

Kupfer (ᷣᵛ) [ahd.: copper; lt. (P⃰ Zypern)] n ⊕ (in 2 mit pl.) 1. copper; chm. (lt.) cuprum (Cu); ſchwefelſaures ~ cupric sulphate, sulphate of copper (= Kupfervitriol); ↓ ein Schiff mit ~ beſchlagen to sheathe (or plate) ... with copper. — 2. ⊙ (mit pl.) (von e-r Kupferplatte abgedruckes Bild) copperplate (engraving or print); mit ~n verſehen to illustrate. — 3. path. (roter Ausſchlag im Geſicht) red pimples, F co. brandy-blossoms pl., ⚯ gutta ros(ac)ea.

Kupfer-ader ⚤ (ᷣ...) f copper-lode, streak (or vein) of copper; ⚥ähnlich a. ⊕ c.-like; ⚯ cupreous; =alau'n m, chm. aluminate of copper; =arbeit f c.-work; =arſe'nik n, chm. arseniate of c.; ⚥artig a. like copper, copperish,...y, ⚯ cupreous; =aſche f c.-ash(es pl.), c.-scales pl.; =ätzung f, typ. half-tone engraving on copper; =auflöſung f c.-solution; =ausſchlag m = Kupfer 3; =barren m c.-bar; =bedachung f c. roof (-ing); =bergwerk n c.-mine; =beſchlag m von Schiffen ꝛc.: c. bottom or sheathing; =blau n blue c.-ore; =blech n c. in sheets, sheet-c., c.-sheet; =block m c.-brick; =blüte f, min. c.-bloom, ⚯ chalcotrichite; =boden m von Schiffen ꝛc.: c. bottom; ⚥bödig a. c.-bottomed; =brand(=erz n) m ⚤ black c.-ore; ⚥braun a. = ⚥farben; =braun m, min. tile-ore; =chlori'd n cupric chloride (CuCl₂); =chlorü'r n cuprous chloride (Cu₂Cl₂); =dorn m c.-thorns pl.; =draht m c. wire; =druck m typ. copperplate (-printing); =drucker m copperplate-printer; =drucke'rei f: a) copperplate printing; b) office or workshop of copperplate-printers; =drucker-preſſe f copperplate printing-press; =druck-papier n plate-paper; =druck-ſchnell-preſſe f, typ. copperplate printing-machine; =druck-ſchwarz n. =ſchwärze f plate-black; =erz ⚤ n c.-ore; =fahl-erz ⚤ n black (or grey) c.-ore; =farbe f c.-colour or -hue, coppery tinge; ⚥farben, ⚥farbig a. c.-coloured, ⚯ cupreous; =feil(icht) n c.(-)filings pl.; =friſch-ofen m c.-finery; =gang ⚤ m c.-lode; =gare f separation of c.; =gar-herd m c.-refining furnace or hearth; =gar-ſchlacke f c.-refining slag; =geld n copper coin(age), c. money, F coppers pl.; =gerät, =geſchirr n copper (cooking-)utensils, F coppers pl.; =geſicht F n, fig. c.-coloured face (vgl. Kupfer 3); =gewinnung f production (or extraction) of c.; =glanz ⚤, =glas n ⚤ (natürliches Kupferſubſulfi'd) c.-glance, vitreous c. (Cu₂S); =glimmer ⚤ m c.-mica; =granalien n/pl. (gekörntes Kupfer) granulated c., bean-shot; =grün n mountain-green, ⚯ chrysocolla; auch = Grünſpan; ⚥haltig a. containing copper, coppery, ⚯ cupreous, cupriferous; =hammer(werk n) m c.-works pl. or -mill; =hammerſchlag m c.-scales pl.; =handel m c.-trade; =haut ↓ f c. bottom; vgl. =beſchlag; =hütte f copper-works pl.; =hütten-arbeiter m c.-smelter; =hütten-prozeß m c.-smelting; =hydroxyd n cupric hydrate, copper-azure (CuH₂O₂).

kupf(e)richt, **kupf(e)rig** (ᷣ(ᵛ)ᷣ) a. ⊕ copper-like; copper-coloured, coppery (auch path. vom Geſichte).

Kupfer-jodü'r (ᷣ...) n ⊕ iodide of copper; =kalk m (Kupferoxyd) cupric oxide; =karbid n copper carbide (CuC₂); =keſſel m copperkettle, größerer: copper; =kies ⚤ m c.-pyrites, yellow c.-ore (CuFeS₂); =knallſäure f, chm.: ⚯ cupro-fulminic acid; =könig m regulus of c.; =laſu'r ⚤ m (f) azure c.-ore, ⚯ azurite; als Farbe: mountain-blue (2CuCO₃·Cu(OH)₂); =legierung f c.-alloy, alloy (or alligation) of c.; =lichtdruck m helio-engraving, heliogravure; =metalle n/pl. chm.: ⚯ cuprides pl.; =münze f copper coin; vgl. =geld.

kupfern (ᷣᵛ) I a. ⊕ (of) copper. — II v/a. ⚥ a. to sheathe with copper.

Kupfer-naſe (ᷣ...) f ⊕ fig. coppernose; =oxy'd n, chm.: ⚯ cupric oxide (CuO); kohlenſaures ~ cupric (or copper) carbonate, =oxyd-hydra't n = =hydroxyd; =oxydu'l cuprous oxide (Cu₂O); =platte f: a) copperplate, Kupferſterecherei: radierte ~ etched plate; b) = =blech; =pol m, elect. negative pole; =probe f copper-assaying or -test, assay of c.-ore; =rauch m c.-smoke; =ring m: a) c. ring; b) c.-ring, c.-syndicate; =rot n red oxide of c.; ⚥rot a. c.-coloured; =röte f c.-colour; =ſalz n, chm. copper salt; =ſammlung f v. Kupferſtichen: copperplate collection; =ſchaum m scum; =ſchiefer m c.-schist; ⚯ cupriferous slate; =ſchlacke f c.-slag; =ſchmelzarbeit f c.-smelting; =ſchmelz-ofen m c.-smelting furnace; =ſchmied m coppersmith, brazier; =ſchmiede f coppersmith's forge or workshop; =ſpeiſe f c.-speiss; =ſtechen n engraving on c.; =ſtecher m copper-plate-engraver, ⚯ chalcographer; =ſtecherei f: a) = =druckerei; b) = =ſtecher-kunſt f copper-plate-engraving; ⚯ chalcography; =ſtich m engraving, ⚯ chalcograph; =ſtich-händler m dealer in engravings, print-seller; =ſtich-kabinett n collection of engravings; =ſtich-platte f copperplate; =ſulfa't n = =vitrio'l; =ſulfid n, chm. cupric sulphide (CuS); =ſulfü'r n cuprous sulphide (Cu₂S); =tafel f = =platte, =blech; =vergiftung f copper-poisoning; =verhüttung f copper-smelting; =vitrio'l m, chm. copper (or blue) vitriol, sulphate of copper (CuSO₄); =ware ⊕ f copper ware; =werk n: a) work (illustrated or adorned) with engravings or copper-plates; b) = =hammer(=werk).

kupfricht, **kupfrig** f. kupfericht, kupferig.

Kupido (ᵛ−⋎−) [It.] npr/m. ⊕ a. myth. (Liebesgott) Cupid, Cupido.

kupieren (−Lᵛ−) [fr. couper] v/a. u. v/n. (h.) ⊕ 1. Kartenſpiel: (abheben) to cut (the cards). — 2. ⌨, &c. Fahr-karten, =ſcheine ⚥ to clip (weitS. to check) the tickets. — 3. ⚔ kupiertes Gelände intersected (or uneven) ground. [cupola-furnace.

Kupol-(hoch)-ofen (ᵛᴸ...) m ⊕ metall.]

Kupon* (−vg̊) = Coupon.

Kuppe (ᷣ) [nbd., *It.] f ⊕ 1. mountain-top, vgl. Koppe. — 2. (Kopf e-s eiſernen Nagels ꝛc.) head of a nail, &c.

Kuppel¹ (ᷣᵛ) f ⊕ = Koppel 1 u. 2.

Kuppel² (ᷣᵛ) f ⊕ arch. (halbkugel-förmig gewölbtes Dach) cupola, dome (-shaped roof); ⚥artig (ᷣᵛ...) a. ⊕ like (or in the style of) a cupola; vgl. ⚥förmig; ~dach n ⊕ = Kuppel².

Kuppelei (ᷣᵛⁿ) f ⊕ match-making; playing the go-between for lovers.

kuppel²-förmig (ᷣᵛ...) a. ⊕ dome-shaped; =gewölbe n ⊕ arch. dome-shaped (or spherical) vault; Att.: ⚯ tholus.

kuppeln¹ (ᷣᵛ) [It. cop(u)la're] I v/n. (h.) und v/a. ⚤ a. 1. (Ehen vermitteln, Pärchen zſ.=bringen) to play the match-maker or go-between; to pair; e-m ein Mädchen ⚥ to procure a girl for a p. — 2. = koppeln 1 u. 2. — II ~ n ⊕ 3. = Kuppelei.

kuppeln² (ᷣᵛ) [Kuppel²] v/a. ⚤ a. arch. to build in the shape of a dome; (mit e-r Kuppel verſehen) to provide with a cupola or dome.

Kuppel²-ofen ⊙ (ᷣᵛ...) m ⊕ = Kupol-ofen; =pelz F m: ſich e-n ~ verdienen to play the match-maker, to bring about a match; =ſtange ⊕ f, mach. coupling-bar, connecting-rod; Wagen-bau: coupling-pole.

Kupp(e)lung (ᷣ(ᵛ)ᷣ) [kuppeln¹ 2] f mach.: (Kuppeln u. Gekuppeltes) coupling (a. ⌨). [(or lop, poll) trees, &c.]

kuppen (ᷣᵛ) v/a. ⚤: Bäume ꝛc. ⚥ to top]

Kuppler (ᷣᵛ) [nhd.] m ⚤, ~in f ⊕ match-maker, go-between; b.s. auch: procurer, f...ess; ehm.: pimp. bawd.

kupplerhaft, kupplerisch (ᷣᵛᵛ) a. ⊕ match-making; procuring.

Kupplung (ᷣᵛ) f. Kuppelung.

Kur¹ (L; Hom. Chur, Cour) [nhd.: cure; *It. cūra] f ⊕ med. cure (a. = Hei-

[Kur] — 631 — [Kurszettel]

lung); e-e ~ gebrauchen to follow a (course of) treatment, to try a cure, durch Brunnentrinken: to drink (or take) the waters (at a spa); e-n in der ~ h., e-n in die ~ nehmen to treat a p. for a complaint; sich in die ~ e-s Arztes begeben to take medical advice, to place o.s. under medical treatment, to call in a doctor; die ~ schlägt an the cure (or treatment) is taking effect; vgl. anschlagen 15.

Kur², **Kür** (⌣́) [ahd.: choice, choose: *kiesen] f ⑯ (Wahl) election; die Kür (Wahl) haben to have the right to elect.

Kurant (⌣⌣́) [nhd.; *fr. courant] n (m) ⑪c. (auch ~geld n ⓶ (Umlaufsmittel) currency; (Landesmünze) coin of the realm; klein ~ small change.

kuranzen P (-⌣́⌣) [*mlt. Kare'nz] v/a. ⑨: e-n (ab=)2 to give a p. a sound thrashing or drubbing; (quälen, schelten) to worry, bother; to scold.

Kurare (-⌣́⌣) [süd=amerik.] n, inv. (Pfeilgift der Indianer, Saft von Strychnos toxi'fera und anderen Pflanzen) curare.

Kur¹-arzt (⌣́⌣⌣) m ⓶ physician at a watering-place or sanatorium.

Küraß ⚔ (⌣́) [nhd.; *fr. cuirasse f Leder=] m ⑪a. (Brustharnisch) cuirass, breast-plate; leichterer: cors(e)let.

Kürassier ⚔ (⌣⌣⌣́) [nhd.; *fr. cuirassier] m ⑪d. cuirassier; ~degen (⌣́...) m ⓶, ~pallasch m heavy straight sword of a cuirassier; ~regime'nt n regiment of cuirassiers, cuirassier-regiment.

Kuratel (⌣⌣⌣́) [mlt.] f ⑯ jur. (Pflegschaft) trusteeship, guardianship; e-n unter ~ stellen to appoint a trustee (or guardian) over a p.

Kurator (-⌣́⌣) [mlt.] n. ⑪ jur. (Pfleger) trustee, guardian, ✱ ~ der Masse (official) administrator (or trustee) of the estate, commissioner in bankruptcy.

Kuratorium (-⌣⌣́(⌣)⌣) [lt.] n ⓶ 1. board of trustees or guardians or governors. — 2. (Verwaltungsrat) board of administration or management, governing body.

Kurbel ⊕ (⌣́⌣) [dim. v. † (ahd.) Kurbe; *fr. courbe] f ⑱: ~ einer Winde, Drehorgel, Presse 2c.: crank, (winch-)handle.

Kurbel-achse ⊕ (⌣́...) f ⓶ crank-axle; =arm m cr.-web, cr.-lever; =bewegung f, =getriebe n cr.-movement.

kurbe(l)n (⌣́⌣) [Kurbe(l)] v/n. (h.) ⓷ (⓶a.) to turn the crank or the (winch-)handle or the switch.

Kurbel-stange (⌣́⌣...) f ⓶ mach. connecting-rod; =umschalter m Fernsp. button-switch; =welle f crank-shaft; =zapfen m crank-pin, trunnion.

kurbettieren (⌣⌣⌣́⌣) [fr. courbetter] v/n. (h.) ⓽ man. (Luftsprünge m.) to curvet.

Kürbis ♀ (⌣́) [ahd.; *lt. cucu'rbita f] m ⑰ ♀ (Pflanze u. Frucht) pumpkin, f. beb. Garten=♀, Flaschen=♀; ♀-ähnlich (⌣́⌣...) a. ⑯, ♀-artig ♀ a. resembling a pumpkin, ⛁ cucurbitaceous; ~baum ♀ m ⓶ gourd- (or calabash-)tree (Crese'ntia cuje'te); ~flasche f gourd (-bottle), calabash; ~frucht ♀ f: ⛁ pepo(nium); ~gewächse ♀ n/pl.: ⛁ cucurbitaceous plants, cucurbit(ac)eæ pl.; ~kern m pip (or seed) of a pumpkin, ♀-kern=förmig a. zo.: ⛁ cucurbitive.

Kur²-brandenburg ♀ (⌣́⌣⌣⌣) n ⓶ (the) Electorate of Brandenburg.

Kurde (⌣́⌣) m ⓸, **Kurdin** f ⓸ Kurd; **kurdisch** a. ⑯ Kurdish; **Kurdistan** ♀ (⌣⌣⌣́) npr/n. ⓷a. (Land Vorder=asiens) Kurdistan; **kurdistanisch** (⌣⌣⌣́⌣) a. ⑯ Kurdish.

küren (⌣́⌣) [nhd.; *for. Kur²] v/a. ⑨, a. ⓸d. altertümlich u. poet. to choose, elect.

Kur²-fürst (⌣́...) m ⓶ elector (f electress); der Große ~ von Brandenburg the Great Elector; =fürstentum n ⑨d. electorate; ♀fürstlich a. ⑯ electoral.

Kur¹-gast (⌣́...) m ⓶ visitor (or guest) at a watering-place; ♀gemäß a. ⑯ according to rules of health; =haus n pump-, well-room, assembly-room (pl.).

Kur²-haus (⌣́...) n ⓶ electoral house; =hessen ♀ n electorate of Hesse.

kurial (-⌣⌣́) [lt.] a. ⑯ = kanzleimäßig; ~ien (-⌣⌣́⌣) n/pl. forensic customs or observances pl.; ~stil (-⌣⌣́...) m ⓶ forensic (or legal, ⛁ curialistic) style.

Kuri-e (⌣́⌣) [it.] f ⑯ 1. röm. Alt.: (Abteilung der Bürger Roms) Versammlungshaus des Senats) curia. — 2. römische ~ (päpstlicher Hof) Roman (or Papal) See or Court.

Kurier (⌣⌣́) [nhd.; *fr. courrier] m ⑪d. (Eilbote) courier, express (messenger); (als) ~ reiten to ride post.

kurieren (⌣⌣́⌣) [lt. cūrā're] v/a. ⑨ (heilen) to cure, mit Arznei: to physic; zu Tode ⚲ to kill by doctoring or with physic; wieder ganz kuriert quite restored.

Kurier-stiefel (⌣⌣́...) m ⓶ jack-boot; =zug 🚂 express (or mail-)train; fast train.

kurios F (-⌣⌣́) [it.] a. ⑯ (D 10) (schnurrig) curious, droll, funny, queer, odd, F rum; furioser Kauz queer fellow, oddity, F rum chap.

Kuriosität (-⌣⌣-⌣́) [it.] f ⑯ 1. curiousness, oddness; der ~ halber as a curiosity. — 2. (et. Kurioses) curiosity, oddity, curious (or F rum) affair.

Kuriositäten-händler (-(⌣)-⌣́...) m ⓶, =liebhaber m dealer in, connoisseur of curios(ities) or rarities.

Kuriosum (-(⌣)⌣́⌣) [it.] n ⓾ curious th. or fact; curiosity.

Kur¹-kosten (⌣́⌣⌣) pl. expense(s pl.) of a cure, charge(s pl.) for medical treatment.

Kurkuma ♀ (⌣́⌣⌣) [ar.] f ⓾ (Gilbwurz) (root of) curcuma; ~gelb n ⓶ chm. = Curcumin; ~papier n (gelbes Reagenspapier) curcuma- (or turmeric-)paper.

Kurland ♀ (⌣́⌣) [Kure, Volk] npr/n. ⓷a. (russische Ostseeprovinz) Courland; **Kurländer(in)** (⌣́⌣⌣) m ⓶ (f ⓸) Courlander, inhabitant of Courland.

Kur¹-liste (⌣́...) f ⓶ list of visitors; =²mainz ♀ n Electorate of Mayence; =mantel m elector's ermine (cloak); =¹methode f, med. method of treatment, cure; =ort m watering-place, health-resort, spa, klimatischer, in Indien 2c.: sanatorium; =²pfalz ♀ f the Palatinate; ♀pfälzisch a. ⑯ Palatine; =¹pfuscher(in f) m quack; =pfuscherei f quackery.

Kurrende (⌣⌣́⌣) [lt.] f ⑯ ehm.: (procession of) poor scholars who go singing before people's houses; ~junge m ⓶, ~schüler m poor chorister or choir-boy.

kurrent (⌣⌣́) [lt. laufend] a. ⑯ current; ~schrift (⌣⌣́...) f ⓶ running-hand.

kurrig ⚮ (⌣́⌣) a. ⑯ 1. lively; (streitsüchtig) quarrelsome, hot-tempered. — 2. (wunderlich) queer, strange, odd.

Kurs (⌣́) [nhd.; *lt. cursus Lauf] m ⓶a. 1. ✱: a) (Umlauf) currency, (rate of) exchange; der ~ ist pa'ri the exchange is at par; der jetzige ~ the current exchange, the present value; b) die Kurse sind gefallen prices have dropped or eased off or receded or gone down; im Kurse steigen to (have a) rise, to go up, to harden, advance, improve; Papiere, die keinen ~ haben stock(s pl.) without official quotation; c) außer ~ setzen to withdraw from circulation, to call in. — 2. ⚓ (Schiffs=)~ course; den ~ ändern to haul; den ~ halten to stand (up)on the course; e-n falschen ~ nehmen, steuern to steer (or take) the wrong course; den ~ nach dem offenen Meere nehmen to head out to sea; den ~ setzen, stellen to shape one's course; fig. der neue ~ (die neue Richtung) the new course or drift (in politics).

Kur¹-saal (⌣́...) m ⓶ = Kur¹-haus.

Kurs-abschlag (⌣́⌣⌣) m ⓶ drop (or fall) in prices.

Kur²-sachsen ♀ (⌣́⌣⌣) n ⓷a. Electorate of Saxony.

Kurs-änderung ⚓ (⌣́...) f ⓾ change of course; ♀anziehend ✱ a. ⑯ Börse: rising, advancing; =bericht m ⓶ market-report; =blatt n list of quotations, (stock-)exchange list; =buch n: a) 🚂 &c. time-table(s pl.), (official) railway-guide, in England a.: Bradshaw; ABC (time-table); b) ✉ post-office guide. [arzt] veterinary surgeon.|

Kur¹-schmied (⌣́⌣⌣) m ⓶ farrier, (Tier=)

Kürschner (⌣́⌣) [nhd.; *slaw.] m ⓶ (Pelzmacher) furrier, skinner; ~arbeiten f/pl. ⓶ furrier's articles or goods pl.

Kürschnerei (⌣⌣⌣́) f ⓾ (Pelzgeschäft) furrier's trade or workshop or establishment.

Kürschner-handwerk (⌣́⌣...) n ⓶ furrier's trade; =innung f in Engl.: Company of Skinners; =ware f peltry, mehr gbr.: furrier's ware, furs and skins pl.

kurs-fähig ✱ (⌣́...) a. ⑯ current, in circulation; ♀habende Papiere n/pl. stocks pl. quoted on the stock-exchange.

kursieren (⌣⌣́⌣) [it.] v/n. (h.) ⑨ Geld, Gerüchte 2c.: to be current or in circulation; Gerüchte 2 lassen to set ... afloat.

Kursiv (⌣⌣́f) [it.] f, ~schrift (⌣⌣́...) f ⓶ typ. (Schrift von dieser Form) italics pl.; mit ~ gedruckt (printed) in italics, italicized.

Kurs-karte ✉ (⌣́...) f ⓶ map of mail-routes; =notierung ✱ f market-quotation, quotation on the stock-exchange or of exchange(s).

kursorisch (⌣⌣́⌣) [it.] a. ⑯ Schule: Le Lektüre cursory reading (ant. sta'ta'risch).

Kurs-schwankung ✱ (⌣́...) f ⓾ fluctuation in the stock-market; =sturz m rapid decline (or fall) of prices, panic; =treiber m (=treiberei f) rigger (rigging) of the market.

Kursus (⌣́⌣) [lt. Lauf] m, inv. u. ⑬ (Lehrgang) course (or series) of lectures, &c.; e-n ganzen ~ durchmachen to go through a complete course.

Kurs-verlust (⌣́...) m ⓶ loss by exchange; =zettel m = =blatt.

⚗ scientific; ♀ botanical; ♀ geography; ⊕ machinery; ⚒ mining; ⚔ military; ⚓ marine; ✱ commercial; ✉ postal; 🚂 railway.

[Kurt] — 632 — [küssen]

Kurt (⁻ ob. ᷉) [Ko(n)r(a)b] *npr/m.* ⊛⊛α. (Br.) Conrad.

Kur¹-taxe (⁻᷉⸜᷉) *f* ⊛ tax imposed on visitors at a spa. [curtain.]

Kurtine ⚹ (⸍⸍) [fr. *courtine*] *f* ⊛ frt.]

Kür-turnen (⁻᷉⸜) *n* ⊛ einzelner Turner: free gymnastic exercises *pl.*

Kurve (᷉ᵐᵛ) [It.] *f* ⊛ math. curve, curved line; ⚹ balliſtiſche ~ (Geſchoßbahn) ballistic curve; ~n-lineaʼl (᷉ᵐᵛ…) *n* ⊛ bow, Schiffbau: curve-templet; ~n-tafel ῶ *f* curve-table.

Kur²-verein (⸍…) *m* ⊛ meeting of the electors; =würde *f* dignity of an elector, electoral dignity.

kurz (᷉) [ahd.: curt; *It. *curtus*] *a.* ⊛ (D²) **1.** Raum: short; ~ u. dick dumpy, thick-set, *a.* podgy; ~ und ſtämmig squat, stumpy; mit ~en Beinen short-legged; ~es Ende Licht short piece (or small bit) of candle; es iſt nur ein ~es Ende bis dahin it is only a short way (or a few steps) from here; ~er Ga-lopp canter; ein ~es Geſicht h. to be short-sighted; ~e Schritte m. to take short (or small) steps; ↓ ~e See chopping sea; ~e Strecke short distance; ⊕ ~e Waren *pl.* small ware; (Metall-waren) hardware, metal ware or goods *pl.*; vgl. Kurzware; mit verbs: ein Pferd ~ halten to tighten a horse's reins; *fig.* e-n ~ halten to keep a tight hand over a p., to keep a p. short (of money); bei et. **zu ~ kommen** to come off badly in a th.; et. ~ u. klein kriegen to pull a th. to pieces; *fig.* et. nicht kurz (ober klein) kriegen können to be unable to understand (or to make out) a th.; zu ~ ſchießen ⚹ to fire (too) short, *fig.* to make an ineffectual (or abortive) attempt; ~ und klein ſchlagen to knock to pieces, to smash (in)to bits or atoms; elect. eine Batterie ꝛc. ~ ſchließen to short-circuit …; ſich (*dat.*) die Haare (zu) ~ ſchneiden laſſen to have one's hair cut (too) short or cropped. — **2.** Zeit, Abfassung ꝛc.: short, brief; ~e (~ gefaßte) Antwort curt (or blunt) answer; ~er Beſuch visit of short duration, flying visit; e-n (raſchen) Entſchluß faſſen, ſich ~ (*adv.*) ent-ſchließen to come to a hasty decision; ein ~es Gedächtnis haben to have a short memory; ~er Hand f. kurzer-hand; (einen) ~en Prozeß mit et. machen to dispatch a th. at once, to make short work of it; ~e Überſicht summary review; eine ~e Weile (for) a short while; mit ~en Worten in a few (short) words, briefly; ~ (ob. ~e Zeit) vorher (nachher) a short time before (after); in ~er Zeit, **in ~em** (with)in a short time, shortly, ere long; die ~e Zeit, die wir zu leben haben the brief (or limited) space (or span) of time that we have to live; ⊛ ~e Sicht short sight or date; ~er Wechſel short-dated bill, short paper, *pl.* oft: shorts. — **3.** in adverbialen Redensarten: **binnen ~em** within a short time or while; **in ~em** (bald) shortly; ſeit ~em for some little time (now); lately, latterly; **vor ~em** a short time (or while) ago, a little time back, lately; bis

vor ~em until quite recently; über ~ oder lang sooner or later; ~-um, ~ und **gut** in a word, in short, the short and long of it is; ~ und bündig con-cise(ly), brief(ly); laconic(ally); ~ und gedrängt succinct(ly), terse(ly), curt(ly); *mit verbs:* alle Beziehungen mit e-m ~ abbrechen suddenly to break off all relations (or connexion[s]) with a p.; e-n ~ abfertigen to cut a p. short; e-e Sache ~ abmachen to dispatch a th. quickly; ~ angebunden f. anbinden III; ſich ~ faſſen to express o.s. briefly, to be brief; um mich ~ zu faſſen, um es ~ zu machen to put it briefly; es ~ m. to be quick in doing a th.; machen Sie es ~! cut it short!; die Tage werden kürzer the days are beginning to draw in, the days are shortening. — **II** *comp.* **3. kürzer:** e-n um e-n Kopf ~ m. to cut a p.'s head off, to behead a p.; den ~(e)n ziehen to get the worst of it, F to come off second best. — **III** *sup.* **4. kürzeſt:** am ~en shortest, most ex-peditiously; aufs, auf das ~e in the shortest (or quickest) way.

kurz-ab (᷉᷉) *adv.* offhand(ishly); =är-melig (᷉…) *a.* ⊛ short-sleeved; =armig *a.* short-armed, with short arms; =at-mig *a.* sh.-winded, *path.*: ⚭ asthmat-ic(al), *vet.* broken-winded, F roaring; =atmigkeit *f* ⊛ short(ness of) breath, ⚭ asthma; =beinig *a.* short-legged; =bauernd *a.* of brief dura-tion, ⊛ short(-dated).

Kürze (᷉᷉) [ahd.] *f* ⊛ (f. kurz) **1.** Raum: shortness. — **2.** Zeit ꝛc.: shortness, brevity, short duration; *gr., pros.* ~ e-r Silbe short syllable; vgl. **3.**; in der ~ (halb) shortly; with due dispatch; die Sache in (der) ~ abmachen to dispatch the matter quickly or promptly or summarily; ſich der ~ im Ausdruck befleißigen to express o.s. briefly, to be brief; in aller ~ erzählen to tell in as few words as possible; Sprichw. ~ iſt des Witzes Würze brevity is the soul of wit. — **3.** *gr., pros.* (kurze Silbe) short (syllable). — [ing-place.)

Kur¹-zeit (⸍⸍) *f* ⊛ season at a water-]

kürzen (᷉᷉) [ahd.; *kurz] **I** *v/a.* ⊛ **1.** = abkürzen I. — **2.** e-m (ſich) die Zeit ~ to make a p.'s (one's) time pass away, to beguile (or to while away) a p.'s (one's) time. — **3.** e-n um ſ-n Lohn, e-m ſ-n Lohn ~ to cut down (F to dock) a p.'s wages or pay. — **II** ~ *n* ⊛ ⚹ *f.* Kürzung.

kurzer-hand (᷉᷉) *adv.* (ohne ſich zu be-ſinnen) without hesitation, offhand, on the spot; abruptly; vgl. k. H.

Kürzer-werden (᷉᷉⸜᷉) *n* ⚹ shortening, shrinking.

kurz-flojjig (᷉…) *a.* ⊛ *ichth.*: micro-pterous; =flüg(e)lig *a.* *orn.* short-winged, ⚭ brevipennate, brachy-pterous; =flügler *m/pl.* *orn.* (Strauß-vögel) ⚭ brachypterus, cursores *pl.*; =füßig *a.* short-footed, ⚭ breviped, brachypodine; =gefaßt *a.* brief(ly worded), concise; =geſchoren *a.* close-shaven, close-cropped; ⊕ von Tuch, Sammet ꝛc.: short-nap(ped); =geſchürzt

a. in short dress(es); =geſchwänzt *a.* sh.-tailed; ⚭ brevicaudate; =haarig *a.* short-haired; =halſig *a.* sh.-necked; =hin (᷉᷉) *adv.* offhand(ishly), abruptly, curtly; =hörnig (᷉…) *a.* sh.-horned; ~es Vieh, *a.* sh.-horns *pl.*; =köpfig *a.* brachycephalic; =köpfigkeit *f* brachy-cephaly; =lebend, =lebig *a.* sh.-lived; =leibig *a.* of short stature; short-waisted. [late; erſt ~ quite recently.]

kürzlich (᷉᷉) *adv.* lately, latterly, of)

kurz-ohrig (᷉…) *a.* ⊛ short-eared; =ſchluß *m* ⊛ *elect.* short circuit; =ſchnä-b(e)lig *a.* *orn.* sh.-billed or -beaked, ⚭ brevirostral; =ſchrift; =ſchreiber *m* shorthand-writer; =ſchrift *f* shorthand(-writing), stenography, brachygraphy; *tel.* code; =ſchwanz *m* short-tailed animal, =ſchwanz-affe *m*, *zo.*: ⚭ brachyuran; =ſichtig *a.*: a) (*ant.* weitſichtig) short- (or near-)sighted, *path.*: ⚭ myopic; b) *fig.* (*ant.* umſichtig) short-sighted, narrow-minded, undiscerning; c) ⊛ ~er Wechſel bill at short sight, short (-dated) bill; =ſichtige([r] *m*) *f* short-sighted person (auch *fig.*), *path.*: ⚭ myops; =ſichtigkeit *f*: a) sh.-sighted-ness, myopy, myopia; b) *fig.* short-sightedness, narrow-mindedness; =ſtielig *a.* short-stalked, ♀: ⚭ subpedunculate, subsessile; =ſtrom *m*, *elect.* short circuit; =um *(᷉᷉) adv.* in short, in a word (ſ. *a.* kurz 3).

Kürzung (᷉᷉) *f* ⊛ **1.** = Ab~. — **2.** *thea.* ~ in Schauſpielen: clipping, cutting down.

Kurz-ware (᷉᷉) *f* ⊛ petty goods or articles *pl.*; (Metallware) hardware, vgl. kurze Waren (kurz 1); =waren-händler(in *f*) *m* small dealer, retailer; dealer in hardware; =weg (᷉᷉) *adv.* curtly, abruptly, offhand(ishly); =weil (᷉…) [mhd.] *f* ⊛ pastime, amusement, entertainment; sport, fun; ~ treiben to disport o.s., to make merry; =wei-lig *a.* amusing, entertaining, sport-ive, funny; weitſ. whiling away the time; =wollig (᷉᷉) *a.* short-nap(ped); =züngig *a.*: ⚭ brevilingual.

kuſchen (᷉᷉) [nhd.; *fr. *coucher*] *v/n.* (h.) u. **ſich ~** *v/refl.* ⊛ **1.** *v.* Hunden: to lie down, to crouch; tuſch!, tuſch' dich! *als int.* lie down!, be quiet!, down, dog! — **2.** *fig.* von Perſonen: to keep quiet, not to stir.

Kuſine* (⸍⸍) *f* ⊛ ſ. Couſine.

Kuß (᷉) [ahd.: kiss] *m* ⊛ *a.* kiss, F buss, ⚭ osculation; e-m einen ~ (ob. eine ~hand) zuwerfen to kiss one's hand to a p., to blow a p. a kiss; Sprichw. ſ. Ehre 4.

Küßchen (᷉᷉) *n* ⊛ dim. v. Kuß.

küſſen (᷉᷉) [ahd.: kiss] **I** *v/a.* u. **ſich ~** *v/rpr.* ⊛ **1.** (ſich) to kiss (one another); e-n (~m) auf die Stirne (Wange) ~ to kiss a p.'s (or a p. on the) forehead (cheek). — **2.** mit Angabe der Wirkung: e-n aus dem Schlafe, e-n wach ~ to rouse a p. with kissing; e-m die Trä-nen vom Antlitz ~ to kiss (away) the tears from a p.'s face. — **3.** *fig. poet.* (leiſe berühren) to kiss, caress. — **II** ~ *n* ⊛ **4.** kissing, *fig.* das iſt zum ~ (prächtig) that is delightful; zum ~ ſchön charm-ing, lovely.

Zeichen (ſ. S. XVII): F familiär; P Volksſprache; Ր Gaunerſprache; ⚹ ſelten; † alt (auch geſtorben); * neu (auch geboren); ⁒ unrichtig.

Küsserei (ˢ⸴ᵘ) f ⊕ constant kissing, F billing and cooing, co. slobbering.

Kuß=finger (ˢ...) m ⊕, =**hand** c, =**händchen** n kissing one's hand to a p. (s. Kuß); fig. etwas mit Kußhand (mit Freuden) tun to do a th. with the greatest pleasure.

Kusso ♀ (⸴...) &c. s. Koso &c.

Küste ⚓ (ˢ⸴) [nbb.: coast; ndl.; fr.; *It. costa Rippe] f ⊕ (sea-)coast; (flaches, oft sandiges Gestade, Strand) (sandy) beach; allg: Meeresufer) shore; an der ~ hinfahren to (sail along the) coast, to hug the shore; die ~ zu Gesicht bekommen to raise the coast or the land.

Küsten=aufnahme ⚓ (ˢ⸴...) f ⊕ =**vermessung**; =**batterie** f shore-battery; =**befestigungen** f/pl. coast- (or shore-)defences; =**beseu(e)rung** f, =**beleuchtung** f lighting (fires along) the coast or beach; =**bewohner** m inhabitant of the coast, a. oft: F seasider; =**fahrer** m (Schiffer und Schiff) coaster, das Schiff auch: coasting vessel; =**fluß** m small river which empties into the sea; =**frachtfahrt** f coasting trade; =**handel** m coasting-trade; =**land** n maritime country, litoral; =**lotse**, =**pilot** m coasting-pilot; =**schiff** (⸴) =**fahrer** m; =**schiffahrt** f coasting(-trade); =**schiffahrts-reeder** m along-shore owner; =**schiffer** m master of a coasting-vessel; =**schutz** m coast-defence; =**stadt** f maritime town, seaside-town; =**strich** m = =**land**; =**telegraph** m: optischer ~ semaphore; =**vermessung** f survey of the coast; =**verteidigung** f defence of the coast; =**wache** f coast-guard; =**wächter** m coast-guard(sman); =**wacht=schiff** n guardship.

Küster (ˢ⸴) [ahd., *mlt. s. Kustos] m ⊕ eccl. sexton; (Kirchendiener) verger; ~ und zugleich Mesner clerk; s. Kuckuck 2; **Küsterei** (ˢ⸴ᵘ) f ⊕ sexton's post or house.

Kustos (ˢ⸴) [lt. custōs] m ⊕ (sg. inv., pl. Kusto'den) 1. e-r Bibliothek, e-s Museums &c. keeper, custodian, curator. – 2. fig., ⊕ typ., &c. (auf das Folgende hinweisendes Wort) catchword, direction.

Kutsch=bock (ˢ...) m ⊕ coach-box, coachman's seat, driving-seat or-box; =**bockdecke** f hammer-cloth.

Kutsche (ˢ⸴) [nhb. 16. sae.; *Kocs (tötsch) ♀ ungar. Dorf] f ⊕, dim. Kütschchen n ⊕ coach, carriage, F trap; zweisitzige offene ~ victoria; (Wagen für Passagiere bsd. ehm.: mail-coach; einspännige (zweispännige) ~ one-horse (two-horse) carriage; ~ und (zwei) Pferde halten to keep one's carriage and pair; in einer Kutsche fahren to ride (or drive) in a coach, F to coach it.

Kutschen=bauer (ˢ⸴...) m ⊕ coach-builder; =**decke** f roof of a coach; =**fabrikant** m = =**bauer**; =**fenster** n carriage-window; =**haus** n coach-house; =**himmel** m top of a coach; =**macher** m = =**bauer**; =**schlag** m carriage-door; =**tor** n large gate for carriages (to pass through); =**tritt** m foot-board of a coach.

Kutscher (ˢ⸴) [Kutsche] m ⊕ coachman; driver (vgl. Droschken2); ~**bock** (ˢ⸴...) m ⊕, ~**sitz** m = Kutschbock; ~**livree** f coachman's livery; ~(=**wein**) F m inferior (or cheap, sour) wine.

Kutsch=feder (ˢ...) f ⊕ coach-spring; =**fenster** n = Kutschen-fenster.

kutschieren (⸴ᴸ) v/n. (su u. h.) ⊕ 1. to drive (or ride) in a coach. — 2. (selbst fahren) to drive (a coach); er kann trefflich 2 he knows how to drive or to handle the reins, he is an excellent whip.

Kutsch=kasten (ˢ...) m ⊕: a) body of a coach; b) boot, box under the seat of a coach; =**pferd** n carriage-horse: =**wagen** m = Kutsche.

Kütt (⸴) m ⊕b. r-r, aber ⚒ = Kitt.

Kutte (ˢ⸴) [mhd.; *Kotze] f ⊕ (Mönchs2) cowl; fig. die ~ anlegen (ablegen) to don (to doff) the monkish garb.

Kuttel, mst ~**n** pl. P (⸴) [nbb.] f ⊕ als Speise: tripe; vgl. Kaldaune.

Kuttel=fleck (ˢ⸴...) m ⊕ = Kuttel.

Kutten=geier (ˢ⸴...) m ⊕ orn. king-vulture (Sarcorha'mphus papa); =**träger** F m, contp. monk, friar.

Kutter ⚓ ⚓ (ˢ⸴) [engl.] m ⊕ cutter.

Kuvert (⸢w⸣) [(+⸢+⸣) fr. couvert] n ⊕c. 1. (Gedeck) cover. — 2. (Umschlag für Briefe) envelope, wrapper; unter ~ under cover.

kuvertieren (⸢w⸣ᴸ) [Kuvert] v/a. ⊕ to (put in an) envelope. [machine.]

Kuvert=maschine ⊕ (⸢w⸣ˢ...) f ⊕ envelope-)

Küvette (⸢w⸣ˢ) [fr.] f ⊕ bei Taschenuhren: inside case of a watch, dust-plate.

Kux ⚒ (ˢ) [nhd.; *tschech.] m ⊕a. share in a mine, mining venture, claim.

☞ **Ky...** f. auch **Cy...**

kyanisieren ⊕ (ˢ⸴...) [Ryan, 1832, Engländer] v/a. ⊕ to kyanize.

Kybele (⸴ᵛᵛ) [grch.] npr/f. = Cybele.

☞ **Kyll...** f. Zyll...

kymrisch (ˢ⸴) a. ⊕ (zu Wales gehörig, auf das Keltische von West-england bezüglich) Cymric.

☞ **Kyn...** f. Zyn... [Cymric.]

Kyrie=eleison (ˢ⸴...)[ᴸᵛᵛᴸᵛᵛ] ⊕, abbr. **Kyrieleis**! (ˢ⸴...) [grch. Herr, erbarme dich!] Lord, have mercy upon us!

☞ **Kyropädie**, **Kyros** f. Cyr...

☞ **Kyst...**, **Kyt...** f. Zyst..., Zyt...

L

L, l (ĕl) n. inv. (Buchstabe) L, l.

l. abbr. = lies read.

l, öft. **l** abbr. = Liter litre.

la (ᴸ ob. ᴸ) int. **1.** ♪: a) (Note) la (= A a); b) (dem Gesange untergelegte Silbe) ○ ○, tra ○ ○, etwa: falderal. — **2.** so ○ ○ (ziemlich), zB. wie geht's? so ○ ○! how are you? pretty well!, F pretty middling!, nothing to boast of!

Lab (ᴸ) [ahd. Brühe] n ⊕c. 1. zo. rennet, a. = ~**magen**. — 2. ♀ = =**kraut**.

Laban (ᴸᵛ) npr/m. ⊕α. bibl. (Schwiegervater Jakobs) Laban; langer ~ tall fellow, F lamp-post, daddy-long-legs.

Labbe (ˢ⸴) [nbb.] f ⊕ heavy, hanging lip, thick lip.

labb(e)rig F (ˢ(⸴)ᵛ) a. ⊕ von Speisen: tasteless, insipid, without flavour; ⚓ 2e Kühlde light breeze.

labbern (ˢ⸴) v/a.u.v/n.(h.)⊕a. **1.**(schlürfen) to lap (up). — **2.** (reden, auch küssen) F to lick, to slobber over. — **3.** (plappern) to blab, babble. — **4.** ⚓ v. Segeln: (schlaff w.) to flap about. [gland(s pl.).]

Lab=drüse (ᵘᴸᴸ) f ⊕, mst pl. ~**n** pepsine-)

Labe (ᴸ⸴) [ahd.; *laben²] f ⊕ poet. = Labsal; trink ihn aus, den Trank der ~ (SCH.) drink up this cup of comfort.

Labe=becher (ᵘ⸴...) m ⊕, =**kelch** m refreshing cup; =**flasche** ⚓ soldier's flask.

laben¹ ⚓ (ᴸ⸴) [Lab] ⊕ **I** v/a. to mix (or treat) with rennet. — **II** v/n. (in) u. sich ⊕ v/refl. to coagulate, to turn.

laben² (ᴸ⸴)[ahd.: lave; *It.lava're baden] **I** v/a. (sich ⊕ v/refl.) ⊕ to regale (o.s.), to refresh (o.s.), to restore (o.s.); (sich) an Speise und Trank ⊕ to partake of refreshments. — **II** ~ n ⊕ s. Labung. — **III** ⊕**d** p.pr. und a. ⊕ refreshing, restorative; (köstlich) delicious, enjoyable. [(gesalzener Kabeljau) salt cod.]

Laberdan (ᴸᵛᴸ) [nbb.; *fr.] m ⊕d. Fischerei:)

Labe=trank (ᵘ⸴...) m ⊕ cooling drink or beverage; =**trunk** m refreshing draught.

Lab=ferment ⚗ (ᵘ,⸴) n ⊕ physiol. rennet-ferment.

labial ⚗ (⸴ᴸ) [lt. Lippen...] a. ⊕ labial; ~**buchstabe** m ⊕ gr. labial (letter).

Labiale (⸴ᵛᴸᵛ) [lt.] f ⊕ ⊕ gr. = Labia'l-buchstabe.

Labiate(n pl.) ♀ (⸴ᵛᴸᵛ) [lt.] f ⊕ = Lippenblütler.

Lab=kraut ♀ (ᵘ⸴) n ⊕ (Ga'lium); echtes (gelbes) ~ Our Lady's bedstraw (G.verum); gemeines (weißes) ~ white bedstraw (G. Mollu'go); kletterndes ~ Klebekr.; =**magen** m, zo. rennet-bag, ⚓ maw, ⚗ abomasus.

Laborant (⸴ᵛˢ) [lt.] m ⊕ chemist('s assistant), analyst.

Laboratorium (⸴ᵛᵛᴸ(⸴)ᵛ) [lt.] n ⊕ chemical, physical, &c. laboratory.

laborieren (⸴ᵛᴸ) [lt.] v/n. (h.) ⊕ **1.** chm. to do laboratory-work, to work in the laboratory. — **2.** F an et. ⊕ (leiden) to suffer from s.th., to be afflicted (or troubled) with s.th.

Labrador ♀ (⸴ᴸ) [port. Ackerland] npr/n. ⊕α. (nordamerik. Halb-insel) Labrador; ~(**feld**=**spat** ⊕) m ⊕d. min. Labrador-feldspar, labradorite.

Labsal (ˢ-) [Labe] n ⊕d. (Erfrischung) refreshment, restorative; (Herzstärkung) cordial, F pick-me-up; (Trost) comfort.

lab=salben ⚓ (ˢ⸴ᵛ) [nbb.] v/a. ⊕**⚒*** (teeren) to (pay with) tar. [Labsal.]

Labung (ᴸ⸴) f ⊕ refreshment; vgl.)

Lab=wein (ᵘ⸴ᴸ) m ⊕ rennet-wine.

Labyrinth (⸴-⸴) [nhd.; *grch.] n ⊕c. (Irrgang) myth., fig., anat. labyrinth, hort., &c. a.: maze; ~**flüssigkeit** (ᵘ...) f ⊕ physiol.: ⚓ endolymph, perilymph; ⚓**fisch** (⸴ᵛᴸᵛ) a. ⊕ labyrinthian, labyrinthine, mazy; ~**wasser** n ⊕ =**flüssigkeit**. [laughter, laughing-fit.]

Lach¹=anfall (ˢ⸴...)[lachen¹] m ⊕ fit of)

[lachbar] [laden]

lachbar (ᵏᶜʰ-) [Lache³] *a.* 66 *for.:* ~er Baum tree which can be tapped for resin, &c.

Lach²-baum (ᵏᶜʰ⸗ᴸ) [Lache³] *m* 62 *for.:* a) notched (or tapped) tree; b) Grenzbaum) boundary-tree.

Lach¹-bruder F (ᵏᶜʰ...) *m* 62 merry (or jovial) fellow who is always laughing.

Lache¹ (ᵏᶜʰ⸗) [lachen¹] *f* 49 laughter (= Gelächter 1); eine (laute oder helle) ~ aufschlagen to set up a loud laugh, to burst into a roar of laughter.

Lache² (ᵏᶜʰ⸗) [ahd. lake] *f* 48 (Pfütze) puddle, pool, slough, (quag)mire, bog.

Lache³ (ᵏᶜʰ⸗) [ahd. Einschnitt] *f* 48 *for.* notch (or incision) made in a tree, blaze; s.th. which marks (off) the boundary.

lächeln (ᵏᶜʰ⸗) [mhd. *lachen¹] 22a. I *v/n.* (h.) to smile (über et. at a th.); einfältig ~ to simper; geziert ~ to smirk (and smile); gnädig ~ to be all (or wreathed in) smiles; das Glück lächelt ihm (zu) fortune smiles upon him. — II *v/a.* sein Auge lächelt Freude his eye (mehr gbr.: face) beams with (or is radiant with) joy; sie lächelt ihm Hoffnung ins Herz her smile instils hope into his heart. — III ~ *n* 23 (f. 1) smile; simper; ein schmerzliches ~ a sickly smile; ein ~ flog über ihre Züge smile passed over her countenance, her features were lit up with a smile.

lachen¹ (ᵏᶜʰ⸗) [ahd.: laugh] 88 I *v/n.* (h.) 1. to laugh (über et. a th.; (plötzlich) aus vollem ~alſe ~ to burst out laughing; gezwungen ~ F to laugh on the wrong side of the mouth; heimlich ~ to snigger; höhnisch ~ to sneer; laut ~ to laugh out loud, to roar with laughter; schadenfroh ~ to chuckle; du hast gut ~ you may well laugh; da ist nichts zu ~ there is nothing to laugh at, it's no laughing-matter; Sie können wohl ~ you may deem (or think) yourself very lucky; sich (*dat.*) ins Fäustchen ~ to laugh in one's sleeve; ~ Gesicht 2; Sprichw. wer zuletzt lacht, lacht am besten he laughs best who laughs last; wer gewinnt, hat gut ~ let him laugh who wins. — 2. *fig.* das Glück lacht ihm fortune smiles upon him or favours him; ein heiterer Himmel lacht über der Gegend ... smiles (or beams down) on the country; ihm lacht das Herz im Leibe his heart leaps for joy, he is beaming with delight, Sprichw. s. bar 3. — 3. (spotten) sie ~ des armen Toren they laugh (or mock) at (or make fun of) the poor fool; sie können über sein wildes Gerede ~ they can make light (or make sport) of his wild talk; man kann nur darüber ~ it only makes one laugh, it's a ridiculous affair. — II *v/a.* u. *sich* ~ *v/refl.* 4. (lachend sagen) ha, lachte er ha, he said laughingly or with a laugh. — 5. mit Angabe der Wirkung: F sich einen Ast (oder Buckel) ~, sich krank (ob. F scheckig) ~ to split with laughter; wir lachten uns (halb) tot we almost died with laughing; e-n aus dem Schlafe ~ to waken (or rouse) a p. with laughing. — III ~ *n* 23 6. laughing, laughter, vereinzeltes ~ laugh; das ist zum ~ it is ridiculous;

schallendes ~ roars *pl.* of laughter, bisw. cachinnation; unter vielem ~ amid much laughter; sich das ~ verbeißen to suppress one's laughter, to keep from laughing; Sprichw. am vielen ~ erkennt man den Narren the loud laugh bespeaks a vacant head, people who laugh much are very empty-headed, a. empty vessels make the most noise. — IV ~d *p.pr.* u. *a.* 66 7. laughing, ~de Erbenjoyful heirs *pl.*; *fig.* ~de Fluren inviting plains *pl.*; ein ~der Himmel a bright sky.

lachen² (ᵏᶜʰ⸗) [Lache³] *v/a.* 66 *for.* 1. e-n Baum ~ (anlachen) to blaze... — 2. Harzbäume ~ (anzapfen) to tap. — 3. e-n Steg durch den Busch ~ to cut a path through the bush.

Lacher (ᵏᶜʰ⸗) *m* 22, ~in *f* 40 laughing person, laugher; die ~ auf s-r Seite haben to have the laugh on one's side.

lächerlich (ᵏᶜʰ⸗) [lachen¹] I *a.* 66 1. (Lachen erregend) laughable, ridiculous; (drollig) ludicrous, comical, droll, (spaßhaft) funny; sich ~ m. to make o.s. ridiculous, to fall into (or to cover o.s. with) ridicule, to make a fool of o.s.; e-n ~ m. to turn a p. into ridicule; Sprichw. f. erhaben II. — 2. F (zum Lachen, vergnügt) es ist mir nicht ~ zumute I do not feel in a laughing (or pleasant) humour or mood. — II ~ e; *n* 67 3. das ~ e the ridiculous; das ~ste daran ist // the most ridiculous part of it is //; ins ~ e ziehen to ridicule, to make fun of; ~er-weise *adv.* in a ridiculous manner, so as to make o.s. ridiculous.

Lächerlichkeit (ᵏᶜʰ⸗⁻) *f* 46 1. o. *pl.* (Zustand des Lächerlichen) ridiculousness. — 2. mit *pl.* (etwas Lächerliches) s.th. ridiculous, (a mere) farce.

lächern ↘ (ᵏᶜʰ⸗) [lachen¹] 1. *v/a.* 9a.: das lächert mich that makes me laugh. — 2. *v/impers.* es lächert mich I feel inclined to laugh.

Lach¹-fähigkeit (ᵏᶜʰ...) *f* ⓒ risible faculty; ~gas *n*, *chm.* u. Zahnheilkunde: (Luftgas) laughing-gas, ⚛ nitrous oxide (N_2O).

lachig (ᵏᶜʰ⸗) [Lache²] *a.* 66 full of puddles or pools; boggy, marshy.

Lach¹-krampf (ᵏᶜʰ...) *m* 62 *path.* paroxysm (or violent fit) of laughter, convulsive (or hysterical) laugh(ter).

Lächler (ᵏᶜʰ⸗) [lächeln] *m* 22, ~in *f* 40 smiling p., stärker: p. wreathed in smiles.

Lach¹-lust (ᵏᶜʰ...) *f* 62 inclination to laugh; j-s ~ erregen to raise a p.'s mirth, to make a p. laugh; ~lustig *a.* 66 fond of laughing; ~möwe *f*, *orn.* laughing-gull, mire-crow, pewit (*Larus ridibundus*); ~muskel *m*, *anat.*: ⚛ risible muscle.

Lachs (ᵏᶜʰs) [ahd.] *m* ⓐ *a. ichth.* salmon (*Salmo salar*); ~ im 1. Jahre skegger.

Lachs-angel (ᵏᶜʰs...) *f* 62 salmon-tackle; ~artig *a.* 66 *ichth.* s.-like, s. salmonoid; ~brut *f* s.-fry; ~fang *m* s.-fishing, s.-catching; ~farbe *f* s.-colour; ~forelle *f*, *ichth.* s.-(or skegger-) trout (*Salmo trutta*).

Lach¹-taube (ᵏᶜʰ⸗ᴸ) *f* 47 *orn.* laughing-dove (*Turtur risorius*, *Columba risoria*).

Lachter (ᵏᶜʰ⸗) [mhd.] *f* 48, *n* 22 ~ Klafter 1 (209,24 cm).

Lack (ᴸ) [mhd., it., *pers.] *m* ⓑ. (*pl.* ~e ⓧ = ~arten) 1. (durch den Stich einer Schildlaus, „Coccus lacca", aus Bäumen Indiens ausschwitzendes Harz) (gum-)lac. — 2. ⓒ (künstlich dargestellter Firnis) (Japan) lacquer, varnish; mit ~ überziehen to lacquer, to japan. — 3. *abbr.* = Siegellack. — 4. *abbr.* ⚛ = Goldlack *b.*

lacken (ᴸ⸗) *v/a.* 88 = lackieren.

Lack-arbeit ⓒ (ᴸ...) *f* 62 lac(quer)-work, japanned work, Japan ware; ~arbeiter *m* lacquerer, japanner; ~artig *a.* 66 like lac(quer), ⚛ laccinic.

Lack-farbe ⓒ (ᴸ...) *f* 62 lake, drop-lake, ostindische: lac-dye; ~firnis *m* lacquer; ~harz *n* (Gummilac) Gum-lac.

Lackier-arbeiten ⓒ (⸗ᴸ⸗) *f/pl.* 62 lacquered (or japanned) goods *pl.*

lackieren (⸗ᴸ⸗) [fr. *laquer*] *v/a.* 93 1. ⓒ to lacquer, to japan; (firnissen) to varnish, Lederzeug ꝛc.: to polish, to shine up. — 2. P e-n (gründlich) ~ (anführen) F to take a p. (thoroughly) in.

Lackierer (⸗ᴸ⸗) *m* 22 lacquerer.

Lack-leder (ᴸ...) *n* ⓒ patent leather.

Lackmus ⚛ (ᴸ⸗) [mhd.; *lt.] *n*, *m*, *inv.* (Saft der ~-flechte) litmus; ~flechte ⚛ (ᴸ⸗...) *f* orchil (*Lecanora tartarea*); ~papier *n*, *chm.* (von Säuren rot, von Basen blau gefärbt) litmus paper; ~pflanze ⚛ *f* turnsol(e) (*Crozophora tinctoria*).

Lack-säure (ᴸ...) *f* 62 *chm.:* ⚛ laccinic acid; ~schild-laus *f*, *zo.* lac-insect (*Coccus lacca*); ~stiefel(chen *n/pl.*) *m/pl.* patent (leather) boots, F patents *pl.*; ~stoff *m*, *chm.*: ⚛ laccin(e); ~waren ⓒ *f/pl.* lacquered goods *pl.*

Ladan (ᴸ⸗) [grch., *ar.] *n* ⓐd., ~gummi (ᴸ⸗...) *n* 60, ~um (ᴸ⸗) *n* 63 *chm.* (Harz der Zistrose) ladanum.

Lade (ᴸ⸗) [mhd.: *laden²] *f* 48 1. (Kasten) trunk, chest, box, für Wäsche ꝛc.: (linen-) press; (Schub-)~ drawer; f. Bundeslade. — 2. (Gewerks-)~ zum Aufbewahren von Urkunden ꝛc.: treasury (or iron chest, safe) of a corporation or company. — 3. ⓒ Weberei: batten; Buchbind.: (Heft-)~ sewing-frame. — 4. ♪ (Wind-)~ der Orgel soundboard. — 5. ~n *pl.* (die zahnlosen Teile der Kinnladen der Pferde) bars.

Lade-baum ⛵ (ᴸ...) *m* 62 derrick, boom; ~brief *m* letter of invitation or citation, gerichtlicher: summons; ~damm ⛵ *m* landing-stage, jetty, quay; ~deckel ⓒ *m* Weberei: pull-to; ~fähig(keit *f*) *a.* = lastig, Lastigkeit; ~frist ⛵ *f* time allowed for lading; ~gebühr *f*, ~geld ⛵ *f* charges *pl.* for lading; ~geschwindigkeit ⚡ *f* speed of loading; ~kette *f*, *phys.* der Elektrisiermaschine: electric chain; ~leere, ~lehre ⚙ *f* gauge of goodsvans; ~maß ⚙ *n* loading-gauge.

Laden¹ (ᴸ⸗) [mhd.: *Latte Brett] *m* 23 u. 20 1. ⓑ shop, offener: stall, größerer: store(s *pl.*), warehouse, emporium; e-n ~ auftun, eröffnen to open (or start) a shop; e-n ~ h. to keep a shop; den ~ öffnen (schließen) to take down (to put up) the shutters. — 2. = Fensterladen.

laden² (ᴸ⸗) [ahd.: *lade, load*] I *v/a.* 85/f. 1. (aufladen) to load, to lade, auf Fracht: to freight, to ship; eine Last auf sich ~ to take a burden upon o.s.

[laden] — 635 — [lagern]

to burden o.s. (with a th.); Waren aus e-m Wagen ⮂ to unload a cart; das Schiff hat zu viel geladen ... is overloaded; F fig. von e-m Trunkenen: er hat schwer (oder schief) geladen he has had quite enough or his full complement, F he is top-heavy; e-m etwas auf den Hals ⮂ to saddle a p. with a th., to pass a th. on to a(nother) p.; jemandes Feindschaft auf sich ⮂ to incur a p.'s enmity; eine große Schuld auf sich ⮂ to commit a grievous offence; eine große Verantwortlichkeit auf sich ⮂ to undertake a great responsibility. — 2. ⚔ to load, to charge; blind (scharf) ⮂ to load with blank cartridge (with ball, with shot); F fig. scharf auf e-n geladen (erzürnt) sein to be highly incensed with a p. — II ~ n ㉓ 3. loading, &c. (f. I); vgl. Ladung.

laden³ (᷾) [ahd.] I v/a. ehm. nur: ⓺, jetzt mst.: Obst. (einladen) e-n zu Tische ⮂ to ask (or invite) a p. to dinner; jur.: vor Gericht ⮂ to cite before a court, to summons, to serve a summons upon; fig. der See ladet zum Bade the lake invites us to (have a) bathe. — II ~ n ㉓ invitation.

Laden¹**-besitzer**(in f) m ⓫ (᷾...) ㉒ shopkeeper; **-buch** n shop-book; **-bursche** m shop-boy; **-dieb(stahl)** m F shop-lifter (-lifting); **-diener** m: a) = **-gehilfe**; b) = **-bursche**; **-einrichtung** f shop-fittings pl. or -furniture; **-fenster** n shop-window or -front, zur Ausstellung von Waren a. show-window; **-flügel** m leaf of a (window-)shutter; **-gehilfe** m shop-assistant, shopman, salesman; vgl. **-schwengel**; **-hüter** m unsaleable article, dead stock; **-jungfer** f = **-mädchen**; **-kasse** f till; **-mädchen** n, F **-mamsell** f shop-girl; **-miete** f rent of a shop; **-preis** m retail price, von Büchern auch: publishing-price; **-schluß** m shutting up shop; **-schwengel**, **-schwung** (F contp. für **-gehilfe**) counter-jumper; **-tisch** m counter.

Lade-platz (᷾᷾) m ⓫: a) ⚓ wharf; b) 🚂 goods-platform.

Lader (᷾) m ⓫ 1. person who loads or lades or charges, bsd. loader, charger. — 2. ⚔ artill. loader.

Lade-raum (᷾᷾) m ⓫: a) space for loading; ⚓ ship's hold; b) ⚔ artill. chamber. [loading or lading.]

Lader-lohn (᷾᷾) m(n) ㉒ charges pl. for ⟩

Lade-schaufel ⚔ (᷾...) f ㉒ artill. gunladle, gunner's ladle; **-schein** ⚓ m bill of lading; **-stock** ⚔ m ramrod, gunrod, artill. loading-plug; **-stockbohrer** ⊕ m pipe-borer; **-vorrichtung** ⚔ f, artill. for Hohlgeschosse: loading-machine; **-zeug** ⚔ n, artill. appliances pl. for loading, side-arms pl.

lädieren (-᷾᷾) [lt. lae'dere] v/a. u. sich ⮂ v/refl. ㉓: (sich) ⮂ to hurt(o.s.) to injure (o.s.); vgl. beschädigen. [dislaw.]

Ladislaus (᷾᷾) npr/m. inv. ⊕γ. La- ⟩

Ladnerin (᷾᷾) f ⓳ shop-girl; woman who keeps a shop.

Lad-stock (᷾᷾) m ㉒ = Ladestock.

Ladung¹ (᷾᷾) f ㊾ 1. = laden² 3. — 2. (zu befördernde Güter) load, freight, consignment, ⚓ a. cargo, shipment, venture; (Wagenvoll) wagonful, vanful (auch 🚂); ~ einnehmen to load, ⚓ to take in cargo, to ship; die ~ brechen (anfangen auszuladen) to break bulk; er hat seine volle ~: a) he has his full freight or cargo; b) F fig. (Wein ob. Prügel) he has had as much as he can carry. — 3. mst ⚔ charge (a. elect.), powder and shot; (Salve) volley; ⚓ eine volle ~ a broadside. — 4. ⊕ ~ e-s Hochofens: furnace-charge.

Ladung² (᷾᷾) f ㊾ jur. summons, citation.

Ladungs¹**-brief** (᷾᷾...) m, ⚓ ⚓ = -schein; **-fähig(keit** f) a. capable (capability) of carrying (a load, a cargo); **-hafen**, **-platz** m port, place of lading; **-schein** m bill of lading, policy of shipment; **-verzeichnis** n ship's manifest; **-wert** m value of the consignment or cargo.

Lafette ⚔ (᷾᷾) [ahd.; * fr. l'affût m] f ㉘ artill. gun-carriage; e-e Kanone (wieder) auf die ~ bringen oder setzen to (re)mount a cannon, von der ~ abheben to dismount.

Lafetten-block ⚔ (᷾᷾...) m ㉒, **-klotz** m carriage-block; **-kasten** m trail-box; **-rahmen** m chassis, gun- slide; **-schwanz** m trail (of a carriage), **-wand** f cheek of a gun-carriage, bracket.

lafettieren ⚔ (᷾᷾) v/a. ㉓ (auf die Lafette bringen) to mount a cannon.

Laffe (᷾᷾) [vgl. ndd. läppisch] m ㊸ fop, dandy, puppy, bsd. ehm.: coxcomb, jetzt: F masher; **laffen-mäßig** a ⓺ foppish, dandified.

lag (᷾) 1. u. 3. Person impf. ind. von liegen.

Lage (᷾᷾) [mhd.: lay; * liegen] f ㊸ 1. situation, position; (Körperhaltung) attitude, a. posture, beim Fechten: guard; ~ eines Hauses c. site, in Hinsicht auf den Anblick: aspect; (Zustand) condition, state; ~ der Dinge state of affairs; das ändert die (ganze) ~ that puts (quite) a new face on things; (Los) lot, fate; in die gehörige ~ bringen to put into the required position; in die rechte ~ bringen to put in(to) proper) order; in der ~ sein, zu // to be in a position to //; wir sind nicht in der ~, zu // we are not able (or prepared) to //; bedrängte ~ distress(ed condition); in eine böse (ob. schlimme) ~ geraten to get into a scrape or a (sad) pickle; in mißlicher ~ sein to be in a (great) predicament. — 2. ♪ die hohen ~n (Töne) the higher notes. — 3. (zsgehörende Dinge) set; geol., min. bed, layer, ⚡ stratum (pl. strata); ⊕ typ. ~ Papier gathering. — 4. ~ (Überzug) von Farben c. coat(ing). — 5. ⚔ artill. e-e ~ Schnellfeuer a volley of (a group of) quick-firing guns; ⚓ ~ tier of cannon; eine volle ~ geben to fire a broad-side.

läge (᷾᷾) 1. u. 3. Person impf. subj. von liegen.

Lägel ⊕ (᷾᷾) [ahd.] n, m (†f ⓲) (kleines Faß) small barrel or cask or keg.

Lagen-bank ⊕ (᷾᷾...) f ㉒ typ. gathering-board; **-weise** adv. in layers or strata or beds, ⚔ artill. (.+.) ㉒ weise Feuer firing in groups.

Lage-plan (᷾᷾) m ⓫ plan of a site.

Lager (᷾) [ahd.: lair; * liegen] n ㉒ 1. (Ruhestätte) couch; (Bett) bed; (Nachtherberge) night's lodging; armseliges, elendes ~ miserable resting-place; ein rauhes ~ a shake-down; ein schlafloses (ob. unruhiges) ~ h. to have (or spend) a sleepless (or restless) night; nach langem ~ (Krankjein) after a long illness; vom ~ (Krankenbett) auffommen, aufstehen to rise from a sickbed or a bed of sickness. — 2. ~ v. Tieren: a) e-s Hundes: kennel; b) hunt. e-s Wildes: lair, vgl. Bau¹ 4. — 3. ⚔ ~ (military) camp or encampment; fliegendes ~ flying camp; ein ~ abstecken to mark out a camp; ein ~ (auf)schlagen (abbrechen) to pitch (to break up) a camp; f. beziehen ⮂. — 4. ~ eines wilden Stammes oder nomadischer Hirten camp, halting- (or resting-) place. — 5. ⊕ ~ im Keller (auf dem die Fässer festliegen) wooden frame or support, auch: stilling; Wein auf ~ bringen to store wine; ein großes ~ von Weinen h. to have a good cellar (or stock) of wine. — 6. ⚓ (Waren-)storehouse, warehouse; (Vorrat von Waren) store, stock, supply; das ~ aufnehmen to take (an inventory of the) stock; aufs ~ bringen to warehouse, to store; auf dem ~ h. to have in stock or on hand; ein gut assortiertes ~ h. to be well stocked, to keep a good stock in hand; wir haben diese Bänder nicht mehr auf ~ we are out of these ribbons. — 7. (Bodensatz) sediment, dregs pl. — 8. ⚛ ~ der Pilze: ⚡ stroma; geol. ~ von Gesteinen c. bed, layer, deposit, stratum (pl. strata). — 9. ⊕ mech. ~ e-r Rolle, Flasche block; mach. (Zapfen-)bearing, carriage, Drechslerei: ~ der Spindel collar. — 10. ⚒ u. geol. bed, deposit, layer.

Lager-apfel (᷾᷾...) m ㉒ winter-apple; **-aufnahme** ⚓ f taking stock, (making the) inventory; **-aufseher** m store- (or stock-) keeper, storeman, warehouseman; clerk in charge of the stores; **-baum** ⊕ m für Fässer gauntree, ga(u)ntry, vgl. Lager 5; **-bestand** ⚓ m stock, inventory; **-bier** n † lager (beer), weits. Bavarian beer or ale; **-buch** ⚓ n stock- (or warehouse-)book; **-diener** m warehouse-clerk; **-faß** n store-cask, stock-barrel; **-fieber** ⚔ n camp-fever; **-frucht** f, agr. corn laid by rain or wind; **-gebühr** f, **-geld** ⚓ n warehouse-charges pl., storage; **-genoß** m: a) bed-fellow; b) ⚔ companion in (the) camp; **-gerät** ⚔ n camp-furniture, equipment of a camp; **-geschäft** n repository (for goods); **-halter** m store-clerk, storekeeper; **-haus** n (Speicher) storehouse, für unverzollte Güter: bonded warehouse, bonding-house; **-hof** m dock(-warehouse); **-hütte** f camphut; vgl. Baracke. [aufseher.]

Lagerist ⚓ (᷾᷾) [btsch.-it.] m ㉒ = Lager-⟩ **Lager-keller** ⚓ (᷾᷾...) m ㉒ store-cellar; **-kunst** ⚔ f art of marking out a camp, Alt. ⚡ castrametation; **-leben** n camp-life; **-miete** f = **-gebühr**.

lagern (᷾᷾) ㉒a. I v/n. (h. u. fn) u. sich ⮂ v/refl. 1. to (lie down to) rest, lang hin-

⚡ scientific; ⚘ botanical; ⊕ geography; ⊕ machinery; ⚒ mining; ⚔ military; ⚓ marine; ⚓ commercial; ✉ postal; 🚂 railway.

[Lagerobst] — 636 — [Lampe]

geſtreckt: to stretch one's limbs; ſich auf das Gras ⸺ to lie (at) full length on the grass; ⸺ ſich ⸺ to encamp, to go into camp, to pitch tents; *fig.* eine dumpfe Schwüle lagerte (ſich) über der Stadt an oppressive heat brooded (or settled) over the town. — 2. *hunt.* to harbour, to couch. — 3. ⊕ *v. Waren*: to be warehoused or stored, *v.* Zigarren, Wein ꝛc.: to season; in den Docks ⸺ to lie (or remain) in dock, unverzollt: to remain in bond; ⸺ laſſen to warehouse, to store. — 4. *geol.* to be deposited in layers or strata. — II *v/a.* 5. to lay down on the ground, to spread out; ⊕ to store (or warehouse) goods; ⸺ to encamp troops. — III ~ n ⑳ 6. = Lagerung.

Lager-obſt (⁻ᵘ...) *n* ⑫ fruit for storing; =**ort**, =**platz** *m*: a) resting-place; b) ⸺ site of a camp, place of encampment; c) *geol.* ſ. Lager 8; =**raum** *m* storage-room, place for storing goods; ⸺, &c. stowage(-room); =**ſchein** *m* (dock-)warrant; =**ſeuche** ⸺ *f* epidemic prevailing in (a) camp; =**ſtatt**, =**ſtätte** *f* resting-place, couch; ⸺ = =**ort** *b*; *geol.* (Erzlagerſtätte) ore-deposit, seam, shoot.

Lagerung (ᵘ⁻ᵛ) *f* ⑯ 1. lying down, &c. (ſ. lagern I u. II). — 2. *geol.*: ⚘ stratification; ⊕ warehousing, storing, storage; ⸺ encampment.

Lager-wache ⸺ (ᵘ⁻ᵛ...) *f* ⑫ camp-watch or -guard; =**wein** ⊕ *m* well-seasoned wine; full-bodied wine (that keeps its quality); =**zins** *m* = =**gebühr**.

Lagune (ᵛ⁻ᵛ) [it.] *f* ⑯ (ſumpfiger Küſtenſtrich) lagoon; ~**n-inſel** *f* ⑫ lagoon-island; ~**n-riff** *n* (Korallen-inſel) atoll; ~**n-ſtadt** *f* (Venedig) City of Lagoons, Venice.

lahm (¹) [ahd.: lame] I *a.* ⊕ 1. lame, *path.* durch mangelnde Innervation: paralysed, bſd. *bibl.* (gichtbrüchig) palsied; (hinkend) halting, limping, F hobbling (along); an (ober auf) einem Beine ⸺ lame of (or on) one leg or foot; ⸺ geh(e)n = hinken; e-n krumm und ⸺ ſchlagen ſ. krumm 3. — 2. *fig.* paralysed; (kraftlos) impotent, weak(-kneed), feeble; (ſchlotternb) loose-jointed, (matt) languishing; (armſelig) poor, wretched; Ler (hinkender) Beweis feeble proof; Le Entſchuldigung lame (or poor, paltry) excuse; Ler Stuhl rickety chair. — 3. *fig.* (unordentlich, ſchlotterig) disorderly, dislocated. — II ~**e**([r]m) *f* ⑯ 4. lame (or paralysed) person, weitS. cripple.

Lähme P *vet.* (¹⁻ᵛ) [ſpan.] *f* ⑯ = Lähmung.

lahmen (¹⁻ᵛ) *v/n.* (h., bisw. a. ſn) ⑳ to be(come) lame, (ſich lahm fortbewegen) to halt, to limp; to be crippled; *fig.* (ſ. lahm 2) to languish, von e-m Beweiſe ꝛc.: to be lame or feeble, to fall flat.

lähmen (¹⁻ᵛ) I *v/a.* ⑳ *path. u. fig.* to (make) lame, to paralyse; (verkrüppelt m.) to cripple; gelähmt paralysed, *path.* auch: struck with paralysis, *fig.* von Geſchäften ꝛc. auch: stagnating, lifeless, languishing, flagging, at a standstill, at a low ebb; *path.* auf der linken Seite gelähmt paralysed on the left side. — II ~ *n* ⑳ paralysing, &c. (ſ. I); *vgl.* Lähmung. [hands.]

lahm-händig (ᵘ...) *a.* ⊕ with paralysed

Lahmheit (¹⁻) *f* ⊕ (ſ. lahm) lameness, paralysed (or paralytic) state (a. *fig.*); *vgl.* Lähmung 1.

lahm-legen (¹⁻ᵛ) *v/a.* ⊕** : ein Geſchäft ⸺ (zum Stocken bringen) to cripple (or paralyse, ruin) a business; =**legung** *f* ⊕ crippling, paralysing (ſ. lahm 2).

Lähmung (¹⁻ᵛ) *f* ⊕ 1. *path.* (gelähmter Zuſtand, bſd. durch Schlagfluß) paralysation, paralysis, bſd. *bibl.* palsy; *vgl.* Lahmheit. — 2. (Erſchlaffung) languishing state, flagging.

Lahn ⊙ (¹) [fr. lame *f*] *m* ⑬c. (dünner Draht) fine wire; (Flitter) tinsel.

Laib (¹) [*Hom.* Leib] (ahd.: loaf] *m* ⑬c. loaf of bread (in England beſteht a whole loaf, a. quartern-loaf, aus 2 zweipfündigen Broten); (ein) ~ Käſe (a) whole cheese.

Laibung (¹⁻ᵛ) *f* ⊕ *arch.* = Leibung.

Laich (¹) [mhd.] *m* ⑬c.: ~ der Fiſche, Fröſche ꝛc.: spawn, der Auſtern: spat; ~=**bett** (⁻ᵘ...) *n* ⊕ spawning-bed.

Laiche (¹⁻ᵛ) [*Hom.* Leiche] *f* ⊕ = Laichzeit.

laichen (¹⁻ᵛ) I *v/n.* (h.) ⊕ to spawn, von Auſtern: to spat. — II ~ *n* ⑳ = Laichzeit.

Laicher (¹⁻ᵛ) *m* ⑫ spawning fish.

Laich-kraut ⚘ (ᵘ...) *n* ⑳ pond-weed (*Potamoge'ton*); =**zeit** *f* ⊕ spawning-time.

Lai-e (¹⁻ᵛ) [ahd.: lay; *lt.* la'icus] *m* ⊕ (Nichtprieſter) layman, (Un-eingeweihter) uninitiated (or unlearned) person; *fig.* novice, outsider; er iſt in dieſen Dingen ein (vollſtändiger) ~, oft: he knows nothing about these things.

Lai-en-brevier (ᵘ⁻...) *n* ⊕ *eccl.* lay-breviary; =**bruder** *m* im Kloſter: lay-brother.

lai-enhaft (¹⁻ᵛᵛ) *a.* ⊕ like a layman or an uninitiated person.

Lai-en-prieſter (ᵘ⁻¹⁻ᵛ) *m* ⑫ lay-priest.

Lai-enſchaft (¹⁻ᵛᵛ) *f* ⊕ laity, lay community or congregation.

Lai-en-ſchweſter (ᵘ...) *f* ⊕ im Kloſter: lay-sister; =**ſtand** *m* laity, laymen *pl.*

Lai-entum (¹⁻ᵛ) *n* ⑨d. laymanship.

Lakai (ᵛ⁻¹) [fr. laquais; *ſpan.*] *m* ⊕ lackey, footman, *fig.* (a. ~**en-ſeele** (ᵛ⁻ᵛ⁻¹⁻ᵛ) *f* ⊕ flunkey, cringer.

lakai-enhaft (ᵛ⁻ᵛᵛ) *a.* ⊕ lackey-like, flunkey-like, cringing; *adv.* like a flunkey. [brine, pickle.]

Lake (¹⁻ᵛ) [ndd.: Lache²] *f* ⊕ (Salzwaſſer)]

Laken (¹⁻ᵛ) [ndd.: hd. (Lei)lach] *n* (m) ⊕ (Leinen) linen; (Leintuch) (linen) sheet, für Tote: shroud.

Lakhnau ⚥ (ᵛ⁻ᵛ) *npr/n.* ⑳α. St. in Oſt-J. Lucknow. [Laccadive Islands.]

Lakkadiven ⚥ (ᵛ⁻ᵛᵛ) *npr/ſpl.* ⑫ Oſt-J.

Lakoni-en ⚥ (ᵛ⁻¹⁻ᵛ) *npr/n.* ⑳α. Alt.: Laconia; **Lakoni-er**(in *f* ⑫) *m* ⊕ Laconian; **lakoniſch** (ᵛ⁻¹⁻ᵛ) *a.* ⊕ laconic; *fig.* (bündig, wie die Spartaner) laconic;

Lakonismus (ᵛ⁻¹⁻ᵛ) *m* ⑳ lacon(ic)ism.

Lakritze (ᵛ⁻¹⁻ᵛ) [mhd.; mlt. *liquiri'tia*; *grch. glycyrrhiza* Süßwurz] *f* ⊕ 1. ⚘ (Spanish) liquorice (*Glycyrrhi'za glabra*). — 2. a. ~**n** *m* ⑳ *pharm.*, &c. (stick of) liquorice; =**holz** (ᵛ⁻¹⁻ᵛ) *n* ⑳ liquorice-root; =**ſaft** *m* li.-juice; =**ſtengel** *m* stick of liquorice; =**wicke** ⚘ *f* li.-vetch (*Astra'galus glycyphy'llus*).

Laktoſe (ᵛ⁻¹⁻ᵛ) [neu-lt.] *f* ⊕ *chm.* (Milch-zucker) lactose ($C_{12}H_{22}O_{11}$).

laſſen (¹⁻ᵛ) [mhd. lauтm.] I *v/n.* (h.) und *v/a.* ⊕ 1. (ſtottern, undeutlich ſprechen) to stutter, stammer, mumble; to speak indistinctly or thick, to babble. — 2. (ohne Worte ſingen) to hum a tune; ein Kind in Schlaf ⸺ to lull ... to sleep. — II ~ *n* ⊕ 3. stuttering, &c. (ſ. I); indistinct or thick, stammering, mumbling) speech.

Lama¹ (¹⁻) [peru.] *n* ⊕ 1. *zo.* llama (*Auche'nia l.*). — 2. ⊕ llama(-wool).

Lama² (¹⁻) [tibet.] *m* ⊕ (Buddhaprieſter in Tibet ꝛc.) lama, Buddhist priest.

Lama-ismus (⁻⁻ᵛ) [Lama²] *m* ⑳ *rel.* Lamaism; **Lama-iſt**(⁻⁻) *m* ⊕ lamaist, follower of the Grand Lama; **lama-iſtiſch**, **lama-itiſch** *a.* ⊕ lamaistic.

Lamantin ⚘ (ᵛ⁻¹) [ſpan.] *m* ⊕d.(⊕) *zo.* (Art Seekuh) manatee (*Mana'tus*).

Lama¹-**wolle** ⊕ (¹⁻ᵛ⁻ᵛ) *f* ⊕ = Lama¹ 2.

Lamberts-nuß ⚘ (ᵛ⁻ᵛ⁻ᵛ) [mhd. Lombarde(ei)] *f* ⊕ filbert (*Co'rylus tubulo'sa*).

Lambris ⊙ (lã-brī') [fr.] *m* ⊕ (*pl. a.* Lambri'en) (Täfelung) wainscoting.

Lamelle ⚘ (ᵛ⁻¹) [it.] *f* ⊕ (Blättchen, Plättchen) lamella, lamel.

lamentieren (⁻ᵛ⁻¹) [it.] *v/n.* (h.) ⊕ (jammern) to lament, wail, moan.

Lamento (⁻¹⁻) [it.] *n* ⊕ (a. *inv.*) (loud) lamentation, great lament or wailing.

Lami-e ⚘ (¹)(ᵛ) [grch.] *f* ⊕ *myth.* (weibl. Schreckgeſpenſt) Lamia.

Laminier-ſtuh ⊙ (ᵛ⁻¹⁻...) [it.] *m* ⊕ z. Strecken der Baumwollbänder: drawing-frame.

Lamm (¹) [ahd.: lamb] *n* ⊕b. 1. *zo.* lamb; *eccl.* ~ Gottes the Holy Lamb, (lt.) agnus dei. — 2. ⸺ white-crested wave. — 3. = Lämmerwolle.

lamm-artig (¹...) *a.* ⊕ lamblike; =**braten** *m* ⊕ roast lamb. [little lamb, lambkin.]

Lämmchen (¹⁻ᵛ) *n* ⑳ (*dim. von* Lamm)]

lammen (¹⁻ᵛ) *v/n.* (h.) ⊕ to lamb, ewe, yean, to bring forth lambs.

Lämmerchen (¹⁻ᵛᵛ) *pl. v.* Lämmchen.

Lämmer-geier (¹⁻ᵛ...) *m* ⊕ *orn.* bearded (auch lamb-) vulture, ϯ lammergeyer, (*Gypa'etus barba'tus*); =**hirt** *a. orn.* = gelbe Bachſtelze; =**junge** *m* shepherd, shepherd-boy tending lambs; =**wolke** (feder-artige Wolke, Schäfchen): ⚘ cirrus, cirro-cumulus; =**wolle** *f* lamb's wool.

Lamm(e)s-geduld (ᵛ(ᵛ)...) *f* ⊕ patience of a lamb.

Lamm-fell (ᵛ...) *n* ⊕ lamb-skin; =**fleiſch** *n* lamb; ⸺**fromm**, ⸺**herzig** *a.* ⊕ (as) gentle as a lamb. [Lämmchen.]

Lämmlein (¹⁻) *n* ⑳ (*dim. von* Lamm) =]

Lamm-wolle ⊕ (ᵛ...) *f* ⊕ lamb's wool; =**zeit** *f* lambing- (or ewing-)time, season for lambing.

Lämpchen (¹⁻ᵛ) *n* ⑳ (*dim. von* Lampe¹) small lamp, zum Illuminieren, auch: Chinese lamp or lantern; *fig.* freut euch des Lebens, weil noch das ~ glüht be merry while you are alive.

Lampe¹ (¹⁻ᵛ) [mhd.: lamp; fr.; *grch.*] *f* ⊕ 1. lamp, weitS. light; bunte ~ coloured lamp (*vgl.* Lämpchen); eine ~ anzünden (auslöſchen) to light (to extinguish) a lamp; e-e ~ putzen to trim a lamp; F *fig.* einen auf die ~ gießen to have a drink, P to wet one's whistle. — 2. *thea.* die ~n zu Füßen der Schauſpieler the footlights *pl.*; ein Stück vor die ~n bringen to put ... on the stage, to stage ...

Zeichen (ſ. S. XVII): F familiär; P Volksſprache; Γ Gaunerſprache; ⸺ ſelten; † alt (auch geſtorben); * neu (auch geboren); ⁺⁺ unrichtig;

[**Lampe**] — 637 — [**Landesvater**]

Lampe² (⌐ᴗ) [ndb. = Lampert] npr/m. ☺☻☹ Tierfabel: (Name des Hasen) Puss.
Lampen=anzünder (⌐ᴗ...) m ⓐ lamp-lighter; **=docht** m (n) wick of a lamp; **=fieber** n, thea. stage-fever or -fright; **=fuß** m foot (or stand) of a lamp; **=geruch** m smell of a l. or of lamps; **=glocke** f globe, l.-shade; **=händler** m dealer in lamps; **=licht** n lamp-light; **=mikroskop** n: ⚛ lucernal microscope; **=öl** n lamp-oil; **=putzer** m l.-trimmer; **=ruß** m = **=schwarz**; **=schein**, **=schimmer** n (soft) light of a lamp; **=schirm** m lamp-shade or -screen; **=schleier** m lace covering for a lamp, auch: lamp-veil; **=schwarz** ☉ n, paint. l.-black; **=teller** m l.-mat; **=zylinder** m chimney (or glass) of a lamp.
Lampert (⌐ᴗ) npr/m. ⓐⓑα. = Lampe².
Lamprete (⌣ᴗ⌣) [ahd.; *mlt. lampe'tra Steinlecker] f ⓑ ichth. lamprey (Petromy'zon) (= Bricke); kleine ~ river-lamprey (P. fluvia'tilis).
Lancier (lɑ-ß̃ᴗ) [fr. Lanzenreiter] m ⓐ Tanz: lancers pl. **[**fling, throw.**]**
lancieren (lɑ-ß̃ᴗ) [fr.] v/a. ⓐ (werfen) to
Land (ˢ) [ahd.: land] n ⓑb., poet. u. 4 a. ⓐb. **1.** (ant. Wasser, Meer) land; festes ~ mainland, continent; auf dem festen ~e, oft: on (it.) terra firma; zu Wasser und zu ~ e by water (or sea) and by land; ans ~ bringen, setzen to (put on) land, to bring to shore; ans ~ steigen to land, to disembark, v. Matrosen ꝛc.: to go on shore; vom ~e eingeschlossen land-locked; vom ~e stoßen to put to sea, ⚓ f. antun 4; ~ bemerken, entdecken to descry (or discover) land; das ~ zu Gesicht bekommen to sight the land; fig. hier ist ~!, etwa: here we are at last! — **2.** (o. pl.) (Erdboden, der bem Ackerbau dient) soil, ground; angeschwemmtes, fruchtbares ~ alluvial, fertile soil; brachliegendes ~ fallow (land); flaches, ebenes, plattes ~ level ground, flat (or open) country, plain; das Land bebauen, urbar m. to cultivate (or till) the land or soil. — **3.** (o. pl.) (ant. Stadt) country; auf das ~ geh(e)n to go into the c.; auf dem ~e wohnen to live in the c., zur Erholung: to ruralize, to rusticate; über ~ geh(e)n to travel across country; F Gottes Wort vom ~e country-parson; Unschuld vom ~e innocent country-girl. — **4.** (fest begrenztes Gebiet; pl. uneinzelnd: Länder, zusammenfassend: Lande) country, land; (Gebiet) dominion, territory; in fernen ~en in far off lands; in fremden Ländern in foreign countries or parts, abroad; bibl. das Gelobte ~, das ~ der Verheißung the Promised Land, the Land of Promise; das Heilige ~ (the) Holy Land; aus aller Herren Ländern from every country in the world, a. from all parts (of the globe); außer ~es sein to be out of the country, auch: to be abroad or in foreign parts; im ~e gemacht (gezogen, gezüchtet) home-made (home-grown, -bred); seitdem sind viele Tage ins ~ gegangen (verstrichen) many a day (or year) has passed since; f. Johann; von einem bekannten

Lande: bei uns zuᴸe in my native country or home, with us; hierzuᴸe in this country of ours, in these parts; das ist des ~es nicht der Brauch it is not the custom with us; e-n ~es verweisen to banish (or exile) a p.; woher des ~es? whence?, from what part(s)?, where do you come (or hail) from?; ~ und Leute kennen lernen to see the (ways of the) world. — **5.** (die Bewohner e-s Landes) das ganze ~ trauert the whole country (or nation) is in mourning. — **6.** fig. = Gebiet, Reich; das ~ der Phantasie the realm (or world) of fancy.
Land=adel (ˢ...) m ⓐ provincial nobility or gentry; **=ammann** m (schwz.) land-amman, (high) bailiff; **=anwachs** m, geol.: ⚛ alluvion; **=arbeit(er** m) f = Feld-arbeit(er); **=armee** ⚔ f land-forces pl.; **=arzt** m country-doctor.
Landauer (ˢ-ᴗ) [Landau ⚥ Stadt der Rheinpfalz] m (Art Wagen) ⛦ landau.
Land=auf=enthalt (ˢ...) m ⓐ stay in the country, ruralizing; ⁈**aus** (ˢ...¹¹), ⁈**ein** adv. from country to country; **=bau** (ˢ...) m agriculture, farming, husbandry; **=bauer** m agriculturist, farmer, husband-man, tiller of the soil; **=bau=erzeugnis** n agricultural produce; **=baumeister** m: a) rural architect; b) county-surveyor; **=besitzer** m land-owner, landed proprietor; **=bewohner** m p. living in the country; countryman (pl. country-people or -folk); **=bezirk** m country-district, rural neighbourhood; **=bote** m: a) c.-messenger; b) = **=tagsabgeordneter**; **=brief=träger** m rural postman or letter-carrier; **=brot** (**=bäcker** m) n (baker who sells) household bread; **=buch** n register of land.
Ländchen (ˢᴗ) n ⓐ (dim. von Land) small country; (Kleinstaat) petty state.
Land=dienst ⚓ (ˢ...) m ⓐ service (or duties pl.) on shore; **=drost** m = Drost.
Lände ⚓ (ˢᴗ) f ⓐ landing-place.
Land=edelmann (ˢ...) m ⓐ provincial nobleman; country-squire, -gentleman; **=eigentum** n landed property; **=eigen(tüm)er** m = **=besitzer**; ⁈**einwärts** adv. (further)inland, up(the) country; **=eis** n coast-ice.
landen ⚓ (ˢᴗ) [ndb.] ⓐ **I** v/n. (h. u. fn) to land, to disembark; to touch at a place; ⚔ auch: to effect a landing; der Kapitän hat (die Mannschaft ist) gelandet the captain (or the crew went on) shore. — **II** v/a. ⚔: ⓐ to land (or disembark) troops, &c. — **III** ~ n ⓐ (f. I) landing; putting to shore; beim ~ on landing; vgl. Landung.
Land=ende (ˢ...) n ⓐ e-s Kabels: shore-end; **=enge** ⓖ f isthmus, neck of land.
Länder (ˢᴗ) f ⓐ (Zaunstange) hedge-stake.
..länder ("...ᴗ) [Land] m ⓐ in Zssgn., zB. Hoch-⁈ highlander.
Länder=beschreiber (ˢ...) m ⓐ: ⚛ chorographer; **=beschreibung** f: ⚛ chorography; **=durst** m = **=sucht**.
Länderei (ˢᴗ¹¹) f, mst pl. ~en landed estates pl. or property, domain(s pl.).
Länder=gier (ˢ...) f ⓐ = **=sucht**; **=kenntnis**, **=kunde** f knowledge of countries, geography; ⁈**kundig** a. ⓐ knowing

many countries, F well up in geography; ⁈**los** a. without lands.
landern, **ländern** (⌐ᴗ) [Länder] v/a. ⓐa. to fence in, to enclose.
Länder=name (ˢ...) m ⓐ name of a country; **=raub** m snatching of provinces, land-grabbling; **=räuber** m usurper, land-grabber; ⁈**reich** a. ⓐ possessing (or containing) many lands; **=sucht** f thirst for (the possession of) new territory, auch: earth-hunger; **=teilung** f partition of territories.
Landes=adel (ˢ...) m ⓐ nobility of the country; **=angehörige** m/pl. denizens pl. of a country; **=angehörigkeit** f nationality, citizenship; **=anleihe** f domestic (or internal) loan; **=art** f: a) custom (or fashion) of a c.; das ist so ~ that's the custom of the country; b) (Beschaffenheit des Bodens) quality of the soil; **=aufnahme** f survey of a country, ⚛ topography; **=ausschuß** m (standing) committee of a diet; **=bank** f national bank of a country; **=beamte(r)** m public functionary, government official; **=brauch** m = **=art** a.; **=direktor** m = **=hauptmann**; **=erzeugnis** n home (or inland) produce, pl. home-made (or home-grown) commodities; **=fabrikat** n home manufacture, home-made article; **=farben** f/pl. national colours pl.; ⁈**flüchtig** a. ⓐ = landsflüchtig; **=fürst(in** f) m reigning prince(ss); sovereign, ruler of the country; ⁈**fürstlich** a. appertaining (or relating) to the sovereign; **=gebiet** n territory; **=gericht** n supreme court of the country; **=gesetz** n law of the land; **=hauptmann** m, etwa: Captain-General of a country; **=herr** (-lich a.) m = **=fürst(lich)**; **=herrlichkeit** f sovereign rule or dignity, sovereignty; **=herrschaft** f: a) sway over a country, sovereignty; b) the reigning prince with his family; **=hoheit** f sovereign power; **=kasse** f exchequer of a country, public treasury; **=kenntnis** f knowledge of a country; **=kind** n native of a country; **=kirche** f national (in Engl.: established) church (nicht zu verwechseln mit Landkirche!); **=kultur** f agriculture; **=kunde** f = **=kenntnis**, ⁈**kundig** a.: a) acquainted with the country; b) = land-k.; ⁈**kundlich** a. geographical; **=münze** f (legal) coinage (or currency) of a country, coin of the realm; **=mutter** f sovereign (princess); **=obrigkeit** f supreme authority in a country; public authorities pl.; **=polizei** f police of a country; **=produkt** n = **=erzeugnis**; **=regierung** f government of a country; **=religion** f national (or established) religion; **=sache** f matter concerning a (whole) country; **=schuld** f national debt; **=sitte** f custom of a country, national custom; **=sprache** f language of a country, vernacular (idiom); **=tracht** f national costume; **=trauer** f public (or general) mourning; ⁈**üblich** a. of universal practice in a country, national; der ⁈e Gruß the customary (or usual) greeting; **=vater** m sovereign (prince) of a country, auch:

♪ Musik; ⚛ Wissenschaft; ☘ Pflanze; ⚥ Geographie; ☉ Technik; ⚒ Bergbau; ⚔ Militär; ⚓ Marine; ⚖ Handel; ✉ Post; 🚂 Eisenbahn.

[landesväterlich] — 638 — [Landtag]

Father of the people; =väterlich a. relating to the sovereign; =e Fürsorge paternal solicitude; =verfassung f constitution of a country; =vermessung f survey of a country; =verrat f =verräter, m treason against (traitor to) one's country; =verräterisch a. treasonable; =verteidigung f defence of the country; =verteidigungs-ausschuß m in Engl. seit 1904: Committee of Defence, Defence Committee; =vertretung f representation (coll. representatives pl.) of a country; =verweisung f banishment from a country, exile; (Achtung) proscription; =verweser m regent; =verwiesene(r) m exile; =zeitung f official gazette.

Land=fahrer (².....) m ② fast † = =streicher; ⁰fern ↓ a. ⑥⑥ far from (the) land; =feste f: a) ✕ = =festung; b) ↓ (Tau zur Befestigung eines Schiffes) mooring-cable, hold-fast; =festung ✕ f inland fortress; =flucht f (Zug vom Lande in die Stadt) migration of country-people into the town(s); ⁰flüchtig a. fugitive; ≈ w. to flee from (F to fly) the country, to escape abroad; =fracht ❀ f freight by land; =frau f countrywoman; =fräulein n young lady from the country; ⁰fremd a. quite foreign or unknown; =friede(n) m: a) public peace; b) bsd. ehm.: laws pl. enforcing (or regulating) public peace; =friedensbruch (=störer) m breach (disturber) of the public peace; =fuhre f: a) conveyance by land; b) (auch =fuhrwerk n) country-carriage; farmer's cart; =fuhr-mann m (pl. =fuhr-leute) carrier; =geistliche(r) m country-clergyman; =gemeinde f (country-) parish; eccl. a. rural congregation; =gericht n: a) provincial court; b) (ant. Stadtgericht) etwa: rural (county-)court; ⁰gerichtlich a. appertaining to a provincial (or rural) court, ehm. =graf m † landgrave; =gräfin f † landgravine; =gräflich a. relating to a landgrave; =grafschaft f landgraviate; ⁰gültig a. valid (or legal) throughout the country; =gut n (country-)estate, country-seat; =haus n country-house or -residence, farm-house; =häuschen n small c.-house, cottage; =heer n = armee; =herrschaft f: a) provincial gentry; b) manor; =jäger m obb. = Gendarm; =jägermeister m grand-master of the chase; =junker m = edelmann, b.s. country-bumpkin; =karte f (geographical) map; =karten-druck ⊕ m map-printing; =kennung f f landmark; =kirche f country-church (nicht zu verwechseln mit Landeskirche!); =kreis m (rural) district; =krieg m war on land; ⁰kundig a. known all over the country, notorious; =kutsche f country-coach, stage-coach; ⁰läufig a. customary in the (whole) country; e-e =e Redensart a current (or common) saying or phrase; =leben n country-life; das ~ schildernd pastoral, bucolic (poem, poetry).

Länd(l)er öst. (ᴊ~) m ② Tanz: slow waltz.
Land=leute (ˢ…ᴸ~) pl. ② country-people or -folk, peasantry, F rustics pl.

ländlich (ᴊ~) a. ⑥⑥ 1. (dem Lande ähnlich) countrylike; (außer der Stadt liegend) rural; (einfach, bäuerisch) rustic (a. ⊕ arch.), simple, countrylike, F countrified; =es Leben country-life. — 2. (im Lande üblich) Sprichw. ≈, sittlich (F co. ≈, schändlich) every country has its (own) customs; in Rome (you must) do as the Romans do.

Ländlichkeit (ᴊ~) f ⑥⑥ countrylike (or rural) character of a scenery, &c.; rusticity (or rustic simplicity) of persons, manners, &c.

Land=liga (ˢ…) f ⑥⑥ pol. bsd. in Irland: land-league; =linie tel. f land-line; =luft f country-air; =luft f pleasures pl. of c.-life; =macht f: a) continental power; b) ✕ land-forces pl.; =mädchen n country-girl or -lass, peasant-girl, young girl from the country; =mann m (pl. =leute, f. ds; nicht zu verwechseln mit Landsmann!) countryman, peasant, rustic; vgl. =bauer; ⁰männisch a. ⑥⑥ like a countryman, peasant-(or farmer-)like; =mark f: a) boundary of a country; b) territory; =marke ↓ f (Kennzeichen, Kennung) landmark; =marschall m, etwa: provincial marshal; =messer m surveyor of land; bsd. ehm. =miliz ✕ f provincial militia, zu Pferde: yeomanry; =nähe ↓ f approach (or looming) of land, landfall; =partie f outing (or trip) in(to) the country; =parzelle f plot of land; =pfarre f country-parsonage or -vicarage; =pfarrer m c.-parson or -vicar; ehm. =pfleger m governor (or prefect) of a province; =plage f universal plague, public calamity or nuisance; =polizei f rural police; =pomeranze F f (einfältiges Landmädchen) unsophisticated country-girl, F c.-miss; =post ✎ f: a) rural post; b) stage-coach; =prediger m = =pfarrer; =rat m: a) in Preußen: administrative head of a district (vereinigt etwa die Pflichten des Lord Lieutenant of the county u. des Sheriff); b) in der Schweiz: cantonal council; ⁰rätlich a. referring to a Landrat (vgl. Landrat); =ratte f: a) zo. (ant. Wasserratte) (common) rat (Mus decumanus); b) ↓ F (ant. Seeratte) landsman, F landlubber; =recht n civil code; das allgemeine ~ in England: Common Law; ⁰rechtlich a. of (or concerning, according to) Common Law; =regen m continuous gentle rain spreading over a wide area, steady downpour; =reise f: a) journey by land, overland; b) journey (or trip) into the (or across) country; =reiter m = Gendarm; =rente f = Boden=r.; =richter m provincial judge; =rücken m ridge of hills or mountains; =saß, =sasse m: a) inhabitant of a country; b) = Landsmann; c) peasant-proprietor, freeholder; ⁰sässig a. settled (or resident) in a country.

Landschaft (ᴊ~) f ⑥⑥ 1. province (of a country); (Bezirk) district, canton. — 2. (Landstände) representative chamber (of a country). — 3. rural outskirts pl.; die Stadt hat e-e reiche ~ ... has

rich (or fertile) surroundings. — 4. künstlerisch: landscape, scenery.

Landschafter (ᴊ~) m ② (Maler) landscape-painter; ~ei (ᴊ~…) f ⑥⑥ landscape-painting.

landschaftlich (ᴊ~) a. ⑥⑥ 1. provincial; =e Ausdrücke provincialisms pl. — 2. = landständig. — 3. paint. (f. Landschaft 4): =e Bilder landscape-paintings pl.

Landschafts=fach (ˢ~...) n ② paint. landscape(-painting); =gärtnerei f landscape-gardening; =maler(ei f) m landscape painter (-painting).

Land=scheide (ˢ...) f = =mark a; =schildkröte f, zo. land-tortoise or -turtle (Testu'do); =schlacht ✕ f battle on land; =schnecken f/pl.: ⌇ geophila pl.; =schreiber m clerk (or registrar) to a provincial court, in Engl.: clerk of sessions; =schule f (=schul-lehrer, =schul-meister m) country-(or village-)school(master); =see m inland lake; =seuche f epidemic (ravaging a country); =sitz m country-house or -seat, villa, weitS. = =gut.

Lands=knecht ✕ (ˢ...) [nhd. 15. sae.] m ② (angeworbener Fußsoldat) lansquenet (a. Kartenspiel), weitS. mercenary, hireling; =mann m, =männin f, pl. =leute: a) aus einem beliebigen Lande: was ist er für ein Landsmann? what countryman is he?, where does he come (or hail) from?; b) aus derselben Heimat: (fellow) countryman, f countrywoman; er ist Ihr Landsmann he is a countryman of yours; =mannschaft f: a) common nationality; b) (Bund von Landsleuten) association of fellow countrymen; c) auf Universitäten: association of students (from the same country).

Land=soldat ✕ (ˢ...) m ② soldier serving on land; =spitze f headland, neck of land, promontory, cape; =stadt f: a) country-town; b) inland (or continental) town; =städtchen n small c.-town; =stand m: die =stände the provincial diet, representative chamber of the province; ⁰ständig a. ⑥⑥ concerning the provincial diet; =e Rechte n/pl., Verfassung privileges pl., constitution of the prov. diet; =steuer f: a) (das ganze Land betr.) general (a. government) taxes pl.; b) (Grundsteuer) land-tax; =straße f: a) highway, high-road, carriage-(or turnpike-)road, main road; b) overland route (ant. Seeweg); an der ~ gelegen by the roadside; =strecke f tract of land; vgl. =strich; =streichen n = =streicherei; ⁰streicher(in f) m vagrant, tramp, vagabond, weitS. wayfarer; =streicherei f vagrancy; =streifen m strip of land; =strich m region, country, in geb. Spr.: clime; vgl. =strecke; =sturm m: a) storm (or gale) on land (ant. Seesturm); b) ✕ last reserve; general levy (of the people); auch: (deutsch) landsturm; ⁰sturmpflichtig a. liable to serve in the landsturm; =sturz m land-slip.

Land=tag (ˢ...) m ② diet, in Deutschland: diet of a (single) federal state; den ~ ausschreiben to convene (or

---

Signs (see page XVII): F familiar; P vulgar; Γ flash; ⟍ rare; † obsolete (died); * new word (born); ⁺⁺ incorrect; ♩ music;

[Landtagsabgeordneter] — 639 — [langen]

convoke) a diet; =tags=abgeordnet(e)r m (=abschied m) member (adjournment) of a diet; =tags=verhandlungen f/pl. debates (or transactions) pl. of a diet; =tiere n/pl. zo. animals pl. living on land, ⌇ terrestrial animals pl.; =transport ✺ m conveyance by land; =truppen pl. landforces pl.

Landung ↓ (⌇) f ⊕ disembarkation; vgl. landen III.

Landungs=armee ↓ (⌇...) f ⊕, etwa: army ready to descend on the coast of the enemy; =brücke f landing-stage, jetty; =damm m quay; =platz m, =stelle f landing-place, pier; =truppen ⚔ pl. troops (ready) for landing.

Land=vögel (⌇...) m/pl. ⊕ orn.: ⌇ terrestrial birds pl.; =vogt m = =pfleger; =vogtei f provincial government (-office); =volk n = =leute; ⌇wärts adv. landward(s), towards land; ⌇ steuern to make for land, to run in-shore; =weg m: a) country-road; parochial road; b) overland route (ant. Seeweg); =wehr ⚔ f: a) (men of the) reserve, in Engl. auch: militia (-force), territorial army, berittene: yeomanry, auch: (deutsch) landwehr; b) (Befestigungen) defences pl. of the country; =wehr=mann m man of the reserve, militiaman; =wein m homegrown wine; =welle f undulated country; =wind ↓ m land-breeze; =wirt m = =bauer; =wirtschaft f: a) (o. pl.) = =bau; ~ treiben to carry on farming, to keep a farm; b) (mit pl.) (Besitztum mit Ackerwirtschaft) country-estate, rural property, farm; ⌇wirtschaftlich a. agricultural, concerning husbandry; ⌇e Gerätschaften, Zwecke farming implements, purposes pl.; =wohnung f rural (or rustic) abode; =zins m rent of land; =zunge f tongue (or neck) of land, headland.

lang (⌇) [ahd.: long: lt. longus] I a. ⊕(D2,7) 1. long, von Menschen ꝛc. auch: tall; etwas ⌇ longish; entsetzlich ⌇ endless (speech, &c.); einen Finger (eines Fingers) ⌇ (of) the length of a finger; vier Meter ⌇ four metres in length; einen Fuß ⌇ (vgl. fuß⌇) a. (or one) foot long; die Länge ⌇ at full length; vgl. Länge 1; gleich ⌇ sein to be equally long, to have the same length; zehn Fuß ⌇ und vier Fuß breit ten feet by four; länger m. to make longer, to lengthen, fig. to prolong, to extend (vgl. breit 1 u. 4). — 2. f. Bank¹ 2; Kocht. ⌇e (verdünnte) Brühe: a) weak broth. F slops pl.; b) fig. f. Brühe 4; ⌇e Finger m. to be long-fingered or light-fingered or F long in the fingers; vgl. Finger 1; ein ⌇es Gesicht m. to make (or pull) a long face; einen ⌇en Hals m. to crane forward; mit ⌇en Händen long-handed, zo.: ⌇ longimanous; mit ⌇er Nase ab=ziehen to go away disappointed or disconcerted; der ⌇en Rede kurzer Sinn ist der ... to cut a long story short ...; Sport: Pferd ꝛc., das lange Strecken läuft long-distance runner; Sprichw. wer ⌇ hat, läßt ⌇ hängen rich people like to show off their finery;

vgl. hangen 4. — 3. zeitlich: vor ⌇en Jahren many years ago or since; eine ⌇e (langwierige) Krankheit a protracted illness; ⌇er Tag jüdisch = Versöhnungsfest; den lieben, ⌇en Tag the livelong day, all day long; eine ⌇e, ewige Zeit an everlasting (or a long, long) time; er kommt auf längere Zeit he comes for a prolonged stay, he intends to stay for some time; so seid Ihr die längste Zeit (lange genug) Abt hier gewesen (BÜRGER) you will not be abbot here much longer; in nicht zu ⌇er Zeit ere (or before) long; ihm wird die Zeit ⌇ time hangs heavy with him. he has much time on his hands; über kurz oder ⌇ sooner or later; ⍟ Wechsel auf ⌇e Sicht, auch: ⌇er Wechsel long(-dated) bill, pl. a. longs. — II ~e(s) n ⊕ (oft klein gschr.) 4. f. breit II; des ⌇en und breiten erzählen to tell with full particulars, to spin a long yarn, F co. to talk a donkey's hind-leg off. — III adv. 5. örtlich: viele Meilen ⌇ (weit) extending (or for) many miles; P den Fluß ⌇ (entlang) along the river. — 6. zeitlich (mehr gebr.: ⌇e): drei Jahre ⌇ for three years; nicht ⌇e darauf a short time after(wards); viele Tage ⌇ for many days together; ⌇e bevor er kam long before he came; das hat nicht ⌇e gedauert it did not last long; das ist schon ⌇e her that was a long time ago; ⌇e hin a long time yet; noch ⌇e nicht not for some time yet; anything but, far from; er ist noch ⌇e nicht fertig he has not nearly finished; (noch) auf lange hinaus for a long time (yet) to come; da können Sie (noch) ⌇e warten, bis das sich wieder bietet you will never have such an opportunity (or such a chance) again; so ⌇e (als) // as long as //; ich kenne ihn schon viele Jahre ⌇ I have known him these many years; seit ⌇em for a long time (past), vgl. 11; wie ⌇e lernen Sie Französisch? how long have you been learning French?; wie ⌇e soll ich denn warten? how long am I to wait, indeed?; bis wie ⌇e sind Sie zu Hause? how long (or until what time) will you be at home? — 7. Beispiele zum comp. u. sup.: ein(en) Tag länger one day more or longer; 1000 Jahre und länger a thousand years and more; je länger, je lieber the longer the better; ich habe es schon länger (seit einiger Zeit) bemerkt I have noticed it for some time (past); ich kann es nicht länger (mehr) ver=schweigen I cannot keep it to myself any longer; wenn er es noch länger so macht if he goes on like this much longer; dieser Mißbrauch hat am längsten gedauert ... will not last much longer. — 8. Nachdruck gebend, oft nicht zu übersetzen, z.B. den muß man nicht erst ⌇e fragen you need not (trouble to) ask him first. — 9. ⌇e, bisw. a. längst mit folgendem neg. = bei weitem, z.B. er ist ⌇e nicht so geschickt he is not nearly so clever. — 10. (hinlänglich, ganz) F das ist für uns ⌇e genug that

is quite sufficient for us. — 11. längst = seit langem, z.B. ich weiß es ⌇ I have known it for a long time or while; ⌇ vergangene Tage bygone days pl., times long past (and gone); das ist ⌇ vorbei that ended (or ceased) a long time ago. — 12. längstens (spätestens) at the latest, (höchstens) at the most.

...lang (...⌇) in Zssgn.: fuß⌇ a foot long; jahre⌇ for years; lebe⌇ for a lifetime.

lang=ährig ↯ (⌇...) a. ⊕ long-eared; =arm=affe m ⊕ zo. long-armed ape, gibbon (Hylo′bates); ⌇armig a. long-armed; ⌇atmig a. long-breathed, mst fig. (lange dauernd) long-winded (speech, &c.), auch: prolix; =atmigkeit f, fig. bjd. der Rede: long-windedness, prolixity; =baum ⊕ m =es Wagens: perch, pole; =bein n l.-legged person, F co. longshanks; ⌇beinig a. l.-legged or -shanked; =bein=Mücke, Schnake daddy-long-legs (Ti′pula); =blätt(e)rig ↯ a. l.-leaved, ⌇ macrophyllous; =duode′z ⊕ n, typ. long twelves pl.

lange (⌇) adv. f. lang, bsd. 6, 8, 9, 10.

Länge (⌇) [length;*lang] f ⊛ 1. length; (Größe) size, v. Personen a.: stature; der Garten hat 20 Meter in der (ob. die) ~ ...is twenty metres long or in length; in die ~ ... nach spalten ꝛc. ... length-ways or lengthwise or longitudinally; et. nach der ~ und Breite ausmessen to measure the length and breadth of a th.; der ~ nach (ob. lang) hinfallen to fall (one's) full length, F to go (down) sprawling; ⚔ der ~ nach be=schießen, bestreichen to enfilade, to rake; ⊕ typ. den Zeilen die richtige ~ geben to adjust the lines; Sport, als Maß: das Pferd siegte mit zwei ~n the horse won by two lengths. — 2. die ~ (Dauer) e=s Aufenthaltes the duration of one's stay or visit; auf die ~ for some (length of) time, in the out, in the long run; in die ~ ziehen to protract, draw out, prolong; e=e Erzählung ꝛc.: to spin out. — 3. pros., gr.: ⌇ e=r Silbe quantity (or length) of a syllable; ~ (lange Silbe) long (syllable). — 4. ⚲, ast.: geographische ~ longitude; unter 10° östlicher ~ at ten degrees East(ern) Longitude (a. abbr. E. L.); astronomische ~ celestial longitude.

Länge=holz (⌇...) ⊕ n ⊛ Bäckerei: rolling-pin; ⌇lang adv. (at) full length.

langen (⌇) [lang]⊛ I v/n.(h.) 1. (ausreichen) to suffice, to be sufficient or enough; das wird nicht weit ⌇ it won't go far; ich kann damit nicht ⌇ (auskommen) I cannot live (or keep myself) on that or F make it do. — 2. nach etwas ⌇ (die Hand ausstrecken) to reach (or to stretch out one's hand) for a th.; in die (a. aus der) Schüssel ⌇ to take from (or out of) the dish; in die Tasche ⌇ to put one's hand in(to) one's pocket (fig. = bezahlen). — II v/a. 3. (nach et. reichen) to seize (or grasp) with outstretched hand; aus der Schublade ⌇ to fetch (or take) out of ...; sie können ihn nicht ⌇ they cannot get hold of him. — 4. (fassen und darreichen) to pass on, to hand.

⌇ scientific; ↯ botanical; ⚲ geography; ⊕ machinery; ⚒ mining; ⚔ military; ↓ marine; ⍟ commercial; ✉ postal; 🚂 railway.

[längen] [Lappen]

längen (⸺) [lang] v/a. und sich ⸺ v/refl. (länger m., w.) **1.** (sich) ⸺ to lengthen, extend, stretch, von Zeug ꝛc. auch: F to give; ⊕ den Teig ⸺ (walzen) to roll. — **2.** ↓ Tau ⸺ (loslassen) to slacken a rope, to pay out more cable.
Längen=achse (⸺...) f ⊕ longitudinal axis; **=ausdehnung** f, phys. linear dimension or expansion; **=bruch, =durchschnitt** m long. fracture, section; **=grad** m ♀ degree of longitude; **=kreis** m ♀, ast. circle of longitude, meridian; **=maß** n long (or linear) measure; **=messung** f measurement of lengths, linear measurement, ⟋ longimetry; **=schnitt** m longitudinal section or incision; **=schwingung** f longitudinal oscillation; **=tal** n long. valley.
lang=entbehrt (⸺) a. ⊕ long missed.
Längen=uhr (⸺...) f ⊕ longitude-watch, time-keeper, chronometer. [for.]
lang=erwünscht (⸺...) a. ⊕ long wished
Lange=schläfer (⸺...) m = Langschläfer.
langettieren ⊕ (⸺) [fr. *languéter* zingeln] v/a. ⊕ Stickerei: (ausbogen) to trim with points.
Lang(e)weile (⸺) f ⊕ weariness of mind, tediousness, boredom, bisw.: (fr.) ennui; aus Lang[e(r)]weile from (mere) dulness, by way of (a) pastime; ~ empfinden, haben to feel bored or dull, to feel the time hang heavy or hang on hand; e-m die ~ vertreiben to amuse (or entertain) a p.; sich (dat.) die ~ vertreiben to pass away the (or to kill) time; fig. s-e Drohungen sind nicht für die ~ (mäßig) his threats are not meant as a joke. [long-stapled.]
lang=faserig ⊕ (⸺) a. ⊕ (bsp. Baumwolle)
Lang=finger F (⸺...) m (Dieb) thief, pilferer, pl. a. long-fingered gentry; **=fing(e)rig** a. ⊕: a) l.-fingered; b) fig. fond of pilfering; **=flüg(e)lig** a. long-winged, ⟋ longipennate, macropteran, ...ous; **=füßig** a. long-footed, ⟋ macropodous, **=geschwänzt** a. zo. l.-tailed, ⟋ longicaudate, macrurous; **=gespitzt** a. gradually running to a point, ♀: ⟋ acuminous, ...ose; **=gestielt** a. with a long stalk, l.-stalked; **=gestreckt** a. lying (or spread out) at full length; **=gewachsen**(er Mensch) a. (person) of tall stature; **=haarig** a. long-haired, ⊕ Baumwolle: longstaple(d); **=hals** m l.-necked person; **=halsig** a. l.-necked; **=händig** a. l.-handed, ⟋ longimanous; **=her** adv. long ago; **=hin** adv. far (and away), for a long distance; **=jährig** a. of many years(' standing or duration); der Freund friend (whom one has known) for many years; ⸺e Freundschaft friendship of long (or old) standing; **=lebig** a. l.-lived, ⟋ macrobiotic; **=lebigkeit** f longevity, ⟋ macrobiosis.
länglich (⸺) a. ⊕ elongated, longish; (mehr lang als breit) oblong (a. ♀ u. math.); **=herzförmig** ♀ a.: ⟋ cordate-oblong; **=rund** a. oval, ♀ oblong-ovate.
Lang=mut (⸺...)[Mut m] f long-suffering nature, forbearance, geh. Spr.: longanimity; ~ üben gegen // to show indulgence to or towards //; **=mütig** a. ⊕ long-suffering, forbearing; adv. with

forbearance; **=mütigkeit** f = =mut; **=nasig** a. long-nosed.
Langobarde (⸺) [bz. Langbart] m ⊕, **Langobardin** (⸺), **langobardisch** (⸺) a. ⊕ hist. Longobard, Lombard.
Lang=ohr (⸺...) m ⊕ (n ⊕)d. [f nhd.]: a) long-eared person or animal; b) (Esel) (jack)ass, F long-ears; f. Esel 2; **=ohrig** a. ⊕ long-eared; **=rund** a. oval.
längs (⸺) [Länge] adv. u. prp. (mit dat., auch mit gen.) = entlang, z.B. ⸺ dem Flusse along (or following the course of) the river; ↓ ⸺ der Küste hinfahren to skirt (or hug) the coast.
langsam (⸺) [ahd.] a. ⊕ **1.** slow, (säumig) tardy, F dawdling, easygoing, (schwerfällig) heavy; der Tod lingering death; ⊕ der Verkauf slack sale; Sprichw. ⸺ kommt auch ans Ziel slow and steady wins the race. — **2.** mit verbs: ⸺ auffassen to be slow (or dull) of comprehension; ⸺ geh(e)n to walk slowly or gently; der geh(e)n to slacken (or moderate) one's pace; die Uhr geht zu ⸺ the watch loses; er ist zu ⸺ he is a slow-coach, he dawdles too much; der m. to retard, to slacken, ↓ to ease the ship; ⸺ sprechen to speak slowly, to be slow of speech; et. ⸺ tun, verrichten to be slow (or F too long) about a th.; ⊕ von Waren: ⸺ abgeh(e)n to go off slowly, to hang on hand. [slackening, retardation.]
Langsamer=werden (⸺...) n ⊕
Langsamkeit (⸺) f ⊕ (f. langsam) slowness, tardiness, slackness; dulness.
Längs=bestreichung ⸺ (⸺...) f ⊕ enfilade.
lang=schattig(e Völker) (⸺...) a. ⊕; ⟋ macroscian(s pl.); **=schiff** n ⊕ arch. einer Kirche nave; **=schläfer**(in f) m person fond of sleep, lie-a-bed, long (or heavy) sleeper; **=schläferei** f excessive sleep (-ing), late rising; **=schnäb(e)lig** a. orn.: ⟋ longirostral; **=schnäbler** m/pl. orn.: ⟋ longirostra pl.; **=schößig** a. long-skirted; **=schwänzig** a. long-tailed; **=schwelle** f ⊕, ⚒, &c. longitudinal (sleeper). [incision.]
Längs=einschnitt (⸺...) m ⊕ longitudinal
lang=sichtig (⸺) a. ⊕: a) (nur in die Ferne gut sehend) long-sighted, ⟋ presbytic (besser: weitsichtig); b) ⊕ v. Wechseln ꝛc.: (von langer Sicht) long-sighted.
Längs=richtung (⸺...) f ⊕ longitudinal direction or sense; **=schnitt** m long. section; **=schwelle** ⚒ f string-piece, stringer; **=streifen** m long. stripe.
längst (⸺) (sup. von lang) f. lang 7, 9, 11 (= seit langer Zeit).
Längs=tal (⸺) n ⊕ longitudinal valley.
längst=begraben (⸺...) a. ⊕ dead and gone; **=bekannt** a. known long ago.
längstens (⸺) adv. f. lang 12 (= spätestens).
lang=stielig (⸺) a. ⊕: a) with a long stalk or handle; b) F fig. =weilig; **=stieligkeit** F f ⊕ =weiligkeit.
längst=lebend (⸺...) a. ⊕ surviving; **~e**(r m) f ⊕ survivor, longest liver.
Languste (⸺) [fr., =It.] f ⊕ zo. spring- (or spiny) lobster (*Palinu'rus vulga'ris*).
Lang=weile ⊕ = Langeweile, **=weilen** ⊕ *** v/a. (f. Langeweile) to weary, tire, bore (zu Tode out of one's life, to death); sich ⸺ v/refl. to

feel tedious or bored or dull; **=weilig** a. ⊕ (f. Langeweile) wearisome, tedious, (verdrießlich) tiresome, v. Personen auch: heavy, humdrum, slow, v. Orten auch: dead-alive; der Mensch, oft: prosy fellow, bore; **=weiligkeit** f ⊕ weari-(some)ness, tediousness, heaviness, dead-aliveness; **=welle** ⊕ f ⊕ =baum; **=wied**(e) f = =baum; **=wierig** a. of long duration, long-lasting, lengthy; vgl. Zweilig; path. lingering, chronic; **=wierigkeit** f long duration, lengthiness, wearisomeness, **=zeher** m, zo.: ⟋ macrodactyl(e); **=zeile** f, pros. long line, bsd. line of twelve syllables; **=ziehen** n lengthening out, elongation; **=züngig** a. long-tongued (a. fig.), zo.: ⟋ macroglossate.
Lanolin ⊕ (⸺) [neu=lt.] n ⊕d. chm. lanoline, wool-fat.
Lanthan ⟋ (⸺) [grch.] n ⊕d. chm. Metall.
Lanze (⸺) [mhd.; fr. *lance*; *It.] f ⊕ **1.** spear, ⚔ lance (f. einlegen 4); e-e ~ mit e-m brechen to break a lance (or to enter the lists) with a p. — **2.** eine Kompagnie von hundert ~n (mit ~n Bewaffneten) ... of a hundred lances. — **3.** ⊕ Walfischfang: harpoon.
Lanzen=brechen ⚔ (⸺...) n ⊕ Mittelalter: tilting, j(o)ust(ing), tournament; **=eisen** n lance-head, spear-head; **=fähnchen**, **=fähnlein** n, **=flagge** f lance-pennon or -flag; **=fisch** m, ichth.: ⟋ acanthurus, ...id; **=förmig** a. ⊕ (shaped) like a lance, spear-shaped, ⟋ lanciform, ♀ lanceolate(d); **=knecht** m ⚔ statt Landsknecht; **=reiter** m lancer, uhlan; **=rennen** n ⚔ =brechen; **=schaft** m shaft of a lance; **=schlange** f rat-tailed serpent (*Bothrops lanceola'tus*); **=schuh** m lance-rest or -bucket; **=spitze** f point of a lance, auch ⸺ =eisen; **=stechen** n = =brechen; **=stich, =stoß** m thrust or wound inflicted with a lance; **=stock** m = =schaft; **=träger** m lance-bearer, lancer, spearman.
Lanzette (⸺) [fr. (dim. zu Lanze)] f ⊕ surg. (Wundnadel) lancet.
Lanzett(en)**=besteck** (⸺...) n ⊕ surg. case with lancets; **=fisch** m lancelet (*Amphi'oxus lanceola'tus*); **=förmig** a. ⊕ lancet-shaped, ⟋ lanceolate(d); **=stich** m prick with a lancet. [late(d)
lanzettlich ♀ (⸺) a. ⊕: ⟋ lanceo-
Laokoon (⸺...) [grch.] npr/m. ⊕ ⊕ a. (trojanischer Priester) Laocoön.
lapidar (⸺) [lt.] a. ⊕ lapidary.
Lapidar=schrift (⸺...) f ⊕, **=stil** m von Inschriften: lapidary style.
Lappali-e (⸺) [nhd.=lt.] f ⊕ trifle, insignificant (or trifling, paltry) matter; vgl. Kleinigkeit.
Läppchen (⸺) n ⊕ (dim. von Lappen³) small rag; ♀, anat.: ⟋ lobule, lobelet.
Lappe (⸺) m ⊕, **Lappin** f ⊕ (Lappländer[in]) Laplander, native of Lapland.
lappen¹ (⸺) [nbd.= lap] v/a. u. v/n. (h.) ⊕ (schlürfen) to lap, to sip.
lappen² (⸺) [Lappen³] v/a. ⊕ nur in p.p. ♀ u. zo. gelappt: ⟋ lobate(d).
Lappen³ (⸺) [ahd.] m ⊕ **1.** piece of cloth, (Fetzen) shred, (Lumpen) rag, pl. a. tatters; zum Wischen: duster, rubber; vgl. Fleck 4. — **2.** hunt. ~ pl. (an einer

[lappenartig] — 641 — [lassen]

Leine befestigte Streifen Leinwand od. Federn) toils pl.; F fig. e-m durch die ~ geh(e)n to escape (or bolt) from a p.. to give a p. the slip. — 3. anat. (weicher Teil e-s inneren Organs): ⚕ lobe (a. ⚕); ⚕ f. Samen-⚕; hunt. ~ pl. (hängende Ohren) des Hundes flap-ears pl.

Lappen³-artig (⚕...) a. ⚕ raglike, ragged, ⚕ lobular, lobulate(d); **=besen** m ⚕ mop; **=bildung** f: ⚕ lob(ul)ation'; **=decke** f patchwork quilt; **=fuß** m, orn. fin-foot, lobe-foot; **=füßig** a. orn. fin-footed, lobe-footed, ⚕ lobiped; **=jagd** f hunting with toils; **=muschel** f. zo. chama; **=qualle** f, zo. nettle-fish, sea-nettle (Acale'pha).

Lapperei (⚕) f ⚕ 1. (Flickerei) patching. — 2. (auch **Läpperei**) = Lappa'lie.

läppern (⚕) [nhd.; *lappen¹] v/a. u. v/n. (h.) ⚕a. 1. = lappen¹. — 2. a. sich ⚕ v/refl. to accumulate by degrees; es läppert sich (durch kleine Ausgaben bald eine große Summe) zusammen petty expenses soon sum (or run. F tot) up to a considerable amount.

Läpper=schulden (⚕...) f/pl. ⚕ petty (or trifling) debts.

lappicht (⚕) [Lappen³] a. ⚕ 1. (looking) like a rag, ragged. — 2. = lappig 1.

lappig (⚕) [Lappen³] a. ⚕ 1. (schlaff) limp, flabby, ⚕ flaccid. — 2. (mit Lappen od. Flicken versehen) patched (or pieced) together; (aus Lappen bestehend) ragged, tattered. — 3. ⚕, zo.: ⚕ lob(ul)ate(d).

läppisch (⚕) [zu mhd. lappe Laffe] a. ⚕ 1. (albern) silly, foolish, nonsensical; (abgeschmackt) insipid, senseless; (kindisch) childish, puerile; ⚕e Reden pl., ~es Zeug twaddle, rubbish, F stuff (and nonsense). — 2. (übermäßig weichlich) too effeminate, coddled; ⚕er Mensch, oft: F milksop, molly(coddle).

Lapp=land ⚕ (⚕) npr/n. ⚕α. (arktisches Land) Lapland; **Lapp=länder** (in f ⚕) m ⚕ Laplander, Lapp; **lapp=ländisch** a. ⚕ Lappish, ...ic, of Lapland.

Lapsus (⚕) [lt. Ausgleiten] m, inv. Lapsus ca'lami slip of the pen; Lapsus li'nguae slip of the tongue.

Lärche ⚕ (⚕; Hom. Lerche) [ahd.: larch; *lt. lăric-] f ⚕ larch-tree or -fir (Larix deci'dua); **lärchen** a. ⚕ (D 9) larchen, of larch-wood.

Lärchen=baum (⚕...) ⚕ m ⚕ = Lärche; **=holz** n zu Bahnschwellen ꝛc.: larch(-tree) wood; **=pech** n pitch of the larch-tree; **=schwamm** ⚕ m female agaric (Poly'porus offici'nalis); **=tanne** ⚕ f = Lärche.

Laren (L⚕) [lt.] pl. inv. röm. Alt.: (Hausgötter) lares, household gods pl. (a. fig.).

larifari! (⚕—⚕—) I int.: ⚕! rubbish!, F stuff and nonsense!, (it's all) bosh! — II ~ n ⚕ (Unsinn) nonsense, twaddle.

Lärm (⚕) [nhd.; *fr. alarme] m ⚕b. 1. noise, hubbub, racket, din, (Geschrei) clamour, (Gepolter) uproar, (Unruhe) bustle, (Getümmel) tumult, row, riot, rioting; (Zank und Schlägerei) brawling; blinder ~ false alarm; großen ~ um et. machen to make a great stir (or fuss) about a th.; wozu all der ~? what is all this noise (or disturbance, row) about?; lauten ~ m. F to kick up a great row or shindy. Sprichw.

viel ~ um nichts much ado about nothing (auch Titel eines Lustspiels von SH.). — 2. ~ blasen, läuten, schlagen to give (or sound) the alarm.

Lärm=apparat ⚕ (⚕...) m ⚕ alar(u)m; **=bläser** m = Lärmmacher b.

lärmen (⚕) ⚕ I v/n. (h.) to be noisy, to make (much) noise, F to kick up a row, (schreien) to shout, to clamour; ⚕d noisy, uproarious, tumultuous. — II v/a. mit Angabe der Wirkung: e-n wach ⚕ to waken (or rouse) a p. with noise or shouting. — III ~ n (m) ⚕ = Lärm.

Lärmer (⚕) m ⚕, ~**in** f ⚕ noisy (or blustering, riotous) person, brawler, rioter, roisterer.

Lärm=glocke (⚕...) f ⚕ alarm-bell, tocsin; **=kanone** f al.-gun; **=macher** m: a) noisy person; b) alarmist; **=platz** ⚕ m al.-post; **=schuß** m, **=trommel** f ⚕ al.-shot, -drum; **=zeichen** n alarm-signal.

Lärvchen (⚕) [Larve 2, dim.] n ⚕ little mask; f. Larve 2.

Larve (⚕) [nhd.; *lt. lărva Gespenst] f ⚕ 1. mask; e-m die ~ abziehen to unmask a p. — 2. (Gesicht, bsd. ein hübsches) (pretty) face, (nice) features pl., oft im dim.: jedes hübsche Lärvchen every pretty (or good-looking, nice-looking) face or girl. — 3. ~n pl. (Geipenster) larvæ, F bogies pl.; unter ~n (Untieren) die einzig fühlende Brust (SCH.) 'mid monsters the only feeling breast. — 4. ent. (Insekten⚕) larva, grub, ⚕ eruca.

larven=ähnlich (⚕...) a. ⚕ zo.: ⚕ larviform; **=blütler** ⚕ m ⚕ personate flower; **=gesicht** n: a) masked face or person; b) ugly (or plain-looking, lantern-jawed) person, F fright; **=taucher** m, orn. mormon, coulter-neb, common puffin (Mormon a'rctica); **=tötend** a. zo.: ⚕ erucivorous.

Laryngoskop ⚕ (⚕⚕) [grch.] n ⚕d. med. (Kehlkopfspiegel) laryngoscope.

las (⚕) 1. u. 3. Person ind. impf. v. lesen.

lasch ⚕, P (⚕) [nhd.] a. ⚕ lax, limp, loose, flabby (= schlaff).

Lasche ⚕ (⚕) [nhd. Lappen] f ⚕ (Verbindungsstück) ⚕ fish(ing)-plate, ⚕, ⚕ sypher-joint; Schneiderei: a) (Zwickel) gusset; b) (Klappe e-r Tasche) flap; Schuhmacherei: latchet; Zimmerei: groove for joining (or lashing) timber.

laschen (⚕) v/a. ⚕ 1. ⚕ for. (anlaschen) to blaze. — 2. ⚕ (mit einer Lasche versehen): Beinkleider ⚕ to provide ... with flaps, Schuhe: to put latchets on; Hölzer: to join (or lash) timber by means of grooves; ⚕ to sling, to lash.

Laschheit (⚕) f ⚕ (f. lasch) laxity.

Lase provc. (⚕) [nhd.] f ⚕ (Krug) pitcher.

läse (⚕) 1. u. 3. Person subj. impf. v. lesen.

Laser=kraut ⚕ (⚕...) [lt.] n ⚕ laserwort (Laserpi'tium); **=saft** m, pharm. laser, ⚕ asadulcis.

lasieren (⚕) ⚕ [Lasur] v/a. ⚕ = glasieren; **Lasier=farbe** f = Lasur.

Läsion ⚕ (-⚕) [lt.] f ⚕ path. (Verletzung) injury, ⚕ lesion.

Laskare ⚕ (⚕⚕) [ar. el asker der Soldat] m ⚕ (ostind. Matrose) lascar.

laß¹ (⚕) imper. von lassen.

laß² ⚕ (⚕) [ahd.] a. ⚕ (D 10) = lässig.

Laß=baum (⚕...) ⚕ m ⚕ for. stand; ehm. **=becken** n, surg. bleeding-basin; **=besitz** m = =gut; **=besitzer** m leaseholder.

Lasse (⚕) m ⚕ (Höriger) bondman.

lassen (⚕) [ahd.: let] ⚕a. I v aux. mit inf. 1. (gestatten) to let, to allow to, to permit, (nicht hindern) not to prevent from (doing a th.); (leiden, dulden) to suffer (or tolerate) a th. (to be done); f. belehren 2; eine Lampe brennen ⚕ to keep a lamp burning; ⚕ Sie sich erzählen // let me (or I must) tell you //; f. fahren 2, gehen 5, gelten 2; ich lasse ihn grüßen I wish to be (kindly) remembered to him; f. handeln 2, hangen 4, hören 2 und 8; laß einmal hören! let me hear what you have to say!; laß ihn kommen! let him come!; wir ⚕ ihn das Buch lesen we allow him to (or we let him) read the book; ⚕ Sie mich nur machen! let me manage it!; ich lasse ihn reden I let him talk; et. sehen ⚕ to show a th.; sich vor einem sehen ⚕ to present o.s. before a p.; vermuten ⚕, daß // to give rise to a belief that //, to cause a suspicion that //; wir ⚕ ihm eine glückliche Reise wünschen will you wish him from us a safe journey (out). — 2. (bewirken) to make, to cause to (be done), to have (done); der König ließ sie vor sich bringen the king ordered them to be (or had them) brought before him; ich ließ die Sachen zu ihm bringen I had ... taken to him; fliegen ⚕ to let fly, Drachen ⚕: to fly; ⚕ Sie den Arzt holen send for the doctor; er läßt sich (dat.) einen Rock machen he has a coat made; ich habe ihn eine Seite lesen ⚕ (st. p.p. gelassen) I have made him read ...; ich habe mir sagen ⚕ (erfahren) I have been told, I have heard; e-n et. tun ⚕ to make a p. do a th. — 3. v/refl.: es läßt sich nicht beschreiben it defies description, it is indescribable; Gold läßt sich dehnen ... is capable of expansion, ... is tensile; das läßt sich denken I should think so; wie läßt sich das sagen as may (easily) be imagined; das läßt sich von ihm erwarten that is the least one may expect from him; der Käse läßt sich kaum essen ... is hardly eatable; Gründe, die sich hören ⚕ plausible reasons pl.; es läßt sich nicht leugnen, daß // it cannot be denied (or it is undeniable, indisputable) that //; lobend: diese Zigarren ⚕ sich rauchen these cigars are (something) worth smoking, schwächer: they are good (enough) to smoke; die Zigarren ⚕ sich nicht rauchen the cigars are not fit to smoke; darüber läßt (od. ließe) sich weiter reden that admits of further discussion; das läßt sich besser sagen als tun that is more easily said than done; sie ⚕ sich leicht schrecken they are easily frightened; hier läßt sich's gut sitzen it's very pleasant sitting here; er läßt sich nicht mit Füßen treten he won't be trampled upon; das Bier läßt sich kaum trinken ... is hardly drinkable; ein Knall ließ sich vernehmen a report could

be heard; es ließe sich wetten, daß one might lay a wager that; das Wort läßt sich nicht übersetzen ... is not translatable. — 4. sein 2: et. sein (ob. bleiben) 2 (unterlassen) to abstain from (doing) a th., to omit (doing) a th.; 2 Sie das (sein)! drop that!, don't think of it (any) more!. drohend: leave it alone!; F u. P e-n sein (in Ruhe) 2 to let (or leave) a p. alone, F to let a p. be. — 5. in Redens-arten mit refl. pron. (oft nicht zu übersetzen): sie 2 sich (dat.) nichts abgehen they don't stint (or pinch) themselves in anything; sich (dat.) et. beigehen, einfallen 2 to devise a th., F to get an idea into one's head: 2 Sie sich belehren! be advised!; f. gefallen² 3, gelüsten I; ich werde mir das gesagt sein 2 I will take it to heart; er ließ sich nichts merken he did not show it; das hätte ich mir nicht träumen 2 I should never have dreamt of such a th.; sich keine Mühe verdrießen 2 to spare no trouble; sich die Lust daran vergeh(e)n 2 to take no further pleasure in a th. — 6. (schildern, sich vorstellen) der Dichter läßt die Helden in der Fremde irren the poet represents ... as wandering in foreign lands; Roman-schriftsteller 2 ihre Heldinnen gern seltsame Abenteuer bestehen novelists are prone to let (or make) their heroines pass through strange adventures; laß ihn nur erst so alt sein wie du bist imagine (or fancy, picture) him as old as you are. — 7. in der ersten Person pl. des imper.: laß (laßt, 2 Sie) uns geh(e)n! let us go or start! (= gehen wir!); 2 wir den Autor selbst sprechen!, etwa: to quote the author's own words! — II v/a. (oft ell.) 8. to leave (undone), to leave off: 2 Sie ihn! leave him (at rest)!, let him alone!; f. frei 2; wo hat er all sein Geld gelassen? what has he done with all his money?; keine Spur 2 (hinterlassen) to leave no trace (behind); die Tür offen 2 to leave the door open; et. unbesprochen 2 to leave a th. unmentioned; e-n unbestraft 2 to let a p. go (scot-) free; eine weiße Stelle 2 to leave a blank. — 9. e-m et. (überlassen) to leave a th. in a p.'s hands, to give s. th. up to a p.; das muß man mir 2 that is (in fairness) due to me; man hat ihm keinen Heller gelassen he hasn't a farthing left, they left him without a penny; wenn Gott mir das Leben läßt provided I am spared or allowed to live; ich lasse Ihnen die Wahl you shall have the choice; sich Zeit 2 to give (or allow) o.s. (sufficient) time; ● ich kann es Ihnen zu dem Preise nicht 2 I cannot let you have it at that price. — 10. mit prp.: keinen guten Faden (ob. kein gutes Haar) an e-m 2 to have not a (single) good word to say for a p.; sich aufs Knie fallen 2 to fall (or drop, go down) on one's knees; nicht aus den Augen 2 never to leave out of (one's) sight; aus den Händen 2 to let slip (from one's

hands); außer acht 2 to take no notice of, to disregard; 2 wir es beim alten! let us keep (or adhere. F stick) to the old customs or ways!; ct. beiseite 2 to leave a th. aside, to pass a th. over; 2 wir diese Scherze beiseite! all joking apart!; e-n in seinem Amte 2 to keep a p. in one's employ or at his post: Fässer in den Keller 2 to haul (or let) down casks into the cellar; 2 Sie mich damit in Ruhe! don't talk about it (any more)!; e-n im Stiche 2 to leave a p. in the lurch; im unklaren über et. 2 to leave in the dark about a th.; Korn vom Boden 2 to bring (or shoot) down corn from the loft; Bier vom Fasse 2 (abzapfen) to draw (off) beer from the cask; f. Stapel; e-n von sich 2 to part with a p., to dismiss a p.; e-n vor sich 2 to admit a p. to one's presence or to an audience; niemand zu sich 2 to admit (or receive) nobody; er läßt niemand zu sich he won't see anybody. — 11. (unterlassen) et. 2 to abstain (or refrain, desist) from (doing) a th.; frei sein zu tun oder zu 2, was man will (to be free) to do as one pleases; ich kann es nicht 2 I cannot help (doing) it; laß den Lärm! stop that noise!; er kann das Rauchen nicht 2 he cannot keep (or wean himself) from smoking; laß das Weinen! leave off crying or weeping or F snivelling. — 12. (verlassen) to leave (behind), forsake, abandon; er mußte Blut 2 he had to bleed or to be bled; das Leben 2 to perish. to lose one's life; das Leben für e-n 2 (hingeben) to give (or lay down) one's life for a p. — 13. (unterbringen) to place, to house, Sachen auch: to deposit; fig. sich vor Freude nicht zu 2 wissen to be beside o.s. with joy. — 14. (hinterlassen) to leave (behind), f-n Erben: to bequeath. — 15. mit bestimmtem s.: e-m Blut 2 to bleed a p.; f. Haar 3; das (ober sein) Wasser 2 to pass one's water, to make water, F to pump ship. — III v/n. (h.) 16. von et. 2 (ablassen) to renounce (or to give up) a th., to desist from a th.; ich kann von ihm nicht 2 I cannot sever (or tear) myself from him; von seiner Meinung 2 to change one's opinion; Sprichw. f. Art¹ 3. — 17. ↖ 2 (aussehen): das läßt schön that is beautiful to look at; die Jacke läßt (steht) ihr gut the jacket suits (or fits) her well. — IV ~ n 23 18. unser Tun und ~ all that we do or neglect to do, oft auch: our commissions and omissions pl. (a. theol.). — V ge-lassen p.p. 19. f. bsd. Art.

lässest ↖ (◡‿) 2. Person sg. des pres. ind. v. lassen, mst läßt.

Laß-gut (◡‿) n 62 land subject to ground-rent, copyhold, leasehold.

Laßheit (◡‿) [laß²] f 46 = Lässigkeit.

lässig (◡‿) [laß²] a. 66 (faul) indolent, lazy, idle, (nachlässig) negligent, neglectful, remiss, (sorglos) careless, (schlaff, träge) sluggish, inactive, lackadaisical; ~keit (◡‿) f 46 indolence, laziness; negligence; carelessness; sluggishness.

läßlich (◡‿) [lassen] a. 66 1. eccl. venial (offence): weitS. (verzeihlich) pardonable. — 2. (nachsichtig) indulgent.

Läßlichkeit (◡‿-) f 46 (f. läßlich) 1. eccl. (mit pl.) venial offence. — 2. (o. pl.) veniality; indulgence.

Lasso (◡‿) [span.] m 23 (Fangseil) lasso; mit e-m ~ fangen to lasso.

laß-pflichtig (◡‿...) a. 66 subject to (a) ground-rent; =reis n 62 for. (stehenbleibender Baum) staddle; vgl. =baum.

läßt (◡‿) 2 u. 3. Person sg., pres.ind. v. lassen.

Laß-zins (◡‿) m 62 ground-rent.

Last (◡‿) [ahd. *ladan] f 46 1. load, (Bürde) burden, fig. auch: encumbrance, charge; (Beschwerde) trouble, bother. nuisance, (great) tax; e-m eine ~ abnehmen to take a burden off a p.'s shoulders, to relieve a p. (of a burden); des Tages ~ und Hitze tragen to bear the burden and heat of the day. — 2. f. fallen 4 gegen Ende und Gemeinde am Schluß; e-m et. zur ~ legen (vorwerfen) to lay a th. at a p.'s door, to charge a p. with a th.; e-m zur ~ liegen to be a burden to a p., to be burdensome (or chargeable) to a p.; ● e-m et. zur ~ schreiben to debit a th. to a p.; wir buchen es zu Ihren ~en we debit it to your account. — 3. (pl. nach Zahlen inv.: nach Ort u. Zeit wechselndes Maß für Wein, Korn, Kohlen ꝛc.) etwa: load; ⚓ (Schiffsfrachtgewicht) load (of two thousand kilograms). — 4. ~en (Abgaben) taxes, imposts, fiscal burdens pl.

Lastadie ⚓ (◡◡‿, bsd. ◡‿(◡‿) [dtsch.-it.; *Last] f 46 wharf(age), quay, jetty; (Fluß-ufer) riverside, riverain land.

lastbar (◡‿) a. 66 1. capable of bearing a burden or of being loaded; Lest-Tier = Lasttier. — 2. (lastend) weighty, burdensome, heavy, cumbersome.

Last-dampfer (◡‿...) m 46 cargo-steamer.

lasten (◡‿) ⊛ I v/n (h.) to weigh (heavily); 2 auf to press down upon, von Schulden: to encumber an estate. — II v/a. poet. = belasten 1. — III ~ n 23 (heavy) pressure or weight.

Lasten-aufzug (◡‿...) m 62 lift (or elevator) for raising goods; 2frei a. 66 free from burdens; =zug ⛟ m 22 (Güterzug) goods-train.

Laster (◡‿) [ahd. Wurzel lah- rügen] n 23 1. vice, weitS. viciousness, depravity. — 2. (schändlicher Mensch) infamous (or low) fellow, miscreant, reprobate, bsd. (schändliches Weib) disgraceful creature, F bad wench; F ein langes ~ a tall piece of unrighteousness, six feet of wickedness.

Läster-allee (◡‿...) f 62 lane of mockers or slanderers; =chronik, =geschichte f (piece of, bits pl. of) scandal, town-talk.

Läster/er (◡‿) m 23, ...in f 40 (f. lästern) slanderer, defamer, reviler, backbiter, scandal-monger; rel. blasphemer.

laster-frei (◡‿...) a. 66 free from vice.

lasterhaft (◡‿) a. 66 vicious, wicked, (verderbt) depraved, corrupt; (unsittlich) immoral, (liederlich) profligate, dissolute, fast; ~igkeit (◡‿◡‿-) f 46 viciousness, wickedness, depravity, immorality, dissoluteness, profligacy.

[Lasterhöhle] — 643 — [Laubsänger]

Laster=höhle (ˈ⏑⏑...) f ⑫ den of iniquity; =**knecht** m slave to vice; =**leben** n life of depravity.
lästerlich (⏑⏑⏑) [mhd.] a. ⑯ 1. (f. lästern) slanderous, defamatory, calumnious, abusive; (gottes=)⏑ blasphemous; (gottlos) wicked. — 2. (schändlich) infamous, disgraceful, scandalous.
Läster=maul (ˈ⏑⏑.¹) n ⑫ slanderous tongue, scandal-monger, slanderer.
lästern (⏑⏑) [ahd.] I v/a. u. v/n. (h.) ⑳a.: e-n ⏑, auch von e-m ⏑ to slander (or defame, revile) a p., to speak ill of a p., (anschwärzen) to backbite; (schmähen) to abuse, to cry (or run) down; den Namen Gottes ⏑, (wider) Gott ⏑ to speak (or utter) blasphemy, to blaspheme. — II ~ n ㉓ = Lästerung.
Läster=rede (ˈ⏑⏑...) f ⑫ slanderous (or defamatory) language; weitS. = Lästerung; =**schrift** f libel(lous pamphlet), lampoon; =**schule** f school for scandal (urspr. Luftspiel v. Sheridan); =**sucht** f love for scandal; =**süchtig** a. ⑯ fond of scandal, slanderous.
Laster=tat (ˈ⏑⏑.¹) f ⑫ infamous action, heinous deed, (villainous) crime.
Lästerung (⏑⏑⏑) f ㊻ (f. lästern) slander (-ing), defamation, abuse, blasphemy.
laster=voll (ˈ⏑⏑.f⏑) a. ⑯ depraved, vicious.
Läster=wort (ˈ⏑⏑...) n ⑫ slander(ous remark), invective, gegen Gott: blasphemy; =**zunge** f slanderous tongue.
Last=esel (ˈ⏑...) n ⑫ = Packesel; =**fracht** ⚓ f freight(age) per ton; =**fuhre** f (heavy) goods-van; =**gebühr** f, =**geld** n ⑫ tonnage, duty per ton.
lastig ⚓ (ˈ⏑⏑) a. ⑯ (ladungsfähig) meist in Zssgn, z.B. zwei=**les** Schiff ship carrying (or with a burden of) two loads.
lästig (ˈ⏑⏑) [Last] a. ⑯ burdensome, onerous, (beschwerlich) troublesome, (verdrießlich) bothersome, irksome, (ermüdend) wearisome, fatiguing; (verhaßt) hateful; e-m ⏑ fallen ob. w. to become a burden (or trouble) to a p., to bore a p.; =**keit** f ㊻ burdensomeness, troublesomeness, irksomeness.
Lastigkeit ⚓ (ˈ⏑⏑⏑) f ㊻ (Ladefähigkeit) ship's tonnage or burden or capacity.
Last=kahn ⚓ (ˈ⏑...) m ⑫ lighter; =**pferd** n pack- (or sumpter-)horse; =**schiff** ⚓ n transport-ship; =**tier** n beast of burden; wie ein ~ arbeiten to drudge, F to work like a nigger, to fag; =**träger** m porter, carrier of parcels, &c.; =**vieh** n beast(s pl.) of burden; =**wagen** m = =fuhre; =**zug** ⚒ m goods-train.
Lasur (⏑ˈ⏑) [mlt.; *perf. ♀ Minen v. Ladschward] I († ob. poet. a. ⏑ˈ⏑) m ⑪d. 1. min. = Lasurstein. — II f ㊻ paint. 2.(Lasierung) colouring blue. — 3. (=farbe) transparent blue coating; vgl. =blau.
Lasur=blau (⏑ˈ⏑...) ⑳ n paint. ultramarine, holländisches: Dutch blue; ⁂**blau** a. ⑯ azure, deep sky-blue; =**farbe** f: a) = =blau; b) (durchscheinende Farbe) transparent colour; =**farben** a. = =blau; =**stein** m, min., paint. azurestone, ⁂ (lt.) (lapis) lazuli, azurite.
Lätare (⏑ˈ⏑⏑) [lt. freue dich!] nur in: Sonntag ~ (4. Fastensonntag) Lætare(Sunday).
Latein (⏑ˈ¹) [lt. latī̆num] n ⑪d. Latin (language or tongue); Ciceronianisches

~ Ciceronian Latin; f. Küchenlatein; fig. mit f=m ~ zu Ende sein (nicht weiter können) to be at one's wits' end or at a standstill or F at a nonplus.
Lateiner (⏑ˈ⏑⏑) m ㊶ 1. m/pl.: a) (Bewohner des alten La'tium) Latini pl.; b) Völker des Westens in den Kreuzzügen: Latin nations pl. — 2. (f. der Latein kennt, spricht) Latinist.
lateinisch (⏑ˈ⏑⏑) [ahd.; *lt.] a. ⑯ 1. Latin; die ⏑e Sprache, das ~(e) n ㊲ the Latin tongue, Latin; ⏑e Brocken scraps pl. of Latin; ⚓ Les Segel lateen; ⏑e Volkssprache low Latin. — 2. Le Buchstaben: a) Latin character(s pl.); b) ⊕ typ. Roman (type or letters pl.); (= Antiqua); italics pl. (= Kursiv).
latein=los* (⏑ˈ⏑.¹) a. ⑯: lateinlose Schule school in which no Latin is taught.
Latein=schule (⏑ˈ⏑.¹⏑) f ⑫ grammar-school. [latent (heat, &c.).]
latent (⏑ˈ⏑) [lt.] a. ⑯ phys. (gebunden)
Laterne (⏑ˈ⏑⏑) [mhd.; *lt. lantĕrna] f ㊻ 1. lantern; (Straßen=) street-lamp. — 2. arch. (durchbrochenes Türmchen) lantern, skylight turret.
Latern(en)=anstecker (⏑ˈ⏑(⏑)...) m ⑫, =**anzünder** m lamplighter; =**arm** m lantern-crank; =**bank** ⊕ f Spinnerei: can-(roving) frame; =**eisen** ⚓ n lantern-braces pl.; =**fabrikant** m lantern-maker; =**halter** m am Fahrrad lamp-bracket; =**pfahl** m lamppost; am ~e aufhängen to hang (or string) up at a lamppost; =**träger** m: a) Person: lantern-bearer; b) = =pfahl; c) ent. lantern-fly (Fu'lgora lanterna'ria).
Latier=baum (⏑ˈ⏑.¹) m ⑫ wagerecht zwischen den Pferdeständen: stable-bar.
Latiner (⏑ˈ⏑⏑) m/pl. ⑫ = Lateiner 1 a.
latinisch (⏑ˈ⏑⏑) [lt.] a. ⑯ of Latium.
latinisieren (⏑ˈ⏑⏑⏑) v/a. ⑳ to Latinize.
Latinismus ⚓ (⏑⏑ˈ⏑⏑) [lt.] m ㉗ (lateinische Spracheigentümlichkeit) Latinism.
Latinist (⏑⏑ˈ¹) m ⑫ (Forscher od. Kenner des Lateinischen) Latinist. [Latinity.)
Latinität (⏑⏑⏑ˈ¹) f ㊻ (lateinischer Stil))
Lätitia (−ˈ⏑ʦ(⏑)⏑) [lt. Freude] npr/f. ⑫㊽a.㉔㊾β. Letitia, Lettice.
Latitudinari=er (⏑⏑⏑⏑ˈ⏑¹(⏑)⏑)[neu=lt.] m ㉑ (Nichtstrenger, Gemäßigter) latitudinarian (a. eccl.); one of broad principles.
Latrine (⏑ˈ⏑⏑) [lt.] f ㊺ = Abtritt 2.
Latsch F (ˈ¹) m ⑳a., ~e¹ m ㊶ (schlaffer Mensch) lackadaisical fellow.
Latsche² (ˈ⏑⏑) f ㊺ 1. (Lappenschuh) shoe (or slipper) down at the heels. — 2. (plumper Fuß, z.B. des Bären) shaggy foot. — 3. F fig. (schlumpiges Weib sloven(ly woman) — 4. ⚒, ⚓ arch. (Unterlage)foundation,patten of a rail,&c.
Latsche³ (ˈ⏑⏑) f ㊺ (Krummholzkiefer) dwarf-pine (Pinus Mughus).
latschen (ˈ⏑⏑) v/n. (h.) ⑪ to have a slouching gait, to shuffle along.
Latschen=öl ⊕ (ˈ⏑⏑.¹) n ⑫ templin-oil.
Latsch=gang (ˈ¹..) m ⑫ (f. latschen) shuffling (or slouching) gait.
latschig (ˈ⏑⏑) a. ⑯ with a shuffling (or slouching) gait; (schlumpig) slovenly, slipshod; (schlaff) lackadaisical.
Latte (ˈ⏑⏑) [ahd.: lath] f ㊺ 1. ⊕ carp., &c. lath; mit ~n beschlagen to lath, to board. — 2. for. (schlanker Schößling)

slender shoot, young tree; F fig. (aufgeschossene Person) = Latsch. — 3. P fig. der Kerl ist dumm wie eine ~ he is a blockhead(ed fellow).
latten ⊕ (ˈ⏑⏑) v/a. ⑱ = belatten.
latten=artig (ˈ⏑⏑..) a. ⑯ (shaped) like a lath; =**gitter** ⊕ n lattice-work, trellis-work; =**holz** n lath-wood; =**kiste** f crate; =**nagel** m lath-nail; =**reißer** ⊕ m lath-splitter; =**verschlag** m partition made of laths or lattice-work; =**werk** n lath- (or lattice-)work; =**zaun** m fence made of laths, wooden fence or paling.
Lattich ♀ (ˈ⏑⏑) [ahd.: lettuce; *lt. lactu'ca f] m ⑫ lettuce (Lactu'ca).
Lattich=salat (ˈ⏑⏑...) m ⑫ garden lettuce (Lactu'ca sati'va); =**säure** f, chm.: ⁂ lactucic acid (aus Lactu'ca viro'sa).
Latt=nagel (ˈ⏑..) m ⑫ = Lattennagel.
Latwerge (⏑ˈ⏑⏑) [mhd.; *lt. elect(u)a'rium n] f ㊺ pharm.: ⁂ electuary.
Latz (ˈ¹) [it. laccio] m ⑫⑦ a. 1. = Brustlatz. — 2. von Kindern: a) bib; b) (Schürzchen) pinafore. — 3. a) (Klappe über e-r Tasche, an Mützen) flap; b) = Hosenlatz.
Lätzchen (ˈ⏑⏑) n ㉓ dim. = Latz 2.
Latz=schürze (ˈ⏑.⏑⏑) f ⑫ = Latz 2 b.
lau (ˈ¹) [ahd.] a. ⑯ lukewarm (a. fig.), tepid; von der Luft: genial; fig. (gleichgültig) indifferent; half-hearted; ⏑ w. to grow lukewarm, fig. a.: to cool down (in one's ardour).
Laub (ˈ¹) [ahd.: leaf] n ⑪(②)c. foliage of a tree; die Bäume bedecken sich mit (verlieren ihr) ~ ... put on (shed) their leaves or foliage; vom Vieh und Wilde: das ~ abnagen to browse.
laub=ähnlich ♀ (ˈ¹..) a. ⑯, ⏑**artig** a. leaf-like, ⁂ foliaceous, phylloid; von Lebermoosen: mit ⏑artigem Thallus: ⁂ frondose; =**baum** m ⑫ tree with (green) foliage; ⏑**bekränzt** a. (sch.) umkränzt wreathed in foliage, leaf clad; =**dach** n leafy roof, canopy of leaves.
Laube (ˈ¹⏑) [ahd.; *Laub] f ㊻ 1. = Gartenlaube. — 2. arch. (Vorhalle) hall, porch; (Säulengang)portico, (Bogengang)arcade.
Lauben (ˈ¹⏑) m ㉓ ichth. (Art Weißfisch) bleak (Albu'rnus lu'cidus).
Lauben=dach (ˈ¹..) n ⑫ roof (or top) of an arbour; =**gang** m: a) arboured walk; b) arcade. — Vgl. a. Laub=...
Lauber=hütte (ˈ¹..) = Laubhütte.
Laub=fall (ˈ¹..) m ⑫ fall of the leaf, ⁂ defoliation; =**flechte** ♀ f: ⁂ frondous lichen; =**förmig** a. ⑯ = =ähnlich; =**frosch** m, zo. green- (or tree-)frog (Hyla arbo'rea); fig. = Jäger; =**futter** n des Viehs: (green) leaves pl. used as fodder; =**gehänge**, =**gewinde** n festoons, (green) garlands pl.; =**holz** n, for. foliage- (⁂ foliaceous) trees pl. (ant. Nadelholz); =**hütte** f: a) arbour clad with foliage; b) der Juden: tabernacle; =**hütten=fest** n feast of (the)tabernacles.
laubicht, mit **laubig** (ˈ⏑⏑) a. ⑯ 1. (belaubt)in (full) leaf, leafy, covered with leaves, clad in foliage. — 2. ⁂ foliaceous.
Laub=knospe (ˈ¹..) ♀ f ⑫ leaf-bud; =**los** a. ⑯ without foliage, leafless; =**moose** ⁂ n/pl.: ⁂ frondiferous mosses, musci pl.; ⏑**reich** a. leafy, full of leaves; =**säge** ⊕ f fret- (or compass-)saw; =**säge=arbeiten** f/pl. fret-saw work; =**sänger** m, orn

⁂ scientific; ♀ botanical; ⊕ geography; ⊕ machinery; ⚒ mining; ⚔ military; ⚓ marine; ⊕ commercial; ✉ postal; ⚒ railway

[**Laubſtreu**] — 644 — [**Läufer**]

wood-wren (*Phyllopneu'ste sibila'trix*); =**ſtreu** *f* litter of leaves; =**taler** *m* ehm. Frankreich: six-franc piece; =**tragend** ⚤ *a.* leaf-bearing, leafy, ⚹ fronde(sce)nt, frondous, frondiferous; =**verzierung** *f*, *arch.*, &c. foliage, leafage; =**wald** *m* leafy wood; =**werk** *n*: a) [Laub] foliage, *paint. a.* trees *pl.*; *arch.*: ⚹ foil, leaf-work, im gotiſchen Stil: ⚹ crocket; b) [Laube] arbour, trellis-work.

Lauch ⚤ (⁴) (=**ich**) [ahd.: leek] m⚤c. (common) leek (*A'llium porrum*); ⚲=**artig** ⚤ (⚹…) *a.* ⚤: ⚹ alliaceous; ⚲=**farben**, ⚲=**farbig**, ⚲=**grün** *a.* leek-green, ⚹ porraceous.

Lauer¹ (¹⁰) [mhd.] *f* ⚤ lurking(-place); (Hinterhalt) ambush, ambuscade; auf der ~ ſein ob. liegen ob. ſteh(e)n to be on the watch *or* on the look-out *for a p.*, to lie in ambush (*or* in wait) *for a p.*

Lauer² (¹⁰) [ahd.: lt. lŏrā *f*] *m* ⚤ (Treſterwein) wine of the second press.

Lau(e)rer (¹⁰) *m* ⚤ lurker, p. on the watch *or* on the look-out *or* in ambush.

lauern (¹⁰) [mhd.: lower] **I** *v/n.* (h.) ⚤ *a.* **1.** auf etwas ⚲ (warten) to wait impatiently for a th. — **2.** to be on the watch, in feindlicher Abſicht: to lie in wait (*or* ambush) *for a p.* — **II** ⚤ ⚹ **3.** impatient waiting, eager expectation; lying in wait; vgl. *Lauer¹*.

Lauf (¹) [ahd.: vgl. laufen] *m* ⚤c. (vgl. aber 4) **1.** (raſche Fortbewegung) run(ning); (Wett-)~ race; v. lebloſen Weſen: course (a. *ast.*); ~ der Geſtirne movement of celestial bodies, (Waſſer in ſ-r Bewegung) current, drift, stream; voller ~ eines Pferdes ꝛc. full career; in vollem ~ at full gallop or speed. — **2.** im ~, während des ~es in (*or* whilst) running; im ~(e) des Monats, Jahres in the course of …; im ~(e) der Zeit in course of time; einer Sache freien ~ geben to let a th. take its (natural) course; den Dingen freien ~ laſſen, oft: to let things slide; ſeinen Gedanken freien ~ laſſen to give full expression (*or* play) to one's thoughts; der Gerechtigkeit freien ~ laſſen to let justice take its course; vgl. *frei 2.* — **3.** (Bahn ob. Kreis, worin ſich et. bewegt) path, track, *ast.* auch: orbit; ~ des Blutes circulation of the blood; das iſt der ~ der Welt that's the way of the world, such is life; ⚓ ~ (Fahrt) course, passage; ſ-n ~ richten nach // to shape one's course for //. — **4.** ♪ (*pl.* oft ⚤c.) (Folge melo'-biſcher Töne) run, ſeltener: roulade. — **5.** *hunt.* (Bein vierfüßiger Jagdtiere) foot, leg. — **6.** ⊕ (Gewehrlauf) barrel; Gewehr mit zwei Läufen double-barrelled gun.

Lauf-achſe ⊕ (¹…) *f* ⚤ an e-m Wagen = Achſe 1; =**bahn** *f*: a) (ebener Raum zum Wettlaufe) (race-)course, für Pferde ꝛc. a.: hippodrome; b) *fig.* (Wirkungskreis) career; eine ~ betreten to enter (upon) a career, to make a start in life; =**brett** ⛴ *n* running board; =**brief** *m*: a) circular (letter); b) =**paß**, =**brücke** *f* narrow wooden bridge, ⚓ pontoon (⚓ gangway; =**burſche** *m* errand-, office-, shop-boy, messenger, light porter.

laufen (¹⁰) [ahd.: leap] haſt **I** *v/n.* (meiſt mit ſn; mit h., wenn die Anſtrengung hervorgehoben wird), *v/a. u.* ſich ⚲ *v/refl.* **1.** (*ant.* gehen)

to run (auch 🚂 von Bahnzügen); ſchnell ⚲ to career, to scud along; ſtärker: to rush, to scamper; ſchneller ⚲ als // to outrun, to outstrip (in running) //; ſ. *gelaufen*, Gerücht 1; **hin und her** ⚲ to run to and fro *or* backwards and forwards; immer hin und her ⚲ to be for ever running about *or* on the move; **in** die Stube hinein ⚲ to run into …, in ſein Verderben ⚲ to rush (headlong) into destruction; **über** Hals und Kopf ⚲ to rush headlong; **um** et. ⚲ to run round a th., von Planeten: to revolve round the sun; um die Wette ⚲ to race (for a wager); ⚲ wie ein Beſenbinder to run like mad; *abs.* das Faß läuft the cask leaks *or* runs; die Züge ⚲ wieder the trains are running again; die Uhr läuft (vor) the watch is (*or* goes too) fast; ſ. *davonlaufen.* — **2.** ſich ⚲ *v/refl.* mit Angabe der Wirkung: ſich außer Atem ⚲ to get out of breath with running; ſich müde (zu Tode) ⚲ to tire (to kill) o.s. with running; ſich (*dat.*) die Füße wund ⚲ to run one's feet sore; *v/impers.* es läuft ſich hier ſchlecht it is bad running (*or* walking, skating) here. — **3.** mit *prp.*: **auf** alle Bälle ⚲ to go (*or* F to run) to all the balls, never to miss a ball; er weiß darauf zu ⚲ he is full of resource or shifts; ⚓ auf den Grund ⚲ to run aground; auf den Strand ⚲ to be stranded *or* cast ashore; **aus** dem Dienſte ⚲ to run away from service; mit dem Kopfe **gegen** die Wand ⚲ to run one's head against the wall (a. *fig.*); **hinter** die Schule ⚲ (ſie heimlich verſäumen) to play (the) truant; e-m **in** die Arme ⚲ to run (*or* rush) into a p.('s arms); das läuft ins Geld that runs into money, it is (very) expensive; ⚓ in den Hafen ⚲ to put into port, to enter the harbour; das Waſſer läuft mir in die Schuhe … runs (*or* soaks) into my boots; alle Welt läuft in dies Stück all the world flock to that piece, everybody rushes to see that play; e-m in den Weg ⚲ to run against (*or* to come across) *a* p.; **um** die Sonne ⚲ to move (*or* revolve) round the sun; **vor** e-m ⚲ (fliehen) to flee before (*or* from) a p.; das läuft **wider** die geſunde Vernunft that runs counter (*or* is contrary) to (all) good sense. — **4.** mit abhängigem Kaſus: a) *gen.*: ſeines Weges, ſeiner Wege ⚲ to run one's course, to go one's way; b) *acc.*: er kann zwei deutſche Meilen in einer Stunde ⚲ he can run (*or* cover) nine English miles (in) an hour; das Pferd läuft einen guten Trab … goes a good trot, … trots well; ⚓ es (unſer Schiff) läuft 12 Knoten die Stunde she makes twelve knots an hour. — **5.** in beſtimmten Verbindungen, meiſt *ell.* (auf) Botſchaft ⚲ to go on an errand, to run errands; ſ. *Bote 1;* Gänge für e-n ⚲ (beſorgen) to run out (*or* on errands) for a p., to do a p.'s errands; ſ. *Gefahr;* Schlittſchuh ⚲ to skate; ⚓ Spießruten ⚲ to run the gauntlet; Sturm ⚲ to (make an) assault, to charge, to storm. — **II** *v/n.* **6.** (fließen, rinnen) to run, to flow, von Kerzen: to gutter; das Blut läuft

durch die (*or* in den) Adern … circulates in the veins; Tränen liefen ihm über die Wangen tears rolled (*or* trickled) down his cheeks; der Wein läuft aus dem Faſſe, *meton.* das Faß läuft the cask leaks. — **7.** *fig.* ein Schauer lief mir über den Rücken I felt a shudder all over me; es läuft mir wie Ameiſen über die Haut I feel a creeping (sensation) all over my skin. — **8.** zeitlich: (vergehen) to pass, elapse, go by; (gültig ſein) to run; die Zinſen ⚲ vom 1. Januar the interest runs (*or* is payable) from the first of January; der Wechſel hat zwei Monate zu ⚲ the bill has two months to run. — **9.** (verlaufen, enden) to end; das läuft auf eins hinaus it comes to the same thing (in the end). — **10.** (ſich erſtrecken) to run, go, extend; in die Höhe ⚲ to run up, to rise; mit et. paralle'l ⚲ to run parallel with (*or* to) a th.; von Gerüchten: (ſich verbreiten) to be current *or* afloat. — **11.** mit „laſſen“: laſſen Sie ihn ⚲: a) let him go *or* F slide; b) (geben Sie ihn auf) don't trouble about him; (ſchicken Sie ihn weg) turn him off, discharge him; (geben Sie ihn frei) let him off; e-n Verhafteten ⚲ laſſen to set free …, to release …; Sprichw. ſ. *Dieb 1;* das Waſſer ⚲ laſſen to let the water run off *or* flow *or* escape; ⚓ ein Schiff vom Stapel ⚲ laſſen to launch …; auf den Strand ⚲ laſſen to beach. — **12.** von Hündinnen: (läufiſch ſein) to be on heat, *hunt.* vom Wilde: to rut. — **III** ~ *n* ⚤ **13.** running, course (ſ. *Lauf*); ins ~ bringen to set going *or* in motion, to give legs to; da ging es an ein ~ then followed a general rush *or* scamper(ing); ich bin des ~s müde I am tired of running (*or* walking) about. — **IV laufend** *p.pr. u. a.* ⚤ **14.** running, z.B. ⚲e Zinſen running interest. — **15.** ⚲e Ausgaben current expenses *pl.*; das ⚲e Jahr the present year; ⚲er Meter metre in length; ⚲e Nummer current number; ⚲e Nummern consecutive numbers *pl.*; ⚲ zum ⚲en Preiſe at the current price; ⚲e Rechnung running (*or* open) account, account-current. — **16.** auf dem ⚲en ſein: a) (Beſcheid wiſſen) to be well posted up, to be quite (fr.) *au fait*; b) ⚤ in den Rechnungsbüchern: to have no arrears, to have one's books in perfect order; e-n (ſich) auf dem ⚲en erhalten to keep a p. (o. s.) well informed *or* posted up.

Läufer (¹⁰) [laufen] *m* ⚤ **1.** von lebenden Weſen (mit *f*): ~, ~**in** *f* ⚤ runner (*a.* von Dienern, Boten ꝛc.); ſie iſt eine gute ~in she runs well, she is a good runner; (Fußgänger[in]) walker, pedestrian; Fußball: half-back, *pl.* halves. — **2.** v. Sachen (ohne *f*): a) Schachſpiel: bishop; b) (Bahnleinwand, ſchmaler Teppich) strip of cloth *or* carpet(ing); (Treppen-)~ stair-carpet; c) ⊕ *mech.* (Schiebering) slider; Schnellwage: = Laufgewicht; *paint.* &c. zum Reiben von Farben: muller, *typ.* brayer; Müllerei: = Läuferſtein. d) *hort.* ~ von Pflanzen: runner, (Ranke) tendril; e) ♪ (Lauf) run, *a.* roulade.

Zeichen (ſ. S. XVII): F familiär; P Volksſprache; ⌐ Gaunerſprache; ⤡ ſelten; † alt (auch geſtorben); * neu (auch geboren); ⁺⁺ unrichtig;

[**Lauferei**] — 645 — [**laut**]

Lauferei (-⌣́ˊ) f ㊻ much running (about); viel ~ von et. haben. oft: F to be kept on the move by a th.; einem unnütze ~en machen, verursachen to send a p. on a great many useless commissions or F on a goose-chase.

Läufer-livree (⌣́ˊ…) f ㊻ runner's (weitS. footman's) livery; =**mühle** ⚔ f vertical mill; =**stein** ⊕ m Müllerei: running stone, runner, upper millstone; =**stoff** m, =**zeug** n cloth (or stuff) for stair-carpets; =**zug** m Schachspiel: move with (or of) the bishop.

Lauf-feuer (⸗…) n ㉒: a) (Feuer von in langer Linie gestreutem Schießpulver) train of powder; fig. die Nachricht verbreitete sich wie ein ~ … like wild fire or with lightning-speed; b) ⚔ (Abfeuern der Gewehre in rascher Reihenfolge) running fire; =**fläche** ❦ f e-r Schiene: upper surface; =**füße** m/pl. orn. feet pl. for running, ⸗ cursorial feet pl.; =**getriebe** ⊕ n, mach. sun-and-planet wheel; =**gewicht** ⊕ n e-r Brückenwage: sliding poise or weight; =**graben** ⚔ m, frt. trench, entrenchment; =**gräben** pl., oft: approaches pl.; =**hund** m, hunt. fast running hound.

läufig (⌣́) **1.** (a. **läufisch**) [laufen 12] a. ㊻ hot, ruttish. — **2.** in Zssgn, zB. bei=, land=, weit=läufig.

Lauf-jagen (⸗…) n ㉒ hunt. coursing, hunting with hounds; =**junge** m = =**bursche**; =**käfer** m, ent.: ⸗ carabid(an), caraboid; =**karren** ⚔ m miner's truck; =**kran** ⊕ m, mach. travelling-crane; =**kugel** f, hunt. small bullet; =**kunde** ⊕ m F chance customer; =**mündung** n. ⚔ f mouth of the cannon, &c.; =**paß** m, iro. dismissal, F sack, P kick-out; e-m den ~ geben to dismiss a p., to turn a p. away or off, F to give a p. the sack; =**rädchen** ⊕ n an Möbeln: caster; =**riemen** ⊕ m, mach. driving-belt, endless strap; =**rolle** f, elect. trolley; =**schicht** ⊕ f, arch. stretching-course; =**schiene** ❦ f flat rail; =**schloß** ⊕ n shutter-latch; =**schreiben** n ⚕ circular letter; =**schritt** m run, ⚔ double-quick (pace or step); =**schütz(e)** m, hunt. huntsman who shoots game whilst running; =**spiel** n racing-sport or =game; =**stuhl** m = =**wagen**. [laufen.]

läuft 2., **läuft** (⌣́)3. Person sg. pres. ind. v.] **Lauft** (⌣́) m Ob. 1. ⸗ hunt. — Lauf 5. — **2.** mst pl. s. Zeitläufte pl.

Lauf-teppich (⸗…) m ㉒ = Läufer 2b; =**treppe** f backstairs pl., private staircase; =**vögel** m/pl. orn. coursers (Cursores); =**wagen** m für Kinder: go-cart, mail-cart; =**werk** n e-r Uhr: movement, works pl.; =**zeit** f: a) zo. (Brunft) rut- (or running-)time; b) ⚕ time which a bill has to run; =**zettel** m: a) ⚕ = =schreiben; b) für Boten: list of errands or commissions; c) ⚒ = =paß.

Laug=… (⸗…) ㉒ = Laugen=…

Lauge (⌣́) [ahd.: lye] f ㊸ lye, ⸗ lixivium; fig. die ~ seines Spottes, Witzes his biting sarcasm, his caustic wit; einem den Kopf mit scharfer ~ waschen to call a p. over the coals, to give a p. a sharp reprimand.

Lauge=… (⸗…) ㉒ = Laugen=…

laugen (⌣́) ⊛ **I** v/a. to soak (or steep) in lye or soda-water, to lixiviate. — **II** v/n. (h.): das Faß laugt … gives a flavour to the wine, &c. — **III** ⸗ n ㉓ chm. u. ⊕ lixiviation; metall. extraction(-work).

laugen-artig (⌣́…) a. ㊻ chm. u. ⊕: lixivial, alkaline; =**asche** f ㊷ alkaline ashes pl.; =**bad** n alkaline bath or liquor; =**blume** ❦ f buck's-horn (Cotula coronopifolia); =**bürste** f, typ. lye-brush; =**bütte** f, =**faß** n: a) lye-vat, leaching-vat, zum Waschen: soda-water tub; b) metall. dissolving-vat.

laugenhaft (⌣́⌣), **laugicht**, **laugig** (⌣́) a ㊻ lixivial (= laugen-artig).

Laugen-salz (⸗…) n ㉒ alkaline salt; =**wasser** n lye, soda-water for soaking.

Lauheit (⌣́=), **Lauigkeit** (⌣́⌣=) f ㊻ (s. lau) lukewarmness (a. fig.), tepidity; fig. auch=. indifference, indifferentism, half-heartedness.

laulich (⌣́⌣) a. ㊻ somewhat lukewarm.

Laune (⌣́) [mhd.; * lt. lū'na Mond(wechsel)] f ㊸ **1.** humour, frame of mind; in guter, schlechter ~ in a good, bad humour or temper; bei lustiger ~ sein to be in a merry mood; ich bin nicht in der ~ zu schreiben I am not (or I do not feel) in the humour (or vein) for writing. — **2.** mst b.s. (Grille) caprice, freak, whim, fancy; sie hat heute ihre ~ she is cross (or ill-tempered) to-day; sobald ihn die ~ anwandelt when (ever) the fit takes him. [p.p. gelaunt, f. ds.]

launen ⸗ (⌣́) v/n. (h.) ⊛, fast nur gbr. im]

launenhaft (⌣́⌣⸗) a. ㊻ (f. Laune 2) capricious, whimsical, full of whims and fancies, fanciful, wayward; (wetterwendisch) changeable, uncertain; **~igkeit** (⌣́⌣⌣⌣=) f ㊻ capriciousness, whimsicality; waywardness.

launig (⌣́⸗) a. ⸗ (stets g.s.; vgl. launisch) humorous, (kurzweilig) entertaining, (komisch) comical, droll, funny; **~keit** f (⌣́⸗=) f ㊻ humorousness; drollness.

launisch (⌣́⸗) a. ⸗ (stets b.s., vgl. launig) **1.** (übler Laune) in a bad humour or temper, ill-humoured, cross. — **2.** = launenhaft.

Laurer (⌣́=) f. Lau(e)rer.

Laurerei (-⌣́ˊ) [lauern] f ㊻ continual watching or waylaying or lying in wait.   [= Steinlorbeer.]

Laurustin(us) ❦ (-⌣́⌣) [it.] m ⊕d. (⊛)]

Laus (⌣́) [ahd.: louse] f ㊸ **1.** zo. (pl. bie Kopf- und Leib-Laus) louse, pl. lice (Pediculus); mit Läusen behaftet lousy. — **2.** P fig. die ~ läuft (ob. kriecht) ihm über die Leber (er ist zornig, mürrisch) he is cross-humoured or out of temper, e-m eine ~ in den Pelz setzen to cause a p. (sore) trouble or vexation.

Laus-bub(e) P derb. (⸗⌣̀=) young scamp, (Lump) ragamuffin.

Lausche (⌣́=) f ㊸ **1.** auf der ~ sein (horchen) to be listening or eavesdropping. — **2.** F (lauschiger Platz) snug (or cosy, quiet) corner.

lauschen (⌣́=) [mhd.: listen] v/n. (h.) ⊛ **1.** auf et. ⸗ (scharf passen) to rivet (or fix) one's (full) attention upon a th.; (horchen) to listen, to be eavesdropping. — **2.** b.s. (lauern) to lie in wait. — **3.** poet. (hervorblicken) to peep forth.

Lauscher (⌣́⌣) m ㉒ **1.** ~, **~in** f ㊵ listener, eavesdropper; Sprichw. der ~ an der Wand hört seine eigne Schand listeners seldom hear good of themselves. — **2.** hunt. ~ pl. (Ohren des Raubwildes 2c.) ears pl.   [catching hares.]

Lausch-garn (⸗…ˋ) n ㉒ hunt. net for]

lauschig (⌣́⸗) a. ㊻ (Lausche 2) snug, cosy, quiet, peaceful, pleasant.

Lausch-platz (⸗…) m ㉒, =**winkel** m snug (or cosy, quiet) corner or nook.

Lause-ding P derb. (⸗…) n ㉒ paltry (or F mucky) thing; =**geld** n trumpery sum, beggarly amount; =**junge** m = =**kerl**; (a. Läuse=) **kamm** m small-tooth comb; =**kerl** m lousy (or filthy, scurvy) fellow or knave, (lumpiger Kerl) tatterdemalion.

Läuse-körner (⸗…) n/pl. ⊛ (Samen des Läuseritterſporns) stavesacre-seeds pl.; =**krankheit** f = (weniger b.s.) **~kraut** ❦ n lousewort (Pedicularis); vgl. =ritterſporn.

lausen P (⌣́⸗) [Laus] v/a. u. sich ⸗ v/refl. ⊛ **1.** e-n (sich) ⸗ to pick a p's (one's) lice, to louse a p. (o.s.). — **2.** fig. e-n (mit Kolben) ⸗ (derb fassen) to give a p. a rough handling or a sound drubbing.

Lause-nest P (⸗⌣́) n ㉒ dirty nest or hole.

Läuse-pulver (⸗…) n ㉒ pharm. powder, ointment used as remedy against lice.

Lauserei (-⌣́ˊ) f ㊻ **1.** (Filzigkeit) meanness. — **2.** (Kleinigkeit) trumpery affair.

Läuse-rittersporn ❦ (⸗…) m ㉒ licebane, stavesacre (Delphinium staphisa'gria); =**salbe** f = =pulver; =**sucht** path. lousy (⸗ pedicular) disease; ⸗ pediculosis, phthiriasis.

Lause-wenzel P derb. (⸗…) m ㉒: a) = **kerl**; b) (schlechter, stinkender Tabak) bad tobacco.

lausig P derb. (⌣́=) a. ㊻ **1.** lousy. — **2.** fig. (erbärmlich) paltry.

lau-sinnig (⸗…ˋ) a. ㊻ indifferent.

Lausitz (⌣́=) [ſlaw.] npr/f. inv. im Südosten Deutschlands: Lusatia; **~er(in** f ㊵) m ㉒, **~er** a. inv., **Lisch** a. ㊻ Lusatian.

laut[1] (⌣́) [ahd.: loud] a. ㊻ (D 1, 6) **1.** (ant. leise) loud, adv. aloud, weniger gbr.: loudly; sehr ⸗ at the top of one's voice; sprechen Sie 2er! speak up!; mit 2er Stimme with (or in) a loud voice, in a loud tone (of voice); ⸗ (adv.) aufschreien to scream aloud, to shout at the top of one's voice; ⸗ denken to think aloud; ⸗ verkünden to proclaim (aloud), to blazon forth. — **2.** (vernehmlich) audible; (klar, bestimmt) clear, distinct; (stark klingend) sonorous, clamorous; (lärmend) noisy, boisterous; 2es Gelächter loud (or F horse-)laugh; s. auflachen; hunt. vom Hunde: ⸗ (it.) to give tongue. — **3.** ♪: ⸗ (it.) forte, sehr ⸗ (it.) fortissimo; phys. intense. — **4.** (öffentlich) public; ich sage es ⸗ I say it before everybody; Stimmen werden ⸗ voices make themselves heard. — **5.** (kundbar) ⸗ werden to become known, to spread abroad; ⸗ m. to make known, to divulge; seine Gefühle ⸗ werden lassen to express (or to give utterance to)…

laut[2] (⌣́) [Laut[3]] prp. (mst mit gen., mit dat. nur bei s/pl. o. art.) in accordance (or conformity) with, in pursuance of, agreeable to; (kraft, vermöge) on the strength (or by virtue) of; ⸗ des

♪ Musik; ⸗ Wissenschaft; ❦ Pflanze; ⚘ Geographie; ⊕ Technik; ⚒ Bergbau; ⚔ Militär; ⚓ Marine; ⚖ Handel; ✉ Post; ⊞ Eisenbahn

[Laut] — 646 — [Lazzaronitum]

Befehls by order; ● ⌁ Bericht (Quittung, Rechnung) as per advice (receipt, account); ⌁ Verfügung as directed, by command.
Laut³ (᷄) [mhd.; *laut¹] m ⓜc. sound, musikalischer: tone, note; keinen ~ von sich geben not to utter a sound, not to breathe; man konnte nicht einen ⌁ hören there was not a sound to be heard, all was hushed (in silence); hunt. (Gebell) ~ geben to give tongue.
Laut=angleichung (᷄᷄·) f ⑫ gr. u. Phonetik: assimilation of sounds.
lautbar (᷄-) a. ⑯ (bekannt) known (to the public), notorious; f. laut¹ 5; es ist ⌁ geworden it has become known, it has got abroad, F it got wind; **~keit** (᷄᷄·) f ⑯ publicity; notoriety.
Laut=bezeichnung (᷄...) f ⑫ gr. u. Phonetik: sound-notation; **=bildung** f notation of sounds.
Laute ♪ (᷄) [mhd.: lute; *ar.] f ㊽ lute (a. fig. als Zeichen des Sängers); die ~ schlagen oder spielen to play the (einmal: on the) lute. [tel. sounder.]
Läut(e)=apparat (᷄(·)᷄᷄·) m ㊷ elect.
Laut=eigenheiten (᷄·᷄᷄·) f/pl. ⑫ phonetic peculiarities pl.
lauten (᷄·) [laut] v/n. (h.) ⑧ 1. to sound (a. gr.), to give forth (or utter) a sound; (laut hallen) to resound; das lautet (klingt) seltsam that sounds strange. — 2. vom Inhalte eines Schriftstücks 2c.: to be expressed or couched, F to run; die Antwort lautet günstig ... is favourable; wie lautet der Brief? what does the letter say?, what is the purport of the l.?; wie lautet das dritte Gebot? what are the words of the third commandment?; das Gesetz lautet so ... is worded (or reads) as follows; sein Urteil lautet dahin, daß // it is his opinion that //; jur. das Urteil lautet auf Tod the sentence is death, it is a death-sentence; wie lauteten seine Worte? what were ...?; ● auf den Inhaber ⌁de (ausgefertigte) Obligation bond (payable) to bearer; auf den Namen ⌁d (payable) to order, not negotiable, not transferable.
läuten (᷄·) [ahd. laut machen] I v/n. (h.), v/a. u. v/impers. ⑨ 1. to ring, to peal; die Glocke (od. es) läutet the bell rings, the (church-)bells are ringing or going (vgl. Glocke 1); die Glocken ⌁ to ring the bells; mit allen Glocken ⌁ to set all (the) bells going; es läutet zur Kirche the bells are ringing for church; es läutet zum zweitenmal the second bells are ringing or out; e-n zu Grabe ⌁ to toll (or ring) the funeral (or passing-)bell at a p.'s burial; fig. f. Glocke 2. — 2. schwach (oder stoßweise) ⌁ to tinkle. — II ~ n ㉓ 3. = Geläut(e) 1 u. 2. — 4. ~ des Totenglöckchens funeral knell, sound (or tolling, passing, ring) of the funeral bell.
Laut(e)ner ♪ (᷄(·)·) ㊷, **Lautenist** (-᷄·) ㊷ m lute-player; a. lut(en)ist.
Lauten=kasten ♪ (᷄...) m ㊷ lute-case; **=macher** ⌁ m lute-maker; **=saite** f lute-string; **=schlagen** n lute-playing; **=schläger(in** f) m = **=spieler(in)**; **=spiel**

n lute-playing; **=spieler(in** f) m lute-player, lutist.
lauter (᷄·) [ahd.] a. I ⑯ (D9) (rein) pure, without admixture, unalloyed, unsullied, Flüssigkeit: clear; (durchsichtig) transparent, Edelstein: flawless; (echt) genuine, (aufrichtig, wahr) candid, true; ⌁es Gold pure (or sterling) gold; das ist die ⌁e Wahrheit that is the real (or plain, unvarnished) truth. — **II** inv. (nichts als; vgl. eitel 2) nothing but; aus ⌁ Bosheit from sheer malice; es sind ⌁ Diebe they are so many thieves; das sind ⌁ Lügen that's nothing but a tissue of lies, it is all a lie; es gibt nicht ⌁ Gelehrte the world is not all made up of scholars; sie ist ⌁ (ganz) Geist she is all mind.
Läuter (᷄·) [läuten] m ⑫ 1. bell-ringer (vgl. Glöckner). — 2. ⊕ elect. ringing-apparatus.
Läuterer (᷄··) [läutern I] m ㉒ 1. purifier, cleanser. — 2. ⊕ refiner.
Läuter=feuer (᷄··) n ㉓ chm., &c. refining fire.
Lauterkeit (᷄·-) f ⑯ (f. lauter I) purity, clearness; transparency; candour, sincerity, truth. [refining.]
Läuter=methode (᷄᷄ ...) f ⑫ method of
läutern (᷄·) [ahd.; *lauter] I v/a. ㉒a. 1. (lauter m.) to purify; (verbessern) to mend; (veredeln) to ennoble, durch Prüfungen: to chasten; (von fremden Stoffen befreien) mst ⊕ to purge, cleanse, depurate, defecate. — 2. Flüssigkeiten: to clarify, durch Destillieren: to rectify; Metalle 2c.: to refine. — II v/a. v. v/n. (h.) 3. jur. eine Partei läutert ein Urteil ... demands the interpretation of a judgment. — III ~ n ㉓ 4. = **Läuterung**.
Läuter=pfanne (᷄᷄ ...) f ⑫ Zuckerfabr.: dissolving-pan; **=trommel** ☒ f washing-cylinder or -drum.
Läuterung (᷄··) f ⑯ (f. läutern I) purification; purging, depuration, defecation; clarification, rectification, refining; ⊕ metall. (Abtreiben) cupellation.
Läuterungs=kessel ⊕ (᷄᷄ ...) m ⑫ clarifier; **=prozeß** m refining-process.
laute=schlagend (᷄᷄ ...) a. ⑯ playing (on) the lute, lute-playing.
Läute=telegraph (᷄᷄ ...) m ⑫ sounder, bell-alarm-telegraph; **=werk** n = **Läut=w**.
Laut=gesetz (᷄·᷄) n ⑫ phonetic law; **⌁getreu** a. corresponding to the sound.
Laut=heit (᷄-) f ⑯ (f. laut¹ 1 u. 2) loudness; distinctness; sonorousness.
lautieren (-᷄·) [dtsch.=lt.; *Laut] I v/a. u. v/n. (h.) ⑬ to spell (and read) phonetically. — II ~ n ㉓ u. **Lautierung** f ⑯, a. **Lautier=methode** f (ant. Buchstabier=m.) phonetic spelling (and reading).
Laut=lehre (᷄·᷄·) f ⑫: ⌁ phonology, phonetics.
lautlich (᷄·) a. ⑯ (und adv.) of (as regards) sound, phonetic(ally).
laut=los (᷄·) a. ⑯ soundless, (still) silent, (stumm) mute, dumb; (bestürzt) F dumbfounded; ⌁lose Stille hushed (or deep) silence; **=losigkeit** f ⑯ (deep) silence; **⌁malend**, **⌁nachahmend**, a. onomatopoetic; **=nachbildung** f imitation of sound, ☒ onomatopœia.
Lautner (᷄·) m f. Lautener.

Laut=physiologie (᷄ ...) f ⑫ physiology of sound; vgl. **=lehre**; **⌁physiologisch** a. relating to the physiology of sound, phonetic(al); **⌁redend** a. vociferating; **=schrift** f phonetic writing; **=sprache** f articulate language; **=system** n phonetic system; **⌁treu** a. = **⌁getreu**; **=verhältnis** n interrelation of sounds; **=verschiebung** f shifting of consonants in Indo-European languages; **Grimmsches Gesetz** der ~ Grimm's law.
Läut=werk (᷄·᷄) n ㉓ electro-magnetic ringing-apparatus.
Laut=zeichen (᷄·᷄·) n ㉓ phonetic sign or symbol, ☒ phonotype.
lau=warm (᷄·᷄) a. ⑯ lukewarm; fig. rel. auch: Laodicean.
Lava (᷄·ᵥ) [mhd., *it.] f ㊽ geol. lava.
lava=ähnlich (᷄·᷄ ...) a. ⑯, **=artig** a. geol. lava-like, ☒ lav(at)ic; **=glas** n ⑫ min. vitreous lava, volcanic glass; **=grus** m volcanic ashes, ☒ lapilli pl.; **=stein** m lava-stone, lavic rock; **=strom** m stream of (red-hot) lava.
Lavendel ♀ (᷄·ᵥ᷄·) [mhd.; it.; *mlt. lavandula] m ⑫ lavender (Lavandula officinalis); gemeiner ~ spike(-lavender) (L. spica); **~blüte** f lavender-blossom; **~geist** m, **~wasser** n lav.-water; **~öl** n essential lav.-oil, oil of spike.
lavieren¹ ↓ (-ᵥ᷄·) [ndl.; *Luv] v/n. (h.), bei Ortsveränderung ⟨n⟩ (einen Seitenwind benutzen) to tack (about), to beat (or put) about, to veer, fig. to shift, to steer a middle course. [to wash.]
lavieren² (-ᵥ᷄·) [fr.] v/a. ⑬ paint., &c.
Lävulose (᷄-ᵥ᷄·) [fr.] v/a. ⑬ [lt. links... (ant. Dextri'n)] f ㊽ chm. fruit-sugar, ☒ levulose ($C_6H_{12}O_6$).
Lawine (-ᵥ᷄·) [schwz.; lt. labi gleiten od. *lau] f ㊽ avalanche; **~sturz** (᷄ ...) m ⑫ fall of an avalanche, snow-slip.
lax (᷄) [lt.] a. ⑯ (locker, schlaff) lax, loose; ⌁e Mora'l, oft: easy morals pl.; ⌁e Sitten licentious manners pl.
Laxheit (᷄-) f ⑯ laxity, laxness, looseness, der Sitten auch: licentiousness.
laxieren (-ᵥ᷄·) [lt.] **I** v/n. (h.) (Abführmittel nehmen) to take an aperient, to loosen (or open) one's bowels; ⌁d laxative, aperient. — **II** v/a. to purge the body with aperients or laxatives. — **III** ~ n ㉓ taking aperients.
Laxier=mittel (-᷄·᷄·) n ㉓ (Abführmittel) purging medicine, laxative.
Lazarett, mst ⚔ (-ᵥ᷄·) [mhd.; it. v. *Lazarus] n ⓜc. (military) hospital or infirmary; ↓ auch: lazaretto; **fliegendes** ~ field-hospital; ambulance.
Lazarett=fieber (-ᵥ᷄ ...) n ⑫ hospital(-) fever; **=gehilfe** m (Sanitätsunteroffizier) orderly at an infirmary; **=krankenwagen** m (field-)ambulance; **=wesen** n hospital- (or ambulance-)service.
Lazarus (᷄᷄··) [lt.; grch.; *hebr. Eleasar] npr/m. ⑯γ. bibl. (Lut. 16, 22) Lazarus (a. fig. Notleidender), fig. (ausfäliger Bettler) lazar.
Lazedämon (-ᵥ᷄·) npr/m. ⑯ α. Alt.: Lacedæmon; **~i=er** (in f ㊼) m ㉒. **Lisch** a. ⑯ Lacedæmonian.
Lazulith ♀ (᷄᷄·) [neu=lt.] m ⓜc. ⑫ min. (Blauspat) lazulite, azure spar.
Lazzarone (-ᵥ᷄·-) [it.; *Lazarus] m ㊸ ⑤⑧ lazzarone; **Lazzaronitum** (-ᵥ᷄·--) n

---

Signs (see page XVII): F familiar; P vulgar; ⌐ flash; ⌁ rare; † obsolete (died); * new word (born); ⌁⌁ incorrect; ♪ music;

[Ldrb.] — 647 — [Lebenselixir]

②d. lazzaronism, leisurely (or lazy) beggar's life. [= Lederrücken.] **Ldrb.** *abbr.* = Lederband; **Ldrr.** *abbr.* **Lea** (´‿) [hebr.] *npr*/*f*. ⓖⓖα.⑨④③. *bibl.* (erste Frau Jakobs) Leah.

Lebe-dame (´‿...)/ⓖ society lady; **-hoch** (´‿–⁀ch) *n* cheers *pl.*, cheering; auf e-n ein ~ ausbringen to give three cheers for a p.; **=lang** (´‿...) *n*: mein (dein ꝛc.) ~ during my (your, &c.) lifetime, all my (your, &c.) life (vgl. lebenslang); **=mann** *m* man of the world or of pleasure, *a.* society man, man about town.

Leben¹ (´‿) [mhd.; *leben² *] *n* ⓓ 1. (*ant.* Tod) life, existence; am ~ sein to be alive or in the land of the living; ihr ~ stand auf dem Spiele their lives were at stake. — 2. mit *prp*. keiner blieb **am** ~ nobody survived or escaped; es ging mir ans ~ my life was in peril or in jeopardy; e-n am ~ strafen to punish a p. with death; ein Kampf **auf** ~ und Tod a life-and-death struggle, a mortal combat; **bei** Leib und ~ (Todesstrafe) under penalty (or on pain) of death; er spielt **für** sein ~ gern he is passionately fond of playing; ich möchte für mein ~ gern reisen I would give anything to travel; ich darf es für mein ~ nicht sagen I dare not for the life of me say it; **im** gemeinen ~ ordinarily; **mit** dem ~ davonkommen to escape with one's life; mit meinem ~ will ich mich dafür verbürgen I will answer for it with my life; mit Leib und ~ with body and soul; e-m **nach** dem ~ trachten to compass a p.'s death, to attempt a p.'s life; **ums** ~ kommen to lose one's life, to perish. — 3. mit *verbs*: sein ~ aushauchen to breathe one's last, to give up the ghost; e-m (sich) das ~ nehmen to take a p.'s (one's) life, to kill a p. (o.s.); e-m das ~ schenken to spare a p.'s life, ⚔ to give quarter to a p.; sein ~ in die Schanze schlagen to fling away (or hazard) one's life, to take one's life in one's hands. — 4. (Lebensweise) manner (or mode) of life; sie führen ein einfaches ~ they lead simple lives or a simple life; (Lebenskraft) biography, life. — 5. (Lebenskraft) vitality, vital power, vigour; (Lebhaftigkeit, Munterkeit) liveliness, cheerfulness, alacrity, animation, F go; es ist kein ~ in ihm there is no life (or spring, F go) in him; neues ~ in eine Sache (F in die Bude) bringen to bring (or infuse) new life into a th.; voller ~, animated, all alive. — 6. (geschäftiges Treiben) movement, stir, animation, bustle; das war ein ~, als er kam there was a commotion (or F to-do) when he came. — 7. (die Wirklichkeit) reality; nach dem ~ zeichnen to sketch (or draw) from (real) life or from nature; et. ins ~ rufen oder setzen to call s.th. into existence, to start a th., ⚓ e-e Gesellschaft ꝛc.: to float, to set on foot; ein Ausdruck des gemeinen ~s an every-day expression. — 8. (lebendes Wesen) living creature or being; manch junges ~ sank dahin many a young life perished, many young

lives were ended. — 9. *zo.*, &c. (die mit dem Gefäßsysteme zsh.hängenden Teile) the (most) vital organs *pl.* of the body. **leben**² (´‿) [ahd.: live] ⓖ **I** *v*/*n*. (h.) 1. to live, to have life, to be alive; to exist; er wird nicht mehr lange ~ his days are numbered, his life is not worth much; (noch) ~ to be (still) alive or in the land of the living; er hat zu ~ he has enough to live upon; davon kann er kaum ~ he can barely exist on that; er hat nichts zu ~ he is destitute; zu ~ wissen (sich fein benehmen) to have good manners, to be well-bred; Sprichw. solange man lebt, so lange man lernt we live and learn; man muß so ~, daß man auch morgen ~ kann (we must) think of the morrow. — 2. (mst *fig.*) flott ~, auf großem Fuße ~, in Saus und Braus ~ to live in (great) style or in luxury; gut (lustig) ~ to lead an easy (a jolly or gay) life; mit ihm ist gut ~ (auskommen) he is a good fellow to live with; kümmerlich ~ (sich ernähren) to lead a precarious existence; Künstler können nicht von der Luft ~ artists cannot live on air; vom Spiele ~ to live by gambling; sie ~ wie Hund und Katze they lead a cat's and dog's life; wie im Himmel ~ to lead a heavenly (or happy) life; zurückgezogen ~ to live in retirement, to lead a retired life. — 3. er lebt (wohnt) in Paris he lives (or resides) ...; wie lange ~ Sie schon in Spanien? how long have you been living ...?; im Auslande ~ to reside (or stay) abroad. — 4. (fortbestehen) s-e Dichtungen werden ewig ~ his poems will live (on) for ever or will never be forgotten; ihr Gedächtnis lebt im Herzen des Volkes her memory is still fresh (or green) in the hearts of the people. — 5. e-n hoch ~ lassen to drink (to) a p.'s health, to cheer a p. (vgl. Lebehoch); ~ und ~ lassen to live and let live; ~ Sie wohl! good bye!, farewell!; es lebe der König! long live the King!; die Damen sollen ~! three cheers for the ladies! — 6. für et. ~, e-r Sache (*dat.*) ~ (sich widmen) to live for a th., to devote o.s. to a th.; *abs.* (das Leben voll genießen) to lead a gay (or jolly) life, *auch*: to live (well); wir ~ der Hoffnung, daß // we live in the hope (or in hopes) that //. — 7. (Leben zeigen, sich regen und bewegen) die Statue lebt ... seems alive or animated; F so et. lebt nicht (noch einmal)! I never!, you don't mean it!; es lebt alles an ihm he is all life; so wahr ich lebe! as sure as I live!, upon my life!; was auf der Erde lebt und webt all that is alive and astir on this earth; *bibl.* in ihm ~ und weben und sind wir in him we live and move and have our being. — 8. (tätig sein) es ist mein Vater wie er leibt und lebt he is the very image (or F the spit) of my father. — **II** *v*/*a*. 9. sein Leben noch einmal ~ to live one's life over again. — **III** *v*/*refl.* mit Angabe der Wirkung: 10. sich satt ~ to get tired of life. — 11. *v*/*impers.* hier lebt es sich gut it is pleasant living here. —

IV Lb *p.pr.* u. *a.* ⓖ 12. als *p.pr.* wild ~de Menschen people leading a savage existence, savages *pl.*; ein hier ~der Freund a friend living here; lange ~d long-lived. — 13. *a.* (lebendig) living, F alive and kicking; keine ~de Seele not a single person, not a living soul; Sprichw. besser ein ~der Hund als ein toter Löwe better a living dog (or ass) than a dead lion. — **V** ~**de**([r] *m*)/14. living *p.*, die einzigen (noch) ~den the only people (still) alive, the only survivors *pl.*; *bibl.* die ~den und die Toten the quick and the dead.

lebendig (-´‿, noch 17. *sae.* ´‿‿) [mhd.] ⓖ **I** *a.* 1. (lebend) living; sie haben zehn ~e Kinder they have ten children living or alive; bei ~em Leibe begraben w. to be buried alive; mehr tot als ~ more dead than alive; ~ machend vivifying; wieder ~ machen to revive, to bring back to life; wieder ~ w. to come to life again. — 2. (von bewegtem Treiben erfüllt) die Gassen sind heute sehr ~ ... are full of life (or bustle) to-day; es wird schon ~ auf der Straße the people are already astir (or begin to move) in the streets. — 3. (von Lebenskraft erfüllt) full of vigour or vitality, F alive and kicking; Ausruf: beim ~en Gotte!, feierlich: by the living God!; *s.* Buchstabe 1. — 4. nur v. Dingen: ~e Blumen natural flowers *pl.*; ~e Hecke quickset hedge; ~e Kohlen live coal(s *pl.*); ⊕ ~e Kraft living force (*a. fig.*). — 5. ⚓ ~es Werk (Schiff unter Wasser) quick work. — **II** ~**e**([r] *m*)/6. = **leben V**

Lebendig-begraben (-´‿...) *n* ⓓ burying a p. alive; **=begraben-werden** *n* being buried alive; **=gebären** *n*, *zo.*: ⚗ viviparousness, viviparity; **=gebärend** *a.* ⓖ: ⚗ viviparous.

Lebendigkeit (-´‿-)/ⓖ 1. being alive and kicking, (Lebenskraft) vitality, vital spark. — 2. = Lebhaftigkeit.

lebendig-machend (-´‿...) *a.* ⓖ vivifying, enlivening; *theol.* ~e Gnade quickening grace; **=machung** *f* ⓖ vivification, quickening; **=werden** *n* ⓓ beginning of (or coming to) life, vivification.

Lebens=abend (´‿...) *m* ⓖ evening (or close, decline) of life; **=abriß** *m* sketch of a p.'s life, biographical notice; **=alter** *n* age, period of l.; **=art** *f* manner (or mode) of l.; feine ~ gentlemanly (or ladylike) manners *pl.*, good breeding; **=aufgabe** *f* task of a p.'s life, l.-task; **=balsam** *m* balm of l., *med.* restorative (drug); **=baum** *m*: a) *poet.* tree of life (*auch bibl.*); b) ♀ (*lt.*) arbor vitæ (*Thuja*); **=bedarf** *m* enough to live on; victuals *pl.*, *vgl.* = **bedürfnisse**; **=bedingung** *f* vital point, essential condition; **=bedürfnisse** *n*/*pl.* necessaries (or wants) *pl.* of life, provisions *pl.*; *vgl.* =**bedarf**; **=beruf** *m* vocation, task in l.; **=beschreibung** *f* life, biography; die ~en des Pluta'rch the lives of Plutarch; **=bild** *n* biographical sketch; **=blut** *n* life-blood; **=blüte** *f* bloom (or prime) of life; **=bühne** *f* stage of l.; **=dauer** *f* duration (or term) of l.; lange ~ longevity; auf ~ for life, to the end of one's life; **=elixir** *n* elixir

---

⚗ scientific; ♀ botanical; ⏚ geography; ⊕ machinery; ⚒ mining; ⚔ military; ⚓ marine; ⓖ commercial; ✉ postal; 🚂 railway.

[Lebensende] — 648 — [Lech]

of life; =ende n end of l.; bis an mein ~ to the end of my days; =erfahrung f practical experience; =erhaltungstrieb m life-preserving instinct; =faden m thread of life; ≗fähig a. capable of living, fit to live; ≗es Unternehmen prosperous (or promising) enterprise; =fähigkeit f vitality; =fahrt f life's pilgrimage; =feuer n (ardent) energy, vital power (s pl.); =flamme f vital flame or spark; =frage f vital question, question of life or death; =freude f enjoyment (or pleasures pl.) of life; =freudigkeit f pleasure of living; vgl. =mut; ≗frisch a. in the freshness of youth, youthful; =frische f freshness of l.; ≗froh a. enjoying (stärker: in the full enjoyment of) life, joyful, joyous; =frühe f dawn (or early part) of life, youth; =frühling m spring (or vernal period) of l.; =führung f conduct in l.; =fülle f fulness (or plenitude) of l.; =funke m =flamme; =gang m: a) process (or evolution) of l.; b) (life-)career; =gefahr f danger to a p.'s life; mit ~ at the peril (or risk) of one's l.; ≗gefährlich a. endangering life, perilous; v. einer Krankheit 2c.: very grave or serious; =gefährte m, =gefährtin f l.-companion; (Gatte, Gattin) partner for life; =geist m: a) meist pl. ~er animal spirits pl.; b) bfd. chm.: (stärkende Esse'nz) elixir (or balm) of life; =genuß m enjoyment of life; =gewohnheiten f pl. habits of l.; von Menschen a. lifelong habits pl.; =glück n happiness of one's life; =göttin f goddess of fate; ~nen pl., a. Destinies; ≗groß a. (as) large as life; ≗es Bild life-size(d) portrait; =größe f l.-size, real size; Bild in. ~ full-length picture; =güter n/pl. earthly possessions pl.; =haltung f standard of life; =hauch m breath of life; bis zum letzten ~ e to one's last (or parting-) breath; =jahr n year of one's life; im 50. 2c. (od. in f-m, meinem 2c. 50.) ~ in one's (his, my, &c.) fiftieth year, at the age of fifty; =klugheit f worldly wisdom, shrewdness; =kraft f vital strength or energy; vgl. Leben¹ 5; ≗kräftig a. full of vital energy, vigorous; =lage f position of life; in jeder ~ at every emergency; ≗lang a. lasting a lifetime; adv. auf ≗ for life; ≗länglich a. lifelong, von Ämtern a. held during life; ≗e Zwangsarbeit penal servitude for life; ≗e Rente annuity for life, life-annuity; =lauf m, =laufbahn f (earthly) career; =lehre f biology; =licht n, poet. (burning) lamp of life; vgl. =flamme; e-m das ~ ausblasen to take a p.'s l., F to put a p.'s light out; =linie f Handwahrsagerei: line of life; =luft f life-sustaining (or vital) air; (Sauerstoff) oxygen (gas); =lust f attachment to(or love of) life; weit S. merriment; vgl. =freude; ≗lustig a. attached to (or fond of) life; gay, jovial, merry; =magneti'smus m, physiol. animal magnetism; =mark n vital marrow, essence of life; =mittel n nourishing substance, sustenance; ~ pl. (articles of) food, provisions, victuals pl., grub;

mit ~n versehen F to provision, to victual; =mittel=händler m provision-dealer; =morgen m = =frühe; ≗müde a. weary (or tired) of life; =mut m courage to face (or endure) life; ≗mutig a. = ≗froh; =odem m breath of life; =ordnung f rules pl. of life; (Gesundheitspflege) regimen, diet; =pfad m path of life; =philosophie f = =weisheit; =prinzi'p n, =proze'ß m vital principle, process; =quelle f source of life; =rad n, opt. Tiere 2c. in Bewegung zeigend: ≗ zoetrope; =regel f rule of life or of conduct; =reise f journey through life; =reiz m charm of life; =rente f l.-annuity; =retter m person who saves life or lives; =rettungs-apparat m l.-saving apparatus, l.-preserver; ≗satt a. = =müde; =stellung f position in l., social status; =strafe f capital punishment; =stufe f stage (or period) of l.; =trieb m vital instinct; =überdruß m satiety of l., (lt.) tædium vitæ; ≗überdrüssig a. sick (or tired) of life; =umstände m/pl. circumstances pl. in l.; =unterhalt m (means f. of) subsistence, livelihood; sich f-n ~ verdienen to earn one's living; =verrichtungen f/pl. vital functions pl.; =versicherung f life-insurance or -assurance; =versicherungs=gesellschaft f life-insurance company; Bureau, Police derselben: life-(insurance) office, life-policy; ≗voll a. full of life or vigour; ≗wahr a. true to life; =wandel m life, (Aufführung) (moral) conduct; =wärme f vital warmth; =wasser n: a) water of life; b) (Branntwein) spirits pl., (lt.) aqua vitæ; =weg m course of l.; =weise f: a) mode of life; b) (Gewohnheiten) habits pl. of life; =weisheit f practical wisdom or philosophy; =wende f turn of l.; ≗wert a. worth living for; =zeichen n sign of l.; kein ~ von sich geben not to stir, (nicht schreiben) to remain silent, not to write; =zeit f lifetime, term of a p.'s (natural) life; auf ~ for life (a. v. Renten), von Ämtern: during life or good behaviour; Lebensversicherung: auf ~ zweier Personen versichern to insure two joint lives; =ziel n goal (or end, aim) of life; =zweck m object of life.
Leber (L~) [ahd.: liver] f ⓰ liver; die Leber betreffend: ≗ hepatic; frei (frisch od. dreist) von der ~ weg reden to speak one's mind, to speak out bluntly or boldly; f. Laus 2.
Leber-anschoppung (~...) f ⓰ path. enlargement of the liver; =balsam ≗ m liver-balsam (Eri'nus alpi'nus); =beschwerde f liver-complaint; =blümchen n liverleaf, hepatica (Hepa'tica no'bilis); =egel m, zo. liver-fluke (Di'stoma hepa'ticum); =entzündung f inflammation of the liver, ≗ hepatitis; ≗farben, ≗farbig a. liver-coloured; =fleck (en pl.) m liver-spot(s pl.), weit S. (Sommersprossen) freckles pl.; =fies m, min. liver-pyrites; ≗krank a. with a diseased liver; =krankheit f liver-complaint, disease of the liver, hepatic disease; =kraut ≗ n liverwort (Marcha'ntia polymo'rpha); =lappen m, anat. lobe of the liver; ≗leidend a. suffering from the liver;

=moose n pl. ≗ (Gattung der Zellensporenpflanzen) liverworts pl. (Hepa'ticæ); =moos-kunde f: ≗ hepaticology; =pilz ≗ m liver-agaric (Fistuli'na hepa'tica); =reim m impromptu doggerel rhyme (in honour of a pike's liver); =rinne f, anat. liver-groove; =stein m, min. liverstone, hepatite; =tran m pharm. &c. cod-liver oil; =wurst f Schlächterei: (German) white (liver-)sausage.
Lebe-welt (⁻~...) f ⓰: die ~ people pl. of the world, society people pl., the world of pleasure; =wesen n living (or animate) being, (living) creature; (mikroskopisches Tierchen): ≗ animalcule; =wohl (L⁻⁻) n ⓴d. ⓰ (a. inv.) farewell; e-m ~ sagen to say good-bye to a p., to bid a p. good-bye or farewell.
lebhaft (L⁻) a. ⓰ 1. lively, vivacious, (voll Lebens) full of life; (feurig) full of fire; ardent, (belebt) animated, brisk, (munter) cheerful, sprightly; v. Bewegungen: quick, impulsive; v. Farben: bright, gay, vivid; v. Schmerzen: acute, smart. — 2. ≗e Erinnerung vivid recollection; ≗e Gesichtsfarbe ruddy complexion; ≗e Straße busy (or much frequented) street; ≗er Wortstreit heated discussion; ≗ w. to become animated or excited or heated; ≗ (adv.) bedauern to regret deeply or keenly; ich kann mir ≗ vorstellen, daß // I can easily (or readily) imagine that //. — 3. ⓰ es war ≗e Nachfrage nach Kaffee there was a strong (or brisk) demand (or inquiry) for coffee, coffee was in great demand.
Lebhaftigkeit (L⁻⁻⁻) f ⓴⓰ 1. o. pl. (f. lebhaft) liveliness, vivacity, fire, animation, briskness, cheerfulness, sprightliness. — 2. mit pl.: (lebhafte Äußerung) lively expression.
...lebig (...⁻L⁻) [leben] a. ⓰ in Zssgn; zB. kurz≗ short-lived.
Leb-kuchen (⁻...) [lt. lib-um] m ⓰ gingerbread; =küchler m gingerbread-baker.
leb-los (⁻...) a. ⓰ lifeless, inanimate, ≗ a. dull, inactive, quiet, flat; =losigkeit f lifelessness, (Empfindungslosigkeit) impassiveness, stärker: coldness, ≗ dulness, stagnation; =tag m (mst pl.) mein(e) ~(e) all (the days of) my life; das habe ich mein ~ nicht gesehen I have never seen anything like that (before); =zeit (⁻⁻·⁻) f (mst pl.) ⓰: bei meinen ~en in my lifetime, as long as I live; bei(zu) ~en meines Vaters during (or in) my father's (life)time; bei ~en schenken to give (away) in one's lifetime.
Lech ↗ (⁻) m (n) ⓭c., mst pl. die ~e (Kupferstein) copper-matte, matte of copper.
lechzen (⁻⁻) [mhd.; *†lech leck] v/n. (h.) ⓰ 1. (start dürsten) to be parched (or dying) with thirst; ≗ to languish from want of water. — 2. fig. nach et. ≗ (heiß verlangen) to have an eager longing (or desire) for, to hanker after, to pant for a th.; nach Blut ≗ to thirst for blood.
leck¹ (⁻) [nbd.: lech(zen)] a. ⓰ leaking, leaky; das Faß 2c. ist ≗ ... leaks, lets in water.
Leck² (⁻) [nbd.: leak] m u. n ⓰c. leakage; outlet for water, &c.; ≗ ein(en) bekommen, stopfen to spring (to stop) a leak.

Zeichen (f. S. XVII): F familiär; P Volkssprache; ℐ Gaunersprache; ↗ selten; † alt (auch gestorben); * neu (auch geboren); ⁺⁺ unrichtig;

[Leckage] — 649 — [Leerheit]

Leckage ⚙ (‿ᴗ‿) [dtsch.-fr.] *f* ⊕ (ausgelaufene Flüssigkeit) leakage, drippings *pl.*
lecken¹ (‿ᴗ) [leck¹] **I** *v/n.* ⊕ **1.** (h.) (undicht sein) to leak, to have a leakage or leak, to let out water, to run. — **2.** (in) (tropfen, rinnen) to leak (or run, ooze) out; (herauströpfeln) to drip (or trickle) out. — **II** ~ *n* ⊕ **3.** leakage.
lecken² (‿ᴗ) [ahd.: lick: lt. *lin'g-ere*] *v/a.* und *v/n.* (h.) und **sich** ⚙ *v/refl.* und *v/recip.* ⊕ **1.** (sich) ⚙ to lick (o.s.); (auf ⚙) to lap up; von der Flamme: **am Dache** ⚙ (emporspringen) to leap up to the roof; **lode Flammen** lambent flames, fiery tongues *pl.* — **2.** mit Angabe der Wirkung: **den Teller rein** ⚙ to lick one's plate clean; **die Katze leckt sich den Pelz sauber ...** cleans(es) itself (or herself) with its (or her) tongue. — **3.** *fig.* **sich** (*dat.*) **die Finger, den Mund nach et.** ⚙ to be greedy (or to hanker) after a th.; **j-s Speichel** ⚙ (j-m untertänig schmeicheln) to cringe (and crawl) before a p., *bibl. u. fig.* to lick the dust before a p.('s feet); **F vorne** ⚙ **und hinten kratzen** to smile to one's face and to stab one in the back, to be double-faced, *vgl.* Katze 3. — **4.** (mit Sorgfalt ausarbeiten) to finish with special care, to do neatly or exquisitely; **das ist wie geleckt** it's as clean as a whistle, (sorgfältig gemacht) it is most neatly finished; **er sieht aus wie geleckt** he looks as smart as a new pin or as if he came out of a bandbox. — **5.** e-n ⚙ (viel küssen) to cover a p. with kisses, F to slobber over a p.
lecken³, *fast* † (‿ᴗ) [mhd.: leg; *vgl.* frohlocken] *v/n.* (h.) ⊕ *bibl.* to skip (about); noch gbr. in: **wider den Stachel** ⚙ to kick against the pricks, *weitS.* to rebel.
Lecker¹ (‿ᴗ) [lecken²] *m* ⊕ **1.** (auch **~in** *f* ⊕): a) one who licks the plates, &c., licker; b) (Schmarotzer, leckere Person) = Speichel-, Teller-⚙; c) (Leckermaul) dainty person. — **2.** als Schimpfwort: (junger Laffe) young fop, milksop, greenhorn. — **3.** F (der viel küßt) slobberer. — **4.** *bsd. hunt.* (Zunge) tongue.
lecker² (‿ᴗ) *a.* ⊕ (D 9) **1.** von Speisen: dainty, delicate, nice (to eat); (köstlich) delicious, luscious; (gaumenreizend) appetizing, relishing, savoury. — **2.** von Personen: (wählerisch im Essen und Trinken) dainty, finical; (schwer zu befriedigen) fastidious, particular.
Lecker-bissen (‿ᴗ‿ᴗ) *m* ⊕ dainty (or delicate) morsel, tit-bit, delicacy, (*fr.*) *bonne-bouche.*
Leckerei (‿ᴗ‿ᴗ¹¹) *f* ⊕ **1.** (Leckerhaftigkeit) daintiness. — **2.** = Leckerbissen. — **3.** (f. lecken² 5) kissing, F slobbering.
Lecker-essen (‿ᴗ‿...) *n* ⊕, **-gericht** *n* dainty (or savoury) food or dish.
leckerhaft (‿ᴗ‿ᴗ) *a.* ⊕ dainty, fastidious; **~igkeit** (‿ᴗ‿ᴗ‿) *f* ⊕ daintiness, fastidiousness.
Lecker-maul (‿ᴗ‿...) *n* ⊕, *dim.* **-mäulchen** *n* dainty (or fastidious, finical) person or feeder, p. fond of delicate food.
leckern (‿ᴗ) [lecken²] *v/n.* (h.) ⊕ *a.:* **nach et.** ⚙ to long for (F to be sweet on) a th.
Leck²**-faß** (‿ᴗ‿ᴗ) *n* ⊕ tub for catching up the drippings of a cask.

Leder (ᴸ‿) [ahd.: leather] *n* ⊕ **1.** (Fell) leather, weiches für Handschuhe 2c. auch: (soft) skin; **lohgares, weißgares ~** tanned, tawed leather or hide; **gemachtes ~** imitation leather; (*f.* Gemsleder u. gerben 1); **zäh wie ~** (as tough as leather; *Sprichw.* aus fremdem **~ ist gut Riemen schneiden** it is easy enough to manage with other people's money. — **2.** Weberei: englisches **~** (satiniertes Baumwollstoff) sateen. — **3.** (Degenscheide) sheath of a sword; **vom ~ ziehen** to draw one's (or the) sword. — **4.** F (die menschliche Haut) **e-m das ~ gerben** to thrash a p., F to curry a p.'s hide.
Leder-abfälle (‿ᴗ‿...) *m/pl.* ⊕ leather waste, leather shavings *pl.*; **-apfel** ⚙ *m* (Goldrenette) l.-coat; **-arbeit(er** *m*) *f* work(er) in leather; **⚙artig** *a.* ⊕ leathery, (as) tough as leather, ⚙ coriaceous; **-band:** a) *m* Buchbinderei: binding in calf, calf (or leather) binding; b) *n* (Riemen) strap; **-baum** ⚙ *m* currier's sumac (*Coria'ria myrtifo'lia*); **-bereiter** *m* leather-dresser, currier; **-bereitung** *f* l.-dressing, curriery; **-beutel** *m* l.-bag; **-blume** ⚙ *f* leather-flower (*Cle'matis vio'rna*); **⚙braun** *a.* tan-coloured, tawny, buff; **-drucker** *m* printer on leather; **-farbe** *f* l.-colour, buff; **⚙farbig** *a.* l.-coloured, buff; **⚙gelb** *a.* buff; **-handel** *m* l.-trade; **-händler** *m* l.-merchant, dealer in l.; **-handschuh** *m* leather-glove; **-haut** *f, anat.:* ⚙ corium, cutis (vera); **des Embryos:** ⚙ chorion; **-hosen** *f/pl.* leather breeches *pl.*; **-koller** *m* leather trunk; **-koller** ⚙ *n* buff-coat; **-leinwand** *f* dowlas(s).
ledern (‿ᴗ) [ahd.] **I** *a.* ⊕ **1.** (of) leather, ⚙ coriaceous; (fest, zäh) leathern, tough. — **2.** [mhd.] *fig.* (philisterhaft) philistine; (langweilig) dull, tedious, humdrum; **ein ⚙er Kerl** F a (dry) stick, a bore. — **II** *v/a.* ⊕ *a.* **3.** = gerben. — **4.** (be⚙) to cover with (or case in) leather.
Leder-narbe ⚙ (‿ᴗ‿...) *f* ⊕ leather-grain; **-pappe** *f* l.-board; **-punze** *f* l.-punch; **-riemen** *m* leather strap; für Rasiermesser 2c.: strop; **-rücken** *m* Buchbind.: leather back; **-schmiere** *f* l.-polish; **-stiefel** *m* (*pl.*) leather boot(s *pl.*); **-streifen** *m* l. thong; **-strumpf** F *npr/m.* in Coopers Indianergeschichten: Leather-stocking; **-stück** *n* piece of l.; **-tapete** ⊕ *f* leather tapestry; **-tuch** *n* (künstliches, vegetabilisches Leder) leather- (or American) cloth; **-überzug** *m* leather covering or case; **-waren** *f/pl.* l. goods or articles *pl.*; **⚙weich** *a.* (as) soft as leather; **-werk** *n* l.-work; l. goods *pl.*; **-zeug** ⚔ *n* l. straps and belts, leathers *pl.*; **-zucker** *m, pharm.* weißer: marsh-mallow paste; schwarzer: liquorice jujubes *pl.*; **-zurichter** ⊕ *m* leather-dresser, currier.
ledig (ᴸ‿) [mhd.] *a.* ⊕ **1.** (entbunden) e-r Sache (*gen.*) oder von et. ⚙ sein to be free (or exempt) from a th. — **2.** e-n los und ⚙ (frei) lassen to let a p. go free, to release a p.; sich von et. los und ⚙ machen to free o.s. from a th., to get rid of a th.; los und ⚙ sein to be absolutely free, to have no ties;

e-n los und ledig sprechen to absolve a p. (entirely). — **3.** (unverheiratet) unmarried, single; ⚙ **bleiben** a) von Mädchen: to remain a spinster, F to be left on the shelf; b) von Männern: to remain a bachelor; ⚙ sein to be single, F co. to live in single blessedness; **Ler Stand** single state, *bsd.* von Männern: celibacy. — **4.** (unbesetzt, leer) unoccupied, empty, von Ämtern 2c.: vacant; **Le Stelle**, auch: vacancy. — **5.** *mst adv.* (rein) purely (and simply), exclusively, solely; **es ist ⚙ (sich)** (ᴸ‿‿) **seine Schuld** it is purely (or solely) his own fault or doing. [free or vacant.]
Ledig-werden (‿ᴗ‿...) *n* ⊕ becoming)
Lee ⚓ (ᴸ) [nbd.: lee Schutz] *f* ⊕ (vom Winde abgekehrte Schiffsseite, *ant.* Luv) lee(-side); **in ~ fallen** to come by the lee, to make leeway; **nach ~ treiben** to drift (or sag) leeward; **~bord** (ᴸ‿...) *m* ⊕ lee-side; **~brassen** *f/pl.* lee-braces *pl.*; **~küste** *f* lee-shore.
leer (ᴸ) [ahd.] **I** *a.* ⊕ **1.** (*ant.* voll) empty; (unbesetzt) unoccupied, vacant, vacated, (geräumt) evacuated; (unbeschrieben) blank, clean; (bedeutungslos) void, (eitel) vain, (unbegründet) unfounded; ⚙ **ausgeh(e)n** to go away empty, to be left out in the cold, *vgl.* ausgehen 2; ⚙ w. to (become) empty or vacant — **2.** **Le Ausflucht, Ausrede** lame excuse; **mit Len Händen** empty-handed; *thea.* **vor e-m Len Hause spielen** to play to an empty house or before a thin audience; **mit Lem Magen** on an empty stomach; **das Nest ist** ⚙, *oft:* the birds are flown; *f.* dreschen 1; **Ler Schein** mere pretence, F empty show; **Le Stelle** vacant situation; **Ler Vorwand** idle (or hollow) pretext; **man sah nichts als die Len Wände** there was nothing but the bare walls; **haben Sie noch ein Zimmer** ⚙? have you any room vacant or to let?; *Sprichw.* **Le Gefäße tönen am meisten** empty vessels give the loudest sound. — **II ~ n** ⊕ *c.* **3.** ⊕ = Lehre 5. — **III** das **~e** ⊕ **4.** vacant (or blank) space, blank, *bsd. phys.* vacuum, *fig.* void.
Leer-darm (ᴸ‿) *m* ⊕ *anat.:* ⚙ jejunum.
Leere (ᴸ‿) *f*; *Hom.* Lehre) *f* ⊕ **1.** (Leerheit) (f. leer) emptiness; vacantness, vacuity; blankness; voidness, void, ⚙ vacuum; eines Vorwandes 2c.: idleness, hollowness. — **2.** ⊕ = Lehre 5.
leeren (ᴸ‿) *v/a.* u. **sich** ⚙ *v/refl.* ⊕ (sich) ⚙ to empty (o.s.); *vgl.* ausleeren 1; (räumen) to vacate, to evacuate; e-n Brunnen ⚙ to pump a well dry; eine Flasche ⚙ to empty (stärker: to drain off, F to finish off) ...; die Schüsseln ⚙ to clear the dishes; der Saal leerte sich in zwei Minuten the hall emptied (or was cleared) ... — **II ~ n** ⊕ emptying, &c. (f. I); evacuation of a country; clearance of a letter-box, &c.
Leer-faß ⊕ (ᴸ‿...) *n* ⊕ emptying-vat; **-gerüst** *n* = Lehrgerüst; **-gesperre** *n*, *arch.* empty truss; **-gut** *n* = Justage.
Leerheit (ᴸ‿) *f* ⊕ **1.** o. *pl.* = Leere 1. — **2.** mit *pl.* (Inhaltloses) s.th. trivial, triviality, geistige: inanity.

♪ Musik; ⚛ Wissenschaft; ☘ Pflanze; ♀ Geographie; ⊕ Technik; ⚒ Bergbau; ⚔ Militär; ⚓ Marine; ⚙ Handel; ✉ Post; 🚂 Eisenbahn.

[Leerholz] — 650 — [Legitimationskarte]

Leer=holz ⊕ (⸗...) n ⓶ = Lehrholz; **=machen** n = leeren II; **=scheibe** ⊕ f groove-disk; **=sein** n: a) empty (or vacant) state; b) (Leere) emptiness, blankness; **=steh(e)n** n (Unbewohntsein) e-r Wohnung: unoccupied (or untenanted) state; **°stehend** a. von Betten, Zimmern: empty, vacant, unoccupied.
Leerung (⸗⸌) f ⓯ = leeren II.
Lee=segel (⸌⸗...) n⓶ studding-sail; **=segelfall** n studding-sail halyard; **=seite** f lee-side; **°wärts** adv. leeward; ⸗ dwars ab on the lee-beam.
Lefze obb. (⸗⸌) [ahd. = nhd. Lippe] f ⓯ poet., anat. und ⊕ lip.
legal (⸗⸌) [lt.] a. ⓰ (gesetzmäßig) legal, lawful; valid in (or before) the law.
legalisier/en (⸗⸗⸌⸌) [lt.] I v/a. ⓰ to legalize, to make legal, to render valid. — II ~ n ⓶, **L̲ung** f ⓯ legalization.
Legalität (⸗⸗⸗⸌) [lt.] f ⓯ (Gesetzmäßigkeit) legality; **legaliter** (⸗⸌⸗⸗) adv. legally.
Legat (⸗⸌) [lt.] I m⓶ (röm. Alt.: Gesandter, ⚔ Unterfeldherr; jetzt: päpstlicher Gesandter, legate. — II n ⓶c. jur. legacy.
Legatar (⸗⸗⸌) [lt.] m ⓭d., **=in** f ⓮ jur. (Vermächtnisnehmer[in]) legatee.
Legation (⸗⸗tẜ(v)⸌) [lt.] f ⓯ (Gesandtschaft) legation, embassy; **~s=rat** (⸌...) m ⓶, **=sekretär** m councillor, secretary to (or of) a legation.
Lege=bohrer (⸌⸗v...) m/pl. ⓶ ent.: ⚐ terebrate pl.; **=büchse** f spring-gun; **=geld** n (Eintrittsgeld) entrance-fee into a society, &c.; **=henne** f laying hen or fowl, (good) layer.
legen [ahd.: lay: liegen] I v/a. und sich ⸗ v/refl. ⓰ 1. (sich) ⸗ to lay (o.s.), weitS. to put (o.s.), to place (o.s.); (hinstrecken) to lay flat down; sich (nieder)⸗, auch ⸗ to lie (flat) down; sich schlafen ⸗ to lie down to sleep, to go to bed; ↧ das Land ist gelegt (unter den Horizont gesunken) the land is laid. — 2. mit Objekt: Eier ⸗ to lay eggs; frisch gelegte Eier new-laid eggs pl.; einen Fußboden, ein Pflaster ⸗ to lay down a floor, a pavement; Geld (in die Kasse) ⸗ to put by..., to deposit...; den Grund(stein) zu et. ⸗ to lay the foundation(-stone) of a th.; e-m die Karten ⸗ to tell a p.'s fortune from (the) cards; (e-n) Rasen ⸗ to put down turf or a lawn; e-n Teppich ⸗ to lay (or put) down a carpet. — 3. agr. Bohnen, Erbsen ⸗ (säen) to sow beans, peas; Senkreiser ⸗ to put layers into the ground. — 4. agr. vom Getreide: sich ⸗ to be beaten (or weighed) down. — 5. mit prp. u. adv.: ad acta ⸗ to put on the shelf; vgl. Akte; an= ea. ⸗ to join (together), to put side by side; et. ans Feuer ⸗ to put a th. to (or near) the fire; (die) Hand an e-n ⸗ to lay hands upon a p.; f. Hand 2; die letzte nachbessernde Hand an et. ⸗ to put the (last) finishing touches (or strokes) to a th.; f. Herz 1 und 2, Kette¹ 1; et. wieder an seinen Platz ⸗ to put a th. back to its (old) place; den Kopf an j-s Schultern ⸗ to rest one's head against a p.'s shoulders; an den Tag ⸗ to show, to evince; an die unrechte Stelle ⸗ to mislay; ↧ sich

Seite an Seite mit e-m andern Schiffe ⸗ to lie alongside another ship; **auf**=ea. ⸗ to lay one on (the top of) the other, to superpose, in Haufen: to pile up; et. auf den Tisch ⸗ to lay (or put, place) a th. on the table; sich aufs Bett ⸗ to lie down on the bed; fig. sich auf die Bärenhaut, auf die faule Seite, aufs Ohr, auf den Rücken ⸗ to take one's ease, to lead an idle life; sich aufs Bitten ⸗ to have recourse to (earnest) entreaty; der Qualm legte sich mir auf die Brust ... settled on my chest; sich auf et. ⸗ to apply (or devote) o.s. to a th.; sich auf die liederliche Seite ⸗ to (begin to) lead a fast life; f. Gewicht am Ende; eine Steuer auf et. ⸗ to put a tax (or duty) on a th.; den Ton, Nachdruck auf et. ⸗ to lay a (great) stress on a th.; großen Wert auf et. ⸗ to attach great importance (or value) to a th.; f. Kante 1 gegen Ende; seine Worte auf die Wagschale ⸗ to weigh every word; Geld auf Zinsen ⸗ to put out money at interest; e-m Worte auf die Zunge ⸗ to put words in(to) a p.'s mouth; ↧ ein Schiff auf die Reede ⸗ (ob. fahren) to put out ... on the road; ein Schiff auf die Seite ⸗ to heel ...; das Schiff legt sich auf die Seite ... heels over, .. lists; etwas **aus** der Hand ⸗ to lay a th. aside or down; et. (Gefaltetes) aus=ea. ⸗ to unfold (or spread out) a th.; **beiseite** ⸗ to lay aside, to put (or lay) by, (aufspeichern) to store up; (verwerfen) to discard; die Sachen **durch** = ea. ⸗ to put things higgledy-piggledy, to jumble (or mix) up things; etwas **hinter** sich ⸗ (sparen) to put s.th. by (for a rainy day); **in** Asche ⸗ to reduce to ashes; Geld in die Bank ⸗ to put ... into the bank; sich ins Bett ⸗ to lie down in bed; in Falten ⸗ to gather up; in Fesseln, Ketten ⸗ to put into irons, chains; f. Geschirr 3; ins Mittel ⸗ to intervene, to step in; e-m Worte in den Mund ⸗ to put words in(to) a p.'s mouth, to attribute words to a p.; f. Hand 2; e-m Hindernisse in den Weg ⸗ to put obstacles in a p.'s way; ⚔ Bresche in et. ⸗ to make a breach in s.th.; e-m Einquartierung, Soldaten ins Haus ⸗ to quarter (or billet) soldiers on a p.; in Kasernen ⸗ to put into barracks; Besatzung in eine Stadt ⸗ to garrison a town; **nach** der Reihe ⸗ to arrange in (proper) order; eine Decke **über** den Tisch ⸗ to spread a cloth over the table; über=ea. ⸗ to put atop of each other, to superpose on one another; den Mantel **um** die Schulter ⸗ to wrap (or draw) the cloak round one's shoulder; et. um et. (herum) ⸗ to surround a th. with s.th.; **unter** Schloß und Riegel ⸗ to put under lock and key; **unter** Siegel ⸗ to seal (up); et. **von** sich ⸗ to lay aside a th., et. das man an sich trägt: to take off a th.; e-m den Kopf **vor** die Füße ⸗ to cut a p.'s head off; ein Schloß **vor** die Tür ⸗ to put a padlock to the door; ⚔ sich **vor** eine Stadt ⸗ to beleaguer (or invest)

a town; ↧ sich **vor** Anker ⸗ to cast (or drop) anchor; **zu**=ea. ⸗ to join to, unite; sich **zu** Bette ⸗ to go to bed, auf längere Zeit: to take to one's bed; f. Grund 6, Last 2; zum übrigen ⸗ to add to the rest; sich (da)**zwischen** ⸗ to intervene, to interfere (between persons). — 6. sich ⸗ (zur Ruhe kommen) vom Winde ꝛc.: to calm (or go, settle) down, to abate, to subside, (langsamer w.) to slacken (down); (aufhören) to cease. — 7. e-m et. ⸗ (unmöglich m.) to stop (or prevent) a p. from doing a th.; f. Handwerk 1. — 8. mit Angabe des Erfolges: et. bereit, fertig ⸗ to keep (or hold) a th. in readiness; f. bloß; ↧ sich fest ⸗ to moor, to berth; hoch, höher ⸗ to raise; lahm (oder matt) ⸗ to paralyse; e-m et. nahe ⸗: a) (so daß er leicht darauf verfällt) to suggest a th. to a p.; b) (ans Herz ⸗) to lay a th. to a p.'s heart, to urge a th. on a p.; schief ⸗ to put crossways, to lay askew; sich schlafen ⸗ to lie down to sleep; trocken ⸗ to dry up, to drain; zurecht ⸗ to arrange. — II ~ n ⓶ 9. laying, &c. (f. I); ~ von Karten zum Wahrsagen fortune-telling.
legendär(isch) (⸗v⸌(v)) a. ⓰ legendary.
Legende (⸗⸌v) [mhd.: *mlt. legēnda] f ⓯ (Heiligen⸗) legend; **~n=buch** (⸌v⸗v tẜ) n ⓶ book of legends, legendary.
legendenhaft (⸗⸌vv⸗) a. ⓰ legendary.
Legenden=sammlung (⸗⸌v...) f ⓯ collection of legends; **=schreiber** m author (or writer) of legends, legendary.
Lege=röhre (⸌v...) f ⓯ ent.: ⚐ ovipositor.
Leger=wall ↧ (⸌⸗⸌) m ⓶ (windfreie Küste) lee-shore.
Lege=zeit (⸌v=⸌) f ⓯ der Vögel: laying-time or -season or -period. [floor.]
Legge (⸌v) f ⓯ (Bleicherei) bleaching-
Leg=henne (⸌⸗⸌v) f ⓯ = Legehenne.
legieren¹ (⸗⸌⸗) [lt.] v/a. ⓰ jur. (hinterlassen, vermachen) to leave (as a legacy), to bequeath, to make over (in one's will).
legieren² ⊕ (⸗⸌⸗) [lt.] I v/a. ⓰ 1. chm., metall. (edlere Metalle mit geringeren versetzen) to alloy. — 2. Kocht.: (verdicken) to thicken gravy with flour. — II ~ n ⓶ u. **Legierung** ⊕ f ⓯ 3. chm., &c. alligation. — 4. nur Legierung chm., &c. (das durch ~ Entstandene) alloy.
Legion (⸗⸌(v)⸌) [lt. lḗgĭō] f ⓯ röm. Alt.: ⚔ legion (f. Fremden⸗); fig. ihr Name ist ~ their name is legion; **~ar**, **~är** (⸗⸌(v)⸗⸌) m ⓭d. legionary.
Legions=kreuz (⸗⸌(v)⸌...) n ⓶ (franz. Orden) cross of the legion of honour; **=soldat** ⚔ m legionary (soldier).
legislativ (⸗⸗v⸗⸌) [lt. gesetzgebend] a. ⓰ legislative, law-making; **Legislative** (⸗⸗⸗⸌vv) f ⓯ legislative power, right to make laws; **legislatorisch** (⸗⸗⸗⸌⸗v) — legislativ.
Legislatur (⸗⸗v⸗⸌) [lt.] f ⓯ legislature, legislative body; **~periode** (⸌...) f ⓯ period of legislature, legislative period. [legitimate, lawful.]
legitim (⸗⸗v⸌) [lt.] a. ⓰ (rechtmäßig)
Legitimation (⸗⸗v⸗tẜ(v)⸌) [lt.] f ⓯ (Ausweis) legitimation; proof of identity; **~s=karte** (⸌...) f ⓯ (Erkennungskarte) card (or ticket) serving for identification;

Signs (see page XVII): F familiar; P vulgar; F flash; ⸜ rare; † obsolete (died); * new word (born); ✚ incorrect; ♪ music;

[Legitimationspapiere] [Lehrerstand]

passport; ~s-papiere n/pl. papers pl. of identification.
legitimieren (-⏑⏑´⏑) [it.] ⓖ I v/a. (gültig m.) to legitim*ate*, ...*ize*. — II sich 2 v/refl. (sich ausweisen) to prove one's identity; können Sie sich 2? auch: have you any papers (to show who you are)? — III ~ n ⏑ u. Legitimierung f ㊻ (f. I) legitim(iz)ation.
Legitimist (-⏑⏑´) [it.] m ㉒, ~in f ⓖ, 2isch a. ⓖ pol. legitimist. [legitimacy.]
Legitimität (-⏑⏑⏑´) f ㊻ (Rechtmäßigkeit)
Leguan ⏑ (-⏑´) [java'nisch] m ⓪d. zo. (Kamm-eidechse) toad-lizard, iguana (Igua'na tubercula'ta); 2artig (´...) a. ⓖ iguan*ian*, ...*iform*. [= Hülsenfrucht.]
Leguminose(n pl.) ⏑ ⚘ (⏑-⏑´⏑) [it.] f ㊻
Legung (´⏑) f ㊻ = legen II.
Lehde provc. (´) [flaw.] f ㊽ (unbebautes Land) waste land, fallow; (Heide) heath.
Lehen (´⏑) [ahd.: loan; *leihen] n ㉓ Feudalwesen: 1. fief, fee, tenure of land, nur auf gewisse Erben übertragbar: conditional fee, estate in fee tail; ein Gut als ~ besitzen ob. zu ~ tragen to possess (or hold) ... in fee; e-m etwas zu ~ geben to invest a p. with land, to enfeoff a p. — 2. (oft im pl. gbr.) die ~ (Belehnung) empfangen to be invested with land or a fief.
leh(e)nbar (´(⏑)-) a. ⓖ Lehenswesen: 1. entitled to hold a fief. — 2. (ein Lehen von e-m tragend) feudatory to a p. — 3. (als Lehen verwaltet) feudal, held in fee.
Leh(e)nbarkeit (´(⏑)⏑-) f ㊻ (f. lehenbar) 1. title for holding a fief. — 2. vassalage, feudal service. — 3. feudality.
Leh(e)n(s)-besitz (´´(⏑)-) m ㉒ fief, feudal tenure, copyhold; -brief m letter of investiture, (bill of) enfeoffment; -buch n roll of fiefs; -dienst m feudal service or tenure; -dienst-pflicht(igkeit) f feudal duty, fealty; -eid m oath of fealty or allegiance; den ~ leisten to take (or swear) the oath of fealty; -einziehung (-erledigung) f forfeiture (falling in) of a fief; -fähig(keit f) a. ⓖ capable (capability) of holding a fief; -fall m escheat of a fief; -folge f: a) feudal succession; b) duty of a vassal to follow his lord (in war); -frei(heit f) a. allodial(ity); -gebühr f, -geld n feudal fine or relief; -gut n feudal estate or holding, fee, fief; -herr m feudal lord or liege, feoffer; -herrlichkeit, -herrschaft, -hoheit f feudal rule or lordship or supremacy, suzerainty; -leute pl. (f. -mann) liegepeople, vassals pl.; -mann m (pl. -männer u. -leute) feuda(to)ry, feudal tenant, vassal, liege(man); 2männisch a. feudatory; -pflicht f feudal duty or obligation, vassalage; die ~ leisten: a) = den -eid leisten; b) to render a vassal's services; -recht n: a) feudal law; b) right of investiture; -sache f feudal affair; -träger m feoffee; vgl. -mann; -treue f feudal loyalty or allegiance, fealty; -verfassung f feudal system; -verhältnis n vassalage; -vertrag m feudal contract; 2weise adv. like (or as) a fief, in fee; -wesen n system of feudal tenure, feudalism; -zins m quit-rent of a farm.

Lehm (´) [ndd.: loam] m ⓪c. (sandiger Ton) loam, oft ⏑⏑ für „Ton": clay, ⏑ argillaceous earth; chm. zum Verkitten: lute.
Lehm-anwurf (´...) m ㉒ Maurerei: coat of loam; -arbeit f Maurerei: mudwalling, pisé-(building); 2artig (´...) loamy, clayey, ⏑ argillaceous; -bau m = -arbeit; -boden m loam (or clay) soil or floor, mud floor; -form(erei) ⊕ f loam-mould(ing); -grube f loam- (or clay-)pit; -grund m loam, clayey soil; -guß ⊕ m loam-casting, -work; -hütte f mud (or clay) cottage.
lehmicht, mst lehmig (´⏑) a. ㊻ loamy, of clay, clayey, ⏑ argillaceous.
Lehm-klecker (´...) m ㉒ = -patzer; -kübel m Maurerei: hod; -mauer f mudwall; -mörtel m clay mortar; -patzer m Maurer: mud-waller; -putzer m loamer; -schicht f loam coat(ing); -stein m clay brick; -wand f loam (or mud) wall, cob-wall; -ziegel m sun-dried brick.
Lehn (´) f ㊻ 2c. = Lehen 2c.
Lehn¹-... (´...) in Zssgn = Lehen-...
Lehn²-bank (´...) [Lehne, lehnen] f ㊻ bench (or seat) with a back to it; (kreisförmiger Diwan) settee; -¹buch n ehm. = Grundbuch.
Lehne¹ (´⏑) [ahd.] f ㊽ 1. ~ einer Bank, e-s Stuhles back; (Seiten)~ in Kutschen, Stühlen xc.: elbow-rest, arm-rest; support; ~ einer Treppe xc. hand-rail. — 2. (sanft geneigter Abhang) gentle slope, inclined plain, declivity. — 3. ⊕ Papierfabr.: ass, gallows pl.
Lehne² (´⏑) f ㊽ (wilde Sau) wild sow.
Lehne³ ⚘ (´⏑) [ahd.] f ㊽ (Spitz-ahorn) Norway maple (Acer platanoi'des).
lehnen¹ (´⏑) [mhd.: lean] ⓖ I v/n. (h.) u. 2 v/refl. mit prp.: to lean; an et. (dat. ob. acc.) 2, sich an et. (acc.) 2 to lean (or recline) against s.th.; sich auf e-n, et. 2 to rest (or support) o.s. (up)on a p., a th. — II v/a. to lean, prop, rest against a th.
lehnen² obb. (´⏑) [:lend] ⓖ = leihen.
Lehn¹-recht (´⏑) n ㉒ f. Lehensrecht.
Lehns-... (´...) f. Lehens-...
Lehn¹-satz (´...) m ㉒ math, phls.: lemma; -²fessel, -stuhl m easy (or arm-)chair, mit zurückgebogener Lehne: reclining- (or lounging-, American) chair, lounge; fahrbarer ~ für Kranke: Bath chair; -¹wort n, gr. borrowed (or naturalized foreign) word.
Lehr ⊕ (´) n ⓪c. = Lehre 5.
Lehr-amt (´...) n ㉒ teacher's (or master's) appointment or post, mastership, Universität: professorship; -anstalt f educational establishment, (Schule) school, college, academy; -apparat m teaching-apparatus; -art f method of teaching or instruction, educational method. [f ㊻ teachableness.]
lehrbar (´⏑) a. ㊻ teachable; ~keit (⏑´⏑-)
Lehr-begier(de) (´...) f ㊻ desire (or eagerness) to teach; -begriff m scientific principle or system; -beruf m scholastic profession, teacher's calling; -bogen ⊕ m, arch. centering; carp., &c. centre; Drechslerei: die ~ aufstellen to set the centres; -bote m apostle, missionary; -brett ⊕ n Maurerei: templet; -brief m indentures pl.

of apprenticeship, articles pl. of indenture; -buch n manual (of instruction), text-book; -bursch(e) m apprentice; -dichter m, -dichtung f didactic poet, poetry.
Lehre (´⏑) [Hom. Leere] [ahd.: lore; *lehren] f ㊻ 1. (Richtschnur) rule, precept, (Wink, Warnung) hint, advice; (Unterweisung) instruction, tuition; ~, die sich aus et. ziehen läßt moral; e-m eine gute ~ erteilen ob. gute ~n geben to teach a p. a good lesson, to give a p. sound advice; lassen Sie sich das eine ~ sein! let that be a warning to you! — 2. (Gesamtheit von wissenschaftlichen, religiösen xc. Lehren) teaching, doctrine; tenets pl.; christliche ~ Christian doctrine; in guter ~ sein to be at (or in) a good school. — 3. (System) system; (Wissenschaft) science, (wissenschaftliche Voraussetzung) theory. — 4. (zunftmäßige Unterweisung) apprenticeship; eine fünfjährige ~ bei e-m besteh(e)n to be articled for five years to a p.; bei e-m in die ~ bringen (ob. geben) to apprentice (or indenture, article) with a p.; in der ~ sein to serve as an apprentice or one's apprenticeship. — 5. ⊕ (auch Leere) (Instrument zur Ausmessung ob. Bestimmung e-s Gegenstandes) gauge, (Schablone) pattern, (Kaliber) calibre, size; (Meßstock) staff, rule; bsd. arch. = Lehrgerüst; Bildhauerei: model; Maurerei = Lehrbrett; Seilerei: laying-top; ⚒ = Nichtschicht.
Lehr-eifer (´´⏑-) m ㉒ zeal for teaching.
lehren (´⏑; Hom. leeren) [ahd.] I v/a. (p.p. bisw. 2) 1. (unterrichten) to teach; e-n (e-m) et. 2 to teach a p. s.th., to instruct a p. in s.th.; e-n lesen (ob. das Lesen) 2 to teach a p. reading or (how) to read; die Folge (oder Zeit) wird es 2 time will show. — II ~ n ㉓ 2. teaching, (imparting) instruction, giving a lesson. — III 2d p.pr. u. a. ㊻ 3. Beb. des inf. — 4. instructive; poet. didactic.
Lehrer (´⏑) [ahd.] m ㉒, ~in f ⓖ teacher (auch f): in e-r Schule: master, f governess; ~ der Mathematik teacher of mathematics, mathematical teacher or master; für Turnen xc.: instructor, f bisw. instructress; in einer Familie: (Erzieher[in]) (private) tutor, f governess; auf der Hochschule: professor, lecturer; sämtliche ~ e-r Schule xc. teaching (Hochschule: professorial) staff; Erster ~ e-r Schule head master, principal; Erste ~in head mistress, head governess.
Lehrer-bildungsanstalt (´´⏑...) f ㉒ training-college for teachers.
Lehrerin (´⏑⏑) f ㊽ f. Lehrer.
Lehrerinnen-examen (´´⏑⏑⏑-...) n ㉒, -semina'r n examination, training-college for governesses.
Lehrer-kollegium (´´⏑...) n ㉒ staff (or body) of teachers; -konferenz f (periodical) meeting of teachers or the teaching staff; -prüfung f examination for teachers.
Lehrerschaft (´⏑⏑) f ㊻ 1. teacher's vocation. — 2. coll. body of teachers.
Lehrer-seminar (´´⏑...) n ㉒ = -bildungsanstalt; -stand m scholastic pro-

⏑ scientific; ⚘ botanical; ⊕ geography; ⊕ machinery; ⚒ mining; ⚔ military; ⚓ marine; ✉ commercial; ✉ postal; 🚂 railway.

[**Lehrerstelle**]

fession; vgl. **Lehrstand**; **=stelle** f an Schulen: mastership, an Hochschulen: chair. **Lehr-fabel** (*"...*) f ⑫: ⚹ apologue; **=fach** n: a) branch of instruction; b) teaching; vgl. =amt; ⚹**fähig** a. ⓑ able to teach; **=fähigkeit** f capacity for teaching; **=form** f: a) mode of teaching; b) poet. didactic form; **=freiheit** f freedom of instruction (ant. =zwang); **=gabe** f gift (or talent) for teaching; **=gang** m (Kursus) course of instruction, als Buchtitel: French, &c. Course; **=gebäude** n system (of instruction); **=gedicht** n didactic poem; **=gegenstand** m subject of instruction, branch of study; **=geld** n: a) premium of apprenticeship; b) fig. ~ bezahlen to pay dearly for one's experience; **=gerüst** ⊖ n (auch Leer=g.) arch. centering. **lehrhaft** (⌣) a. ⓑ v. Sachen: instructive, didactic (a. v. Dichtungen); v. Personen: fond of (or apt or clever at) teaching. **Lehr-herr** (*"...*) m ⑫ master (of an apprentice); **=holz** ⊖ (auch Leerholz) n, carp., &c. centre; **=jahre** n/pl. years pl. of apprenticeship; seine ~ besteh(e)n to serve one's appr.; **=junge** m =bursche; **=körper** m teaching staff, einer Hochschule: professoriate; **=kraft** f qualified teacher; ausgezeichnete =kräfte excellent teachers or professors pl.; **=kunst** f art of teaching, pedagogics. **Lehrling** (⌣) m ⓓd. (Lehrbursche) apprentice; weitS. (Neuling) novice, beginner, tyro; als ~ ein Handwerk lernen to be apprenticed to a trade; **~s-stand** (*"...*) m ⑫, **~s-verhältnis** n apprenticeship. **Lehr-mädchen** (*"...*) n ⑫ girl apprentice; ⚹**mäßig** a. ⓑ dogmatic, doctrinal; **=meinung** f, theol. dogma, tenet; **=meister** m: a) = =herr; b) (Hofmeister) tutor; **=methode** f method of instruction; **=mittel** n/pl. educational appliances pl., means pl. of instruction; **=personal** n = =körper; **=plan** m plan of instruction, (school-) curriculum; **=punkt** m point of doctrine; ⚹**reich** a. instructive; **=saal** m class-room; **=satz** m proposition, math. a.: theorem; weitS. doctrine, tenet, theol. dogma; **=schriften** f/pl. didactic writings pl.; **=spruch** m sentence, maxim, aphorism, ⚹ apophthegm; **=stand** m: a) coll. (ant. Nähr- und Wehrstand) body of teachers, scholastic profession; b) teacher's vocation; **=stil** m dogmatic (or didactic) style; **=stoff** m matter of instruction; **=stuhl** m professorial chair, professorship; ~ für Chemie ⚹c. chair for chemistry, &c.; **=stunde** f teacher's lesson. professor's lecture; **=tätigkeit** f teacher's (or professorial, educational) work; **=ton** m dogmatic(al) tone; **=vertrag** m = =brief; **=weisheit** f scholastic wisdom; ⚹**widrig** a. contrary to an accepted doctrine or dogma, heterodox; **=zeit** f (term of) apprenticeship; vgl. Lehre 4; **=zimmer** n class-room; **=zwang** m: a) compulsory education; b) theol. (dogmatic[al]) restrictions pl. placed upon free teaching (ant. =freiheit).

...lei (...") [fr. loi] Anhängesilbe zur Bildung von a. zB. allerlei (of) all sorts. **Leib** (⌣; Hom. Laib) [ahd.: life Leben] m ⓂÖc. 1. (Körper) body; toter ~ dead body, corpse, e-s Tieres: carcass; ~ und Seele body and soul; als hätte sie (die Ratte) Lieb' im ~e (G.) as though love's frenzy filled her frame; rel. unser irdischer ~ our mortal clay or tenement; ~ und Leben wagen to stake one's life, to risk life and limb. — 2. mit prp.: es ging ihm **an** ~ und Leben his life was in jeopardy or at stake; am ~e strafen to inflict corporal punishment upon; am ganzen ~e zittern to tremble all over (one's body); kein Hemd(e) **auf** dem ~e h. to have not a shirt to one's back; e-m (hart) auf den ~ rücken to press a p. hard, to attack a p.; (**bei** ~e) beileibe (i.dS.), bei ~esleben nicht! by no means, on no account!; (um keinen Preis) not for the world!, not for the life of me!; bei lebendigem ~e (while still) alive; er hat keine Ehre im ~e he is devoid of all honourable feeling; kein Herz im ~e h. to be heartless or without a heart; fig. das Herz im ~e lacht einem it gladdens one's heart, F it does one's heart good; er hat den Teufel im ~e he is a tricky (or wily, wicked) fellow, F he has old Nick in him; er ist **mit** ~ und Seele dabei he is (with all his) heart and soul in it; er hat sich ihm mit ~ und Seele verkauft he has given himself over to him body and soul; e-n **um** den ~ fassen to put one's arm round a p.('s waist); das Pferd wurde ihm **unter** dem ~e erschossen his horse was shot under him; sich einen **vom** ~e halten to keep a p. at a distance; bleib mir damit vom ~e! don't trouble me with that!; drei Schritt vom ~e! don't come near me!, stand off!; e-m nicht vom ~e geh(e)n to keep close (or hang on) to a p.; e-m **zu** ~e geh(e)n to assault a p.; e-m zu ~e wollen to have a design upon a p. — 3. (Bauch, Unterleib) belly, abdomen; sich et. am (eigenen) ~e abdarben to stint o.s. of a th.; Grimmen im ~e h. to have a stomach-ache, F sich das Essen in den ~ jagen to bolt one's dinner or food; j-n ~ pflegen, j-m ~e Gutes (oder et. zugut[e]) tun to look well after o.s., to pamper o.s.; F sich den ~ voll schlagen F to fill one's belly; gut bei ~e (beleibt) sein to be stout or corpulent; med. offenen ~ h. to have regular (or easy) motions; harten, verstopften ~ h. to be costive or constipated. — 4. ~ (als Sitz des zu Gebärenden) womb; gesegneten ~es sein to be with child or F in the familyway; von Mutter ~e an from one's birth; s. Mutterleib. — 5. = Leben, m. dem es oft in Verbindung tritt; s. Leben¹ 2. **Leib-arzt** (*"...*) m ⑫ physician in ordinary to His Majesty, &c.; **=batterie** ⚹ f in Preußen: first company in the artillery regiment of the Guards; **=binde** f sash, in Indien ⚹c. = kummerbund; aus Flanell: belly-band, flannel waistband; surg. abdominal bandage; **=bürge** m (Geisel) hostage.

Leibchen (⌣) n ㉓ (dim. v. Leib) 1. small body. — 2. (small) bodice of a dress; (Schnürbrust) corset(s pl.). **Leib-chirurg** (*"...*) m ⑫ surgeon in ordinary; ⚹**eigen** a. (held) in bondage; ⚹ m. to enthral; **eigene([r]** m) f (ant. Freie) bonds-(wo)man, serf, thrall; ehm. villain; **eigenschaft** f bondage, serfdom; ehm. villainage. **leiben** (⌣) v/n. (h.) ⑧: ~ und leben i. leben⁼ 8; da ist er wie er leibt und lebt there (or that) is the exact likeness of him, F that's he to a T, that's him exactly or all over. **Leibes-beschaffenheit** (*"...*) f ⑫ state of the body, (bodily) constitution; (Temperame'nt) temperament; (Äußeres) physique; **=beschwerde** f (bodily) infirmity; **=bewegung** f bodily exercise; sich ~ m. to take exercise; **=erbe** m legitimate heir or offspring; ohne ~n sterben to die without issue; **=fehler** m = =gebrechen; **=frucht** f: ⚹ fetus, embryo; **=gebrechen** n bodily defect, deformity; **=gefahr** f = Lebensgefahr; **=gestalt** f shape of the body, figure, F build; **=größe** f size of the body, stature; **=kraft** f bodily (or physical) strength; aus =kräften with all one's might; aus =kräften schreien to shout at the top of one's voice; **=länge** f length of the body; **=leben** ⚹ n: bei ~ during one's life-time, while alive; **=nahrung** f nourishment for the body; ~ und **=notdurft** food and clothing, necessaries pl. of life; **=öffnung** f open (or openness of the) bowels pl.; **=pflege** f care bestowed on the body, physical culture; **=schwäche** f (physical) infirmity. **Leib-essen** (*"...*) n ⑫ = Leibgericht. **Leibes-stellung** (*"...*) f ⑫ posture. attitude; **=strafe** f: a) corporal punishment; b) bei ~ on pain of death; **=übung** f bodily exercise; (Turnen) gymnastics; **=umfang** m corpulence; **=verstopfung** f constipation. costiveness. **Leib-farbe** (*"...*) f ⑫ fig. favourite colour; **=fluß** m. path. diarrhœa; **=garde** ⚹ f bodyguard, in Engl.: Life Guards pl.; **=gardist** m life-guardsman; **=gedinge** n life-annuity, settlement; (Wittum) jointure; **=geleit** n safe conduct; **=gericht** n favourite dish; **=gurt**, **=gürtel** m waist-belt. **leibhaft(ig)** (-⌣(⌣)) a. ⓑ endowed with a body, embodied, (zu Fleisch geworden) incarnate; (personifiziert) personified; (wirklich) real, true; (selbst) he himself, f she herself, auch (it.) in pro'pria perso'na; ein Les Ebenbild a living likeness or image; der Le Teufel the devil incarnate, Old Nick himself; **leibhaftig** (adv.) erscheinen to appear in the flesh or in person. **...leibig** (..."⌣) a. ⓑ in Zssgn, zB.: drei-Leibig, with three bodies, three-bodied. **Leib-jäger** (*"⌣⌣) m ⑫ (fr.) chasseur. **leiblich** (⌣) a. ⓑ 1. (den Körper betr.) of the body, corpor(e)al, ⚹ somatic. — 2. (irdisch) earthly, worldly. — 3. = leibhaft(ig). — 4. (eigentlich) von Verwandten: ihr Ler Bruder her own brother, Ler Vetter full cousin, cousin-german.

Zeichen (s. S. XVII): F familiär; P Volkssprache; P Gaunersprache; ⚹ selten; † alt (auch gestorben); * neu (auch geboren); ⚹⚹ unrichtig.

[Leibpacht] — 653 — [Leichtsinn]

Leib-pacht (¨...) f ⑫ tenure (or lease) for life; **=page** m page in ordinary; **=regime'nt** ⚔ n sovereign's own regiment; **=rente** f life-annuity; **=rentner** m life-annuitant, pensioner; **=rock** m: a) fast † dress-(or evening-)coat; b) (langer Rock der katholischen Priester) soutane; **=schmerz(en** pl.) m, **=schneiden** n stomach-ache, F gripes pl., P belly-ache, path. colic; **=schüssel, =speise** f = **=gericht**; **=stück** n: a) des Frauenrocks: bodice; b) ♪ favourite tune or air. **Leibung** ⊕ (¹⁄) f (¹⁄) arch.: ~ (Innerseite) eines Bogens: intrados, soffit.

Leib=wache (¨...) f ⑫ = **=garde**; **=wäsche** f body-linen, underwear; **=weh** n = **=schmerzen**; **=zucht** f = Nießbrauch; **=züchter** m = Altsitzer; **=zwang** m. path. costiveness. ¶ (Gedicht u. Tonstück) lay.

Leich¹ ♪ (¹⁄) [ahd.] m ⓐc. im Mittelalter:

Leich²**=dorn** (¨.♪) [Leiche] m ⓑ corn (= Hühnerauge).

Leiche (¹⁄) [ahd.] f ⑭ **1.** corpse, milderd: dead body, contp. carcass; ♂ cadaver; zur ~ m. to kill, P to corpse: fig. eine lebendige ~ a living (or walking) skeleton. — **2.** (Bestattung) funeral (procession); zur ~ bitten to invite to a funeral; zur ~ geh(e)n to go to (or to attend) a funeral or burial. — **3.** ⊕ typ. (Ausgelassenes) omission, s.th. omitted or left out, F out.

Leichen=acker (¨⁻...) m ⑫ = Gottesacker; **=alkaloid(e** pl.) n, chm. cadaveric alkaloid(s pl.); **=artig** a. ⑫ like a corpse, cadaverous; **=ausgrabung** f exhumation (of a body); **=bahre** f bier; **=begängnis** n funeral (procession); (Trauerfeier) obsequies pl.; **=begleiter** m mourner; **=begleitung** f procession of mourners; funeral train; **=beschauer** m coroner; **=besichtigung** f post-mortem examination; **=besorger, =bestatter** m undertaker, funeral furnisher; **=bestattung** f = **=begängnis**; **=bestattungsverein** m burial-club; **=besteller** m person who organizes a funeral, undertaker; **=bitter** m p. who invites to a funeral; **=bitter=gesicht** n, **=miene** f F fig. funereal (or woebegone) countenance; **=blaß** a. (as) pale as death, deadly pale; **=blasses** Gesicht a. face as white as a sheet; **=blässe** f deathlike pallor; **=buch** n register of burials; **=dieb** m body-snatcher, ehm.: resurrection-man; **=fahl** a. livid, F cadaverous-looking; **=farbe** (**=farbig** a.) f (of a) cadaverous hue or colour; **=feier(lichkeit)** f funeral rites or obsequies pl.; **=feld** n field strewn with dead bodies, field of carnage; **=fett** n: ♂ adipocere; **=fledderer** F m pickpocket who robs people in their sleep; **=frau** f woman who lays out the dead; **=geruch** m cadaverous smell; **=gerüst** n = Grabgerüst; **=gesang** m = Grablied; **=gesicht** n cadaverous face, funereal countenance; **=gewölbe** n family-vault; **=gift** n, med. virus of dead bodies, ♂ cadaverine; **=gruft** f family-tomb.

leichenhaft (¹⁄⁻⁻) a. ⑫ like a corpse, like (or of) a dead body, cadaverous.

Leichen=halle (¨⁻...) ⑫ f, **=haus** n: a) beim Kirchhofe: mortuary, F dead-house; b) = **=schauhaus**; **=hemd** n shroud, winding-sheet; **=kalt** a. ⑫ like a corpse, icy cold; **=kammer** f death-chamber, anat. dissecting-room; **=kasse** f burial-fund; **=klage** f mourning (or wailing) for the dead; **=kosten** pl. funeral expenses pl.; **=mahl** n fun. repast; **=öffnung** f opening (or dissection) of a dead body, med.: ♂ autopsy, vgl. **=schau**; **=predigt** f funeral sermon; **=räuber** m: a) = dieb; b) one who strips dead bodies; **=rede** f funeral oration or discourse; **=schändung** f desecration of dead bodies or of the dead; **=schau** f inquest on a dead body, post-mortem examination, coroner's inquest; **=schauer** m coroner; =(**=schau**) **=haus** n zur Ausstellung v. Verunglückten etc.: morgue; **=schmaus** m = **=mahl**; **=starre** f, med.: ♂ cadaveric rigidity, a. (lt.) rigor mortis; **=stein** m tomb-stone; **=träger** m bearer of a coffin, a. undertaker's man; **=tuch** n: a) (Tuch zum Einhüllen der Leiche) shroud; b) (Bahrtuch) pall; **=untersuchung** f = **=schau**; **=verbrennung** f cremation; **=verbrennungsofen** m furnace for cremating the dead, cremator; **=wache** f watching by a dead body, a. death-watch, in Irland: wake; **=wachs** n = **=fett**; **=wagen** m hearse, funeral carriage; **=zug** m funeral procession.

Leichnam (¹⁄⁻) [ahd. Leichenhemd(d) „fleischliche Hülle"] m ⓐd. dead body, corpse, mortal remains pl.; F co. seinen ~ pflegen to pamper o.s., to coddle o.s., F to look well after number one.

leicht(¹⁄)[ahd.: light] a. ⓐ **1.** (von geringem Gewichte; ant. schwer) light, of small weight; F ² wie ein Schneider (as) light as a feather; ♂ zu ² under weight; zu ² (von Münzen etc.) too light, reduced in weight, worn; ²es Backwerk light pastry; ²en Fußes sein to be light-footed or nimble; eine ²e Hand h. von Barbieren, Malern etc.: to have a light touch; ²e (dünne) Kleidung light (or thin) clothing, chm. ²e Metalle light metals pl.; ⚔ ²e Reiterei light horse pl.; ²e Zigarre light (or mild) cigar; ² machen to lighten; den Kopf ² m. to clear one's head or brain; sich ² m. (entleeren) to relieve o.s. or one's bowels. — **2.** fig. (geringe Mühe verursachend; ant. a. hart) easy (task), light (matter), slight (exertion); f. Achsel ²; ²en Kaufes davonkommen to get off cheaply; mit ²er Mühe with little trouble; ²en Sinnes of an easy temper, easy-going, vgl. Leichtsinn; mit dem werde ich ²es Spiel h. I shall manage (or beat, persuade) him easily; ein ²er (gefälliger) Stil a light (or an easy) style; ²er Vorwurf gentle (or slight) rebuke; es ist ² mit ihm auszukommen; es ist ² gesagt, doch schwer getan it is more easily said than done; Cicero ist ² zu versteh(e)n ... is easy to understand; es wird ihm alles ² he shows great ease in everything; ²(er) machen to render easy or less difficult, to facilitate; er macht sich's ² he treats it lightly, F he takes it easy; das ist ihm ein ²es it is an easy (or a trifling) matter to him; ♎ ²en Absatz finden to meet with a ready sale. — **3.** nur adv.: a) (Geneigtheit bezeichnend) Sie können ² denken you may easily (or readily) imagine; sich ² erkälten to be subject to colds; etwas ² nehmen to make light of a th.; wie ² ist ein Unglück geschehen how easily (or soon) an accident can happen; man irrt sich sehr ² one is very apt (or liable) to make a mistake; das kommt nicht ² wieder vor such a thing is not likely to occur again; ² verdaulich light (or easy) of digestion; b) bloße Möglichkeit bezeichnend: es könnte ² sein daß // it could well be that /; das wird nicht ² geschehen that is not likely to happen, that won't easily occur.

leicht=bedeckt (¨⁻...) a. ⑫ lightly covered; **²beflügelt**; **²beschwingt** a. light-winged; **²bewaffnet** ⚔ a. (~e[r] m ⑰) light-armed (soldier); **²blütig** a. sanguine, excitable, mercurial, buoyant (in spirit); vgl. **²fertig**; **=blütigkeit** f sanguineness, excitableness, buoyancy (of spirit).

Leichter ♻ (¹⁄) m ⑫ etc. = Lichter¹ etc.

leicht=faßlich (¨...) a. ⑫ easy to understand, plain; **²fertig** a. light-hearted; (unbedachtsam) thoughtless, unthinking; (ohne inneren Halt) frivolous, (oberflächlich) superficial; (unbeständig) fickle; (mutwillig) wanton, skittish, (locker) loose, fast, giddy; ²es Frauenzimmer fast (or gay) woman; et. ² (adv.) behandeln to treat a th. lightly, to make light of a th.; **=fertigkeit** f light-heartedness, levity, thoughtlessness, frivolity, wantonness, looseness, fastness; **²flüssig** a. chem., &c. easily fusible; **=fuß** m (nur fig.) giddy fellow, gay young spark, madcap; vgl. Bruder 5; **²füßig** a.: a) light-footed, nimble; b) fig. = **²fertig**; **=füßigkeit** f: a) lightness of foot; b) fig. = **=fertigkeit**; **²geschürzt** a. with tucked-up clothes, bibl. with girt-up loins; **²gläubig** a. easy of belief, credulous, F gullible; **=gläubige(r]** m f credulous person; **=gläubigkeit** f credulity, F gullibility.

Leichtheit (¹⁄⁻) [leicht 1] f ⑭ lightness.

leicht=herzig (¨⁻...) a. ⑫ light-hearted, cheerful; **=herzigkeit** f ⑫ light-heartedness; **²hin** adv. lightly.

Leichtigkeit (¹⁄⁻) f ⑫ **1.** (f. leicht 1) lightness (in weight); ~ der Bewegung, oft: lightness of foot, nimbleness, agility. — **2.** fig. (f. leicht 2) easiness, ease, facility.

leicht=lebig (¨...) a. ⑫ easy-going, F happy-go-lucky; **=lebigkeit** f ⑫ easy (or easy-going) temper.

leichtlich (¹⁄⁻) adv. lightly; easily, without (much) trouble; vgl. leicht 3.

Leicht=matrose ♻ (¨...) m ⑫ ordinary seaman; **=sinn** m: a) levity; (Sorglosigkeit) carelessness; vgl. **=fertigkeit**; b) (=sinniger Mensch) oft: gay or giddy, reckless, F non-carish fellow;

♪ Musik; ♂ Wissenschaft; ♀ Pflanze; ⌂ Geographie; ⊕ Technik; ⚒ Bergbau; ⚔ Militär; ♻ Marine; ♎ Handel; ✉ Post; 🚂 Eisenbahn.

[leichtsinnig] — 654 — [leihen]

ſinnig a. light-minded, (forglos) careless; (vgl. ꝛlebig u. ꝛfertig); ꝛer Menſch = ꝛſinn b: ꝛerweiſe adv. thoughtlessly, F non-carishly; light-heartedly; =ſinnigkeit f = ꝛſinn a; ꝛverſtändlich a. easy to understand, easily understood.

leid¹ (ʹ) [ahd.: loath] I a. ⓖ inv.: es tut (oder iſt) mir ꝛ, daß ǁ, ʓu ǁ; a) I feel (or I am) sorry that ǁ, to ǁ (inf.); b) (bedaure) I regret (ſtärker: I am very grieved) that ǁ, to ǁ (inf.); das tut mir ꝛ: a) it grieves (or pains) me; b) (ich kann es nicht ändern) so much the worse, I cannot help it; es tut mir um Ihretwillen ꝛ I am sorry for your sake, it grieves me on your account; e-m et. ꝛ m. to make a p. regret a th.; es iſt mir noch nicht ꝛ geworden I have not repented (of) it yet; es wird dir eines Tages ꝛ werden you will one day rue it; es ſich nicht ꝛ ſein l. not to rue (or repent) a th. — II n ⓖ nichts (kein) ꝛes tun to do no harm.

Leid² (ʹ) [ahd.: leid¹] n ⓖc. 1. injury, (Unrecht) wrong, ſtärker: outrage; keinem zuꝛe und keinem zuliebe without respect of persons; ſich (dat.) ein ꝛ(es) (an)tun to lay hands upon o.s.; Erlkönig hat mir ein ꝛs getan (G.) the Fairy King has wrought me some harm; es ſoll Ihnen kein ꝛ widerfahren you shall suffer no harm or injury. — 2. (Unglück) misfortune, calamity; (Betrübnis) grief, sorrow, (Bedauern) regret; (Schmerz) pain; in Lieb' und ꝛ in good and evil days; in Freud' und ꝛ in joy and sorrow, Trauungsformel: for better for worse. — 3. ꝛ tragen (trauern) to be in mourning; um e-n Toten ꝛ tragen to mourn for a p., to bewail a p.'s death.

Leide=form (ʹ-ʹ) f ⓖ gr. passive (voice).
leiden¹ (ʹ-) [ahd.] ⓖc. I v/n. (h.) und v/a. 1. to suffer; an der Gicht ꝛ to suffer from (or to be afflicted with) gout; er leidet an der Leber, am Magen his liver is out of order, his stomach is deranged; ſie leidet an den Nerven she has a nervous complaint, her nerves are upset; an Ohnmacht(en) ꝛ to be subject to fainting fits; woran leidet er? what does he ail from? ſeine Geſundheit litt (ſtark) darunter it (seriously) affected his health. — 2. (über ſich ergehen laſſen) großen Schaden ꝛ to suffer (or sustain) a great loss or injury, von Dingen: to suffer great damage, to get seriously damaged; Schiffbruch ꝛ to suffer shipwreck, to be shipwrecked; Strafe ꝛ to suffer (or undergo) punishment. — 3. (erlauben, zulaſſen; mögen) to allow, to permit; to like; das Schießen wird hier nicht gelitten … is not allowed (or tolerated) here; die Sache leidet keinen Aufſchub … admits of (or brooks) no delay; ſie litt nicht, daß er beſtraft würde she would not allow (or consent to) his being punished; ſie können ihn nicht (vor Augen) ꝛ they cannot bear (the sight of) him; ſie mag ihn in der Seele nicht ꝛ she can-

not endure him, she utterly dislikes (or abhors) him; er iſt bei uns wohl gelitten he is a great favourite with us or of ours. — 4. v impers. es leidet ihn hier nicht länger he cannot endure to (or F he won't) stay here any longer. — II ⁓ n ㉓ 5. suffering; das ⁓ Chriſti the sufferings pl. (or Passion) of Christ; F er ſieht aus wie das ⁓ Chriſti he looks a picture of misery. — 6. mit pl. (was oder woran man leidet) affliction, (Trübſal) tribulation; Werthers ⁓ (G.) Sorrows pl. of Werther, (Krankheit) ailment, complaint; ſchweres ⁓ grave malady. — Vgl. a. Leid² 2. — III ꝛd p.pr. und a. ⓖ 7. in den Bed. des inf. — 8. (kränklich) sickly, ailing; er iſt ſehr ꝛd he is a great sufferer; s. der, die ꝛ ⓖ the sufferer, patient, invalid. — 9. gram. ꝛde Form passive (voice).

Leiden² ⓖ (ʹ-) npr/n. (ndl. St.) Leyden; ⁓er (a. inv.) Flaſche f (Cunäus (1746) in ⁓] elect. Leyden jar.

leiden¹=frei (ʹ- …) a. ⓖ free from suffering or pain or trouble.

Leidenſchaft (ʹ- -) [nhd. *(lt. passio)] f ⓖ passion, deep emotion; edle ⁓, oft: sacred fire; wilde ⁓ towering rage, fury; ſ-n ⁓en frönen to give way (or full license) to one's passions.

leidenſchaftlich (ʹ- - -) a. ⓖ passionate (mood, character), impassioned (speech), vehement (gesture), ardent (longing), burning (desire), enthusiastic (admirer); ꝛ w. to fly into a passion, F to boil over (with anger); ꝛ (adv.) lieben to be passionately fond of, to love to distraction; ⁓keit f ⓖ passionateness, vehemence, ardour; (Ungeſtüm) violence, quick (or hot) temper, impetuous spirit.

leidenſchafts=frei (ʹ- - - …) a. ⓖ free from passion; ꝛlos a. dispassionate; (unempfindlich) callous, apathetic, cool(-blooded); =loſigkeit f ⓖ dispassionateness; callousness, apathy; cool-bloodedness; (Unparteilichkeit) impartiality, fair-mindedness.

Leidens=gefährte (ʹ- …) m ㉒, =gefährtin f, =genoſſe m, =genoſſin f fellow-sufferer, companion in misfortune or adversity; =geſchichte f history of a p.'s sufferings, sorrowful tale, tale of woe; ⁓ Jeſu passion of (the Lord) Jesus; =jahr n year of suffering or misfortune; =kelch m, fig. cup of bitterness or sorrow; =probe f trial; =ſtation f, eccl.: die zwölf ⁓en the twelve Stations of the Cross; =ſtätte f place of suffering, fig. u. rel. Mount Calvary, Golgotha; =woche f week of woe or tribulation, eccl. Passion-week.

leider (ʹ-) [ahd. comp. v. leid] int. ꝛ!, ſtärker: ꝛ Gottes! alas!; es iſt ꝛ nur zu wahr it is unfortunately only too true; daran iſt ꝛ kein wahres Wort sad to relate (or to say) there is not a word of truth in it; ꝛ iſt er noch krank I am sorry (or grieved) to say he is still ill.

leidig (ʹ-) [Leid²] a. ⓖ pitiful, miserable; (unangenehm) unpleasant, disagreeable;

troublesome; (verbrießlich) vexatious; (verderblich) fatal, pernicious; Le Geſchichte unfortunate affair; der Le Mammon cursed (or baleful) Mammon.

leidlich (ʹ-) [leiden] a. ⓖ (ziemlich) bearable, tolerable, endurable, sufferable; (halbwegs gut) passable, mediocre, indifferent, F middling; ꝛ ſein, oft: to pass muster; es geht mir ſo ꝛ (adv.) I am getting on fairly well, F things are pretty middling with me; ich bin noch ſo ꝛ weggekommen I got off pretty easily or cheaply; ⁓keit f ⓖ tolerableness, passableness, mediocrity.

Leid=tragende (ʹ- …) s. ⓖ mourner, person in mourning; die ⁓n pl., auch: the bereaved family; ꝛvoll ⁓ a. ⓖ sorrowful, full of mourning; =weſen n sorrow, grief, ſtärker: affliction; zu meinem (großen) ⁓ to my (great) disappointment or regret or sorrow.

Leier (ʹ-) [ahd.; lt.; *grch. lyra] f ⓖ 1. ♪: a) bſd. poet. lyre; die ⁓ ſchlagen to touch the (cords of the) lyre; b) P = ⁓kaſten. — 2. ast.: ⚷ (nördliches Sternbild) Lyra. — 3. fig. alte ⁓ humdrum (or well-worn) tune; die alte ⁓ (dieſelbe Geſchichte) the same old tune.

Leierei (-ʹ-) f ⓖ = Geleier.
Leierer P (ʹ--) m ㉒, Lei(r)erin f ⓖ organ-grinder.

leier=förmig (ʹ- …) a. ⓖ lyre-shaped, ⚷ lyriform, ♀ lyrate(d); =gang ⓖ m der alte ⁓ the old slow (or humdrum) course, the old jog-trot or groove; =kaſten m barrel- (or street-)organ; =(kaſten)mann morgan-man; vgl. Leierer; =leiern (ʹ-) I v/n. (h.) u. v/a. ⓖa. 1. ♪ to play (on) the lyre; to grind on a barrel-organ; fig. immer dasſelbe ꝛ (ſagen) to be for ever harping on the same string; e-m die Ohren voll ꝛ to din one's talc into a p.'s ears; vgl. ableiern. — 2. (eine Kurbel drehen) to turn a crank or handle. — 3. fig. (ſich einförmig und langſam bewegen) to potter about, to go one's slow and even pace, to crawl quietly along; Sprichw. geleiert iſt beſſer als gefeiert (it is) better to do just a little than to rest altogether. — II ⁓ n ㉓ 4. = Geleier.
Leier=naſe (ʹ- …) f ⓖ zo. (Art Fledermaus) lyre-bat (Megade'rma lyra); =ſchwanz m. orn. lyre-bird (Menu'ra supe'rba); =ſpieler(in f) m lyrist; =ſtück P n street-organ tune.

Leih=amt (ʹ-…) n ㉒, =anſtalt f = =haus; =bank f loan-office.
leihbar (ʹ-) a. ⓖ loanable.
Leih=bibliothek (ʹ-…) f ⓖ circulating library, ſtädtiſche: lending-library.
leihen (ʹ-) [ahd.: lend] I v/a. ⓖ 1. to lend (auch ſo: to loan; (vermieten) to let out; (liefern) to provide, to supply; das Geliehene the thing(s pl.) lent. — 2. et. von e-m ꝛ: a) (entlehnen) to borrow a th. of a p.; b) (mieten) to hire a th. from a p.; geliehenes Geld borrowed money; geliehenes Pferd hired horse; Bücher aus einer Leihbibliothek ⁓ to borrow (or get) books from …; ich habe es mir geliehen ob. ꝛ laſſen I had it lent me, mietweiſe: I took it on hire; fig. e-m,

Signs (see page XVII): F familiar; P vulgar; F̌ flash; ⚹ rare; † obsolete (died); * new word (born); ++ incorrect; ♪ music.

[Leiher] — 655 — [Leistung]

e-r Sache sein Ohr 2 to lend an (or to open one's) ear. — II ~ n 23 3. (s. 1) loan; (s. 2) borrowing.
Leiher (¹⁻) m 22, **~in** f 47 (s. leihen) 1. lender. — 2. borrower.
Leih=haus (¹⁻...) n 62 pawnshop, pawn-broker's shop; ins ~ tragen, oft: to put in(to) pawn or F up the spout; =kasse f loan-office; =schein m pawn-ticket; =weise adv. (F a. a.) in the shape (or by way) of a loan; (mietweise) on hire.
Leit¹ ⌁ (¹) [ndb.] n ②c. ship's carcass.
Leit² ⌁ (¹) n ②c. = Lief.
Leilach (¹⁻ᴄʰ) [mhd. lei(nen)es Laten] n 23d. (linen) sheet, linen cloth.
Leim (¹) [ahd.: lime] m ②c. ⊕ glue; (Gallerte) jelly; (Vogel=)~ bird-lime; dünner ~ zum Planieren 2c.: size; tierischer ~ für feines Schreibpapier: animal sizing; aus dem ~(e) geh(e)n to get out of joint, to fall to pieces; fig. auf den Leim geh(e)n (sich anführen l.) to go (or fall) into a trap, F to be taken in.
leim=artig (¹⁻...) a. ⊕ glue-like, ⚕ glutinous, colloid; =druck m 62 typ. collotype.
leimen (¹⁻) I v/a. ⊕ 1. ⊕ (mit Leim zs.=fügen) to glue (together); (mit Leim überziehen) to dress with) glue, to size; Buchbinderei: den Rücken e-s Buches 2 to glue up the back ... — 2. hunt. einen Vogel (mit der Leimrute) 2 to lime ...; fig. einen Gimpel 2 (betrügen) to entrap (or cheat, catch) a jay; geleimt w., a. to go into a snare or a trap. — II ~ n 23 3. gluing; sizing; ⚒ Papierfabr.: ~ in der Bütte sizing in the vat.
Leimer (¹⁻) m 22 1. gluer, sizer, one who glues or sizes. — 2. = Kleiber 1.
Leim=farbe (¹⁻...) f ⊕ distemper, glue-water colour; paint. size-colour; =grund m Vergolderei: glue-priming; =gut n Gerberei: glue-materials pl.
leimicht, leimig (¹⁻) a. ⊕ = leimartig.
Leim=kocher (¹⁻...) m ⊕ =sieder a; =kraut ⚕ n catch-fly, ⚕ silene; =pinsel m glue-brush; =rohstoff m glue-stock; =rute f, hunt. lime-rod or -twig; =sieden n glue-boiling; =sieder m: a) glue-boiler; b) F fig. (langweiliger Mensch) dull (or humdrum, prosy) fellow, slow-coach, bore; =stoff m, chm.: ⚕ gluten; =tiegel, =topf m glue-pot; =überzug m glue-coat; =wasser n, paint. glue-water; =zucker n, chm.: ⚕ glycocoll, glycocin ($C_2H_5NO_2$); =zwinge f, join. glue-press.
..lein (...¹) [ahd.] n 23 dim. Endung, 3B. Lämmlein lambkin.
Lein (¹) [ahd.] m (bisw. a. n) ②c. 1. ⚕ flax (Linum); echter ~ common flax (L. usitati'ssimum). — 2. = ~samen. — 3. poet. linen = ~wand.
Lein=acker (¹⁻...) m 62 flax-field; =bau m cultivation of flax; =blüte ⚕ f flax-blossom; =boden m flax-soil; =dotter ⚕ m gold-of-pleasure (Cameli'na sati'va).
Leine (¹⁻) [ahd.: line] f ⊕ 1. line, cord, (thin) rope; (Wasch=)~ clothes-line; (Leitriemen der Wagenpferde) driving-rein; hunt. (Koppelriemen) leash, slip; ⌁ (dünnes Tau) line, thin rope. — 2. fig. e-n an der ~ haben to keep (or have) a p. in tow or in hand.

leinen (¹⁻) [ahd.; *Lein] I a. 66 (of) linen; 2e Unterkleider pl. linen underwear sg. — II ~ n 23 linen, zum Hausgebrauche: house-linen (vgl. Leinwand); ⊕ (Weißware) linen ware or goods pl.
Leinen=band ⊕ u. ⊕ (¹⁻) n 62 tape; Buchbind.: ~ m linen binding; =damast m linen-damask; =garn n linen yarn or thread; =gewebe n linen texture or woof; =industrie f linen-industry; =tuch n linen cloth; =ware(n pl.) f linen goods pl. or ware, =waren=handel m linen-trade; =zeug n linen.
Leine=weber (¹⁻ᵘ⁻) = Leinweber.
Lein=feld (¹⁻...) n 62 =acker; =fink m, orn. flax-finch (Fringi'lla lina'ria); =grau a. 66 flaxy (grey); =kraut ⚕ n (Lina'ria), gemeines ~ toad-flax (L. vulga'ris); =kuchen m linseed- (or oil-) cake; =laken n = Leilach; =öl n linseed-oil; das ~ betreffend: ⚕ linoleic; =öl=firnis m boiled linseed-oil; =pfad m (=Leine) an Flüssen: tow (-ing)-path; =pflanze ⚕ f flax (Linum); =saat f, =samen ⚕ m linseed, fl.-seed; =samen=mehl n linseed-meal or -flour; =seide ⚕ f = Flachs=s.; =straße ⌁ f = =pfad; =tuch n linen cloth, Bettuch: sheet.
Leinwand ⊕ u. ⊕ (¹⁻) [mhd.] f, inv. linen (cloth); für Ölgemälde: canvas, (un)gebleichte ~ (un)bleached linen; Buchbind.: in ~ gebunden bound in cloth.
Leinwand=band ⊕, ⊕ (¹⁻...) m 62 Buchbinderei: cloth binding; volume bound in cloth; =bleiche f bleaching-ground for linen; =handel m linen-trade, linendrapery; =händler(in f) m linen-draper; =kittel m linen frock; =laden m linendraper's shop.
Lein=waren ⊕ (¹⁻...) f/pl. 62 linen goods or articles pl.; =weber ⊕ m linen-weaver; =weber=stuhl ⊕ m linen-weaver's loom; =zeug ⊕ n linen; =zieher ⌁ [Leine] m tower, tracker.
leis (¹) a. 66(D 10) = leise.
leise (¹⁻) [ahd.] a. 66 (ant. laut) 1. (kaum hörbar) low, under one's breath; mit 2r Stimme in a low voice or tone, in an undertone; 2 sprechen to speak in a low voice or under one's breath. — 2. (wenig merkbar) soft, gentle, hardly perceptible; (zart) delicate; nicht die 2ste Ahnung not the faintest idea; adv. 2 auftreten to tread softly or noiselessly; nur 2 berühren to touch lightly; nicht im 2sten zweifeln not to doubt in the least, not to have the slightest doubt. — 3. 2s (scharfes) Gehör good (or quick) hearing; 2 (adv.) schlafen, einen 2n (nicht festen) Schlaf haben to be a light sleeper, to have a light sleep.
Leise=treter F (¹⁻ᵘ⁻...) m 62 sneak, sneaking fellow, eavesdropper; =treterei f sneaking, eavesdropping.
Leist ⊕ (¹) m ⓐ a. (hölzerne Fußform) last.
Leistchen (¹⁻) n 23 (dim.: Leiste¹) small ledge; arch.: plattes ~: ⚕ bandelet.
Leiste¹ (¹⁻) [ahd.: list] f ⊕ 1. ⊕ ledge, border, margin; arch., Tischlerei 2c. auch: moulding, fillet, bracket, listel, reglet; typ. (Verzierung) flourish; Weberei: (Sal=)~ selvedge, list. — 2. provc. = Leite.

Leiste² [erst nhd.] f 48 anat. groin.
leisten¹ (¹⁻) [ahd.] I. v/a. ⊕ 1. (tun) to do one's duty, (verrichten) to perform a piece of work; (ausführen) to carry out, to execute, (wirklich m.) to realize, make good, effect, (erfüllen) to accomplish, to fulfil; (liefern, schaffen) to provide, procure, supply. — 2. Bsd. Verbindungen: Bürgschaft für e-n 2 to go bail (or be security) for a p.; Buße 2 to do penitence; s. Dienst 1, Eid, Folge 5, gehorsam II; e-m Genugtuung 2 to give a p. satisfaction; s. Gesellschaft 2, Gewähr¹; e-m hilfreiche Hand 2, Hilfe 2 to lend a p. a helping hand, to give a p. assistance; Huldigung 2 to render (or do) homage; Sicherheit (Kaution) 2 to give security; auf et. Verzicht 2 to give up (or to waive) one's claim to a th.; ⊕ Vorschuß 2 auf // to advance money on //; e-m Widerstand 2 to make opposition to a p., to resist a p.; eine Zahlung 2 to make a payment. — 3. mit allgemeinem Objekte: er wird nie etwas oder et. Ordentliches 2 he will never do much (for himself); er sucht das Höchste zu 2 he aspires to a high level (or pitch) of excellence; er hat sein möglichstes geleistet he has done his best or F his level best; leistet so viel wie zwei andere Mädchen she does the work of two other girls; diese Schüler 2 Tüchtiges im Lateinischen ... are doing well (or showing great proficiency) in Latin; im Zeichnen habe ich nie viel geleistet I have never been clever (or F a good hand) at drawing; Vorzügliches 2 to do excellently well, to achieve excellent results; sich et. 2 to treat o.s. to a th.; ich kann mir das nicht 2 I cannot afford it. — II ~ n 23 4. = Leistung 1.
Leisten² ⊕ (¹⁻) [mhd.: last] m 23 (shoemaker's) last; zum Ausweiten: boot-tree, block; auf (ob. über) den Leisten schlagen to put (or mount) on the block; fig. alles über einen ~ schlagen to treat all things alike; F sie sind sämtlich über einen ~ geschlagen they are all of a kidney or tarred with the same brush; Sprichw. Schuster, bleib bei deinem ~! the cobbler must stick to his last!, every jack to his trade!
Leisten³=beule (¹⁻...) [Leiste²] f ⊕ anat. u. path. swelling in the groin, bubo; =bruch m, path.: ⚕ inguinal rupture, bubonocele; =bruch=band n, surg.: ⚕ inguinal bandage; =drüse f: ⚕ inguinal gland; =gegend f groin, ⚕ inguinal region; =²hobel ⊕ [Leiste¹] m (Simshobel) rabbet-, ogee-plane; =²holz ⊕ n wood for lasts; =macher m last-maker; =³ring m: ⚕ abdominal ring; =²schneider m last-cutter; =²tür f batten-door; =werk n moulding, bordering, beading.
Leistung (¹⁻) f 48 1. (s. leisten¹) doing, performance; execution, accomplishment. — 2. (das Geleistete) work done (auch ⊕ mach.), mech. &c. (Effekt) effect (or result) produced; service(s pl.) rendered; ~ e-s Künstlers artistic performance; trefflich ~ eines Arbeiters excellent workmanship or piece of

---

⚕ scientific; ⚘ botanical; 🜨 geography; ⊕ machinery; ⚒ mining; ⚔ military; ⌁ marine; ⊕ commercial; ✉ postal; 🚂 railway.

[leistungsfähig] — 656 — [Leoniden]

work; seine ~en in der Mathematik 2c. his attainments pl. in ...; ⊕ ~ in Geld und Naturalien disbursement in money and in kind.
leistungs=fähig (ᴵᴵ~·ᴸ~) a. ⓖ capable of producing, able to perform one's work, &c., productive; ⊕ solvent, solid; (tüchtig) efficient; **~keit** f ⓖ productive power, ability to perform one's work, &c.; ⊕ mach. mechanical power or force; ⊕ financial position, engS. solvency; (Tüchtigkeit) efficiency.
Leit-artikel ᵀ (ᴵᴵ...) m ⓖ einer Zeitung: leading article, leader; **=artikelchen** n leaderette; **=artikel=schreiber** m leader-writer; **=band** = Gängelband.
leitbar (ᴸ~) a. ⓖ dirigible, tractable.
Leit-block ↓ (ᴵᴵ,ᴸ) m ⓖ für ein Tau: leading-block.   [slope, declivity.]
Leite (ᴸ~) [ahd.] f ⓖ (Halde) (mountain-)
leiten (ᴸ~) [ahd.: lead] 1 v/a. ⓖ 1. (führen) to lead, to conduct, steuernd: to steer; auf unbekannten Wegen: to guide, auf die rechte Bahn: to direct, to put right or in the right way; f. irre=2: sich schwer 2 lassen to be difficult to manage; er läßt sich ganz von ihnen 2 he is quite in their hands; ⊕ Wasser 2c. durch Röhren 2 to convey ... through (or by means of) tubes; Kloakenwasser in das Meer 2 to drain sewage into the sea. — 2. (beaufsichtigen, verwalten) to direct, control, manage; et. als Hauptperson 2 to be at the head of a th.; e-n Gottesdienst 2 to conduct (or to officiate at) a service; den Staat 2 to rule (or to be at the helm of) the state; eine Versammlung 2 to preside over a meeting. — **II ~ n** ⓖ 3. = Leitung 1. — **III** 2d p.pr. und a. ⓖ 4. (f. I) leading, conducting (a. phys.), &c.; elect., &c. non-conducting. — 5. fig. 2de Kreise leading (or influential) circles, ruling (or governing) classes pl.; 2de Persönlichkeiten chief personages, head (or principal) men, F great swells or guns pl.
Leiter¹ (ᴸ~) [leiten] m ⓖ 1. v. Personen: **~(in** f ⓖ) leader, conductor, guide, director, e-s Geschäfts: manager(ess f), e-r Schule: principal, head master, a. head, e-r Partei: wire-puller, Am. boss. — 2. v. Sachen: phys. conductor of electricity, &c.
Leiter² ⊕ (ᴸ~) [ahd.: ladder] f ⓖ ladder, (Steh=)~ (pair of) steps pl., f. anlegen 1; mit ~n ersteigen to mount with ladders, ⚔ to scale.
Leiter²=baum ⊕ (ᴵᴵ~...) m ⓖ ladder-beam; **=ersteigung** f mounting of (or with) ladders, ⚔ scaling; **=förmig** a. ⓖ ladder-shaped, ?: ⚔ scalariform; **=sprosse** f rung (or step) of a ladder; **=wagen** m rack-wagon, mehr gbr.: open van or wagon, feinerer Art: break.
Leit-faden (ᴵᴵ...) m ⓖ: a) myth. ~ der Ariadne clue; b) fig. (Lehrbuch) introduction to grammar, &c.; **=feuer** ⚔ n bei Minen: train of powder; ↓ leading fire; **=hammel** m Schafzucht: bell-wether; fig. ringleader; **=hund** m, hunt. bsb. ehm.: lime-hound; (Stöberhund) tufter; **=kurve** ⊕ f Wasserbau: guide-blade; **=motiv** ♪

leitmotiv; **=riemen** m f. Leine 1; **=rolle** ⊕ f guide-pulley; **=satz** m guiding principle; **=schiene** f ⚙ guide-rail, safety-rail; ⚔ der Kammer am Gewehr: directrix; **=seil** n: a) guide-rope or -cord; b) hunt. für Spürhunde: leash; **=stern** [mhd.] m, ast. (Mittelpunkt des Sternenhimmels) polar star, ✱ lode-star; fig. guiding star; **=strahl** m, math.: ⚙ radius vector; **=tier** n, hunt. leader; **=ton** ♪ m leading note.
Leitung (ᴸ~) f ⓖ 1. (das Leiten) lead(ing), conduct(ing), guidance, direction; control, management; die ~ in die Hand nehmen to take the management (or the reins of government) into one's (own) hands; alles steht unter f-r ~ everything is under his control or is managed by him. — 2. ⊕ e-r Maschine: guiding-bar, (Übertragung) transmission; elect., &c. conduction, tel. line, wire. — 3. (Weg für Strömendes) conduit(-pipe).
Leitungs=draht ⊕ (ᴵᴵ...) m ⓖ tel. connecting wire, (telegraph-)wire; ein Haus 2c. mit elektrischen =drähten versehen to wire ...; **=fähig** a. ⓖ fit to be guided or conducted, phys. conductible, ...ive; **=fähigkeit** f, phys. conductibility, ...ivity; **=gang** m für Kabel 2c.: subway; **=gewebe** ♀ n der Pflanzen: tissue of ducts; **=kraft** f conducting power; **=rohr** n, **=röhre** ⊕ f conduit-pipe, für Gas, Wasser: gas-, water-pipe; **=vermögen** n = =kraft.
Leit-walze ⊕ (ᴵᴵ~,ᴸ~) f ⊕ guide-roller.
Lektion (~tß(ᵛ)ᴸ) [lt.] f ⓖ (Lehrstunde und das zu lernende Pensum) lesson; fig. (Verweis) lecture, f. lesen 4.
Lektions=katalog (ᴸ...) m ⓖ syllabus (or list) of lectures; **=plan** m, **=tabelle** f time-table, routine of a school; **=verzeichnis** n = =katalog.
Lektor (ᴸ~) [lt. Leser] m ⓖ univ.: ~ der neueren Sprachen (university-)lecturer of modern languages; **~stelle** (ᴸ~·ᴸ~) f appointment (or post) of a lecturer.
Lektüre (~ᴸ~) [fr.] f ⓖ (Lesung, Lesestoff) reading; nach der ~ e-s Werkes after the reading (or perusal) of a work.
Lemming (ᴸ~) [norweg.] m ⓖ d. zo. lemming (Myodes Lemmus).
lemnisch (ᴸ~) (♀ Lemnos) a. ⓖ Lemnian; 2e Erde Lemnian (or Turkish) earth.
Lemur (ᴸ~) [lt.] m 1. myth. ~en (~ᴸ~) pl. (Nachtgeister) lemures, weitS. ghosts, spirits pl. — 2. zo. (Affen-art) maki (Lemur).
Lemuride(n pl.) (~ᴸ~ᴸ~) m ⓖ lemuridæ.
Lenchen F (ᴸ~) [Lene, dim.] npr/n. ⓖ a. etwa: Nell, Nelly, Nellie.
Lende (ᴸ~) [ahd.(: loin, *fr.)] f ⓖ 1. ~n pl. (Nierengegend) loin, ⚙ lumbar region; f. gürten 2. — 2. weitS. (Hüfte) hip, haunch; (Schenkel) thigh.
Lenden=blutader (ᴸ~ᴸ~) f ⓖ anat.: ⚙ lumbar vein; **=braten** m Kocht.: roast loin, vom Rinde auch: sirloin of beef; **=gegend** f: ⚙ lumbar region; **=gicht** f, path.: ⚙ sciatica; **=knochen** m hipbone, ⚙ ischium; **=lahm** a. ⓖ lame in the hips or haunches, ⚙ lumbaginous; vgl. kreuzlahm; **=muskel** m, anat.: ⚙ lumbar muscle, psoas; zum ~ gehörig: ⚙ psoadic; **=stück** n Kocht.:

piece of the loin, loin-steak, rumpsteak; **=tuch** n in tropischen Ländern: waistcloth; **=weh** n, path.: ⚙ lumbar pain, lumbago; **=wirbel** m, anat.: ⚙ lumbar (vertebra). — Vgl. auch Hüft-....
...lendig (...ᴸ~) a. ⓖ ...loined, zB. dick2 thick-loined, with large thighs.
Lene F (ᴸ~)[(Magda)lene; (He)lene] npr/f. ⓖ d. f. (Bn.) Maud, Helen, Ellen.
lenkbar (ᴸ~) a. ⓖ guidable, governable, manageable, tractable; 2es Luftschiff steerable balloon, navigable (or dirigible) airship; **~keit** f ⓖ manageableness, tractability; navigability.
lenken (ᴸ~) [mhd.; *† Lanke] I v/a., v/n. (h.) u. sich 2 v/refl. ⓖ 1. (sich) (wenden) to turn, to bend; in neue Bahnen (ein=) 2 to take a new departure. — 2. (f. leiten I) to lead, conduct, guide; e-n Kriegswagen 2 to drive a chariot; ein Schiff 2 (steuern) to steer ..., als Lotse: to pilot; weitS. (verwalten, regieren) to direct, control, manage, govern; (beherrschen, meistern) to master, rule, subdue; ⚙ directing, directive, ruling; j-s Aufmerksamkeit auf et. 2 to draw (or call) a p.'s attention to a th.; die Aufmerksamkeit auf sich 2 to attract (people's) attention; er weiß sein Roß zu 2 he knows how to manage (or control, rein) his steed; sich 2 lassen to be manageable or tractable; Sprichw. f. denken 1b. — **II ~ n** ⓖ 3. = Lenkung.
Lenker (ᴸ~) m ⓖ, **~in** f ⓖ 1. = Leiter¹ 1; rel. der ~ des Weltalls the Lord of the Universe; der ~ unserer Herzen He who guides (or directs) our hearts. — 2. (Rosse=)~: a) charioteer; b) F co. coachman, (Droschkenkutscher) F cabby. — 3. ⊕ mach. nur m guide-bar, guiding-rod. [Wagenpferde: reins pl.]
Lenk-riemen (ᴸ~) (ᴸ~,ᴸ~) m/pl. ⓖ für
lenksam (ᴸ~) a. ⓖ easy of guidance; easy to manage (vgl. lenkbar); (biegsam) flexible, pliable, (geschmeidig) supple, (nachgiebig) yielding, tractable.
Lenksamkeit (ᴸ~·ᴸ~) f ⓖ manageableness; flexibility, suppleness.
Lenk-scheit (ᴸ...) n ⓖ am Wagen: sway- (or sweep-)bar; **=stange** f einer Dampfmaschine: radius-bar.
Lenkung (ᴸ~) f ⓖ (f. lenken I) guidance; direction (or management) of affairs; ruling (or rule, sway) over men, an empire, &c., pol. lead(ership).
Lenore (~ᴸᴸ~) npr/f. ⓖ d. f. = Leonore.
Lenz (ᴸ) [ahd.: Lent] m ⓖ a. spring(-tide) (= Frühling); ~ des Lebens bloom (or spring) of life, youth.
lenzen ↓ (ᴸ~) v/n. ⓖ (vor schwerem Sturm mit dicht gerefften Segeln laufen) to scud; vor Topp und Takel 2 to scud under bare poles.
Lenz¹=freuden (ᴸ...) f/pl. ⓖ, **=genüsse** m/pl. vernal joys, enjoyments pl.; **=monat** m month of March.
Lenz²=pumpe ↓ (ᴸ~,ᴸ~) f ⓖ bilge-pump; 2pumpen ↓ v/n. (h.) ⓖ (mit der Lenzpumpe leerpumpen) to free the ship.
Leonhard (ᴸ~) npr/m. ⓖ ⓖ ⓖ ⓖ a. (Bn.) Leonard, dim. Len(nie).
Leoniden (~ᴸᴸ~ᴸ) [leo Löwe] pl., inv. ast. (November-meteor-schwarm, vom Sternbilde des Löwen ausgehend) Leonides pl.

Zeichen (f. S. XVII): F familiär; P Volkssprache; Γ Gaunersprache; ✱ selten; † alt (auch gestorben) * neu (auch geboren); ‥ unrichtig

[leoninisch] — 657 — [Lettergut]

leoninisch (⏑⏑⎯⏑) [Leo(nius), Dichter, um 1150] *a.* ⑯ *pros.*: Le Verse (abwechselnd Hexameter u. Pentameter, in Mitte und Ende sich reimend) leonine verse. [**Leonora.**]
Leonore (⏑⎯⏑⏑) [S²] *npr/f.* ⑨⑧β. (Vn.)
Leopard (⎯⏑) [mhd.; *It. Löwenparder] *m* ㉒ und ⓒ.C. *zo.* (a. *her.* schreitender Löwe, der das volle Gesicht zeigt) leopard (*Felis leopa'rdus*); ~ zum Jagen = Gepard.
Leoparden-fell (⏑⎯⏑⏑...) *n* ㉒ leopard's skin; =**weibchen** *n* leopardess.
Lepidolith ⚗ (⏑⏑⎯⏑) *m* ⑨d.㊷ *min.* (Schuppenstein, Art Lithionglimmer) lepidolite.
Lepidoptere (*n pl.*) ⚗ (⏑⏑⎯⏑⏑) [grch.] *f* ⑨ *ent.* (Schmetterlinge) lepidopters *pl.*
lepontinisch ♀ (⎯⏑⎯) Lepo'ntier, altes rätisches Volk] *a.* ⑯: =e Alpen *pl.* Lepontine (or Helvetic) Alps *pl.*
Lepra (⎯⏑) [grch. ♀⎯] *f*, *inv. path.* (Aussatz) leprosy.
Lerche (⎯⏑; *Hom.* Lärche) [ahd.: lark] *f* ⑨ 1. *orn.* (sky-)lark (*Alau'da*); =n streichen to catch (sky-)larks with a net. — 2. F *fig.* eine ~ schießen (stürzen) F to go a cropper.
Lerchen-falke (⎯⏑...) *m* ㉒ *orn.* hobby (*Falco subbu'teo*); =**fang** *m* catching (or snaring) of larks; =**garn** *n* net for catching larks; =**gesang** *m* singing (or warbling) of sky-larks; =**herd** *m* decoy for larks; =**netz** *n* = =**garn**; =**pfeife** *f*, *hunt.* lark-call; =**sporn** ♀ *m* hollowwort, ⚗ corydalis; =**streichen** *n*, =**strich** *m*: a) flight (or passage) of larks; b) netting of larks.
lernäisch (⎯⏑) [grch.] *a.* ⑯ Lernæan.
lernbar (⎯⏑) *a.* ⑯ learnable.
Lern-begierde (⎯⏑...) *f* ㉒ desire (or eagerness) to learn, studiousness; ⁀**begierig** *a.* ⑯ desirous of learning, eager to learn, studious; =**eifer** *m* zeal for learning, eagerness to learn.
lernen (⎯⏑) [ahd.: learn; *lehren] I *v/a.*, *v/n.* (h.) u. *v/refl.* ⑱ 1. to learn, (studieren) to study; (üben) to practise; F *u.* P (auch *G.* u. *L.*) statt lehren = to teach; Englisch ⁀ to learn (or study) English; auswendig ⁀ to learn by rote, e-e Rolle rc.: to get up (or off) by heart; bei einem Lehrer ⁀ to be under a master; gelegentlich ⁀ to pick up; Französisch gründlich ⁀ to acquire (or master) French thoroughly; er hat et. Tüchtiges gelernt he has applied himself to his studies, he is a good scholar; ich habe das von ihr gelernt I learnt that from her; so et. lernt sich bald such things are soon learnt; f. kennen I; lesen ⁀ to learn reading or to read; *fig.* wir haben ihn achten ⁀ (oder gelernt) we have come to esteem him; Sprichw. lerne was, so kannst du was learn, and you will know; knowledge must be acquired (by learning); es will alles gelernt sein everything has to be learnt. — 2. (in der Lehre sein) to serve one's apprenticeship with a master, to be apprenticed to a trade. — II ~ *n* ㉓ 3. (f. 1) learning; study (-ing); acquisition of knowledge; das ~ wird ihm schwer he is slow in learning or dull of apprehension.—4. (f. 2) apprenticeship. — III **ge-lernt** *p.p.* und *a.* ⑯ 5. Beb. des *inf.* — 6. (zunft-

mäßig geschult) knowing a trade or craft; 2er Schuster shoemaker by trade.
Lernende(r) (⎯⏑⏑) *s.* ⑰ one who learns, scholar, pupil; ● *u.* Handwerk = learner; apprentice, F new hand (vgl. Lehrling).
Lern-fleiß (⎯...) *m* ⑨ application to one's studies; =**gegenstand** *m* subject of study, matter to be learnt or acquired; ⁀**lust(ig** *a.* ⑯) *f* = =**begier(ig)**; =**zeit** *f*: a) =Lehrzeit; b) time for study.
Les-art (⎯,⎯) [lesen] *f* ㉒ Philologie: reading, *pl. auch:* variants, *fig.* die gewöhnliche ~ the ordinary version.
lesbar (⎯⏑) [lesen] *a.* ⑯ 1. (leserlich) legible, (entziffernd) decipherable. — 2. (lesenswert) readable, worth reading.
Lesbarkeit (⎯⏑⎯) *f* ⑯ 1. legibility. — 2. readableness, readability.
Lesbi-er (⎯(⏑)⏑) [Lesbos, grch. Insel] *m* ㉒, =**in** ㊼, **lesbisch** (⎯⏑) *a.* ⑯ Lesbian.
Lese (⎯⏑) [lesen] *f* ⑨ 1. von Früchten: gathering, picking, gleaning, von Trauben: vintage; f. Ähren=, Blumen= lese. — 2. = Auslese.
Lese-abend (⎯⏑...) *m* ㉒ evening gathering for reading (purposes); =**bibliothek** *f* circulating library; =**brille** *f* glasses *pl.* for reading, reading-glasses *pl.*; =**buch** *n* reading-book, reader (auch für Sprachunterricht); =**fibel** *f* first reader, primer; vgl. Fibel; =**freund(in** *f*) *m* person fond of reading, great (stärker: voracious) reader; =**früchte** *f/pl.* selections (or gleanings) *pl.* from various authors; =**gesellschaft** *f* literary society; =**halle** *f*, =**kabinett** *n* reading-room (*pl.*); =**holz** *n* (small) picked-up wood; =**kränzchen** *n* society for reading; =**lehrer(in** *f*) *m* teacher of reading; =(**lehr=)methode** *f* method of teaching (the art of) reading; =**lust** *f* love (or taste) for reading; ⁀**lustig** *a.* ⑯ fond of reading.
lesen (⎯⏑) [ahd. (2 1 nach *It. le'gere)] I *v/a.*, *v/n.* (h.) und *v/refl.* ⑨a.. 1. to read, mit Mühe: to spell; für sich ⁀ to read to o.s.; eine schlechte Handschrift ⁀ (entziffern) to decipher ...; ich kann es nicht ⁀, oft: I cannot make it out; nicht zu ⁀(d) illegible; sie liest sehr viel she reads a great (stärker: an immense) deal, she is a great (stärker: an omnivorous) reader; lies (*abbr.* l.) read; er hat 6 Wochen an der Erzählung gelesen it took him (or he took) six weeks to read the tale (through); man kann es in ihren Augen ⁀ one can read it in her eyes; vgl. ableben 1; in den Sternen ⁀ to read in the stars; zwischen den Zeilen ⁀ to read between the lines; ein viel gelesener Schriftsteller a much read (or very popular) author; ⊙ *typ.*: eine Korrektur ⁀ to read a proof; *Cath.eccl.* Messe ⁀ to say mass. — 2. *v/refl.* das liest sich wie ein Roman that reads like a novel; der Brief läßt sich (nicht) ⁀ ... is (il)legible; das Buch läßt sich (nicht) ⁀ ... is (un-)readable; ich habe mich müde gelesen I have tired myself with reading; sich blind ⁀ to read o.s. blind. — 3. auf Hochschulen: (Lehrvorträge halten) to give (or deliver) lectures; er liest (über) Geschichte he lectures on history;

heute wird nicht gelesen (there will be) no lecture(s) to-day. — 4. F *fig.* e-m die Epistel, das Kapitel, die Lektion, die Leviten, den Psalter, den Text ⁀ (einen Verweis geben) to reprimand (or rebuke) a p., F to lecture (or sermonize) a p., to give a p. a (good) set-down. — 5. (auflesen) to pick up, Ähren: to glean; (sammeln) to gather; (aussuchen) to pick, select, cull; Erbsen, Salat rc. ⁀ (reinigen, sondern) to pick (or clean) ... —
II ~ *n* ㉓ 6. (f. 1) lautes ~ loud reading; ~ e-r schlechten Handschrift decipherment; ~ von den Lippen lip-reading; mit ~ beschäftigt (engaged in) reading; (f. 3) lecturing; (f. 5) picking (up), (in-)gathering; von Trauben: vintage.
lesens-wert (⎯⏑⎯) *a.* ⑯ worth reading.
Lese-probe (⎯⏑...) *f* ㉒ *thea.* reading-rehearsal; =**publikum** *n* reading public; =**pult** *n* (*m*) reading-desk.
Leser (⎯⏑) *m* ㉒, ~**in** *f* ㊼ 1. (f. lesen 1) reader; ein fleißiger ~ a hard reader; der (geneigte) ~ the gentle (or courteous) reader; die (geneigte) ~in the fair reader. — 2. (f. lesen 5) picker, gleaner, gatherer, vintager.
Lese-ratte, =ratze F (⎯⏑...) *f* ⑨ bookworm.
Leserei (⏑⏑⎯) *f* ⑨ desultory reading, (constant) poring over books.
Leser-kreis (⎯⏑⎯) *m* ㉒ circle of readers, circulation; *Kipling* hat einen weiten ~ ... is extensively (or widely) read.
leserlich (⎯⏑⏑) *a.* ⑯ easy to read, legible.
Leserlichkeit (⎯⏑⏑⎯) *f* ⑯ legibility.
Leserschaft (⎯⏑⎯) *f* ⑯ all the readers *pl.*
Lese-saal (⎯⏑...) *m* ⑧: a) =**halle**; b) lecture-hall; =**schule** *f* elementary school; =**schüler(in** *f*) *m* boy (*f* girl) who learns reading, abecedarian; =**stoff** *m* reading; =**stücke** *n/pl.* select pieces *pl.* for reading, v. Gedichten auch: anthology; =**stunde** *f* reading-lesson, lesson in reading; =**sucht** *f* mania (or passion, craze) for r.; ⁀**süchtig** *a.* ⑯ madly (or passionately) fond of r.; =**übung** *f* r.-exercise, =**unterricht** *m* instruction in r.; =**welt** *f* reading public, (world of) readers *pl.*; =**wut** *f* = =**sucht**; =**zeichen** *n* a) *gram.* (Satzzeichen) stop; b) bookmark, (book-)marker; =**zeit** *f*: a) gathering-in (or harvesting-)time; b) time devoted to reading; =**zimmer** *n* = =**halle**; =**zirkel** *m* circle (or society, party) of readers, reading-club.
Lesung (⎯⏑) *f* ⑨ = lesen II; bei ~ Ihres Namens on reading your name; *parl.* ~ eines Gesetzvorschlages reading of a bill; der Entwurf kam zur ersten ~ the bill was read for the first time.
Lethargie ⚗ (⎯⏑⎯) [grch.] *f* ⑨ (Schlafsucht) lethargy (a. *fig.*).
lethargisch (⎯⏑⏑) *a.* ⑯ lethargic(al).
Lethe (⎯⏑) [grch.] *npr/f.* ⑨⑧β. (*m* ⑨⑭a.) *myth.* (Fl. der Vergessenheit in der Unterwelt) Lethe; ~ trinken to drink of the river Lethe. [variegated) clay.]
Letten (⎯⏑) [ahd.] *m* ㉓ Geognosie: red (or **letten-artig** (⎯⏑...) *a.* ⑯ clayey; =**boden** *m* red clay-soil, clayey soil.
Letter (⎯⏑) [fr. *lettre*] *f* ⑨ (Buchstabe) letter, character; ⊙ *typ. a.* type.
Letter-gut (⎯⏑⎯) *n* ㉓ type-metal.

♩ Musik; ⚗ Wissenschaft; ⚘ Pflanze; ♀ Geographie; ⊙ Technik; ⚒ Bergbau; ⚔ Militär; ⚓ Marine; ⊛ Handel; ✉ Post; 🚂 Eisenbahn.

Lettern-druck (⌣‿...) m ㊂ printing, letter-press; **-gießmaschine** f type-founding machine; **-metall** n = Lettergut.
lettich, lettig (⌣‿) [Letten] a. ㊅ clayey.
Lett(n)er (⌣‿) [lt.] m ㊁ eccl. reading-desk, lectern; gallery of a church.
letzen (⌣‿) [ahd.; *Letze Raft] v/a. u. sich ~ v/refl. ㊇ 1. (sich) ~ = (sich) er-quicken; weitS. (erfreuen) to gladden; sich an et. ~ to enjoy a th. — 2. sich mit Freunden ~ (den Abschiedsschmaus halten) to give a farewell dinner.
letzt (‿) [ahd.: late, last; *laß] **I** a. ㊅ (ant. erste) 1. last, ultimate; (am Ende) final, extreme; die ~e (unterste) Abteilung the lowest (or F bottom) division; f. Atem-zug; e-m die ~e Ehre erweisen to pay a p. the last tribute of respect, to attend a p.'s funeral; er war im ~en Grunde froh darüber he was at the bottom of his heart (or in real truth) glad of it; bis auf den ~en Mann to the last man, to a man; Cath. eccl.: ~e Ölung extreme unction; ~er Versuch last (or supreme) effort; sein ~er Wille his last wishes pl., feierlicher: his last will and testament; er will immer das ~e Wort haben he always wants (to have) the last word; seine ~en Worte his last (e-s Sterbenden: his dying) words pl.; in der ~en Zeit f. 6; in den ~en Zügen liegen to be breathing one's last. — 2. im comp. der, die, das ~ere, ~erer ㊅ [:latter] (the) latter; im ~eren Falle in the latter case, f. erste 3. — **II** ~e(r) m, ~e f, ~es n ㊂ 3. der (die) ~e the last (one); das ist der ~e, dem ich trauen möchte he is the last person (that) I would trust; f. erste 2; der ~e in der Klasse sein to be the last in (or at the bottom of) one's class; der ~e des Monats the last day of the month; der ~e seines Stammes the last (repre-sentative) of his race; Sprichw. den ~en beißen die Hunde the devil take the hindmost; bibl. die Ersten werden die Letzten sein f. erste 2. — 4. das ~e the last thing, (das Ende) the end; (das Äußerste) the last extremity; er gäbe das ~e hin he would give his last (penny) or his very life; zum ~en greifen to take extreme measures, to cling to the last straw. — **III** adv. 5. in the end, last of all, finally; der (die) ~ Eintretende the last comer. — 6. ~ ob. letztens, letzthin, letztlich (in der ~en Zeit) latterly, lately, of late, in these latter days; (neulich) the other day, recently, a short time ago. — 7. letztens: a) = ~ 6; b) auch: zum ~en, in Aufzählungen: erstens, zweitens :c., ~ens lastly, in the last place. — **8. am** (ob. **zum**) ~en (bisw. = zuletzt) finally; at last, ultimately; auf Auktionen: zum (dritten und) ~en Male for the (third and) last time; es ist mit ihm (Matthä'i) am ~en it is all over (or up) with him, he is on his last resources or F legs. — **IV Letzt(e)** f, inv. 9. auf die ~ in the end, ultimately; zu guter ~ as a finish, in the end, in conclusion, to finish up with, last not least.
Letzt-bietende(r) (‿...) m ㊇ last and highest bidder.

letztens (⌣‿) adv. f. letzt 6 u. 7.
letzter (⌣‿) comp. von letzt (f. ds 2).
letzt-erwähnt (‿...) a. ㊅ last mentioned; **-hin** (⌣‿) f. letzt 6; **-jährig** a. last year's, of last year; **-lebende(r)** s. survivor.
letztlich (⌣‿) adv. f. letzt 6. [adv. by will.
letzt-willig (‿⌣) a. ㊅ testamentary;
Leu (́) [lt. leo] m ㊁ † ob. poet. = Löwe.
Leucht-boje ⌄ (⌣‿) f ㊇ light buoy.
Leuchte (⌣‿) [ahd.] f ㊇ 1. luminous body, light, fig. luminary (or shining light, star) in science, art, &c. — 2. (Late'rne) lamp, lantern; ⌄ u. ✕ beacon.
leuchten (⌣‿) [ahd.; *Liecht] **I** v/n. (h.) ㊈ 1. (Licht geben) to (give) light, to shine (forth); (blinken) to glitter, to gleam, (strahlen) to beam, to radiate, (funkeln) to sparkle; ⌄ vom Meere: to phos-phoresce. — 2. fig. das leuchten in die Augen (ist einleuchtend) that is (self-)evident or obvious; bibl. sein Licht ~ lassen to let one's light shine before men. — 3. die Blitze ~, der Himmel leuchtet, v/impers. es leuchtet the sky is lit up with flashes of lightning, it lightens. — 4. mit persönlichem Subjekt: e-m ~ (damit er sehen kann) to hold the light (or a candle) for a p., bsd. ehm.: to light a p. to the door, &c.; e-m (ob. v/a. e-n) nach Hause ~: a) to see a p. home with a lantern; b) F fig. = heimleuchten. — **II** ~ n ㊄ 5. (f. 1) shin-ing, &c.; illumination, radiation, phys.: ⌒ coruscation, luminosity; ⌄ des Meeres: phosphorescence. — **III** 2d p.pr. u. a. ㊅ 6. in den Bed. des inf. — 7. luminous, bright, lustrous; ~des Beispiel brilliant example; ~der Him-melskörper luminary.
Leuchter (⌣‿) m ㊁ candlestick; mehr-armiger: chandelier; vgl. Kron~.
Leuchter-arm (⌣‿...) m ㊁ bracket of a chandelier; **-einsatz** m socket of a candlestick; **-gehänge** n crystals pl., (Glasprismen) lustres pl.; **-knecht** m save-all; **-säule** f, **-tisch** m chandelier-stand, pier-table; **-träger** m candle-stand; **-tülle** f = -einsatz.
Leucht-fackel ✕ (⌣‿...) f ㊇ torch; **-farbe** ⊙ f luminous paint; **-feuer** ✕ u. ⌄ n beacon, signal-fire; **-gas** n (lighting- or coal-)gas, chm.: ⌒ carburetted hydrogen; **-käfer** m glow-worm, fire-fly (Lampy'ris noctilu'ca); **-kraft** f illumin-ating power of gas, &c.; **-kugel** ⊙ f Feuerwerk: fire- (or light-)ball; **-öl** n illuminating oil, für Lampen: lamp-oil; **-pilz** ⚘ m phosphorescent agaric; **-rakete** f light-rocket; **-schiff** ⌄ n light-ship; **-stoff** m luminous matter; chm. ~ der im Dunkeln leuchtenden Tiere: ⌒ noctilucin; **-tiere** n/pl. ent. phos-phorescent (or luminous, noctilucent) animals pl.; **-tonne** ⌄ f = -boje; **-turm** ⌄ m light-house (mit Drehfeuer with revolving light); **-turm-wächter** m lighthouse-man, lighthouse-keeper.
Leuchtung (⌣‿) f ㊇ (f. leuchten II) (flashes pl. of) lightning.
Leucht-wurm (⌣‿) m ㊁ = -käfer.
Leucin ⌒ (⌣‿) [grch.] n ⓪ d. chm. (Käsefynd) leucine ($C_6H_{13}O_2N$; = Apofepedi'n).
leugn/en (⌣‿) [ahd. *lügen] **I** v/a. ㊅b. to deny; (in Abrede stellen) to disavow,

(bestreiten) to contest; (ablengnen, nicht anerkennen) to disown, (widerrufen) to retract, to recant; et. rundweg (steif und feft) ~ flatly (most positively) to deny a th.; fie ~ (nicht), daß er es ge-tan hat they (do not) deny (or dispute) his having done it; es ist nicht zu ~, daß // it cannot be denied (or is un-deniable) that // — **II** ~ n ㊄ f. L/ung.
Leugner (⌣‿) m ㊁, **~in** f ㊇ one who denies, &c. (f. leugnen I); denier.
Leugnung (⌣‿) f ㊇ (f. leugnen I) denial; disavowal; retract(at)ion.
leugſt, leugt ⚘ (/) poet. u. altertümlich 2 u. 3. Person des pres. ind. von lügen.
Leumund (⌣‿) [ahd.: laut] m ⓪d. (Ruf) reputation, repute, renown; böser ~ ill fame; in bösen ~ bringen to bring into disrepute, to defame; **~s-erforschung** f ㊇ inquiry into a p.'s character; **~s-zeugnis** n certificate of good con-duct, für Dienstboten :c. (good) character.
Leutchen (⌣‿) pl. ㊃ (dim. von Leute) good people or folk(s) pl.; hört, ihr ~! listen, my friends!
Leute (⌣‿) [ahd.] m/pl. ⓒ. 1. people, persons, folk(s) pl.; allerlei ~ all sorts and conditions of men pl.; unsere ~ (Partei :c.) our (own) people or men or set; seine ~ his people or men, (Diener-schaft) his domestics or (establish-ment of) servants pl., (Arbeiter) his (field- or factory-)hands pl.; die armen und die reichen ~ both the poor and the rich people pl.; man muß seine ~ kennen you must know your customers or whom you are dealing with; so sagen alle faulen ~ thus say all lazy people or the lazy ones; das sind die rechten ~ those are the right sort (of people); Sprichw. kleine ~, große Herzen some small folks have big hearts. — 2. coll. (Menge Personen) the world, the (general) public; die ~ sagen people say, it is said; was werden die ~ sagen? what will the world (or F Mrs. Grundy) say?; f. Ge-rede 2; f. bringen 8; gar nicht unter die ~ geh(e)n to see nobody, to shun society; er ist unter den ~n gewesen he has seen the world or mixed with people or been in society. — 3. (Men-schen) der Krieg hat viel ~ gekostet ... has cost many lives; es sind ~ (Besuch) bei ihm he has visitors (at his house); iro. das sind schöne ~ they are a fine set (of people or of fellows). — 4. (Er-wachsene) aus Kindern werden ~ boys will be men.
Leute-betrüger (⌣‿...) m ㊁ common (or notorious) cheat; **-placker, -plager,** **-scherer** m = **-schinder;** **-schinder** m tormentor, oppressor, petty tyrant, F nigger-driver, workmen's sweater; ✕ martinet; (Wucherer) extortioner; **-schinderei** f oppression, F sweating.
Leutnant (⌣‿) [uhd. 15. sac.; *fr. lieutenant „Statthalter"] m ⓪e. ㊁ bsd. ✕ (ehm. Sekonde-~) second lieutenant; ⌄ ~ zur See: a) (ehm. Unter-2 z. S.) sub-lieutenant; b) † = Ober-2 z. S.; Herr ~! Anrede: lieutenant!, mehr gbr.: sir!; Frau ~ lieutenant's wife, als Anrede: Mrs. N.; **~(s)-epauletten** f/pl. lieutenant's

[Leutnantsstelle]

shoulder-knots or epaulettes pl.; ~s-stelle f lieutenant's commission, lieutenancy. [secular priest.
Leut-priester (̈́ʹ‿) m ⊕ (Weltgeistlicher)
leut-selig (̈́ʹ‿) a. ⊕ affable, familiar, (herablassend) condescending, (artig) courteous, pleasant, gentle, kind; ~keit f ⊕ affability, familiarity; condescension, courtesy, pleasant (or gentle) ways pl., kindness.
Leuzit ⚒ (‿ʹ) [grch.] m ⊕c. min. leucite, amphigene, white garnet.
Levante ♀ (‿⌣‿) [it. (Sonnen-)Aufgang] f ⊕ Levant, East, Orient.
levantisch (‿⌣‿) a. ⊕ Levantine; die 2e Sprache, das ~(e) n ⊕ (it.) lingua franca. [täm] Leviathan (auch fig.).)
Leviathan (-w(‿)ʹ‿) m ⊕d. bibl. (Unge-)
Levit (-wʹ) [Levi, 3. Sohn Jakobs] m ⊕, ~in f ⊕ bibl. Levite; F fig. j. lesen 4; ~ikus (-wʹ‿‿) m ⊕ (das 3. Buch Mosis) Leviticus; 2isch (-wʹ‿‿) a. ⊕ levitical.
Levkoie, a. Levkoje(‿ʹ‿) [grch. Weißveilchen] f ⊕ stock (Matthi'ola); bsd. (Winter-)~ (stock-)gillyflower (M. inca'na).
lexikal(isch) (⌣‿ʹ(‿)) [grch.] a. ⊕ like (or relating to) a dictionary, ⚒ lexical.
Lexikograph ⚒ (⌣‿ʹ‿) [grch.] m ⊕ (Wörterbuchschreiber) lexicographer; ~ie (⌣‿‿ʹ) f ⊕ lexicography; 2isch (⌣‿‿ʹ‿) a. ⊕ lexicographic(al).
Lexikon (ʹ⌣‿) [grch.] n ⊕ (⊕) (Wörterbuch) dictionary, von gelehrten Sprachen auch:
Lfg. abbr. = Lieferung. [lexicon.]
L'hombre (lɔbr) [fr.; *span.] n ⊕ = Lomber. [pflanze) liana.}
Liane ♀ (-‿ʹ) [fr., *span.] f ⊕ (Schling-)
Lias ⚒ ⚒ (laí‐äs) [engl.] m u. f, inv. geol. (untere Juraformation) Lias; ~formation f ⊕ Lias(sic) formation or system; liassisch (laí‐‿) a. ⊕ Liassic.
Libanon ♀ (ʹ‿‿) [syr. weißes Gebirge] npr/m. ⊕α. (Mount) Lebanon.
Libation (-‐tsʹ‿) [it.] f ⊕ Alt. (Trankopfer) libation, drink-offering.
Libell (‿ʹ) [lt.] n ⊕d. (Schmähschrift) libel.
Libelle (‿ʹ‿) [lt. dim. zu libra Wage] f ⊕ 1. ⊕ surv. (Wasserwage) (water-)level, libella. — 2. ent. (Wasserjungfer) dragonfly (Libe'llula).
libellieren (‿‿ʹ‿) [Libell] v/a. ⊕ jur. to libel; Libellist (‿‿ʹ) m ⊕ libeller.
liberal (‿‐ʹ) [lt.] a. ⊕ liberal, pol. Liberal; die ~en the Liberals pl.; ~ismus (‐⌣‿ʹ‿) m⊕ pol. Liberalism; ~ität (‐⌣‿ʹ) f ⊕ (Freigebigkeit) liberality, generosity.
Librettist ♪ (‿⌣ʹ) [it.] m ⊕ librettist.
Libretto ♪ (‿ʹ‿) [it.] n ⊕⊕ book (or words pl., text) of an opera, libretto; ~schreiber (‿ʹ‿‿) m ⊕ = Libretti'st.
Liby-en ♀ (ʹ(‿)‿) [lt. Li'bya] npr/n. ⊕α. (Nordafrika) Libya; Liby-er(in f ⊕) m ⊕, libysch (ʹ‿) a. ⊕ Libyan; Libysche Wüste Libyan desert.
...lich (...⌣) [ahd.] ...ly (like) a. ⊕ u. adv., zB. glücklich lucky; grünlich greenish; schrecklich dreadful.
Licht¹ (⌣) [ahd.: licht] n ⊕ u. (~5) ⊕b. 1. light, (Helle) brightness, lustre (Tageslicht) day-light, (Beleuchtung) illumination; paint. ~er und Schatten pl. lights and shadows pl.; ~ des Mondes, e-r Kerze: moon-light, candle-light; ~er eines Diamanten rc.: lustre, fire sg.; bibl.

Gott sprach: Es werde ~, und es ward ~ ... Let there be light, and there was light. — 2. meist fig. das ~ der Welt erblicken to see the light, to come into the world; e-m ein ~ aufstecken über etwas to open a p.'s eyes to the real facts of a th.; ~ in etwas bringen to throw light upon a th., to clear a matter up; mir geht ein ~ auf a light dawns upon me, I begin to see clearly; ein ungünstiges ~ auf e-n rc. werfen to put a p., a th. in an unfavourable light; Sprichw. wo viel ~ ist, da ist viel Schatten strong light casts deep shadows. — 3. abhängig v. prp.: an: ans ~ bringen, fördern to bring to light; (bekanntmachen) to make known, to publish; ans ~ kommen (offenbar w.) to come to light, to become known; ans ~ treten to see daylight; ans ~ ziehen to cast light upon; gehen Sie mir aus dem ~e! get out of my light; bei ~e arbeiten rc. ... by candle- (or gas-)light; ct. bei ~e besehen to examine a th. closely; bei ~e betrachtet: a) (if) closely scanned; b) fig. taking a general view (of the case); gegen das ~ halten to hold to the light; hinter: e-n hinters ~ führen (täuschen) to mislead (or trick, cheat) a p.; in: et. ins rechte ~ setzen to put a th. in the right light (a. fig.); et. in helles ~ setzen to throw a strong light upon a th.; alles in rosigem ~e sehen to see everything in a rosy light, to look only at the bright side of things; e-m im ~e steh(e)n to be (or stand) in a p.'s light, way (auch fig.); fig. Sie steh(e)n sich selbst im ~e you are acting against your own interest; im besten ~e zeigen to show up to the best advantage; zwischen ~ und Dunkel in the twilight, between two lights. — 4. (leuchtender Gegenstand) luminous body; (Gestirn) luminary; fig. er ist kein großes ~ he is no great light or genius; von den Phasen des Mondes: das neue ~ the new moon; ⚓ (Leuchtfeuer) beacon. — 5. (Kerze) (Talg-)~ tallow (or dip-)candle, (Stearin-, Wachs-)~ wax candle; ~e ziehen to dip candles; P fig. er zieht ~e his nose is running; bibl. sein ~ (nicht) unter den Scheffel stellen (not) to put one's light under a bushel, weit. (not) to hide one's talent. — 6. hunt. ~er (Augen des Wildes) eyes pl. licht² (⌣) [ahd.: licht] a. ⊕ 1. light, stärker: bright, luminous, (glänzend) shining; von Farben: light(-coloured), pale; bei 2em Tage in full (or broad) day-light; es ist heller, 2er Tag it is broad daylight; es wird 2 the day (or it) is dawning; fig. 2e Augenblicke e-s Irrsinnigen: lucid intervals or moments pl. — 2. (durchsichtig) der Edelstein ist 2 (adv.) gefaßt ... is set transparently or (fr.) à jour; 2e Fassung, auch: clear setting; (mit weiten Zwischenräumen) clear; 2e Stelle: a) am bewölkten Himmel: break in the clouds; b) im Walde: clearing, glade, open space; e-n Wald 2 m. to clear ...; ⚒ 2e Reihen thin (or narrow) lines or ranks pl.; die Reihen 2en lassen to thin the ranks; typ. 2e Schrift con-

[Lichtleimdruck]

tour (or outline) face. — 3. ⊕ arch., &c.: das ~e clear space; im ~en (im Innern gemessen) in the clear.
Licht¹-arbeit (⌣...) f ⊕ working (or work done) by candle-light; ₂arm a. ⊕ wanting in light; =äther m, phys.: ⊕ luminiferous ether; =auge n, vet. wall-eye of a horse; =beugung f, phys. refraction; =bild ⊕ n photograph, bisw.: sun-picture; farbiges: heliochrom(otyp)e, in Kupfer rc. gravierte: photogravure; ₂bildlich a. photographic; =bildner m = Photograph; ₂²blau a. light (or pale) blue; =¹blick m flash (or gleam, ray) of light; (lichte Stelle am Himmel) bright spot, fig. auch: bright ray; =bogen ⊕ m, elect. luminous arc; ₂²braun a. light brown; =¹brechung f, phys. refraction of light.
Lichtchen (⌣‿) n ⊕ (dim. von Licht) small candle, rush-light.
Licht¹-dämpfer (⌣...) m ⊕ extinguisher; fig. s. Dämpfer 1; =docht m wick of a candle; =druck ⊕ m: a) =farbendruck; b) phototypy; c) (die Platte, das Bild) phototype, photogravure; =druckmanier f phototypic process; =effekt m, phys. luminous effect, paint. effect of light (on the picture); =eindruck m, =empfindung f impression, sensation caused by light; ₂empfindlich a. sensitive to light, phot. sensitive (paper), sensitized (plate, &c.).
lichten¹ (⌣‿) [Licht] I v/a. u. sich 2 v/refl. ⊕ to clear a forest; ⚒ to thin the ranks; die Reihen lichteten sich the ranks grew thin(ner) or were reduced; sich 2 to (become) clear. — II ~ n ⊕ = Lichtung 1.
lichten² ⚓ (⌣‿) [ndd. leicht machen] v/a. ⊕: den (oder die) Anker 2 (heben) to weigh anchor, to trip the anchor(s); ein Schiff 2 (leichten) to light(en) a ship.
Licht¹-engel (⌣‿‿) m ⊕ angel of light.
Lichter¹ ⚓ (⌣‿) [lichten²] m ⊕ (flaches Fahrzeug zum Ausladen großer Schiffe) lighter, barge.
Lichter² (⌣‿) pl. v. Licht¹. [v. Lichtchen.]
Licht(er)chen (⌣‿‿), Licht(er)lein (⌣‿) pl.}
Lichter²-glanz (⌣...) m ⊕ bright illumination of candles; 2loh adv.: 2 brennen to be in a blaze or ablaze or all aflame, to flare (or blaze) up.
Licht¹-erscheinung (⌣...) f ⊕: a) luminous appearance; b) brilliant meteor; =farbe f colour (or shade) of light; =farben-druck ⊕ m heliograph(ic impression); =feind m, fig. obscurantist; =form ⊕ f des Lichtziehers: candle-mould; =freund m enlightened person; ₂gebend a.: ⚒ luminiferous; =gestalt f radiant form; =gießer m candle-maker; =glanz m brilliancy of light; ₂²grau a. light grey; ₂hell a. brilliant, bright(ly lit up); =¹hof m court (covered over) with a glass roof; =holz n = Laubholz; =hut m, =hütchen n extinguisher; =kabel n, elect. electric-light cable; =kegel m, phys. cone (or pencil) of light; =knecht ⊕ m save-all; ₂kräftig a. phot. giving off strong light, luminous; =kreis m luminous circle, photic halo; =kupferdruck ⊕ m heliogravure; =lehre f, phys. photology; (Sehkunde) ⚒ optics; =leimdruck m = =druck.

⚒ scientific; ♀ botanical; ♀ geography; ⊕ machinery; ⚒ mining; ⚔ military; ⚓ marine; ⊕ commercial; ✉ postal; 🚂 railway.

[Lichtlein] — 660 — [Liebesbriefchen]

Lichtlein (⌐-) n ⓔ = Lichtchen.
Licht¹-loch ⊕ (⁸...) n ⓔ arch. light, loophole, in Gewölben: lunette; ²los a. ⓔ without (or devoid of) light, (totally) dark; =malerei f photochromy; =manschette f paper or glass ornament for candlesticks; =masse f, =meer n mass, ocean (or sea) of light, a. beides: one blaze; =meß, =messe f (katholisches Fest, 2. Februar) Candlemas; =messer m, phys. Instrument: ⊘ photometer; =meßkunst, =messung f photometry; =motte f, ent. (Günsler): ⊘ pyralid; =mühle f, phys.: ⊘ radiometer; =nelke ⁊ f campion (Lychnis); =pausverfahren n, phot. heliographic caulking; =punkt m, phys. luminous point, ⊘ focus; vgl. =blick; =putze, =(putz-)schere f snuffers pl.; =schacht m day- (or light-)shaft (auch ⁊); =schein m gleam of light, ray of candle-light; =schere f = =putze; ²scheu a. shunning the light (auch fig.), path.: ⊘ photophobic; fig. walking in the dark, obscurantist; =scheu f: ⊘ photophobia; =schimmer m =schein; =schirm m screen; =schnuppe f snuff of a candle; ²schwach a. phot. giving off feeble light, dull; =seite f luminous (or sunny) side, fig. bright side; =sphäre f der Sonne: ⊘ photosphere; =spieß ⊕ m candle-broach; =spur f luminous track; =stärke f intensity of light, candle-power; =stoff m lumin(ifer)ous matter; =strahl m ray (or beam) of light (auch fig.); =strahlen-brechung f, phys. refraction of light; =strom m stream (or flood) of light; =stumpf m candle-end; =talg m tallow; =telegraphie f: ⊘ phototelegraphy; =therapie f: ⊘ phototherapeutics; ²umflossen, ²umstrahlt a. bathed in light, radiant.
Lichtung (⁊-) f ⓔ 1. clearing; ⁊ thinning of the ranks. — 2. for. clearing, open space; lawn, a. vista; (Ausbau) glade.
licht¹-voll (⁸...) a. ⓔ full of light, bright, luminous, fig. auch lucid; =weite ⊕ f ⓔ arch. open space, inner width; =welle f, phys. wave of light; =wesen n celestial being; =wirkung f luminous effect, cloud; =zerstreuung f, phys. dispersion of light; =ziehen ⊕ n dipping (or making) of candles; =zieher(in f) m candle-maker, chandler; =zieh-maschine f candle-dipper. [⊕c. eyelid.]
Lid (¹; Hom. Lied) [ahd.: lid Deckel] n ⌐
Liderung ⊕ (¹⌐⌐) [Leder] f ⓔ mach.: ~ (Dichtung) eines Kolbens rc.: leathering, packing, washer; =⁊-deckel (⁊⌐...) m ⓔ, =⁊-scheibe f packing-washer; =⁊-zieher m packing-drawer.
lieb (¹) [ahd.: lief] I a. ⓔ 1. attributiv: (teuer, wert) dear; esteemed; (zärtlich geliebt) beloved, cherished; das ⌐e (tägliche) Brot the daily bread; s. Frau 6; um des ⌐en Friedens willen for peace and quietness' sake; der ⌐e Gott the (good) Lord; du ⌐er Himmel! good gracious!, feierlich: good heavens!; das weiß der ⌐e Himmel! Heaven only knows!, er hat kaum das ⌐e Leben his is a bare existence, he has only just enough to live upon or to keep body and soul together; wir hatten unsere ⌐e Not mit ihm we had a nice (or fine) trouble with him; er arbeitet den ⌐en langen Tag ... all day long; du ⌐e Zeit! dear me!, oh, goodness!, F oh, my (eye)! — 2. prädikativ: (angenehm) agreeable, pleasant; (liebenswürdig) amiable, charming; es ist mir ⌐, daß // I am pleased (to see) that //; das ist mir ⌐ und auch leid it both pleases and grieves me; es ist mir gar nicht ⌐ zu hören, daß // I am anything but pleased that //, I'm very sorry (to hear) that //; es wäre mir ⌐, wenn // I should be glad if //; wenn Ihnen Ihr Leben ⌐ ist, so schweigen Sie! as you value (or prize) your life, don't speak!; sich et. ⌐ (genügend) sein lassen to make shift with a th.; er ist uns ⌐ geworden we have become attached to him; bisw. ohne dat.: das Kind ist gar zu ⌐ it's a sweet (or lovable) child. — 3. ⌐er (comp. zu lieb u. zu gern) more agreeable; adv. more willingly, (eher) rather, sooner; je länger, je lieber s. lang 7; ⌐er haben, mögen, sehen, wollen to like better; ich möchte ⌐er nicht hingehen I had (or would) rather not go there. — 4. ⌐st (sup. zu lieb und zu gern): meine ⌐ste Beschäftigung my (most) favourite occupation; das habe ich am ⌐sten I like that best of all; s. allerliebst. — II s. 5. ⌐e([r] m) f ⓔ mein ⌐er! meine ⌐e! my dear fellow! my dear woman or girl or lady!, auch: my dear!; meine ⌐en my dear (or beloved) ones, als Anrede: (my) dear friends, F zärtlich: my dears pl. — 6. ~(chen n ⓔ) m ⓔ [nhd.] love, beloved one darling, sweetheart. — 7. das ~e, et. ~es n ⓔ pleasant (or agreeable) thing(s pl.); nicht wissen, was man e-m (alles) ⌐es antun soll to bestow the most loving care upon a p., to overwhelm (or kill) a p. with kindness; e-m viel Gutes und ⌐es erweisen, erzeigen to show a p. great kindness or affection, to be very kind to a p.; e-m zu⌐e et. tun ... out of affection(ate regard) for a p., schwächer: for the sake of a p.; s. Leid² 1. — 8. der, die ⌐ste mst = Geliebte(r); poet. die ⌐ste sein his lady love, his beloved (one); in der Anrede: ⌐ste(r)! my darling or pet!). 9. das ⌐ste ⓔ the most precious (or beloved) thing (that) one possesses, what one loves (or cherishes) most; das wäre mir das ⌐ste I should like that best of all.
Lieb-äugelei (¹⌐⌐⌐) f ⓔ amorous glances pl.; ogling; ²äugeln (⁊¹⌐⌐) v/n. (h.) ⓔ a. *,* to cast amorous glances (or F to make sheep's eyes at) a p., to ogle a p.
Liebchen (¹⌐⌐) n ⓔ s. lieb 6.
Liebden (¹⌐⌐) f, inv. ehm. Anrede fürstlicher Personen unter⌐ea.: Euer (Ew.) ~! etwa: your Dilection?
Liebe (¹⌐⌐) [ahd.: ⁊lieb] f ⓔ (pl. mst Liebschaften) 1. (ant. Haß) love, affection; (Anhänglichkeit) attachment; (Zuneigung) fondness (or liking) for. kindliche: filial affection, christliche: Christian charity, abgöttische: idolatry, eigennützige: cupboard-love; ~ zum Nächsten love for one's neighbour, weiter: philanthropy; ~ zum Vaterlande love of one's country, patriotism; Heirat aus ~ love-match; fleischliche, sinnliche ~ carnal, sensual love; eine unglückliche ~ an unfortunate love-affair; eine unerwiderte ~ an unrequited attachment; s. Leib 1; e-m eine heftige ~ einflößen, e-n mit heftiger ~ erfüllen to fill (or inspire) a p. with a passionate love or a deep passion; fig. eine alte ~ an old sweetheart or F flame; (Liebesgott) (God of) Love, Cupid, Eros. — 2. Sprichw. s. alt¹ 2 am Schluß; kalte Hände, warme ~ a cold hand, a warm heart; die ~ ist blind love is blind; mit ~ erreicht man mehr als mit Gewalt a little kindness goes a long way, soft words do more than hard blows; Lust und Lieb' zum Ding macht Müh' und Arbeit gering where there is a will there is a way. — 3. (Gefälligkeit) tun (od. erweisen) Sie mir die ~ do me the favour or the kindness; s. zuliebe; Sprichw. eine ~ ist der andern wert one good turn deserves another; s. brennen 13.
Liebe-diener(in f) m (¹⌐...) ⓔ fawning (or obsequious, F carneying) person, toady; =dienerei f ⓔ obsequiousness; ²dienerisch a. ⓔ obsequious, fawning, cringing; ²glühend a. burning (or aglow, kindled) with love; ²leer a. (de)void of (or lacking in) love.
Liebelei (⌐⌐¹) f ⓔ (trifling) love-affair, flirtation, sweethearting, amour.
liebeln (¹⌐) v/n. (h.) ⓔ a. to carry on a flirtation, to flirt; to dally with a girl.
lieben (¹⌐) [ahd.; *lieb] I v/a., v/n. (h.) u. sich ⌐ v/refl., v/recip. ⓔ (ant. hassen): (sich, ea.) ⌐ to love (o.s., one another, each other); (Zuneigung h.) to show affection (ate regard) for, to be fond of, to be attached to, to cherish; weiter: to like, esteem, fancy; närrisch ⌐ to dote upon, F to idolize; unglücklich ⌐ to be crossed in love; fig. die Veilchen ⌐ den Schatten violets like (or prefer) the shade; mit Objektsatz: sie ⌐ es, ihren Reichtum zu entfalten they are fond of (or delight in) exhibiting their wealth. — II ⌐ n ⓔ s. Liebe. — III ⌐d p.pr. und a. ⓔ loving, affectionate; Briefschluß: Deine Dich innigst ⌐de Schwester Your very affectionate (or fond) sister; die ⌐den the two lovers pl. — IV ge-liebt p.p. u. a. ⓔ (be)loved; ⌐e Eltern dearest parents pl.; s. ~e(r).
liebens-wert (¹⌐...) a. ⓔ worthy of love, deserving to be loved; ²würdig a. lovable, amiable; =würdigerweise adv. amiably, in a kind (or an amiable) spirit; =würdigkeit f ⓔ: a) lovableness; b) amiability.
Liebes-abenteuer (¹⌐...) n ⓔ love-adventure; auf ~ ausgeh(e)n to go in search of galla'nt adventures; =apfel ⊕ m love-apple, mehr gbr.: tomato (Lycope'rsicum escule'ntum); =band n bond of love, tie of affection; =bedürfnis f desire for (s.th. to) love; =beteu(e)rung f protestation of love; =bewerbung f love-suit; =blick m loving (or amorous) glance; =bote m, botin f messenger of love; =brief m love-letter; =briefchen

n, dim. (fr.) billet-doux; =dichter m poet of love-songs, erotic poet; =dichtung f amatory (or erotic) poetry; =dienst m kind (or loving) service; charitable (or kindly) office; e-m einen ~ erweisen to do a p. a good turn; =erklärung f declaration of love; =feuer n ardour of love; =fieber n feverish love, (hot) fit of love; =flamme f flame of love; =gabe f loving (or charitable) gift; =gedicht n love-poem, amatory (or erotic) poem; =genuß m enjoyment of love; =geschichte f love-tale or -story; =gespräch n lovers' discourse; =geständnis n confession of love; =glück n happiness of love (rs); =glut f = =feuer; =gott m, myth. (god of) Love, Cupid, Eros; =götter cupids pl.; =göttin f goddess of Love, Venus; =handel m love-affair, amour, intrigue; =hof m = Minnehof.

liebe=siech (ᴗ-ᴵ) a. ⑥ love-sick.

Liebes=klage (ᴵᴵᴗ...) f ⑫ amorous (com-)plaint; =knoten m (true) love-knot; =kummer m lover's grief; =kuß m loving kiss; =lied n l.-song; =liedchen n love-ditty; =lust f pleasure (or joy, delight) of love; =mahl n loving feast, der ersten Christen: ⚄ agape; Festmahl der Offiziere ꝛc.: banquet of kindred souls, brotherly repast; =not f = =pein; =paar n loving pair or couple; =pein f torment of love, love-woe; =pfand n love-token, (Kind) pledge of love; =pfeil m Cupid's dart; =pflicht f loving (or charitable) duty; =poesie f amatory (or erotic) poetry; =qual f = pein; =rausch m short ecstasy (or transport) of love; =roman m l.-tale, sinnlicher Art: erotic novel; =sache f l.-affair; =schmerz m love-pang; =schwur m lover's oath; =seufzer m lover's sigh; =spiel n amorous sport, flirtation; vgl. Liebelei; =sprache f language of love, amatory speech; ⚄toll a. ⑥ mad with (or madly in) love; =trank m l.-potion, auch: (fr.) philtre; ⚄trunken a. intoxicated with love; =verhältnis n = Liebschaft; =wahnsinn m love's frenzy; =werke n/pl. works pl. of charity; =wonne f = =lust; =wut f frenzy of love, path.: ⚄ satyriasis; =zauber m love-spell; =zeichen n love-token.

liebe=voll (ᴵᴵᴗᵗᵇ) a. ⑥ affectionate, loving, kind (-hearted); Ɛe Fürsorge loving care, tender solicitude.

Lieb=frauen=kirche (ᴵᴵᴗᴗ,ᴗᴗ) f ⑫ St. Mary's (church); in Frankreich: Notre Dame.

lieb=gewinnen (ᴵᴵ...) v/a. ⓐa (b)*/*: e-n, et. ⚄ to take a fancy (or a liking) to ...; ⚄haben v/a. ⓐb**: e-n, et. ⚄ to be fond of ..., to like ...; bibl. wen Gott ⚄hat, den züchtigt er whom God loveth he chasteneth.

Lieb=haber (ᴵᴵ...) m ㉒: a) eines Mädchens: lover, sweetheart, admirer, auch: follower; poet. swain, (Buhle) paramour; thea. Erste(r) ~(in f ㊼) one who plays the leading lover's part(s), a. leading gentleman (f lady); b) s. der et. gern hat) lover (or admirer) of a th.; fancier of dogs, &c., connoisseur of pictures, &c.; ~ des Rennsports turfite, racing man, von hohen Herren: patron of the turf; =haberei f ㊻ fancy (or taste, stärker: passion) for a th., weitS. favourite pursuit; =haber=rolle f lover's part; =haber=theater n amateur (or private) theatricals pl.

lieb=kosen (ᴵᴗ) v/a. u. v/n. (h.) ⓾*, *.*: e-n (e-m) ⚄ to caress (or fondle) a p.; =kosung f ㊻ caresses pl., fondling.

lieblich (ᴸᵛ) a. ⑥ pleasing to the senses; agreeable; Ɛes Mädchen lovely (or graceful, F sweet) girl; Ɛe Gegend delightful (or charming) neighbourhood; Ɛer Geschmack delicious (or savoury) taste; ⚄ (adv.) duftend sweet-scented; ⚄ klingend melodious; ~keit f ㊻ loveliness, gracefulness, F sweetness; delightfulness, charm; deliciousness; v. Tönen: melodiousness.

Liebling (ᴸᵛ) m ⓶d. (a. für f) darling, pet; (Günstling) favourite; minion.

Lieblings=beschäftigung (ᴵᴵᴗ...) f ⑫ favourite occupation; =dichter m favourite poet; =hund m pet-dog; =sohn m, =tochter f favourite (or darling) son, daughter; =sünde f besetting sin; =wunsch m greatest (or fondest) wish.

lieb=los (ᴵᴵ...) a. ⑥ unloving, unkind, stärker: uncharitable, unfeeling; =losigkeit f ㊻ lack of affection, unkindness, uncharitableness; Ɛreich a. loving, affectionate, (freundlich) kind (-hearted); affable; =reiz m ⚄ charm, attractiveness, (Anmut) gracefulness, fascination, F sweetness; Ɛreizend a. charming, attractive, lovable; graceful, fascinating, F sweet.

Liebschaft (ᴸᵛ) f ㊻ love(-affair), amour, flüchtige: flirtation, (Buhlschaft) (amor-) **Liebste(r)** (ᴸᵛ) s. f. lieb 8. [ous) intrigue.

Lieb=stöckel (ᴸᴗᴵᴗ) n [ahd. (P); mlt. libi'sticum; *lt. ligu'sticum] ⚄ m, n ⚄ lovage (Ligu'sticum levi'sticum).

Lied (ᴸ, Hom. Lid) [ahd.] n ㉔c. 1. song; (Weise) tune, air, melody; (Jubel=)~ carol; (Volks=)~ ballad; mehrstimmiges: glee; kirchliches ~ hymn; ein ~ anstimmen to intone a song; wollen Sie uns ein ~ zum besten geben? will you favour us with (or give us) a song? — 2. (Gedicht) poem; romance; bibl. s. Hohelied. — 3. fig. ein anderes ~ anstimmen to change one's tone; das ist das Ende vom ~ that's the end (or upshot) of the matter; davon kann ich auch ein ~(chen) singen (aus Erfahrung mitreden) I know a little (or I could tell a tale) about that, I have been through the mill myself.

Liedchen (ᴸᵛ) n ㉔ (dim. von Lied) short song or tune, ditty; s. Lied 3.

lieder=artig (ᴵᴵᴗ...) a. ⑥ song-like; in (the) form of a song, ⚄ cantabile; =buch n ⚄ song-book, eccl. hymn-book; =dichter m song-writer, lyrical poet; =dichtung f song-writing, lyrical poetry.

Liederjahn F (ᴵᴗᴵ) [liederlich] m ⓐd. fast (or loose) fellow; stärker: rake, debauchee.

Lieder=komponist (ᴵᴵᴗ...) m ⚄ composer of songs; =kranz m: a) = =saal; b) = =tafel.

liederlich (ᴸᵛᵛ) [mhd.: Lotter..., ledig] a. ⑥ 1. (nachlässig) careless, negligent, in der Kleidung u. Arbeit: slovenly; (unordentlich) disorderly; ⚄ (adv.) arbeiten F to scamp one's work. — 2. (aus-schweifend) dissipated, stärker: debauched, dissolute; Ɛes Frauenzimmer fast (or gay, loose) woman, F lady of easy virtue, P bad' un; Ɛer Kerl, a. Hans ~ rake, scapegrace, F one (who has) gone to the bad, P bad lot; ein Ɛes Leben führen to lead a profligate (or loose, fast) life, to live in debauchery.

Liederlichkeit (ᴸᵛᵛ-) f ㊻ (s. liederlich) 1. carelessness, negligence, slovenliness. — 2. dissipation, looseness, debauchery; profligacy.

lieder=reich (ᴵᴵᴗ...) a. ⑥ rich in song(s), melodious, tuneful; =sammlung f collection of songs; =sänger(in f) m ballad-singer; =spiel n musical play; =tafel f etwa: choral society; =zyklus m cycle of romances.

lief(e) (ᴵᵛ) impf. ind. (subj.) v. laufen.

Lieferant ⚄ (-ᵛᵈ) [it. livrante] m ⚄, ~in f ㊼ purveyor, (wholesale) contractor; ~ von Lebensmitteln auch: provider, caterer, von Möbeln &c.: furnisher, v. Kleidungsstücken: outfitter.

lieferbar ⚄ (ᴸᵛ) a. ⑥ to be delivered.

Lieferer (ᴸᵛᵛ) m ⚄ = Liefera'nt.

liefern (ᴸᵛᵛ) [nhd.; *fr. livrer] I v/a., v/n. (h.) und sich ⚄ v/refl. ⓐa. 1. e-m et. ⚄ to deliver a th. to a p.; (beschaffen) to supply (or provide, furnish) a p. with a th.; s. Beweis 1; e-e gute Ernte ⚄ to yield a good crop; eine Schlacht ⚄ (schlagen) to fight a (or to give) battle; ⚄ an Herrn N. zu ⚄ to be delivered to Mr. N.; in acht Tagen an Bord zu ⚄ deliverable on board within a week; Buchhandel: in Heften ⚄ to publish (or issue) in numbers. — 2. F fig. e-n ⚄ (verderben) to ruin a p.; er ist geliefert he is lost or undone or done for. — II ~ n ⚄ 3. = Lieferung.

Lieferung (ᴸᵛᵛ) f ㊻ (das Liefern u. das Gelieferte) delivery; supply(ing), providing; yielding; ⚄ für das Heer: issue; ~en für ein Regiment besorgen to make issues to a regiment; e-e ~ ausschreiben to put up a contract for open competition; f. Afford 2; ⚄ zahlbar bei ~ payable on delivery; Buchhandel: in ~en erscheinen to appear (or come out) in numbers or (serial) parts; auf ~ kaufen to purchase for delivery.

Liefer(ungs) ⚄ (ᴸᵛ(ᵛ)...) n ⚄ tender; =bedingungen f/pl. terms pl. of delivery; =frist f = =zeit; =geschäft n business (or job) undertaken on contract; (Zeitgeschäft) time-bargain; =kontrakt m = =vertrag; =preis m contracted price; =schein m receipt (for goods delivered), bill of delivery; =tag m day of (or fixed for) delivery; (Abrechnungstag) settling-day; =vertrag m contract for future delivery; =zeit f time of delivery.

Liege=geld ⚄, ⚓ (ᴵᴵᴗᴵ) n ⚄ demurrage.

liegen (ᴸᵛ) [ahd.: lie; vgl. legen] ⓐ I v/n. (h., subb. sn) 1. to lie (or rest) on the floor, on the table, &c.; weitS. to be placed or situated, (sich befinden) to be; das Buch liegt hier ... is (lying) here; da liegt es there it lies or is; es liegt zwei Fuß hoher Schnee the snow lies (or is) two feet deep; die Stadt liegt nördlich von Berlin ... lies (to the)

[liegen] — 662 — [Liese]

north of Berlin; hier liegt der Hase im Pfeffer, der Knoten there's the rub, that's where the difficulty lies; auf Grabschriften: Hier liegt // Here lies //; wie die Sache jetzt liegt as matters stand at present. — 2. mit abhängiger prp.: dicht an et. anderem ≈ to touch (or join) a th. closely; an j-s Brust ≈ to lie on a p.'s breast; das Kind liegt an der Erde ... is lying on the ground; er liegt an Fieber krank oder danieder he is down (or laid low) with a fever; v. Hunden: an der Kette ≈ to be chained up; die Ursache liegt am Tage ... is quite evident; fig. das liegt mir am Herzen, an der Seele it is nearest to my (or I have it at) heart; mir liegt et. an dieser Sache I am concerned about (or interested in) this matter; mir liegt nichts (P ein Dreck) daran it does not (much) matter to me, F I don't care a fig; was liegt Ihnen daran? what does it matter (or what is that) to you?; es liegt mir daran, Sie zu überzeugen it is my great wish (or I am anxious) to convince you; an wem liegt das? whose fault is it?; es liegt an ihm the fault lies (or rests) with him; soviel an mir liegt as far as (it) lies in my power; ↓ hart am Winde ≈ to sail close to the wind; auf: s. Bärenhaut; auf dem Bauche (Rücken) ≈ to lie on one's stomach (back), s. flach 1 und 2; der Wein liegt auf Flaschen ... is in bottles; e-m (ewig) auf dem Halse ≈ to pester (or bore) a p.; auf e-m Haufen ≈ to lie in a heap, to be piled up; s. Knie 1, Lauer¹; die ganze Last liegt auf mir oder auf meinen Schultern the whole burden rests on my shoulders; der Ton liegt auf der letzten Silbe the accent rests (or is) on the last syllable; es ≈ viele Bücher auf dem Tische the table is littered up (or covered) with books; er lag auf den Tod krank he was not expected to live, he was at death's door, bibl. he lay sick unto death; fig. es liegt mir auf der Brust I feel heavy on the chest; s. Hals 3; das liegt ihm schwer auf dem Herzen that greatly troubles (or grieves) him; das Geld liegt auf der Straße money can be picked up in the street; das Wort lag mir auf der Zunge the word was at the tip of my tongue; aus dem Fenster ≈ to lean (or look) out of the window; das liegt außer meinem Wege (Bereiche) that lies (or is) out of my way (beyond my province); das Buch liegt bei den übrigen ... is (or can be found) with the others; durch=ea. ≈ to be in a state of confusion or at sixes and sevens; das Land liegt gegen (ob. gen) Süden ... lies to the south; das Haus liegt gegen Süden ... faces the south, ... has a southern aspect; in: (ziehend) im Anschlage ≈ to aim (or present) a gun; in den Armen ≈ sich beide (SCH.) the two are linked in each other's arms; die Stadt liegt in Asche, in Trümmern ... is reduced to ashes, lies in ruins; im (oder zu) Bette ≈ to lie in bed or F abed, als Kranker: to keep (to) one's bed, to be laid up with gout, &c.; das liegt im Blut (in der Familie) that runs in the blood (in the family); ✕ von Truppen: im Felde ≈ to be encamped in the field; es liegt eine starke Besatzung in der Festung the fortress is strongly garrisoned; im Hinterhalte liegen to lie in ambush; die Wahrheit liegt in der Mitte truth lies half-way; im tiefsten Schlafe ≈ to be in a deep sleep; im Sterben ≈ to be dying or at death's door; beständig in den Wirtshäusern ≈ to be for ever in the pub(lic house); fig. das lag nicht in meiner Absicht that was not my intention; es liegt mir schwer wie Blei in den Gliedern I feel as heavy as lead; s. Haar 3; das liegt in meiner Macht that lies (with) in my power; der Leichtsinn liegt einmal im Menschen well, a light heart is part of human nature; e-m in den Ohren ≈ to fill a p.'s ears (or to bore a p.) with complaints; das liegt mir im Sinne it is always in (or never out of) my thoughts; es liegt ein tiefer Sinn darin there is a deep meaning implied (or contained) in it; mit=ea. im Streite ≈ to be engaged in a (long) contest; die Gefahr, welche darin lag, daß er blieb the danger which arose from (the fact of) his staying; mit dem Bauche auf der Erde ≈ to lie on one's belly or stomach; das Haus liegt mit der Front nach dem Markte ... faces (or fronts) the market-place; nach Osten ≈ to face the East, to have an Eastern aspect; das Zimmer liegt nach dem Hofe zu ... overlooks (or looks upon, looks out upon) the yard; dicht neben et. ≈ to lie close (or to be adjacent) to a th.; fig. immer über den Büchern ≈ to be for ever poring over (one's) books, to be a regular bookworm; unter der Erde ≈ to rest in one's grave, to be bedded under ground or beneath the sods; unter Schloß und Riegel ≈ to be under lock and key; das Dorf liegt zwei deutsche Meilen von der Stadt the village lies nine English miles from the town; es liegt ein Garten vor dem Hause there is a garden in front of the house; ↓ vor Anker ≈ to lie (or ride) at anchor; ✕ mit dem Heere vor einer Stadt ≈ to lay siege to a town; zu Bette ≈ to keep (or to be confined) to one's bed; zu j-s Füßen, e-m zu Füßen ≈ to lie (or to be prostrate) at a p.'s feet; s. zugrunde≈, Last 2; zu tage ≈ to be obvious or evident. — 3. mit adv. der Art und prädikativer Bestimmung, zB. ausgestreckt ≈ to lie (at) full length; das Geld liegt bereit ... is ready (at hand); nichts liegt mir ferner als // nothing is further from my mind than //; wie hingegossen ≈ to recline negligently or with (charming) ease; wie liegt die Sache? how do matters stand?; Sie sehen jetzt, wie die Sache liegt you now see how things are, you now understand the state of the case; ✱ das Tuch liegt zwei Ellen breit ... is (or measures) two yards in width. — 4. ohne abhängige Bestimmung: a) ell. statt zu Bette ≈ (f. 2); b) (zu Boden ≈, von et., das früher stand) to be overthrown or floored, to lie prostrate; c) fig. (stocken) to languish, to be at a standstill; d) von Tieren: (sich lagern) to couch (down); e) ≈ bleiben to remain (or continue) in a lying (or recumbent) position or in bed; unterwegs ≈ bleiben to break down on the way, to come to a dead stop or halt (a. 🚂); unter e-r Last: to sink under a burden; die Sache muß einstweilen ≈ bleiben the matter must stand over for a while; ✱ v. Waren: to be unsaleable, to remain on one's hands, F to hang on hand; f) Wein ≈ haben to have (a good stock of) wine in the cellar; g) et. ≈ lassen to let a th. lie or rest, aus Vergeßlichkeit: to leave a th. behind; fig. e-n links ≈ (unbeachtet) lassen to give a p. the cold shoulder, stärker: to cut a p.; e-n für tot ≈ lassen to leave a p. for dead. — II sich ≈ v/refl. 5. mit Angabe der Wirkung: sich (acc.) wund ≈, sich (dat.) den Rücken wund ≈ = sich durchliegen. — III ~ n ⊕ 6. lying; (f. 8) recumbency, reclining (or recumbent) position; prostration; bin das ~ (oder des ~s) müde I am tired of lying (on my back) or of (lying on) my couch. — IV ≈d p.pr. u. a. ⊕ 7. lying; situated, placed. — 8. (in ruhender Lage) recumbent, reclining on the couch, &c.; (hingestreckt) prostrate, auf dem Bauche: prone, auf dem Rücken: supine; ≈: ⚔ procumbent; her. couchant; ⊕ typ. ≈ de Schrift italics pl. — 9. ≈ de (ant. bewegliche) Güter oder Gründe landed (or real) estate(s pl.) or property. — 10. ⚒ ≈ de Schicht = Liegendflöz; das ~ de n ⊕ (ant. das Hangende) footwall, hanging wall. — V. ge-legen p.p. und a. ⊕ 11. s. bsd. Artikel.

Liegen=bleiben (⁻ᵛ⌣ᵛ) n ⊕ discontinuance, stoppage; 🚂, &c. (f liegen 4e) break-down.

Liegend=flöz ⚒ (⁻ᵛ…) n ⊕ (ant. Hangendflöz), =schicht f (ant. Hangendschicht) floor of a seam or lode.

Liegen=lassen (⁻ᵛ⌣ᵛ) n ⊕ (f. liegen 4 g) leaving a th. behind.

Liegenschaft (⁻⌣⌣) f ⊕: ~(en pl.) real estate(s pl.), landed property.

Liege=platz (⁻ᵛ…) m ⊕ berth; =tage m/pl., =zeit ↓ f time which has to elapse before a ship may unload or disembark; demurrage.

lieh(e) (¹(⌣)) impf. ind. (subj.) von leihen.

Liek ↓ (¹) n (m) ⊕c. (Saum eines Segels) bolt-rope; stehendes: leech-rope.

Lienhard (⁻⌣) npr/m. ⊕⊕⊕α. (Bn.) Leonard. [abbr. l.

lies (¹: Hom. ließ) imper. von lesen;

Liesch ♀ (¹) [nbd.] n ⊕a., ~e f ⊕ cat's-tail (or timothy-)grass (Phleum prate'nse).

Lieschen (⁻⌣) npr/n. ⊕α. (dim.) Lizzy, **Liesch=gras** (⁻⌣) n ⊕ = Liesch. [Lizzie.

Li(e)se¹ (⁻⌣) [(S)lisa(beth)] npr/f. ⊕⊕β. 1. Bess(ie), Betty, Lisa(bel). — 2. fig. dumme ~ silly goose; vgl. Klatsch=≈.

Liese² (⁻⌣) f ⊕ 1. fat(ty portion) of the inside of an animal. — 2. (enge Kluft) narrow fissure.

Signs (see page XVII): F familiar; P vulgar; ꞘꞘ flash; ⟡ rare; † obsolete (died); * new word (born); ₊ incorrect; ♪ music;

lies(e)t u. **lies(e)t** (´(‿) 2. u. 3. Person pres. ind. von **lesen**. [von **lassen**.]
ließ(e) (´(‿); Hom. lies) impf.ind.(subj.)|
Liga (´‿) [it. Bündnis] f ⊕ league.
Ligatur (‿‿´) [lt.] f ⊕ 1. ♪ (Bindung), surg. (Unterbindung) ligature. — 2. ⊙ typ. (Doppelbuchstabe) ligature, double type or letter (z.B. æ).
Lige (´‿) [fr. ligue] f ⊕ = Liga.
Ligist (‿´) [++fr.] m ⊕, **~in** f ⊕ hist. leaguer; **Lisch** a. ⊕ of the league.
Lignin ⚛ (-´) [lt.] n ⊕d. (Holzfaser) lignine ($C_6H_{10}O_5$). [lignite.]
Lignit ⚛ (-´) [lt.] m ⊕c. (Braunkohle)|
Ligroin ⚛ (‿´‿) n ⊕d. (Erdöl) ligroin.
Liguster ♀ (‿´‿) [lt.] m ⊕ common privet (Ligu'strum vulga're); **~schwärmer** (´...) m ⊕ ent. (Schmetterling) privet-hawkmoth (Sphinx ligu'stri).
liieren (‿´‿) [fr.] I v/a. u. sich ⊕ v/refl. ⊕ to unite; sich mit e-m ⊕ to form (or to enter into) an alliance with a p. — II ~ n ⊕ und **Liierung** f ⊕ (forming an) alliance.
Likör (‿´) [fr. liqueur] m ⊕d. liqueur, cordial; **~bonbon** m (n) brandy-ball; **~fabrik** f liqueur-distillery; **~fabrikant** m liqueur-distiller; **~gestell** n liqueur-stand; **~glas** n liqueur-glass.
Liktor (´‿) [lt.] m ⊕ röm. Alt. (Beamter e-r Magistratsperson) lictor; **~en-bündel** n/pl. (Zeichen amtlicher Macht) (lt.) fasces pl.
Lila (´‿) [span. *pers. lilak ♀ Flieder] n ⊕ und **lila** a. inv., auch **~farbig** a. ⊕ lilac (colour), pale violet.
Lili-e ♀ (´(‿)) [ahd. : lily; *pers.] f ⊕ lily (Li'lium); weiße **~** white lily (L. ca'ndidum); her. die drei **~n** (Wappen der ehemaligen fr. Könige) the three lilies; fleur-de-lis, flower-de-luce.
lili-en-ähnlich (´(‿)...) a. ⊕, **~artig** a. like a lily, ⚛ liliaceous; **~arm** m ⊕ arm as white as a lily; **~beet** n bed of lilies; **~busen** m lily-white bosom; **~stengel** m stem of a lily; **~weiß** a. lily-white, (as) white as a lily; **~weiße** f whiteness (or colour) of a lily.
limitieren (‿‿´‿) v/a. ⊕ to limit.
Limonade (‿‿´‿) [fr.; it.; *Limone] f ⊕ lemonade; **~n-pulver** n ⊕ sherbet.
Limone ♀ (‿´‿) [pers.] f ⊕ = Zitrone.
Linchen (´‿) npr/n. ⊕a. little Lina.
lind (´) [ahd.: lithe: lt. len(t)-] a. ⊕ gentle, soft; vgl. gelind(e).
Linde ♀ (´‿) [ahd.: linden, lime] f ⊕ lime(-tree), linden(-tree) (Ti'lia).
linden (´) a. ⊕ (D 9) of lime-wood.
Linden-allee (´‿‿...) f ⊕ = **~gang**; **~bast** m bast of the lime-tree; **~baum** ♀ m = Linde; **~blüte** ♀ f lime-blossom; **~blüten-tee** m, pharm. lime-blossom tea; **~gang** m lime-tree walk or avenue; **~hain** m lime-grove; **~holz** n lime-wood; **~schwärmer** m, ent. (Schmetterling) lime-hawkmoth (Smeri'nthus ti'liae); **~weg** m = **~gang**.
Lind(e)rer (´(‿)‿) m ⊕, **Lind(r)erin** f ⊕ one who allays (or assuages, soothes) pain, soother, comforter.
lindern (´‿) [lind] I v/a. und sich ⊕ v/refl. ⊕a. (mildern) to soften; (erleichtern) to ease, alleviate, soothe; (mäßigen) to moderate, (beruhigen) to calm, appease, pacify; Armut ⊕ to

relieve poverty; Schmerzen ⊕ to allay (or ease, assuage) pain; Übel ⊕ to mitigate evils; die Krämpfe ⊕ sich the spasms are abating or diminishing; med. ⊕des Mittel, ⚛ lenitive (remedy); vgl. Linderungsmittel. — II ~ n ⊕ u. **Linderung** f ⊕ softening; easing; alleviation; relief; mitigation; abatement; path.: ⚛ palliation.
Linderungs-mittel (´(‿)...) n ⊕ med. soothing remedy, ⚛ lenitive, palliative, demulcent. [Gelindheit.]
Lindheit (´-), **Lindigkeit** (´‿-) f ⊕ =|
Lind-wurm (´‿) [ahd.: lithe] m ⊕ dragon, griffin.
Lineal (‿‿´) P ⊕(i)‿) [nhd.; *lt. (*Linie)] n ⊕d. ruler, zum Messen a. rule; ⊙ typ. guide; **~geometrie** (‿‿´´...) f ⊕ geometrical drawing.
linear (‿‿´) [lt.] a. ⊕ linear; **~perspekti've** (‿‿´´...) f ⊕, **~zeichnung** f linear perspective, drawing.
...ling (...´) m ⊕d. dient zur Bildung v. s/m., z.B. Dichterling poetaster.
...lings (...´) adv.in Zssgn: blind ⊕ blindly.
Lingual-buchstabe (‿g(‿)´...) [lt. Zungen-] m ⊕, **~laut** m gram. lingual (letter).
Linguist (‿g(‿)´) [lt.] m ⊕ (Sprachenkenner) linguist; **~ik** f ⊕ linguistics, study of languages; **Lisch** a. ⊕ linguistic.
Lini-e (´(‿)‿) [ahd.: line; *lt. li'nea] f ⊕ 1. line, typ. rule; gerade, krumme **~** straight, crooked (math. curved) line; dicke **~** beim Schreiben: thick stroke; in e-r **~** (Reihe) aufstellen to draw (or march) up in a line, to aline (auch: ✕); **~** halten to keep in (or to) the line, typ. to line, beim Schreiben: to write straight; fig. sich auf gleiche **~** mit e-m stellen to put o.s. on the same footing with a p.; in erster **~** (vor allem) first of all, above all. — 2. ✕ a) (Aufstellung in einer Reihe neben-ea.) Kompagnie in **~** company drawn up in (close) line; b) **~ Linien-truppen**; in der **~** dienen, steh(e)n to serve in the line. — 3. ♀ = Aqua'tor; die **~** passieren to cross the line. — 4. (Stamm, Geschlecht) lineage, descent; in gerader **~** abstammend, Abstammende(r) lineally descended, lineal (or direct) descendant.
Linien-blatt (´(‿)...) n ⊕ beim Schreiben ink- (or transparent) lines pl.; **~för-mig** a. ⊕ linear (auch ⚛); **~manier** f Kupferstecherkunst: line-engraving; **~papier** n ruled paper; **~richter** m Fußballspiel: linesman, touch-judge; **~schiff** ⚓ n vessel of the line, liner, battle-ship; **~soldat** ✕ m linesman; **~system** n diatonic scale; **~truppen** f/pl. (Truppen pl. of) the line, regulars pl.; **~umschalter** ⊕ m, tel. commutator, switch; **~ziehen** n ruling; **~zieher** m: a) (Person) person who rules paper, &c.; b) (Reißfeder) ruling-pen.
...linig (...´‿) [Linie] a. ⊕ i. Zssgn: gerad ⊕ rectilinear. [for ruling.]
Liniier-brett ⊙ (-(‿)´...) n ⊕ board|
liniieren (-(‿)´‿) [lt.] v/a. ⊕ Papier ⊕ to rule...; rot liniiert ruled with red lines.
Liniier-feder(-(‿)´´...) f ⊕ ruling-pen; **~maschine** f ruling-machine.
Liniierung (-(‿)´‿) f ⊕ ruling.

Liniment ⚛ (‿‿´) [lt. lini're schmieren] n ⊕ d. med. (Salbe) liniment.
link (´) [ahd.] (ant. recht) I a. ⊕ 1. left, her. sinister; die **~e** Seite the left(-hand) side, the left, des Pferdes: near side; des Schiffes: port, ehm.: larboard; in Handlungsbüchern: the debtor's (or debit-) side; **~er** Fuß, **~e** Hand des Reiters, oft: stirrup-foot, bridle-hand. — 2. ⊕(s) ein (die **~e** Hand gebrauchen) to be left-handed; du bist wohl mit dem **~en** Beine zuerst aufgestanden you must have got out of bed the wrong way; v. Fürsten: sich zur **~en** Hand trauen l. to contract a morganatic marriage. — 3. **~e** (innere) Seite: a) des Tuches ꝛc.: wrong side; b) e-s Kragens, einer Münze ꝛc.: reverse (side). — II **~e** f ⊕ 4. left side or hand; zu seiner **~n** on (or at) his left (side); parl. opposition; Radical party or section. [the left (hand or side).]
linker-hand (´‿...), **~seits** adv. on|
Link-hand (´...) m ⊕ left-handed person; **~händig** a. ⊕ left-handed; **~händigkeit** f ⊕ left-handedness.
linkisch (´‿) a. ⊕ awkward, clumsy.
links (´) adv. 1. on the left(-hand) side, to the left of a th.; on the wrong (or reverse) side (f. link 3); von, nach ⊕ from, to the left; ✕ ⊕ abgeschwenkt! left wheel!; Zum! left about!; fig. f. liegen 4 am Ende. — 2. fig. ⊕ (auf dem unrechten Wege) sein to be on the wrong track; Sie sind weit ⊕ (im Irrtume) you are far out (of your reckoning). — 3. = linkisch.
Links-drehung (´...) f ⊕: ⚛ sinistration, opt. Polarisation: ⚛ levogyration.
link-seitig (´‿...) a. ⊕ left-sided.
links-gewunden (´‿...) a. ⊕ sinistral; **~her**, **~hin** adv. from, to the left; **~hörnchen** n, zo.: ⚛ clausilia; **~rheinisch** a. on the left bank of the Rhine; **~seitig** a. = link-s.; **~um** adv. f. links 1.
Linnen (´‿)[nhd.] n ⊕, ⊕ a. ⊕ = Leinen.
Linnésch (‿´) [Linné, schwed. Botaniker, 1707—78] a. ⊕ Linnæan, of Linné.
Linoleum ♀ (-(‿)´‿) [neu-lt. Leinöl=] n ⊕ linoleum; **~teppich** (‿´‿) m ⊕ (Korkteppich) carpet of a linoleum (pattern).
Linon ♀ (‿´ng) [fr.] m ⊕ French lawn.
Linse (´‿) [ahd.: *lt. lens] f ⊕ 1. ♀ Pflanze und Samen: echte **~** lentil (Lens escule'nta); **~** des Auges crystalline lens. — 2. ⊙: a) opt. lens; b) phys. eines Pendels: bob.
linsen-ähnlich (´(‿)...) a. ⊕ lentil- (or lens-)shaped, ⚛ lenticular, lentiform; **~artig**, **~förmig** a. = **~ähnlich**; **~gericht** n ⊕ dish of lentils; bibl. (1. Mose 25, 34) **~** Jakobs pottage of lentils; **~glas** n, opt. lens; **~klöße** m/pl. lentil-fritters pl.; **~mal** n, path.: ⚛ lentigo; **~mehl** n meal of lentils; **~suppe** f lentil-soup.
Lippe (´‿) [nhd. (hd. Lefze]: lip] f ⊕ lip, ent., &c.: ⚛ labrum; dicke, aufgeworfene **~** pouting lip; wulstige **~** F blubber-lip; fig. die **~n** aufwerfen to purse up one's mouth; f. beißen 1; fig. an j-s **~n** hangen to hang upon a p.'s words or lips; die **~n** hangen lassen (maulen) to mope; über die **~n**

⚛ scientific; ♀ botanical; ♁ geography; ⊕ machinery; ✕ mining; ⚔ military; ⚓ marine; ⊛ commercial; ✉ postal; 🚂 railway.

bringen to utter, to give mouth to; das soll nicht über m-e ~n kommen that shall not pass my lips.

Lippen-bär (⌣◡…) m ㊂ zo. Indian bear (*Ursus labia'tus*); =**blume** f, =**blüt-**(l)er m ♀: ⚹ labiate(d) flower, labiate, pl. auch: (lt.) Labiatæ; ⚹**blütig** a. ㊅: ⚹ labiatifloral; =**buchstabe** m, gram. labial (letter); ⚹**förmig** a. lipshaped, ♀: ⚹ labiate(d); =**füßer** m, zo.: ⚹ chilopod, =**laut** m, gr. labial (sound); ⚹**los** a. lipless, ♀: ⚹ acheilous, …ary; =**pomade**, =**salbe** f, pharm. lip-salve.

Lipp=fisch (⌣◡) m ㊂ ichth. wrass(e) (*Labrus*); gemeiner ~ cook-wrass(e) (*L. mixtus*); ⚹**fisch-artig** a. ㊅: ⚹ labroid.

lippig (⌣◡) a. ㊅ 1. lipped, ♀ und zo. labial, labiate(d). — 2. …**lippig** in Zssgn, z.B.: dünn=⚹ with thin lips.

liquid ❀ (⌣◡) [lt. flüssig] a. ㊅ (nicht geregelt) not settled, unpaid; ♀e Schulden debts owing, liabilities pl.

Liquida (⌣◡◡) [lt.] f (sg. inv., pl. …dä) gram. (ant. Muta) liquid consonant; vgl. flüssig 2.

Liquidation (◡◡=tz(◡)⌣)[lt.]f㊉ ♀ jur. (Abrechnung) liquidation; Börse: settlement.

Liquidations=bureau (⌢…) n ㊂ ❀ Börse: Stock-exchange clearing-house; =**tag**, =**termi'n** m day of settlement, settling day; =**verfahren** n beim Bankrott: winding-up (of the estate).

Liquidator (◡◡⌣◡) [lt.] m ㊈ jur. liquidator, administrator (of the estate).

liquidier|en, meist ❀ (◡◡⌣◡) [lt.] **I** v/a. ㊈ (abrechnen) to liquidate, to settle, to clear accounts; von Zahlungs-unfähigen: to wind up one's affairs. — **II** ~ n ㊃ u. ⚹**ung** f ㊉ = Liquidation.

Lira (⌣◡) [it.] f ㊂ (pl. Lire) (it. Münze) lira (= about 9.5 pence).

Lisbeth (⌣◡) [(S)li(s)(a)beth] npr/f. ㊅㊅α, ㊉㊅β. (Vn.) = Li(e)se.

lisch (◡) imper., ⚹**e(st** (◡) 2. u. ⚹**t** (◡) 3. Person sy. pres. ind. von † ob. poet. löschen¹ **II.** [arch. pilaster-strip.]

Lisene (◡⌣◡) [corr. fr. lisière Saum] f ❀]

Lisp(e)ler (⌣(◡)◡) m ㊆, **Lispl̠erin** f ㊅ lisper, lisping person; whisperer.

Lispel=laut (◡◡⌣) m ㊂ lisped (or whispered) sound.

lispeln (⌣◡) [dim. v. ahd. lispan: lisp] **I** v/n. (h.) u. v/a. ㊃a. **1.** von Wind, Schilf ꝛc.: to whisper (softly), von Gewässern auch: to murmur, ripple, purl; (plätschern) to splash. — **2.** (mit der Zunge, bes. bei f und z, anstoßen) to have a lisp. — **II** ~ n ㊃ **3.** (f. I) whisper(ing), murmur(ing), lisp(ing); ⚹ susurration, susurrus.

Lispel=ton m = =laut; **Lispler(in)** f.=Lispeler.

Lissabon (⌣◡◡) npr/n. ㊅α. (Hauptstadt und Hafen Portugals) Lisbon.

List (◡) [ahd.: *lehren] f ㊉ cunning; (Verschmitztheit) craft(iness), F depth; (Verschlagenheit) astuteness; (Kunstgriff) artifice, ruse, underhand work or trick; ~ anwenden to employ (or resort to, use) cunning or trickery; frei von ~ guileless, ingenuous; Sprichw. ~ gegen ~, etwa: diamond cut diamond.

Liste (⌣◡) [nhd.: list; *fr., it.] f ㊉ list, amtliche: register; f. Geschworenen=~; (Steuer-ꝛc. Register) roll (a. ⚹); (beschrei-

bendes Verzeichnis) catalogue; in eine ~ aufnehmen, eintragen to (enter in a) register, to enrol; to catalogue.

Listen¹=führung (⌣◡⌣◡) [Liste] f ㊉ keeping of lists or registers, registration.

listen²=reich (⌣◡⌣) [List] a. ㊅ (full of) cunning, crafty.

listig (⌣◡) [ahd.; *List] a. ㊅ cunning, crafty, astute, F deep; artful, underhand, tricky; wily, sly; ♂er Mensch artful fellow, F (old) sly-boots, sly fox.

listiger=weise (⌣◡◡⌣◡) adv. cunningly, in a cunning (or artful) way.

Listigkeit (⌣◡=) f ㊉ cunningness, craftiness, astuteness; artfulness.

Litanei (◡◡⌣) [grch. Anflehung] f ㊉ **1.** eccl. litany. — **2.** fig. lange ~ long story or rigmarole or yarn.

Litauen ♀ (⌣◡◡) npr/n. ㊅α. Lithuania.

Litauer(in f ㊆) m ㊈ (⌣◡◡◡), **litauisch** a. ㊅ Lithuanian.

Liter (⌣◡ a. ◡⌣) [fr.; *grch.] n (m) ㊂ (abbr. **l.**, öft. **l**) Hohlmaß ¹⁄₁₀₀₀ cbm litre (= 1.76 engl. od. 2.113 U.S. pints).

Litera (⌣◡◡) [lt. li't(t)ĕrä] f ㊂ (pl. a. …ä) (Buchstabe) letter; sub litera A under the letter (or heading) A.

Literär=geschichte (◡◡⌣◡◡◡) f ㊉ history (and bibliography) of literature.

Literar=historiker (◡◡⌣◡◡⌣◡◡) m ㊂ historian of literature.

literarisch (◡◡⌣◡) [lt.] a. ㊅ literary; ♂er Diebstahl: a) von Schriftstellern: plagiarism; b) von Buchdruckern: (literary) piracy; ein ♀ (adv.) gebildeter Mann a man of letters.

Literat (◡◡⌣) [lt.] m ㊂, bisw. ~**in** f ㊆ literary man, pl. a. literati, F co. literary gents pl., knights pl. of the pen; (Schriftsteller) writer, author (ess f); ~**entum** (◡◡⌣◡◡) n ㊃d.: a) literary vocation, authorship; b) coll. literary men or people, world of letters.

Literatur (◡◡◡⌣) [fr., *lt.] f ㊉ **1.** (Schrifttum) literature, weitS. letters pl. — **2.** (Verzeichnis der benutzten Schriften): ⚹ bibliography.

Literatur=blatt (◡◡◡⌣…) n ㊂ literary review or magazine; =**geschichte** f literary history, history of literature; =**zeitung** f = =blatt.

liter=weise (⌣◡⌣◡) adv. (F auch a. ㊅) by the litre.

Litewka (◡⌣◡) [poln. Litauer…] f ㊆ (Uniformbluse) patrol.

Litfaß=säule (⌣◡⌣◡) [L., Berliner Buchdrucker, † 1874] f ㊉ (Anschlagsäule) (Berlin) advertising (or advertisement-) pillar.

Lithium ⚹ (⌣◡◡) [lt., *grch.] n ㊄ Metall: lithium (Li); ~**oxyd** n ㊄ lithia (Li₂O).

Lithograph (⌣◡⌣) [grch.] m ㊂ lithographer; ~**ie** (◡◡⌣) f ㊉ (Steindruck) lithography, als Bild: lithograph(ic print); =**ieren** (◡◡⌣◡) v/a. ㊈ to lithograph; ⚹**isch** (◡◡⌣◡) a. ㊅ lithographic(al); ♂ische Anstalt lithographic printing-office or establishment.

litt(e) (◡(◡)) impf. ind. (subj.) v. leiden.

Liturgie (◡◡⌣) [grch.] f ㊉ eccl. (Anordnung des Gottesdienstes) liturgy; **liturgisch** (◡⌣◡) a. ㊅ liturgic(al).

Litze (⌣◡) [mhd.; *lt. li'cium Faden] f ㊆ **1.** Posamentier= (Besatzschnur) lace, cord, braid, tape; (Tresse) galoon. —

2. Seilerei: (die zs.-gezwirnten Garnfäden) strand of a rope. — **3.** Weberei: heddle.

Litzen=besatz ⊙ (⌣◡…) m ㊂ braiding, lace-trimming; =**zwirn** m Weberei: heddle-thread or yarn.

Livland ♀ (⌣◡) [finn. Liven pl. (Volk)] npr n. ㊅α. (ruff. Ostseeprovinz) Livonia; **Livländer(in** f ㊆)m㊈, **livländisch** (⌣◡◡◡), **livonisch** (◡⌣◡) a. ㊅ Livonian.

Livree (li-wre') [fr.] f ㊄ livery; eine ~ tragen to wear a livery; ~=**bediente**(r), ~=**diener** m ㊂ li.-servant, footman in livery, F (boy in) buttons; ~=**borte** f li.-lace; ~=**knopf** m button of a livery.

Lizentiat (◡◡=tz(◡)⌣) [lt.] m ㊂ licentiate (in England jetzt Titel für Ärzte ꝛc., z.B. Licentiate of the College of Surgeons, &c.).

Lizenz (◡⌣) [lt.] f ㊉ (dichterische) (Freiheit) poetic(al) license.

l. J. abbr. = laufenden Jahres.

Llanos ♀ (lja'-noß) [span.] m/pl. inv. (Steppen im nördl. Süd-amerika) llanos pl.

Lloyd ⊤ ♃ (loid) [Edward ~, Besitzer eines Kaffeehauses mit Schiffsbörse in London 17. saec.] m ㊂ Schiffahrtsgesellschaft, bsd.: der Norddeutsche ~ (in Bremen, 1857) the North German Lloyd.

l. M. abbr. = laufenden Monats.

Lob (⌣) [ahd.] n ㊇b. (meist ohne pl.) (ant. Tadel) **1.** (pl. oft: Lobes-erhebungen) praise, (Lobrede) eulogy, laudation, encomium; (Empfehlung) commendation; (Beifall) applause; (Ruhm) glory, fame; spärliches ~ faint praise; übertriebenes ~ exaggerated praise, puff(ing); f. auspofaunen, erhaben 3; e-m zum ~e gereichen to redound to a p.'s credit, to be a feather in a p.'s cap; vgl. gottlob!; es gereicht ihm sehr zum ~e, daß // it does him great credit that //. — **2.** Schule: (bisw. mit pl.) ein ~ einschreiben to enter a good mark. — **3.** allg. (Urteil über e-n) ein ~ ein gutes (schlechtes) ~ erteilen to bestow great (poor) praise upon a p., to speak well (ill) of a p., to give a p. a good (bad) character.

Lob=begier(de) (♂…) f ㊉ love of praise, striving after fame; ⚹**begierig** a. ㊅ desirous of praise or commendation.

loben (⌣◡) [ahd.: love: lieben] **I** v/a. sich ♀ v/refl., v/recip. ㊈ **1.** (sich) ♀ to praise (o.s.); (empfehlen) to commend; (rühmen) to extol, eulogize, glorify, panegyrize; übermäßig ♀ to laud (or praise up) to the skies, F to crack up, bsd. ❀ Waren: to puff; was sich an ihm ♀ läßt what is praiseworthy (or commendable) in him; Sprichw. gute Ware lobt sich selbst good wine needs no bush; man soll den Tag nicht vor dem Abend ♀ don't whistle before you are out of the wood, F don't crow too soon; das Werk lobt den Meister the work commends the workman, the skill of the master is proclaimed by his work. — **2.** mit ethischem dat.: sich et. ♀ to praise (or commend) a th.; da lobe ich mir den Mann! he is one after my own heart!, F he is the man for me!; ich lobe mir ein gutes Seebad give me (or there's nothing like) … — **II** ~ n ㊃ praise; commendation.

lobens=wert (⌣◡…) a. ㊅, ⚹**würdig** a. praiseworthy, deserving praise.

[Lober] — 665 — [log]

Lober (˘ˇ) *m* 22, **~in** *f* 47 praiser, eulogizer, extoller; *vgl.* Lobredner.

lobesam (˘ˇ-) *a.* 66 worshipful; *ehm. als Titel nach dem s.:* Kaiser Rotbart 2 the worthy emperor Barbarossa.

Lobes-erhebung (ˇ˘˘ˇ) *f* 22 (*f.* Lob 1) (high) praise, encomium.

Lob-gedicht (ˇ...) *n* 22 poem in praise of a p., laudatory lines *pl.*; **=gesang** *m* song of praise, hymn of thanksgiving; **=hudelei** *f* (vile) adulation, exaggerated (or fulsome) praise; **=hudeln** *v/a.* ˇˇ*ˇ*** to praise to the skies or in a fulsome measure, to overpraise, belaud; **=hudler (in** *f*) *m* adulator, base flatterer.

löblich (ˇˇ) [loben] *a.* 66 praiseworthy, commendable, laudable, als Titel etwa: worshipful; **~keit** *f* 46 praiseworthiness, commendableness, laudableness.

Lob-lied (ˇ...) *n* 22 = **=gesang**; **=preisen** *v/a. u. sich* 2 *v/refl.* 90** (*inf. u. p.p.*), *** (*pres. u. imper.*): (sich) 2 to glorify (o.s.), to extol (o.s.); *eccl.* lobpreiset den Herrn praise (or sing praises unto) the Lord; **=preisung** *f* laudation, glorification; **=rede** *f* laudatory oration, *geh. Spr.:* panegyric; *vgl.* Lob 1; **=redner** *m* eulogist, panegyrist; **=rednerisch** *a.* 66 eulogistic, ɔ encomiastic; **=singen** *v/n.* (h.) 90ˇˇ (*inf., p.p.*), *** (*pres. u. imper.*) einem 2 to sing a p.'s praises, to extol a p.; **=spruch** *m* eulogium.

Loch (˘ch) [ahd.: lock Verschluß] *n* 2c. 1. hole (a. *fig.* elende Wohnung); (Öffnung) opening, aperture; (Höhlung) hollow, cavity, cave, (Lücke in einer Mauer) breach; (Bohrung) bore- (or drill-)hole; gepunztes ~ punched hole; *hunt.* = Bau[1] 4; ein ~ ausfüllen to stop a gap; Löcher im Strumpfe haben to have holes in one's stockings; sich ein ~ in den Kopf fallen to break one's head by a fall. — 2. F *fig.* auf dem letzten ~e pfeifen to be on one's last legs; aus einem andern ~e pfeifen to change one's tone; das macht ein ~ in den Beutel that makes a hole in one's pocket; e-m ein ~ in den Leib fragen to torment a p. with one's questions, F to pump a p. (dry); er säuft wie ein ~ he can drink like a fish; e-m zeigen, wo der Zimmermann das ~ gemacht (oder gelassen) hat (die Türe weisen) to show a p. the door. — 3. Kinderspiel: f. Fuchs[2]; Billard: pocket; ins ~ stoßen: to pocket. — 4. (Sackgasse) blind alley. — 5. F (Gefängnis) jail, lock-up, F quod, limbo, ✕ black hole; ins ~ spazieren to (have to) go to prison; ins ~ stecken to lay by the heels, to clap into jail, F to put in(to) quod.

Loch-beitel ☉ (˘ch...) *m* 22 = **=meißel**; **=billard** *n* billiard-table with pockets; **=bohrer** *m:* a) Person: driller; b) ☉ Werkzeug: auger, piercing-drill; **=eisen** ☉ *n* punch(eon); **Löchelchen** (ˇˇˇ) *n* 23 (*dim.:* Loch) small hole or aperture, (Grübchen) dimple.

lochen ☉ (˘ch˘) *v/a.* 89 to pierce (holes), to make holes; to perforate, punch.

Locher (˘ch˘) *m* 22 punch(eon), piercer.

löch(e)richt ✳, mst **löch(e)rig** (ˇˇ˘ˇ) [Loch] *a.* 66 full of holes, F co. holy; (durchlöchert) perforated; ☉ metall., &c. honeycombed; (porös) porous, ɔ foraminiferous.

Löcherigkeit (ˇ˘˘˘-) *f* 46 perforated (or honeycombed) state; porosity.

Löcher-pilz ɤ (ˇˇ...) *m* 22, **=schwamm** ɤ *m:* ɔ polyporus, (Röhrenpilz) ɔ boletus; **=zahl** *f* number of holes. — *Vgl.* Loch.

Loch-koralle (ˇch...) *f* 22 *zo.:* ɔ madrepora, porite; **=maschine** ☉ punching-bear; **=meißel** *m* mortise-chisel; **=säge** *f* keyhole- (or table-, piercing-)saw; **=scheibe** *f* Schlosserei: bolster; **=zange** *f* punch-pliers *pl.*

Löckchen (ˇˇˇ) *n* 23 (*dim.:* Locke) little curl, ringlet; *bfd. ehm. auch:* kiss-me-quick.

Locke (˘ˇ) [ahd.: lock] *f* 22 1. (Haar-)lock, curl, ringlet, wie ein Korkzieher gedrehte: F corkscrew curl; e-m ~n brennen to curl (or frizzle) a p.'s hair with curling-tongs, to frizzle (up) a p.'s hair. — 2. ☉ ~n *pl.* (gröberer Teil der Wolle) locks *pl.*

locken[1] (˘ˇ) [Locke] *v/a. u. sich* 2 *v/refl.* 89 Haar: (sich) 2 to curl, to form locks; gelocktes Haar curly (or wavy) hair.

locken[2] (˘ˇ) [ahd.] I *v/a. u. v/n.* (h.) 89 1. *hunt.* to bait, to decoy. Vögel durch Nachahmung ihrer Stimme: to call, einen Hund: to whistle to. — 2. *fig.* (an sich ziehen) to attract, allure, entice, (verführen) to seduce; e-n durch Versprechungen 2 to tempt a p. with promises; e-m das Geld aus der Tasche 2 to get money out of a p., stärker: to fleece a p.; f. Hund 2; einem Tränen aus den Augen 2 to draw tears from a p.'s eyes (*vgl.* entlocken); ✕ sich in einen Hinterhalt 2 lassen to be drawn into an ambush. — II **~** *n* 3. f. Lockung.

löcken, fast † (˘ˇ) *v/n.* (h.) 89 = locken[3].

Locken[3]**-haar** (˘ˇ...) [Locke] *n* 22 curly hair; **=kopf** *m* curly head, c.-headed person; **=papier** *n* curl-paper; **=perücke** *f ehm.:* (full) wig with flowing ringlets, full-bottomed wig. [decoy-duck.]

Lock-ente (˘ˇˇ) [locken[2]] *f* 22 *hunt.*

Locken[3]**-wickel** (˘ˇ...) *m* 22 curl-paper; **=wulst** *m* dense (mass of) curly hair.

Locker[1] (˘ˇ) [locken[2]] *m* 22, **~in** *f* 47 enticer, (Verführer) seducer; *vgl.* Lockvogel.

locker[2] (˘ˇ) [nhd.] *a.* 66 (D9) 1. (*ant.* fest) loose, not (very) firm or solid or dense, vom Boden auch: light; (nicht straff) slack, not (very) tight, (nicht blicht) not compact (enough), (nachgebend) giving (way), crumbling (away); (wackelnd) shaky, rickety; (porös) porous, von Brot &c.: spongy; 2 machen to make loose, *vgl.* lockern; 2 werden to (be)come loose (auch von Zähnen); F *fig.* er läßt nicht 2 he won't give in, he never yields. — 2. *fig.* (ohne sittlichen Halt, schmähend als „liederlich") lax (morals), demoralized (state), stärker: dissolute (habits); 2 (*adv.*) leben, ein 2es Leben führen to lead a disorderly (or loose, extravagant, gay and easy) life; ein 2er Vogel od. Zeisig a loose fellow or F fish, a scapegrace.

Lockerheit (˘ˇ-) *f* 46 (f. locker[2]) 1. looseness; slackness; sponginess. — 2. laxity, demoralization; extravagance.

lockern (˘ˇ) 89a. I *v/a., v/n.* (ſn) to loosen; to slacken; to make shaky; *fig.* to demoralize. — II sich 2 *v/refl.* to loosen, to come loose; to give way; *fig.* to relax. — III **Lockerung** *f* 46 relaxation.

Lock-flöte (˘ˇ...) *f* 22 = Lockpfeife.

lockig (˘ˇ) [Locke] *a.* 66 curly, curled, in curls or locks or ringlets.

Lock-mittel (˘ˇ...) *n* 22 bait; temptation, inducement; **=pfeife** *f, hunt.* decoywhistle, bird-whistle or =call; **=ruf** *m, hunt.* call of a decoy-bird, *fig.* alluring call; **=speise** *f, hunt.* bait, lure (a. *fig.*); **=spitzel** F [ſchwz.] *m* Polizei: (fr.) *agent provocateur*.

Lockung (˘ˇ) *f* 46 (f. locken[2] I) bait(ing); attraction, allurement, enticement, (Verführung) seduction; temptation.

Lock-vogel (˘ˇ...) *m* 22: a) *hunt.* decoybird (a. *fig.*); b) *fig.* allurer, tempter.

Lode *prove.* ɤ (˘ˇ) [ahd.] *f* 22 (Schößling) sprig, spray, shoot.

Loden[1] ☉ (˘ˇ) [ahd. Zotte] *m* 23 Tuchfabrikation: rough woollen cloth, unfulled cloth, shag.

loden[2] (˘ˇ-) *a.* 66 (D9): der Rock (a. **Loden**[1]**-rock** (˘ˇˇ) *m* 22) rough cloth coat, shag coat.

Loder[1] (˘ˇ) *m* 22 (Lodenweber) weaver of coarse woollen materials or stout carpets. [for-nothing.]

Loder[2] *bayr.* (˘ˇ) *m* 22 (Tunichtgut) good-

Loder[3] *prove.* (˘ˇ) [: lather Schaum] *n* 22 lather. [asche] light ashes *pl.*

Loder[4]**-asche** (˘ˇˇ) [lodern] *f* 22 (Flug-

Loderer (˘ˇˇ) *m* 22 = Loder[1].

lodern (˘ˇ) [ndd.] I *v/n.* (h.) 89a. von der Flamme: to flare (up), to blaze (up), to burst forth; *fig.* (glühen) to burn (in Liebesglut with love). — II **~** *n* 23 flaring, blazing; flare, blaze.

Löffel (ˇˇ) [ahd.] *m* 22 1. spoon, zum Kochen und Vorlegen: ladle, *vgl.* Eßlöffel. — 2. *fig.* f. barbieren I; tun, als ob man die Weisheit mit ~n gegessen hätte to make a great show (or pretence) of wisdom or learning. — 3. *hunt.* (Ohr des Hasen, co. des Menschen) ear.

Löffel-blech (ˇˇ...) *n* 22: a) in welches Löffel gesteckt werden: spoon-rack; b) ☉ Klempnerei: tin to make spoons of; **=bohrer** ☉ *m* wimble, auger, well-borer, spitzer: spoon-bit; **=ente** *f, orn.* broad-bill, shoveller (*Spa'tula clypea'ta*); **=förmig** *a.* 66 spoon-shaped, ɔ cochleariform; **=gans** *f* ☉ *orn.*: a) = **=ente**; b) = **=reiher**; **=garde** F *f, co.* ill-trained (or undisciplined) soldiers *pl.* more fond of feasting than fighting; **=korb** *m:* a) für Löffel u. Gabeln: plate-basket; b) zum Wegtragen vom Speisetische: spoon-tray, mehr gebr.: knife-and-fork tray; **=kraut** ɤ *n* spoonwort (*Cochlea'ria*); echtes ~ scurvygrass (*C. officina'lis*).

löffeln[1] (ˇˇ) *v/a.* 89a. 1. to ladle out. — 2. to eat (or F gobble) up with a spoon.

löffeln[2] fast † (ˇˇ) [Löffel † = Laffe] *v/n.* (h.) 89a. (lieben) to be flirting or spooning or sweethearting or courting.

Löffel-reiher (ˇˇ...) *m* 22 *orn.* spoonbill (*Plata'lea leucoro'dia*); **=stiel** *m* spoon-handle; **=voll** *m* spoonful; **=weise** *adv.* by spoonfuls or ladlefuls; **=reiher**.

Löffler (ˇˇ) *m* 22 *orn.* = Löffel-ente.

log[1] (ˉ) *impf. ind.* von lügen.

♪ Musik; ɔ Wissenschaft; ɤ Pflanze; ♀ Geographie; ☉ Technik; ✕ Bergbau; ✕ Militär; ⚓ Marine; ● Handel; ✉ Post; 🚂 Eisenbahn.

Log² ⚓ (ʼ) [schwd.] n [S]d. (Fahrtmesser) log; das ~ auswerfen to heave the log.
Logarithmen-rechnung (ᵕᵕʼᵕ...) f [S], -syste'm n, *math.* logarithmic calculation, system; -**tafeln** f pl. logarithmic tables *pl.* [logarithmic(al).
logarithmisch (ᵕᵕʼᵕ) [grch.] *a.* [S] *math.*
Logarithmus (ᵕᵕʼᵕ) [lt., *grch.] m [W] *math.* logarithm; ~en, oft *abbr.*: logs *pl.*
Log²-brett ⚓ (ʼ...) n [S] log-boat (a. Logscheit); -**buch** n (Schiffstagebuch) log-book.
Loge (ʼᵕ) [fr.; *dtsch. Laube] f [S] 1. *arch.* (Bauhütte) lodge. — 2. *thea.* box, ersten Ranges: dress-box. [lügen.
löge (ʼᵕ) 1. u. 3. Person *impf. subj.* von
Logen-billett (ʼᵕ...) n [S] *thea.* ticket for a box; -**bruder** m (Freimaurer) member of a masonic lodge, brother mason; -**gang** m, *thea.* lobby; -**meister** m master of a masonic lodge; -**schließer(in** f) m, *thea.* box-keeper, attendant at a theatre, f auch: girl usher.
loggen ⚓ (ʼᵕ) [Log²] v/n. (h.) [S] to (heave the) log. [glass.
Log²-glas ⚓ (ʼʼ) n [S] (Sanduhr) (log-)
Logier-besuch (ᵕʼᵕ...) [logieren] m [S] staying company, visitors (or guests) *pl.* staying at the house.
logieren (ᵕʼᵕ) [fr.; *Loge] [S] I v/n. (h.) (wohnen) to lodge (or stay) with a p. — II v/a. (aufnehmen) to lodge, to harbour, to put up (for the night).
Logier-zimmer (ᵕʼᵕ...) n [S] spare room.
Logik (ʼᵕ) [grch.] f [S] *phls.* (Denklehre) logic; ~er (ʼᵕᵕ) m [S] logician.
Logis (ᵕʼ) [fr.; *Loge] n [S] (Wohnung) lodgings, apartments *pl.*; s. Kost.
logisch (ʼᵕ) [grch.] *a.* [S] logical.
Log²-leine ⚓ (ʼ...) f [S] log-line; -**scheit** n = Logbrett.
loh (ʼ) [Lohe²] *a.* [S] s. lichterloh.
Loh¹-bad ⚙ (ʼ...) [Lohe¹] n [S] Gerberei: bark-stove; -**ballen** m tan-ball; -**beet** n. *hort.* tan-bed; -**beize** f tanning.
Lohe¹ ⚙ (ʼᵕ) [ahd.] f [S] Gerberei: (Fichten- oder Eichen-rindenmehl) tanner's bark, tanning-bark, tan.
Lohe² (ʼᵕ) [mhd.: lt. *lūc-*] f [S] (helle Glut) blaze, blazing fire, F flare; in lichter ~ brennen to be all ablaze.
Loh¹-eiche ⚘ (ʼʼᵕ) [Lohe¹] f [S] common oak (*Quercus robur*).
lohen¹ ⚙ (ʼᵕ) [Lohe¹] v/a. [S] Gerberei &c.: to (treat with) tan.
lohen² (ʼᵕ) [ahd.; *Lohe²] v/n. (h. u. sn) [S] to blaze (or flare) up, to be in flames.
Loh¹-farbe (ʼ...) f [S] tan-colour; ²**farben**, ²**farbig** *a.* [S] tan-coloured, tawny; -**faß** n tan-vat; -²**feuer** [Lohe²] n blazing (or flaring) fire; ²¹**gar** ⚙ *a.* (bark-)tanned; ² machen to tan; -**gerber** m tanner; -**gerberei** f: a) Gewerbe: tanner's trade, tanning; b) Ort: tanner's yard, tannery; s. auch -haus; -**grube** f tan- (or bark-)pit; -**haus** n tan-house; -**kuchen** m tan-brick, -cake, zum Brennen: tan-turf; -**mühle** f tan-mill, oak-bark mill.
Lohn (ʼ) [ahd.: lt. *lucrum*] m (P oft n) [T]c. 1. o. *pl.*: (Entgelt) compensation, (good or bad) return; (Belohnung) reward, recompense; seinen ~ empfangen to receive one's desert, to get one's due; er hat schlimmen ~ empfangen he was ill requited (or rewarded) for his trouble; *bibl.* sie haben ihren ~ dahin they have their reward; Sprichw. Undank ist der Welt ~ ingratitude (that) is the way of the world. — 2. (P oft n) mit *pl.*: (Arbeitslohn) salary, (Zahlung) payment, (Gebühr) fee; ~ der Dienstboten &c.: wages *pl.*; wöchentlicher &c. ~ weekly, &c. pay (a. ⚔, vgl. Löhnung); (Vergütung) gratification, remuneration; ~, bei dem man leben kann living wage; in j-s ~ steh(e)n to be in a p.'s pay or service; Sprichw. s. Arbeit 7, Arbeiter 1.
Lohn-arbeit (ʼ...) f [S] paid (or hired) labour; -**arbeiter(in** f) m hired labourer, paid workman, f workwoman; -**auszahlung** f payment of wages; -**bediente(r)**, -**diener** m (occasionally engaged) valet; -**buch** n wages-book; -**drückerei** f sweating.
lohnen (ʼᵕ) [ahd.; *Lohn] I v/a., v/n. (h.), v/impers. u. sich ² v/refl. [S] 1. e-m et. ² to compensate (or remunerate, reward, recompense) a p. for a th.; Gott lohn' es dir! God bless you (for it)!; einem mit Undank ² to repay a p. with ingratitude. — 2. mit sachl. *acc.* (od. *gen.*): dort lohnt man die Arbeit besser als hier there workmen receive better wages than here; wieviel lohnt die Arbeit? how much does the work bring in?; es lohnt (sich) nicht der Mühe (*gen.*) it is not worth while, F it does not pay; *iro.* das lohnte auch gerade die (od. sich der) Mühe that's not worth the trouble, the game is not worth the candle. — 3. mit persönlichem *acc.*: den Arbeiter ² to pay ... — 4. *abs.* (Vorteil bringen) to be profitable or remunerative; die Sache lohnt (sich) it is a paying (or profitable) concern, it pays; würde sich das für Sie ²? would that be worth your while?, would it pay you? — II ²d *p.pr.* u. *a.* [S] 5. Bed. des *inf.* — 6. profitable, remunerative; advantageous; lucrative.
löhnen (ʼᵕ) [mhd.; *Lohn] I *v/a.* [S] to pay wages to servants, workmen, &c., ⚔ to pay soldiers. — II ~ n [S] s. Löhnung 1.
Lohn-fuhre (ʼ...) f [S] ride in a hackney-carriage; -**gesetz** n: ehernes ~ iron (or fixed) law of wages; -**herr** m employer; -**kellner** m waiter engaged for the day; -**kutsche** f hackney-carriage, cab, fly; -**kutscher** m hackney-coachman, cabman; -**lakai** m = -diener; -**satz** m rate of pay; -**tag** m pay-day.
Löhnung (ʼᵕ) f [S] 1. payment of wages. — 2. ⚔ soldier's pay.
Löhnungs-tag (ʼᵕʼ) m [S] pay-day.
Lohn-zahlung (ʼ-ʼᵕ) f [S] payment of wages. [tanning.
Loh¹-rinde (ʼ-ʼᵕ) f [S] oak-bark for
lokal (ᵕʼ) [lt.] I *a.* [S] local; ~e(s) n [S] in Zeitungen: local news. — II ~ n [S]d. (Örtlichkeit) locality; (Bier-)~ public(-)house, F pub, beer-shop; (Geschäfts-)~ business-premises *pl.*, place of business; office, shop; (Tanz-)~ dancing-room(s *pl.*), feinerer Art: assembly-rooms *pl.*
Lokal-bahn 🚂 (ᵕʼ...) f [S] local (or suburban) railway; -**behörde** f local authorities *pl.*; -**berühmtheit** f local celebrity; -**blatt** n l. paper; -**farbe** f, *paint.* u. *fig.* e-s Romans &c.: l. colouring.
lokalisier|en (ᵕ-ᵕʼᵕ) [lt.] I *v/a.* [S] (örtlich beschränken, bestimmen) to localize, to locate. — II ~ n [S] und ²**ung** f [S] localization, location.
Lokalität (ᵕ-ᵕʼ) [lt.] f [S] (Örtlichkeit) locality; ~en *pl.* (Räumlichkeiten) eines Hauses &c. whereabouts (or rooms) *pl.* ...
Lokal-kenntnis (ᵕʼ...) f [S] knowledge of a place; -**kenntnisse** sammeln to study (or look about) a place; -**miete** f office- (or shop-)rent; -**nachricht** f local news; -**patrioti'smus** m local patriotism, parochialism; -**veränderung** f change of premises or address; -**verhältnisse** *n/pl.* local circumstances *pl.*; die ~ kennen to know (the ins and outs of) a place; -**verkehr**, -**zug** 🚂 m local traffic, train; -**zeitung** f local paper.
Lokativ (ʼ-ʼ) [lt.] m [S]d. *gr.* (Ortsfall bsd. älterer Sprachen) locative (case).
Loko-geschäft ✱ (ʼᵕ-ᵕʼ) n [S] spot-business.
Lokomobile ⚙ (ᵕᵕᵕʼᵕ) [lt.] f [S] (Straßenlokomotive) traction-engine, zum Pflastern: steam-roller. [🚂 (locomotive) engine.
Lokomotive ⚙ (ᵕᵕᵕʼᵕ) [lt.] f [S] bsd.
Lokomotiv-führer (ᵕᵕᵕʼ...) m [S] engine-driver or -man; -**pfeife** f steam-whistle of an engine; -**schuppen** m engine-shed or -house. [spots *pl.*
Loko-ware(n *pl.*) ✱ (ʼᵕ-ʼᵕ) f spot-goods,
Lokus F (ʼᵕ) [lt. *lŏcŭs*] (Ort) m, *inv.* und [S] water-closet (= Abtritt 2).
Lolch ⚘ (ʼ) [mhd., * lt.] m [S]b. darnel (-grass) (*Lo'lium*); s. Taumel-².
Lombard (ᵕʼ) [fr.] m, n [S]c. 1. (Leihhaus) pawnshop; (Pfandschein) pawn-ticket. — 2. ✱ (deposit-)bank; ~-**bestände** (ᵕʼ...) *m/pl.* [S] deposits *pl.*
Lombardei ♀ (ᵕᵕʼ) *npr/f.* Lombardy.
Lombard-geschäft n [S] deposit-business.
lombardisch (ᵕʼᵕ) *a.* [S] Lombard(ic).
Lomber (ʼᵕ) [fr. *l'hombre* m] n [S] Kartenspiel: (l'h)ombre, omber.
Londoner (ʼᵕᵕ) I m [S], ~in f [S] Londoner, F cockney. — II *a. inv.* (of) London, Metropolitan; ~ Spracheigentümlichkeit Londonism, F cockneyism.
Longe (ʼᵕ) [fr.] f [S] *man.* (Longierleine) allonge. [lunge.
longieren (ᵕʼᵕ) [fr.] *v/a.* [S] *man.* to
Loos, loosen, Lootse s. Los, losen, Lotse.
Lorbeer (ʼ-, ↘ ʼ-) [ahd.; *lt. *laurus*] m [S]d. ⚘ laurel(-tree), bay(-tree) (*Laurus no'bilis*); *fig.* auf s-n ~en ausruhen to rest on one's laurels; mit ~(en) kränzen to crown with laurel(-wreaths); Beere des ~(baum)s bayberry.
lorbeer-artig ⚘ (ʼ-...) *a.* [S]: ♪ lauraceous; -**baum** ⚘ m [S] = Lorbeer; ²**bekränzt** *a.* laurel-crowned, *poet.* auch laureate; -**blatt** n bay-leaf; -**blüte** f bay-flower; -**hain** m laurel-grove; -**kranz** m wreath (or crown) of laurel; -**öl** ✱ n bay-oil; -**zweig** m laurel-branch. [top (*Helve'lla*).
Lorchel ⚘ (ʼᵕ) f [S] Pilz: eatable turban-
Lord ⚘ (ʼ) [engl.] m [S] lord, als Anrede: my lord, mylord; ~-**Mayor** m Lord Mayor; ~**schaft** (ʼᵕ) f [S] (his, your, &c.) lordship. [(Bn.) Nora, Nelly.
Lore¹ (ʼᵕ) [L(eon)ore] *npr/f* [S] [B].
Lore² ⚘ 🚂 (ʼᵕ) [engl.] f [S] lorry, truck.
Lorenz (ʼᵕ) ... [lt.] *npr/m.* (Bn.) Laurence, Lawrence;

[Lorenzstrom] — 667 — [lösen]

~strom ♂ m: der ~ in Nord-amerika the St. Lawrence. [courtesan, gay woman.]
Lorette (⌣⌣) [fr.] f ⊕ (feine Buhlerin),
Lorgnette (lör-njĕ'-t⁴) [(⁺⌣) fr.; * dtsch. lauern] f ⊕ eye-glasses pl., für ein Auge (auch **Lorgnon** (lör-nją') n ⊕) eye-glass, monocle.
lorgnettieren (lör-nj⌣⌣)v/a. ⊕ to observe (or quiz) through an eye-glass.
Lori¹ (⌣⌣) [span., *malai.] m ⊕ zo. (Faul-affe) loris (stenops); orn. (Papagei) lory.
Lori² ⊤ ⊞ (⌣⌣) [engl.] ⊕ = **Lore²**.
Lork (⌣) [ndd. Lurch] m ⊕b. zo. = Kröte.
Los¹ (⌣) [ahd.: lot] n ⊕a. 1. lot; durchs ~ entscheiden to decide by lot; das ~ ist gefallen the die is cast, F we (they, &c.) are in for it; das ~werfen (ziehen) to cast (to draw) lots (über et. for a th.). — 2. fig. (Geschick) fate, destiny, lot; chance; sein ~ ist nicht zu beneiden his position (or lot) is not an enviable one; sie teilten ihr ~ mit-ea. they shared the same fate. — 3. Lotterie (Zettel, Schein) lottery-ticket; (Gewinn) prize; das große ~ gewinnen to draw (or win) the first prize. — 4. weitS. (Anteil) lot, share, portion; ⊕ (Partie Waren) lot, parcel; agr., &c. (Stück Land) allotment, piece of ground; ⚒ (Erzhaufen) heap of ore.

Los² (⌣) [ahd.: loose] I prädikatives a. ⊕ (D 10) (als attributives a. f. lose²) 1. ohne Ob-jekt: loose, slack, free, disengaged; die Kette ist ⌣ is detached or off; der Gefangene ist ⌣ the prisoner is free; der Hund ist von der Kette ⌣ the dog is off (or free from) the chain or un-chained. — 2. F fig. et., nicht viel ⌣ haben to know s.th., very little; es ist et. ⌣ there is something (import-ant) going on or in the wind; es ist mit ihm, mit seinem Wissen nicht viel ⌣ F he (or his knowledge) is not up to much; da war der Teufel ⌣ F there was a devil (or a deuce) of a row, it was like hell let loose; was ist ⌣ (was gibt's)? what is the matter or F the row?, F what is up here? — 3. ⌣ sein von et. ob. mit gen., auch acc. (e-r Sache ⌣ und ledig sein) to be rid of a th.; mein Geld bin ich ⌣ I have lost (or I am done out of)…; et. ⌣ w. to get rid of (durch Verkauf) to part with) a th.; ⌣ von Rom! away from Rome! — 4. ell. ⌣! (angefangen) go (it)!, F fire away!, look alive!; Tennis ꝛc.: play!; d(a)rauf ⌣! go it!, at it!, on to it!, don't be afraid!; laß ⌣! let go! — II adv. los-… als Vorsilbe mit v., immer trennbar(**), bz.⌣5.Loslösung, Befreiung ex, zB. ⌣drehen v/a. to detach (or loosen) by turning. — 6. plötzliches Hervorbrechen, zB. auf e-n, et. ⌣stürzen v/n. (fn) to rush at (or upon) a p., a th.; to make a dash at a p., a th. — 7. Ziel, Richtung auf etwas hin, zB. auf et. ⌣marschieren (⌣rennen) v/n. (fn) to march (to run) straight towards a th.; auf e-n ⌣schlagen (h.) to belabour (or pitch into) a p. — 8. Anfang e-r Handlung: tüchtig d(a)rauf ⌣essen u. ⌣trinken to eat and drink to one's heart's content, to cram o.s. with eating and drinking (f. darauf 2).

— III …los (…"¹) [ahd.: …less] 9. in Zssgn mit vorangehendem s. bz. Fehlen, Mangel, zB. hoffnungs⌣ hopeless.
los² =ankern (⌣…) v/a. ⊕a** to unmoor (auch fig.); ⌣arbeiten ⊕** v/a. u. sich ⌣ v/refl. to work off, to get off with great effort(s); sich ⌣ to get loose, to extricate (or disengage) o.s. with difficulty; v/n. (h.) tapfer d(a)rauf ⌣ to work away (or hard) at a th.
lösbar (⌣¹⌣) a. ⊕ soluble, solvable (auch math.); **Lösbarkeit** (⌣¹⌣) f ⊕ solubility.
los² =bekommen (⌣…) v/a. ⊕**/*: a) ⌣bringen; b) F fig. to begin to under-stand, F to get (into) the knack of; ⌣binden ⊕** v/a. to untie, unbind, uncord, undo, unfasten, ⌣ to unfurl; ~ n untying, &c., detachment; ⌣bitten v/a. ⊕**: (einen) ⌣ to beg (a person) off, to effect by one's en-treaties a p.'s release; ⌣brechen ⊕a** v/a. to break (or pull) off; v/n. (fn) to come off or undone; fig. to break loose, to burst forth; ⌣brennen v/a. ⊕b**=⌣feuern; ⌣bringen v/a. ⊕** to get off or away or free, to disengage; ⌣bröckeln v/a., v/n. (fn) u. sich ⌣ v/refl. ⊕a** to crumble away.
losch (⌣) impf. ind. v. löschen. [station.]
Lösch¹=anstalt (⌣…) [löschen¹] f ⊕ fire-
löschbar (⌣-) a. ⊕ extinguishable, vom Durste: quenchable. [ting-paper.]
Lösch¹=blatt (⌣⌣) n ⊕ (sheet of) blot-]
lösche (⌣⌣) impf. subj. von löschen.
Lösch¹ =eimer (⌣⌣) m ⊕: a) fire-bucket; b)⊕Schmiede: quenching-tub or-bucket.
Löschen (⌣⌣) [Los¹, dim.] n ⊕ small lot.
löschen¹ (⌣⌣) [ahd.] I v/a. ⊕ (⌣ ⊕b(e)ft) 1. to extinguish (or put out) a light, a fire, to quench the flames; bei Feuersbrünsten: to play with the hose upon a burning roof; den Durst ⌣ to quench (or slacken) one's thirst; ⊕ Kalk ⌣ to slake lime. — 2. Ge-schriebenes, Gemaltes ⌣ (tilgen) to efface…, to blot out …; fig. (verwischen) to ob-literate; jur. eine Hypothek ⌣ to pay off a mortgage. — 3. ⊕ Posten im Buche ⌣ to strike off entries; eine Forderung: to cancel, to liquidate. — II v/n. (fn) ⊕b(e)ft (⌣ ⊕) 4. poet. = er⌣. — 5. v. Papier: ⌣ (Tinte einziehen) to blot. — III ~ n 6. = Löschung¹.
löschen² ⌣ (⌣⌣) [ndb. nbl.; *los] v/a. ⊕ (ausladen) ein Schiff ⌣ to unload (or unlade, discharge, clear, lighten) a ship; Waren ⌣ to unship (or land) goods or a cargo.
Löscher¹ (⌣⌣) [löschen¹] m ⊕ 1. = Lösch-horn. — 2. (aufgerolltes Löschpapier) (roll-)blotter.
Löscher² ⌣ (⌣⌣) [löschen²] m ⊕ unloader, discharger, docker, stevedore.
Lösch² =geld ⌣ (⌣…) [löschen²] n ⊕ charges pl. for unlading, wharfage; =¹gerät(schaften f/pl.) ⊕ appliance(s pl.) for extinguishing fire; =²hafen ⌣ m port of discharge; =¹haken ⊕ m fire-hook; poker; =horn, =hütchen n ⊕ extinguisher; =kalk ⊕ m slaked lime, quicklime; =kohle f extinguished coal(s pl.), cinders pl.; =kübel m = =eimer b; =mannschaft f fire-brigade or -staff, (corps of) firemen; =papier

n blotting-paper; Buch von ~ blotting-case, blotter; =²platz ⌣ m: a) (Platz zum Ausladen) place for unloading, dis-charging-wharf or -berth, port of discharge; b) (Bestimmungshafen des Schiffes) ship's destination.
Löschung¹ (⌣⌣) f ⊕ (zu löschen 1:) ex-tinction; (zu 2:) effacement, obliteration; (zu 3:) liquidation of a debt.
Löschung² ⌣ (⌣⌣) f ⊕ (f. löschen²) un-loading, &c.
Lösch²-vorrichtung (⌣…) f ⊕ = =gerät; =wesen n system of fire-brigades.
los² =donnern (⌣…) v/n. (h.) ⊕a** to thunder away, fig. to burst forth (with a thundering noise); ⌣drehen v/a. ⊕** to twist (or wrench) off, vgl. ⌣schrauben; f. a. los² 5; ⌣drücken v/a. ⊕** to push (or squeeze) off, ein Ge-wehr: to fire, to discharge, e-n Pfeil: to shoot off, to let fly.
Lose¹ ⌣ (⌣⌣) f ⊕ bight (or slack) of a rope.
lose² (⌣⌣) [los] I a. ⊕ (D 10) 1. = locker² 1. — 2. (ohne Zsf.-hang) incoherent; (be-weglich) movable, shifting; ⌣s Geld loose cash, (small) change; ⌣s Haar loose (or dishevelled) hair; ⊕ ⌣ Waren loose goods, loosely packed articles pl.; ⌣ werden: a) von Ge-leimtem: to come untied; b) von Ge-schürtem: to come unglued. — 3. (ohne inneren Wert) of base alloy, (schlecht) bad, inferior; (ungebunden) loose, (leicht be-weglich) fickle, volatile, free (and easy); (lüderlich) dissipated, fast; ⌣s Gesindel vagrants, tramps pl.; ⌣ Reden pl. loose (or incoherent, foolish) talk sg.; ⌣r Streich naughty trick; ⌣r Vogel waggish (or gay) person; einen ⌣n Mund, ein ⌣s (böses) Maul h. to have a sharp (stärker: malicious, loose, F long) tongue. — II ~([r] m) f 4. rogue, wag(gish person); gay (or fast) p.
Löse-geld (⌣⌣⌣) n ⊕ ransom.
los² =eisen (⌣¹⌣⌣) v/a. ⊕** to clear of ice; fig. to obtain with difficulty, Geld: to squeeze (or screw) … out of a p.
losen¹ (⌣⌣) [los] I v/n (h.), v/a. u. v/refl. ⊕ to draw (or to decide by) lots; Tennis: to toss; um et. ⌣ to raffle (or draw lots) for a th.; ⚔ sich fest (frei) ⌣ to draw a bad (good) number (as a conscript). — II ~ n ⊕ drawing (of lots). [listen, hearken.]
losen² obb. (⌣⌣) v/n. (h.) ⊕ (lauschen) to]
lösen (⌣⌣) [ahd.: lose; *los] I v/a. und sich ⌣ v/refl. ⊕ 1. to loosen, to part asunder (sich ⌣ to get loose); Ge-schnürtes, Geknüpftes: to untie, unbind, unknot (sich ⌣ to come untied); (ab-trennen) to sever, to detach; (aus-ea. machen) to undo, to take apart or to pieces (sich ⌣ to come undone); der Schlaf löst die Glieder sleep relaxes (or unbends) the limbs; e-m die Zunge ⌣ to cut the ligament of a p.'s tongue, fig. to loosen a p.'s tongue; fig. den Knoten im Drama ⌣ to un-ravel the plot; med. die Arznei löst den Schleim von der Brust … loosens the phlegm, … eases the chest. — 2. e-e Verbindlichkeit ⌣ to cancel (or set aside) an obligation, a contract; eccl. die Macht zu binden und zu ⌣ the

⚗ scientific; ❀ botanical; ♁ geography; ☉ machinery; ⚒ mining; ⚔ military; ⚓ marine; ⊕ commercial; ✉ postal; 🚂 railway.

power to bind and unbind; sein Verhältnis zu e-m ≈ to give up (or discontinue) all connexion with a p. — 3. (schmelzen) (sich) ≈ to (dis)solve, to melt; Jodkalium läßt sich in Wasser leicht ≈ potassium iodide is easily dissolved in water. — 4. eine Aufgabe, Gleichung &c. ≈ to solve …; Zweifel ≈ to clear up … — 5. (aus-, ein-lösen) ein Pfand ≈ to redeem a pledge; sein Versprechen ≈ to redeem (or keep) one's promise; an der Kasse sein Billett ≈ to take (or buy) one's ticket; einen Gewerbeschein ≈ to take out a license. — 6. Geld ≈ (für Waren einnehmen) to make money out of (or by selling) a th.; ❀ wir haben heute nur wenig gelöst our takings (or receipts, returns) have been very small (or poor) today. — 7. = losfeuern. — II ~ n [23] 8. = Lösung 1.

Loser (´⏑) [losen²] m [22] (Ohr[en] des Wildes) ear(s *pl.*) of a deer or other game.

Löser¹ (´⏑) m [22] one who loosens or unties or solves, loosener; *fig.* = Erlöser.

Löser² (´⏑) m [22] *zo.* = Blättermagen; **~-dürre** (″⏑-`⏑) f [62] *vet.* = Rinderpest.

los²-fahren (″…) *v/n.* (sn) [85]b**: a) auf et. ≈ to rush upon a th.; ⚓ gerade auf das Land ≈ to make straight for land; b) (sich plötzlich ablösen) to fly off; c) *fig.* to burst forth; auf e-n ≈ to make a sudden onslaught on a p.; **≗feuern** [92]a** *v/a.* to fire a shot, to discharge a pistol; *v/n.* (sn) von e-m Schusse: to go off; ~ n [23] discharge; *v/n.* (h.): auf e-n ≈ to fire at a p.; **≗geben** *v/a.* [82]c** to release, set free, let off, liberate, discharge; **-gebung** f release, discharge, v. Sklaven &c.: emancipation; **≗geh(e)n**: *v/n.* (sn) [94]**: a) auf e-n ≈ to go straight up to a p.; frisch auf et. ≈ to take a th. vigorously in hand, to set to with a will; ⚔ auf den Feind ≈ to march against the enemy; auf-ea. ≈ to attack (F to go for) each other; *abs.* burschikos: sie sind ≗gegangen they fought a duel; b) F (anfangen) to commence, to start; fertig, es kann ≈! ready, go!; da ging der Spektakel los then came (or began) the row; wann soll's ≈? when is it to come off?; c) von Feuerwaffen: to go off, nicht ≈ to miss fire; d) (sich ablösen) to come off or unfastened, (locker w.) to get loose; **≗gürten** *v/a.* [89]** to ungird, to unbelt; **≗haben** *v/a.* [70]b** s. los² 2; **≗haken** *v/a.* [88]** to unhook; **≗hauen** [87]c**: *v/a.* to knock (or strike) off; *v/n.* (h.) F auf e-n ≈ to knock (or batter) a p. about; e-m **≗helfen** *v/n.* (h.) [73]b** to aid (or assist) a p. in getting free, to help to extricate a p.

…losigkeit (…″´⏑-) [vgl. los² III, …ig u. …keit] f [46] in Zssgn: Farb≈ colourlessness.

Los²-kauf (″…) m [62] buying off, redemption, ransom(ing) of prisoners, &c.; **≗kaufen** [88]** *v/a.* to buy, to redeem, Gefangene &c.: to ransom; sich ≈ to buy o.s. out, to purchase one's liberty; ~ n [23] = -kauf; **≗käuflich** *a.* [66] redeemable, ransomable; **-kauf-summe** f purchase-money, bisw. smart-money; Feudalrecht: scutage; **-kaufung** f = -kauf; **≗ketten** *v/a.* [89]** to unchain, to free from chains; **≗knüpfen** *v/a.* [88]** to unknot, to untie; **≗kommen** *v/n.* (sn) [84]** to get (or come) off or loose; (frei w.) to become free, aus Gefangenschaft: to be released or set free; von et. ≈ (es los-w.) to get rid of a th.; **≗koppeln** *v/a.* [92]a** *hunt.* to unleash hounds; **≗kriegen** F *v/a.* [88]**: a) = ≗bringen; b) (lernen) F to get into a th., to twig a th.; vgl. ≗bekommen; **≗kuppeln** ⚙ *v/a.* [92]a** *mach.* to disconnect, to disengage, 🚂 to uncouple; **≗lassen** [86]a** *v/a.*: a) to let go, to leave hold of; lassen Sie nicht los! hold fast or tight!; b) Gefangene ≈ to release, set free, liberate; *fig.* eine Spottschrift gegen e-n ≈ to launch (or publish) a lampoon against a p.; *v/n.* (h.) = ≗gehen d; ~ n [23] u. **-lassung** f [46] release, liberation; **≗leben** *v/n.* (h.) [88]** F d(a)rauf-≈ to live thoughtlessly on; **≗legen** F *v/n.* (h.) [88]** to set about doing a th., to set to (work).

löslich (´⏑) *a.* [66] dissolvable; *chm.*: (leicht) ≈ soluble, easily dissolved; **~keit** f [46] dissolvability; *chm.* solubility.

los²-lösen (″…) *v/a.* [90]** (pleonastisch für: lösen) to loosen, to detach; (trennen) to sever; **sich** ≈ *v/refl.* to come off, (sich abschälen) to peel off; *fig.* to sever (or free) o.s. from; **≗machen** *v/a.* [89]** und **sich** ≈ *v/refl.*: a) to undo, unfasten, untie, detach; Hindernisse wegräumend: sich ≈ to disengage (o.s.) (von et., e-m from a th., a p.); b) (freimachen) (sich) ≈ to make (o.s) free, v. vormundschaftlicher &c. Gewalt: to emancipate (o.s.), von lästigen Dingen: to extricate (o.s.), to disentangle (o.s.); ~ n u. **-machung** f undoing, &c.; emancipation; extrication, disentanglement; **≗marschieren** *v/n.* (sn) [93]*/* s. los² 7; **≗platzen** *v/n.* (sn) [90]** to burst off or asunder, *fig.* to blurt out (with) a th.; **≗reden** *v/n.* (h.) [89]**: d(a)rauf-≈ to talk on and on or at random; **≗reißen** [80]a** *v/a.* u. **sich** ≈ *v/refl.*: (sich) ≈ to tear (o.s.) away, et. Geklebtes, Genähtes: to tear off, to pull off; ⚓ sich ≈ to break adrift, vom Anker: to part anchor; *v/n.* (h.) to break off; **≗rennen** *v/n.* (sn) [96]b** s. los² 7.

Löß (`) m [8]a. *geol.* ⊤ loess.

los²-sagen (″…) *v/n.* (sn) [96]b** u. **sich** ≈ *v/refl.* to renounce a th.; sich von e-m ≈ to sever o.s. from a p.'s cause, to break with a p.; ~ n u. **-sagung** f renunciation; **-scheibe** ⚙ f loose pulley; **≗schießen** [75]c(e)st** *v/a.* u. *v/n.* (h.): a) to fire (or discharge) a gun, &c., to fire away, to let fly; *fig. abs.* (bisw. auch **sich** ≈ *v/refl.*) (sich aussprechen) to give one's opinion; b) et. ≈ to shoot a th. off; *v/n.* (sn): auf e-n ≈ (stürzen) to (make a) rush at a p.; ~ n discharge of a gun; **≗schlagen** [85]b** *v/a.*: a) to knock off with a hammer, &c.; b) ❀ Waren: to sell (or clear) off, spottbillig: to sell off cheaply or at a sacrifice or for a mere song; *v/n.* (h.): a) auf e-n ≈ to give a p. a (sound) thrashing; s. auch los² 7; b) to strike the first blow, to open the attack; **≗schnallen** *v/a.* [88]** to unbuckle; **≗schneiden** *v/a.* [80]c** to cut off or away; **≗schnüren** *v/a.* [88]** to unlace, to untie; **≗schrauben** ⚙ *v/a.* [88][77]c** to unscrew, to screw off; **≗sein** [70]a** s. los² 1, 2 und 3; **≗spannen** *v/a.* [88]** e-n Bogen &c.: to unbend; ein Pferd: to unyoke; **≗sprechen** *v/a.* [73]a**: a) to absolve (a. *rel.*); jur. to acquit, to discharge, von einer Verbindlichkeit: to release; b) (freimachen) to (set) free, to liberate, v. väterlicher &c. Gewalt: to emancipate, e-n Lehrling: to declare free; **-sprechung** f absolution; acquittal, discharge, release; **≗sprengen** [88]** *v/a.* to burst off, to loosen by blasting; *v/n.* (sn): auf e-n ≈ to gallop towards a p.; **≗springen** *v/n.* (sn) [71]st**: a) to jump off; v. Dingen: to snap (or burst) off; b) auf e-n ≈ to spring upon a p.; **≗spülen** *v/a.* [88]** to wash away a riverbank, &c.; **≗steuern** *v/n.* (sn) [92]a**: auf et. ≈ to make (straight) for a th.; ⚓ auf das Land ≈ to make for land, to stand in or inshore; **≗stürmen** *v/n.* (sn) [88]**: auf et. ≈ to (take by) storm; auf seine Gesundheit ≈ to ruin one's health with reckless living; **≗stürzen** *v/n.* (sn) [90]** s. los² 6.

Los¹-topf (″-`) m [62] etwa: lottery-urn.

los²-trennen (″-`⏑) [88]** *v/a.* und **sich** ≈ *v/refl.*: (sich) ≈ to sever (o.s.), to separate (o.s.); Genähtes: to unstitch, to unsew; ~ n, **-trennung** f separation.

Losung¹ (´⏑) [ahd.; *losen¹] f [46] (Werfen des Loses) casting lots.

Losung² ❀ (´⏑) [Lösung] f [46] (Tageseinnahme, Erlös) takings, receipts *pl.*

Losung³ (´⏑) [mhd.] ⚔ (Parole) f [46] watch- (or pass-)word, battle-cry (a. *fig.*); Sprichw. Geld ist die ~ money is the thing (nowadays).

Losung⁴ (´⏑) [los²] f [46] *hunt.* (Kot des Wildes) droppings, fumets *pl.*; dung.

Lösung (´⏑) f [46] 1. loosing, &c. (s. lösen I); severance; solution (auch *chm.*, *math.*). — 2. *chm.* (Flüssigkeit, worin etwas aufgelöst ist) solution.

Losungs³-wort n watchword, rallying-cry.

Los-von-Rom-Bewegung (´-s⏑-″-⏑´⏑) f [62] in Österreich: secession from Rome or the Romish Church; s. los² 3.

los²-weichen (″…) [88]** *v/a.* to get off by soaking; *v/n.* (sn) to come off after (or through) soaking; **≗werden** *v/n.* (sn) [70]c** s. los² 3 gegen Schluß; **≗wickeln** [92]a** *v/a.* und **sich** ≈ *v/refl.* to unwind, to unwrap; *fig.* sich ≈ to disentangle o.s.; **≗winden** *v/a.* [71]** to unwind, to untwist, *fig.* to extricate; **≗ziehen** [76]b** *v/a.* to pull (or wrench) off or away; *v/n.* (h.) auf (gegen, über) e-n, et. ≈ to inveigh against a p., to gird at a p., F to run a p. down; *v/n.* (sn): auf et. ≈ to march towards a th.; ~ n [23] invective, abuse.

Lot (´) [mhd.: lead Blei] n [11]c,6. 1. a) (ehm. Gewicht von 1/32 oder 1/30 Pfund) half an ounce; b) jetzt: (Neu-)~ ten grammes. — 2. ⚙: a) (Bleigewicht an e-r Schnur, ⚓ Senkblei) plumb-line, plummet, lead; ⚓ das ~ besetzen to man the lead; das ~ werfen (loten) to take soundings; b) (Lötmetall) solder. — 3. *geom.* perpendicular (or vertical) line; ein

[Lotblei] — 669 — **[Luft]**

~ fällen to drop a perpendicular (line); vgl. errichten I; fig. zwischen ihnen ist nicht alles im ~e matters between them are not what they should be.
Lot=blei (ˊˉ) n ⊙ = Bleilot.
Löt=block ⊙ (ˊˉ...) m ⊙ soldering-block; =**brett** n s.-board.
Löte ⊙ (ˊˇ) f ⊙ solder, soldering.
Löt=eisen ⊙ (ˊˌˇ) n ⊙ soldering-iron or -tool or -hammer.
loten (ˊˇ) [Lot 2] v/n. (h.), v/a. ⊙ 1. ⊕ arch., &c. to plumb, to (set to the) plumb-line, to make perpendicular with the aid of the plummet. — 2. ⇩ (die Tiefe messen) to take soundings, to sound, to (heave the) lead; noch ⇩ können to be in soundings; nicht mehr ⇩ können to lose (or get out of, be out of) soundings; ⇩der Matrose leadsman.
löten ⊙ (ˊˇ) [mhd.; *Lot 2] I v/a. ⊙ to solder. — II ~ n ⊚ = Lötung.
Löter ⊙ (ˊˇ) m ⊙ solderer, tel. jointer.
Lot=gast ⇩ (ˊˌˇ) m ⊙ leadsman; =**gewicht** n half-ounce weight.
Löt=haken ⊙ (ˊˌˇ) m ⊙ joint-hook.
Lothar (ˊˊ) [ahd.] npr/m. ⊙⊙α. Lothario.
Lothringen ♀ (ˊˇ) [Lothar II., 855] npr/n. ⊙α. Lorraine, chm.: Lotharingia;
Lothringer (in f ⊕) m ⊙, **lothringisch** a. ⊙ Lotharingian, a. auch Lorrainese.
lötig [Lot] a. ⊙ 1. weighing half an ounce or ten grammes. — 2. (vollwichtig) ⇩es Silber pure (or fine) silver. — 3. in Zssgn mit vorangehender Zahl, z.B.: vierzehn=⇩es Silber (wovon die Mark [= 16 Lot] 14 Lot feines Silber enthält) silver 12 dwts. (= pennyweights) W. (= worse), alloy of fourteen parts of silver and two of copper.
Lötigkeit (ˊˇ) f ⊙ fineness of silver.
Löt=kolben ⊙ (ˊˉ) m ⊙ soldering-club, copper-bit; vgl. =eisen; =**lampe** f soldering-lamp.
Lot=leine ⇩ (ˊˌˇ) f ⊙ sounding- (or plumb-)line, plummet.
Lotophage(n pl.) ⚔ (ˉˊˇ) [grch., nach Homer: Lotosesser] m ⊕ lotus-eater, pl. auch: Lotophagi.
Lotos ♀ (ˊˉ) 2c. f. Lotus 2c.
Lot=perlen (ˊˉ...) f/pl. ⊙ (sehr kleine Perlen) ounce-pearls pl., ⇩**recht** a. ⊙ perpendicular, vertical, plumb (= senkrecht). [b) chm. blow-pipe.⟩
Löt=rohr (ˊˌˊ) n ⊙ : a) soldering-pipe;⟩
Lotse (ˊˇ) [ndd.; nbl.; *engl. lodesman Geleitsmann] m ⊕ 1. ⇩ pilot. — 2. ichth. = Lotsenfisch.
lotsen ⇩ (ˊˇ) v/a. ⊙ 1. to pilot a ship, to serve as pilot. — 2. F fig. (mit= schleppen) to pull (or drag) along.
Lotsen=boot ⇩ (ˊˇ...) n ⊙ pilot(ing)- boat; =**fisch** m, ichth. pilot-fish (Naucrates ductor); =**gebühr** f, =**geld** n pilot's fee or due or charge, pilotage.
Lottchen (ˊˇ) npr/n. ⊙α. (dim. von Lotte, Charlotte) Lottie, Lotty.
Lotte[1] (ˊˇ) npr/f. ⊙⊙β. Charlotte.
Lotte[2] ⚔ (ˊˇ) f ⊕ = Lutte.
Lotter=bett ⚔ (ˊˇ...) [lottern] n ⊙ (lazy) couch; =**bube** m young rascal or blackguard, idle vagabond.
Lotterei (ˊˇˇ) f ⊙ vagrant life; (Trägheit) laziness, idleness, (Liederlichkeit) dissipation, loose (or dissipated) life.

Lotterie (ˊˇˊ) [nhd.; fr.; *dtsch Los[1]] f ⊙ lottery; in die ~ setzen to put in(to) the lottery. to take a lottery-ticket.
Lotterie=anlehen ⊛ (ˊˇˇ...) f ⊙ lottery-loan, loan with periodical drawings; =**einnehmer** m = Kollekteu'r; =**gewinn** m prize in the lottery; =**kollekte** f l.-office; =**kollekteur** m p. who keeps a l.-office; =**los** n l.-ticket; =**plan** m scheme for a lottery; =**spiel** n (playing in the) lottery; =**spieler**(in f) m person who plays in the l.; =**zettel** m = =**los**.
lotterig (ˊˇˇ) a. ⊙ (schlotternd) tottering, shaky; (unordentlich) slovenly, disorderly, (liederlich) dissipated, rakish, debauched, loose, fast.
Lotter=leben (ˊˇˌˊˇ) n ⊙ loose (or idle, dissipated) life, life of dissipation.
lottern (ˊˇ) [ahd.: loiter] I v/n. (h.) ⊙a. (schlottern) to totter, (liederlich leben) to lead a dissipated (or fast) life, (sich müßig umhertreiben) to idle (or F lazy) about, to lead a loose (or vagrant) life. — II ~ n ⊙ dissipated (or fast, idle, lazy, vagrant) life.
Lotto (ˊˉ) [it.; *dtsch. Los] n ⊙, a. ~ **spiel** (ˊˉˌˊ) n ⊙ (Zahlenlotterie) (game of) lotto. [casting the lead.⟩
Lotung ⇩ (ˊˇ) f ⊙ plumbing, sounding,⟩
Lötung (ˊˇ) f ⊙ soldering; =**s=**... [= =**blume**.⟩
Lotus ♀ (ˊˉ) [lt., *grch.] m, inv.: ~ der Alten⟩
Lotus=baum ♀ (ˊˉ...) m ⊙ = Wegedorn; =**blume** f (Egyptian) lotus (Nymphae'a lotus); =**essend** a. ⊙ lotus-eating; =**esser** m = Lotopha'g(e); =**klee** ♀ m lotus, bird's-foot trefoil (Lotus). [plummet-)level.⟩
Lot=wage ⊙ (ˊˌˊ) f ⊙ plumb- (or⟩
Löt=wasser ⊙ (ˊˌˊˇ) n ⊙ chlorate of zinc.
lot=weise (ˊˌˊ) adv. by the half-ounce, by half-ounces.
Louis (lūˊˉi) [fr.] npr/m. ⊙γ. (Bn) Louis, Lewis; P (Zuhälter) bully.
Louisdor (lūˊˌˉbōˊr) [+fr. le louis)] m ⊙d(⊙)6. (fr. Goldmünze) louisd'or.
Löwe (ˊˇ) [ahd.; *lt. leō] m ⊕, **Löwin** f ⊙ zo. lion(ess f) (a. fig.), ast. Leo; junger ~ young lion, lion's cub or whelp, a. lionet, her. lion(c)el; fig. ⇵ der ~ des Tages the lion (or hero) of the day; wie wenn der ~ Blut geleckt hat like the lion (or tiger) when he has tasted blood; Gasthoftitel: im ~n at the Lion Hotel.
Löwen=äffchen (ˊˊ...) n ⊙ zo.: rotes ~ silky tamarin (Midas rosa'lia); =**anteil** m lion's share; ⇩**artig** a. ⊙ lion-like, ⚔ leonine; =**bändiger** m lion-tamer; =**garten** m lion-garden; =**grube** f lion's den.
Löwen=haut (ˊˊ...) f ⊙ lion's skin; =**herz** n lion's heart; Richard ~ Richard Lion-heart or the Lion-hearted or Cœur de Lion; ⇩**herzig** a. ⊙ (as) brave as a lion; =**jagd** f, =**jäger** m lion-hunting, -hunter; =**maul** n: a) lion's mouth or jaw; b) ♀ snapdragon (Antirrhi'num); großes ~ bucranion (A. majus); kleines ~ calf's-snout (A. Oro'ntium); =**mut** m lion's courage; ⇩**haben** to be as brave as a lion; ⇩**stark** a. (as) strong as a lion; =**tatze** f lion's paw; =**zahn** m: a) lion's tooth; b) ♀ (gemeiner) ~ dandelion (Leo'ntodon tara'zacum).

Löwin (ˊˇ) f ⊙ f. Löwe.
loyal (loāˊl) [fr.] a. ⊙ loyal.
Loyalität (loāˊl-ˇ) [fr.] f ⊙ (Biederkeit, Treue) loyalty, faithful attachment.
L. S. abbr. = loco sigilli [lt. an Stelle des Siegels] at the place of the seal.
lübisch (ˊˇ) [Lübeck ♀, Hansestadt] a. ⊙ of (or belonging to) Lübeck or Lubeck.
Luch (ˊch) f ⊙ (n⊙.) (Bruch) marsh, bog.
Luchs (ˊchs) [ahd.] m ⊙ zo. lynx/ ⊙a., **Luchsin** f ⊙ 1. zo. lynx (Felis lynx). — 2. fig. cunning (or artful) person.
luchs=artig (ˊchs...) a. ⊙ lynx-like, ⚔ lyncean; =**auge** n ⊙ lynx-eye; ⇩**äugig** a. lynx- (or keen-)eyed, ⚔ lyncean.
luchsen F (ˊchs) v/n. (h.) und v/a. ⊙ 1. to keep a sharp lookout; to be keen-eyed. — 2. fig. (stehlen) to pilfer.
Luci=e (ˊtsi(ˇ)ˉ) npr/f. ⊙⊙β. (Bn) Lucy, Luce; ~**n=holz** ♀, ⊙ n ⊙ wood of the mahaleb cherry-tree (Ce'rasus ma'haleb).
Lücke (ˊˇ) [ahd.; *Loch] f ⊙ : ~ in den Zähnen 2c., gap, ⚔ hiatus, (Riß, Bruch) breach, opening; (offene Stelle) void, blank; (Zwischenraum) interstice, interval, (Unterbrechung) break, (Auslassung) omission; im Texte e-s Autors: ⚔ lacuna; ⚜ eine ~ in die feindlichen Reihen reißen to open a breach (or make a gap) in the enemy's ranks; ~ in e-r Kasse: deficit, deficiency; eine ~ ausfüllen to fill up a gap, fig. eine empfindliche ~ ausfüllen to supply a long-felt want; eine ~ lassen to leave an open space or a blank.
Lücken=büßer (ˊˇˌˊˇ) m ⊙ stop-gap; (Füllwert) expletive, padding (auch literarisch); (Notbehelf) makeshift.
lückenhaft (ˊˇˇ) a. ⊙ with many gaps; (unvollständig) incomplete, defective, imperfect, v. Werken a. fragmentary; ~**igkeit** (ˊˇˇˇ) f ⊙ incompleteness, defectiveness, imperfection.
lücken=los (ˊˇˌˊ) a. ⊙ without a gap or a break, unbroken, uninterrupted.
lud (ˊ), **lüde** (ˊˇ) impf. ind., subj. v. laden.
Ludel ⚔ †, ⚔ (ˊˇ) [nbl. Röhrchen] f ⊙ (Zündpulver) priming-powder; ~=**faden** (ˊˇˌˊˇ) (Schnur) quick-match.
Luder (ˊˇ) [mhd.] n ⊙ 1. = Aas 1; hunt., &c. = Aas 2. — 2. fig. (et. Abscheu Erregendes) abomination; P unter allem ~ below criticism, unspeakably bad, ineffable, abominable, execrable. — 3. P Schimpfwort: verdammtes ~! horrid beast!, damned wretch!; von Frauen: (low) hussy!, good-for-nothing baggage!, accursed wench!; bisw. liebkosend, scherzend: das ~(chen n ⊙) the young rascal or Turk or monkey; das ~ von Uhr the beast of a watch.
Lüderjahn (ˊˇˇ), **lüderlich** (ˊˇˇ) f. Liederjahn, liederlich.
Luder=leben (ˊˇ...) n ⊙ dissolute (or disorderly, debauched, profligate) life; ⇩**mäßig** adv. wretchedly, F devilishly.
ludern (ˊˇ) v/a. ⊙a. hunt. to bait.
Ludwig (ˊˇ) [ahd. Ruhmkämpfer] npr/m. ⊙⊙α. (Bn) Lewis, Louis.
Luf (ˊ) [nbl.] 2c. f. Luv 2c.
Luffa (ˊˇ) [neu=lt.; ar. lūfa] f ⊙ (Schwammkürbis) luffa.
Luft (ˊ) [ahd.; loft, lift] f ⊙ 1. air; (luftförmige Substanz) gas; frische ~

♪ Musik; ⚔ Wissenschaft; ♀ Pflanze; ♁ Geographie; ⊙ Technik; ⚒ Bergbau; ⚔ Militär; ⇩ Marine; ⊛ Handel; ✉ Post; 🚂 Eisenbahn.

[Luftart] — 670 — [lügen]

schöpfen to breathe fresh air, to take the air; in freier ~ in the open air, outdoors; an die ~ bringen to air; F fig. e-n an die ~ setzen to turn a p. out; es liegt et. in der ~ there is s.th. in the air or on the cards. — 2. (leichter Wind, Luftzug) (gentle) breeze, draught (of air); es weht kein Lüftchen there is not a breath of air (stirring); die Zigarre hat gute ~ ... draws well. — 3. (Atem) wieder ~ bekommen to breathe again, a. to get one's second wind; keine ~ h. to be out of breath; wieder ~ schöpfen to breathe again, to recover one's breath, vgl. 1. — 4. Redensarten: in die ~ fliegen, sprengen to blow up, to be blown up; beides auch: to explode; das hängt (ob. schwebt) in der ~: a) it has no real foundation; b) (ist noch zu entscheiden) it is uncertain or undecided; ~ machen (erleichtern) to ease, relieve, unburden; f-n Gefühlen, f-m Herzen, sich ~ machen to give vent to one's feelings, to open one's heart, to unbosom o.s.; aus der ~ gegriffen: a) (haltlos) without any foundation, unfounded; b) (erfunden) invented, fictitious, fabricated; fig. die ~ ist rein (niemand da) the coast is clear.

Luft-art (ᵇ...) f ⓔ kind of air or gas; =artig a. ⓔ aeriform, gaseous; =bad n air-bath; =ballon m air-balloon; in einem ~ aufsteigen to go up (or ascend) in a balloon; =behälter m: a) orn. air-sac; b) ⓔ u. chm. air-vessel or -chest; vgl. =kammer; =bereitung f, chm. aerification; =beschaffenheit f condition of the air or atmosphere; =beschreibung f meteorology, ☞ aerography; =bett ⓔ n air-bed; =bild n phantom, vision; =bildung f: ☞ aerification; =blase f (air-)bubble; ⚕: ☞ vesicle; ichth. air-bladder; =bläschen n/pl. anat.: ☞ pulmonary vesicles pl.; =bremse ⓔ f atmospheric brake.

Lüftchen (⋃⋃) n ⓔ (dim. v. Luft) breath of air, gentle breeze; f. Luft 2.

luft-dicht (ᵇ...) a. ⓔ air-tight, impervious to air; ⓔ (adv.) verschlossen hermetically closed or sealed; =dichtheit f ⓔ air-tightness; =dichtigkeit f density of the air; =dichtigkeits-messer m, phys.: ☞ manometer; =druck m, phys.: ☞ atmospheric pressure; =druck-bremse ⓔ, ⚒ f atmospheric (railway-)brake; =druck-(eisen)bahn ⓔ f atmospheric railway; =druck-maschine f, =werk n ⓔ pneumatic engine; =druck-messer m, phys.: ☞ barometer; =eisenbahn ⓔ f aerial railway; =elektrizität f atmospheric electricity.

lüften (⋃⋃) [ahd.: lift] I v/a. u. sich ⓔ v/refl. ⓔ 1. = aus² I. — 2. durch Luftzutritt: to ventilate. — 3. sich ⓔ: a) körperlich: to go into (or to take) the air; b) geistig: to pour out one's heart, to unburden one's mind. — 4. et. Verdeckendes ⓔ (in die Höhe heben) to lift up, to raise; den Hut, die Mütze ⓔ to raise (or take off) one's hat, cap (to a p.); den Schleier eines Geheimnisses ⓔ to unveil (or reveal) a secret. — II ~ n ⓔ 5. airing; ventilation, vgl. Lüftung, Luftreinigung.

Luft-erscheinung (ᵇ...) f ⓔ aerial meteor, atmospheric phenomenon; =erscheinungs-lehre f, phys.: ☞ meteorology; =fahrer m aeronaut, balloonist; =fahrt f balloon-excursion or -ascent, aerial voyage; =fang ⓔ m ventilator; =förmig a. ⓔ aeriform, chm. gaseous; =gang m, ⚕ u. zo. aerial duct; =gebilde n: a) aerial form; b) = =bild; =gefäß n ⚕ u. zo. air-vessel or -sac or -vesicle; =geist m aerial spirit, sylph, Theosophie: astral spirit; =gestalt f aerial shape; phantom; =gleichgewichts-lehre f aerostatics; =gütemesser, =messung f, phys.: ☞ eudiometer, eudiometry; =hauch m breath of air; =heizung f heating with hot air; =heizungs-apparat ⓔ m hot-air stove or apparatus.

luftig (⋃⋃) a. ⓔ 1. (aus Luft bestehend, in der Luft schwebend) aerial, airy; (gasartig) gaseous; (nebelhaft) vaporous, hazy, nebulous; (der Luft ausgesetzt) exposed to the air, airy, von Orten auch: breezy; (viel Luft habend) well aired. — 2. (leicht) (as) light (as air), unsubstantial; (durchsichtig) transparent; Les Gewand light (or loose) garment. — 3. fig. (flatterhaft) (highty-)flighty, giddy; volatile, F gasy.

Luftikus (⋃⋃⋃) [dtsch.-lt.] m, inv. ob. ⓔ F co. (Windbeutel) windbag, gas-bag.

Luft-kammer ⓔ (ᵇ...) f ⓔ air-chamber; =kanal m air-passage; =kissen n air-cushion or -pillow; =klappe ⓔ f air-valve; ventilator; =körper m aerial body, Theosophie: astral body; =kraftmaschine ⓔ f hot-air engine or motor; =kreis m atmosphere; =kugel f globe filled with air, phys.: ☞ æolipile; =kunde f: ☞ aerology; =kur-ort m health-resort, in Indien ꝛc.: sanatorium; =leer a. ⓔ void of air; phys.: e-n Len Raum herstellen to produce a vacuum, to exhaust (or pump out) the air; im Len Raume: ⋃ in vacuo; =leere f vacuum; =lehre f: ☞ aerology; =leitung ⓔ f, tel. aerial connexion, overhead wire; =linie f aerial line; in der ~ (auf dem kürzesten Wege) in a bee-line, as the crow flies; =loch n air-hole, ⓔ arch., &c. a. vent-hole; (Zugloch) blow-hole, am Gebläseofen: air-drain, am Ofen: register, ent.: ☞ stigma, spiracle; vgl. =röhre c; =mantel ⓔ m air-casing; =maschine ⓔ f atmospheric engine or machine; =matratze f air-mattress or -cushion; =meer n aerial ocean, (vast) expanse of air; =messer m, phys.: ☞ aerometer; =meßkunst, =messung f aerometry; =perspektive f aerial perspective; =pflanze ⚕ f aerophyte; =pumpe f, phys. air-pump; =pumpen-glocke f receiver of an air-pump; =raum m space filled with air, aerial region, atmosphere, heaven(s pl.); =reich n kingdom of the air, aerial space; =reinigend a. purifying the air, disinfecting; =reiniger m disinfectant; =reinigung f purification of the air, disinfection; ⚒, ⚒, &c. ventilation; =reise f = =fahrt; =rohr ⓔ n Dampfmasch.: vacuum-pipe, zur Lüftung: air-tube, ventilator; =röhre f: a) zur Zimmerlüftung: ventilator; b) ⓔ air-tube

or -pipe; c) ⚕, zo. air-vessel, anat., zo.: ☞ trachea, bei Menschen a. windpipe; =röhren-äste m/pl. bronchial ways, ☞ bronchia pl.; =röhren-deckel m epiglottis; =röhren-katarrh m, path. bronchitis, bronchial catarrh; =röhren-schnitt m, surg.: ☞ tracheotomy, laryngotomy; =röhren-schwindsucht f, path.: ☞ bronchial consumption; =sack m =behälter; =salz n, chm. saline particles pl. (contained) in the air; =säule f, phys. column of air; =schacht ⚒ m air-shaft, ventilating-shaft; =scheu a. afraid of (fresh) air; =schicht f layer of air; =schiff n air-ship, balloon, ☞ aerostat(ic vessel); =schiffahrt f aerial navigation or voyage, ☞ aerostation; =schiff(fahrts)-kunde, -kunst f: ☞ aeronautics; =schiffer m aeronaut, balloonist; =schifferabteilung ⚔ f ballooning detachment, aeronautic section; =schloß n airy fabric; =schlösser bauen to build castles in the air; =spieg(e)lung f, phys. Fata Morgana, (fr.) mirage; =springer m caperer, tumbler, acrobat; =sprung m caper(ing), somersault; =sprünge m. to cut capers, to throw somersaults; =stein ⓔ m = =ziegel; =stoß m gust of air; =streich m stroke in the air; =strich m atmospheric region; =strom m, =strömung f, phys. current of air; =trocken ⓔ a. dried (or seasoned) in the air.

Lüftung (⋃⋃) f ⓔ = Aus², lüften II.

Lüftungs-apparat (⋃⋃⋃⋃⋃) m ⓔ ventilator; (Luftklappe) air-valve.

Luft-veränderung (ᵇ...) f ⓔ change of air; =verdichter ⓔ m der Dampfmaschine: air-condenser; =verdünnung f rarefaction of the air; =wage f, phys. air-poise; aerometer; =weg m: a) aerial course or path; b) ⓔ aerial duct or passage; =welle f, phys. air-wave; =widerstand m resistance of the air, atmospheric resistance; =wurzel ⚕ f aerial root; =zelle ⚕ u. zo. f air-cell; =ziegel ⓔ m air-dried brick; =zieher ⓔ m ventilator; =zug m draught, current of air; ventilation; ⚔ air-funnel, ⓔ im Herde: flue; =zutritt m access (or supply) of air.

Lug¹ (ᴸ) m ⓐc. (o. pl.) = Lüge; mit ~ und Trug lying and cheating.

Lug² (ᴸ) n ⓐc. (Öffnung) opening, aperture; (Gucloch) peep-hole, spy-hole.

Lug-aus (⋃ᴸ) m, inv. lookout, ⚓ watch.

Lüge (ᴸ⋃) [ahd.: lie] f ⓔ lie, falsehood, untruth, F cram(mer), story, (Erfindung) fable, fabrication; vgl. Flunkerei; grobe ~ gross falsehood, pure invention, F whacking (or thumping) lie; harmlose ~ white lie; es sind lauter ~n it's (nothing but) a pack of lies, it's all a lie; e-n einer ~ bezichtigen (zeihen) to accuse a p. of telling lies; e-n ~n strafen to give a p. the lie (ins Gesicht to his face); Sprichw. ~n haben kurze Beine lies have short wings.

lugen (⋃⋃) [ahd.: lo(ok)] v/n. (h.) ⓔ to look out, to spy about, peep, pry.

lügen (ᴸ⋃) [ahd.: lie] I v/n. (h.), v/a. u. v/refl. ⓔd. 1. to tell a) lie, to tell lies, to tell a falsehood, to speak (or

Signs (see page XVII): F familiar; P vulgar; F flash; ⋋ rare; † obsolete (died); * new word (born); ✝ incorrect; ♪ music;

[**Lügenfürst**] — 671 — [**Lurch**]

tell) an untruth; F to tell stories or crammers; (aufbinden, weismachen) to (tell a) fib; et. 2 (erdichten) to invent (or fabricate) a th. — 2. er lügt wie gedruckt he lies like truth; in seinen Hals hinein 2 to lie in one's throat; Sprichw. wer (gern) lügt, der stiehlt auch lying and thieving go together; f. einmal 1 am Schluß. — 3. (falsch vorgeben) to pretend, to sham. — 4. mit Angabe des Erfolges: F e-m die Ohren, F Jacke, Haut (P Hucke) voll 2 to cram a p. with lies; sich in j-s Vertrauen 2 to worm o.s. into a p.'s confidence by telling lies. — II ~ n ⑫ 5. lying, telling lies, F story-telling, fibbing, als Laster: mendacity.
Lügen-fürst (⁻ᵘ...) m ⑫ (Teufel) father of lies or mischief; =**geist** m bold (or consummate) liar; vgl. =fürst; =**gewebe** n tissue of lies or falsehoods.
lügenhaft, =ig (ᴸᵛᵛ) a. ⑯ v. Personen: lying, mendacious, (betrüglich) deceitful; v. Sachen: untruthful, (erdichtet) invented, fictitious, fabricated.
Lügenhaftigkeit (ᴸᵛᵛᵛ) f⑯ lying spirit, mendacity, deceitfulness; untruthfulness, fictitiousness.
Lügen-maul P (ᴸᵛ...) n ⑫ = Lügner(in); =**netz** n tissue of lies; =**prophet** m false (or lying) prophet; =**schmied** m forger (or fabricator) of lies.
Lug-ins-land (ᴸ,ᵛ,ᵛ) m, inv. (Wartturm) watch-tower.
Lügner (ᴸᵛ) [ahd.] m ⑫, ~**in** f ⑯ liar, F story-teller; (Betrüger) impostor; zum ~ an e-m w. to deceive (or beguile) a p. by one's lies; e-n zum ~ m. to prove a p. (to be) a liar, to expose a p.'s lies or falsehoods.
lügnerisch (ᴸᵛᵛ) a. ⑯ mendacious, lying, milder: untruthful. [Louise.}
Luise (⁻ᴸᵛ)[fr.;*btschLudwig]npr/f.⑰⑭β.)
Luk ↓ (ᴸ) n ⓑc. (Luke) hatchway; die ~e verschließen to close down the hatches.
Lukas (ᴸᵛ) npr/m.⑲γ. (a.Bn.) Lucas; der Evangelist ~, Sankt = St. Luke; Evangelium Lucä Gospel according to St. Luke.
Luke (ᴸᵛ) [nbd.: Lücke, Loch] f⑯ 1. dormer- (or garret-)window. — 2. ↓ = Luk.
Luken-deckel (ᴸᵛ...) m ⑫ lid (or cover) of the hatchway; =**kappe** f companion.
lukrativ (-ᵛᴸf) [lt.] a. ⑯ (einträglich) lucrative. [to (make a) profit.}
lukrieren (-ᴸᵛ) [lt.] v/n. (h.) und v/a. ⑬)
lukullisch (-ᵛᴸ) a. ⑯ like (or of) Lucullus; fig. sumptuous, luxurious.
lullen (ᴸᵛᵛ) [nbd.: lull, lautm.] v/a. u. v/n. (h.) ⑱ to lull to sleep; **Lull-gesang** (ᴸᵛ-ᵛ) m ⑫ für Wiegenlieder: lullaby.
Lumen F (ᴸᵛ) [lt. Licht] n ⑭⑩ fig. (a. iro.) e. großes ~ a shining light. [mot (U'ria).}
Lumme¹ (ᴸᵛ) f⑯ orn.(Tauchervogel)guille-)
Lumme² ⊙ (ᴸᵛ) f ⑯ (Riegel) bolt.
Lümmel (ᴸᵛ) [ahd.] m ⑫ lout, uncouth (or saucy) fellow, boor, F booby.
Lümmelei (ᴸᵛᴸ) f ⑯ 2c. f. Flegelei 2c.
lümmelhaft (ᴸᵛᵛ) a. ⑯ loutish, lubberly, uncouth, boorish, saucy.
lümmeln (ᴸᵛᵛ) v/n. u. v/refl. ⑫a. sich 2 to slouch, to have a slouching gait.
Lump (ᴸ)[nbd.; *Lumpen] m⑫.⑫ 1. (zerlumpter Mensch) ragamuffin, tatterdemalion, ragged (or beggarly) fellow,

person of beggarly appearance; (jämmerlicher Kerl) wretch(ed fellow), (miserable) scamp, (gemeiner Mensch) low (or common) fellow, (Schurke) knave, rascal, blackguard; F dieser ~ von Kerl that scamp of a fellow, this rascally fellow. — 2. = Lumpfisch.
Lumpen¹ (ᴸᵛ) [(nhd.) nbd.] m⑫1.(Lappen) rag, bsd. ehm.: clout; pl. oft: rags and tatters. — 2. fig. (Wertloses, Verächtliches) lumber, rubbish(y stuff), trumpery thing, trash.
lumpen² (ᴸᵛ) v/refl. ⑱: sich nicht 2 lassen to act (F to come down) handsomely; er will sich nicht 2 lassen he won't be (called) shabby, he means to do the proper thing.
Lumpen-brei ⊙ (ᴸᵛᵛ...) m ⑫ Papierfabr.: pulp, first stuff; =**ding** n trumpery (or paltry) thing or concern; F von Kindern x.: (little) scrub; =**frau** f = =**sammlerin**; =**geld** n trumpery sum (of money); für ein ~ kaufen to buy dirt-cheap or for a mere song; =**gesindel** n rabble, riffraff, dregs pl. of the population; vgl. =**pack**; =**handel** ⑬ m: a) rag-trade; b) miserable dealing or business; =**händler(in** f) m dealer in rags, rag-and-bone (wo)man; =**hund**, =**kerl** m = Lump¹; =**kram** m: a) rag-and-bone shop; b) trumpery (or wretched) stuff; vgl. Lumpen 2; =**mann** m: =sammler; =**mäßig** a. ⑯ miserable, wretched; =**nest** n wretched place, F (dirty) hole; =**pack** n F tag-rag and bobtail; =**papier** ⊙ n paper made of (linen) rags; =**sack** m rag-and-bone man's sack or bay; =**sammler(in** f) m rag-picker; =**volk** n = =gesindel; =**wolle** ⑬ f shoddy; =**zeug** n flimsy material, inferior stuff; a. = =wolle; =**zucker** † m lump-sugar.
Lumperei (ᴸᵛᴸf) f ⑯ trumpery (or paltry) concern or affair, trash, rubbish, (Kleinigkeit) trifle, F (mere) flea-bite.
Lump-fisch (ᴸ,ᵛ) m ⑫a. ichth. lump-fish or -sucker (Cyclo'pterus lumpus).
lumpicht, mst **lumpig** (ᴸᵛ) a. ⑯ ragged, tattered, in rags (and tatters); (ärmlich) shabby, scurvy, (erbärmlich) paltry, miserable; **Lumpigkeit** (ᴸᵛ) f⑯ ragged (or tattered) state, raggedness, shabbiness, paltriness.
Luna (ᴸᵛ) [lt.] npr/f.⑭β.⑯⑯α. myth. (Mondgöttin) Luna; ₂**tisch** (ᴸᵛ) a. ⑯ lunar; ₂**tisch** a. ⑯ (mondsüchtig) lunatic.
Lund (ᴸ) m ⑫b. orn. puffin (Mormon a'rctica). [lunette, demi-lune.}
Lünette ⫻ (-ᴸᵛ) [fr. fl. Mond] f ⑯ frt.)
Lunge (ᴸᵛ) [ahd.: lung] f ⑯ 1. anat. die ~(n pl.) the lungs pl.; seine rechte ~ ist angegriffen his right lung is affected; von Tieren auch: lights pl. — 2. fig. eine starke ~ haben to have good (F cast-iron) lungs; aus voller ~ schreien to shout at the top of one's voice or with all one's might; F sich die ~ aus dem Leibe (ob. wund) schreien to scream one's lungs out.
Lungen-abszeß (ᴸᵛᵛ...) m⑫ path. abscess in the lungs; =**ader** f pulmonary blood-vessel; =**blutung** f hæmorrhage of the lungs; =**drüse** f, anat.: =**bronchial gland**; =**entzündung** f, path.

inflammation of the lungs; =**enzian** ⚘ m lung-flower, marsh-gentian (Gentia'na Pneumona'nthe); =**fäule** f, vet. dry-rot; =**fieber** n, path. pulmonary fever; =**flechte** ⚘ f lungwort (Sticta pulmona'ria); =**flügel** m, anat. lobe of the lungs; =**geschwür** n ulcer (or abscess) in the lungs; =**hasche** n = =mus; =**hieb** m thrust into the lungs, fig. home-thrust; =**katarrh** m, path. catarrh in the lungs; ♀**krank** a. ⑯ suffering from the lungs, vet. lung-sick; =**kranke(r)** s.: ⫻ pulmonic (patient); =**krankheit** f pulmonary disease; =**kraut** ⚘ n lungwort, pulmonary (Pulmona'ria); =**lappen** m = =flügel; =**leidend** a. suffering from the lungs; =**mittel** n, med.: ⫻ pulmonic; =**mus** n Kochkunst: hash made of calf's lights; =**muskel** m, anat. inspiratory muscle; =**ödem** n, path.: ⫻ œdema of the lungs; =**probe** f testing the lungs of an infant; =**schlag** m, path. apoplexy of the lungs; =**schnecke** f, zo.: ⫻ pulmonate; ~n pl.: ⫻ pulmonata pl.; =**schuß** ⚔ m lung-shot; =**schützer** m respirator; =**(schwind)sucht** f, path. pulmonary consumption; ♀**(schwind)süchtig** a. ⑯ suffering from pulmonary consumption, consumptive; =**tuberkulose** f, path.: ⫻ tuberculosis (of the lungs). [loafer.}
Lungerer (ᴸᵛᵛ) m ⑫ idler, lounger,}
Lunger-leben (ᴸᵛ,ᴸᵛ) n ⑫ lazy (or idle, roving, vagrant) life.
lungern (ᴸᵛᵛ) [nbd.: lounge, linger] v/n. ⑫a. 1. (h. u. fu) to loiter (or lounge, loll) about, to lead a vagabond life. — 2. (h.) nach et. 2 (verlangen) to long for a th., to covet a th.
Lünse ⊙ (ᴸᵛ) [nbd.: linch] f ⑯ Wagnerei: linch- (or axle-)pin.
Lunte (ᴸᵛ) [nbl.] f ⑯ 1. ⚔ artill. u. ⚒ bgb. ehm.: slow match; fig. ~ riechen (Gefahr wittern) to scent danger, mehr gebr.: to smell a rat. — 2. hunt. (Schweif des Fuchses u. Wolfes) brush, tail.
Lunten-gewehr ⚔ (ᴸᵛᵛ...) n ⑫ match-lock (gun); =**schloß** n match-lock; =**stock** m linstock, match-staff.
Lupe (ᴸᵛ) (fr. loupe) f ⑯ Optik: (Vergrößerungsglas) magnifying glass, pocket-lens; durch die ~ betrachten to examine under a magnifying glass, fig. to scrutinize (closely).
Luperkali-en (-ᵛᴸ(ᵛ)ᵛ)[lt.] pl.inv.röm.Alt.: (Fest des Lupe'rkus-Pan) Lupercalia pl.
lupfen, lüpfen (ᴸᵛ) [nhd.] v/a. ⑱ to lift gently, to raise slightly.
Lupine ⚘ (-ᴸᵛ) [lt. Wolfs(bohne)] f ⑯ lupine (Lupi'nus); ~**n-klee** (-ᴸᵛ,ᴸ) m ⑬ lupinaster (Trifo'lium Lupina'ster).
Luppe ⊙ (ᴸᵛ) (fr. loupe) f ⑯ metall. lump (or ball) of wrought iron, loop, bloom; ~**n-eisen** (ᴸᵛ,ᴸᵛ) n ⑫ malleable iron. [(Hopfenbitter) lupulin.}
Lupulin ⚘ (-ᵛᴸ) [neu-lt.] n ⑭d. chm.}
Lupus (ᴸᵛ) [lt. Wolf] I m, inv. ob. ⑯: a) path. (fressende, Perlsucht-flechte) lupus; b) ast. (südliches Sternbild) Lupus. — II Lupus in fa'bula, etwa: if you speak of the angels the angels appear.
Lurch (ᴸ) [: Lorf] m ⑬b. zo.: ⫻ batrachian; ~e pl. (frosch-artige Tiere): ⫻ batrachia pl.

⫻ scientific; ⚘ botanical; ⚥ geography; ⊙ machinery; ⚒ mining; ⚔ military; ↓ marine; ⬤ commercial; ⚫ postal; 🚃 railway.

[Lusitanien] — 672 — [L.Zug]

Lusitani-en (-ᴗ́-ᴗ) npr/n. ⓑ α. Alt.: (Portugal) Lusitania; **Lusitani-er**(in f ④) m ㉒, **lusitanisch** (-ᴗ́ᴗ) a. ⑯ Lusitanian.

Lust (⁵) [ahd.: lust] f ⑩ (pl. nur in 2) 1. (Verlangen) desire; (Neigung) disposition, inclination; wenn ihn die ~ anwandelt when(ever) he is in the mood or vein, F when the maggot bites him; s-e ~ an et. (vollauf) befriedigen, seine ~ (od. sein Lüstchen) büßen to satisfy one's desire (to the top of one's bent); ich bekomme ~ zu // I feel inclined to //; s. benehmen 1; ~ haben zu // to have a mind to //; haben Sie ~ auszugehen? do you care (or would you like) to go out?; ganz wie du ~ hast, nach deines Herzens ~ just as you like, do as you please; ich habe die ~ (dazu) verloren, mir ist alle ~ vergangen I have lost all liking for it, my fancy (for it) is gone; es stieg in ihm die ~ auf sich zu baden he was seized with a desire to take a bath, he felt in the humour (or mood) for a bath; mit ~ und Liebe with heart and soul, with a will; er betreibt es, die Arbeit mit ~ und Liebe he puts his whole heart into it or his work, his whole heart is in it; Sprichw. s. Liebe 2. — 2. mit pl. (sinnliche Begierde) lust (of the flesh), carnal desire or appetite, cupidity; rel. (fleischliche Lüste, a. concupiscence sg.; seinen Lüsten frönen to serve (or gratify) one's evil passions. — 3. (Wohlgefühl) pleasure, delight; (Genuß) enjoyment; (Fröhlichkeit) merriment, mirth, (Freude) joy, (Freudenbezeigung) rejoicing; seine ~ an et. haben (sehen, hören) to take a delight (or a pleasure) in (seeing, hearing) s.th.; er ist ihre ganze ~ he is her only joy or her all; es ist eine wahre ~, sie zu sehen it is quite delightful (or it does one's heart good) to see them; er arbeitet, daß es eine ~ ist it is a treat (or a pleasure) to see him work.

Lustbarkeit (ᴗ́-) f ⑯ diversion, merriment, F jollification, high jinks; (Fest) festivity, fête, revelry. F gala.

Lüstchen (ᴗ́) n ㉓ (dim. v. Lust, s. ds 1): ein ~ zu et. h. to feel inclined for a th.

Lust-birne (⁵...) f ⑫ prostitute, street-walker; **=empfindung** f pleasant (or pleasurable) sensation.

lüsten (ᴗ́) [ahd.: list] ⑱, a. **lüstern** ⑫a. v impers. u. v/n. (h.) = gelüsten.

Lüster (ᴗ́) [fr., it.] m ㉒: a) (Glanz, Zeug) lustre; b) (Kronleuchter) chandelier.

lüstern (ᴗ́) [Lust] a. ⑯ hankering (or eager) after, longing (or pining) for; fleischlich: lewd, lascivious, lustful, prurient; Le Erzählung slippery (or racy, spicy) tale; auf (od. nach) et. ~ sein to have a strong passion (or desire) for a th.; mit Len Augen ansehen to cast longing eyes at, to leer at; **~heit** (ᴗ́-) f ⑯ hankering; lewdness, lasciviousness, lustfulness, pruriency; raciness of a tale.

lust-erweckend (⁵...) a. ⑯ appetizing, savoury; **=fahrt** f ⑫ pleasure-trip, excursion; **=feuer(werk)** n fireworks pl.; **=gang** m: a) delightful walk; b) (Allee) avenue; **=garten** m pleasure-garden or -grounds pl.; **=gärtner** m ornamental gardener; florist; **=gas** n, chm. (Stickstoffoxydu'l) laughing-gas; vgl. Lachgas; **=hain** m = **=wäldchen**; **=haus, =häuschen** n summer-house, in Zeltform: pavilion; (Laube) arbour.

lustig (ᴗ́) [ahd.: lusty; *Lust] a. ⑯ 1. gay, joyous; (fröhlich) merry, mirthful, jolly, von Natur: jovial, cheerful; (belustigend) amusing, laughable, funny; (drollig) droll, comical; thea. Le Person comical character, die grobe Späße macht: low comedian; Ler Scherz fine fun, F (great) lark; Ler Streich bit of fun, merry trick, F jolly lark; sich (dat.) einen Len Tag machen to make a jolly day of it; s. leben² 2; L werden to cheer up, to grow merry; Bruder ~ vgl. Bruder 5. — 2. (lächerlich) ridiculous, ludicrous; sich über e-n L m. to make fun (or game) of a p.; alles macht sich über ihn L he is the laughing-stock of everybody. — 3. (hurtig, flink) nun L an die Arbeit! now then, to your work!, set to!, cheer up!, F wire in!, P buck up! — 4. ...L in Zssgn mit vorangehendem s. taking a pleasure in, z.B.: arbeits-L fond of work.

Lustigkeit (ᴗ́-) f ⑯ (s. lustig) gaiety; merriment, mirth, jollity, joviality, cheerfulness; fun; drollness, comicality.

Lustig-macher (ᴗ́-ᴗ-ᴗ) m ㉒ buffoon, jester, merry Andrew; (Spaßmacher) wag.

Lust-lager (⁵·ᴗ́) n ⑯ holiday-camp, e-s Fürsten: princely pleasure-camp.

Lüstling (ᴗ́) [Lust] m ⓓd. voluptuary, sensualist, debauchee, profligate (man or fellow), libertine.

lust-los (⁵...) a. ⑯ Börse: lifeless, inanimate, dejected; Lose Stimmung, Tendenz dull tone; **=losigkeit** f ⑯ dulness, flatness (of the market); **=mord** m ㉒ murder preceded by rape; **=ort** m place of amusement, recreation-grounds pl.; **=partie** f pleasure-party, outing. [lustring.)

Lüstrin (ᴗ́) [fr.] m ⓓd. (Glanzzeug)

Lust-ritt (⁵·⁵) m ㉒ excursion (or outing) on horseback.

Lustrum (ᴗ́) [lt. ᴸ·ᴸ] n ㉘ ㉚ Alt. u. poet. (Zeit von fünf Jahren) lustrum.

Lust-schiff ⅃ (⁵·ᴗ) n ㉒ pleasure-boat or -yacht; **=schloß** n country-seat; **=seuche** f. path. venereal (or syphilitic) disease, syphilis; **=spiel** n comedy; **=spiel-dichter** m comedy-writer; **=wäldchen** n shrubbery, park, grove; ᴸwandeln v/n. (h.) ㉒ a.*.* to take one's walks (abroad), to promenade, to stroll (or saunter) about; **=wandler**(in f) m p. enjoying a walk, stroller, saunterer.

Luteolin ⟨ᴗ (-ᴗᴗᴸ) [lt. (Rese'da) lute'ola ⟨ᴗ-) ⓓ. chm. gelber Farbstoff: luteol(e)ine ($C_{15}H_{10}O_6$).

Lutheraner (ᴗ́-ᴗ) (Martin Luther, dtsch. Reformator, 1483–1546) m ㉒, **~in** f ④ Lutheran; **lutherisch** (ᴗ́ᴗ, mst ᴗ-ᴗ) a. ⑯ of Luther, Lutheran; **Luthertum** (ᴗ́-) n ⓓ chm. Lutheranism. [to lute.)

lutieren ⟨ᴗ (ᴗ-ᴸ) [lt.] v/a. ⑱ chm. (titten)

Lutsch-beutel (⁵·ᴗ) m ㉒ für Säuglinge: sucking-bag, mit Zucker ec.: titty-bag.

lutschen (ᴗ́ᴗ, a ᴗ-) [lautnachahmend] v/a. u. v/n. ⑩ (saugen) to suck.

Lutte ✕ (ᴗ́) f ⑱ (Abzugsrinne) drain.

Lutter ⊙ (ᴗ́) [fr.] ⑱ [lauter] m ㉒ Branntweinbrennerei: (Vorlauf) singlings pl.

Lüttich ♀ (ᴗ́) npr/n. ⓑ α. (belgische Provinz und Stadt) Liége; **~er** a. inv. of L.

Luv ⅃ (⁵f) [ndl.] f ⑯ (windige Seite) luff, weather-side or -gauge; ~! keep your (or her) luff or weather-side!; **~baum** m ⑯ luff-timber; **Len** ⅃ (ᴸ·ᴗ) v/n. (h.) ⑱ = anluven; **=gierig** a. ⑯ weatherly; **~gierigkeit** f ⑯ weatherliness; **=seite** f = Luv; **~wall** m (windige Küste) weather-shore; **Lwärts** adv. to windward; am meisten L weathermost.

luxuriös (ᴗᴗ-(ᴗ)ᴸ) [fr.] a. ⑯ (D 10) (verschwenderisch) luxurious, sumptuous.

Luxus (ᴗ́ᴗ) [lt. lúxŭs] m, inv. (Aufwand) luxury, sumptuousness, extravagance.

Luxus-artikel ⚙ (⁵...) m ㉒ article of luxury, fancy-article; **=ausgabe** f e-s Buches costly (or richly got-up) edition, (fr.) édition de luxe; **=band** m rich (or luxurious) binding; **=gesetz** n sumptuary law; **=papier** n fancy-paper; **=steuer** f duty on luxuries; **=ware** ⚙ f fancy-goods pl. or -article; **=zug** ⟂ m luxuriously fitted-up train, (fr.) train de luxe.

Luzern ♀ (-ᴗ) [lt. Leuchtturm] npr/n. ⓑ α. (schwz. Stadt und Kanton) Lucerne.

Luzerne ♀ (-ᴗ́-) [fr.] f ⑱ agr. lucern(e), purple medic(k) (Medica'go [sati'va]).

Luzifer (ᴗ́-ᴗ) [lt.] npr/m. ⓑ α. Lucifer.

Lwbd. abbr. = Leinwandband.

Lyddit-granate ⟨ ✕ (ᴗᴸ·ᴸ·ᴗ) [Lyd St. in Kent] f ⑱ lyddite shell.

Lydia (ᴗ́-ᴗ) npr/f. ⓑ ⓑ α. Lydia.

Lydi-en ♀ (ᴗ́-(ᴗ)ᴗ) npr/n. ⓑ α. Alt.: (Landschaft in Klein-asien) Lydia; **Lyd(i-)er**(in f ④) m ㉒, **lydisch** a. ⑯ Lydian.

Lykurg ⟨ᴗ npr/m. ⓑ α. grch. Alt.: (Gesetzgeber v. Sparta, 884 v. Chr.) Lycurgus; Lisch a. ⑯ Lycurg(e)an, of Lycurgus.

lymphatisch ⟨ᴗ (-fᴸ-) [lt. lympha (Quellwasser)] a. ⑯ physiol. lymphatic.

Lymph-bereitung ⟨ᴗ (⁵f...) f physiol. lymphosis; **=drüse** f lymphatic gland or ganglion.

Lymphe (ᴗ́f-) [lt.] f ⑱ med. (helle Blutflüssigkeit) lymph; (Impfstoff) vaccine.

Lymph-gefäß (⁵...) n physiol., med. lymphatic vessel or duct, pl. a. lymphatics; **=gefäß-entzündung** f, path.: lymphangitis; **=herz** n bei niederen Wirbeltieren: lymph-heart; **=körperchen** n lymph-corpuscle.

Lynch ⟨ (lĭ'n(t)sch) f ⑯ (Volksjustiz) lynch.

lynchen (ᴗ́(t)sch-) v/a. ⑯ to lynch.

Lyncher (ᴗ́t)sch-) m ㉒ lyncher.

Lynch-gesetz (⁵...) n ㉒, **=justiz** f (Volksjustiz) lynch-law, mob-law.

Lyon ♀ (lĭ-a') npr/n. ⓑ α. (fr. Stadt) Lyons.

Lyra (ᴗ́) [grch. lýra] f ⑱ ⑯ 1. ♪ (Leier) lyre. — 2. ast. Lyra.

Lyrik (ᴗ́-) f ⑯ lyric(al) poetry or verse; **~er** m ㉒ lyric(al) poet, ᴸ lyric.

lyrisch (ᴗ́-) a. ⑯ lyric(al).

Lyze-um (ᴗ́-ᴗᴸ) [lt.; *grch. Lý'keion in Athen, wo Aristo'teles lehrte] n ㉘ (sg. auch inv.) lyceum; (Gelehrtenschule) college.

Lyzi-en ♀ (ᴗ́-(ᴗ)ᴗ) npr/n. ⓑ α. Alt.: (Landschaft in Klein-asien) Lycia; **Lyzi-er**(in f ④) m ㉒, **lyzisch** (ᴗ́-) a. ⑯ Lycian.

L-Zug abbr. = Luxuszug.

M

M, m (ö'm) *m, inv.* (Buchstabe) M, m.
M. *abbr.*: a) = Monat; b) ⊕ = Mittel=
M abbr. = Mark³. [ſorte.ſ
m. öſt. m *abbr.* = Meter; m², m³ öſt.
abbr. = Quadrat=, Kubik=meter.
m *abbr.* = Maſkulinum masculine.
μ *abbr.* = Mikron.
M.=A. *abbr.* = Miniatu′r=ausgabe.
M.A. *abbr.* = *Magi′ster a′rtium*)
mä (ˈ) *int.* = mäh. [ſ. Magi′ſter.ſ
Maal=brief ⚓ † (ˈ⸗ˈ) *m* ⊕ (Schiffsbau=
kontrakt) shipbuilding-contract.
Mäander (=˘˘) [grch.] *m* ⊕ **I** ♀ *npr.*
(Fluß in Kleinaſien) Mæander. — **II**
fig. meander(ing stream, road, &c.;
(Irrgang) maze; *arch.* Vitruvian scroll.
mäandrisch (=˘˘) [grch.] *a.* ⊕ meander-
ing, meandrian, serpentine, winding.
Maas ♀ (ˈ; *Hom.* Maß) *npr*/*f. inv.* die ~
(linker Nebenfluß des Rheins) the Meuse.
Maat (ˈ; *Hom.* Mahd) [ndd., ndl.] *m* ⊕c.
1. (Kamerad) mate, comrade. F pal. —
2. ⚓ (Marine=unteroffizier) (ship's) mate.
Maatjes=hering ⊕ (ˈ⸗ˈ˘) *m* ⊕d. (junger
Hering) white herring, matie, maty.
Maatſchaft ⚓ (ˈ˘) *f* ⊕: a) ship's crew
or company; b) mateship.
Mäcenas (=tsˈ⸗) *npr*/*m.* ⊕γ. (Freund des
Auguſtus, † 8 v. Chr.) Mæcenas.
Mache (˘˘) [machen] *f* ⊕ **1.** (Anfertigung)
manufacture, make; (Art, wie et. ge=
macht iſt) workmanship, make, style,
fashion; Ihr Rock iſt in der ~ ... is
being made or is in hand. — **2.** F *fig.*
e-n in der ~ haben to pull a p. about,
to maltreat a p.; et. in die ~ nehmen
to take a th. in hand; einen in die
~ nehmen: a) (verfeinern) to polish a p.,
F to lick a p. into shape; b) (bearbeiten)
to handle a p. roughly, to pitch
into a p.; c) (prügeln) to belabour
a p.; er verſteht ſich auf die ~ (die
Reklame, ſein Handwerk) he knows how
to puff his goods, he is up to the
tricks (or dodges) of the trade, F he
knows a thing or two; Sprichw.
wie die ~, ſo die Sache, etwa: as the
bake so the cake; like carpenter
like chips.
machen (˘˘) [ahd.: make] ⊕ **I** *v*/*a.* u.
ſich ~ *v*/*refl.* **1.** meiſt: to make; ſ. Bett 1;
~ Sie ein anſtändiges Gebot! make a
decent (or fair) offer!; 20 Schilling(e)
~ ein Pfund twenty shillings make
(or go to) a pound; ſich (*dat.*) ein Ver=
mögen ~ to make one's fortune; ſ.
laſſen; zu et. ~ to convert (or change)
into a th., (einen zu ſeinem Freunde ~
to make a friend of a p., to befriend
a p.; e-n zum General ~ (ernennen) to
m. (or appoint) a p. general; ſich (*dat.*)
et. zur Geſetze ~ to m. a strict rule of
a th.; ſich zum Herrn (ob. Meiſter) e-s
Landes ꝛc. ~ to make o.s. master (or
lord) of a country, &c.; ein Herzog=
tum zum Königreiche ~ to raise a
duchy into a kingdom; *arith.* die
Pfennige zu Mark ~ to reduce pfennigs

to marks. — **2.** a) mit *pron.* als
Objekt: **das** macht man ſo that's how
it's done; das mußt du anders ~ you
must manage that differently; es e-m
~ wie den andern to treat all alike;
was ~ Sie? what are you doing?,
geſundheitlich: how are you?, how do
you do?; was iſt zu ~? what is to be
done?; ich weiß nicht, was ich aus ihm,
der Sache ~ ſoll I don't know what
to make of him, of it; was (ob. wieviel)
macht die Rechnung? what does the
bill amount to?; wieviel macht alles
zuſammen? what does the sum total
amount (or come) to?; b) mit *a.* zur Be=
ſtimmung des Objekts: to make, mit beſchränk=
terer Verwendung, bſd. um e-n Wandel des Zu=
ſtandes anzudeuten: to render; arm ~
to m. a p. poor, to impoverish a p.;
ſ. fett 1, flüſſig 3; et. glaubwürdiger ~ to
render (or make) a th. more plausible;
das macht mich (ſie macht ihn) glücklich
it makes me (she makes him) happy;
einen jung ~ to m. a p. (feel) young
(again); ſich krank ~ (ſtellen) to pretend
to be ill, to sham illness; ſie ~ es
möglich (unmöglich) they render (or
make) it possible (impossible); einen
ſchlecht ~ (verdächtigen) to cast suspicions
on a p., F to run a p. down; c) mit
adv.: er macht's mal nicht anders
that's his way of doing things; ich
kann es nicht anders ~ I cannot do it
any other way; ſ. arg 5; geſund ~ to
restore to health, to cure; ſ. lang 7;
niemand kann es ihm recht ~ nobody
can satisfy him; wie haben Sie es ge=
macht? how did you do (or manage)
it? — **3.** a) mit *acc.* und *inf.*: er hat
die Kinder glauben ~ (oder gemacht) he
imposed on the (credulity of) children;
b) mit *part. pres.* ſtatt des *inf.*: e-m et.
einleuchtend ~ to m. a th. clear to a
p.; c) mit *p.p.* ſtatt des *inf.* im paſſiven
Sinne: ſich gefürchtet ~ to m. o.s. feared
or an object of fear; d) ~, daß et. zu=
ſtande kommt to make a th. come to
pass, to manage (or accomplish) a th.
— **4.** (ſchaffen) to create, (bilden) to
form; (fabrizieren) to manufacture; (er=
richten, aufbauen) to erect, to construct;
(verurſachen) to cause; *arith.* (zum Pro=
dukte haben) to make; viermal 5 macht
20 four times five is twenty; *thea.*
(ſpielen) to perform (or play) a part, to
represent a p.; Anſpruch auf et. ~ to
lay claim to a th.; einem Appetit ~ to
give a p. an appetite; ſie ~ gute Ar=
beit they do (or produce) good work;
Billard: e-n Ball ~ to make (or pocket,
score) a ball; ſ. Begriff 1; ſich (*dat.*)
viel Bewegung ~ to take a great deal
of exercise; F den Doktor ~ to
obtain a doctor's degree or diploma;
einem Durſt ~ to m. a p. thirsty; ſ.
Finger 2; e-m Freude ~ to give a p.
pleasure; das macht einem allerlei
Gedanken it makes one think all

sorts of things; ſ. Gelegenheit 1,
Geſchäft 1, Geſchrei 1, Geſicht 2 und 3;
einem (ſich) das Haar ~ to do a p.'s
(one's) hair; e-m graue Haare ~ to m.
a p.'s hair turn (white); ein Haus ~
to keep an open house, to live in
(great) style; Holz (klein) ~ to split
(or chop) wood; ein Komma ~ to put
a comma; Licht ~ to strike a light,
to light the candle, gas, &c.; ſ.
Männchen 4; e-m viel Mühe ~ to put a
p. to great trouble; es macht mir viel
Mühe zu gehen I find it a great trouble
to walk; e-m Mut ~ to instil courage
in a p., to encourage a p.; das macht
(ſchadet) nichts it's of no consequence;
da iſt nichts zu ~ nothing can be done,
it cannot be helped; einem viel Not
(oder viel zu ſchaffen) ~ to give a p. a
good deal of trouble or anxiety; eine
Rechnung ~ to make a calculation, F to
do a sum; Schulden ~ to m. (or contract) debts; ✕ Schwenkung ~ to wheel
round; e-m Verdruß ~ to cause annoyance (or vexation) to a p., to annoy
(or vex) a p.; e-m Vorwürfe ~ to reproach a p.; e-m et. zu tun ~ to give
a p. work to do. — **5.** mit *prp.*: einen
Pfropfen **auf** die Flaſche ~ (ſtecken) to
put a cork on the bottle; ſich **aus** e-r
Sache et. ~ to lay weight upon a th.; ich
mache mir nichts daraus (aus ihm) I do
not trouble about it (care about him);
vgl. 2a Mitte; Flecken aus der Wäſche
~ (wegbringen) to take (F get) stains
out of the linen; es iſt **bei** der Sache
(ob. dabei) nichts zu ~ there is nothing
to be gained by it; **mit** ihm (damit)
iſt nichts zu ~ with him (with it) we
can do nothing; ⊕ ſie ~ 10% mit
dem Gelde they make ten per cent. out
of it; einen **zum** Doktor ~ to confer a
doctor's hood (or degree) upon a p.;
vgl. 1. — **II** ſich ~ *v*/*refl.* **6.** von Sachen:
ſich ~ (geſchehen) to happen, to come
about; (fortſchreiten) to progress, advance, get on; wie geht's? — F es macht
ſich (ja)! how are you getting on?
— pretty well!, F pretty middling!;
es wird ſich ſchon alles ~ all will
come (or be) right (in the end); es
wird ſich alles von ſelbſt wieder ~ all
will come round again (in time); von
Kranken: ſich wieder ~ to be getting
better, to improve, to mend. — **7.** mit
prädikativer Beſtimmung: ſ. 1 am Schluß,
2 b am Schluß, 5 u. 6. — **8.** (erſcheinen)
to appear; der Kopfputz macht ſich (gut)
... does (or looks) well, ... is very
becoming; es macht ſich gut, wenn //
it sounds well if //. — **9.** mit *prp.*:
an e-n (heran)~ to get near (to) a p.,
to accost (F to tackle) a p.; ſich **auf**
den Weg, auf die Beine ~ to get on
one's way; ſich daran zu ſtudieren to
set about studying, to begin to study;
ſich über et., e-n her ~ to fall (or rush)
upon a p.; ſich **aus** dem Staube ~ to

♪ Muſik; ⚚ Wiſſenſchaft; ♀ Pflanze; ♀ Geographie; ⊙ Technik; ⚒ Bergbau; ✕ Militär; ⚓ Marine; ⊕ Handel; ✉ Poſt; 🚂 Eiſenbahn.

[Machenschaft] — 674 — [mag]

decamp, F to make off, to hook it; sich zum Herrn e-s Landes 2 to m. o.s. (the) master of a country, to conquer a country. — III v/n. (h.) 10. (tun) to do; wie macht der Hund? — wau-wau! what does the dog say? — bow-wow!; macht, daß ihr bald zurück seid! see that you are back soon!; sie 2 lange (bis sie kommen) they are a long time coming; mach', daß du ins Bett kommst! be off to bed at once!; mach flink, auch abs. mach'! (spute dich!) make haste!, look sharp! — 11. (örtlich verändern) linksum 2 to turn (or wheel) round to the left. — 12. ⊛ in einem Artikel ꝛc. 2 to deal in ...; in Kaffee wird wenig gemacht there is little dealing (or doing) in coffee; F co. in Patriotismus 2 to dabble in patriotism; sie 2 stark in Sozialismus they are working socialism for all it is worth. — 13. e-n 2 (gewähren) lassen to let a p. do as he pleases; laßt mich nur 2!, oft: I will see (or attend) to it! —14. f. 2 c u. 3 d.— IV ~ n ⊛ 15. making, &c. (f. I—III); make; f. Mache. — V ge-macht p.p. u. a. ⊛ 16. in den Bed. des inf. — 17. (unecht) artificial. — 18. (vollendet) accomplished, perfect(ed); ein 2er Mann a man whose fortune is made, F a made man. — 19. das ist wie für Sie 2 (geschaffen) it's as good as if it were (or F it's like) made for you, it fits you to a T.

Machenschaft (ˇˇˇˇ) f ⊛ (bsd. im pl. gbr.) machination, intrigue, manœuvre.

Macher (ˇˇ) m ⊛ 1. (Verfertiger) maker, producer. — 2. F (Hauptkerl) leader, F big pot; pol. (Leiter) wirepuller. — 3. in Bssgn m. vorangehendem s., z.B. Stuhl-2 maker (or manufacturer) of chairs.

Macherei (ˇˇ–́) f ⊛ making, (inferior) make; (Pfuscherei) amateurism, bungling, blundering; pol. wire-pulling.

Macher-lohn (ˇˇ-́) m (n) ⊛ cost of making a th.; manufacturing-price.

Machination (ˇˇ–tsjˇ-́) [lt.] f ⊛ (listiger Anschlag) machination, deep plot, manœuvre, intrigue.

Machsen (ˇˇ) [ar.] m ⊛ (Regierung des Sultans von Marokko) Maghzen.

Macht (ˇˇ) [ahd.: might] f ⊛ 1. power, might, geistige: ascendency, gesetzmäßige: authority; (Herrschaft) sway, empire; (Fähigkeit) faculty, (Kraft) force, (Stärke) strength; die himmlischen Mächte the heavenly powers pl. (f. a. himmlisch 1); f. kriegführend; Englands ist e-e bedeutende ~ ... is a great power; auf dem Gipfel der ~ steh(e)n to have reached the zenith (or meridian) of one's power; vgl. Gipfel; ~ über Leben und Tod power over life and death; ~ über e-n, et. haben to hold a p., a th. in one's power or hands; e-m ~ (und Gewalt) zu etwas geben to empower (or authorize) a p. to do a th.; zu etwas (Fug und) ~ haben to have full power (or authority) to do a th.; Sprichw. ~ geht vor Recht might before right. — 2. mit prp.: aus eigener ~ on one's own responsibility; das steht nicht in meiner ~ it is not (or it does not lie) in my power; sich in der ~ haben to keep o.s. (or one's passions) under control; mit aller ~ auf einen eindringen to attack (or press) a p. with all one's might; über ~ beyond one's strength. — 3. (Heer) military force(s pl.), troops pl.; bewaffnete ~ armed force. — 4. poet. (mächtiger Herr) König Rudolfs heilige ~ (SCH.) his sacred Majesty King Rudolph.

Macht-befugnis (ˇcht...) f ⊛ full power or authority, competency; =bereich m, n sphere of power or influence; =fülle f fulness (or plenitude) of power; =geber(in f) m person who gives authority; =gebot n authoritative (stärker: despotic) order; =haber m person in power; ruler, lord, paramount chief; f. a. Gewalthaber; ?ha-berisch a. ⊛ lordly; despotic, dictatorial; =handlung f despotic act.

mächtig (ˇˇ) [ahd.: mighty] I a. ⊛ 1. powerful, mighty, authoritative. — 2. (bedeutend) considerable, (sehr groß) very great, extensive, ✕ thick, rich; (gewaltig) immense, huge; (nachdrücklich) emphatic, intense; hoch und 2 high and mighty; als adv. (auch 2(ich) considerably, very (much); e-n 2 bedrängen to press a p. very hard. — 3. e-r Sache, Person 2 sein to be master (or lord) of (or over) a th., a p., to have authority (or mastery, sway) over a th., a p.; einer Sprache 2 sein to have full command over a language; nur eines Armes 2 sein (L.) to have the use of only one arm. — II ~e(r) s. ⊛ 4. powerful person, die ~en the powerful or mighty (ones) pl.

Mächtigkeit ✕ (ˇˇ–́) f ⊛ (f. mächtig 2) ~ e-s Ganges thickness (or richness, size, width) of a lode or vein.

mächtiglich (ˇˇˇ) adv. f. mächtig 2.

macht-los (ˇcht...) a. ⊛ powerless, impotent; (schwach) weak; =losigkeit f ⊛ powerlessness, impotence, weakness; =probe f ⊛ trial of strength; =spruch m authoritative decision or decree; einen ~ tun to give a peremptory order, to speak with the voice of authority; =stellung f eines Staates ꝛc. power(ful position), ascendency, predominance; =verhältnis n balance of power; =vollkommenheit f plenitude of power, absolute power; aus eigener ~ of one's own authority; vgl. =fülle; =wort n: a) = =spruch; b) (mächtig wirkendes Wort) powerful (or strong) utterance, words pl. of great force or effect, emphatic expression.

Mach-werk (ˇch-́) n ⊛c. s.th. (indifferently) made; armseliges ~ clumsy (or bungling, inferior) work, v. e-m Buch ꝛc.: poor piece of work.

Mack F (ˇ) n f. Hack.

Madagaskar ♀ (ˇˇˇˇ) [port.] npr/n. ⊛α. (südafr. Insel in fr. Besitz) Madagascar.

Madam (ˇˇ) [fr.] ⊛e/⊛, ~chen (ˇˇ) n ⊛ dim., etwa: (dear) madam, F ma'am.

Mädchen[1] (ˇ-́) [nhd.; *Maid, dim.] n ⊛ 1. (ant. Bube, Junge) girl, in geh. Spr.: maid, maiden; (Fräulein) miss, F co. (young) damsel; fast poet. (young) lass; f. ausgelassen 2 am Schluß; F co. altes ~ old maid; junges ~ young lady, amtlich: young woman, ⊛ auch: young person; süßes ~ sweet girl, F co. jam, tart. — 2. = Dienstmädchen; ~ für alles maid-of-all-work. — 3. das ~ aus der Fremde (SCH.) The Fair Stranger. — 4. = Geliebte. [maggot or mite.]

Mädchen[2] (ˇ-́) [Made, dim.] n ⊛ little]

Mädchen[1]-**anstalt** (ˇˇ...) f ⊛ = =schule; =erziehung f education of girls or young ladies; =gymnasium n college (or High School) for girls.

mädchenhaft (ˇˇˇ) a. ⊛ girlish, girl-like, maidenly; fig. (schüchtern) bashful, modest, coy; ~igkeit (ˇˇˇˇ–́) f ⊛ girlishness, girl-like (or maidenly) nature; bashfulness.

Mädchen[1]-**handel** (ˇˇ...) m ⊛ traffic in young girls, white slavery; =heim n, =hort m home for young girls; =jäger F m one who runs (or hunts) after girls; =kammer f servant's bedroom; =lehrer(in f) m teacher (nur f: governess) for girls; =name m girl's name, e-r Frau: maiden-name; =raub (=räuber m abduction (abductor) of young girls =schule f school for girls, young ladies' boarding-school; =stand m girlhood; =turnen n callisthenics; =volk n, co. girls, (young) maidens pl.

Made (ˇ-́) [ahd.] f ⊛ zo. im Käse ꝛc.: maggot, (cheese-)mite; (Larve) grub.

Madegasse (ˇˇˇˇ) [Madagaskar] m ⊛, **Madegassin** f ⊛, madegassisch a. ⊛ Madagascan, Malagasy. [young girl.]

Mädel F (ˇ-́) n ⊛ F (⊛) (dim. v. Mädchen)]

Maden-**fraß** (ˇˇ...) m ⊛ food for maggots or worms; =fresser m, orn. ani (Crotophaga ani); =hacker m, orn ox-bird, beef-eater (Buphaga); =sack m, contp. vom Menschenleibe: (miserable) carcass, bag of worms; =wurm m pin-worm (Oxyuris).

Madera (ˇˇ–́) [port.] I ♀ npr/n. ⊛α.: (Insel) ~ (island of) Madeira. — II m ⊛ (auch =wein m ⊛) Madeira (wine).

madig (ˇ-́) a. ⊛ 1. maggoty, full of maggots or mites, von Früchten: worm-eaten. — 2. F fig. e-n 2 machen (schelten) to scold a p., F to blow a p. up; ein 2er Kerl a paltry fellow, a cad.

Madjar (ˇ-́, bff. als ˇ–́) ⊛, a. ~e (ˇ-ˇ) ⊛ m, ~in (ˇˇ-́) f ⊛ u. Lisch (ˇ–́) a. ⊛ Ungarn: Magyar; Lisieren (ˇˇ–́ˇ) v/a. ⊛ to magyarize.

Madonna (ˇˇ–́) [it.] f ⊛⊛ 1. the Virgin (Mary), the Holy Virgin, the Madonna. — 2. = Madonnenbild.

Madonnen-**bild** (ˇˇˇ-́) n ⊛ (Marienbild) image of the Virgin (Mary). [like.]

madonnenhaft (ˇˇˇˇ) a. ⊛ Madonna-]

Madonnen-**kultus** (ˇˇˇ...) m ⊛, =verehrung f adoration (stärker: worship) of the Virgin (Mary). [koralle) madrepora.]

Madrepore ⚘ (ˇ–́ˇ-́) [it.] f ⊛ (Löcher-]

Madrid ♀ (ˇ-́) [it. Maioritum] npr/n. ⊛α. (span. Hauptstadt) Madrid; ~er(in f) m ⊛ inhabitant of Madrid, Madrilenian. [(bichtchen) madrigal.]

Madrigal (ˇˇ-́) [it.] n ⊛d. (zierliches Ge-]

Madura-**fuß** (ˇˇˇ-́ˇ) m ⊛ path. Ost-J.: fungus-foot, ⚘ mycetoma.

Mag. abbr. f. Magister. [mögen.]

mag (ˇ) 1. u. 3. Person sg. pres. ind. von]

Signs (see page XVII): F familiar; P vulgar; ⸢ flash; ⤡ rare; † obsolete (died), * new word (born); +† incorrect; ♪ music)

[Magazin]

Magazin (⏑–⏑´) [nhd. *ar.] n ⓓ. (Lager) warehouse, storehouse, repository, storage-room (s pl.); im ~ aufspeichern to warehouse, to store; schwimmendes ~ für Petroleum ꝛc. floating warehouse; ✉ (Laderaum des Postwagens) space for parcels; ⚔ Proviant, Pulver- ꝛc.: stores pl., depot, magazine; ⊕ ⚔ Gewehr-⸗ magazine; magnetisches ~ magnetic magazine or battery.

Magazin-gewehr ⚔ (⏑–⏑´...) n ⓑ magazine-rifle; **=verpflegung** ⚔ f provisioning troops from depots; **=verwalter** m warehouse-(or store-)keeper, 🚂 manager of the goods-department.

Magd (–´) [ahd.: maid(en)] f ⓰ (bienende Person) maid-servant, servant-girl, (female) servant, P slavey; (die) Hausfrau und (die) ~ mistress and maid; bibl. siehe, ich bin des Herrn ~ (Lukas 1, 38) behold the handmaid of the Lord; poet. die holde ~ the fair maiden.

Magdalena, ...ne (⏑⏑–⏑) [hebr.] **I.** npr f. 💮 a., 💮 f. (Mary) Magdalen, als Bn.: Magdalene, Maudlin. — **II. ...n**⸗ f ⓰ (Büßerin) penitent woman, sinner repenting her ways, magdalen.

Magdalenen-stift ⚲ (⏑⏑–⏑´,⸗) n ⓑ Magdalen asylum or home, magdalen.

mägdehaft (–⏑⏑) [Magd] a. ⓑ after the manner of a servant-girl, like a servant, servant-like.

Mägde-heim (–⏑...) n ⓑ, **=herberge** f home (or lodging-house, boarding-house) for servant-girls; **=stube** f servants' room.

Mägdlein (–⏑) [f. Mädchen¹] n ⓑ little girl or maiden, bsd. schott.: lassie.

Magen (–⏑) [ahd.: maw] m ⓑ (P oft ⓐ) stomach, von Tieren a. maw, orn., &c. gizzard; e-n guten ~ haben to have a good digestion, fig. to swallow insults easily; fig. et. im ~ haben to be sick (and tired) of a th.; F fig. den Kerl habe ich im ~ I cannot bear (the sight of) that fellow, he is my aversion; schwer (wie Blei) im ~ liegen to lie heavy (or like lead) on one's stomach; sich (dat.) den ~ überladen to overload one's stomach, to overeat (or gorge) o.s.; sich (dat.) den ~ verderben to upset one's stomach or digestive organs; er hat sich den ~ verdorben, auch: his stomach (or liver) is out of order.

Magen-beschwerde (–⏑...) f ⓑ indigestion, liver-complaint; **=bitter(er)** m bitter cordial (for the stomach); **=brennen** n heart-burn, ⚕ pyrosis; **=bruch** m, path. rupture of the stomach, ⚕ gastrocele; **=drücken** n pressure on the stomach; **=elixier** n: ⚕ stomachic (drops pl. or elixir); **=entzündung** f, path. inflammation of the stomach, ⚕ gastritis; **=fieber** n gastric fever; **=gegend** f epigastric region; **=geschwür** n, path. gastric ulcer; **=katarrh** m cold in the stomach, ⚕ gastric catarrh; **=knurren** n rumbling in the bowels, ⚕ borborygmus; **=krampf** m spasm in the stomach, ⚕ gastrodynia; **=krebs** m cancer in the st.; **=leiden** n gastric complaint or disease; **=mund** m (upper) orifice of the stomach, ⚕ cardia; **=pflaster** n: a) plaster for the st.; b) fig. substantial meal, large piece of bread and butter; **=pförtner** m lower orifice of the stomach, ⚕ pylorus; **=pumpe** f stomach-pump; **=saft** m gastric juice; **=säure** f acidity (on the stomach); **=schmerzen** m/pl. pains in the stomach, st.-ache; **=schnitt** m: ⚕ gastrotomy; **=schwäche** f: ⚕ dyspepsia; **=stärkend** a. ⓑ strengthening the digestion, ⚕ stomachic, tonic; **=stärkung** f, **=tropfen** m/pl. (bitter) cordial or drops pl.; **=weh** n = **=schmerzen**.

mager (–⏑) [ahd.: meagre: It. mácer] **I** a. ⓑ (D⑨) **1.** lean, thin, in geh. Spr.: attenuated (form); (schlant) slender, bisw. lank; (dürr) spare, fleshless, emaciated, ill-conditioned (vgl. hager); bsd. fig. meagre; ⚕e Kost frugal diet, slender fare; typ. ⚕e Schrift lean-faced type, lean-face; ⚕(er) werden to grow thin, to lose (in) flesh, bsd. vom Vieh: to fall away. — **2.** fig. (ärmlich) poor, v. Schriften a. prosy, dry, jejune; Sprichw. ein ⚕er Vergleich ist besser als ein fetter Prozeß a poor compromise is better than costly litigation. — **II** das **~e**, **~es** n ⓑ **3.** the lean (part) of the meat; das **~e** und das Fette the lean as well as the fat.

Magerkeit (–⏑–) f ⓰ (f. mager) leanness; slenderness; spareness; meagreness; fig. poorness, prosiness, dryness.

Mager-milch (–⏑,⸗) f ⓰ (ant. Vollmilch) skimmed milk.

magern (–⏑) v/n. (h. u. sn) ⓑ a. to grow lean or thin; to lose flesh.

Mager-werden (–⏑...) n ⓑ growing lean.

Magie (⏑–´) [lt., *perf.] f ⓑ (Zauberei) magic art, occult science.

Magi-er (–⏑⏑) m ⓑ **1.** Alt.: (persischer Priester) Magus; mehr gbr. als pl.: Magi. — **2.** (Zauberer) magician, wizard.

Magiker (–⏑⏑) m ⓑ magician.

magisch (–⏑) [lt.] a. ⓑ magic(al).

Magister (⏑–⏑) [lt.] m ⓑ (auch **~in** f ⓑ) (school)master; (atade´mische Würde) ~ der freien Künste, ehm. lt. magi´ster a´rtium, jetzt: Master of Arts (abbr. M. A. ob. A. M.); Frau **~(in)** nur: madam.

Magister-diplom (⏑–⏑...) n ⓑ diploma (or parchment) of a Master of Arts.

Magistrat (⏑⏑–´) [lt.] m ⓑ municipal (or town-)council or authorities pl., ~ engl. Städte auch: Corporation.

Magistrats-mitglied (⏑⏑–⏑...) n ⓑ, **=person** f town-councillor; **=sitzung** f meeting of the municipal council; **=würde** f town-councillorship.

Magistratur (⏑⏑–´) [lt.] f ⓑ municipal council; **~ =beamte(r)** (–´...) m ⓑ municipal officer; official appointed by the town-council or corporation.

Magnat (–´) [lt.] m ⓑ magnate, weltS. grandee; **~en-herrschaft** (⏑–⏑...) f ⓑ government by magnates; **~enschaft** (⏑–´) f ⓑ body of magnates; **~entafel** f ⓑ chamber of magnates.

Magnesia ⚕ (⏑–´(⏑)⏑) [grch. St. in Kleinasien] f ⓑ chm. (Magnesium-oxyd) magnesia (MgO); gebrannte ~ burnt magnesia; kohlensaure ~ carbonate of magnesia (MgCO₃); schwefelsaure ~ = Bittersalz.

Magnesit ⚕ (⏑–´) m ⓑc. min. (Talkspat) magnesite, rhomb-spar.

Magnesium ⚕ (⏑–´(⏑)⏑) n ⓑ chm. (Metall) ⊕ magnesium (Mg); vgl. Chlor⸗.

Magnesium-chlorid (–´...) n ⓑ = Chlormagnesium; **=draht** m magnesium-wire; **=licht** n magnesium-light; **=oxyd** n magnesium oxide, magnesia.

Magnet (⏑–´) [grch. St. Magne´sia] m ⓑc. (㊶) magnet (auch fig.), natürlicher lodestone; f. bestreichen 3, Armatur 2.

Magnet-berg (⏑–´...) m ⓑ magnetic mountain, in Fabeln a. lodestone-rock; **=eisen(erz)** n, **=(eisen)stein** m magnetic iron-ore or -stone, lodestone; **⸗elektrisch** a. ⓑ phys. magneto-electric; **=elektrizität** f, phys. magneto-electricity.

magnetisch (⏑–´⏑) a. ⓑ phys. magnetic; e-n Körper ⸗ m. to magnetize a body; ⸗e Kraft magnetic force, magnetism; ⸗er Schlaf magnetic (or mesmeric) trance; ⸗er Wind magnetic storm.

Magnetiseur (⏑–⏑–fö´r) [fr.] m ⓓ. magnetizer, mehr gbr.: mesmerizer.

magnetisierbar (⏑–⏑–´) a. ⓑ magnetizable; **~keit** f ⓑ magnetizability.

magnetisier/en (⏑–⏑–´⏑) **I** v/a. ⓑ Eisen ꝛc.: to magnetize; e-e Person: to mesmerize, to hypnotize. — **II** ⚕ **/te(r)** m f ⓑ mesmerized (or hypnotized) person. — **III** ~ n ⓑ u. ⚕/ung f ⓑ magnetization; mesmerization.

Magnetismus ⚕ (⏑–´⏑⏑) [grch.] m ⓑ phys. magnetism; zo. tierischer ~ animal m.; **~=messer** ⊕ m ⓑ = Magnetome´ter.

Magnet-kies (⏑–´...) m ⓑ min. magnetic pyrites; **=nadel** f magnetic (or compass-)needle; f. abweichen² 2.

magneto-elektrisch ⚕ (⏑–⏑–...) a. ⓑ magneto-electrical; ⸗e Maschine magneto(-machine); ⸗er Telegraph magneto-telegraph; **=elektrizität** f ⓑ magneto-electricity; **=induktion** f magnetic induction; **Magnetometer** ⚕ (⏑–⏑–´) n (m) ⓑ phys. (Messer der magnetischen Kraft) magnetometer.

Magnet-stab (⏑–´...) m ⓑ bar-magnet.

Magnifizenz (⏑⏑–´) [lt.] f ⓑ als Titel von Universitätsrektoren ꝛc., etwa: His, Your Magnificence.

Magnoli-e ⚘ (⏑–´(⏑)⏑) [Magnol, fr. Botaniker, † 1715] f ⓑ magnolia (Magno´lia).

magst (–´) 2. Person sg. pres. ind. v. mögen.

Magus (–⏑) [lt.] m ⓑ(⓰) = Ma´gier 1.

Magyar ꝛc. = Madjar ꝛc.

mäh (–´) int. (Geblöt der Schafe) ⸗! bah!

Mahagoni ⊙ (⏑⏑–⏑) [indian.] n ⓑ mahogany (wood); **~=baum** ⚘ (–´...) m ⓑ mahogany(-tree) (Swiete´nia mahago´ni); **=block** m block of mah.; **=furniere** ⊙ n/pl. mahogany veneer(ing); **=holz** n = Mahago´ni; **=möbel** n/pl. mahogany furniture; **=tisch** m mah. table.

Maharadscha ⚔ (⏑⏑–´) [fr. Großkönig] m ⓑ (ost-ind. eingeborener Fürst) Maharajah.

mähbar (–´⏑) a. ⓑ mowable, ready (or fit) for mowing.

Mahd (–´) [ahd.: (das Mähen) mowing; b) (Heuernte) haycrop, hay-harvest; c) (Schwaben) swath; d) day's work of a mower.

Mäh(d)er (–´⏑) m ⓑ agr. mower.

...mähdig (...–´⏑) [Mahd] a. ⓑ in Zssgn: ein⸗, zwei⸗ von Wiesen: that may be

[...mähdig]

⚕ scientific; ⚘ botanical; ⊙ geography; ⊕ machinery; ⚒ mining; ⚔ military; ⚓ marine; ⊛ commercial; ✉ postal; 🚂 railway.

[Mahdist] — 676 — [majorenn]

mown once, twice; giving (or yielding) one, two crops of hay.
Mahdist (ᵛᵈ⁻) [ar. Mahdi] m ⓶ Mahdist.
mähen¹ (ᴸᵛ) [ahd.: mow] v/a. u. v/n. (h.) ⑱ agr. to mow (auch fig.), to cut grass, corn. &c., to reap.
mähen² F (ᴸᵛ) [mäh] v/n. (h.) ⑱ von Schafen: to (cry) bah. to bleat.
Mäher (ᴸᵛ) m ㉒, **~in** f ㊼ mower, reaper, harvester; **~lohn** m ㉒ mower's (or harvester's) wages pl. or pay.
Mahl¹ (ᴸ; Hom. Ma(a)l) [mhd.: meal] n ⓰ u. ㉒c. (Gastˎ, ~zeit) meal, repast, F feed; festliches: feast, banquet.
Mahl²... (ᴸ...) [mahlen] f. Mahlfläche 2c.
mahlen (ᴸᵛ) [ahd.: mill] meist ⓰ I v/a., v/n. (h.) und v/impers. refl. (p.p. gemahlen) to grind, Korn 2c. auch: to mill; (zerquetschen) to crush, zu Pulver: to pulverize; gemahlener Kaffee ground coffee; Sprichw. f. kommen 1, mit zwei harten Steinen mahlt es sich schlecht it is difficult to grind with two hard stones, fig. two strong natures cannot agree. — II **~n** ㉓ grinding, &c. (f. I); pulverization.
Mahl-fläche (ᵈ...) f ㊽ eines Mühlsteins: rubbing-surface; **=gang** ⓰ m Müllerei: set of millstones; run; **=gast** m miller's customer; **=geld** n miller's fee; multure; **=gerinne** n, **=graben** m milltail or -trench; **=gut** n grist. [all.].
mählich † ᙭ (ᴸᵛ) [(ge)mächlich] adv. =
Mahl²-knecht (ᵈ...) m ㉒ miller's assistant or man; **=korn** n corn to be ground; **=lohn** m (n), **=metze** f = **=geld**; **=mühle** f flour-mill, a. grinding- (Am. grist-)mill; **=recht** n right to (use a) mill; **=¹schatz** m dowry; **=statt** [ahd.], **=stätte** f meeting-place; **=²stein** m millstone; **=steuer** f duty paid on each sack of corn ground into flour; **=strom** ⓺ ↯ m maelstrom, whirlpool; **=¹zeit** f meal, repast; (ich wünsche Ihnen eine) gesegnete ~! (als Wunsch in England nicht üblich), etwa: I trust you have made a good dinner; F iro. ja, pros(i)t ~! don't you wish you may get it!; da haben wir die (Proste)~! here we are (in a fine pickle)!, F we're in a nice mess!; seine vier ordentlichen **~en** halten to take (or have) four square meals (a day).
Mäh-maschine ⓞ (ᵈ..ᵛᴸ) f ㉒ agr. mowing- (or reaping-)machine.
mahnbar (ᴸ-) a. ⓺ Schuld: demandable.
Mahn-brief (ᵈ...) m ㉒ a) letter of exhortation, eccl. monitory epistle; b) (Aufforderung zum Zahlen) request of payment, a. dunning letter.
Mähne (ᴸᵛ) [ahd.: mane] f ㊽ e-s Löwen, Pferdes: mane, zo.: ⚮ juba; co. v. Menschen: (good) head of hair, F mob, umbrella.
mahnen (ᴸᵛ) [ahd.: moan] I v/a. u. v/n. (h.) ⑱ 1. e-n an et. 2 to remind a p. of a th., to (re)call a th. to a p.'s mind, to put a p. in mind of a th.; 2ᵈ monitorial, monitory. — 2. e-n zu et. 2, an et., daß er et. tue to exhort (or urge) a p. to do a th. — 3. e-n um (ob. wegen) et. 2 (um es zurückzuerhalten) to ask a th. back of a p.; e-n wegen e-r Schuld 2 to press a p. for payment, to dun a p. — II **~n** ㉓ 4. = Mahnung.

Mähnen-robbe (ᵈ~...) f ㉒ maned seal (Ota'ria iuba'ta); **=schaf** n maned sheep. aoudad (Ovis trage'laphus).
Mahner (ᴸᵛ) m ㉒, **~in** f ㊼ one who reminds (or exhorts) a person, monitor, admonisher; lästiger ~ (Gläubiger) importunate creditor, dun(ner).
Mahn-glocke (ᵈ...) ⓶ f ㉒ warning bell; **=ruf** m cry of warning.
Mahnung (ᴸᵛ) f ㊽ (f. mahnen I) reminder, exhortation, ⚮ monition; demand of payment, &c., lästige: dunning.
Mahn-wort (ᵈ...) n ㉒ word of exhortation; **=zettel** m reminder.
Mahomed (ᴸᵛᵛ) npr/m. = Mohammed.
Mahr (ahd.: (night)mare] m ⓶c. (Alp[drücken]) nightmare.
Mähre¹ (ᴸᵛ) [Hom. Märe] [ahd.: mare] f ㊽: a) contp. (Pferd) jade, F old crock; b) (Stute) mare.
Mähre² (ᴸᵛ) [March, Fl.] m ㊵, **Mährin** f ㊼ Moravian, **Mähren** ♀ npr. n. ㉓ a. Österreich: Moravia.
mährisch (ᴸᵛ) a. ⓺ Moravian; eccl. ~e Brüder m/pl. Moravian Brethren pl.; vgl. a. Böhmische Brüder u. Herrnhuter; ♀ f. Gesenke.
Mäh-zeit (ᵈ..ᴸ) f ㉒ mowing- (or harvest-)time, harvesting(time).
Mai (ᴸ) [ahd.: May; *It. Māius] m ㉓ ⓰ b. (obb. ㊷) (month of) May; fig. (Frühlingszeit) spring-(tide); (Blüte) flowering-season; des Lebens ~ blüht einmal und nicht wieder (SCH.) life's vernal season is but one short spell; Sprichw. ~ kühl und naß füllt dem Bauer Scheuer und Faß a cold and showery May makes farm and vineyard pay.
Mai-baum (ᵈ...) m ㉒ = Maienbaum; **=blume** ♀ f: a) große ~ common Solomon's seal (Polygona'tum multiflo'rum); b) = **=glöckchen**; **=bowle** f = **=trank**; **=butter** f butter made in May, spring-butter.
Maid (ᴸ) [: Magd] f ㊽ (ohne pl.) poet. für Mädchen: maid(en).
Mai-e (ᴸᵛ) [Mai] f ㊽ (m ㊽) 1. = Mai. — 2. for. (jährlicher Safttrieb) yearly shoot. — 3. grüne Zweige als Festschmuck) green boughs pl. as decoration (auf dem Tanzplatze aufgerichteter Baum) May-pole.
Mai-en-baum (ᵈ...) m ㉒ (Stange, Birke, um die am Maifeste getanzt wird) May-pole, vgl. Maie 3; **=licht** n: im holden ~ (U., Des Sängers Fluch) in the golden light of May; **=zeit** f May-time.
Mai-fest (ᴸ..) n ㉒ May-day; **=fisch** m ichth. = Alse; **=frost** m frost in May; **=glöckchen** n lily-of-the-valley (Convalla'ria maia'lis); **=grün**: a) Farbe: a. u. n celadon; b) Laub: first foliage or verdure; **=käfer** m, ent. cockchafer (Melolo'ntha vulga'ris); **=kätzchen** ♀ n catkin of birches, &c.; **=königin** f May-(-)queen.
Mailand ♀ (ᴸᵛ) [(P) lt. Mediola'num] npr/n. ㉓ α. (it. Provinz u. Stadt) Mila'n.
Mailänder (ᴸᵛᵛ) I m ㉒, **~in** f ㊼ Milanese. — II a. inv., a. **mailändisch** (ᴸᵛᵛ) a. ⓺ of Milan, Milanese.
Mai-lüftchen (ᵈ...) n ㉒, F **=lüfterl** n soft (or vernal) breeze; **=monat**, **=mond** m month of May.
Main ♀ (ᴸ) npr/m. ⓰ α.: der ~ (Nebenfluß des Rheins) the Main; f. Frankfurt; **~gau** (ᵈ...) m ㉒ valley of the Main;

~linie f, etwa: Main (boundary-)line, between North and South Germany.
Mainz ♀ (ᴸ) [lt. Mogunti'acum] npr n. inv. (St. in Hessen u. deutsche Reichsfestung am Rhein) Mayence, Mainz.
Mainzer (ᴸᵛ) I m ㉒, **~in** f ㊼ inhabitant (or native) of Mayence. — II a. inv. of Mayence.
Mairan ♀ (ᴸ-) = Meiran, f. Majoran.
Mais (ᴸ) [mhd.: *haitisch] m ⓵ a. (a. inv.) ♀ und agr. maize, Am. Indian corn. Südafr. 2c.: mealies pl. (Zea Mais); **~brei** m, Am. hominy; **~brot** n bread made of maize, Am. pone.
Maisch-behälter (ᵈ...) m ㉒ ⓞ Brauerei: mash-charger; **=bottich** m mash(ing)tub or -tun or -vat.
Maische ⓞ (ᴸᵛ) [mhd.: mash; *mischen] f ㊽ Brauerei: mash, Destillation: wash.
maischen (ᴸᵛ) v/a. ⑨ to mash.
Maisch-holz (ᵈ...) n ㉒ mash-staff or -stick; **=kühler** m mash-cooler; **=maschine** f mash-machine or -pulper; **=würze** f mash-wort.
Mais-dieb (ᵈ...) m ㉒ orn. maize-bird (Qui'squalus versi'color); **=feld** n maize-field, Süd-afr. mealie-field; **=hülse** f, Am. corn-husk; **=kleber** m, chm.: ⚮ zein(e); **=kolben** m, Am. corn-cob; **=mehl** n, Am. Indian meal.
Maisur ♀ (ᴸ-) npr n. ⓰ α. Ost-J.: Mysore.
Mai-trank (ᵈ..ᴸ) m ㉒ (in England unbekannt) wine seasoned (or flavoured) with woodruff.
Maitresse (mäᴸᵛ) f. Mätresse.
Mai-wein (ᵈ...) m ㉒ = Maitrank; **=wurm** m, ent. (Ölkäfer) oil-beetle (Me'loe).
Majestät (ᵛᵛᴸ) [lt.] f ㊽ majesty; ~! als Anrede an Könige, Königinnen (Kaiser[innen]): Your Royal (Imperial) Majesty!; f. geruhen; **majestätisch** (-ᵛᴸᵛ) a. ⓺ majestic; full of majesty; awe-inspiring.
Majestäts-beleidigung (-ᵛᵈ...) f ㉒ offence against the sovereign (prince); jur. auch: lese-majesty; **=brief** m Royal (or Imperial) charter, letters pl. patent, hist. (Imperial) charter of toleration, granted to the Bohemian Utraquists, 1609; **=plural** m „We" used by sovereigns; **=recht** n sovereign's prerogative; **=verbrechen** n = **=beleidigung**; **=verbrecher** m offender against the sovereign.
Majolika ⓞ (ᵛᴸᵛᵛ) [it. (Majo'rka ♀)] f ㊽ Töpferei: majolica (ware or pottery).
Major [lt. größerer] m I (ᵛᴸ) ⓵.(S) ✕ major; Herr ~! Major!; Frau e-s ~s, Frau **~in** f ㊼ major's wife, in der Anrede nur: Madam. — II (ᴸᵛ) ⓛ Logik (Obersatz) major proposition.
Majoran (ᵛᵛᴸ, F ᴸᵛᵛ) [mlt.] m ⓶ ♀ marjoram (Ori'ganum maiora'na).
Majorat (ᵛᵛᴸ) [it.] n ⓶c. (Erstgeburtsrecht) (right of) primogeniture; **~s-erbe** m heir by right of prim., eldest son; **~(s-)gut** n estate devolving by primogeniture, entail(ed estate); **~s-herr** m tenant in tail, owner of entailed property or an entailed estate.
Majordomus (ᴸᵛᴸᵛ) [it.] m inv. hist. mayor (or steward) of the palace; F co. major-domo.
majorenn (ᵛᵛᴸ) [it.] a. ⓺ (volljährig, in Engl. 21 Jahre alt) of (full) age; **~ität** (ᵛᵛᴸᴸ) f ㊻ (age of) majority.

[majorisieren] — 677 — [malerisch]

majorisieren (ᵛᵛᵘᴵᵛ) [lt.] v/a. ⑬ (durch Stimmenmehrheit schlagen) to beat by a majority (of votes).
Majorität (ᵛᵛᵛᴵ) [lt.] f ㊻ (Mehrheit; ant. Minorität): (absolute) ~ (absolute) majority; mit e-r ~ von zehn Stimmen schlagen to beat by a majority of ten (votes); ~s-beschluß m ㉒ resolution carried by a majority (of votes).
Majors-ecke (ᵛᴵᴵ...) f ㊷ critical period in an officer's career; -rang m, -stelle f major's rank, commission; majorship.
Majuskel (ᵛᵘᴵᵛ) [lt.] f ㊽ (ant. Minuskel) capital letter or initial. ⊖ typ. a. cap.
Makadam ᵀ (ᴵᵛᵛ) [Mac Adam, schott. Ingenieur, 1756–1836] m, n ⑨ d. ⊖ Straßenbau: macadam; **makadamisieren** ⊖ (ᵛᵛᵛᴵᵛ) I v/a. ⑬ Straßenbau: (mit Steinschutt bewerfen) to macadamize. — II ~ n ㉓ und **M=ung** f ㊻ macadamization.
Makako (ᵛᴵᵛ) m ㊿ zo. Affe: macaco (Lemur maca'co).
Makao (ᵛᴵᵛ) m ㊿ orn. Papagei: macaw.
Makassar-öl (ᵛᵛᴵᴵ. F ᵛᵘᵛᴵ) [r-r Mangkassar (St. u. Staat auf Celebes)] n ㉒ Macassar oil (von Schlei'chera tri'inga ♀).
☞ **Makedon...** f. Mazedon...
Makel (ᴵᵛ) [mhd.; *lt. mā'cula f Fleck] m ㉒ stain, spot, blot, blur; fig. auch: blemish, flaw, shortcoming, defect, fault; ohne ~ immaculate.
Mäkelei (-ᵛᴵ) [mäkeln²] f ㊻ carping (or ill-natured) criticism or critique, fault-finding; weitS. censoriousness; im Essen: daintiness.
makel-frei (ᴵᵛᵛᴵ) a. ㊿ = makellos.
mäkelig (ᴵᵛᵛ) a. ㊿ fault-finding; censorious; (wählerisch) overnice, particular, F fussy, im Essen: dainty.
makel-los (ᴵᵛᴵ) a. ㊿ stainless, spotless, unblemished; immaculate (a. theol.).
Makel-losigkeit (ᴵᵛᴵᵛ-) f ㊻ stainlessness, spotlessness.
makeln, mäkeln¹ ⊛ (ᴵᵛ) [ndd.: machen 12] v/n. (h.) ⑬ a. (Geschäfte vermitteln) to act as (or to play the) broker or middleman; fig. mit seinem Gewissen ⓛ to (strike a) bargain with one's conscience.
mäkeln² (ᴵᵛ) [Makel] I v/a. u. v/n. (h.) ⑬ a.: (an) et. ⓛ to find fault with (F to pick holes in) a th., beim Essen: to be very fastidious or dainty, F to pick one's food about; an allem ⓛ (et. aussetzen) to carp (or cavil) at everything; mäkle nicht zu viel! don't be always finding fault! — II ~ n ㉓ = Mäkelei.
Maki ⚯ (ᴵᵛ) [afrik.] m ⑨ zo.: a) (Fuchsaffe) maki (Lemur); b) (j) (Fledermaus) f. Flatterkatze.
Makkabäer (ᵛᵛᴵᵛ) [hebr. Hammer] npr/m. ㉒ bibl. Maccabee; Bücher n/pl. der ~ Books pl. of Maccabees; **makkabäisch** a. ㊿ Maccabean. [macaroni.]
Makkaroni (ᵛᵛᴵ-) [it.] m/pl. inv. Kocht.⌋
makkaronisch (ᵛᵛᴵᵛ) [it.] a. ㊿ Schrifttum: (bunt gemischt) macaronic.
Makler, Mäkler¹ ⚯ (ᴵᵛ) [mäkeln¹] m ㉒ broker (a. Börse); für Warenhandel a.: (commission-)agent, factor; weitS. (Vermittler) middleman; fig. „der ehrliche Makler" (Bismarck) the honest broker.
Mäkler² (ᴵᵛ) [mäkeln²] m ㉒ fault-finder; censorious (or carping) critic.
Maklerei ⚯ (-ᵛᴵ) f ㊻ broker's dealings pl., commission business.

Makler-gebühr ⚯ ("ᵛ...) f ㉖; -lohn m brokerage, broker's (or agent's) commission or fee; -geschäft n broker's business. [like) a broker.⌋
maklerisch, mäklerisch ⚯ (ᴵᵛᵛ) a. ㊿ of (or⌋
Makrele (ᵛᴵᵛ) [mhd., ndl., *fr.] f ㊺ ichth. mackerel (Scomber scomber): ~n-fang ("...) m ㉒ mackerel-catching; ~n-fänger ⇓ m (Boot) mackerel-boat.
Makrobiotik ⚕ (ᵛᵛᵛᴵᵛ) [grch.] f ㊺ (Kunst, das Leben zu verlängern) macrobiotics.
Makrokosmus ⚙ (ᵛᵛᴵᵛ) [grch.] m ㉗ (Weltall) macrocosm. [macaroon.⌋
Makrone (ᵛᴵᵛ) [fr., it.] f ㊽ Zuckerbäckerei:⌋
Makuba ⚯ (ᵛᴵᵛ) [fr., St. auf Martinique] m ㊿ (Schnupftabak) maccoboy.
Makulatur (ᵛᵛᵛᴵ) [lt.] f ㊺ bsd. typ. waste paper, fig. schlechtes Buch worthless old book; ~-bogen ("...) m ㉒ waste sheet, spoilt sheet.
Mal¹ (*: Hom. Maal, Mahl) [mhd.: mole] n ⑫ ⓒ. 1. (Mutter-) mole, (birth)mark, spot. — 2. (Denk-, Merk-, Zeichen) (lasting) sign or token, (Pfahl) post, (Grenze) boundary; Spiel: start(-ing point), home; Fußballspiel ꝛc. (Ziel): goal.
Mal² (ᴵ) [ahd.] I n ⓒ. mst klein gschr.: time (vgl. einmal); alleⓏ (f. bs) ein für alleⓏ once for all; das and(e)re ~, ein and(e)res ~, ein anderⓏ another time; diesesⓏ, diesⓏ, für diesesⓏ this time, for once; dreiⓏ three times, thrice; drei= bis vierⓏ three or four times; ein= bis zweimal once or twice; ein ~ über das and(e)re over and over again; ein ~ umsⓏ and(e)re alternately, by turns; mit einem ~e (plötzlich) all at once, all of a sudden (vgl. a. einⓏ); das dieses eine ~ this once; einigeⓏ (f. bs) das einzige ~ the only time; nicht ein einzigesⓏ not a single time, not once; zum (beim) erstenⓏe the first time, F at the first go; das ersteⓏ the first time; jedesⓏ (f. bs) fast jedesⓏ nearly each time; keinⓏ (f. bs) das letzteⓏ the last time; letztⓏs, zum letztenⓏ for the last time; manchesⓏ (manchⓏ f. bs) many a time, manch liebesⓏ many and many a time; mehrereⓏe (mehrereⓏ, mehrⓏ[s]) several times; ein paarⓏ a few times; zu verschiedenen ~en, zu wiederholten ~en repeatedly, time after time, again and again; vielⓏ(s) many times; zweiⓏ twice; zum zweitenⓏe (ob. zum zweitenⓏ) the second time. — II F **mal** adv. = einmal B, zB. es warⓏ ein Kaiser once (upon a time) there was ...; es istⓏ nicht anders it can't be helped, F co. such is life; sie ist nichtⓏ hübsch she is not even pretty; seit beim imper.: sagⓏ an! now just (or do) tell me!
...mal (...ᴵ) [Mal²] adv. in Zssgn, zB.: dreiⓏ (f. Mal²) done (or repeated, happening) three times.
Malachit ⚒ (ᵛᵛᴵ) [grch.] m ⓒ. min. (Kupfersmp) malachite, green copperore; ~-grün ("=ᴵ) n ㉒ malachite-green.
Malaga (ᴵᵛᵛ) [~ ⚒, span. St.] m ⑤. ~-wein m ㉒ malaga (wine).
Malai-e (ᵛᴵᵛ) m ⑭, **Malai-in** f ㊵ Malay(man, f woman).
malai-isch (ᵛᴵᵛ) a. ㊿ (dasⓏe) Malay(an); ⚒ der ~e Archipe'l(agus) Malaysia; ~-

polynesisch a. ㊿ Malayopolynesian, Malay-Polynesian.
Malak(k)a ⚒ (ᵛᴵᵛ) npr/n. ⑨ a. Hinterindien: Halbinsel ~ Malacca (Peninsula), Malay Peninsula; ~-rohr, -röhrchen ⚛ n Malacca cane (von Ca'lamus scipio'num).
Malaria (ᵛᴵ(ᵛ)ᵛ) [it.] f, inv. med. (Sumpfluft, -fieber) malaria.
malbar (ᴵ-) (malen) a. ㊿ suitable (subject) for painting or the artist's brush; which can be painted, auch: paintable; ~keit f ㊺ suitableness for painting or the artist's brush.
Malchen (ᴵᵛ) [(A)ma'lie, dim.] npr/n. ⑬ a. (f Bn.) Milly.
Maleachi (ᵛᵛᴵᵛ) [hebr.] npr/m. ⑨ ⓒa. bibl. Malachi.
maledeien ⊛ (ᵛᵛᴵᵛ), **maledizieren** ⊛ (ᵛᵛ-ᴵᵛ) [mhd., *lt.] v/a. (versluchen) to curse.
Mal(e)diven ⚒ (-ᵛᴵᵛᵛ, -ᴵᵛᵛ) npr. f/pl. ㊸ (Inselkette im Indischen Ozean) Maldive Islands, auch: Maldives pl.; **mal(e)divisch** a. ㊿ Maldivian.
Malefikant (ᵛᵛᵛᴵ) m ㊷, **Malefikus** (ᵛᴵ-ᵛᵛ) m ㉜ od. inv. [lt. übeltäter] malefactor, evildoer; **Malefiz-kerl** (ᵛᵛᴵᴵ) m ㉒ devil of a fellow, (deuced or confounded) rascal, clever dodger.
malen (ᴵᵛ; Hom. mahlen) [*Mal¹] I v/a. 1. to paint; weitS. to portray, sketch, depict; (zeichnen) to draw, weitS. to delineate, leicht und flüchtig: to dash off; an e-m BildeⓏ to be at work on a picture, to be painting a picture; inⓏ Email to anneal, to enamel; in Öl, Wasserfarben ⓛ to paint in oils, in water-colours; in (ob. mit) Tusche ⓛ to paint in Indian ink, to wash (with Indian ink); nach der Naturⓛ to paint from nature, to sketch from life; er hat sichⓛ lassen he has sat for his portrait or picture. — 2. fig. man muß den Teufel nicht an die Wandⓛ talk of the devil, and his imps appear; iro. man wird ihm wasⓛ he may go and whistle for it; du kannst dir wasⓛ (you won't) catch me doing it. — II sichⓛ v/refl. 3. sich selbstⓛ to paint o.s. — 4. (sich zeigen, darstellen) der Himmel malt sich im Wasser the sky is reflected in the water; Freude malt sich in s-n Zügen joy is depicted in his features. — III ~ n ㉓ 5. painting; zumⓛ schön bildschön. — IV **ge-malt** p.p. u. a. ㊿ 6. Bed. des inf.: 7. dies ist wieⓛ this looks (like) a picture, it is perfect.
Maler (ᴵᵛ) m ㉒. ~-in f ㊷ painter (auch = Tüncher), mehr gbr.: artist; weitS. (Darsteller) delineator; ~-in f female painter, lady artist, auch: paintress.
Maler-akademie (ᴵᵛ...) f ㉖ academy of painters; -atelier n painter's (or artist's) studio.
Malerei (-ᵛᴵ) f ㊻: a) (Malen) painting; schlechte: daubing; (Malerkunst) art of painting; b) (Gemälde) painting, picture.
Maler-farbe (ᴵᵛ...) f ㉖ painter's colour; -firnis ⚙ m painter's varnish; -gerätschaften ⊖ f/pl. painter's tools pl.; -gold ⊖ n painter's gold, ormolu.
malerisch (ᴵᵛᵛ) a. ㊿ pictorial, graphic(al), (schön) picturesque, artistic, tasty; dasⓏe ⓒ the picturesque(ness).

Maler=kunst (⁻ᵘ⌣...) f ⓶ = Malerei a; **=leinwand** ⊖ f painter's canvas; **=muschel** f, zo. painter's gaper (U'nio picto'rum); **=pinsel** ⊖ m painter's brush; **=scheibe** f palette; **=schule** f: a) school for painters; b) Flemish, &c. school of painters; **=silber** ⊖ n silver powder; **=staffelei** f easel; **=stock** m ⚔ maul-, mahl-stick; **=stuhl** m sketching-stool.

Mal²=gerätschaften (⁻ᵘ...) [malen] f/pl. ⓶ painting-utensils pl.; **=¹graben** [Mal¹] m boundary-ditch.

Malheur (mä-lö'r) [fr. Unglück] n ⓷d. ⓹ misfortune; er hat viel ~ gehabt he has been very unfortunate or unlucky.

Malice (⌣¹ᴸ⌣) [fr.] (ⓢBosheit) malice.

...malig (...⁻ᴸ⌣) [Mal²] a. ⓶ in Zssgn mit vorangehender Zahl, z.B.: **drei=²** taking place (or happening) three times.

maliziös (⌣⌣⌣ᴸ) [fr.] a. ⓶ (D 10) (bös-willig) malicious, ill-natured, spiteful.

Mal²=kasten (⁻ᵘ...) m ⓶ paint-box; **=¹mark** f Fußball: touch-in-goal.

Mall ⚓ ⌣ (⌣) n ⓷b. bend-, sheer-mould.

Malon=säure ⚗ ⌣ (⁻⁻ᴸ⌣) [lt. Apfel-] f ⓶ chm. malonic acid (C₃H₄O₄).

...mals (...⁻ᴸ) [Mal², gen.] in Zssgn **mehr=²** several times.

Mal¹=säule (⁻ᵘ...) f ⓶ = Grenzsäule; **=stein** m = Grenzstein.

Malta ♀ (⌣⌣) npr/n. ⓷α. (englische Insel im Mittelmeere) (Isle of) Malta.

Malter (⌣⌣) [ahd.; *mahlen] m u. n ⓶ (Maß): a) für Getreide (in Preußen ehm. = 650,54 Liter) about 2²/₇ Imperial quarters; b) für Holz (= 80 Kubikfuß) etwa: cord; **~holz** ⌣ ⓶ wood sold by cords.

maltern (⌣⌣) v/a. ⓷d.: Holz ² to stack wood in cords.

Malteser (⌣⌣ᴸ⌣) [Malta] I m ⓶ 1. (auch **~in** f ⓷) Maltese. — 2. = ~ritter. — II a. inv. 3. Maltese (= maltesisch).

Malteser=erde (⌣⌣ᴸ⌣...) f ⓶ min. earth of Malta, Maltese clay; **=kreuz** n cross of Malta, Maltese cross (✠); **=ritter** m knight of Malta, vgl. Johanni'ter.

maltesisch (⌣⌣ᴸ⌣) [Malta] a. ⓶ Maltese.

Maltose ⚗ (⌣⌣ᴸ) f ⓶ = Malzzucker.

malträtieren (⌣⁻⌣⁻ᴸ⌣) [fr.] v/a. ⓷ (mißhandeln) to maltreat.

Malvasier (⌣⌣¹(⌣)⌣, ⌣⌣⌣ᴸ) [Malvasi'a. grch.St.] m ⓶ malmsey (wine), malvasia.

Malve ♀ (⌣⌣) [lt.] f ⓶ mallow (Malva); nordische, rundblättrige ~ dwarf mallow (M. rotundifo'lia); **=n=artig** ⓷ (⌣⁻⌣⌣...) a. ⓹: ⌣ malvaceous; **~n=baum** ♀ m ⓶ tree-mallow (Lavate'ra arbo'rea); **~n=blatt** n mallow-leaf; **~n=farbe** f, **=n=farbig** a. mauve.

Malz ⊖ (⌣) [ahd.: malt] n ⓷a. Brauerei ꝛc.: malt; s. Hopfen.

Malz=bereitung ⊖ (⌣⁻...) f ⓶ malting, maltage; **=bier** n malt-beer, ale; **=boden** m malt-loft; **=bottich** m malt-tub or -vat; **=darre** f malt-drier or -kiln.

Mal¹=zeichen (⁻⌣ᴸ⌣) n ⓶ mark (of distinction); memorial (stone).

malzen, mälzen ⊖ (⌣⌣) [Malz²] v/a. und v/n. (h.) ⓹ Brauerei: to (make) malt.

Malz=entkeimungs=maschine ⊖ (⌣⁻⌣⌣...) f ⓶ malting-machine.

Mälzer (⌣⌣) m ⓶ maltster, maltman.

Mälzerei (⌣⌣⁻) f ⓸: a) malting; b) malt-house or -shed.

Malz=extrakt (⌣⁻...) m (n) ⓶ extract of malt; **=händler** ⊛ m maltster; **=trücke** f malt-rake, -scoop; **=mühle** ⊖ f, **=quetsche** f malt-mill; **=schrot** m od. n ground (or bruised) malt; **=staub** m malt-dust; **=steuer** f duty on malt, maltage; **=tenne** f malt-floor; **=treber** f /pl. malt-residue sg., brewer's dregs; **=trank** m malt-liquor.; **=zucker** m, chm. ⌣ maltose.

Mama (⌣⌣ᴸ, südd. u. md. ⌣⌣) [nhd., *fr.] f ⓹ Kindersprache: mamma, F ma.

Mameluck ⚔ (⌣⌣⌣) [ar.] m ⓶ (ehm. äg. Leibwache, 9. sae. bis 1811) mameluke.

Mammon (⌣⌣) [nhd.; *hebr. Schatz] m ⓶ bibl. Mammon; fig. worldly riches pl., mammon, money, pelf; dem ~ dienen to serve (or worship) Mammon; **~s=diener** (⌣⁻⌣...) m ⓶, **=knecht** m worshipper of M.; **~s=dienst** m mammon-worship, worship of the golden calf; **~s=tempel** m temple of Mammon.

Mammut ⚗ ⌣ (⁻⌣) [russ.] n ⓷d. ⓶ zo. (ausgestorbenes Riesentier) mammoth (E'lephas primige'nius); **~baum** ♀ (⌣⁻...) m ⓶ mammoth tree (Sequo'ia gigante'a); **~elfenbein** n aus den russischen Seen: mammoth (or fossil) ivory; **~zahn** m mammoth tusk.

Mamsell (⌣⌣) [Mademoiselle] f ⓹ (⌣) miss, young woman or lady, F damsel; nordb. (Köchin) cook; a. = Büfett².

man¹ (⌣) [Mann] indef. pron. (nur als Subjekt gbr.; sg. dat. einem, acc. einen) one, somebody; they, people; oft passivisch übersetzt: ² weiß nicht, was e=m begegnen kann one never knows what may happen (to one), mehr gbr. ⌣ you never know what may happen (to you); ² muß es tun it must be done; ² holte ihn he was fetched; ² kann nicht sagen (wissen), ob // there is no telling (knowing) whether /; ² sang und schrie there was singing and shouting; wenn ² ihn hört, sollte ² glauben // to hear him one would think //; in Vorschriften, z.B.: ² läute(t) zweimal! ring twice!; ² verbinde die Punkte let ... be joined, join ...

man² P (⌣) [nbd.] = nur; ² bloß nothing but; ² nicht flunkern! don't tell fibs!

Man¹ (⌣) [ind.] n ⓶ 6. Gewicht: maund (= 82²/₇ lb. avdp. = 37¹/₃ kg).

Mänade (-⌣ᴸ) [grch. Rasende] f ⓹ myth. (Bacchantin) u. fig. maenad.

Manasse (⌣⌣ᴸ⌣) npr/m. ⓷α. bibl. (ältester Sohn Josephs; Kg. v. Juda) Manasseh.

Manati ⚗ ⌣ (⌣⌣ᴸ⌣) m ⓶ zo. = Lamantin.

manch (⌣) [ahd.: many; *Menge] a. ⓶ (A³†, B*) (vor a. mit s. und vor s/n. oft inv.) und indef. pron. ²er m, ²e f, ²es n 1. many a; ²es Mal (f. ²mal), ²liebes Mal (full) many a time; ² eine(r), ² ein Mensch many a one; ² Bürschchen zog dahin many a young lad went forth; ²e reiche (⌣⌣ ... en) Leute (a great) many rich people; ...hat ²en Sturm erlebt has lived through many a storm; schon ²er hat gelitten (a great) many have suffered; in ²em hat er recht in many things he is right. — 2. verstärkt durch „so" oder „gar": so ²er a good many (people); so ²es Jahr for many a year or many years; ich habe Ihnen gar ²es zu erzählen I have so much (or so many things) to relate to you, I have plenty (or a great deal) to tell you. — 3. ²e pl. several; many; ²en schien er toll to some (or many) he appeared mad.

mancherlei (⌣⌣⌣) inv. I a. divers, different, many; auf ² Art in sundry (or various) ways. — II ~ n all sorts (or many kinds) of things.

manch=mal (⌣,ᴸ) adv. sometimes, many a time, many times, often.

Mandant (⌣⌣ᴸ) [lt. Auftraggeber] m ⓶, **~in** f ⓷ jur. † (Vollmachtgeber) client: pol. constituent; ⓹ customer.

Mandarin (⌣⌣ᴸ) [port., *ind., aber chin. kwan] m ⓷d. ⓶ mandarin.

Mandarine ♀ (⌣⌣ᴸ⌣) f ⓹ (sehr kleine Apfelsine) mandarin (Citrus no'bilis).

Mandarinen=amt (⌣⌣⌣⌣) n ⓶, **=würde** f mandarinate; **=herrschaft** f mandarin rule, mandarinism.

mandarinisch (⌣⌣⌣⌣) a. ⓹ mandarin. mandarinic. of mandarins.

Mandat (⌣⌣ᴸ) [lt. Auftrag] n ⓷c. jur. brief, authorization; (Erlaß) decree; pol. mandate; sein ~ niederlegen to resign (or vacate) one's seat; **~ar** (⌣⌣⌣ᴸ) m ⓶ (Beauftragter) authorized person or agent. mandatory.

Mandel¹ (⌣⌣) [ahd.; mlt. ama'ndola; *grch. amygdä'le] f ⓹ 1. (Frucht) almond; gebrannte ~ sugared almond. — 2. ♀ = **~baum**. — 3. anat. ~n pl. (Drüsen am Halse) tonsils pl.

Mandel² (⌣⌣) [nhd.; *mlt.] f ⓹ 6. set of fifteen; agr. shock of sheaves; 3 ~ Eier forty-five eggs pl.

mandel=artig (⌣⌣...) a. ⓹ like almonds, ⌣ amygdaline; **=baum** ♀ m ⓶ almond-tree (Prunus Amy'gdalus); **=blüte** f al.-blossom; **=brot** n al.-biscuit; **=entzündung** f, path. mumps pl., ⌣ amygdalitis, tonsillitis; vet. f. Feifel; **=förmig** a. almond-shaped, ⌣ amygdaloid; **=kern** m almond; **=kleie** f al. mond-powder; **=krähe** f. orn. roller (Cora'cias ga'rrulus); **=kuchen** m al.-cake; **=milch** f, pharm., &c. al.-milk.

mandeln (⌣⌣) [Mandel²] v/a. ⓹a. to arrange in sets of fifteen; agr. to set up sheaves of corn in shocks.

Mandel¹=öl (⌣⌣...) n ⓶ (sweet) almond-oil; vgl. Bittermandel=öl; **=pfirsich** ⚗ m al.-peach (Amy'gdalus commu'nis per'sica); **=seife** f al.-soap; **=stein** m, min. amygdaloid; **=torte** f = **=kuchen**; **²²=weise** (⌣⌣...) adv. in sets of fifteen.

Mandoline ♪ (⌣⌣ᴸ⌣) [it.] f ⓹ (fl. Laute) mandolin; **~n=spieler(in** f) m mandolinist.

Mandrill (⌣⌣) [afrik.] m ⓷d. zo. Affe: mandrill (Cynoce'phalus mormon).

Mandschu (⌣⌣) ⓶ 1. m inhabitant of Manchuria, Manchu. — 2. n Sprache: Manchu(rian); **~dynastie** (⌣⁻...) f ⓶ Manchu dynasty.

Mandschurei ♀ (⌣⁻⌣⁻ᴸ) npr/f. ⓷α. (chin. Prov.) die ~ Manchuria.

mandschurisch (⌣⌣ᴸ⌣) a. ⓹ Manchurian.

Manege (⌣⌣ᴸ⌣) [fr.] f ⓹ horsemanship; riding-school.

Manen (⌣⌣) [lt.] pl. inv. (Geister der Verstorbenen) manes pl., shades (or spirits, souls) pl. of the departed.

mang P norbb. (⚓) [nbb.] prp. among.
Mangan ⚛ (⚘¹) [grch.] n ⚙d. min. u. chm. (schweres Metall) manganese (Mn).
Mangan=blende ⚛ (⚘¹...) f ⚒ min. alabandite; **=chlorī'b** n, chm. manganic chloride (Mn_2Cl_6); **=chlorǖ'r** n manganous chloride ($MnCl_2$); **=dioxy'b** n = =superoxy'b; **=erz** n manganese-ore; **=glanz m = =blende**; **⚶haltig** a. ⚒ manganiferous, ...esian, ...ic.
Manganit ⚛ (⚘¹) n ⚙c. min. manganite, grey manganese-ore.
Mangan=oxy'b ⚛ (⚘¹...) n ⚙ chm. manganic oxide (Mn_2O_3); **=oxybu'l** n manganous oxide (MnO); **=oxybu''loxy'b** n manganous-manganic oxide (Mn_3O_4); **⚶sauer** a. ⚒ manganic; **⚶saures Salz** manganate; **=säure** f manganic acid (H_2MnO_4); **=schaum** m wad (H_2MnO_3); **=spat** m manganous carbonate ($MnCO_3$); **=superoxyb** n (Braunstein) manganese dioxide, peroxide (or black oxide) of manganese (MnO_2); a. pyrolusite.
Mange(l¹) ⚛ (⚘⚘) [mhb., *grch.] f ⚒ (Zeugrolle) mangle; (Tuchpresse) calender.
Mangel² (⚘⚘) [mhb.; *mangeln] m ⚙ (Fehler) defect, fault, flaw, shortcoming; (Nichtvorhandensein) absence, lack, want, deficiency; (Spärlichkeit) scarcity; **aus ~** an for (or from) want of, in default of; **~ an Geld** impecuniosity; **~ an Lebensart** lack of (good) manners, ill-breeding; **~ an Lebensmitteln** shortness (or dearth) of provisions, famine; **gänzlicher ~ an Wasser** water-famine; **einem drigenden ~ abhelfen** to supply a much-felt want; **Mängel** (Schäden) aufdecken, an Licht bringen to show up defects or imperfections, to bring the shortcomings of a th. to light; **~ an allem h.** to be short of everything; **~ (Not) leiden** to be destitute, to live in poverty or (a state of) indigence; **sie litten großen ~** they were in great distress or utter destitution.
Mangel¹=brett ⚛ (⚘⚘...) n ⚒ mangling board; **⚶frei** a ⚒ faultless.
mangel²haft (⚘⚘⚘) a. ⚒ (s. Mangel²) defective (a. gr.), faulty, deficient, (unvollkommen) imperfect; (unvollständig) incomplete, (ungenügend) insufficient; ⚶ (adv.) verschlossen not properly locked; **~igkeit** (⚘⚘⚘⚘) f ⚒ defectiveness (a. gr.), faultiness; imperfection; incompleteness.
Mangel¹=holz ⚛ (⚘⚘...) n ⚒ roller for mangling; **=maschine** f mangling-machine, mangle.
mange(l)n¹ (⚘⚘) v/a. ⚒a. = mangen.
mangeln² (⚘⚘) ⚶a.: mangle; *It. mancus verstümmelt; vgl. Manko/ v/n. (h.) ⚒a. to be deficient (or lacking, wanting) in a th.; ⚶b wanting, deficient; **wegen 2den Raumes** for lack of space; **es mangelt mir an et.** I am in want (or I am short) of a th., I lack a th.; **sie lassen es sich an nichts ~** they do not deny themselves any thing, they take good care of themselves; **an mir soll es nicht ⚶** I shall spare no pains, I will do my part or all I can (vgl. fehlen 4).
mängeln (⚘⚘) ⚒a. **I** v/n. (h.) u. v/a. = mäkeln² I. — **II** v/a. = bemängeln.
mangels (⚘⚘) prp. mit gen. in default of.

mangen ⚛ (⚘⚘) [Mange] v/a. ⚒: bie Wäsche ⚶ to mangle the linen.
Mang=futter (⚘⚘...) n ⚒ mixed grain; **=gut** n inferior metal or alloy; **=korn** n bread-corn. — Vgl. Meng=...
Mango=baum ⚛ (⚘⚘⚘...) m ⚒ mango(-tree) (Mangi'fera i'ndica); **=frucht** f mango.
Mangold ⚛ (⚘⚘) [mhb.] m ⚙d. T mangel-wurzel (Beta vulga'ris macrorrhi'za); **roter ~** (Runkelrübe) beet(-root) (Beta vulga'ris).
Mango=pflaume ⚛ f = Mangofrucht.
Mangostane ⚛ (⚘⚘⚘) f ⚒ mangosteen (Garci'nia Mangosta'na und ihre Frucht).
Manichäer (–⚘⚘) m ⚒ **1.** [Mani, Stifter der Sekte, 215/6—276] eccl. Manichæan, ...ee, ...ist. — **2.** [P: mahnen] F bursch.: (Gläubiger) creditor, hart bedrängender: dun.
Manie (⚘¹) [grch.] f ⚒ (Sucht) mania.
Manier (⚘¹) [mhb.; *fr.manière] f ⚒ (Weise) manner, mode, fashion; **in solcher ~** in such a way; **sie hat angenehme ~en** she has pleasant manners, she has a nice way with her; **er hat schlechte ~en** (Lebensart) he has bad (stärker: shocking or no) manners, he is ill-bred; **das ist keine ~** that's not the proper thing to do; **et. mit guter ~** (bereitwilligst) tun to do a th. readily or with a good grace.
maniert (⚘¹) a. ⚒ (geziert) affected, stilted, F put on; **~heit** (⚘¹⚘) f ⚒ affectation, mannerism.
manierlich (⚘¹⚘) a. ⚒ well-mannered, well-bred; (höflich) courteous, polite, civil; **sich ⚶** (adv.) betragen to be polite or on one's best behaviour; **~keit** f ⚒ courtesy, politeness, civility.
Manifest (⚘⚘⚘) [It.] n ⚙a. (öffentliche Erklärung) manifesto.
Manifestation (⚘⚘⚘-(⚘)⚙) [It.] f ⚒ (Kundgebung) manifestation, demonstration; **~s=eid** m ⚒ = Offenbarungs-eid.
manifestieren (⚘⚘⚘⚘) [It.] v/a. ⚒ **1.** (bekunden) to manifest. — **2.** ⚒ jur. to swear an affidavit on one's insolvency. [manicure.]
Manifur (⚘⚘¹) [fr.] f ⚒ (Handpflege))
Manila (⚘¹⚘) [⚓ größte Philippinen-insel, jetzt Luzon, u. ihre Hauptstadt] ⚒ f ⚒ (⚶igarre) **~=zigarre**; **=hanf** ⚛ (⚘⚘...) m Manila hemp or fibre, Siam hemp, Menado hemp (von Musa te'xtilis); **⚶i=garre** f Manila cigar or cheroot, manila.
Maniok ⚛ (⚶(⚶)⚘) [brasil.] m ⚒ (Brotwurzel) manioc; **~=mehl** (⚴...) n ⚒ cassava.
Manipel (⚘⚶¹) [It.] ⚒ **1.** m ⚙ röm. Alt.: (Abteilung von 60 Mann) maniple. — **2.** n, Cath. eccl. (Armbinde des Meßpriesters) maniple.
Manipulation (⚘⚶⚘⚘-tz(⚘)⚙) [fr.] f ⚒ (Handhabung) manipulation; **manipulieren** (⚘⚶⚘⚘⚘) v/a. ⚒ (handhaben) to manipulate, handle; fig. (to know how) to work a th.
Manko ⚛ (⚘⚶) [it.; vgl. mangeln] n ⚒ (Fehlbetrag) deficiency; (Kassenbefelt) deficit, shortness (of cash).
Mann (⚶; Hom. man) [ahb.: man] m ⚙d., poet. a. ⚶, pl. a. inv. **1.** (ant. Weib) man; **er ist nicht der ~ dazu** he is not the man to do it; **er ist ~s genug dafür** he is quite the man for it, he is well capable of it; **sich als ~ zeigen** to show o.s. a man; **alter (junger) ~** old (young)

man; **feiner ~** (perfect) gentleman; **ganzer ~** quite (or every inch) a man, F fine fellow; **gebildeter ~** man of culture; **der rechte ~** the right sort (of man); **ein vielseitiger ~** an all-round man; **~ bei (ob. für) ~** man for man; **each one, individually, singly**; **⚶ drei ~ hoch** three men deep; **~ und Roß** horse and rider, man and horse; **5000 ~ zu Fuß und zu Pferd** five thousand foot and horse; **⚓ alle ~ hoch!** all hands aloft!; **alle ~ auf Deck!** all hands on deck!; **Sprichw. ein Wort ein Wort, ein ~ ein ~** an honest man's word's as good as his bond; **honour bright!** — **2.** mit prp.: **seine Ware an den ~ bringen** to dispose of one's goods; **wenn Not an (den) ~ geht ob. kommt** (ob. wenn Not am ~ ist) if the worst comes to the worst, in case of emergency or need; **ich halte mich an (ihn als) meinen ~ (Bürgen)** I must look to (him as) my security; **an den unrechten ~ kommen** to come (F to get) to the wrong man or F party, shop; **die Kosten betragen auf den ~ fünf Mark** the expenses are five shillings a head or F a piece; **bis auf den letzten ~ fallen** to perish to the last (or to a) man; **bs. jur.: durch den dritten ~ gehen** to be done by proxy or attorney; **für einen ~ stehen** to stand up for each other; **to be as one man**; **"(Für) Männer" auf Bahnhöfen ⚓**: (For) Gentlemen!, Gentlemen's Lavatory!; **~ gegen ~ kämpfen** to fight man against (or to) man; **⚓ mit ~ und Maus untergehen** to go down with every soul (or all hands) on board; **zum ~ heranwachsen** to grow up to manhood or to be a man. — **3.** fig. **Sie sind ein (ob. ein Kind) des Todes, wenn //** you are lost (or a dead man) if //; **er wird seinen ~ schon finden** he will find his match yet; **Gott einen guten ~ sein lassen s. Gott 2**; **f-n ~ stehen** to hold one's ground; **Sprichw. selbst ist der ~** every tub must stand on its own bottom, oft: **help yourself!**; **ein ~, ein Vogel** one (for) each. — **4.** = **Ehemann**; **grüßen Sie mir Ihren ~** my kind regards to your (good) husband; **~ und Frau** man (or husband) and wife; **einen ~ bekommen** to get married; **seine Tochter an den ~ bringen** to find a husband for ..., F to get ... off; **e-n ~ nehmen** to marry; **sie ist der ~ (Herr) im Hause** she is master, F she wears the breeches. — **5.** j-s ~ (Spielgehilfe) sein to be a p.'s partner; **den vierten ~ m.** to take the fourth hand. — **6.** coll. **der gemeine ~** the common folk or people pl., auch: the man in the street. — **7.** (Lehnsmann; pl. ~en) vassal, follower; ⚔ warrior, soldier; **mit allen s-n ~en** with all his (fighting) men or his merry men.
Manna (⚶⚘) [hebr. (Himmels-)Gabe] f ⚒, n ⚒ (Saft der Mannaesche ⚓.) manna.
Manna=esche ⚛ (⚘⚘...) f ⚒ manna-ash, flowering ash (Fra'xinus Ornus); **⚶gebend** a. ⚒: ⚛ manniferous; **=gras** ⚛ n manna-grass (Glyce'ria

---
⚛ scientific; ⚘ botanical; ⚶ geography; ⚙ machinery; ⚒ mining; ⚔ military; ⚓ marine; ⚒ commercial; ⚶ postal; ⚒ railway.

[Mannagrütze]

flu'itans); =grütze f (geschrotene Körner des =grases) manna-groats pl.; =klee ♀ m: echter ~ agul (*Hedy'sarum alha'gi*); =zucker m ❀ manna-sugar, *chm.* mannite ($C_6H_{14}O_6$).

mannbar (ᵇ-) a. ⑥ marriageable, having attained to (wo)manhood; ~ werdend pubescent; **~keit** (ᵇ⁻) f ㊻ marriageable age, (wo)manhood, (wo)man's estate, v. Jünglingen auch: puberty; **~werden** n ㉓ pubescence.

Männchen (ᵇ⁻) n ㉔ (*dim.* v. Mann) **1.** little man, manikin; (Knirps) whipper-snapper. — **2.** liebkosend: (Ehemann) mein liebes ~! my dear hubbie! — **3.** von männlichen Tieren: male, von Hasen, Kaninchen ꝛc. auch: buck; von Kühen, Seehunden, Walfischen ꝛc.: bull, v. Vögeln: cock; ~ und Weibchen male and female, auch: he and she. — **4.** von Hasen ꝛc.: ~ machen to stand (up) on the hind-legs; weitS. to frisk (or caper) about, to cut capers.

Männerchen (ᵇ⁻⁻) n/pl. ㉔ (*dim.* von Männer pl.) little men, manikins pl.

Männer=chor ♪ (ᵇ⁻...) m ㊱ men's choir, *thea.* chorus of men; **=gesang=verein** ♪ m men's choral society.

...männ(er)ig ♀ (...ᵇ(⌣)⁻) [Mann] a. ⑥ i. Zssgn: vielⁿ polyandrian, ...ous.

Männer=mord ♪ (ᵇ⁻...) m ㊱ murder of men; **=mordend** a. ⑥ *poet.* homicidal; **=scheu** a. afraid (F timid) of men; **=treu** ♀ f creeping forget-me-not (*Omphalo'des verna*), auch = Mannstreu.

Mannes=alter (ᵇ⁻...) n ㉒ (years pl.) of manhood, man's estate; im besten ~ in the flower of manhood, in the prime of life; **=art** f man's ways pl.; **=kraft** f, **=mut** m man's (or manly) strength, courage; **=stamm** m male line (of descendants); **=stolz** m manly pride; **=wort** n (honest) man's word; **=würde** f manly dignity; vgl. Manns=...

mannhaft (ᵇ⁻) a. ⑥ manly, manful, virile; (entschlossen) resolute; (tapfer) brave; **~igkeit** (ᵇ⌣⁻) f ㊻ manliness, virility; resoluteness.

Mannheit (ᵇ⁻) f ㊻ **1.** (Männlichkeit) masculinity, masculineness. — **2.** (was Männern eigen ist) manliness, manly nature. — **3.** (Zeugungsfähigkeit) virility.

...männig ♀ (...ᵇ⁻) a. ⑥ f. ...männ(er)ig.

mannig=fach (ᵇ⁻...) [many: manch] a. ⑥, **=faltig** a. manifold, multifarious, multiple, varied; **=faltigkeit** f ㊻ manifoldness, multifariousness, multiplicity, variety.

männiglich (ᵇ⁻⁻) [ahd.] indef. pronoun *inv.* altertümlich = jedermann.

Männin (ᵇ⁻) [f zu Mann] f ㊼ woman, (Mannweib) virago; **...männin** (...ᵇ⁻); B. Landsⁿ (fellow) countrywoman; **...männisch** (...ᵇ⁻) a. ⑥ i. Zssgn: see ꝛc.

Mannit ⚗ (ᵇ⁻⁻) m ⓓ*c*. = Mannazucker.

Männlein (ᵇ⁻) n = Männchen 1—3.

männlich (ᵇ⁻) [Mann] a. ⑥ **1.** (ant. weiblich) male; *gram.* masculine (auch: stark wie ein Mann). — **2.** (einem Manne zukommend) ꝛe Kleidung man's clothing, male habiliment or garments pl.; ꝛes Wesen manliness, virility. — **3.** *pros.* ꝛer (einsilbiger) Reim male (or masculine, single) rhyme.

— 680 —

Männlichkeit (ᵇ⌣⁻) f ㊻ **1.** masculinity (a. *gram.*). — **2.** = Mannheit 3.

Mann=loch ⊕ (ᵇ⌣ch) n ㊵ am Dampfkessel: man-hole.

Manns=bild F (ᵇ⁻) n ㊷ (Mann) man, male, F one of the male sex.

Mannschaft (ᵇ⌣) f ㊻ **1.** body (für gemeinsame Arbeiten a. gang) of men. — **2.** ✕ squad (of men), troops pl., junge ~ young recruits, fresh levies pl.; die alte ~ (seasoned) veterans pl.; sämtliche ~en all the men or troops pl.; Fußball: team. — **3.** ⚓ (ship's) crew or company. — **~s=anwerbung** ✕ u. ⚓ (ᵇ⌣...) f ㊷ enrolment of men; **~s=rolle** f muster-roll.

manns=dick (ᵇ⁻...) a. ⑥ (as) stout (or big) as a (full-grown) man; **=erbe** m ㊷ Lehnswesen: male heir; **=gestalt** f man's figure, form of a man; **=hand** f man's hand or handwriting; **=hemd(e)** n (man's) shirt; **=hoch** a. of a man's height or stature; **=leute** pl. men pl., the male sex, male folk; **=name** m man's name; **=person** f man, male; **=pflicht** f: a) duty of a man; b) husband's (or marital) duty; **=schild** ♀ ♀ sea-navelwort (*Andro'sace*); **=schneider** m gentlemen's tailor; **=stamm** m male line; **=stimme** f man's voice; **=toll** ꝛc. = manntoll ꝛc.; **=tracht** f man's dress, male costume; **=treu** f eryngo (*Ery'ngium*); auch = Männertreu; **=volk** n = =leute; **=zucht** ✕ f (military) discipline; an ~ gewöhnen to discipline; ohne ~ undisciplined.

mann=toll (ᵇ...) a. ⑥ very fond of (stärker: mad after) men, ⚕ nymphomaniac; **=tollheit** f ㊻ passion for men, ⚕ nymphomania, andromania, uterine fury; **=weib** n ㊷ virago.

Manometer ⚕ ⊕ (⌣ⁿ⁻⌣) [grch.]n(m)㉒*mach.* &c. (Luft=, Dampfdruckmesser) manometer, pressure-indicator, steam-gauge.

Manöver (⌣ᵇ⌣v) [fr.] n ㉒ (Kunstgriff) knack, trick; ✕ (Heeresübung) manœuvre, field-practice, ⚓ (Schiffsübung) naval manœuvre or evolution; (Scheingefecht) sham fight; **~=anzug** m ㊷ field-dress, -uniform; **~=krieg** m sham warfare.

manövrieren (⌣⁻w⌣) [fr.] **I** v/n. (h.) ㉓ bsd. ✕ und ⚓ to manœuvre, to carry on sham warfare, to practise (tactical evolutions). — **II** ~n㉓ manœuvring, manœuvres pl., practice, field- (⚓ naval) operations pl.

Manövrier=fähigkeit ✕ u. ⚓ (⌣⁻w⌣⁻...) f ㊷ capacity of manœuvring or operating (in the field, ⚓ on sea); **=unfähig** a. ⑥ unable to manœuvre, unfit for manœuvring.

Mansarde (⌣ᵇ⌣) [fr.] f ㊻ (Dachwohnung) garret, attic, top floor.

mansard(en)=artig (⌣ᵇ(⌣)⁻) a. ⑥ garret-like; **=dach** n ㊷ mansard- (or curb-) roof; **=fenster** n attic-window; **=wohnung** f lodging(s pl.) in a garret or on the top floor; **=zimmer** n garret-chamber, top room, F *co.* skyloft.

Mansch P (ᵇ) [mengen] m ⓓa., **~e** (ᵇ⁻) f ㊸ mixture, medley, hodge-podge, F (nasty) mess; **~en** v/n. (h.) u. v/a. ⑨ to mix, to splash (about); **~er** m ㉒ splasher, F messing fellow; **~erei** f

[Manufakturwaren]

㊻ (nasty) mixture or stew or compound or F mess, hodge-podge.

Manschester ❀ ⛏ (⌣ᵇ⌣) [Manchester, *engl.* St.] m ㉒ (Sammet aus Baumwolle) cotton velvet, velveteen, geköperter: corduroy; **=n** a. ⑥ of Manchester, ❀ of cotton velvet; **~partei** (ᵇ...) f ⑫ Manchester school of free-traders.

Manschette (⌣ᵇ⌣) [fr. *manchette*] f ㊸ **1.** a) (lose Stulpe) cuff; b) am Hemb=ärmel befestigte: wristband. — **2.** F *fig.* ~n h. to be frightened (out of one's life), F to be (very) funky or in a blue funk; e-m ~n machen to frighten (or alarm) a p., to make a p. nervous.

Manschetten=fieber (⌣ᵇ⌣...) F n ㊷ *co.* abject fear, F funk(iness); **=knopf** m stud (for a cuff), a. wrist-stud; durch Gelenk verbundene doppelte =knöpfe links pl.

manschig (ᵇ⌣)[Mansch]a.⑥sloppy, slushy.

Mantel (ᵇ⌣) [ahd.= mantle; *mlt. mantellum*] m ⑲ **1.** cloak (a. ✕), mantle; den Mantel umhängen (ablegen) to put on (to take off) one's cloak; ✕ gerollter ~ cloak slung over the shoulder; *fig.* den ~ nach dem Winde hängen (sich in die Zeit schicken) to temporize, to be a time-server, to trim one's sails to the wind; to accommodate o.s. to circumstances; den ~ auf beiden Schultern tragen to hold with both sides or parties, F to sit on the fence; mit dem ~ der Liebe zudecken to cover with the cloak of charity, to draw a veil over. — **2.** *math.* e-s Zylinders, Kegels: convex surface. — **3.** ⊕ case (a. ✕ e-s Geschosses), casing, jacket; e-s Kamins: mantel, eines Hochofens ꝛc.: shell; *arch.*, Gießerei: cope. — **4.** *zo.* ~ (Überzug) der Weichtiere: ⚕ mantle.

Mäntelchen (ᵇ⌣⁻) n ㉓ (*dim.* v. Mantel) short cloak or mantle, auch: mantlet; cape; *fig.* einer Sache ein ~ umhängen to palliate (or veil, hush up) a th.

Mantel=kragen (ᵇ⌣...) m ㊸ cape; **=riemen** m cloak-strap; **=sack** m portmanteau, ✕ valise; **=stoff** m = =tuch; **=takel** ⚓ n runner-purchase; **=tasche** f pocket in a cloak; **=tier**, *zo.*: ⚕ tunicary, tunicate; **=träger** m, *fig.* time-server, temporizer. bsd. *pol.* trimmer, wabbler, opportunist; **=tuch**, **=zeug** ❀ n mantling; **=und=Degen=stück** n, *thea.* cloak-and-sword piece or play.

Mantille (⌣ᵇ⌣lje) [fr., *span.*] f ㊸ bsd. *chm.*: mantilla.

Mantisse ⚕ (⌣ᵇ⌣) [lt. Zugabe] f ㊸ *math.* (*ant.* Kennziffer) mantissa, decimal part of a logarithm.

☞ **Man(t)sch** ꝛc. f. Mansch ꝛc.

Manual ♪ (⌣⁻ᵇ) [lt.] n ⓓd. **1.** ✡ memorandum- (or note-) book. — **2.** ♪ Orgelbau: (Klaviatur) key-board, manual; **~akten** pl. *jur.* manuals pl.

Manufaktur (⌣⌣ᵇ⁻) [lt. *manu factum* et. mit der Hand Gemachtes] f ㊷ manufacturing, ...e; (Fabrik) (manu=)factory; **~arbeiter(in** f) m factory-hand; **~er=zeugnis** n manufacture(d goods pl.).

Manufakturist ♪ (⌣⌣ᵇ⌣⁻) m ⓓ **1.** manufacturer, factory-(or mill-)owner. — **2.** dealer in manufactured goods.

Manufaktur=waren (⌣⌣ᵇ⁻⁻...) f pl. ㊷ manufactured goods pl., engS. cloths pl.

Zeichen (f. S. XVII): F familiär; P Volkssprache; ℱ Gaunersprache; ↘ selten; † alt (auch gestorben); * neu (auch geboren); ⸚ unrichtig;

[Manuskript] — 681 — [markhaltig]

Manuskript (⸌⸌⸌) [lt. Handschrift] n ⓦb.:
a) (Handschrift eines Werkes ꝛc.) manuscript
(abbr. MS., pl. MSS.); b) ⊕ typ. für
den Setzer: (printer's) copy, matter; ~
berechnen to cast up copy; kein ~ mehr
haben to be out (or short) of copy;
gedrucktes ~ manuscript-work, book
printed for private circulation; den
Bühnen gegenüber als ~ gedruckt right
of acting reserved.

Manzanilla-baum ♀ (⸌⸌⸍-jä-⸍) [span.] m
⑫ manchineel (Hippo'mane mancine'lla).

Mappe (⸌⸍) [nhd.: map; *fr. mappe
Plan; lt. (*pun.) mappa Tuch] f ㊽ zum
Tragen: portfolio (a. für Zeichnungen ꝛc.),
album, zum Umhängen: satchel; (Schul-
tornister) school-bag.

Mär (⸍) f ㊻ = Märe.

Marabu (-⸌⸍) [fr., *ar.] m ㊾ orn.
marabou(-stork) (Lepto'ptilus cru:me'nifer).

Maräne (⸌⸍) [lt.] ✽ ichth. marena (Core'-
gonus marae'na). [(Ce'rasus mara'sca).]

Maraska-kirsche ♀ (⸌⸌-⸍-⸍) ✽ marasca

Marasmus ⚕ (⸌⸍⸍) [grch.] m ㊷ path.
(Abzehrung) marasmus, wasting.

Marbel, Märbel (⸌⸍) [fr. marbre Marmor]
m ⑫ zum Spielen: marble.

marbeln ⊕ (⸌⸍) [fr.] Glashütte: v/a. ㉘ a.
(den Fluß auf der Platte rollen) to marver.

Märchen (⸌⸍) [nhd.; *Mär(e) dim.] n ㉓
fairy-tale; fiction, fable, romance;
(Gerücht) rumour, (Stadtgespräch) scandal;
(Lüge) fabulous (or cock-and-bull)
story, fabrication; ~ aus Tausendund-
einer Nacht Arabian Night tales or
Nights, a. Ar. Nights' Entertain-
ments pl.; **⸝-artig** (⸌⸍...) a. ㊻ like a
fairy-tale; **~buch** n ⑫ book of fairy-
tales; **~erzähler(in** f) m story-teller.

märchenhaft (⸌⸍⸍) a. ㊻ fictitious,
fabulous, romantic, legendary; **~ig-
keit** f ㊺ fictitiousness, fabulousness.

Märchen-schatz (⸌⸍...) m ⑫ collection
of fairy-tales, folk-lore; **welt** f, etwa:
world of romance; fabulous world.

Marconigramm* (⸌⸍⸌) [Guglielmo
Marco'ni, geb. 1874, it. Physiker] n ⓒc.
(Funkspruch) marconigram.

marconisch (⸌⸍⸍) a. ㊻ [Marco'ni]: das
~e System der drahtlosen Telegraphie
Marconi's (or the Marconi) system of
wireless telegraphy.

Marcus (⸌⸍) [lt.] npr/m. ⓑγ. (Bn.), bibl.
Evangelist: Evangelium Marci Gospel
according to St. Mark; vgl. Markus.

Marder (⸌⸍) [ahd.] m ㉒ zo. marten
(Muste'la); f. Haus-2; **⸝-artig** (⸌⸍...) a.
㊻ like a marten, ⚒ musteline; **~falle**
f ㊽ trap (set) for martens; **~fell** n =
~pelz; ~hund m, zo. racoon-dog (Canis
procyonoi'des); **~pelz** m marten(-skin).

Mardocha-i (⸌⸌-⸍) [hebr.] npr/m. ⓑα.
bibl. (Oheim der Esther) Mardocheus.

Märe (⸍⸍) [Hom. Mähre] [ahd.] f ㊽
1. frohe ~ glad tidings pl. or news;
(Gerücht) rumour, report. — 2. (über-
lieferte Erzählung) old tale or story or
tradition, (Märchen) fairy-tale.

Marelle ♀ (⸌⸌) [Amarelle] f ㊽ 1. =
Amare'lle. — 2. small yellow apricot.

Margareta, ...e (⸌⸌⸍) [grch.] npr/f. ㊻α.,
㊴β. (Bn.) Margaret Marguerite.

Margareten-blume ♀ (⸌⸌⸌⸍...) f ㊷: a) =
Maßlieb; b) künstlich gezogene: marguerite.

Margarin ⚒ (⸌⸍) [fr., *grch.] n ⓓd.,
~e (⸌⸌⸍) f ㊽ (Kunstbutter) margarine.

Margarin-butter ❀ (⸌⸍⸍...) f ㊷ margarine, F und P oft: margerine; **fett** n
margarine, ⚒ glycerine margarate;
⸍sauer a. ㊻.: ⚒ margaric; **⸍saures**
Salz margarate; **⸍säure** f margaric
acid ($C_{17}H_{34}O_2$).

Marginali-en (⸌⸌⸍(⸍)) [lt.] ㉙ pl. inv.
(Randnoten) marginal notes pl.

Maria (⸍⸌⸍) [grch., *hebr.] npr/f. ㊴ξβ.
㊻㊷α. (rel. oft mit lt. gen. Mari'ä)
Mary, Maria; rel. die heilige Jungfrau ~ the Holy Virgin, the Virgin
Mary, the Madonna; Mariä Reinigung (Feast of the) Purification of
the Virgin Mary.

Mariage (⸌⸍⸍Q(⸍)) [fr. Heirat] f ㊽, bsd.
Kartenspiel: marriage, matrimony.

Marianen ♀ (⸌⸍(⸍)) npr/f/pl. ⓕα. (seit
1899 deutsche Inselgruppe im Stillen Ozean)
Marian Islands pl. [anne,PMaryAnn.]

Marianne (⸌⸍⸍) [fr.] npr/f. ㊴㊷β. Mari-⸍

Marie (⸌⸍⸍) [hebr.] npr/f. ㊴㊷β. = Maria;
hist. die Blutige ~ Bloody Mary.

Mariechen (⸌⸍⸍) npr/n. ㉘α. (dim. von
Marie) little Mary, Polly, in Irland
auch Molly.

Marie-n-anbetung (⸌(⸍⸍)...) f ㊷ eccl.
Mariolatry; vgl. **⸍dienst; ⸍bad** n
bsd. chm. water-bath; **⸍bild** n, eccl.
image of the Virgin Mary; **⸍blatt**
n (Frauenminze) ale-cost, costmary
(Tanace'tum Balsami'ta); **⸍dienst** m,
eccl. worship of the Holy Virgin;
⸍distel ♀ f lady's-thistle (Ca'rduus
Maria'num); **⸍fäden** m/pl. gossamer;
⸍fest n (25. März) Lady-day; **⸍flachs** ♀
m toad-flax (Lina'ria vulga'ris); **⸍glas** n,
min. (blätteriger Gips) isinglass, ⚒ mica;
⸍glöckchen ♀ n Coventry-bell (Campanula me'dium); **⸍hähnchen** n, **⸍käfer**,
zo. lady-bird (Coccine'lla); **⸍kirche** f,
eccl. St. Mary's church, church of
St. Mary; **⸍kultus** m Mariolatry; **⸍tag**
m = **⸍fest; ⸍würmchen** n = **⸍käfer**.

Marille ♀ (⸌⸍⸍) f ㊽ = Marelle.

Marine ⚓ (⸌⸌⸍) [fr.; *lt. See-...] f ㊽
(Kriegsflotte) navy, naval forces pl.,
fleet of war-(or battle-)ships; auch:
war-fleet; bei der ~ dienen (eintreten)
to serve in (to enter) the navy, to
belong to (to enter) the naval service.

Marine-amt (⸌⸌⸍...) n ㉘ naval
board; **⸍arsenal** n = **⸍werft; ⸍artillerie**
f naval artillery, Blue Marines pl.;
⸍blau a. u. n marine-blue; **⸍etat** n
naval estimates pl.; **⸍infanterie** f
Red Marines pl.; **⸍ingenieur** m naval
engineer; **⸍maler** m marine-painter,
sea(scape)-painter; **⸍minister** m
minister of naval affairs, in Engl.:
First Lord of the Admiralty, U.S.
Secretary of the Navy; **⸍ministerium**
n ministry of naval affairs, in Engl.:
(the) Admiralty, U.S. Naval Board;
⸍stück n, paint. marine painting, sea-
piece, seascape; **⸍soldaten**, **⸍truppen**
⚓ pl. marines pl.; **⸍verwaltung** f
administration of the navy; **⸍werft**
n (f) navy-yard, auch government
dockyard; **⸍wesen** n naval affairs pl.;
⸍zahlmeister m paymaster of the
navy. — Vgl. auch See-...

marinieren (⸌⸌⸍⸍) [fr.] v/a. ㊷ Kochkunst:
(einlegen) to pickle fish, to put in
vinegar, to cure, bisw. to marinate.

Marionette (⸌(⸍)-⸍) [fr.] f ㊽ (Drahtpuppe)
marionette, (wire) puppet; **~n-spiel**
n ⑫ puppet-play; **~n-spieler** m puppet-
man; **~n-theater** n puppet-show,
englisches: Punch and Judy (show).

mariottesch (⸌⸌⸍tsch) [Mariotte, fr. Physiker, † 1684] a. ㊻: **~es** Gesetz Mariotte's
law.   [betr.) maritime.]

maritim (⸌⸌⸍) [lt.] a. ㊻ (das Seewesen

Mark¹ (⸌) [ahd.: marrow] n ⓦb.: Knochen-
~ marrow, ⚒ medulla; im Holze: pith,
von Früchten: pulp; fig. (das Wertvollste,
die beste Kraft) the very marrow or pith
or essence; vigour, mettle, backbone;
bis ins ~ to the quick; morsch bis ins
~ rotten to the core; f. Bein 2.

Mark² (⸌) [ahd.] f ㊽ ⓒ 1. (Grenz-) ~ boundary, border-land, frontier-country,
bsd. ehm. a. marches pl., z.B. the Welsh
Marches pl.; ~ Brandenburg March
(or Electorate) of Brandenburg. —
2. (Ländereien einer Gemeinde) land belonging to a parish, village-bounds
pl. — 3. fig.: touch.

Mark³ (⸌) [mhd.: mark] f ㊻ 6. (pl. mst
~stücke) 1. ⓩ (Gewicht für edle Metalle,
$1/2$ Pfund) mark, six ounces. — 2. (Sil-
berstück = 100 Pfennig; abbr. ℳ) mark;
eine ~, in Engl. eines: one shilling, F u.
P a bob; U.S. twenty-four cents;
$2\frac{1}{2}$ ~, in Engl. two (shillings) and
sixpence, half-a-crown.

Marke ⊕ (⸌) [mhd.: mark; fr. marque;
*dtsch] f ㊽ 1. mark, token, sign;
zur Kontrolle v. Personen, Gepäck ꝛc.: pass,
check; ~ auf Briefen: stamp, zum Spiele:
counter; Schule: good, bad mark; ⊕
zum Schutze von Waren: trade-mark.
— 2. ⊕ (Güte) sort, quality, bsd. des
Weines: growth, vintage; die besten
~n (Sorten) Zigarren ꝛc. best brands pl.
Marken-album (⊕...) n ⓦ stamp-album;
⸍nachmacher ⊕ m forger of trade-
marks; **⸍sammler** m stamp-collector,
philatelist; **⸍schutz** m protection of
trade-marks; **⸍schutzgesetz** n in Engl.
Merchandise Marks Act.

Märker (⸌⸍) [Mark²] m ⑫, **~in** f ㊺ inhabitant of the marches, engS. native
of Brandenburg, Brandenburger.

mark¹-erschütternd (⸌⸍⸍⸌⸌⸍) a. ㊻ shaking
the very marrow, thrilling.

Marketender ⚔ (⸌⸌⸍) [nhd.; *it.
mercata'nte] m ㉒, **~in** f ㊺ canteen-
(wo)man; caterer (f cateress) for
soldiers, sutler; **~bude** (⸌⸍⸍) f ㊽
canteen; **~ei** ⚔ (⸌⸌⸌⸍) f ㊺ catering
for troops, sutlership; (Wirtschaft) canteen,
soldiers' bar; **~wagen** (⸌⸌⸌-⸍) m ⑫
sutler's wagon or van.

Marketerie ⊕ (⸌⸍⸍) [fr. marquet(t)erie]
f ㊽ (Holzmosaik) marqueterie, ...try.

Mark¹-gefäß (⸌⸍...) n ㉘ anat.: ⚒
medullary vessel; **²gerechtigkeit** f
right of enclosure; **³gewicht** n in
England: troy weight; ehm. **²graf** m,
⸍gräfin f ⚛ margrave, f margravine;
²gräflich a. ㊻ referring to a margrave,
margravial; **²grafschaft** f, **²graf(en)tum** n margrav-
iate; **²haltig** a. anat. containing
marrow, ⚒ medullary.

markicht (⌣⌣) [Mark¹] a. ⑯ marrow-like, ⚭ medullary; *fig.* pithy, strong.
markier/en (⌣⌢⌣) [fr.] *v*/*a.*— ⑨ 1. to mark goods, linen, &c.; ⚔ m/ter Feind (im Manöver) marked enemy. — 2. (hervortreten laſſen) to accentuate, to emphasize; v. Schauſpielern: to play with great feeling or expression, to show off; gut m/t clearly (or well) defined; m/ter Strich clearly marked line; ſcharf m/te Züge well-marked (or well-cut) features *pl*. — 3. F = aufſpielen II.
markig (⌣⌣) [Mark¹] a. ⑯ = markicht; *fig.* ⸗er Ausdruck vigorous (or racy) expression.
märkiſch (⌣⌣) [Mark²] a. ⑯ belonging to the marches or to Brandenburg.
Markiſe (⌣⌢⌣; *Hom.* Marquiſe) [fr. *marquise*] f ㊽ (Sonnendach) outside (window-) blind; (Zelt) marquee, awning.
Mark¹-klößchen (⌢⌣...) n/*pl.* ㊾ Kochkunſt: marrow-balls *pl.*; ⸗knochen m Schlächterei: marrow-bone; ⸗²linie f Fußball: touchline; ⸗²los a. ⑯ marrowless, *fig.* without strength or backbone, pithless.
Markomanne (⌣⌣⌣) [Mart²mann(en)] m ㊹ *hist.* meiſt ⸗n *pl.* (germaniſcher Stamm) Marcomanni *pl.*; **markomanniſch** a. ⑯ Marcomannic.
Markör (⌣⌢) [fr. *marqueur*] m ⑨d. (Zähler beim Billard⸗, Ballſpiele ⁊c.) marker, scorer; (Aufwärter) waiter.
Mark²-ordnung (⌢⌣...) f ㊷ rules *pl.* respecting borders and boundaries; ⸗ſcheibe f boundary-line between mines, parishes, &c.; ⸗ſcheibe-kunſt f surveying of mines, &c.; ⸗ſcheider m surveyor of mines, &c.; ⸗ſcheidung f delimitation of mines, &c.; ⸗ſtein m boundary-stone, land-mark; *fig.* epoch; ⸗¹ſtoff m, *chm.*: ⚭ medullin(e); ⸗ſtrahlen m/*pl.* des Holzes: medullary rays *pl.*, silver-grain *sg.*; ⸗ſtück n Schlächterei: piece of a marrow-bone; ⸗²ſtück n mark- (or shilling-) piece, F u. P bob; ⸗²ſubſtanz f, *anat.*: ⚭ medullary substance.

Markt ⚹ (⌣) [ahd.: market; *lt. mercatus*] m ⑨b. 1. (Jahr⸗) fair. — 2. (Tages⸗, Wochen⸗)~(daily, weekly) market; auf dem ~ in the market; wir haben dreimal ~ we have market-day three times a week; den ~ beſchicken to send goods to market; zu ⸗e bringen to offer for sale; zu ⸗e gehen to go to (the) market, (Einkäufe machen) to go marketing. — 3. (Handel, Geſchäft) trade, business; ~ für Korn, Wolle ⁊c. corn-, wool- &c. market; unſer ~ iſt ſehr belebt (flau) our market is (mehr gbr.: markets are) very active or brisk (dull, lifeless); eine Anleihe auf den ~ bringen to put a loan on the market, to issue a (new) loan; e-m den ~ verderben to spoil a p.'s trade or market. — 4. *fig. et. zu* ⸗e bringen, mit et. zu ~ kommen (etwas vorbringen) to come forward with a th.; ſ. Haut 2. — 5. (Handelsplatz) market, market town; emporium, trade-centre, staple. — 6. (freier Platz) market-place, (open) square. — 7. = ~⸗flecken.

Markt-bauer ⚹ (⌢...) m ㊷ farmer who attends the markets; ⸗bericht m market-report; ⸗beſuch m marketing; ⸗bude f booth (or stall, stand) in the market or at a fair.

markten (⌣⌣) v/n. (h.) u. v/a. ⑨ 1. um et. ⸗² to bargain for a th. — 2. to deal (or sell) in the market.

Markt-flecken (⌢...) m ㊷ small market town; ⸗frau f = ⸗weib; ⸗freiheit f right of holding a (or of selling in the) market; ⸗gänger m m.-man, dealer in the m.; ⸗²gängig a. ⑯ customary in the market; (verkäuflich) marketable, salable; Der Preis current price; ⸗geld n: a) = Budengeld; b) money to be spent in the market or at a fair; ⸗geſchäft n m.-business, business done in the market; ⸗halle f covered market; ⸗helfer m packer (or porter) in a market or at a fair; ⸗karren m m.-cart; ⸗korb m m.-basket; ⸗kurſe m/*pl.* m.-quotations *pl.*; ⸗leute *pl.* m.-folk, frequenters *pl.* of a fair; (Budenleute) stall-keepers *pl.*; ⸗meiſter m inspector of the market; ⸗ordnung f rules *pl.* of the m., m.-regulations *pl.*; ⸗ort m, ⸗platz m = Markt 6; ⸗polizei f m.-police; ⸗preis m m.-price; ⸗recht n: a) = ⸗freiheit; b) = ⸗ordnung; ⸗ſchiff n m.-boat; ⸗ſchreier m (Quackſalber) quack, mountebank, Cheap Jack; (Reklamemacher) puffing advertiser; ⸗ſchreierei f quackery; (Reklame) puffing (advertisement); lauter ~ nothing but puff and boast; ⸗ſchreieriſch a. like a quack or mountebank; puffing; Des Anpreiſens puff(ing), booming; ⸗tag m market-day; ⸗verkehr m traffic (or business) in the market; offener ~ open market, market overt; ⸗vogt m = ⸗meiſter; ⸗weib n market-woman; ⸗zettel m list of m.-quotations; *vgl.* ⸗bericht; ⸗zoll m m.-toll or -due.

Markung (⌣⌣) f ㊻ = Mark², bſb. 2.

Markus (⌣⌣) [lt.] *npr*/m. ⑯γ. (chriſtlicher u. jüdiſcher Vn.) Mark; *vgl.* Marcus.

Markus-kirche (⌢⌣⌣⌣) f ㊻ church of St. Mark, St. Mark's church.

marlen ⚹ (⌣) [fr.] v/a. ⑧: Taue ⸗² (umwickeln) to marl(ine).

Marl-leine (⌢⌣⌣) f ㊻, **Marling** (⌣⌣) [ndl. v. *marren* binden u. *Leine*] f ㊺ marline.

Marmara-meer (⌢⌣⌣⌣⌣) *npr*/n. ⓿ zwischen Dardanellen und Bosporus: Sea of Marmora. ⎱
⎰— 2. = Marbel.⎰

Marmel (⌣⌣) m ㊷ 1. † *poet.* = Marmor.

Marmelade (⌣⌣⌣) f ㊻ ⁕*port. marme'lo* Quitte (v. grch. *melö'meli* Honig-apfel)] ⚹ (Frucht-, Schachtel-mus) jam, v. Apfelſinen: marmalade.

Marmel-stein (⌢⌣⌢) m ㊷ *poet.* = Marmor.

Marmor (⌣⌣) [lt.] m ⑨d. marble; künſtlicher ~ impastation.

Marmor-ader (⌢⌣...) f ㊻ vein in marble; ⸗arbeit f m.-work; ⸗arbeiter m worker in marble, m.-cutter; ⸗²artig a. like marble, ⚭ marmoraceous, ...ean, ...eal; ⸗bild n marble statue; ⸗bildwerke n/*pl.* marble monuments, *auch*: marbles *pl.*; ⸗block m m. block; ⸗bruch m m.-quarry, *poet.* snowy bosom, m. breast; ⸗büſte f m. bust; ⸗²glatt a. (as) smooth as m.; ⸗glätter ⊕ m Werkzeug: m.-rubber; ⸗grube f m.-pit; *vgl.* ⸗bruch; ⸗hart a. (as) hard as m.; ⸗herz n, *poet.* heart of flint.

marmorier/en ⊕ (⌣⌣⌢⌣) v/a. ⑨ to marble; m/tes Papier marble(d) paper; Buchb.:

mit m/tem Schnitt marble-edged.

Marmorierer(in f ㊺) m ㊷ marbler.

Marmor-imitation ⊕ (⌢⌣...) f ㊷ impastation; ⸗²kalt a. ⑯ (as) cold as marble; ⸗mühle ⊕ f marble-mill.

marmorn (⌣⌣) a. ⑯ (of) marble (a. *fig.*), ⚭ marmorean.

Marmor-palaſt (⌢⌣...) m ㊷ marble-palace; ⸗papier ⊕ n marble(d) paper; ⸗platte f marble slab; ⸗ſäule f m.-column; ⸗ſchleifer ⊕ m m.-grinder, -cutter, -polisher; ⸗ſchleiferei, ⸗ſchneide-mühle f marble-(cutting) works *pl.*; ⸗ſchnitt ⊕ m Buchb.: marbled edges *pl.*; ⸗ſtein m marble; ⸗tafel f = ⸗platte; ⸗tiſch m m. table; ⸗treppe f m. staircase, m. stairs *pl.*; ⸗waren f/*pl.* m. ware(s *pl.*).

marode (⌣⌢⌣) [fr.] a. ⑯ (matt) exhausted, worn (F fagged) out, dead-beat, **Marodeur** ⚔ (⌣⌢⌣'r) [fr.] m ⑨d. (Plünderer) marauder; **marodieren** (⌣⌣⌢⌣) v/n. (h.) ⑨ (plündern) to maraud, to pillage.

Marokkaner (⌣⌣⌢⌣) I m ㊷, ~in f ㊺ inhabitant of Morocco. — II *a. inv.* a. **marokkaniſch** (⌣⌣⌢⌣) a. ⑯ (of) Moroccan. — **Marokko** ⚲ (⌣⌣⌣) [span. *ar.*] *npr*/n. ⑯α. Morocco; ~⸗leder ⊕ n ㊷ morocco leather (= Maroquin).

Marone ⚲ (⌣⌢⌣) [it.] f ㊾ (Eßkastanie) edible (or sweet) chestnut; ~n-baum (⌣⌣...) m ㊷, ~n-kaſtanie f Spanish (or sweet) chestnut-tree (*Castanea vesca*).

Maroquin ⊕ (⌣⌣⌢') [fr.; *Marokko*] m ⑨d. (Saffian) Morocco leather, morocco; ⸗ieren (⌣⌣⌢⌣) v/a. ⑨ to morocco.

Marotte (⌣⌢⌣) [fr.] f ㊻ caprice, whim, fancy; (Steckenpferd) hobby, fad.

Marquis (⌣⌢') [fr.] *m* ⑬, **Marquiſe** (⌣⌢⌣; *Hom.* Markiſe) f ㊽ *ob.* **Marquiſin** f ㊺ marquis, f marchioness.

Mars¹ ⚲ (⌣) [it.] *npr*/m. ⑯γ. *myth.* (Kriegsgott u. *ast.* Planet) Mars; den ~ betreffend Martian; Bewohner des ~ inhabitant of Mars, *auch*: Martian.

Mars² ⚹ (⌣) [ndl. Korb; ⁕lt.] m ⑬, f ㊻ (Maſtkorb) top, masthead.

Mars²-braſſen ⚹ (⌣⌢⌣) f/*pl.* ㊷ top-braces *pl.*

Marſch¹ (⌣) [fr. *marche* f] I m ⑨a. 1. march; ~ im Geſchwindſchritt quick march; ſich auf den ~ begeben, ſich in ~ ſetzen to (set out on one's) march, to move off; auf dem ~e ſein to be on the march; ⚔ in eiligen (ob. forcierten) Märſchen vorrücken to advance in forced marches; bem Feinde einen ~ abgewinnen to steal a march upon ...; ♪ (Militär-)~ military march. — 2. *fig.* e-m den ~ blaſen ob. machen: a) (e-n wegweiſen) to turn a p. away, to send a p. to the right-about(s); b) (e-n herunter machen) to give a p. a good scolding; F to blow a p. up. — II **marſch!** *int.* 3. a) ⚔ vorwärts ⸗! forward, march!; b) (pack dich!) be off, F clear off!, P sling your hook!; c) ⸗² hinaus! out you go!

Marſch² (⌣) [ndb.: marsh] f ㊻ (fruchtbare Niederung, *ant.* Geeſt) marsh(y land).

Marſchall (⌣⌣) [fr.; *ahd.* Mähre = Schalt, Pferdeknecht] m ⑨d., ~in f ㊺ marshal; die Frau ~(in) the Marshal's spouse or lady; *vgl.* Hof-².

Marschall(s)=amt (⌣⌣...) n ⓶ marshal's office or post; **=stab** m m.'s staff or baton; **=würde** f m.'s dignity or rank, marshalship.

Marsch¹=anzug ⚔ (⌣...) m ⓶ marching-kit; **=bataillo'n** n battalion on the march; **=befehl** m marching-order(s pl.); ~ haben to be under marching-orders; ²**bereit** a. ⓺ ready to march; **=bereitschaft** f readiness (or fitness) for marching; **=²boden** m marshy soil; ²**fähig** a. fit for marching; ²**fertig** a. = ²bereit; **=²fieber** n marsh-fever; **=¹geschwindigkeit** f (marching-) pace.

marschieren (⌣⌣) [fr.] v/n. (fn u. h.) ⓶ to march; ⚔ auf eine Stadt (los=)⚯ to march on a town; F du kannst ⚯! (you can) be off!, F take your hook!

marschig (⌣⌣) a. ⓺ marshy, boggy.

Marsch¹=kolo'nne ⚔ (⌣...) f ⓶ marching column of an army; **=²land** n marshy land, fenland, fens pl., F co. bogland (auch = Irland); **=länder(in** f) m native of a marshy country; F co. bog-lander (auch = Ire, Irin); **=¹lied** n (song for soldiers on the) march; ²**mäßig** a. ⓺ u. adv. in marching-order or -style; **=ordnung** f order of march, marching-order; **=quartier** n quarters pl. for moving-troops; **=richtung** f direction of a march or of marching troops; **=route** f route (of marching troops), line of march; **=tag** m day of marching, marching-day; **=verpflegung** f provisioning (or commissariat) of troops on the march.

Mars²=fall (⌣...) n ⚓ topsail halyard; **=¹feld** n, hist. (Tagung der Franken im März) (fr.) champ de Mars; **=²late'rne** f top-lantern; **=¹priester** m priest of Mars; **=²rahe** f topsail yard; **=schote** f topsail sheet; **=segel** n topsail.

Mars²=stenge ⚓ (⌣⌣) f ⚓ topmast.

Marstall (⌣⌣) [mhd. Mähre + Stall] m ⓸c. royal or princely stud.

Marter (⌣) [ahd.; *grch=lt. marty'rium] f ⓺ 1. torment, torture; excruciating pain, agony (a. fig.). — 2. = Folter.

Marter=bank (⌣...) f ⓺ rack; **=gerät** n instrument(s pl.) of torture. [turer.⌃

Mart(e)rer (⌣⌣) m ⓶ = tormentor.⌃

Märterer (⌣⌣) m ⓶ = Märtyrer.

Marter=holz (⌣...) n ⓶ eccl. Christ's cross; **=kammer** f = Folterkammer; **=leben** n life of torment.

martern (⌣⌣) [ahd.; *Marter] I v/a. und sich ⚯ v/refl. ⓶a. to torment (o.s.), to torture (o.s.); (foltern) to (put to the) rack; um des Glaubens willen: to martyr; gemarterte Heilige martyred saints pl.; fig. sein Gehirn ⚯ to rack (or cudgel) one's brain; zu Tode ~ to torment to death. — II ~ n ⓷ = Marter.

Marter=pfahl (⌣...) m ⓶ stake to which a p. to be tortured is tied; **=tod** m martyr's death, death by torture.

Martertum, Märtertum (⌣⌣) n ⓶d. martyrdom; **martervoll** (⌣⌣) a. ⓺ tormenting, excruciating, agonizing.

Marter=werkzeug (⌣...) n ⓶ = =gerät; **=woche** f = Karwoche.

Martha (⌣⌣) [hebr. die Betrübte] npr/f. ⓹ⓑ. ⓺α. Martha.

Marthchen (⌣⌣) n ⓶α. Marty, Patty.

martialisch (⌣tʃ⌣⌣) [lt.; *Mars¹] a. ⓺ (kriegerisch) martial, warlike.

Martin (⌣-) [lt. *Mars¹...] npr/m. ⓹ⓐα. (Bn.) Martin; **~i** (⌣⌣) [lt. gen.* ⌣ v. Tours † 400] n, inv. (11. Nov.) ehm.: Martinmas.

Martins=fest (⌣-...) n ⓶ = Martini; **=gans** f Martinmas goose; **=tag** m = Martini.

Märtyrer (⌣⌣) [ahd.; *grch. Zeuge] m ⓶, **~in** (auch ⌣⌣⌣) f ⓵ martyr for one's faith; **~chronik, ~geschichte** (⌣...) f ⓶ history of martyrs, ⚯ martyrology; **~krone** f crown of martyrdom; **~tod** m martyr's death; den ⁓sterben to suffer martyrdom.

Märtyr(er)tum (⌣⌣(-)-) n ⓶d., auch **Märtyrium** (⌣⌣⌣⌣) n ⓶ martyrdom.

Märtyrin (⌣⌣) f ⓵ = Märtyrerin.

Marunke (⌣⌣) [corr. lt. malus arme-ni'aca] f ⓺ red egg-plum.

März (³) [ahd.; *lt. Ma'rtius] m ⓶a. ⓵ ⓶ (month of) March; **~(en)=bier** (³⌣...) n ⓶ March ale, March beer; **~hase** m March hare.

Marzipan (⌣⌣⌣) [lt/hd., *it.] m (n) ⓶d. marchpane; **Zen** (⌣⌣⌣) a. ⓺ of marchpane. [(or in) March.⌃

märzlich ⚙ (⌣⌣) a. ⓺ March-like, of ⌃

März=monat (³...) m ⓶ month of March; **=schnee** m snow in March; Sprichw. ~ tut den Saaten weh March snow to crops brings woe; **=veilchen** ♀ n sweet violet (Vi'ola odora'ta).

Masche (⌣⌣) [ahd.: mesh] f ⓺ mesh, stitch; eine ~ aufheben (fallen lassen) to pick up (to drop) a stitch.

Maschen=grund (⌣⌣...) m ⓶ v. Spitzen 2c. meshed work; ²**weise** adv. stitch by stitch; **=werk** n mesh- (or net-)work; **=zahl** f number of stitches.

maschig (⌣⌣) a. ⓺ in (or formed of) meshes, meshy, ⚯ reticulate.

Maschine (⌣⌣⌣) [nhd., fr., *grch.] f ⓶ mst ⓷ machine, engine (vgl. Dampf=, Näh=⚯); (**~werk**) machinery; (Apparat) apparatus, mechanical contrivance; mit der ~ gemacht machine-made; F co. dicke, schwere ~ (Person) clumsy, heavy person, mountain of flesh, whacker.

Maschinen=arbeit ⓷ (⌣⌣⌣...) f ⓶ machine-work; durch ~ hergestellt oder erzeugt mach.-made; **=arbeiter** m machinist; **=bauer** m machine-maker, (mechanical) engineer; **=bau-kunst** f construction of machines, (art of) engine- (or machine-)building; **=bau(meist)er** m constructor of machinery, engine-builder; **=bau=schule** f engineering-school; **=bau=werkstätte** f machine-shop; **=betrieb** m working of machines or machinery; **=dreh=bank** f power-lathe; **=druck** m, typ. machine-impression, mit der Schnell-presse: steam-printing; **=fabrik** f engine- (or engineering-, machine-)works pl., machine-factory or -shop; **=garn** ♀ n machine-spun yarn; **=gebäude, =haus** n engine-house or -shed; **=gerüst** n frame(-work) of a machine; **=geschütz** ⚔ n machine-gun; ²**glatt** a. ⓺: ⚯es Papier mill-finished paper; **=hammer** m power-hammer; **=ingenieur** m mechanical engineer; **=kunde, =lehre** f (science of) engineering; **=macher** m = =bauer; ²**mäßig** a. machine-like, mechanical; weits. automatic, in-

stinctive; **=meister** m: a) 🚂 superintendent (or manager) of the rolling-stock; b) thea. stage-manager; c) typ. machine-minder, pressman; vgl. Maschinist 1; **=mode'll** n model of a machine; **=papie'r** n (ant. Büttenpapier) machine-made paper; **=pflug** m plough with mechanical traction, engS. steam-plough; **=raum, =saal** m room (set apart) for machines; engine-room; typ. press-room; **=schacht** m engine-shaft; **=schmierer** m lubricator; **=schmier=öl** n mach.-oil; lubricant; **=schreiber(in** f) m (female or girl or lady) typewriter or typist; **=seide** ♀ f / mach.-twist; **=setzer** m, typ. machine-operator; **=techniker** m machine-constructor or -maker; **=telegraph** m engine-telegraph; **=wärter** m, typ. mach.-minder; **=webstuhl** m power-loom; **=wechsel** 🚂 m change of engines; **=werk** n driving-gear of a machine or of machinery; **=wesen** n engineering.

Maschinerie (⌣⌣⌣⌣) [fr.] f ⓶ machinery; fig., pol. wheel within a wheel.

Maschinist (⌣⌣-⌣) m ⓶ 1. thea. manager of the machinery; scene-shifter. — 2. ⓷ engine-man, machinist; 🚂 engine-driver.

Maser (⌣⌣) [ahd.] 1. f ⓵ u. m ⓶ knotty (or gnarled) wood; (Faser des Holzes) grain of the wood. — 2. ~n f/pl. ⓵ path. (Hautausschlag) measles, ⚯ morbilli pl.; die ~n haben to have (or to suffer from) the measles. — 3. m ⓶ (Flecken) speck; (Ader) vein.

Maser=fleck ⓷ (⌣⌣...) m ⓶ join. mark (or speck) in the wood, &c.; **=holz** n veined (or finely marked) wood.

maseric̆ht, =ig (⌣⌣⌣) a. ⓺ von Holz 2c.: veined, (finely) marked, speckled.

maser=krank (⌣⌣⌣) a. ⓺ path. suffering from the measles.

masern¹ ⓷ (⌣⌣) I a. ⓺ v. Holz 2c.: veined, (delicately) marked. — II v/a. ⓶a. to grain; gemasert = maseric̆ht.

Masern² (⌣⌣) f. Maser 2; ²**=artig** (⌣⌣⌣⌣) a. ⓺ path. like (or resembling) measles, ⚯ morbilliform.

Maske (⌣⌣) [nhd. 18. sae., fr., it., *ar.] f ⓺ 1. mask; für Fechter 2c. auch: visor, fig. e-m die ~ abnehmen, abziehen, herunterreißen to unmask (or expose) a p. — 2. fig. (trügerischer Schein) blind, cloak, pretext; unter der ~ der Frömmigkeit under the cloak of piety.

Masken=anzug (⌣⌣...) m ⓶ fancy-dress; **=ball** m masked (or fancy-dress) ball; **=blütler** ♀ m (Larvenblütler) personate flower; **=fest** n carnival; **=freiheit** f license enjoyed at a masquerade.

maskenhaft (⌣⌣⌣) a. ⓺ like a mask.

Masken=kleid (⌣⌣) n ⓷ fancy-dress; **=scherz** m mummery; fun at a fancy-dress ball; **=tanz** m dance in a fancy-costume; **=tracht** f fancy-costume; **=verleiher(in** f) m p. who lets out fancy-costumes, costumier; **=zug** m fancy-dress procession, masquerade.

Maskerade (⌣⌣⌣⌣) [fr.; *Maske] f ⓺ masquerade; fancy-dress fête or ball, mummery, carnival.

maskieren (⌣⌣⌣) [fr.] I v/a. u. sich ⚯ v/refl. ⓶ to mask (auch fig. u. ⚔ in der

---
⚯ scientific; ♀ botanical; ⚘ geography; ⓷ machinery; ⚒ mining; ⚔ military; ⚓ marine; ⚭ commercial; ✉ postal; 🚂 railway.

[**Maskierung**]

Feuerwirkung hindern); sich 2 to put on a mask; (sich) 2 (verkleiden) to disguise (o.s.). — II **Maskierung** f ⓖ masking (a. ⚔), masquerade. [masculine form.
Maskulin-form (⌢‑ᴵᴵ‑˘) f ⓖ gram.
maskulinisch (˘‑ᴵ˘) a. ⓖ (und adv. männlich) (as a) masculine.
Maskulin(um) (⌢‑ᴵ(˘)) [lt. männlich] n ⓖd. (⓹⓪) gram. masculine (form). [messen.
maß¹ (ᴵ) 1. u. 3. Person sg. ind. impf. v.
Maß² (ᴵ) [ahd.: mete; *messen] n ⓖa, 6. (f.3) 1. measure; (Verhältnis) proportion, rate; (Ausdehnung) extent, dimension; (Größe) size, ⚔ a.: height, measurement; (Grenzen) bounds pl.; alles hat sein ~ und Ziel there is a limit to everything; er hat sein volles ~ ... full measure, ... fill; vgl. maßhalten u. häufen I; (das) ~ zu e-m Rocke nehmen to take the measurement(s pl.) for a coat; e-m das ~ nehmen to measure a p. for a suit, &c.; das ~ überschreiten to exceed all bounds (of moderation); das ~ vollmachen to fill the cup to the brim or to overflowing. — 2. mit prp.: in dem ~e als ‖ in the same measure (or proportion) as ‖; according as ‖; in dem ~e, daß ‖ to such a degree (or so far) as to ‖ (inf.); in hohem (ober reichem) ~e in a high degree, highly, richly, amply; in höherem ~e in a higher degree, to a larger (or fuller) extent; im höchsten ~e in the highest degree, to the utmost limit; in vollem ~e to the full, fully, abundantly; Sprichw. alles mit ~(en) everything in moderation, nach ~ angefertigt made to measure. — 3. (Eich-)~ gauge; f ⓖ eine ~ Bier (zwei Seidel) a quart (or pot) of beer; zwei ~ (inv.) two quarts; ~ bsd. für Arznei: dose.
Massage (⌢ᴵʳᵛ) [fr.] f ⓖ med. (Kultur) massage, massaging, kneading, im Dampfbade: shampooing.
massakrieren (˘˘‑ᴵ˘) [fr.] I v/a. ⓖ (niedermetzeln) to massacre. — II ~ n ⓖ und **Massakrierung** f ⓖ massacre.
Maß²-analyse (ᴵᴵ...) f ⓖ chm.: ✧ volumetric analysis; **-arbeit** f s.th. made to measure; **-bestimmung** f measurement.
Masse (˘˘) [ahd.: mass; *lt.] f ⓖ mass, bulk, volume; (Menge) quantity; die große ~ (das Volk) the multitude, the masses pl., F the million; in großer ~ in large numbers; ⊕ weiche (Papier-)~ pulp; teigige ~ dough, paste; ✧ Falliten-2: die ~ verwalten to administer a bankrupt's estate.
Maße † (ᴵ˘) f ⓖ (Art u. Weise) manner.
mäße (ᴵ˘) 1. u. 3. Person sg. subj. impf. v. messen.
Massen-... (˘˘...) = **Massen**-... [ment.
Maß²-einheit (ᴵᴵ‑ᴵ‑) f ⓖ unit of measure-
Massel (˘˘) [lt.] f ⓖ metall. pig.
Maßen¹ (ᴵ˘) [pl. v. Maß²]: mit ~ s. Maß² 2; ohne ~ without moderation or restriction; ohne ~ schön exceedingly beautiful; über die (ob. alle) ~ beyond all bounds, excessively; über alle ~ glücklich supremely happy.
maßen² fast † (ᴵ˘) [mhd. dat. pl. v. Maß] cj. (weil) seeing that; inasmuch as.
...maßen (...ᴵ˘) [gen. pl. v. Maße] adv. meist klein geschrieben und mit dem vorhergehenden Worte verbunden, z.B. anerkannter-

— 684 —

2 as generally acknowledged; vgl. anerkannt; bekannter- notoriously; vgl. bekanntlich; der 2 so much, in such a degree; dieser 2 in this way; einiger-2, folgender 2 s. die bsd. Artikel; gebührender 2 as by rights, duly; gewisser 2 to a certain extent, in a measure; solcher 2 in such a manner or degree, so much; unverdienter 2 undeservedly; versprochener 2 as promised.
Massen-aufgebot ⚔ (˘˘...) n ⓖ general levy; vgl. Landsturm b; **-bildung** ⚔ f massing of troops; **-ernährung** f provisioning (or feeding) of large numbers; **-feuer** n ⚔ general volley; **-gebirge** n, geol. mountain-mass.
massenhaft (˘˘ᴵ) a. ⓖ 1. massed together, massy, voluminous. — 2. (zahlreich) numerous; sie kamen 2 (adv.) ... in crowds or shoals or large numbers; vgl. massenweise. [abundance.
Massenhaftigkeit (˘˘˘˘‑) f ⓖ massiness.
Massen-kurator (˘˘...) m ⓖ = verwalter; **-mord** m wholesale murder, (general) massacre; **-versammlung** f mass meeting; **-verwalter** jur. m official receiver (or administrator) of a bankrupt's estate; 2weise adv. in masses or (large) numbers; in the bulk, in a lump.
Masseur (˘ᴵʳ) [fr.] m ⓖd., ~in f ⓖ, F **Masseuse** (˘ᴵʳ˘) = Massierer(in).
Maß²-gabe (ᴵᴵ...) f ⓖ proportion; nach ~ seiner Leistung according to his work; 2gebend a. ⓖ authoritative, decisive; 2e Kreise influential (or leading) circles pl.; das kann nicht 2 für uns sein that can be no guide (or criterion) for us; **-gefäß** n vessel of standard capacity; **-geschäft** n für Herrengarderobe: tailoring business for clothing made to measure; 2halten v/n. (h.) ⓖa** to keep within bounds; weder Maß noch Ziel halten to go too far; to go to extremes; das rechte Maß halten to observe moderation, to steer the right course; 2haltend a. moderate, keeping within bounds; **-haltung** f moderation; **-holder** ♀ m = Feld-ahorn.
massieren (˘ᴵ˘) [fr.] med. I v/a. ⓖ: den Körper 2 (durch-arbeiten, kneten) to massage ..., to knead .... (reiben) to rub, im Bade: to shampoo ... — II ~ n ⓖ massage, shampoo(ing).
Massierer (˘ᴵ˘) m ⓖ, ~in f ⓖ med. (Kneter[in]) masseur f/masseuse); ⊕ rubber, im Bade: shampooer. [solid.
massig (˘˘) [Masse] a. ⓖ massy, bulky.
mäßig (ᴵ˘) [ahd.: *Maß] a. ⓖ 1. moderate, im Essen u. Trinken: frugal, bsd. im Trinken: temperate, sober, abstemious (vgl. mittel-2); 2 (adv.) genießen to enjoy in moderation. — 2. (billig) cheap; zu 2em Preise at a reasonable (or moderate) price or figure. — 3. in Zssgn: a) mit vorangehender Zahl, z.B. (ein-)2 measuring one quart; b) mit s., z.B. helden-2 like a hero, heroic.
mäßigen (ᴵ˘˘) I v/a. u. sich 2 v/refl. ⓖ 1. (sich) 2 to moderate (o.s.). — 2. (mildern) to soften (down), assuage, mitigate; (sich) 2 (in Grenzen halten) to contain (o.s.), to restrain (o.s.), to check (o.s.); (beschränken) to keep (with)in bounds (a. refl.); vermindern to lessen,

[**masten**]

to diminish (a. refl.); (langsamer m.) to slacken; ♀ gemäßigte Zone temperate zone. — II ~ n ⓖ 3. = Mäßigung.
Mäßigkeit (ᴵ˘˘) f ⓖ (s. mäßig) moderation; frugality, temperance, sobriety, abstemiousness; ⓖ reasonableness (or cheapness) of prices.
Mäßigkeits-apostel (ᴵ...) m ⓖ apostle of temperance; **-verein** m temperance-society, im Heer: blue-ribbon army; **-verein(l)er** m (total)abstainer, teetotaller.
Mäßigung (ᴵ˘˘) f ⓖ (s. mäßigen I) moderation; mitigation; restriction, check(ing); limitation.
massiv (˘ᴵ) [it.] I a. ⓖ 1. = gediegen. — 2. massive. — II **Massiv** n ⓖd. 3. geol. (Gebirgsstock) massif.
Massiv-bau (˘ᴵ‑ᴵ) m ⓖ massive structure. [ness, solidity.
Massivität (˘‑w˘ᴵ) [it.] f ⓖ massive-
Maß²-kanne (ᴵᴵ...) f ⓖ quart-can or -pot; **-krug** m quart-jug; **-lieb(chen)** [ndl. fl. Lieb] ♀ n: a) (Gänseblümchen) daisy (Bellis perennis); b) großes (Wucherblume) ox-eye daisy (Chrysanthemum Leucanthemum); 2los a. ⓖ boundless, als adv. beyond all bounds, Charakter: immoderate, reckless; **-losigkeit** f ⓖ boundlessness; Charakter: want of moderation, recklessness; **-nahme** f taking (one's) measure; **-nehmen** n ⓖ, **-nehmung** f ⓖ = nahme; **-regel** f step; (Auskunftsmittel) expedient, proviso, remedy; seine ~n treffen to take one's measures or precautions; 2regeln v/a. ⓖa*‑*‑*: a) to regulate; b) e-n Beamten 2c. to reprimand ..., to inflict disciplinary punishment on ...; **-reg(e)lung** f: a) regulation; b) reprimand, disciplinary punishment; **-stab** m: a) zum Messen kleiner Längen: rule(r), yard-measure; b) ~ beim Zeichnen 2c.: scale (auch von Karten); vergrößerter ~ enlarged scale; verjüngter ~ reduced scale; im größten (in groß-artigem) ~e on the largest (on a grand) scale; fig. einen verschiedenen ~ an etwas anlegen to apply a different standard to a th.; **-stock** ⊕ m carpenter's (foot-)rule; = **und Gewichtskunde** f knowledge of weights and measures. ✧ metrology; **-verhältnisse** n/pl. dimensions pl.; 2voll a. moderate, discreet; 2weise adv.: 2 verkaufen ... in quarts; **-werk** n, arch. carved work, tracery.
Mast¹ ⚓ (ᴵ) [ahd.: mast] m ⓖa. mast (a. aufgepflanzter Baum); vgl. Großmast; mit ~en versehen or takeln; f. kappen.
Mast² (ᴵ) [ahd.: mast] ⓖ food, von Eicheln 2c.: mast; (Fettmachen) fattening of cattle, (over-)feeding of poultry, &c.
Mast¹-band ⚓ (ᴵ...) n ⓖ mast-hoop; **-baum** ⚓ m mast; **-²darm** m.anat. great (or straight) gut, ✧ rectum; **-darmentzündung** f, path.: ✧ inflammation of the rectum, rectitis; **-darmfistel** f, path.: ✧ anal fistula, fistula recti; **-darm-spiegel** m. med.: ✧ rectoscope; **-darm-vorfall** m, path.: dropping (or bearing-down) of the rectum, ✧ prolapsus recti or ani.
masten ⚓ (˘˘) [Mast¹] v/a. ⓖ to mast; bsd. p.p. (hoch-)gemastet high-masted.

Zeichen (f. S. XVII): F familiär; P Volkssprache; ⌐ Gaunersprache; ⌐ selten; † alt (auch gestorben); * neu (auch geboren); ++ unrichtig:

[mästen] — 685 — [Matthias]

mästen¹ (⌣⌣) [Mast²] v/a., **sich ~** v/refl. u. v/n. (h.) ⓲ to fatten, to feed (well); fig. sich ~ (üppig leben) to live well; sich von der Arbeit anderer ~ to fatten (or grow fat) on the labour of others.

Masten=knecht ⌄ (⌣⌣...) m ⓺² knight; =**kran** m sheers pl.; =**macher**, =**setzer** m mast-maker; =**reich** a. ⓺⓺ abounding in masts or ships; =**stütze** f = Maststütze.

...**master** ⌄ (..."⌣) [Mast¹] m ⓺² in Zssgn, zB. Zwei=~ two-master; f. Drei=~.

Mäster (⌣⌣) m ⓶² fattener of cattle.

Mast²=futter (⌣...) n ⓺² agr. food for fattening; =**gast** ⌄ m mastman; =²**hühnchen** n fattened chicken, fat pullet.

mastig¹ ⌄ (⌣⌣) [Mast¹] a. ⓺⓺ in Zssgn, zB. hoch=~ high-masted.

mastig² (⌣⌣) [Mast²] a. ⓺⓺ fat, corpulent, (schwerfällig) heavy; tretet nicht so ~ (adv.) auf wie Elefantenkälber! (G.) do not bump upon the ground as though you were young elephants!, trip it lightly!

Mastix ⌘ (⌣⌣) [It., grch.] m ⓶⓺a. (gum-) mastic; geringer ~ mastic in sorts.

Mastix=baum ⚘ (⌣...) m ⓺² mastic-tree (Pista'cia lenti'scus); =**distel** ⚘ f m.-thistle (Carli'na gummi'fera); =**firnis** ⌘ m m.-varnish; =**zement** m mastic(-cement).

Mast²=kalb (⌣...) n ⓺² fattened calf; =¹**korb** ⌄ m (round) top (of a mast), mast-head (= Mars²); =²**los** a. ⓺⓺ mastless, dismasted; ~ machen to dismast; =**losigkeit** f dismasted state; =²**ochs**, =**ochse** m: a) fattened (bibl. stalled) ox; b) Pfig. heavy (or clumsy) fellow.

Mastodon ⌘ (⌣⌣) [grch.] n ⓺² (pl. auch =ten) geol. (fossiler Elefant) mastodon.

Mast²=schwein (⌣...) n ⓺² fat(tened) pig; Pfig. dickes ~ fat sow or hog; =¹**spur** ⌄ f mast-step or -trunk; =²**stall** m, agr. feeding- (or fattening-)stall; =¹**stange**, =**stenge** ⌄ f (main)top-mast; =**stütze** f mast-prop, outrigger; =**topp** m masthead.

Mastung, Mästung (⌣⌣) f ⓵⓺ (Fettwerden) fattening; vgl. Mast².

Mast²=vieh (⌣...) n ⓺²: a) cattle to be fattened; b) fattened cattle; =¹**wache** f lookout (man); =**wächter** m top-man; ~**wärts** adv. (naut.) aback; =**werk** n the masts (and yards) pl. of a ship; =²**zeit** f fattening-period for cattle.

Masurek (⌣⌣) [poln.] m ⓹⓺. **Masurka** (⌣⌣) [russ.] f ⓹⓺ Tanz: mazurka.

Matador (⌣⌣⌣) [span.] m ⓸d. (⓶, ⓹): a) (Stiertöter im Stiergefechte) matador; b) eminent person, F great swell, big gun, (Hauptperson) top sawyer; c) (ausgezeichneter Spieler) crack player, champion; d) (hohe Karte, Trumpf) master card, trump card.

Mate ⚘ (⌣⌣) [paraguay'isch] f ⓸⓺ Brazil tea, maté (von Ilex paraguay'nsis).

Mater ⚙ (⌣⌣) [lt.] f ⓶ typ.: a) justierte ~ matrix; b) unjustierte ~ drive.

Material (⌣⌣⌣) [lt.] n ⓶⓺ 1. (Stoff) material, substance; (Ausrüstung; ant. Persona'l) equipment, plant; ⊞ **rollendes ~** rolling-stock. — 2. ~**ien** pl. (Rohstoffe) raw material; (Arzneiware) drugs pl.; (Spezerei) spices pl., grocery (ware).

materialisieren (⌣⌣⌣⌣⌣) [fr.] v/a. ⓺⓺ (verkörpern) to materialize.

Materialismus ⌘ (⌣⌣⌣⌣) [lt.] m ⓶⓻ phls. Weltanschauung: materialism.

Materialist (⌣⌣⌣⌣) [lt.] m ⓸⓶ 1. ⓺⓺ = Materialwarenhändler. — 2. ⌘ phls. materialist.

materialistisch (⌣⌣⌣⌣⌣) [lt.] a. ⓺⓺ materialistic, relating to matter.

Material=ware(n pl.) ⓺ (⌣⌣⌣") f ⓺² groceries pl., drugs pl. (vgl. Material 2); =**waren=geschäft** n, =**waren=handlung** f grocer's business or shop, grocery-stores pl., weitS. colonial warehouse; für Arzneiwaren: drug-stores pl.; =**warenhändler** m grocer; (Arzeneihändler) (wholesale) druggist.

Materi-e (⌣⌣⌣)[mhd.: matter; *lt.] f ⓺ (Stoff) Gegenstand der Behandlung; med. Eiter; matter, subject; vgl. Material 1.

materi-ell (⌣⌣⌣⌣) [fr.] a. ⓺⓺ matérial; phls. ~e (ant. formale) Ursache material (or intrinsic) reason; ~ (adv.) gesinnt of a material (or wordly) mind, bent on (physical or sensual) enjoyment.

Mate-tee (⌣⌣⌣) m ⓺² = Mate.

Mathematik (⌣⌣⌣⌣⌣) [grch.] f ⓺ mathematics; reine (angewandte) ~ pure (applied) mathematics.

Mathematiker (⌣⌣⌣⌣⌣) m ⓶, ~**us** m ⓹ (⓺⓺) mathematician.

Mathematik=lehrer (⌣...) m ⓺² mathematical teacher or master.

mathematisch (⌣⌣⌣⌣) a. ⓺⓺ mathematical; ~**er** Satz: a) mathem. proposition; b) typ. composition of algebra; ~**e** Geographie astronomical geography.

Mathilde (⌣⌣⌣) [Mechthild] npr/f. ⓺⓺β. Mathilda, Matilda.

Matinee (⌣⌣⌣) [fr. Morgen] f ⓺⓺ thea., &c. (Frühvorstellung) matinee.

Matjes=hering f. Maatjes=hering.

Matratze (⌣⌣⌣) [mhd., lt., *ar.] f ⓺⓺ mattress, mit Sprungfedern: spring-mattress; ~**n=macher(in** f) m (⌣⌣...) ⓶² mattress-maker or -manufacturer.

Mätresse(-⌣⌣)[fr.maîtresse]f⓺⓺mistress, kept woman; ~**n=wirtschaft** (⌣...) f ⓺² reign (or influence) of mistresses.

Matrikel (⌣⌣⌣) [lt.] f ⓺⓺ (Verzeichnis der e-r Gemeinschaft Zugehörigen) register, roll, ⌘ matricula; in die ~ eintragen to (enter in the) register, to matriculate.

Matrikular=beitrag (⌣⌣⌣"⌣) m ⓺² proportionate payment, quota.

Matrize ⚙, typ., mint. (-⌣⌣) [lt.] f ⓺⓺ Schriftgießerei: matrix; Stereotypie, Galvanoplastik: mould. [stereo-flong.]

Matrizen=papier (⌣⌣⌣⌣⌣⌣)n⓶⓺Stereotypie.

Matrone (-⌣⌣) [lt. ältere Frau] f ⓺⓺ matron.

matronenhaft (-⌣⌣⌣) a. ⓺⓺ matronly.

Matrose ⌄ (⌣⌣⌣) [mhd., *fr. matelot] m ⓸⓺ (common) sailor, seaman, a. (ship's) hand, F blue jacket, jack-tar, tar; weitS. mariner; befahrener, erfahrener ~ able (or experienced) seaman. F old salt; als ~ dienen to serve as a sailor or before the mast.

Matrosen=art ⌄ (⌣⌣⌣...) f ⓺² sailor-fashion; auf ~ s.-like; =**handwerk** n seamanship, sailor's calling; =**hose** f sailor's breeches pl.; =**hut** m s.'s hat; (Südwester) southwester; =**jacke** f s.'s (pea-)jacket; =**kleider** n/pl. s.'s clothes, F slops; =**lied** n s.'s tune, mariner's song; =**schenke** f sailors' inn or pub;

=**sold** m sailor's (or seaman's) pay or wages; =**streich** m sailor's trick; =**tanz** m s.'s hornpipe; =**werber** m crimp.

Matsch¹ (⌣) [= Mansch] I m ⓺a. (breiweiche Masse) pulp, squash; (schleimiger Kot) slush, slop, (slimy) mud, mire; (Pfütze) puddle; die Kirschen sind zu ~ geworden ... are squashed (up); F es ist ein ~ zum Versinken the mire (or mud) is enough to drown one (in). — II ~ a. ⓺⓺ (breiweich) squashed, mashed.

Matsch² (⌣) [it. marcio faul] m ⓺a. Spiel: ~ machen (alles gewinnen) to sweep the board; ~ werden (verlieren) to lose heavily. [to squash, to mash.)

matschen¹ (⌣⌣) v/a. ⓺⓺ to turn into pulp,)

matschen² (⌣⌣) v/a. ⓺⓺ Spiel: to make most (or all the) tricks.

matschig (⌣⌣)a.⓺⓺pulpy;(schmierig)slushy, muddy, F squashy, messy, sloppy.

matt (⌣) [mhd.:mat(e); *perf. tot] a. ⓺⓺(D⓺) 1. meist Schachspiel: mate; e-n ~ machen oder setzen to checkmate a p.; Schach und ~ check and mate; auch s/n. ein ~ a mate. — 2. fig. v. Personen: (erschöpft) exhausted, worn (or F fagged) out, jaded, (kraftlos) feeble, enfeebled; vor Hunger ~ sein to feel faint (with hunger); ~ sein, werden to languish; schwach und ~ (as) weak as a rat. — 3. von Sachen: (kraftlos) flabby (auch vom Stile), limp; (glanzlos) without lustre, lustreless, mat, von Metallen: tarnished; (trübe) turbid; (geistlos) insipid, dull, heavy; ~e Augen dim eyes pl.; ~e (geschäftslose) Börse lifeless (or dull, flat, inactive, stagnant) market; ~es Echo feeble echo; ~e Farben subdued colours pl.; ~es oder ~ (adv.) geschliffenes Glas opaque ground glass; ~es Gold dead gold; ⚔ ~e Kugel spent ball; ~es Licht subdued light; ~e Stimme faint (or feeble) voice; ~er Witz tame (or stale, F poor) joke.

matt=äugig (⌣...) a. ⓺⓺ with dim (or lustreless) eyes, dim-eyed; ~**blau** a. of a dull blue.

Matte¹ ⚘ (⌣⌣) [mhd.: mead(ow); *mähen] f ⓺⓺ meadow(-land), poet. mead, lea; (Alpenwiese) Alpine meadow; (Weide) pasture(-land); die grünen ~n the green fields pl.

Matte² ⊖ ⓺ (⌣⌣) [ahd.: mat; *lt.] f ⓺⓺ (Flechtwerk) mat(ting), aus Stroh: straw-mat, aus Kokosnuß: cocoanut mat(ting); ~ vor der Tür door-mat.

Matten=flechter(in f) m (⌣...) ⓶ mat-maker; straw-plaiter; =**händler(in** f) m dealer in mats; =**macher(in)** = ~**flechter(in)**; =**werk** n matwork.

matt=grün (⌣...) a. ⓺⓺ of a dull green.

Matthäus (⌣⌣⌣) [grch., *hebr.] npr/m. ⓺⓺γ. (a. Bn.) Matthew; Evange'lium Matthä'i Gospel according to St. Matthew; f. letzt 8.

Matt=heit (⌣...) f ⓸⓺ (f. matt 3) lassitude; flabbiness;lackoflustre;dulness;dimness, ⓺ lifelessness, deadness, flatness of prices, stagnancy of the market.

matt=herzig (⌣⌣⌣) a. ⓺⓺ faint-hearted; (feig) cowardly; ~**keit** (⌣⌣⌣) f ⓸⓺ faint-heartedness;cowardliness,cowardice.

Matthias (⌣⌣⌣) [hebr.] npr/m. ⓺⓺γ. (Bn.) Matthew, bisw. a. Matthias.

Mattigkeit (⌣‐) f ⑤ (s. matt 2) exhaustion; feebleness; faintness; languor.
Matt=setzen (⌣...) n ㉓ Schachspiel: checkmating; ₂**vergoldet** ⊙ a. ⑥ dead-gilt; ₂**weiß** a. dull white, whitish.
Maturitäts=examen (‐‐⌣ᵘ...)[lt. Reife=]n ㉒ auf deutschen höheren Schulen: leaving-examination; vgl. Abiturientenexamen (die entsprechende englische Prüfung für den Grad eines „Bachelor of Arts" wird auf der Universität abgelegt); ₂**zeugnis** n certificate (or diploma) of maturity granted to a student on passing the final examination of a German first-class secondary school.
Matz (⌣) m ⑪Ⓐ. F npr. ⑤ₐ. (Bn.) — Matthias; fig. (einfältiger Schwätzer) chatterbox, F jabberer, babbler; (Dummkopf) simpleton, F duffer, mug, juggins; s. Hans 2 u. Piepmatz.
Mätzchen (⌣) n ⑭ (dim.: Matz) dunce, young fool or simpleton, F little silly (a. losend); ~ machen to play the fool.
Matze(n m ㉓) f ⑥ (⌣) [nhd., *hebr.] unleavened (or Passover) bread.
mauen (⌣) [mhd.] = miauen.
Mauer ⊙ (⌣) [ahd.; *lt. *mūrus m*] f ⑥ arch. wall, aus Backsteinen: brick w., aus Stein: stone w., ohne Fenster: dead w.; s. chinesisch I; mit ~n umgeben to wall in; innerhalb (außerhalb) der ~n e-r St. gelegen intramural (extramural); fig. fest wie eine ~ (as) firm as a rock.
Mauer=abdeckung (⌣...) f ⑫ coping; ₂**absatz** m offset; ₂**ähnlich** a. ⑥ mural; ₂**anker** m wall-clamp; ₂**anschlag** m mural advertisement, bill posted on a wall; poster; ₂**arbeit** f building (of) walls; brick-(layer's) work; masonry; ₂**biene** f, ent. mason-bee (O'smia); ₂**blümchen** F n, co. auf Bällen: wall-flower; ₂**brecher** ⚔ m Alt.: battering-ram; ₂**bruch** ⚔ m breach (in a wall); ₂**dicke** f thickness of a wall; ₂**ecke** f: (☗) quoin, coin.
Mauerei (‐⌣⌣) [mauern] f ⑥ = Maurerei.
Mauer=eidechse (⌣...) f ⑫ zo. wall-lizard (Lace'rta mura'lis); ₂**feld** n pane of a wall; ₂**fest** a. ⑥ (as) firm as a rock, like a solid wall; ₂**förmig** a. ⚚ muriform; ₂**gerste** ⚘ f wall-barley (Ho'rdeum muri'num); ₂**grund**(=masse f) m foundation of a wall; ₂**kalk** m mortar; ₂**kappe** f coping; ₂**kelle** f (bricklayer's) trowel; ₂**kitt** m w.-cement; ₂**klammer** f = ₂anker; ₂**krone** f Alt.: ⚚ mural crown; ₂**lattich** ⚘ m w.-lettuce (Lactu'ca mura'lis); ₂**loch** n, ₂**lücke** f hole, gap, opening in a w.; ₂**meister** m = Maurermeister.
mauern (⌣) v/n. (h.) u. v/a. ⑥ₐ. 1. arch. to build (or construct) walls; to wall in; to build in stone or in brick. — 2. beim Kartenspiel: not to risk anything.
Mauer=nische (⌣...) f ⑫ niche (in a wall); ₂**öffnung** f = ₂loch; ₂**pfeffer** ⚘ m stonecrop (Sedum), scharfer ~ wall-pepper (S. acre); ₂**polier** m bricklayer's foreman; ₂**raute** ⚘ f tentwort, wall-rue (Asple'nium ruta mura'ria); ₂**ritze** f chink (or crevice) in a wall; ₂**salpeter** m, chm. w.-saltpetre; ₂**schwalbe** f, orn. black martin, swift (Cy'pselus apus); ₂**stein** m (Ziegel) brick; ₂**bricklaying**.
Mauerung (‐⌣⌣) f ⑥ building walls,

Mauer=verband (⌣...) m ㉒ bond; ₂**verkleidung** f lining of a wall; ⚔ frt. revetment; ₂**werk** n stone- (or brick-)work, masonry, vgl. ₂arbeit; ₂**zinne** ⚔ f, frt. battlement (of a wall), pinnacle. — Vgl. a. Maurer=...
Maute (⌣) [(mhd.) nbd.] f ⑥ 1. vet. (ausschlag-artige Fußkrankheit) malanders pl. — 2. (Versteck) hiding-place.
Maul¹ (⌣) [ahd.] n ⑨c. 1. [(großer Mund) (large) mouth; (Schnauze) snout, muzzle, co. v. Menschen: F chops pl., jaw, P potato-trap; sich et. am ~e abbrechen to stint o.s. of a th.; s. aufsperren 1; das ~ nicht auftun not to open one's lips; einem übers ~ fahren, e-m eins aufs ~ geben: a) to cut a p. short; to talk sharply to a p.; b) fig. (ihn Lügen strafen) to give a p. the lie; er ist nicht aufs ~ gefallen he is never at a loss for a word or an answer, he is not tongue-tied; s. Fleck 1 am Schluß; (immer) das große ~ haben to talk everybody down, F to lay down the law; ein böses (oder loses) ~ haben to have a loose (or wicked, malicious, flippant) tongue; ein großes ~ haben to talk big, to boast and brag; das ~ halten to hold one's tongue; halt's ~! F shut up!, hold your gab!, P stash it!; das ~ hängen lassen to be down in the mouth; to pout (one's lips), to sulk; in der Leute Mäuler kommen to become the talk of the town; ein schiefes ~ machen = maulen; das ~ gar zu voll nehmen to talk very big; e-m nach dem ~ reden to chime in with a p.; s. Brei 2 fig.; sich selbst aufs ~ schlagen to contradict o.s.; das ~ steht ihr keinen Augenblick still her tongue is never at rest or goes nineteen to the dozen, she has an everlasting clack (with her); einem das ~ stopfen to stop a p.'s talk or F gab; sich (dat.) das ~ verbrennen to speak (out) too freely; das ~ wässert ihm danach it makes his mouth water; Sprichw. mancher meint, die Tauben werden ihm gebraten ins ~ fliegen many a one thinks that he is living in a fools' paradise. — 2. mit a. (Person), ⑳ die bösen Mäuler der Stadt the scandalmongers (or gossips) of the town.
Maul²... (⌣...) s. Maulbeerbaum 2c.
Maul³... (⌣...) s. Maulesel 2c.
Maul⁴... (⌣...) s. Maulwurf.
Maul¹=affe (⌣...) [(P) Maul offen] F m ⑫ one who stands gaping about, F Jackanapes, booby; ~n feil=haben oder =halten, a. **₂affen** v/n. (h.) ⑥ *.* to stand gaping about, to lounge (or F hang-slang) about; ₂**afferei** f lazy life; ²**beer**(₌**baum**) ⚘ [ahd.; *lt. mor(um) u. Beere] m mulberry-tree (Morus); ₌**baum=pflanzung** f mulberry plantation; ₂**beere** f ⚘: a) (Frucht) mulberry; b) (Baum) = ₂beer(=baum).
Mäuschen (⌣) n ⑭ (dim. von Maul) 1. little mouth; ein ~ machen to point (or pout) one's lips, to pucker (up) one's mouth or lips; vgl. maulen. — 2. F (Kuß) kiss.
Maul¹=christ F (⌣...) m ⑫ professing Christian; ₌**diarrhöe** F f, co. ceaseless

chatter(ing); die ~ haben to have an intolerable clack or gab; ₂**drescher** F m great (or inveterate) talker.
maulen (⌣) v/n. (h.) ⑬ to pout (one's lips), F to make a mouth, P to pull a long mug; (schmollen) to sulk, to be sulky or in the sulks.
Maul³=esel(in f) m (⌣...) ⑫ [ahd.: mule; *lt. mūlus: a) zo. (Bastard von Pferdehengst und Eselin) mule (f she-mule), genauer: hinny (Equus hinnus); wie ein ₌esel mulish; b) burschikos: freshman not yet entered in the university-register; ₌**esel=treiber**, ₌**wärter** m mule-driver, muleteer; ₂¹**faul** F a. ⑥ too lazy to speak, slow of speech; taciturn; ₂**fäule** f, vet. der Pferde flaps pl.; ₌**fertigkeit** f loquacity; ₌**hänger**(in f) m F sulky_ (or moody, moping) person; ₌**hängerei** f sulking, sulks ⑫_, moping; ₌**held** P m inveterate (F everlasting) talker; (Prahler) braggart, big talker, F braggadocio; ₌**heldentum** P n (boasting and bragging, big talk.
...**mäulig**(...⌣) ₌ⓑ.hart²hard-mouthed.
Maul¹=korb (⌣...) m ⑫ für Tiere: muzzle; mit e-m ~e versehen to (provide with a) muzzle; ₂³**pfad** m path for mules; ₌¹**schelle** [Maul¹, schallen] f slap in the face, box on the ear, F chop(s pl.) (= Ohrfeige); ₌**schell**(**ier**)**en** v/a. ⑥ *.* to box a p.'s ears, to slap a p.'s face; ₌**seuche** f, vet. flaps pl.; ₌**sperre** f, path. lock-jaw, ⚚ trismus; ₌**spitzen** F n: da hilft kein ~ (es muß gepfiffen sein), etwa: there is no (such) getting (or backing) out of it, you are in for it; ₌**stück** ⊙ n des Gebisses: mouthpiece; ₌**tasche** F f: a) = ₌schelle; b) large-mouthed person; ₌³**tier** n, zo. (Bastard von Eselhengst und Pferdestute) mule (Equus mulus); ₂¹**tot** F a. ⑥ reduced to silence; F mum; e-n ~ machen to silence a p.; ₌**trommel** ♪ f jew's harp; ₌ **und Klauenseuche** f foot-and-mouth disease; ₌**voll** n mouthful; ₌**werk** F n: ein gutes ~ haben to have the gift of the gab.
Maul⁴=wurf (⌣...) [mhd. (P) mūu.(„Erd=") (auf)werfer] m ⑨c. zo. mole(warp), provv. mouldwarp (Talpa); blind wie ein ~ (as) blind as a bat; **Maulwurfs=falle** (⌣...) f ⑫ mole-trap; ₌**fang**, ₌**fänger** m mole-catching, -catcher; ₌**fell** n mole-skin; ₌**grille** f, zo. mole-cricket (Gryllota'lpa vulga'ris); ₌**haufen**, ₌**hügel** m molehill; ₌**loch** n mole-hole; ₌**maus** f, zo. mole-rat (Spalax typhlus).
Maure (⌣) [lt., *phön.: Mohr] m ⑥, **Maurin** f ⑥ Moor(ish woman f); bisw. auch: Moresco.
Maurer(⌣)[mauern] m ⑫ 1. brick-layer, brick-mason, mason; weiß. builder; (Gipser) plasterer. — 2. = Freimaurer.
Maurer=arbeit ⊙ (⌣⌣,⌣) f ⑫ brick-laying, brick(layer's) work; F brick-and-mortar (work).
Maurerei (‐⌣⌣) f ⑥ 1. bricklayery (or mason's, weiß. building-)trade. — 2. = Freimaurerei.
Maurer=gesell(**e**) (⌣⌣...) m ⑫ journeyman mason; ₌**handwerk** n bricklayer's (or builder's, building-)trade.
maurerisch (⌣⌣) a. ⑥ = frei².

Signs (see page XVII): F familiar; P vulgar; 🗡 flash; ⚊ rare; † obsolete (died); * new word (born); ⁓ incorrect; ♪ music.

Maurer=kelle (⁻ᵘ⌣...) f ⚙ bricklayer's trowel; =**kunst** f masonry; =**meister** m master mason or builder; =**pinsel** m mason's brush; =**polier** = Mauerpolier; =**zunft** f masons' guild, company of masons. [Mt.: Mauritania.

Mauretani=en ⚲ (⌣⌣(⌣)⌣) npr/n. ᴅα.

maurisch (⌣⌣) a. ⚙ Moorish; *arch.* Der Baustil Moorish (or Moresque) style of architecture; Der Bogen Moorish (or horseshoe) arch.

Maus (⌣) (ahd.: mouse: lt. *mūs*: grch. *mys*) f ⚙ 1. *zo.* mouse (*Mus*); die Mäuse pfeifen oder quieken the mice squeak. — 2. *fig.* f. Mann 2 gegen Schluß und beißen I am Schluß; er hat Mäuse (Grillen) im Kopfe he is a maggoty fellow, he is full of whims and fancies; sie leben wie Mäuse in der Speckseite they live like fighting-cocks; das ist den Mäusen gepfiffen (nutzlos) that's a waste of breath or time. — 3. Sprichw. f. Katze 3; wenn die ~ satt ist, schmeckt das Mehl bitter, *etwa*: it's not easy to tempt a full stomach; mit Speck fängt man Mäuse good bait catches fine fish. — 4. tosend = Mäuschen 2. — 5. *anat.* thick part of the thumb, ⚕ thenar (muscle).

maus=artig (⌣⌣⌣) a. ⚙ like a mouse, mouse-shaped, ⚕ murine, muriform.

Mauschel (⌣⌣) [Moses] m ⚙ *contp.* (Jude) (low-class) Jew, P mouchey, Ikey; ~**ei** (⌣⌣⌣) f ⚙ Jewish speech or bargaining; **2n** (⌣⌣) v/n. (h.) ⚙ a. to speak (or haggle) like a Jew.

Mäuschen (⌣⌣) n ⚙ (*dim.* von Maus) 1. little mouse, F mousie. — 2. F tosend: mein ~! little duckie or darling!, my love!, my pet!

mäuschen=still (⌣⌣⌣) a. ⚙ (as) quiet as a mouse; es war 2 there was a dead silence, one might have heard a pin drop; sich 2 (adv.) verhalten to keep very quiet, F to be mum.

Mause (⌣) [ahd., *lt.] f ⚙ = Mauser².

mäuse=artig (⌣⌣...) a. ⚙ *zo.* like mice, ⚕ murine; =**bussard** m ⚙ *orn.* common buzzard (*Bu'teo vulga'ris*); =**dorn** § m butcher's-broom (*Ruscus acula'tus*); =**dreck** m mice-dung or -dirt.

Mause=, Mäuse=falle (⌣⌣...) f ⚙ mouse-trap; ~**n=händler** m mouse-trap dealer.

Mäuse=fang (⌣⌣...) m ⚙ catching mice; von Katzen: mousing; =**fänger** (**in** f) m mouse-catcher, *vgl.* Mausekatze.

Mäuse=farbe (⌣⌣...) f ⚙ mouse-colour, dun; =**farben** a. ⚙ m.-coloured, dun.

Mäuse=fraß (⌣⌣...) m ⚙ things *pl.* eaten or nibbled by mice; =**gift** n ratsbane.

mause=grau (⌣⌣...) a. ⚙ drab; =**kätzchen** F n ⚙ tosend: mein ~! my little pet!; =**katze** f good mouser; =**loch** n, **Mäuse=loch** n mouse-hole; *fig.* ins ~ kriechen (Angstl.) F to be shivering in one's shoes.

mausen¹ (⌣⌣) [mhd.; *Maus] ⚙ I v/n. 1. (h.) von Tieren, *bfb.* Katzen: to catch mice. — 2. (h. u. fn) (heimlich schleichen) to sneak about. — II v/a. 3. F (entwenden) to pilfer, to filch, P to nick, prig, pinch; das geht wie gemaust that goes like steam. — III ~ n ⚙ 4. = Mauserei; aufs ~ ausgehen to go pilfering, P to be on the make; Sprichw. f. Katze 3.

mausen² (⌣⌣) ⚙ = mausern.

Mäuse=nest (⌣⌣...) n ⚙ mouse-nest; nest of mice; =**not** f plague of mice; =**ohr** n: a) ear of a mouse; b) ⚲ a. =**öhrchen** mouse-ear scorpion-grass (*Myoso'tis palu'stris*).

Mauser¹ (⌣⌣) [mausen (⌣)] m ⚙, ~**in** f ⚙ pilferer, P prig(ger), (area-)sneak.

Mauser² (⌣⌣) [ahd. f. mausern] f ⚙ der Vögel &c.: moult(ing-season); in der ~ sein to be moulting.

Mauserei (⌣⌣⌣) [mausen¹ II] f ⚙ pilfering, filching, P prigging.

Mauser³=gewehr ⚔ (⌣⌣⌣⌣) [Wilh. Mauser, 1834–82] n ⚙ Mauser rifle.

mausern (⌣⌣) [ahd.: mo(u)lt; *lt. *mūtāre* wechseln] v/n. (h.) u. sich 2 v/refl. ⚙ a. to moult, to mew; F *fig.* von Personen: to start a new life, to turn over a new leaf.

Mauser²=zeit (⌣⌣⌣) f ⚙ moulting-time.

Mause=schwanz (⌣⌣) m ⚙: a) tail of a mouse; b) F *fig.* thin plait of hair.

mäuse=still (⌣⌣⌣) a. ⚙ = mäuschenstill.

mause=tot (⌣⌣⌣) a. ⚙ stone-dead, (as) dead as mutton, *ehm. auch*: (as) dead as a door-nail. [little tooth.

Mäuse=zahn (⌣⌣⌣) m ⚙, =**zähnchen** n]

maus=farbig (⌣⌣⌣) a. ⚙ = mausefarben.

mausig¹ (⌣⌣) [Maus] a. ⚙ smelling of mice, F (smelling) mousy.

mausig² (⌣⌣) [mausern] a. ⚙ F *fig.*: sich 2 m. (sich zu viel herausnehmen) to take (great) liberties, to assume an air of importance; er soll sich nicht 2 machen he must not put on airs, he should keep his station or his place.

Mäusle(in) (⌣⌣, ⌣⌣) n ⚙ = Mäuschen.

Maus=loch (⌣⌣) n ⚙ = Mauseloch.

Mausole=um (⌣⌣⌣) [König Mauso'lus von Karien, dem seine Gemahlin Artemi'sia in Halikarnassus 351 v. Chr. ein berühmtes Grabbenkmal erbaute] n ⚙ mausoleum.

maus=tot (⌣⌣⌣) a ⚙ = mausetot.

Maut *südd.* ⚙ (⌣) [ahd. Zoll] f ⚙ 1. duty, (Akzise) excise, (Wegegeld) toll. — 2. = Maut=amt.

Maut=amt ⚙ (⌣⌣...) *südd.* n ⚙ (Zoll=amt) custom-house; =**aufseher, =beamte(r)** m custom-house officer; ⚙**frei** a. ⚙ free of duty. [officer or official.

Mautner *subb.* ⚙ (⌣⌣) m ⚙ custom-house]

Max (⌣) [Max(imilian)] npr/m. ⚙ ᴅγ. (Bn.) Maximilian, Max. [masternote.

Maxima ♪ (⌣⌣⌣) [It.] f ⚙ (Leitnote)]

Maximal=betrag (⌣⌣⌣⌣...) m ⚙ maximum, highest amount, =**limit, =geschwindigkeit** f greatest (or maximum) velocity or speed; =**preis** ⚙ m maximum (or highest) price.

Maxime (⌣⌣⌣) [fr.] f ⚙ (Grundsatz) maxim.

Maximilian (⌣⌣(⌣)⌣) [lt.] npr/m. ⚙ ᴅα. (a. Bn.) Maximilian.

Maximum (⌣⌣⌣) [lt.] n ⚙ (Höchstbetrag); *ant.* Mi'nimum) maximum (amount); ~**und=Minimum=thermometer** n (m) ⚙ *phys.* maximum-and-minimum (or self-registering) thermometer.

Mayonnaise (⌣⌣ˈnäˑ⌣) [fr. (*Mahon, St.)] f ⚙ Kochkunst: mayon(n)aise.

Mazedoni=en (⌣⌣⌣(⌣)⌣) [grch.] npr/n. ᴅα. (Land nördl. v. Griechenland) Macedonia; **Mazedoni=er**(**in** f ⚙) m ⚙, **mazedonisch** a. ⚙ Macedonian.

Mäzen (⌣ˈtsɛ̄n) [Freund d. Augustus, † 8 v. Chr.] m ⚙d. *Alt.* Mæcenas (a. *fig.* Beschützer der Künste); ~**atentum** (⌣⌣⌣ˈ⌣⌣) n ⚙d. patronage of arts and letters; Lisch (⌣⌣⌣) a. ⚙ of Mæcenas.

mazerieren ⚗ (⌣⌣⌣⌣) [It.] v/a. ⚙ *chm.* (durch Flüssigkeit ausziehen) to macerate.

M. d. R. *abbr.* = Mitglied des Reichstags member of the Reichstag. [erachten II.

m. E. *abbr.* = meines Erachtens, f. bs unter]

Mechanik (⌣⌣⌣⌣) [grch.] f ⚙: a) *phys.*, &c. (Bewegungs- u. Gleichgewichts-lehre) mechanics; b) (a. ⚙) (Triebwerk) mechanism, (Vorrichtung) contrivance; ~**er** ⚙ (⌣⌣⌣⌣) m ⚙, ~**us** (⌣ˈ⌣⌣⌣) m ⚙ mechanician, instrument-maker; (Optikus) optician; **mechanisch** a. ⚙: a) (auf Mechanik gegründet), b) (handwerks-, maschinen-mäßig): mechanical, automatic; *phys.* Des Wärme-äquivalent equivalent of heat in units of work; *adv.* mechanically, automatically, like clock-work; et. 2 hersagen F to say a th. off mechanically or by rote;

Mechanismus (⌣⌣ˈ⌣⌣) m ⚙ mechanism, einer Uhr &c. auch: works *pl.*

Mecheln ⚲ (⌣⌣) npr/n. ⚙ α. (belgische Fabrikstadt) Mechlin, Malines.

meckern (⌣⌣) [nhd. *lautm.*] v/n. (h.) ⚙a. von der Ziege: to bleat; von Personen: to speak (or sing) with a thin and shaky (or with a tremulous) voice.

Meckerstimme (⌣⌣...) f ⚙ feeble and tremulous voice; =**ton** m, *med.* bei Brustfell=entzündung ⚙ ægophony.

Medaille (⌣ˈdäˑl-jˑ⌣) [nhd.; *fr.] f ⚙ medal; die Kehrseite der ~, *oft*: the dark side of the question or picture; Inhaber e-r goldenen (silbernen, bronzenen) ~ gold (silver, bronze) medallist; ~**n=kenner, =sammler** m medallist; ~**n=stecher** m (a. **Medailleur** (⌣ˈdäl-jōˑr) m ⚙) engraver of medals.

Medaillon (⌣ˈdäl-jɑ̃ˈ) [fr.] n ⚙ medallion, (Kapsel für ein Bildchen &c.) locket.

Mede(i)a—(⌣⌣⌣) [grch.] npr/f.⚙. ᴅα.*myth.* (Gemahlin des Jason, Zauberin) Medea.

Meder (⌣⌣) m ⚙ *Alt.*: Mede; ~**reich** (⌣⌣⌣) n ⚙ Median kingdom.

Media ⚕ (⌣⌣⌣) [It. *mēˑdia*] f (*sg. inv.*, *pl.* ...iä) *gr.* Laut b, d, g) media (1 letter).

medial (⌣⌣⌣) [Medium 2] a. ⚙ *grch. gr.* of (or in) the middle voice. [*papier.*

Median ⚙ (⌣(⌣)⌣) [lt.] n ⚙d. = Median=]

Median=ader (⌣ˈ(⌣)⌣ˈ...) f ⚙ *ent.* von Schmetterlingsflügeln: ⚕ median vein; =**fo'lio, =okta'v** ⚙ n (Papierformat) demi-folio, -octavo; =**papier** ⚙ n (engl. Druckpapier: 18 × 28 inches, Schreibpapier: 17½ × 22 inches) medium (paper).

Mediante (⌣⌣⌣⌣) ♪ [It.] f ⚙ mediant.

Median=vene f ⚙ *anat.* ⚕ median vein.

Mediat=gebiet (⌣⌣⌣⌣⌣) n ⚙ (nicht reichs-unmittelbares Land) mediate territory.

mediatisier=en (⌣⌣⌣(⌣)⌣⌣) [It.] I v/a. ⚙ *pol.* to mediatize. — II ~ n ⚙ u. **M./ung** f ⚙ mediatization.

mediäval (⌣⌣⌣ᵐ⌣) [It.] a. ⚙ (mittelalterlich) medieval; ~(=**schrift**) f, *typ.* old style.

Medice=er (⌣⌣⌣⌣⌣) m ⚙, *bisw. auch:* ~**in** f ⚙ Medicean, prince of the house of (the) Medici; ~**e Venus** Venus dei Medici.

Medi=en¹ ⚲ (⌣(⌣)⌣) npr/n. ⚙α. *Alt.* (*asia*tische Landschaft) Media.

Medi=en² (⌣(⌣)⌣) *pl.* von Medium.

[Medikament] — 688 — [mehr]

Medikament (⏑‒⏑‒)[lt.] n ①c. (Heilmittel) medicine, medical remedy, drug, physic, bisw. auch: medicament.
Medikaster (⏑⏑‒⏑)[mlt.] m②contp. quack.
Medikus (‒⏑⏑) [lt.] m ⑤⑧ medical man or practitioner, physician.
Medina-wurm (‒‒⏑‒⏑) m ⑥② Guinea-worm (*Filaria medinensis*).
medisch (‒⏑) [Me'dien¹] a. ⑥⑥ Median.
meditieren (⏑⏑‒⏑) [lt.] v/a. ⑨③ (nachsinnen) to meditate.
Medium (‒⏑(⏑)‒) [lt.] n ② 1. *phys.*, Spiritismus ꝛc.: (Mitte und vermittelnde Person) medium. — 2. *grch. gr.* middle-voice.
Medizin (⏑⏑‒) [lt. *medicīnă*] f ⑥⑥ (Heilkunde, -mittel) medicine; ~ einnehmen to take medicine or physic, to physic o.s.; ~ studieren to study medicine, von Studenten: to walk the hospital (as a medical student); Doktor der ~ doctor of medicine (*abbr.* M. D.).
Medizinal-beamte(r) (⏑⏑‒‒⏑‒) m ⑥② medical officer; =gewicht n apothecaries' weight; =kollegium n Board of Health; =kräuter *n/pl.* medicinal herbs *pl.*; =rat m medical councillor or adviser, als Titel: officer of health; =rechtswissenschaft f medical jurisprudence; =verordnung f sanitary regulation or by-law; =waren *f pl.* (medicinal) drugs *pl.*; =wesen n medical affairs *pl.*
Mediziner (⏑⏑‒⏑) [lt.] m ⑥② 1. medical student. — 2. (Arzt) medical man.
Medizin-glas (⏑⏑‒‒⏑) n ⑥② phial; (Arzneiflasche) medicine-bottle.
medizinieren (⏑⏑‒‒⏑) [lt.] v/n. (h.) ⑨③ to take medicine or physic.
medizinisch (⏑⏑‒⏑) [lt.] a. ⑥⑥ (ärztlich) medical, (arzneilich) medicinal, (heilend) sanitary, curative; s. Fakultät.
Medizin-karren (⏑⏑‒‒⏑) m ⑥②, =wagen ⅄ m ambulance(-wagon) with drugs and medicines; =mann m (Ärzt. Wahrsager, Zauberer der Indianer) medicine-man.
Medusa (⏑‒⏑) [grch.] npr/f. ⑲ ⑤⑥ *myth.* (eine der Gorgonen) Medusa.
Meduse ⚭ (⏑‒⏑) [grch.] f ⑥⑥ *zo.* (Schirmqualle) jellyfish, ⚭ hydrozoon (*Medusa*); Schwimmglocke e-r ~ medusa-bell.
medusen-artig (⏑‒⏑‒⏑), **medusenhaft** (⏑‒⏑‒) a. ⑥⑥ gorgonian, adv. like Medusa; *zo.*: ⚭ medusan, medusoid.
Medusen-haupt (⏑‒⏑‒⏑) n ② *myth.* (dessen Anblick versteinerte) head of Medusa, Gorgon's head; *vgl.* Gorgonenhaupt.
Meer (‒; *Hom.* mehr) [ahd.: mere: lt. *mărĕ*] n ⓐc. (*ant.* Land) sea, (Welt-) ⓛ ocean, F the briny; das offene ~ the offing, the main, the high seas *pl.*; das tiefe ~ the deep (sea); am (im) ~e befindlich maritime (marine); auf dem Meere (out) at sea, on the main; jenseits des ~s, über dem ~e (befindlich) transmarine, over-sea.
Meer-aal (‒‒) m ⑥② *ichth.* conger(-eel) (*Conger vulgaris*); =anwohner m inhabitant of a seaside town, dweller on the sea-shore; ²artig a. sealike, marine; =äsche f, *ichth.* grey mullet (*Mugil cephalus*); =barbe f, *ichth.* surmullet (*Mullus*); =beherrscher(in f) m ruler of the sea or the main or the waves; =beschreibung f: ⚭ hydro-

graphy; =bewohner m: a) inhabitant of the sea; b) = =tier; =bohne f sea-bean (*Entada scandens*); =busen m bay, gulf; =eichel f, *zo.*: ⚭ balanid (*Balanus*); =enge f strait(s *pl.*), narrow sea or channel; =engel m, *ichth.* angel-fish (*Squatina angelus*).
Meeres-arm (‒‒⏑) m ⑥② arm (or branch, inlet) of the sea; =boden m = =grund; =brandung f surf (of the sea), breakers *pl.*; =bucht f bay, bight; =flut f: a) sea-waves *pl.*; b) high tide or water; =grund m sea-bottom, bottom of the sea; =küste f sea-coast, shore; *vgl.* =strand; =spiegel m surface (or level) of the sea, sea-level; =stille ↓ f calm (at) sea, calmness of the sea; =strand m beach, sea-border; *vgl.* =küste; =strömung f ocean-current, oceanic current, current of the sea; =ufer n = =strand; =welle, =woge f sea- (or ocean-)wave, hohe: billow.
Meer-fahrt (‒‒) f ⑥② kürzere: sea-trip, cruise, längere: (sea-)voyage; (Überfahrt) passage; =farbe a. ⑥⑥ sea-colour or -green; ²farben a. ⑥⑥ sea-green; =fenchel f m samphire, crest-marine, sea-fennel (*Crithmum maritimum*); =frau f, =fräulein n mermaid, siren; =gewächs n marine plant or growth; =gott m, =gottheit f sea-god, marine deity, *myth.* Neptune; =göttin f sea-goddess; =gras f n sea-grass (*Zostera marina*); ²grün a. sea-green; =grundel m, *ichth.* goby, sea-gudgeon (*Gobius*); =katze [(P) aus indisch *marcati*] f: a) *zo.* (Affe) long-tailed monkey (*Cercopithecus*); b) *fig.* (häßliche Person) monkey-face(d person); =kohl f m sea-kale or -cabbage (*Crambe maritima*); =lattich f m sea-lettuce (*Ulva lactuca*); =leuchten n phosphorescence (of the sea); =mädchen n mermaid; =nebel m sea-fog; =nessel f, *zo.* = Qualle; =nymphe f. *myth.* Nereid; =ohr n. *zo.* (Muschel) (common) sea-ear (*Haliotis*); =rettich f [ahd. P st. Mähr(e)=] m horse-radish (*Cochlearia Armoracia*); =salz n sea-salt; =sand m sea-sand; =schaum m: a) sea-froth, foam; b) *min.* f meerschaum; =schaumpfeife f meerschaum (pipe); =schaumspitze f meerschaum cigar-holder; =schwein n. *zo.* porpoise, sea-hog (*Phocaena*); =schweinchen n, *zo.* guinea-pig (*Cavia cobaya*); =senf f m sea-rocket (*Cakile maritima*); =spinne f, *zo.* sea-spider, king-crab (*Maia squinado*); =strands-winde f f sea-withwind or -bells *pl.* (*Convolvulus soldanella*); =strom m sea-current; =strudel m (marine) whirlpool or eddy; =tier n marine animal; ²umflossen, ²umschlungen a. sea-girt, encircled (or surrounded by the sea); =ungeheuer n sea-monster; =wasser n sea-water; =weibchen n, *myth.* = =frau; =wunder n wonder(ful growth) of the sea; *fig.* (Staunen erregendes) prodigy, marvellous occurrence; ²zwiebel f (echte) squill, sea-onion (*Scilla maritima*).
Meffert F (⏑‒) npr/m. ⑳ α. (ein Beliebiger, Namenloser) Mr. What's-his-name.
Megafarad ⚭ (⏑⏑‒) n ⑥c. *elect.* (1 Million Farad) megafarad (*ant.* Mikrofarad).

Megäre (⏑‒⏑) [grch.] f ⑥⑥ 1. *myth.* Megæra, Fury. — 2. *fig.* (böses Weib) fury, dragon, termagant, vixen.
megarisch (⏑‒⏑) [Megara] a. ⑥⑥ Alt.: Megarian; ²e Schule Megaric school.
Megatherion ⚭ (⏑⏑‒(⏑)‒) [grch.] n ② (fossiles Riesenfaultier) megathere.
Meg-ohm (‒‒) [grch.-dtsch.] n ⑥. (a. *inv.*) *elect.* (1 Million Ohm; s. Ohm³) megohm.
Mehl (‒) [ahd.: meal¹; *mahlen] n ⓐc. flour, gröberes: meal; mit ~ bestreuen to strew (or sprinkle) with flour, to flour (over); (et. Staub-artiges) dust, powder(ed substance).
mehl-arm (‒‒) a. ⑥⑥ yielding little flour; ²artig a. like flour, farinaceous; =baum ⊙ a. ⑥⑥ Mühle: meal-bench; =beer-baum f m beam-tree (*Pirus* oder *Sorbus Aria*); =beere f: a) = =beerbaum; b) (Frucht vom Weißdorn) haw; =beutel m: a) flour-bag; ⊙ f Müllerei: bolter, sifter; =börse ⊛ f flour-exchange; =brei m pap (or paste) made of flour; =faß n flour-barrel, meal-tub; ²haltig a. containing flour, mealy, farinaceous; =handel ⊛ m flour-trade; =händler m flour-merchant or -dealer, corn-chandler; a. mealman, mealmonger.
mehlicht, mehlig (‒⏑) a. ⑥⑥ floury, flour-like, farinaceous; mealy, meal-like.
Mehl-käfer (‒‒) m ent. meal-beetle (*Tenebrio molitor*); =kasten m flour- (or meal-)chest; *vgl.* =faß; =kleister f m paste; =kloß m Kocht.: flour-ball, plain dumpling; =mühle ⊙ f flour-mill; ²reich a. ⑥⑥ floury; *vgl.* ²haltig; =sack m: a) flour-bag; F *fig.* (dicker, plumper Mensch) heavy (F lumpy) person; a. F tub; =sieb n flour-sieve; =speise f allg. farinaceous food; engS. (süße Speise nach Braten) pudding, sweets *pl.*, pastry; =suppe f soup made of flour; F *fig.* er sieht aus wie (eine) ~ he looks (like) a milksop; =tau m f. Meltau; =teig m dough; =wurm m, ent. meal-worm; =zucker m powdered sugar; =zünsler m, ent. meal-moth (*Asopia farinalis*).
mehr (‒; *Hom.* Meer) [ahd.: more] *comp.* von viel. **I** *adv.* (*ant.* minder) 1. more; ² als ich sagen kann more than I can say; ² Freunde als Feinde more friends than enemies *pl.*; ich habe zwei ² erhalten als Sie I received two more than you; ² groß als klein rather tall than short; ² verdrießlich als zornig more vexed than angry; je ² man ihm gibt, desto ² verlangt er the more one gives him the more he asks (for); er ist ² Geschäftsmann als Politiker he is more of a business-man than (of a) politician; ² und ² more and more; vor Zahlwörtern: ² als (über) zwanzig Mark more than twenty shillings; ² als ein Dutzend upwards of a dozen; vier Augen sehen ² als zwei four eyes see more than two; sie ist ² als fünfzig Jahre alt she is on the wrong (or shady) side of fifty; ² als zuviel more than enough, more and to spare; mit *gen.*: es gibt deren ² als zuviel there are too many of them (already). — 2. mit Negationen: es dauert nicht ² lange it won't last

Zeichen (f. S. XVII). F familiär; P Volkssprache; Ҏ Gaunersprache; ⚹ selten; † alt (auch gestorben); * neu (auch geboren); ⚌ unrichtig;

[mehrarmig] — 689 — [meinesteils]

much longer; er ist nicht 2 als ich he is no(thing) better than I am; das ist nicht 2 als meine Schuldigkeit that's no(thing) more than my duty; es ist nichts 2 da there is nothing else left; ich kann nicht 2! F I am done (up)!; 2 kann man nicht verlangen nothing more can be expected, that's all one can expect; er lebt nicht 2 he is no longer alive, he is not living now; seine Tränen 2! no more tears!; das tut er nicht 2 wie gern (er tut's sehr gern) he is most willing (or only too glad) to do it; niemand wollte 2 spielen nobody wanted to continue the game. — **3.** und andere 2 and some (or a few) others; und dergleichen 2 and the like, and such like (abbr. u. a. [m.], u. dgl. [m.]); F das schmeckt nach 2 it tastes of more; er hat Geld, sein Bruder hat noch 2 ... has even more; immer noch 2 still more and more; ja, was noch 2 ist nay, what is more; wer noch 2? who else?; um so 2 als // all the more as //; viel 2 much (F a lot or a precious sight) more; ein paar Mark 2 oder weniger ... more or less, ... F up or down. — **4.** (sonst, weiter) was will er 2? what else does he want?; was bringst du 2? what's the news or the latest?; was ist denn nun 2 (weiter)? what else is there? — **II** Mehr n, inv. **5.** greater part, majority, ❀ over; (Vermehrung) increase; (Überschuß) surplus, excess.

mehr=armig (⸚...) a. ⓖ with several arms; vgl. Leuchter; **=aufwand** m ⓖ **=ausgabe** f: a) increased expense, additional expenditure; b) ⦾ von Wertpapieren: over-issue; **=betrag** m surplus; **=bieter(in** f) m higher bidder; **=blumig** ⚘ a. with several flowers or blossoms, ⚘ pluriflorous; **=deutig** a. ambiguous; **=deutigkeit** f ambiguity; **=einnahme** f additional receipts pl.

mehren (⸚) [ahd.; *mehr] **I** v/a. und sich 2 v/refl. ⓖ to multiply, increase, augment; sich 2, auch: to grow (apace), to rise. — **II** ~ n ㉓ multiplication, increase; growth, rise.

mehren=teils (⸚⸚⁀) adv. for the most part, generally, usually.

Mehrer (⸚⸚) m ⓖ multiplier, increaser; Herrschertitel: all(e)zeit ~ des Reiches perpetual enlarger of the Empire.

mehrere (⸚⸚⸚) [ahd.] a. ⓖ A 2, 3: 2mal, 2 Male several times; 2 gute (*...ein) Leute several (or some) good people; 2 von ihnen rauchten some (or a few) of them smoked; unbestimmtes Zahlwort: 2 (ant. ein) several, a few, more than one; (verschiedene) divers, sundry, different; a. als s/n. (ein) 2⁊ 🟋 divers (or sundry) matters pl.

mehrer=lei (⸚⸚⁀) a. inv. of several (or sundry) kinds, divers, sundry.

mehr=erwähnt (⸚...) a. ⓖ repeatedly mentioned; aforesaid; **=fach** a. manifold, bsd. math.: ⚛ multiple; 2e Telegraphie multiplex telegraphy; das ~e e-r Zahl the multiple of a number; adv. on several occasions, repeatedly; **=farben=druck** m ⓖ colour-printing; **=farbig** a.; ⚛ polychromatic; **=gebot** n

higher bid; **=gewicht** n excess of weight; **=glied(e)rig** a.: a) ⚚ of several ranks; b) math. of several terms.

Mehrheit (⸚⁀) f ⓖ **1.** plurality, bei Wahlen ꝛc.: majority. — **2.** gr. plural (number).

Mehrheits=beschluß (⸚⸚⸚⸜) m ⓖ resolution by a majority; durch ~ by a majority of votes, v.s. by a plurality.

mehr=jährig (⸚...) a. ⓖ several years old; **=lader** ⚔ m magazine-rifle (ant. Einlader); **=malig** a. repeated, reiterated; **=mal(s)** adv. several times, more than once; **=phasen=strom** m, elect. polyphase current; **=seitig** a. with several sides or faces; fig. multifarious; **=silbig** ⚘ of several syllables, ⚘ polysyllabic; **=stellig** a. von Zahlen: of several places; **=stimmenrecht** n, pol. plural vote; **=stimmig** ♫ a. (arranged) for several voices; 2er Gesang part-singing; **=teilig** a. (consisting of several parts, complex.

Mehrung (⸚⁀) f ⓖ = mehren **II**.

Mehr=wert (⸚...) m ⓖ surplus value; **=zahl** f: a) greater part; die große 2 the great majority, the greater number; b) gr. plural (number).

meiden (⸚⁀) [ahd.] **I** v/a. und sich 2 v/recip. 🞉: (sich, ea.) 2 to shun or avoid (each other), to steer clear (F to fight shy) of (one another); sorgfältig 2 to give a wide berth to; rel. das Böse 2 to shrink (or flee, depart) from evil, to eschew evil. — **II** ~ n ㉓ shunning, avoidance.

Meidinger (⸚⸚⸚) [~, npr. (1783)] m ⓖ (alter Witz) stale joke, F Joe Miller.

Meier (⸚⁀) [lt. maior] m ⓖ, **~in** f ⓖ **1.** steward (or bailiff) of an estate. — **2.** ehm. (Haus2) major-domo. — **3.** (Pächter) tenant of a farm, tenant-farmer.

Meierei (⸚⸚⸚) f ⓖ (dairy-)farm; **~=erzeugnisse** n/pl. ⓖ dairy-farm produce.

Meier=gut (⸚⸚⸚) n ⓖ, **=hof** m (dairy-)farm.

meiern F (⸚⸚) v/a. ⓖ a. (anführen) to bamboozle, diddle, do; der Gemeierte the victim, the jay. [of a farm.⟩

Meier=zins (⸚⸚⁀) m ⓖ farm-rent, rent⟩

Meile (⸚⁀) [ahd.: mile; *lt. mi'lia (pl. v. mille) 1000 (Schritte)] f ⓖ mile; deutsche (Reichs= ob. metrische) (= 7500 m) German (metrical) mile; [eine deutsche ~ etwa = 4½ English miles]; geographische ~ (deutsche = 7420,44 m, englische = 1855 m) geographical (or nautical) mile.

meilen=breit (⸚...) a. ⓖ, **=lang** a. one mile (or some miles) wide, long; **=geld** n ⓖ mileage; **=länge** f length of a mile; **=säule** f mile- (or milliary) column; **=stein** m milestone; **=weit** a. u. adv. extending for (several) miles, many miles away or distant, fig. 2 davon entfernt sein, et. zu tun to be very far (removed) from doing a th.; **=zahl** f number of miles, a. mileage; **=zeiger** m mile-post, mile-stone.

Meiler ⦿ (⸚⁀) [mhd.; *lt.] m ⓖ Köhlerei: charcoal-kiln or -pile; (kleiner: charcoal-stack; **~=holz** (⸚...) n ⓖ wood for charcoal; **~=kohle** f charcoal.

mein (⸜) [ahd.: mine, my: lt. me-us] **I** gen. von ich ⓖ A **1.** †, noch poet. meiner; gedenke 2 remember me; vergiß 2 nicht do not forget me. —

2. (mir angehörig, vgl. dein 2) das Buch ist (F gehört) 2 the book is mine or belongs to me. — **II** [2 I] a. u. possessive pron. 2(e f) m, n ⓖ C. (poet. oft inv. und dem s. nachgestellt) **3.** my; 2 (und euer) Buch my book (and yours); dieser 2 Sohn this son of mine, bibl. this my son; 2 Fuß tut (mir) weh my foot aches; 2e liebe Frau Base my dear cousin; 2 Herr Wirt my (F co. mine) host; die Ehre ist ganz auf 2er Seite the honour is entirely mine or on my side; ich kenne ihn 2er Treu nicht I assure you (feierlicher: on my soul, bsd. irisch: [by my] faith) I do not know him; 2es Wissens as far as (or for aught) I know, to the best of my knowledge; poet. geliebte Freunde 2! beloved friends! — **III 4.** a) 2er, 2e, 2es ⓖ A 2.; b) mit dem bestimmten art. der (die, das) **~(ig)e** ⓖ mine; die ~(ig)en my family or people; ich habe das ~e getan I have done all I can, I've done my best. — **IV** ~ n, inv. **5.** f. dein **IV**. — **V** int. [ell. 2 Gott!] **6.** 2!, ei du 2!; dear me!, good gracious!; F oh, my!, did you ever?

Mein=eid (⸚...) [ahd.] m ⓖ perjury, false oath; **=eidig** a. ⓖ perjured; 2 werden to perjure (or forswear) o.s., jur. to commit perjury; **=eidige([r]** m) f ⓖ perjurer.

meinen (⸚⁀) [ahd.] v/a. u. v/n. (h.) ⓖ **1.** to think, (glauben) to believe, fancy, imagine; (behaupten) to assert; 🞉 (der Ansicht sein) to be of opinion, to opine; viele 2, sie sei ein Schatz many fancy her a treasure; das will ich wohl 2! I quite believe it!; das sollte ich doch 2! I should think so (, indeed)!; was 2 Sie dazu? what is your opinion about it?; ich meine nur so it only just strikes me; ja, meinte er, wenn // yes, said he, if //. — **2.** (als Ziel im Auge haben) to mean, to have in view, to aim at; to purpose; 2 Sie das ernstlich? do you really mean it?; damit sind Sie gemeint that's meant for you; so ist's nicht gemeint it's not intended like that, that's not the drift (or purpose) of it. — **3.** (gesinnt sein) er hat's nicht böse gemeint he meant no harm; es war nicht böse gemeint it was meant for the best; er meint es gut he means well, his meaning is good; sie 2 es gut mit uns they have good intentions towards us, they have our welfare at heart; die Sonne meint es gut the sun is hot or shines brightly. — **4.** 🞉 mit inf. und „zu" (beabsichtigen): ich meine nicht (oder mehr gbr. ich bin nicht gemeint) zu // I am not in a mind to // (inf.). — **5.** 🞉 (minnen, lieben) Freiheit, die ich meine Freedom that I love. [mein **1.** — **II** s. mein **III.**⟩

meiner (⸚⁀) **I** gen. von ich ⸺ mir; vgl.⟩

meiner=seits (⸚⸚⁀) adv. on my part; as far as I am concerned, as to myself.

meines=gleichen (⸚⸚⸚⁀) pron. inv. (people) like me, the like(s) of me; my equals, pol. auch: my peers pl.; **=teils** (⸚⸚⁀) adv. on my part.

♪ Musik; ⚛ Wissenschaft; ⚘ Pflanze; ⚘ Geographie; ⚙ Technik; ⚒ Bergbau; ⚔ Militär; ⚓ Marine; ⚖ Handel; ✉ Post; 🚂 Eisenbahn.

[meinethalben] — 690 — [melieren]

meinet=halben (⸺...), ⸗wegen, ⸗willen for my sake; um ⸗willen on my behalf or account; ⸗halben mag er es tun he may do it for all I care.
meinige (⸺) f. mein III.
Meinung (⸺) [ahd.: meaning (f. 2); *meinen] f ⓮ 1. opinion, view; idea; (Glaube) belief; meiner ~ nach in my opinion, to my way of thinking, as I take it; ich habe ihm derb meine (ober die) ~ gesagt I gave him a bit of my mind; ich bin ganz seiner ~ I quite agree with him; falsche, irrige ~ wrong (or erroneous) opinion, misconception; es herrscht nur eine ~ darüber there is a general consensus of opinion about it; vorgefaßte ~ prejudice; die öffentliche ~ public opinion; eine zu gute ~ von sich h. to have too good an opinion (or to think too much) of o.s. — 2. (Absicht) meaning, intention; (Wunsch) wish.
Meinungs=äußerung (⸺...) f ⓮ expression of one's opinion; ⸗austausch m interchange of views or ideas; comparing notes; ⸗verschiedenheit f divergence (or difference) of opinion; disagreement, dissension; ⸗wechsel m change of (one's) opinion or views or mind; (Bekehrung) conversion.
Meiran ♀ (⸺) m ⓭d. f. Majoran.
Meirich ♀ (⸺) m ⓭d. chickweed (Alsine).
Meise (⸺) [ahd.: (tit)mouse] f ⓮ orn. titmouse (pl. titmice), tomtit (Parus); vgl. Hauben= und Kohl=meise.
Meißel ⊙ (⸺) [ahd.] m ⓮ chisel; ~bohrer (⸺) m ⓮ pitching-borer.
meißeln ⊙ (⸺) I v/a. u. v/n. (h.) ⓮a. to (work with the) chisel, to carve (out); (wie) gemeißelt sculpturesque. — II ~ n ⓮ chiselling, chisel-work.
meist (⸺) [ahd.: most] sup. von mehr: I a. ⓮ 1. mit s. im pl.: most of //; die Len Schüler lesen gut most of the pupils read well; die Len Menschen most (or the majority, F the generality of) people (vgl. 3). — 2. bei Abstrakten: die Le Geschicklichkeit the greatest skill; s-e Le Zeit most (or the greater part) of his time. — II s. ⓯ 3. die Len pl. the greater number, the (great) majority, F the generality (of people); die Len von ihnen (uns ꝛc.) most of them (us, &c.). — 4. das Le the greater (or best) part, most (F the bulk) of it. — III adv. 5. am Len most (highly). — 6. Ⅼ(ens), Len=teils, ⸗hin (in den Len Fällen) mostly, in most cases or instances, in the majority of cases, for the most part.
Meist=begünstigungs=klausel (⸺...) f ⓮ in Handelsverträgen: most-favoured nation clause; ⸗betrag m highest (or maximum) amount; ⸗bietend a. ⓮ bidding (or offering) most; adv.: Ⅼ verkaufen to sell to the highest bidder or without reserve; ⸗bietende(r) m highest bidder.
meistens (⸺), **meisten=teils** (⸺⸺, ⸺⸺) adv. f. meist 6. auch: generally, usually.
Meister (⸺) [ahd.: master; *lt. magi=ster] m ⓮, ~in f ⓮ 1. master (man), bsd. in Zssgn, zB. Bäckermeister master baker; ~in (auch Frau ~) f master's wife;

Sprichw. fein ~ fällt vom Himmel no man is born a master of his craft. — 2. ~ vom Stuhle Master of the Lodge, in der Anrede: worshipful master. — 3. fig. großer ~ im Schach= spiele first-class chess-player, great master at (or of) chess, a. chess(-)master; er hat seinen ~ gefunden he has found his match; j-s, e-r Sache ~ w. to master a p., a th.; seiner Gefühle ~ werden to restrain (or curb) one's feelings; f. machen 1 gegen Schluß; Sprichw. f. loben 1; Übung macht den ~ practice makes perfect. — 4. f. Hämmerlein 2.   [b) = ⸗werk.)
Meister=arbeit (⸺⸺) f ⓮: a) = ⸗stück;)
Meisterer (⸺) [meistern] m ⓮ one who plays the master; (Tadler) critic.
Meister=gesang (⸺...) m ⓮ song (or poetry) of a German mastersinger or meistersinger; ⸗grad m = ⸗recht.
meisterhaft (⸺⸺) a. ⓮ masterly, accomplished; adv. in a masterly manner, to perfection.
Meister=hand (⸺⸻) f ⓮ master's (skilled or experienced) hand, master-hand.
meisterlich (⸺⸺) a. ⓮ = meisterhaft.
meister=los (⸺⸻) a. ⓮ without a master.
meistern (⸺) [ahd.; *Meister] v/a. u. v/n. (h.) ⓮a. 1. e-n, etwas Ⅼ to master (or conquer, subdue) a p., a th.; poet. wenn dein Finger durch die Saiten meistert (sch.) when your fingers sway the tuneful chords. — 2. (übertreffen) to excel, surpass, outdo, outstrip. — 3. (zurechtweisen) to admonish; b.s. = hofmeistern; weit S. (rügen) to cavil (or carp) at, to find fault with.
Meister=recht (⸺...) n ⓮ der Handwerker freedom of a company; ⸗sang m = ⸗gesang; ⸗sänger m (deutscher Zunft= dichter) mastersinger, ⁊ meistersinger.
Meisterschaft (⸺⸺) f ⓮ 1. coll. (Gesamtheit von Meistern) guild, company; auch: the masters pl. of a trade. — 2. (überlegenheit, Geschick) mastership, mastery, masterly (or consummate) skill, excellency, superiority, great perfection. — 3. = Meisterrecht. — 4. Sport: championship; sich um die ~ bewerben, um die ~ streiten to compete for the championship; ~s=fahren (⸺...) ⓮, ⸗rennen n race for a championship, championship-meeting.
Meister=schuß (⸺...) m ⓮ best (or excellent, capital) shot; ⸗singer m = ⸗sänger; ⸗spiel n masterly play(ing) or performance; ⸗spieler m high-class player or performer, a. crack player, professional (artist); ⸗streich m master-stroke; ⸗stück n der Handwerker u. allS. masterpiece, (fr.) chef-d'œuvre; ⸗werk n, a. fig. masterwork, masterly achievement; ⸗würde f mastership.
Meist=gebot (⸺⸺) n ⓮ highest bid.
Mekka ♀ (⸺) npr/n. ⓮a. (ar. St., Geburts=ort Mohammeds, Pilger=ort) Mecca; ~balsam m ⓮ pharm. opobalsam(um), carpobalsamum.   [($C_{10}H_{10}O_4$).)
Mekonin ⌀ (⸺⸺) n ⓭d. chm. meconin(e))
mekon=sauer (⸺⸺) [grch. Mohn=] a. ⓮ chm. meconic; ⸗saures Salz meconate; ⸗säure f ⓮ meconic acid ($C_7H_4O_7$).

Melancholie (⸺⸻) [grch. Schwarzgalligkeit] f ⓮ (Schwermut) melancholy, (mental) gloom; **Melancholiker** (⸺⸻) m ⓮ melancholy person; **melancholisch** (⸺⸻) a. ⓮ (schwermütig) melancholy, gloomy, stärker: hypochondriac, (grübelnd) contemplative, pensive.
Melanesi=en ♀ (⸺⸻) [grch.] npr/n. ⓮a. (von Negritos bewohnter Teil Ozeaniens) Melanesia; **Melanesi=er(in** f ⓮) m ⓮, **melanesisch** (⸺⸻) a. ⓮ Melanesian.
Melange (⸺⸻) [fr. m] f ⓮ (Mischung) mixture; ~kaffee m coffee with milk.
Melanose ⌀ (⸺⸻) [grch. melan= schwarz] f ⓮ med. (Schwarzsucht) melanosis.
Melasse (⸺⸻) [fr., span.] f ⓮ (brauner Zuckersirup) molasses pl., treacle.
Melchisedek (⸺⸺) [hebr.] npr/m. ⓮⓯a. bibl. Melchizedek, Mechisedec.
Melde¹ ♀ f ⓮ or(r)ach (A'triplex).
Melde²=amt (⸺...) [melden] n ⓮ office for registration (gibt's in England nicht); vgl. Zivilstandsamt; ⸗brief ✉ m letter of advice; ⸗dienst ⚔ m intelligence service.
melden (⸺) [ahd.:] ⓮ I v/a. u. v/n. (h.) 1. e-m etwas Ⅼ to advise (or inform, apprise) a p. of a th.; (ankündigen) to announce a th. to a p., schriftlich: to inform a p. in writing, amtlich: to notify a th. to a p., dienstlich: to report a th. to a p.; e-m et. telegraphisch Ⅼ to acquaint a p. by telegraph (or wire) of a th., to telegraph (or wire) a th. to a p.; e-m Ⅼ lassen to send a p. word. — 2. Kartenspiel: wie viele Stiche haben Sie zu Ⅼ? how many tricks can you call or make?; Solo=Whist: ein Solo (5 Stiche) Ⅼ to call a solo (vgl. ansagen 3). — 3. (erwähnen) to mention; (sagen) to tell, to relate; wie bereits gemeldet as previously stated; mit Ehren, mit Respekt zu Ⅼ with all due respect to you, ehm.: save your reverence. — II sich Ⅼ v refl. 4. to report o.s. (auch ⚔); to give (or send) in one's name (vgl. anmelden 2); sich krank Ⅼ to report o.s. ill; ☙ von Gläubigern: to come forward; fig. das Alter meldet sich bei ihm age is telling on him; der Winter meldet sich winter is setting in (fast). — 5. sich zu (ob. für) et. Ⅼ to apply for a th., zum Examen: to enter one's name for an examination, zu einer Stelle: to compete (or to put up) for an appointment. — III ~ n ⓮ 6. = Meldung. [reporting or mentioning.)
meldens=wert (⸺⸻) a. ⓮ worth)
Melde=reiter ⚔ (⸺⸻) m ⓮ mounted messenger, (fr.) estafette; ⸗schiff ⚓ n advice-, dispatch-boat; ⸗stelle f für Feuersbrünste: fire-station. a. -watch; ⸗zettel m registration-form; f. anmelden.
Meldung (⸺⸻) f ⓮ 1. (f. melden I) advice, information, announcement, notification; report(ing); mention(ing); telegraphische ~ telegraphic message, wire; Tennis: entry. — 2. (f. melden II) report(ing o.s.); (making) application; competing, competition.
Meldungs=... (⸺⸻) in Zssgn = Melde=...
melieren (⸺⸻) [fr.] v/a. u. sich Ⅼ v/refl. ⓯ (mengen, mischen) to mix, to mingle; ☙ meliertes Tuch pepper and salt.

Signs (see page XVII): F familiar; P vulgar; ⌐ flash; ⸱ rare; ÷ obsolete (died); * new word (born); ⸝⸜ incorrect; ♪ music;

Meliloten-klee ♀ (⌣⌣ˌ⌢ˌ‿) m ⑫ = Steinklee.
Melinit (-⌣ˌ)·[fr. *mélinite*] m ⓓc. ⚔ *chm.* (Pikrinsäurepräparat, Sprengstoff für Hohlgeschoße) melinite.
meliorieren (⌣(⌣)⌣⌣ˌ⌣) [lt.] v/a. ⑬ (verbessern, veredeln) to (a)meliorate.
Melis ⓑ (⌣ˌ) [fr. *mélis*; *It. *melite'nse* Malta*] m, *inv.* (coarse) loaf-sugar.
melisch (⌢⌣) [grch. *mēlikós*] a. ⓖⓖ: Le Poesie lyric (bisw. melic) poetry.
Melisse ♀ (⌣⌢⌣) [grch.] f ⓖⓖ melissa, balm-mint or -gentle (*Meli'ssa officina'lis*); ~n-geist (⌣⌢⌣...) m ⑫ Carmelite water; ~n-öl n, *pharm.* melissa-oil.
Melis-zucker (⌢⌣⌢⌣) m ⑫ = Melis.
Melitose ♀ (⌣⌢⌣) [grch.] f ⓖⓖ *chm.* (Zucker aus Eukaly'ptusmanna) melitose.
melk (⌢) [ahd.], **melkbar** (⌢⌣) a. ⓖⓖ bsd. v. Kühen: giving milk, in milk.
Melk-eimer (⌢⌣⌣ˌ⌣) m ⑫ milking-pail.
melken (⌢⌣) [ahd.: milch] ⑬ u. Tb. I v/a.: Kühe ⚘ to milk cows; frisch gemolkene Milch milk fresh from the cow; *fig.* (aussaugen) to drain. — II v/n. (h.) (Milch geben) to give (or yield) milk. — III ~ n ⑳ milking; *fig. a.* draining a p.'s resources, fleecing a p.
Melker (⌢⌣) m ⑫, ~in f ⑭ milker, person who milks, f a. milk-maid.
Melkerei (⌣⌣⌣ˌ) f ⑭ 1. milking. — 2. (Milchwirtschaft) dairy(-farm).
Melk-faß (⌢...) n ⑫, **-kübel** m milking-tub; **-kuh** f milk-cow; **-maschine** ⊕ f milker; **-röhre** f milking-tube; **-schemel** m m.-stool; **-zeit** f m.-time.
Melodie ♪ (⌣⌣⌣ˌ) [grch.] f ⑭ (Weise) melody, air, tune; jämmerliche ~ miserable tune, F the tune the old cow died of; nach der ~ von // to the tune of //.
Melodik ♪ (⌣⌢⌣) f ⑭ melodics.
Melodion ♪ (⌣⌢⌣⌣) n ⑳ melodeon.
melodiös (⌣-(⌣)⌢), **melodisch** (⌣⌢⌣) a. ⓖⓖ (klangvoll) melodious.
Melodrama (⌣⌣⌢ˌ) [grch.] n ⑳ (Singspiel) melodrama; **-tisch** (⌣⌣⌢⌣) a. ⓖⓖ melodramatic.
Melone ♀ (-⌢⌣) [it. „großer Apfel", *grch.] f ⑭ (echte) melon (*Cu'cumis melo*).
Melonen-baum ♀ (⌣⌢⌣...) m ⑫ melontree (*Ca'rica papa'ya*); **-beet** n melonbed; **-förmig** a. ⓖⓖ melon-shaped, ⚘ meloniform; **-kaktus** ♀ m meloncactus or -thistle (*Meloca'ctus commu'nis*); **-kern** m melon-seed.
Meltau ♀ (⌢ˌ) [ahd.: mildew] m ⓑb.(o.pl.) mildew, blight, rust, ⚘ rubigo; von ~ befallen mildewy, blighted.
Membran(e) ⚘ (⌣⌢ˌ(⌣)) [lt.] f ⑭ (⑭) (Häutchen) membrane; des Telephons: diaphragm.
Memme (⌢⌣) [mhd. weibliche Brust] f ⑭ (Feigling) coward, poltroon; **memmenhaft** (⌢⌣⌣) a. ⓖⓖ cowardly.
Memoire ⚘ (⌣*mã'r*) [fr.] n ⑳ (Denkschrift) mst *pl.* ~n Denkwürdigkeiten) memoir; **~n-schreiber** (⌣*mã'r*-⌣...) m ⑫ writer (or author) of memoirs, memoirist.
Memorial(e) (⌣⌣(⌣)ˌ(⌣)) [lt.] n ⓓd. (㉙) 1. (Eingabe) memorial, petition. — 2. (Tagebuch) day-(or memorandum-)book.
memorieren (⌣⌣⌣ˌ⌣) [lt.] v/a. ⑬ to commit to memory, to learn by rote; eine Rolle ⚘ to get up one's part.
Memorier-stoff (⌣⌣ˌ...) m ⑫ things *pl.* to be committed to memory.

Menage (⌣ˈɡ⌣) [fr. (2. u. 3. ⌢ˌ fr.)] f ⑭ 1. (Haushalt) household, housekeeping. — 2. (Essigschüsseln) set of dishes. — 3. (Ölständer) (set of) casters *pl.*
Menagerie (⌣-ɡ⌣ˌ) [fr.] f ⑭ (Tierbude) menagerie, menagery; **~-wagen** (⌢...) m ⑫ travelling menagerie, † caravan.
menagieren (⌣-ɡ⌣ˌ⌣) [fr.] ⑬ I v/a. (mit Schonung behandeln) to manage; (sparen) to economize. — II sich ⚘ v/refl. (sich mäßigen) to moderate o.s.
Menge (⌢⌣) [ahd.: manch: many] f ⑭ 1. quantity, great (or large) number; (Vielheit) multitude, (Schwarm) swarm, crowd, (Haufe) heap; eine ~ Fleisch plenty (or a great deal) of meat; eine ~ Geld a lot (F heap, lump) of money; eine ~ Menschen a great many people; Freunde die ~ scores of friends, friends galore; Obst die ~ a (large) quantity of fruit, fruit in abundance; die ~ muß es bringen the number must do it; in (großer) ~ in (great) abundance, (most) plentiful(ly); F schwere ~ great quantity, *iro.* e-e schöne ~ a fine (or pretty) lot. — 2. die ~ (Volksmasse) the masses *pl.*, the multitude, the million.
mengen (⌢⌣) [ahd.: mingle] I v/a. und sich ⚘ v/refl. ⑬ 1. to mix (together), seltener: to (inter)mingle; (zf.-passen) to blend; (verwirren) to embroil, F to muddle (up); unter-ea. ⚘ to jumble together. — 2. sich in eine Sache ⚘ to meddle (or interfere) in a th.; er mengt sich in alles he puts (F pokes) his nose in everywhere, he is most interfering; *poet.* wie wenn Wasser mit Feuer sich mengt (SCH.) as if water with fire commingled (or embraced); sich unter die Leute ⚘ to mingle (or mix) with the crowd. — II ~ n ⑳ 3. (f. I) mixing, mixture; blend(ing).
Mengerei (⌢⌣⌣ˌ) f ⑭ (endless) mixing or F muddling or messing.
Meng-futter (⌢...) n ⑳ mixed food, für Vieh *auch:* mash; **-gestein** n, *geol.* conglomerate; **-korn** n, *agr.* (Weizen und Roggen) wheat and rye mixed; **-saat** f für Winterfutter: mixed seeds *pl.*
Mengsel (⌢⌣) [mengen] n ⑳ (odd) mixture, medley, hotchpotch, mess.
Mengung (⌢⌣) f ⑭ = mengen II.
Meng-werk (⌢ˌ⌣) n ⑳ medley, mixture.
Meniskus (⌣⌢⌣) [grch. fl. Mond] m ⑫ *anat., zo., phys. u. opt.* meniscus.
Mennig (⌢⌣) [ahd.; *lt. *mi'nium*] m ⓓd., **~e** f ⑭ *min., chm., &c.* (rotes Bleioxy) minium, red oxide of lead (Pb_3O_4); **~en** ⊕ v/a. ⑬ to paint with minium; **~-rot** (⌢⌣ˌ) a. ⓖⓖ miniate.
Mennonit (⌢⌣ˌ⌢) [Menno Simons, 1492-1559] m ⑫, **~in** f ⑭ *eccl.* Mennonite.
Mensch (⌢) [ahd.:*Mann] I m ⑫ 1. human being, bsd. *bibl.* man; die ~en mankind; (einzelner) person, individual, (Sterblicher) mortal, (denkendes Wesen) rational being, *auch:* head; (Arbeiter) oft: hand; (Kerl) fellow; junger ~ young man, youth; zum (gesitteten) ~en m. to humanize; *bibl.* des ~en Sohn the Son of Man; ~ werden to be made flesh; *Sprichw.* s. denken I b. — 2. eine Menge ~en a great many people, a

large crowd; viele ~en, *auch:* many folks *pl.*; viele ~en kamen ums Leben many (people) lost their lives, many lives were lost; in London wohnen 7 Millionen ~en London has seven million inhabitants; unter die ~en kommen to go into society; kein ~ würde es wagen nobody (or no one) would venture; kein einziger ~ not a (single) soul; jeder ~ everybody, everyone, stärker: every living soul, all the world. — II n ⓐa. [mhd. Magd] 3. (gemeines Weib) (common) wench or hussy, troll, F baggage; derbes ~ F bouncer, strapper, whacker.
Menschen-affe (⌢⌣...) m ⑫ *zo.* anthropomorphous ape; **-ähnlich** a. ⓖⓖ like a human being, ⚘ anthropomorphous, anthropoid; **-ähnlichkeit** f resemblance to a human being, ⚘ anthropomorphism; **-alter** n age of man; generation; **-antlitz** n human face or countenance; **-art** f: a) = **-schlag**; b) das ist ~ (menschliche Weise) that's the way (or those are the ways) of the world, it's human nature; **-blut** n human blood; **-dasein** n human existence; *vgl.* **-leben**; **-familie** f human race; **-feind** m: a) enemy of mankind; b) misanthropist; **-feindlich** a. misanthropic(al); **-feindlichkeit** f misanthropy; **-fleisch** n human flesh; **-fresser(in** f) m man-eater, cannibal, ⚘ anthropophagist; **-fresserei** f cannibalism, ⚘ anthropophagy; **-freund** m friend of mankind, philanthropist; **-freundlich** a. philanthropic(al); (leutselig) affable, genial, kind; (wohlwollend) benevolent, humane; **-freundlichkeit** f philanthropy; affability, geniality; benevolence, humaneness; **-furcht** f fear of men; **-gebot** n human ordinance or law; **-gedenken** n: seit ~ within the memory of man; **-gerippe** n human skeleton; **-geschlecht** n h. species or race, mankind; **-gestalt** f h. shape or form; Jesus Christus nahm ~ an the Lord was made like unto man; er ist ein Teufel in ~ he is a devil incarnate, he has the very devil (or F Old Nick) in him; **-gewühl** n crowd (or throng) of people; **-glück** n human happiness; **-haar** n h. hair; **-hai** m, *ichth. s.* Hai; **-hand** f human hand; **-handel** m traffic in human flesh, *engS.* slave-trade; **-haß** m hatred of mankind; **-hasser** m = **-feind**; **-herz** n human heart; **-jäger** m man-hunter; **-kenner** m one who knows mankind, (keen) observer (or discerner, judge) of human nature; **-kenntnis** f knowledge of mankind, (deep) insight into human character; **-kind** n = Mensch; *bibl.* die ~er *pl.* the children of men; *b.s.* ein sonderbares ~ a queer fellow; **-leben** n h. life, life of man; es kostete viele ~ it cost many lives, many lives were sacrificed; **-leer** a. deserted; **-liebe** f human love; love of mankind, philanthropy; **-masse** f, **-menge** f crowd of people; **-möglich** a. within the power (or reach) of man; feasible; das ⚘e (alles) all that is

humanly possible, F every mortal thing; =mord m homicide; böswilliger= murder; =mörder m homicide, murderer; =opfer n human sacrifice; =pack n rabble, low set (of people); =pocken f/pl. ᵣath. small-pox; =raffe f race of people; =raub m man-stealing, kidnapping; =räuber m kidnapper; =recht n law of mankind; ~e pl. rights of man, human rights pl.; =fatzung f h. institution; vgl. =gebot; =fcheu f shyness, unsociableness; ²fcheu a. shy, unsociable; =fchlag m race of men; =feele f human soul; es war keine ~ da not a (living) soul was there; =fohn m, bibl. Son of man; =ftrom m (dense) crowd of people.

Menfchentum (˘˘) n ⓓ. 1. human race. — 2. = Menfchlichkeit.

Menfchen-verächter (˘˘...) m ⓶ one who despises mankind, cynic; =verftand m human understanding; gefunder ~ common sense; =volk n people pl., mankind; =werk n work of man; =würde f human dignity; ²würdig a. ⓖ worthy of a human being.

Menfchheit (˘-) [ahd.] f ⓘ 1. human nature or form. — 2. (Menfchengefchlecht) mankind. — 3. = Menfchenmaffe.

Menfchlein F (˘-) n ⓶ (dim. v. Menfch) (little) manikin, F hop-o'-my-thumb.

menfchlich (˘˘) a. ⓖ 1. human; das ~e human affairs pl.; ² m. to humanize; nach ᵣem Ermeffen as far as human judgment goes, humanly speaking; nach ᵣer Vorausficht as far as we can tell the future; das überfteigt die ᵣen Begriffe that is beyond human conception, it transcends all h. ideas or notions; euph. wenn mir was ~es begegnet should anything (unforeseen) happen to me; ihm ift was ~es begegnet: a) he has paid his tribute to nature, he is dead; b) he has made a mistake; Sprichw. f. irren IV. — 2. (ᵣer Sitte gemäß) conventional; (erträglich) tolerable. — 3. (² fühlend) humane; poet. er fühlt ein ²es Rühren human compassion stirs his breast.

Menfchlichkeit (˘˘-) f ⓕ 1. humanity, human nature or frailty. — 2. humaneness. [carnation of our Lord.⁾

Menfch-werdung (˘˙˘) f ⓖ theol. in-⌋

Menfel (˘˘) [lt. Tifchchen] f ⓘ = Meßtifch.

Menftruation (˘˘—tsˇ˘)ᵘ) [lt.] f ⓜ med. (Monatsfluß); ⚋ menstruation; vgl. Regel; **menftruieren** (˘˘˘˙) v/n. (h. u. ſn) ⓑ F to be poorly, ⚋ to menstruate.

Menfur (˘˙) [lt.] f ⓘ 1. ♪ (Orgelpfeifenmaß) diapason; fenc. (Fechterabftand) proper distance. — 2. burfchlos: fencing- (or duelling-)ground; auf die ~ geh(e)n, auf der ~ ſteh(e)n to fight (out) a (student's) duel.

Menthol ⚋ (˘˙) [lt. Minz-öl] n ⓓ. chm. menthol ($C_{10}H_{20}O$).

Mentor (˘)[grch.]npr/m.ⓓa.myth.(Führer des Te'lemach) Mentor; ⓼ fig. (Erzieher, Berater)mentor, tutor, faithful adviser.

Menü (˘˙) [fr.] n ⓢ (Speifenfolge) bill of fare, (fr.) menu. [(ⓢ) minuet.⌋

Menuett (˘˘˘)[fr. „klein"fchriftung]nⓒ.⌋

Mephifto, **~pheles** (-f˘, -f˘l˘)[hebr. Verberber u. Lügner] m ⓒ. (Teufel, bſd.

G. Fauft) Mephistopheles; **²phelifch** (-f˘˘f˘) a. ⓖ Mephistophelean.

Mergel (˘˘) [ahd., *lt.] m ⓶ geol. marl.

Mergel-ablagerung (˘˘˙...) f ⓖ bed (or layer) of marl; ²artig a. ⓖ marly, ⚋ marlaceous; =boden m, agr. marly soil; =düngung f marling; =erde f earthy marl; =grube f marl-pit.

merg(e)lig (˘˘˘) a. ⓖ marly.

Mergel-kalk (˘˘˙) m ⓖ marly limestone. **mergeln** (˘˘) [mhd.] v/a. ⓖa. agr. (mit Mergel düngen) to (manure with) marl.

Mergel-fchiefer (˘˘...) m ⓖ min., geol. slaty marl; =ftein m marlstone. =ton m: ⚋ argillaceous marl.

merglig (˘˘) a. ⓖ f. mergelig.

Meridian ⚋ (˘-(˘)˙) [lt.] m ⓓ. ast. ☿ (Mittagskreis) meridian (line); durch den ~ geh(e)n to culminate; den ~ paffieren to cross the meridian.

meridional ⚋ (˘-(˘)˘˙) [lt.] a. ⓖ ast. (mittägig) meridional.

Merino (-˙-) [fpan.] m ⓢ 1. zo. ~(=fchaf n) merino(-sheep). — 2. ⓢ ~(=wolle f) merino(-wool).

Merk ⚘ (˙) m ⓓb. skirret (sium); breiter ~ water-parsnip (S. latifo'lium).

merkantil, **²ifch** ⚘ (˘˘˘˙(˘)) [lt.] a. ⓖ (kaufmännifch) mercantile, commercial; ~ fyftem (˘˘˙˘˙) n ⓒ mercantile system.

Merk-band (˙˙) n ⓖ (Lefezeichen) book mark(er).

merkbar (˘˘) a. ⓖ perceptible, noticeable; ~keit (˙-) f ⓕ perceptibility.

Merk-buch (˙˙h) n ⓖ memorandum- (or note-)book.

merken (˘˘) [ahd.: mark; f. Marke] v/a. ⓑ 1. (bezeichnen) to mark, (aufzeichnen) to note (down). — 2. fich (dat.) et. ² (einprägen) to impress a th. on one's memory, to retain (or remember) a th.; ² Sie fich, daß // mark (or mind, take note) that //; das werde ich mir ² I will bear that in mind; als warnendes Beifpiel: that shall be a lesson to me; wohl zu ²! now remember!, now mark! — 3. et. ² u. v/n. (h.) auf et. ² (achten) to pay attention to a th., to heed a th. — 4. (wahrnehmen) to perceive, notice, observe; er merkt et., oft. he can smell a rat; ich merkte lange, wo er hinauswollte I knew at once what he was driving at; ich habe es fchon gemerkt, daß // I am fully aware that //; man merkt es an feiner Art, daß // his manner shows one that //. — 5. ² laffen (verraten) to betray, to divulge, F to let out; er ließ mich ², daß // he gave me to understand that //; et. nicht ² laffen not to divulge (or betray) one's knowledge of a th., to keep a th. snug; laß dir (laffen Sie fich nichts) ²! don't appear to know anything!, F don't give yourself away!

merkens-wert (˘˘˙) a. ⓖ worthy of notice; remarkable, notable.

Merker (˘˘) m ⓶, ~in f ⓘ 1. one who marks, marker, scorer; bſd. bei den Meifterfängern: judge, critic. — 2. F er hat den richtigen ~ (Verftand, Spürfinn) he has all his wits about him.

merklich (˘˘) a. ⓖ perceptible, noticeable; (fichtlich) visible, (augenfcheinlich)

evident, obvious; ein ²er Unterfchied a marked difference, a sharp contrast.

Merk-mal (˙...) n ⓖ mark (of distinction), attribute, property; (Anzeichen) sign, badge; (Eigentümlichkeit) characteristic (a. ⚘, zo., &c.), (particular) feature; =fpruch m popular saying.

Merkur (˘˙) [lt.] ⓖⓑa., ~ius (˘˙(˘)˘)ⓖf. I npr/m. myth. (Götterbote u. ♄gott) u. ast. (Planet) Mercury. — II ⚋ m ⓓd. chm., &c. (Queckfilber) mercury, quicksilver.

Merkurial-kur (˘˙-(˘)˙...) f ⓖ med. mercurial treatment; =falbe f (graue Salbe) (grey) mercurial ointment.

Merk-wort (˙...) n ⓖ catch-word, key-word, thea. cue; ²würdig a. ⓖ noteworthy, remarkable, (denkwürdig) memorable; (feltfam) strange, curious; ²er-weife hat er gewonnen marvellous (or curious) to relate, he won; =würdigkeit f: a) o. pl.: remarkableness, memorableness; marvellousness; b) mit pl.: remarkable thing; e-m die ~en einer Stadt zeigen to show a p. the sights (or lions) of a town; =zeichen n (distinctive) sign or mark; mit einem ~ verfehen to mark (with s.th.); vgl. Merkmal. [(Gadus merla'ngus).⌋

Merlan (˘˙) [fr.] m ⓓd. ichth. merling⌋

Merle (˘˘) [fr., *lt.] f ⓘ orn. (Amfel) blackbird, ousel, merle.

Merlin (˘˙) [flt.] m I npr. ⓖⓑa. (Zauberer)Merlin.—II⚋ m ⓓ, auch ~falke m ⓖ orn. merlin (Falco ae'salon).

Merowinger (-˘˘˘˘) m/pl. ⓖ (fränkifche Könige, 5. sae. bis 752) Merovingians pl.; **merowingifch** a. ⓖ Merovingian.

merzen (˘˘) [März] ⓢ f. aus².

merzerifieren ⚋ ⊙ (˘˘˘˙˙) [Mercer, 1844] v/a. ⓑ: Baumwolle ² (mit Kalilauge behandeln) to mercerize.

Merz-fchafe (˘˙...) n/pl. ⓖ cast-off sheep pl. which are sold in the autumn; =vieh n rejected cattle. [Mißheirat.⌋

Mesalliance (me-ſä-li-a'ß) [fr.] f ⓖ =⌋ **mesmerifieren** (˘˘˘˙˙) [Mesmer, dtfch. Arzt 1733—1815] v/a. ⓑ to mesmerize.

Mesmerismus (˘˘˘˘) m ⓘ mesmerism, animal magnetism.

Mesner (˘˘) [lt. mansiona'rius (+˙+: Meffe¹)] m ⓖ eccl. 1. sacristan, weitS. sexton. — 2. priest saying mass.

Mesopotami-en ☿ (˘˘˘˙(˘)˘) [grch.] npr/n. ⓑa. (Land zwifchen Euphrat und Tigris) Mesopotamia; **Mesopotami-er** (=in f ⓘ) m ⓶, **mesopotamifch** (˘˘˘˙˙) a. ⓖ Mesopotamian.

Meß¹ ⚘ ⨀ ☾ (˙) f ⓖ (Offiziers²) mess.

Meß²-amt (˙...) [Meffe¹ 1] n ⓖ eccl. (service of the) mass; =³band [meffen] n (measuring-)tape, tape-measure. [~keit f ⓖ measurableness.⌋

meß³bar (˘) [meffen] a. ⓖ measurable;⌋

Meß²-befucher (˘...) [Meffe¹ 2] m ⓖ visitor at a fair; =³bildverfahren n: ⚋ photogrammetry; =brief ⚓ m über den Raumgehalt des Schiffes : bill of tonnage; =²buch n mass-book, missal; =bude f booth (or stall) at a fair; =diener m = Meſner 1, auch: acolyte, server.

Meffe¹ (˘˘) [ahd.: mass; *lt. missa = entlaffen] f ⓖ 1. Cath. eccl. mass; die ~ lefen to say (or celebrate, read) mass; in die ~ gehen to go to mass. — 2.

[Messe] — 693 — [...meter]

(Jahrmarkt) fair; die ~ beschicken (beziehen) to send goods (to go) to the fair. **Messe**² 𝆕 (ᴗ́ᴗ) f 🜨 = Meß. [mass.] **Messe**¹-lesen (ᴗ́ᴗ.ᴗ́ᴗ) n 23 eccl. saying **messen** (ᴗ́ᴗ) [ahd.: mete] I v/a., v/n. (h.) u. sich 2 v/refl. 🜨 **1.** 2 to measure, to take the measurement of; f. Elle; mit einer Schnur 2 to cord; 🜨 (nivellieren) to level; (ausmessen, eichen) to gauge; Land 2 to survey land; *fig.* er kann das Geld mit Scheffeln 2 F he has heaps (or tons, loads) of money. — **2.** *fig.* sich mit e-m 2 to measure one's strength against another p.'s, to try conclusions (or a fall) with a p.; sich mit e-m nicht 2 können to be no match for a p. — II ~ n 23 3. = Meßung. **Messenie-n** ♀ (ᴗ́(ᴗ)ᴗ) npr/n. 23 α. Alt.: (Landschaft im Peloponnes) Messenia; **Messeni-er(in** f 🜨 47) m 22, **messenisch** (ᴗ́ᴗ) a. 🜨 Messenian. **Messer**¹ (ᴗ́ᴗ) [messen] m 22 **1.** (messende Person) measurer. — **2.** (zum Messen dienendes Werkzeug) in Zssgn, meist: ⚗ ...meter, 3B. Luftdruckmesser barometer. **Messer**² (ᴗ́ᴗ) [ahd.] n 22 knife; ~ mit doppelter Klinge double-bladed knife; ~ zum Fischessen fish-knife; ~ zum Beschneiden der Äste pruning-knife; Krieg bis aufs ~ war to the knife; f. Kehle 1; *fig.* das ~ sitzt ihm an der Kehle he is put to his last shifts or trumps. **messer**²-**artig** (ᴗ́ᴗ...) a. 🜨 like a knife; **=bänkchen** n 22 (in England nur für Vorlege-messer u. -gabel) knife-rest; **=besteck** n knife-case; **=brett** n zum Putzen der Messer: knife-board. **Messerchen** (ᴗ́ᴗᴗ) n 23 (*dim. v.* Messer²) little (or small, tiny) knife. **messer**²-**förmig** (ᴗ́ᴗ...) a. 🜨 knife-shaped, ⚗ cultriform; **=gras** ♀ n 22 knife-grass (*Sele'ria latifo'lia*); **=griff** m, **=heft** n kn.-handle; **=händler(in** f) m cutler; **=held** m = **=stecher**; **=klinge** f blade of a kn.; **=korb** m kn.-basket; **=rücken** m back of a knife; **=schärfer** m (Werkzeug) knife-sharpener; **=scheide** f: a) case of a kn.; b) zo. razor-shell or fish (*Solen vagi'na*); **=schmied(e** f) m 🜨 cutler('s workshop); **=schmiede**-**handwerk** n, **=waren** f/pl. cutlery; **=schmiede**-**werkstatt** f cutler's workshop; **=schneide** f edge of a knife; **=spitze** f point of a knife; **=stecher** m cutthroat; **=stich** m thrust (or stab) with a knife; **=stiel** m knife-handle. **Meß**³-**fahne** (ᴗ́...) f 22 surveyor's flag (-pole); **=fremde** m/pl. merchants (or strangers) pl. attending a fair; **=gehilfe** f. **=diener**; **=gerät** n, *eccl.* appointments pl. for the celebration of mass, *auch*: mass-requisites pl.; **=geschenk** n present bought at a fair, bfd. ehm.: fairing; **=gewand** n, *eccl.* priestly vestment; chasuble; **=glöckchen** n bell calling to mass, mass-bell; **=gut** n, *coll.* goods (or articles) pl. sent to a fair; **=hemd(e** n, *eccl.* alb.

Messiade (ᴗ́ᴗ)ᴗ) f 48 die ~ (religiöse Dichtung v. Kl.) the Messiad. **messianisch** (ᴗ́(ᴗ)ᴗ) [Messi'as] a. 🜨 Messianic. **Messias** (ᴗ́ᴗ) [hebr. der Gesalbte] m 26 γ. *rel.* Messiah; ~**amt** n 22 Messiahship.

Messing 🜨 (ᴗ́ᴗ) [mhd.] n 🜨 d. (Legierung aus Kupfer u. Zink) brass, ehm.: latten. **Messing-arbeit** 🜨 (ᴗ́ᴗ...) f 22 brass-work; **=beschlag** m brass mounting; **=blech** n sheet-brass, br. plate; **=draht** m br. wire; **=ecke** f br. corner. **messingen** (ᴗ́ᴗᴗ) a. 🜨 (D9) (of) brass, brazen. **Messing-feilicht** (ᴗ́ᴗ...) n 22 brass filings pl.; **=gerät**, **=geschirr** n brass utensils pl. or battery; *auch*: brasses pl.; **=gießer** m br.-founder; **=hammer** m: a) hammer for beating brass; b) = **=hütte**; **=hütte** f br.-foundry; **=linie** f 22 *typ.* brass rule; **=nagel** m br. nail; **=platte** f, **=schild** n br. plate; **=schläger** m; **=schmied** m brazier; **=schlag-lot** n br.-solder; **=schrift** f, *typ.* brass type; **=ware** f brass ware, braziery. **Meß**³-**instrument** (ᴗ́...) n 22 = **=werkzeug**; **=²katalog** m Buchhandel: catalogue of books sold at the (Leipzig) fair; **=kelch** m chalice; **=³kette** f surveyor's (or measuring-) chain; **=krämer** m stall-keeper at a fair; **=³kunde** f practical surveying or mensuration; **=kunst** f (art of) surveying; **=künstler** m surveyor; **=latte** f surveyor's (or station-) staff or pole; **=²lesen** n saying mass; **=leute** pl. people (or traders) pl. attending a fair; **=³maschine** f measuring-machine; **=²opfer** n sacrifice of the mass; **=priester** m priest celebrating mass, mass-priest; **=pult** n desk for the mass-book; **=³rad** n measuring-wheel; **=rute** f = **=latte**; **=stange** f offset-staff; **=stock** m yard-measure; **=tisch** m surveyor's (or plane-, plain-) table; **=trichter** m measuring-funnel; **=²tuch** n, worauf der Kelch bei der Messe steht: corporal(-cloth). **Messung** (ᴗ́ᴗ) [mhd.; *messen] f 46 measurement. *math.* mensuration. **Meß**²-**wein** (ᴗ́...) m 22 sacramental wine; **=³werkzeug** n instrument for measuring or surveying or gauging; **=²zeit** f time appointed for a fair. **Mestize** (ᴗ́ᴗᴗ) [span. Mischling v. Weißen od. Kreolen u. Indianern] m 44, **Mestizin** f 47 mestizo. [🜨c. (Honigwein) mead.] **Met** (ᴗ́) [ahd.: mead: grch. *methy*] m] **Metall** (ᴗ́ᴗ) [grch.] n 🜨d. **1.** metal; (un)edles ~ precious (base) metal. — **2.** (Klang der Stimme) metallic ring, musical quality, timbre (of the voice). **Metall-ader** (ᴗ́ᴗ...) f 22 metallic vein or lode; **²ähnlich**, **²artig** a. 🜨 resembling metal, metallic, ⚗ metalloid; **=arbeiter** m metal-worker, metalman, metallist; **=asche** f metallic ashes pl.; **=bearbeitung** f working of metal(s), metal-work; **=beschickung** f alligation, alloyage; **=beschreiber** m; ⚗ **=metallographer**; **=beschreibung** f: ⚗ metallography; **=blättchen** n metallic leaf or foil; **=chemie** f: ⚗ metallo-chemistry; **=draht** 🜨 m metal(lic) wire. **Metallerz** (ᴗ́ᴗ...) [Metall-lehre] f 🜨 metallurgy. [metallic.] **metallen** (ᴗ́ᴗᴗ) a. 🜨 (D9) (of) metal,] **Metall-färbung** (ᴗ́ᴗ...) f 22 metallic colour(ing), elektrolytisch erzeugte: **=metallochromie**; **=geld** n specie, (hard) cash; **=gemisch** n (metallic) composition, alloy;

=glanz m metallic lustre; **=guß** m casting metal, metal cast; **²haltig** a. 🜨 metalliferous, metalline. **Metalliderung** (ᴗ́ᴗᴗᴗ) [Metall-liderung] f 🜨 metal packing. **metallisch** (ᴗ́ᴗᴗ) a. 🜨 metallic. **metallisier/en** 🜨 (ᴗᴗᴗ́ᴗ) I v/a. 🜨 to metallize, to impregnate wood, &c. with metal(lic solutions). — II ~ n 23 u. M/ung f 🜨 metallization. **Metall-knopf** (ᴗ́ᴗ...) m 22 metal button; **=kunde** f metallography; (Hüttenkunde) metallurgy; **=kundige(r** m metallurgist; **=lehre** f f. Metallehre; **=liderung** f f. Metalliderung. **Metallo-id** ⚗ (ᴗᴗᴗ́) [grch.] n 🜨d. *chm.* metalloid, non-metallic element. **Metall-oxyd** (ᴗ́ᴗ...) n 🜨 *chm.* metallic oxide; **=platte** f metal plate or sheet; **=probe** f assay; **²reich** a. 🜨 metalliferous, von der Stimme: with a metallic ring, sonorous; **=salze** n/pl. *chm.* metallic salts pl.; **=spektrum** n, *phys.* spectrum of a metal; **=spiegel** m metal mirror; **=stange** f metal rod. **Metallurg** (ᴗᴗᴗ́) [grch.] m 22 metallurgist; **~ie** (ᴗᴗᴗᴗ́) f 48 metallurgy; **~isch** (ᴗᴗᴗ́ᴗ) a. 🜨 metallurgic(al); Börse: **~ische Werte** mining shares pl. **Metall-waren** 🜨 (ᴗ́ᴗ...) f/pl. hardware. **Metamorphose** (ᴗᴗᴗ́ᴗ) f 48 (Umwandlung) metamorphosis, transformation; **metamorphosieren** (ᴗᴗᴗᴗᴗ́ᴗ) v/a. 🜨 (umwandeln) to metamorphize, transform. **Metapher** ⚗ (ᴗ́ᴗᴗ) [grch.] f 🜨 *rhet.* (bildlicher Ausdruck) metaphor(ical expression), figure of speech; **Metaphoriker** (ᴗᴗᴗ́ᴗ) m 22 metaphorist; **metaphorisch** (ᴗᴗᴗ́ᴗ) a. 🜨 metaphorical, figurative. **Metaphosphor-säure** (ᴗᴗᴗ́ᴗᴗ) f 🜨 metaphosphoric acid ($H_2O \cdot P_2O_5$). **Metaphysik** ⚗ (ᴗᴗᴗ́, a. ᴗᴗᴗ́ᴗ) [grch.] (Lehre vom Übersinnlichen) metaphysics; **~er** (ᴗᴗᴗ́ᴗᴗ) m 22 metaphysician, ...ist; **metaphysisch** (ᴗᴗᴗ́ᴗ) a. 🜨 metaphysical. **Metastase** ⚗ (ᴗᴗᴗ́ᴗ) [grch.] f 48 *physiol., path., &c.* (Krankheitswanderung) metastasis. [(Stabenversetzung) metathesis.] **Metathesis** (ᴗᴗᴗ́ᴗ) f 🜨 *gr.* (Buch-] **Metazentrum** ↧ (ᴗᴗᴗ́ᴗ) [grch.-lt.] n 28 (Schwankpunkt) metacentre. **Metempsychose** ⚗ (ᴗᴗᴗ́ᴗ) [grch.] f 48 (Seelenwanderung) metempsychosis. **Meteor** ⚗ (ᴗᴗᴗ́) [grch.] n 🜨d. *ast.* (Lufterscheinung) meteor; **²artig** a. 🜨 meteor-like, meteoric; **~eisen** n 22 meteoric iron; **²haft**, **²isch** ⚗ (ᴗᴗᴗ́ᴗ) a. 🜨 meteoric, seltener: meteorical; **~it** (ᴗᴗᴗ́) m 🜨c. ~**stein**; **~kugel** f: ⚗ bolide. **Meteorolog** ⚗ (ᴗᴗᴗᴗ́) m 22, **~e** 44 meteorologist; **~ie** (ᴗᴗᴗᴗᴗ́) f 48 (Wetterkunde) meteorology; **~isch** (ᴗᴗᴗᴗ́ᴗ) a. 🜨 meteorological; **~ische Station** meteorological observatory or station. **Meteor-stein** (ᴗᴗᴗ́...) m 22 meteor(ol)ite, aerolite, ...th.; **=stern** m Sternschnuppe. **Meter** (ᴗ́ᴗ) [fr. *mètre* m; *grch. *métron* n Maß] n (m) 22 (Grundmaß des dezimalen Maßsystems, zehnmillionster Teil des Erdmeridianquadranten; abbr. **m**, öft. **m**) metre (= 1·0936 yards or 39·37 inches). **...meter** ⚗ [grch.] **1.** 🜨 (...)ᴗ́ᴗ) n (m) 22 in Zssgn: Baro² barometer. — **2.** (...)ᴗ́ᴗ) m 22 pros.: Hexa² hexameter.

♪ Musik; ⚗ Wissenschaft; ♀ Pflanze; ⚱ Geographie; 🜨 Technik; ⚔ Bergbau; ⚔ Militär; ⚓ Marine; ✉ Handel; ✉ Post; 🜨 Eisenbahn.

Meter=kerze (⏑‒⏑...) f ⓑ elect. metre-candle; =**kilogramm** n, phys. kilogrammetre; ⏑**lang** a. ⓑ a metre long; =**maß** n metric measure(ment); ⏑**weise** adv. (F a. a.) by the meter.

Methan ⚥ (‒⏑) [grch.] n ⓓd. chm. (Sumpf=, Gruben=gas) marsh-gas, ⚥ methane (CH₄).

Methode (⏑‒⏑) [fr.,*grch.] f ⓑ (Verfahren) method, (Art u. Weise) mode, manner, way; bewährte ~ approved method.

Methodik (⏑‒⏑) f ⓑ methodics, methodology; ~**er** (⏑‒⏑⏑) m ⓑ methodizer.

methodisch (⏑‒⏑) a. ⓑ methodical; ⏑e Anordnung methodization.

Methodist ⏉ (⏑‒⏑) m ⓑ, ~**in** f ⓑ eccl. engl. Settierer[in]: Methodist; ~**en mission** f ⓑ Methodist mission; ~**en prediger** m Methodist preacher; ⏑**isch** (⏑‒⏑) a. ⓑ eccl. Methodistical.

Methusalem (⏑‒⏑⏑) [hebr.] npr/m. ⓓa. bibl. (fig. m ⓓ) Methuselah.

Methyl ⚥ (‒⏑) [grch.] n (m) ⓓd. chm. (Radikal des Holzgeistes) methyl (CH₃); ~ enthaltend, mit ~ gemischt methylated; ~**alkohol** (⏑⏑‒...) m ⓑ = Holzgeist; ~**ami'n** n methylamine (NH₂CH₃); ~**äther** m methylic ether (C₂H₆O).

Methylen ⚥ (⏑‒⏑) [grch.] n ⓓd. chm. methylene (CH₂); ~**blau** (⏑‒‒) n ⓑ methylene-blue (C₁₆H₁₈N₃SCl).

Metier (-tič') [fr. métier m] n ⓑ (Hand werk, Beruf) trade, profession, calling.

Metöke ⚥ (⏑‒⏑) [grch.] m ⓑ grch. Alt.: (Schutzverwandter) metic, alien resident.

Metonymie ⚥ (⏑⏑⏑‒) [grch. Namenvertauschung] f ⓑ rhet. metonymy; **metonymisch** (⏑⏑‒⏑) a. ⓑ metonymic(al).

Metope ⊕ (⏑‒⏑) [grch. Stirn] f ⓑ arch. (Zwischenfeld zw.Dreischlitzen)metope, space between triglyphs of a Doric frieze.

Metrik ⚥ (‒⏑) [grch.] f ⓑ (Verslehre) metrics, metrical art; versification.

Metriker (‒⏑⏑) m ⓑ metrist; **metrisch** a. ⓑ metrical; ⏑es Maßsystem metrical system of measurement.

Metro=logie ⚥ (⏑⏑⏑‒) [grch.] f ⓑ (Maßkunde) metrology. [meſſer] metronome.]

Metronom ♪ (⏑⏑‒) [grch.] n ⓓd. Takt=

Metropole (⏑⏑‒⏑) f ⓑ, **Metropolis** (⏑‒⏑⏑) f ⓑ [grch. Mutterstadt] metropolis (a. = Hauptstadt, in England = London).

Metropolit (⏑⏑⏑‒) [grch.] m ⓑ (Erzbischof in der gr. Kirche) metropolite, ...an; ~**a'n kirche** f metropolitan church (in England = Londoner Kirche). [maß] metre.]

Metrum ⚥ (‒⏑) [grch.] n ⓑ ⓑ pros. (Vers=

Mette (⏑⏑) [ahd.; *lt. matuti'na (hora)] f Cath. eccl. (Frühmesse) matins pl.

Metteur ⊕ (‒tö'r) [fr.] m ⓑ d. typ. maker-up (of the columns in a newspaper, &c.), ehm. a. clicker; foreman of the composing room.

Mett=wurst (⏑⏑⏑) [ndb. Mett=: meat Speise] f ⓑ Bologna, German sausage.

Metze¹ (⏑⏑) [ahd.: mete; *messen] f ⓑ 1. (ehm. Hohlmaß = 3,44 Liter) etwa: three quarts. — 2. = Metzengelb.

Metze² (⏑⏑) [mhd. (Kf. v. Mechthild)] f ⓑ (gemeine Dirne) common wench; prostitute, street-walker.

Metzelei (⏑⏑‒) ⊕ = Gemetzel.

metzeln (⏑⏑) [mhd.; † (ahd.) metzen] v/a. ⓑ a. (schlachten) to slaughter; (niederhauen) to massacre, butcher, cut down.

Metzen=geld (⏑⏑⏑) [Metze¹] n ⓑ (Mahlgeld) miller's fee for grinding.

Metzger prov. (⏑⏑) [mhd.] m ⓑ butcher (= Fleischer, Schlächter).

Metzgerei prov. (⏑⏑‒) f ⓑ butcher's trade or business, butchering.

Meuchel=mord (⏑⏑‒) [mhd.] m ⓑ assassination; =**mörder(in)** m assassin; (hired) bravo; ⏑**mörderisch** a. ⓑ assassin-like. [ⓑa. to assassinate.]

meucheln (⏑⏑) [ahd.] v/a. und v/n. (h.)]

Meuchler (⏑⏑) [ahd.] m ⓑ, ~**in** f ⓑ assassin; hired murderer; **meuchlerisch** (⏑⏑⏑) a. ⓑ assassin-like; (verräterisch) treacherous, insidious.

meuchlings (⏑⏑) [mhd.] adv. treacherously, insidiously, in an underhand way, slily, F on the sly.

Meute (⏑⏑) [nhd. 15. sae.; *fr. meute] f ⓑ hunt. pack of hounds.

Meuterei (‒⏑‒) [nhd.; *fr. émeute Aufstand] f ⓑ bsd. ⚔ und ⚓ mutiny, weitS. sedition, plot; **Meuterer** (‒⏑⏑) m ⓑ mutineer, plotter; **meuterisch** a. ⓑ mutinous, weitS. seditious.

meutern (‒⏑) v/n. (h.) ⓑa. to (cause a) mutiny. [kanisch a. ⓑ Mexican.]

Mexikaner (⏑‒⏑) [nhd.] m ⓑ, ~**in** f ⓑ, **mexi Mexiko** ☿ (⏑‒⏑) npr/n. ⓓa. (Republik u. St. in Nord=amerika) Mexico.

Mezzanin (⏑⏑‒) [it.] n ⓓd. arch. (Halbgeschoß) intermediate story.

Mezzo=sopran ♪ (mě'd=so...) [it.] m ⓑ (Stimme zw. Sopra'n u. Alt) mezzo-soprano.

mg, öft. **mg** abbr. = Milligramm.

mhd. abbr. = mittelhochdeutsch.

Miasma (-⏑⏑) [grch.] n ⓑ med. (Ansteckungsstoff) infectious substance, ⚥ miasma; ⏑**tisch** (-⏑‒⏑) a. ⓑ miasmatic(al).

miau (⏑‒) int. Katze: mew!; ⏑**en** (⏑‒⏑) v/n. (h.) ⓑ to mew, to cater-waul.

mich (⏑) [ahd.: me; lt. me] acc. von ich: me; er kennt ⏑ he knows me; ⏑ selbst myself; ich kenne ⏑ I know myself; ich freue ⏑ I am glad, I rejoice; ich fürchte ⏑ nicht I am not afraid; ich ziehe ⏑ an I am dressing (myself); ich setzte ⏑ I sat down. [Micah.]

Micha (‒⏑) [hebr.] npr/m. ⓓa. bibl.]

Micha=el (⏑⏑⏑) [hebr.] npr/m. ⓓa. (auch Bn.) Michael; ~**i(s)** inv. (29. September, engl. Quartalstag) Michaelmas; ~**i=fest** n, ~**i=tag** m Michaelmas(-day); ~**i=messe** f Michaelmas-fair.

Michel (⏑⏑) npr/m. ⓑ ⓓa. 1. [Mi'cha=el] (Bn.) Mick, Mike. — 2. [ahd.: mickle groß (P)] fig. (Tölpel) clumsy (or unmannerly) fellow; (Bauer) yokel, clodhopper; (Dummkopf) stupid fellow; der deutsche ~ honest (but slow) German or Teuton; ~**s=tag** m = Michaeli(s).

mied(e) (⏑(⏑)) impf. ind. (subj.) v. meiden.

Mieder (⏑⏑) [mhd.] n ⓑ tightly fitting bodice, (corset-like) vest.

Miene (⏑⏑) [Hom. Mine] [nhd.; *fr. mine] f ⓑ air, countenance, mien; (Gesichtszug) feature; (Musschen) look; f. ernsthaft; e=m eine finstere (od. saure) ~ m. to look black (or to frown, to glower) at a p.; eine kecke ~ aufsetzen, oft: to put on a bold front; ohne eine ~ zu verziehen without moving a muscle (of one's face), without wincing, f. gut 4 gegen Schluß.

Mienen=deuter (⏑⏑‒...) m ⓑ physiognomist; =**deuterei, =kunde** f (art of) physiognomy, physiognomics; =**spiel** n, =**sprache** f play (or expression) of the facial muscles or the features; pantomime, mimicry, dumb show.

Miere ⚲ (⏑⏑) f ⓑ chickweed (Alsi'ne).

Mies=muschel (‒⏑⏑) f ⓑ zo. common (or eatable, edible) mussel or muscle (My'tilus edu'lis).

Miet=ausfall (‒⏑⏑) m ⓑ loss of rent.

mietbar (‒⏑) [Miete¹] a. ⓑ rentable, on hire; tenantable.

Miete¹ (‒⏑) [ahd.: meed] f ⓑ 1. (Geld für et. Gemietetes) (house-) rent, weitS. hire; die vierteljährliche ~ ist fällig the quarter's rent is due (to-day); rückständige ~ overdue (or arrears pl. of) rent. — 2. (Verhältnis des Mieters) tenancy, lease; zur ~ geben: to let out (on hire); Diener: to engage, Pferde: to job; ⚓ ein Schiff: to charter, to freight; monatlich ⏑ to take a room, &c. by the month. — II ~ n ⓑ renting, &c. (f. I); engagement of servants. [stack, store.]

mieten² (⏑⏑) [ahd.] f ⓑ agr. (aufschichten) to]

Miet=entschädigung (⏑‒⏑⏑⏑) f ⓑ allowance for house-rent.

Mieter (⏑⏑) [Miete¹] m ⓑ, ~**in** f ⓑ: ~ einer Wohnung tenant of a dwelling-house; ⚓ ~ e=s Schiffes: charterer, freighter.

Miet=frau (‒...) f ⓑ: a) landlady; b) (Mieterin) female tenant or lodger; ⏑**frei** a. ⓑ rent-free; (zu vermieten) to be let (with immediate occupation); =**fuhre** f hackney-carriage; =**gaul** m = =**pferd**; =**geld** n: a) = =**zins**; b) (Handgeld) earnest(-money); =**haus** n house let (out) to a tenant, auch = =**kaserne**; =**herr** m: a) landlord; b) tenant; (gentleman)lodger; =**kaserne** f large house inhabited by several (or many) families, Am. a. tenement-house; =**kontrakt** m = =**vertrag**; =**kutsche** f hackney-coach; =**kutscher** m hackney-coachman; (Jauberer)jobber; =**leute** pl. tenants, lodgers pl.

Mietling (‒⏑) m ⓓd. bsd. ⚔ mercenary, hireling; ~**s=schar** (⏑⏑‒) f ⓑ band (or troop, gang) of mercenaries.

Miet=pferd (‒...) n ⓑ hired (or livery-) horse, job(bed) horse, hack(ney-horse); =**preis** m (house-)rent.

Miets=mann (‒⏑⏑) m ⓑ tenant, lodger, occupier; **Miets=...** f. **Miet=...**

Mietung (⏑⏑) f ⓑ = mieten¹ II.

Miet=vertrag (‒...) m ⓑ agreement between tenant and landlord, für längere Zeit: lease; =**wagen** m hackney-carriage; ⏑**weise** adv. on (or by way of) hire; =**wohnung** f(hired) lodgings pl.; =**zeit** f time of hire, term of an agreement or a lease; =**zins** m (house-)rent.

[Miez] — 695 — [Militärmütze]

Miez (́) f ⚥, **~e** (́̆) f ⚥, *dim.* **~chen** n ⚥ 1. *npr/f.* = Marie(chen). — 2. Lockruf für die Katze: puss, pussy, tib, tibby.
Migräne (̆́̆) [fr., *grch.] f ⚥ *path.* sick (or bilious) headache, (fr.) migraine; **~hemicrania**; **~stift** (́̆⌣̆⌣̆) m ⚥ *pharm.* headache-pencil.
Mikado (-́-) [jap.] m ⚥ (Kaiser) Mikado.
Mikrobe ⚕ (-́⌣) [fr.; *grch. kurzlebig] f ⚥, **Mikrobion** (-́(⌣)⌣) n ⚥ = Bakterie.
Mikro=farad ⚕ (́⌣.⌣̆) [grch.-engl.] n ⚥ d. ($1/1\,000\,000$ Farad, *ant.* Megafarad) microfarad. [(Kugelbatterie) micrococcus.]
Mikrokokkus ⚕ (-́⌣́-) [grch.] m ⚥ Biologie:
Mikrokosmus ⚕ (-́⌣́-) [grch.] m ⚥ microcosm, man (as a world in himself).
Mikrometer ⚕ (-́⌣̆́-) n (m) ⚥ *phys., ast.* micrometer; **~schraube** f micr.-screw.
Mikron ⚕ (́-) [grch.] n ⚥ (*abbr.* μ = $1/1000$ mm) micron.
Mikronesi=en ♀ (-́⌣(⌣)⌣) [grch.] *npr/n.* ⚥ α. Inseln im Großen Ozean: Micronesia.
Mikronesi=er/in (́⌣) m ⚥ Micronesian.
Mikroorganismus ⚕ (́-⌣⌣⌣⌣̆-) [lt., *grch.] m ⚥ Biologie: micro-organism.
Mikrophon ⚕ (-̆́⌣) [grch.] n ⚥ d. microphone. [f ⚥ microphotography.]
Mikrophotographie ⚕ (́-⌣̆⌣-⌣̆-) [grch.]
Mikroskop (-̆́-) [grch.] n ⚥ d. *phys.* (Vergrößerungsglas) microscope; **~ie** (-⌣̆-́) f ⚥ microscopy; **~iker** (-⌣́-⌣⌣) m ⚥ microscopist; **Zisch=** (-⌣́-) a. ⚥ microscopical; Zisches Präparat microscopic slide.
Mikrozephale ⚕ (-⌣⌣⌣́⌣) [grch. Kleinkopf] m ⚥ microcephalous being.
Milan (⌣́-) [fr., *It.] m ⚥ d., **~e** (⌣́⌣) f ⚥ *orn.* kite (*Milvus*).
Milbe (́⌣) [ahd.] f ⚥ zo. mite (*A'carus*); **milbig** *a.* ⚥ full of mites.
Milch (⚥) [ahd.: milch; *melken] f ⚥ (o. *pl.*) 1. milk; dicke (a. saure) ~ curdled (or sour) milk; f. abrahmen¹ und abschöpfen 1; die ~ ist geronnen the milk has curdled or turned sour; ~ erzeugend milk-producing, ⚕ lactific; *fig.* aussehen wie ~ und Blut to have a complexion like lilies and roses; die ~ frommer Denkungsart (SCH. der frommen Denkart) the milk of human kindness. — 2. *ichth.* bisw. *a.* m ⚥ b. (Samen männlicher Fische; *ant.* Rogen) soft roe, milt.
Milch=ader (⚥...) f ⚥ *anat.*: ⚕ lacteal-vein; **=artig** *a.* ⚥ milky, ⚕ lacteal; **=artigkeit** f: ⚕ lactescence; **=bart** F m: a) downy beard; b) *fig.* beardless youth, b.s. (Gelbschnabel) F greenhorn, milksop; **=brei** m milk- (or milky) porridge; **=brötchen** n French roll; **=bruder** m: a) der dieselbe Amme gehabt hat: foster-brother; b) (man who is) fond of milk; **=bureau** n creamery, dairy; **=drüse** f, *anat.*: ⚕ mammary (or lactiferous) gland; **=einer** m milk-pail.
milchen¹ (́⌣) *a.* ⚥ (D9) 1. of milk, milky. — 2. *ichth.* with soft roe.
milchen² (́⌣) *v/n.* (h.) ⚥ 1. vom Milchvieh: to give milk; ²de Kuh milch cow, cow in milk. — 2. ⚕ to yield (or give) a milky juice, to be lactescent.
Milcher (́⌣) m ⚥ 1. = Milchner. — 2. *a.* ~in ⚥ = Melker(in).
Milch=farbe (⚥...) f ⚥ colour of milk, milky colour; **=fieber** n, *path.* milk-fever, ⚕ lacteal fever, galactopyretus; **=frau** f woman who sells milk; dairy-woman; vgl. **=händler**; **²gebend** *a.* ⚥ giving milk, ⚕ lactiferous, lactescent; **=gefäß** n: a) vessel for milk, milk-jug; b) *anat.* **=e** *n/pl.*: ⚕ lacteal (or galactophorous) vessels *pl.*; **=gesicht** n, *fig.*: a) (child's) soft face; b) pasty (or white) face; α. whey-face; **=glas** n: a) milk-(white) glass, opal(escent) glass; b) ⚕ =pumpe; **=güte=prober** m Werkzeug: lactoscope; vgl. =messer.
milchhaft, milchicht, milchig (́⌣) *a.* ⚥ milky, like milk, ⚕ lacteal; milchige Beschaffenheit milkiness, ⚕ lactescence.
milch=haltig (⚥...) *a.* ⚥: ⚕ lactiferous, lactescent; **=handel** ⚒ m ⚥ milk-trade; **=händler** m dairy-man; milk-man (in England bringt meistens ein Mann die Milch ins Haus); **=händlerin** f = =frau; **=kaffee** m coffee with milk; **=kammer** f dairy; **=kanne** f: a) metallene: milk-can; b) milk-jug; **=kraut** n milk-tare (*Glaux mari'tima*); **=kuh** f milch cow, cow in milk; **=kur** f, *med.* milk-cure or -diet; **=mädchen** n, **=magd** f milk-maid; dairy-maid; **=mangel** m shortness of milk, *med.* bei Wöchnerinnen: ⚕ agalactia; **=mann** m = =händler; **=messer** ⚙ m milk-gauge, ⚕ (ga)lactometer.
Milch(n)er (⚥...) [Milch 2] m ⚥ *ichth.* (Männchen der Fische, *ant.* Rogner) soft-roe(d) fish, milter.
Milch=prober ⚙ (⚥...) m ⚥ = =messer; **=pumpe** f, *med.* breast-glass or -fountain; **=rahm** m cream; **=reis** m rice boiled in milk, rice-pudding; **=saft** m: a) ♀ milky juice; b) *physiol.*: ⚕ chyle; **=sauer** *a.* ⚥ *chm.*: ⚕ lactic; ²saures Salz lactate; **=säure** f ⚕ lactic acid ($C_3H_6O_3$); **=schwester** f: a) foster-sister; b) woman (who is) fond of milk; **=speise** f milk-diet; **=stern** ♀ m star-of-Bethlehem (*Ornitho'galum*); doldiger ~ six-o'clock flower (*O. umbella'tum*); **=straße** f, *ast.* Milky Way, ⚕ galaxy; **=suppe** f milk-soup; **=topf** m milk-pot or -pan; **=vieh** n cattle which give milk; **²weiß** *a.* (of a) milky white; *ent.*: ⚕ lacteous; **=wirtschaft** f dairy-farm(ing); **=zahn** m, *anat.* milk-tooth; **=zucker** m, *chm.* sugar of milk, ⚕ lactin(e), lactose ($C_{12}H_{22}O_{11}$).
mild, ²e¹ (́⌣) [ahd.: mild] *a.* ⚥ (*ant.* hart, herb, streng) mild (climate, weather, taste), soft (air, rain, words), gentle (breezes, rebuke), mellow (wine, fruit); (nachsichtig) indulgent, lenient, (gut-mütig) good-natured; (barmherzig) charitable, (wohlwollend) benevolent, kind; (freigebig) liberal; f. Gabe 1; seine ²e Hand auftun to give with an open hand, to loosen one's purse-strings; ²es Klima mild (or genial) climate; ²e Stiftung charitable endowment; foundation, charity; ²e Strafe slight punishment; ²e (*adv.*) beurteilen to judge leniently, to criticize mildly, to make allowance(s) for, beschönigend: to gloss over.
Milde² (́⌣) f ⚥ (f. mild) mildness, softness, gentleness, mellowness; indulgence, leniency; benevolence, kindness, charitableness; des Wetters oft: geniality, clemency, balminess.
mildern (́⌣) I *v/a.* u. **sich ²** *v/refl.* ⚥ *a.*: (sich) ² to make (to grow) mild or mellow or gentle; to soften; (ermäßigen) to moderate, mitigate, temper; (lindern) to soothe, assuage, alleviate; (menschlicher machen) to humanize; vom Wetter: sich ² to grow milder or more genial; gemilderter Ausdruck qualified statement; *pharm.*(versüßen) to sweeten, *chm.* to correct; *jur.* ²de Umstände extenuating circumstances *pl.* — II ~ n ⚥ u. **Milderung** f ⚥ softening, &c. (f. I); mitigation of evils; alleviation or pain; humanization of men; qualification of a statement; *chm.* correction.
Milderungs=grund (⚥⌣⌣...) m ⚥ mitigating cause; **=mittel** n. *med.* lenitive, corrective; **=wort** n euphemism.
mild=gesinnt (⚥...) *a.* ⚥ of gentle disposition; **²herzig** *a.*: a) tender- (or kind-)hearted; b) charitable, bountiful; **=herzigkeit** f ⚥: a) tender- (or kind-)heartedness; b) charitableness; **²reich, ²tätig** *a.* charitable, open-handed; **=tätigkeit** f charity.
Milieu* (mi-liö') [fr. Mitte] n ⚥ Schrifttum u. Kunst: (Umgebung) surroundings *pl.*, sphere, (Hintergrund) background; (Färbung, Ton) (local) colour, (general) tone.
Militär ⚔ (⌣⌣́) [fr. ~ *militaire*; *It. militar-*] I n ⚥ d. (o. *pl.*) (Soldatenstand; *ant.* Zivil) the military (profession), soldiery; (Heer) army; unter das ~ geh(e)n to join the army or the ranks. — II m ⚥ (*ant.* Bürger) military man, soldier; man of the sword.
Militär=anwärter ⚔ (⌣⌣́-⌣...) m ⚥ soldier entitled to civil employment; **=arzt** m army-surgeon, -doctor; **=attaché** m military attaché; **=beamte(r)** m official attached to the army, commissary; **=behörden** f/pl. military authorities *pl.*; **=budget** n = =etat; **=dienst** m military service; **²dienst=frei** *a.* ⚥ exempt from mil. service; vgl. ²frei; **=(dienst=)pflicht** f liability to serve in the army; **²(dienst=)pflichtig** *a.* liable to mil. service, bound to serve in the army; **=dienst=tauglichkeit** f fitness for military service; **=dienst=zeichen** n badge showing a soldier's time of service; **=eisenbahnwesen** n (all that concerns) strategic railways; **=etat** m army-budget or -estimates *pl.*; **²frei** *a.* free (or discharged) from mil. service; **²fromm** *a. v.* Pferden: trained to the sounds of battle, accustomed to (the noise of) firing; **=gericht** n mil. court; **=grenze** ♀ f mil. frontier; **=herrschaft** f mil. rule, militarism.
Militaria ⚔ (⌣⌣́-⌣) [lt.] *pl. inv.* military affairs or matters, army-matters *pl.*; auf Brief=adressen: on service.
militärisch ⚔ (⌣⌣́-⌣) *a.* ⚥ (*ant.* bürgerlich) military, soldierlike, soldierly; (kriegerisch aussehend) martial. [ism.)
Militarismus (⌣⌣⌣́⌣) [ult.] m ⚥ militar-)
Militär=kapelle (⌣⌣́⌣...) f ⚥ military band; **=macht** f mil. power; **=maß** n mil. standard; **=musik** f music of a mil. band; auch martial music; **=mütze** f soldier's cap; für den Felddienst:

⚕ scientific; ♀ botanical; ♀ geography; ⚙ machinery; ⚒ mining; ⚔ military; ⚓ marine; ⚖ commercial; ✉ postal; 🚂 railway.

foraging-cap; =pflicht f liability to serve (in the army); pflichtig a. liable to mil. service; =pflichtige(r) m one liable to mil. service or bound to serve in the army; =staat m mil. state; =stand m = Militär I; auch: profession of arms; =straße f military road; =tuch n army-cloth; =verwaltung f army administration; (Kriegsrat: in England seit 1895) Army Board; =vorlage f, parl. army-bill; =wesen n military questions or affairs pl.; =wirtschaft f militarism.

Miliz [it.] (Bürgersoldaten) in Engl.: militia, berittene: yeomanry.

Millennium [lt. -Jahrtausend] n millennium; millenary.

Milliarde [fr.] f (tausend Millionen = 1 000 000 000) milliard.

Milli-gramm [fr.] n d, 6. (1/1000 Gramm = 0'0154 troy grains; abbr. mg, öft. mg) milligram(me); =meter n (m) (1/1000 Meter = 0'03937 of an inch; abbr. mm, öft. mm) millimetre.

Million [nhd., *fr.] f million; drei =en Menschen three million(s of) people; ~är m d. millionaire; =en-fach, -mal a million times.

million(s)t ord. numb. millionth; ~el n millionth part; elect. ein 2el Ampere (Farad) microampere (microfarad). [spleen.]

Milz [ahd.: milt] f anat. milt,

Milz-blut-ader f anat. splenic vein; =brand(ig a.) m, vet. (suffering from) anthrax; =farn m spleenwort, ceterach (Asplenium ceterach); =krank a. splenetic, =krankheit f, path.: splenopathy; =kraut n golden saxifrage (Chrysosplenium oppositifolium); =stechen n stitch in the side, splenalgia; =sucht f, path. spleen, hypochondria(sis); =süchtig(er m) a. splenetic, hypochondriac (als a. a. ...al).

Mime [grch.] m thea. Alt.: (Schauspieler) actor, stage-player, weiterS. mimic; Mimik f mimic art, mimics, mimicry; Mimiker m mimic; mimisch a. mimical.

Mimose [it.] f (Sinnpflanze) sensitive plant, mimosa (Mimo'sa).

Minarett [ar. Leuchtturm] n d. arch. (Moscheenturm) minaret.

Minchen [Mine³, dim.] npr/n. a. (Bn.) Minnie, Wilmot.

minder [ahd.: lt. minor] comp. von wenig, gering, auch klein (ant. mehr) I adv. 1. less; 2 gut of lower (or inferior) quality. — II a. (D9), bisw. inv. 2. less(er), (kleiner) smaller; (weniger bedeutend) inferior, minor; 2e Anzahl = Minderzahl. — 3. als s/n. das ~ minor quantity. — 4. s/m. der ~e the inferior man. — Vgl. a. gering, wenig.

Minder-betrag m less (or smaller) amount; deficiency, shortness (of cash); =einnahme f (=ertrag m) smaller (or falling-off in the) receipts (returns) pl.; =gewicht n shortness in weight.

Minderheit f minority.

minder-jährig a. jur. under age; ~e(r) m jur. minor, jur. auch: infant; ~keit f minority.

mindern I v/a. u. sich v/refl. a.: (sich) to make (to grow) less; to lessen, diminish, decrease; sich a.: to fall off; (herabsetzen) to abate, to reduce; vgl. mildern I; die Schnelligkeit to slacken speed; die Segel to shorten sail. — II ~ n und Minderung f diminution, decrease, falling-off; abatement, reduction.

Minder-wert m inferiority; =wertig a. of inferior (or lower) value, inferior, a. low-priced; =wertigkeit f inferior value, inferiority, a. inferior (or lower) quality; =zahl f lesser (or smaller) number, beim Abstimmen: minority.

mindest sup. v. minder. I adv. least; smallest, lowest; 2ens, zum 2en, aufs 2e, zu2 at the (very) least, to say the least; nicht im 2en not in the least, not in the slightest degree. — II a. u. s. the least; nicht das 2e not the smallest amount, F not a bit (of it), not the least bit; er hat nicht die 2e Aussicht he has not the slightest (F not the ghost of a) chance.

Mindest-betrag m lowest (or minimum) amount or sum; =bietend(e[r m] f) a. (p.) making the lowest offer or bid; =fordernd(e[r m] f) a. (p.) asking (or charging) the lowest price; =gehalt: a) m lowest percentage; b) minimum salary or pay.

Mine¹ Hom. Miene [nhd.; *fr.] f 1. = Bergwerf. — 2. frt. (Sprenggrube, Sprengvorrichtung) mine; ~n streuen to lay (submarine) mines, to put down mines; fig. alle ~n springen lassen to use every possible effort, to leave no stone unturned.

Mine² [grch.] f Alt.: (Gewicht und Münze: 1/60 Talent = 100 Drachmen) mina.

Mine³ npr/f. Bß. (Bn.; abbr. von Wilhelmine) Mina, vgl. Minchen.

Minen-auge [Mine¹] n entrance to a mine or gallery; =bau m construction of mines, mining operations pl.; =besitztümer n/pl. mining properties pl.; =feld n (mit Minen belegtes Gewässer) mine-field; =gang m gallery; =gräber m miner, sapper; =gründe m/pl. mining plots pl.; =hals m outlet to a gallery; =kammer f chamber of a mine; =krieg m subterraneous (or subterranean) war; =ladung f charge of a mine; =netz n araign(ée); =schacht, =trichter m shaft, funnel of a mine; =zündung f firing of mines (durch elektrische Drähte by means of electric wires); =zweig m branch of a mine, side-gallery.

Mineral [mlt.] n d. (ant. Pflanze, Tier) mineral; reich an ~ien rich in minerals, well mineralized.

Mineral-bad n mineral bath; =brunnen m =quelle; =gelb n (basisches Chlorblei) mineral yellow; =grün n (arsenitsaures Kupfer) mineral green.

Minerali-en-kabinett n, =sammlung f cabinet, collection of minerals; =kunde f mineralogy.

mineralisch a. mineral; 2e Reichtümer pl. mineral wealth sg.

Mineral-lager n mineral deposit.

Mineralog m, ~e mineralogist; ~ie (Mineralienkunde) mineralogy; Lisch a. mineralogical.

Mineral-öl n mineral oil, petroleum; =öl-quelle f oil-spring; =quelle f mineral spring, spa, warme: thermal spring; =reich n (ant. Tier-, Pflanzen-reich) min. kingdom; =reichtum abundance of minerals; =wasser n min. water; =wässer pl.: mineralsp pl.

Mineur [fr.] m d. = Minierer, (a.) Minengräber. [miniature.]

Miniatur [fr.] f (Kleinmalerei)

Miniatur-ausgabe f Buchhandel: miniature (or pocket-)edition; =band m miniature volume; =bild, =gemälde n min. picture; =maler(ei f) m min. painter (painting). [ant.

Minier-ameise f ent. mining

minieren und [fr.] v/a. to sap; to (under)mine; Minierer m sapper; miner.

Minier-kunst f art of mining, underground engineering, art of laying submarine mines; =pflug subsoil plough; =spinne f, zo. trap-door spider (Ctenʹiza); =werkzeuge n/pl. miner's tools pl.

Minimal-betrag m = Mindestbetrag; =fläche f minimum area or space; =gewicht n minimum weight; =preis, =satz m lowest (or minimum) price or rate.

Minimum [lt.] n (Mindestbetrag; ant. Maximum) minimum (a. math.), auf ein ~ bringen to minimize.

Minister [lt. Diener] m , ~in f minister; (Staatssekretär) secretary of state; Frau =(in) minister's wife, als Anrede: Madam //; s. äußere 3, inner 3, Finanz-, Kolonial-, Kriegs-, Kultus- 2.

Ministerial-beamte(r) m (permanent) official of a ministerial department; =befehl, =erlaß m pol. ministerial order or edict, in Engl.: order of the Privy Council; =gebäude n (building containing) government offices pl.; =rat m, etwa: permanent head of a ministerial department; =sekretär m secretary (or clerk) in a ministerial office.

ministeri-ell [fr.] a. ministerial; ~e(r) m, pol. ministerialist.

Ministerium [lt.] n ministry (in England heißen die das Kabinett bildenden Ersten Minister Cabinet Ministers, das Kabinett b); pol. Anhänger des ~s supporter of the ministry, ministerialist; im ~ sein to be in the ministry or in office; ins ~ treten to enter the ministry, mit Portefeuille: to accept a seat in the cabinet; s. äußere 3, inner 3, Finanz-, Kolonial-, Kriegs-, Kultus- 2.

Minister-konferenz f conference of ministers; vgl. =rat; =krisis f ministerial crisis; =portefeuille n, etwa: seat in the cabinet; vgl. =stelle; =präsident m President of the Council; (Erster Minister) Prime Minister, Premier; =rat m Council of Ministers, Cabinet Council; =resident m minister resident; =stelle f ministerial office; =verantwortlichkeit f ministerial

responsibility; **=wechsel** m change of (or in) the ministry.
Ministrant (ᴗ‿ᴗ)[lt.] m ⓐ vgl. Mesner 1.
ministrieren (ᴗ‿ᴗᴗ) [lt. dienen] v/n. (h.) ⓐ bsd. eccl. to minister, to officiate.
Minne (´ᴗ) [ahd.: mind] f ⓐ mst poet. (Liebe) love; (Werbung) lover's wooing.
Minne=(ge)sang (´ᴗ...) m ⓐ love-song (or -poetry); **=glück** n happiness of love(rs); **=hof** m court of love; **=lied** n love-ditty; **=lohn** m lover's meed; **=sold** m lover's reward. [to love, to woo.
minnen (´ᴗ) v/a. u. v/n. (h.) ⓐ mst poet.
Minne=sang (´ᴗ...) m ⓐ = =gesang; **=sänger** m, **=singer** m (deutscher Lyriker im 12. u. 13. sae.) † minnesinger; **=sold** m lover's reward.
minnig(lich) (´ᴗ(ᴗ) a. ⓐ 1. (lieblich) lovely, charming; (Minne erregend) love-inspiring. — 2. (liebend) loving, enamoured.
minorenn (ᴗᴗ´) [lt.] a. ⓐ (minderjährig) under age; **=e(r)** m f ⓐ minor; **=ität** f ⓐ (years pl. of) minority.
Minorit (ᴗᴗ´) [lt.] m ⓐ eccl. Minor(ite).
Minorität (ᴗᴗᴗ´) [lt.] f ⓐ (ant. Majorität) minority, s. Minderzahl.
Minotaur(os) (-´ᴗ(ᴗ) [grch.] m ⓐd. (②) myth. (Stiermensch) Minotaur.
Minstrel † (´ᴗ) [engl.] m ⓐ minstrel.
Minuend (ᴗᴗ´) [lt.] m ⓐ arith. (ant. Subtrahend) minuend.
minus (´lt.] bsd. math. **I** adv.: 6 ⁒ 4 (gschr. 6—4) six minus four. — **II Minus** n, inv. (Ausfall) deficiency, ⓐ deficit, shortness; **=betrag** m = Minderbetrag.
Minuskel (ᴗ´ᴗ) [lt.] f ⓐ (ant. Majuskel) small letter, minuscule (a. ⊙ typ.).
Minus=zeichen (´ᴗ.ᴗ) n ⓐ math. minus sign, sign of subtraction (—).
Minute (ᴗ´ᴗ) [lt.] f ⓐ Zeit= und Winkelmaß: minute; auf die ~ at (or to) the (very) minute; in ein paar ~n in a few minutes; in der nächsten ~e in another minute, a minute after; wart' eine ~! wait a moment (P abbr. a mo.)!
minuten=lang (ᴗ´ᴗ...) a. ⓐ lasting a minute or for minutes, of a min.'s duration; **=uhr** ♀ f ⓐ minute-watch; **=weise** adv. (F a. a.) by minutes, (happening) every minute; **=werk** ⊙ n in Uhren ꝛc.: minute-works pl.; **=zeiger** ⊙ m minute-hand. [(genau) minute.
minuziös (ᴗ-tß/ᴗ´) [lt.] a. ⓐ (D 10)⎬
Minze ⚹ (´ᴗ) [grch.] f ⓐ mint (Mentha).
Miozän ⚷ (-ᴗtß´) [grch.] n ⓐ d. miocene.
mir (´) [ahd.: me: lt. mihi] dat. von ich:
1. to me, me; er gab es mir ob. ⒉'s he gave it (to) me; das braucht ⒉ niemand zu sagen nobody need tell me that; ⒉ ist's kalt I feel cold; ich wusch ⒉ die Hände I washed my hands; ein Freund von ⒉ a friend of mine; jetzt ist es an ⒉ now it is my turn. — 2. Redensarten: (nur so) ⒉ nichts, dir nichts (ohne weiteres) without ado or ceremony, quite coolly or unceremoniously; als dati'vus e'thicus, meist nicht zu übersetzen, ⒊B.: laßt ⒉ das bleiben! leave (or let) that alone!, don't do that!; vgl. bleiben 8; Sprichw. s. heute 1; wie du ⒉, so ich dir tit for tat; as you treat (or do to) me, so I (shall) treat (or do to) you.
Mirabelle ⚹ (-ᴗ´ᴗ) [fr.] f ⓐ (gelbliche Pflaume) (small) yellow plum.

Mirakel (-´ᴗ) [lt.] n ⓐ (Wunder) miracle; im Mittelalter: **~=spiel** (-´ᴗ.ᴗ´) n ⓐ (christlich-religiöses Drama) miracle-play.
Nirban=essenz, **=öl** (´ᴗ...) n ⓐ nitrobenzene, nitrobenzol ($C_6H_5NO_2$).
Misanthrop (-ᴗ´) [grch.] m ⓐ (Menschenfeind) misanthrope; **=ie** (-ᴗᴗ´) f ⓐ misanthropy; **=isch** (-ᴗ´ᴗ) a. ⓐ misanthropical.
Misch=art (´ᴗ´) f ⓐ mongrel race, cross-breed; vgl. Mischvolk.
mischbar (´ᴗ) a. ⓐ mixable.
Mischbarkeit (´ᴗ‿) f ⓐ mixability.
Misch=butter ⚹ (´ᴗ...) f ⓐ adulterated butter, margarine; **=dünger** m, agr. compost; **=ehe** f mixed marriage.
Mischel (´ᴗ) m, n ⓐ = Mischkorn.
mischen (´ᴗ) [ahd.: mix: lt. misce're] **I** v/a. und sich ⒉ v/refl. ⓐ **1.** = mengen I; chm. to combine, ⊙ metall. to alloy; Wein mit Wasser ⒉ to mix wine with water; unter et. ⒉ to jumble up with s.th. — 2. die Karten ⒉ to shuffle (F to make) the cards; betrügerisch: F to doctor the cards; wer muß ⒉? F who makes the cards? Sie müssen ⒉ F it's your make. — **3.** sich in fremde Angelegenheiten ⒉ to interfere in (or meddle with) other people's affairs; sich ins Gespräch ⒉ to take part (or join) in a conversation. — **II** ~ n ⓐ 4. = Mischung 1. — **III ge=mischt** p.p. u. a. ⓐ 5. mixed; eine ⒉e Gesellschaft a mixed (or miscellaneous) company; ⒉e Schule mixed school (for boys and girls); System der ⒉en Schulen bsd. Am. u. schott. co-education; arith. ⒉e Zahl (ganze Zahl und Bruch) mixed number. — 6. (gefälscht) adulterated, F doctored.
Misch=farbe (´ᴗ...) f ⓐ mixed colour; **=futter** n mixed fodder or provender; **=gefäß** n vessel for mixing; **=korn** n wheat and rye mixed; **=krug** m = =gefäß.
Mischling (´ᴗ) m ⓐd. hybrid, mongrel, (Kreuzung) cross- (or half-)breed, auch F cross, vgl. Blendling.
Misch=masch (´ᴗ...) m ⓐ a. medley, hodgepodge; (Heap of) confusion; **=metall** ⊙ n ⓐ composition, compound (metal); (Legierung) alloy; **=rasse** f = =art; **=sprache** f mixed (or hybrid) language; **=trank** n mixture.
Mischung (´ᴗ) f ⓐ **1.** mixing, &c. (s. mischen I) mixture. — 2. chm. combination, composition; (Legierung) alloy.
Mischungs=gewicht (´ᴗ...) n ⓐ chm. combining- (or atomic) weight; **=rechnung**, **=regel** f, arith. rule of alligation; **=verhältnis** n ratio of combination or components, combining-ratio.
Misch=volk (´ᴗᴗ) n ⓐ mixed race or breed; vgl. Misch=art.
miserabel (ᴗᴗ´ᴗ) [lt.] a. ⓐ (D9) miserable, wretched.' [wretchedness.⎬
Misere (ᴗ´ᴗ) [fr. Elend] f ⓐ misery.
Miserere (ᴗᴗ´ᴗ) [lt. erbarme dich!] n ⓐ (inv.): a) Cath. eccl. Bußpsalm (Pf. 51); b) path. (Kot=erbrechen bei Darmverschlingung) miserere.
Misogyn (-ᴗ´) [grch.] m ⓐ (⓪d.), **~e** ⓐ (Weiberfeind) misogynist, woman-hater.
Mispel ⚹ (´ᴗ) [ahd.] f ⓐ **1.** (Frucht) medlar. — 2. **=baum** (´ᴗ.ᴗ´) m ⓐ medlar-tree (Me'spilus germa'nica).
miß¹ (´) imper. von messen.

miß²=..., **Miß²=...** (´...) [ahd.: mis...] Bestimmungswort zu s., a. und v. mit der Grundbedeutung des Verfehlens, Nichttreffens, des Unrechten, Falschen. Bei nouns (ausgenommen verbal nouns auf ...ung) und adjectives liegt der Hauptton auf miß, zB. ~brauch (´ᴗ´), ⒉günstig (´ᴗᴗ); ebenso bei verbs mit einer Vorsilbe, zB. ⒉behagen (´ᴗ.ᴗ´), ⒉braucht (´.. ge=braucht); einfach zs.=gesetzte verbs haben doppelte Betonung (den Ton auf dem Verbalstamme), zB. ⒉deuten: a) (´ᴗ.ᴗ), besser b) (ᴗ´ᴗ); zu a: p.p. ⒉"gedeutet, inf.: miß"zudeuten, zu b: p.p. ⒉deu"tet, inf.: zu ⒉deu"ten.
miß²=achten (´ᴗ.ᴗ´) v/a. ⓐ* (*.*) **I** to disregard, despise, neglect; (geringschätzen) to disdain, undervalue; (nicht befolgen) to disobey. — **II Miß²=achtung** f ⓐ disregard, neglect, disdain.
Missal (ᴗ´) [lt.] **I** f ⓐ typ. Schriftgrad: (44 Punkte) canon. — **II** ~(e) n ⓐd. (②) Cath. eccl. (Meßbuch) missal.
miß²=arten (´ᴗ...) v/n. (fn.) ⓐ*.* (p.p. ⒉geartet) to degenerate; ⒉art p.p. */*, sonst *.* to displease, v/impers. ⓐ es behagt mir I am ill at ease, I feel uncomfortable; ~ n ⓐ uncomfortable feeling; (Unzufriedenheit) discontent; (Unlust) dislike; ⒉behaglich (´ᴗᴗ) a. ⓐ uncomfortable; displeasing; sich ⒉ fühlen to feel uncomfortable or ill at ease; **=belieben** n ⓐ displeasure, dislike; ⒉bilden (´ᴗᴗ) v/a. ⓐ*(*.*) to shape badly, to misshape, stärker: to disfigure; **=bildung** (´ᴗᴗ´) f: a) malformation (auch ♀ u. zo.), stärker: disfigurement, deformity; b) deficient education; ⒉billigen (´ᴗᴗᴗ) v/a. ⓐ*(*.*) to disapprove (of), to discountenance; (nicht gutheißen) to disallow, disavow, condemn; (verwerfen) to reject, to object to; ⒉d p.pr. u. a. ⓐ (u. adv.) disapproving(ly); ~ n ⓐ; **=billigung** f ⓐ disapproval, disapprobation; rejection, objection; **=brauch** (´ᴗch) m abuse, wrong (or improper) use; jur. misprision; **=brauchen** (´ᴗᴗᴗ´) v/a. ⓐ*(*.*): et. (bisw. e-r Sache [gen.]) ⒉ (zu bösen Zwecken verwenden) to abuse a th.; (unrichtig gebrauchen) to misuse a th., to make wrong use of a th.; j-s Güte ⒉ to take advantage of (or to trespass upon) a p.'s kindness; bibl. den Namen Gottes ⒉ to take the name of the Lord in vain; ⒉bräuchlich (er=weise adv.) (´ᴗ.ᴗ) a. ⓐ founded (or resting) on abuse, wrong; ⒉deuten (ᴗ´ᴗ u. ´ᴗ.ᴗ) v/a. ⓐ*(*.*) to misinterpret, misconstrue, misrepresent; ~ n ⓐ u. **=deutung** f ⓐ misinterpretation, misconstruction, misrepresentation.
missen (´ᴗ) [ahd.: miss] v/a. u. v/n. (h.) ⓐ to miss; e=n, et. ⒉ (entbehren) auch: to (have to) do without (or to dispense with) a p., a th.; wir ⒉ ihn ungern we grieve to (have to) lose him or to part with him; er läßt sich leicht ⒉ he can be easily spared.
missest (´ᴗ) ⒉. Person pres. ind. a) von messen; b) von missen.
Miß²=erfolg (´ᴗ...) m ⓐ ill success, want of success; **=ernte** f bad harvest or crop, failure of crops.
Misse=tat (´ᴗ´) [ahd.] f ⓐ misdeed; (Verbrechen) crime.

[**Missetäter**] — 698 — [**mit**]

Misse=täter(in f ㊵) m ㉒ (◡◡⌣◡) evil-doer, malefactor, criminal, jur. felon. **miß²=fallen** (◡◡, ◡◡) v/n. (h.) ㊸a*: e-m ≈ to displease a p., mir ≈fällt die Sache, oft: I am not pleased with it; ~ n ㉓ displeasure; j-š ~ erregen to displease a p.; ≈fällig (◡◡, a. ◡◡) a. ㊻: a) displeasing, unpleasant, disagreeable; (anstößig) offensive, shocking; e-m ≈ werden to displease a p.; to incur a p.'s displeasure; b) adv. sich ≈ (absprechend) über et. äußern to speak unfavourably (or disparagingly) of a th., to find fault with a th.; =**fälligkeit** f㊻ disagreeableness, displeasure; offensiveness; ≈förmig (◡...) a. mis-shapen, deformed; ≈geartet a. degenerate; ≈gebildet a. malformed; =**geburt** f: a) (Fehlgeburt) miscarriage; misconception, false conception; b) (mißgestaltetes Geschöpf) deformity; fig. ~ der Hölle infernal monster; =**geschick** n misfortune; ill(or bad)luck; fatality, adverse fate, adversity; (Unfall) misadventure, accident, mishap; =**gestalt** f deformity; (Scheusal) monstrosity, monster; ≈gestalt(et), ≈gestaltig a. misshapen, (entstellt) deformed; ≈gestimmt a. f. ≈stimmen; ≈glücken (◡◡, ◡◡) v/n. (in, bisw. a. h.) ㊸* to meet with ill success, to miscarry; der Plan ist ihm mißglückt, a. his plan has failed; ~ n ill success, failure; ≈gönnen (◡◡, ◡◡) v/a. ㊸*: e-m et. ≈ to (be)grudge (or envy) a p. a th.; ~ n =**gunst**; =**griff** (◡◡) m: a) ♪ touching a wrong key or note; b) fig. =Fehlgriff; =**gunst** (◡◡) f disfavour; envy, jealousy; ill-will, grudge; ≈günstig (◡◡) a. envious, jealous (auf etwas of a th.); ≈**handeln** (◡◡, ◡◡) v/a. ㊸a*(*,*) to maltreat, to ill-treat, to treat (or use) badly; to brutalize; (◡◡) v/n. (h.) to act wrongly; =**handlung** f maltreatment, ill-treatment, ill-usage; jur. tätliche ~ assault (and battery); =**heirat** (◡◡) f ill-assorted match, (fr.) mésalliance; ≈**hellig** (◡◡) a. discordant (a. fig.); (uneins) dissentient; at variance; =**helligkeit** f discord, dissension; (Zwistigkeit) disagreement, misunderstanding.

Mission (◡◡L) [lt.] f㊻ eccl. mission; ~ar, ~är (◡◡⌣ll) [fr.] m ㊹d. eccl. missionary, evangelizer of the heathen(s). **Missions=anstalt** (◡◡ll...) f㊻ mission-house; =**gesellschaft** f = =verein; =**haus** n training-college for missionaries; =**verein** m missionary society; =**wesen** n missionary affairs pl. or work.

Miß²=jahr (◡...) n ㊷ bad year or harvest, year of failure; =**klang** m ♪ wrong note; jarring sound, jangle; dissonance, discord, disharmony (a. fig.); =**kredit** m discredit, disfavour; in ~ bringen to discredit, to bring into ill repute; =**laut** m discordant (or unpleasant) sound; ≈**leiten** (◡◡) v/a. ㊸* to mislead, misguide, misdirect; to lead astray.

mißlich (◡◡) [ahd. verschieden] a. ㊻ (ungewiß) uncertain, doubtful; (unbequem) awkward; (bedenklich) critical (point), precarious (state), (heikel) delicate

(question), (schwierig) difficult (task); in der Lage in a critical position, F in a tight corner, in a pickle. **Mißlichkeit** (◡◡) f㊻ uncertainty; awkwardness; precariousness, difficulty. **miß²=liebig** (◡...) a. ㊻ unpopular, not much liked, in ill favour; objectionable, obnoxious; et. ≈ (adv.) aufnehmen to take a th. amiss; =**liebigkeit** f ㊻ unpopularity; ≈**lingen** (◡◡, ◡◡) v/n. (in) ㊸* not to succeed, (fehlschlagen) to fail, to prove abortive, to fall through; eine (ganz) ≈lung(e)ne Sache a (dead) failure; ≈lung(e)ner Versuch abortive attempt, a. flash in the pan; ~ n =**glücken**; =**mut** (◡L) m ill-humour, cross mood or temper, discontent; ≈**mutig**, ≈**mütig** a. ill-humoured, cross (-tempered), discontented; ≈**raten** (◡L) v/n. (in) ㊸a*: ≈lingen; ≈rat(e)nes Kind ill-bred child; v/a. (a. ᵟL): e-m et. ≈ to dissuade a p. from a th.; ~ n = ≈glücken; =**stand** (᛬*) m inconvenience, bad (or improper) state; (Fehler) defect; (Beschwerde) grievance; =stände beseitigen to remedy (or remove) abuses; ≈**stimmen** (◡◡, ◡◡) ㊸*, p. p. u. inf. a. ㊸** m (h.) to be discordant; v/a. to put out of tune; fig. to put in ill humour; ≈gestimmt p.p. u. a. discordant; fig. in bad humour, ㊸ depressed, dejected; =**stimmung** f ㊻ discordance; fig. ill-humour, ㊸ depression.

mißt (⌣; Hom. Mist) 2. u. 3. Person pres. ind. v. messen u. missen.

Miß²=ton (◡...) m ㊷ wrong (or false) note; vgl. =klang; ≈tönend, ≈tönig a. ㊻ discordant, grating on the ear, out of tune; ≈**trauen** (◡◡, ◡L◡) v/n. (h.), v/a. u. v/refl. ㊸*(*,*): e-m, et. ≈ to distrust (or mistrust) a p., a th.; to have no confidence in a p., a th.; sich (seinen Fähigkeiten) ≈ to be diffident, to lack (in) self-confidence; ~ (ᵟL) n ㉓: a) distrust, mistrust, want of confidence; gegen sich selbst: diffidence; ~ in e-n, et. setzen to distrust a p., a th.; b) (Argwohn) suspicion; =**trauens=votum** n, parl.,&c. want-of-confidence vote, mehr gbr.: vote of censure; e-m ein ~ ausstellen to pass a vote of censure upon a p.; ≈**trauisch** (ᵟL◡) a. distrustful, (argwöhnisch) suspicious; =**vergnügen** (◡◡L) n displeasure; (Unzufriedenheit) dissatisfaction, discontent; (Bedauern) regret; ≈**vergnügt** (◡◡L) a. displeased, dissatisfied (mit oder über et. with a th.); ✕, pol.,&c.: disaffected, malcontent; (mätelnd) fault-finding; ~e([r] m) f㊻ disaffected person, malcontent, grumbler; =**verhalten** (◡◡◡) n misconduct; =**verhältnis** (◡◡◡) n: a) disproportion(ateness), want of proportion, (Ungleichheit) disparity, incongruity; b) (Zerwürfnis) disagreement, unpleasantness; =**verstand** m =verständnis a.; ≈**verständlich** (◡◡◡) a. mistaken, erroneous, adv. by mistake; =**verständnis** (◡◡◡) n: a) misunderstanding, misapprehension; (falsche Auffassung) misconstruction; b) (Zwist) dissension; ≈**versteh(e)n** (ᵟL(◡) v/a. ㊸*, inf. u. p. p. ㊸*(*) to

misunderstand, to misapprehend; j-š Absichten ≈ to mistake (or misconstrue) a p.'s intentions; =**wachs** (◡◡ts) m scarcity of crops, vgl. =ernte; =**weisung** f der Magnetnadel: aberration of the needle. **Mist¹** (⌣; Hom. mißt) [ahd.] m ㊶b. 1. dung, manure; F muck; fig. fa reine ~ mere rubbish or dirt or trash. — 2. (Kot von Menschen und Tieren) excrements pl., v. Pferden 2c.: droppings pl. **Mist²** T (⌣) m ㊶b. (Nebel) mist, fog. **Mist¹=bauer** (⌣...) m ㊷ driver of a dung-cart; fig. clodhopper, low rustic; =**beet** n, hort. hot- (or forcing-)bed; =**beet=fenster** n forcing-frame; =**beet=kultur** f forcing-bed (or forced) culture. [mistletoe (Viscum album).] **Mistel** ♀ (◡◡) [ahd.: mis(t)le(toe)] f㊻ **Mistel=beere** ♀ (◡◡...) f ㊷ berry of the mistletoe; =**drossel** f, orn. mistle-thrush (Turdus visci'vorus); =**zweig** m mistletoe bough.

misten (◡◡) [Mist¹] ㊸ I v/n. von Tieren: to dung. — II v/a. (den Stall fegen) to clean (or clear) the stable(s).

Mist¹=fink (◡◡...) m ㊷: a) orn. brambling (Fringi'lla montifringi'lla); b) fig. (schmutziger Mensch) dirty(-looking) person, F mud-lark; =**fuhre** f dung-cart; (Fuhre Mist) load of manure; =**gabel** f dung-fork, pitch-fork; =**grube** f dung-hole or -pit; =**hafen** m dung-hook; =**haufe(n)** m dung- (or manure-)heap, dunghill, F muck-heap. [like manure, F mucky.] **mistig¹** (◡◡) [Mist¹] a. ㊻ dung-like,] **mistig²** ↓ (⌣) [Mist²] a. ㊻ (nebelig) misty, foggy; thick (air, atmosphere).

Mist¹=jauche (◡...) f ㊷ liquid manure, drainings pl. of manure; =**käfer** m, ent.: ㉗ coprophagan, dor(-beetle) (Geotru'pes stercora'rius); =**karren** m dung-, manure-cart; =**lache** f, =**pfuhl** m, =**pfütze** f puddle (or pool, bog) formed by liquid manure. **Miszellane=en** (◡◡◡) [lt.], **Miszellen** (◡◡) f/pl. ㊸ (Vermischtes) miscellanies pl. **mit** (⌣) [ahd.: grch. metá'] 1 prp. mit dat. 1. with; ≈ea. with each other, vgl. mit-ein-an-der; (in Begleitung von) in the company of; die Axt, ≈ welcher er den Baum gefällt hat ... with which he felled the tree, ... he felled the tree with; ich ging ≈ ihnen I went (along) with them; ≈ Öl braten (essen) to fry (to eat) with oil. — 2. (voll von) ein Beutel ≈ Datteln a bag (full) of dates. — 3. mit nouns: ≈ Absicht intentionally, with full intention; ≈ den Augen e-n Wink geben F to wink one's eye(s); ≈ blauen Augen with blue eyes, blue-eyed, f. blau 2; ≈ Bleistift schreiben to write in pencil; ≈ voller Dampfkraft at full steam; ≈ dem Degen in der Hand (with) sword in hand; f. Einschluß; ≈ der Eisenbahn by rail; ≈ der elektrischen Bahn by the electric car; ≈ dem Finger auf et. zeigen to point one's finger at a th.; ≈ dem Fuß aufstampfen to stamp one's foot; ≈ offener Gewalt by main force; ≈ den Glocken läuten to ring the bells; f. bewaffnen III; ≈ Lebensgefahr at the peril (or risk) of one's life; einen ≈ Namen nennen to call a p. by his name; ≈nichten by no means, not at all, in no way; ≈ dem

[mit...] — 699 — [Mithilfe]

Omnibus by (omni)bus; ~ der Post by post; ~ Protest under protest; ~ lauter Stimme in a loud voice or tone; ~ der Straßenbahn by tram; ~ einem Worte in a word. — 4. mit *adjectives*: zufrieden ~ // satisfied (or contented) with //; geizig, sparsam ~ // sparing with or of. — 5. mit *verbs*: f. anfangen 2 u. 3; ~ et. bedecken to cover with a th.; sich ~ et. beeilen to make haste with a th.; ich fühle (Mitleid) ~ ihm I feel for him, I sympathize with him; sie geht ~ ihm (ihrem Liebhaber) she goes out (or is keeping company) with him; wie geht es ~ ihm? how is he (getting on)?; wie geht es ~ Ihrer Gicht? how is your gout?; ~ diesen Dingen geht es wie ~ // it is with those things as with //; vgl. unten 10 unter „mit"; ~ einem das gleiche Alter haben to be of the same age as a p.; was ist ~ ihm? what is the matter (F what's up) with him?; es ist ~ seiner Freundschaft nur Verstellung his friendship is a mere sham; wie weit sind Sie ~ Ihrer Arbeit? how far have you advanced with your work?; ~ den Worten spielen to play on words; Böses ~ Gutem vergelten to return good for evil; was hat er ~ ihm vor? what does he intend doing with him? — 6. zeitlich: ~ dem Abend towards (or in the) evening; ~ ehestem with the first (or at the next) opportunity; f. ein 6 am Schluß; alle ~ ea. all at the same time; ~ der ersten Gelegenheit at the first opportunity; sie trennen sich ~ heute they part from this day forth; mit 15, 20 Jahren at (the age of) fifteen, twenty; ~ einem Male all at once, all of a sudden; ~ dem (Glocken-) Schlage zwölf on the stroke of twelve; ~ Tagesanbruch at day-break; ~ diesen Worten with (or at) these words; ~ der Zeit in (the course of) time. — II *adv.* 7. also, likewise; ~ anwesend (oder dabei) sein to be there (or to attend) as well, to form (or make) one of the party; f. anfassen II, anlegen 1; das gehört ~ dazu that belongs to it, that's part and parcel of it.

mit-... (*...) Vorsilbe (immer betont, ausgenommen vor Parti'keln, wie ~ hin) bz. in Bssgn. mit *s. u. v.* Gemeinschaft, Mitwirkung, Gleichzeitigkeit: I mit *nouns*, oft: fellow-...; co(-)..., col..., com..., con...; part-...; (gemeinschaftlich) common; (gleichzeitig) simultaneous; a.: participation in ... — II mit fast allen *verbs*, immer trennbar (**), oft: jointly, together; co..., col..., com..., con...; (gemeinschaftlich) in common (with); (along) with others; (gleichzeitig) simultaneously; at the same time; a. durch die *verbs*: (teilnehmen) to join (or participate, share, take part) in; (helfen) to aid (or assist) in. **Mit-angeklagte([r] m) f** (*...) a. ⓖ jur. co-defendant; =**arbeit f** ⓖ co-operation; =**arbeiten** v/n. (h.) ⓖ** to take part (or to assist) in a work, to collaborate, to co-operate in a th.; to be a fellow-labourer or co-worker; an einer Zeitung: to contribute to; =**arbeiter(in** f ⓖ) m ⓖ fellow-labourer, co-worker,

assistant, collaborator, Zeitung ꝛc.: contributor; =**arbeiterschaft f** ⓖ Zeitung ꝛc.: contributor's office or post, auch: collaboration; =**beklagte(r)** = =angeklagte(r); =**bekommen** v/a. ⓖ**/** to receive at the same time or on departing; von einer Braut: to receive as dowry; =**belehnen** v/a. ⓖ**/** Feudalwesen: to invest (or enfeoff) simultaneously; ~ n ⓖ und =**belehnung f** ⓖ co-investiture; =**belehnte(r)** s. ⓖ co-feoffee; =**besitz** m ⓖ a. co-proprietorship, joint possession or property; =**besitzen** v/a. ⓖ**/** to possess in common (with others), to be (a) joint owner of a th.; =**besitzer(in** f ⓖ) m ⓖ joint proprietor (f ...tress), owner; =**beteiligt** a. ⓖ participating (or taking part) in, interested in; er war dabei nicht ~ he had no part (or share) in it; =**beteiligte([r] m) f** ⓖ jur. interested person or party, ⓖ partner in a firm; =**bevollmächtigte([r] m) f** ⓖ joint proxy; fellow-commissioner; **sich** =**bewerben** v/refl. ⓖ b*/*: sich um et. ~ to compete for a th.; ~ n ⓖ u. =**bewerbung f** ⓖ competition; rivalry; =**bewerber(in** f ⓖ) m ⓖ competitor, rival; =**bewohner(in** f ⓖ) m ⓖ co-inhabitant, eines Hauses: fellow-lodger; =**bezahlen** v/a. und v/n. (h.) ⓖ**/** to pay one's share; ich werde für dich ~ I will pay for you as well; =**bringen** v/a. ⓖ** to bring (or take) with one, Sachen auch: to carry (along) with one; als Heiratsgut: to bring as dowry; er hat uns nichts =gebracht he has brought us no present; =**gebrachte(s)** n ⓖ (Heiratsgut e-r Frau) marriage-portion, (wife's) dowry; =**bruder** m ⓖ fellow, colleague; (fr.) confrère; *pl.* oft: brethren; =**brüderschaft f** ⓖ fellowship, brotherhood, fraternity; =**bürge** m ⓖ joint security; =**bürger(in** f ⓖ) m ⓖ fellow-citizen or -townsman, f bisw.: fellow-townswoman; =**bürgerschaft f** ⓖ: a) fellow-citizenship; b) *coll.* fellow-citizens *pl.*; =**christ(in** f ⓖ) m ⓖ fellow-Christian, brother (f sister) in Christ; =**dasein** n ⓖ coexistence; =**dürfen** v/n. (h.) ⓖ** (*ell.* = mitgehen dürfen) to be allowed to go (or to come along) with a p.; =**eigentum** n ⓖ d. joint property; =**eigentümer(in** f ⓖ) m ⓖ joint owner; =**einander** (ˋ‿ˋ‿, ˊ‿ˊ‿) *adv.* with one another, together, (con)jointly; =**einbegriffen**, =**eingeschlossen** (ˋ‿‿‿) a. ⓖ included, inclusive; 25 Mart, Frühstück ~ ... including breakfast, breakfast included; =**empfinden** (ˋ...) v/a. ⓖ**/** to feel with (or for) others, to sympathize with a p.; ~ n u. =**empfindung f** fellow-feeling, sympathy; =**erbe** m ⓖ, =**erbin f** ⓖ jur. coheir(ess f), fellow- (or joint) heir(ess f); =**erben** v/n. (h.) ⓖ** to be joint heir(ess), to come into one's share; =**essen** ⓖ** v/n. (h.) to dine (or to sit down to dinner) with a p., to partake of a p.'s dinner or repast; v/a. alles ~ to eat up everything; =**esser** m ⓖ *path.* (Hautfinne) grub, maggot; =**esser(in** f ⓖ) m ⓖ (fellow-) boarder; =**fahren** v/n. (fn) ⓖ a** to

join a p. in a drive or ride or cycling-tour or sail, to ride in a carriage (or motor-car, &c.) with others; er ließ mich ~ he gave me a ride; =**fangen** v/a. ⓖ b** to catch (or capture) with others; Sprichw. ⓖ gefangen (ob. ⓖ gegangen), ⓖ gehangen etwa: caught to gether, hanged together; **sich** =**freuen** v/refl. ⓖ*** to share (in) the joy of others, to rejoice with others; =**fühlen** v/n. (h.) ⓖ*** to feel for others (= =empfinden); =**führen** v/a. ⓖ*** to taken (along) with one; v. Flüssen: Gold ~ to carry gold; ⓖ unser Reisender führt Proben mit ... has (a good selection of) samples with him; =**gabe** f ⓖ = =gift; =**geben** v/a. ⓖ c**: e-m et. ~ to give a p. s.th. to take (along) with him; e-m einen Führer ~ to send a guide (along) with a p.; e-m Proviant ~ to provision a p.; als Mitgift: to give as a marriage-portion or dowry; =**gebrachte(s)** n ⓖ f. mitbringen; =**gebrauch** m ⓖ d. joint use; =**gefangene([r] m) f** ⓖ fellow-captive or -prisoner; (prisoner's) chum; =**gefühl** n ⓖ d. fellow-feeling, sympathy; (Mitleid) compassion; ohne ~ unsympathetic, devoid of compassion; =**geh(e)n** v/n. (fn) ⓖ*** to go (along) with a p., to accompany a p.; geh(e)n Sie mit? are you coming with us or me?; Sprichw. f. mitfangen; Spiel: to take part (in a game); et. ~ heißen (stehlen) to pocket a th., to help o.s. to s.th.; F (leidlich sein) das geht so mit that will do at a pinch, it may pass; =**genießen** v/a. ⓖ d.*/* to partake in the enjoyment of a p., to enjoy with others; =**genießende([r] m) f** ⓖ p. who rejoices (or enjoys s.th.) with others; =**genoß**, =**genosse** m ⓖ, ⓖ (co)partner, associate; comrade, F chum; =**genossenschaft f** ⓖ (co)partnership, association, comradeship; *coll.* associates *pl.*; =**genuß** m ⓖ a. participation in the enjoyment of others or another person; =**geschöpf** n ⓖ b. fellow-creature; =**gesell(e)** m ⓖ (ⓖ) fellow-journeyman, auch: mate, pal; =**gift** f ⓖ marriage-portion, dowry; =**glied ⓖ** ⓖ d. member of a society; vgl. korrespondieren; ~ e-r Gemeinde, e-s Kirchspiels parishioner; ~ des Reichstags (*abbr.* M. d. R.) member of the Reichstag; ~ des Unterhauses member of the House of Commons, member of parliament (*abbr.* M. P.); =**gliedschaft f** ⓖ membership; =**haben** v/a. ⓖ b** *ell.* (mitgenommen h.) to have (taken) with one; =**halten** v/a. ⓖ a** to hold (or keep) in common with others or another person; ein Fest ~ to join in a celebration; wir halten die Zeitung mit we take ... in together; ich halte mit I will join (you) or take part, I'll make one of the party; =**helfen** v/n. (h.) ⓖ b** to give aid or assistance, to lend a (helping) hand; to co-operate with others; =**helfer(in** f ⓖ) m ⓖ person who helps, aider (and abettor); jur. a. accessory, accomplice; =**herausgeber** m ⓖ co-editor; =**herrschaft f** ⓖ co-regency; joint rule or dominion; =**herrscher** m ⓖ co-regent, fellow-ruler; =**hilfe f** ⓖ aid,

---

⓿ scientific; ❦ botanical; ⚹ geography; ⊙ machinery; ⚒ mining; ⚔ military; ⚓ marine; ⚖ commercial; ✉ postal; 🚂 railway.

[mithin] — 700 — [Mitte]

assistance, help; co-operation; ₂**hin**(⌣⌣) adv. hence, therefore, consequently; (also) thus, so, then; =**hör=taste** (⌣...) f ㊽ Fernsprecher: listening key; =**inhaber** m ㉒ fellow-proprietor or -occupier; ₂**kämpfen** v/n. (h.) ⑱*** to take part in a combat or struggle; =**kämpfer** m ㉒ fellow-combatant; =**kläger(in** f ㊼) m ㉒ co-plaintiff, party to a suit or a prosecution; ₂**kommen** v/n. (jn) ⑥⑪*** to come (along) with a p.; wollen Sie ₂? will you come with us?; Schule: er kommt mit: a) he can follow, he is getting on; b) he will be (re)moved or promoted; ₂**können** v/n. (h.) ⑱*** ell. = mitgehen können to be able to get (or come) along with a p.; ₂**kriegen** F v/a. ⑱*** = ₂**bekommen**; ₂**lachen** v/n. (h.) ⑱*** to laugh as well; er lachte mit he joined in the laugh; ₂**lassen** v/a. ⓖa** ell. = mitgehen ɪc. lassen: to allow to join; ₂**laufen** v.n. (jn) ⓢaft** to run (along) with a p.; a. = ₂**gehen** F; =**läufer** m ㉒ pol. camp-follower; =**laut(er** ㉒) ⓓd. m, gr. (ant. Selbstlaut(er) consonant; =**leid** n ⓒc. compassion; (Erbarmen) commiseration, pity. (Mitgefühl) sympathy; aus bloßem ~ merely out of pity, out of pure charity; mit e-m ~ h. to have compassion with (or on) a p., to take pity on a p., F to feel for a p.; ~ erregend, erweckend piteous, pitiful; voll ~ compassionate; ₂**leiden** v/n. (h.) ⑥c** to suffer with others, to be a fellow-sufferer; path. to be in sympathy; ~ n ㉓ = =**leid(enschaft)**; =**leidenschaft** f ㊻ sympathy (a. path.), common suffering; in ~ ziehen to affect, to involve, to implicate; e-n zur ~ ziehen to make a p. contribute (his share); ₂**leidens=wert. =würdig** a. ⑥ deserving pity, pitiable; ₂**leidig** a. ⑥ compassionate to(wards); charitable to; adv. a. pitifully; =**leids=bezeigung** f ㊻ condolence; =**leid(s)=los** a. ⑥ pitiless, without compassion, void of pity or feeling, unfeeling; =**leid(s)=losig= keit** f ㊻ pitilessness; =**leid(s)voll** a. ⑥ compassionate, full of pity, pitiful; tender-hearted; ₂**lernen** v/a. ⑱*** to learn with others; to learn at the same time; ₂**lesen** v/a. ⓖa** to read with a p.; e-e Zeitung: to take in together; ₂**machen** v/a. ⑱*** to participate (or share, join) in the doings of others; sie macht alle Bälle mit she goes to every dance, she does not miss a single ball; alles ₂ to take part in everything, to be ready (F game) for anything; die Mode ₂ to follow (F to go with) the fashion; ein Spiel Whist ₂ to take a hand at (a game of) whist; er hat viel ₂ge= macht he has seen (or gone through) a great deal; er hat vier Feldzüge ₂gemacht he has been through (or in) four campaigns; v/n. (h.) to be one of a party; willst du ₂? will you make one of us?; =**mensch** m ㊷ fellow-man or -being or -creature, bibl. neighbour; ₂**mögen**, ₂**müssen** v/n. ⑱*** ell. = mitgehen mögen, müssen: to feel inclined, to be obliged to go

with a p. or to join others; =**nahme** f ㊽ taking (along) with one; ₂**nehmen** v/a. ⓐa** to take (along or away) with one, e-e Sache, a. to carry away, to bear off; e-n im Schiff, im Wagen ₂ to give a p. a sail, a ride; fig. et. ₂ to avail o.s. of a th.; das ist immer ₂zu= nehmen that's no ill store, it's not to be refused or F sneezed at; auf der Reise einen Ort ₂ to touch (or to call at) a place; e-n Verdienst (nebenbei) ₂ to make a profit by the way; eine Stunde ₂ to partake of a lesson; er will Chemie ₂ he wants to join the chemistry class; arg oder hart ₂ (anfassen) to deal harshly with, to treat severely; (bekritteln) to carp at, F to pull to pieces, to be hard on; (erschöpfen) to exhaust, to wear (out); e-n gehörig ₂ F to give it a p. well; die Krankheit hat ihn (schlimm) ₂genommen the illness has pulled him down (very much) or (seriously) told on him; ₂**nichten** (⌣⌣) f. mit 3; =**pächter** m ㉒ jur. co-tenant, co-lessee.

Mitra (¹⁻) [grch.] f ㊽⑲ Cath. eccl. mitre. **mit=raten** (⌣...) v/a. ⓐa** f. ₂taten; ₂**rechnen** ⑫b** v/a. to reckon (or count) with the rest; a. = hinzurechnen; (einrechnen) to include in the account; die Kosten mitgerechnet including (or inclusive of the) cost(s); v/n. (h.) das rechnet (zählt) nicht mit that does not count; ₂**reden** v/n. (h.) und v/a. ⑱*** to join in a conversation or discussion, to put in a word (or two); Sie haben hier nichts ₂zureden you have nothing to say in this matter, it's no concern of yours; ein Wort ₂, oft: to have one's say; ein Wort bei et. ₂zureden h. to have a voice in the matter; =**reeder** ⊥ m ㉒ part-owner of (or copartner in) a ship; =**regent(in** f ㊼) m ㉒ co-regent; ₂**reisen** v/n. (jn.) ⑥⑪** to travel (along) with a p.; to join (a party of) travellers; =**reisende([r]** m) f ㊱ fellow-traveller or passenger; ₂**reiten** v/n. (jn) ⑥b** to accompany others on horseback; ₂**sammen** (⌣⌣) adv. = ₂ein= ander; ₂**samt** (⌣⌣) prp. (together) with; ₂**schicken** (⌣...) v/a. ⑱**: a) to send with a p., a th.: in Briefen ɪc.: to enclose; b) to send at the same time; ₂**schleppen** v/a. ⑱*** to drag along with one, ⊥ to tow along; ₂**schreiben** v/n. (h.) ⑥⑪*** to write (or note down) with others; =**schuld** f ㊻ complicity; ₂**schuldig** a. ⑥ implicated in an offence; =**schuldige([r]** m) f ㊱ accessory (to a crime), accomplice; =**schuldner(in** f ㊼) m ㉒ jur. co-debtor, joint debtor; =**schüler(in** f ㊼) m ㉒ school-fellow, schoolmate, fellow-pupil, F chum (at school); =**schwester** f ㊽ im Kloster: fellow-nun, another sister; ₂**segeln** v/n. (jn) ⓐa** to sail (along) with, to join in a sail; ₂**sein** v/n. ⓐa** to be with others; ell. er ist mit (₂gegangen, ₂gereist) he went with the others, he joined (or made one of) the party; ₂**singen** v/n. (h.) u. v/a. ⓓft**: a) to join in singing, den Kehrreim ₂: to join in the chorus; b) (begleiten) to ac-

company with one's voice; ₂**sollen** v/n. (h.) ⑱*** ell. = mitgehen sollen: to be obliged to go with a p.; ₂**speisen** v/n. (h.) ⑨⑪** to dine (or sup) with a p.; ₂**spielen** v/n. (h.) u. v/a. ⑱*** to join in a game, to take part in a play; nicht mehr ₂ to give up playing, von Karten, a. to throw up the cards; F fig. nicht mehr ₂ (genug h.) to withdraw, retire, resign; e-m arg (hart, grausam, schlimm, übel) ₂ to play a p. a nasty trick, F to play Old Gooseberry with a p.; =**spieler** (=**in** f ㊼) m ㉒ one who joins in a game or play, bsd. v. Kindern: playmate, playfellow; von derselben Partei der Spielenden: partner; ₂**sprechen** v/n. (h.) ⓐa** a) = mitreden; b) Fernsprecher: to be in contact, to emit confused (or mixed) sounds; ₂**stimmen** v/n. (h.) ⑱*** to take part in an election, to vote with; =**streiter** m ㉒ brother-in-arms; vgl. Mitkämpfer.

Mittag (⌣⌣) [ahd.: midday] m ⓓd. 1. midday, noon(day), noontide; des ~s f. ₂s; heute ₂ at noon to-day; es ist ~ it is twelve o'clock; fig. er hat den ~ des Lebens hinter sich he has crossed the meridian of life. — 2. meist n, abbr. für ~s=essen, zB. zu bleiben to stay to dinner; viel (wenig) zu ~ essen to make a good (a poor) dinner; ~ halten, zu ~ essen, speisen to dine, to have (one's) dinner.

mittäg=ig, =lich (⌣⌣⌣) a. ⑥ 1. (of) midday, of (or happening at) noon, ⚹ meridian. — 2. (südlich) southerly, southern.

mittags (⌣⌣) adv. 1. at midday, at noon, at twelve o'clock. — 2. at dinner(time).

Mittag(s)=blume ♀ (⌣⌣...) f ㊽ midday-flower, fig-marigold (Mesembryanthemum); =**brot**, =**essen** n dinner, vgl. =**mahl**; nach dem ~ geschehend postprandial (speech, &c.); =**gast** m dinner-guest; =**gesellschaft** f dinner-party; =**glocke** f dinner-bell; =**glut**, =**hitze** f midday (or noonday) heat; =**höhe** f, ast. meridian altitude; =**kreis** m, ast. meridian (circle); =**linie** f, ast. meridian (line); =**mahl** n, **mahlzeit** f midday meal; =**predigt** f afternoon sermon; =**punkt** m, ast.: ⚹ meridional point; =**rast**, =**ruhe** f midday (or noonday) rest; =**schlaf** m, =**schläfchen** n after-dinner nap, siesta; ein =**schläf= chen** halten F to have one's forty winks; =**sonne** f midday-sun; =**stunde** f noon(tide), dinner-hour; =**tafel** f, =**tisch** m dinner(-table); freien =**tisch** h. to have one's dinners free; ₂**wärts** adv. towards (the) south, southward; =**zeit** f noontide, dinner-time; um die ~ towards noon.

mit=tanzen (⌣...) v/n. (h.) ⑱*** to take part in a dance, to dance with others; ₂**taten** ⦁ v/n. (h.) ⑱*** = ₂**tun**; Sprichw. wer nicht mittatet, auch nicht mitratet, those who pay may have their say; =**täter** m accessory, accomplice; ₂**tätig** a. ⑥ taking an active part, assisting.

Mitte (⌣⌣) [ahd.: mid] f ㊽ (poet. auch gen. u. dat. ~n) 1. middle, midst, (Mittelpunkt) centre; (gegen) ~ Juni (about) the middle of June; ~ des

Zeichen (f. S. XVII): F familiär; P Volkssprache; ☇ Gaunersprache; ⦁ selten; † alt (auch gestorben); * neu (auch geboren); ⁺⁺ unrichtig;

[Mittefünfziger] — 701 — [Mittnacht]

Sommers (des Winters) midsummer (midwinter); aus ihrer ~ from their midst, from among them; in unserer ~ in our midst; Fußballspiel: ~! centre!; nach der ~ stoßen to centre; ♀ Reich der ~ (China) central kingdom. — 2. fig. die goldene ~ the golden mean; die rechte ~ the happy medium; ✕ in die ~ nehmen to attack from both sides, to take between two fires.

Mitte-fünfziger(in f) m (ˇ˘…) ⓜ (wo)man half-way between fifty and sixty (years of age).

mit-teilbar (ˇ˘-) a. ⓜ communicable; von Krankheiten: contagious, infectious; ~**keit** (ˇ˘˘-) f ⓜ communicability; contagiousness, infectiousness.

mit-teilen (ˇ˘-) v/a. u. sich ⓢ v/refl. ⓜ** to communicate a th. to a p.; e-m et. ⓢ: a) (zu wissen tun) to inform (or acquaint, apprise) a p. of a th., ⓜ to advise a p. of a th.; b) (zukommen lassen) to convey a th. to a p., to let a p. partake of (or have) a th.; ⓜ to break a th. to a p.; e-m f-e Ansicht ⓢ to give (or tell) a p. one's opinion; amtlich ⓢ to notify a p. of a th.; vertraulich ⓢ to impart a th. to a p.; die Bewegung teilt sich den Rädern mit the motion passes on (or is imparted) to the wheels; sich e-m ⓢ to open one's heart to a p. **mit-teilsam** (ˇ˘-) a. ⓜ communicative; ~**keit** (ˇ˘˘-) f ⓜ communicativeness.

Mit-teilung (ˇ˘˘) f ⓜ (f. mitteilen) communication; information, ⓜ advice, statement; amtliche: intelligence, notification; vertrauliche ~ confidential (or private) communication.

mittel¹ (ˇ˘) [ahd.: middle] I a. ⓜ (D9) nur attributiv gbr., ↘ im Positiv: 1. (ant. hintere I) (situated in the) middle; (im Mittelpunkte gelegen) central; (zwischen zwei Dingen liegend) intermed*iary*. …iate; (halb gut, halb schlecht) middling, of medium quality, medium (auch ⓜ); Börse: die Weizenernte ist unter ⓢ the wheat-crop is below the average; im mittleren, von mittlerem Alter middle-aged; von mittlerer Größe of middle (or medium, average) size, ⓜ medium-sized; *math.* mittlere Proportionale mean proportional. — 2. f. mittlerweile. — II ~ f, inv. 3. = Mittelschrift.

Mittel² (ˇ˘) [mhd.] n ⓜ 1. means, expedient, contrivance; bedeutende ~ large means or resources *pl.*; alle erdenklichen ~ anwenden to use (or try) every possible means; neue ~ anwenden to change one's method or tactics; die ~ besitzen, (F ++ um) et. auszuführen to be in a position to carry out a th.; f. erlauben 1; ~ und Wege für et. finden to contrive (or manage) a th.; f. heiligen 1; kein ~ unversucht lassen to leave no stone unturned. — 2. (Heilmittel) remedy, (Arznei) medicine; unfehlbares ~ safe cure, specific. — 3. sich ins ~ legen od. schlagen, ins ~ treten to interpose, intervene, interfere, mediate. — 4. *math.* arithmetisches (geometrisches) ~ arithmetical (geometrical) means; im ~ (durchschnittlich) on an average. — 5. *phys.* (zwischenliegender Stoff) medium.

Mittel¹-afrika ♀ (ˇ˘…) n ⓜ Central Africa; =**alter** n, *hist.* Middle Ages *pl.*, medieval period; ⓢ**alt(e)rig** ↘ a. ⓜ middle-aged; ⓢ**alterlich** a. medieval; =**amerika** ♀ n Central America; =**arrest** ✕ m (solitary) cell; =**art** f = =**sorte**.

mittelbar (ˇ˘-) a. ⓜ indirect, (inter-)mediate; ~**keit** (ˇ˘˘-) f ⓜ indirectness, mediateness, (inter)mediate position.

Mittelchen (ˇ˘˘) n ⓢ slight remedy.

Mittel¹-deck (ˇ˘…) ⬇ n ⓜ middle deck; =**deutschland** ♀ n Central Germany; =**ding** n cross (or intermediary) between two things; =**europa** ♀ n Central Europe; ⓢ**europäisch** a. ⓜ: Ze Zeit Central European time; =**farbe** f intermediate (or neutral) colour; ⓢ**fein** ⓜ a. middling (fine), medium; =**feld** n, *arch.* &c. centre-field; =**fell** n, *anat.* zwischen beiden Brustfellhöhlen: ⊘ mediastinum; =**finger** m middle finger; =**fleisch** n, *anat.*: ⊘ perineum; =**form*** f, *gr.* participle; =**fuß** m: a) middle-sized foot; b) *anat.*: ⊘ metatarsus; =**gang** m: a) average pace; b) central walk; =**gattung** f intermediate species or kind; =**gebäude** n central building; =**gebirge** n intermediate (or secondary) chain of mountains; =**glied** n: a) *anat.* e-s Fingers: middle joint or phalanx; b) *Logik* u. *math.*: middle term; ⓢ**groß** a. medium-sized, of middle size; =**größe** f middling (or intermediate) size; =**grund** me-s Bildes: centre-ground; ⓢ**gut** ⓜ a. of medium (or average) quality; =**gut** ⓜ n medium goods *pl.*; =**hand** f: a) *anat.*: ⊘ metacarpus; b) beim Kartenspiel: second hand; =**hand-knochen** m: ⊘ metacarpal (bone); ⓢ**hochdeutsch** a. u. ~(e) n ⓜ Middle High German; =**klasse** f des Volkes: middle classes; =**kraft** f, *mech.* resultant (force); ⓢ**ländisch** a. ♀ inland; das ~e Meer the Mediterranean (Sea); =**latein** n (600-1500) Low (or Medieval) Latin; ⓢ**lateinisch** a. Low Latin; =**linie** f, *geom.* bisecting line, bisector; *phys.* des Magneten: neutral zone; *Tennis*: half-court line; ⓢ²**los** a. without means or resources; destitute, penniless; =**losigkeit** f lack of means; destitution; =¹**mann** m: a) average man; b) = Mittelsmann; =**maß** n medium size, average; ⓢ**mäßig** a. mediocre, indifferent; ⓜ middling, medium, fair; Ze Begabung moderate ability; =**mäßigkeit** f mediocrity; =**mauer** f partition- (or party-)wall; =**meer** n: a) = Binnenmeer; b) ♀ Mediterranean (Sea); =**partei** f, *parl.* central (or intermediate) party; vgl. Zentrum 2; =**pfeiler** m central pillar; =**punkt** m, *math.*, *mech.*, &c. centre, central point; im ~e der Stadt ꝛc. in the heart of the town, &c.; *mech.* nach dem ~e strebend centripetal; vom ~e wegstrebend centrifugal; =**rippe** ♣ f e-s Blattes: midrib.

mittels (ˇ˘) [Mittel²] *prp.* (mit gen.) by means of, with the aid (or assistance) of, through (the medium of).

Mittel¹-satz (ˇ˘…) m ⓜ *Logik* ꝛc.: middle term; =**schiff** n, *arch.* e-r Kirche: middle aisle; =**schlag** m = =**sorte**; =**schrift** ⊙ f, *typ.* English; =**schule** f intermediate (or secondary) school.

Mittels-mann (ˇ˘˘) m ⓜ: a) = Mittler; b) ⓜ middleman, go-between, broker.

Mittel-sorte ⓜ (ˇ˘…) f ⓜ medium quality, average sort; seconds *pl.* **Mittels-person** f = =**mann**. [mittel¹.] **mittelst** (ˇ˘) 1. = mittels. — 2. *sup. v.*

Mittel¹-staaten (ˇ˘…) m *pl.* ⓜ states *pl.* of secondary importance; =**stadt** f second-rate town; =**stand** m middle class(es *pl.*), (fr.) bourgeoisie; =**stelle** f: a) central place; b) (vermittelnd) intermediate station; =**stimme** ♪ f: a) zwischen Sopra'n u. Alt: mezzo-soprano; b) zw. Tenor und Baß: barytone; c) ~n *pl.* (begleitende Stimmen) accompanying (or choral) voices *pl.*; =**straße** f: a) central road or route; b) *fig.* middle course, happy medium; die goldene ~ the golden mean; =**stück** n middle piece; Schlächterei: middle cut; =**stufe** f: a) middle step; b) intermediate grade or degree; =**stürmer** m Fußball: centre-forward; =**ton** m bsd. ♪ mediant; Kunst u. *typ.* =**töne** e-s Holzschnitts ꝛc.: half tints *pl.*; =**treffen** ✕ n main body of an army; =**wand** ⊙ f: a) *arch.* partition-wall; b) ♣ der Schotenfrüchte: ⊘ mediastinum; =**weg** m = =**straße**; e-n ~ einschlagen to steer a middle course, to adopt a compromise; =**wort** n, *gr.* participle; =**zeit** f: a) mean time; b) *gr.*, *pros.* mean (or doubtful) quantity; ⓢ**zeitig** a. ⓜ *gr.*, *pros.* doubtful, common.

mitten (ˇ˘) [nhd. (aus in Mitten): mid] *adv.* meist mit *prp.*: ⓢ an, auf, in, unter in(to) the midst of, amid(st); ⓢ auf der Straße in the open street; ⓢ aus der Versammlung from the midst of the assembly; ⓢ durch right across; ⓢ in der Luft in mid-air; ⓢ in der Nacht in the middle of the (or in the dead of) night; ⓢ im Winter in the depth of winter; ⓢ ins Herz right into the heart; vgl. in².

mitten-dar-unter (ˇ˘˘…) *adv.* in the very midst or centre, in among them; ⓢ**durch** *adv.* right across; =**ent-zwei** *adv.* (broken right) in two or in the middle; ⓢ**hindurch** *adv.* right across; ⓢ**inne** *adv.* = darunter.

Mitternacht (ˇ˘˘ ˘t) [ahd. (zu) Mitt'er Nacht] f ⊙ d. midnight; des ~s, ⓢs, um ~ at m.; gegen ~ (Norden) towards the north; Schlaf vor ~ beauty-sleep.

mitter-nächtig, ⓢnächtlich (ˇ˘˘˘) a. ⓜ taking place at midnight; (nächtlich) nightly, nocturnal; (nördlich) northerly.

Mitternachts-sonne (ˇ˘˘…) f ⓜ in arktischen Ländern: midnight sun; =**stunde**, =**zeit** f midnight (hour); die gespenstische ~ the witching midnight hour.

mittewegs (ˇ˘˘) *adv.* midway. [Lent.]

Mitt-fasten (ˇ˘˘) f /sg. u. *pl.* ⓜ *eccl.* Mid-

Mittler¹ (ˇ˘) m ⓜ, ~**in** f ⓜ mediator (f mediatress, bisweilen: mediatrix), intercessor (beide auch *rel.*), negotiator, auch: third party; ⓜ middleman.

mittler² (ˇ˘) a. ⓜ u. *comp.* f. mittel¹.

Mittler¹-amt (ˇ˘…) n ⓜ office of mediator; =**tod** m, *rel.* (sacrificial) death of our Mediator; ⓢ²**weile** *adv.* (in the)meanwhile or meantime, all the while, ⓜ &c. during (or in) the interim.

Mitt-nacht fast✝ (ˇ˘ ˘ℓ) f = Mitternacht.

mit-tönen (ˈ...) v/n. (h.) ⊛** to sound simultaneously or in unison with; **₂tragen** v/a. ⊛b** to carry (or bear) jointly or with others; Verluste 2c.: to share; **₂trinken** v/a. ⓓi** to drink (F to booze) with a p. or others.

mitt-schiffs ↓ (ˊˇ) adv. amidships; Ruder 2! helm amidships!

Mitt-sommernacht(s-traum m ⳁ SH.] (ˇˇˇch(ˊ) f ⑫ Midsummer-Night('s Dream). [assist, help in doing.]

mit-tun (ˊˊ) v/n. (h.) ⊛** to join (or)

Mitt-woch (ˊˊˊ) [ahd.] m ⓓd., **~e** r ⓔ Wednesday; **₂lich** a. u. adv., (des)**-s** every Wednesday, on Wednesdays.

mit-unter (ˇˊˇ) adv. now and then, now and again, from time to time, sometimes, occasionally.

mit-unterschreiben (ˊ...) ⊛*/*, **₂unterzeichnen** ⊛b*/* v/a. u. v/n. (h.) to add one's signature to, to countersign; **₌unterzeichner(in/**④**)** m⑫co-signatory; **₌urheber** m ⑫ joint author; **₌ursache** f ⑱ secondary (or additional) cause, concurrent reason; **₂verantwortlich** a. ⑮ responsible (or sharing the responsibility) with others; **₌verbrecher** (**₌in** f ④) m ⑫ accomplice, accessory to a crime; **₌verschwor(e)ne([r]** m) f ⑰ fellow-conspirator, p. implicated in a plot; **₌vormund** m ⓓd., **₌vormünderin** f ④ jur. co-guardian; **₌welt** f ⑯: die **~** the living generation, our contemporaries pl., auch: the age (or time) we live in, our (present) age; die Geschichte der **~** the history of our time, contemporary history; **₂wirken** v/n. (h.) ⊛**: bei, zu et. 2 to co-operate in a th., to contribute towards a th.; bei einer Vorstellung 2c. 2 to take part in ..., to assist in (or at) ...; bei e-m Schriftwerke 2 to contribute to ...; **~** n ⳻ = **₌wirkung**; 2d p.pr. u. a. ⑯ co-operating, co-operative, concurrent; **~de([r]** m) f ⑰: a) thea. performer; b) literarisch: contributor; **₌wirkung** f ⑯ co-operation, concurrence, participation, assistance; **₂wissen** v/n. (h.) ⊛**: um et. 2 to know of a th., to be privy to a th.; **~(schaft** f ④) n ⳻ knowledge; ohne sein **~** without his knowledge or cognizance, unbeknown to him; **₌wisser(in** f ④) m ⑫ person who is in the secret, P one in the know; **₂wollen** v/n. (h.) ⊛** sep., ell. = mitgehen, mitreisen wollen: to want to go (or leave, start, travel) with others; **₂zahlen** v/n. (h.) ⊛** to pay (or contribute) one's share; **₂zählen** ⊛** v/a. to take into account; v/n. (h.): das zählt nicht mit that does not count; er zählt nicht mit he is of no account, F he's not in it; **₂zechen** v/n. (h.) ⊛** to join in a carousal or drinking-bout; **₌zeuge** m ④ fellow-witness; **₂ziehen** ⓑb** v/a. to pull with others; to draw (or drag) along with one; v/n. (in) to travel (or journey, march) with others; **₌zweck** m ⓓd. additional purpose or object.

Mixtur (ˇˊ) [mhd.,* lt.] f ④ 1. (Gemisch) mixture; pharm. auch: draught. — 2. ♪ (Register zur Verstärkung des Tones) furniture(-stop).

mlt. abbr. = mittellateinisch.
mm, öst. mm abbr. = Millimeter.
mm², **mm³** öst. = Quadrat-, Kubikum öst. abbr.= Myriameter. [millimeter.]
Mnemonik ɔ(-ˊˇ) [grch.] f ⑯ (Gedächtnislehre) mnemonics, mnemotechnics; **~er** (-ˊˇˇ) m ⑫ mnemonician; **mnemonisch** a. ⑯ mnemonic.
Mnemo-technik ɔ (ˊˇˇ) [grch.] f ⑯ mnemotechnics, mnemonic art.
Moabiter (-ˇˊˇ) m ⑫, **~in** f ④ [Moab, Sohn Lots, 1. Mos.] bibl. Moabite.
Möbel (ˊˇ) [fr. meuble m] n ⑫ (pl. F a. ⑳ u. ⑫) 1. piece of furniture, pl. (household) furniture, F sticks pl. — 2. F fig. altes **~** old fogey, fixture.
Möbel-arbeiter ⊙ (ˊˇ...) m ⑫ furniture-maker; **₌händler** ⓢ m ⑫ fu.-dealer; **₌kattun** ⓢ m chintz, cotton damask; **₌lager**, **₌magazin** n fu.-warehouse; **₌politur** f fu.-polish, French polish; **₌tischler** ⊙ m cabinet-maker; **₌transport-geschäft** ⓢ n firm of furniture-removers; **₌wagen** m fu.-van.
mobil (-ˊ) [fr.] a. ⑯ 1. ⚔ (schlagfertig) mobile, ready to take the field; 2 m. to mobilize troops. — 2. (rüstig, flink) nimble, active, mobile; munter u. 2 in good health and cheer, hale and hearty.
Mobiliar (-ˇˊ) [lt.] n ⓓd. (household) furniture, auch: movables, household goods pl.; **~erbe** m ⑫ jur. heir to the personal estate; **~vermögen** n jur. personal estate or property.
Mobilie-n (-ˊ(ˇ)ˇ) [lt.] pl. inv. (bewegliche Habe; ant. Immobilien) movables, goods and chattels pl.
mobilisier/en ⚔ (-ˇˊˇ) I v/a. ⑬ (kriegsbereit m.) to mobilize. — II **~** n ⑬ u. **M/ung** f ⑯ mobilization. [tion.]
Mobil-machung (-ˊˊˇˇ) f ⑯ mobiliza-)
Mobilmachungs-geld (ˊˊ...) n ⑫ increase of pay at the beginning of a campaign, field-allowance; **₌plan** m plan of mobilization; **₌zulage** f = **₌geld**.
möblieren (-ˊˇ) [fr. meubler] v/a. ⑬ to furnish, to fit up rooms, offices, &c.
Möblierer (-ˊˇ) m ⑫ upholsterer.
mochte (ˊchˇ), **möchte** (ˊˇ) [ahd.: might] impf. ind., subj. von mögen.
Modalität ɔ (--ˊ) [lt.] f ⑯ phls. (Art und Weise des Seins) modality.
Mode (ˊˇ) [fr.] f ⑯ fashion; die neueste **~** the latest craze or fad; aus der **~** sein to be out of fashion; in die **~** bringen to bring into fashion or vogue; aus der **~** kommen to go (or grow, F get) out of fa., to become antiquated; sich nach der neuesten **~** kleiden to dress fashionably or according to the latest fashion or F up to date; in der **~** sein to be in fa. or in vogue; Spitzen sind jetzt **~**, oft: F ... are now all the rage; es wird **~** it is coming into (or becoming the) fashion.
Mode-artikel ⓢ (ˊˇ...) m ⑫ fancy-article; neue **~** pl. novelties pl.; **₌ausdruck** m = **₌wort**; **₌bild** n = **₌kupfer**; **₌dame** f fashionable (or fine) lady; **₌dichter** m popular poet, poet of the day; **₌farbe** f fashionable colour; **₌händler(in** f) m ⓢ dealer in fancy-goods or millinery; milliner; **₌herr** m, **₌herrchen** n fashionable gentleman,

dandy, fop; F masher; **₌journal** n ladies' magazine; vgl. **₌zeitung**; **₌krankheit** f fashionable complaint; **₌kupfer** n fashion-plate.
Model ⊙ (ˊˇ) [lt. moˊdulus] m (n) ⑫ und ⑳ 1. arch. module; math., mech.: ɔ modulus. — 2. Zeugdruck: block.
Modell (-ˊ) [it.] n ⓓd. 1. paint., sculp., &c.: (Vorbild für Künstler und körperliche Darstellung im verjüngten Maßstabe) model; lebendes **~** living model; **~** steh(e)n to stand (or serve) as model. — 2. ⊙ (Form) mould; a. = Guß-2; ausgeschnittenes **~** (Muster) (paper) pattern.
Modelleur (ˇˇˊr) m ⓓd. = Modellierer.
modellieren (ˇˇˊˇ) [Modell] v/a. ⑬ sculp., &c. to model, to mould.
Modellierer (ˇˇˊˇ) m ⑫ modeller, moulder; pattern-maker.
Modellier-kunst (ˇˇˊˇˊ) f ⑯ art of modelling or moulding.
Modell-sammlung (ˇˊ...) f ⑯ collection of models; **₌stecher(in** f) m (artist's) model; **₌zeichnen** n model-drawing, drawing from the cast.
modeln (ˊˇ) [Modell] v/a. ⑬a. 1. ⊙ Weberei: (Figuren einwirken) to work figures into, to figure. — 2. (nach einem Modell formen) to model; to mould, fashion, shape.
Mode-narr (ˊˇ...) m ⑫ slave of fashion; vgl. **₌herr**; **₌närrin**, **₌puppe** f fine(ly dressed) doll. [vgl. Modewelt.]
Moden-welt (ˊˇˇˊ) f ⑯ world of fashion;)
Moder (ˊˇ) [ndd.] m ⑫ 1. (Schlamm) mud, bog. — 2. (dumpfe Luft) musty air. — 3. (Fäulnis) rottenness, putrefaction; mould(ering), mustiness; in **~** zerfallen to crumble and moulder away.
Moderator ⊙ (-ˇˊˇ) m ⑫ mach. (Geschwindigkeitsmesser) moderator, governor.
Moder-duft (ˊˇ...) m ⑫ = **₌geruch**; **₌erde** f mould, soil made up of decayed substances; **₌flecken** ⓢ m in Papier: mildew; **₌geruch** m musty (or mouldy, fusty) smell or odour; (leichen-artiger Geruch) cadaverous smell.
modericht (ˊˇˇ) a. ⑯ = moderig.
moderig (ˊˇˇ) a. ⑯ mouldy, musty, fusty; (faulend) decaying, putrid; **~** werden to go mouldy.
Moder-luft (ˊˇˇ) f ⑯ = Moder 2.
modern¹ (ˊˇ) [Moder] I v/n. (su. u. h.) ⑳a. (faulen) to rot, decay, putrefy; to moulder, to go mouldy. — II **~** n decay, putrefaction; mouldering.
modern² (ˇˊ) [fr.] a. ⑯ 1. (der Neuzeit angehörig) modern. — 2. (neumodisch) fashionable, after the latest fashion.
modernisieren (ˇˇˇˊˇ) [fr.] v/a. ⑬ to modernize, to bring up to date.
Modernität (ˇˇˇˊ) f ⑯ modernness.
Moder-wasser (ˊˇˇˇ) n ⑫ muddy (or putrid) water.
Mode-schriftsteller (ˊˇ...) m ⑫ fashionable (or popular) writer; **₌stoff** ⓢ m novelty (of the season); **₌sucht** f mania (or craze) for fashions; **₌tracht** f fashionable costume or wear; **₌waren** f pl. fancy-goods pl.; (Putzwaren) millinery; **₌waren-geschäft** n fancy-business; millinery-warehouse; für Damenkleider: ladies' outfitting warehouse; **₌welt** f fashion-

[Modewort] — 703 — [Moiré]

able world; vgl. Modenwelt; =wort n fashionable expression; =zeitung f fashion-journal, ladies' magazine.
Modi (⌣⌣) pl. von Modus.
modifizier/en (⌣⌣⌣⌣) [lt.] **I** v/a. ⓑ (abändern) to modify; e-n Ausdruck: to qualify. — **II** ~ n ⓐ u. **M/ung** f ⓰ modification; qualification.
modisch (⌣⌣) a. ⓰ fashionable, stylish.
Modist ⚥ (⌣⌣) [fr.] m ⓐ, ~in f ⓰ milliner, als m oft: man-milliner.
Modul (⌣⌣) m = Model.
modulieren ♪ (⌣⌣⌣⌣) [lt.] v/a. ⓑ to modulate.)
Modus (⌣⌣) [lt. módus Maß] m ⓐ mode; fashion, manner; gram. mood.
Mogelei F (~⌣¹) f⓰ trickery, cheating;
mogeln (⌣⌣) v/n. (h.) ⓑa. to trick, cheat.
mögen (⌣⌣) [ahd.: may] **I** v/aux. ⓑ
1. als wahrscheinlich hinstellend: **a)** er mag krank sein he may (possibly) be ill; das mag wohl sein that's very likely; sie möchte zwölf Jahre alt sein she might be twelve years old; einräumend: er mag wohl recht h. he may (possibly) be right; mag er auch Geld haben though he may have money; verallgemeinernd: er mag sagen was er will let him say what he likes or chooses, whatever he may say; s. meinethalben; er mag fortgehen oder bleiben whether he leaves or stays; ich möchte wollen oder nicht whether I liked it or not; was ich auch immer tun mag (oder ich mag tun was ich will), so ist es dir nicht recht whatever I may do or contrive ...; wie sie auch sein mag of what(so)ever kind she may be; wo er auch sein mag wherever he may be; ⁂ sie noch so wohlhabend sein may they (or let them) be ever so wealthy; mag daraus werden was da will come what may, whatever may become of it; **b)** elliptisch: er mag nun zusehen (mich kümmert's nicht), wie er durchkommt let him pull through the best way he can; mag es tun wer es kann let anybody do it who can; er mag sich in acht nehmen! let him beware!; das mag der Teufel tun, etwa: you won't catch me doing it; **c)** in unbestimmten Fragen: wo mag sie das gehört haben? where can she have heard it?; wie mag's dem Kranken geh(e)n? how may the patient be?; **d)** im impf. subj. mildernd: das möchte nicht ganz leicht (zu tun) sein (I fear or I am afraid) that might not be quite easy (to accomplish); hören Sie auf, oder ich möchte böse werden stop, or I might grow angry; das möchte leicht zu Wasser w. (I fear) it could easily come to nothing. — 2. zustimmend: das mag er immerhin tun he may do so if he likes; Sie ⁂ mitgeh(e)n you are welcome to go with us; es mag geschehen let it be so. — 3. wünschend: ich möchte laut aufjauchzen I should like to (or I feel as if I could) shout for joy; ich möchte fliegen I wish I could (altertümlich: I would fain) fly; ich möchte ein Vogel sein I wish I were a bird; ich (er) möchte wohl wissen, ob // I should (he would) be glad to know whether //; das hätte

ich sehen ⁂ (st. p. p. gemocht) I should like to have seen that. — 4. ablehnend (mst mit neg.): ich mag ihn nicht sehen I don't want to see him; er mag nicht nach Hause (gehen) he does not care (or wish) to go home; ich hätte nicht (gern) zusehen ⁂ I should not have cared to look on; unwillig: das möchte ich doch einmal sehen! I should like to see him do it! — 5. ben Konjunktiv, Optativ, Imperativ umschreibend: ich wünsche (wünschte), daß er kommen möge (möchte) I wish(ed) that he may (might, would) come; ⁂ sie sich darüber beklagen! let them complain of it!; möchte ich ihn wohlbehalten wiedersehen! would I might (or I trust I may) see him return safe and sound!; sage ihm, er möge (oder möchte) nach Hause geh(e)n tell him to (or bid him) go home; ich möchte rasend werden! it's enough to drive one mad!; ich möchte beinahe fortlaufen I feel half inclined to run away; das Herz möchte mir zerspringen my heart is ready to burst; iro. es möge ihm wohl bekommen! much good may it do him! — **II** v/a. 6. (gern) ⁂ to be fond of or partial to; nicht ⁂ to dislike; sie ⁂ mich nicht (leiden) they don't like me, they can't bear me; ich mag (es) nicht I don't care for it; lieber ⁂ to like better, to prefer; ich möchte lieber I would (or had) rather. — **III** ~ n ⓐ 7. (Wünschen) wishing, wish, willingness, desire; (Können) ability, power; (Neigung) inclination, liking.
möglich (⌣⌣) [mhd.: *mögen] a. ⓰
1. possible; es ist ⁂, daß er kommt he may (possibly) come; ich will es ihm ⁂ machen zu entrinnen I will make it possible for him (or enable him) to escape; ich werde alle ⁂e Sorgfalt anwenden oder alles ⁂e aufbieten I shall do everything (that's) (with)in my power, I will do my very utmost; alle ⁂en Unglücksfälle all sorts of accidents; et. mit der ⁂ten Eile (oder ⁂t eilig) betreiben to do a th. with the utmost (or the greatest possible) dispatch; den höchst erreichbaren Grad bezeichnend: so bald als (nur irgend) ⁂ as soon as (ever) possible; sobald es Ihnen ⁂ ist at your earliest convenience; soviel als ⁂ as much as possible; so gut als ⁂ s. gut 2; macht so wenig Lärm als nur ⁂ make as little noise as you can; alles ⁂e versuchen to try everything possible or conceivable or imaginable, to use all possible means; sein ⁂tes tun to do one's utmost, to exert o.s. to the uttermost, to strain every nerve; in Bssgn, zB.: bestmöglich (r-r: ⁂t gut, so gut wie ⁂) the best possible, in the best possible way. — 2. (ausführbar) feasible, practicable; (etwaig) eventual; ⁂ machen to render feasible; wie soll ich (oder man) es ⁂ m.? how is it to be done or managed?; es war mir nicht ⁂ it was beyond my ability or power, it was more than I could do, I was unable to do it.

möglichen=falls(⌣⌣⌣⌣)adv. in case of possibility, if (it be) possible or feasible.
möglicher=weise (⌣⌣⌣⌣⌣) adv. possibly; ⁂ gefallen sie ihm they may perhaps (or it is possible that they may) suit him.
Möglichkeit (⌣⌣⌣) [mhd.] f ⓰ possibility, ⚛ potentiality; phls. in der ~: ⚛ in posse, potentially; (etwas Mögliches) s.th. possible or feasible; (möglicher Fall) eventuality, contingency; (Ausführbarkeit) practicability, feasibility; nicht die entfernteste ~ not the remotest chance; nach ~ as far as (or in the best way) possible; es ist die ~ vorhanden, daß // it is just possible (F it's on the cards) that //; F ist's die ~? really?, well, I never!, you don't say so!; ich sehe keine ~, es zu erreichen I see no chance (or way) of attaining it.
Mogul (⌣⌣) [ar.: *Mongole] m ⓐ ⓐ der (Groß=)~ the (Grand) Mogul.
Mohammed (⌣⌣⌣) [ar. Mu-ha'med der Gepriesene] npr/m.ⓑa. (bsd. der Stifter des Islams, † 632) Mohammed, ++ Mahomet; ~aner(in f ⓰) m ⓐ, 2anisch a. ⓰ Mohammedan, ++ Mahometan; ~anismus (~⌣⌣⌣⌣) m ⓐ Mohammedanism, ++ Mahometanism; Islamism.
Mohär ⛉ (⌣¹) [ar.] m ⓓd. = Mohr².
Mohn ⚥ (⌣¹) [ahd.] m ⓑc. poppy (Papa'ver); wilder ~ = Klatschmohn.
mohn=artig ⚥ (⌣¹...) a. ⓰; ⚛ papaver(ace)ous; =blatt n ⓐ poppy-leaf; dünn wie ein ~, etwa: (as) thin as a wafer; =blume ⚥ f opium-poppy (Papa'ver somni'ferum); =gewächse ⚥ n/pl.: ⚛ papaveraceæ pl.; =kopf m poppy-head; =kuchen m kind of seed-cake; =öl n poppy-oil; =saft m, pharm. poppy-juice; opium; =same(n) m poppy-seed; =säure f, chm.: ⚛ meconic acid ($C_7H_4O_7$).
Mohr¹ (⌣¹; *Hom. Moor)[ahd.; mlt. *Maure] m ⓑ, ~in f ⓰ 1. a) (Schwarze[r]) Moor(ish woman f); (Neger[in]) negro, f negress, F blackie, darkie, blackamoor; b) fig. von vergeblicher Arbeit: e-n ~en weiß waschen wollen = (try to) wash an Ethiop(ian) white. — 2. ehm. chm. pharm. (schwarzes Schwefelmetall) mineral æthiops.
Mohr² ⚥ (⌣¹) [fr. moire f; *ind.] m ⓑc. (schwarzer Stoff) mohair, tabby; (Wasser=) **Mohr³**=... s. Mohrrübe. [glanz) moire.)
Möhre ⚥ (⌣⌣) [ahd.] f ⓑ = Mohrrübe.
möhren=farbig (⌣⌣⌣⌣) a. ⓰ carroty.
Mohren=fürst (⌣⌣...) m ⓐ Moorish prince; =gesicht n F blackamoor's face.
mohrenhaft (⌣⌣⌣), **mohrisch** (⌣⌣) a. ⓰ Moorish, Moresque; like a negro.
Mohren=hirse ⚥ (⌣⌣...) f ⓑ Caffre-corn (Sorghum vulga're); =kopf m Moor's (or negro's) head; =land ⚥ n: a) negroland; b) country of the Moors.
Möhren=same (⌣⌣⌣⌣) m ⓑ carrot-seed.
Mohren=sklave (⌣⌣...) m ⓑ black slave; =tanz m Moorish dance, in Engl. ehm.: morris (dance); =weib n Moorish woman; (Negerweib) negress, black (or negro) woman.
Mohr²=kleid (⌣⌣⌣) n ⓑ mohair dress.
Mohr³=rübe ⚥ (⌣⌣⌣) [Möhre] f ⓑ (gelbe Rübe) carrot (Daucus caro'ta).
Moira (⌣⌣) [grch.] f ⓰ myth. = Möre.
Moiré ⚥ (mia-re') [fr.] m, n ⓑ = Mohr².

⚛ scientific; ⚥ botanical; ⛉ geography; ⓐ machinery; ⚔ mining; ⚔ military; ⚓ marine; ⚥ commercial; ⚬ postal; 🚂 railway.

[moirieren] — 704 — [monologisch]

moirieren ⊕ (mȧ⌣´) [fr. *moirer*] v/a. ⓢ (wässern) to cloud, water, wave.
mokant (⌣⌣) [fr. *moquant*] a. ⓢ (spöttisch) mocking, sneering, sarcastic.
Mokassin † (⌣⌣´) m ⓢ (Indianerschuh aus Wildleder ohne harte Sohle) moccasin.
mokieren (⌣⌣´) [fr. *moquer*] v/refl. ⓢ: sich ⌐ über to sneer at, to mock.
Mokka ⚥ (⌣´) [ar. *Mucha*] I npr/n. ⓢ α. (arab. St.) Mocha. — II ⚤ m ~(=kaffee) m ⓢ Mocha(-coffee).
Molasse (⌣⌣´) [fr.] f ⓢ geol. (feinkörniger grauer Sandstein) molasse.
Molch (⌣) [ahd. Eidechse] m ⓢb. zo. salamander (*Salama'ndra*).
Moldau ⚥ (⌣´) [Moldava, Fl.] npr/f. ⓢα. (Donaufürstentum, Teil Rumäniens): die ~ Moldavia; ~er(in) f ⓢ) m ⓢ, Lisch a. ⓢ Moldavian.
Mole¹ (⌣´) [fr. *môle m*; *it. (Molo)] f ⓢ (Hafendamm) jetty, mole, pier.
Mole² ⚥ (⌣´) [lt., *grch.] f ⓢ med. (Mondkalb, Wind=ei) mole, false conception.
Molekül ⚥ (⌣⌣´) [fr. *molécule f*] n ⓢd. chm. u. phs. (kleinstes Stoffteilchen) molecule; weitS. (Atom) atom.
Molekular=gewicht ⚥ (⌣⌣⌣´...) n ⓢ molecular weight; **=kräfte** f/pl. molecular forces pl. [= belästigen.)
molestieren (⌣⌣´) [fr.] v/a. ⓢ
molk ⚲ (⌣) imp. ind. v. melken.
Molke (⌣´) [mhd.; *melken] f ⓢ whey.
Molken=kur (⌣´...) f ⓢ med.: die ~ gebrauchen to drink whey medicinally; **=werk** n, **=wirtschaft** f dairy(-farm).
Molkerei (⌣⌣´) f ⓢ dairy-farm(ing); **~=genossenschaft** f ⓢ dairy-farmers' association. [wheyish, ⓢ serous.)
molkicht, mst **molkig** (⌣´) a. ⓢ like whey,)
Moll¹ † ⚥ (⌣) m ⓢc. u. ⓢ Zeug: mull, mulmul, India(n) muslin. [(key).)
Moll² ♪ (⌣) [it.] n, inv. (ant. Dur) minor)
Molla (⌣´) [ar. *Herr*] m ⓢ (mohammedanischer Priester) Mullah, Mollah.
Moll² **=akkord** ♪ (⌣⌣´) m ⓢ minor chord.
Möller=haus ⚒ (⌣⌣´) n ⓢ ore-house.
möllern ⚒ (⌣´) I v/n. (h.) ⓢa. (gattieren) to mix the ores. — II ~ n ⓢ u. **Möllerung** f ⓢ mixing the ores.
mollig F (⌣´) a. ⓢ 1. pleasant, comfortable; hier ist's recht ⌐ it's very snug (or cosy) here. — 2. (weich anzufassen) soft. [=ton=leiter f minor scale.)
Moll²=**ton(art)** f m ♪ (⌣⌣´(⌣)) ⓢ = Moll²;)
Molluske ⚤ (⌣´) [lt.] f ⓢ zo. (Weichtier))
Molo (⌣´) [it.] m ⓢ = Mole¹. [mollusc.)
Moloch (⌣ch) m ⓢd. (a. *inv.*) (Gott der Phönizier in Stiergestalt) Moloch.
molossisch ⚥ (⌣⌣´) [grch.] a. ⓢ pros.: der Versfuß, **Molossus** (⌣⌣´) m, inv. u. ⓢ molossic metre (---).
Molukken(=inseln) ⚥ (⌣⌣´(⌣)) [malai.] npr/f/pl. (Gewürz=inseln im Malai'schen Archipel) Moluccas, Spice Islands pl.
Molybdän ⚥ (⌣⌣´) [grch.Blei...] n ⓢd. chm. molybdenum (Mo); ⚥=sauer a. ⓢ molybdic; ⚥=saures Salz molybdate; **~=säure** f ⓢ molybdic acid (H_2MoO_4).
Moment (⌣⌣´) [lt. *momēntum n*] ⓢc. I m 1. = Augenblick 2; der entscheidende ~ the critical moment; im rechten ~ at the right moment. — II n 2. (Haupt=ursache) chief reason or consideration; (Beweggrund) motive; (Haupt=)~ main

point. — 3. mech. (Produkt aus Masse u. Geschwindigkeit) momentum of a force.
momentan (⌣⌣´) a. ⓢ = augenblicklich.
Moment=aufnahme (⌣⌣´...) f ⓢ, **=bild** n instantaneous photograph, F snapshot.
Monade ⚥ (⌣⌣´) [grch.] f ⓢ phls. (unteilbare Substanz) monad; **~n=lehre** f ⓢ v. Leibniz x. monadology, monadism.
monadisch ⚥ (⌣⌣´) [grch.] a. ⓢ phls. (einheitlich, unteilbar) monadic.
Monarch (⌣⌣´) [grch.] m ⓢ, **~in** f ⓢ monarch, sovereign; **~ie** (⌣⌣⌣´´) f ⓢ monarchy; Lisch (⌣⌣´) a. ⓢ monarchical; **~ist** (⌣⌣´) m ⓢ monarchist.
Monat (⌣´) [ahd.: month] m ⓢd, 6. month, *poet.* moon; am 10. dieses ⓢ des laufenden Monats on the tenth of this month, ⚤ on the 10th instant (*abbr.* inst.); am Ersten des nächsten, vorigen ~s on the first of next, last month, ⚤ on the first *proximo*, *ultimo*; in drei ~en, drei ~(e) nach heute (with)in three months, *genauer*: this day three months; vor anderthalb ~en six weeks ago; Le=lang a., adv. lasting for months.
(...)monatig (...)(⌣⌣´) a. ⓢ in Zssgn: drei2 (3 Monate dauernd ob. alt) lasting three months, three months old; vier2es Kalb four months' calf.
monatlich (⌣⌣´) a. ⓢ 1. (sich jeden Monat wiederholend) monthly, adv. every (or by the) month. — 2. physiol. Le Reinigung, das ~e (auch Monatsfluß m) monthly courses or F visitors pl., F poorly time, ⚥ menstruation, menstrual flux or flow. — 3. in Zssgn. z.B.: drei2 (alle 3 Monate) every three months, quarterly.
Monat(s)=abschluß (⌣⌣´⌣...) m ⓢ, **=bericht** ⚤ m monthly balance, report; **=fluß** m f. monatlich 2; **=frist** f one month's time or grace; in ~ within (the space of) a month; **=geld**, **=gehalt** n monthly salary or pay or allowance; **=heft** n monthly part of a new work; **=lieferung** f monthly number of a periodical, &c.; **=rose** ⚥ f monthly rose (*Rosa damasce'na*); **=schrift** f monthly journal or review or periodical or publication; ~en pl., oft: monthlies pl.; **=tag** m day of the month, date; **=übersicht** f monthly return(s pl.).
monat=weise (⌣´⌣⌣) adv. by the month.
Mönch (⌣) [ahd.: monk; *grch. *monacho's* Einsiedel] m ⓢb. 1. monk, friar. — 2. ⓢ a) *arch.* ~ (Mittelpfosten) e-s Fensters: mullion; b) *mach.* (Stempel) punch of a cutting-press.
Möncherei (⌣⌣´´) f ⓢ monkery, weitS. monasticism; **mönchisch** (⌣´) a. ⓢ monkish, monastic, ehm.: friarlike.
Mönchlein (⌣´) n ⓢ (*dim.* von Mönch) little monk, ehm. *contp.* shaveling.
Mönchs=kappe (⌣´...) f ⓢ monk's hood, cowl; **=kloster** n monastery; **=kolben** ⚥ m, *mach.* plunger; **=kutte** f monk's frock, cowl; die ~ anlegen to turn monk; **=latein** n monkish Latin; **=leben** n monkish (or monastic) life; **=orden** m monastic (or religious) order; **=schrift** f, *typ.* pointed black letter; **=wesen** n monkish affairs pl., monasticism; **=zelle** f friar's cell; **=zucht** f monastic discipline.

Mönchtum (⌣´) n ⓢd. = Mönchswesen.
Mond¹ (⌣) [: month, moon] m ⓢb. 1. moon (*poet.* ⓢ b. ⓢ = Monat); halber ~ crescent; voller ~ full moon; der ~ nimmt ab (zu) the moon is waning (waxing); der ~ ist voll it is full moon; der ~ scheint the moon is shining, it is moonlight; der Mann im ~ the man in the moon (a. *fig.*); den ~ betreffend ⚥ lunar; unter dem ~e (befindlich) ⚥ sublunary. — 2. die ~e pl. des Jupiter the satellites of J.
Mond=alter (⌣´...) n ⓢ age of the moon; **=auge** n, *vet.* (Augenübel v. Pferden) moon-eye; **=bahn** f moon's (or lunar) orbit; **⚥=beglänzt** a. ⓢ illumined by the moon, lit up by moonshine; **=beschreibung** f: ⚥ selenography; **=blindheit** f, *vet.* moon-blindness. [= Mond=...)
Monden=..., **Mond(e)s=...**(⌣´(⌣)...)in Zssgn)
Mond=finsternis (⌣´...) f ⓢ lunar eclipse; **=fläche** f moon's disk; **⚥förmig** a. ⓢ moon- (or crescent-)shaped, ⚥ luniform; ⚥ lunate(d); **=gebirge** n, *ast.* Lunar Mountains pl.; **=göttin** f Luna, Cynthia, Selene; ⚥**hell** a. moon-lit; **=jahr** n lunar year; **=kalb** n, *physiol.* false conception; **=karte** f moon-chart, ⚥ selenographic chart; **=klee** n = moon-trefoil (*Medica'go arbo'rea*); **=licht** n moonlight; **=mo'nat** m lunar month; **=phase(n pl.)** f phase(s pl.) of the moon; **=raute** ⚥ f moonwort (*Botry'chium luna'ria*); **=same** ⚥ f moon-seed (*Menispe'rmum palma'tum*); **=scheibe** f lunar disk or orb; **=schein** m moonshine; **=sichel** f crescent; **=stein** m, *min.* moonstone, ⚥ selenite; **=sucht** f, *path.* somnambulism; ⚥**süchtig** a. moonstruck; somnambulous, walking in one's sleep; **=viertel** n quarter of the moon; **=viole** ⚥ f = lunary (*Luna'ria bio'nnis* oder *a'nnua*); **=wechsel** m, *ast.* change of the moon, ⚥ lunation.
Moneten F (⌣⌣´) [lt. *mōne'tă*] pl. ⓢ (Geld) money, (ready) cash, F tin, P oof.
Mongo/le (⌣⌣´) m ⓢ, **M/lin** f ⓢ Mongol(ian); M/lei ⚥ (⌣⌣´´) npr/f. ⓢα. Mongolia; M/lentum ⓢd. the Mongols pl.; **mongolisch** (⌣⌣´) a. ⓢ Mongol(ic).
monieren (⌣⌣´) [lt.] v/a. ⓢ: a) (benachrichtigen) to inform; b) (tadeln) to blame, criticize, censure; c) (vermerken) to note.
Monismus ⚥ (⌣⌣´) [grch.] m ⓢ phls. (Lehre von der Einheit in den Erscheinungen) monism; **monistisch** a. ⓢ monistic(al).
Monitor (⌣⌣´) [lt.] m ⓢ 1. (Mahner) monitor. — 2. zo. (Warneidechse) monitor (*Mo'nitor*). — 3. † ⚓ (auch ⓢ) monitor.
Monitorium (⌣⌣⌣´´) n ⓢ (Ermahnungs=schreiben) (letter of) admonition; reminder. — **Monitum** (⌣´⌣) n ⓢ admonition; (Verweis) censure.
Monochord ♪ (⌣⌣´) [grch.] n ⓢc. phys. (Tonmesser) monochord, sonometer.
Monogamie ⚥ (⌣⌣⌣´) [grch.] f ⓢ (Ein=ehe) monogamy; **monogamisch** (⌣⌣´⌣) a. ⓢ monogamous. [monogram.)
Monogramm ⚥ (⌣⌣´) [grch.] n ⓢd. =)
Monokotyledone(n pl.) ⚥ ⚥ (⌣⌣⌣⌣´(⌣)) [grch.] f ⓢ (einsamenlappige Pflanze) monocotyledon (= Spitzkeimer).
Monolog (⌣⌣´) [grch.] m ⓢd. (Selbst=gespräch) monologue, soliloquy.

Zeichen (f. S. XVII): F familiär; P Volkssprache; P Gaunersprache; ⚲ selten; † alt (auch gestorben); * neu (auch geboren); ⟋ unrichtig;

[Monopol] — 705 — [mordsmäßig]

Monopol (⌣⌣́) [grch.] n ⑪d. (Alleinhandel) monopoly; (Vorrecht) (exclusive) privilege; **monopolisier/en** (⌣⌣⌣́⌣) v/a. to monopolize; ~ n ㉓ u. **M/ung** f ㊻ monopolization.

Monothe-ismus (⌣⌣⌣́⌣) [grch.] m ㉗ rel. (Glaube an einen Gott) monotheism. **Monothe-ist** (⌣⌣⌣́) [grch.] m ㊷ monotheist; **/isch** (⌣⌣⌣́) a. ⑥⑥ monotheistic. **monoton** (⌣⌣́) [grch.] a. ⑥⑥ (eintönig; langweilig) monotonous; humdrum, slow. **Monotonie** (⌣⌣⌣́) [grch.] f ㊻ monotony. **Monster-petition** T (́⌣⌣⌣–tś(⌣)́) f ⑫ monster petition. [monstrance, pyx.] **Monstranz** (⌣́) [lt.] f ㊻ Cath. eccl. **monströs** (⌣́) [lt.] a. ⑥⑥ (D 10) monstrous. **Monstrosität** (⌣⌣⌣́) [lt.] f ㊻ monstrosity. **Monstrum** (⌣́) [lt.] n ㉘㊾ (Ungeheuer, Mißgeburt) monster. monstrous creature. **Monsun** ↯ (⌣́) [ar.] m ⑪d. (ostindischer Passatwind) monsoon; in einen ~ geraten to strike a monsoon. **Montag** (́⌣) [ahd.: Monday; *Mond] m ⑪d. Monday; f. blau 2; ~ abend Monday evening; (des) ~s every Monday. on Mondays. **Montage** ⊕ (mɑ́ɡ⌣) [fr.] f ㊽ (Aufrichtung, Aufstellung) mounting of machines, &c., fixing-up of machinery, of a plant. **montägig** (́⌣⌣) a. ⑥⑥ (happening) on a Monday; **montäglich** a. ⑥⑥ taking place every Monday. [post or mail. **Montags-post** (́⌣⌣) f ㊻ Monday's **Montan-aktien** ✪ (⌣́) [lt. Berg-] f pl. = -werte; **-industrie** f ⑫ mining-industry; **-werte** m/pl. mining shares pl. **Montenegriner** (⌣⌣⌣́) [Montene'gro ⚲; *it., Fürstentum der Balkanhalbinsel] m ㉒, ~in f ㊼, **montenegrinisch** a. ⑥⑥ Montenegrin. [elect., &c. mounter, fitter. **Monteur** ⊕ (mɡ-tö́r) [fr.] m ⑪d. mach., **Montgolfi-ere** ehm. (mɑ(⌣)́⌣) [fr. Montgolfier, Erfinder 1783] f ㊽ montgolfier, balloon inflated with heated air. **montier/en** (⌣́⌣) [fr.] I v/a. ⑨⑨ 1. ⊕ (aufstellen, anlegen) to mount, to fit (up). — 2. ⚔ to mount a gun; (ausrüsten) to equip (or fit out) troops; (beritten m.) to provide cavalry with horses or mounts; schlecht montiert miserably mounted. — 3. ↯ ein Schiff ⚲ (bemannen) to man ... — II ~ n ㉓ ⚔ = M/ung 1 4. — **Montierung** (⌣́⌣) f ㊻ (Montage) 1. mounting; equipment; manning. — 2. ⚔ (Kleidung) soldier's clothing or outfit or accoutrements or regimentals pl. **Montierungs-depots** ⚔ (⌣⌣…) n/pl. ⑫, **-kammer** f stores pl. (or depot) of army-clothing; **-stücke** n/pl. mountings, (soldiers') uniforms pl.; **-werkstatt** f fitting-shop. **Montur** (⌣́) [fr.] f ㊻ 1. öft. ⚔ soldier's clothing (Montierung 2). — 2. livery **Monument** (⌣⌣́) [lt. Denkmal] n ⑪d. monument; **Mal** (⌣⌣́) a. ⑥⑥ monumental; **-bau** m ⑫ monumental structure or edifice, geh. Spr.: noble pile. **Moor** (́, Hom. Mohr) [ndd.: moor] n ⑪(⑦)c. fen, bog, swamp, marsh(es pl.) (moor bz. mst „Heideland"; ⚲B. the Scotch Moors). **Moor-bad** (́…) n ㉓ mud-bath; **-boden** m marshy soil; **-erde** f peaty soil, bog-earth; **-gegend** f, **-grund** m = -land;

-hahn m, orn. gorcock; **-henne** f, orn. gorhen; schottisches **-huhn** n, orn. moorfowl or -game, Scotch ptarmigan (Lago'pus sco'ticus); **-ig** a. = -hahn, -henne. **moorig** (́⌣) a. ⑥⑥ boggy, marshy. **Moor-kohle** (́…) f ⑫ geol. moor-coal; **-kolonie** f moorland colony; **-land** n moor(land), fen-country, marshy (or boggy) district; **-schnepfe** f, orn. small (or jack, half) snipe (Gallina'go od. Sco'lopax galli'nula); **-wasser** n marshy (or muddy) water. — Vgl. Sumpf... **Moos**¹ (́) [ahd.: moss] n 1. ♇ bu-s; irländisches ~ (Knorpeltang) Irish (or carrageen) moss (Chondrus crispus); isländisches ~ Iceland moss (Cetra'ria isla'ndica). — 2. südd. ⓐ a. = Moor. **Moos**² P (́) [f jüd. meo(s) Pfennig(e) n, inv. (Geld) cash, F tin, chink, oof, ooftish, Am. spondulics pl. **Moos-achat** (́…) m ⑫ min. moss-agate; **-ähnlich** a. ⑥⑥, **-artig** a. moss-like, mossy, ⚕ muscoid; **-bank** f moss-bank; (moosige Bank) moss-covered seat; **-bedeckt** a. moss-clad; **-beere** ♇ f moorberry, mossberry cranberry (Vacci'nium oxyco'ccus); **-bewachsen** a. moss-grown; **-binse** ♇ f moss-rush (Iuncus squarro'sus). **moosicht, moosig** (⌣́) [Moos¹] a. ⑥⑥ mossy, covered (or overgrown) with moss. **Moos¹-kapsel** (́…) f ⑫ ⚕ pyxis, pyxidium; **-kunde, -lehre** f ⚕ muscology; **-rose** f moss-rose (Rosa musco'sa); **-tierchen** n, zo. moss-animalcule or -coral (Bryozo'on od. Polyzo'on); **-überzug** m moss covering. **Mops** (́) [ndd., ndl.] m ⑧a. 1. (Hunderasse) pug(-dog); sich langweilen wie ein ~ to be bored to death. — 2. F fig. (Dummkopf) blockhead, stupid fellow; (Murrkopf) grumbler; growler. **mopsen** P (⌣́) ⑨ I v/a. (stibitzen) to pilfer. — II sich ⚤ v/refl. (sich langweilen) to feel bored or dull. **Mops-gesicht** (⌣́…) n ⑫ pug-face. **mopsig** (⌣́) [Mops] a. ⑥⑥ like a pug or pug-dog; pug- (or flat-)nosed. **Mops-nase** (⌣́…) f ⑫ pug-nose. **Moral** (⌣⌣́) [lt. morāl- Sitten-] f ㊻ 1. (Sittenlehre, Sittlichkeit) morality, (good) morals pl. — 2. (Nutzanwendung) moral; F co. und die ~ von der Geschicht' // and the moral (or outcome, upshot) of the matter is …. **moralisch** (⌣⌣́) [lt.] a. ⑥⑥ 1. (sittlich) moral. — 2. ⚖ Betrachtungen anstellen to moralize; **-e(r)** m, ell. f. Katzenjammer. **moralisieren** (⌣⌣⌣́) [lt.] v/n. (h.) ⑨ (Moral predigen) to moralize. **Moralist** (⌣⌣́) [lt.] m ㊷ (Sittenrichter) moralist, moral philosopher. **Moralität** (⌣⌣⌣́) [lt.] f ㊻ a) (o. pl. Sittlichkeit) morality; b) (pl. **-en**) † thea. mst pl. moralities. **Moral-philosophie** (⌣⌣́…) f ㊻ moral philosophy. ethics; **-predigt** f sermon on morality, moral lecture; **-wissenschaft** f moral science. **Moräne** (⌣⌣́) [fr. moraine] f ㊽ geol. (Gletschergeröll) moraine. **Morast** (⌣⌣́) [ndd.: morass; *fr. marais] m ⑪⑦b. (tiefsotige, schwarze Erde) rich swampy soil; (Sumpfloch) bog, (Moor) fen, (Kot) mud. (Sumpfgegend) marsh(y

place or district), a. morass; sich aus dem ~ herausarbeiten to get out of the mud or mire (a. fig.); im ~e stecken bleiben to stick in the mud (a. fig.). **morastig** (⌣⌣́) a. ⑥⑥ 1. (kotig) muddy, covered (or bespattered) with mud. — 2. (voller Moräste) marshy, swampy, boggy; Les Land auch: fen-country. **Morast-loch** (⌣⌣́…) n ㉓ muddy (or marshy) hole, puddle, slough. **Moratorium** ⚖ (⌣⌣⌣́(⌣)) [lt. Verzug morātōr-] n ㉙ jur. (letter of) respite. grace. **Mor-braten** (́…) [ndd. mürbe] m ㉒ Kocht.: (Lendenbraten) roast-loin. **Morchel** ♇ (⌣́) [ahd.: *Möhre] f ㊼ morel (Morche'lla escule'nta); vgl. Herbst⚲, Stock⚲. **Mord** (́) [ahd.: murder: lt. mort-Tod] m ⑪b. 1. (Tötung mit oder ohne Absicht) homicide, manslaughter; dort gab es ~ und Totschlag it ended in bloodshed, it was a sanguinary affair. — 2. zeter und ⚲(io) schreien to cry murder, to raise an outcry. F to kick up a hullabaloo; P es ist der reine ~! F it's an awful business! **Mord-anfall** (́…) m ㊻, **-anschlag** m murderous assault, plot, or attempt; **-axt** f murderer's axe, im Krieg: battle-axe; **-brenner(in** f) m incendiary; **-brennerei** f incendiarism; **-brennerisch** a. ⑥⑥ incendiary; **-bube** m assassin; **-element!** int goodness alive! **morden** (⌣́) ⑨ I v/n. (h.) to commit murder(s) or a murder. — II v/a. — ermorden I; (töten) to kill, to slay; (niedermetzeln) to massacre, slaughter, butcher. — III ~ n ㉓ = Mord 1; (Gemetzel) massacre. **Mörder** (⌣́) [mhd.: *Mord] m ㉒, ~in f ㊼ murderer (f murderess); slayer; gedung(e)ner ~ hired assassin, bravo; **-grube, -höhle** f ㊻ den of murderers or cutthroats; fig. er macht aus seinem Herzen keine -grube he is very open-hearted or frank or outspoken. **mörderisch** (⌣́) a. ⑥⑥ murderous; homicidal; (blutdürstig) bloodthirsty; (blutig) sanguinary; (tödlich) deadly, fatal. **mörderlich** a. ⑥⑥ (schrecklich) terrible, frightful, awful (a. fig.); (grausam) cruel, F fig. (groß, gewaltig) enormous, F fearful; sie haben ihn ⚲ verhauen they beat him within an inch of his life. **Mord-fliege** (́…) f ⑫ ent. ⚕ tachina (-fly); **-geschichte** f tale (or story) of a murder, a. murderous tale; **-geschrei** n: a) cry of murder; b) loud shouting or screaming, F ein ~ erheben to raise a terrible outcry, vgl. (-⚲)lärm; **-gesell** m assassin('s accomplice); **-gewehr** n murderous (or deadly) weapon; **-gier** f homicidal passion, bloodthirstiness; **-gierig** a. ⑥⑥ bent on murder; bloodthirsty, sanguinary. **mordio** (́(⌣)⌣) int murder!; f. a. Mord 2. **Mord-keller** ⚔ (́…) m ⑫ frt. casemate; **-lust** f murderous lust; f. -gier; **-lustig** a. = -gierig; **-nacht** f night of (a) murder. **Mords-gaudium** (́…) n ⑫ loud rejoicing; **-kerl** F m devil of a fellow; q.s. (regular) trump or brick; **-lärm** F m deafening noise. fearful uproar, hell let loose; F hullabaloo, (rare) shindy; **-mäßig** a. ⑥⑥ awful; enormous.

[Mordspektakel] — 706 — [Motette]

Mord=spektakel (″...) m ⓢ dreadful row, terrific noise; vgl. Mords=lärm; =stahl m murderous steel or sword.
Mord=tat (‵...) f ⓢ murder(ous deed), homicidal act; =versuch m attempt at murder; =waffe f murderous weapon.
Möre (‵⌣) [s. Moira] f ⓢ myth. (Schicksalsgöttin) (goddess of) Fate; Fatal Sister.
Morelle ⚥ (⌣‵⌣) [fr., it.] f ⓢ 1. = Aprikose. — 2. Amarelle, Schwarzkirsche) morello.
Mores F (‵⌣) [lt. pl. Sitten] pl. inv. (good) behaviour, manners pl.; ich werde ihn ~ lehren I'll teach him manners, I'll make him behave himself.
morganatisch (⌣⌣‵⌣) [mlt.; *ditsch „Morgengabe"] a. ⓢ: ⅜e Ehe eines Fürsten morganatic marriage ...; vgl. a. linf 2.
Morgen (‵⌣) [ahd. morn(ing), morrow] I m ⓢ 1. (ant. Abend) morning; poet. a. morn; der anbrechende ~ the dawn of day, day-break; des ~s (vgl. 2§) in the morning; diesen ~ this morning; gegen ~ towards the morning; nächsten ~ the next (or following) morning; eines schönen ~s some (or one) fine morning; es wird ~ the day is breaking, it's getting light; es war schon ~ it was daylight, the day had already broken; heute 2 this morning; Sonntag 2 on Sunday morning; um 1 Uhr 2s (des Nachts) at one in the morning. — 2. guten ~! Grußformel: good morning!; e-m einen guten ~ wünschen to wish (or bid) a p. a good morning. — 3. Himmelsgegend: (Osten) East, Orient, Levant. — 4. ehm. (größeres Feldmaß, meist = 25,5 Ar) nearly an acre; 5 ~ Land five acres of land. —
II **morgen** (‵⌣) [dat. sg. von Morgen] adv. 5. to-morrow; 2 früh (2 abend, 2 nachmittag) to-morrow morning (evening or night, afternoon); 2 über acht (vierzehn) Tage to-morrow week (fortnight); iro. ja, 2! (warum nicht gar) don't you wish you may get it!; Sprichw. 2, 2, nur nicht heute, sprechen alle faulen Leute, etwa: to-morrow, not to-day, all the lazy people say. —
III ~ n ⓢ 6. the morrow, the coming (or following) day; sorget nicht für das ~ do not trouble about (bibl. give no thought for) the morrow.
Morgen=andacht (‵⌣...) f ⓢ morning-devotion or -prayers pl.; =anzug m m.-dress or -garb; vgl. =kleid; =ausgabe f e-r Zeitung: m.-edition; =besuch m m.-call or -visit; =blatt n m.-paper.
morgend (‵⌣) [morgen] a. ⓢ of to-morrow; der 2e Tag to-morrow; die 2e Zeitung to-morrow's (news)paper.
Morgen=dämmerung (‵⌣‵⌣⌣...) f ⓢ early dawn, dawn of day, day-break; in der ~ in the early twilight.
morgendlich (‵⌣⌣) a. ⓢ of (or in) the morning, matutinal.
Morgen=gabe (‵⌣...) f ⓢ: a) ehm.: gift of the bridegroom to his bride on the morning after the nuptials; b) (Mitgift) dowry; =gebet n morning-prayer or -devotion; =glocke f m.-bell; =grauen n: beim ~ at the break of day; =gruß m early greeting, m.-salute; =kleid n m.-gown, (fr.) deshabille; =land ⚥ n Orient, East, Levant; bibl.

die drei Weisen aus dem ~e the wise men from the East, the three Magi; =länder(in f) m Oriental; 2ländisch a. ⓢ Oriental, eastern; 2er Handel eastern trade, trade with the East; =licht n m.-light; =luft f m.-air; =musik f early music or concert; =post f early mail; =rock m dressing-gown; vgl. =kleid; =rot n, =röte f red m.-sky, aurora; fig. ~ der Freiheit dawn of liberty.
morgens (‵⌣) adv. in the (F of a) morning, every morning; früh=2 quite early (in the morning); vgl. früh 1.
Morgen=sonne (‵⌣...) f ⓢ morning-sun; =stern m, ast. m.-star, (the planet) Venus; =strahl m m.-ray; =stunde f m.-hour; zu früher ~ in the early morn(ing); Sprichw. ~ hat Gold im Munde, etwa: the early bird catches the worm; =tau m m.-dew; =trunk m early draught; =wache f (von 4–8 Uhr morgens) morning-watch; 2wärts adv. eastward; =wind m: a) m.-breeze or -wind; b) east(erly) wind; =zeit f m.-hours pl.; =zeitung f m.-paper.
morgig (‵⌣) a. ⓢ = morgend.
Morgue (‵g) [fr.] f ⓢ (Leichenschauhaus) morgue; mortuary, deadhouse.
Morin ⚥ (‵⌣) n ⓢ d. chm. (Farbstoff aus Fustikholz) morin(e), moric acid (C₁₂H₈O₅).
Morinde ⚥ (⌣‵⌣) f ⓢ (Färber)=~ morinda.
Mor(i)nell (‵⌣‵) [span.] m ⓢ d. orn. morinel, dotterel (Eudromias morinellus).
Moriske (⌣‵⌣) [span.] m ⓢ (Abkömmling der Mauren in Spanien) Morisco.
Moritz (‵⌣) [lt. Mauritius] npr/m. ⓢ ⓖγ. (Vn.) Maurice.
Mormone ⚥ (⌣‵⌣) [amer. 1830] m ⓢ, **Mormonin** f (⌣‵⌣) m, pl. a. Latter-day saints; **Mormonentum** (⌣‵⌣⌣) n ⓢ d. mormonism; **mormonisch** a. ⓢ Mormon.
moros (⌣‵) [lt.] a. ⓢ (D10) morose.
Morpheus (‵⌣) [grch.] npr/m. ⓢ γ. myth. (Gott des Schlafes) Morpheus; in ~ Armen in the arms (or lap) of M.
Morphium (‵f(⌣)) [grch.] n ⓢ chm., med. (Alkaloid des Opiums) morphia, ...ium, ...ine (C₁₇H₁₉NO₃); =esser(in f) m (‵f(⌣)...) ⓢ path. morphia-eater, ⚥ morphiophage; =krankheit f, path.: ⚥ morphinism; =sucht f, path. morphia habit, ⚥ morphi(n)omania.
morsch (ndd.: Mörser] a. ⓢ rotten, decayed, decaying, decomposed, vom Obst a.: pulpy; (hinfällig) frail, fragile, F rickety, (brüchig) brittle, (schabhaft) damaged, (verfallen) dilapidated; 2er Zahn carious tooth; 2 w. to decay, to rot; =heit f ⓢ rottenness, decay(ed state); frailness, brittleness.
Morse (‵⌣, ‵⌣[⌣]) [Morse, Verbesserer der elektrischen Telegraphie, 1791 bis 1872]; ~ Alphabet (‵...) n ⓢ Morse alphabet.
Morselle (⌣‵⌣) [it.] f ⓢ pharm. lozenge.
Mörser (‵⌣) [ahd.; *mlt. mortarium] m ⓢ: a) Gefäß zum Zerstoßen: mortar; b) ✠ artill. Art Geschütz: mortar(-piece), shell-gun; =batterie ✠ (‵⌣...) f ⓢ mortar-battery, battery of mortars; =block m = =lafette; =keule f pestle (of a mortar), brayer; =lafette ✠ f carriage of a mortar(-piece).
Morse=schlüssel (‵⌣..., ‵⌣[⌣]...) m ⓢ; =taster m Morse key.

Mortalität (⌣⌣‵) [lt.] f ⓢ (Sterblichkeits=verhältnis, =ziffer]) mortality.
Mörtel (‵⌣) [mhd.; *mlt. morta'rium] m ⓢ Bauwesen: mortar; (Bewurf, Stuck) plaster; vgl. Gipsmörtel; ~ anmachen, bereiten to prepare (or make up, mix up) mortar; mit ~ bewerfen to plaster, to rough-cast.
mörteln ⓢ (‵⌣) [Mörtel] v/a. ⓢ a. Bauwesen: to (bind with) mortar.
Mortifikation ⓢ (‵⌣⌣=tsj(⌣)‵) [lt.] f ⓢ, ~s=erklärung f ⓢ (Kraftlos-erklärung) amortization; ~s=schein m bill of am.
Mosa=ik ⓢ (⌣⌣‵) [fr., it., *ar.] n ⓢ (ⓢ)d., f ⓢ (eingelegte Arbeit) mosaic, tessellated (or inlaid) work, tessellation, inlay; ~=arbeit f ⓢ = Mosaik; ~=arbeiter m mosaicist, inlayer; ~=fußboden m tessellated pavement; =pflaster n fancy-pavement. [(law,&c.), of Mos s.
mosa=isch (⌣‵⌣) [Moses] a. ⓢ Mosaʼ
Moschee (⌣‵) [ar. masdschid Betort] f ⓢ mosque. [inv. musk (= Bisam).
Moschus (‵⌣) [lt., ar., *ind. Hode] m, =beutel m ⓢ des Moschustieres: musk-bag; =bock m, ent. musk-beetle (Callichroma moscha'ta); =drüse f des männlichen Moschustieres: musk-gland; =geruch m scent of musk, musky odour; =hyazinthe ⚥ f musk-hyacinth (Muscari moscha'tum); =rose ⚥ f musk-rose (Rosa moscha'ta); =schafgarbe ⚥ f m.-milfoil (Achillea moscha'ta); =tier n, zo. m.-deer, moschus (Moschus moschiferus).
Mosel ⚥ (‵⌣) npr/f. ⓢ a. (Fl.) the Moselle; ~wein (″⌣‵) m ⓢ Moselle (wine).
Moses (‵⌣) [hebr.] npr/m. ⓢ γ. bibl. Moses; die fünf Bücher Mosis ⓢ d. Mose (gen.) the Pentateuch (s. Buch 4); ~ (oder Mosen) und die Propheten haben: a) bibl. to have Moses and the prophets; b) [Moos] fig. (Geld h.) to have plenty of money or F of the needful.
Moskau ⚥ (‵⌣) [Moskwa, Fl.] npr/n. ⓢ α. (russische Stadt) Moscow; 2isch (‵⌣‵) a. ⓢ of Moscow, Muscovite.
Moskito (⌣‵⌣) [span.] m ⓢ ent. (Stechmücke) mosquito (bsd. Culex mosquito); ~=netz n ⓢ m.-net; =stich m m.-bite.
Moskowiter (⌣⌣‵⌣⌣) m ⓢ, ~in f ⓢ: a) Bewohner[in] von Moskau; b) weitS. Russe, Russin: Muscovite; **moskowitisch** (⌣⌣‵⌣⌣) a. ⓢ Muscovite.
Moslem (‵⌣) [ar.] m ⓢ (pl. a. ~in ″⌣) Moslem, Mussulman (pl. Mussulmans).
Most (‵) [ahd.: must; *lt. mustum n] m ⓢ b. 1. (Trauben=)~ grape-juice, new wine, ✚ must; bibl. s. fassen 3; Sprichw. s. Barthel. — 2. sübd. (Obstwein) home-made (or British) wine; cider, perry,&c.
mosteln ⓢ a. I v/n. (h.) to taste like new wine. — II v/a., mst **mosten** (‵⌣) ⓢ: Trauben 2 to press grapes; Obst 2 to make home-made wine.
Moster (‵⌣) m ⓢ (Arbeiter, der Most preßt) person who works the wine-press.
Mostert ✚ (‵⌣) [mhd.; *Most] = Mostrich.
Most=kelter ⓢ (‵⌣...) f ⓢ wine- (or cider-) press; =presse f ⓢ = =kelter.
Mostrich (‵⌣) [nhd. P. v. Mostert] m ⓢ d. mustard (= Senf); =büchse f, =näpfchen, =töpfchen n ⓢ mustard-pot.
Most=wage ⓢ (‵⌣) f ⓢ must-gauge.
Motette ♪ (⌣‵⌣) [fr., it. m] f ⓢ motet.

Signs (see page XVII): F familiar; P vulgar; ✠ flash; ⚥ rare; † obsolete (died); * new word (born); ++ incorrect; ♪ music;

Motion (-ts(ᵕ)ˊ) [lt.] *f* ⑯ 1. (Leibesbewegung) (bodily) exercise; sich (eine kleine) ~ m. to take exercise *or* a walk. — 2. † *parl.* motion. — 3. *gr.* inflexional change indicating the gender of a substantive.

Motiv (-ˊf) [lt.] *n* ⓔd. 1. (Triebfeder) motive, incentive; (zugrunde liegende Tatsache) underlying fact. — 2. in der Kunst: subject, theme, ♪ *a.*: † leitmotiv.

motivier/en (-ᵕwˊᵕ) [lt.] I *v/a.* ⑳ to state the motive of, to allege the reasons (*or* a reason) for, bisw. *a.*: to motivate (vgl. begründen 1 c). — II **M/ung** *f* ⑯: mit der ~, daß // on the plea that //.

Motor ⚙ (ˊᵕ, P -ˊ) [lt. Beweger] *m* ⑳ (Kraftmaschine) motor.

Motor=boot (ˊ...) *n* ⑫ motor-boat; **=brille** *f* F motor-goggles *pl.*; **=droschke** *f* motor cab; **=fahrzeug** *n* = Selbstfahrer.

motorisch (-ˊᵕ) [lt.] *a.* ⑯ motor.

Motor=omnibus (ˊ..., P ˊˊ...) *m* ⑫ motor (omni)bus; **=wagen** *m* motor (-car); im ~ fahren to go in a) motor.

Motte (ˊᵕ) [(mhd.) ndd.: moth] *f* ⑯ *ent.* moth (*Ti'nea*); vgl. Kleidermotte; F *fig.* man möchte die ~n davon kriegen!, etwa: it sorely tries one's patience!, F it gives one the hump!

Motten=fraß (ˊᵕ...) *m* ⑫ damage done by moths; **ℒfräßig** *a.* ⑯ moth-eaten; **=pulver** *n* insect-powder, insecticide.

Motto (ˊ-) [it. Wort] *n* ⓔ(⑳) (Denkspruch) motto, ⚘ epigraph.

moussieren (mūˊᵕ) [fr.] *v/n.* (h.) ⑳ (schäumen) to effervesce, froth, F fizz(le); ℒd, *a.* effervescent (spring, &c.), sparkling (wine, &c.); (kohlensäurehaltig) carbonic.

Möwe (ˊᵕ) [ndd.: mew] *f* ⑯ *orn.* gull, sea-gull, (sea-)mew, ⚘ larid (*Larus*).

Mskr. *abbr.* = Manuskript; engl.: M.S.

Muck (ˊ) *m* ⓔb. feeble (*or* faint) sound *or* noise; keinen ~ tun not to utter a sound; nicht ~ sagen not to say a word *or* a syllable, to be mum.

Mücke (ˊᵕ) [ahd.: midge] *f* ⑯ 1. *ent.*: (Stech=)~ gnat (*Culex*); (Zuck=)~ midge (*Chiro'nomus*); obd. = Fliege 1; ~n fangen: a) to catch flies; b) *fig.* to stand gaping; *fig.* s. Elefant und Kamel 1. — 2. ⚙ ~ e-s Gewehres = Fliege 5.

Mucken[1] (ˊᵕ) [ndd. = Mücke (vgl. Grille)] *f/pl.* ⑯ 1. sullen (*or* sulky) mood; (Laune) whim, caprice, fancy, freak; der Gaul hat seine ~ it's a tricky (*or* a vicious) horse; F die Sache hat ~, s. mucken[2] 4. — 2. ~ (Grimassen) m. od. ziehen to make grimaces, F to pull faces.

mucken[2] (ˊᵕ) [nhd. lautm.] *v/n.* (h.) ⑳ 1. to utter a (faint) sound, aus Unzufriedenheit: to mutter, growl, grumble; (mürrisch sein) to be sulky *or* cross *or* F in the sulks, F to have the hump; mucke nicht!, nicht gemuckt! don't argue!, keep quiet!, not a word! (vgl. aufℒ). — 2. (still sein, sich ducken) to be silent *or* glum *or* cowed down. — 3. von einem dumpfen Schmerz: meine Zähne ℒ (auch muckern) I feel a gnawing pain in my teeth. — 4. F die Sache muckt, es muckt mit der Sache (sie hat ihre Schwierigkeiten) the matter is hanging fire *or* at a standstill.

Mücken=fett (ˊᵕ...) *n* ⑫ *co.* (et. Albernes, Unmögliches) mare's nest; **=schwarm** *m* swarm of gnats; **=seiger** *m* gnat-strainer, F fidgety (*or* fussy) person; **=stich** *m* sting of a gnat; vgl. Fliegen=...

Mucker[1] (ˊᵕ) [mucken] *m* ⑫, **~in** *f* ⑯ sulky (*or* F cross-tempered) person.

Mucker[2] (ˊᵕ) [nhd.; *munkeln] *m* ⑫, **~in** *f* ⑯ (Scheinheilige[r]) sanctimonious (F saintly) person; vgl. Duckmäuser(in), Frömmler(in); **~ei** (ᵕᵕˊ) *f* ⑯ = Frömmelei; **ℒhaft, ℒisch** (ˊᵕᵕ) *a.* ⑯ sanctimonious, F saintly; canting, hypocritical. shamming (piety).

muckern[1] (ˊᵕ) *v/n.* (h.) ⓐa. to play the saint *or* the hypocrite, to sham.

muckern[2] (ˊᵕ) *v/n.* (h.) ⓐa. = mucken 3.

Muckertum (ˊᵕ-) [Mucker[2]] *n* ⓔd. sanctimoniousness, F saintliness; canting, false piety, hypocrisy, bigotry.

muckisch (ˊᵕ), F **mucksch** (ˊ) [Mucke] *a.* ⑯ sulky, peevish; whimsical, capricious.

Mucks (ˊ) *m* ⓔa. = Muck.

mucksen (ˊᵕ) [ahd.] *v/n.* (h.) u. **sich ℒ** *v/refl.* ⑳ to stir; er darf sich nicht ℒ he dare not say a word. [mum.]

muck(s)-still F (ˊˊ) *a.* ⑯ quite still,

müde (ˊᵕ) [ahd.; *Mühe] *a.* ⑯ 1. weary, tired, v. übermäßiger Bewegung: fatigued, exhausted, F knocked up, fagged (out); zum Umfallen ℒ dead-beat(en); ℒ m. to tire out, fatigue, weary; bei (oder durch) et. ℒ w., sich ℒ m. to grow weary (F to get tired) in (*or* by) doing a th.; sich ℒ schreien to tire o.s. out with shouting. — 2. mit *gen.* und *acc.* = überdrüssig; z.B. des Lebens ℒ sein to be tired (*or* weary) of life; ich bin es ℒ, immer dasselbe zu hören I am tired (*or* sick) of always hearing the same thing; ich bin es jetzt ℒ (satt) I have had enough (*or* my fill) of it.

Müdigkeit (ˊᵕ-) *f* ⑯ (s. müde) weariness, tired state, fatigue, exhaustion, in geh. Spr.: lassitude; vor ~ umfallen (nicht weiter können) to drop down from (sheer) exhaustion, F to be done up (with fatigue).

Muff[1] (ˊ) [ndd.] *m* ⓔb. growling (*or* snarling) dog; F *fig.* = Maulhänger.

Muff[2] (ˊ) [ndl.] *m* ⓔb. (Schimmel) mouldiness, mustiness; (dumpfiger Geruch) fusty (*or* musty, mouldy) smell.

Muff[3] (ˊ) [ndd., ndl.] *m* ⓔb., auch **~(e)** (ˊ(ᵕ)) *f* ⑯ (⑳) 1. (Pelz zum Wärmen der Hände) muff. — 2. ⚙ *mach.* (Hülse): a) der Wellenkuppelung: coupling-box; b) e-s Rohres: socket, muff.

Müffchen (ˊᵕ) *n* ⑳ (*dim.* von Muff[3]) small muff; (Fausthandschuh) mitten.

Muffe (ˊᵕ) *f* ⑯ s. Muff[3].

Muffel[1] (ˊᵕ) [Muff[1]] *m* ⑫: a) (Schnauze) snout, muzzle; bisw.: muffle; b) *arch.* (Tier-, bsd. Löwen-gesicht) ornament in (the) shape of a lion's, &c. face; c) F (Mund) mouth, P mug, potato-trap; d) *fig.* (mürrischer Mensch) growler.

Muffel[2] (ˊᵕ) [fr. *moufle m*] *f* ⑯ *chm.*, *metall.*, &c.: (feuerfester (Erz=)Schmelztiegel) muffle.

Muffel[2]**=farben** ⚙ (ˊᵕ...) *f/pl.* ⑫ burnt-in colours *pl.*; **=**[1]**gesicht** F *n* pudding-face(d person), P ugly mug.

muff(e)lig (ˊ(ᵕ)ᵕ) [Muff[1]] *a.* ⑯ sulky, sullen; (verbrießlich) vexed, cross.

muffeln (ˊᵕ) [*provc.* Muffel = Mundvoll] *v/a.* u. *v/n.* (h.) ⓐa: a) (ohne Zähne od. mit wenigen Zähnen kauen) to munch; b) (mit vollen Backen kauen) to eat heartily; c) (unvernehmlich reden) to mumble.

Muffel[2]**=ofen** ⚙ (ˊᵕ...) *m* ⑫ *chm.*, &c muffle-furnace; **=platte** ⚙ *f*, *metall.* bib; **=**[3]**schaf**, **=tier** *n*, *zo.* = Mufflon.

muffen[1] (ˊᵕ) [Muff[1]] *v/n.* (h.) ⑳ to grumble, to be sulking *or* in the sulks.

muffen[2], **müffen** (ˊᵕ) [Muff[2]] *v/n.* (h.) ⑳ to smell mouldy *or* fusty *or* faint.

Muffen[3]**=kupp(e)lung**, **=verbindung** ⚙ (ˊᵕ...) [Muff[3] 2] *f* ⑫ *mach.* socket-joint.

muffig (ˊᵕ) *a.* ⑯ 1. [Muff[1]] (mürrisch) sulky. — 2. [Muff[2]] (faulig riechend) (smelling) mouldy *or* fusty; v. Fleisch *a.* faint.

mufflig (ˊᵕ) *a.* ⑯ s. muffelig.

Mufflon (ˊᵕ) [fr.] *m* ⓢ (sardinisches Schaf) *mouflon* (*Ovis mu's(i)mon*).

Mufti (ˊ-) [ar. Rechtsprecher] *m* ⓢ (mohammedanischer Gelehrter) *mufti.*

mug(e)lig ⚙ (ˊ(ᵕ)ᵕ) *a.* ⑯ Goldschmied: (mit gewölbter Fläche) convex.

muh (ˊ) [lautm.] *int.* v. Kühen: moo.

Müh= (ˊ...) in Zssgn s. Mühe=...

Mühe (ˊᵕ) [ahd.; s. mühen] *f* ⑯ trouble; (Arbeit) labour, toil, (Anstrengung) exertion, effort; sich ~ mit et. geben to take pains over (*or* with) a th., to bestow pains (up)on a th.; es macht mir ~, ihm das zu sagen it pains me to (have to) tell him that; **mit großer** (od. vieler) ~ with much trouble *or* difficulty, by dint of great exertion; mit leichter ~ easily, without (much) difficulty; die Sache ist wohl der ~ wert, (ver)lohnt sich der ~ (*gen.*) it is worth the trouble *or* worth (one's) while; er läßt sich keine ~ verdrießen he does not mind any trouble; e-m viele ~ und Kosten verursachen to put a p. to great trouble and expense.

mühe=los (ˊᵕ...) *a.* ⑯ without trouble; easy; **=losigkeit** *f* ⑯ immunity from (all) trouble; ease, facility.

muhen (ˊᵕ) [mhd.; *muh lautm.] *v/n.* (h.) ⑳ von Rindern: to moo, to low.

mühen (ˊᵕ) [ahd. quälen] *v/a.* und **sich ℒ** *v/refl.* ⑳ = bemühen I u. II. [difficult.]

mühe=voll (ˊᵕ,ˊ) *a.* ⑯ troublesome,

Mühe=waltung (ˊᵕ,ˊᵕ) *f* ⑫ trouble, taking (great) pains, exertion, (great) effort.

Mühl=bach (ˊ...) *m* ⑫ mill-brook, -stream; **=bursche** *m* miller's assistant *or* boy.

Mühle (ˊᵕ) [ahd.: mill; *lt. mŏlī'nă] *f* ⑯ 1. ⚙ mill. — 2. *fig.* das ist Wasser auf seine ~ that's grist to his mill, that's just what he wanted. — 3. (Turn-Übung am Reck) grinder.

Mühlen=bau ⚙ (ˊᵕ...) *m* ⑫ construction of mills, mill-wrighting; **=bauer** *m* mill-wright; **=berg** *m* hill crowned with windmills; **=besitzer** *m* mill-owner; **=gerinne** *n* = Mühlgerinne; **=haus** *n* cage of a windmill; **=meister** *m* owner of a mill, (master) miller; **=pferd** *n* mill-horse; **=sandstein** *m* millstone-grit; **=wehr** *n* = Mühlwehr; ehm. **=zwang** *m* compulsory employment of a mill, in Schottland: thirlage; vgl. Mühl=...

Mühl=gang (ˊ...) *m* ⑫ mill-course, set of m.-stones; **=gerinne** *n* m.-race, m.-trench, leat; vgl. =bach; **=graben** *m*

= =bach; klapper f mill-clapper or -clack; knappe, knecht m miller's man or assistant; lauf m drum; rad n mill-wheel; rad=schaufel f jaunt of a mill-wheel; schleuse f mill-sluice; stein m millstone; oberer: upper millstone, runner, unterer: nether (or lower) millstone; französischer ~ burstone; teich m mill-pond; wasser n mill-race; wehr n mill-weir, -dam; werk n mill(-work), mill-shaft.
Mühmchen (⌐ᵕ) n ㉓ (dim. von Muhme) little aunt or cousin, aunty.
Muhme (⌐ᵕ) [ahd. Mutterschwester] f ④ aunt; female (or girl) cousin.
Mühsal (⌐ᵕ) [mhd.; *Mühe] n ⑬ d.. f ⑲ trouble(some work); (beschwerliche Sache) hardship, toil, difficulty; (Strapaze) fatiguing work, fatigue; (Sorgen) cares pl., distress, grief, worry.
mühsam (⌐ᵕ) a. ⑥ 1. troublesome; (ermüdend) fatiguing, wearisome; (schwer) difficult, hard; (anstrengend) laborious, toilsome; sich ♀ (adv.) ernähren to struggle for a living: ♀ verdientes Geld hard-earned money. — 2. (eifrig sich mühend) painstaking, assiduous.
Mühsamkeit(⌐ᵕ⌐)/⑭(s.mühsam)troublesomeness; difficulty; assiduity.
mühselig (⌐ᵕ) [Mühsal + -ig] a. ⑥: a) (voll Mühsal) troublesome, laborious, b) (mit Mühsal beladen) full of trouble, (elend) wretched; ~keit f ⑯: a) e-r Sache, trouble or troublesomeness of a th.; b) (et. Mühseliges) hardship, toil.
Müh=waltung (⌐ᵕ⌐) s. Mühewaltung.
Mulatte (-ᵕ⌐) [span.] m ㊹, **Mulattin** f㊽ mulatto (woman f); f a. mulattress; **mulattenhaft** (-ᵕ⌐), **mulattisch** a. ⑥ like a mulatto, like mulattoes.
Mulde (⌐ᵕ) [mhd.; *lt. mulctra Melkkübel] f ㊽ 1. (flachrundes Holzgefäß) wooden tray or trough; fig. es gießt wie mit ~n it's raining cats and dogs. — 2. ⊕ metall. (Blei=)~ pig of lead. — 3. ⚒ ♀ (Vertiefung, Tal) depression (of the ground), valley, pocket, hollow.
Mulden=blei ⊙ (⌐ᵕ ...) ⊙ metall. piglead; ~förmig (⌐ᵕ ...) a. trough- (or basin-)shaped; geol. Le Biegung einer Schichtenreihe: ⚒ synclinal (fold), syncline; =see m lake which fills a valley.
Mull¹ f ⊕ [engl.: *ind. malmal] m u. n ⑭b. Weberei: (feiner Musselin) mull (-muslin), mulmul.
Mull², mst **Müll** (⌐) [mahlen] n (m) ⑭b. dust, mould; (Kehricht) rubbish, refuse, waste, garbage; sweepings pl.
Mullah (⌐ᵕ) [ar.] m ㊺ = Molla.
Müll=eimer (⌐ᵕ⌐ᵕ) m ㊷ dust-bin.
Müller (⌐ᵕ) [ahd.: mhd.: *mlt. molinārius] m ㉓ 1. ~(in f ㊹) m miller's wife or daughter f). — 2. ent. mealbeetle (Tenebrio molitor).
Müller=blau (⌐ᵕ ...) n ⑳ u. ⊙blau a. ⑥ light blue; =bursch(e) m miller's man or assistant. [craft.]
Müllerei (⌐ᵕ⌐) f ㊽ miller's trade or
Müller=esel (⌐ᵕ ...) m ㊷ miller's donkey; =gesell(e) m miller's (journey-)man; =knappe, =knecht m =gesell.
Müll=grube (⌐ᵕ⌐)/ ㊽ dust-hole; ash-pit; =haufen m dust-heap; =kasten m =eimer.
Mull¹=kleid (⌐ᵕ) n ㊷ fine muslin dress.

Müll=verbrennung (⌐ᵕf⌐ᵕᵕ) f ㊷ combustion of the refuse or dust.
Mulm (⌐) [ndd.; *malmen mahlen] m ⑭b. 1. light (or dusty) earth. — 2. (faulendes Holz) decaying (or rotten) wood. — 3. (Verwitterung, Fäulnis) decay, rot(tenness), mouldiness.
mulmen (⌐ᵕ) ⊕ I v/a. to pulverize, to reduce to powder. — II v/n. (su) to crumble away, to fall to powder.
mulmicht, mst **mulmig** (⌐ᵕ) a. ⑥ dusty, mouldy, (wurmstichig) worm-eaten; F fig. precarious; die Sache ist ♀ it's a rotten affair or case.
Multe=beere ♀ (⌐ᵕ,⌐ᵕ) f ㊷ cloudberry (Rubus Chamaemorus).
mult(e)rig prov. (⌐(ᵕ)⌐) a. ⑥ 1. (smelling) mouldy or fusty. — 2. = mulmicht.
Multiplikand ⚒ (⌐ᵕᵕ⌐) [lt.] m ㊷ arith. multiplicand, factor.
Multiplikation ⚒ (⌐ᵕᵕ-tẕ(ᵕ)ⁿ) [lt.] f ㊻ math. (Vervielfachung) multiplication; ~s=zeichen n sign of multiplication(×).
Multiplikator ⚒ (⌐ᵕᵕ⌐ᵕ) [lt.] m ㊸ arith. und phys. multiplicator, multiplier.
multiplizieren (⌐ᵕᵕ⌐ᵕ) I v/a. ⑨ (vervielfältigen) to multiply; 5 mit 2 multipliziert gibt 10 five (multiplied) by two makes (or is) ten; mit sich selbst ♀ (to raise to the) square. — II ~ ㉓ und M=ung f ㊻ multiplication.
Mumi=e (⌐(ᵕ)⌐) [mlt.; *pers. mūm Wachs] f ㊽ mummy: nhaft (⌐(ᵕ)ᵕᵕ) a. ⑥ mummy-like, mummified.
mumifizieren (-ᵕᵕ⌐ᵕ) [Mumie] I v/a. ⑬ to mummify. — II ~ n ㉓ und **Mumifizierung** f ㊻ mummification.
mum(m) (⌐) int. (schweig[t] still!) mum!
Mumm F (⌐) m, inv. er hat keinen ~ (keine Lust, keinen Mut) he has no inclination, no pluck, no go.
Mumme¹ (⌐ᵕ) [~, npr. Bierbrauer, 1492] f ㊽: Braunschweiger ~ (dides, starkes Bier) Brunswick mum(me) or beer.
Mumme² (⌐ᵕ) [ndl., fr., span.] f ㊽ (Larve) mask; (verlarvte Person) masked p.
Mummel¹ (⌐ᵕ) [mumme(l)n²] m ㉓ (Schreckgespenst) bogey, bugbear. [Seerose.]
Mummel² ♀ (⌐ᵕ) [Muhme dim.] f ㊽—]
mummeln¹ (⌐ᵕ) [lautm.] v/n. (h.) ㊷ a. to mumble, mutter, murmur.
mumme(l)n² (⌐ᵕ) [Mumme²] v/a. ⑬ (㊸a.) (einhüllen) to muffle up.
Mummen=schanz (⌐ᵕ⌐) [Mumme² u. fr. chance] m ⑭a. masquerade, fancy-dress ball, carnival.
Mummerei (⌐ᵕ⌐) [Mumme²] f ㊻ masquerade, masked (or fancy-dress) ball, (Verkleidung) mummery, disguise: fig. (Verstellung) feint, sham(ming).
Mumpitz (⌐ᵕ) [nhd.] m ⑭a. ⑯ (Unsinn) nonsense, rubbish.
München ♀ (⌐ᵕ) [Mönch=(stadt)] npr n. ㉓α. (Hauptstadt von Bayern) Munich.
Münch(e)ner (⌐ᴄh(ᵕ)ᵕ) I m ㉓ ~ in f ㊹ inhabitant of Munich. — II a. inv. (of) Munich: ~ Bier Munich (or Bavarian) beer.
Münchhausiade (⌐ᴄh-(ᵕ)⌐ᵕ) [* Freiherr v. Münchhausen, 1720—97] f ㊸ Baron Munchausen's tale, traveller's yarn, wonderful (or impossible) story.
Mund¹ (⌐) [ahd.: mouth] m ⑪ (⑦) ⑭b. 1. mouth, (Lippen) lips pl.; zo.: ⚒ stoma

(vgl. Maul): einen ~ voll a mouthful; der ~ wässert ihm danach it makes his mouth water; Sprichw. s. Herz 1 am Schluß. — 2. als Objekt von verbs: den ~ aufsperren to stand gaping; vgl. aufsperren 1; den ~ auftun to open one's mouth or lips; er tut den ~ nicht auf he keeps his mouth shut, he does not say a word; s. halten 4; den ~ spitzen to screw up one's mouth; sich (dat.) den ~ verbrennen to speak one's mind too freely, F to put one's foot in (it); e-m den ~ (ver)stopfen to stop a p.'s mouth; den ~ voll nehmen to talk big, to boast (and brag). — 3. nach prp.: an den ~ führen ob. setzen to put to one's mouth; sich et. am ~e absparen to stint o.s. of a th.; nicht auf den ~ gefallen sein to have a ready tongue; er war wie auf den ~ geschlagen he was dumbfounded; wir haben es aus seinem eigenen ~e we have it from his own mouth or lips; Sie nehmen mir das Wort aus dem ~e you take the very words out of my mouth, I was going to say the very same thing; aus dem ~e riechen to have a bad (or foul) breath; s. Hand 4 unter aus; in aller ~e sein to be in everybody's mouth; e-m Worte in den ~ legen to attribute words to a p.; e-m die Bissen in den ~ zählen to grudge a p. every morsel; nur mit halbem ~e lachen to laugh on one side of the mouth, to put on a sickly smile; s. Hand 4 unter mit; e-m nach dem ~e reden to agree (or to chime in) with a p.: von ~ zu ~e geh(e)n to pass from mouth to mouth, to be in everybody's mouth, to be the talk of the town; e-m das Brot vor dem ~e wegnehmen to take the bread out of a p.'s mouth; s. Blatt 9 u. führen 1. — 4. ⊕ (Mündung) v. Geschützen 2c.: muzzle, mouth; (Luftloch) vent; (Öffnung) opening, aperture; anat. ~ des Magens 2c. orifice. [Vormund.]
Mund² (⌐) [ahd.] f ⑱ nur in Zssgn, z. B.
Mund¹=art (⌐ᵕ...) f ㉒ dialect; (Besonderheit der Sprache) idiom, landschaftliche: provincialism; irische ~ (Irish) brogue; ♀artlich a. ⑥ dialectal, provincial, F ~ bedarf m provisions, victuals pl., F grub.
Mündchen (⌐ᵕ) [Mund¹ dim.] n ㉔ little mouth. [muzzle-cap, tampion.]
Mund¹=deckel (⌐ᵕ⌐ᵕ) ⚔ m artill.]
Mündel (⌐ᵕ) [ahd.; *Mund²] m n. n ㉓, \ f ㊷ ward; (Minderjährige[r]) minor.
Mündel=gelder (⌐ᵕ...) n/pl. ㉒ money belonging to a ward, weitS. trustmoney; =sache f affair of a ward or minor; =sicher ♀ a. ⑥ v. Geldanlagen: sufficiently safe for investment of trust-money; =stand m pupilage.
munden (⌐ᵕ) [Mund¹] v/n. (h.) ㊸ to be to one's taste, F to go down with a relish; weitS. to please a p.; das Mundet mir nicht I do not like (or relish) it, that's not to my taste.
münden (⌐ᵕ) [Mund¹] v/n. (h.) u. sich ♀ v/refl. ⑨: a) v. Gewässern: to fall (or flow) into; Flüsse, die in das Stille Meer ♀, a. rivers which empty (or discharge) themselves into the Pacific; b) von Straßen: to run into;

Zeichen (s. S. XVII): F familiär; P Volkssprache; Ր Gaunersprache; ⧹ selten; † alt (auch gestorben); * neu (auch geboren); ⁺⁺ unrichtig;

[Mundentzündung] — 709 — [mürben]

die in den Ganges oden Flüsse the affluents (or tributaries) of the Ganges; *anat.* ineinander 2d: ⚕ inosculating, anastomosing.
Mund¹-entzündung (ℨ...) *f* ⚕ *path.*: ⚕ stomatitis; ²faul *a.* ⚕ = maul= faul; =fäule *f*, *path.*: ⚕ stomacace, scorbutic stomatitis, bſd. bei Säug= lingen: thrush; ²gerecht *a.* fit for eating or drinking, palatable, weitS. suitable; *fig.* e-m et. 2 machen to adapt (or suit) a th. to a p.'s taste or fancy; =geſchwür *n*, *path.* ulcer in the mouth; =harmonika 🎵 *f* harmo= nica, mouth-organ; vgl. Maultrommel; =höhle *f*, *anat.* cavity of the mouth, ⚕ (It.) cavum oris.
mundier/en (◡◡) [It.] I *v/a.* ⚕ to make a fair copy of, *jur.* to engross (deeds). — II M/ung *f* ⚕ engrossment.
mündig (◡◡) [mhd.; *Mund²] *a.* ⚕ *jur.* of age; 2 ſein (werden) to be (to come) of age; er ward für 2 erklärt he was declared (or pronounced) of age; ~keit *f* ⚕ (coming of) age, ma= jority; ²=ſprechen (ℨ...) *v/a.* ⚕a ** to declare of age; ~ſprechung *f* ⚕ e-r Perſon: declaring a p. (to be) of age.
Mund¹-klemme (ℨ...) *f* ⚕ *path.* lock-jaw, ⚕ trismus; =loch *m*, =löchin *f* cook (nur *m* chef) to a p. of (high) rank; =lack, =leim *m* lip- (or mouth-)glue.
mündlich (◡◡) [Mund¹] *a.* ⚕ oral; 2e Prüfung, *a.* viva-voce examination; 2e Abmachung verbal agreement; *adv.* by word of mouth; personally; in Briefen: 2 mehr I will tell you more when we meet; ~keit (ℨ◡) *f* ⚕ *jur.* oral procedure; ~keit des Verfahrens oral method of procedure.
Mund¹-loch (ℨ...) *n* ⚕ mouth, orifice, vent, blow-hole, einer Flöte: blowing-hole; 2los *a.* ⚕ mouthless, ⚕ asto= matous; =öffnung *f*: a) opening of the mouth; b) = =loch, =portion *f* ration; =raub *m* theft of food or provisions; 2recht *a.* = 2gerecht; =ſchenk *m* cup-bearer; =ſchwamm *m*, =ſchwämmchen *n*, *path.* bei Kindern: milk-thrush, ⚕ aphthæ *pl.*; =ſperre *f* = =klemme; =ſpiegel *m*, *surg.* zur Unterſuchung der Mundhöhle: ⚕ stomatoscope, (It.) spe= culum oris; =ſtellung *f* position of the (several parts of the) mouth in voicing a sound, &c.; =ſtück *n* mouthpiece, des Blaſebalges c.: nozzle, an Blas-inſtrumen= ten: mouthpiece, mouthpipe; *man.* am Zaume: bit; ²¹tot *a.* without a voice; 2 m. to (reduce to) silence; ²²tot *a. jur.* dead (or incapacitated) in the eyes of the law; =tuch *n* (table-)napkin.
Mündung (◡◡) *f* ⚕ eines Fluſſes: mouth, den Gezeiten unterliegende: estuary, firth; e-r Flaſche c.: mouth, opening; e-r Röhre c.: orifice; ✕ *artill.* muzzle (or mouth) of a cannon; 🚂 terminus of a railway.
Mündungs-arm (ℨ...) *m* ⚕ branch of an estuary; =deckel ✕ *m* muzzle-cap; =gebiet ⚕ *n* e-s Fluſſes: delta; =weite *f* e-s Geſchützes: bore.
Mund¹-verpflegung ✕ (ℨ...) *f* ⚕ pro= visioning of an army, commissariat; =voll *m* mouthful; =vorrat *m* store of provisions, food; =waſſer *n* water for

rinsing one's mouth, gargle; *med.*: ⚕ collutorium; =werk *n* mouth, (voluble or glib) tongue; ein gutes ~ haben to have the gift of the gab or a well-oiled tongue or a good flow of lan= guage; =winkel *m* corner of the mouth.
Munifizenz (◡◡◡) [lt.] *f* ⚕ (große Frei= gebigkeit) munificence.
Munition ✕ (--tᵗⁱ͜o͡n_L) [lt.] *f* ⚕ (Kriegs= bedarf) ammunition (of war).
Munitions-kaſten ✕ (--tᵗⁱ͜o͡n_U...) *m* ⚕ ammunition-box; =kolonnen *f/pl.* am= munition-columns *pl.*; =wagen *m* ammunition-wagon or -cart.
munizipal (-◡ᵗⁱᴵ) [lt.] *a.* ⚕ (ſtädtiſch) municipal; urban.
Munizipal-beamte(r) (-◡ᵗⁱᴵ...) *m* ⚕ municipal officer; =behörde *f* munici= pality, municipal authorities *pl.*, cor= poration; =garde *f* municipal guard.
Munizipalität (-◡ᵗⁱ◡-ᵗⁱᴵ) [lt.] *f* ⚕ (ſtädtiſche Behörde) municipality.
Munkelei (◡◡ᴵᴵ) *f* ⚕ vague rumour(s *pl.*)
munkeln (◡◡) [nhd.: meucheln] *v/n.* (h.) und *v/a.* ⚕a. to mutter, to whisper; man munkelt davon, es wird davon gemunkelt it is rumoured abroad, a report of it has been set afloat; Sprichw. im Dunkeln iſt gut 2, etwa: night cloaks lovers and dark deeds.
Münſter (◡◡) [ahd.; *lt.-grch. monaste'= rium n*] *n* (m) ⚕ cathedral, minster; ~-turm (ℨ◡◡) *m* ⚕ spire of a cathedral.
munter (◡◡) [ahd.] I *a.* ⚕ (D9) lively, brisk, sprightly, wide-awake; (fröh= lich) merry, cheerful, blithe, gay, F jolly; (rüſtig) vigorous; 2 und geſund hale and hearty; safe and sound; 2 wie ein Eichhörnchen, wie ein Fiſch im Waſſer (as) merry as a lark, as jolly as a sandboy; 2 (wach) bleiben to watch; 2 erhalten to keep awake; 2 werden to awake from sleep. — II *int.* 2! cheer (or wake) up!, F look alive!
Munterkeit (ℨ◡◡) *f* ⚕ (ſ. munter) liveli= ness, briskness, sprightliness; mirth, cheerfulness; vigour; watchfulness.
Münz-abdruck ⊙ (ℨ...) *m* ⚕ impres= sion (⚕ ectype) of a coin; =abfall *m* scissel (from the planchets); =amt *n*, =anſtalt *f* mint(-office); =arbeiter *m* workman employed at a mint, bisw.: minter; =aufſeher *m* inspector of the mint; =beamte(r) *m* official (or officer) of a mint; =beſchickung *f* mixture of metals for the purposes of coinage, alloyage; =beſchneider *m* coin-clipper; =beſchreibung *f*: ⚕ numismatography; =direktor *m* master of the mint; =druck= werk *n* coining-, minting-mill.
Münze¹ (◡◡) [ahd.: mint; *lt. mone'ta*] *f* ⚕ 1. coin(age), (piece of) money; ab= genutzte ~ defaced (or worn) coin; falſche ~ false (or counterfeit) coin; geſetzliche ~ legal tender, coin of the realm; klingende ~ hard cash, specie; engS. (kleine) ~ (*ant.* hartes Geld, ſ. hart 5) (small) change, silver and copper (coins *pl.*); geben Sie mir für eine Krone ~ give me change for a crown-piece. — 2. (Denk=, Schau=)~ medal. — 3. *fig.* ſ. bar 3 am Schluß; einen mit gleicher ~ bezahlen to pay a p. (back) in his own coin, to serve a p. the

same trick, to give a p. tit for tat. — 4. (Münzſtätte) mint.
Münze² ♀ = Minze.
Münz-einheit (ℨ◡ᴵ) *f* ⚕ monetary uni(formi)ty.
münzen (◡◡) [ahd.; *Münze¹] I *v/n.* (h.) u. *v/a.* ⚕ 1. ⊙ to coin (or stamp, issue) money, to mint coin; gemünztes Gold specie; in gemünztem Golde in specie. — 2. *fig.* das iſt auf ihn gemünzt, etwa: it is meant (or intended) for him. — II ~ *n* ⚕ 3. coinage, minting.
Münzen-ſammler(in *f*) *m* (ℨ◡...) ⚕ collector of coins or medals; =ſamm= lung *f* collection of coins or medals, coin-collection.
Münzer ⊙ (◡◡) [münzen] *m* ⚕ coiner, bisw.: minter; ehm.: moneyer.
Münz-fälſcher (ℨ...) *m* ⚕ false coiner; =fälſchung *f* making counterfeit coin; =freiheit *f* right of coinage; =fuß *m* monetary standard; =gebühr *f* mint-age; =gehalt *m* (intrinsic) value of a coin; =gepräge *n* mint-stamp; =gerech= tigkeit *f* = =recht; =geſetz *n* in England: coinage act; =gewicht *n* standard weight of money; =gold *n* standard gold; =herr *m* lord who enjoys the right of coinage; =juſtierer *m* mint-assayer; =kabinett *n* collection of coins or medals, numismatic collec= tion; =kenner *m* expert on coins, ⚕ numismat(olog)ist; =koſten *pl.* cost of coinage, mintage; =kunde *f*: ⚕ numis= matics, numismatology; =kundige(r) *m* = =kenner; =liebhaber(in *f*) *m* col= lector of coins or medals; =ordnung *f* mint-regulations *pl.*; =prägung *f* coinage, monetization; =probe *f* assay (-ing) of coins; =recht, =regal *n* right of coinage; =ſchlag(en *n*) *m* coinage; =ſchreiber *m* clerk to the mint; =ſchrift *f* inscription (or legend) on a coin; =ſilber *n* standard silver; =ſorten *f/pl.* species *pl.* of money; =ſtadt *f* town which has the right of coinage; =ſtätte *f* mint; =ſtempel *m* coiner's die; =ſyſtem *n* monetary system; =ver= brechen *n*, =verfälſchung *f* false coin= ing; =vertrag *m* monetary conven= tion; =wage *f* adjusting-balance; =währung *f* monetary standard; =wardein *m* mint-warden, assayer of the mint; =wert *m* mint-price; =weſen *n* coinage; =zeichen *n* coiner's (or mint-)mark; =zuſatz *m* alloy.
Muräne (-ᴵ◡) [lt.; *grch. mȳ'raina*] *f* ⚕ *ichth.* muræna (*Mur*[*a*]*e'na he'lena*).
mürb, 2e (ℨ, ℨ◡) [ahd.: morſch] I *a.* ⚕ von Fleiſch, Obſt: tender, soft; (zart) delicate; (ſehr reif) mellow; *vgl.* morſch; (gut durchgekocht) well boiled or done; (auf der Zunge zergehend) melting on the tongue; (bröckelig, knuſperig) short; 2er Kuchen short-cake; Fleiſch 2e m. to make meat tender; F *fig.* e-n 2e (nach= giebig) machen to curb a p.('s spirit), to make a p. pliable; 2e w.: a) von Fleiſch: to grow tender; b) *fig.* to grow weary, (nachgeben) to give in, yield, relent. — II ~e *f* ⚕ = Mürbheit.
Mürb-braten (ℨ-ᴵ◡) *m* ⚕ = Mörbraten.
mürben (◡◡) *v/n.* (ſn) ⚕ to grow tender or soft or mellow.

♪ Muſik; ⚕ Wiſſenſchaft; ⚘ Pflanze; ⚭ Geographie; ⊙ Techni.; ⚒ Bergbau; ✕ Militär; ⚓ Marine; ⚖ Handel; ✉ Poſt; 🚂 Eiſenbahn.

[**Mürbheit**] — 710 — [**Muße**]

Mürbheit (⌣-), **Mürbigkeit** (⌣-) f ⑯ (s. mürb(e) tenderness, softness; mellowness; shortness; vgl. Morschheit.
murksen F (⌣) [: mar] ⑳ **I** v/a. (heimlich töten) to murder, dispatch. — **II** v/n. (h.) (sich vergeblich abmühen) to labour in vain. [㉒ zum Spielen: marble.)
Murmel F (⌣) [Marmel, *Marmor] m\
murmeln (⌣) [lautm.] **I** v/n. (h.) u. v/a. ㉒a. to murmur; der 2de Bach the purling (or murmuring, babbling) brook. — **II** ~ n ㉓ murmur(ing).
Murmel¹-spiel (⌣...) [Murmel] n ㉒ game of (or at) marbles; **-²tier** [ahd. P; *lt. mur- (Maus) montis (des Berges)] n, zo. marmot, mountain-rat (*Arctomys marmo'ta*); fig. schlafen wie ein ~ to sleep like a dormouse or a top, to be a sound sleeper.
Murner (⌣) [= Murrende(r)] m ㉒, auch: **Murr** (⌣) m ⑳ in der Tierfabel: (Kater) tomcat, tom(mie); Grimalkin.
murren (⌣) [nhd. lautm.] **I** v/n. (h.) u. v/a. ㉒ to murmur, to grumble (über et. about a th.); to mutter, to growl. — **II** ~ n ㉓ murmurs pl., grumbling; muttering; ohne ~ without a murmur, ungrudgingly.
mürrisch (⌣) [murren] a. ⑯ (verdrießlich) ill-humoured or -tempered, sullen, sulky, glum; (brummig) grumbling, surly, F grumpy, cantankerous; (unfreundlich) morose, F crabby, crusty; 2er Mensch grumbler, growler.
Murr-kopf (⌣...) m ㉒ peevish (or cross-tempered) person, grumbler; **2köpfisch** a. ⑯ peevish, grumbling; **-sinn** m cross humour, grumbling mood.
Mus (¹) [ahd.] n ⑪ (⌣③)a. pap, von Früchten: jam, von Apfelsinen: marmalade; F fig. zu ~ schlagen to beat (or knock) (in)to a jelly (vgl. Brei 1 und 2).
Musaget (-⌣¹) [grch. Musenführer] m ㊷ myth. (Apollo) Musagetes.
mus-artig (⌣...) a. ⑯like jam, squashed.
Muschel (⌣)[ahd.: mussel; *lt. mu'sculus m Mäuschen] f ㊽ 1. zo. Tier u. Schale: mussel, Tier: shell-fish, vgl. Mies2 u. ~tier; (Schale allein) shell, ⇒ conch; kleine ~, Müschelchen n ㉓ little shell. — 2. anat. = Ohrmuschel.
muschel-ähnlich (⌣...) a. ⑯, **²artig** a. ⑯ shell-like, conchyl(i)aceous; **-bank** f ⑫ shell-bank; **-erde** f, geol. tertiary deposit richly intermixed with shells, shell-marl; **²förmig** a. musselshaped; vgl. 2ähnlich; **-geld** n cowrie; **-gold** n = Goldbronze; **-hut** m derPilger: cockle-hat.
musch(e)licht, mst **musch(e)lig** (⌣(⌣) a. ⑯ shell-like, shelly, ⇒ conchoidal.
Muschel-kabinett (⌣...) n ㉒ = -sammlung; **-kalk(stein)** m, geol. shell lime (-stone); **-kenner** m: ⇒ conchologist; **-krebs** m, zo. water-flea, ⇒ cypris, ostracode; **-kunde**, **-lehre** f: ⇒ conch(yli)ology; **-linie** f, math. conchoid; **-marmor** m, min. shell-marble, lumachel(la); **-mergel** m, agr. shell-marl; **²reich** a. ⑯ abounding in shells, shelly; **-sammler(in** f) m collector of shells; **-sammlung** n ㉓ collection of shells; **-sand** m shell- (or shelly) sand; **-schale** f shell, ⇒ conch; **-seide** f, zo.: ⇒ byssus; **-silber** n. paint. shell-silver; **-tier** n, zo. shell-fish, ⇒ conchifer; ~e pl. auch: conchylia pl.; **-vergiftung** f poisoning (caused) by mussels; **-werk** n shell-work.
Muschik (⌣) [russ. tl. Mann] m ⑮ (russ. Bauer) muzhik, a. mo(u)jik.
Muse (⌣) [grch.] f ㊽ myth. (Göttin der künstlerischen Begeisterung) Muse.
Muselman (⌣⌣) [corr. ar. Moslemin pl.] m ㊷, ~**in** f ㊼, auch **Musel-mann** ⑳c., **-männin** ㊼, **musel-manisch, -männisch** (⌣⌣) a. ⑯ Mussulman, Moslem.
Musen-almanach (⌣...) m ㉒ almanac of the Muses; **-berg** m Mount Parnassus or Helicon; **-freund** m friend of the Muse(s), patron of poets; **-gott** m, myth. god (or leader) of the Muses, Apollo; **-quell** m Castalian (or Pierian) fount; **-roß** n hippogriff, Pegasus; **-sitz** m seat of the Muses; weitS. university; **-sohn** m son of the Muses, poet; oft für Student. [museum.)
Muse-um (-¹⌣) [grch. Musen(tempel)] n ㉙
musiert (-¹) [Mosaik] a. ⑯ arranged like mosaic, inlaid with squares of glass, marble, &c.
Musik ♪ (-¹, südd. ¹⌣) [grch.] f ㊻ music; in ~ setzen to set to music; fig. ohne ~ abziehen to steal away unobserved, to take French leave; F da ist (oder liegt) ~ drin there is some sense in that, F that's the (proper) thing.
Musik-akademie ♪ (-⌣⌣⌣¹) f ㊻ musical academy. [(pieces pl. of) music.)
Musikali-en ♪ (-⌣¹(⌣)⌣) [mlt.] pl. ㉙
Musikali-en-halter ♪ (-⌣¹¹(⌣)⌣...) m ㉒ music-rack; **-händler** m music-seller; **-handlung** f music-shop; **-leih-institut** n circulating library for music.
musikalisch ♪ (-⌣¹⌣) [mlt.] a. ⑯ musical, of music; ² sein to be musical, to like (or to be fond of) music; 2er Vortrag musical recital or performance.
Musikant (-⌣⌣) [mlt.] m ㊷, ~**in** f ㊼ 1. ♪ low-class (or itinerant) musician, indifferent fiddler or player, member of a brass-band, bandsman; ~**in** musician's wife, female musician; fahrende (böhmische, Nürnberger) ~en pl. German band sg. — 2. F fig. da sitzen die ~en: a) an die Tasche schlagend: (ba ist das klingende Geld) there is the ready cash; b) (ba liegt die Schwierigkeit) there's the rub.
Musikanten-bande ♪ (-⌣⌣⌣...) f ㊻ band of musicians, street-band; **-knochen** F m am Ellbogen: funny-bone; **-tisch** F m (Nebentisch) side-table for servants, &c.
Musik-aufführung ♪ (-¹¹...) f ㊻ musical performance; **-bande** f band of musicians; **-direktor** m chief conductor; **-dirigent** m band-master, conductor; **-dose** f musical box.
Musiker ♪ (¹⌣⌣) [it.] m ㉒ (Tonkünstler) musician, professional player; (Mitglied einer Kapelle) bandsman.
Musik-fest ♪ (-¹¹...) n ㉓ musical fête or festival; **-freund(in** f) m friend of music; **-instrument** n musical instrument; **-kenner(in** f) m connoisseur of music; **-korps** n orchestra; vgl. **-bande; ☒ e-s Regiments:** (regimental or military) band; **-lehrer(in** f) m music-teacher, m auch music-master;

²liebend a. ⑯ fond of music; **-liebhaber(in** f) m lover of m.; **-notensatz** m, typ. (type for) music-printing; **-probe** f musical rehearsal; **-schule** f school of music, conservatoire; **-stück** n piece of music; **-stunde** f music-lesson; **²treibend** a. cultivating music; **-unterricht** m teaching of (or instruction in) music.
Musikus ♪ (¹⌣⌣) [lt.] m ⑤⑱ musician.
Musik-verein ♪ (-¹¹...) m ㉒ musical (or philharmonic) society; **-verleger** m music-publisher; **-verständige(r)** s. musical expert; **-werk** ☉ n automatic (musical) instrument.[by the Muses.)
musisch (¹⌣) a. ⑯ favoured (or inspired))
Musiv-arbeit ☉ (-¹¹...) f ㊻ mosaic work; **-gold** ☉ n mosaic gold.[inlaid.)
musivisch ☉ (-¹⌣) [grch.] a. ⑯ mosaic,)
musizieren ♪ (-⌣¹¹⌣) [mlt.; *Musik] v/n. (h.) ㉓ to play music; bei ihnen wird viel musiziert they play a good deal on the piano, &c., they are fond of music; des Abends wurde musiziert u. getanzt in the evening there was (or they had) music and dancing.
Musje P (⌣¹) [fr. *monsieur*] m ⑤ fellow.
Muskat (-¹) [mlt.; *Moschus] m ⑳c., ~**e** (⌣¹⌣) f ㊽ starkes Gewürz: nutmeg.
Muskat-baum ⚘ (⌣¹¹...) m ㉒ = **-nuß-baum**; **-blüte** ⚘ f mace; **-butter** ⚘ f nutmeg-butter.
Muskateller (⌣⌣¹⌣) [it. *moscatello*] m ㉒ 1. ⚘ (Traube v. würzigem Geschmack) muscadel (grape). — 2. muscadel (wine); ~**birne** ⚘ (¹...) f ㊽ musk-pear; **-traube** ⚘ f muscadel-(or muscadine-)grape.
Muskat-nuß(**-baum** m, **-öl** n) f (⌣¹¹...) nutmeg (-tree, -oil) (*Myri'stica fragrans*); **-traube** ⚘ f = Muskateller 1; **-wein** m = Muskateller 2.
Muskel (⌣) [nhd.; * lt. mu'sculus m Mäuschen] m ㉒, f ㊽ anat. muscle.
Muskel-anstrengung (⌣...) f ㊻ muscular exertion; **-band** n, anat. m. ligament; **-bau** m m. structure, contexture of muscles; **-beschreibung** f: ⇒ myography; **-bewegung** f muscular movement; **-faser** f m. fibre; **-haut** f muscular membrane.
muskelig (⌣⌣) a. ⑯ muscular.
Muskel-kraft (⌣¹...) f ㊻ muscular strength; **-schmerz** m pain in the muscle(s), ⇒ myalgia, myodynia; **-schwund** m, path. atrophy of the muscles; **-spiel** n play of the muscles; **²stark** a. ⑯ muscular; **-stärke** f muscularity; **-tätigkeit** f muscular activity; **-zerlegung** f: ⇒ myotomy.
Muskete ⚔ (⌣¹⌣) [fr., it.] f ㊽ (alte Flinte) musket, F brown bess.
Musketier ⚔ (⌣⌣¹) [fr.] m ⑳d. (†; ant. Füsilier, Grenadier) musketeer.
Muskulatur (⌣⌣¹) [it.] f ㊻ anat. muscular system, musculature.
muskulös (⌣⌣¹) [it.] a. ⑯ (D10) muscular.
muß (⌣) **I** 1. u. 3. Person *pres. ind.* v. müssen. — **II Muß** n, inv. (absolute or dire) necessity; es ist kein ~ dabei there is no (real) necessity (or need) for it; sprchw. ~ ist ein bitter(es) Kraut f. Kraut 3. Nuß oder ein bitter(es) Kraut f. Kraut 3.
Muße (¹⌣) [ahd.; *müssen] f ㊽ leisure, spare time, holiday(-time); F off-

---

Signs (see page XVII): F familiar; P vulgar; ⌐ flash; ⌐ rare; † obsolete (died); * new word (born); ‡ incorrect; ♪ music;

[Musselin] — 711 — [mutieren]

time; ~ für et. finden to find (spare) time for s.th.; mit ~ at (one's) leisure, leisurely (als *adv.*, besser: in a leisurely way).

Musselin ⚥(ᵕ‿ᴗ̀)[it.; *Mosul ⚥ St.] *m* ⓓ. muslin; 2en (ᵕ‿ᴗ̀) *a.* ⓰ (of) muslin.

müssen (ᵕ́) [ahd.: meet, must angemessen sein] **I** *v/aux.* ⓰ 1. (durch die Umstände genötigt sein) to be obliged, to have to (must kommt fast nur im *pres. ind.* vor!); ich, er muß I, he must; wir 2 es tun we must do it; er mußte abreisen he had to leave; er handelt, wie er muß he acts as he should (act); ich muß mit ihm sprechen I must (or want to) speak to him; Sie 2 wissen you ought to know; Sie 2 sich von ihm nichts befehlen lassen don't let him order you about; warum mußten Sie das sagen? what obliged you to (or made you) say that?; das müßte noch heute geschehen that ought to be done this very day; er hätte schwerer arbeiten 2 (st. *p. p.* gemußt) he must have worked harder; wir hätten bezahlen 2 we should have had (or it would have devolved upon us) to pay; er hätte schneller reisen 2 (sollen) he ought to have travelled faster. — 2. (gezwungen sein) to be forced or compelled to do a th., to be under the necessity of doing a th.; die Briefe 2 sofort geschrieben w. ... require to be written at once; das ist, als müßte es so sein that seems as if it must be so or could not be otherwise; sie 2 bald kommen they are bound to come soon; ich muß lachen, wenn // I am obliged to laugh when //; ich mußte weinen, als ich ihn sah I could not help crying when I saw him; es muß ihn doch freuen, daß // he cannot but rejoice that //; ich muß weg I must (needs) be going or be off; muß das wirklich geschehen? is it really necessary to do that?, must it needs be done?; alle Menschen 2 sterben all men must (or are doomed to) die; wenn es sein muß ob. müßte on (or at) a pinch; eine Frau, wie sie sein muß a pattern of a woman, a model wife; das mußte nun einmal so sein fate (or necessity) would have it so; *v.* Ungewißheit aftem: das muß wahr sein it is undoubtedly true; bei Vermutungen: sie 2 wohl krank sein (surely) they must be ill, I suppose they are ill; welches Vergnügen müßte es sein // what a pleasure it would be //; wie sie gelitten haben 2! how (much) they must have suffered! — 3. *ell.*: die Briefe 2 zur Post the letters must be posted; ich muß fort I must be off; er muß aufs Land he must go into the country; in Fragen: wer muß es ihm gesagt haben? (s. muß es gesagt h., aber wer?) who can (or may) have told him? — 4. in Wünschen: die Bösen 2 zuschanden w.! may (or let) the wicked be confounded!, confound the evil ones! — 5. im *impf. subj.* mit „denn": das tue ich nicht, er müßte es mir denn selbst befehlen ... unless he gave me the order himself. — **II** ~ *n* ⓘ 6. = muß II.

Muße-stunde (ᵕ‿ᴗ̀...) *f* ⓶ leisure-hour; -zeit *f* = Muße.

müßig (ᵕ́) [ahd.; *Muße] *a.* ⓰ 1. idle, lazy; disengaged; 2e Zeit unemployed time; 2 (*adv.*) geh(e)n to idle (about); ⚥ *v.* Geldern: 2 liegen to lie idle. — 2. (überflüssig) superfluous; 2es Geschwätz useless (or idle, frivolous) talk.

Müßig-gang (ᵕ‿ᴗ̀...) *m* ⓶ idleness, laziness, stärker: sloth(fulness) Sprichw. ~ ist aller Laster Anfang idleness is the root of all evil; -gänger (-in *f*) *m* idler, lazy person, loafer, F lazybones; 2gängerisch *a.* ⓰ idling, lazy, stärker: F bone-lazy.

mußt (ᵕ́) 2. Person *sg. pres. ind.*, 2e (ᵕ́) *ind. u.* **müßte** (ᵕ́) *subj. impf. v.* müssen.

Muster (ᵕ́) [it. *mostra f*] *n* ⓶ 1. model, (Vorbild) paragon, (Urbild) type, (Richtschnur) standard, (Ideal) (beau-)ideal; sie ist ein ~ der Höflichkeit she is the pink (or essence) of politeness; als ~ hinstellen to hold up as a model or pattern; sich e-n zum ~ nehmen to take a p. for one's model, to follow a p.'s example. — 2. ⊙ (Zeichnung, Form v. Kleidungsstücken *zc.*) pattern, design; nach dem ~ arbeiten to work from a pattern; nach e-m ~ gemacht made to pattern. — 3. ⚥ (Probe von Waren) sample, specimen; ⚭ ~ *pl.* ohne Wert samples *pl.* of no value.

Muster-anstalt (ᵕ‿ᴗ̀...) *f* ⓰ model school; -bild *n* = Muster 1; -buch *n*: a) standard work; b) ⚥, &c. book of patterns or samples.

Musterer ⚔ (ᵕ‿ᴗ̀) *m* ⓶ inspector of troops, inspecting officer.

muster-gültig (ᵕ‿ᴗ̀...) *a.* ⓰ (fit to serve as a) model; typical, standard, classical; ideal; -keit *f* ⓰ classicism.

musterhaft (ᵕ‿ᴗ̀) *a.* ⓰ exemplary, perfect, model; ein 2er Arbeiter a pattern (or model) of a workman; **~igkeit** (ᵕ‿ᴗ̀) *f* ⓰ exemplariness, perfection.

...musterig (ᵕ‿ᴗ̀) *a.* ⓰ in Zssgn, *zB.*: groß-2 with large designs.

Muster-karte ⚥ (ᵕ‿ᴗ̀...) *f* ⓶ paper of patterns, sample-card; -kasten ⚥ *m* box of samples; -knabe *m* model boy, Schule *zc.*: show-boy; -lager ⚥ *n* stor(ag)e (or stock) of samples; -mensch *m* pattern of excellence, model of a man or woman.

mustern (ᵕ‿ᴗ̀) **I** *v/a.* ⚥ *a.* 1. to examine, to inspect, to (pass in) review, mit den Blicken: to eye; alles gut 2 to take stock of everything; ⚔ und ↓ to muster, to review. — 2. (tadeln) to criticize, to censure. — 3. ⊙ Weberei *zc.*: (mit einem Muster versehen) to figure, wie Damast: to damask. — **II** ~ *n* ⓘ 4. = Musterung. — **III** ge-mustert *p.p.* und *a.* 5. (fancy-)figured; 2es Zeug fancy-material or -cloth.

Muster-platz ⚔ (ᵕ‿ᴗ̀...) *m* ⓶ muster-place, place of review; -reisende(r) ⚥ *m.contp.* -reiter *m* commercial traveller, F bagman; -riß ⊙ *m* working-design; -rolle ⚔ *f* muster-roll or file, ↓, ⚔ the (ship's) articles *pl.*; -sammlung *f*: a) Schrifttum: selection from standard authors; b) ⚥ collection of samples; -schrift *f*: a) model writing; copy (for writing);

b) classical work; -schriftsteller(in *f*) *m* standard writer or author(ess *f*); -schule *f* = -anstalt; -schüler(in *f*) *m* model pupil; -schutz *m* protection of (or copyright in) designs; -stück *n* (piece which can serve as a) model, (fine) specimen; deutsche ~e extracts *pl.* from German classics.

Musterung (ᵕ‿ᴗ̀) *f* ⓰ examination, inspection, review; ⚔ muster; ⚔ e-e ~ halten to hold a review, to muster (or review) troops; die ~ bestehen to pass muster (auch *fig.*); **~s-geschäft** ⚔ *n* ⓰ recruiting (business); **~s-tag** *m* day of inspection, field-day.

Muster-weberei ⊙ (ᵕ‿ᴗ̀...) *f* ⓰ fancy-weaving; -werk *n* standard (or classical) work; -wirtschaft *f* model farm; -wohnhaus *n* model residence; -wort *n*, *gr.* paradigm; -zeichner (-in *f*) *m* designer of patterns; -zeichnung *f* design(ing) carton; -zimmer *n* sample (or show-)room.

Mut[1] (ᵕ́) [ahd.: mood] *m* ⓒ. 1. courage; (Kühnheit) boldness, hardihood; (Herzhaftigkeit) heart, mettle, pluck; spirit(edness); kriegerischer ~ valour, bravery; moralischer ~ moral courage, assurance, in Widerwärtigkeiten: fortitude; e-m den ~ benehmen to damp a p.'s courage, to discourage a p., F to take the heart (or pluck) out of a p.; ~ fassen to take courage, to sum up pluck; e-m ~ m. to fill (or inspire) a p. with courage, to encourage a p.; den ~ sinken lassen oder verlieren to lose courage or heart, to get discouraged; ihm sank der ~ his courage failed (or deserted) him, he lost heart; nur ~ (gefaßt)! have courage!, be plucky!, pluck up (courage)!, never say die! — 2. (Gemütszustand) mood, frame of mind; getrosten, gutes ob. ...n ~(e)s sein to be of good cheer; wie ist Ihnen zu 2? how do you feel?; mir ist gar nicht lächerlich zu 2 I am not in a laughing humour or mood; mir ist schlecht zu 2 I feel ill at ease or out of sorts; ihm ist (dabei) nicht wohl zu 2 he is not at his ease, it makes him feel uncomfortable; du kannst dir denken, wie mir zu 2 war you may imagine what I felt or suffered. — 3. oft *dim.* Mütchen (ᵕ́) *n* ⓘ (Groll, Zorn) rancour, wrath; *s.* kühlen 2.

Mut[2]... ("...) [muten 2] *s.* Mutschein *zc.*

Muta (ᵕ́) [it.] *f* (*sg. inv.*, *pl.* Mutä) *gram.* (*ant.* Li'quida) mute (consonant).

mut[1]-**beseelt** (ᵕ‿ᴗ̀) *a.* ⓰ full of courage, (high-)spirited; *vgl.* 2voll.

Mütchen (ᵕ́) *n* ⓘ *s.* kühlen 2.

muten (ᵕ́) [Mut] **I** *v/a. u. v/n.* (h.) ⓰ 1. ⊙ † to aspire to a mastership. — 2. ⚒ to sue (or apply) for a mining-concession or -patent. — **II** ~ *n* ⓘ 3. = Mutung 1. — **III** ge-mut(et) *p.p.* *u. a.* ⓰ 4. (gestimmt) disposed, inclined; wohl gemutet sein to be well disposed or in a good humour; bsd. in Zssgn, *zB.* froh-gemut(et) with a joyous heart, in a gay mood.

mut[1]-**erfüllt** (ᵕ‿ᴗ̀) *a.* ⓰ = 2beseelt.

mutieren (-ᵕ́) [it.] **I** *v/n.* (h.) ⓰ Stimme: to break. — **II** ~ *n* ⓘ mutation.

[mutig] — 712 — [Nabelbruch]

mutig (ᴗ́ᴗ) [ahd.] *a.* ⑥ courageous, im Kampfe: brave; (kühn) bold; Sprichw. dem ~en gehört die Welt courage conquers the world, fortune favours the brave.
...mütig (...″ᴗ́) [Mut¹] *a.* ⑥ i. Zsfgn, z.B.: einmütig unanimous.
mut¹=los (″ᴗ...) *a.* ⑥ without courage, disheartened, dejected; ♀ m. to discourage, to dishearten; **=losigkeit** *f* ⑯ despondency, dejectedness; lack of courage; ♀**maßen** v/a. ⃰*⃰* to presume; ♀**maßlich** *a.* probable, (anzunehmen) putative, supposed; (scheinbar) apparent; *adv.* auch: to all appearance; ♀er Erbe heir presumptive to the throne, &c.; **=maßung** *f* ⑫ presumption, conjecture (über et. about a th.); supposition, surmise; ~en anstellen to form conjectures, to conjecture.
Mut²=schein ⚒ (″ᴗ́ᴧ) *m* ⑯ license (or permit) for working a mine.
Mutter (ᴗ́ᴗ) [ahd.: mother] *f* ㉑, *v. art.* ㉙ (vgl. 3) **1.** mother (*a. fig.*); (Erzeugerin) progenitress, progenitrix; *v. Tieren*: dam; wie eine ~ motherly; zur ~ m. to get with child; *poet.* ~ Erde mother earth; *rel.* die ~ Gottes the Madonna. — **2.** *anat.* = Gebärmutter. — **3.** ☉ (hohler Raum) cavity, hollow (space); (Schrauben=)~ nut of a screw; *typ.*, &c. (Gieß=) ~ matrix.
Mutter=auge (ᴗ́ᴗ...) *n* ⑫ mother's eye; **=band** *n, anat.*: ⇝ uterine ligament; **=beschwerde** *f*: ⇝ uterine complaint, hysterics, hysteria; **=biene** *f, ent.* queen-bee; **=boden** *m, agr.* native (or original) soil; **=bruder** *m* mother's brother, maternal uncle.
Mütterchen (ᴗ́ᴗᴗ) [*dim. v.* Mutter] *n* ㉓ **1.** little mother. — **2.** (bejahrte Frau) (steinaltes) ~ little old woman, F (little) granny.
Mutter=erde (ᴗ́ᴗ...) *f* ⑫: a) *hort.*, *agr.* (garden-)mould; b) (Heimat)native soil; **=gottes-bild** *n* image of the Holy Virgin; **=harz** *n* galban(um) (v. Fe′rula); **=herz** *n* mother's heart; **=kind** *n*: a) = Menschenkind; b) (verzogenes Kind) spoilt (or pet) child; **=kirche** *f* mother-church; **=korn** ? *n*: a) ergot, spur (Sclero′tium clavus); b) blighted (or smutted) corn; *pharm.* (Franzer Roggen) spurred rye (Seca′le cornu′tum); ♀**krank** *a.* ⑥ hysterical; **=krankheit** *f* hysterics; **=kraut** ♀ (..″ᴗ) *n* in feverfew (Chrysa′nthemum parthe′nium); **=kuchen** *m, anat., zo.*: ⇝ placenta; **=lamm** *n* ewe-lamb; **=land** *n*: a) native country; b) (Stammland e. Kolonie)mother-country;

=lauge *f. chm.* mother-liquor, -lye; **=leib** *m* womb, ⇝ uterus; vom ~e an from one's birth.
Mütterlein (ᴗ́ᴗ-) *n* ㉓ = Mütterchen.
mütterlich (ᴗ́ᴗᴗ) [ahd.; *Mutter] *a.* ⑥ motherly, motherlike, maternal; Oheim, Tante von Ler Seite maternal uncle, aunt; **Ler=seits** *adv.* from (or on) the mother's side; **~keit** *f* ⑯ motherliness.
Mutter=liebe (ᴗ́ᴗ...) *f* ⑫ motherly love; **=loge** *f* mother-lodge; ♀**los** *a.* ⑥ motherless; **=mal** *n* birth-mark, mole, ⇝ nævus; **=milch** *f* mother's milk; mit der ~ einsaugen to imbibe from (one's) infancy; **=mord, =mörder(in)** (″...) matricide; **=pferd** *n* mare; **=pflicht** *f* maternal (or mother's) duty; **=schaf** *n* ewe.
Mutterschaft (ᴗ́ᴗᴗ) *f* ⑯ maternity.
Mutter=scheide (ᴗ́ᴗ...) *f* ⑫ *anat.* passage of the womb, ⇝ vagina; **=schmerz** *m*: ⇝ hysteralgia; **=schoß** *m* mother's lap or womb; **=schraube** ☉ *f* hollow screw, nut-screw; **=schwein** *n* sow; **=schwester** *f* mother's sister, maternal aunt; **=seele** *f* = Mensch(enkind); es war keine ~ da not a (living) soul was there; ♀**seelen=allein** F *a.* ⑥ quite lonely or forlorn; **=söhnchen** *n* mother's boy or pet, F milksop; **=sole** *f* = =lauge; **=spiegel** *m, med.*: ⇝ uterine speculum, (lt.) speculum uteri; **=sprache** *f* mother-tongue, native language, vernacular(speech); **=stadt** *f*: a) (Geburtsstadt) native town; b) (Hauptstadt) metropolis, von Ansiedlern a. mother-city; **=stamm** *m* parent stock; **=stelle** *f* mother's place; ~ bei e-m vertreten to be like a (second) mother to a p.; **=teil** *n* maternal portion or inheritance; **=witz** *m* motherwit; **=wurz** ♀ *f* arnica; a. = Fenchel; **=wut** *f, path.*: ⇝ nymphomania, uteromania; **=zäpfchen** *n, anat.*: ⇝ suppository; **=zelle** *f, biol.* parent (f. cell, ⇝ cytula.
Mutung (ᴗ́ᴗ) [mhd.] *f* ⑯: **1.** aspiring, &c. (f. muten). — **2.** ⚒ claim.
mut=voll (″ᴗ́) *a.* ⑥ courageous, plucky.
Mut=wille (″ᴗ́ᴗ) [ahd.] *m* ㉙: a) *g. s.* playfulness, sportiveness; (Ausgelassenheit) exuberance of spirit, excessive gaiety; b) *b.s.* wantonness; (*bibl.*: Frevelmut) temerity, rashness, c) (Bosheit) malice, wickedness; (Schelmerei) waggery, waggishness; (ausgelassener Streich) mischievous prank, F larking.
mutwillig (..ᴗ́.) *a.* ⑥ playful, sportive; gay; wanton; malicious, wicked; waggish;

mischievous; *adv.* a. wilfully; ♀ in sein Verderben rennen to run blindly (or headlong) into destruction; ☞ Ler Bankero′tt fraudulent bankruptcy.
Mütze (ᴗ́ᴗ) [mhd., neu-lt., *ar.] *f* ㊽ **1.** (Kopfbedeckung) cap(für Frauen = Haube), weit ♀. head-gear; die ~ vor e-m abziehen to take off (or to doff) one's cap to a p.; vgl. Kappe 1. — **2.** (f. der eine ~ trägt, bsd. in Zsfgn) die Rot=~n *pl.* the red caps. — **3.** *zo.* (zweiter Magen der Wiederkäuer) bonnet (= Haube 5). — **4.** ♀ (Haube der Moose): ⇝ calyptra.
Mützen=fabrikant(in) *f) m* (ᴗ́ᴗ...) ⑫ capmaker; ♀**förmig** *a.* ⑥ cap-shaped, ⇝ mitriform; **=futter** *n* lining of a cap; **=macher** *m* cap-maker; **=schirm** *m* peak of a cap.
Myrmidonen (ᴗᴗᴗ́ᴗ) [grch.] *m/pl.* ㊹ Alt.: (thessalisches Volk) Myrmidons *pl.*
Myrobalane ♀ (-ᴗᴗᴗ́ᴗ) [grch.] *f* ⑫ *pharm.* myrobalan (Frucht v. Termina′lia Che′bula).
Myron=säure ⇝ (-ᴗ́ᴗᴗ) *f* ⑫ *chm.* aus schwarzem Senf: myronic acid.
Myrrhe ♀ (ᴗ́ᴗ) [grch., *semit.] *f* ⑫ balsamisches Gummiharz: myrrh; **~n-tinktur** (ᴗ́ᴗᴗᴗᴗ́) *f* ⑫ *pharm.* tincture of myrrh.
Myrte ♀ (ᴗ́ᴗ) [grch.] *f* ㊽ myrtle (Myrtus).
Myrten=baum (ᴗ́ᴗ...) *m* ㉙ = Myrte; **=beere** *f* myrtle-berry; ♀**förmig** *a.* ⑥ ⇝ myrtiform; **=kranz** *m* myrtle-wreath or -crown; **=strauch** *m* = Myrte; **=wäldchen** *n* myrtle-grove; **=zweig** *m* myrtle bough or branch.
Mysteri-en (ᴗᴗ́(ᴗ)ᴗ) [grch.] *n/pl.* ㉘ Alt.: *rel.* (geheime Gebräuche) mysteries *pl.*
mysteriös (ᴗᴗᴗᴗ́) [fr., *grch.] *a.* ⑥ (D 10) (geheimnisvoll) mysterious.
Mysterium (ᴗᴗ́(ᴗ)ᴗ) *n* ㉘: a) mystery (f. Mysterien); b) [+ft. Ministe′rien] im Mittelalter: (religiöses Schauspiel) miracle-play.
Mystifikation (ᴗᴗᴗ-tsᴗ́) [grch.-lt.] *f* ⑫ **mystifizieren** (ᴗᴗᴗᴗ́) *v/a.* ⑬ (täuschen, hintergehen) to mystify, hoax.
Mystik (ᴗ́ᴗ) [grch.] *f* ⑯ *rel.* (Geheimlehre) mysticism; **~er(in** *f* ⑯) *m* ㉗ mystic; **mystisch** *a.* ⑥ mystical; **Mystizismus** (ᴗᴗᴗ́ᴗ) *m* ㉗ mysticism.
Mythe (ᴗ́ᴗ) [grch.] *f* ㊽ (Sage) myth.
Mythen-bildung (ᴗ́ᴗ...) *f* ⑫ formation of myths; **=forschung, =kunde** *f* mythology.
mythenhaft (ᴗ́ᴗᴗ), **mythisch** (ᴗ́ᴗ) *a.* ⑥ mythical, fabulous. [tion of myths.]
Mythen-sammlung (ᴗ́ᴗᴗ́ᴗ) *f* ⑫ collec-
Mytholog (ᴗᴗᴗ́) *m*, **~e** *m* ⑱ mythologist; **~ie** (-ᴗᴗ́) *f* ㊽ (Götterlehre) mythology; **Lisch** (-ᴗ́ᴗ) *a.* ⑥ mythological.
Mythos (ᴗ́ᴗ) [grch.], mst **Mythus** (ᴗ́ᴗ) *m* ㉗ myth, fable, (ancient) legend.

N

N, n (ɛ) *n, inv.* Buchstabe: N, n.
N *abbr.* auf Eisenbahnfahrplänen: (Zeit von 12 Uhr mittags bis 12 Uhr nachts): = nachmittags) p. m. [*abbr.* = post meridiem].
N, öst. **N.** *abbr.* = Nord(en).
N *chm.* Symbol für Nitrogen (= Stickstoff).
na! F (ᴗ ..ᴗ́) [nhd.] *int.* auffordernd: ♀, mach! now, then!, look sharp!; begü-

tigend: ♀, werden Sie nur nicht böse! ob. ♀ ♀, nur nicht hitzig! there, don't excite (or heat) yourself!; zögernd: ♀, ich will denn nur weiter gehen well then, I'll proceed!; ♀ (nun), was hat er gesagt? well, ...? *iro.* ♀ das wäre! (I) don't believe it!; ♀ ob! I shouldn't I! rather!; P ♀ nu! well, I never!; ♀ warte nur! just wait a minute!

Nabe (ᴗ́ᴗ) [ahd.: nave] *f* ㊽ ☉ e-s Rades: nave, hub; ↓ der (Dampf=) Schiffsschraube: boss.
Nabel (ᴗ́ᴗ) [ahd.: navel] *m* ⑲ **1.** navel, *her.* (Mittelpunkt des Schildes) nombril, ♀ (Samen=)~ eye, speck, ⇝ hilum. — **2.** ♀ *arch.* (Schlußstein) keystone.
Nabel-binde (ᴗ́ᴗ...) *f* ⑫ *surg.* umbilical bandage; **=bruch** *m, path.* umbilical

---

Zeichen (s. S. XVII): F familiär; P Volkssprache; Г Gaunersprache; ⚹ selten; † alt (auch gestorben); * neu (auch geboren); ⁺⁺ unrichtig

[nabelförmig] — 713 — [Nachbestellung]

hernia, ⚕ omphalocele; ⚕förmig *a.* ⚕ navel-shaped, ⚕ umbiliform, umbilicate(d); =**gegend** *f, anat.* umbilical region; =**kraut** ⚘ navel-wort(*Cotyle'don*); gemeines ~ penny-wort (*C. umbili'cus*). **nabeln** (¹ᵛ) I *v/a.* ⚕a.: ein Kind ⚯ to arrange (or dress, bind up) the navel of a child. — II **ge-nabelt** *p.p. u. a.* ⚕ von Schilden: ⚕ umbonate(d).

Nabel-schnur (¹ᵛ...) *f* ⚕ =strang; =**schwein** *n, zo.* tajassu, peccary (*Dico'tyles torqua'tus*); =**strang** *m, anat.* navel-string, umbilical cord, funicle; zum ~ gehörig funicular.

Naben-büchse ⊙ (¹ᵛ...) *f* ⚕ nave-box; ⚕förmig *a.* ⚕ n.-shaped; =**loch** *n* n.-hole; =**ring** *m* äußerer: n.-hoop; innerer: n.-ring.

Nabob (¹ᵛ) [ar.(*pl.*) Statthalter] *m* ⚕ (⚕d.) Titel in Ost-J.: nabob(*a. fig.*=Geldfürst).

nach (¹ch) [ahd.; *nahe] (*Syn.* zu, bis, *ant.* vor) I *prp.* mit *dat.*, oft *adv.* dem *dat.* nachgesetzt. 1. (Richtung, Streben): a) to(wards), for; eine Reise ⚯ Frankreich a journey (or tour, trip) to France; ⚯ Hause geh(e)n to go home, to make for home; ⚯ rechts to the right; ⚯ jeder Richtung in every direction; ⚯ der Straße hin facing the street; ⚯ Süden (Westen) to the South (West), southward(westward); ⚯ vorn liegen to lie (or be) in the front; bfd. ⚯ dort = dorthin, nach hier = hierher; b) mit *verbs* und *adjectives*: ⚯ Amerika abreisen to start for (or to go to) America; f. aussehen 4 b, begierig; ⚓ ⚯ Japan bestimmt bound for Japan; ⚯ der Heimat homeward-bound; f. erkundigen, fragen 1 u. 2; ⚯ Wasser gehen to go for (or to fetch) water; f. greifen 6; ⚯ Deutschland reisen to leave for Germany; ⚯ dem Arzte schicken to send for the doctor; ⚯ e-m schießen to shoot at a p.; ⚯ Brot schreien to cry for bread; ⚯ Indien segeln to sail for India; sich ⚯ et. umsehen to look about for a th.; et. ⚯ et. werfen to throw (or fling) s. th. at a th. — 2. (Reihenfolge, Zeit) after, subsequent to; next to; ⚯ Ablauf der Frist at the expiration of the appointed time; ⚯ getaner Arbeit after (or when) the work was (or is) done; f. Christus (n. **Chr.** [**G.**]); ⚯ =ea. successively; gleich ⚯ =ea. in close (or quick) succession; ⚯ Empfang f-s Briefes (up)on receipt...; ⚯ dem Gottesdienste after divine service; noch ⚯ Jahrhunderten even in centuries to come; fünf Minuten ⚯ eins five minutes past one; *gr.* das Wort steht ⚯ dem Verb the word stands after (or follows) the verb; ⚯ ⚯ Sicht at sight; ⚯ genau (bff. genau ⚯) 10 Minuten exactly (or just) ten minutes later. — 3. (Art und Weise, Maß, Vorbild): according to, in accordance or conformity with, agreeably to; ⚯ dem Alphabet alphabetically; f. Anschein 1; meiner Ansicht ⚯ in my opinion; ⚯ ihrer Aussage from (or according to) their account; seinem Aussehen ⚯ to judge from his looks; f. belieben III, Buchstabe 1; ⚯ der Diät leben to keep to one's diet; f. Diktat; ⚯ der Elle verkaufen to sell by the yard; Lust-

spiel ⚯ dem Französischen comedy (taken or copied) from the French; ⚯ dem Gedächtnisse from memory; ⚯ deutschem Gelde in German money; ⚯ dem neuesten Geschmacke according to the latest fashion, in up-to-date style; ⚯ englischem Gesetz according to English law; ⚯ dem Gewichte by the weight; f. Handwerk 1; ⚯ Herzenswunsch (according) to one's heart's desire; f. Maßgabe; m-r Meinung ⚯ in my opinion; e-n nur dem Namen ⚯ kennen to know a p. only by name; F der Nase ⚯ straight ahead; ⚯ Noten: a) spielen to play from notes; b) *fig.* (gehörig) (thoroughly) well, in capital style; ⚯ alphabetischer Ordnung in alphabetical order; ⚯ Rosen riechen to smell of roses; ⚯ der Reihe, der Reihe ⚯ in turn, by turns; ⚯ dem Scheine urteilen ... from the outside or from appearances; ⚯ dem Takte spielen to play in time; je ⚯ Umständen, Verhältnissen according to circumstances; ⚯ seiner Weise in his usual (or accustomed) way; ⚯ bestem Wissen to the best of one's knowledge; ⚯ f-m Zeugnisse according to his evidence; ⚯ Zwiebeln schmecken to taste of onions; ⚯ wenn es ⚯ dem Verfasser ginge if one may believe (or trust) the author; ✪ (je) ⚯ dem Werte (it.) *ad valorem.* — II *adv.* **4.** im Sinne der *prp.* dem *dat.* nachgesetzt (f. I); bisw. *ell.*: mir ⚯! after me!, follow me!; wir wollen ihnen ⚯ we will go (or run) after them. — **5.** f. nachgerade u. hintennach; **nach und nach** gradually, by degrees, little by little; in the course of time; **nach wie vor** just the same (as before), now (the same) as ever, without (a) change; as usual.

nach..., Nach... (¹ch...) Vorsilbe in Zffgn I mit *verbs*, die immer trennbar sind (**) und als *v/n.* meist den *dat.* regieren, bz. **1.** Folgen, Verfolgen, zB. e-m ⚯ **drohen** to pursue a p. with threats. — **2.** zeitliche Reihenfolge, zB. ⚯ **dröhnen** to rumble after(wards) or subsequently. — **3.** Wiederholung, zB. Worte ⚯ **stottern** to repeat... in a stammering voice.— **4.** Nachahmung, zB. ⚯ **zeichnen** to draw from a copy. — II mit *nouns*: **5.** bz. mst: nachträgliches Tun, zB. ⚯ **sitzung** *f* aftermeeting. — III mit *adjectives*: **6.** (zeitlich nachfolgend) oft: post..., zB. ⚯ **apostolisch** *a.* post-apostolic.

nach-achten (¹ch...) *v/n.* (h.) ⚕⚕**: einer Sache (*dat.*) ⚯ to observe a rule, to act according to (or in conformity with) a law; ~ *n* ⚕, mehr gbr. =**achtung** *f* ⚕ observance of a rule, conformity with a law; dies diene Ihnen zur ~ let this serve you as (a) guide or guidance; ⚯**äffen** *v/a. u. v/n.* (h.) ⚕⚕**: e-m (ob. e-n) ⚯ to ape (or copy, imitate) a p., *co.* to mimic a p.; ⚯**d** mimicking, mimetic; die Vornehmen ⚯**d** snobbish; ~ *n* ⚕ aping, mimicry, (stupid) imitation or copy; =**äffer(in** *f* ⚕) *m* ⚕ mimic, (stupid) imitator, ape; *~ der* Vornehmen snob; =**äfferei** *f* ⚕ mimicry, (silly) imitation or copying; =**äffung** *f* ⚕ =**äffen**; ⚯**ahmen** [nhd.; *Ohm*²] *v/a. u. v/n.* (h.) ⚕⚕*** to imitate; e-n ⚯ (nachmachen) to copy a p.; e-m ⚯ (nachstreben)

to emulate a p.; in betrüglicher Absicht: to counterfeit, to forge, schriftstellerisch: to plagiarize; ⚯**geahmt** imitated, copied (künstlich) artificial or imitation (jewel, &c.), counterfeit (coin); ⚯**geahmter** Diamant paste diamond; ⚯**d** imitative, durch Gebärden: mimic; ~ *n* ⚕ f. =ahmung; ⚯**ahmenswert** *a.* ⚕ worthy of imitation, exemplary; =**ahmer(in** *f* ⚕**)** *m* ⚕ imitator, copyist; forger, plagiarist; =**ahmerei** *f* ⚕ systematic imitation or copying or forgery, (continued) plagiarism; =**ahmung** *f* ⚕ imitation, copy(ing), durch Gebärden: mimicry; (Fälschung) forgery; (Entlehnung) plagiarism.

Nach-ahmungs-gabe (¹ch⊥...) *f* ⚕ =talent; =**sucht** *f* mania for imitating or copying; =**talent** *n* imitative talent or gift or faculty; =**trieb** *m* imitative instinct; ⚯**wert** *a.* ⚕ worthy of imitation = nachahmenswert.

nach-apostolisch (¹ch...) *a.* ⚕ f. nach=... III; =**arbeit** *f* ⚕ subsequent (or later) work, verbessernde: (last) finish, finishing touches *pl.*; ⚯**arbeiten** ⚕** *v/n.* (h.) to work after or later; e-m Muster ⚯ to work from (or after) a pattern or model; *v/a.* (nachbilden) to copy; das Versäumte ⚯ to make up for lost time; (nachträglich verbessern) to (a)mend, touch up, retouch; ⚯**arten** *v/n.* (h.) ⚕** e-m ⚯ to take after a p., to be like a p.

Nachbar (¹ch) [ahd.; ∗Bauer] *m* ⚕ neighbour = „Nahbauer"] *m* ⚕, ~**in** *f* ⚕ neighbour, one who dwells near (by), im Nebenhause od. Nebenzimmer: next-door neighbour; ~**haus** (⚯...) *n* ⚕ neighbouring (or adjoining) house; er wohnte im ~hause he lived next door; ~**land** *n* neighbouring country; ⚯**lich** *a.* ⚕ neighbourly; ⚯**liche** Beziehungen *pl.* neighbourly intercourse; mit e-n ⚯**lich** (*adv.*) verkehren to be (or live) on neighbourly terms with a p.; ~**ort** *m* neighbouring locality or place; die ~**orte** the surroundings *pl.*; ~**schaft** *f* ⚕ neighbourhood (a. Gesamtheit der Nachbarn); (Nähe) proximity; in nächster ~f. von // in close vicinity (or in the immediate neighbourhood) of //; gute ~f. halten to have friendly intercourse with one's neighbours; ~**s-frau** *f* neighbour, lady living next door; ~**s-leute** *pl.* neighbours *pl.*, F nextdoor people; ~**s-mann** *m* neighbour, (gentle-)man living next door (to one); ~**staat** *m*, ~**stadt** *f* neighbouring state, town.

Nach-bau (¹ch...) *m* ⚕*c.* additional building or wing or premises *pl.*; ⚯**bedenken** *v a.* ⚕*/* to consider afterwards or after the event; Sprichw. vorgetan und ⚯**bedacht** hat manchem schon groß Leid gebracht ill-considered action will cause dissatisfaction; ⚯**behalten** *v/a.* ⚕*/* in Schulen: to keep in (after school), to detain; ⚯**bellen** *v/n.* (h.) ⚕**: e-m ⚯ to bark after a p.; ⚯**bessern** *v/a.* ⚕*/* to mend, to finish, to touch up, to retouch; to improve, to make improvements in; ⚯**bestellen** *v/a.* ⚕*/* to order afterwards or subsequently; ~ *n* ⚕ u. =**bestellung** *f* ⚕ subsequent (or additional) order;

[nachbeten] — 714 — [Nachfrage]

²beten v/n. (h.) u. v/a. ⓈⒶ**: e-m ² to pray after a p.; F fig. (nachplappern) to repeat mechanically, F to rattle off (like a parrot); ~ n ㉓ = Nachbetung; =beter(in f ㊼) m ㉒ one who re-echoes another person's words or sentiments; blind adherent or follower; F parrot; =beterei f ㊻ = =betung; auch: blind adherence; =betung f ㊻ mechanical repetition; ²bewilligen v/a. ⓈⒶ*/* to grant (or vote) subsequently or additionally; ~ n ㉓ u. =bewilligung f ㊻ additional grant or vote, supplementary (or extra) credit; ²bezahlen v/a. ⓈⒶ*/* to pay afterwards or later (on); (noch et.) ² to pay extra; ~ n ㉓ u. =bezahlung f ㊻ subsequent (or extra) payment; =bild n ④c. copy (or imitation) of a picture, &c., betrügliches: forgery; phys. auf der Nethaut: impression left on the retina, ocular spectrum; ²bilden v/a. ⓈⒶ**: ein Kunstwert ꝛc. ² to copy (or imitate) ...; scherzhaft ² to parody; v/refl. er will sich ² he wants to finish (or complete) his education; ~ n ㉓ u. =bildung f ㊻ copying, imitation, scherzhafte: parody; nur =bildung copy, reproduction, genaue: facsimile; ²blättern v/a. u. v/n. (h.) Ⓐa** to turn over the leaves of a book, to search for (or to hunt after) a passage; ²bleiben v/n. (fn) ⓇⒹ** (zurückbleiben) to remain (or lag) behind; (übrigbleiben) to be left over, to remain; Schule: to be detained or kept in, to stop after school, to stay in; ² lassen to detain, to keep in (after school); (überleben) to survive; ~(=lassen) n ㉓ detention; ²blicken v/n. (h.) ⓈⒶ**: e-m ² to follow a p. with one's glances; =blüte f ㊸ second bloom or blossom (-ing), belated flower(ing); ²bohren v/a. ⓈⒶ** to bore again; ein Loch ² to enlarge an opening, to rebore a hole; ²bringen v/a. Ⓖ⁷*: Fehlendes ² to supply (or supplement) a deficiency; einen Schüler ² to push on a pupil, to bring him to the level of the class; e-m (der weggegangen ist) et. ² to carry (or take) a th. after a p.; ²datieren v/a. ⓈⒶ*/* to postdate; =datum n ㉘ ㊿ postdate.

nach=dem (⁼ch⁻) I adv. 1. ⁓ afterwards (= nachher). — 2. (f. 3) je ² according as. — II cj. 3. Maß und Grad bezeichnend: according as; oft ell. je ² (die Umstände sind od. es sich trifft) according to circumstances, (just) as it may happen, F it all depends. — 4. zeitlich: after, when; ² Gallien erobert war after Gaul had been (or when Gaul was) conquered; ²Napoleon geflohen war, ergab sich das Heer Napoleon having fled the army surrendered; bei gleichem Subjekt: ² er gespeist hatte, schlief er after having dined (or after dining) he slept. — 5. prov. (öft.) because (=weil).

nach=denken (⁼ch⁻) v/n. (h.) Ⓖ⁷*: über etwas ² to reflect (or meditate) on a th.; vgl. ²grübeln; einem ² to follow up a p.'s thought(s); ~ n ㉓ reflexion, meditation; (deep) thought, beschauliches: contemplation, brütendes: rumination; nach reiflichem ~ after mature consideration; e-n zum ~ antreiben to set a p. thinking; ²d p.pr. u. a. ⓈⒶ reflecting, reflective; vgl. ²denklich; =**denklich** a. ⓈⒶ (bedächtig) meditative, thoughtful; (in Gedanken versunken) (deep) in thought, pensive, pondering, ruminating, F in a brown study; (ernst) grave, serious; =**denklichkeit** f ㊻ meditativeness, thoughtfulness; pensiveness; ²der=hand adv. (später) after the event, later on; ²dichten ⓈⒶ** v/a. (ganz dicht m.) to tighten; e-m ² to imitate (or copy) a poet('s style or work); v/n. (h.) to become tight, to tighten; ²drängen v/n. (h.), v/a. und sich ² v/refl. ⓈⒶ** to crowd (or press) after, to push from the back; sich ² to push (or force) one's way in; ²dringen v/n. (fn) Ⓓfⁿ** to press after; e-m ² auch: to pursue a p.; ²drohen, ²dröhnen v/n. (h.) ⓈⒶ** 1, 2; =**druck** m: a) ⓉⒸ. (Tatkraft) vigour, energy; (Festigkeit) firmness; (Gewicht) weight; mech. u. phys. intensity, rhet. emphasis, forcibleness; mit ~ emphatically, urgently; et. mit ~ sagen to emphasize (or urge) a th.; ~ auf et. legen to lay stress upon a th.; b) Ⓣc.: Ⓣ typ. reprint(ing), reproduction; ungesetzlicher: pirating, piracy; ~ verboten all rights reserved; Buch: reprint; pirated edition; ²drucken Ⓣ v/a. ⓈⒶ** typ. ein Buch: to reprint, to reproduce, ungesetzlich: to pirate; ²gedrucktes Buch reprint; ²drücken v/a. ⓈⒶ** to press (or squeeze) again; meist Ⓢ. to push forward; =**drucker** Ⓣ m ㉒ (f. Nachdruck b) piratical printer or publisher; =**druckerei** f ㊻ printing (of) pirated editions; ²drücklich a. ⓈⒶ (f. =druck a) vigorous, energetic, firm; rhet. emphatic, impressive; ²e Sprache, auch: strong or forcible language; adv. vigorously, energetically, with great force or emphasis; =**drücklichkeit** f ㊻ = druck a; ²drucksvoll a. ⓈⒶ = ²drücklich; ²dunkeln v/n. (h.) Ⓐa** paint. to darken (in); von Farben: to deepen; =**eiferer** m ㉒, =**eif(r)erin** f ㊼ emulator, rival; competitor; ²eifern v/n. (h.) Ⓐa**: e-m ² to emulate a p.; to vie (or compete) with a p.; ²d emulative; ~ n ㉓ und =**eiferung** f ㊻ emulation; competition; ²eilen v/n. (fn) ⓈⒶ**: e-m ² to hasten (or run) after a p., to pursue a p.; ~ n ㉓ (hasty) pursuit; ²ein=ander adv. one after the other, after each other; by (or in) turns, successively; =**empfängnis** f ⓕ physiol. superconception, superfetation; =**empfinden** v/n. (h.) u. v/a. Ⓖ¹*/* = ²fühlen; =**empfindung** f: a) physiol. after-sensation; b) poet. subsequent impression.

Nachen (⁼ch⁻) [ahd.: It. nav-: grch. nau-] m ㉓ (small) boat, skiff, (flaches Boot) punt, (Barte) barge, (Fähre) ferry (-boat); ²=**förmig** a. ⓈⒶ boat-shaped, ꝛ navicular, cymbiform; ~=**führer** m boatman, ferryman.

Nach=erbe (⁼ch⁻...) m ㊹, =**erbin** f ㊼ inferior (or second) heir(ess f), residuary legatee; =**ernte** f ㊸ agr. aftercrop, von Heu: aftermath; vgl. Ährenlese; ²**erzählen** v/a. ⓈⒶ*/*: e-m et. ² to relate a th. (or to tell a tale) after a p.: dem Englischen ²erzählt adapted from the English; meist b.s.: e-m et. ² to tell tales of a p., to repeat slanderous reports about a p.; es werden ihm schreckliche Dinge ²erzählt some terrible reports are being circulated about him; ²**essen** v/a. u. v/n. (h.) ⓈⒶ** to dine after the others; et. ² (hinterbrein essen) to eat after s. th. else; ~ n ㉓ after-dish; dessert; ²**exerzieren** ꝛ v/n. (h.) ⓈⒶ*/* als Strafe: to do extra drilling; fig. to do an extra task or an imposition, co. beim Essen: to dine after the others; ²**exilisch** a. ⓈⒶ hist. post-exilian; =**fahr** [mhd.] m ㉖ (ant. Vorfahr) descendant; ²**fahren** Ⓢb** v/n. (h.): e-m ² to drive (or cycle, motor, sail) after a p., to follow a p. in a carriage, &c.; v/a. e-m seine Sachen ² to cart (or convey, carry, send) a p.'s things after him; =**fall** Ⓡm following; ²**färben** Ⓥ v/a. ⓈⒶ** to redip, to dye (or colour) again; =**feier** f ㊺ after-celebration, extra (days pl. of a) fête; ²**feiern** v/a. Ⓐa** to celebrate after the event; ²**feilen** Ⓥ v/a. ⓈⒶ** to file again; fig. to retouch, to polish (up); ²**feuern** v/n. (h.) Ⓐa** to fire at; to fire after(wards) or a second time; to replenish (or keep up) a fire; ²**fliegen** v/n. (fn) Ⓑafⁿ** to fly after; F fig. du wirst gleich ² you will be turned (or kicked) out next or after them; =**folge** f ㊸ in einem Amte ꝛc.: succession; (Anwartschaft auf eine Stelle) reversion of a post; (Nachstreben) emulation; rel. ~ Christi imitation of Christ; (Reihenfolge) sequence; ²**folgen** v/n. (fn) ⓈⒶ** räumlich und zeitlich: to follow (after), to come later; (verfolgen) to pursue; e-m auf den Fersen ² to be at a p.'s heels; e-m im Amte, in der Würde ² to succeed a p. in his office, to take a p.'s place; e-m als Muster ² to tread in a p.'s footsteps, to emulate (or imitate) a p.; ~ n ㉓ = =folge; ²d p.pr. und a. ⓈⒶ following, nur von Sachen: subsequent, ensuing; bes. coll. the attendants pl., the suite; =**folger(in** f ㊼) m ㉒ successor to a p., auch aftercomer; (Anhänger[in]) follower, adherent; (Jünger[in]) disciple; ²**fordern** v/a. Ⓐa** to claim subsequently, to demand (or charge) extra; ~ n ㉓ und =**forderung** f ㊻ extra charge; ²**formen** v/a. ⓈⒶ** = ²bilden; ²**forschen** v/n. (h.) Ⓖ¹**: einem Dinge, e-m ² to search for a th., a p.; (nachfragen) to inquire (or dive) into a th., to investigate a th., sorgfältig: to examine a th., sehr genau: to scrutinize a th.; ~ n ㉓ = =**forschung**; =**forscher(in** f ㊼) m ㉒ inquirer, investigator; =**forschung** f ㊻ search, inquiry, investigation, examination, scrutiny; eines Gelehrten: research; =**frage** f ㊸ (Erkundigung) inquiry after (or about) a th.; über e-n ~ halten to make inquiries (or investigations) about a p.; Ⓢ (Begehr) demand; die ~ nach Wolle ist wenig belebt there is little demand (or inquiry) for ..., the market for

Signs (see page XVII): F familiar; P vulgar; ⌐ flash; ⌋ rare; † obsolete (died); * new word (born); ⁓ incorrect; ♪ music;

[nachfragen] — 715 — [Nachlassenschaft]

... is flat or slack; es herrscht starke (effektive) ~ nach Butter there is a brisk (a real) demand for butter, butter is in great (in actual) demand; **fragen** v/n. (h.) ⑧ (P ⁂ ⑤b)**: e-m Dinge ² to inquire after (or for, into) a th., to ask for a th., to investigate a th.; **=frist** f ⑯ prolongation of time; **=frost** m ⓒc. late frost; **=frühling** m ⓒd. second (or after-)spring, late spring; **=fühlen** v/a. ⑧** to feel subsequently; e-m et. ² to feel with a p.; ich kann es ihm so recht ² I can quite enter into his feelings about the matter; **=füllen** v/a. ⑧**: die Fässer ² to fill up ..., to replenish ...; **=gaffen** v/n. (h.) ⑧**: e-m ² to stare (or gaze) after a p.; **=gären** v/n. (h.) ⓒa** to ferment again; ~ n ㉓ u. **=gärung** f ⑯ second fermentation; **=geben** v/a. ⑫c** to give subsequently; eine Stunde ² to make up (for) a lesson; noch Geld ꝛc. ² to add, to pay in addition; v/n. (h.) (nicht standhalten) to give (way); (erschlaffen) to relax, to stretch; e-m ² (nicht widerstehen) to give in (or to yield) to a p., to comply (or to fall in) with a p.'s wish(es); aus Achtung: to defer to a p.'s judgment, &c.; aus Nachsichtigkeit: to indulge or humour a child, &c.; e-m in et. nicht(s) ² (nicht nachstehen) to be in no way inferior to a p. in a th.; ~ n ㉓ relaxation; compliance; **=geboren** p.p. u. a. ⑯ (D9) (nach des Vaters Tode geboren) posthumous; (jünger) born after, younger, junior; **=gebor(e)ne([r])** m f ⑰ posthumous child; **=gebot** n ⓒd. later bid; **=geburt** f ⑯ physiol. und Geburtshilfe: afterbirth, ⚭ secundine; **=geh(e)n** v/n. (jn) ⑭**: e-m ² to follow (or go after) a p.; s-n Geschäften ² to attend to one's business; dem Geschäft geht alles andere nach business first, pleasure afterwards; auch: business before pleasure; dem Vergnügen ² to seek (or pursue) pleasure; von der Uhr: to be slow or behind (the time); to lose; jeden Tag zwei Minuten ² to lose ... a day; meine Uhr geht nach gegen die Bahnhofsuhr my watch is (F I am) slower than the station-clock; **=gehends** adv. (später) afterwards; **=gelassen** p.p. v. ²lassen u. a. ⑯(D9): ²e Werke posthumous works pl.; **=gemacht** s. ²machen; **=gera'de** adv. by degrees, little by little; by this time, (endlich) at last; das müßtest du ² wissen you should know that by now; **=gesang** m ⓒc. bsd. in den Chören des grch. Dramas: ² epode; **=geschmack** m ⓒc. (o.pl.) after-taste; fig. bitterer ~ bitter consequences pl.; **=gewiesener=maßen** adv. as has been proved or shown; **=giebig** a. ⑯ flexible, pliable; (zum Nachgeben bereit) yielding, compliant, easy-going; (unterwürfig) submissive, obsequious; (gefällig) obliging, accommodating; (nachsichtig) indulgent, forbearing; **=giebigkeit** f ⑯ flexibility, pliability; yielding (or easy-going) nature; submissiveness; indulgence, forbearance, complaisance; aus Ehrerbietung: deference; **=gießen** v/a. ⓒd** to pour (in) after, to add to a fluid;

=glanz m ⑦ⓒa. (pl. ⚄) reflexion; **=graben** v/a. ⓒb** to dig for, to excavate; ~ n ㉓ u. **=grabung** f ⑯ excavation; **=grübeln** v/n. (h.) ⓒa**: e-m Dinge ² to muse on a th., to ponder (or brood) over a th., to turn a th. over (or to revolve a th.) in one's mind; ~ n ㉓ musing, &c. (s. v/n.); close (or deep) thinking; meditation, reflexion, F brown study; **=gucken** F v/n. (h.) ⑧**: e-m ² to follow a p. with one's eyes; **=guß** m ⓒa. replenishing (or refilling) with a fluid; ⊕ cast from a copy; **=hall** m ⓒc. reflected (or re-echoed) sound, echo, reverberation, phys. resonance; **=hallen** v/n. (h.) ⑧** to resound, re-echo, reverberate; v/a. Töne ² to reflect (or re-echo) sounds; **=halten** v/a. ⓒa** to hold (or keep) later (on), ein Fest: to celebrate afterwards; eine Stunde ² to give ... afterwards or another time; v/n. (h.) to hold out (well), to last (well), to be durable; **=haltig** a. ⑯ lasting (well), enduring, durable; (ausdauernd) persevering; **=haltigkeit** f ⑯ durableness, perseverance; **=hand** f ⑩ = Hinterhand b u. c; **=hangen**, P **=hängen** v/n.(h.) ⑧b**: e-m Dinge ² to be(come) addicted (or to give o.s. up) to a th.; seinen Gedanken ² to give free play to one's thoughts, to be lost in thought; **=hauen** v/n. (h.) ⑫c**: e-m ² to strike (or slash) at a p.; fenc., abs. to parry and cut; ⚔ von verfolgender Kavallerie: to pursue the enemy with drawn swords; **=hause=geh(e)n** n ㉓ walk(ing) home; beim ~ on the way home; **=heilen** v/a. (h.) ⑧** to heal afterwards or later on; **=heizen** v/a. u. v/n. (h.) ⑨**** to heat a second time; to make up the fire; **=helfen** v/n. (h.) ⑧b**: e-m ² to give a p. assistance or F a lift, to help a p. on; e-m Schüler ² to assist a pupil; e-m Dinge ² to push a th. on or forward; to touch a th. up; **=her**(¹ʰᴸ) adv. after that, afterwards; (darauf) then, subsequently; (später) later on; bald ² soon after (that), presently; **=herbst** m ⓒa. latter part of the autumn; end (or last weeks pl.) of autumn; **=herig** a. ⑯ later, subsequent; (später eintretend) posterior; (folgend) following; (künftig) future; **=hieb** m ⓒd. second blow; fenc. cut; after parrying; **=hilfe** f ⑯ assistance, aid; **=hilfe=schule** f school for backward pupils; **=hilfe=stunde** f private lesson given to a backward pupil; ~ n pl. a. private coaching sg.; e-m ~ n geben to help a p. on by private teaching or lessons, a. to coach a p.; **=hinken** v/n. (jn) ⑧**: e-m ² to limp (or F hobble) after a p.; fig. e-m ² to imitate a p. in a clumsy (or half-hearted) way; **=holen** v/a. ⑧**: et. ² to fetch s.th. missing, Versäumtes: to recover; to make up for time, to retrieve (or recover) a loss; eine (Unterrichts-)Stunde ² to give (or take) a lesson later (on); **=hülfe** ꝛc. s. **=hilfe** ꝛc.; **=hut** f ⑯ agr. second pastur(ag)e; ⚔ Arrieregarde; **=jagen** v/n. (jn) ⑧**: e-m ² to chase a p., to pursue a p. in

hot haste; fig. dem Ruhme ² to hunt (or race) after glory; v/a. to send in pursuit of a p.; e-m eine Kugel ² to send a bullet (or to fire a shot) after a p.; **=kauen** v/a. ⑧** to chew again; fig. e-m et. ² to say (or repeat) a th. after a p.; **=klang** m ⓒc. lingering note; echo; phys. resonance; fig. reminiscence; **=klettern** ⓒa**, **=klimmen** ⓒa (⑧)** v/n. (jn): e-m ² to climb after a p.; **=klingen** ⓒf** v/n. (h.) to linger in the ear; to (re-)echo, to resound; ⚄ v/a. to (re-)echo; ~ n ㉓ =klang; **=komme** m ⑭ descendant; ohne ~n sterben to die without offspring or issue, to die childless; **=kommen** v/n. (jn) ⑭**: e-m ² to follow a p., to come up with (or to overtake) a p.; fig. to act in conformity with a th.; to comply with an order; to accede to a request; to do one's duty; s-n Verbindlichkeiten ² to discharge (or meet) one's liabilities; s-m Versprechen ² to keep (or fulfil) one's promise; e-m beim Trinken ² to respond to a p.('s pledge); (sich später einstellen) to come later or too late; **=kommenschaft** f ⑯ offspring, issue, progeny; posterity, descendants pl.; **=kömmling** m ⓒd. descendant; **=können** v/n. (h.) ⑧** ell. = ²kommen können to be able to follow; **=kriechen** v/n. (jn) ⓒdf**: e-m ² to creep (or crawl) after a p.; **=kur** f ⑯ med. completion (or after-effect) of a cure; second course of treatment; stay at another health-resort; **=laß** m ⑧ⓒa. (verminderte Anspannung) relaxation; ohne ~ arbeiten ... without cessation or intermission, ... incessantly; (Ablassen von e-r Forderung, Strafe ꝛc.) remission; (Ermäßigung) diminution; allowance; ⚭ abatement, reduction, deduction; unter ~ von 5 Prozent Rabatt allowing (or deducting) a discount of five per cent.; = **Hinterlassenschaft**; **²lassen** ⑧a** v/a. to leave behind, als Erbstück: to bequeath; s. **²gelassen**; (nachfließen l.) to pour after; ein straffes Seil ² to slacken ..., to let go ...; e-e Schraube ² to loosen; von e-r Forderung, Strafe ² to remit a claim, fine; von s-n Forderungen et. ² to abate one's demands; ⚭ et. vom (oder am) Preise ² to make a deduction, to take (or F knock) off s.th.; F to ask a lower figure; bei e-m Handel beiderseits et. ² to split the difference; v/n. (h.) (von et. abstehen) to desist (or abstain) from; mit (oder in) der Verfolgung ² to slacken in a pursuit; (die Spannkraft verlieren) to slacken; (lose w.) to relax; (milder w.) to soften, to relent; (sich beruhigen) to calm (down); (sich vermindern) to diminish; (schwach w.) to grow feeble, (lau, matt w.) to grow lukewarm, languid, (kühl w.) to cool down, to flag; (aufhören) to cease; in s-m Eifer, Fleiße ² to flag (or relax) in one's zeal, industry; der Regen hat ²gelassen ... has abated or subsided; der Wind hat ²gelassen ... has calmed (or settled, gone) down; ~ n ㉓ = **=lassung**; **=lassenschaft** f ⑯ in-

⚭ scientific; ✿ botanical; ⚲ geography; ⊕ machinery; ⚒ mining; ⚔ military; ⚓ marine; ⚫ commercial; ✉ postal; 🚂 railway.

[nachlässig] — 716 — [nachschiffen]

heritance; ≈lässig *a.* ⑥⑥ (ohne Sorgfalt) negligent, neglectful, (lässig) careless, indolent, lazy, (schlaff) remiss, F non-carish, (ungenau) inaccurate, (unaufmerksam) inattentive, (unfleißig) without application; *adv.* auch ≈er= weise in a careless (or perfunctory) manner; ≈ gekleidet dressed in a slovenly (or negligent) fashion; =lässigkeit *f* ④⑥ negligence, neglect; carelessness, indolence, laziness, remissness; want of attention or application; =laß=pfleger, =verwalter *m* ㉒ administrator of an estate; =lassung *f* ④⑥ (s. ≈lassen) bequest; remission, abatement; deduction; desistance, abstention; relaxation; diminution; flagging; cessation; subsidence; =lauf ⊕ *m* ⑦d. Branntweinbrennerei: second running(s *pl.*); ≈laufen *v/n.* (sn) Gast=**: e-m, e-r Sache ≈ to run after (or follow, pursue) a p., a th.; den Frauenzimmern ≈ to run (madly) after women or girls; Billard: e-e Kugel ≈ I. to run a ball through; ~ *n* ㉓ running after, pursuit, chase; =läufer(in *f* ㊵) *m* ㉒ one who runs after a p., a th.; ≈leben *v/n.* (h.) ⑧** to live later or after; (überleben) to outlive; (im Leben befolgen) to live up to; weitS. to conform to; j-s Rate ≈ to live in accordance (or conformity) with a p.'s advice; ~ *n* ㉓ continuation of (one's) life; conformity in one's (manner of) life; ≈legen *v/a.* ⑧** to add; zum Heizen: to put on (more) coal, wood, to replenish (or make up) the fire; =lese *f* ㊽ agr.: a) (das Nachlesen) gleaning; ~ halten to glean; b) (das Gelesene) gleanings *pl.*; *fig.* (nachträgliche Auswahl) later (or second) selection; ≈lesen *v/a.* u. *v/n.* (h.) ⑧a** *agr.* to glean; e-m ≈: a) to imitate a p.'s (manner of) reading; b) to follow a p. in reading; Versäumtes: to read passages previously missed; (noch einmal lesen) to read (over) again; bfd. ⊕ ≈ ⑧**: to look up ..., to refer to ...; ~ *n* ㉓ = =lese; second perusal; beim ~ des Briefes on reading the letter again or once more; ≈liefern *v/a.* ⑧a**: a) später: to deliver subsequently or (too) late; b) vervollständigend: to deliver as supplementary stock; ~ *n* ㉓ u. =lieferung *f* ④⑥ subsequent (or supplementary) delivery; ≈machen *v/a.* ⑧**: et. ≈ to do a th. after(wards); e-m et. ≈ to imitate (or copy) a p. in s.th.; das soll mir einer ≈ I defy anybody to do it like me; (fälschen) to counterfeit, forge; ~ *n* ㉓ ≈. =machung ≈gemacht *p.p.* und *a.* ⑥⑥ imitated; (gefälscht) counterfeit(ed), forged, spurious; (künstlich) artificial; ≈ gemachte Waren imitation goods *pl.*; =macher *m* ㉒ imitator; (Verfälscher) counterfeiter, forger; =machung *f* ④⑥ imitation, copy(ing); =mahd *f* ④ *agr.* aftermath; ≈malen *v/a.* ⑧**: ein Bild ≈ to copy ...; eine Unterschrift ≈ to forge ...; ≈malig *a.* ⑥⑥ = ≈herig; ≈mals *adv.* afterwards, subsequently, later on; since (then); ≈messen *v/a.*

⑧*** to measure again, Felder ⅽ.: to resurvey; ~ *n* ㉓ resurvey. **Nach=mittag** (ⁿch̑ᵍ=, ¹ch̑ᵍ=) *m* ⑦d. afternoon; heute ≈ this afternoon, (nach dem Mittagessen) after dinner; ≈mittäg= lich *a.* ⑥⑥ taking place in the afternoon, ⚇ postmeridian; ≈mittags *adv.* in (or during) the a., auf Fahrplänen ⅽ. p. m. (= *post meridiem*). **Nachmittag(s)=gottesdienst** (ⁿch̑ᵍ=...) *m* ⑫, =prediger *m* afternoon service, preacher; =schlaf *m*, =schläfchen *n* siesta, F after-dinner nap; =sitzung *f*, *parl.* afternoon sitting; =unterricht *m* afternoon lessons *pl.*; =zeit *f* afternoon, ⚇ postmeridian time. **nach=müssen** (ⁿch̑=...) *v/n.* (h.) ⑧** *ell.* = ≈folgen müssen; e-m ≈ to be obliged to follow (or to go after) a p.; =nahme ⚹ *f* ④⑧ reimbursement; ⤳ (in England nicht üblich) prepayment made by the post-office, cash on delivery; ≈nehmen *v/a.* ⑧a** to take after or again; ⚹ to reimburse o.s. for the value of goods, &c. forwarded; to send goods for cash on delivery; ≈pfeifen *v/a.* u. *v/n.* (h.) ⑧b**: et. ≈ to whistle a tune, &c. which one has heard; e-m ≈ to whistle after a p.; F *iro.* ich kann m-m Gelde ≈ I may whistle for my money; ≈pflanzen *v/a.* u. *v/n.* (h.) ⑧** to plant after; to finish planting; ≈pfuschen *v/a.* u. *v/n.* (h.) ⑧** to copy (or imitate) in a clumsy (or bungling) manner, to bungle; ≈pin= seln ⊕ *v/a.* ⑧a** *paint.* to paint again, nachbessernd: to retouch, to touch up; ≈plappern, ≈plaudern *v/a.* u. *v/n.* (h.) ⑧a** to repeat mechanically or like a parrot; ≈polieren *v/a.* ⑧*/* to polish afterwards or again, to finish polishing; =porto ⚹ *n* ⑭⑧ surcharge (or additional charge) on letters, &c., additional (or excess) postage; ≈prägen *v/a.* ⑧** to coin later or again, to recoin; Münzen betrügerisch ≈ to counterfeit coin; =raum *m, for.* chips *pl.* of felled trees; =rechnen *v/a.* und *v/n.* (h.) ⑧b** to calculate (or reckon) afterwards or again; prüfend: to check (or verify, examine, revise) accounts; wir können es ihm leicht ≈ we can easily check his calculations or figures; ~ *n* ㉓ f. =rechnung; =rechner *m* ㉒ revisor (or controller) of accounts, auditor; =rech= nung *f* ④⑥ checking (or verification, examination, revision) of accounts; =rede *f* ④⑧ closing (or final) remark, e-s Buches: epilogue; report, rumour, gossip, üble: defamation, slander (-ous talk), calumny, libel; in üble ~ bringen to bring into bad repute, to slander, to backbite; ≈reden *v/n.* (h.) u. *v/a.* ⑧**: a) e-m ≈ to imitate a p.'s manner of speech, to talk like a p.; b) e-m alles auf Treu' und Glauben ≈ to swear by a p.'s words; c) e-m et. (übles) ≈ to speak ill of a p., to defame (or slander, libel) a p.; ≈reifen *v/n.* (sn) *hort.* von Früchten ⅽ.: to ripen (or mature) after being gathered; ~ *n* ㉓ subsequent ripening (or maturing) of gathered fruit, &c.; ≈reisen

v/n. (sn) ⑨**: e-m ≈ to travel (or start, leave, depart) after a p., (folgen) to follow a p. travelling; ≈reiten *v/n.* (sn) ⑧b**: e-m ≈ to ride after a p., to pursue a p. on horseback; ≈rennen *v/n.* (sn) ⑧b**: e-m ≈ to run after a p.; =richt [nhd. 17/18. sae.; vgl. Bericht] *f* ④⑥ news, über Personen oft: tidings *pl.*; (Wink) hint, advice; (Bericht) report, account, kurzer: notice, (Auskunft) (piece of) information, intelligence, briefliche: communication, telegraphische: telegram, F wire, verspätete: belated post; vermischte ~en in Zeitungen: miscellaneous items or news, miscellanies *pl.*; von et. ~ ein= ziehen to make inquiries about a th.; e-m ~ von et. geben to give a p. advice (or to advise a p.) of a th., amtlich: to notify a th. to a p.; =richten= dienst ⚔ *m* intelligence-service [an der Spitze des ⚔ Nachrichtendienstes steht in Engl. der Director of Intelligence]; =rich= ter *m* ㉒ (Scharfrichter) executioner; (Henker) hangman; ≈richtlich *a.* ⑥⑥ serving as advice, by way of information; ≈rücken *v/n.* (sn) ⑧**: e-m ≈ to follow in a p.'s wake or footsteps; in eine höhere Stelle: to move (higher) up; *v/a.* to promote; =ruf *m* ⑦d. call after a person; ein ~ konnte ihn nicht mehr erreichen he was out of call or beyond the reach of our voices; ~ an einen Geschiedenen speech (or poem) in honour of a deceased person or a departed one, in Zeitungen: obituary (notice); e-m e-n ~ widmen to write s.th. in memory (or in praise) of a dead p.; (Ruf, den j. zurückläßt) memory; ≈rufen *v/n.* (h.) u. *v/a.* ⑧b**: e-m ≈ to shout (or call) after a p.; e-n ≈ to ask a p. to follow; =ruhm *m* ⑦d. posthumous fame, lasting renown or glory or fame; ≈rühmen *v/a.* ⑧**: e-m et. ≈ to say a th. in praise of a p.; ≈rutschen *v/n.* (sn) ⑨** von Erde, Geröll ⅽ.: to slip after; e-m ≈ to drag o.s. (or to roll down) after a p.; ≈sagen *v/a.* ⑧**: et. ≈ to say a th. over again, to repeat a th.; e-m et. ≈ = ≈reden b u. c; =satz *m* ⑦a. *gr.* concluding sentence, ⚇ apodosis; *log.* conclusion; ≈schauen *v/n.* (h.) ⑧**: e-m ≈ to follow a p. with one's eyes or glances; *abs.* to (go and) look after; ≈schicken *v/a.* ⑧** to send (or forward) a th. after a p.; Briefe, Telegramme ⅽ.: to reforward, to readdress; to send later (on) or afterwards; ≈schieben *v/a.* u. *v/n.* (h.) ⑧c** to push (F to shove) after; weitS. to help (or push) on or along; ≈schießen ⑧c(e)fi** *v/a.* (auch *abs.*): a) e-m (eine Kugel) ≈ to shoot (or fire) after a p.; b) to fire later (on); ⚹ Gelder ≈ to pay (in) an additional sum (of money), to supply the funds required; *v/n.* (sn) (schnell nachfolgen) to rush (or dart, dash, fly) after a p., a th.; v. et. Sprießendem: to shoot (or spring) up later (on); ≈schiffen ⑧** *v/n.* (sn) e-m ≈ to follow (verfolgend: to pursue or chase) a p. by boat, to sail (or steam) after a p.; *v/a.* to ship

[Nachschlag] — 717 — [nachstehen]

later (on); =ſchlag m ⊙d. second blow; afterclap; ♪ complementary note; =ſchlage-buch n ㉒ book (or work) of reference; ⸗ſchlagen ⓖb** v/a. u. v/n. (h.): e-m ⸗ to strike a blow at a p. departing; ♪ to strike (or mark) a note after another; ein Buch ⸗, in e-m Buch ⸗ to consult (or refer to) a book; e-e Stelle ⸗ to look up (or out) a passage; v/n. (in): e-m ⸗ (gleichen) to take after a p.; ~ n ㉓: beim ~ e-s Werkes on reference (or referring) to a work; ⸗ſchleichen v/n. (ſn) ⓖaſt**: e-m ⸗ to sneak (or steal, skulk) after a p., bſd. ſpähend: to shadow a p.; ⸗ſchleifen v/a. ⓖb**: ein Meſſer ꝛc. ⸗ to grind (or sharpen, whet) … again; einen Fuß ꝛc. ⸗ to drag … after; ⸗ſchleppen ⓖ** v/a. u. v/refl. to drag (or trail) after; ſich mühſam ⸗ to drag o.s. after, to crawl after; ⚓ ein Schiff ⸗ to take … in tow; v/n. (h.) to drag, to trail (on the ground); ⸗ſchlüſſel m ㉒ master-key, (Dietrich) skeleton-key, picklock; ⸗ſchmecken v/n. (h.) ⓖ** to leave a taste behind; ⸗ſchmieren v/a. ⓖ** to grease (or oil, lubricate) again; to copy in a slovenly way, F to scribble off; ⸗ſchneiden v/a. ⓖc** to cut (or carve) again; noch Brot ⸗ to cut more …; eine Feder ⸗ to make … afresh, to mend …; ⸗ſchreiben v/a. u. v/n. (h.) ⓖ** to write from (or under) a p.'s dictation; einen Vortrag ⸗ to take down (notes of) a lecture; ⸗geſchrie-b(e)nes Heft note-book containing (notes taken down during) a lecture; to write later (on) or subsequently; eine Vorſchrift ⸗ to write from a copy; e-m ⸗ to imitate a p.'s hand-writing or style, b.s. to plagiarize a p.'s writings; ⸗ſchreiber m ㉒ copyist; ⸗ſchreien v/n. (h.) u. v/a. ⓖ**: e-m ⸗ to shout after a p.; e-m Schimpfworte ⸗ to pursue a p. with invectives; =ſchrift f ㊻: a) writing from a dictation or copy; b) (Nachgeſchriebenes) dictated passage, dictation; c) (Abſchrift) copy, transcript; (Anhang zu e-m Briefe) postscript; ⸗ſchub m ⊙d. Bäckerei: new batch; ✠ v. Truppen u. Verpflegung: fresh force, reinforcements, supports pl.; ♛ Kegelſpiel: ich habe den ~ I have the next throw, I come next; ⸗ſchüren v/a. u. v/n. (h.) ⓖ** to poke (or make up, stir) the fire; =ſchuß m ⓖa. ⚜ fresh (or additional) payment or instalment; ⚜ new shoot; ⸗ſchütten v/a. ⓖ** to pour after, to add to a liquid; Kohlen ⸗ to put fresh coal(s) on the fire, to make up the fire; =ſchwarm m ⊙c. Bienenzucht: second (or later) swarm; ⸗ſchwatzen v/a. ⓖ** to talk after (or like) a p.; to repeat tales,&c.; ⸗ſchwimmen v/n.(ſn)ⓖa(b)**: e-m ⸗ to swim (or float) after a p.; ⸗ſchwören v/a. u. v/n. (h.) ⓖb**: e-m ⸗ to swear after a p.; ⸗ſegeln ⚓ v/n. (ſn) ⓖa** to sail after another ship; verfolgend: e-m Schiffe ⸗ to give chase to a ship; ⸗ſehen v/n. (h.) und v/a. ⓖa**: e-m ⸗ = ⸗ſchauen (nach etwas ſehen) a) et. ⸗ to look after (or into)

a th.; to look up in a book; (prüfen) to examine, investigate; ein Schriftſtück, a. to look over; (beauſſichtigen) to inspect; ⸗, ob // to (go and) see whether //; ſieh nach, wer da iſt! see who is there!; b) ✠ ſeine Beſtände ⸗ to make an inventory of one's stock; Rechnungen: to revise; e-m et. ⸗ (hingehen l.) to excuse (or overlook, condone) a p.'s mistakes, b.s. to connive at a p.'s faults; ~ n ㉓: du wirſt das (leere) ~ ob. nichts als das ~ h. you will have your trouble for nothing or be too late in the field; (Prüfung) examination, investigation; inspection; (Hingehen-l.) making excuses for, connivance; ⸗ſein v/n. ⓖa** ell. = ⸗gekommen ſein, zB. er iſt ihm nach he is after him, he has reached (or overtaken) him; (zurück ſein) to lag behind, to be behind-hand; ⸗ſenden v/a. ⓖa** = ⸗ſchicken; ✉ ⸗zuſenden! to be forwarded (on), please forward; =ſendung f㊻ forwarding. (verſpätete Sendung) belated (or late) consignment; ⸗ſetzen v/a. ⓖ**: et. e-m Gegenſtande ⸗ to put (or place) a th. after a th.; (hintanſetzen) to think less of, to set less store by or less value upon; (nachträglich ſetzen) to put later (on), to add, Bäume ꝛc.: to plant later on, Spiel: (noch einſetzen) to stake once more; v/n. (ſn): e-m ⸗ (nach-eilen) to hurry (or rush, run, career, gallop) after a p., to pursue (or chase) a p.; ~ n ㉓ und =ſetzung f ㊻ hot pursuit, chase; =ſicht f ㊻ indulgence; (Nachgiebigkeit) forbearance, complaisance; (Duldung) toleration, leniency; (Mitleid) pity, commiseration; ~ h., mit ~ verfahren to be indulgent to(wards) a p., to have patience (or to be lenient or patient) with a p., to forbear (mehr gebr.: to bear) with a p.; ~ gegen-ea. üben to bear with each other, to bear and forbear; Sprichw. Vorſicht iſt beſſer als ~ prevention is better than cure; ⸗ſichtig a. ⓖⓖ (ſ. =ſicht) indulgent; for-bearing; lenient, patient; adv. auch: with indulgence or forbearance; =ſich-tigkeit f ㊻ forbearing (or tolerant) spirit; =ſichts-tage ✠ m/pl. ㉒ days pl. of grace or respite; ⸗ſichtsvoll a. ⓖⓖ full of indulgence (= ⸗ſichtig); =ſilbe f ㊸ gr. suffix, affix; ⸗ſingen v/a. ⓖſt**: etwas ⸗ to sing (or chant) after; ein Lied: to repeat; ⸗ſinken v/n. (ſn) ⓖſt** to sink (in) after, to dip in after; ⸗ſinnen v/n. (h.) ⑦²**: einer Sache ⸗, über et. ⸗ to reflect (or meditate) (up)on a th.; ~ n ㉓ reflexion; ⸗ſitzen v/n. (h.) ⑦⁴** in der Schule: to be detained or kept in; ~ n ㉓ detention; =ſitzung f ㊻ later meeting or sitting, vgl. nach=… II; =ſommer m ㉒ late summer; second (or return of) summer; ⸗ſpähen v/n. (h.) ⓖ**: e-m ⸗ to spy after a p., to watch a p.; (Geheimniſſen ⸗ to dive into mysteries; ⸗ſpiel n ⊙d. thea.: a) afterpiece; b) (Schluß) conclusion of the play; ♪ postlude; fig. after-event, further action, sequel; ⸗ſpielen v/n. (h.): e-m ⸗ to imitate a p.'s play(ing); to play after a p.; v/a. Karten: eine Farbe

⸗ to follow (or return) the partner's lead; eine andere Farbe ⸗ to follow with another suit; ♪ ein Stück nach dem Gehör ⸗ to play … by ear; ⸗ſprechen v/n. (h.) u. v/a. ⓖa**: e-m et. ⸗ to say a th. after a p., to repeat a p.'s words; ⸗ ⸗beten F fig.; e-m ⸗ to mimic a p.'s voice; ~ n ㉓ repetition; mimicking, mimicry; ⸗ſprengen v/n. (ſn) ⓖ⸗**: e-m ⸗ to gallop after a p.; ⸗ſpringen v/n. (ſn) ⓖſt**: e-m ⸗ to leap (or jump, skip) after a p.; ⸗ſpüren v/n. (h.) ⓖ**: e-m ⸗ to track (or trace) a p., auf Schritt u. Tritt: to dog a p.'s foot(steps); ⸗d inquisitional; hunt. to scent; e-m Haſen ꝛc. ⸗, auch: to pursue … (by its tracks); v/a. et. ⸗ (ſpäter verſpüren) to feel the after-effects of a th.; ~ n ㉓ und =ſpürung f ㊻ tracking; pursuit.

nächſt (¹) [ahd.: next] I a. ⓖⓖ 1. (Ent-fernung, Beziehung) nearest; der ⸗e Weg the nearest (or shortest) route or cut; die ⸗en Beziehungen the closest (or most intimate) relationship sg.; der ⸗te (erſte) beſte the first comer; ſ. Nähe; die ⸗en Verwandten the nearest relations, the next of kin. — 2. (Zeit, Reihenfolge) next; im ⸗en Augenblick the next moment, a moment afterwards; bei ⸗er Gelegenheit at the first opportunity (given); am ⸗en Tage the next day, on the following day; ✠ am Erſten des ⸗en Monats on the first prox. (= proximo); Sprichw. jeder iſt ſich ſelbſt der ~e charity begins at home. — II der (die, das) ~e s. ⓖⓣ 3. ſ. 2. Sprichw. — 4. der ~e (Mitmenſch) one's neighbour or fellow-man; bibl. liebe deinen ~en wie dich ſelbſt! thou shalt love thy neighbour as thyself! — 5. das ⸗e the nearest(or next) thing; das ⸗e (zu tun) wäre the next thing to be done would be; ✉ in meinem ~en in my next (letter). — III adv. 6. am ⸗en nearest, next; er kommt ihm am ⸗en he comes next to him (an Größe in size); ſeine Kinder ſtehen ihm am ⸗en his children are nearest to his heart or his first care; fürs ⸗e for the present, for the time being. — 7. ⸗ens, mit ⸗em next time, (bald einmal) (very) shortly. very soon, presently; one of these days; (ſpäter) later on. — IV prp. mit dat. 8. (auch adv. mit örtlicher prp., ganz nahe) ⸗ (bei, zu) ihr next (or close) to her. — 9. ⸗ (unmittelbar nach) Gott danke ich Ihnen meine Erhaltung next to God I owe my preservation to you.

nach-ſtammeln (″ch⌣⌣) v/a. ⓖa** to stammer (or stutter) after.

nächſt-beſt(e) (″…) a. u. s.: a) the next in quality; b) (der nächſte beste) the first comer; ⸗dem adv. after (or next to) that, besides; immediately after.

nach-ſtechen (″ch⌣) v/a. ⓖa** to counterfeit an engraving, to forge a stamp.

nach-ſteh|n (″⌣)(⌣) v/n. (h.) ⓖa** to stand after, to follow; das Prädikat ſteht dem Subjekt nach the predicate comes (or is placed) after the subject; ⸗des Abenteuer the following adventure; die ⸗de Liſte the subjoined

♪ Muſik; ⚛ Wiſſenſchaft; ⚘ Pflanze; ⚲ Geographie; ⊙ Technik; ⚒ Bergbau; ✠ Militär; ⚓ Marine; ✠ Handel; ✉ Poſt; 🚂 Eiſenbahn.

[nachstellen] — 718 — [Nachtrupp]

list; ⓐ die ⚏d verzeichneten Waren the goods *pl.* mentioned (or specified) below; in ⚏dem (im ⚏den) in the following (passage), in what follows; e-m im Range ꝛc. ⚏ to be inferior to a p., to rank below a p.; er steht dir in vielem nach he is below (or behind) you in many things; feinem ⚏d second to none; ~ *n* ㉓ inferiority.

nach-stellen (″ch...) ⓧ** *v/a.* to put after, to place behind; eine Uhr ⚏ to put ... back; *v/n.* (h.): e-m ⚏ to lay snares (or set traps) for a p.; F to be after a p., *vgl.* auflauern; ~ *n* ㉓ =stellung; **=steller** *m* ㉒ snarer; (Verfolger) persecutor; **=stellung** *f* ㊻ snaring, trapping; (Verfolgung) persecution; hinterlistige ~en ambuscades *pl.*

Nächsten-liebe (″ch=L″) [nächst 4] *f* ㊻ love for (or of) one's neighbour, charity.

nächstens (L‿) f. nächst 7.

Nach-steuer (″ch...) *f* ㊸ additional tax, extra duty; ⚏steuern *v/n.* (h.) ⓐa** to pay extra duty.

nächst-folgend (″=‿) *a.* ㊻ next (in order), immediately following; der ⚏e Tag the morrow; ~e(r) *m* f ㊼ one following (or coming) next.

Nach-stich (″ch‿) *m* ⓪d. copy of an engraving. [at hand, adjacent.]

nächst-liegend (″=L‿) *a.* ㊻ lying nearest

nach-stöbern (″ch...) *v/n.* (h.) ⓐa** to rummage (or search, hunt) for or after; **=stoß** *m* ⓪a. second thrust, mit dem Fuße: second kick; *fenc.* auch: counter-thrust; ⚏stoßen *v/a.* und *v/n.* (h.) ⓐa** to push after; to thrust again, mit dem Fuße: to kick again; *fenc.* auch: to parry and thrust; ~ *n* ㉓ = =stoß; ⚏streben *v/n.* (h.) ⓧ**: e-m Dinge ⚏ to strive after a th., to aspire to a th., to pursue a th.; e-m ⚏ to emulate a p.; ⚏strömen *v/n.* (sn) ⓧ** to stream (or flow, rush) after; *fig.* to follow in a crowd or in throngs, to stream (or crowd) after; ⚏stürmen *v/n.* (sn) ⓧ**: e-m ⚏ to rush (or hurry, race) after a p.; ⚏stürzen *v/n.* (sn) ⓧ**: e-m Dinge ⚏ to fall (or tumble) after a th.; e-m ⚏ = ⚏stürmen; *v/a.*: noch ein Glas Wein ⚏ to gulp down (F to tipple off) another glass of wine.

nächst-vergangen (″...) *a.* ㊻ just past, in the immediate past; ⚏vorhergehend *a.* immediately preceding.

nach-suchen (″chL‿) **I** *v/a.* u. *v/n.* (h.) ⓧ** 1. to search after, to look for; in f-r Tasche ⚏ to search (or rummage) in one's pocket. — 2. (um) et. ⚏ = ansuchen I, auch: to sue for a th. — **II** ~ *n* u. **Nach-suchung** *f* ㊼ 3. (f. 1) search; (f. 2) auch: suit, petition.

Nacht (cht) [ahd.: night] *f* ⓾ (ant. Tag) night; bei dunkler ~ in the darkness (or gloom) of night; bei ~ und Nebel under (the) cover of night or darkness; Sprichw. f. Katze 3; bis tief in die ~ far into the night, till late at night; des ~s ob. ⚏s, bei ~, in der ~ (at or in the, during the) night; die ganze ~ hindurch all night long; ganze Nächte lang whole nights (together); vgl. nächtelang; heute ⚏ to-

night; in der Stille der ~ in the silence (or at dead) of night; mitten in der ~ in the middle of the night, in the depth of night; über ~ over night, *fig.* unexpectedly; wie Tag und ~ verschieden as different as day and night or as chalk from cheese; schwarz wie die ~ (as) dark as pitch, (as) black as coal; es ist ~ it is nighttime; es wird ~ night is setting in or coming on or approaching, it is growing (F getting) dark; *fig.* es wird ~ vor m-n Blicken my eyes are darkening, my senses are going; e-m gute ~ wünschen to wish (or bid) a p. good night; zu(r) ~ essen to take supper, to sup.

Nacht-angel ⊙ (cht...) *f* ㊻ night-angle-line; **=angeln** *n* night-angling; **=angriff** *m* n.-attack; **=anzug** *m* nightdress, vgl. Zeug; **=arbeit** *f* n.-work, eines Gelehrten: lucubration; **=blindheit** *f* night-blindness; ⚬ nyctalopy, hemeralopia; **=bogen** *m, ast.* (ant. Tag=b.) nocturnal arc; **=dienst** *m* n.-duty.

Nach-teil (″chL) [nhd.] *m* ⓪d. disadvantage, drawback, detriment; (Beschädigung) injury, prejudice, (Schaden, Verlust) damage, loss; e-m ~ bringen to injure (or prejudice) a p., to do a p. harm; ohne ~ für f-e Ehre, f-n Ruf without detriment (or prejudice) to his honour, his repute; das würde mir zu großen ~e gereichen it would be very detrimental to me; ⓐ mit ~ verkaufen to sell at a loss.

nach-teilig (″chL‿) [nhd.] *a.* ㊻ (ant. beförderlich) disadvantageous, detrimental, injurious, prejudicial, derogatory; der Gesundheit ⚏ (*dat.*) injurious (or detrimental) to one's health, unhealthy (occupation, &c.), unwholesome (food, &c.); e-n ⚏ (*adv.*) beeinflussen to have an unfavourable influence on a p.

Nach-teiligkeit (″chL‿) *f* ㊻ disadvantageousness; injuriousness.

nächte-lang (‿‿) *adv.* for nights together, night after night.

nachten (‿ch) *v/n.* (h.) ⓐ ⚏ *v/impers.*: es nachtet it is growing dark, night is falling or setting in, night is at hand.

nächten (‿‿) [Nacht] ⓐ **I** *v/n.* (h.) = übernachten. — **II** *v/a.*: e-n ⚏ to receive (or put up) a p. for the night.

nächtens *poet.* (‿‿) *adv.* = nachts.

Nacht-essen (cht...) *n* ㊻ supper; **=eule** *f*: a) *orn.* (night-)owl (*Strix*); b) F *fig.* von e-r häßlichen Person: fright; **=falter** *m. ent.* night-butterfly or -flutterer; **=frost** *m* night-frost; **=geschirr** *n* chamber-pot, F (fr.) pot; **=gespenst** *n* ghost, nocturnal vis(itat)ion; **=gleiche** f. Tagundnachtgleiche; **=glocke** *f* night-bell; **=haube** *f* (woman's) night-cap; **=hemd(e)** *n* night-shirt, der Frauen: chemise, chm.: shift; **=herberge** *f* lodging-house. [vgl. nächtlich.]

nächtig (‿‿) *a.* ㊻ like night, gloomy;

Nachtigall (‿‿‿) [ahd.: nightingale *Nacht* u. gellen] *f* ㊻ nightingale (*Lusci'nia philome'la*); ⚏enhaft *a.* ㊻ like a nightingale; ~en-schlag *m* warbling (or song) of the nightingale.

nächtigen (‿‿‿) *v/n.* (h.) ⓐ = übernachten.

Nacht-imbiß (cht...) *m* supper.
Nach-tisch (″ch‿) *m* ⓐa. dessert, last course; beim ~ at dessert.

Nacht-jacke (cht...) *f* ㊻ night-jacket; **=kerze** *f*: a) = =lampe; b) ♃ eveningprimrose (*Oenoth'era bien'nis*); **=kleid** *n* night-dress or -gown; **=lager** *n* (das Übernachten) night's rest; (Ort) night's lodging; rasch hergerichtetes: F shakedown; **=lampe** *f* night-lamp; **=leuchter** *m* bedroom candlestick.

nächtlich (‿‿) [Nacht] *a.* ㊻ 1. taking place at night, nocturnal; vgl. all⚏; bei ⚏er Weile oder ⚏er-weile at (or in the) night-time. — 2. *f. fig.* (finster) gloomy, dark, dismal; (schwarz) black.

Nacht-licht (cht...) *n* ㊻ night-light; **=luft** *f* night-air; **=mahl** *n* = Abendmahl 1 u. 2; **=mahr** *m, provc.* (Alpdrücken) nightmare; **=marsch** *m* night-march; **=musik** *f* serenade; **=mütze** *f*: a) nightcap; b) F *fig.* (schläfrige Person) dullard, sleepy-headed person.

nach-tönen (″ch‿) *v/n.* (h.) ⓧ** to sound after, to resound, to (re-)echo; von Noten auch: to linger.

Nacht-pfauen-auge (cht...) *n* ㊻ *ent.* emperor-moth (*Satu'rnia pavo'nia*); **=quartier** *n* (=lager).

Nach-trab ⚔ (″chL) *m* ⓪d. rear(-guard); *fig.* im ~ fein to be behind the times.

Nacht-rabe (cht‿L) *m* ㊻ *orn.* nightheron (*Nycti'corax gri'seus*).

nach-traben (″ch...) *v/n.* (sn) ⓧ** to trot after, to follow (or pursue) at a trot; ⚏trachten *v/n.* (h.) ⓧ** = ⚏streben; **=trag** *m* ⓪d. zu einer Schrift: supplement, zu e-m Testament: codicil, zu e-m Briefe: postscript; als ~ supplementary; *a.* = =tragszahlung; ⚏tragen *v/a.* ⓑb**: e-m et. ⚏ to carry a th. after a p.; *fig.* e-m et. (eine Beleidigung ꝛc.) ⚏ to harbour a grudge (or to bear a resentment, to have a spite) against a p.; noch Holz ⚏ to carry in (or to fetch) more ...; (zufügen) to add as supplement, to append; ⓐ einen Posten ⚏ (später eintragen) to book an omitted item; ⚏ *p.pr.* u. *a.* ⓐ, ⚏trägerisch *a.* ㊻ resentful, spiteful, vindictive; ⚏träglich *a.* ㊻ (später nachfolgend) additional, further, belated; (ergänzend) supplementary; *adv.* auch: after the event, subsequently; ultimately, in the end; **=trags-artikel** *m* ㊻ additional (or supplementary) article; **=trags-etat** *m, parl.* supplementary estimates *pl.*; **=trags-zahlung** ⓐ *f*: a) payment to be made after a certain date; b) (neue Einzahlung) new capital paid in; c) (Zahlung von Rückständen) payment of arrears; ⚏treten *v/n.* (sn) ⓓd**: e-m ⚏ to step after a p., to follow in a p.'s footsteps; **=treter** *m* ㉒ (servile) follower; (Anhänger) adherent; **=trieb** ✚ *m* ⓪d. *agr.* fresh shoot; ⚏trillern *v/a.* u. *v/n.* (h.) ⓐa** to trill after; ⚏trinken *v/a.* u. *v/n.* (h.) ⓓt** to drink after; to respond to a toast.

Nacht-rock (cht...) *m* ㊻ night- or dressing-)gown; **=ruhe** *f* night's rest; **=runde** ⚔ *f* patrol.

Nach-trupp ⚔ (″chL) *m* ⓾(⓪d.) = =trab.

Signs (see page XVII): F familiar; P vulgar; F flash; ⚞ rare; † obsolete (died); * new word (born); +⁺ incorrect; ♩ music.

[nachts] — 719 — [Nadelgeld]

nachts (ˢchtz) adv. j. Nacht
Nacht=schatten (ˢcht...) m ⌗: a) shade of night; b) ⚘ nightshade (Sola'num); =schatten=artig ⚘ a. ⌗: ⚗ solan(ac)eous; =schatten=gewächse ⚘ n/pl.: ⚗ solanaceæ; =schicht ⚔ f night-shift or -task; =schlafend F a. nur in: bei der Zeit at night when everybody's asleep; =schmetterling m, ent. = =falter; =schwalbe f, orn. = Ziegenmelker b; =schwärmer m: a) nightly reveller; b) = =falter; =schwärmerei f night-revelling; =ständchen n = =musik; =stuhl m night-stool, commode; =tier n nocturnal animal; =tisch(chen n) m bedside table, night-table; =topf m = =geschirr; =trunk m F night-cap; =übung ⚔ f night practice.
nach=tun (ᵘcht¹) v/n. (h.) u. v/a. ⌗**: 1. to imitate (or copy) a th.; es einem ⚘ to come up to a p., to be a p.'s equal; es e-m ⚘ wollen to emulate a p., to set up a rivalry with a p. — 2. to do later (on).
Nacht=viole ⚘ (ˢcht...) f: a) night-smelling rocket (He'speris [tristis]); b) dame's violet (H. matrona'lis); =vogel m: a) night-bird; b) = =falter; =wache f n.-watch; =wächter m: a) n.-watch (-man); F fig. das ist unter dem ~ that's beneath contempt or one's notice; b) F lackadaisical person; =wandeln v/n. (in, a. h.) ⌗*.* path. to walk in one's sleep; ⚘d a. ⌗ somnambulistic; walking in one's sleep, somnambulism; =wandler(in f) m somnambulist; =wind m night-wind or -breeze; =zeit f n.-time; bei dunkler ~ in the dark hours of night; =zeug n clothing for the night; night-dresses or -things pl.; (Flanellkostüm: Unterhose u. Jacke) pyjamas pl.; =zug 🚂 m night-train.
Nach=urlaub (ᵘcht...) m ⌗d. additional (or extra-)leave or holiday or ⚔ furlough; =verlangen v/a. ⌗*/* to demand subsequently or in addition; =versichern ⚘ v/a. ⌗*/* to reinsure, to insure for a larger amount; ~ n ⌗ u. =versicherung f ⌗ reinsurance; =verzollen ⚘ v/a. ⌗*/* to pay an additional duty on goods; =wachsen v/n. (jn) ⌗b** to grow after or later or again or afresh; es wachsen ihm andere Zähne nach he is having (F getting) new (or fresh) teeth; fig. to succeed, to follow; das ⚘de Geschlecht the growing (or rising) generation; ~ n ⌗ after-growth, new (or fresh) growth; =wägen v/a. = nachwiegen; =wahl f ⌗ second (or final) choice or election; (Ersatzwahl) by-election; =weh n ⌗c. (meist im pl. gbr.) subsequent pain; fig. ~en (traurige Folgen) sad (or evil) consequences or after-effects pl.; (Geburtshilfe) ~en after-pains pl.; =weinen v/n. (h.) u. v/a. ⌗**: e-m (Tränen) ⚘ to cry after a p., to bewail (or deplore) a p.('s death), to mourn (over) the loss of a p.; =weis m ⌗a. information; vgl. Nachweisung; =weis=bar a. ⌗ demonstrable, traceable; (bekannt) notorious, (offenbar) manifest; =weisbarkeit f ⌗ demonstrability, traceability; =weise=amt ⌗ =anstalt f, =bureau n inquiry-office, für Arbeiter: labour-bureau. für Dienstboten ꝛc.: registry-office, für Lehrer: scholastic (or educational) agency; =weisen v/a. u. v/n. (h.) ⌗**: e-m et. ⚘ (was er sucht) to inform a p. about a th.; to point out (or indicate) a th. to a p.; (beweisen) to prove, als echt: to authenticate; e-m Arbeit ⚘ to obtain (or get) work for a p.; einem Irrtümer ⚘ to demonstrate a p.'s mistakes; jur. e-m ein Verbrechen ⚘ to convict a p. of a crime; urkundlich nachgewies(e)ne Rechte rights proved (or attested) by documentary evidence; ~ n ⌗ = =weisung; =weiser m ⌗ indicator, index; als Buch: vork of reference, für Adressen: directory; =weise=zahl ⚘ f ⌗ folio-number; =weise=zeichen n in Büchern: sign of reference, index; =weislich a. ⌗ demonstrable; traceable; =weisung f ⌗ information, indication, proof, demonstration; (Verweisung) reference; =welt f ⌗ (ohne pl.) after-ages or -times pl.; posterity, future generations pl.; der ~ überliefern to hand down to posterity, to pass on to future ages; =werfen v/a. ⌗b**: e-m et. ⚘ to throw (or fling) a th. after (or at) a p.; noch Kohlen ꝛc. ⚘ to put on more...; =wiegen v/a. ⌗c** to weigh after or again, to reweigh; =winter m ⌗: a) end of the winter; b) second (spell of) winter; =wirken v/n. (h.) ⌗** to produce an after-effect, to take effect afterwards or later (on); von einer Arznei: to act (or operate) afterwards; ~ n ⌗, mst =wirkung f ⌗ after-effect; ultimate effect; =wollen v/n. (h.) ⌗**: einem ⚘ ell. für e-m nachfolgen wollen to wish (or desire) to follow a p.; ich will ihm nach I will go after him; =wort n ⌗c. (brief) epilogue; =wuchs m ⌗a. = Nachwachsen; (Nachwachsendes) fresh (or new) shoot, young wood; (neues Geschlecht) rising (or new) generation; F co. young branches or offshoots pl.; =zahlen v/a. und v/n. (h.) ⌗** to pay afterwards or in addition; 🚂, thea.: für einen besseren Platz ⚘ to secure a better seat by paying more; ⚘ auf Aktien ⚘ to pay a further call on shares; ~ n ⌗ = =zahlung; =zählen v/a. ⌗** to count over again, to recount; in Banken: to check; =zahlung f ⌗ additional payment; ⚘ fresh call (made) on shares; =zeichnen v/a. ⌗b** to draw from a model, to copy; vgl. nach=... 4; ~ n ⌗ und =zeichnung f ⌗ drawing from a model, copy(ing); =ziehen v/a. ⌗b** to draw (or pull) after, to pull along; ⚓ am Schlepptau ⚘ to (take in) tow; Striche ꝛc. ⚘ to go over (or trace) lines, &c.; v/n. (jn): a) e-m ⚘ to (re)move to the same locality with a p.; b) to follow (after) a p., to go in search of a p.; Schach: to move next; =zins m ⌗a. quit-rent; =zotteln P v/n. (jn) ⌗a**: einem ⚘ to toddle after a p.; =zucht f ⌗ (pl. ⚘) late hatching or rearing; last brood of chickens, &c., last swarm of bees; =zug m ⌗c. marching (or moving) after; ⚔ rear(-guard) Schach: next (or following) move; =zügler, meist ⚔ m ⌗ camp-follower, straggler, (Plünderer) marauder.
Nacken (⚘) [ahd.: neck] m ⌗ 1. nape (of the neck), P scruff of the neck, ⚗ cervix, nucha; zum ~ gehörig: ⚗ cervical, nuchal. — 2. Redensarten (meist fig.): j. beugen I; e-m auf dem ~ liegen od. sitzen to be at (or to hang on) a p.'s heels. to press (or harass) a p., stärker: to be (like) a millstone (hung) round a p.'s neck; den ~ hoch tragen to bear (or carry) one's head high; e-n (od. den) Schelm im ~ h. to have a roguish (or waggish) nature or disposition.
nackend (⚘) a. ⌗ = nackt.
Nacken=haar (⚘...) n ⌗ back-hair; =schlag m blow from the back; fig. =schläge bekommen to be in great trouble or tribulation; =stück n neck-piece; Schlächterei: scrag-end; bsd. Mode. =wulst, =zopf m chignon.
...nackig (...⚘) [Nacken] a. ⌗: kurz⚘ short-necked.   [stiff-necked.]
...näckig (...⚘) [Nacken] a. ⌗: hart⚘
nackt (⚘) [ahd.: naked] a. ⌗ (stark) naked, bare, undressed, bsd. paint. nude; co. in nature's garb; (ohne Federn) without plumage, unfledged; (ohne Haare) hairless, bald, ⚗ psilodermatous; einen ⚘ ausziehen to strip a p. naked or to the skin; fig. um das ⚘e Leben for bare life; die ⚘e Wahrheit the plain (or bare, unvarnished) truth; mit ⚘en Worten in plain words, plainly.
nackt=beinig (⚘...) a. ⌗ bare-legged; =blumig ⚘ a. nudiflorous, ⚗ gymnanthous; =blütig ⚘ a.: ⚗ achlamydeous; =früchtig ⚘ a.: ⚗ gymnocarpous.
Nackt=heit (⚘...) f ⌗ (j. nackt) nakedness, bareness, (state of) nudity, baldness.
Nackt=keimer (⚘...) m ⌗ acotyledon; =kiemig a. ⌗ nudibranchiate, gymnobranchiate; =samenpflanze ⚘ f: ⚗ gymnosperm; =samig ⚘ a. ⌗ gymnogenous, gymnosperm•al,...ous; =schnecken f/pl. zo.: ⚗ limacidæ; =sporig ⚘ a. gymnosporous.
Nadel (⚘) [ahd.: needle; *nähen] f ⌗ 1. needle (a. min. spitzer Körper in Kristallen u. ⚔ Zündnadel; vgl. Atz-, Haar-, Magnet-, Sicherheits-⚘, Zünd-⚘, Radier-⚘) ~ der Kupferstecher dry-point; (Steck-) ~ pin; mit ~n feststecken to pin (fast); sich auf die ~ versteh(e)n to be clever at needlework. — 2. ⚘ e-r Konifere: needle-leaf, ⚗ acicular (or acerose) leaf; zo. bei Schwämmen ꝛc.: ⚗ spicule. — 3. fig. wie auf ~n geh(e)n od. sein to be (or sit) on thorns, to be on tenter-hooks; mit der heißen ~ gemacht made in hot haste, F (only) blown together, run up in a hurry.
Nadel=arbeit (⚘...) f ⌗ needlework; =blatt n = Nadel 2; =bolzen ⚘ m n.-bolt; =brief m paper of needles or pins; =buch n n.-book; =büchse f box for needles and pins; =draht ⚘ m needle (or pin-)wire; =erz n, min. n.-ore, ⚗ acicular bismuth; =fabrik ⚘ f n.-factory or -mill; =fisch m, zo. (Seenadel) n.-fish (Syngna'thus acus); =förmig ⚘ a. n.-shaped, ⚗ acicular; =führer ⚘ m e-r Nähmaschine: n.-guide; =futteral n n.-case; =geld n: a) bsd. ehm.: pin-money;

⚗ scientific; ⚘ botanical; ⚘ geography; ⚘ machinery; ⚔ mining; ⚔ military; ⚓ marine; ⚘ commercial; ⚘ postal; 🚂 railway.

[Nadelholz] — 720 — [Näherrecht]

b) (Trinkgeld für Dienstboten) (female) servant's tip(s pl.); =holz (,=hölzer pl.) ⚲ n (ant. Laubholz) conifers, coniferous trees pl.; fir-,pine-wood; =holz=baum ⚲ m f. Konifere; =kerbel ⚲ m needle-chervil (Scandix pecten Ve'neris); =kissen n pincushion; =k(n)opf m pin's head; =k(n)opf=schneider ⊕ m pin-header, workman who heads pins; =loch n f.-öhr.

nadeln (⌣⌣) v/a. ⓐa. 1. to supply with needles. — 2. to fasten with pins.

Nadel=öhr (⌣⌣...) n ⓔ eye of a needle; =schaft ⊕ m, =spitze f shaft, point of a needle or pin; =stechen n pricking with pins or needles, surg., med.: ⚲ acupuncture; =stich m: a) prick of a needle or pin; b) beim Nähen: stitch; =telegraph ⊕ m, tel. needle-telegraph or -instrument; =waldung f =holz.

Nadir ⚲ (⌣, ⌣⌣) [ar.] m ⓝ (o. pl.) ast. (Fußpunkt) nadir (ant. Zenit).

Nadler ⊕ (⌣⌣) m ⓔ needler, needle- (or pin-)maker; ~ei ⊕ (⌣⌣⌣) f ⓕ needle-(or pin-)making; ~handwerk (⌣⌣...) n ⓔ needler's trade, needle-making; ~ware f pins and needles pl.

Nagel (⌣⌣) [ahd.: nail] m ⓔ 1.(hornartige Decke der Finger, Zehen) nail, ⚲ unguis; f. fauen 1; sich (dat.) die Nägel putzen (schneiden) to clean (to cut) one's nails; keinen ~ breit not an inch; ⚲ mit einem ~ (zo. mit Nägeln) versehen: ⚲ unguiculate(d); fig. das Feuer (ob. es) brennt mir auf die Nägel oder den Nägeln I am hard driven or pressed, I am in a tight corner. — 2. ⊕ (spitzer, keilförmiger Körper) allg.: nail, geschmiedeter: wrought nail, geschnittener: cut nail, kleiner: (tin-)tack, großer: spike; ohne Kopf: brad, hölzerner: peg, plug, ↓ tree-nail, trennel; f. beschlagen 1, einschlagen 1; fig. et. an den ~ hängen (aufgeben) to give up (or abandon) a th., to put (or lay) it aside or on the shelf; den ~ auf den Kopf treffen to hit the right nail on the head; e-n (hohen, gewaltigen) ~ haben to be (very) conceited, to have a great idea of o.s.; e-n ~ im Kopfe h. to have queer notions or a bee in one's bonnet; das ist ein ~ zu meinem Sarge (großer Kummer) that is a nail in my coffin, that will be the death of me.

Nagel=auszieher ⊕ (⌣⌣...) m ⓔ nail-drawer or extractor; =baum ⚲ m = Flieder (Syringe); =bein n, anat. des menschlichen Schädels: nail-bone; =bohrer m gimlet; =bürste f nail-brush.

Nägelchen (⌣⌣⌣), Näg(e)lein (⌣⌣⌣-) [Nagel, dim.] n ⓔ 1. little nail. ⓔ a. (tin-)tack. — 2. ⚲: a) = Nelke; b) mit pl. = Gewürz⚲; c) = Flieder (Syringe).

Nagel=eisen (⌣⌣...) n ⓔ nail-rod or -bore; =feile f für Fingernägel: nail-file or trimmer; =fest a. ⓔ nailed (fast), immovable; f. niet- und nagelfest; =fleck m nail-spot; =fluh f, geol. (Tertiärformation) ⚲ nagelfluh, gompholite; =form f nail-mould; =geschwür n, path. whitlow, ⚲ paronychia; =kopf(=artig a.) m nail-head(ed); =krankheit f. path.: ⚲ onychosis; =mal n mark of a nail.

nageln ⊕ (⌣⌣) v/a. ⓐa. to nail, to spike.

nagel=neu (⌣⌣...) a. ⓔ = funkel(nagel)=neu; =probe f ⓔ chm.: supernaculum; die ~ machen to drink to the last drop; =schere f: a) für die Fingernägel: nail-scissors pl.; b) der Nagelschmiede: nail-shears pl.; =schmied m nail-smith or -maker; =verkrümmung f, path.: ⚲ gryposis; =wurzel f root of a nail; =zange f nail-nippers pl.; =zieher m nail-extractor, claw-hammer.

nagen (⌣⌣) (ahd.: gnaw) I v/a. u. v/n. (h.) ⓔ to gnaw, (beknabbern) to nibble; ätzend: to eat into, to corrode; an e-m Knochen ⚲ to pick a bone; f. Hungertuch; sie h. nichts zu ⚲ noch zu beißen they haven't a morsel (of anything) to eat; fig. das nagte ihm am Herzen it preyed upon his mind; it rankled in his breast. — II ⚲d p.pr. u. a. ⓔ gnawing (a. fig.); zo. ⚲ rodent; ⚲der Hunger ravenous appetite, ⚲der Kummer poignant grief, poet. carking care.

Nager (⌣⌣) m ⚲ 1. ~(in f ⓕ) p. who gnaws, nibbler. — 2. ~ pl. zo.: ⚲ rodents pl.

Nage=tier (⌣⌣...) n ⓔ gnawer, ⚲ rodent.

Näglein (⌣⌣-) n ⓔ f. Nägelchen.

Nagler (⌣⌣) [Nagel 2] m ⓔ nail-maker.

nah(e) (⌣⌣) [ahd.: nigh, near] a. ⓔ und adv., comp. näher (f. ds.), sup. nächst (f. ds.) 1. (ant. fern) near; räumlich, auch: nigh, F handy; (anstoßend) adjoining, adjacent; von ⚲ und fern far and near; ⚲ bei der Kirche near (or close to) the church; ⚲ bekannt intimately acquainted; ⚲ an 50 nearly (or close upon) fifty; es waren ihrer ⚲ an die hundert there were nearly (or close upon) a hundred of them, they numbered just upon a hundred; ganz ⚲ an=ea. close together or to each other; er war ⚲ daran zu ertrinken he was on the point of drowning; es war ⚲ daran, daß // it nearly happened that //; ich war ⚲ daran nachzugeben I very nearly yielded, I was about to give in; ⚲ verwandt closely related; sie sind ⚲ verwandt they are near relatives; wie ⚲ sind Sie verwandt? what degree of relationship is there between you?; ⚲e Gefahr imminent (or impending) danger; in ⚲er Aussicht near at hand. — 2. mit verbs: einen ⚲ berühren to come home to a p.; ⚲ bevorsteh(e)n to be impending or imminent; ⚲ bringen f. bringen 7; vgl. naheleg(e)n; ⚲ an et. grenzen to adjoin a th., be adjacent to a th., to border on a th.; vgl. nahekommen; e-m zu ⚲ kommen to offend a p.; vgl. nahe-legen, ⚲liegen; ⚲ näher rücken to approach; dem Tode ⚲ sein to be near (one's) death or one's end; ⚲ setzen, ⚲ stellen to put (or place) near; dem Hofe (sehr) ⚲ steh(e)n to be (intimately) connected with the court; fig. einem zu ⚲ treten, rücken, kommen to give offence to a p., to hurt a p.'s feelings; j-s Ansehen zu ⚲ treten to encroach upon a p.'s authority; vgl. nahetreten.

Näh=arbeit (⌣⌣...) f ⓔ needlework, sewing; =beutel m (lady's) work-bag.

nahe (⌣⌣) a. ⓔ u. adv. f. nah.

Nähe (⌣⌣) [ahd.: *nah(e)] f ⓕ nearness, proximity, closeness, örtlich auch:

vicinity; (Anstoßen) contiguity; (Umgebung) surroundings pl.; zeitlich auch: imminence; propinquity (auch von Verwandtschaft); aus größter ~ schießen to fire at close quarters or point-blank; es ist ganz in der ~ it is close by or near at hand; in der ~ der Stadt near the town; et. in der ~ besehen to look closely at a th., to examine a th. closely; in unmittelbarer ~ in the immediate neighbourhood, close by.

nahe=bei (⌣⌣...) adv. near by, close by, close at hand; ⚲geh(e)n v/n. ⓔ** (zu Herzen gehen): e-m ⚲ to affect (or grieve) a p.; sein Tod geht mir nahe ... is a great grief to me; sich et. (zu) lassen to take a th. to heart; ⚲hin adv. nearly, almost, well-nigh; ⚲kommen v/n. (jn) ⓔ** to come (or draw) near; der Wahrheit ⚲ kommen to get at the truth; komm(t) mir nicht zu nahe! keep your distance!, stand off!; ⚲legen v/a. ⓔ**: e-m et. ⚲ (zu verstehen geben) to give a p. s.th. to understand; fig. einem et. ⚲ to urge a th. (up)on a p.; ⚲liegen v/n. (h.) ⓔ** to lie close by, be near at hand; fig. das liegt nahe that is obvious or very natural or easy to understand; es liegt (sehr) nahe zu glauben one easily believes; ⚲d a. ⓔ (näher=, nächst=liegend) (lying) near at hand, adjacent; fig. obvious, manifest; aus ⚲den Gründen from reasons not far to seek.

nahen (⌣⌣) v/n. (jn) u. sich ⚲ v/refl. ⓔ to approach, to come (or draw) near.

nähen (⌣⌣) [ahd.: lt. u. grch. nēō ich spinne] v/a. ⓔ to sew, (heften) to stitch (a. surg.) to do sewing or needlework, mit weiten Stichen: to baste, überwendlich: to overcast; sich die Finger wund ⚲ to make one's fingers sore with sewing, to sew the flesh off one's bones.

näher¹ (⌣⌣) comp. v. nah(e): mit e-m ⚲ bekannt w. to become closely (or intimately) acquainted with a p.; fig. um einer Sache näher zu kommen (in order) to get to the bottom of a th.; treten Sie näher! please step this way!; bei ⚲er Betrachtung on further consideration; gram. ⚲es Objekt direct object; ⚲e Umstände, ~e(s) n ⓔ particulars, details pl.; ⚲es folgt further particulars will follow; des ⚲(e)n auseinandersetzen to explain fully; ich kann mich des ~(e)n nicht entsinnen I cannot remember all the circumstances (connected with it); das ~e wollen Sie ersehen aus // you will find further (or fuller) particulars (or information) in //.

Näher² (⌣⌣) [nähen] m ⓔ, ~in f ⓔ one who sews; f seamstress, † sempstress, needlewoman.

Näherei (⌣⌣⌣) f ⓕ sewing, needlework, v. Weißzeug: plainwork; (feine Handarbeit) fancy-work; ⚲ (⌣⌣) patchwork.

nähern (⌣⌣) [näher¹] I v/a., sich ⚲ v/refl. ⓐa. to bring (or F get) near; sich e-m, einer Sache ⚲ to come nearer (or closer) to a p., a th., to approach a p., a th.; sich dem Ende ⚲ to draw to a close. — II ~ n ⓔ = Näherung.

Näher=recht (⌣⌣⌣) n ⓐc. jur. prior (or better) claim.

[Näherung] — 721 — [Napoleondor]

Näherung (⌣⌣⌣) f ⊕ approach; *math.* approximation; ~s-wert (⌣⌣⌣⌣) m ⊕ *math.* approximate value.

nahe-stehend (⌣⌣⌣) a. ⊕ (näher-, nächststehend) closely connected; ⁰treten v/n. (jn) ⊕d**: e-m ⁰ to come into (close) contact with a p., to approach a p.; ⁰zu ⁰hin.

Näh-garn ⊕ (⌣-⌣) n ⊕ sewing-cotton or -thread. [fight.)

Nah-kampf ⚔ (⌣-⌣) m ⊕ hand-to-hand

Näh-kästchen (⌣...) n ⊕ lady's workbox; -kissen n sewing-cushion; -kloben ⊕ m Sattlerei: sewing-clamp or -block; -korb m (lady's) work-basket; -kränzchen n = -verein.

nahm (¹) ind. impf. von nehmen.

Näh-mädchen (⌣...) n ⊕, -mamsell f needlewoman, seamstress; -maschine ⊕ f sewing-machine; auf der ~ arbeiten to work (with) a sewing-machine.

nähme (⌣⌣) subj. impf. von nehmen.

Näh-nadel (⌣-⌣) f ⊕ (sewing-)needle.

Nähr-boden (⌣-⌣⌣) m ⊕ fostering soil; Batteriologie: ~ für Bazillen agar (or medium) for the culture of bacilli.

nähren (⌣⌣) [ahd.: (ge-)nesen] ⊕ I v/a. und sich ⁰ v/refl. 1. (sich) ⁰ to feed (o.s.), to provide (o.s.) with food; (Nahrung gewähren) to nourish; (säugen) to suckle, to nurse; vgl. ernähren 2; sich ⁰ von to live on; sich kümmerlich ⁰ to earn a scanty living; *fig.* der von ihm genährte Verdacht the suspicion entertained by him. — II v/n. (h.) 2. (nahrhaft sein) to nourish, to be nourishing. — III ~ n ⊕ 3. feeding, nourishment, nutrition; vgl. Ernährung 2. — IV ⁰d p.pr. u. a. ⊕ 4. Beb. des inf. — 5. = nahrhaft.

Nährer (⌣⌣) m ⊕, ~in f ⊕ = Ernährer.

nahrhaft (⌣⌣) [ahd. nara Erhaltung] a. ⊕ nourishing, nutritive, nutritious, nutrient, bisw.: alimental, ...ary; v. Speisen a. substantial (fare, meal), strengthening (food), rich (diet); (den Unterhalt liefernd) productive (soil); ~igkeit (⌣⌣⌣) f ⊕ nutritiousness, substantialness, richness; productiveness.

Näh-ring (⌣-⌣) m ⊕ sewing-ring.

Nähr-kraft (⌣...) f ⊕ nutritive power; -mutter f = Pflegemutter; -präparat n patent food; -salz n, mst ~e pl. nutritive salts pl.; -stand m (ant. Lehr- u. Wehr-stand) working class(es pl.) or population; (Bauern) peasantry.

Nahrung (⌣⌣) [ahd.; *nähren] f ⊕ (Speise und Trank) food, nourishment, nutriment, diet; (Unterhalt) maintenance, support, sustenance, bisw.: aliment, F keep; (Mittel des Unterhalts) means of subsistence, daily bread, livelihood, living; geistige ~ food for the mind, mental nutriment or pabulum; e-m ~ und Kleidung geben to find a p. in board and clothing; genügende ~ zu sich nehmen to take sufficient nourishment or food, to eat enough; e-n in ~ setzen to give a p. employment or work, to engage a p.; zur ~ gehörig nutritional, pabular.

Nahrungs-bedürfnis (⌣⌣...) n ⊕ *physiol.* want of nourishment or food; -brei m, *physiol.*: ⚕ chyme;

-kanal m, *anat.* alimentary canal; -lehre f s. Diätetif; ⁰los a. ⊕ without food; weits. without means or resources, (arm) poor, starving; (unfruchtbar) unproductive; ⁰lose Zeiten pl. hard times pl.; -losigkeit f lack of food or means; starvation; des Bodens: unproductiveness, hardness; -mangel m lack of provisions, scarcity of food; -mittel n article of food, pl. auch: provisions, victuals; -mittel-fälschung f adulteration of food; -mittel-lehre f, *physiol.*: ⚕ sit(i)ology; -pflanze ⚘ f food-plant; -saft m, *physiol.*: ⚕ chyle; -sorge f care caused by the struggle for life; ~n haben to make a precarious living; -steuer f duty on provisions; -stoff m, *physiol.* nutritious (or nutritive) substance; -wert m = Nährwert; -zufuhr f taking nourishment, alimentation; -zweig ⚐ m branch of industry; livelihood; (Handwert) trade, craft, business. [or quality.)

Nähr-wert (⌣-⌣) m ⊕ nutritive value)

Näh-schraube ⊕ (⌣...) f ⊕ sewing-bird; pin-cushion vice; -schule f school for needle-work; -seide ⚘ f sewing-silk; -stunde f sewing-lesson.

Naht (¹) [ahd.; *nähen] f ⊕ (⚔ ⊕) (Saum der Zf.-nähung, Vereinigungsstelle zweier Flächen, *arch.*, Gießerei ⚙.) seam, ⊕ auch: joint; *anat.* am Schäbel: ⚕ suture, commissure; f. aufgehen 5, aufreißen 2; F *fig.* e-m auf die ~ fühlen to sound a p., to test (or try) a p.

Nähter(in) (⌣⌣(⌣)) ⚙. f. Näher(in) ⚙.

Näh-tisch (⌣...) m ⊕ sewing-table, Buchbinderei: s.-press; -tischchen n (lady's) work-table; -verein m zu wohltätigen Zwecken: ladies' working party, auch: Dorcas-meeting or -society; -zeug m sewing-implements or -utensils, F sewing-things pl.

na-iv (⌣⌣f) [fr.] a. ⊕ ingenuous, simple-minded, unsophisticated, (fr.) naive; ~ität (⌣⌣⌣⌣) f ⊕ ingenuousness, simple-mindedness, (fr.) naïveté.

Najade (⌣⌣⌣) [grch.] f ⊕ *myth.* Naiad.

Name (⌣⌣) [ahd.: name] m ⊕, a. -n m ⊕ 1. name; (Benennung) denomination, appellation; (Ruf) renown, reputation; f. falsch 3; irrtümlicher ~ misnomer, misappellation; mit ~n Hans called Jack, Jack by name; sich (dat.) einen ~n m. to make o.s. a name; die ~n verlesen to call the roll. — 2. et. (F das Kind) beim rechten ~n nennen to call a spade a spade; wer darf das Kind beim rechten ~n nennen? (g.) who dare call things by their right names?; in Gottes ~n: a) feierlich: in God's name; b) (immerhin) just as you like; geht in Gottes ~n! then go (if it so pleases you)!; F in des Teufels ~n! (go and be damned!, hang it (all)!; e-n dem ~n nach kennen to know a p. by name; wie ist sein ~? what's his name?

Namen-buch (⌣...) n ⊕ register (or dictionary) of names; -gebung f naming, giving a name to, christening, ⚕ nomenclature; -liste f list of names, roll, für Wahlen auch: poll, ⚕ nomenclature;

⁰los a. ⊕: a) nameless, anonymous; b) (ruhmlos) inglorious; c) (unaussprechlich) inexpressible, unspeakable; als adv. oft: utterly; ⁰lose([r] m) f ⊕ anonymous p.; -losigkeit f nameless-ness, anonymousness; -papier ⚐ n (ant. Inhaberpapier) stock (or scrip) payable to order; -register n = -liste.

namens (⌣⌣) 1. (mit Namen) ein Mädchen ⁰ Liese a girl named (or by the name of) Lizzie. — 2. prp. mit gen. (im Namen) in the name of; ⁰ unserer Gesellschaft on behalf of our association.

Namens-änderung (⌣⌣...) f ⊕ change of name; -aufruf m calling over the names, ⚔ &c.: roll-call; -fest n, -tag m name-day; (saint's) festival; -unterschrift f signature; -verwechs(e)lung f confusion of names; -vetter m: mein ~ my namesake; -zeichnung f signature; -zug m sign manual, signature; (Schnörfel) flourish.

namentlich (⌣⌣⌣) a. ⊕ u. adv. 1. by (his, her, &c.) name; ⁰ anführen to mention individually, to specify. — 2. (besonders) especially, particularly, in particular. — 3. parl. ⁰e Abstimmung (unter Nennung des Namens) (voting by) call.

Namen-verzeichnis (⌣⌣...) n ⊕ = -liste; -wechsel m = Namensänderung.

namhaft (⌣⌣) a. ⊕ 1. named, known by name; ⁰ m. to name, to mention by name. — 2. (berühmt) notable, noted, renowned; (bedeutend) considerable.

Namhaft-machung (⌣⌣⌣⌣) f ⊕ mentioning (or giving) the name of a p.

...namig (...⌣⌣) [Name(n)] a. ⊕ in Zssgn., zB.: viel⁰: ⚕ polyonymous.

nämlich (⌣⌣) [ahd.] I a. ⊕ 1. der ⁰e Mensch the same (seltener: selfsame) person, F the identical fellow; das ⁰e the (very) same thing. — II adv. 2. die Großmächte, ⁰ Deutschland, England ⚙. the great powers, namely ..., that is (to say) ..., viz. (= videlicet) ..., to wit ... — 3. meist begründend nach dem v.: ich traf ihn nicht, er war ⁰ krank ... because (or for you must know) he was ill.

Näni-e ⚙ (⌣(⌣)⌣) [grch.] f ⊕ Alt.: (Klagelied bei Begräbnissen) nenia, (funeral) dirge.

Nanking (⌣⌣) m ⊕d.⊕ (Art Baumwollstoff) nankeen; ⁰en a. ⊕ (of) nankeen.

nannte (⌣⌣) ind. impf. von nennen.

nanu F (⌣⌣) [na na] int. f. na.

Napf (¹) [ahd.] m ⊕b.⊕.1. (Schale) bowl, basin, dish, für Suppe: soup-tureen; (Becher) cup, zylinderförmiger mit Henkel: mug. — 2. ⚘ (napfförmiger Kelch) ⚕ cupule, ...a.

Näpfchen (⌣⌣) n ⊕ (dim. von Napf) 1. small bowl or basin. — 2. ⚘ cup of acorns, ⚕ cupule.

napf-förmig (⌣...) a. ⊕ cup-shaped; -kuchen m ⊕ pound-cake; -schnecke f, zo. limpet, cup-shell (Patella).

Naphtha (⌣f-) [grch., *hebr.] n ⊕ u. f ⊕ min. (Steinöl) naphtha, rock-oil.

Naphthalin (⌣f-⌣) n ⊕d. *chm.* (Steinkohlenteerkampfer) naphthalene ($C_{10}H_8$); ~rot (⌣-⌣) n ⊕ naphthalene red.

Napoleon (⌣⌣(⌣)⌣, ⌣⌣⌣) I npr/m. ⊕ a. Napoleon. — II ~(dor) m ⊕d(⊕)⊕. *num.* (16 Mart) twenty-franc piece.

[napoleonisch]

napoleonisch (‿-(‿)ᴸ‿) *a.* ⑥ Napoleonic.
Narbe (‿‿) [ahd.] *f* ⑱ **1.** *med.* ~ einer Wunde: scar, mark, ⌑ cicatrice, e-s Schwerthiebes, auch: gash, slash; mit ~n von Blattern bedeckt pitted with the small-pox; eine ~ ansetzen to put on a scar, to heal up. — **2.** ¿ (Griffel-ende): ⌑ stigma. — **3.** *agr.* (oberste Bodenschicht) top-soil. — **4.** ⊕ ~ des Saffians: grain.
narben (‿‿) *v/a.* und **sich** ⌒ *v/refl.* ⑱ **1.** von Wunden: (sich) ⌒ to (form a) scar, ⌑ to cicatrice. — **2.** *agr.* to take off the top-soil. — **3.** ⊕ Gerberei: to grain, to shagreen.
Narben=bildung (‿‿...) *f* ⑫ formation of a scar, ⌑ cicatrization; =**leder** ⊕ *n* shagreen; ₂**los** *a.* ⑯ scarless, without a scar; =**seite** *f* des Leders grain-(or hair-)side of leather; ₂**tragend** ¿ *a.*: ⌑ stigmatiferous; ₂**voll** *a.* scarred.
narbicht, mst **narbig** (‿‿) *a.* ⑯ **1.** scarred, marked with scars, ⌑ cicatrized. — **2.** ⊕ von Leder 2c. : grained.
Narde ¿ (‿‿) [grch.] *f* ⑭ (spike)nard (*Valeria'na ce'ltica*, &c.); ~n=**öl** (‿‿...) *n* ⑫ nard, spike(nard)-oil; ~n=**salbe** *f* nard.
Nargileh (‿⌣⌣) [pers.] *n* ⑩ (türkische Wasserpfeife) narghile. [narcotism.]
Narkose ⌑ (‿‿) [grch.] *f* ⑭ narcosis,
Narkotin ⌑ (‿⌣‿) *n* ⑩ d. chm. (Alkaloid des Opiums) narcotine (C₂₉H₂₃NO₇).
narkotisch ⌑ (‿ᴸ‿) [grch.] *a.* ⑯ *med.* (betäubend): 2(es Mittel) narcotic.
narkotisier/en ⌑ (‿⌣⌣ᴸ‿) [fr.] **I** *v/a.* ⑰ (betäuben) to narcotize. — **II** ~ *n* ㉓ und **N/ung** *f* ⑯ narcotization.
Narr (‿) [ahd.] *m* ⑫, **Närrin** *f* ⑯ **1.** fool (als engl. Schimpfwort sehr beleidigend!), milder: foolish (wo)man; ~ von Geburt born fool; sich wie ein ~ benehmen to act the (or like a) fool; e-n zum =en haben (halten oder machen) to make a fool of a p.; (verwirren) to mystify a p.; sich zum =en hergeben to play the fool, to be made a laughing-stock of. — **2.** *fig.* u. Sprichw.: s. fressen 3, lachen III u. Kappe 2; die alten =en sind die schlimmsten there is no fool like an old one; ein ~ macht viele one fool makes many; wenn die =en zu Markte gehen, lösen die Krämer Geld a fool and his money are soon parted.
Närrchen (‿‿) *n* ㉓ (*dim. v.* Narr) little fool or F silly; von Mädchen auch: silly little goose, silly young thing.
narren (‿‿) ⑱ **I** *v/n.* (h.) to play (or act) the fool. — **II** *v/a.* to fool, to make a fool of, to make game (or sport) of.
Narren=fest (‿‿...) *n* ⑫ ehm. fool's fête, (1. April) All-Fools' Day; =**geschwätz** *n* foolish talk; =**hände** *f/pl.* ⋅ Sprichw. ~ beschmieren Tisch und Wände, etwa: white walls are a fool's writing-paper; =**haus** *n* mad-house; =**jacke** *f* fool's (or harlequin's) dress, ehm.: motley; =**kappe** *f*: a) fool's cap, ehm.: cap and bell; b) *zo.* Muschel: foolscap (*Isoca'rdia cor*); =**kleid** *n* = =jacke; ₂**mäßig** *a.* like a fool, foolish; =**seil** *n*: e-n am ~ führen to lead a p. by the nose; =**spiel** *n* fool's play or game, tomfoolery.
Narrens=possen (‿‿...) *f/pl.* ⑫ buffoonery, tomfoolery; ~ treiben to play the fool, to fool about.

Narren=streich (‿‿...) *m* ⑫ foolish trick; ~e *pl. m.* to do foolish things, to make a fool of o.s.; =**teiding** *m*(*n*) = Narretei.
Narretei (‿⌣ᴸ) *f* ⑯ folly; buffoonery, tomfoolery; (piece of) madness.
Narrheit (‿‿) *f* ⑯ folly (als Handlung, auch: piece of folly), foolishness; (überspanntheit) eccentricity; (Verrücktheit) craziness, F daftness.
Närrin (‿‿) *f* ⑯ s. Narr.
närrisch (‿‿) [Narr] *a.* ⑯ foolish; (überspannt) eccentric, odd, (verrückt) mad, crazy, F off one's head or chump, daft, cracked; (possierlich) funny, droll; (schäkernd) skittish.
Narwal (‿‿) [schwd.] *m* ⑪ d. *zo.* narwhal, sea-unicorn (*Mo'nodon mono'ceros*).
Narzisse ¿ (‿ᴸ‿) [grch.] *f* ⑱ (*Narci'ssus*): weiße ~ poet's narcissus (*N. poe'ticus*); gelbe ~ daffodil (*N. pseudonarci'ssus*); ₂**n=artig** *a.* ⑯: ⌑ narcissine.
nasal (‿ᴸ) [lt.] *a.* ⑯ *gr.* (durch die Nase tönend) nasal; ~**ität** (‿‿‿ᴸ) *f* ⑯ nasality; ~**laut** *m* ⑫ nasal sound. [of sweets.]
Nasch=dose (‿‿) *f* ⑫ box for (gefüllt.)
naschen (‿‿) [ahd.: nähren; (ge)nesen] *v/n.* (h.) u. *v/a.* ⑩ to eat on the sly, to pilfer (delicacies or dainty bits); weits. to enjoy forbidden things or pleasures; gern ⌒ to have a sweet tooth.
Näschen (ᴸ‿) *n* ㉓ *dim. v.* Nase.
Nascher, Näscher (‿‿) [naschen] *m* ⑫, ~**in** *f* ⑯ p. fond of sweet things or F with a sweet tooth, pilferer (of dainties); ~**ei** (‿‿ᴸ) *f* ⑯ **1.** eating (or taking) dainties on the sly. — **2.** = Naschwerk.
naschhaft (‿‿) *a.* ⑯ fond of dainties; ⌒ sein, oft: F to have a sweet tooth; ~**igkeit** (‿‿‿) *f* ⑯ fondness for dainties.
Nasch=kätzchen (‿...) *n* ⑫, =**katze** *f*: a) thievish cat; b) *fig.* (Näscher[in]) person fond of (pilfering) dainties; =**lust** *f* love for (forbidden) dainties; =**maul**, =**mäulchen** *n* = Leckermaul; =**sucht** *f* daintiness; =**werk** *n* dainties, sweetmeats, sweets, lollypops, titbits *pl.*
Nase (ᴸ‿) [ahd.: nose: lt. *nāsus*, *nāres*] *f* ⑱ **1.** nose; vgl. Geruchswerkzeug; (Rüssel) snout, ⌑ proboscis; ~ e-s Pfluges 2c. beak of a sock, &c.; ⊕ ~ e-s Hobels horn of a plane; ~ einer Schwanzschraube tang of a screw. — **2.** Redensarten (mst *fig.*): F alle 2n(lang) every few steps; eine feine ~ (einen scharfen Geruch) haben to have a sharp nose or a keen scent; eine ~ (einen Verweis) bekommen to get a reprimand or F a good wigging; e-m eine ~ drehen F to take a sight at a p.; e-m e-e ~ geben to give a p. a sharp talking-to, to rebuke a p.; die ~ hoch tragen to put up one's nose, to carry one's head high; immer der ~ nach geh(e)n to go straight ahead, auch: to follow one's nose; die ~ rümpfen, runzeln ob. ziehen to turn up one's nose; seine ~ in allem haben, in alles stecken to poke one's nose into everything; die ~ in die Bücher stecken to pore over one's books. — **3.** mit *prp.* (mst *fig.*): e-m et. **an** der ~ ansehen to (be able to) tell (or judge) by a p.'s face; e-m et. an (ob. auf) die ~ binden ob. heften (verraten) to blurt (or blab) a th. out to a p.; fassen (ob.

[nasführen]

zupfen) Sie sich doch an Ihre(r) eigene(n) ~! mind your own business!; an (ob. bei) der ~ herum=führen, =ziehen to lead by the nose; to bamboozle, to trick; e-m **auf** der ~ spielen ob. tanzen to make game (or sport) of a p.; er blutet **aus** der ~ his nose is bleeding; vgl. bluten 1; e-m die Würmer **aus** der ~ ziehen to worm the secrets out of a p., F to pump a p. (dry); **bei** der ~ = an der ~; **durch** die ~ atmen to breathe through the nose; Wasser 2c. durch die ~ einziehen to sniff up ...; durch die ~ sprechen = näseln 2; etwas **in** die ~ bekommen (riechen, spüren) to smell (or scent) a th.; v. Gerüchen: in die ~ steigen to get up one's nose; das sticht ihm in die ~ (reizt sein Verlangen) it makes his mouth water, it excites his greed; mit der ~ gegen et. rennen to run right into a th.; f. abziehen II am Schluß u. heimschicken b; e-n mit der ~ **auf** etwas stoßen to bring a th. forcibly under a p.'s notice; er hat sich viel Wind **um** die ~ wehen lassen he has boxed the compass, he has seen a good deal of the world; e-m et. **unter** die ~ reiben to cast a th. in a p.'s teeth, to rub a th. into a p.; es liegt **vor** s-r (ob. ihm vor der) ~ it lies under his very eyes or nose; e-m et. vor der ~ wegnehmen to snatch a th. (away) from a p.('s grasp); e-m die Tür vor der ~ zumachen to slam the door in a p.'s face.
Näseler (ᴸ‿‿) [näseln 2] *m* ⑫, **Näslerin** *f* ⑯ p. who speaks through the nose.
näseln (ᴸ‿) [Nase] *v/n.* (h.) ⑫ *a.* **1.** (schnüffeln) to sniff, to scent. — **2.** (durch die Nase sprechen) to speak through the nose, to have a nasal twang; 2d nasal.
Nasen=affe (ᴸ‿...) *m* ⑫ *zo.* proboscis-monkey, kahau (*Nasa'lis larva'tus*); =**bär** *m*, *zo.* coati (*Na'sua na'rica*); =**bein** *n*, *anat.* nasal bone; künstliche =**bildung** *f*, *surg.*: ⌑ rhinoplasty; =**bluten** *n* bleeding of (or at) the nose; =**buchstabe** *m*, *gr.* nasal letter; =**flügel** *m* side of the nose; =**höhle** *f*, *anat.* nasal cavity or fossa; =**klemmer**, =**kneifer** F *m* eyeglass(es *pl.*), (fr.) pince-nez; =**knorpel** *m*, *anat.* nasal cartilage; =**laut** *m* nasal sound; =**loch** *n* nostril; =**polyp** *m*, *path.* nasal polypus; =**popel** P *m* nose-dirt; =**quetscher** F *m*: a) = =klemmer; b) (Sarg mit flachem Deckel) flat coffin; =**ring** *m* ring through the nose, nose-ring; =**rücken** *m* bridge of the n.; =**rümpfen** *n* turning up one's nose; =**scheidewand** *f*, *anat.* column of the nose, (lt.) septum narium; =**schleimhaut** *f*, *anat.*: ⌑ pituitary membrane; =**spitze** *f* tip of the nose; =**stüber** *m* rap on the nose, fillip; 2**stübern** *v/a.* ⑫ a.*.* to fillip; =**ton** *m* nasal tone, twang; =**wärmer** *m*: a) (Halstuch) comforter; b) (kurze Pfeife) short (clay) pipe; =**wurzel** *f* root of the nose.
nase=weis (ᴸ‿‿ᴸ) *a.* ⑯ (D 10) pert, forward, prying; (zudringlich) impertinent, obtrusive; F junge Frau (ob. Jungfer) ~ Miss Pert; (Herr) ~ *m* ⑫ *a.* meddler, auch oft: Paul Pry; ~**heit** *f* ⑯ pertness; impertinence.
nas=führen (ᴸᴸ‿) *v/a.* ⑯ a.*.* to lead by the nose; er wurde von ihnen genasführt he was fooled by them.

Signs (see page XVII): F familiar; P vulgar; ⌐ flash; ⌏ rare; ⊤ obsolete (died); * new word (born); ⁒ incorrect; ♪ music;

[Nashorn] — 723 — [Naturselbstdruck]

Nas=horn (⁻⁻ʹ) n ⚙ zo. rhinoceros, nasicorn (Rhino'ceros).
Nashorn=käfer (⁻⁻ʹ…) m ⚙ ent. rhinoceros-beetle (Ory'ctes nasico'rnis); **=vogel** m, orn. rh.-bird or =hornbill (Bu'ceros rhino'ceros).
…nasig (…"ᴸᵛ) a. ⚙ in Zssgn, z.B.: adler= with an aquiline nose; fig. auch **…näsig**, z.B.: hoch=² supercilious, F stuck-up.
naß (ʲ) [ahd.: netzen] **I** a. ⚙ (D 4, 10) 1. wet; (feucht) damp, moist; chm., &c. humid; Analyse auf nassem Wege humid analysis; (sich) ² m. to wet (o.s.); ² w. to become (F get) wet; fig. nasser Bruder tippler; nasses Grab watery grave. — 2. bis auf den letzten Faden (ob. bis auf die Haut) ² wet (or soaked) to the skin; durch und durch ² wet through, thoroughly drenched, soaking (wet), v. Kleidern a. wringing wet. — **II** Naß n ⓐa. 3. liquid, fluid; (Getränk) beverage; poet. Naß der Tränen flow of tears.
Nassauer (ᴶ⁻ᵛ) m ⚙, ~in f ⚙ 1. inhabitant of Nassau, Nassovian. — 2. F fig. (j. der nicht bezahlt, blinder Teilnehmer) sponger, F deadhead; **nassauern** F v/n. (h.) ⓐa. to sponge (bei e-m in a p.), F co. to pross. [sovian.]
nassau-isch (ᴶ⁻ᵛ) a. ⚙ of Nassau, Nas-]
Nässe (ᴶᵛ) [ahd.; *naß] f ⚙ wet, bisw. wetness; damp(ness), moisture; chm., &c. humidity; auf Paketen: vor ~ zu bewahren! to be kept dry!
nässen (ᴶᵛ) ⚙ **I** v/a. 1. to wet, (befeuchten) to damp, to moisten; in Wasser ² to soak in water. — **II** v/n. (h.) 2. v/impers. es näßt it drizzles, F there is a damp falling. — 3. surg. eine Wunde näßt … discharges. [rot.]
Naß=fäule (ᴶ·ᴸᵛ) f ⚙ der Kartoffeln: wet]
naß=kalt (ᴶ⁻ᵛ) a. ⚙ wet (or damp) and cold, raw, dank.
Nation (-tz(ᵛ)ᴸ) [fr., *It.] f ⚙ nation.
national (-tz(ᵛ)⁻ᴸ) a. ⚙ (Volks…) national.
National=charakter (⁻ᵗᶻ(ᵛ)⁻"…) m ⚙ national character.
Nationale (⁻ᵗᶻ(ᵛ)⁻ᴸ⁻) [It.] n ⓘ (⚙, ⚙) full particulars pl. of persons.
National=farbe (⁻ᵗᶻ(ᵛ)⁻ᴸ⁻) f ⚙ national colour(s pl.); **=flagge** f nat. flag, englische: union-jack; **=garde** f nat. guard, in England: territorial army; **=gardist** m soldier of the nat. guard, citizen-soldier, in England: militiaman, volunteer; **=hymne** f national hymn.
nationalisier/en (⁻ᵗᶻ(ᵛ)⁻⁻ᴸᵛ) **I** v/a. ⚙ to nationalize. — **II** ~ n ⚙ u. N/ung f ⚙ nationalization. [ality.)
Nationalität (⁻ᵗᶻ(ᵛ)⁻⁻ᴸʲ) f ⚙ nation-]
National=konve'nt (⁻ᵗᶻ(ᵛ)⁻"…) m ⚙ f. Konvent 2; **²liberal(e[r]** m) a. pol. National-Liberal; **=literatu'r** f national literature; **=ökonomie** f m political economist (economy), auch: social philosopher (philosophy); **=schuld** f national debt; **=tracht** f nat. costume; **=verein** m nat. league; **=versammlung** f nat. assembly.
Nativität (⁻ᵛ⁻ʷᴸ) [It.] f ⚙ Astrologie: nativity; e-m die ~ stellen to cast a p.'s horoscope.
Natrium ⚙ (ᴸᵛᵛ) [Natron] n ⚙ chm. sodium (Na).

Natrium=hydroxyd (⁻ᴸᵛᵛ…) n ⚙ sodium hydroxide (N₁OH); **=oxy'd** n f. Natron=oxy'd=hydra't n = hydroxyd.
Natron (ᴸᵛ) [semit.] n ⚙ chm. (Natriumoxyd) soda (Na₂O); kaustisches ~ (Ätznatron) caustic soda, sodium hydroxide or hydrate (NaHO); (zweifach) kohlensaures ~ (bi)carbonate of soda, sodium (bi)carbonate; schwefelsaures ~ sodium sulphate, f. Glaubersalz.
Natron=glas (ᴸᵛ…) n ⚙ soda-glass; **²haltig** a. ⚙ sodic; **=lauge** f solution of sodium hydroxide or caustic soda; **=salpeter** m (Chilisalpeter) soda-nitre, cube-nitre, (commercial) nitrate of sodium (NaNO₃); **=salz** n sodium (or sodic) salt; **=seife** f soda-soap.
Natter (ᴶᵛ) [ahd.] f ⚙ 1. zo. adder, viper, poet. asp; Familie der ~: ☿ colubridæ. — 2. fig. (giftige Person) venomous (or spiteful, ill-natured) person; serpent, snake (in the grass).
Natter(n)=biß (ᵛ…) m ⚙ bite (or sting) of an adder; **=brut** f nest of vipers; **=kopf** m: a) head of an adder; b) ♀ viper's bugloss, blueweed (E'chium vulga're); **=wurz(el)** ♀ f adder's-wort, bistort (Poly'gonum bistor'ta); **=zunge** ♀ f adder's-tongue (Ophioglo'ssum vulga'tum).
Natur (ᵛᴸ) [ahd., *It.] f ⚙ 1. nature; (Leibesbeschaffenheit) constitution, (Gemüts=anlage) temper(ament); (Gefilde, Wiesen u. Wälder) (natural) scenery; Gottes freie ~ the temple (or realm) of nature, the open fields pl.; e-e gute ~ haben: a) to have a good constitution; b) to be good-natured; verliebter ~ sein to be of an amorous disposition; der ~ f-e Schuld (ob. f-n Tribut) zahlen (sterben) to pay the debt of nature, to go the way of all flesh; es liegt in der ~ der Sache it is in the nature of things, it is quite natural; nach der ~ zeichnen to draw (or sketch) from nature or life; Eis ist seiner ~ nach kalt ice is cold by nature; von ~ schwächlich constitutionally weak; sie ist von ~ sehr schüchtern she is by nature (or naturally) very timid, she is of a very timid disposition; es geht mir wider die ~ it goes against the grain; es ist ihm zur zweiten ~ geworden it has become a second nature with him, it has grown upon him. — 2. (einzelnes Wesen) being, person; hitzige ~en hot (or fiery) natures.
Naturali-en (ᵛ⁻ᴸ(ᵛ)⁻) [It.] f/pl. inv. 1. natural produce, fruits pl. of the soil. — 2. (Bestandteile e-r naturgeschichtlichen Sammlung) natural (history) objects pl.
Naturali-en=kabinett (⁻…) n ⚙, **=sammlung** f natural history collection.
Naturalisations=gesuch (ᵛ⁻⁻⁻ᵗᶻ(ᵛ)"ᴸ) n ⚙ petition (or application) for naturalization.
naturalisier/en (ᵛ⁻⁻⁻ᴸᵛ) [It.] **I** v/a. ⚙ to naturalize; sich ² lassen to become naturalized. — **II** ~ n ⚙ u. N/ung f ⚙ naturalization. [naturalism.)
Naturalismus ⚙ (ᵛ⁻⁻⁻ᴸᵛ) [It.] m ⚙ phls.)
Naturalist (ᵛ⁻⁻⁻ᴸᵛ) [It.] m ⚙ person living according to the rules (or in a state) of nature, bisw.: naturalist; **²isch** a. ⚙ naturalistic.

Natural=leistung (ᵛ⁻"…) f ⚙ payment in kind; **=verpflegung** f (✕ nur „Verpflegung" genannt) supply of provisions, ✕ maintenance of troops (by the population); **=zins** m rent paid in (farm=)produce.
Natur=anlage (ᵛ⁻"…) f ⚙ natural disposition, **=arzt** m nature-doctor, one who cures disease without drugs; **=beobachtung** f observation (or study) of nature; **=beschreibung** f description of nature; vgl. =geschichte; **=butter** f (ant. Kunstbutter) real (or genuine) butter; **=dichter** m born poet; **=dichtung** f nat. poetry; **=dienst** m =verehrung.
Naturell (ᵛ⁻ᴶ) [fr.] n ⓓd. natural disposition, temper, nature.
Natur=ereignis (⁻ᴶʲ…) n ⚙, **=erscheinung** f natural phenomenon; **=erzeugnisse** n/pl. nat. produce; **=forscher** m nat. philosopher, investigator of nature; **=forschung** f natural philosophy or science; **=gabe** f nat. gift; **²gemäß** a. ⚙ u. adv.: in conformity with nature, natural; b) *,+,+ = natürlich(erweise); **=genuß** m enjoyment of nature; **=geschichte** f natural history; **²geschichtlich** a. descriptive of nature; **²es Museum** natural history museum; **=gesetz** n law of nature, natural (or physical) law; **²getreu** a. true to nature; life-like; **=heil-kunde**, **=lehre** f treatment by natural remedies; **=heilung** f, **=heilverfahren** n cure effected by natural methods; **²historisch** a. referring to nat. history; vgl. =geschichtlich; **=kenner** m student of n.; **=kenntnis** f =kunde; **=kind** child of nature, unsophisticated (or uneducated) p.; **=körper** m physical body; **=kunde** f knowledge of nature, natural science, bsb. physics; **=laut** m natural sound; **=lehre** f = =kunde.
natürlich (ᵛᴸᵛ) [Natur] a. ⚙ 1. natural; according to nature; f. Auslese; das ging nicht mit den Dingen zu there was s.th. supernatural (or miraculous) about it; e-s den Todes sterben to die a natural death; auf ² Weise erklären to give a natural (or rational) explanation of; **²er=weise** adv. naturally, of course; er möchte ² (adv.) die Welt sehen he would naturally like to see the world; will er Geld ? — ²! does he want money? — of course or to be sure or Prather! — 2. (ungekünstelt) natural, unaffected, artless; (einfach) simple, simpleminded, primitive, homely; (unbefangen) ingenuous, unsophisticated; et. ²es s.th. natural; es ist nichts ²es an f-m Stil there is nothing natural in his style, his style has s.th. unnatural (about it). — 3. (unehelich) illegitimate.
Natürlichkeit (ᵛᴸᵛ⁻) f ⚙ (f. natürlich) naturalness, unaffectedness, artlessness; simplicity.
Natur=mensch (ᵛ⁻"…) m ⚙ natural man; vgl. =kind; **=notwendigkeit** f physical necessity; **=pflicht** f natural duty; **=philosoph** m nat. philosopher; **=philosophie** f nat. philosophy, naturalism; **=recht** n nat. right; **=reich** n realm of nature; **=religion** f natural religion, naturalism; **=schönheit** f nat. beauty; **=selbstdruck** m nature-printing, ⚙

⚙ scientific; ♀ botanical; ⚙ geography; ⚙ machinery; ✕ mining; ✕ military; ⚓ marine; ● commercial; ✉ postal; 🚆 railway.

physiotypy, phytoglyphy; =ſpiel n freak of nature; =ſtudien n/pl. Kunſt: studies from nature; =trieb m nat. instinct; =verehrung f worship of nature; =volk n primitive race; people living in a natural state; =wahr(heit f) a. ⑥ true (truth) to nature; ⚣widrig a. contrary to n.; =wiſſenſchaften f/pl. natural sciences pl.; =wiſſenſchaft(l)er m student of natural science, weitS.: man of science; ⚣wiſſenſchaftlich a. belonging to nat. science, physical; Ler Verein philosophical society; =wolle f native wool; ⚣wüchſig a. of natural growth, spontaneous, untutored; (gerade heraus) blunt; (eigentümlich) original; =wüchſigkeit f nat. growth, spontaneousness; bluntness; originality; =wunder n prodigy; =zuſtand m nat. state; =zweck m purpose of nature.

Naue ſübd. ⚓ (⌣⌣) [mhd.; *lt. nāvis] f ⓢ, ~n m ㉓ (kleines Ruder-, Segel-ſchiff) small rowing-boat, skiff, yawl; a. = Motorboot.

Nautik ⚓ (⌣⌣) [grch.] f ㊻ (Schiffahrtskunde) nautical science, navigation.

nautiſch ⚓ (⌣⌣) [grch.] a. ⑥ nautical; Les Jahrbuch n. almanac.

Navigations-akte ⚓ (⌣⌣⌣⌣⌢) f ㊷ navigation act, ehm. Act of Navigation; =offizier m navigating lieutenant; =ſchule f school of navigation, naval school.

Nazarener (-tş⌣⌣) [Na′zareth] m ㉒, ~in f ㊻, nazareniſch a. ⑥ Nazarene.

NB. abbr. = nota bene (engl. abbr. **N. B.**).

n. Chr. (**G.**) abbr. = nach Chriſto (nach Chriſti Geburt) after Christ, mſt A. D. (= anno domini: im Jahre des Herrn.)

(')**ne** P u. poet. (⌣) indef. art. = eine.

Neapel ☉(⌣⌣) [grch.] npr/n. ⓢ a. (it. Stadt u. ehemaliges Königreich) Naples; ~er m ㉒ u. a. inv. Neapolitan; ~gelb ⊕ (⌣⌣⌢) n ㉒ Naples (or antimony) yellow.

nearktiſch ⚔ (⌣⌣⌣) [grch.] a. ⑥ Le (weſtliche gemäßigte) Region Nearctic region.

Nebel (⌣⌣) [ahd.: lt. nē′bŭla: grch.: nēphē′lē] m ㉒ **1.** mist, dichter: (thick) fog, leichter: (light) haze, naſſer: Scotch mist, vom Meere aufſteigend: sea-fog; Staubregen: drizzle; ſ. Nacht; ast. = =fleck; in ~ gehüllt wrapt in fog, shrouded in mist; befogged (mſt fig.). — **2.** fig. (den Blick Verſchleierndes) mist, veil, cloud; ⚣(zweifel) doubt, uncertainty.

Nebel-bank (⌣⌣⌣) f ㊷ fog-bank; =bild n hazy scene or picture; künſtlich hergeſtellte ~er dissolving views pl.; =decke f = =ſchleier; =ferne f hazy distance; =fleck m: a) ast.: ⚔ nebula; b) path. im Auge: spot (in the eye), ⚔ nebula; ⚣grau a. ⑥ u. s. misty grey.

nebelhaft (⌣⌣⌣) a. ⑥ mistlike; bſd. fig. (ohne feſte Geſtalt) nebulous, hazy, vague, dim; (dunkel) obscure; =igkeit f ㊻ mistiness, fogginess, vaporousness, haziness.   [(Sirene) siren.]

Nebel-horn (⌣⌣⌣) n ㉓c. fog-horn; **neb(e)licht** ⚓, mſt **neb(e)lig** (⌣⌣⌣) a. ⑥ misty, foggy, enshrouded in fog, hazy; (bewölkt) cloudy; (mit Dünſten beladen) damp, full of moisture, vaporous.

Nebel-kanone ⚔ (⌣⌣⌣⌢) f ㊷ fog-gun; =kappe f: a) um Berge: hood of mist enshrouding a mountain; b) in der

Sage: magic hood which makes its wearer invisible; =Tarnkappe); =krähe f, orn. hooded (or bunting-)crow (Corvus cornix); =land n land of fog; =monat m foggy month, auch: November.

nebeln (⌣⌣) I v/n. (h.) ⚣ a. **1.** to be misty or foggy; bſd. v/impers. es nebelt, a. there is a mist or a fog. — **2.** fig. (bei Ortsveränderung mit ſu): a) to float like a cloud (um et. around a th.); b) (faſeln) to ramble. — II ~ n **3.** mist(iness), fog(giness); ~ u. Schwebeln haphazard conjectures, phantastic ideas, hazy notions pl.

Nebel-regen (⌣⌣⌣) m ㉒ drizzling rain; =ſchicht f fog-bank; =ſchleier m misty veil; =ſchwaden m damp fog; =ſignal n fog-signal; =ſtern m, ast.: ⚔ nebula; =ſtreif m misty cloud; =wetter n foggy weather; =zerteiler m fog-dispeller, (Knallgeräuſch) mist-puffer.

neben (⌣⌣) [ahd.; *in eben] I prp. mit dat. und acc. **1.** by the side of, beside, alongside (of); ſie ging 2 ihm she walked by his side; 2 dem Hauſe close to ..., near ...; 2=ea.: a) örtlich: side by side; b) zeitlich: simultaneously (with). — **2.** (verglichen mit) = gegen 5. — **3.** (nebſt) besides, in addition to, independently of. — **II** adv. **4.** = da 2 1; bſd. gbr. in Zſſgn (ſ. dſe).

Neben-abſicht (⌣⌣⌣) f ㊷ additional (or simultaneous) purpose; =achſe f, math.: ⚔ conjugate (or secondary) axis; =allee f side-walk; =altar m side-altar; =amt n additional (or subsidiary) office; ⚣a'n adv. by the side, close by, next door; auf Schriftſtücken: on the margin; =arbeit f: a) extra work; b) work done in spare hours; =artikel m additional (or subordinate) article; =ausgaben f/pl. = =koſten; =ausgang m side-entrance or -door; =bahn ☛ f. (ant. Vollbahn) branch line or railway, (side-)branch; local line; =bedeutung f secondary meaning; =begriff m subordinate notion; ⚣bei adv.: a) = ⚣an; b) (beiläufig) by the way, in passing, incidentally; 2 bemerken to remark parenthetically or by way of parenthesis; c) (außerdem) besides, moreover; (along) with it; =beruf m, =beſchäftigung f occupation (or business) pursued in spare hours, F by-play, hobby; =beweis m additional (or collateral) proof; =bewohner m = =wohner; =blatt ⚤ n er-Blüte: ⚔ bract(ea); =blättchen ⚤ n: ⚔ stipule, ...a; mit ~ verſehen ⚔ stipulated; =buhler(in f) m (female) rival or competitor; ⚣buhleriſch a. ⑥ rival(ling), competing; =buhlerſchaft f rivalry, rivalship; =bürgſchaft f jur. collateral security or bail; =draht m, elect. secondary wire.

neben-einander (⌣⌣⌣⌢⌣) adv. side by side; abreast; 2 beſtehend co-existing; ⚣ſtellen to put side by side, vergleichend: to compare; ⚣ 2 wachſend: ⚔ apposite; 2 wohnend living next door to each other; ~ſtellung f ㊻: ⚔ juxtaposition.

Neben-eingang (⌣⌣⌣⌣) m ㉒ side-entrance; =einkünfte, =einnahmen f/pl. additional income, perquisites, F extras, pickings pl.; =fach n subordinate (or subsidiary) branch or department; =flügel u, arch. side-wing; =fluß m tributary, affluent, feeder; =gang m side-passage; =gaſſe f: a) adjacent street; b) by-street, lane; =gebäude n, arch. side-wing, outhouse, outbuilding, annexe; =gedanke m simultaneous thought, subordinate idea; vgl. =abſicht; =gericht n Kochkunſt: side-dish; (fr.) entremets; =geſchäft n subsidiary (or subordinate) business; vgl. =beruf; =geſchöpf n = Mitgeſchöpf; =gewinn m incidental profit or gain; =handlung f (minor) episode, by-play; ⚣her, ⚣hin adv.: a) by his (her) side; b) = ⚣bei b u. c; =koſten pl. extra costs or expenses, extras, incidental charges pl.; =linie f: a) parallel line; b) ⚣ Genealogie: collateral line, branch; c) = =bahn; =mann m next man (a. ⚔); =menſch m fellow-man or -creature; =mond m, ast. mock moon, ⚔ paraselene; =niere f, anat.: ⚔ (supra)renal gland or capsule, paranephros; =ordnung f co-ordination; =perſon f person of no consequence, F outsider; thea. = =rolle; ſ. a. Figura(n)t; =pforte f side-gate; =poſten ⚥ m incidental item; =produkt n by- (or residual) product; =raum ⊕ m auf Münzen ꝛc.: exergue; =rolle f subordinate rôle or character; thea. ~n ſpielen to take (or play) subordinate parts; =ſaal m adjoining hall; =ſache f: a) subordinate (or accessory) matter, secondary consideration; ganz ~ ſein to be of no consequence; b) Schrifttum: padding; ⚣ſächlich a. ⑥ subordinate, accessory; accidental, incidental; =ſatz m, gr. subordinate sentence or clause; =ſchiff n, arch. einer Kirche: side-aisle; =ſchluß m, elect. shunt; =ſchlüſſel m second key; =ſchoß, =ſchößling m side-shoot, sucker; =ſonne f, ast. mock sun, ⚔ parhelion, anthelion; =ſpeſen f/pl. = =koſten; ⚣ſtehend standing by, annexed; (am Rande) marginal; in 2em on the (⚥ as per) margin; das ~e ⑥ the note on the margin; =ſtrang ☛ m side-rail or -track; =ſtraße f adjacent street, by-street; =ſtrom ⊕ m, tel. induced current; =tiſch m side-table; =titel m additional title, subtitle; =ton m: a) ♪ second; b) gr. secondary accent or stress; =treppe ⊕ f, arch. backstairs pl.; =tür(e) f side- (or neighbouring) door; =umſtand m accessory (circumstance) (minor) detail, bſd. Schrifttum: (minor) incident; =urſache f secondary (or incidental) cause; =verbienſte m/pl. incidental or casual earnings pl.; vgl. =einkünfte; =vormund m co-guardian, =vorteil m incidental advantage or gain; =wand ⊕ f, arch. side-wall; =weg m by-road or -path; =wind ⚓ m side-wind; =winkel m, math. adjacent angle; =wohner m neighbour; =wort n word of secondary importance; gr. adverb.; =zimmer n adjoining room, (fr.) boudoir; =zweck m subsidiary (or subordinate) aim or purpose.

neblicht, ...ig (⌐) f. nebelicht, ...ig.
nebst (´) [mhd.] *prp. mit dat.* besides, along (or together, conjointly) with; (noch hinzu) in addition to; added to.
nebst=bei (-´) *adv.* = nebenbei.
Nebukadnezar (---´-) *npr/m.* ⑮ ⑯ α. Alt.: Nebuchadnezzar, Nabuchodonosor, Nebuchadrezzar. [dressing-case.]
Necessaire (-ß-ä´r) [fr. Notwendiges] *n* ⑩
necken (⌐) [mhd.] **I** *v/a. u. v/recip.* ⑱ (sich ea. oder mit e-m) to tease (each other), to chaff (one another); heraus= fordernd: to rile, taunt, jeer, spottend: to mock, to quiz, F to chip; sie neckt gern she is fond of teasing, she's a (great) teaser. — **II** ~ *n* ㉓ = Neckerei.
Necker (⌐) *m* ㉒, ~in *f* ㊵ teaser, p. fond of chaff(ing); mocker, quiz(zer).
Neckerei (⌐-´´) *f* ㊻ (f. necken) teasing, chaff(ing), banter, raillery; taunt (-ing), jeering; mockery, quiz(zing).
neckisch (⌐) *a.* ⑯ 1. teasing, fond of chaffing or quizzing; (drollig) droll, comical; full of quips and pranks. — 2. (tückisch) malicious; full of taunts and jeers. [name,]
Neck=name (⁹-´-) *m* ㉒ (Spitzname) nick-]
Neffe (⌐) [ahd.] *m* ㉒ nephew (*fr.): lt. *nepos* Enkel] *m* ㉒ nephew. [negation.]
Negation (⌐-tß(´)´) [lt. Verneinung] *f* ㊻
negativ (⌐²⌐f) [lt. verneinend] (*ant.* positiv) **I** *a.* ⑯ *math., phys., phot.* negative; 2e Elektrizität negative (or resinous) electricity; der Pol negative pole. — **II** ~ *n* ⑩d., auch: ~*bild* (⌐...) *n* ⑫ *phot.* negative (proof or picture); ~*druck m* negative print(ing).
Neger (⌐) [fr. span.; *lt. niger* schwarz] *m* ㉒, ~in *f* ㊵ negro (*f* negress; *contp.* nigger, F blackie, darkie (*f* oft: negro woman, black woman), co. Sambo, bit of ebony; die ~ *pl.* the black (or coloured) population *sg.*; ²=artig(´...) *a.* ⑯negro-like; ~*aufseher m* ⑭negro-(Fnigger-)driver; ~*gitarre ♪ f* banjo; ~*handel* ⑳ *m* traffic with (or in) negroes, *a.* slave-trade; ~*hirse f* = Mohrenhirse; ~*knabe m*, ~*mädchen n* negro (F nigger) boy, girl; ~*rasse f* negro-race; ~*schiff ↓ n* slave-ship or -dhow; ~*sklave m* black slave; ~*tanz m* negro-dance.
negieren (⌐²⌐) [lt. verneinen] **I** *v/a.* ⑭ to deny. — **II** Regierung *f* ㊻ negation.
Negligé (-´gë´) [fr.] *n* ⑩ (loses Kleid) négligé, deshabille; undress, morning- garb (vgl. Hauskleid); ~*haube* (⌐...) *f* ⑫ lady's morning-cap.
nehmen (⌐) [ahd.] ⓐ *a.* **I** *v/a.* 1. to take (away); ⚔ to capture, carry; Dargebotenes: to receive, accept; (entwenden) to abstract, (fortschaffen) to remove, to carry away; (sich aneignen) to appropriate; ⚔e-e Stellung ⚔ to take (or capture) a position; mit Sturm ⚔ to (take by) storm. — 2. *mit s. als Objekt: eccl.* das Abendmahl ⚔ to receive the Holy Communion; f. Abrede 1, Abschied 2 u. 3, Anstand 3, Anstoß 4, Aufenthalt 2; die Bahn ⚔ to take the train, to go by rail or train; Sport: Hindernisse ⚔ (oder überspringen) to take a fence, to jump (or leap) over a ditch, &c.; vgl. Einsicht 2; ein Ende ⚔ to come to an end; ein ehrenvolles Ende ⚔ to die an honourable death; ⚔ wir den Fall, daß // let us assume (or suppose) //; f. Frau 2, Freiheit 1; e-m alle Hoffnung ⚔ to deprive a p. of all hope; f. Leben 3; sich die Mühe ⚔ to take the trouble; sie ⚔ sich beide nichts (they are worthy of (or a match to) each other; F das wird sich nichts ⚔ it's all the same; den Omnibus nach A. ⚔ to take the omnibus (or F to ride by bus) to A.; er läßt sich nichts von s-m Rechte ⚔ he won't have his rights encroached upon; f. Reißaus, Rücksicht, Schaden 2; Kartenspiel: e-n Stich ⚔ to make a trick; ⚔ Sie e-e Tasse Kaffee? will you have (or take) a cup of coffee?; Urlaub ⚔ to take a holiday; ⚔ to go on furlough; das nimmt mich w. nicht that astonishes me; er wollte sich nicht die Zeit ⚔ he would not give (or allow) himself the time; das lasse ich mir nicht ⚔ I won't be talked out of it. — 3. *mit prp.*: et. **an** sich ⚔: a) to take care of a th.; b) Gefundenes: to pocket a th.; e-n **an** seinen Tisch ⚔ to receive a p. at one's table; nehmt ein Exempel d(ar)an! let it serve you as an example!; eine Last **auf** die Schultern ⚔ to take a burden on one's shoulders; aufs Korn ⚔ to take aim at; et. **auf** sich ⚔ to undertake (to do) a th.; die Folgen **auf** sich ⚔ to (a)bide (or bear) the consequences; Geld **aus** s-r Börse ⚔ to take ... from one's purse; *fig.* e-m eine Bemerkung **aus** dem Munde ⚔ to take the words out of a p.'s mouth; *hort.* Pflanzen **aus** der Erde ⚔ to take (or dig, grub) ... out of the ground; e-n **aus** der Schule ⚔ to remove a p. from (a) school; e-n **beim** Kragen ⚔ to collar a p.; e-n **beim** Worte ⚔ to take a p. at his word; et. **für** ein günstiges Zeichen ⚔ (halten) to take (or consider) a th. as a good omen; ⚔ Sie es nicht **für** ungut, wenn // don't think it unkind (or be offended) if //; **in**: f. Acht am Schluß, Angriff 1, Anspruch, Arbeit 1, Augenschein, Empfang 2, Gebet 2; in die Hand ⚔ to take in hand; sieh Mitte 2, Obacht, Obhut; in Pacht ⚔ to (take on) lease; e-n in seinen Schutz ⚔ to take a p. under one's protection; et. **mit** Gewalt ⚔ to take a th. by main force; et. mit **nach** der Stadt ⚔ to take a th. to town (with one); et. **vom** Tische ⚔ to remove a th. from the table; **zur** Ehe ⚔ to take in marriage, to marry; e-n **zum** Gehilfen ⚔ to engage a p. as assistant; sich et. **zu** Herzen (ob. **zu** nahe) ⚔ to take a th. to heart; e-n **zu** sich (ins Haus) ⚔ to receive (or harbour) a p., ein Kind: to take charge of; Speise **zu** sich ⚔ to take food; er hat nichts **zu** sich genommen he has not eaten a morsel; sich **zum** Vorbilde ⚔ to take for a model. — 4. *mit a. und adv.*: f. buchstäblich; es ernst mit et. ⚔ to be in earnest about a th.; f. fest ⚔, fürlieb; im ganzen genommen taking it all round; f. gefangen, genau 1; leicht 3; wenn man's so ⚔ will if you take it in that light; et. streng ⚔ to take a th. in the strict sense of the word; streng genommen strictly speaking; den Mund recht voll ⚔ to talk very big; wie man's nimmt according as one takes it, F it (all) depends. — **II** ⚔ *v/refl.* 5. = sich aus=, be=nehmen. — **III** ~ *n* ㉓ 6.(f.1)taking; acceptance, acceptation; Sprichw. Geben ist seliger denn ~ it is more blessed to give than to receive.
Nehmer (⌐) *m* ㉒, ~in *f* ㊵ bsp. ⚭ buyer, purchaser (= Käufer, Käuferin).
Nehm=fall (´´-´) *m* ⑫ *gr.* Ablativ.
Nehrung ☿ (⌐) [ndd.] *f* ㊻ long and narrow tongue of land which separates a haff from the sea, Nehrung; Frische ~ Frische Nehrung.
Neid (´) [ahd.] *m* ⑩c. envy; (Mißgunst) jealousy; aus ~ gegen // from envy towards or of //; bei e-m ~ erregen to excite a p.'s envy; f. hegen 4; vor ~ vergehen to die (F to burst) with envy.
Neider (⌐) *m* ㉒, ~in *f* ㊵ envier, mehr gebr. envious (or jealous) person; Sprichw. besser ~ als Mitleider better (to be) envied than (to be) pitied.
neid=erfüllt (⌐´...) *a.* ⑯ filled with (or full of) envy; =*hammel m* ㉒, =*hart m* ⑩c. = Neider.
neidisch (⌐) *a.* ⑯: auf e-n, et. ⚔ sein to be envious (or jealous) of a p., a th.; er ist ⚔ auf unser Glück he is envious of (or he envies us) our good fortune, he (be)grudges us our luck; mit den Augen mit envious (or jealous, jaundiced) eyes.
neid=los (⌐´...) *a.* ⑯ free from envy, unenvious, ungrudging; =*nagel m* ⑫ agnail (= Niednagel).
Neige (⌐) [neigen] *f* ㊻ 1. (Verbeugung) bow. — 2. (Senkung) depression of the ground; auf der ~ on the slope, aslant, v. Fässern &c.: atilt. — 3. *fig.* (Abnahme) decline; (Ende) end; auf die (ob. zur) ~ geh(e)n to (be on the) decline, to run low, to draw to an end; es geht mit ihm auf die ~ he is in a bad way; ⚭ unser Lager geht auf die ~ we are running short (of stock). — 4. (Rest v. Flüssigkeiten): a) im Fasse: tiltings, dregs *pl.*; b) im Glase: heel-tap.
neigen (⌐) [ahd.] **I** *v/a.* to bend, to incline; (niederbeugen) to bow (down); ein Faß: to tilt; sein Ohr (zu) e-m ⚔ to lend an (*bibl.*, &c., *a.* to incline one's) ear to a p. — **II** sich ⚔ *v/refl.* to bend, to incline, v. e-r Ebene: to slope, to slant, *phys.* v. d. Magnetnadel: to dip; die Sonne, der Tag neigt sich (zum Abend) the sun goes down, the day is drawing to a close; der sich ⚔de Tag the departing day; sich vor e-m ⚔ to bow to a p., (e-n Knicks m.) to (drop a) curtsy to a p.; sich zum Ende (oder Untergange) ⚔ to (be on the) decline or wane. — **III** *v/n.* (h.) = **II**; *fig.* ⚔ to lean to; zur Schwindsucht ⚔ (Anlage h.) to incline to consumption; zum Trunke ⚔ (Hang h.) to have a liking (or propensity, weakness) for drink (vgl. geneigt 4).
Neigung (⌐) *f* ㊻ (f. neigen) 1. (geneigte Lage) zB. einer Fläche: incline, slope, slant, declivity, ⚔ gradient, ⚔ dip, hade; *phys.* ~ der Magnetnadel dip

♫ Musik; ⚙ Wissenschaft; ⚘ Pflanze; ⚱ Geographie; ⊙ Technik; ⚒ Bergbau; ⚔ Militär; ↓ Marine; ⚭ Handel; ✉ Post; 🚂 Eisenbahn.

[Neigungsebene] — 726 — [Nesthäkchen]

of the needle. — 2. (Verbeugung) bow, curtsy. — 3. (Vorliebe für) inclination, liking (or preference) for, leaning (or bias) towards; (Hang zu) propensity for, (Lust zu) taste for, (Streben nach) tendency towards; (Empfänglichkeit für) disposition to; er hat keine ~ dazu he has no bend (or is not bent) that way; ● die Preise haben ~ zum Fallen (Steigen) prices show a downward (an upward) tendency. — 4. (Wohlwollen gegen) good-will (or kind intention) towards, affection(ate regard) for; eine tiefe ~ für e-n fassen to take a strong liking for a p., to fall deeply in love with a p.

Neigungs-ebene (⁻ᵕ...), -fläche f ⓬ incline(d plane), slope; -kompaß m, -nadel f, phys. dipping-needle, inclination-compass, inclinatorium; -messer m: ⚹ clinometer; -winkel m, math. angle of inclination; ⚹ dip.

nein (¹) [ahd.] no(ne) nie ein] **I** adv. (ant. ja) no, bsp. ehm.: nay; aber ⚹!, but no!; ⚹ doch! indeed so!; ⚹ und abermals ⚹! a thousand times no!; bekräftigend: ⚹, das ist doch ein Jammer! well (stärker: upon my soul), that's wretched, indeed!; liest er? — ⚹! is he reading? — no, he is not!; haben Sie gerufen? — ⚹! have you called or did you call? — no, I have not or I did not!; mit ⚹, mit einem ~ antworten to reply in the negative; da sage ich nicht ⚹ I won't say nay, I won't refuse; das Ja und das ~ the yea and the nay; parl. die mit ja und ⚹ Stimmenden the ayes and the noes pl. — **II** ~ n ⓬ no, (Leugnung) denial.

Nein-sagen (⁻ᵕ⁻ᵕ) n ⓬ saying no, (Weigerung) refusal.

Nekrolog (ᵕᵕ⁻) [grch.] m ⓭ (Nachruf) obituary (notice), ⚹ necrology; ~schreiber (⁻....) m ⓬ writer of obituary notices, necrologist.

Nekromant (ᵕᵕ⁻) [grch.] m ⓬, ~in f ⓮ (Geisterbeschwörer[in]) necromancer; ~ie (ᵕᵕᵕ⁻) f ⓮ necromancy.

Nektar (⁻ᵕ) [grch.] m ⓭. = Göttertrank; ⚹isch (ᵕ⁻ᵕ), ⚹n a. ⓰ nectareous, ...an; ~ine (ᵕ⁻ᵕ) f ⓰ Pfirsich-abart: nectarine; ~ium ⚹ f (ᵕ⁻(ᵕ)ᵕ) n ⓯ (Honigdrüse) nectary, nectar-gland.

Nelke ⚹ (⁻ᵕ) [ndd. Nägelchen] f ⓬ 1. pink, carnation, gillyflower (Dia'nthus); rauhe ~ sweet William (Sile'ne Arme'ria ob. D. Arme'ria); vgl. Gartennelke. — 2. ● (Gewürznägelein) clove.

nelken-artig ⚹ (⁻ᵕ...) a. ⓰: ⚹ caryophyllaceous; -baumholz ⚹ n f ⓮ clove-tree wood (v. Caryophy'llus aroma'ticus); -beet n bed of pinks or carnations; -blüte ⚹ f clove-blossom; -öl ⚹ n (essential) oil of cloves; -pfeffer ⚹ m pimento, allspice, Jamaica pepper (von Pime'nta acris); -stock m, hort. pink (or gillyflower) plant; -wurz ⚹ f (echte ~ herb) bennet, avens (Geum urba'num).

neme-isch (ᵕ⁻ᵕ) a. ⓰ Nemean. [Gerechtigkeit) Nemesis.]

Nemesis (⁻ᵕᵕ) [grch.] npr/f. inv. (strafende

nennbar (⁻ᵕ) a. ⓰ namable, mentionable, denominable; nicht ⚹ unmentionable, inexpressible, unspeakable.

nennen (⁻ᵕ) [ahd.; *Name] **I** v/a. und sich ⚹ v/refl. ⓰b. 1. to name, to call, to denominate; Rennsport: ein Pferd ⚹ (fürs Rennen anmelden) to enter a horse (for a race); schimpfend: to nickname; f. Name 2; ein Kind nach dem Vater ⚹ to name (or call, christen) the child after the father; sich ⚹ 2 to be named or called; das nenne ich mir Spaß that's what I call fun, F there's fun for you. — 2. (anführen) to mention, to quote; (betiteln) to style, to term; er nennt sich Graf R. his name (or title) is Count R.; sich als Verfasser ⚹ to declare (or acknowledge) o.s. the author. — **II** ~ n ⓬ 3. = Nennung; das bloße ~ seines Namens the (mere) mention(ing) ...; Tennis: entry. — **III** ge-nannt p.p. u. a. ⓰ 4. Karl, ⚹ der Kühne Charles surnamed the Bold; der, die oben ~ the above-mentioned person. — 5. f. sogenannt. [ing.]

nennenswert (⁻ᵕ⁻ᵕ) a. ⓰ worth mention-

Nenner (⁻ᵕ) m ⓬ math. (ant. Zähler) denominator; (größter) gemeinschaftlicher ~ (greatest) common denominator.

Nenn-fall (⁻...) m ⓬ gr. = Nominativ; -form f Infinitivo.

nennte (⁻ᵕ) f subj. impf. v. nennen.

Nennung (⁻ᵕ) f ⓮ naming, &c. (f. nennen I); ohne ~ der Quelle without giving the source; Tennis, Rennsport: entry.

Nenn-wert (⁻...) m ⓬ nominal value; ● Börse: zum ~ at par; -wort n, gr. (Hauptwort) noun, substantive.

Neokom ⚹ (ᵕᵕ⁻) [(Neuenburg, Neuchâtel i. d. Schwz.)] n ⓭d. geol. lower greensand formation, ⚹ Neocomian.

Neolog, -e (ᵕᵕ⁻(ᵕ)) [grch.] m ⓬, ⚹ neologist; -ismus (ᵕᵕᵕ⁻ᵕ) m ⓭ (neuer Ausdruck) neologism. [Neotropical region.]

neotropisch (ᵕᵕ⁻ᵕ) a. ⓰: ⚹e Region

Nephrit ⚹ (ᵕ⁻) [gr.] m ⓭c. min. (Beilstein) nephrite, jade, kidney-stone.

Nepotismus ⚹ (ᵕᵕ⁻ᵕ) [it.] n ⓭ (Begünstigung von Verwandten) nepotism.

Neptun (ᵕ⁻) [lt.] npr/m. ⓭ γ. myth. (Meergott), ast. (Planet) Neptune; ⚹isch ⚹ (ᵕ⁻ᵕ) a. ⓰ Neptunian; ⚹isches Gestein Neptunian rocks pl.; ~ismus (ᵕ⁻ᵕ) m ⓭ (Lehre v. der Bildung der Erde durch Wasser; ant. Plutoni'smus) Neptunian theory; ~ist (ᵕ⁻) m ⓬ Neptunist; ⚹istisch (ᵕ⁻ᵕᵕ) a. ⓰ Neptunist; ~trabant (ᵕ⁻...) m ⓬ ast. satellite of Neptune.

Nere-ide (-ᵕ⁻ᵕ) [grch.] f ⓮ 1. myth. (Tochter des Nereus) Nereid. — 2. zo. ~n pl. (Meerwürmer) nereids (Nerei'dae).

neronisch (ᵕ⁻ᵕ) [Nero, röm. Kaiser, † 68 nach Chr.] a. ⓰ of Nero, Neronian.

Nerv (ᵕf) [nhd., *lt.] m ⓭ (pl. a. ⁻ᵕᵕ) 1. nerve; das fiel ihm auf die ~en that affected (F it got on) his nerves; an den ~en leiden to suffer from (or to be troubled with) the nerves; es hat sich bei ihr auf die ~en geschlagen she has it on her nerves; j. der starke ~en hat a p. of strong nerve; vgl. angreifen 4. — 2. ⚹ (Ader eines Blattes) vein(s pl.) of a leaf.

Nervchen (⁻ᵕ) [dim. v. Nerv] n ⓭ tiny nerve; dünnes ~ nervule.

Nerven-anfall (⁻ᵕ..., auch ⁻ᵕᵕ...) m ⓬ path. nervous fit; -aufregend a. ⓰ exciting the nerves; -aufregung f nervous excitement, irritation of the nerves; -beschreibung f: ⚹ neurography; -entzündung f, path.: ⚹ neuritis; -faser f, anat. nerve-fibre; -fieber n, path. nervous fever, ansteckendes: typhus; -geflecht, -gewebe n, anat.: nerve-tissue; -heil-anstalt f neurotic establishment; -knoten m, anat.: ⚹ ganglion; -krank a. neuropathic; -krankheit f, path. neurosis, neurotic (or nervous) disease; -kunde, -lehre f: ⚹ neurology; -leiden n nervous complaint or affection; -mittel n: ⚹ nervine, neurotic; -reiz m nervous irritation; -schlag-fluß m, path. apoplexy; -schmerz m, path.: ⚹ neuralgia; -schnitt m, anat.: ⚹ neurotomy; -schwach a. of weak nerves, nervous; -schwäche f nervous debility or prostration, nervousness, ⚹ neurasthenia; -stärkend a. strengthening the nerves, med.: ⚹ neurotic; ⚹es Mittel tonic, F pick-me-up; -system n nervous system; -tätigkeit f, physiol. nerve-function; -zentrum n, anat. nerve-centre; -zerrüttung f shattered (state of the) nerves; -zucken n nervous spasms or twitches pl.

nervicht, nervig (⁻ᵕ, ⁻ᵕ) a. ⓰ 1. nervous. — 2. fig. vigorous, strong, pithy, terse (style). — 3. ⚹ nerved, nervate.

nervös (ᵕ⁻) [fr.] a. ⓰ (D 10) path. nervous, excitable; e-n ⚹ machen to make a p. nervous or irritable, to fidget a p.; ⚹ sein to be nervous or troubled with the nerves, to have weak nerves; nervöser Zustand (auch: **Nervosität** (ᵕᵕ⁻ᵕ) f ⓮) nervous state, nervousness.

Nerz (ᵕ) [russ.] m ⓭a. zo. (Art Wiesel) mink (Puto'rius lutre'ola); ●-felle n/pl. minks.

Nessel ⚹ (⁻ᵕ) [ahd.: nettle] f ⓭ nettle (Urti'ca); taube ~ f. Taub-⚹; ⚹-artig ⚹ (⁻ᵕ...) a. ⓰: ⚹ urticaceous; ~-ausschlag m ⚹ ~-fieber; ~-brand m burning sensation produced by nettles; ~-faden m, ⚹ der Lappenquallen: nettle-thread; ~-falter m, ent. nettle-butterfly (Vane'ssa urti'cae); ~-fieber, ~-friesel n, ⚹ ~-sucht f, path. nettle-rash, ⚹ urticaria; ~-tuch ⚹ n nettle-cloth, (Musselin) muslin.

Nest (⁻) [ahd.: nest; lt. nīdûs] n ⓭b. 1. nest, großer Raubvögel: eyrie, aerie, ~er ausnehmen to go bird('s)-nesting; er fand das ~ leer he found the bird(s) flown; ein ~voll a nestful, a brood (fig. a. viele Kinder). — 2. F b.s. (erbärmliche Wohnung) (miserable) hole or den. — 3. F (Bett) bed; sich ins ~ legen to go to bed, F to go to roost.

Nest-bau (⁻ᵕ) m ⓭ building (of) nests.

Nestchen (⁻ᵕ) n ⓭ dim. little nest.

Nest-ei (⁻ᵕ) n ⓭ nest-egg.

Nestel (⁻ᵕ) f ⓮ (n ⓭) (Senkel zur Befestigung v. Kleidungsstücken) lace, string; ⚹n (⁻ᵕ) v/a. ⓰a. to lace (up), to fasten with a string; ~-nadel f bodkin; ~-stift m tag.

Nester-bau (ᵕᵕ⁻) [Nester, pl. v. Nest] m ⓬ building of nests, ⚹ nidification.

Nest-feder (⁻ᵕ...) f ⓮ down; -flüchter m (ant. -hocker) orn.: ⚹ autophagous bird, pl. a. (lt.) autophagi; -häkchen

---

Signs (see page XVII): F familiar; P vulgar; F flash; ⚹ rare; † obsolete (died); * new word (born); ✚ incorrect; ♪ music;

[Nesthocker] — 727 — [neulich]

n = ⸗küchlein; ⸗hocker m (ant. ⸗flüchter) orn.: ⚘ insessorial bird, pl. a. (lt.) insessores; ⸗küchlein n last (bird) of a brood, nest-chicken, F fig. youngest child, baby, pet (child).
Nestlein (⸗) n ⓚ = Nestchen.
Nestling (⸗) m ⓓd. young bird still in the nest, nestling; a. = Nesthäkchen.
nett (⸗) [nhd.,*fr.] a. ⓖ (zierlich) elegant, (sauber) neat, tidy, (hübsch) pretty, spruce; (gemütlich) jolly; das ist nicht 2 von ihm that's not nice of him, iro. Sie sind mir ein 2er Mensch, ein ~er you're a fine (or pretty) sort of fellow; ~heit (⸗), ~igkeit (⸗) f ⓖ elegance, neatness, tidiness, prettiness, spruceness; jollity.
netto ⓖ (⸗) [nhd., *it.] (rein, nach Abzug der Unkosten ꝛc.; ant. brutto) I adv. net, clear; Sie bekommen 2 zehn Mark you receive ... net. — II **Netto** n ⓖ — ⸗gewicht, ⸗preis.
Netto-betrag ⓖ (⸗...) m ⓖ net amount, clear balance; ⸗einnahme f, ⸗ertrag m net receipts, proceeds pl.; ⸗gewicht n net weight; ⸗gewinn m clear gain; ⸗preis m net price.
Netz (⸗) [ahd.: net] n ⓐa. 1. net, zum Fischen: fishing-net; hunt. toils pl.; ~ v. Eisenbahnen: railway-net, network of railways; ⊕ ~ von Fäden im astronomischen Fernrohr: ⚘ retic(u)le, v. Quadraten über e-r Zeichnung: ⚘ graticule; surv. trigonometrisches ~ trigonometrical survey, triangulation; anat. (Bauchfelleinstülpung) caul, ⚘ mesentery, omentum, epiploön. — 2. ein ~ aufstellen to spread (or put up) a net; ein ~ auswerfen to cast (out) one's net; ins ~ gehen to go into the net, v. Fischen ꝛc. a.: to be netted, fig. auch to be ensnared or entrapped; ins ~ locken to draw into one's net or toils, to entice, to decoy; e-m ein ~ stellen to lay a snare (or to spread one's toils, to set a trap) for a p.
Netz-arbeit (⸗...) f ⓖ netting; vgl. ⸗werk; ⸗artig a. ⓖ net-like, vgl. ⸗förmig; ⸗ballspiel n lawn-tennis; ⸗bruch m, path.: ⚘ epiplocele. [net.]
Netzchen (⸗) n ⓖ (dim. v. Netz) small)
Netz-druck (⸗...) m ⓖ Autotypie.
netzen¹ (⸗) [ahd.; *naß] v/a. ⓖ to wet.
netzen² (⸗) [Netz] v/a. ⓖ (netzartig stricken) to knit like a) net.
Netz-fischerei (⸗...) f ⓖ net-fishery, casting the net(s); ⸗flügler m/pl. ent. lace-fly neuroptera(ns) pl.; ⸗förmig a. ⓖ net-like, ⚘ reticular, reticulated; ⸗haut f, anat.: a) der Eingeweide: caul; vgl. Netz 1 am Schluß; b) des Auges: ⚘ retina; ⸗haut-entzündung f, path. im Auge: ⚘ retinitis; ⸗koralle f, zo.: ⚘ retepore; ⸗magen m, zo. der Wiederkäuer: honeycomb (stomach) (= Haube 5); ⸗nadel f netting-needle; ⸗punkt m, surv. station; ⸗spannung* f, elect. (electric) main; ⸗spiel n Tennis: net-play; ⸗spinne f, zo.: ⚘ retiary (spider), retilerian; ⸗steller(in f) m, hunt. one who spreads the toils or lays the snares; ⸗stricker(in f) m ⓖ net-knitter or -maker; ⸗strickmaschine ⊕ f netting machine; ⸗werk n network, netting; ⊕ arch. reticulated work, reticulation.

neu (⸗) [ahd.: new: lt. nŏv-: grch. nĕF] I a. ⓖ 1. (ant. alt) new; (2 erfunden, eingeführt) original, lately discovered, novel; ganz 2 brand-new, Sprichw. f. Besen 1; bibl. der ~e Bund the New Covenant or Testament; das 2e Jahr the new year; einem zum ~en Jahre (vgl. ⸗jahr) Glück wünschen to wish a p. a happy New Year; ⚥ ~e Hebriden New Hebrides pl.; ⚥ 2es Kapital fresh (or additional) capital; 2e Kräfte gewinnen to recover (or recruit) one's strength; f. Mode; ein 2er Rock a new coat; 2en Stiles of new style, f. n. St.; das ~e Testament (N. T.) the New Testament, the Gospel; 2e Unruhen further disturbances pl.; 2er Wein: a) (diesjähriger) new wine; b) (aus e-m frisch angestochenen Fasse) fresh tap; ⚥ die ~e Welt the New World; mir ist die Sache 2 I am new (or unused) to it; 2 machen to restore, to renovate; 2 (adv.) einkleiden to dress (up) afresh or anew. — 2. (vor kurzem geschehen) recent, (unserer Zeit angehörig) modern, (im Entstehen begriffen) rising; ein 2er Mensch a new man (auch theol.); die 2e(ste) Mode the latest fashion; 2en Mut schöpfen to take fresh courage; 2e Nachrichten f/pl. latest news or intelligence; 2ere Sprachen modern languages pl.; thea. 2es Stück fresh piece or play; in 2erer Zeit of late years, in recent (or modern) times. — II s. ⓖ 3. das ~e new (or fresh) thing, the latest; was gibt es ~es? what is the (latest) news? es gibt nichts ~es there is no news, there's nothing fresh or stirring; das ist mir et. (nichts) ~es that's s.th. (nothing) new to me; ⓖ et. ganz 2e, von 2em afresh, anew. — 4. ein ~er: a) = Neuling; b) (der Ankömmling) new comer or arrival; comp. die ~er(e)n (Modernen) the moderns, men of our own time, our contemporaries pl.; das ~(e)ste f-r Art the latest thing of its kind. — III adv. 5. (f. 1 und 3 am Schluß); (wieder) 2 erbauen to build afresh, to rebuild. — 6. (vor kurzem) lately, of late, recently; (neuerdings) latterly. — 7. 2(e)stens adv. quite lately or of late or recently; latterly.
Neu-angekommene(r) (⸗...) s. ⓖ newly (or recently) arrived; ⸗angeworbene(r) ⚔ m (fresh) recruit; ⸗anschaffung f von Möbeln ꝛc.: new purchase of furniture, &c.; 2aufgelegt a. ⓖ von Büchern: reissued, republished, reprinted; ⸗auflage f new edition, fresh issue; reprint; 2backen a.: a) new(ly baked), fresh; b) fig. new-fangled, lately introduced; ⸗bau m new construction, rebuilding, reconstruction; ⸗bauten m/pl. new buildings or premises pl.; 2bekehrt a., ~e([r] m) f new convert, ⚘ neophyte; ⸗bewaffnung f rearmament; ⸗bildung f new formation, reproduction; ⸗blau ⊕ n Wollfärberei: Saxon blue; ⸗braunschweig ⚥ npr/n. New Brunswick; ⸗bruch m, agr. virgin soil; ⸗buch n f. S. XXXIX; ⸗deutsch(e

Sprache f) a. modern German; ⸗druck ⊕ m eines Buches: reprint; ⸗england ⚥ n (Nord-osten der U.S.) New England; ⸗englisch a. u. n modern English; 2erbaut a. newly built.
neuerdings (⸗) [neu und Ding] adv. 1. latterly; recently, lately, of late. — 2. öft. (aufs neue) afresh, anew, again.
Neu(e)rer (⸗(⸗)⸗) [neu] m ⓖ, **Neu(e)rin** f ⊕ innovator; (Sprach⸗)~: ⚘ neologist.
neuerlich (⸗⸗) adv. lately, f. neu 6.
neuern (⸗) v/a. u. v/n. (h.) ⓖ a. to renovate; to make innovations.
Neu(e)rung (⸗(⸗)⸗) f ⓖ innovation; (Änderung) (recent) change, (Besserung) reform; daraus Entstandenes: a. novelty; sprachliche: neologism.
Neu(e)rungs-geist (⸗(⸗)⸗...) m ⓖ spirit of innovation; ⸗liebe, ⸗lust, ⸗sucht f passion (or mania) for innovation, modernism; 2lustig, 2süchtig a. ⓖ fond of (or bent on) innovation(s)
neuestens (⸗⸗) f. neu 7. [or change(s).]
Neu-fundland ⚥ (⸗.⸗.⸗) npr/n. ⓖa. (Insel in Britisch Nord-amerika) Newfoundland; ⸗fundländer m ⓖ: a) Newfoundlander; b) Hund: Newfoundland dog; 2gebacken (⸗...) a. ⓖ: a) = 2backen a.; b) fig. iro. (seit kurzem zu einer Würde erhoben) lately created; 2er Adel upstart (or mushroom) nobility; 2geboren a. new-born; sich wie 2 fühlen to feel like a new man or another being; ⸗geburt f ⓖ theol. new birth; 2gemacht a. renovated; 2geschaffen a. newly created; ⸗gestaltung f ⓖ reorganization, (Abänderung) modification; ⸗gier, ⸗gierde f curiosity, inquisitiveness; 2gierig a. curious, inquisitive; (vorwitzig) prying; e-n 2 m. to arouse a p.'s curiosity; 2 auf et. sein to be curious (or eager) to know a th.; ⸗grieche m modern Greek; 2griechisch a. modern Greek, neo-Greek, neo-Hellenic; ⸗guinea ⚥ n größte Insel Melanesiens: New Guinea.
Neuheit (⸗⸗) f ⓖ 1. newness, freshness, (Ursprünglichkeit) originality; (frisches Anbenken) recentness; (et. Neues) s.th. new, novelty, F thing of the day. — 2. ⓖ, ⊕ novelty, latest invention or fashion.
neu-hochdeutsch a. ⓖ (abbr. nhd.), ~(e) n ⓖ modern High German; ⸗holland ⚥ n (ehm. = Australien) New Holland.
Neuigkeit (⸗⸗) f ⓖ 1. (piece of) news; die ~ des Tages the news (or event) of the day; in Zeitungen: auswärtige ~en news from abroad, foreign items pl. — 2. ⓖ, ⊕ ‡‡ = Neuheit 2.
Neuigkeits-jäger (⸗⸗...) m ⓖ person who hunts for news, gossip, busybody; ⸗krämer(in f) m newsmonger.
Neu-jahr (⸗...) n ⓖ New Year('s Day) (f. neu 1); ⸗jahrs-abend m New Year's Eve; ⸗jahrs-brief m, etwa: New Year's card; ⸗jahrs-geschenk n New Year's gift; ⸗jahrs-tag m New Year's Day; ⸗jahrswunsch m good wishes pl. for the New Year; ⸗kaledonien ⚥ fr. Inseln im Stillen Ozean: New Caledonia; 2lateinisch a. neo-Latin, modern Latin.
neulich (⸗⸗) I a. ⓖ recent, late. — II adv. recently, lately, of late; the other day; 2 abends the other evening.

⚘ scientific; ⚘ botanical; ⚥ geography; ⊕ machinery; ⚒ mining; ⚔ military; ⚓ marine; ⓖ commercial; ✉ postal; 🚊 railway.

[Neuling] — 728 — [Nichtraucherabteil]

Neuling (⌣̄) m ⑪d. (auch von e-r Frau) novice at a th.; (new) beginner, new hand, tyro, F greenhorn.
Neu-lot ❂ (″…) n ⑫ decagram; ⁍modiſch a. ⑯ after the latest fashion, fashionable, new-fangled, F up to date; ⁍mond m new moon.
neun (⌣́) [ahd.: nine: lt. novem] I card. numb. (o. s. a.: 2e) nine; wir sind unser 2(e) there are nine of us; Kegelspiel: alle 2(e), eine ~, einen ~er ſchieben ob. werfen to throw all the ninepins; F alle 2e! (wenn j. Geſchirr zerſchlägt) there goes!, bang!; ⚹ Klaſſe der Pflanzen mit 2 Staubfäden: ⚘ enneandria. — II (die Zahl) ~ f ⑯ (number) nine.
Neun-auge (″…) n ㉖, f ⑱ ichth. river-lamprey (Petromy'zon fluvia'tilis); ⁍eck n ⑪c. math.: enneagon, nonagon; ⁍eckig a. ⑯ nine-angled, ⚘ enneagonal.
Neuner (⌣̄) m ㉒: a) one of nine (persons); b) (die Zahl 9) number nine; c) soldier of the niuth regiment.
neuner-lei (⌣̄) a. inv. of nine (different) kinds or sorts.
Neuner-probe (″⌣̄) f ⑫ arith. für e-e Multiplikation: casting out the nines, die ~ machen to cast out the nines.

neun-fach (″…) a. ⑯, ⁍fältig a. nine-fold; ⁍flach n ⑪d. math.: ⚘ ennea-hedron; ⁍flächig a. bounded by nine planes; ⁍hundert numer. a. nine hundred; ⁍hundertſte(r) a. u. s. nine-hundredth; ⁍jährig a. nine years old; ⁍jährlich a. (recurring) every nine years, ⚘ novennial; ⁍mal adv. nine times; ⁍malig a. done nine times; ⁍männig a. ⚘ enneandrian, …ous; ⁍monatlich a. of (or once in) nine months; ⁍ſchwänzig a. ſ. Katze 6; ⁍ſeitig a. geom. n.-sided; ⁍ſtündig a. of nine hours; ⁍tägig a. of nine days, nine days old; ⁍täglich a. every nine days; med.: ⚘ enneatic.
neunte (⌣̄) [ahd.] ord. numb. ⑯⑰ ninth; der 2 Januar (gſchr. 9. Januar) the ninth of January, January the ninth (gſchr. January 9th); ⁍halb (″⌣̄) a. inv. (= 8½) eight and a half; ~(⌣́) n ㉒, ㉑ a. inv. ninth (part); 2ns (⌣̄) adv. ninthly, in the ninth (9th) place.
Neun-töter (″…) m ⑫ orn. nine-killer (Enneo'ctonus collu'rio); ⁍undneunzigerm F co.(Apotheker)chemist; ⁍zahl/:⚘ennead.
neunzehn (⌣́) numer. I card. numb. inv. nineteen. — II (die Zahl) ~ f ⑯ (number) nineteen. — 2te (⌣̄) ord. numb. ⑰ nineteenth; ~tel n ㉒, 2tel a. inv. nineteenth (part); 2tens adv. in the nineteenth (19th) place.
neunzig (⌣̄) numer. I card. numb. inv. ninety; neunundz⚘ ninety-nine. — II (die Zahl) ~ f ⑯ (number) ninety.
Neunziger (⌣̄⌣) I m ㉒ 1. (a. ~in f ㊲) p. (over) ninety years old, nonagenarian. — 2. soldier of the ninetieth regiment. — II 2 a. inv. 3. in den 2er Jahren in the nineties (of last century).
neunzig-fach (″…) a. ⑯, ⁍fältig a. ninetyfold; ⁍jährig a. of ninety years, ninety years old; nonagenarian; ⁍jährige(r) s. ⑰ nonagenarian.
neunzigſte (⌣̄⌣) ord. numb. ⑰ ninetieth; das 2 Jahr erreichen to live to

(the age of) ninety; ~l n ㉒, ㉑ a. inv. ninetieth (part); 2ns adv. in the ninetieth (90th) place.
Neu-philolog(e) (″…) m ⑫ modern-language student; ⁍platoniker m Neoplatonist; ⁍platoniſch a. ⑯ Neo-platonic; neo-Platonic.
Neuralgie ⚘ (⌣⌣́) [grch.] f ⑱ path. (Nervenſchmerz) neuralgia; **neuralgiſch** (⌣⌣́) a. ⑯ neuralgic. [Nervenſchwäche.)
Neuraſthenie ⚘ (⌣⌣́) [grch.] f ⑱
Neurer, Neurung ſ. Neuerer, Neuerung.
Neu-ſatz ❂ (″…) m ⑫ typ. reset; ⁍ſcheffel ❂ m half a hectolitre; ⁍ſchottland ⚥ n Provinz von Kanada: Nova Scotia; ⁍ſee-land ⚥ n auſtral. Inſelgruppe: New Zea-land; ⁍ſeeländer m New Zealander; ⁍ſilber ❂ n German silver; ⁍ſprachler m = ⁍philolog; ⁍ſprachlich a. relating to modern languages; ⁍ſtadt f new (part of a) town.
neuſtens (⌣̄) ſ. neu 7.
Neuſtri-en ⚥ (⌣⌣⌣) npr/n. ⓥa. hist. weſtfränkiſches Reich, 6.—8. sae.: Neustria.
Neu-ſüd-wales ⚥ (″⌣̄″li) npr/n. inv. in Auſtralien: New South Wales.
neu-teſtamentlich (″⌣́⌣⌣̄) a. ⑯ of the New Testament.
neutral (⌣⌣́) [fr.] I a. ⑯ 1. neutral (auch pol., chm., phys., &c.); 2 bleiben to remain neutral, to observe neutral-ity. — 2. gr. (ſächlich) neuter. — II bſd. pol. ~e(r) m ㊶ 3. neutral party.
neutraliſieren (⌣⌣⌣̄) I v/a. ⑬ to neu-tralize (a. chm.). — II ~ n ㉓ u. **Neu-traliſierung** f ㊻ neutralization.
Neutralität (⌣⌣⌣́) [lt.] f ㊻ neutrality; ⁍s-erklärung f, pol. declaration of neutrality.
Neutrum (⌣̄⌣) [lt.] n ㉓㊴ (ſächliches) neuter noun or adjective or verb.
neu-vermählt (″⌣̄) a. ⑯ newly (or lately) married; ~e f ⑯ bride, ~e(r) m ⑰ bridegroom; die ~en the bridal couple, the newly married pair.
Neu-york ⚥ (⌣̄⌣) n ⓥa. New York; ⁍yorker (⁍in f) m, ⁍yorkiſch a. New Yorker.
Neu-zeit (″…) f ⑯ modern times pl.; ⁍zeitlich a. ⑯ of (or in) modern times, modern; ⁍zoll m centimetre. [Neva.)
Newa ⚥ (⌣̄⌣, ruſſ. ⌣⌣̄) npr/f. inv. (ruſſ. Fl.)
nhd. abbr. = neuhochdeutſch.
nicht (⌣́) [ahd.: nie=(Ge)wicht] I adv. 1. not; mit verſtärkenden Zuſätzen: auch 2 neither, not either, nor; wir auch 2 nor we either; gar 2 not at all; ganz und gar 2 not in the least; durchaus 2 by no means, on no ac-count; 2 eben, 2 viel scarcely (any); 2 doch: a) certainly not!; b) pray don't (trouble)!; 2 mehr no more, no longer; ſ. noch 2; nur 2 ängſtlich! never fear!; nur das 2! anything but that!; ſchlechterdings 2, ſicher(lich) 2 decidedly not, surely not; 2 wenig not a little; 2 wenige not a few; 2 weniger als ein Pfund no(t) less than a pound; 2 weniger als 200 no fewer than two hundred; wo 2 unless, if … not; ell. das 2 that's not the case, no such thing; 2 daß ich wüßte not that I know of; 2 daß mich das wun-derte not that it astonishes me; je nach der Stellung: 2 alle kamen not all came; alle kamen 2 not any (of them)

came. — 2. bei verbs: ſchreibt er 2? does he not write?, is he not writ-ing?; ich hatte es 2 I had it not, F I didn't have it, I hadn't (got) it; fürchtet euch 2! don't be afraid!, in geh. Spr.: be not afraid!, bibl. auch: fear not!; ſie ſah es 2, ich auch 2 she did not see it, neither (or no more) did I; er käme gern, wäre er nur 2 krank … if it were not for his illness, … but for his illness; er reiſt 2 mehr he has given up travelling; wir gingen 2 weiter we went no further, we did not go any further; es gibt keinen, der das 2 zugibt there is nobody but admits it; vgl. nur 3. — 3. 2 wahr? is it not so?, F isn't that so? = gelt!; er iſt hier, 2 wahr? he is here, is he not?; Sie treffen ihn 2 oft, 2 wahr? you don't often meet him, do you? — II ~ 4. als s. †: — ⁅s; nur in Verbindungen: ſ. mit 3; zunichte m. to annihilate; (zu-grunde richten) to ruin, destroy; (unwirk-ſam m.) to undo; (vereiteln) to frustrate, zunichte w. to come to nothing or to grief, to fall to the ground.
Nicht-achtung (″…) f ⑫ want of re-spect, disrespect; ⁍annahme f non-acceptance; ⁍anweſenheit f absence, fortgeſetzte: absenteeism; ⁍ausführung f non-performance; ⁍befolgung, ⁍be-obachtung f non-observance, (Vernach-läſſigung) neglect; ⁍bezahlung f non-payment, e-s Wechſels: dishonouring a bill; ⁍chriſt m non-Christian; pagan; ⁍duldung f intolerance.
Nichte (⌣́⌣) [ndd.] f ⑯ niece; Gatte der ~ nephew by marriage.
Nicht-erfolg (″…) m ⑫ = ⁍gelingen; ⁍erfüllung f non-fulfilment; ⁍erſchei-nen n non-appearance, absence, vor Gericht: non-attendance, default; ⁍fertig a. ⑯ unready; ⁍gelehrte(r) m unlearned (or unlettered) person; ⁍gelingen n want of success, failure; ⁍gewöhnung f want of habit, unac-customedness; ⁍haltung f: a) einer Sitzung: adjournment; b) = ⁍befolgung.
nichtig (⌣́⌣) [nicht] a. ⑯ unreal, (eitel) vain, frivolous; (nichtsſagend) futile, empty, hollow (excuse), flimsy (pre-text); (vergänglich) perishable, fleeting, transitory; (wirkungslos) ineffectual; (ungültig) invalid; (leer) void, empty; jur. null und 2 null and void; ſ. er-klären 3; null und 2 m. to quash, annul'l, to set aside; ~keit f ⑯ unre-ality; vanity; futility, flimsiness, perishableness; jur. nullity, voidness.
Nichtigkeits-beſchwerde (″⌣…) f ⑫, ⁍klage f plea of nullity; ⁍erklärung f annulment, nullification; jur. quash-ing a verdict, reversing a sentence.
Nicht-kenner (″…) m ⑫ non-connoisseur; ⁍kombattant ⚔ m non-combatant; ⁍leitend a. ⑯ elect. non-conducting, insulating; ⁍leiter m non-conductor, insulator; ⁍leuchtend a.non-luminous; ⁍metall n, chm. metalloid; ⁍militä'r m civilian; ⁍organiſiert a. ⑯: ⁍er Arbeiter non-unionist; ⁍raucher m non-smoker; ☜ Aufſchrift: für ~! smoking (is) not allowed!; ⁍raucher-abteil n compartment for non-smokers.

Zeichen (ſ. S. XVII): F familiär, P Volksſprache, ⌐ Gaunerſprache; ⧵ ſelten; † alt (auch geſtorben); * neu (auch geboren); ⫶⫶ unrichtig;

[nichts] — 729 — [Niederlage]

nichts¹ (ˢ) [nhd.; *nicht] I indef. pron., inv. (ant. etwas) 1. nothing, nought, not any(thing); ⁂ Näheres no particulars pl., no detailed information; ⁂ Neues nothing new; er sagte ⁂ he said nothing, he did not say anything; mit verstärkenden Zusätzen: ⁂ (an)d(e)res als nothing but; ⁂ and(e)res nothing else; ⁂ mehr no(thing) more, not any more; fast gar ⁂ hardly anything; (ganz und) gar ⁂ nothing at all, nothing whatever; sonst ⁂? nothing else?; iro. (wouldn't you like) anything else?; so viel wie ⁂ next to nothing; um (ob. für) ⁂ und wieder ⁂ for nothing, without any reason; weiter ⁂ n. further; weiter ⁂? is that all?; ⁂ weniger als das anything but that; ⁂ da! nothing of the kind!; ⁂ davon! don't talk about it! (f. mir 2). — 2. ⁂ ahnend without any foreboding(s), unsuspecting; f. dafür 5; es ist ⁂ damit there is nothing in it; vgl. damit 2; das ist ⁂ für mich that's of no use to me, it's not in my line; hier ist ⁂ zu lachen it's nothing to laugh at; ⁂ wert (oder nutz) sein ... of no value or use; es wird ⁂ daraus nothing will come of it; zu ⁂ w. to come to nought, to fail; wenn es weiter ⁂ ist if that be (or is) all (f. anfangen 2, machen 4). — II ~ n, inv. (f. Nichts²) auch mit art. (pl. bisw. Nichtse) 3. (das Nichtsein) nothingness, phls. (ant. Etwas): ⁂ nonentity; (Leere) void; er hat ihn aus dem ~ hervorgezogen he raised him from a mere nothing or from utter obscurity. — 4. (Geringfügigkeit) insignificance; (Wertlosigkeit) uselessness; in seines ~ durchbohrendem Gefühle (SCH.) in the crushing knowledge of his nothingness. — 5. (bloße Einbildung) mere shadow or fancy or phantom; (etwas Geringes) a (mere) nothing, a trifle; Sprichw. aus ~ wird ~ from nothing nothing comes, f. Kaiser 2, Lärm 1.

Nichts² (ˢ) [(P)grch. (o)nychī'tis] n, a. m, inv., chm. weißes ~ (flockiges Zinkoxyd) zinc-flowers pl., ⁂ (lt.) nihilum album.

nichts¹-bedeutend (ˢ...) a. ⓖ insignificant; ⁂**desto-minder**, **-weniger** adv. nevertheless, notwithstanding; despite (or of) that; [ity; vgl. nichts¹3].

Nicht-fein (ˢ,¹) n⑫ non-existence; null-

Nichts-nutz (ˢ...) m ⓐ a.good-for-nothing, of no use; ⁂**nutz(ig)** a. ⓖ, ⁂**nützig** a. naughty, wicked; ⁂**er Mensch** good-for-nothing (fellow), scamp; **-nutzigkeit** f naughtiness; wickedness; ⁂**sagend** a. insignificant, meaningless, futile; (farblos) colourless; **-tuer(in** f) m idle person, idler; **-tuerei** f idleness, inactivity; **-tuerisch** a. idle, inactive; **-wisser** m ignorant person, F ignoramus; ⁂**würdig** a. worthless, futile, (niederträchtig) base, vile, contemptible, infamous, villainous; ⁂**er Mensch, ~e(r)** m ⓔ villain, wretch; **-würdigkeit** f worthlessness, futility, baseness, vileness, contemptibleness, villainy.

Nicht-teilnahme (ˢ...) f⑫ non-participation; lack of sympathy; **-verantwortlichkeit** f irresponsibility; **-verbind-**

lichkeit f immunity (from an(y) obligation); **-verbotensein** n permissibleness; **-vollziehung** f non-execution; **-vorhandensein** n: a) absence, (utter) lack; b) phls. non-existence; **-wissen** n ignorance; **-wollen** n unwillingness; **-zahlung** f non-payment; **-zulassung** f non-admission.

Nick (ˢ) m ⓐ b. nod(ding of the head).

Nickel¹ (ˢ˯) m ⑫ (dim. von Nikolaus) Nicholas; auch n ⑫ contp. (gemeiner Mensch) low (or mean, nasty, contemptible) fellow, cad; auch = Knirps.

Nickel² (ˢ˯) [schwd.] ⑫ 1. m u. n, min., chm. nickel (Ni); mit ~ bekleidet nickel-cased or -mounted ⓖ mit ~ plattiert nickel-plated. — 2. m, num. nickel (coin), (10-Pf.-Stück) nickel penny.

Nickel²-blüte (ˢ˯...) f ⓐ min. Nickel-bloom, arseniate of nickel; **-chlorür** n, chm. nickelous chloride (NiCl₂); **-glanz** m nickel-glance (Ni S₂ Ni (As₂); **-haltig** a. ⓖ nickelic, nickel(iferous; **-hydroxydul** n nickel-hydrate (H₂ Ni O₂); **-münze** f nickel coin; **-oxydul** n nickelous oxide (NiO); **-oxydulsalz** n nickelous salt; **-platierung** f nickel-plating; **-stahl** ⓖ m für Schiffspanzer ꝛc.: nickel steel; **-sulfür** n, chm. nickelous sulphide (Ni S).

nicken (ˢ˯) [ahd.; *neigen] ⓐⓐ I v/n. (h.) 1. v. lebenden Wesen: to nod (one's head); als Gruß: to bow, als Wink: to beckon; aus Müdigkeit: to drop one's head, (einschlummern) to drop off to sleep, F to (have a) snooze. — 2. von leblosen Dingen: to droop; (baumeln) to dangle; ⁂ ⁂: ⁂ nutant. — II ~ n ⑫ 3. (f. 1) nod(ding), bow(ing); (Schläfchen) F nap, forty winks pl.

Nicker (ˢ˯) m ⑫ nodder; **-chen**, **-lein** n ⑫ F (Schläfchen) nap, snooze.

Nickhaut (ˢ...) f ⑫: ⁂ nictitating membrane; **-krampf** m nodding spasm.

nie (ˡ) [ahd. nie-je] adv. never, at no time; fast ⁂ hardly ever; ⁂ und nimmer(mehr) never (to the end of one's days), never more; ich habe ⁂ in meinem Leben so etwas gesehen I have never in (all) my life seen (türger: I never saw) anything like it.

Nie-besessene(s) (ˢ˯...) n ⓔ s.th. never (previously) possessed or owned.

nieder (¹˯) [ahd.: nether] I a. ⓐ (D9) fast nur attributivisch gebr. 1. low; (unedel) base; (gemein) common, vulgar; von ⁂er Geburt of mean (or low) birth or descent, low-born, of humble origin; ⁂e Jagd shooting (of) small game. — II als s. ⓐ 2. ein ~er a low fellow; Hohe und ~e, hoch und ⁂ high and low. — III adv. 3. low (down); f. auf 11; als Ausruf: ⁂ mit den Verrätern! down with the traitors! — 4. ⁂ ell. das Haus ist ⁂(gebrannt) ... is burnt(down) to the ground. [Alps pl.]

Nieder-alpen ⁂ (¹¹˯ˡ˯) pl. ⓐ lower]

nieder-beugen (¹¹˯...) v/a. ⓐ⁑⁑: a) to bend (or bow) down; b) fig. j-s Mut ⁂ to damp a person's courage, to discourage a p.; ⁂**biegen** v/a. ⓐ⁑⁑ to turn down; ⁂**blicken** v/n. (h.) ⓐ⁑⁑ to look (or glance) down; ⁂**brechen** ⓐa⁑⁑ v/n. (sn) to fall down; v/a. to

pull (or pluck) down; ⁂**brennen** ⓐb⁑⁑ v/n. (sn) to burn (or to be burnt) down, von Häusern auch: to be destroyed by fire; v/a. to burn down; ⁂**bringen** v/a. ⓐ⁑⁑ to bring a p. to the ground, F to floor a p.; ⁂**brüllen** v/a. ⓐ⁑⁑ to howl down; ⁂**bücken** v/a. und sich ⁂ v/refl. ⓐ⁑⁑ to bow down, v/refl., auch: to stoop down; ⁂**deutsch** a. ⓐ, ⁂**e** (Sprache) Low German; **-deutsche(r)** s. ⓐ North German; **-deutschland** n ⑫ Lower (or North) Germany; ⁂**donnern** ⓐa⁑⁑: v/n. (h.) to come down with a crash; v/a. fig. to talk down; ⁂**drehen** v/a. ⓐ⁑⁑ die Lampe ꝛc.: to turn down, elektrisches Licht: to switch off; ~ n ⑫ des Dochtes the turning down of the wick; **-druck** ⓐ m, mach. low-pressure; **-druck-dampf** ⓐ m low-pressure steam; ⁂**drücken** v/a. ⓐ⁑⁑: a) to weigh down; to depress (a. ⓐ v. Preisen); b) fig. den Geist ⁂ to weigh on (or oppress) the mind, (tief betrümmern) to grieve; **-druck-kessel** ⓐ m low-pressure boiler; **-druck-maschine** ⓐ f Dampfm.: low-pressure engine; ⁂**drückung** f depression; ⁂**fahren** ⓐb⁑⁑ v/n. (sn): a) to drive down in a carriage, &c.; b) to shoot down; ⁂**gefahren zur Hölle** descended into hell; ~ n, ⁂**fahrt** f descent; **-fall** m down-fall; ⁂**fallen** v/n. (sn) ⓐa⁑⁑ to fall (or drop) down or to the ground; vor e-m (auf die Knie) ⁂ to fall (or to throw o.s.) at a p.'s feet; **-gang** m: a) going down; b) der Gestirne: setting; c) (Westen) West; d) ⓐ mach. des Kolbens: down-stroke; e) fig. decline; ⁂**gebrochen**, p.p. v. ⁂**brechen** u. a. ⓐ (D9) broken-down; ⁂**gedrückt** a. ⓐ depressed, dejected; **~heit** f depression; ⁂**geh(e)n** v/n. (sn) ⓐ⁑⁑ to go down; (abnehmen) to subside; über dem Dorfe ging ein heftiges Gewitter nieder a violent thunderstorm burst (or broke) over the village; ⁂**gehockt** p.p. = ⁂**hockend**; ⁂**geschlagen** f. ⁂**schlagen**; **-geschlagenheit** f dejection, despondency; (Mutlosigkeit) low spirits pl.; ⁂**halten** v/a. ⓐa⁑⁑: a) to keep down or under; b) fig. to curb (or suppress) a rebellion, &c.; ⁂**hangen**, P ⁂**hängen** v/n. (h.) ⓐb⁑⁑ to hang down, to droop; ⁂**hauen** v/a. ⓐc⁑⁑ to hew (or knock) down, to lay low, ⁂ auch: to cut (or mow) down; ⁂**hocken** v/n. (sn) und sich ⁂ v/refl. ⓐ⁑⁑ to cower down; ⁂**hockend** p.pr. crouching (down); ⁂**holen** ↓ v/a. ⓐ⁑⁑ to haul down; **-holz** n, for. underwood, brush-wood, copse; ⁂**kämpfen** v/a. ⓐ⁑⁑ to subdue, f-e Leidenschaften: to master, to get the better of; ⁂**klappen** v/a. ⓐ⁑⁑ to turn down; ⁂**knien** v n. (sn) u. sich ⁂ v/refl. ⓐ⁑⁑ to kneel down; ⁂**kommen** v/n. (sn) ⓐ⁑⁑: a) to come down, to descend; b) v. Frauen: to be confined; mit Zwillingen ⁂ to be confined (or delivered) of twins; **-kunft** f ⓐ⑩: a) ⁂ descent; b) confinement, child-bed or -birth, zu frühe: miscarriage; **-lage** f: a) depositing; warehousing; (Deponiertes) deposit; b) ⓐ Ort: depository, re-

♪ Musik; ⁂ Wissenschaft; ♀ Pflanze; ♀ Geographie; ⓐ Technik; ⚒ Bergbau; ⚔ Militär; ↓ Marine; ⓔ Handel; ⁂ Post; 🚂 Eisenbahn.

[Niederlagsgebühr] — 730 — [niesen]

pository; warehouse, storehouse; c) ❋ (Nebengeschäft) branch establishment of a firm; d) ✕ defeat, discomfiture; eine schwere ~ erleiden to sustain (or suffer) a crushing defeat; (wilde Flucht) rout; =lags=gebühr f fee for warehousing, warehouse-rent; die =lande ⚥ pl. the Low Countries, the Netherlands pl.; =länder(in f) m Dutch(wo)man; =ländisch a. Dutch; lassen ⓐa** v/a. to let down, to lower; sich v/refl.: a) to settle (von Vögeln: to perch) down, to alight; b) (sich setzen) to sit down; c) (f-n Wohnsitz nehmen) to take up one's domicile, to establish (or locate) o.s.; =lassung f lowering; (das Sichniederlassen) domiciliation, establishment; (Ort der Niederlassung) settlement, v. Ansiedlern: colony; =lassungs=recht n right of domicile; =lausitz ⚥ f Lower Lusatia; legen ⓑ** v/a.: a) to lay (or put) down, ein Kind: to put ... to bed; sich v/refl.: a) to go to bed, to lie down (to rest); b) (hinterlegen) to deposit (auch ❋ von Geld); ❋ Waren im Speicher to warehouse goods; c) sein Amt to resign one's office, ein Geschäft: to retire from business; die Krone: to give up the crown, to abdicate (the throne); ✕ die Waffen to lay down arms; ~ n, =legung f laying down, depositing; resignation, retirement, abdication; liegend ⚥ a.: ⚶ decumbent; machen v/a. ⓑ**: a) to scold; b) (fällen) to cut down; c) = metzeln; metzeln v/a. ⓐa** to massacre, butcher, slaughter; ~ n, =metz(e)lung f massacre, slaughter; =österreich ⚥ npr/n. Lower Austria; reißen ⓐa** v/a. to tear down, Gebäude ꝛc.: to pull down, to demolish, ✕ to raze, to dismantle; =reißung f pulling down, demolition; reiten v/a. ⓑb** to ride down; rennen v/a. ⓑb** to run down; =rhein m Lower Rhine; rheinisch a. of the Lower Rhine; ringen v/a. ⓐi** to force down, to overpower; rollen v/n. (fn) ⓑb** to roll down; thea.: der Vorhang rollt nieder the curtain drops; säbeln ✕ v/a. ⓐa** to sabre, to mow down with the sword; =sachsen ⚥ npr/n. Lower Saxony; schießen ⓒ(e)ft** v/n. (fn) to shoot (or rush) down; v/a. to shoot down, to knock down by a shot or in shooting; =schlag m: a) ♩ beim Tafte: thesis; b) chm. (Bodensatz) precipitate, sediment; c) feuchte =schläge precipitations pl. (of the atmosphere); schlagen ⓑb** v/n. (fn): chm. (aus e-r Flüssigkeit zu Boden fallen) to precipitate, to settle down; v/a.: a) die Augen (senken) to cast down one's eyes; b) Bäume (fällen) to fell (or cut down) trees; ein to knock a p. down, to lay him low; c) Wallungen des Blutes (beruhigen) to calm down ...; med. d refrigerant; d) (aufhören m.) to suppress (or quell) a rising, &c.; e-e Untersuchung: to quash (or stop) proceedings; e) (bekümmern) to depress, afflict, aggrieve, grieve; j-s Mut to discourage (or

dishearten) a p.; f) chm. e-n Körper aus e-r Flüssigkeit to precipitate ...; geschlagen p.p. u. a.: a) in den Bed. des inf.; b) bsd. zu e: depressed, dejected, cast down, low-spirited; ~ n, =schlagung f felling of trees, suppression of a rising, quashing of a lawsuit; chm. precipitation; =schlags=gefäß n, =schlags=kessel m ⊙ chm. precipitation-vessel, -pan; schlucken v/a. ⓑ** to swallow (down); schmettern v/a. ⓐa** to dash to the ground; de Worte crushing ...; schreiben v/a. ⓑ* to write down, to put (or take) down in writing; to pen; schreien v/a. ⓑ** to shout down; =schrift f writing down, (Geschriebenes) writing, copy; senken ⓑ** v/a. to let down; (niedriger m.) to lower; sich v/refl. to sink down; die Nacht senkt sich nieder ... is falling or setting in; setzen v/a. u. sich v/refl. ⓑ**: a) to set down, to deposit; sich to sit down, von Vögeln a. to perch down; b) thea. ! (wenn die Vorderen aufstehen) sit down!, c) fig. sich zwischen zwei Stühle to sit between two chairs; sinken v/n. (fn) ⓑft** to sink (or go) down, im Wasser a. to go to the bottom; sie sank erschöpft nieder she dropped down exhausted; sitzen ⓐ** v/n. (h. und fn) to sit down; v/a. to flatten a th. by sitting on it; spülen v/a. ⓑ** to wash down. niederste (ᴸ⌣⌣) [sup. v. nieder] a. ⓐ nethermost, lowest.
nieder=stechen (ᴵᴵ⌣...) v/a. ⓐa** to cut down with a sword, to stab; steigen v/n.(fn) ⓑ** to step down, to descend; ⊙ de Bewegung e-r Pumpe ꝛc.: downstroke; ~ n ⓐ descent; stoßen ⓐa** v/a.: a) to knock (or push) down; b) = stechen; v/n. (fn): auf et. to pounce down upon a th.; strecken v/a. und sich v/refl. ⓑ**: a) (sich) to stretch (o.s.) on the ground; b) = hauen; stürzen ⓐ** v/n. (fn) to have a heavy fall, to tumble (down) v/a. = to hurl down; =tracht f =trächtigkeit; trächtig v/a. vile, base, mean; eine e Geschichte an infamous affair; =trächtigkeit f vileness, baseness, infamy; als Handlung: villainous (or mean) act, villainy; treten v/a. ⓐd** to tread under foot, to trample down; seine Schuhe hinten to run down one's heels; tropfen v/n. (fn) ⓑ** to drip (or trickle) down. Niederung (ᴸ⌣⌣) f ⓐ low country or ground, lowland, plain, flat country. Nieder=wald (ᴵᴵ⌣...) m ⓑ: a) = =holz; b) npr. ⚥ am Rhein-ufer: Niederwald; wärts adv. down(wards); werfen v/a. und sich v/refl. ⓑb**: (sich) to throw (o.s.) down; e-n Aufstand: to put down ...; sich vor e-m stehend to throw o.s. at a p.'s feet, to prostrate o.s. before a p.; =werfung f overthrow, eines Aufstandes: suppression; ziehen v/a. ⓑb** to draw (or pull) down; (niedriger m.) to lower. niedlich (ᴸ⌣) [mhd.] a. ⓐ neat, nice, (zierlich) elegant, (anmutig) graceful; (hübsch) pretty; F iro. das ist ja ! that's

a pretty state of things!; ~keit f ⓐ neatness, nicety; elegance; prettiness. Nied=nagel (ᴵᴵ⌣) m ⓐ agnail, hangnail. niedrig (ᴸ⌣) [nieder] I a. ⓐ 1. low, von Stand auch: lowly, humble, obscure, (gemein) base, vulgar, mean; (verworfen) abject; er lower; bsd. nach Range nach: inferior. — 2. adv. er hängen, setzen, stellen to hang, set, place lower (down); sitzen to sit low or on a low chair, to have a low seat; spielen to play for small (or low) stakes; ♩ er singen to pitch lower; fig. gesinnt low-minded. — 3. ❋ e Preise stellen oder berechnen to ask moderate ...; zu erem Preise at a lower (or reduced) ...; zum sten Preise at the lowest (or F bottom) price or rate; die Kurse gingen er (adv.) prices went down or fell or receded or dropped. — II ein ~er m ⓐ 4. a person of mean birth or low station; Hohe und ~e, hoch und high and low, rich and poor. Niedrigkeit (ᴸ⌣⌣) f ⓐ (s. niedrig) low(li)ness, der Geburt a. humbleness of origin; der Gesinnung: baseness, vulgarity; ❋ ~ der Preise: lowness, moderateness, depression. ni=ellieren ⊙ (⌣⌣ᴸ⌣) v/a. ⓐ Goldarbeit: to niello; Ni=ello (⌣ᴸ⌣) [it. schwärzlich] n ⓐⓑ(ⓢ) niello-engraving or -work; Ni=ello=schmelz m ⓐ niello-enamel. niemals (ᴸ⌣) adv. = nie; Sprichw. besser spät als better late than never. niemand (ᴸ⌣) [ahd. nie + Mann] indef. pron. m ⓐA2a. (dat. u. acc. ß inv.) nobody, no one, none, no(t a single) person; F not a soul; als none (or no one) but; anders nobody (or no one) else; ausgenommen no one excepted, without (a single) exception; da? anybody there?; Fremdes no stranger; bei Versteigerungen mehr? no other (or higher) bid? Niere(ᴸ⌣)[ahd.: (kid)ney; grch. nephrōs] f ⓐ anat. kidney; Kochkunst: ~n kidneys pl.; bibl. (Psalm 7,10) Gott prüft die Herzen und ~en God trieth the hearts and reins; F fig. das geht ihm an die ~en it touches him very near, cuts him to the quick. Nieren=beschwerde (ᴵᴵ⌣...) f ⓐ path. kidney complaint, vgl. =krankheit; =braten m Schlächterei: loin of veal, &c.; =bruch m, path.: ⚶ nephrocele; =entzündung f, path.: ⚶ nephritis; =fett n = =talg; förmig a. ⓐ kidney-shaped, ⚶ reniform, renal; =grieß n f. Grieß 3; =kartoffel f kidney (-potato); krank a. suffering from the kidneys; =krankheit f, =leiden n, path. disease of the kidneys, ⚶ nephritic (or renal) disorder or complaint; =schmerz m, path. pain in the kidneys, ⚶ nephralgia; =stein m, path. stone in the kidneys; =stück n = =braten; =talg m kidney-suet; weise ✕ adv. in nodules, in pockets. nierig ✕ (ᴸ⌣) a. ⓐ = nierenweise. Niese=... (ᴵᴵ⌣...) in Zssgn = Nies=... niesen (ᴸ⌣) [ahd.] I v/n.(h.) ⓐ to sneeze. — II ~ n ⓐ sneezing, ⚶sternutation, ~ erregend: ⚶ sternutatory, ptarmic.

Nies-holz ⚕ (⸗...) n ⓶ sneezewood (*Ptaero'xylon u'tile*); =**mittel** n:⚕ sternutatory; =**pulver** n sneezing-powder.
Nieß-brauch (⸗...) [(ge)nießen] m ⓶ bsd. jur. usufruct; reversion (for life); =**braucher(in** f ⓱) m ⓶ = =**nutzer(in)**; =**brauchs-recht** n right of usufruct; =**nutzer(in** f) m usufructuary.
Nies-wurz ⚕ (⸗ᴗ) f ⓶ hellebore (*Helle'borus*); schwarze ~ Christmas-rose (*H. niger*).
Niet ⊕ (⸗) [mhd.; *nieten] n (m) ⓰c. rivet; (Vernietung) clinch; (Bolzen) pin.
Niet-bank (⸗...) f ⓶, =**blech** n riveting-bench, -plate; =**bolzen** m clinch-bolt.
Niete (⸗ᴗ) [ndl. nichts] f ⓲ Lotterie: (Fehllos) blank. [clinch.]
nieten ⊕ (⸗ᴗ) [ahd.] v/a. ⓺⓺ to rivet, to]
Niet-hammer (⸗...) m ⓶, =**kluppe** f riveting-hammer, -clamp; =**keil** m rivet-pin; =**nagel** m: a) rivet; b) ++ = Niednagel.
niet- und nagel-fest (⸗ᴗ⸗ᴗ⸗) a. ⓺⓺ (clinched and) riveted; nailed (or made) fast, solid (ly fixed), (as) firm as a rock.
Nietung (⸗ᴗ) f ⓲ (s. nieten) riveting.
Niftel (⸗ᴗ) f ⓲ obb. = Nichte.
Nigriti-en ⚕ (⸗ᴸtʃ(ᴗ)⸗)[lt. s. Neger] npr/n. ⓶α. (Land in Nord-afrika) Nigeria.
Nihilismus ⚕ (⸗⸗⸗ᴸ⸗) [lt.] m ⓶ phls. (Ansicht, daß alles zu nichts führe) nihilism.
Nihilist(in f ⓱) m ⓶ nihilist; **nihilistisch** a. ⓺⓺ nihilistic.
Nikobaren ⚕ (⸗ᴗᴸᴗ) [sft. 9 Inseln] npr/f/pl. ⓶α. (britische Inselgruppe im Bengalischen Meerbusen) Nicobar Islands pl.
Nikodemus (⸗ᴗᴸᴗ) [grch.] npr/m. ⓰γ. bibl. (Pharisäer u. Verehrer Jesu) Nicodemus.
Nikola(u)s (⸗ᴸᴗᴗ) [grch.] npr/m. ⓰γ. (Vn.) Nicholas. Sankt ~ Santa Claus.
Nikotin ⚕ (⸗ᴗᴸ) [Jean Nicot † 1600, Einführer des Tabaks in Frankreich] n ⓺d. chm. (Alkaloid b. Tabaks) nicotin(e) ($C_{10}H_{14}N_2$); mit ~ sättigen, vergiften to nicotinize; =**frei** (⸗ᴗ⸗) a. ⓺⓺ free from nicotine; =**säure** f ⓶ nicotinic acid ($C_5H_4N[CO_2H]$); =**vergiftung** f nicotine-poisoning, ⚕ nicotinism.
Nil ⚕ (⸗) npr/m. ⓰⓰α.: der ~ Strom Ägyptens) the Nile; zum ~ gehörig Nilotic; =**delta** (⸗...) n ⓶ delta of the Nile; =**flut** f Nile flood.
Nilgau (⸗⸗) [perf.] n ⓹ zo. (große indische Antilope) nilgau (*Portax pictus*).
Nil-messer (⸗ᴸ⸗ᴗ) m ⓶ nilometre; weitS. (selbsttätiger Flußhöhenmesser) nilometer.
nilotisch ⚕ (⸗ᴸᴗ) a. ⓺⓺ Nilotic, of (or relating to) the Nile.
Nil-pferd (⸗...) n ⓹ zo.: hippopotamus; =**pferd-peitsche** f Südafr.: sjambok; =**strom** m ⚕ = Nil.
Nimbus (⸗ᴗ) [lt., *grch.] m ⓰ paint. (Heiligenschein) nimbus, aureole, halo, glory; *fig.* (Vorrang) prestige; (Ansehen) authority; von e-m strahlenden ~ umgeben surrounded by a brilliant halo.
nimm (⸗) *imper.* von nehmen.
nimmer (⸗ᴗ) [ahd. nie mehr] adv. 1. = nie. – 2. starke Verneinung: nun und ⚕(=mehr) by no means, not at all, nowise; feierlich: nevermore.
nimmer=mehr (⸗ᴗ⸗ᴸ) adv. nevermore, F at the blue moon; vgl. nimmer 2; =**mehrs-tag** F(⸗ᴗ⸗ᴗ⸗) m ⓶: am ~e at the Greek Calends, when two Sundays come together; =**satt**: a) a. insatiable; b) m ⓰c. von Personen: ravenous person, glutton, P greedy-guts; =**wiedersehen** n: auf ~ never to meet again; farewell for ever!
nimmst, nimmt (⸗) pres. ind. v. nehmen.
Nimrod (⸗ᴗ) npr/m. ⓰⓰⓺⓺α. bibl. Nimrod (auch *fig.* ⓺d. nach 1. Mos. 10,9: großer Jäger). [Nimeguen.]
Nimwegen ⚕ (⸗ᴗ⸗) npr/n. ⓶α. (Holl. St.)]
Ninive ⚕ (⸗ᴗᴗ, ⸗ᴸf⸗) [assyr.] npr/n. ⓶α. Alt.: Hauptstadt Assyriens: Niniveh; **ninivitisch** (⸗ᴗᴸᴗ) a. ⓺⓺ Ninevitical.
Niob-säure ⚕ (⸗ᴗᴸᴗ) [Rio'bium] f ⓶ chm. niobic acid (H_2NbO_4).
Nipp (⸗) m ⓰b.: e-n ~ tun to take a sip.
nippen (⸗ᴗ) [ndd.] I v/n. (h.) u. v/a. ⓺⓺ to (take a) sip, to drink in small draughts or sips; *fig.* to graze, to skim. – II ~ n ⓶ (much) sipping or tippling.
Nippes (nipß) [fr.] f/pl. = Nippsachen.
Nipp¹-flut ⚓ (⸗⸗ᴸ) [nippen] f ⓶ (ant. Springflut) neap (tide).
Nipp²-sachen (⸗ᴸ...) [Nippes] f/pl. trinkets, knickknacks pl.; =**tisch** m table (or stand) for knickknacks, whatnot, fancy-table, canterbury.
nirgend(s) (⸗ᴗ⸗) [mhd. nie irgend(s)], ⚕(=) wo (hin) adv. nowhere, not anywhere.
...nis (...ᴗ) f ⓲ u. n ⓹ Suffix: Fäulnis f, vgl. foulness; Gleichnis n, vgl. likeness.
Nische (⸗ᴸ⸗) [fr. *niche*] f ⓲ arch. (Wandvertiefung) niche, recess (in the wall); ~n-gewölbe (⸗ᴗ...) n ⓹ niche-vaulting.
Niß (⸗) f ⓲, **Nisse** (⸗ᴗ) f ⓲ [ahd.: nit] *ent.* (Ei e-r Laus) nit; **nissig** a. ⓺⓺ full of nits, bisw. auch: nitty.
nisten (⸗ᴗ) [ahd.: nestle; *Nest] I v/n. (h.) u. v/refl. ⓺⓺ to (build a) nest. – II ~ n ⓶ building of a nest or of nests, ⚕ nidification.
Nist-kästchen (⸗⸗...) n ⓶, =**kasten** m nest-box; breeding-cage.
Nitrat ⚕ (⸗ᴸ) [grch. ni'tron; *semit. Natron] n ⓰c. chm. (Salpetersäuresalz) nitrate. [säure behandeln) to nitrate.]
nitrieren ⚕ (⸗ᴸᴗ) v/a. ⓺⓺ (mit Salpeter=]
Nitro-benzin ⚕ (⸗ᴗ⸗ᴸ) [grch. Salpeter f. Nitrat], bff. =**benzol** n, chm. nitro-benzene, nitrobenzol(e) ($C_6H_5.NO_2$).
Nitrogen ⚕ (⸗ᴗᴸ⸗) n ⓺d. chm. (Stickstoff, Hauptbestandteil der Luft) nitrogen (N).
Nitro-glyzerin ⚕ (⸗ᴗ⸗ᴗ⸗) n ⓹ (Nobelsches Spreng-öl) nitroglycerine ($C_3H_5N_3O_9$); =**schwefel-säure** f nitro-sulphuric acid.
Niveau (⸗ᴸ⸗) [fr. *niveau* m] n ⓹ (wagerechte Ebene) level (surface); ~-**differenz** (ᴸ...) f ⓶ difference of level; ~-**übergang** 🚂 m level-crossing.
nivellier/en ⚕ (⸗ᴗᴸ⸗) [fr. *niveler*] I v/a. ⓺⓺ surv., arch., &c. (ebenen) to (make) level. – II ~ n ⓶ = N/ung.
Nivellierer ⊕ (⸗ᴗᴸ⸗ᴗ) m ⓶ leveller.
Nivellier-fernglas ⊕ (⸗ᴗᴸ...) n ⓹ telescope-level; =**instrument** n, =**maßstab**, =**pflug** m levelling-instrument, -rule, -plough; =**scheibe** f sliding-vane.
Nivellierung ⚕ (⸗ᴗᴸᴗ) f ⓺⓺ levelling operation(s pl.), levelment.
Nivellier-wage ⊕ (⸗ᴗᴸᴗ) f ⓶ surv., arch., &c. spirit-level.
Nix (⸗) [ahd.: Nick] m ⓰a., ~**e** (⸗ᴗ) f ⓲ (Wassergeist) water-sprite, f a. nymph; *dim.* **Nixchen** n ⓹ little fairy.

Nizäa ⚕ (⸗tʃ⸗ᴸ⸗) npr/n. ⓶α. Alt.: (Stadt in Klein-asien) Nicaea; Konzil zu ~ (325 u. 787) Council of Nicaea; **nizäisch** a. ⓺⓺ Nicaean or Nicene (creed, &c.).
Nizza ⚕ (⸗ᴗ) npr/n. ⓶α. (fr. Seebad an der Riviera) Nice. [Monats.]
n. J., n. M. *abbr.* = nächsten Jahres,] **NO**, öst. **NO.** *abbr.* = Nordost. [Noachian]
noachitisch (⸗ᴗᴸᴗ) [Noah] a. ⓺⓺ of Noah;]
Noah (⸗) [hebr.] npr/m. ⓶α. bibl. Noah; die Arche ~(s) ob. (lt.) Noä Noah's ark.
nobel (⸗ᴸ⸗) [fr.] I a. ⓺⓺ (D9) 1. (vornehm) noble; (freigebig) liberal, generous; (fein) elegant, stylish. — II ~ m ⓶ 2. (ehm. engl. Münze, 16 bis 19 Mark) noble. — 3. (König) ~ (der Löwe im „Reineke Fuchs") Noble.
Nobelsch (⸗ᴸ⸗) [Nobel, schw. Ingenieur, 19. sae.] a. ⓺⓺ of Nobel; ~**es Sprengöl** = Nitroglyzerin.
noch¹ (⸗ch) [ahd. nu(n) auch] adv. 1. still; er ist ⚕ immer unwohl he is still indisposed; ⚕ besser even better; er kommt ⚕ he will yet come; er wird es ⚕ bereuen he will rue it yet; ⚕ an demselben Tage on the very same day; ⚕ bis jetzt to this very hour; ⚕ dazu in addition to that; vgl. dazu 4; wir müssen es ⚕ erst abwarten we must first of all wait; er soll ⚕ erst die Prüfung besteh(e)n he is yet (or before that) to pass the examination, ⚕ et. something else, one thing more; ⚕ gestern only (or but) yesterday; zehn oder ⚕ mehr ten or even more; er hat nur ⚕ 10 Mark he has only ten shillings left. — 2. mit *neg.*: ⚕ nicht not yet, Tennis: not ready; ⚕ lange nicht not by a long way; ⚕ nichts nothing yet; ⚕ nie never yet; ⚕ ist keiner (ob. niemand) erschienen as yet no one has appeared. — 3. (hinzutretend, außerdem) besides, in addition to (that); ⚕ ein Versuch one more (or another) attempt; ⚕ einmal once more; ⚕ einmal so viel (so hoch) as much (as high) again, twice as much (as high); ⚕ oben (dr)ein besides, moreover, over and above that. – 4. einräumend: ⚕ so // ever so //; sei es ⚕ so klein be it (or let it be) ever so small; wäre er auch ⚕ so reich though he may be (or were he) ever so rich, however rich he may be.
noch² (⸗ch) [ahd. nie auch] cj. weder ... ⚕ ... neither ... nor ..., zB. weder reich ⚕ arm neither rich nor poor; er hat weder Geld ⚕ Freunde he has neither money nor friends, he is without either money or friends.
noch¹-mal (⸗ch...) adv.: a) once more; b) (⸗ch⸗ᴸ) ⚕ (zweimal) so breit as wide again, double the width; ⚕**malig** a. ⓺⓺ repeated, reiterated; bei ⚕ er Durchsicht on (a) second inspection, on re-examination; bei ⚕ er Überlegung on second consideration or thoughts; ⚕**mals** adv. once more, again.
Nock ⚓ (⸗) [ndl.] n ⓰b.: a) ~ e-r Rahe yard-arm; b) ~ e pl. e-s Segels upper cringles pl. of a sail.
Nock-gording ⚓ (⸗...) f ⓶ outer leech-line; =**takel** n yard-tackle.
nölen F *prov.* (⸗ᴸ⸗) v/n. (h.) ⓺⓺ to dawdle.
Nöl-peter (⸗ᴸ⸗ᴗ) m ⓶ dawdler.

⚕ scientific; ⚘ botanical; ⚕ geography; ⊕ machinery; ⚒ mining; ⚔ military; ⚓ marine; ⚕ commercial; ✉ postal; 🚂 railway.

[Nomade] — 732 — [Not]

Nomade (⌣‒⌣) [grch.] n ⊕ nomad; **Zn=haft** (⌣‒⌣⌣) = nomadisch; **~n=leben, =volk** (⌣ʺ...) n ② nomadic life, tribe.

nomadisch (⌣‒⌣) a. ⊕ nomadic, migrating, migratory, wandering.

nomadisieren (⌣⌣‒⌣) v/n. (h.) ⊕ (wandern) to lead a nomadic (or roving) life.

Nomen (‒⌣) [lt.] n ⊕ gram. (Hauptwort) noun, substantive.

Nomenklatur ⚡ (‒⌣‒) [lt.] f ⊕ (Namenverzeichnis) nomenclature.

nominal (‒⌣‒) [lt. dem Namen nach] a. ⊕ nominal; **~=betrag** (‒⌣‒...) m ② nominal value; **~ismus** (‒⌣‒⌣) [lt.] m ㉗ phls. nominalism; **~ist** (‒⌣‒) m ② (Scholastiker, dem Begriffe nur Namen sind, ant. Realist) nominalist; **~wert** m = ~=betrag.

Nominativ (‒⌣‒⌣f) [lt. nomen] m ⊕ d., **~us** (‒⌣‒⌣w) m ⑬ gr. (Nennfall) nominative (case); subject. [nach] nominal.)

nominell (⌣⌣‒) [+=fr.] a. ⊕ (dem Namen

Nonchalance (ng'=schǎ-la'ß) [fr.] f ⊕ (Rücksichtslosigkeit) nonchalance, inconsiderateness, **nonchalant** (ng'=schǎ-laŋ) a. ⊕ (nachlässig) careless, bisw. nonchalant; (rücksichtslos) cavalierly, inconsiderate.

None (‒⌣) [ahd.; *lt. 9.] f ⊕ 1. Cath. eccl.: **~n** pl. (Gottesdienst in der 9. Tagesstunde, d. h. um 3 Uhr nachmittags) nones pl. — 2. im alt=römischen Kalender: **~n** pl. (3. März, Mai, Juli, Okt.; der 5. in den anderen Monaten) nones pl. — 3. [it.] ♪ ninth.

Nonius (‒⌣⌣) [Nuñez, port. Mathematiker, 16. sae] m, inv. ast., surv. (Rechenlineal) nonius. slide-(orsliding-)rule, vernier.

Nonkonformist ⚡ (⌣⌣⌣) [engl.] m ② Nonconformist.

Nonne (⌣⌣) [ahd.: nun; *ägyptisch] f ⊕ 1. nun; ~ werden, oft: to take the veil, to go into a nunnery. — 2. orn. weiße ~ (Art Taucher) nun (Mergus albe'llus). — 3. ent. (Fichtenspinner) black arches (Ocne'ria od. Li'paris mo'nacha).

Nonnen=chor (⌣ʺ...) m ⊕ choir of nuns; **=kloster** n nunnery, convent; **=leben** n convent-life; **=schleier** m veil of a nun; **=taube** f. orn. = Schleiertaube; **=weihe** f taking the veil; **=zelle** f nun's cell.

Nonpareille ⊕ (ng=pă=rö'ĭ(e)) [fr. Unvergleichliche] f 50, auch **~=schrift** f ⊕ typ. (Schrift von 6 Punkten) nonpareil.

Non-plus-ultra (⌣⌣⌣‒⌣) [lt. nicht darüber hinaus] n, inv. acme, top, height of folly &c.; ❦ (lt.) ne (or non) plus ultra.

Noppe ⊕ (⌣⌣) [ndd., ndl., *fr.] f ⊕ Weberei: (Wollknötchen am Zeuge) burl, nap.

Nopp=eisen ⊕ (⌣‒⌣) n ⊕ burling-iron.

noppen ⊕ (⌣⌣) v/a. ⊕ Weberei, Tuchfabrikation: (ausrauhen) to burl, to nap.

Nopper (⌣⌣) m ⊕, **~in** f ④ burler.

Nopp=maschine ⊕ (⌣‒⌣⌣) f ⊕ Weberei: burling-machine.

Nord (⌣) [ahd.: north] m ⊕ c., (abbr. N.) 1. north (abbr. N.); ~ und Süd north and south; ↓ ~ gewinnen (machen) to gain (to make) northing. — 2. = Nordwind

Nord=afrika ⚥ (⌣ʺ...) n ② North Africa; **=amerika** ⚥ n North America; **=amerika'ner**(in f) m, **⚥amerika'nisch** a. ⊕ North American; **=armee** ⚥ f army of the North; **=bahn** 🚂 f northern railway; **⚥deutsch** a.. **=deutsch(e)r** s. North German; **=deutschland** ⚥ n North Germany.

Norden (⌣⌣) m ㉓ (bes. mit art. = Nord); gegen (od. nach) ~ to(wards) the north, in a northerly direction, northward; im ~ von // in (or to) the north of //.

nordisch (⌣⌣) a. ⊕ northerly, northern, belonging to the north, poet. boreal, hyperborean; (altnormannisch) Norse; ~(e) n ⊕ Sprache: the Norse language.

Nord=kap (⌣...) n ⊕ (nördlichste Spitze von Europa) North Cape; **=kaper** m, zo. Art Wal: northern whale, bsd.: grampus (Orca gladia'tor); **=land** n: a) **=länder** pl. northern countries pl.; b) (Namen skandinavischer Gebiete) Nordland; **=länder**: a) pl. v. **=land**; b) **=länder**(in f) m p. living in a northern (or an arctic) country; northerner; **=land=fahrt** f, **=land=reise** f arctic expedition.

nördlich (⌣⌣) [Nord] a. ⊕ northerly, northern, of (or in) the north; arctic; 2e Breite north latitude (a. ↓ u. ⚥); das ~e Eismeer the Arctic Ocean; 2e Lage northerliness, northern aspect; 2 (adv.) liegen von ... to lie (to the) north of ...

Nord=licht (⌣...) n ⊕ phys. northern light(s pl.), (lt.) aurora borea'lis; vgl. **=schein**; **=ost** m (abbr. NO.) northeast (abbr. N.E.); ~ zu Nord northeast by north; **=ostering** ↓ f (östliche Mißweisung) easterly variation; **⚥östlich** a. ⊕ northeast(erly); **=ostsee=kanal** ⚥ m Baltic Canal; **=ost=wind** m northeast(erly) wind, ↓ northeaster; **=pol** ⚥ m North Pole; **=pol=expedition, =fahrt** f polar expedition; **=pol=fahrer** ↓ m arctic explorer; **=schein** m zodiacal light; vgl. **=licht**; **=see** ⚥ f North Sea, German Ocean; **=seite** f north side; **=sonne** f northern sun; vgl. Mitternachtssonne; **=staaten** m/pl. der U.S. Northern States pl.; **=stern** m northern star, bsd. polar star; **⚥wärts** adv. northward; **=west** m (abbr. NW.) northwest (abbr. N.W.); ~ zum West northwest by west; **=westering** ↓ f (westl. Mißweisung) westerly variation; **⚥westlich** a. northwest(erly); **=west=wind** m northwest(erly) wind, ↓ northwester; **=wind** m north-wind, poet. Boreas.

Nörgelei F (⌣‒⌣) f ⊕, **nörg(e)lig** (⌣‒⌣) a. ⊕ grumbling, nagging, faultfinding, teasing, worrying.

nörgeln F (⌣‒) [erst nhd.] ⊕ a. I v/n. (h.) to grumble, to nag, to find fault. — II v/a. to tease, to worry.

Nörgler (⌣⌣) m ㉒, **~in** f ④ grumbler.

norisch ⚥ (‒⌣) [No'riker, alt. Volk] a. ⊕: ~e Alpen Noric Alps pl.

Norm (⌣) [lt.] f ⊕ 1. (Regel) rule; (Vorbild) model, pattern, bsd. ⚡ a. norm(a); als ~ gelten to serve as a standard. — 2. ⊕ typ. (Bogenzeichen) sheet signature.

normal (‒⌣) [lt.] a. ⊕ (regelmäßig) normal, standard; regular.

Normal=(arbeits=)tag (‒⌣...) m ⊕ ordinary (working-)day; **=bahn** 🚂 (Hauptbahn) main line; **=etat** m, parl. ordinary budget; **=fuß** m standard foot; **=geschwindigkeit** f average (or ordinary) speed; **=gewicht** n standard weight; **=höhe** f, typ. standard type; **=kerze** f standard candle; **=klasse** f Tennis: scratch (vgl. Über-, Unter-); **=lehrplan** m normal routine for a fixed type of (German) schools; **=maß** n standard; **=mäßigkeit** f normality; **=maß=stab** m proof-staff; **=satz** ❦ m limit; **=schriftlinie** f, typ. standard line; **=schule** f training-college; **⚥spurig** 🚂 a. ⊕ of the standard (or ordinary) gauge; **=spur=weite** f standard gauge; **=uhr** ⊕ central (electric) clock; **=weingeist** m proof-spirit; **=zeit** f mean time.

Normandie ⚥ (‒⌣‒) [Normannen (911)] npr f. ⊕: die ~ (nordfr. Provinz) Normandy. [(Nord=mann(en)) Norman.]

Normann. **=e** (⌣‒⌣) m ⊕, ⊕, **~in** f ④

normannisch, normännisch (‒⌣‒⌣) a. ⊕ 1. hist. (skandinavisch) Norman, of the Normans; 2e Eroberung Englands (1066) Norman Conquest. — 2. ⚥ (auf die Normandie bezüglich) (of) Normandy, ⚥ ~e Inseln (im Ärmelmeer) Channel Islands pl.

normieren (⌣‒) [lt.] v/a. ⊕ (bemessen) to regulate, to gauge; (feststellen) to fix.

Norm=zeile (⌣‒⌣) f ⊕ typ. standard line.

norsch (⌣⌣) a. ⊕ Norse.

Norwegen ⚥ (⌣⌣‒) [Nord=weg (= =land)] npr/n. 23 a. Norway; **Norweger**(in f) ⊕ m ㉓, **norwegisch** a. ⊕ Norwegian.

Nörz (⌣) m ⊕ a. zo. = Nerz.

Nößel (⌣) [nhd.] n u. n ⊕ ehm. kleines Flüssigkeitsmaß: pint.

Not (‒) [ahd.: need] f ⑩ (pl. nur in 3 u. 6) 1. (Zwang) necessity, compulsion; (Dringlichkeit) urgency, exigency; im Falle der ~ in case of need, on an emergency; wenn ~ an Mann geht (kommt) if need be, when the worst comes to the worst; Sprichw. f. erfinderisch, Gebot[1] 1. — 2. (Mühsal) trouble, (Anstrengung) effort, exertion, (Kummer) grief, affliction, tribulation, (Sorge) sorrow, care; (Leiden) suffering; höchste ~ great distress or calamity; viele ~ (f seine Liebe) ~ haben to be greatly troubled or bothered or harassed; er macht uns viele ~ he gives us great trouble. — 3. (große Gefahr) (great) danger, (imminent) peril, jeopardy, bsd. ↓ distress; in (Ängsten und) Nöten sein to be hard pressed; Sprichw. f. Holland. — 4. (drückender Mangel) need, want, an Lebensmitteln: famine; (Dürftigkeit) indigence; gänzliche= (utter) destitution; (Elend) misery; in ~ geraten to become destitute, F to get low (in the world); in ~ sein to be destitute, to be in want (of common necessities); in großer ~ sein to be (very) hard up or in great straits; mit der ~ (dem Hunger) kämpfen to keep the wolf from the door; ~ leiden to suffer want, to be in distress, F to feel the pinch; vgl. Leidend; Sprichw. Freunde in der ~ gehn hundert auf ein Lot a poor man has no friends; ein Freund in der ~ ist ein Freund im Tod a friend in need is a friend indeed; ~ ist der Liebe Tod when poverty comes in at the door love flies out at the window; wenn die ~ am größten, ist Gottes Hilfe am nächsten man's extremity is God's opportunity; when things are at their worst they are sure to mend; f. Eisen[2] 1 am Schluß. — 5. f. Schwerenot. — 6. mit adjektivischem oder adver-

Zeichen (f. S. XVII): F familiär; P Volkssprache; ⚡ Gaunersprache; ❦ selten; † alt (auch gestorben); * neu (auch geboren); ++ unrichtig;

biellem Charakter (oft klein gschr.): a) eins ist 2 one thing is needful or needed; mir ist et. 2 (nötig), bisw. es ist mir um et. I am in need of (or F hard up for) a th.; b) ich habe ~ (Mühe), alles unterzubringen I find it a difficult task to dispose of everything; es hat ~ (hält schwer), daß // it is a difficult (or hard) matter to // (inf.); c) es tut 2 (ist nötig), daß // it is needful (or necessary) that //; es täte 2, ich ginge selbst hin it would be best if I went myself; ihm tut es 2 (auf den Abtritt zu gehen) he (badly) wants to ease nature or F to do something; d) aus prp.: **aus** ~ from necessity; *fig.* aus der ~ eine Tugend machen to make a virtue of necessity; **in** s. 3 u. 4; **mit** ~, mit Müh' und ~ barely, with difficulty; mit genauer (harter oder knapper) ~ narrowly, only just; mit knapper ~ entrinnen to have a narrow escape; **ohne** ~ without necessity, unnecessarily, needlessly; (ohne Ursache) without (any) cause; **über** ~ more than needful or required; über ~ essen to eat to excess or more than enough; ich habe etwas **vonnöten** (bedarf es) I am in need of a th., I require a th.; das ist vonnöten that is a matter of necessity; **zur** ~ (als Notbehelf) on an emergency.

Nota (*ᴸ*ˇ) [lt.] *f* ⑳ **1.** ✱ note; (kurz ausgestellte Rechnung) short memorandum or bill. — **2.** a) sich et. ad notam nehmen to take not(ic)e of a th.; b) als *imper.* nota bene [lt. merke wohl]! mark well!, take notice!, mind!

Notabeln (ˇᴸˇ) [lt.] *m/pl.* (Standespersonen) notabilities, notable people *pl.*

Notabene (ˇˇᴸˇ) [lt.; f. Nota 2b] *n* ⑳ (a. *inv.*) (abbr. **NB.**) nota bene (**N.B.**).

Notabilität (ˇˇˇᴸ) [lt.] *f* ⑳: a) notability; b) ~en *pl.* (angesehene Leute) notabilities, distinguished people *pl.*, F big (or great) guns, swells *pl.*

Not-achse ⊕ (ˇˇ...) *f* ⑳ temporary (or spare) axle-tree; **-adresse** ✱ *f* address for case(s) of need.

notam (*ᴸ*ˇ) f. Nota 2a.

Not-anker ⚓ (ˇˇˇˇˇ) *m* ⑳ spare anchor, sheet-anchor (auch *fig.*).

Notar (ˇᴸ) [lt. *nŏtā́rius* Zeichen-, Geschwindschreiber] *m* ⑳ d. jur. (public) notary, als Verfasser gesetzlicher Urkunden: solicitor, v. Abtretungsurkunden: conveyancer.

Notariat (ˇ-(ˇ)ᴸ) [lt.] *n* ⑳ c. (Amt, Geschäft e-s Notars) notary's office; von ~s wegen by order of a notary.

Notariats-gebühren (ˇ-(ˇ)ᴸ...) *f/pl.* ⑳ notarial (or notary's) fees *pl.*; **-instrument** *n* legal document, solicitor's deed; **-siegel** *n* notary's seal.

notariell (ˇ-(ˇ)ˇ) [+ fr.] *a.* ⑳ notarial, attested (or drawn up) by a notary.

Not-ausgang (ˇˇ...) *m* ⑳ thea., &c. emergency door or exit; vgl. -tür; **-auswurf** ⚓ *m* (Ausgeworfenes) jetsam; **-bau** ⊕ *m* temporary structure; **-behelf** *m* (make)shift, stop-gap, last resource; (Auskunftsmittel) expedient; **-bremse** ✱ *f* brake for emergency-cases; **-brücke** *f* temporary bridge; **-brunnen** *m* water-tank (or well) for

cases of fire or of emergency; **-damm**, **-deich** ⊕ *m* temporary dike; **-dringend** *a.* ⑳ urgent; **-durft** *f* (utmost) necessity, exigency, pressing need; seine ~ verrichten to ease (or relieve) nature, to make o.s. comfortable; **-dürftig** *a.*: a) (knapp) scanty; b) (darbend) necessitous, needy, F hard up; **-dürftigkeit** *f* need(iness), indigence, distress.

Note (*ᴸ*ˇ) [lt. *nŏtă*] *f* ⑳ **1.** note (a. ♪); ~n *pl.* a. music; ♪ ganze ✱ semibreve (○); halbe ~ minim (♩); schwarze (Viertel-)crotchet (♩); geschwänzte (Achtel-)quaver (♪); eine Melodie in ~n setzen to set a tune to music; ~n abschreiben to copy music; *fig.* nach ~n (gehörig) properly, thoroughly; vgl. nach 3; F es kommt ihm auf eine Handvoll ~n (eine Kleinigkeit) nicht an he is not over-particular. — **2.** Schule: mark for conduct, industry, &c. — **3.** (Anmerkung) note, remark, zu e-m Werke: annotation, auf den Rand geschriebene: marginal note; ✱ memorandum; (Banknote) banknote. — **4.** Diplomatie: note, short (or brief) communication, (fr.) communiqué.

Noten-ausgabe (*ᴸ*ˇ...) *f* ⑳ issue of banknotes; **-austausch** *m* exchange of notes; **-bank** *f* bsd. chm.: issuing bank, jetzt in Engl.: issue-department of the Bank of England; **-beilage** *f* einer Zeitung: musical supplement; **-bezeichnung** ♪ *f* musical notation; **-blatt** *n* sheet of music; **-buch** *n* music-book; **-drucker** *m*, *typ.* music-printer; **-format** ⊕ *n*, *typ.* oblong quarto; **-fresser** ♪ F *m* humdrum player or musician; **-gestell** *n* music-stand; **-halter** *m*: a) music-clamp or -rack; b) = **-mappe**; **-heft** *n* = **-buch**; **-inhaber** ✱ *m* bearer, holder; **-lesen** ♪ *n* music-reading; **-leser(in** *f*) *m* one who reads music well, badly, &c.; **-linie** ♪ *f* line of the staff; vgl. **-system**; **-linien-zieher** ⊕ *m* music-pen; **-mappe** *f* m.-holder or -folio; **-papier** *n* m.-paper; **-pult** *n* m.-desk; **-schlüssel** ♪ *m* clef; **-schreiben** *n* music-writing; ♪ musicography; **-schreiber** *m* music-copyist; **-stecher** ⊕ *m* m.-engraver, engraver of music; **-stimme** ♪ *f* (musical) part; **-stück** *n* piece of music; **-system** *n* (die fünf -linien) staff; **-typen** ⊕ *f pl.* m.-type; **-umlauf** ✱ *m* circulation of (bank)notes; **-zeichen** ♪ *n* note.

Not-erbe (ˇˇ...) *m* ⑳ jur. lawful heir; **-fall** *m* case of necessity or emergency; im ~e in case of need, F at a pinch; **-feuer** *n*: a) alarm-fire; b) [:ahd. nuan reiben] needfire; **-flagge** ⚓ *f* flag of distress; **-gedrungen** *p.p.* und *a.* ⑳ driven by necessity; compulsory, forced, *adv.* auch: from sheer necessity; needs; **-geschrei** *n* cries *pl.* of distress; ein ~ erheben to raise an alarm; **-hafen** ⚓ *m* harbour of refuge; **-helfer** *m* person who comes to the rescue, deliverer; **-hilfe** *f* succour.

notier/en (ˇᴸˇ) [lt.] I *v/a.* ⑳: (anmerken) to note, to put down (in writing), to make a note (✱ a memorandum) of, ✱ to book; (flüchtig aufschreiben) to jot down, bei Spielen: to score: ✱ die notierten Preise the prices quoted. — II ~ *n* ⑳ und **N/ung** *f* ⑳ noting, ⚓ u.

♪ notation; ✱ booking, entry; ~ der Effekten (market-)quotation.

Notifikation (ˇˇˇ-tf(ˇ)ᴸ) [lt.] *f* ⑳ (Anmeldung) notification. [notify a th. to a p.]

notifizieren (ˇˇˇᴸˇ) *v/a.* ⑳ (anmelden) to

nötig (*ᴸ*ˇ) [ahd.; *Not] I *a.* ⑳ **1.** necessary, required; unbedingt, unumgänglich 2 absolutely needed or wanted, indispensable; es ist nicht 2, daß du schreibst there is no need (or occasion) for you to write; *adv.* f. nötigenfalls. — 2 ich habe et. 2, mir tut et. 2 (ich brauche et.) I am (or stand) in need of a th., I require (or want) a th.; I am hard up for money, &c.; was hatte er 2, sich da einzumengen? what need (or occasion, business) had he to interfere? — II das ~e *n* ⑳ **3.** the necessary thing, the thing required; (Geld) the needful.

nötigen (*ᴸ*ˇ) [ahd.] I *v/a.* ⑳ **1.** e-n 2, et. zu tun to oblige (or force, compel) a p. to do a th.; durch die Umstände genötigt driven (or compelled) by circumstances. — 2. (dringend bitten) to press, to urge; (einladen) to invite, to ask; lassen Sie sich nicht 2, greifen Sie zu don't wait to be asked, help yourself (*pl.* yourselves); ich lasse mich nicht (lange) 2 I require no (or very little) pressing. — II ~ *n* ⑳ **3.** f. Nötigung.

nötigen-falls (*ᴸ*ˇˇ,ᴸ) *adv.* in case of need or necessity or emergency, F at a pinch; (beziehentlich) eventually.

Nötigkeit (*ᴸ*ˇˇ) *f* ⑳ necessity; urgency.

Nötigung (*ᴸ*ˇˇ) *f* ⑳ (f. nötigen I) forcing, compulsion; pressing, (pressing) invitation; urgent request.

Notiz (ˇᴸ) [fr., *lt.*] *f* ⑳ **1.** ~ (Kenntnis) von et. nehmen to take notice (or cognizance) of a th. — 2. (schriftlicher Vermerk) note, memorandum; sich ~en machen to take (or jot) down notes.

Notiz(en)-buch (ˇᴸ(ˇ)-ᴸ*ch*) *n* ⑳ note-book, memorandum-book.

Not-jahr (ˇˇ...) *n* ⑳ year of scarcity or distress; **-klausel** ✱ *f* emergency clause; **-lage** *f* distress(ed condition), calamity, vgl. **-stand**; **-leidend** *a.* ⑳: a) necessitous, indigent; b) suffering, distressed, c) ✱ der Wechsel blieb 2 ... remained dishonoured; **-leidende([r]** *m*) *f* person in distress, sufferer; **-leine** ✱ *f* communicator, bell-cord or -pull; **-lüge** *f* white lie, fib; (Dienstlüge) official lie; **-mast** ⚓ *m* jury-mast; **-mittel** *n* = **-behelf**; **-nagel** *m*: a) nail which serves in case of need; b) *fig.* = **-behelf**.

Notori-etät (--(ˇ)ᴸ) [lt.] *f* ⑳ notoriety. **notorisch** (ˇᴸˇ) *a.* ⑳ (offenkundig) notorious. **not-peinlich** (ˇˇ...) *a.* ⑳ *tu.* criminal, penal; **-pfeife** ⊕ *f* danger-whistle; **-pfennig** *m* savings *pl.*; money put by against a rainy day; **-reif** *a.* ripe before the time, forced; **-ruder** ⚓ *n* preventer-rudder; **-ruf**, **-schrei** *m* cry of distress; **-schuß** *m* shot of distress; **-signal** *n* signal of distress; ✱ &c. a. danger-signal; **-seine**; **-stall** *m*: a) provisional stable, für widerspenstige Pferde: trave; b) ⊕ brake for shoeing vicious horses; **-stand** *m* = **-lage**, auch: critical state, urgent case; **-stands-gesetz** *n*, *parl.* bill passed in time(s) of

[Nottaufe] — 734 — [nur]

distress; =**taufe** f private baptism; ₂**taufen** v/a. ⊛*⁎* to baptize privately; =**tür(e)** f (fire-)escape.
Notturno ♪ (‿‑) [it.] n ⓰ (Nachtmusik) notturno, (fr.) nocturne.
Not=verband (″...) m ⓬ surg. provisional dressing; =**wehr** [nhd.] f self-defence; aus ~ in self-defence; ₂**wendig** a. ⓰ [nhd.] necessary, requisite; das ~**fte, die** ₂**ten Bedürfniſſe** necessaries, requisites, the most indispensable wants pl.; **ſchlechterdings** (ob. unvedingt, unumgänglich) ₂**absolutely necessary, indispensable;** (unvermeidlich) inevitable, fated; =**wendigenfalls** adv. in case of need or necessity; ₂**wendigerweise** adv. necessarily, of necessity; =**wendigkeit** f: a) necessity; (Verhängnis) fatality; b) thing required, requirement; in die ~ **verſetzt zu** // compelled (or forced) to //; =**werk** indispensable (or pressing) work, urgent task; =**zucht** [nhd.] f (gewaltsame Behandlung) rape, ravishment; jur. auch: indecent assault; ₂**züchtigen** [urſpr. zu Not ziehen] v/a.⊛*⁎* to ravish, jur. to assault; =**züchtigung** f = =**zucht**.
Novelle (‿‑‿) f ⓰ 1. [it., ſpan.] (Erzählung) short novel or tale. — 2. [it.] jur., parl. (Nachtragsgeſetz) supplementary law; ~**n von Juſtinian** Novels pl.
novellen=artig (‿‑‿...) a. ⓰ in (the) form of a short novel; =**ſchreiber** m ⓬ writer of short novels or tales, weitS. writer of fiction.
Novelliſt (‿‑‿) m ⓬ = **Novellenſchreiber; ~in** (‿‑‿‑) f ⓰ short novels pl., (works of) fiction; ₂**iſch** (‿‑‿) a. ⓰ novelistic, fictional.
November (‿‑‿) [lt. der 9. Monat der alten Römer] m ⓬ (a. inv.) November; im ~ in the month of) November.
Novität (‿‑‿‑) [lt.] f ⓰ (Neuheit) thea. new play; Buchhandel: =**en** new (or latest) publications pl.
Novize (‿‑‿) [neu=lt. Neuling] m ⓬, f ⓰ eccl. probationer; bſd. weitS. a. novice.
Noviziat (‿‑‿‑)[neu=lt.] n ⓰ c.eccl., &c. (Probezeit) novitiate, probationership.
Nowaja Semlja ♀ (‑‿‿ ‑‿) [ruſſ. Neuland] npr/n. ⓑα. ruſſ. Inſelgruppe im Nördlichen Eismeer: Nova Zembla.
Nr., № abbr. = **Nummer, Numero**.
N. S. abbr. = **Nachſchrift.**
n. St. abbr. = **neuen Stiles** of new style (gregorianiſcher Kalender).
N. T. abbr. = **Neues Teſtament.**
nu (‑) [ſ. nun] I int. P = nun; nu also, die Sache macht ſich now (or well) then, things are looking up. — II **Nu** m, n, inv. moment; **im Nu** in an instant, in a trice, F in no time, in a jiffy.
Nuance (nü‑a'ß‑ᵊ) [fr.] f ⓰ (Schattierung) shade (a. fig.), paint., &c. a. tinge, tint.
nuancieren (nü‑g‑ß‑L‿) [fr.] v/a. ⓰ to shade off, ♪ to modulate.
Rubi=en ♀ (‑(‿)‿) npr/n. ⓑα. Land in Nord=afrika: Nubia. [(‑L‿) a. ⓰ Nubian.
Rubi=er (‑(‿)‿) npr/m. ⓬ ⓰, **nubiſch**)
nüchtern (‑‿) [ahd.] a. ⓰ 1. ₂, **mit dem Magen** empty, with (or on) an empty stomach, fasting, bſd. fig. jejune; ich bin noch ₂ I have not partaken of any food, I have not broken my fast or not breakfasted. — 2. (ant. trunken) sober; ₂ **machen** to (make) sober; ₂ **werden** to become sober, bſd. fig. to sober down; ganz ₂ as sober as a judge. — 3. (mäßig) abstemious, moderate, temperate; frugal. — 4. fig.: a) (klug) prudent; (beſonnen) cool (-headed), calm; (vernünftig) sensible; (leidenſchaftlos) dispassionate; **der Menſch prosy** (or humdrum) fellow; **des Urteil sober** (or sound) judgment; b) (langweilig) prosy; (geiſtlos, ant. pikant) jejune, dry, dreary. — 5. **von Speiſen**: insipid, stale, **vom Stil auch**: vapid.
Rüchternheit (‑‿‑) f ⓰ (zu nüchtern 1:) emptiness of the stomach, fasting condition; (zu 2:) sober state, sobriety; (zu 3:) abstemiousness, temperance; (zu 4:) prosiness; jejuneness; dryness.
Nücke, Nücke F (‑‿) [nhd.] f ⓰ 1. (Laune) caprice; ~**n h.** to have (one's) whims and fancies. — 2. (Tücke) malice.
Nudel (‑‿) [nhd. 16. sae.] f ⓰ 1. Kochkunſt: **deutſche ~n** (in England unbekannt), etwa: strips pl. of dough or paste; italieniſche ~**n** maccaroni, (Fadennudeln) vermicelli. — 2. (Teig zum Stopfen der Gänſe) fattening-ball. [a ball.
nudel=dick F (″...) a. ⓰ (as) round as)
Nud(e)ler (‑(‿)‿) m ⓬ fattener.
Nudel=holz (″...) n ⓬ rolling-pin; =**macher** m vermicelli-maker.
nudeln (‑‿) v/a. ⓬ a. Federvieh: to fatten; fig. (vollſtopfen) to cram (with food).
Nudel=ſuppe (″‑‿‑‿) f ⓰ vermicelli-soup.
Nudität (‑‿‑) [lt.] f ⓰ (Nacktheit) nudity.
null (‿) [lt.] a. inv. null; **Tennis**: scratch; ₂ **und nichtig** null and void; ſ. **erklären** 3 u. **nichtig.**
Null (‿) [it.] f ⓰ 1. arith. zero (auch in e-r Skala), cipher, F nought. — 2. (Nullpunkt) **das Thermometer ſteht auf ~ ...** stands (or is) at zero, ... registers zero; **unter ~** below zero. — 3. fig. (Wertloſes) **er iſt die reine ~ ...** a mere cipher or a (mere) nobody or a (perfect) nonentity; **das Ergebnis war gleich ~** the result was a mere nothing or F was nil.
Null=grad (ᵦ‑) m ⓬ des Thermometers ꝛc.: zero; (Gefrierpunkt) freezing-point.
Nullität (‿‑‑) f ⓰ nullity, invalidity.
Null=partie (ᵦ...) f ⓰ Tennis: love-set; =**punkt** m = =**grad**; =**ſpiel** n Tennis: love-game; =**ſtrich** m zero-mark.
Numerale (‿‿‑‿) [lt.] n ⓬ (pl. a. ...a'lia) (Zahlwort) numeral (adjective).
Numeri (‑‿‑) [lt. pl. v. nu'merus] m/pl. ⓰ (4. Buch Moſis) (book of) Numbers.
numerier/en (‿‿‑‿) [lt. zählen] I v/a. ⓰ to (mark with a) number; ⊛ (bezetteln) to ticket. — II ~ n ⓬ u. ₂**ung** f ⓰ (e)numeration, math. auch: ◯ notation.
numeriſch (‿‑‿) [lt.] a. ⓰ numerical.
Numero (‑‿‑) [dat. ob. abl. von lt. nu'merus] n ⓬, meiſt abbr. = **Nummer**, zB. ~ **3** number three.
Numerus (‑‿‿) [lt. nu'mĕrŭs Zahl] m ⓬ gram. number; math. number (corresponding to a logarithm).
Numidi=en ♀ (‿‑L‿) npr/n. ⓑα. röm. Alt. in Nord=afrika: Numidia. **Nu'mider** (in f ⓰), **numi'diſch** a. ⓰ Numidian.
Numismatik ◯ (‿‿‑‿) [grch.] f ⓰ **Münzkunde**; =**er** (‿‿‑‿‑) m ⓬ numismat(olog)ist; **numismatiſch** (‿‿‑‿) a. ⓰ numismatical, numismatic.
Nummer (‑‿) [lt. nu'mĕrŭs m] f ⓰ 1. (Zahl) number (auch Lotterie u. ⊛); ~ **einer Zeitung** ꝛc.: copy, issue; Buchhandel: **fortlaufende ~n** pl. series sg.; **in monatlichen ~n erſcheinen** to appear in monthly parts. — 2. ⊛ (Größe, zB. von Handſchuhen) size; (Güte) quality. — 3. F fig. ~ **Sicher** place of safety; (Gefängnis) lock-up, jail; **in ~ bringen** to put under lock and key.
Nummer=pfahl (ᵦ‿...) m ⓬ ⛁, surv., &c. number-peg, =**poſt**; =**ſtein** m milestone; =**ſtempel** m numbering-stamp; =**zettel** ⊛ m auf eingeſchriebenen Briefen: label marked with 'R' (= Registered).
nun (‑) [ahd.: now] I adv. 1. (jetzt) now, at the present moment; **da er ₂ hier iſt** now (that) he is here; ₂ **erſt geſtand er** only then (or now at last) ...; **von ₂ an**: a) (in Zukunft) henceforth, in (the) future; b) (in der Vergangenheit) from that time forth, ever since then; **als ₂** // now when //; ſ. **nimmer 2**. — 2. (unter den Umſtänden) then, as things now stand or then stood; vgl. **erſt 3**. — 3. **eine Rede fortſetzend**: well now; why; auch **bei Folgerungen**: hence, so; ₂ (aber) now since; ₂, **das iſt doch** on my word, that is too bad; ₂ **ja!** yes, indeed! — 4. oft nicht zu überſetzen, zB. **er mag ₂ kommen oder nicht** whether he comes or not; **da es ₂ einmal ſo iſt** since things are as they are. — 5. **fragend**: ₂? (wie ſteht's?) well, how are things?; ₂ **und?** well, and after that? — 6. **als int.**, anſpornend: now, then!; ₂ **los!** now, go it!; ₂ **gut!** well, then!, that's settled!; **begütigend**: ₂ ₂! (nicht ſo hitzig!) gently!, come, come!, don't be so rash! — II ~ cj. 7. ₂ — da, zB. ₂ **du mich kennſt** now that you know me.
nun=mehr (″‑, ‑‿″) biśw. ₂**mehro** (‑‿″‑) adv. u. cj. now, at the present time, by this time, (von jetzt ab) henceforth: ₂**mehrig** (‑‿″‑) a. ⓰ = **jetzig**.
Nunziatur (‿ᵗᶻ(‿)‿″) [it.] f ⓰ (Amt ꝛc. e-s **Nunzius**); **Nunzius** (‿ᵗᶻ(‿)‿) m ㉗ (Geſandter des Papſtes) nuncio.
nur (‑) [ahd. (wenn) nicht wäre] adv. 1. **ausſchließend**: only, solely (immer vor dem zu beſchränkenden Ausdrucke), zB. **hat ₂ Freunde an dieſem Orte** he has only (or nothing but) friends in this place; **er hat Freunde ₂ an dieſem Orte** he has friends only in this place, his only friends are in this place; **das beweiſt ₂, daß** // it only (or solely, merely) proves that //; **ſie hat ₂ Gutes empfangen** she received nothing but kindness; **er pfiff ₂** he only (or simply) whistled; **er ſpielt ₂** (immer fort) he does nothing but play, all that he does is playing; ₂ **er entkam** he alone (or no one but he) got off; **das Stück iſt ₂ klein** the piece is but (or quite) small. — 2. **mit anderen** adv.: ₂ **etwa** only about; ₂ **noch** (öſt., ſüdd. ₂ **mehr**) only just; **faſt ₂ noch** hardly any (-thing) but; ₂ **zu ſehr** only too much or too well; **nicht ₂** //, **ſondern auch** // not only //, but also // — 3. bſd. **mit**

Signs (see page XVII): F familiar; P vulgar; ꟊ flash; ⟍ rare; † obsolete (died); * new word (born); ⧺ incorrect; ♪ music;

neg. oder Zahlwörtern; f. nicht 2; fie flohen alle, 2 er nicht all fled but he; alles, 2 nicht der Tod all excepting (or save) death, death alone excepted; alles, 2 dies nicht anything rather than this; mit 2 wenigen Ausnahmen with but few exceptions; fie hat 2 eine Tochter she has but one daughter; ich bin ärmer, 2 daß ich feine Familie habe ... except (in so far as) I have no family. — **4.** bedingend: hier haft du 100 Marf, 2 schweige! here are five pounds (for you), but not (or don't say) a word!; wenn 2 // provided that //; wenn fie mich 2 in Ruhe ließen if they would only let me alone. — **5.** wünschend: wenn 2 was fäme would that something might (or if only s.th. would) come. — **6.** bewilligend: er mag 2 gehen he may go (if he likes); 2 zu! do as you please! — **7.** verftärfend: geh 2! then, go!; go, by all means!; fieh 2, was er tut! only (or just) look what he is doing!; wart 2, ich fomme dir! just wait (or wait a bit), I'll be after you!; verfaufe es 2 ja nicht! don't sell it on any account!; oft nicht überfetzt, zB. laß mich 2 machen! (do) let me manage! — **8.** zweifelnd: wie fam er 2 hierher? how on earth did he get here?; was follen wir 2 fagen what are we really to say?, what on earth shall we say?; was er 2 damit fagen will! I wonder what he means by it! — **9.** verallgemeinernd: was 2 what(so)ever, wer 2 who(so)ever; wo 2 where(so)ever; wohin 2 wherever, feltener: withersoever; soviel ich 2 fann as much as ever I can; er hat es so gut (wie) man es 2 haben fann he is as well off as ever anybody could (wish to) be; die schönsten Blumen, die man fich 2 denken fann the finest flowers (that) one could possibly imagine.

Nürnberg ♀ (ˊ˘) npr/n. ⊕ a. (bayr. St., ehm. freie Reichsstadt) Nuremberg.

Nürnberger (ˊ˘˘) **I** m ⊕, ~**in** f ⊕ inhabitant of Nuremberg. — **II** a. inv. (of) N.; ehm. (16. sae.) ~ Ei (dicke Taschenuhr) Nuremberg egg; ~ Trichter, twa: patent method of teaching dullards.

nuseln (ˊ˘) v/n. (h.) ⊕ a. (tröbeln) to dawdle; (undeutlich reden) to mumble.

Nuß¹ (ˊ) [ahd.: nuz] f ⊕ **1.** ♀ nut (auch ⊕), ♀ engS. = Haselnuß; welsche ~ (large) walnut; in die Nüsse gehen to go (a-)nutting; ⊕ ~ am Gewehrschloß: tumbler. — **2.** fig. das ift nicht e-e (taube oder hohle) ~ wert that's not worth a straw or a rush; harte ~ hard nut (to crack), F poser; f. fnacken II.

Nuß² (ˊ) f ⊕ = Kopfnuß b.

Nuß¹-baum (ˊ...) ♀ m ⊕ (wal)nut-tree (Iuglans); ⸗baumen a. ⊕ of (wal)nutwood; ⸗baumholz n walnut (wood); ⸗blätter n/pl. leaves pl. of a nut-tree; ⸗bohrer m, ent. nut-weevil (Balani'nus); ⸗braun a. nut-brown, vom Haar, auch: auburn, von den Augen: hazel.

Nüßchen (ˊ˘) n ⊕ (dim. von Nuß) little (or tiny) nut, ♀: ⊕ nucule.

Nuß¹-häher (ˊ...) m ⊕ orn. nutbreaker, nutcracker, ✐ nucifrage (Nuci'fraga caryocata'ctes); ⸗hafen m nut-hook; ⸗fern m kernel of a nut; ⸗fernmehl n nutmeal; ⸗fnackend a. ⊕ zo.: ✐ nucifragous; ⸗fnacker m: a) (Werkzeug) nutcracker; b) F alter ~ old fogey; ⸗muschel f, zo.: ⊕ nucula; ⸗schale f: a) nutshell; b) (kleiner Kahn) mere nutshell, canoe; ⸗schraube ⊕ f nutscrew; ⸗strauch ♀ m = Haselstrauch; ⸗tragend a. nut-bearing, ✐ nuciferous.

Nüster (ˊ˘) [nbd.: nostril] f ⊕ (meift im pl. gbr.): ~n pl. nostrils.

Nut ⊕ (ˊ) [mhd.] f ⊕, ~**e** (ˊ˘) f ⊕ groove, rabbet; ~ und Zapfen mortise and tenon; ~**eisen** (ˊ˘˘) n ⊕ plough-bit.

Nuten-bohrer ⊕ (ˊ...) m ⊕ slotting-auger; ⸗stoß-maschine f sl.-machine.

Nut-hobel ⊕ (ˊ˘˘) m ⊕ grooving-plane, rabbet-plane or -plough.

nutz¹ (ˊ) [ahd.: *(ge)nießen] auch: **nutze**, **nütze** a. (nur prädikativ gbr.) useful, profitable; nichts 2 fein to be of no use; zu nichts 2, zu nichts nütze good for nothing, useless, worthless.

Nutz² (ˊ) m ⊕ a. oder inv. usefulness, utility, profitableness; sich et. zunutze machen to profit (or to avail o.s.) of a th., to turn a th. to account; zu Nutz und Frommen der Menschheit for the good of mankind.

Nutz-anwendung (ˊ˘˘˘) f ⊕ practical application, utilization.

nutzbar (ˊ˘) a. ⊕ useful; (Gewinn tragend) profitable, productive; zu et. 2 machen to utilize, to turn to (good) account; ~**feit** f ⊕ usefulness; profitableness.

Nutzbar-machung (ˊ˘ˊ˘) f ⊕ (f. nutzbar) utilization.

Nutz-bäume (ˊ...) m/pl. ⊕, ⸗**baum-hölzer** n/pl. ⊕ timber (for building); ⸗**berechnung** ✐ f valuation of the profits; ⸗**bringend** a. ⊕ profitable, useful, advantageous; productive.

nutze, nütze (ˊ˘) a. ⊕ f. nutz¹.

Nutz-effekt (ˊ˘˘˘) m ⊕ = ⸗leistung.

Nutzen¹ (ˊ˘) [ahd.: f. genießen] m ⊕ (pl.⸗) mft: use, utility; (Gewinn) profit, gain; (Vorteil) advantage; (Ertrag von etwas) fruit, emolument; ~ bringen to yield a profit; von ~ fein to be of (great) use or advantage; mit ~ verkaufen to sell with (or at) a profit; ~ ziehen aus to derive advantage from, to make the most of, to make a profit out of.

nutzen² (ˊ˘) [ahd.] ⊕ **I** v/n. (h.) zu et. 2 (dienen) to serve (or to be useful) for a th.; wozu nutzt das? what is the use for that?; was kann es ihm 2 fich zu grämen? what can it profit (or benefit) him to worry?; das nutzt (nichts) und schadet nichts it is neither useful nor hurtful. — **II** v/a. = nützen.

nützen (ˊ˘) [ahd.] ⊕ **I** v/a.: et. 2 (aus et. Nutzen ziehen) to utilize a th., to put a th. to account; die Gelegenheit 2 to avail o.s. of (or to use) the opportunity; er nützt sein Gut jährlich auf 3000 Mark his estate brings him in £ 150 a year or per annum. — **II** v/n. = nutzen.

Nutz-garten (ˊ...) m ⊕ kitchen-garden; ⸗**gewächs** n kitchen-plant; ⸗**holz** ⊕ n (ant. Brennholz) timber (for building); ⸗**leistung** ⊕ f, mach. effective (or mechanical) power.

nützlich (ˊ˘) a. ⊕ useful, of use; 2 für, a.: conducive to health, &c.; (frommend) profitable, advantageous, (dienlich) serviceable, of service, available.

Nützlichkeit (ˊ˘˘) f ⊕ use(fulness), utility; profitableness, advantage, advantageousness; serviceableness.

Nützlichkeits-prinzip (ˊ˘˘...) n ⊕ utilitarian principle; ⸗**rücksichten** f/pl. utilitarian considerations pl.; ⸗**system** n utilitarian system; ✐ utilitarianism.

nutz-los (ˊ...) a. ⊕ useless, unprofitable, unavailing; 2loses Kapital dead capital; ⸗**losigkeit** f ⊕ uselessness, unprofitableness; ⸗**nießen** v/a. ⊕*⸪* to derive (or enjoy) the profits of; jur., auch: to usufruct; ⸗**nießer**(in f) m usufructuary; ⸗**nießung** f usufruct.

Nutzung (ˊ˘) f ⊕ **1.** = Be⸗2. — **2.** (Ertrag von et.) yield, produce, revenue.

Nutzungs-anschlag (ˊ˘˘...) m ⊕ estimate of (the) revenue; ⸗**recht** n jur. right of usufruct; ⸗**wert** m value of the produce, (amount of) revenue.

NW, öft. **NW.** abbr. = Nordwest.

Nymphe (ˊ˘) [grch.] f ⊕ **1.** myth. (Elfe) u. poet. nymph. — **2.** ent. (Puppe) chrysalis; ✐ pupa.

nymphenhaft (ˊ˘˘˘) a. ⊕ nymph-like.

O, o (ˊ) n, inv. (Buchstabe) O, o; vgl. A.
O, öft. **O.** abbr. = Oft(en).
O chm. Symbol für Oxygen (= Sauerstoff).
o! int.: **a)** Anruf: oh!; **b)** Ausruf der Bewunderung, Freude ꝛc.: oh!, ah!; o wie köstlich!(oh) how delicious!; des Schmerzes, Verdrußes ꝛc.: o des Schurfen! what a scoundrel!; **c)** in Wunschfätzen: o daß er doch bald käme! (how) I wish (that) he would soon come, feierlicher: would (to God) that he might soon come!; **d)** vor Wörtern, die e-n Satz erseßen: o ja! oh yes!, yes, indeed!, P rather!; o doch! on the contrary!; o nein! oh no!, not at all!, far from it!; o weh! oh dear (me)!, in geh. Spr.: woe (is) me!; **e)** Vokativ: o König! oh king!, o Himmel! good Heavens!

Oase (ˊ˘ˊ) [grch., *äg.] f ⊕ (fruchtbare Stelle inmitten e-r Wüste) oasis; die ~ betreffend oasal; ~**n-bewohner**(in f ⊕) m ⊕ (ˊ˘˘˘) inhabitant of an oasis.

ob¹ (ˊ) [ahd.: if] cj. **1.** whether, if; ell. ob er wohl wiederkommt? I wonder whether (or if) he will come back?; wer weiß, ob er nicht hier ift? who knows but what he may be here?;

✐ scientific; ♀ botanical; ♁ geography; ⊕ machinery; ✕ mining; ✕ military; ⚓ marine; ⊛ commercial; ✉ postal; 🚂 railway.

willst du es haben? na ob (selbstverständlich)! …? of course!, (most) certainly!, I should think so!, P rather!; ob er gewinnt oder nicht whether he wins or not; vgl. 3. — 2. als ob as if, as though; er tat, als ob er mich nicht sähe he pretended not to see me; es ist mir, als ob ich weinen möchte I feel as if I could cry; nicht als ob es mir leid täte not that I am sorry for it. — 3. ob … ob: ob Ihr sie anerkennt, ob nicht // whether you acknowledge them or not //. — 4. ob auch although, bisw.: albeit; ob er auch droht(al)though he may threaten, despite his threats.

ob² (⌣) [ahd.: (ab)ove] *prp*. **1.** (nur in geh. Spr.) = über. — **2.** ⚥ (jenseit) beyond.

Ob³ (⌣) *npr/m*. ⓜa. der ~ (ein großer sibirischer Fluß) the (river) Obi.

Ob-acht (⌣cht) [ob²] *f* ⓜ = Acht³, z.B. auf et. ~ geben to pay attention (or heed) to a th.; et. in ~ nehmen to guard a th.

Obadja (-⌣-) *npr/m*. ⓜa. *bibl*. Obadiah.

ob²-bemeldet, ⸗benannt, ⸗berührt, ⸗besagt (⌣…) *a*. ⓜ abovementioned, auch aforementioned, aforesaid.

Ob-dach (⌣ch) [ob²¹] *n* ⓜd. (*pl*. ⬆) shelter; (Wohnstätte) dwelling, lodging; e-m ~ gewähren to harbour a p.; unter ~ bringen to put (or get) under shelter.

ob-dach-los (⌣…) *a*. ⓜ without shelter, homeless; ⸗lose[r] m) *f* ⓜ homeless person, tramp; Asyl für ⸗lose casual-ward; ⸗losigkeit *f* ⓜ homelessness.

Obduktion (⌣-iz(⌣)") [lt.] *f* ⓜ jur. med. (Leichenschau)post-mortem examination.

obduzieren (⌣-⌣-⌣) [lt.] *v/a*. ⓜ to hold an inquest on (the dead body of).

O⸗Beine F(⌣.⌣) *n/pl*. ⓜ bandy (or bow-)legs. ⌊obelisk.⌋

Obelisk (⌣⌣) [grch.] *m* ⓜ (Spitzsäule)

oben (⌣-) [ahd.: (ab)ove] **I** *adv*. (ant. unten) **1.** above, im Hause: upstairs, im Himmelsraume: aloft, on high; (zu Häupten) overhead; in Büchern: wie ⓞ angegeben as previously mentioned; et. ⓞ abschöpfen to skim the surface of a th. (a. *fig*.); das ⓞ Gesagte what was previously mentioned, the statement(s) made above; da, dort ⓞ up there; weiter ⓞ further (or higher) up. — **2.** mit prp.: ⓞ an (oder ⓞ-an, f. ds) auf der Liste at the top of the list; auf dem Dache on the top of the roof; nach ⓞ (up) on high; von ⓞ herab condescendingly; uppishly; e-n von ⓞ herab ansehen to look down upon a p.; e-n von ⓞ herab behandeln to treat a p. offhandishly or haughtily; *rel*. alles Gute kommt von ⓞ all blessings come from above; e-n von ⓞ bis unten besehen to look at a p. from head to foot. — **3.** *fig*. den Kopf ⓞ behalten to keep one's head, to keep calm; mir steht die Wirtschaft bis hier ⓞ (an den Hals) I am sick and tired of it (all). I am disgusted with the affair.
— **II** ~ *n* ⓶ **4.** top, surface.

oben⸗ab (⌣…) *adv*. from the top or the surface; ⸗an *adv*. (an der Spitze) at the top or head, (in erster Stelle) in the first place; ⸗auf *adv*.: a) uppermost; on the surface or top, atop; b) ⓞ (in gehobener Stimmung) in a buoyant spirit

or vein; ⸗aus *adv*. out above; *fig*. ⓞ wollen to have high-flying schemes or high notions; ⸗benannt *a*. ⓜ abovenamed; ⸗da(r)auf *adv*. = ⸗auf a.; ⸗d(r)ein *adv*. over and above; (mit in den Kauf) into the bargain; ⸗erwähnt, ⸗genannt *a*. abovementioned; ⸗her, ⸗hin *adv*. superficially, perfunctorily; et. ⸗hin abtun to half-do (or scamp, skip, botch) a th.; ⸗hinaus *adv*. = ⸗aus; ⸗werk ⬇ *n* eines Schiffes: part of a ship above water.

ober (⌣) [ahd.: over] **I** *a*. ⓜ (D9) nur attributivisch, ohne *comp*., im Positiv mit komparativer Bed. **1.** superior; örtlich: higher, more elevated, loftier; (was etwas anderem befindlich) upper; die ⓞen Klassen einer Schule, der Gesellschaft: the upper classes *pl*.; ♪ die ⓞen Töne the higher notes *pl*. — **2.** ⓢt *sup*. topmost, highest; (vornehmster) chief, principal, (höchster) supreme, sovereign; ⓞste Gewalt, auch supremacy; *a*. prädikativ: er ist der ⸗ste (oder *adv*. er sitzt zu ⓞst) in seiner Klasse he is at the head (or top) of his class; der ⓞste Schüler the first boy, the head boy, einer großen Schule: the captain; *adv*. alles zu unterst und zu ⓞst (oder das Unterste zu ⓞst) kehren, das ⸗ste zu unterst kehren to turn everything upside down or topsy-turvy. — **II** *s*. ⓞ **3.** *s/n*. das ~e the upper parts *pl*., the top. — **4.** *s/m*.: a) der ~e the chief, the head; b) *eccl*. Vorgesetze[r] e-s Klosters, dazu als *f*: ⸗in *f* ⓞ (lady) superior; c) ~ste(r) highest (or supreme) chief; die ⸗sten des Volkes the leaders *pl*. of the people. — **III** ~ *m* ⓜ **5.** in bisch. Karten Figur zw. dem Könige u. Unter (f. ds). etwa: first knave.
— **6.** * F = (Ober-)Kellner.

Ober⸗admiral (⌣"…) *m* ⓜ high admiral; ⸗ägypten ⚥ *n* Upper Egypt; ⸗amtmann *m* high-bailiff; ⸗appellations⸗gericht(s⸗rat *m*) *n* jur. (judge attached to a) High Court of Appeal or Supreme Appellate Tribunal; ⸗arm *m* upper (part of the) arm; ⸗arzt *m* head physician or surgeon; ⸗aufseher(in *f*) *m* chief overseer, senior inspector; ⸗aufsicht *f* general superintendence; ⸗aufsichts⸗behörde *f* supreme board of control, central office; ⸗bau ⓞ *m*: a) *arch*. structure above ground, superstructure; b) 🚂 permanent way; ⸗bauch⸗gegend *f*, *anat*.: ⍺ epigastrium, epigastric region; ⸗bayern ⚥ *n* Upper Bavaria; ⸗befehl (bib. ⚔) *m* chief (or supreme) command; den ~ führen to have the chief command; ⸗befehlshaber ⚔ *m* commander-in-chief; ⸗befehlshaber⸗schaft *f* chief command(ership); ⸗berg⸗amt ⚒ *n* board of mines; ⸗berg⸗hauptmann *m* Inspector General of (the) Mines; ⸗berg⸗rat *m*, etwa: adviser of the board of mines; ⸗bett *n* coverlet, aus Daunen: eiderdown (quilt); ⸗bibliothekar *m* chief librarian; ⸗blatt *n* top sheet; ⸗boden *m* top loft or garret; ⸗bürger⸗meister *m* chief burgomaster, in Engl.: Lord Mayor; ⸗deck ⬇ *n* upper-deck; ⸗deutsch *a*. ⓜ und ~(e) *n* ⓞ: a) = hochdeutsch; b) South

German (dialect); ⸗deutsche([r] *m*) *f* ⓜ South German; ⸗deutschland ⚥ *n* Upper Germany.

Obere(r, s) (⌣⌣) *m*, *n* ⓜ f. ober 3 u. 4.

Ober⸗examinations⸗kommission (⌣"…) *f* ⓜ supreme examining board, für engl. Beamte, a.: Civil Service Commissioners *pl*.; ⸗faul *a*. ⓜ quite rotten (a. *fig*.); ⸗feld⸗herr ⚔ *m* ⌣ = ⸗befehlshaber; ⸗feldzeug⸗meister ⚔ *m* master-general of ordnance; ⸗feuerwerker ⚔ *m* laboratory-serjeant; (erster Kanonier) chief gunner; ⸗fläche *f* (*ant*. Grund) surface, *math*. auch: superficies; (Flächeninhalt) area; auf der ~, oft: on the outside; ⸗flächen⸗leitung *f*, *elect*. surface-conduction; ⸗flächlich *a*.: a) (*ant*. gründlich) superficial, shallow; ⓞe Kenntnis slight knowledge, smattering; b) *fig*. et. ⓞ (*adv*.) behandeln, auch: to treat a th. in a perfunctory manner; ⸗flächlichkeit *f* superficiality, shallowness; ⸗förster *m* upper forester or ranger; ⸗forst⸗rat *m* Commissioner of Woods and Forests; ⸗franken ⚥ *n* Upper Franconia; ⸗gärig (es Bier) ⊙ *a*. (beer) brewed by surface fermentation; ⸗gärtner *m* head gardener; ⸗gärung ⊙ *f* Brauerei: surface fermentation; ⸗gehilfe *m* chief assistant; ⸗gericht *n* high court of justice, superior court; ⸗geschoß *n* upper story; ⸗gewalt *f* supremacy, supreme power or authority; ⸗glied *n*, *phls*. major term; ⸗halb [ahd.] *prp*. (*ant*. unterhalb) mit *gen*. above; ⸗hand *f*: a) back of the hand; b) *fig*. predominance; die ~ haben, behalten to prevail; die ~ gewinnen to get the upper hand or F the whip-hand of a p., to get the best of it, to carry the day; ⸗handels⸗gericht *n* supreme commercial court; ⸗haupt *n* chief, head, sovereign; e-r Partei leader of a party; ⸗haus *n*: a) upper part of a house; b) im engl. Parlamente: Upper House, House of Lords; ⸗haut *f* top-skin, *anat*.: ⍺ epidermis; ⸗haut(zell)gewebe *n*, *anat*.: ⍺ epidermal tissue; ⸗hemd *n* day-shirt; ⸗herr *m* supreme lord, liege-lord; vgl. ⸗haupt; ⸗herrin *f* lady sovereign; ⓞherrlich *a*. lordly, sovereign (power, &c.), bsd. ehm. a. seignorial; ⸗herrlich⸗keit *f* lordship. sovereignty, ehm. auch seigniory; ⸗herrschaft *f* lordly sway, dominion, zur See: naval supremacy; ⸗hirt(e) *m*. *eccl*. (lord) bishop, prelate; ⸗hof⸗marschall *m* Lord Marshal; ⸗hof⸗meister *m* Lord High Steward; ⸗hof⸗meisterin *f* Mistress of the Robes; ⸗hof⸗prediger *m* First Chaplain in ordinary; ⸗hoheit *f* = ⸗gewalt; ⸗holz *n*: a) timber; b) branches *pl*. of a tree.

Oberin ⌣ *f* ⓜ f. ober 4b.

Ober⸗inn⸗tal ⚥ (⌣"…) *n* ⓜ valley of the Upper Inn; ⸗irdisch ⊙ *a*. ⓜ overground; *elect*. ⓞe Drahtleitung overhead wire; ⸗italien ⚥ *n* North of Italy; ⸗jäger ⚔ *m* corporal of riflemen; ⸗jägermeister *m* Master of the Hunt or of the Buckhounds; ⸗kammer⸗herr *m* Lord High Chamberlain; ⸗kellner *m* head-waiter; ⸗kiefer, ⸗kinn⸗backen *m* upper jaw; ⸗kirchen⸗rat *m*:

Zeichen (f. S. XVII): F familiär; P Volkssprache; P̄ Gaunersprache; ⬆ selten; † alt (auch gestorben); * neu (auch geboren); ⁒ unrichtig,

[**Oberklassen**] — 737 — [**Observationskorps**]

a) high consistory(-court); b) member of a high consistory; **=klassen** f pl. higher classes pl., e-r Schule auch. senior forms pl.; **=kleid** n upper (or outside) garment; **=kommandierende(r)** ⚔ m = Befehlshaber; **=kommando** ⚔ n = Befehl; **=körper** m upper part of the body; **=kriegsgerichtsrat** ⚔ m († General-auditeur) Judge-Advocate-General; **=land** n upland, upper country; ♀ das Berner ~ the Bernese Oberland or Highlands or Plateau; **=landesgericht** n court of appeal of a country or province; **=lastig** ⚓ a. ⑥ top-heavy; **=lauf** m upper course of a river; **=lausitz** ♀ npr/f. Upper Lusatia; **=leder** ☉ n Schuhmacherei: upper leather, uppers pl.; **=lehns=herr** m lord paramount. suzerain (lord); **=lehns=herrlichkeit** f suzerainty; **=lehns=recht** n right of suzerainty; **=lehrer** m (senior) master of a secondary school, professor; **=leib** m = Körper; **=leitung** f supreme direction. management; **=leutnant** ⚔ m († Premier-leutnant) (first) lieutenant; ⚓ ~ zur See (ehm. Leutnant z. S.) lieutenant; **=licht** n top- (or sky-) light, über e-r Tür fan-light (auch das betr. Fenster); **=lippe** f upper lip; **=maschinen=meister** 🚂 m superintendent of the engine-room; **=matrose** ⚓ m leading seaman; **=meister** m master of a corporation; **=militär=prüfungskommission** f supreme examining board for army candidates; **=münz=wardein** ⚔ m Master of the Mint; **=österreich** ♀ n Upper Austria; **=pfalz** ♀ f Upper Palatinate; **=pfarre** f vicarage, rectorship; **=pfarrer** m vicar, rector; **=post=amt** n chief (or general) post office; **=post=direktion** f (**=direktor** m) administration (manager) of the general post office; **=post=meister** m Postmaster-General; **=präsident** m, etwa: Lord Lieutenant of a Prussian province; **=priester** m high-priest, auch: pontiff; ♀ **priesterlich** a. pontifical; **=priestertum** n pontificate; **=prima** f senior (or highest) form of a college, in Engl. etwa: (higher division of the) sixth form; **=primaner** m student of the highest form, in Engl.: sixth-form boy (in the higher division); **=quartier=meister** ⚔ m Quartermaster-General; **=rabbiner** m chief rabbi; **=rechnungs=kammer** f in England etwa: Imperial Audit-office; **=rhein** ♀ m Upper Rhine; **=rheinisch** a. of the Upper Rhine; **=richter** m senior judge; **=rinde** f outer bark, upper crust; **=rock** m der Männer: over-coat, der Frauen: skirt of a dress; **=sachsen** ♀ n Upper Saxonia; **=satz** m: a) first principle; b) log. (ant. Untersatz) major (premise); **=schaffner** m 🚂, &c. head-guard; **=schale** f = =tasse; **=schenkel** m, anat. upper thigh; **=schiedsrichter** m first umpire, Sport: chief referee; ♀ **schlächtig**, ♀ **schlägig** ☉ a. Mühlenbau: overshot (mill); **=schlesien** ♀ n Upper Silesia; **=schule** f upper school; **=schulrat** m senior inspector of schools; **=schwelle** ☉ f, carp. e-r Fenster-, Türöffnung: lintel; **=see** ♀ m, U.S.: Lake Superior.

oberst¹ (¹⌣) f. ober 2.
Oberst² ⚔ (¹⌣) [sup. v. ober] m ⑫ colonel.
Ober=staats=anwalt (⌣⌣...) m ⑫ in Engl. Attorney-General. Solicitor-General; **=stabs=arzt** m Surgeon-Major-General; **=stadt** f upper town; **=stall=knecht** m stud-groom; **=stall=meister** m equerry to the Royal (Imperial. &c.) stud; **=standes=beamte(r)** m Registrar-General; ♀ **ständig** ⚓ a. ⑥ superior; **=statthalter** m. etwa: Governor-General. viceroy (of Ireland. India, &c.).
Oberste(r) (¹⌣⌣) m f. ober 4 c. [the mine.]
Ober=steiger ⚒ (⌣¹⌣) m ⑫ foreman of]
=Obersten=stelle (⌣⌣⌣) f ⑫ colonelcy.
Ober=steuer=direktor (⌣¹...) m ⑫. **=steuer=einnehmer** m Receiver-General of taxes; **=steuer=mann** ⚓ m first mate; **=stimme** ♪ f treble, soprano.
Oberst=inhaber ⚔ (¹⌣...) m ⑫ honorary colonel of a regiment; **=leutnant** m Lieutenant-Colonel.
Ober=stube (⌣¹...) f ⑫: a) arch. top-room, garret; b) F fig. = Kopf. meist nur im dim., zB. bei ihm ist's im **=stübchen** nicht richtig he is queer in the attic. he is touched in the upper story; **=stufe** f upper (or higher) grade.
Oberst=wachtmeister (¹⌣...) m ⑫ (nur noch in der Anrede statt „Major"): Herr ~! Major!
Ober=tasse (¹⌣...) f ⑫ cup; ~ und Untertasse cup and saucer; **=teil** m u. n upper part; **=tribunal** n supreme (or superior) court (of justice); = **und Unter=haus** n, parl. in Engl.: Upper and Lower House, the two Houses of Parliament; **=verdeck** ⚓ n upper deck; **=veterinär*** ⚔ m († Roß-arzt) army veterinary surgeon; **=vormund** m jur. chief guardian; **=vormundschaft(s-gericht** n) f in England: (High) Court of Chancery; **=wade** f, anat. thick (part) of the calf; **=wallis** ♀ n (Schweiz) Haut-Valais; ♀ **wärts** adv. in an upward direction. towards the top; **=wasser** n: a) ☉ Mühle: overshot water; b) fig. ~ (die Oberhand) h. to get the upper hand; bis seine Leidenschaft wieder ~ bekam until his passion again obtained the mastery (over him) or got the better of him; **=welt** f upper world; **=wind** m upper current of air; **=zahn** m upper tooth; **=zeremonienmeister** m Grand Master of the Ceremonies. in Engl. auch: Usher of the Black Rod; **=zeug** n (an Kleidern; ant. Futter²) cloth (for the outside). (Oberkleid[er]) outer garments pl.; **=zoll=einnehmer** (**=zoll=inspektor**) m Receiver-General (Inspector-General) of customs.
obgleich (⌣¹) cj. (al)though, auch oft: albeit; ♀ er nichts weiß (al)though he knows nothing or may not know anything, ignorant as he is, though he (may) be ignorant.
Ob=hut (⁰¹) f ⑯ guard(ianship), (Beschirmung) protection; (Sorgfalt) care; j-s ~ anvertrauen to commit to a p.'s care. to give into a p.'s charge; e-n et. in seine ~ nehmen to take (the) charge of a p., a th.
obig (¹⌣) a. ⑥ abovementioned, aforesaid. foregoing, previously mentioned or referred to; im ⌣en (weiter oben) in the

above; der, das ~e (der, das oben Erwähnte) the abovementioned (person, matter).
Objekt (⌣¹) [lt.] n ⓒ c. **1.** object. — **2.** gr. (Ziel eines transitiven v.) object; direktes (oder näheres) ~ direct object, accusative. [(for examining objects).)
Objekten=tisch (⌣¹⌣⌣) m ⑫ opt. stage)
objektiv [lt.] **I** (⌣⌣¹) a. ⑥ objective; f. Tatbestand. — **II** (⌣⌣¹) ~ n ⓒ d., a. ~**glas** n ⑫ opt. object-glass.
Objektivität (⌣⌣⌣w⌣¹) [lt.] f ⑯ phls. objectivity, objectiveness.
Oblate (⌣¹⌣, südd. a. ⌣⌣) [mhd.; *lt. obla'ta, zu offerre opfern] f ⑱ **1.** eccl. host, consecrated wafer. — **2.** (Mundlack; a. ein Backwerk) wafer.
Oblaten=bäcker (⌣¹⌣...) ☉ m ⑫ wafer-maker; **=dose** f wafer-box; **=petschaft** n wafer-seal; **=tellerchen** n wafer-dish, Cath. eccl. paten.
ob=liegen (⁰¹⌣) v n. (h.) ⓒ** **1.** e-m Werte ♀ to apply o.s. to a task, to attend to one's work; der Kunst ♀c. **2.** to study (or cultivate, pursue) art, &c. — **2.** mit sachlichem Subjekt: e-m (als Pflicht) ♀ to devolve upon a p., to fall to a p.'s duty; es liegt mir ob, zu || it is incumbent upon me to ||, I am in duty bound to || (inf.).
Ob=liegenheit (⁰¹⌣⌣) f ⑯ (Verpflichtung) obligation, incumbency; (Pflicht) duty; (Amt) office.
ob=ligat (⌣⌣¹) [lt.] a. ⑥ **1.** (verpflichtet) in duty bound. — **2.** ♪ (hauptstimmig) ob(b)ligato.
Obligation (⌣⌣⌣w=tsĭ⌣ōn) [lt.] f ⑯ (Verpflichtung) obligation; (Schuldverschreibung) bond, obligation.
ob=ligatorisch (⌣⌣w⌣¹⌣) [lt.] a. ⑥ (verpflichtend; ant. fakultativ) obligatory (subject, &c.), compulsory (attendance, &c.).
Obligo ☣ (⌣¹⌣) [it. o'bbligo] n ⓝ (Verbindlichkeit) obligation to pay; ohne ~ without prejudice, free from liability.
Ob=long(um) (⁰¹⌣) [lt. länglich] n ⑬ (⑱ ⑥) math. (Recht-eck) oblong, rectangle.
Ob=macht (⁰¹⌣ct) f ⑯ superior (or supreme) power.
Ob=mann (⁰¹⌣) m ⓒ c. **1.** (Oberster) chief; (Vorsitzender) chairman; ~ der Geschworenen foreman of the jury. — **2.** (Schiedsmann) umpire.
O=bo=e (-¹⌣) ♫c. f. Hoboe ♫c.
Obolus (¹⌣⌣) [grch.] m, inv. ob. ⑫ Alt.: (¹⁄₆ Drachme) obol(us); (Scherflein) mite.
Obrigkeit (¹⌣⌣) f ⑯ (public) authorities pl.. government, magistracy; bibl. es ist keine ~ ohne von Gott (Römerbrief XIII, 1) the powers that be are ordained of God.
obrigkeitlich (¹⌣⌣⌣) a. ⑥ governmental, magisterial; adv. auch: by (public) authority.
Obrist ⚔ (⌣¹) m ⑫ f. Oberst². [authority.)
ob=schon (⁰¹) cj. = obgleich. [obsequies pl.)
Obsequi=en (⌣¹⌣) [lt.] pl. ⑱ (Totenfeier))
Observanz (⌣⌣w⌣¹) [lt.] f ⑯ bfd. eccl. (Gepflogenheit) observance, custom, rule; (Konfession) denomination, faith; ♀ **mäßig** (⌣¹...) a. ⑥ in conformity with the rule(s), according to custom.
Observation (⌣⌣⌣w-tsĭ⌣ōn) [lt.] f ⑯ (Beobachtung) observation, zB. ~s=**heer**. ~s=**korps** ⚔ n flying corps, mobile column; army of observation.

♪ Musik; ⚛ Wissenschaft; ❦ Pflanze; 🏆 Geographie; ☉ Technik; ⚒ Bergbau; ⚔ Militär; ⚓ Marine; ☣ Handel; ✉ Post; 🚂 Eisenbahn.

Observatorium n (Sternwarte) observatory. [obsidian.]
Obsidian m ⟨d. min.⟩
ob-siegen v/n. (h.) p.p. u. inf. ⟨**, sonst ⟨*: seinen Feinden 2 to carry the victory (or to triumph) over one's enemies; e-r Sache (dat.) 2 to conquer (or carry) a th.
obskur a. (dunkel, bsd. fig. unbekannt) obscure; F der Mensch nonentity.
Obskurant m⟨ = Finsterling 1; ~ismus m ⟨ obscurantism.
obsolet a. (veraltet) obsolete, (gone) out of fashion, antiquated.
Ob-sorge f ⟨ (Aufsicht) control, care.
Obst n ⟨ahd.⟩ a. fruit; (eatable) fruits pl. of trees, shrubs. &c.
Obst-bau m ⟨ fruit-culture, growing (of) fruit(-trees); **=baum** m fruit-tree; **=baum-zucht** f = bcu, a.: ⟨ pomiculture; **=baum-züchter** m grower of fruit-trees, cultivator of fruit; **=boden** m loft for drying fruit; **=branntwein** m fr.-brandy; **=brecher** ⟨ m (Werkzeug) hook (or implement) for gathering fruit, auch: fruit-gatherer; **=bude** f fr.-stall; **=darre** f fr.-kiln; **=ernte**(**=zeit**) f fr.-crop, fruit-gathering (season); **=frau** f woman selling fruit; **=garten** m orchard, fruit-garden; **=gärtner** m fruit-grower or -gardener; **=göttin** f goddess of fruit, Pomona; **=handel** ⟨ m fruit-trade; **=händler**(**in** f) m fruiterer, dealer in fruit; vgl. **=höker**(**in**); **=handlung** f fruit-shop or -business; **=höker**(**in** f) m costermonger. [stinate.
obstinat [lt.] a. (eigensinnig) ob-
Obst-jahr n ⟨ fruit-year; good, bad year for fruit; **=kammer** f fr.-loft; fig. fr.-country; **=keller** m fruit-cellar; **=kenner** m: a) pomologist; (kleinerer:) kernel (or stone) of fruit, kleinerer: pip; **=korb** m fr.-basket; **=kultur** f = **=bau**; **=kunde**, **=lehre** f: ⟨ pomology; **=markt** m fr.-market; **=messer** n fr.-knife; **=most** m new home-made wine, v. Äpfeln: new cider; **=mus** n jam, aus Apfelsinen: marmalade; **=pflanzung** f nursery (or plantation) of fr.-trees; **=reich** a. abounding in fruit.
obstruieren [lt.] v/a. ⟨ parl. (verschleppen) to obstruct; med. (hartleibig m.) to constipate. [struction.
Obstruktion [lt.] f ⟨ parl. ob-
Obst-schralle f ⟨ garlic pear (Crataeˈvagynaˈndra); **=stück** n. paint. fruit-piece; **=wein** m home-made (or British) wine, bsd. (Apfelwein) cider; **=werk** n fruit(ery); **=zeit** f fruit-season; **=zucht** f = **=bau**; **=züchter** m = **=gärtner**.
obszön [lt. obs-c(a)eˈnus totig] a. ⟨ (unzüchtig) obscene, smutty; **~ität** f ⟨ obscenity, smut, smuttiness.
ob-walten v/n. (h.) ⟨** 1. mit persönlichem Subjekt: to rule (over a th.); e-m Dinge 2 to control a th. — 2. mit sachlichem Subjekt: to exist, to be in actual existence; da Gefahr obwaltete as there was danger (ahead); bei (ober unter) den Oben Umständen under the prevailing circumstances, as things are or were.
ob-wohl, öft. **ob-zwar** cj. = obgleich.

Ochlokrat m (Anhänger der ~ie) ochlocrat; **~ie** f ⟨ (Pöbelherrschaft) mobocracy; **2isch** a. ⟨ ochlocratical.
Ochs (Ochs) m ⟨, **Ochse** m ⟨ [ahd.: ox] 1. ox, bullock; der ~ brüllt the ox bellows; f. Berg 2. — 2. F fig. (dummer, plumper Kerl) clumsy fellow, blockhead; (grober Lümmel) boor, bear.
ochsen F v/n. (h.) ⟨ = büffeln.
ochsen-artig a. ⟨ ox-like, ⟨ bovine; **=auge** n ⟨ bull's eye = ⟨ arch.), ox-eye; **2äugig** a. ox-eyed; **=bauer** m farmer who tills his land with oxen; **=blase** f ox-bladder; **=blut** n blood of an ox; **=braten** m Kocht. (joint of) roast beef; **=darm** m bullock's gut; **=fleisch** n beef; **=galle** f. pharm. ox-gall, (lt.) fel bovinum; **=geschlecht** n breed of oxen, ⟨ bovine genus; **=gespann** n team of oxen.
ochsenhaft a. ⟨ ox-like; (plump) heavy, clumsy, (dumm) stupid.
Ochsen-handel m ⟨ cattle-trade; **=händler** m cattle-dealer, drover; **=haut** f ox- (or bull's) hide; **=herz** n Fleischerei: bullock's heart; **=hirt**(**e**) n neatherd; **=kalb** n bull-calf; **=kopf** m: a) bullock's head (auch fig. bei Pferden): b) P fig. (Dummkopf) blockhead, dunce; **=leder** n ox-leather, neat's leather; **=markt** m market for oxen or bullocks; **2mäßig** a. ⟨ = ochsenhaft; F fig. adv. a. immensely, enormously; **=schwanz** m ox-tail; **=schwanz-suppe** f Kocht.: ox-tail soup; **=stall** m ox-stall or -house; **=treiber** m driver of oxen, drover, oxman; **=treib-stock** m ox-goad; **=ziemer** m: a) bull's pizzle; b) zum Prügeln: cowhide, horsewhip; **=züchter** m breeder of oxen; **=zunge** f: a) Fleischerei: ox-tongue; b) ⟨ echte ~ ox-tongue, bugloss (Anchuˈsa officinaˈlis).
ochsig a. ⟨ 1. = ochsenhaft. — 2. F fig. enormous, huge, tremendous.
Ocker [mhd.: *grch. ochra f] m ⟨ min. (eisenhaltiger Ton) (yellow) ochre; **2-artig**, **2-farbig** a. ⟨ ochr(ac)eous; **~gelb** n ⟨ min. yellow earth; ob. abbr. = oder. [**2-haltig** a. ochry.]
Odaliske [türk. odalyˈk Stuben-...(mädchen)] f ⟨ odalisque.
Ode [fr.: *grch. Sang] f ⟨ ode.
öde¹ [ahd. leer] a. ⟨ deserted, desolate, dreary, (unbewohnt) uninhabited, (unbebaut) uncultivated, waste; (einsam) solitary, (still) silent.
Öde² [ahd. Wüste] f ⟨ 1. desertedness, desolation, dreariness. — 2. (öde Gegend) desert(ed country), solitude; waste.
Odem [mhd.] m ⟨ (o. pl.) † und jetzt noch bibl. ob. poet. = Atem.
Odem ⟨ [grch. Geschwulst] n ⟨d. path. (Wassergeschwulst) oedema.
oden-artig [...] ⟨de pl.] a. ⟨ odic; **=dichter** m ⟨ writer of odes, a. odemaker, weits. lyric poet.
Ode-on [grch.] n ⟨ = Odeum.
oder [ahd.] cj. or (f. auch 2 am Schluß); eins 2 das andre either one thing or the other; 2 (aber) (sonst) otherwise, (or) else; in the contrary (or opposite) case. — Vgl. entweder.

Odermennig f ⟨ [mhd. (P)] lt. agrimoˈnia f; *grch. argēmōˈnē] m ⟨ agrimony, feverfew.
Ode-um [lt., *grch.] n ⟨ Alt.: (Gebäude für musische Wettkämpfe) odeon, odeum.
Öd-feld n ⟨ barren (or waste, untilled) field.
Ödigkeit f ⟨ solitariness.
Odin [isländ.] npr/m. ⟨a. myth. (höchste german. Gottheit) Odin, Wodan, Woden.
Öd-land n ⟨b. barren (or waste) land.
Odyssee [grch.] f ⟨ Homerisches Epos: Odyssey, f. Irrfahrt.
Ofen [ahd.: oven] m ⟨ 1. (Heizraum) fire-place, (Stuben-) ~ stove; (immer) hinter dem ~ hocken to coddle (or snuggle) over the fire, never to stir from the corner of one's chimney. to be a home-bird; fig. den Hund vom ~ zu locken wissen to know how to manage things, to be very knowing or F up to snuff. — 2. ⊙ zum Brotbacken: oven, zum Kalkbrennen: kiln; (Fabrik, Gebläse, Schmelz-) ~ furnace; den ~ abstechen to tap the furnace; rauchverzehrender ~ smoke-consuming furnace; (Koch-) ~ kitchener; bibl. der feurige ~ the fiery furnace.
Ofen-arbeiter ⊙ [...] m ⟨ oven-man; **=aufsatz** m cornice (or top-piece) of a stove; **=bank** f bench by (the side of) a stove; **=blech** n: a) plate serving as guard in front of a stove; b) oven-tin for baking, &c.; **=gabel** f oven-fork or -rake; **=gekrätz** n furnace-ends pl.; **=gitter** n guard; **=haken** m = **=gabel**; **=heizer** m furnace-feeder; **=herd** m hearth; **=hocker**(**in** f) F stay-at-home (bird); (verfrorene Person) F coddle, chilly subject; **=kachel** f = Kachel; **=klappe** f register (of a stove); **=krücke** f = **=gabel**; **=loch** n, **=mund** m oven-mouth; **=rechen** m furnace-rake; **=röhre** f: a) a. **=rohr** n stove-pipe, flue; b) (in den Ofen eingebauter Raum zur Wärmung von Speisen zc.) oven; **=rost** m grate of a stove or an oven; **=ruß** m soot from an oven; **=sau** f, metall. furnace-pig; **=schaufel**, **=schippe** f oven-peel; fire-shovel; **=schirm** m fire-screen; **=schlacke** f furnace-slag; **=schwärze** f black-lead, mit ~ putzen to black-lead; **=setzer** m one who puts up ovens, stove-fitter; **=sohle** f furnace-bed; **=tür**(**e**) f oven-door, door of a stove; **=vorsetzer** m fender.
offen [ahd.: open] a. ⟨ (D9) 1. open; bei den Türen with open doors; 2 stehen to stand open; die Tür steht halb 2 ... is ajar (vgl. Stech(c)n); fig. (ohne Hinterhalt) frank, (aufrichtig) sincere; (treuherzig) candid, ingenuous; adv. 2 gesagt frankly speaking; frei und 2 handeln to act straightforwardly; 2 mit der Sprache herausrücken to speak plainly or without reserve; 2 (unbeschrieben) lassen to leave blank; f. Hintertür; die Jagd ist 2 the shooting season has opened; die Wahl steht ihm 2 he has the choice, he is free to choose; jungen Leuten steht die Welt 2 young people have the world before them. — 2. mit s.: der Blick open face or countenance; des Geständnis frank (or full) ad-

Signs (see page XVII): F familiar; P vulgar; ſ flash; ⟨ rare; † obsolete (died); * new word (born); ++ incorrect; ♪ music;

[offenbar] — 739 — [ohne]

mission; ein Les Haus h. to keep open house; Ler (heller) Kopf clear intellect, clever head; Ler Kredit unlimited (or blank) credit; Ler Leib open (or loose) bowels pl.; ↓ Le See high sea, offing; auf Ler See in the offing, on the open sea, on the main; Le Stelle: a) in e-r Hecke ꝛc.: opening, gap; b) vacant post, vacancy; Le Straße public road or thoroughfare; auf Ler Straße in the open street; 2 zutage liegen to be obvious or evident or patent; *fig.* mit Lem Visier openly, above board. — 3. ● Le Rechnung current (or running) account; Ler Wechsel blank cheque; 2 (*adv.*) bleibender Posten uncovered amount.

offenbar (ˇ˘‿) [ahd.] *a.* ⊕ (*ant.* geheim) manifest; (in die Augen springend) obvious, evident, (handgreiflich) palpable; (sichtbar) visible, plain, (klar) clear; (allgemein bekannt) notorious, public; Le Beleidigung downright insult; 2 werden to become known, to get wind, F to leak out; er hat sich 2 (*adv.*) geirrt he is evidently (or clearly) mistaken.

offenbaren (˘‿‿) I *v/a.* u. sich 2 *v/refl.* ●* (*.*.*): (sich) 2 to (become) manifest, to make (o.s.) known, *theol.* to reveal (o.s.); ein Geheimnis ꝛc. 2 to disclose or unveil …, F to let out …; e-m sein Herz 2, sich e-m 2 to open one's heart or to unbosom o.s. to a p. — II **offenbart**, *theol.* **ge-offenbart** *p.p.* u. *a.* ⊕ (made) public; offenbarte Heimlichkeit open secret; die geoffenbarte Religion revealed religion.

Offenbarung (˘‿‿) *f* ⊕ (f. offenbaren) manifestation, revelation (a. *theol.*); disclosure; publication; *bibl.* die ~ Johannis the Revelation of St. John, the Apocalypse.

Offenbarungs=eid (˘‿‿…) *m* ⊕ *jur.* oath of manifestation; **=glaube** *m* (=gläubige[r] *s.*) belief (believer) in revealed religion.

offen=halten (ˇ‿,ˇ‿) *v/a.* ⊕* (vorbehalten) to reserve.

Offenheit (ˇ‿‿) *f* ⊕ (f. offen) openness, frankness, open-heartedness; candour.

offen=herzig (ˇ‿…) *a.* ⊕ open-hearted, frank, outspoken; (aufrichtig) candid, sincere; **=herzigkeit** *f* ⊕ open-heartedness, frankness; candour; F *co.* sein Rock hat einige ~en (Risse) … is torn in several places, *co.* … is more holy than righteous; 2**kundig** *a.* well-known, manifest, notorious, public; (frech) barefaced; =kundigkeit *f* notoriousness, publicity; 2legen *v/a.* ●** to lay open; 2leibig *a.* with open bowels; 2sichtlich* *a.* manifest.

offensiv ˟ (˘‿‿ˊ) [neu=lt.] *a.* ⊕ (*ant.* defensiv) offensive; ~**=bündnis** *n* ⊕ offensive alliance; ~**e** ˟ (˘‿‿ˊ˘) *f* ⊕ (*ant.* Defensive): die ~e ergreifen to take (or assume) the offensive, to (open the) attack; ~**=krieg** *m* offensive war.

offen=steh(e)n (ˇ‿ˊ‿) *v/n.* (h.) ●** *fig.* (freistehn, gestattet sein) to be allowed, to be open to, vgl. offen 1 Anfang und Schluß; 2**stehend** *p.pr.* u. *a.* ⊕ (standing) open; obvious; (klaffend) yawning, (aufspringend): ⚛ dehiscent.

öffentlich (ˇ˘‿) [ahd.] *a.* ⊕ (*ant.* geheim) public; 2 (*adv.*) bekannt m. to publish, to make public; Le Bekanntmachung public announcement, publication, der Obrigkeit: proclamation, e-r Partei ꝛc.: manifesto; vor Lem Gericht in (the) open court; auf Ler Straße in a public thoroughfare, in the open street; 2 2 (*adv.*) verkaufen to sell by public auction.

Öffentlichkeit (ˇ˘‿‿) *f* ⊕ publicity; an die ~ treten to come (or appear) before the public, to appear publicly.

offerieren (˘‿‿ˊ) [it.] *v/a.* ⊕ (anbieten) to offer; **Offert(e** *f*) ⊕ *n* ⊕c. (˘ˊ(˘) (Anerbieten) offer, *sup.* tender, proposal, ● auch: tender.

Offizial (˘ˇ(˘)ˊ) [it.] *m* ⊕d. *Cath. eccl.* (weltlicher Vertreter eines Bischofs) official.

Offiziant (˘ˇ(˘)ˊ˘) [it.] *m* ⊕ *Cath. eccl.* (diensttuender Priester) officiating priest.

offiziell (˘ˇ(˘)ˊ) [fr.] *a.* ⊕ — amtlich.

Offizier (˘ˇ‿ˊ) [fr.; *It. offi′cium*] *m* ⊕d. 1. ˟ u. ↓ officer; ältester, jüngster ~ dem Range nach: senior, junior officer; höherer ~ superior officer; ~ unterm Hauptmann subaltern; vom Gemeinen zum ~ emporsteigen to rise (or to be raised) from the ranks, vgl. Pike; zur Disposition gestellter ~ (mit Pension) half-pay officer; ~ vom Dienst († du jour) officer on duty. — 2. Schach: ~e *pl.* (Figuren außer Bauern) the best men or pieces *pl.*

Offizier=korps ˟ (˘ˇ‿ˊ,ˊ) *n* ⊕ body (or staff) of officers.

Offiziers=aspirant ˟ und ↓ (˘ˇ‿ˊ…) *m* ⊕ = Fahnenjunker b; **=bursche** *m* officer's man; **=degen** *m* officer's sword; **=examen** *n* examination qualifying for a(n officer's) commission; **=kasino** *n* officers' club; **=patent** *n* commission; **=stand** *m* military profession; officers *pl.*

Offizier=verein (˘ˇ‿ˊ,˘ˊ) *m* ⊕ army-and-navy club; Bedarfshaus, Warenlager des ~s army-and-navy stores *pl.*

Offizin (˘ˇ‿ˊ) [it.] *f* ⊕ workshop; eng=S.: a) *pharm.* (Laboratorium) laboratory; (Apotheke) chemist's shop; (Aufbewahrungsort der Drogen) drug-stores *pl.*; b) (Buchdruckerei) printing-office or =establishment or -house.

offizinell (˘ˇ‿‿ˊ) [fr.=It.] *a.* ⊕ *pharm.* (vorgeschrieben) officinal; Le Kräuter *n/pl.*, auch: medicinal herbs *pl.*

offiziös (˘ˇ‿ˊ) [fr.=It.] *a.* ⊕ (D10) (halbamtlich) semi-official (paper, &c.).

öffnen (ˇ‿) [ahd.; *offen*] I *v/a.*, *v/n.* (h.) u. sich 2 *v/refl.* ●b. to open, et. Verkorktes: to uncork a bottle; et. Versiegeltes: to unseal a letter; durch Einschlagen: to stave in a cask, durch Bohren: to bore open a case, &c.; mit dem Dietrich: to pick a lock; *fig.* e-m die Augen 2 to open a p.'s eyes, to undeceive (or disillusion) a p.; die Tür 2 to open the door for a p., von Dienstboten: to answer the door; *fig.* dem Laster Tür und Tor 2 to give full license (or scope) to vice; e-m die Wege 2 to pave the way for a p.; *med.* einen Abszeß 2 to lance an abscess; den Leib 2 to open (or loosen) the bowels; e-e Leiche 2 to dissect a (dead) body;

♀ von Kapseln: sich 2 ⚛ to dehisce. — II ~ *n* ⊕ = Öffnung 1.

Öffner (ˇ‿) *m* ⊕, ~**in** *f* ⊕ opener.

Öffnung (ˇ‿) [ahd.] *f* ⊕ 1. (das Öffnen) opening, &c. — 2. (offene Stelle) opening, aperture, in einem Walde: glade; (Loch) hole; (Eingang) entrance, (Mündung) mouth, orifice; (Spalt, Riß) chink, gap, crack, (Schlitz) slit; in e-m Briefkasten ꝛc.: slot, in einer Glasröhre, einem Fasse ꝛc.: leakage. — 3. = Leibes=öffnung; keine ~ h. to be constipated or costive or bound. — ~**s=mittel** (ˇ‿,˘ˊ) *n* ⊕ *med.* aperient, medicine for loosening the bowels.

oft (ˊ) [ahd.] *adv.* oft(en) (ˇ a. ⊕), *comp.* öfter, *sup.* öftest 1. *adv.* (häufig) frequent; (vielmal) many times; **ebenso** 2 wie // as often as //; **sehr** 2 very often, many (F scores of) times; ich habe es dir so 2 gesagt, daß // I have told you so often (or again and again) that //; vgl. sooft; Ausruf: **wie** 2 //! how many times //!; wie 2 ist 2 in 6 enthalten? how many times is two contained in six?; nur zu 2 only too often. — 2. **öfter** *comp.*, bisw. doppelt gesteigert: öfterer: a) ich sehe ihn öfter als dich I see him oftener (or more often) than you; je öfter ich ihn treffe, desto mehr // the oftener I meet (or the more I see of) him the more //; b) ohne Vergleich in der Zahl: **öfter(s)**, des (ob. zum) **öfter(e)n** (manchmal) oftentimes, (pretty) often, frequently; c) als *a.*: ein öfteres Kommen frequent (or numerous) visits *pl.* — 3. im *sup.* **am** (ob. **zum**) **öftesten** most frequently, bisw. auch: oftenest.

oft=malig (ˊ…) *a.* ⊕ frequent, repeated; 2**mals** *adv.* often, oftentimes, frequently, repeatedly.

Oger (ˊ‿) [fr.] *npr/m.* ⊕ (Riese) ogre.

oh (ˊ) *int.* u. **Oh** n ⊕: 2! oh! (alleinstehend,) **oha!** (‿ˊ) *int.* hallo! [sonst o! f. das.]

Oheim, Ohm¹ (ˊ(‿) [ahd.] *m* ⊕d. uncle.

Ohm² † (ˊ) [ahd.; lt. (h)ama *f*, *grch. ȧ′me* Eimer] *m*, *n* ⊕b, 6, *f* ⊕ 6 (137,4 Liter) aam.

Ohm³ (ˊ) [bisch. Physiker Ohm, 1787–1854] *n* ⊕ 6. (a. *inv.*) *elect.* (Einheit des elektrischen Widerstandes) † ohm, † ohmad; 4 ~ four ohm; nach ~ gemessen ohmic; **ohmsch** *a.* ⊕: Ohmsches Gesetz Ohm's law.

Ohm = **Oh(ei)m**. [(*Mono′tropa unifto′ra*).)

Ohn=blatt ♀ (ˊ‿) *n* ⊕ tobacco-pipe)

ohne (ˊ‿) [ahd.; *arch. a′neu*] I *prp.* mit *acc.* 1. without, F minus; 2 Arbeit without (or out of) work; 2 Bedeutung of no consequence; 2 Gefühl devoid of feeling; 2 Geist lacking in wit; 2 Geld hard up for money, impecunious; 2 seine Hilfe wäre ich nicht hier I should not be here but for his assistance or had it not been for him; 2 Stelle without a situation, out of employment; 2 weiteres without (more or further) ado; 2 mein Wissen unbeknown to me; 2 Zweifel, zweifels2 without (a) doubt, undoubtedly. — 2. *ell.* das (oder die Sache) ist nicht (so ganz) 2: a) (nicht ohne Grund) it is not unlikely, F there's something in that; b) (hat viel für sich) there's a great deal to be said for it; der Mensch ist nicht 2 (Geschick ꝛc.)

⚛ scientific; ♀ botanical; ⚲ geography; ⊕ machinery; ✕ mining; ˟ military; ↓ marine; ● commercial; ✉ postal; 🚂 railway.

[ohnedas] — 740 — [Oktavianus]

the fellow has some good (stuff) in him, he is not a fool, he is not half bad. — II *conj.* 3. ⌾ daß //, bei gleichem Subjekt auch: ⌾ zu // (*inf.*) but that //; ⌾ daß ich ihn kenne without my knowing him, P (nicht nachzuahmen!) without I know him; er lief ⌾ einzuhalten he ran without stopping; ⌾ daß (außer wenn) ich es sehe (ob. ⌾ es zu sehen), kann ich es nicht glauben unless I see it ...

ohne-das (⌴...), ⌾**dem** †, ⌾**dies** *adv.* without (or apart from) that; (außerdem) besides, moreover; ⌾**gleichen** *a.* unequalled, unparalleled, matchless, *adv.* uniquely; ⌾**hin** = ⌾**das**; =**hose(n** *pl.*) *m* ⓱ *hist.* Sansculotte. =**maßen** *adv.* beyond measure, exceedingly; =**sorge** *m* child (or person) without (a) care; F happy-go-lucky (chap).

ohn-geachtet (⌴⌵⌣) [+. st. un=] = ungeachtet. [ungefähr (f. das).}

ohn-gefähr (⌴⌵||) [mhd.] †, nhd. ⇢=

Ohn-macht (⌴...) [ahd.] *f* ⓱ a) impotence, powerlessness, (Schwäche) weakness, b) *path.* (Bewußtlosigkeit) unconsciousness, mit Herabsetzung der Herztätigkeit: fainting fit, seltener: swoon, *path.* syncope (of the heart); s. fallen 4; es wandelte ihn eine ~ an a (feeling of) faintness came over him or seized him, F he felt faint; ⌾**mächtig** *a.* ⓱: a) infirm, weak; impotent, powerless, ⌾ (*adv.*) schimpfen, biswl. to bark at the moon; b) *path.* unconscious, faint (-ing), in a faint, seltener: swooning; ⌾ w. to faint (away), to have a fainting fit, *a.* to swoon, F to go off (in a dead faint); ⌾**maßen** = ohnemaßen.

oho (⌣⌴) *int.* ⌾! oho!, Pyah!; s. ho.

Ohr (⌴) [ahd.: ear: lt. *auris*] *n* ⓲c.
1. Körperteil: ear; äußeres ~ external ear, ⌵ auricle; s. Eselsohr *fig.*; musikalisches ~ (Gehör) musical ear, ear for music; vgl. a. Öhr. — 2. Redens-arten: bei e-m ein geneigtes (offenes oder williges) ~ finden to obtain a favourable hearing from a p.; die ~en steif halten to keep up one's spirits or courage; mir klingen die ~en he my ears tingle (a. *fig.* = es wird von mir gesprochen); e-m ein geneigtes (oder williges) ~ leihen to lend one's (or to give) ear to a p., to listen to a p.; tauben ~en predigen to preach to deaf (or unwilling) ears; einem die ~en voll schreien to deafen a p. with (one's) shouting; ganz ~ sein to be all ear or attention; die ~en (horchend) spitzen to prick up one's ears; einem Hunde die ~en stutzen to crop a dog's ears; sich die ~en zuhalten to close (or shut up, stop up) one's ears; *bibl.* wer ~en hat zu hören, der höre he that has ears to hear let him hear; Sprichw. die Wände haben ~en walls have ears, von kleinen Kindern: little pitchers have long ears. — 3. nach *prp.* (oft *fig.*): e-m **an** (oder beim) ~e zupfen to pull a p.'s ears (for him); er hört nicht gut **auf** dem rechten ~e he is slightly deaf on the right ear; sich aufs ~ legen to lie down (to rest), to take a nap; e-n **bei** den ~en fassen (sich festhalten) to collar a p.; sich **hinter** den ~en kratzen to scratch one's ear; er ist hinter den ~en

noch nicht trocken (er ist jung, unerfahren) he is a greenhorn; er hat es dick (oder den Schalk) hinter den ~en (sitzen) he is a (bit of a) wag or rogue, he is a sly fellow or F sly-boots; sich (*dat.*) etwas hinter die ~en schreiben to take particular notice of (or to note) a th.; e-m et. **in** das ~ flüstern to whisper a th. in(to) a p.'s ear; e-m in den ~en liegen (mit Reden zusetzen) to keep dinning in(to) a p.'s ears, to talk a p. to death; e-m einen Floh ins ~ setzen (et. Verdrießliches sagen) to put a flea in a p.'s ear; et. **mit** gespanntem ~e anhören to listen to a th. with the closest attention; eins übers ~ bekommen to receive a box on the ear, F to get one's ears boxed; f. hauen 2; einem das Fell über die ~en ziehen to fleece a p.; bis über die ~en up to one's ears; bis über die ~en rot werden to blush up to one's eyes; bis über die ~en in Schulden stecken (verliebt sein) to be over head and ears (or to be deeply, hopelessly) in debt (in love); **vor** seinen ~en in his hearing; e-m et. **zu** ~en bringen to inform (or apprise) a p. of a th.; es ist mir zu ~en gekommen it has come to my ears or my knowledge, I have been told, I have heard, I understand; zu e-m ~ hinein, zum andern (flugs) heraus in at one ear, (and) out at the other.

Öhr ⓞ (⌴) [ahd.: *Öhr] *n* ⓲c.: a) eye of a needle; ~e schlagen to perforate needles; b) ~ für e-n Haken: catch for a hook; c) ~ eines Bolzens ⦆c.: eyelet, d) (Henkel) handle; e) (Loch zur Aufnahme des Stiels in Hämmern ⦆c.) eye.

Ohr-bammel (⌴...) *f* ⓱, =**baumel** *f* = Ohrgehänge.

Öhrchen (⌴) *n* ⓳: a) (*dim.* von Ohr) little ear, auricle; b) ⓞ (*dim* von Öhr) little eye, eyelet; small catch for a hook.

Ohr-drüse (⌴...) *f* ⓱ = Ohrspeicheldrüse.

ohren (⌴) *v/a.* ⓱ (mit Ohren versehen) to provide with ears; bsd. im *p.p.* ge**ohrt** eared, ⌵ auriculate(d); von Gefäßen: (provided) with handles; oft in Zssgn, z.B. langgeohrt long-eared.

öhren ⓞ (⌴)*v/a.*⓱: Nadeln ⌾ (mit e-m Öhr versehen) to eye (or perforate) needles.

Ohren-arzt (⌴...) *m* ⓱ specialist for ear-diseases, ⌵ aurist, otologist; =**beichte** *f*, *eccl.* auricular confession; =**bläser(in/**)*m*tell-tale, scandalmonger, slanderer; =**bläserei** *f* scandal, slander; =**brausen** *n* = sausen; =**entzündung** *f* inflammation of the ear *or* otitis; =**fluß** *m*, *path.* running from the ear, eitriger: ⌵ otorrhoea, blutiger: ⌵ otorrhagia =**kitzel** *m* tickling in one's ears; *fig.* curiosity; =**klingen** *n* singing in the ear(s), ⌵ tinnitus, ⌵ aural disease, otopathy; =**kunde** *f*, *med.*: ⌵ otology; =**leiden** *n* = =krankheit; =**reißen** *n*, *path.*: ⌵ otodynia; =**sausen** *n*, *path.* buzzing in the ear(s); =**schmalz** *n* ear-wax, ⌵ cerumen; =**schmaus** *m* feast (or treat) for the ears, musical treat, sweet melodies *pl.*; =**schmerz** *m* = =zwang; =**spiegel** *m*, *med.* auriscope, otoscope; =**wärmer** *m* cover (or wrap) for the ears, ear-flap;

=**zeuge** *m* auricular (or ear-)witness; =**zwang** *m*, *path.* earache, otalgia.

Ohr-eule (⌴...) *f* ⓱ *orn.* (bsd. Uhu) horned (or horn-)owl (*Bubo ma'ximus*); =**feige** *f* [nhd., P(ndl. *veeg* Schlag)] box on the ear, smack (or slap) in the face; ⌾**feigen** *v/a.* ⓱***: e-n ⌾ to box a p.'s ears, to smack (or slap) a p.'s face; =**förmig** *a.* ⓱ ear-shaped, ⌵ auriform, auricular, ⌵ u. zo.: ⌵ auriculate(d); =**gehänge** = **geschmeide** *n* ear-drops, pendants *pl.*; =**höhle** *f*, *anat.* cavity of the ear; =**holz** ↓ *n* bollard-timber. =**..ohrig** (...⌴) *a.* ⓱: lang=⌾ long-eared, (provided) with long ears, flap-eared (horse), ⌵ aurite, macrotous.

Ohr-kissen (⌴...) *n* ⓱ small pillow; =**läppchen** *n* lob(ul)e (or flap, tip) of the ear; =**leiste** *f* = =schnecke; =**loch** *n* ear-hole; e-m =**löcher** stechen to pierce a p.'s ears; =**löffel** *m* ear-pick, ⌵ auriscalp; =**muschel** *f*, *anat.* shell (or exterior part) of the ear, external ear, ⌵ auricle, (It.) concha, =**öffnung** *f* ear-hole; =**ring** *m* ear-ring; =**schmuck** *m* ear-ornament; =**schnecke** *f*, *anat.*: ⌵ auricle (*Auri'cula*); =**speichel-drüse** *f*, *anat.*: ⌵ parotid gland; =**speichel-drüsen-entzündung** *f*: ⌵ paroti(di)tis; =**trompete** *f*, *anat.* Eustachian tube; =**wurm** *m*, *ent.* ear-wig or =piercer (*Forfi'cula*); ⌾**zerreißend** *a.* =ear-splitting (music, &c.). [gracious!]

oje(mine) (⌴) (⌵⌣) *int.* dear me!, good)

Okapi (⌴) *n* ⓱ zo. okapi.

Okarina (⌴⌵⌣) [it.] *f* ⓱ ocarina.

Okkultismus (⌵⌣⌴⌣) [it.] *m* ⓱ (geheime Wissenschaft) occultism, occult science(s *pl.*)

okkupieren (⌵⌣⌴⌣) [it.] **I** *v/a.* ⓱ (innehaben) to occupy. — **II** ~ *n* ⓱ u. **Okkupierung** *f* ⓱ occupation.

Ökonom (⌣⌴) [grch. Haushalter] *m* ⓱ (good or economical) housekeeper, (Verwalter) steward, bailiff, manager, (Landwirt) (gentleman-)farmer, wissenschaftlich gebildeter: agriculturist; ⌶ Speisewirt; vgl. Nationalökonom.

Ökonomie (⌣⌴⌵) [grch.] *f* ⓲ (Sparsamkeit) economy; (Kunst der Haushaltung) art of housekeeping; weitS. = Landbau.

Ökonomie-gebäude (⌴...) *n*/*pl.* ⓱ *agr.* farm-building(s *pl.*); =**verwalter** *m* steward of a farm.

ökonomisch (⌣⌵⌴) [grch.] *a.* ⓱: a) (sparsam) economical, thrifty; ⌾ (*adv.*) umgehen mit to economize; b) weitS. = landwirtschaftlich.

Okta-eder (⌴⌵⌴) [grch. *oktō* acht] *n* ⓱ *math.* (Achtflach) octahedron. [hedral.]

okta-edrisch (⌵⌴⌵) *a.* ⓱ (achtflächig) octa=)

Oktant (⌵⌴) [It.] *m* ⓱ *math.* (Kreisbogen von 45 Grad) ⌵ octant (a. ↓ Winkelmeßinstrument). [(d. *typ.* (8⁰) octavo.]

Oktav ⓞ (⌵⌴*f*) [It. *octav-us* achte(r)] *n*)

Oktav-band (⌵⌴*f*...) *m* ⓱ *typ.* octavo (volume); =**blatt** *n* octavo sheet; =**brief-papier** ⓶ *n* octavo post.

Oktave ♪ (⌵⌴⌵) [It.] *f* ⓱ octave; eine ~ höher, tiefer an octave higher, deeper. [octave-stop.]

Oktav-register (⌵⌴⌵...) ⓱ = Orgel)

Oktav-format (⌵⌴*f*...) *n* ⓱ = Oktav.

Oktavia (⌵⌴⌵⌣) *npr/f.* ⓳⌵ *a.* röm. Alt.: Octavia; **Oktavian(us)** (⌣⌵⌴⌣...)

[Oktavius] — 741 — [operativ]

npr/m. ⑮⑯α(γ). Octavianus; **Oktavius** (⌣́⌣(⌣́)) npr/m. ⑯γ. Octavius.
Oktett ♪ (⌣́) [it.] n ⓝc. (8 stimmiges Stück, 8 zj.-spielende Musiker) octet.
Oktober (⌣⌣́) [lt.] m ㉒ (a. inv.) (month of) October. [n, typ. octodecimo.]
Oktodez-band ⊕ (⌣́⌣⌣) ... m ㉒. = format/
Oktogon (⌣⌣⌣́) [grch.] n ⓝd. math. (Achteck) octagon (a. ⚔ frt.).
Oktro-i (⌣⌣ά) südd. [fr. octroi m] m, n ㉝ (Stadtsteuer) excise paid to the town.
oktroyieren (⌣⌣(a)ı⌣́⌣) [fr. octroyer] v/a. ㉓ (gewähren) to grant a charter, &c.; (aufnötigen) to press on, to dictate to.
Okular (⌣⌣́) [lt.] n ⓝd., a. ~**glas** (⌣⌣), opt. in e-m Fernrohre: eye-piece, -glass, ocular; ~**inspektion** f ocular inspection.
okulieren (⌣⌣⌣́⌣) [lt.] hort. I v/a. ㉓ to inoculate, graft, bud. — II ~ n ㉓ f. Okulierung. — **Okulier-messer** (⌣⌣́...) n ㉖ grafting- (or budding-)knife; ~**reis** n grafting-twig. — **Okulierung** (⌣⌣⌣́) f ㊻ inoculation, grafting.
Okulist (⌣⌣⌣́) [lt.] m ㉒ = Augenarzt.
ökumenisch (-⌣⌣́) [grch.] a. ⓖⓖ Cath. eccl.: Les (allgemeines) Konzil œcumenical (or ecumenical) council.
Okzident (⌣⌣⌣́) [lt.] m ⓝc. (o. pl.) 1. = Westen. — 2. = Abendland. [ländisch.]
okzidentalisch (⌣⌣⌣⌣́) a. ⓖⓖ = abend-
ö. L. abbr. = östliche Länge (j. Länge 4).
Öl (́) [ahd.: oil; *lt. o'leum] n ⓝc. (pl. Ölabrikate ⦿) oil (j. ätherisch u. fett 1); mit ~ schmieren, tränken to lubricate (with) oil; paint. in ~ malen to paint in oil(s); fig. ~ aufs Wasser (oder auf die Wogen) gießen to throw (or pour) oil upon the (troubled) waters; ~ ins Feuer gießen to add fuel to the fire.
Öl-anstrich (́...) m ㉒ coat of paint; =**bad** n, chm. oil-bath; =**baum** ♀ m olive-tree (O'lea europae'a), wilder: ▽ oleaster (O'lea olea'ster); =**baum-harz** n elemi, =**baum-pflanzung** f olive-plantation; =**beere** ♀ f: a) berry containing oil; b) olive; =**behälter** ⊕ m e-r Lampe &c.: vessel containing the oil, lamp-fount; einer Maschine: oil-cup; größerer: oil-tank; =**berg** ♀ m, bibl. bei Jerusalem Mount of Olives; =**bild** n oil-painting; ⦿**bildend** a. ⓖⓖ chm. = oleifiant; =**blatt** n olive-leaf; =**bogen** m, typ. offset-sheet; =**druck** = =farbendruck.
Oleander ♀ (⌣⌣⌣́) [fr., *it.] m ㉒: gemeiner ~ oleander (Ne'rium olea'nder).
Oleaster ♀ (⌣⌣⌣́) [lt.] m ㉒ (wilder Ölbaum) oleaster (O'lea olea'ster).
Ole-in ▽ (⌣⌣́) [lt.] n ⓝd. chm. olein(e) $(C_{18}H_{33}O)_2C_3H_5O_3$; ~**säure** (⌣⌣́...) f ㊻ oleic acid $(C_{18}H_{34}O_2)$.
ölen (́⌣) [mhd.: *Öl] I v/a. ㉓ to oil, ⊕ auch: to lubricate; (salben) to anoint (with oil). — II ~ n ㉓ = Ölung.
Öl-ernte (́,⌣) ♀ f ㊻ olive-season.
Ole-um P (́⌣⌣) [lt. o'leum vitri'oli] n ㉝ = Schwefelsäure.
Öl-fabrik (́...) f ㉕ oil-factory; vgl. =**mühle**; =**farbe** f oil-colour; paint; mit ~n malen to paint in oil(s); =**farben-druck** m: a) Kunst: oleography, chromolithography; b) Bild: oleograph. chromolithograph; =**farben-händler** ⦿ m oilman; =**faß** n: a) leeres: oil-cask or -barrel; b) volles: cask of

oil; =**flasche** f oil-flask; =**fläschchen** n zu Salat &c.: oil-cruet; =**fleck(en)** m stain of oil, oil-stain; =**gemälde** n = =bild ; =**geschmack** m oily taste; =**götze** F m, co. (Dummkopf) blockhead, duffer; wie ein ~ dasteh(e)n to stand dumbfounded; =**handel** ⦿ m oil-trade; =**händler** m oil-merchant, im kleinen: oilman.
ölicht, ölig (́⌣) a. ⓖⓖ oily, ▽ oleaginous, oleose, oleose, (salbungsvoll) unctuous.
Oligarch (⌣⌣⌣́) [grch.] m ㉒ oligarch; ~**ie** (⌣⌣⌣́) f (Herrschaft weniger) oligarchy; **Lisch** (⌣⌣⌣́) a. ⓖⓖ oligarchical.
Öligkeit (́⌣⌣) f ㊻ oiliness.
olim (́⌣) [lt. adv.] — ehemals; als s.: seit, zu Olims Zeiten in the days of yore or of old, in olden times.
Olive ♀ (⌣́⌣⌣) [mhd.: *lt.] f ㊸: a) (die Frucht) olive; b) = Ölbaum.
Oliven-baum (⌣⌣́...) m ㉒ olive-tree; ♀**braun** a. ⓖⓖ = ♀**farben**; =**ernte**(=**zeit**) f olive-harvest or -season; =**farbe** f olive-colour; ♀**farben**, ♀**farbig** a. olive-coloured or -green, ▽ olivaceous; =**grün** n olive-green; =**hain** m ol.-grove; =**holz** n ol.-wood; =**öl** n ol.-oil, sweet oil; =**wäldchen** n ol.-grove.
Öl-käfer (́...) m ㉒ ent. (Maiwurm) oil-beetle (Me'loë); =**kännchen** n, =**kanne** f oil-can, ⊕ mach. auch: oil-feeder, oiler; =**kelter** f = =**presse**; =**krug** m, =**krüglein** n, bibl.: ~ der Witwe the widow's cruse of oil; =**kuchen** m oilcake; als Viehfutter a. linseed-cake; =**laden** m oil-shop; =**lampe** f oil-lamp.
Olm (́) [ndd.] m ⓝb. zo. (Art Molch): ▽ proteus (Pro'teus angui'neus).
Öl-malerei (́...) f ㊻ painting in oil; =**mühle** ⊕ f oil-mill or -works pl.; =**müller** m manufacturer of oil; =**palme** ♀ f oil-palm (Elae'is); =**papier** n oil-paper, zum Durchzeichnen &c.: transparent paper; =**pflanzen** ♀ f/pl. oleiferous plants pl.; =**presse** ⊕ f oil-press; =**pumpe** ⊕ f oil-pump; =**same** m oil-seed; ♀**sauer** a. ⓖⓖ chm.: ▽ oleic; ♀**saures** Salz oleate; =**säure** f = Oleinsäure; =**schiefer** m, min. oil-shale; =**schläger** ⊕ m oil-presser; vgl. =**müller**; =**schlange** ⊕ f, typ. beim Walzenguß: oil-streak; =**stein** ⊕ m für feine Schleiferei: oilstone, oil-rubber; =**strauch** ♀ m olive-wood (Elaeode'ndron orienta'le); =**süß** n, chm. = Glyzerin; =**trester** ⊕ pl. oil-greaves, olive-husks pl.; =**tuch** ⦿, ↓ n zu Matrosenjacken: oilcloth.
Ölung (́⌣) [ölen] f ㊻ oiling, ⊕ a. lubrication, (Salbung) anointment, Cath. eccl.: Letzte ~ extreme unction.
Öl-weide (́⌣) ♀ f ㉒: oleaster, wild olive-tree (Elaea'gnus).
Olymp (⌣́) [grch.] ⓖⓐ. I npr/m. (a. ~**us** (⌣⌣) inv.) ♂ u. myth. (Berg im Norden v. Thessalien, Göttersitz) Olympus. — II F m, thea. gallery, F the gods pl.
Olympiade (⌣⌣́⌣(⌣)) [grch.] f ㊸ grch. Alt.: (Zeitraum von 4 Jahren) Olympiad.
Olympi-er (⌣⌣́⌣(⌣)) [grch.] m ㉒, ~**in** f ㊼ myth. (Bewohner[in] des Olympus: Gott, Göttin) Olympian (god, f goddess).
olympisch[1] (⌣⌣́⌣) [Olymp] a. ⓖⓖ of Olympus, Olympian.
olympisch[2] (⌣) [Oly'mpia] a. ⓖⓖ of Olympia, Olymp-

ian; grch. Alt.: (die) Le(n) (Wett=)Spiele the Olympian games pl.
olynthisch (⌣⌣́) [grch. Olynth(us) Stadt auf Chalki'dike] a. ⓖⓖ ♀ Alt.: Olynthian, ...ac.
Öl-zeug (́...) n ㉒ = =tuch; =**zucker** m, chm.: ▽ oleosaccharum; a. = Glyzerin; =**zweig** m olive-branch, twig of an olive-tree.
Omelett (⌣⌣́) [fr. omelette f] n ⓝc., ~**e** (⌣⌣́⌣) f ㊸ (Eierkuchen) omelet.
Omen (́⌣) [lt.] n ㉖ (gutes, böses Vorzeichen) omen, foreboding. [evil augury.]
ominös (-⌣́) a. ⓖⓖ (D 10) ominous, of
Omnibus (́⌣⌣) [fr. 1823; *lt. für alle] m ⑰ (a. inv.) omnibus, F bus; elektrischer = electric (omni)bus; mit dem ~ fahren to go by (or to take an) omnibus to a place, a. F to bus it. **Omnibus-fahrt** (⌣⌣́...) ⊕ f ㉒ journey by omnibus; =**kondukteur** m =**schaffner**; =**kutscher** m omn.-driver; =**passagier** m passenger of an omn.; F auch: fare; =**schaffner** m omnibus-conductor.
Onanie (-⌣⌣́) [Onan, 1. Mos. 38] f ㊸ (Selbstbefleckung) onanism, self-pollution, masturbation; **onanieren** (-⌣⌣́) v/n. (h.) ㉓ to commit onanism or self-pollution; **Onanist** (-⌣⌣́) m ㉒ onanist.
Onanth-äther ▽ (́...) m ㉒, =**säure** f, chm. œnanthic ether, acid.
Onkel (́⌣) [fr. oncle] m ㉒ uncle; ~**chen** n ㉓ (dim.) (dear) little uncle; e-n ~ betreffend, e-m ~ gehörig avuncular.
onomato-po-etisch ▽ (⌣⌣⌣́...) [grch.] a. ⓖⓖ (laut-malend, =nachahmend) onomatopoetic, **Onomato-pöie** (⌣⌣⌣.́.) f ㊸ (Laut-, Ton-nachahmung) onomatopœia.
Ontologie (⌣⌣⌣́) [grch.] f ㊸ phls. (Lehre vom Sein) ontology.
Onyx (́⌣) [grch. „Nagel" (farbig)] m ⓝd ⓖⓖ a. min. (Art Chalzedon) onyx.
Oolith (-⌣́) [grch. „Rogenstein"] m ⓝc ㊷ geol. (Art Kalksteinbildung) oolite, amnite; **oolithisch** (-⌣⌣́) a. ⓖⓖ oolitic.
opak (⌣́) [lt.] a. ⓖⓖ (undurchsichtig) opaque.
Opal (⌣́) [lt.; *ft. Stein] m ⓝd.min. opal; ♀-**artig** (⌣́...) a. ⓖⓖ resembling opal, opaline; ~**blau** n opal-blue; **Leisieren** = Lisieren; ♀-**glänzend** a. opalescent; ~**glas** n ⓖ opal (or iridescent) glass; **Lisieren** (⌣⌣⌣́) v/n. (h.) ㉓ (schillern) to opalesce; ~**jaspis** m, min. opal-jasper, jasper-opal.
Oper (́⌣) [mhd. 17. sae.; *it. (j. Opus 2)] f ㊸ thea. ㉒ (Singspiel) opera; eine ~ geben, darstellen to perform (or give) an opera; in die (große) ~ gehen to go to the (grand) opera. — 2. (Gebäude zur Aufführung v. Opern) opera-house.
Operateur (⌣⌣⌣⌣́) [fr.] m ⓝd. operator; surg. operating surgeon.
Operation (⌣⌣⌣⌣́) [fr., *lt.] f ㊸ ⚔ u. surg. operation; surg. c-e ~ bestehen to undergo an operation.
Operations-basis (⌣⌣⌣⌣́...) ⚔ f ㉒ basis of operation(s); =**feld** n field (or scene) of operation; =**lehre** f. surg. operative surgery; =**linie** ⚔ f line of operation; =**objekt** n, =**plan** m object, plan of operation; =**saal** m. surg. operating-room or -theatre; =**tisch** m, surg. operating-table or -board.
operativ (⌣⌣⌣́f) [fr., *lt.] a. ⓖⓖ ⚔ und surg. operative.

♪ Musik; ▽ Wissenschaft; ♀ Pflanze; ⚲ Geographie; ⊕ Technik; ⚒ Bergbau; ⚔ Militär; ↓ Marine; ⦿ Handel; ⦿ Post; ⊞ Eisenbahn.

[Operette] — 742 — [ordentlich]

Operette (⏑⏑⏑⏑) [fr.] f ⓖ operetta.
operieren (⏑⏑⏔) [fr., *lt.] v/n. (h.) u. v/a. ⓖ surg. u. ⚔ to operate (upon); surg. sich ⚓ lassen to be operated upon, to submit to an operation, Medizinerslang: to be laid straight.
Operment (⏑⏑⏑) [mhd.; *Auripigment] n ⓓ. (Rauschgelb) orpiment.
Opern=abend (⏑⏑...) m ⓖ opera-night; ⸗artig a. ⓖ operatic, adv. in the style of an opera; ⸗buch n = ⸗text; ⸗dichter m writer of (a book for) an opera, librettist; ⸗glas n, ⸗gucker m (pair of) opera-glasses pl., binocular.
opernhaft (⏑⏔⏑) a. ⓖ = opernartig.
Opern=haus (⏑⏑...) n ⓖ opera-house; ⸗komponist m composer of an opera; ⸗musik f (ant. Kammermusik a) opera- (or operatic) music; ⸗sänger(in f) m opera-singer; ⸗text m book (or words pl.) of an opera, seltener: libretto.
Opfer (⏑⏑) [ahd.; *opfurn] n ⓖ 1. offering, sacrifice, geh. Spr. a. immolation, oblation; ein ~ bringen to make a sacrifice. — 2. (geopfertes Tier, fig. duldende Person) victim; (Märtyrer) martyr; er fiel als ~ seines Glaubens he fell a martyr to his faith.
Opfer=altar (⏑⏑...) m ⓖ sacrificial altar; ⸗binde f fillet.
Opferer (⏑⏑⏑) m ⓖ sacrificer.
Opfer=fest (⏑⏑...) n ⓖ sacrificial feast; ⸗flamme f flame consuming the victims; ⸗fleisch n flesh of the (offered) victims; ⸗freudig(keit f) a. willing (-ness) to make sacrifices, self-sacrificing (spirit); ⸗gabe f offering; ⸗gebet n, Cath. eccl. offertory; ⸗gebrauch m sacrificial custom or rite; ⸗gefäß n sacr. vessel; ⸗geld n money-offering; ⸗kasten m poor-box; ⸗lamm n: a) sacrificial lamb; eccl. the Lamb (Jesus); b) fig. innocent victim; ⸗mahl n = ⸗schmaus; ⸗messer n sacrificial knife.
opfern (⏑⏑) [ahd.; *lt. opera'ri (gute Werke tun)] I v/a. v/n. (h.) u. sich ⚓ v/refl. ⓐa. : (sich) ⚓ to sacrifice (o.s.), to offer (o.s.) as a victim, geh. Spr.: to immolate (o.s.) on the altar of duty, &c.; sein Leben für das Vaterland ⚓ to offer up (or give, lay down) one's life for one's country. — II ~ n ⓖ = Opferung.
Opfer=priester (⏑⏑...) m ⓖ sacrificer; ⸗schale f offering-cup; basin (or dish) for the victim's blood; ⸗schmaus m sacrificial repast; ⸗stock m = ⸗kasten; ⸗tier n victim (a. fig. v. Menschen); ⸗tisch m altar; ⸗tod m sacrificatory death; ~ am Kreuze sacrifice (or expiation) on the cross; ⸗trank m libation.
Opferung (⏑⏑⏑) f ⓖ sacrificing, sacrifice, immolation.
Opfer=wein (⏑⏑...) m ⓖ eccl. sacramental wine; ⚓willig a. ⓖ willing to make sacrifices, auch: devoted.
Ophthalmie ⚓ (⏑⏑⏔) [grch.] f ⓖ (Augenentzündung) ophthalmia.
Opiat ⚓ (⏑⏑⏔) [grch.] n ⓓc. pharm. (Schlaftrunk) opiate.
Opium (⏔⏑) [lt.; *grch. ó'pion] n ⓖ (getrockneter Mohnsaft) opium.
Opium=esser (⏔⏑...) m ⓖ opium-eater; ⚓haltig a. ⓖ containing opium, opiated; ⚓es Mittel opiate; ⸗handel ⚡

m opium-traffic or -trade; ⸗raucher m opium-smoker; ⸗spelunke f op.-den; ⸗tinktur f, pharm. tincture of opium, mit Spiritus bereitete, auch: laudanum.
Opodeldok (⏑⏑⏑) m, n ⓓ pharm. (Einreibemittel aus Seifenspiritus) opodeldoc.
Opossum ⚓ (⏑⏑) [indian.] n ⓖ zo. (virginische Beutelratte u. ihr Fell) opossum, F Am. possum (Dide'lphys virginia'na).
Opponent (⏑⏑⏔) [lt.] m ⓖ (Gegner bei e-r Disputation ꝛc.) opponent, adversary.
opponieren (⏑⏑⏔⏑) [lt.] I v/a. to oppose, to resist. — II v/n. (h.) u. sich ⚓ v/refl. to make (or offer) opposition to.
opportun (⏑⏑⏔) [lt.] a. ⓖ (gelegen) opportune; (coming) in good time; **Opportunität** (⏑⏑⏑⏔) f ⓖ opportuneness.
Opposition (⏑⏑⏔⏔) [lt.] f ⓖ (Widerspruch, Gegnerschaft) opposition; gegen et. ⚓ machen to oppose a th., coll. die ~ ward überstimmt the opposition were outvoted; ⚓ell (⏑⏑⏑⏔) a. ⓖ oppositional, of the opposition.
Oppositions=blatt (⏑⏑⏑⏔...) n ⓖ opposition paper or journal; ⸗geist m spirit of opposition; ⸗mann m opponent, member of the opposition; ⸗partei f opposition (party).
Optativ (⏑⏑⏔) [lt.] m ⓓd. grch. gr. (Wunschform des Zeitworts) optative (mood).
optieren (⏑⏔⏑) [lt.] I v/n. (h.) ⓖ (wählen) to choose, F auch: to opt (between); (sich entscheiden für) to decide for. — II ~ n ⓖ u. **Optierung** f ⓖ optation.
Optik ⚓ (⏑⏑) [grch.] f ⓖ (Lehre vom Licht) optics; ~er (⏑⏑⏑) m ⓖ, ~us m ⓖ (Verfertiger optischer Instrumente) optician, optical instrument-maker.
Optimat (⏑⏑⏔) [lt. o'ptimus beste] m ⓖ aristocrat, röm. Alt.: ⸗en pl. (die Vornehmen) (lt.) optimates pl.; ⸗en=herrschaft (⏑⏑...) f ⓖ oligarchy.
Optimismus (⏑⏑⏑⏑) [neu-lt.] m ⓖ (Neigung, alles gut zu finden) optimism.
Optimist (⏑⏑⏔) [neu-lt.] m ⓖ, ⚓isch (⏑⏑⏑) a. ⓖ optimist(ic).
optisch (⏑⏑) [grch.] a. ⓖ (das Sehen betr.) optical; ⚓e Täuschung optical delusion.
opulent (⏑⏑⏔) [lt.] a. ⓖ (begütert) opulent, wealthy; (herrlich) sumptuous; **Opulenz** f ⓖ (Wohlstand) opulence, wealth.
Opus (⏔⏑) [lt.] n (sg. inv., pl. O'pera) 1. allg.: (Werk) work, production. — 2. bsd. ♪: ~ 12 (abbr. op. 12) opus 12.
Orakel (⏑⏔⏑) [lt.] n ⓖ Alt.: (göttlicher Spruch) oracle (jetzt auch fig.: untrügliche Person); ~(be)fragen n, ~einholung f consultation of the oracle; ⚓haft a. ⓖ: ⚓h. (adv.) sprechen, auch: ⚓n v/n. (h.) ⓐa. to speak oracularly or in oracles or in riddles; ⚓mäßig a. oracular; ~spruch m oracle, oracular sentence.
Orange (⏑⏔⏑) [mhd., *fr.] I f ⓖ orange; süße ~ (Apfelsine) sweet (or China) orange; bittere ~ (Pomeranze) Seville orange. — II orange a. ⓖ, ~ n, inv. (Farbe) orange (colour).
Orange=admiral (⏑⏑...) m ⓖ zo. orange-admiral (Conus aurisi'acus); ⚓farben, ⚓farbig a. ⓖ orange(-coloured); ⸗gelb a. u. s/n. orange(colour).
Orangen=baum ⚓ (⏑⏔"...) m [Orange] m ⓖ orange-tree (Citrus Aura'ntium); ⸗blüte f orange-blossom or -flower

(bsd. für Brauttränze gbr.); ⸗blüten=öl n, chm. neroli, neroly; ⚓farbig a. ⓖ = orangefarbig; ⸗schale f orange-peel; ⸗schalen=öl n, chm. Portugallo-oil.
Orangerie (⏑⏔⏑⏔) [fr.] f ⓖ, ~haus n, hort. orangery, orange-house.
Orang-Utan (⏑⏔⏑⏔) [malai-isch Waldmensch] m ⓓd. ⓖ zo. orang-outang, r-r. orang-utan (Pithe'cus sa'tyrus).
Orani-en ⚓ (⏑⏔⏑) [Orange, fr. St.] npr/n. ⓑa. (Fürstenhaus): Prinz von ~ (Titel holl. Prinzen) Prince of Orange.
Oranje=fluß=kolonie f, ehm. **Oranje=Frei=staat** ⚓ (⏑⏑...) [Oranien] m ⓖ in Südafrika: Orange River Colony [1854-1900 Orange Free State], auch: Oranja.
oratorisch (⏑⏑⏔⏑) [lt.] a. ⓖ oratorical.
Oratorium (⏑⏑⏔⏑⏑) [lt.] n ⓖ 1. (Betsaal) oratory. — 2. ♪ (geistl. Tonstück) oratorio.
Orchester ♪ (⏑⏔⏑), oft ⏑⏔⏑ ob. ⏑⏔⏑ [fr., *grch.] n ⓖ (Musikkorps) orchestra; band; ~begleitung f ⓖ orchestral accompaniment, orchestration; ~diener m attendant of the orchestra; ~musik f music of an orchestra or a band (Partitur) score; ~satz m orchestrated piece.
orchestrier=en ♪ (⏑⏑⏔⏑) I v/a. ⓖ to orchestrate, to score. — II ~ n ⓖ u. ⚓ung f ⓖ orchestration, scoring.
Orchide=e ⚓ (⏑⏑⏔⏑) [grch.] f ⓖ orchid; ⚓n-artige Gewächse orchid(ac)eæ pl.
Orchis ⚓ ⚓ (⏑⏑) f, inv. = Knabenkraut.
ord. abbr. = ordinär, ordentlich.
Orden (⏑⏑) [ahd. *lt. ordin-] m ⓖ 1. (Mönchs-, Ritter=) order; in einen geistlichen ~ eintreten to enter a religious order. — 2. (Auszeichnung) order, decoration, ⓓ auch: distinction, (Denkmünze) medal.
Ordens=band (⏑⏑...) n ⓖ: a) ribbon of an order; b) ent. (Schmetterling) underwing (Cato'cala); ⸗bruder m member of an order, eccl. a. friar, monk; ⸗fest n anniversary of the institution of an order; ⸗geistliche(r) m ecclesiastic, member of the (regular) clergy; ⸗geistlichkeit f regular clergy; ⸗gelübde n, eccl. monastic vow or profession; ⸗gesellschaft f order; geistliche ~ congregation; ⸗insignien pl. insignia of an order; ⸗kleid n, eccl. monastic garb or gown; ⸗kreuz n cross of an order; ⸗meister m master of an o.; ⸗regel f rule (or statute) of an o.; ⸗ritter m knight of an o.; ⸗schwester f, eccl. sister, nun; ⸗tracht f = ⸗kleid; ⸗verbrüderung f confraternity of the members of an order; ⸗verleihung f conferring (of) an o.; ⸗zeichen n badge of an o.; ⸗zucht f monastic discipline.
ordentlich (⏑⏑⏑) [ahd., *Orden 1] a. ⓖ 1. (gewöhnlich) ordinary; der Lehrer (regularly) appointed teacher; die Mahlzeit proper meal; der Professor professor in ordinary. — 2. (ordnungs=mäßig) orderly; sein Zimmer ist ⚓ (adv.) gehalten ... is kept in good order. ... is well kept; ⚓ erzählen to relate in proper order; et. ⚓ tun to do a th. properly or in proper order. — 3. (achtbar) der Kerl decent fellow; der Mensch person of orderly habits, steady person; ein der Mensch w. to steady (or settle) down, to become a useful member of society; des Mädchen re-

Signs (see page XVII): F familiar; P vulgar; ⌐ flash; ⚓ rare; † obsolete (died); * new word (born); ++ incorrect; ♪ music;

[**Ordentlichkeit**] — [**Orkan**]

spectable girl. — 4. (tüchtig, gehörig) regular, downright, F awful; wir bekamen nichts ~es zu essen we had no proper (or regular) meals, we were kept without proper (or substantial) food. — 5. oft adv.: (wirklich) real(ly); (allen Ernstes) seriously, thoroughly, F with a vengeance; ein 2er Schimpf, oft: quite a disgrace; eine 2e Schlacht a pitched battle; 2e Schläge bekommen to get a sound beating; der Wind hat 2 (adv.) geheult the wind howled furiously or tremendously or F awfully; 2er=weise adv. in an orderly manner, properly.

Ordentlichkeit (᷄⏑⏑⏑-) f ⑯ (f. ordentlich 2 u. 3) orderliness, good (or proper) order or style; des Charakters: steadiness, respectability.

Order f. [fr. ordre m Auftrag] f ⑮: a) order, commission, (Befehl) command, injunction; F ~ parieren to obey orders; bis auf weitere ~ until further orders; b) ⊕ Ihrer (Bestellung) gemäß in conformity with your order; in Indossamenten: für mich an die ~ des // pay to the order of //; ~buch n ⑫ order-book; ~hafen ↓ m port of call.

Ordinale (⏑⏑᷄⏑) [lt.] n (sg. inv., pl. ...a'lia), **Ordinal=zahl** (⏑⏑᷄⏑) f ⑫ gr. (Ordnungszahl, zB. der achte) ordinal number, auch: ordinal.   [lich.)

ordinär (⏑⏑᷄) [(+.) fr.] a. ⑯ = gewöhn-)

Ordinariat (⏑⏑-(⏑)᷄) [lt.] n ⑩c. (Stellung eines Ordina'rius): a) Schule: classmaster's position or appointment; b) eccl. etwa: diocesan court.

Ordinarium (⏑⏑᷄⏑) [lt.] n ㉙ Finanzwesen: ordinary budget.

Ordinarius (⏑⏑᷄(⏑)⏑) [lt.] m ㉗ 1. univ. professor in ordinary. — 2. Schule: (regular) class-master. — 3. eccl. etwa: diocesan overseer; (Kirchensprengelbischof) suffragan (bishop) of a diocese.

Ordinate ⓩ (⏑⏑᷄⏑) [lt.] f ⑱ math. (Hilfslinie für mathmatische Bestimmung; ant. Abszisse) ordinate; ~n=achse (ⓩ...) f ⑫ axis of ordinates.

Ordination (᷄⏑-tß(⏑)᷄) [lt.] f ⑯ eccl. (Weihe, Einsegnung) ordination.

ordinieren (⏑⏑᷄) [lt.] I v/a. ⓐ 1. eccl.: e-n 2 (als Priester weihen) to ordain a p.; sich 2 l. to take holy orders. — 2. med. Arznei 2 (verschreiben) to prescribe ... II ~ n ㉓ u. O/ung f ⑯ 3. eccl. ordination; med. prescription.

ordnen (᷄⏑) [ahd.; *lt. ordina're] I v/a., v n. (h.) u. sich 2 v/refl. ⓐb. to put in(to) order, to set in order or to rights, to put straight; (regeln, einrichten) to regulate, arrange, organize, settle, supervise; (entwirren) to disentangle; die Sache läßt sich leicht 2 that's easily settled or managed, it's soon set right; alphabetisch (ob. nach dem Alphabet) 2 to arrange alphabetically or in alphabetical order; grammatisch 2 to construe; systematisch 2 to systematize; nach Klassen 2 to classify. — II ~ n ㉓ = Ordnung 1. — III ge=ordnet p.p. u. a. ⑯ orderly, systematic; in 2er Reihenfolge in proper order; 2e Verhältnisse, Zustände proper (or orderly, decent) state of affairs.

Ordner (᷄⏑) m ㉒, ~in f ㉔ person who creates order; regulator, organizer, supervisor; nach Klassen: classifier.

Ordnung (᷄⏑) f ⑯ 1. (f. ordnen I) putting (or setting) in order, regulation, arrangement, organization; disentanglement. — 2. order; aus der ~ bringen to derange, disarrange, confuse, disturb; aus der ~ kommen to get out of order; in bester ~, oft: in excellent trim or condition, F in apple-pie order; ⚔ in zerstreuter ~ in scattered (or loose) formation; et. in ~ bringen (stellen ob. setzen) to put a th. in order; wieder in ~ bringen to rearrange; ich finde das ganz in der ~ I think it quite right or proper; alles ist in ~: a) (wie es sein soll) everything is in order or as it should be; b) (ist abgetan) all is right or settled; der ~ nach in due order; parl. zur ~ rufen to call to order. — 3. (Abteilung) division, class; (Aufeinanderfolge) succession; ehemalige (neue) ~ der Dinge old (new) regime or style. — 4. arch. = Säulenordnung.

Ordnungs=liebe (᷄⏑...) f ⑫ orderliness, tidiness; 2liebend a. ⑯ orderly, tidy, methodical; 2los a. disorderly; (zuchtlos) unruly; 2mäßig a. in due (or good) order, orderly, regular; (gesetzlich) lawful; =mäßigkeit f orderliness, regularity, lawfulness; =ruf m, parl. call to order; =strafe f punishment (or fine) for contravention of a bylaw or regulation; 2widrig a. contrary to order, irregular; vgl. 2los; =widrigkeit f irregularity; =zahl f, gr. ordinal number.

Ordonnanz (᷄⏑⏑᷄) [(+.) fr. ordonnance] f ⑯ 1. (Dienstbefehl) order, ordinance. — 2. ⚔ (zu Meldungen kommandierter Soldat) orderly (man); auf ~ on orderly duty.

Ordonnanz=dienst ⚔(᷄⏑-⏑)m ㉔ orderly duty; den ~ h. to be on orderly duty; =offizier m orderly officer; 2widrig a. ⑯ contrary to orders; (nymphe) oread.)

Oreade ⓩ (⏑⏑᷄⏑) [grch.] f ⑯ myth. (Berg-)

Organ (⏑᷄) [grch. Werkzeug] n ⑩d. organ.

Organisation (᷄⏑⏑-tß(⏑)᷄)[fr.,*grch.] f ⑯ (Gestaltung) organization; **Organisator** (᷄⏑⏑⏑᷄) m ㉒ (Veranstalt[end]er) organizer, auch: organizing spirit.

organisch (⏑᷄⏑) [fr., *grch.] a. ⑯ (zu e-m Körperteil gehörig, belebt) organic.

organisieren (᷄⏑⏑⏑᷄)[fr., *grch.] I v/a. (gestalten, einrichten) to organize, set on foot, arrange. — II ~ n ㉓ u. O/ung f ⑯ organization.

Organismus (᷄⏑⏑⏑) [lt.. *grch.] m ㉗ organism, organic body.

Organist ♪ (᷄⏑᷄⏑) [fr., *grch.] m ㉒, ~in f ㉔ (Orgelspieler[in]) organist; f auch: a) lady organist; b) organist's wife.

Organsin (᷄⏑᷄)[it.] m ⑩d. (⑪). ~=seide f (Kettenseide) organzine, thrown silk.

Orgeade ⓩ (⏑Ga᷄) [+ fr.] f ⑯, **Orgeat** (⏑Ga') [fr.] m ⑩c. (Mandelmilch mit Zucker) orgeat.

Orgel ♪ (᷄⏑) [ahd.; *grch. o'rgana n pl.] f ⑯ organ; (Dreh-)~ barrel-organ; die ~ spielen to play (on) the organ.

Orgel=balg ♪ (᷄⏑...) m ⑫ bellows pl. of an organ; =bau m organ-building; =bauer m o.-builder; =chor n(m) o.-loft.

Orgelei (᷄⏑⏑᷄) f ⑯ incessant organ-playing or -grinding, dull music.

Orgel=gehäuse ♪(᷄⏑...) n ⑫ organ-case; =harmonium n o.-harmonium; =kasten m = =gehäuse; =klang m sound (or swell) of an organ; =konzert n organ-recital.

orgeln (᷄⏑) v/n. (h.) ⓐa. to play (on) an organ, to turn (or grind) a barrel-organ.

Orgel=pfeife (᷄⏑...) f ⑫: a) ♪ organ-pipe; b) fig. ~en pl. (Kinder von geringem Unterschiede der Größe) F little steps pl.; **2pfeifen=artig** a. ⑯ like organ-pipes; in gradual succession; =punkt m (lange gehaltene Note) organ-point; =register n register (or stop) of an organ; =spieler(in f) m organ-player, organist; =stimme f notes pl. of an organ; vgl. =register; =stück n piece for the organ; =treter m = Balgentreter; =werk n works pl. of an organ; =zug m organ-stop; vgl. =register.

Orgi=e (᷄⏑(⏑)) [grch.] f ⑯ (wüstes Gelage) orgy. [Osten. — 2. = Morgenland.)

Ori=ent (᷄(⏑)᷄, a. ᷄(⏑)᷄) [lt.] m ⑩d. 1. =)

Ori=entale(᷄(⏑)᷄⏑)m ㉔, **Ori=entalin** f ㉔ 1. = Morgenländer(in). — 2. F = Jude.

ori=entalisch (᷄(⏑)᷄⏑)a. ⑯ 1. = morgenländisch; F = jüdisch. — 2. Hochschule: 2es Semina'r school for Oriental languages; pol. die 2e Frage the Eastern question.

Ori=entalist (᷄(⏑)⏑⏑᷄) [neu=lt.] m ㉒ Oriental scholar, student (or professor, teacher) of Oriental languages.

Ori=ent=express=zug 🚂 (᷄(⏑)᷄...) m ⑫ Oriental express.

ori=entier=en (᷄(⏑)᷄) [fr.] I v/a. u. sich 2 v/refl. ⓐ (often, örtlich bestimmen) to locate, fix, survey; sich 2 (sich umsehen) to look about, (sich zurechtfinden) to find one's bearings or latitude, to find one's way (about); sich nicht (mehr) 2 (können) to have lost one's bearings, F to be all at sea or out of one's reckoning. — II O/ung f orientation.

Ori=entierungs=sinn (᷄(⏑)᷄...) m ⑫, =vermögen n ability to find one's way (about); vgl. Ortssinn.

Ori=ent=post 🚂 (᷄(⏑)᷄...) f ⑫ Oriental (or Eastern) mail.

Original (᷄⏑⏑᷄) [fr.] I n ⑩d. 1. (das Ursprüngliche) original; (Urtext) original text, (Urschrift) autograph (letter, &c.). — 2. (Sonderling) original (person); b.s. queer(-headed) person, peculiar (or F rum) person. — II 2 a. ⑯ 3. original; (anerschaffen) innate, inborn, inherent. F bred in the bone.

Original=ausgabe (᷄⏑-⏑᷄...) f ⑫ original edition; =band m original binding; =gemälde n original painting; =hand=schrift f autograph (letter).

Originalität (᷄⏑-⏑᷄) [lt.] f ⑯: a) (Ursprünglichkeit) originality; b) (Eigenheit) peculiarity, oddity, singularity.

Original=manuskript (᷄⏑-⏑᷄...) n ⑫ = Original; =mensch m: ein wahrer 2 quite a character, F a cure; =zeichnung f original drawing or draft.

originell (᷄⏑⏑᷄) [(+.) fr.] a. ⑯ original; (eigentümlich) singular, (seltsam, wunderlich) strange, queer (, peculiar, odd).

Orkan (⏑᷄, ♪) [fr.] m ⑩d. (heftiger Sturm) hurricane, violent gale.

⚛ scientific; 🌿 botanical; ♀ geography; ⊕ machinery; ⚒ mining; ⚔ military; ↓ marine; ⊛ commercial; ⧫ postal; 🚂 railway.

Orkus (⌣◡) [lt.] *m, inv. myth.* (Unterwelt) Orcus, Hades.

Orlean ⊙ (◡◡) [fr.; *It. (*Bixa*) orella'na* ♀] *m, inv.* (⑪ d.) (gelbroter Farbstoff) anatta; rocoa, rocoe, rocou. [⑥⑥ Orleanist.]

Orleanist (◡–◡̈) *m* ㊷, **Lisch** (◡–◡) *a.*

Orlog (◡) [ndl.] *m* ⑪d. ⑬ = Krieg; **~deck** ⌄ (◡...) *n* ㊷ ÷+ = Orlopdeck; **~schiff** ⌄ *n* = Kriegsschiff. [orlop.]

Orlop=deck ⌄ [⁻–◡] (ndl. überlauf) *n* ㊷

Ornament (◡◡–) [lt. --◡̈...] *n* ⑪d., bsd. *arch.* (Verzierung) ornament; **Lieren** *v/a.* ㊸ to ornament, to decorate; **~ik** (◡◡̈–) *f*⑥⑥ ornamentation, decoration.

Ornat (◡–) [lt. ōrnāt-] *m(n)* ⑪d., bsd. *eccl.* (clerical) robes, canonicals *pl.*; official garb; in vollem ~ *F co.* in full fig.

Ornitholog ʒ (◡◡–◡) [grch.] *m* ㊷, **~e** ㊹ (Vogelkenner) ornithologist; **~ie** (◡◡–◡̈–) *f* ㊽ (Vogelkunde) ornithology; **Lisch** (◡◡–◡̈) *a.* ⑥⑥ ornithological.

Orographie ʒ (◡◡–◡̈–) *f* ㊽ (Beschreibung der Gebirge) orography; **orographisch** (◡◡–◡̈–) *a.* ⑥⑥ orographical. [orology.]

Orologie (◡◡–◡̈–) *f* ㊽ (Gebirgskunde)

Orphe-um (◡̈ʹ◡̈) [lt., *grch.] *n* ㉗: a) (Tonhalle) music-hall; b) (Gesangverein) choral society. [melodious.]

orphisch (◡̈ʹ◡̈) *a.* ⑥⑥ Orphean (melodisch)

Orseille (◡̈ ē'l-jē̊) [fr., von *Oricella'ri, it. Färber um 1300] *f* ㊽ (Farbstoff aus der Färberflechte) archil, orchil, orseille.

Ort¹ (◡) [ahd.] *m* ⑭ ⑪b. 1. place, locality, spot; *math.* geometrischer ~ locus; an allen ~en (aller=Ös, -öen) everywhere; ein gewisser ♀ a certain place, *euph.* (Abtritt) closet, W.C., lavatory; ⚔ Seitengewehr an ~ return arms!; hiesigen ~(e)s in this place, in our town; am unrechten ~e in the wrong spot, out of place; ⚔ (auch *n*) ⑫ d. (Ende des Grubenbaues): vor Ort in (or near the end of) the drift. — 2. meist *fig.*: an ~ und Stelle on the (very) spot; an ~ und Stelle gelangen to arrive at (or to reach) one's destination; das ist hier sehr am ~e that's most appropriate or befitting, F it fits in admirably; der Plan ist höheren ~(e)s genehmigt worden ... has been approved of by the authorities; et. gehörigen ~(e)s melden to lodge information of a th. with the proper authorities or in the proper quarter. — 3. ⊙ *m u. n* ⑪b. (Schuster=ahle) awl.

Ort² (◡) [mhd.:*ndl. = ¼] *m* ⑪b, 6. (als Maß *pl. inv.*; vierter Teil gewisser Münzen, Maße, Gewichte) fourth part.

Ort¹=band ⚔ (◡–) *n* ㊷ c-r Degenscheide: chape of a leather-scabbard. [place.]

Örtchen (◡̈◡) [*dim. v.* Ort] *n* ㉔ small

örtern ⊙ (◡̈◡) [Ort¹] *v/a.* ㊷a. (die Ecken abstoßen) to plane off the corners, to chamfer. [Mauer: tail-bay.]

Ort¹=fach ⊙ (◡–◡) *n* ㊷ *carp.* zunächst der

orthodox (◡◡–) [grch.] *a.* ⑥⑥ (rechtgläubig) orthodox; **~ie** (◡◡–◡̈) *f* ㊽, **~ismus** (◡◡–◡̈◡) *m* ㉗ orthodoxy.

Ortho-epie ʒ (◡◡–◡̈–) [grch.] *f* ㊽, **Ortho-epik** (◡◡–◡̈) *f* ㊽ (richtige Aussprache) orthoepy.

Orthographie (◡◡–◡̈–) [nhd. 16. *sae.*; *grch.] *f* ㊽ (richtige Schreibweise) orthography, right (or correct) spelling.

orthographisch (◡◡–◡̈–◡̈) [grch.] *a.* ⑥⑥ orthographic(al); ♀ (*adv.*) schreiben to spell correctly.

Orthoklas ʒ (◡◡–) [grch.] *m* ⑪a. *min.* (Kalifeldspat) orthoclase.

orthopädisch (◡◡–◡̈–) [grch.] *a.* ⑥⑥ (auf Heilgymnastik bezüglich) orthopædic(al).

örtlich (◡̈◡) [Ort¹] ⑥⑥ local; ⊙ u. *med. a.* topical; **~keit** *f* ㊽ locality, place, (Gegend) vicinity, neighbourhood.

Ortolan (◡̈◡–) [it. Garten=] *n* ㉒, **~ammer** *f, orn.* ortolan (*Emberi'za hortula'na*).

Orts=adverb (◡...) *n* ㊸ *gram.* adverb of place; **=angabe** *f* indication of a place, direction, address; **=arme([r]** *m) f* der von f-m Orte unterhalten werden muß pauper maintained by the parish; **=behörde** *f* local authorities *pl.*; **=beschaffenheit** *f* nature of a locality; **=beschreibung, =bestimmung** *f* ʒ topography; **=bewegung** *f:* ʒ locomotion.

Ortschaft (◡̈◡) *f* ㊽ (inhabited) place, borough, township, village.

Ort¹=scheit ⊙ (◡–◡) [nhd.] *n* ⑪d. Wagenbau: swingle-tree, swing-bar, splinter-bar.

Orts=gedächtnis (◡...) *n* ㊷ memory for places; **=geistliche(r)** *m* local clergyman or minister; **=gemäß** *a.* ⑥⑥ local; **=geschichte** *f* local history; **=kenntnis** *f* knowledge of a place, **=kenntnisse** *pl.* *h.* to know (the whereabouts of) a place; **=frankenkasse** *f* local sick-fund; **=kunde** *f* = **=kenntnis**; **=kundig** *a.* acquainted with a locality; **=pfarrer** *m* vicar, local parson; **=polizei(=behörde)** *f* local police (authorities *pl.*); **=sinn** *m* sense (Phrenologie: bump) of locality; **=statut** *n* local by-law.

Ort¹=stein (◡–◡) *m* ㊷ = Raseneisenerz.

orts=üblich (◡̈...) *a.* ⑥⑥ customary in a place; **=veränderung** *f* ㊷ change of place, ʒ locomotion; für Kranke *zc.*: change of scenery; **=vorsteher** *m* headman (or chief magistrate) of a place; **=wechsel** *m* = **=veränderung**; **=zeit** *f* (die für den Meridian eines Ortes geltende Zeit) local (or meridional) time.

Öse ⊙ (◡̈–) [nhd.; *Ohr] *f* ㊸ *arch.*: a) = Öhr; *a.* loop; Haken und ~ hook and eye; b) (Ring v. Metall) metal ring.

Osiris (◡̈–◡̈–) [ägyptisch] *npr/m.*⑥⑥γ. Osiris. **osirisch** (◡̈–◡̈) *a.* ⑥⑥ Osirian. [⑮⑥α. Oscar.]

Oskar (◡̈◡) [schwd. = Asen=ger] *npr/m.]

Osker (◡̈◡) *m* ㊷, **~in** *f* ㊼, **oskisch** *a.* ⑥⑥ röm. Alt.: Oscan. [= Osmanli; *a.* Ottomane.]

Osmane (◡̈◡) [Osman I., 1288-1326] *m* ㊹

osmanisch (◡̈◡) *a.* ⑥⑥ Ottoman; ~es Reich *n* (Türkei) Ottoman Empire.

Osmanli (◡̈◡–) [Osman I., †1326] *m* (*pl.*) *inv.* Osmanli, (true) Turk(s *pl.*).

Ost (◡) bisw. ○, [nhd.; *Osten] *m* ⑪b. (*abbr.* O(.) 1. ⚓ *ast.*, ♀ East (f. Osten). — 2. = Ostwind.

Ost=afrika (◡̈...) *npr/n.* ⑥⑥ East Africa; ♀**afrikanisch** *a.* ⑥⑥ East African; **=angeln** ♀ *npr/n.* (jetzige engl. Grafschaften Norfolk u. Suffolk) East Anglia; ♀**anglisch** *a.* East Anglian; **=asien** *npr/n.* Eastern (or East of) Asia.

Osten¹ (◡̈◡) [ahd.: east] *m* ㉓ East (*abbr.* E.), Orient, *poet. a.* morning.

osten² * (◡̈◡) [Ost] *v a.* ㊽ f. orientieren.

Ostende (◡̈◡–) *npr/n.* ⓶*a.* Ostend.

Ost=ende² (◡̈.◡̈◡) *n* ㊷ East End.

ostensibel (◡̈◡–) [fr.] *a.* ⑥⑥ (offenkundig) ostensible. [(Knochenlehre) osteology.]

Osteologie (◡̈◡◡◡̈–) [grch.] *f* ㊽ *anat.*

Oster=abend (◡̈...) [Ostern] *m* ㊷ Easter-eve; **=ei(er** *pl.*) *n* E.(-)egg(s *pl.*); **=feiertage** *m/pl.* E.(-)holidays *pl.*; **=fest** *n* E.(-) festival; **=hase** *m* fabulous hare that lays the E.(-)eggs; **=kerze** *f. Cath. eccl.* E.(-)taper; paschal candle; **=lamm** *n* E.(-)lamb, der Juden: paschal lamb.

österlich (◡̈–◡) [mhd.: *Östern] *a.* ⑥⑥ (of or referring to) Easter, paschal.

Osterluzei ♀ (◡̈◡–◡̈) [nhd. (P.); *It.] *f* ㊽ birth-wort (*Aristolochi'a clemati'tis*).

Oster=messe (◡̈...) *f* ㊷ Easter(-)fair; **=monat** *m* (month of) April; **=montag** *m* Easter(-)Monday.

Ostern (◡̈–◡) [ahd.: Easter] *f/pl.* ㊹, *f, inv.* oder *n* ㉓: a) christliche(s) ~ Easter; zu ~ at Easter; b) jüdische(s) ~ (Jewish) Passover.

Österreich ♀ (◡̈–◡) [ahd. Ost=reich] *npr/n.* ⓶α.: *hist.* ehm. Haus Habsburg in Deutschland u. Spanien, ♀ Kaiserreich und Erzherzogtum: Austria.

Österreicher (◡̈–◡̈◡) *m* ㊷, **~in** *f* ㊼, **österreichisch** *a.* ⑥⑥ Austrian; **österreichisch=ungarisch(e** Monarchie) Austro-Hungarian (monarchy).

Österreich=Ungarn ♀ (◡̈–◡.◡̈◡) *npr/n.* ⓶ Austro-Hungary.

Oster=sonntag (◡̈...) *m* ㊷ Easter(-) Sunday; **=woche** *f* E.(-)week, holy week; **=zeit** *f* Eastertide; **=zyklus** *m ast.*, Chronologie: paschal cycle.

Ost=europa ♀ (◡̈...) *npr/n.* ⓶ Eastern (or East of) Europe; **=friesland** ♀ *npr/n.* East Frisia; **=gote** *m*, **=gotin** *f* East Goth, Ostrogoth; **=grenze** *f* eastern frontier or boundary; **=indien** ♀ *npr/n.* (East) India, *geh.* Spr.: East Indies *pl.*; ehm. **=indien=fahrer** ⚓ *m* East-Indiaman; **=indier(in** *f) m*, **=indisch** *a.* ⑥⑥ East Indian; *auch:* Hindoo; De Gesellschaft (1600–1858) East India Company; **=kap** ♀ *n* Asiens: East Cape.

östlich ♀ (◡̈◡) [Ost] *a.* ⑥⑥ eastern, easterly, Oriental; De Länge East Longitude (E.L.); *adv.* ♀ von Frankreich (to the) east of France.

Ost=london ♀ (◡̈...) *npr/n.* ⓶ East London; **=mark(en** *pl.) f* ♀ (Posen *zc.*) Eastern Marches *pl.*; **=nord=ost** *m (abbr.* ONO(.) East-North-East; **=preuße** *m*, **=preußin** *f* East Prussian; **=preußen** ♀ *npr/n.* East Prussia.

Ostrazismus (◡̈◡–◡̈◡) [grch.] *m* ㉗ *grch.* Alt.: (Scherbengericht) ostracism.

ost=römisch (◡̈...) *a.* ~es Reich Empire of the East, *a.* Byzantine Empire; **=see** *f* ㊷ (the) Baltic (Sea); **=see=provinzen** ♀ *f/pl.* Rußlands: Baltic provinces *pl.*

Ostung * (◡̈◡) *f* ㊽ = Orientierung.

ost=wärts (◡̈...) *adv.* ⑥⑥ eastward; **=wind** *m* ㊷ east(erly) wind.

oszillieren (◡̈◡–◡̈–) [lt.] I *v/n.* (h.) ⑲ (schwingen) to oscillate. — II ~ *n* ㉓ und **Oszillation** *f* ㊽ oscillation.

Ottaverime (◡̈◡–◡̈◡̈–) [it. Stanze von acht Versen] *f/pl. inv. pros.* ottava rima.

Otter¹ (◡̈◡) [ahd.: otter; grch. Hydra] *m* ㊷ (*f* ㊸) *zo.* (Fisch♀) otter (*Lutra*).

Otter² (◡̈◡) [ndd.: adder: Natter] *f* ㊸ *zo.* adder (*Viperi'na*).

Zeichen (s. S. XVII): F familiär; P Volkssprache; Г Gaunersprache; ⚡ selten; † alt (auch gestorben); * neu (auch geboren); ÷+ unrichtig;

[Otternbalg] — 745 — [Packen]

Otter(n)=balg (⌣⌣...) m ❻❷ otter's skin; **=fang** (=fänger) m catching (catcher) of otters; **=²gezücht(e)** n, fig. bibl. generation of vipers; **=¹jagd** f otter-hunting.

Ottili-e (⌣⌣(⌣)⌣) [ahd.] npr/f. ❸❾ ❻❽. (Bn.) Ottilia.

Otto (⌣⌣) [ahd.] npr/m. ⑮❻α. (pl. auch Ottonen: ⌣⌣⌣) (Bn.) Otto, Otho.

Ottomane (⌣⌣⌣⌣) [türk.] **I** m ❹: **~n** pl. Ottoman. — **II** [fr.] f ❽ (türk. Sofa) ottomane.

ottomanisch (⌣⌣⌣⌣) a. ❻❻ = osmanisch.

Ouvertüre (u-w⌣⌣) [fr.] f ❽ (Einleitungs-spiel) overture.

oval (-w⌣) [lt.] **I** a. ❻❻ (eirund) oval. — **II ~** n ⓐd. oval.

Oval-drehbank (-w⌣...) f ❷, **=werk** n Drechslerei: oval lathe.

Ovarium ⚡ (-w⌣(⌣)⌣) [lt.] n ❷❽ anat. u. ⚥ (Eierstock) ovary.

Ovid (⌣w⌣) [lt. Schäfer] npr/m. ⑮⑯❷❹α. (röm. D., † 17 n. Chr.) Ovid(ius); **Lisch, ~isch** a. ❻❻ Ovidian.

ö. W. abbr. = österreichische Währung Austrian currency.

Oxal-äther ⚡ (⌣⌣...) [grch.] m ❻❷ chm. oxalic ether $(C_2[C_2H_5]O_4)$; **=säure** f = Kleesäure; **=säure=salz** n oxalate.

Oxhoft (⌣⌣) [ndl. Ochsenhaupt] n ⓐc,6. (Maß inv.) (ehm. dtsch. Flüssigkeitsmaß = 1½ Ohm, f. Ohm²) hogshead. [chloride.]

Oxychlorid ⚡ (⌣⌣t⌣⌣) n ⓐd. chm. oxy-

Oxyd ⚡ (⌣¹) [grch.] n ⓐd. chm. (höhere Sauerstoffverbindung; ant. Oxydul) oxide, oft durch das Suffix ...ic bezeichnet, z.B. Kupfer=oxyd cupric oxide; mit Wasser verbundenes ~ hydroxide; in ein ~ verwandeln to oxidize.

Oxydation ⚡ (⌣⌣⌣-tß⌣⌣) f ❹❻ = oxydieren II; **~s=flamme** f ❻❷ oxidizing flame; **~s=mittel** n oxidizing agent, oxidizer.

Oxyd=beschlag ⚡ (⌣⌣...) m ❻❷, **=häutchen** n, chm. layer, film of oxide; **=hydrat** n hydroxide.

oxydierbar ⚡ (⌣⌣⌣⌣) a. ❻❻ chm. oxid(iz)able; **~keit** f ❹❻ oxidability.

oxydier/en ⚡ (⌣⌣⌣⌣) **I** v/a., v/n. (sn) und sich ⚡ v/refl. ❾❸ (mit Sauerstoff verbinden, ein Oxyd bilden) to oxidize. — **II ~** n ❷❸ u. O/ung f ❹❻ oxidation, oxygenation, des Eisens ꝛc. auch: rusting.

Oxydul ⚡ (⌣⌣⌣) [grch.] n ⓐd. chm. (niedere Sauerstoffverbindung; ant. Oxyd, Super-oxyd) lower oxide, protoxide, oft durch das Suffix ...ous bezeichnet, z.B. Kupfer=oxydul cuprous oxide.

Oxygen ⚡ (⌣⌣¹) [grch.] n ⓐd. (Sauerstoff) oxygen (O); **~gas** n ❻❷ oxygen gas.

Oxytonon ⚡ (⌣⌣⌣⌣) [grch.] n ❺❾ grch. gr. (Wort mit Akut auf der letzten Silbe) oxytone.

Ozean (⌣⌣) [grch.] m ⓐd. (großes Meer) ocean; **~iden** (-⌣⌣-⌣) f/pl. ❽ (Töchter des Okeanos) Oceanides pl.; **~i-en** ⚥ (-⌣¹(⌣)⌣) npr/n. ❷❸α. = Australien; **ozeanisch** (⌣⌣⌣⌣) a. ❻❻ oceanic.

Ozelot (⌣⌣¹) [mer.] m ⓐd. zo. (Pardel-tatze) ocelot (Felis pa'rdalis).

Ozokerit ⚡ (⌣⌣-¹) [grch. Riechwachs] m ⓐc. min. chm. = Erdwachs.

Ozon ⚡ (⌣¹) [grch. riechend] n ❺❶ chm. (freier Sauerstoff) ozone; in ~ verwandeln to ozonify; **L=erzeugend** ⚡ (⌣⌣⌣...) a. ❻❻ ozoniferous; **L=haltig** a. ozonic, ozoniferous; **L(is)ieren** ⚡ (⌣-(⌣)⌣) v/a. ❾❸ (mit Ozon versetzen) to ozonize; **~messer** m ❻❷ ozonometer; **~messung** f ozonometry; **L=reich** a. rich in ozone.

P

P, p (¹) n, inv. (Buchstabe) P, p.
P chm. Symbol für Phosphor.
P. abbr. = Pater; Pastor.
p. (bfd. ♩) abbr. = piano; a. = pag.
p. a. abbr. = pro anno [lt. jährlich] annually; auf Briefen: per Adresse.

Pään (¹-) [grch.] m ⓐd. Alt.: (Triumph-lied) pæan, song of victory.

Paar [ahd.: pair; *lt. pār gleich] **I** n ⓐc,6., dim. **Pärchen** (¹⌣) n ❷❸ (zwei zsf-gehörige Dinge, Personen derselben Art) pair; (zwei gleichartige, mit-ea. verbundene Dinge, auch Personen bsd. verschiedenen Geschlechts) couple; ein ~ Schuhe, sechs ~ Handschuhe a (or one) pair of boots, six pair(s) of gloves; ein liebendes (ein verehelichtes) ~ a loving (a married) couple; es tanzten 6 ~e six couples were dancing; sie sind ein ~ geworden they became man and wife, they made a match of it; ein ~ Ochsen a pair (or yoke) of oxen; ein ~ Reb-hühner ꝛc. a brace of partridges. &c.; adv. ~ und ~, ~ bei ~, bei (od. zu) ~en by twos, two and two, in pairs or couples; zu ~en treiben [corr. aus zum Barren (zur Krippe zurück) treiben] to put to flight, to rout. — **II paar** a. ❻❻: a) (zsf.=gehörig) forming a pair; die Handschuhe sind nicht ~e the gloves are odd, they are odd gloves; Spiel: ~ oder un~? even or odd?; b) von Zahlen: (durch zwei ohne Rest teilbar) even.— **III** unbestimmtes Zahlwort: ~ inv. (nicht viel, einige) a few; ein ~ Fälle some (or a) few cases; deine ~ Sachen what few things you have; in ein ~ Tagen (with-) in a few days; ein ~ tausend Menschen some thousands of people; mit ein ~ Worten with (or in) a few words; ein ~ Zeilen schreiben to write a line or two; schreiben Sie mir ein ~ Zeilen! drop me a line!

paaren (¹⌣) ❽❽ **I** v/a. 1. Tauben ꝛc. ⚡ (zu e-m Paare verbinden) to pair ..., Handschuhe ꝛc.: to match; (gleich zu gleich gesellen) to couple, to assort; (vereinigen) to join, to unite, (hinzugesellen) to associate. — **II sich** ⚡ v/refl., bisw. ⚡ v/n. (h.) 2. to pair, to form a couple; (sich begatten) to pair, mate, copulate; (sich vereinigen) to join, to unite. — **III ~** ⚡ ❸. = Paarung. — **IV gepaart** p.p. u. a. ❻❻ 4. paired, coupled. — 5. (paarweise vorhanden) in twos, twinned; anat., math..&c.: conjugate, ⚡: geminate, geminous, didymous.

paarig (¹⌣) a. ❻❻ in pairs or couples; ⚡ ⚡ (adv.) gefiedert: ⚡ paripinnate; ⚡ geteilt: ⚡ dichotomous.

paar=mal (¹⌣¹) adv.: ein ~ a few times.

Paarung (¹⌣) f ❹❻ pairing, matching; coupling; union; (Begattung) copulation.

paar=weise (¹⌣¹⌣) a. ❻❻ u. adv. in pairs or couples, by twos; ⚡ geh(e)n to walk two and two, to march in double file; ⚡ ordnen to arrange in pairs, to pair; ⚡ ⚡ wachsend: ⚡ didymous.

Paar=zeher (¹⌣...) m ❻❷ zo.: ⚡ artiodactyl; **=zeit** [paaren] f pairing-time, season for pairing (birds, &c.).

Pacht (⌣t) [ndd.; *lt. pacta] f ❹❻ (m ⓐb.): a) tenure of land, tenancy (vgl. ~=vertrag); in ~ geben (nehmen) to let out (to take) on lease; in ~ h. to farm, rent; b) = Pachtgeld. [of a lease.]

Pacht=anschlag (⌣cht=¹⌣) m ❻❷ valuation

pachtbar (⌣cht-) a. ❻❻ leasable.

Pacht=besitz (⌣cht...) m ❻❷ leasehold (property); **=brief** m ⚡=vertrag.

pachten (⌣cht) **I** v/a. ❻❶ to take on lease, to farm, rent. — **II ~** n ❷❸ = Pachtung 1.

Pachter (⌣cht⌣), mst **Pächter** (⌣⌣) [pachten] m ❷❷, **~in** f ❹❼ farmer (wife), (female) tenant, leaseholder, lessee.

Pacht=geld (⌣cht...) n ❻❷ rent of a farm, farm-rent, zu hohes: rack-rent; **=gut** n leasehold estate, farm (ed land); **=herr** m owner (of a farm); **=hof** m farm; **=kon-trakt** m =vertrag; **=schilling** m =geld.

Pachtung (⌣cht⌣) f ❹❻ 1. taking on lease, &c. (f. pachten I), tenancy. — 2. = Pachtgut.

Pacht=vertrag (⌣cht...) m ❻❷ lease(hold deed); **L=weise** adv. on lease; **=zeit** f term of lease; nach Ablauf der ~ at the expiration of the lease, when the lease expires; **=zins** m rent(al).

Pachulke (⌣ch⌣⌣⌣)[poln. ⚥ pacho'lek Knappe] m ❹❹ typ. (Gehilfe) printer's devil.

Pack (⌣) [ndd.= pack] **I** m (n) ⓐⓒc,6. 1. packet, package, parcel, ⊕ (Ballen) bale; ~ Papiere pile (or bundle) of papers. — 2. (bestimmte Menge) parcel; ~ von 20 Stück score. — 3. (Gepäck) luggage; mit Sack und ~ (urspr. ⚥) with bag and baggage. — **II** n ⓐc. (o. pl.) 4. (gemeines Volk) rabble; Sprichw. ~ schlägt sich, ~ verträgt sich cads' fighting when ended is very soon mended.

Pack=an P (⌣¹) m ❺❶ ob. inv.: a) policeman, P copper; b) big (watch-)dog, a. Holdfast; **=bengel** (⌣...) m ❻❷ (Stock zum Schnüren von Warenballen) packing-stick, woolder; **=bind-faden** m packing-cord, twine.

Päckchen (⌣⌣) n ❹❹ (dim. v. Pack) small package or parcel; Sprichw. jeder hat sein ~ zu tragen each one (of us) has his burden to carry or his own troubles.

Pack=eis (⌣¹) n ❻❷ pack-ice.

Packen¹ (⌣⌣) m (n) ❷❸ large packet or parcel or bundle or bale.

♩ Musik; ⚡ Wissenschaft; ⚥ Pflanze; ⚥ Geographie; ⊕ Technik; ⚡ Bergbau; ⚔ Militär; ⚓ Marine; ⚡ Handel; ⚡ Post; 🚂 Eisenbahn.

packen² (⁵ᵛ) ⑧ **I** v/a. **1.** to pack (up), to do up in parcels, in Haufen: to pile up; in e-n Koffer ℒ to pack up in a trunk or box — **2.** a) (seine) Koffer ℒ, sein Felleisen ℒ, abs. ℒ to pack up, to be off, to clear out; b) die Taschen ꝛc. voll ℒ to cram (or fill) one's pockets, &c. — **3.** (derb fassen) to seize (roughly), to lay hold of, to clutch, beim Kragen: to collar, mit den Krallen: to claw, von Raubvögeln: to pounce upon; fig. er versteht es, seine Zuhörer zu ℒ he knows how to work up (or impress) his audience; ℒd darstellen to depict in a striking manner, to hold up to life; thea. ein ℒdes Stück a powerful (or sensational) play, F a fetching piece; e-e ℒde Szene a touching (or thrilling, stirring) scene. — **II** sich ℒ v/refl. **4.** F (sich eilig davon m.) to decamp, F to bundle off, to hook it; packt euch! be off!, out you go! — **III** ~ n ㉓ **5.** f. Packung 1 u. 2.

Packer (⁵ᵛ) m ㉒ **1.** packer. — **2.** Schwarzwald, v. Uhrenhändlern: commission-agent. — **3.** hunt. (Hund, der die Beute anpackt) large boar-hound or coursing-dog.

Packerei (⁵ᵛ˲ᴵ) f㊻ (das Packen) packing; das ist eine schlechte ~ that's badly packed.

Päckerei (⁵ᵛ˲ᴵᴵ) f ㊻ = Gepäck.

Packer=lohn (⁵ᵛ˲ᴵ) m (n) ㉒ packer's wages pl., cost of packing.

Pack=esel (⁵ᵛ˲ᴵ) m ㉒: a) sumpter-mule; b) fig. drudge, slave. [tupfer) pakfong.]

Packfong (⁵ᵛ) [chin.] n ㊿ (chinesisches Weiß-

Pack=garn (⁵ᵛ...) n ㉘ = bindpagen; **=haus** n, **=hof** m ㉒: a) in Fabriken: yard for packing; b) Zollwesen: bonded warehouse, docks pl.; **=kammer** f: a) ⓟ packing-room; b) 🚂 goods-office; **=kasten** m packing-case; **=knecht** m packer; **=korb** m hamper, für Porzellan ꝛc.: crate; **=kosten** pl. charges for (or cost of) packing; **=laken**, **=leinen** n, **=leinwand** f, **=linnen** n pack- (or sack-)cloth, canvas for packing, sacking; **=maschine** ○ f packing-machine, bundle-press; **=meister** m ℬ und ⚡ foreman of packers; **=nadel** ⚏ f packing-needle; **=papier** n packing-paper, brown paper; **=pferd** n pack- (or baggage-)horse, sumpter; **=raum** m: a) packing-room; b) eines Wagens: boot; c) ⚓ stowage(-room); **=riemen** ⚏ m saddle-strap; **=sattel** m pack-saddle; **=träger** m porter; **=tuch** ○ n packing-cloth.

Packung (⁵ᵛ) f ㊻ **1.** (zu packen² 1:) packing (up); eines Wagens: loading. — **2.** (zu 3:) seizure, collaring. — **3.** ○ mach. (Liederung) packing(-tow). — **4.** Wasserkur (Einpackung) packing.

Pack=wagen (⁵ᵛ...) m ⓔ luggage- (or goods-)van (a. 🚂); ⚏ baggage-cart; **=wesen** n packing (🚂 luggage) department; **=zeug** n things pl. used for packing; **=zwirn** m pack-thread.

Pädagog, **~e** (˲ᴵ˲ᴵ) [grch. Knabenleiter] m ㊷, ㊹ (Erzieher) pedagogue, educationist, b.s. pedant; **~ik** (˲ᴵ˲ᴵ) f ㊻ pedagogics, educational science; **~isch** a. ㊻ pedagogical, educational; **~ium** (˲ᴵ(ᵛ)˲) n ㉘ educational establishment; (höhere Schule) college.

Padde P (⁵ᵛ) f ㊺ nordd. (Frosch) frog; (Kröte) toad, ehm.: paddock.

paddeln F (⁵ᵛ) v/n. (h.) ⚡a. to paddle.

Päderast (˲˲ᴵ) [grch. Knabenlieber] m ㊷ pederast, sodomite; **~ie** (˲˲ᴵ) f ㊸ pederasty, sodomy.

Padischah (˲ᴵ˲ᴵ) [pers.] m ㊾ (Großherr, Titel des Sultans u. Schahs) padishah.

paff (⁵) (lautnachahmend) **I** int. **1.** (bsd. e-n Schuß nachahmend) bang!, pop!; F fig. ganz ℒ sein to be astounded or flummoxed or struck of a heap. — **II** Paff m ⓑh. **2.** (Schuß) report of a gun. — **3.** (Zug beim Tabakrauchen) whiff.

paffen (⁵ᵛ) [ndd.] v/n. (h.), bisw. v/a. ⑧ to whiff, (stark rauchen) to puff away at one's pipe; F fig. daß es nur so pafft with a vengeance or vehemence; drauf los ℒ (schießen) to pepper (or pop) away.

pag. abbr. = pa'gina [lt. Seite].

Page (ᴵG˲) [fr.] m ㊹ **1.** page. — **2.** dress-holder (= Aufschürzer).

Pagen=dienst (˲G˲...) m ㊹ duties pl. of a page; **=streich** m page's frolic or trick; ~e pl., auch: boyish pranks pl.

Pagina (˲ᴵ˲˲) [lt.] f ㊻ (Seite) page, ⊗ pagina, ⊙ typ. folio.

paginier|en (˲˲ᴵ˲˲) [lt.] **I** v/a. ⑧ ein Buch: to paginate, to mark the pages of. — **II** ~ n ㉓ u. **P.ung** f ㊻ pagination.

Paginier=maschine ○ (˲˲ᴵ˲˲˲˲) m ㊷ paging-machine.

Pagode (˲˲ᴵ) [indisch] f ㊺ (b. a. ㊹): a) indischer, chinesischer Götzentempel; b) Nickfigur; c) ehm. ind. Goldmünze: pagoda; **ℒn=artig** a. ㊻ (auch ℒnhaft (˲˲˲˲) a. ㊻) pagoda-like. [law!, pshaw!]

pah (ᴵ, ˲) [tautm.] int. ℒ! pooh!, lo!,

Pair (pär) [fr.] m ㊿; **~in** (˲ᴵ) f ㊷ (Mitglied der Adelskammer) peer, f peeress.

Pairschaft (pä'rʃ) f ㊻ peerage.

Pairs=kammer (pä'rʃ...) f ㊷ Chamber of Peers, House of Lords; **=schub** m batch (or wholesale creation) of peers; **=würde** f peerage.

Paket (˲ᴵ) [fr. paquet m; *Pack] n ⓑc.ⓢ. packet, parcel; ~e pl., oft: packages pl.; ~ Nadeln paper of needles; typ. = setzen to compose in slips; ~ Roheisenschienen: faggot.

Paket=ausgabe (˲ᴵ˲˲) f ㊺ parcel-delivery; **=beförderung** f carriage of parcels; **=beförderungs=gesellschaft** f parcel-delivery company (in Engl. oft: Pickford's); **=boot** ⚓ n (Postdampfer) packet(-boat), mail-boat, auf dem Atlantischen Ozean: Transatlantic liner; **=porto** ⚡ n postage (or carriage) for parcels; **=post** ⚡ f parcel-post; **=wagen** m parcel-delivery van.

Pakfong öst. = Packfong.

Pako (ᴵ˲) n ㊿ zo. (peruanische Kamelziege) alpaca (Auche'nia pacos).

Pakt (⁵) [lt.] m ⑧ⓑ., **~um** (⁵ᵛ) n ㉘ [lt.] (Abmachung) compact, agreement; e-n ~ schließen, auch **paktieren** (˲˲˲ᴵ˲˲) ⓐ u. v/n. (h.) ⑧ to agree upon; to make a compact or an agreement, to come to terms, to settle (matters) (ausbedingen) to stipulate, to covenant, to claim, to demand.

Paladin (˲˲ᴵ) [it.] m ⓑd. (Held bsd. im Gefolge Karls des Großen) paladin.

Palais (˲ᴵã) [fr.] n ㊿ = Palast.

Palankin (˲˲ᴵ, a. ⁵ᵛ˲] [ʃft. Bett] m ⓑd. (Sänfte mit Seiten=öffnung) palankeen.

Paläo=graph ⊗ (˲˲ᵛ˲ᴵf) [grch.] m ㊹ (Kenner alter Schrift=arten) palæographer, ... ist; **~ie** (˲˲ᵛ˲f˲ᴵ) f ㊹ palæography; **ℒisch** a. ㊻ palæographic(al).

paläolithisch ⊗ (˲˲ᵛ˲ᴵ˲) [grch.] a. ㊻ (die ältere Steinzeit betreffend) palæolithic.

Paläontolog, **~e** ⊗ (˲˲ᵛ˲ᴵ˲(˲)) [grch.] m ㊷, ㊹ palæontologist; **~ie** (˲˲ᵛ˲ᴵ˲f) f ㊸ (Urweltkunde) palæontology.

Palast (˲ᵛ˲) [nhd.; fr. palais; *lt. Palá'tium (röm. Kaiser=ℒ auf dem Palatinischen Hügel)] m ⓑb. palace; **ℒ=artig** a. ㊻ palatial; **~dame** f ㊺ lady of the court.

Palästina ⚥ (˲˲ᵛ˲ᴵ˲˲) [Philister] npr/n ⓑa. (Land West=asiens) Palestine; **palästinisch** a. ㊻ Palestinian, Palestinean.

Palästra (˲˲ᵛ˲ᴵ) [grch.] f ㊺ Alt.: (Ringschule) palæstra. [court-revolution.]

Palast=revolution (˲ᵛ˲˲wℒ=tß(˲)ᴵ) f ㉒]

palatal ⊗ (˲˲˲ᴵᴵ) a. ㊻ [lt. Gaumen...] a. ㊻ palatal; **~laut** m ⓔ palatal sound.

Palatin (˲˲ᴵ) [lt.] m ⓑd. **1.** röm. Alt.: (hoher Beamter) palatine. — **2.** = Pfalzgraf. [Berg m Palatine Hill.]

palatinisch (˲˲ᴵ˲) a. ㊻ palatine; **~er**]

Pala=u=inseln ⚥ (˲ᴵ˲˲) npr/pl. (deutsch, bei den Karolinen) Pelew Islands pl.

Paletot (˲ᵛ˲ᴵō) [fr. †, *ndl.] m ⓑ (Überzieher) overcoat, greatcoat, top-coat: **~marder** F m ㉒ stealer of overcoats.

Palette (˲ᵛ˲˲) [fr.] f ㊺ paint. (Farbentafel) palette.

Palimpsest ⊗ (˲˲ᵛ˲ᴵ) [grch. wieder abgekratzt] m, n ⓑa. (zweimal beschriebenes Pergament) palimpsest.

Palingenesie ⊗ (˲˲ᴵ˲˲˲ᴵᴵ) [grch.] f ㊸ (Wiedergeburt) palingenesis.

Palisade, mit ⚏ (˲˲ᵛ˲ᴵ˲) [nhd.; fr. palissade; *It. Pfahl] f ㊺ frt. (Schanzpfahl) palisade; **~n=reihe** (˲˲ᴵ...) f ㊺ row of palisades; **~n=verschanzung** f stockade.

palisadier|en ⚏ (˲˲ᵛ˲ᴵᴵ˲) [fr.] **I** v/a. ⑧ to palisade, to stockade. — **II** ~ n ㉓ und **P.ung** f ㊻ palisading.

Palisander(=holz n) (˲˲˲ᵛ(˲ᴵ) [brasil.] m ㉒ rosewood, palisander (Jacara'nda).

Palladium (˲˲ᴵ(˲)˲) [grch.] n ㉘ **1.** myth. u. fig. (schützendes Heiligtum) palladium. — **2.** ⊗ chm. (bläulich=weißes Metall) palladium (Pd); **~säure** f ㊺ palladic acid.

Pallas (⁵ᵛ) [grch.] npr/f. inv.: a) myth. ~ Athe'ne Pallas (Athene), Minerva; b) ast. Planetoide: Pallas.

Pallasch ⚏ (⁵ᵛ) [ruff.] m ⓑa. cut-and-thrust sword, broadsword.

Palliativ (˲ᵛ˲ℒ˲˲f) [lt. Bemäntelung] n ⓑd. bsd. med. palliative; **~maßregel** f palliative measure; **~mittel** n palliative.

Pallium (⁵˲˲) [lt.] n ㉘ Alt.: (Obergewand) u. eccl. (Erzbischofsmantel) pallium.

palm=artig (⁵ᵛ...) a. ㊻ ⊗ palmaceous; **=baum** ⚥ m ⓔ palm-tree; **=blatt** ⚥ n palm-leaf (a. arch.); **=bohrer** m, ent. palm-borer or -weevil (Cala'ndra pal'ma'rum); **=butter** f palm-butter.

Palme ⚥ (⁵ᵛ) [ahd.; *It. palma] f ㊺ **1.** (Palmbaum) palm(-tree) (Palma). — **2.** (Palmzweig) palm(-branch); fig. die ~ des Sieges erringen to carry off (or bear away) the palm. — **3.** = Palmwedel.

palmen ⚓ (⁵ᵛ) [It.] v/a. ⑧ ein Tau ℒ to haul a cable hand over hand.

[Palmenfarne] — 747 — [Papier]

Palmen=farne ♃(ˇ˘...) m/pl. ⚘: ⚚ cycadaceæ; =**hain** m grove of palm-trees, palm-grove; =**haus** n ſ. Palmhaus; =**kohl**, =**lilie** ꝛc. ſ. Palm=...; =**wespe** f, ent. palm-wasp (Poly'bius palma'rum).

Palmette (˘ˇ˘) [fr.] f ⚘ arch. (palmblattartige Verzierung) palmette, (decorative or conventional) palm-leaf.

Palmetto=palme ♃(˘ˇ˘⸗˘) [span. palmito] f ⚘ palmetto (Chamae'rops palme'tto).

Palm=haus (ˇ⸗) n ⚘ palm-house, palmery, palmetum.

palmig (ˇ˘) a. ⚘ palmy, palmiferous, covered (or grown) with palms.

Palmin (˘ˇ) [neu=lt.] n ⚘d. (Kokosnußbutter) coco(a)nut butter; **Palmitin** ⚚ (˘˘ˇ) n ⚘d. chm. (fester Bestandteil des Palmöls) palmitin(e) $(C_3H_5[C_{16}H_{31}O_2]_3)$; ~**säure** f palmitic acid $(C_{16}H_{32}O_2)$.

Palm=kern (ˇ⸗) m ⚘ palm-kernel or -nut, =**kern=öl** ⚘ n palm-oil; =**kohl** m (Gipfelknospe der Kohlpalme) palm-cabbage; =**lilie** ♀ f yucca; =**öl** ⚘ n palm-oil; =**ölseife** f palm-soap; ♀**reich** a. = palmig; =**sonntag** m, eccl. Palm Sunday; =**wachs** ♀ n palm-wax (von Cero'xylon andi'cola; Süd=amerika); =**wäldchen** n grove of palm-trees; =**wedel** m palm-branch or -frond; =**weide** ♀ f English palm, goat-willow, sallow (Salix ca'prea); =**wein** ⚘ m p.-wine, toddy; =**zucker** m p.-sugar, Oſt=J. jaggery; =**zweig** m branch of a palm(-tree).

Pampas ♀ (ˇ˘) [span.; *perua. Ebene] f/pl. ⊕ Südamerika: pampas pl.

Pamphlet (˘ˇ) [fr., *engl.] n ⚘c. (Flugschrift) pamphlet; =**ist** (˘ˇ˘) m ⚘, ~**schreiber** m ⚘ pamphleteer.

Pan (ˉ) [grch. Weidender] npr/m. ⚘⚘α. myth. (grch. Hirtengott) Pan.

Panama ♀ (ˇ˘˘) npr/n. ⚘α. Panama. Land=enge von ~ in Zentral=amerika Isthmus of Panama; ~**hut** m ⚘ Panama (hat); ~**kanal** m Panama Canal.

Panathenäen ⚚ (˘˘ˇ˘) pl. inv. grch. Alt.: (Fest der Athene in Athen) Panathenæa pl.

Panazee (˘˘ˇ) [fr., ✱grch.] f ⚘ (Mittel für alles) panacea, universal remedy.

Pandämonium (˘˘ˇ˘˘) [grch.] n ⚘ (Wohn=ort böser Geister) pandemonium.

Pandekten (˘ˇ˘) [grch.] pl.inv. (Hauptteil des Korpus juris) Pandects pl.; a. = Digeſten.

Pandemie ⚚ (˘˘ˇ) [grch.] f ⚘ (über ein ganzes Volk verbreitete Krankheit) pandemia.

Pandora (˘ˇ˘) [grch.] npr/f. ⚘β.⚘α. myth. Pandora; ~**büchse** f ⚘ aus der alles menschliche Unheil entsprang: Pandora's box.

Pandschab ♀ (ˇ˘) [ind. pandsch(s)-ab Fünfſtrom(land)] npr/n. ⚘α. Nordindien: Punjab, Panjab.

Pandur (˘ˇ) [Bande'rium od. ~ (St.)] m ⚘ ehm. ⚔ (ungarischer Infanteriſt) pandoor, pandour; fig. (Marodeur) marauder.

Paneel ⊕ (˘ˉ) [ndl.; fr. panneau; mlt.; dim. v. *lt. panis Futter] n ⚘d., carp. (Füllung e=r Tür ꝛc.) panel; wainscoting; ~**bekleidung** ⊕ (...) f ⚘ e=s Perſonenwagens: panel-furring.

paneelieren (˘˘ˇ˘) v/a. ⚘ carp. to panel.

Panegyrikus (˘˘ˇ˘˘) [lt., ✱grch.] m ⚘ panegyric (= Lobrede). [pipes pl.]

Pan=flöte ♪ (ˇ⸗˘) ⚘ Pan-pipe, Pandean)

Panier (˘ˇ) [mhd.; ✱fr. bannière f; v. ✱Banner] n ⚘d. = Banner².

panieren (˘ˇ˘) [fr. paner; ✱lt. panis] v/a. ⚘ Kocht. (mit Ei u. geriebenem Brot beſtreuen) to cover (or dress, sprinkle) with eggs and bread-crumbs.

Panik (fr. ˘ˇ, bſſ. ˉ˘) [fr. von grch. Pan als Dämon plötzlichen Schreckens] f ⚘⚘ panic, stampede (a. ⚜); von e=r ~ ergriffen werden to be seized with a panic; ♀**=artig**, **panisch** (ˇ˘) a. ⚘ panicky; **panischer Schrecken** panic (fear).

Pankratius (˘ˉ˘˘) ♂γ.npr/m. eccl. (Eisheiliger) Pancras.

Pankreas ⚚ (ˇ˘˘) [grch. Ganzfleiſch] n, inv. anat. (Bauchspeicheldrüse) pancreas.

Panne ✱ (ˇ˘) [fr.] f ⚘ Automobilweſen: (Nichtmehrvorwärtskommen) eine ~h., in der ~ ſein to come to a standstill or a dead stop.

Pannoni=en ♀ (˘ˇ(˘)) npr/n. Da. Alt.: (röm. Donauprovinz zw. Save u. Donau) Pannonia; **Pannoni=er** (in f ⚘) ⚘; **pannonisch** (˘ˇ˘) a. ⚘ Pannonian.

Panorama (˘˘ˉ˘) [grch.] n ⚘ (Rundbild) panorama; **panoramisch** a. ⚘ panoramic (view, &c.).

panſchen (ˇ˘) v/n. (h.) u. v/a. ⚘ = manſchen.

Panſcher (ˇ˘) m ⚘ 1. = Manſcher. — 2. oft in Zſſgn für (Ver=)Fälſcher, ſ. zB. Weinpan(t)ſcher.

Panſe (ˇ˘) [ndd.: pa(u)nch; ✱fr. panse f] f ⚘, mſt ~n m ⚘ 1. zo. (erſter Magen der Wiederkäuer) farding-bag, ⚚ runen. — 2. weitS. = Panzen.

Panſlawismus (˘˘ˇ˘) [grch.] m ⚘ (ſlawiſche Einheitsbeſtrebung) panslavism.

Panſlawiſt (˘˘ˇ) m ⚘, ♀**iſch** (˘˘ˇ˘) a. ⚘ Panslavist, a. auch: Panslavic.

Panthe=ismus (˘˘ˉ˘) [grch.] m ⚘ phls. (Glaube, daß das Welt=all Gottſei) pantheism.

Panthe=iſt (˘˘ˉ) m ⚘, ~**in** f ⚘ pantheist; **pantheiſtiſch** (˘˘ˇ˘) a. ⚘ pantheistic.

Pantheon (ˇ˘˘) [grch.] n ⚘ (Alt.: Tempel aller Götter; jetzt: Ruhmeshalle) Pantheon.

Panther (ˇ˘) [ahd.; ✱grch.] m ⚘ zo. panther (Felis pardus); schwarzer ~ black leopard (Felis melas); ♀**=artig** (˘ˇ˘...) a. ⚘ panther-like; ~**fell** n ⚘ panther's skin; ~**katzen** f/pl. zo.: ⚚ pardina pl.; ~**tier** n. zo. = Panther.

Pantine nordd. (˘ˇ˘) [fr. patin m] f ⚘ (Holzschuh) patten, clog.

Pantoffel (˘ˇ˘) [ndh.; it. panto'fola f; ✱grch.] m ⚘ (oft ⸗+ ⚘) 1. slipper; in ~n gehen to go about in slippers, to wear (thin) house-shoes; dem Papſte den ~ küſſen to kiss the Pope's toe. — 2. fig. unter dem ~ (der Herrſchaft der Frau im Hauſe) ſteh(e)n to be under petticoat-government; er ſteht unter dem ~, ſie hält ihn unter dem ~, a. he is henpecked or wife-ridden or F too much married, she has him under her thumb.

Pantoffel=blume ♀ (˘ˇ˘...) f ⚘: ⚚ calceolaria; ♀**förmig** a. ⚘ shaped like a slipper; =**held** m henpecked husband (vgl. Pantoffel 2); =**holz** n cork(-bark); =**macher** m maker of slippers; =**regiment** n ſ. Pantoffel 2; =**ritter** m = =held.

Pantomime (˘˘ˇ˘) [grch.] f ⚘ (Gebärden(ſchau=)ſpiel) pantomime, dumb show. **pantomimiſch** a. ⚘ pantomimical; ♀ darſtellen to act in dumb show.

pantſchen (ˇ˘) = panſchen.

Panzen (ˇ˘) m ⚘ 1. (Wanſt) paunch, belly. — 2. = Panſen.

Panzer (ˇ˘) [mhd., ✱it.] m ⚘ cuirass, coat of mail (vgl. Harniſch 1); ⚓ e=s Schiffes: armour, iron (or steel) casing.

Panzer=ärmel (ˇ˘...) m ⚘ vambrace; =**batterie** ⚔ f protected battery; =**deck** ⚓ n armoured deck; =**dreh=turm** bſd. ⚓ m revolving armoured turret; =**flotte** ⚓ f fleet of ironclads, ironclad fleet; =**fregatte** ⚓ f armoured (or ironclad) frigate; =**geschwader** ⚓ n squadron of ironclads; =**granate** ⚔ u. ⚓ f armour-piercing shell, armour-piercer; =**handſchuh** m mail glove, gauntlet; =**hemd** ⚔ n mail-shirt; =**hoſen** ⚔ f/pl. breeches pl. of mail; =**kette** ⊕ f Uhrmach.: curb-chain; =**krebſe** m/pl. zo.: ⚚ palinuridæ pl.; =**kreuzer** ⚓ m armoured cruiser.

panzern (ˇ˘) v/a. und ſich ♀ v/refl. ⚘a. to dress in mail, to arm with (a coat of) mail; ⚓ to armour, to plate, to (en)case in steel; ſich ♀ to put on mail or (an) armour; fig. to arm o.s. to get ready (for a contest); **gepanzert** mail-clad, clad in mail or in armour, ⚓ armoured, iron-clad, steel-clad, zo.: ⚚ loricate; **mit gepanzerter Fauſt** with the mailed fist; **gegen alle Widerwärtigkeiten gepanzert** steeled (or armed) against all reverses.

Panzer=platte ⚔ (ˇ˘...) f ⚓ armour-plate or -plating; =**reiter** ⚔ m cuirassier; =**ring** m mail; =**rock** ⚔ m coat of mail, mail(coat); =**schiff** ⚓ n armour-clad (or armoured, ironclad) ship, ironclad; =**ſchild** ✱ ⚔ für Geſchütze: protecting shield; =**tier** n, zo. armadillo (Da'sypus); =**turm** m: a) ⚔ frt. armoured (or armour-plated) turret; b) = Drehturm; =**turm=geschütz** ⚔ n turret-gun; =**turmſchiff** ⚓ n turret-ship, ehm. monitor.

Panzerung (ˇ˘˘) f ⚘ (dressing in) mail, ⚓ armour(ing), steel-casing, -plating.

Panzer=wangen (ˇ˘...) f/pl. ⚘ ichth. mailed-cheeks pl. (Familie Cataphra'cti); =**zug** m ⚂ ⚔ armoured train.

Päon (ˉ˘) [grch. -ˉ] m ⚘d. pros. (Versfuß aus 3 kurzen und 1 langen Silbe: -˘˘˘) pæon.

Päoni=e ♀ (-ˉ(˘)˘) [grch. *Päon Götterarzt] f ⚘ (Pfingſtblume) peony (Paeo'nia).

Papa (˘ˉ, ſüdd. ˇ˘) [ndh.; *fr.] m ⚘ (dim. ~**chen** (˘ˇ˘, ˘˘ˇ) n ⚘) papa, pa, F dad(dy).

Papagei (˘˘ˉ) [ndl., fr., *ar.] m ⚘c. u. ⚘ orn. parrot (Psi'ttacus), F Poll(y): ſchwatzen wie ein ~ to chatter (or jabber) like a parrot; ♀**=artig** (ˇ...) a. ⚘ parrot-like; ~**fiſch** m ⚘ ichth. parrot-fish (Scarus); ~**grün** ⊕ n parrot-green; ~**taucher** m, orn. puffin, coulter-neb (Mormon a'rctica oder frate'rcula).

Papageno=flöte ♪ (˘˘ˉ˘...) f ⚘ Papageno's magical flute. [Poll(y).]

Päpchen (ˇ˘) n ⚘ (dim. von Papagei) F)

Papier (˘ˇ) [mhd.; *lt.: paper; fr. *Papyrus] n ⚘d. 1. paper (ſ. Bogen 7, Buch 5); buntes ~ coloured paper; geleimtes ~ sized paper; liniiertes ~ ruled paper; zu ~ bringen to put on (or to commit to) paper, to write down; Sprichw. ſ. geduldig. — 2.

⚚ scientific; ♀ botanical; ♀ geography; ⊕ machinery; ⚔ mining; ⚔ military; ⚓ marine; ⊕ commercial; ✉ postal; ⚂ railway.

[Papierabfälle] — 748 — [Parallaxe]

(Wert=)~ paper; russische (spanische) ~e Russian (Spanish) bonds pl., auch Russians, Spaniards pl.; schlechte ~ worthless stock, F rubbish; (Staats=) ~e government bonds or securities pl.; die ~e steh(e)n gut (schlecht) the stocks are high (low).

Papier=abfälle (⌣͞⌣…) m/pl. ⑫, =abgänge m/pl. waste paper; =adel m = Brief=adel; ⁀artig a. ⑯ like paper, ⌒ papyraceous, …itious; =blume f: a) ⚥: ⌒ xeranthemum; b) künstliche: artificial paper flower; =bogen m sheet of paper; =boot n = nautilus; =brei ⊙ m paper-pulp; =drache m (paper) kite; =drucker ⊙ m paper-stainer.

papieren (⌣͞⌣) a. ⑯(D9) **1.** (of) paper; — 2. fig. (existing only on) paper; imaginary; ⁀er Stil prosy style.

Papier=fabrik(ant m) f(⌣͞⌣…) ⑫ paper-manufacture(r); =fetzen m scrap of paper; =form ⊙ f paper-mould; =format n size of paper; =geld ⊛ n (ant. hartes Geld) paper money; vgl. währung; =geschäft ⊛ n: a) paper-trade; b) dealing in stocks; =handel ⊛ m paper-trade; =händler(in f) m paper-merchant, im kleinen: stationer; =handlung f stationer's shop; =kohle ⚘ f paper-coal, ⌒ papyraceous lignite; =korb m paper-basket; =tragen m p.-collar; =laden m = =handlung; =maché ⊙ (pä-pjē' mä-schē") [fr.] n ⓾ ⑫ (hart gewordener Papierteig) papier mâché; Teebrett aus ~ papier-mâché tray; =macher(in f) m(⌣͞⌣…) ⑫ paper-maker; =maulbeer=baum ⚘ m paper-mulberry (Broussone'tia papyri'fera); =messer n paper-knife; =mühle ⊙ f paper-mill; =narzisse ⚘ f paper-narcissus (Narci'ssus papyra'ceus); =nautilus m, zo. p.-nautilus (Argonau'ta argo); =prüfer ⊙ m Maschine: paper-tester; =prüfung f p.-testing; =schere f large scissors pl. (for cutting paper); =schirm n paper screen; =schneide=maschine ⊙ f paper-cutting machine, p.-cutter; =schnitzel n/pl. p.-shavings pl.; =stereotypie ⊙ f paper stereo-process. p. stereotyping; =stoff m, =teig m = =brei; =streifen m strip (or slip) of paper; =tapete ⊙ f wallpaper, paper-hanging; =tüte ⊙ f paper bag; =umlauf ⊙ m p.-circulation; =valuta ⊛ f p.-value; =währung ⊛ f p.-currency; =wäsche ⊙ f paper collars and cuffs pl.; =wickel f curl-paper.

Papilionazee(n pl.) ⚘ ⊙ - (-⌣'-⌣--) [it.] f ⑱ = Schmetterlingsblume(n).

Papillar=drüse ⌒ (⌣͞⌣…) f ⑫ papillary gland; =körper m, zo. papillary body.

Papille ⌒ (⌣͞⌣)[it.] f ⑱ anat. u. ⚘ ⚶ papilla.

Papillote (⌣͞⌣¹)[fr.] f ⑱ (Haarwickel) curling-paper.

papinisch (⌣͞⌣¹) [Denis Papin. fr. Physiker, 1647—1710] a. ⑯: ⁀er Topf (Dampfkochtopf) Papin's digester.

Papismus (⌣͞⌣') [mlt.] m ② papistry; b.s. popery; **Papist**(in f ⓭) m ⑫ (Anhänger[in] des Papstes) papist; **papistisch** (⌣͞⌣') ⓰ papistic(al). papal.b.s. Popish.

Papp (⌣) m ⓪ b. = Pappe 1 u. 2.

Papp=arbeit ⊙ (⌣'…) f ⑫ cardboard (or paste-, pasteboard-)work; =arbeiter(in f) m worker in cardboard

or pasteboard; =band m Buchbind.: pasteboard binding; (book in) boards; =bogen ⚥ m sheet of cardboard; =deckel m pasteboard (= Pappendeckel).

Pappe (⌣') [mhd., ndd.: pap; *it.] f ⑱ 1. (Mehlbrei) pap. — 2. (Kleister) size, paste. — 3. ⊙ (Pappdeckel) pasteboard, dünnere: cardboard, geformte: millboard; F das ist nicht von ~! that's not (half) bad or to be sneezed at.

Pappel¹ ⚘ (⌣') [mhd.: poplar; *lt. po'pulus] f ⑱ poplar(-tree) (Po'pulus); schwarze ~ black poplar (Po'pulus nigra).

Pappel² ⚘ (⌣')[ahd.; dim. v. *lt. pappus Samenkrone] f ⑱ (Malve) mallow.

Pappel¹=allee (⌣'…) f ⑫ avenue of poplars; =baum ⚘ m = Pappel¹; =holz n poplar wood; =knoppern f/pl. pharm. poplar-galls pl.

pappeln (⌣') a. ⑯ of poplar wood.

päppeln (⌣') [Pappe 1] v/a. ⑫ a: ein Kind ⚲ to feed a child with pap, to bring it up by hand or with the bottle.

Pappel¹=öl (⌣'…) n ⑫ oil of the poplar bud; =salbe f = =öl; =weide ⚘ f (Schwarzpappel) black poplar. [pasteboard.]

pappen¹ (⌣') a. ⑯(D9) of cardboard or

pappen² (⌣') v/a. u. v/n. (h.) ⑱ 1. (zu Pappe 2:) to (stick with) paste. — 2. (zu Pappe 3:) to do cardboard-work.

Pappen=blume ⚘ (⌣'…)[ndd. Pfaffenblume] f ⑫ (Löwenzahn) dandelion; =¹deckel m pasteboard, vgl. Pappe 3; =fabrikation ⊙ f cardboard (or pasteboard) manufacture; =form ⊙ f mould for pasteboard.

Pappen=heimer (⌣'--⌣') m ⑫ hist. Dreißigjähriger Krieg: soldier of (General) Pappenheim; Sprichw. (nach SCH., Wallensteins Tod) daran erkenn' ich meine ~. etwa: I know my men by that, F I know my customers.

Pappen¹=macher ⊙ (⌣'…) m ⑫ pasteboard-maker; =³stiel F (Stiel der Pappenblume) m (et. Geringes) trifle; für (ob. um) e-n ~ for a mere song.

papperlapapp (⌣⌣⌣') int. abweisend: (what) nonsense!. fiddle-sticks!, rubbish!

pappicht. mst **pappig** (⌣') [Pappe 1] a. ⑯ pasty; (klebrig) sticky.

Papp=kasten (⌣'…) m ⑫, =schachtel f box (made) of cardboard, für Hüte ꝛc.: bandbox; =stoffel F m clumsy (or awkward) fellow; =waren f/pl. pasteboard goods or wares pl.

Paprika ⚘ (⌣⌣') [madj.] m ⑩ (spanischer Pfeffer) Cayenne pepper. capsicum.

Papst (⌣') [ahd.: pope; *lt. pāpa] m ⑦ a. (Titel ⓺⓹) eccl. Pope, Pontiff. Holy Father; ~ Gregor Pope Gregory.

Papst=gläubige(r) (⌣'--⌣) s. ⑫ Papist.

Päpstin (⌣') (von Papst) f ⑫ female Pope; hist. ~ Johanna Pope Joan.

päpstisch (⌣') [Papst] a. ⑯ b.s. Popish.

Papst=krone (⌣'…) f ⑫ (Pope's) triple crown, tiara. [Popery.]

Päpstler (⌣') m ⑫ Papist; ~ei (-⌣') f ⑫

päpstlich (⌣') [Papst] a. ⑯ papal, papist, pontifical, b.s. Popish; ehemaliges ⁀es Gebiet St. Peter's Patrimony. Papal States pl.; ⁀e Krone Papsttrone, ⁀er Stuhl Holy See; ⁀e Würde papal dignity, papacy.

Papst=tum (⌣') n ⓶d. papacy, pontificate, b.s. Popery, Popedom.

Papst=wahl (⌣'…) f ⑫ election of a Pope; conclave (of cardinals); =würde f papal dignity. papacy.

Papua (⌣⌣') [malaiisch kraushaarig] m ⑤, ~neger(in f ⓭) m ⑫ Papuan.

Papyrus ⚘ (⌣⌣') [lt., *grch. f] m ⓰ u. ⓾ Alt. (ägyptische Pflanze, daraus bereitetes Papier) papyrus; ~rolle f ⑫ p. (scroll); ~staude ⚘ f p.(-plant)(Cy'perus papy'rus).

Parabel (⌣⌣') [grch.] f ⑱: a) (Gleichnis) parable, simile; b) ⌒ math. (Kegelschnitt parallel e-r Mantellinie): ⌒ parabola. ~kurve (⌣⌣'…) f ⑫ parabolic curve.

parabolisch ⌒ (⌣⌣⌣') [grch.] a. ⑯ parabolic(al) (auch math.); (bildlich) allegorical, symbolical.

Parade (⌣⌣') [nhd., fr., *span.] f ⑱ 1. ⚔ (Musterung) review; die ~ abnehmen to hold a review; bei der ~ on parade; ↓ ~ anlegen to dress ship. — 2. (Prunk) display; ~ machen to make a show. — 3. fenc. = Deckung 1.

Parade=anzug ⚔ (⌣⌣'…) m ⑫ (ant. Kommißanzug) full-dress uniform; =bett n bed of state: auf dem ~e liegen to lie in state: =marsch ⚔ m march past; =pferd n horse for review; fig. object (serving) for show; in Schulen: picked scholar, F show-boy; =platz ⚔ m parade-ground; =schritt ⚔ m parade-step: slow (or ordinary) pace: =stück(chen) n piece for show, show-piece: (Steckenpferd) hobby; =zimmer n state-apartment.

paradieren (⌣⌣'⌣) [fr.] v/n. (h.) ⑬ (prunken) to parade; mit etwas ⚲ to show a th. off, to exhibit a th., to make a show (or an exhibition) of a th.

Paradies (⌣⌣') [ahd.; grch.] *pers. Garten] n ⓺ a. 1. bibl. u. fig. paradise. — 2. thea. co. gallery. F the gods.

Paradies=apfel ⚘ (⌣⌣'…) m ⑫ (Liebesapfel) tomato (Lycope'rsicum escule'ntum); =bewohner(in f) m inhabitant of paradise; =feige ⚘ f banana (Musa paradisi'aca); =fisch m, ichth. paradise-fish (Polyne'mus paradi'seus).

paradiesisch (⌣⌣'⌣) [Paradies] a. ⑯ of paradise, paradisaic(al). paradisean; fig. (wonnig) delightful, blissful, delicious; (entzückend) charming.

Paradies=körner ⚘ (⌣⌣'…) n/pl. ⑫ grains pl. of paradise (von Amo'mum granum paradi'si); =vogel m. orn. bird of paradise (Paradi'sea apo'da).

Paradigma ⌒ (⌣⌣'⌣) [grch.] n ⓶ (⓺⓺) gr. (Musterwort) paradigm; ⁀tisch (⌣⌣-⌣'⌣) a. ⑯ paradigmatic; paradigmatical.

paradox (⌣⌣') [grch.] a. ⑯ (widersinnig) paradoxical; ~ie (-⌣') f ⑫ paradoxy; ~on (⌣⌣'⌣) n ⓹⓽ paradox.

Paraffin (⌣⌣') [neu-lt. parum affi'nis wenig verwandt] n ⓪d. chm.(fettiges Produkt der trockenen Destillation von Holz, Kohlen ꝛc.) paraffin; ~kerze (⌣⌣'…) f ⑫, ~licht n paraffin-candle; ~öl n paraffin-oil.

Paragraph (⌣⌣') [grch.] m ⑫ (Abschnitt) paragraph. oft: article; (abbr. §); ⁀ieren (-⌣'-⌣) v/a. ⑬ to arrange in paragraphs. to paragraph.

parallaktisch ⌒ (⌣⌣⌣') [grch.] a. ⑯ parallactic(al); **Parallaxe** f ⑱ (scheinbare Verschiebung e-s Gegenstandes bei veränderter Stellung des Beobachters) parallax(is).

Zeichen (f. S. XVII): F familiär, P Volkssprache, Γ Gaunersprache, ⚲ selten; † alt (auch gestorben) ; * neu (auch geboren); ⸸ unrichtig

[parallel] — 749 — [Parteieifer]

parallel (⌣⌣⌢)[grch.] a. 🌐 bid. math. (gleich-laufend, gleisig) parallel (to or with); 2 (adv.) laufen mit to run parallel with.
Parallele (⌣⌣⌢) [grch.] f 🌐 (🌐) 1. math. (parallele Linie, Gleise) parallel line. — 2. fig. (Vergleichung) parallel; eine ~ bilden to form a parallel case, F to be on all fours; eine ~ ziehen mit to establish a comparison with.
Parallelepiped(on) ⌢ (⌣⌣⌢⌣⌣⌢, ⌣⌣⌢⌣⌢) [grch.] n🌐c.(🌐)math.(v.🌐Parallelogrammen begrenzt, Gleised) parallelepiped(on).
parallelisieren (⌣⌣⌣⌢)[fr. *grch.] v.a. 🌐 to make parallel, a. to parallelize.
Parallelismus ⌢ (⌣⌣⌢⌣) [it., *grch.] m 🌐 math., &c. parallelism.
Parallel-kreis (⌣⌣⌢…)m🌐ast. parallel; ≈laufend a. 🌐 running parallel with; ≈lineal ⊖ n parallel ruler; ≈linie f geom. parallel line.
Parallelogramm ⌢ (⌣⌣⌣⌢) [grch.] n🌐d. math., phys. (Gleised) parallelogram; ~ der Kräfte parallelogram of forces; Wattjches ~ Watt's parallel motion.
Parallel-schaltung ⊖ (⌣⌣⌢…) f 🌐 elect. connexion in parallel; ≈stelle f e-s Buches: parallel passage; ≈trapez n, geom.: ⌢ trapezoid. [paralysis.]
Paralyse ⌢ (⌣⌣⌢) [grch.] f 🌐 (Lähmung)
paralysieren ⌢ (⌣⌣⌢⌣) [fr.] v/a. 🌐 (lahm machen) to paralyse.
paralytisch ⌢ (⌣⌣⌢⌣) [grch.] a. 🌐 (ge-lähmt) paralytic. paralysed.
Para-nuß (⌢⌣⌢) [brasil. Para' ♀] f 🌐 Brazil-nut (Frucht v. Bertholle'tia exce'lsa).
Paraphe(⌣⌢⌣)[fr.parafe m;*grch.para-graph-] f 🌐, m 🌐 (Namenszug) flourish, paraph. [schreibung) paraphrase.]
Paraphrase ⌢ (⌣⌣⌢) [grch.] f 🌐 (Um-]
paraphrasieren(⌣⌣⌣⌢⌣)v/a.🌐(umschreiben) to paraphrase; **paraphrastisch** ⌢ (⌣⌣⌢⌣) a. 🌐 paraphrastic(al).
Parasit ⌢ (⌣⌣⌢) [grch.] m 🌐 (Schmarotzer) parasite; **Lenhaft** (⌣⌣⌢⌣), **Lisch** (⌣⌣⌢) a. 🌐 parasitic(al) (auch ♀).
parat (⌣⌢) [it.] a. 🌐 (bereit) ready.
Pärchen (⌢⌣) n🌐 dim. von Paar. [goes!]
pardauz F (⌣⌢) int. bang!, crash!, there/
Pardel, a. **Parder** (⌢⌣) [ahd.; *It.-grch. pa'rdalis] m 🌐 zo. leopard, panther, perd (Felis pardus); ~katze f = Ozelot.
Pardon (⌣⌢) [fr.] 🌐 m 🌐 1. (Verzeihung) pardon; (Begnadigung) (free) pardon; Ausruf: ~! I beg (your) pardon! — 2. 🌐 (Schonung des Lebens) ~ gewähren to give quarter; keinen ~ geben to give (or extend) no quarter, to show no mercy. [(starkes Tau) backstay.]
Pardun ⌄ (⌣⌢) [ndl.] n🌐d. u. 🌐. ~e f 🌐/
Par-enchym ⌢ (⌣⌣⌢) [grch.] n 🌐d. anat., ♀ (lockeres Zellgewebe) parenchyma, ..e.
Parenthese (⌣⌣⌢) [grch.] f 🌐 (Klammer) parenthesis; **parenthetisch** a. 🌐 paren-thetical; adv. a. by way of parenthesis.
Parforce-hund ⌢ (⌣fo͞"rß(⌣)…) [(+·+) fr.] m 🌐 hound (used for coursing); ≈jagd f hunting (on horseback), hunt, coursing; ≈kur f violent cure; ≈peitsche f hunting-whip; ≈ritt m ride or race on horseback) at full speed, F mad career. [perfume, scent.]
Parfüm (⌣⌢) [fr.] n 🌐d. (Wohlriechendes)/
Parfümerie (⌣⌣⌣⌢) [fr.] f 🌐 ≈ per-fumes, scents pl.; perfumery. ~ge-

schäft n perfumer's business; ~händ-ler(in f) m perfumer, dealer in scents.
Parfüm-fläschchen (⌣⌢…) n 🌐 (small) scent-bottle; **handlung** f perfumer's business. [scent-fountain.]
Parfümier-apparat 🌐 (⌣⌢⌣⌣⌢) m 🌐/
parfümieren (⌣⌢⌣) [fr.] v/a. und sich 2 v/refl. 🌐: (sich) 2 to perfume (o.s), to (sprinkle o.s. with) scent; stark par-fümiert strongly scented up.
pari 🌐 (⌢) [it. gleich] adv. und ~ n 🌐 (Rennwert, 100 Prozent): 2 stehe(e)n to be at par; über ~ above par. at a pre-mium; unter ~ below par. at a discount.
Paria (⌢⌣⌣) [tamulisch] m 🌐 (a. inv.) (Hindu o.Kaste, weit 🌐.Ausgestoßener)pariah.
parieren[1] (⌣⌢⌣) [It. pare're gehorchen] I v/n. (h.) 🌐 to obey (orders); f. Order. — II ~ n 🌐 obedience.
parieren[2] (⌣⌢⌣) [fr.] I v/a. u. v/n. (h.) 🌐 1. [fr. parier] (wetten) to (lay a) wager, to (make a) bet. — 2. [fr. parer] man. (sein Pferd) 2 (plötzlich anhalten) to stop short; das Pferd pariert (hebt die Vorder-füße) ~ reclines on its haunches. — 3. fenc. to parry a thrust, to ward off a blow. — II ~ n 🌐 u. **Parierung** f 🌐 4. wagering, bet(ting); fenc. parrying.
Parier-stange (⌣⌢…) [parieren[2] 3] f 🌐 fenc. am Säbelgefäße: cross-bar of a sword-hilt, cross-guard.
parisch (⌢⌣) [Paros ♀ grch. Insel] a. 🌐 of Paros, Parian (marble, &c.).
Pariser (⌣⌢⌣) [Pari's ♀, fr. Hauptst.] I s. 1. m 🌐, ~in f 🌐 Parisian (f oft: (fr.) Parisienne); inhabitant of Paris. — 2. (Haus-, Morgenschuh) slipper. — II a., inv. 3. Parisian, of Paris: ~ Mode f Paris(ian) fashion(s pl.); ~ Schrift f, typ. = Parisienne.
Pariser-blau 🌐 (⌣⌢⌣⌢) n 🌐 Paris (or paris) blue, pure Prussian blue.
Parisienne (⌣⌣(⌣)⌢) [Pari's] f 🌐 typ. sehr kleine Schriftgattung: ruby, Am. agate.
parisisch (⌣⌢⌣) a. 🌐 Parisian.
Parität (⌣⌣⌢) [It.] f 🌐 (Gleichheit) equal-ity, auch: parity.
paritätisch (⌣⌣⌢⌣) [It.] a. 🌐 on a footing of equality; 2e Schule undenominational (or unsectarian) …; 2er Staat … with religious equality.
Pari-wert 🌐 (⌢⌣⌢) m 🌐 par value.
Park 🌻 (⌢) [mhd.; fr., engl. (f. Pferch)] m 🌐b. (🌐) (Gartenanlage und ⚔) park.
park-ähnlich (⌣⌢…) a. 🌐, 2artig a. 🌐 like a park; ≈anlage f 🌐 park.
Parkett 🌐 (⌣⌢) [fr. parquet m] n 🌐c. a) carp. inlaid floor; b) thea. (Sperrsitze) stalls, reserved seats pl.
Parkett-besucher (⌣⌢…) m/pl. 🌐 thea. people (or spectators) pl. in the stalls; ≈(fuß)boden m inlaid floor; parquetry.
parkettieren 🌐 (⌣⌣⌢) [fr. parqueter] v/a. 🌐 carp. (austäfeln) to inlay a floor. [stall.]
Parkett-platz m 🌐 thea. (orchestra-)/
parkieren ⚔ (⌣⌢⌣) v/a. u. v/n.(h.)🌐 to park.
Park-tor (⌢…) n 🌐 park-gate; ≈wache ⚔ f guard to a park of artillery.
Parlament (⌣⌣⌢) [fr. parlement⌢] n 🌐c. (Volksvertretung) parliament; das ~ auf-lösen (vertagen) to dissolve (to pro-rogue) parl.; Auflösung (Vertagung) des ~s dissolution (prorogation) of parl.; vgl. Auflösung; ein ~ berufen to

convoke (or convene, summon) a parl.; im ~ sitzen to be (or sit) in parl., to be a member of parl. (abbr. an M.P.).
Parlamentär ⚔ (⌣⌣⌣⌢) [fr.] m🌐d. (Unter-händler) officer bearing the flag of truce; ~-flagge (⌢…) f 🌐 flag of truce.
Parlaments-ier (⌣⌣⌣⌢(⌣)⌣) m 🌐 member of parliament, parliamentariar
parlamentarisch (⌣⌣⌣⌢) a. 🌐 pol. parliamentary, hist. (unter Karl I. von England) parliamentarian (army, &c.).
Parlamentarismus (⌣⌣⌣⌢⌣) [neut.-lt.] m 🌐 parliamentary government or system. parliamentarism.
parlamentieren ⚔ (⌣⌣⌣⌢) [fr.parlemen-ter] v/n. (h.) 🌐 (unterhandeln) to parley.
Parlaments-akte (⌣⌣⌣⌢) m 🌐 pol. act of parliament, ≈anhänger m parlia-mentarian, hist. (unter Karl I. v. England) auch: pl. Roundheads; ≈ferien pl. re-cess (of parliament); ≈gebäude n (houses pl. of) parl.; ≈mitglied n mem-ber of parl. (M.P.); ≈ordnung f stand-ing orders pl.; ≈redner m speaker in parliament; ≈sitzung f sitting of parl.; ≈tagung f (parliamentary) session; ≈ver-handlung f parliamentary debate.
parlieren(⌣⌢⌣) [fr. parler] v/n.(h.) u. v/a. 🌐 to chat(ter), to gabble, F to jaw; (fließend sprechen) to speak fluently.
Parnaß ♀ (⌣⌢) npr/m. 🌐a. grch. Alt.: (Musenberg in Phokis) der ~ (Mount) Parnassus. [(or on) Parnassus.]
parnassisch (⌣⌢⌣) a. 🌐 Parnassian, of/
Parochial-kirche (⌣⌣(⌣)⌢…) f 🌐 (Pfarr-kirche) parochial (or parish-) church.
Parodie (⌣⌣⌢) [grch.] f 🌐 poet. (scherz-hafte Umbildung) parody; burlesque; Schreiber, Verfertiger von ~ n parodist.
parodieren (⌣⌣⌢⌣) v/a. 🌐 to parody, travesty, burlesque, F to take off.
parodistisch (⌣⌣⌣⌢) a. 🌐 parodic(al).
Parole ⚔ (⌣⌢⌣) [(+·+) fr.] f 🌐 (Losung) watchword, password, parole; die ~ ausgeben to pass the watchword.
Parole-befehl (⌣⌢⌣…) m 🌐 order given at the muster; ≈buch n book of orders.
Paroli (⌣⌢⌣, ++⌣⌢) [fr. par au lit ob. it., span.?] n 🌐 urspr. im Pharospiel, dann fig.: ein ~ bieten (r-r biegen) to pay back, to repay in kind, to give tit for tat; einem ein ~ bieten to challenge a p.
Paroxysmus ⌢ (⌣⌣⌢⌣) [grch.] m 🌐 path. (krampfhafte Aufregung) paroxysm.
Parse (⌢⌣) m 🌐, **Parsin** f 🌐 (Anhänger[in] der Lehren Zoroasters) Parsee (woman f).
parsisch (⌢⌣) a. 🌐 Parsee: ≈e Religion (auch **Parsismus** (⌢⌣⌣) m 🌐) Parsee religion, Parseeism.
Part (⌢) [it.] m u. n 🌐c. 1. (Anteil) share, portion; f. halb2.. — 2. ♪ (Rolle, Stimme) part. — 3. ⚓ m stehender ~ = Holpart.
Partei (⌣⌢) [mhd.; *fr. parti m] f 🌐 1. politisch zc.; party; b.s. faction, set; f. ergreifen 2; sich zu j-s ~ schlagen to take a p.'s side, to espouse a p.'s cause; pol. sich zwischen den ~en halten to sit on the fence. — 2. vor Gericht: party, side. — 3. F drei ~ en in dem-selben Hause three households (or F parties) under the same roof.
Partei-eifer (⌣⌢…) m 🌐 partisan zeal, zeal shown in the service of one's party; 2eifrig a. 🌐 factious.

[parteien] — 750 — [passen]

parteien (⌣́⌣) [Partei] I v/a. u. **ſich** ⚥ v/refl. ⊛: (ſich) ⚥ to (be) split up into parties or groups; to form cliques. — II ~ n ㉓ = Parteiung 1.

Partei-farbe (⌣́⌣…) f ㊵ party-colour; =**führer** m leader (or head) of a party, party-leader; =**gänger** m: a) partisan; b) ⚔ military adventurer; =**geiſt** m party- (or factious) spirit, party-feeling; =**genoſs** m partisan, political associate; =**gruppe** f Fraktion.

partei-iſch (⌣́⌣) a. ㊿ partial, biassed, taking sides; one-sided.

Partei-kampf (⌣́⌣…) m ㉒ party-strife or -warfare; =**leidenſchaft** f violent

parteilich = parteiiſch. [party-feeling.]

Parteilichkeit (⌣́⌣⌣) f ㊵ partiality, bias.

partei-los (⌣́…) a. ㊿ neutral, pol. auch: independent; =**loſigkeit** f ㊵ neutrality; independence; =**mann** m ㉒ partisan; =**nahme** f espousing a cause; =**programm** n (party-)platform, Am. ticket; =**regierung** f party government; =**rückſichten** f pl. considerations pl. of party; =**ſucht** f factious spirit, factiousness; =**ſüchtig** a. factious; =**treiben** n factious agitation.

Parteiung (⌣́⌣) f ㊵ 1. formation of parties or cliques. — 2. party, faction, clique; a. group, set, b.s. gang.

Partei-weſen (⌣́⌣…) n ㉒ party doings, concerns pl.; cliquism; =**wut** f frenzy of (contending) parties; =**zwecke** m/pl. objects of a party; ~ **dienen** to serve party purposes.

Parterre (⌣⁻tä'r) [fr. m] n ㉓ 1. [⁎.[⁺.fr.] (Erdgeſchoß) groundfloor; ⚥ (adv.) **wohnen** to live on the groundfloor. — 2. thea. (Zuſchauerraum zu ebener Erde) pit. — 3. (Blumenbeet) flower-bed.

Parterre-beſucher(in f) m (⌣…) ㉒ thea. pitster, one who sits in the pit; =**loge** f, thea. pit-stall; =**publikum** n, thea. the pit; =**wohnung** f(=**zimmer** n) apartments pl. (room) on the ground-floor.

Parthenogenesis ⚿ (⌣⌣⌣́⌣) [grch. Jungfernzeugung] f ⓰ biol. parthenogenesis.

Parther (⌣́⌣) m/pl. ㉒ Alt.: (aſiatiſches Volk) Parthians pl.; **Parthi-en** ♀ (⌣⌣⌣) npr/n. ㉓ α. Alt.: (Landſchaft in Perſien) Parthia;

parthiſch (⌣́⌣) a. ㊿ Parthian.

Partie (⌣⌣́) [fr.] f ㊸ 1. (Geſellſchaft) party, company; (Land=) excursion, outing; **eine ~ machen** to have an outing, to go on an excursion. — 2. (Heirats=) match; **eine gute ~ machen** to make a good match; **eine ~ ausſchlagen** to refuse an offer. — 3. ♟ parcel; **in ~n von 10 Ellen** in lots of ten yards (each). — 4. (Kartenſpiel) game, (Ballſpiel) game, match, Tennis: set; **eine ~ Schach ſpielen** to play a game of chess.

Partie-geld (⌣⌣́…) n ㉓ Billard: charge for the use of the (billiard-)table.

parti-ell (⌣tiě̆l) [fr. partiel] a. ㊿ (teilweiſe) partial; adv. part(ial)ly, not entirely.

partien-weiſe ✿ (⌣⌣́⌣) adv. (F a. a. ㊿) in (small) lots or parcels.

partieren (⌣⌣́⌣)[fr.] v/a. ㉓ (teilen) to share; to distribute; to mete (or dole) out.

Partierer (⌣⌣́⌣) m ㉒ distributer; engl. S. (Hehler) receiver of stolen goods.

Partikel (⌣⌣́) [lt. Teilchen] f ㊽ gram. (unveränderliches Wort) particle.

Partikelchen (⌣⌣́⌣) n ㉓ (small) particle, (a) mere dust, atom.

Partikular-beſtrebung (⌣⌣⁼⌣́⌣⌣) f ㊵ pol. separatist movement.

Partikularismus (⌣⌣⌣⁻⌣́) [lt.] m ㉗ pol. u. rel. particularism, separatism.

Partikulariſt (⌣⌣⌣⁻⌣́) m ㉒, **partikulariſtiſch** a. ㊿ particularist, separatist.

Partiſan (⌣⌣́) [fr., it.] m ⑳d., ~e¹ (⌣⌣́⌣) ㊹ (Parteigänger) partisan. [partiſan.]

Partiſane² ⚔ (⌣) [fr.] f ⓮ ehm. (Art Spieß)

partitiv (⌣⌣́f) [lt. verteilend] a. ㊿ gram. **Der Artikel** partitive article. [score.]

Partitur ♪ (⌣⌣⌣́) [it.] f ㊶ (Stimmbuch)

Partizip (⌣⌣ti̱p) [lt. teilhabend (an Verb u. Nomen)] n ⑳d. gr.: ~**ium Präſentis** (Perfekti) participle present or present participle (part. past or past part.).

Partizipial-konſtruktion (⌣⌣ti̱p⁻⌣⌣⌣́…) f ㊵ gram. participial construction.

partizipieren (⌣⌣⌣⁻⌣́⌣)[lt.] v/n.(h.)⑬(teilnehmen) to participate (or take part) in.

Partizipium (⌣⌣ti̱p(⌣)⌣) n ㉓㊴ = Partizip.

Partner Ƭ (⌣́⌣) m ㉒, ~**in** f ㊷ Spiel u. ⚭ (Teilhaber) partner.

Partnerſchaft (⌣⌣́⌣) f ㊻ partnership.

partout (⌣⌣tū) [fr. überall] = **durchaus**.

Partout-billett (⌣tū…) n ㉓ thea. ticket (or card) admitting to all performances, auch: free pass.

Parvenü (⌣⌣⌣́) [fr.] m ⑳ (Emporkömmling) upstart, (fr.) parvenu (e f).

Parze (⌣́⌣) [lt.] f ㊶ myth. (Schickſalsgöttin) (goddess of) Fate or Destiny, one of the three Parcæ or sisters.

Parzelle (⌣⌣́⌣) [fr. parcelle] f ㊶ (Stück, bſd. v. Land) lot, allotment.

parzellieren (⌣⌣⌣́⌣) [fr.] v/a. ㊾ to divide into lots, to allot; to parcel out.

Paſch (ǎ) [fr. passe-dix] m ⑳ㅇa. (Würfel) dice pl.; (Wurf, bei dem zwei Würfel gleich viel Augen haben) doublets pl.; **einen ~ werfen** to throw doublets.

Paſcha (⌣́) [türk. Haupt] m ⓹ pasha.

Paſchalik (⌣⌣́) n ⑳d. ㊴ pashalic.

Paſcha-wirtſchaft (⌣⌣⁻⌣́⌣) f ㊵ misgovernment of pashas, arbitrary rule.

paſchen¹ (⌣́) [Paſch] v/n. (h.) ⑬ to play at dice; to throw doublets.

paſchen² (⌣́) [nhd. 18. sae. F; * (die Grenze) paſſieren] v/a. ⑬: **Waren ~** (ſchmuggeln) to smuggle goods, to (carry) contraband.

Paſcher (⌣́) [paſchen] m ㉒ smuggler, contrabandist; ~**ei** (⌣⌣́) f ㊵ (system of) smuggling, contraband(ism).

Paſigraphie ⚿ (⌣⁻⌣⌣́) [grch.] f ㊸ (Schrift für alle Völker) pasigraphy.

Paſpel ♀ (⌣́) [fr. passepoil m Litze] m ㉒, f ㊸ braid (or hem, border) of a dress.

paſpelieren (⌣⌣⌣́⌣) [fr.] v/a. (einfaſſen) to braid, hem, bind.

Pasquill (⌣⌣́) [it.] n ⑳d. (Schmähſchrift) lampoon, libel; ~**ant** (⌣⌣⌣́) m ㉒ lampooner, libeller; **Lieren** (⌣⌣⌣́⌣) v/n. (h.) u. v/a. ⑬ to lampoon, to libel.

Paß (ǎ) [nhd., nld., *lt.] m ⑳a. 1. (Durchgang) passage; (enger Übergang über ein Gebirge) pass, (narrow) defile; vgl. a. Eng., Gebirgs=paß. — 2. [fr. passeport] (obrigkeitlicher Geſelſchein) passport, biſw. papers pl.; **e-m e-n ~ ausſtellen** to make out a passport for a p. — 3. (Maß) measure. — 4. man. auch ~**gang** amble, ambling pace. — 5. adv. nordd.: a) **der Rock iſt ihm zu** ⚥, auch: iſt **ihm** ⚥ … fits him well or like a glove; b) fig. **zu** ⚥, **zupaſſe kommen**.

paſſabel (⌣⌣́) [fr.] a. ㊿ (leidlich gut) passable, tolerable.

Paſſage (⌣⌣G̱⌣) [fr. m] f ㊵ 1. a) Durchgang, Überfahrt; b) ꕥ Stelle in einem Buche: passage; c) (mit Glas bedeckter Gang) auch: arcade. — 2. ♪ run (ſ. Lauf 4).

Paſſage-inſtrument (⌣⁻G̱⌣⁻⌣⁻) n ㉓ ast. transit-instrument.

Paſſagier (⌣⌣G̱⌣́) [fr.] m ⑳d.(㈷), biſw. ~**in** f ㊷ (Fahrgaſt) passenger, in Mietswagen: fare; **blinder ~** (der nicht bezahlt) deadhead, ↯ stow-away (passenger).

Paſſagier-boot ↯ (⌣⌣G̱⌣́⌣) n ㉓ passenger-boat or -steamer; =**geld** n fare, ↯ auch: passage(-money); =**gut** n (passengers') luggage or effects pl.; =**kammer** ↯ f auf e-m Dampfer: state-room; =**liſte** f list of passengers; =**ſchiff** ↯ n = =**boot**; =**ſtube** f waiting-room; =**verkehr** m passenger-traffic; =**zettel** ⚙ m waybill; =**zimmer** n = =**ſtube**; =**zug** 🚂 m passenger-train. [(Oſtern) Passover.]

Paſſah (⌣́) [hebr.] n ⑳, meiſt ~=**feſt** n ㉓

Paß-amt (ǎ⁻⌣) n ㉓ passport-office.

Paſſant (⌣⌣́) [fr.] m ㊸ passer-by.

Paſſat ↯ (⌣⌣́) [it.], ~=**wind** m ⑳c. trade-wind, bſd. im Indiſchen Ocean: monsoon.

paſſen (⌣́) [ndl., *fr. passer] ⑬ I v/n. (h.) 1. (auf ⚥) to lie in wait, to watch; (harren, warten) to wait; ſ. Dienſt 4. — 2. [fr.] (nicht ſpielen) to pass. — 3. (ſf. ⚥) to tally, to harmonize, to go well (or agree) together, to be in keeping; **der Rock paßt ihm gut** … fits him well; **das Kleid paßt nicht** … is a bad fit or a misfit; **der Deckel paßt nicht auf die Kanne** the lid does not fit the jug; **es paßt nicht hierher** it's not(hing) to the purpose; **der Ausdruck paßt nicht in die Rede** the expression is not suited to the speech; **ſie paßt in eine Geſellſchaft** she is fit for (or can mix with) any society; **ſie** ⚥ **gut zu-ea.** F they jog on (or gee in) well together; **Grün und Blau** ⚥ **ſchlecht zu-ea.** … do not blend well; **er paßt nicht zum Arzte** he is not fit to be (or cut out for) a medical man; **die beiden** ⚥ **nicht zuſammen** the two are ill matched or F do not hit it off well; ſ. Kram 4; Sprichw. ſ. Fauſt¹ am Schluß. (**recht ob. genehm ſein**) to be suitable or convenient; **das paßt mir** that suits me or will do for me; **wie das paßt! how convenient! — II ſich** ⚥ v/refl. 4. (ſich ziemen) to be convenient or meet or befitting or seemly or proper or appropriate; **das würde ſich für eine Dame nicht** ⚥ that would not become (or be becoming for) a lady. — III v/a. 5. (paſſend machen) to adjust; **an** (oder **auf**) **et.** ⚥ to adapt (or accommodate) to a th.; (meſſen) to measure. — IV ⚥ p.pr. u. a. ㊿ 6. (ſ. 3) harmonizing, in keeping; well matched, to the purpose; suitable. — 7. convenient, &c. (ſ. 4); ⚥ **de Bemerkung** timely (or apposite) remark; ⚥ **de Zeit für** ‖ seasonable (or right) time for ‖; **für** ⚥ **halten** to think proper or fit or suitable; **in ſich ſchlecht** ⚥ out of

Signs (see page XVII): F familiar; P vulgar, F flash; ⚡ rare; † obsolete (died); * new word (born); ++ incorrect; ♪ music;

[**Passepartout**] proportion, incongruous, ill matched or proportioned.

Passepartout (pä'ß-pär-tū'...) [fr. überall passend] m ⊕, ~**billett** n ⊕ thea. free pass.

Paß=gang (ß...) m ⊕ f. Paß 1; =**gänger** m, man. ambling horse; =**glas** ⊕ n graduated jar or glass.

passierbar (⌣́⌣...) a. ⊕ = gangbar 1.

passier/en (⌣́⌣) [fr.] I v/n. (ſu), a. v/a. ⊕ 1. (überschreiten) to cross, to pass; mag 2 (durchgehen) it will (just) do; 2 laſſen to (let) pass (a. ×); für et. 2 (gehalten werden) to pass for s.th. — 2. (begegnen, zuſtoßen) to happen, occur, take place; ſo etwas paſſirt nicht alle Tage such things do not happen every day, that's not an every-day occurrence; wenn mir et. Schlimmes 2 ſollte if anything untoward should befall me, if I should meet with an accident, F das kann e-m 2, der Frau u. Kinder hat such things (can) happen in the best-regulated family. — II ~ n ⊕ u. P/ung f ⊕ 3. (ſ. 1) crossing, passage.

Passier=gewicht ⊕ (⌣́⌣...) n ⊕: Münze: allowance, deduction; =**schein** ⊕ m pass(-bill), permit; =**stein** m = =**gewicht**; =**zettel** m = =**schein**.

Passion (⌣v̌) [lt.] f ⊕ = Leiden(ſchaft).

passionieren (⌣⌣-́⌣) I v/refl. ⊕ ſich für et. 2 to be passionately fond of (or deeply interested in) a th. — II **passioniert** p.p. u. a. ⊕ (leidenſchaftl.) impassioned, passionate(ly fond of).

Passions=betrachtung (⌣v)̌v... f ⊕ eccl. meditation for Passion-week; =**blume** ♀ f passion-flower (*Passiflo'ra*); =**buch** n, eccl. passionary; =**christ** m Passion of our Lord; =**kreuz** n, her. passion-(or Latin) cross; =**predigt** f, eccl. p.-sermon; =**spiel** n bſd. ehm.: p.-play; =**woche**, =**zeit** f Passion-week, -tide.

passiv (⌣́f) [mlt. leidensfähig, leidend] I a. ⊕ 1. (ant. aktiv) passive (a. gr. u. chm.). — II (a. -́f) ~ n ⊕d. 2. gr. passive (voice or verb). — 3. bſd. ⊕, ~**en** pl. (Schulden, ant. Aktiva) liabilities pl.

Passiv=handel (⌣́f-⌣v) m ⊕ import-trade.

passivisch (⌣́⌣) [lt.] a. ⊕ (leidend) passive, adv. a. in the passive; **Passivität** (⌣v-⌣́) f ⊕ (ant. Aktivität) passivity.

Passiv=seite (⌣́f-⌣) f ⊕ in Handelsbüchern: left (or wrong) side of the ledger.

Passivum (⌣-́⌣v) [lt.] n ⊕ = passiv II.

Paß=karte (ß...) f ⊕: a) passport; b) Kartenspiel: ~n bad cards pl.; =**kugel** f, hunt. bullet which only just fits the bore of the gun, auch: proof-ball.

paßlich (⌣́v) [passen II] a. ⊕ convenient.

Paß=pflicht (ß...) f ⊕ obligation to carry (or take out) a passport; vgl. =**zwang**; **2recht** a. ⊕ u. adv. fitting exactly; =**schererei** f vexatious passport-system.

Passung (⌣́v) f ⊕ mach. agreement between different parts of a machine.

Passus (⌣́v) [lt.] m, inv. (Stelle) passage.

Paß=wesen (ß...) n ⊕ passport-concerns pl.; =**wort** n = Parole; =**zwang** m compulsory passport-system; vgl. =**pflicht**.

Paste (⌣́v) [it.] f ⊕ 1. (teig-artige Maſſe) paste. — 2. ⊕ (falſche Edelſteine) paste, imitation jewelry or gems pl.

Pastell (⌣v)́ [it.] m u. n ⊕d. paint. (Farbenſtift) pastel, (coloured) crayon; =**bild** (⌣v́...) n ⊕ pastel (picture); =**farbe** f pastel- (or coloured) crayon; =**gemälde** n pastel (painting); =**maler** m pastel(l)ist; =**malerei** f pastel-painting; =**stift** m pastel-crayon.

Pastetchen (⌣v́⌣) n ⊕ (dim. v. Paſtete) small pie, patty, mit Obſt: tartlet.

Pastete (⌣v́⌣) [mhd.; *mlt.; *Paſte] f ⊕ mit Fleiſch: pie, mit Obſt: tart [Am. dagegen a.: Obſt2 = pie]; F fig. da h. wir die~ (Beſcherung)! we are in a nice mess or stew!, that's a pretty state to be in!

Pasteten=bäcker(in f) m (⌣v́v...) ⊕ pastry-cook; =**bäckerei** f pastry-cook's (shop); =(**back**)**werk** n pastry; =**fleisch** n mince-meat; =**händler** m pie-man; =**kruste** f pie-crust; =**schüssel** f pie-dish.

Pasteurisation (⌣tß̌-tß̌-́⌣)[Louis Paſteur, fr. Chemiker, 1822—95] f ⊕ (Verhütung der Pilzbildung in Wein, Milch ꝛc.) pasteurization; **pasteurisieren** (⌣tß̌-́⌣) v/n. to pasteurize; **Pasteur'sch** (⌣tß̌ʹrsch) a. ⊕ of Pasteur, Pasteurian. [(le).]

Pastille (⌣v)́ [lt.] f ⊕ (Plätzchen) pastil-f

Pastinake ♀ (⌣⌣-́⌣) [lt.] f ⊕: gemeine ~ parsnip (*Pastinaʹca satiʹva*).

Pastor (v́, P ⌣ʹv) [lt. pāstor Hirte] m ⊕ (P nordd. a. ⊕ ⊕ ⊕ ⊕ d.), ~**in** (⌣v́⌣) f ⊕ pastor, (Proteſtant) minister; anglit. Pfarrer u. Pfr. a. ~(**s**)**frau** f pastor's (or minister's, vicar's) wife.

Pastoral=brief (⌣-v́-́⌣) m ⊕ Cath. eccl. (Hirtenbrief) pastoral (letter).

Pastorale (⌣-v́-⌣) [it., it.] n ⊕: a) (Hirtenſpiel, -muſit) pastoral(e); b) Cath. eccl. (Hirtenbrief) pastoral (letter).

Pastoral=konferenz f ⊕ (⌣-v́-⌣...) clerical meeting, conference of the clergy; =**theologie** f pastoral divinity.

Pastorat (⌣-v́-́) [lt.] n ⊕c. (Pfarramt) clerical office or living or appointment, als Gebäude: parsonage, vicarage.

Patagoni=en ♀ (⌣-v-́⌣-⌣) npr/n. ⊕ ×. (Land auf der Südſpitze von Amerika) Patagonia; **Patagoni=er(in** f ⊕) m ⊕ [port. Tatzenfüßler], **patagonisch** (⌣⌣v)́ a. ⊕ Patagonian.

Pate (⌣́v) [mhd.; *lt. pater] m ⊕, **Patin** f ⊕ eccl. 1. (Tauſzeuge) godfather; godmother; a. sponsor. — 2. (Täufling) godson, f goddaughter; a. godchild.

Paten=brief (⌣́v-́) m ⊕ invitation to act as godfather (or godmother) to a child. [paten.]

Patene (⌣v́⌣) [lt.] f ⊕ eccl. (Hoſtienteller)f

Paten=geld (⌣́v...) n ⊕, =**geschenk** n christening-present; =**kind** n godchild; =**stelle** f sponsorship; bei e-m Kinde ~ vertreten to act as (or to stand) godfather (or godmother) to a child.

Patent (⌣v)́ [fr. offener (Brief)] I n ⊕c. 1. (landesherrlicher Brief) letters pl. patent. — 2. × (Beförderungs=urkunde) (officer's) commission. — 3. (Urkunde für den Schutz e-r Erfindung) patent; ein ~ anmelden to give notice of a patent; ein ~ erlangen to obtain (or to be granted) a patent; ein auf et. löſen ob. nehmen to take out a patent for a th. — II 2 [nhd. burſch.] F a. ⊕ 4. (fein gestriegelt) stylish, elegant; der Kerl smart fellow.

Patent=amt (⌣v́...) n ⊕ patent-office; =**anwalt** m patent-agent; =**brief** m = Patent 1; =**bruch** m infringement of (a) patent; =**geber** m patentor; =**gebühr** f royalty; =**gesetz**(**gebung**) f patent-law(s pl.).

patentierbar (⌣⌣-́⌣) a. ⊕ patentable.

patentieren (⌣⌣-́⌣) [fr.] I v/a. ⊕ to (protect by) patent; **patentiert** patent(ed). — II ~ n ⊕ und **Patentierung** f ⊕ patenting an invention, &c.

Patent=inhaber (⌣v́...) f ⊕ patentee; =**nadel** f safety-pin; =**register** n register of patents, patent-rolls pl.; =**schutz** m protection of patents or patented inventions; =**schutz=gesetz** n law for the protection of patents, patent-law.

Pater (⌣́v) [lt. pāter Vater] m (sg. ⊕, pl. Pa'tres) (reverend) father; pater peccavi ſagen to confess (one's sins), F to cry peccavi.

Paternoster (⌣v⌣́v) [lt.] n ⊕: a) (Vaterunſer) paternoster, Lord's prayer; b) (Roſenkranz) chaplet, beads pl.; ~ **baum** ♀ (z̀...) m ⊕ bread-tree (*Meʹlia azeʹdarach*); ~**kraut** ♀ n wild liquorice (*Aprus precatoʹrius*); ~**kunst** f, ~**werk** n ⊕ chain-pump.

pathetisch (⌣-v́⌣) [grch.] a. ⊕ (rührend, schwungvoll, leidenſchaftlich) pathetic(al).

Patholog, ~**e** ⊠ (⌣⌣-v)́ [grch.] m ⊕, ⊕ pathologist; ~**ie** (⌣⌣v-)́ f ⊕ (Krankheitslehre) pathology; **2isch** (⌣-v́⌣) a. ⊕ pathological.

Pathos (⌣́v) [grch. päʹthos Leiden] n, inv. (Sprache, Ausdruck der Leidenſchaft) pathos.

Patience (pa-ſīʹß) [fr. Geduld] f ⊕, ~**spiel** (⌣⌣́...) n ⊕ patience.

Pati=ent (⌣tß(v)́) [nhd.; *lt.] m ⊕, ~**in** f ⊕ (Kranke[r]): mit Bezug auf den Arzt: patient, z.B. er heilt wenige ſeiner ~en he cures few of his patients; ſonſt: invalid; ich bin noch immer ~ I am still under medical treatment or F under the doctor or on the sick-list; ~**en=stube** f sick-room, im Hoſpital: ward; ~**en=zahl** f number of patients.

Patin (⌣v́) [Pate] f ⊕ ſ. Pate.

Patina ⊕ (⌣́v⌣) [it. (*It. Pfanne)] f ⊕ (Edelroſt) patina.

patinieren (⌣⌣-́⌣) [fr.] v/a. ⊕ to overlay with patina.

Patois (pä-tŭä́) [fr.] n ⊕ (Volksmundart) provincial dialect.

Patriarch (⌣⌣v)́ [grch.] m ⊕ (Erzvater) patriarch; 2(**al**)**isch** (⌣⌣-v́, -v́-⌣) a. ⊕ patriarchal; ~**at** (⌣⌣v-́) n ⊕c. patriarchate; ~**en=kreuz** (⌣v̌v...) n ⊕ her. patriarchal cross; ~**en=würde** f patriarchal dignity; patriarchate.

Patrimonial=gericht(**sbarkeit** f) n (⌣v-́(v)v́...) ⊕ [lt. ererbt] patrimonial jurisdiction; =**güter** n/pl. patrimonial estates pl.

Patrimonium (⌣v-́⌣(v)⌣) [lt.] n ⊕ (Erbgut) patrimony; ~ Petri eccl. ehm. St. Peter's Patrimony, Papal States pl.

Patriot (⌣v)́ [nhd. 16. sae.; *fr.; *grch.] m ⊕, ~**in** f ⊕ (Vaterlandsfreund[in]) patriot; 2**isch** (⌣v́⌣) a. ⊕ patriotic; ~**ismus** (⌣v-́v) m ⊕ (Vaterlandsliebe) patriotism.

Patristik (⌣v́⌣) [grch.] f ⊕ (Lehre von den Kirchenvätern) patristic learning or theology, patristics; **patristisch** (⌣v́⌣) a. ⊕ patristic.

Patrize ⊕ (⌣v́⌣) [lt.] f ⊕ Schriftgießerei: (Schriftſtempel) punch(eon), counter-die.

⚛ scientific; ♀ botanical; ⚥ geography; ⊕ machinery; ⚒ mining; ⚔ military; ⚓ marine; ⊕ commercial; ✉ postal; 🚂 railway.

[Patriziat] — 752 — [Pechvogel]

Patriziat (⌣⌣(⌣)⌣) [lt.] n ⓵c. (Stellung, Gesamtheit der Patrizier) patriciate.
Patrizi-er (⌣⌣(⌣)⌣)[lt.*patri'cii* Adlige]m㉒, ~in f ㊼ (ant. Plebe'jer[in]) patrician; ⸗haft a. ㊅㊅ patrician; ~⸗herrschaft f patrician rule; ~⸗stolz m patrician pride; ~tum n ②d.: a) patricianism; b) coll. patricianspl.; **patrizisch**(⌣⌣⌣) a. ㊅㊅patrician, weit⸗S. of the upper classes.
Patron (⌣⌣) [lt. pătrō'nus] m ㊵d., ~in f ㊼ 1. a) Alt.: (Schutzherr der Klienten), b) (i. der bevorzugt ist, Stellen zu besetzen): patron; (kirchlicher Schutzherr) advowee; c) eccl. (Schutzheiliger) patron saint; d) (Schiffs⸗eigentümer) master (or owner) of a ship; ~in f patroness. — 2. F = Person, Bruder, Kerl, z.B. lustiger ~ jolly fellow; auch: merry body or soul; iro. ein sauberer ~ a (regular) scamp.
Patronat(⌣⌣⌣)[lt.] n(⌣m) ⓵c. pol., eccl. patronage, einer Pfründe auch: advowson; ⸗S⸗berechtigt (⌣...) a. ㊅㊅ having the right of patronage; ~s⸗pfarre f living in the gift of a (private) patron; ~s⸗verhältnis n patronage.
Patrone (⌣⌣⌣) [fr. patron m] f ㊼ 1. ⊕ (Modell) model, pattern, zum Durchmalen: stencil; mit ~n malen to stencil. — 2. cardboard casing; ✕ u. hunt. cartridge; blinde (scharfe) ~ blank (ball-) cartridge.
Patronen⸗bandelier ✕ (⌣⌣⌣⌣) n ⓶ cartridge-bandoleer; ⸗hülse ⊕ ✕ f cartridge-case; ⸗leere f, ⸗lehre f cartridge-gauge; ⸗tasche f = Patron⸗tasche; ⸗wagen m cartridge-wagon.
patronisieren (⌣⌣⌣⌣) [Patron] v/a. ⑨㉓ (in Schutz nehmen) to patronize, protect.
Patron⸗tasche ✕ (⌣''⌣⌣) f ㊶ cartridge-box; pouch (for cartridges).
Patronymikum (⌣⌣⌣⌣) [grch.] n ㉒㊲ (Geschlechtsname) patronymic; **patrony⸗misch** (⌣⌣⌣⌣) a. ㊅㊅ patronymic(al).
Patrouille ✕ (⌣'trŭl'i-⌣) [fr.] f ㊼ (Runde) patrol; ~⸗dienst ✕ m ㊶ patrol-duty; **patrouillieren** (⌣trŭl-ji'⌣) v/n.(h. u. sn)㉓ to patrol, to go (or make) the round.
Patsch¹ (⌣) [lautm.] m ⓵a. smack.
patsch² (⌣) [lautm.] int. flop!, slap!, dash!, splash!
Patsche¹ (⌣⌣) [lautm.] f ㊼ 1. (schallender Schlag) smack, slap. — 2. oft im dim. **Pätschchen** n ㉓ (Hand) hand, F paw.
Patsche² (⌣⌣) f ㊼ (Pfütze) puddle, pool; fig. in der ~ (Klemme) sein to be in a dilemma or a (fine) mess; e⸗n in die ~ bringen to get a p. into a scrape; in die ~ geraten to get into a hobble, to put one's foot in; da sitzen wir nun in der ~! here we are in a nice fix!
patschen (⌣⌣) [ndd.] ⑪ I v/n. (h., wenn der Schall, sn, wenn die Ortsveränderung hervorgehoben wird) u. v/impers. 1. = klatschen 1. — 2. (klatschend gehen) im Kote ² to (s)plash through the mud. — II v/n. (h.) u. v/a. 3. (klatschend schlagen) to smack, slap. — 4. e⸗m Wasser ins Gesicht ² (spritzen) to splash water in a p.'s face. — 5. (gelinde schlagen) to pat.
Patsch⸗hand F (⌣..) f ㊶, ⸗händchen n = Patsche¹ 2; ⸗naß a. ㊅㊅ soaked to the skin, wet through.
Patschuli (⌣⌣⌣) [ind.] n ㉓: a) ♀ patchouli (Pogoste'mon Pa'tchouli); b) ⊕ ~⸗essenz f, ⸗parfüm n ㉒ patchouli (scent).

patt (⌣) [fr., *it.] a. inv. (nur prädikativ gbr.) Schach: ² sein (machen od. setzen) to be (to make) stalemate; ² werden to be stalemated. [b. Uniform) flap.」
Patte (⌣⌣) [fr.] f ㊼ (Pfote) paw; ✕ Aufschlag a.」
patzig F (⌣⌣) [nhd.] a. ㊅㊅ pert, saucy, impudent, F cheeky; (trotzig) insolent; ~keit f pertness, boldness, sauciness, impudence, F cheek; insolence.
Paukant(-⌣)[paufen] m ㊶ burschikos: duelling student. [ing students' duels.
Pauk⸗arzt (⌣..) m ㉒ surgeon attend⸗」
Pauke (⌣⌣) [mhd.] f ㊼ 1. ♪ kettle-drum, tympano; mit ~en und Trompeten with beating of drums and sounding of trumpets, triumphantly, gaily; iro. ignominiously, utterly; fig. der ~ ein Loch m. (suddenly or abruptly) to break off a th. — 2. anat. (mittleres Ohr): ⚕ tympan(um). — 3. f fig. (feierliche Rede) (set) speech, oration; (Predigt) sermon, eine ~ halten to speechify, to hold forth.
pauken (⌣⌣) [mhd.] v/n. (h.) u. v/a. ⑧⑧ 1. ♪ to beat the kettledrum(s); auf dem Klaviere ² to thump (or strum) on the piano. — 2. bursch.: (reden) to make a speech, to speechify, F to sputter, rant, Moral ² to talk morality. — 3. (schlagen) er pauft die Kanzel he thumps (on) the pulpit; e⸗n gehörig ² to give a p. a sound drubbing. — 4. bursch. (fechten) mit e⸗m ², a. v/refl. sich ² to fight a duel with a p.
Pauken⸗fell (⌣''...) n ㉒: a) ♪ skin of a kettledrum; b) anat. = Trommelfell; ⸗klang ♪ m sound of the kettledrum; ⸗klöpfel, ⸗schlegel ♪ m kettledrum stick; ⸗schall, ⸗schlag m = ⸗klang; ⸗schläger ♪ m kettledrummer; ⸗wirbel ♪ m roll of the kettledrum.
Pauker (⌣⌣) m ㉒ 1. ♪ kettledrummer. bisw. auch: tympanist. — 2. = Paukant.
Paukerei F (⌣⌣⌣) f ㊼ students' duelling; weit⸗S. (Prügelei) fight, row.
Pauk⸗handschuhe (⌣''...) m/pl. ㉒ gauntlets for fencing; ⸗wichs m get-up of a student for fencing or duelling.
Paul (⌣) npr/m. ⑮⑭⑬㉝α. (Bn.) Paul; ~a (⌣⌣) npr/f. ⑨⑭⑧㊽⑯㉝α. (Bn.) Paula; ~chen (⌣⌣) npr/n. Bx. dim.: a) v. Paul: little Paul; b) v. Paula: little Paula; ~ine (⌣⌣⌣) npr/f. ⑨⑭⑧. (Bn.) Paulina.
paulinisch (-⌣⌣) a. ㊅㊅ Pauline, of (or relating to) Paul; ~e Briefe (Schriften) epistles (writings) pl. of (St.) Paul.
Paulinismus ⚕ (-⌣⌣⌣) m ㊳ (Festhalten an der Paulinischen Lehre) Paulinism.
Pauls⸗kirche (⌣..⌣⌣) f ㊶ in London: St. Paul's (Cathedral).
Paulus (⌣⌣) npr/m. ⑯γ. Paul(us); bibl. der Apostel ~ Paul the Apostle of the Gentiles, auch: St. Paul.
Pauperismus (-⌣⌣⌣) [neu⸗lt.] m ㊲ (Verarmung) pauperism, pauperized state.
Paus⸗back F (⌣''..) m ⓵c. chubby-faced person; ⸗backe(n m) f ㊷ chubby face; ⸗backig, ⸗bäckig a. ㊅㊅ chubby-faced.
Pauschale (-⌣⌣) [dtsch.⸗lt.] ⚕ (⸗Bausch) n ㉙ bulk, F whole lot; **Pausch(al)⸗quantum** n, ⸗summe f ㊶ lump sum.
Pause¹ (⌣⌣) [mhd., fr., *grch.] f ㊼ (Aufhören) pause, stop, a. interval; e⸗e ~ m. to (make) a pause or stop; to (take) rest;

♪ (bar of) rest; ganze (a. Viertel⸗) semibreve rest; halbe ~ minim rest; die ~n zählen to count the rests.
Pause² (⌣⌣) [nhd.; *pausen²] f ㊼ (Durchzeichnung) tracing, pouncing; (Durchgezeichnetes) traced design.
pausen¹ (⌣⌣) [lt. pausieren] v/n. (h.) ㊾ to (make a) pause, to stop.
pausen² ⊕ (⌣⌣) [fr. poncer] v/a. ⑨ (durch²) to trace, to pounce.
pausieren (⌣⌣⌣) [lt.] a. ㊅㊅ = **pausen**¹.
Paus²⸗papier (⌣''...) n ㉓ tracing-paper.
Pavian (⌣'w(⌣)⌣) [ndl.; *fr. babouin] m ⓵d.: a) zo. baboon (Cynoce'phalus); b) fig. (Ged) fop; (Dummkopf) duffer.
Pavillon (⌣'w⌣) [fr.] m ㊵ (Zelt, Gartenhaus) arch. pavilion.
Pazifikation (-⌣⌣⌣⸗tsj(⌣)⌣) [lt.] f ㊼ (Friedensstiftung) pacification. [the Pacific.」
pazifisch ⚕ (⌣⌣⌣) a. ㊅㊅: ♀ der ~ Ozean」
pazifizieren (-⌣⌣⌣⌣) [lt.] I v/a. ⑨ (versöhnen) to pacify. — II ~ n ㉓ und **Pazifizierung** f ㊼ pacification.
pazisieren (⌣⌣⌣⌣) [lt.] v/n. ⑨ jur. (e⸗n Vergleich eingehen) to come to terms.
p. c. abbr. = pro centum [lt. v. Hundert].
p. Chr. (n.) abbr. = post Christum (natum) [lt. nach Christo, nach Christi Geburt] after Christ, engl. mehr gbr. A. D. (= anno domini — im Jahre des Herrn).
Pech (⌣) [ahd.: pitch: *lt. pic·] n ⓵c. 1. ⊕ pitch; (Schuster⸗)~ cobbler's wax; es klebt wie ~ an ihm it sticks like glue to him; Sprichw. s. angreifen 1. — 2. [nhd. bursch.] F (fatale Lage) unfortunate position; (Unglück) ill (or bad) luck; fig. e⸗n ins ~ bringen to bring misfortune (or trouble) upon a p.; ~ geben (ausreißen) to run away, F to hook it, to bolt; ~ haben to be unlucky or F down in one's luck; das ist doch großes ~! that's hard lines!; tief im ~ sitzen to be dead out of luck.
Pech⸗artig (⌣'...) a. ㊅㊅ pitch-like, pitchy, ⚕ piceous; ⸗blende f ㊶ min. pitchblende or -ore; ⸗brenner m p.-maker; ⸗draht m p.-thread, wax- (or waxed) end, shoemaker's thread.
pecheln (⌣⌣⌣) a. I v/n. (h.) to make pitch. — II v/a. e⸗n Baum ² s. härzen 2.
Pech⸗fackel (⌣'...) f ㊵ pitch-torch; ⸗faden m pitched thread; vgl. ⸗draht; ⸗finster a. ㊅㊅ (as) dark as pitch; ²⸗e Nacht pitch-dark night; ⸗haube f pitch-cap; ⸗hütte f pitch-hut.
pechicht, mst **pechig** (⌣⌣) a. ㊅㊅ pitchy.
Pech⸗kelle (⌣'...) f ㊶ pitch-ladle; ⸗kessel m pitch-boiler; ⸗kohle f, min. pitch-coal, bituminous coal; (Gagat) jet; ⸗kranz m p.-ring; ⸗krücke f Küferei: p.-scraper; ⸗kugel f Goldarbeiter: p.-ball.
Pechler ⊕ (⌣⌣⌣) m ㉒ pitch-maker.
Pech⸗nelke ♀ (⌣'...) f ㊶ catch-fly (Lychnis Visca'ria); s. a. Nelke (rauhe); ⸗pfanne f pitch-pan; ⸗pflaster n. pharm. p.-plaster; ²⸗schwarz a. ㊅㊅ (as) black as pitch or as a coal; jet-black; ⸗sieden n pitch-boiling; ⸗sieder m = Pechler; ⸗stein m, min. pitchstone, ⚕ retinite; ⸗tanne f spruce-(fir) (Pi'cea excel'sa); ⸗tonne f pitch-barrel; ⸗torf m black (or bituminous) peat; ⸗vogel F m, fig. (ant. Glücks⸗kind, ⸗pilz) unlucky (or unfortunate) fellow.

Pedal (⏑´) [lt. *pedāl-* Fuß-] *n* ⓓ d.: a) ♪ Orgel ꝛc..: (Zug) pedal; b) ☉ am Fahrrade: (Trittbrett) pedal; in die ~e treten to work the pedals, to pedal; c) ~e *pl.* F *co.* (Füße) feet, F trotters *pl.*

Pedal-harfe ♪ (⏑´...) *f* ⑫ pedal (or double-actioned) harp; **=taste** *f* der Orgel: pedal-key.

Pedant (⏑´)[fr., it. *)*grch.] *m* ⑫, **~in** *f* ㊷ (Schulfuchs) pedant; **~erie** (⏑⏑⏑´) *f* ㊸ pedantry; **~isch** (⏑´⏑) *a.* ㊻ (kleinlich, steif) pedantic; (peinlich genau) most precise.

Pedell (⏑´) [neul.: *)*Büttel] *m* ⓓ d. ㊷ beadle, mace-bearer, apparitor, in Cambridge u. Oxford: proctor's man or F bulldog; in Schulen: attendant, school-porter. [cure.

Pedikur (⏑´⏑´) [lt.] *f* ㊻ (Fußpflege) pedi-

Pegasus (´⏑⏑) [grch.] npr/m. ⑯ *a.* myth. (Flügelroß der Musen) Pegasus; den ~ besteigen, sich auf den ~ schwingen to mount Pegasus, to be inspired by the muses, to write poetry.

Pegel (´⏑) [ndd.: pail] *m* ㉒ (Flutmesser) water-gauge; **~höhe** (´´...) *f*, **~stand** *m* ㉒ water-level; **pegeln** *v/a. u. v/n.* (h.) ㉒ *a.* (die Tiefe des Wassers bestimmen) to sound, to take soundings.

peilen ⚓ (´⏑) [Peil = Pegel] I *v/a.* ㉘ to sound; (messen) to gauge; das Land ⚓ to take the bearings of the land or coast, to bear the land; die Sonne ⚓ to take the altitude of the sun. — II ~ *n* ㉓ = Peilung 1.

Peil-kompaß ⚓ (´´...) *m* ㉒ bearing-compass; **=lot** *n* plummet, sounding-lead; **=rohr** *n* einer Pumpe: sounding-pipe; **=stange** *f*, **=stock** *m* sounding-rod.

Peilung (´⏑) *f* ㊻ 1. sounding, taking the bearings. 2. bearing(*s pl.*); e-e ~, ~en nehmen ... a bearing, the bearings.

Pein (´) [ahd.: pain; *)*lt. *poena*; *)*grch. *poinē*] *f* ㊻ (*pl.* ⚹) (Schmerz) pain; (Leiden) suffering(*s pl.*);(Qual) torment, torture.

peinigen (´⏑⏑) [Pein] I *v/a.* ㉘ to inflict pain on; to torment, torture; (foltern) to rack. — II ~ *n* ㉓ = Peinigung.

Peiniger (´⏑⏑) *m* ㉒: a) *a.* **~in** *f* ㊷ Person: tormentor, torturer; b) Ding: (et. Qualbringendes) torment.

Peinigung (´⏑⏑) *f* ㊻ torment(ing), torturing, torture.

peinlich (´⏑) [Pein] *a.* ㊻ 1. *jur.* (kriminal) penal, criminal, ₂e Frage (Folter) torture; ₂e Gerichtsbarkeit criminal jurisdiction; ₂ (*adv.*) befragen to torture, to rack. — 2. (peinigend) painful; (quälend) tormenting, worrying, agonizing. — 3. (von ängstlicher Sorgfalt erfüllt) very particular; pedantic, punctilious; F fidgety; ₂ (*adv.*) genau very scrupulous or precise; die Sache hat uns ₂ berührt the matter has pained us or made a painful impression upon us.

Peinlichkeit (´⏑⏑) *f* ㊻ (zu peinlich 2:) painfulness; agony; (zu 3:) punctiliousness, F fidgetiness; scrupulousness.

pein-voll (´´*f*) *a.* ㊻ = peinlich 2.

Peitsche (´⏑) [poln.] *f* ㊺ whip; (Reit-) horsewhip; (Geißel) scourge; *f.* Knallen ㉒; mit der ~ schlagen, **peitschen** *v/a. u. v/n.* (h.) ⑨ to (horse)whip, scourge, lash, flog; to apply the whip (to).

Peitschen-beschlag (´´...) *m* ㉒ whip-mounting; **=förmig** *a.* ⑯ whip-shaped; **=geknall** *n* cracking of a whip or of whips; **=griff** *m* = *)*stiel; **=hieb** *m* cut (or flick) with a whip; **=macher** *m* whip-maker; **=riemen** *m*, man. thong of a whip; **=schlange** *f. zo.* whip-snake (*Dry'ophis*); **=schmitze** *f* whip-lash; **=schnur** *f* whip-cord; **=stiel**, **=stock** *m* whip-handle, whip-stick.

Peitschung (´⏑) *f* ㊻ whipping.

Pekari ⚷ (´´-) [amerif.] *n* ⓓ *zo.* (Nabelschwein) peccary, tajassu (*Dico'tyles torqua'tus*). [laced coat.

Pekesche (´⏑´) [poln.] *f* ㊸ (Schnürenrock)

Peking ⚲ (´⏑) [chin. Nordhof] ⓓ *a.* I npr/n. (Hauptst. v. China) Peking, Pei-Ching. — II *m* ㉒ Seidenstoff: pekin.

Pekko-tee ⚲ (´-´) [chin.] *m* ㉒ pekoe.

Pektin ⚷ (-´) [grch. *pēktē* geronnene Milch] *n* ⓓ d. chm. (Pflanzengallerte) pectin ($C_4H_6O_4$); **=säure** *f* ㉒ pectic acid.

pekuniär (⏑-(⏑)´) [fr.] *a.* ㊻ pecuniary (aid, profit, &c.).

pekzieren (⏑´⏑) [lt. *pecca're*] *v/n.* (h.) u. *v/a.* ㉘ (sich vergehen, et. verschen) to put one's foot in, to commit o.s.; et. ~ to do s.th. (bad); was hat er pekziert? what (mischief) has he been up to?

Pelargoni-e ⚘ (⏑⏑´(⏑)⏑) [grch. Storch-] *f* ㊸ pelargonium (*Pelargo'nium*).

Pelasger (⏑´⏑) [grch.] *m* ㉒ (Ureinwohner Griechenlands) Pelasgian, *pl. a.* Pelasgi.

pelasgisch *a.* ㊻ Pelasgian, Pelasgic.

pelemele (păl-mäl) [fr.] *adv.* (durch-ea.) pell-mell, helter-skelter.

Pelerine (⏑⏑´) [fr. *pèlerine*] *f* ㊸ (Frauenumhang) pelerine, aus Pelz *a.* fur-tippet.

Pelide (-´⏑) [grch. Sohn des Königs Peleus von Jolkos] npr/m. ㊺ (Achilles) Pelides.

Pelikan (´⏑´) [mhd.; *)*grch. *pěleka'n*] *m* ⓓ d. 1. *orn.* pelican (*Peleca'nus*). — 2. ☉ (Art Zahnstange, Art Haken; Destillierapparat) pelican.

Pelle (´⏑) [ndd.; *)*lt. *pellis* Fell] *f* ㊸ peel, skin; *fig.* e-m auf die ~ rücken to press a p. hard. [to peel, to skin.]

pellen (´⏑) [Pelle] *v/a. u. v/n.* (h.) ㉘)

Pell-kartoffeln (´´⏑⏑) *f/pl.* ㊸ potatoes *pl.* in their jackets or skins.

Pelopide (⏑´⏑⏑) [grch. Nachkomme des Pelops] *m* ㊹ grch. *myth.* Pelopid.

Peloponnes ⚲ (⏑⏑⏑´) [grch. *f* Pelops-insel] npr/m. ⑪ ⓓ d. (⚓ *f*, *inv.*) Alt.: (jetzt More'a) Peloponnesus; **Peloponnesi-er** (=in *f* ㊷) *m* ㉒ (⏑⏑⏑´(⏑)⏑), **peloponnesisch** (⏑⏑⏑´⏑) *a.* ㊻ Peloponnesian.

Peloton ⚔ (⏑⏑*t*ǫ´...) [fr. Knäuel] *n* ⓓ platoon; **~feuer** (´´...) *n* ㉑ platoon-fire.

pelusisch (-´⏑)[Pelu'sium ⚲, St. in Ägypten] *a.* ㊻ Pelusiac.

Pelz (´) [ahd.: pelt; mlt. *pelli'cia f*; *)*lt. *pellis* Fell] *m* ⓓ a. 1. pelt, mehr gbr.: fur (a. v. zubereiteten Fellen); weit S. skin, hide; a. = **~mantel**, **=rock**; ☉ mit ~ besetzen (füttern) to trim (to line) with fur; *fig.* e-m Läuse in den ~ setzen, etwa: to play a p. an underhand trick. — 2. F *co.* von Menschen: (Haut, Leib), *z*B. e-m den ~ ausklopfen, e-m die Motten aus dem ~ klopfen to give a p. a sound thrashing or a good jacketing; e-m eins auf den ~ brennen to fire (F to pot) at a p.; *f.* pfeffern; e-m auf den ~ rücken to press a p. hard; e-m den ~ waschen (derb zusetzen) to give a p. a good scolding or rub-down. — 3. (Haut über Flüssigkeiten) skin, furring.

Pelz=art (´´...) *f* ㊻ species of fur; **=besetzt** *a.* ㊻ fur-lined, trimmed with fur.

pelzen (´⏑) *a.* ㊻ of fur, furred.

Pelz=flatterer (´´...) *m* ㉒ *zo.* flying lemur (*Saleopithe'cus*); **=fresser** *m*, *ent.*: ⚷ mallophagan; **=futter** *n* fur (lining); **=handel** *m* fur-trade, trade in furs; **=händler** *m* furrier; **=handschuhe** *m/pl.* fur(red) gloves *pl.*

pelzicht ⚹, *mst.* **pelzig** (´⏑) *a.* ㊻ 1. clothed in fur; like fur, furry, ⚹ nappy; vgl. filzig 1. — 2. von Flüssigkeiten: covered with fur(ring). — 3. F von Händen od. Füßen: numb, asleep.

Pelz=jacke (´´...) *f* ㊸ fur jacket; **=jäger** *m, Am.* fur-trapper; **=kappe** *f* fur cap; **=kragen** *m*: a) fur collar; b) (Damenkragen) fur cape; **=mantel** *m* fur cloak; **=motte** *f, ent.* clothes-moth (*Tinea pellione'lla*); **=mütze** *f* fur cap; **=rock** *m* fur(red) coat; **=sam(me)t** *m* (Felbel) feathershag; **=stiefel** *m/pl.* fur boots *pl.*; **=tiere** *n/pl.* fur-bearing animals *pl., coll.* fur; **=verbrämung** *f* fur trimming or bordering; **=ware** *f*, **=werk** *n* furriery, fur goods, furs *pl., ehm. a.* peltry.

Penaten (⏑´⏑) [lt.] *pl. inv.* röm. Alt.: (Hausgötter) Penates, household gods *pl.*

Pendant (*pã*-*dă*´) [fr. *m*] *n* ⓓ (Gegenstück) counterpart, pair (to); (Seitenstück) companion piece or picture, (fr.) pendant.

Pendel (´⏑) [fr. *pendule m*] *m* u. *n* ㉒ *mech., phys.,* ☉ Uhrmacherei: pendulum; **~länge** (´´...) *f* ㊻ length of a pendulum; **~linse** *f* pendulum bob.

pendeln (´⏑) *v/n.* (h.) ㉒ *a.* to oscillate; F *fig.* (bummeln) to saunter (or stroll) about.

Pendel=schlag (´´...) *m* ㉒, **=schwingung** *f* oscillation; **=uhr** *f* pendulum-clock.

Pendschab ⚲ Pandschab. [clock.]

Pendüle (*pã*-´) [fr.] *f* ㊸ mantel-piece.

penibel (⏑´⏑⏑)[fr. *pénible*] *a.* ㊻ (peinlich) painful; (schwer zu befriedigen) (very) particular, fastidious, difficult to please, fussy.

Pennal (⏑´) [mlt. *penna'le*] I *n* ⓓ d. 1. (Federbüchse) pen(cil)-case. — 2. Schulsl. = Gymnasium; aufs ~ gehen to attend a classical state-school. — II *m* ⓓ d. 3. Schulsl. = Gymnasiast; univ. fast † = Fuchs 5.

Pennäler (⏑´⏑) *m* ㉒ = Pennal 3

Pennalismus (⏑-´⏑⏑) *m* ㉗ (Bedrückung jüngerer Schüler durch ältere) fagging (system).

Penn-bruder P (´´-⏑) [Penne] *m* ㉒ homeless tramp, loafer who camps out in the open.

Penne P (⏑´) [?] *f* ㊸ (Herberge niedrigster Art, Nachtasyl) doss-house.

pennen P (´⏑) *v/n.* (h.) ㉒ = schlafen.

penninisch ⚲ (⏑´⏑) [lt.; *)*flt.] *a.* ㊻: ~e Alpen *pl.* Pennine Alps *pl.*

Pennsylvani-en ⚲ (´⏑*w*´⏑/⏑) [W.Penn, 1681 in den Wäldern (lt. *silvae*) gegründeter Staat] npr/n. ㉓ *a.* (nordamerikan. Freistaat) Pennsylvania; **Pennsylva'ni-er**(in *f* ㊷) *m* ㉒, **pennsylvanisch** (⏑⏑*w*´´⏑) *a.* ㊻ Pennsylvanian.

Pensee (*pã*-*sē*´) [fr.] I *n* ⓓ ⚘ pansy (= Stiefmütterchen). — II ⚹ *a. inv.,* auch **=farbig** (´´´⏑) *a.* ㊻ pansy-coloured.

[Pension] — 754 — [Perlmuschel]

Pension (pą-į(v)ᴸ, südd. v(v)ᴸ) [fr.] f ㊻: a) jur. (Ruhegehalt) pension, ⚔ für Offiziere: retired pay; mit ~ verabschiedet pensioned off; b) (Kostgeld) board; im Gasthofe: ~ 6 Mark täglich inclusive terms six shillings a day; c) (Kosthaus) boarding-house or establishment, (fr.) pension; d) (Kostschule für Mädchen) boarding-school (for young ladies); die ganze ~ (sämtliche Zöglinge) all the boarders pl.; sich in ~ geben bei // to board (out) with //.
Pensionär (pą-į(südd.v)į(v)v²ᴸ)[fr.] m ⑪d.(㊾): a)(Empfänger e-s Ruhegehaltes) pensioner; b) ~in f ㊼ (Kostgänger[in], Kostschüler[in]) boarder, pupil at a boarding-school.
Pensionat (pą[südd.v]į(v)v²) [fr.] n ⑪c. boarding-school (for young ladies).
pensionier/en (pą[südd.v]į(v)v²ᴸ) I v/a. ㉝ to pension off, ⚔ Offiziere: to put on the retired list or on half-pay; p/t, a.: retired (officer, &c.). — II ~ n ㉓ und P/ung f ㊻ pensioning off; retirement.
Pensions=anstalt (pą-į(v)ᴸ...) f ㊷ boarding-school; =**beitrag** m superannuation-money; =**berechtigung** f title (or claim) to a pension; =**fonds** m, =**kasse** f superannuation-fund; =**liste** ⚔ f retired list; =**preis** m charge for boarding, board; =**stand** m: in ~ treten to be pensioned off; =**vorsteher(in** f) m: a) keeper (or owner) of a boarding-house; b) principal of a b.-school.
Pensum (v²) [lt. ᴸv Aufgabe] n ㉓ ㉙ task, lesson; (Straf-arbeit) imposition.
Penta-eder ↗ (v⁻ᴸv) [grch.] n (m) ㉒ geom. (Fünfflach) pentahedron.
Pentagon ↗ (vv²ᴸ) [grch.] n ⑪d. geom. (Fünfeck) pentagon.
Pentagramm ↗ (vvᴸ) [grch.] n ⑪d. (Drudenfuß) pentacle; das ~a macht dir Pein? (G., Faust) does the pentacle annoy (or upset) you?
Pentameter ↗ (v⁻ᴸvv) [grch.] m ㉒ pros. (⏑ ⏔ | ⏔ ⏑ | ⏑⏑ ⏑⏑ ⏓) pentameter; **pentametrisch** (v⁻ᴸv) a. ㊻ pentametric(al). [Bücher Mosis) Pentateuch.]
Pentateuch (vv⁻ᴸ) [grch.] m ⑪c. (die 5
Pentathion=säure ↗ (vv⁻ᴸ...) [grch.] f ㊷ chm. pentathionic acid (H₂S₅O₆).
Peping (²ᴸv) [fr. *pépin*] m ㊹ Apfel: pippin.
Pepini-ere ⚔ (-v(v)⁻ᴸv) [fr. Samen...] f ㊺ (Pflanzschule) college for(preparing) army-surgeons, army medical college.
Pepsin ↗ (v⁻ᴸ) [grch.] n ⑪d. chm. (Verdauungsstoff des Magens) pepsin; ~**drüse** (v⁻ᴸv) f ㊼ anat. peptic gland.
Pepton ↗ (v⁻ᴸ) [grch.] n ⑪d. chm. (durch den Magensaft verdauter Eiweißstoff) peptone; =**erzeugend** a. ㊻ peptogenic.
per (ᴸ) [lt.] prp. (bsd. ⚭ u. F) statt „mit, in": f. Achse 1; ² Adresse (des) Herrn N. (to the) care of (abbr. c/o) Mr. N.; ² Dampf by rail, by steamer; ² Eisenbahn, ² Bahn by rail, by train; bei ihnen geht alles ² „du" they call everybody 'thou'; ² Kassa in (or for) cash; ² Pfund per pound; ² Post by post; ² Saldo per balance; ² sofort gesucht ein flotter Verkäufer required immediately (or at once) a smart salesman; verteilend: zweimal ² Jahr twice a year; 100 Mark ² Monat (Jahr) £ 5 per month (per annum).

pereat (²⁻vv) [lt. es vergehe] I int. ²! confusion (or death) to!; ² Pedanterie! away (or down) with pedantry!; mit Subjekt im pl.: **pe'reant**, ³B. pereant die Philister! three groans to all Philistines! — II ~ n ㊹: e-m ein ~ bringen to bring three groans to a p.
peremtorisch (vv⁻ᴸv) [lt.] a. ㊻ (endgültig) peremptory.
perennierend (vv⁻ᴸv) [lt.] a. ㊻ ⚘, ent., &c. (jährlich wiederkehrend) perennial.
perfekt (v⁻ᴸ) [lt. vollkommen] I a. ㊻ perfect; (vollendet) accomplished. — II ~ (a. ⁻vv) n ⑪c. gr. perfect (tense); ~**bildung** f ㊷ formation of the perfect (tense); ~**um** (ᴸvv) n ㊾ = perfekt II.
perfid (v⁻ᴸ) [fr.] a. ㊻ (treulos, tückisch) perfidious; **Perfidie** (vv⁻ᴸ) f ㊺ perfidy.
Perforation, mst ⊙ (⁻v⁻v-tj(v)⁻ᴸ) [lt.] f ㊻ (Durchlöcherung) perforation; **perforieren** (vv⁻ᴸv) v/a. ㉝ (durchlöchern) to perforate.
pergamenisch (vvv⁻ᴸv) [Pergamon] a. ㊻: a) Trojan; b) of Pergamum.
Pergament (vvv²) [Pergamon a b] n ⑪c. parchment, aus Kalbfell: vellum; ²=**ähnlich** (ᴸv...) a. ㊻, ²=**artig** a. parchmentlike, membranous; ~**band** m ㊷ parchment (or vellum) binding or covering or volume; ²**en** (⁻ᴸv) [lt.] a. ㊻ (of) parchment; ~**fabrikation** f manufacture of parchment; ²**=farben** a. parchment-coloured; ~**form** f der Blattgoldschläger: cutch; ~**haut** f, anat. med. parchment-like membrane or skin, ↗ xeroderm(i)a; ~**leim** m parchment-glue; ~**macher** m parchment-maker; ~**papier** n parchment- (or vellum-) paper; ~**rolle**, ~**tafel** f scroll, tablet of parchment; ~**schabsel** n parchment-parings pl.
Pergamon ♀ (⁻ᴸvv) npr/n. ⑪a. grch. Alt.: a) (Troja) Troy; b) (jetzt: Bergama) St. in Mysien; Pergamum, ...on, ...os.
perhorreszieren (vvv⁻ᴸv) [lt.] v/a. ㉝ to shudder at, to reject with horror; jur. to challenge witnesses, jurymen, &c.
Perigäum ↗ (vv⁻ᴸv) [lt., *grch.] n ㉙ ast. (Erdnähe) perigee.
Peri-hel(ium) ↗ (vv⁻ᴸ(v)v) [lt., *grch.] n ⑪d.(㉘) ast. (Sonnennähe eines Planeten) perihelion, ...um.
perikle-isch (vv⁻ᴸv)[Pe'rikles, athen. Feldherr u. Redner, † 429 v. Chr.] a. ㊻ Periclean.
Perikope ↗ (vv⁻ᴸv) [grch.] f ㊺ eccl. (Auswahl aus den Evangelien oder Episteln) pericope.
Periode ↗ (v-(v)⁻ᴸv) [grch.] f ㊽ 1. a) Kreislauf; b) Zeit=abschnitt; c) gr. Satzgefüge: period. — 2. physiol. bei Frauen: menstruation, F poorly time. — 3. math. bei Dezimalbrüchen: repeating (or circulating) figures pl. of a decimal.
Perioden=bau (v⁻(v)⁻ᴸv) m ㉒ gram. structure of periods.
periodisch (v⁻(v)⁻v) [grch.] a. ㊻ (regelmäßig wiederkehrend) periodical; math. Der Dezimalbruch repeating (or circulating, recurring) decimal, repeater; **Periodizität** (v⁻(v)-v²ᴸ) f ㊺ periodicity.
Periöke(n pl.) ↗ (vv⁻ᴸv) [grch. Umwohner] m ㊹ grch. Alt.: Pericœci pl.
Peripatetiker ↗ (vvv⁻ᴸvv) [grch. Umherwandler] m ㉒ phls. Alt.: (Anhänger des Aristoteles) Peripatetic; **peripatetisch** (vvv⁻ᴸv) a. ㊻ peripatetic.

Peripetie ↗ (vvv⁻ᴸᴸ) [grch.] f ㊹ (Lösung des Knotens im Drama) unravelling (of) the plot, (fr.) *dénouement*.
Peripherie ↗ (v-f⁻ᴸ) [grch.] f ㊹ (Umkreis) circumference, bisw.: periphery; ~=**winkel** (...) m ㉒ angle at the circumference of a circle.
peripherisch (vv⁻ᴸv) a. ㊻ peripheric(al).
Periphrase ↗ (vv⁻ᴸv) [grch.] f ㊹ (Umschreibung) periphrase, periphrasis.
Perispomenon ↗ (vv⁻ᴸvv) [grch.] n ㊾ grch. gr. (Wort mit Zirkumflex auf der letzten Silbe) perispome(non).
Peristyl ↗ (vv⁻ᴸ) [grch.] n ⑪d. arch. (Säulengang) peristyle.
Perkal ↗ (v⁻ᴸ) [fr., *ind.] m ⑪d. ㊿ (Baumwollgewebe) percale.
Perkussion (vv(v)⁻ᴸ) [lt.] f ㊻ (Erschütterung) percussion (a. med.).
Perkussions=gewehr ⊙ (⁻v(v)⁻ᴸ...) n ㉒ percussion-gun; =**hammer** m, med. perc.-hammer; =**schloß** ⊕ n perc.-lock; =**zünder** m percussion-fuse.
perkutieren ↗ (vv⁻ᴸv) [lt.] I v/a. ㉝ bsd. med. (beklopfend untersuchen) to percuss. — II ~ n ㉓ percussion.
Perl ⊙ (ᴸ) [fr.] f, inv. = Perlschrift.
perl-artig (⁻ᴸv...) a. ㊻ pearl-like, pearly; =**asche** ⚗ f ㊷ (kalzinierte Pott-asche) pearl-ash; =**boot** n, zo. pearl-nautilus (Nau'tilus pompi'lius).
Perlchen (⁻ᴸv) n ㉓ (dim. von Perle) little (or tiny) pearl.
Perle (⁻ᴸv) [ahd.: *roman. *pi'rula* Birnchen] f ㊹ pearl; (Glas=)bead; f. aufreihen; ~n fischen to fish (or dive) for pearls; fig. eine ~ unter den Frauen a jewel (or pearl) among women; bibl. (seine) ~n vor die Säue werfen (Matth. 7,6) to cast (one's) pearls before swine. [pearly.]
perlen[1] (⁻ᴸv) a. ㊻ (made) of pearls,
perlen[2] (⁻ᴸv) I v/n. (h.) ㊴ von Getränken: to rise in pearls, to effervesce, sparkle; (glänzen) to glisten, to glitter; ²der Wein sparkling wine; ♪ ²d (adv.) rein spielen to pearl a passage. — II ~ n ㉓ (f. I) effervescence, sparkling; ♪ pearling.
Perlen[3]=**aloe** ⚘ (⁻ᴸv...)[Perle pl.] f ㊷ pearl-aloe (*A'loë margina'ta*); =**bank** f bank of pearl-oysters; =**besatz** m pearl-edging; =**erzeugend** a. pearl-producing, ↗ margaritiferous; =**fischer(ei** f) m pearl-fisher (-fishing or -fishery); =**glanz** m (soft) lustre of pearls; =**händler** m dealer in pearls; =**küste** ⚓ f, Venezuela: Pearl-Coast; =**muschel** f Perl-m.; ²=**reich** a. rich (or abounding) in pearls; =**schmuck** m pearl-ornaments pl.; =**schnur** f string of pearls or beads; =**stickerei** f embroidery in pearls, bead-work, beading.
perl-farben (⁻...) a. ㊻ pearl-coloured; ²**förmig** a. pearl-shaped; =**gerste** f ㊷ = graupen; =**geschwulst** f, path. pearl-tumour; =**gras** ⚘ n p.-grass (*Me'lica*); ²**grau** a. p.-grey; =**graupen** f/pl. p.-barley; =**huhn** n. orn. guinea-fowl or -hen (*Nu'mida melea'gris*).
perlicht. ...**ig** (⁻ᴸv) a. ㊻ = perlartig.
Perl=muschel (⁻ᴸ...) f ㊷ zo. pearl-oyster, oriental pearl-mussel (*Avi'cula marga-riti'fera*); ~n pl.: ↗ margaritaceæ pl.

Signs (see page XVII): F familiar; P vulgar; F flash; ↘ rare; † obsolete (died); * new word (born); ⸫ incorrect; ♪ music;

[Perlmutter] — 755 — [Petersilie]

Perlmutter (⌣⌣) [Mutter der Perle] f ⑬ mother-of-pearl, ⚛ nacre; ⁓artig (⌣⌣...) a. ⑯ like mother-of-pearl, nacreous; ⚛ margaritaceous, margaritaceous; ⁓=falter m ⑫ ent. F fritillary (Argy'nnis); ⁓=glanz m nacreous lustre; ⁓n a. ⑯ (of) mother-of-pearl.

Perl-rundstab ⊕ (⸋...) m ⑫ = =stab; =sago ⊛ m pearl-sago; =schnur f = Perlenschnur; =schrift ⚁ f, typ. pearl; =spat m, min. p.-spar; =stab m, arch. bead moulding, chaplet; =sucht f, vet. des Rindviehs: tuberculosis; =süchtig a. ⑯ vet. tuberculous; =tee ⊛ m pearl-tea; =weiß ⊛ n (Wismut-oxychlorid) pearl-powder; =zwiebel ⚘ f pearl-onion (A'llium ophiosco'rodon).

permanent (⌣⌣') [lt.] a. ⑯ (dauernd) permanent, (ever)lasting; sich 2 erklären to declare o.s. in permanence.

Permanenz () f ⑯ ohne pl. permanence, permanency. [permutation.)

Permutation ⚛ (⸋⸋⸏⸋)[lt.] f⑯math.)

permutier/en (⸋⸋') [lt.] I v/a. ⑯ math. (versetzen) to permute. — II ⁓ n ⑬ u. P/ung f ⑯ permutation.

Peroration (⌣⸋⸏⸋⸋) [lt.] f ⑯ (Redeschluß) peroration; (Schulrede) school-speech; **perorieren** (⌣⌣⸋⸋') v/n. (h.) ⑬ (mit Nachdruck sprechen) to hold forth, to speechify, F to spout, to rant.

Perpendikel (⸋⸋⸋⸋⸋)[lt. n] m, n ⑬ 1. math. (Senkrechte) perpendicular (line). — 2. (Pendel der Uhr) pendulum; ⁓=schlag m period of oscillation of a pendulum.

perpendikular, ...lär (⸋⸋⸋⸋⸋⸋⸋) [lt.] a. ⑯ (senkrecht) perpendicular (auf on).

perpetuell (⌣⌣⸋⸋) [lt.], **perpetuierlich** (⸋⸋⸋⸋⸋) a. ⑯ (fortdauernd) perpetual.

Perpetuum mobile (⸋⸋⸋⸋⸋⸋⸋⸋⸋) [lt. beständige Bewegung] n ⑫ (pl. a. Perpe'tua mobi'lia) perpetual motion.

perplex (⸋⸋') [lt.] a. ⑯ (verblüfft) perplexed, dumbfounded, F flummuxed.

Perron ⚒ † (⸋') [(⸋.) fr.] m ⑩ (Bahnsteig) (railway-)platform; vgl. Inselperron.

Persenning ⚓ (⸋⸋) [ndl.] f ⑯ (geteertes Segeltuch) tarpaulin.

Perser (⸋⸋) m ⑫, ⁓in f ⑰ Persian.

Persi-en ⚘ (⸋⸋') npr/n. ⑬α. Persia.

Persiflage (⸋⸋ⓖ') [fr. m] f ⑬ mockery, satire; **persiflieren** (⸋⸋⸋⸋') v/a. ⑬ (verspotten) to mock, ridicule, take off.

Persiko (⸋⸋⸋) [it. Pfirsich] m ⑩ (Pfirsich-fernbranntwein) persico.

persisch (⸋⸋⸋) a. ⑯ Persian; ⚘ ⁓er Meerbusen Persian Gulf; die 2e Sprache, das ⁓(e) n ⑰ (the) Persian (language).

Person (⸋⸋') [lt.] f ⑯ person; hervorragende: (great) personage, F big gun or pot; einzelne: individual, bei et. beteiligte: party; thea. (Rolle) rôle, character; stumme ⁓ dumb part; ich für meine ⁓ for my (own) part, I for one; in (eigener) ⁓ in person, personally; die Ehrlichkeit in ⁓ honesty itself, the personification of honesty; der Teufel in (eigener) ⁓ the devil incarnate; s. Ansehen² 3; zehn Mark pro ⁓ ten shillings a head; groß (klein) von ⁓ sein to be of great (small) size or stature; e-n von ⁓ kennen to know somebody personally, to be personally acquainted with a p.

Personal (⸋⸋⸋⸋) [lt.] n ⑩d. (ant. Material) staff, employees pl., eines Bureaus: office-staff; (Bühnen-)⁓ performers pl., cast (of a play); (Dienstboten) establishment of servants.

Personal-arrest (⸋⸋⸋⸋⸋...) m ⑫ attachment of a person; =beschreibung f (accurate) description of a person in a warrant, &c.; =frage f personal question.

Personali-en (⸋⸋⸋⸋⸋⸋) [lt.] pl. inv. particulars pl. of a person; (Angriffe) personalities, personal attacks pl.

Personal-pronomen (⸋⸋⸋⸋⸋...) n ⑫ gram. personal pronoun; =stand m = Personenstand; =union f personal union of several states under one sovereign; =verzeichnis n list (or register) of persons employed, list of employees.

Persönchen (⸋⸋⸋⸋) n ⑬ (dim. v. Person) small (or short) person, F little dot; schnurriges ⁓ funny little (wo)man.

Personen-aufzug ⊕ (⸋⸋⸋⸋...) m ⑫ (ant. Lastenaufzug) lift for persons, Am. passenger-elevator; =bahnhof ⚒ m passenger-station; =beförderung f conveyance of passengers; vgl. =verkehr; =beschreibung f: ⚛ prosopography; s. auch Personalbeschreibung; =dampfer ⚓ m passenger-(steam)boat; =frage f personal question; =halle ⚒ f (roofed) hall for passengers; =post f stage-coach; =stand m statistics of the population; = und Güter-verkehr ⚒ m passenger-and-goods traffic; =verkehr m passenger-traffic; =verzeichnis n, thea. (it.) dramatis sonæ pl.; =wagen m: a) stage-coach; b) ⚒ passenger-carriage or Am. -car; =wechsel m in Ämtern: personal changes pl., rotation of office; =zug ⚒ m passenger-train. — Vgl. a. Personal-...

Personifikation (⸋⸋⸋⸋⸋⸋) [lt.] f ⑯ personification; **personifizieren** (⸋⸋⸋⸋⸋⸋) v/a. ⑬ (persönlich erkennen, darstellen) to personify, impersonate, embody; die personifizierte Bosheit the personification (or incarnation, embodiment) of wickedness.

persönlich (⸋⸋⸋') [Person] a. ⑯ personal, ⚖. es Fürwort personal pronoun; (leibhaft) personified, in person; 2e Meinung private opinion; meiner 2en Meinung nach in my (own) opinion; 2 w. to make personal remarks; auf Briefen: 2 private; 2 (adv.) erscheinen to appear in person; 2 haften to be personally (or individually) answerable; ⁓keit f ⑯ personality, personal appearance; (Einzelwesen) individuality; hochstehende ⁓keit eminent person(age).

Perspektiv (⸋⸋⸋⸋⸋) [fr., *lt.) n ⑩d. opt. (Fernrohr) field- (or spy-)glass, telescope; ⁓e (⸋⸋⸋⸋⸋) f ⑬ Zeichenkunst: perspective; fig. (Aussicht), auch: prospect; 2isch a. ⑯ perspective (drawing, plan, &c.); fig. prospective, adv. auch: in perspective or prospect; ⁓schnecke (⸋⸋⸋⸋⸋⸋) f ⑫ zo. perspective shell (Sola'rium perspecti'vum).

Pertinens (⸋⸋⸋) [lt.] n ⑳ (Zubehör): das Haus mit den Pertine'nzien ... (all) the appurtenances or appointments.

Pertinenz (⸋⸋⸋) f ⑯ (Zugehörigkeit) accessoriness, dependence.

Peru ⚘ (⸋⸋) [span. 1524] npr/n. ⑩a. süd-amerikan. Republik: Peru.

Peruaner (⸋⸋⸋⸋) I m ⑫, ⁓in f ⑰ Peruvian.— II a. inv., auch **peruanisch** a. ⑯ of Peru, Peruvian.

Peru-balsam (⸋...⸋, oft ⸋⸋) m ⑫ pharm. Peruvian balsam.

Perücke (⸋⸋') [fr. perruque] f ⑬ wig, bsd. ehem. a. periwig; eine ⁓ tragen to wear a wig; ⁓n-baum ⚘ (⸋⸋⸋...) m ⑫ wig-(or smoke-)tree (Rhusco'tinus); ⁓n-futter n lining of a wig; ⁓n-macher m wig-maker; ⁓n-netz n caul of a wig; ⁓n-stock m wig-block. [vian bark.)

Peru-rinde (⸋⸋..., oft ⸋⸋...) f ⑫ Peru-

pervers (⸋⸋') [lt.] a. ⑯ (D10) (verkehrt) perverse; perverser Mensch cross-grained fellow; **Perversität** (⸋⸋⸋⸋⸋⸋') f ⑯.

Perzent ⊛ = Prozent; ⁓ual a. ⑯ per cent; ⁓uell, ⁓ualiter a. ⑯ percentage.

Pessimismus (⸋⸋⸋⸋)[neu-lt.] m ⑫ (Schwarzseherei) pessimism; **Pessimist** (⸋⸋⸋') m ⑫ pessimist, F croaker; **pessimistisch** (⸋⸋⸋') a. ⑯ pessimist(ic), F croaking.

Pest¹ ⚘ (⸋') [slav. Ofen] npr/n. ⑩a. Pesth, bsd. Budapest.

Pest² (⸋') [nhd.; fr. peste; *lt. pēstīs] f ⑯ path. pestilence, plague; (Seuche) epidemic; wahre ⁓ (böse Dünste) pestilential vapours or effluvia pl.; daß dich die ⁓ (hole)! a plague (or curse) upon you!, the devil take you!; fig. (et. Verdrießliches) pest, bore, nuisance.

pest²-ähnlich (⸋...) a. ⑯, 2artig a. pestilential, contagious; =artigkeit f ⑫ contagiousness; =arzt m physician to plague-stricken patients; =beschreibung f: ⚛ loimography; =beule f plague-boil, ⚛ bubo; fig. plague-spot; =flecken m plague-spot; =geruch m, =hauch m pestilential smell, breath; =haus n, =hof m plague-hospital.

Pestilenz (⸋⸋⸋)[mhd.; *lt.] f ⑯ = Pest²; 2ialisch (⸋⸋⸋⸋⸋⸋) a. ⑯ pestilential.

pest²-krank (⸋...) a. ⑯ infected with (or suffering from) the plague; =luft f ⑫ pestilential (or foul) air; =mal n plague-mark; =ordnung f regulations pl. for plague-stricken districts; =stoff m plague-virus; =wurz ⚘ f pestilence-weed or -wort, Indian plantain (Petasi'tes u. Adenosty'les).

Petarde (⸋⸋') [fr. pétard m] f ⑬ ⚔ artill. (Spreng-büchse, -geschoß) petard; ⚒ (Knallsignal) fog-signal; **Petardier(er)** (⸋⸋⸋⸋) m ⑫ petarderer, petardier. [tioner.)

Petent (⸋⸋') [lt.] m ⑫ (Bittsteller) peti-

Peter (⸋⸋') [s. Petrus] npr/m. ⑫α. (Bn.) Peter; Sankt ⁓ St. Peter; fig. dummer ⁓ stupid fellow, duffer, jackass; langweiliger ⁓ slow fellow, dullard, bore; schwarzer ⁓ (Kartenspiel, in Engl. unbekannt) black Peter; ⁓chen (⸋⸋') npr/n. ⑫α. dim. little Peter, Peterkin.

Petersburg (⸋⸋') npr/n. ⑩α. (russ. Hauptstadt) (Sankt-)⁓ St. Petersburg; ⁓er(in f ⑰) m ⑫ inhabitant of St. Pet.

Petersili-e ⚘ (⸋⸋⸋⸋⸋) f ⑬ (abg.) parsley; grch. Stein-eppich] f ⑱ parsley (Petroseli'num sati'vum); F fig. von Mädchen: ⁓ pflücken to have to sit out a dance, to find no partner (to dance with); ihm ist die ⁓ verhagelt he has had (a stroke of) bad luck or a misadventure; 2n-blätt(e)rig (⸋⸋⸋) a. ⑯ parsley-

---

⚛ scientific; ⚘ botanical; ⚘ geography; ⊕ machinery; ⚒ mining; ⚔ military; ⚓ marine; ⊛ commercial; ⚒ postal; ⚒ railway.

[Petersilienwein] — 756 — [Pfännerschaft]

leaved; ~n-wein ⚥ m ⓶ parsley-leaved vine (*Vitis lacinio'sa*).
Peters-kirche (⌣⌣...) f ⓶ in Rom: St. Peter's (Church); **=pfennig** m (Spende an den Papst) coll. Peter's pence pl.
Petit ⊙ (p'ti⌣) [fr.] f, inv., ⚹ ⓷⓺ typ. Schriftgrad v. 8 Punkten: brevier.
Petition (⌣‐tß(v)⌣) [lt.] f ⓸⓺ (Bittschrift) petition; **Lieren** (⌣‐tß(v)⌣⌢⌣) v n. (h.) ⓽⓷ to (make a) petition.
Petitions-recht (⌣‐tß(v)⌣...) n ⓶ right of petition; **=weg** m: auf dem ~e by way of (or in a) petition.
Petit-schrift (p'ti⌣⌢) f ⓶ = Petit.
peträ-isch (⌣⌣⌣) [lt.] a. ⓺⓺: das ~e Arabien Arabia Petræa, Stony Araby.
Petrefakt ⚇ (⌣⌣⌣) [grch.‐lt.] m, n ⓷⓸c. *geol.* (Versteinerung) petrifaction, fossil; **~en-kunde** f ⓺⓶ palæontology.
Petri (⌣⌣) *gen.* von Petrus.
petrinisch (⌣⌣⌣) a. ⓺⓺ *theol.* relating to (St.) Peter, Petrine.
Petrographie ⚇ (⌣⌣⌣f⌣) [grch.] f ⓸⓼ (Felsbeschreibung) petrography.
Petroleum (⌣⌣(v)⌣) [grch.‐lt.] n ⓷⓸ mineral‐oil; **~äther** m (⌣...) m ⓶ *chm.* petroleum‐ether, naphtha; **~-droschke** f petrol‐cab; **~-koch-apparat, ~-kocher, ~-koch-ofen** m petroleum‐stove; **~-lampe** f petroleum‐lamp; **~-omnibus** m petrol‐driven omnibus; **~-quelle** f petroleum‐spring; **~-raffinerie** f petroleum‐refinery; **~-schacht** ⊙ m petroleum‐works pl.; **~-weib** n z. 3. der Kommune in Paris 1871: (fr.) petroleuse.
Petrus (⌣⌣) [lt.; *grch.] npr/m. ⓶⓼. *bibl.* Peter (the Apostle).
Petschaft (⌣⌣) [mhd. (P.) ⌣tschech.] n ⓶e. seal, signet; **~-stecher** ⊙ (⌣⌣...) m ⓶ seal‐engraver.
petschieren (⌣⌣⌣)[Petschaft] v a. ⓸⓼ to seal.
petto (⌣⌣) [it. Brust]: in ⚹ haben to have in petto or F up one's sleeve.
Petuni-e ⚥ (⌣⌣(v)⌣) [brasil.] f ⓸⓼ petunia.
Petz (⌣) [mhd.] m ⓶a.: in Märchen ⌣. Freund ~, Meister ~ (Bär) Bruin.
Petze (⌣⌣) f ⓶ 1. (Bärin) she‐bear, (Hündin) bitch. — 2. F = Petzer.
petzen F (⌣⌣) [ndd.] v/a. u. v n. (h.) ⓽⓶ to tell tales of, to inform against; F to peach on, bsd. in Schulen: to sneak against.
Petzer F (⌣⌣) m ⓶, **~in** f ⓸⓻ tell‐tale, informer, sneak.
Pf. *abbr.* = Pfennig.
Pfad (⌣) [ahd.⌣ path] m ⓶c. path, narrow way; krumme ~e pl. sinuous paths, bsd. *fig.* crooked ways pl.
Pfad-finder (⌣...) m ⓶ path‐finder; *fig.* die Wissenschaft als ⌣finderin ... as pioneer; **=los** a. pathless; (unwegsam) inaccessible; **=sucher** m pioneer.
Pfaffe (⌣⌣) [ahd.; *grch. pa'ppas Papa] m⓸⓺contp. parson, cleric, P sky‐pilot.
Pfaffen-feind (⌣-freund) (⌣⌣...) m ⓶ enemy (friend) of the clergy or priests; **=herrschaft** f clerical (or priestly) dominion; **=knecht** m slavish adherent of the clergy; **=latein** n monkish Latin; **=list** f priestcraft.
Pfaffentum (⌣⌣) n ⓶d. 1. clericalism, clerical (or priestly) rule. — 2. *coll.* parsons, priests pl., P black brigade.
Pfaffen-wesen (⌣⌣) n ⓷, **=wirtschaft** f clerical doings or machinations pl.

pfäffisch (⌣⌣) [Pfaffe] a. ⓺⓺ sacerdotal, priestly, priestridden. [priest.]
Pfäfflein (⌣⌣) [Pfaffe, dim.] n ⓶⓷ little]
Pfahl (⌣) [ahd.: pole, pale; *lt. *palus*] m ⓶c. 1. stake, pile; (Baumstütze) prop, (Pfosten) post; (Stange) pole, zum Feldmessen, Absteden a. rod, picket; (Schand-)pillory; *coll.* Pfähle, a. paling; Pfähle einrammen to drive (or ram) piles into the ground. — 2. *fig.* in (oder zw.) meinen vier Pfählen within my four walls, in my (own) home; *bibl.* ein ~ im Fleische a thorn in the flesh.
Pfahl-bau (⌣...) m ⓶: a) ⊙ Bauwesen: building erected on piles, pile‐work; b) ~ten pl. aus der Vorzeit lake‐ (or lacustrine) dwellings or habitations pl.; **=bauer** m pile‐builder; lake‐dweller; **=brücke** f pile‐bridge; ehm. **=bürger** m suburban dweller, *contp.* cit; **=dorf** n (Dorf aus Pfahlbauten) lake‐village.
pfählen (⌣⌣) [Pfahl] v a. ⓸⓼ 1. to fence with stakes; ⊙ Wasserbau: (Grundpfähle in die Erde rammen) to drive piles into the ground. — 2. *hort.* Pflanzen ⚹ to prop (up) ..., to support ... with props. — 3. (als Todesstrafe) to impale, to pierce with a sharp stake; gepfählt with a stake through the heart.
Pfahl-graben (⌣...) m ⓶ ditch fenced (or fortified) with stakes; **=hecke** f fence made up of stakes; **=mühle** ⊙ f mill built on piles (ant. Schiffsmühle); **=werk** n paling, pile‐work; ⚹ *frt.* palisade, stockade; **=wurm** m, *zo.* ship‐worm (*Tere'do nava'lis*); **=wurzel** ⚥ f tap‐root; **=zaun** m paling.
Pfalz (⌣) [ahd.: *lt. *pala'tium* n] f ⓸⓺ *hist.* (e‐m Pfalzgrafen verliehenes Land) palatinate; ⚲ die ~ the Palatinate; i. Ober‐, Rhein‐⌣.; *hist.* Kurfürst von der ~ Elector Palatine.
Pfälzer (⌣⌣) [Pfalz] I m ⓶ 1. (a. **~in** f ⓱) inhabitant of the Palatinate. — 2. (~ Wein, ~ Tabak) wine, tobacco grown in the Palatinate. — II a. *inv.* 3. = pfälzisch.
Pfalz-graf m (f **=gräfin**) (⌣...) ⓶ Count (‐ess f) Palatine, auch ⚜ Palsgrave (f Palsgravine); **=gräflich**, **=gräflich** a. ⓺⓺ of (or belonging to) a Count Palatine; **=grafschaft** f Palatinate, County Palatine.
pfälzisch (⌣⌣) [Pfalz] a. ⓺⓺ Palatine, of the Palatinate.
Pfand (⌣) [ahd.: pawn] n ⓶b. 1. pledge, ⚲ deposit; (Bürgschaft) security; e‐m verschriebenes mortgage; ein ~ einlösen to redeem a pledge; in ~ nehmen to take in pawn; zum ~e setzen to (put in) pawn, seine Ehre: to pledge one's honour; ich setze mein Leben zum ~e I stake my life (upon it). — 2. Pfänderspiel: forfeit; die Pfänder ausrufen to call the pledges; was soll der tun, dem dies ~ gehört? what shall he do to whom this (pledge) belongs?
pfandbar (⌣⌣) a. ⓺⓺ *jur.* fit to serve as a pledge; mortgageable.
pfändbar (⌣⌣) a. ⓺⓺ *jur.* distrainable, seizable, attachable.
Pfand-brief (⌣⌣) m ⓶: a) ⚲ *jur.* mortgage‐deed; b) ⚲ mortgage‐bond, debenture; **=bürge** m (Geisel) hostage.

pfänden (⌣⌣) [ahd.; *Pfand] I v a. ⓸⓽: et. ⚹ to seize a th. as a pledge or a security; Vieh ⚹ to pound cattle; e‐m Schuldner die Möbel ⚹ lassen to levy a distress upon a debtor; *vgl.* auspfänden I. — II ~ n ⓷⓷ = Pfändung.
Pfänder¹ (⌣⌣) m ⓶ = Exekutor.
Pfänder²-spiel (⌣⌣⌣) [pl. v. Pfand 2] n ⓶ game of forfeits.
Pfand-geber(in) f m (⌣...) *jur.* = Schuldner(in); **=geld** n money obtained by pawning or on mortgage; **=gläubiger** m mortgagee; **=gut** n mortgaged property; **=haber** m holder of a pledge or mortgage; pledgee, mortgagee; **=haus** ⚥ n = Leihhaus; **=inhaber** m = ‐haber; **=leihe** f, **=leih-geschäft** n pawnbroker's business or shop; **=leiher** m pawnbroker, F *co.* Mr. Two‐to‐one [wegen der 3 goldenen Kugeln, die das Haus des engl. Pfandleihers schmücken]; seine Uhr ist beim ~ his watch is in pawn or F *co.* at my uncle's or P up the spout; **=lösung** f taking out of pawn, redemption of a pledge; **=nehmer** m = ‐haber; **=objekt** n pawned (or pledged) article, pledge; **=recht** n *jur.* lien; **=rechtlich** a. ⓺⓺ hypothecary; **=schein** m pawn‐ticket; **=schuld** f hypothecary debt; **=schuldner(in** f) m person who pledges (or pawns, mortgages) s. th.; pledger, mortgager; **=sicherheit** f hypothecary security; **=stall** m *jur.* pound; in den ~ einsperren to pound.
Pfändung (⌣⌣) f ⓸⓺ = Auspfändung; gerichtliche ~ a. attachment; **~s-befehl** (⌣...) m ⓶ *jur.* warrant of distress.
Pfand-verschreibung (⌣...) f ⓶ = **=brief**; **=vertrag** m mortgage‐deed; **=weise** adv. by way of a pledge or of security.
Pfännchen (⌣⌣) n ⓶⓷ [dim. von Pfanne] little pan, auch: pannikin.
Pfanne (⌣⌣) [ahd.: pan] f ⓸⓺ 1. Gefäß zum Backen ⌣.: pan, zum Braten: frying‐pan, zum Schmoren ⌣.: saucepan; eine ~ voll a panful. — 2. (großes Metallgefäß zum Sieden) copper. — 3. *fig.* den Feind in die ~ hauen to cut the enemy to pieces, F to chop them into mincemeat. — 4. *anat.* = Gelenk‐, Knochen‐⚹. — 5. ⊙: a) *mech.* ~ e‐s Zapfenlagers: brass, seat; b) ehm. Büchsenmacherei: ~ eines Steinschlosses (priming‐)pan; Pulver auf die ~ schütten to prime a gun.
Pfannen-blech ⊙ (⌣⌣...) n ⓶ iron plates pl. for pans; **=dach** n (pan)tiling; **=deckel** m: a) lid of a saucepan or copper; b) ehm. Büchsenmacherei: ~ e‐s Steinschlosses: hammer; **=flicker** m tinker; **=gericht** n *Kochk.*: s. th. cooked (or dish prepared) in a pan; **=kolben** m am Vorderladergewehr: pan‐borer; **=meister** m *Saline*: inspector of salt‐works; **=salz** n *Saline*: pan‐scrapings pl.; **=schloß** ⚹ n am Gewehr: hammer; **=schmied** m maker of sauce‐pans, tinsmith; **=stein** m: a) *Saline*: panscales pl.; b) sediment in boilers, (Kesselstein) fur; **=stiel** m handle of a (frying‐)pan or saucepan, pan‐handle.
Pfänner ⊙ (⌣⌣) [Pfanne] m ⓶ *Saline*: owner of salt‐works, (Salzwirker) salt‐maker; **~schaft** (⌣⌣⌣) f ⓸⓺ ownership (*coll.* proprietors pl.) of salt‐works.

Zeichen (f. S. XVII): F familiär; P Volkssprache; ☠ Gaunersprache; ⚹ selten; † alt (auch gestorben); * neu (auch geboren); ⌣⌣ unrichtig;

[**Pfannkuchen**] — 757 — [**Pferchschlag**]

Pfann-kuchen (⌣-⌣) m ⓶ pancake, mit Obstschnitzeln: fritter; ~ backen to make pancakes; Berliner ~ dough-nut.
Pfarr-amt (⌣...) n ⓶ clergyman's (or clerical) living, bsd. bei Dissidenten: ministry, pastoral office; weitS. (Seelsorge) cure of souls; =**amtlich** a. ⓺ parochial; =**amts-vertreter** m =helfer; =**besetzungs-recht** n = Patronat; =**bezirk** m parish; =**buch** n parochial register; =**dorf** n village forming a parish.
Pfarre (⌣⌣) [ahd.: parish; mlt. parochia; *grch. paroiki'a] f ⓸ **1**. Amt: clerical office, Stelle: clerical living, bei Dissidenten: ministry, pastorate, pastorship; Sprichw. erst die ~, dann die Quarre ob. Knarre first a rich post, then the squalling host. — **2**. = Pfarr-haus, =kirche, =sprengel. [a. ⓺ parochial.]
Pfarrei (⌣⌣) f ⓺ = Pfarre; **pfarreilich** (⌣⌣⌣)
Pfarrer (⌣⌣) [ahd.: parson; *Pfarre] m ⓸, ~**in** f ⓸: a) der engl. Staatskirche: rector, vicar; clergyman; b) der Dissidenten: minister, pastor; c) weitS., oft contp. parson; ~in vicar's (or minister's) wife.
Pfarr-gebäude (⌣...) n/pl. = church buildings pl.; =**gemeinde** f parish; =**genoß** m, =**genossin** f parishioner; =**haus** n rectory, vicarage, parsonage, in Schottland: manse; =**helfer** m curate; =**herr** m der engl. Staatskirche: rector, vicar; =**kind** n parishioner; =**kirche** f parish-church; =**land** n glebe-land; =**sprengel** m parish; =**stelle** f = Pfarre 1; =**stübchen** n vestry.
Pfau (⌣) [ahd.; *lt. pavo'] m ⓺(ⓑ)b. orn. peafowl, ⚥ pavo, her. pawn; mehr gbr.: m peacock, f peahen (Pavo crista'tus); der ~ schlägt ein Rad the peacock spreads his feathers or train; junger ~ = Pfauchen¹. [⚥ pavonian, pavonine.]
pfau-ähnlich (⌣⌣) a. ⓺ like a peacock;
Pfauchen¹ (⌣⌣) n ⓶ peachick.
pfauchen² (⌣⌣) v/n. = fauchen.
Pfauen-auge (⌣⌣...) n ⓶: a) peacock's eye; b) ent. (Tagpfauenauge) peacock- (or argus-)butterfly (Vane'ssa io); (Abendpfauenauge) eyed hawk-moth (Smeri'nthus ocella'tus); =**blau** peacock-blue; =**feder** f peacock's feather; =**gerste** ⚘ f battledore-barley (Ho'rdeum Zeo'crithon); =**schwanz** m peacock's tail; =**taube** f fan-tail(-pigeon) (Colu'mba li'via latican'da).
Pfau-fasan (⌣...) m ⓶ orn. argus-pheasant (Argus giganteus); =**hahn** m peacock; =**henne** f =**hahn** n peahen.
Pfd. (St.) abbr. = Pfund (Sterling).
Pfeffer (⌣⌣) [ahd.: pepper; *lt. piper] m ⓶ **1**. pepper (bsd. Frucht von Piper nigrum); gemahlener (oder gestoßener) ~ ground pepper; spanischer ~ Cayenne pepper (Frucht von Ca'psicum a'nnuum, frute'scens, &c.). — **2**. fig. und Sprichw.: das ist starker ~ that's (a bit) too strong; im ~ sein ob. liegen to be in straits or in distress; s. Hase 3; ich wollte, er wäre wo der ~ wächst I wish him at Jericho (and a thousand miles beyond) or at the bottom of the sea.
Pfeffer-baum ⚘ (⌣⌣...) m ⓶ pepper-tree (Piper); =**brühe** Kocht. peppered sauce; =**büchse**, =**dose** f pepper-box or -cruet; =**fäßchen** n = -büchse; =**fraß**, =**fresser** m, orn. p.-bird, toucan (Rhampha'stos piperi'-

vorus); =**gurke** f gherkin; =**korn** n pepper corn, grain of pepper; =**kraut** ⚘ n pepperwort, pepper-grass (Lepi'dium); =**kuchen** m gingerbread; =**kuchen-bäcker**, =**küchler** m gingerbread-baker.
Pfefferling (⌣⌣) m ⓑ d. = Pifferling.
Pfeffer-minze ⚘ (⌣⌣...) f ⓶ peppermint (Mentha piperi'ta); =**minz-küchel** (=chen), =**plätzchen**, =**zeltchen** n peppermint(drop); =**minz(schnaps)** m peppermint-liqueur; =**mühle** f pepper-mill.
pfeffern (⌣⌣) v/a. ⓶ a. Kocht.: to pepper, stärker: to devil (up); fig. (beißend, pita'nt m.) to make spicy or piquant; F e-m den Pelz ⌣, e-n ⌣ to give a p. a set-down, to pitch into a p., weitS. = prügeln; auf e-n los ⌣ to pepper (or fire) away at a p.; stark gepfeffert very peppery, highly seasoned, fig. von Worten 2c.: rather strong; gepfefferte Geschichte highly spiced tale; gepfefferte Rechnung exorbitant bill.
Pfeffer-nuß (⌣⌣...) f ⓶ ginger(bread)-nut; =**pflanzen-artig** ⚘ a. ⓺: ⚥ piperaceous; =**rohr** ⚘ n = -staude; =**rohr-stock** m pepper-tree cane; =**sack**: a) pepper-bag; b) contp. = Krämer; =**staude** f, =**strauch** m ⚘ pepper-plant or -shrub or -vine (Piper).
Pfeifchen (⌣⌣) n ⓷ (dim. von Pfeife) little whistle or pipe.
Pfeife (⌣⌣) [ahd.: pipe; *mlt. pipa] f ⓸ **1**. a) ♪ whistle, little flute, zum Locken: bird-call, der Orgel: organ-pipe; b) ⚔ (Quer-)~ fife. — **2**. fig. u. Sprichw.: es muß alles nach s-r ~ tanzen everybody has to obey him, he plays first fiddle in everything; sich ~n schneiden, während man im Rohre sitzt to make hay while the sun shines. — **3**. (Tabaks-)~ (tobacco-)pipe. — **4**. (Röhre) tube.
pfeifen (⌣⌣) [ahd.; *mlt. pipa're, lautm. wie piepen] ⚥ Obst **I** v/n. (h.) **1**. (vom Winde, von flötenden Tönen) to whistle, v. Mäusen auch: to squeak, vom Winde auch: to whiz; auf der Querpfeife ⌣ to fife, to pipe; auf e-r Lockpfeife ⌣ to call; thea. (zischen) to hiss; fig. also daher pfeift der Wind? the wind's in that quarter, eh? — **2**. F fig. tanzen müssen, wie j. pfeift to have to do as a p. bids (one), to be at a p.'s beck and call; das soll anders ⌣ I will lead you a nice dance. — **II** v/a. **3**. ein Lied ⌣ to whistle a tune. — **4**. P einen ⌣ (eins trinken) to wet one's whistle or clay, to have a drink; dem Herrgott sei (es) getrommelt und gepfiffen! thank God or Goodness!; ich will ihm was ⌣ he may whistle for it; s. Loch 2; auf etwas ⌣ (keinen Wert legen) not to care a button (or a straw) for a th. — **III** ~ n ⓷ **5**. whistling, &c. (s. I).
Pfeifen-beschlag (⌣⌣...) m ⓶ mounting of a pipe; =**bohrer** ⊕ m pipe-borer; =**deckel** m lid of a pipe-bowl; =**erde** f = =ton; =**fabrikant** m: a) pipe-maker; b) whistle- (or fife-)maker; =**form** f pipe-mould; =**gestell** n stand for (tobacco-)pipes; =**kopf** m pipe-bowl; =**macher** m = =fabrikant; =**räumer** ⊕ m pipe-clean(s)er or -picker; =**rohr** n pipe-stick or -tube; =**spitze** f mouthpiece of a pipe, a. pipe-tip; =**stiel** m

a) pipe-stem; keinen ~ wert not worth a (brass) farthing; b) F fig. ~e pl. (dünne Beine) broom-sticks pl.; =**stopfer** m pipe-stopper; =**strauch** ⚘ m: wohlriechender ~ (vgl. Jasmin) (white) syringa (Philade'lphus corona'rius).
Pfeif-ente (⌣⌣...) f ⓸ orn. whistling (or whistle-)duck (Anas pene'lope).
Pfeifen-ton (⌣⌣...) m ⓶ pipe-clay; =**zünder** m pipe-light, spill.
Pfeifer (⌣⌣) m ⓸, ~**in** f ⓸ **1**. whistler. — **2**. ♪ (Querpfeifenspieler) fife-player.
Pfeil (⌣) [ahd.: pile; *lt. pilum n Wurfspieß] m ⓑ c. arrow, geh. Spr.: bolt, dart; mit ~ und Bogen schießen ... with (a) bow and arrow. [sagittal.]
pfeil-artig (⌣⌣) a. ⓺ arrow-like, ⚥)
Pfeiler ⊙ (⌣⌣) [ahd.: pillar; *mlt. pila'rius] m ⓶ arch. pillar (a. fig. = Stütze); (Säule) column; (Brücken-, Strebe-)~ pier; (starke Grundmauer) strong foundation(-wall); (Pfosten) post, prop.
Pfeiler-bogen ⊙ (⌣⌣...) m ⓶ arch. pier-arch; =**brücke** f bridge resting on piers or pillars; ⚥**förmig** a. ⓺ arch. pillar-shaped; =**haupt** n Wasserbau: cut-water; =**schaft** m shaft of a pillar; =**spiegel** m pier-glass; =**stein** m = Basalt; =**tisch** m pier-table; =**weite** f, arch. (Raum zwischen zwei Pfeilern) intercolumniation.
pfeil-förmig (⌣...) a. ⓺ arrow-shaped, ⚥ sagittate; ⚥**gerade** (⌣⚥**geschwind**) a. (as) straight (swift) as an arrow; =**gift** n ⓶ arrow-poison; =**hagel** m shower (or flight) of arrows; =**kraut** ⚘ n arrow-head (Sagitta'ria sagittifo'lia); =**naht** f, anat.: ⚥ sagitta(l suture); =**sack** m, zo. der Lungenschnecken: dart-sac; =**schanze** f, frt. flèche, redan; =**schuß** m arrow-shot; =**schütze** m archer, bowman; =**spitze** f arrow-head; =**wurm** m, zo. ar-worm, sagitta (Sagi'tta); =**wurz(el)** ⚘ f ar.-root (Mara'nta arundina'cea); =**wurzel-mehl** n ar.-root.
Pfennig (⌣⌣) [ahd.: penny] m ⓑ d. c. (ehm. 1/12 ob. 1/10 Groschen, jetzt 1/100 Mark) pfennig, nearly half-a-farthing; 6 ~ six pfennig(s), nearly three farthings pl.; 1 M. 50 ~ (a. 50 ⚥) eighteenpence; vgl. Fünfzigpfennigstück; fig. s. Heller; er hat keinen ~ he hasn't a farthing, he hasn't a penny (to bless himself with); ohne einen ~ without a rap; Sprichw.: ersparter ~ ist verdienter ~ a penny saved is a penny got or earned.
Pfennig-fuchser F (⌣⌣...) m ⓶ pinch-penny; =**fuchserei** f mean economy, niggardly spirit, stinginess; ⚥**fuchsern** v/n. (h.) ⓺⚥* to scrape money together; =**kraut** ⚘ n: a) moneywort (Lysima'chia nummula'ria); b) penny-cress (Thlaspi arve'nse); =**licht** n farthing-candle; =**meister** m treasurer, purser; =**stück** n penny-piece; =**weise** adv. by penny-worths, weitS. in small doles.
Pfenning (⌣⌣) m ⓑ d. = Pfennig.
Pferch (⌣) [ahd.: park] m ⓑ b. agr. (sheep)fold, pen, penfold, pinfold.
pferchen (⌣⌣) agr. v/a. (⓺): Schafe 2c. ⌣ to pen (or fold)...; fig. (eng zs.-sperren) to pack closely, to cram into a narrow space.
Pferch-hütte (⌣⌣...) f ⓶ shepherd's cot; =**schlag** m penning (or folding) of cattle, pen (or fold) for cattle.

Pferd (¹) [ahd.: palfrey; *It. paraverēdus] n ⓑ b. **1.** horse, Kindersprache: gee-gee (f. Gaul); schlechtes (altes) ~ jade (crock); f. beschlagen 1; ein ~ besteigen, sich aufs ~ setzen to mount a horse or on horseback; **vom** ~ **absteigen** to dismount; **von** ~**en gezogen** drawn by horses, horse-drawn, horsed; **zu** ~**e** on horseback; Schutzmann zu ~e mounted constable; zu ~e steigen to mount (on horseback), to get into the saddle; ✕ **an die** ~**e**! stand to your horses!; 500 Mann zu ~e five hundred horse or cavalry. — **2.** fig. u. Sprichw.: sich aufs hohe ~ setzen (stolz reden) to ride the high horse, to give o s. (great) airs; das ~ beim Schwanze aufzäumen, das ~ hinter den Wagen spannen to put the cart before the horse; sein ~ (meist Steckenpferd) reiten to ride one's hobby(-horse); vom ~e auf den Esel kommen to go from bad to worse. — **3.** ⚓ foot-rope, horse. [horse, pony.]
Pferdchen (L~) [Pferd, dim.] n ㉓ small
Pferde=ameise (ᴗ~...) f ⓔ ent. large black ant (Formi'ca hercula'nea); =**arbeit** f: a) work done by horses; b) fig. wie für ein Pferd: very hard (or rough) work; =**artig** a. ⓖ horsy, =**artigkeit** f horsiness; =**arz(e)nei** f horse-physic; =**arzt** ↘ m = Roßarzt; =**ausfuhr-verbot** n prohibition to export horses; =**bahn** f tramway, tram-line; =**bahn=wagen** m (horse-drawn) tram-car; =**behang** m trappings pl. of a horse, harness; =**betrieb** ⓖ m von Straßenbahnen ꝛc.: horse-traction; =**bohne** f ♀ horse-bean, tick (Vi'cia faba); =**bremse** f, ent. horse-fly (Gastro'philus equi); =**decke** f horse-rug or -cloth or blanket; =**dieb** m h.-thief or -stealer; =**egel** m, zo. h.-leech (Haemo'pis sangui-so'rba); =**eisenbahn** f ꝛc. f. =bahn ꝛc.; =**fleisch** n horse-flesh; =**fliege** f = =bremse; =**fuß** m: a) horse's foot; b) (Klumpfuß) club-foot; =**futter** n horse's fodder; =**geschirr** ⓖ n horse-furniture, harness; =**getrappel** n tramping of horses; =**haar** n horse-hair; =**handel** ⓜ m trade in horses, horse-dealing; ~ treiben to deal in horses; =**händler** m horse-dealer; =**huf** m horse's hoof; =**jude** P m Jewish h.-dealer; =**junge** m stable-boy; =**kamm** m h.-comb; =**kenner** m = =kundige(r); =**knecht** m h(o)stler, groom; =**kopf** m horse's head; =**kraft** f horse-power (a. mech., abbr. HP.); Maschine von dreißig =**kräften** thirty-horse-power machine; =**krippe** f crib, manger; =**kum(me)t** ⓖ n horse-collar; =**kunde** f knowledge of horses, ⚚ hippology; =**kundige(r)** m good judge of horses or horse-flesh, ⚚ hippologist; =**länge** f length of a horse; Sport: um 2 ~n by two lengths; =**last** f h.-load; =**liebhaber** m horse-fancier, ⚚ hippo-phile; =**liebhaberei** f fancy for horses; =**mähne** f horse's mane; =**makler** ⓜ m horse-broker; =**markt** ⓜ m h.-fair; ≗ =**mäßig** a. like a horse; adv. fig. excessively, F tremendously; =**milch** f mare's milk; =**mist** m horse-dung, h.-droppings pl.; =**philister** F m: a) job-

master; b) = =händler; =**putzeug** ✕ n horse-kit; =**rennbahn** f race-course; =**rennen** n h.-race; =**saat** ♀ f: hohle ~ water-dropwort (Oena'nthe fistulo'sa); =**schwanz**, =**schweif** m h.-tail, h.'s tail; =**schwemme** f h.-pond; =**stall** m horse's stable; =**ställe** pl. in Gäßchen hinter herrschaftlichen Gebäuden: mews pl.; =**stärke** f strength of a horse, a. = =kraft; =**stehlen** n h.-stealing; =**striegel** ⓖ m currycomb; =**tränke** f = =schwemme; =**trans-port=)wagen** ⓜ m horse-box, -car; =**verleiher**, =**vermieter** m livery-man, job-master; =**wechsel** m change of horses, relay; =**zucht** f horse-breeding; =**züchter** m breeder of horses. — Vgl. Roß=...
Pfette ⓖ (ᴗ~) [nhd.] f ⓖ carp. purlin.
pfetzen (ᴗ~) **1.** = petzen. — **2.** südd. = zwicken.
pfiff¹ (ˣ) impf. ind. von pfeifen.
Pfiff² (ˣ) [pfiff¹] m ⓑ b. **1.** (das Pfeifen) whistling, whistle; einen ~ tun to (blow a) whistle. — **2.** fig. (et. Geringes) a (mere) nothing, zeitlich: moment, twinkle. — **3.** (Kunstgriff) trick, ruse, stratagem; er hat ihn manchen ~ gelehrt he gave him many wrinkles or tips; den ~ verstehen to know the tricks of the trade.
Pfifferling (ᴗᴗ) [mhd.; *Pfeffer] m ⓓ d. **1.** ♀ (Pilz) chanterelle (Canthare'llus ciba'rius). — **2.** [nhd.] fig. (etwas Geringes) keinen ~ wert not worth a rush; ich mache mir keinen ~ daraus I don't care a fig (for it).
pfiffig (ᴗ~) [F Pfiff² 3] a. ⓖ cunning, artful, crafty, sly, F deep, up to snuff; ~**keit** f ⓖ cunning, artfulness, craftiness, slyness, F depth.
Pfiffikus F (ᴗᴗᴗ) [bursch. 17. sae.. dtsch.-lt.] m ⓖ cunning (or sly) fellow, F sly-boots.
Pfingst=abend (ˣ...) m ⓖ eve of Whitsunday; =**blume** f = =rose.
Pfingsten (ᴗ~) [ahd.; *grch. pentekoste' 50ter (Tag nach Ostern)] n ㉓, a. f, inv., mit art. mst pl. Whitsun(tide), eccl. a. Pentecost. [a.: (feast of) Pentecost.)
Pfingst=fest (ˣ...) n ⓖ Whitsuntide, eccl.)
pfingstlich (ᴗ~) a. ⓖ of Whitsun(tide), eccl. Pentecostal.
Pfingst=montag (ˣ...) m ⓖ Whit-Monday; ehm. ochſe m ox festively adorned and led through the streets at Whitsuntide; P geputzt wie ein ~ F dressed up to date or to the nines; =**rose** ♀ f peony (Paeo'nia): echte ~ common peony (P. officina'lis); =**sonntag** m Whit-Sunday; =**woche** f Whitsun-week; =**zeit** f Whitsun(tide).
Pfirsich ♀ (ᴗ~) [ahd.; *It. pe'rsicum] **1.** m ⓓ d. = =baum. — **2.** ~(e) (ᴗ~) f ⓘ (⓾) Frucht: peach (Prunus pe'rsica).
Pfirsich=baum ♀ (ᴗ~...) m ⓖ peach-tree (Pe'rsica vulga'ris); =**blüte** f peach-blossom; ♀**blüten(=farbig)** a.ⓖ peach (blossom) colour; =**garten** m, =**haus** n peachery; =**kern** m peach-stone; =**rost** ♀ mp.-\
pflanzbar (ᴗ~) a. ⓖ plantable. [blight.]
Pflänzchen ♀ (ᴗ~) n ㉓ (dim. v. Pflanze) little plant, plantlet, herblet, ♀ planticle, plantule; fig. tender plant.
Pflanze (ᴗ~) [ahd.: plant; *It. planta Setzling] f ⓘ (ant. Tier, Mineral) **1.** plant, aus Samen gezogene: seedling; weiß. vegetable (growth), ⚚ vegetal; auf

andern ~n lebende ~ (Luftpflanze) aerial plant, epiphyte; schmarotzende ~ parasitic plant, parasite. — **2.** F iro. eine saub(e)re (nette oder rare) ~ (Person) a pretty (or nice) article.
pflanzen (ᴗ~) [lt.] **I** v/a. ⓚ to plant (auch fig.); vgl. an², auf²; ✕ Geschütze auf eine Anhöhe ∠ to plant (or mount) cannon on an elevation; fig. etwas in j-s Herz ∠, e-m et. ins Herz ∠ to implant (or inculcate, instil) a th. into a p. — **II** ~ n ㉓ = Pflanzung 1.
Pflanzen=abdruck (ˣ...) m ⓖ imprint (or impression) of a plant, auf Steinen: herborization, arborization; =**ähnlich** a. ⓖ plant-like, ⚚ phytoid, phytiform; =**alkali** n, chm.: ⚚ vegeto-alkali; =**anatomie** f: ⚚ phytotomy; ≗**artig** a. vegetable- (or plant-) like; =**beet** n bed of plants; =**beschreibung** f: ⚚ phytography; =**buch** n herbal; =**chemie** f: ⚚ phytochemistry; =**entstehungs-lehre** f phytogenesis, ...y; =**erde** f vegetable earth or. mould; =**esser(in** f) m vegetarian; =**faser** f vegetable fibre; =**faser-stoff** m f. Zellulose; ⚚**fressend** a. zo.: ⚚ herbivorous, graminivorous, ⚚ phytophagous; =**fresser** m herbivorous animal, herbivore, ⚚ phytophagan; =**garten** m botanical garden; =**geo-graphie** f botanical geography, ⚚ phytogeography; =**gift** n vegetable poison; =**kenner** m botanist, ⚚ phytologist; =**kost** f vegetable diet; =**kunde** f botany, ⚚ phytology; =**leben** n vegetable life, vegetation; ein ~ führen to vegetate; =**lehre** f: a) = =kunde; b) (Buch darüber) book on botany; =**leim** m, chm.: ⚚ gliadin(e); =**natur** f vegetable nature; =**physiologie** f vegetable physiology, ⚚ phytonomy; =**presse** f botanical press; =**reich** n (ant. Mineral-, Tier-reich) vegetable kingdom; ≗**reich** a. rich in plants or vegetation; =**saft** m: a) ♀ sap; b) pharm. juice of plants; =**sammeln** n collecting plants, botanizing, herborization; =**sammler** m collector of plants, herbalist; =**sammlung** f collection of plants, herbarium; =**schimmel** m mildew; =**schleim** m, chm.: ⚚ mucilage; =**seide** ⓖ f vegetable silk; =**speise** f vegetable food; =**stecher** ⓖ m planter(-tool), dibble; =**stoff** m vegetable matter; =**tiere** n/pl. zo.: ⚚ vegeto- (or plant-) animals, phytozoans, zoophytes pl.; =**wachs** ⓖ n vegetable wax; =**wachs-tum** n vegetable growth, vegetation; =**welt** f vegetable world or kingdom; =**zelle** f vegetable cell; =**züchtung** f cultivation of plants.
Pflanzer (ᴗ~) m ⓖ (=in f ⓥ) **1.** planter, (wo)man who plants. — **2.** (Ansiedler) settler, colonist. — **3.** owner of a plantation, planter('s wife f).
Pflanz=garten (ˣ...) m ⓖ nursery, seed-plot; =**gärtner** m nursery-gardener, nurseryman; =**holz** n = =stock.
pflanzlich (ᴗ~) a. ⓖ of (or relating to) plants, vegetable, ⚚ vegetal.
Pflänzling (ᴗ~) m ⓓ d. young plant, seedling; fig. nursling, foster-child.
Pflanz=ort (ˣ...) m ⓖ settlement; =**reis** n, hort. slip for planting, scion;

Signs (see page XVII): F familiar; P vulgar; ʄ flash; ↘ rare; † obsolete (died); * new word (born); ⁺⁺ incorrect; ♪ music;

[**Pflanzschule**] — 759 — [**pflügen**]

=**schule** f, hort. nursery; fig. seminary, training-college; =**staat** m, =**stadt** f colony, settlement; =**stätte** f: a) place for planting (s.th.); b) settlement; =**stock** m, hort., agr. setting, stick, dibble.

Pflanzung (⌣‿) f ⊕ **1.** planting. — **2.** a) (bepflanztes Gefilde, Plantage) plantation; b) (Ansiedlung) settlement, colony.

Pflanz=volk (‿...) n ⊕ colonial people, nation of settlers; =**wetter**, =**zeit** f, agr., hort. weather, season for planting.

Pflaster (⌣‿) [: plaster; *grch. empla'str=] n ⊕ **1.** [ahd.] a) pharm. plaster; englisches ~ court-plaster; s. Blasen= pflaster; ein ~ auflegen to apply a plaster, fig. to heal a sore; ein ~ streichen to spread a plaster; b) ⊕ Büchsenmach.: (Kugel=)~ (greased) patch for a rifle-bullet. — **2.** ⊕ [nhd.] pavement, im Hause: paved floor, aus Fliesen: flagging; s. Mosaik=~; das ~ aufreißen to tear (or take) up the pavement; fig. ein teures ~ an expensive place (to live in); F ~ treten (sich umhertreiben) to loaf about, to walk the streets; aufs ~ werfen to turn out (into the street), to kick (or P chuck) out, Arbeiterspr.: to lock out.

Pflaster=arbeit ⊕ (⌣‿‿‿) f ⊕ paving, pavior's work.

Pfläſterchen (⌣‿‿) n ⊕ (dim. v. Pflaster) small plaster; Schönfleden aus schwarzem Taft) little black patch for the face.

Pflasterer ⊕ (⌣‿‿) m ⊕ pavior, paver.

Pflaster=fliese (⌣‿...) f ⊕ paving-tile; =**geld** n: a) (charge for) pavage; b) (right of) passage; =**kasten** m: a) case with plasters; b) P fig. (Chirurg) surgeon, F sawbones; =**lohn** m = =geld a; =**meister** m master pavior.

pflastern (⌣‿) I v/a. ⊕ a. **1.** [Pflaster 1] surg. eine Wunde ꝛc. ⊕ to plaster (up) ...; to patch — . **2.** ⊕ [Pflaster 2] die Straße ⊕ to pave, mit Fliesen: to flag the road, mit Holz: to wood-pave. — II ~ n ⊕ **3.** = Pflasterung.

Pflaster=ramme ⊕ (⌣‿...) f ⊕ paving-beetle, pavior's rammer; =**schmierer** m = =streicher; =**setzer** m = Pflasterer; =**stein** ⊕ m paving-stone; =**streicher** m one who spreads plasters, spöttisch: chemist, surgeon; =**treter** F m loafer, idler, f co. inspector of pavements; =**treterei** f loafing, idling.

Pflasterung (⌣‿) f ⊕ **1.** plastering. — **2.** ⊕ paving, flagging, wood paving.

Pflaster=ziegel (⌣‿...) m ⊕ paving-brick.

Pflaume ♀ (⌣‿) [ahd.: plum; *mlt. pruna] f ⊕ plum, gedörrte: prune; ge= schmorte ~n stewed prunes pl.

Pflaumen=baum ♀ (⌣‿...) m ⊕: (echter) ~ plum-tree (Prunus [dome'stica]); ⊕**farbig** a. ⊕ plum-coloured; ⊕**förmig** a.: ⊕ pruniform; =**kern** m plum-stone; =**kuchen** m, etwa: open plum-tart (plum-cake mst „Rosinenkuchen"; s. Kuchen 1 b) =**mus** n pl.=jam; =**schlehe** ♀ f bullace (Prunus insiti'tia); =**stein** m = =kern; =**torte** f (als engl. Gericht) plum-tart; ⊕**weich** a. (as) soft as a (ripe) plum or as butter, fig. very yielding, weak-minded; contp. ein ~er ⊕ a soft one, pol. a waverer, a wabbler.

Pfleg=amt (⌣‿‿) n ⊕ board of guardians.

Pflege (⌣‿) [ahd.; *pflegen] f ⊕ care, attention, e=s Kranken: nursing; e=s Kindes: fostering, rearing; der Künste, e=s Gartens ꝛc.: culture, cultivation; (Verwaltung) administration; (Leitung) direction, superintendence; (Bevormundung) tutelage; einem Kranken gute ~ angedeihen lassen to nurse a patient well, to take great care of an invalid; gute ~ h. to have good nursing, to be well looked after; ein Kind in ~ .geben to put ... out to nurse; ein Kind in f=e ~ nehmen to take charge of ...

pflege=bedürftig (⌣‿‿...) a. ⊕ needing care or attention; =**befohlene([r]** m) f ⊕ (person committed to somebody's charge, (fr.) protégé(e f); vgl. =kind.

Pflege=eltern (⌣‿...) pl. ⊕ foster-parents pl.; =**kind** n foster-child; (Mündel) ward.

Pflege=mutter (⌣‿...) f ⊕ foster-mother; (Beschützerin) patroness, protectress.

pflegen (⌣‿) [ahd.: play] I v/a. u. sich ⊕ v/refl. ⊕ (a. mit gen.): e=r oder j=s. et. od. einer Sache ⊕ to attend to a p., a th.; to bestow care on a p., a th.; sich ⊕ to nurse o.s., to take care of o.s.; s. hegen 3. — II v/a. und oft mit gen., meist ⊕b.: et. od. einer Sache ⊕ (ihr obliegen) to apply o.s. to a th.; (betreiben) to carry on, to exercise, (verwalten) to administer; (der) Freundschaft mit e-m ⊕ to cultivate a p.'s friendship; süßer Liebe ⊕ to enjoy (or indulge in) the sweets of love; Rat(s) ⊕ to keep counsel, to deliberate, nach gepflog(e)nem Rate after due deliberation; der Ruhe ⊕ to take one's ease; Umgang mit einem ⊕ to keep up (or carry on) a friendly intercourse with a p. — III v/n. (h.) ⊕ mit inf. (gewöhnlich vorfallen, gewohnt sein): das pflegt (bisw. pleonastisch: gewöhnlich, in der Regel, meistens) zu geschehen that is usually the case or often the way, it generally (or mostly) happens like that; er pflegte früh aufzustehen he was accustomed (or used, wont) to rise early; er pflegt sich nicht anzustrengen he is not in the habit of exerting himself; sie pflegte jedesmal zu sagen she would (or it was her custom to) say each time; wie man so zu sagen pflegt as people usually say, as the saying goes.

Pfleger (⌣‿) m ⊕, ~**in** f ⊕ one who takes care (or charge) of a p., a th., weit S. = Pflege=vater, =mutter; ~**in** v. Kranken nurse; fig. (Förderer) promoter; Athen war die ~in der Künste Athens was the patroness of (the fine) arts. — **2.** jur. administrator, guardian, trustee.

Pflege=sohn (⌣‿...) m ⊕, =**tochter** f foster-son, -daughter; =**vater** m f.-father.

Pflegling (⌣‿) m ⊕d. = Pflegebefohlene(r).

Pflegschaft (⌣‿) f ⊕ jur. guardianship.

Pflicht¹ (‿) [ahd.: plight; *pflegen] f ⊕ duty (a. Abgabe); (Amt) office, (Verpflichtung) obligation, liability; s.obliegen 2; seine ~ (gut) erfüllen, seine volle ~ tun to fulfil one's duties, to do one's duty to the utmost or to the last; auf ~ und Gewissen with a good conscience, conscientiously; er hält es nicht für seine ~ zu // he does not think it his duty to //, he does not feel called upon to //; **in** ~ (ob. in Eid u. ~) nehmen to bind by oath; s. anhalten 3; e=m etwas **zur** ~ machen to impress (or urge) a th. on a p.

Pflicht² ⌑ (‿) [ahd.] f ⊕: a) (Vorderdeck) forepart of the deck; b) = Flicht¹.

Pflicht²=anker ⌑ (‿...) m ⊕ sheet- (or main-)anchor; =**anteil** m, =**beitrag** m quota, an Soldaten ꝛc.: contingent; =**eifer** m zeal; ⊕**eifrig** a. ⊕ zealous in one's duty.

Pflichten=lehre (⌣‿...) f ⊕ phls. doctrine of moral obligations, weit S. ethics; =**streit** m conflict of duties.

Pflicht¹=erfüllung (‿...) f ⊕ performance of a duty; =**exemplar** n presentation copy (to be) supplied to the authorities; ⊕**frei** a. ⊕ exempt from duty; =**gebot** n call of duty, moral obligation; =**gefühl** n sense of duty; ⊕**gemäß** a. ⊕ conformable to (one's) duty, incumbent; vgl. ⊕**mäßig**; ⊕**getreu** a. = ⊕**treu**; ⊕**leistung** f: a) performance of a duty; b) payment of dues; c) oath of allegiance; ⊕**mäßig** a. ⊕ dutiful; vgl. ⊕**gemäß**; ⊕**schuldig** a. in duty bound, obligatory; ⊕ adv. duly, deferentially; =**teil** m u. n jur. lawful (or legitimate) portion; ⊕**treu** a. devoted to (one's) duty, dutiful; =**treue** f devotion to (one's) duty, dutifulness; ⊕**vergessen** a. forgetful of one's duty, undutiful, disloyal; =**vergessenheit** f dereliction of (one's) duty, disloyalty; =**versäumnis** f neglect of duty; ⊕**widrig** a. contrary to one's duty, undutiful; =**widrigkeit** f undutifulness.

Pflock ⊕ (‿) [ndd.: plug] m ⊕b. (hölzerner Nagel, Zapfen, Döbel) peg, wooden plug or pin; mit Pflöcken befestigen to peg; mit Pflöcken versehen to plug. [pegging-awl.]

Pflock=ahle ⊕ (‿‿) f ⊕ Schuhmacher:

pflöcken (⌣‿) [Pflock] v/a. ⊕ to fasten with pegs, to peg, to plug.

Pflock=holz (‿‿) n ⊕, a. Pflöck=holz n, carp. peg-wood. [v. pflegen.]

pflog (‿), **pflöge** (⌣‿) impf. ind., subj.

pflücken (⌣‿) [ahd.: pluck; *mlt.] v/a. ⊕ **1.** Blumen, Früchte ꝛc. ⊕ to pick (or gather, pluck) ...; mit der Zeit pflückt man Rosen everything comes to those who (can) wait; Salat ⊕ to gather (or pick) salad. — **2.** Geflügel ⊕ (rupfen) to pluck a goose, &c.; fig. s. Hühnchen 2.

Pflücksel (⌣‿) n ⊕ s. th. picked (or pulled) to pieces, (small) morsel or shred.

Pflug (‿) [ahd.: plough] m ⊕c. plough, Am. plow; bibl. die Hand an den legen to put one's hand to the plough or one's shoulder to the wheel; Land, das unter dem ~e ist arable (or ploughed) land, ploughland.

Pflug=arbeit (‿...) f ⊕ ploughing, ploughman's work; =**balken**, =**baum** m plough-beam or -shaft.

pflugbar (‿‿) [Pflug] a. ⊕ ploughable, ready for the plough, arable.

Pflug=eisen (‿...) n ⊕ = =messer, =schar.

pflügen (⌣‿) [Pflug] v/a. u. v/n. (h.) ⊕ **1.** agr. to plough; s. Kalb 1; heimlich mit e=m ⊕ to have a secret understanding (or to plot) with a p.; den

🔬 scientific; ❦ botanical; ♀ geography; ⊕ machinery; ⚒ mining; ⚔ military; ⚓ marine; ⊛ commercial; ✉ postal; 🚂 railway.

[Pflüger] — 760 — [phantasiereich]

Sand 2 (sich vergebens abmühten) to plough the sand(s). — 2. = furchen I.
Pflüger (‿‿) m ② ploughman.
Pflug-handhabe (‿...) f ② = ‑sterz; ‑haupt n plough-head; ‑holz n plough-beam; ‑karren m plough-truck; ‑land n ploughland, land under cultivation; ‑macher m = ‑schmied; ‑messer n coulter; ‑ochsen m/pl. oxen used for ploughing, plough-oxen pl.; ‑rad n plough-wheel; ‑reitel m, ‑reute f, ‑rodel m zum Reinigen der Pflugschar plough-raker or -staff; ‑schar f [ahd.] ploughshare; ‑schar-bein n, anat. Knochen der Nase, ⚕ vomer; ‑schleife f plough-drag; ‑schmied m plough-wright; ‑schuh m plough-shoe; ‑sterz(e f) m plough-tail or -neck or -handle; ‑treiber m ploughboy, ploughman.
Pfort-ader (‿‿‿) f ② anat.: ⚕ portal (or port-)vein. ▌gate, or door, wicket.▐
Pförtchen (‿‿) [Pforte, dim.] n ㉓ little
Pforte (‿‿) [ahd.: port, porch; *lt. porta] f ⑭ 1. gate, (Tür) door; die (Hohe) ~ (türk. Regierung) the Sublime Porte; bibl. die ~n pl. der Hölle the Gates of Hell; gehet ein durch die enge ~ enter ye in at the straight gate; vor den ~n der Ewigkeit before the gates (or portals) of eternity, on the brink of the grave. — 2. ⚓ (verschließbare Öffnung in den Planken des Schiffes) port(-hole) (‑Stück=) gunport.
Pfort-luke ⚓ (‿‿‿) f ② port.
Pförtner (‿‿) [Pforte] m ㉒, ~in f ㊼ 1. gatekeeper, doorkeeper, (hall-) porter, F co. janitor; ~in gatekeeper's (or porter's) wife; bisw.: portress. 2. (Schließer in Gefängnissen) warder, turnkey, jailer. — 3. anat. (Magen-mund): ⚕ pylorus.
Pförtner-haus (‿‿...) n ②, ‑wohnung f keeper's (or porter's) lodge; ‑klappe f, anat.: ⚕ pyloric valve.
Pfoste (‿‿) f ⑭, mst ~n m ㉓ [ahd.: post; *lt. postis m] post, jamb, aus Stein auch: mullion; Tennis posts pl.
Pfötchen (‿‿) n ㉓ (dim. v. Pfote) little paw; zum Hund: gib ~! give your paw!
Pfote (‿‿) [ndd.: paw] f ⑭ 1. (tierischer Fuß, auch F P Hand, Fuß des Menschen) paw; e-m auf die ~n klopfen to give a p. a rap on the knuckles; iro. reich mir die ~! F tip us your fist or your fin! — 2. F (schlechte Handschrift) scrawl, scribbling, scribble.
Pfriem¹ ⊙ (‿) m ⑭c., ‑e (‿‿) f ⑭ u. ‑en¹ (‿‿) m ㉓ [mhd.] Schuhmacherei: awl; (Loch-eisen) punch(eon), puncher; typ. (Ahle) bodkin.
Pfriem² ⊙ (‿) [ahd.] m ⑭c., ‑en² (‿‿) m ㉓ = Pfriem(en)kraut
pfriemen³ (‿‿) [Pfriem¹] v/a. ⑱ to pierce with an awl or a bodkin.
pfriem(en)¹-**förmig** (‿...) a. ⑥ ⊙ awl-shaped, ⚕ ent. subuliform, ⚘ subulate(d); ‑gras ⚘: spanisches ~ esparto (grass) (Stipa tenacissima); ‑kraut ⚘ (deutscher Ginster) German broom; ²-spitzig a.: ⚕ subulose.
Pfrille (‿‿) ⚓ ichth. minnow (Pho'xinus).
Pfropf (‿) [ahd.: f. propa'go Setzling] m ⑭ b.: 1. a) hölzerner ~ zum Schließen e‑s Gefäßes: plug, e‑s Fasses: bung, e‑r Ge-

schützmündung: tampion; b) ✕ artill. (Lade-)‿ wad(ding); c) path. ~ in Blut-gefäßen: ⚕ thrombus; surg. ~ v. Watte, Schwamm ꝛc.: tampon. — 2. = Pfropfen¹.
Pfropf-bastard (‿‿‿) m ⑭ hort. graft-hybrid. ▌(Kork) stopper, cork.▐
Pfropfen¹ (‿‿) [f. Pfropf] m ㉓ (Stöpsel,
pfropfen² (‿‿) [mhd.; *lt. f. Pfropf] I v/a. ⑱ hort. to graft, in die Rinde: to graft in the rind or shoulder, in den Spalt: to splice, to graft in the slit. — II ~ n ㉓ grafting, in die Rinde: shoulder-grafting, in den Spalt: splicing, slit- (or stock-)grafting.
pfropfen³ (‿‿) [Pfropf] v/a. ⑱ 1. (mit e‑m Pfropfen verschließen) to cork, to plug; to stop up. — 2. (stopfen, stark anfüllen) to cram (into), to stuff (full of); sich den Magen mit Speisen voll‿ to overload one's stomach; gepfropft voll crammed, chock-full, filled to overflowing; der Saal war gepfropft voll ... was crammed (full), ... was packed (with people), ... was crowded to overflowing.
Pfropfen¹-**geld** (‿‿...) n corkage; ‑zieher m = Korkzieher.
Pfröpfling ♀ (‿‿) m ⑭d. graftling, grafted tree, slip for grafting.
Pfropf-messer (‿...) n ⑭ hort. grafting-knife; ‑reis n graft(ing-twig), scion; ‑säge f grafting-saw, grafter; ‑schnitt m slit for grafting; ‑wachs n grafting-wax.
Pfründe (‿‿) [ahd.; *mlt. praebe'nda] f ⑭ eccl. prebend, mehr gbr.: benefice, living; ohne Seelsorge: sinecure.
Pfründen-besetzungs-recht (‿‿...) n ⑭ eccl. patronage of a living, advowson; ‑besitzer m = Pfründner; ‑inhaber m beneficiary, beneficed clergyman, incumbent; ‑wucher m traffic in benefices, simony.
Pfründ-haus (‿‿...) n ⑭ 1. = Pfarrhaus. — 2. (Stift) foundation, almshouses pl.
Pfründner (‿‿) [Pfründe] m ⑭ eccl. prebendary, beneficiary, incumbent.
Pfuhl (‿) [ahd.: pool] m ⑭c. pool, puddle; fig. sink of corruption, &c., slough of despond, &c.; (Hölle) bottomless pit.
Pfühl (‿) [ahd.: pillow; *lt. pulvi'nus m] m u. n ⑭c. 1. (Kopfkissen) pillow, bolster; (größeres Kissen) cushion. — 2. arch. (Glied an Säulenstühlen) torus.
pfuhlicht (‿‿) a. ⑥ pool-like.
pfui (‿) [vgl. lt. phui] int. ②! pish!, faugh, ugh, phew, mehr gbr.: fie!, for (or what a) shame!; ‿über ihn! fie upon him!; ‿ rufen (a. ‿en (‿‿) v/a. ⑱) über ... to cry shame upon.
Pfui-ruf (‿‿) m ⑭ cry of shame.
Pfund (‿) [ahd. 1/2. sae.: pound; *lt. pondo] n ⑭,⑥. (abbr. Pfd. ℔) 1. a) Gewicht: pound; (vgl. Fußpfund). b) Rechnungsmünze: 4 ~ Butter four pounds of butter; ~ Sterling pound sterling (abbr. Pfd. St., £ = libra). — 2. fig. bib. bibl.: sein ~ vergraben to bury (or hide) one's talent.
Pfund-bärme (‿‿‿) f ⑭ German yeast.
...**pfünder** (...‿‿) [Pfund] m ⑭ in Zssgn mit Zahlwörtern: ...pounder, zB. ✕ artill. so und so viel Pfund schießend: Zehn-‿ ten-pounder.

Pfund-geld (‿...) n ⑭ poundage; ‑gewicht n pound-weight; ‑hefe f = ‑bärme.
pfundig, pfündig (‿‿) a. ⑥ 1. of (or weighing) one pound; weitS. heavy, weighty. — 2. in Zssgn mit Zahlwörtern: (ein-)pfündiger Hecht pike weighing one pound; ✕ artill. zehn-‿s Geschütz (vgl. ...pfünder) ten-pounder.
Pfund-leder ⊙ (‿...) n ⑭ sole-leather; ‑weise adv. (F a. a.) by the pound.
Pfusch-arbeit (‿‿...) f ⑭ bungling (work), botching, blunder(ing), spoilt (F scamped) work; (schlechtes Bauen) jerry-building.
pfuschen (‿‿) [mhd. lautm.] I v/n. (h.) v. a. ⑱ (schlecht arbeiten) to bungle, botch, blunder; to spoil (F to scamp) one's work; in et. ② to dabble in (or meddle with) a th.; f. Handwerk 1. — II ~ n ㉓ bungling, &c. (f. I); inferior work(manship).
Pfuscher (‿‿) m ⑭, ~in f ㊼ (schlechter Arbeiter) bungler, botcher, blunderer; inferior workman; (Marktschreier) quack.
Pfuscherei (‿‿⁰) f ⑥ = Pfusch-arbeit.
pfuscherhaft (‿‿‿) a. ⑥ like a bungler or botcher or quack; unworkmanlike, unskilful, unprofessional; adv. a. in a bungling (or perfunctory) manner.
pfuschern (‿‿) v/a. ⑲a. to trick, cheat.
Pfütze (‿‿) [ahd.; *lt. pu'teus m Brunnen] f ⑭ puddle, pool (of mud or slush), quagmire, mud-hole, ehm. auch: slough; ⛏ water in (the workings of) a pit.
Pfütz-eimer ⛏ (‿‿‿) m bucket for baling (out) water.
pfützen-naß (‿‿‿) a. ⑥ dripping (or soaking) wet, wet (or soaked) through; ‑wasser n ⑭ muddy water, slush.
pfützig (‿‿) a. ⑥ full of puddles or pools, muddy, slushy, sloppy.
Phäake (‿‿‿) m ⑭. **Phäakin** f ㊼, **phäakisch** a. ⑥ myth. bsd. in der Odyssee: Phæacian.
Pha-ethon (‿‿‿) [grch.] m ⑲ 1. npr. myth. Phaethon. — 2. Art Wagen: phaeton.
Phalanx (‿‿) [grch. Schlachtordnung] f ⑯ (pl. Phala'ngen) Alt.: ✕ phalanx.
Phanerogame ⚘ ⚭ (‿‿‿‿) [grch.] f ⑭ (Blütenpflanze) phanerogam(ic plant), pl. phanerogamia; **phanerogamisch** a. ⑥ phanerogamic, ...ian.
Phänologie ⚭ (‿‿‿‿) [grch.] f ⑭ (Lehre von den periodischen Erscheinungen im Tier- und Pflanzen-reich) phenology.
Phänomen ⚭ (‿‿‿‿) [grch.] n ⑭d., ([Natur-]Erscheinung, Wunder) phenomenon; ²al (‿‿‿‿) a. ⑥ (außerordentlich) phenomenal; ~ologie (‿‿‿‿‿‿) f ⑭ (Lehre von den Erscheinungen) phenomenology; ~on n (‿‿‿‿) n ㊴ = Phänomen.
Phantasie, poet. a. ...**sei** (‿‿‿‿) [mhd.; *grch.] f ⑭ 1. (Einbildungskraft) imagination, fancy, poet. a.: fantasy. — 2. (Traumbild) (fantastic) vision; ~n pl. reverie, (day-)dreams pl.; (Laune, Einfall) fancy, freak; ~n e‑s Fiebernden: ravings, rambling speeches pl. — 3. a) (leichte Erzählung) light (or fantastic) tale; fiction; b) ♪ fantasia, reverie.
Phantasie-anzug (‿‿‿...) m ⑭ fancy costume or dress; ‑gebilde n creation of the mind, fanciful picture; ²reich a. ⑥ = ²voll.

Zeichen (f. S. XVII): F familiär; P Volkssprache; ⸢ Gaunersprache; ⟋ selten; † alt (auch gestorben); * neu (auch geboren); ⁺⁺ unrichtig;

[phantasieren] — 761 — [Phrase]

phantasieren (f~⌣⌣) **I** v/n. (h.) u. v/a. 1. to dream; to indulge in fancies or (day-) dreams or reveries; (Unsinn schwatzen) to ramble, to rave; path. im Fieber ♫ to be delirious or light-headed or raving. — 2. ♪ to play extempore, to improvise. — **II** ~ n 3. reveries pl., raving(s pl.), path. delirium; ♪ extempore play(ing) or recitation, improvisation.

Phantasie-stück ♪ (f~⌣⌣...) n = Phantasie 3b; **=voll** a. endowed with a strong imagination, imaginative, inventive, creative; fanciful.

Phantasma (f~⌣⌣) [grch.] n phantasm, delusion, conception of fancy.

Phantasmagorie (f~⌣⌣~⌣) f (Gaukelbild) phantasmagory, ...ia, fancy picture.

Phantast (f~⌣) [mhd., *grch.] m ~in f fantastic(al) person, fantast(ic). dreamer, visionary; **~erei** (f~⌣⌣~⌣) f fantastic(al) manner or ideas pl.; (Grille) fancy, caprice; **2isch** (f~⌣⌣) a. fantastic(al); visionary; (grillenhaft) fanciful, capricious, whimsical.

Phantom (f~⌣) [grch.] n (Trugbild) phantom, delusive vision; (Gespenst) ghost.

Pharao (f~⌣) [hebr.; *äg. Hohe Pforte] m α. **I** npr/m. (mit art.: sg. inv., pl. Pharaonen) Alt.: (ägyptischer König) Pharaoh. — **II** n Spiel: = Pharo.

pharaonisch (f~⌣~⌣) a. Pharaonic, of Pharaoh. [Ichneumon.]

Pharao(ns)-ratte (f~⌣⌣,⌣⌣) f zo. =

Pharisäer (f~⌣~⌣) [hebr. Abgesonderter] m bibl. Pharisee (auch fig. = Scheinheiliger); **~tum** (f~⌣~⌣) n pharisaism; sanctimoniousness; **pharisä-isch** a. pharisaic(al); sanctimonious; shamming piety.

Pharmako-gnosie (f~⌣⌣⌣⌣~⌣) [grch.] f (Arzneiwarenkunde) pharmacognosy, ...stics; **-logie** (f~⌣~⌣) f (Arzneimittellehre) pharmacology; **-pöe** (f~⌣~⌣) f (Arzneibuch) pharmacopœia, dispensatory.

Pharmazeut (f~⌣~⌣) [grch.] m (Apotheker) (pharmaceutical or dispensing chemist; chemist's assistant; student of pharmacy; **2isch** a. pharmaceutical; **Pharmazie** f pharmacy.

Pharo (f~⌣) [Pharao] n Hasardspiel: faro. [(Leuchtturm) lighthouse.]

Pharus (f~⌣) [lt., *grch. ⌣⌣] m, inv. od.

Phase (f~⌣; Hom. Fase) [grch.] f (Wandlung) phase; (Stufe) stage; **phasisch** a. phasic. [Karbolsäure.]

Phenol (f~⌣) (f~') [fr., *grch.] n ⊕d. =

Phenyl (f~⌣) (f~') [grch.] n ⊕d. chm. phenyl (C₆H₅, wenn frei: C₁₂H₁₀); **~alkohol** (f~''...) m phenyl alcohol (=Phenol); **~amin** n phenylamine (= Anilin); **~wasserstoff** m = Benzol.

Philanthrop (f~⌣~⌣) [grch.] m, **~ie** (f~⌣~⌣') f, **2isch** (f~⌣~⌣) a. = Menschenfreund, =freundlichkeit, 2freundlich; **~ismus** (...⌣⌣) m philanthropism.

Philatelie (f~⌣⌣~⌣') [grch.] f philately; **Philatelist** (f~⌣⌣~⌣') [grch.] m (Briefmarkensammler) philatelist, stamp-collector.

Philharmonie (f~⌣⌣~⌣) [grch.] f (Konzerthaus) Philharmonic Hall; **philharmonisch** (f~⌣~⌣) a. philharmonic.

Philhellene (f~⌣~⌣) [grch.] m = Griechenfreund.

Philipp (f~⌣) [grch. Pferdefreund] npr m. (Bn.) Alt. mst **~us** (⌣⌣~) γ. Philip.

Philipper (f~⌣~) [Philippi ♀ Stadt in Mazedonien] m Philippian.

Philippika (f~⌣⌣⌣) f (heftige Rede [des Demosthenes gegen Philipp von Mazedonien], a. fig.) j. philippisch.

Philippinen ♀ (f~⌣~⌣) [span. (1543)] *Philipp II.] f pl. Ost-asien: Philippine Islands, Philippines pl.

philippisch (f~⌣⌣) [grch.] a. Philippian; ~e Reden des Demosthenes: Philippics pl., orations against Philip(pus); fig. 2e (heftige) Reden philippics pl.

philistä-isch (f~⌣~⌣) [hebr.] a. of the Philistines. Philistine.

Philister (f~⌣~) [hebr.] m **I** npr. Alt. bes. bibl. Volksname: Philistine. — **II** bursch. : philistine, townsman, cit; (Hauswirt des Studenten) student's landlord; fig. (lederner Mensch) F dry stick, muff. humdrum fellow; vgl. Pferde-♫; **~ei** (f~⌣~⌣') f philistinism. narrow-mindedness. pedantry. fogyism; **2haft** (f~⌣~⌣), **2iös** a. = philiströs; **~ium** (f~⌣~(⌣)⌣) n ⊕d. ordinary citizen's life; humdrum existence, every-day routine; **philiströs** (f~⌣~⌣) a. (D10) philistine, narrow-minded, humdrum.

Philolog (f~⌣~) [grch.] m. **~e** (Sprach- u. Altertums-forscher) philologist; **~en-versammlung** (f~⌣~⌣~⌣) f philological congress; **~ie** (f~⌣~⌣') f philology; **2isch** (f~⌣~⌣) a. philological.

Philomele (f~⌣~⌣) [grch.] npr f. myth., poet. (Nachtigall) Philomela.

Philosoph (f~⌣~) [grch.] m ♀, **~in** f (Weltweise[r]) philosopher; **~em** (f~⌣~f') n ⊕d. philosophical argument or problem; **~en-schule** (f~⌣~f'...) f philosophical school; **~ie** (f~⌣~⌣') f philosophy; **2ieren** (f~⌣~⌣~⌣) v/n. (h.) ♀ to philosophize, to speculate (über et. on a th.); **2isch** (f~⌣~f) a. philosophical; 2ische Fakultät phil. faculty.

Philotten (f~⌣~) [mhd.] pl. (eingerammte Balken) piles pl. rammed into the earth.

Phiole (f~⌣~) [fr. fiole; *grch.] f (Fläschen) phial, vial.

Phlegma (f~⌣) [grch. ⌣⌣ Verschleimung] n (Schwerfälligkeit) phlegm; (Faulheit) sluggishness. indolence; **~tiker** (f~⌣~⌣) m phlegmatic person; **2tisch** (f~⌣~⌣) a. phlegmatic; (faul) sluggish, indolent, lazy.

phlogistisch (f~⌣~⌣) [grch.] a. chm. phlogistic; **Phlogiston** (f~⌣~⌣) n (angeblicher Brennstoff) phlogiston.

Phlori(d)zin (f~⌣~⌣) r. v. **Phlorrhizin** (f~⌣~⌣') [grch.] n ⊕d. chm. (Stoff in der Wurzelrinde der Obstbäume) phlorizin (C₂₁H₂₄O₁₀).

Phöbus (f~⌣) [grch.] m npr/m. γ. myth. (Sonnengott) Phœbus (Apollo).

Phonetik (f~⌣~) [grch.] f (Lautlehre) phonetics; **~er** (f~⌣~⌣) m phonetician; **phonetisch** a. phonetic(al); **phonisch** (f~⌣) a. (lautlich) phonic.

Phönix (f~⌣) [grch.] m ⊕α. myth. äg.: (fabelhafter Vogel) phœnix (a. fig. et. Einziges in seiner Art).

Phönizi-en (f~⌣~⌣) npr/n. α. Alt. Küstenlandschaft Vorder-asiens: Phœnicia; **Phönizi-er** (in f) m, **phönizisch** (f~⌣~) a. Phœnician.

Phonograph ♫ (f~⌣~f) [grch. Lautschreiber] m phonograph. [lehre) phonology.]

Phonologie ♫ (f~⌣~⌣') [grch.] f (Laut-

Phosgen (f~⌣') [grch.] n ⊕d. chm. phosgen(e) (COCl₂).

Phosphat (f~⌣~') [neu-lt.; *Phosphor] n ⊕c. chm. (phosphorsaures Salz) phosphate.

Phosphor (f~⌣~, a. f~⌣~) [grch. phósphŏrŏs Lichtträger] m ⊕d. chm. phosphorus (P).

Phosphor-brei (f~⌣~...) m ♫ zum Töten von Ungeziefer: phosphorus paste; **=bronze** ⊙ f phosphor-bronze; **=eisen** n phosphide of iron. [phosphorescence.]

Phosphoreszenz ♫ (f~⌣~⌣~') f phys.

phosphoreszieren (f~⌣~⌣~⌣) v/n. (h.) phys. chm. (im Dunkeln leuchten) to phosphoresce; 2d phosphorescent.

phosphor-haltig (f~⌣~⌣~⌣) a. phosphoric, phosphorized.

phosphorig ♫ (f~⌣~) a. chm.: 2e Säure phosphorous acid (H₃PO₃); 2-sauer a. phosphorous: 2-saures Salz phosphite; **~säure-anhydrid** n phosphorous anhydride, phosphorus trioxide (P₂O₃).

phosphorisch ♫ (f~⌣~⌣) a. phosphoric.

phosphorisieren ♫ (f~⌣~⌣~⌣) [neu-lt.] v/a. chm. (mit Phosphor verbinden) to phosphorate. phosphorize.

Phosphorit ♫ (f~⌣~') [neu-lt.] m ⊕c. min. phosphorite, phosphate of lime.

Phosphor-metall (f~⌣~⌣) n ⊕ phosphide; **=pentachlorid** n phosphorus pentachloride, phosphoric chloride (PCl₅); **2sauer** a. phosphoric; 2saurer Kalk phosphate of lime (Ca₃[PO₄]₂); 2saures Salz phosphate, basisch 2saures Salz subphosphate, basic phosphate; **=säure** f phosphoric acid (H₃P₃O₄); **=säure-anhydrid** n phosphoric anhydride, phosphorus pentoxide (P₂O₅); **=trichlorid** n phosphorus trichloride, phosphorous chloride (PCl₃); **=wasserstoff** m phosphoretted hydrogen, hydric (or hydrogen) phosphide (PH₃); **=zündhölzchen** n phosphorus (or phosphoric) match.

Photochemie ♫ (f~⌣~⌣') [grch.] f photochemistry. [electric(al).]

photo-electric (f~⌣~⌣~⌣) a. phys.

Photogramm ♫ (f~⌣) [grch.] n ⊕d. (Lichtbild) photograph, bisw.: photogram.

Photograph (f~⌣~f) m photographer.

Photographie (f~⌣~f') [grch. Lichtschrift] f a) Kunst: photography, photographic art; b) Bild: photograph, (photographic) likeness, F photo, in Kabinettformat: cabinet photo(graph); lebende ~n animated photographs or pictures pl.; **~album** n photographic album; **~rahmen** m photograph-frame.

photographieren (f~⌣~⌣~⌣) v/a. to (take a) photograph; sich ♫ (aufnehmen lassen) to have one's photo(graph) taken, to sit for one's photo(graph) or likeness.

photographisch (f~⌣~f) a. photographic(al); 2e Aufnahme taking a photograph; photograph(ic view); vgl. Atelier u. aufnehmen 10.

Photogravüre (f~⌣~w~⌣') [grch.-fr.] f = Heliogravüre. [n ⊕d. photophone.]

Photophon (f~⌣~) [grch. Lichtsprecher]

Phrase (f~⌣) [grch. phrásis] f (Redensart) phrase; leere ~n hollow phrases pl., empty talk or words pl., claptrap.

♪ Musik; ♫ Wissenschaft; ♃ Pflanze; ♀ Geographie; ⊙ Technik; ⚔ Bergbau; ⚔ Militär; ⚓ Marine; ⚖ Handel; ✉ Post; 🚂 Eisenbahn.

phrasenhaft (f⌣⌣) a. ⓺ phraseologic(al); *fig.* meaningless, empty.

Phrasen-held (f⌣...) m ⓶. =**macher** m phrase-monger, great talker, F gasbag; =**macherei** f empty talk, F gasing.

Phraseologie ⚤ (f⌣⌣⌣⌣) [grch.] f ⓸ (Ausdrucksweise) phraseology; **phraseologisch** (f⌣⌣⌣⌣) a. ⓺ phraseologic(al).

Phrenesie ⚤ (f⌣⌣⌣) [grch. *phrēnēsis* v. *phrēn* Zwerchfell, Seele] f ⓸ (Wahnsinn) frenzy. [phrenetic, frantic.)

phrenetisch (f⌣⌣⌣) [grch.] a. ⓺ (wahnsinnig)

Phrenolog ⚤, ~**e** (f⌣⌣⌣(⌣)) [grch.] m ⓶, ⓸ phrenologist; ~**ie** (f⌣⌣⌣⌣) f ⓸ (Schädellehre) phrenology; **Zisch** (f⌣⌣⌣) a. ⓺ phrenologic(al).

Phrygi-en ♀ (f⌣(⌣)⌣) [grch.] *npr/n.* ⓶⓺. Alt., Landschaft in Klein-asien: Phrygia; **Phrygi-er**(in f ⓸) m ⓶, **phrygisch** (f⌣⌣) a. ⓺ Phrygian.

Phthal-säure ⚤ (f⌣⌣⌣) [(Na)phthal(in)] f ⓸ phthalic acid $(C_8H_6O_4)$.

Phylloxera ⚤ (f⌣⌣⌣⌣, bff. als f⌣⌣⌣) [grch.] f ⓺ u. ⓸ ent. = Reblaus.

Phys-harmonika ♪ (f⌣⌣⌣⌣) [grch. Wind-harmonika] f ⓸ harmonium.

Physik (f⌣⌣, ⌣⌣) [grch. *physik*= Natur-] f ⓸ (Naturlehre) physics, natural science.

physikalisch (f⌣⌣⌣⌣) a. ⓺ physical; ⚤ In-strumente philosophical instruments *pl.*; ⚤=**chemisch** a. physico-chemical.

Physikat (f⌣⌣⌣) n ⓓc. medical officer's district or appointment.

Physiker (f⌣⌣⌣) [grch.] m ⓶ (Kenner, Lehrer der Physik) physicist, natural philosopher, student of science; teacher of physics.

Physikum (f⌣⌣⌣) n ⓹ medical student's first examination (in natural science).

Physik-unterricht (f⌣⌣⌣⌣⌣) m ⓶ instruction (or lesson) in physics, science-teaching. [= Kreisarzt.)

Physikus (f⌣⌣⌣) [it., *grch.] m ⓶ⓓ(ⓢ) †]

Physiognom ⚤ (f⌣(⌣)⌣⌣) [grch.] m ⓶ physiognomist; ~**ie** (f⌣(⌣)⌣⌣) f ⓸ (Gesichts-ausdruck) physiognomy, facial expression, countenance; P *phiz*; ~**ik** (f⌣(⌣)⌣⌣) f ⓸ physiognomics; **Zisch** a. ⓺ physiognomic(al), relating to the physiognomy.

Physiolog ⚤, ~**e** (f⌣(⌣)⌣(⌣)) [grch.] m ⓶, ⓸ physiologist; ~**ie** (f⌣(⌣)⌣⌣) f ⓸ (Lehre von den Lebensgesetzen) physiology, **Zisch** (f⌣(⌣)⌣⌣) a. ⓺ physiological.

physisch (f⌣⌣) [grch.] a. ⓺ physical; ⚤ (*adv.*) unmöglich physically impossible.

Phyto-chemie ⚤ (f⌣⌣⌣) f ⓸ (Pflanzenchemie) phytochemistry; **phyto-chemisch** (f⌣⌣⌣) a. ⓺ phytochemical.

Pianino ⚤ (⌣⌣⌣) [it. nur *adv.*] n ⓹ cottage-pianino.

pianissimo ♪ (⌣⌣⌣⌣) [it. sehr leise] *adv.* (*abbr. p.p.*). **Pianissimo** *n.inv.*pianissimo.

Pianist (⌣⌣⌣) [it.] m ⓶, ~**in** f ⓸ (Klavierspieler[in]) pianist, piano-player.

piano ♪ (⌣⌣⌣) [it. leise] **I** *adv.* (*abbr. p.*) *piano*, softly. — **II Piano** n ⓹ (leise gespielte Stelle) *piano*.

Piano(forte) ♪ (⌣⌣⌣(⌣)) [it.] n ⓹ (*a.inv.*) (Art Klavier) piano(forte); ~**sessel** m music-stool; vgl. Fortepiano.

Piano-zug ♪ (⌣⌣⌣) m ⓶ piano pedal.

Piassava ♀ (⌣⌣⌣⌣) [port., *brasil.] f ⓸ (Bahia) bast-palm, coquilla-nut palm (*Attale̅a funi̅fera*); ~**besen** (f"...) m ⓶

piassava (or **piassaba**) **broom**; ~**faser** f piassava (fibre), Bahia bast.

Piaster (⌣⌣⌣) [it.] m ⓶ (ägyptischer etwa 20, türk. 18 Pfg.; span. etwa 4¹/₄ Mart) piastre.

Pichel (⌣⌣) m ⓶ (Geifersahl) bib.

Pich(e)ler (⌣(⌣)⌣) m ⓶ tippler.

picheln F (⌣⌣) *v/n.* (h.) und *v/a.* ⓶ a. to tipple, to imbibe, F to booze.

pichen (⌣⌣) [Pech] *v/a.* u. *v/n.* (h.) ⓼ **1.** ⓹ (mit Pech verschmieren) to pitch, ⚓ to pay. — **2.** (wie Pech kleben) to stick like glue.

Pichler (⌣⌣) m ⓶ s. Picheler.

pick¹ (⌣) [lautm.] *int.* ⚤! pick!, tick!

Pick² (⌣) m ⓓb. e-s Vogels: peck, picking.

Picke ⚤ (⌣⌣) [picken] f ⓸ pick(axe).

Pickel¹ (⌣⌣) m ⓶ **1.** (*pl.* ⌣+ a. ~n ⓺) path. pimple. — **2.** ⚤ = Picke.

Pickel²-flöte ♪ (⌣⌣⌣...) [it.] f ⓶ piccolo; =**haube** k[mhd.Becken-h.]chm.:skull-cap, jetzt: spiked (or infantry-)helmet; =**hering** ⚥ [Pökel-] m: a) pickled herring; b) (Hanswurst) Merry Andrew; clown, chm.=pickle-herring. [full of pimples.)

pick(e)lig (⌣(⌣)⌣) a. ⓺ path. pimpled,)

picken (⌣⌣) [ndd.] *v/a.* und *v/n.* (h.) ⓼ to pick, v. Vögeln a.: to peck.

Pick(e)nick (⌣(⌣)⌣) [ndh.; *fr.] n ⓓd. ⓹ picnic; ein ~ veranstalten to make (or get) up a picnic party.

Pi-edestal (pi-⌣⌣) [fr., it. Fußgestell] n ⓓd. *sculp.*, *arch.* pedestal.

Piek ⚓ (⌣) [Hom. Pik] f [= Pike] f ⓸: a) e-s Schiffes; b) einer Gaffel: peak.

pieken (⌣⌣) *v/a.* ⓼ **1.** ⚓ die Riemen ⚤ (zum Salutieren hoch nehmen) to toss the oars. — **2.** F nordd. = stechen.

Pi-emont ♀ (⌣⌣⌣) [fr. Fuß der Berge] *npr.n.* ⓶⚤. (nord-ital. Landschaft) Piedmont; ~**ese** (⌣⌣⌣⌣) m ⓸, ~**esin** f ⓸, **Zesisch** a. ⓺ Piedmontese.

piep (⌣) *int.* **1.** ⚤! (Schrei der Küchlein) peep! — **2.** (a. **Piep** m ⓓc.) nicht Piep (kein Wörtchen) sagen not to utter a word.

piepen (⌣⌣) [ndh. lautm. wie It. s. Pfeife] *v/n.* (h.) ⓶ von jungen Vögeln: to pipe, to chirp, von Mäusen ꝛc.: to squeak.

Pieper (⌣⌣) m ⓶ *orn.* pipit-(lark) (*Anthus*).

piepicht, piepig, piepisch (⌣⌣) a. ⓺ **1.** ⚤e Stimme piping (or squeaky) voice. — **2.** bsd. **piepig**: (schwächlich) weakly, (kränklich) sickly, puling.

Piep-matz (⌣⌣...) m ⓶, =**mätzchen** n Kindersprache: (Böglein) dicky (bird).

pieps (⌣) = piep; **piepsen** (⌣⌣) *v/n.* (h.) ⓓ = piepen; **piepsig** (⌣⌣) a. ⓺ (schwächlich) peaky, vgl. piepig 2.

Pier nordd. (⌣) [ndd.] m ⓓc. (Wurm) lob-worm (*Areni̅cola mari̅na*).

Pi-eriden (⌣⌣⌣⌣)[grch.]f/*pl.*⚸myth.(Musen) Pierides, Muses *pl.*; **pi-erisch** (⌣⌣⌣) a. ⓺ Pierian, of the Muses. [torment.)

piesacken P (⌣⌣⌣) *v/a.* ⓼ (quälen) to)

Pi-etät (⌣⌣⌣) [it.] f ⓸: a) (Ehrfurcht) reverence; b) (kindliche Liebe) filial love or regard; c) (Frömmigkeit) piety; ⚤(s)=**los** (⌣"...) a. ⓺ without reverence, irreverent; ~(s)=**voll** (⌣⌣⌣) a. ⓺ reverent.

Pi-etismus (⌣⌣⌣⌣) [it.] m ⓶ (Frömmelei) false piety, bigotry, cant(ing).

Pi-etist (⌣⌣⌣) [it.] m ⓶, ~**in** f ⓸ (Eiferin) bigot, devotee, F saint; ~**erei** (⌣⌣⌣⌣) f ⓸ sanctimoniousness, **Zisch** a. ⓺ bigoted, sanctimonious, F saintly.

piff (⌣) [lautm.] *int.* ⚤, **Zpaff!** (Schuß) bang!; ping!

Pigment ⚤ (⌣⌣) [lt.] n ⓓc. = Farbstoff; ~**druck** (⌣⌣...) m ⓶ pigment-printing; ~**fleck** m, *zo.* und ♀ pigment-spot; ~**geschwulst** f, *med.*: ⚤ melanoma; **Zieren** (⌣⌣⌣) *v/a.* (h.) ⓼ to treat with pigment, to colour. [(Bergspitze) peak.)

Pik¹ (⌣; Hom. Piek) [fr. *pic*] m ⓓc. ⓹)

Pik² (⌣) [fr. *pique* f] m ⓓc. (Groll) rancour, bisw.: pique; e-n ~ auf e-n h. to have a grudge (or spite) against a p.

Pik³ (⌣) [fr. *pique* m] n ⓹ (*a.inv.*) (schwarze Farbe des fr. Kartenspiels) spades *pl.*

pikant (⌣⌣) [fr.] **I** a. ⓺ (anziehend, reizend, *ant.* nüchtern) piquant, spicy, F saucy, racy, Kochkunst: highly seasoned or flavoured, hot; (prickelnd) pungent. — **II** das ~**e** n ⓺ piquancy; piquant (or spicy) flavour; pungency. [spades.)

Pik-as (⌣"...) n ⓹, =**dame** f ace, queen of)

Pike (⌣⌣) [fr. *pique* Spieß] f ⓸ a. ⚔ F **1.** pike; *fig.* von der ~ auf dienen to rise (or serve) from the ranks; Offizier, der von der ~ auf gedient hat officer who has served from the ranks, F ranker. — **2.** = Pik².

Pikee (⌣⌣) [fr. *piqué*] m ⓹ (Kattun mit erhabenem Muster) piqué.

Piken-träger (⌣"...) m ⓶ (auch **Pikenier** (⌣⌣⌣⌣) [fr. *piconnier*] m ⓓd.) pike-man.

Pikett (⌣⌣) [fr. *piquet* m] n ⓓc.: a) ⚔ ✝ (Vorposten-estadron) picket; b) Kartenspiel: piquet; ~**pfahl** (⌣⌣⌣) ⚔ m ⓶ picket.

pik-fein (⌣⌣) [ndh.; *ndl.] a. ⓺ very fine or smart or elegant; stylish.

pikieren (⌣⌣⌣) [fr. *piquer*] ⓼ **I** *v/refl.* sich ⚤ (s-e Ehre darein setzen) et. zu tun to make it a point (of honour) to do a th. — **II** *v/a.* (empfindlich berühren) to pique, nettle; **pikiert** (⌣⌣) a. ⓺ nettled, offended.

Pikkolo (⌣⌣⌣)[it. kleiner] m ⓶ **1.** (a. ⓼⓼) = Diener, Kellner. — **2.** (*a.n*) ♪ = Pickelflöte.

pikrin-sauer ⚤ (⌣⌣"...) [grch.] a. ⓺ *chm.* picric; ⚤=**saures Salz** picrate; =**säure** f ⓸ picric acid $(C_6H_3N_3O_7)$.

Pikten (⌣⌣) [ilt.] m/*pl.* ⓸ *hist.* ♀ Picts *pl.*

Pilaster (⌣⌣⌣) [fr.] m ⓶ *arch.* pilaster.

Pilatus (⌣⌣⌣) *npr.m.* ⓶✝. *bibl.* Pontius ~ Pontius Pilate. [~**in** f ⓸ pilgrim.)

Pilger (⌣⌣) [ahd.; *it. *peregrīnus*]m⓶,)

Pilger-fahrt (⌣⌣...) f ⓸ pilgrimage; =**flasche** f pilgrim's gourd-bottle; =**hut** m pilgrim's (chm. a. cockle-)hat; =**kleid** (=**ung** f) n pilgrim's garb or dress; =**leben** n (earthly) pilgrimage.

pilgern (⌣⌣) [Pilger] *v/n.* (h. und sn) ⓶ a. to go (or start) on a pilgrimage.

Pilgerschaft (⌣⌣⌣) f ⓸ pilgrimage.

Pilger-schar (⌣⌣...) f ⓸ host (or party, troop) of pilgrims; =**stab** m pilgrim's staff; =**tasche** f pilgrim's wallet or scrip; =**zug** (a. ⓶) m pilgrim's train.

Pille (⌣⌣) [mhd.; *lt. *pi̅lula*] f ⓸ *pharm.* pill; ~n drehen to make pills; *fig.* das ist e-e bitt(e)re ~ that's a bitter pill (to swallow); eine ~ verzuckern (übergolden) to sugar (to gild) a pill.

Pillen-dose (⌣⌣...) f ⓶ pill-box; =**dreher** m, *co.* (Apothe'ter) pill-monger, -driver; =**farn** ♀ m pillwort, pepper-grass (*Pilu-la̅ria pili̅lifera*); ⚤=**förmig** a. pill-shaped; =**käfer** m, *ent.* pill-beetle (*Byrrhus*); =**kraut** ♀ n pillwort (= =**farn**); =**masse**

Signs (see page XVII): F familiar; P vulgar; ⚑ flash; ⟋ rare; † obsolete (died); * new word (born); ⁺⁺ incorrect; ♪ music;

[Pillennessel] — 763 — [Plage]

pulp from which pills are made, pilular mass; **=nessel** ⚘ f Roman nettle (*Urti'ca piluli'fera*); **=schachtel** f = =dose.
Pilot ⚓ (‿ˊ) [ndl.; fr. *pilote*; *grch.] m ㊷ (Lotse) pilot.
Pilz ⚘ (‿) [ahd.; *lt. *bōlē'tus*] m ①a. mushroom, ⚕ fungus, größerer, mst giftiger: toadstool; (Blätter=)~ agaric; in die ~e geh(e)n: a) to go mushroom-gathering or -picking; b) F *fig.* (verloren gehen) to get lost, to go to the dogs; (sich davon m.) to run off; sie wachsen wie ~e aus der Erde they grow (or shoot) up like mushrooms.
pilz=ähnlich (ˊ‿…), ≈artig *a.* ㊻ mushroom-like, ⚕ fungous, fungoid, mycelioid; ≈förmig *a.:* ⚕ fungiform.
pilzhaft ⚘, **pilzicht** ⚘, mst **pilzig** (ˊ‿) *a.* ㊻ = pilzähnlich.
Pilz=hut ⚘(ˊ…)m㊷:⚕pileus; **=kenner** m: ⚕ fungologist; **=spore** f fungus-spore.
Piment (‿ˊ) [port.; *lt. *pigme'ntum*] m, n ㊶c., ~=**pfeffer** m ㊷ pimento, allspice.
Pimpelei F (‿‿ˊ) f ㊺ 1. (Klägerei) lamentations *pl.* — 2. (Verweichlichung) coddling (ways *pl.*), pampering; effeminacy.
Pimpel=fritz(e) F (ˊ‿‿) m ㊷ =(**liese** f) sickly (or delicate) fellow (woman, girl).
pimp(e)lig F (ˊ‿(‿)) *a.* ㊻ (kränklich) sickly, peaky; (weichlich) delicate, effeminate.
pimpeln F (ˊ‿) v/n. (h.) ㊸ *a.* to be sickly or peaky or delicate or weakly.
Pimpernell (‿‿ˊ) [Pimpinelle] m ①d. burnet (*Pote'rium*); ~=**wurzel** f ㊷ great burnet-saxifrage (*Pimpine'lla magna*).
Pimper=nuß (ˊ‿…) f ㊷, =**nuß=baum** m bladder-nut (tree) (*Staphylae'a*).
Pimpinelle ⚘ (‿‿ˊ) [fr.] f ㊸ = Pimpernell.
pimplig (ˊ‿) *a.* ㊻ s. pimpelig. [nell.]
Pinakothek ⚕ (‿‿‿ˊ) [grch.] f ㊺ picture-gallery, pinacotheca. [boat.]
Pinasse ⚓ (‿ˊ) [fr.] f ㊸ pinnace, long-
pindarisch (ˊ‿‿) [Pindar, grch. Lyriker 522 bis 448 v. Chr.] *a.* ㊻ Pindaric.
Pinguin (‿‿ˊ) [ft. Fett=…] m ①d. *orn.* (Fettgans) penguin (*Apteno'dytes*).
Pini-e ⚘ (ˊ(‿)‿) [it.] f ㊸ 1. (Baum) nut-, stone-pine (*Pinus Pi'nea*). — 2. (Pignole) pine-kernel. [=**zapfen** m pine-cone.]
Pinien=nuß (ˊ‿(‿)…) f ㊷ = Pinie 2.
pink (ˊ) [lautm.] *int.* ≈ ≈! ting! ting!; ping! ping! [od. Würfelspiel) stake.]
Pinke (ˊ‿) [pink] f ㊸ (Einsatz beim Hasard=)
pinken (ˊ‿) [lautm.] v/n. (h.) ㊸ 1. ⊕ (schmieden) to forge (on an anvil). — 2. to sing like a finch.
Pink=salz (ˊ‿) n ㊷ *chm.* (Ammoniumzinnchlorid) pink salt (Sn Cl$_4$ + 2 NH$_4$ Cl).
Pinne ⊕ (ˊ‿) f ㊸ [ndb.; als *lt. *pinna*] (Zwecke) peg; (spitzer Stift) tack, (Zapfen) tenon, pivot; ⚓ ~ des Kompasses: centre-pin; ⚓ ~ des Steuerruders: tiller.
pinnen (ˊ‿) v/a. ㊸ to pin (fast), to fasten (or fix) with pegs or tacks.
Pinscher ⚬ (ˊ‿) [engl.] m ㊷ *zo.* Hundeart: kind of fox-terrier, (fr.) griffon.
Pinsel[1] (ˊ‿) [mhd.: pencil; *lt.] m ㊷ 1. Malerei, Tüncherei c.: (artist's or painter's) brush, feinerer, zum Tuschen c., *a.* (hair-)pencil. — 2. (Haarbüschel bei Tieren) tuft of hair, eines Wales: pizzle.
Pinsel[2] (ˊ‿) [ndb. Pinn=suhle = Schuster =ahle] F *fig.* (Einfalts=)~ dunce, duffer, simpleton, F ninny, flat, juggins.

Pinselei (‿‿ˊ) f ㊺ 1. (schlechte Malerei) daub(ing). — 2. F *fig.* (Eselei) stupid act.
Pins(e)ler (ˊ‿(‿)) m ㊷, ~**in** f ㊵ 1. ⊖ brush-maker. — 2. (Farbenkleckser) dauber, F knight of the brush.
pinsel[1]=**förmig** (ˊ‿…) *a.* ㊻: brush- (or pencil-) shaped, ⚕ penicillated, penicilliform; **=führung** f ㊶ *paint.* handling of the brush, (manner of) laying on the colours, touch (of the brush).
pinselhaft, pinselig F (ˊ‿‿) [Pinsel[2]] *a.* ㊻ like a dunce, stupid, foolish.
pinseln ⊕ (ˊ‿) [Pinsel[1]] v/n. (h.) u. v/a. ㊸ a. to handle (or to touch up with) the brush; to paint, oft *b.s.* to daub, to plash; sich (*dat.*) den Hals ≈ to paint one's throat.
Pinsel[1]=**stiel** (ˊ‿…) m ㊷, =**stock** m brush-handle, handle of the brush; *vgl.* =**führung**; =**strich** m, *paint.* stroke of the brush; *vgl.* =**führung**; =**trog** ⊕ m, *paint.* pot for washing the brushes (in).
Pinsler(in) (ˊ‿(‿)) s. Pinseler(in).
Pinzette (vᴀ-ᵦˊ‿, ‿‿ˊ) [fr.] f ㊸ (feine Zange) pincette; *typ.*, &c. nippers, pincers *pl.*
Pionier (‿‿ˊ) [fr. *pionnier*] m ①d. ⚔ engineer, (Schanzgräber) sapper; *fig.* pioneer. [pipe, butt; *a.* = Faßhahn.]
Pipe[1] ⚓ (ˊ‿) [span.] f ㊸ (großes Faß)
Pipe[2] (ˊ‿) f ㊸ nordd. = (Tabaks=)Pfeife.
Piperin ⚕ (‿‿ˊ) [lt. *Pfeffer=*] n ①d. *chm.* piperin(e) (C$_{17}$H$_{19}$NO$_2$).
Pippau ⚘ (ˊ‿) [slaw.] m ㊶ = Feste 4.
Pips (ˊ) [ndb. (ahd.): pip; *lt. *pitui'ta* Schleim] m ①a. (Krankheit der Vögel) pip; v. fränklichen Personen: er hat einen ~ weg he has a weak (or sickly) constitution; *vgl.* piepsig; **pipsig** (ˊ‿) *a.* ㊻ having (or suffering from) the pip.
Piqu… s. Pif…
Pirat (‿ˊ) [grch.] m ㊷ = Seeräuber.
Pirä-us ⚓ (‿ˊ‿) [it., *grch.] *npr./m.* ⑯γ. alter Hafen von Athen: (the) Piræus.
Piroge ⚓ (‿ˊ‿) [karibisch] f ㊸ (schmales Boot) pirogue, Indian canoe.
Pirol (‿ˊ, ˊ‿) [lautm. ob. *grch. feuerfarben] m ①d. ㊵ *orn.* (golden) oriole (*Ori'olus*).
Pirsch (ˊ) [alt=fr.] f ㊺ *hunt.* (Beschleichen des Rotwildes) deer-stalking; auf die ~ gehen, **pirschen** (ˊ‿) v/a. u. v/n. (h.) ㊸ to go deer-stalking or -shooting.
Pirsch=gang (ˊ…) m㊷ stalking; **=gerechtigkeit** f shooting-licence; **=jäger** m deer-stalker; **=pulver** n fowling-powder.
Pisang ⚘ (ˊ‿) [malai.] m ①d. ㊵ plantain, banana-tree (*Musa*); Frucht: plantain, banana, tum-tum; ~=**fresser** (ˊ‿,‿ˊ‿) m ㊷ *orn.* plantain-eater.
pisch (ˊ) *int.* ≈! hush!, 'sh! (= pst).
Pisé-bau ⊕ (‿ˊ‿) [fr.] m ①b. (Lehmstampfbau) pisé, coffer-work.
Pisolith ⚕ (‿‿ˊ) [grch. Erbsenstein] m ①c. ㊷ *min.* peastone, ⚕ pisolite. [whisper.]
pispern (ˊ‿) [lautm.] v/n. (h.) ㊸ a. to
Pisse P (ˊ‿) [ndb.] f ㊸ urine; ≈**n** v/n. (h.) to piddle, piss; *vgl.* harnen.
Pissoir (‿ˊ) [fr. †] n ①d. ㊸ urinal, urinary, anständiger: lavatory.
Piß=topf (ˊ…) m ㊷ = Nachtgeschirr; =**winkel** m unanständig: pissing-place, anständiger: urinal, lavatory.
Pistazi-e ⚘ (‿ˊ‿(‿)) [grch., *pers.] f ㊸ 1. (Frucht) pistachio(-nut). — 2. echte ~ pistacia, pistachio-tree (*Pista'cia vera*).

Pistazi-en=baum (‿ˊ(‿)‿…) m ㊷ = Pistazie 2; =**grün** ⚘ n pistachio-green; =**holz** n pistacia-wood; =**mandel, =nuß** f = Pistazie 1.
Pistill (‿ˊ) [it.] n ①d.: a) des Mörsers: pestle; b) ⚘ (=Stempel) ⚕ pistil.
Pistol (‿ˊ) [fr.] n ①d. = Pistole[1].
Pistole[1] (‿ˊ‿) [fr.; *Pistoja ⚘ it. St.] f ㊸ (Waffe) pistol; e-m die ~ auf die Brust setzen to put a pistol (or a revolver) to a p.'s head, *fig. a.* to force a p. by (violent) threats; sich auf ~n schlagen to fight (a duel) with pistols; *fig.* wie aus der ~ geschossen like a flash of lightning, F (off) like a shot; point-blank.
Pistole[2] (‿ˊ‿) [fr., span.] f ㊸ (ältere span. Goldmünze, etwa 15 M.) pistole.
Pistolen=duell (‿ˊ…) = [Pistole[1]] m ㊷ duel (fought) with pistols; =**forderung** f challenge to (fight) a duel with pistols; =**griff** m butt-end of a pistol; =**holfter** m pistol-case (at the saddle-bow), holster; =**lauf** m barrel of a pistol; =**schuß, =schütze** m pistol-shot; e-n ~ schuß weit within pistol-shot; =**stand** m pistol-gallery.
Piston ⊕ (‿ˊ) [fr.] n (m) ㊶ 1. ⊕ (Kolbenstange) piston-rod. — 2. ♪ (bff. Kornett) cornet (à pistons); ~=**bläser** (‿ˊ‿‿) m ㊷ cornet(t)ist, cornet-player.
Pita-faser ⚘ (ˊ‿‿‿) f ㊸ (als Zwirn 2c. gebraucht) pita(-flax or -fibre or -hemp) (von *Aga've america'na*). [soaking wet.]
pitsch=naß F (ˊ‿ˊ) *a.* ㊻ wet through,
pittoresk (‿‿ˊ) [it.] *a.* ㊻ (malerisch) picturesque. [Drehpunkt) pivot.]
Pivot ⚔ (ˊ=vo') [fr.] m u. ⊕ (Zapfen,
placieren (‿ˊ‿‿) [fr. stellen, setzen] v/a. ㊸: e-n ≈ to place a p., to find a situation (or berth) for a p.
Plack(en)[1] (ˊ‿) [ndb.] m ㊷ ①b.㉓ 1. (Fleck) spot. — 2. (Flicken) patch. — 3. (ebene Fläche) plain (surface).
placken[2] (ˊ‿) [plagen] v/a. ㊸ to harass; e-n ≈ und plagen to torment (or worry) a p., to ill-use (or maltreat) a p.; das Volk ≈ (bedrücken) to oppress …; (mißhandeln) to maltreat; *a.* v/refl. sich ≈ (und plagen) to work very hard, to (be a) drudge, to slave.
placken[3] (ˊ‿) v/a. ㊸ 1. an die Wand ≈ (kleben) to stick (or attach) to the wall; (verkleiben) to line. — 2. (fest stampfen) to flatten (or beat, stamp) down.
Placker (ˊ‿) [placken[2]] m ㊷ tormentor, oppressor, F nigger-driver; ~**ei** (‿‿ˊ) f ㊺ harassing; oppression, petty tyranny; (Erpressung) exaction, extortion; (Beschwerde) trouble, toil.
plackern ⚔ (ˊ‿) v/n. (h.) (einzelne Schüsse abfeuern) to take random shots.
plädieren (‿ˊ‿‿) [fr. *plaider*] v/n. (h.) ㊸ (als Verteidiger auftreten) to plead a cause, to act as counsel (for the defence).
Plafond (‿ˊ) [fr.] m ㊶ (Zimmerdecke) ceiling, (fr.) plafond.
Plage (ˊ‿) [ahd. plague; *lt. *plāga* Schlag] f ㊸ 1. torment, vexation, annoyance, bother; (quälende Sorge) harassing care, worry; Sprichw. jeder hat seine eig(e)ne ~ we all have our troubles; *bibl.* es ist genug, daß ein jeglicher Tag seine eigene ~ habe sufficient unto the

⚕ scientific; ⚘ botanical; ⚓ geography; ⊕ machinery; ⚒ mining; ⚔ military; ⚓ marine; ⚬ commercial; ✉ postal; 🚂 railway.

[**Plagegeist**] — 764 — [**platt**]

day is the evil thereof. — 2. (beschwerendes Übel) nuisance, grievance; (Land=)~ plague, calamity, pest.

Plag(e)=geist (⁻⌣...) m ⓺ mischievous spirit; von Personen: tormentor, bore, pest; ?los a. ⓺ free from vexation.

plagen (⌣⌣) [mhd.; *Plage] v/a. u. sich ⁀ v/refl. ⓺ to torment, vex, annoy, bother, durch Necken: to tease, mit Bitten ɜc.: to importune, to pester (vgl. placken²); sich sehr ⁀ (abarbeiten) to work very hard or F like a nigger, F to fag; von der Gicht geplagt troubled (or afflicted) with the gout.　[fiend.]

Plage=teufel (⁻⌣⌣⌣) m ⓺ tormenting)

Plagge ⓞ (⌣⌣) [ndd.] f ⓽ agr. (Rasenstück) sod (of turf); ⅋n v/a. ⓼⓼ to take up turf.

Plagiar (⌣⌣¹) m ⓸d., ~ius (⌣⌣⌣⌣) [lt.] m ⓶ (schriftstellerischer Dieb, Abschreiber) plagiarist; **Plagiat** (⌣⌣¹) [lt.] n ⓸c. (schriftstellerischer Diebstahl) plagiarism; ein ~ begeh(e)n to plagiarize.

Plagiator (⌣⌣¹⌣⌣) m ⓶ = Plagiar.

Plakat (⌣⁻) [dtsch (*placken³)=lt.] n ⓸c. placard (= Anschlag 4); ~=anzeiger m advertising sheet; ~=säule f = Anschlagsäule; ~=schrift f. typ. poster-type; ~=wagen m advertising van.

plakieren ⓞ (⌣¹⌣) [fr.] v/a. ⓼ (mit Gold od. Silber plattieren, belegen) to (overlay with) plate; **plakiert** plated.

Plan¹ (¹) [fr.] m ⓸c. 1. plan; (Absicht) design, intention; (Vorhaben) project, scheme (vgl. durchkreuzen 2, entwerfen 2); es war im ~ it was planned or proposed. — 2. (genaue Karte): a) ⨯ topographical map; b) plan of a town, harbour, fort, &c.

Plan² (¹) [mhd.: plain; *lt. plānum n] m ⓸c. (Ebene) (open) plain, level ground; (Lichtung im Walde) glade; (Kampfplatz) arena, battle-field.

plan³ (¹) [lt.] a. ⓺ (eben) plain, level; fig. straightforward; (einfach) simple.

Plane ⓞ (¹⌣) [Blahe] f ⓽: ~ über e-m Wagen (a. ⅋) tilt, awning, geteert: tarpaulin.

Pläne=macher (⁻⌣⌣⌣) = Planmacher.

planen (¹⌣) [Plan¹] v/n. (h.) u. v/a. ⓼⓼ to plan, to scheme; (planmäßig entwerfen) to project, to scheme, heimlich: to plot; ⨯ geplanter Angriff (well-)planned attack; was ⁀ Sie für morgen? what are your intentions (or plans) for tomorrow?; sorgfältig geplant carefully thought (or worked) out.

Planet ⚹ (⌣¹) [grch. Wandel(stern)] m ⓶ ast. planet, kleiner: planetoid, asteroid.

planetarisch ⚹ (⌣⌣⁻⌣) a. ⓺ planetary.

Planetarium ⚹ (⌣⌣⁻¹⌣) [lt.] n ⓶ (die Planetenbewegung darstellendes Kunstwerk) planetarium, ehm.: orrery.

Planeten=bahn ⚹ (⌣⁻⌣...) f ⓹ ast. orbit of a planet; =jahr n, =karte f planetary year, chart; =lauf m, ast. course of a planet; =rad n ⓞ planet-wheel; =raum m planetary space; =stand m position of planets, astrol. aspect (of planets); =system n, ast. planetary system.

Planeto=ide ⚹ (⌣⌣⌣¹⌣) [grch.] m ⓶ ast. (Pt. Planet)planetoid, asteroid, small planet.

plan¹=gemäß (⁻⌣¹) a. ⓺ = planmäßig.

Planier=amboß ⓞ (⌣⁻¹⌣⌣) m ⓶ planishing-stake, flattening-anvil.

planieren ⓞ (⌣¹⌣) [fr.] v/a. ⓼ 1. bei Erdarbeiten: (ebenen) to level. — 2. metall. getriebene Gegenstände ⁀ (schlichten) to planish. — 3. Buchbinderei: (Druckbogen durch Leimwasser ziehen) to size the sheets.

Planierer ⓞ (⌣¹⌣) m ⓶ Wegebau: leveller; Buchbinderei: sizer.

Planier=hammer ⓞ (⌣¹⌣...) m ⓶ planishing-stake, -hammer; =kessel m Buchbind.: size-copper or -kettle; =kolben m der Klempner ɜc.: planisher; =kreuz n, =presse f Buchbinderei: size-cross, -press.

Plani=glob ⚹ (⌣¹¹) [lt.] m ⓶, ~ium (⌣¹⌣⌣) n ⓶ planisphere.

Plani=metrie ⚹ (⌣⌣¹¹) [lt.=grch.] f ⓽ (Flächenlehre) planimetry, mehr gebr.: plane geometry.

plani=metrisch ⚹ (⌣⌣⁻⌣) a. ⓺ planimetric(al), of plane geometry.

Plan¹=kammer ⨯ (⌣⁻⌣) f ⓽ (room containing the) stock of military maps.

Planke (⌣⌣) [mhd.: plank; *mlt. planca] f ⓽ plank, (thick) board.

Plänkelei ⨯ (⌣⌣¹) f ⓽ skirmish(ing).

Plänk(e)ler ⨯ (⌣(⌣)⌣) m ⓶ skirmisher, scout.　[⓽a. to skirmish (a. fig.).]

plänkeln ⨯ (⌣⌣⌣) [vgl. plackern] v/n. (h.))

planken ⓞ (⌣⌣) v/n. (h.) ⓼⓼ to plank, board.

Planken=gang ⚓ (⌣⌣⌣...) m ⓶ strake, -streak; =gerüst n ⓼ scaffolding; =werk n boarding; =zaun m boarding, wooden fence, Bauwesen: boarding.

Plänkler ɜc. f. Plänkeler ɜc.

plan²=konkav, ⁀konvex (⁻...) a. ⓺ opt. plano-concave, -convex.

Plankung (⌣⌣) f ⓽ planking.

plan¹=los (⁻...) a. ⓺ without a fixed plan or purpose; desultory, (aufs Geratewohl) at random; =losigkeit f ⓽ lack of a (regular) plan; desultoriness; =macher m ⓶ schemer, projector; =macherei f ⓽ scheming, projecting; ⁀mäßig a. systematic, (well-)planned methodical; =mäßigkeit f methodicalness; systematical arrangement.

planschen F (⌣⌣) v/n. (h.) u. v/a. ⓴ to splash, paddle.　[paddling.]

Planscherei (⌣⌣⁻¹) f ⓽ splashing,)

Plan²=spiegel (⁻¹⌣⌣) m ⓶ opt. plane mirror.　[plantation.)

Plantage (⌣¹ᴳ⌣) [fr. m] f ⓽ (Pflanzung))

plantschen = planschen.

Planum ⛯, ⨯ (¹⌣) [lt.] n ⓾ bei Erdarbeiten: (Oberfläche) surface of the formation.

plan¹=voll (⁻¹⁻) a. ⓺ carefully planned.

Plan⁴=wagen (⁻¹...) [Plane] m ⓶ covered van, tilt-wagon; =zeichnen n designing (of maps), field-sketching; =zeichner(in f) m designer.

Plapperei F (⌣⌣¹¹) f ⓽ chatter(ing), babble, prattle, silly talk, F mag.

Plapp(e)rer (⌣(⌣)⌣) m ⓶, **Plapperin** (⌣⌣⌣) f ⓸⓻ babbler, prattler.

plapperhaft F (⌣⌣⌣) a. ⓺ garrulous, loquacious; voluble; ~igkeit (⌣⌣⌣⌣) f ⓽ garrulity, loquacity; volubility.

Plapper=maul F (⌣⌣...) n ⓶, =mäulchen (⌣⌣⌣) n chatterbox, babbler, prattler.

plappern F (⌣⌣) [lautm.] I v/n. (h.) und v/a. ⓽a. (gedankenlos schwatzen) to chat, chatter, babble, prattle, jabber, gabble. — II ~ n ⓶ = Plapperei.

Plapper=tasche F (⌣⌣...) = Plappermaul.

Plapperer(in f). Plapperer, Plapperin.

plärren F (⌣⌣) [mhd. lautm.] v/n. (h.) und v/a. ⓼ to pule, flennend: F to snivel, blubber, singend: to bawl (out), predigend: to rant; (herleiern) to rattle off.

Pläsier F (⌣¹) [fr. plaisir m Vergnügen] n ⓸d. pleasure; ~chen (⌣⌣) n ⓸⓻: Sprichw. jedes Tierchen hat sein ~chen, etwa: each little beast has its (own) little feast.　[able, delightful.)

pläsierlich (⌣¹⌣) a. ⓺ amusing, enjoy-)

Plastik (¹⌣) [grch.] f ⓺ (Bildhauerkunst) plastic art.

plastisch (⌣⌣) a. ⓺ (bildsam) plastic.

Plastizität (⌣⌣⌣¹) f ⓽ plasticity.

Platä=er (⌣¹⌣) m ⓶, ⁀in f ⓽ Platæan, (inhabitant) of Platææ or Platæa.

Platane ⚹ (⌣¹⌣) [grch.] f ⓽ plane(-tree) (Pla'tanus); abendländische ~ Occidental plane-tree, North American sycamore (Pt. occidenta'lis); morgenländische ~ Oriental plane-tree, chenar (Pt. orienta'lis).

Plateau (⌣¹ᵗᵒ) [fr. m] n ⓹⓺ (Hochebene) plateau, table-land, elevated-plain.

Platin (⌣¹, ¹⌣) [span. plati'no m „Silber-"] n ⓸d., ~a (¹⌣⌣) n ⓸⓻ chm. (edles, seltenes Metall) platinum, platina (Pt).

Platin=blase (⌣...) f ⓽ für Schwefelsäuredestillation: platinum retort; =blech n platinum foil; =chlorid n platinic chloride (PtCl₄); =chlorür n platinous chloride (PtCl₂); =draht m platinum wire; =druck m, phot. platinotype.

Platine (⌣¹⌣) [fr.] f ⓽ Weberei: (Hebehaken für die Kettenfäden) lifting-wire, lifter; Strumpfwirkerei: sinker, plate.

Platin=feuerzeug ⓞ n ⓶ Doebereiner's lamp; =haltig a. ⓺ platiniferous.

platinier/en (⌣⌣¹¹) [Platti'n] I v/a. ⓽ to platinize, to coat with platinum. — II ~ n ⓶ u. ⁀ung f ⓽ platinization.

Platin=oxyd (⌣⌣¹..., ¹⌣...) n ⓶ chm. platinic oxide (PtO₂); =schwamm m spongy platinum, pl.-sponge; =schwarz n, chm. pl.-black or -mohr; =tiegel m platinum crucible; =zink=element n, elect. Grove's element or cell; =zündmaschine f = feuerzeug.

Platoniker (⌣¹⌣⌣) [Plato, grch. Philosoph, 427—347 v. Chr.] m ⓶ follower of Plato, Platonic philosopher, Platonist, Platonizer; **platonisch** (⌣¹⌣) a. ⓺ Platonic; ⁀e Liebe Platonic love; ~es System Platonism.

platsch (⌣) [lautm., vgl. platzen, plan(t)schen] int. (s)plash!, plump!, flop!; **platschen** (⌣⌣) v/n. (h.) ⓴ to (s)plash, F to (fall) plump into the water.

plätschern (⌣⌣) [platschen] v/n. (h.) ⓽a. v. fließendem Wasser: to ripple, murmur, plash; gegen das Ufer ⁀ to wash (against) the shore; von Personen: im Wasser ⁀ to paddle (or splash about) in the water; die ⁀den Wellen poet. the murmuring (or babbling) waves pl.

platt (⌣) [ndd.; fr. plat] a. ⓺ 1. (flach) flat, (eben) level, even; (gleichförmig eben) unbroken, plain; (abgeplattet) flattened (out), (eingedrückt) depressed, (niedrig) low; ⁀ drücken, machen, schlagen to flatten (out); sich ⁀ (adv.) auf den Bauch (od. den Boden) legen to lie down flat on the ground or F on one's belly; auf der ⁀en Erde liegen to lie on the bare ground. — 2. fig. das ⁀e (reine) Gegenteil quite (or just) the contrary or opposite; die ⁀e Wahrheit

[plättbar] — 765 — [Pleite]

the plain truth; (abgeschmackt) flat, stale, insipid; adv. 2 (gerade) heraus sagen to speak out plainly or F straight, to tell frankly; et. 2 abschlagen to refuse a th. flatly. — 3. sprachlich: a) = plattdeutsch; 2e Sprache, auch Platt ⊙ = Plattdeutsch; b) von nichtdeutschen Sprachen: dialectal, provincial, im Englischen: broad.

plättbar ⊙ (ˇ-) *a.* ⓜ metall. (streckbar) laminable; **~keit** *f* ⑯ laminability.

Plätt-bolzen ⊙ (ˇ..) [plätten] *m* ⑫ = Bolzen 3; **=brett** *n* ironing-board; (dürr) wie ein ~ (as) flat as a board.

Plättchen (ˇ⌣) *n* ㉓ (dim.: Platte) **1.** (little or thin) plate. — **2.** ♀ *u. zo.*: ⊘ lamella. — **3.** arch. (Leistchen) list(el), fillet.

Platt-decke (ˇ...) *f* ⑫ arch. plain ceiling; **2deutsch** *a.* ⓜ *u.* **-deutsch(e)** *n* ㊹ (ant. hochdeutsch) Low German.

Platte [mhd.: plate; *platt] *f* ⑯ **1.** = Glatze. — **2.** (nackte Stelle) bare place or spot; (Waldblöße) glade; ↓ (Bank) sand-bank. — **3.** (Blatt, Blech) plate, dünne: sheet, foil, aus Schiefer, Stein, Holz ꝛc.: slab; (Fliese) flag, (Kachel) tile; *phot.* (photographic) plate, *typ.* (stereotype-)plate; *arch.* (zur Wandbekleidung) abacus; (Säulen-)~ plinth. — **4.** (Präsentierteller) tray, waiter; salver.

Plätte (ˇ⌣) *f* ㊽: a) (Plätten der Wäsche) ironing; b) = Plätt-eisen.

Platteis (ˇ-)[ndl.; *mlt. platessa] *m* ⓐ.

Platteise (ˇ⌣) *f* ⑯ *ichth.* = Plattfisch.

Plätt-eisen ⊙ (ˇ-ˇ-) *n* ⑫ flat-iron, smoothing-iron.

platten, plätten[1] (ˇ⌣) [platt] *v/a.* ⓾ **1.** auch *v/refl.* (sich) 2 to flatten. — **2.** (ebenen) to level.

plätten[2] (ˇ⌣) [platt] *v/a.* ⓾ **1.** (Wäsche) 2 (bügeln) to iron (linen). — **2.** ⊙ *metall.* to laminate, plate. — **3. ~n** ㉓ flattening, &c. (f. 1); ⊙ *metall.* lamination.

Platten-abzug ⊙ (ˇ⌣...) [Platte] *m* ⑫ *typ.* stereotype(d) proof; **=druck** *m, typ.* stereotype-printing; **=formerei** *f, metall.* plate-moulding; ⊘ **förmig** *a.* plated, ⊘ laminiform; **=halter** *m, phot.* plate-holder or -vise; **=kiel** ↓ *m* plate-keel; **=korrektur** *f, typ.* stereo(type)-correction, correction of stereotype; **=kultur** *f* Bakteriologie: plate-culture; **=panzer(ung)**, **=rüstung** ⚔ *f* plate-armour; **=schrift** *f* stereotype. [ironer.]

Plätter ⊙ (ˇ⌣) *m* ⑫, **~in** *f* ㊹ der Wäsche:

Platt-erbse ♀ (ˇ⌣ˇ) *f* ⑫ chickling (pea or vetch) (*La'thyrus*).

platter-dings (ˇ⌣ˇ) [platt u. Ding] *adv.* absolutely, decidedly, flatly; 2 nicht by no means; 2 unmöglich utterly (or altogether, absolutely) impossible.

Plätterei (ˇ⌣ˇ) *f* ⑯ ironing.

Plätterin (ˇ⌣⌣) *f* ㊹ f. Plätter.

Platt-fisch (ˇ...) *m* ⑫ *ichth.* flat fish, ⊘ pleuronectid; **=form** [fr. *plate-forme*] *f, arch.* platform, flat roof.

Plätt-frau (ˇ⌣ˇ) *f* ⑯ ironer.

Platt-fuß (ˇ...) *m* ⑫: a) flat foot, b) (Sohle) sole of the foot; **füßig** *a.* ⓜ flat-footed.

Plattheit (ˇ-) *f* ⑯ **1.** (f. platt) flatness, geistig *a.* staleness, insipidity. — **2.** (einfältige Rede) platitude, trivial remark.

platt-hufig (ˇˇˇ-) *a.* ⓜ *zo.* flat-hoofed.

plattier/en ⊙ (⌣ˇ⌣) **I** *v/a.* ⓼ Kupferblech ꝛc. 2 (mit Gold od. Silber überziehen) to plate; p/tes Geschirr, p/te Waren plate(d goods *pl.*), electro-plate. — **II ~n** ㉓ plating.

Plattierer ⊙ (⌣ˇ⌣) *m* ⑫ plater, plategilder; *galvanisch*: ~ electro-plater.

Plattierung (⌣ˇ⌣) *f* ㊻ plating. [table.]

Plättisch(⊙ˇ)[Plätt=tisch]*m*ⓐ.ironing-

Platt-kopf (ˇˇ) *m* ⑫ flat-head.

Platt-menage (ˇ⌣...) [(⌣+) *fr.*] *f* ⑫ cruetstand; **=mönch** *m, orn.* black cap (*Sy'lvia atricapi'lla*); **=nase** *f* flat nose; **2nasig** *a.* ⓜ flat-nosed, ⊘ platyrhine, platyrhinian. [the irons.)

Plätt-ofen (ˇ⌣ˇ⌣)*m* ⑫ stove for heating)

Platt-schiene (ˇ...) *f* ⑫ plate-rail; **=schmeißen** ↓ *v/a.* 2 werfen; **=schote** ♀ *f* flat pea (*Platylo'bium*); **2schwänzig** *a.* ⓜ *zo.*: ⊘ platurous. [iron.)

Plätt-stahl (ˇ-ˇ) *m* ⑫ heater (of a flat-)

Platt-stich ⊙ (ˇ...) *m* ⑫ Näherei: broad stitch; **=stickerei** *f* flat (or plain) embroidery; **=stück** *n, carp.* capping-piece or -plate.

Plätt-tisch (ˇ...) *m* ⑫ f. Plättisch; **=tuch, Plättuch** *n* ironing-blanket or -cloth; **=wäsche** *f* fine linen that has to be ironed or which requires ironing.

platt-weg (ˇ...) *adv.* flatly, roundly, downright; 2werfen ↓ *v/a.*: die Riemen 2 to feather the oars; **=würmer** *m/pl.* flatworms, ⊘ plat(y)helminthes *pl.*; **=ziegel** ⊙ *m* flat tile.

Platz[1] (ˇ) [mhd.: place; *grch. platei'a f*] *m* ⓐ. **1.** (Ort, Stelle) place, (Fleck) spot; (Lage) site, locality; (Raum) room, space; freier ~ (public) square; *thea.* reservierte Plätze reserved seats *pl.*; ⚔ fester, befestigter ~ fortified place, fortress. — **2.** Redensarten: einem ~ machen to make room (or to clear the way) for a p.; nehmen Sie ~! take a seat, be seated, (will you) sit down!; es ist kein ~ (mehr) there is no room (left) or no vacancy; am (un)rechten ~e sein to be in the right (wrong) place; ⚔ auf dem ~e bleiben (fallen) to fall (or perish) in battle; *thea.* &c. Plätze nehmen to book seats.— **3.** *fig.* a(n f-)m ~e sein to be in one's (or in the right) place; nicht am ~e out of place; am ~e sein to be opportune; immer auf dem ~e (gerüstet, bereit) sein to be always ready or handy, F to be game for anything; f-n ~ behaupten to stand one's ground; ~ greifen (Wurzel fassen) to take root or effect, (eintreten, stattfinden) to take place, to come to pass; beides hat bei mir ~ both apply to me. — **4.** ✱ (Stadt) auf Ihrem ~e in your town or city; am ~e on the spot.

Platz[2] obd. (ˇ) [mhd.: *tschech. u. poln. Fladen] *m* ⓐ. (raisin-)cake.

platz[3] (ˇ) [lautm.] *int.* crash!, smash!

Platz[1]-**adjutant** (ˇ⌣...) ⚔ *m* town-adjutant; **=angst** *f* v. Nervenkranken: dread of open spaces, ⊘ agoraphobia; **=bedarf** ✱ *m* local wants *pl.*

Plätzchen[1] (ˇ⌣) *n* ㉓ small space or seat, snug (little) place.

Plätzchen[2] (ˇ⌣) *n* ㉓ *pharm.* lozenge.

platzen (ˇ⌣) [mhd. lautm.; vgl. plauz] *v/n.* ⓾ **I 1.** (h.) (krachen) to crack, to crash, vom Feuer: to crackle; es regnet, daß es platzt it is pouring in torrents. — **2.** (sn): a) to burst = bersten **I**; die geplatzte Bombe the exploded bomb; b) (plötzlich hervorkommen) to burst forth, to rush out; mit et. hervor od. heraus 2 (nicht länger zurückhalten können) to blurt out a th.; *fig.* wenn die Geister auf-ea. 2 when (hostile) spirits clash, in the conflict of opinions. — **II ~ n** ㉓ **3.** = bersten **II**; *med.* auch: rupture.

plätzen (ˇ⌣) *v/a. u. v/n.* (h.) ⓾ **1.** (knallend schießen) to pop; (ohnmächtig schlagen) to smack. — **2.** *for.* Bäume 2 (anlaschen) to blaze …

Platz[1]-**furcht** (ˇ...) *f* ⑫ = angst; **=geschäft** ✱ *n* local business; **=karte** 🚂 *f* ticket for a reserved seat; **=kommandant** ⚔ *m* commandant; **=major** [fr.] ⚔ *m* major in command of a town; **=patrone** ⚔ *f* blank cartridge; **=regen** [ndl.] *m* heavy shower, pelting (or torrential) rain, F downpour; **=reisende(r)** ✱ *m* town-traveller; **=stoß** *m* Fußball: place-kick; **=verkauf** ✱ *m* sale on the spot; **=wechsel** *m*: a) change of place; ✱ local bill.

Plauderei (⌣-ˇ) *f* ㊽: (gemütliche) ~ (cosy) chat; geistlose: prattling, tittle-tattle, small talk; (Klatscherei) gossip(ing).

Plaud(e)rer (ˇ(⌣)⌣) *m* ⑫, **Plauderin** (ˇ⌣-ˇ) *f* ㊹ chatterer, prattler; mst *b.s.* gossip, babbler, nur *b.s.* scandalmonger.

plauderhaft (ˇ⌣-ˇ) *a.* ⓜ fond of a chat or of prattling or F magging; talkative, garrulous; **~igkeit** (ˇ⌣⌣⌣-) *f* ㊽ talkativeness, garrulity.

Plauder-hans (ˇ⌣ˇ) *m* ⑫ = tasche.

Plauderin (ˇ⌣⌣) *f.* Plaud(e)rer ꝛc.

Plauder-liese *f.*=matz *m,* =maul *n* = tasche.

plaudern (ˇ⌣-) [mhd. lautm.] **I** *v/n.* (h.) *u. v/a.* ⓐ. a. to chat, chatter, prattle, prate; to have a chat, F to mag; mst *b.s.* to gossip, babble, blab; aus der Schule 2 to tell tales out of school. — **II** *v/a. u. v/refl.* mit Angabe der Wirkung: e-m die Ohren von et. voll 2 to drub a th. into a p.'s ears; sich müde 2 to weary o.s. with gossiping or prattling. — **III ~ n** ㉓ = Plauderei.

Plauder-ort (ˇ⌣...) *m* ⑫ cosy corner; **=stübchen** *n* cosy room; **=stündchen** *n* hour for a nice chat; (an hour's) chat; **=tasche** *f* chatterbox, prattler, gossip.

Plaudrer(in *f*) *m* (ˇ(⌣)⌣) *f.* Plaud(e)rer ꝛc.

plauschen (ˇ⌣) [mhd.] *v/n.* (h.) ⓾ bayr.-öst. = plaudern.

plausibel (⌣-ˇ) [fr.] *a.* ⓜ (D9) (einleuchtend) plausible; 2 m. to make plausible, to give colour (or support) to.

plauz (ˇ) *int.* smash!, flop!, bang!

Plauze P(ˇ⌣) [poln. *pluca*] *f* ㊽ = Bauch.

Plebejer (⌣-ˇ⌣) [it.] *m* ⑫, **~in** *f* ㊹ röm. *Alt.*: (*ant.* Patrizier[in]) plebeian; **~tum** (-ˇ⌣) *n* ㉘ d.: a) (all) the plebeians *pl.*, the populace; b) plebeian order or estate, plebeianism; **plebejisch** *a.* ⓜ plebeian, (gemein) low, vulgar.

Plebiszit (⌣⌣-ˇ) [it. *plebi-scit…*] *n* ㉘ (Volksabstimmung) (general) plebiscite, röm. *Alt.*: plebiscitum.

Plebs (ˇ) [lt.] *f* ⑱, *m* ⓐ. (o. *pl.*) bsd. röm. *Alt.*: plebs; weit.: (Pöbel) rabble, mob.

Pleite F (ˇ-ˇ) [jüd. Flucht] *f* ㊽ = bank(e)rott **I** u. **II**; ~ m., 2 geh(e)n to go bankrupt, to fail (in business).

[Pleitegeier] — 766 — [Pocke]

Pleite-geier (⸗′⸍‚⸍) [corr. (P) ndd. Pleitegeher] m: F co. der ~ krächzte über dem Unternehmen misfortune dogged (or bank-ruptcy ruined) the enterprise.
Plejade(n pl.) (-′⸍) [grch.] npr/f. ⑱ myth. u. ast. Pleiad, pl. a. Pleiades.
Plempe F (⸍⸣) f ⑱ **1.** (Degen) sword. — 2. a. ~l m ⑫ (schwaches Gesöff) slops, swipes pl., water bewitched.
plempern F (⸍⸣) v/n. (h.) und v/a. ⑭a. 1. im Wasser ⚲ to splash in the water; (herumlungern) to lounge about. — 2. (tneipen) to tipple, F to booze.
Plenar-sitzung (-′‚⸍⸍) f ⑫ (Vollversammlung) full sitting or session, ⊕ general meeting of shareholders.
Plenum (⸍⸣) [lt.] n ㊿ (Gesamtheit) totality (or entire body) of (the) members; jur. in pleno in full session or court.
Pleonasmus ⚙ (⸣‿⸍⸣) [grch.] m ㉗ rhet. (Wort-überfluß) pleonasm.
pleonastisch (-⸍⸣) [grch.] a. ⑥ pleonastic.
Plethi (′-) s. Krethi.
Pleuel-stange = Bleuelstange.
Pleuresie (-⸣⸍) [grch.] /⑱, **Pleuritis** (-′⸍) f, inv. path. (Brustfell-entzündung) pleurisy.
plieren (′⸍) v/n. (h.) ⑧ nordd. to peer.
Plinius (′⸣⸣) npr/m. ⑯ γ. röm. Alt.: ~ der Ältere († 79 n. Chr.) Pliny the Elder; ~ der Jüngere († um 114 n. Chr.) Pliny the Younger.
plinkern (⸍⸣) v/n. (h.) ⑭a. nordd. to blink; mit den Augen ⚲ to blink one's eyes.
Plinse (⸍) [russ. blin(ec)] f ⑱ Kocht.: pancake filled with jam.
Plinthe (⸍⸣) [grch. plinthos Ziegel] f ⑱ arch. (Platte unter den Säulen) plinth.
Pliozän ⚙ (-⸣‚⸍′) [grch.] n ⑭d. geol. (jüngere tertiäre Stufe) Pliocene.
Plissee ⊕ (⸣⸍) [fr. plissé m gefältelt] n ㊿ pleating, kilting.
Plombe (⸍⸣) [‚+. fr.] f ⑱: a) ⊕ (Bleisiegel) lead(en seal); b) Zahnheilkunde: stopping (or filling) of a decaying tooth; stoppage.
plombieren (⸣⸍⸣) [fr.] v/a. ⑬: a) Zollwesen: to affix a lead to, to lead goods; b) Zahnheilkunde: to stop (or plug) a tooth.
Plongier-schuß ⚔ (pl⚙-G⸢⸍′) [fr.] m ⑫ plunging fire. [(Leucis̀cus ru′tilus).]
Plötze (⸍⸣) [poln. ploć] f ⑧ ichth. roach)
plötzlich (⸍⸣) [mhd.; lautm. vgl. *plauz!] a. ⑥ sudden, (blitzschnell) instantaneous, (un-erwartet) unexpected, unforeseen; adv. a. all of a sudden; (schroff) abruptly, offhand(ishly).
Plötzlichkeit (⸍⸣-) f ⑱ suddenness.
Pluder-hose(n pl.) (⸍‚⸍⸣) [pludern sich aufblähen, schlottern] f ⑱ wide (a. sailor's) breeches pl. [eiderdown quilt.)
Plumeau (plü-mo′) [fr.] n ⑨ (Federbedbett))
plump (′) [ndd.] a. ⑥ coarse, blunt, (schwerfällig) clumsy, heavy, unwieldy, awkward, F lumpy; fig. vom Stile: ponderous. [Seerose) water-lily.)
Plumpe (⸍⸣) f ⑱ a = Pumpe; b) ⚲ (weiße)
plumpen (⸍⸣) v/n. (su) ⑨ = plumpsen.
Plump-heit (′-) f ⑱ (s. plump) coarseness, clumsiness; fig. ponderousness.
plumps (′) I int. plump!, thump!, flop!, bang! — II ~ m ⑭a. heavy fall, thud, thump(ing noise).
Plump-sack (′⸍⸣) m ⑫: a) in Schülerspielen: knotted handkerchief; dreh dich nicht um, der ~ geht rum! don't

turn about, the knot's going round!; b) fig. clumsy fellow.
plumpsen (⸍⸣) v/n. (h. u. su) ⑩ to fall with a heavy thud or thump, to plop.
Plum-pudding ┬ (′⸣⸣‚⸍) [engl.] m ⑭d. (㊿) (Kloß mit Rosinen) plum-pudding.
Plunder (⸍⸣) [ndd.] m ⑫ lumber, F sticks (of furniture) pl.; (Lumpen) rags, castoff clothes pl.; (Bettel) (old) rubbish, trumpery stuff.
Plünderei (⸍⸣⸣) f ⑱ bsd. ⊕ plundering, pillaging, sacking, der Nachzügler: marauding; (Raub) depredation, spoliation.
Plünd(e)rer (⸣⸍⸣) m ⑫, **Plünd(r)erin** f ㊿ pillager, (Nachzügler) marauder; depredator, despoiler.
Plunder-kammer (⸍⸣‚...) f ⑫ lumber-room; =kasten m, =kiste f chest with old clothes or lumber; =kram m = Plunder; =mann, =matz F m rag- (and-bone) man; =markt m rag-fair.
plündern (⸍⸣) [ndd.: plunder; *ndl.] I v/a. u. v/n. (h.) ⑭a. to plunder; e-n Reisenden: to rob (or strip) a traveller, to rifle a p.'s pocket, eine Stadt, meist ⚔.: to pillage, sack, loot; einen Baum, Bienenstock ⚲c. ⚲ to strip (or despoil) ...; fig. beim Kartenspiel wurde er förmlich geplündert at cards he was regularly fleeced or bled or robbed. — II ~ n ⑤⚲ und **Plünderung** f ㊿ plundering, &c. (s. I); vgl. Plünderei; der ~ preisgeben to give up to pillage, to allow to be sacked or looted.
Plünderungs-sucht (⸍⸣⸣⸣...) f ⑫ eagerness to plunder, rapacity; =süchtig a. ⑥ bent on pillage, rapacious.
Plündrer ⚲c. s. Plünderer.
Plural (′-, auch: -′) [lt.] m ⑭d. gram. (Mehrzahl) plural (number).
Plural-bildung (⸍...) f ⑫, =endung f formation, termination of the plural.
Pluraletantum ⚙ (-′⸣⸣⸍′) [lt.] n ㊿ (pl. a. Pluralia'ntum) gram. word used in the plural only.
Pluralis (′⸍⸣) m ⑬ = Plural. [plural.)
pluralisch (′⸍⸣) [lt.] a. ⑥ (in the))
Pluralismus ⚙ (-⸣⸍⸣) [lt.] m ⑫ (Gemeinsinn) pluralism, public spirit.
Pluralität (-⸣⸣′) [lt.] f ⑱ plurality.
plus (′) [lt. ′] I adv. math., zB. 6 2 4 (meist gspr.: 6 + 4) six plus four. — II **Plus** n, inv. Rechenkunst: ein Plus (=zeichen: +) a plus (mark); Geldwesen: (Überschuß) surplus.
Plus-betrag (⸍⸣‚⸍) m ⑫ surplus.
Plüsch ⊕ (′) [fr. peluche f] m ⑭a. (pl. ⊕ ~arten) Weberei: plush.
plüsch-artig (⸣‚′⸍) a. ⑥ plush-like, plushy, shaggy.
plüschen (⸍⸣) a. ⑥ (of) plush.
Plüsch-kragen (′..., ⸍..) m ⑫ für Damen plush cape; =sofa n plush sofa; =teppich m velvet-pile carpet, in Engl. bsd. Wilton or Axminster carpet.
Plus-macher(ei f) m (⸍...) ⑫ maker of (making up) a fictitious surplus.
Plusquamperfekt(um) (⸣‿⸍⸣(′)) [lt.] n ⑭c.(⑨) gram. (Vorvergangenheit) pluperfect, past perfect.
plust(e)rig nordd. (⸣(⸣)⸣) a. ⑥ (bauschig) baggy, (gedunsen) puffed out.
Plus-vorgabe (n pl.) (′...) f ⑫ Tennis: received odds pl.; =zeichen n s. plus II.

Plutarch (-′) npr/m. ⑮⑯α. (grch. Geschichtschreiber, 1. Jahrh. n. Chr.) Plutarch; ~s Biographien Plutarch's Lives pl.
Plutokratie ⚙ (-⸣⸣′) [grch.] f ⑱ (Herrschaft der Reichen) plutocracy.
plutonisch ⚙ (-′⸍⸣) [grch.]; *Pluto, Gott der Unterwelt] a. ⑥ bsd. geol. (durch Feuer gebildet) Plutonic, ...ian.
Plutonismus ⚙ (--⸣⸍) [lt.] m ⑫ (Lehre von der Bildung der Felsen durch vulkanische Tätigkeit; ant. Neptunismus) geol. Plutonism, Plutonic theory.
Plutonist ⚙ (--′⸍) [lt.] m ⑫ Plutonist.
Pneumatik ⚙ [grch. pneuma Hauch] f ⑱ phys. 1. (-′⸍) (Lehre vom Druck der Flüssigkeiten) pneumatics. 2. ~ (=reifen) m (-⸣′) am Fahrrad ⚲c.: pneumatic (tyre).
pneumatisch ⚙ (-′⸍) [grch.] a. ⑥ pneumatic; chm. Se Wanne (zum Auffangen von Gasen unter Wasser ⚲c.) pneumatic trough.
Po ♀ (′) [it.] npr/m. ⑯α. the (river) Po; diesseits (jenseits) des Po Cispadane (Transpadane).
Pöbel (′⸣) [mhd.: people; *fr. peuple Volk] m ⑫ common (or low) people, populace, rabble; ~ei (-⸣′) f ⑱ vulgar doings or ways pl. [beian.)
pöbelhaft (′⸣⸣) a. ⑥ vulgar, low, plebeian.
Pöbelhaftigkeit (′⸣⸣⸣-) f ⑱ vulgarity, lowness, plebeian character.
Pöbel-haufe (′⸣‚...) m ⑫ (vulgar) mob; =herrschaft f ochlocracy, F mobocracy; =justiz f bsd. Am. lynch law; =sprache f vulgar (or low) language; =wort n vulgarism, low (or slang) word.
Poch (′ch) [pochen] m ⑭c. 1. (Klopfen) knock, rap. — 2. = Pochspiel.
Poch-brett (′ch...) n ⑭ scoring-board for the „Pochspiel" (s. ds); =eisen ⚒ n stamp-head(ing), bucking-iron.
pochen (′ch⸣) [mhd.: poke] I v/n. (h.) u. v/a. ⑱ **1.** to knock, to rap, v. Herzen: to beat, to throb; lärmend: to make a rattling noise, stampfend: to stamp one's feet, hämmernd: to thump. — 2. ⊕ (hämmern) to pound, to batter; ⚒ Erz ⚲ (zerstampfen) to stamp (or break) ore. — 3. auf et. ⚲ (sich stützen) to rely on a th.; (stolz sein) to boast (or brag) of a th., to presume on a th.; auf sein gutes Recht ⚲ to stand on one's rights. — 4. (s. Pochspiel) to play poker. — II ~ n ⑤ 5. = klopfen III. — 6. (s. 2) ⊕ pounding; ⚒ stamping. — 7. (s. 3) reliance; presumption.
Pocher (′ch⸣) m ⑫ **1.** one who knocks (or raps) at the door, &c.. — 2. (Prahler) boaster, braggart. — 3. im Pochspiele: (3 ob. 4 gleiche Karten) poker. — 4. a) ⊕ Arbeiter: pounder; b) ⚒ = Poch-hammer, =werk.
Pocherei (′ch⸣′) f ⑱ (s. pochen) 1. repeated knocking. — 2. loud boasting.
Poch-erz ⚒ (′ch...) n ⑭ ore ready for stamping, in Goldminen: battery-stone; =hammer m: a) ore-hammer; b) = =mühle; =mehl n stamped ore; =mühle f stamping-mill; =satz m battery of stamps, stamp-battery; =schlamm m, =schlick m wet slick, slime; =schuh m stamping-shoe; =spiel n Kartenspiel, bsd. Am. poker; =stempel ⚒ m stamp(ing-bar); =stempel-batteri'e f = =satz; =werk n pounding-machine; vgl. =hammer.
Pocke (⸍⸣) [ndd.] f ⑱ = Blatter.

Signs (see page XVII): F familiar; P vulgar; ⚡ flash; ⚲ rare; † obsolete (died); * new word (born); ⚛ incorrect; ♪ music;

[pockenartig] — 767 — [Pollen]

pocken-artig (ᴗ...) *a.* resembling (the) smallpox, variolous, ...oid; ♀ u. *ent.* 2 genartet: variolate; **-gift** *n* virus of (the) smallpox, vaccine (variolous) virus; **-grube** *f* pockmark; **-impfung** *f* = Blattern-impfung; ♀**krank** *a.* ill with (or suffering from the) smallpox; **-kranke[r]** *m* *f* smallpox patient; **-krankheit** *f* smallpox, *vet.* der Schweine: measles *pl.*; **-lymphe** *f*: variolo-vaccine; **-narbe** *f* pockmark; ♀**narbig** *a.* pock-marked, pitted with (the) smallpox. [(= Guajakholz).]
Pock-holz ♀ *u.* ⊕ (ᵉ,ᵋ) *n* ②*a.* pockwood/
pockicht, pockig (ᴗ) *a.* 1. = blatternarbig. — 2. = pocken-artig.
Podagra (¹ᴗᴗ) [grch. ᴗᴗ] *n* ⑤ *path.* gout in the feet (= Fußgicht).
podagrisch (ᴗ¹ᴗ) *a.* *path.* gouty.
Podagrist (ᴗᴗ¹) *m* ② gouty patient.
Podest ⊕ (ᴗ¹) [grch.] *m* u. *n* ②*a.* *arch.* (Treppen-absatz) landing (of a staircase).
Podex (¹ᴗ) [lt.] *m* ①⑤*a.* (Gesäß) posterior.
Podium (¹(ᴗ)ᴗ) [lt.] *n* ② podium; auch = Bühne 2. [poem.)
Po-em (ᴗ¹) [lt., *grch.] *n* ⑤*d.* (Gedicht)/
Po-esie (ᴗᴗ¹) [lt., *grch.] *f* ⑤ (ant. Prosa): a) poetry (= Dichtkunst); b) poem, piece of poetry (= Dichtung, Gedicht).
po-esie-los (ᴗᴗ¹ᴗ) *a.* without poetry, unpoetical, prosy, matter-of-fact.
Po-et (ᴗ¹) [lt., *grch.] *m* ②, **~in** *f* ④⑦ poet(ess *f*) (= Dichter[in]).
Po-etaster *F* (ᴗᴗ¹ᴗ) *m* ② = Dichterling.
Po-et(ast)erei (ᴗ-(ᴗ)ᴗ¹) *f* ④⑥ (dabbling in) poetry; rhyming, versifying.
Po-etik (ᴗ¹ᴗ) [lt., *grch.] *f* ④⑥ poetics, art (or theory) of poetry.
po-etisch (ᴗ¹ᴗ) [lt., *grch.] *a.* poetic(al), *adv.* poetically, in poetic form; eine Le Ader haben to have a poetic vein or a turn for poetry.
Pogge *provc.* (ᴗ) [ndd.] *f* ⑥ (Frosch) frog.
Point (pēā̊) [fr. Punkt] *m* ⑤ Kartenspiel: (Stich, Auge) point; die **~s** anschreiben to score the points (made); bei Prüfungen: mark; die vollen **~s** bekommen to obtain full marks; ⚔ **~** zum Einrichten bei der Parade: field-colours *pl.*
Pointe (pēā̊´-t̊) [fr.] *f* ④⑧: **~** (Spitze) eines Witzes ꝛc. point (or pith) of a joke, ꝛc.
pointieren¹ (pēā̊-) [Pointe] *v/a.* ⑧: e-n Witz ꝛc. ⚓ to bring to a point, to give poignancy (or piquancy) to.
pointieren² (pēā̊´¹ᴗ) [Point] *v/n.* (h.) ⑧ Kartenspiel: (setzen) to punt.
Pokal (ᴗ¹) [nhd., (+.)it.; *grch.] *m* ②*d.* (Humpen) goblet, gefüllter: bumper.
Pökel (¹ᴗ) [ndd.] *m* ② Kocht.: pickle, brine.
Pökel-faß (¹ᴗ...) *n* ⑥ pickling-, salting-tub; **-fleisch** *n* salt-meat; vgl. **-rindfleisch**; **-hering** *m* smoked herring, bloater.
pökeln (¹ᴗ) *v/a.* ⓑa. to pickle, to salt.
Pökel-rindfleisch (¹ᴗ...) *n* ⑥ salt beef; corned beef; **-schweinefleisch** *n* pickled pork; brawn.
pokulieren (-ᴗ¹ᴗ) [lt.] *v/n.* (h.) ⑧ (bechern) to drink freely, to carouse, F to booze.
Pol¹ (¹) [grch.] *m* ⓓd. pole; *elect.* positiver **~** positive pole, anode; negativer **~** negative pole, cathode.
Pol² ⊕ (¹) *m* ⓹⓪ = Pole².
Polack (¹ᴗ, ᴗ¹) [poln.] *m* ④⑧, **~e** (ᴗ¹ᴗ) *f* ④⑥ *b.s.* für Pole: Pole.

Polackei (ᴗᴗ¹) *f, inv., contp.* für Polen: Poland; Polen aus der **~** (HEINE), etwa: true-born Poles *pl.*
polar (ᴗ¹) *a.* *ast., math.* polar.
Polar-bär (ᴗ¹ᴗ¹) *m* ④⑦ polar bear.
Polare (ᴗ¹ᴗ) [Pol¹] *f* ⑧ *math.*: **~** e-s Punktes in Bezug auf eine Kurve: polar.
Polar-eis (ᴗ¹ᴗ...) *n* ⑥ polar ice; **-expedition** *f*, **-fahrt** *f* polar expedition; **-fuchs** *m,* zo. arctic fox (*Vulpes lago'pus*); **-gegend** *f* polar region.
Polarisation (ᴗ-ᴗᴗ-¹) [lt.] *f* ⑥ *phys.* (Licht-, Strahlen-drehung) polarization; **~s-ebene** *f* ⑧ plane of polarization; **~s-winkel** *m* polarizing angle.
Polarisator (ᴗ-ᴗ¹ᴗ) *m* polarizer. [able.)
polarisierbar (ᴗ-ᴗ¹ᴗ) *a.* ⑥ *opt.* polariz-/
polarisieren (ᴗ-ᴗ¹ᴗ) I *v/a.* ⑧ *phys.* to polarize. — II **~** *n* ② und **Polarisierung** *f* ⑥ = Polarisation.
Polariskop (ᴗ-ᴗ¹) [grch.] *n* ⓒ. *opt.* polariscope, polarimeter. [polarity.)
Polarität (ᴗ-ᴗ¹) [lt.] *f* ⑥ *phys.*/
Polar-kreis (ᴗ¹ᴗ...) *m* ② polar circle; **-licht** *n* = Nordlicht; **-meer** ♀ *n*: Nördliches (Südliches) **~** Arctic (Antarctic) Ocean; **-stern** *m,* *ast.* polar star, *poet.* auch: lodestar, polaris; **-strömung** *f* polar current; **-zone** *f* frigid zone.
Polder (¹ᴗ) [ndl.] *m* ② (eingedämmte Niederung; *ant.* Helder) polder, land reclaimed from the sea.
Pol²-draht ⊕ (¹ᴗ¹) *n* ⑥② pile-wire.
Pole¹ (¹ᴗ) [Polen²] *m* ④, **Polin** *f* ⑥ Pole, seltener: Polander.
Pole² ⊕ (¹ᴗ) [fr. *poil*] *f* ⑧ Weberei: 1. v. Samt, Tuch; pile, nap. — 2. am Webstuhl: bar.
Polei ♀ (-¹) [ahd.: poly; lt. *pule'ium n* Flohkraut] *m* (*n*) ⓒc., *f* ⑥ pennyroyal (*Mentha pule'gium*).
Polemik (ᴗ¹ᴗ) [grch.] *f* ⑥ (Fehde) polemics, controversy, schriftstellerische: literary feud; **~er** (ᴗ¹ᴗᴗ) *m* ② controversialist; **polemisch** (ᴗ¹ᴗ) *a.* ⑥ polemic(al); **polemisieren** (ᴗᴗ-¹ᴗ) *v/n.* (h.) ⑧ to carry on a controversy with a *p.*
polen ⊕ (¹ᴗ) *v/a.* ⑧ *metall.* das Kupfer ♀ (mit saftiger Holzstange umrühren) to pole (or toughen) copper.
Polen² ♀ (¹ᴗ) [slaw. Feld] *npr/n.* ②*a.* Poland; Sprichw. noch ist **~** nicht verloren still there is hope (for Poland).
Polen-aufstand (¹ᴗ,¹ᴗ) [Pole¹] *m* ② Polish rising.
Pol¹-ende (¹,¹ᴗ) *n* ② *elect.* einer galvanischen Kette: ⊕ electrode. [Poland.)
Polen-land (¹ᴗ...) *n*, **-reich** *n* [Pole¹]/
Polentum (¹ᴗᴗ) *n* ⓓd. Polonism.
Pol¹-höhe (¹,¹ᴗ) *f* ⑥ *ast.* altitude (or elevation) of the pole, latitude.
Police ♀ (-¹ᵇᴗ) [fr.] *f* ⑥ (Versicherungs-schein) (insurance-)policy; Inhaber e-r **~** policy-holder.
Policinello (ᴗᴗᴗ¹ᴗ) [it. Däumling] *m* ⑤ u. ⑦ Punch(inello).
Polier ⊕ (ᴗ¹) [corr. aus Parlierer] *m* ⓓd. (Obergeselle) foreman. [bench.)
Polier-bank ⊕ (ᴗ¹ᴗ¹) *f* ⑥② polishing-/
polierbar (ᴗ¹ᴗᴗ) *a.* ⑥ polishable.
Polier-bürste (ᴗ¹ᴗ...) *f* ⑥② polishing-brush; **-eisen** *n* = **-stahl**.
polieren (ᴗ¹ᴗ) [lt.] *v/a.* ⑧ to polish, to burnish (blank *m.*) to furbish (up) (glätten) to smooth; (sichten) to planish.

Polierer (ᴗ¹ᴗᴗ) *m* ②, **~in** *f* ⑥ 1 (French-) polisher, burnisher. — 2 = Polier.
Polier-feile ⊕ (ᴗ¹ᴗ..) *f* ⑥② polishing- (or smoothing-)file; **-hammer** *m* pol.-hammer; **-kunst** *f* art of polishing; **-lappen** *m* polishing-rag; **-maschine** *f* polishing- (or burnishing-)machine; **-pulver** *n,* **-scheibe** *f* pol.-powder, -wheel; **-stahl** *m* polishing- (or burnishing-)steel, burnishing-stick, burnisher; **-stein** *m,* **-wachs** *n,* **-zahn** *m* polishing-stone, -wax, -tooth.
Poliklinik (ᴗ¹¹ᴗ, ᴗᴗ¹ᴗ) [grch. Stadt-kl.] *f* ⑥ *med.* clinical hospital; ambulatory clinic.
Polin (¹ᴗ) *f* ④ s. Pole¹.
Politik (ᴗᴗ¹) [grch.] *f* ⑥ politics, (Welt-klugheit) policy; über **~** sprechen to talk politics; **~er** (ᴗ¹ᴗᴗ) *m* ② politician; **~us** *F* (ᴗ¹ᴗᴗ) *m* ⑥ (Schlaukopf) sly-boots, clever dodger.
politisch (ᴗ¹ᴗ) *a.* ⑥ political (a. *fig.*): Ler Flüchtling political refugee; Ler Verbrecher political offender.
politisieren (ᴗ-ᴗ¹ᴗ) I *v/n.*(h.) ⑧ to discuss (or debate, talk) politics. — II **~** *n* ② political discussion or argument.
Politur (ᴗᴗ¹) [fr.] *f* ⑥ 1. ⊕: a) (durch Polieren bewirkter Glanz) polish, gloss, lustre; b) Tischlerei: (Firnis) varnish, French polish. — 2. *fig.* (feine Lebensart) polish(ed manners *pl.*), refinement.
Polizei (ᴗᴗ¹) [fr.; *grch. *politei'a* Staat] *f* ⑥ police (auch Behörde und ihr Lokal).
Polizei-agent (ᴗᴗ¹ᴗ...) *m* ② police-agent; **-amt** *n* pol.-station; **-aufsicht** *f* pol. supervision; **-beamte(r)** *m* police-officer; **-behörde** *f* police (authorities *pl.*); **-diener** *m* policeman, (police-)constable, F bobby, P copper; **-gefängnis** *n,* **-gewahrsam** *m,* *n, f* pol.-cell, lock-up; **-gericht** *n* pol.-court; **-kommissar, ...är** *m,* **-leutnant** *m* inspector of police.
polizeilich (ᴗᴗ¹ᴗ) *a.* ⑥ of (or issued by, referring to) the police, unter Ler Aufsicht under police supervision; 2 (*adv.*) einschreiten to cause intervention of the police.
Polizei-minister (ᴗᴗ¹ᴗ...) *m* ② in Engl. etwa: Home Secretary; **-ordnung** *f* police regulations *pl.*; **-präsident** *m* in England: Chief (Commissioner) of the Police; **-richter** *m* pol. magistrate; **-sache** *f* pol. affair; **-spion, -spitzel** *m*: a) pol.-spy; b) = Geheimpolizist; **-staat** *m* state ruled by the police; **-stunde** *f* closing-hour for licensed houses; **-truppe** ⚔ *f* bsd. in überseeischen Kolonien: military police-force; **-vergehen** *n* offence against police regulations; **-verordnung** *f* police regulation(s *pl.*); **-wache** *f* = -amt; **-wacht-meister** *m* police-sergeant; **-wesen** *n* pol.-department; 2**widrig** *a.* ⑥ contrary to police regulations; **-wirtschaft** *f* doings *pl.* of the police.
Polizist (ᴗᴗ¹) *m* ② policeman; vgl. Polizeidiener; **~** in Zivil plain-clothes man; vgl. Geheimpolizist.
Polizze ♀ (ᴗ¹ᴗ) [it.] *f* ⑥ öft. = Police.
Polka (¹ᴗ) [tschech.] *f* ⑥ polka (a. ♪); **~** tanzen to dance a polka.
Pol²-kette ⊕ (¹,¹ᴗ) *f* pile-warp. [pollen.)
Pollen ♀ (¹ᴗ) [lt.] *m* u. *n* ② (Blütenstaub)/

scientific; ♀ botanical; ♀ geography; ⊕ machinery; ⚒ mining; ⚔ military; ⚓ marine; ⓪ commercial; ✉ postal; 🚂 railway

Poller ⊥ (⏑⏑) *m* ㉒ zum Festmachen der Taue: bollard, im Walfischboot: billet head.
Poll-mehl ⏑ (⎯⏑) *n* ㉖ (mittelfeines Weizenmehl) middle-fine wheat-flour.
Pollux (⏑⏑) *npr/m. inv.* f. Kastor¹.
polnisch (⏑⏑, *a.* ⎯⏑) *a.* ⑥⑥ Polish; die ²e Sprache, das ~(e) *n* ⑥⑦ the P. language, Polish; *hist.* der ²e Reichstag the Polish Diet. *fig.* the reign of confusion; *fig.* ²e (unordentliche) Wirtschaft a disorderly household.
Polonäse (⏑⎯⏑⎯) [fr.] *f* ㊽ (Tanz) polonaise. ❦ [m.] to Polonize.⟩
polonisieren (⏑⎯⏑⎯⏑) [fr.] *v/a.* ⑬ (polnisch)
Pol¹-schuh ⊙ (″...) *m* ㉒ *tel.* pole-piece; **=spannung** *f. elect.* polar tension.
Polster (⏑⏑) [ahd.: bolster] *n* (*m*) ② 1. (Füllhaar) stuffing for chairs, &c.; (Wattierung) pad(ding); ⚥ (Blattkissen): ⏑ pulvinus. — 2. stuffed seat, e-s Sofas: squab; (Unterlage für das Kopfkissen) bolster; (Fußkissen) hassock, cushion.
Polster-bank ⊙ (⏑⏑...) *f* ㉒ rout-seat; **=bett** *n* divan, ottoman; **=förmig** *a.* cushion-like, ⚥: ⏑ pulviniform. *arch.*: ⏑ pulvinate(d); **=macher(in** *f*) *m* ① upholsterer; **=möbel** *n/pl.* upholstered (articles *pl.* of) furniture.
polstern ⊙ (⏑⏑) *v/a.* ⑭a. to stuff (or upholster) chairs, &c.; (wattieren) to pad.
Polster-sessel (⏑⏑...) *m* ㉒, **=stuhl** *m* stuffed chair.
Polsterung (⏑⏑⏑) *f* ㊻: a) stuffing of chairs, &c.; b) upholstery.
Polter-abend (⏑⏑⏑) [poltern] *m* ㉒ in Deutschland: eve of the wedding.
Polterer (⏑⏑⏑) *m* ㉒ blustering (or noisy) fellow, ill-tempered man.
Polter-geist (⏑⏑⏑) *m* ㉒: a) = Polterer; b) (Kobold) hobgoblin; **=kammer** *f* = Plunderkammer.
poltern (⏑⏑) [Völler] I *v/n.* (h. u. sn) und *v/a.* ⑭a. 1. (h.): a) to make a (loud and) rumbling noise, von Personen auch: to make a disturbance, F to kick up a row; b) an der Tür (hämmern) to rap hard (or to give a loud knock) at the door; c) (spuken) es poltert in der Kammer there are ghosts (or goblins) in the room; d) (heftig schreien und zanken) to bluster and storm. — 2. (sn) to come rumbling along. — II ~ *n* ㉓ 3. rumbling noise; bluster(ing).
polyandrisch ⏑ (⏑⏑⏑) [grch.] *a.* ⑥⑥ (vielmännig: mit mehr als 10 Staubfäden) polyandrian.
polychrom ⏑ (⏑⎯⏑) [grch. vielfarbig] *a.* ⑥⑥ polychrome; **~ie** ⏑ ⊙ (⏑⏑⎯⏑) *f* ㊽ (Bemalen mit bunten Farben) polychromy.
Polyeder ⏑ (⏑⎯⏑⏑) [grch.] *n* ㉓ *math.* (Vielflach) polyhedron.
Polygamia ⏑ ⚥ (⏑⏑⎯⏑⏑) [grch.] *f* ㊾ (23. Klasse nach Linné) polygamia.
Polygamie ⏑ ⚥ (⏑⏑⎯⎯) [grch.] *f* ㊽ = Polygamy; **polygamisch** (⏑⏑⏑⏑) *a.* ⑥⑥ (vielehig) polygamous; ⚥ mit Zwitterblüten neben eingeschlechtigen: polygamian; ²e Pflanze polygam.
Polyglotte ⏑ (⏑⏑⎯⏑) [grch.] *f* ㊽ (Werk in mehreren Sprachen) polyglot work; **~n-bibel** (″...) *f* ㉒ polyglot bible.
Polygon ⏑ (⏑⏑⎯) [grch.] *n* ⑪d. *math.* (Viel-eck) polygon (auch ⚔ *frt.*).

Polygonal-zahl ⏑ (⏑⏑⎯″⎯) *f* ⑫ *math.* polygonal number.
Polyhistor ⏑ (⏑⏑⎯⏑) [grch.] *m* ㉑(⑭) (Vielwisser) polyhistor, all-round scholar.
Poly(hy)mnia ⏑ (⏑(⏑)⎯⏑⏑) [grch.] *npr/f.* ㉛㊻ *myth.* (Muse der Lyrik) Polyhymnia.
polymer ⏑ (⏑⏑⎯) [grch.] *a.* ⑥⑥ *chm.* polymeric; **~ie** (⏑⏑⎯⎯) *f* ㊽ (gleiche chem. Zssg bei ungleichen Äquivalenten) polymerism.
Polynesi-en ⚥ (⏑⏑⎯⏑(⏑)⏑) [grch.] *npr/n.* ㉓α. (die australischen Inseln) Polynesia; **Polynesi-er(in** *f*) *m* ㉒, **polynesisch** (⏑⏑⎯⏑⏑) *a.* ⑥⑥ Polynesian.
Polynom ⏑ (⏑⏑⎯) [grch.] *n* ⑪d. *math.* (vielgliedrige Größe) polynome; ²isch (⏑⏑⎯⏑) *a.* ⑥⑥ polynomial; ²ischer Satz polynomial theorem.
Polyp (⏑⎯) [grch. Vielfuß] *m* ㊷ 1. ⏑ *zo.* polyp, polypus, fossiler: polypite. — 2. ⏑ *path.* polypus, fleshy (or rank, spongy) excrescence or growth. — 3. *bursch.* = Polizist od. Pedell.
Polypen-arm ⏑ (⏑⎯⏑...) *m* ㉒ *zo.* arm of a polyp(us); **²artig** *a.* ⑥⑥ *zo.* und *path.* like a polyp(us), polyp**ous**, ...iform. ...oid; **=gehäuse** *n, zo.* polypide, polypier; **=qualle** *f, zo.* jelly-fish (*Medu'sa*); **=stock** *m, zo.* polyp-stem or -stock, polypifer.
polyphon, ²isch (⏑⏑⎯(⏑)) [grch.] *a.* ⑥⑥ (vielstimmig) polyphonic.
Polyphonie ♪ ⏑ (⏑⎯⎯) *f* ㊽ polyphony.
Polytechniker (⏑⏑⏑⏑) [grch.] *m* ㉒ pupil of (or student at) a polytechnic(al school); **Polytechnikum** *n* ㉘㉙ polytechnic(al school or institute), in höherem Sinne: technical university; **polytechnisch** (⏑⏑⏑⏑) *a.* ⑥⑥ polytechnical.
Polythe-ismus (⏑⏑⎯⏑⏑) [grch.] *m* ㊼ (Vielgötterei) polytheism.
Polythe-ist (⏑⏑⎯⏑) [grch.] *m* ㊷ polytheist; **polythe-istisch** *a.* ⑥⑥ polytheistic.
Pomade¹ (⏑⎯⏑) [fr. *pommade*] *f* ㊽ (Haarsalbe) pomade, ehm. pomatum.
Pomade² F (⏑⎯⏑) [pomadig] *f* ㊽ *bursch.* (Ruhe) calm, quiet; das ist mir ganz ~ (gleichgültig)! that's all the same to me!
Pomaden¹-büchse (⏑⎯⏑...) *f* ㊽ pomade-pot; **=stange** *f* stick of pomade or cosmetic.
pomadig (⏑⎯⏑) [poln. *pomalu*] *a.* ⑥⑥ phlegmatic, slow, (faul) indolent; *adv. auch:* quite at one's ease.
pomadisieren (⏑⎯⏑⎯⏑) [Pomade¹] *v/a.* ⑬ to (grease with) pomade.
Pomeranze ⚥ (⏑⎯⏑⏑) [it. *pomo* Apfel u. *arancia* Orange] *f* ㊽ Seville (or bitter) orange (*Aura'ntia ama'ra*); vgl. Land-².
Pomeranzen-baum ⚥ (⏑⎯⏑⏑...) *m* ㉒ orange-tree (= Orangenbaum); **=blüte** *f* orange-blossom; **=blüten-öl** *n, chm.* neroli-oil; **=farben** *a.* ⑥⑥, **=farbig** *a.* orange-coloured; **=händler(in** *f*) *m* or.-(wo)man; **=saft** *m* or.-juice; **=schale** *f* or.-peel, eingemachte: candied or.-peel.
Pommer (⏑⏑) *m* ㉒, **~in** *f* ㊼: a) (Bewohner[in] Pommerns) Pomeranian; b) Hunderasse, Art Spitz: Pomeranian dog (*Canis pomera'nus*); ²(i)sch (⏑⏑(⏑)) *a.* ⑥⑥ Pomeranian; ~**n** ⚥ [slaw. *po (am) morje* (Meere)] *npr/n.* ㉓α. preuß. Provinz: Pomerania.
Pomolog (⏑⎯⎯) [it.=grch.] *m* ㊷ (Obstbau-kundiger) pomologist; **~ie** (⏑⎯⏑⎯) *f* ㊽ pomology; ²isch (⏑⎯⏑) *a.* ⑥⑥ pomological.

Pomp (⎯) [fr. *pompe* *f*, *grch.*] *m* ⑪b. (Gepränge) pomp, state, splendour; (Prachtentfaltung) brilliant display or show.
Pompadour † (⏑⏑⎯dur) [fr.] *npr.* *m* ⑪d.⑳ (Strickbeutel) knitting-bag.
Pompejaner (⏑⎯⎯⏑) [it.] I *m* ㉒, **~in** *f* ㊷: a) Anhänger des Pompejus; b) Bewohner[in] von Pompeji: Pompeian. — II *a. inv.* auch **pompej(an)isch** *a.* ⑥⑥ Pompeian.
Pompeji (⏑⎯⏑) *npr/n.* ㉓α. Alt.: (vom Vesuv 79 n. Chr. verschüttete St.) Pompeii.
Pompejus (⏑⎯⏑) *npr/m.* ⑥γ. Alt.: (röm. Feldherr, 106—48 vor Chr.) Pompey.
Pompelmus (⏑⏑⎯) [ndl., *ind.*] *m* ⑪a., **...se** ⚥ ㊽ (Baum u. Frucht) pampelmoes; pompelmoose, pompelmous, *Am.* grape-fruit (*Citrus decuma'na*).
pomphaft (⎯⏑) *a.* ⑥⑥ pompous, stately, showy, ostentatious; **~igkeit** (⏑⏑⏑⎯) *f* ㊻ pomposity, stateliness, ostentation.
pompös (⏑⎯) [fr.-lt.] *a.* ⑥⑥ (D 10) (prächtig) magnificent; *bib. fig.* = vortrefflich.
Pön (⎯) [lt.] *f* ㊽ (Strafe) penalty; **~ale** (⏑⎯⏑) *n* ㉙ (Bußgeld) fine.
Ponderabilien (⏑⏑⏑⎯⏑⏑) [lt.] *n/pl.* (wägbare Stoffe) ponderable substances *pl.*
ponieren F (⏑⎯⏑) [lt.] *v/a.* ⑬ *burschikos* e-m etwas ² (zum besten geben) to treat (or F stand) a p. to a th.
Pontifex (⏑⏑⏑) [lt.] *m* ⑪a.⑥ röm.Alt.: (Oberpriester) pontiff, *pontifex*; high priest.
pontificalibus (⏑⏑⎯⎯⏑⏑) [lt.] *adv.*: in ² in pontifical garb, in pontificals.
Pontifikat (⏑⏑⏑⎯) [lt.] *n* ⑪c. (Alt. Oberpriestertum, jetzt: päpstliche Würde) pontificate, pontifical office.
pontinisch (⏑⎯⏑) [it.] *a.* ⑥⑥ Alt.: die ~en Sümpfe in den Süden der römischen Campagna: the Pontine Marshes *pl.*
Pontius (⏑ti(⏑)) [lt.] *npr/m.* ⑥γ. Pontius; f. Pilatus; *fig.* von ~ zu Pilatus, etwa: from post to pillar.
Ponton (pą-tg', ⎯tg) [fr.] *m* ⑪ mst ♆ (Brückenkahn) pontoon; **~brücke** (⎯...) *f* ㉒ pontoon-bridge; **~ier** ♆ (⏑⎯) *m* ⑪d. (Soldat zum Brückenschlagen) ponton(n)ier, bridge-maker; **~karren** *m* == wagen; **~train** *m* pontoon-train; **~wagen** *m* pontoon-carriage or -wagon.
Pontus (⏑⏑) [lt.] *npr/m.* ⑥γ. röm. Alt.: 1. (Königreich in Klein-asien) Pontus. — 2. ~ Euxi'nus (das Schwarze Meer) the Euxine (Sea); the Black Sea.
Pony ⚥ (⏑⏑) [engl. ⎯⏑] *m*, *n* ⑪ (kl. Pferd) pony; F ~s *pl.* (~haare) bang(s *pl.*).
Popanz (⎯⏑) [tschech. *bubák*] *m* ⑪a. bogey, bugbear, (Scheuche) scarecrow; wie ein ~ aussehen F to look a fright or a guy; ein leerer ~ a mere dummy.
Pope (⎯⏑) [slaw.; *it. papa*] *m* ⑳ (russ. Priester) pope, priest of the Greek church in Russia.
Pop(e)lin ⚥ (⏑(⏑)⎯) [fr.] *f* (*n*) ⑪⑯ (wollseidenes Gewebe) poplin, bengaline.
Popo F (⏑⎯) [nhd. *Po(der)* *m* ⑪e. ⑳ Kinderspr.: posterior, behind, P bum, rump, backside.
populär (⏑⏑⎯) [fr.-lt.] *a.* ⑥⑥ (volkstümlich) popular; sich ² machen to make o.s. a (general) favourite, to ingratiate o.s. with the people; ²-wissenschaftliche Vorlesung scientific lecture for the general public.

[popularisieren] — 769 — [Post

popularisier/en (⌣⌣–⌣⌣) [fr.] **I** v/a. ⓖ to popularize, to make popular. — **II** ~ n ㉓ u. **P/ung** f ㊻ popularization.
Popularität (⌣⌣–⌣⌴) [lt.] f ㊻ (Volkstümlichkeit, Beliebtheit) popularity.
Pore (⌴⌣) [grch. pó'rŏs m Öffnung] f ㊵ anat., ♀, phys., zo. pore; **porig** f. **porös**.
Porling ♀ (⌴⌣)[Pore]m ⓓ.: ⌒ polyporus.
porös (⌴⌴) a. ㊺ (D 10) porous.
Porosität (⌣⌣–⌣⌴) f ㊻ porousness, porosity.
Porphyr (⌴f¹) [grch.] m ⓓ.min., geol. (von Feldspat ꝛc. durchsetzte Fels-art) porphyry; **♀-artig** (⌴...), **♀-haltig** a. ㊺: ⌒ porphyritic(al), porphyraceous; **~felsen** m ㉒ porphyritic rock; **♀ig**, **♀isch** (⌴f⌣) a. = **♀-artig**; **~vase** f porphyry vase.
Porree, **Porrei** ♀ (⌴–) [lt. porrum n] m ⓔ (Lauch) leek (Allium porrum).
Porsch, a. **Porst** ♀ (⌴)[Borste]m ⓓ.a. marsh- (or wild) rosemary (Ledum palu'stre).
Port (⌴) [lt. Hafen] m ⓓb. port; vom sichern ~ läßt sich's gemächlich raten (SCH.) it's easy to advise when safe in port.
Portal (⌣⌴) [lt.] n ⓓ. arch. porch.
Portechaise (vört-schä'-f³) [fr.] (†) m Tragsessel f ⓸ (Sänfte) sedan-chair; **~n=träger** m ㉒ bearer of a sedan-chair.
Portefeuille (vör-t(s)-fö(l)j) [fr. m] n ㊵: a) (Mappe) portfolio; b) = Minister-♀; **~träger** m ㉒ cabinet minister.
Portemonnaie (vört-mö-nē') [fr. n] n ㊵ (Börse, Geldbeutel) purse, money-bag.
Portepee ⚔ (vört-ē-pē') [(⌣⌣) fr. m] n ㊵ sword-knot; **~fähnrich** (⌴...) m ㉒ (†, jetzt Fähnrich) ehm. ensign.
Portier (vör-tiē') [(⌣⌴) fr.] m ㊵ = Pförtner; stiller ~ (Tafel mit dem Namen der Hausbewohner) tablet with the names of the occupants.
Portiere (vör-tiä'-r⁵) [fr.] f ㊵ (Türvorhang) curtain before a door.
Portikus (⌴⌣⌣) [lt.] m, inv. (a. ⓰) arch. (Säulenhalle) portico, porch.
Portion (⌣tß(⌣)⌴) [lt.] f ㊻ (Gericht, Essen) dish; (Anteil) portion, allowance; knappe ~ pittance; ⚔ ↓ tägliche ~ ration; bei Tische: zwei ~en Fleisch ꝛc. two helpings (or plates, platefuls) of meat, &c.; im Hotel: drei ~en Salat ꝛc. salad, &c. for three; **♀en-**, a. **♀-weise** adv. in rations, by the plateful.
Portland-vase ⚱ (⌴...) [Portland, Vorgebirge in Dorsetsh.] f ㉒ Portland vase; **=zement** m Portland cement.
Porto ✉ (⌴–) [it.] n ㊵⓸ postage, payment (or prepayment) for letters, &c.
Porto=einnahme (⌴–...) f ㊻ revenue (derived) from postage; **=ermäßigung** f reduction of postage; **♀frei** a.: a) free of po.; b) (im voraus bezahlt) (pre)paid, auf Paketen: carriage paid; Aufschrift: Ꝛe Dienstsache On His Majesty's Service; **=freiheit** f exemption from po.; **=gebühr** f (fee paid for) postage; **♀pflichtig** a. subject to (the payment of) po.; **=satz** m rate of po.; **=tarif** m, **=taxe** f postal tariff; **=vergütung** ⚙ f sum allowed (or repaid) for postage, refunding of po.; **=zuschlag** m additional (or extra) postage.
Porträt (vrä(t) [fr. portrait m] n ⓓc. (Bildnis) portrait, likeness, a. picture.
porträtieren (⌣–⌴⌴) v/a. ㉓ to portray, to paint the portrait of.

Porträt=maler (⌣trä(t)"...) m ㉒ portrait-painter, portraitist; **=malen** n, **=malerei** f portrait-painting; **=rahmen** m picture-frame.
Portugal ♀ (⌴⌣⌣) [lt. portus Ga'lliae Hafen Galliens] npr/n. ⓓα. Portugal;
Portugiese (⌣⌴⌣⌣) m ㊹, **...sin** f ㊵,
portugiesisch a. ㊺ Portuguese.
Portulak ♀ (⌴⌣⌣) [lt.] m ⓓd. purslain, purslane (Portula'ca olera'cea). [wine.
Port=wein (⌴⌴) [Porto ♀] m ㉒ port-
Porzellan (⌣tß⌴) [it. porcella'na] n ⓓd.: a) echtes: porcelain, real china; chinesisches ~ Chinese porcelain; Delfter ~ Delft ware; Dresdener (auch Meißner) ~ Dresden china; b) unechtes: (common) china, earthenware.
porzellan=artig (⌴...) a. ㊺ like china, porcel(l)an(e)ous; **~blümchen** ♀ n ㉒ London pride (Saxi'fraga umbro'sa).
porzellanen (⌣tß⌴⌣) a. ㊺ (made of) porcelain or china.
Porzellan=erde (⌣tß⌴⌴...) f ㊵ porcelain-clay, kaolin(e); **=fabrik** ⚒ f porcelain- (or china-) manufactory; **=fabrikant** m manufacturer (or maker) of china; **=geschirr** n china ware, crockery; **=handel** ⚖ m ch.-trade; **=händler** (=in f) m dealer in china; **=handlung** f ch.-shop; **=jaspis** m, min. porcel(l)anite; **=maler** (in f) m painter on china; **=malerei** f painting on china; **=masse** f porc.-paste; **=niederlage** ⚖ f china-warehouse; **=ofen** m porc.-kiln; **=schnecke** f, zo. cowry (Cyprae'a mone'ta); **=tasse** f china cup; **=teller** m china plate; **=tiegel** m, chm. porc. crucible; **=waren** f/pl. china (or porcelain) ware; **=ziegel** ⚒ m glazed brick, fire-brick.
Posament(e[n] pl.) ⚖ (⌣-⌴⌣⌴) [fr. passements Borten] n ⓑc. lace-work.
Posamenten=kragen m ㉒ lace collar.
Posamentier ⚖ u. ⚒ (⌣–⌴⌴) m ⓓd. lace-maker, weit S. haberdasher; **~arbeit** f ㊻, **~handwerk** n lace-making; **~er** F (⌣–⌴⌴⌴) m ㉒ = ~; **~erei** ⚒ (⌣–⌣⌴⌴⌴) f ㊻ haberdashery; **~ware** f lace-work, trimmings pl., haberdashery.
Posaune ♪ (⌣⌴⌴) [nhd.; *lt. bu'cina] f ㊸ 1. trombone, † sackbut; weit S. (a. bibl.) (large) trumpet; fig. die ~ des Weltgerichts the last trumpet, the trump of doom; in die ~ blasen od. stoßen (um et. laut zu verkünden oder anzupreisen) to sound the trumpet. — 2. (stärkste Zungenstimme der Orgel) trombone-stop of an organ.
posaunen ♪ (⌣⌴⌴) v/n. (h.) u. v/a. ㉓ to (play on the) trombone, to sound the trumpet.
Posaunen=bläser ♪ (⌣⌴⌴...) m ㉒ trombonist; **=engel** m, co. angel with puffed (or chubby) cheeks; **=klang**, **=ruf**, **=schall** m sound of trombones or trumpets; bibl. beim letzten **=rufe** at the last trumpet-call. [♪ ㊵ trombonist.]
Posauner (⌣⌴⌴) m ㉒, **Posaunist** (⌣–⌴) m
Pose¹ (⌴⌣) [fr.] f ㊸ paint. (Stellung) pose (or attitude) of a model, &c.; eine ~ annehmen, machen to strike (up) an attitude, to pose.
Pose² (⌴⌣) [ndd.] f ㊸ (goose-)quill; F co. nach ~n reisen (zu Bett gehen) to go to Bedfordshire.

Position (⌣⌣tß(⌣)⌴) [lt.] f ㊻ (Stellung) position; **~s-geschütz** ⚔ (⌴...) n ㉒ heavy (piece of) ordnance; **~s-lichter** ↓ n/pl. ship's (side-)lights pl.
positiv (⌴⌣⌴) [lt.] (ant. negativ) **I** a. ㊺ positive (auch elect., &c.); (bejahend) affirmative; ♀e Philosophie positive philosophy, positivism; ♀es Wissen solid knowledge; er behauptet es ganz ♀ (adv.) he asserts it most positively, he is most positive about it. — **II** ~ m ⓓd. gr. positive (degree). — **III** ~ n ⓓd.: a) phot. (a. **~bild** n) positive (picture); b) ♪ chamber-organ.
positiv-elektrisch (⌴⌣–⌴⌴) a. ㊺ phys. positively electric(al).
Positur (⌣⌣⌴) [lt.] f ㊻ (Haltung) posture; sich in ~ setzen to strike (up) an attitude, to attitudinize; sich in ~ stellen fenc. to take one's guard, beim Boxen: to square up.
Posse (⌴⌣) [nhd. 18. sae.; *Possen] f ㊸: a) farce, buffoonery, drollery; (Spaß) joking, fun, sport; (Albernheit) tomfoolery; ~n! (dummes Zeug) nonsense!, rubbish!, fiddlesticks!; ~n reißen to play antics; ~n treiben to fool (or F lark) about; b) thea. (derbtomisches Stück) farce, (fr.) burlesque.
Possekel (⌴-⌴⌴, mst +⌴ ⌴⌴) [ahd.] m ㉒ large sledge-hammer.
Possen (⌴⌣) [nhd. 16. sae.; *fr. bosse f (grotesker) Relief] m ㉓ trick, prank; e-m e-n ~ spielen ob. tun to play (or serve) a p. a (nasty) trick; e-m zum ~ etwas tun to do a th. to spite (or in spite of) a p.
Possen=dichter (⌴⌣...) [Posse] m ㉒ author (or writer) of farces.
possenhaft (⌴⌣⌣) [Posse(n)] a. ㊺ farcical, comical, clownish, ludicrous.
Possenhaftigkeit (⌴⌣⌣⌣⌴) f ㊻ farcicality, comicality, clownishness.
Possen=macher (⌴⌣...) m ㉒, **=reißer** m buffoon, droll (or funny, comical) fellow, clown, bsd. ehm.: (court-)jester; **=reißerei** f buffoonery; antics pl.; vgl. Posse a.; **=schreiber** m = **=dichter**; **=spiel** n farcical acting; vgl. Posse b.; **=spieler(in** f) m low comedian.
possessiv (⌴⌣⌴f) [lt.] **I** a. ㊺ gram. (besitzanzeigend) ~(es Fürwort) possessive (pronoun). — **II** ~ n ⓓd., **~um** (⌣⌴⌣⌴) n ㊵ possessive adjective or pronoun.
possierlich (⌣⌴⌣) [Posse] a. ㊺ droll, laughable (vgl. possenhaft); (sonderbar) singular, queer, odd.
Possierlichkeit (⌣⌴⌣⌴) f ㊻ drollness (vgl. Possenhaftigkeit); singularity, oddity.
Post¹ ✉ (⌣) [nhd. 16. sae.: post; *it. (mlt. pó'sita Stand-ort)] **I** f ㊵ **1.** a) Wagen: mail-coach (auch für Briefe und Pakete), ehm. stage-coach; ~ nehmen (mit der ~ tutsche fahren) to take the (or to travel by) mail-coach, to take post-horses; b) sämtliche mit der ~ ankommenden oder abgehenden Briefe ꝛc.: mail; mit umgehender (oder wendender) ~ by return of post, by the next mail; sobald die ~ ankommt as soon as the mail comes in. — **2.** Anstalt: post office (P.O.); für Briefe, Pakete auch: letter-, parcel-post; fahrende ~ travelling post office (T. P.O.); f. auf ♀ legen Schluß: auf die ~ geben to post, to drop in(to) the letter-

[post] — 770 — [Prachtzimmer]

box; mit der ~ schicken to send (or dispatch) by post; die ~ betreffend postal. — 3. (Nachricht) news, intelligence; schlimme ~ bad news, in geh. Spr.: evil tidings pl. — II f ⑯, m ⓐ a. 4. = Posten 2. — III [fr. postes f/pl.] m ㉒ 5. hunt. (Reh=)~en pl. (kleine Kugeln) buckshot sg.

post² (⌣) [It. = nach] f. p. Chr. (n.).

Post¹=adreßbuch (⌣⌣⌣) f ㉒ postal directory; =agentur f postal agency.

postalisch (⌣⌣⌣) a. ⑯ postal.

Postament (⌣⌣⌣) [neul.] n ⓓc. arch. pedestal (f. Fußgestell).

Post¹=amt (⌣⌣) n ㉒: a) als Ort: post office (P.O.); b) als Stellung: situation at (or in) the P.O.; =annahme f receiving-house for letters or parcels; =anschluß m postal connexion; =anstalt f post office; =anweisung f money-order, post-office order (P.O.O.); =auftrag m (in England unbekannt) postal order for collecting money; =beamte(r) m post-office clerk; =bediente(r) m porter at the P.O.; =beförderung f carriage (or conveyance) by post, mail-service; der Zug hat ~ ... carries the mails; =behörden f/pl. post-office authorities pl.; =beutel m post-, mail-bag; =bote m postman, letter-carrier; =briefkasten m postal letter-box, in Engl. a.: pillar-box; =bureau n post office.

Pöstchen (⌣⌣) n ㉓ dim. v. Posten¹ (f. s. 2).

Post¹=dampfer (⌣⌣) m ㉒, =dampfschiff n ↧ mail-steamer; =dampferlinie ↧ f line of mail-steamers.

post²=datieren (⌣⌣⌣⌣) v/a. ㉓ to postdate.

Post¹=debit (⌣⌣) m sales pl. (effected) by the P.O.; =diebstahl m post-office theft; =dienst m postal service; =direktion f management of the P.O.; =direktor m postmaster; =eleve m = =praktikant.

Posten¹ (⌣⌣) [It. posto; *It. po'situs] m ㉓ 1. a) post; (Anstellung) a situation, berth; einträglicher ~ remunerative post, snug berth; b) ⚔ (Schildwache auf) ~ sentry, zu Pferde: mounted sentry; verlor(e)ner ~ forlorn hope; (auf) ~ steh(e)n to be (or stand) on sentry(-go) or on guard; fig. immer auf dem ~ sein to be always at one's post or on the alert; c) ↧ quarters pl.; seid (wachsam) auf eurem ~! keep good quarters! — 2. mst ⚈: a) (Partie Waren) lot, parcel; b) (Betrag) amount, sum; eingetragener ~ entry; kleiner ~ (a. Pöstchen) small item.

Posten² (⌣⌣) m/pl. hunt. f. Post¹ III.

Posten¹=kette ⚔ (⌣⌣⌣) f ㉒ chain of posts; =lauf m line of posts; ²weise adv. (F a. a. ⑯) in parcels or lots.

Post¹=expedition (⌣⌣⌣) f ㉒: a) post office; b) =beförderung; ²fähig a. ⑯ mailable; ²frei a. prepaid, seltener: post paid; =freiheit f exemption from postage; =gefälle n/pl. revenue of the P.O.; =gehilfe m post-office assistant; =geld n: a) für Briefe: postage; b) für Personen: fare for the mail-coach; =gut n goods pl. carried by the post; =halter(ei f) m post-master('s house); =hand=buch n postal (or post-office) guide; =haus n post(ing)-house; =horn ♪ n postillion's (or postboy's) horn.

postieren (⌣⌣⌣) [fr.] v/a. und sich ² v/refl. ㉓: (sich) ² (aufstellen) to post (o.s.), to station (o.s.), to place (o.s.).

Postille (⌣⌣⌣) [It. post illa (verba) nach jenen (Worten)] f ㊽ book of homilies, collection of sermons.

Postillion (⌣⌣⌣⌣) [fr.] m ⓓd. postilion, postboy, driver of a mail-coach.

Post¹=karte (⌣⌣) f ㊽: a) (Karte der Postverbindungen) postal (or travelling-) map; b) list of letters, &c. contained in a mail; c) (Korrespondenzkarte) post card; ~ fürs Ausland foreign post card; ~ mit Ansicht picture (or pictorial) post card; =kasten m (letter-)box; =knecht m postillion; =kutsche f = Post 1; ²lagernd adv. auf Briefen: to be (left till) called for, poste restante; =mandat n = =auftrag; =marke f = Briefmarke; =meister m postmaster; =nachnahme ⚈ (in Engl. nicht gbr.) advance made by the P.O.; money collected by the post; =note f postal order or note.

post²=numerando (⌣⌣⌣⌣) (ant. pränumerando) adv.: ² bezahlen (a. ²numerieren v/a. ㉓) to pay on receipt; to settle at the end of the month, &c.

Posto (⌣⌣) [It.] n ⓓ nur gbr. in: ~ fassen to post o.s., to take (up) one's stand.

Post¹=ordnung (⌣⌣⌣) f ㉒ post-office regulations pl.; =paket n parcel sent by post; =papier ⚈ n note-paper, seltener: post(-paper); =pferd n post-horse; =praktikant m learner at the P.O.; p. qualifying for a (higher) p.-o. appointment; =recht, =regal n post-office monopoly; =reisende([r]m)/mail-coach passenger; =reiter m courier; =sache f postal matter; =säule f mile-stone; =schaffner m conductor (or guard) of a mail-coach; =schein m: a) postal receipt; b) ticket for a mail-coach; =schiff ↧ n mail- (or packet-)boat; =schluß m: vor ~ during post-office hours, previous to the departure of the mail; =sekretär m post-office clerk.

Post²=skript(um) (⌣⌣⌣) n ⓓc.(㊾) (abbr. P.S.) (Nachschrift zu e-m Briefe) postscript.

Post¹=sparkasse (⌣⌣) f ㊽ post-office savings bank; =station f post-stage or -station or -town; =stempel m post-mark; =straße f = Heerstraße b; =stube f post office; =stück n postal parcel; =stunden f/pl. post-office hours pl.; =tag m mail-day; fig. e-n ~ zu spät a day after the fair; =taube f = Brieftaube.

Postulat (⌣⌣⌣) [It.] n ⓓc. = Forderung 1 u. Heischesatz.

postulieren (⌣⌣⌣⌣) v/a. ㉓ to postulate.

Post¹=verband (⌣⌣) m ㉒, =verbindung f postal union, communication; =vertrag m postal treaty or convention; =verwaltung f postal administration, coll. heads pl. of the post office; =vorschuß m = =nachnahme; =wagen m = Post 1, ⚊ mail-van; =wechsel m change of post-horses, relay; ²wendend adv. by return of post; =wertzeichen n postage-stamp; =wesen n postal affairs pl.; =zahlschein m postal order; =zeichen n postmark, date-stamp; =zeitungs=dienst m postal newspaper-service; =zug ⚊ m mail-train.

Pot=asche 2c. f. Pottasche 2c.

Potentat (⌣⌣⌣) [fr., *It.] m ㊷ (Herrscher) potentate.

potential ⓩ(⌣⌣(⌣)⌣)[It.] I a. ⑯ phls., &c. (möglich) potential, possible. — II ~ ⓓd. elect. (elektrische Wirkungsfähigkeit in der Umgebung elektrischer Körper) potential.

Potenz (⌣⌣) [It.] f ⑯ math. power; auf die fünfte ~ erheben to raise to the fifth power; vgl. auch Kubus und Quadrat; ~=exponent m ㊷ index.

potenzier/en (⌣⌣⌣⌣) I v/a. ㉓ math. to raise to a higher power. — II ~ n ㉓ u. P/ung f ㊻ involution.

Potpourri ♪ (pō't-pū-rī) [fr. m] n ⑪ (musikalisches Allerlei) musical selection.

Pott=asche (⌣⌣) [ubd. Topf...] f ⑯ chm. (kohlensaures Kali) potash (K_2CO_3) =fisch, =wal m sperm(aceti)-whale, cachalot (Ca'todon, Physe'ter macroce'phalus).

potz (⌣) [für „Gottes" int. goodness (alive)!, ² Blitz!, Tausend, ² Wetter! the deuce!, damn (or hang) it all!, good gracious!, well, I never!, goodness alive! [Billard: pool.⟩

Poule (pūl) [fr.] f ㊽ (auch ~=spiel n ㉒)

poussieren (pū⌣⌣) [fr.] v/a. und sich ² v/refl. ㉓ 1. (sich) ² to push (one's way). — 2. bursch.: ein Mädchen ² to court ..., to flirt (or spoon) with ..., F to mash ...

Pozzuolan-erde (⌣⌣⌣⌣⌣)[it.; * Pozzuoli ♀, St. bei Neapel] f ⑯ min. pozz(u)olana.

Ppb. abbr. = Pappband boards.

P.P. abbr. = praemissis praemittendis.

Pr.=A. abbr. = Pracht-ausgabe.

Prä F (¹) [It.] n, inv. (Vorrang): das ~ h. to have the preference, to rank first.

Präbende (⌣⌣⌣) [It.] f ㊽ = Pfründe.

Pracht (⌣t) [ahd.: bright] f ⑯ (o. pl.) splendour, magnificence, tostpflege: luxury, feierliche: pomp, state, auffällige: ostentation, (outside) show, rich array, überladene: gorgeousness.

Pracht=aufwand (⌣t...) m ㉒ sumptuousness, luxury, gorgeous display; =auf=zug m gorgeous procession or array; =ausgabe f Buchhandel: (abbr. Pr.A.) handsome edition, (fr.) édition de luxe; =bau m magnificent building, geh. Sprache: noble pile; =(ein)band m Buchb.: magnificent volume (binding); =exemplar n splendid specimen, handsome copy.

prächtig (⌣⌣) a. ⑯ (f. Pracht) splendid, magnificent, luxurious; pompous; gorgeous; (köstlich) delicious; (reizend) charming, enchanting; ein ²er Fahnenschmuck a brave show of flags; ein ²er Mensch, oft: a fine (or nice) fellow, F a brick.

Pracht=käfer (⌣t...) m ㉒ ent.: ⚃ buprestid(an); =kerl m F splendid fellow, F brick, trump; =liebe f love of display or splendour; ²liebend a. ⑯ fond of show or display, ostentatious, pompous; ²los a., =losigkeit f = prunklos, Prunklosigkeit; =mädchen n splendid girl, F brick of a girl; =stück n choice piece, fine specimen; F (a) beauty; =sucht f (²süchtig a.) = =liebe(nd); ²voll a. magnificent, glorious; vgl. prächtig, weitS. (sehr schön) ²e Musik splendid (or very fine) music; =wagen m state-carriage; =werk n splendid (or elegant) work; =zimmer n magnificent room, state-room.

Signs (see page XVII): F familiar; P vulgar; ꜰ flash; ↘ rare; † obsolete (died); * new word (born); ++ incorrect; ♪ music;

[**Prädestination**] — 771 — [**präparieren**]

Prädestination ⚯ (-ˬˑ-tsi̯(ˇ)ⁿ) [lt.] *f* ㊻ *theol.* (Gnadenwahl) predestination; **~s-lehre** ⚯ (″...) *f* ㊷ doctrine of pr.
prädestinieren ⚯ (-ˬˑˑ) [lt.] *v/a.* ㊚ (vorherbestimmen) to predestinate (auch *theol.*).
Prädikant (-ˬˊ) *m* ㊷ (Prediger) preacher.
Prädikat (-ˬˊ) [lt.] *n* ⓝc. 1. *gram.* predicate. — 2. (Titel) title. — 3. Schule: ~ für einzelne Leistungen der Schüler: mark; Gesamt-₂, etwa: (term's) report.
prädikativ (-ˬˑˑ-ɨ̯) [lt.] *a.* ㊻ predicative.
Prädikats-adjektiv (-ˬˑ.ˬ-ɨ̯) *n* ㊷ *gram.* predicative adjective.
prädisponieren ⚯ (-ˬ-ˑˑ) [lt.] *v/a.* ㊚ (vorher anordnen, anlegen) to predispose.
prädominieren (-ˬˬˑˑ) [lt.] *v/n.* (h.) ㊚ (vorherrschen) to predominate.
Präfekt (-ˊ) [lt.] *m* ㊷⑴b. röm. Alt. und jetzt in Frankreich: prefect.
Präfektur (-ˬˊ) [lt.] *f* ㊻ prefecture.
Präfix ⚯ (-ˊ) [lt. -ˊ] *n* ⑪a., a. **~um** (-ˬˑ) *n* ㊾ *gram.* (Vorsilbe) prefix.
Prag ♀ (ˊ) [tschech. *Praha* Untiefe] *npr/n.* ㊚α. Hauptstadt v. Böhmen: Prague.
Präg-anstalt (″(ˬ)...) *f* ㊷ mint; **-druck** *m*, *typ.* raised impression or printing.
prägen (ˊˬ) [ahd.; *brechen*] **I** *v/a.* ㊚ 1. ⊙ to stamp; Münzen ₂ to coin money. — 2. *fig.* to imprint, to implant; sich et. ins Gedächtnis ₂ to impress a th. on one's memory. — **II** ~ *n* ㉓ 3. = Prägung.
Präge-ort (ˊ″...) *m* ㊷ place of coinage; **-presse** ⊙ *f* coining press.
Prager (ˊˬ) **I** *m* ㉒, **~in** *f* ㊼ inhabitant of Prague. — **II** *a. inv.* of Prague; ~ (Musikanten) *pl.* German band *sg.*
Präger ⊙ (ˊˬ) *m* ㉒ mint. coiner.
Präge-satz (ˊ″...) *m* ㊷ mintage; **-stätte** *f* minting- (or stamp-) room; **-stempel**, **-stock** *m* s. Prägstock; **-werk** *n* coining press or engine.
Präg-maschine ⊙ (″-ˬˑ) *f* ㊷ stamping (or embossing) press; *mint.* = Prägewerk.
pragmatisch ⚯ (ˬˊˬ) [grch. geschäftskundig] *a.* ㊻ pragmatic(al); ²e (den Zj.-hang der Ereignisse erforschende) Geschichtschreibung pragmatic history.
prägnant (-ˬ) [lt.] *a.* ㊻ (inhaltsvoll) pregnant; full of meaning, (kräftig) pithy, (genau) exact, precise, (bezeichnend) significant; **Prägnanz** *f* ㊻ pregnancy, pithiness; significance.
Prägstock (ˊ″ˬ) *m* ㊷ matrix, die.
Prägung (ˊˬ) *f* ㊻ stamping; coinage.
prähistorisch (ˬˑˬˬ) [lt.] *a.* ㊻ (vorgeschichtlich) prehistoric(al).
prahlen (ˊˬ) [mhd.] **I** *v/n.* (h.) ㊚ 1. mit persönlichem Subjekt: (sich rühmen) to boast, brag, vaunt (mit et. of a th.), to make a boast of; *abs. auch:* to be vainglorious, to talk big, (großtun) to swagger, (prunken) to show off. — 2. mit sachlichem Subjekt: (auffallen) to attract attention, als Schaustück: to make a show; (glänzen) to shine; ²de Farben gaudy (or loud) colours *pl.* — **II** ~ *n* ㉓ 3. = Prahlerei 1.
Prahler (ˊˬ) *m* ㉒, **~in** *f* ㊼ boaster, braggart, F braggadocio, swaggerer; (ruhmrediger Mensch) vainglorious p.
Prahlerei (-ˬˊ) *f* ㊻ 1. (das Prahlen) boasting, bragging, swaggering, (Aufschneiden) exaggeration, (Flunkern)

throwing the hatchet; (das Prunken) ostentation. — 2. (prahlende Äußerung) boast, brag, seltener: vaunt. bsd. Am. (bit of) bluff.
prahlerisch (ˊˬˬˬ) *a.* ㊻ boastful; (ruhmredig) vainglorious, talking big, F big in one's talk; (prunkend) ostentatious, showy; ● ²e Ankündigung puff(ing advertisement).
Prahl-hans (″...) *m* ㊵ boaster, swaggerer, F braggadocio; **-hanserei** *f* ㊻ boasting, swaggering, brag; **-sucht** *f* ㊻ boastfulness, vainglory; ²**süchtig** *a.* ㊻ boastful, vainglorious.
Prahm ⚓ (ˊ) [ndb.; *slaw.*] *m* ⑪(⑦)c., **~e** (ˊˬ) *f* ㊷ pram, punt, flat-bottomed boat; **~spritze** *f* ㊷ floating engine.
Präjudiz (--ˊ) [lt.] *n* ⑩a.: a) (Vorentscheidung) precedent; b) (Nachteil) prejudice.
präjudizieren (--ˬˊ) *v/n.* (h.) u. *v/a.* ㊚: a) *jur.* to prejudge a case; b) to prejudice, to act prejudicially.
präjudizierlich (..) *a.* ㊻ prejudicial.
präkludieren (--ˬˊ) [lt.] *v/a.* ㊚ (ausschließen) to exclude; *jur.* (für verfallen erklären) to foreclose a mortgage; **Präklusion** (--(ˬ)ˊ) *f* ㊻ = Ausschließung; **Präklusiv-frist** (--″ˬˊ) *f* ㊷ time allowed for proving claims.
Praktik (ˊˬ) [grch.] *f* ㊻: a) (*pl.* -ˬˬ) (Brauch) practice; b) *b.s.* **~en** (P -ˬˊ) *pl.* (Kniffe) (sharp) practices, dodges, tricks *pl.*
praktikabel[1] (-ˬˬˊ) *a.* ㊻ practicable.
Praktikabel[2] (ˬ) [fr. *practicable m*] *n* ㊿(㉒) *thea.* (Versatzstück) movable piece.
Praktikant (-ˬˊ) *m* ㊷ a) (ausübender Arzt) medical practitioner; b) (Beamter in der ersten Stelle) probationer.
Praktiker (ˊˬˬ) *m* ㉒ (*ant.* Theoretiker) practician, practical person.
Praktikus (ˊˬˬ) *m* ⑥㊻ practical fellow, practised hand, F old stager.
praktisch (ˊˬ) [grch.] *a.* ㊻ 1. (*ant.* theoretisch) practical; (nützlich) useful, serviceable, (zweckdienlich) well adapted; ² (*adv.*) erlernen to learn by practice, to get a practical (or technical) training in s. th.; sich ² bewähren to prove very useful *or* great utility. — 2. (geübt) practised; (geschäftskundig) business-like, (verständig) sensible; ²er Arzt medical (wenn auch Chirurg: general) practitioner.
praktizieren (-ˬˊˬ) [lt.] *v/a.* u. *v/n.* (h.) ㊚ 1. vom Arzte: to practise (medicine), to follow the medical profession. — 2. (geschickt wegnehmen, hinbringen) e-m et. aus der (in die) Tasche ² to slip a th. cleverly out of (into) a p.'s pocket.
Prälat (-ˊ) [lt.] *m* ㊷ *eccl.* (vornehmer Geistlicher) prelate; **~ur** (--ˊ) *f* ㊷ (Amt e-s Prälaten) prelacy, prelateship.
Präliminar-friede (--ˬ″-ˬˊ) *m* ㊷ preliminaries *pl.* of peace.
Präliminari-en (--ˬˊ(ˬ)ˬ) [lt.] *n/pl.* ㉙ (Vorverhandlungen) preliminaries *pl.*
Praliné (-ˬˊ) [fr. *chocolat praliné m*] *n* ㊿ Konditorei: chocolate-cream.
prall[1] (ˊ) [ndb.] *a.* ㊻ (straff) tight(ly stretched or fitting), ↓ taut; (voll und rund) well-rounded, stout, plump, F crumby; ²e Backen chubby cheeks *pl.*
Prall[2] (ˊ) *m* ㊚b. (heftiger Stoß) shock, collision; (Rückprall) rebound, *elect.*, &c. back-stroke.

prallen (ˊˬ) [mhd.: *prellen*] *v/n.* (h. u. sn) ㊚ to bound (or bounce, dash) against; (zurück-)² to rebound, ⚔ *artill.*: to ricochet, *phys.* to be reflected.
Prallheit (ˊˬ) *f* ㊻ (s. prall¹) tightness, tension; roundness, stoutness.
Prall-kraft (ˊ″...) *f* ㊷ elasticity; **-schuß** *m* = Prellschuß; **-stoß** *m* = prall²; **-winkel** *m*, *phys.* angle of reflexion.
präludieren ♪ (--ˬˊ) [lt.] *v/n.* (h.) ㊚ (als Einleitung spielen) to prelude; **Präludium** (--ˊ(ˬ)ˬ) *n* ㉘ (Vorspiel) prelude.
prämeditieren (-ˬˬˊ) [lt.] *v/a.* ㊚ (vorher erwägen) to premeditate.
Prämi-e (ˊ(ˬ)ˬ) [lt. *prae'mium* Belohnung] *f* ㊷ 1. Schule ꝛc.: prize; *vgl.* Preis¹ 2. — 2. ●: a) (Versicherungs-)~ premium of insurance, F insurance (-money); b) Börse: (Überschuß des Wertes über Pari) premium, value above par; c) (Zuschuß zur Beförderung der Industrie ꝛc.) bounty; d) (Extradividende) bonus.
Prämi-en-anleihe ● (ˊ(ˬ)ˬ(ˬ)ˬ...) *f* ㊷ issue of lottery-bonds; **-geschäft** *n* time-bargain, option; **-papiere** *n/pl.* lottery-bonds *pl.*; **-schein**, **-zettel** *m* lottery-bond, drawn bond.
prämiier-en (-(ˬ)ˊˬ) [lt.] *v/a.* ㊚ to award a prize to; *p/t* = preisgekrönt.
Prämisse (-ˬˊ) [lt.] *f* ㊷ Logik: premise.
prangen (ˊˬ) [mhd.] **I** *v/n.* (h.) ㊚ 1. a) von Sachen: to be resplendent with; to make a fine (or magnificent) show; to glitter, to shine; die Bäume ² in vollem Blätterschmucke ... exhibit (or look beautiful in) their leafy garb; b) von Personen: to look fine; in der Blüte der Jugend ² to shine forth in the splendour of youth; in kostbaren Gewändern ² to show off one's (or to array o.s. in, to dress up in) costly garments. — 2. ⚓ (alle Segel aufspannen) to carry a full press of sail. — **II** ~ *n* ㉓ 3. = Prunk.
Pranger (ˊˬ) [ndb.] *m* ㉒ (Schandpfahl) pillory, whipping-post; an den ² stellen (to put into the) pillory, *fig.* a. to expose, disgrace, dishonour.
Pranke (ˊˬ) [mlt. *branca*] *f* ㊸ (Klaue) claw; (Tatze) clutch, paw.
pränumerando (-ˬˬˊˬ) [lt.] *adv.* (im voraus [bezahlend]) (paying) in advance.
Pränumerant (-ˬˬˊ) *m* ㊷ subscriber.
Pränumeration (-ˬˬˬ-tsi̯(ˇ)ⁿ) [lt.] *f* ㊻ (Vorauszahlung) subscription (auf et. to a th.); **~s-liste** *f* ㊷ list of subscribers.
pränumerieren (-ˬˬˬˊ) [lt.] *v/n.* (h.) u. *v/a.* ㊚ (*ant.* postnumerieren) to pay in advance; auf et. ² to subscribe to a th.
Präparand (-ˬˊ) [lt.] *m* ㊷ candidate for admission to a training-college; **~en-anstalt**, **-schule** (ˊ″...) *f* ㊷ training-college for elementary teachers.
Präparat (-ˬˊ) [lt.] *n* ⓝc. *anat.*, *chm.*, *pharm.* preparation, compound; mikroskopisches ~ microscopic slide.
Präparation (-ˬˬ-tsi̯(ˇ)ⁿ) [lt.] *f* ㊻ bsd. Schule: preparation (auf ... for ...); **~s-heft** *n* ㊷ note- (or copy-)book for preparations.
präparieren (-ˬˊˬ) [lt.] **I** *v/a.* u. sich ² *v/refl.* ㊚: (e-n auf et. ² (vorbereiten) to prepare (a p. for) a th.; sich für die Schule ² to prepare (or do) one's lessons (for school); *phot.* präpariertes

---

⚯ scientific; ♦ botanical; ♀ geography; ⊙ machinery; ⚒ mining; ⚔ military; ⚓ marine; ● commercial; ✉ postal; 🚂 railway.

[**Präposition**] — 772 — [**preisgekrönt**]

Papier sensitized paper. — II ~ n ㉓ = Präparation.
Präposition (-⏑⏑tᵴ(⏑)ᴸ) [lt.] f ㊺ (Verhältniswort, Vorwort) preposition.
Prärie (-ᴸ) [fr.] f ㊺ (große Gras-ebene) prairie; ~**fuchs** (-ᵘ...) m f. Kittfuchs; ~**huhn** n prairie-hen (*Tetrao cupido*); ~**hund** m prairie-dog (*Cynomys ludovicianus*).
Prärogativ (-⏑-ᴸf)[lt.]n㊀c., ~**e** (-⏑-ᴸw⏑) f ㊽ (Vorrecht) prerogative.
Präsem ⸗ (ᴸ) [mlt.] m ㉓ min. prase.
Präsens (ᴸ) [lt.] n (sg. inv., pl. Präse'ntia) gr. (Gegenwart) present (tense).
Präsent (-⏑) [fr.] n㊀b. (Geschenk) present, gift; ~**ation** (-⏑-tᵴ(⏑)ᴸ) f ㊺ presentation.
präsentierbar (-⏑ᴸ-) a. ㊂ presentable.
Präsentier-brett (-⏑ᴸ⏑) n ㉓ tray, waiter, (silver) salver.
präsentieren (-⏑ᴸ⏑) [lt.] v/a. und sich ⸗ v/refl. ㊽ 1. (sich) ⸗ to present (o.s.); sich gut ⸗ to present (or have) a good appearance, to have a good address; ⬩ der präsentierte Wechsel the presented bill (of exchange). — 2. ⚔ präsentiert das Gewehr! present arms!
Präsentier-teller f. Präsentierbrett.
Präsenz (-⏑) [lt.] f ㊺ (Anwesenheit) presence; ~**liste** (-⏑...) f ㉓ list of persons present, ⚔ roll; ~**stand** ⚔ m effective (or actual) strength; ~**stärke** ⚔ f effective force.
Praser ⸗ (ᴸ⏑) m ⸗ Prasem.
Präservativ (-⏑w-ᴸf) [lt.] n ㊀d., ~**mittel** n ㊅ (Schutzmittel) preservative.
Präses (ᴸ⏑) [lt.] m, inv. (pl. auch Präsi'den) ⸗ Präsident.
Präsident (-⏑ᴸ) [lt.] m ㊷ (Vorsitzender) president, chairman, im Unterhause: Speaker; ~**in** f ㊺ auch: presiding lady, bisw.: chairwoman; zum ~en wählen to elect as president, to vote into the chair; ~**(en)schaft** (-⏑⏑(⏑)ᴸ) f ㊺, ~**ur** (-⏑⏑ᴸ) f ㊺ presidency, presidentship; ~**en-stelle** f ㊅ presidency; im Unterhause: speakership; ~**stuhl** m presidential chair; den ~ besteigen to take the chair; ~**entum** ⸗ ~enschaft.
präsidieren (-⏑ᴸ⏑) [lt.] v/n. (h.) ㊾ to preside over, abs. a. to be in the chair.
Präsidium (-ᴸ(⏑)⏑)[lt.]n㉓ presidency, chair(manship), (Vorrang) precedence; das ~ übernehmen to take the chair.
prasseln (ᴸ⏑) [mhd.: prattle] I v/n. (h. u. s.) ㊚a. 1. (h.) bsd. vom Feuer: to crackle, vom Regen ꝛc.: to patter (up, kirschen, knistern). — 2. (s.) to move (or come down, fall) with a rustling (or pattering) noise. — II ~ n ㉓ 3. crackling, ꝛc. (Snattern) crepitation.
prassen (ᴸ⏑) [ndd., ndl.] I v/n. (h.) ⑨⓪ to lead a gay (or debauched, dissipated) life, to live in luxury, engS. to be feasting and revelling. — II ~ n ㉓ gay (or debauched, dissipated) life.
Prasser (ᴸ⏑) m ㊷ gay (or debauched) p., reveller, rake, spendthrift; ~**ei** (⏑⏑ᴸ) f ㊺ ⸗ prassen II, auch: debauchery, dissipation, revelry, feasting.
präsumieren (-⏑ᴸ⏑) [lt.] v/a. ㊾ (mutmaßen) to presume; **Präsumtion** (-⏑tᵴ(⏑)ᴸ) f ㊺ presumption.
Präsumtiv-erbe (-⏑ᴸf,⏑⏑) m ㊷ heir presumptive to an estate, to the throne, &c.

Prätendent (-⏑⏑ᴸ) [lt.] m ㊷, ~**in** f ㊺ pretender to a throne, claimant to a title, &c.; ~**(en=)schaft** (-⏑⏑ᴸ(⏑)⏑) f ㊺ pretendership; **prätendieren** (-⏑⏑ᴸ⏑) v/a. ㊾ (beanspruchen) to pretend, to claim; **Prätension...tion** (-⏑(⏑)ᴸ)/㊺(Anmaßung) pretension; (Anspruch) claim; **prätentiös** (-⏑tᵴ(⏑)ᴸ) a. ㊂ (D 10) pretentious.
Präteritum (-ᴸ⏑⏑) [lt. -⏑⏑] n ㊾ gr. (Vergangenheit) preterite, past (tense).
praeter propter (ᴸ⏑ ᴸ⏑) [lt.] adv. (meist abbr. pr. pr.) (ungefähr, nahezu) nearly, about, approximately.
Prätor (ᴸ⏑) [lt.] m ㊶ röm. Alt.: prætor.
Prätorianer (-⏑(⏑)ᴸ⏑) m ㊷ röm. Alt.: (Soldat von der kaiserlichen Leibwache) prætorian; **prätorianisch** a. ㊂ prætorian.
Prätor=würde (ᴸ⏑⏑⏑) f ㊺ prætorship, office of prætor.
Prätur (-ᴸ) [lt.] f ㊺ prætorship.
Präventiv=maßregeln (-w⏑ᴸf...) [lt. vorbeugend] f pl., ~**mittel** n/pl. preventive measures pl.
Praxis (ᴸ⏑) [grch. ᴸ⏑] f, inv. 1. (ant. Theorie) practice, (Übung) exercise; (Brauch) usage. — 2. (Patienten e-s Arztes) practice, patients pl.; (Klienten eines Anwalts) clients pl.; (Geschäftskreis) connexion; customers pl. [denzfall.]
Präzedens (-ᴸ⏑) [lt.] n ㉚ ⸗ Präze=**Präzedenz** (-tᵴ-ᴸ) f ㊺ (Vorrang) precedence; ~**fall** (ᴸ...) m ㊷ jur. (früherer ähnlicher Fall) precedent; ohne ~ without(a) precedent, unprecedented; ~**streit** m dispute about precedence.
Präzeptor (-tᵴ-ᴸ⏑) [lt. Lehrer] m ㉛ preceptor, mehr gbr.: tutor, teacher.
Präzipitat ⸗ (-tᵴ⏑-ᴸ) [lt.] n (m) ㊀c. pharm., chm. (Niederschlag) precipitate.
präzis (-tᵴᴸ) [lt.] a. ㊂ (genau) precise, exact, accurate; **Präzision** (-tᵴ-(⏑)ᴸ) f ㊺ precision, exactness; accuracy; ~**s=gewehr** (ᴸ...) n ㊅ precision-gun.
Prchtb. abbr. ⸗ Prachtband.
predigen (ᴸ⏑⏑) [ahd.: preach; *mlt. prædica're*] I v/n. (h.) u. v/a. ㊽ 1. to preach, außerhalb der Kirche: to rant; (ein Langes und Breites reden) to hold forth, to discourse; gegen et.: to declaim against s.th.; tauben Ohren ⸗ to preach to deaf ears. — 2. fig. (schelten) to sermonize, to lecture; Sprichw. Gelehrten ist gut ⸗ a word to the wise is enough. — II ~ n ㉓ 3. preaching; wozu all das ~? what's the use of these sermons or this sermonizing?
Prediger (ᴸ⏑⏑) [predigen] m ㊷, ~**in** f ㊺ 1. preacher, nicht kirchlicher: ranter; bibl. eine Stimme e-s ~s in der Wüste the voice of one crying in the wilderness. — 2. (protestant. Geistlicher) pastor, clergyman; die Frau ~(in) the clergyman's wife. — 3. (Buch des Alten Testaments) ~ Salomo(nis) Ecclesiastes.
Prediger(=)frau (ᴸ⏑⏑) f ㊅ pastor's wife; ~**mönch** m preaching friar; Dominican (friar); ~**schule** f, ~**seminar** f college for theological students or students of divinity, für engl. Dissidenten auch training-college for ministers, pastors' college; ~**stelle** f ⸗ Pfarr=amt; ~**stuhl** m pulpit; ~**talar** m clergyman's gown.
Predigt (ᴸ⏑) [ahd., *predigen*] f ㊺ sermon (auch F fig. langweilige Ermahnung);

(Auslegung der Bibel) a.: (simple) homily eine ~ halten to preach a sermon fig. e-m eine ~ halten to give a p. a lecture (vgl. predigen I); ~**amt** (ᴸ...) n㊅ preacher's office; ministry; zum ~amt berufen to call to the ministry; ~**amts=kandidat** m candidate for the ministry or for holy orders; ~**buch** n collection of sermons; ~**entwurf** m skeleton-sermon; ~**stuhl** m pulpit.
prei-en ⸗ (ᴸ⏑) v/a. ㊾: ein Schiff ⸗ (anrufen) to hail ..., to speak ...
Preis[1] (ᴸ) m ㊀a. [nhd.: price, prize, praise; *lt. prétium*] 1. (was ein Ding kostet) price; (Gebühr) fee; (Fahrgeld) fare; um jeden ~ at any price or sacrifice, at all costs; um keinen ~ not at any price; e-n ~ auf j-s Kopf setzen to set a price on a p.'s head; ⬩ die Preise halten sich prices keep steady or are well maintained; im Preise steigen to rise (in price), to go up; unter dem Preise verkauft sold below cost (-price) or its value; zu billigem (hohem) Preise at a cheap (high) rate, F at a low (high) figure; zum Preise von // at the rate of //; f. fallen 6 u. 16 und fest 3 ⬩. — 2. für „Prämie", bsd. 1: e-n ~ ausschreiben to offer a prize; e-n ~ in der Schule ꝛc. davontragen to carry off (or to take, bei Losen: to win) a prize. — 3. mit gen. (das Beste seiner Art) du, o ~ der Dichter! thou, foremost (or prince) among poets ! — 4. (hohes Lob) praise, glory, eulogium, eulogy.
Preis[2] (ᴸ) [it. *presa* Prise] f. preisgeben.
Preis[3] (ᴸ) m ㊀a. (Einfassung) border(ing).
Preis[1]=**abschlag** ⬩ (ᴸ...) m ㊷ reduction (or deduction) in price(s), abatement, =**angabe** f, =**ansatz** m quotation; =**aufgabe** f subject proposed for a prize-competition, a. prize-question; =**aufschlag**, =**aufstieg** m rise (or advance, improvement) in price(s); =**ausschreibung** f prize-competition; =**ausstellung** f distribution of prizes; =**bericht** ⬩ m market-report; =**bewerber** m competitor; =**bewerbung** f prize-competition.
Preise (ᴸ⏑) f ㊺ ⸗ Preis[3]. [petition.]
Preisel=beere ⸗ (ᴸ⏑...) [tschech.] f ㊺ red whortleberry or bilberry, cowberry (*Vaccinium Vitis Idaea*).
preisen (ᴸ⏑) [nhd.: praise; *fr. priser*] v/a. ㉛ (f. Preis[1] 4) to praise, glorify, eulogize, erhebend: to extol, to exalt, to laud to the skies, empfehlend: to commend; e-n glücklich ⸗ to call a p. happy; Gott sei gepriesen! Heaven be praised!, glory be to God!
Preiser (ᴸ⏑) m ㊷ praiser, eulogist.
Preis[1]=**ermäßigung** ⬩ (ᴸ...) f ㊺ (trade-) discount; deduction in price, abatement; =**frage** f = =**aufgabe**; ⬩[2] **geben** v/a. u. sich ⸗ v/refl. to abandon (or to surrender, to hand over) a p., a th. to a p.; alles ⸗ to sacrifice (or give up) everything; den Winden und Wellen ⸗gegeben (drifting) at the mercy of the winds and waves; sich ⸗ to abandon o.s.; von Weibern: to prostitute o.s.; sich dem Gelächter ⸗ to expose o.s. to ridicule; =**gebung** f abandonment, surrender; prostitution; ⬩[1] **gekrönt** a. ㊂ who (or which) has carried

Zeichen (f. S. XVII): F familiär; P Volkssprache; ⸎ Gaunersprache; ⸌ selten; † alt (auch gestorben); * neu (auch geboren); ⟊ unrichtig;

[**Preisgekrönter**] — 773 — [**Prima**]

off the prize; **=gekrönte(r)** m prizeman; **=herabsetzung ♦** f shrinking of prices; **=kurant** m **=verzeichnis**.
preislich (⸗‐) a. ⓺ 1. = preiswürdig. — 2. F = lobesam.
Preis¹=liste ♣ (″…) f ⓷ price-list, list of prices; **=medaille** f prize-medal; Inhaber e-r ~ prize-medallist; **=richter** m awarder of prizes, umpire, juror; **=schießen** n rifle-competition; **=schrift** f prize-essay; **=schwankung ♦** f fluctuation in prices.
Preißel-beere ♀ = Preiselbeere.
Preis¹=spiel (″…) n ⓷ Tennis: event; **=sturz ♦** m collapse (or sudden fall) of prices; **=verderber ♦** m one who cuts the prices, cutting tradesman; **=verteilung** f distribution of prizes; **=verzeichnis** n = **=liste**; ⸗**wert** a. ⓺, ⸗**würdig** a.: a) (lobenswert) praiseworthy; b) worth the money, moderate in price, cheap (at the price); **=würdigkeit** f: a) praiseworthiness; b) e-r Ware: moderate price, cheapness; **=zettel ♦** m label showing the price of an article; **=zuschlag ♦** m addition to the price (originally charged).
prekär (‐⸗) [fr. *précaire*] a. ⓺ (unsicher) precarious.
Prell-bock ⛟ (⸗,⸗) m ⓷ bulkhead.
prellen (⸗⸗) [prallen] ⓷ **I** v/n. (h. u. ſn) 1. = prallen. — **II** v/a. 2. to make rebound. — 3. bſd. hunt. e-n Fuchs ⸗ (auf prall angezogenem Tuche in die Höhe ſchnellen) to toss a fox in a blanket. — 4. fig. (betrügen) to cheat, dupe, bamboozle, F to take in, to diddle; (überfordern) to overcharge; einen um et. ⸗ to cheat (or swindle, F do) a p. out of a th. — **III** ~ n ⓷ 5. = Prellerei.
Preller (⸗⸗) m ⓷ 1. Perſon: (f. prellen 3 u. 4) tosser; fig. (Betrüger) cheat, swindler. — 2. Sache: a) = prall²; b) = Prellſchuß.
Prellerei (⸗⸗″) f ⓸ (f. prellen 4) cheating, bamboozling, imposition, F u. P take-in, (dead) sell, (awful) do.
Prell-pfahl ⊙ (⸗…) m ⓷ fender; **=schuß** ⚔ m, artill. ricochet; **=stein** m curbstone, kerbstone, guardstone; **=stoß** m Fußball: drop-kick; e-n ~ m. to drop.
Premiere (prᵊ-mjã'-rᵊ) [fr.] f ⓸ thea.: a) (erste Aufführung eines Stückes) first night; (zum erstenmal aufgeführtes Stück) first-nighter; b) = Primadonna.
Premier(=leutnant) ⚔ † (prᵊ-mjẽ″…) m ⓷ = Oberleutnant; **=minister** m prime minister, premier.
Presbyter (⸗‐⸗) [grch.] m ⓷ eccl. (Ältester) presbyter, mehr abs.: elder.
Presbyterial-verfassung (⸗‐ᵥ(ᵥ)″…) f ⓷ eccl. presbyterian constitution.
Presbyterianer (⸗‐ᵥ(⸗)″) m ⓷, ~**in** f ⓸, **presbyterianisch** a. ⓺ Presbyterian.
Presbyterium (ᵥ-⸗(ᵥ)ᵥ) n ⓷ (Kirchenrat) presbytery, council of elders.
preschen nordd. (⸗⸗) [fr. *presser*] v/n. (h. u. ſn) ⓷ to hurry, to scurry. to pelt, to tear along.
Presenning ⛵ (ᵥᵥ⸗) f ⓸ = Persenning.
preß¹ (⸗) [fr.] a. ⓺(D 10) close together; Kleider: ⸗ (an)liegen, ſitzen to fit tightly.
Preß²=angelegenheit (⸗…) [Presse] f ⓷ press-affair; **=¹balken** ⊙ m/pl. typ. press-cheeks pl.

preßbar (⸗‐) [pressen] a. ⓺ compressible; ~**keit** (⸗‐) f ⓸ compressibility.
Preß¹=baum ⊙ (⸗…) m ⓷ press-beam or -lever; **=bengel** m, typ. u. Buchbinderei: press-jack or -stick, bar of the handpress; **=beutel** m Ölfabrikat.: pressing-bag; **²bureau** m editorial office; **=¹deckel** m, typ. tympan.
Presse (⸗⸗) [ahd. Kelter: press; *fr.] f ⓸ 1. typ., &c. press, weitS. the Press, a. journalism; Vertreter der ~ representative of the Press, reporter, pressman; eben **aus** der ~ fresh from the press; **in** die ~ geh(e)n to go to press; **unter** der ~ in the press. — 2. ⊙ Spinnerei: ~ an einer Vorſpinnmaſchine clasp; ~ mit Zahnſtange rack-and-pinion press. — 3. ⊙ Tuchfabr.: (Appretur) lustring, lustre, gloss, dressing. — 4. F fig. = Fähnrichspresse.
Preß¹=eis (⸗‐‐) n ⓷ compressed (or machine-made) ice.
pressen (⸗⸗) [ahd.: press; *lt. *pressa're*] **I** v/a. ⓷ 1. to press (auch = feltern); (zſ.-drücken) to compress, (aufrücken) to impress; (klemmen) to pinch, (quetſchen) to squeeze; durch ein Tuch ⸗ to strain; Tuch ꝛc. heiß ⸗ to hot-press…; in Falten ⸗ to goffer; gepreßtes Glas = Preßglas. — 2. fig. (niederdrücken) to depress; in gepreßter Stimmung in a dejected (or downcast) mood; e-n ⸗ (drängen) to urge a p.; das preßt ihm Tränen aus den Augen it draws tears from his eyes; ein Land, ſeine Untertanen ⸗ (bedrücken) to oppress…; der Saal war gepreßt (gedrängt) voll … was (over-)crowded (with people) or crammed (full); ⛵ Matroſen ⸗ to (im)press seamen. — 3. ⛵ den Wind ⸗ to sail close to the wind. — **II** ~ n ⓷ 4. = Pressung.
Presser (⸗⸗) m ⓷, ~**in** f ⓸ one who presses or urges; oppressor.
Preß²=fehde (⸗…) f ⓷ Press-feud, journalistic war; **=¹flügel** m Spinnerei: presser-flyer; **=²freiheit** f liberty of the press; bſd. ehm. **=¹gang** ⛵ m press-gang; **=²gesetz** n press-law; **=¹glanz** m Tuchfabr.: gloss from the press; **=glas** n moulded glass; **=hefe** f press-yeast.
pressieren (⸗‐⸗) [fr. *presser*] v/n. (h.) ⓷ to be urgent; es pressiert nicht there is no hurry; preſſiert ſein to be pressed for time or in a hurry.
Preß¹=kohle ⊙ (⸗…) f ⓷ briquette; **=kolben** m press-ram; **=kopf** m Kochkunst: brawn; **=¹kosak** m, contp. servile pressman; **=¹kurbel** f, typ. press-pin; **=luft** f compressed air; **²ordnung** f press-regulations pl.; **=¹platte** ⊙ f pressing-plate; **=²prozeß** m action against a newspaper (for infringement of the press-laws); **=revision** f, typ. revise(d proof); **=sachen** f/pl. affairs pl. of the Press; **=¹schiene** f, typ. press-hoop; **=schraube** f pressing-screw; **=¹span** m glazed board; **=stange** f, mint. press-bar; **=²tätigkeit** f der Zeitungs-preſſe: activity of the Press.
Pressung (⸗⸗) f ⓸ (f. pressen I) pressing, pressure, compression; impression; squeezing, squeeze; oppression; crowding of people.

Preß²=vergehen (⸗…) n ⓷ offence against the press-laws; **=¹walze** ⊙ f press-roll; **=ziegel** m press-brick; **=²zwang** f restriction imposed on (F gagging of) the Press.
Pretiosen (⸗t(ᵥ)⸗‐) [lt.] pl. inv. (Kostbarkeiten) valuables, precious stones pl.
Preuße (⸗‐) [lt.] m ⓶, **Preußin** ♀ f ⓸ Prussian; **Preußen** ♀ (‐‐) npr/n. ⓷α. Königreich u. Provinz: Prussia; **Preußenkönig** (⸗‐‐‐) m ⓶ king of Prussia.
Preußentum (‐‐‐) n ⓷d.: a) Prussianism. Prussian ways pl.; b) das geſamte ~, auch: all (the) Prussians pl.
preußisch (⸗‐) a. ⓺ Prussian.
Preußisch=blau (⸗‐…) n ⓷ chm. prussian blue; **=polen** ♀ n Prussian Poland.
preziös (‐(ᵥ)⸗) [fr. *précieux*] a. ⓺ (D 10) (koſtbar) precious. [von Troja: Priam.]
Priamus (⸗‐ᵥ) npr/m. ⓷γ. myth. König
priape-isch ⚤ (⸗‐⸗‐) [grch.] a. ⓺ pros.: Der Vers Priapean metre.
Priapus (ᵥ⸗‐) [lt., *grch.] npr/m. ⓷γ. myth. (zeugende Naturkraft) Priapus.
prick(e)lig (⸗(ᵥ)‐) a. ⓺ pungent.
prickeln (⸗‐) [ndd.: prick(le)] **I** v/n. (h.) u. v/a. ⓶a. 1. to prick. — 2. (lebhaft reizen) to prickle, to sting, vom Champagner: to effervesce, vom Senf: to be hot; das prickelt im Halſe that burns one's throat; ⓶d, a. pungent, sharp. — **II** ~ n ⓷ 3. prickling (or prickly, stinging) sensation, hot (or burning) taste; pungency.
Priel ⛵ (⸗) [ndd.] n ⓷c., ~**e** (‐‐) f ⓷ (Fahrrinne) (narrow) channel.
Priem (⸗); Hom. Prim) [ndl.] m ⓷c., ~**chen** (⸗‐) n ⓷, ~**e** f ⓷ (Stückchen Kautabak) quid (or chew) of tobacco.
priemen (⸗‐) [Priem] v/n. (h.) ⓷ to chew tobacco. [von preiſen.]
pries (⸗) ind., **priese¹** (⸗‐) subj. impf.
Priese² (⸗‐; Hom. Priſe) f ⓷ (Einfaſſung, Schnur) border. (Saum am Kleid) hem.
Priester (⸗‐) [ahd.: priest, pres(by)ter; *grch.] m ⓷, ~**in** f ⓸ priest(ess f).
Priester=amt (⸗‐‐) n ⓷ priestly office, priesthood; **=binde** f Alt.: fillet; **=ehe** f marriage of priests or clergymen; **=hemd** n alb; (Chorhemd) surplice; **=herrschaft** f priestly rule, hierarchy, theocracy; **=hut** m clerical hat; **=käppchen** n, Cath. eccl. calotte; **=kleid** n priestly garment or garb.
priesterlich (⸗‐‐) a. ⓺ eccl. priestly, of priests, sacerdotal, weitS. clerical.
Priester-rock (⸗‐‐) m ⓷ cassock.
Priesterschaft (⸗‐‐‐) f ⓸ 1. = Priestertum. — 2. (Gesamtheit von Prieſtern) body of priests, clergy, F the black cloth, P the black brigade.
Priester-seminar (⸗‐…) n ⓷ training-college (or seminary) for (Roman Catholic) priests; **=stand** m (Klerus) priesthood, sacerdotal order.
Priestertum (⸗‐‐) n ⓷d. priesthood.
Priester-volk (⸗‐…) n ⓷ priests pl., weitS. clergy; **=weihe** f ordination of a priest; **=würde** f priestly (or sacerdotal) dignity.
Prim (⸗) [lt.] f ⓸ fenc. (Kopfhieb) prime (guard), cut at the top of the head.
Prima (‐‐) [it. erſte] **I** f ⓸ 1. Schule: first (or highest) class, engl. Gymnaſien:

♪ Muſik; ⚛ Wissenschaft; ✿ Pflanze; ♀ Geographie; ⊙ Technik; ⚒ Bergbau; ⚔ Militär; ⛵ Marine; ♦ Handel; ✉ Post; ⛟ Eisenbahn.

[Primadonna] — 774 — [Probe]

sixth form. — 2. ✱ = **Primawechsel**.
— II ♀ als *a. inv.* 3. (feinste, beste Sorte) of prime (or best) quality; A 1, A one.
Prima=donna (⌣⌣⌣⌣) [it.] *f* ⊕ (erste Opernsängerin) prima donna, leading lady.
Primage ↓ ✱ (⌣ʟ⌣) [fr. *m*] *f* ⊕ (dem Schiffskapitän entrichteter Prozentsatz von der Fracht) primage (= Kaplaken).
Primaner (⌣ʟ⌣) *m* ⊕ student of the highest class, in England: sixth-form boy. [buch) day-book.
Prima Nota öst. ✱ (⌣ʟ⌣) [it.] *f* (Tage=)
Prima=qualität *f* = =sorte.
primär (⌣ʟ) [fr. *primaire*] *a.* ⊕ primary; *elect.* 2er Draht primary wire.
Primär=schule (⌣ʟ...) *f* ⊕ primary school; vgl. Elementarschule; =strom *m*, *elect.* primary current.
Primas (⌣ʟ) [lt.] *m, inv. (pl. auch* Prima'ten) *eccl.* (oberster Bischof) primate.
Prima=sorte (⌣ʟ⌣⌣) *f* ⊕ prima quality, firsts *pl.* [primateship.]
Primat (⌣ʟ) [it.] *m* u. *n* ⊕c. *eccl.* primacy,
prima vista ♪, ✱ (⌣ʟ⌣) [it.] *adv.* at (first) sight.
Prima=ware ✱ (⌣ʟ...) *f* ⊕ first-class (or first-rate) goods *pl.*; =wechsel ✱ *m* first of exchange.
Prime (⌣ʟ; *Hom.* Prieme) [it.] *f* ⊕
1. = **Prim**. — 2. *eccl.* (erste Betstunde) prime.
Primel ♀ (⌣ʟ) [lt. Erstling (des Frühlings)] *f* ⊕ primrose, cowslip (*Pri'mula*); ~**n=bund** (⌣ʟ⌣) *m* ⊕ (engl. Bund konservativer Männer u. Frauen) PrimroseLeague (1883).
Primen=blatt (⌣ʟ⌣) *n* ⊕ *typ.* first page.
Prim=geld ↓ ✱ (⌣ʟ) *n* ⊕ = **Primage**.
primitiv (⌣⌣ʟ) [lt.] *a.* ⊕ (ursprünglich) primitive; (einfach) simple.
Primiz (⌣ʟ) [lt.] *f* ⊕⊕ *Cath. eccl.* (erste Messe e-s Priesters) first mass of a newly-ordained priest. [geburt] primogeniture.
Primogenitur (⌣⌣⌣ʟ) [mlt.] *f* ⊕ (Erst=)
Primus (⌣ʟ) [lt. Erster] *m* ⊕ Schule: head boy of a form; Primus omnium [lt. Erster von allen] captain of a school.
Prim=zahl (⌣ʟ) *f* ⊕ *arith.* prime number.
Prinz (ʟ) [mhd.; fr. *prince*; *lt. princeps*] *m* ⊕ prince (von königlichem Geblüt of the Blood [Royal]).
Prinzen=erzieher (⌣⌣...) *m* ⊕, =**hof=meister** *m* tutor (ehm.: governor) of (or to) princes or a prince.
Prinzessin (⌣⌣ʟ) *f* ⊕, *a.* **Prinzeß** (⌣ʟ) *f* ⊕ [fr.] princess (von königlichem Geblüt of the Blood [Royal]).
Prinz=gemahl (ʟ⌣ʟ) *m* ⊕ Prince Consort (in England bsd. Prinz Albert, † 1861).
Prinzip (⌣ʟ) [lt.] *n* ⊕ ⊕d. (Grundsatz) principle; aus ~ on principle; im ~ einig sein to agree in principle.
Prinzipal ✱ (⌣⌣ʟ) [lt.] *m* ⊕d., ~**in** *f* ⊕ principal('s wife *f*); chief, head, F governor, boss (urspr. *Am.*); (Brotherr [=in]) employer; master, *f* mistress; (Dirigent[in]) manager, *f* manageress.
prinzipi=ell (⌣⌣⌣ʟ) [lt.] *a.* ⊕ und *adv.* on principle; ♀ einverstanden agreed in principle.
Prinzipi=en=frage (⌣⌣ʟ⌣...) *f* ⊕ question of principle; =**reiter** F *m* dogmatist, stickler (for pr.) pedant; =**streit** *m* dispute (or wrangling) about principles.
Prinzlein (ʟ⌣) *n* ⊕ (dim. von Prinz) little (or young) prince, princelet.

prinzlich (ʟ⌣) *a.* ⊕ princely.
Prinzlichkeiten (ʟ⌣⌣⌣) *f*/*pl.* ⊕ party of princes, in Engl.: Royalties *pl.*
Prinz=metall (ʟ...) *n* ⊕ metall. (Legierung von Kupfer und Zint) Prince's (or Prince Rupert's) metal; =**regent** *m* Prince Regent.
Prior (ʟ⌣) [lt.] *m* ⊕, ~**in** (⌣ʟ⌣) *f* ⊕ *eccl.* eines Klosters: prior(ess *f*).
Priorat (⌣ʟ) [lt.] *n* (*m*) ⊕c.: a) (Priorwürde) priorship; b) (a. **Priorei** *f* ⊕ (Wohnung eines Priors) priory.
Priorität (⌣⌣ʟ) [lt.] *f* ⊕ (Vorrang) priority, preference; precedence; ~**en** *pl.* ✱ (Aktien) preference shares *pl.*
Prioritäts=aktie ✱ (⌣⌣ʟ⌣...) *f* ⊕ einer Eisenbahn: preference-share; =**anleihe** ✱ *f* mortgage-loan; =**anspruch** *m* prior (-ity-)claim; =**obligation** ✱ *f* mortgage-bond, debenture; =**papiere** ✱ *n*/*pl.* preference stock(s *pl.*); =**streit** *m* dispute about priority or precedence.
Prischen (ʟ⌣) [Prise, *dim.*] *n* ⊕ small pinch (of snuff).
Prise (ʟ⌣; *Hom.* Priese;) [fr.] *f* ⊕ 1. ↓ prize, capture(d ship); eine ~ machen to secure (or take) a prize. — 2. eine ~ Tabak a pinch of snuff; eine ~ nehmen (a. **prisen** *v*/*n.* (h.) ⊕) to take (a pinch of) snuff.
Prisen=gelder ↓ (ʟ...) *n*/*pl.* ⊕ prize-money *sg.*; =**gericht** *n* prize-court.
Prisma ⚡ (ʟ⌣) [grch.] *n* ⊕ *math., phys.* (Körper mit zwei kongruenten und parallelen Grundflächen und so viel Seitenflächen, als jene Seiten haben) prism.
prismatisch (⌣ʟ⌣) *a.* ⊕ prismatic(al); 2e (durch das Prisma erzeugte Grund=) Farben prismatic(al or elementary) colours *pl.*; doppelt ♀ diprismatic.
Pritsche (ʟ⌣) [ndd.; *Brett*] *f* ⊕ 1. harlequin's wooden sword; (3untrute) schoolmaster's rod. — 2. (Schlagholz) bat; auch = Bleuel. — 3. (hölzerne Lagerstatt) ⚔ guard-bed; in Gefängnissen: plank-bed. — 4. (Sitz hinten am Schlitten) back-seat of a sledge. — 5. ⚔ (leichter Reitfattel) English hunting-saddle.
pritschen (ʟ⌣) [Pritsche 1] *v*/*a.* ⊕ to beat, drub, slap; F *fig.* ich bin (schön) gepritscht I am (nicely) done or in a (pretty) fix.
Pritsch(en)=meister (ʟ(⌣)ʟ⌣) [mhd.] *m* ⊕ harlequin who drubs the people, weit. clown.
Pritstabel *provc.* (⌣ʟ⌣) [russ. *pristaw*] *m* ⊕ (Fischerei=aufseher) inspector of fisheries.
privat (⌣ʟ) [lt.] *a.* ⊕ (nicht öffentlich) private; (vertraulich) confidential.
Privat=abkommen (⌣ʟ...) *n* ⊕, =**abmachung** *f* private agreement or arrangement; =**angelegenheit** *f* private affair or business; vgl. =**sache**; =**dozent** *m* unsalaried lecturer of a German university who receives only the students' fees.
Privat=eigentum (⌣ʟ...) *f* ⊕ private property; =**erziehung** *f* home-education; =**fuhrwerk** *n* private carriage; =**gebrauch** *m*: für den ~ for private use; =**gelehrte(r)** *m* savant without official appointment; =**haus** *n* private (dwelling-)house.
Privatier (⌣⌣⌣tje') [+, fr.] *m* ⊕, ~**e** (⌣⌣⌣tjä') *f* ⊕ = **Privatperson**.

privatim (⌣⌣ʟ) [lt.] *adv.* 1. in a private way, privately, confidentially; sich ♀ zu e-r Prüfung vorbereiten to prepare (o.s.) for an examination by private study. — 2. *univ.* ein Kolleg ♀ (stärker : **privati'ssime**) lesen to lecture to (paying)students either at the Professor's private residence or in the University buildings. [interest.]
Privat=interesse (⌣⌣ʟ⌣⌣⌣) *n* ⊕ private
privatisieren (⌣⌣⌣ʟ⌣) *v*/*n.* (h.) ⊕ to live in privacy or on one's private means.
Privatissimum (⌣⌣ʟ⌣⌣⌣) [lt.] *n* ⊕ *univ.* Professor's (private) lecture (s. privatim 2).
privativ (⌣⌣ʟ) [lt. beraubend] *a.* ⊕
Privat=kasse (⌣ʟ...) *f* ⊕ e-r fürstl. Person: privy purse; =**kolleg(ium)** *n* university lecture for paying students; =**leben** *n* private life; =**lehrer(in** *f*) *m* private teacher; =**lektüre** *f* pr. reading; =**leute** *pl.*pr.persons or individuals *pl.*; =**mann** *m* (private) gentleman; =**meinung** *f* pr. (or individual, unofficial) opinion; =**mitteilung** *f* pr. communication; =**person** *f* pr. person; =**recht** *n* civil law; ♀**rechtlich** *a.* ⊕ according to civil law; =**rücksicht** *f* private consideration; aus ~ on personal grounds; =**sache** *f* private matter; =**schule** *f* private (adventure-)school; =**sekretär** *m* pr. secretary, eines Gelehrten: amanuensis; =**stunde** *f* pr. lesson; =**theater** *n* pr. theatricals *pl.*, amateur theatre. dramatic club; =**unterhaltung** *f* private conversation; =**unterricht** *m* pr. teaching or instruction; =**verhältnisse** *n*/*pl.* pr. affairs or concerns *pl.*; =**weg** *m*: auf dem ~e in a pr. way; =**wohnung** *f* pr. residence; =**zimmer** *n* pr. room; =**zweck** *m* pr. purpose, personal end or object, individual aim.
Privileg (⌣⌣ʟ) [lt.] *n* ⊕ = **Privilegium**.
privilegieren (⌣⌣⌣ʟ⌣) [lt.] *v*/*a.* ⊕ (berechtigen) to privilege, empower; *jur.* privilegierteForderungprivileged debt.
Privilegium (⌣⌣ʟ(⌣)⌣) [lt.] *n* ⊕ (Sonderrecht(e) privilege; (Konzession) license, licence.
pro (ʟ) [lt. *prp.*] **I** *prp.* (für) for; s. pro forma; so viel ♀ Kopf so much per head or a head; ✱ ♀ Stück a piece; ♀ Mille per thousand, per mille. —
II Pro *n, inv.* s. Kontra.
probat (⌣ʟ) [lt.] *a.* ⊕ (bewährt) approved, well tried; (recht gut) excellent.
Pröbchen (ʟ⌣) [Probe, *dim.*] *n* ⊕ small sample.
Probe (ʟ⌣) [mhd.: proof; *it. prova*] *f* ⊕ 1. (Versuch) trial, experiment; metall. assay, auf dem Probierstein: touch; s. ablegen 5; auf ~ on probation, on trial; eine ~ mit et. (auch e-m) anstellen to try (or test) a th. (a p.), to give a th. (a p.) a trial; e-n auf die ~ stellen to put a p. to the test or on his mettle; auf eine harte ~ stellen, oft: to tax to the utmost. —
2. *arith.* (Beweis für die Richtigkeit e-r Rechnung) proof; die ~ machen to do the proof, to prove a sum or one's working. —
3. *thea.* (Vor=itzung) rehearsal, im Kostüm: dress-rehearsal; ~ halten to have a rehearsal, to rehearse. —
4. ✱ ~ von Waren ⚡: sample, specimen;

Signs (see page XVII): F familiar; P vulgar; ⚡ flash; ⚡ rare; † obsolete (died); * new word (born); ⚡ incorrect; ♪ music;

[Probeabzug] — 775 — [Prohibitorium]

(Muster) pattern; laut (ob. nach) ~ as per sample; F nicht die ~! not a bit of it!, not in the least! — 5. (Beweis) ~n von Mut ablegen to show (or prove one's) courage. — 6. 🌑 (Zeichen, Stempel) (trade-)mark, brand, der Goldschmiede: hall-mark.

Probe-abzug ⊕ (ᵘ⁻…) m ㉒ *typ.* proof (-slip or -impression); **=arbeit** f specimen (of one's work); **=blatt** n, **=bogen** m proof-sheet; **=blatt** e-r neuen Zeitung ꝛc.: specimen copy; **=druck** ⊕ m, *typ.* = **=abzug**; **=exemplar** n specimen copy; **=fahrt** f trial trip, maiden trip, experimental trip; ♀**fest** a. ㊌ proof; **=gewicht** n standard weight; **=haltend**, ♀**haltig** a. proof, standard; (echt) genuine; von Gold ꝛc. sterling; **=heft** n specimen part; **=jahr** n year of probation, probationary year; **=kandidat** m probationer at a school; **=kiste** f sample-box; **=kolumne** f, *typ.* specimen page; **=lektion** f trial-lesson; **=loch** ⊕ n Töpferei: trial hole; **=maß** n = Eichmaß; ♀**mäßig** a. according to sample or pattern; **=münze** ⊕ f, mint. proof-coin.

proben (⸮) [Probe] v/a. ㊳ 1. = probieren, ♪ und *thea.* to rehearse. — 2. Gold u. Silber ♀ (als probehaltig stempeln) to hall-mark …

Proben-buch (ᵘ⁻…) n ㉒ *typ.* specimen book; **=karte** f sample-card; **=nehmer** 🌑 m sampler; **=schneider** ⊕ m sample-cutter; **=stecher** m f. Getreide: sampling-stick. [number; vgl. **=heft**.]

Probe-nummer (ᵘ⁻…) f ㉒ specimen)

Proben-zimmer 🌑 n ㉒ sample-room.

Probe-papier (ᵘ⁻…) n ㉒ *chm.* test-paper; **=platte** ⊕ f, mint. trial-plate; **=präparat** n, *opt.* test-object; **=predigt** f trial-sermon.

Prober (⸮) m ㉒ tester, assayer.

Probe-rennen (ᵘ⁻…) n ㉒ Sport: heat; **=ritt** m trial-ride; **=rolle** f. *thea.* (minor) part for a beginner; **=schießen** n trial-shooting; **=schrift** f specimen of handwriting; **=schuß** m trial-shot, a. sighting shot, sighter; **=seite** f, *typ.* specimen page; **=sendung** 🌑 f sample (or parcel) sent on approval; **=stange** ⊕ f beim Stahlbrennen: assaying-beam; **=stecher** m Zuckerfabr.: proofstick; **=stück** n specimen (or sample) of work(manship), ⊕ trial (or assay-)piece; (Versuch) trial; ♀**weise** adv. by way of trial, on probation; F a. ⚗. experimental; **=zeit** f time of probation, probationership.

probieren (⸮) [It. *probā're*] I v/a. ㊳ to try, to (put to the) test; Speisen ꝛc.: to taste, Wein ꝛc. auch to sample; *metall.* to assay; *thea.* to rehearse (f. Probe 3); F er hat's zu oft probiert he tried it once too often. — II ~ n ㉓ = Probe 1 und 3, Sprichw. ~ geht über Studieren practice goes before theory, F the proof of the pudding is in the eating.

Probierer (⸮) m ㉒ one who tries or tests, ⊕ *metall.* assayer, assay-master.

Probier-gefäß ⊕ (ᵘ⁻…) n ㉒ assay-test; **=gläschen** n test-tube; **=hahn** m: a) *mach.* try- (or gauge-)cock; b) an Fässern: sample-spigot; **=hammer** m

assayer's hammer; **=korn** n assay-grain; **=kunst** f assayer's art; **=mamsell** f in Konfektionsgeschäften: show-room lady or girl; **=methode** f method of testing or assaying; **=nadel** f der Goldschmiede: touch(ing)-needle; **=ofen** m assay-furnace; **=plättchen** n assay-plate; **=stein** m der Goldschmiede: touchstone; **=tiegel** m assay-crucible; **=wage** f assay-balance. — Vgl. Probe=…

Problem (⸮) [grch.] n ⓓ. (Aufgabe) problem; **Latisch** (⸮) a. ㊌ (ungewiß) problematic(al); uncertain.

Produkt (⸮) [lt. -⸮… Erzeugnis] n ⓓc. 1. product(ion), des Bodens ꝛc.: agricultural produce or yield. — 2. *math.* (Ergebnis e-r Multiplikation) product.

Produkten-ausstellung (⸮…) f ㉒ oft: agricultural show; **=börse** f produce-exchange; **=handel** m (=händler m) trade (dealer) in agricultural produce; **=makler** m produce-broker.

Produktion (⸮…ᵗⁱˢ(ᵛ)⁻…) [It.] f ㊻ production (auch jur.); (Ertrag) yield, return, einer Mine: output.

produktiv (⸮⁻ᵘ f) [lt.] a. ㊌ (hervorbringend, ertragsfähig) productive.

Produktiv-assoziation (⸮…ᵘ…) f ㉒, **=genossenschaft** 🌑 f co-operative association or society.

Produktivität (⸮…ᵛ⁻…) f ㊻ productiveness, productivity, fertility. [value.]

Produktiv-wert (⸮…f=…) m ㉒ productive

Produzent (⸮…) [lt. Erzeugender] m ㊷ (*ant.* Konsument) producer, *agr.* grower, 🌑 maker, manufacturer.

produzieren (⸮⁻…) [It.] I v/a. u. sich ♀ v/refl. ㊳ 1. (hervorbringen, auch vorzeigen) to produce; *agr.* to grow, vom Boden: to yield; der in Kanada produzierte Weizen the wheat grown in Canada; ein Land, das Weizen (Kohlen, Gold) produziert a wheat-growing (coal-producing, gold-bearing or auriferous) country; im Lande selbst Produziertes home-produce; sich ♀ (öffentlich auftreten) to exhibit (or show) o.s. (in public); sich zum erstenmal ♀ to appear (or perform) for the first time. — 2. jur. (Beweismittel beibringen) to furnish evidence. — II ~ n ㉓ und

Produzierung f ㊻ 3. production.

Prof. abbr. = Professor.

profan (⸮) [It. ⸮] a. ㊌ (nicht heilig) profane, secular; **~geschichte** (⸮⁻…ᵛ) f ㉒ profane history.

profanieren (⸮⁻…) I v/a. ㊳ (entheiligen) to profane. — II ~ n ㉓ und **Profanierung** f ㊻ profanation.

Profeß (⸮) [It.] m I ⓓa. *rel.* = Ordensgelübde; ~ tun to take the vow(s), to go into a monastery or convent. — II ㊷ (in die Ordensgeheimnisse Eingeweihter [Jesuit]) professed Jesuit.

Profeß-haus (⸮⁻…) n ㉒ professed house.

Profession (⸮⁻(ᵛ)⁻…) [It.] f ㊻ (Handwerk) trade, business; (Beruf) profession, vocation; von ~ by trade or profession; **Lell** (⸮⁻(ᵛ)⁻…) a. ㊌, **Liert** (⸮⁻(ᵛ)⁻…ᵘ) (gewerbsmäßig) a. ㊌ professional, by trade; Lierte Gauner professional (or experienced) rogues, old hands *pl.*; **~ist** (⸮⁻(ᵛ)⁻…) m ㊷ = Handwerker; **Lsmäßig** a. ㊌ (u. *adv.*) professional(ly).

Professor (⸮⁻ᵛ⁻) [lt.] m ㉛, ㊹㊻, **~in** (⸮⁻ᵛ⁻) f ㊻ (= Universitätslehrer; als verliehener Titel in England unbekannt) professor, ordentlicher ~, etwa: full prof.; außerordentlicher ~ assistant prof.; **~enkollegium** n professorial lecture; **~enschaft** (⸮⁻ᵛ⁻…) f ㊻ staff of professors, professoriate; **~stelle** f = Professur; **~(en)titel** m title of professor.

Professorin (⸮⁻ᵛ⁻…) f ㊻: a) lady professor; b) professor's wife; Frau Professor(in) N., einfach: Mrs. N.

Professur (⸮⁻ᵛ⁻) [lt.] f ㊻ professorship, professoriate.

Profil (⸮⁻ⁱ) [fr. m] n ⓓ*d. paint., arch., &c.* (Seitenansicht) profile; im ~ zeichnen to (draw in) profile; **~bild(nis)** n ㉒ profile-likeness; **~brett** ⊕ n Geschützfabr.: profile-board; **Lieren** (⸮⁻ᵛ⁻) v/a. ㊳ (im Durchschnitt zeichnen) to (sketch in) profile; **~messer** ⊕ n profile-cutter.

Profit (⸮⁻ⁱ) [fr.] m ⓓc. (Nutzen) profit; **Label** (⸮⁻ᵛ⁻) a. ㊌ (D 9) profitable; **~chen** (⸮⁻ᵛ⁻) n ㉓ *dim.* small profit.

profitieren (⸮⁻ᵛ⁻…) [fr.] v/n. (h.) und v/a. ㊳ to (make a) profit; bei e-m Handel ♀ to profit by a bargain, to make a bargain; **profitlich** (⸮⁻ᵛ⁻) a. ㊌ profitable, advantageous, yielding a profit.

pro forma (⸮⁻ ⸮⁻ᵛ⁻) [lt.] *adv.* pro *forma*, as a matter of form; **Proforma-wechsel** 🌑 m ㉒ accommodation-bill.

Profos, a. **Profoß** ⚔ (⸮⁻ᵛ⁻, a. ⸮⁻ᵛ⁻) [nhd.; fr. Propst] m ⓓa. ㊷ (ehm. Handhaber der Militär-polizei) provost of the army.

Prognose ♋ (⸮⁻ᵛ⁻) [grch.] f ㊻ *med.* (Vorausbestimmung) prognosis; **Prognostikon** (⸮⁻ᵛ⁻…) n ㉘㊾ (Vorzeichen) prognostic; **prognostisch** (⸮⁻ᵛ⁻) a. ㊌ prognostic(al); **prognostizieren** (⸮⁻ᵛ⁻…) v/a. ㊳ (voraussagen) to prognosticate, to predict.

Programm (⸮⁻ᵛ) [fr.; *grch.] n ⓓd. *thea.*, ♪ ꝛc. programme; *pol.* auch: platform, *Am.* ticket; e-r Schule: prospectus; annual report; ein ~ aufstellen to draw (or make) up a programme.

programmäßig (⸮⁻ᵛ⁻…) [programmäßig] a. ㊌, **programm=gemäß** a. according to programme, (ohne Störung, glatt) without a hitch; ♀ abwickeln to go off as previously arranged.

Programmusik ♪ (⸮⁻ᵛ⁻) [Programmusik] f ㊻ programme music, illustrative (or descriptive) music.

Progression ♋ (⸮⁻(ᵛ)⁻…) [lt.] f ㊻ *math.* arithmetische, geometrische, harmonische ~ (Reihe) arithmetical, geometrical, harmonical progression.

Progressist (⸮⁻ᵛ⁻) m ㊷ *pol.* (Fortschrittler) progressist; **Lisch** a. ㊌, **progressiv** (⸮⁻ᵛ⁻f) a. ㊌ (fortschrittlich) progressive, in favour of progress; **Progressiv=steuer** f ㉒ progressive tax or assessment.

Progymnasium (ᵘ⁻…ⁱ(ᵛ)⁻) [It.-grch.] n ㉘ grammar school of the second rank.

prohibieren (-⸮⁻ᵛ⁻) [lt. *prŏhibē're*] v/a. ㊳ (abhalten, ver)hindern) to prohibit.

prohibitiv (-⸮⁻ᵛ⁻ f) [lt.] a. ㊌ prohibitive (regulation, &c.); **~maßregel(n** pl.) f ㊷ prohibitive measures *pl.*; **~system** n prohibitionism; **~zölle** m/pl. (Schutzzölle) prohibitory duties *pl.*

Prohibitorium 🌑 ↓ (⸮⁻ᵛ⁻(ᵛ)⁻) [lt.] n ㉘ writ of prohibition.

⚗ scientific; ♀ botanical; ♀ geography; ⊕ machinery; ⚒ mining; ⚔ military; ⚓ marine; 🌑 commercial; 🌐 postal; 🚂 railway.

[Projekt] — 776 — [Proszenium]

Projekt (⌣́⌣) [lt.] *n* ⓦb. (Plan) project, scheme, design, plan; **~en=macher**(in *f*) *m* projector, schemer, designing p.
projektieren (⌣⌣́⌣) [lt.] *v/a.* ⑬ to project (a. math.), to scheme, to make plans.
Projektil ⌣́ (⌣⌣́) [fr.] *n* ⑬d. projectile.
Projektion (⌣⌣tß(⌣)́) [lt.] *f* ⑯ geom., ast., Zeichenk: projection.
projizieren (-⌣⌣́⌣) [lt.] *v/a.* ⑬ bfb. geom. und Zeichenkunst: to project.
Proklamation (⌣⌣-tß(⌣)́) [lt.] *f* ⑯ (Bekanntmachung) proclamation; ⸰ = Aufgebot; **proklamieren** (⌣⌣⌣́⌣) *v/a.* ⑬ to proclaim; ⸰ = aufbieten.
Proklitikon ⌣ (⌣́⌣) [grch.] *n* ⓢ *gr.* (Wort, das sich im Tone an das nachfolgende anlehnt) proclitic.
Prokonsul (-⌣́⌣) [lt.] *m* ㉖ Alt.: proconsul; **Larisch** (-⌣́⌣⌣) *a.* ⓺ proconsular; **~at** (-⌣́⌣⌣́) *n* ⓜc. proconsulship.
Prokrustes (⌣⌣́⌣) [grch.] *npr/m.* ⓺γ. *myth.* Procrustes; **~=bett** (⌣́⌣) *n* ⑫ (Folterbett) Procrustean bed.
Prokura ⊛ (⌣́⌣) [it.] *f* ⑯ procuration, seltener: proxy; per ~ by (or per) procuration; ~ erteilen to give the proc.; die~h.to have the proc., to sign for the firm; **~=führer** (⌣⌣́⌣⌣⌣) *m* =Prokurist.
Prokurator (⌣-⌣́⌣) [lt.] *m* ㉛ **1.** röm. Alt.: (Vertreter des Kaisers) procurator; Staats-= Staatsanwalt. — **2.** jur. (bevollmächtigter Sachwalter) proxy.
Prokura=träger (⌣⌣⌣⌣́⌣)*m*㉔=Prokurist.
Prokurist ⊛ (⌣-⌣́) *m* ㊷ junior partner who signs for the firm; weit=S. head clerk, managing (or confidential) clerk.
Proletariat (-⌣-⌣́(⌣)) *n* ⓜc. (besitzlose Bevölkerung) proletariat, rabble; **Proletari-er** (-⌣́(⌣)⌣) [lt. Kinder=erzeuger, von *proles*] *m* ㉒ (Alt.: Bürger der untersten Klasse, jetzt: Besitzloser) proletarian; **proletarisch** (-⌣́⌣⌣) *a.* ⓺ proletarian.
Prolog (⌣⌣́) [grch. Vorwort] *m* ⓜc. prologue; den ~ sprechen to prologize.
Prolongation ⊛ (⌣⌣-tß(⌣)⌣) [it.] *f* ⑯ (Verlängerung) Börse: carry(ing)-over; **~s=gebühr** *f* ⑯ (Kostgeld) continuation-rate, contango; **~s=geschäft** *n* (Kostgeschäft)continuation, contango-business.
prolongieren (⌣⌣⌣́⌣) [lt.] *v/a.* ⑬: Wechsel ꝛc. ⸰ (verlängern) to renew ..., to extend (the time for payment of) ..., auch: to prolong ...
Promenade (⌣⌣⌣́⌣) [fr.] ⸰ (Spazierweg) promenade, (Spaziergang) walk, stroll;
promenieren *v/n.* (ſn) ⑬ (luſtwandeln) to take a walk or a ramble or a stroll, to promenade (about), to ramble (or stroll) about.
Promesse (⌣⌣́⌣) [fr. Versprechen] *f* ㊽ (Schuldverschreibung) promissory note.
promethe-isch (⌣-⌣́⌣) [Prome'theus, Titan, der das Feuer vom Himmel holte u. dafür Strafe erlitt] *a.* ⓺ *myth.* Promethean, of Prometheus; Des Ringen Promethean (or Titanic) struggle.
Promille ⊛ (⌣⌣́⌣) [it.] *n, inv.* per thousand (*abbr.* per thou.).
Promotion ⌣ (⌣-tß(⌣)⌣) [lt.] *f* ⑯ univ. graduation, taking a (doctor's) degree.
promovieren (⌣-w⌣́⌣) [lt.] ⑬ **I** *v/a.* to confer a (doctor's) degree upon. — **II** *v/n.* (h.) to graduate, to pass (or take) a (doctor's) degree.

prompt (⌣́) [lt.] *a.* ⓺ (flink) prompt, quick, ready (at hand); *adv.* promptly, readily; ⊛ bezahlen, a. to pay (in) ready cash; **~heit** (⌣́-) *f* ⓯ promptness, promptitude.
promulgieren (⌣⌣⌣́⌣) [lt.] *v/a.* ⑬ (veröffentlichen) to promulgate.
Pronomen ⌣ (⌣⌣́) [lt.] *n* ⑰ *gr.* pronoun (= Fürwort); **pronominal** (⌣-⌣⌣́) *a.* ⓺ pronominal.
Propädeutik ⌣ (⌣-⌣́⌣) [grch.] *f* ⑯ (Vorstufe) propædeutics, introduction; **propädeutisch** *a.* ⓺ (vorbereitend) propædeutic(al), preparatory.
Propaganda (⌣-⌣́) [it.] *f* ⑯ (*pl.* ⸰) (Ausbreitung e-r Lehre ꝛc.) propaganda; ~ für et. m. to make pr. for a th., to propagate a th., *pol.* a. to canvass for a th.
Propagandist (⌣-⌣́) *m* ㊷, **Lifch** *a.* ⓺ propagandist; *s. pol.* a. canvasser.
Proparoxytonon (⌣-⌣⌣́⌣) [grch.] *n* ⓢ grch. *gram.* (Wort mit Aku't auf der drittletzten Silbe) proparoxytone.
Propatria=papier (⌣-⌣⌣́⌣⌣⌣) [lt.] *n* ⑫ German foolscap (paper).
proper (⌣́⌣) f. *propre*.
Properispomenon (⌣⌣⌣⌣́⌣⌣) [grch.] *n* ⓢ grch. *gram.* (Wort mit Zirkumflex auf der vorletzten Silbe) properispome(non).
Prophet (⌣f⌣́) [grch.] *m* ㊷, **~in** *f* ㊼ prophet(ess *f*); mohammedanisch: Allah ist Allah (Gott ist Gott) und Mohammed ist sein ~ Allah is Allah (there is no God but God), and Mohammed is his Prophet; Sprichw. der ~ gilt nichts in f-m Vaterlande a prophet has no honour (Lukas 4, 24: no prophet is accepted) in his own country; F *fig.* Moses (f. de) und die ~en (Bargeld) ready cash; **~en=gabe** (⌣f⌣́...) *f* ⑫ prophetic gift or power; **~enschaft** (⌣f⌣́⌣) *f* ⑯, **~entum** (⌣⌣́⌣) *n* ⑬d. prophetic mission; *coll.* (all) the prophets *pl.*; **~en=schule** *f* school of prophets; **Lisch** (⌣f⌣́) *a.* ⓺ prophetic(al).
prophezeien (⌣f⌣⌣́) [nhd. von † mhd. Prophezei] **I** *v/a.* ⑬ (⑱) (weissagen) to prophesy; (voraussagen) to predict, to foretell. — **II** ~ *n* ㉓ und **Prophezeiung** *f* ⑯ prophecy, prediction.
prophylaktisch ⌣ (⌣f⌣́) [grch.] *a.* ⓺ *med.* (vorbeugend) prophylactic, preventive; **Prophylaxis** *f, inv.* prophylaxis.
Proponent(⌣⌣⌣́) [lt.] *m*㊷ (Vorschlagender) proposer; **proponieren** (⌣⌣⌣́⌣) *v/a.* ⑬ (vorschlagen) to propose.
Proportion ⌣ (⌣⌣tß(⌣)⌣́) [lt. Verhältnis] *f* ⑯ proportion (a. math.); in umgekehrter ~ in inverse proportion or ratio; (Beziehung) relation(ship); **Lal** (-⌣tß(⌣)⌣́) *a.* ⓺ proportional; umgekehrt ⸰ inversely proportional; **~ale** (⌣⌣tß(⌣)⌣́⌣) *f* math.: mittlere ~ mean proportional; **Liert** *a.* ⓺ proportionate; **~s=rechnung** (⌣́...) *f* ⑫ *arith.* (rule of) proportion.
Proposition (-⌣⌣tß(⌣)⌣́) [lt.] *f* ⑯ (Vorschlag) proposition, proposal.
Prop̈rätor (-⌣́⌣) [lt.] *m* ㉛ Alt.: (Statthalter e-r römischen Provinz) proprætor.
Prop̈rätur (-⌣⌣́) [lt.] *f* ⑯ proprætorship.
propre (⌣́p̈⌣) [nhd.: proper; *fr. eigen*] clean, neat, tidy; **~=geschäft** *n.* ⸰ **handel** *m* ⑫ ⓺ (Geschäft für eigene Rech-

nung) business (conducted) on one's own account.
Propri-etät (⌣⌣⌣́) [lt.] *f* ⑯ (Eigentum) property; ⨯ öft. **~en** *pl.* (Puggegenstände u. sonstige kleine Erfordernisse des Soldaten): soldier's own outfit of small articles for his accoutrement.
Propst (⌣́) [ahd.; *lt. propo'situs* Vorgesetzter] *m* ⑦a., **Pröpstin** *f* ㊼: a) *Cath. eccl.* provost of a chapter; **Pröpstin** etwa: Lady Superior; b) evangeliſche Kirche: (Geistlicher unter dem Superintendenten) dean; Pröpstin dean's wife; **Propstei** (-⌣́) *f* ⑯: a) provost's office, provostship; b) pr.'s residence; **propsteilich** (-⌣́⌣), **pröpstlich** (⌣́⌣) *a.* ⓺ relating to the provost.
Propyläen (⌣⌣⌣́⌣) [grch.] *pl.* (Vorhalle der Burg von Athen) the Propylæa *pl.*
Prorektor (⌣⌣́) [lt.] *m* ㉛ prorector.
Prorektorat (-⌣⌣⌣́) *n* ⓜc. prorector's office, prorectorate.
prorogieren (-⌣⌣́⌣) [lt.] *v/a.* ⑬ *parl.* (vertagen) to prorogue.
Prosa (⌣́⌣) [lt.] *f* ⑯ (*ant.* Poeſie) prose.
Prosa-iker (-⌣́⌣⌣) *m* ㉒ prose-writer.
prosa-isch (-⌣́⌣) *a.* ⓺ in prose; (unpoetisch) prosy; (nüchtern) matter-of-fact, jejune.
Prosa-ist (--⌣́) *m* ㊷ = Prosaiker.
Prosa-schriften (⌣́⌣...) *f/pl.* ⑫, **=schrift=steller**(in *f*) *m* prose-writings *pl.*, -writer; **=stil** *m* prose-style.
Prosektor (⌣⌣́) [lt.] *m* ㉛ *anat.* assistant professor of anatomy.
Proselyt (⌣⌣́) [grch.] *m* ㊷, **~in** *f* ㊼ (Neubekehrte[r]) proselyte, convert; **~enmacher** *m* proselytizer; **~en=macherei** *f*, **~ismus** (⌣⌣-⌣́) *m* ㉗ proselytism.
Proserpina (⌣⌣́⌣⌣) [röm. Name der Perse'phone] *npr/f.* ⓺β. ⓺. *myth.* Proserpine.
pros(i)t (⌣́⌣) [lt.] **I** *int.* ⓶! (wohl bekomm's!) much good may it do you!; *iro.* ja ⓶! (daraus wird nichts) F don't you wish you may get it!; you may (go and) whistle for it! — **II** ~ *n* ⓢ good wishes *pl.* [to proscribe, to outlaw.]
proskribieren (⌣⌣⌣́⌣) [lt.] *v/a.* ⑬ (ächten)
Proskription (⌣⌣tß(⌣)⌣́) [lt.] *f* ⑯ (Ächtung) proscription; **~s=liste** (⌣́...) *f* ⑫ list of proscribed persons.
Prosodie ⌣ (⌣⌣-⌣́) [grch.] *f* ㊽, **Prosodik** (⌣⌣́⌣) *f* ⑯ (Lehre v. Versmaßen, a. als Buch) prosody; **prosodisch** *a.* ⓺ prosodic(al).
Prosopopöie ⌣ (⌣-⌣-⌣⌣) [grch.] *f* ㊽ *rhet.* (Personifikation von leblosen Dingen) prosopopeia, prosopopœia.
Prospekt (⌣⌣́) [lt.] *m* ⓦb. **1.** (Aussicht) prospect; (Fernsicht) perspective, (distant) view. — **2.** (a. **~us** ⑬) (Anzeige von et., das erscheinen soll) prospectus (a. ⊛).
prosperieren (⌣⌣⌣́⌣) [lt.] *v/n.* (h.) ⑬ (gedeihen) to prosper, to thrive; **Prosperität** (⌣⌣⌣́) *f* ⑯ prosperity.
prost (⌣́) *int.* ⓶! ⓝ ⓜ b. f. *prosit*; **Prostemahl=zeit** *f* f. Mahlzeit am Ende.
prostituieren (⌣⌣⌣́⌣) [lt.] **I** *v/a.* u. **sich** ⓶ *v/refl.* ⑬: (der Schande preisgeben) (sich) ⓶ to prostitute (o.s.). — **II** ~ *n* ㉓ u. **Prostituierung** *f*, **Prostitution**(⌣⌣-tß(⌣)⌣́) *f* ⑯ prostitution. verhüllend: social evil; **Prostituierte** *f* ㊺ prostitute.
Proszenium (⌣⌣́(⌣)⌣) [lt.; *grch.*] *n* ㉘ *thea.* (Vorbühne) proscenium; **~s=loge** (⌣́...) *f* ⑫ proscenium-(or stage-)box.

Zeichen (f. S. XVII): F familiär; P Volkssprache; Γ Gaunersprache; ⸰ selten; † alt (auch gestorben); * neu (auch geboren); ⁑ unrichtig;

Protagonist (-ᴗ-ᴗ) [grch.] m ㊷ Alt.: (Vorkämpfer) protagonist; weitS. (Hauptperson) principal person.

protegieren (-ᴗ-ᴠ) [fr. *protéger*] v/a. ⓽ (begünstigen) to patronize.

Prote-in ⚷ (-ᴗ-) [grch.] n ⓪d. *chm., physiol.* (Grundstoff im Eiweiß ꝛc.) protein.

prote-isch ⚷ (-ᴵᴗ) [Proteus] a. ⓺⓺ (die Gestalt leicht ändernd) Protean.

Protektion (ᴗ-tᵏ(ᴗ)ᴸ) [lt.] f ㊺ (Schutz) protection, (Gönnerschaft) patronage; ~ist (ᴗ-tᵏ(ᴗ)ᴵᴗ) m ㊷ (Schutzzöllner) protectionist; **Listisch** a. ⓺⓺ protectionist.

Protektor (ᴗ-ᴗ) [lt.] m ㉛ (Gönner) protector, patron; ~at (ᴗᴗ-ᴵ) n ⓫c., ~schaft (ᴗᴗᴗ) f ㊺ (Schutzherrschaft) protectorate, protectorship.

Protest (ᴗ-ᴗ) [it. *prote'sta f*] m ⓫b.
1. (Einwendung) protest; ~ (Verwahrung) gegen et. einlegen to enter a protest against (or to raise an objection to) a th.; ~ (Einspruch) erheben to protest. —
2. ⨁ f. Nichtannahme; mit ~ zurückkommen to be returned under protest.

Protestant (ᴗ-ᴗ) [lt.] m ㊷, ~in f ㊼ *eccl.* Protestant; ~en-verein m Pr. union; **Lisch** (ᴗ-ᴗᴗ) [lt.] a. ⓺⓺ Protestant; Elisabeth wurde Lisch erzogen Elizabeth was brought up in the Protestant faith or as a Protestant; ~ismus (ᴗᴗᴗᴗ) m ㉗ Protestantism.

Protestation (ᴗᴗ-tᵏ(ᴗ)ᴸ), ~s-schrift jur. u. ⨁ f ㊺ protest (in writing).

protestieren (ᴗᴗ-ᴵᴗ) [lt.] ⓽ **I** v/n. (h.): gegen et. ⚹ (sich verwahren) to protest against (or to object to) a th. —
II v/a. ⨁ e-n Wechsel ⚹ to protest a bill. — **III** ~ n ㉓ protest(ation).

Protest-kosten ⨁ (ᴗ-ᴗ-ᴗᴗ) [s. Protest 2] pl. ⓹⓶ jur. protest-charges.

Protestler (ᴗ-ᴗᴗ) m ㊷ protester, objector.

Protest-spesen (ᴗ-ᴗᴵᴗ) pl. = -kosten.

Proteus (ᴵ-) [grch.] *npr/m.* ⓺ᵞ. *myth.* (Meergott von wandelbarer Gestalt) Proteus; **proteus-artig** a. ⓺⓺ Protean.

Protokoll (-ᴗᴗ-) [grch. vorgesetzt] n ⓪d.
1. record (or report) of proceedings, resolutions, &c.; minutes *pl.* of a meeting, &c.; eines Gerichts: register; ein ~ aufnehmen to draw up the minutes; to take down evidence; das ~ führen to draft the report; to keep the minutes or the register; jur. zu ~ geben to state in evidence, to depose; zu ~ nehmen to take down evidence, &c. —
2. ~ e-r diplomatischen Konferenz: protocol.

Protokollant (-ᴗᴗ-ᴗ) [lt.] m ㊷ = **Protokollführer**; **protokollarisch** (-ᴗᴗᴗᴗᴗ) a. ⓺⓺ of (or according to) the minutes.

Protokoll-aufnahme (-ᴗᴗᴗ...) f ㊷ drafting (of) the report or the minutes; **-buch** ⨁ n minute-book; **-führer** m one who keeps the minutes, e-s Gerichts: (recording) clerk of the court; (Altmar) registrar.

protokollieren (-ᴗᴗᴗᴵᴗ) [Protokoll] **I** v/a. u. v/n. (h.) ⓽ (beurkunden) to enter in (or to keep) the minutes of, to take down (on record); to register; ⚹ lassen to leave (or place) on record. —
II ~ n ㉓ und **Protokollierung** f ㊺ (Beurkundung) entry, registration.

protokoll-mäßig (-ᴗᴗᵎᴵᴗ) a. ⓺⓺ according to the minutes or evidence.

Protophyten ⚷ (-ᴗfᴸᴗ) [grch.] *pl.* (allereinfachste Pflanzen) protoph*ytes,* ...ta *pl.*

Protoplasma ⚷ (-ᴗᴗᴗ) [grch.] n ㉘ (Urstoff, lebendiger Inhalt der Zelle) protoplasm.

Prototyp (-ᴗᴵ) [grch.] n ⓪d., ~e f ㊻ (Urbild) prototype. [tierchen) protozoon.〕

Protozoon ⚷ (-ᴗᴗᴵ) [grch.] n ㉘ (Ur-

Protuberanz ⚷ (ᴗ-ᴗᴗ) [lt.] f ㊻ *anat.* (Vorwölbung) u. *ast.* (Lichterhöhung in der Hülle der Sonne) protuberance.

Protz¹ (ᴵ) [nhd.] m ㊷ swell, proud man, F stuck-up fellow; vgl. Geldprotz.

Protz²**-achse** ⨶ (ᴵ-tᴸᴗ) [Protze] f ㊷ limber-axle. [gun-carriage, limber.〕

Protze ⨶ (ᴵᴗ) [it. Barutsche] f ㊸ *artill.*〕

protzen (ᴵᴗ) v/n. (h.) ⓽⓪ (stolz tun) to put on airs, to be (purse-)proud.

protzenhaft (ᴵᴗᴗ) a. ⓺⓺ = protzig.

Protzentum (ᴵᴗᴗ) n ⓪d, **Protzerei** (ᴗᴗᴵ) f ㊻ moneyed man's pride or ways *pl.*

Protz²**-gestell** ⨶ (ᴵᴗ...) n ㊷ limber-body; **-haken** m pintle-hook.

protzig (ᴵᴗ) a. ⓺⓺ 1. (purse-)proud, F stuck-up. — 2. (schmollend) sulky.

Protz²**-kasten** ⨶ (ᴵᴗ...) m ㊷ ammunition-chest; **-loch** n pintle-hole, trail-eye; **-ring** m trail-ring or -eye; **-schemel** m limber-bolster; **-wagen** m = Protze.

Provenzale (ᴗᴗᴗᴵᴗ) [Provence ♀] m ㊷, **...lin** f ㊼ Provençal, inhabitant (or native) of the Provence; **provenzalisch** a. ⓺⓺ (zum Sprachgebiet der Provenzalen gehörig) Provençal.

Proviant (ᴗᴗ(ᴗ)ᴸ) [nhd.: provender; *it. provia'nda f*] m ⓫c. (Lebensmittel) (store of) provisions, victuals *pl.*; für Tiere: forage; mit ~ versehen to provision, to victual; to forage.

Proviant-amt ⨶ (ᴗᴗ(ᴗ)ᴗ-ᴗ) n ㊷ victualling-office; **-ausgabe** f issue of provisions; **-beamte(r)** m commissariat officer; **-boot** ⚓ n provision-boat or -hoy, F bum-boat.

proviantieren (ᴗᴗ(ᴗ)ᴵᴗ) [Proviant] v/a. ⓽ to provision, to victual, to supply with provisions or victuals or food.

Proviant-kolonne ⨶ (ᴗᴗ(ᴗ)ᴗ...) f ㊷ victualling-column; **-magazin** ⨶ n provision-stores ⓹; **-meister** m: a) ⨶ commissary of stores; b) ⚓ purser; **-schein** ⚓ m victualling-bill; **-schiff** ⚓ n victualling-ship; **-wagen** m victualling-wagon; **-wesen** ⨶ n commissariat.

Provinz (ᴗᴗᴵ) [lt.] f ㊺ province, im Gegensatz zur Hauptstadt, auch: country; Verwandte, Vettern aus der ~ relations from the country, auch country-cousins *pl.*; thea. Gastrollen in der ~ geben to go starring (or touring) in the provinces. [provincial.〕

Provinz-bewohner(in f) m (ᴗᴗᴗ...) ㊷〕

Provinzial (ᴗᴗᴗᴗᴵ) [lt.] **I** m ⓪d. *rel.* (Ordens-)~ provincial of an order. —
II ♀ a. ⓺⓺ (landschaftlich) provincial; ~e(r) (ᴗᴗ(ᴗ)ᴵᴗ) m ㊼ provincial, countryman. [vincial paper.〕

Provinzial-blatt (ᴗᴗᴗ(ᴗ)ᴵᴗ) n ㊷ pro-〕

Provinzialismus (ᴗᴗᴗᴗᴗᴗ) m ㉗ (Spracheigentümlichkeit e-r Provinz) provincialism.

Provinzial-regierung (ᴗᴗᴗ(ᴗ)ᴵᴵ...) f ㊷ provincial government; **-schulkollegium** n educational board of a province; **-schulrat** m inspector of schools of a province; **-stadt** f provincial town;

-stände *m/pl.* provincial diet; **-synode** f prov. synod; **-theater** n prov. theatre.

provinziell (ᴗᴡ(ᴗ)ᴸ) a. ⓺⓺ provincial.

Provinzler (ᴗᴡᴗ) m ㊷, ~in f ㊼ (Kleinstädter[in]) provincial.

Provision ⨁ (ᴗᴡ-(ᴗ)ᴸ) [lt.] f ㊺ (Gebühr) commission, F com.; e-s Maklers: brokerage; **Ls-frei** ⨁ (ᴗᴡ-(ᴗ)ᴸ...) a. ⓺⓺ free of commission; **-s-reisende(r)** m ㊷ traveller on commission; **Ls-weise** *adv.* on commission.

Provisor P (ᴗᴡᴸᴗ) [lt.] m ㉛ (Apothekergehilfe) chemist('s assistant).

provisorisch (ᴗᴡ-ᴵᴗ) [lt.] a. ⓺⓺ (einstweilig) provisional, temporary; **Provisorium** (ᴗᴡ-ᴵ(ᴗ)ᴗ) [lt.] n ㉘ (vorläufige Einrichtung) provisional (or temporary) arrangement or state.

Provokation (ᴗᴡᴗ-tᵏ(ᴗ)ᴸ) [lt.] f ㊺ (Herausforderung) provocation.

provozieren (ᴗᴡᴗᴵᴗ) ⓽ **I** v a.: e-n, et. ♀ to provoke a p... a th. — **II** v/n. (h.): auf et. ♀ (sich berufen) to refer to a th.

Prozedere ⚷ (ᴗᴵᴗᴗ) [lt.] n ⓹⓪ *chm.* (Verfahren) process.

prozedieren ⚷ (ᴗ-ᴵᴗ) [lt.] v/n. ⓽ (vorgehen) to proceed.

Prozedur (ᴗ-ᴵ) [neu-lt.] f ㊻ (Verfahren) procedure, (manner of) proceeding at law.

Prozent (ᴗᴵ) [neu-lt. für Hundert] n ⓪b, ⓺ (abbr. ⁰⁄₀) per cent(.); zu 5 ~ at five per cent(.); zu hohen ~en at a high percentage or rate of interest.

...prozentig (..."ᴵᴗ) a. ⓺⓺ in Zssgn mit Zahlwörtern, zB.: drei-Ze Rente, Papiere three per cent(.) stock, three per cents *pl.*

Prozent-rechnung (ᴗᴵ...) f ㊷ interest account; **-satz** m percentage, rate per cent(.), rate of interest.

prozentual (ᴗᴵᴗ) [neu-lt.] a. ⓺⓺ (nach Prozenten berechnet) per cent(.), expressed as percentage; **~-gebühr(en** *pl.*) (ᴵ...) f ㊷ percentage.

Prozeß (ᴗᴵ) [lt.] m ⓫a. 1. *jur.* (Klage) action, (Rechtsstreit) lawsuit, (Verhör) trial, (Rechtsgang) legal process; f. anfangen 1; e-m e-n ~ anhängen to take (legal) proceedings against a p., to bring (or lay) an action against a p., f. führen 8; im ~ mit e-m liegen to be involved in a lawsuit with a p.; e-m den ~ m. to put a p. on (his) trial, to try a p. for s.th., to bring a p. to justice; der ~ schwebt noch the case is still pending or (lt.) sub judice; *fig.* kurzen ~ machen to act quickly; to deal summarily with a th., to cut a matter short; mit et. (e-m) kurzen ~ machen to make short work of a p., a th.; Sprichw. s. mager 2. —
2. allg.: (naturgemäßer Vorgang) (natural) process, (Verfahrungsweise) (mode of) procedure, operation.

Prozeß-akten (ᴗᴵ...) *pl.* ㊷ *jur.* papers connected with (or records of) a lawsuit, pleadings *pl.*; **-form(el)** / form of procedure; **-führer** m litigant, plaintiff's counsel; **-führung** f conduct (or management) of a case.

prozessieren (ᴗᴗ-ᴵᴗ) [lt.] **I** v/a. (h.) ⓽ to carry on a lawsuit (or to litigate) with a p.; **~de(r)** s. litigant, suitor.
II ~ n ㉓ going to law, litigation.
— **III ~de(r)** s. litigant, suitor.

Prozession (ˇ‿(ˇ)ˊ) [lt.] f ㊻ (feierlicher Zug) procession; eine ~ halten to hold a (or to go in) proc.; **~s-spinner** m ⑫ ent. processionary caterpillar (Cnethoca'mpa processio'nea).

Prozeß-kosten (ˇˊ...) pl. ㊷ jur. costs pl. of a lawsuit, law-costs pl.; **=ordnung** f forensic procedure, auch: rules pl. of (the) court; **=sache** f legal case or business; **=sucht** f litigiousness; **=süchtig** a. ㊶ litigious.

prozessualisch (ˇ‿ˇ‿ˊ) a. ㊶ jur. connected with a lawsuit or trial.

Prozeß-verfahren (ˇˊ...) n ⑫ jur. procedure; ein ~ gegen e-n einleiten to institute proceedings (or to proceed) against a p.; **=wesen** n forensic (or law-)business; **=wut** f = **=sucht**.

prüde (ˊ‿) [fr.] a. ㊶ (zimperlich) prudish, (spröde) coy, v. Jungfern: old-maidish.

Prudelei prove. F (‿ˊ‿) f ㊻ (pfuscherei, botching, botched work; **prudeln** (ˊ‿) v/n. (h.) ⓶a. (pfuschen) to botch, bungle.

Prüderie (‿ˊ‿) [fr.] f ㊻ (Zimperlichkeit) prudishness, (Sprödigkeit) coyness.

prüfen (ˊ‿) [mhd.: prove; *fr. prouver] I v/a. u. sich ⓶ v/refl. ㊾ 1. (erforschen) (sich) ⓶ to examine (o.s.), gründlicher: to scrutinize (o.s.); (besichtigen) to inspect, to look into; (erproben) to try, to (put to the) test, ⊙ metall. to assay; (genau untersuchen) to sift, to investigate; F to con (over); j-s Kenntnisse ⓶ to test a p.'s knowledge; e-e Rechnung ⓶ to check (amtlich: to audit) an account; die Richtigkeit von et. ⓶ to verify a th.; Wein ꝛc: to taste; *bibl.* prüfet alles //! prove all things //!; *fig.* die Herzen (und Nieren) ⓶ *bibl.* to try the hearts (and reins); ⓶der Blick searching glance.—2. *bibl.*, ꝛc. (durch Trübsal läutern) to visit, to afflict.—II ~ n ㉓ 3. f. Prüfung.—III ge-prüft p.p. und a. ㊶ 4. in den Bed. des *inf.*; vom Schicksal schwer geprüft severely tried (or sorely afflicted) by fate.—5. Der Lehrer certificated teacher.

Prüfer (ˊ‿) m ⑫ **~in** f ㊼ examiner, tester, ⊙ metall. assayer.

Prüfling (ˊ‿) m ⓶d. p. to be examined, examination-candidate, examinee.

Prüf-stein (ˊ‿ˊ) m ⑫ = Probierstein.

Prüfung (ˊ‿) f ㊻ 1. (zu prüfen 1): examining, &c., examination, scrutiny; probation, investigation, verification; f. bestehen 1 u. 5.—2. (zu 2 u. 3) visitation, affliction; harte (oder schwere) ~ severe (or sore, hard) trial.

Prüfungs-arbeit (ˊ‿...) f ㊻ examination-paper; **=behörde** f examining board, board of examiners, für engl. Beamte = Civil Service Commissioners pl.; **=kommission** f = **=behörde**; **=ordnung** f regulations pl. for the conduct of an examination; **=tag** m day of examination; **=zeit** f: a) time of examination; b) time of (sore) trial; **=zeugnis** n certificate, diploma, für Lehrer ꝛc., auch: parchment. [probation.]

Prüf-zeit (ˊ‿ˊ) f ⑫ time of trial or

Prügel (ˊ‿) [mhd.] m ⑫ 1. cudgel, (hard) stick.—2. ~ pl., auch Tracht ~ (derbe Schläge) hard blows, stripes pl., good hiding, sound cudgelling or beating or thrashing or flogging; (eine Tracht) ~ bekommen to get a good beating, F to come in for a good licking or hiding.

Prügelei (‿ˊ) f ㊻ 1. = Prügel 2.—2. (Schlägerei) (street-)fight, scuffle.

Prüg(e)ler (ˊ(‿)‿) m ⑫ cudgeller.

Prügel-holz (ˊ‿...) n ⑫ = Prügel 1; **=junge**, **=knabe** m whipping-boy, (Sündenbock) scapegoat.

prügeln (ˊ‿) [Prügel] v/a. to cudgel, beat, thrash, flog, pommel, auch: to belabour, mit dem Rohrstocke: to cane; e-n beinahe tot ⓶ to beat (or thrash) a p. within an inch of his life; sich (ea.) ⓶ v/recip. to (have a) fight, to come to blows.

Prügel-strafe (ˊ‿...) f ⑫ corporal punishment, mit dem Rohrstocke: caning, Rute: birching; **=suppe** F f = Prügel 2.

Prünelle (‿ˊ‿) [++ fr.] f ㊻ (getrocknete Schälpflaume) prunello, ⓐ auch oft: prune.

Prunk (ˊ) [ndd.: prangen] m ⓶b. magnificence, splendour, pomp; (Aufwand) luxury; in reichem ~ in great state; bsd. b.s. (Schaugepränge) fine show, gorgeous display.

Prunk-bett (ˊ‿ˊ) n ⑫ bed of state.

prunken (ˊ‿) [Prunk] I v/n. (h.) ㊾ 1. to exhibit great splendour or wealth, to make a fine show or display, F to show off, to cut a dash, to do the grand or the swell; mit et. ⓶ to boast of a th.—II ⓶d p.pr. u. a. ㊶ 2. in den Bed. des *inf.*—3. = prunkvoll.

Prunk-essen (ˊ‿...) n ⑫ (Bankett) banquet; **=gemach** n state-, drawing-room; **=gewand** n gorgeous dress, costly garment.

prunkhaft (ˊ‿) a. ㊶ = prunkvoll.

Prunk-liebe (ˊ‿...) f ㊻ love of display; **=liebend** a. ㊶ luxurious; fond of show or display, vgl. **=süchtig**; **=los** a unostentatious, unadorned simple; **=losigkeit** f unostentatiousness, simplicity; **=mahl** n banquet; **=rede** f pompous speech; declamation; **=redner** m pompous orator; **=stück** n spectacular performance, F show-piece; **=sucht** f love of splendour, ostentatiousness, pomposity; **=süchtig** a. ostentatious, pompous; vgl. **=liebend**; **=voll** a. splendid, gorgeous, meist b.s. pompous, showy; **=zimmer** n = **=gemach**.—Vgl. a. Pracht=...

prusten (ˊ‿) [ndd.] v/n. (h.) ㊾ 1. von Katzen: to spit.—2. F von Personen: (heftig niesen) to sneeze aloud; (laut lachen) to burst out laughing.

Prytane (‿ˊ‿) [grch.] m ㊹ Alt.: (obrigkeitliche Person) prytanis.

Prytane-um (‿ˊ‿ˊ) [grch.] n ㉓ Alt.: (Rathaus der Fünfhundert in Athen) prytaneum.

P. S. abbr. a) = postscriptum [lt. Nachschrift] postscript; b) = Pferdestärke.

Psalm (ˊ) [grch.] m ⓶c. bibl. psalm.

Psalmen-buch (ˊ‿...) n ⑫ book of psalms, psalter; **=dichter**, **=sänger** m psalm(od)ist; **=gesang** m, **=singen** n singing of psalms, psalmody.

Psalmist (‿ˊ) m ㊷ = Psalmendichter.

psalmodisch (‿ˊ‿) a. ㊶ psalmodic, relating to psalmody.

Psalter (ˊ‿) [grch.] m ⑫ 1. Alt.: Saiteninstrument: psaltery.—2. bibl. (Buch der Psalmen) Psalter.—3. zo = Blättermagen.

pseudonym[1] (‿ˊ‿) [grch.] a. ㊶ (unter erdichtetem Namen auftretend) pseudonymous.

Pseudonym[2] (‿ˊ‿) n ⓶d. pseudonym.

pst (ˊ) int. pist!, hush!, 'sh!, silence!

Psyche (ˊ‿) [grch.] I npr/f. ㊾㉝. myth., ast. Psyche.—II f ㊻ (Seele) soul.

Psychiatrie ⚡ (‿(‿)ˊ) [grch.] f ㊻ (Seelenheilkunde) psychiatry. [psychical.]

psychisch (ˊ‿) [grch.] a. ㊶ (seelisch) psychic,

Psycholog ⚡, **~e** (‿ˊ‿) [grch.] m ⑫, f ㊻ (Seelenforscher) psychologist; **~ie** (‿‿ˊ) f ㊻ (Seelenforschung) psychology. **=isch** (‿ˊ‿) a. ㊶ psychological.

p. t. abbr. = pro te'mpore [lt. für jetzt] (abbr. pro tem., p. t.)

Ptolemäer (‿‿ˊ‿) [v-r Ptolomä'er] m/pl. ⑫ Alt.: die ~ (äg. Könige, 323–30 v. Chr.) the Ptolemies pl.

ptolemäisch (‿‿ˊ‿) [Ptolemäus] a. ㊶ Ptolemæan, Ptolemaic; **Des Weltsystem** Ptolemaic system of astronomy.

Ptolemäus (‿‿ˊ‿) npr/m. ㊹ γ. (Astronom u. Geograph zu Alexandrien, 2. sae. n. Chr.) Ptolemy. [bartet) puberty.]

Pubertät (‿‿ˊ) [lt.] f ㊻ physiol. (Mann-]

publice (ˊ‿tß-) [lt.] adv. publicly.

Publikandum (‿‿ˊ‿) [lt.] n ㉓ (Anschlag) public announcement, poster.

Publikation (‿‿‿tß(‿)ˊ) [lt.] f ㊻ (Bekanntmachung) publication.

Publikum (ˊ‿‿) [lt.] n ㉓ 1. public; das große (oder allgemeine) ~ the general public, the public at large, F the million; (Zuhörerschaft) audience.—2. (auch ㊾) univ. (öffentliche Vorlesung) public (gratis) lecture(s pl.).

publizieren (‿‿ˊ‿) [lt.] I v/a. ㊾ (veröffentlichen) to publish;—II ~ n ㉓ u. **Publizierung** f ㊻ publication.

Publizist (‿‿ˊ) [lt.] m ㊷ political writer; **~ik** f (‿ˊ‿) f ㊻ pol. writing, journalism; **=isch** a. ㊶ journalistic.

Publizität (‿‿‿ˊ) [lt.] f ㊻ (Öffentlichkeit) publicity. [SH., &c. auch: Puck.]

Puck (ˊ) [ndd.] m ㉓ (Kobold) hobgoblin,

puckern prove. u. F (ˊ‿) v/n. (h.) ⓶a. (dumpf pochen) to (produce a dull) throb.

Pud (ˊ) [russ. put m] n ⓶c.6. (russ. Gew. = 40 russ. ℔ = 16,375 Kilogr.) pood.

Puddel-arbeiter ⊙ (ˊ‿...) m ⑫ metall. puddler; **=hütte** f forge; **=luppe** f puddled ball; **=maschine** f mechanical puddler, puddling-machine.

puddeln ⊙ (ˊ‿) [engl.] v/a. ㊾a. metall. (im Flammofen frischen, umrühren) to puddle.

Puddel-ofen ⊙ (ˊ‿...) m ⑫ metall. puddling-furnace; **=roheisen** n forge-pig; **=schlacke** f puddling-slag; **=stahl** m puddle-steel; **=walzwerk** n rolling-mill. [pudding.]

Pudding ⚡ (ˊ‿) [engl.] m ⓶d. ㊽ Kocht.:

Puddler ⊙ (ˊ‿) m ⑫ metall. puddler.

Pudel (ˊ‿) [ndd.] m ⑫ 1. (Hund mit trauszottigem Haare) (French) poodle.—2. fig. (f. der niedrige Dienste leistet) menial (servant), drudge; wie ein begossener ~ dasteh(e)n to stand quite abashed or ashamed or dumbfounded, vgl. begießen III; f. Kern 2.—3.—~-kopf weiß. (schlumpige Frauensperson) slut, sloven(ly creature).—4. Kegelspiel: (Fehlwurf) miss, F boss; (Versehen) blunder,

Signs (see page XVII): F familiar; P vulgar; ꜰ flash; ❋ rare; † obsolete (died); * new word (born); ✠ incorrect; ♪ music;

[pudeldick] — 779 — [Punkt]

pudel-dick (ᵘ⌣...) *a.* ⊙ very thick; (sehr satt) quite full of eating and drinking; sich 2 essen to eat one's fill, to gorge o.s. (with food); **-hund** *m* ⊙ = Pudel 1; **-kopf** *m* dishevelled hair, F mop; **-mütze** *f* fur cap.

pudeln (⌣ᴸ) *v/n.* (ju) ⊙ *a.* Kegelspiel: (nicht treffen) to miss, F boss; *fig.* to blunder.

pudel-närrisch F (ᵘ⌣...) *a.* ⊙ very droll or funny; quite crazy; **-naß** *a.* soaked, drenched (to the skin).

Puder (ᴸ⌣) [fr. *poudre f*] *m* ⊙ powder for the face or hair; **-beutel** (ᵘ⌣...) *m* ⊙ powder-bag; **-büchse** *f* powder-box.

pud(e)rig (ᴸ⌣⌣) *a.* ⊙ powdered.

Puder-mantel (ᵘ⌣...) *m* ⊙ beim Haarschneiden: barber's haircutting cloth.

pudern (ᴸ⌣) *v/a. u.* sich 2 *v/refl.* ⊙ *a.:* e-n (sich) 2 to powder a p.'s (one's) hair.

Puder-quaste (ᵘ⌣...) *f* ⊙ powder-puff; **-zucker** *m* powdered sugar.

pudrig (ᴸ⌣) f. puderig.

puff¹ (⌣) [lautm.] *int.:* 2! bang!, pop!

Puff² (⌣) [puff¹] I *m* 1. ⊙ (Knall) bang, crash, pop, e-s Gewehrs ꝛc.: report. — 2. = paff 3. — 3. ⑪ ⊙c. (Stoß) cuff, thump, blow, knock; *fig.* er kann einen guten ~ vertragen he can stand a good deal, he is very tough; das kann einen harten ~ schon vertragen that will bear some rough handling or hard knocks. — 4. burſch. = Bordell. — 5. ⊙c. (Bausch) puff of a sleeve, &c.; s.th. puffed up or inflated; small round cushion. — 6. (Richtiges, Täuschendes) deception, fraud, als Reklame: puff. — II *n* ⊙c. 7. = Puffſpiel.

Puff²-ärmel (⌣...) *m* ⊙ puff (or leg-of-mutton) sleeve; **-bohne** ⚥ *f* horsebean (Vi'ciafaba); **-brett** n backgammon-board.

Puffe (⌣) *f* ⊙ 1. = Puff² 5. — 2. (in Falten gelegter Besatz) fluted trimming.

puffen (⌣) [ndd.: puff; *puff¹] *v/n.* (h.) u. *v/a.* ⊙ 1. to puff; *fig.* daß es nur so pufft (tüchtig, gehörig) thoroughly (well), with a vengeance. — 2. (knallend schießen) to bang away. — 3. e-n 2 (derb schlagen) to cuff (or thump, pommel) a p., F to bang (or knock) a p. about. — 4. (sich aufblähen) to puff o.s. out. to swell out. — 5. (bauschig m.) to puff up. — 6. (Puff spielen) to play backgammon.

Puffer (⌣) *m* ⊙ 1. (s. puffen 3) thumper. — 2. = Puff² 3. — 3. (kleines Gewehr) small gun, pop-gun. — 4. Kochkunst: potato-pancake. — 5. ⊙ 🚂 buffer.

Puffer-apparat (⌣...) ⊙ *m* ⊙ = Puffer 5; **-federn** 🚂 *f/pl.* buffer-springs *pl.*; **-scheibe**, **-stange** *f* buffer-disk, -rod; **-staat** *m, pol.* buffer State.

puffig (⌣) *a.* ⊙ 1. puffed (out). — 2. F prov. (ungart) indelicate; (derb) rough.

Puff-otter (⌣...) *f* ⊙ Süd-afrika: puff-adder (*Clotho arie'tans*); **-spiel** *n* (game of) backgammon.

puh (ᴸ) *int.* pooh!, P yah! [bottle.]

Pulle (⌣) [ndd.; *lt. (am)pulla*] *f* ⊙

Puls (⌣) [mhd.;*lt. Schlag] *m* ⊙ *a. physiol., path., med.* pulse; seine Pulse flogen his pulse was beating (or hammering) fast; e-m den ~ fühlen to feel a p.'s pulse (*a. fig.*); j-s ~ zählen to take a p.'s pulse; die Glocken läuteten in drei Pulsen the bells gave three peals.

Puls-ader (⌣...) *f* ⊙ *anat.* artery; **-ader-geschwulst** *f, path.:* ⚕ aneurism.

pulsen (⌣) (h.) ⊙ = pulsieren. [glass.]

Puls-hammer (⌣...) *m* ⊙ *phys.* pulse-

pulsieren (⌣ᴸ⌣) [Puls] I *v/n.* (h.) ⊙ vom Blute: to pulsate, to throb; das Blut pulste (ob. pulsierte) heftig in seinen Adern the blood throbbed (or hammered) lustily in his veins. — II ~ *n* ⊙ pulsation, throbbing.

puls-los (⌣...) *a.* ⊙ pulseless; **-messer** *m* ⊙: ⚕ pulsmeter, sphygmometer.

Pulsometer (⌣⌣ᴸ⌣) [lt.-grch.] *n* (*m*) ⊙ *mech.* (Pumpe mit Dampfdruck) pulsometer.

Puls-schlag (⌣...) *m* ⊙ beating (or throbbing) of the pulse, pulsation; **-stockung** *f* stoppage (or intermission) of the pulse; **-wärmer** *m* cuff, mitten; **-welle** *f, physiol.* pulse-wave.

Pult (⌣) [mhd.; *lt. pu'lpitum *n* Tribüne] *n* (*m*) ⊙ a. desk; (Schreib-~) writing-desk; *ecol.* (Chor-) ~ pew (or seat) in the chancel; reading-desk, lectern; **-dach** (⌣ᴸ⌣) *n* ⊙ *arch.* lean-to roof.

Pulver (⌣⌣)[mhd.;*lt.*pulver-* m] *n* ⊙ 1. (Staub-ähnliches) powder (*a. pharm.*); in ~ verwandeln, zu ~ reiben to (reduce to, grind to) powder, to pulverize; (Schieß-)~ gunpowder; rauchschwaches ~ smokeless powder, cordite, Am. indurite; ~ und Blei powder and shot; ⚔ sie haben noch kein ~ gerochen they have never been under fire. — 2. *fig.* er (das) ist keinen Schuß ~ wert he (it) is not worth powder and shot, he (it) is worthless; er hat das ~ nicht erfunden he is no great light or luminary, he will never set the Thames on fire; sein ~ unnütz verschießen to waste one's powder, to labour in vain; sein ~ verschossen h. to have spent one's substance or strength; to be impotent.

pulver-artig (⌣⌣..., ᴸ⌣...) *a.* ⊙ powdery, pulverous, ⚕ und *zo.* pulveraceous, ...ulent; **-beutel** ⚔ *m* ⊙ powder-bag.

Pülverchen (⌣⌣⌣, ᴸ⌣...) *n* ⊙ (*dim. v.* Pulver) a) little powder; b) poison, drug.

Pulver-dampf (⌣⌣..., ᴸ⌣...) *m* ⊙ powder-smoke; **-explosion** *f* gunpowder explosion; **-fabrik** ⊙ *f* = **-mühle**; **-fabrikant** *m* = **-müller**; **-faß** ⚔ *m* powder-barrel; **-fege** *f* powder-sieve; **-flasche** *f* powder-flask, bsb. ehm. **-horn** *n* powder- (or priming-)horn.

pulv(e)rig (⌣⌣⌣, *a.* ᴸ⌣⌣⌣) *a.* ⊙: a) like powder; b) containing powder.

pulverisierbar (⌣⌣⌣ᴸ⌣, ⌣⌣⌣ᴸ⌣) *a.* ⊙ pulveriz(iz)able.

pulverisier/en (⌣⌣⌣ᴸ⌣, ⌣⌣⌣ᴸ⌣) I *v/a.* ⊙ to (reduce to) powder, to pulverize; *chm., pharm.* (schlämmend zerreiben) ⚕ to levigate. — II ~ *n* ⊙ u. **P/ung** ⊙ powdering, pulverization; ⚕ levigation.

Pulver-kammer (⌣⌣⌣..., ᴸ⌣...) ⚔, ⚓ *f* ⊙ powder-chamber or -room; **-karren** *m* = **-wagen**; **-kasten** ⚔ *m* powder-chest; **-korn** *n* grain of gunpowder; **-kuchen** *m* mill (or press) cake; **-ladung** *f* gunpowder charge; **-lufe** ⚔, ⚓ *f* powder-scuttle; **-magazin** *n* powder-magazine; **-masse** *f* powder-composition; **-mine** *f* powder-mine; **-mühle** ⊙ *f* powder-works *pl.* or -mill; **-müller** *m* gunpowder-maker.

pulvern (⌣⌣, ᴸ⌣) ⊙*a.* = pulverisieren.

Pulver-presse ⊙ (⌣⌣..., ᴸ⌣...) *f* ⊙ gunpowder-press; **-probe** ⊙ *f* powder-trial or -test(ing); **-prober** *m*, **-probier-maschine** *f* powder-prover; **-rauch** *m* = **-dampf**; **-sack** *m* p.-sack; **-scheu** ⚔ *a.* afraid of gunpowder, *fig.* cowardly; **-schlag** ⊙ *m* cracker; **-schwärmer** *m* cracker; **-sieb** ⊙ *n* powder-sieve; **-staub** *m* powder-dust; **-turm** *m* = **-magazin**; **-wagen** ⚔ *m* powder-cart.

Puma (ᴸ⌣)[peru.] *m* ⊙ *zo.* (Silberlöwe) puma, catamount, coug(o)uar (*Felis co'ncolor*).

Pump¹ F (⌣) [pumpen] *m* ⊙ b. burſch.⊙: einen ~ anlegen to run up a bill; auf ~ (Borg) leben, nehmen to live, to take on credit or F on tick. [pump-well.]

Pump²-brunnen (⌣⌣⌣) [pumpen] *m* ⊙

Pumpe ⊙ (⌣⌣) [ndd.; *span. bomba*] *f* ⊙ pump (*auch* ⊥) (*vgl.* Bier-, Druck-, Luft-); die ~ faßt, zieht the pump draws; Wasser in eine ~ gießen, eine ~ ansaugen lassen to fetch a pump, to get a pump to suck; ⊥ die ~ peilen to sound the pump.

pumpen (⌣⌣) *v/a.* ⊙ 1. [Pumpe] to pump. — 2. F [burſch. 18. *sae.*] to take (or give) on tick (f. borgen 1 und 2).

Pumpen-bohrloch ⊙ (⌣⌣...) *n* ⊙ pump-bore; **-eimer** *m* lower pu.-box; **-gerät** *n* pu.-gear; **-gestänge** ⛏ *n* pu.-spears *pl.*; **-hub** *m* pu.-lift; **-kasten** *m* pu.-cistern or -box or -stock; **-klappe** *f* = **-ventil**; **-koker** *m* pu.-casing; **-kolben** *m* pu.-piston or -bucket; **-macher** *m* pu.-maker; **-rohr** *n*, **-röhre** *f* pipe of a pump; *vgl.* **-stiefel**; **-schuh** *m* pu.-sock, sucker (of a pump); **-schwengel** *m* pu.-handle or -lever or -brake; **-sod** ⊥ *m* pu.-well; **-spake** ⊥ *f* pu.-handle; **-stange** *f* pump-rod or -spear, piston-rod; **-stiefel** *m* pump-barrel, body of a pump; **-stock** *m* pu.-staff; **-stütze** *f* pu.-cheeks *pl.*; **-ventil** *n* pu.-valve; **-wärter** ⛏ *m* waterman, pitman; **-werk** *n* = Pump-w.

Pumpernickel (⌣⌣⌣⌣) [ndd.] *m* ⊙ (Westphalian) rye-bread, ⚔ brown tommy.

Pump-haken ⊙ (⌣⌣...) *m* ⊙ pump-hook; **-hose**(*n pl.*) *f* = Pluderhose; **-maschine** ⊙ *f* pumping-engine; **-satz** *m* lift of pumps; **-station** *f* water- (or pumping-)station; **-wage** *f, phys.* pump-areometer; **-werk** *n* pu.-work; ⚒ **-pumptier** or -tyer; **-zylinder** *m* = Pumpenstiefel. — Mgl. Pumpen-... [Carthaginian.]

Puni-er (⌣⌣⌣) *m* ⊙, **~in** *f* ⊙. Alt.: **punisch** (ᴸ⌣) [lt.] *a.* ⊙ Alt.: Punic, Carthaginian; die ~en Kriege the Punic Wars; *vgl.* Treue.

Punkt (⌣) [lt. *punctum* *n* „Stich"] *m* ⊙ b. 1. point (*a. typ.* als Maßeinheit); *typ.* full stop (*vgl.* Pünktchen; auf dem ~e stehen, et. zu tun to be on the point of doing a th.; bis auf den ~ (ganz genau) zutreffen to be exactly the case; bis zu e-m gewissen ~e up to a certain point, to some extent; ~ für ~ gehen to examine in detail; in vielen ~en in many respects; *fig.* höchster ~ des Ruhmes ꝛc.: highest pitch, climax, zenith, apogee; springender ~ [(lt. Punctum sa'liens]] main (or chief) point; wesentlicher, wichtiger ~ im-

---

⚕ scientific; ⚘ botanical; 🜨 geography; ⊙ machinery; ⚔ mining; ⚔ military; ⊥ marine; ⊙ commercial; ✉ postal; 🚂 railway.

[Punktanordnung] — 780 — [Putz]

portant point or matter or item. — 2. ~ 1 Uhr punctually at one o'clock, at one precisely or F sharp.
Punkt-anordnung (⸺) f ⓺ Kristallographie: arrangements of points.
Punktation (-tß(⸺)¹) [lt.] f ⓸⁶ 1. draft of a treaty or deed. — 2. = Abmachung.
Pünktchen (⸺) n ㉓ (dim. v. Punkt) small point; dot, jot, bsd. bibl. tittle.
punkt-förmig (⸺) a. ⓺ punctiform.
punktieren (⸺¹) [mlt. puncta're] I v/a. ⓽³ 1. to point, to dot, durch Stiche: to puncture, to prick; gr. to punctuate; sich die Haut 2 to tattoo o.s.; punktiert dotted; Kupferstecherei: (durch Punkte darstellen) to stipple; punktierte Arbeit stippled engraving; typ. punktierte Linie dotted rule. — 2. (durch die Punktierkunst erforschen) to trace by geomancy. — 3. den Frieden 2 (die Punktation dazu machen) to draw up the preliminaries of peace. — II ~ n ㉓ 4. = Punktierung.
Punktierer ⊙ (⸺) m ㊷. ~in f ㊼ 1. Stechkunst: stippler, one who engraves by stippling. — 2. Punktierkunst: geomancer. — 3. typ. pointer.
Punktier-feder ⊙ (⸺) f ⓺ dottingpen; =kunst f: ⫶ geomancy; =manier f dotted manner, stipple; =maschine f stippling-machine; =nadel f der Gravure u.: dotting-needle; =rad, =rädchen n dotting-wheel; =stichel m stipple-graver, stippler.
Punktierung (⸺¹) f ⓸⁶ (s. punktieren I) pointing, dotting; gr. punctuation.
...punktig (...⸺) a. ⓺ in Zssgn mit a., B.: fein=2 marked with fine dots.
pünktlich (⸺) [Punkt] a. ⓺ punctual; (genau) exact, accurate; der Gehorsam strict obedience; 2 wie ein Uhrwerk like clockwork; aufs Ꝛste besorgen to carry out to the letter; 2 zahlen to pay promptly; **Pünktlichkeit** f ⓸⁶ punctuality; exactness, accuracy.
Punkt-linie (⸺) f ⓺² dotted line.
Punktum (⸺) [lt.] n ㊾ 1. gr., typ. full stop. — 2. fig. (Ende) ein ~ hinter et. m. to put an end to a th. ; das ist genug, (und damit) ~!, a. ~, streu Sand d(a)rum that's enough, and there's an end of it!; now, that's settled!
Punktur (⸺¹) [lt.] f ⓸⁶ 1. surg. (Stich) puncture, puncturation, punction; typ. ~en stops pl. — 2. ⊙ typ. (zum Festhalten des Druckbogens) point.
Punktur-loch (⸺...) n ⓺² point-hole; =schraube f ⓺ point-screw; =spitze f p.-spur; =zange f pincers pl.
punkt-weise (⸺) adv. point for point, (lt.) punctuatim.
Punsch T (⸺) [ind. fünf (: Arrak, Tee, Zucker, Wasser, Zitrone)] m ㊹ⓐ. punch; ~=bowle (⸺) f ⓺² punch-bowl, (hot) negus.
punschen (⸺) v/n. (h.) ⓺¹ to (drink)punch.
Punsch-essenz (⸺...) f ㊷ essence of punch, punch-extract; =gesellschaft f party of punch-drinkers; =glas n, =löffel m punch-glass, -ladle.
Punze (⸺) [it. punzo'ne m] f ㊽, mst ~n¹ m ㉓ Goldarbeiter, Klempner ꝛc.: punch(eon) (Stempel) stamp; **punzen²** (⸺) ⓽⁰, **punzieren** (⸺¹) v/a. ⓽³: a) to punch (out); to stamp; b) metall. (auf den Feingehalt prüfen und stempeln) to (hall-)mark.

Pupill (-⸺) [lt.] m ㊷ = Pupille I; Ꝛar(isch) (-⸺¹(⸺) a. ⓺⁶ jur. pupillary.
Pupille (-⸺) [lt. Püppchen] I m ㊹, f ㊽ jur. = Mündel. — II f ㊽ anat., &c. (Augenstern) pupil (of the eye).
Pupillen-erweiterung (=verengerung) (-⸺...) f ⓺² enlargement (contraction) of the pupil, ⫶ mydriasis (myosis).
Püppchen (⸺) n ㉓ (dim. v. Puppe) little doll. als Kosewort für Kinder u. Frauen: (little) darling or pet or F duckie.
Puppe (⸺) [mhd. puppy; lt. pūpa] f ㊽ 1. doll. a. fig. niedliche Frauengestalt); bewegliche zum Puppenspiel: puppet (a. fig. leicht zu lenkende Person); Schachspiel: die ~n pl. (Figuren) the (chess)men, the pieces pl. — 2. von Personen: a) g.s. darling (child); b) b.s. gezierte ~ affected creature. — 3. F fig. über alle ~n (ungemein) beyond all bounds or all measure, exceedingly; das geht bis in die ~n (hat keine Grenze) it exceeds (or passes) all bounds, that beats all. — 4. ⫶ ent. pupa, chrysalis, nymph; des Seidenspinners: cocoon.
puppen (⸺) v/n. (h.) u. sich 2 v/refl. ⓼⁸ 1. to play with dolls, to dress a doll. — 2. ent. (sich) 2 (bsd. von Raupen) to change into a pupa or chrysalis.
Puppen-bildung (⸺...) f ⓺² ⫶ pupation, change into the pupa- (or chrysalis-)state; ²fressend a. ⓺⁶ ent.: ⫶ pupivorous; =gesicht, =haus n doll's face, house; =macher(in f) m maker (or dresser) of dolls, doll-maker; =räuber m, ent.: ⫶ pupivorous insect; =spiel n: a) playing with dolls; b) puppet-show; fig. (Gaukelei) jugglery; das reine ~ quite a pantomime, a mere farce; =spieler m Punch-and-Judy man; =theater n Punch-and-Judy show; =zeug n doll's clothes pl.; =zustand m, ent. chrysalis-stage or -state.
pur (⸺¹) [lt.] a. ⓺⁶ (rein) pure; aus Ꝛer Neugierde from sheer curiosity.
pure (⸺) [lt.] adv. etwas 2 ablehnen to refuse a th. point-blank.
Püree (-⸺¹) [fr. purée f] n ㊾ u. ㊹ (Brei) mashed potatoes, &c.
Purganz (⸺) [lt.] f ⓸⁶ (Abführmittel) purgative, aperient.
purgieren (⸺¹) [lt.] ⓽³ I v/a. 1. = reinigen. — 2. med. = abführen 5. — II v/n. (h.) 3. med. to take aperients. — III ~ n ㉓ 4. med. purgation.
Purgier-gurke (⸺...) f ⓺² = Koloquinte; =körner n/pl. pharm.: a) (Samen v. kroton) tilly-seed, croton-seeds pl.; b) (v. Ri'cinus commu'nis) castor-beans pl.; =kroton ⚥ m purging-croton (Croton ti'glium); =mittel n aperient, purgative; =pille f, =pulver, =salz n purging (or purgative) pill, powder, salt.
purifizieren (-⸺¹) [lt.] I v/a. ⓽³ (reinigen) to purify. — II ~ n ㉓ u. **Purifizierung** f ⓸⁶ purification.
Purismus (-⸺) [neu-lt.] m ㉗ purism.
Purist (-⸺) m ㊷ (Sprachreiniger) purist; **puristisch** (-⸺) a. ⓺⁶ purist(ic).
Puritaner (-⸺¹) m, ~in f ㊼ hist. u. eccl. Puritan; **puritanisch** a. ⓺⁶ Puritan. Puritanical.
Purpur (⸺) [lt.; *grch.] m ㊾ 1. (=farbe) Alt.: aus dem Saft der ~schnecke: purple

(dye or colour). — 2. (=gewand) purple (gown or robe or garment); in ~ geboren born in the purple; von Kardinälen: den ~ tragen to wear the purple.
purpur-bekleidet (⸺...) a. ⓺⁶ clad (or robed) in purple. =farbe f ⓺² = Purpur 1; ²farben, ²farbig a. purple (-coloured); =fieber n, =friesel n (m. f) path. purples pl.; =gewand, =kleid n = Purpur 2; =holz n purple-wood.
Purpurin ⫶ (⸺¹) [neu-lt.] n ⑪ chm. purpurin(e) ($C_{14}H_5O_2(HO)_3$).
Purpur-lippen (⸺) f/pl. ⓺² purple lips pl.; =mantel m purple cloak.
purpurn a. ⓺⁶ purple, of purple colour.
Purpur-rot (⸺) n ⑪ u. ² a. ⓺⁶ purple; sie wurde 2 her face became quite purple or F as red as a turkey(-cock); =röte f purple (colour); ²sauer a. chm.: ⫶ purpuric; ²saures Salz purpurate; =säure f, chm. purpuric acid ($C_8H_5N_5O_6$); =schnecke f, zo. purple (-fish) (Purpura); =weide ⚥ f red osier, bitter willow (Salix purpu'rea).
purren (⸺) [ndl.] ⓼⁸ I v/a. (h.) = burren. — II nordd. v/a. to poke the fire.
Purzel¹ (⸺) m ㊷ stout little man.
Purzel²-baum (⸺...)[purzeln] m ㊷, =bock m somersault; s. a. Bock 3; e-n =baum machen (ob. schlagen, schießen) to (throw a or turn a) somersault. [tumble.
purzeln (⸺) [Bürzel] v/n. (in) ㊆a. to)
Purzel²-taube (⸺...) f ⓺ orn. tumbler (Colu'mba li'via gyra'trix).
pusseln F (⸺) v/n. (h.) ㊆a. to bustle (or potter) about, F to mess about.
Puszta, öst. **Puszta** (⸺) [slaw. puszta] f ⓽ (ungarische Steppe) Hungarian steppe.
Puste P (⸺) nordd. (Atem) breath, F puff; die ~ ging ihm aus he was out (or short) of breath.
Pustel (⸺) [lt. pu'stŭla] f ㊽ path.: ⫶ pustule; ²-artig (⸺...) a. ⓺⁶ pustular; ~=bildung f ⓺²: ⫶ pustulation.
pusten F (⸺) [ndd.] v/n. (h.) ㊇ 1. to breathe (hard), to (puff and) blow. — 2. Damenspiel: to huff.
Pust(e)rohr P (⸺¹) n = Blaserohr.
put (⸺), a. **putt** (⸺) int. (Lockruf für Hühner) 2! 2! chick! chick! chuck! chuck!
Putchen (⸺) n ㉓ 1. (dim. von Pute) small turkey. — 2. fig. tosend: mein ~! (my) duckie!, my darling or pet!
Pute (⸺) [ndb.] f ㊽ turkey-hen.
Puten-braten (⸺...) s. Puter=...
Puter (⸺) [Pute] m ㊷ turkey-cook.
Puter-braten (⸺...) m ㊷ roast turkey; =hahn m = Puter; ²rot a. ⓺⁶ (as) red as a turkey(-cock). [Puter.]
Put-hahn (⸺...) m ㊷, =hähnchen n =)
Putsch (⸺) [schwz.] m ⓐa. (mißlungener Aufstand) unsuccessful (or abortive) insurrection or rising; (Krawall) riot; **putschen** v/a. u. v/n. (h.) ㊆ to (raise a) revolt, to create a disturbance; to riot; (aufreizen) to incite, to goad (or egg) on.
Püttings-band ⚓ (⸺...) n ⓺² futtock-hoop; =bolzen m chain-bolt; =taue n/pl., =wanten f/pl. futtock-shrouds pl.
Putz (⸺) [ndl.] m ⓐa. 1. a) (das Putzen) dressing, adornment, toilet; b) (feine Kleidung) finery, elegant attire, stylish dress; (Kleidungsstücke) articles pl. of dress, apparel; (Modewaren) millinery;

Zeichen (s. S. XVII): F familiär; P Volkssprache; ℱ Gaunersprache; ⸜ selten; † alt (auch gestorben); * neu (auch geboren); ⚠ unrichtig;

[Putzarbeiten] — 781 — [Quadratzoll]

im (vollen) ~ in full dress, F in full fig. — 2. ⊕ arch. (Mauerbewurf) plaster. **Putz-arbeiten** (⸗...) f/pl. ②: a) der Putzmacherin: = ⸗artikel; b) ⊕ Maurerei: plaster-work; **⸗artikel** m/pl. millinery; **⸗bürste** ⚔ f polishing-brush; **⸗däumchen** n lady fond of dress(ing) or finery. **putzen**[1] (⸗⌣) [mhd.; *ndl. *poetsen*] I v/a. u. sich ⸗ v/refl. ⊕ 1. to clean, to cleanse, (scheuern) to scour; Kocht.: to pick (salad, &c.); (glänzend m.) to shine (up), to polish; to furbish up; sich (dat.) den Bart ⸗ to trim one's beard; hort. Bäume ⸗ f. ausputzen 2; Geschirr ⸗ to wash (or scour) the dishes; Kleider ⸗ (bürsten) to brush clothes; e-e Klinge ⸗ to furbish (up) a blade; Knöpfe ⸗ to shine up buttons; eine Lampe ⸗ to trim a lamp; ein Licht ⸗ to snuff (a candle; Metalle ⸗ to burnish metals; sich (dat.) die Nase ⸗ to blow (or wipe) one's nose; sich die Schuhe, Stiefel ⸗ to wipe one's ..., (wichsen) to clean (or polish) one's ...; sich die Zähne ⸗ to clean (or wash) one's teeth. — 2. ein Pferd ⸗ (bürsten, striegeln) to clean (or brush or rub) down ..., to groom ..., to curry ... — 3. (schmücken) to adorn, to decorate, bes. Personen: to dress, deck out, attire; sich ⸗ to smarten (or dress) o.s. up; fein geputzt elegantly (or smartly, stylishly) dressed. — 4. metonymisch, ohne Objekt: Diamanten ⸗ sehr ... are very ornamental or F dressy. — 5. F co. das Essen vom Teller rein (weg)⸗ to clear the plate. — 6. F e-n ⸗ (hubeln) to reprimand a p. — 7. ⊕ Maurerei: s. abputzen 2. — II ~ n ② 8. clean(s)ing, &c. (s. 1 u. 2). — 9. (s. 3) adornment, attire. — 10. ⊕ = abputzen 5.

Putzen[2] ⊕ (⸗⌣)[Butz(e)²] m ② typ. (tl. Teilchen Farbe 2c., Schmutz aus Buchstaben) pick. **Putzer** (⸗⌣) [putzen¹] m ② 1. (auch ~*in* ⊕) clean(s)er. — 2. = Putzlappen. — 3. F (Verweis) reprimand. **Putz-gemach** (⸗...) n ②: a) dressing-room; b) = ⸗stube; **⸗geschäft** ⊕ n, **⸗handel** m milliner's (or millinery-)business; **⸗händler** m man-milliner; **⸗händlerin** f milliner; **⸗handlung** f milliner's shop. **putzig** (⸗⌣) [Butz(e)¹] a. ⊕ (possierlich) droll, comical, funny. **Putz-kästchen** (⸗...) n ⊕ dressing- (or toilet-)case; **⸗kram** m = Putz 1 b; **⸗laden** m milliner's shop; **⸗lappen** m rag for cleaning, rubber; **⸗liebend** a. fond of dress or finery; **⸗macherei** f milliner's trade; **⸗macherin** f milliner; **⸗pulver** n polishing-powder; **⸗sachen** f/pl. = Putz 1 b; **⸗schere** f für Lichter: snuffers pl.; **⸗stube** f best room or parlour; **⸗sucht** f passion(ate love) for dress or finery; **⸗süchtig** a. (passionately) fond of dress; **⸗tisch** m dressing-table; **⸗tuch** n polishing-cloth; **⸗waren** ⊕ f/pl. articles pl. of dress, millinery; **⸗werk** n ornaments pl.; **⸗wolle** ⊕ f wool(len) refuse for cleaning (or polishing, scouring) machines; **⸗zeug** ⚔ n cleaning-utensils pl.; **⸗zimmer** n = ⸗stube. **Puzzolan-erde** (⸗⌣...) = Pozzuolan-erde. **Pygmäe** (⸗⌣) [grch.] m ⊕ myth. pygmy (a. fig. winziges Männchen); **pygmäenhaft** (⸗⌣⌣), **pygmäisch** (⸗⌣) a. ⊕ (zwerghaft) pygmean, dwarfish. **pyramidal** (⸗⌣⌣´) [lt.] a. ⊕ pyramidal, in the shape (or form) of a pyramid fig. (groß-artig) huge, enormous; **~zahl** (⸗⌣´...) f ⊕ math. pyramidal number.

Pyramide (⸗⌣⌣´) [grch., *äg.*] f ⊕ 1. pyramid (auch math.). — 2. ⚔ die Gewehre in ~n setzen to pile arms. **pyramiden-förmig** (⸗⌣⌣...) a. ⊕ pyramidal, ...ic; **⸗gruppe** f ⊕ group of pyramids; **⸗pappel** ⊕ f Lombardy poplar (*Po'pulus pyramida'lis*); **⸗schnecke** f, zo. pyramid-shell; ~n pl.: zo. pyramidellidæ; **⸗stumpf** m, math.: zo. frustum of a pyramid. **Pyrenäen** ⚥ (⸗⌣⌣´) [flt.] npr/pl. inv. die ~ (Gebirge zw. Frankreich u. Spanien) the Pyrenees pl.; **pyrenäisch** a. ⊕ Pyrenean; Pyrenäische Halbinsel (Spanien u. Portugal) Iberian Peninsula. **Pyrogallus-säure** ⚛ (⸗⌣⌣´⌣) f ⊕ chm. pyrogallic acid ($C_6H_6O_3$). **pyro-phosphor-sauer** ⚛ (⸗´⌣⸗´⌣) a. ⊕ chm. pyrophosphoric. **Pyro-schlein-säure** ⚛ (⸗⌣´⌣) f ⊕ chm. pyromucic acid. **Pyrotechnik** ⊕ (⸗⌣⌣´) [grch.] f ⊕ (Feuerwerkerei) pyrotechnics, ...y; **~er** (⸗⌣⌣´⌣) m ⊕ pyrotechnist; **pyro-technisch** (⸗⌣⌣´⌣) a. ⊕ pyrotechnical. **Pyrrhus** (⸗⌣) npr/m. ⊕ γ. (bsd. König von Epirus, † 272 v. Chr.) Pyrrhus; **~sieg** m ⊕ (Erfolg, der, wie der Sieg des ~ über die Römer 279 v. Chr. bei A'sculum, mit großen Verlusten errungen ist) dearly-bought victory or success. a. Pyrrhic victory. **Pythagore-er** (⸗⌣⌣´⌣) m ⊕ Pythagorean (philosopher), follower of Pythagoras. **pythagore-isch** ⚛ (⸗⌣⌣´) [Pyta'goras, grch. Philosoph, 6. sae. v. Chr.] a. ⊕ Pythagorean; ~e Lehre Pythagorism; math. Der Lehrsatz 47ten proposition of the first book of Euclid, F co. (lt.) *pons asinorum*. **pythisch** (⸗⌣) [Py'thia, Priesterin des Apollo zu Delphi] a. ⊕ Die Spiele (zu Delphi gefeierte) Pythian games.

Q

Q, q (⸗) n, inv. Buchstabe; meist mit folgendem u: Q, q./ Q. abbr. = Quadrat. [dem u : Q, q./ q öst. abbr. = Quintal. **qcm, qdcm, qkm, qm, qmm** = Quadratzenti-, ⸗dezi-, ⸗kilo-, ⸗meter, ⸗milli-meter. **Quabbe** (⸗⌣) f ⊕ 1. (Fettwulst) wen, fatty, growth. — 2. ⚛ zo. = Quappe. **Quabbel** (⸗⌣) m ⊕ 1. (Moor) marsh(y soil), bog. — 2. = Quabbe 1. **quabb(e)lig** (⸗(⌣)⌣) a. ⊕ flabby, wabbling, quaking, von Menschen und Körperteilen: podgy, F crumby; mir ist ⸗ (übel) (zu Mute) I feel sick or F qualmy. **quabbeln** (⸗⌣) [ndd.] v/n. (h.) ⊕ a. von gallert-artigen Massen: to quiver (or shake) like jelly, to quake, F to wabble, von moorigem Boden: to move; von Wangen 2c.: to be flabby or limp. **Quackelei** F (⸗⌣⸗´) f ⊕ 1. (Unentschlossenheit) irresolution, wavering, shilly-shallying, F wabbling; (Tändelei) trifling, dallying. — 2. (wertloses Zeug) rubbish, trash, stuff, F rot. [wabbly.] **quackelig** F (⸗⌣⌣) a. ⊕ irresolute, F/ **quackeln** (⸗⌣) [ndd.: quakeln] v/n. (h.) ⊕ a. to waver, F to wabble; (schwatzen) to prattle, jabber, babble.

Quacksalber (⸗⌣⌣) [ndl.: kwakzalver] ⊕ quack (doctor), mountebank, empiric; **~ei** (⸗⌣⌣´) a: a) quackery, empiricism; b) quack medicine. **quacksalbern** (⸗⌣⌣) v/n. (h.) ⊕ a. to play the quack, to practise quackery; an e-m herum⸗ to physic (or doctor) a p. with quack remedies. **Quader** ⚥ (⸗´⌣)[mhd.; it. *quadro'ne* m; *lt. vier-eckig*] m ⊕, f ⊕ Bauwesen: square (or hewn) stone, freestone, ashlar. **Quader-bau** ⊕ (⸗´⌣...) m ⊕ freestone structure; **⸗bruch** m quarry of freestone; **⸗mauer** f freestone wall, ashlaring. **quadern** (⸗´⌣) [Quader] v/a. ⊕ a. Steine ⸗ to square (or dress, hew) ... **Quader-stein** (⸗´⌣...) m ⊕ = Quader; **⸗werk** ⊕ n freestone work or masonry. **Quadragesima** (⸗⌣⌣´⌣⌣) [lt.] nur in: Sonntag ... mä (erster Fastensonntag) Quadragesima Sunday. **Quadrant** (⸗⌣´) [lt.] m ⊕ ↕, ast., math. (Viertel eines Kreises) quadrant. **Quadranten-elektrometer** (⸗⌣´⌣...) n (m) ⊕ elect. quadrant-electrometer; **⸗elektroskop** n, phys. quadrant-electroscope.

Quadrat (⸗´) [lt.] I n ⊕ c. 1. (Geviert) square; auf das (oder zum, ins) ~ erheben to (raise to the) square. — 2. ♪ (Wiederrufungszeichen) natural. — II m ⊕ 3. ⊕ typ., meist im pl.: ~en quadrats pl. **Quadrat-bein** (⸗´...) n ⊕ zo. (Schädelknochen) quadrate; **⸗förmig** a. ⊕ square, quadratic; ~fuß m sqare foot. **quadratisch** (⸗´⌣) [lt.] a. ⊕ square; math. quadratic; ⸗e Gleichung quadratic (equation); Lehre von den ⸗en Gleichungen (theory of or chapter on) quadratics. **Quadrat-kilometer** (⸗´...) n (m) ⊕ (abbr. qkm, öst. km^2) square (kilo)metre; **⸗meile** f square mile; **⸗meter** n (m) (abbr. qm, öst. m^2) square metre; **⸗millimeter** n (m) (abbr. qmm, öst. mm^2) square millimetre. **Quadratur** (⸗⌣´) [lt.] f ⊕ 1. math., &c. quadrature (or squaring) of the circle. — 2. astrol. quartile. **Quadrat-wurzel** (⸗´...) f ⊕ math. square root; die ~ ausziehen to extract the sq. root; **⸗zahl** f, math. square number; **⸗zentimeter** n (m) (abbr. qcm, öst. cm^2) sq. centimetre; chm. **⸗zoll** m sq. inch.

♪ Musik; ⚛ Wissenschaft; ⚥ Pflanze; ⚘ Geographie; ⊕ Technik; ⚒ Bergbau; ⚔ Militär; ⚓ Marine; ⚖ Handel; ⚐ Post; ⚞ Eisenbahn.

[quadrieren] — 782 — [quasseln]

quadrieren (⌣⌢⌣) [lt.] ⑱ **I** v/a. math. to (raise to the) square. — **II** v/n. (h.) mit et. 2 (ʒf.-paſſen) to fit (with) a th.
Quadriga (⌣⌢⌣) [lt.] f ㊾ röm. Alt.: (Viergeſpann) quadriga, four-horse chariot.
Quadrille (tå-brĭ'l-jĕ) [fr. m, ſpan.] f ㊽ Tanz: quadrille (auch ♪); ~ tanzen to dance a quadrille.
Quadrillion (⌣⌣(⌣)⌣) [neu=lt.] f ㊻ (engl. und dtſch.: 1 mit 24 Nullen) quadrillion.
Quadrupel (⌣⌣⌣) [lt.] m ㊷ (etwas Vierfaches) quadruple; ~=allianz (⌢,...) f ㊶ (Vierbund) quadruple alliance.
Quagga ⚤ (⌣⌣) [hottentottiſch] n ㊿(⑬) zo. quagga (Equus quagga).
quah (⌣) int. Schrei des Raben) croak!
Quai (tä) [fr.] m ㊿ = Kai.
quaken (⌣⌣) [lautm.] v/n. (h.) ⑱ von Fröſchen: to croak, v. Enten: to quack; fig. **quäken** to squeak.
Quaker (⌣⌣) [quaken] m ㉒ croaker.
Quäker ✝ (⌣⌣) [engl. Zitterer] m ㉒, ~in f ㊼ rel. Quaker(ess f).
Quäker-bund (⌣⌣⌢) m ㊻ Selbſtbenennung der Quäker: Society of Friends.
Quäkerei (-⌣⌣) f ㊻ croaking, quacking.
Quäkerei (-⌣⌣) f ㊻ Quakerism.
Quäker=gemeinde (⌣⌣⌣⌢) f ㊻ congregation (or brotherhood) of Quakers.
quäkeriſch (⌣⌣⌣) [Quäker] a. ㊻ of (or like) Quakers, Quakerish.
Quäkertum (⌣-⌣) n ② Quakerdom.
Qual (⌣) [ahd.: qualm] f ㊻ (intense) pain or suffering; torment, torture, agony; great affliction or distress; große ~(en) erdulden oder erleiden to suffer excruciating pain or great agony or F a martyrdom.
qual=beladen (⌣⌣⌣⌢) a. ㊻ full of aches and pains.
quälen (⌣⌣) [ahd.] **I** v/a. u. ſich 2 v/reflx. ⑱ **1.** (ſich) 2 to torment (o.s.); (foltern) to torture; zu Tode 2 to kill by (slow) torture, fig. to worry to death; ſich zu Tode 2 to work o.s. to death, to drudge (or slave) one's life out; er hat ſich umſonſt gequält he has toiled to no purpose, he laboured in vain. — **2.** fig. = plagen; (ſehr langweilen) to bore; (beläſtigen) to molest. — **II** ~ n ㉓ **3.** = Quälerei. — **III** 2d p.pr. u. a. ㊻ **4.** = qualvoll.
Quäler (⌣⌣) m ㉒ tormentor, torturer; (läſtiger Menſch) bore, F affliction.
Quälerei (-⌣⌣) f ㊻ torment, torture; fig. worry(ing), vexation, molestation.
quäleriſch (⌣⌣) a. ㊻ tormenting, worrying, annoying. [torment.]
Quäl=geiſt (⌣⌢) m ㊷ tormentor, F]
Qualifikation (-⌣⌣-tſĭ(⌣)⌣) [lt.] f ㊻ (Befähigung) qualification, fitness, capacity; ~s=atteſt (⌢,...) n ㊻ certificate qualifying for an appointment.
qualifizierbar (-⌣⌣⌣⌢) a. ㊻ qualifiable.
qualifizieren (-⌣⌣⌣⌣) [lt.] **I** v/a. (bezeichnen) to qualify. — **II** ſich 2 = eignen **I**; qualifiziert qualified, jur. v. Verbrechen: with aggravating circumstances.
Qualität (-⌣⌣, ⌣⌣) [lt.] f ㊻ (Beſchaffenheit) quality; (Sorte, Art) sort, kind; erſter, zweiter ~ first-, second-rate; ⊛ die beſſeren (mittleren) ~en (Sorten) the better (medium) sorts or brands pl.
qualitativ (⌣⌣⌣-f) [lt.] a. ㊻ qualitative.

Qualle (⌣⌣) [ndd., ndl. (zee)kwal] f ㊺ zo. jelly-fish, sea-jelly, ⚤ medusa; (Lappen)~ sea-nettle, ⚤ acaleph.
Qualm (⌣) [ndd.: qualm] m ㊶b. dense smoke or mist or vapour, (reeking) fumes pl.
qualmen (⌣⌣) ⑱ **I** v/n. (h.) to rise in fumes, to (give forth dense) smoke, v. der Lokomotive 2c.: to puff (up clouds of smoke), von einem Raucher: to puff away at one's pipe. — **II** v/a.: den Rauch gen Himmel 2 to send up puffs of smoke. [inveterate smoker.]
Qualmer F (⌣⌣) m ㉒ (ſtarker Raucher)]
qualmicht, mſt **qualmig** (⌣⌣) a.㊻ **1.** smoky, (nebelig) misty, (dunſtig) vaporous. — **2.** filled with smoke or fumes.
Quäl=ort (⌣⌢⌣) m ㊷ place of torment.
Qualſter F (⌣⌣) [ndd.: Qualle] m ㊷ spittle, phlegm; **qualſt(e)rig** (⌣(⌣)⌣) a. ㊻ like spittle, viscous.
qualſtern (⌣⌣) v/n. (h.) ㉖a. to spit phlegm, to expectorate. [menting.]
quäl=ſüchtig (⌣⌢⌣) a. ㊻ fond of tor-]
qual=voll (⌣-f⌢) a. ㊻ very painful; tormenting, agonizing, excruciating, racking; harrowing, distressing.
Quantität (⌣⌣⌣, ⌣⌣) [lt.] f ㊻ (Menge) quantity, amount; in kleinen ~en, oft: in driblets or little bits or small lots.
quantitativ (⌣⌣⌣-f) [lt.] a. ㊻ chm., &c. quantitative (analysis, &c.); adv. auch: as to (or as regards) quantity.
Quantum (⌣⌣) [lt.] n ㉘㊾ (Menge) quantum, quantity.
Quappe (⌣⌣) [ndd.] f ㊺ zo.: a) ichth. eel-pout; b) tadpole (= Kaulquappe).
Quarantäne (t⌣⌣⌣) [fr. quarantaine; *it.] f ㊺ ⑯b. ⚓ (Geſundheitsprobe) quarantine; ~ halten to pass (or perform, v. Schiffen auch: to ride at) quarantine.
Quarantäne=anſtalt (⌢,...) f ㊻ = =haus; =aufſeher m quarantine-officer; =haus n quarantine-station or -hospital.
Quark (⌣) [ndd. (uhpd.); ruſſ. twăro't] m ⑪ ㊶b. **1.** curds pl.; cream-cheese; fig. den alten ~ aufrühren to stir up old (forgotten) stories. — **2.** F contp. (etwas Wertloſes) trash, rubbish (vgl. Plunder); da liegt der ~! there goes (the lot)!, there's a mess! [cream-cheese.]
Quark=brot (⌣⌣⌢) n ㊷ bread with]
quarkig (⌣⌣) [Quark] a. ㊻ curdy; (geringfügig) trifling, trashy.
Quark=käſe (⌣⌢) m ㊷ cream-cheese; =kuchen m curd-cake.
Quarre F (⌣⌣) [lautm.] f ㊺ (weinendes Kind) squalling child; Sprichw. f. Pfarre.
quarren F (⌣⌣) [lautm.] v/n. (h.) ⑱ Kinder: to squall, scream; e-m die Ohren voll 2 to din (or shout) into a p.'s ears.
quarrig (⌣⌣) a. ㊻ (fond of) squalling; Les Kind fretful child, auch: cry-baby, F u. P squeaker.
Quart (⌣) [mhd., fr., it. 1/4] **I** n ⑪b, 6. **1.** (ehm. Flüſſigkeitsmaß, in Preußen 1 1/8 Liter) etwa: quart. — **2.** ⊕ typ. (Format gleich einem Viertelbogen) quarto (volume or book). — **II** f ㊾ **3.** (4. Ton vom Grundton aus) fourth, Alt.: diatessaron. — **4.** fenc. (Bruſt innen) carte.
Quarta (⌣⌣) [lt. 4. Klaſſe] f ㊺ fourth (or third lowest) form of a German secondary school.

Quartal (⌣⌣) [lt.] n ⑪d. **1.** = Vierteljahr. — **2.** (Anfangs- oder Schlußtag eines ~s) quarter-day.
Quartal(s)=abonnement (⌣⌢...) n ㊷ quarterly subscription; =abſchluß ⊛ m quarterly balance; =kündigung f quarterly notice; =miete f quarter's rent; =rechnung f quarterly bill; =tag m quarter-day; ⦵weiſe adv. (F a. a.) quarterly, by the quarter.
Quartaner (⌣⌣⌣) [Quarta] m ㉒ pupil of the "Quarta", third-form boy.
Quartan=fieber (⌣⌣⌣⌣) n ㊷ path. (viertägiges Fieber) quartan fever.
Quartant (⌣⌣) [lt.] m ㊷ = Quartband.
Quart=band ⊕ (⌣⌢) m ㊷ typ. volume in quarto; =blatt n quarter of a sheet; =buch n, typ. book in quarto.
Quarte (⌣⌣) [lt.] f ㊾ **1.** quarter (= Viertel). — **2.** ♪ u. **3.** fenc. f. Quart II.
Quarter=deck ⚓ (⌣⌣-⌢) n ㊷ quarter-deck.
Quarteron(e) (⌣⌣⌣⌣) [ſpan.] m ⑪d. (㊷), f ㊽ (Miſchling von Meſtizen u. Europäern) quarteroon, quadroon.
Quartett ♪ (⌣⌣)[it. m] n ⑪c. quartet(te); ~=muſik ♪ (⌣⌢...) f ㊷ music of a q.
Quart=flaſche (⌣⌢...) f ㊷ quart-bottle; =format n, typ. quarto; in ~ in quarto.
Quartier (⌣⌢) [mhd.; *fr. m] n ⑪d. **1.** quarters pl.; (Wohnung) lodging(s), rooms, apartments pl.; wo wird er ſein ~ aufſchlagen? where will he take up his quarters? ein ~ nehmen to take lodgings; ⚔ in ~ legen bei to billet soldiers upon; bei e-m im ~ liegen to be quartered (or billeted) upon a p.; ~ machen to prepare quarters. — **2.** ⚓ (vierſtündige Wache) watch; ~ rufen to call (up) the watch.
Quartier=amt ⚔ (⌣⌣...) n ㊷ = commissariat-office; =billett n = =zettel; **quartieren** (⌣⌣) v/a. ⑱ = einquartieren.
quartier=frei (⌣⌣...) a. ㊻ exempt from the duty of receiving billeted soldiers; =geber m ㊷ host; =geld n fee paid for each billeted soldier, billet-money; =macher, =meiſter m quartermaster; =verpflegung f board and lodging; =wirt ⚔ m host, landlord; =zettel m billet.
Quarto (⌣⌣) [it.] n ㉓ ⊛ = Quartformat.
Quart=ſeite (⌣⌣⌢) f ㊷ page in quarto.
Quarz ⚤ (⌣⌣) [mhd.] m ⑪(⑦)a. (natürliches Kieſel=oxyd, SiO₂, im Granit 2c.) ☌ quartz, rock-flint, glashell = rock-crystal, opt. f. Brillen: pebble; 2=ähnlich, 2=artig a. ㊻ quartzy, quartzous,...ose; ~=druſe f ㊺ quartz(y) druse, geode of quartz; ~=fels m quartz-rock, ⚤ quartzite; 2=haltig a.: ⚤ quartziferous, quartzose; ſig (⌣⌣) a. ㊻ quartzy; ~=kriſtall m rock-crystal; ~=mühle ⊕ f quartz-crusher; ~=ſand m ⚤ arenaceous quartz; ~=ſandſtein m quartzy sandstone; ~=ſinter m: ⚤ quartz-sinter.
quaſi (⌣⌢) [lt.] adv. quasi, mſt. as it were, so to speak, F in a sort of way.
Quaſi=künſtler (⌣⌣...) m ㊷ would-be (or sham) artist; =modo'gniti eccl. Sonntag ~ (Sonntag nach Oſtern) Quasimodo(geniti)(Sunday), a. Low Sunday; =vertrag m so-called agreement.
quaſſeln F nordd. (⌣⌣) v/n. (h.) u. v/a ㉖a. to talk nonsense; vgl. quatſchen **3.**

Signs (see page XVII): F familiar; P vulgar; ┌ flash; ⟍ rare; † obsolete (died); * new word (born); ⧺ incorrect; ♪ music;

[Quassia] — 783 — [Quertal]

Quassia ⚗ ⚘ (‥‿) [Quassi, Neger in Surinam] f ✪ = Bitterholz(baum).
Quast (ˇ) [ahd. Laubschürze] m ⓤ(⑦)a. 1. tuft, knot. — 2. oft: ~e (ˇ) f ✪ (Büschel von Fäden und Fransen) tassel.
quasten=förmig (ˇ‥ˇ) a. ✪ like a tuft or tassel, ⚗ aspergilliform.
quastig (ˇ‿) a. ✪ tasselled.
Quästor (ᴸ‿) [lt.] m ⑫ röm. Alt.: quaestor.
Quästur (‿ᴸ) f ✪ quaestorship.
Quatember (‿‿‿) [lt. *quatuor tempora*] m ⑫ 1. = Quartal 2. — 2. Cath. eccl. (am ersten Mittwoch, Freitag u. Sonnabend des Vierteljahres zu beachtende Fasten) bzh. ehm. ~=fasten n ember-days pl. or =fast.
quatsch F (ˇ) [lautm.] I int. 1. squash!, smash!, splash!, quitsch, ʔ! flip-flop! slap-bang! — II ~ m ⓐa. 2. (lauter Schlag) smack, slap. — 3. (breiweiche Masse) squash. — 4. (unsinniges Gerede) foolish talk, twaddle, bosh, F rot. — III a. ⑤. (albern) foolish; (dumm) silly.
quatschen F (ˇ‿) [quatsch] ⑪ I v/n. (h. und sn) 1. = klatschen 1. — II v/a. 2. (zu e-m Brei zerdrücken) to squash; weitS. = quetschen. — 3. (a. v/n.) (unsinnig reden) to talk foolishly, to twaddle, babble, jabber, chatter.
Quecke ⚘ (‿ˇ) [ndd.] f ✪ couch- (or quick-, dog-)grass (*Triticum repens*).
Quecken=gras ⚘ (ˇ‿‥) n ✪, **=weizen** m, **=wurzel** f, **Queck=gras** f ✪ = Quecke.
Queck=silber (ˇ‥ˇ) [ahd. nach lt. *argentum vivum*] n ⑫ quicksilver, bsd. chm., med., &c. mercury (Hg); ⊕ und chm. mit ~ verbinden, legieren to amalgamate; fig. wie ~ (unruhig, beweglich) sein to be like quicksilver, to be mercurial or F fidgety.
quecksilber=artig ⚗ (ˇ‥ˇ‥) a. ✪ like quicksilver, mercurial; **=chlorid** n ✪ chm. mercuric chloride (HgCl₂); **=chlorür** n, chm. mercurous chloride, calomel (Hg₂Cl₂); **=erz** n, min. quicksilver ore, mercurial ore; **=fulminat** n (Knallquecksilber) fulminate of mercury; **=gefäß** n des Barometers: mercury-cup; **=haltig** a. mercurial, ...ic; **=jodid** n, chm. mercuric iodide, red iodide of mercury (HgJ₂); **=jodür** n, chm. mercurous iodide (Hg₂J₂); **=kügelchen** n globule of mercury; **=kur** f, med. mercurial treatment; **=leber=erz** n, min. (Brand=erz) hepatic mercurial ore; **=legierung** f amalgam; **=luftpumpe** f, phys. mercurial air-pump.
queck=silbern (ˇ‥ˇ) a. ✪ (consisting of) quicksilver, mercurial; F fig. v. Personen, a. restless, F fidgety.
Quecksilber=oxyd (ˇ‥ˇ‥) n ✪ chm. mercuric oxide (HgO); rotes ~ red oxide of mercury; **=oxydul** n, chm. mercurous oxide (Hg₂O); **=pflaster** n; **=salbe** f, pharm. mercurial plaster, ointment; **=säule** f column of mercury; **=vergoldung**, **=versilberung** f amalgam gilding, silvering; **=wanne** f: pneumatische ~ chm. mercury-trough.
Quehle ⚔ (ᴸ‿) f ✪ (Schurfgraben) trench.
Quell (ˇ) m ⓑb. bsd. poet. = Quelle 1.
Quell=bezirk (ˇ‥ˇ) m ✪ country containing (or home of) the sources of a river; **=bottich** ⊕ m Brauerei: steeping-vat or -trough.

Quelle (ˇ‿) [ahd.: quellen¹] f ✪ 1. source, fountain, e-s Flusses a. head; (Brunnen) well. — 2. fig. source, fountain-head, origin; eine ~ für Neuigkeiten &c. abschneiden to stop the channel; aus guter ~ h., wissen to know from good authority; aus der besten ~ schöpfen to draw from the best sources.
quellen¹ (ˇ‿) [ahd.] v/n. (in, bisw. h.) ⑦b. von Flüssigkeiten: to gush (forth), to well, bsd. v. Quellen: to arise, to spring; (fließen) to flow; (i-n Ursprung haben) to originate, to emanate (in et. from a th.); das Blut quoll aus seiner Wunde the blood gushed (or flowed, trickled) from his wound.
quellen² (ˇ‿) [ahd.] I v/n. (in) ⑦b. to swell; die Erbsen ❋ im Wasser peas swell up in water; die Augen quollen ihm aus den Höhlen his eyes started from their sockets. — II v/a. ⑧ (durch Feuchtigkeit anschwellen m.) to swell; Brauerei: Gerste ❋ to steep the barley; Gerberei: die Häute ❋ to soak the hides.
Quellen=entdecker (ˇ‥ˇ‥‥) m ✪, **=finder** m water-finder; **=forscher** m investigator of the (original) sources; **=forschung** f study of the authorities, original research; **=mäßig** a. ✪ according to the (best) sources or authorities, weitS. authentic; **=moos** ⚘ n water-moss (*Fontinalis*); **=reich** a. ✪ rich (or abounding) in springs or fountains; **=schrift** f source, authority; **=studium** n = =forschung. [(*Salicornia herbacea*).]
Queller ⚘ (ˇ‿) [ndd.] m ✪ glasswort⌋
Quell=fluß (ˇ‥ˇ) m ✪: die Flüsse der Donau: the sources of the Danube; **=gebiet** n = =bezirk; **=säure** f, chm.: ⚗ crenate; **=wasser** n spring- (or fountain-)water.
Quendel ⚘ (ˇ‿) [ahd.: lt. *cunila* f; * grch. *kynílē*] m ✪: a) wild thyme (*Thymus serpyllum*); b) = Kalaminthe.
Quengelei F (‿‿ᴸ) f ✪ 1. bother(ation). — 2. (Murren) grumbling, (Kritteln) fault-finding, nagging; (weinerliches Klagen) lamentation, F snivelling.
Quengel=fritze F (ˇ‥ˇ‥) m ✪, **=hans** m grumbler; F sniveller.
queng(e)lig (ˇ(‿)‿) a. ✪ grumbling, fault-finding.
quengeln F (ˇ‿) [ndd.] v/n. (h.) ⓑa. to grumble, find fault, lament.
Quengler (ˇ‿) m ✪ grumbler.
quenglig (ˇ‿) f. quengelig.
Quent (ˇ) [mhd., *lt.] n ⑪, ~chen, ~lein n ㉓ (ehm. kleines Gewicht = 1,66 g) etwa 1¼ scruple.
quer (ˇ) [ndd.: queer] a. ✪ 1. ⒧ (hindurch gehend) cross, transversal, transverse; (schräg) slanting, oblique; fig. ❋e Wege cross ways pl. — 2. adv. crosswise, athwart, vgl. Kreuz 5; (nach der Diagonale) diagonally; ❋ über (right) across; ❋ übers Feld (die Straße) geh(e)n to go across country (the street), to cross the fields (the street); ❋ über=ea. legen to put crossways, to cross; ⓜ co. ❋ schreiben to accept a bill (of exchange); fig. perversely; e-n ❋ anblicken to look askance at a p.; die Sache geht ❋ (verkehrt) ... is going wrong; das kommt mir ❋ (störend) that puts me out or thwarts me or crosses my purpose.
Quer=achse (ˇ‥ˇ‿) f ✪ transverse axis; **=ader** ⚔ f cross-lode; **=axt** ⊕ f, carp. twibill; **=balken** m: a) ⊙ cross-beam, transom; b) her. bar, fess(e); **=band** n cross-band or -rail; **=bau** ⚔ m cross-working; **=baum** m: a) vor e-m Tore: bar; b) ⚔ Turngerät: horizontal bar (= Reck); c) ⚓ cross-tree; **=brett** n in Schränken: shelf; **=bruch** m, surg. transversal fracture; **=damm** m cross-dike; **=durch** adv. right (or straight) across; **=durchschnitt** m transverse section.
Quere (ᴸ‿) [quer] f ✪ transverse (or diagonal) direction, meist im gen., acc., mit prp.: die (od. der) ~, in die ~, der ~ nach crossways, transversely, across, aslant, slantwise; s. Kreuz 5; fig. die Sache geht der Quere ... is taking a wrong turn; e-m in die ~ kommen to cross a p.'s path or purpose, to traverse (or thwart, balk) a p.'s plans; es ist ihm et. in die ~ gekommen something has gone wrong (or awry) with him.
quer=feld=ein (ˇ‿ᴸ‿) adv. across country, across the (open) fields.
Quer=flöte ♪ (ˇ‥ˇ...) f ✪ traverse flute; **=folio** n oblong folio; **=format** n, typ. broadsheet, broadside; **=frage** f cross-question; **=furche** f transverse furrow; **=gang** m cross-way, ⚔ crosscutting, traverse; **=gasse** f (little) street across; **=gäßchen** n cross-cut or -lane; **=griff** m eines Stockes: cross-handle; **=hieb** m cross-cut; **=hin** adv. crossways; **=holz** ⊙ n cross-rod, traverse, vgl. =balken a; **=kluft** ⚔ f crossbar; **=kopf** m: a) ⊕ = Brettnagel; b) F fig. queer fellow, crank; **=köpfig** F a. ✪ wrong- (or queer-)headed or odd, cranky; **=köpfigkeit** f wrong- (or queer-)headedness; **=laufend** a. transversal; **=leiste** f join. cross-piece or -rail; **=linie** f cross (or diagonal) line; **=muskel** m, anat.: ⚗ transversal muscle, transverse; **=naht** f: a) cross-seam; b) anat. des Schädels: ⚗ transverse suture; **=pfeife** ♪ f fife; **=pfeifer** m fifer; **=profil** ⊙ n cross-section; **=riegel** ⊙ m: a) = =stück; b) am Wagen: cross-bar; **=riß** m rent (or crack) across or crossways; **=sack** m wallet; **=säge** ⊕ f cross-cut saw; **=sattel** m lady's side-saddle; **=schiff** n, arch. einer Kirche: cross-aisle, transept; **=schnitt** m transverse section; **=schott** ⚓ n transverse bulkhead; **=schreiben** ⓜ v/n. (h) ⑪** to endorse a bill; **=schwelle** ⊙ f: a) 🚂 traverse sleeper; b) Wasserbau: cross-sleeper; **=sparren** ⊙ m, carp. cross-rafter; **=sprung** m cross-caper; **=stange** ⊙ f cross-bar or -pole; **=straße** f street across, cut; **=streifen** m cross-stripe; **=strich** m: a) cross-line, -bar, dash, stroke (a. ⊙ typ.); b) fig. (Widerwärtigkeit) disappointment; e-n ~ durch etwas machen to thwart a th.; **=stück** ⊙ n, carp. cross-piece; mittleres ~ einer Tür: lock-rail; **=summe** f einer Zahl total of the digits of a number; **=tal** n transversal valley;

⚗ scientific; ⚘ botanical; ⚱ geography; ⊕ machinery; ⚔ mining; ⚔ military; ⚓ marine; ⓜ commercial; ✉ postal; 🚂 railway.

[Quertreiberei] — 784 — [Rachbegierde]

=treiberei f intriguing, plotting; Quer=über adv. across; f. auch quer 2.
Querulant [lt.] m, ~in f querulous p., litigator; grumbler; querulieren v/n. (h.) to be querulous or litigious; to grumble.
Quer=wall m frt. traverse; =wand f, arch. partition- (or traverse-)wall; =weg m cross-cut or -way.
Quese f nordd. (Blase auf der Hand ꝛc.) blister.
Quetsche f 1. pinch; fig. Klemme 2. — 2. (Presse) crusher, für Erz: ore-crusher. — 3. = Zwetsch(g)e.
quetschen [mhd.: squeeze] I v/t. u. sich v/refl. 1. to pinch, bruise, squeeze, crush, path. auch: to contuse; zu einem Brei 2 to mash; sich 2 to get a pinch or bruise, sich (dat.) den Finger 2 to pinch (or jam) one's finger. — 2. Billard: e-n Ball an die Bande 2 to cushion a ball. — II ~ n 3. = Quetschung 1.
Quetsch=hahn m chm. pinchcock; =kartoffeln f pl. Kocht.: mashed potatoes pl.; =laut m Phonetik: a) (ch in chop) hiss(ing sound); b) (j, g in jar, age) buzz(ing sound).
Quetschung f 1. pinching, &c. (f. quetschen 1). — 2. (Verletzung) pinch, bruise, contusion; von Obst ꝛc.: mashing.
Quetsch=wunde f wound caused by a pinch or bruise or contusion.
Queue (tö) [fr. queue f] 1. n (Billardstock) cue, billiard-stick. — 2. f (× † = Ende): ~ machen to bring up the rear; thea. ~ bilden to stand in file, auch: to form a queue.
quick¹ [: quick] (lebendig) quick, alert.
Quick² m = Quecksilber.
Quick²=beutel m metall. amalgamating-skin; =¹born m nbd. (Jungbrunnen) fountain of youth; =²brei m amalgam; =erz n = Queck=silbererz; =gold n gold-amalgam; =mühle f amalgamating-mill; =¹sand m (Flugsand) quicksand; =²wasser n zum Vergolden: quick-water, mercurial solution.

Quidam [lt. jemand] m quidam, a somebody, a certain person.
Quidproquo [lt. et. für et.] n (Verwechslung) quidproquo.
quiek int. squeak!
quieken [lautm.] v/n. (h.) von Ferkeln, Mäusen ꝛc.: to squeak, to squeal; quiekig a. squeaky, squealing.
qui=eszieren [lt.] I v/n. (h.) (ruhen) to quiesce. — II v/a. (in den Ruhestand versetzen) to pension off; qui=esziert a. pensioned (off).
Qui=etismus [lt.] m bsd. theol. Art Mystik: quietism; Qui=etist m quietist.
quietschen [: quieken] v/n. (h.) to squeak; ²des Geräusch squeaky noise.
quill imper., quillst 2., quillt 3. Person pres. v. quellen. [stehend) quinary.]
quinär a. (aus 5 Elementen be=
Quinquagesima [lt. fünfzigster (Tag vor Ostern)] nur in: Sonntag ...mä Quinquagesima (Sunday).
Quint f [lt. fünfte Klasse] fifth, Mit.: diapente; (höchste Saite einer Geige) E-string of a violin.
Quinta [lt. fünfte Klasse] f fifth (or last but one) form of a German secondary school; ~ner m scholar of the "Quinta". [zentner.]
Quintal öft. [fr.] m d. = Doppel=
Quinte f f. Quint. [pranks pl.]
Quinten pl. Kniffe, Streiche) tricks,
Quintessenz [lt. fünftes Wesen] f (Hauptsache) quintessence, most essential thing; pith of the matter.
Quintett [it. quinte'tto m] n c. (5stimmiges Tonstück) quintet(te).
Quint=fagott n basson quinte.
Quiproquo [lt.] n (Verwechslung von Personen) confusion of persons.
Quirinal [lt. Quirinā'lis] npr/m. d. bsd. Alt.: (e-r der Hügel Roms, jetzt kgl. Palast) Quirinalis.
Quirite [lt.] m (alt-röm. Bürger) Quirite, Roman burgess.
Quirl [ahd.: twirl] m b. 1. twirling-stick. — 2. for. (Trieb von Nadelhölzern) shoot of conifers. — 3. (quirlförmiger Stand) whirl, verticil. — 4. F fig. (unruhiger, quirliger Mensch) restless (F fidgety) fellow. [flower.]
Quirl=blume f verticillate
quirlen v/a. to twirl (round); Eier 2 (zu Schaum schlagen) to whisk eggs; typ. gequirlter Satz broken matter.
quirl=förmig a. whorled, verticillate; quirlig a. mercurial, restless; quirl=ständig a. (kreisförmig um die Achse geordnet) verticillate(d).
quitt a. [mhd.: quit; *fr. quitte] (nur als Prädikat gbr.) even; 2 sein mit e-m to be quits (or even) with a p.
Quitte f [ahd.: quince; *grch. kydon(ischer Apfel) f]: a) Frucht: quince; b) Baum: quince-tree (Cydo'nia vulga'ris).
Quitten=baum m = Quitte b; =blüte f quince-blossom; =farben =gelb a. (as) yellow as a quince or a saffron bag; =kern m pip of a quince; =mus n quince-preserve.
quittieren [fr. quitter] v/a. 1. eine Rechnung 2 to receipt (or to give a receipt for) a bill; dankend quittiert received with thanks; oft: paid; quittierte Rechnung receipted bill. — 2. (aufgeben, verlassen) to quit, to give up, to leave; × † den Dienst 2 to quit (or leave) the service.
Quittung f (Empfangsbekenntnis) receipt, acquittance, discharge; f. ausstellen 4; ~s=buch n receipt-book; ~s=stempel m receipt-stamp.
Quivive (ki-wī'w) [fr. wer da?] n, inv. : auf dem ~ sieh(e)n to be on the alert or on the qui vive.
Quodlibet [lt.] n (Allerlei) medley, bsp. selection.
quoll ind., quölle subj. impf. von quellen.
Quote [lt.] [lt.] f (Bruchteil) quota, (Anteil) share, portion, F whack.
Quoti=ent [lt.] m arith. (Ergebnis einer Division) quotient.
quotisier/en [lt.] I v/a. (Anteile berechnen) to allot shares. — II ~ n u. Q/ung f allotment of shares.

R

R, r n, inv. Buchstabe: R, r.
r. abbr. = rund.
R abbr. = Reaumur.
Raa ꝛc. f. Rahe ꝛc.
Rabatt m [nhd.: rebate; *fr. rabat (mst. rabais)] m c. (Abzug) (mercantile) discount, abatement, allowance, deduction; bei Barzahlung 5 Prozent ~ geben to allow five per cent(.) discount for cash (vgl. Diskont). — NB. In Rechenbüchern unterscheidet man Rabatt in Hundert (= mercantile discount) von Diskonto oder Rabatt auf Hundert (= true discount).
Rabatte [nhd.] [ndl. (fr. rabat n)] f 1. Schneiderei: facing. — 2. hort. (Beet) bed, border. [deduct, allow, take off.]
rabattieren v/a. to discount,
Rabatt=marke f discount ticket; =rechnung f discount sum.

Rabau f [ndl. rabauw] m b. kind of apple. [rabbi.]
Rabbi [hebr. mein Meister] m (a.inv.)
Rabbinat n c. = Rabbinen=amt.
Rabbinen=, Rabbiner=amt n, =würde f rabbi's office, rabbinate; =wohnung f rabbi's residence.
Rabbiner m (jüd. Geistlicher) rabbi; rabbinisch a. rabbinical.
Rabe [ahd.: raven] m orn. raven (Corvus corax); fig. weißer ~ (ct. sehr Seltenes) rare bird, rarity, curiosity, (lt.) rara avis; stehlen wie ein ~ to steal like a magpie.
Raben=aas n oft fig. carrion; =art f: a) species of raven; b) raven-like (or rapacious) nature; conduct of unnatural parents; 2artig a. raven-like, corvine; 2artige Vögel corvidæ; =eltern pl. unnatural parents pl.; =feder f raven- (or crow-) quill; =gekrächz(e) n croaking of ravens; =haar n raven-black hair; =krähe f, orn. carrion-crow (Corvus co-ro'ne); =mutter f unnatural (or cruel) mother; =schnabel m raven's beak; 2schnabel=förmig a. anat.: coracoid; =schnabel=fortsatz m am Schulterblatte: coracoid (process); 2schwarz a. (as) black as a crow, jetblack; =stein m place of execution, gibbet; =vater m unnatural (or cruel) father; =vögel m/pl. orn.: corvidæ.
rabiat [it. arrabia'to] a. (wütend) rabid, raving, furious.
Rabulist [lt. rä'bula Schreier] m =erei f pettifoggery; 2isch (-isch) a. pettifogging.
Rach=begierde f = Rachgier.

Zeichen (s. S. XVII): F familiär; P Volkssprache; ̸P Gaunersprache; ⚹ selten; † alt (auch gestorben); * neu (auch geboren); +* unrichtig;

Rache (´ch˘) [ahd.: wreak] *f* [48] revenge, als Strafe, auch *bibl.*: vengeance; ~ an e-m nehmen to wreak one's vengeance upon a p.; ~ für et. nehmen to take (one's) revenge for a th., to avenge a th.; ~ schnauben to breathe vengeance.

Rache=akt (˝ch˘...) *m* [62] act of revenge; **=durst** 2c. s. Rachsucht 2c.; **=engel** *m* avenging angel; **=geist** *m* spirit of revenge, vindictive spirit; **=göttin** *f* avenging goddess; Fury; (grch.) Erinnys; die ~nen *pl.* the Eumenides *pl.*

Rachen (´ch˘) [ahd.] *m* [23] (Schlundkopf) throat, ⚗ pharynx; (Mundhöhle) cavity of the mouth; (weit aufgerissenes Maul) jaw; den ~ aufsperren to open one's jaw or mouth, to gape, yawn; *fig.* chasm, abyss; aus dem ~ des Todes befreien to save from the jaws of death.

rächen (´˘) [ahd.: wreak] **I** *v.a.* u. **sich** ~ *v/refl.* [88] († u. bisw. noch *poet. p.p.* gerochen) **1.** mit persönlichem Subjekt: to avenge; sich für et. ~ to take revenge (or to revenge o.s.) for a th.; sich wegen et. an e-m ~ to wreak one's vengeance upon a p. for a th. — **2.** mit sachlichem Subjekt: sich ~ (gestraft w.) to meet with (one's) punishment, to be atoned for; das wird sich an ihm ~ that will come home to him, he will have to suffer for it. — **II** ~ *n* [23] **3.** = Rache.

Rachen=blume (˝ch˘...), **=blüte** ⚘ *f* [62]: ⚗ ringent corol(la); ~**blütig**, ~**förmig** ⚘ *a.* [66]: ⚗ ringent, labiate; **=bräune** *f*, *path.* quinsy, ⚗ pharyngitis; vgl. Bräune 2; **=drüse**, **=höhle** *f*, *anat.*: ⚗ pharyngeal gland, cavity; **=katarrh** *m* cold in the throat, ⚗ pharyngeal catarrh; **=putzer** F *m* (saurer, billiger Wein) sourish (or inferior) wine; (Fusel) bad spirits *pl.*

Rächer (´˘) *m* [22], **~in** *f* [47] avenger; (Verteidiger[in]) vindicator.

rach=erfüllt (˝ch=˘´) *a.* [66] full of resentment, revengeful.

rache=schreiend (˝ch˘...) *a.* [66] calling for vengeance; **=schwur** *m* [62] oath to revenge o.s., threatening oath.

Rach=gefühl (˝ch...) *n* [62] resentment, revengefulness; **=gier** *f* craving for revenge, vindictiveness; ~**gierig** *a.* [66] vindictive, resentful.

Rachitis ⚗ (˘ch´˘) [grch.] *f*, *inv.*, *path.* (englische Krankheit) rickets, ⚗ rhachitis.

rachitisch ⚗ (˘ch´˘) *a.* [66] rickety.

Rach=lust (˝ch...) *f* [62], ~**lustig** *a.* [66] = =gier(ig); **=sucht** *f* thirst for revenge; ~**süchtig** *a.* thirsting for revenge.

Rack ⚓ (´) *n* [22]: ~ (Beifuß) e-r Rahe parrel of a yard.

Racke (´˘) [lautm.] *f* [48], **Racker**¹ (´˘) *m* [22] *orn.* roller (*Coracias*).

Racker² F (´˘) [ndd.] *m* [22] **1.** *provc.* (Schinder) knacker. — **2.** *fig.* als (leichtes) Schimpfwort: rogue; von Kindern: young Turk, little rascal, F pickle.

rackern F (´˘) *v/n.* (h.) und **sich** ~ *v/refl.* [92]a. to (toil like a) drudge, F to fag.

Rack=klote ⚓ (˝...) *f* [62] parrel-truck; **=taljen=aufholer** *m* parrel-halyard.

Rad (´, ´, *pl.* ´˘) [ahd.; *klt.] *n* [2]c. **1.** ⊙ am Wagen 2c.: wheel; s. beschlagen 1, flechten I; (Rolle) truckle, trundle; ~ am Sporn rowel; ⊙ *mech.* kleines ~ zwischen zwei größeren pinion; ~ und Welle, ~ an der Welle wheel and axle (s. Kammrad); (Treib=) ~ driver. — **2.** (Kreisfigur) ein ~ schlagen (vgl. ~schlagen) to throw (or turn) somersaults, to turn and tumble, Turnerei: to throw hand-springs; der Pfau schlägt ein ~ the peacock spreads his tail. — **3.** cycle, F wheel (= Fahrrad). — **4.** *fig.* s. fünfte 2.

Rad=achse ⊙ (˝..., ˝...) *f* [62] axle-tree; vgl. =welle; ~**ähnlich** *a.* [66] like a wheel; **=arm** ⚓ *m* paddle-arm.

Radau F (˘´) [berlin.; *russ. *ra'dawatj* fröhlich sein, lärmen] *m* [11]b. roaring noise, row.

Radau=brüder (˘˝=´˘) *m/pl.* [62] rowdies; roysterers *pl.*, F rowdydowdy lot.

Rad=band(age *f*) *n* ⊙ (˝...) [62] tire; **=bewegung** *f* = =lauf; **=bogen** *m* Uhr: rim; **=bremse** *f* wheel-lock; **=büchse** *f* box of a carriage-wheel, wheel-box.

Rädchen (´˘) [Rad *dim.*] *n* [24] little wheel, an Sporen 2c.: rowel, an Möbeln: castor.

Rad=dampfer ⚓ (˝...) *m* [62] paddle-steamer; **=deckel** *m* splasher.

Rade ⚘ (´˘) [ndd.; *roden] *f* [48] corn-campion, cockle (*Agroste'mma githa'go*).

rade=brechen (˝˘=´˘) *v/a.* [88]*⁎*: a) [mhd.] = rädern 2; b) *fig.* eine Sprache ~ (mangelhaft sprechen) to speak a language badly or imperfectly; englisch ~ to murder the King's (or Queen's) English, to speak broken English.

Rade=hacke (˝˘...) *f* [62], **=haue** ⊙ *f*, *agr.* mattock.

radeln (´˘) *v/n.* (h. u. sn) [92]a. = radfahren.

rädeln ⊙ (´˘) [Rad] *v/a.* [92]a. to mill, to gnarl; to (furnish with a) rim.

Rädels=führer (˝˘=´˘) [nhd. 16. *sae.*] *m* [22] ringleader.

Rade=macher (˝˘=´ch˘) ⊙ *m* [62] wheel-wright, cartwright.

Raden ⚘ (´˘) *m* [23] = Rade.

Räder=boot (˝˘...), **=dampf=schiff** ⚓ *n* [62] = Raddampfer; **=gehäuse** ⊙ *n* e-r Uhr: frame (or case) of a clock.

...räd(e)rig (...˝´(˘)˘) *a.* [66]: vier~ four-wheeled.

rädern (´˘) [Rad] *v/a.* [92]a. **1.** to supply (or furnish) with wheels, to put on wheels. — **2.** Verbrecher ~ (mit dem Rade zerschmettern) to break ... on the wheel; *fig.* ich bin wie gerädert I am quite knocked (or done) up or F dead-beat.

Räder=schneid=maschine (˝˘...) ⊙ *f* [62] teeth-cutting machine; **=tierchen**, **tiere** *n/pl.*, *zo.* wheel-animalcules, ⚗ rotatories, rotifers, rotatoria *pl.*; **=werk** ⊙ *n* wheel-work, gearing; ~ einer Uhr clock-work. — Vgl. Rad(e)=...

rad=fahren (˝...) *v/n.* [85]b** (h. u. sn) to cycle, to ride (on) a bicycle or tricycle, F to bike, to wheel, in rasender Eile: to scorch; **=fahrer(in** *f*) *m* [62] cyclist; bicyclist, tricyclist; F wheel(wo)man, dahinsausende(r): scorcher; **=fahrer=bahn** *f* (bi)cycling-ground, F cinder-track or -path; **=fahrer=klub** *m* cycling club; **=fahr=sport** *m* cycling (sport); **=felge** *f* felly, felloe, jaunt; **=felgen=kranz** *m* rim; **=fenster** *n*. *arch.* wheel- (or rose-)window; ~**förmig** *a.* wheel-shaped, ⚗ rotiform; **=gehäuse** ⚓ *n* paddle-box; **=geleise** *n* track of a wheel, rut; **=gestell** *n* wheel-frame.

Radial=bohrmaschine (˘(˘)˝...) [lt.] ⊙ *f* [62] radial drilling-machine; **=muskel** *m*. *anat.* radial muscle; **=system** *m* beim Kanalbau: radialization of canals.

Radi-en (´(˘)˘) *pl.* v. Radius; **~=winkel** (˝...) *m* [62] *math.* = Zentriwinkel.

radieren (˘´˘) [mhd.; *lt. *rä'dere* schaben] **I** *v/a.* [93] **1.** to grate, to scrape; (auskratzen) to erase. — **2.** ⊙ Kupferstecherei: (mit der Radiernadel einreißen) to etch. — **II** ~ *n* [23] **3.** = Radierung 1.

Radierer ⊙ (˘´˘) *m* [22] etcher.

Radier=firnis ⊙ (˘˝...), **=grund** *m* [62] etching-varnish, -ground; **=gummi** *n* (*m*) (vulcanized) india-rubber; **=kunst** *f* etching; **=messer** *n* eraser, penknife; **=nadel** ⊙ *f* etching-needle, (Punktiernadel) dry needle.

Radierung (˘´˘) *f* [46] **1.** (das Radieren) grating, erasure; ⊙ etching. — **2.** Bild: etching, etched plate.

Radies ⚘ (˘´) [fr. *radis* **m**] *n* [11], mst **~chen** (-´˘) *n* [23] radish (*Ra'phanus sati'vus*).

radikal (-˘´) [fr.; *lt. *radix* Wurzel] **I** *a.* [66] **1.** radical (a. ⚲ *pol.*). — **II 2.** ~ *n* [11]d. *chm.* (Grundbestandteil) radical. — **3.** **~e(r)** *m* [67] *pol.* Radical, Liberal.

Radikalismus (-˘-´˘) *m* [27] radicalism.

Radikal=kur (-˘˝...) *f* [62] radical cure; **=wort** *n* radical word, (Stamm) stem.

Radikand ⚗ (-˘´) *m* [42] *math.* (Größe, aus der die Wurzel gezogen w. soll) radicand.

radio=aktiv ⚗ (´(˘)˘=˘˝f) *a.* [66] *phys.* radio-active; **Radio=aktivität** (´(˘)˘-˘-w˘˝) *f* [62] radio-activity.

Radium ⚗ (´(˘)˘) [neu=lt. Strahl...] *n* [53] *chm.* 1903 entdecktes Element: radium.

Radius (´(˘)˘) [lt. Strahl, Stab] *m* [27] *math.*, *ast.*, &c. (Halbmesser) radius; **~=vektor** *m* [62] radius vector.

radizieren (-˘´˘) [lt.] *math.* **I** *v/a.* [93] (die Wurzel ausziehen) to extract the root of. — **II** ~ *n* [23] evolution.

Rad=kasten ⊙ (˝...) *m* [62] wheel-case; **=kasten=balken** ⚓ *m* paddle-beam; **=kranz** *m* rim; vgl. =reif(en); **=lauf** *m* rota(to)ry motion, rotation.

Radler (´˘) *m* [22], **~in** *f* [47] cyclist (= Radfahrer(in).

Rad=linie (˝...) *f* [62] *math.*: ⚗ cycloid, trochoid(al curve); ~**linig** *a.* [66]: ⚗ cycloidal; **=macher** *m* = Rademacher; **=nabe** ⊙ *f* wheel-nave, hub; **=reif(en)** *m* tire (or P tyre) (of a wheel); pneumatischer ~ pneumatic tire (or P tyre); **=rennen** *n* (bi)cycle-race.

Radscha (´-) [indisch] *m* [51] (eingeborener Fürst) Raja(h).

Rad=schaufel ⊙ (˝...) *f* [92] paddle-board (a. ⚓); **=schiene** *f* wheel-band; vgl. =reif(en); ~**schlagen** *v/n.* (h.) [85]b** s. Rad 2; ~ *n* turning somersaults; F *fig.* das ist zum ~ that's enough to drive one silly or to make a parson swear.

Radschput(e) (˘´(˘)) *m* [42]([44]), **Radschputin** *f* [47] Abkömmling der alten indischen Kriegerkaste: Rajpoot.

Rad=schuh ⊙ (˝...) *m* [62] = Hemmschuh; **=speiche** *f* spoke of a wheel; **=sperre** *f* = Hemmschuh; **=sport** *m* cycling(-sport); ~**sportlich** *a.* [66] relating to cycling (as a sport); **=spur** *f* = =geleise; **=stube** *f* Wassermühle: wheel-race or -box; ~**tragend** *a.* [66] *zo.*: ⚗ rotiferous; **=welle** *f* wheel-shaft or -spindle, ⚓ am Dampfschiffe: paddle-shaft; **=wett=fahren** *n* cycling-race; **=zahn** *m* cog (of a wheel); **=zapfen** *m* trunnion (or pivot, spindle) of a wheel.

[Raffael] — 786 — [rangieren]

Raffa-el (⌣⌣) [it. *Raffaello*, Maler, 1483—1520] *npr/m.* ⑯α. Raphael.
Raffel (⌣) *f* ⑱ 1. = Klapper, Plaudermaul. — 2. (Fiſchnetz) raffle-net.
raffen (⌣⌣) [mhd.: rap] *v/a.* ⑱ 1. to pick (or snatch, gather) up, to carry off hastily, to sweep (together). — 2. das Kleid ≗ to hold up (Näherei: to take up, to let in) one's dress.
Raff-gier (⸗...) *f* ⑫ rapacity; ≗gierig *a.* ⑯ rapacious; ≗gut *n* stolen article; ≗holz *n* gathered wood.
Raffinade ⊕ (⌣⌣⌣) [fr.] *f* ⑱, ~zucker (⸗...) *m* ⑫ refined sugar. [ment.]
Raffinement (⌣⌣mã') [fr.] *n* ⑱ refine-
Raffinerie (⌣⌣⌣) [fr.] *f* ⑱ refinery.
Raffineur ⊕ (⌣⌣nö'r) [fr.] *m* ⊕d. refiner.
raffinier/en (⌣⌣⌣) [fr. verfeinern] ⑬
I *v/a.* ⊕ Zucker, Öl ꝛc.: to refine; *fig.* raffiniert *p.p.* u. *a.* ⑯ cunning, designing, crafty; raffinierte Grauſamkeit refined (or exquisite) cruelty. — II *v/n.* (h.): auf (ob. über) et. ≗ (ſinnen) to speculate on a th. — III ~ *n* ㉓ u. R/ung *f* ㊻ ⊕ refining, refinery.
Raffinierer ⊕ (⌣⌣⌣) *m* ⑫ refiner.
raffiniert (⌣⌣⌣) ſ. raffinieren I; ~heit *f* ㊻ cunning, craftiness, refined cruelty.
Raff-zahn (⸗...) *m* ⑫ *vet.* projecting front-tooth, snag-tooth. [por=, hervor=ragen.]
ragen (⌣⌣) [mhd.: regen] *v/n.* (h.) ⑱ = em=
Ragout (⌣gu') [fr. *ragoût* m.] *n* ㉔ stew, hotch potch, hash(ed meat), (fr.) ragout.
Rag-wurz ⚥ (⌣⌣) *f* ㊻ (Stendelwurz) orchis; einknollige ~ musk-orchis (*Hermi'nium mono'rchis*).
Rahe ⚓ (⌣⌣) [ndd.] *f* ⑱ yard; große ~ main-yard; mit bloßen ~n (ohne Segel) under bare poles. [Jakobs] Rachel.]
Rahel (⌣⌣) [hebr.] *npr/f* ⑮⑯α. (zweite Frau
Rah-jolle ⚓ (⸗...) *f* ⑫ yard-rope; ≗kette *f* yard-chain; ≗lief *n* e-s Segels: head-rope or -line.
Rahm(⌣) [mhd.: ream] *m* ⑯c. (Milchrahm) cream; *a. fig. u. chm.* den ~ abſchöpfen to take off the cream, to skim the milk; ~ anſetzen to form (a) cream.
Rähmchen (⌣⌣) *n* ㉓ (*dim. v.* Rahmen) 1. little (or small, tiny) frame. — 2. ⊕ *typ.* am Preßbeckel: frisket.
Rahme (⌣⌣) *f* ⑱ *typ.* (Rahmen) form-chase.
rahmen[1] (⌣⌣) [Rahm] ⑱ I *v/n.* (h.) (Rahm anſetzen) to form cream. — II *v/a.* Milch ≗ to skim ...
rahmen[2] (⌣⌣) [Rahmen][3] *v/a.* ⑱ (in e-n Rahmen ſpannen) to (put into a) frame.
Rahmen[3] (⌣⌣) [ahd.] *m* ㉓ frame (*a.* ⊕), Tuchmacherei: tenter-frame, Pulvermühle: shaking-frame; eines Schuhes: welt; (Fenſter=)~ window-frame, casement; (Stick=)~tambour-frame; ⚙e=Getriebeſchacht: shaft-frame; weitſt. (Einfaſſung) edge, border; *fig.* in engem ~ within a narrow (or small) compass, within narrow bounds.
Rahmen=einfaſſung ⊕ (⸗...) *f* ⑫ *typ.* framing=, ≗ſpiegel *m* framed mirror; ≗ſtickerei *f* frame-embroidery, tambour-work.
rahm[1]**-farben** (⸗...) [Rahm] ≗farbig *a.* ⑯ cream-coloured; ≗fanne *f* ⑫ cr.-pot; ≗käſe *m* cr.-cheese; ≗kelle *f* cr.-slice; ≗löffel *m* cr.-ladle; ≗meſſer ⊕ *n* (Gerät) creamometer; ≗reich *a.* rich in cream,

creamy; ≗ſpeiſe *f* dish prepared with cream; ≗²ſpiegel, ≗ſtickerei ſ. Rahmen[3]; ≗¹topf *m* cream-pot; ≗törtchen *n* custard, ≗torte *f* cream-tart or -puff.
Rah-nock ⚓ (⸗...) *f* ⑫ e-s Segels: yard-arm; ≗ſegel *n* squaresail; ≗tau *n* = ≗lief.
Rai-gras ⚕ ⚓ (⸗⌣) *n* (⸗⌣) *n* ㉑ rye-grass, red darnel (*Lo'lium pere'nne*).
Raimund (⌣⌣) *npr/m.* ⑮ (a.Vn.) Raymond.
Rain(⌣) [rein] [ahd.] *m* ⑯c. ridge between two fields, balk, (Grenze) limit, border.
Rain-farn ⚕ (⸗...) *n* ⑫ (common) tansy (*Tanace'tum vulga're*); ≗kohl *m* dock-cress, nipplewort (*La'mpsana commu'nis*); ≗weide ⚕ *f* privet (*Ligu'strum vulga're*).
Rajah (⌣⌣) [türf. *ar.*] *m* ⑫ (nichtmohammedaniſcher Untertan) raya(h).
rajolen ⊕ (⌣⌣⌣) = rigolen.
Rakete (⌣⌣⌣) [(++) it. *rocchetto* m Spule (*Rocken)] *f* ⑱ Feuerwerkerei: rocket.
Raketen-feuer (⸗⌣...) *n* ⑫ rocket-practice; ≗hülſe *f* ro.-case; ≗ſatz *m* ro.-composition; ≗ſtab *m* ro.-stick; ≗ſtock *m* ro.-mould.
Rakett (⌣⌣) [fr. *raquette f*] *n* ⑯c. ~e *f* ⑱ (Schlagnetz) racket, Federball≗ battledore.
Ralle (⌣⌣) [fr. *râle m*] *f* ⑱ *orn.* (Rohrhuhn) (water-)rail (*Rallus aqua'ticus*).
Ramie ⚕ (⌣(⌣)⌣) [malai.] ⚕ China-grass (*Boehme'ria ni'vea*); ~faſer *f* ramie-fibre.
Ramm-arbeit ⊕ (⸗⌣⌣) [rammen] *f* ⑱ piling (-work). [⚙ piling-machine.]
Rammaſchine ⊕ (⸗...) [Ramm-maſchine.]
Rammbär (⸗...) *m* ⑫, -b(l)ock *m*, ≗kloz *m* ⊕ bſd. Waſſerbau: pile-driver, pile-driving engine; ram(mer).
Ramme (⌣⌣) *f* ⑱ a) Bauweſen: = Rammbär; b) (Hand-)~ der Pflaſterer: paving-beetle, paver's rammer; c) F *fig.* Mann bei der ~ man at the wheel, reliable man.
rammeln (⌣⌣) [ahd.] ⑱a. I *v/a.* 1. to ram (into the ground). — II *v/n.* (h.) 2. von Haſen, Kaninchen ꝛc.: to buck, rut, copulate. — 3. (ſich unruhig bewegen) to toss (or fidget, roll) about.
rammen (⌣⌣) *v/a.* ⑱ 1. = einrammen. — 2. den Boden ≗ (feſtſtampfen) to beat (or stamp) down the soil. — 3. ⚓ (mit dem Bug anrennen) to ram.
Rammler (⌣⌣) [mhd.; *rammeln 2*] *m* ⑫ *huni.* buck, male hare or rabbit.
Ramm-ſchiff ⚓ (⸗...) *n* ⑫ ram-ship.
Rampe (⌣⌣) [fr.] *f* ⑱: a) *arch., tet.* (Auffahrt) ramp, ascent; b) ⚓, &c. (Landungsſtelle) landing(-place), 🚂 auch platform; c) *thea.* (*a.* ~n-lichter *n/pl.*) footlights *pl.*; vor der ~ (auf der Bühne) erſcheinen to appear before the footlights.
ramponieren (⌣⌣⌣⌣) [(++) it.] *v/a.* ⑱ bſd. im *p.p.* ramponiert (beſchädigt) damaged, spoilt, knocked about. ⚓ v. Schiffen *a.*: disabled, (zertrümmt) creased, crumpled.
Ramſch ⊕ (⌣) [ndd.; *fr. ramas*] *m* ⑯a. job lot; refuse; im ~ kaufen (*a.* ramſchen (⌣⌣) ⑱) to buy in the bulk or in the lump or in (large) parcels.
Ramſch-ware (⸗⌣⌣) *f* ⑫ job lot (of goods), cheap stuff.
(')**ran** F (⌣) *abbr. für* heran; ich komme morgen ≗ I shall call to-morrow.
Rand (⌣) [ahd.] *m* ⑯b. 1. ~ eines Gefäßes ꝛc.: rim, e-s Hutes ꝛc. auch: brim; e-s Ufers ꝛc.: edge, e-s Abgrundes ꝛc.: brink, e-r Fels-

wand: ledge; e-s Buches, Heftes ꝛc.: margin, *ast.* der Sonnen-, Mond-ſcheibe ꝛc.: limb; (Einfaſſung, Grenze) border; blaue Ränder um die Augen h. to have blue rings round (or under) one's eyes; voll bis an den ~ full to the brim, brimful; Papier mit ſchwarzem ~e black-edged paper. — 2. *fig.* am ~e des Grabes, des Verderbens on the verge (or brink) of the grave, of destruction; er iſt am ~e ſ-r Mittel angekommen his means are coming to an end; P das verſteht ſich am ~e (von ſelbſt) that's understood; ſ. Band 2 ⁷; mit et. ~e (Ende) kommen to accomplish a th. — 3. burſch.: den ~ (Mund) halten to hold one's tongue, F to shut up.
Randal F (⌣⌣) [mhd.] *m* ⊕d. burſchikos: row, uproarious noise; ~ ſchlagen (a. Zieren (⌣⌣⌣) *v/n.* (h.) ⑬) to kick up a row or F a shindy. ~macher (⌣⌣...) *m* ⑫ blustering fellow.
Rand-bemerkung (⸗⌣⌣) *f* ⑫ marginal note; ≗dukaten *m*, *num.* ring- (or round-edged) ducat.
rändeln ⑱a., **randen** ⑱ (⌣⌣) = rändern.
Rand-erklärung (⸗⌣⌣⌣) *f* ⑫ marginal gloss. [border; to mill coins.]
rändern (⌣⌣) *v/a.* ⑱a. to rim, edge,
Rand-gebirge ⚴ (⸗...) *n* ⑫ mountain-chain bordering on a plateau; ≗gloſſe *f*: *a.* ≗bemerkung; b) *fig.* ≗gloſſen m. über zu comment (unfavourably) upon; ≗härchen *n/pl.* cilia *pl.*; ≗leiſte ⊕ *f* ledge, *arch.* auch: ribbon; ≗note *f* = ≗bemerkung; ≗ſchnecke *f*, *zo.*: ⚥ mar ginella; ≗ſchrift *f* marginal writing or inscription, einer Münze: legend; ≗ſtein m curb-stone; ≗vermerk m = ≗bemerkung; ≗verzierung *f* marg. adornment. ⊕ am Buchbeutel: edge-roll; ≗zeichnung *f* marginal (or border-) drawing or sketch.
Ranft (⌣) [ahd.] *m* ⊕b. crust of bread; (Anſtoß am Brote) kissing-crust; *a.* = Rand; *dim.* **Ränftchen** (⌣⌣) *n* ㉓ small crust.
Rang¹ (⌣) [mhd.: rank; *fr.* (v. dtſch. Ring)] *m* ⊕b. 1. rank (auch ⚔); (Würde) dignity; (Stellung) station, position; (Stand) vocation; dem ~ nach in rank; vom erſten, höchſten ~e of the highest standing or eminence, first-rate (*a.* ⊕); einen hohen ~ bekleiden to be of high rank, to occupy a high position. — 2. *thea.* row of seats, tier of boxes; erſter ~ dress-circle; zweiter ~ upper circle.
Rang² (⌣) [++ ft. Rank] *m* ⊕b. e-m den ≗ ablaufen to get ahead (or the better) of a p. to outrun (or outstrip) a p.
rang³ (⌣) *impf. ind.* von ringen.
Range (⌣⌣) [mhd.; *ringen] *m* ⑭, *f* ⑱ (großer Bengel) big unmannerly boy, lout; (wilder Junge) young scamp, auch (wildes Mädchen) tomboy, romp.
ränge (⌣⌣) *impf. subj.* von ringen.
Rang¹**-erhöhung** (⸗⌣⌣⌣) *f* ⑫ elevation in rank. F step up the ladder.
Rangier-bahn-hof 🚂 (rg-Gi"r⌣⌣) *m* ⑫ shunting-station or -yard.
rangieren (rg-Gi⌣⌣) [fr.] ⑱ I *v/a.* to arrange; 🚂 e-n Zug ≗ to shunt a train, auch abs. ≗ to shunt; (nach der Größe rangiert ſein (ob. *v/n.* ≗) to be classed according to height. — II *v/n.* (h.): a) ſ. I; b) to (take) rank

---

Signs (see page XVII): F familiar; P vulgar; ⌐ flash; ⌙ rare; † obsolete (died); * new word (born); ⁎ incorrect; ♪ music;

(vor e-m before a p.); c) ⚔ 2 mit // to be ranked (or classed) with //.
Rangierer 🚂 (ra-ᵭĭ') m ⊕ shunter.
Rangier=geleise 🚂, =gleis (ra-ᵭĭ'r...) n ⊕ siding; =maschine f shunting- (or switching-)engine or -locomotive.
Rangierung (ra-ᵭĭ') f ⊕ (f. rangieren) arrangement; ranking, classing.
Rang¹=klasse (⁵...) f ⊕ class; =liste ⚔ f army-list; =loge f, thea. im ersten Range box in the dress-circle; ⁢mäßig a. ⊕ according to rank; =ordnung f order of rank, gradation, gesellschaftliche, auch: social scale or hierarchy; =stolz m pride of rank; =streit(igkeit f) m quarrel (or dispute) about rank or precedence; =stufe f degree, grade, order (of rank); zu einer höheren ~ befördert w. to be promoted (to a higher grade), F to take (or gain) a step up; =sucht f craving for (high) rank; =süchtig a. desirous of (high) rank; =unterschied m distinction of rank.
rank¹ (⁵) [: rank] I a ⊕: 2 (und schlank) slender, slim; ⚓ (übermastet) crank.
Rank² (⁵) [mhd.: wrench] m ⑦b. südd. (krummer Weg) winding road; (Kehre) turn, (Vorrang) precedence; vgl. Rang².
Ranke ♀ (⁵⌣) [nhd.: Rank²] f ⊕ tendril, clavicle, clasper, ⚔ cirrus; shoot (or branch) of a vine.
Ränke (⁵⌣) [mhd.: pl. v. Rank²] m/pl. ⑦ (geheime Umtriebe) intrigues pl.; (Kunstgriffe) tricks, dodges, artifices, machinations pl.; ~ schmieden oder spinnen to set intrigues on foot, to hatch plots, to intrigue, to plot; voller ~ und Kniffe full of dodges and devices, F up to every move.
Ränke=geist (⁵⌣...) m ⊕ intriguing spirit; =macher(in f) m F = =schmied.
ranken (⁵⌣) [Ranke] v/n. (h. u. ſn) u. ſich 2 v/refl. to creep, climb, shoot, run; to send forth tendrils or shoots or runners; 2d creeping.
ranken=artig (⁵⌣...), =förmig a. ⊕: ⚇ cirrose, cirrous, capreolary, capreolate; (wurzelrankig) ⚇ sarmentose, sarmentous, sarmentaceous; =fuß(ler) m ⊕ zo.: ⚇ cirriped(e); =gewächs n creeping (⚇ cirrose) plant, creeper.
Ränke=schmied (⁵⌣...) m ⊕ intriguer, plotter, schemer; trickster; artful person; =spiel n intrigue(s pl.); =sucht f = =geist; =süchtig, =voll a. ⊕ intriguing, plotting, scheming, designing; full of tricks or dodges, tricky, artful.
rankig ♀ (⁵⌣) a. ⊕ (rankend) creeping, (provided) with tendrils or runners.
rann (⁵)ind., **ränne** subj. impf. v. rinnen.
rannte (⁵) ind. impf. von rennen.
Ranunkel (-⁵⌣) [lt. m Fröschchen) f ⊕ crowfoot, buttercup (Ranu'nculus).
Ränzel (⁵⌣) n (m) ⊕ (dim. v. Ranzen 1) (small) knapsack; (Schultasche) satchel.
Ranzen (⁵⌣) [nhd., ⌐ 16. sae.] m ⊕ 1. wallet, travelling-bag (vgl. Ränzel); F den ~ schnüren to pack (and be) off. — 2. P (Bauch) belly, paunch.
ranzig (⁵⌣) [nbl., fr. rance] a. ⊕ v. verborbenem Fett ᴑ., rancid, (übelriechend) rank; etwas 2: ⚇ rancescent, rankish; 2 werden to turn rancid; ~keit f ⊕ rancidness, rancidity, rankness.

Ranzion (⌣⌣¹) [fr. rançon) f ⊕ (Lösegeld) ransom; **2ieren** (⌣⌣-¹⌣) v/a. ⊕ to ransom; (abgegelb fordern) to demand a r.
Ränzlein (⁵-) n ⊕ (dim. von Ranzen) 1. = Ränzel. — 2. = Ranzen 2; ... hatte sich ein ~ (Bäuchlein) angemäst('t), als wie der Doktor Luther (G.) ... had filled his paunch and portly sides like unto Doctor Luther.
Rapee (⌣-¹) [fr. râpé] m ⊕ (Schnupftabak) rappee, (coarse and) strong snuff.
Rapier (⌣-¹) [nhd. 16. sae.; *fr. rapière f] n ⊕d. fenc. zum Hauen: rapier, zum Stoßen: foil; er führte ein gutes ~ /focht gut) he was a good swordsman.
rapiert (⌣-¹) [fr. râper reiben] p.p. u. a. ⊕ (gerieben, zerrieben) ground, grated.
Rapillen ⚇ (⌣⌣¹) [corr. v. lt. lapilli m/pl. Steinchen] pl. inv. (vulkan. Schlackensteinchen) rapilli pl.
Rappe (⁵⌣) [mhd.; *Rabe] m ⊕ black horse; F fig. auf Schusters ~n reiten (zu Fuße gehen) to ride (or go) on Shank's pony, P to pad the hoof.
Rappel F (⁵⌣) [nbd.: rappeln²] m ⊕ fit of madness, (wunderliche Laune) mad freak or whim; den ~ haben to be off one's head, F to have a crazy fit.
rapp(e)lig (⁵(⌣)⌣) a. ⊕ mad, crazy, whimsical, F cracked, daft.
Rappel-kopf F (⁵⌣...) m ⊕ madcap, crazy Jack; =köpfisch a. ⊕ = rappelig.
rappeln¹ (⁵⌣) [nbd. lautm.: rap: Raffel] v/n. (h.) ⊕ a. to make a rattling noise.
rappeln² F (⁵⌣) [nbd.: rave; *fr.] ⊕ a. v/impers. es rappelt bei ihm (im Oberstübchen) he is wrong in the upper story, he has taken leave of his senses.
rappeln³ F provc. (⁵⌣) [nbd.] sich 2 v/refl. ⊕ a. (sich sputen) to make haste, to hurry (along).
rapplig (⁵⌣) s. rappelig.
Rapport ⚔ (⌣⌣¹) [fr.] m⊕c. (Bericht) report; **2ieren** (⌣⌣-¹⌣) v/a. ⊕ to (make a) report.
Raps ♀ (⁵) [lt. rapi'cium] m ⊕a. (Ölfrucht) rape(-seed), colza (Bra'ssica Napus).
Raps=feld (⁵...) n ⊕ field of rape-seed; =saat f rape-seed.
Raptus (⁵⌣) [lt.] m ⊕ = Rappel.
Rapünzchen ♀ (⌣⌣-¹) [mlt. rapu'ncium] n ⊕, **Rapunze**(lm⊕, f ⊕) f ⊕ corn-salad, lamb's-lettuce (Valeriane'lla olito'ria).
Rapunzel-glocke(nblume) (⌣⌣⌣¹-⌣) f ⊕ (garden-)rampion, Coventry-rape (Campa'nula rapu'nculus).
Rapuse (⌣-¹⌣) [mhd.; *tschech. rabuše Kerbholz] f ⊕ scramble, scrimmage; in die ~ geben, werfen to throw money, &c. to be scrambled for.
rar (⁻) [fr. rare] a. ⊕ (selten) rare, scarce, (vorzüglich) exquisite, uncommon, ⊛ at a premium; sich 2 machen to make o.s. scarce; 2 werden to grow rare or scarce or obsolete; s. Pflanze 2.
Rarität (-⌣¹) [lt.] f ⊕: a) (Seltenheit) rarity, scarcity; b) rare thing or F bird, curiosity, F curio; ~en-kabinett n ⊕, ~en-kammer f, ~en-kasten m cabinet of curios(ities), raree-show.
rasaunen F provc. (⁵⌣.(⌣.)¹) ⊕ a. to riot.
rasch¹ (⁻) [ahd.: rash] v/a. ⊕ (D 1,6) als a. meist v. Tieren u. Dingen: quick, brisk, nimble (vgl. schnell), 2e Antwort: a) mst mündlich: quick repartee, ready answer; b) mst brieflich: speedy (or prompt)

reply; 2e Entscheidung hasty (or hurried) decision; 2es Pferd fleet (or swift) horse; ⊛ 2er Umsatz quick returns pl.; sich 2 (adv.) besinnen to make up one's mind in a hurry.
Rasch² ⊛ (⁵) [Arras ⚑, fr. St.] m ⊕a. (glatter Seiden- ob. Wollen=stoff) ras; serge.
rascheln (⁵⌣) [lautm.] v/n. ⊕ a. 1. (h.) to rustle, (knistern) to crackle. — 2. (ſn) (sich mit Geräusch bewegen) to move (or glide) along with a rustling (or crackling) noise, to whiz along.
Raschheit (⁵-) f ⊕ (f. rasch) quickness, briskness, readiness; speed, promptness; fleetness, swiftness; (Eile) haste.
rasch¹=hin (⁵⁵) adv. briskly, lightly; 2lebig (⁵...) a. ⊕ fast (living).
Rasch²=macher ⊛, ⊛ (⁵,⁵⌣) m ⊕ manufacturer of serge.
Rasen¹ (¹⌣) [mhd.; *nbd. wrase] m ⊕ (green) sward, turf; gestochenes Stück ~ sod; ~ stechen to cut (sods of) turf.
rasen² (¹⌣) [nbd. (LU.): race] ⊕ I v/n. (h.) 1. (toben) to rave, to rage; (irre reden) to be delirious, (außer sich sein) to be beside o.s. or out of one's mind, (tobsüchtig sein) to be frantic or raving mad. — 2. (sich ungestüm bewegen, bei Ortsveränderung: ſn) to rush (about); sie haben beim Tanzen ᴑ. gerast they danced, &c. like mad; es rast der See und will sein Opfer haben (sch.) the storm-swept lake is calling for its prey. — II v/a. 3. to utter in a fit of frenzy or madness. — III ~ n ⊕ 4. = Raserei; zum ~ verliebt desperately (or madly) in love, love-sick. — IV 2b p.pr. u.a. ⊕ 5. raving (mad), delirious, (toll) out of one's mind or sense, beside oneself; frantic, distracted; e-n 2b machen to drive a p. mad or F silly, to enrage a p.; ich möchte 2b werden I shall go out of my mind; vgl. Rasendwerden. — 6. metonymisch: 2der Automobilfahrer scorching motorist, P road-hog; in 2der (größter) Eile at a tearing pace, in hot haste; ich habe e-n 2den (gewaltigen) Hunger I have a ravenous appetite, I am desperately hungry; ich habe 2des Kopfweh I have a distracting (or splitting) headache; sie hat 2de Schmerzen she suffers agony or agonizing pain.
Rasen¹=bank (¹⌣...) f ⊕ grassy bank, bank of turf; =bekleidung ⚔ f e-r Böschung: (turf) revetment of a slope; =bleiche ⊛ f: a) bleaching on grass; b) Platz dazu: bleaching-ground; =decke f einer Wiese: grassy surface, turf.
Rasend=werden (¹⌣...) n ⊕ es ist zum 2 it is enough to drive one mad or silly, it drives one to distraction.
Rasen¹=eisen-erz (¹⌣...) n ⊕, =eisenstein m, min. meadow-(or swamp-)ore; =hügel m grassy mound or hill; =mäh-maschine ⊕ flawn-mower; =platz m lawn, grass-plot, green; =spaten ⊕ m turfing-iron or -spade; =stechen n turf-cutting; =stecher ⊛ m turf-(or sod-)cutter; =stein m = =eisen-erz; =teppich m, hort. velvet(y) lawn, (soft) green sward.
Raserei (-⌣¹) f ⊕ 1. (das Rasen) raving, rage, frenzy, fury, madness. —

[Rasierbecken] — 788 — [Rätsel]

2. (Handlung eines Rasenden) mad(man's) act or doing.
Rasier=becken (⸺) n ⓖ shaving-basin.
rasieren (⸺) [nhd.: raze; * fr. *raser*] v/a. ⓖ 1. to shave, F to trim one's beard; sich ⸺ l. to get shaved, F to have a shave. — 2. ⚔ frt. to raze, ⚓ to cut down; ⚓ rasiertes Linienschiff razee.
Rasierer (⸺) m ⓖ barber.
Rasier=messer ⊖ (⸺) n ⓖ razor; =pinsel m, =pulver n, =seife f shaving-brush, -powder, -soap; =zeug n shaving-utensils or F -things pl., co. shaving-tackle.
rasig (⸺) a. [Rasen¹] ⓖ grassy, turfy, covered with grass or turf.
Räson (-fg') [nhd.: reason;* fr. *raison*] f ⓖ (Vernunft) reason; er will keine ⸺ annehmen he won't listen to reason; **~eur** (-⸺r) m ⓖd. litigating p., grumbler.
räsonieren (⸺) [fr. *raisonner*] I v/n. (h.) ⓖ 1. (auseinandersetzen) to reason, to argue. — 2. (schimpfen) to grumble; (streiten) to quarrel, dispute, wrangle, litigate. — II ⚓ p.pr. u. a. ⓖ 3. argumentative, litigating. [ing-iron.}
Raspel¹ ⊖ (⸺) f ⓖ rasp; (Reib=eisen) grat- }
Raspel²=brot ⊖ (⸺) [raspeln] n ⓖ grated bread; =feile f rasp(-file); =maschine f rasping-machine.
raspeln (⸺) [† (ahd.) raspen] v/a. ⓖ a. 1. ⊖ to rasp, Brot; to grate; (schaben) to scrape. — 2. F fig. Süßholz ⚓ to flirt, to spoon, to do the la-de-da (or to talk soft nonsense) to a lady. [ings pl.}
Raspel²=späne ⊖ (⸺) m/pl. ⓖ rasp- }
Rasse (⸺) [nhd.: race; * fr. *race*] f ⓖ race, von Tieren: breed, stock; von reiner (gekreuzter) ⸺ thoroughbred (cross-bred); das liegt in der ⸺ that runs (F that's) in the blood.
Rassel (⸺) f ⓖ rattle. [rhonchus.}
Rassel=geräusch (⸺) n ⓖ med.: ⚓ }
rasseln (⸺) [nhd.: rattle] I v/n. (h. u. sn) ⓖa. 1. (h.) to rattle, to make a rattling noise; (klirren) to clash (auch von Waffen), to clank (auch von Ketten); b) (sn) to come rattling along. — 2. = röcheln. — II ~ n ⓖ 3. = Gerassel.
Rassen=kampf ⊖ (⸺) [Rasse] m ⓖ racial struggle, conflict of races; =kreuzung f cross-breeding.
rassig (⸺) [Rasse] a. ⓖ racy, bsd. von Tieren: of a good (or pure) breed.
Rast (⸺) [ahd.: rest] f ⓖ 1. rest, repose; (Erholung) recreation, relaxation; eine kurze ⸺ m. to make a short halt or stay; ohne Ruh(e) und ⸺ restlessly, never at rest or at peace; ⚔ (auf dem Marsch) halt. — 2. (Station) halting-place (a. ⚔), stage, station. — 3. ⊖ am Hochofen: boshes pl.
Rastel=binder (⸺) [Rastell] m ⓖ (Siebmacher) sieve-maker, (slowakischer Kesselflicker) Slovak tinker. [(Rechen)rake.}
Rastel(l) (⸺) [it.] n ⓖd. (Gitter) railing; }
rasten (⸺) [Rast] v/n. (h.), v/a. u. sich ⸺ v/refl. ⓖ: (die Glieder) ⚓, sich ⚓ (take) rest, to repose, auf dem Marsche: to (make a) halt, to stop; Sprichw. rast' ich, so rost' ich resting is rusting.
rast=los (⸺) a. ⓖ restless, (zappelig) fidgety, (unermüdlich) indefatigable; =losigkeit f restlessness, fidgeti-

ness, F fidgets pl.; indefatigableness; =ort m ⓖ = Rast 2.
Rastral ♪ (⸺) [neu=lt.] n ⓖd. music-pen.
Rast=tag ⚔ (⸺) m ⓖ (= Ruhetag) day of rest or relaxation, ⚔ halting-day, a day's halt.
Rasur (⸺) [lt.] f ⓖ erasure.
Rat (⸺) [ahd.: raten] m ⓖc. 1. (pl. meist Ratschläge) counsel, advice; auf j-s ⸺ on (or by) a p.'s advice, at a p.'s suggestion; mit ⸺ und Tat (unterstützen to assist) by word and deed; f. annehmen 3, erholen 2, folgen 2; e-n (wieder) um=fragen to (re)consult a p.; e-m ⸺ geben to give a p. advice, to advise a p.; Sprichw. habe ⸺ vor der Tat look before you leap; guter ⸺ kommt über Nacht, etwa: our pillow is our best adviser, it is better to sleep on it; kommt Zeit, kommt ⸺ all in good time, time heals all things; vgl. auch kommen 3 am Schluß. — 2. (Beratung) consultation, deliberation; mit e-m ⸺ über et. halten, ⸺(s) pflegen, ratschlagen, zu ⸺e geh(e)n to consult (or deliberate) with a p.; e-n zu ⸺e ziehen to take a p.'s advice, to consult a p., einen Anwalt: to take counsel's opinion. — 3. (pl. Räte): a) (Ratgeber) counsellor, adviser; b) (Rechtskonsulent) counsel, legal adviser; c) Mitglied einer Ratsversammlung, oft bloßer Titel) councillor, member of a council; f. geheim 3; als f hierzu: Frau ⸺ ob. **Rätin** councillor's wife, meist nur Mrs. mit dem npr.; d) (Kollegium) council, board, body of (town-)councillors, corporation; f. geheim 3 und hoch 2. — 4. (Mittel) remedy, means, expedient; für et. ⸺ schaffen to provide for an emergency, to find ways and means; dazu kann ⸺ werden that may be managed; keinen ⸺ wissen not to know what to do, to be at one's wits' ends; hier ist guter ⸺ teuer that's a difficult (or a thorny) matter, the situation is critical. — 5. et. zu ⸺e halten (sparsam brauchen) to be sparing with (or of) a th., to economize (or save) a th., to husband a p.'s resources.
rät (⸺) pres. ind. von raten.
Rata (⸺) [lt.] f ⓖ = Rate.
Rate (⸺) [it.] f ⓖ (An=, Teil=zahlung) instalment; auf Aktien: call on shares, in ⸺n bezahlen to pay by instalments.
raten¹ (⸺) [ahd.: read] I v/n. (h.), v/a., bisw. a. v/refl. ⓖa. 1. e-m et. (ob. zu einer Sache) ⚓ to advise a p. on (or respecting) a th.; man hat mir geraten zu reisen I have been advised to travel; wozu ⚓ Sie mir? what do you advise me to do?, what do you think I had better do?; er läßt sich von niemand(em) ⚓ he takes nobody's advice; Sprichw. wem nicht zu ⚓ ist, dem ist nicht zu helfen he that won't be advised must expect no help, freier: if you won't be led you must suffer instead. — 2. (tätlich beistehen) to help, aid, assist; sich nicht zu ⚓ (noch zu helfen) wissen not to know what to do or what course to pursue; vgl. helfen 5; damit ist mir nicht geraten that does not (or F won't) help (or

avail) me much. — 3. = erraten; hin und her ⚓ to cast about for an answer, to make random guesses; das war gut geraten that was a good guess; e-m et. zu ⚓ (auf)geben to give a p. a nut to crack or a task to do. — II v/n. ⓖ 4. (ant. taten): ⚓ und taten to advise and to act; ~ n ⓖ (f. 1) advice; (f. 3) guess(ing).
raten²=weise (⸺) [Rate] adv. by instalments; =zahlung f ⓖ payment by instalments.
Rater (⸺) [raten] m ⓖ, ~in f ⓖ 1. guesser, person who guesses or divines. — 2. = Ratgeber(in).
rätern ⊖ (⸺) v/a. ⓖa. (sieben) to screen.
Rat=fragen (⸺) n ⓖ consultation; =geber(in f) m counsellor, adviser, in Rechtssachen: counsel; =haus n town hall.
Räti=en ⚓ (⸺) npr. ⓖ Alt. (jetzt etwa Graubünden und Westtirol) Rhætia; **Räti=er** (in f) m ⓖ Rhætian.
Ratifikation (⸺) [neu=lt.] f ⓖ (Bestätigung[surkunde]) ratification.
ratifizieren (⸺) [neu=lt.] v/a. ⓖ (bestätigen) to ratify, to confirm.
Rätin (⸺) f ⓖ f. Rat 3 c.
Ration ⚔ (⸺) [fr., * lt.] f ⓖ für Pferde: ration, portion, allowance, in (kleinen) ⸺en austeilen to dole out.
rational (⸺) [lt.] a. ⓖ 1. math. rational. — 2. = rationell.
Rationalismus (⸺) m ⓖ phls., rel. (Vernunftglaube) rationalism.
Rationalist (⸺) m ⓖ rationalist; ⚓=isch (⸺) a. ⓖ rationalist(ic).
rationell (⸺) [fr.] a. ⓖ (vernünftig) rational, reasonable.
rätisch (⸺) a. ⓖ Rhætian; ⚓ =e Alpen (Teil der Zentral=alpen) Rhætian Alps pl.
rätlich (⸺) [Rat] a. ⓖ advisable; (förderlich) expedient, useful; ~keit f ⓖ advisability; expediency.
rat=los (⸺) a. ⓖ: a) without advice, unadvised; b) (sich nicht zu helfen wissend) perplexed, embarrassed; =losigkeit f ⓖ perplexity, embarrassment.
räto=romanisch (⸺) a. ⓖ: die ⚓e Sprache, das R/e, ⸺ n ⓖ (Dialekt in Graubünden) Rhæto-Romanic.
ratsam (⸺) a. ⓖ = rätlich; (zu empfehlen) commendable, (heilsam) wholesome; (geeignet) fit; **Ratsamkeit** (⸺) f ⓖ advisability; wholesomeness; fitness.
rats=bedürftig (⸺) a. ⓖ in need of advice; =bote m ⓖ messenger, beadle of the town-council.
ratsch (⸺) int. f. ritsch. [drill.}
Ratsch=bohrer ⊖ (⸺) m ⓖ ratchet- }
Ratsche, a. **Rätsche** (⸺) f ⓖ (child's, policeman's, &c.) rattle.
ratschen, a. **rätschen** (⸺) [mhd.] v/n. (h.) ⓖ (knarren) to rattle.
Rat=schlag (⸺) m ⓖ counsel, advice; f. Rat 1; ⚓schlagen [ahd.] v/n. (h.) ⓖ * * * to deliberate; =schlagung f deliberation; =schluß m resolution, decision, decree; die unerforschlichen =schlüsse Gottes the inscrutable ways of God, the unfathomable decrees of Heaven; =schreiber m f. Ratsschreiber.
Rats=diener ⸺ m ⓖ = Ratsbote.
Rätsel (⸺) [nbd.: riddle] n ⓖ riddle (f. aufgeben 5), puzzle, schwer zu lösen-

[**Rätselaufgabe**] des: enigma, scherzhaftes: conundrum; das ist mir ein ~ it puzzles me.
Rätsel=aufgabe (⁻ʹ⋃⋃…) f ② problem; **=buch** n book of riddles; **=dichter** m composer of riddles, ⚯ enigmatographer; **=frage** f puzzling (or enigmatic) question, conundrum, F puzzler, poser.
rätselhaft (⁻⋃⋃) a. ⑥⑥ puzzling, enigmatical; (unverständlich) unintelligible, mysterious; **~igkeit**(⁻⋃⋃⋅) f⑥⑥ puzzling nature of a th.; mysteriousness.
rätseln (⁻⋃) v/a. ②a. to speak in riddles.
Rätsel=spruch (⁻ʹ⋅⋅ʹ⑥) m ② enigmatical (or puzzling) sentence.
Rats=geschlecht (⁻ʹ…) n ② patrician family; **=herr** m council-man, councillor, alderman, weitS. patrician; **⚲herrlich** a. ⑥⑥ alderman*like*, …*ly*; **=kammer** f council-chamber; **=keller** m cellar of the town hall; **=kollegium** n town-council; (body of) aldermen pl.; **=mann** m (pl. ② u. =**leute**) = **=herr**; **=mitglied** n member of a council.
Rat(s)=saal (⁻ʹ…) m ② council-hall; **=schreiber** m town-clerk; **=sitzung** f sitting of a council; **=stelle** f councillorship; **=stube** f = Ratskammer.
rätst (⁻ʹ) 2. Person sg. pres. ind. von raten.
Rats=tafel (⁻ʹ…), **=tisch** m councilboard; **=versammlung** f meeting of a council or board; **=wage** f in Deutschland: stamped scales pl. of the town (-council); **=wahl** f election of town-councillors, municipal election; **=zimmer** n = **=kammer**.
Ratte (⁻⋃) [ahd.: rat] f ⑥ zo. rat (Mus rattus); fig. wie eine ~ schlafen to sleep like a dormouse, mehr gbr.: to sleep like a top.
Ratten=falle (⁻⋃…) f ⑥ rat-trap; **=fänger(in** f) m rat-catcher; **=fänger von Hameln** der deutschen Sage: Pied Piper of Hamelin; **=gift** n rat-poison, a. ratsbane; **=jagd** f rat-hunting; auf die ~ gehen to go ratting; **=kahl** P a. ⑥⑥ = radikal; **=könig** m rats pl. grown together by the tails; **=loch** n rats' hole; **=nest** n rats' nest; **=pulver** n = **=gift**; **=schlange** f, zo. rat-snake (Ptyas muco'sus); **=schwanz** m: a) rat's tail; b) vet. (Krankheit des Pferdeschwanzes) u. c) (kleine Rundfeile) rat-tail; **⚲schwänzig** a. rat-tailed; **=tod** m = **=gift**.
Rätter ⚒ (⁻⋃) m ② (Sieb) screen.
rattern (⁻⋃) [ndd.] v/n. (h.) ⑧ to rattle.
Rat=versammlung (⁻ʹ…) f ② = Rats….
Ratz (⁻ʹ) m ⓐ a. 1. zo. = Hamster. — 2. hunt. = Iltis. — 3. bayr. = Ratte.
Ratze P (⁻⋃) [mhd.] f ⑥ 1. zo. = Ratte. — 2. Regelspiel: = Pudel 4.
Raub (⁻ʹ) [ahd. f. rauben] m ③c. (pl. mst Raubtaten, Räubereien) 1. (das Rauben) robbing, robbery, in gehobener Spr.: rap(in)e.(Straßen=)~highway robbery, brigandage, (Kinder=, Weiber=)~ kidnapping, abduction; röm. Alt.: ~ der Sabinerinnen rape of the Sabine women; (Plündern) pillaging, ⚔ a. looting, sacking; depredation; (Beraubung) spoliation; (Unterschlagung) embezzlement; gewaltsamer ~ theft with violence; auf ~ ausgehen to go thieving or plundering or in quest of booty, bsd. von Tieren: to prowl (about). — 2. (Beute) prey (auch von Tieren), des Siegers: spoils pl.; (Geplündertes, Erjagtes) booty; j-s ~ werden, e-m zum ~ w. to fall a(n easy) prey (or a victim) to a p.; ein ~ der Flammen werden to be consumed by the flames, to be destroyed by fire.

Raub=anfall (⁻ʹ…) m ② predatory attack, auf der Landstraße: highway robbery; **=ausgabe** f Buchhandel: pirated edition; **=bau** m ⚒ u. ⊕ agr. careless (or unmethodical) working of a mine or a farm; **=begier(de)** f = **=gier**.
rauben (⁻⋃) [ahd.: reave] ⓔ I v/a.: e-m et. ② to rob (or deprive) a p. of a th., to take a th. from a p.; Kinder ⚒. ② to kidnap …, to abduct …; e-m j-n guten Namen ② to take away a p.'s good name, to defame a p.; es raubt mir zu viel Zeit it takes up too much of my time. — II v/n. (h.) to commit robberies, plündernd: to go pillaging or marauding. — III ~ n ② = Raub 1.
Räuber (⁻⋃) [ahd.] m ②, **~in** f ④ 1. one who robs (or deprives) a p. of s.th., despoiler; gewerbsmäßiger: robber; (Straßen=)~ highwayman, brigand, zu Fuße: footpad; (See=)~ pirate; per ~ seiner Ehre his detractor. — 2. a) fig. = Dieb 2; b) hort. eines Baumes: sucker.
Räuber=bande (⁻ʹ⋃⋅⋃ʹ⋃) f ② band (or gang) of robbers or brigands; vgl. Raubgesindel. [brigandage; pillage.]
Räuberei (⋃⁻ʹ⋃) f ④⑥ system of robbery,]
Räuber=geschichte (⁻ʹ⋃⋃⋅⋃ʹ⋃⋃) f ②: a) tale of robbers or brigands; b) F fig. cock-and-bull story, penny-dreadful.
räuberhaft (⁻⋃⋃⋅) a. ⑥⑥ = räuberisch.
Räuber=hauptmann (⁻ʹ⋃⋃…) m ② captain of brigands, robber-chief; **=höhle** f den of robbers or thieves.
räuberisch (⁻⋃⋃⋃) a. ⑥⑥ of (or like) robbers or brigands; predatory.
räubern (⁻ʹ⋃) v/n. (h.) ②a. 1. to go robbing and thieving, to commit (highway) robberies. — 2. Tennis: to poach.
Räuber=nest (⁻ʹ⋃…) n ② = **=höhle**; **=schar** f, **=volk** n set(or pack, gang) of robbers or thieves; **=wesen** n brigandage, brigandism.
Raub=fisch (⁻ʹ…) m ② ichth. fish of prey; **=fliege** f, ent. hornet-(or robber-, hawk-)fly (Asi'lus); **=gesell** m robber, highwayman, brigand; **=gesindel** n gang of thieves, troop of marauders; vgl. Räuberbande; **=gier** f rapacity; vgl. =**lust**; **⚲gierig** a. ⑥⑥ rapacious; **=gut** n booty, stolen goods pl.; **=krieg** m war of plunder, predatory war (-fare); **=lust** f lust of booty; vgl. **=gier**; **=mord** m murder (attended) with robbery; **=mörder** m one who commits a murder with robbery; **=möwe** f: a) langschwänzige: arctic-bird (Lestris longicau'da); b) große: skua(-gull) (Lestris catarrha'ctes); **=nest** n haunt (auch nest) of robbers, den of thieves; ehm. =**ritter** m robber-knight or =baron; **=schiff** ⚓ n pirate(-ship), corsair, privateer; **=schloß** n castle of a robber-baron, robber-knight's castle; **=staat** m: a) piratical state, country of brigands; ehm. die ~en in Nordafrika: the Barbary States pl.; b) iro. small country; **=sucht** f = **=gier**; **⚲süchtig** a. = **⚲gierig**; **=tat** f robbery with violence; **=tier** n, zo. beast of prey, rapacious animal; ~e ⚯ carnivora; **=vogel** m bird of prey; **=zeug** n, hunt. (Jagdtiere) animals which live by hunting, beasts pl. of prey; (Ungeziefer) vermin; **=zug** m pillaging-(or marauding-)expedition, raid.

Rauch[1] (⁻ʹ⋅) [ahd.: reek] m ③c. u. ⑦c. (pl. ⋅⋅ʹ) 1. smoke (vgl. Dampf 1 und Dunst 1); Fleisch ⚒. in den ~ hängen to smoke(-dry) …; nach ~ schmecken to taste of smoke, to have a smoky taste; in ~ aufgehen to be consumed by fire, fig. to end in smoke, to come to nothing. — 2. (Ruß) soot. [tabak ⚒.]
Rauch[2]… (⁻ʹ…) [rauchen] f. Rauch=]
rauch[a] (⁻ʹ⑥) [mhd.] a. ⑥⑥ = rauh; (haarig) hairy; furred; (zottig) shaggy; ⚭: ⚯ hirsute; f. Rauch=handel, =ware, =werk.
Rauch[1]=altar (⁻ʹ⑥…) m ② der Juden ⚒.: incense-altar; vgl. Opferaltar.
rauchbar (⁻ʹ⑥⋅) a. ⑥⑥ smokable. [abteil.\]
Rauch[2]=coupé 🚂 (⁻ʹ⑥⋃) n ② = **Raucher=\]
rauchen [Rauch¹] I v/n. (h. und sn), a. v/impers., v/a. ⑧ 1. to smoke (vgl. dampfen I u. II und dunsten I); gern ② to be fond of smoking or of a cigar or of one's pipe; haben die Damen et. dagegen, wenn wir ②? do the ladies object to (or mind) our smoking?; darf hier geraucht werden? is smoking here allowed?; es raucht there is smoke (rising); fig. daß e-m der Kopf raucht (mit Anstrengung des Geistes) (so as) to make one's head ache or split, with a vengeance; chm. ②de Schwefelsäure fuming sulphuric acid. — 2. v/a. mit Angabe der Wirkung: e-n Pfeifenkopf braun ② = anrauchen 2; die Stube voll Dampf ② to fill the room with smoke. — II ~ n ② 3. smoking; das ~ ist (hier) verboten! smoking is not allowed (here)!, (please) do not smoke!
Raucher (⁻ʹ⑥⋃) m ②, **~in** f ④ smoker, person who smokes; ein starker ~ a great (or inveterate) smoker.
Raucher=abteil 🚂 (⁻ʹ⑥⋃⋅⋃ʹ⋅) m ② smoking-compartment, F smoker.
Räucher=apparat (⁻ʹ⑥⋃…) m ② fumigator. [bloaters, &c.; perfumer.\]
Räucherer ⊖ (⁻⋃⋃) m ② smoker of]
Räucher=essenz (⁻ʹ⑥⋃…) f ② strong scent, fragrant essence; **=essig** m aromatic vinegar. [smoke; reeking, reeky.\]
räucherig (⁻ʹ⋃⋃) a. ⑥⑥ smoky, tasting of]
Räucher=kammer ⊖ (⁻ʹ⑥⋃…) f ② smoking-chamber for meat, &c.; **=kerzchen** n, **=kerze** f fumigating-candle; pastil(le).
räuchern (⁻ʹ⋃) [Rauch] ②a. I v/a. to (expose to) smoke, Schinken, Würste ⚒. auch: to smoke-dry, Heringe ⚒.: to cure, kranke Glieder, zum Krankenzimmer ⚒.: to fumigate, eccl. den Altar ⚒.: to cense (vgl. beräuchern); (mit Wohlgeruch erfüllen) to perfume, to scent; Bienen(stöcke): to smoke out; ⊖ geräucherter Hering smoked(or cured, red)herring, bloater. — II v/n. (h.) to burn incense on an altar, before an idol, fig. before a p. — III ~ n ② = Räucherung.
Räucher=papier (⁻ʹ⑥⋃…) n ② fumigating paper; **=pfanne** f = Rauchfaß; **=pulver** n fumigating powder.

[Räucherung] — 790 — [Raupentöter]

Räucherung (‿‿) f ⓴ (s. räuchern I) smoking; fumigation.
Räucher=werk (‿‿‿) [mhd.] n ⓶ perfumes, scents pl., perfumery; (Weihrauch) frankincense.
Rauch¹=fang ⊙ (″ch…) m ⓶ Bauwesen: flue; (Schornstein) chimney; vgl. =mantel; =fangkehrer m chimney-sweep(er), F sweep; ²farben a. ⓺ smoke-coloured; =faß n, eccl. censer, ☿ thurible; =fleisch ⚥ n smoked meat; ²frei a. = =los; =³fuß m foot covered with hair or feathers; ²füßig a. hairy-legged, orn.: ☿ plumiped; ²gar ⊙ a. Kürschnerei: (von Fellen) dressed with the hair (on); ²¹gar a. (vom Fleische) well (or thoroughly) smoked; ²gelb a. smoky yellow; ²geschwärzt a. smoke-stained; =glas ⊙ n smoked glass; ²grau a. smoky grey, dun; ²handel m, ²händler m = Pelz=handel, =händler.
rauchig (‿ch‿) [: reeky] a. ⓺ smoky.
Rauch²=kabinett (″ch…) n ⓶ =zimmer; =¹kammer f: a) ⊙ einer Dampfmaschine: smoke-box, e-r Lokomotive: smoke-arch; b) = Räucherkammer; =²kater m (Katzenjammer v. Rauchen) sick headache produced by smoking; =¹loch n: a) ⊙ smoke-hole; b) (räucherige Stube) smoky room or F hole; =²lokal n: a) smoking-room, -saloon; =²los a. ⓺ smokeless; ⚔ f. ²schwach; =mantel ⊙ m chimney-hood; =massen f/pl. volumes pl. of smoke; =opfer n incense-offering; =plage f: i. Fabrikstädten: smoke-nuisance; =säule f column (or pillar) of smoke; ²schwach ⚔ a.: ²es Pulver smokeless powder; =schwalbe f, orn. chimney-swallow (Hirundo rustica); =³seite f hairy side of a skin; =²stube f =zimmer; =tabak m tobacco for smoking); =¹topas m, min. smoke-quartz; =topf m = =faß; ²verzehrend a. ⓾ smoke-consuming or -burning, lumivorous; =verzehrung f consumption (or burning) of smoke; =verzehrungs=apparat ⊙ m smoke-consumer; =³ware(n pl.) ⊛ f, =werk [mhd.] n = Pelzware; =¹wirbel m wreath(s pl.) of smkoe; =wolke f cloud of smoke; =²zimmer n smoking-room.
Raude ⚕, mst **Räude** (‿‿) [ahd.] f ⓾ path. (Grind) scab, der Haustiere auch: mange, der Schafe: rubbers pl.
räudig (‿‿) [ahd.] a. ⓺ scabbed, mangy; fig. ²es Schaf (the) black sheep of the family, &c.; ~keit (‿‿‿) f ⓾ manginess.
(')**rauf** F (‿) abbr. = herauf.
Rauf²=bold (″…) [raufen] m ⓶ brawler, bully, pugnacious fellow, rowdy; =degen m: a) rapier, long sword; b) = =bold.
Raufe (‿‿) [mhd.] f ⓾ 1. ⊙ = Flachshechel. — 2. (stable-)rack; ⚔ rack for guns.
raufen (‿‿) [ahd.] v. reap: rupfen] v/a. u. sich ⟲ v/recip. u. v/n. (h.) ⓼ to pluck, to pull (vgl. ausraufen I); sich das Haar (ob. die Haare) aus dem Kopfe ⟲ to tear (out) one's hair; (sich) mit e-m ⟲ (balgen) to fight (or scuffle, tussle) with a p., spielend: to romp (together or with each other), to have a romp.
Raufer (‿‿) m ⓶ = Rauf=bold, =degen; ~ei (‿‿‿) f ⓾ fight, scuffle, tussle, row.

Rauf²=lust (″…) f ⓺, ²lustig a. ⓺ = =sucht; ²süchtig; =messer ⊙ n (double-edged) hair-scraper; =sucht f pugnacity, combativeness; ²süchtig a. pugnacious, combative, full of fight.
Rau=graf (″‿) [mhd.] m ⓶ ehm. Titel von Adelsfamilien am Oberrhein: ⑇ raugrave.
rauh (‿) [ahd.: rough] a. ⓺ 1. (ant. glatt) rough (s. rauch³); von Gegenden, Wegen ꝛc.: rugged; (wild) wild; ⟲ im Halse hoarse; Tennis: ⟲ ob. glatt? rough or smooth? — 2. (streng) severe, stern, vom Tone: rough, harsh, von der Kälte: biting, bitter, vom Wetter: raw, bleak, inclement; einen ⟲ (adv.) anfahren to talk roughly (or harshly) to a p. — 3. (aus dem groben gearbeitet, ant. fein) raw, unfinished, (ungehobelt) unpolished; fig. ²e Sitten coarse (or rude, rustic, primitive) manners pl.
Rauh=bank ⊙ (″…) f ⓺ Tischlerei: trying-plane; =bein F m (roher Kerl) cad, blackguard; low fellow, ruffian, plebeian, bei Studenten = Knote, Philister; ²beinig a. ⓺ rough, caddish, low, plebeian; ²blätterig(e Gewächse) ꝑ a.: ☿ asperifolious (plants pl.); =borsten ⊙ f/pl. coarse (or unsorted) bristles pl.
Rauhe prov. (‿‿) f ⓾ = Mauser².
Rauheit (‿‿) f ⓾ (s. rauh) roughness, ruggedness, der Stimme: hoarseness, harshness, des Charakters: sternness, des Wetters: bleakness, inclemency; der Sitten: coarseness, rudeness.
rauhen (‿‿) ⓼ I v/a. to (make) rough, to roughen, ⊙ das Tuch: to tease(l), card, nap. — II v/n. (h.) und sich ⟲ v/refl. von Vögeln: (mausern) to moult.
Rauher ⊙ (‿‿) m ⓶ Tuchfabrikation: teaseler; ~ei (‿‿‿) f ⓾ teaseling.
Rauh=frost (″…) m ⓶ = =reif; =futter n coarse food or fodder, hay and straw; =graf m = Raugraf; =haare n/pl. rough bristles pl.; ²haarig a. ⓺: ☿ hirsute.
Rauhigkeit (‿‿‿) f ⓾ = Rauheit.
Rauh=reif (″…) m ⓶ hoar-frost; =schlei=fer m rough-grinder; =wolle f skin-wool.
Raufe ꝑ (‿‿) [mhd.] f = rocket; *It. eruca* f ⓺ hedge-mustard (Sisymbrium).
Raum¹ (‿) [ahd.: room: It. rus Land] m ⓓc. 1. room, space, freier ⟲ open space; in engem ~e within a narrow compass; (Ausdehnung) expanse; (Platz zu e-m Hausbau ꝛc.) plot; hohler ~ eines Gefäßes ꝛc.: capacity, ⚓ e-s Schiffes: ship's (Spiel=)~ scope; (Unterkommen) accommodation; =ist in der kleinsten Hütte für ein glücklich liebend Paar (SCH.) the meanest hut is amply large for a happy loving couple. — 2. (Räumlichkeit) locality; Räume e-s Hauses: rooms, conveniences pl.; (Abteilung) compartment (a. ⛴); arch. ~ im Lichten area. — 3. phys. luftleerer ~ vacuum. — 4. fig. e-r Bitte ~ geben to grant (or to comply with) a request, e-m Gedanken: to give way to a thought, der Hoffnung: to live (or indulge) in hope.
raum² ⚓ (‿) [ahd.] a. ⓺ = geräumig; ⚓ ²e See open sea, offing; ²er Wind quarter-wind.
Raum¹=anker ⚓ (″…) m ⓶ spare anchor; =balken ⚓ m hold-beam; =einheit f unit of space.

räumen (‿‿) [ahd.; *Raum¹] I v/a. und v/n. (h.) ⓼ 1. (fortschaffen) to remove; an die Seite (oder beiseite) ⟲ to clear away obstacles, &c.; to push aside, to put out of the way; e-n aus dem Wege ⟲ (durch Mord ꝛc.) to dispatch (or kill) a p., to make away with a p.; oder Objekt: sie räumt den ganzen Tag she's tidying up (or F putting things straight) all day long. — 2. (säubern) to clean (up); in e-n Hafen ꝛc. ⟲ to dredge ... — 3. ⊛ das Lager ⟲ to clear off old stock (vgl. aufräumen 2); Ausverkauf, um mit dem Lager zu ⟲ clearance-sale. — 4. e-n Ort ⟲ (aufgeben, verlassen) to give up (or leave, quit) a place, to remove from a house; ⚔ das Feld ⟲ to quit the field, to retreat; eine Festung ⟲ to evacuate ... — 5. ⚓ der Wind räumt (wird günstiger) ... veers aft. — II ~ n ⓶ 6. s. Räumung.
Räumer (‿‿) m ⓶ 1. (s. der räumt) person who clears away; clean(s)er. — 2. ⚔ u. ⊙ = Räumnadel.
Raum¹=ersparnis (″…) f ⓶: der ~ wegen to save room, to gain space; =größe f geometrical quantity or value.
räumig (‿‿) [Raum¹] a. ⓺ = geräumig.
Raum¹=inhalt (″‿‿) m ⓶ volume, (solid) contents pl., ⚓ e-s Schiffes: tonnage.
räumlich (‿‿) [Raum¹] a. ⓺ of (or in, relating to) space, spatial.
Räumlichkeit (‿‿‿) f ⓾: a) phls., &c. spatiality; b) = Raum¹ 2.
raum¹=los (″…) a. ⓺ spaceless; =mangel m ⓶ lack of room, want of space; =meter n (m) (abbr. rm) cubic metre.
Räum=nadel ⊙ (‿‿‿) [räumen] f ⓾ wire-riddle, pin (a. ⚔, f. Ausräumer 2).
Räumte ⚓ (‿) [ndd.] f ⓾ high sea(s pl.), main, (freier Seeraum) offing, open sea; die ~ gewinnen to gain the offing; die ~ suchen to make for the main.
Räumung (‿‿) f ⓾ 1. (zu räumen 1:) removal, clearance. — 2. (zu 4:) nächtliche ~ e-r Wohnung: nocturnal removal, F co. moonlight flit; ⚔ e-r Festung: evacuation.
Räumungs=frage ⚔ (″…) f ⓶ question of evacuation; =öffnung ⊙ f manhole of a cesspool, &c. [space-perception.
Raum¹=wahrnehmung (″‿‿‿) f ⓶ phls.]
raunen¹ (‿‿) [ahd.: roun(d): grch. ereunā'n] I v/n. (h.) u. v/a. ⓼ to whisper (softly) in(to) a p.'s ear. — II ~ n ⓷ (soft) whisper(ing).
raunen² (‿‿) v/n. (h.) ⓼ hunt. v. Hasen: (Seitensprünge machen) to double.
Raupe (‿‿) [ndd.] f ⓾ 1. ent. caterpillar; fig. ~n (Launen) whims, fancies, F maggots pl.; (hochfahrende Gedanken) high (or proud) notions pl. — 2. ⊛ Posamentier: (Sammetschnur) chenille; ⚔ ~n pl. eines deutschen Generals ꝛc.: thick fringes pl. of the epaulettes.
raupen (‿‿) v/a. ⓼ to pick caterpillars from (or off) trees or shrubs or plants.
Raupen=ablesen (″…) n ⓶ picking (of) caterpillars; =fraß m damage done by (or blight of) caterpillars; =helm ⚔ m padded helmet of the Bavarians; =nest n nest of caterpillars; =schere f, hort. gardener's pruning-shears pl.; =töter m, ent. ichneumon-fly.

Signs (see page XVII): F familiar; P vulgar; ⚑ flash; ⚐ rare; † obsolete (died); * new word (born); ⁜ incorrect; ♪ music;

[Rauper] — 791 — [Rechenschüler]

Rauper (´‿) [raupen] m ⌬ p. who picks caterpillars.
raupig (´‿) a. ⊙ full of caterpillars.
(')**raus** F (´) abbr. für heraus (f. dS); er hat's ⸺ he knows a thing or two, he has all his wits about him.
Rausch¹ (´) [nhd.; *rauschen] m ⒯a. 1. tipsiness, tipsy fit, stärker: intoxication, drunkenness; sich einen Rausch antrinken to get fuddled (with drink); s. ausschlafen II; einen ~ haben to be tipsy or intoxicated, F to be boozed or well on; wer niemals e-n ~ gehabt he who ne'er was half-seas-over, freier: he who ne'er felt flushed with liquor; im ~e while intoxicated; in one's cups. — 2. fig. ~ der Liebe ꝛc.: passionate glow (or heat) …, ecstasy …, frenzy …, F mad fit …
Rausch²**-beere** ⚘ (´‿…) [it. rosso rot] f ⊙ crake-, crow-berry (Empetrum nigrum).
Räuschchen (´‿) n ⌬ dim. v. Rausch.
rauschen (´‿) [ndd.: rush] ⓴ I v/n. (h. u. ſn) 1. (h.) to rush, stärker (bes. von Wind u. Wellen) to roar; sanft ⸺: a) von Bächen, Quellen: to murmur, gurgle, purl, von Wellen: to swirl; b) v. Winde in den Blättern: to rustle, to sough; c) von seidenen Stoffen: to rustle. — 2. (ſn) Ortsveränderung bezeichnend: to rush (or roar) past. — II v/a. 3. poet. mit Angabe der Wirkung: der Wald hat mir die alte Zeit wach gerauscht … has called up within me memories of the past. — III ~ n ⌬ 4. rushing, &c. (f. I); roar(ing noise), uproar; murmur(s pl.). — IV ⓸ p.pr. u. a. ⊙ 5. in mir Bed. des inf. — 6. = geräuschvoll; Oder Beifall thundering applause, ringing cheers pl.; Ode Freude exuberant joy.
Rauſch²**-gelb** ⊙ (´‿…) n ⊙ min. (Auripigment) orpiment, arsenious sulphide (As₂S₃); **-gold** [rauſchen] n brass-foil, Dutch gold; vgl. Flittergold; **-rot** n, min. = Realgar; **-ſilber** ⊙ n leaf-silver.
räuspern (´‿) [mhd.] I v/n. (h.) u. ſich ⸺ v/refl. ⓶a. to hawk (up the phlegm); to hem, mehr gbr. to clear one's throat; wie er ſich räuspert und wie er ſpuckt // (SCH. Wallensteins Lager) how he hems and how he spits //. — II ~ n ⌬ = Geräusper.
Raute¹ ⚘ (´‿) [ahd.: rue; *It. ruta] f ⊙ rue (Ruta graveolens); Familie der ~n: ⚘ Rutaceæ.
Raute² (´‿) [mhd.] f ⓭ lozenge (-shaped figure), a. diamond, math. rhomb(oid); Steinschneiderei: facet; arch. quarrel; s. Rauten-glas ꝛc. -stab.
rauten¹ (´‿) [Raute²] v/a. ⓰ to cut in the shape of a lozenge or rhomb(oid).
Rauten²**-diamant** (´‿…) [Raute²] m ⓭ Steinschneiderei: brilliant; **-feld** n bes. her. lozenge; **-fläche** ⊙ f von Glas und Steinen: facet; **-förmig** a. ⊙ lozenge- (or diamond-)shaped, lozenged, math. rhombic, rhomboidal, ⚘ rhombiform; ⸗er Muskel anat. am Schulterblatt: ⚘ rhomboid; **-glas** ⊙ n Glaserei: glass-lozenge, faceted glass; **-öl** [Raute¹] n (essential) oil of rue; **-spat** m, min. rhomb-spar; **-stab** ⊙ m, arch. lozenge-fret or -moulding; **-viereck** n rhomb; **-weise** a. lozengewise; in facets.

rautig (´‿) [Raute²] a. ⊙ lozenged.
Rayon (ra-joɴ') [fr.] m ⓰(⊙d.) fr. ⓰ (Umkreis) radius; (Bereich) range.
Razzia (´‿‿) [fr.; *ar. ghazīja Heldenstück] f ⓰⓴⓽ (Überfall, bes. der Polizei) raid; eine ~ halten to (make a) raid.
Rbl. abbr. = Rubel.
Reagens (‿´‿) [neu=lt.] n ⓾ chm. (Prüfungsmittel) test, a. reagent.
Reagens- (´‿‿…), meist -‿ **Reagenz-glas** (‿´…) n ⓰ test-glass, test-tube; **-papier** n test-paper, violettes, auch: litmus-paper, gelbes: curcuma-paper.
reagieren (‿‿´‿) [lt.] I v/n. (h.) ⓽ to react upon; F fig. auf et. nicht ⸺ not to respond to a th. — II ~ n ⌬ = Reaktion.
Reaktion (‿‿tß(‿)´) [lt.] f ⓰: a) chm. (Wirkung); b) pol. (Rückgang): reaction.
reaktionär (‿‿tß(‿)ɴ´) a. ⊙ reactionary; ~ m ⓰d. pol. reactionist.
real¹ (‿´) [neu=lt.] I a. ⊙ (sachlich) substantial, material, (tätlich) actual, (wirklich) real. — II das **Reale** n ⓶ reality, real fact; vgl. auch Real'ien 1.
Real² (‿´) [span.] m ⓰d. (vort. pl. Reis (span. Münze = 20 Pf.) real.
Real³ öst. typ. (‿´) n ⓰d. = Regal¹.
Real⁴ (‿´) f ⓰ typ. Schriftgrad: eight-line pica. [cyclopædia.)
Real¹**-enzyklopädie** (‿´‿‿´‿‿) f ⓰ (en-)
Realgar ⸗ (‿´‿) [ar.] n ⓰ min. realgar.
Real¹**-gymnasium** (‿´‿…) n ⓰ (German) secondary school for modern subjects, sciences and Latin.
Reali-en (‿´(‿)‿) n/pl. inv. 1. (Tatsächliches) real (or actual) facts pl. — 2. = Realkenntnisse; engS. knowledge of modern facts and things.
Real¹**-injurien-klage** f) (‿´…) f/pl. ⓰ (action for) assault and battery.
Realisation ⓰ (‿‿‿tß‿´) f ⓰ Börse: realization; **-lust** (⸺…) f ⓰ eagerness to realize or to sell.
realiſier/en (‿‿‿´‿) I v/a. ⓳: a) verwirklichen; b) zu Gelde machen: to realize. — II ~ ⌬ n. R/ung f ⓰ realization.
Realismus (‿‿´‿‿) m ⓵ phls. realism.
Realist (‿‿´) m ⓰, **-iſch** (‿‿´‿) a. ⊙ Kunst, phls. (ant. Nominaliſt) realist.
Realität (‿‿‿´) f ⓰ (Wirklichkeit) reality.
realiter (‿‿´‿) adv. in reality.
Real¹**-kenntniſſe** (‿´…) f/pl. ⓰ historical and scientific knowledge; **-klaſſen** f/pl. modern side of a college; **-lehrer** m teacher at a "Realschule" (f. =ſchule); **-lexikon** n dictionary of arts and sciences; **-ſchule** f (German) secondary school for modern subjects and sciences; weitS. modern school; **-ſchüler** m pupil of a "Realschule"; **-ſchulweſen** n affairs pl. of the "Realschulen"; weitS. modern system of school-education or teaching; **-wert** m actual value; **-wörterbuch** n = =lexikon.
Réaumur (re'-ō-mǖr)[Réaumur, fr. Physiker, 1683—1757. Verbeſſerer des Thermometers] npr. m. ⊙a. (abbr. R) Réaumur; ~ſche Skala Réaumur's scale; 3° ~ three degrees R. [vines; **-auge** ⚘ n vine-bud.)
Reb-acker (´‿‿) m ⓰ field planted with)
Rebe (´‿) [ahd.] f ⓰ (Wein-)~: a) (Weinstock) vine; b) (Ranke) tendril, shoot.
Rebekka (‿´‿) npr/f. ⓽⓰, ⓶⓶ ⓸a. (Frau Isaaks) Rebecca, Rebekah, auch F Bec(ca).

Rebell (‿´) [lt. rebellis] m ⓰ (gen. sg. a. ~s), **~in** f ⓰ rebel; vgl. Aufrührer.
rebellieren (‿‿´‿) [nhd.; *lt.] v/n. (h.) ⓽ to rebel, revolt, rise.
Rebellion (‿‿(‿)´) [lt.] f ⓰ rebellion.
rebelliſch (‿‿´‿) [lt.] a. ⊙ (aufrühreriſch) rebellious, revolutionary; mutinous (conduct); seditious (speech).
reben=bekränzt (´‿…) [Rebe] a. ⊙ vine-clad; **-blatt** ⚘ n ⓰ vine-leaf; **-blut** n = -saft; **-dolde** ⚘ f earth-nut (Oena'nthe); **-gelände** n vine-clad country; **-geländer** n trellis-work for vines; **-holz** n wood of a vine; **-hügel** m vineyard (on a hill); **-laub** n foliage of a vine, vine-leaves pl.; **-meſſer** ⊙ n pruning-knife; **-reich** a. rich in vines; **-saft** m grape-juice, wine; **-stab** m, myth. thyrsus; **-unsorm** a. vine-clad; **-züchter** vine-grower, ⚘ viticulturist.
Reb¹**-gewinde** (´‿‿‿)[Rebe] n ⓰ garland (or festoon) of vine-branches.
Reb²**-hahn** (‿´) [f. Rebhuhn] m ⓯c. orn. u. hunt. cock-partridge.
Reb¹**-hügel** (´‿‿) m ⓰ hill planted (or covered) with vines.
Reb²**-huhn** (‿´) [ahd.; *slaw.] n ⓾ orn. partridge (Perdix cine'rea); s. Kette²; **~jagd** (‿´…) f ⓰ partridge-shooting.
Reb¹**-land** (´‿…) n ⓰ land planted (or covered) with vines; **-laus** f, zo. phylloxera (Phyllox'era vasta'trix); **-laus-krankheit** f vine-disease. [shoot.)
Rebling (´‿) m ⓰d. (Rebenschößling) vine-)
Reb¹**-pfahl** (´‿…) m ⓰ vine-prop; **-schere** ⊙ f pruning-shears pl.; **-schoß** ⚘ m vine-shoot or -branch; **-stock** m = Rebe a.
Rebus (´‿) [lt. durch Dinge (dargeſtellt)] m u. n, inv. u. ⓰ (Bilderrätsel) rebus, mehr gbr.: picture-puzzle.
Rechen¹ ⊙ (´‿) [Rechen¹ = rake] m ⓰ 1. obb. (Harke) rake. — 2. (Kleider=)~ rack, clothes-rail, peg-board.
rechen² ⊙ (´‿) [Rechen¹] v/a. ⓸ to rake.
Rechen³**-aufgabe** (‿´‿‿) [rechnen] f ⓰ (arithmetical) problem, mehr gbr.: (arithmetical) sum; **-brett** n ehm. counting-board; vgl. =tisch; **-buch** n arithmetic-book; **-exempel** n = =aufgabe; **-fehler** m miscalculation, arithmetical mistake; **-heft** n sum-book, exercise-book for arithmetic; **-knecht** m ready reckoner; **-kunst** f (art of) arithmetic, ciphering; **-künstler(in** f) m arithmetician; **-lehrer(in** f) m teacher of arithmetic; **-lineal** n s. Nonius; **-maschine** f calculating machine, (mechanical) calculator; **-meister** m (clever) arithmetician; **-münze** f nominal (or fictitious) coin; **-pfennig** m counter.
Rechenschaft (´‿‿) [rechnen] f ⓰ account; ~ ablegen (ob. geben) von etwas to give (or render) an account of a th., to account for a th.; e-n wegen et. zur ~ ziehen to call a p. to account (or F to book) for a th.
Rechenschafts=ablage (´‿‿…) f ⓰, **-bericht** m statement of accounts, account rendered; **-legung** f rendering (or giving) an account; **-pflichtig** a. ⊙ accountable.
Rechen³**-schule** (´‿…) f ⓰ ciphering-school; **-schüler(in** f) m pupil in

⚛ scientific; ⚘ botanical; ⚕ geography; ⊙ machinery; ⚒ mining; ⚔ military; ⚓ marine; ⚖ commercial; ✉ postal; 🚂 railway.

[**Rechenstiel**] arithmetic, arithmetic-pupil; =¹**stiel** ⊕ *m* handle of a rake; =³**stift** *m* slate pencil; =**stunde** *f* arithmetic-lesson; =**tafel** *f*: a) (Schiefertafel) slate; b) (Schultafel) black-board; c) multiplication-tables *pl.*; =**tisch** *m* abacus; *vgl.* =**brett**; =**unterricht** *m* instruction in arithmetic, arithmetical teaching; =**virtuose** *m* (Schnellrechner) arithmetical genius or prodigy. [investigation, inquiry.] **Recherche** (~ˈsch~ˈsch~)[fr.] *f* ⑳ (Nachforschung) **rechnen** (~ˈv~) [ahd.: reckon] **I** *v/a.* und *v/n.* (h.) ⑳b. **1.** to count; (zf.=zählen) to reckon (up), to cast (or sum) up; (ausrechnen) to calculate, to compute; (Aufgaben lösen) to do sums (in arithmetic), to do ciphering; (veranschlagen) to estimate, to value; im Kopf ⌒ to reckon in one's head, to work out mentally; er kann gut ⌒ he is good (or clever) at arithmetic or sums, he is quick at figures. — **2.** Redens=arten: eins zum andern ⌒ to add (or sum) up; eins ins andere ⌒ to take one thing with another; alles in allem gerechnet taking all in all; gegen=ea. ⌒ (vergleichen) to compare; alles mit dazu ⌒ to include everything; sie sind, hoch (oder gut) gerechnet, zwei Meilen it is two miles at the most; ohne die Zeit zu ⌒ without counting (or not to mention) the time; wir ⌒ es uns zur Ehre, daß // we reckon (or consider, think, deem) it an honour that //. — **3.** auf e=n oder etwas ⌒ (sich verlassen) to reckon (or depend, rely) on a p. or a th.; wir ⌒ zuversichtlich auf eine gute Ernte we have sanguine hopes (or we are sanguine) of a good crop. — **II** ~ ㉓ (s. I) **4.** counting, calculation, computation; ciphering; arithmetic. — **5.** = Rechnung.

Rechnen... (~ˈv~...) ++ = Rechen³...
Rechner (~ˈv~) *m* ㉒, **~in** *f* ㊸ calculator, arithmetician (vgl. Berechner).
Rechnerei (~ˈvˈl~) *f* ㊻ continued reckoning, long account or calculation.
Rechnung (~ˈv~) [mhd.: reckoning] *f* ㊻ **1.** a)=rechnen 4; b) (Ausführung einer Rechenaufgabe) working (or doing) a sum (in arithmetic); s=e ~ stimmt nicht he is wrong (or out) in his calculation or account. — **2.** (Aufstellung e-r Schuld) account, bill, kurz gefaßte: memorandum, beim Restaurateur auch: check, im Wirtshause: score; Tennis: score; (Faktura) invoice; *fig.* die ~ ohne den Wirt *m.* to reckon without one's host; mach deine ~ mit dem Himmel, Vogt! (SCH.) settle (or square) your account with Heaven, bailiff! — **3.** ⊕ f. abschließen 4; auf eigene ~ on one's own account; auf ~ kaufen to buy on credit; auf j-s ~ stellen to place (or carry) to a p.'s account; s. gemeinschaftlich, ausgleichen 3; j-s ~ mit etwas belasten to debit a p. with a th., to put a th. to a p.'s debit; s. bringen 8 unter „auf" u. „in"; ~ führen to keep an account, als Buchhalter: to keep the accounts; mit e-m (fortlaufend) in ~ stehen to have an (a running) account with a p. — **4.** (Annahme) supposition; das stimmt nicht mit meiner ~ that does not agree with my calculation. — **5.** *fig.* s=e ~ (s-n Vorteil) bei et. finden to derive (an) advantage from a th., to make a profit by a th.; dabei finden wir unsere ~ nicht we lose (or are losers) by it; sich ~ auf et. m. to reckon (or count, depend) upon a th., e-m e-n Strich durch die ~ m. to cross (or thwart) a p.'s plan(s); den Umständen ~ tragen to act according (or to accommodate o.s.) to circumstances; ⊛ den Wünschen der Käufer ~ tragen to comply (or fall in) with the wishes of the customers.

Rechnungs=ablage ⊛ (~ˈv~...) *f* ㊷ rendering of accounts; =**abnahme** *f* audit (-ing of accounts); =**abnehmer** *m* auditor (of accounts); =**abschluß** *m* closing (or balancing) of accounts; =**art** *f* method of calculation; die vier =arten the four species; *vgl.* Grundrechnungs=arten; =**auszug** *m* abstract (or short statement) of an account (-current); =**beamte(r)** *m* accountant; =**beleg** *m* voucher; =**buch** *n* account-book; =**fehler** *m* mistake in calculation; *vgl.* Rechenfehler; =**führer** *m* book-keeper; =**führung** *f* keeping of accounts; =**jahr** *n* financial year; =**kammer** *f* chamber of accounts, audit-office; ⌒ **mäßig** *a.* ⑳ u. *adv.* in conformity with the books; =**münze** *f* fictitious coin; =**probe** *f* proof; =**prüfung** *f* checking (or overhauling) of accounts; =**rat** *m,* etwa: member of a chamber of accounts; =**revision** *f* audit; =**revisor** *m* controller (of accounts), auditor; =**überschlag** *m* rough estimate; =**wesen** *n* (system of) accounts.

recht¹ (⌒) [ahd.: right] *a.* ⑳ ohne *comp.* **1.** [mhd.] (ant. linf): a) right, her. dexter; *s.* rechter=hand, ⌒seits; ⌒e Seite right side, eines Pferdes: off-side; b) *s/f.* die ~**e** (rechte Hand) right hand; *pol.* (konservative Seite) Conservative side in Parliament; zur ~en (geh(e)n) (to walk) on the right hand or right-hand side; c) *adv.* ⌒s on (or at) the right (side); sich ⌒s halten (wenden) to keep (to turn) to the right; ⚔ Augen ⌒s! eyes right!; es schließt euch! close to the right!; ⌒s um (sieht), nach ⌒s! right turn!, to right in file!; F a. *prp.* mit *gen.* ⌒s der Donau on the right bank of the Danube. — **2.** (ant. schief) *math.* der Winkel, **~er** right angle. — **3.** (der Regel, den Wünschen gemäß) right; (richtig) correct; (gerecht) just, (schicklich) proper, suitable, befitting, (wie sich's gehört) as it should be; das ist nicht mehr als ⌒ und billig that's only right and proper; Sprichw. f. billig 1. — **4.** meist mit *nouns:* der ⌒e Mann, der **~e** the right man or one or F sort; an den ~en kommen to find (or meet) one's match; *iro.* du bist mir der ~e, ein ~er! you are a nice (or fine, pretty) fellow!; am ⌒en Orte in the right (or proper) place; F vor die ⌒e Schmiede gehen to come to the right shop, to apply in the right quarters; zum ~en sehen to see (or attend) to a th.; (genau) zur ⌒en Zeit (exactly) in (due) time, in the (very) nick of time; *fig.* und Sprichw. f. Ding 4, Fleck 1. — **5.** meist mit *verbs.* oft *adv.:* ⌒ haben to be right; er hat ⌒ daran he is justified in doing so; das ist ⌒!, so ist es ⌒!, ell. ⌒!, ⌒ so!, ganz ⌒! that's right!, quite right!; ⌒ so! (Befehl, geradeaus zu steuern) right ahead!; Tennis: ⌒! all right!; es ist ⌒ von Ihnen, daß Sie kommen it is right of you to come; you are right in coming; wenn (oder wo) mir ⌒ ist if I am not (or unless I be) mistaken; bist du nicht ⌒ hier (auf die Stirn zeigend)? are you in your right senses?; mir ist nicht ⌒ (zu Mute, zu Sinne) I feel queer or low-spirited, F I don't feel up to much; gehe ich hier ⌒ (oder ist das der ⌒e Weg) nach X.? am I on the right way to X.?; es geschieht ihnen ganz ⌒ it serves them quite right; habe ich ⌒ gehört? did I understand rightly?; verstehe ich Ihnen ⌒? I'm not inconveniencing (or disturbing) you(, I hope)?; *vgl.* kommen 8; ⌒ tun to do the right (or correct) thing, to do right; Sprichw. tue ⌒ und scheue niemand do right and defy the world. — **6.** (wirklich, echt) real, genuine; der ⌒e Erbe the legitimate (or rightful) heir; meine ⌒e Mutter my own (or real) mother; *adv.:* a) = sehr, vor *a.* u. *adv.:* ⌒ gut very good, quite well; ich bin ⌒ begierig zu erfahren I am rather anxious to learn; ⌒ gern most gladly or willingly; es tut mir ⌒ leid I am very (or right, stärker: extremely) sorry; es ist ⌒ schade it is a great pity; (so) ⌒ als ob // quite as if //; b) meist vor *verbs:* (allerdings) indeed; (genau) exactly, quite, et. ⌒ erfassen, verstehen to understand a th. rightly or fully; ich weiß nicht ⌒, was ich tun soll I hardly know what to do; o bitte ⌒ sehr!; a) abwehrend: pray don't mention!; b) vorwurfsvoll: I beg your pardon!, stärker: what do you mean? — **7.** mit „erst" steigernd: nun schreien sie erst ⌒ now they shout all the more; (nun) erst ⌒ nicht (now) less than ever; *vgl.* erst¹ 5. — **8.** (gehörig, tüchtig) downright, solid, thorough; er hat etwas ~es gelernt he has applied himself, he possesses good (or sound) knowledge; er weiß nichts ~es he does not know anything worth mentioning, he is a poor scholar; es ist nichts ~es an ihm there is nothing to be proud of; *iro.* das ist (auch) was ~(e)s! that's a pretty concern or F a fine go! (*vgl.* 4). — **9.** (angenehm) mir ist's (ganz) ⌒, mir kann (ob. soll) es (ganz) ⌒ sein I am (quite) agreeable to it; wenn es Ihnen ⌒ ist if you agree to it; ihm ist alles ⌒ he puts up with anything; es e-m ⌒ m. to do a th. to a p.'s satisfaction; Sprichw. man kann es nicht allen ⌒ machen one cannot please (or satisfy) everybody.

Recht² (⌒) [recht¹] *n* ⑪b. (gen. in einigen Verbindungen: ~ens, s. 2.) **1.** right; (Vorrecht) privilege; ~ auf Arbeit right to work; ~ über Leben u. Tod power over life and death; er hat ein ~ dazu he has a right (or title) to it (*vgl.* recht h. bei recht¹ 5): mit (ohne) ~ (un)justly; mit gutem (ob. vollem) ~ for good reason(s);

[Rechte]

f. Fug; mit um so größerem ~e with all the more reason; mit ~ oder Unrecht whether rightly or wrongly; Sprichw. f. Kaiser. — 2. (Gerechtigkeit) justice, (Befugnis) competence; siehe Doktor 1; bürgerliches ~ civil law; gemeines ~ common law; geschriebenes ~ statute-law; f. Gnade 2; den Weg ~ens ergreifen to take legal (or law-) proceedings; es ist ~ens it is lawful; im Wege ~ens by legal process or proceedings or means; ~ sprechen to administer justice; die ~e pl. (Jura) studieren to study for (or to follow) the law; sich selbst ~ verschaffen to take the law into one's own hands; im ~(e) sein to be in the right; von ~s wegen (v.R.w.) by right(s), according to justice or to (the) law; zu ~ besteh(e)n to be (legally) valid, von Gesetzen: to be in force; zu ~ erkennen to judge (or find) according to law; vgl. zurechtkommen. — 3. oft klein gschr.: behalten to be right in the end or after all; to carry one's point; f. geben 2; 2 haben, 2 tun f. recht¹ 5. **Rechte** (⌐): **1.** m, f, n 67 f. recht¹ 1b. — 2. n/pl. f. Recht² 2.
Recht¹-eck (⌐...) n 62 math. rectangle; 2eckig a. 66 rectangular.
rechten (⌐) [Recht²] v/n. (h.) 69 to go to law, to litigate; jur. to plead; fig. = hadern 1.
Rechtens (⌐) gen. von Recht² (f. d² 2.).
Rechte(r) (⌐) m 67 f. recht¹ 2 u. 4.
rechter-hand, 2seits (⌐·', ·'·) [recht¹] adv. on the right hand or side.
Rechte(s) (⌐) n 67 f. recht¹ 8.
recht²-fertigen (⌐...) [mhd.] 66*.*: a) v/a. to justify, to warrant, (verteidigen) to defend, to vindicate; nicht zu 2(d) unjustifiable; b) sich 2 v/refl. to clear o.s. or one's character, to exculpate o.s.; **-fertigung** f 46 justification, vindication; exculpation; **-fertigungs-schrift** f apology; 2gläubig a. 66 orthodox; **-gläubige(r)** m f 67 orthodox person, true believer; **-gläubigkeit** f 46 orthodoxy; **-haber(in** f 47) m 62 disputatious (or dogmatical) person; **-haberei** f 46 disputatiousness, dogmaticalness; 2haberisch a. 66 disputatious, dogmatical, positive; 2¹händig a. right-handed; 2läufig a., bsd. ast. of normal course.
rechtlich (⌐) [ahd.] a. 66 **1.** = rechtschaffen a. — **2.** (gesetzlich) legal, lawful; (zu Recht bestehend) juridical (vgl. gerichtlich); (billig) fair (and just); ⌐er Beistand legal aid or assistance or advice, als Person: counsel; 2e Gültigkeit validity in (or before the) law.
Rechtlichkeit (⌐·) f 46 **1.** = Rechtschaffenheit. — **2.** (Gesetzlichkeit) legality, lawfulness; (Gültigkeit) validity.
recht²-liebend (⌐...) a. 66 loving (right and) justice, fair-minded; 2¹linig a. geom. rectilineal, ...ar; 2²los a.: a) without rights, outlawed; 2lose Leute outlaws pl.; b) (rechtswidrig) unlawful, illegal; **-losigkeit** f 46 (total) absence of rights; unlawfulness, illegality; 2mäßig a. 66 lawful, legal, vom Besitzer, Erben ⌐c. auch: rightful,

legitimate; (billig) fair (and just); **-mäßigkeit** f 46 lawfulness, legality, legitimacy, fairness.
rechts¹ (⌐) [recht¹]: a) prädikatives a. = rechtshändig; b) adv. f. recht 1c.
Rechts²-altertümer (⌐...) [gen. v. Recht²] n/pl. 62 legal antiquities pl.; **-angelegenheit** f law-business, legal matter; **-anspruch** m legal claim or title; **-anwalt** m = Advokat. vgl. **-beistand** f, **-anwaltschaft** f = Anwaltschaft; **-ausdruck** m legal (or law-)term; 2beflissen a. 66 studying (or learned in) the law; **-beflissene(r)** m law-student, lawyer; **-beistand** m: a) counsel; b) legal advice; 2beständig a. legally valid; **-beugung** f defeating the ends of the law; **-¹bewegung** ⌐ f movement to the right; **-²brauch** m lawful custom.
recht¹-schaffen (⌐...) [recht geschaffen] a. 66 (D9): a) honest, just, bsd. rel. righteous; (geraden Sinnes) upright (vgl. ehrlich 1); b) bsd. als adv. (gehörig) thoroughly (well); er hat sich 2 geplagt he has worked very hard; F co. er ist 2 dumm he's awfully stupid; **~heit** f 46 honesty, righteousness, uprightness.
Recht¹-schreibung (⌐...) f 46 orthography, spelling; **-schrift** f (richtige Schreibung) right spelling.
Rechts¹-drall ⌐ (⌐...) m 62 der Züge eines Gewehres right-handed twist; 2drehend a. 66 opt. vom polarisierten Lichte: ⌐ dextrogyrate; **-²einwand** m demurrer.
recht¹-seitig (⌐·'·) a. 66 rectilineal.
rechts²-erfahren (⌐...) a. 66 versed (or learned) in law; 2fähig a. 66 legally competent; **-fähigkeit** f 46 legal competence or standing; **-fall** m 62 legal case, case in court; vgl. **-handel**; **-form**, **-frage** f legal form, question; **-freund** m = **-beistand** a; **-gang** m legal procedure or process; **-gelehrsamkeit** f jurisprudence; 2gelehrt a. learned in (the) law; **-gelehrte(r)** m jurist, bsd. röm. Alt.: jurisconsult; weitS. lawyer; **-geschäft** n law-business; **-gewohnheit** f judicial (or legal) custom; **-gleichheit** f equality before the law; **-grund** m legal title or argument; **-grundsatz** m legal maxim; 2gültig a. legal, valid in law; **-gültigkeit** f legality, validity; **-gutachten** n counsel's opinion; **-handel** m lawsuit (legal) action; vgl. **-fall**; 2hängig a. pending, (lt.) sub judice; 2her, 2hin adv. from. to the right; **-hilfe** f legal redress; **-kenner** m jurist; **-kenntnis** f knowledge of the law; vgl. **-kunde**; **-kniff** m legal quibble. lawyer's trick or dodge; **-konsulent** m (Ratgeber) barrister (practising) in chambers; weitS. counsel; **-kraft** f validity, legal force; 2kräftig a. valid, legal; 2 machen to make valid; 2 werden to become legally binding, to pass into law; **-kunde** f jurisprudence; **-kundig(er** m) a. = 2gelehrter; **-lehre** f jurisprudence; **-lehrer** teacher of the law, professor of jurisprudence; **-mittel** n legal remedy; **-nachfolger** m assign; **-pflege** f administration of justice; **-philosophie** f philosophy of the law;

[Rede]

Rechts²-sprechung (⌐·⌐·) f 62 administration of justice.
Rechts²-punkt (⌐...) m 62 point in (or of) law; **-¹rheinisch** ⚥ a. 66 (situated) on the right bank of the Rhine; **-²sache** f legal affair; vgl. **-handel**; **-satz** m legal maxim; **-schule** f law-school; **-schulen** pl. in Lo. Inns pl. of Court, Temple; **-schutz** m legal protection; **-schutzverein** m legal aid society, für Kinder, in Engl.: society for the prevention of cruelty to children; **-sprache** f legal terminology; **-spruch** m in Strafsachen: sentence, in Zivilsachen: judgment, von Geschworenen: verdict; **-staat** m constitutional state; **-streit** m legal contest or dispute; vgl. **-handel**; **-titel** m legal title; 2¹um adv. meist ⌐ right about; **-²verbindlichkeit** f legal obligation; **-verdreher** m pettifogging lawyer; **-verdreherei**, **-verdrehung** f straining the law, pettifogging action or spirit; **-verfahren** n = **-gang**; **-verfassung** f judicial system, ebm. judiciary; **-verhandlungen** f/pl. legal proceedings pl.; **-verständig(er** m) a. = **-gelehrt(er)**; **-verweigerung** f denial of justice; **-vorbehalt** m, **-vorschrift** f legal reservation, prescription; **-weg** m: den ~ beschreiten oder einschlagen to take legal steps, to go to law; 2wegen ⌐·· adv. f. Recht² 2 am Schluß; 2widrig a. 66 contrary to law, illegal; **-wissenschaft** f science of the law; **-wohltat** f benefit of the law; **-zuständigkeit** f f. Gehörigkeit 2.
recht¹-winke(e)lig (⌐...) a. 66 math. right-angled, rectangular; 2zeitig a.: a) opportune, seasonable; b) adv. a. in (the nick of) time, in due (or right) time. punctually; 2 zum Schiff, zum Zuge gelangen, kommen to catch the boat, the train; **-zeitigkeit** f 46 opportuneness, seasonableness; von Zügen ⌐c.: punctuality. [zontal bar.
Reck¹ (⌐) [ndd.] n ⌐b. Turnerei: hori-
Recke (⌐·) [ahd.: wretch] m 44 brave warrior, valiant hero, mighty swordsman.
Reck²-eisen ⌐ (⌐·'·) [recken] ⌐ 62 der Gerber: stretching-iron, stretcher.
recken (⌐·) [ahd.: rack] v/a. und sich 2 v/refl. 68 to stretch (a. ⌐ metall.), to draw (or flatten) out, to rack; die Glieder 2. sich 2 (und strecken) to stretch one's limbs or o.s.; den Hals nach et. 2 to crane one's neck to see a th.
reckenhaft (⌐·) [Recke] a. 66 like one of the heroes of old, brave, valiant.
Reck¹-übung (⌐·⌐·) f 62 Turnerei: exercise on the horizontal bar.
Redakteur (⌐·⌐·r) [fr. rédacteur] m ⌐d. (Schriftleiter einer Zeitung ⌐c.) editor.
Redaktion (⌐·⌐·ts(⌐·)·n) [neu-lt.] f 46: a) (das Leiten) editing, editorial work; (Fassung) wording; b) das Personal: editorial staff; c) das Bureau e-r Zeitung ⌐c.: editorial (or newspaper-)office.
redaktionell (⌐·⌐·ts(⌐·)⌐·ll) a. 66 editorial.
Redaktrice (⌐·⌐·ts·) [fr.] f 48 editress.
Rede (⌐·) [Hom. Reede] [ahd.: *lt. rătĭō] f 48 **1.** speech; (~weise) language, elocution; f. binden 11; (Gespräch) discourse, talk, (Unterhaltung) conversation, F palaver; (Äußerung) utterance; (Vortrag) speech,

[Redeaktus] — 794 — [Reflexbewegung]

feierlicher: oration; Ansprache: address, eccl. allocution of the Pope, &c. (f. Anrede 1); angenehme, leere ~en pleasant, empty words pl.; in der alltäglichen ~ (~weise) in common parlance; erste ~ eines Abgeordneten ꝛc. maiden-speech; f. lang 2; schwülstige ~n bombastic sentences, hollow phrases pl., big talk sg.; e-m in die ~ fallen to interrupt a p.('s speech), to cut a p. short; eine ~ halten to make a speech, to deliver an address; es kam die ~ auf das Wetter the conversation turned upon ...; nach seiner ~ zu urteilen to judge from what he says; davon ist keine ~ that is not the question, (das ist selbstverständlich) that is understood; vergessen Sie Ihre ~ nicht do not (F don't) forget what you were saying or going to say; nicht der ~ wert not worth talking about or mentioning; wovon ist die ~?: a) what are you (they, &c.) discussing or speaking of?; b) (um was handelt es sich?) what is the point in question? — 2. (Gerücht) rumour, report; es geht die ~ davon, daß // it is (being) rumoured that //, people say that //. — 3. (Rechenschaft) account; e-m ~ (Antwort) steh(e)n to render (or give) a p. an account of a th., to (have to) answer for a th.; e-n über et. zur (zu) ~ stellen to call a p. to account (or to take a p. to task) for a th.

Rede-akt(us) (ᴜ...) m ⑫ in Schulen: recitations pl., Tag dafür: speech-day; =akzent m rhetorical accent; =blume f = figur; ⚹fertig a. ⑯ of ready speech, of glib tongue; =fertigkeit f readiness of speech, glibness of tongue; =figur, =floskel f figure of speech, metaphor(ical expression); =fluß m fluency of speech, flow of words; =freiheit f liberty of speech; =gabe f gift of speech or F of the gab; eloquence; =gesang m recitative, ...o; ⚹gewandt a. gifted in speech; vgl. ⚹fertig; =kunst f art of speaking, oratory, rhetoric; =künstler m orator, b.s. rhetorician, word-spinner; =lust f loquacity, talkativeness; ⚹lustig a. loquacious, talkative.

reden (ᴸ~) [ahd.; *Rede] I v/n. (h.) u. v/a. ⑧⑨ 1. to speak to a p.; (sich unterhalten) to talk to a p., to converse (or chat) with a p.; (vorbringen) to utter, to say; vor Gericht: to plead, vor der Öffentlichkeit: to speak in public, F to speechify; zu der Menge ⚹ to harangue the mob; jetzt redet er ganz anders he talks in quite a different strain (or tone) now; f. gut 6, klug 2; ⚹ Sie nur weiter! go on (talking)! — 2. Redens-arten mit prp.: aus ihm redet die Verzweiflung his is the language of despair; e-m ins Gewissen ⚹ to appeal to a person's conscience; in den Wind ⚹ to speak to no purpose; um mit dem Dichter zu ~ to use the words of the poet; mit sich ⚹ lassen to be open to (good) advice, to listen to reason; f. Mund¹ 3; (ein) langes und breites über et. ⚹ to make a long rigmarole (or story) of a th.; über

Politik ⚹ to talk politics; wir wollen **von** et. anderem ⚹ let us change the subject; von seinem Geschäfte ⚹ F to talk shop; f. Leber; viel von sich ⚹ machen to cause a great stir (in the world). — 3. v/a. u. v/refl. Böses über Leute ⚹ to talk ill of people; mit Angabe der Wirkung: **sich heiser** ⚹ to talk o.s. hoarse; sich einen Prozeß an den Hals ⚹ to become involved in an action by one's talk(ing). — II ~ n ㉓ 4. (f. I) speaking, speech; talk; all ihr ~ ist umsonst all their words are (spoken) in vain; sein ~ ist schlimmer als sein Tun his bark is worse than his bite; Sprichw. ~ ist Silber, Schweigen ist Gold speech is silver, silence is gold; a still tongue makes a wise head. — 5. viel ~s von et. m. to make much noise (or fuss) about a th. — III 2d p.pr. u. a. ⑯ 6. speaking; 2de Person interlocutor. — 7. von Sachlichem: (ausdrucksvoll) expressive; 2de Künste (Dichtkunst und Beredsamkeit) rhetorical arts pl.

Redens-art (ᴹᴜ=ᴸ) f ㊻ (mode of) expression; eine allgemeine (oder gewöhnliche) ~ a common saying or phrase; eigentümliche ~ peculiar (or idiomatic) phrase; das ist nur so eine ~ that's merely a (polite) way of putting it; höfliche ~ complimentary words pl.); lange ~en machen to spin a long yarn; sprichwörtliche ~ proverb (-ial saying); nur keine ~en! please no fuss or ceremony!

Rederei (~ᴸ) f ㊻ (idle) talk, prattle.

Rede-satz (ᴹᴜ...) m ㊷ period; ⚹scheu a. taciturn; =schwall, =schwulst, =strom m bombast (of words), exuberance of speech, verbiage; =teil m, gr. part of speech; =ton m: a) debating tone; b) = =akzent; =übung f exercise in speaking or debating; =weise f manner of speech, mode of expression, parlance, (Stil) diction; vgl. Rede 1.

redigieren (ᴗ⁻ᴸᴗ, a. fr. ~ᴳ⁻ᴸᴗ) [fr. *rédiger*] I v/a. ⑬ ein Blatt ⚹ (leiten) to edit ... — II ~ n ㉓ = Redaktion a.

redlich (ᴸᴗ) [ahd.; *Rede] a. ⑯ upright, honourable (vgl. ehrlich 1); (aufrichtig) open, candid, straightforward; er meint es ⚹ (adv.) he means well, he is honestly inclined; ~keit (ᴸᴗ~) f ㊻ uprightness, honourableness (vgl. Ehrlichkeit); openness, candour, straightforwardness, frankness.

Redner (ᴸᴗ) [ahd.; *reden] m ㉒, ~in f ㊼ (public) speaker, orator, politischer auch: platform - speaker, F contp. stump-orator, religiöser: ranter. **Redner-bühne** (ᴹᴜ...) f ㊷ platform, für Wahlreden auch: hustings pl.; =gabe f gift of speech, eloquence.

rednerisch (ᴸᴗᴗ) a. ⑯ oratorical, rhetorical; declamatory.

Redner-kunst (ᴹᴜ...) f ㊷ oratory, rhetoric art; =talent n =gabe; =ton m declamatory tone.

Redoute ⚹ (~būt-ᴸ) [fr.] f ㊽ 1. frt. (Schanze) redoubt. — 2. ✝ = Maskenball.

red-selig (ᴹᴸ/~) a. ⑯ talkative, loquacious, garrulous; ~keit (ᴹᴸᴗᴗ) f ㊻ talkativeness, loquacity, garrulity.

Reduktion (ᴹᴗ/tß(ᴗ)ᴸ) [lt.] f ㊺: a) math. ~ von Ausdrücken, Gleichungen ꝛc. u. b) metall., chm. ~ eines Oxydes ꝛc.: reduction; ~³ **tabelle** (~...) f ㊷ table of reduction.

Reduplikation (ᴹᴗᴗ~tß(ᴗ)ᴸ) [lt.] f ㊺ (Verdoppelung) reduplication.

reduzierbar (ᴗ⁻ᴸ~) a. ⑯ bsd. ⚹ chm. und math. auf etwas ⚹ reducible to a th.; **Reduzierbarkeit** f ㊺ reduc(t)ibility. **reduzieren** (ᴗ⁻ᴸᴗ) [lt.] I v/a. u. sich ⚹ v/refl. ⑬ to reduce, to diminish; sich ⚹ (abnehmen) to be(come) reduced, to decrease; fig. er sieht sehr reduziert (abgerissen) aus he appears (to be) very much down in the world, he looks very shabby. — II ~ n ㉓ au. **Reduzierung** f ㊺ reduction.

Reede ⚹ (ᴸ~; Hom. Rede) [ndd.: road: reiten] f ㊸ (Ankerplatz) roadstead, roads pl.; auf der ~ liegen to lie in the roadstead, to ride at anchor in the roads.

Reeder (ᴸ~) m ㉒ freighter, shipper; (Schiffseigentümer) shipowner.

Reederei (~~ᴸ) f ㊺ freighting, shipping (-business); equipment (or rigging) of merchantmen; ⚓ ~ betreiben to be (engaged) in the shipping-trade a. ⚹-line; ~betrieb m ㉒ shipping-trade.

Reef ⚹ (ᴸ) [ndd.] n ⑩c. (eingebundener Teil eines Segels) reef; **reefen** (ᴸ~) v/a. ⑯ to (take in a) reef.

re-ell (~⁻ᴸ) [fr. *réel*] a. ⑯ 1. (wirklich) real; 2er Gewinn solid gain. — 2. ⚹ (zuverlässig) respectable, honourable, fair-dealing; 2e Ware sound (or high-class) goods pl.; ⚹ (adv.) bedienen to serve fairly, to give a p. good value (for his money); **Re-ellität** (~ᴸ~ᴸ) f ㊺ respectability of a firm; fairness (in dealing); good quality.

Reep ⚹ (ᴸ) [ndd.] n ⑩c. (Tau) rope; ~er**bahn** f ㊷ rope-walk; ~schläger(ei f) m rope-maker(s') work.

Refektorium (ᴗᴗᴸ(ᴗ)ᴸ) [lt.] n ㉘ (Speisesaal in Klöstern) refectory. **Referat** (ᴗᴗᴸ) [neu-lt. ⚹] n ⑨c. (Bericht) [report.]

Referendar (ᴗᴗᴗᴸ) [neu-lt.] m ⑩d., auch: ~ius (ᴗᴗᴸ(ᴗ)~) m ㉗ Preußen ꝛc.: (angehender Assessor) young barrister attending the courts and qualifying for the post of an „Assessor". [reporter.]

Referent (ᴗᴗᴸ) [lt.] m ㉒ (Bericht-erstatter) **Referenz** ꝉ ⚹ (ᴗᴗᴸ) f ㊺ (Empfehlung) reference; (Auskunft) information.

referieren (ᴗᴗᴸᴗ) [lt.] v/a. ⑬ (berichten) to (send in a) report.

Reff¹ (ᴸ) [ahd.: rip] n ⑩b. basket for the back, ehm. auch: dorser, dosser.

Reff² ⚹ (ᴸ) [lt.] n ⑩b. = Reef.

reffen ⚹ (ᴸ~) = reefen. [purchaser.] **Reflektant** ⚹ (ᴗᴗᴸᴗ) [lt.] m ㉒ intending] **reflektieren** (ᴗᴗᴸᴗ) [lt.] ⑬ I v/a. phys. 1. Lichtstrahlen ꝛc. (zurückstrahlen) to reflect ... — II v/n. (h.) 2. auf et. ⚹ (sein Augenmerk richten) to have a th. in view, ⚹ to think of purchasing a th. — 3. über et. ⚹ (nachdenken) to reflect upon a th. — III ~ n ㉓ 4. reflexion (a. phys.).

Reflektor ⚹ (ᴗᴗᴸ) [lt.] m ㉛ phys. (Lichtspiegel) reflector (auch ☉).

Reflex ⚹ (ᴗᴸ) [lt.] m ⓪a. phys. (Widerschein) reflexion; ~bewegung (ᴗᴸ~ᴗᴗᴸ) f ㊷ physiol. reflex (or involuntary) movement or action.

Signs (see page XVII): F familiar; P vulgar; Г flash; ⚹ rare; † obsolete (died); * new word (born); ++ incorrect; ♪ music;

[**Reflexion**] — 795 — [**Regiment**]

Reflexion ⚲ (⌣(⌣)⌣) [lt.] f ㊻ phys., &c. reflexion, a. reflection; **~s=kreis** (⌣...) m ㊷ ast. reflecting circle; **~s=winkel** m, phys. angle of reflexion.
reflexiv ⚲ (⌣⌣⌣) [lt.] a. ㊺ gr. (rückbezüglich) reflexive (pronoun).
Reform (⌣⌣)[fr.]f㊻(Umgestaltung) reform. **Reformation** (⌣⌣⌣⌣) [lt.] f ㊻ (Besserung) reformation; **~s=zeit** (⌣..⌣) f ㊷ hist. (16. sae.) time of the Reformation.
Reformator (⌣⌣⌣⌣) [lt.] m ㉛ bisw. a. **~in** (⌣⌣⌣⌣) f ㊸ reformer; **Tisch** a. ㊺ reformatory (movement, &c.).
Reform=bestrebungen (⌣⌣⌣⌣⌣) f/pl. reformatory efforts pl.
reformieren (⌣⌣⌣⌣) [lt. neu bilden] I v/a. ㊽ to reform; die reformierte Kirche the Reformed (or Calvinistic) Church. — II **~** n ㉓ reformation. — III **Reformierte**[r] m) f ㊿ member of the Reformed Church, Calvinist.
Reform=partei (⌣⌣⌣⌣) f ㊷ party of reformers, reform-party.
Refrain (vfg⌣) [fr.] m 50 (Kehrreim eines Liedes) burden (of a song).
Refraktor ⚲ (⌣⌣⌣) [lt.] m ㉛ ast. Art Fernrohr: refractor, refracting telescope.
Regal[1] (-⌣) [dtsch=lt. *Riege ob.* it. *riga*] n ⑪ c. (Bretterfach)shelves pl.; am Schreibtisch: pigeon-holes pl.; ⊕ typ. rack, frame.
Regal[2], **~e** (-⌣⌣) [lt.] n ㉓ (Hoheitsrecht) royal prerogative, royalty, pl. regalia.
regalieren (⌣⌣⌣⌣) [fr. régaler] v/a. u. sich ⌣ v/refl. ㊽ (bewirten) to entertain, F to treat to a th.; sich ⌣ (schmausen) to regale o.s. with a th., to feast on a th.
Regatta ⌣ (-⌣⌣) [nhd., *it.] f ㊾ (㊻) (Bootwettfahrt) regatta.
rege (⌣⌣) [nhd.; *regen] a. ㊺ moving, stirring, astir, active; (lebendig) brisk, lively, alive, animated; (munter) nimble, alert, quick; (wach) awake, astir; (tätig) active, up and doing; ⌣ Kauflust brisk demand; ⌣ Sorgfalt vigilant care; ein 2r Verstand a keen (or an active) mind; ⌣ m. to stir up, rouse, incite; (wecken) to awaken; ⌣ werden to awake, to be (a)roused; der Wunsch wurde in ihm ⌣ he was seized with a desire.
Regel (⌣⌣) [ahd.: rule; *lt. *regŭla*] f ㊻ 1. rule, (Vorschrift) regulation, precept; in der **~** as a rule, generally (speaking); (gewöhnlich) usually, ordinarily; der **~** nach according to the rule; eine **~** aufstellen (beobachten) to lay down (to observe) a rule; es ist **~**, daß // it is a rule that //. — 2. (oft **~**n pl.) = Menstruation.
Regel=buch (⌣⌣⌣ch) n ㉓ book of rules.
Regeldetri (-⌣⌣⌣) [lt.] f. inv. arith. rule of three; proportion.
Regeling ↓ (⌣⌣) f ㊻ = Reling.
regel=los (⌣⌣...) a. ㊺ without rules and regulations, irregular; (unordentlich) disorderly; **=losigkeit** f㊻ irregularity, disorderliness; **⌣mäßig** a. u. adv. regular, (geregelt) regulated, orderly; (mustergültig) normal; adv. er kommt ⌣ (immer) zu spät he is always late; **=mäßigkeit** f ㊻ regularity.
regeln (⌣⌣) [nhd. 18. sae. ; *Regel] I v/a. u. sich ⌣ v/refl. ㊺a. (regulieren) to regulate, adjust; (bestimmen) to arrange,

settle, order, (feststellen) to fix; sich ⌣ nach // to be regulated (or ruled) by //; geregelt (well) regulated; ein geregeltes Leben führen to lead an orderly (or a steady) life. — II **~** n ㉓ = Regelung.
regel=recht (⌣⌣⌣) a. ㊺ according to the rules, correct; methodical; F ein 2er Kampf a regular fight, ⚔ a pitched battle.
Reg(e)lung (⌣(⌣)⌣) [regeln] f ㊻ (Regulierung) regulation, adjustment; (Bestimmung) arrangement, settlement.
regel=widrig (⌣⌣⌣⌣) a. ㊺ contrary to the rules, irregular; anomalous, abnormal; Sport: foul; **~keit** f ㊻ irregularity.
regen[1] (⌣⌣) [mhd.; *ragen] I v/a. u. sich ⌣ v/refl. ㊽ (in Bewegung setzen) to stir, set astir, move, rouse, agitate; sich ⌣ to bestir o.s., to be astir or moving or alive; v. Gefühlen: to spring up (or take rise) in one's heart or breast; es regte sich nur ein leises Lüftchen only a gentle breeze was astir. — II **~** n ㉓ = Regung.
Regen[2](⌣⌣)[ahd.: rain]m㉓ rain(f.fein1); starker **~** heavy shower, F downpour, soaker; f. a. Land=, Platz=, Staub=regen; wir bekommen (a. es gibt) heute **~** we shall have rain to-day; Sprichw. aus dem **~** in die Traufe kommen, etwa: to fall out of the frying-pan into the fire, to get from bad to worse; auf **~** folgt Sonnenschein after rain comes sunshine, after a storm comes a calm.
Regen²=bad (⌣⌣...) n ㉓ shower-bath, (cold) douche; **=bogen** [ahd.] m rainbow; **=bogen=farben** f/pl. colours pl. of the rainbow, prismatic colours pl.; Schillern n in den **~** iridescence; **=bogen=farben=druck** ⊙ m prismatic-colour printing; **=bogen=farbig** a. ㊺ in (all) the colours of the rainbow, (schillernd) iridescent; **=bogen=haut** f, anat.: ⚲ iris; **=bringend** a. von Wolken: full of rain, rainy; **=dach** n penthouse; **=dicht** a. rain-proof, waterproof.
Regeneration (⌣⌣⌣=tß(⌣)⌣) [lt.] f ㊻ (Wieder=erzeugung) regeneration.
Regenerator ⊙ (⌣⌣⌣⌣) [lt.] m ㉛ regenerator, regenerating (or regenerative) chamber; **~ofen** ⊙ (⌣..⌣) m ㊷ regenerator-furnace.
regenerier/en (⌣⌣⌣⌣) [lt.] I v a. ㊽ (wieder erzeugen) to regenerate.— II **~** n ㉓ u. R/ung f ㊻ regeneration.
Regen²=fall (⌣⌣...) m ㊷ rainfall; **=fang** m cistern; **=faß** n water-butt; **=frei** a. ㊺ free from rain; **=galle** f (zweiter Regenbogen) rain-gall; **=gott** m f. Jupiter Pluvius; **=guß** m heavy shower, F downpour of rain, vgl. **=strom**; **=hut** m water-proof hat; **=jahr** n rainy year; **=karte** f rain-chart, ⚲ hyetograph(ic map); **=kunde** f: hyetology; **=leder** ⊙ n am Wagen: cornice; **=los** a. without rain; **=mangel** m drought; **=mantel** m waterproof (cloak), mackintosh; **=menge** f amount of rain, (total) rain-fall; **=messer** m rain-gauge, ⚲ pluviometer; **=messung** f: ⚲ pluviometry; **=monat** m rainy month; **=pfeifer** m, orn. plover (*Chara'drius pluvia'tilis*); **=rock** m mackintosh; **=schauer** m shower (of rain), gelinder: sprinkling (of rain); vgl. **=guß**; **=schirm** m umbrella; **=schirm=**

fabrikant, =macher m umbrella-maker; **=schirm= gestell** n umbrella-frame; **=schirm=ständer** m umbrella-stand; **=schwanger, =schwer** a. v. Wolken: full of rain; **=sterne** m pl. ast.: ⚲ Hyades pl.; **=streifen** m im Sonnenspektrum: rainband; **=strom** m torrential rain, vgl. **=guß**.
Regent (⌣⌣)[lt.] m㊷, **~in** f㊸(Herrscher[in]) sovereign, ruler; engS. (der, die an Stelle des Fürsten Waltende) regent.
Regen²=tag (⌣⌣) m ㊷ day of rain.
Regenten=tugend (⌣⌣⌣⌣) f ㊷ virtue becoming to a ruler. [rain.]
Regen²=tropfen (⌣⌣⌣⌣) m ㊷ drop of
Regentschaft (⌣⌣⌣) f ㊻ regency.
Regen=wasser (⌣⌣...) n ㊷ rain-water; **=wetter** n rainy weather; **=wind** m rainy wind; **=wolke** f rainy cloud, ⚲ nimbus; **=wurm** m, zo. earth- (or dew-)worm (*Lumbri'cus terre'stris*); **=zeit** f rainy (or wet) season.
Regie (⌣Gi⌣, a. ⌣⌣) [fr. régie] f ㊻ 1. (Verwaltung v. Staatseinkünften) administration of public funds; (Staatsmonopol) state-monopoly. — 2. thea. management.
regierbar (⌣⌣⌣) a. ㊺ governable.
regieren (⌣⌣⌣) [lt. re'gere] ㊽ I v/a. to reign (or rule) over, to govern; (lenken, leiten) to direct, conduct, guide; ein Pferd etc.: to manage, ein Schiff: to steer. — II v/n. (h.) (herrschen) to reign, to rule; v. Ministern: to govern, to be at the head of affairs or at the helm (of the state); der 2de Fürst the reigning prince. — III **~** n ㉓ = Regierung 1. [ment.]
Regiererei (⌣⌣⌣⌣) f ㊻ b. s. misgovern-
Regierung (⌣⌣⌣) [regieren] f ㊻ 1. reign, rule, government; direction, guidance, management; in der **~** folgen to succeed on the throne; unter der **~** von ⌣ in the time of //, under //; zur **~** gelangen: a) von Fürsten: to come to the throne; b) von Ministern: to assume (or get into) office, to come into power. — 2. (Gesamtheit der Staatslenker) government, administration.
Regierungs=antritt (⌣⌣...) m ㊷ accession to the throne; **=beamte(r)** m government official, civil-service clerk; **=bezirk** m administrative district or area; **=blatt** n government (or ministerial) paper, official gazette; **=form** f form of government, a. (fr.) régime; **=freundlich** a. ㊺ governmental; **=gebäude** n government offices pl.; **=gewalt** f supreme (or sovereign) power; **=kunst** f art of government; **=präsident** m in Preußen: president (or governor) of an administrative district (mit größerer Macht als ein englischer Lord Lieutenant e-r Grafschaft!); **=sekretär** m permanent undersecretary; **=sitz** m seat of government; **=sorgen** f/pl. cares pl. of government; **=system** n system of government; **=wechsel** m change of ruler or government; **=zeit** f reign.
Regiment[1] (⌣⌣⌣) [lt.] n ⑪c. government; persönliches **~** personal government; das **~** h. ob. führen, am **~**e sein to rule, to command; sie (die Frau) führt das **~** she rules the house, F she wears the breeches.

⚲ scientific; ♀ botanical; ⚲ geography; ⊙ machinery; ⚒ mining; ⚔ military; ⚓ marine; ⊛ commercial; ⚘ postal; 🚂 railway.

[Regiment] — 796 — [reichlich]

Regiment² ⚥ (⚌⚍) [fr.] n ④c. (v. einem Obersten geführte Truppenschar) regiment; ein ~ betreffend regimental; **regimenter=weise** (⚌⚍⚐,⚑) adv. in regiments.
Regiments²=adjutant ⚥ (⚌⚍...) m ⑫ adjutant of a regiment; =**inhaber** m honorary colonel of a regiment; =**kasse** f regimental chest; =**kommandeur** m commander of a r.; =**lazarett** n (field-) hospital of the regiment; =**musik** f band of a reg., regimental band; =**stab** m regimental staff (of officers); =**tambour** m drum-major; =**tisch** m (officers') mess; =**uniform** f uniform of a reg., regimentals pl.; =**unkosten** pl.: co. auf ~ leben to live at public (or at other people's) expense. [(Qu.) Regina.
Regina, ...e (-⚑⚑) npr/f. ㊵ ㊿α., ㊴ ㊽.
Region (⚐(⚑)⚑) [lt.] f ㊻ (Gegend) region.
Regisseur (-Gi-ßö'r) [fr. régisseur] m ①d. thea. stage-manager.
Register (⚌⚐⚑) [mlt.] n ㉒ 1. register (a. ⊕ typ.), record; (Steuer=)~ register of ratepayers, (alphabetisches Verzeichnis) index; table of contents, (Katalog) catalogue, (Liste) list; ins ~ eintragen to (enter in the) register. — 2. F fig. ins alte ~ gehören to be superannuated or out of date or F on the shelf; er steht im schwarzen ~ he is in the black book or a marked man. — 3. ⊕ (Ofenklappe) register, damper. — 4. ♪ ~ e-r Orgel: register, organ-stop.
Register=ofen (⚌⚐..), =**rost** ⊕ m ㉒ register-stove, -grate; =**stimme** ♪ f = Register 4; =**tonne** ⚓ f (= 1000 engl. Kubikfuß = 2,8316 cbm) register ton; =**zug** m = Register 4.
Registrator (⚌⚐⚑⚑) [lt.] m ㉛ registrar, recorder; **Registratur** (⚌⚐⚑⚑) f ㊻ registrar's office, registry, für Urkunden: record-office. [gistering apparatus.]
Registrier=apparat ⊕ (⚌⚐⚑⚑,⚑⚑) m ㉒ re-
registrieren (⚌⚑⚑⚑) I v/a. ⑬ to register, to reco'rd, to enter (on re'cord), jur. a. to file; registriert † f. eintragen 2 a. — II ~ n ㉓ u. **Registrierung** f ㊻ registration; jur. † = Beurkundung.
Reglement (-⚑⚑⚐') [fr. règlement m] n ⑨ regulation(s pl.); (Verordnung) by-law; ⚒=**mäßig** (⚒=**widrig**) a. according (contrary) to rules and regulations.
Regler (⚐⚑) [regeln] m ㉒ regulator.
Reglette (⚐⚑⚑) [fr. réglette] f ⑭ typ. reglet.
reg=los (⚑,⚑) a. ㊻ motionless.
regnen (⚐⚑) [ahd.: rain] v/n. (h.) ㉒b. to rain, fein: to drizzle, to sprinkle; es regnet stark, in Strömen it rains (or is raining) fast, in torrents.
regnerisch (⚑⚑⚑), **regnicht** (⚑⚑) a. ㊻ rainy, threatening (or full of) rain; es ist ⚒es Wetter it is rainy weather, F it is showery.
Regreß (⚐⚑) [lt.] m ①a. jur. recourse, (legal) remedy; (Schaden=ersatz) recovery (of damages); ~**nehmer** (⚐⚑) m ㉒ recoverer; ~**recht** n right of recovery.
regsam (⚑⚑) a. ㊻ active, agile, mobile (f. rege); ~**keit** (⚑⚑⚑) f ㊻ activity; briskness, alertness; agility; ~ des Geistes a. keenness of (the) mind.
regulär (⚐⚑⚑) [lt.] a. ㊻ regular; ⚒ Engl.: ⚒e Armee regular army, regulars pl.
Regulativ (⚐⚑⚑⚑) [lt.] n ①d. regulation.

Regulator ⊕ (-⚐⚑⚑) [lt.] m ㉛ mach., mech. 1. (steuernde ob. ordnende Vorrichtung) regulator, governor, Papierfabrik: pulp-meter. — 2. (Uhr) regulator.
Regulier=apparat ⊕ (-⚐⚑⚐⚐,⚑⚑) m ㉒ regulating apparatus, regulator.
regulieren (-⚑⚑⚑) [mlt.] I v/a. ⑬ (ordnen) to regulate, to adjust, to (set in) order. — II ~ n ㉓ f. Regulierung.
Regulier=(füll=)ofen ⊕ (-⚑⚑(⚑⚑,)⚑⚑) m ㉒ = **Füll=ofen**.
Regulierung (-⚑⚑⚑) f ㊻ regulation, adjustment, ⚒ Börse: settlement.
Regulus (⚑⚑⚑) [lt.] m, inv. u. ㊸ 1. ast. (Stern) Regulus. — 2. ⊕ metall., chm. (Metallkönig) regulus, button.
Regung (⚑⚑) [regen] f ㊻ 1. stirring, moving, movement, motion. — 2. des Gemüts: emotion, heftige: agitation, excitement; (Anwandlung) impulse.
Regungs=kraft (⚑⚑...) f ㊶ motor force; =**los** a. ㊻ motionless; =**losigkeit** f ㊻ motionlessness, immovability.
Reh (⚑) [ahd.: roe] n ⓒc. zo. und hunt. roe (Capre'olus caprae'a), männliches: roebuck, weibliches: doe; weiß⚒. deer, z.B. ein Rudel ~e a herd of deer.
Rehabeam (-⚑⚑⚑) [hebr.] npr/m. bibl. (Kg. v. Juda, 953—932 v. Chr.) Rehoboam.
rehabilitier=en (⚌⚑⚑⚑⚑) [neu=lt.] I v/a. ⑬ (wieder zu Ehren bringen) to rehabilitate, to reinstate. — II ~ n ㉓ u. **Rung** f ㊻ rehabilitation, reinstatement, auch: restitution.
Reh=blatt (⚑⚑) n ㉚ hunt. shoulder of a roe; =**bock** m roebuck; =**braten** m roast venison; =**braun** a. ㊻ fawn-coloured.
Rehe¹ (⚑⚑) f ⚕vet. founder. [plough-tail.]
Rehe² ⊕ (⚑⚑) f ⓐ agr. (Pflugsterz) ⚒
Reh=fell (⚑⚑...) n ㉚ doeskin; =**geiß** f doe; =**kalb** n ob. =**kitze** f roe-calf, fawn; =**keule** f leg (or haunch) of venison; =**leder** n = =**fell**; =**posten** m/pl. buckshot; =**pirsch** f: auf die ~ geh(e)n to go deer-stalking; =**schlegel** m = =**keule**; =**wild**(bret) n venison; =**ziege** f doe; =**ziemer** m loin of venison.
Reib=ahle ⊕ (⚑⚑,⚑⚑) f ⓐ carp. reamer- (or opening-) bit, rimer.
Reibe ⊕ (⚑⚑) f ⓐ grater.
Reib=eisen ⊕ (⚑⚑,⚑⚑) n ⓐ grater. [(sound).]
Reibe=laut (⚑⚑,⚑⚑) m ⓐ gr.: ⚐ fricative
reiben (⚑⚑) [ahd.] I v/a., v/n. (h.) u. sich ⚒ v/refl. ⑪ 1. (sich) ⚒ to rub (o.s.); (sich) wund ⚒ to gall (o.s.); auf dem Reib=eisen ⚒ to grate, im Mörser: to bray; Farben 2c.: to grind; fig. e-m et. unter die Nase ⚒ to cast a th. in a p.'s teeth, to tell a p. s.th. to his face; sich an e-m ⚒ to tease (or chaff) a p., herausfordernd, reizend: to provoke (or irritate) a p. — 2. mit Angabe der Wirkung: klein (ob. fein, zu Pulver) ⚒ to powder, to pulverize, ⚐ to triturate; sich die Hände wund ⚒ to chafe one's hands; sich die Tränen aus den Augen ⚒ to wipe the tears from one's eyes. — II ~ n ㉓ = Reibung 1 u. 2. — III gerieben 4. p.p. Bed. des inf. — 5. a. ⓐ (durchtrieben) cunning, artful. F deep.
Reiber (⚑⚑) m ㉒ 1. (a. =**in** f ㊼) person who rubs or grates; (Farben 2c.) ~ grinder. — 2. ⊕ sachlich: typ. rubber.
Reiberei (-⚑⚑) f ㊻ (constant) friction.

Reib=gummi ⊕ (⚑...) n (m) ⓑ indiarubber; =**keule** f pestle; =**kissen** n der Elektrisiermaschine: cushion rubber; =**scheibe** f friction-plate.
Reibsel (⚑⚑) n ㉓ gratings pl.
Reib=stein (⚑,⚑) m ㉓ für Farben: grindstone, typ. ink-block.
Reibung (⚑⚑) f ㊻ 1. rubbing, &c. (f. reiben 1), friction. — 2. (f. reiben 2) pulverization, ⚐ trituration. — 3. fig. friction, (Zwist) difference (of opinion), dissension, (Streit) conflict, (Zf.=stoß) collision, clash(ing).
Reibungs=elektrizität ⊕ (⚑...) f ⓐ mach., phys. frictional electricity; =**koeffizient** m coefficient (or index) of friction; =**rad** n friction-wheel; =**winkel** m angle of friction or resistance.
Reib=zeug (⚑...) n ⓑ = =**kissen**; =**zündhölzchen** n (lucifer-)match, friction-match.
reich¹ (⚑) [ahd.: rich; *Flt.] I a. ㊻ rich, (vermögend) wealthy, opulent; (reichlich) abundant; ⚒ an Wild, Fischen 2c.: abounding in ...; ⚒e Gabe bountiful gift; ⚒e Jahre pl. years of plenty; ⚒es Mahl sumptuous repast; ⚒ m. to enrich. — II der **Reiche** (ein **Reicher**) ㊼ the (a) rich person, pl. die Reichen the rich (people), the wealthy (classes), the well-to-do (folk); f. arm² II.
Reich² (⚑) [ahd., *Flt.] n ⓒc. empire; realm (a. fig.); (Königreich) kingdom (a. in der Naturgeschichte); hist. das Heilige Römische ~ (Deutscher Nation) the Holy Roman Empire; ~ der Mitte (China) Middle Kingdom, Celestial Empire.
reich²=blütig ⊕ (⚑...), ⚒**blütig** ⚒ a. ㊻ ⚐ multiflorous; ⚒**busig** a. f. busig b.
reichen (⚑⚑) [ahd.: reach] ⓐ I v/n. (h.) 1. (sich erstrecken) to reach, to extend, in die Höhe: to go up to, in die Tiefe: to go down to; soweit das Auge reicht as far as one can see; soweit der Blick (die Stimme) reicht within sight (hail); soweit der Vorrat reicht as long as the provisions last; das Wasser reichte bis hierher ... came up to here. — 2. fig. c.t et. ⚒ (ihm gleichkommen) to come up to ⚑ th., to be equal (or a match) to a th. — ⚐. nach et. ⚒ (langen) to stretch out one's hand after a th. — 4. = ausreichen 1 u. langen 1. — II v/a. 5. e-m et. ⚒ (hinlangen) to reach (mehr gbr.: to pass, to hand) a th. to a p.; (darbieten) to present (vgl. darreichen I); f. Hand 2; den Armen Nahrung ⚒ to serve out food to the poor; als Aufschrift: hier wird nichts (kein Almosen) gereicht! no alms given (here)!; fig. er kann ihm nicht das Wasser ⚒ he cannot be compared with him, F he is not a patch on him; F e-m eine ⚒ (eine Ohrfeige versetzen) to box a p.'s ears, to smack a p.'s face; to punch a p.'s head, P to land a p. one.
reich¹=haltig (⚑...) a. ㊻ rich, copious, abundant, plentiful, von Büchern: full of matter; =**haltigkeit** f ㊻ richness, copiousness, abundance; ⚒**illustriert** a. richly (or profusely) illustrated.
reichlich (⚑⚑) a. ㊻ (ant. karg) abundant, copious, plentiful; sehr ⚒ in profusion, profuse, mit e-r Mahlzeit 2c. sich

Zeichen (f. S. XVI): F familiär; P Volkssprache; Γ Gaunersprache; ⚊ selten; † alt (auch gestorben); * neu (auch geboren); ⁺ unrichtig;

[Reichlichkeit] — 797 — [Reimgeklingel]

nehmen to partake of a substantial (or heavy) meal; sein 2es Auskommen h. to make (or earn) a good living; adv.: 2 genug h. to have plenty; 2 so breit fully (or quite) as wide; et. 2 ersetzen to make ample compensation for a th.

Reichlichkeit (⌐˘-) f ㊻ abundance, copiousness, plenty, profusion.

Reichs-abschied (⌐...) m ㉒ hist. recess of the Imperial Diet; =acht f: in die ~ erklären to put under the ban of the empire; =adel m nobility of the empire; =adler m imperial eagle; =amt n Imperial Ministry; =angehörigkeit f imperial citizenship or franchise; =anzeiger m German Imperial Gazette; =apfel m imp. globe; =bank ⚙ f Imp. Bank, auch: Reichsbank; =bote m =tags-abgeordnete(r); =druckerei f imperial printing-office; =einheit f unity of the empire; =eisenbahn-amt n imperial railway-board; =erb-amt n hereditary office of the empire; 2feindlich a. ㊻ hostile to the empire; 2frei a. hist. bound in fealty (or subject) to the Emperor alone; ehm. =freiherr m baron of the Empire; 2freundlich a. friendly to the empire, Imperialist; =fürst m prince of the Empire; =gericht n Supreme Court (of Justice) of the Empire; =gesetz n law of the empire, in Engl. law enacted by the Imperial Parliament, kürzer: Act of Parliament; =hauptstadt f Imperial City, capital of the Empire; =heer ⚔ n imperial army; =hilfe f aid given (or subsidy paid) to the empire; =kammergericht nehm. Imperial Court of Chancery; =kanzlei f Imperial Chancery; =kanzler m Imperial Chancellor; =kleinodien n/pl. imp. crown-jewels; =krone f imp. crown; =kurs-buch 🚂 n imp. railway-guide; =land n territory of the empire; die =lande (Elsaß und Lothringen) the Imperial Provinces of Alsace and Lorraine; =lehen n imp. fief; =marine-amt n a) German Naval Board; b) England: Admiralty; =münze f (current) coin of the empire; =ober-haupt n (supreme) head of the empire; =post f imp. post; =post-amt n imp. post office; =post-dampfer ⚓ m imp. mail-steamer; =rat m council of the empire; =ritter(schaft f) m knight(hood) of the e.; =schatz-amt n Imperial Treasury; =schwert n imperial sword; =stadt f imp. city; freie =städte free imp. cities pl.; =tag m Imperial Diet, Reichstag; =tags-abgeordnete(r) m member of the Reichstag; =tags-beschluß m resolution of (or passed by) the Imperial Diet; ehm. =taler m, num. rix-dollar; 2treu a. ㊻ loyal to the empire; =truppen ⚔ f pl. imp. troops pl.; 2unmittelbar a. = 2frei, a. immediate; =unmittelbarkeit f. hist. immediacy of a German prince or city; =verfassung f constitution of the empire; =verweser m vice-regent of the empire; =währung f standard currency of the e.; =wappen n imp. coat-of-arms; =zepter n imperial sceptre.

Reichtum (⌐-) m ②d. riches pl.; (Wohlstand) wealth, opulence; (Überfluß) abundance, profusion; Sprichw. =macht nicht immer glücklich wealth does not insure happiness.

reich-verziert (⌐-ˇ-⌐) a. ㊻ richly adorned, profusely decorated, Baustil: florid.

reif¹ (⌐) [ahd.: ripe] a. ㊻ ripe, mature, (mürbe) mellow; (voll entwickelt) fully developed or grown; vgl. mannbar; in 2eren Jahren: a) of mature age, middle-aged; b) (hochbejahrt) in the fulness of years, aged; von Geschwüren: 2 werden to come to a head.

Reif² (⌐) [ahd.: rope] m ⓒc. ㊷ ring, am Faß, Eimer ꝛc.: hoop, am Rande: tire, tyre; (Kreis) circle; Spiel: einen ~(en) schlagen oder laufen lassen to trundle (or bowl, drive) a hoop.

Reif³ (⌐) [ahd.] m ⓒc. hoar-frost, white frost, ⚘ rime; (Duft auf Pflaumen, Pfirsichen ꝛc.) bloom. [hoops.]

Reif²-binder ⊙ (⌐...) m ㉒ maker of
Reifchen (⌐ˇ) n ㉓ (dim. von Reif²) little hoop or circle, circlet.

Reife (⌐ˇ) [reif¹] f ㊽ ripeness, maturity, mellowness; vgl. Mannbarkeit; zur ~ bringen to ripen, to (make) mature; zur ~ kommen to ripen, to (become) mature.

Reif³-eis (⌐...) n ㉒ hoar-frost; =²eisen n band- (or hooping-) iron.

reifeln ⊙ (⌐ˇ) I v/a. ㉞a. 1. arch. = ausfehlen I. — 2. Büchsenmacherei: (Züge in ein Gewehr m.) to rifle a gun. — II ~ n ㉓ und **Reif(e)lung** (⌐ˇ) f ㊽ 3. = ausfehlen II.

reifen¹ (⌐ˇ) [ahd. ⚘ *reif¹] ⊙ I v/n. (h.) 1. (ausreitigen) to ripen, mature, to grow ripe or mellow or to maturity, von Geschwüren: to gather. — 2. von Personen: (mannbar w.) to attain the age of (wo)manhood; der Jüngling reift zum Manne ... grows to man's estate; s. a. heranreifen. — II v/a. (zur Reife bringen) 2. to ripen, to mature, to bring to maturity (a. fig.). — III ~ n ㉓ 4. v. Früchten: fructescence.

reifen² ⊙ (⌐ˇ) [Reif²] v/a. ㊽ Fässer ꝛc.: to hoop, to furnish with hoops.

reifen³ (⌐ˇ) [Reif³] v/n. impers. (h.) ㊽: es reift there is (or we are having) a hoar-frost or white frost.

Reifen⁴ (⌐ˇ) m ㉓ = Reif².

Reifen⁴-bahre (⌐ˇ...) f ㊷ surg. cradle (for a broken limb); =bruch m rupture (or twisting) of a tire or tyre; =schlagen, =spiel n trundling (or driving, bowling) a hoop; =springen n skipping (through a hoop).

Reife-prüfung (⌐ˇ-⌐ˇ) f ㊷ (Maturitätsprüfung) leaving-examination.

reifig (⌐ˇ) [reif²] a. ㊻ circular.

reiflich (⌐ˇ) [reif¹] a. ㊻ mature; nach 2er Überlegung e-r Sache on mature consideration of a th., after thinking a matter well over.

Reifung (⌐ˇ) f ㊽ f. Reifelung.

Reif²-macher (⌐...) m ㉒ = =binder; =²monat m November; =²rock m ehm. farthingale, hoop-petticoat, in neuerer Zeit: crinoline; =²schlagen n, =²spiel n = Reifenschlagen; =²springen n = Reifenspringen; =²treiber m, =²zwinge f ⊙ Böttcherei: hoop-driver, -cramp.

Reigen (⌐ˇ) [mhd.] m ㉓ 1. party of dancers; den ~ eröffnen to lead the dance, to open the ball (a. fig.). — 2. (auch ~-tanz m ㉒) round dance with musical accompaniment. — 3. dance(-music); Lied: song.

Reihe (⌐ˇ) [mhd.: row] f ㊽ 1. v. Häusern, Personen ꝛc.: row, von Bergen: range, von Zimmern: suite, math. u. von Werten: series; lange ~ von Kindern ꝛc.: long string, von Ahnen ꝛc.: long line, F eine ganze ~ von Schriftstellern a great number (or a long list) of authors; in einer ~ in a row or a line; senkrechte ~ column, von Personen auch: file; ⚔ in Reih' und Glied in rank and file; in Reih' und Glied treten to fall in(to) line; in dichten ~n in close (or serried) ranks. — 2. (Aufeinanderfolge) succession; rotation; die ~ ist an mir, ich bin an der ~ it is my turn; an wem ist die ~? whose turn is it?; Sie werden bald an die ~ kommen your turn will soon come; nach der ~ (a. **reih-um** adv.) in (or by) turns, alternately, in succession; der ~ nach successively, in rotation, seriatim; in, außer der ~ in turn, out of one's turn; außer der ~ fragen, bsd. in Schulen: to dodge. [of the foot.]

Reihen¹ (⌐ˇ) m ㉓ (Rücken des Fußes) back/
Reihen² (⌐ˇ) [mhd.] m ㉒ poet. = Reigen.
reihen³ (⌐ˇ) [ahd.] v/a. u. sich 2 v/refl. ㉞ 1. to put in a row or a line, to range; an-ea. 2 to link (together); vgl. 2; sich 2 to form a row; to rank. — 2. Perlen auf e-e Schnur (ob. an-ea.) 2 to string ... — 3. ⊙ (heften) to stitch, baste.

Reihen⁴-folge (⌐ˇ-...) [Reihe] f ㊷ succession, sequence; alphabetische: alphabetical order (vgl. Reihe 2); =marsch ⚔ m march(ing) in columns or files; =sämaschine f, agr. ridge-drill; 2weise adv. (F a. a.) in rows; 2geordnet serial.

Reiher (⌐ˇ) [mhd.] m ㉓ orn. (Sumpfvogel) heron (A'rdea); ~-beize ⊙ f hunt. heron-hawking; ~-busch m aigret(te) (made of heron's feathers); ~-feder f heron's feather; ~-jagd f = ~-beize; ~-schnabel ⚘ m (gemeiner) stork's-bill (Ero'dium cicuta'rium).

...reihig (..."⌐ˇ) [Reihe] a. ㊻ in Zssgn, z. B. zwei-² two-rowed, ⚘ distichous.

reih-um (-⌐) adv. s. Reihe 2.

Reim (⌐) [ahd. Reihe. mhd. (*fr. rime f) Vers, nhd. seit Opitz: Gleichklang] m ⓒc. pros. rhyme, ⚘ rime; s. männlich 3 u. weiblich 3; ~e machen ob. schmieden to make rhymes, to rhyme, to write poetry.

Reim-art (⌐ˇ-⌐) f ㊷ kind (or form) of rh.
reimbar (⌐-) a. ㊻ forming a rhyme.
Reim-chronik (⌐ˇ-⌐ˇ-ˇ) f ㊷ rhymed (or rhyming) chronicle.

reimen (⌐ˇ) ⊙ I v/n. (h.) u. sich 2 v/refl. 1. to (be in) rhyme with. — 2. (Reime m.) to make rhymes. — II v/a. 3. to rhyme. — 4. fig. (in Einklang bringen) to make things agree or tally. — III ~ n ㉓ 5. rhyming, making rhymes.

Reimer (⌐ˇ) m ㉓ rhym(est)er, contp. inferior poet; ~-ei f ㊻ rhyming; (making) inferior poetry.

reim-frei (⌐...) a. ㊻ = 2los; =gedicht n ㉒ poem in rhymes; =geklingel n

♩ Musik; ⚘ Wissenschaft; ♀ Pflanze; ♀ Geographie; ⊙ Technik; ⚒ Bergbau; ⚔ Militär; ⚓ Marine; ⚙ Handel; ✉ Post; 🚂 Eisenbahn.

[Reimkunst] — 798 — [Reisetasche]

jingling of rhymes; =kunst f art of rhyming; =los a. rhymeless; =lose Verse m/pl. blank verse sg.; =schmied m rhym(est)er; =silbe f rhyming syllable; =wörter-buch n rhyming-dictionary.
rein¹ (¹⁄) [ahd. gesiebt] I a. ⊕ 1. pure, von Metallen, a. unalloyed; (keusch) a. chaste; (sauber) clean (linen, &c.), (unbefleckt) unsullied (honour), untarnished (fame); (ordentlich) neat, tidy, proper. — 2. =it nouns: der Bogen Papier blank sheet (of paper); das Deutsch pure (or correct) German; der Ertrag, Gewinn net gain or profit; das Gemüt pure (or unpolluted, untainted) mind; das Gewissen clear conscience; des Herzens with a pure heart, bibl. pure in heart; den Mund halten to hold one's tongue; den Tisch m. to clear the table, fig. er machte den Tisch mit ihnen he made a clean sweep of them; die Wahrheit plain (or unvarnished) truth; das Wasser clear water; Diamanten vom 2ten Wasser diamonds of the first water; der Wein pure (or unadulterated) wine; fig. s. einschenken u. Luft 4 am Ende. — 3. mit verbs: 2 halten to keep clean, (scheuern) to scrub, (fegen) to sweep; sich (dat.) das Gesicht 2 waschen to wash one's face clean; fig. sich 2 waschen od. brennen to clear o.s., to establish one's innocence; vgl. brennen 9b. — 4. fig. (vollständig, bloß, ganz und gar) downright, mere; aus dem Mitleid out of sheer compassion; F der 2e Hohn pure (or undisguised) mockery; fig. 2e Wirtschaft m. to make a clean sweep (of it); adv. quite; 2 ableugnen (abschlagen) to deny (to refuse) flatly; F 2 alle clean gone; 2 aufessen to eat (or clear) up to the last; 2 nichts nothing at all; s. unmöglich; 2 verrückt stark mad. — II s. ⊕ 5. der, die ~e the pure (wo)man; bibl. den (ob. meist dem) ~en ist alles 2 (un)to the pure all things are pure. — 6. a) das ~e what is pure or clean; b) et. ins 2e schreiben to make a clean (or fair) copy of a th., Attenstücke: to engross; c) ins (oder aufs) 2e bringen to put (or set) in order, to clear up; darüber muß ich ins 2e kommen I must get to the bottom of it; mit e-m ins 2e kommen to come to an arrangement (or a settlement) with a p.; mit et. (mit einem) im 2en sein to have come to a clear understanding about a th. (with a p.).
(')rein² F (¹) abbr. für her-ein; s. hb. Herein-fall, 2fallen, 2legen, 2reiten etc.
Rein¹-druck ⊕ (¹,⁰) m ⊕ typ. clean (or fair) proof.
Reineclaude ♀ (rän-tlō'-b⁻) [fr.] f ⊕ grüne Pflaumenart: greengage, P gage.
Reineke (¹⁻⁻) npr/m. ⊕a. Re(y)nard.
Rein¹-ertrag ⊕ (¹...) m ⊕ net proceeds pl. or produce; =gewinn m clear gain or profit; =gold n fine gold. [nard.]
Reinhard (¹⁻) npr/m. ⊕a. (Bn) Rey-
Reinheit (¹⁻) f ⊕ (s. rein¹ 1 u. 2) pureness, purity; clean(li)ness; neatness, tidiness; unpollutedness, clearness; (Unschuld) innocence. [Reginald.]
Reinhold (¹⁻) npr/m.⊕a.(Bn.) Reynold.

reinigen (¹⁻⁻) [mhd.; *rein¹] I v/a. u. sich 2 v. refl. ⊕ (sich) 2 to clean(se) (o.s.), fig. to purify (o.s.), to purge (o.s.) of sin, &c., to clear (o.s.) of a crime, &c.; (scheuern) to scrub, to scour, (fegen) to sweep, (spülen) to rinse, to wash; (putzen) to tidy up; e-m Kinde das Gesicht 2 to wash a child's face; metall. to refine a metal; chm. to purify a chemical substance, to rectify alcohol, &c.; med. to cleanse a wound, &c., to disinfect a room, &c. — II ~ n ⊕ s. Reinigung 1. — III 2d p.pr. u. a. ⊕ cleansing, purifying, &c. (s. I); bsd. med.: ⊘ abluent, abstergent, detergent, purging, aperient.
Reiniger (¹⁻⁻) m ⊕, ~in f ⊕ cleaner; (Läuterer) purifier; refiner; reformer.
Reinigung (¹⁻⁻) f ⊕ 1. (s. reinigen I) clean(s)ing, purification, purgation; metall. refining; chm. rectification. — 2. a) monatliche ~ = Menstruation; b) Mariä ~ (katholisches Fest) Purification; c) P = Züchtigung.
Reinigungs-eid (¹⁻⁻...) m ⊕ oath of purgation; =maschine ⊙ f clean(s)ing (or scouring) machine, für Korn: separator; =mittel n bsd. med.: ⊘ abluent, abstergent, detergent, (Abführmittel) purging medicine, purgative, aperient; =opfer n röm. Alt.: lustration; =rohr ⊙ n, mach. blow-through pipe.
Rein¹-kultur (¹,⁻) f ⊘: ⊘ culture of bacilli, bacilliculture.
reinlich (¹⁻) a. ⊕ clean(ly); (schmuck) neat, tidy; äußerst 2 scrupulously clean.
Reinlichkeit (¹⁻⁻) f ⊕ cleanliness, neatness, tidiness; ein Muster von ~ the pink of cleanliness; Sprichw. ~ ist's halbe Leben cleanliness is next to godliness.
Rein¹-mache-frau (¹⁻...) f ⊕charwoman; =machen n cleaning, scouring; =schrift f fair copy; 2weg F (¹⁻) adv. right away, clean gone, fig. highly delighted.
Reis¹ ♀ (¹) [mhd.; it. riso; ar.; *sft.] m ⊕a. (Pflanze u. Korn) rice (Ory'za sati'va); ~ in Hülsen Ost-J.: paddy.
Reis² (¹) [ahd.; *rauschen] n ⊕a. twig, sprig; (Pfropfreis) scion, (Rute) rod, (Zweig) bough, ⊘ virgule; vgl. Absenker; dünne Reiser für Feuer: faggots pl., small fire-wood, brushwood.
Reis¹-bau (¹⁻...) m ⊕ growth (or cultivation) of rice; =besen ⊕ m birch-broom; =branntwein ⊕ m (a)rack; =brei m Kochkunst: rice boiled in milk; =²bündel n faggot, auch: fagot.
Reise (¹⁻) [ahd.] f ⊕ journey, kürzere: tour, trip, excursion, F u. P run; auf dem Fahrrade: cycling tour, im Automobil: motoring tour, zur See: voyage, längere: travel(s pl.), des Staatsoberhauptes: (royal) progress; (Überfahrt) passage to America, &c.; sich auf die ~ machen to set out on a journey, to go on one's travels, ins Ausland: to go abroad; immer auf ~n sein to be for ever travelling or on the move; wo geht die ~ hin? where are you going (to)?, whither are you bound?
Reise-abenteuer (¹⁻...) n ⊕ adventure; =anzug m travelling-costume; vgl. =kleid; =apotheke f medicine-

chest (for travelling); =bedarf m travelling-necessaries pl.; =begleiter m travelling-companion; =beschreiber m (=beschreibung f) writer (book) of travels; =besteck n travelling-case; =bibliothek f travelling-library; =buch n itinerary, traveller's guide or handbook, tourist's, cyclist's, &c. vademecum or road-book; =bureau n (office of a) tourist agency; =decke f travelling-rug, railway-rug; =eindrücke m/pl., =erinnerungen f/pl. travelling-impressions, -reminiscences pl.; ²fertig a. ⊕ fully equipped for travelling, ready to start (on a journey); =fieber n excitement preceding (or caused by) a (long) journey; =führer m = =buch; =gefährte m. =gefährtin f travelling-companion; =gefolge n (travelling-)suite; =geld n money for travelling; =gepäck n luggage, a. (it.) impedimenta pl.; =gesellschaft f party (or company) of (fellow-)travellers; =hand-buch n = =buch; =karte f map for travellers, itinerant map; =kästchen n travelling-case; =kleid n travelling-dress, -garb; =koffer m travelling-box, -trunk, kleiner: portmanteau; =kosten pl. travelling-expenses pl.; =lust f: a) pleasure derived from travelling; b) passion (or mania) for travelling, roaming spirit; ²lustig a. fond of (or bent on) travelling; =mantel m travelling-cloak; =marschall m officer supervising a prince's travelling arrangements; =mütze f travelling-cap.
reisen (¹⁻) [ahd.] I v/n. (sn; ohne Rücksicht auf das Ziel a. h.), v/refl. u. v/impers. ⊕ to (make a) journey to, to be bound for, to go to (s. abreisen); ohne Angabe des Ziels: to travel (about), to be (or go) on one's travels, to be (or go) touring; ⊗ die Firma läßt nicht 2 the firm employs no travellers; ein weit gereister Mann a great traveller; gereiste Leute travelled people pl.; 2d travelling, on one's travels, itinerant, roaming; desselben Weges, einen Weg 2 to travel by (or to follow) the same route; mit prp.: auf das Land 2 to go into (or to start for) the country; durch einen Ort 2 to pass (through) a place; mit der Eisenbahn 2 to travel (or go) by rail; über Brüssel 2 to go over (or by, viâ) Brussels; von Ort zu Ort 2 to journey (or travel) from one place to another, to move (or shift) from place to place; zu Fuße 2 to go on foot, to walk (it), F to tramp it; zur See 2 to go by sea; sich müde 2 to tire o.s. with travelling; mit der Post reist es sich bequem it is pleasant travelling by coach. — II ~ n ⊕ journeying; travelling.
Reisende([r) m) f (¹⁻⁻) ⊕ railway-, &c. traveller; (Wanderer) wayfarer; (Fahrgast) passenger, zur See: voyager; vgl. Ausflügler, Handlungs-, Vergnügungs-reisender.

Reise-paß (¹⁻...) m ⊕ traveller's passport; =pfennig m (it.) viaticum; =prediger m itinerant preacher; =route f route (taken in travelling); =tasche

Signs (see page XVII): F familiar; P vulgar; P flash; ⊻ rare; † obsolete (died); * new word (born); ⁺⁺ incorrect; ♪ music.

[Reisewagen]

f travelling-bag, bsd. ehm. a.: carpet-bag; =**wagen** *m* tr.-coach; =**wetter** *n*: gutes ~ fine (or pleasant) weather for travelling; =**ziel** *n* (traveller's) destination; B. ist mein ~ I am bound for B.

Reis¹=**feld** (*"*=*⸗*) *m* ⊕ rice-field, Ost-J. paddy-field.

reisig¹ (*¹⌣*) [mhd.; *Reise] I *a.* ⊕ ehm. ⚔, noch in geh. Spr. (kriegsgerüstet) equipped (for war); (beritten) mounted. — II ehm. ⚔ **Reisige(r)** *m* ⊕ horse-soldier, trooper.

Reisig² (*¹⌣*) [ahd.; *Reis²] *n* (*m*) ⊕d. 1. faggots *pl.* — 2. brushwood; vgl. **Buschholz.** [bundle of fire-wood.]

Reisig-bund (*"⌣*...) *n* ⊕, =**bündel** *n*

Reis¹-käfer (*"*...) *m* ⊕ ent. rice-weevil (*Calandra oryzae*); =**läufer** ehm. ⚔ [Reise] *m* schwz. = Söldner; =**papier** *n* rice-paper.

Reiß-ahle ⊕ (*"*...) *f* ⊕ scribe; =**aus** (*¹"*) F *m*, *n*: ~ nehmen to take to one's heels; vgl. **ausreißen** 3; =**blei** *n* black-lead; vgl. **Graphit**; =**brett** *n* drawing-board.

reißen (*¹⌣*) [ahd.: write (vgl. **Reiß-feder** 2c.)] ⊕a. I *v/a.* u. sich ⸗ *v/refl.* 1. to tear; (fortziehen) to drag (along), pull, tug; (ab-, los-)⸗ to tear (or pull) off; an sich ⸗ to grasp, to seize, *fig.* to usurp, e-n Geschäftszweig: to monopolize, ● to form a corner in cotton, &c., to corner wheat, &c.; einem et. **aus** den **Händen** ⸗ to snatch a th. from (or out of) a p.'s hands; **zu Boden**, **zur Erde** ⸗ to pull down. — 2. **entzwei** (oder in Stücke) ⸗ to tear in two or apart, to pull to pieces. — 3. mit dem durch Reißen Entstehenden als Objekt: ein Loch ⸗ to tear a hole; sich (*dat.*) Löcher in die Strümpfe ⸗ to tear (or make) holes in one's stockings; sein Tod reißt eine große Lücke ... makes a great gap. — 4. Federn ⸗ to split feathers or pens or quills; Kochkunst: einen Fisch ⸗ (aufschlitzen) to cut open ..., to gut ...; *hunt.* vom Wolf ⸗: ein Tier ⸗ to tear ... (to pieces), to fall upon ... — 5. e-n ⸗ (ritzend verwunden) to scratch; sich an e-r Nadel ⸗ to scratch o.s. with a pin or needle. — 6. *fig.* Grimassen ⸗ to make grimaces or faces; Possen, schlechte Witze ⸗ to make (or crack) bad jokes; Zoten ⸗ to say smutty things, to talk smut. — II sich ⸗ *v/refl.* 7. sich **um** et. ⸗ (eifrig bemühen) to compete eagerly for a th., to scramble (or fight) for a th.; man reißt sich um ihn he is very much sought after. — III *v/n.*: a) (h.) 8. **an** et. ⸗ to pull at a th.; *fig.* ins Geld ⸗ (viel kosten) to run into money. — 9. *v/impers.* (von rheumatischen 2c. Schmerzen) es reißt mir in allen Gliedern I have racking (or shooting) pains in all my limbs, all my limbs are aching; b) (sn) 10. (brechen) to break, to snap (auch von Fäden), von Zeug, Kleidern: to tear, F to get torn; (sich spalten) to chink, crack, split; (bersten) to burst; die Geduld reißt mir I am losing all (or I am out of) patience; wenn alle Stränge ⸗ if nothing (else) avails, if the worst comes to the worst. — IV ~ *n* ⊕ 11. tearing, &c. (s. I); (s. 9) ~ in den Gliedern: acute (rheumatic) pains *pl.*; im Leibe, im

— 799 —

Magen: colic, F gripes *pl.*; (s. 10) break(age), tear(ing); split(ting). — **V** ⸗**d** *p.pr.* u. *a.* ⊕ 12. von Tieren: ravenous, rapacious; (fleischfressend) carnivorous; ⸗**des Tier** beast of prey. — 13. *path.* ⸗**de Schmerzen** racking (or violent) pains *pl.* — 14. (ungestüm eilend) impetuous, rapid, hurried; ⸗**de Fortschritte machen** to make rapid progress; ⸗**der Strom** torrent; ⸗**d** (*adv.*) schnell rapidly, swiftly; ● die Ware geht ⸗**d** (oder in ⸗**der Weise**) ab ... sells quickly, ... has a rapid sale, F ... goes off like steam or wild-fire. — **VI** ge-**rissen** *p.p.* und *a.* ⊕ (D9) 15. Bed. des *inf.* — 16. F *fig.* (pfiffig) artful, sly; vgl. **durchtrieben.**

Reißer (*¹⌣*) *m* ⊕ 1. (a. ~**in** *f* ⊕) (e-r der Dinge an sich reißt) grasping p., grasper. — 2. F *thea.* (zündendes Wort) kindling word, fetching phrase, F draw. — 3. ⊕ Tischlerei: cutting-point; vgl. **Reißstift.**

Reiß-feder (*"*...) *f* ⊕ drawing-, ruling-pen; =**kohle** *f* charcoal crayon or pencil; =**nagel** *m* Zeichnen: drawing-pin.

Reis¹-speise (*"=*¹⌣) *f* ⊕ rice-pudding.

Reiß-schiene ⊕ (*"*...) *f* ⊕ drawing-rule(r), mst T-square; =**spitze** *f* = =**ahle**; =**stift** *m* tracing-point; vgl. **Reißer** 3.

Reis¹-stärke (*"*...) *f* ⊕ rice-starch; =**suppe** *f* rice-soup.

Reiß-werk ⊕ (*"*...) *n* ⊕ cutting-frame; =**wolf** ⊕ *m* Wollspinnerei: willowing- (or tearing-)machine; =**zahn** *m*, *anat.*: ⸗ laniary tooth; =**zeug** *n* (case of) mathematical instruments; =**zirkel** *m* drawing-compasses *pl.*

Reis¹-vogel (*"*=*¹⌣*) *m* ⊕ *orn.*: javanischer ~ paddy-bird (*Padda oryzivora*).

Reit-anzug (*"*...) *m* ⊕ riding-costume or -suit; vgl. =**kleid**; =**bahn** *f* riding-ground, der Kunstreiter: circus.

reitbar (*¹⌣*) *a.* ⊕ ridable, fit for riding; ⸗**er Weg** good road for riding; vgl. **Reitweg.** [(Schabracke) housings *pl.*]

Reit-decke (*"*=*⸗*) *f* ⊕ saddle-cloth;

reiten (*¹⌣*) [ahd.: ride] ⊕b. I *v/n.* (h.; bei Ortsveränderung sn) 1. (ant. gehen, fahren) to ride (on horseback), to go on horseback; gut (schlecht) ⸗ to be a good (bad) rider, to sit a horse well (badly); durch (oder über) einen Ort ⸗ to pass through ... on horseback; Galopp ⸗ to gallop; vgl. galoppieren; Schritt ⸗ to pace, to amble; Trab ⸗ to trot; spazieren ⸗ to take a ride (or to ride out) on horseback; auf e-m Pferde ⸗ to be mounted (or to ride) on horseback; s. **Rappe**; geritten kommen to come (along) on horseback; ⚓ vor Anker ⸗ to ride at anchor; (stampfen) to ride hard. — II *v/a.* 2. ein Pferd ⸗ to mount (or ride, bestride) ...; ein Pferd **ins Freie** ⸗ to exercise ..., to give ... open-air (or outdoor) exercise; ein Pferd in die Schwemme ⸗ to ride (or take) ... into the horsepond; e-n **über den Haufen** (oder zu Boden) ⸗ to ride a p. down, to ride over a p.; ein Pferd **zu Schanden** ⸗ to founder (or overwork) ..., auch: to ride ... off his mettle; sich (*dat.*) e-n Wolf ⸗ to chafe o.s. in riding. — 3. *fig.* ein Prinzip ⸗ to have a fad; F e-n in die Tinte ⸗ to

[Reiz]

get a p. into a scrape or into trouble; ● **Wechsel** ⸗ to circulate (worthless) bills, F to fly kites. — 4. *fig.* der Alp reitet ihn he has (or suffers from) the nightmare; der Teufel muß ihn ⸗ he must have the (very) devil in him. — III ~ *n* ⊕ 5. riding (on horseback), horse-riding, bisw.: equitation; vgl. **Reitsport.** — IV ⸗**d** *p.pr.* u. *a.* ⊕ 6. on horseback; s. **Artillerie**; ⸗**de Gendarmerie** mounted police; ¤ ⸗**des Blatt**: ⸗ equitant leaf.

Reiter¹ (*¹⌣*) [ahd.; *reiten] *m* ⊕ 1. (a. ~**in** *f* ⊕) horseman (*f* horsewoman, auch: lady [who rides] on horseback): s. **Kunstreiter(in).** — 2. ⚔ (Soldat z. Pferde) horseman (*pl.* horsemen, col. horse); vgl. **Kavallerist.** — 3. ⊕ (Drahtgewicht einer Waage) rider. — 4. ⚔ *frt.* (erhöhte Bastion) cavalier; spanischer ~ cheval (*pl.* chevaux) de frise.

Reiter² (*¹⌣*) [ahd.; riddle] *f* ⊕ (a. *m* ⊕) (grobes Sieb) coarse sieve, riddle.

Reiter¹-aufzug ⚔ (*¹"*...) *m* ⊕ cavalcade; =**dienst** *m* horse-soldier's (or trooper's) duty, cavalry-service.

Reiterei (-*⌣¹*) *f* ⊕ 1. ⚔ cavalry, horse; horsemen, mounted troops *pl.* — 2. *contp.* (inferior) style of riding.

Reiter¹-fahne ⚔ (*¹"*...) *f* ⊕ standard; =**fähnrich** *m* cornet; =**gefecht** *n* cavalry-fight or -engagement; =**haufen** *m* troop of horse or cavalry; =**künste** *f/pl.* equestrian feats or tricks *pl.*

reitern obb. (*¹⌣*) [Reiter²] *v/a.* ⊕a. (sieben) to riddle, to screen.

Reiter¹-regiment (*¹"⌣⌣⌣*) *n* ⊕ regiment of horse, cavalry-regiment.

Reiterschaft (*¹"*...) *f* ⊕ body of horsemen

Reiters-mann (*¹"*,*⸗*) *m* ⊕c. horseman.

Reiter¹-standbild (*¹"*...) *n* ⊕, =**statue** *f* equestrian statue; =**stiefel** *m* = **Reitstiefel**; =**stückchen** *n* bsd. im Kriege: horseman's (daring) feat, trooper's adventure; =**zug** *m* cavalcade.

Reit-gerte (*¹"*...) *f* ⊕ horseman's switch; vgl. =**peitsche**; =**handschuh** *m* riding-glove or -gauntlet; =**hose** *f* ri.-breeches *pl.*, (Lederhose) leather breeches; =**institut** *n* = =**schule**; =**jacke** *f* ri.-jacket; =**kissen** *n* pillion; =**kleid** *n* für Frauen ri.-habit; =**knecht** *m* groom; =**kunst** *f* horsemanship; =**künste** *pl.* equestrian tricks *p..*; =**lehrer** *m* riding-master; =**lehrerin** *f* ri.-mistress; =**mantel** *m* ri.-cloak; =**peitsche** *f* ri.-whip, horsewhip; e-m die ⸗ geben to horsewhip a p.; =**pferd** *n* saddle-horse, mount; =**platz** *m* ri.-ground; =**post** *f* (mail sent by a) courier; =**rad** *n* cycle; =**rock** *m* riding-coat; =**sattel** *m* ri.-saddle; =**schule** *f* ri.-school; =**schüler** *m* ri.-pupil; =**sport** *m* equestrian sport, equestrianism; (Rennsport) the turf; =**stall** *m* stable for saddle-horses; =**stiefel** *m* riding- (or top-, jack-)boot; =**stunde** *f* ri.-lesson; =**unterricht** *m* instruction in riding; =**weg** *m* horse- (or bridle-)path or -road; =**zeug** *n* bsd. ⚔ harness of a saddle-horse, riding-equipment.

Reiz (*¹*) [nhd.; *reizen] *m* ⊕a. 1. (Erregung) excitement, stärker: irritation (s. Reizmittel); (Kitzel) tickling, itching. — 2. (Lockung) enticement, allure-

⚛ scientific; ¥ botanical; ♀ geography; ⊕ machinery; ⚒ mining; ⚔ military; ⚓ marine; ● commercial; ✉ postal; 🚂 railway

[reizbar] — 800 — [Rendant]

ment, (Zauber) charm, (Anziehung) attraction, attractiveness, fascination; (Anmut) grace(fulness).
reizbar (⸗́⸗) a. 66 (ſ. Reiz 1) irritable, (jähzornig) irascible, (empfindlich) sensitive, touchy; **~keit** (⸗́⸗-) f 46 irritability; (Zähzornigkeit) irascibility; (Empfindlichkeit) sensitiveness, touchiness.
reizen (⸗́⸗)[ahd.; *reißen] I v/a. u. v/n. (h.) 93 1. e-n zu et. 2 (anregen) to stimulate (or incite, instigate, rouse) a p. to (do) a th. (vgl. aufreizen); zur Wut 2 to exasperate; gereizt irritated, angry; in gereizter Stimmung in an irritable (ſtärker: in a savage) mood. — 2. (erregen) to excite, to stir up; den Appetit 2 to whet (or sharpen) the appetite; den Gaumen 2 to tickle the palate; den Durſt 2 to produce thirst. — 3. (locken) to entice, to allure, (bezaubern) to charm, (anziehen) to attract, to fascinate; (in Verſuchung führen) to tempt. — II ~ n 23 4. ſ. Reizung. — III 2d p.pr. u. a. 66 5. (ſ. 2) exciting; den Appetit 2d appetizing; (ſ. 3) enticing, charming, attractive, bewitching; (köſtlich) delightful, delicious.
Reizker ℛ (⸗́⸗) [ſlaw. Rötling] m 22 Pilz: orange-agaric (*Lacta'rius delicio'sus*).
reiz=los (⸗́⸗) a. 66 charmless, without charms, unattractive; (fade) insipid; **=loſigkeit** f 46 unattractiveness, charmlessness; insipidity; **=mittel** n 62 incentive, stimulus, inducement, *med.* stimulant.
Reizung (⸗́⸗) f 46 1. (ſ. reizen 1) stimulation, incitement, instigation; irritation, provocation. — 2. = Reiz 2.
reiz=voll (⸗́⸗) a. 66 charming, attractive; fascinating, enticing.
rekapitulieren (⸗⸗⸗́⸗) [lt.] I v/a. 93 (kurz wiederholen) to recapitulate. — II ~ n 23 recapitulation.
Rekel P (⸗́) [ndd.: rake] m 22 = Flegel 2; **~ei** f 46 = Flegelei.
rekeln (⸗́⸗) [Rekel] v/refl., bisw. v/n. (h.), a. v/a. 92a.: ſich (a. ſeine Glieder) 2 to stretch o.s. (or one's limbs) in an unmannerly way, to loll about.
Reklamation (⸗⸗-tsi(⸗)́) [lt.] f 46 (Zurückforderung) reclamation, (Einwand) auch: objection, protest, (Klage) complaint.
Reklame (⸗́⸗) [fr. *réclame*] f 46 (puffing) advertisement; ~ m. to advertise, to puff one's goods. weitS. to sound one's trumpet; **~macher(in** f) m (⸗⸗⸗...) 62 puffing advertiser or trader; **~mann** m sandwich-man; 2(n)haft a. 66 after the style of an advertisement, puffing; **=ſchild** n advertising board, hoch auf Dächern ꝛc. angebrachtes: sky-sign; **~wagen** m advertising van.
reklamieren (⸗⸗⸗́⸗) [lt.] v/a. u. v/n. (h.) 93 ([zurück]fordern) to (re)claim; (Einwand erheben) to object, wegen et.: to complain (or to make complaints) about a th.
rekognoſzier/en (⸗⸗⸗́⸗) [lt.] I v/a. 93 bſd. ℳ u. ⚓ (erkunden) to reconnoitre. — II ~ n 23, R/ung f 46 reconnaissance.
rekommandieren (⸗⸗⸗́⸗) [fr., *lt.] I v/a. 93 (empfehlen) to recommend, ✉ ſ. einſchreiben 1. — II ~ n 23 recommendation.
Rekonvaleſzent (⸗⸗w⸗⸗́) [lt.] m 42, **~in** f 46 (Wiedergeneſende[r]) convalescent.

Rekonvaleſzenz (⸗⸗w⸗⸗́) [lt.] f 46 (Wiedergeneſung) convalescence. [record.]
Rekord ⊺ (⸗́) ⓖⓓ. (unübertroffene Leiſtung)
Rekrut ℳ (⸗́) [fr. *recrue* f] m 42 recruit (auch *fig.*), neu angeworbener: raw recruit, newly enlisted soldier.
Rekruten=ausbildung (⸗⸗⸗⸗́⸗...) f 46 drilling of recruits; **=aushebung** f recruiting; **=unteroffizier** m drill-serjeant.
rekrutier/en ℳ (⸗⸗⸗́⸗) [fr. *recruter*] 93 I v/n. (h.) to recruit, to enlist (fresh) recruits. — II v/a. u. ſich 2 v/refl.: ein Regiment 2 to recruit ..., to bring ... to its full complement; ſich 2 to draw recruits from, to be recruited from. — III ~ n 23 und R/ung f 46 recruiting, enlistment (of soldiers).
Rekrutierungs=detachement ℳ (⸗⸗⸗⸗⸗́⸗...)n 62 recruiting party.
Rektaſzenſion 🜨 (⸗⸗(⸗)́) [lt.] f 46 *ast.* right ascension.
rektifizier/en (⸗⸗⸗́⸗) [lt.] I v/a. 93 (berichtigen) *chm.* deſtillieren) to rectify. — II ~ n 23 u. R/ung f 46 rectification.
Rektion (⸗tsi(⸗)́) [lt.] f 62 *gram.* (Nachſichziehen e-s Kaſus ob. Modus) government.
Rektor (⸗́⸗) [lt. Lenker] m 41: a) e-r Hochſchule: rector; b) einer Bürgerſchule ꝛc.: head master, principal; **~at** (⸗⸗́) ⓓⓒ., **~ſtelle** (⸗́⸗...) f 46: a) rectorship; b) headmastership.
Rekurs (⸗́) m 41a. *jur.* (Berufung) appeal; ~ einlegen to appeal.
Relais ⸮ (rĭ-lä') [fr.] n 65 ⚙, ℳ (Vorſpann, Pferdewechſel), *tel.* (Übertrager) relay.
Relation (⸗⸗tsi(⸗)́) [lt.] f 46 1. (Bericht) report. — 2. (Beziehung) relationship.
relativ (⸗⸗́ɾ) [lt.] I a. 66 (*ant.* abſolut) relative; *gram.* Des Fürwort relative pronoun. — II **~pronomen** 62) n ⓓⓓ., auch (lt.) **~um** (⸗⸗⸗́w) n 69 *gram.* (zurückbezügliches Fürwort) relative pronoun.
Relativ=ſatz (⸗⸗́⸗...) m 62 *gr.* relative (or adjective) clause or sentence.
Relegation (⸗⸗-tsi(⸗)́) [lt. *rēleg*...] f 46 expulsion from a university or school.
relegieren (⸗⸗⸗́⸗) [lt.] v/a. 93 Studenten, Schüler: to expel students from college.
Reli=ef ⊕ (⸗(⸗)́) [fr.] n 62 ⓓⓓ. (erhabene Arbeit) relief; vgl. Baß=, Haut=relief.
Reli=ef=druck ⊕ (⸗(⸗)́..) m 62 relief printing; **=globus** m embossed globe; **=karte** f relief-map, embossed map; **=ſtickerei** f raised embroidery.
Religion (⸗⸗(⸗)́)[nhd.16.sae.;*lt. *relĭ'giō*] f 46 religion, confession; die chriſtliche ~ annehmen to embrace the Christian faith, to turn Christian.
Religions=änderung (⸗⸗(⸗)́...) f 62 =wechſel; **=angelegenheit** f religious affair or concern; **=bekenntnis** n rel. profession; **=duldung** f rel. toleration; **=eifer** m rel. zeal; **=freiheit** f rel. freedom; **=friede(n)** m rel. peace, peace between rel. parties or sects; **=gebrauch** m rel. rite; **=geſchichte** f history of religion; **=krieg** m rel. war; **=lehre** f rel. instruction or teaching; (Gottesgelehrſamkeit) divinity; **=lehrer** m teacher of religion, religious teacher; (Gottesgelehrter) divine; 2los a. 66 irreligious; **=loſigkeit** f irreligion, irreligiousness; **=partei** f religious party; **=ſchwärmer(ei** f) m (rel.) fanatic(ism); **=ſtifter**

m founder of a religion; **=ſtreit(igkeit** f) m rel. controversy; **=ſtunde** f religious (or Bible) lesson; **=trennung** f schism; **=übung** f: a) (freie) ~ (free) exercise of religion, (free) public worship; b) **~en** rel. exercises pl.; **=unterricht** m = lehre; **=verbeſſerung** f rel. reform, reformation; **=wechſel** m change of religion, conversion; **=wiſſenſchaft** f science of religion, engS. theology, divinity; **=zwang** m intolerance.
religiös (⸗⸗(⸗)́) [fr.=lt.] a. 66 (⊳ 10) religious; (fromm) pious; **Religioſität** (⸗⸗(⸗)-⸗́) f 46 religiousness; piety.
Reliktien (⸗⸗́) [lt.] m/pl. 44 (die Hinterbliebenen) the bereaved, the survivors, the heirs pl., ſeltener: the relicts pl.; *biol.*, *geol.* relics (of former ages or periods) pl.; **~geſetz** n law safeguarding the rights of heirs. [breast-rail.]
Reling ⚓ (⸗́) f 46 (m ⓓⓓ.) (Schiffsbrüſtung)
Reliqui=e (⸗⸗́⸗) [lt. *relĭ'quĭae*] f 48 relic
Reliqui=en=dienſt (⸗⸗́⸗...) m 62 adoration of relics; **=käſtchen** n, **=kaſten** m, **=ſchrank** m, **=ſchrein** m shrine containing relics, reliquary.
Remen ⚓ (⸗́) [ndd.] m 23 = Ruder.
Reminiſzenz (⸗⸗⸗́) [lt.] f 46 (Erinnerung) reminiscence, recollection; **Reminiſzere** (⸗⸗⸗́⸗) [lt.gedenke! (Pſalm 25,6)] m (i. Faſtenſonntag) second Sunday in Lent.
remis (⸗mi') [fr.] prädikatives a.: das Spiel (Schach) iſt 2 (unentſchieden) it is a drawn game; **Partie remise** f, *inv.* drawn game. [coach-house.]
Remiſe (⸗́⸗) [fr.] f 46 (Wagenſchuppen)
Remittent 🕮 (⸗⸗́) [lt.] m 42 remitter.
remittier/en (⸗⸗́⸗) [lt. *rĕmĭt'tĕre*] I v/a. 93: a) (zurückſenden) to send back (or return) goods; b) (Geld einſenden) to send a remittance, to remit money. — II ~ n 23: a) returning goods; b) remittance of money. [Kocht.: salad-cream.]
Remoladen=ſauce (-⸗⸗w⸗-fō-β⸗) [fr.] f 62
Remonſtration (⸗⸗-tsi(⸗)́) [lt.] f 46 (Einwendung) remonstrance; **remonſtrieren** (⸗⸗⸗́⸗) v/n. (h.) 93 to remonstrate.
Remonte ℳ (⸗⸗́,vmg⸗́)[fr.] f 46 (Ergänzung der Pferde) remount(ing); **~depot** (⸗́...) n 62 remounting-depot; **~pferde** n/pl. remount(-horses pl.).
remontieren (⸗⸗⸗́⸗,vmg⸗́⸗)[fr.] v/n. (h.) 93 ℳ (nochmals blühen) to blossom again. **Remontierung** ℳ (⸗) f 46 remounting.
Remontoir=uhr ⊕ (⸗mɔ-tōá"r⸗́) [fr.] f 62 keyless (or stem-winding) watch.
Remorkör ⚓ (⸗⸗⸗́) [fr. *remorqueur*] m ⓓⓓ. (Schleppdampfer) tug-boat.
removieren (⸗⸗⸗́⸗)[lt.] v/a. 93 (entfernen) to remove; (abſetzen) to dismiss.
Rempelei F (⸗⸗⸗́) f 46 (Knuff, Krawall) F rumpus; **rempeln** (⸗́⸗) [ndd.; *Rampe] v a. 92a.: e-n (an) 2 to jostle (or push) a p.
Rem(p)ter (⸗́⸗) [corr. Refectorium] m (n) 22 in Klöſtern, Burgen: refectory.
remunerier/en (⸗⸗⸗́⸗) [lt.] v/a. 93 (belohnen) to remunerate. — II ~ n 23 und R/ung f 46 remuneration.
Renaiſſance (r⸗⸗nä-zá'β(⸗)́) [fr. Wiedergeburt (der Künſte)] f 48 Renaissance, (period of) revival; **~ſtil** (⸗́⸗) m 62 Kunſt, *arch.* Renaissance style.

Rendant (⸗⸗́) [lt.] m 42 accountant; **~ur** (⸗⸗́) f 46 ac.'s post, accountantship.

Zeichen (ſ. S. XVII): F familiär; P Volksſprache; Γ Gaunerſprache; ⸮ ſelten; † alt (auch geſtorben); * neu (auch geboren); ⁺⁺ unrichtig;

[Rendezvous] — 801 — [Reservezimmer]

Rendezvous (ra'-dĕ-wū) [fr. m Begegnung] n ⑤ meeting, appointment, rendezvous, ⚔ † = Sammelplatz, Versammlung.

Renegat (‿‿́) [nhd.; * neu-lt.] m ㊷, ~**in** f ㊼ bsd. rel. (Abtrünnige[r]) renegade.

Renette (‿̆‿̆) [fr. reinette] f ❀ rennet (-apple), russeting, bisw.: golding.

renitent (‿‿́) [lt.] a. ㊺, **Renitenz** (‿‿́) f ㊻ = widerspenstig, Widerspenstigkeit.

renken (‿̆) [ahd.: wrench: ringen] v/a. ❀ to wrench, ein Gelenk: to sprain.

Renkontre (ra-tg'-t'r) [fr. rencontre f (+ m)] n ㊼ (feindliches 3i.-treffen) (hostile) encounter.

Renn-arbeit ⚒ (‿‿́...) f ⓜ manufacture of iron by the direct process; =**bahn** f Sport: race-course; cinder-path; bei Wettrennen: die ~ frei! clear the course!; =**berge** ⚒ m/pl. heaps of crushed ore (ready for smelting); =**boot** ⚓ n racing boat.

rennen (‿̆) [ahd.: run] ⓑ b. **I** v/n. (jn) 1. to run; (vorwärts stürzen) to rush (forward); alles rennet, rettet, flüchtet (SCH.) all rush and rescue and hurry away; in sein Verderben 2 to rush headlong into destruction; mit e-m um die Wette 2 to race a p. for a wager; mit dem Kopfe gegen die Wand 2 to run one's head against the wall; nach et. 2 (jagen) to hunt after a th.; Sport: ein Pferd 2 lassen to run ... — **II** v/a. u. v/refl. 2. mit Angabe der Wirkung: **sich außer Atem** 2 to run o.s. out of breath; **sich fest** 2 to (run and) stick fast. — 3. (rennend stoßen) e-n zu Boden 2 to knock a p. down in running; e-m den Degen durch den Leib 2 to run a p. through with a sword, to run a sword through a p.('s body). — **III** v/a. 4. ⚙ metall.: Eisen 2 (schmelzen) to smelt ... — **IV** ~ n ㉓ 5. running; racing, race; Sport: ~ ohne Hindernisse flat race, mit Hindernissen : steeple-chase.

Renner (‿̆) m ㊷ 1. runner, person who rushes or runs. — 2. race-horse.

renn(e)te (‿̆(‿̆)) subj. impf. v. rennen.

Renn-fahrt (‿̆...) f ⓶ race (of motor cars); =**jacht** ⚓ f racing yacht; =**pferd** n race-horse, runner; =**platz** m =**bahn**; =**reiten** n horse-racing; =**schiff** ⚓ n racing yacht; =**sport** m racing; the turf; =**stahl** ⚒ m natural steel; =**stall** m racing-stud, stable for race-horses; =**tier** [P.+.; * altnordisch hrein] n, zo. reindeer (Ra'ngifertara'ndus); =**tierflechte** ⚘ f reindeer-moss (Clado'nia rangife'ri'na); =**wagen** m Alt.: chariot for racing, jetzt: racing car; =**wolf** m (Tretschlitten beim Eis- und Schnee-sport) (Swedish) sleigh; =**ziel** n winning-post.

Renommage (‿‿́) [‿‿ fr.] f ㊸: (blasse) ~ (Prahlerei) boast(ing), brag(ging), swagger(ing), big talk.

Renommee (‿‿́) [fr. renommée f Ruf] n ㊾ (ohne pl.) reputation; (Ruhm) renown.

renommieren (‿‿́) [(++) fr.] I v/n. (h.) ❀ burschikos: to boast, to brag (mit et. of a th.); to talk big, F to throw the hatchet. — **II** ~ n ㉓ = Großsprecherei. — **III** renommiert p.p. u. a. ㊻ (weit bekannt) well known, stärker: renowned, famous (wegen et. for a th.).

Renommist (‿‿́) [nhd. 17. sae.; + † fr.] m ㊷ burſch.: boaster, braggart, stärker: bully; ~**erei** f (‿‿‿́) f ㊺ = Großsprecherei.

Renonce (rö-ng'-ß) [fr. f] I f ❀ Kartenspiel: (Nichtbekennen einer Farbe) renounce, renouncing; ~ sein not to be able to follow suit. — **II** m ㊹ bursch. freshman of a "Corps".

renovieren (‿‿́w‿́) [lt.] v/a. ❀ (ausbessern) to renovate, repair, do up.

rentabel (‿‿́) [Rente] a. ㊻ (D 9) (einträglich) lucrative, profitable; ein rentables Geschäft a paying business.

Rentabilität (‿‿‿́) f ㊼ (Einträglichkeit) lucrativeness, profitableness.

Rent-amt (‿‿́) n ㊷, etwa: revenue-office.

Rente (‿̆) [nhd.; * fr.] f ㊺ revenue, income; (Leib-)~ annuity; von seinen ~n leben to live on one's private income or one's means.

Rentei (‿‿́) f ㊻ = Rentamt.

Renten-ablösung ❀ (‿‿...) f ⓶ amortization (or liquidation) of an annuity; =**anstalt**, =**bank** f annuity-office; =**gut** n estate held in perpetuity against payment of a fixed rental. [Rentner(in).]

Renti-er(e) f) m (‿̆ti'̌(‿̆') [fr.]

rentieren (‿‿́) v/n. (h.) u. **sich** 2 v/refl. ❀ to bring in revenue, to yield an income, ❀ von e-m Geschäfte: to pay (its way).

Rent-kammer (‿́...) f ㊷ = Rentamt; =**meister** m (Vorsteher eines Rentamtes) superintendent (or collector) of the revenue; (Verwalter) steward, bailiff.

Rentner (‿̆) m ㊷, ~**in** f ㊼ [Rente] p. living on his (f her) private means, independent gentleman (f lady).

reorganisier/en (‿‿‿́) [lt.] **I** v/a. ❀ (neugestalten) to reorganize. — **II** ~ n ㉓ und **R/ung** f ㊺ reorganization.

Reparatur (‿‿‿́) [mlt.] f ㊼ (Ausbesserung) repairing, repairs pl.; (mending of boots, &c.; ⚓-**bedürftig** a. ㊻ in need of repair; ~-**kosten** pl. ㊷ (cost of) repairs.

reparieren (‿‿́) [lt.] v/a. ❀ to (put into good) repair, ein Haus ic. auch: to do up.

repartier/en (-‿́‿́) [fr. répartir verteilen] **I** v/a. ❀ to allot, Steuern: to assess; (teilen) to share. — **II** ~ n ㉓ u. **R/ung**, **Repartition** f ㊺ allotment, assessment.

Repertoire (‿‿ä'r) [fr. répertoire m] n ⓪, **Repertorium** (‿‿‿́) [lt.] n ㉘ thea. (Spielplan) selection (or stock) of plays.

Repetent (‿‿́) [lt.] m ㊹ Universität 2c.: private tutor or coach, F crammer.

repetieren (‿‿‿́) [fr. répéter wiederholen] **I** v/a. u. v/n. (h.) ❀ to repeat, to do (over) again. — **II** ~ n ㉓ repetition.

Repetier-gewehr ⚔ (‿‿́...) n ㊷, =**telegraph** m, =**uhr** f repeater.

Repetition (‿‿‿́) [lt.] f ㊺ (Wiederholung) repetition, recapitulation; ~-**kreis** (‿̆...) m ⓶ ast., surv. repeating circle or instrument.

Repetitorium (‿‿‿́(‿̆)) [lt.] n ㉘ short course (or survey) of lectures for examination-candidates, &c.

Replik (‿‿́) [fr.réplique f ㊼ jur. (Erwiderung) rejoinder; Kunst 2c.: (Kopie) replica; **replizieren** (‿‿‿́) v/a. ❀ (erwidern) to reply.

reponieren (‿‿‿́) [lt. wieder (an die Stelle) setzen] ❀ ⚕ surg. ein gebrochenes Glied: to (re)set, einen Bruch: to reduce.

Report ❢ ❀ (‿‿́) m ⓐc.⑤ Börse: contango (ant. Deport backwardation).

Reporter ❢ (‿‿́) [engl.] m ㊷ (Berichterstatter; vgl. bs) reporter.

Report-geschäft (‿‿́...) n ㊷ (Schiebungsgeschäft) carrying-over, contango-business. [brett] (set of) book-shelves.]

Repositorium (‿‿‿́(‿̆)) [lt.] n ㉓ (Bücher-)

Repp-hahn (‿‿́) 2c. s. Rebhahn 2c.

Repräsentant (‿‿‿́) [lt.] m ㊷, ~**in** f ㊼ (Vertreter[in]) representative; ~**enhaus** n, Am. House of Representatives.

Repräsentations-kosten (‿‿‿tſ(‿̆)‿̆́) pl. inv. expense(s pl.) incurred by (or cost of) representation.

Repräsentativ-system (‿‿‿́f...) n ㊷ parl. representative system; =**verfassung** f constitution (on representative principles). [treten) to represent.]

repräsentieren (‿‿‿́) [lt.] v/a. ❀ (ver-)

Repressali-e (‿‿́(‿̆)) [neu-lt.] f ㊺ (Vergeltung) reprisal; ~**n ergreifen gegen** // to make reprisals on //.

Repressiv-maßregeln (‿‿‿́f...) [lt.] f/pl. ㊷ repressive measures pl.

Reproduktion (‿‿‿tſ(‿̆)́) [lt.] f ㊺ (Nachbildung) reproduction; ⚓-**fähig** (‿̆...) a. ㊻ able to reproduce; ~**s-verfahren** n process of reproduction.

reproduktiv (‿‿‿́f) [lt.] a. ㊻ reproductive.

reproduzieren (‿‿‿́) v/a. ❀ to reproduce.

Reps[1] ❀ (‿́) m ⓐa. = **Raps**.

Reps[2] ❢ (‿́) m ⓐa. ❀ = **Rips**[1].

Reptil (‿‿́) [lt. kriechend] n ⓐd. ㊷ zo. reptile (a. fig. b.s. Kriecher).

Reptilien-fonds (‿‿́(‿̆)...) m ㊷ pol. contp. secret-service fund; =**presse** f servile government-press.

Republik (-‿‿́) [fr.; * lt. res pu'blica] f ㊺ (Freistaat) republic, bsd. ehm. auch: commonwealth; ~**a'ner**(in f) m ㊷, ~**a'nisch** a. ㊻ republican; **Lanisieren** (-‿‿‿́) v/a. ❀ to republicanize; ~**anismus** (-‿‿‿́) m ㊷ republicanism.

Repuls (‿‿́) [lt.] m ⓐa., **Repulsion** (‿‿‿́) [lt.] f ㊺ (Zurückweisung) repulse.

Reputation (‿‿‿tſ(‿̆)́) [lt.] f ㊺ (Ruf) reputation, repute; **reputierlich** (‿‿‿́) a. ㊻ reputable, respectable.

Requi-em (‿‿̆‿̆) [lt.] n ⓑ Cath.eccl. u. ♪ (Totenmesse) requiem (mass).

requirieren (‿‿‿́) [lt.] v/a. ❀ bsd. ⚔ (anfordern) to requisition, in Südafrika 2c.: to commandeer.

Requisit (‿‿́) [lt.] n ㉓Ⓑ c. (Erforderliches) requisite; thea. ~**en** pl. (Zubehör eines Stücks) properties, F props pl.; ~**en-meister** m thea. = Garderobenmeister.

Requisition (‿‿‿tſ(‿̆)́) [lt.] f ㊺ bsd. ⚔ (Anforderung) requisition.

Reseda ❀ (‿‿́) [lt. still(e)!] f ㊽, ...**de** f ㊺ (Wau) mignonette (Rese'da odora'ta).

Reservage ⊙ (-‿w‿́) [fr. réservage m] f ⓶ Zeugdruckerei: (Schutzbeize) resist-paste.

Reservation (‿‿w‿tſ(‿̆)́) [lt.] f ㊺ (Vorbehalt) reservation. [right(s pl.).]

Reservat-recht (‿‿w‿́) n ㊷ reserved

Reserve (‿‿́) [fr. réserve] f ㊺ (Vorrat, ⚔ Ersatzmannschaft; ant. aktiv) reserve; die ~ einberufen to call out the reserve.

Reserve-anker ⚓ (‿‿w...) m ⓶ spare anchor; =**fonds** m reserve-fund; =**mann** = Reservist; =**mannschaft** ⚔ f (body of) reserve; =**mast** ⚓ m spare mast; =**offizier** ⚔ m officer in the reserve; =**segel** ⚓ n spare sail; =**truppen** f/pl. ⚔ reserve forces, reserves pl.; =**zimmer** n spare room.

[reservieren] — 802 — [Rettungsschlauch]

reservieren (⏑–⏑ᴸ⏑) [lt.] v/a. ⓐ (aufbewahren, sparen) to (keep in) reserve, to put by, a. = ausbedingen 2; fig. **reserviert** (zurückhaltend) reserved, F buttoned-up, stand-offish; thea., &c. reservierter Platz reserved seat.

Reservist ⚔ (⏑–⏑ᵛ) [fr. *réserviste*] m ⓐ reserve-man, reservist.

Reservoir (–⏑vā'r) [fr. *réservoir* m Behälter] n ⓐd. (⑤) reservoir, tank.

Resident (⏑–ᵛ) [lt.] m ⓐ resident (minister). [(princely) residence.)

Residenz (⏑–ᵛ) [fr. *résidence*] f ⓐ

Residenzler (⏑–⏑ᵛ) m ⓐ, ~in f ⓐ inhabitant of a capital.

Residenz-stadt (⏑–ᵛ...) f ⓐ place of residence, des Staatsoberhauptes: capital; =theater n theatre attached to a royal, &c. residence; (chief) theatre of a capital. [to reside (in a town).)

residieren (⏑–⏑ᴸ⏑) [lt.] v/n.(h.) ⓐ (wohnen))

Residuum ⚔ (⏑–ᴸ⏑⏑) [lt. überrest] n ⓐ bsd. chm. residue, residuum.

Resignation (⏑⏑–tß(⏑)ᴸ) [lt.] f ⓐ (Verzicht, Abdankung) resignation.

resignieren (⏑⏑–ᴸ⏑) [lt.] ⓐ I v/n. (h.): auf etwas ⚔ (verzichten) to resign a th.; resigniert resigned (to one's fate). — II v/refl. sich in et. ⚔ (ergeben) to resign o.s. to a th. — III ~ n ⓐ u. **Resignierung** f ⓐ resignation.

reskribieren (⏑⏑–ᴸ⏑) [lt.] v/a. ⓐ (verordnen) to decree; **Reskript** (⏑–ᴸ) n ⓐc. rescript.

resolut (⏑⏑–ᴸ) [lt.] a. ⓐ (entschlossen) resolute, determined; **Resolution** (⏑⏑–tß(⏑)ᴸ) [lt.] f ⓐ (Beschluß) resolution.

resolvieren (⏑⏑–ᴸ⏑) [lt.] v/a. und sich ⚔ v/refl. ⓐ: a) (sich) ⚔ (auflösen) to dissolve; b) (sich) ⚔ (beschließen) to resolve.

Resonanz (⏑⏑–ᵛ) [lt.] f ⓐ ♪, phys. (Widerhall) resonance, reverberation; ~boden (⏑⏑–ᵛ...) m ⓐ sounding-board; =kasten m resonance-box or -chamber.

resorbieren ⚔ (⏑–ᴸ⏑) [lt.] v/a. ⓐ (wieder aufsaugen) to reabsorb; **Resorption** (⏑⏑–tß(⏑)ᴸ) [lt.] f ⓐ reabsorption.

Resorzin ⚔ (⏑⏑–ᴸ) [neut-lt.] n ⓐd. chm. resorcin, resorcine ($C_6H_6O_2$).

resp. abbr. = respektive.

Respekt (⏑–ᵛ) [lt.] m ⓐb. (Ehrfurcht) respect; (Achtung) esteem; e-m ~ einflößen to inspire a p. with awe or dread; gewaltigen ~ vor e-m h. to hold a p. in great respect, to stand in (great) awe of a p.; mit ~ zu melden with all due respect (or deference) to you; if I may say so; vgl. melden 3; sich ~ verschaffen to secure respect, to make o.s. respected.

respektabel (⏑⏑–ᵛ) [lt.] a. ⓐ (D9) (angesehen) respectable; **Respektabilität** (⏑⏑–⏑ᴸ) f ⓐ respectability.

Respekt-blatt (⏑–ᵛ...) n typ. fly-leaf.

respektieren (⏑⏑–ᴸ⏑) [lt.] v/a. ⓐ (achten) to respect, to esteem, ⓐ Wechsel (nicht) ⚔ to (dis)honour ...; **respektierlich** (⏑⏑–ᴸ⏑) a. ⓐ respectable, honourable.

respektiv (⏑⏑–ᴸf) [lt.] a. ⓐ respective.

respektive (⏑⏑–ᴸ⏑v) adv. (beziehungsweise) respectively (abbr. resp.).

respekt-los (⏑–ᵛ...) a. ⓐ without (proper) respect; =losigkeit f ⓐ want of respect.   [be held in respect.)

Respekts-person (⏑–ᵛ...) f ⓐ person to

Respekt-tage ⚔ (⏑–ᵛ...) m/pl. ⓐ (Frist) days pl. of grace; =voll a. ⓐ respectful; =widrig a. disrespectful; =widrigkeit f ⓐ disrespect(fulness).

respirieren (⏑–ᴸ⏑) [lt.] v/n.(h.) ⓐ to breathe.

Responsorium (⏑–ᴸ(⏑)ᴸ) [lt.] n ⓐ Liturgie: responses pl.; ♪ responsory (song).

Ressen ⚔ (⏑ᵛ) m ⓐ washing-trough.

Ressort (⏑ßō'r) [fr. m] ⓐ 1. m (Springfederaufschwung) spring. — 2. n (Geschäftskreis, ⚔ jur. † Verwaltungszweig) department, (administrative) province or sphere; das gehört nicht zu meinem ~ it's beyond (or outside) my province.

ressortieren (⏑⏑–ᴸ⏑) [fr. *ressortir*] v/n. (h.) ⓐ to appertain (or belong) to a th.

ressort-mäßig (⏑ßō'r-ᴸ⏑) a. ⓐ jur., pol. departmental.

Ressource (⏑ßü'r-ß⏑) [fr.] f ⓐ 1. (Hilfsmittel) resource; expedient, remedy. — 2. (geschlossene Gesellschaft) club.

Rest (ᵛ) [fr. *reste*] m ⓐb. und (f. 2b) ⓐb. 1. (das übrige) rest, remaining part, math., &c. remainder, jur., chm., &c. residue, path. e-r Krankheit: dregs pl.; j-s irdische ~e a p.'s earthly remains pl., eines Heiligen ⚔c.: relics pl. — 2. ⚫: a) (Zahlungsrest) balance; b) ~er pl. (Schnittwaren ⚔c.) remnants, odds and ends pl. — 3. fig. seinen ~ bekommen to receive the finishing stroke.

Restant ⚔ (⏑–ᵛ) [lt.] m ⓐ (mit der Zahlung Rückständiger) person in arrears, defaulter; ~en-liste (⏑–⏑ᵛ⏑) f ⓐ list of defaulters.   [ⓑ = Restauration 2.)

Restaurant (⏑ßto[Pßtau]-ra') [fr. m] n)

Restaurateur (⏑ßto[Pßtau]rä-tö'r) m ⓐd. restaurant-keeper, keeper of a restaurant.

Restauration (⏑ßto[Pßtau]⏑tß(⏑)ᴸ) [+f fr.] f ⓐ 1. (Wiederherstellung) restoration. — 2. (Speisehaus, Bier- und Weinlokal, Wirtschaft) restaurant, dining-rooms pl., 🚃 refreshment-room; für Milch, Kaffee, Tee ⚔c.: creamery, tea-rooms pl.; niederer Art: coffee-shop.

Restaurations-essen (⏑...) n meal (or mealing, dining) at a restaurant; =kellner m waiter at a restaurant; =wagen 🚃 m dining-car.

restaurieren (⏑ßto[Pßtau]ᴸ⏑) [fr., * lt.] v/a. ⓐ (wiederherstellen) to restore; sich ⚔ (durch Speise und Trank erquicken) to partake of refreshments.

Rest-betrag (ᵛ...) m ⓐ remainder.

Restchen (ᴸ⏑) n ⓐ (dim. von Rest) small remainder or balance or remnant.

Rester-handlung ⚫ (ᴸ⏑⏑⏑) [Rester, pl. f. Rest 2b] f ⓐ shop for remnants.

restieren (⏑–ᴸ⏑) [lt.] v/n. (h.) ⓐ to remain, to be left over, von Schulden: to be still due, to be still owing.

restituieren (⏑⏑–ᴸ⏑) [lt. zurückerstatten, wiederherstellen] I v/a. ⓐ to restore, bisw.: to restitute. — II ~ n ⓐ und **Restituierung** f ⓐ restitution.

Restitution (⏑⏑–tß(⏑)ᴸ) [lt.] f ⓐ (Wiederherstellung) restitution; ~s-edikt (ᴸ...) n ⓐ hist. (1629) Edict of Restitution.

rest-los (ᵛ...) a. ⓐ u. adv. without a remainder; * fig. sich ⚔ (gründlich) mit etwas befassen to devote o.s. thoroughly (or unsparingly) to a th.   [resultant.)

Resultante (⏑⏑–ᵛ⏑) [fr.] f ⓐ mech., phys.)

Resultat (⏑⏑–ᴸ) [fr. *résultat* m] n ⓐc. (Ergebnis) result, outcome, arith. auch: answer; ~los a. ⓐ without result.

resultieren (⏑⏑–ᴸ⏑)[fr.]v/n.(h.) ⓐ to result.

Resümee, öst. **Resumee** (–⏑ᴸ) [fr. *résumé* m] n ⓐ (Übersicht) summary, (fr.) résumé.

resümieren (–ᴸ⏑) [fr. *résumer*] v/a. u. sich ⚔ v/refl. ⓐ (zsfassen) to sum up (auch vom Richter), to summarize, to recapitulate; das resümiert sich leicht that's easily reckoned up.

retablieren (–ᴸ⏑) [fr. *rétablir*] v/a. (u. v/refl. sich ⚔) ⓐ to re-establish (o.s.).

Retentions-recht (⏑⏑–tß(⏑)ᴸ⏑ᴸ) [lt.] n ⓐ jur. right of retention, lien.

Retirade (⏑⏑–ᴸ⏑) [fr.] f ⓐ 1. fast † od. co. ⚔ retreat. — 2. [⏑+ fr.] = Abtritt 2.

retirieren (⏑⏑–ᴸ⏑) [fr.] v/n. (fn) u. sich ⚔ v/refl. ⓐ: (sich) ⚔ to (effect a) retreat.

Retorsion (⏑⏑–ᴸ) [fr. *rétorsion*] f ⓐ (Wiedervergeltung) retorsion; ~s-zölle (⏑⏑(⏑)ᴸ...)m/pl. ⓐ retaliation duty sg.

Retorte (⏑–ᴸ⏑) [fr.] f ⓐ chm. retort.

Retorten-kohle ⚔ (⏑ᵛ⏑ᴸ⏑) f ⓐ metall. cylinder-charcoal.

retour (⏑tū'r) [fr.] adv. (zurück) back; ~(en pl.) f ⓐ ⚫ = Rücksendung(en).

Retour-billett 🚃 (⏑tū'r–...) n ⓐ (Rückfahrkarte) return-ticket; =fracht ⚫ f return- (or home-)freight; =kutsche f: a) return-chaise; b) F fig. repartee couched in the same form as the original joke of the assailant.

retournieren ⚫ (⏑tū–ᴸ⏑) [fr.] v/a. ⓐ (zurücksenden) to return, to send back.

Retour-waren ⚫ (⏑tū'r–ᴸ⏑) f/pl. ⓐ returned goods, F returns pl.

rettbar (ᴸ–) a. ⓐ savable.

retten (ᴸ⏑) [ahd.: rid] I v/a. und sich ⚔ v/refl. ⓐ: (sich) ⚔ to save (o.s.); sich ⚔ auch: to (make good one's) escape; (befreien) to deliver, rescue, (set) free, aus dem Feuer, Wasser ⚔c. ⚔ to snatch from ..., Güter ⚔c.: to recover; er ist nicht zu ⚔ ... (irretrievably) lost; rette sich, wer kann!, look out for yourselves!, each (one) for himself!, (fr.) sauve qui peut! — II ~ n ⓐ = Rettung.

Retter (ᴸ⏑) m ⓐ, ~in f ⓐ deliverer (f bisw.: deliveress), rescuer; (Heiland) Saviour, Redeemer.

Rettich (ᴸ⏑) [ahd.; * lt. *rādīc-* Wurzel] m ⓐd. (black) radish (Ra'phanus sati'vus).

rett-los ⚔ (ᵛ...) a. ⓐ (außerstande, See zu halten) disabled, unseaworthy.

Rettung (ᴸ⏑) f ⓐ (s. retten) saving; deliverance, rescue, salvation (auch rel.); von Gütern: recovery, ⚔ salvage; (Entkommen) escape.

Rettungs-anker (ᴸ⏑...) m ⓐ ⚔ spare anchor, fig. sheet-anchor; =anstalt f establishment for saving life; =apparat m life-saving apparatus; =boje ⚔ f life-buoy; =gürtel m life-belt; =insel f auf den Straßen: island; =kahn ⚔ m life-boat; =leine ⚔ f life-line; =leiter ⊙ f fire-escape; =los a. (adv.) verloren irretrievably lost, irrecoverable; =losigkeit f hopeless state; irretrievableness; =medaille f medal (received) for saving life; =mittel n means of safety, refuge; vgl. Hilfsmittel; unser letztes ~ our last straw; =sack, =schlauch

Signs (see page IX): F familiar; P vulgar; ⌐ flash; ⚔ rare; † obsolete (died); * new word (born); +| incorrect; ♪ music;

[Rettungstuch] — 803 — [rhombisch]

m chute; **=tuch** *n* = Sprung=, Rutsch=tuch; **=versuch** *m* attempt at saving (or rescuing) a p.; **=werk** *n* work of rescue.
Retusche (⌣⌣)[fr. *retouche*] *f* ⊕ *phot.* (überarbeitung) retouching. [**Retuschierer.**
Retuscheur (⌣⌣⇂ʳ)[fr.] *m* ⒹD. (⊙) =
retuschieren (⌣⌣⇂⌣)[fr. *retoucher*] *v*/*a*. ⊙ ein Gemälde, Lichtbild ꝛc. ⚷ (überarbeiten) to retouch ..., to touch up ...
Retuschierer (⌣) *m* ⊕ bsd. *phot.* retoucher.
Reue (⇂⌣)[ahd.: *reuen*] *f* ⊕ repentance (über of), über begangene Sünden: penitence, compunction; ~ über et. empfinden to feel remorse at a th., to repent (of) a th.
Reu(e)=gefühl (⇂⇂,⌣⇂) *n* ⊕ remorse.
reu(e)=los (⇂⌣...) *a*. ⊕ remorseless; **=losigkeit** *f* ⊕ remorselessness.
reuen (⇂⌣)[ahd.: rue] *v*/*a*. u. *v*/*n*. (h.), oft *v*/*impers*. ⊙ to repent (of) a th.; es reu(e)t mich, dies getan zu haben, diese Tat reut mich, geh. Spr. es reut mich dieser (*gen.*) Tat I repent having done it, I regret (or feel sorry for) my action; er wird es sich noch ⚷ laßen he will yet rue (or be sorry for) it.
reue=voll (⇂⌣⇂⚶) *a*. ⊕ = reuig.
Reu=geld (⇂⇂⚶) *n* ⊕ forfeit.
reuig (⇂⌣)[ahd.] *a*. ⊕ repentant; *rel*. (bußfertig) penitent; *adv*. auch: with a penitent (or contrite) heart. [*a*. ⊕ = reuig.
Reu=kauf (⇂⇂...) *m* ⊕ forfeit; **⚷mütig**
Reuse ⊙ (⇂⌣) [ahd.: Rohr] *f* ⊕ (Bunge) für Krebsfang ꝛc.: bow-net, für Aalfang: eel-pot or -basket.
Reute ⊙ (⇂⌣) *f* ⊕ = ausroden II; **reuten** (⇂⌣) *v*/*a*. ⊙ = ausroden I.
Reut=feld ⊙ (⇂⇂...) *n* ⊕ land newly cleared or hoed; **=hacke, =haue** *f* grubbing-axe, mattock. (Mehr gbr. Rode=...).
Revanche (⌣wa-ʃč⌣, ⚶⚶ -G⌣) [fr. *Rache*] *f* ⊕ revenge (auch *fig*. vom Kartenspiel).
revanchieren (⌣wa-ʃč⇂⌣, ⚶⚶ ... G⇂⌣) [fr.] *v*/*refl*. ⊙ sich ⚷ to take (or have) one's revenge, *g*. *s*. to return.
Reveille ⚔ ↓ (⌣wḗ'l-jə) [fr. *réveil m*] *f* ⊕ (Wecken) reveille.
Reverbere ⊙ (-w⇂(⌣) [fr. *réverbère m*] *vn* ⊕(⊕) (⚶⚶ *f* ⊕) (Lampe mit Scheinwerfer) reverberator, lamp with a reflector.
reverberieren (-⌣⚶⇂⌣)[fr.]*v*/*a*.⊙*phys.*,&c. (zurückstrahlen) to reverberate, to reflect.
Reverenz (⌣w⚶) [lt.] *f* ⊕ 1. = Ehrerbietung. — 2. (Verbeugung) bow, ehm.: obeisance; (Knicks) curtsy.
Revers (⌣wē'rß) [lt.] *m* ⒹDa. 1. *num*. reverse, &c. (= Rückseite; *ant*. Avers). — 2. *jur*. (Gegenschein) counter-bill.
Reversions=pendel (⌣w⇂(⌣)⇂⚶⚶) [lt.] *m*, *n* ⊕ *phys*. reversible pendulum.
revidieren (⌣w⚶⇂⌣) [lt.] *v*/*a*. ⊙ (auf Richtigkeit prüfen) ⊕ to check, examine, audit; ⊕ *typ.* Druckbogen: to revise.
Revier (⌣w⇂ʳ) [mhd. Ufergelände; * (⚶⚶ fr. *rivière f* Fluß] *n* ⒹD. (Bezirk) district, der Polizei: beat, der Briefträger: walk, round; ⚔ country; *hunt.* hunting- (or shooting-)ground; ein ~ abgeh(e)n, durchsuchen to beat a cover, to shoot over an estate; ⚔ = bekommen to get sick-leave, to be put on the sick-list.
Revier=förster (⌣wʳ...) *m* ⊕, **=jäger** *m* quarter-ranger; **=kranke(r)** ⚔ *m* invalid(ed) soldier in private quarters.

Revision (⌣w-(⌣)⇂) [lt.] *f* ⊕ ⚶, *jur*. (Prüfung betreffs der Richtigkeit) revision, revisal (auch ⊕ *typ*.); von Rechnungen: checking, auditing, overhauling; zoll=amtliche: examination of luggage.
Revisions=bogen ⊙ (⌣w-(⌣)⇂⇂) *m* ⊕ *typ*. revised proof-sheet, auch: revise; **=hof** *m* *jur*. court of revision.
Revisor (⌣w⇂⇂) [lt.] *m* ⊕ ⚶, &c. (f. der durchsieht, auf die Richtigkeit prüft) reviser, controller, auditor (of accounts).
Revolte (-w⌣⚶) [fr. *révolte*] *f* ⊕ (Aufruhr) revolt, rising; **revoltieren** (-w⌣⇂⌣) *v*/*n*. (h.), bisw. auch sich ⚷ *v*/*refl*. ⊙ to revolt.
Revolution (⌣w⚶-tß(⌣)⇂) [lt. Umwälzung] *f* ⊕ *ast.*, *fig.*, *pol*. revolution.
revolutionär (⌣w⚶-tß(⌣)⚶⇂) [lt.-fr.] I *a*. ⊕ revolutionary. — II ~ *m* ⊕(⊕) (Umstürzler) revolutionist, revolutionary.
revolutionieren (⌣w⚶-tß(⌣)⚶⇂⌣)[fr.]*v*/*a*.⊙ (umstürzen, aufwiegeln) to revolutionize.
Revolutions=geist (⌣w⚶-tß(⌣)⇂⇂...) *m* ⊕ revolutionary spirit; **=held** *m* revolutionist; **=krieg** *m* revolutionary (or civil) war, rebellion; **=mann** *m* = =held.
Revolver ⚰ (⌣w⇂w⌣) [amer. (*It.)] *m* ⊕ (Drehpistole) revolver; sechsläufiger ~ six-chambered revolver.
Revolver=kanone ⚔ (⌣w⇂w...) *f* ⊕ revolving cannon, machine-gun; **=presse** *f*, *b.s.* etwa: press conducted by rowdies.
revozier/en (⌣w⇂⌣) [lt.] I *v*/*a*. ⊙ (widerrufen) to revoke, retract. — II ~ *n* ⊕ u. **R/ung** *f* ⊕ revocation, retractation.
Revue (⌣wü⇂) [(⚶⚶⚶ fr.] *f* ⊕ (Musterung) review (a. ⚔); ⚔ =passieren to pass muster.
Rezensent (⌣⌣⇂) [lt.] *m* ⊕ reviewer, critic; **rezensieren** (⌣⌣⌣⇂) *v*/*a*. ⊙ (kritisch beurteilen) to review, to criticize.
Rezension (⌣w(⌣)⇂) [lt.] *f* ⊕ (kritisches Urteil) review, criticism. [viewer's copy.]
Rezensions=exemplar (⌣"...) *n* ⊕ re-
Rezepisse (⌣-⌣-) [lt.] *n* ⊕ *ob. inv.* receipt.
Rezept (⌣⌣) [lt.] *n* ⒹDb.: a) Kocht. ꝛc.: receipt; b) *med*., prescription, recipe.
rezeptieren (⌣⌣⇂⌣) [neu-lt.] *v*/*n*. (h.) ⊙ *med.*, *pharm*. (Arzeneien nach Vorschrift bereiten) to make up prescriptions, to dispense medicines or drugs; **Rezeptier=kunst** (⌣⌣,⚶) *f* ⊕ *med*., *pharm*. art of prescribing or dispensing (medicines).
rezeptiv (⌣⌣⇂ʳ) *a*. ⊕ (empfänglich) receptive.
Rezeptivität (⌣⌣-w⇂) [neu-lt.] *f* ⊕ receptivity. [Einnehmer.]
Rezeptor (⌣⌣⇂) [lt.] *m* ⊕ receiver; f. a.]
Rezeptur (⌣⌣⇂) [neu-lt.] *f* ⊕ 1. receivership. — 2. *pharm*. die ~ h. to dispense.
Rezeß (⌣⌣) [lt.] *m* ⒹDa. 1. + *parl*. (Ferien) recess. — 2. (Vertrag) agreement, treaty.
Rezidiv (⌣⌣⇂ʳ) [lt.] *n* ⒹDd, *a*. ~e (⌣⇂⌣w) *f* ⊕ *jur.*, *path*. (Rückfall) relapse.
Rezipient (⌣⌣⇂⌣⇂) [lt.] *m* ⊕, *chm*. recipient, receiving vessel.
reziprok ⚰ (⌣⌣⇂) [lt.] *a*. ⊕ (gegenseitig) reciprocal; **Reziprozität** (⌣⌣⌣⇂⇂) *f* ⊕ reciprocity. [tation.]
Rezitation (⌣⌣-tß(⌣)⇂) [lt.] *f* ⊕ reci-
Rezitativ (⌣⌣⇂ʳ) [lt.] *n* ⒹDd. (Redegesang) recitative, ...o. [to recite.]
rezitieren (⌣⌣⇂⌣) [lt.] *v*/*a*. ⊙ (vortragen)
Rhabarber ⚘ u. *pharm*. (⌣⌣) [(ʰ)[ihd. 16. sae.] *it. raba'rbaro*] *m* ⊕ rhubarb (*Rhe'um*); englischer ~ = Garten=⚷; indischer (echter) ~ *official* (or medicinal) rh.

(*Rh. officina'le*); **=tinktur** (⌣⚶⌣...) *f* ⊕ *pharm*. tincture of rhubarb; **=torte** *f* Kocht.: rhubarb tart.
Rhapsode (⌣⇂⌣) [grch.] *m* ⊕ Alt.: (wandernder Sänger) rhapsodist; **Rhapsodie** (⌣-⇂) *f* ⊕ (epischer Vortrag) rhapsody; **rhapsodisch** (⌣⇂⌣) *a*. ⊕ rhapsodical; **Rhapsodist** (⌣-⌣) *m* ⊕ rhapsodist.
Rhede ↓ (⇂⌣) ꝛc. f. Reede ꝛc.
Rhein ⚥ (⇂⌣) *npr/m*. ⒹDa.: der ~ the Rhine; Sprichw.: Waßer in den ~ tragen, etwa: to carry coals to Newcastle.
Rhein=brücke (⇂⇂...) *f* ⊕ bridge across the Rhine; **=bund** *m*, *hist*. unter Napoleon I. Rhenish Confederation; **=dampfer** *m* steamer on the Rh.; **=fahrt** *f* tour (or trip) on the Rh.; **=fall** *m* bei Schaffhausen: Falls *pl*. of the Rh.; **=gau** *npr/m(n)*. Rheingau; ehm. **=graf** *m* Rhinegrave; **=hessen** ⚥ *npr/n*. Rhenish Hessia.
rheinisch (⇂⌣) *a*. ⊕ = rheinländisch.
Rhein=land (⇂"...) *n* ⒹDa, **=lande** *n*/*pl*. Rhine country, *a*. Rhineland; **=länder** *m*: a) inhabitant of the Rh. country; b) (Tanz) schotti'sche; **=ländisch** *a*. ⊕ of the Rhineland, Rhenish; **=pfalz** ⚥ *npr/f*. Palatinate (of the Rhine); **=provinz** *f* Rhenish Prussia, Rhine Province; **=reise** *f* journey along (or on) the Rhine; vgl. =fahrt; **=schiffahrt** *f* navigation on the Rhine; **=strom** *m* river Rhine; **=tal** *n* Rhine valley; **=ufer** *n* bank of the Rh.; **=wein** *m* Rhenish (or Rhine) wine, auch: hock.
Rheochord ⚙ (-⌣⇂) [grch.] *m* ⒹDc. *elect*. (Widerstandsmesser) rheochord.
Rheostat ⚙ (-⇂⇂) [grch.] *m* (*n*) ⒹDc. *elect*. (Stromwiderstandsmesser) rheostat.
Rhetor (⇂⌣) [grch.] *m* ⒹD bsd. Alt.: (Redner) rhetor(ician).
Rhetorik (-⇂⌣)[grch.]*f*⊕ rhetoric(al art).
Rhetoriker (-⇂⌣⌣) *m* ⊕ rhetorician.
rhetorisch (-⇂⌣) *a*. ⊕ rhetorical. [mus]
Rheuma (⇂⌣) [grch. Fließen] *n* ⊕ = Rheumatis=
rheumatisch (-⇂⌣) *a*. ⊕ rheumatic(al).
Rheumatismus (-⌣⌣⌣) [grch.] *m* ⊕ *path*. (Reißen der Glieder) rheumatism; am ob. an ~ leiden to suffer from rheumatism; am ~ leidend afflicted (or troubled) with rheumatism, rheumatic(al).
Rhinozeros (-⇂⌣⌣) [grch. Nashorn] *n*, *inv*. u. ⒹD ꝛo. (Nashorn) rhinoceros (auch *fig*. als Schimpfwort); **=fell** (⌣...) *n* ⊕ rhinoceroshide. [cyanate.]
Rhodan ⚗ (-⇂) [grch.] *n* ⒹD *chm*. sulpho-
Rhodan=kalium ⚗ (⌣⇂...) *n* ⊕ potassium sulphocyanate (CNKS); **=waßerstoffsäure** *f* sulphocyanic acid (CNSH).
Rhodesien ⚥ (-⇂(⌣)⌣) [Cecil Rhodes, gest. 1902] *n* ⊕ Süd=afr. Rhodesia.
Rhodi=er (⇂⌣⌣) *m* [Rhodus] ⊕, **~in** *f* ⊕ ehm. (Bewohner[in] von Rhodus) inhabitant of Rhodes, Rhodian.
rhodisch (⇂⌣) *a*. ⊕ Rhodian.
Rhodiser (⇂⌣⌣) [Rhodus] I *m* ⊕, **~in** *f* ⊕ jetzt (Bewohner[in] von Rhodus) Rhodian. — II *a*. *inv*. Rhodian; bsd. ehm. ⚷ Ritter knight of Rhodes.
Rhododendron ⚘ (⌣⌣⌣) [grch. Rosenbaum] *n* ⊕ (Alpenrose) rhododendron.
Rhodus ⚥ (⇂⌣) *npr/n*. *inv*. (jetzt türkische Insel) (Isle of) Rhodes.
rhombisch ⚗ (⇂⌣) [grch.] *a*. ⊕ rhombic.

⚶ scientific; ⚘ botanical; ⚥ geography; ⊕ machinery; ⚔ mining; ⚔ military; ↓ marine; ⚙ commercial; ✉ postal; 🚂 railway.

[Rhomboeder] — 804 — [Riechbarkeit]

Rhombo-eder ⚬ (⌣⌣⌣́⌣) [grch.] n ㉒ math. (verschobener Würfel) rhombohedron.
Rhombo-id ⚬ (⌣⌣́⌣) n ⑪c. math. (verschobenes Rechteck) rhomboid; **⌀isch** (⌣⌣́⌣) a. ⑯ (rautenförmig) rhomboid(al).
Rhombus ⚬ (́⌣⌣) [grch.] m ㉗ geom. (Raute) rhombus, a. rhomb ⟨◇⟩.
Rhythmik (́⌣⌣) [grch.] f ㊻ rhythmics.
Rhythmiker (́⌣⌣) [grch.] m ㉒ rhythmist.
rhythmisch (́⌣⌣) a. ⑯ (taktmäßig) rhythmical. [mäßige Bewegung) rhythm.
Rhythmus (́⌣⌣) [lt., *grch.] m ㉗ (taktf
Richard (́⌣⌣) npr. m ⑮ a. (a. Bn.) Richard, F Dick; f. Löwenherz.
Richt-balken ⊕ (⌣...) m ㉒ Brückenbau: traverse-beam; **=baum** m: a) = Hebebaum; b) carp. pulley-beam, beam with pulley for lifting building-material c) ⚔ artill. traversing handspike; **=beil** n executioner's (or headsman's) axe; **=blei** ⊕ n = Bleilot; **=block** m für Hinrichtungen: executioner's block.
Richte (́⌣⌣) [ahd.] f ㊽ **1.** = Richtung. — **2.** (gerader Weg) straight line; in die ~ geh(e)n to take the shortest route or cut. — **3.** (richtige Lage) right position; et. in die ~ bringen to put a th. straight or right, to right a th. — **4.** = Richtschnur.
Richt-eisen ⊕ (⌣́...) n ㉒ straightenerf
richten (́⌣⌣) [ahd.; *recht] I v/a., bisw. ohne Objekt oder v/n. (h.) u. sich ⌞ v/refl. ㊾ **1.** et. Krummes, Schiefes ⌞ oder gerade ⌞ (bsd. ⊕) to set a th.; in die Höhe ⌞ to raise (or lift) up; sich in die Höhe ⌞ to raise o.s., to rise (up); nach der Setzwage ⌞ to plumb; ⚓ die Segel nach dem Winde ⌞ to trim one's sails according to the wind (a. fig.); ⚔ richt euch! fall in!; fig. nach et. ⌞ to adjust (or accommodate) to a th.; sich (sein Verhalten) nach etwas ⌞ to conform with a th.; sich nach den Umständen ⌞ to act according to circumstances; ❋ der Preis richtet sich nach der Ware ... depends on (or is in keeping with) the goods; gram. das Prädikat richtet sich nach dem Subjekt the predicate agrees with the subject. — **2.** ⚙ carp. ein Haus ⌞ to set up the roof of a house; den Zeiger der Uhr (metonymisch: die Uhr) ⌞ to regulate the watch or clock. — **3.** (lenken, wenden) to direct (gegen etwas against a th.); feine Aufmerksamkeit auf et. ⌞ to turn (or direct) one's attention to a th.; fig. eine Bitte, einen Brief an e-n ⌞ to address ... to a p.; den Blick gegen den (ob. gen) Himmel ⌞ to cast one's eyes (up) to heaven; ein Fernrohr rc.: to level (or point) ...; eine Frage an e-n ⌞ to put a question to a p., to ask a p. a question; feine Gedanken auf etwas ⌞ to turn one's thoughts to(wards) a th., to give one's mind to a th.; ⚔ ein Geschütz ⌞ to lay (or train) a gun; seine Wut auf e-n ⌞ to direct one's fury against a p., to vent one's rage upon a p. — **4.** Präpositionelle Redensarten: sich auf et. ⌞ (gefaßt halten) to keep (o.s.) ready for a th.; das war gegen mich gerichtet that was intended for me; etwas ins Werk ⌞ to carry a th. into execution

or effect, to accomplish a th.; e-n zugrunde, zu Schaden ⌞ to ruin a p. — **5.** jur. (Urteil sprechen) (über) e-n ⌞ to pass (or pronounce) sentence on a p., to sentence a p.; bibl. richtet nicht, auf daß ihr nicht gerichtet werdet judge not, and ye shall not be judged. — **6.** = hin⌞ c. — II ~ n㉓ **7.** (f. 1) adjustment; (f. 2) regulation; (f. 5) sentencing, sentence, judgment; vgl. Richtung.
Richter (́⌣⌣) [ahd.; *richten] m ㉒, **~in** f ㊸ **1.** judge; oberster ~ supreme judge, in Engl.: Lord Chief Justice; vorsitzender ~ presiding judge; (Polizei-)~ police-magistrate; sich zum ~ aufwerfen to constitute o.s. judge; zum ~ ernannt werden to be made a judge, to be called to the Bench; Sprichw. wo kein Kläger ist, ist auch kein ~ no accuser (or no complainant), no judge. — **2.** ⊕ (f. der et. gerade richtet) straightener, adjuster.
Richter-amt (́⌣⌣..) n ㉒ judge's office, judicature. [censorious.
richterisch (́⌣⌣⌣) a. ⑯ like a judge;f
Richter-kollegium (́⌣⌣⌣́⌣⌣) n ㉒ body (or conclave) of judges, a. the Bench.
richterlich (́⌣⌣⌣) a. ⑯ of (or like a) judge, judicial; (gerichtlich) judiciary; Des Urteil sentence, judgment.
Richter-schwert (́⌣⌣...) n ㉒ sword of justice; vgl. Richtschwert; **=spruch** m judge's sentence; f. a. Bescheid 2; **=stand** m judicial calling, a. oft coll. the Bench; Am. the Judiciary; **=stuhl** m judge's seat or chair, tribunal; das gehört nicht vor seinen ~ that's not within his jurisdiction; rel. vor dem ~ des Allerhöchsten before the judgment-seat of the Almighty.
Richt-feier (́⌣...) f ㉒, **=fest** n = **=schmaus**; **=holz** n der Nadler: straightening-board.
richtig (́⌣⌣) [ahd.; *recht] a. ⑯ **1.** right, correct, (genau) exact, accurate; (geeignet) suitable; (gerecht) just, fair; (echt, wirklich) genuine, real; ein Der Engländer a true(-born) Briton, an Englishman bred and born; f. Fährte; das Le Maß halten to keep within (due) bounds; ein Des Urteil haben to have a sound judgment; das ⌞e treffen to hit upon the right thing; tue stets das ⌞e (you should) always do the correct (or proper) thing. — **2.** adv. geht Ihre Uhr ⌞? is your watch right?, does your watch keep good time?; et. ⌞ be-zahlen to pay ... in full, to discharge ... honestly; wir haben die Ware ⌞ empfangen we duly received ..., we received ... in due course; ich hatte es ⌞ vergessen ... certainly forgotten it. — **3.** (in Ordnung) in order, arranged; alles ist ⌞ all is settled, F it's all right or O. K. [aus all correct]; et. ⌞ m. to set a thing right or to rights, to adjust a th.; eine Rechnung: to pay (or clear) off. — **4.** Ausruf: ⌞! right!, that's the thing!, just so!; ganz ⌞! quite right!, quite so!; F das ist die ⌞e Sorte that's the sort or the kind!; oft vorher Gesagtes bestätigend, zB. ich sagte: „er kommt bald", und ⌞, da trat er ein!...and, behold (or lo, and behold), he stepped in!; mit Negation:

das ist nicht ⌞ that's not as it should be; das geht nicht ⌞ (adv.) zu, das geht nicht mit Den Dingen zu there is something wrong (or extraordinary) about it; es ist hier nicht ⌞ the place is haunted; es ist nicht ganz ⌞ (adv.) mit ihm, er ist nicht ganz ⌞ (im Kopfe) he is not quite right in the upper story or in his head.
Richtig-(be)finden (́⌣⌣(⌣)́⌣) n ㉒ verification; ❋ nach ~ if found correct.
Richtigkeit (́⌣⌣⌣) f ㊻ (f. richtig) rightness, correctness, exactness; accuracy; justness, fairness; truth; et. in ~ bringen to set a th. right or to rights or in order; das hat seine ~, die Sache hat ihre ~ it is quite right or true, it is a real fact.
Richtig-machung (́⌣⌣...) f ㉒ arrangement, settlement; **Qstellen** v/a. ⑱** to put (or set) right, to rectify; **=stellung** f rectification.
Richt-keil ⚔ (́⌣...) m ㉒ artill. quoin for pointing a gun; **=klotz** m = **=block**; **=korn** ⊕ n e-s Gewehres: sight, ⚔ artill. dispart-sight; **=maschine** f: a) ⊕ straightening-machine; b) ⚔ artill. contrivance used in training guns; **=maß** n standard (of measurement), gauge; **=platte** ⊕ f, metall. straightening-plate; **=platz** m place of execution; **=schacht** ⚒ m vertical shaft; **=scheit** ⊕ n (jointing-)rule, straightedge; **=schmaus** ⊕ m, carp. treat (given) to builders' workmen on setting up the roof of a new house; **=schnur** f: a) ⊕ plumb-line; b) fig. rule of conduct; e-m zur ~ dienen to serve for a p.'s guidance; **=schraube** ⚔ f, artill. elevating-screw; **=schwert** n executioner's sword; **=stätte** f = **=platz**; **=stock** ⊕ m zum Messen: yard-measure; **=stuhl** m = Richterstuhl; **=tag** m day fixed for an execution.
Richtung (́⌣⌣) [ahd.] f ㊽ **1.** = richten II. — **2.** (das Wohin) direction; (Linie, Weg) line, route, course; bent, drift (a. fig.); die ~ verlieren to lose one's bearings; ⚔ gerade ~ alinement; fig. neue ~ in der Poesie rc. new school (or line of thought) in poetry, &c.; politische ~ political opinion: radikale ~ radicalism. — **3.** mit prp.: **in** derselben Richtung weiter gehen to pursue the same course; in gerader ~ in a straight line, straight on; in entgegengesetzter ~ in the opposite direction, directly opposite; nach allen ~en in all directions; nach beiden ~en both ways, this way and that, hither and thither.
Richtungs-fahne (́⌣⌣...) f ㉒ ⚔ u. surv. zum Markieren: field-colours pl.; **=linie** f line of direction; **=winkel** ⚔ ⚓ m angle of elevation.
Richt-visier ⊕ (́⌣...) n ㉒ sight; **=wage** ⊕ f level; **=weg** m straight (or direct) route or road, short cut.
Ricke (́⌣⌣) [nhd.; * Reh] f ㊸ hunt. doe.
riech (⌣) (́⌣) impf. ind. (subj.) v. reiben.
riechbar (́⌣⌣) a. ⑯ perceptible by the smell, smellable; (wohlriechend) odor(ifer)ous; **~keit** f ㊻ etwa: distinct(ness of) odour; odor(ifer)ousness.

Zeichen (f. S. XVII): F familiär; P Volkssprache; Γ Gaunersprache; ⚹ selten; † alt (auch gestorben); * neu (auch geboren); ++ unrichtig.

[**Riechbüchse**] — 805 — [**Rikoschettfeuer**]

Riech-büchse (ᴗ-ˊ⁀ᴗ) f ⊕ scent-box.
riechen (ˊᴗ) [ahd.: Rauch] ☉c. I v/n. (h.) 1. to smell; gut (übel) ~ to have a(n un)pleasant smell or a sweet (nasty) odour; köstlich ~ to have a delicious scent; er riecht aus dem Munde his breath smells, he has a foul breath; nach Wein ꝛc. ~ to smell of ... — 2. von faulenden Stoffen: to smell (faint), P to stink, whiff, hum; ſtark 2d tainted, rank, v. toten Körpern: putrid, decomposed; v/impers. es riecht (hier) nach Talg it smells (or there is a smell) of tallow; im p.pr. bisw. mit dem adv. verſchmelzend: wohl2d odor(ifer)ous, scented. — II v/a. v/n. (h.) 3. (durch den Geruchsſinn wahrnehmen) to (perceive by the) smell, (ſchnüffeln) to sniff, (wittern) to scent; ſein ob. ſcharf ~ to have a keen scent; F fig. den Braten, die Lunte ~ to smell a rat. — 4. (vertragen) ich kann es nicht ~ I cannot endure (or bear) the smell (of it); F fig. ich kann ihn nicht ~ I cannot bear (the sight of) him; er kann das Pulver nicht ~ he is a coward. — 5. an einer Roſe ꝛc. ~ to smell (at) a ...; F fig. als berber Beſcheid: daran kann er ~! he can put it in his pipe and smoke it! — III ~ n ⊕ 6. smell(ing), odour; (Geruchsſinn) olfactory organ, ⚕ olfaction, rhinæsthesia; (Witterung) scent.
Riecher (ˊᴗ) m ⊕ 1. one who smells (or scents, sniffs out) things; feiner ~ person with a fine nose, keen-scented (or F nosy) person. — 2. F (Naſe) nose, (Geruch) smell.
Riech-eſſig (ᴗ-ˊᴗ) m ⊕ aromatic vinegar; **=fläſchchen** n scent- (or smelling-) bottle; **=holz** n scented (or fragrant) wood; **=kiſſen** n scent-bag; **=kolben** P m large red nose, bottle-nose; **=nerv** m, anat. olfactory nerve; **=organ** n = **=werkzeug**; **=ſalz** n smelling-salt(s), sal volatile (= Hirſchhornſalz); **=ſtoff** m, **=waſſer** n scent; **=werkzeug** n, anat. olfactory organ; (Naſe) nose.
Ried (ˊ) [ndd.: reed] n ☉c.: a) marsh (grown with reeds); ~ (Schilf, Rohr) reed(-grass); **~antilope** (ᴗ-ˊ...) f, **~bock** m, zo. reedbuck, rietbok (Eleotragus arundina'ceus); **~gras** ♃ n: a) (Segge) sedge (Carex); b) reed bent-grass (Calamagro'stis). [rufen.)
rief (ˊ) ind., **riefe** 1 (ˊᴗ) subj. impf. von)
Riefe 2 ⊕ (ˊᴗ) [ndd.] f ⊕ groove, channel, flute; **riefe(l)n**, **Rief(e)lung** = **reifeln**, **Reif(e)lung**, **riefig** (ˊᴗ) a. ⊕ grooved, fluted, arch. auch channelled.
Riege (ˊᴗ) [ahd.: Reihe] f ⊕ Turnerei: section, squad, division; Fußball: team.
Riegel (ˊᴗ) [ahd.: Ragel; * lt. rē'gula f] m ⊕ 1. ⊕ Schloſſerei: bolt, weit S. fastening, am Türſchloß: key-bolt; ~ mit Feder spring- (or catch-)bolt; den ~ vorſchieben to shoot (or put up) the bolt; hinter Schloß und ~ under lock and key, (safely) locked up; fig. e-m (e-r Sache) e-n ~ vorſchieben to put an obstacle in a p.'s way (a stop to a th.). — 2. ~ (langes recht-eckiges Stück) Seife bar of soap. — 3. = **Kleiderriegel**. — 4. ⊕ Glasfabr.: (Roſt) sleeper;

carp. (Querſtab) crossbar, rail, am Streichmaß: stem; **arch.** (Quer-)transom; **mach.** ~ am Balancier der Dampfmaſch.: spring-beam.
Riegel-bohrer ⊕ (ˊᴗ...) m ⊕ bar-wimble; **=feder** f bolt-spring; **=feſt** a. ⊕ bolted (and barred); **=holz** ⊕ n, carp. cross-bar.
riegeln (ˊᴗ) v/a. ☉a. = verriegeln.
Riegel-ſchloß ⊕ (ˊᴗ...) n ⊕ Schloſſerei: stock-lock, lock without spring; **=ſtück** n, carp. framing-piece, -timber; **=wand** f = **Fachwand**; **=werk** n = **Fachwerk**.
Riegen-turnen (ˊᴗ-ˊᴗ) n ⊕ an Geräten: gymnastic exercises pl. (carried out) in sections or squads.
Riem (ˊ) m ☉c. = **Riemen** 1.
Riemen 1 ⊕ (ˊᴗ) [ahd.] m ⊕ (leather) strap, ſtärker: thong; zum Zuſchnüren der Schuhe: boot-lace, bibl., &c. latchet; zum Zſ.-ſchnüren von Akten ꝛc.: tape; mit ~en binden, peitſchen to strap, to lash; Sprichw. aus anderer Leute Haut iſt gut ~ ſchneiden it's easy to pay with other people's money.
Riemen 2 ↓ (ˊᴗ) [lt. rē'mus] m ⊕ (Ruder) oar, zum Wriken: scull; die ~ klar machen to ship the oars; die ~ platt werfen to feather; die ~ auf! up oars!
Riemen-blume ♃ (ˊᴗ...) f loranth (Lora'nthus europæ'us); **=halter** m strap-clamp; **=leiter** m strap-guide; **=leitung** f belt-gearing, belting; **=pferd** n, man. leader; **=ſcheibe** f strap-wheel, rigger, der Nähmaſchine: strap-disk; **=ſchneider** m = **Riemer**; **=tang** ♃ m sea-tangle (Lamina'ria sacchari'na); **=welle** f strap-rod; **=werk** n leather straps pl.; (Sattelzeug) harness(ing); **=wurm** m, zo. strap-worm (Li'gula).
Riemer ⊕ (ˊᴗ) m ⊕ strap- (or harness-, belt-)maker, leather-cutter; **~arbeit** f (a. **~ei** (-ᴗˊ) f) ⊕ harness-making.
Riem-pferd, -ſchneider, -werk f. **Riemen-...**
Ries ⊕ (ˊ) [mhd.: it. (*ar. Bündel) risma f] n ☉a.: ~ (20 Buch) Papier ream of paper.
Rieſe 1 (ˊᴗ; Hom. Riſe) [ahd.] m ⊕: a) v. Perſonen: ~, **Rieſin** ⊕ f giant(ess f), F co. a.: son of Anak, Goliath; als Menſchenfreſſer(in), in Märchen: ogre(ss f); b) weit S. a. v. Sachen: (et. übergroßes) monster, colossus, v. Menſchen u. Sachen: F whacker.
Rieſe 2 (ˊᴗ) Ryſe, Verfaſſer eines Rechenbuches, 1523 npr/m. ⊕a. co. nach Adam ~ according to Cocker. [for timber.)
Rieſe 3 ⊕ (ˊᴗ) f ⊕ (Holzrutſchbahn) slide)
Rieſel 1 (ˊᴗ) [ahd.] m ⊕ purl, ripple.
Rieſel 2 **-feld** (ˊᴗ-ˊ) [rieſeln] n ⊕ irrigated (or irrigational) field.
rieſeln (ˊᴗ) [mhd.: *reiſen] I v/n. (h. u. ſn) ☉a. 1. (ſanft rinnen) to purl, gurgle. — 2. v/imp. es rieſelt (regnet fein) it drizzles. — II ~ n 3. = **Geriesel**. [(fine) rain.)
Rieſel-regen (ˊᴗ-ˊᴗ) m ⊕ drizzling)
Rieſ(e)lung (ˊᴗ) f ⊕ irrigation.
Rieſel 2 **-wieſe** (ˊᴗ-ˊᴗ) f ⊕ irrigated meadow or pasture-land.
Rieſen-ameiſe (ˊᴗ...) [Rieſe 1] f ⊕ ent. great black ant; **=arbeit** f gigantic (or herculean) task, F tremendous (piece of) work; **=artig** a. ⊕ giant-like; vgl. **=groß**; **=bau** m gigantic structure or building, auch oft: noble pile; **=farn** m, geol. foſſiler: ⚕ megaphyton; **=faultier** n, geol.: ⚕ megatherium;

megalonyx; **=förmig** a. gigantic, of enormous shape; **=gebirge** ♀ npr/n. zwiſchen Böhmen und Schleſien: Riesengebirge; **=geiſt** m mighty (or powerful) intellect; **=geſchlecht** n race of giants; **=geſtalt** f gigantic (or enormous) figure or form or shape; colossus; **=groß** a. of gigantic stature or size, gigantic; **=größe** f gigantic stature or size.
rieſenhaft (ˊᴗᴗ) a. ⊕ = **rieſig** a; **~igkeit** f ⊕ gigantic (or colossal, enormous, stupendous) size or proportions p¹.
Rieſen-hai (ˊᴗ...) m ⊕ ichth. basking shark (Se'lache ma'xima); **=hirſch** m geol. foſſiler: ⚕ megaceros; **=kampf** m bſd. myth. battle of giants; **=kraft** f gigantic (or Herculean) strength; **=mäßig** a. ⊕ = **=artig**; **=ſchlange** f, zo.: a) python; b) boa constrictor; **=ſchritt** m giant-stride, giant's step; mit ~en at a rapid (or F tremendous) pace; **=ſchwung** m Turnerei: giant-swing; **=ſtark** a. of gigantic (or herculean) strength; **=ſtärke** f = **=kraft**; **=tier** n huge beast; **=werk** n = **=arbeit**.
rieſig (ˊᴗ) [Rieſe 1] a. ⊕: a) gigantic, colossal, enormous; b) mſt F fig. (ganz ungeheuer) immense, prodigious; Der Fehlgriff, Irrtum stupendous mistake; ~ (adv.) dumm extremely (F awfully) stupid; **~keit** f ⊕ ✻ = **Rieſenhaftigkeit**.
Rieſin (ˊᴗ) f ⊕ f. **Rieſe** 1.
Riesling (ˊᴗ) m ⊕d. Traubenſorte: riesling.
Rieſter ⊕ (ˊᴗ) [nhd.] m (n) ⊕ Schuhmacherei: (aufgeſetzter Flicken) patch.
rieſtern (ˊᴗ) v/a. ☉a. to patch, mend.
ries-weiſe (ˊᴗ-ˊᴗ) adv. in reams.
Riet 1 ꝛc. f. **Ried** ꝛc.
riet 2 (ˊ) ind., **~e** (ˊᴗ) subj. impf. v. **raten**.
Riff ↓ (ˊ) [ndd.: reef] n ⊕b.: (Felſen-)reef, (Sandbank) sandbank, sands pl.
Riff-auſter (ˊ...) f ⊕ zo. reefer; **=bildner** m, zo. (Korallentier) reef-builder.
Riffel 1 (ˊᴗ) [mhd.: Raffel] I ⊕ f ⊕ Spinnerei: zum Abſtreichen der Knöpfe vom Flachſe) ripple. — II F m ⊕ = **Rüffel**.
Riffel 2 **-kamm** (ˊᴗ...) [riffeln] m ⊕ = **Riffel** I; **=maſchine** f fluting-machine.
riffeln (ˊᴗ) [: ripple] v/a. ☉a. 1. ⊕ den Flachs: to ripple. — 2. F fig. = rüffeln. [fluted roller.)
Riffel 2 **-walze** (ˊᴗ-ˊᴗ) f ⊕ Spinnerei:)
Riff-piraten (ˊᴗ-ᴗˊᴗ) [ar. rif Küſtenſtrich] m/pl. in Marokko Riff(ian) Arabs or Pirates pl. [railway or line.)
Rigi-bahn (ˊᴗᴗ) f ⊕ Schweiz: Rigi)
Rigole ⊕ (ᴗˊᴗ) [fr.] f ⊕ agr. (tiefe Furche) deep furrow, trench; (Abzugskanal) culvert, **rigolen** v/a. ⊕ to trench-plough, **Rigol-pflug** m trench-plough.
Rigorismus ⚕ (ᴗˊᴗᴗ) [lt.] m ⊕ (Sittenſtrenge) rigorism; **Rigoriſt** (ᴗᴗˊ) m ⊕ (ant. Latitudinarier) rigorist; **rigoriſtiſch** (ᴗᴗˊᴗ) a. ⊕ rigorist(ic).
rigoros, rigorös (ᴗᴗˊ) [lt.] a. ⊕ (D 10) (ſtreng) rigorous, strict.
Rigoroſum (ᴗᴗˊᴗ) [lt.] n ⊕ ⊕ rigorous examination (or severe test) of candidates for a doctor's degree.
Rikchen (ˊᴗ) n ☉a., **Rike** (ˊᴗ) [(Friede)rike] f ⊕ ⊕. F npr/f. (Vn.) Frederica.
Rikoſchett ⚔ (ᴗᴗˊ) [fr. ricochet] m ⊕ (Prell-ſchuß) ricochet (shot); **~feuer** (ᴗᴗˊ-ˊᴗ) n ⊕ ricochet fire.

[**rikoschettieren**] — 806 — [**Rippenfleisch**]

rikoschettieren ⚔ (‿‿‿́‿) [+.+.fr. *ricocher*] v/n.(h.)⑱ (abprallen) to ricochet, rebound.
Rikoschett=schuß ⚔ (‿‿́‿,‿) m ⑫ ricochet (or rebounding) shot.
Rille (‿́‿) [nhd.: T rill] f ㊽ ⊕ groove, die ~n und Risse im Boden ꝛc. the furrows and cracks. [**riefe**(l)**n**.]
rillen (‿́‿) v/a. ㊳ to groove (vgl. **Riefe**¹,)
rillig (‿́‿) a. ㊺ marked with grooves, fluted, ⚹ sulcate.
Rimesse ⓞ (‿‿́‿) [it.] f ㊽ (Geldsendung) remittance; ~n machen to make remittances, to provide funds; ~=buch (‿‿́‿‿‿́) n ㉒ book of remittances.
Rind (‿́) [ahd.] n ⓸b. zo. neat, engS. a. ox, cow (*Bos*); weitS. head of cattle; ~er pl. horned cattle; bovine race.
Rinde (‿́‿) [ahd.: rind: Rand] f ㊽: (Baum=)~ bark; ~ (*ant*. Krume) des Brotes, e-r Pastete ꝛc.: crust, am Käse ꝛc.: rind.
rinden (‿́‿) a. ㊻ (made) of bark.
rinden=artig (‿́‿...) a. ㊻ bark-like, ⚹ cortical, corticose; =**dach** n ㉒ roof made of bark; =**koralle** f, zo. fan-coral, ⚹ corticifer.
Rinder=braten (‿́‿...) [Rind pl.] m ⑫ roast beef; =**bremse** f, ent. gadfly (*Taba'nus*); =**brust** f Kocht.: brisket of beef; =**herde** f herd (or drove) of cattle; =**hirt** m neat-herd, cow-keeper, bsd. Am. cow-boy; =**pest** f, =**seuche** f, vet. cattle-plague, pleuro-pneumonia in cattle, in Süd-afrika: T rinderpest; =**pökel=fleisch** n corned beef; =**talg** m beef-suet; =**zunge** f = Rindszunge. [boiled beef.]
Rind=fleisch (‿́‿‿) n ⑫ beef, ausgekochtes:)
rindig (‿́‿) [Rinde] a. ㊻ covered with a bark, crusty, crusted, ⚹ corticose.
Rind=leder, =ledern = Rinds=...
Rinds=blase (‿́‿...) [Rind gen.] f ⑫ bullock's bladder; =**keule** f shin (vom Hinterteile: round) of beef; =**leder** n cow-hide, neat's leather; ⒵**ledern** a. ㊻ (made) of neat's leather; =**talg** = Rindertalg.
Rinds=stück (‿́‿...) n ㉒ ⊕ beefsteak. [tongue.]
Rinds=zunge (‿́‿‿) f ㊽ ox-, neat's)
Rind=vieh (‿́‿) n ⑫: a) horned (or neat, black) cattle; b) P Schimpfw. blockhead.
Ring¹ (‿́) [ahd.: ring] m ⓪b. 1. ring (am Finger on one's finger), von Draht, a. coil; kleiner ~ (a. **Ringel** m (n) ㉒, **Ringelchen, Ringlein** n ㉓) ringlet, little circle, circlet, annulet; goldene ~e in den Ohren golden ear-rings pl.; arch. ~ um eine Säule: ⚹ astragal; orn. ~ um den Hals e-r Taube: ruff; ent. ~e am Bauch der Insekten: segments pl. — 2. (Kreis) circle, round; f. Jahresring, (dunkle) ~e um die Augen haben to have dark rings under (or round) the eyes, to look dark round the eyes; anat. ~ um die Brustwarzen: ⚹ areola, corona; Meteorologie: ~ um Gestirne: T halo; ast. ~e des Saturn rings pl. of Saturn. — 3. ⊕ ~ (Glied) e-r Kette link of a chain; (Zwinge) ferrule; (Dreh=)~ swivel. — 4. (Kreis von Personen): a) circle, b.s. clique; b) T [engl.] ⊖ ring (a. **** ring), trust, syndicate, pool.
Ring²...(‿́) [ringen²] f. Ringkampf ꝛc.
Ring³=**amsel** (‿́‿‿) f orn. ring-ousel (*Turdus torqua'tus*); ⓶**artig** a. ㊻ r.-like, annular; =**bahn** f ⧫ circular railway;

Züge e-r ~ circle-trains pl.; =**bein** n, vet. der Pferde: ring-bone.
Ringel (‿́‿) [nhd.] m (n) ② f. Ring¹ 1; Weberei: mail; (Löckchen) ringlet; ~=**blume** (‿‿́‿) ⚘ f ㉑ marigold (*Calendula*).
Ringelchen (‿́‿‿) n ㉓ f. Ring¹ 1.
Ringel=gans (‿́‿...) f orn. brent-goose (*Ber'nicla brenta*); =**gedicht** n rondeau, roundelay; =**haar** n hair in ringlets, curled hair.
ring(e)licht, ...ig (‿́‿)(‿) a. ㊻ like a ring or ringlet or curl; (sich ringelnd) curling, coiling; (ring=artig) annular.
Ringel=locke (‿́‿...) f ㉑ ringlet, curl.
ringeln (‿́‿) [ahd.] ㉒ a. I v/a. 1. (in Ringel legen) to curl; geringelt curled, in ringlets. — 2. to provide with a ring or with rings. — 3. Bäume ~ (damit sie absterben) Am. to girdle ... — II v/n. (h. u. sn) u. sich ~ v/refl. 4. to curl, to coil, von Rauch ꝛc.: to wreathe, sich schlängelnd: to wind, to meander, spiral=förmig: to form (into) a spiral.
Ringel=natter (‿́‿...) f ㊿ zo. ring-snake (*Tropidono'tus natrix*); =**reigen, =reihen** m dancing in a ring; =**reim** m = =gedicht; (Wiederholungsreim) burden of a song; =**rennen** n, =**stechen** n tilting at the ring; =**stück** ♪ n rondo; =**tanz** m circular dance, dancing in a ring; =**taube** f, orn. ring-dove, cushat, wood-pigeon (*Palum'bus torqua'tus*); =**wurm** m, zo. ringed worm; =**würmer** pl.: ⚹ annelids, ...ides, ...idæ, ...id(i)ans.
ringen¹ (‿́‿) [ahd.; *Ring] v/n. (h.) ㊸ (Ringe bilden) to form rings.
ringen² (‿́‿) [ahd.: (w)ring] ⓪ft I v/a. u. sich ~ v/refl. 1. (windend drehen) to twist; die Hände ~ to wring one's hands; e-m eine Pistole aus der Hand ~ to wrest (or wrench) ... from a p.'s hand. — II v/n. (h.), v/a. u. sich ~ v/refl. 2. (sich gegenseitig niederzuwerfen suchen) to wrestle with a p., to try a fall with a p.; e-n zu Boden (ob. nieder) ~ to throw a p. in wrestling; mit et. ~ to struggle (or grapple) with a th.; mit dem Tode ~ to be in the grip (or the throes) of death or in one's last agony. — 3. (sich mühen) nach et. ~ to strive for (or after) a th.; mit e-m und et. ~ to contend with a p. for a th. — III ~ n ㉓ 4. (f. 1) twisting, &c.; (f. 2) wrestling(-match); (Kampf) struggle, contest, mit dem Tode: (last) agony. [weitS. athlete.]
Ringer (‿́‿) [ringen²] m ② wrestler,)
Ring¹=**faser** (‿́‿...) f ㊽ annular marking; =**finger** m ring-finger; ⓶**förmig** a. ㊻ ring-shaped, annular; ⚹ orbicular, anat. cricoid, armillary; vgl. ⒵**artig**, =**förmigkeit** f annularity; =**gefäß** ⚘ n annular duct; =**gewölbe** n, arch. ann. vault; =**haken** m ring-hook; =⒵**kampf** [ringen²] m wrestling-match; =**kämpfer** m wrestler; =**kanal** m ⚘ u. zo. der Stachelhäuter u. Pflanzentiere: ring-canal; =**kästchen** n, =**kasten** m ring-(weitS. jewel-)case; =**knorpel** m, anat. des Kehlkopfes: annular (or cricoid) cartilage; =**kolben** ⊖ m annular piston; =**kragen** m, ehm. gorget; =²**kunst** f art of wrestling, Alt.: palæstric art.
Ringlein (‿́‿) n ㉓ dim. v. Ring¹, f. bf 1.
ringlicht, ...ig (‿́‿) a. f. ringelicht, ...ig.

Ring¹=**mauer** (‿́‿...) f ㉑ wall enclosing (or encircling) a town; =**ofen** ⊖ m annular kiln or furnace; ehm. =**panzer** m ring-mail; =²**platz** m wrestling-ground; =¹**reiten**, =**rennen** n tilting (or riding) at the ring.
rings (‿́) [Ring¹] adv.: ~, ~her(um), ~um(her) round about, right round, all around, in a circle; (überall) everywhere; (von allen Seiten) on all sides, from every quarter.
Ring¹=**schraube** ⊖ (‿́‿...) f ㉑ ring-screw; =²**schule** f Alt.: palæstra.
rings=herum (‿‿́‿) f. rings.
Ring¹=**spindelbank** ⊖ (‿́‿...) f ㉑ ring-frame; =**stopper** ⚓ m für die Ankerkette: r.-stopper; =**straße** f circular road.
rings=um(=her) (‿́‿(‿́)) f. rings.
Ring¹=**wechsel** (‿́‿...) m ⑫ bei Trauungen ꝛc.: exchange of rings; ⒵**weise** adv. in a circle or round; =**zylinder** = =kolben.
Rinke (‿́‿) [ahd.] f ㊽, ~n m ㉓ (Schnalle, Spange) buckle, metal ring or hoop.
Rinne (‿́‿) f ㊽ 1. (Leitungsröhre) conduit, pipe; (Wasserabzug) gully, sewer; f. Dachrinne. — 2. (Furche) groove, channel. — 3. ⊕. a) arch. (Schaft=)~ an Säulen: flutes pl.; b) Büchsenmacherei: ~ für den Gewehrlauf: rifle; c) Gießerei: ~ zum Gießen casting gutter.
rinnen¹ (‿́‿)[ahd.: run: rennen]I v/n.(sn,) h.) ㊹ ⓑ(a). 1. to flow, run; (strömen) to gush, rush; (tröpfeln) to trickle, drip; von der Stirne heiß ~ muß der Schweiß (*SCH*.) the hot brow be wet with honest sweat. — 2. (h.) (lecken) to leak. — II ~ n ㉓ 3. flow(ing); (Lecken) leakage.
Rinnen²=**eisen** ⊖ (‿́‿...) [Rinne] n ⑫ channel-iron; ⓶**förmig** a. ㊻ in (the) form of a channel, ⚹: ⚹ canaliculate(d); =**pflug** ⊖ m draining-plough; =**schiene** f, Am. trough-rail.
rinnig (‿́‿) a. ㊻ running. [cyma.]
Rinn=leiste ⊖ (‿́‿‿) f arch. (straight))
Rinnsal (‿́‿) [rinnen¹] n ⓪d. water-course, rill; (Mühlbach) mill-stream; (Flußbett) river-bed.
Rinn=stein (‿́‿) m ⑫: a) in der Straße: gutter, ehm.: kennel; b) in der Küche: sink; c) arch. culvert, drain-pipe; sewer; =**stein=kehrer** m sewerman.
Rippchen (‿́‿) n ㉓ (dim. v. Rippe) small rib; Kochkunst: cutlet, chop.
Rippe (‿́‿) [ahd.: rib] f ㊽ 1. rib, anat., &c.: ⚹ costa; wahre (falsche) true (false or floating) rib: e-m (ob. alle) ~n im Leibe entzweischlagen to break every bin in a p.'s body; ⚹ den ~n gehörig: ⚹ costal; zwischen (unter) den ~n befindlich: ⚹ inter-costal (subcostal). — 2. ⚘ rib, nerve of a leaf, &c.; arch. ~ eines Gewölbes: groin, nervure; (Spante) frame; ⚓ die ~n e-s Schiffes the frame- (or timber-) work of the (ship's) hulk.
rippen¹ (‿́‿) I v/a. ㊳ to rib. — II ge=**rippt** p.p. u. a. ㊻ f. bs u. vgl. Rips¹; ⊖ arch. ꝛc Decke groined ceiling.
Rippen²=**braten** (‿́‿...) [Rippe] m ⑫ roast ribs pl. or fore-quarter; =**bruch** m, surg. fracture of a rib or of ribs; =**farn** m moon-fern (*Botrychium Luna'ria*); =**fell** n, anat.: pleura; =**fell=entzündung** f, path.: ⚹ pleurisy; =**fleisch**

Signs (see page XVII): F familiar; P vulgar; F flash; ⚔ rare; † obsolete (died); * new word (born); +.+ incorrect; ♪ music;

Schlächterei: meat on the ribs; =gegend f. anat.: ⚕ costal region; =schmerz m =weh; =speer m Kocht.: roast ribs pl. of pork; =stoß m nudge, F dig (or poke) in the ribs; =stück n Schlächterei: piece of the ribs; =weh n, path. pain in the ribs or sides, ⚕ pleuralgia.
Rippe=speer (ˊˇˇˊ) = Rippenspeer.
rippig (ˊˇ) [Rippe] a. ⊕ ribbed; in Zssgn: vier2 ꝛc. [velvet.]
Ripp=sam(me)t ⊕ (ˊˇˊ(ˇ)) m ⊕ ribbed
Rips¹ (ˊ) [fr. reps(sg.); *engl. reps pl.] m ⓐ. (geripptes Baumwollenzeug) rep.
Rips²! (ˊ) int. 2!, raps! snip-snap.
ripuarisch (ˇˇˊˇ)[lt.Ufer:] a.⊕ Ripuarian.
Risalit ⊕ (ˇˇˊ) [it.] m ⓒ. arch. (Vorsprung) projection.
risch (ˊ) a. ⊕ quick, swift. [long veil.]
Rise (ˊˇ; Hom. Riese) f ⊕ (langer Schleier)
Risiko (ˊˇˇ)[nhd.17.sae.;*it.ri'schio m] f ⓐ(a.inv.)(Wagnis) risk, venture, ⚓ auch: adventure; (Gefahr) peril; auf eigenes ~ at one's own risk or peril (a. ⚓).
riskant (ˇˊ) [+ˊfr.] a. ⊕ risky, venturesome, perilous, hazardous.
riskieren (ˇˊˇ)[fr. risquer] v/a. ⊕ (wagen) to risk, venture, hazard, jeopardize.
Rispe ⚘ (ˊˇ) [ahd.] f ⊕ Art Blütenstand: panicle; ⚘n=förmig ⚘ (ˊˇ...) a. ⊕ panicled, paniculate(d); ~n=gras n ⊕ meadow-grass (Poa).
riß (ˊ) impf. ind. von reißen.
Riß² (ˊ) [ahd.: writ; *riß¹] m ⓐa. 1. (das Entzweireißen) rending, tearing; e-n ~ in et. m. to rend (or tear) a th. — 2. (Lücke) gap; (gerissenes Loch) rent, tear, hole; torn part; (Spalt) chink, crevice, fissure, in e-r Mauer: breach; (Sprung) crack, flaw, (Schlitz) slit; fig. (Spaltung) split, disunion, auch: rift in the lute, eccl. schism; Risse bekommen to tear; vgl. reißen 10. — 3. fig. in (ob. vor) den ~ (eigentl.: Wallbruch) treten to step into the breach, to fill (up) the gap; sein Tod hat einen großen ~ gemacht ... has left a great blank. — 4. F bsd. im pl. Risse (Hiebe) blows pl.; Risse bekommen to get a (good) thrashing or hiding. — 5. (entworfene Zeichnung) draft, drawing, sketch, design; vgl. Bauriß.
risse (ˊˇ) impf. subj. von reißen.
rissig (ˊˇ) [Riß] a. ⊕ full of rents or holes or chinks or flaws, cracked, split; ⚘: ⚕ rimose;2 werden = reißen 10.
Rist (ˊ) [mhd.: wrist] m (n) ⓐa.: a) back of the hand; (Handgelenk) wrist; b) (Spann d. Fußes) instep.
Ritornell ♪ (ˇˇˊ)[it.m] n ⓓ.(Begleitung e-r Arie durch ein Orchester) ritornello.
Ritratte ⚓ (ˇˊˇ) [it.] f ⊕ (Rückwechsel) redraft, re-exchange.
ritsch (ˊ, ˊ) int. ⊕, ratsch!, etwa: slap, bang!; slish, slash!; crash!
ritt¹ (ˊ) ind. impf. v. reiten.
Ritt² (ˊ) [mhd.; *ritt¹] m ⓒ. 1. ride (on horseback; kurzer, schneller ~ short gallop, sprint; einen ~ machen to take a ride, to go out on horseback. — 2. fig. in einem ~e with one (mighty) effort or pull, F at one go.
ritte (ˊˇ) subj. impf. v. reiten.
Ritter (ˊˇ) [ndd. = Reiter] m ⊕ 1. knight, weitS. cavalier; fahrender

ob. irrender ~ knight-errant; der ~ von der traurigen Gestalt (Don Quichotte) the knight of the rueful (or sorrowful) countenance; e-n zum ~ schlagen to dub (or make, create) a p. a knight, jetzt in Engl.: to knight a p.; co. ~ von der Elle knight of the thimble, Snip; ~ von der Feder knight of the pen. — 2. fig. zum ~ werden (obsiegen) to carry the victory; an e-m zum ~ werden to win one's spurs by vanquishing a p. — 3. Kocht.: s. Armeritter.
Ritter=akademie (ˊˇ...) f ⊕ boarding-school for sons of the aristocracy; =alter n = =zeit; =brauch m knightly (or chivalrous) usage; =burg f knight's castle; ⚘bürtig a. ⊕ of knightly birth or descent; =dienst m: a) knight-service; b) chivalrous wooing; =fahrt f ⊕ knightly expedition; =geist m spirit of chivalry; =geschichte f history of chivalry; =gut n (ant. Bauerngut) baronical land or property, manor(ial estate); =guts=besitzer m owner of a manorial estate, lord of the manor; =haus n knightly (or noble) house; =hof m knightly residence; vgl. =gut; ehm. =lehen n land held by knight-service, knight's fee; vgl. =gut.
ritterlich (ˊˇˇ) [Ritter] a. ⊕ knightly; (e-m Ritter gemäß) chivalrous, chivalric; ga'llant; (mutig) valiant, brave; ~keit (ˊˇˇ-) f ⊕ chivalrousness, chivalry; gallantry, valour.
ritter=mäßig (ˊˇ...) a. ⊕ knight-like, chivalrous, weitS. of noble bearing; =orden m ⊕ order of knighthood; f. deutsch; =pflicht f knight's (or cavalier's) duty; =roman m novel dealing with (the age of) chivalry; =saal m hall of the knights.
Ritterschaft (ˊˇˇ) f ⊕ knighthood, chivalry; coll. (body of knights pl., jetzt auch weitS. baronetcy, gentry; (Adel) nobility; bibl. (LU.) military service; ⚘lich (ˊˇˇˇ) a. ⊕ appertaining to knighthood, relating to the (whole body of) knights.
Ritter=schlag (ˊˇ...) m ⊕ dubbing, knighting; den ~ empfangen to be (-come) knighted; =schloß n = =burg; =sinn m chivalrous spirit; =sitte f knightly (or courteous) manners pl.; vgl. =brauch; =sitz m = =gut.
Ritters=mann (ˊˇˇ) m ⊕ knight.
Ritter=spiel (ˊˇ...) n ⊕ tournament, tilting; =sporn m: a) knight's spur; b) ⚘ larkspur (Delphi'nium); =stand m: a) röm.Alt.: equestrian order; b) Mittelalter: knighthood, jetzt auch: gentry; =tracht f knight's garb or armour.
Rittertum (ˊˇˇ) n ⊕d. knighthood, (system of) chivalry (vgl. Ritterschaft).
Ritter=wesen (ˊˇ...) n ⊕ chivalry; =würde f dignity of a knight, knightly rank; =zeit f age of chivalry, chivalric age or times pl.; =zug m knightly expedition.
rittlings (ˊˇˇ) adv. astride, astraddle.
Ritt=meister ⚔ (ˊˇˊˇ) m ⊕ cavalry-captain, captain of horse; ~ werden to be promoted to captain (of horse), auch F: to get one's troop. [ritual.]
Ritual (ˇˇˊ) [it.] n ⓓ. (Kirchen-ordnung)

Ritualismus (ˇˇˊˇˇ) [it.] m ⓖ ritualism.
Ritualist (ˇˇˊˇ) [it.] m ⓖ ritualist.
rituell (ˇˇˊ) [fr. rituel] a. ⊕ relating to rites (and ceremonies), ceremonial.
Ritus (ˊˇ) [it.] m ⓖ ob. inv. (kirchlicher Brauch) rite, form of worship.
Ritz (ˊ) [mhd.: *ritzen] m ⓐa., ~e (ˊˇ) f ⊕ 1. cleft, fissure, rift, cranny, e-r Gasröhre ꝛc.: flaw, crack (vgl. Schlitz). — 2. (Schramme) scratch, slight cut or wound, ⚕ excoriation; (Sprung in der Haut) chap.
ritzen (ˊˇ) [ahd.: reißen] I v/a. u. sich ⚓ v/refl. ⊕ to crack, (schlitzen) to slit, (kratzen) to scratch; (abschürfen) to graze, ⚕ to excoriate; sich (an der Haut) ⚓ to scratch (or graze) o.s. or one's skin. — II ~ n ⓖ = Ritzung.
ritzig (ˊˇ) a. ⊕ full of crannies or cracks or scratches, flawed, cracked.
Ritzung (ˊˇ) f ⊕ scratching; vgl. Ritz.
Rival (ˇˊ) [fr.] m ⓓ.⊕, ~e m ⊕ (Nebenbuhler) rival.
rivalisieren (ˇˇˇˊˇ) [fr. rivaliser] v/n. (h.) ⊕ (wett=eifern) to rival, to enter into rivalry, to compete (mit e-m with a p.).
Rivalität (ˇˇˇˊ) [fr.=it.] f ⊕ (Nebenbuhlerschaft, Wettbewerb) rivalry, competition.
Rizinus ⚘ (ˊˇˇ) [it. ri'cinus; ++ a. aus grch. (*äg.) kiki] m, inv. castor-oil plant (Ri'cinus commu'nis); ~öl ⚘ n ⊕ castor-oil; ~pflanze f = Rizinus.
rm abbr. = Raummeter.
Roastbeef ⚓ (rō̆st-, ṗ mst röst-bī̆f) [engl.] n ⓖ (Rostbraten) roast beef.
Robbe (ˊˇ) [ndd.] f ⊕ zo. seal, a. sea-calf (Phoca, bsd. Phoca vituli'na).
Robben=fang (ˊˇ...) m ⊕ seal-hunting or -fishery, sealing, sealery; =fänger m sealer, ⚓ sealing-vessel; =fell n sealskin; =jagd f = =fang; =schläger m seal-killer or -hunter; =speck m seal-blubber; =tran ⚓ m seal-oil.
Robber ⚓ (ˊˇ) [engl.] m ⊕ Whistspiel: (Doppelpartie) rubber.
Robe (ˊˇ) [fr.] f ⊕ lady's gown, robe.
Robert (ˊˇ) [fr. =dtsch Rupert] npr/m. ⓐα. (Vn.) Robert, F Bob(bie).
Robot (ˊˇ) [slaw. rabo'ta: Arbeit] f ⊕, m ⓒ. (Frondienst) (fr.) corvée.
robust (ˇˊ) [lt. eichen] a. ⊕ (stark, stämmig) robust, F strapping, whacking.
roch (ˊch) impf. ind. von riechen.
Roche¹ (ˊˇch) m ⊕ = Rochen¹.
Roche² (ˊˇch, a. ˊsch)[mhd., it., *ar.pers.] m ⊕ Schachspiel: (Turm) castle, rook.
röcheln (ˊˇ) impf. subj. von riechen.
röcheln (ˊˇ) [lautm.] I v/n. (h.) ⊕a. to rattle or to have the rattles) in one's throat. — II ~ n ⓖ (death-)rattles pl.
Rochen¹ (ˊˇ)[ndd.] m ⊕ ichth. ray(Raja); elektrischer ~ electric ray (Torpe'do).
rochen² (ˊˇ) [Roche²], mst rochieren (ˇˊˇ) [++fr.roquer] v/n. (h.) ⊕ Schach: to castle.
Rock (ˊ) [ahd.] m ⓞb. 1. für Männer: coat (s. Leib=, Über=rock), den bunten ~ anziehen (v. Soldaten) to don the King's colours, to enlist; f. ausklopfen. — 2. ~ des (Frauen=)Kleides (ant. Taille) skirt.
Röckchen (ˊˇˇ) n ⓖ (dim. v. Rock) little (or child's) coat or frock.
Rocken ⊕ (ˊˇ) [ahd.] m ⓖ (Spinn2) distaff.
Rocken=bolle ⚘ (ˊˇˇˇˇ) f ⊕ (Graslauch) rocambole (A'llium scorodo'prasum).

⚕ scientific; ⚘ botanical; ⚱ geography; ⊕ machinery; ⚒ mining; ⚔ military; ⚓ marine; ⚓ commercial; ⚓ postal; 🚂 railway.

[Rockfalte] — 808 — [rollen]

Rock-falte (⁵...) f ⓖ fold in a coat; plait (or pleat) of a dress; **-futter** n lining of a coat or skirt; **-kragen** m collar of a coat; **-schoß** m coat-tail; am Frauenrock: front (part) of a skirt; fig. der Mutter am ~ hängen to be tied to one's mother's apron-strings; **-tasche** f coat-pocket; **-zipfel** m lappet of a coat.
Rode-hacke ⊙ (ᵘ...) [roden] f ⓖ agr. grubbing-hoe, mattock; **-land** n (newly) cleared land, (as)sart.
roden ⊙ (ᴸ˘) [md., ndd. = reuten] I v/a. u. v/n. (h.) ⓢ agr. to clear land. — II ~ n ⓒ u. **Rodung** f ⓕ clearance of land.
Rogate (ᵛᴸ˘) [lt. bittet!] m. ecel. (5. Sonntag nach Ostern) Rogation Sunday.
Rogen (ᴸ˘) [ahd.: roe] m ⓒ (ant. Milch) spawn, (hard) roe. [= Rogenfisch.]
Rog(e)ner (ᴸ(˘)˘) m ⓒ (ant. Milchner).
Rogen-fisch (ᴸ˘) m ⓒ ichth. spawner; **-stein** m, min. roe-stone, ⊕ oolite.
Roggen ♃ (˘˘) [ndd.: rye] m ⓒ agr. rye (Seca'le cerea'le).
Roggen-brot (˘˘...) n ⓖ rye-bread; **-fliege** f, ent. rye-worm (O'scinis pumi'lio'nis); **-korn-brand** ♃ m ustilago (Ustila'go seca'lis); **-land** n rye-land; **-mehl** n rye-flour; **-stroh** n rye-straw, zum Dachdecken: thatch.
Rogner (ᴸ˘) f. Rogener.
roh (ᴸ) [ahd.: raw] a. ⓖ 1. raw (cotton, egg, flesh); ²es (unbroschiertes) Buch book in loose sheets; ²er Diamant rough diamond; ²es Erz crude ore; ²es Fell undressed (or untanned) hide or skin; ²er Kalk, Schwefel native lime, sulphur; ²es Kupfer unwrought copper (ant. gar); fig. e-n behandeln wie ein ²es Ei (schonend, zart) to treat a p. with great delicacy or care; vgl. Rohheit 1 u. 3. — 2. Reitkunst: ²es (unzugerittenes) Pferd fresh (or unbroken) horse. — 3. fig. von Personen: rough, uncultured, uneducated, (derb) rude, coarse, (ungeschliffen) unpolished, vulgar, ill-bred; (viehisch) brutal, (wild) savage, fierce; ²e Sitten coarse (or unpolished, unrefined) manners pl.; ²es Volk barbarous nation (vgl. Rohheit 2). — 4. ⊕ (brutto) gross.
Roh-arbeit ⊙ (ᵘ...) f ⓖ metall. raw smelting; **-bau** m bare (or rough) brickwork; **-baumwolle** ♃ f raw cotton; **-einnahme** ♃ f gross receipts or takings pl.; **-eisen** ⊙ n unforged (or unwrought) iron, pig-iron.
Roheit (ᴸ˘) f ⓕ 1. (roher Zustand) raw (or crude) state, rawness, crudeness. — 2. fig. (rohes Benehmen) roughness, rudeness, coarseness, ill-breeding, brutality. — 3. (rohe Handlung) coarse (or brutal) act; (roher Ausdruck) rude expression or saying. [or revenue.]
Roh-ertrag ♃ (ᴸ˘ᵘ˘) m ⊙ gross income.
roher-weise (ᴸ˘˘ᵘ˘) in a rude (or coarse) manner, rudely, coarsely, brutally.
Roh-erz ✕ (ᵘ...) n ⓖ crude (or native) ore; **-erzeugnisse** ♃ n/pl. raw products pl. or produce sg.; **-gewicht** ⊙ n gross weight; **-häute** f/pl. Gerberei: raw (or green, untanned) skins pl.; **-kost** f (Köstler m vegetarian living on) uncooked food; **-material** n raw material; **-metall** n crude metal; **-ofen** m, metall.

furnace for smelting native ore; **-petroleum** ♃, ⊙ n native naphtha; **-produkte** ⊙ n/pl. = erzeugnisse; **-putz** ⊙ m Maurerei: rough cast(ing).
Rohr (ᴸ) [ahd.: Röhre, Reuse] n ⓔc. 1. allg.: cane. — 2. ♃ (Schilf) reed (Phragmi'tes commu'nis). — 3. ♃ coll. spanisches ~ ratan (von Ca'lamus). — 4. ⊙ (hoher Zylinder) tube, pipe, e-s Ofens a. flue, e-s Gewehres: barrel, stock; e-n auf den ~ (Korn) h. to have a spite (or grudge) against a p. — 5. ♪ (zylindrisches Blasinstrument, bsd. Schalmei) shawm, shalm.
Rohr-ammer (ᵘ...) f ⓖ orn. reed-bunting or -sparrow (Emberi'za schoe'niclus); **-ansatz** ⊙ m am Leuchter ꝛc.: socket; **-artig** a. ⓖ reed-like, reedy, ♃: ⊕ arundinaceous. [fountain.]
Röhr-brunnen (ᵘ˘˘) m ⊙ running.
Röhrchen (ᴸ˘) n ⓒ dim. v. Rohr u. Röhre.
Rohr-dach (ᵘ...) n ⓖ reed-covered roof; **-dickicht** n thicket (or bed) of reeds; vgl. -gebüsch; **-dommel** f, orn. bittern, mire-drum (Botau'rus stella'ris); **-drossel** f, orn. reed-thrush (Acroce'phalus turdoi'des).
Röhre (ᴸ˘) [ahd.: Rohr] f ⓖ 1. tube; channel, anat., &c. auch: duct (f. eustachisch); ~ einer Dachrinne: spout, an Gefäßen ꝛc. auch: nozzle; (Leitungs-)~, auch: pipe, conduit, connexion(-pipe). — 2. ⊙ Ofenröhre b.
rohren¹ (ᴸ˘; Hom. roren) a. ⓖ (made) of reed. [... of reed(s).]
rohren² (ᴸ˘) v/a. ⊛: den Teich ♃ to clear.
röhren¹ ⊙ (ᴸ˘; Hom. rören) (mit Röhren versehen) to fit with tubes or pipes.
Röhren²-anlage (ᵘ...) f [Röhre] ⓖ **-leitung**; **-bohr-maschine** ⊙ f/pipe-boring machine; **-brücke** f tubular bridge; **-brunnen** m = Röhrbrunnen, -tiefscher: tube-well; **-dorn** ⊙ m Kesselfabr.: tube-mandrel; **-federei** f scroll-springs pl.; **-förmig** a. ⓖ tubular, ⊕ tubiform; **-kessel** ⊙ m einer Dampfmaschine: tube-boiler; **-klammer** ⊙ f t.-clamp; **-knochen** m hollow cylindrical bone; **-legung** f laying (down) of pipes; vgl. Rohrlegen; **-leitung** f (connexion by means of) pipes, conduit; **-meister** ⊙ m manager of waterworks; **-muschel** f, zo. tube-shell, ⊕ tubivalve (Gastrochae'na); **-pilz** ♃ m: ⊕ boletus; **-qualle** f, zo.: ⊕ siphonophore; **-spinne** f, ent. tube-weaver (Familie Tubitela'riae); **-system** n system of pipes or tubes; **-wasser** n conduit-water; **-werk** n conduit; drain(age-system); **-wurm** m, ent. tube-worm (Tubi'cola).
Rohr-flechte (ᵘ...) f, **-flechten** n ⓖ **-geflecht**; **-flöte** ♪ f e-r Orgel: reed-flute; **-förmig** a. ⓖ tubular; **-gebüsch** n reed-bank or -bed; cane-brake, vgl. -dickicht; **-geflecht** n cane-plaiting.
röhricht¹ (ᴸ˘) a. ⓖ = rohrartig.
Röhricht² (ᴸ˘) [ahd.] n ⓔd. reed-plot; vgl. Röhricht.
rohrig, röhrig (ᴸ˘) [Rohr] a. ⓖ 1. grown with reeds. — 2. ⊙ tubular.
Röhr-kasten (ᵘ...) m ⓖ cistern (of a fountain); **-knochen** m, anat. tubular (or hollow) bone.
Rohr-kolben (ᵘ...) m ⓖ reed-mace (Typha); **-legen** ⊙ n pipe-laying;

-leger ⊙ m pipe-layer; **-matte** f reed- (or rush-)mat; **-pfeife** f reed-flute; **-pflanzung** f = gebüsch; **-post** ⊕ f pneumatic (or tubular) post or dispatch; **-postbrief** m, **-postkarte** f etwa: pneumatic-tube letter, card; **-poströhre** f pneumatic tube; **-rücklauf** m, artill. recoil-barrel; **-rücklaufschütz** ✕ n, artill. recoil-barrel gun; **-sänger** m, orn. reed-warbler (Acroce'phalus); **-sparrow** = Rohrammer; **-schmied** ⊙ m gun-barrel maker; **-spalt-maschine** ⊙ f cane-splitter; **-spatz, -sperling** m: a) = ammer; b) fig. schimpfen wie ein -spatz to use strong language, fluchend: to swear like a trooper; **-stock** m cane, bamboo (stick); **-stuhl** m cane-bottom(ed) chair, cane-chair; **-weih(e** m, f) m, orn. marsh-harrier. moor-buzzard or -hawk (Circus rufus); **-weite** ✕ f bore (of a barrel); **-werk** ♪ n Orgel: reed-stop; **-zucker** ♃ m cane-sugar.
Roh-schiene (ᵘ...) f metall. puddle-bar; **-seide** ♃ f raw silk; **-stahl** m raw steel; **-stahl-eisen** n, metall. steel-pig; **-stoff(e)** ♃ m raw materials pl.; **-walzwerk** ⊙ n puddle rolling-mill; **-zucker** ⊙ m raw sugar. [⊛ to row.]
rojen ⚓ (ᴸ˘) [ndd. = rudern] v/n. (h.).
Rokoko (ˇ˘˘) [fr.] n ⊙, ♃ a. inv. (Kunststil des 18. sae.) rococo. **~-geschmack, ~-stil** m rococo style, style of Louis XV.
Roland (ᴸ˘) [ahd. Ruhmland] npr/m. ⓖ α. (Neffe Karls des Großen) Roland, als Vn. auch: Rowland, Orlando; **~s-lied** (ᵘ...) n ⓖ song of Roland; **~s-schwert** n Roland's sword, auch: Durandal.
Rollladen (ᵛᴸ˘) [Roll-laden] m ⓢ blind.
Roll-angel ⊙ (⁵˘˘) f ⓖ trolling-rod; mit der ~ angeln od. fischen to troll.
rollbar (⁵˘) [rollen] a. ⓖ rollable.
Roll-bett ⊙ (⁵...) n ⓖ truckle- (or trundle-)bed; **-binde** f, surg. roller, roll-bandage; **-brett** ⊙ n mangling-board; der Lichtzieher: rolling-board; **-brücke** f roller- (or turning) bridge.
Röllchen F (⁵˘) n ⓓ (dim. v. Rolle) cuff (fastened to the shirt-sleeve).
Rolle (⁵˘) [mhd.: roll; *fr. rôle] f ⓖ 1. roll, ⊕ auch: truckle, trundle, an der Angelrute: reel, spool, unter Möbeln: caster, am Flaschenzuge, zum Ziehen und Heben: pulley, zum Pressen von Tuch: calender; (Mange) mangle (vgl. Roll-holz); anat. ~ des Ober-armknochens; ⊕ trochlea. — 2. ~ Papier, Pergament (sc)roll of paper, of parchment. — 3. (Register) roll, register. — 4. thea. ~ e-s Schauspielers, Sängers part, rôle; aus der ~ fallen to forget (or not to keep to) one's part; f. besetzen 3; e-e große ~ spielen to act (or play) an important part, F fig. to do the swell, to cut a great dash; F fig. das Geld spielt keine ~ ... plays no part, ... is no consideration.
rollen (⁵˘) [mhd. f. Rolle] ⓢ I v/n. (h., b.) Ortsveränderung f) to roll; (vom Donner) to rumble; vgl. Donner; ⚓ die See rollt the sea is rolling, there is a heavy swell (on). — II v/a.: a) to roll, to trundle (along); aus ea. 2 to unroll, to unfold; ✕ den Mantel gerollt tragen to carry one's cloak slung over

Zeichen (s. S. XVII): F familiär; P Volkssprache; ſ Gaunersprache; ⚆ selten; † alt (auch gestorben); * neu (auch geboren); ++ unrichtig;

[Rollenbesetzung] column:

one's shoulder; b) ⊕ Wäsche ♃ to mangle ..., Tuch ♃ to calender ... — III sich ♃ v/refl. to roll, to turn over (and over); sich ♃ I. to be (or run) on casters or wheels; der Stuhl läßt sich ♃ ... can be wheeled (along). — IV ~ n ㉓ roll(ing), &c. (f. I und II), ~ der See auch: heavy swell.

Rollen-besetzung (ᵛ⁻ᴗ...) f ㉒ thea. casting of (the) parts; =fach n, thea. kind of character (or part) filled by an actor or actress; ♀förmig a. ⑥ in the shape of a (sc)roll, ⚗ trochlear, trochleate, trochoid(al); =papier ⊕ n endless web of paper; =system m, elect. trolley-system; =tabak ⚓ m = Rolltabak; =verteilung f = =besetzung; =zug ⊕ m = Flaschenzug.

Roller (ᴵ⁻ᴗ) m ㉒ 1. person who rolls or mangles, ⊕ Tuchfabr.: calenderer. — 2. ⥥ (Sturzsee) rolling (or heavy) sea.

Roll-fleisch (ᵛ⁻...) n ㉒ Kocht.: collared beef; =fuhr-geschäft ⚓ n carrier's business; =fuhrmann ⚓ m drayman, carter, carrier; =geld n: a) ⚓ für Rollfuhren: cartage, carrier's fee or charge(s pl.); b) money (paid) for mangling; =gut ⥥ n (Kisten und Fässer) rolling freight, cases and casks pl.; =handtuch n jack- (or endless) towel; =holz ⊕ n der Hutmacher und Bäcker: rolling-pin.

Rollini-e (ᵛᴵ⁻(ᴗ)) [Roll=linie] f ㉔ geom. rolling curve.

Roll-kammer (³⁻...) f ㉒ mangling-room; =kloben m pulley-block; =knecht m carter's man; =kupfer n, metall. sheet-copper in rolls; =kutscher m = =fuhrmann; =laden m f. Rolladen; =lini-e f f. Rollinie; =maschine f calender(ing-machine); =material ⚓ n rolling stock; =mops n collared herring, prove. = =wagenjunge; =muskel m, anat. der Augen: ⚗ trochleary (or pathetic) muscle; =rad, =rädchen n truck-wheel, an Möbeln: castor; =scheibe f sheave; (schlitt=)schuhe m/pl. roller-skates pl.; (schlitt=)schuh-bahn f skating-rink; =schnecke f, zo. butterfly-shell, ⚗ volute (Volu'ta); =schwanz m trundle-tail; =schwanz-affe m, zo. sapajou (Cebus); =stein m, geol. erratic block; =stuhl m arm-chair on casters, auch: rolling- (or wheel-)chair, für Kranke: Bath chair; =system ⚓ n, elect. trolley-system; =tabak m tobacco in rolls, twist(ed tobacco); =tuch n cloth in which linen is mangled; =vorhang m roller-blind; =wagen m: a) (auch =wägelchen n) children's go-cart or perambulator or mail-cart; b) für Frachtgüter: truck, dray(-cart); vgl. Güterwagen; =wagen-junge m truckman; vgl. =mops; =wäsche f linen which has to be mangled.

Rom ♀ (ᴵ) [It.] npr/n. ㉒a. Rome; Sprichw. f. erbauen 1; alle Wege führen nach ~, etwa: there are many roads that lead to Rome or many ways leading to the same goal.

Roman (ᵛᴵ) [nhd.; *fr.: ursprgl. Erzählung in „romanischer" Sprache] m ⑪d. novel, romance, weitS. work of fiction; kurzer ~ novelette; ihre Lebensgeschichte ist ein wahrer ~ her life is quite a romance.

roman-artig (ᵛ⁻ᴵ...) a. ⑥ like a novel or romance, novelistic; vgl. romanhaft; =dichter(in f) m ㉒ romancer.

Romane (ᵛᴵ⁻) [Rom] m ㊹, mst pl. ~n (Franzosen, Italiener ꝛc.) the Romance (or neo-Latin) people(s) or nations pl.

romanhaft (ᵛᴵ⁻ᴵ) a. ⑥ romantic, fictitious, adventurous, vgl. romanartig.

Roman=held(in f) (ᵛ⁻ᴵᴵ⁻ᴗ(ᴗ)) m ㉒ hero (heroine f) of a novel.

romanisch (ᵛᴵ⁻ᴵ) a. ⑥ Philologie: Romance, neo-Latin, arch. Romanesque; ⸗er Spitzbogenstil transition style.

romanisieren (ᵛᴗᴵ⁻ᴵ) [neu=lt.] v/a. ⑬ (römisch machen) to Romanize.

Romanismus (ᵛᴗᴵ⁻) [neu=lt.] m ㉒: a) Römertum, b) Romanentum, romanisches Volkstum ꝛc.: Romanism.

Romanist (ᵛᴗᴵ⁻) m (ᵛᴵ⁻) (Kenner des Romanischen) Romance scholar or student, one versed in Romance languages.

Roman=leser(in f) (ᵛ⁻ᴵᴵ⁻...) m ㉒ novel-reader; =literatur f works pl. of fiction, a. fictional reading; =schreiber(in f) m, =schriftsteller(in f) m novel-writer or F -scribbler, novelist, weitS. writer (or author) of fiction.

Romantik (ᵛᴗᴵᴵ) [neu=lt.] f ㊺ romantic poetry or style, romance(s pl.); ~er(in f) ㊵) m ㉒ romantic writer, romanticist.

romantisch (ᴗ) a. ⑥ romantic, fanciful.

Romanze (ᵛᴗᴵ) [fr.] f ㊺ (modernes Epos) romance; (Ballade) ballad; ~ro (ᵛᴗᴵ⁻ᴗ) [span.] m ㊽ (Sammlung v. ~n) romancero.

Roman-zeitung (ᵛ⁻ᴵᴵ⁻ᴵ) f ㉒ journal for fiction, fictional magazine.

römeln (ᴵ⁻ᴗ) [Rom] v/n. (h.) ㉟a. eccl. to lean to Rome, to Romanize.

Romeo ♂ (ᴵ⁻ᴗ⁻) npr/m. ⑪㉒a. f. Julia.

Römer¹ (ᴵ⁻ᴗ) [ahd.; *Rom] m ㉒, ~in f ⑪ Roman.   [claret-glass.

Römer² (ᴵ⁻ᴗ) m ㉒ (grünes Weinglas) green

Römer¹=brief (ᴵᴵ⁻ᴗ...) m ㉒ bibl. (Paul's) Epistle to the Romans; =brücke f Roman bridge; =zug m, hist. Mittelalter: expedition or journey of a German Emperor to Rome there to be crowned by the Pope.

Rom=fahrt (ᴵᴵ⁻ᴵ) f ㉒ journey to Rome.

römisch (ᴵ⁻ᴗ) [ahd.] a. ⑥ Roman, Kirche (f. alt=♃) ⸗e Ziffern (a. typ.) roman numerals pl.; ♃-katholisch a. Roman Catholic, b.s. Romish (doctrine, &c.).

Römling (ᴵ⁻ᴗ) [Rom] m ⑪d. rel. b.s. Papist, Romanist, Roman Catholic.

Ronde (ᴵ⁻ᴗ, a. rg=bᵈ) [fr.] f ㊹ bsd. ⚔ (Rundgang) round; die ~ geh(e)n oder tun to go the round(s).   [rinnen.)

ronne (ᴵ⁻ᴗ) 1. u. 3. Person subj. impf. von

Röntgen=apparat (ᵛ⁻...) [R., 1895, dtsch. Physiker, *1845] m ㉒ Röntgen apparatus; =aufnahme f, =bild n Röntgen ray photogram or photograph.

röntgenisieren (ᴗᴗᴗᴵ⁻) v/a. ⑬ med. to treat with Röntgen rays.

Röntgen=röhre (ᵛ⁻...) f ㉒ Röntgen tube; =strahlen m/pl. Röntgen (or Röntgen) rays, X-rays pl.; =verfahren n Röntgen treatment.   [to roar.)

roren¹ ♀ (ᴵ⁻ᴗ; Hom. rohren) v/n. (h.) vet.

roren², mst **rören** (ᴵ⁻ᴗ; Hom. röhren) [ahd.] v/n. (h.) ⑭ hunt. v. Hirsch: to troat, to bell.

Rosa (ᴵ⁻ᴗ) [lt. rösa Rose] I n ⑮ pink (colour). — II ♃ a. inv., a. ♃=farben, ♃=farbig pink; ~band n pink-ribbon.

[right column, rosenwangig:]

Rosali-e (ᵛ⁻ᴵ(ᴗ)ᴗ) [neu=lt.; *Rosa] npr/f. ⑪㊸. (Bn.) Rosalie. [(Bn.) Rosamond.)

Rosamunde (ᴵ⁻ᴗᴗ⁻ᴗ) [lt.=dtsch.] npr/f. ⑪㊸

Rosanilin ⚗ (ᴗᴗᴗᴵ) n ⑪d. chm. rosaniline ($C_{20}H_{21}N_3O$). [blüter) Rosaceæ pl.)

Rosaze-en ᛭ (ᵛ⁻ᴗ(ᴗ)) [lt.] f/pl. ⑭ (Rosen-

Röschen¹ (ᴵ⁻ᴗ) [Rose dim.] n ㉓ little rose; poet. (ein) ~ rot (a) red little rose.

Röschen² (ᴵ⁻ᴗ) npr/n. ㉓α. (dim. v. Rosa) (Bn.) little Rosa or Rose, Rosy.

Rose (ᴵ⁻ᴗ) [ahd.: rose; lt.; grch. *ῥέον;} f ⑭ 1. ᛭ rose (Rosa); gelbe ~ Austrian brier (R. lu'tea); hundertblätterige ~ cabbage-rose (R. centifo'lia); weiße ~ white rose (R. alba); wilde ~ dog-rose, wild brier (R. cani'na); f. Jericho; Krieg der ~n = Rosenkrieg; fig. wir sind nicht auf ~n gebettet it is not all honey with us; keine ~ ohne Dornen no rose without a thorn; mit der Zeit pflückt man (die) ~n ob. Zeit bringt ~n everything comes to the man who can wait (for it). — 2. arch. (Rosen-fenster) rose-window. — 3. hunt. (kreisförmige Erhabenheit am Hirschgeweih) bsd. ehm.: bur(r). — 4. path. (Rotlauf) ⚗ erysipelas; f. kaltes Antoniusfeuer.

Röse (ᴵ⁻ᴗ) npr/f. ⑪㊸. Rosa, Rose.

Rösel (ᴵ⁻ᴗ) npr/n. ㉓α. = Röschen².

Rosen-apfel (ᴵᴵ⁻...) m ㉒ = =schwamm; ♃artig a. ⑥ rose-like, like a rose, ᛭: ⚗ rosaceous; =baum m rose-tree; =beet n bed of roses; =blatt n rose-leaf; =blüter m/pl., =blütige Gewächse ᛭ n/pl. Rosaceæ pl.; =busch m rose-bush; =duft m fragrance (or perfume) of roses; =essig m rose-vinegar; =farbe f rose-colour, rosiness; ♃farben, ♃farbig a. rose-coloured, rosy; =fenster n = Rose 2; =fest n festival of roses; =finger m rosy finger; =fingerig a., bsd. poet. in Homer ꝛc.: die ♃e Eos rosy-fingered Eos or Aurora; =garten [ahd.] m garden of roses, rosery; =geruch m smell of roses; =hain m, =hecke f grove, hedge of roses; =honig m, pharm. rose-honey; =käfer m, ent. r.-beetle (Ceto'nia aura'ta); =knospe f rose-bud; =kohl ᛭ m brussels (or Brussels) sprouts pl. (Bra'ssica olera'cea, var. gemmi'fera); =kranz m: a) garland (or wreath) of roses; b) Cath. eccl. rosary, chaplet; f. beten 3; =kreuzer m/pl. (Mystiker des 17. sae.) Rosicrucians pl.; =krieg m engl. hist. (1455–1485) Wars pl. of the Roses; =lauch ᛭ m rose-garlic; =lippen f/pl. rosy lips pl.; =lorbeer ᛭ m: a) = Alpenrose; b) = Oleander; =mädchen n: a) girl selling roses; b) rosy maid; =monat, =mond m month of roses, June, July; =mund m rosy mouth; =öl ⊕ n attar of roses; =pappel ᛭ f vervain-mallow (Ma'lva a'lcea); =pfad m path strewn with roses; =quarz m, min. rose-quartz; ♃rot a., =rot n rosy red; =salbe f, pharm. rose-liniment; =schwamm m rose-gall; =sonntag m Lätare; =stahl ⊕ m, metall. rose-steel, superfine steel; =star m, orn. rose-ousel (Pastor ro'seus); =stein ⊕ m Juwelier: rose, rose-diamond; =stock, =strauch m (standard) r.-tree; wilder ~ wild brier; =strauß m bunch of roses; =wange f rosy cheek; ♃wangig a. rosy-

[Rosenwasser] — 810 — [Rotlauf]

cheeked; =wasser n rose-water; =zucht f growing (or cultivation) of roses; =züchter m grower (or fancier) of roses.
Rosette (⌣⌣́) [fr.] f ⊕ rosette, rose-knot; ⊙ arch. u. Diamantschleiferei: rose.
rosettieren (⌣⌣́⌣) v/a. ⊙ Diamantschleiferei: to cut in rosettes or as a rosette.
rosicht ⟋, mst **rosig** (⌣́⌣) [Rose] a. ⊕ rosy, roseate, like a rose; in Ler Laune ob. Stimmung sein to be in a merry humour or in high glee; alles in Lem Lichte sehen to see everything (fr.) couleur de rose, to look at the best (or brightest) side of things.
Rosine¹ (⌣⌣́) [mhd.: raisin; *fr. raisin m] f ⊕ (getrocknete Weinbeere) größere: raisin, ⁓ bsd. im Pudding, auch: plum; kleinere, ohne Kerne: sultana (vgl. Korinthe); fig. große ⁓n im Sacke haben to be full of brag, to talk big; to have grand ideas or high notions. [Rosina.)
Rosine² (⌣⌣́) [Rosa¹] npr/f. ⊕⊕ (Bn.)
Rosinen=kuchen (⌣⌣́⌣⌣) [Rosine¹] m ⊕ f. Kuchen, =pudding m raisin-(or plum-) pudding, =wein m raisin-wine.
rosin=farben (⌣́⌣⌣) a. ⊕ raisin-coloured.
Röslein (⌣́⌣) n ㉓ = Röschen¹.
Rosmarin (⌣⌣⌣́) [mhd. (P); *lt. Meertau] m ⑦d. rosemary (Rosmari'nus); ⁓=öl (⌣⌣⌣⌣́⌣) n ㉓ pharm. rosemary-oil.
Roß (⌣́) [ahd.: horse] n ⓐa. horse; Spr. edles ⁓ noble steed or charger; ⁓ und Reiter horse and (horse)man; hoch zu ⁓ mounted on horseback.
Roß=arznei=kunde (⌣́⌣⌣) f ⊕ veterinary surgery; =arzt m ⚼ † = (Ober-) Veterinär; = (ob. Rosse=)bändiger m horse-breaker or -tamer.
Rosse=lenker (⌣⌣́⌣) m ⊕ charioteer, F (Kutscher) coachman, cabman, cabby.
Rössel=sprung (⌣́⌣⌣⌣) [nhd.] m ⊙c. Schachspiel: knight's move.
Roß=haar (⌣́⌣) n ⊕ horsehair; =haar= matratze f horsehair mattress; =härren a. ⊕ (made) of horsehair.
rossig (⌣́⌣) [Roß] a. ⊕ v. d. Stute: in heat.
Roß=käfer (⌣́⌣⌣) m ⊕ ent. dor(-beetle) (Geotru'pes stercora'rius); =kamm m: a) curry-comb; b) [it. cambio Tausch] horse-dealer, F h.-faker; vgl. täuscher; =kastanie ♀ f horse-chestnut; =kasta= nien=baum m horse-chestnut tree (Ae'sculus hippoca'stanum); =leder n horse-leather. [(or small) horse.)
Rößlein (⌣́⌣) n ㉓ (dim. von Roß) little}
Roß=markt (⌣́⌣) m ⊕ horse-market or -fair; =schlächter m h.-slaughterer or -butcher; =schlächterei f slaughtering of horses; (Ort dazu:) knacker's yard; =schweif m horse's tail; =täuscher m [mhd.] horse-dealer or F-chanter; vgl. =kamm b; =trappe f imprint (or mark) of a horse's hoof. — Vgl. auch Pferde=
Rost¹ (⌣́) [ahd.: rust: rot] m ⓐb. 1. (Eisen= oxyd) rust (auch fig.); edler ⁓ verd= antique, bisw. auch: ⊙ ærugo. — 2. ♀ u. agr. = Brand 7.
Rost² ⊙ (⌣́, † od. provc.⌣) [ahd.] m ⓐ(⑦)b. 1. (gitterartige Unterlage für Feuerung) grate of an oven or a hearth or a furnace, fire-grate, furnace-grate, zum Braten: gridiron, grill; auf dem ⁓ braten to grill. — 2. metall. (Erz zum Rösten) roasting-charge; (einmaliges Rösten)

roasting. — 3. arch. (Pfahl=)⁓ pile-work, (pile-)grating.
Röst=arbeit ⊙ (⌣́⌣⌣, bisw. ⌣⌣⌣́) f ⊕ metall. roasting-process.
Rost²=braten (⌣́⌣) m ⊕ Kocht. roast joint; ⚬¹**braun** a. ⊕ rusty brown.
Röste (⌣́, ⌣ ⌣) f ⊕ 1. (Rösten, Rotten v. Flachs ꝛc.) steeping; Ort= place for steeping flax, &c. — 2. metall. batch (or heap) of ore to be roasted; vgl. Rost² 2.
rosten (⌣́⌣) [Rost¹] ⊕ I v/n. (h. u. ſn) to rust, to grow (F to get) rusty, chm.: ⚯ to oxidize; fig. to wear away; Sprichw. f. alt¹ 2 am Schluß. — II v/a. to cause to (or to make) rust. — III ⁓ n ㉓ rusting, chm.: ⚯ oxidation.
rösten¹ (⌣́, bisw. ⌣ ⌣) [ahd.; *Rost²] I v/a. ⊕ Kochkunst: to roast (auch ⊙ metall.), auf dem Bratrost: to grill, in der Pfanne: to fry (vgl. braten¹ 1); Brot 2 to toast, Kaffee: to burn; geröstete Kartoffeln fried potatoes. — II ⁓ n ㉓ roasting, grilling, frying, &c. (I.)
rösten² ⊙ (⌣́⌣) [: ret (rot)] v/a. ⊕: Flachs, Hanf ꝛ (rotten) to steep (or to ret)...
Rost¹=farbe (⌣́⌣) f ⊕ colour of rust; ⚬**farben**, ⚬**farbig** a. ⊕ rust-coloured, ⚯ rubiginose; =fleck(en) m iron-mould; ⚬**fleckig** a. iron-mouldy; machen to iron-mould; =**fleisch** n Kocht. grilled (or roast) meat; ⚬**förmig** a. (shaped) like a gridiron, gridiron-shaped; =**gebratenes** n = =braten.
rostig (⌣́⌣) [Rost¹] a. ⊕ rusty; ⚬ w. to grow rusty, to rust, fig. auch: to rest, to grow idle. [furnace.)
Röst=ofen ⊙ (⌣́⌣) m ⊕ metall. roasting-}
Rost¹=papier (⌣́⌣⌣) n ⊕ polishing-paper for rusty metal; =**pendel** ⊙ n (m) Uhr: gridiron-, compensation-pendulum.
Röst=pfanne (⌣́⌣) f ⊕ frying-pan.
Rost¹=pilz ♀ (⌣́⌣) m ⊕: ⚯ uredo.
Rostral ♪ (⌣⌣́) [lt.] n ⓐd. = Rastral.
Rost²=rinder=braten (⌣́⌣⌣) m ⊕ Kocht. roast beef; =**rippchen** n grilled cutlet.
Rost²=stab (⌣́⌣) m ⊕ e-s Herdes: grate-bar, e-s Hochofens: furnace-bar, =**träger** ⊕ m im Schmelzofen: bearer- (or bearing-)bar.
Röstung (⌣́, ⌣ ⌣) f ⊕ = rösten¹ II.
Rost²=werk (⌣́⌣) n ⊕ = Rost¹ 2.
rot (⌣́) [ahd.: red, ruddy] I a. ⊕ (D2, bsd. fig. a. D1, 6) 1. red; (hoch=⚬) vermilion, von d. Gesichtsfarbe: ruddy; (er= hitzt) flushed; (rötlich) reddish (a. von der Nase), (tupferig) coppery, ⚯ rubicund; auch = rothaarig, vgl. fahl=⚬, karmesin=⚬, kirsch=⚬; Le Haare (ob. Les Haar) haben to have red(dish) (or F carroty, sandy) hair, to be red-haired or F carroty, co. to be on fire; ⁓e Erde = Westfalen; f. Heller, Kreuz 1; ♀ ⁓es Meer Red Sea; f. Rübe; path. Le Ruhr: ⚯ dysentery; ⚬ werden to turn red, to redden; (erröten) to blush, to colour up; vor Zorn ⚬ w. to flush with anger; Sprichw. f. heute 1. — II s. ⑦ 2. das ⁓ n red (a. als Kartenfarbe), red dye; lebhaftes ⁓ bright red, crimson, (Schminke) rouge, (red) paint; zu viel ⁓ auflegen to lay on the rouge too thick. — 3. das **Rote** the red (colour), crimson, ruby. — III **Rote(r)** m 4. v. Personen: a) ruddy-looking person; a. = **Rotkopf**: b) (der Republikaner) red-

hot (or extreme) republican. — 5. F = Rotwein. [rattan (Ca'lamus).)
Rotan, ⌣⌣́⌣ ♀ (⌣⌣́) [malaiisch] m ⓐd. ⊛}
Rotation ⚬ (⌣⌣⌣tß(⌣́)⌣) [lt.] f ⊕ (Umlauf) rotation, revolution; ⁓s=**achse** f axis of rotation; ⁓s=**maschine** ⊕ f, typ. rota(to)ry machine or press; ⁓s=**pumpe** ⊕ f rota(to)ry pump.
Rot=auge (⌣́⌣) n ⊕: a) red eye; b) red-eyed person or animal; c) ichth. = Plötze u. =**feder**; ⚬**bäckig** a. ⊕ red-cheeked, with ruddy cheeks; =**bart** m: a) red beard; b) red-bearded person; Kaiser ⁓ (Friedrich I.) Frederick Barbarossa; ⚬**bärtig** a. red-bearded; =**blindheit** f: ⚯ daltonism; ⚬**blond** a. auburn; ⚬**braun** a. red(dish)-brown, sorrel, bay; ⚬**brüchig** a. vom Eisen: red-short; =**buche** ♀ f red-beech, copper-beech (Fagus ferrugi'nea); =**dorn** ♀ m (rotblühende Abart des Weißdorns) red blowing hawthorn; =**drossel** f, orn. redwing (Turdus ili'acus).
Röte (⌣́) [ahd. ⁓: rot] f ⊕ 1. redness, red colour (auch des Haares) (leuchtend rote Farbe) vermilion (vgl. Fleischfarbe); die ⁓ stieg ihr zu Gesicht the colour rose to her face, she coloured up. — 2. ♀ = **Färberröte**. — 3. = **Rotlauf**.
Rot=eisen=erz (⌣́⌣⌣) n ⊕: =**eisen=stein** m, min. red iron-ore; f. a. Blutstein; =**eisen=ocker** m, min. red ochre.
Rötel (⌣́) [mhd.: ruddle; *rot] m ⊕ red chalk, reddle, ruddle; ⁓=**erde** (⌣⌣́⌣) f ⊕ min. Adamic earth.
Röteln (⌣́⌣) [rot] pl. inv., path. German measles, rose-rash, ⚯ roseola.
Rötel=stift (⌣́⌣⌣) m ⊕ red chalk pencil.
röten (⌣́⌣) [ahd.; *rot] ⊕ I v/a. 1. to paint (or dye) in red; gerötete Wangen flushed cheeks pl. — 2. ⊙ = rösten². — II sich ⚬ v/refl. 3. to redden, to turn red, vom Gesichte auch: to colour (up), to get flushed.
Rot=erle ♀ (⌣́⌣) f ⊕ = Schwarz=e.; =**fahl** a. ⊕ pale red; =**feder** f, ichth.: a) rudd (Scardi'nius erythrophtha'lmus); ⚬**fleckig** a. red-spotted, with red stains; =**fuchs** m: a) = Fuchs; b) bay (or chestnut) horse; ⚬**gar** ⊕ a. = lohgar; ⚬**gelb** a. orange-coloured; =**gerber** ⊕ m tanner; =**gerberei** f tannery; =**gießer** ⊕ m brazier; =**gießerei** f brazier's work or work-shop; ⚬**giltig=erz** n = =**güldig=erz**; ⚬**glühend** a. red-hot; =**glüh= hitze**, =**glut** ⊕ f, metall. red-heat; =**güldig=erz** n, min. red silver-ore; =**guß** ⊕ m red brass; bronze; ⚬**haarig** a. red-haired, F carroty, sandy; =**haut** f (Indianer) Red Indian, red man, red-skin; =**holz** ♀ n Brazil-wood (von Cae= salpi'nia Sappan); =**huhn** n, orn. redlegs, red-legged partridge (Ca'ccabis rufa).
rotieren ⚯ (⌣⌣́⌣) [lt.] v/n. (h.) ⊕ (sich drehen) to rotate, to revolve.
Rot=käppchen (⌣́⌣) n ⊕ im Märchen: (Little) Red Riding Hood; =**kehlchen** n, orn. robin (redbreast) (Eri'thacus rube'culus); =**kohl** ♀ m red cabbage; =**kopf** m red-haired person, F carrots, ginger, sandy; ⚬**köpfig** a.: a) red-headed; b) = ⚬**haarig**; =**kupfer=erz** n, min. red copper-ore; =**lauf** m, path.: a) = Rose 4; b) (rote Ruhr): ⚯ dysentery; c) vet. der

Signs (see page XVII): F familiar; P vulgar; F̄ flash; ⟋ rare; † obsolete (died); * new word (born); ⁓ incorrect; ♪ music;

[rotlaufartig] — 811 — [Rückennerv]

Schweine: red murrain; ²lauf=artig a.: ⚕ erysipelatic, ...ous.
rötlich (¹⸜) [rot] a. ⓺ reddish, rubicund, rubescent, vom Gesichte auch: florid (f. rot 1); ²=braun a. russet.
Rot=liegende(s) (¹‿‿‿) n ⓶ geol. lower strata pl. of new red sand-stone.
Rötling (¹⸜) m ⓭. = Rotschwanz.
rot=nasig (¹‿...) a. ⓺ red-nosed; =rock m ⓶ (engl. Soldat) F redcoat; =schecke f, =schimmel m roan (horse); =schmied = =gießer; =schwanz m, orn. redstart, fire-tail (Rubici'lla phoenicu'ra); =stift m red-chalk pencil; ²streifig a. red-striped; =tanne ♀ f = Fichte 1; =tannen=holz n = red deal.
Rotte (⸜⸜) [mhd.; *alt=fr.] f ⓺ 1. troop, band, gang; (Schwarm) swarm, flock; b.s. clique, set, ring, F tribe; (Pöbel) rabble, mob; (Partei) faction. — 2. hunt. = Rudel; ~ Wölfe pack of wolves. — 3. ⚔: a) ehm. battalion; b) jetzt: (die hinter=ea. aufgestellten Leute) file; (Trupp) squad; Kommando: in ~n links! file left!; in ~n marschieren to march in file.
rotten (⸜⸜) [Rotte]: sich ² v/refl. ⓻ to flock together, to assemble, b.s. to conspire, to plot.
Rotten=aufmarsch ⚔ (⸜⸜...) m⓶ deployment in file(s); =feuer n file-firing; =führer m file-leader, corporal; =geist m factious spirit; =liste ⚔ f squad-roll; ²weise adv. in gangs, ⚔ in files.
Rotunde (⸜¹⸜) [It.] f ⓺ (Rundbau) rotunda.
rot=wangig (¹...) a. ⓺ = ²bäckig; =wein m ⓶ red wine; französischer: claret; portugiesischer: port; =wein=bowle f claret-cup; =wein=farbe f claret-colour; ²welsch [mhd.: Rot ⌐ = Bettler] n (beggars') cant, thieves' language or F lingo, gibberish; =wild n, hunt. (Hirsche) red deer or venison.
Rotz (⸝) [ahd.] m ⓭a. (ohne pl.): a) (Nasenschleim) (nasal) mucus, F nosedirt, P snot; b) vet. glanders (= Druse 2); ²behaftet a. ⓺ vet. glandered.
rotzig (¹⸜) a. ⓺: a) with a dirty nose, P snot-nosed; b) vet. glandered.
rotz=krank (¹...)a.⓺=rotzbehaftet; =krankheit f ⓶ = Rotz b; =löffel m, =näschen n, =nase/P:a)dirty(or running)nose;b)fig. (Schimpfwort) saucy (F cheeky) boy, girl.
Roué (ru-e') [fr. Geräderte(r)] m ⓷ (Wüstling) rake, (fr.) roué. [= Rollfleisch.]
Roulade (ru⸜¹) [fr.] f ⓶ (Kochkunst)
Rouleau (ru-lo') [(+,+)fr. m] n (m) ⓶ (pl. auch ~⸝: ru-lō'ß) (roller-)blind, äußeres: sun-blind; das ~ aufziehen (herunterlassen) to pull up (let down) the blind.
Roulett (ru⸜¹) [fr. roulette f] n ⓶c., ~e (ru⸜⸜) f ⓶ (Hasardspiel) roulette; ~ spielen to play roulette.
Route (rū'⸝) [fr.] f ⓶ (Weg) route.
Routine (rū⸜¹) [fr.] f ⓶ (Übung, Geschäftsgang) routine; round of business, daily practice; routiniert (rū-⸜¹) a. ⓺ smart in business; (erfahren) experienced, practised, bsd. ⓶ versed (F well up) in business(-routine).
royal (rõa⸜j¹) [fr.] a. ⓺ (königlich gesinnt) royal; ~ismus (...j⸜⸜) m ⓵ royalism; ~ist (...j⸜⸜) m ⓶ royalist; ²istisch (...j⸜⸜) a. royalist, loyal to the king; ~papier n ⓶ royal paper, paper-royal.

rrum (⸝) [lautm.] int. (Trommelwirbel) rataplan, rubadub!
Rübchen (¹⸜) n ⓶ (dim. v. Rübe) small turnip or carrot; fig. e-m Rüben ob. ein ~ schaben (höhnend mit dem Zeigefinger der Rechten über den der Linken streichen), etwa: to jeer (or flout, tease, taunt) a p.
Rübe (¹⸜) [ahd.] f ⓺ 1. ♀ agr. bsd. weiße (ob. Stoppel=) ~ turnip (Bra'ssica rapa); gelbe ~ (Möhre) carrot (Daucus caro'ta); rote ~ (Runkel²) beet(-root) (Beta vulga'ris). — 2. fig. = Kraut 3; Rübchen.
Rubel ⓼ (¹⸜) [russ. „Hack"(silber) m ⓶ (abbr. Rbl.; etwa 2,16 Mark) rouble.
Rüben=acker (¹‿...) m ⓶ agr. turnip-field, field of turnips; =bau m cultivation of turnips; =ernte f, agr. root-crop; =feld n = =acker; ²förmig ♀ a. ⓺: ⚕ napiform; =heber ⚙ m turnip-lifter; =kohl ♀ m = Kohlrabi; =kraut ♀ n turnip-tops pl.; =zucker ⚙ m beet-root sugar.
(')rüber F (¹⸜) abbr. = herüber.
Rübezahl (¹⸜‿) [mhd. Ruwi(Rauh=)zagel: tail Schwanz] ob. *Rlt.] npr/m. ⓺⓺a. (Berggeist im Riesengebirge) Mountain Sprite, Old Nip. [(Edelstein: ruby.)
Rubin (⸜¹) [mhd.; *lt. Rot...] m ⓭d. min.
Rubin=farbe (¹‿...) f ⓺ ruby-colour; ²=farben, ²=farbig, ²=rot a. ⓺ ruby-coloured, ruby. [colza-)oil.]
Rüb=öl ⚙ (¹‿) n ⓶ rape-seed (or Rubrik (⸜¹) [mhd.; *lt. rote...] f ⓺ (Überschrift) rubric, heading; (Spalte) column of a page; rubrizieren (⸜⸜¹⸜) v/a. ⓺ to provide with headings, to head; to arrange (or set out) in columns.
Rüb=saat (¹...) f ⓺, =same(n) m = Rübsen.
[Stoppelrübe) rape-seed.]
Rübsen ♀ (¹⸜) m ⓶ agr. (Samen der ruchbar (²ch⸜) [ndd.: (Ge)rücht] a. ⓺ notorious, public; ² machen to make (publicly) known, to spread about; ² werden to become known, to be noised abroad or bruited about; ~keit (²ch⸜¹) f ⓺ notoriety, publicity.
Ruch=gras (²ch⸜¹) n ⓶ (Ge)ruch] ♀ ⓶ sweet vernal-grass (Anthoxa'nthum odora'tum).
ruch=los (²ch⸜¹) [ahd.: reckless] a. ⓺ wicked, nefarious, malicious; Ruch=losigkeit (²ch⸜¹⸜) f ⓺ wickedness, nefariousness, malice; profligacy.
Ruck (⸝) [ahd.: rücken²] m ⓭b. sudden push, jerk, F shove; einen ~ tun to make a move or start; auf einen ~, mit einem ~ at one pull or F go.
Rück¹... (⸝...) [Rücken¹] f. Rückgrat 2c.
Rück²=abtretung (²...) [(zu)rück²] f⓺ retrocession; =anspruch m jur. counterclaim; =antwort f, =äußerung f reply; =berufung f recall; =bewegung f retrograde movement; ²bezüglich a. ⓺ (des' Fürwort) reflexive (pronoun); =bleibende(r) s. one who remains (or lags) behind; oft: dawdler; ²bleibend n ⓶ remnant, rest, residue; =blick m ⓶ retrospect(ive view); einen ~ werfen auf to cast a retrospective glance at; =bürge m, =bürgschaft f meist ⓶ counter-security; =einfuhr ⚓ f reimportation.
rucken¹ (⸜⸜) v/n. (h.) ⓻ f. rücken² 3 b.
rucken² (⸜⸜) v/n. (h.) ⓻ v. Tauben: to coo.
Rücken¹ (⸜⸜) [ahd.] (ridge) m ⓶ 1. back, ⚕ dorsum der Nase, eines

Berges: ridge, ⚔ eines Heeres: rear; anat., zo. zum ~ gehörig: ⚕ dorsal; ~ gegen ~, mit dem ~ gegen=ea. gekehrt back to back, her. addorsed. — 2. mit verbs: den ~ beugen, e-n krummen ~ machen to bend one's back, to bow (down), to stoop, b.s. to cringe; e-m den ~ decken to cover a p.'s rear, sich den ~ frei halten to secure one's (line of) retreat; e-m den ~ kehren to turn one's back upon a p.; sobald ich den ~ wende ober e-m darf nur den ~ wenden as soon as I (or I need only) turn my back. — 3. mit prp.: sich selbst eine Rute auf den ~ binden to make a rod for one's own back; auf den ~ fallen to fall backward or on one's back, fig. to be taken aback; auf dem ~ liegend prostrate, ⚕ supine; auf dem ~ schwimmen to swim (or float) on one's back; hinter j-s ~ oder e-m hinterm ~ (ant. ins Gesicht) behind a p.'s back; f. ansehen 3; ⚔ dem Feinde in den ~ fallen, den Feind im ~ angreifen to attack the enemy in the rear; es läuft mir eiskalt über den ~ I feel a cold shiver (running) up (or down) my back, it makes my flesh creep, I shudder.
rücken² (⸜⸜) [ahd.: rock] ⓻ I v/a. 1. to (re)move, von sich fort: to push (away), näher zu sich: to bring nearer or closer, to draw (or pull) towards one; den Topf vom Feuer ² to take ... off the fire; den Zeiger der Uhr (metonymisch: die Uhr) ² to regulate the watch. — II v/refl. 2. sich nicht ² und rühren (mehr nicht von der Stelle ²) not to stir, F not to budge (an inch). — III v/n. 3. (h.): a) an (ob. mit) etwas ² to (re)move a th.; b) meist rucken: elektrische Schläge rucken (fahren stoßweise) durch den Körper electric shocks send a jerk (or thrill) through the body. — 4. (ſn) to move, näher: to draw near, to approach, dicht an=ea.: to draw close together (f. herauf=, heraus=²); an j-s Stelle ² to take a p.'s place; f. Bude; ⚔ aus dem Lager ² to leave (or quit) the camp; f. Feld 3; durch ein Dorf ² to march (or advance) through a village; in ein Land ² to invade (or march into) a country; vor eine Stadt ² to lay siege to a town; e-m zu Leibe ² to press a p. hard. — 5. F berliniſch: (heimlich ausziehen) to take a moonlight flit, to shoot the moon. — IV ~ n ⓶ 6. (f. 1) removal; (f. 4) march(ing); (f. 5) F moonlight flit.
Rücken²=bein ✝ (⸜⸜...) [ahd.] n ⓶ anat. = Rückgrat; =blatt ⚙ n, arch. des Altarstückes: back of an altar-piece; =darre f = =marksschwindsucht; =flosse f ichth. dorsal fin; =halter m back-board; =lehne f = Rücklehne; =mark n spinal marrow or cord; =märker F m, co. = =marksleidende(r); =marks=darre f = =marksleidende; =marks=leidende(r) s., path. person suffering from a spinal disease, spinal patient; =marks=schwindsucht f, path. spinal consumption or disease; =muskel, =nerv m, anat.: ⚕ dorsal muscle, nerve;

⚕ scientific; ♀ botanical; ⚲ geography; ⚙ machinery; ⚒ mining; ⚔ military; ⚓ marine; ⓶ commercial; ⚜ postal; 🚆 railway.

[Rückenschild] — 812 — [Ruder]

=schild m, zo. der Krabben ꝛc.: ⚔ carapase; =schlag m blow (or slap) on the back; =schmerz m, path. pain in the back, backache, ⚔ notalgia; =seite f back part (nicht: backside); =stück n back-piece or -part, e-s Schlachttieres a. chine; =weh n = =schmerz; =wehr ✕ f, frt. parados; =wirbel m, anat.: ⚔ dorsal vertebra; =wirbel=säule f, anat. spinal (or vertebral) column; =wirbeltier n, zo. vertebrate animal.

Rück=erinnerung (⸗...) f ⊛ (besser: Erinnerung) reminiscence; =fahr-karte f, =fahr-schein m return-ticket; =fahrt f return-journey or -trip; auf seiner ~ on his return (home); =fall m: a) jur.: = Heimfall; b) in e-n früheren Zustand, e-n Fehler, e-e Krankheit ꝛc.: relapse, return, new fit or attack; =fällig a. ⊛: a) jur. = heimfällig; b) in e-n Fehler ꝛc.: relapsing; v. Verbrechern: previously convicted, resuming one's criminal habits; =fluß m flowing back, reflux; =forderung f counter-demand or -claim; =fracht ⚓ f: a) return-freight or -cargo or -goods pl.; b) inward charges pl. or freight; =frage f counter-question or -inquiry; bei e-m ~ halten to inquire (again) of a p.; =fuhre f return-carriage or -conveyance; =gabe f giving back, restitution; bei der ~, oft: on returning a th.; =gang m: a) (das Zurückgehen) return(ing), retreat, retreating; b) (Rückwärtsgehen) walking (or marching) backwards, ast.: ⚔ retrogradation, retrogression; mech. return-movement; c) ⊛ von Wertpapieren: going down, retrograde (or downward) movement, decline; d) (schlechtes Gelingen) ill success, failure; fig. = Krebsgang; ⚔gängig a. going back(ward), retrograde; ein Verlöbnis, einen Handel ⚔ machen ⚔ to undo (or cancel) a bargain; ⚔ werden to come to nothing, von Heiraten: to be broken off; =gängig-machung f breaking off, cancelling; =gewährung f counter-concession; =¹grat n, m, anat. backbone, spine, ⚔ vertebral column; =gratskrümmung f, path. curvature of the spine; =grats-nerv m, anat. spinal nerve; =grats-wirbel m: ⚔ vertebra; =halt m: a) [Rückenhalt] ✕ reserve (-force); support, prop, (main) stay; an e-m ~ h. to be backed (up) by a p.; b) =²halt [Zurückhaltung] reserve(d manner); ohne ~ (a. ⚔haltlos a.) without reserve or restraint, unreservedly, openly; plainly; =haltlosigkeit f unreservedness, plainness; Tennis: (mit) =hand f (gespielt) back-hand; =kauf m mst ⊛ repurchase; (Einlösung) redemption; ⚔käuflich a. redeemable; =kaufs-recht n right of repurchase or redemption; =kaufs-weise adv. by way of repurchase; =kehr, =kunft f return (-journey), home-journey; bei meiner ~ nach Hause fand ich ... on returning home ...; =ladung f = =fracht a.; =lage f, jetzt oft für Reservefonds: reserve; =lauf m: a) run(ning) back, return, fig. recurrence; b) ast. retrogradation; c) ✕ e-s Geschützes: drawback; d) ↓ e-r

Schiffsmaschine: slip; ⚔läufig a. running back; fig. recurrent; bsd. ast. retrograde; =lauf-tau ↓ n gun-breeching; =lehne f e-s Stuhles: back to (or of) a chair; =leiter m, =leitung f, elect. return-current, ⊛ tel. return-wire; =lieferung ⊛ f redelivery.

rücklings (⸗̣⸣) [ahd.] adv. **1.** backwards; sich ⚔ bewegen (⚔ gehen) to move (to walk) backwards. — **2.** ⚔ (auf dem Rücken) liegen to lie on one's back, to be in a recumbent position; ⚔ fallen to fall backwards.

Rück²=marsch (⸗...) m ⊛ meist ✕ march (-ing) back or home, countermarch; vgl. =zug a.; =porto ✉ n postage on returned letters; =prall m rebound, recoil, repercussion; reaction (auch fig.); =reise f (ant. Hinreise) return-journey, journey (↓ voyage) back or home, ↓ return-(or home-)voyage; auf der ~ on the return-journey; bound for home, homeward bound (a. ↓); =ruf m recall.

Ruck=sack (⸗̣⸣) m ⊛ knapsack to be slung over the shoulder.

Rück²=schein (⸗...) m ⊛: a) reflexion; b) ⊛ receipt on delivery; =schlag m: a) =wirkung f; b) (Schlag, durch den et. zurückgeworfen wird) back-stroke (a. ⊛ elect., &c.), rebound, recoil, von Gewehren: kick, elect. return-shock, Tennis: first stroke; fig. reverse; c) (Zurückartung, Rückbildung): ⚔ atavism; =schläger m Tennis: striker out; =schluß m conclusion (a posterio'ri); =schreiben n reply; (Bescheid) a. rescript; ⚔schreitend a. retrograde; =schritt m step (or going) back, fig. re(tro)gression, (opp.) reaction; =schrittler m, ⚔schrittlich a. reactionary; =schritts-partei f, pol. reactionary party; =¹seite f back, wrong side, reverse; vgl. Kehrseite; ~ e-r Münze: reverse, ✕ tail (ant. head).

rucksen (⸗̣⸣) [mhd.] v/n. (h.) ⊛ = rucken².

Rück²=sendung (⸗...) f ⊛ sending back, return of goods, &c.; =sicht f regard, consideration; (Achtung) respect, deference; auf et. ~ nehmen to have regard (or consideration) for a th.; keine ~ nehmen auf to pay no heed to, to be regardless of; in (aus ob. mit) ~ auf out of regard for, in consideration of, in deference to; ohne ~ auf die Kosten regardless of expense; bestimmende, leitende ~en pl. (Beweggründe) guiding motives pl.; ⚔sichtlich adv. mit gen. with regard to, in respect (or in consideration) of; regarding, concerning, as to; =sicht-nahme f (taking into) consideration, considerateness for; ⚔sichts ✕ adv. u. prp. mit gen. = ⚔sichtlich; ⚔sichts-los a. without consideration for other people; inconsiderate, (gefühllos, rauh) unfeeling, uncouth; ⚔ sein to show no consideration; =sichts-losigkeit f lack of consideration, inconsiderateness; ⚔sichts-voll a. full of (kind) consideration, considerate, thoughtful; =sitz m im Wagen ꝛc. back-seat; für Rückwärtssitzende: seat with one's back to the horses or to the engine; =sprache f conference, con-

sultation; mit e-m ~ nehmen ober halten to confer (or consult, parley) with a p., to have a talk (or chat) with a p.; =sprung m leap-back; =stand m: a) von Geldzahlungen ꝛc.: arrears pl.; im ~ sein to be in arrears with one's payments or work; =stände (ausstehende Gelder) outstanding debts, F outstandings pl.; b) chm. &c.: ⚔ residue, ...um; c) ⚒ tailings pl.; ⚔ständig a.: a) von Personen: in arrears, behindhand; b) von Geldern: outstanding, (still) due; ⚔e Arbeit, Zahlung ꝛc., a. back-work, -payment, &c.; c) chm. &c.: ⚔ residuary; d) * fig. (veraltet) backward, behind the times; ⚔e Anschauungen antiquated notions pl.; =stoß m rebuff, ✕ artill recoil; vgl. =schlag b; =stoß=apparat ⚓ m rebuffing-apparatus; =strahlung f, phys. reflexion, reverberation; =strom ⊛ m, tel. return-current; =tratte ⊛ redraft; =tritt m step(ping) back (-wards); (das Sichzurückziehen) withdrawal, retirement, retreat (v. et. from a th.), von e-m Amte: resignation of an appointment, von Ministern: going out of office; =vergütung f reimbursement, repayment of money laid out; =versicherer ⊛ m reinsurer; ⚔versichern v/a. ⚓ a* to reinsure; =versicherung f reinsurance; =¹wand f back, (Hinterwand) back-wall; ⚔²wärtig a. ⊛ a) retrograde; b) in the background, behindhand; ⚔wärts adv.: backwards, back; ⚔ geh(e)n to walk (or go) backwards; ↓ ⚔ fahren! back water!; ⚔ und zo. ⚔ gebogen: ⚔ retrorse; =wärts-bewegung f backward (or retrograde) movement; =wärtser m = Rückschrittler; =wärts-geh(e)n v/n. (fn) ⊛** fig. (sich verschlechtern) to retrograde, von Geschäften auch to fall off, to go down; =wechsel ⊛ m re-exchange; =weg m way back or home; den ~ antreten to set out for (or to return) home.

ruck=weise (⸗̣⸣) adv. (F a. ⊛) by jerks, intermittently, (nach Laune) by fits and starts, capriciously, F co. as the maggot bites.

rück=wirkend (⸗...) a. ⊛ reacting, retroactive; ⚔e Kraft retrospective force or effect, =wirkung f ⊛ reaction, eines Gesetzes: retrospectiveness of a law; ⚔zahlbar a. repayable, von Anlehen: redeemable; =zahlung f paying back, reimbursement; =zoll ⊛ m b. Wiederausfuhr: drawback; =zoll-güter n/pl. debentured goods pl.; =zoll-schein m debenture; =zug m: a) bsd. ✕ retreat, eilig den ~ antreten to beat a hasty retreat; zum ~e blasen to sound the r.; b) ⚒ back-(or return-)train.

rüd, ⚔e¹ (⸗̣⸣) [fr. rude roh] a. ⊛ rude, rough, coarse; (gemein) low, vulgar.

Rüde² (⸗̣⸣) [ahd.] m ⊛ **1.** large hound. — **2.** male dog or fox or wolf.

Rudel (⸗̣⸣) [mhd. 18. sae.] n (m) ⊛ troop, crowd of people; hunt. herd of deer, pack of wolves; ⚔=weise (⸗̣⸣,⸣) adv. (F a.) in herds or flocks or gangs or troops.

Ruder (⸗̣⸣) [ahd.: rudder; *rojen] n ⊛ ↓ oar (s. Riemen²); (Steuer-) rudder, helm; am ~ sein ob. sitzen

Zeichen (s. S. XVII): F familiär; P Volkssprache; ⸗ Gaunersprache; ✕ selten; † alt (auch gestorben); * neu (auch geboren); ✚ unrichtig.

[Rudera] — 813 — [ruhen]

das ~ führen to be at the helm, to steer (the boat), *fig.* to be at the head of affairs, to carry on the government; ↓ das ~ umlegen to shift the helm; *fig.* aus ~ kommen to come into office or power.
Rudera (⌣⌣) [lt.] *n/pl. inv.* fragments, remains *pl.*; (Trümmer)debris,wreckage.
Ruder-apparat ↓ (‒⌣...) *m* ⌬ rowing-tackle; =**bank** *f* seat for rowers; =**barke** *f*, =**boot** *n* rowing-barge, -boat; =**ente** *f, orn.* ruddy duck (*Erismatu'ra*).
Rud(e)rer ↓ (⌣(⌣)⌣) *m* ⌬ 1. rower, oarsman, boatman. — 2. in Zssgn mit Zahlwörtern, zB. Drei=⌣ galley with three benches of rowers, *Alt.*: trireme.
Ruder-fahrt ↓ (‒⌣...) *f* ⌬ boating-excursion, F row (on the river, lake, &c.); =**förmig** *a.* ⌬ oar-shaped, ⚇ remiform; =**fuß** *m, zo.* webbed foot; =**füß(l)er** *m*: ⚇ remiped; =**gatt** *n* oar-lock; =**griff** *m* oar-handle; =**klampe** *f* rowlock; =**klub** *m* rowing-club; =**knecht** *m* rower, *ehm. a.* galley-slave; =**kunst** *f* oarsmanship.
rudern (⌣⌣) I *v/a. u. v/n.* (h. u. jn) ⌬a. 1. ↓ to row a boat, to pull or ply an oar, to paddle a canoe; mit allen Kräften ⌣ to ply the oars, to pull with all one's might or strength; sich fest ⌣ to run aground in rowing. — 2. *fig.* beim Schwimmen: to strike out with one's arms; mit den Armen ⌣ (beim Gehen schlenkern) to wave one's arms (about). — II ~ *n* ⌬ 3. rowing &c. (f. I).
Ruder-nagel ↓ (‒⌣...) *m* ⌬, =**pflock** *m* thole(-pin); =**pinne** *f* tiller; =**schiff** *n* = =**barke**; =**schlag** *m* stroke of the oar(s); =**schnecke** *f, zo.* ⚇ pteropod; =**spi(e)ker** *m* rudder-nail; =**sport** *m* rowing-(or boating-)sport; =**wett-fahrt** *f* rowing-match, größere boat-race.
Rüdiger (⌣⌣) *npr/m.* ⌬a. (a. Vn.) Roger.
Rudimente (⌣⌣⌣) [lt.] *n/pl.* ⌬c. (Anfangsgründe) (first) rudiments, elements *pl.*
Rudolf (⌣⌣) [ahd. Ruhmwolf] *npr/m.* ⌬⌬ *a.* (*a. Vn.*) Rudolph, weniger genau Ralph.
Ruf (⌣) [ahd.] *m* ⌬c. 1. (Schrei) cry, shout. — 2. (Zeichen, daß j. kommen soll) call. — 3. (Berufung zu einem Amte) summons; er hat e-n ~ als Professor nach B. erhalten he has been offered a professorship at (the University of) B., *auch:* he has received a call to B. — 4. (Schall, bsd. von Blasinstrumenten) signal, sound. — 5. (*o. pl.*) (Gerücht) rumour, report; es geht der ~, daß // it is rumoured (or reported) that //. — 6. (*o. pl.*) (öffentliches Urteil über e-n) reputation, *auch:* standing, credit; weitverbreiteter ~ renown, fame; (Berühmtheit) celebrity; ~ bekommen to acquire fame, to rise in public esteem or into public notice; einen, et. in ~ bringen to bring a p., a th. into repute or vogue; e-n in den ~ bringen, daß (od. als ob) er geizig sei od. geizig zu sein to give a p. the character of a miser; in üblen ~ bringen to defame, to cry (or F run) down; e-n großen ~ erlangen to rise into fame or high repute; sie sind viel besser als ihr ~ they are far better than they are reputed (or said) to be; in gutem (üblem) ~e stehen bei e-m to be in good (bad) repute (or omen) with a p., to be in a p.'s good (bad) books; Mann von ~ famous (or well-known, distinguished, noted, eminent) man, *auch:* man of great distinction or note.
rufen (⌣⌣) [ahd.] ⌬b. I *v/n.* (h.) 1. (laut erschallen lassen) to cry (out), to shout; ⚔ ins Gewehr ⌣ to call to arms; um Hilfe ⌣ to cry (or shout, call) for help; mit *dat.*: e-m ⌣ to warn a p. by shouting, *geh. Spr.* — e-m ⌣ to call (to) a p. — II *v/a.* 2. e-n ⌣ to call a p.; beiseite ⌣ to call aside; e-m et. ins Gedächtnis ⌣ to recall a th. to a p.'s mind, to remind a p. of a th. f. Leben 17; wieder ins Leben ⌣ to recall (or restore) to life, to resuscitate; e-n zu sich ⌣ to bid a p. come near, feierlich: to summon a p. into one's presence. — 3. *fig.* wie gerufen kommen to come in the nick of time or at the right moment, von Dingen *auch:* to fit the occasion. — 4. e-n wach ⌣ to rouse a p. from his sleep; *v/refl.* sich heiser ⌣ to shout o.s. hoarse. — III ~ *n* ⌬ 5. shouting, &c. (f. I u. II), shouts *pl., thea.* call, encore.
Rufer (⌣⌣) *m* ⌬ 1. (*a.* =**in** *f* ⌬) person who shouts or calls; (Schreier) crier. — 2. *a)* ⌘ am Fernsprecher = **Wecker**; *b)* ↓ (Sprachrohr) speaking-trumpet.
Ruf-fall (‒⌣) *m* ⌬ *gram.* vocative case.
Rüffel F (⌣⌣) [mhd.; *rüffeln] *m* ⌬ reprimand, F wigging (vgl. Rüge).
rüffeln (⌣⌣) [mhd.] [riffeln hecheln] *v/a.* ⌬a. to reprimand, to scold, F to blow up.
Ruf-glocke (‒...) *f* ⌬ electric, &c., call-bell; =**name** *m* name by which a p. is called; =**pfeife** *f* bird-call; =**station** *f Fernspr.* call-office; =**taste** ⌘ *f Fernspr.* call-button,bell-button or -push; =**weite** *f*: in ~ within call or ear-shot or hail.
Rüge (⌣⌣) [mhd.] *f* ⌬ 1. reproof (vgl. Rüffel); (Tadel) reproach, blame; (Warnung) admonition, öffentliche: censure; eine ~ bekommen to be reprimanded, F to get a good blowing-up or wigging; einem eine ~ für et. erteilen to reprove (or censure) a p. for a th. — 2. ältere Rechtssprache, noch bisw. gbr.: *a)* denunciation of a crime; *b)* (Vergehen) offence; *ehm.* ~=**amt**, ~=**gericht** *n* (inferior) court of justice, jetzt bsd.: police-court.
rügen bsd. nordd. (⌣⌣) [ahd.] *v/a.* ⌬ 1. e-n wegen et. ⌣ to reprimand (or reprove, blame, stärker: censure) a p. for a th. — 2. *ehm. jur.:* a) to denounce; b) (richten) to sentence; (strafen) to punish, fine.
rügens=wert (‒⌣⌣.) *a.* ⌬ deserving a reprimand, liable to censure.
Rüge-richter (‒⌣...) *m* ⌬ magistrate; =**sache** *f* police-court affair.
Ruh (⌣) *f* ⌬ = **Ruhe**.
Ruh-... (‒...) in Zssgn = **Ruhe-...**
Ruhe (⌣⌣) [ahd.] *f* ⌬ 1. rest, repose, (Erholung) recreation; (Stille) quiet, silence; sich zur ~ begeben to go to rest; vgl. begeben 2; ~ seiner Asche!, ~ sei mit ihm! (Nachruf) peace be with him!, may he rest in peace!; ~ ist die erste Bürgerpflicht the first duty of a citizen is orderliness or peacefulness; meine Ruh ist hin (*G., Faust*) my peace is flown; keine Ruh bei Tag u. Nacht! in Mozarts Don Juan: no peace by day or night!, F co. no rest for the wicked! — 2. mit *verbs:* e-m Hunde ~ bedeuten to make a dog be quiet; dem Geiste ~ gönnen to rest one's mind or brain; einem keine ~ gönnen to give a p. no rest, to be for ever bothering a p.; er hat auf keinem Flecke ~ he cannot rest (or does not stay) anywhere; ich habe keine ~ vor ihm he gives me no peace; F jetzt hat die Liebe (*od.* arme) Seele Ruh! now there's nothing left (to worry about)!, that's all!, it's all over!; (haltet) ~! be quiet!, hush!, silence!; sein Leiden läßt ihm keinen Augenblick ~ his complaint does not allow him a moment's respite; seine Gläubiger, Verfolger ⚇. lassen ihm keine ~ ... leave him no rest, ... press him hard; F Sie werden uns doch die ~ nicht **mitnehmen!** do not leave without having sat down (a minute), F don't hurry (away)!; f. pflegen II; e-m ~ **wünschen** to wish a p. a good night's rest. — 3. mit *prp.*: es ist nicht **aus** seiner ~ zu bringen he is not easily put out, nothing disturbs the balance of his mind, he is imperturbable; **in** aller ~ very calmly, with great composure or self-possession; lassen Sie mich in ~! leave me at rest!, let (or leave) me alone!; laß mich damit in ~! don't trouble (or bother) me with that!; ohne ~ und Rast, ohne Rast und Ruh without any rest or peace; e-n **zur letzten** ~ begleiten, bestatten to lay a p. to rest; zur ~ bringen to pacify, calm, quiet, hush; f. eingehen 3; zur ~ gehen: *a)* (schlafen) to go (or retire) to rest; *b)* (sterben) to pass away, to enter into rest, *rel.* to go to one's eternal home; zur ~ setzen to pension off; sich zur ~ setzen to retire from business or into private life. — 4. = **Ruhestätte**. — 5. ⚔ den Hahn e-s Gewehres in ~ setzen to half-cock a gun; eine Maschine in ~ setzen to stop (or ungear) ..., to bring ... to a dead stop.
Ruhe-bank (‒⌣...) *f* ⌬ bench (for the weary); settee; f. =**bett**; =**bett** *n* bed of ease; comfortable lounge, couch, sofa; =**gehalt** *n* (retiring-)pension; =**kissen** *n* (soft) pillow; Sprichw. f. Gewissen; =**lager** *n* = =**bett**; ⌣**los** *a.* ⌬ restless, (unruhig) disquieted; =**losigkeit** *f* restlessness, disquietude.
ruhen (⌣⌣) [ahd.] ⌬ I *v/n.* (h.) 1. to rest (o.s.), to take (one's) rest, to repose; (stillsitzen) to sit still; (nichts tun) to be doing nothing, to rest (or remain) idle, (stillstehen) to be at a standstill; im Grabe ⌣ to rest in the grave, *auch:* to sleep in peace; sanft ruhe seine Asche may he rest in peace; auf Leichensteinen: hier ruht (in Gott) ... here lies ..., *auch:* here sleeps in Jesus ...; ⌘ ⌣des Kapital dead (or unemployed) capital; Sprichw. f. Arbeit 7; höfliche Redensart: (ich) wünsche (Ihnen) wohl geruht zu haben I trust you have had (or enjoyed) a good night's rest. — 2. eine Arbeit ⌣ **lassen** to leave a task unfinished, to cease one's labour; Ihre Erfolge lassen ihn

[Ruheort] — 814 — [Rumelier]

nicht 2 ... will not let him sleep; eine Sache 2 laffen to drop a matter; laffet die Toten 2! honour (or respect) the peace of the dead! — 3. fig. ich werde nicht eher 2, als bis es durchgeführt ist I shall not rest (or cease, stop) until it is carried through. — 4. auf et. 2 (begründet sein) to rest on a th., to be based (or founded) on a th.; auf Säulen 2 to be supported by pillars; Gottes Segen ruht auf God's blessing is (or rests, dwells) upon it. — II v/a. 5. den Geist 2c. 2 to rest ... — III v/refl. sich 2 6. to (take) rest, feierlich: to repose; hier ruht sich's sanft here one finds gentle rest or sweet repose.—IV ~ n 23 7. rest(ing), repose, jur. des Verfahrens: suspension.

Ruhe-ort (ᴵᵛ...) m 12 = =platz; =pause f pause (for rest), F slack moment; =platz m, =plätzchen n: a) = =ftätte; b) arch. auf einer Treppe: landing; =poften m = =ftätte a; =punkt m point of (or where to) rest; ♪, &c. auch: pause, pros.: ⁊ cæsura; phys. fulcrum; =feffel m lounge, lounging-chair; vgl. Lehnfeffel; =fitz m: a) in e-m Garten: (garden-) seat, bench; b) (Wohnfitz) (quiet) residence, country-seat; =ftand m: a) state of rest or repose; b) (Stand j-s, der sich zur Ruhe gesetzt hat) retirement; in den — versetzen to superannuate, to pension off, auch: to put on half-pay; =ftätte f: a) place (or haven, harbour) of rest, resting-place; retreat; b) oft fig. letzte ~ last resting-place, grave; =ftelle f = =ftätte a; =ftifter m peace-maker; =ftörer(in f) m disturber of the peace, brawler, rioter; =ftörung f breach of the peace, disturbance; brawl(ing), riot(ing); =ftunde f hour of rest or recreation, leisure-hour; f. Feierabend b; =tag m day of rest, holiday, F day off, off-day; =zeichen ♪ n rest, pause; f. a. Fermate; =zeit f time of rest or repose, leisure; =zuftand m = =ftand a.

ruhig (ᴸᵛ) [mhd.] a. 66 1. at rest; quiet, (ftill) still, (leidenschaftslos) calm, tranquil; (friedliebend) pacific, peaceful; (heiter) serene; (kaltblütig) cool (and collected); (beruhigt) reassured; (behaglich) easy, at ease; fei 2, mein Kind! hush, baby!, be quiet, child!; fei 2, es wird fich schon alles machen! don't worry, all will come right! — 2. bei dem Blute, bei der Überlegung when calm(ly considered), F das läßt mich 2 that does not trouble me; 2 (adv.) schlafen to sleep soundly; F Sie können das 2 (getroft) unterzeichnen you may safely sign it; ♃ die See calm (or smooth, unruffled) sea, poet. halcyon sea; vom Winde: 2 werden to (fall) calm, to come to a dead calm, to go down.

Ruhm (ᴸ) [ahd.] m ⓒc. 1. glory; (Preis) praise; hoher ~ celebrity, great renown or name or fame; sich mit ~ bedecken, großen ~ erwarten to cover o.s. with glory, to win great fame. — 2. = Ruf 6, z.B. sein ~ ist nicht fein his reputation is not of the best.

ruhm-bedeckt (ᴵᴵ...) a. 66, =bekränzt a. covered (or crowned) with glory;

=(be)gier(de) f ⓐ desire of glory; vgl. =fucht; 2(be)gierig a. desirous of glory. **rühmen** (ᴸᵛ) [ahd.; *Ruhm] I v/a. u. sich 2 v/refl. 88 1. sich e-r Sache 2, sich wegen (ob. mit) etwas 2 to boast of a th., to pride o.s. on a th., mit Stolz: to glory in a th., to talk proudly (or to be proud) of a th.; ohne mich zu 2 without boasting, auch oft: though I say it. — 2. (empfehlen) to commend; (loben) to praise, to sing the praises of, to speak highly of; (erheben) to extol, to glorify; für Geschäftszwecke: to puff, to advertise; man rühmt ihn als tapfer he is reputed to be brave; 2d erwähnen to make honourable mention of. — II ~ n 23 3. (f. 2) commendation, praise(s pl.); glorification; viel ~s von et. m. to speak in the highest terms of a th., F to make a great fuss about a th.

rühmens-wert (ᴵᴵᵛᴸ) a. 66 praise-worthy, commendable, laudable.

Ruhmes-glanz (ᴵᴵ...) m 12 lustre of glory, prestige; =halle f, =tempel m temple of glory, pantheon. [glory.\ **ruhm-gekrönt** (ᴵᴵᵛᴸ) a. 66 crowned with/ **rühmlich** (ᴸᵛ) [ahd.] a. 66 glorious, honourable; vgl. rühmenswert.

Rühmlichkeit (ᴸᵛ-) f 46 gloriousness; praiseworthiness.

Ruhm-liebe (ᴵᴵ...) f 12 love of glory; =los a. 66 inglorious, unknown to fame, obscure; =lofigkeit f ingloriousness; =redig a. vainglorious, boastful; =redigkeit f vainglory, boastfulness; =reich a. = =voll; =fucht f passion (or thirst) for glory, (inordinate) ambition; =füchtig a. thirsting after (or greedy of) glory, (very)ambitious; =voll a. glorious; =würdig a. praiseworthy, meritorious; =würdigkeit f praiseworthiness, meritoriousness.

Ruhr (ᴸ) [ahd.; *rühren] f 46 1. path. (Abführen) diarrhœa; rote ~ (blutiger Stuhlgang) dysentery. — 2. agr. turning up the soil or the earth or the ground. **Ruhr-anfall** (ᴵᴵ...) m 12 path. attack of dysentery; 2artig a. 66 dysenteric. **Rühr-ei** (ᴸᵛᴸ) n 2 Kocht.: scrambled eggs pl. **rühren** (ᴸᵛ) [ahd.: rear] 88 I v/n. (h.) 1. to stir, to move. — 2. = herrühren, z.B. der Gebrauch rührt daher the custom originates from that (circumstance). — II v/a. 3. to stir; die Beine 2 to use one's legs, to move about nimbly, to trot along; kein Glied 2 können to be unable to move (or stir) a limb. — 4. ♪ die Trommel 2 (schlagen) to beat the drum; die Laute 2 to touch (or play) the lute. — 5. ⸺ = an=, berühren. — 6. (plötzlich und heftig treffen) to strike (hard); der Schlag hat ihn gerührt he has had an apoplectic stroke; vom Schlag gerührt struck with apoplexy; f. Donner. — 7. (um=) 2 to stir (round), to twirl. ⊙ to rake; Eier ~ to beat up eggs; Kalk 2, Mörtel 2 to tew mortar. — 8. innerlich 2 to touch; es hat ihn tief gerührt it deeply affected him; zu Tränen 2 to move to tears. — III sich 2 v/refl. 9. oft: sich und regen to bestir o.s., to be astir, bsd. von geschäftiger Tätigkeit: to be up and doing; ich kann mich vor Müdigkeit

nicht 2 I am too tired to move or to stir; rührt euch!: a) look alive!; b) ᚷ stand at ease! — 10. fig. sein Gewissen rührt sich his conscience is (a)roused or awakened. — IV ~ n 23 11. = Rührung; er fühlt' ein menschlich ~ he felt a touch of human sympathy. — V 2b p.pr. u. a. 66 12. touching, affecting; (ergreifend) pathetic, thrilling, emotional, heart-stirring.

Rühr=faß ⊙ (ᴵᴵ...) n 12 churn. **rührig** (ᴸᵛ) [ahd. ge2] a. 66 astir, busy, active; (munter) alert; (flint) agile, nimble; **~keit** (ᴸᵛ-) f 46 stir, activity; alertness; agility.

Rühr=kelle (ᴵᴵᵛᴸ) f 12 = Rührlöffel.

ruhr-krank (ᴵᴵ...) a. 66 path. suffering from dysentery; =kranke([r] m) f ⊕ dysenteric patient; =kraut ♀ n 12 cudweed (Gnapha'lium); falbes ~ Jersey livelong (G. lu'teo-a'lbum).

Rühr=krücke ⊙ (ᴵᴵ...) f 12 stirrer; =löffel m Küche: (pot-)ladle; =mich-nicht-an ♀ n balsam, touch-me-not (Impa'tiens noli me ta'ngere); 2fam (ᴸᵛ) [ndd.] a. 66, 2felig a. sentimental, emotional; =scheit n, =fpatel m ⊕ Brauerei: mash-staff or -stick; chm., pharm. spatula; =ftück n, thea. sensational piece, melodrama; =fzene f, thea. touching (or moving, pathetic) scene.

Rührung (ᴸᵛ) [rühren] f 46: a) unter ~ der Trommeln with drums beating; b) (Gemütsbewegung) (deep) emotion; er sah ihn mit großer ~ an he looked at him with deep compassion or emotion; vor ~ nicht sprechen können to be too deeply moved to speak, a. to feel a lump in one's throat.

Ruin (ᵛᴸ) [fr. ruine f] m ⓐd. ruin, destruction, (Verfall) decay, (Sturz) (down)fall; dem ~ nahe sein to be nearly ruined; er ist dem ~ sehr nahe he has ruin staring him in the face; dem ~ zusteuernd on the road to ruin.

Ruine (ᵛᴸ) [fr.] f 46 ruin (von Gebäudetrümmern: ruins pl.), wreckage, debris, fig. v. Menschen auch: wreck.

ruinen-artig (ᵛᴸᵛᴸ), **ruinenhaft** (ᵛᴸᵛᴸ) a. 66 in ruins; decayed; als Attribut auch: tumble-down, dilapidated.

ruinieren (ᵛᵛᴸᵛ) [fr. ruiner] v/a. u. sich 2 v/refl. 98: e-n 2 to ruin a p., to compass (or cause) a p.'s ruin, F to do for a p., Kleider: to spoil; ♣ ruiniert, oft: lost, broken, done for, F smashed (up), up the tree, P broke.

Rülp(s) P(ᴸᵛ) m ⓐa. derb (Aufstoßen v. Speisen) belch(ing), ⸺ (e)ructation; F fig. coarse (or rude, saucy) fellow, lout. **rülpsen** P(ᴸᵛ) v/n. (h.) 90 to belch, to break wind.

(ˀ)**rum**[1] F (ᴸ) adv., abbr. = herum. **Rum**[2] ᛋ (ᴸ) [ndd., *engl.] m ⓓd. (aus Zuckerrohr bereiteter Branntwein) rum. **Rumäne** f ⓓ R(o)umanian m 12. **Rumänien** ♀ (-ᴸ(ᵛ)-) npr/n. 23α. (Königreich, vereinigte Walachei und Moldau) R(o)umania.

Rumäni=er(in f ⓓ) m 12, rumänisch (-ᴸ-) a. 66 Roumanian. [distillery.\ **Rum²-brennerei** (ᴱᵛᴸ-) f ⓓ rum-/ **Rumeli=en** ♀ (-ᴸ(ᵛ)-) [türk.] npr/n. 23α. (türk. Provinz) R(o)umelia. **Rumeli-er(in**

Signs (see page XVII): F familiar; P vulgar; ⌐ flash; ⸺ rare; † obsolete (died); * new word (born); ⁺⁺ incorrect; ♪ music;

[Rumeliot] — 815 — [Russe]

f ⑳ m ㉒, a. **Rumeliot**(in f ⑳) (--(◡)ᴸ) m ㉒, **rumelisch** (-ᴸ◡) a. ⑯ R(o)umelian.
Rum²-fabrik(⚜◡ᴸ) f ㊷ = Rumbrennerei.
Rummel (⚜◡) [ndd.: rumble] m ㉒ 1. = Gerümpel; (Lärm) loud noise, row, uproar; (Auflauf) riot. — 2. = Gerümpel. — 3. ⚘ (et.) im ~ (in Bausch und Bogen) kaufen, auch: den ganzen ~ kaufen to buy (s.th.) in the bulk or the lump, F to buy the (whole) lot. — 4. F fig den (ganzen) ~ (Kram) kennen to know all about a th.; er kennt den ~ schon he knows the ropes or what's what; den ~ (die Pfiffe) verstehen to know a trick or two, F to be up to snuff.
rummeln (⚜◡) [f. Rummel] = rumpeln.
Rumor (-ᴸ) [mhd.; *it. *rumo're*] m ⑳d. noise, row, hubbub; (Gelärm) riot, rioting, uproar, F rumpus.
rumoren (-ᴸ◡) [Rumor] v/n. (h.) ㊸ to make a noise or a hubbub, F to kick up a row or a rumpus. [person.]
Rumorer (-ᴸ◡) m ㉒ noisy (or riotous)
Rumpelei (⚜◡ᴸᴵ) f ㊷ rumbling (noise).
rumpelig F (⚜◡◡) a. ⑯ = holperig.
Rumpel-kammer (⚜◡...) f ㊷ lumber-room; fig. in die ~ kommen to be put (or laid) on the shelf; **=kasten** m box full of old lumber; F fig. (alte Kutsche) rumbling (or lumbering, shaky, jolting) old coach, F co. rattletrap.
rumpeln (⚜◡) [mhd.: rumble] I v/n. ㉒a. 1. (h.) to rumble, to make a rumbling (or rattling) noise. — 2. (in) der Wagen ist über die Brücke gerumpelt (2b gefahren) ... rumbled (or lumbered, jolted) across the bridge. — 3. bisw. v/a.: alles durch~ea. ㊷ to toss everything upside down, F to jumble up things. — II ~ n ㉓ 4. rumbling (noise).
Rumpf (⚜) [mhd.: rump] m ⓂⒷb. trunk, body, e-r Statue: torso; ⓔ e-r Mühle: (mill-)hopper, ↓ eines Schiffes: hull of a ship.
Rumpf-baum ⊙ (⚜...) m ㊷ Müllerei: trimmer; **=beugen und =strecken** n bending and stretching of the body.
rümpfen (⚜◡) [ahd.] v/a. ㊺ to wrinkle, to curl; die Nase ㊷ to turn up one's nose; den Mund (oder das Maul) ㊷ to pucker up (or to draw) one's mouth.
Rumpf-leiter (⚜...) f ㊷ = **=baum**; **=parlament** ⑨ n, hist.: englisches ~ unter Cromwell, Mitte des 17. sae. Rump (Parliament), the Rump.
Rum²-punsch (⚜◡ᴸ) m ㊷ rum-punch.
rund (⚜) [mhd.: round; fr. *rond*; *lt. *ro-tu'ndus*] I a.⑯(D1,6)1.round,mſt◡◡zo.☝ rotund(ate); (abgerundet) rounded (off); (kreisförmig) circular; (kugelig) globular, spherical; (walzenförmig) cylindrical, ☝ terete, das ist mir zu ㊷ (schwer verständlich) that's beyond me; ein 2es, volles Dutzend a good round dozen; in 2er Zahl in round numbers; 2 m. to round (off); fig. (vollständig m.) to complete, to accomplish; ㊷ (und dick) w. to grow plump or fat or stout or sleek. — 2. adv. ㊷ abschlagen to refuse flatly; e-m ㊷ heraus sagen to tell a p. roundly or openly, to speak plainly; sagen Sie es mir ㊷ und nett tell me frankly and plainly; ㊷ um et. herum round about a th.; acht Kilometer ㊷ umher for five miles (a)round or in circumference.

— II ~ n ①b. 3. (etwas Rundes) round (vgl. Kreis, Kugel), bſp. = Erdenrund.
rund-bäckig (⚜...) a. ⑯ chubby(-faced), round-cheeked, plump (in the face);
=bau m ㉒ arch. round (or circular) building; **=beet** n, hort. round bed;
=bild n = gemälde; **=blätt(e)rig** a. ☝ round-leaved, ☝ rotundifolious; **=blick** m view all round, panorama; **=bogen** ⊙ m (ant. Spitzbogen) arch. Norman (or Roman) arch; über Türen u. Fenstern: round-head; **=bogenstil** m Norman (or Roman) style (of architecture);
=brenner ⊙ m round burner.
Runde (⚜◡) [rund] f ㊷ 1. (Kreis, kreisförmige Bewegung) round, circle, circular motion, von Tanzenden a. ring, von Zechbrüdern: company, party; die ~ m. to go the round; den Becher die ~ machen l. to send (or hand) the cup round; in der ~ = rund umher (f. rund 2 am Ende). — 2. [nhd.; *fr. f. Ronde] ⚔ (Rundgang der Wache) round, inspection of sentinels or pickets.
Ründe (⚜◡) [rund] f ㊷ 1. a) roundness, rotundity, einer Kugel: globosity, sphericity; b) fig.(Abgerundetsein) roundness. — 2. ⊙ arch. (Bogenrundung) vault, arched shape. [iron.]
Rund-eisen ⊙ (⚜ᴸ◡) n ㊷ round bar-
Rundell (◡⚜) [(⚜+) fr. *rondelle* f] n ①c. hort. (rundes Beet) round bed, roundel.
runden, ⚘ **ründen** (⚜◡) I v/a. u. sich ㊷ v/refl. ㊾: (sich) ㊷ to (grow) round.
— II ~ n ㉓ rounding (off), fig. finish(ing).
rund-erhaben (⚜...) a. ⑯ convex, auf beiden Seiten: biconvex; **=erhabenheit** f ㊷ convexity; **=fahrt** f drive (or ride) round a town, &c.; vgl. **=reise**;
=gang m: a) (Umlauf) rotation; b) bſp. ⚔ round (vgl. Runde 2); **=gebäude** n rotunda; vgl. **=bau**; **=gemälde** n panorama, panoramic view; **=gesang** m glee, roundelay, komisches: catch.
Rundheit (⚜-) f ㊷ = Ründe 1. [about.]
rund-herum (⚜◡ᴸ) adv. all around, round
Rund-holz ↓ (⚜ᴸ◡) n ㊷ round timber.
Rundigkeit (⚜◡-) f ㊷ = Ründe 1.
Rund-kopf (⚜...) m ㊷: a) round head; b) **=köpfe** m/pl., hist. (engl. Puritaner) Round Heads pl.; **=köpfig** a. ⑯ round-headed; **=lauf** m ㊷: a) = Kreisbewegung; b) Turnerei: giant stride.
rundlich (⚜◡) a. ⑯ roundish; (geschweift) rounded off, sinuous; ⊙ cambered;
=keit f ㊷ roundishness, sinuosity.
Rund-maul (⚜...) n ㊷ ichth. round-mouth; **=mäuler** pl. auch: ☝ cyclostomata pl.; **=mäulig** a. ⑯ round-mouthed; **=reim** m = Kehrreim; **=reise** f circular tour or trip, Am. a. round trip; e-s engl. Richters: circuit; auf einer politischen ~ begriffen on the stump; **=reise-billett** n, **=reise-karte** f tourist ticket, combination ticket; **=säge** ⊙ f circular saw; **=säule** f round column, cylinder;
=schau f: a) panorama, ☝ ⚘ periscope; b) in e-r Zeitung: politische ~ political review or summary; **=schild** ⚔ m round shield, ehm. auch: roundel; **=schnur** f round bobbin; **=schreiben** n circular (letter); **=schrift** f Kalligraphie: round-hand, (fr.) ronde; **=stab** ⊙ m, arch. astragal, round, am Säulenfuße: tore;

=stäbchen ⊙ n, arch., &c. beading; **=stab-leiste** f bead-line; **=tanz** m round dance;
=trunk m drink(ing) all round; ꝙum (a. ⚜◡⚜) adv. round about, all around.
Rundung, ⚘ **Ründung** (⚜◡) f ㊷ 1. = runden II. — 2. = Ründe. — 3. = rund II. — 4. (Aufbauschung) swelling, puffiness, inflation.
Rund-weg (⚜ᴸ) m ㊷ circular path or road; ꝙweg (⚜◡, ⚜ᴸ) adv. plainly, flatly, bluntly; **=wurm** m, zo. round-worm (A'scaris); **=zange** ⊙ f round-nosed pliers pl. [runic letter.]
Rune (ᴸ◡) [nhd.; *stand.: raunen] f ㊷
Runen-alphabet (ᴸ◡...) n ㊷ futhorc, futhark; **=schrift** f (älteste germanische Schrift) runic character or writing; **=stab** m runic wand; **=stein** m rune-stone.
Runge ⊙ (⚜◡) [nhd.: rung] f ㊷ Wagenbau: ~ einer Kutsche: coach-standard, e-s Leiterwagens: stud-stave, e-s Karrens 2c.: (iron) support for the sides.
Runkel-rübe ♀ (⚜◡ᴸ◡) f ㊷ beet(-root) (*Beta vulga'ris* var. *Rapa*); vgl. Mangold;
=rüben-zucker ♀ m beet-root sugar.
Runzel (⚜◡) [ahd.] f ㊷ wrinkle, fold, rumple, um den Mund a. pucker, ~n um die Augen a. F crows' feet pl.
runz(e)lig (⚜(◡)◡) a. ⑯ wrinkled, puckered; (zſ.-geschrumpft) shrivelled(up)
runzeln (⚜◡) v/a. und sich ㊷ v/refl. ㊾a. to wrinkle, to form wrinkles; die Stirn ㊷ to knit one's brows, to frown.
Rüpel F (ᴸ◡) [nhd.; *Rup(recht) *dim.] m ㉒ (Flegel) coarse (or rude) fellow.
Rüpelei (◡◡ᴸ) [Rüpel] f ㊷ coarseness, stärker: brutality. [stärker: brutal.)
rüpelhaft (ᴸ◡◡) a. ⑯ coarse, rude,
rupfen (⚜◡) [mhd.; *raufen] v/a. ㊸ to pull up or out, Blumen: to pick, Vögel: to pluck; fig. e-n ㊷ (um sein Geld bringen) to rob a p. (of his money), to fleece a p.
Rupfer (⚜◡) m ㉒, **~in** f ㊵ plucker, person who plucks geese, &c.
Rupi-e (ᴸ(◡)◡) [ſft. Silber] f ㊷ (indische Münze von ungefähr 1,35 ℳ Wert) rupee.
ruppicht ☝, mſt **ruppig** (⚜◡) [ndd.] a. ⑯ tattered (and torn), shabby(-looking), (armſelig) paltry; (roh) rude.
Ruppigkeit (⚜◡-) f ㊷ tattered state, shabbiness; paltriness; rudeness.
Rupp-sack F (⚜ᴸ) m ⓒc.: a) shabby fellow; b) naughty child.
Ruprecht (ᴸ◡) npr/m. ⑮ Rupert, Robert; Knecht ~ (der zu Weihnachten umgeht) etwa: (Old) Father Christmas, Santa Claus.
Ruprechts-kraut ♀ (ᴸ◡◡ᴸ) n ㊷ herb-robert (*Gera'nium Robertia'num*).
Rusch (⚜) [ndd.] m ⑪(⚜)a.: ~ und Busch brambles (or briers) pl. and brush-wood. [Damenkleider 2c.) ruche.)
Rüsche (ᴸ◡) [fr.] f ㊷ (gefältelter Besatz für
ruscheln F (⚜◡) v/n. (h.) ㊸ Wa. = huscheln; weiſS. to scamp one's work.
Ruß (⚜) [ahd.] m ⓐa. 1. soot, einer Lampe: lamp-black. — 2. ⚘ = Rußbrand.
ruß-artig (⚜...) a. ⑯ sooty, ☝ fuliginous; **=brand** ♀ m im Getreide: burnt-ear, smut (*Ustila'go carbo*); **=braun** n sooty brown, zum Tuſchen: bistre; **=druck** ⊙ m Stecherkunſt: smoke-proof.
Russe (⚜◡) [stand.] m ㊹, **Russin** f ㊵ 1. Russian, auch: Muscovite (Moskauer). — 2. F (Küchenschabe) black beetle.

⚜ scientific; ♀ botanical; ⚷ geography; ⊙ machinery; ⚒ mining; ⚔ military; ↓ marine; ⚘ commercial; ☝ postal; 🚂 railway.

Rüssel (⌣⌢) [mhd.: root wühlen] m zo. des Elefanten, Tapirs ꝛc.: trunk, des Schweines: snout, der Insekten ꝛc.: proboscis.
rüssel-artig (⌣⌢...), -förmig a. like a trunk or proboscis, trunk-shaped, proboscidiform.
Rüssel-käfer (⌣⌢...) m ent. weevil (Familie Curculio'nidae); **-maus** f, zo. (Desman) Muscovitic rat, musk-rat (Myo'gale moscha'ta); **-tier** n animal with a trunk or proboscis; **-tiere** n/pl., zo.: proboscidians pl.
rußen (⌣⌣)[Ruß] I v/n. (h.) to produce (or give off) soot, Lampe ꝛc.: to smoke. — II v/a. to (blacken with) soot.
Russen-freund (⌣⌢...) m , -freundlich a. Russophile; **-freundlichkeit** f Russophilism; **-furcht** f Russophobia.
Ruß-farbe (⌢...) f = -braun; -farben a. sooty brown, paint. bistre; **-fleck** m speck of soot, smut.
russifizieren (⌣⌣⌣⌣⌣) [neu-lt.] v/a. (russisch m.) to Russianize.
rußicht a., mst **rußig** (⌣⌣) a. sooty, fuliginous. — 2. agr. vom Getreide: (brandig) smutty, smuttied.
russisch (⌣⌣) a. Russian, of Russia, auch: Muscovite; -es Pelzwerk Muscovy fur; die -e Sprache, das ~(e) n the Russian language, Russian; ~-japanischer Krieg (1904—5) Russo-Japanese war; -türkisch (⌣⌣⌣⌣) a. Russo-Turkish; die ~-türkischen Kriege the Turco-Russian wars pl.
Ruß-kohle (⌢...) f min. sooty coal; **-kreide** f black-chalk. ‖Russia.‖
Rußland ⚲ (⌢⌣) [Russen-land] npr/n.
Ruß-schreiber Ⓞ (⌢...) m tel. carbon-recorder; **-schwarz** n = Kienruß.
Rüst-anker ⚓ (⌢...) [rüsten] m sheet-(or waist-)anchor; **-baum** Ⓞ m scaffolding-pole; **-bock** m sc.-trestle, jack; **-brett** n sc.-plank.
Rüste (⌣⌣) [ndd.: Rast] f = Ruhe; die Sonne geht zu(r) ~ (geht unter) the sun is setting; zu(r) ~ geh(e)n (zu Ende gehen) to come to an end; das Jahr geht zur ~ the end of the year is fast approaching.
rüsten (⌣⌣) [ahd.] I v/a. u. sich ~ v/refl. (sich) ~ zu (zu bereiten (o.s.) for; e-n mit et. ~ to equip (or fit, provide) a p. with a th.; ⚔ ein Heer ~ to mobilize..., to put ... on war-footing; sich zum Kriege ~, auch abs. ~ to prepare (or get ready) for war, to mobilize. — II v/n. (h.) Ⓞ arch., ⚒ (ein Gerüst m.) to raise (or put up) a scaffolding. — III ~ n = Rüstung 1.
Rüster ⚘ [nhd.: Rot] f agr.1 elm (Ulmus); **rüstern** a. (made) of elm wood.
Rüst-haus (⌢...) n = -kammer; **-holz** n wooden prop or support.
rüstig (⌣⌣) [ahd.; *rüsten] a. (voll Kraft) vigorous, robust, hale (and hearty); (hurtig) active, alert, nimble; **-keit** f vigour, robustness; activity; unimpaired strength.
Rüst-kammer ⚔ (⌢...) f armoury, weitS. arsenal; ehm. **-knappe** ⚔ m armourer; ehm. **-meister** m ⚔ armourer, keeper of an arsenal; **-platz** ⚔ m place of arms, **-saal** ⚔ m armoury; **-stange** f = -baum; **-tag** m day (set apart) for preparation(s); (Vorabend) eve of a (Jewish) feastday.
Rüstung (⌣⌣) [ahd.; *rüsten] f 1. (f. rüsten I) preparation (or equipment) for, mit Waffen: armament; ⚔ mobilization, (making) warlike preparations pl. — 2. a) (Gerät) utensils, implements pl., ⚓ tackling; b) (Baugerüst) scaffold(ing); c) bsd. ehm. ⚔ (Harnisch) armour; volle ~ panoply (of war); die ~ anlegen to put on (or don) one's armour.
Rüst-wagen (⌢...) m = Leiterwagen; **-woche** f holy week; **-zeug** n armour, weitS. (Werkzeuge) set of tools, Bauwesen: parts of a scaffold(ing); bibl. auserwähltes ~ des Herrn chosen vessel of the Lord.
Rute (⌣⌢) [ahd.: ro(o)d] f 1. rod, wand, (Birkenreis) birch, (Gerte) switch; (Peitsche) whip, (Fuchtel) scourge; e-n eine ~ binden to lay (or have) a rod in pickle for a p.; sich selbst eine ~ binden to make a rod for one's own back; e-m Kinde die ~ geben to give a child the rod or the birch or a whipping (s. Rücken¹ 2 am Schluß); bibl. wer die ~ spart, verzieht das Kind spare the rod and spoil the child. — 2. hunt. (Schwanz vom Hund, Fuchs, Wolf ꝛc.) brush.
Ruten-bündel (⌢...) n bundle of rods, röm. Alt.: ~ pl. der Liktoren (lt.) fasces pl.; -förmig a. rod-shaped,

virgate; **-gänger** m (Quellensucher) dowser; **-hieb**, **-schlag**, **-streich** m stroke (or cut) with a rod.
Ruthene (⌣⌢⌣) m , **Ruthenin** f Ruthenian; **Rutheni-en** ⚲ (⌣⌢⌣⌣) npr/n. Ga. (Teil Galiziens) Ruthenia; **ruthenisch** a. Ruthenian.
Ruthenium ⚛ (⌣⌢⌣⌣)[neu-lt.] n chm. (seltenes Platinmetall) ruthenium (Ru); ~-säure (⌢⌣⌣) f ruthenic acid. [(TiO₂).]
Rutil ⚛ (⌣⌢)[neu-lt.rot]m ⚒d.min.rutil.(⌣)
Rutsch (⌣⌢) m Ⓐ a.: a) slide, v. Erde: landslip, co. (= Fahrt; vgl. rutschen 2) F im ~ in a twinkling, in a trice; b) crumbling ground (of a slope).
Rutsch-bahn (⌢...) [rutschen] f slide (Berg- und Talbahn) switchback (railway); a. = Eisbahn; **-berg** m (künstlicher Eisberg) (artificial) slide.
rutschen (⌣⌣) [mhd.] v/n. (h. u. sn) Ⓐ 1. to slide, to glide, vom Erdreich: to roll (down), von Personen: to slip; von Kleidern: in die Höhe ~ to ride up; Holz ~ lassen to slide wood (down a hill or an inclined plain); Ⓞ metall. v. den Gichten im Hochofen: to shift, sink, settle (down). — 2. F fig. aufs Land ~ (im Flug reisen) to pay a flying visit to the country; die Sache rutscht (geht voran), the matter is progressing or making headway.
Rutscher (⌣⌣) m 1. person who slides or slips. — 2. (schneller Tanz) gallop(ade).
Rutsch-güter ⚙ (⌢...) n/pl. goods pl. (packed) in sacks or boxes; **-partie** f slide, F auch: short, trip; **-tuch** n bei der Feuerwehr: chute(-escape), fire-chute.
Rüttel-fischer (⌢...) m orn. ceryle; **-herd** m. metall. moving board; **-holz** Ⓞ n tool for pressing down seams.
rütteln (⌣⌣) [mhd.] v/a. u. v/n (h.) Ⓐ a. 1. to shake, to jog; (umschütteln) to shake up, to toss (up); vom Wagen beim Fahren: to jolt; e-n aus dem Schlafe ~ to rouse a p. by shaking (him); fig voll gerütteltes Maß full (or good) measure. — 2. fig. an et. ~ (mit feindlicher Absicht tasten) to attack (or undermine) a th.; an der bestehenden Ordnung ~ to upset (or revolutionize) the existing order; daran ist nicht zu ~ that's a well established fact; that cannot be altered.

𝕾

S, s, am Schlusse e-s Wortes: ß (eß) n, inv. Buchstabe: S, s.
S. abbr. a) = Seite; b) = (it.) San, Sant', Santa, Santo.
f. abbr. = sich(e).
ß für auf s ausgehende Formen des def. art., z.B. fürs (= für das) Geld for the money; ins (= in das) Haus into the house.
's für das pron. es, z.B. ist's wahr? is it true?; seid ihr's? is it you?
S. öft. S. = Süd(en).
Sa. abbr. = Summa [It. Summe].
sa (ßa) [mhd.; *fr. ça] int. ho!, there!; ~ ~! cheer up!, look alive!
Sä- ... (⌢...) in Zssgn = Säe-...

Saal (⌢) [ahd.] m Ⓓc.: a) größerer, für öffentliche Zwecke: hall; dim. Sälchen (f. dß); b) eleganter, kleinerer: drawing- (or reception-)room; ~-einrichtung(⌢...) f fittings and appointments pl. of a hall; drawing-room furniture; ~-theater n theatre established in a hall; ~-tür(e) f drawing-room door.
Saat (⌢) [ahd.: seed; *jäen] f agr.1. (das Säen) sowing (the seed), a. seeding (the land). — 2. (das Ausgesäete) seed(s pl.), grain (or crop) sown. — 3. (das Hervorsprossende) young crop(s pl.); (Getreide) grain; die ~ steht schön the crops look well.

Saat-bestellung (⌢...) f = Saat 1; **-feld** n field sown with corn, seed- (or corn-)field; **-gans** f, orn. bean-goose (Anser se'getum); **-gerste** f barley for sowing; **-kartoffel** f seed-potato; potato-seed; **-korn** n seed(-corn or -grain), grain for sowing; **-krähe** f, orn. rook (Corvus frugi'legus); **-lerche** f, orn. field- (or sky-)lark; **-pflug** m seeding-plough; **-rauke** ⚘ f (garden-rocket (Eru'ca sati'va); **-wechsel** m rotation of crops; **-zeit** f seed(ing)- (or sowing-)time.
Sabäer (⌣⌣⌣) m , ~in f Ⓖ: a) Volk: Sabean; b) christliche Sekte: Sabian;

Zeichen (s. S. XVII): F familiär; P Volkssprache; ✗ Gaunersprache; ⟍ selten; † alt (auch gestorben); * neu (auch geboren); ✕ unrichtig;

[Sabäismus] — 817 — [Säckel]

Sabäismus (⌣-⌣) (Sternbienſt) m ㉗ Sabianism, Sabaism, a. Sabæ(an)ism.
ſä=bar (⌐) [ſäen] a. ⓺ sowable.
Sabbat (⌣) [hebr. Ruhe] m ⓐc. Sabbath, chriſtlich: Sunday, Lord's day; den ~ (ent)heiligen to keep (to break) the Sabbath; **~=feier** (⌣...) f ㉒ keeping the Sabbath; ehm. **~=jahr** n (bei den Juden jedes 7. Jahr) sabbatical year.
ſabbatlich (⌣⌣) a. ⓺ of (or relating to) the Sabbath or Sunday, Sabbatarian; adv. on the Sabbath or Sunday.
Sabbat=ruhe (⌣...) f ㉒ quiet (or stillness) of the Sabbath, Sunday rest; **=ſchänder(in** f) m Sabbath-breaker; **=ſchändung** f desecration (or breaking) of the Sabbath; **=ſtille** f = =ruhe; **=tag** m = Sabbat.
Sabbel ⁊c. ſ. Sabber ⁊c.
Sabber F (⌣) m ㉒ = Geifer 1; **~ei** (⌣⌣) f ⓺ drivelling, slobbering; F fig. (Geſchwätz) babble; **~er** (⌣) m ㉒ driveller, F slobberer, slaverer; **~=latz** m ㉒ = Geifertuch; **~=liſe** f, **~=matz** m = Sabberer; ⁑n (⌣) v/n. (h.) ⓶a. = geifern 1; **~=tuch** n = Geifertuch.
Säbel ⚔ (⌐) [ruſſ. sa'bl'a f; ⁕orientaliſch] m ㉒ Hiebwaffe: sabre, broadsword, kurzer cutlass, türkiſcher: scimitar.
Säbel=bajonett ⚔ (⌐...) n ㉒ sword-bayonet; **=beine** F n/pl. bandy legs, bow-legs pl.; ⁑**beinig** a. ⓺ bandy- (or bow-)legged; **=duell** n duel with sabres; ⁑**förmig** a. sabre-shaped, ♀: ⁊ ensiform; **=gehenk** ⚔ n = =koppel; **=geraſſel** n rattling (or clanking) of swords; **=herrſchaft** f sword-law, military rule; **=hieb** m sabre-cut, sword-cut; **=klinge** f blade of a sabre or scimitar, sabre-blade; **=koppel** ⚔ n, f um den Leib: sabre- (mehr gbr. sword-)belt; **=korb** ⚔ m basket-hilt. [sabre.]
ſäbeln (⌐) v/a. ㉒a. to (cut with a) f
Säbel=ſchnäbler (⌐...) m ⁊ orn. avocet(ta), ⁊ recurviroster; **=taſche** ⚔ f sabretache; **=troddel** ⚔ f sword-knot.
Sabiner (⌣⌣) [lt.] m ㉒, **~in** f ⓺ röm. Alt.: Sabine; vgl. Raub 1; **ſabiniſch** a. ⓺ Sabine, of the Sabines. [of facts.]
Sach=angabe (⌣⌣-⌣) f ㉒ statementſ
Sacharimeter ⁊ (⌣⌣⌣) [grch.] n (m) ㉒ (Zuckermeſſer) saccharimeter.
Sacharin ⁊ (⌣⌣) [grch.] n ⓐd. (Zuckerſtoff) saccharine (C₇H₅NSO₃). [Zechariah.]
Sacharja (⌣⌣⌣) npr/m. ⓑ bibl. Prophet:
Sach=bemerkung (⌣ch...) f ㉒ comment on the subject (in hand), pertinent (or weighty) remark; **=beweis** m material evidence or proof; ⁑**dienlich** a. ⓺ serving its (appointed) purpose, relevant, pertinent, appropriate, serviceable, suitable.
Sache (⌣ch⌣) [ahd.: sake] f ⓮ 1. (Gegenſtand) matter, thing, object, article; (Geſchäft) affair, concern; (Umſtand) circumstance; (Tatſache) fact; die ganze ~ the whole matter or concern. — 2. Redensarten: ſ. abziehen II am Schluß; das iſt eine ~ für ſich that's a thing (or a matter) for itself; ſ-r ~ gewiß ſein to be sure of one's facts, to know what one is about; ich weiß noch ganz andere ~n ... (even) better things than that; eine ~ von vielen Jahren a matter (or

work) ... — 3. mit prp.: ich muß wiſſen, was **an** der ~e iſt ... the real state of the case or the real truth of it; ſich an die ~ und nicht an die Worte halten to keep to facts and not to words; mit ganzer Seele **bei** der ~ ſein to be (all) heart and soul in a th.; nicht bei der ~ ſein: a) not to keep to the point; b) mit ſ-n Gedanken: to be absent-minded; ſ. bleiben 4 unter bei; **von** der ~ abſchweifen to stray from the subject; **zur** ~! keep (or come) to the point!, parl. auch: question!; ſ. gehören 2 unter zu; nicht zur ~ gehörig beside the question, irrelevant; vgl. gehörig 2. — 4. (beſtimmter Gegenſtand) mſt pl.: ſind meine ~n angekommen? have my things arrived?; dieſe ~n (Briefe ⁊c.) müſſen zur Poſt these things must be posted; fig. ſ-e ſieben ~n (a. Siebenſachen) (all) one's belongings or personal effects or goods and chattels pl.; ~n (Möbel) furniture, F co. sticks pl. — 5. (Angelegenheit, Handel) eine abgefartete ~ a got-up affair, F a (regular) plant, P u. F a put-up job; in ~n der Religion in matters of religion, in religious affairs; ſich in fremde ~n miſchen to interfere with other people's affairs; mit=e-m gemeinſchaftliche ~ m. to make common cause with a p.; das iſt meine ~ that's my business or concern or look-out; das iſt nicht ſeine ~ that's no business of his, it has nothing to do with him; er iſt ſeiner ~ ſicher he feels sure about it, he knows what he is about; ſo ſteht die ~ that's how matters stand; ſeine ~n ſtehen gut his affairs are going on well, he is doing well; ſ-e ~n ſtehen mißlich, ſchlecht his affairs are in an unsatisfactory state, it's a bad look-out for him; wie ſteht's mit der ~? how are matters progressing or getting on?; ſ. andere II. — 6. (Rechtshandel) lawsuit, (legal) case; die ~ e-s andern führen to conduct (or plead) another p.'s cause; jur. in ~n (des N.N. wider ... in re N.N. versus ... — 7. verhüllend: ſ-e ~n (Notdurft) verrichten to do one's business, to ease nature.
Sächelchen (⌣⌣) n ㉓ (dim. v. Sache): a) little thing, small affair; b) pl. pretty little things, knickknacks pl.
Sach=erklärung (⌣ch...) [Sache] f ㉒ (ant. Worterklärung) definition of the (real) substance or matter; **=führer** m: a) appointed agent; (Vertreter) representative; b) = =walter; **=gedächtnis** n memory for things or facts; ⁑**gemäß** a. ⓺ = ⁑dienlich; **=kenner** m connoisseur, expert, good (or competent) judge of things or of a thing; **=kenntnis**, biſw. **=kunde** f practical (or professional, special) knowledge, auch: pract, experience; ⁑**kundig** a. practically acquainted with a th., versed (or thoroughly experienced) in a th.; **=lage** f state (or condition) of affairs, circumstances pl. (of the case).
ſachlich (⌣ch⌣) [Sache] a. ⓺ concerning the matter or subject; real; (im Weſen begründet) essential, positive; (gegenſtändlich) objective, material.

ſächlich (⌣ch) [Sache] a. ⓺ gr. neuter; ein ⁑es Dingwort a neuter (noun); gr. ⁑es Geſchlecht neuter gender.
Sachlichkeit (⌣ch⌣) f ⓺ (ſ. ſachlich) reality; essentiality; objectivity.
Sach=regiſter (⌣ch-⌣⌣) n ㉒ index (= Inhaltsverzeichnis). [ⓐa. (Meſſer) knife.]
Sachs ehm. (⌣ch) [ahd.: lt. saxum Stein] m
Sachſe (⌣ch⌣) [ahd.: ⁕Sachs] m ⓮, **Sächſin** f ㊵ Saxon; **ſächſeln** v/n. (h.) ⓶a. to speak in the Saxon dialect.
Sachſen ♀ (⌣ch⌣) [(zu den) ⁑dat.pl.] npr/n. ㉓α. (kingdom of, province of) Saxony.
Sachſen=gänger (⌣ch⌣...) m/pl. ㉒ (Arbeiter aus dem öſtlichen Preußen, die weſtlich ziehen) labourers pl. from the East of Prussia who try to find work in the Saxon lands; **=Koburg(=Gotha)** npr/n. Saxe-Coburg(-Gotha); **=Meiningen** npr/n. Saxe-Meiningen; **=ſpiegel** m, von Eike v. Repgow im 13. sae. verfaßte Geſetzſammlung old Saxon law-code; **=Weimar(=Eiſenach)** npr/n. Saxe-Weimar. [Schweiz.]
ſächſiſch (⌣ch⌣) [Sachſe(n)] a. ⓺ Saxon; vgl.ſ
ſacht (⌣ch), ⁑e (⌣ch⌣) [ndd.: = ſanft] a. ⓺ bjb. adv.: a) a. F dim **⁑chen** (leiſe) adv. softly, gently; (vorſichtig) cautiously; b) (allmählich) gradually, by degrees, ⁑e! gently!, don't hurry!, not so fast!; (nicht zu böſig) don't flurry yourself!
Sach=verhalt (⌣ch...) m ㉒ = =lage; der wahre ~ the true (or real) facts pl. (of the case); den ~ darlegen to explain how matters stand; **=verhältnis** n = =verhalt; ⁑**verſtändig** a. ⓺, **~e(r)** m ⓺ expert, a. specialist, authority on a subject; ~e zu Rate ziehen to call in experts; **=walter** m legal adviser, counsel, attorney, weitS. advocate; **=wert** m real (or substantial) value or worth; **=wörterbuch** n (en)cyclopædia.
Sack (⌣) [ahd.: sack; lt. saccus; ⁕ſemitiſch] m ⓑb,G. 1. sack; ~ (voll) Korn sack(ful) of corn; ~ Wolle pack of wool; ⁑ inkluſive ~ sack(s) included; bibl. im ~ und in der Aſche Buße tun ob. trauern to do penance or to mourn in sackcloth and ashes; fig. ſ. Pack 3. — 2. baggy (or loose) gown or garment or overcoat. — 3. (Taſche) pocket; (Geldbeutel) money-bag, purse; fig. ~ voll Neuigkeiten bagful (or budget) of news. — 4. = Sackgaſſe. — 5. anat. u. zo.: sac; ⁊ vgl. Sackgeſchwulſt. — 6. fig. ſ. Eſel 2; die Katze aus dem ~e laſſen to let the cat out of the bag; e-n im ~e h. to have (or hold) a p. in one's clutches; ſ. Fauſt 12; Lachen und Weinen in einem ~e h. to laugh and cry at the same time; ſ. Katze 2, Roſine¹; e-n in den ~ ſtecken (urſpr. von dem beim Ringkampfe Beſiegten, den man in e-n ~ ſchob) to get the better of a p., to overmatch a p.; ſchlafen wie ein ~ to sleep like a top; voll ſein wie ein ~ to be as drunk as a fiddler or a lord, to be dead (P blind) drunk. — 7. jübb. = Taſche.
Sack=bahn 🚂 (⌣...) f ㉒ loop-line; **=band** n sack-string or -tie.
Säckchen (⌣⌣) n ㉓ (dim. von Sack) little (or small) sack or bag or pouch or purse, ⁊, anat.: ⁊ saccule.
Säckel (⌣⌣) [ahd.] m ㉒ (dim. von Sack) 1. = Säckchen. — 2. (Geldbeutel

♪ Muſik; ⁊ Wiſſenſchaft; ⚘ Pflanze; ♀ Geographie; ⊕ Technik; ⚒ Bergbau; ⚔ Militär; ⚓ Marine; ⊛ Handel; ✉ Poſt; 🚂 Eiſenbahn.

[Säckelmeister] — 818 — [sagen]

money-bag, purse; (Kasse) cash-box; ~meister m, prov. cashier, treasurer, ehm.: purse-bearer.
säckeln (ˇ‿) v/a. ⓐa. to collect in bags.
sacken¹ (ˇ‿) [Sack] ⓼ I v/a. 1. Korn ꝛc. ⓶ to put ... into sacks, to sack ... — 2. = säcken. — 3. (packen) to pack (in bags), to bag. — 4. (an sich raffen) to sack off, to pocket; den Bauch, den Wanst (a. v/refl. sich) voll ⓶ to gorge o.s., to fill one's belly. — II sich ⓶ v/refl. 5. f. 4. — 6. to (form a) bag, to bulge (out); sich die Taschen voll ⓶ to cram one's pockets; von Kleidern ꝛc. auch: to puff out, to be baggy.
sacken² (ˇ‿) [ndd.: senken] sich ⓶ v/refl. und v/n. (ſu) ⓼⓽ von Gebäuden: to settle, von der Erde ꝛc.: to sink, to give way; ⊥ = zurückbleiben, a. sinken.
säcken (ˇ‿) v/a. ⓼⓼ ehm.: e-n Verbrecher ⓶ (in e-m Sacke ertränken) to drown ... in a sack.
sacker F (ˇ‿, ₴ˇ‿) [fr. sacré geheiligt] int., mst ⓶lot (‿ˇˇ), ⓶ment (‿ˇ‿) [Sakrament], etwa: the deuce!, bother(ation)!;
Sackerlöter (~‿ˇ‿), Sackermenter (~ˇ‿) m ⓶ deuced (or devil of a) fellow, devilish(ly smart) person.
sack=förmig (ˇ‿...) a. ⓼⓼ in (the) shape of a sack or a bag, baggy, ⚹ sacciform; =garn ⚈ n ⓼⓶ = =zwirn; =gasse f blind alley or lane, (fr.) cul-de-sac, fig. deadlock, (fr.) impasse; =geschwulst f, path.: ⚹ encysted tumour; ⓶grob F a. exceedingly rude; like a bear; =hüpfen n racing in sacks, sack-race.
sackig (ˇ‿) a. ⓼⓼ baggy.
Sack=jackett (ˇ‿...) n ⓼⓶ loose jacket. =laufen n = =hüpfen.
Säcklein (ˇ‿) n ⓼⓷ = Säckchen.
Sack=leinen n ⓼⓶, =leinwand f sacking, sackcloth.
Säckler südd. (ˇ‿) m ⓼⓶ purse-maker.
Sack=linnen (ˇ‿...) n ⓼⓶ = =leinen; =nadel f pack(ing)-needle; =paletot m = =überzieher; =pfeife f bagpipe (s pl.); =pfeifer m bagpiper; =pistole f südd. pocket-pistol; =rutsche ⊕ f sack-shooter; ⓶siebe=grob a. ⓼⓼ u. adv. = ⓶grob; ⓶tragend a. u. zo.: ⚹ sacciferous; =träger m: a) sack-heaver, porter; Sprichw. ein Esel schilt den andern ~, etwa: the pot calls the kettle black; b) ent.: ⚹ sacciferous larva (Psyche); =tuch n: a) = =leinen; bengalisches ~ gunny; b) südd. = Taschentuch; =überzieher m sack-coat, wide (or loose) overcoat; =voll m sackful; f. a. Sack 1 u. 3; ⓶weise adv. (F a. a.) in sacks, by bagfuls; =zwirn ⚈ m sack-thread or -twine.
Sadduzäer (‿ˇ‿) [hebr.] m ⓼⓶ bibl. Anhänger e-r jüd. Sekte: Sadducee; sadduzäisch (‿ˇ‿) ⓶ Sadducean; Sadduzäismus (‿ˇ‿) m ⓼⓻ Sadduceeism.
Sade=baum ⚹ (ˇ‿‿) [corr. *It. Sabinerˉ(traut)] m ⓼c. savin (Sabi'na [officina'lis]).
Säe=mann (ˇ‿...) m ⓼ sower, agr. auch: seeder; =maschine f. Sämaschine.
säen (ˇ‿) [ahd.: sow] I v/a., v/n. (h.) u. v/refl. ⓼⓼ agr. to sow (seed), to seed (the land), in Furchen oder Reihen: to drill; f. breitwürfig; gesät (ant. wild wachsend) grown (or sprung) from seed; fig. Zwietracht ⓶ to sow (the seeds of) discord; dünn gesät scattered,

scarce. — II ~ n ⓼⓷ sowing, (a. Ein=~) seeding (the land). [plough.)
Säe=pflug (ˇ‿...) (ˇ‿ˇ) m ⓼⓶ agr. drill=ˉSäer (ˇ‿) [säen] m ⓼⓶, ~in f ⓽⓷ sower.
Säe=tuch (ˇ‿...) n ⓼⓶ seed-cloth; =wetter n weather for sowing; =zeit f = Saatzeit.
Saffian ⊕ (ˇ‿)‿) [St. Saffi ⚹ in Marotto] m ⓼d. Leder=art: morocco, Morocco leather, saffian; =bereiter (ˇ‿ˇ‿...) m ⓼⓶ = =fabrikant; =bereitung f morocco-dressing; =einband m Buchbind.: m.-binding; =fabrikant, =gerber, =macher m maker of morocco, m.-dresser; =papier n m.-paper.
Saflor ⚹ (‿ˇˇ) [alt=fr. saflor; alt=it. asfiore; *ar. usfur] m ⓼d. safflower, bastard saffron (Ca'rthamus tincto'rius).
Saflor=öl (‿ˇ‿...) n ⓼⓶ safflower-oil; =rot ⊕ n: ⚹ carthamin(e).
Safran ⚹ (ˇ‿) [mhd.; fr.; *ar. za'farān (*pers. safra gelb)] m ⓼d. ⚹ saffron, crocus (Crocus sati'vus); ⓶ Färberei: (die getrockneten gelben Narben des ⚹=s) saffron; ⓶=artig a. ⓼⓼ saffron-like, ⚹ croceous; ~=farbe f ⓼⓼ saffron-colour; ⓶=gelb a. (as) yellow as saffron, s.-coloured, saffron(y); ~=gelb n, chm.: ⚹ safranin; ~=pflanzung f saffron-plantation.
Saft ⚹ (ˇ‿) [ahd.: sap] m ⓼b. 1. sap of trees, &c., juice of fruit, meat, &c.; f. Himbeer=, Milch=saft; ~ der Trauben grape-juice; ~ e-r Zitrone lemon-juice; (Sauce) gravy; (Flüssigkeit) liquid, fluid, (Feuchtigkeit) moisture, anat.: ⚹ succus; Säfte pl. des Körpers, a. humours of the body; med. fehlerhafte Mischung der Säfte vitiated state of the blood, ⚹ dyscrasia, cachexy; ~ führend: ⚹ succiferous; voll ~ juicy, succulent; von Bäumen: im ~ in sap. — 2. (bisw. dim. Säftchen (ˇ‿) n ⓼⓷) eingedickter Saft von Pflanzen inspissated juice, syrup. — 3. fig. weder ~ noch Kraft haben, ohne ~ und Salz sein to be without strength and flavour or without goodness, to be pithless or marrowless or insipid or flabby.
Saft=behälter ⚹ (ˇ‿...) m ⓼⓶ = Honigbehälter; =farbe f, paint. sap-colour; =fülle f abundance of sap or juice; =gang m, =gefäß n: a) ⚹ sap-duct or -tube, a. -vessel; b) physiol.: ⚹ chyliferous vessel; =grün n, paint. sap-green.
saftig (ˇ‿) a. ⓼⓼ saftreich; fig. a. (zotig) juicy, spicy, (unzüchtig) lewd, obscene; ~keit f ⓽⓼ juiciness, succulence; fig. juiciness, lewdness, obscenity.
saft=leer (ˇ‿...), ⓶los a. ⓼⓼ sapless, juiceless, (ausgedörrt) dried up, desiccated; fig. a. pithless, marrowless, insipid, flabby, F wishy-washy; =losigkeit f ⓽⓼ lack of sap or juice or goodness; insipidity, flabbiness; ⓶reich, ⓶strotzend a. rich in juice, juicy, succulent, med. plethoric.
Säg=(ˇ‿...) = Säge=.
Sagapen(=gummi) (‿‿ˇ‿...) [grch.] n ⓼d. (⓼) pharm.: ⚹ sagapen(um).
sagbar (ˇ‿) [sagen] a. ⓼⓼ utterable; meist negativ: es ist nicht ⓶, wie // it cannot be expressed in words (or it's not possible to say) how //.
Sage (ˇ‿) [ahd.: saw; *sagen] f ⓼⓼ (Gerücht) rumour, report; (Überlieferung) tradition,

fable, myth, religiöse: legend, altnordische: saga; es geht die ~, daß // the story goes (or they say, people say) that //.
Säge (ˇ‿) [sägen] f ⓼⓼ saw; *sägen [⓶ ⓼ saw, ⚹ serra, eine ~ ausfeilen to notch a saw; ~ v. Ende endless saw, belt-saw.
säge=artig ⊕ (ˇ‿...) a. ⓼⓼ saw-like, ⚹ serrate(d); ₴ ⓶ gezähnt a.: ⚹ serrate-dentate; =blatt n ⓼⓶ blade of a saw; ⓶blätt(e)rig ⚹ a.: ⚹ serratifoliate; =block m log to be sawn; =bock ⊕ m sawing-jack or -trestle; =fisch m, ichth. sawfish (Pristis); ⓶förmig a. = =artig, anat. Zer Muskel saw-muscle; ₴ ⓶ gezähnt: ⚹ dentate-serrate; orn. mit zem Schnabel saw-billed or -beaked, ⚹ odontorhynchous; =gestell ⊕ n frame of a saw, saw-frame; =griff m saw-handle; =grube f sawpit; =maschine f saw-engine; =mehl n sawdust; =mühle f sawmill; =müller m owner (or manager) of a sawmill.
sagen (ˇ‿) [ahd.: say] I v/a. u. v/n. (h.) ⓼⓼ 1. to say s.th. to a p., to tell a p. s.th.; du darfst keinem ein Wort ⓶ you must not say a word to anybody, oder: you must not tell anybody (anything); ich sagte es ihm I told him (of it) (nie: I told it him); sie ⓶ täglich zu mir: „Du bist toll!" they say to me daily, 'you are mad!'; sie ⓶ (sagten) mir oft, ich sei toll they often tell (told) me I am (was) mad; man sagt, er sei blind they say (that) he is blind, he is said to be blind; das (ob. so etwas) sagt man nicht (schickt sich nicht) that's not the proper thing to say; er weiß auf alles et. zu ⓶ (zu erwidern) he has an answer ready to everything; ich kann dasselbe von uns ⓶ I can apply the same to us; ich muß ⓶ (zugeben), daß // I must admit that //; befehlend: ⓶ Sie ihm, daß er es holen soll tell him to fetch it; er hat dabei nichts zu ⓶ he has no(thing) to say in the matter; vgl. 8 am Ende. — 2. meist eingeschoben: er ist reich — wohlhabend, wollte ich ⓶ he is rich — or rather, well-to-do; sie ist nicht schön, ich kann sogar ⓶, sie ist häßlich ... I might (venture to) say that she is ugly; mit Erlaubnis zu ⓶ with due deference to you, begging your pardon; wenn ich so ⓶ darf if I may so express myself; sozu⓶ so to speak. — 3. im p.p. oft eingeschoben: beiläufig gesagt by the by, by the way; er ist — offen (ob. gerade heraus) gesagt — ein Spitzbube he is — in plain language — a thief; im Vertrauen (ob. streng unter uns) gesagt speaking confidentially, between you and me; richtiger gesagt more correctly speaking, to be more exact; gesagt, getan, auch: so gesagt, so getan no sooner said than done; oft als n: das Gesagte bleibt unter uns what I have told you is (spoken) in strict confidence; aus dem Gesagten erhellt, daß // from what has been mentioned it appears that //. — 4. (ausdrücken, beschreiben) e-m Dank ⓶ to give (or render, return) thanks to a p.; das will ich nicht gesagt haben I don't mean (or want to imply)

[sägen] — 819 — [Saldo]

that; er sagt nur so (es ist nicht sein Ernst) that's only his way of speaking, he does not mean it; seine Meinung über et. 2 to utter (or express, give) one's opinion on (or about) a th.; es ist nicht zu 2, es läßt sich nicht 2, was in mir vorging it cannot be expressed in words ..., it is inexpressible ... — 5. Redensarten: ich hätte bald was gesagt I wasn't far off saying s.th.; ich hätte es beinahe gesagt I had it on the tip of my tongue; s. Gesicht 2; e-m et. ins Ohr 2 to whisper a th. in a p.'s ear; was ich 2 wollte (ich muß mich darauf besinnen) what was I going to say?; was Sie (nicht) 2! (Sie erstaunen mich) now, really!, you don't say so or mean it!; e-m gute Nacht 2 (wünschen) to bid (or wish) a p. good night; Sie können von Glück 2 you may deem (or call) yourself fortunate or lucky; Sie haben mir nichts zu 2 (zu befehlen) F I won't be ordered about by you; da soll einer 2, was eine Sache ist you can never tell (what a thing is like); wie gesagt as I said before; was wollen Sie damit 2? what do you mean by it?; s. ja 5, nein. — 6. mit lassen: ich habe mir (erzählen) lassen, daß // I have been told (or been given to understand) that //; ich ließ es mir nicht zweimal (oder lange) 2 I did not wait to be told a second time; lassen Sie sich et. 2 (raten) take my advice, believe me; ich ließ ihm 2, sie sei krank I sent him word (or a message) that she was ill; dagegen läßt sich nichts 2 nothing can be said against that, there is no denying (or gainsaying) that. — 7. mit a.: für et. gut 2 to be (or stand) security for a th. — 8. (von Bedeutung sein) to signify; (das) hat nichts zu 2 it does not (much) matter, a. no harm has been done; das will viel 2 that is saying a great deal; das will nicht viel 2 there is not much (meaning) in that; er hat bei ihnen nicht viel zu 2 his word has no great weight with them, he has not much influence with them. — II ~ n ⑨ 9. saying, words pl. [(cut with a) saw.]
sägen ⊕ (᷄᷅) [ahd.: saw] v/a. ⓺ to
Sagen-dichtung (᷄᷅...) [Sage] f ⓬ legendary (or cyclic, epic) poetry; =forschung f study of legends, legendary research; =geschichte f legendary (or mythical) history, folk-lore.
sagenhaft (᷄᷅) [Sage] a. ⓺ legendary, traditional, fabulous, mythical.
Sagen-kreis (᷄᷅...) m ⓬ legendary (or mythical) cycle; =kunde f leg. lore, mythology; ⓺reich a. ⓺ rich in legends; =reich n = Märchenwelt; =schatz m e-s Volkes: folk-lore.
Sägen-schmied (᷄᷅᷅᷅) m ⓬ maker (or cutter) of saws. [age of fairy-tales.]
Sagen-zeit (᷄᷅᷅᷅) f ⓺ mythical period,]
Säger (᷄᷅) m ⓬ 1. ⊕ saw(y)er. — 2. orn. merganser, sawbill (Mergus).
Säge-rahmen ⊕ (᷄᷅...) m ⓬ saw-frame.
Sägerei (᷄᷅᷅᷅) f ⓺ continuous sawing.
Säge-schmied (᷄᷅...) m ⓬ = Sägen-s.;
=späne m/pl. =mehl, a. scobs pl.;

=werk ⨯ n, frt. indented line, (Flesche) redan; =zahn m tooth of a saw; ⓺zähnig a. ⓺ saw-toothed, ⚄ serrate(d).
Sago (᷄᷅) [Papua: Brot] m ⑳ sago; westindischer ~ tapioca; =baum (᷄᷅᷅...) m ⓬ = =palme; =grütze f, =mehl n sago-powder; =palme ⚄ f sago-tree or -palm (Cycas); =suppe f sago-soup.
sah (᷄) ind. impf. von sehen.
Sahara (᷄᷅) [ar.] npr/f. ⓺a. die (Wüste) ~ in Nord-afrika the (desert of) Sahara.
sähe (᷄᷅) subj. impf. von sehen.
Sahne (᷄᷅) [ndd.] f ⓺ cream.
sahnen (᷄᷅) ⓺ I v/a. to fill with cream; die Milch (ab=)2 to skim ... — II v/n. (h.) (Sahne geben) to (give off) cream.
Sahnen-gießer (᷄᷅...) m ⓬ cream-jug; ⓺haltig a. ⓺ creamy; =käse m cream-cheese; =kuchen m cream-tart; =topf m cream-pot; =töpfchen n cream-jug.
sahnig (᷄᷅) a. ⓺ creamy.
Saibling (᷄᷅) [Salmling] m ⓬d. ichth. char (Salmo salveli'nus).
Saison (sä-, sä-zõ') [fr.] f ⓺ ([richtige] Jahreszeit) season; stille, tote ~ dead (or silly) season, off-season; =arbeiter (᷄᷅...) m ⓬ workman engaged for the season; =karte f season ticket.
Saite (᷄᷅) Hom. Seite) [ahb.: Sei(l)] f ⓺ 1. ♪ string of a musical instrument, music-string, auch: c(h)ord (vgl. Darmsaite); eine ~ anschlagen to touch a string; mit ~ n beziehen to string. — 2. fig. s. aufziehen 5 und gelinde; seine ~n zu hoch spannen to aim too high.
Saiten-bezug ♪ (᷄᷅...) m ⓬ set of strings; =brett n tail-piece of a violin; =draht ⊕ m music-wire, wire string; =instrument n stringed (or string-) instrument; =klang m sound of strings, string-music; =messer ⊕ m string-gauge, chordometer; =spiel n: a) =instrument, bsd. (Leier) lyre, (Laute) lute: b) string-music, music of (or on) a stringed instrument; =spieler(in f) m lute- (or harp-)player.
saitig ♪ (᷄᷅) a. ⓺ furnished with strings; bsd. in Zssgn, zB.: sieben=2 seven-stringed. [= Saccharimeter.)
Sakcharimeter (᷄᷅᷅᷅᷅) [grch.] n (m) ⓬)
Saker-falk(e) (᷄᷅᷅᷅(᷄)) [engl., *ar.] m ⓬ saker (Falco sacer ob. lania'rius).
Sakrament (᷄᷅᷅᷅) [mhd., *lt.] n ⓬c. eccl. sacrament, a. = Abendmahl 2; Sal (᷄᷅᷅᷅), ⓶lich (᷄᷅᷅᷅) a. ⓺ sacramental, ...arian. ~(s)=häuschen n tabernacle.
Sakristan (᷄᷅᷅) [mlt.] m ⓬d. eccl. sexton (vgl. Küster); **Sakristei** (᷄᷅᷅) f ⓺ vestry.
Säkular-feier (᷄᷅᷅᷅᷅) [lt. 100jährig] f ⓬ centennial celebration.
säkularisier/en (᷄᷅᷅᷅᷅᷅) [neu=lt.] I v/a. ⓺ (verweltlichen) to secularize. — II ~ n ⓺ u. ⓺ung f ⓺ secularization.
Säkular-klerus (-᷄᷅᷅᷅) m⓬ (Weltgeistliche) secular clergy. [century.]
Säkulum (᷄᷅᷅) [lt. Jahrhundert] n ⓬)
...sal[1] (᷄...) n ⓬d., f ⓺ Anhängesilbe zur Bildung v. nouns, ⓺ Mühsal [Mühe] f trouble, Labsal [Lab(e)] n refreshment; **Sal**[2]... (᷄᷅) [ndd. P aus *Selb=ende, (f. bs)] s. Sal-band, =leiste.
Sal[3]... (᷄᷅) [ahd.: sale, sell] s. Sal-buch, =hof. [s. Salweide.)
Sal[4]... (᷄᷅᷅) [ahd.: sallow: lt. salix)

Salamander (᷄᷅᷅) [mhd.; grch. salamándra f; *pers. samandra] m ⓬ 1. zo. salamander (Sala'mandra). — 2. Univ. richter Salomon in Bonn 1840/50] bursch. e-n ~ reiben to drink a general toast.
Salame (᷄᷅) [it.] m ⓺ ⓺ = Salami.
Salami (᷄᷅) [it.] m ⓺ a. inv. ob. f ⓺ kind of Italian sausage, salame.
Salär (᷄᷅, a. ⓺᷄᷅) [fr.] n ⓬d. salary; vgl. Gehalt 4; **salarieren** (᷄᷅᷅᷅) v/a. ⓺ to pay a salary to; vgl. besolden 1.
Salat (᷄᷅) [mhd.; fr. salade f; *it. insalata f „gesalzen"] m ⓬c. 1. Kochk.: salad; den ~ anmachen to dress (the) salad; F fig. da h. wir den ~! there's a pretty state of affairs! — 2. ⚄ = Lattich.
Salat-beet (᷄᷅...) n ⓺ hort. lettuce-bed; =blatt n lettuce-leaf; =topf m head of lettuce; =napf m salad-bowl; =öl n salad-oil; =pflanze f lettuce-plant, ⚄ acetarious plant; =sauce f salad-cream; =schüssel f salad-dish, -bowl.
Salbader (᷄᷅᷅) [mhd.] m ⓬ (langweiliger Schwätzer) chatterer, (silly) prattler; ~ei (᷄᷅᷅!) f ⓺ chattering, twaddle, (silly) prattling; **salbadern** (᷄᷅᷅᷅) v/n. ⓺a. (h.) to chatter, twaddle, prattle, to talk nonsense or rubbish.
Sal[2]=**band** (᷄᷅) [s. Sal[2]...] n ⓬c.: a) Tuchfabr.: list, selvedge; b) ⚒ wall of a lode; hängendes ~ hanging wall.
Salbe (᷄᷅) [ahd.: salve] f ⓺ 1. pharm., med. ointment, salve. — 2. (wohlduftendes Öl, Fett zum Einreiben des Körpers) scented oil for anointing the body, balm; vgl. Pomade[1]; s. Sprichw. unter Dose[2]. — 3. ⚓ (Schmiere) coat for a ship's bottom.
Salbei ⚄ (᷄᷅, ᷄᷅) [lt. sa'lvia f] m ⓺b., f ⓺ sage (Sa'lvia); echte(r) ~ common sage (Sa'lvia officina'tis); lavendelblütige(r) ~ vervain sage (S. verbena'ca).
salben (᷄᷅) [ahd.: salve; *Salbe] I v/a. u. sich 2 v/refl. ⓺ 1. to rub (o.s.) with oil or grease; e-n zum Könige zc. 2 to anoint a p. king, &c.; e-n Toten 2 to embalm a dead body. — 2. med. to rub with ointment or salve. — 3. ⚓ to coat a ship's bottom. — 4. fig. e-n, e-m die Hände 2 (e-n bestechen) to bribe a p., bisw.: F to grease a p.'s palms. — II ~ n ⓺ 5. = Salbung 1.
Salben-büchse (᷄᷅...) f ⓺ ointment- (or salve-)box; =händler, =krämer m vendor of (or dealer in) ointments or salves; =topf m gallipot.
salbicht ⚄, mst **salbig** (᷄᷅) a. ⓺ greasy; auch = salbungsvoll.
Salb-öl (᷄᷅) n ⓺ oil for anointing; eccl. geweihtes ~ consecrated oil, chrism, chrismal oil.
Sal[3]=**buch** (᷄᷅ch) n ⓺ ehm. = Grundbuch.
Salbung (᷄᷅) f ⓺ 1. = der Priester, Könige zc.: anointment ... — 2. fig. beim Reden: unction, pathos; ⚄=voll (᷄᷅᷅᷅᷅) a. ⓺ unctuous, pathetic, smug, adv. auch: with unction or pathos.
Sälchen (᷄᷅) n ⓺ dim. v. Saal.
saldier/en (᷄᷅᷅) [it.] I v/a. ⓺ eine Rechnung 2: a) (abschließen) to balance ...; b) (begleichen) to settle (or F square)... — II ~ n ⓺ u. S/ung f ⓺ balancing or (settlement) of accounts.
Saldo ⚖ (᷄᷅) [it.] m ⓺⓬⓺ (Rest) balance, remainder; per ~ quittieren to (give

⚛ scientific; ⚕ botanical; ⚲ geography; ⊕ machinery; ⚒ mining; ⚔ military; ⚓ marine; ⚖ commercial; ⚘ postal; 🚂 railway

[Saldobetrag] — 820 — [...sam]

a) receipt in full; per ~ trassieren to draw per appoint; ~=betrag (ᵇᵛ...) m ⑫ amount of balance; ~=übertrag m balance from former account, amount carried forward; ~=wechsel m draft for the balance; ~=zahlung f payment per appoint.
Salem f. Selam. [pharm. salep, salop.
Salep (ᴸᵛ) [ar. sahleb] m ⑩ ⚥ u.]
Sal³=hof (ᵘ‚ᵛ) m ⑫ free-hold farm.
Saline ⊕ (ᵛᴸᵛ) [lt.] f ⑱ (Salzwert) saltworks pl. or -pit; salinisch a. ⑥⑥ saline.
salisch (ᴸᵛ) [salische Franken] a. ⑥⑥ hist.: ~es Gesetz, das Töchter von der Thronfolge ausschließt: Salic law.
Salizin ⚥ (ᵛᴸtẑ¹) [lt. sălix Weide] n ⑩d. chm. (Weidenbitter) salicine ($C_{13}H_{18}O_7$).
Salizyl ⚥ (ᵛᴸtẑ¹) [lt.-grch.; *Salizin] n ⑩d. chm. salicyl; =ieren v/a. ⑬ to impregnate with salicylic acid; ²=sauer (ᵛᴸtẑ"...) a. ⑥⑥ chm. salicylic; ²=saures Salz salicylate; ~=säure f ⑫ salicylic acid ($C_7H_6O_3$); ~=watte f salicylic cotton. [band.
Sal²=leiste (ᵘ‚ᴸᵛ) f ⑫ oberfächisch = Sal-
Salm¹ (ᵛ) [mhd., lt. *flt.] m ⑩b.(⑫) ichth. salmon = Lachs).
Salm² nordd. (ᵛ) [ahd.; *Psalm] m ⑩b.(⑫) fig. langer.~ long rigmarole or yarn.
Salmiak ⚥ [lt. sal (ammon)i'acus] m ⑩d. chm. sal ammoniac, ⚥ ammonium chloride, hydrochlorate of ammonia (NH_4Cl); =geist (ᴸ...) m ⑫ (Ammoniakflüssigkeit) liquid (or spirit of) ammonia; ~=spiritus m = =geist. [= Saibling.
Salmling, Sälmling (ᵛ‚ᵛ) [Salm¹] m ⑩d.]
Salomo (ᴸᵛ‚) [hebr.] npr/m. ⑩a. (gen. oft Salomo'nis, pl. auch Salomo'ne nach ⑪) bibl. Solomon (Kg. v. Israel, 1018—978; a. fig. = weiser König); Sprüche ~(ni)s Proverbs pl.; der Prediger ~ Ecclesiastes; das Hohelied ~(ni)s the Song of Solomon, the Song of Songs.
salomonisch (-ᵛᴸᵛ) a. ⑥⑥ of Solomon.
Salomons=siegel ⚥ (ᵘᵛ‚ᴸᵛ) n ⑫ Solomon's-seal (= echte Weißwurz).
Salon (ᵛᴸᵒ) [fr.] m ⑭ (Putzzimmer) drawing-room, auf Schiffen ꝛc.: saloon; ²=fähig (ᵛᴸᵒ...) a. ⑥⑥ fit for (good) society; ~=held, ~=löwe m ⑫ carpet-knight; ~=wagen ⬛ m saloon-carriage or -car, Pulman car.
salopp (ᵛᴸ) [fr. salope] a. ⑥⑥ (schmutzig, nachlässig) slovenly, sluttish. [slut.
Saloppe F (ᵛᴸ) f ⑱ (schlumpiges Weib)]
Salpe ⚥ (ᵛᴸ) [grch.] f ⑱ zo. (Manteltier, Art Molluske) salp (Thalia'cea).
Salpeter (ᵛᴸᵛ) [mlt. sal petrae Felsensalz] m ⑫ chm. (salpetersaures Kali) saltpetre, nitre, ⚥ potassium nitrate (KNO_3); vgl. Chili=.; in ~verwandeln to nitrify.
salpeter=artig (ᵛᵘᵛ...) a. ⑥⑥ chm. nitrous; =äther m ⑫ nitrous ether; =äther(wein)geist m = =geist b; =bildung f formation of saltpetre or nitre, ⚥ nitrification; =blumen f/pl. wall-saltpetre, nitrous efflorescence sg.; =dampf m nitric fumes pl.; =erde f nitrous earth; =erzeugung f = =bildung; ²=führend a. saltpetrous, ⚥ nitriferous; =geist m: a) chm. = =säure; b)versüßter (alkoholische Lösung v.Salpetersäureäther) sweet spirit of nitre; =grube ⊕ f nitre-bed; ²=haltig a. nitrous, nitric;

vgl. ²=führend; =haltigkeit f: ⚥ nitrosity; =hütte ⊕ f saltpetre-(or nitre-) works pl., nitrifying-shed; saltpetre-house.
salpet(e)rig (ᵛᴸ(ᵛ)) a. ⑥⑥ chm.: ⚥ nitrous; ²e Säure nitrous acid (HNO_2).
salpet(e)rig-sauer (ᵛᴸ"(ᵛ)"...) a. ⑥⑥ chm.: ⚥ nitrous; ²saures Kali potassium nitrite (KNO_2); =säure =äther m ⑫ nitrous ether ($C_2H_5NO_2$); vgl. Salpetergeist b.
Salpeter=plantage (ᵛᵘᵛ...) f ⑫ nitriary; =salzsäure f = Königswasser; ²sauer a. ⑥⑥ chm. nitric; ²saures Kali (KNO_3) = Salpeter; ²saures Natron ($NaNO_3$) = Chilisalpeter; ²saures Salz nitrate; ²saures Silber nitrate of silver ($AgNO_3$), (Höllenstein) lunar caustic; =säure f nitric acid (HNO_3); rauchende ~ fuming nitric acid; =schwefel=säure f: ⚥ nitro-sulphuric acid; =sieder m saltpetre-maker; =siederei f = =hütte.
Salto (ᵛ-) [it. Sprung] m ⑭⑱: ~ morta'le ⑫ (pl. a. Salti morta'li) break-neck leap.
Salut ⚔, ⚓ (ᵛᴸ) [fr., *lt.] m ⑪c. salute; ~ schießen to fire a salute; salutieren (ᵛᴸᵛ) v/a. u. v/n. (h.) ⑬ (grüßen) to salute.
Salut=schießen (ᵛᴸ...) n ⑫, =schuß m (firing a) salute, saluting (with cannon).
salve¹ (ᵛw-) [mhd.; *lt. sei gegrüßt] int. hail (to you)!; (be thou) welcome!
Salve² ⚔, ⚓ (ᵛw) [fr., *lt. s. salve¹] f ⑱: a) (Absfeuern v.Geschütz als Ehrengruß) (firing a) salute; b) (gleichzeitiges Feuern) volley (of musketry), salvo; round (a. fig.), ⚓ a. broadside.
Salvei ⚥ (ᵛw¹) m u. f = Salbei.
Salven=feuer ⚔, ⚓ (ᵛwᵛ‚ᴸᵛ) n ⑫ firing volleys, firing at command.
salvieren (ᵛw-) [mhd.: sa(l)ve; *mlt.] v/a. u. sich ² v/refl. ⑬: (sich) ² (retten) to save (o.s.); bsd. ⚡ sich ² to secure o.s., to be on the safe side, to get off without a loss. [ca'prea).
Sal⁴=weide ⚥ (ᵘ‚ᴸᵛ) f ⑱ sallow (Salix]
Salz (ᵛ) [ahd.: salt: lt. sal] n ⑩a. 1. salt, bsd. = Kochsalz; ~e pl., oft: ⚥ saline bodies pl., chm. salts pl.; flüchtiges ~ zum Riechen: smelling-salts pl. — 2. fig. (Würze) seasoning, (Witz) wit; attisches ~ Attic salt; ohne ~ u. Schmalz without seasoning; tasteless, insipid.
Salz=abgabe (ᵛ...) f ⑱ = =steuer; =ader f salt-vein; ²=ähnlich a. ⑥⑥: ⚥ haloid; =amt n salt-office; =arbeiter m s.-maker; ²=artig a. ⑥⑥ saline; =äther m, chm.: ⚥ hydrochloric (or light muriatic) ether; =berg=werk n salt-mine; vgl. =grube; ²=bildend a.: ⚥ halogenous; =bild(n)er m, chm. halogen; =bildung f formation of salt, salification; =blumen f/pl. flowers pl. (or efflorescence) of salt; =born ⊕ m f. Born 1; =brühe f brine, pickle; =brunnen m salt-spring.
salzen (ᵛ) [ahd.; *Salz] I v/a. u. v/n. (h.) ⑭ (p.p. mst, fig. nur: gesalzen) 1. to salt, to season (or pickle) with salt; gesalzene Butter salt butter; zu stark ² to salt too much, to oversalt; f. schmalzen 1. — 2. fig. die Unterhaltung mit Witz (attischem Salz) ² to season (or interlard, intersperse, enliven) the conversation with wit(ty remarks); gesalzen piquant, spicy, F strong; das ist gesalzen (zu stark, zu viel) I call that

too strong or too much or exorbitant; ein gesalzener Seemann an old salt or sea-dog. — II ~ n ⑳ 3. salting, seasoning; zu starkes ~ oversalting.
Salz=faß (ᵛ...) n ⑫: a) =fäßchen n auf dem Tische: salt-cellar; b) hölzernes ~ wooden salt-box; =fisch m, =fleisch n salt-fish, -meat; =flut f s. sea(-water); =gehalt m proportion (or percentage) of salt; =gehalts-messung f: ⚥ halometry; =geschmack m salt (or briny) taste, vom Seewasser auch: brackishness; =glasur f Töpferei: salt-glaze; =graf m. etwa: owner (or manager) of a salt-mine; =grube f salt-pit; =gurke f cucumber pickled in salt; ²=haltig a. ⑥⑥ saliferous, saline; =handel ⚖ m salt-trade; =händler m salt-merchant, -man, dealer in salt; =haus n: a) salt-loft, -stores pl.; b) ⊕ (Ort zum Salzkochen) house (or shed) for salt-making.
salzicht, mst salzig (ᵛᵛ) a. ⑥⑥ salt(y), von Flüssigem a. briny, von stehendem Wasser: brackish. (Salzteilchen enthaltend) saline; etwas ² saltish, brinish; die Suppe schmeckt sehr ²... tastes very salt; =Salzigkeit f ⑱ saltness, salty taste.
Salz=industrie (ᵛ...) f ⑫ salt-making (industry); =kasten m, =kiste f salt-box; =klumpen m lump of salt; =korn n grain of salt; =kote f salt-cote; vgl. =grube; =kraut ⚥ n saltwort (Sa'lsola kali); =krebs (=chen n) m. zo. brine-shrimp (Arte'mia sali'na); =krücke f salt-stirrer, scraper; =kuchen m. chm., &c. cake (or crust) of salt; =lake, =lauge f = =brühe; -lecke f für das Vieh: salt-lick, lick-stone; =löffel(chen n) m salt-spoon; =messer ⊕ m Werkzeug: salinometer; =meste f = =faß b; =morast m salt-marsh; =napf m = =faß a; =niederschlag m saline deposit or precipitate; =ordnung f regulations pl. respecting the making (or selling) of salt; =pfanne ⊕ f salt-pan; =pfänner m overseer of the salt-pans; =pflanzen f/pl.: ⚥ halophytes pl.; =probe f s.-test(ing); =quelle f salt-spring; =rinde f rind (or crust) of salt; ²=sauer a. ⑥⑥ chm.: ⚥ hydrochloric. bsd. =saures Natron; ²saures Natron (Chlornatrium) sodium chloride; =säule f, bibl. pillar of salt; =säure f, chm. (Chlorwasserstoff: HCl) hydrochloric (or muriatic) acid; =säure=gas n hydrochloric acid gas; =schreiber m clerk to salt-works; =see m salt-lake; =sieder ⊕ m salt-maker; =siederei ⊕ f salt-making; vgl. =werk; =sole f salt-spring; =speicher m = =haus a.; =steppen f/pl. ♀ salt-steppes pl.; =steuer f salt-duty or -tax; =verwaltung f administration of salt-pits or -works; =wage ⊕ f brine-gauge; =wasser-teich m brine-pond; =werk n salt-works pl.; =wirker ⊕ m workman employed in salt-works; =wirkerei ⊕ f salt-making.
...sam (...'-) [ahd.:...some] a. ⑥⑥ Anhängesilbe zur Bildung von adjectives und adverbs, ...samkeit (...'ᵛ) f ⑱ zur Bildung von nouns, bedeutet: a) Vorhandensein oder Besitz, zB.: furchtsam possessed (or filled) with fear, timid, bisw.: fearsome; Furchtsamkeit timidity; b) Fähigkeit oder Geneigtheit, zB.: wachsam ready (or

Zeichen (f. S. XVII): F familiär; P Volkssprache; Γ Gaunersprache; ⚡ selten; † alt (auch gestorben); * neu (auch geboren); ++ unrichtig;

able) to watch, vigilant; Wachsamkeit vigilance; c) Ähnlichkeit, zB.: wundersam like a miracle, miraculous, wonderful, marvellous.

Sä=mann (⏑,⸍) *m* s. Säe=mann.

Samariter (⏑⏑⸍⏑) *m* [22], **~in** *f* [47] Samaritan; *bibl.* der barmherzige ~ the Good Samaritan; **~=dienst** *m* [62] Samaritan duty; **~tum** *n* [2]d. Samaritanism.

samaritisch (⏑⏑⸍⏑) *a.* [66] Samaritan.

Sä=maschine ⚙ (⏑=⏑⸍⏑) *f* [62] seeding- (or sowing-) machine, seeder, corn-drill.

Sambesi ♁ (⏑⸍⏑) [afrik.] *npr*/*m.* [53]α. Fl. in Süd=afrika: Zambezi.

Same (⸍⏑) [ahd.: lt. *semen*; *säen] *m* [37], a. **~n** *m* [23] **1.** a) seed, v. Tieren a. sperm, v. Menschen a. (lt.) semen, P spunk; vgl. Fischlaich; (Eier der Seidenwürmer 2c.) silkworms', &c. eggs *pl.*; b) *fig.* seed, (Keim) germ, (Quelle) source. — **2.** *hort.* aus ~n ziehen to raise from seed(s); in ~n schießen to run to seed. — **3.** bsd. *bibl.* Abrahams ~ A.'s seed or offspring.

Samen=ader (⏑⏑...) *f* [62] *anat.* = =gefäß; **=anlage** *f*: ⚗ ovulum, gemmula; **=behälter** *m*, **=behältnis** *n* ⚘ seed-vessel; **=bläschen** *n*, *anat.*: ⚗ spermatocyst; **=blatt**, **=blättchen** ⚘ *n* seminal leaf; vgl. =lappen; **=ergießung** *f*, **=erguß** *m*, *zo.*, *physiol.* seminal discharge or emission, spermatism; vgl. =fluß; **⁓erzeugend** *a.* [66]: ⚗ seminific(al), *physiol.* spermatic; **=fach** ⚘ *n* seed-compartment; **=fluß** *m*: ⚗ spermatorrhœa; vgl. Tripper; **⁓führend** *a.* = ⁓tragend; **=gang** *m*, *zo.*, *anat.*: ⚗ spermatic duct, spermaduct; **=gefäß** *n*, *anat.* spermatic vessel; **=gehäuse** ⚘ *n*: ⚗ pericarp; vgl. =hülle, =hülse; **=handel** ✱ *m* seed-trade; **=händler** *m* seedsman, seed-merchant; **=haut** ⚘ *f* seed-coat, ⚗ episperm; **=hülle** ⚘ *f* seed-case, ⚗ perisperm, spermoderm; **=hülse** ⚘ *f* seed-pod, husk, hull; **=kapsel** ⚘ *f* seed-pod, ⚗ seminal capsule; **=katalog** ✱ *m* catalogue of seeds; **=kelch** ⚘ *m* seed-cup; **=kern** *m*, *physiol.* sperm-nucleus; **=knospe** *f* = =anlage; **=korn** *n*, *agr.* grain of seed, seed-grain; **=krone** ⚘ *f* down, ⚗ pappus; **=kuchen** ⚘ *m*: ⚗ placenta; **=lappen** ⚘ *m* seed-leaf or -lobe, ⚗ cotyledon; **=lehre** *f*: ⚗ spermatology; **⁓los** *a.* seedless; **=pflanze** *f*, *hort.* seedling; **=pflanzen** *pl.* ⚘: ⚗ phanerogamous plants *pl.*; **=schule** *f*, *hort.* seed-plat or -plot, nursery (for seedlings); **=staub** ⚘ *m*: ⚗ pollen; **=strang** *m*: a) ⚘ seed-stalk; b) *anat.* spermatic cord; **=tier(chen)** *n* Biologie: spermatic animalcule, spermule, spermatozoon, *pl.* a. spermatozoa; **⁓tragend** *a.*: ⚗ seminiferous, *physiol.* auch spermatophorous; **=träger** ⚘ *m*: ⚗ spermaphore; vgl. =kuchen; **=zelle** *f*, *physiol.* sperm-cell, ⚗ spermule.

Sämerei (⏑⏑⸍) [Same] *f* [46] meist *pl.* ~en seeds *pl.*, (different kinds of) grain; **~=handel** (⏑⏑⏑,⏑) *m* [62] = Samenhandel.

...samig (...⏑) [Same] *a.* [66] in Zssgn, zB.: einsamig one-seeded, ⚗ monospermous.

sämig (⸍⏑) *a.* [66] = dickflüssig.

samisch (⸍⏑) [Samos ♁, grch. Insel] *a.* [66] of (the Isle of) Samos, Samian.

sämisch ⚙ (⸍⏑) [fr. *chamois*] *a.* [66] chamois-dressed; vgl. gerben I.

Sämisch=gerben ⚙ (⏑⏑...) *n* [62] chamois-dressing, shamoying; **=gerber** *m* chamois-dresser; **=gerberei** *f* = =gerben, auch: oil-leather manufactory; **=leder** *n* chamois(-), shamoy(-), shammy(-leather), auch: oil- (or wash-)leather.

Sämling (⸍⏑) [Same] *m* [1]d. *hort.* seedling, plant raised from seed.

Sammel=becken ⚙ (⏑⏑...) *n* [62], **=behälter** ⚙ *m* reservoir; **=biene** *f*, *ent.* working bee; **=fleiß** *m* industry (shown) in collecting (or compiling) material for a work, &c.; **=frucht** ⚘ *f* collective fruit; **=glas** *n* = =linse; **=kasten** ⚙ *m*, *arch.* reservoir; **=linse** *f*, *opt.* condensing-lens.

sammeln (⏑⏑) [mhd.: samt, (zu)sammen] [92]a. **I** *v*/*a.* **1.** (zf.=bringen) to gather, für einen bestimmten Zweck: to collect coins, stamps, &c., in Haufen: to heap (or lay, pile, treasure) up, to accumulate wealth, &c., in Massen: to amass riches, &c.; (einernten) to gather, pick, harvest; Kenntnisse ⁓ to store (or garner) knowledge; neue Kräfte ⁓ to gather new strength, F to pick up again; (versammeln) to assemble, bsd. ⚔ wieder ⁓ to rally fugitive soldiers, &c. — **2.** ⚘ Pflanzen ⁓, oft: to herborize, botanize; *opt.* in einem Brennpunkte ⁓ to focus rays of light. — **II** *v*/*n.* (h.) **3.** für Arme 2c. ⁓ to raise a subscription (or collection) for ..., to collect money for ..., to club together for ...; ich habe lange daran gesammelt I have been a long time collecting them; aus fremden Büchern ⁓ to compile. — **III sich** ⁓ *v*/*refl.* (s. I) **4.** to gather, collect, accumulate; (sich versammeln) to assemble, meet, ⚔ a. to rendezvous, to rally round the colours, &c. — **5.** (seine Gedanken ⁓) to collect one's thoughts, to compose o.s., nach einem Schrecken: to recover (o.s.), nach e-r Ohnmacht: to come to. — **IV** ~ *n* [23] **6.** = Sammlung 1.

Sammel=name (⏑⏑...) *m* [62] = =wort; **=platz**, **=punkt** *m* place of appointment or assembly, meet(ing-place), ⚔ auch: rendezvous; **=ruf** ⚔ *m* assembly; **=stelle** *f* bsd. ⚔ central depot; **=surium** F (⏑⏑⏑(⏑)⏑) [dtsch.=lt.] *n* [28] medley, omnium-gatherum; **=werk** *n* compilation; auch: (en)cyclopædia; **=wort** *n*, *gram.* collective noun; **=zylinder** ⚙ *m*, *mech.*, *phys.* accumulator.

Sam(me)t (⸍(⏑)) [mhd.; grch. *hexa'miton* 6fädenig; P v. ar. *Schâmi* ♁ Damaskus] *m* [1]c. ⚙ Weberei u. ✱ velvet; baumwollener ~ velveteen; in ~ und Seide kleiden to dress (or clothe) in silk(s) and satin(s).

sam(me)t=artig (⸍(⏑)...) *a.* [66] ⚙, ✱ velvet-like, velvety; **=band** *n* [62] velvet ribbon; **=blume** *f*: a) flower made of velvet; b) ⚘ amarant(h) (*Amara'ntus*); aufrechte ~ African marigold (*Tage'tes ere'cta*); **=bürste** *f* velvet-brush.

sam(me)ten (⸍(⏑)⏑) *a.* [66] velvety.

Sam(me)t=handschuh (⸍(⏑)...) *m* [62] velvet glove; *fig.* e-n mit ~en anfassen to handle a p. very delicately or gently; **=hut** *m* velvet bonnet; **=kleid** *n*, **=kragen** *m* velvet dress, collar; **=manschester** *m* cotton-velvet, velveteen; **=mütze** *f* velvet cap; **=pfötchen** *n* von der Katze: ~ machen to draw in the claws (a. *fig.*); **=rock** *m* velvet coat; **=schwarz** ⚙ *n* (Art Beinschwarz) velvet-black; **=stoffe** *m*/*pl.* velvet(ing)s *pl.*; **=tapete** *f* velvet tapestry or hangings *pl.*; **=teppich** *m* Brussels carpet; **=weber** *m* velvet-maker; **=weberei** *f* velvet-weaving; **=webstuhl** *m* velvet-loom; **⁓weich** *a.* [66] (as) soft as velvet.

Sammler (⏑⏑) [sammeln] *m* [22] **1.** **~(in** *f* [47]) gatherer, gleaner, collector (vgl. Briefmarken=⁓), aus fremden Büchern: compiler, von Altertümern: antiquary, v. Schätzen: hoarder (or amasser) of wealth, *bibl.* one who lays up treasures; (e-r der eine Kollekte macht) p. who collects subscriptions or makes a collection. — **2.** ⚙: a) = Sammelbecken; b) *elect.* accumulator.

Sammlung (⏑⏑) [ahd.; *sammeln] *f* [46] **1.** gathering, &c. (s. sammeln I); ~ zu wohltätigen Zwecken subscription (or collection) for charitable purposes; ⚔ ~ assembly; ~ um die Fahne rallying round the colours. — **2.** a) (Gesammeltes) collection, compilation; (Blütenlese) selection, anthology; b) (Fassung, Ruhe) collectedness, composure, equanimity, balance of mind.

Sammlungs=... (⏑⏑...) = Sammel=...

Samniter (⏑⸍⏑) [Sa'mnium ♁, it. Landschaft] *m* [22] (a. **Samnite** *m* [44]), **~in** *f* [47], **samnitisch** *a.* [66] röm. Alt.: Samnite.

Samoaner (-⏑⸍⏑) [Samo'a ♁, Inseln in Polynesien] *m* [22], **~in** *f* [47] inhabitant of Samoa, Samoan (islander).

Samojede (-⏑⸍⏑) [russ.] *m* [44], **...jedin** *f* [47] Nord=asiate finnischen Stammes: Samoyed.

Sams=tag *provc.* (⸍=⸍) [ahd.; *Sabbat=s] *m* [1]c. Saturday; (des) ~s on Saturdays.

samt[1] (⸍) [ahd.: same] **I** *adv.* = alle⁓; ⁓ u. sonders each and all, all and sundry, jointly and severally, all together, F *co.* every man jack. — **II** (mit)samt *prp.* mit *dat.* together with; das Pferd (mit)samt dem Reiter horse and rider.

Samt[2] (⸍) 2c. *m* [1]b. s. Sam(me)t 2c.

sämtlich (⸍⏑) [mhd.; *samt[1]] *a.* [66]c. all (together); (vollständig) complete; die⁓e Bürgerschaft the whole (or entire) body of citizens; des Dichters ⁓e Werke the poet's collected works *pl.*, a complete edition of the poet's works; sie sind ⁓ ertrunken they (or all) went down in a body or to a man, every one of them was drowned.

Samu-el (⸍⏑⏑) [hebr. Gott erhört] *npr*/*m.* [1][66]α. *bibl.* (a. Vn.) Samuel, Koseform: Sam, *dim.* Sammy.

Samum (⸍⏑) [ar.] *m* [1] (heißer Wüstenwind) simoom, simoon, samiel (wind).

San (⸍) [it. u. span.] vor Konsonanten, außer Sp... u. St... = Sankt (*abbr.* S.).

Sanatorium ⚗ (-⏑⸍(⏑)⏑) [lt.] *n* [28] (klimatische Heil=anstalt) sanatorium.

Sand (⸍) [ahd.: sand] *m* [1]b. **1.** sand, grober: grit; mit ~ bestreuen to (strew with) sand; s. Punktum 2; ⚓ auf den ~ geraten oder laufen, auf dem ~e sitzen bleiben to run aground (on the sands); auf dem ~e sitzend stranded. — **2.** *fig.* auf den ~ bauen to build on the sands; e-n auf den ~ setzen (besiegen) to unhorse a p., *fig.* to nonplus

[Sandaal] — 822 — [Saphir]

a p., to get the better of a p.; auf dem ~e sitzen oder sein to be in great distress or F on one's last legs; einem ~ in die Augen streuen (et. vorspiegeln) to throw dust in a p.'s eyes; bibl. ihrer sind wie ~ am Meere their number is as the sand of the sea. — 3. ↓ = Sandbaum.
Sand=aal (ˇ‿¹) m ⑫ sand-eel (Ammo'dytes).
Sandale (‿ˊ‿) [grch. sa'ndalon n; *pers.] f (Schnürsohle) sandal; mit ~n bekleidet sandalled. [dals, ⚥ sandaliform.]
sandalen=artig (‿ˊ‿ˇ) a. ⓖⓖ like san-
Sandarak (ˇ‿‿) [grch.] m ⓓ. pharm. (Harz von ♃ Ca'llitris quadriva'lis) sandarach.
sand=artig (ˇ...) a. ⓖⓖ sand- (or gravel-)like, ⚥ arenaceous, arenose; **=bad** n ⑫ für Bäder ɾc.: sand-bath (a. chm.); **=bank** s.-bank, sands pl., bar; s. a. Bank¹ 4; **=berg** m = **=hügel**; **=blatt** ♃ n: a) = Huflattich; b) am Tabak: shrub; **=boden** m, agr. sandy soil or ground; **=büchse** f für Streusand: s.-box; **=dorn** ♃ m sea-buckthorn (Hippo'phaë); **=dünen** f/pl. sandy beach, sands pl.
Sandel=holz (ˇ‿...) [lt. sa'ndalo m; grch. sa'ntalon n;*skt. chandana] n ⓝsandal-wood; **=holzbaum** ♃ m sandalwood-tree (Sa'ntalum album); **=(holz=)öl** n sandal-oil.
Sander (ˇ‿) [Zahn] m ⑫ ichth. perch-pike (Luciope'rca sandra). [**=läufer.**]
Sanderling (ˇ‿‿) m ⓓ. orn. = Sand=
Sand=erze (ˇ...) n/pl. ⑫ min. sand-ores pl.; **=faß** n: a) barrel for sand; b) = **=büchse**; **=fläche** f sandy plain; **=floh** m, ent. sand- (or earth-)flea, chigoe (Pulex pe'netrans); **=form** ⊕ f Gießerei: sand-mould; **=former** m sand-moulder; **=formerei** f sand-moulding; **=führend** a. ⓖⓖ ⚥ sabulous; **=gebirge** n sand-hills or -mountains pl.; **=gebläse** ⊕ n sand-jet; **=gegend** f sandy country or neighbourhood; **=gießerei** f, **=guß** m ⊕ sand-casting; **=glas** n = **=uhr**; **=grieß** m gravel, grit; **=grube** f s.-pit; **=grund** m sandy ground, e-s Flusses ɾc.: sandy bottom; **=hase** m: a) zo. hare (living) in a sandy country; b) Kegelspiel: in ~n schieben (nichts treffen) to miss; **=haufen** m heap of sand; **=hose** f sand-spout; **=hügel** m sand-hill, down.
sandig (ˇ‿) a. ⓖⓖ (s. Sand) sandy, gritty, ⚥ sabulous; full of sand; vgl. sandartig.
Sand=junge (ˇ...) m ⑫ sand-boy; **=käfer** m, ent. tiger-beetle (Cicinde'la); **=korn** n, **=körnchen** n grain of sand; **=läufer** m, orn. Sanderling, sandpiper (Ca'lidris arena'ria); **=loch** n sand-pit; **=mann** m sand-man; F co. bei dir kommt der ~ (du bist schläfrig) the sand-man is coming, mehr gbr.: the dustman's in your eyes; **=meer** n sea of sand, sandy desert; **=nelke** ♃ f sand-pink (Dia'nthus are-na'rius); **=papier** ⊕ n sand-paper; **=pumpe** f für Brunnen ɾc.: sand-pump or -ejector; **=rohr** ♃ n sand-reed, beach-grass (Ammo'phila); **=rücken** m sand-ridge; **=sack** m sand-bag; **=schaufel** f sand-shovel; **=schicht** f layer (or stratum) of sand; **=stein** m sandstone, freestone; **=stein=arbeit** f sandstone work; **=stein=formation** f, **=gebirge**, **=gewände** n, geol. sandstone formation; **=strahlapparat** ⊕ m sand-jet; **=sturm** m sand-storm.

sandte (ˇ‿) ind. impf. von senden.
Sand=tiegel ⊕ (ˇ...) m ⑫ sand-crucible; **=torte** f Madeira cake; **=ufer** n sandy shore or bank; **=uhr** ⊕ f sand-, hour-glass, zum Eierkochen: time- (or egg-)boiler; **=viper** f, zo. sand-natter (Eryx); **=weg** m sandy path or road; **=wespe** f, ent. sand-wasp (Ammo'phila sabulo'sa); **=wirbel** m sandspout; **=wurm** m, zo. sandworm (Areni'cola); **=wüste** f sandy desert or waste; **=zucker** ⚭ m brown (or moist) sugar; **=zunge** ↓ f sand-spit.
sanft (ˇ) [ahd.: soft] a. ⓖⓖ (weich) soft, (glatt) smooth; (milde) gentle, mild, (ruhig) calm, placid; (lieblich) lovely; vom Charakter: sweet; (gutmütig) good-natured; e-s ~en Todes sterben to die an easy death, to come to a peaceful end; Jer werden to soften, to relent; 2 (adv.) ansteigende Höhe gently rising ground, gentle slope; Sprichw. Gewissen am Schluß.
Sänfte (ˇ‿) [ahd.;*sanft] f ⓒ (Tragsessel) sedan (-chair), für Kranke auch: stretcher, ambulance; litter.
Sänften=träger (ˇ‿‿) m ⑫ sedan-chairman; bearer of a stretcher.
sanft=gesinnt (ˇ‿ˇ) a. ⓖⓖ = **=mütig**.
Sanft=heit (ˇ‿) f ⓖⓖ softness, smoothness; vgl. Sanftmut. [vgl. besänftigen.]
sänftigen (ˇ‿‿) [sanft] v/a. ⓖⓖ to soften.]
sänft(ig)lich (ˇ‿)(‿) adv. softly, gently.
Sanft=mut (ˇ...) f ⑫ gentleness (or mildness, sweetness) of character; meekness; **=mütig** a. ⓖⓖ gentle, sweet, meek, F contp. soft; bibl. selig sind die ~en blessed are the meek.
sang¹ (ˇ) ind. impf. von singen.
Sang² (ˇ) [ahd.: song;*sang¹] m ⓓ b. singing, chant(ing), song; s. Klang I.
sangbar (ˇ‿) a. ⓖⓖ singable, fit for singing; (melodisch) melodious, tuneful.
Sangbarkeit (ˇ‿‿) f ⓖⓖ singableness, melodiousness, tunefulness.
sänge (ˇ‿) subj. impf. v. singen.
Sänger (ˇ‿) [ahd.; *Sang] m ⑫, **~in** f ① 1. (singende Person) singer, vocalist (a. thea.), weit S. songster (auch v. Vögeln); vgl. Chor-, Kirchen=sänger; (Opern=) (=in) opera-singer, f auch: primadonna, diva; weit S. professional singer; die ~ des Waldes the warblers pl. of the wood. — 2. geh. Spr. = Dichter. — 3. orn. warbler (Sy'lvia. &c.).
Sänger=bund (ˇ‿...) m ⑫, etwa: union of singers or minstrels: singing club or fraternity; **=chor** m s. Chor 2.
Sängerei (ˇ‿ˊ) f ⓖⓖ: a) g.s. professional singing; b) b.s. bad (or inferior) singing, bawling.
Sänger=fest (ˇ‿ˇ) n ⑫ = Gesangfest.
sängerhaft (ˇ‿ˇ) a. ⓖⓖ after the manner of singers or minstrels.
Sängerschaft (ˇ‿ˇ) f ⓖⓖ **Sängertum** (ˇ‿) n ⓓ. 1. (art of) singing, singer's profession or vocation; minstrelsy. — 2. coll. (company of) singers pl.; (body of) minstrels pl.
Sanges=bruder (ˇ‿‿) m ⑫ member of a singing club; fellow-minstrel.
sang(es)=froh (ˇ‿)(...) a. ⓖⓖ, ⚥ lustig a. fond of singing or warbling.
Sanguinifer (‿gā‿‿) [neu=lt.] m ⑫ sanguine person.

sanguinisch (‿gā‿) [neu=lt.] a. ⓖⓖ (leichtblütig) sanguine (temperament, &c.).
Sanhedrin (‿‿ˊ) [hebr.; *grch. Synedrium] m ⓓ d. Alt.: (Hoher Rat der Juden) Sanhedrim, ...in.
Sanherib (ˇ‿‿) npr/. m. ⓓ ⓖ a. (assyr. König, 700 v. Chr.) Sennacherib.
sanieren (‿ˊ‿) [lt.] I v/a. ⓖ (gesund m.) to cure, to restore to health; ⚭ Finanzen, Geldverhältnisse ⚤ to put finances, financial matters on a healthy (or sound) basis. — II ~ ⓖ u. **Sanierung** f ⓖⓖ restoration (to health), v. Dingen: sanitation.
Sanikel ♃ (‿ˊ‿) [lt. f Heil=] m ⑫ sanicle (Sani'cula Europae'a).
sanitär (‿‿ˊ) [fr.] a. ⓖⓖ sanitary.
Sanität (‿‿ˊ) [lt.] f ⓖⓖ (gesunder Zustand) health(y condition), sanitation; **Lich** (‿‿ˊ) a. ⓖⓖ (gesundheitlich) sanitary.
Sanitäts=beamte(r) (‿‿ˊˇ...) m ⑫ sanitary officer or inspector, a. health-officer; **=behörde** f san. board or authorities pl.; **=kollegium** n board of health; **=kolonne** ⚔ f ambulance-corps; **=mäßig** a. ⓖⓖ = sanitary, hygienic; **=offizier** ⚔ m medical staff officer; **=offizier=korps** ⚔ n medical staff; **=polizei** f sanitary police; **=rat** m: a) member of a board of health; b) Titel etwa: medical adviser; **=wache** f public (or free) dispensary (and surgery); **=wagen** m ambulance(-cart); **=wesen** n sanitary (or hygienic) matters pl.
sank¹ ↓ (ˇ) [sinkend] a. ⓖⓖ heavier than water; Les Holz wood of greater specific gravity than water.
sank² (ˇ) impf. ind. von sinken.
Sankt (ˇ) [lt. heilig] a. inv. (abbr. St.) I vor npr. von Heiliggesprochenen: saint (abbr. St.), z. B. ~**Bartholomäus** St. Bartholomew, ~ **Bernhard** St. Bernard, ~ **Johannes** St. John, ~ **Paul(us)** St. Paul. — II in ♀ Namen, z. B. der Große ~ **Bernhard** Alpenberg: the Great St. Bernard; ~ **Gallen** n schwz. Stadt: St. Gall; s. Gotthard, Petersburg. — III in andern Verbindungen, z. B. ~**Bartholomäus=Nacht** s. Bartholomäusnacht; ~**=Elmsfeuer** s. Elmsfeuer.
Sanktion (‿tsĭ(‿)ˊ) [lt.] f ⓖⓖ (Bestätigung) sanction; vgl. pragmatisch.
sanktionieren (‿tsĭ‿ˊ‿) [lt.] v/a. ⓖⓖ (bestätigen) to sanction.
Sanktuarium (‿‿ˊ(‿)‿) [lt.] n ⓓ rel., arch. (Heiligtum) sanctuary. [sinnen.]
sann (ˇ) ind., **sänne** (ˇ‿) subj. impf. v.)
Sansculotte (ßã-tü-lot) [fr. ohne Hosen] m ⓖⓖ (fr. Republikaner oder Soldat Ende des 18. sae.) sans-culotte. [culottism.]
Sansculottismus (ßã-tü-‿‿) m sans-)
Sansibar ♀ (‿‿ˊ) [ar. Schwarzenland] npr. n ⓓ α. (ost=afrik. Insel u. Stadt) Zanzibar; **~er** (‿‿) m ⓖⓖ, **~in** f ⓖ Zanzibari, inhabita. t (or native) of Zanzibar.
Sanskrit (ˇ‿, ‿ˊ) [skt. Literatur...] n ⓓ ⓒ. (ohne pl.) (alte heilige Sprache der Hindus) Sanskrit; **Lisch** (‿ˊ‿) a. ⓖⓖ Sanskritic; **~ist** (‿‿ˊ) m ⓖⓖ Sanskritist.
Sapan=holz (‿‿ˊ,...) [malai.] n ⓓ (rotes Farbholz von Caesalpi'nia Sappan) sapan-wood.
Saphir (ˇ‿ˊ) [mhd.; *hebr. sapīr] m ⓓ d. min. (Edelstein, meist blau) sapphire; grüner ~ green corundum; roter ~

Signs (see page XVII): F familiar; P vulgar; ſ flash; ⚲ rare; † obsolete (died); * new word (born); ⁺⁺ incorrect; ♪ music;

[Sappe] — 823 — [Sattlerware]

oriental ruby; **Sen** (ˊˌˇ) *a.* ⊕ of sapphire, sapphirine. [sap, trench.)
Sappe ⚔(ˊˇ)[fr.*sape*]*f*⊕*frt.*(Laufgraben).
sapperlot (ˊˇⁿ), **Sapperlöter** *m* ㉒, **sapperment** (ˊˇˇˇ) *int.*, **Sappermenter** *m* ㉒ = sackerlot ꝛc.
Sappeur ⚔(ˊˇ) *m* (f.... ob. ɦ͜v ͜p͜oʼr) [fr. *sapeur*] *m* ⑪d. ㉚ (Schanzgräber) sapper.
sapphisch (ˊˇ) [Sappho, lesbische Dichterin, um 600 v. Chr.] *a.* ⊕ of Sappho, Sapphic; ≈e Strophe, ≈es Versmaß Sapphic metre or verse.
sappieren ⚔(ˇˊˇ)[fr. *saper*]*v/a. u. v/n.*(h.) ⊕ (grabend aushöhlen) to sap, to undermine (a. *fig.*); **Sappierer** *m* ㉒ sapper.
Sara (ˊˇ) [hebr. Fürstin] *npr/f.* ⊕ ㊾ß. ⊕ㆇa. (auch Vn.) *bibl.* Sarah.
Sarazene (ˇˇˊˇ) [ar. Orientale] *m* ㊹, **Sarazenin** *f* ㊼ Saracen; **Sarazenentum** *n* ㉒d. (Mohammedanismus) Saracenism; **sarazenisch** *a.* ⊕ Saracenic.
Sard-achat ⊓ (ˊˇ-ch-) [grch.] *m* ⊕ *min.* (rötlicher Achat) sardachate.
Sardanapal (ˇˇˊˊ) *npr/m.* ⑪d.*α.* Alt.: (letzter assyrischer König, †883 v. Chr.) Sardanapalus; *fig.*(Schwelger) debauchee, epicure.
Sardelle (ˇˊˇ) [*it. „aus Sardinien"] *f* ㊽ *ichth.*: a) echte ~ anchovy (*Engrau'lis enchrasi'cholus*); b) = Sardine.
Sardellen-brötchen(ˇˊˇ…)*n* ㉒anchovy-sandwich; **-butter**, **-paste** *f* anchovy-paste; **-sauce** *f* anchovy-sauce.
Sardine (ˇˊˇ) [it. *sardi'na*; *Sardinien] *f* ㊽ *ichth.* sardine, pilchard (*Clu'pea pilcha'rdus*); ⚓ ~n *pl.* in Öl (tinned) sardines *pl.* preserved in oil.
Sardini-en ⚑ (ˇˊ(ˇ)ˇ) [it.] *npr/n.* ㉓*α.*: it. Insel und ehm. Königreich: Sardinia; **Sardini-er** (in *f* ㊼) *m* ㉒, **sard(in)isch** (ˇˊˇ, ˊˇ) *a.* ⊕ Sardinian.
sardonisch (ˇˊˊˇ) [grch. v. *Sardoa*?] *a.* ⊕: ≈es (gezwungenes) Lachen sardonic laugh or smile; *path.* bei Tetanus ꝛc.: canine (or unnatural, spasmodic) laugh.
Sard-onyx ⊓ (ˊˊˇ, r-r ˇˇˇ) [grch.] *m* ⑪a. ⑯ *min.* Edelstein: sardonyx.
Sarg (ˊ) [ahd.; *Sark(ophag)] *m* ⑦b. coffin (↓ a. = altes Schiff); einfacher(ob. provisorischer) ~ shell. [(=Beerentang).)
Sargasso ⚑ (ˇˊˇ) [port.] *m* ㊿ gulf-weed)
Sarg-beschlag (ˊˇ…) *m* ㉒ coffin-mounting or -furniture; **-deckel** *m* coffin-lid; ≈förmig *a.* ⊕ coffin-shaped; **-nagel** *m* coffin-nail; **-platte** *f* mit Namen des Toten coffin-plate; **-tuch** *n* pall.
Sarkasmus (ˇˊˇ) [grch.] *m* ㉗ (beißender Spott) sarcasm, sarcastic expression;
sarkastisch *a.* ⊕ sarcastic(al).
Sarkophag (ˇˊˇⁿ) [grch. Fleischverzehrer] *m* ⑪d. (Steinsarg) sarcophagus, stone coffin or vault.
Sarmat/e (ˇˊˇ) *m* ㊹, **≈in** *f* ㊼ Alt.: Sarmatian; **Sarmati-en** ⚑ (ˇˊˇß, ˇˇ) *npr/n.* ㉓ *α.* (ehm. nord-östl. Europa) Sarmatia; **sarmatisch** *a.* ⊕ Sarmatian.
Saron ⚑ (ˊˇ) [hebr.] *npr/n.* ⊕d. *bibl.* (fruchtbare Ebene in Palästina) Sharon. Rose zu ~ (Hohelied 2, 1) Rose of Sharon.
saronisch (-ˊˇ) *a.* ⊕ Alt.: ⚑ ≈er Meerbusen im Ägäischen Meere: Saronic Gulf.
Sarraß ⚔(ˊˇ)[poln.]*m*⑳a. heavy sabre.
Sarsaparille ⚘ (ˇˇˊˇ) [span.] *f* ㊽ sarsaparilla (*Smilax*); **Sarsaparill-wurzel** ⚘ (ˇˇˊˇ, ˊˇ) *f* ㊲ *pharm.* sarsaparilla.

Sarsche¹ (ˊˇ) *f.* Serge. ~² *f.* Zarge.
Sarsenett ⚘ (ˇˇˊ) [fr. *sarsenet m*] *m* ⊕ *m* ㊷ = Sasse. [⊕c. sarcenet.)
saß¹ (ˊ) *ind. impf.* von sitzen.
Sassafras ⚘(ˊˇˇ)[span.]*m,inv.* sassafras.
Sassaparille ꝛc. (ˇˇˊˇ) *f.* Sarsaparille ꝛc.
Sasse (ˊˇ) *m* ㊹, **Sassin** *f* ㊼ occupant, tenant; (Besitzer[in] e-s Grundstückes) owner of (freehold) land; *vgl.* Insaß.
säße (ˊˇ) *subj. impf.* von sitzen.
sässig (ˊˇ) *a.* ⊕ settled; *vgl.* ansässig.
Sassin (ˊˇ) *f* ㊼ f. Sasse.
Satan (ˊˇ) [ahd.; *hebr. Feind] *m* ⑪ⓓd. ㊿, ~**as** (ˊˇˇ) *m* ⑯ *rel.* Satan; *fig.* ein wahrer ~ the veriest devil or demon or fiend; **satanisch** (ˇˊˇ) *a.* ⊕ of Satan, satanic (teuflisch) diabolic(al).
Satans-kerl F (ˊⁿ…) *m* ㊷ devil (or demon) of a fellow; **-tücke** *f* fiendish malice or cunning; **-weib** F *n* devil in petticoats. [Planeten) satellite.)
Satellit ⊓ (ˇˇˊ) [lt.] *m* ㊷ *ast.* (Mond e-s
Satin ⊛ (ˇˊ) [fr. „Seiden-"] *m* ㊿ (Seiden atlas) sateen. [satinet.)
Satinett ⊛ (ˇˇˊ) [fr.] *m* ⊕c. (Halb-atlas))
satinieren ⊛ (ˇˇˊˇ) [fr.] I *v/a.* ⊕ Papierfabr.: to glaze, to satin, *typ.* to calender; satiniertes Papier super-calendered paper. — II ~ *n* ㉓ glazing, satining.
Satinierer ⊛ (ˇˇˊˇ) *m* ㉒, ~**in** *f* ㊼ Papierfabr.: glazer.
Satinier-maschine ⊛ (ˇˇˊⁿ…) *f* ⊕ glazing-machine, *typ.* rolling-machine; **-walzen** *f/pl.* glazing-rolls *pl.*
Satire (ˇˊˇ) [lt. *sä'tira*] *f* ⊕ (Spottschrift) satire; lampoon; ~**n-dichter** (ˇˇˇ…)*m* ㊷ satirical poet; **Satiriker** (ˇˊˇˇ) *m* ㊷ satirist, satirical writer or poet; **satirisch** *a.* ⊕ satirical, mocking.
Satisfaktion (ˇˇˇß(ˇ)ˊ) [lt.] *f* ㊻: Genugtuung; e-m ~ geben to give a p. satisfaction; ≈s-fähig (ˊˇˊ) *a.* ⊕ qualified to give satisfaction or to fight a duel.
Satrap (ˇˊ) [grch., *pers.] *m* ㊷ (alt-pers. Statthalter) satrap (a. *fig.*); ~**enschaft** (ˇˇˊ) *f* ㊻, ~**ie** (ˇˇˊ) *f* ⊕ satrapy.
satt (ˊ) [ahd.: *sad*: lt. *satis*] *a.* ⊕ (D1,6) 1. satisfied (gesättigt) satiated, full, *a.* sated; *chm.*, &c. saturated, *v.* Farben *a.* deep, rich, intens(iv)e; *fig.* ≈ und genug more than ample. — 2. mit *v/refl.* sich ≈ essen to eat one's fill; ich habe mich ≈ gegessen I have had (or eaten) enough; sich ≈ lachen (trinken) to laugh (or drink) to one's heart's content or to the top of one's bent; wir haben uns ≈ gesehen we have seen enough or had enough of sight-seeing; er kann sich daran nicht ≈ sehen he never gets tired of gazing at it, *a.* he cannot take his eyes off (it). — 3. mit nicht-reflexiven *verbs*: er ist nicht ≈ zu bekommen he is insatiable; et. ≈ bekommen, et. ob. e-r Sache (*gen.*) ≈ w. to grow (or get) tired (or weary) of a th., to have had enough of it; et. ≈ h. to be tired (or sick) of a th.; e-n ≈ m. to give a p. enough to eat or as much as he can eat; ≈ sein to feel satisfied or full. [pan or -bowl.)
Satte (ˊˇ) [ndd. (sich) setzen] *f* ⊕ milk-)
Sattel (ˊˇ) [ahd.: *saddle*] *m* ⑲ ㉑ 1. saddle (auch ⚓ u. ⚔); *anat.* (Nasen-

rücken) bridge of the nose; ⚑ ~ eines Berges (*ant.* Grat) depression between two peaks; ⊕ *arch.* (Querholz) crossbeam; ♪ upper saddle of a violin, &c. — 2. Redensarten: (im Turnier ꝛc.) e-n aus dem ~ heben to unhorse (or throw) a p., *fig.* to take a p.'s place; fest im ~ sitzen to have a good (or firm) seat (*vgl.* sattelfest); *fig.* to be firmly established or safely settled; *fig.* in allen Sätteln gerecht sein to be ready for any emergency, to be fit for any task, to be an all-round man.
Sattel-band ⊕ (ˊˇ…) *n* ㊷ saddle-band; **-baum** *m* saddle-tree; **-blech** *n* witherband; **-bogen** *m* saddle-bow; **-bügel** *m* tree of a pack-saddle; **-dach** *n, arch.* saddle- (or span-, ridged) roof; mit rechtem Winkel: square roof; **-decke** *f* saddle-cloth (= Schabracke); **-druck** *m, vet.* sore caused by the saddle, *a.* s.-gall; ≈**fertig** *a.* ⊕ ready to mount; ≈**fest** *a.*: ≈ sein to sit (one's horse) well or firmly, *fig.* to know one's business thoroughly, to be master of one's trade; ≈**förmig** *a.* saddle-shaped; **-gurt** *m* s.-girth; **-holz** *n* Wasserbau: s.-beam; **-kammer** *f* s.-room; **-kissen** *n* s.-cushion, pillion, für Kutschpferde: s.-pad; **-knecht** *m* groom; **-knopf** *m* pommel (of a saddle).
satteln (ˊˇ) I *v/a.* ㉒a. *man.* ein Pferd ꝛc. ≈ to saddle…, to put the saddle on … — II ~ *n* ㉓ saddling, ⚔ zum ≈ blasen to sound boot(s) and saddle(s).
Sattel-pausche ⊕ (ˊˇ…) *f* ⊕ cantle; **-pferd** *n* near horse, auch near sider; *vgl.* **-seite**; ehm. **-pistole** *f* horse-pistol; **-platz** *m* bei Rennen: saddling-place; **-polster** *n* pillion; **-rost** *m, metall.* saddle-grate; **-seite** *f* (linke Seite) des Pferdes: near side; **-steg** ⚔ *m* cross-beam of a saddle; **-stück** *n* (Fleisch) saddle (of mutton, &c.); **-tasche** *f* saddle-bag.
Sattelung (ˊˇˇ) *f* ㊻ saddling.
Sattel-wagen ⚔ (ˊˇ…) *m* ㊷ *artill.* platform-carriage; **-waren** ⊛ *f/pl.* saddlery *sg.*; **-zeug** *n* saddle and harness(ing).
Sattheit (ˊˇ) *f* ㊻ (f. satt) satiety, satiated (or satisfied) state; fulness (of the stomach); (übersättigung) repletion.
sättig/en (ˊˇˇ) [mhd.; *satt] I *v/a., v/n.* (h.) u. sich ≈ *v/refl.* ⊕ 1. to satisfy, to sat(iat)e; e-n (sich) ≈ to appease a p.'s (one's) hunger, F to fill a p.'s (one's) stomach or belly; übermäßig ≈ to glut (or cram, sate) with. — 2. *chm.*, &c. to saturate with a gas, &c.; sich ≈ to become saturated. — II ~ *n* ㉓ = ≈ung.
Sättigung (ˊˇˇ) *f* ㊻ appeasing a p.'s hunger, &c. (f. sättigen 1); (Speisung) feeding; *chm.*, &c. saturation of a solution, &c. [of saturation.)
Sättigungs-punkt (ˊˇˇⁿ…) *m* ㊷ point)
Sattler (ˊˇ) [ahd.; *satteln] *m* ㉒ saddler, jetzt mehr gbr.: harness-maker.
Sattler-arbeit(ˊˇˇ…)*f* ㊷ saddler's work.
Sattlerei (ˊˇˊˇ) *f* ㊽ saddler's (or harness-maker's) trade or workshop.
Sattler-gesell(e) (ˊˇ…) *m* f. Gesell(e) 2; **-handwerk** *n* saddler's trade; **-meister** *m* master harness-maker; **-ware** *f* harnessing, *a.*: saddlery.

㊼ scientific; ⚘ botanical; ⚑ geography; ⊕ machinery; ⚔ mining; ⚔ military; ↓ marine; ⊛ commercial; ⚓ postal; 🚂 railway.

[**sattsam**] — 824 — [**Sauerwerden**]

sattsam (˘-) a. ⑯ (bsd. adv.) sufficient(ly), stärker: abundant(ly); (genug) enough; **~keit** (˘˘-) f ⑯ sufficiency. [*Satureia*].

Saturei ̧ (---́) [mhd., *it.] f ⑯ savory

Saturn (-s) [lt.] npr/m.⑪α., a.: **~us** (-˘) ⑯γ.: a) *myth.* Jupiters Vater: Saturn(us); b) *ast.* Planet: Saturn; **~ali-en** (-˘⁄-˘˘) m/pl.inv. röm. Fest im Dezember: Saturnalia pl.; **˘isch** a. ⑯ Saturnine, Saturnian; **˘ischer Vers** Saturnian verse.

Satyr (˘˘) [grch.] m ㉔(㉖) *myth.* (Waldgott mit Bocksfüßen) satyr; **˘artig** a. ⑯ satyric, satyrical; **~-drama** n ㉒, **~spiel** n grch. Alt.: satyric drama.

Satz (ˇ) [ahd.: set; *sitzen, saß] m ⑪a. **1.** (Sprung) leap, bound, (Anlauf) dash; in einem Satze at (or with) one leap or jump; in Sätzen by (leaps and) bounds; e-n ~ m. to take a leap, to jump, to bound; to dash forward. — **2.** = Bodensatz. — **3.** F (Schmaus) e-n ~ geben to stand treat. — **4.** (zugehörige Dinge) set of weights, tools, &c.; ~ Brot ⁊c. batch of bread, &c.; Tennis: set; *phys.* galvanischer ~ galvanic pile; ⊛ ~ Waren assortment (or lot, parcel) of goods. — **5.** *hunt.* von Hasen ⁊c.: breeding; ~ Kaninchen nest of rabbits; vgl. Brut 2; Fischerei: (young) fry of fish. — **6.** ⊛ *typ.* (Arbeit des Setzers) setting up (of) type, compositor's work; (zu Setzendes) copy, (Gesetztes) matter. — **7.** (bestimmte Geldsumme) fixed amount, sum agreed upon; ↯ in diesem Geschäfte hat alles seinen festen ~ ... everything has its fixed price; zu niedrigen (hohen) Sätzen at low (high) rates. — **8.** (in Worte gefaßter Gedanke) sentence (a. *gr.*), proposition (a. *log. u. math.*); vgl. Lehrsatz; (Glaubens)~ article of faith, ⊘ dogma; ~ aus der Sittenlehre tenet, (kurzer Denkspruch) aphorism; s. abhängig 2; zs.-gesetzter ~ complex sentence, period. — **9.** ♪: a) (Kunst Tonstücke zu setzen) composition; b) (Teil eines Tonstücks) (musical) phrase or movement.

Satz-akzent (ˇ...) m ⑫ *gr., rhet.* tonic stress; **˘artig** a., *chm.* like a sediment; **-bau** m, **-bildung** f, *gram.* structure, formation of sentences.

Sätzchen (˘˘) n ㉓ (dim. von Satz) short leap; *gr.* short sentence, phrase.

Satz-fehler (ˇ...) m ⑫ *typ.* printing-mistake, misprint; **-fügung** f, *gr.* = -gefüge; **-fügungs-lehre** f = Satzlehre; **-gefüge** n structure (or construction) of a sentence; **-glied** n = -teil; **-lehre** f syntax; **-teich** m für (junge) Fische: stockpond; **-teil** m, *gr.* part of a sentence.

Satzung (˘˘) f ⑯ statute, (Vorschrift) precept; (Gesetz) law; (Glaubenssatz) dogma; (feste Regel) fixed rule, ordinance, (Einrichtung) institution; organization; **˘s-gemäß, ˘mäßig** (ˇ˘...) a. ⑯ (u. adv.) statutory (in a stat. way).

Satz-wage ⊛ (ˇ...) f ⑫ spirit-level; **˘weise** adv. (F a. a.): a) by leaps or jumps, (unregelmäßig) by fits and starts; b) *gr., rhet.* sentence by sentence; **-zeit** f, *hunt.*, wo das Rot-, Reh- ⁊c. wild Junge bringt: breeding-time or -season.

Sau (¹) [ahd.: sow: lt. *su-s*] f ⑩, *hunt.* ⑯ **1.** (*pl.* Säue) sow, (Schwein) hog; s. Perle. — **2.** *hunt.* (*pl.* Sauen) wild sow. — **3.** P *fig.* (unsaubere oder unflätige Person) slut, dirty (or filthy) trollop or beast; von einem Manne: filthy (or nasty, smutty) fellow. — **4.** (Tintenfleck) ink-blot. — **5.** (Versehen) blunder. — **6.** burschikos: ~ (Glück) haben to be lucky or fortunate, bsd. beim Spiel: to be in luck's way. — **7.** ⊕ *metall.* (Eisen-)~ am Boden des Hochofens: sow of melted iron; (Gemisch von Schlacken- und Schmelz-eisen) (ferriferous) bear.

Sau-arbeit F (ˇ...) f ⑫ dirty (or filthy) work; (schwere Arbeit) drudgery; **-balg** m sow-bane (*Chenopodium rubrum*); **-bär** m (das männliche Schwein) boar.

sauber (˘˘) [ahd.: sober] a. ⑯ (D9) clean (shirt, &c.), tidy (room, &c.); (niedlich) neat, (hübsch) pretty; ˘e Arbeit careful work(ing), *iro.* fine doings *pl.*; *iro.* ˘es Bürschchen young scapegrace or hopeful; ˘es Früchtchen, ˘e Person promising young scamp, pretty article; *fig.* ˘er Stil clear (or lucid) style; ˘ (adv.) abschreiben to make a clean (or fair) copy of; **~keit** (˘˘-) f ⑯ clean(li)ness, tidiness, neatness; clearness (or lucidity) of style.

säuberlich (˘˘˘) a. ⑯: ˘, oft fein ˘ = sauber; (anständig) decent, proper.

säubern (˘˘) [ahd.: *sauber] I v/a. und sich ˘ v/refl. ⑨a.: (sich) ˘ to clean(se) (o.s.), von Schlechtem: to purge (o.s.) of evil (vgl. reinigen I). — II ~ n ⑬ u. **Säuberung** f ⑯ = Reinigung 1.

Sau-bohne ̧ (ˇ...) f ⑫ broad (or horse-) bean (von *Vicia faba*); **-borste** f hog's bristle; **-brot** ̧ n schwz. (Alpenveilchen) sowbread (*Cyclamen Europaeum*).

Sauce (sō-ß) [fr. "Sülze", "Salz"] f ⑫ (Tunke) sauce; vgl. Brühe 1 u. 2 u. Soße.

Saucischen (sō-ßi'ß˘) [fr. *saucisse* u. dtsch *-chen*] n ㉓ small sausage.

Sau-distel ̧ (ˇ...) f ⑫ sow-thistle (*Sonchus oleraceus*).

sauen (˘˘) [Sau] v/n. (h.) ⊛ to do (or say) piggish (or filthy, dirty) things; e-n (sich) voll ˘ to befoul (or F mess over) a p. (o.s.).

sauer (˘˘) [ahd.: sour] a. ⑯ (D9) (*comp.* saurer; *sup.* sauerst) **1.** (*ant.* süß) sour, acid (*a. chm.; ant.* basisch); (herb) tart; ˘ wie Essig as sharp (or sour) as vinegar; saure Gurken pickled cucumbers *pl.*; s. Hering, ̧ saure Kirsche = Sauerkirsche u. -weichsel; ˘ m. to (make) sour, to turn milk, &c., ˘ to acidify; ˘ w. to turn sour or acid; die Milch wird ˘, auch: ... is curdling; *iro.* die Trauben sind ˘ he finds (or they find) the grapes too sour, auch: sour grapes, said the fox, when he could not reach them; F *fig.* das können Sie sich ˘ kochen lassen! put that in your pipe and smoke it!; s. aufstoßen 5. — **2.** *agr.* saurer Boden sour (or marshy) soil. — **3.** *fig.* (Mühe verursachend) troublesome, harassing, F fagging; saure Arbeit hard work, laborious task; saurer Verdienst hard earnings *pl.*; es kommt mir ˘ an it comes very hard to me, it goes against the grain; e-m das Leben ˘ m. to embitter a p.'s life, to worry (the life out of) a p.; das Gehen wird ihm ˘ walking is (becoming) a trouble to him; er läßt es sich ˘ w. he works very hard or like a slave, he takes great pains. — **4.** *fig.* (mürrisch) morose, peevish; ˘ aussehen, ein saures Gesicht m. to make (or put on) a sour face, to look cross or surly or sour-tempered; ein saures Gesicht zu et. machen to make (or F pull) a long face over a th.; mit saurer Miene sour-faced, surly-looking. — II ~ n ㉒. **5.** = Säure. — **6.** *typ.*, *chm.* F (vorausbezahlte Arbeit) advance on wages, dead horse.

Sauer-ampfer ̧ (ˇ˘˘) m ⑫ sorrel (*Rumex*); echter ~ a. true sorrel, sharp (or sour) dock (*R. acetosa*); kleiner ~ a. field- (or sheep-)sorrel. [able.

säuerbar (˘˘-) a. ⑯ *chm.*: ⊘ acidifi-

Sauer-braten (˘˘...) m ⑫ Kochkunst: meat soaked in vinegar previous to roasting; **-brunnen** m acidulous spring or fountain or water; **-dorn** ̧ m barberry-bush (*Berberis vulgaris*).

Sauerei F (-˘-) f ⑯ hoggishness, uncleanliness, beastliness, Rede.: smuttiness, obscenity; vgl. Sauwirtschaft.

Sauer-kirsche (˘˘...) f ⑫ common cherry (*Prunus Cerasus*); **-klee** ̧ m wood-sorrel (*Oxalis acetosella*); **-klee-salz** n, *chm.* salt(s) of lemon or sorrel, ⊘ potassium binoxalate; vgl. Kleesalz; **-klee-säure** f = Kleesäure; **-kohl** m, **-kraut** n Kochkunst: (chopped and) fermented cabbage, a. ↯ sauerkraut.

säuerlich (˘˘˘) [sauer] a. ⑯ sourish, tartish, *chm.* acidulous, acidulated, a. acetose; ˘ m. to acidulate; **~keit** (˘˘-) f ⑯ sourishness, ⊘ acescence.

säuerlich-süß (˘˘˘) a. ⑯ = sauersüß.

Säuerling (˘˘˘) m ⑪d. **1.** acidulous water; vgl. Sauerbrunnen. — **2.** (saurer Wein) sour(ish) wine.

Sauer-milch (˘˘˘...) f ⑫ curdled milk.

sauern (˘˘) v/n. (h. u. sn) ⑨a. **1.** to turn (or become) sour. — **2.** (ärgern, verdrießen) to vex, to annoy; Sprichw.: was nicht sauert, süßt nicht no gains without pains.

säuern (˘˘) I v/a. ⑨a. **1.** to make sour or acid; das Brot, den Teig ˘ to leaven ...; ˘d: ⊘ acescent. — **2.** *chm.* (mit einer Säure verbinden) to combine with an acid, ⊘ to acidify (oxydieren) to oxidize. — II ~ **3.** s. Säuerung.

Sauer-quelle (˘˘...) f ⑫ = -brunnen; **˘sehend** a. ⑯ sour-looking or -faced; **-stoff** m, *chm.*: ⊘ oxygen (O); mit ~ verbinden to oxidize; **-stoff-gas** n oxygen gas; **˘stoff-haltig** a: ⊘ oxygenated, oxidized; **-stoff-messer** m für die Luft: ⊘ eudiometer; **-stoff-pol** m, *phys.* anode; **-stoff-verbindung** f oxide; **˘süß** a. sour(ish)-sweet, sweetish-sour; **-teig** m Bäckerei: leaven, yeast; **-topf** F m, *fig.* sour-tempered (or morose, peevish, F crabby) person; **˘töpfisch** a. sour-tempered.

Säu(e)rung (˘(˘)˘) f ⑯ des Brotes: leavening; *chm.*: ⊘ acidification; oxidation; **˘s-fähig** (˘˘˘...) a. ⑯ acidifiable.

Sauer-wasser (˘˘...) n ⑬ acidulous (or acidulated) water; **-weichsel** ̧ f Art Kirsche: morello (*Cerasus morasca*); **-werden** n turning sour, *chm.*: ⊘ acetification.

Zeichen (s. S. XVII): F familiär; P Volkssprache; ſ Gaunersprache; ⸗ selten; † alt (auch gestorben); * neu (auch geboren); ⁓ unrichtig;

[**Sauessen**] — [**Säumigkeit**]

Sau=essen F (″...) n filthy (or nasty) food; **=fang** m catching (or spearing, sticking) the wild boar; vgl. **=hatz**; **=fänger** m = **=rüde**.

Sauf=aus P verb (″...) m (pl. co. **=ausse**), **=bold** m = Säufer; **=bruder** m: a) fellow-tippler, boon-companion, bottle-friend; b) = Säufer.

Sau=feder (″⌣) f hunt. um Sauen abzufangen: hog-spear.

saufen (⌣) [ahd.] I v/a., v/n. (h.) und mit Angabe der Wirkung auch v/refl. Gf. von Tieren: to drink, F v. Menschen: to drink immoderately or excessively, a. to tipple, to carouse, F to booze, guzzle, imbibe; abs. to be addicted to (hard) drinking, to be a (confirmed) drunkard; er säuft wie ein Loch he drinks like a fish; Pferden ꝛc. zu ♃ geben to water …; sich tot ♃ to drink o.s. to death; sich voll ♃ to drink to excess, to get drunk or F boozed. — II ~ n (ſ. I) (hard) drinking, tippling, carousing, drunkenness; F boozing.

Sau=fenchel ⚘ (″⌣) m sow-fennel (*Peuce'danum officina'le*).

Säufer (⌣) m, **~in** f hard drinker, drunkard, toper, tippler, F boozer, guzzler, *path.* inebriate, ⚕ dipsomaniac.

Säuferei (–⌣⌣) [saufen] f 1. excessive drinking. — 2. = Saufgelag(e).

Säufer=nase (″⌣...) f copper-nose; vgl. Schnapsnase; **=wahnsinn** m (lt.) delirium tremens.

Sauf=gelag(e) (″...) n drinking-bout, carousal, F booze; **=genosse** m = **=bruder** a; **=gesellschaft** f party of tipplers or boozers; **=gurgel** f = Säufer.

Sau=finder (″⌣⌣) m = Saurüde.

Sauf=kompagnie (″...) f = **=gesellschaft**; **=lied** n (low) drinking-song; **=lustig** a. fond of tippling or boozing.

Sauf=fraß P verb (″⌣) m = Sauessen.

Sauf=schwester (″⌣⌣) f = Säuferin.

säufst, säuft (⌣) pres.ind. von saufen.

Saug=ader (″⌣) f anat.: absorbent (blood-)vessel.

Säug=amme (″⌣⌣) f wet-nurse, nurse engaged to suckle a child.

Sau=garten (″⌣⌣) m hunt. preserve for wild boars.

Saug=brunnen ⚙ (″⌣⌣) m well fitted with a suction-pump.

säugeln (⌣) v/a. = absäuge(l)n.

saugen (⌣) [ahd.: suck(le)] I v/a., v/n. (h.) u. v/refl. ⚙c. (⑧) 1. to suck, von Kindern: an der Brust ♃ to take (or suck) the breast; ♃b: ⚕ sugent; an sich ♃ to suck up, to absorb; in sich ♃ to suck (or draw, drink) in, to imbibe; mit Angabe der Wirkung: sich fest ♃ to attach o.s. by sucking or suction; sich satt ♃, sich voll ♃ to suck o.s. full, to suck one's fill. — 2. fig. sich (dat.) et. aus den Fingern ♃ to invent or fabricate a th. or a tale; F Hungerpfoten ♃, an den Klauen ♃ to have nothing to eat, to be starving. — II ~ n 3. sucking, suction, absorption.

säugen (⌣) [ahd. saugen l.] I v/a. ein Kind ♃ to suckle (or nurse) …, to give … the breast, bisw.: to) give suck to … — II ~ n (Stillen e-s Kindes) suckling, nursing, ⚕ lactation.

Sauger (⌣) [saugen] m, **~in** f 1. sucker (a. ⊙). — 2. *agr.* suckling, sucking young, bſp. = Sauglamm. — 3. (Gummischlauch mit Pfropfen an einer Saugflasche) sucking-tube and tit of a child's bottle.

Säuger (⌣) [säugen] m, **~in** f 1. ~in f suckling mother; a. = Säugamme. — 2. zo. mst pl. = Säugetier.

Säuge=tier (″⌣...) n zo.: ⚕ mammal (pl. a. mammalia), mammalian, mammifer; **=tier=kunde** f. zo.: ⚕ mammalogy, mastology; **=tier=kundige(r)** m: ⚕ mammalogist; **=zahn** m, anat. milk-tooth.

Sauge=zeit (″⌣⌣) f sucking-period, period of suck(l)ing, ⚕ lactation.

Saug=flasche (″...) f, **=fläschchen** n baby's sucking- (or feeding-)bottle; **=füßchen** n, zo. der Seeigel: sucker-foot; **=heber** m, *phys.* siphon; **=kalb** n sucking calf; **=kolben** ⊙ m = r Pumpe: valve-piston; **=lamm** n suckling lamb; **=leder** n sucker.

Säugling (⌣) [nhd.] m ⑬d. suckling, (sucking) infant, mehr gbr.: child (or babe) at the breast or in arms, weitS. (young) baby, infant child; **~s= bewahranstalt, =krippe** (″⌣...) f (fr.) crèche.

Sau=glocke (″...) f fig. die ~(n) läuten to make smutty (or loose) jokes or remarks; **=glück** F n verb: unexpected (or undeserved) good luck.

Saug=magen (″...) m zo. sucking-stomach; **=maschine** ⊙ f exhauster, aspirator; **=mündung** f, zo. eines Eingeweidewurmes: ⚕ osculum; **=muskel** m: ⚕ suctorial muscle; **=öffnung** f, zo. = **=werkzeug**; **=pumpe** ⊙ f suction- (or sucking-)pump; **=rohr** ⊙ n, **=röhre** f, *mach.* suction-pipe or -tube, sucker; **⚒ windbore**; **=rüssel** m, ent.: ⚕ proboscis; **=scheibe** ⊙ f sucking-disk, sucker; **=ventil** ⊙ n e-r Pumpe: suction- (or rucking-)valve; **=warze** f nipple; **=werkzeug** n, zo.: ⚕ suctorial (or sugescent) organ, ent. auch: siphon.

Sau=hatz (″...) f, **=hetze** f boar-hunt; **=hieb** m, *fenc.* irregular cut; **=hirt** m swine-herd; fig. (unflätiger Mensch) filthy fellow; **=igel** F m verb: filthy (or dirty, smutty, disgusting) fellow.

säu=isch (⌣) [Sau] a. hoggish, piggish, swinish; - (unsauber) filthy, dirty; (sotig) smutty.

Sau=jagd (″...) f = **=hatz**; **=kerl** m = **=igel**; **=koben** m = **=stall**.

Saul (″) [hebr.] npr/m. ⑮α. (1. König v. Israel, 11. sae. v. Chr.) Saul. [(to wallow in.)

Sau=lache (″⌣) f pool for swine

Säulchen (⌣) n (dim. v. Säule) *arch.* small column or pillar; ⚘, zo.: ⚕ columella

Säule[1] (⌣) [ahd.: Schwelle] f 1. column (vgl. Bildsäule); *arch.* (Pfeiler) pillar, support (auch *fig.*), ohne Sims: cippus; (Pfosten) post, jamb; *cryst.* (Prisma) prism. — 2. voltaische (ob. galvanische) = voltaic (or galvanic) pile. — 3. ♃ die ~n des Herakles the Pillars of Hercules.

Säule[2] (⌣) [ahd.: Saum[1]] f = Ahle.

Sau=leben P (″...) n: ein ~ führen to lead a piggish (or disgusting) life; **=leder** ⊙ n hog's (or pig's) leather.

Säulen=apostel (″⌣...) m = **=heiliger**; **=artig** a. = ?förmig; **=bau** m: a) columnar architecture; b) building supported by columns; **=förmig** a. *arch.* column- (or pillar-)shaped, columnar, columniform; **=fuß** m foot (or base) of a column, pedestal; **=gang** m colonnade, eines Tempels: ⚕ peridrome; vgl. **=reihe**; **=halle** f pillared (or columnated) hall, vor e-m Gebäude: portico; **=heilige(r)** m, *eccl. hist.* pillarist, ⚕ stylite; **=knauf** m, *arch.* capital of a column; **=koppel** f coupled columns *pl.*; **=ordnung** f order of columns; **=platte** f plinth. abacus; **=reihe** f row of columns, ⚕ peristyle, runde: ⚕ monopteron; vgl. **=gang**; **=schaft** m shaft of a column; **=stellung** f arrangement of columns; vgl. **=weite**; **=stuhl** m pedestal, ⚕ stylobate; **=stumpf** m truncated column; **=weite** f intercolumniation; **=werk** n colonnade.

säulig (⌣) a. 1. = säulenförmig. — 2. resting on columns, columned. — 3. in Zs.-ſſetzgn mit a... zB.: acht=♃ with eight columns, eight-columned.

Saulus (⌣) npr/m. ⑯α. Kirchengeschichte: (der spätere Paulus Paulus) Saul.

Saum[1] (⌣) [ahd.: seam] m ⓄC. 1. Näherei: seam; hem of a dress, &c.; (Franse) fringe. — 2. weitS. edge, edging, margin; ~ e-s Waldes borders (or outskirts) *pl.* of a forest.

Saum[2] *prov.* (⌣) [ahd.: *grch. sagma* n] m ⓄC, 6. (Ladung eines Packtiers) load of a beast of burden, mule-load.

Sau=magen (″...) m ⓄC: a) hog's paunch; b) F = **=igel**; **=mäßig** a. hoggish, piggish, beastly; schwäbisch = heidenmäßig.

saumen, säumen[1] (⌣) [Saum[2]] v/a. (durch Saumtiere befördern) to convey on mules; ein Lasttier ♃ to put a packsaddle (or load) on …. to saddle …

säumen[2] (⌣) [Saum[1]] v/a. Näherei: to hem, edge, border; (mit Fransen versehen) to fringe, ⚕ to fimbriate; ⊙ Bretter ♃ (von der Rindenseite befreien) to dress (or square) boards.

säumen[3] (⌣) [ahd.] I v/n. (h.) u. v/refl. (sich) ♃ to tarry; (zaudern) to hesitate before doing a th., to delay doing a th.; (hinten bleiben) to linger (or stay, lag) behind; ohne einen Augenblick zu ♃ without a moment's delay. — II ~ n tarrying; dawdling, hesitation, delay.

Sau=mensch P verb (″⌣) n = Sau 3; (Hure) prostitute, bad wench.

Saumer (⌣) [säumen] m man who keeps (or guides) sumpter-mules.

Säumer[1] (⌣) [säumen[2]] m 1. Person: ~ (in f) person who hems or edges. — 2. ⊙ Werkzeug der Nähmaschine: hemmer, hemming-rule.

Säumer[2] (⌣) [ahd.: summer; *Saum[2]] m beast of burden; a. = Saumer.

Säumer[3] (⌣) [säumen[3]] m lingerer, laggard, dawdler, loiterer, im Zahlen: slow payer; **~ei** (–⌣⌣) f long (or frequent) delay, slow work, dawdling.

Saum=esel (″...) m sumpter mule; **=holz** ⊙ n Brückenbau: curb-beam.

säumig (⌣) [ahd.: säumen[3]] a. **~keit** f = saumselig, Saumseligkeit.

♪ Musik; ⚕ Wissenschaft; ⚘ Pflanze; ♁ Geographie; ⊙ Technik; ⚒ Bergbau; ⚔ Militär; ⚓ Marine; ⚖ Handel; ✉ Post; 🚂 Eisenbahn.

[Saumnaht] — [Schachteinfahrt]

Saum¹-naht (ᵘʳᴸ) f ㊷ Näherei: hem.
Säumnis (ᴸᵛ) f ⑱, n ⑰ 1. mit f (Verzug) delay, stay, stoppage. — 2. mst n (Hindernis) hindrance, impediment.
Saum²-pfad (ᵘ...) m ㊷ mule-track; **=pferd, =roß** n = Packpferd; **=sattel** [mhd.] m pack-saddle.
saumselig (ᵘᴸᵛ) [mhd. † Saumsal + -ig] a. ㊌ tardy, slow, sluggish, dilatory; (zu spät kommend) lagging behind, hanging back; (nachlässig) negligent, (lässig) lazy, careless, heedless; F don't-carish; **~keit** (ᵘᴸᵛ-) f ㊺ tardiness, dilatoriness; negligence, laziness.
Saum²-stieg (ᵘ...) f ㊷ =pfad; **=stich** m Näherei: hemstitch; **=²tier** n beast of burden, sumpter-horse, -mule.
Säumung (ᴸᵛ) f ㊺ = säumen³ II.
Saum-weg (ᵘᴸ) m ㊷ = Saumpfad.
Sau-nest F (ᵘ...) n ㊷ fig. (garstige Wohnung, Stadt) dirty place, filthy hole; **=nickel** F m = =igel.
Säure (ᴸᵛ) [ahd.; *sauer] f ㊺ 1. als Eigenschaft: sourness, chm., &c. acidity (auch des Magens); (Herbheit) tartness; fig. der Gemütsstimmung: sour temper, sourness, acrimony, moroseness, F crabbiness. — 2. chm. (saure Verbindung, ant. Base²) acid; mit ~ versetzen to add acid to.
säure-bildend (ᵘᵛ...) a. ㊌ chm. acidifying, acidific; **=bildner** m ㊷ acidifier; **=frei** a. free from acid(ity).
Sauregurten-händler (ᴸᵛᵛ...) m ㊷, etwa: pickle-merchant; **=zeit** f (Spätsommer) dead (or silly) season.
säure-haltig (ᵘᵛ...) a. ㊌ chm. containing acid, acidiferous, acidific; **=messer** m ㊷ ↻ acidimeter; **=messung** f acidimetry.
Sauri-er ↻ (ᴸᵛᵛ) [grch.] m/pl. ㊷ zo. (Familie der Eidechsen) saurians pl.
Sau-rüde (ᵘᴸ...) m ㊷ hunt. boar-hound.
Saus (ᴸ) [sausen] m ⓐ. (ohne pl.) 1. = Sausen II. — 2. (rauschende Lust) whirl of pleasure, noisy revelling, boisterous gaiety; f. Braus 2.
Sause-fahrt (ᴸᵛ...) f ㊷ rapid drive, race, F scorching; **=laut** m, gr. sibilant.
säuseln (ᴸᵛ) [nhd. dim. v. sausen] ㊺ a. I v/n. 1. (h.) vom Winde ꝛc.: to rustle, to whisper gently through the leaves, &c.; auch: to sigh, to sough; (summen) to hum, (schwirren) to whiz. — 2. (sn) (sich ⬦ bewegen) to move with a soft murmur; to buzz along. — II v/a. 3. (⬦ aussprechen) to hum, to whisper. — 4. mit Angabe der Wirkung: e-n in Schlaf ⇵ to hum (or buzz) a p. to sleep.
sausen (ᴸᵛ) [ahd.] I v/n. ⓐ 1. (h.) vom Wasser: to rush, to swish, vom Winde: to roar, whistle, blow hard, von Kugeln ꝛc.: to whiz; es saust mir in den Ohren I have a singing (or buzzing) in my ears. — 2. (sn) (sich ⬦ [durch die Luft] bewegen) to rush (or whiz) along, vom Winde ꝛc. auch: to come blustering along; die Bomben kamen durch die Luft gesaust the shells came whizzing (or hurtling) through the air. — II v/n ㉓ 3. (f. I) rush(ing), roaring (noise).
Sause-wind (ᵘᴸ, ᴗ) m ㊷ = Brausewind.
Sau-spieß (ᵘ...) m ㊷ hunt. boar-spear; **=stall** m shed for swine, hog-sty; fig. (schmutziges Loch) filthy hole; **=trank** F m hog's wash; **=trog** m hog-trough;

=wetter F n filthy weather; **=wirtschaft** F f, fig. disorderly (or dirty) household, wretched management, auch = Sauerei; Zwohl a. ㊌ burschikos: mir ist 2 I feel awfully jolly.
Savanne (ᵛᵛ) [span.] f ㊾ (Gras-ebene am Missouri ꝛc.) savanna.
Savoyarde(r)-ᵛ/ᵛ)[Savoyen]m㊼,...din f ㊼ Savoyard, inhabitant of Savoy.
savoyardisch (ᵛ..) a. ㊌ (of) Savoy.
Savoyen ⚥ (ᵛ)(ᵛ-)ᵛᵒⁱᵛ) npr/n. ⓑ a. (ehm. it., seit 1860 fr. Provinz) Savoy.
Savoyer (ᵛ)ᵛᵒⁱᵛ) I m ㉒, ~in f ㊼ = Savoyarde. — II a., inv., a. **savoyisch** ㊌ (of) Savoy; Savoyer Kohl savoy.
Sax-horn ♪ (ᴸᵛ) [Adolphe Sax, Pariser Instrumentenmacher, 1814—94] n ㊷ saxhorn.
Sayette ☙ (ᵇᵛjɛ't) [fr. sayette, mst saie] f ㊼ (halb seidenes, halb wollenes Zeug) sayette; **Sayett(en)-garn** (ᴸᵛ) n ㊷ worsted yarn.
Sbirre (ᵛᵛ) [it.] m ㊶ sbirro (= Häscher).
☞ Sch... vgl. Ch... u. Sh...
sch! int. Schweigen gebietend: 'sh!, hush!
Schab-... (ᴸ...) in Zssgn f. Schabe-...
Schabbes (ᵛᵛ) m, inv. jüdisch = Sabbat.
Schabe (ᴸᵛ) [ahd.; *schaben] f ㊼ 1. = Kakerlak 1; Motte. — 2. = Schab-eisen.
Schäbe (ᴸᵛ) (Flachsabfall) refuse of flax.
Schab(e)-baum (ᴸ(ᵛ)...), **=block** m, **=brett** n ㊷ Gerberei: scraping-block, leather- (or hide-)dresser's horse.
Schab-eisen (ᴸᵛ) n ㊷ scraper, shaving-iron or -knife or -tool.
schaben¹ (ᴸᵛ) [ahd.: shave] v/a. ㊸ 1. to shave skins, &c., to scrape carrots, potatoes, &c.; auf dem Reib-eisen: to grate, to rasp; (traßen) to scratch; (streifen) to graze (vgl. abschaben I). — 2. ↻ Stechkunst: Abzug (Blatt) in geschabter Manier mezzotint print (plate). — 3. fig. f. Rübe 2; ein geiziger schabt und kraßt a miser saves and scrapes (the money) together.
Schaben²-kraut ☙ (ᵘᵛᴸ) [Schabe] n ㊷ moth-mullein (Verbascum Blattaria).
Schab(e)-polier-stahl ↻ (ᴸ(ᵛ)...) m ㊷ scraper-burnisher.
Schaber (ᴸᵛ) m ㊷ 1. Person: scraper. — 2. ↻ = Schab-eisen, =messer.
Schaber-nack (ᴸᵛ,ᵛ) [mhd. zu neden] m ⓒ. mischievous (or ill-natured) trick, practical joke, hoax, F lark(s pl.); e-m e-n ~ spielen, a. e-n Zen (ᴸᵛᵛᵛ) v/a.㊸ *⁎* to play a p. a (nasty) trick, to play a practical joke upon a p.; e-m et. zum ~ tun to serve a p. a nasty trick, to hoax a p.; uns zum ~ to our annoyance. [wolle.]
Schabe-wolle (ᴸᵛᵛ,ᵛ) f ㊷ = Rauh-ᶠ
Schab-hobel ↻ (ᴸ,ᴸᵛ) m ㊷ Tischlerei: spoke-shave, scraping-plane.
schäbig (ᴸᵛ) [mhd.; *schaben] a. ㊌ 1. = räudig. — 2. (kahl, abgescheuert) bare, bald — 3. (abgenußt) shabby (-looking), worn (out); (abgerissen) tattered and torn. — 4. fig. (knauserig) shabby, mean.
Schäbigkeit (ᴸᵛ-) f ㊺ (f. schäbig) shabby appearance; fig. shabbiness, meanness.
Schabin ↻ (-ᴸ) [dtsch-lt. schab(en) + -in] n ⓒᵈ. metall. gold-beater's waste.
Schab-klinge ↻ (ᴸᵛ,ᵛ) f ㊷ = scraper.
Schablone ↻ (ᵛᴸᵛ) [nbl.; *schaben] f ㊺ Modell; zum Durchmalen stencil; nach der ~ by routine, in a mechanical fashion.

schablonen-artig (ᵛᴸᵛ...) a. ㊌ (u. adv.) after a certain mould or pattern, routine-like, stereotyped, mechanical(ly); **=drucker(ei)** ㊷ = =maler(ei); **Zhaft** = Zartig; **=maler** ☉ m stenciller; **=malerei** f stencilling; **Zmäßig** a. = Zartig; **=stechmaschine** f stencil-pen; **=wesen** n routine. [stencil.]
schablon(is)ieren ☉ (ᵛ-(ᵛ)ᴸᵛ) v/a. ㊹ to
Schab-manier (ᴸ.../) ☉ ㊷ Kupferstich in ~ mezzotint(o); **=messer** ☉ n scraping-knife, scraper; Gerberei: shaving-knife, shaver. [(Amboßstock) anvil-bed.]
Schabotte ☉ (-ᴸᵛ) [fr. chabotte] f ㊼ᶠ
Schabracke ☙ ᵛ(ᴸᵛ) [türk.]/㊼(kostbare Pferdedecke) shabrack, mehr gebr.: caparison; (Sattel-decke) saddle-cloth; mit e-r reichen ~ geschmückt richly caparisoned.
Schabsel (ᴸᵛ) f ㊷ shavings, scrapings, parings pl., ⚥ abrasure.
Schabzieger (ᴸᴸᵛ) m ㊷ (schwz. Kräuterkäse) green cheese; **~klee** ☙ m blue melilot (Melilotus caerulea).
Schach (ᴸ) [pers. schâh König] n ⓒ.ⓑ 1. a) ~(spiel) (game of) chess; b) = Schachbrett; c) (Bedrohung d. Königs) ~ (dem Könige) check!; ~ bieten to give check (to the king), fig. a. to bid defiance to a p., to set a p. at defiance; in ~ halten to keep in check (auch fig.); ~und matt! (check)mate! (s. schachmatt). — 2. (Quadrat) square.
Schach-aufgabe (ᴸᵛ...) f ㊷ chess-problem; **=brett** n chess-board; Zbrett-artig a. ㊌ tessellated, chequered, in squares; des Muster check.
Schacher (ᴸᵛ) [hebr.] m ㊷ (Jew's) trade, bartering, huckstering, (higgling and) haggling, chaffering; politischer ~ political jobbery; vgl. Kuhhandel.
Schächer (ᴸᵛ) [ahd.] m ㊷ 1. fast † robber, malefactor; noch bibl. der ~ am Kreuze (mit Jesu gekreuzigter Missetäter) the thief on the cross. — 2. fig. armer ~ (Mensch) poor wretch, F poor devil.
Schacherei (ᵛᵛᴸ) f ㊺ = Schacher.
Schacherer (ᴸᵛᵛ) m ㉒ haggler, peddling (or old-clothes) Jew, low-class trader or dealer or huckster.
Schacher-handel (ᴸᵛᵛ) m = Schacher; **=jude** m = Schacherer; Zmäßig a. ㊌ u. adv. in a bartering (or haggling, chaffering) way.
schachern (ᴸᵛ) [Schacher] v/n. (h.) ㊺ a. to barter, haggle, chaffer; to carry on a small (or petty) trade.
Schach-feld (ᴸᵛ...) n ㊷ square of a chess-board; **=figur** f chess-man, piece; sämtliche ~en set of chess-men; Zförmig = Zbrettartig; Zmatt [f. matt] a. (check)mate, fig. tired (or worn) out, dead tired, F dead-beat; ² machen to check-mate; **=meisterschaft** f chess-championship; **=partie** f game of chess; **=spiel** n: a) (das Spielen) playing chess; b) = =brett; **=spieler** m chess-player.
Schacht (ᴸ) [nbd.] m ⓒⓑ. 1. square hole, bsp. ⚒ shaft, pit (s. abteufen); ~ e-s Hoch-ofens: fire-room. — 2. (Schlucht) gorge, ravine; (Höhlung) hollow; (Senkung) depression, dip; **=arbeiter** ⚒ m ㊷ pitman; **=bühne** f landing-stage; **=einfahrt** f pit-mouth.

Signs (see page XVII): F familiar; P vulgar; ꟻ flash; ↘ rare; † obsolete (died); * new word (born); ⁺⁺ incorrect; ♪ music;

[**Schachtel**] — [**Schaffel**]

Schachtel¹ (ˇǎcht~) [mhd.,*it. (f. Schatulle)] f ⑱ box, für Damenhüte ꝛc.: bandbox. **Schachtel²** F (ˇǎcht~) [mhd. altes Weib] f ⑱: alte ~ old spinster or maid or woman, F old frump. [of a box.] **Schachtel¹-boden** (ˇǎcht~.⌣) m ⑫ bottom; **Schächtelchen** (⌣⌣) n ㉓ (dim. v. Schachtel¹) little box; wie aus dem ~ (sorgsam gekleidet) as if (s)he came out of a bandbox. **Schachtel¹-deckel** (ˇǎcht~...) m ⑫ lid of a box; **=³halm** ♀ [ndd. ... = Schaft(el)-] m shave- (or pewter-)grass, horse-tail or -willow, toad-pipe (*Equise'tum*); **=händler(in** f) m dealer in boxes; **=heu** n = halm; **männchen** n jack-in-the-box; **=mus*** n = Marmelade. **schachteln** ⊕ (ˇǎcht~) v/a. ⓐ a. (mit Schachtelhalm schleifen) to polish with shave-grass. **Schachtel¹-satz** (⌣⌣) m ⑫ bsd. im Deutschen: gr. involved period. **schachten** ⚒ und ⊕ (ˇǎcht~) [Schacht] v/n. ⑱ = ausschachten. **schächten** (ˇǎ~) [hebr. *šachat* schlachten] v/a. ⑱ to kill (or slaughter) according to Jewish rites; **Schächter** m ㉒ Jewish (auch: kosher) butcher. **Schacht-futter** ⚒ (ˇǎcht...) n ⑫ shaft-lining; **=geviere** n shaft-frame; **=hut** m miner's cap; **=meister** m superintendent of a mine or pit, Bahn-, Kanal-bau: foreman of navvies; **=ofen** m pit-kiln or -furnace; ⊕ metall. shaft-furnace; **=öffnung** f pit-mouth or -head; **=senker** m shaft-sinker; **=steuer** f shaft-rent. **Schächtung** (ˇǎ~) f ⑯ kosher butchering. **Schach-turnier** (ˇǎch~.⌣)) n ⑫ chess-tournament. **Schacht-verkleidung** ⚒ (ˇǎcht...) f ⑫ = futter; **=zimmerung** f shaft-timbering. **schach=weise** (ˇǎch...) adv. in squares, chequered; **=zug** m ⑫ move at chess, geschickter ~ clever move (a. *fig.*). **Schadchen** (⌣⌣) [jüd.] m, n ㉓ (Heiratsvermittler) (Jewish) marriage-broker. **Schade¹** (⌣⌣) [ahd.] m ⑱ fast † = Schaden². **schade²** (⌣⌣) prädikative u. c. (es ist recht) ♃, jammer♁, daß // it is a great pity that //; es ist (sehr) ♁ um ihn it's a (great) pity for him, I pity him (very much); dafür ist es zu ♁ (zu gut) it's too good for that. **Schädel** (⌣⌣) [ndd.: skull] m ㉒ anat. brain-pan, skull, ⚕ cranium. **Schädel-beschreibung** (⌣⌣...) f ⑫: ⚕ craniography; **=bohrer** m, *surg.* trepan; **=bruch** m fracture of the skull; **=form** f shape of a skull; **=haut** f, anat.: ⚕ pericranium; **=höhle** f cranial cavity; **=kenntnis**, **=lehre** f: ⚕ craniography, craniology, phrenology; **=meßkunst**, **=messung** f: ⚕ craniometry; **=naht** f, anat.: ⚕ coronal suture; **=stätte** f, bibl. (Hinrichtungsstätte in Jerusalem) place of skulls, Calvary, Golgotha; **=zange** f, *surg.* cranioclast. **schaden¹** (⌣⌣) [ahd.; *Schade¹*] v/n. (h.) ⑱ 1. to injure, to hurt; e-m, e-r Sache ♁ (nachteilig sein) to prejudice (or to be prejudicial to) a p., a th.; Ehrlichkeit kann niemals ♁ ... can never do harm, ... never comes amiss; e-m bei e-m andern ♁ to prejudice (or set) a p. against a p.; j-m (eigenen) Rufe ♁ to

injure (or blast) one's (own) reputation; sich selbst ♁ to stand in one's own light. — 2. das schadet (F schad't) nichts (ist kein Hindernis) that won't hurt, there is no harm in that; it does not matter or signify; es kann (ob. könnte nicht(s) ♁, wenn // it would not be amiss if //; was schadet es? what does it matter?, F what's the odds?; was schadet es, wenn //? what harm is there (F what's the odds) if //? — 3. das schadet ihm nichts (geschieht ihm recht) that serves him right. **Schaden²** (⌣⌣) [f. Schade¹] m ㉙ 1. damage, durch Verheerung: ravages pl., havoc; (Nachteil, Abbruch) detriment, prejudice, harm, jur. tort; (Verlust) loss, (Unheil) mischief, (Verletzung) injury, hurt; innerer ~ internal injury or complaint; offener ~ open sore; (Gebrechen) infirmity. — 2. mit verbs: wenn man den ~ genauer (ob. bei Licht) besieht on closer examination, looking at the matter more closely; e-m ~ bringen to injure (or hurt) a p.; sich seines ~s erholen, s-m ~ wieder nachkommen to recover (or recoup) one's loss(es); ~ erleiden to suffer (or sustain) injury; bei Geschäften ~ haben, leiden to suffer (or have) losses, to be a loser; er hat an seiner Gesundheit ~ gelitten he has suffered in health, his health has suffered or has been impaired; ~ leiden ob. nehmen to come to grief; es soll dein ~ nicht sein you shall not regret it or lose anything by it; sich (*dat.*) ~ tun to injure (*path., &c.:* to rupture) o.s.; er wird seiner Gesundheit ~ tun that will injure his health; er will deinen ~ nicht he means no harm to you; e-m ~ zufügen to inflict injury on a p., to wrong a p. — 3. *mit prp.* **gegen** ~ durch Feuer und Wasser versichern to insure against loss by fire or water; e-n **in** ~ bringen, stürzen to bring losses upon a p., to ruin a p.; **mit** ~ verkaufen to sell at a loss or under cost-price; fort mit ~! let it go!, (it's) a good riddance!; **zu** m-m ~ to my detriment, at my cost; **zu** ~ kommen to come off a loser. — 4. *Sprichw.* durch ~ wird man klug adversity is the school of wisdom; wer den ~ hat, braucht für den Spott nicht zu sorgen the loser is always laughed at (vgl. ~: to add injury to insult). **Schaden²=ersatz** (⌣⌣...) m ⑫ jur. indemnification, compensation, als Geldstrafe: damages pl.; ~ leisten to make amends for; auf ~ klagen to sue for damages; **=ersatz=klage** f action for damages; **=feuer** n destructive fire, fire which does considerable damage; **=freude** f malicious joy (at the misfortune of others); **=froh** a. ⑯ rejoicing at (stärker: gloating over) other people's misfortunes; malicious. **schadhaft** (⌣⌣) a. ⑯ damaged, (schlecht geworden) deteriorated, decayed, wasted; (mangelhaft) faulty, defective, (verdorben) spoilt, spoiled, v. Zähnen: carious, v. Gebäuden: dilapidated; ♁ werden to get damaged or spoilt; to decay, to go to waste or ruin; **~igkeit** (⌣⌣~) f ⑯

damaged (or decayed, dilapidated) state, defectiveness. **schädigen** (⌣⌣) [mhd.] I *v/a.* ⑱ 1. † ob. geh. Spr. = beschädigen. — 2. e-n ♁ to prejudice (or wrong) a p., (verletzen) to injure a p. — II ~ n ㉓ u. **Schädigung** f ⑯ 3. damage done to a p. or a th., prejudice; ohne ~ seiner Interessen without prejudice to his interests. **schädlich** (⌣⌣) [ahd.; *Schade¹*] a. ⑯ injurious, hurtful, v. Giften ꝛc.: noxious; (nachteilig) prejudicial, detrimental, (gefährlich) dangerous, (verderblich) pernicious; (bösartig) malignant; der Gesundheit ♁ injurious to health, unwholesome; **~keit** f ⑯ injuriousness, hurtfulness, noxiousness; perniciousness; malignancy, malignity. **Schädling** (⌣⌣) m ⑫ d. dangerous (or noxious) creature, tierischer a. vermin. **schad=los** (⌣⌣...) a. ⑯ unhurt, uninjured, (entschädigt) indemnified; e-n ♁ halten to indemnify (or compensate) a p. for a th.; sich ♁ halten to repay (or indemnify o.s., to recover one's loss(es); **=los-haltung** f indemnification, compensation; **=losigkeit** f uninjured condition. **Schaf** (⌣) [ahd.: sheep] n ⑪c. 1. sheep (*Ovis*); (weibliches ~) ewe (ant. Hammel, Widder). — 2. *fig.* v. Personen: er ist ein ~ (gutmütiger, dummer Mensch) he is a good-natured simpleton or a weak-minded fool; f. räudig, Sprichw. der geduldigen ~e gehen viele in einen Stall a patient flock (or crowd) can be packed into a very small space. **schaf=artig** (⌣...) a. ⑯ sheep-like, ⚕ ovine, *fig.* ⑫ = pocken; **=bock** m ram; **=bremse** f, *ent.* sheep-bot, bot-fly of the sheep (*Oestrus ovis*). **Schäfchen** (⌣⌣) n ㉓ (*dim. v. Schaf*) 1. little sheep; (Lämmchen) lamb(kin); *fig.* sein ~ scheren, sein ~ [P aus ndd. Schiffchen] ins Trockene bringen to make one's fortune, F to feather one's nest, to coin money. — 2. ♆ das Meer hat ~ (Schaumwellen) ... has crested waves or white horses. — 3. ~ (**=wolke** f) fleecy cloud, mare's tail(s *pl.*), ⚕ cirrocumulus; Himmel mit ~(-wolken) curdled sky. **Schaf=darm** (⌣...) m ⑫ sheep's gut; **=diebstahl** m sheep-stealing. **Schäfer** (⌣⌣) [ahd.; *Schaf*] m ㉒, **~in** f ⑰ shepherd(ess f), geh. Spr.: swain; **♁=artig** (⌣⌣.⌣) a. ⑯ pastoral, Arcadian. **Schäferei** (⌣-) f ⑯ sheep-farm. **Schäfer-gedicht** (⌣⌣...) n ⑫ pastoral (or bucolic) poem; **=hund** m shepherd's (or shepherd-)dog; **=hütte** f sh.'s hut or hovel; **=junge** m shepherd's (or shepherd-)boy; **=karren** m sh.'s cart or watch-box; **=kittel** m sh.'s frock; **=knabe** = =junge; **=leben**, **=lied** n pastoral life, song; **=mädchen** n young shepherdess (f); **=pfeife** f shepherd's pipe or flute; **=poesie** f bucolic poetry; **=roman** m pastoral romance; **=spiel** n pastoral play; **=stab** m shepherd's staff or crook; **=stunde** f happy hour spent by lovers; **=tasche** f shepherd's scrip. **Schaff** (⌣) [ahd.: Scheffel] n ⑪(②b. (Gefäß) flat tub; (Eimer) pail. **Schaf=fäule** (⌣...) f ⑯ sheep-rot; **=fell** n sheepskin, mit der Wolle: fleece.

⚕ scientific; ♀ botanical; ⚲ geography; ⊕ machinery; ⚒ mining; ⚔ military; ♆ marine; ⬤ commercial; ⬤ postal; 🚂 railway.

[schaffen] — 828 — [schälen]

schaffen (⌣‿)[ahd.: shape: schöpfen] **I** v/a. u. v/n. (h.) ⓢa. **1.** (erschaffen) to create, to call into existence or life; (hervorbringen) to bring forth, produce, make; für et. (wie) geschaffen sein to be made (or born, most fitted) for a th.; 2d creative, productive; neu geschaffen newly created, recently produced; alles Geschaffene everything created, all creation. — **II** v/a. u. v/n. (h.) ⓢ **2.** (beschäftigt, geschäftig sein) to be active or busy or occupied; (arbeiten) to work, (wirken) to act, (tun) to do. — **3.** e-m zu ⌢ geben to give a p. (some) work to do; zu ⌢ haben to have s.th. to do, to be engaged; ich habe nichts damit zu ⌢ it does not concern me; er will nichts damit zu ⌢ haben he won't have anything to do with it; e-m viel zu ⌢ (Sorge) **machen** to give (or cause) a p. (great) trouble or bother; sich zu ⌢ m. to be busy, to potter (or tinker) about; sich mit et. zu ⌢ m. to be busy with s.th., to concern o.s. about a th.; die Gicht macht ihm viel zu ⌢ the gout troubles him a great deal. — **4.** mit „daß": ⌢ (sorgen) Sie, daß das Essen früh fertig ist see that the dinner is (or be) ready in good time. — **5.** — verschaffen, zB. Geld ⌢ to provide funds, ⓢ to find the money; Hilfe ⌢ to render assistance, to procure help; Linderung ⌢ to bring relief; Rat ⌢ to devise means or a remedy; da werde ich schon Rat ⌢ I will see to it; er weiß immer Rat zu ⌢ he is full of resource, he is never at a loss; abs. das schafft (fördert) that helps, F that's a lift. — **6.** mit Angabe: a) des Erfolges: et. fertig ⌢ to achieve (or finish, accomplish) a th.; b) der Ortsveränderung: an Ort und Stelle ⌢ to convey (or bring) to the spot; etwas auf die Seite (od. beiseite) ⌢ to put a th. aside, to hide a th., betrügerisch: to embezzle money; aus dem Hause ⌢ to remove from the house; et. aus dem Wege ⌢ to put (or get) a th. out of the way; e-n aus dem Wege, aus der Welt ⌢ to make away with (or to dispatch) a p.; s. Hals 3 am Schluß. — **7.** prove. (befehlen) to command; südd. — machen. — **8.** ↓ = essen. — **III** ~n ⓝ **9.** (s. I) creation; production. — **10.** (s. II) activity; work(ing).

Schaffens=drang (⌣‿...) m ⓜ creative impulse or instinct, desire to create or to produce; =freudigkeit f, =lust f delight in creating (works of art); ⌢lustig a. ⓜ creative, desirous of creating or producing.

Schaffer (⌣‿)[ahd.] m ⓜ (Schöpfer) creator; ↓ steward on a man-of-war.

Schafferei ↓ (‿‿⌣) f ⓜ bread-room.

Schaf=fleisch (⌣‿) n ⓜ mutton.

Schaffner (⌣‿)[mhd.; *schaffen] m ⓜ, ~in f ⓜ **1.** ~ e-s Landgutes, Haushaltes: steward, manager; ~in f stewardess, manageress; housekeeper. — **2.** 🚆 (railway=guard); Post, Pferdebahn, Omnibus 2c.: conductor.

Schaffnerei (‿‿⌣) f ⓜ steward's residence or situation or employment.

Schaffung (⌣‿) f ⓜ = schaffen III.

Schaf=garbe ? (⌣‿...) f ⓜ (common) milfoil, tansy, yarrow (Achillea Millefolium); =geblök n bleating of sheep; =gras ? n = schwingel; =haut f: a) sheepskin; b) a. =häutchen n, physiol. innerste Haut um den Fötus: caul, ⊽ amnion; =herde f flock of sheep; =hirt m shepherd; =hürde f sheep-fold or =cot(e), pen; =husten m ohne Auswurf: dry cough; =kamel n = Lama¹; =knecht m shepherd's man; =kot m = mist; =lamm n ewe-lamb; =laus f = zecke; =leder n sheep's skin, sheepskin; vgl. =fell; fig. s. ausreißen 3; =leder=einband m sheep(skin) binding; ⌢ledern a. ⓜ (made) of sheepskin.

Schäflein (⌣‿) n ⓜ = Schäfchen.

schaf=mäßig (⌣‿...) a. ⓜ: a) sheep-like, like a sheep; b) fig. (dumm) sheepish; =milch f ewe's milk; =mist m sheep's dung or crottels; fig. iro. ein schöner ~ a nice mess; =mutter f ewe.

Schafott (‿⌣)[fr. échafaud m; *Katafalk] n ⓜ. (Blutgerüst) scaffold; das ~ besteigen to mount the scaffold.

Schaf=pelz (⌣‿...) m ⓜ sheepskin fur or coat; =pocken f/pl. vet. sheep-pox.

Schafs=auge (⌣‿...) n ⓜ: a) sheep's eye; b) fig. dull eye; =bart ? m sheep's-beard (Arnopogon).

Schaf=schere (⌣‿...) f ⓜ agr. sheep-shears pl.; =scherer(in f) m sh.-shearer; =schur f sh.-shearing; =schwemmen f sh.-washing; =schwingel ? m sheep's-fescue (Festuca ovina).

Schafs=gesicht (⌣‿...) n ⓜ sheepish (or stupid) face or p.; =kleid n, fig. ein Wolf im ~ a wolf in sheep's clothing; =kopf m: a) sheep's head, sheepshead; b) fig. (Dummkopf) blockhead.

Schaf=stall (⌣‿...) m ⓜ shed for sheep; =stand m stock (or flock) of sheep.

...schaft (...⌣): [: ...ship] f ⓜ Anhängesilbe zur Bildung von weiblichen Dingwörtern: **1.** abstract nouns, zB.: Freundschaft (friendship) aus Freund m; Wissenschaft (knowledge) aus wissen v/a.; Eigenschaft (property) aus eigen a. — **2.** collective nouns, zB.: Priesterschaft (priesthood) aus Priester m. — **3.** den Stand bz., zB.: Jungfer(n)schaft (virginity) aus Jungfer f. — **4.** e-e Örtlichkeit bz., zB.: Grafschaft (county) aus Graf m.

Schaft (⌣) [ahd.: shaft; *schaben] m ⓑ. ~ e-r Lange, Säule 2c.: shaft..., e-r Fahne: stick, e-r Handfeuerwaffe: gunstock, e-s Stiefels: leg, e-s Baumes: trunk, e-r Blume: stalk, stem, ? (laubloser Sproß) scape (a. orn. e-r Feder), ⊙ an e-m Maschinenteil, Schlüssel 2c.: shank, des Webstuhls: leaf; Nadlerei: stem, shank, length.

schäften (⌣‿) **I** v/a. ⓜ to provide with a shaft, &c. (s. Schaft); ⊙ Büchsenmacherei: eine Flinte ⌢ to stock (or mount) a gun; Schuhmacherei: einen Stiefel ⌢ to leg a boot. — **II** geschäftet, ge=schaftet p.p. und a. ⓜ stocked; for. ein gut geschäfteter Baum tree with a fine, long trunk.

Schäfter (⌣‿) m ⓜ gun-stocker.

schaft=förmig ⊙ (⌣‿...) a. ⓜ shaft-like; =halm ? m ⓜ = Schachtelhalm; =holz n wood for gunstocks; =leisten f Schuhmach.: boot-tree or =last.

Schaf=trift (⌣‿) f ⓜ sheepwalk, sheeprun, Am. auch: sh.-ranch; vgl. =weide.

Schaft=rinne (⌣‿...) f ⓜ ? einer Säule: groove, fluting; =stiefel m/pl. top-boots, Wellington boots pl.

Schaf=wasser (⌣...) n ⓜ physiol.: ⊽ amniotic fluid; =weide f pasture for sheep, sh.-way; vgl. =trift; =wolle f sheep's wool; =zecke f, ent. sheep-louse or =tick (Melophagus ovinus); =zucht f sh.-breeding or =farming; =züchter m sh.-breeder or =farmer, sheepman.

Schah (⌣) [pers. König] m ⓜ shah.

Schakal (‿⌣, ‿⌣) [fr. chacal; *türk., pers.] m ⓑd. (ⓜ) zo. jackal (Canis aureus).

Schake prove. ⊙ (‿⌣) f ⓜ link of a chain.

Schäkel ↓ (‿⌣) m ⓜ (zu öffnendes Kettenglied) shackle; ~=bolzen m ⓜ shackle-bolt.

Schaken=kette ⊙ (‿‿⌣) f ⓜ als Uhrkette: oval-linked chain.

Schäker (‿⌣) [mhd.; *hebr. Lügner] m ⓜ, ~in f ⓜ playful person; (Spaßmacher) jester, joker; (Schelm) wag; ~ei (‿‿⌣) f ⓜ play; jesting, joking, dallying, fun; (Schelmerei) ⌢mund m ⓜ, Schäk(e)rin f ⓜ jester; **schäkerhaft** (‿‿⌣) a. ⓜ playful; jocose; waggish, roguish, facetious, sportive; **schäkern** v/n. (h.) ⓜa. to play; to jest, to joke; (tändeln) to dally, to sport.

schal¹ (⌣) [mhd.: shallow] a. ⓜ insipid, unsavoury; (abgestanden) stale, dead; fig. auch: flat, vapid; (leicht) shallow.

Schal² F (⌣)[engl., *perl.] m ⓑd. ⓜ shawl.

schälbar (‿⌣) a. ⓜ easy to peel.

Schal=brett ⊙ (‿⌣) [Schale] n ⓜ Bauwesen: outside plank. [muffler.]

Schälchen¹ (‿⌣) n ⓜ (dim. von Schale²); **Schälchen²** (‿⌣) n ⓜ (dim. von Schale²) small bowl or basin or dish.

Schale¹ (‿⌣) [ahd.: shell: Scholle] f ⓜ **1.** ~ v. Eiern, Nüssen, Austern 2c.: shell, v. Früchten: peel, skin, v. Samen: husk, hull; (Schote) pod, (Rinde) bark, rind. — **2.** zo. ~ (harte Bedeckung) der Konchylien, Schildkröten 2c.: crust, test, ⊽ testa; hunt. ~ n pl. (Hufe des Wildes): cloven hoofs pl.; vet. ring-bone. — **3.** ⊙ ~ e-r Wage: scale, e-s Löffels: bowl, e-s Messers: sheath (or casing, plate) of a knife-handle. — **4.** ↓ ~ n (ob. Wangen) zur Verstärkung e-s Maftes, e-r Rahe: fishes pl. — **5.** fig. outer covering, outside, (Querfläche) surface; unter e-r rauhen ~ verbirgt er einen gesunden Kern he hides his sterling qualities under a rough outside. he is a rough diamond.

Schale² (‿⌣) [ahd.] (Trink2) bowl, basin, dish, vessel; s. Frucht=, Opfer=schale; (Untertasse) saucer; ⊙ metall. (gußeiserne Form) chill; bibl. die ~s Zornes über e-n ausgießen to pour (or open) the vials of one's wrath upon a p.; goldene Äpfel in silbernen ~n apples of gold in pictures of silver.

schalen ⊙ (‿⌣) v/a. ⓜ to line with planks or boards, to board (up).

schälen (‿⌣)[Schale¹] ⓜ **I** v/a. ⓜ to remove the skin (or bark) from; Hülsenfrüchte: to shell, to husk; Obst und Kartoffeln: to peel, to skin, Bäume: to bark, ⊽ to decorticate; agr. to peel off the turf; fig. s. Ei 2 gegen Schluß. — **II** sich ⌢ v/refl. to (cast one's) shell; Baum=

Zeichen (s. S. XVII): F familiär; P Volkssprache; Г Gaunersprache; ↘ selten; † alt (auch gestorben); * neu (auch geboren); ✢ unrichtig;

[Schaleneisen] — 829 — [Schande]

to shed the bark; **Haut:** to peel (off), scale, come off. — **III** ~ n 23 = Schälung.
Schalen-eisen ⊕ (*ʺ*...) n ⊕ metall. aus dem Maffelgraben: sow-iron, metal-cake; **=gehäuse** n, zo. shell; **=guß** ⊕ m, metall. chill-casting; **=haut** f j. Haut 1; **=obst** n shell-fruit.
Schalheit (*ʹ*-) f ⊕ (f. schal¹) insipidity; staleness; flatness, vapidity.
Schäl-hengst (*ʺʹ*) [ahd. schël Hengft] m ② (Zuchthengft) stallion.
Schal³-holz ⊕ (*ʺ*ʹ) n ⊕ Bauwefen: outside of a tree (cut into planks).
schalig (*ʹ*ᵕ) [Schale¹] a. ⊕ 1. provided with a shell or skin; shelled, ⚥: ⚙ tunicated, zo.: ⚙ crustaceous, testaceous. — 2. in Zssgn, z.B.: dick-⚥ thick-skinned.
Schalk (*ʹ*) [ahd. Knecht] m ⑪ ⑦b., **Schälkin** (*ʹ*-) f ① 1. b.s. (vgl. Schelm 1) knave, f etwa: vixen. — 2. g.s. (vgl. Schäfer) rascal; der kleine ~ (auch von Mädchen) the little rogue or scamp. — 3. = Schalkhaftigkeit, z.B. den ~ verdecken to be very sly or cunning; fig. er hat den ~ im Nacken he is a sly-boots or sly-fox; vgl. Schelm 4.
schalkhaft (*ʹᵕ*) a. ⊕ roguish, waggish, arch; sly, cunning, **~igkeit** (*ʹᵕ*-), **Schalkheit** (*ʹ*-) f ⊕ roguishness, waggishness, archness, slyness, cunning; bibl. b.s. knavery, villainy.
Schäl-knötchen (*ʺʹᵕ*) n/pl. ⊕ path. (Zahn-ausfchlag der Säuglinge) tooth-rash.
Schalks-auge (*ʹ*...) n ⊕ rogue's (or roguish) eye; **=freund** m ⊕ false (or deceitful) friend, **-knecht** m, bibl. wicked (or unfaithful) servant; **=narr** m ⊕ ⚙ buffoon; **=streich** m ⊕ roguish (or sly, artful) trick.
Schall (*ʹ*) [ahd.: schallen] m ⊕ ⑦ c. sound, der Glocken: ring(ing), peal(ing); (Widerhall) reverberation, echo; (Geräufch) noise.
Schall-becken ♪ (*ʹ*...) n ⊕ cymbal; **=boden** m sound(ing)-board; **=brechung** f refraction of sound; **=brechungs-lehre** f: ⚙ diacoustics; **=brett** n, arch. louver-board; **=bach** f = Deckel; **=dämpfer** ♪ m sourdine; **=deckel** m, arch. über einer Kanzel ꝛc.: sound-board, reflector. [acoustics.
Schall-lehre (*ᵕʹ*) [Schall-lehre] f ⊕ phys.]
schallen (*ʹᵕ*) [ahd.: schellen] ⁷⁵ a. ⊕ **I** v/n. (h., bei Angabe der Richtung: fn) to (give a) sound, (widerhallen) to resound, v. Glocken ꝛc.: to ring, to peal; es schallt fehr in diefem Saale there is a strong echo in this hall. — **II** ~ n ㉓ sounding, sound, ring(ing). — **III** ℨd p.pr. u. a.⊕ (re)sounding, sonorous, resonant, ringing, pealing; f. Gelächter 1.
Schall-fänger (*ʹ*...) m ⊕ ear-trumpet or -tube; **=fenster** n, arch. e-s Glockenturms: louver-window; **=gewölbe** n, arch. acoustic vault; **=hemmung** f durch große Gegenstände: sound-shadow; **=kasten** ♪ m e-r Violine: body; **=lehre, =loch** f. Schallehre, Schalloch; **=messer** m: ⚙ phonometer. [Gitarre ꝛc.: (sound-)hole.
Schalloch (*ʹᵕ*) [Schall-loch] f ⊕ neutr.
Schall-rohr (*ʹ*...) n ⊕ speaking-trumpet; **=schwingung** f acoustic vibra-

tion, **=strahl** m ray of sound; **=stück** n = **=trichter**; **=telegraph** m acoustic telegraph; **=trichter** m ♪ e-s Hörrohrs ꝛc.: mouth-piece, bell-mouth; **=welle** f sound-wave; **⚥zurückwerfend** a. ⊕: ⚙ phonocamptic; **=zurückwerfungs-lehre** f: ⚙ phonocamptics.
Schäl-maschine ⊕ (*ʺᵕʹᵕ*) f ⊕ peeling-(or shelling-)machine.
Schalmei ♪ (ᵕʹ) [mhd.; *fr. chalumeau m] f ⊕ shawm, shalm.
Schal-obst (*ʺ*...) n ⊕ fruit which can be peeled; **=ohr** n, vet. ear of too great (a) width.
Schalotte ⊘ (ᵕʹᵕ) [mhd.; *fr. échalot(t)e] f ⊕ shallot (A'llium ascalo'nicum).
Schäl-pflug ⊕ (*ʺ*...) m ⊕ agr. paring-plough; **=seife** f kitchen-soap.
schalt¹ (*ʹ*) ind. impf. v. schelten.
Schalt²-brett ⊕ (*ʹᵕʹ*) [schalten] n ⊕ elect. switchboard.
schalten (*ʹᵕ*) [↓ ein Schiff (ab)stoßen, dann: lenken] ⊕ **I** v/n. (h.) to command, to rule; ich bin frei ⚥ (und walten) to do as one likes with a th., to be master (f mistress) over a th.; e-n ⚥ und walten l. to let a p. do as (s)he likes, to give a p. full power or control. — **II** v/a. = einschalten I; ⊕ elect. to connect, to join (up). — **III** ~ n ㉓ = Schaltung.
Schalter (*ʹᵕ*) [schalten] m ㉒ 1. ruler, master. — 2. a. f⊕ (Schiebefenfter) sliding window, ➡, &c. booking-office, ticket-office, -window; ⚥ am ⚥ aufgeben to post at the counter. — 3. elect. switch.
Schalter-brief ➡ (*ʹᵕ*...) m ⊕ letter handed in at the counter; **=fenster** n = Schalter 2; **=öffnung** f opening of the ticket-office.
Schal-tier (*ʺʹ*) n ⊕ zo. shell-fish, ⚙ testaceous (or crustaceous) animal, pl. a.: ⚙ conchylia.
Schaltier-kenner (*ʺʹ*...) m ⊕: ⚙ conchologist; **=kunde** f: ⚙ conchology; **=versteinerung** f fossil shell.
Schalt²-jahr (*ʹ*...) [ahd. Zahr, in das ein Tag eingefchaltet ift] n ⊕ agr. gemeines Zahr) leap-year; **=knochen** m, anat. (Zwickelbein): ⚙ intercalare; **=monat, =tag** m: ⚙ intercalary month, day.
Schaltung (*ʹᵕ*) f ⊕ (zu schalten I:) command, rule; (zu II:) elect. connexion.
Schalt²-vorrichtung (*ʹ*...) f ⊕ elect. switch; **=wort** n interpolated word.
Schälung (*ʹᵕ*) f ⊕ shelling, &c. (f. I), von Bäumen: decortication.
Sch(a)luppe ⚓ ↓ (ᵕ)(*ʹᵕ*) [fr. chaloupe *ndl.] f ⓮ sloop; große ~ long-boat.
Schal-wand ⊕ (*ʺ*...) f ⊕ wooden partition; **=werk** n plank-lining.
Scham (*ʹ*) [ahd.: shame: Schande] f ⓮ (o. pl.) 1. (Scheu) bashfulness, modesty, (mit Gram und Zerknirfchung) shame; vor ~ erröten to blush for (or with) shame; f. abbeißen 2; aller ~ bar fein, alle ~ abgelegt h., F keine ~ im Leibe h. to be devoid of all (sense of) shame. — 2. (Gefchlechtsteile) privy parts, genitals pl., bfd. bibl. (Nacktheit) nakedness; männliche ~ penis, ⚙ membrum virile; weibliche ~: ⚙ vulva, pudendum.
Schamade ⚔ (ᵕʹᵕ) [fr. chamade] f ⓮ (Signal zur Unterhandlung) chamade; ~ schlagen to beat (or sound) a parley.

Schamane (-ʹᵕ) [ind. Büßer] m ⓮ (mongolifcher Priefter) Shaman; **schamanisch** a. ⊕ Shamanic; **Schamanismus** (--ᵕʹᵕ) m ㉗ Shamanism.
Scham-bein (*ʺ*...) n ⓮ anat. share-bone, pubic bone, ⚙ (lt.) (os) pubis; **=bein-bogen** m, anat.: ⚙ pubic arch, arch of the pubis; **=blume** ⚥ f pea-flower (Clito'ria); **=bug** m, anat. groin; **=drüse** f, anat.: ⚙ inguinal gland.
schämen (*ʹᵕ*) [Scham] ⓯ **I** sich ⚥ v/refl. to feel abashed, (erröten) to blush at a th.; sich halbwegs (oder ein wenig) ⚥ to be half ashamed (of o.s.); sie ⚥ sich meiner they are ashamed of me; sie brauchen sich deshalb nicht zu ⚥ there is nothing in it (that) they need be ashamed of; sich e-r Sache (gen.), sich über et., e-r Sache wegen (oder halber) ⚥ to feel ashamed of a th.; sie ⚥ sich vor mir they are ashamed to appear (or stand) before me; ich würde mich zu Tode ⚥ (ob. mir die Augen aus dem Kopfe [vgl. II]) ⚥ I should die for shame, I should not survive the disgrace; schämt euch! shame upon you!, for shame! — **II** v/a. ich würde mir die Augen aus dem Kopfe ⚥ I should be too much ashamed to look any one in the face (vgl. I am Ende).
scham-erregend (*ʺ*...) a. ⊕ filling with shame; **=gefühl** n ⊕ sense of shame; **=gegend** f, anat.: ⚙ pubic region; **=glied** n = Scham 2.
schamhaft (*ʹᵕ*) a. ⊕ bashful, shame-faced, modest; (fpröde) prim, coy, shy; (keusch) chaste; **~igkeit** (*ʹᵕᵕ*-) f ⊕ bashfulness, modesty, coyness, primness, shyness; chastity.
Scham-hügel (*ʺʹᵕ*) m ⊕ anat.: pubes, (lt.) mons Veneris.
schämig (*ʹᵕ*) a. ⊕ bashful, abashed.
Scham-knochen (*ʺ*...) m ⊕ = **=bein**; **=lefzen, =lippen** f/pl. anat. wings (or lips, ⚙ labia) of the vulva; **=leiste** f ⊕ = **=bug**; **=los** a. ⊕ shameless, unabashed, unblushing, (unverfchämt) impudent, brazen-faced, barefaced; (lafterhaft) profligate; **=losigkeit** f/shamelessness; impudence, profligacy.
Schamotte ⊕ (ᵕʹᵕ) [dtfch-it. *Scherben pl. +-otte] f ⊕ (feuerfefter Ton) fire-clay; **~-stein, ~-ziegel** m ⊕ fire-brick.
schampu(nier)en ⚓ (ᵕ-ʹᵕ, ᵕʹᵕ) [ind. kneten] v/a. ⊕ ⑬ to shampoo.
Scham-ritze (*ʺ*...) f ⊕ anat.: ⚙ (fissure of the) vulva; **=rot** a. ⊕ blushing, ⚥ machen to put to the blush; ⚥ werden to colour (up); **=rot** n, **=röte** f blush; **=seite** f = **=bug, =teile** m/pl. = Scham 2, a.: ⚙ (lt.) pudenda pl.; **=zünglein** n, anat.: ⚙ clitoris.
schandbar (*ʹᵕ*) a. ⊕ infamous; **~-keit** (*ʹᵕᵕ*-) f ⊕ infamy (vgl. fchändlich ꝛc.).
Schand-blatt (*ʹ*...) n ⊕ abominable (or scandalous) paper; **=bube** m infamous fellow, scoundrel, villain; **=buch** n infamous book; **=deckel** m (Deckmantel der Schande) cloak (to hide one's shame).
Schande (*ʹᵕ*) [ahd.: Scham] f ⓮, auch (bfd. poet.) ⊕ 1. shame; (Unehre) dishonour, disgrace, discredit, (Ent-

[**Schandeckel**] — 830 — [**scharf**]

ehrung) ignominy, infamy; (Schimpf) opprobrium, (Beschimpfung) outrage, insult. — 2. ~ auf sich laden to draw down disgrace upon o.s., to disgrace o.s.; f. gereichen; e-m ~ m., e-n in ~ bringen to bring discredit (or shame) upon a p.; zu m-r ~ muß ich gestehen to my shame I must confess; Sprichw. Armut ist keine ~ poverty is no disgrace. — 3. f. zuschanden.

Schan=deck(el m) n ↓ (♂.♀.(~) ⊕ (Deckbalken über den Spanten) gunwale.

schänden (♂~) [ahd.: Schande] I v/a. und **sich** ⚲ v/refl. ⊕ 1. (an der Ehre verletzen) to dishonour; (sich) ⚲ to disgrace (o.s.); (tränken) to insult, durch Nachrede: to defame; (besudeln) to soil, to sully; (brandmarken) to brand, (entweihen) to profane, desecrate, violate; einen guten Namen ⚲ to bring disgrace (or dishonour) upon a good name; den Sabbat ⚲ to break the sabbath; ein Weib: to ravish. — 2. (verunstalten) to disfigure, to deform; (verderben) to spoil. — II ~ n ⚲ 3. f. **Schändung**.

schande(n)=halber (♂~.♀~) adv. for shame's sake, for the sake of (or to save) appearances.

Schänder (♂~) [mhd.] m ⚲ (f. schänden 1) one who dishonours, &c.; profaner, violator; ravisher; ~ des Sabbats sabbath-breaker.

Schand=fleck (♂...) m ⚲ blemish, stain, slur, taint, blot; vgl. =mal; =**gedicht** n: a) infamous poem; b) (Spottgedicht) lampoon; =**geld** n: a) price of infamy; b) paltry sum; =**gesell** m = =**bube**; =**kauf** m: a) disgraceful purchase; b) cheap bargain; =**leben** n disgraceful life.

schändlich (♂~) [ahd.] a.⊕1.shameful,disgraceful, despicable; (Schande bringend) ignominious; infamous, scandalous; ⚲es Verbrechen, Vorhaben foul (or base, atrocious, abominable) crime, plot; das ist (höchst) ⚲ von ihm it is (most) disgraceful of him or a (great) disgrace to him. — 2. F fig. (ungemein) das ärgert mich ⚲ (adv.) I am greatly (or exceedingly, extremely, F awfully) annoyed about it, it vexes me very much; **~keit** (♂~) f⊕ shamefulness, disgrace(fulness); ignominiousness, ignominy; baseness, atrociousness.

Schand=lied (♂...) n ⚲ ribald song; =**mal** n mark (or brand) of infamy, stigma; vgl. =**fleck**; =**maul** n scandalous tongue; foul-mouthed person; =**pfahl** m = =**säule**; =**preis** m ridiculous price; =**säule** f pillory, whipping-post; =**schrift** f libel, libellous publication; =**tat** f infamous (or shameful, mean) act(ion), misdeed.

Schändung (♂~) f ⊕ (zu schänden 1:) insult(ing), defamation; profanation; breaking the sabbath; ravishing a woman; (zu 2:) disfigurement.

Schand=weib (♂...) n ⊕ vile woman or creature; =**wort** n abominable (or smutty) word; =**zunge** f = =**maul**.

Schanghai (♂~) npr/n. ⊕α. chines. Hafenstadt: Shanghai.

Schank (♂) [mhd.: *schenken] m ⊕b. 1. license for retailing beer, wine or spirits, publican's license.— 2. (Verkauf) retail(trade) of alcoholic liquor(s). — 3. (Ort, wo Bier ꝛc. verzapft wird) bar, tap-room, F pot-house.

Schank=berechtigung (♂...) f ⊕ = Schant 1; =**bier** n beer from the tap, beer sold on the premises.

Schanker (♂~) [fr. chancre] m ⚲ path. chancre, F the (venereal) disease.

Schank=gerechtigkeit (♂...) f ⊕ = Schant 1; =**geschäft** n: a) licensed victualler's trade; b) = Schant 3; =**steuer** f = Schant 1; =**tisch** m bar; =**wirt(in** f) m publican (f a. woman keeping a pub); retailer of beer, wine or spirits; licensed victualler; =**wirtschaft** f pub(lic house), licensed house, F beer-shop; vgl. Schank 3; eine ~ haben to keep a pub.

Schanz=arbeit ⚔ (♂...) f ⊕ frt. (throwing up) earthworks or entrenchments, palisading; =**arbeiter** m trencher, sapper; =**bekleidung** f gabion(n)ade; =**deck** ↓ n f. Dahlbord.

Schanze[1] (♂~) [mhd.: entrenchment, earthwork; geschlossene ~ redoubt; e-e ~ aufführen to throw up trenches or earthworks, to entrench o.s.

Schanze[2] (♂~) [mhd.: chance; *fr. chance] f ⊕: in die ~ schlagen (aufs Spiel setzen) to hazard, venture, jeopardize, risk; sein Leben in die ~ schlagen to stake (or imperil) one's life.

schanzen (♂~) [Schanze] ⊕ I v/a. to (en)trench. — II v/n. (h.) to work (or dig) at a trench, to throw up entrenchments, F fig. (schwer arbeiten) to work hard, to drudge, F to sweat, to slave, to fag (one's life out). — III ~ n ⚲ entrenchment; F fig. hard work, drudgery, slaving. [arbeit ꝛc.]

Schanzen=bau (♂~.♂) m ⊕ ꝛc. = Schanz-**Schanzer** (♂~) m ⊕ = Schanz-arbeiter.

Schanz=gerät ⚔ (♂...) n ⊕ utensils (or implements) pl. used for entrenching or palisading; =**gräber** m = =**arbeiter**; =**kleid** ↓ n bulwark; =**korb** m gabion, kleiner: corbeil; =**korb=bekleidung**, =**brücke**, =**lehre** f gabion-revetment, -bridge, -form; =**pfahl** m palisade; mit =pfählen umgeben to palisade; =**wehr** f barrier; =**werk** n entrenchment; =**zeug** n entrenching tools pl.

Schar[1] (♂¹) [ahd.: share] f ⊕ 1. ⚔ troop, squad; (Heer) host; feindliche ~en hostile forces pl. — 2. weit.= Menge.

Schar[2] (♂) f ⊕ († ⊕c.) = Pflug-⚲.

Scharade (♂~) [fr.] f (Silbenrätsel) charade; ~n aufführen to act charades.

Schar=arbeit (♂...♂~) f = Fron-arbeit.

Scharbe (♂~) [ahd.] f⊕ orn. =Kormoran-⚲; schwarze ~ common cormorant.

Scharb(e)=brett ⊕ (♂(~)...), =**messer** n ⊕ chopping-board, -knife.

scharben, schärben (♂~) [ahd.] v/a. ⊕ Kochkunst: Gemüse ꝛc. ⚲ to chop (up) ..., to cut ... small.

Scharbock (♂~) [(P) lt. Scorbut] m ⊕c. (o.pl.) path. scurvy; mit dem ~ behaftet scurvy, scorbutic; Mittel wider (oder gegen) den ~: =**antiscorbutic**; ~**s=kraut** ♀ (♂~.♀) n ⊕ figwort (Ficaria verna).

Schäre (♂~) [schwd.: schären] f ⊕ meist pl. ~n ♀ (Felsen=inseln und Klippen, bsd. in der Ostsee) Schären, rocky islands pl. in the Baltic.

scharen (♂~) [ahd.: Schar¹] v/a. u. **sich** ⚲ v/refl. ⊕: (sich) ⚲ to form troops or gangs, to congregate, to flock together, to assemble.

Scharen=führer (♂...) m ⊕ leader of a troop or gang; =**weise** adv. (F a. a.) in troops or gangs or bands.

scharf[1] (♂) [ahd.: Schar¹] a. ⊕ (comp. schärfer, sup. schärfst) 1. (ant. stumpf) sharp, cutting, fig. auch: trenchant, keen; (geschliffen) sharpened; (spitz zulaufend) pointed, acute, ⚲: ⚔ acuminate; ⚲e Gesichtszüge sharp(ly) cut features pl.; ⚲ m. to make sharp; to sharpen, auf e-m Schleifstein: to grind, to whet; Sprichw. allzu ⚲ macht schartig too much cunning overleaps itself or defeats its own purpose; excessive severity breeds discontent. — 2. (ant. sanft, milde): a) allgemein: rough, harsh; (ätzend) caustic, corrosive, mordant; ⚲es Gift strong (or violent) poison; ⚲er Spott bitter mockery; ⚲er Wind biting (or piercing) wind; ⚲e Zunge sharp tongue; gr. ⚲er Akzent acute accent; med. ⚲e Säfte acrid humours pl.; b) für den Geschmack: sharp, pungent; (gepfeffert) peppered, hot; ⚲er Essig strong vinegar; c) fürs Gehör: piercing, shrill; d) geistig: (streng) severe, rigorous; (heftig) violent; (bitter) bitter, harsh; (satirisch) satirical, biting, caustic; ⚲e Bemerkung cutting remark; ⚲er Verweis severe reprimand; ⚲e Zucht rigid (F iron) discipline; e-n ⚲ (adv.) anlassen to talk roughly to a person; es ging (daselbst) ⚲ her there was rough (or hot) work, ⚔ was a hot fight; auf das schärfste untersuchen to make the strictest (or most searching) investigation; e-n ⚲ zurechtweisen to give a p. a sharp (or good) talking to, F to pull a p. up sharp(ly). — 3. fig. (bestimmt hervortretend) salient; (sich stark äußernd) pronounced; ⚲ (adv.) ausgeprägt clean-cut, chisselled (out); ⚲ begrenzt strictly limited; ⚲ abrupt, steep; et. ⚲ betonen, hervorheben to emphasize (or accentuate) a th.; ⚲ hervortretend standing out in bold relief. — 4. (rasch wahrnehmend) keen; ⚲er Beobachter acute (or close, shrewd) observer; ⚲es Gedächtnis faithful memory; ein ⚲es Gesicht h., ⚲ (adv.) sehen to be keen- (or sharp-) sighted, to have a good sight; e-n ⚲ ansehen to fix one's glances (or eyes) upon a p.; ⚲ hören to be quick of hearing, to have a quick ear. — 5. (sorgfältig und genau) exact, precise; ⚲e Prüfung searching examination, close scruting; e-n ⚲ (adv.) bewachen to watch a p. closely or narrowly; es mit e-m ⚲ nehmen to be very strict with a p. — 6. (rasch, mit Wucht) ⚲er Schritt smart (or quick) pace; ⚲ (adv.) fahren to drive (or go) at a sharp pace or trot; ⚲ gehen to walk fast or (at) a good pace; ⚲ reiten to ride in hot haste or at full speed; e-m ⚲ auf den Leib rücken ob. ⚲ zu Leibe gehen to

Signs (see page XVII): F familiar; P vulgar; ⚐ flash; ⚲ rare; † obsolete (died); * new word (born); ⁺⁺ incorrect; ♪ music;

[Scharf] — 831 — [Schattenbild]

press a p. very closely or hard; ⚓ hinter et. her sein to be keenly bent on a th., to be eager after a th. — 7. a) **man.** ⚓ (adv.) beschlagen to rough(shoe); b) ⚔ ⚓ (ant. blind) schießen to use ball-cartridge; ⚓e Patro'ne ball-cartridge; ⚓er Schuß shot with ball or bullet.

Scharf² ⚓ (⚓) n ⓌGeogr. (scharf zulaufender Schiffsboden) sharp bottom, rising floor; hinteres ~ run; vorderes ~ entrance (of a vessel); vgl. Schärfe 2.

Scharf¹=blick (⚓...) m ⚙ penetrating glance, quick eye, keen observation; fig. acuteness, penetration; ⚓**blickend** a. ⚙ =⚓sichtig.

Schärfe (ahd.; *scharf) f ⚙ 1. (zu scharf 1:) sharpness, fig. trenchancy, keenness; acuteness; (zu 2:) causticity, corrosiveness, mordancy; acridity, acrimony; pungency; severity, rigour, harshness; (zu 3:) saliency, emphasis; (zu 5:) exactness, precision (vgl. Scharfblick, =sinn). — 2. (scharfe Ecke, Kante) sharp corner, edge; ~ (Schneide) e-s Messers rc. (sharp) edge ...; ⚓ eines Schiffes am Bug: entrance; vgl. Scharf².

scharf¹=eckig (⚓⚓) a. ⚙ with sharp corners, acute-angled.

schärfen (⚓) [ahd.; *scharf] v/a. u. sich ⚓ v/refl. ⚙ 1. ⚓ ein Messer, eine Klinge ⚓ to sharpen ...; ⚙ (wetzen) to whet, (schleifen) to grind, (abziehen) to set, to give an edge to; (zuspitzen) to point, e-n Bleistift a. to cut, e-n Mühlstein: to freshcut; e-m Pferde die Eisen ⚓, metonymisch: ein Pferd ⚓ to rough(shoe) a horse. — 2. (stärken) to strengthen, fortify, intensify; e-m das Gehör (den Verstand) ⚓ to make a p. quicker (or keener) of hearing (of understanding); sich ⚓ to grow stronger or keener or more intense. — 3. (erhöhen, vermehren) to increase, augment, raise, enhance. — 4. (schärfer hervortreten l.) to heighten the effect of, to put into fuller relief. — 5. P gestohlene Sachen: a) (hehlen) to receive; b) (verkaufen) to sell.

scharf¹=gebaut ⚓ (⚓...) a. ⚙ Schiff: pointed, clipper-built; ⚓**geladen** a. ⚙ Schußwaffe: charged with ball-cartridge, loaded with bullets or a bullet; ⚓**kantig** a. with sharp edges, sharp-edged; ⚓**klauig** a. with sharp claws; =**macher** m: a) ⚙ millstone-dresser; b) pol. (Wühler) intriguing politician, political agitator; =**macherei** f, pol. political intriguing or agitation; =**richter** m headsman, executioner; =**richter=amt** n, a. =**richterei** f executioner's office; =**schießen** n firing with ball or bullet; ⚓**schmeckend** a. having a sharp (or pungent, hot) taste; =**schuß** m shot with ball or bullet; =**schütz(e)** m: a) good marksman, splendid (or dead) shot; b) ⚔ sharpshooter; =**schützen=korps** n corps of sharpshooters; =**sicht** f quickness (or keenness) of sight or vision; vgl. =**blick**; ⚓**sichtig** a. sharp- (or quick-, keen-)sighted, fig. acute, penetrating; =**sichtigkeit** f =**sicht**; =**sinn** m sagacity, acumen, penetration; (Urteilskraft) discrimination, discernment, judgment; ⚓**sinnig** a. sagacious, (a)cute,

discerning. (erfinderisch) ingenious; =**sinnigkeit** f sagacity, ingeniousness.

Schärfung (⚓) f ⚙ sharpening.

scharf=züngig (⚓,⚓) a. ⚙ sharp-tongued.

Scharlach(⚓=ch)[mhd.P(ge)schor(nes)Lat(en); fr. écarlate f; it. scarla'tto m; *perf.] m (n) ⓌGeogr. 1. a) Farbe: scarlet (colour or dye); b) (scharlachroter Stoff) scarlet cloth. — 2. path. = Scharlachfieber. scharlach=**artig** (⚓=ch...) a. ⚙ like scarlet, ⚓ scarlatinoid; =**baum** ⚘ m ⚙ =Kermeseiche. [— 2. (scharlachrot) scarlet.]

scharlachen (⚓...)(D⚓) 1. (of) scarlet.

Scharlach=farbe (⚓=ch...) f ⚙ scarlet (colour or dye); ⚓**farben** a. ⚙ scarlet; =**färber** ✪ m scarlet-dyer; =**fieber** =**friesel** n, path. scarlet fever, milderer Art: scarlatina; =**kraut** ⚘ n clary (Sal'via scla'rea); ⚓**rot** a. scarlet; =**rot** n, auch: =**röte** f scarlet (colour), cochineal.

Scharlatan (⚓) [mhd. fr. charlatan; *it. ciarlata'no] m ⓌGeogr. (auch D) charlatan, quack (-doctor), mountebank; ~**erie** (⚓⚓) f ⚙, ~**ismus** (⚓⚓) m ⚙ charlatanry, charlatanism, quackery.

Scharlei ⚘ (⚓) [mhd.; *mlt.] m ⓌGeogr.species of elecampane (I'nula o'culus Christi); ~ **salbei** ⚘ (⚓...) m, f = Scharlachkraut.

scharmant (⚓) [fr.] a. ⚙ charming.

scharmieren F (⚓) [(+) fr. charmer] v/n. ⚙: mit e-m ⚓ F to carry on (a flirtation) with a p., to flirt with a p.

Scharmützel ⚔ (⚓) [mhd.; it. scaramu'ccia f; *dtsch schirmen] n ⚓ skirmish, trifling engagement; ⚓**n** v/n. (h.) ⓌGeogr. to skirmish, to have a brush with the enemy.

scharmutzieren (⚓) v/n. (h.) ⚙: a) ⚔ to skirmish; b) = scharmieren.

Scharmützler ⚔ (⚓) m ⚙ skirmisher.

Scharn (⚓) [ndd.] m ⓌGeogr.: a) (Brotbank) bread-stall; b) (Fleischbank) butcher's stall. [ⓌGeogr. hinge, joint.]

Scharnier ⚙ (⚓) [fr. charnière f] n **Scharnier=band** ⚙ (⚓...) n ⚓ jointframe; =**feile** f joint-file; =**gelenk** n rule-joint, anat.: ⚓ ginglymus; ⚓**gelenk=artig** a. ⚙ ginglymoid, ginglyform; =**säge** f joint-saw; =**stift** m jointpin, joint-wire; =**ventil** n flap-valve; =**zange** f joint-pliers pl.; =**zirkel** m joint-compasses pl.

Schärpe (⚓) [mhd.; fr. écharpe; *dtsch] f ⚙ scarf, sash, surg. (Binde) sling.

Scharpie (⚓) [fr. charpie] f ⚙ surg. lint.

Scharpie=bausch (⚓...) m ⚙ surg. zum Verbinden: roll of lint; =**pfropf** m zur Stopfung von Blutungen rc.: tampon; =**rolle** f dossil; =**wiefe** f zum Offenhalten von Wunden rc.: tent, bunch of lint.

Scharre (⚓) [ahd. Striegel] f ⚙ raker, scraping-iron, scraper.

Scharr=eisen ⚙ (⚓...) n ⚓ scraping-iron, scraper. [m ⚓ f. Scharn.]

Scharren¹ (⚓) [ndd. = hd. Schranne]

scharren² (⚓) [mhd.] v/n. (h.) ⚓ to rake, scrape, scratch; auf e-n Haufen ⚓ to rake into a heap, et. in die Erde ⚓ to bury a th. in the ground; mit den Füßen ⚓: a) v. Hühnern: to scratch (in) the ground; b) v. Menschen: to scrape (or shuffle with) one's feet; c) v. Pferden: to paw the ground; ein Loch in die Erde ⚓ to scratch a hole in the ground.

Scharrer (⚓) m ⚓ 1. raker, scraper, scratcher. — 2. orn. ~ pl. = Scharrvögel.

Scharr=fuß (⚓.) m ⚓ = Kratzfuß. [pin.] **Scharr²=riegel** ⚙ (⚓...)m⚓ ploughshare-**Scharr=netz** ⚓ (⚓...) n ⚓ trawl, dragnet; =**vögel** m/pl., orn. (Hühnervögel) scratchers, ⚓ rasores pl. [maker.] **Scharr²=schmied** ⚙(⚓...)m⚓ploughshare-**Scharte¹** (⚓) [mhd.; *scheren] f ⚙ 1. in e-m Schneidewerkzeuge: notch, dent; f. auswetzen; ~n bekommen to become notched or dented or jagged. — 2. bfd. ⚔ (Schieß=)~ loophole, embrasure, crenelle. — 3. (Einschnitt in Bergen) gap, depression, dip; vgl. Schlucht.

Scharte² ⚘ (⚓, ⚓) f ⚙ common sawwort (Serra'tula tincto'ria).

Schartefe (⚓) [mhd.] f ⚙: a) (altes Buch) old (or second-hand) book; b) (Schund) old lumber, trash; c) F co. (altes Weib) old frump or crock, P old geezer; ~**n=händler** (⚓...) m ⚓ dealer in old books and curios; ~**n=jäger** m bookhunter, curio-hunter.

Scharten=mauer ⚔ (⚓⚓) [Scharte¹ 2] f ⚓ loopholed (or crenellated) wall.

schartig (⚓, ⚓) [Scharte¹ 1] a. ⚙ von Schneidewerkzeugen: notchy, dented, jagged; Sprichw. f. scharf 1; **Schartig=keit** f ⚙ notchiness, jaggedness.

Schartung (⚓) f ⚙ geol. dip (or indenture) in elevated ground; vgl. Scharte¹ 3.

Schar¹=wache (⚓...) f ⚙ patrol; =**wächter** m man belonging to a patrol, watchman; ⚓**weise** adv. =scharenweise.

Scharwenzel (⚓) m ⚓ 1. = Kratzfuß. — 2. (Person, die sich zu allerlei schickt) jack-of-all-trades, handy man; (Speichellecker) toady, flunkey; (Sache, die zu allem zu gebrauchen ist) handy thing. — 3. deutsches Kartenspiel: scherwenzel; beggar-my-neighbour.

scharwenzeln (⚓) v/n. (h.) ⚓a. (Kratzfüße m.) to bow and scrape; (untertänig kriechen) to (play the) toady; to (cringe and) crawl, to fawn, F to carney.

Schar=werk ⚓ (⚓...) n ⚓: a) ehm. statutelabour; b) Bauhandwerk: jobbing (work), job-work; =**werken** v/n. (h.) ⚓*.* to do jobbing or job-work; (sich placken) to work hard, to toil and slave; =**werker** m ⚓ jobbing man, common labourer, navvy. [jagen) to expel (from school).]

schassen (⚓) [: chase; *fr.] (Schul=sl. weg=)

schatten¹ (⚓) [Schatten²] ⚓ I v/n. (h.): auf et. ⚓ to cast a shadow upon. — II v/a. ⚓ to overshadow, to darken.

Schatten² (⚓) [ahd.: shade, shadow] m ⓌGeogr. 1. a) mst angenehm, kühlend: shade (a. paint.); b) dunkel, düster, a. lästig: shadow; (Zwielicht) twilight, (Dunkel) darkness, gloom; es war heiß, selbst im ~ ..., even in the shade; einen ~ werfen to cast a shadow upon a th.; fig. in den ~ stellen to eclipse, to put in (or to throw into) the shade; bloßer ~ des Königtums: mere shadow (or semblance) of royalty; vgl. Denkungsart. — 2. myth. (Bewohner der Unterwelt) shade; departed spirit or soul.

schatten²=artig (⚓...) a. ⚙ = schattenhaft; =**bild** n ⚓: a) (shadowy) outline; b) =**riß**; c) (wesenloses Bild) phantom;

⚓ scientific; ⚘ botanical; ⚓ geography; ⚙ machinery; ⚒ mining; ⚔ military; ⚓ marine; ⚓ commercial; ⚓ postal; 🚂 railway.

[Schattenblümchen] — 832 — [Schauermann]

=blümchen ⚹ n bifoliate lily of the valley (Maia'nthemum bifo'lium); =fürst m, myth. ruler of the shades, (it.) Pluto; =gang m shady walk or avenue; =gebung f, paint. shading.
schattenhaft (⌣⌣⌣) a. ⑥⑥ shadowy, like a (mere) shadow, shadow-like.
Schatten²=hut (⌣⌣...) m ⑥② (breitrandiger Hut) broad-brimmed hat; =kegel m, ast.: ⚹ umbra; =könig m sham (or nominal) king; =königtum n mock royalty; =licht n dim light, paint. (it.) chiaroscuro; =lini=e f (shadowy) outline; =los a. ⑥⑥ without shadow or shade; shadowless, shadeless; =pflanze ⚹ f plant thriving in the shade; =probe f, opt. shadow-test, ⚹ skiascopy; =reich a. shady, umbrageous; =reich n, myth. realm of shades, (grch.) Hades; =riß m shadow-figure, ⚹ skiagraph(y); als Bild auch: silhouette; her. umbration; fig. hasty sketch; =seite f shady side (auch fig.); (Nordseite) north(ern) aspect; fig. ~ e-r Sache: dark side of a picture, seamy side of a th.., drawback of a th.; =spender m s.th. giving (or affording) shade; =spiel n: a) chinesisches ~ oder ~ an der Wand Chinese shades pl.; b) fig. phantasmagoria; =verteilung f, paint. gradation of shades, distribution of lights and shades; ⚹werfend a. casting a shadow, giving shade; =wesen n phantom, vision; auch = Schatten² 2; =zeiger m Sonnenuhr: hand of a sundial.
schattier=en (⌣⌣⌣)[dtsch=lt.] I v/a, v/n.(h.) ⑨③ paint. &c. to shade (off), to tint; als v/n. diese Farben ⚹ gut ... blend (or harmonize) well. — II ~ n ㉓ = Sch/ung 1.
Schattierung (⌣⌣⌣) f ⑯ 1. shading, tinting, paint. auch: distribution of lights. — 2. (Farbenübergänge) shades pl. (vgl. Schattenverteilung); typ. pressure.
schattig (⌣⌣) a. ⑥⑥ 1. shady, giving (or affording) shade; (beschattet) umbrageous, shaded, her. umbrated; das Schattige the shadiness. — 2. paint. (Schatten bildend) shaded.
Schatulle (⌣⌣⌣) [(+⁺)] it. sca'tola Schachtel] f ⑧ 1. (Geldkasten) cash-box, strong-box. — 2. (Privatvermögen eines Fürsten) privy (or private) purse.
Schatull(en)=gelder (⌣⌣(⌣)...) n/pl. ⑥② private revenue (or income) of a prince; vgl. Schatulle 2; =güter n/pl. private domain, crown property pl.
Schatz (⌣) [ahd.] m ⑦a. 1. treasure (s. heben 1); (Reichtum) riches pl., wealth; s. heben 1; ~ (reiche Fülle) von Kenntnissen rich store of knowledge; sie ist ein wahrer ~ she is a real gem or F brick. — 2. als Kosewort: mein ~ my darling!, my love!; sein (ihr) ~ his (her) sweetheart or beloved (one), bsd. Am. his (her) best girl (boy).
Schatz=amt (⌣...) n ⑥② treasury, exchequer; =anweisung f treasury-warrant, -bill.
schätzbar (⌣⌣) a. ⑥⑥ estimable, precious; mein ⚹er Freund my worthy (or esteemed) friend; seine ⚹en Dienste his valuable (or valued) services pl.
Schätzbarkeit (⌣⌣⌣) f ⑯ estimableness, estimable qualities pl.; worthiness, worth; valuableness.

Schatz=bon ⚹ (⌣...) m ⑥② treasury-bond or -bill or -note.
Schätzchen (⌣⌣) n ㉓ (dim. von Schatz, s. ds, bsd. 2): sein ~ his lady love, his (little) sweetheart, F his (best) girl.
schatzen (⌣⌣) [ahd.] I v/a. ⑨⓪ to tax, to impose (or levy) taxes on; vgl. brandschatzen. — II ~ n ㉓ s. Schatzung.
schätzen (⌣⌣) [mhd.; *Schatz] I v/a., v/n.(h.), v/refl. ⑨⓪ to esteem, behufs Besteuerung: to assess, durch Berechnung: to value, to appraise; durch geistige Prüfung: to appreciate; zu hoch ⚹ to overrate, to overestimate (s. gering 5, hochachten); wie alt ⚹ Sie ihn? how old do you take him to be or do you think he is?; wir ⚹ es für eine (ob. uns zur) Ehre zu // we deem it an honour to //; er schätzt sich für den feinsten aller Kenner he considers himself the best of judges; vgl. glücklich I; geschätzter Freund! my dear (or worthy) friend!; ⚹ wir ⚹ Sie im Besitz unserer Briefe we trust you are in receipt of our letters; das geschätzte Ihrige vom // your esteemed lines (or your favour) of //. — II ~ n ㉓ s. Schätzung.
schätzens=wert (⌣⌣⌣) a. ⑥⑥ worthy of esteem, to be esteemed, estimable; vgl. schätzbar. [schätzer.]
Schätzer (⌣⌣) m ㉒ valuer; auch = Ab=
Schatz=gräber (⌣...) m ⑥② person digging for treasures, treasure-seeker; =haus n treasure-house; =kammer f treasury, exchequer, bibl. treasure-house; =kammer=schein ⚹ m treasury- (or exchequer-)bill or note; =kanzler m (engl. Finanzminister) Chancellor of the Exchequer; =kästchen n = =kästlein; =kasten m treasure-(or money-)chest; =kästlein n: a) jewel-case or -box, casket; b) Buchtitel etwa: choice selection; =meister m treasurer; =meister=amt n, =meisterei f treasurer's office, treasurership; ⚹pflichtig a. ⑥⑥ tributary; =schein ⚹ m treasury-bill.
Schatzung (⌣⌣) f ⑯ imposition of taxes.
Schätzung (⌣⌣) f ⑯ (s. schätzen I) estimation, estimate, assessment, valuation, appreciation; ~s=wert (⌣⌣⌣) m ⑥② estimated (or assessed) value.
Schau (⌣) [mhd.: show; *schauen] f ⑯ (Besichtigung) view, inspection; (Ausstellung) show, exhibition; mst ⚹ (passing in) review, muster (vgl. Schauspiel, in Artikel); nur zur ~ dienen to serve merely for (outside) show; zur ~ steh(e)n to be on view, to be exposed to the public gaze; zur ~ stellen to exhibit, prunkend: to make a show of; vgl. ausstellen 2; zur ~ tragen to make an exhibition of, to display, to parade, heuchelnd: to sham, feign, put on.
Schaub (⌣) [ahd.: sheaf; *schieben] m ①⑦c. (Strohbund) wisp of straw.
schau=begierig (⌣⌣⌣⌣) a. ⑥⑥ eager (or anxious) to see.
Schau=bild (⌣...) n ⑥② exhibited picture; =brot n, bibl. show-bread; =bude f show(-booth); =budenbesitzer m showman; =bühne f stage; vgl. =gerüst.
Schauder (⌣⌣) [nbd.; *schaudern] m ⑥② shudder(ing); (Zittern, Beben) trembling, shaking, vor Kälte: shivering, F (fit of)

shivers, vor Entsetzen: horror, terror, fright, mit Haarsträuben: ⚹ horripilation.
schauder=erregend (⌣...) ⑥⑥ horrifying; vgl. schauderhaft; =geschichte f ⑥② awful (or dreadful, thrilling) story.
schauderhaft (⌣⌣⌣) a. ⑥⑥ horrible, awful, dreadful, terrible, shocking; (abscheulich) abominable, atrocious, F fig. ganz ⚹e (gewaltige) Ausgabe fearful (or awful, tremendous) expense.
Schauderhaftigkeit (⌣⌣⌣⌣) f⑯(s. schauderhaft) horribleness, awfulness, dreadfulness; atrociousness.
schaudern (⌣⌣) [nbd.: shudder = (er)schüttern] I v/n. (h. u. sn) u. v/a. ⑨②a. 1. (Schauder erregen): a) to make a p.'s flesh creep, to send a thrill through a p.; b) v/impers. es schaudert mich (ob. mich schaudert's) vor et. I shudder at a th., I have a horror of a th. — 2. (Schauder empfinden) to shudder (vor etwas at a th.); (beben) to tremble (or shiver) at a th.; mir schaudert die Haut oder es schaudert mir I shudder, I feel my flesh creep; ⚹d in die Höhe fahren to start with a shudder. — II ~ n ㉓ 3. = Schauder.
Schauder=szene (⌣...) f ⑥② scene of horror, dreadful (or horrible) scene or sight; ⚹voll a. ⑥⑥ = schauderhaft.
schauen (⌣⌣) [ahd.: show] I v/n. (h.), v/a. u. v/refl. ⑧⑧ (sehen, erblicken) to see, behold, perceive, observe; (auf et. blicken) to look (or gaze, peep) at; (aufmerksam betrachten) to view, (besichtigen) to inspect, examine, scrutinize; auf et. ⚹ (achthaben) to pay regard (or heed) to a th.; auf et., einen (als Richtschnur) ⚹ to take a th., a p. as model; gen Himmel ⚹ to look up to heaven; in die Zukunft ⚹ to look (or peer) into the future; zu tief ins Glas ⚹ to take a drop too much; um sich ⚹ to look about (one), to spy all (a)round. — II ~ n ㉓ (f. I) observation; view(ing); inspection; nach innen: intuition.
Schau=ende ⚹ (⌣⌣) n ⑥② v. Tuch: sample.
Schauer¹ (⌣⌣) [schauen] m ㉒ 1. looker-on, spectator, eye-witness.—2. (prüfender Beamter) inspector, examiner.
Schauer² (⌣⌣) [ahd.: shower] m ㉒ 1. = Schauder; bsd. heiliger ~ sacred awe, wholesome dread, bodily fear; heimlicher ~ secret horror; toller ~ mad fit. — 2. path. (heftiger Anfall) violent fit, paroxysm, spasm. — 3. (Unwetter) storm; (Regenguß) shower, downpour (of rain), mit Graupeln: heavy fall of rain and sleet.
Schauer³ prove. (⌣⌣) [: Scheuer] n (a. m) ⑥² a) (Schutz gegen Unwetter) shelter; b) (offener Schuppen) open shed, pent-house.
Schauer⁴ ⚹ (⌣⌣) [nbd.] m ㉒ (Hafen-arbeiter) wharfinger, docker. [douche.]
Schauer²=bad (⌣⌣⌣) n ⑥② shower-bath.
schau(e)rig (⌣(⌣)⌣) a. ⑥⑥ = schauerlich.
Schauer⁴=leute ⚹ (⌣⌣⌣) m/pl. von Schauermann.
schauerlich (⌣⌣⌣) a. ⑥⑥ causing a shudder, thrilling, ghastly, gruesome, weird (vgl. schauderhaft); ~keit (⌣⌣⌣⌣) f ⑯ thrilling nature, ghastliness, gruesomeness; atrociousness.
Schauer⁴=mann (⌣⌣⌣) m ⑥② = Schauer⁴.

Zeichen (s. S. XVII): F familiär; P Volkssprache; ⌐ Gaunersprache; ⚹ selten; † alt (auch gestorben); * neu (auch geboren); ⁺⁺ unrichtig;

[ſchauern] — 833 — [Scheibenblume]

ſchauern (´⌣) [Schauer²] v n. (h.) ⚘ 1. = ſchaudern 2. — 2. v impers. vom Wetter: **es ſchauert** it is pouring (with rain). it's showery, (es graupelt) there is (rain and) sleet falling.

Schauer²-nacht (´⌣...) f ⚘ night of horror(s), awful night; **=roman** m ghastly novel, F blood-freezer or -curdler, penny-dreadful; **=tat** f atrocious deed, horrible (or awful, ghastly) crime. atrocity; ⚘**voll** a. ⚘ full of horror; vgl. ſchauderhaft.

Schaufel (´⌣) [ahd.: shovel; *ſchieben] f ⚘ 1. shovel (a. hort. zo., &c.), zum Schöpfen: scoop; eine ~ voll a shovelful (vgl. Spaten). — 2. ☉: a) ~ e-s Waſſerrades: paddle- (or ladle-)board, float; b) ~ e-s Ruders: blade; c) ~ e-s Ankers: palm, fluke. — 3. hunt. (Gehörn des Dam- und Elen-wildes ꝛc.) palm(ate antler).

Schaufel-band (´⌣...) n ⚘ Schlosserei: dovetail hinge; **=brett** ☉ n am Mühlrade: jaunt. a. = Schaufel 2a; **=förmig** a. ⚘ shovel-shaped; **=füßig** a., zo. shovel-footed; **=gehörn, =geweih** n, hunt. palmed head; vgl. Schaufel 3; **=hirſch** m, hunt. buck of the fallow deer more than two years old.

ſchauf(e)lig (´⌣(⌣)) a. ⚘ shovel-shaped.

ſchaufeln (´⌣) v a. und v/n. (h.) ⚘ a. to (work with a) shovel (vgl. ſchöpfen): **ein Grab ⚘** to dig a grave.

Schaufel-pflug ☉ (´⌣⌣) m ⚘ shovel-, scoop-plough; **=rad** n an Dampfſchiffen: paddle-wheel; **=rad-nabe** f paddle-wheel boss; **=raum** ⚓ m für Kohlen: shovelling-flat; ⚘**voll** a. ⚘ shovelful; **=zahn** m der Wiedertäuber: broad incisor.

Schau-fenſter ♥ (´⌣...) n ⚘ show- (or shop-)window, shop-front; im ~ ausſtellen to display in the (shop-)window.

Schaufler (´⌣) m ⚘ 1. ☉ shoveller, labourer (or man) using a shovel. — 2. = Schaufelhirſch.

Schau-gefecht (´⌣...) n ⚘ sham-fight, röm. Alt.: gladiatorial combat; **=gericht** n show-dish, (Tafelauſſatz) table-ornament; **=gerüſt** n: a) stage, platform, bei Wettrennen: grand stand; b) für e-n Sarg: catafalque; **=haus** n für Leichen: (public) mortuary, (fr.) morgue; **=kaſten** m, **=käſtchen** n show-case.

Schaukel (´⌣) [ndd. shake] f ⚘ (Sitzbrett an Stricken) swing; (Wippwapp) seesaw; ruſſiſche ~ swingboat; eine ~ anbringen to put up a swing.

Schaukel-brett (´⌣...) n ⚘ seesaw; **=gerät** n Turnen: swinging-apparatus.

ſchaukeln (´⌣) [Schaukel] ⚘ a. I v/n. (h.) to rock (to and fro), to swing, auf und nieder: to see-saw; mit dem Körper ⚘ (wackeln) to sway, to waddle; ⚓ vom Schiffe: to roll, to pitch. — II v/a. und ſich ⚘ v/refl. to rock, to swing; ſich auf e-n Stuhle ⚘ to balance o.s. on a chair; ein Kind auf den Knien ⚘ to dance (or dangle) ... on one's knees.

Schaukel-pfanne ☉ (´⌣...) f Zuckerfabr.: seesaw pan; **=pferd** n rocking-horse, **=politik** f = ſyſtem; **=reck** n Turnerei: trapeze; **=stuhl** m rocking-chair, rocker; **=ſyſtem** n, pol. political seesaw, trimming (one's sails to the wind), F wobbling, sitting on the fence.

Schaukler (´⌣) m ⚘, **~in** f ⚘ 1. p. who swings or rocks or sways. — 2. phot. (Vorrichtung) ~ für die Platten rocker.

Schau-luſt (´⌣...) f ⚘ love for sight-seeing, curiosity; ⚘**luſtig** a. ⚘ fond of sight-seeing, curious.

Schaum (´) [ahd.: scum, skim] m ⚘ c. 1. foam of the sea, &c.; (Giſcht) spray; ~ auf Bier, Champagner ꝛc.: froth, head, auf Seifenwaſſer: lather; (Abſchaum) scum; path. (Geifer) foam, a. spume; Eiweiß zu ~ ſchlagen to whisk (or beat up) the white of an egg. — 2. fig. bubble; zu ~ werden to vanish (into space), to dissolve into thin air; to come to naught; Sprichw. Träume ſind Schäume dreams are idle fancies or (mere) shadows.

ſchaum-artig (´⌣...) a. ⚘ foam-like, frothy; ⚘**bedeckt** a. covered with foam; **=bier** n ⚘ sparkling ale; **=blaſe** f bubble.

Schau-meiſter † (´⌣...) m ⚘ inspector.

ſchäumen (´⌣) [ahd., *Schaum] v/n. (h.) ⚘ to foam, to froth; von Wein ꝛc. to sparkle, to effervesce, F to fiz(zle), von Seifenwaſſer: to lather (vgl. abſchäumen I); fig. vor Wut ⚘ to boil over with rage; ⚘ d foaming, frothy, ⚘ spumescent, von Getränken: sparkling, effervescent, poet. der ⚘de Pokal the flowing (or sparkling) cup or bowl.

ſchaum-geboren (´⌣...) a. ⚘ (D 9) risen (or sprung) from the foam; myth. die ~e (Venus) Aphrodite, Anadyomene; **=gold** n ⚘ = Blattgold.

ſchaumig (´⌣) a. ⚘ foaming, frothy.

Schaum-kalk (´⌣...) m ⚘ min. ⚘ aphrite; **=kelle** f skimming-ladle; **=kette** f e-s Zaumes: slavering-chain; **=kraut** ♀ n cardamine; bitteres ~ cuckoo-flower (Cardami'ne prate'nsis); **=krone** f v. Meereswellen: white crest; **=löffel** m = **kelle**; ⚘**los** a. ⚘ foamless, without froth, von Bier ꝛc.: without a head; flat, dead; **=ſchläger** m: a) = Barbier; b) fig. a. **~in** f puffing shopkeeper or trader; **=tierchen** n = ȥirpe.

Schaum-münze (´⌣...) f ⚘ medal.

Schaum-wein (´⌣...) m ⚘ sparkling wine; champagne, F fiz(z); **=ȥirpe** f, ent. frog-hopper (Aphro'phora spuma'ria).

Schau-pfennig (´⌣...) m ⚘ = **münze**; **=platz** m scene (of action), stage, e-s Krieges: seat of war.

Schau-ſpiel (´⌣) n ⚘ d.: a) spectacle, scene, sight (vgl. Schauſtellung); b) thea. play, performance; drama; **=p. bürgerlich** ⚘; ehm. geiſtliches ~ miracle-play.

ſchauſpiel-artig (´⌣...) a. ⚘ dramatic, theatrical; **=dichter(in** f) m ⚘ dramatic poet(ess f), dramatist, playwright; **=dichtung** f drama, dramatic poetry; **=direktor** m manager of a theatre, a. theatrical manager.

Schau-ſpieler (´⌣⌣) m ⚘, **~in** f ⚘ actor (f actress), player, performer, F contp. board-strutter; ~ für komiſche (tragiſche) Rollen: comedian (tragedian); herumziehender ~ strolling (jetzt meist: touring) actor; **~ei** (⌣⌣´⌣) f ⚘ acting or performing (on the stage), histrionism; fig. affectation; **~geſellſchaft** f ⚘ (provincial) company of actors; a. touring company; ⚘**iſch** (´⌣⌣) a. ⚘ theatrical, histrionic; **~kunſt** f dramatic (or histrionic) art, histrionics; **⚘n** (´⌣...) v/n. (h.) ⚘ a. to act (on the stage), to play a part; fig. to sham; **~truppe** f = **geſellſchaft**.

Schauſpiel-haus (´⌣⌣´) n ⚘ playhouse, theatre, thea. auch: house.

Schau-ſtellung (´⌣...) f ⚘ exhibition, show, pageant(ry); **=ſtück** n: a) show-piece, specimen; b) = **münze**.

Schaute (´⌣) = Schote³. [tragen (j. ds).

ſchau-tragen (´⌣´⌣) v/a. ⚘ b.** = zur Schau **Schau-turm** (´...) m ⚘ look-out (or watch-)tower; **=turnen** n gymnastic display; ⚘**würdig** a. ⚘ worth seeing.

Schech (´) [ar. Greis, Lehrer] m ⚘ (arabischer Häuptling) sheik(h).

Scheck¹ ♀ (´) [engl.] m ⚘ c. ⚘ (Anweisung auf eine Bank) cheque; durchkreuzter ~ crossed cheque; an den Inhaber zahlbarer ~ open cheque.

Scheck² (´) [ahd.] m ⚘ = Schecke.

Scheck¹-buch (´⌣...) n ⚘ cheque-book.

Schecke (´⌣) [ſ. Scheck²] f ⚘ (geflecktes Pferd) dappled (or piebald) horse. [cheque.]

Scheck¹-formular (´⌣⌣⌣) n ⚘ blank **ſcheckig** (´⌣) [mhd.; *Scheck²(e) od. fr. échec] a. ⚘ dapple(d) or piebald (horse, &c.), brindle(d) (cow, cat, &c.), mottled (soap, &c.); spotted, speckled, checkered; F fig. ſich ⚘ lachen to burst (or split) with laughing.

Scheck¹-inhaber (´⌣⌣) m ⚘ bearer.

ſcheel (´) [ndd. LU. (dafür (a.)hd. ſchelb): grch. skoliós: ſchielen] a. ⚘ ⚘ cross- (or squint-, F boss-)eyed, squint(ing); ⚘ zu et. ſehen, et. mit ⚘en Augen anſehen to look at a th. with jealous eyes. auch: to look askance (or awry) at a th.

Scheel-auge (´⌣...) n ⚘ squint- (F boss-)eye; ⚘**äugig, ⚘blickend** a. ⚘ = ſcheel; **=ſucht** f envy, jealousy; ⚘**ſüchtig** a. envious, jealous.

Scheffel (´⌣) [ahd.; *Schaff dim.] m ⚘ (Getreidemaß, bſd. ehm. in Preußen 54.96 Liter) etwa: 1½ bushels; bibl. ſein Licht unter einen ~ ſtellen to hide one's light under a bushel.

Scheffel-maß (´⌣...) n ⚘ bushel; **=ſack** m sack holding one bushel; ⚘**weiſe** adv. (F a. a. ⚘) (taken) by the bushel.

Scheibchen (´⌣) n ⚘ small disk or slice.

Scheibe (´⌣) [ahd.; *ſcheiben: grch. skoipós Töpferſcheibe] f ⚘ 1. disk (a. der Sonne ꝛc.), bſd. ast. (lunar, &c.) orb; ~ (Schnitte) Brot, Wurſt, eines Apfels ꝛc.: slice; ~ Fleiſch, ~ Wachs, Harz ꝛc. cake of wax, resin, &c.; ~ von Tauwerk coil of rope; in ~n ſchneiden to slice. — 2. ~ (Zifferblatt): a) eines Kompaſſes: card of the compass, b) einer Uhr: dial of a watch. — 3. (Ziel fürs Wettſchießen) target; nach der ~ ſchießen to shoot at a target. — 4. = Fenſterſcheibe. — 5. ☉ (Töpfer-)~ (potter's) wheel; mach., mech. (runde) ~ sheave (of a block); pulley; ~ und Tau whip; zwei ~n und Taue whip tackle.

ſcheiben-artig (´⌣...) a. ⚘ in shape of a disk, disk-like, ⚘ discoid, orbicular; **=bank** ☉ f ⚘ Drahtzieherei: draw(ing)-bench; **=blei** n Glaserei: window-lead; **=blume** ♀ f; ⚘ discoid

♪ Muſik; ⚘ Wiſſenſchaft; ♀ Pflanze; ♀ Geographie; ☉ Technik; ⚒ Bergbau; ⚔ Militär; ⚓ Marine; ⚘ Handel; ✉ Poſt; 🚂 Eiſenbahn.

[Scheibenbüchse] — 834 — [Scheitel]

flower; =büchse f rifle for target-firing; ℈förmig a. disk-shaped, ⚔ discous; =gatt ↓ n sheave-hole; =glas n sheet-glass; =honig m honey in combs; =könig m. etwa: winner of the first prize at a shooting-match; =maschine f: a) disk-engine; b) phys. plate-machine; =pulver n fine gun-powder; =qualle f. zo.: ⚔ disco-medusan; =rad ⚙ n disk-(or plate-)wheel; =reißen Ⓞ n. metall. taking off the cakes; =schießen n target-practice (auch ⚔); (Wettschießen) rifle- (or shooting-)match; =schütze m marksman; =stand ⚔ m butt(s pl.); =telegraph ⚡ m, tel. disk-telegraph ; = und =seil=werk Ⓞ n sheaves pl. and cordage; ℈weise adv. in slices; =werfen n throwing the disk; =wickelung Ⓞ f, elect. disk-armature.

scheibig (ᴗ́ᴗ) a. ⚙ = scheiben-artig, ℈weise.

Scheich (ᴗ́) = Schech.

Scheid-... (ᴗ́...) in Ifign = Scheide-...

scheidbar (ᴗ́-) a. ⚙ separable, chm.: ⚔ decomposable, analysable; ~keit f ⚙ separability. chm.: ⚔decomposability.

Scheide¹ (ᴗ́ᴗ) [ahd.: sheath] f ⚙ 1. line of separation, border-line, parting; (Grenze) frontier. — 2. (Futteral für schneidende Werkzeuge) sheath (a. ⚔ u. zo.), für Schwert, Dolch ꝛc. auch: scabbard, case; in die ~ stecken to sheathe, ein Schwert auch: to put up; aus der ~ ziehen to unsheathe (or draw) one's sword, &c. 3. anat. = Mutterscheide.

Scheide²-bank ⚒ (ᴗ́-...) [scheiden] f ⚙ sorting-table for ore; =blick m parting glance, farewell look; =brief m: a) farewell letter; b) law: bond of separation; divorce; =erz ⚒ n rich (or paying) ore; =gruß m farewell (greeting); =kunst f (analytical) chemistry; =kuß m parting-kiss; =linie f = Grenzlinie; =mauer m party- (or partition-)wall; =münze f (kleines Geld) small coin, change.

scheiden (ᴗ́ᴗ) [ahd.: It. scin'dere] ⚙ (e)ft I v/n. (jn) sich ℈ v/refl. 1. (sich) ℈ to separate (o.s.); sie schieden (von-ea.) they parted (company); das ℈de Jahr the parting year; die Milch scheidet sich (gerinnt) ... is turning or curdling; meist rel. aus diesem Leben ℈ to depart this life. — II v/a. 2. to separate, gewaltsam: to sever, trennend: to part, to disconnect, teilend: to divide, sondernd: to sunder (vgl. absondern); sie sind geschiedene Leute they are estranged from each other; ⚙ Zuckerfabr.: Rübensaft ℈ to defecate beet-root juice; Zuckerrohrsaft ℈ to clarify (or clear) cane-root sugar; chm. Verbindungen ℈ to decompose (or analyse) ... — 3. Eheleute ℈ to divorce a married couple; sich ℈ l. to sue for a (judicial) separation or a divorce. — III ~ n ⚙ 4. parting; vor seinem ~ previous to his departure or his death. — IV Geschiedene(r) s. ⚙ 5. divorced man (f wife), f bisw. divorcee.

scheiden-artig (ᴗ́ᴗ...), ℈förmig a. ⚙ sheath-like, ⚔ vaginal; =mündung f ⚙ anat.: ⚔ orifice of the vagina; =schnabel m, orn. sheath-bill (Chi'onis).

Scheide-punkt (ᴗ́ᴗ.ᴗ́) m ⚙ point of divergence.

Scheider Ⓞ (ᴗ́ᴗ) m ⚙: Person u. Werkzeug separator; (Arbeiter b. Erzscheiden) sorter (or picker and culler) of ore.

Scheide-stunde (ᴗ́ᴗ...) f ⚙ parting-hour, hour of separation or death; =trunk m parting-cup; =wand f: a) = mauer; b) ♀, zo., anat., &c.: ⚔ septum. in Samengehäusen, in der Nase ꝛc.: ⚔ dissepiment; (Zwerchfell) diaphragm (⚔ elect.); ↓ bulk-head; =wasser n, chm. (lt.) aquafortis (= Salpetersäure); =weg m: a) parting-way, (Kreuzweg) cross-road or -way; b) fig. am ~ steh(e)n to have a difficult choice to make; Herkules am ~e Hercules at the cross-way, a. Hercules' choice.

Scheidung (ᴗ́ᴗ) [ahd.] f ⚙ 1. (zu scheiden 1 u. 2:) separation; chm. decomposition, (chemical) analysis. — 2. (zu 3:) ~ von Eheleuten: (judicial) separation, stärker: divorce.

Scheidungs-erkenntnis (ᴗ́ᴗ...) n ⚙ jur. decree nisi; =grund m ground (on which to sue) for a divorce; =klage f divorce-suit or -proceedings pl.; =pfanne Ⓞ f Zuckerfabrikation: defecator, defecating-pan.

Scheit(h) (ᴗ́) = Schech.

Schein (ᴗ́) [ahd.: shine; *scheinen] m ⓜc. 1. (mattes Licht) subdued (or gleam of) light, F shine, poet. sheen; (Glanz) brilliancy, shining light (vgl. Heiligenschein). — 2. fig. (ant. Wirklichkeit) appearance, semblance; (Aussehen) air, look, (Außenseite) outside, mere show; (Vorwand) pretence, pretext; äußerer ~ outward appearance; dem ~e nach to all appearance(s), apparently; unter dem ~e der Freundschaft under the cloak (or disguise, mask) of friendship; sich den ~ geben, als ob // to feign (or pretend) as though //; zum ~e, des ~es wegen, a. (lt.) pro forma, for form's sake, for the sake of appearance (vgl. Anschein); das ist alles nur ~ (Verstellung) that's nothing but a feint or blind or make-believe; F it's all (a) sham, Sprichw. der ~ trügt appearances are (often) deceptive or delusive. — 3. (Bescheinigung) certificate, weitS. bill; (Quittung) receipt; (Formular) form.

Schein-andacht (ᴗ́ᴗ...) f ⚙ false devotion; =angriff m: a) ⚔ feigned attack; b) fenc. feint.

scheinbar (ᴗ́-) a. ⚙ seeming, (augenscheinlich) apparent, (angeblich) ostensible; (durch den Schein blendend) specious (pretext, &c.); (einleuchtend) plausible (reason, &c.); (wahrscheinlich) likely (motive, &c.); sein ℈er Reichtum his fictitious (or make-believe) wealth; ast. ℈er Horizont apparent horizon; ~keit f ⚙ seemingness; appearance; speciousness; plausibility; likelihood.

Schein-behelf (ᴗ́ᴗ...) m ⚙ specious pretext, makeshift; =beweis m sham proof; =bild n delusion; (Schemen) phantom; =ding n imaginary (or fictitious) object, chimera; =ehe f fictitious marriage.

scheinen (ᴗ́ᴗ) [ahd.: shine] I v/n. (h.) ⚙ 1. to shine, to give light; (glänzen) to glitter; (blenden) to dazzle; (wärmen) to give off warmth or heat; der Mond, die Sonne scheint the moon, the sun shines or is shining; die Sonne scheint heiß ... is hot. — 2. (den Schein v. et. h.) to seem, to appear; sie ℈ reich zu sein od. es scheint, sie sind reich (od. als ob sie reich seien) they seem (or appear) to be rich, weniger bestimmt: it seems as though they were rich; er scheint ein braver Mensch (zu sein) he looks an honest fellow; wenn es Ihnen recht scheint if you deem it right, if you approve of it; das scheint nur so that's only an illusion, it only looks like that; das will mir nicht so ganz ℈ (einleuchten) I don't quite see (or understand) that; Sprichw. ein anderes ist ℈, ein anderes ist sein seeming and being (or appearance and reality) are (two) different things. — II ~ n ⚙ 3. (f. 1) shining; light, brilliancy; (f. 2) semblance, appearance, look of a. th.

Schein-freund (ᴗ́ᴗ...) m ⚙ false friend; =freundschaft f false (or pretended) friendship; =friede m hollow (or patched-up) peace; =fromm a. ⚙ shamming piety; vgl. ℈heilig; =frömmigkeit f sham piety, false devotion; (Heuchelei) hypocrisy; =frucht ℉ ⚙ collective fruit; =gefecht ⚔ n shamfight; =gelehrsamkeit f pseudo-learning, smattering (of knowledge); =geschäft ⚙ n fictitious bargain; =grund m fictitious (or apparent) reason, phls. sophism; (Vorwand) pretext; ℈heilig a. sanctimonious, canting, F saintly; (heuchlerisch) hypocritical; =heilige(r) s. hypocrite, F saint; =heiligkeit f sanctimoniousness, F saintliness; =kampf ⚔ m mock combat; =kauf m fictitious purchase; =körper m delusive body; vgl. =wesen; =krankheit f feigned (or sham, shammed) sickness; =krieg m mimic warfare; =leben n semblance of life, fig. useless existence; =quittung f sham receipt; =tod m semblance of death, suspended animation, trance, med.: ⚔ asphyxia(tion); ℈tot a. seeming(ly) dead, (lying) in a trance, fig., auch von Dingen: dead-alive; =verhör n mock trial; =vertrag m sham contract; =wechsel ⚙ m accommodation-bill; =welt f, etwa: world of visions or fictions; =werfer m: elektrischer ~ auf Schiffen ꝛc.: search-light; =wesen n imaginary (or fictitious) being; vgl. =bild. [shit, turd.

Scheiß-dreck P (ᴗ́.ᴗ́) m ⚙ unanständig.

Scheiße P (ᴗ́ᴗ) f ⚙ unanst. shit, human excrements pl.; **scheißen** (ᴗ́ᴗ) (h.) und v/a. ⚙a. to shit; **Scheißerei** (ᴗᴗᴗ́) f ⚙ shitting; (Abführen) diarrhoea.

Scheiß-haus (ᴗ́...) n ⚙ unanst. = Abtritt 2; =kerl m nasty (or cowardly) fellow.

Scheit (ᴗ́) [ahd.; *scheiden] n ⚙ ④c.: ~ Holz log (or piece) of wood, billet; (Brettchen) thin board; (Splitter) splinter; zu ~ern gehen = scheitern.

Scheitel (ᴗ́ᴗ) [ahd.; *scheiden] m ⚙, a. f ⚙ 1. crown (or top) of the head, ⚔

Signs (see page XVII): F familiar; P vulgar; ℉ flash; ⚲ rare; † obsolete (died); * new word (born); ₊₊ incorrect; ♪ music;

[Scheitelabstand] — 835 — [schenken]

Scheitel; vom ~ bis zu den Fußsohlen from top to toe, from head to heels or foot; den ~ betreffend, zum ~ gehörig vertical. — 2. *geom.* e-s Winkels: vertex; *math.* (Ausgangspunkt der Koordinaten einer Kurve) origin. — 3. (Teilung des Haupthaares) parting of the hair.

Scheitel-abstand (ⁿ...) *m* ⊕ *ast.* zenith-distance; **-bein** *n*, *anat.*: ⚔ parietal bone; **-fläche** *f* vertical plane; **-haar** *n* top-hair; **-käppchen** *n* little cap covering the crown of the head, *auch*: skullcap; **-kreis** *m* vertical circle, *ast.*: ⚔ azimuth; **-lini-e** *f*, *ast.* Zeichnen: vertical line.

scheiteln (¹⌣) *v/a.* und sich ² *v/refl.* ⊕ a. die Haare ² to part the hair, to make a parting; von den Haaren: sich ² to form a parting, to part.

Scheitel-punkt (ⁿ⌣...) *m* ⊕: a) (*ant.* Fußpunkt): ⚔ vertex, *ast.* auch: zenith; a. = Scheitel 2; b) *fig.* (Gipfelpunkt) apex; **-recht** *a.* ⊕ (senkrecht) vertical; **-winkel** *m/pl.*, *math.* vertical and opposite angles *pl.*

Scheiter-haufe(n) (ⁿ⌣⌣) [Scheit] *m* ⊕ (funeral) pile, pyre; für Lebende: stake; auf dem ~ hinrichten, verbrennen to burn at the stake.

scheitern (¹⌣) [Scheit] I *v/n.* (ſn u. h.) ⊕ a. ⚓ (ſtranden) to run aground, to be stranded; (auf Klippen in Stücke gehen) to split on rocks, to be wrecked, to suffer shipwreck; (untergehen) to founder, to be lost, *fig.* to go to pieces or F to smithereens; to fail, to miscarry; *fig.* daran ſcheitert ſ-e ganze Kunſt it baffles him altogether, that's beyond him or his ability; geſcheitert frustrated (scheme), abortive (attempt). — II ~ *n* ⊕ running aground; shipwreck, foundering, *fig.* failure, miscarriage.

Scheit-holz (ⁿ...) *n* ⊕ wood in logs or billets, logs *pl.* of wood; **-recht** *a.* ⊕ *arch.* (geradlinig) forming a straight line.

Schelch (⌣) *m*, *n* ⊕ b. (Boot) barge.

Schelde ♀ (⌣) *npr/f.* ⊕ die ~ (belgischer Fluß) the Shelde, the Scheldt.

Schelfe (⌣) [ahd.: shelf; *Schale¹] *f* ⊕ (Fruchthülſe, Schale) husk, shell.

Schellack (⌣) [ndd. Schalen-lack] *m* ⊕ c. (Harz des Gummilackbaumes) shellac.

Schelle (⌣) [ahd.; *ſchallen] *f* ⊕ 1. little bell, die zu Tiſche lädt: dinner-bell, in der Schule: school-bell, (Klingel) hand-bell, *bibl.* wie eine klingende ~ (1. Kor. 13, 1) as a tinkling cymbal; *vgl.* anhängen 1. — 2. ~ *n pl.* = Handfesseln. — 3. = Maulschelle. — 4. ~ *n¹ pl.* Farbe im Kartenspiel: diamond(s *pl.*).

ſchellen² (⌣) [mhd.; *Schelle] I *v/n.* (h.) ⊕ to ring (the bell), to pull the bell. — II ~ *n* ⊕ ringing (the bell), pull (or ring) of the bell, sound of a bell.

Schellen¹-baum ⚔ (⌣...) *m* ⊕ crescent; **-bube** *m* Karte: knave of diamonds; **-ente** *f*, *orn.* garrot; **-geläut(e)** *n*: a) (ringing (or tinkling) of bells; b) *coll.* (set of) bells, e-s Pferdes: bell-harness; an Schlitten: sleigh-bells *pl.*; *vgl.* Glockenſpiel; **-hals-band** *n* bell-collar; **-kappe** *f* fool's cap with bells; **-schlitten** *m* sledge with bell-harness; **-trommel** ♪ *f* tambourine; **-zug** *m* bell-pull or -wire.

Schell-fiſch (⌣⌣) [(nicht = shell-fish!) ndd., ndl. Schalenfiſch] *m* ⊕ a. *ichth.* haddock (*Gadus Aegleſinus*).

Schell-hengſt (⌣⌣) [ahd. scëlo = Zuchthengſt] *m* ⊕ a. stallion.

Schell-kraut (⌣⌣) [grch. *chelidō'n* Schwalbe] *n* ⊕ c. celandine (*Chelidonium majus*).

Schelm (⌣) [ahd. Peſtilenz] *m* ⊕ b., obb. ⊕, ~**in** *f* ⊕ 1. *b.s.* rogue; (Schurke) scoundrel, knave, (Böſewicht) villain, F bad one, P bad'un; ~**in** / female rogue; cunning woman, vixen, F huzzie; an e-m zum ~ werden to play a p. a knavish trick, to act the villain to a p.; ſ. Hans 2; Sprichw. auf einen ~ (gehören) anderthalbe pay rogues in their own coin; ein ~, der mehr gibt als er hat you cannot give more than you have; ein ~, der mehr tut als er kann you cannot do impossibilities; ein ~, der Schlechtes dabei denkt! (*fr.*) honni soit qui mal y pense; je größer (ob. je ärger) ~, je größer Glück the greater the rogue the greater his luck. — 2. (Ausdruck des Bedauerns) der arme ~ the poor fellow or F devil. — 3. *g.s.* = Schalk 2. — 4. = Schelmerei, *zB.*: *fig.* er hat einen ~ im Nacken ober hinter den Ohren he is a cunning rogue or a sly fellow or F an artful dodger (*vgl.* Schalk 3).

Schelmen-geſicht (⌣⌣...) *n* ⊕ knave's (or knavish) face; **-lied** *n* frivolous (or fast, F flash) song; **-pack** F *n* set of rogues; **-roman** *m* frivolous (or racy, F fast) novel; **-ſtreich** *m*, **-ſtück** *n* knavish (or roguish, villainous, base) trick; (Schurkerei) villainy.

Schelmerei (⌣⌣ⁿ) *f* ⊕ (Weſen eines Schelmes) roguery, knavery, villainy; ~ treiben to play the rogue or the knave.

ſchelmiſch (⌣⌣) [Schelm] *a.* ⊕ *g.s.* (ſchalkhaft) roguish, (durchtrieben) arch.

Schelm-ſtreich, **-ſtück** (⌣...) ſ. Schelmen-...

Schelpe (⌣) [ndd.] *f* ⊕, *mſt. pl.* ~**n** small shells *pl.* found on the beach.

Schelte (⌣) [ahd.; *ſchelten] *f* ⊕ scolding, (words of) reprimand; ~ bekommen to get a scolding or F a blowing-up or (a good) talking-to.

ſchelten (⌣) [ahd.: scold] I *v/a.*, *v/n.* (h.), *v/recip.* ⊕ c. 1. e-n wegen ſ-s Betragens (ober über ſein Betragen) ², j-s Betragen ² to scold (or blame, chide, ſtärker: rebuke, revile) a p. for his conduct; (heruntermachen) to reprimand, F to blow up, (ſchimpfen) to abuse; als *v/n.*: den ganzen Tag ² to be scolding all day long; auf e-n, et. ² to inveigh against (or to find fault with, F to run down) a p., a th. — 2. e-n einen Dummkopf oder als dumm ² to call a p. a blockhead or a duffer. — II ~ *n* ⊕ 3. scolding, rebuke; reprimand, abuse, invective.

Schelter (⌣) *m* ⊕ scolder, reviler.

Schelt-name (⌣...) *m* ⊕ nickname; **-rede** *f* diatribe, philippic; **-wort** *n* abusive term, invective.

Schema (¹⌣) [grch. Geſtalt] *n* ⊕ ⊕: a) (Muſter) model, pattern; ~ F (gedankenloſes Handeln nach der Vorſchrift) mere routine-work, mechanical drill; nach ~ F by rule of thumb; b) = Formular, *bſd.* 2; **-tiſch** (⌣ⁿ⌣) *a.* ⊕ schematic, in accordance with a certain model or formula; **-tiſieren** (⌣⌣ⁿ⌣) *v/a.* ⊕ to schematize; **~tismus** (⌣⌣ⁿ⌣) *m* ⊕ (Form[en]weſen; [Perſonal-] Verzeichnis) schematism; **~tiſt** (⌣⌣ⁿ) *m* schematist.

Schemel (¹⌣) *m* ⊕ *It. scamĕll-um n* ⊕ (niedriges Stühlchen) stool, für die Füße: footstool, gepolſterter: hassock.

Schemen (¹⌣) [mhd.: ſcheinen] *m* ⊕ phantom, (mere) shadow, delusion, *bibl.* vain show; **ſchemenhaft** (¹⌣⌣) *a.* ⊕ like a phantom, shadowy, delusive.

Schenk (⌣) [ahd.; *(ein)ſchenken] *m* ⊕. **~in** *f* ⊕ 1. cup-bearer. — 2. bar-keeper; *vgl.* Schankwirt(in).

ſchenkbar (⌣⌣) *a.* ⊕ 1. fit to be given away or to be presented. — 2. (Getränk) fit to be retailed, *weitS.* saleable.

Schenke (⌣) [mhd.; *ſchenken] *f* ⊕ ale- (or beer-) house, public-house, bar, inn, tavern, F pub, pot house, an der Landſtraße: half-way house.

Schenkel (⌣) [ahd.] *m* ⊕ 1. *anat.*: a) (Ober-)~ (bis zum Knie herab) thigh, ⚔ femur; b) (Unter-)~ shank; (Bein) leg; zum ~ gehörig: ⚔ femoral, crural; *man.* ſ. anſchließen 6. — 2. ⊕ shank, leg, side-piece, foot, e-s Hufeiſenmagnets: limb, ⚔ *artill.* ~ eines Hebezeugs: pry-pole, gin-cheek; ⚓ ~ (Tau-ende) pendant. — 3. *geom.* ~ eines Winkels side of an angle.

Schenkel-(blut)ader (⌣⌣...) *f* *anat.*: ⚔ femoral (or crural) blood-vessel; **-bruch** *m*: a) *surg.* fracture of the thigh(-bone); b) *path.* (Vorfall) femoral hernia; **-druck** *m* pressure of the thighs; **...ſchenk(e)lig** (...⌣⌣) *a.* ⊕ in Zſſgn mit *a.*, *zB.*: a) dick-² having big thighs; b) *math.* gleich-²: ⚔ isosceles.

Schenkel-knochen (⌣⌣...) *m* ⊕ *anat.* thigh-bone; **-muskel** *m*: ⚔ crural muscle; **-schlag-ader** *f*, *anat.*: ⚔ femoral (or crural) artery; **-zirkel** ⊕ *m* (pair of) compasses *pl.*

ſchenken (⌣⌣) [ahd. = einschenken] *v/a.* u. *v/refl.* ⊕ 1. a) to pour out; das Glas voll ² to fill the glass (to the brim); b) von Schankwirten: (reichen, verkaufen) to retail (alcoholic) liquor, to sell (at the bar), *abs.* to keep a bar or a public-house. — 2. (geben) to give a p. a th., als Geſchenk: to present a p. with a th., to make a p. a present of a th.; er hat es geſchenkt bekommen ob. F gekriegt he has had it as a gift, he has been presented with it; et. zu Weihnachten geſchenkt bekommen to get a th. as a Christmas-present (von Dienſtperſonen ꝛc.: as a Christmas-box); das Haus habe ich beinahe geſchenkt bekommen I bought the house for next to nothing or for a mere song; ich möchte es nicht geſchenkt h. I would not have it for a gift; e-m die Freiheit ² to bestow freedom upon a p., to give a p. his liberty, to set a p. free; ſ. Glaube 1; e-m das Leben ² to grant a p. his life, e-m Verurteilten: to pardon a p.; wenn Gott mir das Leben ſchenkt if God spare me, please God I am

⚔ scientific; ♣ botanical; ♀ geography; ⊕ machinery; ⚒ mining; ⚔ military; ⚓ marine; ⊕ commercial; ✉ postal; 🚂 railway.

[**Schenkenamt**] — 836 — [**Scheurer**]

spared; sich (selbst) et. 2 to treat o.s. to a th. — 3. (erlassen) to acquit a p. of a th.; e-m e-e Strafe für et. 2 to pardon a p. s.th., to let a p. off without punishment (for a th.); es soll dir diesmal geschenkt sein I'll let you off this time; es ist ihm nicht geschenkt he shall not be spared, he shall pay for it; Sprichw. f. Gaul. — II ~ n 23 4. presentation; f. Schenkung.

Schenken-amt (*....*) n 62 ehm. an Fürstenhöfen: cup-bearer's office.

Schenker (*....*) m 22, ~in f 40 giver, donor, p. who gives, &c. (f. schenken 2).

Schenk-gerechtigkeit (*....*) f 62 publican's license, vgl. Schank 1; =haus n = Schenke; =kanne f beer-can, pot, pint; =mädchen n, =mamsell F f bar-maid; =stube f tap-room, (public) bar; =tisch m bar; vgl. Büfett 1.

Schenkung (*....*) f 46: a) (das Schenken u. Geschenkte) donation; vgl. schenken II; b) (Geschenk) gift, present; reiche ~ rich gift, bsd. ehm. largess(e); ~s-akte (*....*) f 62, =brief m, =urkunde f jur. deed of donation; =weise adv. (F a. a.) by way of donation, (bestowed or received) as a gift.   [Schankwirt(schaft).

Schenk-wirt(schaft f) (*....*) m 62 = **Scher-baum** (*....*) m 62: a) Weberei: Garnbaum; b) Wagenbau: f. Schere 3.

Scherbe (*....*) [ahd.: scharf] f fragment (or piece) of glass, china, &c.; shard, potsherd; weitS. ~n pl. (Trümmer) debris sg. ob. pl.; = (Blumentopf) flower-pot.

Scher-becken (*....*) n 62 = Barbierbecken.

Scherbel prove. (*....*) m 22 = Scherbe.

Scherben-gericht (*....*) n 22 grch. Alt.: ostracism; =kobalt ⚔ m, min. native flaky arsenic, fly-powder.

Scherbett (*....*) [türk.: *ar. Trank] n ⓤc. (limonaden-artiges Getränk) sherbet.

Scher-beutel fast † (*....*) m 62 (barber's) shaving-bag or -case; =blatt n shearblade; =block m Seilerei: warping-block.

Schere (*....*) [ahd.: shears] f 8 1. (pair of) scissors pl., größere: shears pl., kleinere für die Nägel: nail-scissors pl. — 2. zo. ~ der Krebse, Skorpionen, Spinnen 2c.: claw. — 3. (Wagen-)~ (Gabeldeichsel) shafts pl. of a carriage, a cart, &c.; ↓ er-w Wage : fork.

scheren (*....*) [ahd.: shear, share] ⓐa. (⑧) I v/a. 1. to shear (or clip) sheep; fig. f. Schäfchen 1. — 2. e-m den Bart 2, e-n 2 to shave a p.; kurz geschoren closeshaven or -cropped; den Rasen 2 to clip the grass, to mow the lawn; fig. f. Kamm 1. — 3. ⊙: a) ⑧ ⓖ Fäden, Seile 2 (ausspannen) to warp ...; ↓ Taue: to extend, stretch; b) geschor(e)ner Sammet cut velvet. — 4. fig. (placken) to vex, torment, tease. — II sich 2 v/refl. 5. sich 2 (fortmachen) to run away, to slope (off); er soll sich zum Henker (ob. Teufel) 2 he may go to hell or P to blazes, let him go and be hanged or damned. — 6. sich um et. 2 (bekümmern) to trouble about a th., to attend (or pay heed) to a th.; sich um nichts 2d reckless, heedless; das sch(i)ert mich nicht (geht mich nichts an) that does not trouble me; was sch(i)ert mich das? what does that matter (or what's that) to me?

— III ~ n 23 7. der Schafe shearing; ⊙ des Tuches 2c. : warping.

scheren² ↓ (*....*) v/n. (jn) 88 (herankommen) to sheer up or alongside.

scheren²-artig (*....*) [pl. v. Schere] a. 66 scissorlike; =block ⊙ m 62 shear-block; =förmig a. scissor-shaped, zo.: 𝔠 forcipate(d); =futteral n scissor-case; =schleifer ⊙ m scissor-, shear- grinder; =schnabel m, orn. scissor(s) bill (Rhynchops); schwarzer ~ cutwater, skimmer.

Scherer ⊙ (*....*) [ahd.] m 22, ~in f 40 shearer, shearman, Weberei: warper.

Schererei (*....*) f 46 (f. scheren¹ 4) vexation, annoyance, worry; e-m viel ~ m. to give a p. much trouble, to cause a p. great bother; =en verursachend vexatious, bothersome.

Scherflein (*....*) [ahd. dim. v. Scherbe] n 23 mite; sein ~ beitragen to give (or throw in) one's mite.

Scherge † ob. fig. b. s. (*....*) [ahd.: *Schar¹] m ⓐ 1. (Polizei-, Gerichts-)diener constable, bailiff, ehm. catchpoll. — 2. = Henker.

Schergen-amt (*....*) n, =dienst m ⓐ of constable's (or bailiff's) office, duty.

Scherif (*....*) [ar. edel] m 50 (Od.) Titel der Nachkommen Mohammeds: sherif, shereef.

Scher-leine ↓ (*....*) f 8 reeving- (or hauling-)line; =maschine f 8 Tuchfabr.: shearing-machine; =maus obb. [ahd. scêro Maulwurf] f = Maulwurf; =messer n: a) ↘razor; b) der Gerber: shaving-knife or -tool; =rahmen m Weberei: shearing-frame; =stube ↘ f barber's shop; =tisch m Tuchmacher: shearing-table; =wange f f. Kloben 5; =wenzel 2c. [fr. servant] f. Scharwenzel 2c.; =wolle f shearings pl.

Scherz (*....*) [mhd.: *scherzen] m ⓐa. (ant. Ernst²) merriment, (Spaß) joking, joke, jest(ing); (Schäferei, Tändelei) sport, fun; quips and pranks, games, F larks pl.; (Neckerei) banter, chaff; ~ beiseite, ohne ~ all joking apart; aus ~, in ~, zum ~e in jest, in (or for) fun, by way of a joke, in a jocose (or laughable) way, facetiously; es war nur ~ it was only (my) fun; ~ mit e-m treiben, f-n ~ mit e-m h. to make sport (or game) of a p.; er kann keinen ~ verstehen he can't stand (or bear) a joke. — II ~ n 23 3. = Scherz; zB. das ist nicht zum ~ that's no joking matter.

Scher-zeug fast † (*....*) n (barber's) shaving-implements pl.; vgl. =beutel.

Scherz-gedicht (*....*) n 62 merry (or comic, humorous, jocular) poem.

scherzhaft (*....*) a. 66 (lustig, heiter) pleasant, merry, jovial; vgl. scherzliebend; (kurzweilig) funny, jocular, facetious, (komisch) comic(al), droll; ~igkeit (*....*) f jocularity, facetiousness, playfulness, waggishness, comicality, drollery.

scherz-liebend (*....*) a. 66 fond of (cracking) jokes, jocular, facetious, playful, frolicsome, waggish, F larky; =lied n 62 comic song; =macher m jester, joker, wag, a. humorist; =name m = Spitzname; =rätsel n humorous riddle; ²weise adv. jestingly, jocularly, in a jocose way, for (a bit of) fun, for a joke; =wort n word (spoken) in jest, a. facetious term or expression, joke.

Scheu¹ (*....*) [scheuen] f 46 (pl.~) shyness; timidity; nervousness, reserve, coyness; ohne ~ without the least fear; (schonungslos) unsparingly; ohne Scham und ~ unabashed; eine (heilige) ~ vor e-m, et. empfinden to have a (wholesome) dread (or fear) of a p., a th., to stand in (great) awe of a p., a th.

scheu² (*....*) [mhd.: shy] a. 66 shy, v. Pferden 2c.: skittish, (easily) shying, wild; (zaghaft) timid, timorous, faint-hearted, nervous; (ungesellig) retired, unsociable, (zurückhaltend) reserved, bashful, coy; 2 m. to startle, frighten, alarm; 2 w. to take fright, v. Pferden a.: to shy, (durchgehen) to run away, to bolt.

Scheuche (*....*) f 48 scarecrow (auch fig.).

scheuchen (*....*) [ahd.: shy, skew] v/a. 88 to scare, to frighten (away), to drive (or chase) away, to expel.

scheuen (*....*) [scheuchen] 88 I v/n. (h.) (scheu w.) to shy, to take fright (vor et. at a th.). — II sich 2 v/refl. sich vor e-m, et. 2 (fürchten) to be in dread (or fear) of a p., a th., (e-n, et. meiden) to fight shy of a p., a th.; to shun (or avoid) a p., a th. — III v/a. e-n, et. 2 = sich vor e-m, et. 2 (f. II.), keine Mühe 2 to spare no trouble or exertion; Sprichw. f. brennen 3; tue recht und scheue niemand do right and fear no one, (sH.) tell truth and shame the devil.

Scheuer¹ (*....*) [ahd.: Schauer²] f 48 1. (Scheune) barn. — 2. (Wetterschutz) shelter, (open) shed.

Scheuer²-besen ⊙ (*....*) [scheuern] m 62, =bürste f scrubbing-brush, hard brush; =faß n wash-up; =frau f scrubber, charwoman; =lappen m house-flannel, ↓ swab; =leiste ⊙ f an Möbeln 2c.: front ledge; =magd f = =frau; a. general servant.

scheuern (*....*) [ndd.: scour; *fr. e'curer] I v/a. u. sich 2 v/refl. ⓐa. 1. (hart reiben) das Hemd scheuert mich auf dem Rücken ober mir den Rücken wund ... chafes (or rubs the skin off) my back. — 2. (reinigen) to scour; Geschirr 2 to wash up crockery or china; den Fußboden 2 to scrub the floor. — II v/n. (h.) 3. das Hemd scheuert ... chafes the skin.

Scheuer²-papier ⊙ (*....*) n 62, =sand m scouring-paper, -sand; =stein m hearthstone; =tag m cleaning-up day; =¹tor n barn-door; =²tuch m, =wisch m = =lappen.

Scheu-klappe ⊙ (*....*) f 62, =leder n am Zaum des Pferdegeschirrs blinker, eye-flap.

Scheune (*....*) [ahd.] f 8 barn; hay-loft.

Scheunen-dach (*....*) n 62 barn-roof; =drescher m = Dresche; f. fressen 1; =tenne f thrashing-floor; =tor n barn-door, gate of a barn.

Scheurer (*....*) m 22, ~in f 40 scourer, scrubber; vgl. Scheuerfrau.

[Scheusal] — 837 — [Schiedsmann]

Scheusal (⌣-) [mhd.; *scheuen] n ⑭d. dreadful (or hideous) object, awful creature, F fright; stärker: monster.

scheußlich (⌣⌣) [mhd.; *scheuch(en)] a. ⑯ 1. dreadful, awful, horrid, horrible, frightful; hideous, ghastly; (widernatürlich) monstrous; (empörend) revolting, atrocious. — 2. fig. für ungemein; adv. das ist mir 2 unangenehm that's exceedingly annoying to me.

Scheußlichkeit (⌣⌣-) f ⑯ (s. scheußlich) dreadfulness, awfulness; als Tat: horrible deed, atrocity.

Schibboleth (⌣⌣-,⸗⸗⌣⌣)[hebr. Ähre, Jungfrau] n ⑭d. ⑳ (Erkennungswort, Losung; Buch der Richter 12, 5 u. 6) shibboleth.

Schicht (⌣) [mhd.: shift; *(ge)schehen] f ⑯ 1. (et. Ausgebreitetes) layer, bed (a. ⚒, geol., min. stratum (a. ♀ und zo.), e-r Flüssigkeit 2c.: film; ⊙ ~ Holz pile (or stack) of wood; fig. die breiten ~en des Volkes the great masses of the people; in den höchsten ~en in the highest walks of life, among the upper ten; die unteren ~en the lower orders or classes pl.; die verschiedenen ~en (Kreise) der Gesellschaft the different classes (or layers, ranks) pl. of society. — 2. ⚒, &c.: a)(bestimmte Arbeit[szeit]) shift, task, turn, job; in einer ~ without a break, at one stretch: b)(Pause) break, pause, rest, breathing-time; ~ m. to make a break, to stop working, F to knock off (work); fig. mit et. ~ m. to put an end to a th.; c) (sf. anfahrende Bergleute) shift, gang of pitmen or miners.

Schicht-arbeit ⊙ (⌣-...) f ⑫ shift, daywork, job-work, task-work; **=arbeiter** m workman paid by the job.

Schichte (⌣⌣) f ⑱ = Schicht 1.

schichten (⌣⌣) ⑯ I v/a. 1. (ordnen) to set in order; (in Schichten aufhäufen) to arrange (or put) in layers or strata or piles, geol.: ⚒ to stratify; nach Klassen: to classify; Holz 2 to stack wood; Meteorologie: geschichtete Federwolke: ⚒ strato-cirrus; geschichtete Haufenwolke: ⚒ strato-cumulus. — 2. ⊙ metall. to charge the furnace. — 3. ⚓ die Ladung 2 (unterbringen) to stow (away) the cargo. — II v/n. (h.) 4. von Menschen: (die Milchzähne verlieren) to lose one's teeth. — III ~ n ㉓ 5. s. Schichtung.

Schichten=bildung (⌣⌣-...) f ⑫ geol. bedding, ⚒ stratification; **=weise** adv. = schichtweise.

Schicht=gestein (⌣-...) n ⑫ min. stratified rock(s pl.); **=holz** n stacked wood; **=lohn** m pay for task-work; **=löhner** m = =arbeiter; **=machen** ⚒ n stopping (F knocking off) work; vgl. Schicht 2 b; **=meister** ⚒ m overseer of pitmen or miners.

Schichtung (⌣⌣) f ⑯ (s. schichten I) arrangement in layers; geol.: ⚒ stratification; nach Klassen: classification.

schicht=weise (⌣-...) adv. (F a. a. ⑯) in layers or strata or piles; **=wolke** f ⑫: ⚒ stratus; **=zahn** m milk-tooth.

Schick¹ (⌣) [mhd. Art und Weise] m ⑪c. 1. = Geschick 1 u. 2; außer ~ kommen to get out of order; et. wieder in ~ bringen to put a th. shipshape or to rights; er hat seinen richtigen ~ (Verstand) nicht he is not quite right in his mind. — 2. [fr. chic; *dtsch Schick] m ⑭ = Geschick 1 u. 2; ~ haben to be (quite) up to the mark, F up to date or up to the knocker; außer ~ kommen F to get old-fashioned; et. wieder in ~ bringen to put a th. in order.

schick² (⌣) [Schick¹ 2] a. ⑯ (meist prädikativ: elegant, fein) fashionable; stylish, swellish, (fr.) chic; das ist sehr 2 F that's very smart or swagger.

schicken (⌣⌣) [ndd.: (ge)schehen] ⑱ I v/a. 1. to send a th., a p. to a place, bsd. ✉ to forward (or dispatch, transmit) goods, &c. to a p., to a place; e-m Geld 2 to remit money to a p.; e-m Nachricht 2 to send a p. word; nach e-m 2 to send for a p. — 2. s. Hals 3 unter auf; e-n auf Reisen 2 to send a p. on (his) travels or on a tour; ein Pferd auf die Weide 2 to put a horse out to grass; s. April; e-n ins Parlament 2 (wählen) to return (or send) a p. to parliament; ein Buch in die Welt 2 to publish a book; e-n zum Henker (Kuckuck od. Teufel) 2 to tell a p. to go to hell or to the devil. — 3. = fügen 2. — II sich 2 v/refl. 4. (sich ereignen) to happen, to come to pass, unvermutet: to chance, zu gelegener Zeit: to come in the nick of time; (je) nachdem es sich schickt (just) as the case may be; wenn es sich gerade so schickt if things so shape themselves, if circumstances (will) allow it. — 5. sich für (od. zu) et. 2 (eignen) to be fit(ted) (or adapted, suitable) for a th.; (damit übereinstimmen) to agree (or harmonize, go well) with a th.; Sprichw.: eines schickt sich nicht für alle what suits one need not suit all, the same tune does not please everybody. — 6. = geziemen I; das schickt sich nicht that's not the proper thing (to do); auch v/impers. es schickt sich nicht (für Sie) zu // it is not becoming (or proper) for you to //, it does not behove you to //. — 7. (sich anschicken) to set about one's work, &c. — 8. sich in et. 2 to accommodate (or reconcile) o.s. to a th., to submit (or to resign o.s.) to a th.; sich in die Umstände 2 to adapt o.s. to circumstances; sich in die Zeit 2 to go with the times, b.s. to be a time-server. — III ~ n ㉓ 9. (s. 1) dispatch; s. Schickung.

schicklich (⌣⌣) a. ⑯ suitable, convenient; becoming, seemly, decent, decorous, proper; **~keit** (⌣⌣-) f ⑯ suitability, convenience; becomingness, seemliness, decency, decorum, propriety.

Schicklichkeits=gefühl (⌣⌣-⌣-) n ⑫ sense of propriety, (good) tact.

Schicksal (⌣-) [ndd.] n ⑭d. = Geschick 3; merkwürdige ~e marvellous adventures; bunt wechselnde ~e vicissitudes or shifting scenes. ups and downs) pl. of life.

Schicksals=fügung (⌣-...) f ⑫ = Schickung 2; **=gefährten, =genossen** m/pl. companions pl. in misfortune, fellow-sufferers pl.; **=glaube** m fatalism; **=göttinnen** f/pl. Destinies, Fates pl.; **=linie** f der Hand: line of Fate; **=prüfung** f sore trial, ordeal; visitation; **=schlag** m heavy blow; reverse; **=tragödie** f tragedy based on fatalism; **=tücke** f malice (or malignity, treachery) of fate; **=wechsel** m change of fortune; vicissitude(s pl.); **=wort** n decree of fate.

Schicksel F (⌣⌣) [jüd. schicksah Christenmädchen; *hebr. schikkus Greuel] n ㉓ Jew(ish) girl.

Schickung (⌣⌣) f ⑯ 1. = Geschick 3. — 2. bsd. rel. divine ordinance or decree; (Heimsuchung) affliction, tribulation; gütige ~ (Gottes, des Himmels) providential coincidence, divine dispensation.

schieb=bar (⌣-) ⑯ sliding, slidable.

Schieb(e)=barri=ere ⛟ (⌣...) f ⑫ sliding barrier; **=bühne** ⛟ f traverse-table; **=fenster** n sash-window.

schieben (⌣⌣) [ahd.: shove] ⑯ I v/a., v/n. (h. u. sn) u. v/refl. ⑯c. 1. to push, to shove; (gleiten l.) to slide, to slip; e-n Karren 2 to wheel a barrow. — 2. Redensarten: et. an die Stelle von et. anderem 2 to put s.th. in(to) the place of s.th. else; die Schuld auf e-n 2 to put the blame upon a p.; e-n, et. beiseite 2 to push (or thrust) a p., a th. aside or out of the way; e-n Stein im Dambrett aufs nächste Feld 2 to move a piece in draughts; der Vorhang hatte sich in die Höhe geschoben ... had moved (or shifted) up; et. in den Mund 2 to slip (or put) s.th. into one's mouth; e-m et. in die Schuhe 2 to lay a th. at a p.'s door, to charge a p. with a th.; vorwärts 2 to shove along, to push forward. — 3. Vagabunden (über die Grenze) 2 to take (or conduct) tramps across the frontier. — 4. zeitlich: von einem Tag auf den andern 2 to put off from day to day or from one day to the next; s. Bank¹ 3. — 5. F auf 2: a) sich weiter 2 to proceed slowly, to shuffle (or crawl) along; ⛟ v. Zügen beim Zs.=stoßen: sich in=ea.= 2 to be telescoped, to telescope; b) = drücken 8; vgl. ab 2 3. — 6. Kegelspiel: Kegel 2 to play (at) ninepins or bowls or skittles; alle neun 2 to throw all nine. — 7. ⓢ to be tricky or F smart. — II ~ n ㉓ 8. s. Schiebung.

Schieber (⌣⌣) m ⑫ 1. (auch ~in f ⑳) p. who pushes. — 2. ⊙ am Regenschirm: slider, runner, am Hochofen 2c.: slide, am Ofen: damper, in der Mühle: slide-plate, ⚔ am Geschütz: tangent-scale; typ. an der Setzmaschine: pusher; Bäckerei: (Ofenschaufel) oven-peel; Dampfmaschine: slide-valve; weitS. (Deckel) (sliding) lid; (Riegel) bolt, bar, fastener.   [pencil-case.)

Schiebe(r)=(blei)stift ⊙ (⌣-(⌣-)⌣) m ⑫)

Schiebe=ring (⌣-...) m ⑫ sliding ring, slide-index, slider; **=tür(e)** f sliding door; **=ventil** n, mach. sliding (or slide-)valve; **=wand** f sliding (or movable) panel or partition.

Schieb=karre(n m) f (⌣-...) ⑫ wheelbarrow, handbarrow; **=kasten** m drawer, chest of drawers; **=lade** f = Schub=l.; **=lehre** f slide- (or sliding-)gauge.

Schiebung (⌣⌣) f ⑯ pushing, &c. (s. schieben I); ⓢ b. s. sharp practices pl., v. Wechseln: kite-flying.   [scheiden.)

schied (⌣) ind., 2e (⌣⌣) subj. impf. v.)

Schieds=gericht (⌣-...) [mhd.: (ent)scheiden] n ⑫ court of arbitration; **=mann** m

♪ Musik; ⚒ Wissenschaft; ♀ Pflanze; ⚲ Geographie; ⊙ Technik; ⚒ Bergbau; ⚔ Militär; ⚓ Marine; ⚖ Handel; ✉ Post; ⛟ Eisenbahn.

[**Schiedsrichter**] — 838 — [**schießen**]

(Friedensrichter) justice of the peace (*abbr.* J. P.); **‑richter** *m* arbitrator, awarder, für Sport und Spiele: umpire, referee; ~ sein to (act as) umpire. **Schied(s)=spruch** (ʼ‑ᵁ‑) *m* ⑫ arbitration, award; umpire's decision; e‑n ~ fällen to arbitrate, to make an award. **schief** (ʼ)[ndd.: askew] *a.*⑥ **1.** (schräg) slanting, *adv. a.* aslant, askance, askew, (nicht senkrecht od. wagerecht) oblique (*a. math.; ant.* recht¹ 2); (abhängig, geneigt) inclined, sloping, shelving; (krumm, verdreht) uneven, crooked, onesided, wry, *adv. a.* awry; s‑e Stiefel 2 laufen ob. treten to tread (or wear) one's boots down at the heels, to run one's boots down on one side; 2 schreiben to write slantingly; ~e Ebene inclined plane, 🚂 gradient, der 2e Turm zu Pisa the leaning tower of Pisa; *math.* 2er Winkel oblique (or bevel) angle; 2 (*adv.*) stehen to (be on the) slant. — **2.** *fig.* 2e Ansicht distorted (or erroneous) view; in einer 2en Lage sein to be in a false position; e‑m ein 2es Maul machen to make wry faces at a p. — **3.** F meist *adv. et.* 2 (verkehrt) anfangen to begin a th. at the wrong end, to go the wrong way to work; s. Buckel² 2; es geht alles 2 bei ihm everything goes wrong with him; et. 2 (übel) nehmen to take a th. amiss; 2(=)gewickelt (falscher Ansicht) sein to be on the wrong track, F to be all at sea. **schief=beinig** (ʼ‑ᵁ‑) *a.*⑥ = krummbeinig. **Schief=blatt** ⚤ (ʼ‑ᵁ) *n* ⑫; ⚕ begonia. **Schiefe** (ʼ‑) *f* ⑱ (s. schief) slant; incline, sloping position; unevenness, crookedness, one‑sidedness; bsb. *ast., phys.* obliquity, *fig.* wrong‑headedness, warped (or misguided) judgment, perversity. **Schiefer** (ʼ‑)[ahd.: Schäbe, schaben] *m* ⑫ *min. u.* ⊕ (gemeiner, blauer) ~ (common) slate, (sich tafelförmig spaltendes Mineral): ⚕ schist; mit ~ decken to slate. **Schiefer=arbeiter** (ʼ‑ᵁ‑) *m* ⑫ slate‑cutter; **‑art** *f*, *min.* variety of slate or schist; **‑bank** *f* bed (or layer) of sl.; **‑blatt** *n* lamina (or thin plate) of sl.; **‑blau** *n*, 2 *a.* ⑥ sl.‑blue; **‑boden** *m* slaty (or schistous) soil; *vgl.* ‑erde; **‑bruch** *m* slate‑pit or ‑quarry or ‑works *pl.*; **‑dach** *n* slate (or slated) roof; **‑decker** *m* slater; **‑erde** *f* slate‑mould *vgl.* ‑boden; **‑farben**, **‑farbig** *a.* slate‑coloured; bluish grey; **‑gebirge** *n* sl.‑mountains *pl.*; **‑griffel** *m* = ‑stift; 2**haltig** *a.* slaty, schistous. **schief(e)richt** ⚲, mst **schief(e)rig** (ʼ(ᵁ)‑) *a.* ⑥ slaty, slate‑like, ⚕ schistous; (mit Schiefer gedeckt) slated, slate‑roofed. **Schiefer=kohle** (ʼ‑ᵁ‑ʼ‑) *f* ⑫ slaty coal. **schiefern** (ʼ‑) **I** *v/n.* (h.) *u.* sich 2 *v/refl.* ⓐ *a.*: (sich) 2 to come off in layers or scales, to scale off, ⚕ to exfoliate. — **II** ~ *n* ㉓ s. Schieferung. **Schiefer=nagel** ⊕ (ʼ‑ᵁ‑) *m* ⑫ der Schieferdecker: slate‑peg; **‑öl** *n* schist‑oil; **‑papier** ⚤ *n* sl.‑paper; **‑platte** *f* slab (or leaf) of slate; **‑schicht** *f*: ⚕ schistous stratum, *vgl.* ‑bank; **‑schwarz** *n u. a.* ⑥ slate‑back; **‑spat** *m* sl.‑spar; **‑stein** *m* sl.‑stone, schist; **‑stift** *m*

sl.(‑)pencil; **‑tafel** *f* §. Schreiben: sl.(‑)board, mehr gbr.: slate; *vgl.* ‑platte; **‑ton** *m* slate‑clay, schistous clay. **Schieferung** (ʼ‑ᵁ) *f* ⑯; ⚕ exfoliation. **Schiefer=wand** (ʼ‑ᵁ‑) *f* ⓕ rock of slate; **‑zahn** *m, vet.* slaty tooth. **schief=geladen** F (ʼ‑‑) *a.* ⑥ *fig.* (betrunken) tipsy, half‑seas over, *a.* full of liquor; **‑gewickelt** *a.*: a) wrapt up awry or the wrong way; b) *fig.* s. schief 3; **‑halsig** *a.* wry‑necked. — 2**=Schiefe**. **Schiefheit** (ʼ‑), **Schiefigkeit** (ʼ‑ᵁ‑) *f* ⑯ **Schief=kopf** (ʼ‑ᵁ‑) *m* ⑫ F *fig.* wrongheaded p.; 2**liegend** *a.* ⑥ on an incline; 2**mäulig** *a.* wry‑mouthed or faced. **schiefricht**, ...**ig** (ʼ‑) *f.* schieferricht. 2**‑rund** (ʼ‑ᵁ‑) *a.* ⑥ (fr.) baroque. **‑segeln** ⚓ *n* ⑫: ⚕ loxodromic sailing; **‑steg** *m, typ.* inclined quoin; **‑steh(e)n** *n* slanting posture or position; **‑werden** ⊕ *n* des Holzes: warping; 2**wink(e)lig** *a., math.* oblique‑angled. **Schiel=auge** (ʼ‑ᵁ‑) *n* ⑫ squint‑ (or cross‑) eye, F boss eye, ⚕ strabismus; 2**äugig** *a.* ⑥ squint‑eyed, F boss‑eyed. **schielen** (ʼ‑) [ahd.: *scheel] **I** *v/n.* (h.) ⑯ to squint, to be cross‑eyed; leicht 2 to have a (slight) cast in one's eye; *fig.* auf (ob. nach) etwas 2 (verstohlen blicken) to cast furtive (or sly or longing) glances at a th., to leer at a th. — **II** ~ *n* ㉓ (s. I) squint(ing), cast in the eye, ⚕ strabism(us). — **III** 2d *p.pr. u. a.* ⑥ squinting, squint‑eyed, *path.*: ⚕ strabism(ic)al. **Schieler** (ʼ‑) *m* ⑫, **~in** *f* ⑱ squinter, squinting p., squint‑ (or boss‑) eye. **Schiel=operation** (ʼ‑ᵁ‑‑tsjʼᵁ‑) *f* ⓕ *surg.*: ⚕ strabotomy. **Schiemann** ⚓ (ʼ‑ᵁ) [ndd.] *m* ⑫. auf holländischen Schiffen: boatswain's mate; **~s=garn** (ʼ‑ᵁ‑ᵁ) *n* ⑫ spun twine or yarn. **schien**¹ (ʼ) *ind. impf.* von scheinen. **Schien=bein** (ʼ‑ᵁ‑) [Schiene¹] *n* ⑫ *anat.* shin‑bone, ⚕ tibia; **‑bein‑bruch** *m, surg.* fracture of the shin‑bone or tibia. **Schiene**¹ (ʼ‑) [ahd.: shin] *f* ⓛ **1.** *surg.* zum Schutz verletzter Glieder: splint; in eine ~ legen to put a broken arm, &c. in a splint, *carp.* ~n einer Jalousie slats of a Venitian blind. — **2.** ⊕ Bauwesen: (Reif, Band) iron hoop or band, tire, tyre; Guß: bar. — **3.** 🚂 rail, *pl.* auch: metals; Lauffläche einer ~ upper surface of a rail; ~ e‑r Zahnradbahn rack‑rail; ~n legen (aufreißen) to lay down (to tear up) rails, aus den ~n kommen to run (or get) off the rails, to leave the metals, to derail; e‑n Zug auf den ~n fahren lassen to run a train on the metals. [scheinen. **Schiene**² (ʼ‑) *subj.*, 2n¹ *pl. impf.* von] **schienen**² (ʼ‑) *v/a.* ⑥ (s. Schiene¹) **1.** *surg.* (put in a) splint, to put in(to) splints. — **2.** ⊕ ein Rad 2 to tire (or tyre) a wheel. — **3.** 🚂 to furnish with rails, to lay down rails on a road, &c. **Schienen=bahn** ⊕ 🚂 (ʼ‑ᵁ‑) [Schiene] *f* ⓕ track, permanent way, weitS.: = Eisenbahn; **‑breite** *f* (broad, narrow, &c.) gauge; **‑eisen** ⊕ *n* iron in bars for tires, rails, &c.; **‑feger** *m* = ‑räumer; **‑kreuzung** *f* crossing of rails; **‑lasche** *f* fish‑plate; **‑leger** *m* rail‑ (or track‑)

plate‑)layer; **‑netz** *n* railway system; **‑räumer** *m* cow‑catcher, track‑sweeper or ‑clearer; **‑stoß** *m* joint; **‑strang** *m* track(‑way), railway‑line; **‑strecke** *f* line (of rails); **‑stuhl** *m* railway‑chair; **‑weg** *m* = ‑bahn; **‑weite** *f* gauge (of) **schier**¹ (ʼ) *f* *imper.* von scheren. [way). **schier**² (ʼ) [ndd.: scharf] *adv.* = fast, beinahe, z.B. er hätte 2 das Leben eingebüßt he all but (or he very nearly) lost his life; 2 dreißig Jahre bist du alt close upon thirty thou art now. **schier**³ (ʼ)[ndd.: sheer; *scheinen] **I** *a.* ⑥ sheer, pure; (schmuck) neat, tidy; das ist eine 2e Unmöglichkeit, das ist 2 unmöglich that's quite (or clearly) impossible. — **II** ~(**=tuch** ⑫) *n* &c. lawn. **Schier=apparat** ⊕ *m* ⑫ zum Durchleuchten v. Eiern: apparatus for candling eggs. **Schierling** ⚤ (ʼ‑) [ahd.: schott. sharn Mist] *m* ⑫d. a) echter ~ hemlock, spotted cowbane (*Coni'um macula'tum*); b) (Wasser‑) ~ water‑hemlock (*Cicu'ta viro'sa*). **Schierlings=becher** (ʼ‑ᵁ‑) *m* ⑫ cup of hemlock; *vgl.* Gift‑; **‑silge** ⚤ *f* hemlock‑parsley (*Conioseli'num tata'ricum*); **‑tanne** ⚤ *f* hemlock‑spruce (*Tsuga Canade'nsis*). **schierst, schiert** (ʼ) *pres. ind.* v. scheren. **Schieß=arbeit** ⚒ (ʼ‑ᵁ‑) [ndd.] *m* ⑫ (Sprengarbeit) blasting‑work; **‑ausbildung** ⚔ *f* der Inf.: musketry‑ (or der Artill. gunnery‑) drill; **‑bahn** *f* ⚔ *artill.* range; verdeckte ~ shooting‑gallery. **schießbar** (ʼ‑) *a.* ⑥ within gunshot or range of a gun, that can be shot at. **Schieß=baumwolle** ⊕ *u.* ⚔ (ʼ‑ᵁ‑) *f* ⓕ Sprengstoff: gun‑cotton, ⚕ pyroxylin(e), trinitro‑cellulose; **‑bedarf** ⚔ *m* ammunition (of war); **‑bereich** ⚔ *m* range. **schießen** (ʼ‑) [ahd.: shoot (scoot)] ⓒ(e)st. **I** *v/a. u. v/n.* (h.) mst mit Schußwaffen: **1.** to shoot (with a gun), to aim (or take) a shot, to fire (auf et., nach et. at a th.); to discharge a gun or an arrow; Fußballspiel: to shoot; daneben 2, vorbei 2 to miss in shooting or firing); s. Bresche, scharf 7b; tot2 to kill a p. with a shot or a bullet, to shoot a p. dead; hinterrücks auf e‑n 2 F to pot (⚔ auch to snipe) at a p.; sich (*dat.*) eine Kugel durch den Kopf 2 to blow out one's brains, to blow one's brains out; e‑m (oder e‑n) in den Arm 2 to shoot a p. in the arm; e‑m eine Kugel in die Brust 2 to fire (or send) a bullet through a p.('s chest); s. Flug 1; in Grund u. Boden 2 to demolish (or to batter down, ⚓ to sink) by firing; nach der Scheibe 2 to shoot at the target; den Vogel ꝛc. von der Stange 2 to knock (or bring) ... down with a shot; e‑n lahm, **zum** Krüppel 2 to lame, to cripple a p. (for life) with a shot; s. Scheibe 3. — **2.** *abs.* ⚔ unaufhörlich 2 to keep up an incessant fire; wie weit 2 die Kanonen? how far do the guns carry?; *hunt.* vor Hunden 2 to shoot over dogs; *fig.* nach e‑m Blick auf e‑n 2 to cast (or dart) a swift glance at a p.; s. Bock 5; fehlgeschossen! there you are wrong!; F 2 Sie los! speak up, F fire away!, go ahead! — **II** *v/n.* (sn) **3.** *fig.*: a) (sich schnell bewegen) to

Signs (see page XVII): F familiar; P vulgar; ⌐ flash; ⚲ rare; † obsolete (died); * new word (born); ⁺⁺ incorrect; ♪ music;

[Schießer] — 839 — [Schiffswesen]

shoot (or rush, run, hurry) along; to dart, to dash, v. Wasser ꝛc. a. to gush; **auf** et. **herab** (sich stürzen) to swoop (or pounce) down upon a th.; ein Gedanke schoß mir **durch** (ob. in) den Kopf a thought flashed through my mind; **in Ähren** (vom Korn) to (put on the) ear; in Blätter, Samen to run to leaf, to seed; das Blut schoß ihr ins Gesicht the blood rushed to her face; **in die Höhe** to shoot (or spring) up (auch v. Bäumen u. Pflanzen); (rasch wachsend) a. to grow (or sprout) rapidly; b) (plötzlich zum Vorschein kommen) to appear (all) of a sudden. — 4. **lassen** to let fly or go, ⊕ Kabel: to pay out; *fig.* e-n lassen (aufgeben) to give up (F to cut) a p.; seinen Begierden den Zügel lassen to give rein (or full licence) to one's passions. — III v/a. 5. s. Purzelbaum. — 6. F (entwenden) to filch, F to nick. — 7. ⊕ Bäckerei: Brot in den Ofen to shove a batch of bread into the oven. — 8. ⚓ den Ballast ins Schiff to ballast the ship. — **IV sich** v/refl. u. v/recip. 9. to fight a duel with pistols. — **V** ~ **n** ㉓ 10. (s. I) shooting, firing, discharge (or report) of a gun or of guns, ⚔ mit Gewehren: musketry-fire, mit Kanonen: artillery-fire; (s. II) shooting, &c. along; rush.

Schießer ( ) m ㉒ shooter; ⚒ (Sprenger) blasting miner.

Schießerei (-) f ㊻ incessant shooting, *b.s.* bad (or indifferent) firing, aimless (or useless) shooting.

Schieß=geld (...) n ㉗ huntsman's remuneration; ⚒ pay for blasting (-operations); **=gerechtigkeit** f right of shooting (over an estate); **=gewehr** n gun, fire-arm; *fig.* mit (dem) ~ **spielen** to play with fire-arms or edge-tools; **=haus** n = **=hütte**; **=hund** m pointer, setter; F *fig.* aufpassen wie ein ~ to listen with great attention, to be all ears; **=hütte** f huntsman's shelter or shed, shooting-box; **=instruktion** ⚔ f (manual of) musketry-instruction; **=loch** n: a) = **=scharte**; b) beim Sprengen: blast-hole; **=patrone** f cartridge; **=plan**, **=platz** ⚔ m shooting-, practice-ground(s pl.), butts pl.; vgl. **=bahn**; **=prügel** m F *fig.* (Flinte) shooting-iron; **=pulver** n gun-powder; **=scharte** ⚔ f loop-hole, embrasure; **=scheibe** f = **Scheibe** 3; **=schule** ⚔ f gunnery-school, school of musketry; **=stand** m shooting-stand, rifle-range; vgl. **=plan**; **=übung** f shooting- (or gun-, rifle-, target-) practice (auch ⚔); **=versuch** m ⚔ u. ⚒ shooting trial; **=vorschrift** f shooting-regulations pl.; **=wolle** f = **=baumwolle**; **=zeit** f shooting-season.

Schiff ( ) [ahd.: ship] n ⊕ b. 1. ⚓ ship, vessel, kleineres: craft; *coll.* ~e, a. shipping; zu ~ versenden to send by boat or by water; zu ~e geh(e)n to take (or to join a) ship, to go on board (ship), to embark. — 2. *arch.* ~ (mittlerer Raum) e-r Kirche: nave. — 3. *anat.* = **Schiffchen** 2 a. — 4. ⊕ (Gefäß) boiler in a kitchener, &c.; Brauerei: s. **Kühlschiff**. Weberei: shuttle, *typ.* (Setz=)~ galley.

Schiffahrer ⚓ ( ) [Schiff=fahrer] m ㉒ seaman, sailor, navigator, mariner, seafaring man. [navigation.)

Schiffahrt ⚓ ( ) [Schiff=fahrt] f ㊺

Schiffahrts=akte (...) f ㊽ navigation-act; **=gesetze** n/pl. navigation-laws pl.; **=kunde** f nautical science, nautics.

schiffahrt=treibend (...) a. ㊻: (es Volk) seafaring (people).

schiffbar ⚓ ( ) a. ㊻ navigable; **~keit** (...) f㊻ navigability, navigableness.

Schiffbar=machung (...) f ㊺ durch Kanäle: canalization.

Schiff=bau ⚓ (...) m ㊷ ship-building, naval architecture or construction; **=bauer** m: a) ship-builder, ship-wright; b) naval architect or constructor; **=bau=hof** m ship-building yard, dockyard, der Marine auch: navy-yard; **=bau=holz** n timber for ship-building, ship-timber; **=bau=kunst** f = **=bau**; **=bau=meister** m = **=bauer** b; **=bau=platz** m = **=bauhof**; **=bau=technisch** a.: e Gesellschaft Institution of Naval Architects; **=bau=werkstätte** f ship-building yard; **=bau=wesen** n ship-building department; **=blech** n ship-sheathing; **=bruch** m shipwreck; ~ leiden to suffer shipwreck, to be shipwrecked or cast away; **brüchig** a. shipwrecked; **=brüchige[r]** (m) f shipwrecked p., castaway; **=brücke** f bridge of boats, floating bridge; vgl. Ponton.

Schiffchen ( ) n ㉓ (*dim.* v. Schiff) 1. ⚓ small ship or vessel or craft or boat; skiff, cutter, yacht. — 2. a) *anat.* des Ohres: ⚡ scapha; b) ♀ der Schmetterlingsblütler: keel, ⚡ carina. — 3. ⊕ Weberei: shuttle. [fly-shuttle race.)

Schiffchen=galerie ⊕ (...) f ㊷ Weberei

schiffen ( ) ⊕ **I** v/n. 1. (sn) ⚓ (zur See fahren) to navigate, to go (or travel) by ship; von H. nach E. to cross (or sail, steam) from H. to E. — 2. F (h.) (harnen) to pump ship, to make water. — **II** ⚓ v/a. 3. (zu Schiff hinschaffen) to ship, to convey by ship or by water. — **III** ⚓ ~ **n** ㉓ 4. (s. I) navigation; (s. II) shipment.

Schiffer ⚓ ( ) m ㉒ mariner; (Schiffsführer, kapitän) master;(Fluß=) boatman, bargee, waterman; weiteS. — Schiffseigentümer; *pl.* oft = Schiffsleute.

Schiffer=ausdruck ⚓ (...) m ㉒ nautical term, boatman's expression; **=hosen** f/pl. sailor's trousers, F slops pl.; **=inseln** ♀ npr/f/pl. = Samoa; **=knabe** m boatman's boy; **=knoten** m sailor's knot; **=lied** n waterman's song; **=sprache** f nautical language.

Schiff=fahrer, **=fahrt**, **=förmig** = Schiffahrer, Schiffahrt, schifförmig.

Schiff=hebewerk (...) n ㊷ machinery for raising (sunken) vessels.

Schifflein ⚓ ( ) n ㉓ = Schiffchen.

Schiff=leine ⚓ (...) f ㊷ (Fangleine) ship's painter, zum Ziehen: tow-line; **=mann** [mhd.] m mariner, sailor; s. a. Schiffsleute, =mannschaft; **=mühle** ⊕ f (ant. Pfahlmühle) ship-mill.

schiffförmig (...) [schiff=förmig] a. ㊻ boat-shaped, ♀, &c.: ⚡ navicular, naviform, cymbiform. [in ships or shipping.)

schiff=reich (...) a. ㊻ rich (or abounding)

Schiffs=angelegenheiten ⚓ (...) f/pl. ㊷ shipping-concerns pl.; **=arzt** m ship's doctor or surgeon; **=ballast** m ship's ballast; **=bau** ꝛc. s. Schiffbau ꝛc.; **=bedarf** m ship-chandlery; **=befrachter** m freighter; **=befrachtung** f ship's freight; **=bekleidung** f planking; **=besatzung** f = **=mannschaft**; **=beschlag** m sheathing, metal casing; **=beute** f prize; **=boden** m ship's bottom or hold; =(**bohr**)**wurm** m, *ent.* bore- (or ship-)worm (*Teredo navalis*); **=boot** n: a) long-boat; b) *zo.* nautilus; **=breite** f breadth of beam; **=brief** m: a) ⚐ ship-letter; b) v. Binnenschiffen: = register; **=dienst** m duty on board; **=eigentümer**, **=eigner** m ship-owner; **=flagge** f flag of a ship; **=fracht** f ship's freight; **=fracht=brief** m bill of lading; **=führer** m s. Schiffer; **=gelegenheit** f shipping opportunity; **=gerät** n ship's rigging; **=gerippe** n ship's carcass; **=geschütz** n, *coll.* ship's guns pl.; **=geschwader** n (naval) squadron; **=grund** m sink (or lowest part) of a ship; **=hafen** m grappling-hook or -iron; **=halter** m, *ichth.* ship-stayer, sucker (*Echeneis*); **=herr** m ship-owner; **=hinterteil** m, n stern, poop; **=journal** n log-book, ship's journal; **=junge** m cabin-boy; **=kanone** f cannon on board a ship; **=kapitän** m ship's captain, e-s kleineren Fahrzeugs: skipper; vgl. Schiffer; **=kessel** m ship's boiler; **=kiel** m keel; **=knecht** m bargee, bargeman; **=koch** m ship's cook; **=kompaß** m ship's compass; **=küche** f (ship's) cook-room; **=kurs** m s. Kurs 2; **=lader** m loader of a ship; **=ladung** f cargo, shipment; **=last** f: a) ship-load; b) (2000 Kilogramm) etwa: last; **=laterne** f ship's lantern; **=lauf** m ship's run; **=lazarett** n sick-bay; **=leute** pl. v. Schiffsmann; **=licht**(**er** pl.) n ship's light(s pl.); **=lieferant** m ship-chandler; **=luken** f/pl. ship's hatches or hatchways pl.; **=maat** m shipmate; **=mäkler** m ship-broker; **=mannschaft** f ship's company or crew; **=maschine** ⊕ f marine engine; **=mühle** ⊕ f = Schiffmühle; **=offizier** m ship's officer; **=papiere** n/pl. ship's papers; **=part** m share in a ship; **=partner** m part-owner of a ship; **=patron** m master of a ship, skipper; **=pech** n common black pitch for ships; **=proviant** m = **=vorräte**; **=raum** m ship's hold; **=reeder** m ship-owner; **=register** n ship's register; **=rolle** f der Handelsschiffe: = Musterrolle; **=rumpf** m ship's hull; **=rüstung** f equipment of a ship; **=schnabel** m: a) cutwater (or prow) of a ship; b) Alt. (it.) rostrum; **=schraube** f ship- (or screw-)propeller, screw; **=soldat** m marine; **=spiegel** m stern; **=spur** m Kielwasser; **=tau** n cable, hawser; **=tauwerk** n rope-work, cord-age; **=treppe** f hatchway; vgl. Kajüten=treppe; **=vermieter** m charterer; **=vermietung** f chartering; **=verzeichnis** n shipping-list; **=volk** n = **=mannschaft**; **=vorderteil** m, n bow, prow; **=vorräte** m/pl. stores (or provisions) pl. of a ship; **=wache** f ship's watch; **=wanten** f/pl. shrouds pl.; **=werft** f ship-builder's yard; vgl. Schiffbauhof; **=wesen** n

⚡ scientific; ♀ botanical; ⚲ geography; ⊕ machinery; ⚒ mining; ⚔ military; ⚓ marine; commercial; ⚐ postal; 🚂 railway.

[Schiffswinde] — 840 — [Schindel]

shipping (-concerns pl.); =winde f capstan; =zimmermann m ship-carpenter, shipwright; =zoll m freightage, lastage; =zertifikat n ship's register; =zwieback m ship-biscuit.

Schi-it(-ˊ) [ar.] m ⊕ (ant. Sunnit)Shiite.

Schikane (⸗⸍⸍) [nhd.; *fr. chicane] f ⊕ (Rechtskniff, böswillige Ränke) chicanery, vexatious trick(ery), underhand dealings pl. or work.

schikanieren (⸗⸍⸍⸌) [fr.] ⊕ I v/a. to vex, annoy, play tricks upon. — II v/n. (h.) to deal in an underhand manner.

schikanös (⸗⸍⸌) a. ⊕(D 10) vexatious.

Schild (ˊ) [ahd.: shield] 1. m ⊕b.: a) × shield (auch ⊕, ⚹), kleiner: buckler, zum Turniere: tilting-shield; b) her. (~ im Wappen, a. Wappen) escutcheon, coat-of-arms; einen Löwen im ~ führen to bear (als Beiwert: to quarter) the lion in one's coat-of-arms; vgl. führen 3; c) zo. shield, ↻ scutum, scute. — 2. [nhd.] n ⊕b. (Zeichen des Gewerbes)bsd. ehm.: sign-(or shop-)board, jetzt meist: (painted) board, name of the firm, messingenes ꝛc. ~ an der Tür: brass plate, door-plate; ~ von Kofferträgern ꝛc.: ticket, badge; ⚫ das ~ aushängen to open business or a shop.

Schild-abteilung (ˊ…) f ⊕ her. quartering; =assel f, zo. shield-centiped (Scutigera); =blume ⚹ f shell-(or tortoise-)flower (Chelo'ne); =bürger m: a) urspr. (alberner Mensch) duffer; ungedeutet auf die Bürger von Schilda (jetzt Schildau) bei Torgau: burgess of Schilda, Gothamite, …ist; =bürger-streich m, =bürgertum n. ct.: silly action, folly.

Schildchen (ˊ) [Schild, dim.] n ⊕ small shield or buckler, bsd. zo.: ↻ scutellum.

Schild-dach × (ˊ…) n ⊕ Alt.: tortoise, ↻ testudo; =drüse f, anat.: ↻ thyroid gland. [Zeugdruck: pencil-blue.]

=blau ⊕ (ˊ…) [Schild] n ⊕ ⌐

Schilderei (ˊ⸍⸌) f ⊕ painting; picture.

Schild(e)rer (ˊ⸍⸌) m ⊕ 1. person who describes, delineator, descriptive writer. — 2. ⊕ (Färber) dyer.

Schilder=haus × (ˊ⸍⸌) [schildern 3] n ⊕ sentry-box. [Aufstand) armed rising.]

Schilder-erhebung (ˊ⸍⸌) f ⊕ (bewaffneter)

Schilder-maler ⊕ (ˊ…) m ⊕ sign-painter; =malerei ⊕ f sign-painting.

schildern (ˊ⸍) [nhd. (* nbl.); * Schild 1] ⊕ a. I v/a. 1. urspr. ⊕ (sonst †) (färben, malen) to colour, dye, paint. — 2. fig. (durch Worte darstellen) to describe, delineate, depict, sketch, portray. — II v/n. (h.) 3. × † = Schildwache (s. d. b) stehen. — III ~ n ⊕ 4. = Schildern 1.

Schild(e)rung (ˊ⸍⸌) f ⊕ 1. (das Schildern) description, delineation, sketching, portraiture.—2.(Geschildertes)(descriptive) sketch, picture, graphic account.

Schild=farn ⚹ (ˊ…) m ⊕ shield-fern (Aspi'dium); ⚹förmig a. ⊕ sh.-shaped, ↻ clypeiform, …eate, ⚹ scutiform, scutellate, scutate, von Blättern auch: peltate(d); =halter m: a) =knappe, b) her. supporter; =käfer m, ent. shield-slater, tortoise-beetle (Ca'ssida); ⚹kiemig a. ichth. sh.-gilled; =knappe, =knecht m sh.-bearer, squire; =knorpel

m, anat.: ↻ thyroid cartilage; ⚹köpfig a. zo. sh.-headed; =krot n ⓜd. tortoise shell; =kröte f, zo. tortoise (Ordnung Chelo'nia); (See-) ~turtle (Testu'do, Chelo'nia, &c.); ⚹kröten-artig a.: ↻ testudinal, …eous, …arious; =kröten-schale f tortoise-shell; =kröten-suppe f turtle-soup; =laus f, ent. shield-louse, cochineal (Coccus); ehm. =lehen n knight's fief or fee entailing services in war (-time); =mauer f, arch. thin wall between two pillars [patt [nbd. Padde = Kröte] ⚫ n ⓜc. tortoise-shell; =patt-kamm m shell-comb; =patt-klauen f/pl. tortoise-hoofs pl.; =patt-knopf m shell-button.   [Schildner, Schildnerung.]

Schildrer (ˊ⸍), Schildrung (ˊ⸍) m ⊕ f.]

Schild=stern (ˊ…) m ⊕ zo. (Art See-igel) ↻ clypeaster; =tierchen n, zo. shield-animalcule (Aspidi'sca); =träger m =knappe; =wache × f: a) einzelner Soldat: sentinel, sentry, zu Pferde: mounted sentry; b) a. =wacht (Wachtdienst) sentry-go; ~ stehen to stand sentry; =wach= platt=form ⚹ f auf Kriegsschiffen: sentry-board; =zapfen ×, artill. trunnion; =zapfen= lager n trunnion - hole; =zapfen-pfanne f trunnion-plate.

Schilf (ˊ) [ahd.] n (m) ⓜb. reed (Phragmi'tes, Aru'ndo); vgl. Binse, Ried.

schilf-artig ⚹ (ˊ…) a. ⊕ reed-like, rush-like, ↻ arundin(ac)eous; ⚹be= kränzt a. crowned with reeds; =dach n ⊕ roof thatched (or covered) with reed(s); =decke f rush-mat.

Schilfe ꝛc. s. Schelfe ꝛc.   [(Carex).]

Schilf=gras ⚹ (ˊ⸌) n ⊕ sedge(-grass)

schilfig (ˊ⸌) a. ⊕ grown (or covered) with reeds, sedgy, a. = schilf-artig, ⚹reich.

Schilf=klinge ⊕ (ˊ…) f ⊕ two-edged hollow-ground blade; =meer n: a) allg. sea (densely) grown with reed; b) ⚹ bibl. npr. Red Sea; ⚹reich a. ⊕ abounding in reeds or rushes, reedy; =rohr n = Schilf.

Schiller (ˊ⸍) m ⊕ 1. changeable (or shot-)colour, play of colours, ↻ iridescence. — 2. Wein: = Schillerwein.

Schiller-falter (ˊ⸍…) [schillern] m ⊕ ent. purple emperor (Apatu'ra Iris); =farbe f iridescent (or changeable) colour.

schillerig (ˊ⸍⸌) a. ⊕ iridescent.

schillern (ˊ⸍) [nhd.; *schielen] I v/n. (h.) ⓜa. to display a variety of colours or hues, to play in different colours, in Regenbogenfarben: to iridesce, wie ein Oval: to opalesce (vgl. changieren 2); ins Rötliche 2 to have a reddish tinge. — II ~ n ⊕ play of colours; iridescence, opalescence, bsd. ehm. a. chatoyancy. — III 2d p.pr. u. a. ⊕ quickly changing colour; iridescent, opalescent; in tausend Farben 2d playing in a thousand colours.

Schillersch (ˊ⸌) a. ⊕ [Friedrich v. Schiller, dtsch. (dramatischer ꝛc.) Dichter, 1759–1805]: die ~en Gedichte Schiller's poems pl.

Schiller=spat (ˊ⸌…) f ⊕ min.: ↻ bastite, schiller-spar; =taff(e)t m ⊕ shot silk or taffeta; =wein m wine (pressed) from black and white grapes mixed.

Schilling (ˊ⸌) [ahd.; *schellen klingen] m ⓜd. 6. mint.: a) ehm. dtsch.(b) engl. shilling.

schilt(st) (ˊ) pres. ind. von schelten.

Schimäre (⸗⸍⸌) [fr. chimère; *Chimära] f ⊕ (Hirngespinst) chimera, phantom.

schimärisch (⸗⸍⸌) a. ⊕ chimerical.

Schimmel (ˊ⸍) [ahd.; *schimmern] m ⊕ 1. ⚹ (Pilzchen) mould, mildew, must (-iness). — 2. (weißes Pferd) white (or greyish) horse; vgl. Apfelschimmel.

schimmel-artig ⚹ (ˊ…) a. ⊕ like or resembling mould or mildew; vgl. Schimm(e)licht; ⚹fleckig a. mildewed; =geruch m ⊕ mouldy (or musty) odour.

schimm(e)licht, schimm(e)lig (ˊ⸍⸌) a. ⊕ mouldy, mildewy, musty; 2 werden = schimmeln; Schimm(e)ligkeit (ˊ⸍⸌) f ⊕ mouldiness, mustiness, ↻ mucor.

schimmeln (ˊ⸍) v/n. (h.(n.)) ⊕ a. to go (or get, turn) mouldy or musty. [mycoderm.]

Schimmel=pilz ⚹ (ˊ⸌…) m ⊕: ↻ oidium,]

Schimmer (ˊ⸍) [nhd.; *schimmern] m ⊕ 1. glimmer, faint light, bsd. poet. a. shimmer; phys., &c. (Aufblitzen) coruscation (vgl. Schein 1). — 2. fig. (blendender Schein) (false) glitter or pomp, empty show. — 3. F fig. = Ahnung 2.

Schimmer-licht (ˊ⸍…) n ⊕ glimmer (-ing light); ⚹los a. ⊕ lustreless, without a gleam (or glimmer) of light.

schimmern (ˊ⸍) [nbd.: shimmer] I v/n. (h.) ⓜa. to glimmer, glitter, glisten, gleam; to shed a faint (or feeble) light; in der Ferne 2 (undeutlich hervortreten) to loom in the distance. — II ~ n ⊕ glimmering, &c. (s. I).

Schimpanse (ˊ⸍) [afrit.] m ⊕ zo. Art Affe: chimpanzee (Si'mia troglo'dytes).

Schimpf (ˊ) [ahd. g.s. = Scherz] m ⓜb. b.s. 1. (Ehrenkränkung) indignity, contumely; opprobrium; (Beschimpfung) insult, affront, stärker: outrage; e-m e-n ~ antun to insult a p., to offer an insult to a p., to put an affront on a p.; einen ~ auf sich sitzen lassen (or. einstecken to swallow (or pocket) an affront. — 2. = Schande 1 u. 2; mit ~ und Schande ignominiously, in a most disgraceful manner.

schimpfen (ˊ⸍) [ahd.; *Schimpf] v/n. (h.) u. v/a. ⊕ to grumble about a th.; abs. f. räsonieren 2; b.s. e-n ⊕ 2 (schmähend beleidigen) to abuse (or insult, affront) a p., to revile a p.; to call a p. hard (or bad, foul) names; e-n e-n Gecken 2 to call a p. a fool; auf e-n, et. (fluchen und) 2 to inveigh (or rail) against a p., a th.

Schimpfer (ˊ⸍) m ⊕, ~in f ⊕ b.s. abusive p., reviler; ⚹ei (ˊ⸍⸌) f ⊕ abuse, reviling, F blackguarding, a. = Schimpfreden.

schimpflich (ˊ⸌) a. ⊕ b.s. opprobrious; insulting; (Schande bringend) ignominious, disgraceful, scandalous, stärker: outrageous; ~keit f ⊕ disgracefulness.

Schimpf=lied (ˊ…) n ⊕ = Schmählied; =name m nickname, geh. Spr.: opprobrious appellation or epithet; =reden f/pl. abusive (or insulting) remarks pl. or language sg.; =wort n abusive (or insulting) word, (term of) invective.

Schind=aas P (ˊ…) n ⊕ carrion; =anger m knacker's yard, carrion-pit, flaying-ground or -yard.

Schindel (ˊ⸍) [ahd.: shingle; *lt. sci'ndula, sca'ndula] f ⊕ 1. ⊕ Dachdeckerei: shingle, wooden tile. — 2. her. (kleine rechteckige Schildfigur) billet.

Zeichen (f. S. XVII): F familiär; P Volkssprache; ℙ Gaunersprache; ⚹ selten; † alt (auch gestorben); * neu (auch geboren); ⁺⁺ unrichtig;

[Schindelbedachung]

Schindel-bedachung ☉ (ˇ˘...) f ㉚ =dach; =beil n shingling-hatchet; =dach n shingle-roof, shingling; =decker m shingler; =macher m shingle-splitter; =messer n shingle-knife.

schindeln ☉ (ˇ˘) v/a. ㉙a. Dächer ⚲ to shingle ..., to cover ... with shingles.

schinden (ˇ˘) [ahd.: skin] v/a., v/n. (h.) und sich ⚲ v/refl. ㉙ (⚓ ㉑) 1. to flay, to skin, ⚗ to excoriate. — 2. fig. seine Leute ⚲ to sweat one's workmen or employees; die Untertanen ⚲ (bedrücken) to oppress (or grind down) one's subjects; von e-m Geizigen: er schindet und schabt he is a skinflint; sich ⚲ und plagen to drudge, to slave (one's life out). — 3. bursch. u. F (et. umsonst h.) to do a th. on the cheap; Kolleg ⚲ to attend (a course of) lectures gratis or without paying (a fee).

Schinder (ˇ˘) [mhd.] m ㉒ 1. = Abdecker. — 2. ⚒ in Flüchen = Henker. — 3. Arbeitersprache: (Leute ⚲) sweater, nigger-driver. — 4. = Schindmähre.

Schinderei (ˇ˘ˑ˘) f ㊻ 1. = Abdeckerei. — 2. fig. (Plackerei): a) oppression, grinding tyranny or system, harsh treatment; b) drudgery, slavery, sweating.

Schinder-karre (n m) f (ˇ˘...) ㉒ knacker's cart; =knecht m knacker's man, schimpfend. low cad; ⚲mäßig a. ㊺ (plackend, bedrückend) oppressive, grinding, harsh.

Schind-grube (ˇ˘...) f ㉒ = =anger; =luder P n = =aas; fig. mit e-m ~ spielen oder treiben (schändlich spielen) to treat a p. disgracefully, to play the deuce with a p.; =mähre f (abgetriebenes Pferd) worn-out (or broken-down) hack, jade, F old crock, P knacker.

Schinken (ˇ˘) [ahd.: Schenkel] m ㉓ 1. bsd. (Schweine=)~: a) von den Vorderbeinen: ham, b) v. d. Hinterbeinen: gammon of bacon, c) über dem Fußgelenk: hock of bacon. — 2. F co. = Bein, Schenkel; bsd. bursch. = Schmöker. a. = Dienstmädchen.

Schinken-bein (ˇ˘...) n ㉒ = ham-bone; =butterbrot n ham-sandwich; =fabrikant ⚘ m ham-curer; =knochen m ham-bone; =muschel f pearl-oyster (Perna); =schnitte f slice of ham.

Schinn (ˇ) [ndd.: skin] m ㉙b., ~e (ˇ˘) f ㊸: ~en pl. scurf, bsd. path. a. dandruff.

Schippe (ˇ˘) [ndd.] f ㊻ 1. ☉ norbb. spade; (Schaufel) shovel. — 2. Kartenspiel: spades pl. (= Pik³). [fig. f. Schüppchen².]

Schippchen ☉ (ˇ˘) n ㉓ (dim. v. Schippe)

schippen (ˇ˘) v/a. ㉘ norbb. schaufeln.

Schippen-As (ˇ˘ˑˇ) n ㉓ ace of spades.

Schirm (ˇ) [ahd. urspr. ⚒] m (P a. n) ㉙b. 1. shelter, (Zuflucht) refuge, safeguard; unter seinem Schutz und ~ under his protection or patronage. — 2. ⚘ (Dolde): ⚗ umbel. — 3. (schützende Vorrichtung) bsd. in Zssgn, oft: shade, screen: f. Augen-, Lampen-, Licht-, Mützen-, Ofen-, Regen-, Sonnen- (2c.) schirm.

schirm-artig ⚘ (ˇ˘...) a. ㊺ : umbellate; ⚒es Gebilde: ⚗ umbraculum; vgl. ⚲förmig; =dach n ㉒ penthouse, (open) shed, ⚓ awning.

schirmen (ˇ˘) [ahd. ⚒; *Schirm] v/a. ㉘ to shield, protect (= beschirmen).

Schirmer (ˇ˘) [ahd. ⚒] m ㉒, ~in f ㊼ protector (f ...tress), patron(ess f).

Schirm-fabrikant (ˇ˘...) m ㉒ umbrella-maker; ⚲förmig a. ㊺ umbr.-shaped, ⚘: ⚗ umbelliform, umbraculiform; =futteral, =gestell n umbrella-case, -frame; =händler m umbrella-man; =herr m protector; patron; =herrschaft f protectorate; =kraut ⚘ n : a) = Siebenstern; b) umbrella-wort (Oxy'laphus); =lafette ⚒ f shielded gun-carriage; =macher m umbrella-maker; =mütze f peaked cap; =palme ⚘ f umbrella-palm (Co'rypha); =ständer m umbrella-stand; =stock m umbrella-stick; =vogel m umbrella-bird (Cephalo'pterus orna'tus); =vogt m: a) = =herr; b) eccl. advowee; =wand f screen(ing) wall; =werke ⚒ n/pl. frt. defences pl.; =zwinge f umbrella-tip.

Schirokko (-ˇ-) [it., *ar.] m ㊵ heißer Südostwind im Mittelmeer: sirocco.

Schirr-kammer ☉ (ˇ˘...) f ㊻, =meister = Geschirr-... [(wollenzeug: shirting.]

Schirting ⚘ (ˇ˘) [engl.] n ⑪d.⑲ Baum-]

Schisma (ˇ˘) [grch. Spaltung] n ㊾⑳㊶ eccl. schism; ~tiker (˘ˑ˘) m ㉒ schismatic; ⚲tisch (˘ˑ˘) a. ㊺ schismatic(al).

Schiß¹ P unanständig (ˇ) [schiß²] m ⑪a. shit(ting); fig. ~ (Angst) h. to be timid or F funky, to show the white feather.

schiß² P unanständig (ˇ) ind. impf. v. scheißen.

schlabb(e)rig (ˇ˘) a. ㊺ (fade) insipid, tasteless; **schlabbern** norbb. (ˇ˘) [ndb.: lautm.: slabber, slobber, slaver] v/n. (h.) ㉙a. (geifern) to slobber; (plaudern) to babble, chat, prattle.

Schlacht¹ ⚒ (ˇcht) [ahd.; *schlagen] f ㊻ battle, kleinere: action, fight, engagement; blutige ~ sanguinary battle; ~ bei Belle=Alliance battle of Waterloo; es kam zur ~ it came to fighting, a battle was fought; eine ~ liefern to fight a battle, to give battle to the enemy; in die ~ ziehen to go into action; ein Schlachten war's, nicht eine ~ zu nennen (SCH.) it was a slaughter, call it not a battle.

Schlacht²=bank ☉ (ˇcht-ˇ) [schlachten¹] f ㉒: a) slaughtering-bench; shambles pl.; b) fig. Truppen zur ~ führen to lead ... into certain destruction, to sacrifice ... (wantonly).

schlachtbar (ˇcht-) a. ㊺ fit for slaughtering, fit to be slaughtered or killed.

Schlacht²=beil (ˇcht...) n ㉒ pole-axe; ⚲bericht ⚒ m report of a battle, account of an action (fought); ⚲block n slaughtering-block. [f. Schlacht²-...]

Schlachte=fest 2c. (ˇch-t˘...) in Zssgn]

schlachten¹ (ˇ˘) [ahd.: schlachter; *Schlacht] ⊙ I v/a. 1. to kill, bsd. größere Tiere: to slaughter, als Opfer: to sacrifice, immolate. — 2. fig. (hinmorden) to butcher; (metzeln) to cut to pieces, to massacre. — II v/n. (h.) 3. v. Schlächter: er schlachtet heute he kills to-day. — III ~ n ㉓ 4. (f. I) slaughtering; fig. butchering; massacre.

schlachten² (ˇ˘) v/n. (h.) ㉙: nach e-m ⚲ (geartet sein) to take after a p.

Schlachten³=bummler ⚒ (ˇcht˘...) [Schlacht¹] m ㉒ camp-follower, hanger-on of an army in the field; =denker m great strategist or tactician; =einheit ⚒ f fighting unit; =glück n

fortune of war; =gott m, myth. god of battle(s), Mars; =göttin f Bellona; =lenker m, bibl. (Lord) God of Hosts; =maler m battle-painter.

Schlachter (ˇch-t-), mst **Schlächter** (ˇ˘) [ahd.; *schlachten] m ㉒ butcher, auf Geschäftsschildern auch: purveyor of meat; in Zssgn = Fleischer=...

Schlächterei (ˇ˘ˑ˘) f ㊻ 1. (Gewerbe, Haus) butcher's trade, shop. — 2. fig. (Gemetzel) butchery, slaughter, massacre.

Schlacht²=essen (ˇcht...) n ㉒ party given when a pig is killed; ⚲feier f fête in commemoration of a battle; =feld ⚒ n battle-field or -ground; ⚲fertig a. ㊺ ready for battle; =fest n =feier; ⚲fest =essen; ⚲flotte ⚓ f fleet of battle-ships; ⚲geld n butcher's fee or pay; ⚲gemälde n battle-picture or -piece; =gesang n =lied; =geschrei n =ruf; =getümmel, =gewühl n din of battle, (fr.) mêlée; im dichten ~ in the thickest of the fight; =glück n = Schlachtenglück; =haufe(n) m body of fighting soldiers; ⚲haus n slaughter-house, abattoir; =hof m slaughtering-yard; ⚲jungfrau f = Walküre; =lied n battle-song; ⚲linie ⚒ f line of battle, fighting line; vgl. =ordnung; ⚲messer n butcher's knife; =ochs, =ochse m ox to be killed; =opfer n victim; ⚲ordnung f battle-array, order of battle; in ~ aufstellen to draw up in battle-array or in line of battle; sie stellten sich in ~ auf they placed themselves in battle-array; =plan m plan of action; ⚲reif a. ㊺ von Schweinen 2c.: ready for slaughtering or killing; ⚲roß n battle-horse, charger; =ruf ⚒ m battle-cry or -shout, bsd. der Indianer: war-whoop; =schiff ⚓ n battle-ship.

Schlachtschitz(en pl.) (ˇ˘ˑˇ) n ㉒ (poln. Adlige) Polish gentry and nobility.

Schlacht²=schwein (ˇcht...) n ㉒ pig (which is) to be killed; ⚲schwert n broadsword, ehm. auch: (double-edged) battle-sword; ⚲steuer f (in England unbekannt) duty on slaughtered (or butcher's) meat; ⚲stück n ⚲gemälde; ⚲tag m ⚒ day of battle; ⚲tag m Schlächterei: slaughtering-day; =und =mahlsteuer f (in Engl. unbekannt), etwa: town-duties pl., (fr.) octroi.

Schlachtung (ˇcht˘) f ㊻ slaughter(ing). **Schlacht²=vieh** (ˇcht...) n ㉒ cattle for slaughter, fattened beasts pl.; =wolle ⚘ f von Schafen: slaughtering-wool; =zeug ⚘ n butcher's implements or tools pl. for slaughtering; =zwang m compulsory use of a slaughter-house.

Schlacke ☉ (ˇ˘) [ndb.: slag; *schlagen] f ㊺ metall. dross (auch fig.), slag, scoria, clinkers pl., vom Puddelofen: tap-cinder.

schlacken¹ (ˇ˘) ☉ v/n. (h.) 1. v/impers. es schlackt it is raining (or pouring) incessantly, F it's sloppy (weather). — 2. ☉ das Erz schlackt ... is drossy.

schlacken²=artig (ˇ˘...) [Schlacke] a. ㊺ metall. drossy, slaggy, scoriaceous, cindery; ⚲bildung f scorification; ⚲förmig a. scoriform; ⚲frei a. drossless; =ofen m slag-furnace; ⚲reich a. scoriaceous; ⚲stein m sl.-stone; =wolle f slag-hair or -wool; ⚲zinn n prill(i)on, block-tin.

♪ Musik; ⚗ Wissenschaft; ⚘ Pflanze; ⚲ Geographie; ☉ Technik; ⚒ Bergbau; ⚒ Militär; ⚓ Marine; ⚘ Handel; ⚘ Post; 🚂 Eisenbahn.

[ſchlackerig] — 842 — [Schlagball]

ſchlack(e)rig (⏑(⏑)⏑) *a.* ⓖ vom Wetter: rainy, F sloppy, slushy, sleety, nasty.
ſchlackern (⏑⏑) *v/n.* (h.) ⓐⓐ. 1. to move limply, to dawdle (or toddle) along, ↓ von Segeln: to flap. — 2. *v/impers.* **es** ſchlackert = es ſchlackt, ſ. ſchlacken 1.
Schlack(er)=wetter (⏑(⏑)⏑⏑) *n* ⓖ² sleety (F sloppy, slushy) weather.
ſchlackicht, ...ig (⏑⏑) *a.* ⓖ 1. = ſchlack(e)rig. — 2. (Schlacken enthaltend) drossy, slaggy, scoriaceous, von Kohlen auch: clinkery.
Schlack=wurſt (⏑⸗⏑) [ndd. Maſtdarm=] *f* ⓖ² kind of German sausage.
Schlaf¹ (⸗) [ahd.: sleep; *ſchlaff] *m* ⓓⓒ. (o. *pl.*) sleep; (Ruhe) rest, repose; feſter ~ sound (or heavy) sleep; einen ſehr leichten ~ haben to be a very light sleeper; magnetiſcher ~ hypnotism; *med.* ~ beförderndes Mittel soporific; im ~e reden (wandeln) to talk (to walk) in one's sleep; es iſt die ganze Nacht kein ~ in meine Augen gekommen I did not sleep a wink all night; in einen tiefen ~ verfallen to fall into a profound sleep, F to go fast asleep; ein Kind in ~ wiegen (ſingen) to rock (to lull) a child to sleep; *fig.* das wäre mir nicht im ~e eingefallen I should never have dreamt of such a thing, it would never have occurred to me; Sprichw. ſ. Gott 4.
Schlaf² (⸗) [ahd.] *m* ⓓⓒ. = Schläfe.
Schlaf¹**=abteil** ⚒ (⸗...) *m* ⓖ² sleeping-compartment; **=ähnlich, =artig** *a.* ⓖ resembling sleep; ²**befördernd** *a.* = ²**bringend**; =**bein** *n* = Schläfenbein; ²**bringend** *a.* soporific, ...ferous, narcotic; =**burſch(e)** *m* night-lodger.
Schläfchen (⸗⏑) *n* ⓒ² (*dim. von* Schlaf¹) short sleep, (light) slumber, nap, nach Tiſch: after-dinner nap, siesta, F forty winks *pl.*, snooze.
Schlaf¹**=deich** ⊙ (⸗⏑) *m* ⓖ² spare dike.
Schläfe (⸗⏑) [Schlaf²] *f* ⓖ *anat.* temple.
ſchlafen (⸗⏑) [ahd.: sleep] I *v/n.* (h.) ⓖⓐ. 1. to sleep; leiſe: to slumber, F to snooze, to have (or take) one's forty winks; feſt: to be fast (or dead) asleep, to lie in a deep (or heavy) sleep; gut: to sleep soundly, to be in a sound sleep; zu lange: to oversleep o.s.; (ruhen) to (take one's) rest; *fig.* von Angelegenheiten: to lie dormant; laß die Sache ~ let the matter rest, leave well alone; lange in den Tag hinein ~ to sleep far into the day or till broad daylight; wünſche Ihnen wohl zu ~ I trust you may have a good night's rest; ~ Sie wohl! (I wish you a good night!; den Schlaf der Gerechten ~ to sleep the sleep of the just. — 2. (übernachten) ſ. auswärts 2, Boden 1; v. Dienſtboten ꝛc.: in (außer) dem Hauſe ~ to sleep in (out); unter freiem Himmel ~ to sleep (or to spend the night) in the open; ~ (zu Bette) gehen, ſich ~ legen to go to bed, to retire to rest; (urſprünglich von Vögeln) to go to roost, Kinderſpr.: to go to bye-bye; Kinder ~ legen to put children to bed. — 3. (fühllos w.) der Arm ꝛc. ſchläft mir I have pins and needles in my arm, &c. (vgl. einſchlafen 3). — II ~ *n* ⓒ² 4. sleep(ing), slumber(ing); ſ. Schlaf¹.

Schläfen=bein (⸗⏑⸗⏑) [Schläfe] *n* ⓖ² *anat.* temporal bone. ǀ bed, retiring to rest.
Schlafen=geh(e)n (⸗⏑⸗⏑) *n* ⓖ² going to
Schlafens=zeit (⸗⏑⸗⏑) *f* ⓖ² bed-time; es iſt ~ it is time to go to bed.
Schläfer (⸗⏑) [mhd.; *ſchlafen] *m* ⓖ², ~**in** *f* ⓕ sleeper; vgl. Lang=, Sieben=, Winter=ſchläfer.
ſchläf(e)rig (⸗(⏑)⏑) [ahd.] ſ. ſchläfrig.
ſchläfern (⸗⏑) [ahd.] ⓐⓐ. *v/impers.*: es ſchläfert mich I feel (or am) sleepy or drowsy. ǀ hypnotic; vgl. ²befördernd.
ſchlaf¹**=erzeugend** (⸗⏑⸗⏑⏑) *a.* ⓖ *med.*
ſchlaff(⸗) [ahd.: ruſſ. sla'bŭ] *a.* ⓖⓘ 1. (ſchlapp) slack (a. ↓ v. Segeln ꝛc.); flaccid, flabby; (loſe) loose, (weich) soft, limp, (herabhängend) drooping; ⓩ *m. ob. w.* to slacken, to relax; vgl. erſchlaffen I. — 2. *fig.* in Sitten, im Stil ꝛc.: lax, loose, careless; enervated, effeminate; (lau, läſſig) languid, half-hearted, negligent, remiss, lackadaisical, (träge) indolent, lazy, sluggish.
Schlaffheit (⸗⏑) [mhd.] *f* ⓕ (ſ. ſchlaff) slackness, flabbiness, looseness, limpness; *fig.* laxity, carelessness, languor, half-heartedness, remissness, indolence, laziness.
Schlaf¹**=gaſt** (⸗...) *m* ⓖ² traveller who sleeps (or puts up for the night) at a hotel; =**gefährte** *m*, =**gefährtin** *f* bed-fellow; =**geld** *n* charge (or pay) for a night's lodging; =**gemach** *n* = =**zimmer**; =**genoß, =geſell** *m* = =**gefährte**; =**gewand** *n* night-dress or -gown.
...ſchläfig (...⸗⏑) [Schlaf¹] *a.* ⓖ v. Betten: ein=² single, zwei=² double.
Schlafittchen, Schlafittich F (⏑⸗⏑) [ndd., d. i. „Schlagfittich" (Flügel)] *n* ⓖ³, ⓖⓓ. nur in: beim ~ nehmen (to seize) by the collar.
Schlaf¹**=kamerad** (⸗...) *m* ⓖ² = =**gefährte**; =**kammer** *f* (small) bed-room; ²**krank** *a.* ⓖ =**ſüchtig**; =**krankheit** *f* sleeping-sickness; vgl. =ſucht; =**lied** *n* song which lulls to sleep; (Wiegenlied) lullaby; ²**los** *a.* sleepless, restless; =**loſigkeit** *f* sleeplessness, restlessness; *path.*: ⓩ insomnia, agrypnia; =**luſt** *f* sleepiness, drowsiness; ²**machend** *a.* = ²**befördernd**; =**mittel** *n* opiate, soporific, soporiferous draught or drug; vgl. =**trank**; =**mütze** *f* nightcap; *fig.* (ſchläfrige Perſon) sleepy (or slow, humdrum) person; ²**mütig** *a.* sleepy, slow, humdrum, lackadaisical, F sleepy-headed; =**pelz** *m* fur-lined cloak or dressing-gown; =**ratz(e** *f*) *m* F *fig.* person fond of sleep, great sleeper, F sleepy-headed person; =**reden** *n* somniloquence.
ſchläfrig (⸗⏑) [ahd.] *a.* ⓖⓘ 1. sleepy, drowsy, somnolent; ²**machen** to make drowsy, F to send to sleep. — 2. *fig.* = ſchlafmütig; (träge) indolent. — 3. (einſchläfernd) lulling to sleep, soporific. — 4. in Zſſgn ſ. ...ſchläfig.
Schläfrigkeit (⸗⏑⏑) *f* ⓕ (ſ. ſchläfrig) 1. sleepiness, drowsiness, somnolence. — 2. *fig.* slowness, indolence.
Schlaf¹**=rock** (⸗...) *m* ⓖ² dressing-gown; =**ſaal** *m* dormitory; =**ſeſſel** *m* = =**ſtuhl**; =**ſofa** *n* sofa-bed(stead); =**ſtätte, =ſtelle** *f*: a) sleeping-place; (Lager) couch, ↓ berth; b) lodging-house, night's lodging, für Vagabunden: casual ward;

=**ſtellen=vermieter(in** *f*) *m* lodging-housekeeper; =**ſtube** *f* = =**zimmer**; =**ſtuhl** *m* easy chair, chair-bedstead; =**ſucht** *f* somnolence, lethargy, ⓩ sopor, stupor, coma; ²**ſüchtig** *a.* ⓖ drowsy, somnolent, lethargic, comatose; =**trank** *m* sleeping-draught, soporiferous potion; =**trunk** *m*: a) = =**trank**; b) (Trank vor dem Schlafengehen) F co. nightcap; ²**trunken** *a.* overcome with sleep, thoroughly drowsy; =**trunkenheit** *f* (great) drowsiness, somnolence; =**wagen** ⚒ *m* sleeping-carriage, bſd. Am. sleeping-car, Pullman car; ²**wandeln** *v/n.* (h.) ⓐ*a*⸗*⸗* to walk in one's sleep; =**wandel(n** *n*) *m* somnambulism; =**zeit** *f*: a) time spent in sleep; b) time to go to bed, bed-time; =**zeug** *n* night-clothes *pl.*; =**zimmer** *n* bedroom, sleeping-apartment or -room.

Schlag¹ (⸗, *pl.* ⸗⏑) [ahd.: ſchlagen] *m* ⓓⓒ. 1. blow (a. *fig.*); (Streich) stroke (auch beim Tennis); (Stoß) concussion, percussion, ~ mit der (flachen) Hand: slap, mit der Fauſt: cuff, punch, mit der Peitſche: lash; leiſer ~ pat(ting), tap(ping), dumpfer: thud, thump, ſtarker: knock, treffender: hit, lauter: bang; elektriſcher: electric shock (vgl. kalt 2); des Pferdes: kick; der Trommel: beat; ~ der Uhr stroke of the clock; ~ zehn (Uhr) at ten (o'clock) precisely or F sharp, punctually at 10; ↓ ~ des Ruders stroke of the oar; Spiel: erſter ~ start, F first go; *fig.* das war ein harter ~ für ihn that was a severe (or crushing) blow to him. — 2. Redensarten: auf einen ~, mit einem ~e at one blow or F go, (SH.) at one fell swoop, weitS. all at once, all of a sudden; ~ auf ~ blow upon blow; (following) in rapid succession; ohne einen ~ zu tun without striking a (single) blow; eine Tracht Schläge bekommen to get a (good) beating or thrashing or Fhiding. — 3. (rhythmiſche Bewegung) ~ des Herzens beating or pulsation, throbbing of the heart; ~ eines Pendels oscillation of a pendulum; einer Taſchenuhr: tick; (Takt) measure, cadence, ♪ time. — 4. (ſchmetternder Geſang) ~ der Lerche ꝛc. warbling, trill(ing), carol(ling). — 5. *path.* paralytic stroke, apoplectic fit; (Gehirn=, Herz=) ~ apoplexy of the brain, of the heart (ſ. rühren 6). — 6. (Tür einer Kutſche) carriage-(or coach-)door; ~ des Tores bar (of a gate); vgl. Schlagbaum; ſ. Taubenſchlag. — 7. *for.* = Hau 2 b u. Holzſchlag b. — 8. *agr.* (beſtelltes Feld) tilled field, land (planted) with a particular crop; in Schläge teilen to parcel (according to) the crops.
Schlag² (⸗, *pl.* ⸗⏑) [mhd. Geſchlecht] *m* ⓓⓒ. 1. kind, sort, F cut; Leute von dieſem ~e people of that stamp or description or F kidney (vgl. Menſchenſchlag); *fig.* ein Mann von m⸗m ~e (wie ich ihn gern habe) a man after my own heart. — 2. (Raſſe) ein ſchöner ~ a fine breed (or stock) of horses, &c.
Schlag=ader (⸗⏑...⸗⏑) *f* ⓖ *anat.* artery (= Puls=ader); =**anfall** *m* = Schlag¹ 5; ²**artig** *a.* ⓖ *path.* apoplectic; =**ball** *m*

Signs (see page XVII): F familiar; P vulgar; ⸗ flash; \ rare; † obsolete (died); * new word (born); ⁺ ⁺ incorrect; ♪ music;

[schlagbar] — 843 — [Schläger]

cricket- (or racket-, tennis-)ball; als Spiel: cricket, racket, tennis.
schlagbar (⸺) *a.* ⊕ *for.* fit for felling.
Schlag¹-baum (⸺, ⸺) *m* ⊕ turnpike; ⸗**bereit** *a.* ⊕ ready to strike; ⸗**block** ⊕ *m* für Ton: batting-block; ⸗**bohrer** ⊕ *m* Schloff.: mandrel; ⸗**bolzen** ⚔ im Hinterlader: striker; ⸗**dame**(⸗spiel *n*) *f* game of draughts in which the winner has to lose all his pieces.
Schlägel ꝛc. f. Schlegel ꝛc.
schlagen (⸺) [ahd.: slay, slog] ⊕ *b.* **I** *v/a.* **1.** (f. Schlag¹ 1) to beat, strike, slap, cuff, punch; to pat, tap, knock, hit, bang (about); vgl. prügeln; vom Pferde: to kick (out), von der Uhr: to strike; *hunt.* v. Raubvögeln: die Beute ≈ (ergreifen) to pounce upon (or strike)... — **2.** Fügung mit *prp.*: **ans** Kreuz ≈ to fix (or fasten, nail) to the cross, to crucify; *univ.* ans schwarze Brett (an)≈ to announce (or placard) on the board; e-m **auf** die Finger ≈ to give a p. a rap (or to rap a p.) on the knuckles; f. Haupt 1, Mund¹ 3; ⊕ die Unkosten auf die Ware ≈ to clap the expenses on (to) the goods; den Boden **aus** dem Fasse ≈ to knock the bottom out of the cask; den Feind aus dem Felde ≈ to rout the enemy, to put the enemy to flight; f. Kopf 8 unter „**aus**"; **durch** ein Sieb ≈ to pass (or strain) through a sieve; et. **entzwei, in** Scherben, in Stücke ≈, in Trümmer, **zu** Trümmern ≈ to knock a th. to pieces or F to smithereens, F to smash a th. (up); e-m (bisw. a. e-n) **hinter** die Ohren ≈ to box a p.'s ears; f. Band 10, Fessel¹¹, Flucht¹ 1; die Augen **in** die Höhe ≈ to raise (*bibl.* to lift up) one's eyes, to look up; in Papier ≈ (wickeln) to wrap in paper; f. Schanze²; *fig.* in den Wind ≈ to pay no heed to, to disregard; e-n **mit** der Peitsche (dem Rohrstock) ≈ to whip (to cane) a p.; *fig.* e-n mit s-n eigenen Waffen ≈ to beat (or defeat) a p. with his own weapons or on his own ground; das Haar **nach** hinten ≈ to push (or comb) back one's hair; die Beine **über**⸗ea. ≈ to cross one's legs; f. Leisten; die Arme **um** e-n ≈ (schlingen) to throw one's arms around a p.; F *fig.* sich (*dat.*) die Welt um die Ohren ≈ to travel (from place to place), F to knock about (the world); vgl. 13; **zu** Boden ≈ to knock (stärker: to strike) to the ground; vgl. Boden 6; die Zinsen zum Kapital ≈ to add the interest to the principal. — **3.** mit *nouns:* f. Alarm; Ball ≈ to play ball or cricket or tennis; den Ball gut ≈ to hit the ball well, beim Kricket: to bat well; e-e Brücke ≈ to make a bridge; vgl. Brücke 1; Eier in die Suppe ≈ to stir (or put) eggs into the soup; Falten ≈ to crease, to pucker; f. Feuer 1, Fliege 2; Holz ≈ to cut (or fell, hew) timber; einen Knoten ≈ to tie a knot; e-n Kreis mit dem Zirkel ≈ to describe a circle ...; f. Klinge 1, Kreuz 1, Lärm 2; e-m ein Loch in den Kopf ≈ to break a p.'s head; e-n Nagel ins Brett ≈ to strike (or knock, drive) a nail into the ...; f. Purzelbaum, Rad 2, Randal, Rat 2,

Schaum 1; eine Schlacht ≈ to fight a battle; Brettspiel: e-n Stein ≈ to take a piece; den Takt ≈ to beat time; *fenc.* eine Terz ≈ to thrust in tierce; Wellen ≈ to throw up waves, v. Meere auch: to be ruffled or rough; Wunden ≈ to inflict wounds; Wurzeln ≈ to strike (or take) root. — **4.** mit Angabe der Wirkung: f. blau 2, breit 2, krumm 3; krumme Nägel gerade ≈ to straighten ...; (kurz und) klein ≈ to knock (or break) to pieces, to smash (up); platt ≈ to flatten (out), to distend; Holz zu Klaftern ≈ to cord ...; f. Ritter 1; Eier zu Schaum, zu Schnee ≈, metonymisch: Schaum, Schnee ≈ to whisk (or beat) the whites of eggs; e-n tot (oder zu Tode) ≈ to kill a p. with a blow or with blows; *fig.* ich ließe mich darauf tot ≈ (ich bin fest davon überzeugt) I could stake my life on it; Geld (die Zeit) tot ≈ to waste (or squander) one's money (one's time); *fig.* sich den Bauch (oder Leib) voll ≈ (tüchtig essen) to fill one's belly or stomach, to gorge o.s., to gormandize, P to have a blow-out; e-n windelweich ≈ to beat a p. to a jelly. — **5.** *fig.* e-n mit Blindheit ≈ (strafen) to strike a p. blind; ein (vom Schicksal) geschlag(e)ner Mann a man crushed by misfortune(s), a ruined (or broken) man. — **6.** ♪ eine Saite ≈ to strike (or touch) a chord; die Harfe, die Laute, die Zither ≈ to play (on) the harp, the lute, the zither. — **7.** ⊕ Öl ≈ to press oil; Hutmacherei: in die Form ≈ to (put into) shape; Schlächterei: e-n Ochsen ≈ to stun an ox; ⚓ ein Tau ≈ (zs.-drehen) to lay a rope; kabelweise ≈ to lay cable-fashion. — **II** *v/n.* (h. u. sn) **8.** to beat, to strike; um sich ≈ to lay about one (vgl. 11), vom Pferde: to kick (or lash) out; vom Puls ꝛc.: to beat, to throb, vom Herzen auch: to palpitate; *fig.* das Gewissen schlägt ihm his conscience pricks him. — **9.** von Singvögeln: to warble, sing, trill, carol; ♪ von einer Harfe ꝛc.: to sound; die Trommel schlug zum Streite (v.) the drum called to battle. — **10.** von der Uhr: to strike, von d. Glocke: to ring; es hat 12, 2 geschlagen it has struck twelve, two; es wird gleich 9 ≈ it (or the clock) is (up)on the stroke of (mehr gbr.: it's close upon) nine; eine geschlagene (volle) Stunde a full (or fully an) hour; *fig.* dem Glücklichen schlägt keine Stunde (the flight of) time does not affect the happy one; seine Stunde hat geschlagen his hour has (or is) come or is at hand; er weiß, was die Glocke geschlagen hat he knows what o'clock it is (vgl. Glocke 3). — **11.** oft mit *prp.:* **a)** mit *prp.* **an** et. ≈ to knock (or strike) against a th.; der Regen schlägt an (oder gegen) das Fenster ... beats (or patters) against the window; liebliche Töne schlugen an mein Ohr ... struck my ear; die Wellen ≈ an den Fels the waves dash against the rock; an⸗ea. ≈ to collide, to come to a collision; fallend **auf** den (*od.* 11) Boden ≈ to strike the ground in falling, to plump down; es schlägt Feuer

aus dem Boden fire leaps (or shoots) up from the ground; aus der Art ≈ to degenerate; die Tinte schlägt **durchs** Papier ... soaks through the paper; mit dem Kopfe **gegen** die Wand ≈ to strike (or knock, F run) one's head against the wall; die Flammen ≈ **gen** Himmel ... flash (or leap) up to heaven, ... rise to the sky; der Blitz hat **in** die Eiche geschlagen the lightning has struck the oak; **in** j-s Fach ≈ to come within a p.'s special department; das schlägt nicht in mein Fach that's not in (or it's out of) my line; e-n **ins** Gesicht ≈ to slap a p.'s face; der Schnee schlägt einem ins Gesicht the snow beats in one's face; es ist mir in die Glieder geschlagen I feel it in every limb; **mit** den Flügeln ≈ to flap one's wings; sie schlägt (artet) sehr **nach** ihrer Mutter she very much takes after (or she favours) her mother; mit Händen und Füßen **um** sich ≈ to strike out (or to struggle) with hands and feet; der kalte Brand ist **zu** der Wunde geschlagen mortification has set in; **b)** mit *adv.:* hinten⸗über ≈ to fall backward; kopf⸗über ≈ to fall (or tumble) headlong (or head foremost). Sport: F to do a cropper; ⚓ v. b. Segeln: rückwärts ≈ to flap backwards. — **III** sich ≈ *v/recip.* u. *v/refl.* **12.** sich im Duell ≈ to do battle, to fight a duel (auf Säbel, Pistolen with swords, pistols); sich (ea.) ≈ to come to blows or to fisticuffs; sich mit e-m (mit Fäusten) ≈ to have a fight (or a box) with a p., F to fight a p.; ⚔ sich mit dem Feinde ≈ to (have a) skirmish with the enemy; sich selbst (oder mit s-n eigenen Worten) ≈ to contradict o.s.; man schlägt sich fast um sie she is eagerly sought after; ⊕ man schlägt sich fast um die Ware the goods are quickly snapped up or eagerly bought or in great demand. — **13.** *fig.* sich links, rechts ≈ (wenden) to turn to the left, to the right; f. Busch 2; sich **auf** die Seite der Verschworenen ≈ to (take) side (or to throw in one's lot) with the conspirators; sich et. **aus** dem Sinne ≈ to put a th. out of one's mind; f. Mittel² 3; sich **zu** einer Partei ≈ to go over to (or to join) a party. — **IV** ~ *n* ⊕ **14.** beating, &c. (f. I u. II); ⊕ einer Brücke construction ...; *for.* e-s Waldes: felling; des Pulses: beating, pulsation, des Herzens: action, palpitation; der Nachtigall: song, trill. — **V** ⊕ *p.pr. u. a.* ⊕ **15.** Bed. des *inf.* — **16.** (treffend) striking; (überzeugend) convincing, forcible, von Gründen auch: cogent, clenching. — **17.** (blitzartig zündend) fulminating; explosive; ⚒ ⸗es Wetter = Schlagwetter.
Schlager (⸺) *m* ⊕ *thea.* (durchschlagendes, erfolgreiches Stück) taking piece, draw, great (theatrical) success or F hit.
Schläger (⸺) [schlagen] *m* ⊕, ~**in** *f* ⊕ **1. a)** p. who beats, &c. (f. schlagen); **b)** (Raufbold) brawler; **c)** (Fechter) fighter; ein guter ~ a fine swordsman; **d)** Kricket ꝛc.: batsman, batter; Tennis: racket. — **2.** Singvogel: warbler. — **4.** Waffe: rapier.

⚡ scientific; ⚘ botanical; ⏣ geography; ⊕ machinery; ⚒ mining; ⚔ military; ⚓ marine; ⊕ commercial; ✉ postal; 🚂 railway.

[**Schlägerduell**] — 844 — [**Schlaraffenleben**]

Schläger-duell (⸗⸗‿⸗) n ⓺ duel with rapiers. [affray, scuffle.
Schlägerei (-‿¹) f ⓯ fight(ing), brawl,
Schläger-mensur (⸗‿⸗¹) f ⓺ (students') duel with rapiers. [fellow, bully.
Schlage-tot (‿¹⸗) m ⓾ big hulking
Schlag¹-feder (⸗...) f ⓺: a) eines Vogels: pinion; b) ⊕ strong steel spring, Gewehrfabrikation: main-spring; ⚥fertig a. ⓺: a) ⚔ ready for fighting or war or battle, in (good) fighting-trim; vgl. ⚥bereit; b) fig. ⚥ sein, den Witz h. to have a quick repartee or a ready wit; =fertigkeit f: a) ⚔ readiness for war; b) fig. quick(ness at) repartee, ready wit; =fluß m = Schlag¹ 5; =gewicht ⊕ n e-r Uhr: striking-weight; =gold n = Blattgold; =holz n: a) for. wood for felling, underwood, copse-wood; b) = Ballfelle; c) ⚥ beetle; =instrument n: a) ⊕ percussor; b) ♪ instrument of percussion; =leiste ⚥ f an Türen und Fenstern: rabbet-ledge; =licht n (ant. =schatten) paint. strong light; fig. glaring light, (full) glare; =lot ⊕ n hard solder; =maschine ⚥ f für Baumwolle 2c.: batting-machine; =mine ⚔ f mine; =netz n: a) zum Vogelfang: clap-net; zum Fischen: seine; b) Ballspiel: racket; =pulver n = Knallpulver; =regen m pouring rain, downpour; =ring n: a) F knuckle-duster; b) ♪ ring for playing (on) the zither, plectrum; =röhrchen n, =röhre f ⚔ artill. percussion-tube; =sahne f whipped cream; =schatten m (ant. =licht) deep shadow produced by an illuminated body, paint. cast-shadow; ehm. =schatz m (Münzgebühr für das Schlagen) mintage; =seite ⚓ f list, lop-side; ~ nach Backbord (Steuerbord) h. to (have a) list to port (starboard).

schlägst (¹) 2. Pers. sg. pres. ind. v. schlagen.
Schlag-stock (⸗‿⸗) m ⓺ Ballspiel: bat; vgl. Schlagnetz b.
schlägt (¹) 3. Pers. sg. pres. ind. v. schlagen.
Schlag-trommel (⸗...) f ⓺ gong, in Indien: tam-tam, tom-tom; =uhr f striking clock or watch; =wald-betrieb m, for. cultivation of copses or underwood; =wasser ⚓ n (Wasser im Schiffsraume) bilge-water; =weite f, elect. striking- (or percussive) distance of electric sparks; =welle f billow, breaker; =werk ⊕ n: a) (Ramme) ram, beetle; b) einer Uhr: striking work(s pl.) or train, F strike; =wetter ⚔ n choke- (or fire-)damp; =wort n catchword, common(place) saying; =worte pl. auch: claptrap; vgl. Stichwort; =zeit f, for. season for felling trees or timber; =zither f t. Zither h.

Schlamassel (⸗‿⸗) [jüd. keinen Stern] m ⓶ (Verlegenheit) scrape, predicament.

Schlamm (¹) [mhd.] m ⓶b. mud, schleimiger: slime, ooze, sandiger: silt, wässeriger: mire, puddle; im ~ stecken (bleiben) to stick in the mud or in the mire (a. fig.).
Schlamm-aal (⸗‿¹) m zo. mud-eel.
Schlämm-apparat (⸗‿⸗¹) [schlämmen] m ⓶ = Schlämmvorrichtung.
Schlamm-bad (⸗...) n ⓶ mud-bath; =bagger ⊕ m mud-drag.
schlämmbar ⊕ (⸗-) a. ⓺ clean(s)able.

Schlamm-beißer (⸗...) m ⓶ ichth. mud-fish (Misgu'rnus fo'ssilis); =boden m muddy (or boggy) soil. [mud.
schlammen (⸗‿) v/n. (h.) ⓼ to deposit
schlämmen ⊕ (⸗: schlemmen) [Schlamm] v/a. ⓼ 1. e-n Hafen, See: (reinigen) to dredge, to clean(se), to clear (of mud or silt). — 2. Erze, Kreide 2c. ⚥ (waschen) to wash !..., Golderz auch: to clean up.
Schlamm-faß (⸗...) n ⓶ dolly-tub; =graben m strake, tye. [pool.
Schlamm-grube (⸗‿⸗) f ⓶ sink; (cess-)
schlammig (⸗‿) a. ⓺ (vgl. Schlamm) muddy, slimy, oozy, silty, miry, puddly, ⚔ uliginous (vgl. fotig).
Schlämm-kasten (⸗...) m ⓶ trunk-buddle; =kreide f prepared chalk, whiting.
Schlamm-netz ⊕ (⸗...) n ⓶ drag-net; =schnecke f, zo. mud-snail, ⚔ limnæa.
Schlämm-vorrichtung (⸗‿‿⸗) ⊕ f ⓶ für Silbererze 2c.: washing-apparatus.
Schlamm-vulkan (⸗...) m ⓶ ⚥ mud-volcano; =werk ⚔ n ore-washing.
Schlämm-werk ⊕ (⸗...) n ⓶ washing-mill.
schlampampen F (⸗‿⸗) [nhd.] v/n. (h.) ⓼ to feast (and revel), to lead a gay (or luxurious, riotous) life.
Schlampe (⸗‿) f ⓸ (schmutziges Weib) slut, trollop, slattern, drab, filthy creature, F draggle-tail; ⚥n v/n. (h.) ⓼ to draggle (along); vgl. schlumpen; ~**rei** (⸗‿¹) f ⓺ slovenliness, sluttishness; **schlampig** a. ⓺ draggle-tailed, slovenly, filthy, F slommikin, v. Nahrungsstoffen: sloppy. [von schlingen.
schlang (⸗) 1. u. 3. Person sg. impf. ind.
Schlange (⸗‿) [ahd.; *schlingen] f ⓺ 1. zo. snake, serpent (a. ast.), ⚔ ophidian; fig. eine ~ am Busen nähren to lay a viper to one's bosom, to lavish one's love on a false creature. — 2. ⚥ long pipe of a pump, &c.; ⚓ water-hose (vgl. Feld-, Kühl-schlange). [v. schlingen.
schlänge (⸗‿) 1. u. 3. Person subj. impf.
schläng(e)licht ⚔, mst **schläng(e)lig** (⸗‿(⸗)⸗) a. ⓺ serpentine, sinuous, von Flüssen a.: meandering, von Pfaden: winding.
schlängeln (⸗‿) [nhd.; *Schlange] ⓺a. I v/a. to coil (up); geschlängelter Weg winding path. — II v/n. (h.) u. sich ⚥ v/refl. to form a sinuous line, to meander, to wind; to crinkle; fig. (schleichen) to sneak, to creep (along); sich um et. ⚥ (schlingen) to wind (or coil) round a th. — III ~ n ⓶ sinuosity.
Schlangen-adler (⸗‿...) m ⓶ orn. snake-buzzard, serpent-eagle (Circa'etus ga'llicus); =anbeter(in f) m snake-worshipper; ⚔ ophiolater; =anbetung f sn.-worship, ⚔ ophiolatry; ⚥artig a. ⓺ sn.-like, serpentine; =balg m slough, cast, skin of a serpent; =beschreibung f ophiography; =beschwörer m sn.-charmer; =beschwörung f sn.-charming; =biß m serpent's (or snake-)bite; =brut f: a) brood of snakes; b) fig. generation of vipers; =bussard m =adler; =dienst m = anbetung; ⚥förmig a. shaped like a serpent, ⚔ serpentiform, ophiomorphus; vgl. ⚥artig; =geschlecht n, zo. = ophidia(ns) pl.; =gezücht n = brut; =gift n snake-poison; ⚥glatt a. as smooth (or slippery) as a serpent.
schlangenhaft (⸗‿⸗) a. ⓺ snake-like.

Schlangen-holz ⚔ (⸗...) n ⓶: a) snake-wood (Strychnos colubri'na); b) serpent-wood (Ophio'xylon serpenti'num); =indianer m Snake Indian, Shoshone; =knoblauch ⚥ m rocambole (A'llium scorodo'prasum); =kopf m: a) serpent's head; b) ichth. ⚔ ophiocephalus; =köpfchen n, zo. viper's-head, cowry (Cyprae'a mone'ta); =kraut n: ⚔ calla; =kunde f ophiology; =lauch ⚥ m serpent's-garlic (A'llium victoria'lis); =linie f serpentine (or sinuous) line; ⚥linig a. ⓺ serpentine, sinuous; =pfad m = =weg; =rohr n, =röhre f (Kühlschlange) winding (or serpentine) tube or pipe, ⓺ für die Destillation auch: worm; =stab m Merkurs: ⚔ caduceus; =stein m, min.: ⚔ ophite; =träger m, ast. Serpentarius; =verehrung f = =anbetung; =weg m winding (or serpentine) path or course or road or track; =windung f sinuosity, winding (or undulating) line, bisw.: serpentry; =wurz(el) ⚥ f virginische: Virginia snake-root, serpentaria (Aristolochi'a serpenta'ria); =zunge ⚥ f serpent's-tongue (Ophioglo'ssum); ⚥züngig a. adder-tongued.
schlänglig (⸗‿) f. schläng(e)lig.
schlank (¹) [nhd.; *schlingen¹] a. ⓺ (D1) 1. slender, slim; (dünn) thin, lean, (lang und mager) (long and) lanky, (fein, zart) slight, delicate; ⚥ wie eine Tanne as slim as a young sapling. — 2. F fig. im ⚥n Trabe at a fast trot. — 3. F fig. (gefällig) accommodating, obliging.
Schlank-affe (⸗‿⸗) m ⚔ semnopithece.
Schlankheit (⸗-) f ⓺ (vgl. schlank) slenderness, slimness; lankiness, slightness, F slight build.
schlank-weg (⸗‿⸗) adv. (ohne weiteres) right away, without ado, F straight (away); etwas ⚥ ablehnen flatly to refuse (or decline) a th.
schlapp¹ prov. (⸗) [ndd. = schlaff] a. ⓺ slack, limp, flabby, vgl. schlaff.
schlapp² (⸗) [lautm.] int. schlipp, ⚥!, etwa: slibber, slobber!, slipslop!
Schlappe¹ bsp. ⚔ (⸗‿) [ndd. = slap] f ⓸ (Niederlage) defeat, discomfiture, check, reverse; (Verlust) loss.
Schlappe² (⸗) prov. (⸗‿) [ndd. = *schlapp¹] f ⓸ (abgetretener Schuh) old slipper, old shoe; in ~n slipshod.
schlappen F (⸗‿) v/n. (h.) ⓼ 1. to flap; es schlappt und hängt alles an ihm his clothes hang on (or about) him like bags. — 2. von Hunden: to lap (up).
Schlappheit (⸗-) f ⓺ slackness, limpness.
Schlapp-hut (⸗‿¹) m ⓺ slouched (or soft felt) hat, wide-awake, broad-brim(med hat).
schlappig (⸗‿) a. ⓺ limp, slack.
Schlapp¹-michel (⸗...) m ⓶ = =schwanz; ⚥ohrig a. ⓺ flap-eared; =schuh m = Schlappe²; =schwanz F m, fig. weakly (or dilly-dally) fellow, F milksop; =seil n slack rope; =werden n, fig. slackening, relaxing.
Schlaps F (⸗) m ⓶a. = Flaps.
Schlaraffe (-⸗‿) [mhd.] = „Schlu(mme)r- (ob. Schl(e)uber²)affe"] m ⓸ sluggard, lackadaisical fellow, idle vagabond, F lazy-bones; ~**n-land** (-⸗‿...) n ⓶ fool's paradise, Utopia, F auch: lubberland; ~**n-leben** n useless and

[Schlaraffia] — 845 — [schleifen]

luxurious life, Utopian (or dreamy, idle, aimless) existence.
Schlaraffia (-ˇ(ˇ)ˇ) = Schlaraffenland.
schlau (ˇ) [ndd.: sly = (ver)schlag(en)] a. ❻ sly; (listig) artful, crafty, cunning, F deep; F ein 2er Kerl ob. Hund wie der an artful dodger (or a sly dog) like him; s. Fuchs 2 u. pfiffig; 2 (adv.) handeln, oft: to act with caution or prudence.
Schlau-berger (ˇˇˇˇ) m ㉒ (auch für f) sly-boots, artful dodger; er ist ein ~ F he knows what's what.
Schlauch (ˇˇ) [ahd.: slough: schlucken] m Ⓓc. **1.** (Sack) bag, v. Bocksfell für Wein u. Öl: goatskin bag; skin; (Röhre zur Leitung von Flüssigkeiten) (leather) tube, e-r Feuerspritze: (leather) hose. — **2.** ♀. ⊘ utricle. — **3.** F fig. (dicke Person) stout fellow; auch = Schlemmer.
schlauch-artig (ˇˇˇ-ˇ) a. ❻ baggy, like a (goatskin) bag; ⊘ utricular, -oid.
Schlauch-frucht ♀(ˇˇ...) f ㉓: ⊘ utricle; **=führer** m manager of the hose of a fire engine; **=maul** n baggy mouth; **=pilze** ♀ m/pl.: ⊘ ascomycetes pl.; **=spritze** f fire-engine (furnished) with a hose; **=wagen** m carriage for the hose.
Schlauder ☉ (ˇˇ) [= Schleuder] f ㊽ arch. (Verankerung) brace, iron tie.
schlaudern¹ (ˇˇ) = schleudern¹ u. ².
schlaudern² ☉ (ˇˇ) v/a. ㉒a. arch. (durch Schlaudern befestigen) to fix with iron ties. [Weise] adv. cunningly, slyly.
schlauer-weise (ˇˇ-ˇˇ) [Schlau gen. +] **Schlauheit** (ˇ-), **Schlauigkeit** (ˇˇ-) f (s. schlau) slyness; artfulness, craftiness, cunning, F depth. [Schlauberger.]
Schlau-kopf F (ˇˇ...) m ㉒, =meier m ②
schlecht (ˇ) [ahd.: slight: schlicht] I a. ❻ (ant. gut) **1.** bad, adv. badly, ill, comp. 2er (schlimmer) worse, sup. 2st (ärgst) the worst. — **2.** mit nouns: 2e Aussicht(en) poor prospect; F schlechtdenken 2, Dank 2 und 6; 2e Entschuldigung lame excuse; 2e Gefährten low (or profligate, depraved, vile) companions pl.; 2es Geld base (or counterfeit) coin or money; 2e Gesundheit ill (or indifferent, poor) health; 2e Luft foul air; 2er Trost poor consolation; 2e Zeiten hard times pl.; phys. 2er Leiter non-conductor of heat, &c.; ✱ s. Absatz 3; 2e Papiere dubious stock; (sehr) 2e Ware (most) inferior goods pl. — **3.** mit verbs, mst adv.: s. anbringen 1, ausfallen 4; v. e-r Uhr: 2 gehen to go badly, to keep bad time; vgl. gehen 8 am Schluß und 9; s. handeln 1, 2 leben to live in a poor (or miserable) way; e-n (durch Reden) 2 m. to speak ill of (F to run down) a p.; mir ist (gesundheitlich) 2 I feel ill or poorly, F I am out of sorts; 2 bei Kasse sein to be hard up (for cash); 2 w. (verderben) to go (or turn) bad, to spoil, moralisch: to grow wicked, to go to the bad; 2er w. to deteriorate; (schlimmer w.) to grow worse, to worsen, to go from bad to worse; 2 (adv.) entzückt von et. sein to be anything but charmed with a th. — **4.** = schlicht, meist durch „und" mit einem a. verbunden, zB. 2 und recht, schlicht und 2 plain and honest. — **5.** nicht 2 (nicht wenig) very much, great(ly); nicht 2 überrascht greatly surprised. — II der, die, das ~e ❻ **6.** der (die) ~e the wicked (or evil) one. — **7.** das ~e the bad thing; evil (things pl.); das ~e an einer Sache the bad side (or worst part) of a th.; alles mögliche ~e von e-m sagen to say everything bad of (or about) a p.
schlechter=dings (ˇˇˇ, ˇˇ) [= schlechter Dinge] adv. (durchaus) absolutely, decidedly, positively, by all means; er will es 2 nicht glauben he is by no means (or not in the least) inclined (or disposed) to believe it, he utterly disbelieves (or discredits) it.
schlecht-gelaunt (ˇˇˇˇ) a. ❻ ill-humoured, in bad humour; 2hin (ˇˇˇ) adv. plainly, simply; (ohne weiteres) without (much) ceremony or fuss.
Schlechtigkeit (ˇˇˇ) f ㊽ (s. schlecht) **1.** Eigenschaft: badness; baseness, sittliche auch: profligacy, depravity, wickedness; ♣ inferiority. — **2.** Tat: evil deed, base (or vile) action, mean (F dirty) trick.
schlecht-weg (ˇˇˇ) = schlechthin.
schlecke(r)n ꝛc. (ˇˇ) = lecke(r)n ꝛc.
Schlegel (ˇˇ) [ahd.: sledge; *schlagen] m ㉒ **1. a)** v. Trommeln ꝛc.: drumstick; **b)** Ballspiel: bat; **c)** ⊙ beetle, mallet, **d)** ✦ (Fäustel) (cat's-head) sledge. — **2.** Koch., Schlächterei: = Keule 3.
Schleh ♀ (ˇ) m Ⓓb. = Schlehe.
Schleh-baum (ˇˇ...), =busch, =dorn ♀ m ㉒ sloe(-tree), blackthorn (Prunus spino'sa).
Schlehe (ˇˇ) [ahd.: sloe] f ㊽ Frucht: sloe, bullace(-plum).
Schlehen-blüte (ˇˇˇ...) f ㊽ sloe-blossom; **=falter** m, ent. sloe-worm (Spina pruni); **=spinner** m, ent. vapourer(-moth) (Or-gy'ia anti'qua); **=strauch** m = Schlehbaum.
schleh-weiß (ˇˇˇ) a. ❻ snow-white.
Schlei (ˇ) [ahd. ꝛc.: Schleie] f ㊽ (m Ⓓb.) ichth. tench (Tinca vulga'ris).
schleichen (ˇˇ) [ahd.: sleek] I v/n. u. v/refl. ㉓ast. to creep (or slip) along, v. Flüssen ꝛc. auch: to crawl along; heimlich 2c. to sneak, to skulk, langsam: to slink (along), im Dunkeln: to prowl about (auch fig.); da kommt er (an-)geschlichen there he comes sneaking (or skulking) along; sich davon 2 to slink (or steal) away; sich in das Haus 2 to steal into the house, vgl. einschleichen; fig. die Bosheit, die im Finstern schleicht wickedness prowling in the dark. — II ~ n ㉓ slow gait or course, furtive movement; fig. = Schleicherei. — III 2d p.pr. u. a. ❻ creeping, &c. along (s. I); (heimlich) furtive, clandestine, adv. on the sly; stealthily; vom Gifte: slow, vom Fieber: (s)low, lingering.
Schleicher (ˇˇ) m ㉒, auch ❻ **1.** creeper, crawler; bsd. fig. (Duckmäuser[in]) sneak, skulker; underhand (or sly) person, intriguer. — **2.** zo. ~ pl. creeping animals, reptiles pl.
Schleicherei (ˇˇ-ˇ) f ㊽ = schleichen II bsd. fig. sneaking, skulking; underhand dealing or manœuvring.
Schleich-fieber (ˇˇ...) n ㉓ path. (s)low fever; **=gut** ♣ n smuggled goods pl., contraband (of war); **=handel** m smuggling, contraband (trade), illicit (or unlawful) trading; ~ treiben to smuggle, to carry (or run) contraband (goods); **=händler(in** f) m smuggler, contrabandist; **=patrouille** ✕ f secret patrol; **=weg** m secret (or hidden) path; auf ~en by crooked means, (verstohlen) stealthily, surreptitiously, furtively.
Schleie (ˇˇ) f ㊽ = Schlei.
Schleier (ˇˇ) [mhd. 13. sae.; *ndl.] m ㉒ **1.** veil; kurzer ~fall; eccl. den 2 nehmen to take the veil, to go into a nunnery; fig. ~ vor den Augen film (or haze) before one's eyes; ~ der Vergessenheit veil of oblivion. — **2.** Weberei: (durchsichtiges Gewebe) lawn.
Schleier-eule (ˇˇ...) f ㊽ orn. barn-owl (Strix flammea); **=flor** ♣ m crape.
schleierhaft (ˇˇˇ) a. ❻ **1.** like a veil. — **2.** veiled; fig. hazy, mysterious.
Schleier-haube (ˇˇ...) f ㊽, **=kappe** f ㊽ (lady's) crape cap; **=leinwand** ♣ f lawn; 2los a. ❻ without a veil; **=macher(in** f) m veil-maker; **=schleifen** (ˇˇ) v/a. ㉒a. to veil (a. fig.); phot. eine Platte 2 to fog a plate.
Schleier-tanz (ˇˇ...) m ㉒ skirt-dance; **=tänzerin** f skirt-dancer; **=taube** f ㊽ orn. nun (Colu'mba li'vea cuculla'ta); **=tuch** n = **=flor**, **=leinwand**.
Schleif²-bahn (ˇˇ...) [schleifen²] f ㊽ auf dem Eise: slide; **=¹bank** f [schleifen¹] f grinding-lathe or -bench; **=brett** n grinding-board, s. Messer: knife-board.
Schleife (ˇˇ) [nhd.; *obd. (mhd.) Schlaufe] f ㊽ **1.** (Schlinge) **a)** sliding (or slip-) knot, an Halsbinden: sailor's knot; a. = Halsbinde; **b)** (zusammengeschlungenes Band zum Putz) bow, in Kreisform: rosette; **c)** ⊙ (Öse) eye; **d)** ~ an geschriebenen Buchstaben, ☉ am Schienenstrang und Telegraphendraht, math. bei Kurven: loop; elect. in einer ~ in the same circuit. — **2.** (schlittenartiges Gestell) sledge, dray; a. = Acker2. — **3.** = Schleifbahn. — **4.** ☉ (Schleifmühle) grinding-mill.
schleifen¹ (ˇˇ) [ahd.] ㉓bst. I v/a. ⊙ **1.** Messer ꝛc. 2 (schärfen, schneidig m.) to grind, to sharpen; (wetzen) to whet; (abziehen) to give an edge to a sword, &c., to set a razor, &c.; (glänzend m.) to polish, Metall a. to burnish, to furbish. — **2.** Diamanten ꝛc. 2 to cut ..., vieleckig: to cut into facets; Glas: to grind ..., aus dem groben: to rough-grind; matt: to rough (down) with sand (vgl. einschleifen²). — **3.** fig. der junge Mann muß erst noch geschliffen w. ... requires polish(ing), F wants licking into shape. — II v/n. (h. u. sn) **4.** auf dem Eise 2 to slide on the ice, beim Tanze: to scrape (or slide) in waltzing. — III ~ n ㉓ **5.** s. Schleifung¹.
schleifen² (ˇˇ) [mhd. = Schleife = nhd. schleppen] I v/a., v/n. (h.) u. v/refl. ㉓ **1.** to drag (or pull) along, v. Gewändern: to trail (along the ground), to draggle (in the mud); (auf einem Schlitten fortschaffen, carry on a) sledge; er schleifte sich mühsam an Krücken he dragged himself along on crutches. — **2.** (dem Boden gleich m.) to level with the ground, Bauten: to demolish, ✕ eine Festung: to raze,

♪ Musik; ⊘ Wissenschaft; ♀ Pflanze; ♁ Geographie; ⊙ Technik; ✦ Bergbau; ✕ Militär; ⚓ Marine; ♣ Handel; ✉ Post; 🚂 Eisenbahn.

[Schleifenfahrt] — 846 — [schleusen]

to dismantle. — 3. ♪. *gr*. Töne. Laute ♀ (verschmelzen, binden) to slur ...; ‖ ~ *n* ㉓ 4. f. Schleifung².
Schleifen²=**fahrt** ⊕ (″...) [Schleife] *f* ⊕ Radsport looping the loop; ‡**probe** *f. tel.* v. Telegraphendrähten: loop-test.
Schleifer (¹‿) *m* ㉒ 1. (Person, die et. schleift) grinder (vgl. Scherenschleifer); polisher, burnisher; *v*. Edelsteinen: cutter. — 2. Tanz: (langsamer Walzer) sliding waltz or step, shuffle. — 3. ♪ (gebundene Note) slurred note.
Schleiferei (‒‿‒¹) [schleifen¹] *f* ㊻ grinding, grinding- (or polishing-) trade.
Schleif²=**feder** (″...) *f* ㊻ *elect.* earth-terminal; =¹**glas** *n* grinding-glass; =³**kanne** [Schleife] *f* (große Kanne mit Henkel u. Deckel) large jug with handle and lid; =²**knoten** *m* slip- (or sliding) knot, ↕ running knot; =¹**maschine**, =**mühle** *f* grinding-machine, -mill; =²**nadel** *f* large hair-pin; =**note** ♪ *f* slurred note; =¹**pulver** *m* grinding-powder, emery-powder; =**rad** *n* grinding- (or polishing-) wheel; =²**ring** *m*, *elect.* segment; =¹**sand** *m* grinding-sand, fine sand; =²**schritt** *m* sliding (or shuffling) step or gait; =¹**stein** *m*: a) nicht drehbarer: whetstone, f. Rasiermesser *2c*.: hone; b) drehbarer: grindstone, grinder, =**trommel** *f* Spinnerei: emery-roller.
Schleifung¹ (¹‿) *f* ㊻ (f. schleifen¹ I) grinding; polish(ing).
Schleifung² (¹‿) *f* ㊻ (f. schleifen² 2) demolition, razing, dismantling; (f. schleifen² 3) slur(ring).
Schleif¹=**zeug** (″...) *n* ㉒ grinding- (or polishing-) implements or tools *pl*.
Schleim (¹) [ahd.: slime] *m* ⓒ. 1. viscous fluid, slimy substance; bsd. *physiol.* ~ im tierischen Körper: phlegm, ☤ mucus, pituita, ...e. — 2. *chm.*, &c. (Pflanzen=)♀ mucilage.
Schleim=**aal** (″...) *m* ㉒ Inger; ♀**absondernd** *a*. ㊻ mucigenous, nuciparous; =**absonderung** *f* = =**auswurf**; =**alge** ♀ *f* nostoc; ♀**artig** *a*. slimy, ☤ mucoid, muciform; pituitous; =**auswurf** *m* ㊻ mucous secretion, expectoration; =**drüse** *f*, *anat.* mucous gland; ♀**eiterig** *a*.: ☤ mucopurulent.
schleimen (¹‿) **I** *v/n*. (h.) 1. (beim Kochen schleimig w.) to form a gruel or a mucilage, to grow viscous or slimy. — 2. (Schleim verursachen) to cause phlegm. — **II** *v/a*. 3. (v. Schleim reinigen) to free from slime or sliminess, Fische a. to clean, Zucker 2c. to scum.
Schleim=fieber (″...) *n* ㊺ *path.* mucous fever; =**fisch** *m*, *ichth.* blenny (*Ble'nnius*); =**fluß** *m, path.* blennorrhœa; =**geschwulst** *f* myxoma; =**haut** *f, anat.* mucous (der Nase auch: pituitary) membrane; =**hautentzündung** *f* mycodermitis.
schleimicht, mst ...**ig** (¹‿) *a.* ㊻ 1. = schleim=artig. — 2. (Schleim enthaltend) slimy, ☤ mucous, bfd. *chm.* mucilaginous.
Schleim=sauer (″...) *a*. ㊻ *chm.* mucic, ♀**saures** Salz mucate; =**säure** *f* ㊺ mucic acid ($C_6H_{10}O_8$); =**stoff** *m* des tierischen Körpers: mucin(e); =**tiere** *n/pl. zo.* (Schnecken, Muscheln, Austern 2c.) molluscs, mollusca *pl*.

Schleiße ↘ (‿‿) [mhd.] *f* ㊻ 1. wooden splint(er). — 2. (Rippe der Feder ohne Fahne) quill of a feather stripped of its beard. — 3. faft ✝ = Scharpie.
schleißen faft ✝ (¹‿) [ahd.: schlitzen] *v/a., v/n.* (fn) u. sich ♀ *v/refl.* ⓐ*a*. 1. to slit, to split; (abnutzen) to wear out; als *v/n.* und *v/refl.* auch: to wear o.s. out. — 2. ⊕ Federn ♀ to strip quills.
Schleißer schleifisch (¹‿) [Schließer(in)] *m* ㉒, ~**in** *f* ㊻ [Hausältester(in)] housekeeper.
Schleiß=feder (″...) *f* ㊻ quill fit for stripping; =**holz** *n* wood for splints.
Schlemihl F (‒¹) [hebr. Selumiel 4 Mos. 1, 6 u. (=Simri) 25, 7—14] *m* ⓒ*d*. = Pechvogel.
Schlemm ✝ (¹) [engl.] *m* ⓒ*d*. ⊕ Whist: ♀ *m*. (alle Stiche *m*.) to make a slam.
schlemmen (¹‿; Hom. schlämmen) [ndd.: *Schlamp m* Schlemmerei] **I** *v/n*. (h.) ⊕ (schmausen und zechen) to eat and drink well, to feast, carouse, revel, gorge, gormandize. — **II** ~*n* ㉓ = Schlemmerei.
Schlemmer (¹‿) [schlemmen] *m* ㉒, ~**in** *f* ㊻ gormandizer, glutton; F high liver; ~**ei** (‒‿‒¹) *f* ㊻ gormandizing, gluttony, revelry, rich (or fine) living.
Schlempe (¹‿) [Schlampe] *f* ㊻ *agr*. (Branntweinspülicht) distiller's wash. [lounger.]
Schlenderer (¹‿‿) *m* ㉒ saunterer,]
Schlender=gang (¹‿‿) *m* ㉒ sauntering (or jaunty) gait or step.
schlendern (¹‿) [ndd.] *v/n*. (h. und fn) ⓑ*a*. to saunter (or lounge, stroll) about; müßig (herum=)♀ to loiter (or F hang, hang-slang) about.
Schlendrian (‒‿‒) [ndd.=lt.; *schlendern*] *m* ⓒ*c*. accustomed routine, humdrum (or old-fashioned) way, amtlicher: redtapism; am alten ~ festhalten to jog on in the old groove.
schlenkern (¹‿) [mhd.; *schlingen*¹] *v/a*. ⓑ*a*. 1. (von fich schleudern) to jerk, fling, toss. — 2. (schlotternd bewegen) to dangle; die Arme ♀, auch *v/n*. mit den Armen ♀ to fling about (or swing) one's arms; die Beine ♀ laffen to dangle one's legs.
Schlepp=anker ↕ (¹‿‿) [schleppen] *m* ㉒ kedger; =**boot** ↕ *n* tug, tow(ing)-boat; =**dampfboot** *n*, =**dampfer** *m*, =**dampfschiff** *n* ↕ steam-tug, tug-boat.
Schleppe (¹‿) [ndd. = schleifen²] *f* ㊻ train (or trail) of a dress; Kleid mit (ohne) ~ trailing (non-trailing) dress or skirt.
schleppen (¹‿) [ndd. = schleifen²] **I** *v/a*. 1. to trail, drag, lug; to draggle in the mud; ein Kleid ♀ (fehr viel tragen) to hack a dress; ein Kleidungsstück entzwei (zuschanden) ♀ to wear out (to ruin) a garment. — 2. ↕ ein Schiff ♀ (bugfieren) to tow ... (along), von e-m andern Schiffe: (es hinter fich herziehen) to tug ...; das Schiff schleppt den Anker ~ drags its anchor. — **II** fich ♀ *v/refl*. (mit Mühe bewegen) 3. to drag o.s. along, to move (or proceed) with difficulty. — 4. fich mit et. ♀ to be burdened (or encumbered, hampered) with a th. — 5. mit Angabe der Wirkung: fich müde ♀ to tire o.s. with dragging (loads, &c.). — **III** *v/n*. (h.) 6. a) (am Boden schleifen) b) (fich hinziehen) to drag (auch *fig*.) c) (↕ vom Anker) fein Kleid ♀ laffen to let one's dress trail or draggle (on the ground); ♀*b*, auch: slow, von der

Sprache: drawling, droning, vom Stile, Gange 2c.: heavy; ♀*de Art*, Methode wearisome (or cumbersome) way, method. — **IV** ~*n* ㉓ 7. (f. I) dragging, lugging, ↕ towing, tugging; (f. III) wearisome way or task. [bearer.]
Schleppen=träger (¹‿‿‿) *m* ㉒ train-]
Schlepper (¹‿) *m* ㉒ 1. a) one who drags; b) ♗ (Kundenwerber) tout(er); F (Helfershelfer) bonnet; c) ⚒ trammer. — 2. ↕ = Schleppdampfer.
Schlepperei (‒‿‒¹) *f* ㊻ = schleppen IV.
Schlepp=kahn ↕ (″...) *m* ㉒ tug, tow-boat; =**kasten** ⚒ *m* sledge, skip; =**kette** ↕ *f* towing-bridle; drag-chain; =**kleid** *n* (long) dress with a train, dress trailing on the ground, trailing skirt; =**lohn** *m* towage; =**netz** ⊕ *n* Fischerei: drag- (or sweep-, trawling-, trail-)net, trammel; mit ~en (Schleppen) to trawl; =**pflug** ⊕ *m*, *agr*. dragplough; =**säbel** ⚔ *m* heavy (cavalry-) sabre, F dangler; =**schiff** ↕ *n* tug(boat); =**schiffahrt** *f* tug-service, towing; =**seil** *n* tow(ing)-rope; =**tau** *n*: a) = =**seil**; b) ↕ towing- (or dragging-) cable, guess-rope or -warp; ein Schiff ins ~ nehmen to take ... in tow; fich ins ~ nehmen laffen (auch *fig*.) to be taken in tow.
Schlesi=en ♀ (¹‿‿) [slaw. Sleza (jetzt. Lohe), Fl.] *npr.n* ㉓ *a*. (preußische Provinz) Silesia.
Schlesi=er (¹‿‿) *m* ㉒, ~**in** *f* ㊻, **schlesisch** (¹‿) *a*. ㊻ Silesian.
Schleuder¹ (¹‿) [mhd. =Schlauder] *f* ㊻ (Riemen zum Schleudern) sling, catapult.
Schleuder²=**arbeit** (¹‿‿‿‿) [schleudern²] *f* ㊻ badly finished work.
Schleud(**e**)**rer**¹ (¹‿‿) [schleudern¹] *m* ㉒ 1. slinger. — 2. ⚔ = Schneller 4.
Schleud(**e**)**rer**² ♗ (¹‿‿) [mhd. nachlässiger Arbeiter] *m* ㉒ (Kaufmann, der spottbillig verkauft) dealer who sells under cost-price, F cutting tradesman.
Schleuder²=**geschäft** ♗ (″...) *n* ㉒ F cutting trade; =¹**maschine** *f*: a) ⊕ centrifugal (drying-)machine; b) ⚔ Alt. = ballista, catapult.
schleudern¹ (¹‿) [Schleuder] ⓑ*a*. **I** *v/a*. to throw with a sling; to fling, hurl, toss, shy; in die Höhe ♀ to toss up; f. Bannstrahl. — **II** *v/n*. (h.) to roll, swing, ⊕ *v*. Maschinenteilen: to have too much play.
schleudern² (¹‿) [mhd. *slûren*] *v/n*. (h.) ⓑ*a*. 1. F (schlecht u. nachläfftg arbeiten) = pfuschen. — 2. ♗ to sell under (or below) cost-price, F to fling (or give) one's goods away, to cut the trade or the prices.
Schleuder²=**preis** ♗ (″...) *m* ㉒ (ruinously) low rate, reduced price; et. zu e-m ~ verkaufen to sell a th. dirt-cheap or at a great (or sweeping) reduction, F to fling a th. away, (almost) to give a th. away; =¹**wurf** *m* throw(ing) with a sling, ☤ jact(it)ation.
schleunig (¹‿) [ahd.] *a*. ㊻ prompt, speedy, ready, quick; *adv*. auch: immediately, at once, in all haste; auf das ♀*te* with the utmost speed or dispatch; most promptly or rapidly.
Schleunigkeit (¹‿‿‿) *f* ㊺ promptness, promptitude, speed.
Schleuße ⊕ (¹‿) [mhd.: sluice; ndl.; *schl*] *f* ㊻ écluse ⊕ Wasserbau: sluice, lock.
schleusen (¹‿) *v/a*. ⓐ to lock a canal, &c.

Signs (see page XVII): F familiar; P vulger; ᚠ flash; ↘ rare; ✝ obsolete (died); * new word (born); ‡ incorrect; ♪ music;

[Schleusenbau] — 847 — [schlimm]

Schleusen-bau ⊕ (ᵘᵛ...) *m* ⑫ construction of sluices or locks; **=boden** *m* bottom of a sluice; **=geld** *n* sluice-(or lock-)dues *pl.*; **=meister** *m* sluice-(or lock-)keeper; **=tor** *n* flood-(or lock-, sluice-)gate, lock; **=wärter** *m* lock-keeper; **=wehr** *n* lock-weir; **=werke** *n/pl.* sluice-works *pl.*, lockage.

Schlich¹ (ˢ) [mhd.; *schlich³] *m* ⑫c. 1. = Schleichweg; alle ~e in e-m Hause kennen to know all the ins and outs (or every nook and corner) of a house. — 2. *fig.* = Kniff 4; ich kenne seine ~e I know his tricks or dodges, F I am up to him; hinter j-s ~e kommen to find out a p.'s artifices.

Schlich² (ˢ) [ahd. = ndd. Schlick] *m* ⑫c. 1. ⊕ *metall.* ⊺ slich, slick (vgl. Erzschlich). — 2. slime, mud, slimy (or muddy) soil, bsd. am Meeresboden: ooze.

schlich³ (ˢ) *ind.*, **schliche** (ˢᵛ) *subj. impf.* von schleichen.

schlicht¹ (ˢ) [ndb. = schlecht] *a.* ⓖ 1. (einfach) plain, simple, homely, unadorned, unpretentious, geistig, a. unsophisticated, ingenuous; ⚔ ⚰er Abschied unceremonious discharge; ⚰e Wahrheit unvarnished truth. — 2. (glatt) smooth; sleek; ⚰es Haar, a. a straight hair.

Schlicht²-beil ⊕ (ˢ·ᴸ) [schlichten] *n* ⑫ *carp., join.* chip-axe.

Schlichte (ˢᵛ) *f* ⑯ 1. = Schlichtheit. — 2. ⊕ a) Weberei: size, dressing; b) Eisengießerei: black-wash.

Schlicht²-eisen ⊕ (ˢ·ᴸ) *n* ⑫ *carp., join.* smoothing-plane iron.

schlichten (ˢᵛ) [ahd.; * schlecht 4] I *v/a.* ⓦ 1. (in Ordnung bringen) to arrange, to adjust; to put straight or right; *fig.* a.: to compose, to accommodate, einen Streit ⚰ to settle a dispute, to make up (or heal) a difference, to close a controversy; einen Prozeß: to (settle by) compromise. — 2. (eben m.) to make even, ⊕ a. to level, to plane, mit dem Schlichthobel: to smooth-plane, mit der Schlichtfeile: to smooth-file. — 3. (glatt machen) to smooth, to polish, ⊕ Weberei *etc.*: to size, dress. — II ~ *n* ㉓ 4. f. Schlichtung.

Schlichter (ˢᵛ) *m* ㉒, **~in** *f* ㊵ 1. (f. schlichten 1) *fig.* eines Streites: peace-maker, mediator. — 2. ⊕ (f. schlichten 3) Weberei *etc.*: sizer, dresser.

Schlicht²-feile ⊕ (ˢ·...) *f* ⓗ smooth-file, noiseless file; ²**haarig** *a.* ⓖ smooth-(or sleek-, straight-)haired; **=²hammer** ⊕ *m* planishing-hammer.

Schlicht-heit (ˢ·) *f* ⑯ (f. schlicht 1) plainness, simplicity, homeliness, unpretentiousness, ingenuousness.

Schlicht²-hobel ⊕ (ˢ...) *m* ⑫ *join.* smoothing-plane; **=maschine** *f* Weberei: dressing-machine; **=stahl** *m* = =eisen.

Schlichtung (ˢᵛ) *f* ㊵ 1. (f. schlichten 1) arrangement, adjustment; *fig. auch:* accommodation, eines Streites: settlement. — 2. ⊕ (f. schlichten 2 und 3) levelling, &c.; sizing, &c.

Schlick (ˢ) [ndd.] *m* ⑫b. (Tonschlamm) mud; **~bank** *f* ⑫ mud bank, a. ⚓ =grund.

schlicken (ˢᵛ) *v/n.* (h.) u. **sich ⚰** *v/refl.* ㊳ to be(come) covered with ooze or mud.

schlick(e)rig (ˢ(ᵛ)·) *a.* ⓖ oozy, muddy.

Schlick=grund ⚓ (ˢ·ᵛ) *m* ⑫ des Meeres: oozy (or slimy) bottom.

schlick(r)ig (ˢᵛ·) = schlickerig.

Schlick=watt (ˢ·ᵛ) *n* ⑫ (bei Ebbe freiliegender Schlammgrund) oozy (or muddy) beach or shore, alluvial ground.

Schlief¹ (ᴸ) *m* ⑫c. (klitschige Stelle im Brote) slack-baked part of a loaf.

schlief² (ᴸ) *ind.*, **schliefe** (ᴸᵛ) *subj.*, **schliefen¹** (ᴸᵛ) *pl. impf.* von schlafen.

schliefen² *prov.* (ᴸᵛ) (ahd.: schlüpfen) *v/n.* (in) ⓓe. to slip; to creep, glide.

schliefig (ᴸᵛ) *a.* bsd. vom Brot: slack-baked, doughy. [in glass.]

Schliere ⊕ (ᴸᵛ) *f* ㊽ Glasmacherei: streak

schließbar ⊕ (ᴸᵛ) *a.* ⓖⓖ 1. which can be shut or locked or closed; (provided) with lock and key. — 2. *log.* deducible, inferable.

Schließ=baum ⊕ (ᵘ...) *m* ⑫ bar, eines Hafens: boom; **=blech** *n* bolt-nab, am Gewehre: locking-plate; **=bolzen** *m* = Schütz².

Schließe ⊕ (ᴸᵛ) *f* ㊽ 1. pin (or bolt) for locking. — 2. = Schütz².

schließen (ᴸᵛ) [ahd.; vgl. Schloß] I *v/a., v/n.* (h.) u. **sich ⚰** *v/refl.* ⓓd. 1. to close, fest: to shut, mit Schloß: to lock, mit Riegel: to bolt; *typ.* to lock up; die Augen ⚰ to close (or shut) one's eyes; den Laden ⚰ to shut up (one's) shop; e-m die Tür vor der Nase ⚰ to shut the door in a p.'s face; um elf Uhr werden die Wirtshäuser geschlossen public houses close (or are closed) *etc.*; e-n krumm ⚰ to bind (or chain) a p. hand and foot; das Fenster schließt nicht ... does not shut (properly); ein Kleid schließt (schmiegt sich dem Körper an) a dress sits (or fits) well; die Wunde hat sich geschlossen ... has closed or healed (up); *man.* der Reiter schließt ob. reitet geschlossen ... grips (or sits) his horse well. — 2. (mit ea. verbinden) e-e Klammer ⚰ to close a bracket or parenthesis, vgl. Klammer 2; *fig.* ein Band (enger) ⚰ to draw a bond tighter; ⚔ die Glieder ⚰ to close (or serry) the ranks; *elect.* die voltaische Säule ⚰ to close the circuit (or to connect the poles of) a Voltaic pile. — 3. meist *fig.* mit örtlicher Bestimmung: einen an die Brust ⚰ to press a p. to one's heart; e-n Hund an die Kette ⚰ to attach ... to the chain; sich eng an-ea. ⚰ to draw close(ly) together; hieran ⚰ wir die Bemerkung, daß // to this we add the remark that //; e-n in seine Arme ⚰ to clasp (or fold, lock) a p. in one's arms; e-n in sein Herz ⚰ to take a great liking (or a fancy) to a p.; et. in sich ⚰ (umfassen) to comprehend (or comprise, imply) a th. — 4. (endigen) to finish a sentence, &c., to conclude a speech, &c.; die Debatte, Verhandlung ⚰ to close the debate or discussion; die Schule ⚰ to break up (school); hier schließt die Geschichte here the story ends; ⊕ j-s Konto ⚰ to close a p.'s account; Börse (von Aktien): Tintos schlossen mit 30 Tintos closed at 30; ⚔ ⚰de (Unter-)Offiziere supernumerary (non-commissioned) officers *pl.* — 5. (zustande bringen)

ein Bündnis ⚰ to form an alliance; vgl. Bund¹ 1; f. Ehe; Freundschaft mit einem ⚰ to form a friendship (or make friends) with a p.; Frieden ⚰ to make peace; e-n Handel ⚰ to strike (or conclude) a bargain; e-n Kreis, e-n Reigen ⚰ to form a circle; einen Vergleich ⚰ to come to an agreement or understanding; e-n Vertrag ⚰ to make a contract. — 6. (folgern) to draw a conclusion, to reason, to argue; aus et. auf et. ⚰ to conclude (or infer) a th. from a th.; wir ⚰ aus f-n Worten, daß // we gather from his words that //; von sich (selbst) auf andere ⚰ to judge others by o.s.; woraus ⚰ Sie das? what do you infer that from?, what makes you think so? — II ~ *n* ㉓ 7. f. Schließung. — III **ge=schlossen** *p.p.* u. *a.* ⓖⓖ (D9) 8. in den Bed. des *inf.* — 9. (eng zs.-gehörig) unbroken; ein ⚰es Ganze(s) a th. complete in itself. — 10. (Unzugehöriges ausschließend) ⚰e Gesellschaft private party or club, select circle; ⚰e Jagd private shooting-ground or preserve; hinter ⚰en Türen with closed doors, *jur.* with exclusion of the public, auch (it.) *in camera*; *hunt.* ⚰e Zeit = Schonzeit.

Schließer (ᴸᵛ) *m* ㉒ 1. (a. ~in *f* ㊵) p. who closes a th., bsd. a) (Pförtner) doorkeeper; b) ~in (Schaffnerin) stewardess, housekeeper, f. Beschließer; c) (Gefangenwärter) jailer. — 2. *anat.* = Schließmuskel. [(or jailer's) post.]

Schließer=amt (ᴸᵛ·) *n* ⑫ doorkeeper's

Schließ=feder ⊕ (ᵘ...) *f* ⑫ spring for locking, an Türen *etc.*: spring-bolt, Uhrmacherei: locking-spring; **=frucht** ⓥ *f*: ⚲ achene; **=geld** *n* des Gefangenwärters: jailer's fee; **=haken** *m* eines Buches *etc.*: clasp; Schlosserei: catch of a lock, bolt (-staple); **=kette** *f* an e-r Tür *etc.*: chain for barring (or fastening) a door, &c.; **=lein** ⓥ *m* common flax (*Linum vulgare*).

schließlich (ᴸᵛ) *a.* ⓖⓖ final, last; (abschließend) conclusive; *adv.* finally, ultimately, in the end, in conclusion.

Schließ=muskel (ᵘ...) *m* ⑫ *anat.*: ⚲ sphincter (muscle), contractor; **=platte** ⊕ *f, typ.* imposing-iron or -stone or -table; **=rahmen** *m, typ.* chase.

Schließung (ᴸᵛ) *f* ㊵ (zu schließen 1:) closing, shutting, &c.; (zu 4:) conclusion, *parl.* e-r Debatte: closure, (fr.) *clôture*; (zu 6:) conclusion; reasoning, inference, vgl. Schluß.

Schließ=zeug ⊕ (ᵘ·ᴸ) *n* ⑫ *typ.* locking-up apparatus.

Schliff¹ (ˢ) [mhd.; *schliff²] *m* ⑫b.: a) = Schleifung; b) (Glätte) polish (auch *fig.*), smooth surface, von Edelsteinen: cut. [schleifen¹.]

schliff² (ˢ) *ind.*, ⚰e (ˢᵛ) *subj. impf.* von

schlimm (ˢ) [ahd.: slim] *a.* ⓖⓖ (D 1) u. *adv.* 1. = schlecht; (übel) evil; er ist ⚰ (am ⚰sten) d(a)ran he is badly (the worst) off; es ist ⚰ für ihn it is hard on him, F it's hard lines for him; desto (ob. um so) ⚰er all (or so much) the worse; immer ⚰er worse and worse; es hätte dir noch ⚰er geh(e)n können you might have fared worse; im ⚰sten Falle (oder ⚰stenfalls) in the worst case, if it

⚲ scientific; ⓥ botanical; ⚹ geography; ⊕ machinery; ⛏ mining; ⚔ military; ⚓ marine; ⊛ commercial; ✉ postal; 🚂 railway.

[Schlingbeschwerde] — 848 — [Schluchzer]

(or if the worst) comes (or came) to the worst; das ~ an der Sache ist // the worst (part) of it is //. — 2. (verdrießend) annoying, (unangenehm) unpleasant, (beunruhigend) disquieting, grave; (verderblich) fatal; eine 2e Geschichte a bad job; 2er Husten, Schnupfen bad (or severe, troublesome) cough, cold; in 2er Lage in a sorry plight, in great straits; alles von der 2(st)en Seite ansehen to look at (or to see) the dark side of everything; das 2ste (ob. dickste) Ende kommt nach the worst (part) is yet to come; aufs (auf das) ~ste gefaßt sein to be prepared for the worst; das ist nicht 2 that does not (much) matter; et. 2er machen to aggravate (or worsen) a th. — 3. (boshaft, böswillig) wicked, malicious; ein 2er Geselle, Kunde a nasty (or bad) fellow, an ugly customer. — 4. F 2 (stark) hinter et. her sein to be bent on (or mad after) a th. — 5. (krank) er ist heute sehr 2 he is very ill (or bad, low) to-day; mir ist 2: a) (zum Erbrechen) I feel sick; b) (nicht wohl) I am not well, F I feel bad or poorly; einen 2en Finger haben to have a bad finger, to suffer from one's finger; ein 2er Hals a sore throat; fig. davor kann e-m 2 und übel werden it makes one heave or (feel) sick, F it makes one feel bad.

Schling=beschwerde (⁸⌣⌣⌣) f ⑫ path. difficulty in swallowing, ⌀ dysphagia.

Schlinge (⁸⌣) [ahd. (bz. Schleuder): sling; *schlingen¹] f ⑱ 1. a) ⚘ (Ranke) tendril; b) (Schleife) running knot, sich zs.-ziehende: noose, hunt. zum Fange: snare; ~n legen to lay snares for wild beasts, &c.; fig. in die ~ fallen, gehen to fall into a trap or an ambush; den Kopf (ob. sich) aus der ~ ziehen to slip one's neck out of the collar, to extricate o.s. (from a difficulty), to (have a lucky) escape. — 2. surg. den Arm in einer ~ tragen to wear one's arm in a sling.

Schlingel F (⁸⌣) [nhd.; *schlingen¹] m ⑫ (impudent or F saucy) fellow, ruffian; von Knaben auch: naughty boy, F young Turk or rascal or rogue, good-for-nothing; fauler ~ sluggard, F lazy-bones; grober ~ rude fellow, boor.

Schlingelei (⁸⌣⌣⁽) f ⑭ impudence, ruffianism; rudeness.

schlingelhaft (⁸⌣⌣) a. ⑥ impudent; naughty, roguish; rude.

schlingen¹ (⁸⌣) [ahd.: sling] v/a. u. sich 2 v/refl. ⓐ st to sling, wind, twist; (flechten) to plait, to (en)twine, in ea.: to intertwine, to interlace; sich um et. 2 to wind (or twine) round a th., von Pflanzen a.: to creep (or climb) round a tree, &c.; ein Band in eine Schleife 2 to tie a ribbon in(to) a bow.

schlingen² (⁸⌣) [nhd. aus † schlinden: Schlund] I v/a., v/n. (h.) ⓐ st to swallow greedily or gluttonously, to gulp (down); to devour, F to gobble up; gefräßig: to gorge. — II ~ n ㉓ ⒥ deglutition; (gieriges Essen) gluttony.

schlingern (⁸⌣) [ndd.; schlingen¹] v/n. (h.) u. v/a. ⓐ a. 1. = schlenkern 2. — 2. ⚓ vom Schiffe: (stark schwanken) to roll

(from one side to the other), to lurch; stampfend und 2d pitching and tossing.

Schling=gewächs (⁸...) n ⑫, =kraut n, =pflanze f creeping (or climbing) plant, creeper. [ing; tying a knot, &c.

Schlingung (⁸⌣) f ⑭ (f. schlingen¹) sling-

Schlippe (⁸⌣) f ⑱ 1. (Feuer=) = Brandgasse. — 2. = Rockschoß.

Schlipper=milch (⁸⌣⌣) f ⑫ curdled milk.

Schlips F (⁸) [(++) engl. slips pl. Schleifen] m ⒜. (narrow) neck-tie (to be tied in a bow). [v. schleißen.]

schliß (⁸) ind., **schlisse** (⁸⌣) subj. impf.

Schlitten (⁸⌣) [ahd.: slide, sled(ge)] m ㉓ 1. sledge, kleinerer: sled (a. ⚔ zur Förderung), bsd. Am. sleigh; ~ fahren to drive (or ride, go) in a sledge or sleigh. — 2. ⊕ mach. sliding-carriage, guide-block, der Sägemühle: chariot, carriage, der Drehbank: slide. — 3. ⚓ zum Stapellauf: ship's cradle.

Schlitten=bahn (⁸⌣...) f ⑫ sledging-path or -road; es wird bald ~ geben there will soon be sledging; **=fahrer** ⚘ m member of a long firm or a gang of commercial sharpers; **=fahrt** f drive in a sledge; **=geläut(e)** n sleigh-bells pl.; **=kufe** ⊕ f sledge-runner; **=partie** f sledging-excursion, bsd. Am. sleighing; **=schieber** m = =fahrer; **=wetter** n weather for sledging.

Schlitter=bahn (⁸⌣⌣ᴸ) [schlittern] f ⑫ slide, bsd. Am. shoot. [slider.]

Schlitterer (⁸⌣⌣) m ㉒, **Schlitterin** f ⑭

schlittern (⁸⌣⌣) [mhd. auf dem Eise gleiten] v/n. (h. u. sn) ⓐ a. to slide.

Schlitt=schuh (⁸⌣ᴸ) [für früheres Schrittschuh] m &c. skate. ~ laufen to skate.

Schlittschuh=bahn (⁸⌣⌣ᴸ...) f ⑫ ice for skating, skating-ground, bsd. für Rollschuhe: skating-rink; **=laufen** n skating; **=läufer(in** f) m skater.

Schlitz (⁸) [ahd.: slit; *schleißen] m ⓐ a. slit; (Spalt) rift, cleft, fissure, zum Geldeinwurf &c.: slot (vgl. Ritz); ~e in et. machen to slit (or slash) a th.

Schlitz=auge (⁸...) n ⑫ der Mongolen: slit eye; **=äugig** a. ⑥ slit-eyed; **=band=muschel** f, zo. slit-shell (Pleurotoma'ria); **schlitzen** (⁸⌣) [mhd.; *schleißen] v/a. ⑨ to slit; geschlitzte Ärmel slashed sleeves pl. (vgl. aufschlitzen).

Schlitz=fenster (⁸...) n ⑫ arch. gap- (or lancet-)window; **=förmig** a. ⑥ like a slit or fissure. [(a. ⚘).]

schlitzig (⁸⌣) a. ⑥ with slits; slashed

Schlitz=messer (⁸⌣...) n ⑫ surg. lancet.

schloh=weiß (⁰ᴸ) [schloh(en)weiß] a. ⑥ snow-white.

Schloß¹ (⁸) [ahd.: slot; *schließ²] n ⓐ a. 1. a) Schlosserarbeit: lock, zum Vorlegen: padlock; f. aufbrechen I und III; unter ~ und Riegel halten to keep under lock and key; der Schlüssel steckt im Schlosse the key is in the door; e-r Tür &c. ein ~ vorlegen to padlock ...; fig. ein ~ vor j-s Mund legen to keep a p.'s lips sealed, to enjoin silence on a p.; b) an einem Buche: clasp, an einem Halsbande: fastening, snap; c) zo. (Scharnier e-r Muschelklappe) hinge of a bivalve; d) ~ am Gewehr: lock. — 2. (mhd.) (herrschaftliches Gebäude) castle, manor-house; vgl. Lustschloß.

Schloß² (⁸) ind. impf. von schließen.

Schloß¹=aufseher (⁸...) m ⑫ keeper (or custodian) of a castle; vgl. =verwalter; **=beamte(r)** m official (or officer) of a castle; **=blatt, =blech** n key-, lock-plate.

Schlößchen (⁸⌣) [dim. v. Schloß] n ㉓ 1. small castle, ehm. auch: castlet. — 2. small lock, an Geldbörsen &c.: snap.

schlösse (⁸⌣) subj. impf. v. schließen.

Schloße mb. (⁸⌣) [mhd.: sleet] f ⑯ (large) hailstone; ~n hail sg.

schloßen mb. (⁸⌣) v/n. (h.) ⑨ to hail.

Schloßen=korn mb. (⁸⌣...) n ⑫, **=stein** m = Schloße; **=wetter** n hail-storm.

Schlosser ⓐ (⁸⌣) [Schloß] m ⑫ locksmith; **=arbeit** f ⑫ locksmith's work.

Schlosserei (⁸⌣⌣ᴸ) ⓐ = Schlosser-arbeit, =handwerk, =werkstatt.

Schlosser=gesell(e) (⁸⌣⌣...) m ⑫ journeyman locksmith; **=handwerk** n locksmith's trade; **=werkstatt** f, **=werkstätte** f locksmith's workshop.

Schloß¹=feder (⁸...) f ⑫ spring of a lock, lock-spring; **=freiheit** f precincts pl. of a castle; **=garten** m garden (or park) round a castle; **=graben** m moat round a castle; **=hauptmann** m governor of a castle; **=herr** m lord of a castle; **=hof** m castle-yard; **=kapelle** f chapel attached to a castle; **=mauer** f castle-wall; **=platz** m square (or open space) in front of a castle or place; **=riegel** m bolt of a lock; **=tor** n, **=turm** m castle-gate, -tower; **=verwalter, =vogt** m castellan; **=wache** f castle- (or palace-)guard.

Schlot mb. (⁽ᴸ) [ahd.] m ⓐ ⓒ. chimney, flue, an Dampfschiffen &c.: funnel, ⊕ auch: funnel-pipe (vgl. Schornstein); **~=baron** F m wealthy manufacturer, cotton-lord; **~=feger** m chimney-sweep(er); **~=junker** m = =baron; **~=kehrer** m = ~feger.

Schlotter (⁸⌣) m ⑫ 1. = schlottern II. — 2. ⊕ Salzsiederei: muddy sediment of salt produced by boiling.

schlotter=beinig (⁸⌣...) a. ⑥ knock-kneed, bandy-legged; **=gang** m ⑫ slouching (or shuffling) gait.

schlott(e)rig (⁸⌣(⌣)) a. ⑥ loose, flabby, (watschelig) waddling, slouching, F wabbly, (wackelig) rickety, shaky, tottering; (nachlässig) slovenly, slipshod; 2 gehen to waddle, to slouch (along); **~=keit** f ⑯ looseness, ricketiness, shakiness; slovenliness.

Schlotter=kopf (⁸...) m ⑫ shaky head; provc. **=milch** f curdled milk.

schlottern (⁸⌣) [mhd.] I v/n. (h. u. sn) ⓐ a. to hang loose(ly), to fit badly; (wackeln) to shake, im Gehen: to waddle, slouch, totter; sein 2des Gebein his shaky bones or limbs pl.; 2 die Knie(e) shaking knees pl.; 2 der Wagen jolting carriage. — II ~ n ㉓ shaking, &c. (f. I).

Schlucht (⁸çt) [nhd.] f ⑯ (poet. a. ⑩) (mountain-)gorge, gully, (Abgrund) chasm, (Hohlweg) hollow, ravine, bsd. ⚔ defile; (enges Tal) glen.

schluchtig (⁸çt⌣) a. ⑥ ravine-like.

schluchzen (⁸çt⌣) [mhd.; *Schluckauf] I v/n. (h.) ⑨ (den Schluck=auf haben) to hiccup or hiccough, to have the hiccups. — II ~ n ㉓, **Schluchzer** m ⑫ sobbing; ⚘ hiccups pl.

[**Schluck**] — 849 — [**schmachten**]

Schluck (´) [mhd.; *schlucken] m ⓗⓂb, 6. (Zug eines Schluckenden) gulp, mouthful, swallow, von Flüssigem: draught, F pull; kleinerer: sip, F drop of brandy, &c.
Schluck-auf (ˇ,¹) m ⓠd. hiccups pl.
Schlückchen (´ⵙ) n ㉓ little draught.
schlucken (ˇⵙ) [mhd.] **I** v/a. u. v/n. (h.), mit Angabe der Wirkung: v/refl. ⓼⓼ **1.** to swallow, gierig: to bolt one's food, rasch: to gulp (down); sich voll 2 to gorge (or cram) o.s. with food; er hat Wasser geschluckt he was nearly drowned. — 2. F fig. in sich 2 to suck up, to absorb; die Einnahme 2 to pocket (F to swallow) the receipts; er wird nicht viel dabei 2 he won't gain much by it. — **II** ~ ㉓ **3.** n swallowing, &c. (f. 1), ⵕ deglutition. — **4.** m = Schluckauf; mit ~ behaftet having the hiccups, ⵕ singultous.
Schlucker (ˇⵙ) m ㉒: **1.** (Fresser) glutton, armer ~ poor (or hungry, starving) wretch or fellow, (half-)starved person, starveling. — **2.** = Schluckauf.
schlucksen (ˇtsⵙ) = schluchzen.
Schluck=vermögen (ˇⵙ...) n ㉒ phys.: ⵕ power of deglutition; ⵕweise adv. (F a.) by gulps or mouthfuls or draughts.
schludern F (ⵡⵙ) = schleudern² 1.
schlug (ⵜ) 1. u. 3. Person sg. ind., **schlüge** (ⵡⵙ) subj. impf. von schlagen.
Schlummer (ˇⵙ) [ndb.: slumber] m ㉒ slumber; (leiser Schlaf) light sleep, nap, dozing, F forty winks.
schlummer=betäubt (ˇⵙ,ⵡ¹) a. ⓶⓶ overcome with drowsiness or sleep.
Schlummerer (ˇⵙ) m ㉒ **1.** slumberer. — **2.** fig. = Schlafmütze.
Schlummer=gott (ˇⵙ...) m ㉒ god of sleep, Morpheus; =kissen n (soft) pillow; =kopf F m sleepy(-headed) fellow (= Schlafmütze fig.); =körner n/pl. poppy-seeds pl.; =lied n lulling tune, für kleine Kinder: lullaby, ♪ hushaby.
schlummern (ˇⵙ) [(mhd.) ndb.] **I** v/n. (h.), v/impers. ⓠa. to slumber, to doze, to (have a gentle) nap, F to take one's forty winks, to (have a) snooze; fig. to lie dormant, to rest. — **II** ~ n ㉓ = Schlummer.
Schlummer=punsch (ˇⵙ...) m ㉒ F nightcap; =rolle f round pillow.
Schlump prov. (´) [ndb.] **I** ⵀ m ⓠb. (Dusel) stroke of luck, lucky chance, fluke. — **II** f ㊻, ~e (ˇⵙ) f ⓠ = Schlampe.
schlumpen prov. (ˇⵙ) [ndb.] v/n. (h. u. fn) ⓼⓼ **1.** ♪ to chance, to succeed by a mere) fluke. — **2.** Kleid: to draggle, to trail (in the mud), to sweep the pavement.
schlumpig ndb. (ˇⵙ) a. ⓶⓶ draggle-tailed.
Schlund (´) [ahd.: schlingen²] m ⓠb. **1.** anat. (Halsöffnung) gullet, gorge, swallow, ⵕ pharynx (Speiseröhre); œsophagus; auch = Gurgel; ⵕ = einer Blumenkrone bisw.: ⵕ rictus. — **2.** fig. (enge Öffnung) mouth of a cave, cannon, &c.; auch = Abgrund.
Schlund=kopf (ˇⵙ...) m ㉒ anat.: ⵕ pharynx; =kopf=spiegel m, med.: ⵕ pharyngoscope; =krampf m, path.: ⵕ pharyngeal spasm; =rohr n, surg. probang.
Schlup(e) (´) ⓘ (ⵡ/ⵙ) f ㊻⑧ = Schaluppe.
Schlupf obb. (ˇⵙ) [mhd.] m ⓠb. **1.** slipping, sliding. — **2.** (Schlupfloch) refuge, cover.

schlüpfen, südd. a. **schlupfen** (ˇⵙ) [mhd.: slip; *schliefen] v/n. (fn) ⓼⓼ to slip, slide, glide; er schlüpfte (schnell) in seinen Schlafrock he (quickly) slipped into (or on) his dressing-gown.
schlüpferig (ˇⵙⵙ) = schlüpfrig.
Schlupf=hafen ⵚ (ˇⵙ...) m ㉒ creek, cove, bight, shelter; =käfer m, ent. = Mehlkäfer; =loch n hiding-place, (Ausflucht) loophole; vgl. Schlupf 2.
schlüpfrig (ˇⵙ) [mhd.: schlupf, schlüpfen] a. ⓶⓶ **1.** slippery (a. fig.); 2 machen to lubricate; 2 machend lubricant (a. ⓞ). — **2.** fig.: a) (mißlich) precarious, delicate, ticklish, critical; (gefährlich) dangerous; b) (zweideutig) ambiguous, equivocal; (anstößig) obscene, lascivious, loose, v. Geschichten etc. a. piquant, racy.
Schlüpfrigkeit (ˇⵙ-) f ㊻ (f. schlüpfrig) **1.** slipperiness; lubricity. — **2.** fig. precariousness; (Anstößigkeit) obscenity, lasciviousness, looseness.
Schlupf=tür (ˇⵙ...) f = Hintertür; =wespe f, ent. ichneumon(ny) (Ichneumon), als Larve: caterpillar-eater; =winkel m lurking-place; (verborgener Winkel) secret nook, hidden corner or recess; b.s. haunt; vgl. =loch.
schlürfen (ˇ [lautn.) v/n. (h.) ⓼⓼ **1.** oft: **schlurfen**, mit den Füßen: to shuffle (along). — 2. mit den Lippen: to sip, to lap.
Schluß (´) [mhd.; *schließen] m ⓠa. **1.** closing, shutting. — **2.** (Ende) close, end, conclusion, termination, (Ergebnis) upshot; Fernspr.: ~! finished!, done!, that's all!; Fußballspiel: ~! no side!; bis zum Schlusse der Aufführung etc.: (right) to the end …; nach ~ der Redaktion before going to press; weit S. at the last moment; ~ einer Rede conclusion (or end, winding-up) of a speech, peroration; (Nachwort) epilogue; =folgt to be concluded in our next; eine Sache zum ~ bringen to bring a matter to a close, to terminate an affair; zum Schlusse in conclusion, finally; bis zum Schlusse (right) to the end. — **3.** (Abschluß) ~ e-r Debatte closing a debate, parl. durch Antrag: closure, F co. guillotine, über e-n bestimmten Gegenstand u. zu bestimmter Zeit: closure by compartments; auf ~ der Debatte antragen to move the question or the closure; ~ e-s Handels, Vertrages etc. conclusion … — **4.** (feste Fügung, genaues Passen) Tür und Fenster haben keinen rechten ~ … do not close (or shut) tightly enough; man. einen guten ~ (am Pferde) h. to grip (or sit) the horse well or firmly. — **5.** geh. Spr., bisw. = Beschluß 1. — **6.** (Folgerung) conclusion, inference; vom einzelnen ausgehend: induction, vom Allgemeinen: deduction; logischer ~ in 3 Sätzen: ⵕ syllogism; zu e-m Schlusse gelangen to arrive at (übersetzt: to jump at) a conclusion; e-n ~ ziehen to draw a conclusion, to conclude, infer.
Schluß=akt (ˇⵙ...) m ㉒ last act; =antrag m, parl. putting (or calling for) the question, auch: moving the closure, F co. putting the guillotine into operation; =art f mode of arguing or reasoning; =bemerkung f final (or concluding) remark.

Schlüssel (ˇⵙ) [ahd.; *schließen] m ㉒ key (a. fig. u. ⵉ = ⵙpunkt), falscher: skeleton-key, picklock; ♪ (Noten=)~ clef.
Schlüssel=bart ⓞ (ˇⵙ...) m ㉒ key-bit, ward of a key; =bein n, anat. key-(mehr gbr.: collar-)bone, ⵕ clavicle; =blech n key-plate, (e)scutcheon; =blume ⵛ f: echte ~ cowslip (Primula officina'lis), hohe ~ oxlip (Pr. ela'tior); =büchse f Spielzeug: pistol made (out) of a key; =bund m = =ring, n bunch of keys; vgl. Bund² 2; =gewalt f, eccl. (Amt der Schlüssel) power of the keys; =haken m key-swivel; =loch n keyhole; durch das ~ gucken to peep through the k.; =punkt ⵉ m key to a position; =ring m key-ring; =rohr n key-pipe or -barrel; =schild n = =blech.
Schluß=ergebnis (ˇⵙ...) n ㉒ final result, upshot; =fall ♪ m cadence; =folge (=rung) f chain (or train, course) of reasoning; argument; auch = Schluß 6; =form f form of a conclusion or a syllogism; ⵑgerecht a. ⓶⓶ conclusive, consistent, logical; =gesang m concluding (or last) song; Alt.: epode.
schlüssig (ˇⵙ) [Schluß] a. ⓶⓶ (entschlossen) resolute, determined; ⵑ w. to form a resolution, to make up one's mind.
Schluß=kette (ˇⵙ...) f ㉒ = =folge(rung); =kurs=notierung ⓦ f closing (or final) quotation; =leiste ⓞ f, typ. tail-piece; =linie f, typ. (fancy-)dash; =note ⓦ f sales-note; =punkt m: a) gr. full stop; b) last point or item; =rechnung f: a) ⓦ final account or settlement; b) arith. rule-of-three; ⵑrecht a. ⓶⓶ = ⵑgerecht; =rede f: a) concluding speech; b) conclusion of a speech; epilogue; ⵑreif a. jur. ready for judgment; =reihe f: a) last line of a page; b) = =folge(rung); =reim m end-rhyme, last rhyme, wiederkehrender: burden of a song; =rennen n Sport: final heat, last event; ⵑrichtig a. = ⵑgerecht; =satz m concluding (or closing) sentence, e-s Syllogismus: ⵕ consequent, ♪ e-s Tonstückes: finale; =schein ⓦ m = =note; =sitzung f final (or last) sitting or meeting; =spieler m Fußball: full-back; =stein m, arch. keystone (a. fig.), des Giebels: crown-stone; =stück n concluding (or last) piece, ♪ auch: finale; =vergleich, =vertrag m final (or ultimate) agreement; =vignette f, typ. tail-piece; ⵑwidrig a. inconsistent, illogical; =wort n concluding (or last) word; summary; f. a. Epilog; =zeichen n final sign(al); gr. full stop, ♪ double bar; Fernspr.: das ~ geben to break off (or stop) the conversation; to ring off; =zeile f concluding (or last) line; =zeit f für die Jagd closing-time; =zettel ⓦ m = =note.
Schmach (´ch) [ahd. Verkleinerung] f ㊻ (pl. †, dafür = Schmähungen) **1.** (Unehre) disgrace, dishonour, ignominy, shame. — **2.** (Beleidigung) affront, offence, insult; e-m eine schwere ~ antun to offer a p. a great insult, in geh. Spr.: to put a grievous affront upon a p.
schmach=bedeckt (ˇⵙ,ⵡ¹) a. ⓶⓶ covered with disgrace or shame; disgraced.
schmachten (ˇchtⵙ) [ahd.: schmähen] **I** v/n. (h.) ⓼⓼ to languish with hunger, love,

♪ Musik; ⵕ Wissenschaft; ⵛ Pflanze; ⊖ Geographie; ⓞ Technik; ⵉ Bergbau; ⵚ Militär; ⵄ Marine; ⓦ Handel; ⵞ Post; ⵟ Eisenbahn.

[**Schmachthans**]   — 850 —   [**schmeichelhaft**]

&c., to be parched with thirst; (sich sehnen) to pine or long (nach et. for a th.); 2 I. to tantalize, to torment with pangs of hunger, &c. — II ~ n 23 languor. — III 2d p.pr. u. a. 66 languishing, languid.

Schmacht-hans (⁵cht=⁵) m 62 = =lappen.

schmächtig (⁵⌣) [mhd.] a. 66 slim, slight, slightly built (vgl. schlank 1); path. delicate, (schwindsüchtig) consumptive.

Schmächtigkeit (⁵⌣-) f 46 slimness; path. delicate constitution or health.

Schmacht-lappen (⁵cht...) m 62 : a) F (Hungerleider) starveling; b) P (Verliebter) love-sick youth or swain; =locke f lovelock, frizzled curl, von Mädchen bsd. ehm. auch: kiss-me-quick; =riemen m, etwa: starveling's belt which can be drawn in round the stomach.

schmach-voll (⁵ch-f) a. 66 disgraceful, ignominious, shameful.

Schmack[1] (⁵) m @c. = Sumach. [smack.]

Schmack[2] ⌣ (⁵) f [ndb.,ndl.], ~e (⁵) f 46]

schmackhaft (⁵⌣) [ahd. † Schmack[3] m Geschmack] a. 66 savoury, palatable, relishing, appetizing, toothsome.

Schmackhaftigkeit (⁵⌣-) f 46 savouriness, palatableness, relish, nice (or pleasant, agreeable) taste.

schmaddern (⁵⌣) [ndb.] v/a. u. v/n. (h.) 92a. to daub, besmear, soil (f. sudeln).

Schmäh-artikel (⁵...) [schmähen] f 62, =brief m defamatory (or libellous, insulting) article, letter.

schmähen (⁵⌣) [ahd. verkleinern: Schmach] I v/a. u. v/n. (h.) 88: einen 2, auf (gegen oder über) einen 2 to abuse (or revile, vilify, libel, vituperate) a p., to inveigh (or rail, speak) against a p., F to run a person down; (verschreien) to defame, slander, backbite, durch Schriften: to lampoon, to libel; 2d abusive, insulting, objurgatory; defamatory, slanderous, libellous.— II ~ n 23 = Schmähung 1.

Schmäher (⁵⌣) m 22, ~in f 46 (f. schmähen) abuser, mehr gbr.: reviler; defamer, slanderer, backbiter, detractor.

schmählich (⁵⌣) [ahd.: Schmach] a. 66 1. disgraceful, ignominious, abusive (vgl. schändlich 1). — 2. F fig. (ungemein) excessively (ly); es ist 2 heiß it is terribly (or awfully, fearfully) hot.

Schmäh-lied (⁵...) n 62 defamatory (or libellous, insulting) song; =rede f libellous speech; abuse, invective, diatribe, pol. a. philippic; =schrift f libel(lous pamphlet), lampoon; =sucht f love of scandal; abusive (or slanderous) spirit, abusiveness; 2süchtig a. 66 abusive, slanderous, insulting.

Schmähung (⁵⌣) f 46 1. abusing, &c. (f. schmähen I). — 2. = Schmährede; auch: objurgation, (Verleumdung) defamation, slander, libel.

Schmäh-wort (⁵...) n 62 insulting word, abusive expression, invective; f.a.=rede.

schmal (⁵) [ahd.: small] a. 66 (D 3,7) 1. narrow; (dünn) thin, slender, slim; 2es Gesicht sharp (or thin, pinched) face; typ. condensed. — 2. fig. (knapp) spare, scant(y), poor, meagre; 2e Bissen small morsels pl.; small pittance; 2e Kost poor fare, short commons pl.

schmal-bäckig (⁵...) a. 66 thin- (bsd. v. Kindern a. weazen-)faced, hollow-cheeked, F lantern-jawed; =blätt(e)rig ♃ a. narrow-leaved, ⚘ angustifolious; =brüstig a. = engbrüstig.

schmälen (⁵⌣) [mhd.; *schmal] v/n. (h.) und v/a. 88 (lästern) to scold, rebuke, chide; auf e-n, et. 2 = schmähen I.

schmälern (⁵⌣) [mhd.; *schmal] I v/a. u. sich 2 v/refl. 92 a. 1. (schmal m.) to (make) narrow, to thin (off), to reduce in width, von Kleidern &c.: to take (or draw) in; sich 2 to grow narrow, to decrease in width. — 2. (verringern) to lessen, diminish, Ausgaben &c.: to curtail, retrench, cut down, j-s Ruf &c.: to derogate (or detract) from, j-s Rechte &c.: to entrench (or encroach) upon, j-s Verdienst: to belittle. — II ~ n 23 u.

Schmälerung f 3. (f. I) narrowing, &c.; lessening, diminution, curtailment, retrenchment. [meister.]

Schmal-hans (⁵...) m 40 62 f. Küchen-]

Schmalheit (⁵-) f 46 (f. schmal) narrowness, slenderness, slimness; fig. (Knappheit) spareness, scantiness, meagreness.

schmal-krempig (⁵...) a. 66 narrow-brimmed (hat); =spur-bahn 🚂 f 62 narrow-gauge railway(-line); 2spurig 🚂 a. narrow-gauge (line).

Schmalt-blau (⁵-) n @c., Schmalte (⁵⌣) [it.] f 48 chm., paint. smalt(-blue).

Schmal-tier (⁵...) n 62 hunt. young hind in her second year, hearse; =vieh n small cattle, such as sheep, goats, &c.

Schmalz (⁵) [ahd.; *schmelzen] n @a. melted-down fat, dripping; bsd. (Schweine-) ~ lard; f. Salz 2.

Schmalz-birne (⁵...) f 62 butter-pear; =brot n (slice of) bread and dripping; =butter f = Schmelzbutter.

schmalzen, schmälzen (⁵⌣) v/a. 90 (p.p. oft F geschmalzen) 1. Kochkunst: to put dripping (or lard, butter, F goodness) into; weder gesalzen noch geschmalzen, etwa: without salt or butter. — 2. ⊙ = einfetten I. [=kuchen.]

Schmalz-gebäck(e)ne(s) (⁵⌣(⌣)⌣) n 62 =]

schmalzig (⁵⌣) a. 66 fatty, greasy.

Schmalz-kuchen (⁵...) m 62 Kocht.: dripping-(or short) cake; =pfanne f Küche: frying-pan; =presse f lard-press.

Schmant prov. (⁵) [mhd., *tschech.] m @b. 1. (Milchrahm) cream. — 2. ⊙ thick cream-like substance or mass.

schmarotzen (⌣⁵⌣) [nhd. 15. Jahr.] I v/n. (h.) 90 93 to sponge upon people, to live at other people's expense, to (play the) toady. — II ~ n 23 sponging (system), toadyism, ⚘ parasitism. — III 2d p.pr. u. a. 66 sponging; zo., ♃ ⚘: parasitic(al).

Schmarotzer (⌣⁵⌣) m 22: a) (a. ~in f 46) sponger; F toady, crawler, sneak; b) zo., ♃: ⚘ parasite; ~ei (⌣⁵⌣⁵) f 46 sponging, ⚘ parasitic(al); ~pflanze (⌣⁵⌣...) f 62, ~tier n: ⚘ parasitic(al) plant, animal; beide auch: parasite.

Schmarre (⁵⌣) [ndb.] f 48 slash, cut (in the face), gash; (Narbe) scar.

Schmarren südb. (⁵⌣) m 23: a) Kocht. kind of omelet; b) fig. (Kleinigkeit) trifle.

schmarrig (⁵⌣) a. 66 slashed, scarred.

Schmatz F (⁵) [mhd.; *schmatzen] m @ 62 a. (auch dim. Schmätzchen n 23) hearty (or smacking) kiss, bisw.: F buss.

schmatzen (⁵⌣) [mhd.; *schmecken] v/n. (h.) 90 to chew with a smacking noise (of the lips), to smack one's lips (in eating); to give a hearty (or smacking) kiss.   [(dense) smoke.)

Schmauch (⁵ch) [mhd.: smoke] m @c.f

schmauchen (⁵⌣) [Schmauch] v/n. (h.) u. v/a. 88 1. to (produce a dense) smoke; Tabak 2 (rauchen) to smoke tobacco; eine Zigarre 2 to puff (away at) a cigar. — 2. (bff. schmäuchen) Bienen aus dem Stock 2 (durch Rauch austreiben) to smoke bees out of the hive. — Schmaucher (⁵ch⌣) m 22 smoker. — Schmauch-feuer (⁵ch-⌣) n 62 smouldering fire.

Schmaus (⁵) [mhd.] m ⊙a. (rich) repast or meal, F (fine) spread, (good) tuck-in; feast, banquet, carousal.

schmausen (⁵⌣) [nhd.] I v/n. (h.) u. v/a. 90 to eat (a good meal), to make a good dinner; to feast, to (sit at a) banquet; (zechen) to carouse; tüchtig 2 to eat heartily, F to have a good tuck-in. — II ~ n 23 feasting, banqueting.

Schmauser (⁵⌣) m 22, ~in f 46 hearty eater, diner; feaster, banqueter, reveller. — 2. = Schmaus. **Schmauserei** (-⌣⁵) f 46 1. = schmausen II.f

schmeckbar (⁵-) a. 66 tastable, noticeable (or perceptible) by the taste.

schmecken (⁵⌣) [ahd.: smack] 88 I v n. (h.) 1. to (have a certain) taste; bitter (angebrannt) 2 to taste bitter (burnt), to have a bitter (burnt) taste or flavour; das Brot schmeckt mir (gut) … is to my taste, I like (the taste of) …; schmeckt Ihnen die Suppe? do you like (or enjoy, relish) the soup?; es hat mir (gut) geschmeckt I have enjoyed my meal or dinner; es sich (gut) 2 I. to eat with a relish, to do full justice to one's dinner; wie schmeckt das Pfeifchen? how do you like your pipe?; Sprichw.: wenn's am besten schmeckt, soll man aufhören you should always leave off with an appetite. — 2. nach et. 2 to taste of a th.; fig. to savour (or smack, remind) of a th.; F co. der Käse schmeckt nach mehr the cheese gives an edge to one's appetite or co. tastes morish. — II v/a. u. v/n. (h.) 3. (durch den Geschmack wahrnehmen, versuchen) to judge by the taste (= kosten[1] 1). — 4. (Geschmackssinn haben) fein 2 to have a delicate taste or a fine palate. — 5. fig. (erdulden) to experience, to undergo, to go through; F to get a taste of; (genießen) to enjoy. — III ~ n 23 6. tasting.

Schmecker (⁵⌣) m 22 1. taster of tea, wine, &c. — 2. person with a fine (or delicate) taste or palate; vgl. Feinschmecker. — 3. F co. organ of taste.

Schmeichelei (-⌣⁵) f 46 flattery, kriechende: adulation, wheedling, fawning, F carneying; liebreiche: coaxing, berückende: cajoling, F butter, soft sawder; (hohes Lob) fulsome praise; high compliments pl.

schmeichelhaft (⁵⌣⌣) a. 66 1. flattering, complimentary, (triechend) adulatory,

---

Signs (see page XVII): **F** familiar; **P** vulgar; **⌐** flash; **⌇** rare; **†** obsolete (died); ***** new word (born); **‡** incorrect; **♩** music;

[Schmeichelkatze] — 851 — [Schmiedegesell]

wheedling, fawning. — 2. von Personen: full of flattery or compliments.
Schmeichel=katze (ᵘ...) f ⊕, **=kätzchen** n coaxer, wheedling (F carneying) person or F pussy; vgl. Schmeichler.
schmeicheln (ᴸᵛ) [mhd.] I v/n. (h.) u. v/refl. ⊕a. 1. to flatter a p. with a th.; lobend: to compliment a p. upon a th., kriechend: to adulate a p., to wheedle round a p., to fawn upon a p., sanft anschmiegend: to coax a p., um et. zu erlangen: to cajole (or F butter) a p.; **sich mit eitlen Hoffnungen ⚲** to buoy o.s. up with vain hopes; er fühlt sich durch Ihre Worte geschmeichelt he feels flattered by your words. — 2. als v/a. mit Angabe der Wirkung: e-m et. aus den Händen ⚲ to coax (or wheedle) a th. out of a p.'s hands. — II ~ n ⚲ 3. (f. 1) flattery, cajolery; vgl. Schmeichelei.
Schmeichel=name (ᵘ...) m ⊕ flattering name, auch = Kosename; **=rede** f, **=wort** n flattering (or coaxing) speech, word, F soft soap, butter, blarney.
Schmeichler (ᴸᵛ) m ⊕ (f. ~in f ⊕ (f. schmeicheln 1) flatterer; adulator (f auch: adulatress), wheedler, coaxer, cringer, cajoler; (Schmarotzer) F toady, crawler; vgl. Schmeichelkatze.
schmeichlerisch (ᴸᵛᵛ) a. ⊕ bisw. = schmeichelhaft, meist mit dem Begriff der Falschheit: adulatory, bland, wheedling, F carneying, crawling.
Schmeiß (ᴸ) [schmeißen²] m ⊕a. fly-dirt.
Schmeiße (ᴸᵛ) f ⊕ = Schmeißfliege.
schmeißen¹ F (ᴸᵛ) [ahd.: smite] v/a. ⊕a. to throw, fling, hurl, F u. P to chuck (= werfen); von Pferden: to kick, to lash out; mit dem Gelde um sich ⚲ to throw away (or squander) one's money; die Tür ⚲ to slam or bang ... ; **schmeißen²** F (ᴸᵛ) [mhd.: smit] v/n. (h.) ⊕(⊕a.) bsd. v. Fliegen: to blow meat, &c., to lay (or deposit) eggs on s.th. ; hunt. v. Raubvögeln: to befoul game, &c.
Schmeiß=fliege (ᵘᴸᵛ) f ⊕ ent. (blaue) ~ bluebottle, blow-fly (Musca vomito'ria).
Schmelz¹ (ᵛ) [ahd.; * schmelzen] m ⊕a. 1. enamel (a. anat. der Zähne 2c.); Töpferei: f. Glasur. — 2. fig. (Jugendblüte) bloom of youth; paint. (Verschmelzen der Farben) blending of colours; ♪ melodischer ~ einer Stimme melodious ring or sweetness ...
Schmelz² ... (ᵛ...) [schmelzen] ⊕ f. Schmelz= butter, =farbe 2c.
Schmelz¹=arbeit (ᵛ...) f ⊕ metall. enamel(ling); (s)melting(-process); **=arbeiter** (in f) m enameller; metall. smelter.
schmelzbar (ᵛᵛ) [schmelzen] a. ⊕ chm., ⊕ metall. fusible, liquefiable; schwer ⚲ difficult of fusion, metall. stubborn; (feuerbeständig) refractory.
Schmelzbarkeit (ᵛ⚲ᵛ) f ⊕ fusibility.
Schmelz¹=blau (ᵛ...) n ⊕ = Schmaltblau; **=²butter** f melted(-down) butter; butter for frying.
Schmelze (ᵛᵛ) [schmelzen] f ⊕ 1. ~ des Schnees 2c.: melting, ⊕ ~ der Metalle, auch: fusion, smelting. — 2. ⊕ (zu schmelzende Masse) charge of the furnace. — 3. ⊕ = Schmelzhütte.
schmelzen (ᵛᵛ) [ahd.: (s)melt] I v/n. (fn) ⊕b(ei)t to melt, in Flüssigkeiten: to dissolve, durch feuchte Luft: ⚲ to deliquesce,

(flüssig w.) to liquefy; (weich w.) to soften (a. fig.); (vergehen) to melt away; geschmolzener Schnee melted snow; geschmolzenes Metall molten metal. — II v/a. ⊕ to melt, Metalle auch: to smelt, fuse; (flüssig m.) to liquefy, liquate. — III ⊕ p.pr. u. a. ⊕ melting, &c. (f. I u. II) fig. (schmachtend) languishing; (rührend) touching; ♪ Töne: melodious, sweet.
Schmelzer ⊕ (ᵛᵛ) m ⚲ melter, metall. auch: smelter, founder. [=hütte.)
Schmelzerei (ᵛᵘᴸᵛ) f ⊕ = Schmelz=arbeit,)
Schmelz¹=farbe ⊕ (ᵛ...) f ⊕ enamel- (or vitrified) colour, vitrifiable pigment; **=gemälde** n enamelled painting; **=glas** n = Schmelz 1; **=²grad** m (Hitze, bei der et. schmilzt) (s)melting-heat; **=herd** m, metall. smelting-hearth; **=hitze** f = **=punkt**; **=hütte** f, **=kammer** f, metall. (s)m.-house, smeltery; foundry; **=laut** m Phonetik: liquid (sound); **=löffel** m (s)melting-ladle; **=¹malerei** f enamelling, enamel-painting; **=²mittel** n, metall. flux; liquefier, ...facient; **=ofen** m, metall. (s)melting-furnace; **=perle** ⊕ f bugle; **=punkt** m melting- (or fusing-)point, point (or temperature) of fusion; **=rohr** n = Lötrohr; **=schicht** f, metall. smelting-shift; **=tiegel**, **=topf** m (s)melting-pot, crucible.
Schmelzung (ᵛᵛ) f ⊕ = Schmelze 1, a. liquefaction, liquation.
Schmelz²=wasser (ᵛ...) n ⊕ melting (or melted) snow; **=werk** n: a) = **=hütte**; b) **=arbeit**; **=zeug** n smelting-gear, smelter's tools pl.
Schmer fast † (ᴸᵛ) [ahd.: smear: schmieren] n (m) ⊕c. fat, grease; (Wagenschmiere) cart-grease; (Talg) suet.
Schmer=bauch (ᵘ...ᴸᵛ) m ⊕ paunch, big (Ppot-)belly, F periphery, P forty-guts.
Schmergel 2c. f. Schmirgel 2c.
Schmerl (ᵛ) [ahd.] m ⊕b., ~e¹ (ᵛ) f ⊕ orn. merlin (Falco ae'salon).
Schmerle² (ᵛᵛ) [mhd.] f ⊕ ichth. groundling, loach (Cobi'tis barba'tula).
Schmerz (ᵛ) [ahd.: smart: schmerzen] m ⊕a. (fast † ⊕) : a) nur körperlich, oft pl. ~en: ache, heftiger, stechender: smart(ing pain); b) auch seelisch: pain; (Leiden) suffering, (Weh) woe, (Kummer) grief; mit ~en (er)warten to (a)wait anxiously; von ~en gequält racked with pain, in torment or agony; iro. haben Sie sonst noch ~en? anything else?, is that all?
schmerz=beladen (ᵛᵛᴸᵛ) a. ⊕ = ⚲erfüllt.
schmerzen (ᵛᵛ) [ahd.: smart] v/n. (h.) u. v/a. ⊕ (meist in der 3. Person) to pain, to cause (or give) pain to, to make suffer; to smart, distress, afflict; nur körperlich: to ache, nur seelisch: to grieve; es schmerzt einen, das zu sagen it pains (or grieves) one (or one feels sorry) to (have to) say so; mich ⚲ alle Glieder all my limbs ache, I ache (or feel pain) in every limb.
schmerzen=reich (ᵛᵛᴸᵛ¹) a. ⊕ deeply afflicted; vgl. schmerzbeladen.
Schmerzens=geld (ᵛᵛ...) [+ gen.v. Schmerz] n ⊕ smart- (or hush-)money; **=kind** n woe-begotten child; **=lager** n bed of suffering; **⚲reich** a. ⊕ = schmerzenreich; **=ruf**, **=schrei**, **=ton** m cry of pain or distress, piteous (or pitiful) sound.

schmerz=erfüllt (ᵛ⚲ᵛ) a. ⊕ full of aches and pains; greatly afflicted, poet. woebegone. [pain.)
Schmerz=gefühl (ᵛ⚲ᵛ¹) n ⊕ feeling of)
schmerzhaft (ᵛᵛ) [mhd.] a. ⊕ painful; afflicting, distressing, agonizing; ⚲e Stelle am Körper: sore place, tender (or sensitive) spot; **~igkeit** f ⊕ painfulness; (state of) agony.
schmerzlich (ᵛᵛ) [mhd.] a. ⊕: a) nur körperlich: aching, smarting; b) auch seelisch: painful; grievous (vgl. schmerzhaft); ⚲es Lächeln sad (or sickly) smile; et. ⚲ (adv.) entbehren to miss a th. sadly or very much, to feel the loss of a th. severely; **~keit** f ⊕ painfulness.
schmerz=lindernd (ᵛ...) a. ⊕ allaying (or assuaging, quieting) pain, soothing; med. lenitive, ⚲ anodyne; **⚲los** a. painless, free from pain; **=losigkeit** f painlessness; **⚲stillend** a. deadening pain; vgl. ⚲lindernd; **⚲voll** a. painful, stärker: agonized, agonizing.
Schmetterling (ᵛᵛ) [mhd.] m ⊕ Schmetten provc. Sahne] m ⊕d. ent. butterfly, ⚲ lepidopter; so bunt wie ein ~ in the bright colours of a butterfly.
Schmetterlings=art (ᵛᵛᵛ...) f ⊕ species of butterflies; **⚲artig** a. ⊕ like a butterfly, ⚲ papilionaceous; **=blumen** f/pl., **=blüt(l)er** m/pl., **⚲blütige Gewächse ⚲**: ⚲ papilionaceous flowers, (it.) papilionaceae pl.; **=brenner** ⊕ m für Gaslicht: butterfly-burner; **=fang** m catching (of) butterflies; **=flügel** m wing of a butterfly; **=kunde** f: ⚲ lepidopterology; **=kundige(r)** m: ⚲ lepidopterist; **=lehre** f = **=kunde**; **=sammlung** f collection of butterflies.
schmettern (ᵛᵛ) [mhd.: smatter] ⊕a. I v/a. 1. to dash (to the ground); in Stücke ⚲ to break to pieces, to shatter, to smash (up). — 2. F e-n ⚲ (trinken) to wet one's whistle or beak. — II v/n. 3. (fn) (krachend stürzen) to fall (or come) down with a crash. — 4. (h.) (laut schallen) to resound, von Lerchen: to warble, von Stimmen: to ring (forth), gellend: to yell; von Trompeten: to blare (out), to bray; von Waffen 2c.: to clang; auch v/a. die Hörner ⚲ lustige Weisen the bugles give forth merry tunes. — III ~ n ⚲ 5. (f. 3) crash; (f. 4) ring(ing sound), v. Trompeten: blare, blast, flourish. [smash.)
Schmetter=schlag (ᵛᵛ⚲ᵛ) ⊕ Tennis:)
Schmicke (ᵛᵛ) f ⊕ whip-lash.
Schmied ⊕ (ᴸ) [ahd.: smith] m ⊕c. smith (f. Grob=, Huf=schmied); fig. author, founder; Sprichw. f. Glück 4.
schmiedbar (ᴸᵛ) a. ⊕ malleable, forgeable, ready to be forged; **Schmied= barkeit** f ⊕ malleability, forgeability.
Schmiede ⊕ (ᴸᵛ) [ahd.] f ⊕ smithy, forge; blacksmith's shop; fig. vor die rechte ~ gehen to apply in the right (or proper) quarter or place, F to go to the right shop; vor die unrechte ~ kommen to get into the wrong box.
Schmiede=amboß ⊕ (ᵘ...) m ⊕ smith's anvil; **=arbeit** f sm.'s work, forging; **=eisen** n wrought (or malleable) iron (ant. Gußeisen); **⚲eisern** a. ⊕ of wrought iron; **=esse** f (smith's) forge, stack; **=gesell(e)** m journeyman smith;

⚲ scientific; ⚹ botanical; ⚱ geography; ⊕ machinery; ⚔ mining; ⚔ military; ⚓ marine; ● commercial; ✉ postal; 🚂 railway.

[Schmiedehammer] — 852 — [schmücken]

hammer *m* smith's hammer, ſchwerer ſ.edge- (or forge-) hammer; =**hand**=**werk** *n* smith's trade; =**herd** *m* = =eſſe; =**kohle** *f* forge-coal; =**meiſter** *m* master smith or blacksmith.

ſchmieden (ᴗ́ᴗ) [ahd.] *v/a.* ⊕ **1.** ⊕ to (make at a) forge; e-n an die Kette (oder in Eiſen) ⁓ to put (or cast) a p. in(to) chains, *fig.* to rivet a p. to the spot. — **2.** *fig.* (anzetteln) to frame, devise, plan, scheme, mſt *b.s.* to concoct; Pläne ⁓ to make schemes; Ränke ⁓ to intrigue, to plot, to hatch (out) plots.

Schmiede-ware ❀ u. ⊕ (ᴗ́...) *f* ⊕ hardware; =**werk**=**ſtatt** *f* smithy, (black)smith's shop, forge; =**zange** *f* (black)smith's tongs *pl.*

Schmiege (ᴗ́ᴗ) *f* ⊕ **1.** (Biegung) curvature, bend. — **2.** ⊕ *arch.* (Winkelpaſſer) bevel.

ſchmiegen (ᴗ́ᴗ) [mhd.: ſchmücken] *v/a.* u. bſd. **ſich** ⁓ *v/refl.* ⊕ **1.** ſich ⁓ to bend, to crouch, unterwürfig: to cringe, crawl, creep; ſich ⁓ und biegen to bow and scrape before people; ſich an e-n ⁓ to cling (or nestle up, F snuggle up) to a p.; ſich an etwas ⁓ to press close against a th.; ſich um einen Baum ⁓ to wind (or twine) round ... — **2.** *arch.* (ſ. Schmiege 2) (ſchiefe Winkel meſſen) to bevel.

ſchmiegſam (ᴗ́ᴗ) *a.* ⊕ flexible, pliant, lithe; *fig.* supple, submissive; ~**keit** *f* ⊕ flexibility, pliancy, *fig.* suppleness.

Schmiele ❀ (ᴗ́ᴗ) [dtſch.-lt.: *ſchmal*] *f* ⊕, **Schmiel-gras** (ᴗ́ᴗ) *n* ⊕ hair-grass (*Aira*).

Schmierali-en F (-ᴗ́ᴗ) [dtſch.-lt.; *ſchmier(en)] n/pl. inv.* scribblings, scrawls, daubs *pl.*

Schmier-apparat (ᴗ́...) *m* ⊕ = =**vor**=**richtung**, =**buch** *n* scribbling-diary, waste-book; =**büchſe** ⊕ *f* grease- (or oil-)box, oil-feeder.

Schmiere¹ (ᴗ́ᴗ) [ſchmieren] *f* ⊕ **1.** ⊕ (Wagen=)~ cart-(or axle-)grease; ~ für Leder dubbing; ↓ stuff, tallow, slush. — **2.** F *fig.*: a) (Prügel) blows *pl.*; die ſchönſte ~ bekommen to come in for a fine thrashing or flogging or hiding; b) (Beſtechung) bribe, bribing, corruption; c) (Geſellſchaft, Bande) die ganze ~ the whole lot or gang or F kit or P shoot; *thea.* company of strolling players, F barn-stormers; low-class theatre, penny-gaff.

Schmiere² F (ᴗ́ᴗ) [hebr. Wache] *f* ⊕: ~ ſteh(e)n (aufpaſſen) to be look-out man, F to bonnet, to stag.

ſchmieren (ᴗ́ᴗ) [ahd.: smear; *Schmer*] **I** *v/a.* ⊕ **1.** to smear, mit Fett: to grease, mit Öl: to oil, to lubricate, mit Salbe: to salve, mit Seife: to soap, mit Teer: to tar, mit Pech: to pitch; Butter auf Brot ⁓ (bſſ. ſtreichen) to spread butter on bread, to spread bread and butter. — **2.** *fig.* e-m den Buckel ⁓ (e-n prügeln) to flog (or thrash) a p.; e-m die Hände ⁓ (e-n beſtechen) to bribe a p., F to grease a p.'s palm; e-m das Maul (mit Honig) ⁓ (ſüße Hoffnung erregen) to buoy a p. up with vain hopes or promises; *vgl.* Honig; das geht wie geſchmiert it goes like clockwork, things go on swimmingly; wie geſchmiert (im Nu) F in a jiffy, *co.* like greased lightning;

Sprichw. wer gut ſchmiert, auch gut fährt if you grease well you speed well; money makes the mare go. — **3.** Wein ⁓ (fälſchen) to adulterate (or F doctor) wine. — **4.** *a. abs.* (flüchtig ſchreiben) to scribble, to scrawl; (ſchlecht malen) to daub; (liederlich arbeiten) to scamp one's work. — **II** ~ *n* ⊕ **5.** (ſ. 1) smearing, &c.; (ſ. 3) adulteration of wine; (ſ. 4) scribbling, scrawl(ing).

Schmierer (ᴗ́ᴗ) *m* ⊕, ~**in** *f* ⊕ **1.** person who greases, &c., lubricator. — **2.** (Sudler) scribbler, scrawler; slovenly worker; (ſchlechter Maler) dauber.

Schmiererei (-ᴗ́) *f* ⊕ **1.** = Geſchmiere. — **2.** (et. Schmieriges) s.th. greasy or messy.

Schmier-faß ↓ (ᴗ́...) *n* ⊕ slush-barrel or -tub; =**fink**(**e**), =**hammel** F *m* dirty (or filthy) fellow.

ſchmierig (ᴗ́ᴗ) *a.* ⊕ greasy, messy, bſw. a.: smeary, (ölig) oily, (klebrig) sticky, viscous, ❀ a.: ⚯ glutinous, (ſchlammig) sloppy, (ſchmutzig) dirty, filthy, *fig.* sordid, stingy; ⁓ m. to besmear, grease, smudge, foul; ~**keit** *f* ⊕ greasiness; stickiness; filth(iness).

Schmier-käſe ❀ (ᴗ́...) *m* ⊕ soft cheese; =**kur** *f*, *med.* treatment with ointment(s); =**lappen** *m*: a) greasy rag; b) F = =fink(e); =**mittel** *n*: a) ⊕ lubricant; b) *pharm.* liniment; =**öl** *n* train-oil, machine- (or engine-)oil; =**ſalbe** *f*, *pharm.* salve; =**ſeife** ❀ *f* soft soap; =**ſtiefel** *m* well-greased leather boot; =**vorrichtung** ⊕ *f* (self-)lubricator; *vgl.* =büchſe.

ſchmilz (ᴗ́) *imper.*, ⁓(**e**)**ſt** (ᴗ́ᴗ) 2. u. 2t (ᴗ́) 3. Perſon *sg. pres. ind. v.* ſchmelzen.

Schmink-beere ❀ (ᴗ́...) *f* ⊕ blite (*Blitum*); =**bohne** ❀ *f*: wilde amerikaniſche ~ kidney-bean (*Phaseolus perennis*); =**büchſe**, =**doſe** *f* paint-box, rouge-box, -pot.

Schminke (ᴗ́ᴗ) [mhd.] *f* ⊕ **1.** paint (for the face, rote: rouge, weißS. (Schönheitsmittel) cosmetic; *thea.* make-up. — **2.** ❀ = Steinſame(n).

ſchminken (ᴗ́ᴗ) *v/a.* u. **ſich** ⁓ *v/refl.* ⊕: (ſich) ⁓ to paint (one's face), to rouge (o.s.), ſich ⁓, a.: to lay on (the) paint or rouge, F to get (or make) o.s. up, to make up (a. *thea.*).

Schmink-läppchen (ᴗ́...) *n* ⊕ rouging-rag; =**mittel** *n*, *paint.* cosmetic; =**pfläſterchen** *n* beauty-patch or -spot; ~**rot** *n* rouge; =**topf** *m* paint- (or rouge-)pot; =**waſſer** *n* wash for the face, cosmetic wash; =**weiß** *n* flake- (or Spanish) white, auch: pearl-powder.

Schmirgel (ᴗ́ᴗ) [it. *smeriglio*] *m* ⊕ min. emery; ⁓**n** ⊕ (ᴗ́) *v/a.* ⊕a. to rub (or polish) with emery-(powder or -paper).

Schmirgel-papier ⊕ (ᴗ́...) *n* ⊕ emery- (or smoothing-)paper; =**ſcheibe** ⊕ *f* emery-wheel.

Schmiß¹ (ᴗ́) [mhd.; *ſchmiß*] *m* ⊕a. (Hieb, Schlag) blow, stroke, lash; Schmiſſe bekommen to get a thrashing; burſchikos: (Wunde von e-r Hiebwaffe) cut; (Narbe) scar.

ſchmiß² (ᴗ́) *ind.,* **ſchmiſſe** (ᴗ́ᴗ) *subj. impf.* von ſchmeißen¹ u. ².

Schmiß (ᴗ́) [ahd. *Fleck*] *m* ⊕a. **1.** = Schmiß¹. — **2.** (Schmutz) smutch, smudge, *fig.* stain, blot. [whip-lash.]

Schmitze (ᴗ́ᴗ) *f* ⊕: ~ einer Peitſchenſchnur

ſchmitzen (ᴗ́ᴗ) [mhd.; *ſchmeißen*] *v/a.* u. *v/n.* (h.) ⊕ **1.** (peitſchen) to whip, to lash. — **2.** (beſchmutzen) to smutch, smudge, splash, *typ.* to blur, to slur.

Schmock F (ᴗ́) *m* ⊕ snob.

Schmöker F (ᴗ́ᴗ) [ndd.: smoker: ſchmauchen] *m* ⊕ worthless (or trashy) old book; antiquated (or second-hand) volume; Schul-sl. (unerlaubte Überſetzung) crib; ⁓**n** *v/n.* (h.) ⊕a. to read old (or old-fashioned, antiquated) books.

ſchmollen (ᴗ́ᴗ) [mhd.: smile] *v/n.* (h.) ⊕ to pout one's lips; (mürriſch ſein) to sulk, to be sulky or F in the sulks; mit e-m ⁓, a.: to look glum (or black) at a p., to scowl at a p.

ſchmollieren (ᴗ́ᴗ) [Schmollis] *v/n.* (h.) ⊕ burſchikos: mit e-m ⁓ (Brüderſchaft trinken) to hobnob (or fraternize) with a p.

Schmollis (ᴗ́ᴗ) [dtſch.-lt.] *n* (m) *inv.* burſchikos: mit-e-m⁓trinken = ſchmollieren; ⁓! your (good) health!

Schmoll-winkel (ᴗ́ᴗ) [ſchmollen] *m* ⊕ sulking-corner, retired nook.

ſchmolz (ᴗ́) *ind.,* **ſchmölze** (ᴗ́ᴗ) *subj. impf. v.* ſchmelzen.

Schmor-braten (ᴗ́ᴗ) *m* ⊕ Kochkunſt: stewed meat; bſd. ehm. auch: beef *à la mode*, alamode beef.

ſchmoren (ᴗ́ᴗ) [ndd.; *ndl.*] ⊕ **I** *v/n.* (h.) **1.** Kochk., vom Fleiſche: to stew. — **2.** (von d. Hitze leiden) to swelter, to be in a stifling heat, to sit in the broiling sun. — **II** *v/a.* **3.** Kochk.: = Fleiſch ⁓ to stew ..., auf dem Roſte: to grill; geſchmorte Pflaumen stewed prunes *pl.*

Schmor-fleiſch (ᴗ́...) *n* ⊕ = =braten; =**früchte** *f/pl.* = Kompott; =**hitze** *f*: a) stifling (or oppressive) heat; b) Kochk.: temperature for stewing or frying; =**kartoffeln** *f/pl.* fried potatoes *pl.*; =**kohl** *m* fried red cabbage; =**pfanne** *f*, =**tiegel**, =**topf** *m* stewing-pan, saucepan.

Schmu F (ᴗ́) [jüdiſch] *m* ⊕ unfair profit or gain, F pickings *pl.*; e-n ~ m. to make a profit, F to pick up a few pence.

Schmuck¹ (ᴗ́) [mhd.] *m* ⊕b. (*pl.* ⁓**e**) ornament; (Putz) adornment, finery, dress, F get-up; (Verſchönerung) embellishment, (Verzierung) decoration; (Juwelen) jewellery; *fig.* ~ der Rede, des Stils flowers *pl.* of speech, (fine) flourishes *pl.*

ſchmuck² (ᴗ́) [ndd.: smug] *a.* ⊕ neat, tidy, trim; (geputzt) smart, spruce, F (finely) got-up; (fein) elegant; ⁓**e** Dirne buxom (or good-looking or bonnie) girl or lass.

Schmuck¹=**anlagen** (ᴗ́...) *f/pl.* ⊕ ornamental grounds *pl.*; =**arbeit** ⊕ *f* jewellery; *vgl.* =ſachen; =**arbeiter** *m* working jeweller.

ſchmücken (ᴗ́ᴗ) [mhd.; *ſchmiegen*; *vgl.* ſchmuck²] **I** *v/a.* u. **ſich** ⁓ *v/refl.* ⊕ **1.** (ſich) ⁓ to adorn (o.s.), to trim (F get) (o.s.) up, to dress (o.s.), to attire (o.s.) in fine clothes; mit Ringen geſchmückt bedizened with rings; ein Zimmer ꝛc. ⁓ to decorate ..., mit Blumenornamenten: to festoon ..., mit Sternen geſchmückt bespangled with stars; *vgl.* ausſchmücken I. — **2.** *fig.* (beſchönigen) to cloak, to palliate, to put in the best (or most favourable) light. — **II** ~ *n* ⊕ **3.** adornment; *vgl.* Schmuck.

Zeichen (ſ. S. XVII): F familiär; P Volksſprache; Γ Gaunerſprache; ↘ ſelten; † alt (auch geſtorben); * neu (auch geboren); ✧ unrichtig;

[Schmuckfeder] — 853 — [Schnarchratze]

Schmuck¹-feder ❀ (*...) f ⓔ plume; **=gegenstände** m/pl. = **=sachen** pl.; **=handel** ● m jewel-trade; **=händler(in** f) m (wholesale) jeweller; **=kästchen** n jewel-case; casket; wahres ~ von e-m Hause ꝛc. quite a gem (or a bijou) of a house, &c.; **=laden** m jeweller's shop; **=los** a. ⓕ without ornament(s), unadorned; (einfach) plain, simple, unvarnished; (nackt) bare, (kahl) bald, in der Kunst auch: austere; **=losigkeit** f unadorned state; plainness, simplicity; bareness; baldness, austerity; **=nadel** f (dress-)pin; (Busennadel) breast-pin, brooch; **=sachen** f/pl. trinkets, knickknacks pl.; (Kleinodien) jewels, gems pl.; (Putz) finery sg.; **=stück** n piece (or article) of jewellery.

Schmückung (ᴗ́ᴗ) f ⓖ = schmücken II.
Schmuck-ware (n pl.) (ᴗ́ᴗ̀ᴗ) f ⓔ jewellery.
Schmuddel nordd. (ᴗ́ᴗ) m ⓔ ꝛc. = Schmutz ꝛc.
Schmuggel ┬ (ᴗ́ᴗ) [ndd., engl., *dän.] m ⓔ, **~ei** (ᴗ́ᴗ̀) f ⓔ = Schleichhandel; **~n** v/n. (h.) u. v/a. ⓑ a. to smuggle; besf. ⚔ to run contraband.
Schmuggler ┬ (ᴗ́ᴗ) m ⓔ, **~in** f ⓕ smuggler (= Schleichhändler[in]); **~-bande** f band (or gang, set) of smugglers or contrabandists; **~-boot** ⚓ n smuggling boat, smuggler; ⚔ blockade-runner.
schmunzeln ┬ (ᴗ́ᴗ) I v/n. (h.) ⓑ a. to smirk (and smile), to wear a smile (of satisfaction) on one's face, to simper. — II ~ n ⓒ (self-satisfied) smile, smirk.
Schmus (¹) [hebr. schemúoth Reden] m ⓐ a. persuasive words pl.; (dummes Geschwätz) silly talk; **schmusen** (ᴗ́ᴗ) v/n. (h.) ⓖ to talk persuasively like a Jewish dealer; to chatter, prattle, babble, jabber, gabble.
Schmuser (ᴗ́ᴗ) m ⓔ prattler, babbler.
Schmutz (ᴗ́, bisw. ¹) [nhd.: smut] m ⓐ a. 1. dirt, filth (auch fig.), F mess(y state); fig. (Zoten) smut, obscene language (vgl. Dreck 1). — 2. obb. = Fett.
Schmutz-ärmel (ᴗ́...) m ⓔ, etwa: protecting sleeve to be worn over a dress or coat during work; **=bartel** F m = **=fink**(e); **=bogen** ⊕ m spoilt (or set-off, soiled) sheet; **=bürste** f mudbrush.
schmutzen (ᴗ́ᴗ, bisw. ᴗ̀ᴗ) [nhd.: smut] v/n. (h.) ⓖ to soil (or tarnish) easily.
Schmutzerei (ᴗ́ᴗ̀ᴗ, bisw. ᴗ̀ᴗ́ᴗ) f ⓖ (schmutzige Arbeit) dirty work; fig. (Zotigkeit) smut, smuttiness, filth, nastiness.
Schmutz-farbe (ᴗ́...) f ⓔ dirty (or dingy, drab) colour; mud-colour; **=fink**(e) F m dirty (or filthy) fellow; **=fleck** m smutch, smudge, stain (or spot) caused by mud, fig. blemish; **=hammel** F m = **=fink**(e).
schmutzig (ᴗ́ᴗ) [:smutty] a. ⓕ 1. dirty, filthy (a. fig.), begrimed; (unreinlich) unclean (auch fig.), besf. durch Elend: squalid; von der Farbe a. dingy, dull, drab, dreary; ²e Wäsche dirty (or foul) linen; es ist ² auf der Straße the streets are muddy or full of mud; ² m., ² w. to soil, to dirty (vgl. dreckig, kotig). — 2. fig. sordid; (geizig) stingy, niggardly, miserly; ²e (zotige) Geschichte smutty (or obscene, indecent) story; ²er (knauseriger) Mensch mean (or shabby, stingy) fellow.

Schmutzigkeit (ᴗ́ᴗ-, bisw. ᴗ̀-ᴗ́-) f ⓖ (s. schmutzig) dirtiness, filthiness (a. fig.); sordidness; smuttiness.
Schmutz-kerl (ᴗ́..., bisw. ᴗ̀...) m ⓔ = **=fink**(e); **=kittel** m der Landleute smockfrock, für Kinder: overall; **=konkurrenz** ❀ f mean competition, underselling, P undercutting; **=kruste** f crust of dirt or mud; **=lappen** m, fig. dirty woman, filthy creature, slut, draggletail; vgl. =fink(e); **=loch** n dirty hole (auch fig. Wohnung); **=papier** m soiled (or waste) paper; **=roman** m filthy novel; **=seite** ⊕ f, typ. sham page; **=titel** ⊕ m, typ. bastard title, halftitle, sham title-page; **=wasser** n dirty water, F slops pl.; **=wort** n foul expression, smutty (or obscene) word.

Schnabel (ᴗ́ᴗ) [ahd.; * schnappen] m ⓓ 1. e-s Vogels: beak, bill, ⚕ rostrum; mit dem ~ picken to pick. — 2. F fig. = Mund; halt' den ~! hold your tongue!, P stop your jaw(ing)!; sie spricht, wie ihr der ~ gewachsen ist she speaks just as she thinks or without the least reserve; das ist nichts für seinen ~ that's not his choice or his taste. — 3. ⊕ ⚓ (Schiffsvorderteil) prow, beak; cutwater.
schnabel-förmig (ᴗ́ᴗᴗ̀ᴗ) a. ⓕ beak-shaped, ⚕ rostriform, rostral, geom. rhamphoid.
schnabelieren (ᴗᴗᴗ́ᴗ) [dtsch.-lt.; * Schnabel] v/a. und v/n. (h.) ⓖ co. to eat heartily (= schmausen).
...schnäb(e)lig (...ᴗ́¹(ᴗ)ᴗ) [Schnabel] a. ⓕ in Zssgn, zB.: rot² red-beaked.
Schnabel-kerfe (ᴗ́ᴗᴗ̀ᴗ) m/pl. ⓔ ent. = Halbflügler; **=los** ❀ a. ⓕ ⚕ erostrate.
schnäbeln (ᴗ́ᴗ) [Schnabel] v/n. (h.) und sich ² v/recip. ⓖ v. Tauben ꝛc.: to bill, fig. v. Menschen: to bill and coo; (küssen) to kiss; geschnäbelt beaked, ⚕ rostrate(d).
Schnabel-schiff (ᴗ́...) n ⓒ ship with beak-shaped prow; **=schuh** m shoe with pointed toes, peaked shoe; **=spitze** f tip (or point) of a bill or beak; **=tier** n, zo. duckbill, tambreet (Ornithorhynchus parado'xus); **=weide** F f delicate (or rich) food, fine dinner, delicacy; **=zange** f, surg. rostrum.
Schnäbler (ᴗ́ᴗ) m ⓔ orn. 1. billing bird. — 2. in Zssgn, zB. Dünn-² bird with a fine beak.
schnabulieren = schnabelieren.
Schnack F (¹) [ndd.: snack] m ⓑ b., G. a. **~e** (ᴗ́ᴗ) m ⓔ prattle, chit-chat, F mag; dummer ~ silly twaddle, (dummer Witz) bad joke; **schnacken** (ᴗ́ᴗ) v/n. (h.) u. v/a. ⓑ to prattle, to chat; **schnackisch** a. ⓕ chatty; auch (meist **schnackisch** a. ⓕ): funny, droll.
Schnada-, **Schnader-hüpfel** südd. F (ᴗ́ᴗᴗ̀ᴗ) n ⓒ (short extempore) Alpine song.
Schnake¹ (ᴗ́ᴗ) m ⓔ und ² f merry jest or joke; fun, F lark; auch = Schnack(e).
Schnake² (ᴗ́ᴗ) [mhd.] f ⓔ ent. gnat (= Stechmücke); langbeinige ~ cranefly, daddy-long-legs (Ti'pula). [...isch.]
schnakig, **...isch** (ᴗ́ᴗ) a. ⓕ = schnackig,]
Schnalle (ᴗᴗ) [mhd.; * schnell(en)] f ⓔ 1. buckle, clasp. — 2. ⊕ Schloss.: (Türfalle) (door-)latch. — 3. (Knips) mit dem Finger) click(ing).
schnallen (ᴗ́ᴗ) [mhd.] v/a. ⓖ to buckle, mit Riemen: to (fasten with a) strap

man. die Bügel länger (höher) ² to lengthen (to shorten) the stirrups; zu eng ² to strap too tightly.
Schnallen-dorn ⊕ (ᴗ́ᴗ...) m ⓔ tongue of a buckle; **=gestell** n buckle-ring; **=haken** m chape; **=loch** n am Riemen: buckle-hole; **=schuh** m shoe with a buckle, buckled shoe; **=zunge** f = **=dorn**.
schnalzen (ᴗ́ᴗ) [mhd. lautm.] v/n. (h.) ⓖ 1. mit den Fingern ² to snap one's fingers; mit der Zunge ² to click one's tongue. — 2. = schmatzen.
Schnalz-laut (ᴗ́.¹) m ⓔ in der Sprache der Kaffern ꝛc.: click.
schnapp (ᴗ́) [lautm.] I int. snap!, bang! — II ~ m ⓑ b. (Happen) mouthful; mit einem ~ at one gulp or draught; beißend: at one bite.
schnappen (ᴗ́ᴗ) [mhd.: snap: Schnabel] v/n. (h.), bisw. v/a. ⓑ 1. = schnalzen. — 2. (a. in) das Brett schnappt (schnellt) in die Höhe ... tips up (into the air); das Taschenmesser, die Feder schnappt ... snaps; das Schloß schnappt ... catches. — 3. nach et. ² (gierig greifen) to snap (or clutch, snatch) at a th.; nach Luft ² to gasp for breath, to pant.
Schnäpper (ᴗ́ᴗ) [schnappen] m ⓔ 1. ⊕ Schlosserei: catch, snap; vgl. Schnappschloß. — 2. surg. bsd. ehm. springlancet, (Schröpfeisen): ⚕ scarificator. — 3. orn. = Fliegenschnäpper.
Schnapp-feder (ᴗ́ᴗᴗ̀ᴗ) f ⓔ ⊕ catchspring; **=hahn** m [mhd.] (mounted) highwayman; **=messer** n clasp-knife; **=sack** m knapsack; **=schloß** n ⊕ spring-(or snap-)lock; vgl. Schnäpper 1; **=schuß**, **=schütze** ⚔ m snapshot; **=verschluß** ⊕ m snap-action.
Schnaps (ᴗ́) [ndd.] m ⓑ 1. small glass (or dram) of strong liquor, F drop (or drain) of something; e-n ~ trinken F to take a drop. — 2. (Branntwein) spirits pl.; gin, whisky, brandy.
Schnaps-bruder (ᴗ́ᴗ...) F m ⓔ = **=säufer**; **=bude** F f = **=kneipe**.
Schnäpschen (ᴗ́ᴗ) n ⓒ (dim. v. Schnaps) small glass of spirits, F small drop of gin or whisky or brandy.
schnapsen F v/n. (h.) ⓖ (s. Schnaps) to drink spirits, tipple gin, liquor up.
Schnaps-flasche (ᴗ́ᴗ...) f ⓔ: a) (leere) gin-, &c. bottle; b) (volle) bottle of gin, &c.; **=glas** n gin-(or liqueur-) glass; **=händler** m spirit-merchant.
schnapsig (ᴗ́ᴗ) a. ⓕ tasting of spirits, alcoholic; smelling of gin, &c.
Schnaps-kneipe (ᴗ́ᴗ...) f ⓔ spirit-house, gin-shop, feinere: F gin-palace; **=laden** m gin-shop; **=nase** F f (tippler's) copper-nose, co. auch: brandy-blossom, strawberry; **=säufer**(in f) m, **=trinker**(in f) m tippler (of spirits), F person fond of his (f her) drops; vgl. Säufer(in).
schnarchen (ᴗ́ᴗ) [mhd.: snore, snort; schnarren] v/n. (h.) ⓖ (im Schlafe geräuschvoll atmen) to snore, F co. to drive one's pigs to market; to snort; ²d snoring, ⚕ stertorous.
Schnarcher (ᴗ́ᴗ) m ⓔ, **~in** f ⓕ snorer; **Schnarcherei** (ᴗ́ᴗᴗ̀ᴗ) f ⓖ snoring.
Schnarch-klappe ⊕ (ᴗ́...) f ⓔ = **=ventil**; **=laut** m snorting sound; **=ratze** F f

♪ Musik; ⚛ Wissenschaft; ❀ Pflanze; ⚲ Geographie; ⊕ Technik; ⛏ Bergbau; ⚔ Militär; ⚓ Marine; ● Handel; ✉ Post; 🚆 Eisenbahn.

— Schnarcher; **=ventil** ⚙ *n*, *mach.* blow-(*or* snifting-, throttle-)valve.

Schnarr=baß ♪ (ˊ…) *m* [12] drone (-bass), rattling bass; **=drossel** *f* mistle-thrush (*Turdus visci'vorus*).

Schnarre (ˊ˘) *f* [49] 1. = Knarre. — 2. *orn.* = Schnarrdrossel.

schnarren (ˊ˘) [mhd. s. schnarchen] I *v/n.* (h.) [88] 1. to rattle; von Spinnrädern *x*c.: to buzz, to whiz (vgl. schnurren). — 2. *ent.*: ⚗ to stridulate; Ⅎd: ⚗ stridulant, stridulatory, stridulous; Ⅎdes Insekt: ⚗ stridulator. — 3. v. Menschen: to speak with a (nasal) twang; (das „R" stark hören lassen) to roll (*or* trill) the r; auch = knurren I. — II ~ *n* [23] 4. (s. I) rattling (noise); strident sound; *ent.*: ⚗ stridulation.

Schnarr=laut (ˊ…) *m* [12] rattling (*or* strident) sound; **=posten** ⚔ *m* single sentry; **=ventil** ⚙ *n* = Schnarchventil; **=wecker** ⚙ *m*, *tel.* trember; **=werk** ♪ *n* Orgelbau: reed-stop(s *pl.*), reed-work, (fr.) bourdon. [of a field.]

Schnat(e) *provc.* (ˊ(˘)) *f* [49] ([49]) boundary

Schnatterei (˘˘ˊ) *f* [49] = Geschnatter.

Schnatter=ente (ˊ˘,ˊ˘) *f* [12] *orn.* gadwall, gadwale (*Anas stre'pera*).

Schnatt(e)rer(ˊ(˘)˘) *m* [22], **Schnatt(r)erin** *f* [47] = Schnatter=gans, =hans.

Schnatter=gans F (ˊ˘…) *f* [12], **=hans** F *m* chatterbox, prattler.

schnatterhaft (ˊ˘˘), **schnatt(e)rig** (ˊ(˘)˘) *a.* [66] chatty, chattering, prattling.

Schnatterin (ˊ˘˘) *f* [12] s. Schnatterer.

schnattern (ˊ˘) [mhd. lautm.] I *v/n.* (h.) [89]a. v. Enten u. Gänsen: to cackle, *fig.* v. Menschen: to chatter (auch von Affen *x*c.), to chat, prattle, gabble. — II ~ *n* [23] cackling, cackle; chatter(ing); gabble.

schnauben (ˊ˘) [mhd.] *v/n.* (h.) u. *v/a.* [88]([87]c.) 1. to snort (auch v. Pferden u. Elefanten); to breathe hard, snort, wheeze; *fig.* vor Wut ≀ to be in a towering (*or* to be mad with) rage, to fret and fume. — 2. (keuchen) to pant, F to puff and blow. — 3. **nach** Luft ≀ to gasp for breath *or* air; *fig.* nach Rache (oder als *v/a.*: Rache) ≀ to breathe vengeance. — 4. die Nase ≀, **sich** ≀ *v/refl.* to blow one's nose.

schnaufen (ˊ˘) [mhd.] *v/n.* (h.) [88] to breathe heavily (vgl. schnauben 1 u. 2); Ⅎde Automobile snorting motors *pl.*

Schnauferl* P (ˊ˘) *n* [22] = Automobil.

Schnauz F (ˊ) *m* [1]a. = Schnauzbart.

Schnauz=bart (ˊ…) *m* [12]: a) moustache (= Schnurrbart); b) F *co.* alter ~ old soldier, ancient warrior; ≀**bärtig** *a.* [66] wearing (*or* with) a moustache, auch: moustached. [little snout.]

Schnäuzchen (ˊ˘) *n* [23] (*dim.* v. Schnauze)

Schnauze (ˊ˘) [ndd. Schnute] *f* [49] 1. snout, muzzle; animal's mouth; P von Personen: die ~ halten F to hold one's jaw; er hat eine tüchtige ~ he has the gift of the gab *or* F plenty of jaw *or* a long tongue. — 2. ⚙ ~ e-r Kanne, e-s Kruges *x*c.: spout, eines Blasebalges: nozzle.

schnauzen F (ˊ˘) *v/n.* (h.) [90] to talk roughly *or* rudely, F to jaw.

Schnauz=krug (ˊ,ˊ) *m* [12] jug (*or* pitcher, ewer) with a spout (to it).

Schnebbe (ˊ˘) *f* [49] = Schneppe 1.

Schnecke (ˊ˘) [ahd.: Schnegel] *f* [49] 1. *zo.*: a) ~ mit Haus: snail, ohne Haus: slug; ~n *pl.*: ⚗ gasteropods *pl.*; eßbare (Weinbergs=) ~ edible (*or* Roman) snail (*Helix poma'tia*); b) nackte ~ slug(-snail) (*Limax*). — 2. *fig.* er geht wie eine ~ he walks (at) a snail's pace *or* trot. — 3. a) *anat.* ~ im Ohr: ⚗ helix, cochlea; b) ⚙ archimedische ~ spiral pump; ~ und Trieb (Getriebe mit endloser Schraube) worm-gear(ing); *arch.* (Spirale) volute, scroll, roll; ionische ~ helix, Ionic scroll; Uhrm.: = Schneckenkegel.

Schnecken=abgleicher ⚙ (ˊ˘…) *m* [12] Uhrmacherei: fusee-tool, -turn; ≀**artig** *a.* [66] snail-like; (gewunden) winding, spiral, ⚗ helical, …ine, …ian, ⚘: ⚗ circinal, …ate, cochleate(d); **=bohne** ⚘ *f* snail-flower (*Phase'olus Caraca'lla*); **=bohrer** ⚙ *m* screw-auger; **=dreh=stift** ⚙ *m* einer Uhr fusee, notching-arbor; **=feder** 🏠 *f* volute-spring; ≀**fett** *a.* very plump, F very crummy; ≀**förmig** *a.* snail-formed, spiral, ⚗ cochleiform, ≀förmig gewunden: ⚗ turbinate; vgl. ≀artig; **=fraß** *m*, *agr.* damage done by snails *or* slugs; **=gang** *m*: a) snail- (*or* snail's) pace, *a. fig.*; b) spiral walk; **=garten** *m* zur Zucht eßbarer Schnecken: snailery; **=gewinde** ⚙ *n* helix; **=gewölbe** *n* snail-formed (*or* spiral) vault; **=haus** *n* (Gehäuse einer Schnecke) snail-shell; **=kegel** ⚙ *m* einer Taschen-uhr: fusee; **=klee** ⚘ *m* snail-clover (*Medica'go scutella'ta*); weitS. medic (*Medica'go*); **=lini-e** *f* spiral, helix; **=post** *f*, *fig.* mit der ~ fahren to go at a snail's trot; **=rad** ⚙ *n* volute-wheel, einer Uhr: snail-wheel; ~ mit Schraube worm and wheel; **=schneide=zeug** ⚙ *n* Uhrm.: fusee-engine; **=stein** *m* snail-stone; **=treppe** *f* winding (*or* spiral) staircase *or* stairs *pl.*; **=übertragung** ⚙ *f* worm-gearing; **=windung** *f* spiral (turning); **=zug** *m*: a) = =gang a; b) spiral stroke.

schnedderengteng(teng) F (˘˘˘ˊ(ˊ)) *int.* vom Trompetengeschmetter: taratantara.

Schnee (ˊ) [ahd.: snow] *m* [1]c. (*pl.* ↘, bisw. ~n) 1. snow; s. ballen² II; im ~ begraben, mit ~ bedeckt snowed up. — 2. Kochk.: milk beaten up with eggs.

Schnee=ammer (ˊ…) *f* [12] *orn.* snow-bunting (*Plectro'phanes niva'lis*); **=bahn** *f* = Schlittenbahn; **=ball** *m*: a) [7]c., *a.* ~en snowball; b) [25] ⚘ snowball, guelder rose (*Vibu'rnum* [*o'pulus*]); ≀**ballen** *v/a.* u. *v/n.* (h.) (sich ≀ *v/recip.*) [88]*,* to throw (to pelt each other with) snowballs, to snowball (each other); vgl. ballen² 2; **=ball=brief** *m*, **=ball=kollekte** *f* snowball collection; ≀**bedeckt** *a.* [66] covered with snow, snow-clad, *poet. a.* snow-capped *or* -capt; **=beere** ⚘ *f* snow-berry (*Symphorica'rpos racemo'sa*); **=berg** *m* mountain covered with snow; ≀**blind** *a.* snow-blind, dazzled by the snow; **=blindheit** *f* snow-blindness, ⚗ niphablepsia; **=blume** *f* = =glöckchen; **=brille** *f* dark glasses *pl.* worn in snowy regions, der Eskimos *a.* snow-eyes *or* -goggles *pl.*; **=bruch** *m*, *for.* breakage of boughs when weighed down by snow; **=dach** 🏠 *n* snow-shed; **=eule** *f*, *orn.* snow-(*or* snowy) owl (*Ny'ctea ni'vea*); **=fall** *m* fall of snow, snowfall; **=feld** *n* snow-field; **=fink(e)** *m*, *orn.* snow-finch, snowbird (*Fringi'lla niva'lis*); **=flocke** *f* flake of snow, snow-flake; **=gans** *f*, *orn.* snow-goose, white brant (*Anser hyperbore'us*); **=gebirge** *n* snow-clad mountains *pl.*; **=gestöber** *n* snow-storm; drifting snow; **=glöckchen** ⚘ *n*: a) snow-drop (*Gala'nthus niva'lis*); b) großes ~ snow-flake (*Leuco'ium* [*aesti'vum*]); **=graupen** *f/pl.* s. Graupe 2; **=grenze** *f*, *phys.* snow-limit *or* -line; **=haufe(n)** *m* heap of snow; **=huhn** *n*, *orn.* ptarmigan (*Lago'pus mutus*).

schnee-icht ↘, mst **schnee-ig** (ˊ˘) *a* [66] 1. snowy, like snow, ⚗ niveous; (schneebedeckt) covered with snow, v. Bergen: snow-clad. — 2. = schneeweiß.

Schnee=könig (ˊ…) *m* [12] = =mann; *fig.* er freut sich wie ein ~ he is as merry as a grig *or* a sand-boy; **=koppe** *f*, **=kuppe** *f* snow-clad mountain-top, snowy peak; **=landschaft** *f* snowy landscape; **=lawine** *f* = Lawine; **=lini-e** *f* = =grenze; **=mann** *m* snow-man; **=masse** *f* mass of snow; **=pflug** *m* snow-plough (auch 🏠); **=rechen** ⚙ *m* snow-rake; **=rutsch** *m* snow-slip, -slide; **=schaufel** *f* snow-shovel; **=schipper** *m* snow-sweeper, p. shovelling (*or* clearing away) snow; **=schläger** *m* Kochk.: whisk for beating up milk and eggs; **=schuh** *m* snow-shoe, schwedischer: ski; **=schuhläufer** *m* p. skating on snow-shoes; **=schüpper** *m* = =schipper; **=schutz=wand** 🏠 *f* snow-shelter; **=staub** *m* fine powdery snow; **=sturz** *m* avalanche; **=treiben** *n*, ↘ **=trift** *f* drifting (*or* heavy fall) of snow; **=verschüttung**, **=verwehung** *f* = =wehe; **=wächte** *f* wall of snow on a mountain-ridge; **=wasser** *n* snow-water *or* -broth, slush; **=wehe** *f* snow-drift; ≀**weiß** *a.* [66] snow-white, (as) white as (the driven) snow; **=wetter** *n* snowy weather, auch =gestöber; **=wittchen** (ˊ,ˊ˘) *n* [12] im deutschen Märchen: Little Snow-white; **=wolke** (ˊ…) *f* cloud full of snow; **=zeit** *f* snowy season. [(Schnecke ohne Haus) slug.]

Schnegel *provc.* (ˊ˘) [: snail] *m* [22]

Schneid (ˊ) *m* [1]c. = Schneidigkeit.

Schneid=... (ˊ…) in Zssgn = Schneide=...

Schneide (ˊ˘) [mhd.] *f* [49] 1. edge of a knife, &c., ⚙ eines Werkzeuges auch: cutting-edge, bit, am Wagebalken *x*c.: knife-edge. — 2. *fig.* (scharf Treffendes) good hit, s.th. cutting *or* sharp.

Schneide=bank ⚙ (ˊ˘…) *f* [12] des Böttchers *x*c.: bench; **=bohnen** *f/pl.* Kochk.: French beans *pl.*; **=bohrer** *m* s. Bohrer 2; **=brett** *n* cutting-board, trencher; **=eisen** *n*: a) *metall.* (in Streifen geschnittenes Eisen) slit(ted) iron *or* rods *pl.*; b) (Werkzeug) edge-tool; vgl. Hackmesser; **=hobel** *m* slitting-plane; **=holz** *n* wood (*or* timber) for sawing; **=klotz** *m* block for cutting (*or* sawing) wood, &c.; **=lini-e** *f* cutting-line; **=lohn** *m* wages *pl.* for sawing *or* chopping; **=maschine**

[**Schneidemesser**] — 855 — [**Schnellphotographie**]

f cutting-engine, cutter, für Häcksel: chaff-cutter or -engine, zum Kleiderausschneiden: cutting-out machine; für Schrauben: bolt-cutter, für Stabeisen: slitting-machine; Buchbinderei = Beschneidemaschine; **messer** *n* cutting-knife, cutter; **mühle** *f* = Sägemühle.

schneiden (*l.v.*) [ahd.] **I** *v/n.* (h.), *v/a.* und sich ² *v/refl.* 30 c. **1.** to cut, in Stücke: to cut up, ganz klein: to mince; (schnitzen) to carve; (hacken) to chop (vgl. beschneiden, bsd. 1 u. 2); ich habe mich (oder mir) in den Finger geschnitten I have cut my finger; in Stücke ² to cut to pieces; in Streifen ² to shred; das Messer schneidet nicht ... does not cut, ... has no (or a blunt) edge. — **2.** mit e-m Objekt: den Braten ² to carve the joint; Bretter ² to saw boards; eine Feder ² to make (or mend) a (quill-)pen; (grünes) Futter ² to (cut) fodder; sich (dat.) die Haare ² lassen to have one's hair cut; Holz ² to saw (or cut up) timber; Korn (Gras) ² to cut (or mow) corn (grass); sich (dat.) die Nägel ² to cut (or clip, pare) one's nails; mint. e-n Prägestock ² to sink a die; surg. den Stein ² to cut (or operate for) the stone; Stroh ² to chop straw; math. die Linien schneiden sich in *A* ... intersect (or cut each other, meet) in *A*. — **3.** fig. f. Cour 2; F e-n ² (beim Begegnen nicht kennen wollen) to cut a p. (dead); Geld ² (verdienen) to earn (F to coin) money; Gesichter, Grimassen ² to make faces or grimaces; f. Kompliment 1; Wein ² (fälschen) to adulterate (or F to doctor) wine; sich gewaltig (F höllisch) ² (täuschen) to make a grievous (or a lamentable) mistake; (enttäuscht sein) to be greatly disappointed; Sprichw. f. Riemen¹; man muß sich Pfeifen ², während man im Rohre sitzt, etwa: make hay while the sun shines (f. a. Pfeife 2). — **4.** ⊙ to cut, (spalten) to cleave, to split; Gravierkunst: in Holz (Stahl) ² to engrave (or carve) in wood (steel); Schlosserei: Schrauben ² to cut (or make, thread) screws. — **5.** Kartenspiel, bsd. Whist: mit der Dame (anstatt e-r höheren Karte) ² to finesse (with) the queen. — **6.** *v/impers.* es schneidet mir im Leibe I have a cutting (or gnawing) pain in my stomach, F I have the gripes; das schneidet mir ins (ob. durchs) Herz, in (ob. durch) die Seele that cuts me to the quick, that sorely grieves me. — **II** ~ *n* ⚙ **7.** cutting, &c. (f. I); surg. incision; ~ im Leibe sharp pain in the stomach, colic, F gripes; math. das (Sich=)~ zweier Linien the intersection of two lines. — **III** 2d *p.pr. u. a.* ⚙ **8.** von Werkzeugen: cutting, sharp, with an edge (on); von der Witterung: 2de Kälte nipping (or biting, piercing) cold; 2der Wind cutting (or keen, piercing) wind; es ist 2d kalt the cold is piercing, it's bitterly cold. — **9.** fig. 2de (grelle) Farben glaring (or loud) colours; 2der (scharfer) Verstand keen (or subtle) intellect, penetrating mind; 2der Widerspruch marked (or striking) contrast. — **IV** geschnitten *p.p. u. a.* ⚙ (D 9) **10.** Bed. des *inf.*; zB.: 2es Eisen = Schneide-eisen a. — **11.** fein 2es Gesicht finely cut (or modelled) face; griechisch 2e Nase Grecian nose or profile; f. Auge 5 u. Gesicht 2.

Schneider (*l.v.*) [mhd.] *m* ⚙, **~in** *f* ⚙ **1.** person who cuts or carves, cutter, carver; bsd. in Zssgn, zB.: Brett=². — **2.** ⊙ (Kleidermacher[in]) tailor(ess), ~in, auch: tailor's wife; (~in) für Damen ladies' tailor (dressmaker); vom ~ gemachtes Frauenkleid tailor-made dress, auf Bestellung arbeitender ~ bespoke tailor. — **3.** fig. co. = Bock¹ 2; (Schwächling) weakling, rickety (or weakly) fellow (f. Gevatter 2). — **4.** Kartenspiel: ~ w. to score less than half the full number of points; aus dem ~ (heraus) sein to have (made) more than half the points, fig. to have reached a mature age. — **5.** zo. = Weberknecht. [work, tailoring.]

Schneider=arbeit (*l.v....*) *f* ⚙ tailor's

Schneiderei (*l.v.*) *f* ⚙ tailoring, tailor's business; für Damen: dressmaking; wir haben heute ~ we have the tailor (or the dressmaker) in the house, we are dressmaking. [man tailor.]

Schneider=gesell(e) (*l.v....*) *m* ⚙ journey-

schneiderhaft (*l.v.*) *a.* ⚙ = schneidermäßig.

Schneider=handwerk (*l.v....*) *f* ⚙ Schneider. [trade.]

Schneiderin (*l.v....*) *f* ⚙ f. Schneider.

Schneider=karpfen (*l.v....*) *m* ⚙ co. (Hering) herring; **=lehrling** *m* tailor's apprentice; **=lohn** *m* tailor's wages *pl.*; **=mamsell** *f* tailoress, dressmaker; **²mäßig** *a.* ⚙ tailor-like, co. sartorial; **=meister** *m* master tailor; **=muskel** *m*, *anat.* tailor's muscle, ⚚ sartorius.

schneidern (*l.v.*) *v/n.* (h.) *u. v/a.* ⚙ a. to do tailoring or dressmaking, to make clothes or dresses.

Schneider=rechnung (*l.v....*) *f* ⚙ tailor's bill; **=seele** *f* coward(ly heart), P funk(y fellow); **=tisch** *m* tailor's shopboard; **=vogel** *m*, *orn.* tailor-bird or -warbler (*Ortho'tomus*); **=werkstatt** *f* tailor's (work)shop; **=zunft** *f* guild (or company) of tailors.

Schneide=säge ⊙ (*l.v....*) *f* ⚙ Streckwerk: cutting-cylinder; **=walze** *f*, **=werk** *n*, metall. slitting-roller or -mill; **=werkzeug** *n* edge-tool, sharp instrument; **=zahn** *m*, anat. incisor, zo. b. Raubtiere: scissor-tooth; **=zeug** *n*: a) *coll.* edge-tools *pl.*; b) einzelnes: (chopping-)blade, cutter, cutting-engine.

schneidig (*l.v.*) *a.* ⚙ sharp(-edged), fig. keen, sharp, smart, F full of go; (entschlossen) determined, resolute; **~keit** *f* ⚙ keenness, sharpness, smartness, F go; fig. determination, resoluteness.

schnei-en (*l.v.*) [ahd.: snow; *Schnee] *v/n.* (⚚ *v/a.*) ⚙ **1.** (h.) to snow; *v/impers.* es schneit it snows, it is snowing, there is snow falling; fig. es hat ihm in die Bude (ob. Hütte) geschneit (er hat Unglück gehabt) s.th. untoward has befallen him, he had a stroke of bad luck. — **2.** (in) fig. sie ist uns ins Haus geschneit (plötzlich auf den Hals gekommen) she suddenly dropped in (to see us), she took us by surprise.

Schneise (*l.v.*) [mhd.; *schneiden] *f* ⚙ **1.** *for.* path cut through (or across) a forest. — **2.** = Dohne.

schneiteln ⊙ (*l.v.*) [mhd.: schneiden] *v/a.* ⚙ a. hort. Bäume ² to lop (or prune) trees.

schnell¹ (*l.v.*) [ahd.] *a.* ⚙ swift (bird, flight, &c.), rapid (stream, &c.), quick (motion, &c.), speedy (action, &c.), fast (steamer, &c.), fleet (horse, &c.), prompt (reply, &c.); (plötzlich) sudden (vgl. rasch¹); zu ² hasty, rash, precipitate, too fast; 2er Puls quick pulse, ⚚ tachycardia; mit 2en Schritten gehen to put one's best leg forward; im 2sten Tempo fahren to run (or drive) at full speed; ⚙ 2er Verkauf brisk (or rapid) sale; 2er (*adv.*) gehen to walk faster, to hasten (or accelerate) one's step; 2! be quick!, hurry on!, look sharp!, make haste!; mach(t) 2! be quick about it!; nicht so 2! gently!; so 2 als möglich as quick(ly) as possible, with the utmost speed. [feder 2c.]

Schnell²=... (*l.v....*) [schnellen] [s. Schnell-

Schnell=lade ⊙ (*l.v....*) [Schnell¹=lade] *f* ⚙ Weberei: fly-shuttle lathe.

Schnell=lade=kanone ⚔ (*l.v....l.v.*) [Schnell=lade-] *f* ⚙ quick-loading gun.

Schnellauf (*l.v.*) [Schnell¹=lauf] *m* ⚙ d. foot-race; im ~ at full speed, posthaste; **Schnelläufer** (*l.v....*) [Schnell¹=läufer] *m* ⚙ (fast) runner.

schnell¹=beschwingt (*l.v....*) *a.* ⚙ on (or with) rapid wings; **=bleiche** ⊙ *f* ⚙ chemical bleaching; **=dampfer** ⚓ *m* fast steamer. [2. f. Stromschnelle.]

Schnelle (*l.v.*) *f* ⚙ **1.** = Schnelligkeit. —

schnellen (*l.v.*) [mhd.; *schnell] ⚙ **I** *v/a.* **1.** to jerk, let fly, flick, fillip; in die Höhe ², in die Luft ² to toss (or kick, tip) up. — **2.** = knipsen. — **3.** F = prellen 2. — **II** *v/n.* (jn) bisw. sich *v/refl.* **4.** to jerk, fly off, bound (up), von einer Feder: to snap (off); von einem Brett, Wagebalken ze. in die Höhe ² to kick up. — **III** ~ *n* ⚙ **5.** jerk(ing), toss(ing).

Schneller (*l.v.*) *m* ⚙ **1.** jerker. — **2.** (Knips) jerk, flick, fillip. — **3.** = Schnellfügelchen. — **4.** ⚚ (Springfaden); ⚚ elater. — **5.** Zählmaß für Garn f. S. XL.

schnell¹=fassend (*l.v....*) *a.* ⚙ quick (of apprehension), quick-witted, sharp; **²feder** *f* ⚙ spring; **=¹feuer** ⚔ *n* quickfiring, running fire; **=feuer=geschütz** *n*, **=feuer=kanone** *f* quick-firing (or machine-)gun, F quick-firer; **=fuhre** *f* fast (or express) carriage; **²füßig** *a.* swiftfooted; **=füßigkeit** *f* swiftness of foot.

Schnelligkeit (*l.v.*-), bisw. **Schnellheit** (*l.v.*-) *f* ⚙ (f. schnell) swiftness, rapidity, speed, fleetness, promptness, suddenness; mech. velocity; zunehmende = accelerated speed; mit großer (geringer) ~ at a quick (slow) rate. — Bgl. auch Geschwindigkeit.

Schnell²=käulchen (*l.v....*) *n* ⚙ = Kugel; **=kraft** *f* springiness, elasticity; **=kugel** *f*, **=kügelchen** *n* Spielzeug: marble; **=¹lade**, **=lauf**, **=lot** f. Schnellade ze.

Schnellot ⊙ (*l.v.*) [Schnell¹=lot] *n* ⚙ d. soft solder.

Schnell¹=photographie (*l.v....*) *f* ⚙: a) als Kunst: instantaneous photography; b) als Bild: inst. photograph, F snap-

---

⚚ scientific; ⚘ botanical; ⚲ geography; ⊕ machinery; ⚒ mining; ⚔ military; ⚓ marine; ⚙ commercial; ✉ postal; 🚂 railway.

[Schnellpost] — 856 — [schnupfig]

shot; =poſt f mail-coach; =preſſe ⊙ f, typ. mechanical (or steam-)press; vgl. Druckmaschine; =ſchreibe-kunſt f: a) rapid writing; b) engS. shorthand, bſd. im Altertum. ⚇ tachygraphy; =ſchreiber m shorthand writer, bſd. im Alt.: ⚇ tachygrapher; =ſchritt ⚔ m quick march; =ſchütz(e) ⊙ m (f) Weberei: fly-shuttle; ⚓ſegelnd ↓ a. fast-sailing; =ſegler ↓ m fast-sailing boat, F fast sailer; =² wage ⊙ f: a) mit Laufgewicht: steelyard, Roman balance; b) mit feſtem Gewicht: Danish balance; =¹zug 🚂 m fast (or express) train; vgl. Blitzzug; =zünder ⚔, ⚡ m quick-match; =züngig a. voluble; =züngigkeit f volubility, fluency of speech.

Schnepfe (⁵) [ahd.] snipe] f ⑱ 1. orn. snipe, woodcock (ſ. Sumpf=, Wald=⁼). — 2. F fig. (Dirne) street-walker.

Schnepfen-dreck (⁵...) n ㉒: a) hunt. snipe's droppings pl. or dirt; b) Kocht.: roast giblets pl. of snipe; =jagd f snipe-shooting; =ſtrauß m ſ. Kiwi; =ſtrich m, hunt.: a) flight (or passage) of woodcocks; b) = =jagd.

Schneuße (⁵) [ahd.] f ⑱ 1. ehm. ~ e-r Haube ꝛc.: peak. — 2. ~ (Ausguß) an Gefäßen: spout (vgl. Schnauze 2).

Schnepper (⁵) ꝛc. = Schnäpper ꝛc.

Schneuße (⁵) ꝛc. = Schneiße.

ſchneuzen (⁵) [ahd.: snot] v/n. (h.), v/a. u. ſich ⚷ v/refl. ⑳ to blow one's nose.

Schnickſchnack F (⁵) [ndd.] m ⓒc. chit-chat, tittle-tattle, gabble, prattle, F mag.

ſchnieben provc. (¹ˬ) = ſchnauben.

ſchniegeln (¹ˬ) [ndd.] v/a. u. ſich ⚷ v/refl. ⓐa.: (ſich) ⚷ to dress (o.s.) up, to smarten (o.s.) up; geſchniegelt und gebügelt looking very smart, F dressed up to the knocker or to the nines.

Schniepel (¹ˬ) m ㉒ F burſch. = Frack.

ſchnipp, ſchnip(p)s (⁵) int. snap!; ſchnipp, ſchnapp! snip-snap!

Schnippchen (⁵) n ㉓: e-m ein ~ ſchlagen to snap one's fingers at a p., fig. to overreach a p.

Schnippel (⁵) [ndd.] m, n (⁵) n ㉓ small piece or bit; snip; ~chen (⁵) n ㉓ wee bit, tiny little scrap; ſchnippeln v/a. u. v/n. (h.) ⓐa. to cut (or chip) into little bits; to snip.

ſchnippen (⁵) v/a. u. v/n. (h.) ⓑ⑧ = knipſen.

ſchnippiſch (⁵) [ndd.] a. ⓖ snappish, pert; (höhniſch ſtolz) disdainful, scornful, F uppish; (herausfordernd) defiant.

ſchnip(p)s (⁵) ſ. ſchnipp.

Schnippſel (⁵) n ㉒ small bit, scrap.

ſchnitt¹ (⁵) ind. impf. v. ſchneiden.

Schnitt² (⁵) [ahd.; *ſchnitt¹] m ⓓb. 1. (das Schneiden) cutting, carving; ~ mit der Sichel (Ernte) crop, reaping, harvest(ing). — 2. F fig. ſeinen ~ (e-n großen Gewinn) bei et. m. to make a large profit on (or over) a th.; ſeinen ~ m. to do a fine stroke of business, to feather one's nest, F to make one's pile. — 3. (Verwundung) cut, ~ ins Fleiſch: flesh-wound, slash, incision, tieferer: stab, gash; surg. operation; (Abnahme e-s Gliedes) amputation. — 4. (durch Schneiden gebildete Vertiefung) incision, (Kerbe) notch. — 5. (durch Schneiden gegebene Form) cut (or make, pattern,

shape) of a dress, &c., build of a coat, &c.; nach dem neueſten ~ after the latest style or fashion; ein Hut, Kleid vom neueſten ~ an up-to-date hat, dress. — 6. (abgeſchnittenes Stück) piece; (Scheibe) slice (= Schnitte). — 7. F (kl. Glas Bier, ³/₁₀ Liter) half-a-pint. — 8. math. section, intersection (= Durchſchnitt). — 9. ⊙: a) Buchbinderei: ~ an e-m Buche edge; geſprengter ~ sprinkled edge; ſ. marmorieren, Goldſchnitt; b) Gravierkunſt: (geflochtene Arbeit) cut; engraving.

Schnitt-bohnen (⁵...) f/pl. = Schneide=b; =brenner ⊙ m für Gas: split burner.

Schnittchen (⁵) n ㉓ (dim. v. Schnitt(e) little (or slight) cut; small (or thin) slice of meat, &c.; ſchmäleres ~: a) Kinderſprache: finger of bread, meat, &c.; b) fig. small profit.

Schnitte (⁵) [ahd.] f ⑱ (abgeſchnittenes Stück) slice of bread, meat, &c.; rasher of bacon; ~ vom Braten cut off the joint; ~ von Ochſenfleiſch ꝛc. steak.

Schnitt-eiſen ⊙ (⁵ˬ) n ㉒ metall. slit(ted) iron, slit rods pl.

Schnitter (⁵) [ahd.] m ㉒, ~in f ⑳ agr. reaper, harvester, mower of grass, &c.

Schnitt-fläche (⁵...) f ㉒ math. plane formed by a cut or a (transversal) section; =fleiſch n Kochkunſt: hash, stew; =handel = Ausſchnitthandel ꝛc.; =lauch ♃ (ˬ) m, hort. chive, scallion (Allium Schoenoprasum).

Schnittling (⁵) m ⓓ.1. = Schnitzel. — 2. hort. (abgetrennter Zweig zur Fortpflanzung) cutting, slip, layer.

Schnitt-lini-e (⁵...) f ㉒ math. intersecting line, am Kreiſe: secant; =meſſer n: a) = Schneidemeſſer; b) surg. bistoury; =muſter n pattern for cutting out a dress, &c.; ⚷reif a. ⓖ ripe (or ready) for cutting; =ſalat ♃ m = Lattich; =waren ⚙ f/pl. = Ausſchnittwaren ꝛc.; ⚷weiſe adv. in cuts or slices; ⚷wunde f = Schnitt 3. — Vgl. a. Schneide=.

Schnitz¹ (⁵) [mhd.] m ⓐa. 1. = Schnippel, auch: chip, cut. — 2. = Schnitzel 2.

Schnitz² =arbeit (⁵...) [ſchnitzen] f ⑳ (wood-)carving, sculpture; =bank f carver's (or chopping-)bench.

Schnitzel (⁵) n (m) ㉒ (dim. v. Schnitz) 1. small chip or cut, scrap, snip. — ⚷ pl. (Abfälle) clippings, shavings, shreds pl.; ſ. Schnitzelsjagd. — 3. Kochkunſt: Wiener ~ (Vienna) veal cutlet.

Schnitzel-bank (⁵...) f = Schnitz=bank; =jagd f paper-chase (die dabei geſtreuten Schnitzel Papier heißen „scents“).

ſchnitzeln (⁵) [ſchnitzen] v/a. u. v/n. (h.) ⓐa. to chip, carve, kunſtvoll: to sculpture.

ſchnitzen (⁵) [ahd.: ſchneiden] v/a. u. v/n. (h.) ⓩ Figuren ꝛc. in Holz ⚷ to carve (or cut) ... into wood.

Schnitzer (⁵) [ahd.; *ſchnitzen] m ㉒ 1. cutter, (wood-)carver. — 2. ⊙ in vielen Handwerken: knife for carving or chipping. — 3. F fig. (Fehler) blunder, slip, mistake, error; ſ. Sprachſchnitzer.

Schnitzerei (⁵ˬ) f (wood-)carving, carved work, sculpture(d articles pl.).

ſchnitzern F (⁵) [Schnitzer 3] v/n. (h.) ⓐa. to blunder, to make a slip or a mistake, to commit o.s., F to trip.

Schnitz²=kunſt ⊙ (⁵...) f ㉒ (art of) carving; sculpture; =meſſer n knife for carving; =waren ⚙ f/pl. carved goods pl. or ware; =werk n = Schnitzerei.

ſchnob (¹) ind., **ſchnöbe** (¹ˬ) subj. impf. ſ. a. ſchnüffeln.

ſchnob(b)ern(⁵ˬ)v/v.(h.)ⓐa.to sniff(le);

ſchnodd(e)rig provc. (¹ˬ) a. ⓖ (frech, vorlaut) saucy, cheeky; ~keit (¹ˬˬ) f ⓖ sauciness, cheek.

ſchnöde (¹ˬ) [mhd.] a. ⓖ 1. (verächtlich) contemptible, despicable, (wertlos) vile; (ſchlecht) bad, (ſchändlich) base, mean, iniquitous; ⚷ Undank erntet to meet with base (or black) ingratitude. — 2. (geringſchätzig) contemptuous, disdainful, scornful; (beleidigend) insulting; e-n ⚷ (adv.) behandeln to treat a p. with contumely, to use a p. badly.

Schnödigkeit (¹ˬˬ) f ⓖ (ſ. ſchnöde) contemptibleness; vileness; baseness; contempt(uousness), scorn.

ſchnop(p)ern(⁵ˬ)v/n.(h.)ⓐa.=ſchnüffeln.

Schnörkel (⁵ˬ) [mhd.] m ㉒: a) scroll, spiral (or twisted, interlaced) ornament; b) Schönſchreiben: flourish; (verſchlungener Namenszug) paraph; c) arch.: ~ am ioniſchen Kapitäl ꝛc.: volute.

Schnörkelei (ˬˬˬ) f ⓖ = Geſchnörkel.

ſchnörkelhaft (⁵ˬˬ) a. ⓖ in (the form of) scrolls or flourishes; weitS. artificial.

ſchnörkeln (⁵ˬ) v/a. u. v/n. (h.) ⓐa. to make (or to adorn with) flourishes, to scroll; geſchnörkelt, a. twisted; vgl. geziert II.

ſchnorren, Schnorrer P (⁵ˬ) [hebr.] v/n. (h.), ⚷ m ㉒ = betteln, Bettler.

Schnucke (⁵ˬ) [ndd.: snug] f ⑱ small sheep; fig. (a. Schnuck(el)chen (⁵ˬˬˬ) n ㉓) koſend: duckey, darling.

ſchnüffeln (⁵ˬ) [ndd.: sniff, snivel] v/n. u. v/a. 1. P auch **ſchnuffeln** (raſch Luft einziehen) to sniff (the air), to snuffle. — 2. fig. (wittern) to smell, to (follow the) scent; (erſpähen) to spy out; (ſpionieren) to spy about, to pry, P to nose; (ſtöbern) to ferret. — 3. (durch die Naſe ſprechen) to speak through the nose or with a twang.

Schnüffler (⁵ˬ) m ㉒, ~in f ⑳ 1. (auch Schnuffler) sniffing person or dog. — 2. fig. spy, F Paul Pry, nosy person.

ſchnupfbar (⁵ˬ) a. ⓖ fit for snuffing.

Schnupfen¹ (⁵ˬ) [mhd.] m ㉓ path. cold (in the head), running (of the) nose, ⚇ (nasal) catarrh, ſeltener: rheum; den ~ haben to have (or to suffer from) a cold (in the head); den ~ bekommen F ſich einen ~ holen to catch (a) cold, to take cold.

ſchnupfen² (⁵ˬ) [ndd.; *ſchnauben] I v/r. (h.) und v/a. ⓑ⑧ 1. (Tabak) ⚷ to take snuff. — 2. fig. das ſchnupft ihm in (ober vor) die Naſe that vexes (or annoys) him, P it sticks in his gizzard. — II ~ n ㉓ 3. (ſ. I) snuffing, taking snuff; ſich das ~ angewöhnen to get into the habit of taking snuff.

ſchnupfen¹=artig (⁵ˬ...) a. ⓖ like a cold, ⚇ catarrhal; =fieber n ㉒ feverish cold, influenza, ⚇ catarrhal fever.

Schnupfer (⁵ˬ) m ㉒, ~in f ⑳ p. (in the habit of) taking snuff, snuff-taker.

ſchnupfig (⁵ˬ) a. ⓖ path. suffering from (or having) a cold (in the head).

[Schnupftabak] — 857 — [schön]

Schnupf-tabak (⠐...) m snuff; **-tabak(s)-dose** f snuff-box; **-tabak(s)-fabrik**, **-mühle** f snuff-mill; **-tuch** n pocket-handkerchief, F co. wipe.

Schnuppe¹ (⠐⠐) [nbd.: snuff] f 1. = Lichtschnuppe. — 2. = Sternschnuppe.

schnuppe² P (⠐⠐) a. inv.: das ist mir ⠐ (gleichgültig) that's all the same (or it matters little) to me. [feln 1 u. 2.]

schnuppern (⠐⠐) v/n. (h.) 2a. = schnüffeln.

Schnur¹ (⠐) [ahd.: snare] f (46) 1. string, cord, line, für Schnürstiefel, Leibchen ꝛc.: lace, zum Einfassen von Kleidungsstücken: braid, tape, trimming; mit ~ besetzen, einfassen to edge with cord, to braid; e-n Rock mit Schnüren besetzen to trim ... with cord or braid. — 2. ~ Perlen string of pearls; ~ Zwiebeln rope of onions. — 3. hunt. (Leitriemen) leash. — 4. fig. über die ~ hauen to run (or rush) into excess(es), to overshoot the mark, to kick over the traces, to exceed the bounds, to go too far.

Schnur² (⠐) [ahd.: lt. nurus] f (46) bibl. daughter-in-law.

Schnur¹-**aufnäher** ⊙ (⠐⠐⠐) m der Näh-maschine: braiding-machine. [stays, &c.]

Schnür-band (⠐⠐) [schnüren] n lace for **Schnür-besatz** (⠐⠐) m braiding; **2 be-setzt** a. trimmed with cord or braid.

Schnür-boden (⠐⠐) m thea. loft for stage-machinery, &c.; ↓ loft; **-brust** f corset(s pl.) = Schnürleib.

Schnürchen (⠐⠐) n (dim. von Schnur¹) thin (or short) string, &c.; fig. seine Lektion am (oder im) ~ haben to know one's lesson by rote, to have it at one's finger's ends.

schnüren (⠐⠐) [ahd.: *Schnur¹] I v/a. u. v/refl. to tie (or fasten, attach) with a string or lace; (fest zj.-binden) to tie (or knüpf) up, Buchbinderei: to tie in; eine Kiste: to cord; (knebeln) to tie fast, to pinion; mit e-m Schnürleibe ⠐ to lace, mit e-m Seile: to rope; sich (eng) ⠐ to lace o.s. (tightly), to wear (tight) stays; fig. es schnürt ein e-m das Herz zj. it makes one's heart wring or wrench or ache; s. Bündel 3. — II ~ n tying, &c. (s.I); das enge ~ ist ungesund tight lacing is injurious to health.

Schnur¹-**feuer** ⊙ (⠐...) n Feuerwerk: line-rocket; **2gerade** a. u. adv. in a straight line, (as) straight as an arrow (flies); (senkrecht) vertical(ly).

Schnür-latz (⠐...) m bodice; a. = -leib; **-leib** m, n, **-leibchen** n corset(s pl.), (pair of) stays pl.; **-leib-macher(in** f) m corset-maker.

Schnürlein (⠐⠐) n = Schnürchen.

Schnür-loch (⠐⠐ch) n eyelet, lacing-hole. [or braid-)maker.]

Schnur¹-**macher** (⠐⠐⠐) m cord-)

Schnür-nadel (⠐⠐⠐) f bodkin.

schnurr int. buzz!, whir!

Schnurr-bart (⠐...) [Schnurre Barthaar] m moustache; e-n ~ tragen, sich e-n ~ stehen lassen to wear (F to sport) a moustache; **2bärtig** a. = wearing a moustache; vgl. schnauzbärtig.

Schnurre (⠐⠐) [mhd.] f 1. comic tale, drollery, buffoonery; ~n erzählen, loslassen to tell amusing stories, to spin (funny) yarns. — 2. (Posse)

farce; (albernes Zeug) silly stuff, rubbish, trumpery things pl. — 3. F fig. (alte Bettel) old hag or crock. — 4. (et. Schnurrendes, z.B.: Hohlkreisel) humming-top; (Spinnrad) spinning-wheel; (Knarre des Nachtwächters) policeman's rattle.

schnurren (⠐⠐) [mhd.: schnarren] I v/n. (h., bei Ortsveränderung beim Fliegen auch sn) 1. von fliegenden Insekten ꝛc.: to buzz, to hum, von Rädern ꝛc. auch: to whir (round), to whiz (round). — 2. von Katzen, als Zeichen des Wohlbehagens: to purr. — 3. F = betteln. — II ~ n 4. buzz(ing), hum(ming), whir(ring), whiz(zing).

Schnurrer F (⠐⠐) m = Bettler.

Schnür-riemen (⠐⠐⠐) m (boot-)lace.

schnurrig (⠐⠐) [Schnurre] a. droll, comical, funny; odd, queer; **~keit** (⠐⠐⠐) f drollness.

Schnür-rock (⠐⠐⠐) m laced coat.

Schnurr-pfeiferei (⠐⠐⠐⠐) f knick-knack, trifle, ehm. auch: kickshaw.

Schnür-schuhe (⠐⠐⠐) m/pl. laced shoes pl.; **-senkel** m tag; ~ = -riemen; **-stiefel** m laced (or lace-up) boot; **-stock** ⊙ m der Teppichweber: upper roller.

schnur¹-**stracks** (⠐⠐⠐) adv.: a) directly, straight(away); b) zuwider diametrically opposed: b) (sofort) on the spot, forthwith, immediately, at once.

Schnürung (⠐⠐) f lacing.

Schnute [ndd.] f = Schnauze 1. [schieben.]

schob (⠐) ind., **schöbe** (⠐⠐) subj. impf. v f

Schober (⠐⠐) [ahd.: Schaub] m shock of sheaves; agr. ~ Heu hayrick, haystack; (Schuppen) (open)shed. [stack.]

schobern (⠐⠐) v/a. 2a. to pile up, to)

Schock (⠐; Hom. Chok) [mhd.] n (b, 6 (60 Stück) threescore; zwei ~ sixscore.

schocken (⠐⠐) [Schock] v/a. u. v/n. (h.) : a) to count by threescores; b) to pile up; c) das Getreide schockt gut (ergibt viel) ... yields well.

Schock-schwere-not! (⠐⠐⠐⠐⠐!) [sehr schwere Not] int. damn (or confound) it!, hang it (all)!, (it's a) damned nuisance!

schock-weise (⠐⠐⠐) adv.(a.) by threescores.

schofel F (⠐⠐) [hebr.] I a. (D9), a. **schof(e)lig** (⠐⠐⠐) (elend, gemein) wretched, paltry; der Kerl mean (or contemptible, shabby) fellow. — II ~ m (n) wretched stuff, refuse, rubbish.

Schöffe (⠐⠐) [ahd.: schaffen, schöpfen] m jur. (Laie als Gerichtsbeisitzer) unpaid magistrate, bisw. assessor.

Schöffen-gericht (⠐...) n , **-stuhl** m (court of) judge and jury, in England: court of aldermen. [f chocolate.]

Schokolade (⠐⠐⠐) [span., *merikanisch])

Schokoladen-baum ♀ (⠐⠐⠐⠐...) m (bff. Kakaobaum) chocolate-tree (Theobro'ma caca'o); **2braun** a. = **2farbig**; **-fabrik** f ch.-mill or -works pl.; **-fabrikant** m ch.-manufacturer or -maker; **2farbig** a. chocolate; **-kanne**, **-maschine** f ch.-pot or -can; **-mehl** n = **-pulver**; **-plätz-chen** n/pl. ch.-drops ꝛc.; **-pulver** n ch.-powder; **-quirl** m ch.-stick or -twirl; **-tafel** f ch.-cake, cake (or square) of ch.; **-tasse** f ch.-cup; **-torte** f ch.-cake.

Scholar † (⠐⠐) [mlt.] m scholar.

Scholarch † (⠐⠐) [mlt.] m: a) inspector of schools; b) schoolmaster.

Scholastik (⠐⠐⠐) [grch. scholē' (gelehrte) Muße] f Mittelalter: phls. scholastic philosophy, scholasticism; **~er** (⠐⠐⠐) m scholastic (philosopher), schoolman, school-doctor.

scholastisch (⠐⠐⠐) a. scholastic; der Theolog(e), auch: school-divine.

Scholiast (⠐⠐⠐) [grch.] m (Scholienschreiber) scholiast, commentator.

Scholi-e (⠐⠐⠐) [grch.] f , a. **~n** (⠐⠐⠐) n/pl. (erläuternde Bemerkung) scholium, commentary.

Scholle¹ (⠐⠐) [ahd.: Schale¹] f 1. lump, (Erdscholle) clod; fig. an der ~ hängen, kleben to stay in one's native country or town, to cling to earthly joys. — 2. = Eisscholle.

Scholle² (⠐⠐) [ndd.] f ichth.: gemeine ~ plaice (Pleurone'ctes Plate'ssa).

Schollen-brecher (⠐⠐⠐)[Scholle¹ 1] m , **-schlegel** m agr. clod-crusher, -beetle; Croskill roller; vgl. Kartoffelpflug.

schollig (⠐⠐) [Scholle¹ 1] a. lumpy, consisting of lumps or clods.

Schöll-kraut ♀ (⠐⠐) n = Schellkraut.

schölte (⠐⠐) subj. impf. von schelten.

schon (⠐) [ahd.; *schön] adv. already; (bis jetzt) by this time, so far, as yet; ⠐ am frühen Morgen schied er he left as soon as the dawn arose; ⠐ am nächsten Tage the very next day; er muß ⠐ dort sein he must be there by this time; ich hätte ⠐ früher geschrieben I should have written long (or much) before this or a long while since; ⠐ längst long ago; wie lange sind Sie ⠐ hier? how long have you now been here?; was ist es (oder gibt's) ⠐ wieder? now what is the matter again?; in Wunschsätzen: wenn er doch nur ⠐ käme! if he would only come now!; tröstend: es wird sich ⠐ finden it will all come right in the end or in good (or in due) time; ich werde ihn ⠐ bezahlen I shall pay him sure enough; (das ist) ⠐ gut! (that's) all right!, that'll do!; das wollen wir ⠐ machen wait, we shall soon do it; einräumend: ich gebe ⠐ (gern) zu, daß // I cannot help admitting that //, I'm quite willing to grant that //; das ist ⠐ wahr, aber // that's true enough, but //; that's all very well, but //; ja, das kennen wir ⠐ yes, that's an old story; hier ist ⠐ Platz genug there is surely room enough here; einschränkend: ⠐ der (bloße) Anblick the bare sight (of it); ⠐ der Gedanke (an sich) even the (very) thought, the mere idea; ⠐ der Höflichkeit halber for mere courtesy, out of sheer politeness; ⠐ die Regeln der Ehre the ordinary (or common) rules of honour; s. ob⠐; F wenn ⠐ denn ⠐ in any case; if it has to be, then let it be.

schön (⠐) [ahd. ansehnlich; *schauen] I a. (ant. häßlich) 1. allg.: beautiful, poet. auch: beauteous; in Gestalt und Zügen: handsome, v. Frauen auch: fair (damsel, lady); ⠐ von Gesicht with handsome features, good-looking; ⠐ von Gestalt fine, well made or built or shaped or formed; (hübsch) pretty, (niedlich) nice; ++ bsf. in Norddeutschland, statt „gut",

♪ Musik; ⚛ Wissenschaft; ♀ Pflanze; ⌘ Geographie; ⊙ Technik; ⚒ Bergbau; ⚔ Militär; ↓ Marine; ⚕ Handel; ✉ Post; ⚙ Eisenbahn.

[**Schönbartspiel**] — 858 — [**schoppenweise**]

zB. ₰es Bier, Brot good (or fine) beer, bread. — 2. mit *nouns*: f. bescheren 3, Dank 4; *fig.* e-e ₰e (günstige) Gelegenheit a good (or favourable) opportunity, a fair chance; *iro.* f. Geschichte 1; das ₰e Geschlecht the fair sex; eine ₰e Handlung a noble action, f. Kunst 1; e-s ₰en Morgens (unerwartet) one fine morning; da kannst du ₰e (tüchtige) Prügel bekommen you may get a good (or sound) thrashing or F hiding; manch ₰es Mal many a time and oft, a good many times; eine ₰e Summe a good round sum. — 3. mit *verbs*: f. anfommen 3; dafür würde ich mich ₰(stens) bedanken I should decidedly decline it; sagen Sie mir, ich bitte ₰ (freundlichst)! will you please, tell me!; do tell me, I beg of you; sie wird sich ₰ (gehörig) erschrecken she will be terribly frightened; grüßen Sie ihn ₰(stens) von mir give him my kind(est) regards; f. heraus sein c; das ist ₰ von ihm that's nice (or kind of him); das ist alles recht ₰, aber // that's all very fine (or very well), but //; das klingt ₰ that sounds well or nice; Sie haben ₰ (leicht) lachen you may well laugh, it's easy for you to laugh; sich ₰ machen to adorn o.s., F to smarten o.s. up; ₰ riechen, schmecken to have a nice (or pleasant) smell, taste; ₰ schreiben to write a nice (or a good, stärker: a beautiful) hand; ₰ tun to be coquettish or affected, to coquet (or flirt) with a p.; *iro.* das wäre noch ₰er! that would be worse still! — 4. F als Antwort: tun Sie das! ₰! ... certainly (, I will)!; F alright or all right (, sir)! — **II** ~e *n* ⑰ 5. das ~e the beautiful; das ~e an diesem Stücke the good part of this play; das ist was ~es! there is a nice thing (a. *iro.*)!; Sie werden was ~es von mir denken you will have a nice opinion of me (meist *iro.*); aufs (ob. auf das) ₰ste, am ₰sten most beautifully, in the finest way possible. — **III** ~e *f* ⓺ 6. eine ~e a beautiful (or handsome) woman, F a beauty; die ~e the fair one. the (fair) damsel; seine ~e his sweetheart, his lady-love; die ~ste auf dem Balle the belle of the ball; die ~ste von allen the fairest (or best-looking) of all.

Schön-bart-spiel (″...) [mhd. (P ˖+)] *Schemen † = Larve, Maske] *n* ⑫ ehm.: fancy-dress ball, mummery.

Schön-druck ⊙ (ˮ ̮) *m* ⑫ *typ.* (einseitig bedruckter Bogen) first form; (einseitiges Drucken) printing the white.

Schöne (ˊ ̮) [ahd.] *f* 1. ⓼ = Schönheit. — 2. ⓺ Person: f. Schöne.

schonen[1] (ˊ ̮) [mhd.; *schön † = rücksichtsvoll] **I** *v/a.* und sich ₰ *v/refl.* ⓼: (sich) ₰ to spare (o.s.), seine Gesundheit 2c. ₰ to take care (or to be careful) of ..., to look well after ...; (sparen) to save, (erhalten) to preserve, (pflegen) to nurse, to mind; seine Mittel ₰ to husband one's resources; sein Geld nicht ₰ to lavish ...; Bäume, Wild 2c. ₰ to preserve ...; — **II** ~ *n* ⑳ f. Schonung. — **III** ₰d *p.pr.* u. *a.* ⓺ careful, tender; (nachsichtig) indulgent, forbearing.

Schonen[2] ⚲ (ˊ ̮) *npr/n.* ⓼ südlichste Provinz Schwedens: Scania, Scane.

schönen (ˊ ̮) [ahd.] *v/a.* ⓼: Wein 2c. ₰ (bsd. mit Hausenblase 2c. klären) to fine wine, &c. (with isinglass), to clarify wine, &c.

Schoner[1] (ˊ ̮) [schonen] *m* ⑬ 1. person who spares. — 2. ~ (Deckchen) für Möbel: tidy, für Sofa und Sessel auch: antimacassar; (Überzug) covering for chairs, &c.

Schoner[2] ⚓︎ ↓ (ˊ ̮) [engl., ndl.] *m* ⑬ (urspr. ein Zweimaster) schooner; als ~ getafelt schooner-rigged.

Schön-färben ⊙ (″...) *n* ⑫ = -färberei; ₰ *v/a.* ⓼** *fig.* to paint in glowing colours, to gloss over; **-färber** ⊙ *m* dyer in fine (or high) colours; **-färberei** ⊙ *f* dyeing in fine colours; **-fleck(en** *n*) *m* = -pfläschen; ₰gebaut *a.* ⓺ finely (or well-) built or made; **-geist** *m* fine scholar; wit(ty writer); *b.s.* prig, *a.* = Blaustrumpf; **-geisterei** *f* fine scholarship, literary aspiration; *b.s.* learned affectation, priggishness; ₰geistig *a.* ⓺ fond of learning or literature; *b.s.* priggish.

Schönheit (ˊ ̮) [mhd.] *f* ⓺ 1. beauty; handsome features, good looks pl., v. Frauen oft: fair face. — 2. metonymisch: (Schöne) beautiful girl, handsome woman, fair lady, fair one; eine berühmte (wahre) ~ a celebrated (regular) beauty. — 3. ~en *pl.* (Artigkeiten) polite (or courteous) phrases, civilities pl.

Schönheits-gefühl (″...) *n* ⑫ sense of (or taste for) the beautiful; **-lehre** *f*, *phls.* æsthetics; **-lini-e** *f* line of beauty; **-mittel** *n* cosmetic; ₰reich *a.* ⓺ of great beauty; **-pflaster** *n* beauty-spot; **-sinn** *m* (artistic) taste; vgl. -gefühl; **-wasser** *n* wash (for the face); auch: beautifying lotion.

Schön-pfläschen (″...) *n* ⑫ = Schönheitspflaster; **-redner** *m* fine (or fluent) speaker; rhetorician; **-rednerei** *f* fine (or fluent) speaking or speech, rhetoric; **-rednerisch** *a.* ⓺ rhetorical; **-schreibe-kunst** *f*, **-schreiben** *n* calligraphy, penmanship; **-schreiber** *m* calligraphist; (j. der schön schreibt) good penman, F a beauty; **-schwäter** *m* good talker; **-sicht** *f* fine view, als Name a. Fair View. (fr.) Bellevue; ₰tuend *a.* (geziert) coquettish, (liebelnd) flirting; **-tuer** *m* **-tuerei** *f* coquetting, flirtation; ₰tun *v/n.* ⓼** to coquet, to flirt.

Schonung (ˊ ̮) [schonen] *f* ⓺ 1. careful (or gentle, tender) treatment; indulgence, forbearance, (Erbarmen) mercy. — 2. *for.* fenced-in district; (Baumpflanzung) nursery; (Jagdgehege) preserve.

Schonungs-brille (ˊ ̮...) *f* ⓺ sight-preservers pl.; ₰los *a.* ⓺ unsparing, relentless, harsh; (v. Erbarmen) merciless, pitiless; **-losigkeit** *f* relentlessness, harshness; ₰voll *a.* full of (kind or gentle, tender) consideration(s); indulgent, considerate, forbearing.

schön-wissenschaftlich (″...) [belletristisch] *a.* ⓺ relating to light (or popular) literature.   [Fischerei: close time.]

Schon-zeit (″...) *f* ⓺ *hunt.* u./

Schopf ⚒︎ [mhd.: Schaub] *m* ⑳ ⒈ 1. (Scheitel) crown, top of the head. — 2. a) (Haarbüschel auf dem Wirbel e-s Menschen) fore-lock; tuft of hair; e-n beim ~e fassen to seize (F to catch hold of) a p. by the hair; *fig.* die Gelegenheit beim ~e fassen (eagerly) to seize the opportunity; b) (Federbusch der Vögel) tuft of feathers, crest. — 3. *for.* eines Baumes top of a tree.

Schöpf-brett ⊙ (ˊ...) *n* ⑫ = Schaufel 2 a; **-brunnen** *m* open well; **-bütte** *f* Papierfabr.: pulp-vat; **-eimer** *m*: a) well-bucket; b) *mach.* piggin, Baggern: bail-scoop.

schöpfen (ˊ ̮) [mhd.: scoop; *schaffen] **I** *v/a.* u. *v/n.* (h.) ⓼ 1. to draw water, &c.; aus derselben Quelle ₰ to draw from the same source; et. aus guter Quelle ₰ to learn (or hear) a th. from a good source, to have a th. on the best authority; Wein in einen Krug ₰ to fill (or put) ... into a jug; ein Faß leer ₰ to empty (out) ... — 2. Atem ₰ to draw (or take) breath, to breathe; tief Atem ₰ to fetch a deep breath; wieder Atem ₰ to recover one's breath, *fig.* to breathe freely; Luft ₰ to draw in air, *fig.* to recover o.s. — 3. *fig.* f. Argwohn, neue Hoffnung ₰ to gather (or conceive) fresh hope. — **II** ~ *n* ⑳ 4. drawing water, &c. (f. **I**).

Schöpfer[1] (ˊ ̮) [ahd.; *schaffen] *m* ⑬. ~in *f* ⓺ creator, producer, maker, originator, author(ess *f*); *rel.* unser ~, oft: our Maker, our Creator.

Schöpfer[2] (ˊ ̮) [schöpfen] *m* ⑬: a) p. who draws water, &c.; b) ⊙ = Schöpfstelle.

Schöpfer[1]**-geist** (ˊ.ˊ) *m* ⑫ creative (or productive) genius.

schöpferisch (ˊ ̮) *a.* ⓺ creative, productive,(Kunst) original;(fruchtbar) fertile; **Schöpfer-kraft** (ˊ...) *f* ⓺ creative (or productive) power; **-wort** *n* word of the creator, creator's fiat.

Schöpf-gefäß (ˊ...) *n* ⑫ = -kelle; **-kanne** *f* can (or jug) for drawing water, &c.; **-kelle** ⊙ *f* dipper, scoop; **-löffel** *m*: a) ⊙ = -kelle; b) Koch.: basting-ladle; **-maschine** ⊙ *f* hydraulic engine or machine; **-napf** *m* = -eimer b; **-rad** ⊙ *n*: a) zum Wasserheben: scoop- (or Persian) wheel, water-wheel, mit Eimern: bucket-wheel; b) Uhrmacherei: (Ausheber) lifter, ratch; **-rahmen** ⊙ *m* Papierfabr.: deckle.

Schöpfung (ˊ ̮) *f* ⓺ (das Schaffen und Geschaffene) creation; (Erschaffenes) creature, production; (die Welt) the universe; co. die Herren der ~ the lords of creation; **~s-geschichte** *f* ⓺ history of creation, mosaische ~ (1. Buch Mosis) Genesis; **~s-tag** *m* day of creation.

Schöpf-werk ⊙ (ˊ.ˊ) *n* ⑫ water-engine.

Schöppchen (ˊ ̮) *n* ⑬ (dim. von Schoppen[2]) small glass of beer, &c.

Schöppe (ˊ ̮) [ndd.] *m* ⑭ = Schöffe.

Schoppen[1] (ˊ ̮) *m* ⑬ = Schuppen.

Schoppen[2] (ˊ ̮) [ndd.] *m* ⑬ ehm. Flüssigkeitsmaß, etwa 1/2 Liter: pint of beer, &c.; **Schoppen-glas** (ˊ ̮.ˊ) *n* ⑫ pint-glass.

Schöppenstedter (ˊ ̮.ˊ ̮) [Schöppen-städt, -stedt ⚲ St. in Braunschweig] *m* ⑬, ~in *f* ⓺ 1. inhabitant of Schoeppenstedt. — 2. *fig.* Gothamite, vgl. Krähwinkler(in).

schoppen[2]**-weise** (ˊ ̮.ˊ ̮) *adv.* by pints.

Signs (see page XVII): F familiar; P vulgar; ℾ flash; ⟍ rare; † obsolete (died); * new word (born); ˖+ incorrect; ♪ music;

[**Schöps**]

Schöps (ˇ) [mhd.; *tschech. Verschnittener] m ⓐa. (㊷) **1.** (Hammel) wether. — **2.** F *fig.* (Dummkopf) simpleton.
Schöpsen-fleisch (ˇ.ˇ) *n* ㊷ mutton.
schor (ˉ) *ind. impf.* von scheren.
Schore ⊙ (ˉˇ) [mhd. schorren ragen] *f* ㊽ *carp.* (Stütze) prop, shore, support.
schöre *subj. impf. v.* scheren.
Schorf (ˇ) [ahd.; *schürfen] *m* ⓑb. *path.* scurf, Kopfschorf a. dandruff, ⚘ eschar.
schorf-artig (ˇ...) *a.* ⓺ *path.* scurf-like, scurfy, ⚘ furfuraceous; **⸗bildend** a. forming scurf or dandruff, ⚘ escharotic; **⸗bildung** *f* ⓺ formation of scurf or dandruff.
schorfig (ˇ) *a.* ⓺ *path.* covered with scurf or dandruff, *a.* = schorf-artig; ⚘ scaly.
Schörl (ˇ) [nordisch] *m* ⓒc. *min.* (Turmalin) ⚘ schorl, black tourmaline, ⚒ cockle; **schörl-artig** *a.* ⓺: ⚘ schorlaceous.
Schorn-stein (ˇˉ) [mhd.; *Schore] *m* ⓒc. chimney, flue, smoke-stack, auf Dampf-schiffen: funnel (vgl. Kamin), *fig.* ich kann es (das mir schuldige Geld) in den ~ schreiben F I may whistle for it, I shan't see the colour of it.
Schornstein-aufsatz (ˇˉ...) *m* ⓺ chimney-pot; **⸗brand** *m* chimney on fire; **⸗fegen** *n* chimney-sweeping; **⸗feger** *m* chi.-sweep(er); **⸗kappe** *f* chi.-pot; **⸗kranz** *m* chi.-top; **⸗rohr** *n*, **⸗röhre** *f* chimney-flue or -shaft.

schoß¹ (ˇ) *ind. impf.* von schießen.
Schoß² (ˇ) ⚘ **I** *f* [ahd.; *schoß¹] *m* ⓐa. (Schößling, Sproß) shoot, sprig, scion. — **II** fast † [mhd.: scot „Zuschuß"] *m* ⓐa. (Abgabe) tax, bsd. ehm., auch: scot.
Schoß³ (ˇ) [ahd.: sheet ⧦ Gehre(n), f. Schote²] *m* ⓐa. **1.** (beim Sitzen entstehendem Bug) lap; auf j-s ~ sitzen to sit in a p.'s lap; *fig.* f. Abraham; es ist ihm in den ~ gefallen it (or luck) has come to him in his sleep or over night; er legt die Hände in den ~ (ist müßig) he sits with his hands before him (doing nothing), he rests on his oars; im ~e (Kreise) s-r Familie in the bosom (or midst) of his family; im ~e der Kirche within the pale of the Church. — **2.** (Mutterleib) womb (a. weitS. das Innere); im ~e der Erde in the bowels of the earth; im ~e der Zukunft in the (dim and) distant future, auch: on the knees of the gods. — **3.** ~ am Mannsrocke tail (or flap) of a coat, coat-tail.
schoßbar fast † (ˇˉ) *a.* ⓺ = schoßpflichtig.
schösse (ˇˇ) *subj. impf. v.* schießen.
Schossee* (ˇˉ) *f* ㊽ = Chaussee.
schossen (ˇˇ) [Schoß²] *v/n.* (h.) ⓺ **1.** *a. v/a.* fast † (steuern) to pay taxes. — **2.** ⁜ (sprossen) to shoot (into blade). [collector.]
Schösser fast † (ˇˇ) [schossen 1] *m* ㉒ tax-]
schoß²-frei fast † (ˇˉ) *a.* ⓺ free from taxes.
Schoß²-hund (ˇˉ) *m* ㉒, **⸗hündchen** *n* lap-dog; **⸗kelle** *f:* a) (Hinterraum am Wagen für Gepäck) boot, (luggage-) basket; b) (Kutscher sitz am Lastwagen) driver's box or seat; **⸗kind** *n* pet (child), darling (child); **⸗länge** *f* length of the coat-tails.
Schößling ⁜ (ˇˇ) [Schoß²] *m* ⓓd. shoot, offshoot, sucker, ⚘ stolon; (Nachwuchs) new growth; (Wurzel-)~ runner.
schoß²-pflichtig (ˇ...) *a.* ⓺ fast † liable to pay taxes; **⸗rebe** ⁜ *f* ㊷ shoot of a vine; **⸗register** *n* fast † register of assessments; **⸗reis** *n* = Schößling.
Schoß³-sünde (ˇ...) *f* ㊷ *theol.* pet (or besetting) sin; **⸗tasche** *f* coat-tail pocket.
Schötchen ⁜ (ˇˇ) [Schote¹] *n* ㉓ small pod, ⚘ silic(u)le, silicula; **⸗artig,** **⸗förmig** *a.* ⓺: ⚘ silicular, ...ose.
Schote¹ (ˉˇ) [mhd.: Scheu-er, Schaum] *f* ㊽ **1.** ⁜ pod, cod, husk, ⚘ siliqua. — **2.** Kocht.: ~ *npl.* (grüne Erbsen) green peas *pl.*
Schote² ⚓ (ˉˇ) [ndd.: sheet ⧦ Schoß³] *f* ㊽ (Segelleine) sheet.
Schote³ (ˉˇ) [hebr.] *m* ㊹ (Narr) fool.
schoten-artig ⁜ (ˉˇ...) [Schote¹] *a.* ⓺ ⚘ = **⸗förmig,** **⸗dorn** *m* ⓺: a) = Akazie; b) virginischer ~ bastard acacia, locust-tree (*Robi'nia pseudaca'cia*); **⸗erbsen** *f/pl.* peas *pl.* in pods; **⸗förmig** *a.* pod-shaped, ⚘ siliquose, ...iform; **⸗früchte** *f/pl. agr.* pulse(-crops *pl.*); **⸗gewächse** *n/pl.:* ⚘ leguminous plants *pl.*; **⸗klee** ⚘ *m* bird's-foot trefoil (*Lotus cornicula'tus*); **⸗tragend** ⚘ *a.* pod-bearing, ⚘ siliquose.
Schott ⚓ **I** [ndd.] *n* ⓒc., ~e (ˉˇ) *f* ㊽ **1.** (Bretterverschlag) wooden partition. — **2.** ⚓ (wasserdichte Scheidewand) bulkhead.
Schotte² (~n¹ *pl.*) (ˉˇ) *m* ㊺, **Schottin** *f* ㊽ Scotchman, f Scotchwoman; *auch:* Scotsman; die Schotten *pl.*, oft: the Scotch (people), meist *hist.* the Scots.
Schotten² öst. (ˉˇ) [ahd.; *schütten] *m* ㉓ (Quark) curds *pl.*
Schotter (ˉˇ) [schütten] *m* ㉒ Straßenbau: metal for (making up) the roads, broken stones *pl.*, ballast; **schottern** (ˉˇ) *v/a.* ⓐa. = beschottern; **Schotter-straße** *f* ㊽ metalled road; **Schotterung** (ˉˇ) *f* ㊻ gravelling, ballasting.
schottisch (ˉˇ) **I** *a.* ⓺ **1.** Scotch, Scottish; vgl. Hochland b; die 2e Sprache, das ~(e) *n* ⓺ the Scotch language, Scotch. — **II** ~ *n* ⓺ **2.** ~(e) *m* Art Walzer: schotti'sche. — **3.** *n, inv.* ⓺ (gewürfelter Tuchstoff) Scotch plaid(ing), tartan. [*poet.* Scotia, Caledonia.]
Schottland ⚐ (ˉˇ) *npr/n.* ⓖg. Scotland,]
schraben (ˉˇ) [ndd.] = schrappen.
schraffieren (ˇˉˇ) [ndl.; *it. f. sgraffito] **I** *v/a. u. v/n.* (h.) ⚃ Zeichenkunst, Kupferstecherei: to hatch, in Kreuz a. to counter-hatch. — **II** ~ *n* ㉓ u. **Schraffierung**, **Schraffur** (ˇˉ) *f* ㊽ hatching, in kreuzweiser Lage auch: counter-hatching, cross-hatching.

schräg (ˉ) [mhd.: Schragen] *a.* ⓺ (ant. gerade) oblique, slant(ing), *adv. auch:* aslant (vgl. schief); (2 laufend) diagonal, (quer hindurchgehend) transversal, *adv. a.* across; ⊙ *carp., &c.* 2 behauen, sägen, zuschneiden to cut slantwise, to bevel.
Schräg-balken (ˉˉ...) *m* her. bend; linker ~ (Zeichen unehelicher Geburt) bar sinister; **⸗beet** *n, hort.* shelving bed.
Schräge (ˉˇ) *f* ㊽ (f. schräg) **1.** obliquity, slant; quer, figure, incline. — **2.** ⊙ (abgestoßene Kante) chamfer.
Schragen¹ ⊙ (ˉˇ) [mhd.: schräg, schränken] *m* **1.** (Gerüst, Gestell mit schrägen Füßen) trestle, (Sägebank) jack, horse. — **2.** ~ der Krämer: stand, stall, P pitch. — **3.** (Ruhebank) couch, chair-bedstead. — **4.** (Totenbahre) bier.
schragen² ⊙ (ˉˇ) *v/a.* ⓺ *carp.* Balken 2 to join ... slantwise or diagonally.

schrägen (ˉˇ) **I** *v/a.* ⓺ (abdachen) to slant, to slope; ⊙ to cut slantwise, to bevel. — **II** ~ *n* ㉓ f. Schrägung.
Schräg-fenster (ˉˉ...) *n* ⓺ für Oberlicht: sky-light; **⸗fläche** *f* incline, slope, e-s Edelsteins *etc.*: bezel.
Schrägheit (ˉˉ) *f* ㊻ = Schräge.
Schräg-hobel ⊙ (ˉˉ...) *m* ⓺ *carp.* bevelling-plane; **⸗kante** ⊙ *f, carp.* chamfer; **⸗kreuz** *n* = Andreaskreuz; **⸗lini-e** *f* diagonal; **⸗maß** ⊙ *n, carp., &c.* bevel-rule; **⸗sägen** *n, carp.* bevelling, chamfering; **⸗steg** ⊙ *m, typ.* inclined quoin; **⸗über** *adv.* aslant.
Schrägung (ˉˇ) *f* ㊻ **1.** ·slanting; ⊙ bevelling. — **2.** = Schräge 2.
schrak (ˉ) **1.** u. **3.** Person *sg. ind.*, **schräke** (ˉˇ) *subj. impf. v.* schrecken³ **I.** [holing.]
Schram ⚒ (ˉ) *m* ⓒc. (Schramme) trench,]
schrämen ⚒ (ˉˇ) *v/a.* ⓺ (Schräme [*pl. v.* Schram] einhauen) to hole, to cut through.
Schräm-häuer ⚒ (ˉˉ...) *m* ⓺ auf Kohlenflözen: holer, hewer of trenches; **⸗maschine** ⊙ *f* coal-cutting machine.
Schramme (ˉˇ) [mhd.] *f* ㊽ (Ritz in der Haut) (slight) scratch or abrasion; (aufgesprungene Haut) crack, (offene Stelle) sore (place), (Narbe) scar.
schrammen (ˉˇ) **I** *v/a.* ⓺ to scratch; to make sore, to graze (or rub) the skin off, to abrade. — **II** *v/n.* (h. u. jn) an et. 2 (anstreifen) to graze, to touch lightly. [scratches or scars.]
schrammig (ˉˇ) *a.* ⓺ covered with]
Schramm-schuß (ˉˉ) *m* ⓺ grazing shot.
Schrank (ˉ) [ahd.; *schränken] *m* ⓑb. cupboard, press, case; f. Bücher, Kleider, Küchen-schrank; f. Porzellan: china-cupboard, für Tafelgerät: sideboard, für Kunstsachen: cabinet, für Reliquien: shrine.
Schränkchen (ˉˇ) *n* ㉓ (*dim. v.* Schrank) small cupboard or press or cabinet.
Schranke (ˉˇ) [mhd.; *schränken] *f* ㊽ **1.** (Querholz) barrier, 🚃 railway-gate; (Einfriedigung) fencing; (Gitter) grating; ~ e-s Gerichtshofes, des Parlamentes bar. — **2.** (umschlossener Raum) enclosure, (Kampf-, Rennplatz) course, Alt.: arena, zum Turnier: lists *pl.*; in die ~n fordern to challenge, weitS. to call to book; in die ~n treten to enter the lists. — **3.** (Grenze) boundary, limit; in ~n halten to keep within bounds, to restrain; einer Sache ~n setzen to put a check on (or to check) a th., to put a limit (or a stop) to a th.
Schränk-eisen ⊙ (ˉˉˇ) [schränk-en] *n* ⓺ saw-set, wrest.
schränken (ˉˇ) [ahd.: shrink: schräg] *v/a.* ⓺ **1.** to put (or lay) crosswise, to cross. — **2.** ⊙ die Zähne einer Säge 2 (richten u. schärfen) to set a saw.
schranken-los (ˉˇ...) [Schranke] *a.* ⓺ boundless, unbounded, unlimited; (maßlos) unmeasured, *fig.* licentious; **⸗losigkeit** *f* boundlessness; *fig.* licentiousness.
Schränker ⊙ (ˉˇ) *m* ㉒ saw-wrester.
Schrank-fach (ˉˉ) *n* ⓺ drawer.
Schränk-stock ⊙ (ˉˉ...) *m* ⓺ saw-clamp or -vice, saw-wrester's block; **⸗zange** *f* saw-set plier.
Schranne südd. (ˉˇ) *f* ㊽ **1.** = Fleischbank. — **2.** (Getreidemarkt) corn-market.

[**Schranne**]

⚛ scientific; ⚘ botanical; ⚐ geography; ⊙ machinery; ⚒ mining; ⚔ military; ⚓ marine; ● commercial; ✉ postal; 🚃 railway.

[Schranz] — 860 — [schreiben]

Schranz(ᵛ)[mhd. Schlitz(kleid); *schrinden] ⑫, ~e (ᵛ) ㊹ m (Höfling) cringing (or fawning) courtier, flunkey, toady.
Schranzen-art(ᵛ⁻ᵛ)f@cringing ways pl.
schranzenhaft (ᵛ⁻ᵛ) a. ㊻ cringing, fawning; flunkey-like, toadying.
schrapen (¹⁻ᵛ) = schrappen.
Schrapnell×(⁻ᵛ)[engl.*OberstShrapnel, 1803] m, n ⓐd. (ⓖ)artill. shrapnel, case-shot; ~schuß m ㉒ round of case-shot.
Schrapp-eisen (ᵛ⁻ᵛ) n ⑫ scrap-iron.
schrapper- (ᵛ⁻ᵛ)[ndd. = hd. schröpfen] v/a. u. v/n. (h.) ㊽ to scrape.
Schrapper ⊕ (ᵛ⁻ᵛ) m ㉒ scraper.
Schrapsel (¹⁻ᵛ) n ㉒ scrapings pl.
Schrat ⑫ [ahd.: (Old) Scratch Teufel] m ⓐc. myth. satyr, faun.
schraub-bar (¹⁻ᵛ) a. ㊻ fit (or adapted) for screwing, screwable.
Schraube (¹⁻ᵛ)[mhd.: screw] f ㊽ ① ①. screw, einer Kelter: pressing-screw, squeezer, an der Schraubenpresse: screw-bar; archime'dische ~, ~ ohne Ende endless (or Archimedean) screw, worm-gear, ↓ an Schraubenschiffen: screw-propeller; einfache (doppelte) ~ single-thread (double-thread) screw; ~n schneiden to cut screws. — 2. F fig. in seinem Kopfe ist eine ~ los he has a screw loose (somewhere), he has not all his buttons on; die ~ ansetzen = schrauben 3; auf ~n stehen (ungewiß sein) to be uncertain; seine Worte auf ~n stellen to give one's words a double meaning, to speak ambiguously; auf ~n gestellt ambiguous, uncertain. — 3. F fig. verdrehte ~ queer fellow; alte ~ old woman or frump or crock.
schrauben (¹⁻ᵛ) [Schraube] v/a. ㊽, ⓒc. ①. to screw; fester (loser) ② to tighten (to loosen) the screw of; die Lampe in die Höhe ② to turn up ..., F to turn ... on (fuller); s. herunter②, fig. seine Hoffnungen niedriger ② to abate one's hopes. — 2. fig. nur ㊽ (übertreiben) to strain, force, overdo; s-n Stil ② to write affectedly; vgl. geschraubt, bfd. Artikel. — 3. fig. seine Forderungen höher (niedriger) ② to raise (to abate) one's demands; ⓢ die Preise zu furchtbarer Höhe hinauf ② to send (or fig) up the prices enormously, to boom the market. — 4. fig. e-n um et. ② (betrügen) to cheat (F to diddle, to do) a p. out of a th. — 5. fig. e-n ② (aufziehen) to tease (or quiz, chaff) a p.
Schrauben-blech ⊕ (¹¹⁻ᵛ...) n ㉒ screw-plate; =**bohrer** m screw-auger, spiral drill; =**bolzen** m sc.-bolt; =**bremse** f sc.-brake; =**dampfer** m (dampf)schiff n sc.-steamer; sc.-propeller; =**flügel** ↓ m propeller-blade; ②förmig a. ㊽ sc.-shaped, ⚘ helical; =**gang** m groove; =**gebläse** n sc.-blower or ventilator; =**gewinde** n sc.-thread, worm; =**kopf** m sc.-head or-knob; =**linie** f. geom., &c. sc.-line, spiral, ⚘ helix; =**mutter** f sc.-nut, female screw; =**nagel** m sc.-nail; =**rahme** f, =**rahmen** m, typ. sc.-chase; =**riegel** m = =bolzen; =**ring** m am Mikroskop: sc.-collar; =**schiff** ↓ n = =dampfer; =**schloß** n am Gewehr: sc.-barrel lock, sc.-lock; =**schlüssel** m sc.-key or -wrench, spanner; =**schneide-**

bank f sc.-cutting lathe; =**schneid-maschine** f sc.-cutter; =**spindel** f: a) male screw; b) Drechsler: sc.-mandrel lathe; =**welle** f propeller-shaft; =**winde** f sc.-jack; =**windung** f spire of a screw, turn; =**zange** f: a) der Schlosser: hand-vice; b) der Zahnärzte: screw-forceps; =**zieher** m sc.-driver; =**zwinge** f vice-pin, screw-clamp.
Schrauberei (⁻ᵛ¹⁻ᵛ¹)f ㊹1.screwing.—2.fig. =Aufziehen.—3.F fig. (Erpressung) (endless) screwing or squeezing, extortion.
Schraub-rahme(n m) f ⊕ (¹¹...) ㉒ typ. = Schrauben-r.; =**stock** m (hand-)vice, screw-vice; =**stock-bank** f vice-bench; =**stock-futter** n vice-grips pl.
Schreck (ᵛ) m ⓐb. = Schrecken¹; s. außer 3.
schreckbar (ᵛ⁻ᵛ) a. ㊻ easily frightened, timid, nervous, F u. P funky.
Schreckbarkeit (ᵛ⁻ᵛ⁻) f ㊹ timidity.
Schreck-bild (ᵛ⁻ᵛ) n ㉒ = Schreckgespenst.
Schrecken¹ (ᵛ⁻ᵛ) [mhd.; *schrecken³] m ㉓ fright, terror, (Entsetzen) horror, dismay; plötzlicher ~ alarm, panic; mit dem (bloßen) ~ davon- kommen to be more frightened than hurt; vgl. davonkommen; e-m ~ einflößen/einjagen to fill a p. with alarm, geh. Spr.: to strike terror into a p.('s breast); von ~ ergriffen terror-stricken, seized with fright; s. erregen I; in ~ setzen to frighten, dismay, alarm.
Schrecken² ↓ (ᵛ⁻ᵛ) pl. (Pfähle) piles pl. to moor rafts to; vgl. Schrickpfahl.
schrecken³ (ᵛ⁻ᵛ) [ahd.: shrug] I v/n. (sn) ⓐa.(impf.schrat)1.to be(come)alarmed; mst in Zssgn, s. auf② I, er② II. — 2. auch sich ② to become (suddenly) chilled. — II v/a. ㊽ 3. (in Schreck setzen) to frighten, dismay, alarm, startle, stärker: to terrify; s. auf② II. — 4. (plötzlich abkühlen) to chill (auch ⊕ metall., &c.), durch kaltes Wasser: to pour cold water upon. — 5. Wasser ꝛc. ② (lau m.) to take the chill off ..., to make ... tepid or lukewarm.
Schreckens-bild (ᵛ⁻ᵛ...) n ㉒ dreadful spectacle, horrible sight; =**bote** m one who brings alarming news; =**botschaft** f terrible (or alarming, disastrous) news; =**herrschaft** f reign of terror; =**jahr** n terrible (or disastrous) year; =**mann** m terrorist; =**nacht** f night of horrors, terrible night; =**ruf** m cry of horror; =**tat** f atrocious deed, horrible crime; ②**voll** = schreckenvoll; =**zeit** f = =herrschaft, auch: terrorism.
schrecken¹-voll (ᵛ⁻ᵛ⁻f) a. ㊻ terrible.
Schreck-gedanke (ᵛ⁻...) m ⑫ terrible thought, alarming idea; =**gespenst** n ⑫, =**gestalt** f terrible vision or phantom, bugbear; bsd. für Kinder: bogy (man).
schreckhaft (ᵛ⁻ᵛ) a. ㊻ 1. = schreckbar. — 2. (schrecklich) fearful.
Schreckhaftigkeit (ᵛ⁻ᵛ⁻) f ㊹ timidity.
schrecklich (ᵛ⁻ᵛ) a. ㊻ terrible, (furchtbar) frightful, fearful, dreadful, formidable (weapon, &c.); (graußig) horrible, horrid, awful, stärker: ghastly (crime, &c.), atrocious (deed, &c.); ② anzusehen fearful to behold, F fig. (oft als adv.) tremendous(ly); (ungemein) exessive(-ly); (ungeheuer) vast(ly), immensely; das tut mir ② leid I am awfully (or extremely) sorry about (or for) that.

Schrecklichkeit (ᵛ⁻ᵛ⁻) f ㊻ (s. schrecklich) frightfulness; awfulness, ghastliness; atrociousness; fig. vastness.
Schrecknis (ᵛ⁻ᵛ) n ⑫ 1. object of terror, a. = Schreckbild. — 2. = Schrecken.
Schreck-schanze ⚔ (ᵛ⁻...) f ㉒ redoubt; =**schuß** m shot in the air intended to alarm people; fig. false alarm, idle threat; =**tuch** n, hunt. toils (or rags) pl. for frightening game.
Schrei¹ (ᵛ) [ahd.] m ⓐc. cry, shout, gellender: yell, yelling, shriek, screeching, der Angst: scream; s. ausstoßen 5.
Schrei²-balg F (¹¹⁻ᵛ) [schrei-en] m ⑫ squalling brat.
Schreib-apparat ⊙ (¹...)[schreib-en]m@tel. indicator; =**ärmel** m = Schmutzärmel; =**art** f manner (or style) of writing; eines Wortes: spelling of a word; =**bedarf** m writing-materials pl., stationery; =**diamant** m glazier's diamond.
Schreibe-brief F (¹¹⁻ᵛ...) m: (langer) (long) epistle; =**buch** n writing-book, s. Schönschreiben: copy-book; vgl. Schreibheft; =**kunst** f s. Schreibkunst.
schreiben (¹⁻ᵛ) [ahd.; *lt. scri'bere] I v/a. v/n. (h.) u. v/refl. ㊽ 1. to write; noch einmal ② to rewrite (s. ab-, nieder-schreiben); gut (schlecht) ② to write a good (bad) hand, meist vom Stil: to be a good (bad) writer; schlecht, unleserlich ② to scribble, to write illegibly; sich et. hinter die Ohren ② to mind (or to take note of) a th.; ins Konzept ② to make a (rough) draft of, to draft; ins reine ② to make a fair copy of; mit Blei(stift) ② to write (or scribble) in pencil; mit der Schreibmaschine ② to typewrite, F to type; mit der Schreibmasch. geschrieben typewritten, F typed; F fig. mit grober Fraktur auf j-s Rücken ② to give a p. a sound thrashing. — 2. mit dem durch Schreiben Erzeugten als Objekt: Aufsätze ② to write essays, Schule: to do composition; seinen Namen ② to sign one's name; seinen Namen unter et. ② to put (or attach) one's name (or signature) to a th.; vgl. 5; Noten (ab-)② to copy music; e-m eine Zeile (ein paar Zeilen) ② to drop a line (a few lines) to a p. — 3. vom Datum: den wievielten ② wir? what is the day of the month?; wir ② heute 1908 we are (living) in (the year) 1908. — 4. (mitteilen) der Standard schreibt ... writes, informs us, a. we read in ...; man schreibt uns aus Paris ... we hear (or receive news) from Paris; e-m ob. an e-n ② to write to a p., to communicate with a p.; sich (dat.) ea. ② to correspond (with each other); bibl. es steht im Buche Hiob geschrieben it is written in the book of Job. — 5. ein Wort richtig ② to spell ... correctly; falsch ② to misspell; das Wort wird mit ll geschrieben ... is spelt with ll; wie schreibt er sich ob. seinen Namen?: a) how does he spell his name?; b) how does he call himself? — 6. ⓢ e-m etwas gut (zur Last) ② to place a th. to a p.'s credit (debit), to credit (to debit) a th. to a p. — 7. metonymisch von Federn: ② schlecht they write badly, those are

---

Zeichen (s. S. IX): F familiär; P Volkssprache; ῤ Gaunersprache; ⸰ selten; † alt (auch gestorben); * neu (auch geboren); ⁺⁺ unrichtig:

[**Schreiber**] — 861 — [**Schriftleitung**]

bad (F shocking) pens (for writing). — 8. ſich von etwas her(=) ⚥ (batteren) to date from; a. = herrühren. — **II** ~ n ㉓ 9. (ſ. I) writing; ſind Sie mit dem ~ fertig? have you done (your) writing?; das ~ wird mir ſauer writing gives me trouble, I find writing difficult. — 10. (Brief) letter, written communication, kürzeres: note, diplomatiſches: dispatch; 🟊 wir haben Ihr geehrtes ~ empfangen your (esteemed) favour has come to hand; in meinem letzten ~ in my previous note, in my last (communication). — 11. = Schreibung. — **III Ge-ſchriebene(s)** n ㉕ 12. writing, written matter; manuscript; eigenhändig Geſchriebenes autograph.

Schreiber (⸗) [ahd.; *ſchreiben] m ㉒; ~in f ㊵ 1. writer, penman; er iſt ein guter (raſcher) ~ he is a good (fast) writer, he writes well (fast); er iſt kein guter ~ he is not a good hand at writing, his penmanship is not good. — 2. mit abhängigem gen.: ~(in) (Verfaſſer[in]) dieſes (Briefes) writer of this (letter) or of the present lines. — 3. (Abſchreiber) copyist. — 4. ~ (Angeſtellter) eines Kaufmanns, Advokaten ꝛc. commercial, solicitor's, &c. clerk; vgl. Amtsſchreiber.

Schreiber-amt (⸗...) n ㉒ = ⸗poſten; ⸗dienſt m clerical (a.: office-) work. **Schreiberei** (⸗⸗) f ㊵ 1. much writing or scribbling; ich habe viel ~en gehabt I have had many letters to write or a great deal of correspondence (to transact). — 2. (Beruf eines Schreibers) clerkship; copying.

Schreiber-poſten (⸗...) m ㉒ clerkship, clerk's post or appointment; ⸗ſeele f, contp. quill-driver; ⸗ſtuhl m office-stool. **ſchreib-faul** (⸗...) a. ㉖ lazy (or slow) in writing, not fond of corresponding; ⸗feder f ㉒ pen; ſ. Feder 2; ⸗fehler m error in writing, clerical mistake, slip of the pen; ⸗fertig a. with a ready pen, skilled with the pen; ⸗fertigkeit f penmanship, (leichter Stil) flowing (or easy) style; ⸗gebrauch m (method of) spelling. ⸗gebühr f, ⸗geld n fee for writing, copying-fee; ⸗gerät n = ⸗bedarf; ⸗griffel m Alt.: stylus, style, vgl. Griffel 1 u. 2; ⸗heft n exercise-book; ⸗kalender m note-book (with almanac); ⸗käſtchen n writing-case, für Federn: pen-case; ⸗krampf m cramp in the hand caused by much writing, path. writer's cramp; ⸗kunſt f art of writing, penmanship; calligraphy; ⸗künſtler m penman; ⸗lehrer m writing-master; ⸗leſe-methode f, ⸗leſen n simultaneous instruction in reading and writing; ⸗luſt f love for writing; ⸗luſtig a. fond of writing; ⸗mappe f: a) portfolio; b) mit Unterlage von Löſchpapier: blotting-book or -case, blotter; ⸗maſchine ☉ f typewriting machine, mehr abs.: typewriter; mit der ~ ſchreiben to typewrite; ⸗maſchinen-bureau n typewriting-office; ⸗maſchinen-ſchrift f typewriter-face; ⸗maſchiniſt(in f) m = Maſchinen-ſchreiber(in); ⸗materialien n/pl. = ⸗bedarf; ⸗materialien-händler ☉ m stationer; ⸗mate-

rialien-handlung f stationer's shop or business; ⸗papier n (ant. Druckpapier) writing-paper; weitS. glazed paper; ⸗pergament n parchment-paper, vellum; ⸗pult n writing-desk; ⸗ſchrift ☉ f, typ. script(-type); ⸗ſchule f: a) school for penmanship; b) set of copies; ⸗ſchüler(in f) m one who learns writing; ⸗ſekretär m (Möbel) secretary; ⸗ſelig a. = ⸗luſtig; ⸗ſeligkeit f = ⸗luſt; ⸗ſtift m = Griffel 2; ⸗ſtube f office, ⸗ = counting-house, einer Behörde ꝛc. auch: bureau, im Hotel ꝛc.: writing-room; ⸗ſtunde f writing-lesson; ⸗ſucht f passion (or mania) for writing; ⸗ſüchtig a. having a mania for writing; ⸗tafel f: a) tablet for writing, b) = Schiefertafel; ⸗tiſch m writing-table; vgl. ⸗pult.

Schreibung (⸗) f ㊵ (mode of) spelling. **Schreib-unterlage** (⸗...) f ㊵ = ⸗mappe b; ⸗utenſilien n/pl. = ⸗bedarf; ⸗verſtändige(r) m expert in (hand)writing; ⸗vorlage, ⸗vorſchrift f copy; headline (of a copy book); ⸗waren n/pl. stationery sg.; ⸗waren-handlung f stationer's shop; ⸗weiſe f = ⸗art; ⸗zeug n writing-case, weitS. = ⸗bedarf; auch necessaries pl. for writing.

ſchreien (⸗) [ahd.; *ſchrei] **I** v/n. (h.), v/a. und v/refl. ㉑ 1. (laut rufen) to (set up a) shout, to cry out, ſtärker: to bawl (out), to vociferate, vom Eſel: to bray, von vielen Menſchen: to clamour (ſ. kreiſchen 1); (knarren) to creak, to crackle. — 2. Redewendungen: ſ. ach II, aus 6; Feuer (Mord) ⚥ to cry fire (murder); um Hilfe ⚥ to cry out for help; ſich (halb) tot ⚥ to scream one's lungs out, to bawl out like mad; e-m in die Ohren ⚥ to bawl (or din) into a p.'s ears, e-m die Ohren voll ⚥ to deafen a p. with one's shouting; zum Himmel ⚥ to cry to Heaven, Sprichw.: wie man in den Wald ſchreit, ſo ſchallt es wieder heraus the echo responds to the call; you get as good as you give. — **II** ~ n ㉓ 3. shout(ing), &c. (ſ. I); F das iſt zum ~ (höchſt amüſant) that's screamingly funny; ☉ ~ des Zinns beim Biegen creaking (or crackling) of tin. — **III** ⚥ p.pr. u. a. ㉖ 4. in den Bed. des inf.; a. clamorous. — 5. fig. (gellend) shrill; ⚥ de Farben pl. glaring (or gaudy, loud) colours pl.; ⚥ de Ungerechtigkeit flagrant injustice, infamous (or burning) shame.

Schreier (⸗)[ahd.] m ㉒, ~in f ㊵ crier, bawler, shouting (or screaming) p. **Schreierei** (⸗⸗) f ㊵ (continued) bawling, (loud) shouting or screaming. **Schrei²-hals** (⸗...) m ㉒ shouting (or screaming) person, auch = ⸗find; ⸗kind n crying (F cry-)baby, squalling child; ⸗maul n = ⸗hals.

Schrein (⸗) [ahd.: shrine; *mlt. scrinium] m ⓒc. (Schrank) press, cupboard, chest, für Reliquien: shrine. **Schreiner(ei)** (⸗, ⸗⸗) ꝛc. ſ. Tiſchler(ei) ꝛc. **Schrei²-puppe** (⸗...) f ㊵ squeaking (or crying, talking) doll; ⸗ſtimme f yelling (or screeching) voice.

Schreit-bein (⸗...) [ſchreit-en] n ㉒ zo.: ⚥ gressorial foot.

ſchreiten (⸗) [ahd.] **I** v/n. (ſn) ⓢb. 1. to stride, to step out, ſtolz: to stalk (along); über et. ⚥ to stride (or step) across a th.; vorwärts ⚥ to progreſs, to advance; weiter ⚥ to proceed, to go on (one's way); zo. ⚥ de Tiere: ⚥ gressorial animals pl. — 2. zu et. ⚥ (daran gehen) to proceed to do a th., to set about doing a th.; zur Abſtimmung ⚥ to vote, to ballot, parl. a. to divide; zum Äußerſten ⚥ to take (or to go to) extreme measures; zu einer zweiten Ehe ⚥ to contract a second marriage. — **II** ~ n ㉓ 3. ſ. Schreitung.

Schreit-fuß (⸗...) m ㉒ = Schreitbein. **Schreitung** (⸗) f ㊵ striding, stepping out; durch ⸗ abmeſſen to step off. **Schrei-vögel** (⸗f⸗) m/pl. ㉒ orn. screechers, ⚥ clamatores pl.

Schrenz ☉ (⸗) [: Schranz] m ㉑a. Buchbinderei (Einſchlagepapier) wrapper. **Schretel** (⸗) m ㉒ = Schrat. **ſchrick** (⸗) imper., 2ſt 2., 2ſt 3. Perſon sg. pres. ind. v. ſchrecken³ I.

ſchrie (⸗) ind. imperf. v. ſchreien.} **ſchrieb** (⸗) ind., 2e (⸗) subj. imperf. v.} **ſchrie-e** (⸗) subj. imperf. v. ſchreien.

Schrick-pfahl ⚓ (⸗...) m ㉒ pile to which a raft is moored; vgl. Schrecken 6.

Schrift (⸗) [ahd.; *lt. scriptum n] f ㊵ 1. (manner of) writing; ſ. Handſchrift. — 2. a) (Schriftzeichen) character; in deutſcher (lateiniſcher) ~ in German (Roman) character(s); b) ☉ typ. print (-ed letters pl.), type; in großer (fetter) ~ in large (fat) type; gotiſche ~ black letter; ſchräge ~ italics pl.; ſ. Abdruck¹ 2. — 3. (Schriftſtück) written notice, agreement, &c.; (Abhandlung) paper; (Veröffentlichung) publication; (Urkunde) document, deed, record, des Gerichts: writ; eine ~ eingeben to present a memorial or a petition. — 4. (geſchriebenes ob. gedrucktes Werk) work; ſämtliche ~ en pl. Kants complete edition of Kant's writings; die Heilige ~ Holy (or Sacred) Writ, the Scriptures pl. — 5. auf Münzen = Schriftſeite b; Spiel: ſ. Kopf 1.

Schrift-art (⸗...) f ㊵ typ. kind of type or letters; ⸗ausleger m expounder of Holy Writ; ⸗auslegung f exposition of the Scriptures, ⚥ exegetics; ⸗beweis m, eccl. Scriptural evidence or proof; ⸗deutſch n literary German. **Schrifttum** (⸗⸗) n = Schrifttum.

Schrift-erklärung (⸗...) f ㊵: ⚥ exegesis; ⸗erz n, min. graphic tellurium, ⚥ sylvanite; ⸗flechte ⚘ f letter-lichen (Graphis scripta); ⸗forſchung f, eccl. Scriptural study or research; ⸗führer m in Verſammlungen ꝛc.: secretary; ⸗garnitur f, typ. series of type; ⸗gattung f = ⸗art; ⸗gelehrte(r) m, bibl. scribe; ⸗gemäß a. = ⸗mäßig; ⸗gießer m type-caster, letter-founder; ⸗gießerei f type-(or letter-)foundry; ⸗gläubig a. believing in the Scriptures; ⸗grad ☉ m size of type; ⸗guß m type-casting, letter-founding, fount, Am. font; ⸗höhe f, typ. height of letters or type; ⸗kaſten m type-case; ⸗kegel m type-block or -body; fo(u)nt; ⸗leiter m (Redakteur) editor; ⸗leitung f (Redaktion) editorship.

♪ Muſik; ⚥ Wiſſenſchaft; ⚘ Pflanze; ⚱ Geographie; ☉ Technik; ⚒ Bergbau; ⚔ Militär; ⚓ Marine; 🟊 Handel; ⚥ Poſt; 🚂 Eiſenbahn.

[ſchriftlich] — 862 — [Schub]

ſchriftlich (⌣́) *a.* ⑯ (*ant.* mündlich) in writing, written; 2̃e Arbeit (written) exercise, e-r Prüfung: examination-paper; 2̃(*adv.*) abfaſſen to draw up (in writing), to draft, to compose; ſich ein Verſprechen ꝛc. 2̃ geben laſſen to ask to have a promise, &c. in black and white; 2̃ mitteilen to inform by letter.

Schrift-magazin (⌣́...) *n* ⑫ *typ.* type-stock room; **=mäßig** *a.* ⑯ *eccl.* according to Holy Writ, Scriptural; **=mäßigkeit** *f* conformity with Holy Writ; **=metall** *n* = zeug b; **=material** *n, typ.* stock of type; **=mutter** *f* Schriftguß: matrix; **=probe** *f* specimen of type; **=ſatz** *m*, **=ſchneide-kunſt** *f* form-cutting; **=ſchneider** *m* letter-cutter; **=ſchnitt** *m* face of type; **=ſeite** *f*: a) page; b) e-r Münze: reverse; **=ſetzer** *m, typ.* compositor, type-setter; **=ſprache** *f*: a) literary language; b) Scriptural language; **=ſtelle** *f* Scriptural passage; **=ſteller(in** *f*) *m* author(ess), writer (of books, &c.); (Literat[in]) literary man (*of* lady), von untergeordneter Art: literary hack, penny-a-liner; **=ſtellerei** *f* authorship, writing (of books, &c.), literary vocation *or* profession; **2̃ſtelleriſch** *a.* (*of adv.* as) an author; literary (career, occupation, &c.); **=ſteller-laufbahn** *f* literary career; **2̃ſtellern** *v/n.* (h.) ⑫a.** to write (books, &c.), to do (*or* to be engaged in) literary work; **=tantieme** *f* author's royalty; **=ſtempel** *m* Schriftguß: punch; **=ſtück** *n*: a) = Schrift 3; b) *typ.* (teilweiſer Satz) packet; **=ſyſtem** *n* system of type bodies; **=text** *m* Scriptural (*or* Biblical) text.

Schrifttum (⌣́−) *n* ⑨d. literature.

Schrift-verdrehung (⌣́...) *f* ⑫ distortion of Scriptural quotations; **=verfälſcher** *m*, **=verfälſchung** *f* forger, forging of writings *or* title-deeds: interpolator, interpolation of manuscripts, &c.; **2̃verſtändig** *a.* ⑯ *eccl.* versed in the Scriptures; **=wart** *m* eines Vereins: secretary; **=wechſel** *m* exchange of communications, correspondence; **=weite** *f, typ.* width (or set) of type; **=werk** *n* (written or printed) work; **2̃widrig** *a. eccl.* contrary to Holy Writ, antiscriptural; **=zeichen** *n* written character *or* letter; **=zettel** *m* Schriftguß: fount of letter; **=zeug** *n* (abgenutzte Schrift) worn type; b) *m* (Schriftmetall) type-metal; **=zug** *m* (written) character; (Schnörkel) flourish.

ſchrill (⌣́) [ndb.: shrill] *a.* ⑯ shrill, yelling, grating on the ear.

ſchrillen (⌣́) *v/n.* (h.) ⑫ to produce a shrill (or yelling) sound or noise.

ſchrinden (⌣́) *v/n.* (in) ⑲ von der Haut: to chap, to crack. [brennen) to smart.]

ſchrinnen (⌣́) *v/n.* (h.) ⑱ =ſchrinden.

Schrippe (⌣́) *f* ⑳ Bäckerei: French roll.

Schritt¹ (⌣́) [ahd.: *scritt²*] *m* ⑨b, 6. 1. step; pace (auch als Maß); langer: (long) stride, langſamer: crawling pace, hörbarer: footstep, footfall; e-m auf ~ und Tritt folgen to dog a p.'s steps, polizeilich: to shadow a p.; bei jedem ~ at every turn; ~ für ~ step by step; mit ſchnellen (langſamen) ~en at a quick (slow) pace; zehn ~(e) geh(e)n to walk ten paces; F er hat einen guten ~ am Leibe he walks a good pace, he takes long strides; ~ halten to keep pace; ſeine ~e lenken nach ob. zu // to bend one's steps (or to wend one's way) towards //; ſ. drei 2. — 2. *fig.* (Maßregel) step; nötige (vorbereitende) ~e *pl.* necessary (preliminary) measures *pl.*; den erſten ~ tun to take the initiative, to move first, to break the ice.

Schritt²(⌣́) *ind.*, **2̃e** *subj. impf. v.* ſchreiten.

Schritt¹-gänger (⌣́...) *m* ⑫ *man.* ambling nag, good stepper, slow trotter; **=länge** *f* length of pace.

ſchritt-lings (⌣́) *adv.* 1. stepping (out) with 2̃. = ſchrittweiſe. — 2. (mit geſpreizten Beinen) straddling, with straddled legs.

Schritt¹-macher (⌣́...) *m* ⑫ Rennſport: pace-maker, auch pacer; **=meſſer** *n* = zähler; **=ſchuh†** = Schlittſchuh; **=wechſel** ⚔ *m* change of step; **2̃weiſe** *adv.* (F auch *a.*) step by (or for) step, by steps; **=weite** *f* (length of) stride; **=zähler** *m*: ⚔ pedometer, stride-meter (a. odometer).

ſchrob (⌣́) *ind.*, **ſchröbe** (⌣́) *subj. impf.* von ſchrauben.

Schrobel ⊕ (⌣́) *m* ⑫ = Schrubbelmaſchine.

ſchrobeln (⌣́) *v/a.* ⑫a. = ſchrubbeln.

ſchroff¹ (⌣́) [mhd.: Schrof(fen)] *a.* ⑯: a) v. Felſen, Bergen: rugged, (jäh, abſchüſſig) steep, precipitous, sheer; b) *fig.* (*ant.* milde) rough; (abſtoßend) blunt, unsociable, (mürriſch) gruff, bearish; (hartherzig) harsh; 2̃er Übergang abrupt transition; e-n 2̃(*adv.*) behandeln to deal harshly (or roughly) with a p., to snub a p. [*m* ㉓ (Klippe) cliff, crag.]

Schrof(f)² *prove.* (⌣́) [mhd.] *m* ⑨c., ~en

Schroffheit (⌣́−) *f* ⑯: a) ruggedness, steepness; b) *fig.* roughness, bluntness, gruffness, harshness.

ſchröpfen (⌣́) [mhd.: ſchrappen] I *v/a.* 1. ehm. *surg.* to cup, to bleed, ⚕ to scarify. — 2. *fig.* e-n 2̃ to fleece (or F bleed) a p. — II ~ *n* ㉓ 3. ſ. Schröpfung.

Schröpfer (⌣́) *m* ⑫, ~in *f* ⑰ ehm. *surg.* cupper, ⚕ scarifier, scarificator.

Schröpf-gerät (⌣́...) *n* ehm. *surg.* cupping-utensils *or* instruments *pl.*; **=kopf** *m* cup(ping-glass); e-m =kopf ſetzen to cup a p.; **=ſchnäpper**, **=ſchnepper** *m* cupping-instrument, scarificator.

Schröpfung (⌣́) *f* ⑯ ehm. *surg.* cupping, bleeding, ⚕ scarification.

Schröpf-zeug (⌣́...) *n* ⑫ = gerät.

Schrot¹ (⌣́) [ahd.: shroud; vgl. 5] *m* u. *n* ⑨c. 1. Müllerei: (grob gemahlenes Korn) bruised (or rough-ground) grain, groats *pl.* — 2. hunt., &c. (Bleiförner z. Schießen) (loaden) shot; dicker ~ buckshot, swan-shot. — 3. *carp.* (Klotz) log (or block) of wood. — 4. mint. (Rauhgewicht) u. *fig.* ſ. Korn 2. — 5. Tuchfabr.: list, selvedge. — 6. (Abfall b. Schroten) clippings, cuttings, chips *pl.* — 7. = Schrotſpeck. — 8. ⚒ tubbing-frame.

Schrot²-axt (⌣́...) [ſchrot-en] *f* ⑫ wood(s)-man's axe; **=beutel** *m* shot-bag, -pouch; **=blatt** *n, typ.* dotted print; **=¹brot** *n* whole-meal bread; **=büchſe** ⚔ *f*: a) ⚕ = =flinte; b) = Kartätſche; **=²eiſen** *n* rugine, Schmiede: priming-iron.

ſchroten (⌣́) [ahd.: shred] *v/a.* ⑱ 1. (*p.p.* geſchroten) a) Schmiede ꝛc.: (zerſchneiden) to hew (or saw) in pieces; b) (zermalmen) to bruise, Getreide, Malz a.: to rough-grind; mit den Zähnen: to crunch; F (tüchtig eſſen) to pack away, to gorge; c) ⊕ *metall.* (aus dem groben hobeln) to rough-plane; d) *mint.* Zaine 2̃ to size (or cut) the blanks for coinage. — 2. (*p.p.* geſchrotet) Laſten 2̃ (ſchiebewälzen) to roll (along) ..., in den Keller: to shoot (or let) down, ↓ to parbuckle.

Schröter (⌣́) [ſchroten] *m* ⑫ 1. *ent.* = Hirſchkäfer. — 2. ⊕: a) wood-cutter; b) = Schroteiſen. — 3. [ſchroten 2̃] drayman, cellar-man, (brewer's) porter.

Schrot¹-flinte (⌣́...) *f* ⑫ shot-gun; für Vögel: fowling-piece; **=form** *f* shot-mould; **2̃förmig** *a.* ⑯ (shaped) like (small) shot; **=gießen** *n*, **=gießerei** *f* shot-casting, -foundry; **=käfer** *m, ent.* ant-fly (*Rha'gium*); **=kleie** *f* coarse bran of groats; **=korn** *n*: a) *hunt.* (grain of) shot; b) ⊕ Müllerei = Schrot 1; **=²leiter** *f* dray- (or drayman's) ladder.

Schrötling (⌣́−) [ſchroten] *m* ⑨d. piece chipped off, chip; *mint.* (ungeprägte Metallplatte) blank, planchet, size of a coin.

Schrot¹-mehl ⊕ (⌣́...) *n* ⑫ coarse meal or flour; **=²meißel** *m* = =eiſen; **=metall** ⊕ *n* shot-metal; **=²mühle** *f* bruising- or rough-grinding-mill; **=ſäge** *f* pit-saw; **2̃ſägig** & *a.* ⑯: ⚕ runcinate; **2̃gezähnt**: ⚕ runcinato-dentate; **=ſchuß** *m, hunt.* shot with small-shot; **=ſeil** *n* = tau; **=¹ſieb** ⊕ *n* sieve for shot-casting; **=²ſpeck** *m* Schlächterei: lean bacon; **=tau** *n* Küferei: drayman's rope, parbuckle; **=turm** *m* Schrotgießen: shot-tower; **=winde** *f* Küferei: windlass.

Schrubbel ⊕ (⌣⌣) *f* ⑱ und *m* Spinnerei: card-comb, fine-tooth card; **~=maſchine** (⌣⌣−⌣́−) *f* ⑫ Tuchmacherei: scribbling-machine, scribbler.

ſchrubbeln ⊕ (⌣⌣) [ndb.] *v/a.* ⑫a. Spinnerei: to card (or comb) wool.

ſchrubben (⌣́) [ndb.: scrub] *v/a.* ⑱ 1. den Fußboden 2̃ to scrub the floor with a hard broom, ↓ to swab, to hog. — 2. ⚔ Tiſchlerei: das Holz 2̃ to rough-plane ...

Schrubber (⌣́) *m* ⑫ scrubbing-brush, scrubber, hard broom (for scrubbing), ↓ swab, hog; **ſchrubbern** *v/a.* ⑫a. = ſchrubben 1. [jack-plane.]

Schrub(b)-hobel ⊕ (⌣́...) *m* ⑫ Tiſchlerei:

Schrulle [ndb.: ſchrill] (⌣́) *f* ⑱ whim, crotchet; vgl. Grille 2; **ſchrullenhaft** (⌣⌣−) *a.* ⑯ whimsical (= grillenhaft).

Schrumpel P (⌣́) [ndb.] *f* ⑱ 1. = Runzel. — 2. alte = wrinkled old woman.

ſchrump(e)lig P (⌣⌣) *a.* ⑯ crumpled, creased; (runzelig) wrinkled; **ſchrumpeln** (⌣⌣) *v/n.* (in) ⑫a. = einſchrumpfen.

ſchrumpfen (⌣́) [mhd.: shrimp, scrimp] *v/n.* (in) u. *v/refl.* = einſchrumpfen.

ſchrumpfig (⌣⌣) *a.* ⑯ = runz(e)lig.

Schrund¹ (⌣́) *ind. imp. v.* ſchrinden.

Schrund² (⌣́) [ahd.: *schrund¹*] *m* ⑨b., meiſt ~e (⌣́) *f* ⑱ crack, chink, crevice, gap; ~en an Händen u. Lippen: chaps *pl.*

ſchrundig, **a. ſchründig** (⌣⌣) *a.* ⑯ cracked, Haut: chapped; 2̃ w. to crack, chap.

Schub (⌣́, ⌣́) [mhd.] shove: ſchieben] *m* ⑨c, 6. (vgl. ~s). 1. pushing, shoving; e-m e-n ~ geben to give a p. a push, to push a p.; mit e-m ~ (Ruck) with one push

Signs (see page XVII): F familiar; P vulgar; ⚡ flash; ↘ rare; † obsolete (died); * new word (born); ⁺⁺ incorrect; ♪ music;

[**Schubbejack**] or effort. — 2. (Haufe sich schiebender Personen) throng; ich kam mit dem ersten ~ hinein I got in with the first set (or batch, lot) of people. — 3. [öft.] Polizei: forcible removal of a p. by the police; e-n auf den ~ bringen to conduct (or remove) a p. to his native parish or home (f. schieben 3), auch: to deport a. p. — 4. Kegelspiel: a) (das Schieben) throw, throwing; ich habe den ~ it is my throw or turn; b) ~ (pl.inv.) (sämtliche Kegel) set of ninepins. — 5. ↘ = **Schublade**. — 6. (pl. inv.: auf einmal in den Ofen geschobenes Brot) batch of bread.

Schubbejack (⌣⌣)[(P.j. der sich mit der Sache schuppt] *russ. schubnja'k* Schafpelz] m ⓜ㊷ ragamuffin; (Kinder) mean (or shabby) fellow; auch = **Schuft**.

Schub-blech ⊙ (B..., ″...) n ㊷ Bäckerei: tin for baking; =**fach** n drawer; =**fenster** n sash-window; =**karre(n** m) f wheelbarrow; =**kärrner** m wheelbarrow man; =**kasten** m, =**lade** f drawer; =**ladenschrank** m chest of drawers; =**leere**, =**lehre** ⊙ f zur Dickmessung: slide-gauge; =**paß** m warrant for removing a p. to his parish; =**riegel** m sliding bolt, sash-bolt; ehm. =**sack** m pocket; =**stange** ⊙ f, mach. connecting-rod; =**tisch** m table with drawers; =**ventil** n = Schiebeventi'l; ⁰**weise** adv.: a) by pushing or shoving; b) in batches; (nach u. nach) by fits and starts, by degrees, little by little.

schüchtern (⌣⌣) (nhd.: scheu] a. ㊺ timid, (verschämt) bashful, coy, (scheu) shy (a. hunt.); ~**heit** f ㊺ timidity, bashfulness, coyness; shyness. [**schaffen**.]

schuf (¹) ind., **schüfe** (¹⌣) subj. impf. v.]

Schuft (⁹)[ndd.: *schieben] m ⓜ㊷ b. rogue, rascal, scoundrel, scamp; dishonest (or bad) fellow; Sprichw. f. **Schelm**; ~**erei** f ㊺ knavish (or mean, dirty) trick.

schuften F (⌣⌣) v/n. (h.) ㊺ to work hard; wir haben riesig geschuftet we did a tremendous amount of work, we worked (or slaved) like niggers.

schuftig, ↘ ...**isch** (⌣⌣) a. ㊺ roguish, rascally; mean, shabby; **Schuftigkeit** f ㊺ (Schurkenstreich) roguery, rascality; mean (or shabby) trick. [ⓜ㊷=**Schuft**.]

Schuftikus (⌣⌣⌣) [dtsch-lt.; *Schuft] m]

Schuh (¹) [ahd.: shoe] m ⓜ c, 6. (f. 4) 1. shoe (auch = Pantoffel), über die Fußknöchel reichender: boot (auch = Stiefel), zum Marschieren: walking-boot; leichter (Tanz-)~ (dancing-)pump; mit guten ~en well-shod; mit niedergetretenen ~en down at heels; ohne ~e unshod. — 2. fig. das habe ich mir längst an den ~en abgelaufen ob. abgetreten that's nothing new to me, I have known that a long time; e-n et. in die ~e schieben, gießen, schütten to lay the fault (for a th.) at a p.'s door, to put the blame (for a th.) upon a p.; ich möchte nicht in seinen ~en stecken I should not like to be in his place or to change places with him; umgekehrt wird ein ~ d(a)raus do the contrary, and you'll do well; Sprichw. f. drücken 3 gegen Ende. — 3. (Huf der Pferde) horse's hoof; (Hufeisen) horse's shoe. — 4. im pl. inv.

Längenmaß: foot. — 5. ⊙ (Eisenbeschlag) iron mounting, ferrule; ↓ (Anker-)~ anchor-shoe; ⚔ f. **Fahnen**-, **Lanzen**-⚔.

Schuh-absatz (″...) m ㊷ heel of a shoe or boot; =**ahle** ⊙ f shoemaker's awl; =**anzieher** m shoe-horn; =**band** n zum Schnüren: boot-lace, ehm. a. shoe-string or -tie; =**bürste** f boot-(zum Wichsen) blacking-)brush. [shoe or slipper.]

Schühchen (¹⌣) n ㊷ (dim. v. **Schuh**) small]

Schuh-creme (″...) f (P m) ㊷ (Nugget's) polish(ing-paste); =**draht** m = Pechdraht; =**eisen** n zum Abkratzen von Schmutz: scraper; =**fabrik** f boot-(manu)factory; =**fabrikant** m manufacturer of boots and shoes; =**fleck**, =**flicken** m patch; =**flicker** m cobbler, contp. vamper; =**knöpfer** m shoe-buttoner, buttonhook; =**laden** m boot-shop; =**macher** m shoemaker, bootmaker; vgl. **Schuster**; =**macherei** f shoemaker's trade, boot-making; =**macher-gesell(e)** m journeyman shoemaker; =**macher-handwerk** n shoemaker's trade, bootmaking; =**markt** m boot-market; =**maß** n shoemaker's measure; =**nagel** m: a) =**pflock**; b) eiserner: hobnail; =**pech** n cobbler's wax; =**pflock** m wooden peg (for boots); =**plattler** m südb. Tyrolese clog-dance; =**putzer** m shoeblack, (Hausknecht) boots sg.; fig. wie e-n ~ (schlecht) behandeln to treat like a slave or like dirt; =**riemen** m boot-lace; bibl. des ich nicht wert bin, daß ich seine ~ auflöse the latchet of whose shoe I am not worthy to unloose; =**schmiere** f grease for boots; zur Erhaltung des Leders: dubbing; =**schnabel** m, orn. shoebeak, shoebill (Balae'niceps rex); =**schnalle** f shoe-buckle; =**schwärze** f (shoe-)blacking; =**sohle**, =**spitze** f sole, point of a shoe or boot. [= Uhu.]

Schuhu (¹⌣) [lautm.] m ⓜd. (⑧) orn.]

Schuh-werk (″...) n ㊷ boots and shoes pl.; weitS. covering for the feet, auch: footgear, footwear; =**wichse** f boot-polish, blacking; =**zwecke** f shoe-peg or -pin or -tack, sparable.

Schul-akt(us) (″...)[Schul-c]m㊷speech-day, in kleineren Schulen: breaking-up; =**amt** n teacher's post; (head) mastership; =**amts-kandidat** m candidate for a mastership or teacher's post; =**anstalt** f educational establishment; school, college; =**arbeit** f task; seine ~arbeiten m. to do (or prepare) one's lessons; =**arrest** m detention (at school); =**atlas** m school-atlas; =**aufseher** m manager of a school; a. = inspector; =**ausgabe** f school-edition; =**ausschuß** m = behörde; =**bank** f form, school-bench; =**behörde** f in England: a) städtische: Education Committee (of the County Council); b) staatliche: Board of Education; =**bekanntschaft** f acquaintance made at school; =**besuch** m school-attendance; =**bezirk** m school-district; =**bibliothek** f school-library; =**bildung** f education(al acquirements pl.), v. Mädchen a. accomplishments pl.; er hat eine gründliche ~ he has had a thorough schooling; =**bube** m school-boy; =**buch** n school (or class-)book; (Leitfaden) text-book, manual; =**bücher**-

=**verlag** m, =**buchhandlung** f (firm of) educational publishers.

Schuld (⁹) [ahd.: shall: sollen] f ㊺ 1. debt (f. fundieren u. schweben III); ~**en** pl.: a) (Geld, das man schuldet) money owing (or due) by a p., liabilities pl. or indebtedness of a p.; b) (ausstehendes Geld) money owing (or due) to a p., ⊕ outstanding debts, assets pl.; drückende ~ heavy debt; frei von ~en free from debt, out of debt, von Gütern: unencumbered; f. abzahlen I: bezahlen 1; in ~en geraten, sich in ~en stürzen to get (or run) into debt; ~en m. to contract (or incur, run up) debts; tief in j-s ~ sein to be deeply indebted (or under a great obligation) to a p., to owe a p. a great debt of gratitude; bis über die Ohren in ~en stecken to be over head and ears in debt; fig. die ~ der Natur bezahlen (sterben) to pay the debt of nature, to die; Sprichw. wer seine ~en bezahlt, verbessert seine Güter a debt paid is money earned; out of debt out of danger. — 2. (Ursache, Veranlassung; Fehler) oft klein (⑨) geschrieben: ohne meine ~ through no fault of mine; e-m in et. ~ geben to lay the blame for a th. on a p. or at a p.'s door; er ist ~ daran he is the cause (or at the bottom) of it, it's his doing; es ist seine (eigene) ~ it's his (own) fault; es ist nicht meine ~, die ~ liegt nicht an mir, ich habe nicht ~ daran it is not my fault, the fault does not lie (or rest) with me; an wem liegt die ~?, wessen ~ ist es? whose fault is it?, who is to blame for it?; sich et. zuschulden kommen lassen to make o.s. guilty of a th.; wir tragen keine ~ daran it is no fault of ours, we are not to blame (or to be blamed) for it. — 3. (Vergehen) offence; (Unrecht) wrong(-doing); im Vaterunser: vergib uns unsere ~(en) forgive us our trespasses.

Schuld-arrest (⁹...) m ㊷ = =**haft**; ⁰**befleckt** a. ㊺ guilt-stained; ⁰**beladen** a. laden with (or steeped in) crime; =**beweis** m proof (or evidence) of guilt; ⁰**bewußt** a. ㊺ conscious of guilt; =**bewußtsein** n consciousness of guilt, guilty conscience; =**brief** m = verschreibung; =**buch** ⊕ n account-book, ledger; fig. unser ~ sei vernichtet! (SCH.) let old wrongs be forgotten.

schulden (⌣⌣) [ahd.; *Schuld] v/a. ㊺ e-m et. ~ to owe a p. a th., meist fig. to be indebted to a p. for a th.

schulden-belastet (⁹...) a. ㊺ loaded (or burdened) with debt; ⁰**frei** a. free from debt, von Gütern 2c.: unencumbered; sich ~ m. to free o.s. from debt, to meet one's engagements; ⁰**halber** adv. owing (or on account of) debts; =**last** f ㊷ (heavy) burden (or load) of debt, auf Gütern 2c.: encumbrance; =**machen** n contracting debts, F running up bills; =**macher(in** f) m person contracting (heavy) debts; =**tilgung** f discharge of debt, liquidation of debts; =**tilgungs-kasse** f für eine Staatsschuld: (office administering a) sinking fund; =**wesen** n debtors' concerns, liabilities pl.

[**Schulderlassung**] — 864 — [**Schulterbein**]

Schuld-erlassung (ˇ...) f ⓔ remission of (a) debt; **=forderung** f claim; (book-)debt; **=forderungs-klage** f = =klage; **=gefängnis** n debtors' jail or prison; **=haft** f imprisonment for debt; **=herr** m creditor.
Schul-diener(ⁿ...) m ⓔ school-attendant; beadle; **=dienst** m scholastic duties pl.
schuldig (ˇ∪) [ahd.; *Schuld] I a. ⓔ 1. a) owing money, (involved) in debt; ich bleibe ihm 100 Mark ≈ I remain his debtor (or in his debt) for five pounds, I still owe him £ 5; e-m Geld ≈ sein to owe a p. money; e-m nichts mehr ≈ sein to be quits (or F square) with a p.; was find wir ≈? how much do we owe (you)? in Hotels auch: please our account!; b) e-m großen Dank (ob. viel) ≈ sein to be under a great obligation to a p.; vgl. Dank 1; das ist man ihm ≈ that (or so much) is due to him; wie ich es ≈ bin, ≈ft as I ought to (do), as I am in duty bound; duly; ≈e Strafe just (or condign) punishment; c) ≈ bleiben fig.: die Antwort ≈ bleiben to make no reply, to return no answer, (verlegen sein) to stand dumbfounded; e-m feine Antwort ≈ bleiben to answer a p. smartly, to give it a p. as good as (s)he sends. — 2. (schuldbeladen) guilty, culpable; f. bekennen 4; die Geschworenen sprachen ihr „schuldig" über ihn aus the jury brought him in guilty. — II ∼e([r¹] m) f ⓔ 3. der, die ∼e the guilty person or party.
Schuldiger² (ˇ∪∪) [mhd.] m ⓔ bibl. = Schuldner; im Vaterunser: wie wir vergeben unsern ∼n as we forgive them that trespass against us.
Schuldig-erklärung (ˇ∪ˇ∪) f ⓔ jur. verdict of guilty, conviction.
schuldiger-maßen (ˇ∪∪ⁿ...) adv. duly, as in duty bound.
Schuldigkeit (ˇ∪ˇ) f ⓔ 1. debt; was ist meine ∼? what is my indebtedness (to you)?; nun fragt' ich nach der ∼ (v.) then I asked what fee was due. — 2. (Verpflichtung) obligation; es ist seine Pflicht und ∼ it is his bounden duty.
schuldigst (ˇ∪) adv. f. schuldig 1 b.
Schul-direktor (ⁿ...) m ⓔ head master, principal (of a school); **=disziplin** f school-discipline.
Schuld-klage (ˇ...) f ⓔ action for the recovery of a debt; **=leute** pl. debtors pl.; ≈los a. ⓔ without guilt, blameless, innocent; **=losigkeit** f blamelessness, innocence.
Schuldner (ˇ∪) [mhd.] m ⓔ, ∼in f ⓔ (ant. Gläubiger²) debtor, person (involved) in debt, p. owing money or a debt.
Schuld-posten ⊛ (ˇ...) m ⓔ sum (of money) due or owing; **=sache** f = =klage; **=schein** m = verschreibung; **=turm** m = gefängnis; **=verpflichtung** f liability, obligation; **=verschreibung** f note of hand, promissory note, a. IOU (= I owe you); ≈voll a. ⓔ guilty, auch = schuldig 2. — Vgl. a. Schulden...
Schule (ˇ∪) [ahd.: school; lt. scholā; *grch. scholé] f ⓔ 1. school; f. Elementarschule; gelehrte ∼ college, grammar-school, public school; f. Gelehrtenschule; Hohe ∼ (Hochschule) university,

academy; die ∼ fängt Montag wieder an school will reopen (or be resumed) on Monday; (Schulunterricht) schooling, teaching, tuition. — 2. oft fig. aus der ∼ schwatzen to tell tales (out of school); hinter (ob. neben) die ∼ gehen, die ∼ schwänzen to play (the) truant; in die ∼ gehen to go to school; f. ab-gehen 6; heute ist keine ∼ there are no lessons (or we have a holiday) to-day; fig. von Dichtern, Künstlern etc.: ∼ bilden, ∼ machen to form a school; durch eine harte ∼ (ober durch die ∼ der Prüfung) gehen to pass through a severe test; auch: to serve one's apprenticeship, F to go through the mill; durch die ∼ gelaufen sein to have a smattering of knowledge; e-n in die ∼ nehmen to take a p. in hand. — 3. Buchtitel: ∼ des Klavierspiels Book of exercises for the piano. — 4. = Baum-, Pflanz-schule. — 5. = Judenschule b.
schulen (ˇ∪) [mhd.] I v/a. u. sich ≈ v/refl. ⓔ 1. to school, instruct, tutor, train; sich ≈ to undergo a (course of) training, to go through a (good) school or schooling. — 2. man. Pferde ≈: a) (zureiten) to break in ...; b) (die Schule gehen lassen) to put ... through their paces. — II ∼ n ⓔ 3. f. Schulung.
Schüler (ˇ∪) [ahd.: scholar; *Schule] m ⓔ, ∼in f ⓔ pupil, einer Schule auch: scholar; schoolboy (f schoolgirl); f. Elementarschüler(in); ∼ eines Gymnasiums grammar-school boy, collegian, älterer student; ∼ e-s großen Meisters, Philosophen etc.: disciple (a. rel.), follower; fig. (Anfänger[in]) novice, tyro; **∼arbeit** f ⓔ (school-)lessons pl., (pupil's) task.
schülerhaft (ˇ∪∪) a. ⓔ like a schoolboy or schoolgirl; fig. like a (mere) novice; inexperienced, blundering, bungling; **Schülerhaftigkeit** f ⓔ lack of experience, blundering ways pl. or style.
Schülerschaft (ˇ∪∪) f ⓔ 1. discipleship. — 2. coll. all the pupils or disciples pl.
Schul-erziehung (ⁿ...) f ⓔ school-education, training at school; **=examen** n = =prüfung; **=feier** f festivity (held) at a school; a. = =akt(us); **=feiertag** m holiday (at school); **=ferien** holidays pl., vacation; **=fest** n school-fête; vgl. =feier; ≈frei a. ⓔ free from school-lessons; ≈er Tag holiday; ≈er Nachmittag half-holiday; **=freund**(in) m school-fellow or -mate or F-chum; **=fuchs** F m pedant; **=fuchserei** f pedantry; ≈füchsig a. pedantic; **=gebäude** n = =haus; **=geld** n school-fees pl., schooling, in höheren Schulen auch: terms pl.; **=gelehrsamkeit** f book-learning, scholastic learning, gründliche: erudition; **=gelehrte**(r) m classical scholar; b. s. = =fuchs; ≈gerecht a.: a) scholastic, weit≈. methodical; auch = kunstgerecht; b) man. des Pferd well-trained horse; **=gesetz** n school-regulation; **=gezänk** n scholastic squabbles pl.; **=grammatik** f school-grammar; **=halter** m proprietor of a school; **=haus** n school-house or -building or -premises pl.; **=heft** n exercise-book; **=hof** m play-ground of a school; **=inspektor** m inspector of schools; **=jahr** n scholastic

year; **=jahre** pl. years pl. spent at school or at college. a. = =zeit b; **=jugend** f school-children pl.; **=junge** m = =bube; **=kamerad** m school-mate; vgl. =freund; **=kenntnisse** f/pl. knowledge acquired at school; **=kind** n child attending (or that goes to) school; **=klasse** f = =stube; **=knabe** m schoolboy; **=kollegium** n: a) staff of teachers, teaching staff, masters pl.; b) school-committee; **=konferenz** f meeting of the teachers of a school; **=krankheit** f: a) disease (or illness) prevailing at a school or at schools; b) sham (or feigned) illness; **=lehrer**(in f) m schoolmaster, (f schoolmistress); **=lehrer-seminar** n training-college for elementary teachers; **=lehrer-stelle** f mastership; **=lokal** n school-premises pl.; eng≈. = =stube; **=mädchen** n schoolgirl; **=mann** m pedagogue, educationist; **=mappe** f school-bag, satchel; ≈mäßig a. = ≈gerecht; **=meister**(in f) m = =lehrer(in); b. s. pedant; **=meisterei** f school-mastering; b. s. pedantry; ≈meisterlich a. school-masterly; b. s. pedantic; ≈meistern v/n. (h.) u. v/a. ⓔ a *,*: a) to teach at a school, to be a school-master; b) b. s. to play the school-master; to be very censorious; ∼ n pedantry; **=meisterton** m magisterial tone; vgl. =ton; **=ordnung** f school-regulations pl. [(mochen) cuttlebone.)
Schulp(ˇ) [ndd.] m ⓑ b., **∼e**(ˇ∪) f ⓔ (Sepia-) **Schul-pferd**(ⁿ...) n ⓔ man. well-trained horse, trick-horse; **=pflicht** f = =zwang; ≈pflichtig a. ⓔ obliged to go to school; **=pflichtigkeit** f obligation to attend (or to send one's children to) school; vgl. =zwang; **=programm** n annual report of a (German) state-school; **=prüfung** f school - examination; **=rat** m: a) coll. educational council or board (vgl. =behörde); b) member of an educational council; a. = =inspektor; **=rede** f address delivered (or speech made) on speech-day; **=reiter**(in f) m Zirkus etc.: manege-rider; **=sache** f school-matter, scholastic concern; **=sattel** m, man. manege-saddle; **=schiff** ⇣ n training-ship; **=schluß** m breaking-up (of a school); **=schrift** f educational pamphlet; bsd. = =programm; **=schritt** m, man. short pace; **=sprache** f: a) language customary in schools, der Schüler: school-slang; b) phls. language of schoolmen; **=staub** m school-dust; **=stube** f school- (or class-) room; **=stunde** f: a) school-hour, eines Lehrers auch: hour of teaching; b) = Lehrstunde; **=tafel** f blackboard; **=tag** m school-day; **=tasche** f satchel.
Schulter (ˇ∪) [ahd.: shoulder] f ⓔ 1. shoulder; e-m auf die ∼ klopfen to tap a p. on the shoulder; breite ∼n h. to be broad-shouldered, to have a broad back; et. auf die ∼ nehmen to take a th. on one's shoulders or upon o.s.; mit den ∼n zucken to shrug one's shoulders; zu eng in den ∼n too narrow in the shoulders or the chest. — 2. fig. f. Achsel 2.
Schulter-band (ˇ∪...) n ⓔ anat. humeral ligament; **=bein** n. anat. shoulder-

[Schulterbinde] — 865 — [Schuß]

bone, ⚕ humerus; =binde f, surg.: ⚕ scapulary; =blatt n, anat. shoulder-blade, ⚕ scapula, omoplate; Schlächterei: blade-bone of mutton; =breite f width of (or between) the shoulders; =gelenk⚔⚔ n shoulder-belt; =gelenk n, anat. shoulder-joint, =höhe f: ⚕ acromion; =knochen m = =bein; =muskel m, anat. humeral muscle.

schultern (⌣⌣) [Schulter] v/a. 🟦a. to shoulder; ehm. ⚔ schultert das Gewehr! shoulder arms!; mit geschultertem Gewehr with arms shouldered.

Schulter=riemen (⌣⌣...) m 🟢 shoulder-strap, vgl. =gehenk; =stück n shoulder-piece (a. ⚔); Schlächterei: shoulder of mutton; vgl. =gehenk; =tuch n f. Humerale; =verrenkung f, surg. dislocation of the shoulder, sprained shoulder, shoulder-wrench; vet. von Pferden auch: sh.-slip; =wehr ⚔ f, frt. epaulement.

Schult=heiß (⌣-) [ahd. Schuldheiß(ender) od. =heisch(ender) = Verpflichtung Befehlender] m 🟢 (Gemeindevorsteher) mayor (of a small town or village), village-mayor.

Schul=theologie (⌣...) f 🟢 scholastic divinity; =ton m dogmatic (or pedantic) tone; =tornister m school-bag; =übung f school-exercise, -task; lesson.

Schulung (⌣⌣) f 🟢 schooling, training.

Schul=unterricht (⌣...) m 🟢 school-teaching or -instruction, schooling; =verfassung f constitution of a school; a. =ordnung; =versäumnis f absence from (or non-attendance at) school; =vorstand m governing body of a school; =vorsteher(in f) m head master (f head mistress) of a school, schoolmaster (schoolmistress); =weisheit f scholastic wisdom or philosophy; =wesen n school- (or educational) matters pl.; public instruction; =wissenschaften f/pl. educational branches or subjects pl.; =witz m schoolmaster's (or schoolboy's) joke; =wörter=buch n school-dictionary.

Schulze (⌣⌣) [mhd.; * Schultheiß] m 🟢 = Schultheiß.

Schul=zeit (⌣⌣) f 🟢: a) school-time;] b) school-days pl. [mayor's office.↓

Schulzen=amt (⌣⌣) n 🟢 village-

Schul=zeugnis (⌣...) n e-s Schülers: school-certificate; =zimmer n = =stube; =zucht f school-discipline; =zwang m compulsory school-attendance.

Schummer (⌣⌣) [ndd.] m 🟢 (Dämmerung) twilight, dawn; ⚓ig (⌣⌣) a. 🟢 (dämmerig) dusky; ⚓n (⌣⌣) 🟦a. a) v/n.(h) dämmern; im ~n (in der Dämmerung) in the dusk or twilight, between the lights; b) v/a. surv. (schattieren) to shade; to hatch, line.

schund¹ (⌣) ind. impf. von schinden.

Schund² (⌣) [nhd.;* schinden¹] m 🟦b. (Abfall) offal, refuse, waste; fig. (schlechtes Zeug) rubbish, trash; ⚓ (schlechtes Tuch) shoddy.

Schund=bauten (⌣⌣⌣) f/pl. jerry-built houses pl.

schünde (⌣⌣) subj. impf. v. schinden.

Schund=literatur (⌣...) f 🟢 worthless (or trashy) literature, =ware(n pl.) 🌱 f low-class (or trashy) goods pl.; F slop-work, von Kleidern auch: P slops pl.

Schuner ⚓⛵ (⌣⌣) m 🟢 = Schoner.

schunkeln prov. (⌣⌣) F = schaukeln.

Schupf (⌣) m 🟦b. (Stoß) push, shove.

schupfen F (⌣⌣) [schieben] v/a. 🟦 to push, shove, mit dem Ellbogen: to elbow; bsd. v/refl. sich ⚓ (kratzen) to scratch o.s.

Schupp (⌣) m 🟦b. (Waschbär) racoon.

Schüppchen¹ (⌣⌣) n 🟢 (dim. v. Schuppe) tiny scale, ⚕ squamella, ...ule, ...ula.

Schüppchen² (⌣⌣) n 🟢 (dim. v. Schüppe): ein ~ machen (weinen) to (set up a) cry, F to (begin to) snivel.

Schuppe (⌣⌣) f 🟢;* schaben] f 🟢 scale, ⚕ squama (f. Kopfschuppen); fig. die ~n sind ihm von den Augen gefallen his eyes have been opened (wide), vgl. bibl. there fell from his eyes as it had been scales.

Schüppe (⌣⌣) [ndd.] f 🟢 = Schippe.

Schuppen¹ (⌣⌣) [ndd.: shop = Schopf] m 🟢 (open) shed, shelter, penthouse; Am. shanty; ~ für Wagen: coachhouse, 🚂 ~ für Lokomotiven: engine-house.

schuppen² (⌣⌣) [Schuppe] v/a. 🟢: einen Fisch ⚓ to (un)scale ...; a. v/refl. die Haut schuppt sich ... scales (or peels) off.

schuppen³ (⌣⌣) v/a. u. v/refl. = schupfen.

schüppen (⌣⌣) v/a. 🟢 nordd. = schaufeln.

schuppen⁴=artig (⌣⌣...) [Schuppe] a. 🟢 like scales, ⚕ squamoid, squamiform.

Schuppen⁴=baum (⌣⌣⌣) m 🟢 ⚕ lepidodendron; =fell n vom Waschbär: racoon fur, Am. coonskin; =flechte f, path: ⚕ psoriasis; =flosser m, ichth.: ⚕ squamipen; =flügler m/pl. f. Lepidopteren; =förmig a. 🟢 = =artig; arch. u. ⚕ auch: ⚕ imbricate(d); =grind m = =flechte; =kette ⚔ f des brit. Helmes, nur noch bei Paraden: scale-chain; ⚓los a. scaleless; =panzer ⚔ m scaly (coat of) mail; =pelz m = =fell; =tanne ⚕ f monkey-puzzle, austral. bunya-bunya (Araucaria imbricata); =tier n, zo.: a) scaly animal, lizard; b) ant-eater (Manis); kurzschwänziges ~ pangolin; ⚓weise adv. in scales.

schuppicht, mst schuppig (⌣⌣) a. 🟢 1. scaly, scaled, covered with scales, ⚕ squamous, squamigerous. — 2. in Bezug mit a., ⚕ blau= ⚓ with blue scales.

Schup(p)s F (⌣) m 🟦a. = Schupf; schup(p)sen (⌣⌣) v/a. 🟢 = schupfen.

Schur (⌣) [mhd.; * scheren¹] f 🟢 1. agr. (Scheren der Schafe ꝛc.) shearing (or clipping) of sheep, &c.; (Wolle) fleece. — 2. hort. ~ einer Hecke ꝛc.: clipping, des Grases ꝛc.: mowing.

Schür=baum (⌣...) m 🟢 [schüren] m stirring-pole; =eisen n poker.

schüren (⌣⌣) [mhd.] v/a. 🟢: das Feuer ⚓ to poke (or mend. rake, stir, trim) ..., durch Luftzug: to fan, durch Heizmittel: to add fuel to (a. fig.).

Schürer (⌣⌣) m 🟢 1. ⚙ stoker, raker; fig. agitator, firebrand. — 2. = Schür=eisen, =haken.

Schurf (⌣) [f. schürfen] m 🟦b. hole dug in the earth; bsd. ⛏ borehole, adit, opening; prospect; Schurf-, Schürf=arbeit ⛏ (⌣⌣...) f 🟢 prospecting (work), digging (or searching) for ore.

schürfen (⌣⌣) [ahd. scharf, Schorf] 🟢 I v/n. (h.) ⛏ to dig (trenches); nach Erz ⚓ to dig (or search, prospect) for ore; weitS. to open (up) a mine. — II v/a. (schrammen) to scratch, to graze. — III ~ n 🟢 f. Schürfung.

Schürfer ⛏ (⌣⌣) m 🟢 prospector.

Schurf-, Schürf=gezäh(e) ⛏ (⌣...) n 🟢 prospecting-tools pl.; =loch n, =schacht m prospect(ing)-shaft; =schein m miner's license for prospecting or boring or trenching or digging.

Schürfung ⛏ (⌣⌣) f 🟢 (f. schürfen I) digging (for ore), prospecting.

Schürge (⌣⌣) [schüren] m 🟢 (Karrenschieber) wheelbarrow-man; ⚓n [ahd.] v/n. (h.) 🟢 (schieben) to push (a wheelbarrow).

Schür=haken (⌣...) m 🟢 fire-hook, (furnace-)rake; =herd m hearth of a kiln.

schurigeln F (⌣⌣⌣) [schürgen] v/a. 🟢a. (ärgern) to vex, worry; (plagen) to plague.

Schurke (⌣⌣) [nhd.] m 🟢 rogue, rascal, stärker: knave, scoundrel, villain; f. abgefeimt II; ~n=leben (⌣...) n 🟢 scoundrel's life; ~n=streich m, ~n=tat f, Schurkerei (⌣⌣⌣) f 🟢 (piece of) rascality, knavish (or scoundrelly, villainous) act or trick; schurkisch (⌣⌣) a. 🟢 rascally, knavish, scoundrelly, villainous.

Schür=loch ⚙ (⌣...ch) n 🟢 metall. stoke-, fire-, flue-hole. [slide for timber.↓

Schurre (⌣⌣) f 🟢 (Gleitbahn für Holz)↑

schurren (⌣⌣) v/n. (h. u. h.) 🟢 to slide (or scrape, shuffle) along. [lumber.↓

Schurrmurr (⌣⌣) prov. (⌣⌣) m 🟦c. (Gerümpel)↑

Schür=schaufel ⚙ (⌣...⌣) f 🟢 fire-shovel.

Schurz (⌣) [ahd.: shirt] m 🟦a. apron, eines Hochschotten: kilt. [fire-)tongs pl.↓

Schür=zange ⚙ (⌣...⌣) f 🟢 chimney- (or↑ Schürzchen (⌣⌣) n 🟢 (dim. von Schürze) short apron. für Kinder: pinafore.

Schürze (⌣⌣) [Schurz] f 🟢 a) = Schurz; eine ~ umbinden to put on an apron, b) fig. (Weib) female, wench; hinter jeder ~ herlaufen, in jede ~ verliebt sein to run after every girl or petticoat, to be mad after women.

Schur=zeit (⌣⌣) f 🟢 shearing-time.

schürzen¹ (⌣⌣) [mhd.; f. Schurz] v/a. und sich ⚓ v/refl. 🟢 1. to tie (up); sich ⚓ to tuck (or pin) up one's dress; bibl. to gird up one's loins (a. fig.). — 2. (bindend schlingen) to entangle; einen Knoten ⚓ to tie ...; fig. den Knoten eines Dramas ꝛc. ⚓ to weave the plot ...; der (fest) geschürzte Knoten the tangled web; der Knoten schürzt sich the plot thickens or ripens.

Schürzen²=band (⌣⌣⌣) n 🟢 apron-string; =herrschaft f petticoat-government; =stipendiat m man living by a woman's vice, P petticoat-pensioner.

Schurz=fell (⌣⌣) n 🟢 leather apron.

Schuß (⌣) [ahd.: sho(o)t; *schießen] m 🟦a. 1. (schießende Bewegung) shooting ahead or along; rapid motion, rush; es ging im ~ vorbei they (or we) galloped past at full speed; in ~ kommen to shoot (or dart, rush) along; wenn er einmal im Schusse ist when once he is started or set going or F on the move; Fußballspiel: ~ (Stoß) aufs Tor shoot. — 2. von Pflanzen: a) (das Emporschießen, Treiben) shooting; b) (Trieb) shoot. — 3. 🟢. mit Feuerwaffen: a) shot; (Knall) report; blinder ~ shot with blank cartridge; f. scharf 7 am Ende; ~ aufs Geratewohl wild (or stray) shot; ~ aus dem Hinterhalt pot-shot, ~ ins Blaue random shot; es fielen Schüsse shots were fired or heard;

♪ Musik; ⚕ Wissenschaft; 🌱 Pflanze; 🌍 Geographie; ⚙ Technik; ⛏ Bergbau; ⚔ Militär; ⚓ Marine; 🛒 Handel; ✉ Post; 🚂 Eisenbahn.

[Schußbereit]

jeder ~ traf each shot went home or took effect or told; **ohne einen ~ zu tun** without firing a shot; b) (Ladung) charge; *fig.* **er ist feinen ~ Pulver wert** ... not worth powder and shot; c) (Schußweite) **außer ~ sein** to be beyond the range of the bullets; *fig.* **e-m in den** (Weg) **kommen** to come across a p., to cross a p.'s path; d) **als Maß im** *pl. inv.*, z.B. *fig.* **ich möchte nicht einen** (zwei)**~ Pulver daran wenden** I would not spend a farthing on it; **ein ~ Kognak im Kaffee** a dash of brandy ...; e) F *fig.* **er hat einen ~** (eine Spur) **deutsches Blut** (bss. deutschen Bluts) **in den Adern** he has a dash of German blood in his veins; **einen ~** (närrische Ansichten) **haben** to have a screw loose, to be (a bit) cracked or F dotty.

schuß-bereit(ˢ...)a.⚔ready to fire; ⚔ **die Gewehre ~ halten** to hold the guns at the ready; **-bühne** f ⚔ **beim Steinsprengen**: shingle. [— 2. jäch. = **Schlitterbahn**.]

Schüffel F *provc.*(ˢ⌣)f ⚔ **harum-scarum.**

Schüffel(ˢ) [ahd.; *lt. scutella] f ⚔ dish (a. Gericht), (earthenware) pan, **große, flache, hölzerne**: platter; (Suppen-)~ tureen, (Napf) bowl, basin.

Schüffel-brett(ˢ⌣ˢ) n ⚔ Küche: a) dresser; b) **zum Abtropfen**: plate- (or dish-)rack.

Schüffelchen (ˢ⌣⌣) n ⚔ 1. small dish or bowl. — 2. ♀ (Flechtenfrucht): ⚔ patella.

Schüffel-förmig (ˢ⌣...) a. ⚔ dish-shaped, ⚔ patelliform, patellate; **-gestell** n ⚔ = **-brett** b; **-glocke** f dish-cover.

schuffelig (ˢ⌣⌣) a. ⚔ light-brained, weak-minded, giddy, fickle.

Schüffel-schrank (ˢ⌣...) m ⚔ china-cupboard; sideboard; **-stürze** f = **-glocke**; **-trage** f tray; **-voll** / dishful; **-wärmer** m dish- (or plate-)warmer; **-wäscherin** f girl (or woman) that washes up (the dishes), scullery-maid.

Schuffer (ˢ⌣) [Schuß] m ⚔ = **Klicker**.

Schuß-feld ⚔ (ˢ...) n ⚔ fire-zone; **im ~e** within range of the guns; ⚔**fertig** a. ⚔ ready to fire; *v. Gewehre*: cocked; ⚔**fest** a. bullet-proof, (unverwundbar) invulnerable; ⚔**frei** a. beyond the reach of the bullets, out of range; *vgl.* Schuß 3c; **-garn** n ⚔ Weberei: weft, woof; **-gatter** ⚔ n flood-gate; ⚔**gerecht** a.: a) (dem Schusse erreichbar) within gunshot; b) von Pferden 2c.: trained to stand fire, accustomed to shooting; c) von Schußwaffen: true.

schußlig (ˢ⌣) a. ⚔ = **schuffelig**.

Schuß-linie ⚔ (ˢ...) f ⚔ artill. firing-line, fire-zone; ⚔**recht** a. ⚔ = **-gerecht**; **-tafel** ⚔ / practice-table; **-waffen** f/pl. fire-arms pl.; ⚔**weise** adv. by fits and starts; **-weite** f range of (the) bullets or guns, fire-zone; **-wunde** f gunshot-wound, auch: bullet-wound.

Schuster (Lˢ, südd. ˢ⌣) [dtsch.-lt. Schuhsutor] m ⚔ (Schuhflicker) cobbler, (Schuhmacher) shoemaker; vgl. Leisten, Rappe.

Schuster-ahle ⚔ (ˢ⌣...)f ⚔ awl; **-arbeit** f cobbler's (or shoemaker's) work, cobbling. [**handwerk.**

Schusterei (⌣⌣ˢ) f ⚔ = **Schuhmacher-**]

Schuster-gesell(e) (ˢ⌣⌣...) m ⚔, **-handwerk** n = Schuhmacher-...; **-junge** n shoemaker's boy; **-kneif** m = **-messer;**

— 866 —

-lehrling m shoemaker's apprentice; **-messer** n ⚔ shoe- (or paring-)knife.

schustern (ˢ⌣) v/n. (h.) ⚔a. to cobble; to make (or mend) boots and shoes.

Schuster-pech ⚔ (ˢ⌣...) n ⚔ cobbler's wax; **-werkstatt** f cobbler's (or shoemaker's) workshop.

Schute, Schüte ⚔ (Lˢ) [ndd.: Schüssel] f ⚔ (Dutch) barge, ehm. scout.

Schutt (ˢ) [nhd.; *schütten] m ⚔ c. rubbish (a. Bauwesen), refuse, **für den Straßenbau**: rubble; (Trümmer) ruins, debris *pl.*, wreckage; **~ abladen** to shoot (or deposit) rubbish.

Schutt-abladeplatz (ˢ...) m ⚔ place where rubbish is shot; public dust-heap; **-ablagerung** f, *geol.*: ⚔ detritus.

Schütt-boden (ˢ⌣ˢ) m ⚔: a) *agr.* cornloft, granary; b) ⚔ Bauwesen: carted earth.

Schütte (ˢ⌣) [nhd.] f ⚔ (⚔) = **Schüttboden**. [**pl.**, cold fits pl. (of fever).)

Schüttel-frost (ˢ⌣ˢ) m ⚔ *path.* shivers]

schütteln (ˢ⌣) [ahd.; *schütten] v/a., v/n. (h.) u. **sich** ⚔ v/refl. ⚔a. (sich) ⚔ to shake (o.s.), vgl. rütteln 1; j. Armel 1; **e-m die Hand** ⚔ to shake hands with a p., to grip a p.'s hand; j. Kopf 2; **den Staub von den Füßen** ⚔ to shake the dust off one's feet; **es schüttelt mich** (macht mich beben) it makes me shiver.

schütten¹ (ˢ⌣) [ahd.: shed] v/a., v/n. (h.) u. v/refl. ⚔ 1. to pour (a. to throw) water, &c.; to shoot corn, &c., (ausgießen, *bib.* 1, 2, 4, 5); **auf den Haufen** ⚔ to heap (or pile) up; **ein Gefäß voll** (leer) ⚔ to fill (to empty) ...; ⚔ **einen Damm** ⚔ (aufwerfen) to throw up a dike; *fig.* **j-n Kummer in j-s Schoß** ⚔ to pour out one's grief to a p.; ehm. ⚔ **Pulver auf die Pfanne** ⚔ to prime a gun; **Pferden** 2c. **Futter** ⚔ to throw (or put) fodder before... — 2. *hunt.* (gebären) to cast (a litter of) young, *v. Hunden* 2c.: to puppy. — 3. *provc. agr. u.* ⚒ = **lohnen** 4. [⚔ = **pfänden**.]

schütten² *provc.* (ˢ⌣) [ndd.: schütten] v/a.]

schüttern (ˢ⌣) [ndd.: shudder] ⚔a. I v/n. (h.) to shake, quake, tremble, shiver, rock. — II v/a. = **erschüttern**. — III ~ n ⚔ u. **Schütterung** f ⚔ shaking, &c. (f. I); vibration. [Dutch pink.)

Schütt-gelb ⚔ (ˢ⌣ˢ) n (gelber Lack)]

Schutt-haufen (ˢ...) m ⚔ rubbish- (or dust-)heap; *fig.* **in einen ~ verwandeln** to lay in ruins; **-karren** m rubbish-(or dust-)cart; tumbrel; **-kärrner** m scavenger, dustman.

Schütt-stall (ˢ...) m ⚔ pound (for cattle); **-stroh** n (long) straw for (making) litters.

Schutt-winkel (ˢ⌣ˢ) m ⚔ dust-bin or -hole, Bauwesen: shoot for rubbish.

Schutz (ˢ) [nhd.: schießen vorspringen] m ⚔ a. 1. protection, (Obhut) shelter, custody, (Schirm) screen, cover; (Stütze) support, (Verteidigung) defence; (Bedeckung) safe-guard, ⚔ escort; (schützender Ort) shelter, (place of) refuge. — 2. Redewendungen: j. **begeben** 2; **e-m ~ gewähren** to afford (or give) a p. shelter, to harbour a p.; **in ~ nehmen** to take under one's protection or F wing; to support, to defend, ⚔ Wechsel: to protect, to honour; **Gott nehme sie in seinen heiligen Schutz** (und Schirm) may the

[Schützenplatz]

Lord keep watch (or guard) over her; j. Schirm 1; **unter dem Schutze der Nacht, der Kanonen** 2c.: under cover ...; **~ unter ... suchen** to seek shelter (or to take refuge) under ..., to stand up under ...; **zu ~ und Trutz** offensive(ly) and defensive(ly); ⚔ **wir werden Ihrer Tratte gebührenden ~ bereiten** we shall duly honour (or pay due honour to) your draft. — 3. ⚔ = **Schütz²**.

Schütz¹ (ˢ) m ⚔ = **Schütze¹**. — **Schütz²** ⚔ (ˢ) n ⚔a. (Schleusenbrett) flood-gate, sluice(-board), shutter; *vgl.* **Schütze²**.

Schutz-amt (ˢ...) n ⚔ protectorship, guardianship; **-bedürftig** a. ⚔ needing (or in want of) protection; **-befohlene**([r] m) f person under one's protection, (fr.) protégé(e f), bsd. röm. Alt.: client; (Mündel) ward; **-blattern** 2c. f/pl. med. = **-pocken** 2c.; **-blech** ⚔ n guard-plate; **-brett** ⚔ n = **Schütz²**; **-brief** m letter of safe-conduct; **-brille** f sight-preserving glasses or spectacles pl.; **-bündnis** n defensive alliance; **-dach** n: a) = **Schuppen**; b) sheltering roof; c) Alt.: ~ **der Belagerer** vinea; **-damm** m: a) protecting dike; b) eng S. inner dike.

Schütz(e) (ˢ(⌣)) [ahd.; *schießen] m ⚔ ⚔ 1. person who shoots; **guter** (schlechter) ~ good (bad) shot or marksman; **vorzüglicher, nie fehlender** ~ crack, dead shot; auch = **Schützenbruder**; j. Armbrustschütze, Bogenschütze. — 2. ⚔ rifleman, sharpshooter, skirmisher. — 3. *ast.* (südliches Sternbild) Sagittarius.

Schütz(e)² ⚔ (ˢ(⌣)) f ⚔(⚔): a) = **Schütz²**; b) (a. m ⚔) (Weberschiffchen) shuttle.

schützen¹ (ˢ⌣) [Schutz] v/a. u. **sich** ⚔ v/refl. ⚔ 1. (sich) ⚔ to protect (o.s.), to defend (o.s.), to (safe)guard (o.s.); ⚔ **eine Tratte** ⚔ **to honour** (or protect) a draft; **gesetzlich geschützt** legally protected, patented. — 2. (unter Obdach bringen) to (put under) shelter, to put in(to) a safe (or sheltered) place. — 3. **e-n gegen** (ob. **vor**, **wider**) et. ⚔ (bewahren) to preserve (or guard, protect) a p. from a th.; **vor Angriffen geschützt** safe from attacks; **vor Erkältung** 2c. ⚔ to fortify (or strengthen) against ..; **gegen Verluste** ⚔ to secure against ..., vor dem Winde ⚔ to screen (or shelter) from ... — 4. ⚔ **das Wasser**, metonymisch: **die Mühle, das Rad** ⚔ (hemmen) to shut off the water. — 5. ⚔ **geschützter Hafen** sheltered harbour; **geschützter Kreuzer** protected cruiser.

Schützen²-bataillon ⚔ (ˢ⌣...) [Schütze¹] n ⚔ battalion of riflemen; **-brigade** ⚔ f rifle-brigade; **-bruder** m member of a rifle-association; **-fest** n (fête on the occasion of a) rifle-match; **-gefecht** ⚔ n skirmish of riflemen, engagement of sharpshooters.

Schutz-engel (ˢ⌣ˢ) m ⚔ guardian (or ministering) angel.

Schützen²-gesellschaft (ˢ⌣...) f ⚔, **-gilde** f rifle-association or -club; **-graben** m ⚔ rifle-pit; **-haus** n, **-hof** m shooting-gallery; **-könig** m winner of the first prize at a rifle-match; champion shot; **-korps** ⚔ n rifle-corps; **-kunst** f marksmanship; **-linie** ⚔ f line of sharpshooters or skirmishers; **-platz** m = **Schießplan**;

Signs (see page XVII): F familiar; P vulgar; F' flash; ⚔ rare; † obsolete (died); * new word (born); ⚔ incorrect; ♪ music;

[Schützenschaft] — 867 — [Schwadroneur]

Schützenschaft (⏑‿) f ⊕ coll. (body of) riflemen pl.; rifle-association.
Schützen³= **schleuse** ⊕ (⏑‿...) [Schütze²] f⏑sluice with sluice-gates; =**schwarm** ⚔ m swarm of skirmishers; =**stand** m = Schieß=plan=stand.; =³**tor** n shutter.
Schützer (⏑‿) m ②, ~**in** f ⓓ protector, f...tress; defender, guardian.
Schutz-gatter (⏑...) n ②: a) = Fallbaum; b) ⊕ Wasserbau: flood-gate; =**gebiet** n: a) protectorate; (Besitzung) possession; b) (deutsche Kolonie) German colony; =**geist** m guardian spirit, tutelary genius; F ⚔+ a. genii sg.; =**geld** n tax paid by protected (or alien) subjects; =**geleit** n safe-conduct, ⚔ escort, convoy; =**gerechtigkeit** f right of (or claim to) protection; =**gott** m, =**göttin** f tutelary god, f goddess; =**gottheit** f tutelary deity; =**hafen** m harbour of refuge; =**heilige(r)** s. patron saint; =**heiligtum** n palladium; =**herr** m protecting lord, protector; (Lehnsherr) suzerain; ♀**herrlich** a. ⓓ protectorial; =**herrlichkeit**, =**herrschaft** f protectorate,...ship; suzerainty; =**hülle** f e-s Kabels: casing (or armour) of a cable; =**hütte** f shelter(ing hut) for Alpine travellers; =**impfung** f vaccination; ehm. =**jude** m Jew (living) under the protection of the authorities; =**kappe** f, elect. protecting cap; =**kind** n charge, (Mündel) ward; =**leute** pl. v. Schutzmann.
Schützling (⏑‿) m ⓓd. (fr.) protégé(e f).
schutz-los (⏑...) a. ⓓ unprotected, defenceless; =**losigkeit** f defencelessness; =**mann** m ② policeman, (police) constable, F bobby, P copper; =**mannschaft** f: a) police (force), bsd. in Irland auch: constabulary (force); b) (Bedeckung) escort; =**marke** ⊛ f trademark; =**marken- gesetz** n in England: Merchandise Marks Act; =**maßregel** f protective measure; =**mauer** f protecting wall, ⚔ rampart, bulwark; =**mittel** n preservative, prevent(at)ive; =**ort** m shelter, (place of) refuge; =**patron(in** f) m, eccl. patron saint (= =**heilige(r)**); =**pocken** f/pl. med. cowpox; =**pocken-impfung** f vaccination; =**pocken- stoff** m vaccine (matter); =**rede** f apology, e-s Advokaten: pleading; =**schild** *⚔ m, artill. shield; mit ~en shielded; =**schrift** f apology, vindication; =**sperre** f, pol. protective tariff; =**truppe** ⚔ f colonial force; = **und Trutz- bündnis** [schwz.] n offensive and defensive alliance; =**verwandte(r)** m alien living under the protection of the authorities; denizen; =**verwandtschaft** f denizenship; =**wache** f (safe)guard; ⚔ (Bedeckung) escort; =**waffe** f defensive arm, weapon of defence (a. fig.); =**wall** ⚔ m, frt. protecting rampart, (fr.) rideau; =**wand** f sheltering wall or partition; =**wehr** f: a) (weapon of) defence; b) ⚔ rampart, bulwark (auch fig.); (Damm) dike; c) fig. safeguard; =**zettel** m = =brief; =**zoll** ⊛ m protective duty; =**zöllner** m (ant. Freihändler) protectionist; prohibitionist; ♀**zöllnerisch** a. protectionist; =**zollpartei** f protectionist party; =**zollsystem** n protection(ist system), protectionism.

Schwabacher ⊕ (⏑‿ⓒ) [Schwabach ♀ bayr. Stadt] f ⓓ, ~(=**schrift**) f, typ. (so: Schwabacher) German italics pl.
Schwabb F (⏑) int. = schwapp.
Schwabbelei F (⏑‿") f ⓓ (leeres Geschwätz) babbling, twaddle, silly talk.
schwabb(e)lig (⏑(⏑)⏑) a. ⓓ wabbling; (geschwätzig) talkative.
schwabbeln (⏑‿) [ndd.] v/n. (h.) ⊛a. 1. = quabbeln. — 2. to babble, twaddle.
Schwabber ⚓ (⏑‿) m ㉓ (Schiffsbesen) swab(ber), kleinerer: squeegee.
schwabbern ⚓ (⏑‿) v/a. ⊛a. (scheuern) das Deck ⚓ to swab the deck.
Schwabe¹ (⏑‿) [ahd.: Sippe] m ⓓ, **Schwäbin** (⏑‿) f ⓓ Swabian, Suabian.
Schwabe² F (⏑‿) f ⓓ = Schabe 1.
schwäbeln (⏑‿) [Schwabe¹] v/n. (h.) ⊛a. to speak (like a) Swabian or in the Swabian dialect.
Schwaben ♀ (⏑‿) [mhd. „(zu den) ~" dat. pl. v. *Schwabe¹ npr/n. ㉓ Teil von Süddtschl., bsd. Württemberg: Swabia, Suabia.
Schwaben-alter (⏑‿...) n ② co. (the) age of forty, weit ㉟. years pl. of discretion or wisdom; =**land** ♀ n = Schwaben; ehm. =**spiegel** [mhd. 1275] m jur. Swabian code of laws; =**streich** m foolish action or trick, (piece of) tomfoolery or folly.
Schwäbin (⏑‿) f ⓓ s. Schwabe¹.
schwäbisch (⏑‿) a. ⓓ Swabian, Suabian; ♀ die ~e Alb the Swabian Alps pl.; das ~e Meer (der Bodensee) the Lake of Constance.
schwach (‿) [mhd.: siech] a. ⓓ (D 2,7) 1. weak (a. gr.); (kraftlos) feeble, infirm; (fein, zart) delicate, tender, adv. a. softly, ♪ piano; (gebrechlich) frail, (dünn) slender, slight, (hinfällig) decrepit, (ohnmächtig) faint, (matt) languishing, (machtlos) powerless; ⚓ ~ bemannt undermanned, short-handed; eccl., thea., &c. ⚓ besucht poorly attended; vom Feuer ⚓ brennen to burn low. — 2. attributiv: ⚓e Bevölkerung sparse (or scanty) population; ⚓e Brust delicate chest; f. Fuß 7 unter stehen; ⚓es Gedächtnis bad memory; ⚓es Licht, ⚓er Schimmer dim light, faint glimmer; ⚓er Magen weak (or poor) digestion; ⚓e Seite f. Schwäche 2; von dem Verstande f. feeble (or weak) intellect; vgl. geistesschwach; ⚓er Versuch feeble attempt; von ⚓er Willenskraft feeble- minded. — 3. prädikativ: f. willig gegen Ende; er war zu ⚓, es zu erlauben he was weak enough to allow it; schwächer sein als // to be inferior (in strength, &c.) to //; ⚓ w. to grow weak, vom Gesichte: to fail; schwächer w. to lose (in) strength, von Kranken: to sink; es wurde ihr ⚓ (sie wurde ohnmächtig) she fainted (away).
schwach=äugig (⏑‿.⏑) a. ⓓ weak- (or blear-)eyed.
Schwäche (⏑‿) [mhd.] f ⓓ 1. (f. schwach) weakness; feebleness, infirmity; frailty, faintness, languor; path. debility, prostration, ⚗ atony; des Geistes: feeble(ness of) intellect, stärker: imbecility. — 2. (schwache Seite) weak point or side, des Charakters: foible; er hat viele ~n he has many failings or faults or imperfections.

schwächen (⏑‿) [schwach] I v/a. u. sich ⚓ v/refl. ⓓⓓ 1. (sich) ⚓ to weaken (o.s.), to enfeeble (o.s.); (entkräften) to debilitate (a. path.), to enervate; (vermindern) to lessen, to diminish; (abstumpfen) to blunt; ⊕ und paint. Farben ⚓ to tone down ...; Fieber schwächte seine Gesundheit ... impaired (or undermined) his health; mit geschwächter Gesundheit with impaired (or broken) health. — 2. fast † ob. bibl.: eine Jungfrau ⚓ to deflower. — II ~ n ㉓ 3. f. Schwächung.
Schwächer-werden (⏑‿.⏑‿) n ㉓ enfeeblement, loss of strength; (Verminderung) diminution, abatement; ~ des Gesichts failure of sight, failing sight.
Schwäche-zustand (⏑‿.⏑‿) m ② weak (or feeble) condition, debility, ⚗ asthenia. |(or little) faith.
schwach=gläubig (‿⏑...) a. ⓓ of weak
Schwachheit (‿ⓒ) [mhd.] f ⓓ 1. = Schwäche 1. — 2. eine ~ (Neigung) für et. haben to have a weakness (or liking) for a th., F fig. bilden Sie sich keine ~en (keine falschen Dinge) ein! don't delude (or deceive) yourself!, don't indulge in such delusions or fancies!
Schwachheits-fehler (‿ⓒ...) m ②, (=**sünde** f) fault due to (or arising from) frailty (or weakness) of mind.
Schwach-herzig(keit f ②) a. ⓓ (‿ⓒ...) faint-hearted(ness); =**kopf** m simpleton, stärker: imbecile; =**köpfig** a. weak- (F soft-)headed, of weak intellect, stärker: imbecile; =**köpfigkeit** f dulness, stärker: imbecility.
schwächlich (⏑‿) [mhd.] a. ⓓ weakly, frail, delicate, von Kindern auch: co. underdone; (kränklich) sickly, infirm, ailing, puling; **Schwächlichkeit** f ⓓ weakly condition, frailty, delicate state of health; sickliness, infirmity.
Schwächling (⏑‿) m ⓓd., **Schwachmatikus** F (⏑‿⏑⏑) [mhd.-lt.] m ⓓ⑤ weakly (or delicate, sickly) p., weakling.
schwach=nervig (‿ⓒ...) a. ⓓ weak-nerved, nervous; ♀**schlagend** ⚓ v. Pulse: low; =**sichtig** a. weak- (or dim-)sighted; =**sichtige(r)** s. ⓓ weak- (or dim-)sighted p.; =**sichtigkeit** f weak-sightedness, ⚗ amblyopia; ♀**sinn** m weakness of mind; =**sinnig** a. = ♀**köpfig**; =**strom** ⊕ m. elect. weak (or low-tension) current; =**strom- kabel** n low-voltage (or low-tension) cable; =**strom-technik** f low-voltage branch of electrical engineering.
Schwächung (⏑‿) f ⓓ weakening, &c. (f. schwächen I); debilitation, enervation, diminution; defloration.
Schwad (‿) [ndd.: swath] m ⓓ, =**en**¹ (⏑‿) m ㉓ agr. swath, row of cut cornsheaves, layers pl. of mown grass.
Schwaden² (⏑‿) [mhd.: sieden] m ㉓ = Brodem; ⚒ (schlagende Wetter) choke- (or fire-)damp, mine-gas.
Schwaden³ ♀ (⏑‿) m ㉓: a) (a. ~**grütze** f) = Mannagras; b) = Fench.
Schwadron ⚔ (⏑‿) f ⓓ nur N. P = (amtlich:) Eskadron.
schwadronen-weise (⏑‿⏑.⏑‿) adv. (F a. a. ⓓ) = schwadrons-weise.
Schwadroneur F (⏑‿n'r) [vgl. schwatzen] m ⓓd. (Schwätzer) (long-winded) talker.

[Schwadronieren] — 868 — [Schwänzchen]

swaggerer, blusterer, F gas-bag; vgl. Großsprecher; **schwadronieren** (⌣⌣⸗⌣) v/n. (h.) ⑧ to talk (too) much, to spin long yarns, to swagger, to bluster, F to gas, to hold forth; vgl. großtun. **schwadrons=weise** (⌣ᵘ⸗⌣) adv. in squadrons or troops. [to twaddle, jabber. **schwafeln** (⌣ᴸ⌣) v/n. (h.) ⓑa. (töricht reden)) **Schwager** (⌣ᴸ) [mhd.: Schwäher, Schwieger] m ⑲ 1. brother-in-law, **Schwägerin** f ㊼ sister-in-law. — 2. weit.S. (Bekannter) friend. — 3. F (urspr. burich., 18. sae.) postilion; coachman. **schwägerlich** (⌣ᴸ⌣) a. ⑯ of (or relating to, like) a brother- or a sister-in-law. **Schwägerschaft** (⌣ᴸ⌣) f ㊻ 1. relationship of brothers (and sisters)-in-law, affinity by marriage. — 2. coll. brothers (and sisters)-in-law. **Schwäher** (⌣ᴸ) [ahd.: lt. socer] m ㉒, **~in** f ㊼ 1. = Schwieger=vater, =mutter. — 2. wir sind ~ (durch unsrer Kinder Ehe verwandt) we are related (or connected) through the marriage of our children. **Schwaige** obb. (⌣ᴸ) f ㊽ (Sennhütte) alpine herdsman's cottage. [herdsman.) **Schwaiger** (⌣ᴸ) m ㉒ (Alpenhirt) alpine **schwajen** ⚓ (⌣ᴸ) [ndd.: sway] v/n. (h.) ⑧ to swing round; v/a. to swing the ship; (vor dem Anker umschwenken) to swing before the anchor. **Schwalbe** (⌣⌣) [ahd.: swalbe] f ㊽ 1. orn. swallow (Hirundo); f. Mauer=, Rauch=schwalbe; Sprichw. eine ~ macht noch keinen Sommer one (or a single) swallow does not make a summer. — 2. F (Ohrfeige) box on the ear. **Schwalben=flug** (⌣⌣...) m ㉒ flight of swallows; **=kraut** ⚥ n: a) = Schellkraut; b) syrisches ~ = Seidenpflanze; **=nest** n swallow's nest, indisches eßbares: edible swallow's nest; =**schwanz** m: a) swallow's tail; b) fig. (langer Frad) dress- (or tail-)coat, F co. swallow-tail coat; c) orn. = Gabelweihe; d) ent. (Schmetterling) swallow-tail butterfly (Papilio machaon); e) ⊕ Tischlerei: dovetail(ing); mit ~ einlassen to dovetail; =**schwanz=feile**, =**verbindung** ⊕ f dovetail-file, -joint; =**stein** m, min. swallow-stone; =**wurz(el)** ⚥ f: a) dog's-bane (Vincetoxicum officinale); b) = Schellkraut. **Schwalch** ⊕ (⌣) [mhd.: swallow; *schwelgen] m ⓑb. Gießerei: furnace-flue, aperture of a furnace through which the flames travel to the ore or metal; ⚥**=en** (⌣⌣) v/n. (h.) ⑧ (blasen, rauchen) to smoulder. **Schwalg** (⌣) m ⓑb. (Gewoge, Flut) surging waves pl., flood (= Schwall). **schwalken** provc. (⌣⌣) [ndd.] v/n. (ſn) ⑧ (herumschwärmen) to lead a roving life. **Schwall** (⌣) [mhd.: schwellen] m ⓑb. swell of the rising water, surging flood or wave; (schwellende Menge) heaving mass; throng, crowd; ~ von Flammen sheet (or torrent) of flames; fig. ~ von Redensarten, Worten flood (or flow, profusion, volume) of words, long rigmarole. **Schwamm¹** (⌣) [ahd.] m ⓑb. 1. sponge, ⚥ porifer; mit e-m ~ waschen, wischen to sponge; mit dem ~ über et. fahren to pass the sponge over a th. (a. fig.); F co. einen ~ im Leibe haben (viel

trinken) to drink like a fish; ~ d(a)rüber! let's have done with it!, no more of that!, let bygones be bygones! — 2. ⚥ (Pilz) mushroom, ⚥ fungus; f. Feuer=, Haus=schwamm. — 3. path. (Wucherung): ⚥ fungus, ...osity; f. Mund=schwamm; Schwämme zerstörend(es Mittel): ⚥ fungicide. — 4. F der ganze ~ the whole lot or F shoot, kit. **schwamm²** (⌣) ind. impf. v. schwimmen. **schwamm¹=artig** (⌣⸗ᴸ⌣) a. ⑯ spongy; auch = schwammicht. **Schwämmchen** (⌣⌣) n ㉓ (dim. von Schwamm) small sponge or ⚥ fungus; path. = Mundschwamm. **schwämme** (⌣⌣) subj. impf. v. schwimmen. **Schwamm¹=fischer(ei)** (⌣...) m ⑫ sponge-fisher(y); =**förmig** a.: ⚥ spongiform; =**gewächs** n = Schwamm 2 u. 3. **schwammicht**, mft ...ig (⌣⌣) a. ⑯ spongy, ⚥ fungous, ...al, ...oid; spongeous, ...iose, ...oid; (porös) porous. **Schwammigkeit** (⌣⌣) f ㊻ sponginess, ⚥ fungosity; porousness. **Schwamm¹=kuchen** (⌣...) m ⑫ sponge-cake; ⚥**=sauer** a. ⑯ chm.: ⚥ fungic; ⚥**=saures Salz**: ⚥ fungate; =**säure** f fungic (or fumaric) acid, =**stein** m, min. mushroom-stone; (versteinerte Madrepore): ⚥ fungite; (fossiler Schwamm): ⚥ spongite; =**taucher** m sponge-diver; =**wülstchen** ⚥ n der Wurzeln: ⚥ spongiole. **Schwan** (⌣) [ahd.: swan] m ①c., (obb.) ㊷ orn. swan (Cygnus); junger ~, auch **Schwänchen** (⌣⌣) n ㉓ cygnet. **schwand** (⌣) ind., **schwände** (⌣⌣) subj. impf. von schwinden. **schwanen** (⌣⌣) [ndd.; *Schwan] I v/n. (h.) ⑧ v/imp. mir schwant etwas I have (dark) forebodings or a (vague) presentiment or a (slight) misgiving, geh. Spr.: s.th. is borne in upon me. — II ~ n ㉓ foreboding, presentiment, (secret) misgiving. **Schwanen=bett** (⌣...) n ⑫ swan's-down bed; =**blume** ⚥ f flowering rush (Butomus umbellatus); =**busen** m snow-white bosom; =**daune**, =**feder** f swan's down, feather; =**fell** n swanskin (a. ♀); =**fluß** ⚥ in West=australien: Swan River; =**gans** f swan-goose (Cygnus cygnoides); =**gesang** m = =lied; =**hals** m swan's neck; =**lied** n swan's song, fig. a poet's dying (or last) song; =**ritter** m (Lohengrin) Knight of the Swan; =**teich** m swannery; ⚥**=weiß** a. ⑯ (as) white as a swan('s down). **Schwang¹** (⌣) [mhd.; schwang²] m ⓑb. (fast nur gbr. mit „in") 1. = Schwingung, Schwung, zB. eine Glocke in ~ bringen to set ... ringing or swinging or in motion. — 2. fig. im ~(e) (Brauch, Gang) sein to be in vogue or fashion, to prevail; in ~ kommen to come into vogue or use. **schwang²** (⌣) ind. impf. von schwingen. **Schwang¹=baum** ⊕ (⌣⸗ᴸ) m ⑫ shaft for a cart or coach or wagon. **schwänge** (⌣⌣) subj. impf. v. schwingen. **schwanger** (⌣⌣) [ahd.] a. ⑯ (D9) 1. von Frauen: pregnant, big with child, in the family-way, feiner: in interesting circumstances, vgl. hochschwanger; ⚥ to fall in(to) the family-way.

2. fig. mit großen Plänen ⚥ gehen to labour with mighty projects, to be hatching (out) great schemes; mit Unglück, Unheil ⚥ overwhelmed with misfortune, big with ruin. **Schwängerer** (⌣⌣⌣) m ⑫ p. who gets a woman in(to) the family-way, ravisher. **schwängern** (⌣⌣⌣) [schwanger] v/a. ⓑa. ein Weib ⚥ to get ... with child or in(to) the family-way or F into trouble; bsd. fig. to impregnate, chm. to saturate. [(period of) gestation.) **Schwangerschaft** (⌣⌣⌣) f ㊺ pregnancy, **Schwängerung** (⌣⌣⌣) f ㊻ getting with child; fig. impregnation, saturation. **Schwang¹=seil** (⌣⸗ᴸ) n ⑫ swinging-rope. **schwank¹** (⌣) [mhd.: schwang; schwingen] a. ⑯ flexible, pliant, pliable; (dünn, schwach) thin, slender, fragile; (unsicher) unsafe, uncertain; ⚥e Brücke frail bridge; ⚥es Rohr wavering reed; ⚥es Schiff rocking (or tossing) boat; ⚥es Seil loose (or slack) rope; ⚥e Schritte faltering (or tottering) steps pl. **Schwank²** (⌣) [mhd.] m ⓑb. merry tale, funny story, (good) joke or jest; drollery; thea. farce, farcical play; er steckt voller Schwänke (Streiche) he is full of (quips and) pranks or of fun, he is very droll or frolicsome or F larky. **schwanken** (⌣⌣) [mhd.: schwingen] I v/n. (h.) ⑧ 1. (sich hin und her neigen) to move (or rock) to and fro, mft fig. to vacillate; (zaudern) to hesitate, to falter, bei einer Wahl: to waver, to be undecided, pol. F to wobble; (wackeln, wanken) to shake, reel, totter, stagger; (zittern) to tremble, von Flammen: to flicker, phys. von der Magnetnadel, b. Barometer ꝛc.: to oscillate; ⚓ vom Schiffe: von einer Seite zur andern ⚥ to roll, toss, pitch; ♁ v. Kursen, Preisen: to fluctuate, to vary, to change (about); ⚥ to rise and fall. — II ~ n ㉓ 2. f. Schwankung. — III ⚥ p.pr. u. a. ⑯ 3. Bed. des inf.; ⚥e Gesundheit precarious health; ⚥e Haltung wavering (or undecided) attitude. — 4. (unentschlossen) undecided, irresolute, (ungewiß) uncertain; unsteady, unsettled (a. ♁ v. Preisen); (unbestimmt) vague, ambiguous. [jester, buffoon.) **Schwank²=macher** (⌣⸗ᴸ⌣) m ⑫ joker, **Schwankung** (⌣⌣) f ㊻ 1. (f. schwanken I) rocking, mft fig. vacillation; (zaudern) hesitation, bei e-r Wahl: wavering, indecision, irresolution; (Ungewißheit) vagueness; phys. oscillation of a magnetic needle, &c.; ♁ fluctuation of prices; (alternate) rise and fall. — 2. ast., phys. (Abweichung) deviation, ⚥ perturbation; ~ der Erdachse: ⚥ nutation. **Schwanz** (⌣) [mhd.; *Schwang¹] m ①a. 1. zo. tail, ⚥ cauda; brush of a fox; ♪ e-r Note flag; e-m Hunde den ~ abschneiden to cut off a dog's tail; den e-s Pferdes stutzen to dock a horse; mit e-m ~ (versehen) tailed. — 2. F fig. e-m den ~ streiche(l)n to fawn on a p., to coax (or cajole) a p.; den ~ zwischen die Beine nehmen to run (or make) off, to sneak away; Sprichw. f. Hund 3. **Schwanz=bein** (⸗ᴸ) n ⑫ = Steißbein. **Schwänzchen** (⌣⌣) n ㉓ (dim. v. Schwanz) little (or short) tail.

Zeichen (f. S. XVII): F familiär; P Volkssprache; Γ Gaunersprache; ⧵ selten; † alt (auch gestorben); * neu (auch geboren); ⁺⁺ unrichtig;

[Schwänze] — 869 — [Schwarzrock]

Schwänze ❀ (⌣) f ⊛ Börse: eine ~ machen = aufschwänzen 3.
schwänzeln (⌣) [mhd.: *schwänzen] v/n. (h.) ⚁ a. 1. von Tieren: to wag (with) the tail. — 2. fig. von Personen: to have an affected gait; to wriggle; wie sie schwänzelt F how she frames herself!, co. how she wags her tail!
schwänzen (⌣) [schwenken u. Schwanz] ⊚ I v/n. (h.) u. v/a. (müßig umhergehen) to saunter (or lounge) about; als v/a. e-e (Schul=)Stunde ☳ (versäumen) to miss (or shirk) a lesson; die Schule ☳ to play (the) truant. — II v/a. to (provide with a) tail (f. III). — III geschwänzt p.p. u. a. ⊛ having (or with) a tail, ☳ caudate; kurz ☳ short-tailed; ♪ ☳e Note crotchet. [of the tail.]
Schwanz=ende (⌣⌣) n ⊛ end (or tip)
Schwänzer (⌣) m ⚁, ~in f ⊛ truant.
Schwanz=federn (⌣…) f/pl. ⊛ orn. tail-feathers, ☳ rectrices pl.; =floſſe f, ichth. tail-fin, ☳ caudal fin; ☳förmig a. ⊛ ☳ caudiform; =haar n hair of a tail; =hammer ⊙ m, metall. tilt-hammer; ☳händig a. zo.: Der Affe prehensile-tailed monkey; =laterne ❀ f hinten am Zuge: tail-lamp; ☳los a. ⊛ tailless, without a tail; =lurch m, zo.: ☳ urodele; =meiſe f, orn. long-tailed titmouse (Parus cauda'tus); =menſch m tailed man; =riemen(=)bügel) m crupper(-loop); =riemen=ring ⊙ m crupper-ring; =ſchraube ⊙ f tail-screw; breech-pin of a gun; =ſtern m comet; =ſtück n piece of a tail, am Fiſch ꝛc.: tail-piece or -part, am Ochſen: rump; =viertel n Schlächterei ꝛc.: hind quarter; =wirbel m, anat.: ☳ caudal vertebra.
ſchwapp F (⌣) int. slap!, smack!, dash!
ſchwapp(e)lig (⌣⌣) a. ⊛ = ſchwabb(e)lig.
ſchwappen F (⌣) v/n. (h.) ⊛: das Waſſer ſchwappt aus dem Eimer … splashes from…; ϸd voll full to overflowing.
ſchwapps! (⌣) int. bang!, there goes!
Schwäre (⌣) [ahd.: ſchwer] f ⊛, ~n[1] m ⊛ path. ulcer, abscess, boil; voller ~n ulcered, ulcerous, vgl. Geſchwür.
ſchwären[2] (⌣) [ahd. f. o.] I v/n. (h. u. ſn) ⦿a. ⦿a. path. to ulcerate, suppurate, fester, gather; to form an ulcer or abscess. — II ~ n ⦾ f. Schwärung.
ſchwärig (⌣⌣) a. ⊛ ulcerated, ulcerous.
Schwarm (⌣) [ahd.: swarm; *ſchwirren] m ⦿b. von Bienen ꝛc.: swarm, v. Vögeln a. flight, v. Fiſchen: shoal, v. anderen Tieren: flock, herd, von Perſonen ꝛc.: crowd, throng, troop, host, multitude.
Schwärm=attacke ⚔ (⌣⌣⌣) f ⦿ attack by skirmishers or in distended order.
ſchwärmen (⌣) [mhd.: *Schwarm] I v/n. (h., bei Ortsveränderung: ſn) ⦿ 1. to run (or fly) to and fro, von Bienen: to swarm, von Jagdhunden: to get off the scent, von anderen Tieren u. v. Menſchen: to rove, wander, stray, flock; ⚔ to skirmish, to move (or attack) in extended (or distended) order; Bienen ☳ (ſchwirren) um den Stock … swarm around the hive; Schmetterlinge ☳ um die Blumen … flit (or flutter) around the flowers; v/impers. es ſchwärmt (wimmelt) von Menſchen auf der Straße the streets are swarming (or crowded) with people. — 2. (in Saus und Braus leben) to lead a gay (or riotous) life. — 3. (begeiſtert ſn) to be full of enthusiasm, F co. to enthuse; (träumen) to fall into reveries, to be a dreamer; für e-n ☳ to be taken (ſtärker: to be smitten or madly in love) with a p., to dote on a p., F to be gone on a p., in idealer Weiſe: to adore (or worship) a p.; von et. ☳ to gush, rave about (or over) a th. — II ~ n ⦿ 4. (ſ. 1) swarming; ⚔ skirmishing; (ſ. 2) gay life; (ſ. 3) enthusiasm; reverie.
Schwärmer (⌣) m ⚁ 1. (auch ~in f ⊛) von Perſonen: a) (flatterhafter Liebhaber) fickle lover; b) (ſ. ſchwärmen 2) p. leading a gay (or riotous) life, reveller; c) (ſ. ſchwärmen 3) enthusiast; dreamer, visionary; d) beſ. rel. fanatic, zealot. — 2. ent. hawk-moth, ☳ sphinx (= Abendfalter). — 3. ⊙ Feuerwerkerei: (fire-)cracker, squib. — 4. ☳ = Schwärmſpore.
Schwärmerei (⌣⌣⌣) f ⦿ 1. (Umherwandern) roaming life; (Schwelgerei) revelry. — 2. (ſ. Schwärmer 1 c u. d) enthusiasm; ardour, (burning) zeal; (Träumerei) reverie; (Verzücktheit) ecstasy; religiöſe ~ fanaticism, zealotism. [zeal.]
Schwärmer=eifer (⌣⌣⌣) m ⦿ fanatical
ſchwärmeriſch (⌣⌣) a. ⊛ (ſ. Schwärmer 1 c u. d) enthusiastic, full of enthusiasm or ardour, F gushing; (überspannt) eccentric, excited; fantastic(al); adv. enthusiastically, with enthusiasm; e-n ☳ verehren to be passionately fond of a p., to adore a p.
Schwarm=geiſt (⌣…) m ⦿ enthusiast(ic mind), fanatic(al spirit); =ſack m der Bienenzüchter: bag for swarming bees.
Schwärm=ſpore ❀ (⌣…) f ⦿ (einzelne Zelle) swarm-cell or -spore, ☳ zoospore; =ſporen=kapſel f: ☳ zoosporange.
ſchwärm=weiſe (⌣⌣⌣) adv. in swarms or flocks or crowds or troops or hosts.
Schwärm=zeit (⌣…) f ⦿ der Bienen: swarming-time; =zelle f = =ſpore.
Schwarte (⌣) [mhd.: sward] f ⦿ 1. rind, (thick or hard) skin; Schweins=, Speck=)~ rind of bacon, gebratene: crackling; F fig. daß die ~ knackt (aufs äußerſte) with a vengeance, thoroughly, vigorously. — 2. (Bucheinband aus Schweinsleder) pigskin binding; (altes Buch) (worm-eaten) old book; F Schule: (verbotene Überſetzung ꝛc.) crib. — 3. (begraſte Ackererde) sod, sward. — 4. ⚒ (Bohle zur Grubenzimmerung) plank.
Schwart(en)=magen (⌣(⌣)⌣) m ⦿ Kochk.: (gefüllter Schweinsmagen) collared head.
ſchwartig (⌣⌣) a. ⊛ thick-skinned.
Schwärung (⌣⌣) f ⊛ ulceration, suppuration, festering, gathering.
ſchwarz (⌣) [ahd.: swart] I a. ⊛ (D 2) 1. black (a. fig.); (geſchwärzt) blackened, durch d. Sonne: swarthy, durch Tinte: inky; (finſter) dark, gloomy; ſo ☳ wie Kohle (as) black as coal or ink, jetblack; fig. von Verbrechen ꝛc.: dark (deed), atrocious (crime). — 2. mit nouns: ☳e Blattern small-pox; ſ. Brett 2, Brot 1, Kunſt 1; ♀ das ~e Meer the Black Sea, ſ. Peter, Star; Der Tod (Peſt im 14. sae.) Black Death; ☳e (ſchmutzige) Wäſche dirty (or foul) linen. — 3. mit verbs: ☳e-n bei e-m ☳ anſchreiben to speak ill of a p. to a p.; ☳ behängen to drape in black; ☳ färben to dye black; ſich ☳ kleiden to dress in black; (ſich) ☳ machen to blacken (o.s.); alles ☳ ſehen to look at the dark side of everything, to take a gloomy view of things; ☳ w. to turn black, durch die Sonne: to tan; F ſich ärgern, daß man ☳ wird to worry o.s. to death. — II s. ⊛⚆ 4. ~ n, inv.: in ~ (gekleidet) (in Trauer) (dressed) in black; in mourning; in ~ geh(e)n to dress in black, to be in mourning; ☳ auf weiß (geſchrieben) in black and white; (gedruckt) in print. — 5. der (die) ~e, ein ~er: a) = Neger(in); b) (ſ. mit ☳en Haaren und dunkler Geſichtsfarbe) dark person; c) Spitzname: die ~en the clerical party, P the black brigade; d) = Rappe. — 6. das ~e ⊛ the black (part or mark or spot); ins ~e (der Schießſcheibe) treffen to hit the bull's-eye or the mark, fig. to make a (good) hit.
Schwarz=auge (⌣…) n ⦿: a) black eye; b) black-(or dark-)eyed person; =äugig a. ⊛ black- (or dark-) eyed; =blau a. ⊛ u. n bluish black, very dark blue; =blech n, metall. (black) sheet-iron; =blech=tafel f plate of sheet-iron; =braun a. brownish black durch die Sonne: swarthy, tanned, tawny; =brot n brown bread,(black)rye-bread; =dorn ❀ m blackthorn (Prunus spino'sa); =droſſel f, orn. = Amſel.
Schwärze (⌣) (ahd.) f ⊛ 1. (ſ. ſchwarz 1) blackness (a. fig.), swarthiness, inkiness; eine ſchöne ~ a fine black (colour); fig. darkness, atrociousness. — 2. ⊙ (Farbe, Wichſe) black(en)ing; typ. printer's (or printing-)ink; ~ auftragen = ſchwärzen 1.
ſchwärzen (⌣) [ahd.] v/a., v/n. (h.) und ſich ☳ v/refl. ⊛ 1. (ſich) ☳ to blacken (o.s.), to make (o.s.) black; ⊙ typ. die Ballen oder Walzen ☳ to ink … — 2. beſ. fig. (verfinſtern) to darken, to spread a gloom over. — 3. ⊛ = einſchmuggeln I.
Schwärzer (⌣⌣) m ⚁ 1. p. who blackens, blackener. — 2. = Schmuggler.
Schwarz=erle ❀ (⌣…) f ⦿ (common) alder-tree (Alnus glutino'sa); =färber(ei f) m dyer (dyeing) in black; ☳gallicht, ☳gallig a. ⊛ melancholy, ☳ atrabilarious, …ian; ☳gar ⊙ a. Gerberei: black-tanned; ☳gelb a. ⊛ a) blackish yellow; b) öſterreichiſche Farben: black and yellow; =geſtreift a. with black stripes; ☳grau a., ~ n greyish black, dark grey; ☳haarig a. black-haired; =holz ❀ n = Nadelholz; =kiefer ❀ f black spruce, Austrian pine (Pinus ni'gricans); =köpfig a. black-headed; orn. ☳e Möwe blackhead (Larus ridibu'ndus); =kümmel ❀ m: türkiſcher ~ fennel-flower (Nige'lla damasce'na); =künſtler m magician, sorcerer, (Geiſterbanner) necromancer; =kupferſchlacke ⊙ f, metall. roaster-slag.
ſchwärzlich (⌣⌣) a. ⊛ blackish, darkish, von der Hautfarbe: swarthy, dusky.
Schwarz=pappel ❀ (⌣…) f ⦿ black poplar (Po'pulus nigra); =plättchen n = Dompfaff; =rauchen n e-r Pfeife: colouring; =rock m: a) black coat; b) =

[**schwarzrot**]

Pfaffe; die =röcke, auch: the clerical tribe, F the cloth, P the black brigade; =rot a. ⑥, ~ n reddish black; =rot=gold(e)nes Banner n (deutsche Farben vor 1866) black, red, and gold; =scheck m, =schecke f (Pferd mit tiefschwarzen Flecken) black pied horse; =schimmel m darkgrey horse; =schmelz ⊕ m der Goldschmiede 2c.: niello; =sehend a. fig. seeing things in the blackest colours; =seher m, fig. pessimist(ic person); =seherei f, fig. pessimism; =sucht f ſ. Melanose; =tanne ſ = Fichte 1.

Schwärzung (´‿) f ㊻ blackening.

Schwarz=wald (´...) m ㉖: a) pine-forest; b) ♀ npr. der ~ the Black Forest; =wälder a. inv.: ~ Uhr Black Forest clock; =wäld(l)er(in f) m inhabitant of the Black Forest; ♀weiß=rot a. u. ~ n jetzige deutsche Farben: black, white, and red; =werden n blackening, darkening, ♋ nigrescence; =wild n, hunt. black game, wild boars pl.; =wurz(el) ♀ f: a) comfrey (Sy'mphytum officina'le); b) spanische ~ viper's-grass (Scorzo'ne'ra hispa'nica).

Schwatz (´) [mhd.] m ⓐa. talk, prattle, chatter(ing), gossip, F mag, blab.

Schwatz=, Schwätz=base (´‿‿) f ㊷ F chatterbox; vgl. Schwätzer.

schwatzen, schwätzen (´‿) [mhd. zu Schwatz] I v/n. (h.) u. v/a. ⑨⓪ to talk, prattle, babble, chatter, gossip; ſ. auch blau 4. — II ~ n ㉓ = Geschwätz.

Schwätzer (´‿) m ㉒, =in f ㊼ (great) talker, prattler, chatterbox, babbler.

Schwätzerei (‿‿") f ㊻ = Geschwätz.

schwatzhaft (´‿) a. ⑥⑥ = geschwätzig; ~igkeit (‿‿‿) f ㊻ = Schwatzsucht.

Schwatz=maul (´...) n ⑥⑥, =michel m = Schwätzer; =sucht f talkativeness, garrulity, loquacity, love of gossip; (Wortreichtum) verbosity.

Schweb=... ⤶ (´...) = Schwebe=...

Schwebe (´‿) [mhd.] f ㊽ (state of) suspense; in der ~ sein to be in suspense, fig. F to hang fire; fig. sein Schicksal hing in der ~ ... hung (or was trembling) in the balance.

Schwebe=bahn ⊕ (´‿...) f ⑥⑥ suspension-railway; =baum m Turnerei: horizontal bar; =bogen m = Schwibbbogen; =fliege f. ent.: ♋ syrphus(-fly) (Bomby'lius); =künstler(in f) m equilibrist.

schweben (´‿) [ahd.: schweißen] I v/n. (h., bei Ortsveränderung: ſn) ⑧⑧ 1. in der Luft ♀ to be suspended (or to float, hover, poise) in mid-air, v. Vögeln: to soar; (hangen) to hang, dangle, balance, ♋ to librate, to pendulate; (hin und her) ♀ to float (or swing) to and fro; durch den Saal ♀ (huschen) to flit (or glide) through ...; bibl. der Geist Gottes schwebte über dem Wasser ... moved upon the face of the waters. — 2. fig. das Wort schwebt mir auf der Zunge ... is on (or at) the tip of my tongue; sein Bild schwebt mir (stets) vor Augen ... is (always) before my eyes, ... is (ever) present to my mind; in Gefahr ♀ to be in jeopardy; in Ungewißheit ♀ to be kept in suspense; zwischen Leben und Tod ♀ to hover between life and death; ♪ der Ton

schwebt zwischen C und Cis the note is half-way between ... — 3. = schwanken; z.B. der Prozeß schwebt the action is pending or F hanging fire; die Sache schwebt noch the matter is still in abeyance. — II ~ n ㉓ 4. suspension. — III ♀d p.pr. und a. ⑥⑥ 5. suspended, floating, fig. a. wavering. undecided; ♀de Brücke suspension-bridge: ♀de Frage pending question; ♀der Schritt light, elastic step; ♀ ♀de Strecke heading; a. ⑥⑥ (ant. fundierte) Schuld floating debt.

Schwebe=reck (´‿...) n ⑥⑥ Turnerei: trapeze; =schritt m balance-step (bſb. ♃); im ~ geh(e)n to balance; =stange f der Seiltänzer: balancing-pole.

Schwebung (´‿) f ㊻: a) Akustik (Schwingung) vibration; b) ♪ (Orgelregister) tremor; vgl. schweben 2 am Ende.

Schwede (´‿) m ㉒, **Schwedin** f ㊼ 1. Swede; F fig. alter ~: a) (ehrlicher Kerl) honest fellow; b) als Anrede: F old boy! — 2. F ohne f: =n pl. (Streichhölzchen) safety-matches pl.

Schweden ⚥ (´‿) npr/n. ㉓α. Sweden.

schwedisch (´‿) a. ⑥⑥ Swedish, of Sweden; ♀e Heilgymnastik Swedish gymnastics; die ♀e Sprache, das ♀(e) n ㉓ the Swedish language. Swedish, agr. ♀e Steckrübe swede; ♀e Zündhölzer Swedish matches, safety-matches pl.

Schwefel (´‿) [ahd.] m ㉒ brimstone (a. bibl.); min., chm. sulphur (S); gediegener ~ native sulphur, ⊕ ~ in Stangen sticks pl. of sulphur.

Schwefel=abdruck ⊕ (´‿...) m ⑥⑥ sulphur impression; =ader ⚒ f vein (or lode) of sulphur; =arsen n, chm. sulphide of arsenic, sulpharsenite. a. = Auripigment; ♀artig a. ⑥⑥ sulphur(e)ous; =äther m sulphuric ether; =auflösung f solution of sulphur; =bad n: a) sulphurated bath; b) (Bade=ort) sulphurous spring (spl.); =bande F f. fig. set of vagabonds; =blausäure f. chm. sulphocyanic acid (CNHS); =blei n lead sulphide, sulphide of lead; =blumen, =blüten f/pl. flowers of sulphur; sublim(at)ed sulphur; =dampf m sulphur(e)ous exhalation, sulphur fumes pl.; =dioxyd n, chm. (Anhydrid der schwefligen Säure) sulphur dioxyde (SO_2); =dunst m = =dampf; =faden m sulphurated match; =farbe f brimstone-colour; ♀farben, ♀farbig a. ⑥⑥ brimstone-coloured; =gang m = =ader; ♀gelb a. ⑥⑥ sulphur-coloured; ♀farbig, =geruch m smell of brimstone, sulphurous smell; =grube f sulphur-(or brimstone-)mine or pit; ♀haltig a. sulphur(e)ous; =holz, =hölzchen n (lucifer) match.

schwef(e)licht (´(‿)) a. ⑥⑥ sulphurated.

schwef(e)lig (‿) a. ⑥⑥: a) = schwef(e)licht; b) chm. ♀e Säure sulphurous acid (H$_2$SO$_3$); ſ. Schwefeldioxyd; ♀=saures Salz: ♋ sulphite.

Schwefel=kalium (´‿...) n ⑥⑥ chm.: einfaches ~ sulphide of potassium, potassium sulphide (K$_2$S); =kammer f, =kasten m ⊕ sulphur-chamber, sulphuring-room; =kies m: ♋ pyrites; =kohlenstoff m, chm. carbonic disulphide (CS$_2$); =kupfer n: a) (Sulfür)

cuprous sulphide (Cu$_2$S); b) (Sulfid) cupric sulphide (CuS); =milch f precipitated sulphur, milk of sulphur.

schwefeln (´‿) ⑨a. I v/a. 1. to dip in (or into) brimstone; ein Faß, Krankenzimmer 2c.: to fumigate (or purify) with burning sulphur. — 2. (mit Schwefel verbinden): a) chm. to combine with sulphur, to sulphurate; b) ⊕ to sulphurize. Kautschuk: to vulcanize. — II v/n. 3. (h.) to smell of sulphur. — III ~ n ㉓ 4. ſ. Schwef(e)lung.

Schwefel=natrium (´‿...) n chm. sulphide of sodium; =pfuhl m. bibl. burning pit, hell-fire; =pulver n powdered sulphur; =quecksilber n sulphide of mercury; ſ. Zinnober; =quelle f sulphur-spring; ♀sauer a. chm. sulphuric, ♀saures Eisen, Kupfer = Eisen=, Kupfervitriol; ♀saures Salz sulphate; =säure f sulphuric acid (H$_2$SO$_4$); ſ. rauchen 1; =säure=anhydrid = =trioxyd; =silber n sulphide of silver (Ag$_2$S); =tellur=erz ⚒ n sulpho-telluride; =trioxyd n, chm. sulphur trioxide (SO$_3$).

Schwefelung (´‿‿) f ㊻ 1. (zu schwefeln I:) fumigation. — 2. (zu 2): a) chm. sulphuration; b) ⊕ sulphurization, vulcanization.

Schwefel=verbindung (´‿...) f ⑥⑥ chm. sulphuret; =wasser n sulphurated (or sulphur) water (s pl.); =wasserstoff(=gas n) m sulphuretted hydrogen (gas), sulphydric acid, hydric sulphide (H$_2$S); =weinsäure f sulphovinic acid; ♀weinsaures Salz sulphovinate; =zyanwasserstoff m = =blausäure.

schweflicht, ...ig ſ. schwefelicht 2c. [fife.

Schwegel ♪ ↑ (´‿) [ahd.] f ㊽ (Flöte) flute, ſ

schwei=en ↧ (´‿) v/n. (h.) ⑧⑧ = schwojen.

Schweif (´) [ahd.: sweep] m ⓐc. (schön-[gefiederter] Schwanz) (fine or full) tail, als Schmuck: train; ~ e=s Kometen: tail.

schweifen[1] (´‿) [ahd.: schweißen] ⑧⑧ I v/n. (h. u. ſn) 1. to ramble, to stray, durch die Felder 2c.: to stroll through ..., in die Weite: to roam, to rove; (immer umher♀) to lead a roving (or vagabond) life; willst du immer weiter ♀? (G.) wilt thou far and farther roam? — II ⊕ v/a. 2. to curve, to slope; ♀ schweifen 1. — III ~ n ㉓ 3. (ſ. I) roving (or vagabond) life. — 4. (ſ. II) curving, sloping.

schweifen[2] (´‿) [Schweif] v/a. ⑧⑧ 1. to (provide with a) tail; schön geschweiftes Pferd ... with a fine tail. — 2. to curve (out); geschweift curved.

Schweif=haar (´...) n ⑥⑥ hair of the tail; =riemen m, man. crupper; =säge ⊕ f bow-saw; =stern m comet.

Schweifung (´‿) f ㊻ (Geschweiftes) curve, slope, sinuosity.

schweif=wedeln (´‿‿) v/n. (h.) ⑨a*⁎ = fuchsschwänzen; =wedler m ㉒ = Fuchsschwänzer.

Schweige=geld (´‿‿) n ⑥⑥ hush-money.

schweigen (´‿) [ahd.] ⑨⓪ I v/n. (h.) to be silent, to keep silence, von Personen auch: to hold one's tongue or peace, not to speak, F to be mum. auf eine Frage: to make no reply; schweigt! silence!, hush!, be quiet!; die Musik schwieg ... ceased (playing); alles

---

Signs (see page XVII): F familiar; P vulgar; ⟍ flash; ⤶ rare; † obsolete (died); * new word (born); ⁓⁺ incorrect; ♪ music;

[**schweigen**]

[Schweiger] — 871 — [schwellen]

(umher) schwieg there was a dead silence (all around); the scene was hushed; ♀ Sie mir davon! don't refer to it!; um zu ♀ von// not to mention //, to say nothing of //; ♀d zuhören to listen in silence; Sprichw. wer schweigt, bejaht silence gives consent. — II v/a. ⊕ mit Angabe der Wirkung: et. tot♀ to hush up a th.; ein (Kunst=)Werk ꝛc. tot♀ to kill ... by a conspiracy of silence. — III ~ n ㉓ silence; ~ bewahren to keep silence; ~ gebieten to command (or impose) silence; f. hüllen 2; zum ~ bringen to reduce to silence; to hush, to quiet; Sprichw. f. reden 4.

Schweiger (⸗⸗) [ahd.] m ㉒ taciturn (or reticent)person,p.who remains silent.

schweigsam (⸗⸗) a. ⓺ silent, quiet; (wortkarg) taciturn, reticent; (verschwiegen) close, discreet, reserved; **~keit** (⸗⸗⸗) f ㊻ taciturnity; closeness, discretion.

Schwein (⸗) [ahd.] n ㉓c. 1. zo. gemeines wildes ~ wild boar (Sus scrofa); zahmes ~ pig, hog (beide a. fig.), pl. auch: swine (a. fig.) (Sus domesticus). — 2. burschikos: ~ (Glück) haben to be lucky or in luck's way; vgl. Sau 6.

Schweinchen (⸗⸗) n ㉓ (dim. v. Schwein) little pig; porkling; vgl. Ferkel.

Schweine=braten (⸗⸗...) m ㉒ Kochk. roast pork; **=fett** n lard; **=fett** n pork dripping; **=fleisch** n pork; **=fraß** m, **=futter** n food for pigs (auch fig.), F fig. auch filthy (or nasty) grub; **=händler** m dealer in pigs; **=hirt** m swineherd, ehm. a. hogherd; **=hund** P m = Schweinhund; **=koben** m pigsty, hogsty; **=markt** m hog-market; **=mast** f food (or mast) for swine; vgl. Eichelmast; **=metzger(ei** f) n =Schlächter(ei); **=pelz** = Schweinpelz; **=pökel=fleisch** n pickled pork.

Schweinerei (⸗⸗⸗) f ㊻ swinishness, piggishness, hoggishness, dirt(iness), weitS. smut(tiness); **~en** smutty (or filthy) jokes or tales pl. [chop.]

Schweine=rippchen (⸗⸗,⸗,) n ㉒ pork-

Schweinerne(s) (⸗⸗⸗) n ㊷ Kochk. pork.

Schweine=schlächter (⸗⸗...) m ㉒ porkbutcher; F co. pigsticker; **=schlächterei** f pork-butcher's shop or business; F co. pig-sticking; **=schmalz** n = =fett; **=schneider** m sow-gelder; **=stall** m: a) = =koben, a. hog-pen; b) F fig. piggery; vgl. Saunest; **=trank** m hogwash (a. fig.); **=treiber** m pig-driver; **=trog** m pig's trough; **=volk** n filthy (set of) people; **=wirtschaft** f = =zeug; **=zeug** n nasty stuff; **=zucht** f: a) agr. breeding of pigs; b) P fig. es ist e-e wahre ~ it's a gross scandal or a great (F a beastly) shame.

Schweinfurter=grün (⸗⸗⸗⸗) [Schweinfurt, ♀ bayr. Stadt] n ⊕ Schweinfurt (or Paris) green.

Schwein=hund P (⸗...) m ㉒ filthy (or nasty)fellow; vgl. =igel b; =igel m: a) zo. = Igel b; b) fig. = Sau 3; a. smutty fellow; **=igelei** f smut, loose (or obscene) talk; **♀igeln** v/n. (h.) ♀a*,* to make smutty jokes or obscene remarks, a. to talk smut(tily).

schweinisch (⸗⸗) a. ⓺ piggish, swinish.

Schwein=pelz F (⸗⸗⸗) m ㉒ smutty (or nasty) fellow.

schweins=äugig (⸗...) a. ⓺ pig-eyed; **=blase** f ㉒ pig's bladder; **=borste** f hog's bristle; **=braten** m f. Schweine=b.; **=brot** ♀ n = Alpenveilchen; **=feder** f, hunt. (Spieß) boar-spear; **=füße** m/pl. pig's trotters pl.; **=hatz** f hog- (or boar-) hunting; **=haut** f pig's (or hog's) skin; vgl. =leder; **=hirsch** m = Hirsch=eber; **=jagd** f = =hatz; **=keule** f leg of pork; **=knöchel(chen)** n/pl., **=knochen** m/pl. pig's pettitoes pl.; **=kopf** m hog's (or boar's) head; **=kotelett** n pork chop; **=leder** n pigskin, hogskin; **=leder=band** m pigskin binding or volume; **♀ledern** a. (of) pigskin; **=ohr** n: a) pig's ear; b) zo. hog's-ear (Mytilus crista galli); **=pocken** f/pl. vet. swine-pox; **=rücken** m Kochk.: pig's back; **=rüssel** m pig's snout, bisw.: pig-nose; **=schwarte** f rind of bacon, gebratene: crackling; **=trüffel** f: ♀ rhizopogon; **=wurst** f pork sausage.

Schweiß¹ (⸗) [ahd.: sweat: schwitzen] m ⓐa. 1. sweat (f. Angesicht 2), feiner: perspiration; in ~ gebadet perspiring profusely or all over, in a bath of perspiration, F u. P all of a sweat; in ~ geraten, kommen to get (or break out) into a persp.; von ~ triefen to be in a bath of (or wet with) persp.; path. der Englische ~ the sweating-sickness; bibl. im ~e deines Angesichtes in the sweat of thy brow; fig. mein saurer ~ the fruit of my labour(s), the results of my (hard) toil(ing); f. fosten³ fig. — 2. (Feuchtigkeit an Fensterscheiben ꝛc.) moisture, steam. — 3. hunt. (Blut) blood as scent of the wounded game.

Schweiß²=arbeit ⊕ (⸗...) [schweißen ⊕] f ㊻ welding; **=¹ausbruch** m profuse perspiration; **=bad** m = Schwitzbad.

schweißbar ⊕ (⸗⸗) a. ⓺ metall. weldable; **~keit** (⸗⸗⸗) f ㊻ weldability.

schweiß=bedeckt (⸗...) a. ⓺ covered with perspiration; **=befördernd** a. = ♀treibend; **=bläschen** n/pl. ㉒ path.: ♀ sudamina pl.; **=blatt** n dresspreserver; **=drüse** f, anat. perspiratory gland; **=²eisen** ⊕ n welded iron.

schweißen (⸗⸗) ⊕ I v/n. (h. und zu) 1. hunt. (f. Schweiß¹ 3) von verwundetem Wilde: to bleed. — 2. ⊕ metall. (von der Glut weich w.) to become weldable, to (begin to) melt. — II v/a. ⊕ 3. Schmiedeeisen ꝛc. ♀ (in der Glühhitze hämmern) to weld (together).

Schweißer (⸗⸗) m ㉒ welder.

Schweiß¹=fieber (⸗...) ⊕ path. sweating-sickness; **=fuchs** m, man. sorrel (or dark chestnut) horse; **=füße** m/pl. perspiring (F sweaty) feet pl.; **=geruch** m smell of perspiration; **=grübchen** n, anat. pore; **=²hitze** f welding-heat; **=¹hund** m, hunt. blood-, sleuth-hound.

schweißig (⸗⸗) a. ⓺ 1. sweaty (feet, &c.), feiner: perspiring, wet (or damp) with perspiration; von Kleidern ꝛc.: F clammy. — 2. hunt. bloody.

Schweiß¹=loch (⸗...) n ㉒ = =grübchen; **=mittel** n, med.: ♀ sudorific, diaphoretic; **=²naht** f welding-seam; **=stahl** m weld-steel, welded steel; **♀¹treibend** a. ⓺ producing perspiration, ♀ sudorific; med. ♀treibendes Mittel = =mittel; **♀triefend** a. dripping with perspira-

tion, perspiring profusely; **=tropfen** m drop of sweat, feiner: bead of perspiration; **=tuch** n handkerchief to wipe off perspiration (with); eccl. ~ Christi holy handkerchief, ♀ sudarium; **=wolle** ⊕ f wool in the grease.

Schweiz ♀ (⸗) [Schwyz] npr/f. inv. die ~ Switzerland, vgl. Helvetien; in der Französischen ~ in French Sw.; die Sächsische ~ Saxon Switzerland.

Schweizer (⸗⸗) I m ㉒ 1. (a. ~in f ㊽) Swiss; fie ist eine ~in a Swiss (woman or girl); die ~ pl. the Swiss (people). — 2. a) (Türsteher) doorkeeper, porter; b) ehm. ⚔ (Leibgardist) Switzer; c) (Meier) dairyman, cow-keeper. — II a. inv. 3. = schweizerisch.

Schweizer=bund (⸗⸗...) m ㉒ Swiss (or Helvetic) Confederation or Confederacy; **=degen** m, typ. compositor who is also a pressman; **=deutsch** n Swiss German. [(Swiss) dairy or creamery.

Schweizerei (⸗⸗⸗) f ㊻ (Milchwirtschaft)

Schweizer=haus (⸗⸗...), **=häuschen** n ㉒ Swiss cottage or chalet.

schweizerisch (⸗⸗⸗) a. ⓺ Swiss, of Switzerland, of the Swiss.

Schweizer=käse (⸗⸗...) m ㉒ Swiss cheese; **=land** n Switzerland; **=tee** m Swiss tea; **=volk** n the Swiss people.

Schwelch=malz ⊕ (⸗⸗⸗) n ㉒ (an der Luft getrocknetes Malz) withered malt.

schwelen (⸗⸗) [ndd.: sweal: schwül] ⊕ I v/n. (h.) to smoulder, to burn slowly and without a flame. — II v/a. ⊕ to burn slowly or by a slow fire; Teer ♀ to distil (or extract) tar.

schwelgen (⸗⸗) [ahd.=swallow: Schwalch] I v/n. (h.) ⊕ to lead a luxurious life, schmausend und zechend: to eat and drink well, to feast and revel, F to live on the fat of the land; meist g.s. in et. ♀ to (take great) delight in a th., to enjoy a th.; er schwelgt in seligen Gefühlen he indulges (or revels) in delightful thoughts. — II ~ n ㉓ luxurious living, revelry.

Schwelger (⸗⸗) m ㉒ person leading (or living) a life of luxury or enjoyment or pleasure. reveller, glutton, F fast (or high) liver.

Schwelgerei (⸗⸗⸗) f ㊻ life of pleasure or enjoyment; revelry, gluttony, feasting, (Ausschweifung) debauchery.

schwelgerisch (⸗⸗⸗) a. ⓺ luxurious; given (or devoted) to enjoyment or revelry or gluttony or feasting; (ausschweifend) debauched.

Schwelle (⸗⸗) [ahd.= Säule] f ㊻ 1. mst ⊕ carp. Bauwesen ꝛc.: beam, (ground-)joist; sill; am Fenster: window-sill, an der Tür: threshold; e-m über die ~ kommen to cross a p.'s threshold, to enter a p.'s door; fig. an der ~ des Grabes stehen to be on the brink of the grave, at death's door. — 2. 🚆 (railway-)sleeper; ~n legen to lay (or put) down sleepers; ⚒ sole.

schwellen¹ (⸗⸗) [ahd.] v/a. (h.) ⊕b. 1. = anschwellen I; das Wasser rauscht', das Wasser schwoll (G.) the water swirled, the water rose; geschwollene Beine ꝛc. swoln (or swollen)legs, &c.; geschwol-

♀ scientific; ⚘ botanical; ⚲ geography; ⊕ machinery; ⚒ mining; ⚔ military; ⚓ marine; ● commercial; ✉ postal; 🚆 railway.

[Schwellenholz] — [Schwert]

lene Gestalt bloated figure; 2d swelling, ⚇ turgescent, tumescent; ⇓ 2de Segel bellying sails pl. — 2. (anwachsen) to increase, grow, extend; der Klang zum Ohre schwoll (v.) rich harmony filled (or fell on) the ear; f. Kamm 3. — II v/a. ⊛ 3. = anschwellen II. 4. (f. 2) to increase, to make grow, to extend. — III ~ n ⓶ 5. f. Schwellung.

Schwellen²-holz (⁸ᵛ⁻) [Schwelle pl.] n ⓶ wood for sleepers.

Schwell-gewebe (⁸…) [schwell-en] n ⓶ anat. spongy (or erectile) tissue; **=ton** ♪ m swelling tone, crescendo.

Schwellung (ᵛ⁻) f ⓸ (f. schwellen¹) swell(ing), inflation, path. a. tumour; (Anwachsen) increase, growth; (geschwollener Zustand) inflatedness, puffiness, bagginess, ⚇ tumefaction; arch. ~ am Säulenschafte: ⚇ entasis.

Schwemme (ᵛ⁻) [mhd.: *schwemmen] f ⓸ 1. für Vieh: watering-place, für Pferde: horse-pond; ein Pferd in die ~ reiten (auch schwemmen) to take (or ride) ... to water, to water ...; Vieh in die ~ treiben to water cattle. — 2. (Kutscherkneipe) low-class restaurant or bar.

schwemmen (ᵛ⁻) [mhd.: swim: schwimmen] v/a. ⊛ 1. to water; to flush (with water); (berieseln) to irrigate; der Regen schwemmt die Erde vom Felde ... sweeps (or washes, carries) the earth off the field; ⇓ Holz ins Tal ⇓ (flößen) to float (or raft) — 2. ein Pferd ⇓ f. Schwemme. — 3. ⊕ Gerber: die Häute ⇓ to soak ... — 4. (anschwemmen) to deposit.

Schwemm-gebilde (⁸…) [schwemm-en] n ⓶ geol. alluvial formation; **=klöße** m/pl. Kocht.: light dumplings pl.; **=land** n, **=sand** m, geol. alluvial land, sand; **=teich** m für Pferde: horse-pond.

Schwengel, mft ⊕ (ᵛ⁻) [mhd.: swingle (-tree); *schwingen] m ⓶ e-r Aufzugsbrücke: bascule, Wagen2: spring-bar, e-r Glocke: bell-crank, swipe (of a bell); clapper, ⊕ Pumpen2: handle, sweep, lever; Schmiede: (Balg-)~ swipe, typ. (Preß-)~ lever (or bar) of the press. Vgl. Laden2.

Schwengel-brunnen ⊕ (⁸…) m ⓶ well with a lever or swipe; **=presse** f, typ. press with a lever or bar; **=pumpe** f pump with a handle, **=werk** f suction-pump (worked) with a lever or swipe.

schweningern (ᵛ⁻) [Schweninger, Bismarcks Arzt] v/n. ⓶a. med. (Entfettungskur gebrauchen) to use a cure for stoutness or obesity, bf. ehm. to go through a course of banting.

Schwenk-becken (⁸ᵛ⁻) [f. schwenken 2] n ⓶ basin for rinsing.

schwenken (ᵛ⁻) [ahd.: schwingen] ⊛ I v/a. u. v/refl. 1. to shake (about), leicht und rasch: to whisk, heftig: to toss (about), den Hut, das Taschentuch ꝛc.: to wave; (hin und her schlenkern) to swing one's arms, &c. to and fro, to brandish (or flourish) a stick, a lance, &c.; den Leib (ob. sich) ⇓ to turn o.s. about; F (von der Schule) ⇓ to expel a pupil. — 2. ein Glas ⇓ (ausspülen) to rinse ... — II v/n. (h.) 3. to turn about, ⚔ to wheel round; ⚔ links schwenkt — marsch! left wheel — march! — 4. fig. (die Gesinnung ändern) to change one's opinion, pol. to change sides, F to rat. — III ~ n ⓶ 5. = Schwenkung 1.

Schwenk-faß (⁸…), **=gefäß** n ⓶ vessel (or tub) for rinsing, Küche: wash-up; **=punkt** ⚔ m = Schwenkungspunkt.

Schwenkung (ᵛ⁻) f ⓸ 1. waving of hats, &c., brandishing of sticks, &c. (f. schwenken I); turning about, &c. (f. schwenken II). — 2. a) ⚔ ⇓ wheel(ing), evolution, manœuvring; b) fig. change of opinion, pol. (f. 4) changing sides, F ratting.

Schwenkungs-punkt ⚔ (⁸ᵛ⁻) m ⓶ pivot, fixed point.

Schwenze ⚇ (ᵛ⁻) = Schwänze.

schwer (¹) [ahd.: sweer] a. ⓺ 1. (⇓ wiegend, ant. leicht) heavy, weighty (beide a. fig.), v. Stoffen a. stout, strong; zwei Pfund ⇓ ... in weight, weighing ...; (schwerfällig) ponderous, clumsy, heavy; ⇓ drückend burdensome, onerous, oppressive; (schlimm) grievous (mistake), hard (times), bad (sore); (mühsam) troublesome (vgl. schwierig); (kräftig) full-bodied, full-flavoured (wine, sauce, &c.), v. Bier, Zigarren auch: strong, heavy, F heady, von Speisen: rich; oben ⇓er als unten, oben zu ⇓ top-heavy; F adv.: ⇓ (sehr) betrunken helplessly (F blind) drunk, F quite boozed or fuddled. — 2. mit nouns: ⇓e Angst great anxiety; ⇓e Arbeit hard drudgery; ⚔ ⇓e Artillerie heavy ordnance; ⇓er Diebstahl great theft or robbery; ⇓es Geld hard cash or coin; das kostet ein ⇓es Geld ... a large (or a good round) sum (of money); ⇓es Gepäck heavy luggage; ⚔ ⇓es Geschütz heavy cannon or guns pl.; mit ⇓em Herzen, ⇓en Herzens with a heavy heart, (most) reluctantly; in a dejected mood; f ⇓er Junge professional thief, mobsman; ⇓er Kampf hard (or severe) struggle, ⚔ a. serious engagement; ⇓e Krankheit serious illness; f. Menge 1, Schwerenot; ⚔ ⇓e Reiterei heavy cavalry or horse; ⇓e See heavy (or rough) sea; ⇓e Strafe severe punishment, an Geld: heavy fine; ⇓es Verbrechen heinous (or shocking) crime; ⇓er Wein full-bodied wine; ⇓e Zeiten hard times pl.; ⇓e Zunge heavy (or slow) tongue. — 3. mit verbs und a.: f. ankommen 6; sich ⇓ ärgern to feel sorely (or greatly) vexed; ⇓ beleidigen to give great offence to; ⇓ büßen to pay dearly (geh. Spr.: fully to atone) for; das wird ihm ⇓ eingehen it will be difficult to make him understand (or see) that; f. fallen 8; ⇓ an et. gehen to go reluctantly to work; ⊕ zu ⇓ geh(e)n (zu wenig Spiel, Flucht h.) to have too little purchase or play; f. halten 15 u. 16. ⇓ hören to be hard of hearing; es liegt mir ⇓ in den Gliedern my limbs feel as heavy as lead, I feel a great heaviness in my limbs; ⇓ im Magen liegen to lie heavy on the stomach, to be hard of digestion; ⇓ daniederliegen to be (lying) dangerously ill; e-m das Herz ⇓ m. to make a p.'s heart sore or sad; to grieve a p.; f. schmelzbar; ⇓ verständlich difficult to grasp, hard to understand; sich ⇓ versündigen an // to offend (or sin) grievously against //; ⇓ verwundet mortally (or dangerously) wounded; ⇓ werden to grow heavy (a. fig. von der Zunge); to increase in weight; e-m ⇓ werden to come difficult to a p.; ⇓ wiegen to be weighty or of great weight (mft fig.); ⇓ zu ersteigen difficult to mount or of ascent; ⇓ zu verdauen (zu erlangen, zu verkaufen) difficult (or hard) to digest (to get at, to sell).

schwer=atmend (¹¹…) a. ⓺⓺ breathing hard; **⇓atmig** a. path. asthmatic(al); **⇓beladen** a. heavily laden, fig. auch weighed down; **⇓betrübt** a. deeply grieved, geh. Spr. sorely afflicted; **⇓bewaffnet** a. heavy-(or heavily) armed.

Schwere (¹ᵛ⁻) f ⓸ (f. schwer) 1. heaviness, weight(iness); ponderousness, clumsiness; des Weins ꝛc.: (full) body or flavour; phys. gravity (auch fig.); vgl. Schwierigkeit. — 2. ~ einer Strafe: severity (or rigour) ..., ~ e-s Verbrechens: gravity (or heinousness, shocking nature) ...; die ganze ~ (Bedeutung) e-s Wortes: the full weight (or import) ...

Schwere=messer (¹¹…) m ⓶ ⚇ gravimeter, für Flüssigkeiten: ⚇ litrameter; **=messung** f bf. der Luft: ⚇ barometry; **=not** f ⓺: a) path. = Epilepsie; es ist um die ~ zu kriegen it's enough to sicken one or to give one the hump; b) in Flüchen: (a. ~ noch einmal! daß dich die ~!) hang (or damn) it (all)!; ~, wo mag er nur stecken? where the devil (or deuce) can he be?; **=nöter** F m ⓶ fast (or gay) young fellow; den ~ spielen, sich auf den ~ aufspielen to play the masher; meift g.s. kleiner ~ young rascal or scamp or Turk, F pickle.

Schwer=erde (¹¹…) f ⓺: a) = =spat; b) = Baryt; **⇓fallen** v/n. ⓺a.** to become difficult or burdensome or a burden; **⇓fällig** a. ⓺⓺ heavy, ponderous; (plump) clumsy, unwieldy, fig. cumbersome (matt, träge) dull, slow; **=fälligkeit** f heaviness, clumsiness; dulness; **⇓flüssig** a. metall. difficult to fuse, refractory; **=flüssigkeit** f refractoriness; **=gewicht** ⇓ n dead weight; **⇓halten** v/n. ⓺a.** to be difficult or a hard task; **⇓hörig** a. = harthörig; **=hörigkeit** f = Hart-h.; **=kraft** f, phys. (force of) gravity, gravitation; der ~ folgen to gravitate.

schwerlich (¹ᵛ⁻) adv. with difficulty; (faft nicht) hardly, scarcely; barely.

Schwer=mut (¹¹…) f ⓺ sad (or dejected) mood, melancholy, path.: ⚇ hypochondria; **⇓mütig**, **⇓mut(s)=voll** a. ⓺⓺ sad, dejected, melancholy; **=mütigkeit** f = =mut; **=punkt** m, mech. centre of gravity (a. fig.); dem ~ zustreben to gravitate; **=spat**, m, min. heavy spar, ⚇ barite, chm. barium sulphate (BaSO₄); **⇓spat=haltig** a.: ⚇ barytic.

Schwert (¹) [ahd.: sword] n ⓸b. sword; f. führen 6, Faust¹¹, Feuer 2 am Schluß; zum ~e greifen to draw (or unsheathe) the (or one's) sword; e-n zum ~e verurteilen to condemn a p. to die by the sword or to be beheaded, auch: to send a p. to the block or scaffold.

Zeichen (f. S. XVII): F familiär; P Volkssprache; ⸗ Gaunersprache; ⸗ selten; † alt (auch gestorben); * neu (auch geboren); ‡ unrichtig;

[**Schwertbruder**] — 873 — [**Schwindelmeier**]

Schwert=bruder (ᴗ́‿ᴗ̀) m 62 ehm. in Livland (1202—1561) Brother of the Sword.
Schwertel ⚘ (́‿) [ahd.] m 22 corn-flag, sword-lily, ⚘ gladiole (*Gladiolus*).
Schwert(er)=geklirr (́ᴗ̀ᴗ...) n 62 clashing of swords; **=tanz** m sword-dance; battle, combat, fight(ing) with swords.
Schwert=feger ⚒ (́ᴗ...) m 62 furbisher; (Waffenschmied) sword-cutler, armourer; **=feger-arbeit** f sw.-cutlery; **=fisch** m: a) *ichth*. sword-fish (*Xiphias*); grampus (*Orca*); b) *ast*. (südl. Sternbild) Dorado; **2förmig** a. 66 sword-like or -shaped, ⚘ ensiform, ensate, ⚘ auch: ⚘ linear-ensate, *anat*.: ⚘ xiphoid; **=fortsatz** m, *anat*.: ⚘ xiphoid; **=geklirr** n ſ. Schwerter; **=hieb** m sw.-cut; vgl. **=streich**; ehm. **=lehen** n (ant. Kunkellehen) male fief; ehm. **=leite** f reception of a squire into (the order of) knighthood; **=lilie** ⚘ f flag, flower de luce (*Iris*), her. fleur-de-lis; gelbe ~ sword-flag, yellow water-flag (*I. pseudacorus*); ehm. **=orden** m Order of the Sword; ehm. **=ritter** m: a) **=bruder**; b) knight of the Order of the Sword; **=schlag** m = **=streich**; **=schwanz** m, zo. sword-tail (*Xiphosu'ra*); **=streich** m stroke with the sword; ohne ~ without (striking) a blow; **=tanz** m sword-dance; vgl. Schwertertanz; **=träger** m sword-bearer.
schwer=verständlich (́ᴗ...) a. 66 difficult to understand; von Schriften ꝛc. auch: abstruse; **2verwundet** a. severely wounded; **2wiegend** a. ſ. schwer 1, fig. a. grave, serious. [ſ. Klosterschwester.]
Schwester (́ᴗ) [ahd.: sister] f 48 sister; **Schwesterchen** (́ᴗᴗ) n 23 (dim. von Schwester) little (or young) sister, F bſd. *Am*. siss(ie), sis.
Schwester=kind (́ᴗᴗ‿̀) n 62 sister's child, meiſt: nephew, f niece.
Schwesterlein (́ᴗᴗ‿) = Schwesterchen.
schwesterlich (́ᴗᴗᴗ) a. 66 sisterly, of a sister, like a sister, ⚘ sororal.
Schwester=liebe (́ᴗᴗ...) f 62 sisterly love; **=mann** m sister's husband, brother-in-law; **=mord**, **=mörder(in** f) m: ⚘ sororicide. [sisters.]
Schwester=paar (́ᴗᴗ‿̀) n 62 couple of **Schwesterschaft** (́ᴗᴗᴗ) f 46 sisterhood; weitS. sisterly friendship or love.
Schwester=sohn (́ᴗᴗ...) m 62 sister's son, nephew; **=sprache** f sister language; **=tochter** f sister's daughter, niece.
Schwib=bogen ⚒ (́ᴗ‿̀ᴗ) [ahd.] m 62 *arch*. arch(way); (Pfeilerbogen) pier-arch; (Strebebogen) flying buttress.
schwichten ⚓ (́ᴗ) v/a. 68: Wanten ℒ (freispannen) to snake the riggings.
Schwicht=leine ⚓ (́ᴗ‿̀) f 62 swifter, swifting-in line, snake; **=(ungs=)talje** f swift(ing-tackle). [schweigen.]
schwieg (‿́) ind., ℒe (́ᴗ) subj. impf. v.ſ
Schwiegel (́ᴗ) m 22 = Schwegel.
Schwieger, faſt † (́ᴗ) [ahd.: Schwäher] m 22, f 48 = Schwieger=vater, =mutter.
Schwieger=eltern (́ᴗᴗ...) pl. 62 parents-in-law pl.; **=kind** n = =sohn od. =tochter; **=mama** F, **=mutter** f mother-in-law; **2mütterlich** a. 66 of a mother-in-law; **2papa** m =vater; **=sohn** m son-in-law; **=tochter** f daughter-in-law; **=vater** m (**2väterlich** a. of) father-in-law.

Schwiele (́ᴗ) [ahd.: schwellen] f 48: a) (harte Haut) horny skin, callosity; b) (blut-unterlaufener Fleck) wale, ⚘ ecchymosis; **2n=artig**, auch **schwielicht**.
schwielig a. 66: a) horny, callous, ⚘ callose; b) marked with wales.
Schwiemel (́ᴗ) m 22 **1.** giddiness, dizziness. — **2.** (a. 50) F auch: **~ant** (‿‿́) m 42 (luſtiger Bruder) gay (or loose, dissolute, fast, rackety) fellow, rake; **~ei** F(‿́) f 46 gay (or dissolute) life; **~er** (́ᴗᴗ) m 22 = Schwiemel 2; **2ig** a. 66 gay, dissolute, rakish; **2n** (́ᴗ) v/n. (h.) 92a. to lead a gay (or dissolute, fast) life, F to go on the spree.
schwierig (́ᴗᴗ) [mhd.; *Schwäre, P: schwer] a. 66 difficult, hard; (heikel) delicate; (mißlich) precarious (position), trying (circumstances); (schwer zu befriedigen) arduous (task); (schwer zu befriedigen) difficult to please, fastidious; (wenig nachgiebig) unyielding, (nicht entgegenkommend) unaccommodating; ℒe Frage intricate (or puzzling) question; ℒer Punkt knotty point; ℒes Unternehmen bold enterprise, F tough job, hard nut (to crack); ℒes Gelände difficult (or broken, intersected) country; das ~ſte haben wir hinter uns we have turned the worst part is over, we have turned the (sharpest) corner.
Schwierigkeit (́ᴗᴗᴗ) f 46 (ſ. schwierig) difficulty, hardness; precariousness; arduousness, intricacy; (nicht) ohne ~ without any (not without some) trouble or friction; ſ. darbieten; das macht gar keine ~ there is no difficulty about that or no obstacle in the way; **~en** m. to raise difficulties, bei etwas: to raise objections to a th.; unnötige **~en** m. to make a(n unnecessary) fuss; auf **~en** ſtoßen to encounter (or meet with) difficulties; F nach der ~ with a vengeance; immensely, enormously. [schwären.]
schwiert (́‿) 3. Perſon sg. pres. ind. von **Schwigt...** ⚓ ſ. Schwicht... [v. schwellen.]
schwill imper., **2ſt**, **2t** (‿́) pres. ind.ſ
Schwimm=anstalt (́ᴗ...) f 62 swimming-baths pl.; weitS. = Bade-anſtalt; **=bad** n swimming-bath; ein ~ nehmen F to have a swim; **=blase** f: a) *ichth*. air-bladder, swim, sound; b) zur Erleichterung des Schwimmens: bladder for swimming; **=dock** ⚓ n floating dock.
Schwimmeister (́ᴗ‿̀ᴗ) [Schwimm-meister] m 22 swimming-master.
schwimmen (́ᴗᴗ)[ahd.: swim] **I** v/n. (h. u. ſn) 92a(b). **1.** a) to swim (ans Land to shore, ashore; unter Waſſer under water, auf dem Rücken (treibend): to float; ℒ lernen to learn swimming or to swim; a. v/refl. ſich frei ℒ to pass in swimming; Verſuch über den Kanal zu ℒ attempt to swim the Channel; b) meiſt von leblosen Dingen: (treiben) to float, to drift, von Schiffen und Flotten a. to be afloat; ℒd, a. afloat, adrift; Schiffchen ꝛc. ℒ I. to swim; c) (undeutlich erscheinen) to present a hazy image. — **2.** Redewendungen: aus Ufer ℒ, das Ufer ℒ reichen to to (the) shore; das Brett ist aus Ufer geschwommen ... drifted (or was carried) to land; mit dem Strome (gegen den Strom) ℒ to swim with (against) the current or the stream (a. fig.); fig. in f-m Blute ℒ to swim (or welter) in one's blood; ihr Auge (oder ſie) schwamm in Tränen she was bathed in tears; im Weine ℒ to be soaked with wine; ✕ ℒde Batterie floating battery; ⚓ ℒde Mine floating mine; ⚒ ℒde Waren goods afloat or carried by bottom or carried by water. — **II** ~ n 3. swimming, floating; ~ im Kopfe = Schwindel 1.
Schwimmer (́ᴗᴗ) m 22 **1.** (a. **~in** f 47) swimmer. — **2.** ⚒ (Widerstandsmesser) float(er), float-gauge or -stick.
schwimm=fähig (́ᴗ...) a. 66 able to swim or to float; **=fähigkeit** f 42 ability to swim or to float; **=fahrt** f = =fest; **=feder** f = floſſe; **=fest** n swimming-match, aquatic sports pl.; **=flosse** f fin; **=fuß** m, zo. webbed (or palmated) foot, web-foot, ⚘ palmiped; **=füßer** m, orn.: ⚘ palmiped; **2füßig** a. web-footed, ⚘ palmiped; **=gürtel** m life-belt or -preserver; **=haut** f, orn. web; **=hose** f bathing-drawers pl.; **=jacke** f swimming-cork-jacket; **=kleid** n bathing-costume; **=kraft** f buoyancy; **2kundig** a. knowing how to swim; **=kunst** f art of swimming; **=lehrer** m swimming-master; **=meister** ſ. Schwimmeiſter; **=niveau** n = Schwimmer 2; **=platz** m place for swimming; **=schnecke** f, zo.: ⚘ nerita; **=schule** f swimming-school; **=stein** m, min. float-stone; **=stoß** m (swimmer's) stroke; **=tier** n swimmer; **=vogel** m, orn. swimming (or web-footed) bird.
Schwinde (́ᴗ) f 48 path. (Flechte) tetter.
Schwindel (́ᴗ) [mhd.] m 62 **1.** giddiness, dizziness, swimming in the head, ⚘ vertigo, vet. staggers pl. — **2.** fig. (Täuschung, Betrug) swindle, deception, fraud, gammon(ing), bubble, F sell, do; es iſt der reine ~ it's a rank fraud; den ~ kenne ich! I know that trick or dodge! — **3.** F der ganze ~ (Kram) the whole lot or kit.
Schwindel=bank ⚒ (́ᴗᴗ‿̀) f 62 bogus bank.
Schwindelei (́ᴗᴗ‿́) [Schwindel 2] f 46 risky (or windy, swindling, F wild-cat) scheme, bogus concern; (commercial or financial) bubble; grobe ~ F (dead) take-in, rank swindle.
schwindel=erregend (́ᴗᴗ‿̀ᴗ) a. 66 = schwindelhaft 1; **=firma** ⚒ f 62 long firm; **2frei** a. not liable to (or free from) giddiness; **=gefühl** n (feeling of) giddiness, giddy sensation; **=geschäft** n swindling business, swindle; **=gesellschaft** f bogus (or bubble-)company; **=hafer** ⚘ m: a) = Lolch; b) = Windhafer.
schwindelhaft (́ᴗᴗᴗ). **schwind(e)lig** (́ᴗ(ᴗ)ᴗ) a. 66 **1.** (Schwindel erregend) causing giddiness, making dizzy; giddy (height). — **2.** (vom Schwindel [1] ergriffen) (feeling) giddy or dizzy; schwindelig w. to turn giddy. — **3.** (auf Schwindel [2] beruhend) deceptive, fraudulent, humbugging; swindling, bogus.
Schwindel=kopf (́ᴗᴗ...) m 62: a) harum-scarum; b) swindler; **2köpfig** a. 66: a) hare-brained; b) humbugging swindling; **=meier** F m swindler, humbug.

♪ Muſik; ⚘ Wiſſenschaft; ⚘ Pflanze; ⚐ Geographie; ⚒ Technik; ⚒ Bergbau; ✕ Militär; ⚓ Marine; ⚒ Handel; ✉ Poſt; ⚒ Eisenbahn.

[ſchwindeln] — 874 — [ſchwül]

ſchwindeln (⌣⌣) [ahd.] v/n. (h.) ⒶA.
1. ich ſchwindle, mein Kopf (ob. Gehirn)
ſchwindelt, der Kopf (mehr gbr. v/impers.
es) ſchwindelt mir I (begin to) feel
giddy or dizzy, my head swims, my
brain reels; *fig.* mir ſchwindelt vor
den Zahlen my head is in a whirl
with figures, the figures make my
head swim; ⚭d *p. pr.*: in ⚭der Höhe
at a giddy height. — 2. (Schwindeleien
treiben) [: swindle] to make bogus
schemes; to swindle (or cheat, gull,
humbug) the public.

Schwindel-ſucht (⌣⌣…) *f* ⓶ *path.*: a) =
Schwindel 1; b) *fig.* eccentricity;
⚭ſüchtig *a.* ⓺ = ⚭köpfig.

ſchwinden (⌣⌣) [ahd.] **I** v/n. (ſn) ⓵
1. (abnehmen) to dwindle, to grow less,
to fall off, (mager w.) to grow thin, to fall
away, (zſ.-ſchrumpfen) to shrink, ⊕
auch: to contract, (welt w.) to wither,
to fade, F to go off, (abſterben) to
perish, to (go to) waste. — 2. (verſchwinden, aufhören) to disappear, vanish,
cease; *fig.* mir iſt aller Mut geſchwun-
den all my courage has deserted me
or has flown (from me); ihr ſchwanden
die Sinne she lost consciousness. —
3. ⚭ laſſen to give up, to forego; ich
mußte alle Hoffnung ⚭ laſſen I had to
abandon all hope. — **II** ~ n ⓸ 4. (ſ. I)
dwindling, &c.; shrinkage; waste;
disappearance, cessation.

Schwind-grube (⌣⌣…) *f* ⓶ = Senkgrube.

Schwindler (⌣⌣) [engl.] *m* ⓶, ~**in** *f* ⓸
swindler, humbug(ging person), ⊕
promoter of bogus companies, (Betrüger) cheat, impostor; ~**bande** *f* gang
of swindlers; ⚭**haft**, ⚭**iſch** (⌣⌣) *a.* ⓺
swindling; humbugging; fraudulent.

ſchwindlig (⌣⌣) *a.* ⓺ ſ. ſchwindelig.

Schwind-maß ⊕ (⌣…) *n* ⓶ Gießerei:
contraction-rule; ⚭**ſucht** *f, path.*
consumption, decline, wasting, ⊕
phthisis, tabes; galoppierende: galloping consumption, rapid decline; vgl.
Lungenſchwindſucht; die ~ bekommen
to go into a consumption, to become
consumptive; ⚭**ſüchtig** *a.* ⓺ consumptive, hectic, ⊕ phthisical, tabetic;
ein ~er a consumptive patient; ⚭**ſüch-
tigkeit** *f* consumptiveness; ⚭**ſuchts-
kandidat** *F m* consumptive (or hectic)
p., p. inclined to consumption.

Schwing-bank (⌣…) *f* für Flachs: swingle-
bench; ⚭**baum** ⚓ *m* swinging-boom;
⚭**brett** *n* für Flachs: swingle-board.

Schwinge (⌣⌣) [mhd.] *f* ⓸ 1. (edler als
„Flügel") ~*n pl.* des Adlers ꝛc.: wings (or
pinions) … 2. ⊕ agr.: a) für das
Getreide: winnow, fan; b) für den
Flachs: swingle(-staff) und für den Hanf:
tewing-beetle; ⎡nerei: wooden horse.

Schwingel¹ (⌣⌣) [ſchwingen] *m* ⓶ Turz;
Schwingel² ♧ (⌣⌣) [mhd.] *m* ⓶ fescue-
grass (*Festuca*), roter ~ creeping (or
red) fescue (*F. rubra*).

ſchwingen (⌣⌣) [ahd.: swing] ⚭ft **I** v/a.
1. to swing (round), to move in
a circle; (ſchaukeln) to balance; die
Füße, die Sohlen im Tanze ⚭, F das
Tanzbein ⚭ to dance, to hop, F to toe
and heel it. — 2. die Lanze, den Speer

⚭ (ſchwenken) to brandish (or wave,
flourish) … — 3. (ſchwingend heben,
ſetzen) er ſchwang ſie auf ſein Pferd he
swung her on his horse. — 4. ⊕
(mit der Schwinge reinigen): a) Getreide:
to winnow, to fan; b) Flachs: to
swingle; c) Hanf: to tew. — **II ſich** ⚭
v/refl. 5. to swing o.s.; auf einer
Schaukel F to have a swing, auf einem
Brette to (have a) see-saw; ſpringend:
to bound, to bounce; ſich aus dem
Sattel ⚭ to leap from …; ſich in den
Sattel ⚭ to vault (or jump) into the
saddle or on horseback. — 6. ſich
auf den Thron ⚭ to ascend (unrechtmäßig: to usurp) the throne. —
III v/n. (h.) 7. von Pendeln ꝛc.: to swing
(to and fro), to oscillate, von Saiten
ꝛc.: to vibrate; ⚭d, a vibratory (motion, &c.); elect. ⚭de Metallzunge, die
e-n Strom öffnet ob. ſchließt: ⚛ vibrator.
— 8. ⚓ das Schiff ſchwingt … swings
or rocks. — **IV** ~ n ⓸ 9. = Schwingung 1. — **V ge-ſchwungen** *p.p. u. a.*
⓺ (D 9) 10. in den Bed. des *inf.*
11. (bogenförmig) arched, curved, sinuous.

Schwing-hang (⌣…) *m* ⓶ Turnerei:
suspension; ⚭**kölbchen** *n*, ⚭**kolben** *m,
ent.* der Zweiflügler: balancer, poiser;
⚭**maſchine** ⊕ *f* für Flachs: swingling-
machine; ⚭**meſſer** *n* zum Reinigen des
Flachſes: swingle, swingling-knife;
⚭**pflug** *m* ohne Räder: swing-plough;
⚭**ſieb** *n*, ⚭**ſtock** *m* swing-sieve, -stick;
⚭**trog** *m* Goldwäſcherei: washing-cradle.

Schwingung (⌣⌣) *f* ⓸ 1. swing(ing), &c.
(ſ. ſchwingen I u. II). — 2. (ſ. ſchwingen III
bſd. mech., phys. oscillation, vibration; vibratory movement; (zitternde
Bewegung) pulsation (a. *physiol.* vom
Herzen ꝛc.); ~en *m* = ſchwingen III;
ein Pendel ꝛc. in ~ ſetzen to set
swinging or going.

Schwingungs-achſe (⌣⌣…) *f* ⓶ e-s Pendels
ꝛc.: axis of oscillation; ⚭**bewegung**
f: ⚛ vibratory motion; ⚭**bogen** *m*
e-s Pendels: arc of oscillation; ⚭**dauer**
f = ⚭**zeit**; ⚭**knoten** *m* einer Saite: ⚛
nodal point; ⚭**meſſer** *m* Inſtrument: ⚛
vibroscope; ⚭**ſchlag** *m* einer Uhr: beat;
⚭**zähler** *m, phys.* siren; ⚭**zeit** *f* time
(or period) of oscillation.

ſchwipp (⌣) **I** *int.* F ⚭! ſchwapp! flip,
flop! — **II** *a.* ⓺ pliant, flexible,
(behende) nimble, agile, mobile.

Schwippe (⌣⌣) [udd.] *f* ⓸ (Gerte) switch.

ſchwippen (⌣⌣) [udd.] ⓼ **I** v/n. (h. u. ſn)
to swing (or balance) o.s., to see-saw.
— **II** v/a. (ſchnellen) to jerk.

ſchwipps¹ (⌣) *int.* F ⚭! smack!

Schwipps² ⚭, mſt **Schwips** (⌣) *m* ⚭a.
1. smack of a switch or whip. —
2. F einen ~ (kleinen Rauſch) h. to be half
fuddled or a little on.

ſchwirbeln (⌣⌣) v/n. (h. u. ſn) ⓶a. to
whirl round.

ſchwirren (⌣⌣) [lautm.: Schwarm] **I** v/n.
(h. u. ſn) ⓼ 1. to whir, von einem
Pfeile ꝛc.: to whiz through the air, von
Inſekten ꝛc.: to buzz, to hum; (ſtrudeln)
to whirl, swirl. — 2. Redewendungen,
umher ⚭ to flit to and fro; die Menſchen ⚭ durcheinander the people are
(in) a confused mass or one whirl;

im Kreiſe herum ⚭ to whirl round;
v/impers. es ſchwirrt mir un die
Ohren, vor den Augen I feel a buzzing in my ears, I see a flickering
(or haze) before my eyes. — **II** ~ n
⓸ 3. whir, whizzing (sound), buzz;
(Strudel) whirl, swirl.

Schwirr-holz (⌣…) *n* ⓶ der Medizinmänner;
a. Spielzeug: bull-roarer.

Schwitz-bad (⌣…) *n* ⓶ vapour-, steam-
bath, F Turkish bath, *med.*: suda-
torium, sudatory; ⚭**bank** *f* sweating-
bench; *fig.* auf der ~ ſitzen to sweat over
one's work; to be in sore trouble.

Schwitze (⌣⌣) *f* ⓸: a) F sweating;
b) ⊕ Gerberei: Häute in die ~ bringen
to pile up …

ſchwitzen (⌣⌣) [ahd.: sweat: Schweiß]
⓵ **I** v/n. (h.), biſw. v/a. 1. to
sweat, feiner: to perspire; (ſtark) am
ganzen Leibe ⚭ to be in a bath of
perspiration, to be all of a sweat;
Ihr habt mich weidlich ⚭ machen (a.),
you have made me sweat profusely;
die Wände ⚭ … are sweaty or humid or
damp; ⊕ Gerberei: die Häute ⚭ l. to
sweat …; vgl. Schwitze b. — 2. biſw.
v/impers. mich ſchwitzt I am perspiring or in a perspiration. — 3. (ſn)
= ausſchwitzen 2. — **II** v/a. 4. et. aus
dem Leibe ⚭ = ausſchwitzen 3 u. 4. —
III~n ⓸ 5. (ſ. I) sweat(ing), perspiration, *med.*: ⚛ sudation, desudation.

ſchwitzig (⌣⌣) *a.* ⓺ = ſchweißig.

Schwitz-kaſten (⌣…) *m* ⓶ sweating-
box, ehm. (*SH.,* &c.) powdering-tub;
fig. (ſtark geheiztes Zimmer) overheated
room; ⚭**kur** *f* sweating cure; eine ~
für et. gebrauchen to drive out s. th.
by means of perspiration, to sweat
a th. out; ⚭**mittel** *n:* ⚛ sudorific;
⚭**prozeß** ⊕ *m* Gerberei ꝛc.: sweat; ⚭**pulver**
n, med.: ⚛ sudorific powder; ⚭**ſtube**
f = ⚭**zimmer** sweating-room, (very) hot room.

Schwof P (⌣) *m* ⓶c. (public) dance, F
shilling-hop; **ſchwofen** (⌣⌣) v/n. (h.) ⓼
to (have a) dance or hop, F to toe it.

ſchwoll (⌣) *ind.,* **ſchwölle** (⌣⌣) *subj. impf.*
v. ſchwellen; **ſchwömme** (⌣⌣) *subj. impf.* v.
ſchwimmen; **ſchwor** (⌣) *ind.,* **ſchwören¹**
pl.) *subj. impf.* von ſchwären u. ſchwören.

ſchwören² (⌣⌣) [ahd.: swear] **I** v/n. (h.),
v/a., a. v/refl. ⓺b. to swear (upon), to
take an oath (upon), to confirm by
oath; ſ. Eid, falſch 3 am Ende, heilig 2;
vor Gericht ⚭ to take the oath, F to
kiss the book; ein Gelöbniß in j-s
Hand ⚭ to make a solemn vow (or
promise) to a p.; Rache ⚭ to vow
vengeance against a p.; mit prp.: auf
et. ⚭ to swear to a th.; ich könnte
(möchte nicht) darauf ⚭ I could (would
not) take an oath upon it; bei et. ⚭
to swear by a th.; zum Katholizismus
⚭ to embrace (or profess) catholicism; ⚔ zur Fahne ⚭ to take one's
military oath. — **II** ~ n ⓸ swearing (a. = Fluchen); (taking an) oath.

ſchwude! (⌣⌣) *int.* = hiſt, har (nach links);
a. *fig.* (auf Abwege) on the wrong track.

ſchwül (⌣) [udd.: ſchwelen] ⓺ 1. (drückend
heiß) stifling (hot), sultry, close. —
2. *fig.* mir iſt (wird) ⚭ (ängſtlich) zumute
oder ums Herz I feel anxious or uneasy.

Signs (see page XVII): F familiar; P vulgar; ℱ flash; ⚭ rare; † obsolete (died); * new word (born); ⁘ incorrect; ♪ music.

[schwüle] — 875 — [Seebad]

Schwüle (⌣–) [schwül] f ④: a) stifling heat, sultriness, closeness; b) fig. (Niedergeschlagenheit) depression, low spirits pl.
Schwulibus F (⌣–⌣) [dtsch.-lt.; *schwül 2]: in ~ (Ängsten) in anxiety, in (sore) trouble, F in a scrape or fix or mess or stew; **Schwulität** F (–⌣⌣́) f ④ anxiety, trouble, F scrape, stew.
Schwulst (–́) [mhd.: schwellen] I m⸗t f ⑩ 1. = Geschwulst. — II m⸗t m ⑥b. 2. (Aufgeblasenheit) pompousness. — 3. ~ im Stile: inflated (or high-flown) speech or style, bombast, grandiloquence.
schwülstig (–́⌣) [Schwulst] a. ⑥⑥ vom Stil: bombastic, grandiloquent, turgid; (hochtönend) high-flown, inflated, pompous; stilted; ~**keit** f = Schwulst 3.
Schwund (–́) m ⑪b. (pl. ⸗) = schwinden II; bsd. path. e⸗s Gliedes: withering, ⊘ atrophy, des Haares: falling off.
Schwung¹ (–́) [mhd.: *schwingen] m ⑥b. 1. swing(ing); vgl. Schwingung; (Anstoß) impulsion, impetus; et. in ~ bringen to set a th. going or in motion; im ~e sein = in full swing (auch fig.). — 2. (Aufschwung) rise, rising; (Aufflug) soaring, flight (of imagination, &c.); ~ des Geistes buoyancy (or elasticity) of mind; mental activity or energy; (Lebendigkeit) briskness, stir; (Erhabenheit) loftiness, sublimeness; (Wärme) warmth, ardour; (Dichterfeuer) poetic fire or inspiration; rapture; diese Verse haben edlen ~ .. have a lofty (or noble) strain or diction; die Sache hat keinen rechten ~ there is no life (or go) in it; Stil ec.: feinen ~ h. to fall flat, to be dull or prosy or dry.
Schwung² P (–́) m ⑥b. = Ladenschwengel.
Schwung¹**-bewegung** (–́⌣...) f ⑥b. phys. oscillation, vibratory motion; **⸗brett** n für Springer: spring-board.
schwünge (⌣–̃) subj. impf. v. schwingen.
Schwung¹**-federn** (–́⌣⌣) f pl. ⑥ orn. pinions, ⊘ remiges pl.
schwunghaft (–́⌣) a. ⑥⑥ 1. full of energy or life or F go; brisk (trade, &c.), flourishing (business, &c.); stirring (speech, &c.) lively (scene, &c.), buoyant (tone, &c.); (begeistert) lofty, sublime, spirited. — 2. (im Schwunge) in vogue; in full swing.
Schwung¹**-kraft** (–́⌣) f ⑥ motor force, phys. centrifugal force; fig. (Tatkraft) energy, spring; (Beweglichkeit) buoyancy; **⸗los** a. ⑥⑥ without stir or life or F go; **⸗rad** ⊙ n, mach. fly-(an Uhren: swing- or balance-)wheel; **⸗reich** a. = schwunghaft; **⸗riemen** m pl. einer Kutsche: main (or check-)braces pl.; **⸗seil** n Turnerei: slack rope; **⸗voll** a. full of fire or energy; vgl. schwunghaft.
schwupp(dich) F (–́⌣) int. = schwipp I.
Schwur¹ (–́) [mhd. (ahd.): *schwören] m ⑦c. 1. oath (= Eid); einen (feierlichen) leisten oder tun to take (or swear) an (a solemn) oath. — 2. bibl. (Fluch) oath.
schwur² (–́) ind. impf. v. schwören.
schwur-brüchig (–́⌣⌣) a. ⑥⑥ = eidbrüchig; **schwüre** (–́⌣) subj. impf. v. schwören.
Schwur¹**-gericht** (–́⌣...) n ⑥② trial by jury, (judge and jury); **⸗gerichtshof** m court of assize; **⸗vergessen** a. ⑥⑥ = eidbrüchig; **⸗zeuge** m ⑫ sworn witness.
Sc.... sc.... s. Sz.... sz..

s. d. abbr. = sich(e) dies.
See. = Seine (Majestät ec.). [Zebulon.|
Sebulon (–́⌣⌣) npr/m. ⑮ bibl. (4. Mose 1, 31)
Sec..., sec... s. Sef..., sef..., Sez..., sez..
Sech ⊙ (–́) [ahd.: Sichel] n ⑩c. (a. f ④) agr. (Pflugschar) ploughshare, coulter.
sechs (–́) [ahd.: sit. lt. sex: grch. hex] numer. I card. numb. (o. s. a. sechse) six; s. sechsundsechzig; mit sechsen (sechs Pferden) fahren to drive (in) a carriage-and-six; um halb 2 (Uhr) at half-past five. — II (die Zahl) ~ f ④, a. Sechse f ④ (number) six; vgl. Sir.
Sechs-achteltakt ♪ (–́⌣...) m ②
six-eight (or sextuple) time; **⸗armig** (–́...), **⸗beinig** a. ⑥⑥ six-armed, -legged; with six arms, legs; **⸗blätt(e)rig** ♣ a. with six leaves, ⊘ hexaphyllous, von Blüten: six-petalled, ⊘ hexapetalous.
Sechse, sechse (–́⌣) s. sechs I u. II.
Sechs-eck (–́...) n ② geom. six-sided figure, hexagon; **⸗eckig** a. with six angles or corners; geom. hexagonal.
Sechser (–́⌣) m ㉒ 1. ehm. nordd. Münze: six-pfennig piece, a. etwa: halfpenny. — 2. the number six. — 3. ✕ soldier of the sixth regiment.
sechser-lei (–́⌣⌣) a. inv. of six kinds or sorts, six kinds of.
sechs-fach (–́⌣...), **⸗fältig** a. ⑥⑥ sixfold, sextuple; das ⸗fache der Zahl: six times the number; **⸗flach** n ② geom. min. hexahedron, cube; **⸗füßig** a.: a) with six feet, zo. ⸗es Tier: ⊘ hexapod; b) pros. ⸗er (daktylischer) Vers: ⊘ hexameter; **⸗jährig** a. six years old, ⊘ sexennial; **⸗läufig** a. six-chambered (revolver, &c.); **⸗mal(ig** a.) adv. (taking place) six times; **⸗männig** ♀ a. (mit 6 Staubgefäßen): ⊘ hexandrous,...ian; **⸗monatlich** a. six-monthly, half-yearly, every six months; **⸗pfünder** ✕ m, artill. six-pounder; **⸗reihig** a. in six rows, six-rowed, ⊘ hexastichous; **⸗saitig** ♪ a. with six strings; hexachord; **⸗seitig** a. six-sided; **⸗silbig** a. of six syllables; ⊘ hexasyllabic; **⸗spänner** m carriage-and-six; **⸗spännig(er Wagen)** a. (coach) drawn by six horses; **⸗stündig** (⸗tägig) a. of (or lasting) six hours (days); **⸗stündlich** (**⸗täglich**) a. (occurring) every (or once in) six hours (days).
sechste (–́⌣⌣) ord. numb. ⑥⑥ (the) sixth; Eduard der ~ (gschr.: VI.) Edward the Sixth (gschr.: VI); Datum: der 2 (am 2en Juni (gschr.: 6. Juni) (on) the sixth of June, June the sixth (gschr.: June 6ᵗʰ); 6. June, Zeitungen ec.: June 6); ⸗**halb** (–́⌣⌣) a. inv. five and a half.
sechs-teilig (–́⌣...) a. ⑥⑥ in six parts.
Sechstel (–́⌣⌣) n ㉒, 2 a. inv. sixth (part); fünf ~ (⁵⁄₆) five-sixths. [(6ᵗʰ) place.|
sechstens (–́⌣⌣) adv. sixthly, in the sixth
sechs-undsechzig (–́⌣...): a) card. numb. sixty-six; b) ~ n (Kartenspiel, in Engl. unbekannt) sixty-six; **⸗viertaltakt** ♪ m ② six-four measure; **⸗weibig** ♀ a. (mit 6 Griffeln): ⊘ hexagynian; **⸗wink(e)lig** a. geom. six-angled; **⸗wöchentlich** a. of (or lasting) six weeks; adv. every (or once in) six weeks; **⸗wöchnerin** f = Kindbetterin; **⸗zeilig** a. of six lines, ⊘ hexastichous.

sechzehn (–́⌣) [ahd.: sixteen] numer. I card. numb. inv. sixteen. — II (die Zahl) ~ f ④ (number) sixteen.
Sechzehn-ender (–́⌣⌣...) m ⑥ hunt. stag with sixteen antlers or points.
sechzehnfach (–́⌣⌣...) a. u. adv. sixteenfold; **⸗jährig** (–́⌣⌣...) a. ⑥⑥ of sixteen years, sixteen years old; **⸗lötig** a. weighing eight ounces; chm. ⸗es Silber unalloyed (or pure) silver.
sechzehnte (–́⌣⌣⌣) ord. numb. ⑥⑥ sixteenth; Ludwig der ~ (gschr.: XVI.) Louis the Sixteenth (gschr.: XVI); der 2 (den 2n April, am 2n April (gschr.: 16. April) (on) the sixteenth of April, April the sixteenth (gschr.: April 16ᵗʰ, 16. April, in Zeitungen ec.: April 16).
Sechzehntel (–́⌣⌣⌣) n ㉒ 1. (a. 2 a. inv.) sixteenth (part); drei ~ (³⁄₁₆) three-sixteenths. — 2. ⌣ Fäßchen von etwa 8 Liter etwa: two-gallon cask.
Sechzehntel-band (–́⌣⌣...) m ㉒, **⸗format** n ⊙ typ. (sheet of) sixteens pl., sedecimo, sixteenmo (abbr. 16mo); **⸗note** ♪ f sixteenth-note, semiquaver; **⸗pause** ♪ f sixteenth-rest.
sechzehntens (–́⌣⌣⌣) adv. sixteenthly, in the sixteenth place.
sechzig (–́⌣) [ahd.: sixty] numer. I card. numb. sixty, threescore. — II (die Zahl) ~ f ④ (number) sixty.
Sechziger (–́⌣⌣) I m ㉒, ~**in** f ④ person sixty (and more) years old, ⊘ sexagenarian; ein hoher ~ (f eine hohe ~in) a (wo)man nearly seventy years old. — II 2 a. inv. die 2 Jahre (Zeitrechnung u. Lebensalter) the sixties pl.
sechzig-jährig (–́⌣⌣⌣) a. ⑥⑥ sixty years old, ⊘ sexagenarian.
sechzigste (–́⌣⌣) ord. numb. ⑥⑥ sixtieth; über das 2 Jahr hinaus sein to be on the wrong (or shady) side of sixty; ~**l** n ㉒, 2 a. inv. sixtieth (part); fünf ~l (⁵⁄₆₀) machen ein Zwölftel five-sixtieths make one-twelfth; 2**ns** (–́⌣⌣) adv. in the sixtieth (60ᵗʰ) place.
Seckel¹ (–́⌣) = Säckel.
Seckel² (–́⌣) = Sekel. [Säure.|
Sedativ-salz (–́–⌣f⌣) [lt.] n ㉒ = Vor-
Sedez ⊙ (–́) ⁽¹⁄₁₆⁾ m ⑥a., ~**ausgabe** f, ~**format** n ⊙ = Sechzehntelformat.
Sedisvakanz (–́⌣⌣⌣) [neul.-lt.] f ④ vacancy of the Papal See.
See (–́) [ahd.: sea] I f ④ ⌘ (Meer) sea, größeres: ocean; an der ~ by the sea or seaside; auf der ~ at sea; s. hoch 2, hochgehend; kabbelige ~ choppy sea; s. offen 2; in ~ gehen ob. stechen f. offen 2; zur ~ geh(e)n to go to sea, to become a seaman or sailor; zur ~ nach Holland gehen to go by sea to ...; s. halten 4; die ~ betreffend, zur ~ gehörig marine, an der ~ gelegen maritime. — II m ㉖ (großes natürliches Wasserbecken) lake, zB. Genfer ~ Lake of Geneva; vgl. Genezareth; kleiner ~ lakelet.
See-adler (–́⌣...) m ㉒ orn. white-tailed eagle (Haliäetus albici'lla); **⸗alpen** f pl. ♀ Maritime Alps pl.; **⸗artig** a. ⑥⑥ u. adv. resembling (or like) the sea or a lake; **⸗ausdruck** m sea-term, nautical term or expression; **⸗bad** n: a) sea-bath, F bathe (or dip) in the sea; **⸗bäder nehmen** to take (a number of) sea-baths,

---

⊘ scientific; ♣ botanical; ♀ geography; ⊙ machinery; ✕ mining; ✕ military; ⌘ marine; ● commercial; ✉ postal; ⑥⑥ railway.

to bathe (regularly) in the sea; b) sea-side resort, weit S. watering-place; =bär m: a) zo. ursine (or fur-)seal, a.: sea-bear (Ota'ria ursi'na); b) F fig. old growler or grumbler; =barbe f, ichth.: gemeine ~ red surmullet (Mullus barba'tus); =barsch m, ichth. sea-perch, bass (Labrax lupus); =bataillon ↓ n battalion of marines; =beben n sea-quake; =becken n sea-basin; =behörde ↓ f: oberste ~ the (Court of or Board of) Admiralty; =beschreibung ↓ f hydrography; =brasse(n) m, ichth. sea-bream (Page'llus); =brief ↓ m sea-letter; ~e ship's papers pl.; =dampfer m, =dampfschiff n ocean (-going) steamer, für regelmäßigen Verkehr: liner; =dienst ↓ m service in the navy, naval service; =einhorn n, zo. narwhal (Mo'nodon mono'ceros); ♀fahrend ↓ a. ⑥ seafaring (people, &c.); maritime (race, &c.); =fahrer m seafarer, seafaring man, berufsmäßiger: mariner, sailor, a. Entdecker: navigator; =fahrt ↓ f: a) = =reise; b) (das Fahren zur See) seafaring, navigation; =fahrt(s)=buch n sailor's book; =fahrt(s)=schule f school of navigation, vgl. =schule a; =fahrzeug ↓ n sea-going vessel, sea-vessel; =feder f, zo. sea-feather or -pen (Penna'tula); ♀fest a.: a) = ♀tüchtig, b) von Personen: able to stand the sea; er (sie) ist (nicht) ♀ he (she) is a good (bad) sailor; c) die Geschütze ♀ machen to secure the guns; =fisch m, ichth. sea- (or salt-water) fish; =fischerei f fishing at sea; =flotte ↓ f: a) allg.: fleet; b) = Kriegsflotte; =fracht ↓ ♣ f freight (across sea); =fracht=brief ↓ ♣ m bill of lading (abbr. B/L); =freibeuter m privateer, vgl. =räuber; =gang ↓ m motion of the sea; hoher ~ rough (or stormy) sea; =gebrauch m maritime (or nautical) custom; =gefecht ↓ n naval fight or action or engagement; =geflügel n, orn. coll. sea-fowl(s pl.); =gegend f maritime country; =gemälde n marine painting; vgl. =stück; =gericht ↓ n = =behörde; =gesetz ↓ n jur. sea-law; =gesetz=buch n maritime code (of laws); =gestade n sea-beach, vgl. =küste; =gewächs n (sub)marine plant or growth; =gras n sea-grass, grass-wrack (Zoste'ra mari'na); =grün a. sea-green; =gurke ⚓ f sea-cucumber or -gherkin (Holothu'ria), eßbare: trepang; =hafen ↓ m seaport; =hahn m: a) orn. = Lumme¹; b) ichth. = =scorpion; =handel ⚓ m shipping-business, ocean- (or oversea) maritime trade; =handlung(s=gesellschaft) f zur Belebung des Außenhandels: oversea trading company; =hase m, zo.: a) ichth. lump-fish or -sucker, sea-owl (Cyclo'pterus lumpus); b) (Schnecke) sea-hare (Aply'sia); =held m naval hero; =herrschaft f naval supremacy; =hospiz n hospital for seamen; =hund m: a) zo. common seal, sea-calf (Phoca); b) fig.: (erfahrener Seemann) old sea-dog, Fold salt; =igel m. zo. sea-hedgehog or -urchin or -egg (Echi'nus); =jungfer ⚓ f mermaid; =kabel n submarine cable; =kadett ↓ m: a) ehm.

(Fähnrich zur See) midshipman; b) jetzt (seit 1899) naval cadet; =kadetten=schule f naval school; =kalb n = =hund; =kampf ↓ m = =gefecht; =karte ↓ f sea-chart, ⚓ hydrographic map; =katze f, zo. sea-monster (Chimae'ra monstro'sa); =kennung ↓ f (intelligence of soundings pl.) ⚓; =zeichen; ♀klar a. v. Schiffen: ready to put to sea; ♀kohl ⚓ m sea-cabbage, -colewort or -kale (Crambe mari'tima); =kompaß ↓ m = Bussole; =könig m, hist. sea-king, viking; =kork m, zo. (Polypengattung) ⚓ alcyonium; ♀krank a. sea-sick; =krankheit f sea-sickness; =krebs m = Hummer; =krieg m naval war (-fare); =kriegs=kunst f naval strategy; =kuh ↓ f, zo. sea-cow, auch: manatee, ...in (Mana'tus); =kunde f knowledge of the sea, naval science; =kürbis ⚓ m sea-gourd (Rhopalodi'na); =küste ↓ f seashore (a. ↓ jur.), seaboard, (maritime) coast; vgl. =gestade; =land npr/n. ♀ a) (dänische Insel); b) (holl. Provinz) Zealand; vgl. Neuseeland; =länder(in f) m Zealander; =laterne ↓ f: a) ship's lantern; b) sea-light, light-house.
Seelchen (ˊ˘) n ㉓ (dim. v. Seele) little soul; das gute ~ the good soul.
Seele (ˊ˘) f [ahd. : soul] f ⑧ 1. soul; eine arme ~ a poor soul; er ist e-e gute ~ (ein guter Mensch) he is a dear good soul or a capital fellow; treue ~ faithful soul or person; F es ist e-e ~ von Kind (s)he is a love of a child; f. Ruhe 2; Sprichw. schöne ~n finden sich kindred spirits meet; f. Herz 2. — 2. es war nicht eine ~, keine (menschliche ob. sterbliche) ~ da not a (living) soul (or creature) was there; 2000 ~n (Menschen) two thousand souls or people. — 3. mit prp.: an: f. krank 2; auf: ich binden 3; das brennt ihm auf der ~ that's preying on his mind; das liegt mir auf der (ob. fällt mir auf die) ~ that weighs on my heart or conscience; Sie sprechen mir aus der ~ you have guessed (or read) my (inmost) thoughts; das geht (schneidet, fährt) mir durch die ~ that cuts me to the quick, it grieves me intensely; et. in tiefster ~ bewahren to keep a th. as the deepest (or greatest) secret; das ist mir in der ~ zuwider I detest it from the bottom of my heart; das tat ihr in der ~ weh that made her heart bleed or ache; mit Leib und ~, mit ganzer ~ body and soul, with all one's might; vgl. Leib 2; von ganzer ~ with all one's heart, candidly. — 4. fig. (das Innerste ob. Wichtigste): a) er ist die ~ des Ganzen ... the life and soul of it all; b) e-r Feder pith of a quill; ~ (weißliches Gefäser im Bauche) e-s Herings gut of a herring; ~ einer Kanone bore of a cannon; ~ e-s Taues core of a cable. ┃faring life.)
See=leben (ˊ⁻ˊ˘) n ㉖ life at sea, sea-┘
Seelen=achse (ˊ˘...) f ㉖ eines Geschützrohrs: axis of the bore; =adel m nobility of soul or mind; =amt n, eccl. service (or office) for the dead; vgl. =messe; =angst f anguish of soul, agony of mind; =arzt m physician (or curer) of souls; =braut f christliche Mystik: bride

of Christ; (die Kirche) the Church; =bund m union of souls; =durchmesser ⚔ m, artill. bore (or caliber) of a cannon; =forscher m: ⚓ psychologist; =forschung f: ⚓ psychology; =freund m bosom-friend; =friede(n) m peace of mind; ♀froh a. ⑥ heartily glad, exceedingly pleased, quite charmed; =größe f greatness of soul; ♀gut a. thoroughly good; =güte f goodness (or kindness) of soul or heart.
seelenhaft (ˊ˘˘) a. ⑥ = seelenvoll.
Seelen=händler (ˊˊ...) m ㉖ = =verkäufer a; =heil n salvation (of a p.'s soul), spiritual welfare; =heilkunde f: ⚓ psychiatry; =hirt m, eccl. pastor, parson, a. shepherd of souls; =hoheit f = =adel; =kraft f strength of mind, mental power; =krankheit f mental disease or suffering; =kunde f = =lehre; =leben n inner (or spiritual) life; =lehre f: ⚓ psychology; =leiden n mental trouble; ♀los a. ⑥: a) soulless; b) lifeless, inanimate; =messe f, eccl. mass for the dead, requiem; =not, =pein, =qual f mental agony; vgl. =angst; =ruhe f peace (or placid state) of mind; =schmerz m = =angst; =stärke f fortitude (of mind); vgl. =kraft; =tag m, eccl. All Souls' Day; ♀vergnügt a. = ♀froh; =verkäufer m: a) kidnapper, man-stealer; (Werber) recruiting sergeant, ehm. F crimp; b) ↓ (leicht umschlagendes Fahrzeug) light and shallow boat, F cockle-shell; ♀verwandt a. congenial (in mind); =verwandtschaft f congeniality (of souls); ♀voll a. full of deep feeling, geh. Spr.: soulful, soul-breathing or -stirring, thrilling; =wand(e)rung f transmigration of souls; ⚓ metempsychosis; =wärmer F m (woollen) comforter or wrap(per); =zustand m state of the soul, spiritual condition.
seel=erfreuend (ˊˊ...) a. ⑥, ♀erquickend a. gladdening, refreshing the soul.
See=leuchte (ˊˊ...) f ㉖ = =laterne; =leute ↓ pl. seamen, mariners pl.
seelisch (ˊ˘) a. ⑥: ⚓ psychic(al).
See=löwe (ˊ⁻ˊ˘) m ㉖ zo. sea-lion (Eumeto'pias Ste'lleri).
Seel=sorge (ˊˊ...) f ㉖ rel. cure of souls, ministerial (or pastoral) office, ministry; =sorger m minister, pastor; ♀sorgerisch a. ⑥ pastoral, weit S. spiritual.
See=luft (ˊˊ...) f ㉖ sea-air; die ~ genießen to enjoy the sea-breezes; =macht f: a) naval forces pl. or strength or equipment; b) (Staat) naval power; =mann ↓ m (pl. a. =leute) seaman; vgl. =fahrer; ♀männisch a. ⑥: a) sailor-like; ♀es Dasein seafaring life, ♀es Personal ship's crew, personnel of a fleet or a navy; b) (die Schiffahrt betr.) nautical; =manns=beine n/pl. F co. sea-legs pl.; =mannschaft f ship's crew or company; =mannskunst f seamanship; =manns=leben n seaman's (or sailor's) life; =manns=schule f naval school; =manns=sprache f language used by seamen; f. Seesprache; =manöver ↓ n naval manœuvre; =marke ↓ f = =zeichen; =meile ↓ f (1855 m) nautical mile; =möwe f, orn. sea-gull

Zeichen (f. S. XVII): F familiär; P Volkssprache; Ϝ Gaunersprache; ⚡ selten; † alt (auch gestorben); * neu (auch geboren); ⚡⚡ unrichtig,

[Seemuschel] — 877 — [Sehachse]

or -mew (*Larus*); =muschel *f*, *zo.* marine shell; =nebel *m* sea-fog; =nessel *f*, *zo.* sea-nettle or -anemone (*Acti'nia*); =nymphe *f*, *myth.* sea-nymph, nereid; =offizier ↓ *m* naval officer; =ohr *n*, *zo.* sea-ear, ear-shell (*Halio'tis*); =otter *f*, *zo.* sea-otter (*E'nhydris*); engS. sea-ape (*E'nhydra mari'na*); =paß ↓ *m* für Handelsschiffe im Kriege: sea-pass; =pferd *n*: a) *myth.* sea-horse; b) *zo.* = Flußpferd und Walroß; =pferdchen *n*, *ichth.* sea-horse (*Hippoca'mpus*); =pflanze ♀ *f* sea-plant; *vgl.* =gewächs; =polyp *m*, *zo.*: ⚷ octopus; =rabe *m*, *orn.* = Kormoran; =rat ↓ *m* = =behörde; =ratte, =ratze *f* (*ant.* Landratte b) (old) mariner; =raub *m* = =räuberei; =räuber *m* sea-rover, pirate, corsair, filibuster; =räuberei *f* sea-roving, piracy; ♀räuberisch *a.* piratical; =räuber-schiff *n* pirate, corsair, privateer; =räubertum, =räuberwesen *n* piracy, filibustering; =raum *m* sea-room, offing; (hohe See) main; =recht ↓ *n* jur. sea-law, maritime law; =reise *f* (sea-)voyage; =reisende(r) *s.* passenger on board ship, geh. Spr.: voyager (across the seas); =richter ↓ *m* judge of the (Court of) Admiralty; =roman *m* sea-novel or -tale; =rose ♀ *f* allg.: water-lily (*Nymphae'a*); gelbe ~ yellow water-lily (*Nuphar lu'teum*); weiße ~ (common) white water-lily (*Nymphae'a alba*); =rüstung *f* naval preparations *pl.* or armament; =sache *f* naval affair or concern; =salz *n* sea-salt; =sand *m* sea-sand; =schaden *m* ↓ *a.* average; =schaum *m* sea-foam; =scheide *f*, *zo.* sea-squirt (*Asci'dium*); =schiff *n* sea-going vessel; =schiffahrt *f* navigation on sea; =schlacht *f* naval battle; =schlange *f* sea-serpent or -monster (*vgl.* Krake); weitS. idle tale, fictitious story; =schule *f*: a) ↓ naval school or academy; b) (engl. Dichterschule: Coleridge, Wordsworth, Southey) Lake School, auch: Lakists *pl.*; =schwalbe *f*, *orn.* sea-swallow, tern (*Sterna*); gemeine ~ common tern (*St. hiru'ndo* oder *fluvia'tilis*); =sieg *m* naval victory; =skorpion *m*, *zo.* sea-scorpion (*Cottus sco'rpius*); =soldat ↓ ⚔ *m* marine; =sprache *f* nautical language; =stadt *f* seaside town, town (lying) by the sea; =stern *m*, *zo.* star-fish, sea-star (*Aste'rias*); =strand *m* seaside, flacher (sea)beach, sandiger: sands *pl.*; =strich *m* track of the sea; =stück *n*, *paint.* sea-piece, sea-scape, marine picture; =sturm *m* (*ant.* Landsturm a) storm at sea; =tang ♀ *m*: a) sea-weed, ⚷ thalassiophyte (*Fucus*, &c.); b) bisw. = =gras; =teufel *m*, *ichth.* sea-devil, (or frog-)fish, angler (*Lo'phius piscato'rius*); =tiefen-messer ⚙ *m* sea-gauge, ⚷ thalassometer; =tier *n*, *zo.* marine animal; =tonne ↓ *f* (Bake) buoy; =treffen *n* = =gefecht; =triften ↓ *f/pl.* articles (or goods) *pl.* washed ashore; (Bradgut) flotsam and jetsam; =trompete *f*, *zo.* Muschel: conch; =truppen ↓ *f/pl.* marines *pl.*; ♀tüchtig ↓ *a.* von Schiffen: seaworthy; =tüchtigkeit *f* eines Schiffes: seaworthiness; =ufer *n*: a) sea-shore, sea-board; b) banks *pl.* (or shore) of a lake; =uhr ↓ *f* (ship's) chronometer; =ungeheuer, =ungetüm *n* sea-monster; ♀untüchtig ↓ *a.* von Schiffen: unseaworthy; =untüchtigkeit *f* unseaworthiness; =verkehr *m* ocean-traffic, maritime traffic; =versicherung ⌘ *f* marine insurance; =vogel *m* sea-bird or -fowl; =volk *n*: a) maritime nation; b) (Mannschaft) ship's crew; =warte ↓ *f*: a) naval observatory; b) = Leuchtturm; ♀wärts *adv.* seaward, ↓ ⚷ anliegen to make (or stand) for the offing; =wasser *n* sea-water, weitS. salt water; =weg *m* (*ant.* Landweg b) sea- (or maritime) route; auf dem ~e by sea; =wehr ↓ ⚔ *f* marine defence or forces *pl.*; =wesen ↓ *n* maritime (or naval) affairs *pl.*; =wind *m* sea-breeze, stärkerer: gale; =wolf *m*, *zo.* sea-wolf (*Ana'rrhichas*); =wurf *m* jettison, jetsam; =zeichen ↓ *n* sea-mark; =zunge *f*, *ichth.* sole (*Pleurone'ctesa so'lea*); gemeine ~ common sole (*So'le vulga'ris*).

Segel (↓~) [ahd.: sail] *n* ⚷ 1. ↓ sail (*fig.* a. für Schiff, mit *pl. inv.*, zB. eine Flotte von 30 ~n a fleet of thirty sail); s. ausspannen 1, beisetzen 3, einziehen 2; mit vollen ~n fahren to carry a (full) press of sail, to crowd all sail; unter ~ gehen to set sail; die ~ streichen to strike sail, *fig.* (nachgeben) to give in, F to come (or climb) down; unter ~ under canvas; unter vollen ~n under full pressure of sail or canvas. — 2. ⊕ (Bekleidung der Windmühlenflügel) sail. — 3. ⚷ (Seitenblättchen einer Schmetterlingsblüte) wing, ⚷ ala.

Segel-anweisungen ↓ (~~...) *f/pl.* ⚷ sailing-directions *pl.*; =baum *m* mast; =boot *n* sailing boat; ♀fertig, ♀klar *a.* ⚷ ready to sail; sich ♀ machen to get under sail; =garn *n* sail-twine; ♀los *a.* sailless, under bare poles; =macher ⊕ *m* sail-maker; =macherei, =macherkunst *f* sail-making; =macher-werkstatt *f* sail-loft; =manufaktur *f* = =macherei; =meister *m*, etwa: master mariner.

segeln, meist ↓ (~~) [mhd.; *Segel] I *v/n.* (h. u. sn), *v/a.* u. *v/refl.* ⚷a. 1. to sail; to make sail for; zehn Knoten in der Stunde ♀ to sail (or make) ten knots an hour; mit *prp.*: am (oder beim) Winde ♀ to sail close-hauled or close to the wind; auf et. los ♀ to head (or make, stand) for a th.; gegen (oder gerade in) den Wind ♀ to sail in the wind's eye; längs der Küste ♀ to sail along (or to hug) the coast; um ein Vorgebirge ♀ to (sail) round (or to double) a cape; vor dem Winde ♀ to sail right before the wind. — 2. mit Angabe der Wirkung: ein Schiff in den Grund ♀ to run down ..., to sink ...; ein Schiff tot ♀ to outstrip (or beat) ... in sailing; sich fest ♀ to run aground. — 3. *fig.* durch die Lüfte ♀ (fliegen) to sail (or float) through the air. — II ~ *n* ⚷ 4. ↓ sailing; weitS. navigation; ~ in einem größten Kreise great-circle sailing.

Segel-order ↓ ⚔ *f* (~~...) *f* ⚷ sailing-orders *pl.*; =ordnung *f* order of sailing; =presenning *f* sail-cover; =schiff *n* sailing vessel or boat; =schiffahrt *f* navigation by sail; =schlitten *m* sleigh carrying sails; =sport *m* sailing-sport; =stange *f* yard; =stellung *f* position of the sails; =tau *n* cable; =tuch *n* ⓓd. sail-cloth, canvas; ♀tüchtig *a.* ⚷ having good sailing qualities; =werk *n*, *coll.* sails *pl.*; =wett-fahrt *f* sailing-match, regatta; =wind *m* (fair or good) wind for sailing, stiff breeze.

Segen (↓~) [ahd.; *It. signum n* (Kreuzes-)Zeichen] *m* ⚷ 1. (*ant.* Fluch) blessing (*bsd. eccl.*), a. benediction; e-m seinen ~ geben, erteilen to give a p. one's blessing, to pronounce one's bl. upon a p.; Gott gebe s-n ~ dazu! God's bl. upon it!, (may the Lord bless it! — 2. *fig.* (Gedeihen) prosperity; (Wonne) bliss; (Ertrag) yield, proceeds *pl.*; der ~ des Ackerbaus, Bergbaus &c. the (rich) produce of agriculture, mining, &c.; das wird ihm keinen ~ bringen that will bring him no luck; dabei ist kein ~ — there is no luck attending it, it's a (dead) failure; Sprichw. s. Gott 4; — 3. den ~ (das Kreuzeszeichen) m. to make the sign of the cross. — 4. ~ (Gebet) vor (nach) Tische grace; den ~ sprechen to say grace. — 5. (Zauberformel) spell.

segen-bringend (↓~...) *a.* ⚷ attended with a blessing, bringing luck, beneficial; =erteilung *f* ⚷ eccl. benediction.

Segens-formel (↓~~.↓~) *f* ⚷ eccl. formula of a benediction or blessing or spell.

segen-spendend (↓~...) *a.* ⚷ (giving one's) blessing; *fig.* fertile, abundant; =sprecher *m* ⚷ = Segner; =spruch *m* s. Segensspruch.

segens-reich (↓~...) *a.* ⚷ full of blessing, blessed, prosperous, lucky; =spruch, =wunsch *m* ⚷ (words of) blessing, kind(est) wishes *pl.* [grass (*Carex*)

Segge ♀ (↓~) [ndd. = sedge] *f* ⚷ sedge-]

Segler (↓~) [segeln] *m* ⚷ 1. ↓: a) von Personen: sailor, navigator; b) von Schiffen: guter (schlechter) ~ good or fast (bad or slow) sailer or sailing vessel. — 2. *fig.* eilende Wolken!, ~ der Lüfte! (SCH.) speeding clouds!, aerial travellers!

Segment ⚷ (~~) [lt.] *n* ⓒc. *geom.* = Kreisabschnitt.

segnen (↓~) [ahd.; *Segen] I *v/a.* u. *sich* ♀ *v/refl.* ⚷b. 1. to bless. — 2. (mit dem Kreuze bezeichnen) to cross; das Kind vor der Stirne ♀ to make the sign of the cross on the child's fore-head; s. kreuzen 1. — 3. (zaubernd beschwören) to conjure with magic words. — 4. *fig.* (verlassen) das Zeitliche ♀ to depart this life, to die. — II ~ *n* ⚷ 5. f. Segnung. — III ge-segnet *p.p.* und *a.* ⚷ 6. in den Bed. des *inf.*, zB. gesegneten Angedenkens of blessed memory; s. Mahlzeit; mit irdischen Gütern gesegnet blessed (or blest) with earthly goods or the (good) things of this life. — 7. verhüllend = schwanger, zB. gesegneten Leibes, in gesegneten Umständen in the family-way, feiner: in interesting circumstances, (fr.) enceinte. [pronounces a blessing.]

Segner (↓~) *m* ⚷ person that blesses or]

Segnung (↓~) *f* ⚷ blessing, benediction.

Seh-achse (↓~.~~) [seh-en] *f* ⚷: ⚷ axis of vision, visual axis.

[sehbar]

sehbar (⌣-) *a.* ⑥ visible, within sight; to be seen; (wahrnehmbar) perceptible.
Sehbarkeit (⌣⌣-) *f* ④ visibleness.
Sehe (⌣) [ahd.] *f* ④ a) = Sehkraft; b) *hunt.* Augen des Hasen hare's eye.
sehen (⌣) [ahd.: see (saw)] ⑧a. **I** *v/n.* (h.) **1.** to see, to be endowed (or gifted) with sight; ich kann nicht mehr ⌣ I can see no longer; gut (schlecht) ⌣ to have good (weak) eyes or a good (a bad) sight: klar, scharf ⌣ to be clear- (or keen-)sighted; et. klar, deutlich ⌣ to see a th. clearly, distinctly. — **2.** a) eingeschaltet: er ist, sehe ich (oder wie ich sehe), nicht hier I see he is not there; b) *imper.*, fast als *int.*, z.B. siehe, da erhob sich ein Sturm behold (or lo), there arose a storm; (ei,) ⌣ Sie mal! look here!, (come and) see!, only look!; ei sieh doch, Sie sind's! well, I declare, it's you; c) verweisend: sieh(e) oben (unten), meist *abbr.* **s. o., s. u.** see above (below); d) F hast du nicht gesehen (im Nu) helter-skelter, in a twinkle, F in a jiffy, F like a shot. — **3.** mit *prp.* (oft *fig.*): **auf** et. ⌣ to look at a th.; aller Augen ⌣ auf ihn all eyes are upon him; einem (scharf) auf die Finger ⌣ to watch a p. (narrowly); auf den Preis ⌣ sie nicht the price is no object (or no consideration) to them; nur auf s-n Vorteil ⌣ to study one's own advantage or F pocket; darauf ⌣, daß // to mind (or take care) that //; nicht **aus** den Augen ⌣ können to be unable to open one's eyes; ihm sieht der Schelm aus den Augen he has a roguish look about him; aus dem Fenster ⌣ to look out of the window; daraus (er)sehe ich, daß // (w)hence it appears to me that //; **durch** die Brille ⌣ to look through one's glasses; s. Brett 9, Brille, Finger ⌣ gegen Ende; **ins** Licht 2c. ⌣ to look into the light, &c.; e-m ins Gesicht ⌣ to look into a p.'s face, stierend: to look a p. (hard) in the face; e-m ins Herz ⌣ to read (in) a p.'s heart; s. Karte 1; ich habe im Tacitus gesehen (gelesen), daß // I noticed in Tacitus that //; weit in die Zukunft ⌣ to see (or dive) into the future, to look far ahead; **nach** et. ⌣ to look (or search) for a th.; (für et. sorgen) to look after a th.; er sieht nach nichts he does not attend to anything; nach dem (od. **zum**) Rechten ⌣ to see that everything is put right; das Fenster sieht nach dem Garten .. overlooks (or looks down upon) the garden; nach der Uhr ⌣ to look at one's watch or at the clock; ↘ **zu** et. ⌣ (achthaben auf) to see to a th. — **4.** meist von Dingen: = heraus-, hervor-sehen, z.B. die Zehen ⌣ ihm aus den Schuhen his toes are (F peep) out of his boots. — **5.** = aussehen, z.B. e-m ähnlich ⌣ to resemble a p., s. ähnlich; F ernst (drein) ⌣ to look serious. — **II** *v/a.* und *v/refl.* **6.** to see, to behold; (wahrnehmen) to perceive, notice, observe; (betrachten) to look at; (erkennen) to recognize; et. nur halb, flüchtig oder undeutlich ⌣ to get only a glimpse of a th.; man sah nichts, man konnte nicht die Hand vor (den) Augen ⌣ (it was so dark that) one could not see anything, one could not see one's hand before one's face; sie will es nicht ⌣ she pretends not to see it, (drückt ein Auge zu) she shuts her eyes upon it. — **7.** zu ⌣ sein to be visible, to show o.s.; es ist dort nichts zu ⌣ there is nothing to be seen (or worth seeing) there; für Geld zu ⌣ sein to be on show or on exhibition. — **8.** von persönlichen Beziehungen: (viel) Gesellschaft bei ⌣ to receive (a great deal of) company; gern bei einem gesehen sein to be welcome (or a welcome visitor) at a p.'s house; man will ihn nirgends ⌣ no one wants to see him, every door is shut against him; ich habe ihn schon seit Jahren nicht mehr gesehen I have not seen (or met) him for years; wir hören und ⌣ nichts mehr von ihm now we neither hear nor see anything of him. — **9.** ⌣ **lassen** (zeigen) to show, to display, (zur Schau stellen) to exhibit; sich ⌣ lassen to show o.s., to appear (in public); (sich einführen) to present o.s.; Sie lassen sich ja nicht mehr ⌣ one never sees you now; sie lassen sich vor niemand ⌣ they won't be seen by (or appear before) anybody; er hat sich nicht wieder ⌣ lassen he has never shown his face again; er kann sich damit ⌣ lassen he need not be ashamed of it, it's most presentable. — **10.** *fig.* das Licht der Sonne ⌣ (noch leben) to be in the land of the living; du wirst dein blaues Wunder ⌣ you will see wonders yet; s. a. blau 2 gegen Ende; alles im rosigsten Lichte ⌣ to see everything in a rosy (or the most favourable) light; s. Baum 2. — **11.** mit abhängigem Satze: a) ich sehe, daß er recht hat I see (that) he is right; F siehst du, wie du bist! that's the man you are!; siehst du, wie er sich quält? do you notice (or observe) how hard he works or struggles?; ich möchte doch ⌣, was Sie an m-r Stelle täten? I should like to see you in my place or position; b) (sich Mühe geben) ich will ⌣, daß (wie oder ob) ich es dir verschaffe oder es dir zu verschaffen I will try to get it for you, F I will see if I can manage it for you; ⌣ Sie, daß er nicht entschlüpft see (or take care) that he does not slip away. — **12.** mit *inf.*: die Sonne aufgehen ⌣ to see ... rise; ich sah es auf der Erde liegen I saw it lying on the ground; im *p.p.* meist sehen, statt gesehen: ich habe es kommen ⌣ I have seen it coming; doppeldeutig: ich habe sie photographieren ⌣: a) die Photographen: I have seen them photograph(ing); b) die Photographierten: I saw them (being) photographed or taken. — **13.** mit Angabe der Wirkung: sich nach et. (fast) blind ⌣ to stare (almost) one's eyes out after a th.; sich (*dat.*) die Augen aus dem Kopfe ⌣ to blind o.s. with gazing or staring. — **14.** sich als Herrn ⌣ to find o.s. master. — **III** ~ *n* ㉓ **15.** seeing, (eye-)sight, *phys.* vision; das ~ mit beiden Augen binocular vision; das ~ hat man umsonst seeing costs nothing; ihm verging Hören und ~ he lost all consciousness. — **IV** ⌒d *p.pr.* u. *a.* ⑥ **16.** seeing; die Blinden ⌒d m. to make the blind see, to restore the sight (*bibl.* to open the eyes) of the blind; wieder ⌒d w. to recover one's sight; *fig.* mit ⌒den Augen blind sn to walk about with one's eyes shut, to make no use of one's eyes.
sehens-wert (⌣⌣-...) *a.* ⑥, ⌒würdig *a.* worth seeing or inspecting, remarkable, curious; =**würdigkeit** ⑥ remarkableness; ~en *pl.* objects of interest, e-r Stadt: sights (or F lions *pl.*) of a town; ~en aufsuchen to go sight-seeing.
Seher (⌣) *m* ㉒, ~**in** *f* ④ **1.** one who sees; *poet.* (Sternseher) astronomer, F stargazer. — **2.** (Prophet[in]) seer, prophet (-ess *f*); (Hellseher[in]) clairvoyant(e).
Seher-blick (⌣⌣-...) *m* ㉒, ⌒**gabe** *f* prophetic eye or gift, *auch*: second sight.
Seh-feld (⌣-...) *n* ㉒ field (or range of) vision; =**kraft** *f* visual power or faculty, sight; =**kunde**, =**kunst**, =**lehre** *f* optics; =**linie** *f*, *ast.*: ⚡ line of collimation; =**linse** *f* = Kristallinse.
Sehne (⌣) [ahd.: sinew] *f* ④ **1.** *anat.* sinew, tendon. — **2.** (Strang, bsd. zum Bogenspannen) string of a bow; mit ~n beziehen to string. — **3.** *math.* (die Endpunkte e-s Bogens verbindende Gerade) chord.
sehnen[1] (⌣) [mhd.] **I** *v/refl.* ⑧: sich nach et. ⌣ to long (or yearn) for a th.; ich sehne mich danach (a. *v.imp.* es sehnt mich) ihn zu sehen I long (or burn) to see him; sich schmerzlich nach e-m, et. ⌣ to grieve (or hanker, pine) after a p., a th.; sich nach der Heimat ⌣ to long for one's native home. — **II** ~ *n* ㉓ longing, yearning, ardent (or keen) desire; grieving after s. th.
Sehnen[2]-**band** (⌣⌣-...) [Sehne] *n* ㉒ *anat.*: ⚡ tendinous ligament; =**vier-eck** *n*, *geom.*: ⚡ quadrilateral (figure) inscribed in a circle or formed by chords (of a circle).
Seh-nerv (⌣-...⌣) *m* ㉒ *anat.* optic nerve.
sehnicht⬩, mst **sehnig** (⌣) *a.* ⑥ **1.** sinewy, sinewed; ⌒es Fleisch, *a.* stringy (or tough) meat. — **2.** (kräftig) muscular or strong (arm, &c.), wiry (person).
sehnlich (⌣) [mhd.; *sehnen] *a.* ⑥ (full of) longing; *adv.* ⌒(st) erwarten to await (most) anxiously.
Sehn-sucht (⌣-...) [sehnen] *f* ㉒ (great) longing or yearning, ardent (or burning) desire; mit ~ erwarten to long (or yearn) for; ⌒**süchtig**, ⌒**suchtsvoll** *a.* ⑥ longing, yearning; ⌒**süchtig** nach et. hankering after (F dying for) a th.
Seh-organ (⌣-...⌣) *n* ㉒ = =werkzeug.
sehr (⌣) [ahd.: sore "empfindlich"] *adv.* **1.** vor *a.* u. *adv.* very, vor mehrsilbigen *a.* u. *adv.* auch: most (delightful(ly), &c.); vgl. hoch 6; s. bald 1; ⌣ viel very much (money, &c.), mehr gbr.: a great (or a good) deal (of trouble, &c.), plenty (of wine, &c.); ⌣ viele a great many. — **2.** mit *verbs*: much, greatly, largely, highly; ebenso ⌣ just as much; so ⌣, daß // so much (or to such a degree) that //; wie ⌣ auch immer however much; wie ⌣ auch zu bleiben wünsche much as I should like to stay.

[sehr]

Signs (see page XVII): F familiar; P vulgar; Γ flash; ↘ rare; † obsolete (died); * new word (born); ‡ incorrect; ♪ music;

[Seh=rohr] — 879 — [Seiltänzer]

Seh=rohr (⁀...) n ⊕ telescope; =strahl m, phys. visual ray; =vermögen n = =kraft; =weite f range of sight, ⚙ visual distance; außer ~ out of sight; =weite= messer m: ⚙ optometer; =werkzeug n organ of sight or vision; eye, F optic; =winkel m visual angle, angle of sight.
sei! (⌣́) imper. u. (ich, er ⚥) subj. v. sein.
Seiber (⌣́), ⚒n = Geifer, geifern.
Seiche P (⌣́) [ahd.] f ⊕ ⚓ ⅏. = Harn ⚓.
seicht (⌣́) [mhd.: sinken] a. ⊕ 1. von Wasser: shallow, low; (durchwatbar) fordable. — 2. fig. shallow (mind, head, &c.), superficial (character, &c.); (fade) insipid (vgl. schal); Se Redens= arten platitudes pl., Ser Mensch, bisw.: platitudinarian, ~heit (⌣́-), ~igkeit (⌣́⌣) f ⊕ (s. seicht) shallowness, geistige, auch: superficiality, insipidity.
seid (⌣́) 2. Person pl. pres. ind. und imper. von sein.
Seide (⌣́) [ahd.; * lt. seta (se'rica)] f ⊕ 1. silk; rohe, ungekochte ob. ungeschälte ~ raw silk; vgl. Sam(me)t; fig. dabei wird er keine ~ spinnen (keinen Vorteil h.) he will not gain (or make) much by that, F it won't do him much good. — 2. ⚘ = Flachsseide.
Seidel¹ (⌣́) [mhd.; * lt. si'tula f] n (bisw. a. m) ⚒ Mah, bsd. für Bier) pint; (Trinkgefäß) pint-mug or -glass.
Seidel²=bast ⚘ (⌣́⌣...) m [mhd. (P ⁀: Seide); *Zeidel Biene) = Kellerhals b; =¹deckel m lid of a (pint-)mug.
seiden (⌣́) a. ⊕ (D9) 1. (von Seide) silk (gown, &c.). — 2. (wie Seide) silken (hair, &c.), a. = seiden=artig, ⚒haarig, ⚒weich.
Seiden=affe (⌣́⌣...) m ⊕, =äffchen n, zo. marmoset (Ha'pale); =arbeit f ⊕ silk= work; ⚒artig a. ⊕ silk-like, silky, ⚙ sericeous; =bau m silk-culture, breed= ing (of) silk-worms, ⚙ seri(ci)culture; =bauer m = =baumwolle ⚘ f silk-cotton; =damast ⊕ m silk-damask; =druck(erei f) m silk-printing (works pl.); =ernte f crop of silk, yield of cocoons; =fabrik ⚙ f silk-mill or -(manu)factory; =fabrikant m silk-manufacturer; =faden m silk (thread); =färber(ei f) m silk-dyer(-dyeing); =garn ⚘ n spun silk, silk yarn; =ge= häuse, =gespinst n cocoon (of a silk-worm); =gewebe n silk tissue; =glanz m silky gloss or lustre; =haar n silken (or silk-like) hair; ⚒haarig a. with silken hair, ⚙ sericated.
seidenhaft (⌣́⌣⌣) = seiden 2.
Seiden=handel ⊕ (⌣́⌣...) m ⊕ silk-trade or -mercery; =händler(in f) m silk-merchant or -mercer or -dealer; =handlung f silk-merchant's business; firm of silk-dealers; =hase m, zo. Angora rabbit (Lepus cuni'culus ango're'nsis); =haspel ⚙ f silk-reel or -winder; =haspler(in f) m s.-reeler; =hut m silk hat; =industrie ⚙ f silk-industry; =kultur f = =bau; =laden ⚘ m shop for silk goods; =leim m, chm.: ⚙ se-ricin; =maler m silk-painter; =manu= faktur f = =fabrik, =mühle ⚘ f s.-mill; =papier ⚘ n silk- (or tissue-) paper; =pflanze ⚘ f silkweed (Ascle-pias Syri'aca); =plüsch ⊕ m silk-shag; =raupe, ent. (Raupe des Seidenspinners)

silkworm; ⚒reich a. ⊕ silky; =sam(me)t ⊕ m silk-velvet; =schmetterling m = =spinner a; =schwanz m, orn. waxwing, chatterer (A'mpelis ga'rrula); =spinner m: a) ent. silk-moth (Bombyx mori); b) ⊕ silk-spinner or -thrower; =spin= nerei f silk-spinning mill; vgl. fabrik; =spitz m (⚒hund): lap-dog with long silky hair; =spitzen ⊕ f/pl. blond(e) lace; =sticker(in f) m silk-embroiderer; =stickerei f silk-embroidery; =stoffe ⊕ m/pl. silks pl.; vgl. =zeug; =strähne f silk-skein; =tüll ⊕ m silk net; =ware ⊕ f silk goods pl. or ware, silks pl.; =waren=geschäft n, =waren= handlung f = Seidenhandlung; =weber ⊕ m silk-weaver; =weberei f silk-weaver's trade; ⚒weich a. (as) soft as silk, silky; =wickler ⊕ m silk-reeler; =winde f = =haspel; =wirker(ei f) m = weber(ei); =wurm m = =raupe; =zeug n silk (cloth or material); vgl. =ware; =zucht f = =bau; =züchter m silkworm-breeder or -grower, ⚙ seri(ci)culturist; =züchterei f silk-nursery; auch = Seidenbau.
seidig (⌣́⌣) a. ⊕ = seiden 2.
Seif=... (⌣́...) in ⚒ssgn s. Seifen=...
Seife (⌣́) [ahd.: soap] f ⊕ 1. soap; weiche (oder grüne) ~ soft (or green) soap; wohlriechende ~ scented soap; ~ kochen ob. sieden to boil (or make) soap; Stück ~ cake of soap. — 2. ⚒ (Erz= wäsche) stream-works pl., dressing-floor; (Sumpfstand) marshy country.
seifen (⌣́) v/a. ⊕ 1. to (rub with) soap. — 2. ⚒ to stream, to dress.
Seifen=abfall (⌣́⌣...) m ⊕ waste of soap; ⚒artig a. ⊕ soapy, ⚙ saponaceous; =asche f soap-ashes pl.; =bad n soap-bath; =balsam m = Opodeldoc; =baum ⚘ m soap-tree (Sapi'ndus sapona'ria); =beere f (Frucht des =baumes) soapberry; =bereitung f soap-making or -boiling; =bildung f, chm.: ⚙ saponification; =blase f s.-bubble; =brühe f s.-suds pl.; =fabrik f s.-works pl.; =form f s.-frame; ⚒haltig a. soapy, rich in soap, sapon= aceous; =handel m soap-trade; =kessel m s.-pan; =kraut ⚘ n soapwort (Sapo-na'ria); =kugel f ball of soap; =lauge f s.-suds pl., soapy liquor; =leim m s.-paste; =masse f mass of soap, soapy mass; =mühle f zum Mahlen trockener Seife: soap-mill; =napf m s.-dish; =pflaster n, pharm. s.-plaster; =probe f s.-test; =pulver n s.-powder; =quetschmaschine ⊕ f soap-crushing machine; =schaum m lather; =sieder m: a) s.-boiler or -maker; b) das denkt wie ein ~ (sch.), they're of a low (or vulgar) way of thinking; F jetzt geht mir ein ~ auf now it dawns upon me, I begin to see clearly; =siederei f: a) soap-boiling; b) (Gebäude) s.-works pl. or house; =sieder=lauge f s.-boiler's lye; =spiritus m, pharm. spirit of soap; =stein m, min. soapstone, saponite; =stoff m, chm. saponin ($C_{32}H_{54}O_{18}$); =wasser (a. Seif=wasser) n soap-suds pl., soapy water; =werk n zum Waschen von Zinnerz: stream-works pl.; =zäpfchen n, med. gegen Verstopfung: suppository; =zinn ⚒ n stream-tin.

seificht, mst seifig (⌣́⌣) a. ⊕ soapy, soap-like, ⚙ saponaceous. [dresser.]
Seifner ⚒ (⌣́⌣) m ⚒ (Erzwischer) ore-
seigen (⌣́) v/a. ⊕ = seihen.
seiger¹ ⚒ (⌣́⌣) a. ⊕ (D9) (senkrecht) perpendicular, vertical.
Seiger² (⌣́⌣) [mhd.] m ⊕ 1. = Perpen= difel 2. — 2. (Sanduhr) hour-glass.
Seiger³=abtreiber ⊕ (⌣́⌣...) [seigern¹] m ⊕, =arbeiter m refiner; ⚒¹gerade ⚒ a. ⊕ u. adv. perpendicular; =³herd ⊕ m refining-hearth, cupelling-furnace; =hütte f refining-shed or -house.
seigern¹ (⌣́⌣) [seigen] ⚒a. I v/a. 1. = seihen; sickern. — 2. ⊕ metall. (aus= schmelzen) to separate silver, &c. from copper, &c. by smelting or liquation, to liquate copper, to refine metals. — II ~ n ⚒ 3. s. Seigerung.
seigern² ⚒ (⌣́⌣) [seiger¹] v/a. ⚒a. to sink a shaft perpendicularly or by the plumb.
Seiger³=ofen (⌣́⌣...) m ⊕ metall. liqua-tion-hearth or -furnace; ⚒¹recht a. u. adv. = ⚒gerade; =³schlacke f, metall. slag of liquation; =⁴teufe f ⚒ e-s Schachtes: perpendicular (or vertical) depth.
Seigerung ⊕ (⌣́⌣⌣) f ⊕ metall. (s. seigern¹ 2) liquation; refining(-process).
Seignette=salz (sën-jö't(⌣-ȳ) n ⊕ pharm. (weinsaures Kalinatron) Rochelle salt.
Seihe (⌣́) [ahd.] f ⊕ 1. strainer, colander; (Filter) filter. — 2. (Rückstand) residue.
Seih(e)=boden (⌣́⌣...) m ⊕ perforated bottom; =gefäß n, =kasten m strainer, filtering-vessel; =korb ⊕ m Zuckerfabr.: straining-basket.
seihen (⌣́) [ahd.] v/a. ⊕ to strain, to filter; fig. Mücken ⚒ s. Kamel 1.
Seiher (⌣́) m ⊕ = Seihe 1.
Seih(e)=sack (⌣́(⌣)...) m ⊕ straining- (or filtering-)bag; =stein m filtering-stone; =trichter m filtering-funnel; =tuch n cloth for straining or filter-ing, strainer.
Seil (⌣́) [ahd.] n ⊕ c. 1. rope, dünneres: line (auch ⚓); (Tau) cable; schlaffes (straffes) ~ für Seiltänzer ⚓. slack (tight) rope (vgl. Strick). — 2. fig. sich am ⚒e führen l. to allow o.s.) to be led by the nose; an einem ⚒e (Strange) ziehen to pull the same way, to pull (well) together, to work (well) together.
Seil=bahn ⊕ (⌣́⌣...) f ⚙ = Drahtseil-bahn; =bohren ⚒ n rope-boring; =brücke f rope-bridge. [ropes.]
seilen (⌣́) v/a. ⊕ to provide with
Seiler ⊕ (⌣́⌣) m ⊕ rope- (or cord-) maker, rope-spinner.
Seiler=arbeit ⊕ (⌣́⌣...) f ⊕ rope-maker's work; =bahn f rope-walk or -yard.
Seilerei ⊕ (⌣⌣⌣́) f ⊕ rope-making, rope-spinning.
Seiler=handwerk ⊕ (⌣́⌣...) n ⊕ rope-maker's trade; =maschine f r.-machine; =meister m master r.-maker; =rad n r.-maker's wheel or reel; =spule f spindle; =waren f/pl. ropes pl., cordage.
Seil=macher ⊕ (⌣́...) m ⊕ = Seiler; =maschine, =pumpe ⊕ f rope-pump; =rolle f, mach. r.-roll; =springen n skipping (the rope), auch: skip(ping)-rope; ⚒tanzen v/n. (h.) ⊕** to walk (on) the tight rope; =tänzer(in f) m rope-

⚙ scientific; ⚘ botanical; ⚱ geography; ⊕ machinery; ⚒ mining; ⚔ military; ⚓ marine; ⊕ commercial; ⚐ postal; ⚒ railway.

[Seiltänzerei] — 880 — [Seite]

dancer, ↘ funambulist; =tänzerei f rope-dancing; ≗tänzerisch a. ⑥⑨ of a r.-dancer, ↘ funambulatory; =tänzer- kunst f = =tänzerei; =tänzer=stange f r.-dancer's pole or balance; =werk n ropes pl., cordage, ↓ a. rigging; =ziehen n Spiel: rope-pulling, tug of war.

Seim (⌐) [ahd.] m ⓜ c. 1. = Honigseim. — 2. (dicker Saft) thick (or glutinous, mucilaginous, viscous) juice.

seimen (⌐⌣) v/n. (h.) ⑱ 1. to strain honey. — 2. to yield a glutinous juice.

seimicht, mit seimig (⌐⌣) a. ⑥⑨ honey-like; (dickflüssig) glutinous, ⌀ mucilaginous.

sein¹ (⌐) [ahd.] I v/n. (in) ⓜa. 1. als Kopula das Subjekt u. Prädikat bindend: to be: a) er ist ehrlich he is honest; sie war 20 Jahre alt she was twenty years old; sie ist ihm von Herzen gut she is very fond of him; sei(d) nicht so ängstlich don't be so timid; s. es 4; b) mit gen.: s. Amt 1 am Ende; ich bin der Ansicht, daß // it is my opinion that //; vgl. Ansicht 2; er ist ganz des Teufels he is quite savage, F he has the very devil in him; Sie sind des Todes, wenn // you are lost (or a dead man) if //; ich bin willens I am willing, it is my intention; wessen ist das Pfand? whose pledge is it?; c) mit „zu" und inf.: sie ist zu beklagen she is to be pitied; er ist nicht zu sprechen he cannot be seen, he is engaged; das Haus ist seit lange(m) zu vermieten the house has been to let for a long time. — 2. als Hilfszeitwort bei vielen v/n.: to have; ich bin ihm begegnet I have met him; es sind viele Fremde angekommen ... have arrived. — 3. in gekürzter Rede mit einer prp. des Ortes zur Bezeichnung einer Bewegung: ist nach Paris (gegangen, gefahren ic.) he has gone to ... — 4. es ist: a) vor a. u. s.: s. es 6; b) vor „zu" u. inf.: es ist zu erwarten, daß // it is to be expected that //; dagegen ist nichts zu sagen there is nothing to be said against it; c) Zeitbestimmung: es ist ein Jahr (her), daß (ob. seit) er abgereist ist it is now a twelvemonth since he left; d) hier ist (es) teuer leben it is expensive living here; wie weit ist es von hier nach Köln? how far (or what distance) is it ...?; bibl. hier ist gut 2 it is good for us to be here (Mart. 9, 5). — 5. (bestehen) to exist, (vorhanden sein) to be there; (leben) to live, to be alive; Sein oder Nichtsein, das ist die Frage to be or not to be, that is the question (SH., Hamlet III, 1). — 6. arith. 5 und 2 sind (machen) sieben five and two are (or is) seven. — 7. es sei!, es mag 2! be it (so)!, let it be so!, granted it (to) be so!; math. es sei x die Unbekannte let x be the unknown; sei es auch noch so wenig! be it ever so little!; dem sei nun, wie ihm wolle be that as it may; sei es im Guten, sei es im Bösen be for good or for evil, for better or (for) worse; es sei denn, daß // except if //, unless //; sei es nun, daß //, oder daß // whether //, or //. — 8. (sich befinden) in Rom 2 to be at Rome; hier ist er! here (there) he is!; bei Kasse 2 to be in funds; was ist Ihnen? what is the matter with you?; wie ist Ihnen? how are you?, how do you feel?; mir ist (wieder) besser I am better (again); ich weiß nicht, wie mir ist I feel I don't know how, I cannot describe what I feel; es ist mir so, als ob ich es schon gehört hätte I imagine (or fancy) I have heard that before. — 9. (stattfinden) to happen, to take place; die Schlacht war am // the battle was fought on the //. — 10. ell. F ist nicht! nothing of the kind!, not at all! — 11. mit „da": s. da¹, bsd. 2, 3, 6. — 12. (sich verhalten) es ist damit wie mit allem it is with that as with all things; gerade so ist es mit mir I am in exactly the same position; wie ist's? how do matters stand?; wäre das nicht so gewesen if that (or such) had not been the case. — 13. (bedeuten) was soll das 2? what does that mean?; ei, das wäre (noch schöner)! well, I never!; ich dachte wunder, was es wäre I thought it (was) something wonderful, I expected (to see) something marvellous. — 14. et. 2 (ungeschehen) lassen to leave (or let) a th. alone. — II ~ n 23 15. being; (Dasein) existence, (Wesenheit) substance, essence, true (or inward) nature; phls. entity.

sein² (⌐) [ahd.: lt. su-us] I ⑥⑥ A 1. gen. v. er 1. †, noch poet. = seiner²; erinnere dich 2 remember him. — 2. (ihm (an)gehörig) die Häuser sind 2 the houses are his; die Kuh ist 2 the cow is his. — II [sein² I]a.u. possessive pron. m sein, f seine, n sein ⑥⑥ C. (poet. oft inv.) 3. his, von (kleinen) Tieren, Dingen ic.: its; mein(e) und 2(e) Freund(in) my friend and his; der Vogel und 2 Nest the bird and its nest; e-r 2er Kunden one of his customers, a customer of his; 2e vielen Jünger his many (or his numerous) disciples; (all) 2 bißchen Geld what little money he has. — 4. von Ländern, Schiffen ic., oft: her; Spanien hat 2e großen Kolonien verloren Spain has lost her large colonies; das Schiff und 2e Mannschaft ... her crew. — 5. mit dem inf.: one's; 2 Glück machen to make one's fortune. — 6. alles zu 2er Zeit everything in due (or at its appointed) time; vgl. seinerzeit. — 7. ~e(r) Königliche(n) Hoheit (of, to) His Royal Highness; ~e(r) Majestät (of, to) His Majesty; ↓ ~er Majestät Schiff (abbr. S. M. S.) His Majesty's Ship (H. M. S.). — III 8.: a) 2er, 2e, 2es ⑥⑥ A 2; b) mit dem bestimmten art. der (die, das) ~e (oder ~ige) ⑥⑥ his (own); er und die ~(ige)n he and his family or people, auch: he and his; (gebt) jedem das ~(ig)e give every one his due; das ~e (seine Habe) retten to save one's belongings or property; das ~ige tun to do one's best or utmost or duty.

seiner¹ (⌐⌣) m s. sein² 8a.

seiner² (⌐⌣) ⑥⑥ A 1 gen. von er (vgl. sein² I): of him; bisw. auch von man: 2 (selbst) nicht mehr mächtig sein to lose (or to have lost) all control over o.s.

seiner=seits (⌐⌣⌐) adv. on his part. with regard to him; er 2=seits he for one; 2=zeit in his (or its) time (vgl. sein² 6).

seines¹ (⌐⌣) n s. sein² 8a.

seines²=gleichen (⌐⌣⌐⌣,⌐⌣⌐)[seines gen.] pron. inv. his equals pl., people like him. the like(s) of him; e-n wie 2 behandeln to treat a p. as one's equal or on an equality with o.s.; er hat nicht 2 he has not his equal. there is no one like (or to match) him.

seinet=halben, 2=wegen (⌐⌣...) a. ⑥⑨ for his sake, on his account; um 2=willen on (or in) his behalf.

Seinige (⌐⌣⌣) s. sein² 8 b.

Seising ↓ (⌐⌣) [fr. saisir] f ⑱ Art Tau: seizing, nipper, gasket.

seismisch ⌀ (⌐⌣) [grch.] a. ⑥⑨ (auf Erdbeben bezüglich) seismic. [mograph.↓ Seismograph ⌀ (⌐⌣⌐) [grch.] m ⑫ seis-

seit¹ (⌐) [ahd.] I prp. mit dat. (ant. bis) since; 2 damals (ever) since then; er ist seit zehn Jahren im Auslande he has been abroad these last ten years; s. Jahr 3 unter seit; 2 kurzem for a short time, latterly (vgl. kurz 3); 2 lange for a long time (past), (now) for some time; 2 wie lange ist er (schon) fort? how long has he been gone? 2 Menschengedenken s. des u. gedenken II; 2 einigen Tagen for some few days (past), these last few days. — II cj. (bisw. 2 daß) since; 2 er abgereist ist (ever) since he left.

seit²=ab (⌐⌣) [Seite] adv. apart, aside.

seit¹=dem (⌐⌣, a. ⌐⌣) a) adv. since (or from) that time, since then, ever since (then), in der Vergangenheit auch: ever after (that); b) cj. = seit II.

Seite (⌐⌣) [ahd.: side] f ⑱ (poet. dat. sg. a. ~n) 1. side, (right, left) flank (a. ⚓ u. arch.), e-s Blattes: page, ⑨ folio; Flügel: wing; (auch ⚔), (Ort, Punkt) point; (Richtung) direction; Kricket (Tennis ic.): side; ~n wechseln to change (over); (Vorder=)~ face, front, e-s Buches ic.: front page (a. ⊕ typ.); behauene ~ eines Steines panel; obere (untere) ~ top (bottom); rechte (linke) ~: a) e-s Pferdes: on (off) side; b) von Zeug ic.: right (wrong) side; verkehrte e-r Münze: reverse; fig. (Partei) party. — 2. mit prp. (oft fig.): ab seiten (s. bs); an j-s ~ by the side of or next to, beside) a p.; an (ob. auf) die ~ gehen to step aside; auf beiden ~n on both sides; auf der einen (andern) ~ on the one (other) side; auf 2en des Volkes on the side (or part) of the people; e-n auf seine ~ bringen to bring (or draw, entice) a p. over to one's side; et. auf (ob. über) die ~ (a. beiseite) bringen (ob. schaffen) (heimlich fortschaffen) to get a th. out of the way, to make away with a th.; s. faul 4, legen 5 unter „an" und „auf"; (schlafend) auf der ~ liegen to lie (or rest) on one's side; e-n auf die ~ (auch beiseite) nehmen to take a p. aside; to talk to a p. in private; auf j-s ~ sein to side with a p.; e-n bei seiner schwachen ~ fassen to tackle (or a.) a man's weak side; beiseite geh(e)n to step aside; etwas beiseite lassen to

Zeichen (s. S. XVII): F familiär, P Volkssprache, P⌐ Gaunersprache, ↘ selten; † alt (auch gestorben); * neu (auch geboren)·⌐+ unrichtig,

[Seitenabriß] — 881 — [selber]

leave a th. (aside); beiseite legen (sparen) to put aside, to save up; allen Haß beiseite legen to lay aside all hatred; vgl. beiseite(e); die Arme (oder Hände) in die ~n stemmen to put one's arms on one's hips, F und ⚓ to stand a-kimbo; Stiche in der ~ haben to have stitches (or a stitch) in one's side; nach allen ~n in all directions; nach (od. von) allen ~n betrachten to look at a th. from all sides; to consider every side of a question; nach dieser ~e hin in this direction; e-n über die ~ schaffen to make away with a p., to get rid of a p.; von allen ~n her on all sides, from every quarter; von der ~ ansehen to look askance at, verächtlich: to look contemptuously at, verführerisch: to cast sidelong glances at; alles von der guten ~ ansehen, nehmen to look on (or at) the bright side of things; et. von der praktischen ~ auffassen to consider a th. from a practical point of view; von dieser ~ habe ich es nie angesehen I never looked at it in that light; e-m nicht von der ~ geh(e)n not to stir (or move) from a p.'s side, to be in constant attendance on a p.; mein Oheim von mütterlicher ~ her oder mütterlicherseits ... by (or on) the mother's side; von seiten des Gerichts on the part of the Court; e-m zur ~ steh(e)n to stand by a p.('s side), to support (or assist) a p.; es steh(e)n ihm gute Zeugnisse zur ~ he can produce good references, he has fine testimonials (to recommend him). — 3. fig. sich vor Lachen die ~n halten to split one's sides with laughing; er hat gute ~n he has his good sides or parts or points; Sprichw. jedes Ding hat seine zwei ~n everything has its two sides, there are two sides to every question. — 4. math. ~ einer ebenen Figur side of a figure, e-s Körpers: face of a solid, e-r Gleichung: side of an equation. — 5. ⊙ Fleischerei: ~ Speck side (or flitch) of bacon. — 6. ⚔ und ⚓ = Flanke.

Seiten=abriß (ᴴᵘ...) m ㉒ profile; =abweichung ⚔ f, artill. infolge Drall: derivation; =achse f, math. = Diagonale; =angriff ⚔ m flank attack; =anmerkung f marginal note; =ansicht f side-view, profile; =aufriß m, arch. side-elevation; =bahn 🚂 f branch-line; =bewegung f lateral movement or motion; =blatt n side-leaf or -flap or -piece (a. ⊙); =blick m sidelong glance, leer; =deckung ⚔ f flank guard; =druck m side-(or lateral) pressure; =erbe m, =erbin f collateral heir(ess f); =erbschaft f collat. succession; =fläche f side-face, eines geschliffenen Edelsteines: facet; =flügel n Gebäudes: side-wing; =front f, arch. side-face; =futter n in Schützen: s.-lining; =gang m s.-passage; =gasse f by-street; =gebäude n (additional) wing of a building; =geleise 🚂 n side-rails pl., siding, shunt; =gewehr ⚔ n side-arm (mst pl.), short sword, sword-bayonet; =grenze f Fußball: touch-line; =hieb m side-blow; (Rippenstoß) F dig in the ribs, fig. mit Worten:

indirect (or sly) attack, innuendo; =kissen n im Wagen: side-cushion; =kulisse f, thea. (side-)wing; =lähmung f. path.: ⚕ hemiplegia, ...y; =lang a. ⓖ filling (whole) pages; voluminous (report, &c.); =lehne f side-rail, e-s Sessels: arm-rest; =licht n, arch. side-light; =linie f: a) ⚓ branch-line; b) eines Geschlechts: collateral line; Fußball: touch, Tennis: side-line; =locke f side-lock; =loge f, thea. side-box; =marsch ⚔ m flank march; =mauer f side-wall; =pfahl, =pfosten m s.-post; =punkt m (col)lateral point; =rand m. typ., &c. margin, innerer: back, äußerer: fore-edge, oberer: head, unterer: tail of a side; =richter m Fußball: touch-judge; =rippe ♎ e-s Blattes: veinlet.

seitens (ᴵᵘ) [Seite] prp. mit gen. (dafür bss.: von) on the part of; ♀ des Vaters on the father's side.

Seiten=schiff (ᴴᵘ...) n ㉒ arch. einer Kirche: (side-)aisle; =schmerz m, path. pain in the side, ⚕ pleuralgia; =schnitt m side-cut, lateral incision; =sprung m s.-leap, gambol; =sprünge m. von Hasen 2c.: to double, weit ♀. to dodge; =ständig ♎ a. ⓖ ⚕ lateral; =stechen n, =stiche m/pl. path. stitch(es pl.) in the side, ⚕ pleurisy; =stoß m thrust (F dig) in the side, lateral push; =stück n side-piece, duplicate of, counterpart to, zu einem Gemälde 2c.: companion picture, &c.; =tafel ⬇ n masttackle; =tal n side-valley, lateral valley; =talje ⚓ f einer Kanone: sidetackle; =tasche f side-pocket; =teil m side-part, lateral portion, eines Rockes: flap; =tisch m side-table; sideboard, =tor n s.-gate; =tür(e) f s.-door; fig. sich eine ~ offen lassen to keep o.s. a loop-hole open; =vermächtnis n special legacy; =verwandte([r] m) f collateral relative or kins(wo)man; =verwandtschaft f collateral-relationship or kinship; =wand f side-wall, partition, thea. = Kulisse; =weg m = Nebenweg; =wendung f turn(ing sideways); =werk ⚔ n, frt. side-(or flanking) work, flank(er); =wind m side-wind; =zahl f: a) number of pages; b) number of the page; mit ~en versehen to pag(inat)e, typ. a. to folio; c) math. Vieleck von ungerader ~ polygon with an odd number of sides; =zimmer n: a) slip-room; b) = Nebenzimmer.

seit=her (a. ᴵᵘ) adv.: a) = seitdem a. b) up to now, thus far; ♀erig a. ⓖ (bis jetzt bestehend) still in force or in use, continuing to exist; vgl. bisherig.

...seitig (...ᴵᵘ) a. ⓖ in Zssgn, bsd. mit Zahlwörtern, z.B. zwölf=♀ twelve-sided.

seitlich (ᴵᵘ) [Seite] a. ⓖ (lying) beside s. th., lateral, auch: collateral.

...seits (...ᴴᵘ) [mhd.] s. Seite 2 gegen Ende; vgl. ab, aller, dies, jen, einer, meinerseits; mütterlicherseits 2c.

seit=wärts (ᴴᵘ) [Seite] adv. sideways, sidelong, laterally; (auf der schmalen Seite) edgeways; ♀ geneigt aslant.

Sekante ⚂ (ᵛᴵᵘ) [lt. Schneidende] f ⚗ math. u. (†) Trigonometrie: (abbr. sec.) secant.

Sekel (ˢᵘ) [hebr. schägel] m ㉒ (altes jüdisches Metallgewicht = 14,55 g; später auch Silbermünze = 2½ Mark) shekel.

Sekonde=leutnant † ⚔ (ᵛˢᵘᴵᵘ) [fr.] m ㉒ second lieutenant (= Leutnant).

Sekret¹ (ᵛᴵᵘ) [lt.] n ⓐ c.; ~e pl. physiol. (Absonderungen aus dem Blute) secretions pl.

sekret² (ᵛᴵᵘ) [lt.] a. ⓖ secret.

Sekretär (---ᴵᵘ) [fr.] m ⓐ d. 1. (Schriftführer, Schreiber) secretary, clerk. — 2. = Schreibtisch; (Kleider-~) wardrobe, clothes-cupboard. — 3. orn. secretary (Gypogeranus secratarius).

Sekretariat (---ᵛᴵᵘ) [neu=lt.] n ⓐ c. secretaryship, clerkship.

Sekt F (ᵛᵘ) [engl. sack (SH. H. IV. I. II. 4)] m ⓐ b. champagne (= Champagner).

Sekte (ᵛᵘ) [lt. abgesonderte] f ⚗ rel. (Glaubensgenossenschaft) sect. [ⓖ sectarian.

Sektierer (ᵛᴵᵘ) m ㉒, Sektiererisch (ᵛᴵᵘᵛ) a.

Sektion (ᵛᵗᵏ(ᵛ)ᴵᵘ) [lt.] f ⓐ 1. (Abteilung) section. — 2. med. (Öffnung u. Untersuchung e-r Leiche) post-mortem examination, ⚕ dissection (of a dead body).

Sektions=befund (ᵛ(ᵗˢ)(ᵛ)ᴵᵘ...) m ⓐ, =bericht m result(s pl.) of (report on) a post-mortem examination; =saal m dissecting room; ♀weise ⚔ adv. (F a. a.) (moving) insections. [(ausschnitt) sector.

Sektor (ᵛᴵᵘ) [lt.] m ⓐ math. (Kreis-, Kugel-)

Sekunda (ᵛᴵᵘ) [lt. zweite] f ⓐ(⚗) second highest form of a German secondary school, in England: fifth form; ~ner (--ᴵᵘ) m ⚗ scholar of the „Sekunda".

Sekundant (ᵛᴵᵘ) [lt.] m ⓐ (Kampfzeuge) second in a duel, b. Bogen: bottle-holder.

sekundär (ᵛᴵᵘ) [neu=lt.] a. ⓖ (untergeordnet) secondary, subordinate; ~bahn 🚂 (ᵛᴵᵘ) f ⓐ branch-line; light railway. [second (bill) of exchange.]

Sekunda=wechsel ⚗ (ᵛᴵᵘᵛᵘ) m ㉒

Sekunde (ᵛᴵᵘ) [lt.] f ⓐ: a) ¹⁄₆₀ Minute, b) ♪ zweiter Ton vom Grundton aus; second; ♀n=lang a. u. adv. for seconds.

Sekunden=pendel ⊙ (ᵛᴵᵘ...) n (m) ㉒ Uhren 2c.: second-pendulum; =uhr f watch with a second-hand; =zeiger m einer Uhr second-hand of a watch.

sekundieren (ᵛᴵᵘᴵᵘ) [neu=lt.] I v. a. ⓐ e-n (ob. e-m) ♀ (e-m helfen, zur Seite stehen): a) fenc. to be second to, to second; b) ♪ to accompany. — II ~ n ㉓ seconding; ♪ accompaniment.

Sekundo=genitur (ᵛᴵᵘ=ᵛᴵᵘᴵᵘ) [lt.] f ⓐ jur. right of a younger son.

Sekundus (ᵛᴵᵘ) [lt. Zweiter] m ⓐ Schule: second boy in a class.

sel. abbr. = selig.

sela (ᴵᵘ) [hebr. ♪ in den Psalmen] int. bibl. selah!; bsd. in der Redensart: abgemacht, ♀! done with it!, vgl. abmachen 3.

Seladon (ᴵᵛᵛ) [fr. Céladon] npr/m. ⓐ (⚗) (schmachtender Liebhaber) Celadon, amorous (or love-sick) swain. [salaam.]

Selam (ˢᵛᴵ) [ar. Friede] m ⓐ Gruß im Orient:

selb (ˢᵘ) [ahd.] a. ⓖ meist verschmelzend mit definite art. (s. derselb(ig)e); zur ♀en (= zu derselben) Stunde at the same hour; im ♀en (= in demselben) Saale in the (very) same hall.

selb=acht(e(r) (ˢᵘ...) a. ⓐ (one) with seven others, eighth of a gang; ♀ander adv. with another; we two; ♀dritt adv. (one) with two others.

selber (ˢᵘ) pronominales adv., oft = selbst I, z.B. ich ♀ I myself, sie ♀ she herself, they themselves.

♪ Musik; ⚂ Wissenschaft; ♎ Pflanze; ♀ Geographie; ⊙ Technik; ⚒ Bergbau; ⚔ Militär; ⚓ Marine; ⚖ Handel; ✉ Post; 🚂 Eisenbahn.

[selbig] — 882 — [selig]

selbig (⌣⌣) *a.* 66 A2. B* = selb; zu ̸der (od. zur ̸sen) Stunde in that very hour.
selbft (´) [selb] **I** *pronominales adv.*
1. (in eigener Person) self. in person; ich 2̸ I myself, er ~ he himself: fie hat (haben) es 2̸ getan she has (they have) done it herself (themselves); beim Zurückgeben eines Schimpfwortes: Schuft! — 2̸ Schuft! rogue! — rogue yourself! — 2. *mit prp.*: die Sache an und für fich 2̸ the thing in itself; aus fich 2̸ of oneself, vgl. von 2̸; mit fich 2̸ reden to talk to oneself; von 2̸ of one's own accord, voluntarily; (maschinenartig) mechanically, automatically; das geht von 2̸ it goes by itself; das versteht fich von 2̸ that is self-understood, that's a matter of course, it goes without saying; wie von 2̸ quite spontaneously; iro. es ift wohl von 2̸ gekommen? F *co.* I suppose, the cat has done it? — **3.** verstärkend: fie ift die Güte 2̸ ... kindness itself; er ift die Höflichkeit 2̸ ... the pink of politeness. — **4.** oft verschmelzend mit *p.p.*: 2̸gebackene Kuchen homemade cakes. — **5.** Sprichw. 2̸ ift der Mann every tub must stand on its own bottom; selbft do self have; 2̸ getan ift wohlgetan self done well done. — **II** *adv.* 6. (sogar) even; seine Freunde 2̸, 2̸ seine Freunde even his friends, his very friends; 2̸ wenn even if, even though, provided even.
— **III** ~ *n* ⓝb. u. (o. *pl.*) *inv.* 7. (one's own) self or individuality or person (-ality); (das 3̸ch) ego. [or -respect.
Selbft-achtung (⌣⌣⌣⌣) *f* 62 self-esteem;
selb-ftändig (⌣⌣) *a.* 66 dependent on oneself, self-reliant; (unabhängig) independent; (fich felbft regierend) autonomous; (ohne Beistand) without assistance, unassisted, unaided; **~keit** *f* 66 independence; autonomy.
Selbft-anlage (⌣...) *f* 62 self-accusation; **2̸auferlegt** *a.* 66 self-imposed; **=aufopferung** *f* self-sacrifice, -immolation; **=befleckung** *f* self-pollution, onanism, masturbation; **=befruchtung** *f* ♀, *zo.* spontaneous generation, ⚹ autogamy; **=beherrschung** *f* self-command or -control; **=bekenntnis** *n* voluntary confession, spontaneous confession; **=beköftigung** *f* paying for (F finding) one's own board, boarding oneself; **=bestimmung** *f* self-determination, *rel.* free agency; **=bestimmungs-recht** *n* (right of) self-government, eines Volkes: sovereign right; **=betrachtung** *f* self-contemplation; **2̸bewegend** ⊕ *a.* 66 automatic, automotor; **2̸bewußt** *a.*: a) self-conscious, b) (stolz) proud; **=bewußtsein** *n* 62: a) self-consciousness, b) (Anmaßung) self-assertion, bisw. auch = Dünkel; **=biographie** *f* autobiography, memoirs *pl.* of one's life; **2̸eigen** *a.* 66 stärker als „eigen": seine 2̸en Kinder his very (own) ...; **=einkehr** *f*, *rel.* self-communion; **=einschätzung** *f* zur Steuer: self-assessment, statement (in respect of) one's income; **=entleibung** *f* suicide; **=entmannung** *f* voluntary castration or emasculation; **=entsagung** *f*

self-denial; **=entzündung** *f* spontaneous combustion; **=erhaltung** *f* self-preservation; **=erkenntnis** *f* knowledge of oneself; **=erniedrigung** *f* self-humiliation; **=fahrer** *m*: a) carriage driven by its owner, a. dog-cart; b) (Automobil) motor car or van; elektrischer ~ electric car; **2̸gebacken** *a.* s. selbft 4; **2̸gefällig** *a.* self-complacent, egotistic(al); **=gefälligkeit** *f* self-complacency, egotism; **=gefühl** *n* s.-reliance; ~ h... *a.* to know one's worth; **2̸gemacht** *a.* 66 self-made; **2̸genügsam** *a.* self-sufficient, self-contained; **=genügsamkeit** *f* 62 self-sufficiency; **=gespräch** *n* soliloquy, monologue.
Selbftheit (⌣-) *f* 46 1. self, one's own person(ality) or individuality; (das 3̸ch) ego. — 2. = Selbftsucht.
Selbft-herr (⌣...) *m* =herrscher; **=herrlich** *a.* 66 sovereign; **=herrlichkeit** *f* 62 sovereignty; **=herrschaft** *f*: a) autocratic rule, autocracy; b) ↘ = Beherrschung; **=herrscher** *m* autocrat(ic ruler); **=hilfe** *f* self-aid or -help; self-defence.
selbftisch (⌣⌣) *a.* 66 egoistic(al).
Selbft-kenntnis (⌣...) *f* 62 self-knowledge; **=kosten-preis** ⊕ *m* = Kosten-preis; **=kritik** *f* self-criticism; **=laut(er)** *m, gr.* (*ant.* Mitlaut(er)) vowel; **=lehrer** *m* self-taught person, bisw.: autodidact; **=liebe** *f* = Eigenliebe. [egotist.)
Selbftling (⌣-) *m* ⓝd. selfish person;(
Selbft-lob (⌣...) *n* 62 = Eigenlob; **2̸los** *a.* 66 unselfish, disinterested; **=losigkeit** *f* unselfishness, disinterestedness; **=mord** *m* self-destruction, suicide; *jur.* (It.) *felo-de-se*; ~ begeh(e)n to commit suicide, to make away with oneself; **=mörder(in** *f*) *m* (p. committing) suicide, *jur.* (It.) *felo-de-se*; **=mörderisch** *a.* suicidal; **=mord-gedanke** *m*: mit ~n umgehen to harbour suicidal thoughts; **=prüfung** *f* self-examination; **=quäler** *m* self-tormentor; **=quälerisch** *a.* self-tormenting; **=rache** *f* private revenge; **2̸redend** *a.* self-evident, vgl. Verständlich; **=reftektant** ⊛ *m*: nur ~en werden berücksichtigt only principals need apply; auch: no agents; **=regierung** *f* self-government; home rule; **2̸regulierend** *a.* mach., &c. self-regulating or -feeding, *phys.*, &c. *a.*: self-registering; **=schrift** *f* autograph; **=schuß** ⊕ *m* spring-gun; **2̸ständig** &c. = selbftständig &c.; **=studium** *n* private study; **=sucht** *f* selfishness, self-seeking; (Reden von fich felbft) egotism; **2̸süchtig** *a.* selfish, self-seeking; egoistic(al); **2̸tätig** *a.*: a) self-acting (auch ⊕), automatic; ⊕ 2̸e Maschine self-actor; b) spontaneous; **=tätigkeit** *f* self-action or -activity; spontaneousness; **=täuschung** *f* self-deception or -delusion; **=überhebung** *f*, **=überschätzung** *f* over-estimating (or over-rating) o.s., conceit, presumption; **=übertrager** *m, elect.* automatic transmitter; **=überwindung** *f* self-conquest; **=unterricht** *m* s.-instruction or -tuition; **=verblendung** *f* = täuschung, auch infatuation; **=verbrennung** *f* = =entzündung; **=verdammung** *f* self-condemnation; **2̸vergessen** *a.* forgetful

of o.s.: **=vergessenheit** *f* self-forgetfulness; **=vergötterung** *f* self-worship or -adulation; **=verlag** *m* Buchhandel: im ~(e) published by the author; **=verleger** *m* author and publisher; **=verleugnung** *f* self-denial; **2̸verftändlich** *a.* self-understood; *adv.* of course, naturally; das ift 2̸ auch: that is understood or a matter of course; it stands to reason; **=verftümmelung** *f* s.-mutilation; **=verteidigung** *f* self-defence; **=vertrauen** *n* self-confidence, -assurance; Mangel an ~ lack of (self-)confidence, diffidence; **=verwaltung** *f* self-administration, autonomy; **=wille** *m*: a) = Eigenwille; b) (Eigensinn) wilfulness; **2̸willig** *a.* wilful; **=zucht** *f* discipline over oneself, self-restraint; **2̸zufrieden(heit** *f*) *a.* = genügsam(keit); **2̸zündend** *a.* self-igniting, ⚹ pyrophoric; **=zünder** *m*, *chm.*: ⚹ pyrophorus, ...e; **=zweck** *m* (forming) one's own object or end.
Selcher *südd.* (⌣-) *m* 62 pork-butcher.
Selch(er)-fleisch *südd.* (⌣(⌣)...) *n* 62, **=ware** *f* smoked meat.
Seldschuke (⌣⌣) *m* 44, **Seldschukin** *f* 47 Glied eines vom 11.—13. sæ. in Oftasien herrschenden türkischen Stammes: Sel(d)juk.
seldschukisch (⌣⌣⌣) *a.* 66 Sel(d)jukian.
Selekta (-⌣⌣) [It.] *f* 49 (96) special class (for senior pupils). [pupil, student.
Selektaner (-⌣⌣⌣) *m* 42, **~in** *f* 62 senior
Selektions-theorie ⚹ (-⌣tsj⌣(⌣)⌣⌣-⌣) [It. Auslese:] *f* 62 Darwin's theory of selection.
Selen ⚹ (⌣⌣) [grch. Mond=, Berzelius 1817] *n* ⓝd. *chm.* Metalloid: selenium (Se).
selen-haltig (⌣⌣⌣⌣) *a.* 66 seleniferous.
selenig ⚹ (⌣⌣⌣) *a.* 66 *chm.*: 2̸e Säure selenious acid (H_2SeO_3); **2̸=sauer** (⌣⌣⌣⌣) *a.* 66: 2̸=saures Salz selenite.
Selenit ⚹ (⌣⌣⌣) [grch. Mond=] *m* 1. ⓜc. *min.* (Gipsspat) selenite. — 2. 42 (Mondbewohner) lunarian.
Selenit-mörtel (⌣-⌣⌣⌣⌣) *m* 62 selenitic mortar. [of copper (Cu_2Se).)
Selen-kupfer (⌣⌣⌣⌣⌣) *n* 62 seleniode
Selenographie ⚹ (-⌣-⌣⌣⌣f) [grch.] *f* 48 (Mondbeschreibung) selenography.
selen-sauer (⌣⌣⌣...) *a.* 66 *chm.* selenic: 2̸saures Salz selenate; **=säure** *f* 62 selenic acid (H_2SeO_4); **=silber** *n* silver selenide (Ag_2Se); **=wasserstoff(gas** *n*) *m* seleniuretted hydrogen (H_2Se).
...**selig**[1] (...⌣⌣) [...ſal + -ig] *a.*, ⁊B. mühselig [Mühsal] toilsome, laborious.
selig[2] (⌣⌣) [ahd.: silly] *a.* 66 **1.** blessed, schwächer: happy; (wonnevoll) blissful; er ift ganz 2̸ ... overjoyed, delighted; ... in the seventh heaven of delight; 2̸ (*adv.*) entschlafen, ein 2̸es Ende nehmen to die as a Christian; Gott habe ihn 2̸! may his soul rest in Heaven (in peace)!; s. Lpreisen; 2̸ werden to go to Heaven, to be saved; Sprichw. s. nehmen III. — **2.** *Cath. eccl.* s. Sprechen. — **3.** *v.* Verstorbenen: deceased, late(ly departed); Ihre 2̸e Mutter your lamented mother; 2̸en Andenkens of blessed memory; nachgesetzt: mein Vater 2̸ my late (F oft: my poor) Father; die ~en the blessed (ones) *pl.*; Aufenthalt der ~en abode of the blessed, realms of bliss, Elysium. — **4.** F 2̸

[Seliggesprochene] — 883 — [Senn]

(betrunken) sein to be elevated or F gloriously drunk.
Selig²-gesprochene([r] m) f (ᴗ́ᴗᴗ́ᴗ) ⓖ⑦ eccl. canonized (or beatified) person.
Seligkeit (ᴗ́ᴗ)[ahd.] ⓖ⑥ blessedness, supreme happiness or delight, felicity, blissful state; theol. ewige ~ salvation; die ewige ~ erlangen, gewinnen to gain eternal bliss or happiness, to enter (the Kingdom of) Heaven.
selig²=machend (ᴗ́ᴗ...) a. ⓖ⑥ beatific, saving (souls); leading to Heaven; s. alleinseligmachend; =macher m ② Saviour; =machung f ⓖ⑥ salvation; **²preisen** v/a. ⓢ①** to call happy, to glorify, eccl. to beatify; =preisung f ⓖ⑥ glorification; **²sprechen** v/a. ⓣa** : e-n ⓛ to canonize (or beatify) a p.; =sprechung f ⓖ⑥ beatification.
Sellerie ⚥ (ᴗ́ᴗᴗ, a. ᴗ́ᴗᴗ́) [fr. céleri m] ⓂⒸ, f ⓖ⑧ celery (A'pium grave'olens); in England viel gegeßener Blattstiel des ~s: celery-stick, stick of celery.
selten (ᴗ́ᴗ) [ahd.: seldom] a. ⓖ⑥(D9) 1. (ant. häufig rare, (spärlich) scarce, sparse; (merkwürdig) curious, remarkable; f ein ²er Vogel a rare bird, a (lt.) rara avis; das ist nichts ²es bei ihm that's nothing unusual (or out of the common) with him; Sie machen sich sehr ² you are making yourself very scarce, we see very little of you; adv. seldom; nicht (eben) ² pretty often; now and again; ich gehe so ² als möglich hin I go there as rarely (or as little) as possible. — 2. (außerordentlich) extraordinary, unusual.
Seltenheit (ᴗ́ᴗᴗ) f ⓖ⑥ 1. o. pl. rareness, rarity, scarcity. — 2. mit pl. rare (or curious, wonderful) thing; curiosity.
Selter (ᴗ́ᴗ) [Selters ⚥, nassauisches Dorf] f ⓖ⑥. inv.: eine (kleine) ~, etwa: a (small) bottle of seltzer (water).
Selter=wasser (ᴗ́ᴗᴗ) n ⑲ seltzer (in England besser bekannt: soda-)water.
seltsam (ᴗ́ᴗ) [ahd.] a. ⓖ⑥ strange, (sonderbar) singular; (eigentümlich) curious, (wunderlich) queer, odd, F u. P rum.
Seltsamkeit (ᴗ́ᴗᴗ) f ⓖ⑥: a) (das Seltsamsein) strangeness, singularity; queerness, oddness; b) (et. Seltsames) curiosity, oddity, F rum object.
Sem (ᴗ́) npr/m. bibl. Sohn Noahs: Shem.
Semester (ᴗ́ᴗᴗ) [lt. 6monatig] n ㉒ (Halbjahr) (term of) six months, half-year; univ. sein erstes ~ his first term; =abschluß (ᴗ́...) m ⓶ univ. end (or close) of the term. [(Strichpunkt) semicolon.]
Semikolon (ᴗ́ᴗᴗ́ᴗ) [lt.=grch.] n ㉛ gr., typ.)
Seminar (ᴗᴗ́) [lt. Pflanz(schule)] n ①㉙d.: a) (Bildungsanstalt für geistliche, Lehrer (=innen) 2c.) training-college for theological students, ministers, (male) teachers, governesses, &c., nur für Theologen: school of divinity; b) univ. mathematical, classical, &c. school; advanced class.
Seminar=bildung (ᴗᴗ́ᴗ...) f ⓖ⑥ education received at a training-college; =direktor m principal of a training-college.
Seminarist (ᴗᴗᴗ́) m ⓶ ⓖ⑥ 1. pupil of a training-college or school of divinity, engS. theological student. — 2. ~in f ⓖ⑥ student of a training-college for governesses or women teachers.

seminar(ist)isch (ᴗᴗᴗ́ᴗ, ᴗᴗ́ᴗ) a. ⓖ⑥: e-e ²e Bildung h., ² (adv.) gebildet sein to have passed through a training-college.
Seminar=kursus (ᴗᴗ́ᴗᴗ) m ⓶ course of studies at a training-college.
Semiotik ⚥ (ᴗᴗ́ᴗ) [grch. Zeichen...] f ⓖ⑥ (Krankheitszeichenlehre) semeiotics.
Semit, ~e (ᴗ́/ᴗ́)[Sem] m ⓶, ⑨, ~in f ⓖ⑥ Semite; engS. = Jude, Jüdin; ²isch (ᴗ́ᴗ) a. ⓖ⑥ Semitic; engS. = jüdisch.
Semmel (ᴗ́ᴗ) [ahd.; *lt. si'mila Weizenmehl] f ⓖ⑧ roll; fig. wie warme ~(n) abgehen to sell (F to go off) rapidly or readily or at lightning-speed.
semmel=blond (ᴗ́ᴗ...) a. ⓖ⑥ very fair, with flaxen hair, F sandy; =klöße m/pl. ⓖ⑧ dumplings pl. made of (fine wheaten) bread; =mehl n fine wheaten flour.
sen. abbr. = senior.
Senar ⚥ (ᴗᴗ́) [lt.] m ⓶d. pros. (sechsfüßiger [iambischer] Vers) six-footed (iambic)line.
Senat (ᴗᴗ́) [lt. Alten=] m ⓒ. (röm. Alt. u. jetzt noch Hoher Rat eines Staates 2c.) senate.
Senator (ᴗᴗ́ᴗ) [lt.] m ⓷⓵ senator.
senatorisch (ᴗᴗᴗ́ᴗ) [lt.] a. ⓖ⑥ senatorial.
Senats=ausschuß (ᴗᴗ́ᴗ...) m ⓖ⑥, =beschluß m committee, decree of the senate; =präsident m president of the senate.
Send=bote (ᴗ́ᴗ...) m ⓖ⑧ messenger; weitS. emissary; delegate; apostle; =brief m epistle; (Rundschreiben) circular (letter).
senden (ᴗ́ᴗ) [ahd.: send] I v/a. ⓖ⑥a. oft als feinerer Ausdruck für schicken I: to send; auf Adressen: nach Ems zu ² to be forwarded (on) to Ems, wenn Adressat verzogen: try Ems. — II ~n ⓷ f. Sendung.
Sender (ᴗ́ᴗ) m ⓶ 1. a. ~in f ⓖ⑥ sender, vgl. Absender. — 2. ⓖ tel. transmitter.
Sendling (ᴗ́ᴗ) m ⓶d. emissary.
Send=schreiben (ᴗ́ᴗᴗ) n ⓶ = Sendbrief.
Sendung (ᴗ́ᴗ) f ⓖ⑥ 1. (das Senden) sending, forwarding; dispatch, transmission. — 2. a) (das Gesandte) s.th. sent or forwarded or dispatched; consignment of goods, parcel, zu Wasser: shipment; b) (Auftrag) (com)mission.
Senegambi=en ⚥ (ᴗᴗ́ᴗᴗ) npr/n. ⓖ⑥α. west=afrik. Landschaft: Senegambia.
Seneschall (ᴗᴗ́) [mhd.; fr. sénéchal; *dtsch. Altknecht] m ⓶d., ~in f ⓖ⑥ seneschal; high steward(ess).
Senf (ᴗ́) [ahd. (*grch.) sinapi] m ⓶b. ⚥ mustard (sina'pis); wilder ~ common charlock (S. arve'nsis); weißer ~ white mustard (S. alba); schwarzer ~ common mustard (S. nigra). — 2. (Moststrich) mustard. — 3. F fig. (Gerede) einen langen ~ von et. machen to make a long rigmarole of a th.; to spin a long yarn about a th.; seinen ~ dazu geben to give one's opinion, to put in a word.
Senf=büchse (ᴗ́ᴗᴗ) f ⓖ⑧ mustard-box; =fabrikant m m.-maker; =gurken f/pl. cucumbers pl. pickled (together) with mustard; =korn n (grain of) m.-seed; =mehl n ground mustard; =öl n oil of mustard; =pflaster n mustard-poultice; =same m m.-seed; =topf m m.-pot; =umschlag m = pflaster.
sengen (ᴗ́ᴗ) [ahd.: singe fingen m.] ⓖ⑧ I v/a. (durch Feuer Fasern, Haare 2c. v. et. entfernen) to singe; (am Feuer ob. in der Sonne dörren) to parch to scorch, F to frizzle, (up); s. brennen 5. — II v/n. (h.) to

be (or get) singed or parched or scorched; to parch, scorch, burn.
sengerig (ᴗ́ᴗᴗ) a. ⓖ⑥ 1. (brändicht) es riecht ² F it smells of burning. — 2. F fig. das (ob. die Sache) riecht ² that's a rotten (or a queer, a strange) case.
Seng(e)=stroh (ᴗ́ᴗ,ᴗ́) n ⓶ straw for lighting the fire.
senior¹ (ᴗ́ᴗ) [lt. älter] a. inv. (abbr. sen.; ant. junior) senior.
Senior² (ᴗ́ᴗᴗ) [lt. Ältere(r)] m ⓷⓵ (Ältester, Vorsitzender) captain (or head) of a students' club; chairman of a (mercantile, &c.) corporation.
Seniorat (ᴗᴗᴗ́) n ⓶c. seniority.
Senioren=konvent (ᴗᴗ́ᴗᴗᴗ́) m ⓶ conference of heads of students' clubs or of chairmen of corporations; parl. standing committee for the regulation of parliamentary business.
Senk=bäume ⚥ (ᴗ́ᴗ...) m/pl. ⓖ⑥ ground-spears pl.; =blei ⚓ n plummet, (sounding-)lead, sinker. [(Schnürband) lace.)
Senkel ⚙ (ᴗ́ᴗ) m ⓶ ; *senken m ⓶)
senkeln (ᴗ́ᴗ) v/a. ⚙ a.: das Mieder ² (schnüren) to lace ... [nadel) bodkin.)
Senkel=stift ⚙ (ᴗ́ᴗ...) m ⓶ tag, (Schnür=)
senken (ᴗ́ᴗ) [ahd.: sink sinken m.] ⓖ⑧ I v/a. 1. to sink, to (put) lower, to let down; (untertauchen) to submerge, to dip; die Augen ² to cast down one's eyes; den Kopf ² (neigen) to incline one's head; gesenkten Hauptes with bent (or drooping) head. — 2. ⓖ hort. — absenken I; ⚒ einen Schacht ² (oft = sinken) = abteufen. — II sich ² v/refl. 3. to sink, drop, droop; to go down; vom Boden, von Gebäuden 2c.: to subside, to give way, von einer Mauer: to sag, von einem Bodensatz: to settle at the bottom. — 4. der Schlaf senkte sich auf seine Augen sleep descended on (or closed) his eyes; sich unter e-e Last ² to sink under a load, to bend under a burden. — III ~n ⓷ 5. f. Senkung.
Senker ⚙ (ᴗ́ᴗ) m ⓶ 1. agr., hort. = Absenker. — 2. ⚙ Schlossergräber: counter-sink. — 3. ⚙ Schachtgräber: sinker.
Senk=grube ⚙ (ᴗ́ᴗ...) f Bauwesen: cesspool, drain; sink-hole; =haue ⚒ f sinker's pick; =nadel f, surg. (Sonde) probe, searcher; =pumpe ⚒ f sinking-pump; =rahmen m ⚒ Wasserbau: sinking-frame; =rebe f Weinbau: layer of a vine, provine, vine-shoot; ²recht a. ⓖ⑥ vertical, by the plumb-line, math. perpendicular; eine ²e Linie (ob. ~e f ⓖ⑥) ziehen, fällen to draw (or drop) a perpendicular (line); ²recht=fertig a. f. ...fertig; =reis n, hort. layer; =schnur f plumb- (or sounding-)line; =schuß ⚔ m plunging fire or shot.
Senkung (ᴗ́ᴗ) f ⓖ⑥ 1. sinking, &c. (f. senken I); unter Wasser: submersion; des Bodens: subsidence. — 2. a) (Vertiefung) depression, hollow (ground); (Neigung) inclination, incline, dip; b) pros. (ant. Hebung) thesis.
Senk=wage (ᴗ́ᴗ...) f ⓖ⑥ = Aräometer; =zeit f, hort. season for layering or taking layers.
Senn schwz. (ᴗ́) [ahd. Hirt] m ⓶b., ~in f ⓖ⑥ Alpine cowherd or herdsman, f Alpine dairy-maid or dairy-woman.

⚥ scientific; ⚘ botanical; ⚥ geography; ⓖ machinery; ⚒ mining; ⚔ military; ⚓ marine; ⓖ commercial; ✉ postal; 🚂 railway.

[Sennalp] — 884 — [setzen]

Senn-alp(e) schwz. (ˊ‿ˊ(‿)) f ⓺ Alpine mountain with dairy-farms.
Senne¹ (ˊ‿) f ⓸ = Sehne. [Sennalp(e).
Senne² (ˊ‿) I m ⓸ = Senn. — II f ⓸ =
Senner schwz. (ˊ‿) m ⓸, **~in** f ⓸ = Senn(in);
~ei (‿‿ˊ) f ⓺ Alpine dairy-farm(ing).
Sennes-blätter (ˊ‿...) [nhd., fr., *ar.] n/pl. ⓺ pharm. senna-leaves pl.;
=strauch ⚥ m senna (Cassia senna).
Senn-hütte schwz. (ˊ‿ˊ‿) f ⓺ Alpine herdsman's cottage.
Sensal (‿ˊ) [it. sensa'le] m ⓵d. (⓶) (vereidigter Makler) sworn broker.
Sensation (ˊ‿tʃ(‿)ⁿ)[neu=lt.] f ⓺ (Aufsehen) sensation; **Zell** (ˊ‿tʃ(‿)ⁿ) a. ⓺ (Aufsehen erregend) sensational; creating (or causing) a sensation; (aufregend) exciting; **2s-bedürftig** (2s-lustig) a. ⓺ wanting (fond of) excitement.
Sensations-nachrichten (ˊ‿tʃ(‿)ⁿ...) f pl. ⓶ sensational news sg.; **=prozeß** m sensational trial or lawsuit, auch: (fr.) cause célèbre; **=roman** m sensational (or exciting) novel, F shilling-shocker, penny-dreadful.
Sense (ˊ‿) [ahd.] f ⓸ agr. scythe; eine ~ dengeln to sharpen a scythe.
Sensen-eisen ⊕ (ˊ‿...) n ⓶. **=klinge** f blade of a scythe; **=mann** m: a) ⚔ man armed with a scythe, auch: scythe-man,-bearer; b) fig. (Tod) Death; **=schmied** m scythe-maker; **=stiel** m scythe-handle; **=träger** m = =mann; **=(wetz)stein** ⊕ m, agr. scythe-stone, whetstone, (feiner Schleifstein) hone.
sensitiv (ˊ‿‿ᵘf) [neu=lt.] a. ⓺ (empfindlich) sensitive; nur von Personen: touchy.
Sensorium ⚥ (‿ˊ(‿)‿) [neu=lt.] n ⓶ physiol., phls. (Sitz des Empfindungsvermögens) sensorium, sensory.
Sensualismus (‿‿‿ˊ‿)[neu=lt.] m ⓶⁷ phls. (Sinnlichkeit) sensualism.
Sentenz (‿ˊ) [lt.] f ⓺ (Denk=, Sinn=spruch) sentence; motto; **2enhaft** (‿ˊ‿‿), **2iös** (‿ˊ‿tʃ(‿)ⁿ) a. ⓺ sententious.
sentimental (ˊ‿‿ᵘf) [fr.] a. ⓺ (empfindsam) sentimental, F soft; **=ität** (ˊ‿‿‿ˊ) f ⓺ sentimentality, ...ism.
separat (‿‿ˊ) [lt.] a. ⓺ (gesondert) separate; (das einzelne betreffend) special, individual; (für sich bestehend) particular.
Separat-ausgabe (‿‿ˊˊ‿‿) f ⓺ separate edition; **=eingang** m separate entrance.
Separatist (‿‿‿ˊ) m ⓶ bsd. pol. separatist, seceder; **2isch** a. ⓺ (Absonderung erstrebend) separatist, seceding.
Separat=konto ⚥ (‿‿ˊˊ‿‿) n ⓶ separate account; **=vertrag** m separate treaty, special agreement.
separier/en (‿‿ˊ‿) [lt.] I v/a. u. sich 2 v/refl. ⓷: (sich) 2 (absondern) to separate (o.s.), to sever (o.s.); ✠ sich 2, auch: to dissolve partnership, pol., &c. to secede; Separierte(r) s. (vom Manne [von der Frau] Getrennte[r]) separated wife (husband). — II **2ung** f ⓺ separation.
Sepia (ˊ‿‿) [grch.] f ⓺ 1. zo. cuttle-fish (Se'pia). — 2. paint. (Tintenfischbraun) sepia. [(or sepic) drawing.
Sepia-zeichnung (ᵘ(‿)‿...) f ⓺ sepia
Sepsis ⚥ (ˊ‿) [grch. sēpsis Fäulnis] f ⓺ (Fäulnis, Blutvergiftung) sepsis.
September (‿‿ˊ‿)[lt.7.Monat der alten Römer] m ⓶ (a. inv.) (month of) September.

Septennat (ˊ‿‿ⁿ) [it.] n ⓵c. (Zeitraum v. sieben Jahren) septennate.
Septett ♪ (‿ˊ) [it.] n ⓵c. (siebenstimmiges Musikstück) septet(te).
Septima (ˊ‿‿) [lt. siebente] f ⓾ preparatory class of a German school; **~ner** (‿‿‿) m ⓶ preparatory pupil.
Septime ♪ (ˊ‿‿) [it.] f ⓺ seventh; **~n-akkord** (ˊ‿‿‿‿ˊ) m ⓺ seventh-chord.
septisch (ˊ‿) [s. Sepsis] a. ⓺ (Fäulnis bewirkend) septic, causing decay.
Septuagesima (‿‿‿ˊ‿‿) [lt.] f, a. **Sonntag** ...mä (3. Sonntag vor den Fasten) Septuagesima (Sunday).
Septuaginta (‿‿‿ˊ‿) [lt. 70 (Übersetzer)] f, inv. bie ~ (oft gefchr.: LXX, grch. Übersetzung des Alten Testaments) Septuagint.
Sequens (ˊ‿) [lt. folgend] m (sg. inv., pl. Seque'ntes) bsd. kirchl.: the following.
Sequenz (‿ˊ) [lt. Reihenfolge] f ⓺ Kartenspiel ꝛc.: sequence; Pikett: ~ von 3 (4) höheren Karten tierce (quart) major.
Sequester (‿ˊ‿) [lt.] ⓶ jur.: a) n (Beschlagnahme) sequestration; in ~ nehmen = sequestrieren; b) m (Verwalter) sequestrator, mehr gbr.: administrator, trustee.
sequestrierbar (‿‿ˊ‿) a. ⓺ sequestrable.
sequestrier/en (‿‿ˊ‿) [lt.] jur. I v/a. ⓷ (unter Zwangsverwaltung stellen) to sequester, to sequestrate, mehr gbr.: to put in trust. — II ~ n ⓶ u. **2ung** f ⓺ sequestration.
Sequoi-e ♀ (ˊ‿two-i-) [Sequo Yah npr. gelehrter Tscherokese] f ⓺ (Mammutbaum) sequoia (Wellingto'nia).
Serail (ʃ)‿ra'j) [fr.; it. serraglio Schloß; *P nach *pers. sarāi Wohnung] n ⓾ ⓵d. (türk. Palast) seraglio.
Serapeion, mst **Serape-um** (‿‿ˊ‿) n ⓾ Alt.: (Serapistempel) Serapeion, Serapeum.
Seraph (ˊ‿f) [hebr. Feuerschlange (Blitz?)] m ⓵d., pl. a. **~im** (ˊ‿f) seraph; **2isch** (‿ˊ‿) a. ⓺ seraphic(al); (engelhaft) angelic.
Serapis (‿ˊ‿) npr/m. inv. Alt.: äg. Gott: Serapis; **~=tempel** m ⓺ = Serapeum.
Serbe (ˊ‿) m ⓸, **Serbin** f ⓸⁷ Servian.
Serbien ⚥ (ˊ(‿)‿) npr/n. ⓶ (Königreich im Norden der Balkanhalbinsel) Servia;
serbisch a. ⓺ Servian. [serenade.
Serenade (‿‿‿ˊ)[fr.,*it.] f ⓺ (Ständchen)
Sereniſſimus (‿‿ˊ‿‿) [lt. heiterst, durchlauchtigst] m ⓷ (Fürst) His Serene Highness. [gewebe) serge.
Serge ✱ (ˊ‿) [fr.] f ⓺, m ⓾ (Wollen-
Sergeant ⚔ (‿‿ˊGä'nt, a. f...)[(f+)fr.sergent] m ⓶ serjeant, sergeant; **~en-stelle** f ⓺ serjeantship, serjeant's post.
Serge-weber ⊕ (ˊ‿‿...) m ⓺ serge-maker; **=weberei** f serge-manufactory.
Seri-e (ˊ‿(‿)) [fr.; *lt. Reihe] f ⓺: a) series; b) ≉ issue; c) Billard: eine ~ (v. guten Stößen) machen to make a break.
Seri-en=los (ᵘ(‿)‿...) n ⓺ serial lottery-ticket; **=ziehung** f serial drawing.
Sermon (‿ˊ) [lt.] m ⓵d. = Predigt, bsd. F co. (tedious) lecture.
serös ⚥ (‿ˊ) [fr.=lt.] a. ⓺ (D 10) physiol. (blutwässerig) serous; **2-eiterig** (‿ˊˊ‿‿) a. ⓺ seropurulent.
Serpentin (‿‿ˊ) [lt. Schlangen=] m ⓵d. min. serpentine, ophite, picrolite; in ~ umwandeln to serpentinize; **2-artig** (‿‿ᵘ...) a. ⓺ serpentinic, ...ous;
~=drechsler m turner of serpentine.

Serpentine (‿‿ˊ‿) [lt. Schlangen=] f ⓺, **~n=straße** (ˊ...) f ⓺ serpentine road; **~n=tanz** m serpentine dance.
Serpentin=stein (‿‿ˊ‿ˊ) m ⓺ min. serpentine- (or snake-)stone.
Serradelle ♀ (‿‿ˊ‿) [port. sägeartig] f ⓺ Kleeart: serradilla (Ornitho'pus sati'vus).
Sersche (ˊ‿) f ⓺ = Serge.
Serubabel (‿‿ˊ‿) npr/m. ⓾ bibl. Zerubbabel. [(Blutwasser) serum.
Serum ⚥ (ˊ‿) [lt. Molke] n ⓶ ⓾ physiol.
servianisch (‿‿(‿)ˊ‿) a. ⓺ bsd. Alt.: of Servius Tullius, auch: Servian.
Service (ʃ..., a. ʃ=wi'ß, Hom. Servis) [fr. m] n ⓶ (gen. u. pl. mit tönendem e) (Tafelgerät) (dinner-, dessert-, &c.) service or set; (Porzellan) china.
servieren (ʃ..., a. ʃ=wiˊ‿) [fr.] v/n. (h. u. ſn) u. v/a. ⓷ 1. (den Tisch, die Tafel) 2 to wait at table, engs.: to lay the cloth or the table. — 2. (dienen) to serve.
Servi-ette (ʃ..., a. ʃ=wi(‿)ˊ‿) [fr.] f ⓺ (Mundtuch) (dinner-)napkin, serviette;
~n=band n ⓶, **~n=ring** m napkin-ring.
servil (‿ˊ‿) [lt. stlavisch] a. ⓺ (knechtisch) servile; **~ismus** (‿ˊ‿‿‿) m, inv., **~ität** (‿‿‿ˊ) f ⓺ servility.
Servis ⚔ (ʃ..., a. ʃ=wi'ß, Hom. Service) [fr. service Dienst] m ⓶ (auch inv.),
~=zulage f ⓺ (Quartiergeld) allowance for a soldier's (or officer's) quarters.
Serviteur (ʃ..., ʃ=wi=tö'r) [fr.] m ⓵d. (⓶) (Vorhemdchen) shirt-front.
Servitut (‿‿ˊ) [lt.] f ⓺ (n ⓵c.) jur. (Dienstbarkeit) servitude; (Verbindlichkeit) obligation.
Sesam (ˊ‿) [ind. samsam] m ⓾ ⓶ 1. ♀ sesame, gingili (Se'samum orienta'le, S. I'ndicum); weißer ~ oily grain, benne (S. orienta'le). — 2. aus „1001 Nacht": ~ tu dich auf! open (thou), sesame!
sesam-artig (ᵘ...) a. ⓺ anat.: ⚥ sesamoid(al); **=beinchen** ⚥ ⓶ anat. des Fußes: ⚥ sesamoid (bone); **=öl** ✱ n sesame-oil.
Seschellen ♀ (‿ˊ‿‿) ⓺: die ~ the Seychelles npr/f/pl.
Sesel ♀ (ˊ‿) [grch.] m ⓶ seseli, cicely (Se'seli). [halb) n ⓺ chm. sesqui-oxide.
Sesqui-oxyd ⚥ (ˊ=‿ˊ) [lt. sēsqui anderst-
Sessel (ˊ‿) [ahd.; *sitzen] m ⓶ easy chair, zum Tragen: sedan(-chair), zum Rollen: Bath chair, zum Zusammenklappen: camp-stool (vgl. Stuhl u. Lehnstuhl); (Sitz)seat.
Sessel-docke (ˊ‿‿...) f ⓶ ⊕ rail of elbow-rest) of an easy chair; **=recht** n ehm. am fr. Hofe: right to sit at Court; **=träger** m sedan-chair man.
seßhaft (ˊ‿) [mhd.: *sitzen] a. ⓺ = säſſig; **~igkeit** (‿‿ˊ‿) f ⓺ Anfäffigkeit.
Session (‿ˊ‿ⁿ) [lt.] f ⓺ (einzelne Sitzung) sitting, (Tagung) session of parliament.
Sester (ˊ‿) [ahd.; *lt. sexta'rius] m ⓶⁶ (ehm. Hohlmaß, oft 15 Liter) sester.
Sesterz (‿ˊ)[lt. seste'rtius brittbalb] m ⓵a. röm. Alt.: num. (2½ As) sesterce.
Sestine (‿ˊ‿) [it.] f ⓺ Dichtkunst: (Stanze v. 6 Zeilen) sestine, sextain.
Setz-angel ⊕ (ˊ‿...) f ⓺ trimmer-hook;
=bord ⚓ m e-s Bootes: wash-board;
=brett ⊕ n, typ. compositor's board;
=ei(er pl.) n Kocht. fried egg(s pl.).
setzen (ˊ‿) [ahd.; *sitzen m..] ⚥ I v/a. u. sich 2 v/refl. 1. (e-m e-n Platz anweisen)

Zeichen (f. S. XVII): F familiär; P Volkssprache; ⌐ Gaunersprache; ✎ selten; † alt (auch gestorben); * neu (auch geboren); +‒ unrichtig;

[**ſetzen**] — **885** — [**Setzmaſchine**]

to seat a p., to assign a place to a p.; (etwas legen, ſtellen) to set (or place, put up) a th.; ſich ₂ to sit down; f. II. — 2. mit *adv.* auf die Frage wohin: e-n obenan ₂ to put (or seat) a p. at the head of the table. — 3. mit *prp.* (oft *fig.*): **an**: an et. ₂ to place (or set, put) near a th.; et. an et. ₂ (aufs Spiel ₂) to stake s.th. on a th.; alles daran (an die Durchführung von etwas) ₂ to move heaven and earth; sein Leben an et. ₂ to risk one's life for a th.; den Topf ans Feuer ₂ to put ... on (the fire); f. Kehle 1; ↓ ans Land ₂ to (put on) land, to disembark; f. Luft 1; an den Mund ₂ to put to one's mouth, ein Glas auch ₂ to raise to one's lips; et. (wieder) an seinen Platz ₂ to put a th. (back) in(to) its place; Knöpfe an den Rock ₂ to sew (or put) buttons on the coat; et. an die Stelle von et. (anderem) ₂ to substitute one thing for another; einen Tiſch an den anderen ₂ to put ... against another; Zeugſtücke ꝛc. an=ea. ₂ (zf.=ſtücken) to piece (or patch) ... together; **auf**: a) mit perſönlichem Objekt: auf dieſer (mſt diese) Bank von Stein will ich mich ₂ (*SCH.*, Tell) on this stone bench will I be seated; e-n auf schmale Diät (ob. Koſt) ₂ to put a p. on a low diet; f. Fuß 7; ſich aufs Pferd ₂ to mount on horseback; f. Sand 2; e-n auf die Straße ₂ to turn a p. out (of doors); auf den Thron ₂ to place on (or to raise to) the throne; v. Vögeln ꝛc.: ſich auf einen Zweig ₂ to perch (down) on ...; b) mit ſachlichem Objekt: et. auf den Boden ₂ to put (or set) a th. (down) on the ground; f. Piſtole¹; Hasardſpiel: Geld auf eine Karte ₂ to stake money on a card; alles auf eine Karte ₂ to put all one's eggs in(to) one basket; Spitzen auf ein Kleid ₂ to put (or sew) lace on a dress; f. Preis¹ 1, Rechnung; et. auf die Seite (ob. beiſeite) ₂ to set a th. aside; aufs Spiel ₂ to risk, hazard, stake, venture; das Frühſtück auf den Tiſch ₂ to put the breakfast on the table, to lay (or serve up) breakfast; Bier auf Wein ₂ (trinken) to drink beer after (F on the top of) wine; **aus**: keinen Fuß aus dem Hauſe ₂ never to move out of the house; den Leuchter aus der Hand ₂ to put ... down; f. Beſitz 3; **außer**: außer Gebrauch ₂ to discontinue the use of, to put aside, to do away with, to abolish; außer Kraft ₂ to invalidate, to annul; f. außer 2; **bei**: beiſeite ₂ to set aside; **gegen**: et. gegen anderes ₂ (vergleichend) to compare one thing with another; ſich gegen (ober wider) et. ₂ to set one's face (F to kick) against a th., to resist (or oppose) a th.; **in**: a) örtlich: den Fuß in ein Haus ₂ to set one's foot inside a house; der Staub ꝛc. ſetzt ſich in die Kleider ... clings to (or settles in) the clothes; ſich in einen Wagen ₂ to get into (or inside) a carriage; in die Zeitung ₂ to put in(to or to insert in) the (news)paper; b) allgemein adverbiell: e-n in Angſt, Furcht, Schrecken ₂ to alarm,

frighten, terrify a p.; ſich bei e-m in Anſehen ₂ to acquire influence with (or over) a p.; f. Beſitz 2, Bewegung 2, erſtaunen III; in Eifer, Feuer, Flamme ₂ to rouse, inflame, incite; in Flammen ₂ to set on fire or ablaze, to set fire to; in Gang ₂ to set going; f. Gunſt, Kopf 8; ⊕ e-m et. in Rechnung ₂ to charge a th. to a p.'s account, to debit a p. s. th.; *thea.* in Szene ₂ to (put on the) stage; to mount a play, &c.; neu in Szene ₂ to revive; e-n in Verlegenheit ₂ to perplex (or embarrass, puzzle) a p.; Kinder in die Welt ₂ to bring children into the world; c) mit ſachlichem Objekt: Holz in Faden, Klafter ₂ to cord wood; d) mit abſtraktem Objekt: Hoffnung in e-n, et. ₂ to set one's hopes upon a p., a th.; Mißtrauen in e-n ₂ to harbour suspicion(s) against a p., to distrust a p.; ſeine Ehre, ſ-n Ehrgeiz, ſ-n Stolz dar(ein) ₂, zu // to make it a point of honour, of ambition to do a th.; to take a pride in doing a th.; e) (verſetzen) et. in die Zeit des Darius ₂ to date a th. from the time of ...; f) ⊕ Glaſerei ꝛc. (einſetzen): Scheiben in ein Fenſter ₂ to put panes into a window; **mit**: ſich mit e-m ₂ (gütlich vergleichen) to come to an arrangement with a p.; **neben**: et. neben et. ₂ to put a th. by the side of a th.; **über**: einen Punkt über das „i" ₂ to dot the "i"; e-n Schüler über die anderen ₂ to move a boy up; e-n über ein Haus (als Aufſeher) ₂ to place a p. in charge of a house; der Schiffer wird uns über das Waſſer ₂ ... will ferry us across the water; **um**: ſich um das Feuer ₂ to sit (or crouch) (a)round...; **unter**: e-n unter die Heiligen ₂ to number (or rank) a p. among ...; ſ-n Namen unter einen Akt ₂ to put (or affix) one's signature to a deed; unter Waſſer ₂ to submerge, to flood; **vor**: er kann keinen Fuß vor den andern ₂ he is not able to put one foot before the other; e-n (e-m den Stuhl) vor die Tür ₂ to turn a p. out (neck and crop); **zu**: a) ſich zu e-m ₂ to sit down beside a p., to sit near a p.; f. Pfand 1; ſich zu Pferde ₂ to mount a horse or on horseback; f. Ruhe 3; ſich zu Tiſch ₂ to sit by the table, zum Eſſen: to sit down to dinner; ſich zur Wehr ₂ to defend o.s.; et. zurecht ₂ to set a th. right, to put a th. in order; b) e-n zum Richter ₂ (machen) to appoint a p. as judge; **zwiſchen**: *fig.* ſich zwiſchen zwei Stühle ₂ to sit between two stools. — 4. mit prädikativem *a.*: e-n (ſich) bequem ₂ to seat a p. (to sit) comfortably; e-n warm ₂: a) to put a p. in a warm (or comfortable) place; b) *iro.* to put a p. in(to) prison or jail. — 5. *v/a.* mit ſachlichem Objekt: a) e-m eine Friſt, e-n Termin ₂ to give a p. (a certain) time; ſeinen Wünſchen ꝛc. Grenzen, ein Ziel ₂ to set a limit to ...; b) e-m ein Denkmal ₂ (errichten) to erect (or raise) a monument to a p.; Grenzſteine ₂ to put up boundary-stones; c) die Füße (gehend, tanzend) ₂ to place one's feet

(in position); d) Interpunktion ₂ to put the stops, to punctuate; e) den Fall ₂ (annehmen) to suppose (s.th. to be the case); vgl. geſetzt 3, bſd. Artikel f) ♪ to compose, to set to music; höher (niedriger) ₂ to raise (to lower) the pitch for; mehrſtimmig ₂ to arrange for several voices; g) Spiel: Geld ₂, *abs.* ₂ to stake (one's) money; to lay; es wurde hoch geſetzt the stakes were (or ran) high; Damenſpiel: eine Dame ₂ to crown a king; h) Junge ₂ to bring forth young (ones), oft *abs.* ₂ to breed, Fiſcherei: to spawn; i) *arith.* ſetze die Einer rechts set down (or arrange) the units on the right (side); *surg.* e-m Blutegel ꝛc. ₂ to apply leeches, &c. to a p.; k) meiſt ⊙: *hort.* Bäume ₂ to plant ...; Hauswirtſchaft: eine Henne ₂ to set ... (on eggs); Töpferei ꝛc.: einen Ofen ₂ to put up (or construct) ...; l) *typ.* Schrift ₂ (a. *abs.*) to compose, to set up (type). — 6. *v/a.* mit perſönlichem Objekt: e-n (feſt) ₂ to put a p. in(to) jail or prison, to lock a p. up. — **II** ſich ₂ *v/refl.* 7. f. 1, 2, 3, 4. — 8. (Platz nehmen) to take a seat; ſetzt euch sit down, take your seats; ₂ Sie ſich sit down, höflicher: (please) take a seat or be seated. — 9. (ſich niederlaſſen) to settle down. — 10. von Flüſſigkeiten: (ſich klären) to clarify, to settle. — 11. von einer Anſchwellung: to go down. — 12. v. Boden ꝛc.: to subside; v. Mauern ꝛc.: (ſacken) to sag. — **III** *v/impers.* 13. es wird Verdruß, böſes Blut ₂ (abgeben) it will breed (or cause) trouble, there will be bad (or ill) blood; es wird Schläge ₂ they will come to blows, it will end in a fight. — **IV** *v/n.* (vgl. a. 4) **14.** (in u. h.) in die Lotterie ₂ to put in(to the lottery); über e-n Fluß ₂ to cross a river; über e-n Graben, e-e Hecke ₂ (ſpringen) to leap (or jump) over (Reitſport: to take) a ditch, a fence; durchs Waſſer ₂ to cross the water. — **15.** ⚒ der Gang ſetzt durch das Geſtein the lode extends through the rock. — **V** ge=ſetzt *p.p.* u. *a.* ⊙ 16. Beb. des *inf.* — 17. f. bſd. Art.

Setzer (⏑—) *m* ㉒, ~**in** *f* ④ **1.** (f. ſetzen 5 g) one who stakes money; layer. — **2.** ⊙ *typ.* compositor (F *abbr.* comp.), *f* auch: compositress; weitS. typographer (F *abbr.* typo).

Setzerei ⊙ (—⏑—) *f* ㊻ *typ.* composing-room, case-department.

Setzer-fehler (⏑—...) *m* ㉒ = Setzfehler; **=lohn** *m* compositor's wages *pl.*; **=ſaal** *m* = Setzerei; **=verrichtungen** *f/pl.* compositor's duties *pl.*

Setz-fehler (⏑—...) *m* ㉒ printer's (or typographical) error, misprint; **=haſe** *m, hunt.* female (or doe of a) hare; **=karpfen** *m* Fiſcherei: young carp put into a pond, fry of carp; **=kaſten** ⊙ *m, typ.* lettercase; **=kunſt** *f*: a) ♪ (musical) composition; b) compositor's art.

Setzling (⏑—) *m* ⓪d. **1.** *agr., hort.* slip, layer. — **2.** Fiſcherei: ~e *pl.* fry.

Setz-linie (⏑—...) *f* ㊷ *typ.* setting-rule; **=maſchine** ⊙ *f, typ.* composing-machine, linotype, (electro)typograph;

♪ Muſik; ⚘ Wiſſenſchaft; ⚘ Pflanze; ⚘ Geographie; ⊙ Technik; ⚒ Bergbau; ⚔ Militär; ↓ Marine; ⚖ Handel; ✉ Poſt; 🚂 Eiſenbahn.

[Setzreis] — 886 — [sichern]

=reis n, agr. slip; vgl. Senkreis; =schiff ☉ n, typ. galley; =stange f: a) eines Zeltes: tent-pole; b) agr. zum Säen, Pflanzen: dibble, stick for planting; =teich m Fischerei: stock-pond.

Setzung (´‿) [setzen] f ⑯ setting.

Setz=wage ⊕ (´‿...) f ⑫ level; =zeit f, hunt. breeding= (Fischerei: spawning-)time.

Seuche (´‿) [ahd.: siech] f ⑱ path. epidemic (disease), contagious (or infectious) malady; plague, pestilence.

seuchen=artig (´‿‿...) a. ⑯ epidemic, contagious; 2frei a. ⑯ free from (an) epidemic; =herd m centre of contagion; =stoff m contagious matter, ⌂ virus.

seufzen (´‿) [ahd.] I v/n. (h.) ⓐ to (heave a) sigh, (ächzen, stöhnen) to groan, to moan; über et. 2 to sigh at (or over) a th., auch: to bemoan a th. — II ~ n sighing, &c. (f. I); unter ~ with (or amid) sighs or groans.

Seufzer (´‿) [mhd.] m ㉒ sigh; (Achzen) groan; einen ~ ausstoßen to heave a sigh, to utter a groan; ~brücke (´‿‿‿) f ⑫ in Venedig: Bridge of Sighs.

Sevennen ♀ (i‿w‿v, auch s...) npr/pl. inv. die ~ (fr. Gebirge) the Cevennes pl.

Sèvres=porzellan (ßä"wr‿‿‿ʼ) [Sèvres ♀, fr. St. unweit Paris] n ㉒ Sèvres china (or porcelain); =vase f Sèvres vase.

Sexagesima (‿‿´‿‿) [lt.] nur in: Sonntag ...mä (2. Sonntag vor Fasten) Sexagesima (Sunday).

Sexta (´‿) [lt. sechste] f ⑭ sixth (or lowest) form of a German secondary school; Sextaner (‿´‿) m ㉒ first-form boy, scholar of the „Sexta".

Sextant (‿´) [lt.] m ㉒ ast., math., ♂ Art Winkelmesser: sextant.

Sexte (´‿) [lt.] f ⑭ 1. ♪ Intervall von sechs Tönen: sixth. — 2. eccl. (Gebet zur sechsten Tagesstunde) sext.

Sextett (‿´) [it. seste'tto] n ⑪c. (sechsstimmiges Musikstück) sextet, sestetto.

Sextole ♪ (‿´‿) [it.] f ⑱ sechs Noten im Werte von vier derselben Art: sextuplet.

Sexualität (‿‿‿´) [lt.] f ⑯ (Geschlechtlichkeit) sexuality.

sexuell (‿‿´) [fr. sexuel] a. ⑯ (geschlechtlich) sexual, of (or relating to) the sex(es).

Sezession (‿‿´‿) [lt. sece'ssio] f ⑯ (Absonderung, Abfall) secession; Sezessionist (‿‿‿´) m ㉒ (a. paint.) secessionist.

Sezessions=krieg (‿‿´‿‿´) m ㉒ U.S. Bürgerkrieg, 1861—65: war of secession.

Sezier=besteck (‿´´‿´) n ⑫ dissecting-case.

sezieren (‿´‿) [lt. seca're schneiden] I v/a. ⑬ anat., surg. (zergliedern) to dissect, a. to open. — II ~ n ㉓ dissection.

Sezier=messer (‿´´‿) n ㉒ surg. scalpel.

s.g. abbr. = sogenannt (bff. sog.).

Sgr. abbr. chm. = Silbergroschen.

Sgraffito (‿´‿) [it. schraffiert] n ⑩⑱ Art Wandmalerei: sgraffito painting.

Shakspeare (schē'k-spīr) npr/m. ⑬α. (englischer Dichter, 1564—1616) Shakespeare; ~=forscher m ㉒ Shakespearian scholar; ~=gesellschaft f Shakespeare Society.

Shakspearisch, fig. 2 (schē't-spīr') a. ⑯ Shakespearian (drama, &c.), of (or relating to) Shakespeare.

Siamese (‿´‿) [Siam ♀, Königreich in Hinter-indien] m ㉔, Siamesin f ⑫, siamesisch a. ⑯ Siamese.

Sibilant (‿‿´) [lt.] m ㉒ gr. (Zischlaut) sibilant.

Sibiri-en ♀ (‿´‿(‿)) npr/n. ㉓ Nordasien: Siberia.

Sibiri-er (‿´‿(‿)) m ㉒, ~in f ⑫, sibirisch (‿´‿) a. ⑯ Siberian.

Sibylle (‿´‿) [grch.; *semit. = S(ch)ibboleth Zungfrau] f ⑫ (Seherin) sibyl; Sibyllinisch, fig. 2 (‿‿´‿) a. ⑯ sibylline; die ~en Bücher the Sibylline Books pl.

sich (´) [ahd.] ⑯ A 1. dat. u. acc. des refl. pron. (oft nicht zu übersetzen) 1. mit verbs: er kleidet 2 an he dresses himself, auch he dresses; 2 befreien to free o.s.; 2 schaden to injure o.s.; das Reh versteckt 2 the deer is hiding (itself); sie trösten 2 they comfort themselves; 2 die Hände waschen to wash one's hands; sie wäscht 2 she washes herself, auch: she washes; in der höflichen Anrede: Sie werden 2 weh tun you will hurt yourself (von mehreren: yourselves); beeilen Sie 2 nicht do not hurry yourself (pl. yourselves). — 2. mit prp. das Ding an 2 the thing in itself; die Sache hat wenig (nichts) auf 2 the matter is of little (of no) consequence; f. außer 3; er (sie) hat ein Gefolge bei 2 he (she) has a suite with him (her); sie haben kein Geld bei 2 they have no money about them; eine Sache für 2 a thing by itself, s.th. apart; das ist eine Sache für 2 that's another matter or story; der König ließ den Ritter vor 2 rufen the king had the knight called before him; er lud sie zu 2 (ins Haus) he invited them to his house; 2 et. zum Muster nehmen to take a th. for one's model. — 3. statt „einander" mit v/recip.: sie prügeln 2 (ea.) they knock each other about, they are fighting. [ment.]

Sich=abfindung (´‿‿‿) n ㉓ (mutual agree-⌐

Sichel (´‿) [ahd.: sickle; *lt. sē'cŭla] f ⑫ 1. agr. sickle, a. reaping-hook, -sickle. — 2. fig. ~ des Mondes crescent.

sichel=artig (´‿‿‿) a. ⑯ = 2förmig; 2beinig a. bow-legged; =form f 2förmig a. sickle-shaped, ⌐ falciform, falcate(d); =klee ⚕ m lucern (Medica'go falca'ta); 2krumm a. curved like a sickle.

sicheln (´‿) v/a. ⑫a to cut (or reap) with a sickle; gesichelt = sichelförmig.

Sichel=wagen (´‿‿´‿) m ㉒ Alt.: (Art Kriegswagen der alten Briten ꝛc.) scythed chariot, chariot (armed) with scythes.

sicher (´‿) [ahd.: secure, sure; *lt. sēcū'r-us ohne Sorge] a. ⑯ (D 9) 1. (außer Gefahr) secure, safe; (frei von Zweifel) sure, positive, (gewiß) certain; (zuverlässig) reliable, trustworthy; F so 2 wie nur was as safe as a house, as sure as a gun; 2 vor secure from or against, safe from, proof against; das 2ste wäre zu // the safest thing would be to //. — 2. mit nouns: 2es Gedächtnis faithful memory; 2es Geleit safe conduct; mit 2er Hand with a steady (or an unfaltering) hand; et. von 2er Hand h. to have s. th. on good authority; 2e Nachrichten pl. reliable news sg. — 3. mit verbs: 2 auf e-n bauen to put full (or entire) confidence in a p.; 2 (den 2sten Weg) geh(e)n to take a safe (the safest) course; er will ganz 2 geh(e)n he wants to make quite sure or to ensure success; er wird 2 kommen he is sure to come; 2 leben to live in security; e-n 2 m. to reassure a p., durch falsche Worte ꝛc.: to lull a p. into security; vor e-m 2 sein to have nothing to fear from a p.; vor Krankheiten ist niemand 2 no one is exempt (or immune) from illness, nobody is proof against disease; man kann sich 2 auf ihn verlassen he can be safely depended on or trusted, you may implicitly rely on him. — 4. mit gen.: einer Sache 2 sein to be sure of a th.; seiner Sache 2 sein to be quite positive, to be on safe (or sure) ground; sie sind ihres Lebens nicht 2 their lives are not safe, their lives are in danger or jeopardy. — 5. öft. = gewiß.

Sicherheit (´‿‿) [ahd.] sicher + -heit] f ⑯ 1. (s. sicher) security, safety; surety, certainty; (Zuverlässigkeit) reliableness, trustworthiness, (Vertrauen) confidence; ~ im Auftreten: assurance, in der Behauptung: positiveness, F cocksureness; f. bringen 8 unter „in"; Sie dürfen mit ~ darauf rechnen od. zählen you may safely depend upon it. — 2. ⚖ security, surety, cover, guarantee.

Sicherheits=anstalt (´‿‿´‿...) f ⑫, etwa: safe shelter, place of safety or refuge; =ausschuß m, pol. committee of public safety; =beamte(r) m, etwa: guardian of the peace; =behörde f police; =dienst m police duty; =geleit n safe conduct; =hafen m harbour of refuge; =hahn ⊕ m safety-cock or -tap; 2halber adv. for safety('s sake); =kette ⊕ f: a) an der Tür: door-chain; b) an der Uhr ꝛc.: guard-chain; =kommissarius F m overcautious fellow; =korb ⊕ m safety-cage; =lampe ⚒ f Davy's, &c. safety-lamp; =leistung f jur. security, gegen ~ entlassen w. to be set free on bail; =maßnahmen, =maßregeln f/pl. measures pl. of precaution, precautionary measures pl.; =nadel f safety-pin; =pfand n security; =rasiermesser n safety-razor; =röhre f. chm. safety-tube; =schiene ⚒ f side-rail; =stellung f v. Geld: placing in safety, (Gewährleistung) safeguarding, guarantee(ing); =ventil n, =vorrichtung f safety-valve, -apparatus; =zündhölzchen n safety-match; ehm. =zweirad n safety-bicycle.

sicherlich (´‿‿) adv. surely, assuredly; certainly; (ohne Zweifel) undoubtedly, without doubt; (ganz bestimmt) decidedly; 2 wissen sie es alle it is certain (or I am sure) they all know it.

sichern (´‿) [ahd.; *sicher] ⊕ a. I v/a. u. sich 2 v/refl. 1. to make safe; to safeguard, secure, ensure; (gewährleisten) to guarantee; (in Sicherheit bringen) to put in safety, to stow away safely; (befestigen) to consolidate, to fortify; sich vor (oder gegen) et. 2 to secure (or protect) o.s. against (or from) a th., im voraus: to guard (or provide) against a th.; ✕ in gesicherter Stellung in a secure (or well-fortified) position, under cover. — 2. ⚔ gesichert sein to be covered.

Signs (see page XVII): F familiar; P vulgar; F flash; ⌐ rare; † obsolete (died); * new word (born); ⌐⌐ incorrect; ♪ music;

[**sicherstellen**] to hold security. — **II** v/n. (h.) 3. *hunt.* vom Wilde: to examine a place of safety. — **III** ~ n ㉓ 4. = Sicherung 1. **Sicher-stellen** (ˇ◡ˇ) ㊿ ** **I** v/a. und sich ♀ v/refl.: c-n ♀ (vor etwas) to secure a p. (against a th.), to shield a p. (from a th.); sich ♀ to protect o.s. against losses, &c. — **II** ~ n ㉓ und **Sicherstellung** (ˇ◡ˇ) f ㊻ making secure; (Gewährleistung) (giving) guarantee; (Schirm und Schutz) safeguard.

Sicherung (◡◡) f ㊻ **1.** safeguarding, &c. (f. sichern I), safeguard; ⚔ protection. — **2.** ⊕ Schlosserei, Büchsenmacherei: slide-bolt or -stop.

Sich-geh(e)n-lassen (ˇ◡ˇ◡...) n ㉓ careless (flackadaisical) way; **=krank-lachen** n: zum ~ f. Krankflachen; **=selbst-überlassen-sein** n being left (entirely) to o.s., abandonment, loneliness.

Sicht (ˇ) [ahd. sight; *sehen] f ㊻ sight; ⚓ auf kurze, lange ~ at short, long sight or date; auf ~ bezahlen to pay at sight; bei ~, bfp. ⚓ in ~ in sight, within view; in ~ bekommen to sight; in ~ kommen to come (or heave, loom) in sight, to loom into view; 10 Tage nach ~ bezahlen to pay ten days after sight or at ten days' sight.

sichtbar (ˇ-) [mhd.] a. ㊿ visible; (wahrnehmbar) perceptible; (augenscheinlich) apparent; (offenbar) evident, obvious, ostensible; ♀ Pflanzen mit ♀en Befruchtungsorganen phanerogamic plants pl.; ♀ w. to become visible, ⚓ to heave in sight, to loom; *fig.* (offenbar w.) to become (or grow) manifest; **~keit** f ㊻ visibleness, perceptibility; obviousness; **♀lich** (ˇ◡ˇ) adv. visibly; evidently, obviously, ostensibly, manifestly; **~=werden** (ˇ◡ˇ◡) n ㉓ appearance of a comet, &c.; ⚓ heaving (or coming) in sight, loom, looming (into view).

sichten[1] ⚓ (ˇ◡) [Sicht] v/a. ㊾ to sight.

sichten[2] (ˇ◡) [nhd.: sift: Sieb] I v/a. ㊾ **1.** ⊕ to sift, Getreide: to winnow (a. *fig.*), Mehl: (beuteln) to bolt. — **2.** *fig.* (ausfondern) to sift, to sort, (untersuchen) to search into, to examine (closely); (läutern) to purify. — **II** ~ n ㉓ **3.** = Sichtung. [sifter, winnower, sorter.]

Sichter (ˇ◡) [sichten[2]] m ㉒, **~in** f ㊷

sichtlich (ˇ◡) a. ㊿ = sichtbar(lich).

Sicht-note (ˇ...) f ㊻ = wechsel; **=tage** m/pl. days of grace or respite.

Sichtung (ˇ◡) f ㊻ [f. sichten[2]] sifting, &c.; search, (close) examination.

Sicht-wechsel (ˇ...) m ㉒ ⬤ bill payable at sight, a.: sight-bill or -draft; **=weite** ⚓ f sighting distance.

Sich-überheben (ˇ◡ˇ◡ˇ) n ㉓ self-exaltation, arrogance.

sickern (ˇ◡) [nhd.] v/n. ㉒a.: a) (fin u. h.) to trickle, drip, drop; (fintern) to ooze (out); b) (h.) das Faß sickert ... leaks.

sideral ᴇᵣ (-◡ˊ), **siderisch** (-ˊ◡) [lt. *sīderi*-Gestirn] a. ㊿ ast. sideral; ♀es Jahr = Sternjahr. [jetzt Saïda) a. ㊿ Sidonian.]

sidonisch (-ˊ◡) [Sidon ♀, St. in Phönizien,]

sie (ˊ; Hom. fieh) [ahd.: she] ㊿ A 1.3 † **I** personal pron. **1.** 3. Person f.sg.: a) von weiblichen Personen und Tieren: she, *acc.* her; fie felbft she herself; von Dingen meift: it; a. personifizierend, bfd. von Ländern und Schiffen: she; b) bfd. ehm. in der Anrede an Untergebene: you (zweite Person pl.); fie foll die Treppe pußen you shall ... — **2.** 3. Person pl. they, *acc.* them; fie kommen they are coming; ich fah fie I saw them; fie felbft they themselves; fie taten es felbst they did it themselves. — **3.** **Sie:** 2. Person pl. in der höflichen Anrede für „du" you (auch *acc.*); Sie wissen felbft you know yourself, von mehreren: yourselves; als Anruf: Sie da! I say, an Geringere: Sie da, Mann! (look) here, my man!; Sie nennen f. fießen. — **II Sie** f ㊻ **4.** v. Personen u. Tieren: the she, the female, von Vögeln auch the hen; f. er 3.

Sieb (ˊ) [ahd.: sieve] n ㉓c. sieve, gröberes: riddle; für Mehl: bolter, für Flüssiges: strainer, für Kohlen, Kies ꝛc.: screen.

sieb=artig ⊕ (ˊˊ...) a. ㊿ sieve-like, cribrate, ...ose, ...iform; **=bein** n ㉖ *anat.*: cribriform (or ethmoid) bone; **=boden** m perforated (or sieve-)bottom.

sieben[1] mft ⊕ (ˊ◡) [mhd.; *Sieb] I v/a. ㊿ (f. Sieb) to (pass through a) sieve, to sift, to riddle, Mehl: to bolt, Kohlen ꝛc.: to screen. — **II** ~ n ㉓ sieving (auch *metall.*), sifting, screening.

sieben[2] (ˊ◡) [ahd.: seven: lt. *septem*] *numer.* **I** *card. numb. inv.* seven, es ist halb ♀ ... half-past six. — **II** (die Zahl) ♀ f ㊻ (number) seven; F böse ~ (regular) witch or termagant or vixen, *SH*, &c. auch: shrew.

sieben-blätt(e)rig ♀ (ˊ◡ˊ◡ˊ◡ˇ) a. ㊿ with seven leaflets, ᴇᵣ heptaphyllous.

Sieben-bürgen ♀ (-◡◡ˇ) npr/n. ㉓a. öft. Kronland: Transylvania; **=bürger(in** f ㊺) m ㉒, **♀bürgisch** a. ㊿ Transylvanian.

Sieben-eck (ˊˊ...) n ㉒ *geom.* seven-sided figure, heptagon; **♀eckig** a. heptagonal.

Siebener (ˊ◡◡) m ㉒ **1.** = sieben[2] II. — **2.** (die Ziffer 7, VII) (the figure) seven. — **3.** member of a council of seven; röm. Alt.: septemvir. — **4.** anything bearing the number seven.

siebener-lei (ˊ◡◡ˊ-) a. *inv.* of seven (different) kinds. [fold.)

sieben-fach (ˊ◡...), **♀fältig** a. ㊿ seven-[

Sieben-gebirge (ˊ◡...) ㉖ ♀ npr/n. nordwestlicher Teil des Westerwaldes: the Seven Mountains pl.; **=gestirn** ♀, *ast.* Pleiades pl.; **=herrschaft** f = Heptarchie; **=hügel-stadt** f (Rom) Seven-hilled City, City of the Seven Hills; **♀jährig** a. ㊿ of (or lasting) seven years, septennial; der ♀e Krieg (1756–63) the Seven Years' War; **♀jährlich** a. taking place once in seven years; **♀mal** adv. seven times; **♀malig** a. happening seven times; **♀männ(er)ig** ♀ a. (mit 7 Staubgefäßen) heptandrian, ...ous; **=meilenstiefel** m/pl. im Märchen: seven-league(d) boots, F seven-leaguers pl.; **=monatskind** n seven-months' child; **=punkt** m, *ent.* = Marienkäfchen; **=sachen** f/pl. a p.'s things or goods and chattels; seine ~ packen to pack up one's traps; **=schläfer** m: a) pl. der Legende (27. Juni): the seven sleepers pl. (of Ephesus); b) = Langschläfer; c) *zo.* = Bilch; **=stern** ⚓ m chickweed (*Trientalis Europaea*)

von Dingen meist: it; a. personifizierend, &c. = ebm. in der Anrede ...

sieb(en)te (ˊ(◡)◡) [ahd.] *ord. numb.* ㊿ the seventh; f. Himmel 1; Datum: der ♀ (am 2n) Mai (gfchr.: 7. Mai) (on) the seventh of May, May the seventh (gfchr.: May 7ᵗʰ); Karl der ~ (gfchr.: VII.) Charles the Seventh (gfchr.: VII); **♀halb** (ˊˊ◡ˇ) a. *inv.* six and a half.

sieben-teilig (ˊ◡ˊ◡) a. ㊿ septempartite.

Sieb(en)tel (ˊ(◡)◡) n ㉒, ♀ a. *inv.* seventh (part); drei ~ (³/₇) three-sevenths.

sieb(en)tens (ˊ(◡)◡) adv. seventhly, in the seventh (7ᵗʰ) place.

sieben-torig (ˊ◡...) a. ㊿ seven-gated, with seven gates; **♀und=zwanzig** twenty-seven, seven-and-twenty; **♀zehn** fast † = siebzehn.

siebenzig fast † (ˊ◡◡) ꝛc. = siebzig ꝛc.

Sieber (ˊ◡) [sieben[1]] m ㉒, **~in** f ㊺ sifter; screener.

sieb-förmig (ˊˊ...) a. ㊿ = ♀artig; **=macher** m sieve-maker; **=mehl** n coarse flour; **=mühle** f bolting-mill; **=platte** f sieveplate (a. *anat.*); **=setzer** m, **=setzmaschine** f ⚒ jigger, jigging-machine; **=staub** m siftings pl.

siebte (ˊ◡) ꝛc. f. siebente ꝛc.

Sieb-trommel (ˊ◡...) f ㊺ Spinnerei: sievedrum; **=tuch** n bolting- (or straining-)cloth, strainer; vgl. Etamin; **=walze** f Papierfabrik: dandy-roller.

siebzehn (ˊ-◡) [ahd.] *numer.* **I** *card. numb. inv.* seventeen. — **II** (die Zahl) ~ f ㊻ (number) seventeen.

siebzehn-jährig (ˊ-◡ˊ◡) a. ㊿ of seventeen years, seventeen years old.

siebzehnte (ˊ-◡◡) *ord. numb.* ㊿ seventeenth; Ludwig der ~ (gfchr.: XVII.) Louis the Seventeenth (gfchr.: XVII); **~l** n ㉒, ♀ a. *inv.* seventeenth (part); ein ~l (¹/₁₇) one-seventeenth; **♀ns** adv. in the seventeenth (17ᵗʰ) place.

Sieb-zeug (ˊ...) n ㉖ Müllerei: bolter.

siebzig (ˊ◡) *card. numb. inv.* seventy.

Siebziger (ˊ◡◡) **I** m ㉒, **~in** f ㊺: ein ~ person seventy (and more) years old, ♀ septuagenarian. — **II** ♀ a. *inv.* die ♀ Jahre (Zeitrechnung u. Lebensalter) the seventies; in den ~n sieh(e)n to be over seventy (years old), F to be going on for eighty.

siebzig-fach (ˊ◡...) a. ㊿, **♀fältig** a. seventy-fold; **♀jährig** a. of (or lasting) seventy years, seventy years old.

siebzigste (ˊ◡◡) *ord. numb.* ㊿ seventieth; **~l** n ㉒, ♀ a. *inv.* seventieth (part); **♀ns** adv. in the seventieth (70ᵗʰ) place.

siech (ˊ) [ahd.: sick] a. ㊿ sick(ly), in ill (or poor) health; (entkräftet) weak, infirm; (matt) languishing, pining (away).

Siech-bett (ˊ◡) n ㉓ sick-bed.

siechen (ˊ◡) [ahd.] v/n. (h.) ㊿ (trant fein) to be sickly or in ill health, auf die Dauer: to be a confirmed invalid; (hinwelken) to languish, to pine (or fade) away. [bfd. hospital for incurables.)

Siechen-haus (ˊ◡ˊ) n ㉖ infirmary,)

Siechtum (ˊ-) n ㉖c. sickliness, lingering illness or malady, protracted suffering; languishing state.

Siede-haus ⊕ (ˊ◡...) [sieden] n ㉖ boiling-house; **=hitze** f boiling-heat; **=hütte** f Salpeterfabrikation: saltpetrehouse; **=kessel** m boiler; **=lauge** f Seifenfabr.: boiling-liquor

---

ᴇᵣ scientific; ♀ botanical; ♀ geography; ⊕ machinery; ⚒ mining; ⚔ military; ⚓ marine; ⬤ commercial; ✉ postal; 🚂 railway.

[Siedelei] — 888 — [Silberblende]

Siedelei (-⸝ᴗ´) [siedeln] f ⑯ settlement.
Sied(e)ler (´⸝ᴗ)ᵥ) m ㉒ settler.
siedeln (´⸝ᴗ) [ahd.] v/a. ㉒a. to settle.
Sied(e)lung (´⸝ᴗ) f ⑯ settlement.
sieden (´⸝ᴗ) [ahd.: seethe] ㊉e(⑧⑨) (p.p. gesotten u. gesiedet) I v/n. (h.) to seethe (auch v. Meereswellen ꝛc.), mehr gbr.: to boil; gelinde: to simmer; das Wasser siedet the water is boiling; fig. ⦵ ebullient. — II v/a. to boil water, &c., gelinde: to let simmer; ich ließ es ⦵ I let it boil, gelinde: I let it (gently) simmer; f. Ei² 1; ⊕ Salz ⦵ to make salt; Seife ⦵ to boil (or make) soap; Zucker ⦵ to refine sugar; Färberei: in Alaun ⦵ to alum; metall., &c. weiß ⦵ to blanch. — III ∼ n ㉓ boiling, &c. (f. I und II), bsd. fig. ebullition; nahe am ∼ nearly boiling, F near (or on) the boil.
siedend-heiß (´⸝ᴗ´) a. ⑯, ⦵warm (´⸝ᴗ´) a. boiling (or seething) hot, scalding.
Siede-ofen ⊕ (´⸝ᴗ…) m ㉒ blanching-furnace, -oven; **=pfanne** f Zuckerfabr. ꝛc.: boiler; Saline: salt-pan; **=punkt** m, phys. e-r Flüssigkeit, des Thermometers ꝛc.: boiling-point. [Zssgn. ꝫB.: Salz-, Seifen-sieder.]
Sieder ⊕ (´⸝ᴗ) m ㉒ one who boils; bsd. in
Siederei (-⸝ᴗ´) f ⑯ = Siede-haus, -hütte.
Siede-rohr ⊕ (´⸝ᴗ…) n ㉒ boiling-tube; **=röhre** f, mach. boiler-tube.
Siedler. Siedlung f. Siedeler, Siedelung.
Sieg (´) [ahd.] m ⑪c. bsd. ⚔ victory; triumph; den ∼ davontragen = siegen; den ∼ über sich selbst erringen to conquer (or master, subdue) o.s.; leichter ∼ easy victory or conquest, parl., &c. auch: walk over.
Siegel (´⸝ᴗ) [mhd.] n ㉒ seal (ahd. Insiegel, f. ds) *It.] n ㉒ (Petschaft und Abdruck davon) seal, königliches ꝛc. auch bisw.: signet; England: kleines (großes) (Staats-) ∼ privy (great) seal; (gerichtlich) unter ∼ legen to put under the seal of the Court; fig. f. Brief 2; das ist für mich ein Buch mit sieben ∼n that's a sealed book (or a puzzle) to me; unter dem ∼ der Verschwiegenheit under the seal of secrecy, in strict confidence.
Siegel=amt (´⸝ᴗ…) n ㉒ signet-office; **=bewahrer** m keeper of the seal; vgl. Großsiegelbewahrer; **=bruch** m breaking a seal (open); **=erde** f, min. Lemnian earth, bole, ⚗ sphragide; **=kapsel** f seal-box; **=kunde** f knowledge of seals, ⚗ sphragistics; **=lack** m u. n sealing-wax; **=lack-fabrikant** m s.-wax manufacturer; **=lack-stange** f stick of s.-wax; ⦵los a. unsealed.
siegeln (´⸝ᴗ) [ahd.; *Siegel] v/a. ㉒a. e-n Brief ⦵ to seal (up)…; amtlich: to put (or affix) a seal to a door, &c., to place a th. under seals. [=stecher m seal-engraver.]
Siegel=ring (´⸝ᴗ…) m ㉒ signet-ring;
Siege(l)ung (´⸝ᴗ) f ⑯ sealing.
Siegel=wachs (´⸝ᴗ…tʃ) n ㉒ wax for sealing.
siegen (´⸝ᴗ) [mhd.; *Sieg] I v/n. (h.) ㉘ to be victorious or triumphant, to conquer; to carry the day; to gain a victory over the enemy; er siegte in jedem Treffen he carried everything before him; die Vernunft wird ⦵ reason will prevail. — II ∼ n ㉓ = Sieg.
— III ⦵d p.pr. u. a. ⑯ victorious, triumphant, conquering (hero, &c.).

Sieger (´⸝ᴗ) m ㉒, **∼in** f ㊼ victor, conqueror, bei einer Preisbewerbung: prize-winner, bei einem Rennen: winner; ∼ bleiben to remain triumphant, to hold the field (f. hervorgehen d).
Sieger=krone (´⸝ᴗ…) f ㉒, **=stolz** m victor's (or conqueror's) crown, pride.
Sieges=aufzug (´⸝ᴗ…) m ㉒ triumphal procession; **=beute** f (victor's) spoils pl.; **=bogen** m triumphal arch; **=botschaft** f = **=kunde**; **=dank-fest** n thanksgiving for a victory, eccl. Te Deum; **=denkmal** n monument commemorative (or in memory) of a victory; **=feier**, **=fest** n (fête in) celebration of a vict.; **=freude** f joy over a victory; **=fürst** m = Sieger; **=gepränge** n triumphal pomp or splendour; **=gesang** m = =lied; **=geschrei** n shout of vict.; ⦵gewiß a. ⑯ sure (or confident) of vict.; **=göttin** f, myth. Victory; **=held** m conquering hero; **=jubel** m jubilation (or rejoicing) over a victory; **=kranz** m crown of vict.; **=kunde** f news of a victory; **=lauf** m victorious career, triumphal progress; **=lied** n triumphal song, chant of victory; **=palme** f palm of vict.; **=preis** m prize (of victory); vgl. **=zeichen**; **=säule** f triumphal column; **=taumel** m flush of victory; ⦵trunken a. flushed (or elated) with victory; **=wagen** m triumphal car; **=zeichen** n trophy; **=zug** m triumphal march or procession.
sieg=gekrönt (´…) (⦵gewohnt) a. ⑯ crowned with (accustomed to) victory.
sieghaft, fast † (´⸝ᴗ) [mhd.] a. ⑯ = siegreich.
Siegler (´⸝ᴗ) [siegeln] m ㉒ sealer.
Sieglung (´⸝ᴗ) f ⑯ f. Siegelung.
Siegmund (´⸝ᴗ) = Sigismund.
sieg=reich (´⸝´) a. ⑯ victorious, triumphant; adv. a. as a conqueror or victor.
sieh (´; Hom. sic), ⦵e (´⸝ᴗ) imper., **siehst** (´) v/a., **sieht** (´) 3. Person sg. pres. ind. v. sehen.
Sieke ⟱, ⊕ (´⸝ᴗ) f ㊽ (Rand, Saum) edge, seam. [anbringen] to crease, to seam.
sieken (´⸝ᴗ) v/n. (h.) ㊹ (schmale Rinnen)
Sieken=draht ⊕ (´⸝ᴗ…) m ㉒ creased wire; **=form** f creasing-die or -tool.
Siel (´) [ndd.] m u. n ⑥c. 1. Wasserbau: sluice. — 2. (Abzugsgraben) sewer, drain, drain-pipe.
Siele ⊕ (´⸝ᴗ) [ahd.: Seil] f ㊽ Sattlerei: (Kummet) horse-collar; fig. es war ihm der Tod in den ∼n (in Ausübung seines Berufs) vergönnt he was allowed to die in harness. [drain.]
sielen ⊕ (´⸝ᴗ) [Siel] v/a. (h.) ㊹ to
Sielen=geschirr ⊕ (´⸝ᴗ…) n ㉒, **=werk** n breast-harness;
Siel=wasser (´⸝ᴗ…) n ㉒ sewage.
Siemens=sch (´⸝ᴗ) [Werner ꝛc. Siemens, deutsche Ingenieure] a. ⑯: ∼e Fabrik Siemens' Works pl.; ∼e Induktionsrolle Siemens armature; ∼e Lampen Siemens lamps pl.; ∼er Stahl Siemens-(Martin) steel. [Mittagsschläfchen.]
Si-esta (ϟ´⸝ᴗ) [span.] f ㊽⑯ siesta (=
siezen F (´⸝ᴗ) [Sie] v/a. ㊐ (ant. duzen): e-n ⦵ (Sie nennen) to call a p. (or to address a p. as) "Sie"
Sigel (´⸝ᴗ; Hom. Siegel) [fr. sigle m] n ㉒ Stenographie ꝛc. (Abkürzungszeichen): ⚗ logogram.

Sigismund (´⸝ᴗᴗ) [Schützer durch Sieg] npr./m. f. a. Sigismund.
Signal (ϟ´´) [lt. sīgn-] n ⑪d. signal; elect. ring of an electric bell; ⚔ das ∼ zum Angriff blasen to sound a charge; ∼ zum Aufsitzen signal for mounting; das ∼ zum Aufsitzen geben to sound to horse.
Signal=apparat (ϟ´´…) m ㉒ signalling-apparatus; **=bude** 🚂 f signal-box; **=dienst** m signal-service.
Signalement (ϟ⸝ᴗ´mɑ̃)[fr.] n ⑪ description of a p. (given) in a police-warrant.
Signal=feuer (ϟ´´…) n ㉒ signal-fire, beacon; **=flagge** f signal-flag; **=glocke** f warning (or signal-)bell; **=horn** n bugle. [anzeigen] to signal.
signalisieren (⸝ᴗ-⸝ᴗ´)v/a. ㊱ (durch Signale)
Signal=leine 🚂 (ϟ´´…) f ㊽ bell-rope, communication-cord; **=licht** n signal-light; **=ordnung** ⚓ f signal-code; **=pfeife** ⦵ f steam-whistle; **=ruf** m signal, call of warning; **=schuß** m signal-gun; **=stange** 🚂 f semaphore; **=wärter** 🚂 m signalman.
Signatar=macht (ϟ´´⸝´ʃt) [lt. unterzeichnend] f ㉒ signatory power.
Signatur (ϟϟ´) [lt.] f ⑯ 1. (Unterschrift,) signature, durch ein Zeichen: sign manual. — 2. ⊕ mark, stamp, brand; (Zettel) label; pharm. (Gebrauchsanweisung) signature. — 3. ⊕ typ.: a) (Bogenbezeichnung) signature; b) (Kerbe in der Letter: ∼rinne f ㉒) nick.
Sigrist obd. (´⸝ᴗ, -´) [ahd.] *It. (f. Sakristan)] m ㉒ sexton.
Sikuler (´⸝ᴗᴗ) [lt. Sĭcŭlus Sizilianer] m ㉒, **∼in** f ㊼, **sikulisch** (´⸝ᴗ) a. ⑯ röm. Alt.: Siculian, jetzt: Sicilian.
Silau ♃ (´⸝´) [lt.] m ㊿ pepper- (or meadow-)saxifrage (Sīlaus pratēnsis).
Silbe (´⸝ᴗ) [ahd.; lt. (*grch.) syllăba] f ㊽ gr. syllable; kurze, lange ∼ short, long syllable, pros. auch: short, long; vorletzte, drittletzte ∼ penult, antepenult; ich verstehe keine ∼ davon I don't understand a word (or syllable) of it; es ist keine wahre ∼ daran there is not a syllable of truth in it; fig. ∼n stechen to quibble (about words), to catch at words, to split hairs.
Silben=akzent (´⸝ᴗ…) m ㉒ syllabic accent; **=fall** m rhythm; **=klauber** m = =stecher; **=maß** n (syllabic) quantity, metre; **=messung** f prosody; **=rätsel** n charade; **=stecher** m quibbler, word-catcher, hair-splitter; **=stecherei** f quibbling, hair-splitting; **=trennung** f splitting up (or division) into syllables, syllabication.
Silber (´⸝ᴗ) [ahd.: silver] n ㉒ silver, chm.: ⚗ argentum (Ag); ☾ ∼ in Barren, Stangen bar-silver, silver in ingots, (silver as) bullion; f. beschlagen 1; mit ∼ gestickt silver-embroidered; Sprichw. f. reden 4.
Silber=ader ⚒ (´⸝ᴗ…) f ㉒ vein (or lode) of silver; **=arbeit** f silver-work; **=arbeiter** m si.-smith; ⦵artig a. ⑯ silvery, ⚗ argentine; **=bach** m, poet. silver(y) stream; **=barre(n** m) f ⚖ bar (or ingot) of si.; **=bergwerk** n si.-mine; **=beschlag** m silver-mounting; ⦵beschlagen a. silver-mounted; **=blech** n silver leaf; **=blende** f, min. ⚗ galena.

Zeichen (f. S. XVII): F familiär; P Volkssprache; Γ Gaunersprache; ⟨ selten; † alt (auch gestorben); * neu (auch geboren); ✠ unrichtig.

[Silberblick] — 889 — [sinken]

of silver, antimonische: pyrargyrite; =blick m, metall. f. Blick 2; fig. gleam (or lightning, fulguration) of silver; =bog(e)ner m one armed with a silver bow; =brenner m silver-refiner; =bromid n, chm. = Bromsilber; =chlorid n, chm. (Chlorsilber) argentic chloride (Ag Cl); =chlorür n, chm. argentous chloride (Ag_2Cl); =diener m an Höfen ꝛc.: keeper of the plate; =dollar m silver dollar; =draht m si. wire; =erz ⚒ n si.-ore; =erz=mühle ⚒ f si.-mill; =faden m silver-thread; =farbe f si.-colour; =farben, =farbig a. silver-coloured, silvery; =fasan m, orn. si.- (or pencilled) pheasant (Gallopha'sis nyc(h)the'merus); =fisch m, ichth. Spielart des Goldfisches: silver-fish; =flotte f bjp. hist. Spanish si.-fleet; =foli-e ⊕ f si.-foil; =fuchs m, zo. silver(-black) fox (Vulpes fulvus); =gehalt m percentage (or proportion) of silver in an alloy; =geld n silver money, kleines: silver change; =gerät, =geschirr n (silver) plate; =gespinst n spun silver; =glanz m: a) lustre (or brightness, brilliancy) of silver; b) min. si.-glance, argentite; =glätte f litharge of silver; =grau a. silver-grey, ehm. =groschen m ($^1/_{30}$ Taler) silbergroschen (= about one penny); =grube f silver-mine; =grund m si.-foundation; =gulden 💰 m si. florin; =haar n, poet. silvery hair; =haltig a. containing silver; argentiferous, argentic; =handel m silver-trade; =hell a. (as) bright as silver; 2er Klang silvery sound; =hütte ⚒ f silver-foundry; =jodid n = Jodsilber; =kammer f plate-room or -chamber; =kämmerer m = =diener; =klang m silvery sound or note; =korn n grain of silver; =krätze f (Abfall) dross of silver; =kuchen m lump of silver; =laden m silversmith's shop; =lahn ⊕ m silver tinsel; =licht n silvery light; =legierung f silver-alloy; =linde ♀ f silver-linden (Ti'lia arge'ntea).
Silberling (⌣⌣) [ahd.] m ⓓ. silver coin. ehm.: silverling; bibl. (Matth. 26,16) um dreißig ~e for thirty pieces of silver.
Silber=locke (⌣⌣..) f ⓮ poet. silver lock; =löwe m f. Puma; =münze f silver coin.
silbern (⌣⌣) a. ⓰ (of) silver; 2e Hochzeit silver wedding; vgl. Schale.
Silber=nitrat (..⌣⌣) n ⓶ chm. = salpetersaures (j. ds) Silber; =oxyd n oxide of silver, argentic oxide (Ag_2O); =oxydsalz n, chm. = Silbersalz; =papier ♀ n silver-paper, silvered paper; =pappel ♀ f white poplar, abele (Po'pulus alba); =plattierung ⊕ f silver-plating; =probe ⊕ f silver-assay or -test; =quell(e f) m, poet. silver-fount or -fountain; =raute ♀ f icy wormwood (Artemi'sia glacia'lis); 2reich a. ⓰ rich in silver; vgl. 2haltig; =reiher m, orn. egret, lesser white heron (A'rdea 'gre'tta); =rein a. (as) pure as silver; =rubel 💰 m silver rouble; =sachen f/pl. articles made of silver. si. objects or things pl.; =salz n, chm. silver-salt; =sand m si.-sand; =schaum m silver-leaf, foliated silver; =scheibe f des Mondes: silver disk of the moon; =scheide-

münze f small silver coin; =schein m silvery lustre; bjp. ehm. =schiff ⚓ n silver-laden ship or galleon; =schimmel m silver-grey horse; =schimmer m = =schein; =schmied ⊕ m silversmith; =schrank m cupboard for plate; =stimme f, poet. silver(y) voice; =stoff ⊕ m silver-cloth or -brocade; =strich m, ent. Schmetterling: silver-washed fritillary (Argy'nnis pa'phia); =stück n = =münze; =stufe f sample of silver-ore; =sulfuret ⚒ n, chm. = Schwefelsilber; =tanne ♀ f = Pechtanne; =ton m = =klang; =tresse f silver-lace; =verwahrer m = =diener; =währung f silver-standard; =waren f/pl. si. goods; vgl. =zeug; =weide ♀ f white willow (Salix alba); 2weiß: a) a. silvery white; b) n silver-white; =welle f, poet. silver(y) wave; =werk n = =gerät; =wirker m silver-weaver; =wirkerei ⊕ f si.-weaving; =zeug n silver plate, silverware. [z.B.: zwei2 dissyllabic.)
...silbig (...⌣) [= Silbe] a. ⓰ in Zsjgn.)
Sile (⌣⌣) f ⓮ = Siele.
Silen(os) (-⌣(⌣) [grch.] npr/m. ⓐa. myth. (Begleiter des Bacchus) Silenus.
Silentium (⌣⌣⌣⌣) [lt. Schweigen] n ⓶ u. int. silence!, (be) quiet!
Silge ♀ (⌣⌣) [lt. (vgl. Petersilie)] f ⓮ milk-parsley (Seli'num Carvifo'lia).
Silhouett/e (si..., a. ßi-lü⌣) [fr.] f ⓮ = Schattenriß; s/ieren (⌣⌣⌣⌣) v/n. (h.) ⓰ to take (or throw off) silhouettes; s/ierer m ⓶ silhouettist.
Silikat ⚒ (⌣⌣⌣) [lt. sílex Kiesel] n ⓶c. chm. (kieselsaures Salz) silicate. [silicium.)
Silizium ⚒ (⌣⌣⌣) [lt. Kiesel] n ⓶ [lt. Kiesel.)
Silo (⌣⌣) [span.] m ⓰ (Kornkeller) silo.
silurisch ⚒ (⌣⌣⌣) [Silu'ren, altes Volk in Wales] a. ⓰ geol. (der unteren Grauwacke angehörig) Silurian.
Silvan(us) (⌣⌣(⌣) [lt.] npr/m. ⓑⓖⓐ. myth. (a. Vn.) Silvanus, Sylvanus.
Silvester (⌣⌣⌣⌣) [lt.] npr/m. ⓶ Silvester, Sylvester; ~abend m (31. Dezember) New Year's Eve. [paste diamond.)
Simili=stein ⊕ (⌣⌣⌣⌣) [lt.-dtsch] m ⓶)
Similor (-⌣⌣) [fr. m] n ⓶ (Kupfer u. Zink) similor, Mannheim gold. [simony.)
Simonie (-⌣⌣) f ⓮ (Apostelgeschichte 8,18))
simonisch (-⌣⌣) a. ⓰ simoniacal.
simpel (-⌣⌣) [fr.] I a. (D 9) simple (s. einfach, ⓶fältig). — II ~ m ⓶ (Einfaltspinsel) simpleton, dunce, F dunce.
simpelhaft (⌣⌣⌣) a. ⓰ simple, silly.
simpeln (⌣⌣⌣) v/n. (h.) ⓶a. to behave like a simpleton; vgl. Fach 2. [simplicity.)
Simplizität (⌣⌣⌣⌣) [lt.] f ⓮ (Einfalt))
Sims (⌣) [ahd.] m, n ⓶a. = Gesims.
Simse (⌣⌣) f ⓮ 1. ♀ (bul)rush (Scirpus); vgl. Binse. — 2. F berlin. = Prügel.
Sims=hobel (⌣⌣⌣⌣) m ⓶ = Leistenhobel.
Simson (⌣⌣) npr/m. ⓑⓐ. bibl. Samson.
Sims=stein (⌣⌣⌣⌣) m ⓶ cornice-stone; =werk n cornice; entablature; =ziegel m cornice-tile.
Simulant (⌣⌣⌣) [lt.] m ⓶, ~in f ⓯ sham patient or invalid, ⚔ a. malingerer.
Simulation (⌣⌣-ti(⌣)⌣) [lt.] f ⓮ (Verstellung, Sichkrankstellen) simulation, shamming illness; ⚔ a. malingering.
simulier/en (⌣⌣⌣⌣) [fr.] v/n. (h.), v/a. ⓰ 1. (sich verstellen) to simulate, feign,

sham, pretend; ⚔ f/ter Rechenschaftsbericht simulated (F cooked, doctored) accounts (pl.). — 2. P auf et 2 (sinnen) to meditate on a th.
simultan (⌣⌣⌣) [lt. gleichzeitig] a. ⓰ simultaneous; ~schule f ⓮ (unkonfessionelle Sch.) undenominational school.
Sina-i ♀ (⌣⌣⌣) [Sin, babyl. Mondgott] npr/m. ⓑa. der ~ (Mount) Sinai.
sind (⌣) 1. und 3. Person pl. pres. ind. v. sein.
Sinekure (⌣⌣⌣⌣) [lt.] f ⓮ (Pfründe ohne Seelsorge; leichtes einträgliches Amt) sinecure.
☞ Sinf.. f. Symph... [academy.)
Sing=akademie (⌣⌣⌣⌣⌣) f ⓮ singing-)
Singapur ♀ (⌣⌣⌣) npr/n. ⓑa. (Insel und Stadt auf Malakka) Singapore.
singbar (⌣⌣) a. ⓰ singable.
Sing=chor (⌣..) ⓶: a) ♪ m choir; b) n, arch. f. Chor 4; =drossel f, orn. common thrush (Tardus mu'sicus).
singen (⌣⌣) [ahd.: sing] I v/n. (h.) u. v/a. ⓶st 1. to sing. langsam u. feierlich: to chant (f. schmettern); das Wasser singt im Kessel (vor dem Kochen) the kettle is singing; fig. mir 2 die Ohren I have a buzzing in my ears; ♪ f. falsch 1 u. Bariton; er singt das hohe C he can sing (or his voice reaches) the high C; mehrstimmig 2 to sing part-songs; s-e Stimme 2 to sing one's part; nach dem Gehör 2 to sing by ear; nach Noten 2 to sing from music; vom Blatte (weg) 2 to read music. — 2. mit Angabe der Wirkung: ein Kind in den Schlaf 2 to sing ... to sleep; auch v/refl. sich heiser (außer Atem) 2 to sing o.s. hoarse (out of breath). — 3. fig. f. Lied 3; das ward mir an meiner Wiege nicht gesungen nobody ever thought (that) I should come to this (state). — II ~ n ⓶ 4. singing, chant(ing); vgl. Gesang; f. Blatt 2 am Ende.
Singer (⌣⌣) [mhd.] m ⓶ ehm.: (Singmeister) singing-master.
Singerei (⌣⌣..) f ⓮ continued (or indifferent) singing, sing-song; F squalling. [for singing.)
Sing=fertigkeit (⌣⌣⌣⌣-) f ⓮ aptitude)
Singhalese (⌣⌣⌣⌣) m ⓸⓸, ...lesin f ⓯ (Bewohner[in] von Ceylon) Cingalese.
Sing=halle (⌣⌣⌣⌣) f ⓮ music-hall; =lehrer, =meister m singing-master; =note ♪ f musical note; =pult n singing-desk.
Sin=grün (⌣⌣) n ⓶c. [rdd. = Immergrün] u. ⓶c. periwinkle (Vinca).
Sing=sang (⌣⌣) m ⓶ sing-song; =schule f, =schüler(in f) m singing-school, -pupil; =schwan m, orn. whistling swan (Cygnus mu'sicus); =spiel n musical comedy or play or farce; (kleine Oper) operetta; =spielhalle f = =halle; =stimme f: a) singing-voice; b) ♪ vocal part; =stück ♪ n (piece of) vocal music, air; =stunde f singing-lesson.
Singular, ~is (⌣⌣⌣(⌣) [lt.] m ⓶d.. ⓢ gr. (Einzahl) singular (number); Lisch (⌣⌣-) a. ⓰ in the singular (number).
Sing=vogel (⌣⌣...) m ⓶ singing bird; auch: songster, warbler; =weise f: a) style of singing; b) air, tune, melody.
sinken (⌣⌣) [ahd.: sink] st I v/n. (in) 1. to sink, to drop. von Schiffen ꝛc.: to go down (to the bottom), auch von

♪ Musik; ⚙ Wissenschaft; ♀ Pflanze; ♀ Geographie; ⊕ Technik; ⚒ Bergbau; ⚔ Militär; ⚓ Marine; 💰 Handel; ✉ Post; 🚂 Eisenbahn.

[Sinn] — 890 — [Sirach]

Personen: to go under, vom Erdboden ꝛc.: to subside, von Preisen ꝛc.: to fall, von Personen: to come down (in the world); (sich vermindern) to decrease, to abate, (verfallen) to decline, to decay; seine Kräfte 2 his strength is failing (him); seine Macht sank bald his power soon diminished or crumbled away; *fig.* er ist tief gesunken he is low down, F he has gone to the dogs. — 2. mit *prp.*: **auf** den (od. zu) Boden 2 to fall (or drop) to the ground; auf einen Stuhl 2 to sink into a chair; e-m **in die** Arme 2 to drop (or sink) into a p.'s arms; in Ohnmacht 2 to faint (away); im Preise 2 to go down in price; in tiefen Schlaf 2 to fall into a deep sleep, to go fast asleep; *fig.* ich hätte vor Scham in die Erde (ver)2 mögen I thought I could have sunk into the earth (for shame). — 3. mst *fig.* den Kopf 2 **lassen** to hang one's head; den Mut, die Flügel nicht 2 l. not to lose courage, to keep up one's spirits; die Stimme 2 l. to drop one's voice. — **II** *v/a.* 4. ⚒ e-n Schacht 2 = abteufen. — **III** ~ *n* 5. sinking, &c. (f. I); ~ des Bodens: subsidence, der Preise: fall, depression, drop; (Verminderung) decrease, abatement, diminution, (Verfall) decline, decay, crumbling (away).

Sinn (²) [ahd.: lt. *sēnsŭs*] *m* ⓑ. 1. sense; e-m in die ~e fallen to occur to (or to strike) a p.; in die ~e fallend striking, perceptible; ihr vergingen die ~e she lost (all) consciousness, Sprichw. f. Kopf 7; *fig.* seine fünf ~e h. to have all one's wits about one; darin ist weder ~ noch Verstand there is no rhyme or reason (or neither rh. nor r.) in that. — 2. (Bedeutung) sense, import, purport: eigentlicher (figürlicher) ~ e-s Satzes ꝛc.: proper or literal (figurative) meaning; im enger(e)n (weiter(e)n) ~e in a narrower (wider) sense; es liegt ein verborg(e)ner ~ darin there is a hidden meaning in that; im wahren ~e des Wortes in the true sense (or acceptation) of the word. — 3. ~ (Empfänglichkeit) für et. taste for a th., (Neigung) liking (or inclination) for a th.; (Anlage) aptitude (or turn) for a th.; (geistiges Empfinden) sensitive faculty; (Verstand) mind, wit, (Einsicht) intelligence, intellect; (Seele, Herz) soul, heart, (Gemütsart) nature, disposition; (Meinung) opinion, (Trachten) tendency, (Absicht) intention, (Wunsch) wish, desire; (Wille) will; f. hart 2; der Graf trug hohen ~ (B.) the count was noble-minded; seinen ~ auf et. richten to turn one's attention to a th.; ~ für das Schöne haben to have an eye for the beautiful; sein ~ steht nach Höherem his mind (or he) is bent on (or aims at) higher things; im *gen.*: demütigen ~es sein to be humble-minded; mit e-m eines (od. gleichen) ~es sein to be one heart and one soul with a p.; to be of the same way of thinking as a p.; andern ~es w. to change one's mind or ideas. — 4. mit *prp.*: **auf** f-m ~ (Willen) beharren to insist on a th.(being carried out); f. beharren 2;

e-m et. **aus** dem ~(e) bringen to talk a p. out of a th.; sich et. aus dem ~(e) schlagen to put (or drive) a th. out of one's mind or one's heart; das will mir nicht aus dem ~(e) I cannot get it out of my head, I cannot shake off the idea; Sprichw. f. Auge 4 am Schluß; **bei** ~en sein to be in one's (right) senses; was fährt Ihnen **durch** den ~? what are you thinking about?; **im** ~(e) behalten: a) (im Gedächtnis bewahren) to retain (in one's memory), to bear in mind; b) (noch immer erstreben) persistently to strive (or aim) at; et. im ~(e) h. to have a th. in view; es kam mir in den ~ it crossed (or flashed through) my mind, it occurred to me; sich et. in den ~ kommen l. to bethink o.s. of a th.; das liegt mir im ~ it is constantly in (or never out of) my mind; das will mir nicht in den ~ I cannot make it out or understand it, I cannot believe it; **nach** j-s ~(e) in agreement with a p.'s views or intentions; wenn es nach m-m ~(e) ginge if I had my (own) way; **ohne** ~ senseless, unmeaning; **von** ~en sein to be out of one's senses or beside o.s.; bist du von ~en? are you out of your mind?, are you mad?; ↘ es kommt mir **zu**~(e) (fällt mir ein) it occurs to me, it comes (in)to my mind.

Sinnau ♀ (³⁻) [nhd. Immertau] *m* ⓒ. alchemilla (*Alchemi'lla*).

Sinn=bild (³...) *n* ⓑ emblem; (Wahrzeichen) outward sign, symbol; (Gleichnis) allegory; **=bildlich** *a.* ⓖ emblematic(al); symbolical, allegoric(al); 2 darstellen to symbolize, allegorize.

sinnen (²~) [ahd.: lt. *sentī're*: senden] **I** *v/n.* (h., ↘ su) u. *v/a.* 1. *abs.* (nachdenken) to meditate, reflect, ponder, cogitate, grübelnd: to speculate, mit Muße: to muse. — 2. auf et. 2 to plan (or plot, scheme) a th.; auf Böses 2 to harbour ill designs; auf Mittel und Wege 2 to devise means and ways. — 3. mit abhängigem Satzes: was sinnt ihr? what are you brooding over?; Gefährliches 2 to hatch dangerous schemes; (auf) Rache 2 to meditate revenge. — **II** ~ *n* 2 4. meditation (*pl.*), reflection(s *pl.*); speculation; all sein ~, all sein Trachten his every thought, his every wish. — **III** 2d *p.pr.* u. *a.* ⓖ 5. meditative, full of thought(s). — **IV** ge=ſonnen *p.p.*, meiſt präd. *a.*: 6. (willens): ich bin 2, es zu tun I feel inclined or disposed or willing ..., I have a good mind ... — 7. ⚹ = geſinnt.

ſinnen=fällig (²~.²~) *a.* ⓖ = ſinnfällig. **Sinnen=genuß** (³~...) *m* ⓑ, **=luſt** f sensual enjoyment, pleasure; **=rauſch**, **=taumel** *m* exuberance of spirits; **=täuſchung** *f* = Sinnestäuſchung; **=welt** *f* physical (or material) world; **=weſen** *n* sentient being. [of the meaning.]

Sinn=erklärung (²~.²~) *f* ⓒ explanation **Sinnes=änderung** (²~...) *f* ⓒ change of opinion or mind, in Religion ꝛc.: conversion; **=art** *f* = Gesinnung; **=richtung** *f* turn of mind; **=täuschung** *f* mental delusion, *path.*: ⌀ hallucination; **=werkzeuge** *n/pl.* organs *pl.* of sense.

sinn=fällig (³~...) *a.* ⓖ obvious; **=gedicht** *n* ⓑ epigram; **=grün** ♀ .₊ ſt. Sinngrün. **sinnig** [ahd.] *a.* ⓖ: a) thoughtful, contemplative (vgl. sinnen III); b) Geschenk ꝛc.: (wohl ersonnen) well devised, ingenious; (anmutig) graceful; c) (bedachtsam) judicious, sensible; d) in Zssgn. f. zB. leichtsinnig ꝛc.; ~keit *f* ⓖ thoughtfulness; ingeniousness; judiciousness.

sinnlich (²~) *a.* ⓖ: a) of (or concerning, affecting) the senses; *phls.* (mit Sinnen begabt) sensuous, sentient, sensitive; b) (wahrnehmbar) perceptible; (körperlich) physical; *phls.* perceptive, material: c) Sinnengenuß betr.: sensual (appetite, &c.), voluptuous (thought, &c.); (fleischlich) carnal (desire, &c.); **Sinnlichkeit** (²~) *f* ⓖ: a) *phls.* sensuousness, sensitive faculty; b) material existence; c) sensuality, voluptuousness.

sinn=los (³...) *a.* ⓖ: a) senseless, unconscious, deprived of one's senses; b) (von Sinnen) out of one's senses or mind; 2 betrunken dead (or helplessly) drunk; c) (nichts bedeutend) void of sense, unmeaning, meaningless; (albern) absurd; **=losigkeit** *f* ⓖ senselessness; (Albernheit) foolishness, absurdity; **=pflanze** ♀ *f* mimosa (*Mimo'sa*); schamhafte ~ sensitive plant (*M. pudi'ca*); **²reich** *a.* (wohlersonnen) ingenious, clever, (geistreich) witty; **=spruch** *m* short (or pithy, witty) saying, ⌀ apophthegm; device, motto; epigram; **²verwandt** *a.*: ⌀ synonymous; 2es Wort synonym; **=verwandtſchaft** *f* synonymy; **²voll** *a.* full of (good) sense, fraught with meaning, auch = ²reich.

Sinolog ⌀ (~⁻´) [Sina✝ = China] *m* ⓒ, **=e** ⓖ (des Chinesischen kundiger) sinologist, sinologue, mehr gbr.: Chinese scholar.

Sinopel (~´~) [Sinope ♀, grch. St.] *m* min. (dunkelroter Eiſenkieſel) sinople.

sintemal(en) fast ✝ (´~´~) [mhd.] *cj.* (weil) since, whereas; *co.* altertümelnd: sintemal und alldieweil inasmuch as.

Sinter (²~) [ahd.] *m* ⓐ: a) *min.* (Tropfstein) ✝ sinter, stalactite; b) ⊙ *metall.* (Hammerschlag) dross of iron (ore), ironsinter; **~=bildung** *f* ⓑ, **~=gebilde** *n*, *min.* formation of stalactite.

sintern (²~) *v/n.* (ſn) ⓑa. 1. a) von verdunſtetem Waſſer: (Tropfstein bilden) to form stalactites; b) (sickern) to trickle, to drip, to ooze (out). — 2. (zusammen=)2 (ſich zusammenballen) to frit (together), to conglobate.

Sint=flut (³~´) [ahd. = große Flut] *f* ⓖ (great) flood, deluge; **sint=flutlich** *a.* ⓖ of the flood, ⌀ diluvian.

Sinto=ismus (~⌴´~) [jap.=lt.] *m* ⓒ (japaniſche Religion und Sittenlehre) Shintoism.

Sinus ⌀ (´~) [lt. *sinŭs* Buſen, Bucht] *m*, *inv.* od. ⓖ *math.* (abbr. sin.) sine.

Sippe (²~) [ahd.: sib] *f* ⓖ = Sippſchaft 2. **Sippſchaft** (²~) [mhd.] *f* ⓖ 1. (verwandtſchaftliches Band) (blood-)relationship, kinship, consanguinity. — 2. *coll.* (Verwandten) (blood-)relations, kindred, kinsfolk *pl.*, kith and kin; vgl. Clique; F die ganze ~ (Bande) the whole kit or set or lot or pack or shoot.

Sirach (´~⌴) [hebr. Springbläſer] *nprim.* ⓕ *bibl.* Sirach; f. Jeſus 2.

Signs (see page XVII): F familiar; P vulgar; ſ flash; ↘ rare; ✝ obsolete (died); * new word (born); ₊₊ incorrect; ♪ music;

[Sirene] — 891 — [sitzen]

Sirene (-⌣–⌣) [grch. *Seirēn*] f ⊕ myth. (Seenymphe) u. phys. Tonmeßinstrument, auch ⚓ (Schallsignalapparat): siren; **~ngesang** m in Homers Odyssee ꝛc.: sirensong, (enticing) song of (the) sirens.

sirenenhaft (-⌣–⌣) a. ⊕ siren-like.

Sirokko f. Schirokko.

Sirup (⌣–) [ar. Trank] m ⊕d. ⊕ Zuckerfabr., *pharm.*, &c.: (Zuckersaft) syrup; (dunkler Zuckerdicksaft) treacle, ※ a. molasses *pl.*; F *fig.* der reine ~ all honey, honeyed words *pl.*; ⚥(§)**=artig** (⌣–⌣) a. ⊕ syrup-like, syrupy, treacly; **~(§)=topf** m ⊕ syrup- (or treacle-)pot.

sistieren (⌣–⌣) [it.] meist jur. **I** v/a. ⊕ **1.** (einstellen) to inhibit, stop, nonsuit (an action). — **2.** e-n ⚥ (vor Gericht bringen) to cite a p. before a court, to summons a p.; (auf die Polizeiwache bringen) to take to the police-station, to lock up. — **II** ~ n ⊕ u. **Sistierung** f ⊕ **3.** (f. 1) inhibition, nonsuit; (f. 2) summons.

Sisyphos, mst ...**us** (⌣–⌣⌣) [grch. der überweise] nprm. ⊕γ. Sisyphus; **~arbeit** (⌣⌣–⌣) f ⊕ (vergebliche Mühe) task of Sisyphus, Sisyphean toil.

Sitte (⌣–) [ahd.] f ⊕ **1.** (das Übliche) custom; (Gewohnheit) habit; (Brauch) usage, use, practice; ~n u. Gebräuche manners and customs *pl.*; feine ~n good manners *pl.*, good breeding *sg.*; das ist bei uns nicht ~ that's not customary (or the custom) with us, we don't do such things; das ist nicht mehr ~ that is not the fashion now, that's out of date; das ist so ihre ~ that's their way (of doing things). — **2.** (Sittlichkeit) morality, morals *pl.*; böse ~n bad (or evil) habits *pl.*; lockere ~n loose morals or principles *pl.*; Sprichw. f. Beispiel am Ende u. Zeit 6. — **3.** P = **~n=polizei**.

Sitten=bild (⌣–⌣...), **=gemälde** n ⊕ picture (or description) of manners or morals; **=gesetz** n moral law, code of morality; **=lehre** f moral philosophy, ethical science, ethics; **=lehrer** m moral teacher, moralist; **=los** a. ⊕ immoral, dissolute, profligate; **=losigkeit** f immorality, dissoluteness, profligacy; **=polizei** f (in Engl. unbekannt) control over (a police regulating) prostitution; **=prediger** m moral preacher, moralizer; **=predigt** f moralizing sermon; **=regel** f moral precept, rule of conduct; **=rein** a. (morally) pure, chaste; **=reinheit** f purity of morals, chastity; **=richter** m moralist, censor; **=spruch** m (moral) maxim or sentence; **=streng** a. austere, puritanical; **=strenge** f austerity (of manners); **=verderbnis** f, **=verfall** m corruption of manners or morals, depravity, demoralization; **=verfeinerung** f refinement of manners, higher culture or civilization; **=zeugnis** n certificate of good conduct; **=zwang** m conventionalism, etiquette.

Sittich (⌣–) [ahd.; *grch. psittakos*] m ⊕d. orn. (kleiner Papagei) par(r)akeet.

sittig (⌣–) [ahd.] a. ⊕ (wohlgesittet) of good manners or morals or breeding, well-bred, well-mannered, well-behaved; (höflich) polite, courteous, civil; (bescheiden) modest; (tugendhaft) virtuous.

sittlich (⌣–) [ahd.; *Sitte] a. ⊕: a) moral; ⚥es Betragen moral conduct, morals *pl.*; b) (üblich) customary; Sprichw. f. ländlich 2.

Sittlichkeit (⌣–⌣) f ⊕ morality, morals *pl.*, auch: moral code.

Sittlichkeits=gefühl (⌣–⌣...) n ⊕ moral sense; **=verbrechen**, **=vergehen** n immoral offence; indecent act or assault.

sittsam (⌣–) [ahd.] a. ⊕ (still u. bescheiden) modest, reserved, (anständig) decent, respectable; (schamhaft) bashful, (keusch) chaste; **~keit** f ⊕ modesty, decency, respectability; bashfulness, chastity.

Situation (⌣⌣–tsj(⌣)–) [fr. *Lage*] f ⊕ situation, auch: position; **~s=plan** (⌣...) m ⊕ arch. plan of a building-estate or (building-)site.

situieren (⌣⌣–⌣) [fr.] v/a. ⊕, bsd. im *p.p.* gut situiert in good (or easy) circumstances, in a comfortable position, well off, well-to-do.

Sitz (⌣) [ahd.: se(a)t: lt. *sēdes*] m ⊕a. **1.** seat (auch im Wagen, Theater ꝛc.); (Platz) place; ~ des Kutschers coachman's seat, box, F dick(e)y; (Stuhl) chair; ~ u. Stimme im Rat haben to have a voice in (or to be a member of) the council. — **2.** (Wohnort) residence, domicile, abode; seat of (the) government; ~ e-s Bischofs episcopal see; seinen ~ an e-m Orte aufschlagen to settle (down) in a place. — **3.** = Gesäß. — **4.** Schneiderei: fit of a dress, &c.; man. fester ~ firm seat.

Sitz=anker ⚓ (⌣...) m ⊕ anchor of rest; **=arbeit** f sedentary work; **=bad** n hip-bath; **=bank** f bench, ⚓ in Booten: seat, thwart; **=bein** n (auch Gesäßbein) anat.: ⚕ ischium.

sitzen (⌣–) [ahd.: sit: lt. *sedē're*] **I** v/n. (h., südd. a. sn) ⊕ **1.** (ant. liegen, stehen) to sit, to be seated, to occupy a seat, v. Vögeln auch: to be perched, to perch; wir ⚥ hier gut we have good seats or places, weit⚥. we are comfortable here; er kann nicht still⚥ he can't sit still, he is restless or fidgety; bibl. Christus ist gesessen (= sitzt) zur Rechten Gottes sits on the right hand of God. — **2.** als v/refl. mit Angabe des Erfolges: sich steif, wund ⚥ to become stiff, sore with sitting; als v/impers. es saß sich so heimlich in der Stube we were so snug (or so comfortably seated) in the room. — **3.** mit prp. (oft *fig.*): oben am Tische ⚥ to sit at the head of the table; an diesen Versen habe ich drei Tage gesessen I have sat ... over these lines (of poetry); e-m auf dem Halse ⚥ to be a (heavy) burden to a p.; e-m auf dem Nacken (F auf dem Dache oder auf der Pelle) ⚥ to keep a strict eye on a p., to keep a p. hard to his work, F. P to hold a p.'s nose to the grindstone; (wie) auf Nadeln, Kohlen, Dornen ⚥ to sit on thorns; auf dem trocknen ⚥ to sit high and dry; f. trocken II; von Hühnern: auf Eiern ⚥ to sit on (or to hatch) eggs; auf dem Pferde ⚥ to sit on horseback; bei Tisch ⚥ to sit at table; hinter Schloß und Riegel ⚥ to sit in jail, to be locked up (in prison), vgl. 6b; in Amt und Würden ⚥ to fill a high position or post; f. Brühe 4, Dreck 2, Patsche²; im Glücke ⚥, wie in Abrahams Schoß ⚥, in der Wolle ⚥ to be in luck's way or in clover; in Prima ⚥ to be a sixth-form boy; im Parlament, im Rate (als Mitglied) ⚥ to have a seat in (or to be a member of) parliament, the council; f. Sattel 2; bis über die Ohren in Schulden ⚥ to be over head and ears in debt; F wie die Made im Speck ⚥ to be as snug as old Pamp or as a bug in a rug; über e-r Arbeit ⚥ to have ⚥. work in hand, to work hard at one's task; über den Büchern ⚥ to be poring over one's books; über einem andern Schüler ⚥ to be above (or to top) another boy; um den Teich (herum) saßen die Frösche around the pond sat ..., the pond was encircled by ...; zu Gericht ⚥ to sit in judgment; zu Pferde ⚥ to be (mounted) on horseback; gut zu Pferde ⚥ to be a good horseman, to sit a horse well, to have a good seat; zu Rate ⚥ to be assembled in council. — **4.** mit *adv.* gut ⚥, stärker: warm und weich ⚥ to be in a comfortable (or good) position; müßig ⚥ to remain idle or lazy. — **5.** mit persönlichem *dat.*: einem Maler (zum Porträt) ⚥ to sit for one's portrait to an artist, to give a painter a sitting. — **6.** *abs.*: a) (Sitzung halten) to hold a meeting; der Rat sitzt heute nicht the Board do(es) not meet to-day; b) (gefangen ⚥) to be in prison, F.u. P to be in quod or in safe keeping, to do time; F er sitzt schon lange he has been in jail for a long time; c) immer zu Hause, hinterm Ofen ⚥ to be a home-bird, to be fond of one's fireside; er sitzt sehr viel he sits a great deal, he leads a very sedentary life; d) (sich aufhalten) to stay, to remain; (wohnen) to reside, to dwell. — **7.** ⚥ lassen to leave (in the lurch), to desert, to abandon; to jilt a girl, a lover; den Hut ⚥ lassen to keep one's hat on (one's head); eine Beleidigung auf sich ⚥ lassen F to swallow (or pocket) an affront. — **8.** von et. voll ⚥ to be full of (or filled with) a th. — **9.** (fest haften) der Hut sitzt auf dem Kopfe ... clings to (or fits) the head; *fig.* da sitzt der Knoten there's the difficulty or the rub; der Nagel sitzt fest ... clinches (or grips, is fixed) well; *fenc.* der Hieb sitzt the thrust (or cut) has gone home; beim Duell: sitzt!, bursch.: hat gesessen! a hit!; mir sitzt Schleim auf der Brust I am troubled with phlegm on my chest; hier sitzt mir's I feel it here; ⚓ das Schiff sitzt fest ob. auf dem Grunde the ship is (or has run) aground. — **10.** von Kleidungsstücken: to fit; die Jacke sitzt ihr wie angegossen the jacket fits her like a glove or to perfection; schlecht ⚥ to fit badly, to be a misfit. — **II** ~ n ⊕ **11.** sitting (position); perching of a bird; des ~s müde tired of sitting; ich komme nie zum ~ I am never able to sit down; e-n zum ~ nötigen to press a p. to (or to make a p.) sit down. — **III** ⚥ *p.pr.* u. *a.* ⊕ **12.** sitting, seated. &c. (f. I), von Vögeln: perching, perched;

[sitzenbleiben] — 892 — [Skupschtina]

die Lebensweise sedentary life. — 13. ♀ ♂es (stielloses) Blatt: ⚥ sessile leaf.

Sitzen-bleiben (⌣⌢...) v/n. (ſn) ⓝ** to keep one's seat, to remain sitting, von e-m Bodensatz: to settle down; von Schülern: in Serta ♀ to remain a second year in the lowest form; von Mädchen: a) (keinen Tänzer finden) to find no partner, F to be a wall-flower; b) (keinen Freier finden) to remain single, F to be left on the shelf; ~ n ㉓ sitting (or sticking) fast, fixed position; (Verlassenheit) forsakenness; =lassen n ㉒ desertion of one's family, &c., abandonment; jilting a sweetheart.

Sitz-fleisch (⌢⌣) n ㉒: er hat kein ~ there is no rest in him, he can't sit still; er hat ~ (Ausdauer bei der Arbeit) he has great perseverance, he is (very) plodding or assiduous; =kasten m seat-box; =kissen n cushion to sit upon, a. seat-cushion.

sitzlings (⌣⌢) adv. in a sitting posture.

Sitz-platz (⌣⌢) m ㉒ sitting-room, seat; =redakteur F m dummy editor who serves terms of imprisonment in lieu of the real editor or author; =reihe f row of seats, tier; =stange f im Vogelbauer: perch.

Sitzung (⌣⌢) f ㊻ sitting (auch des Parlaments, eines Rates, Gerichtshofes ꝛc.; vgl. Session); f. abhalten 4 am Schluß; eine lange ~ bei Tische ꝛc. halten to sit a long time at table, over dinner, &c.; die ~ begann um 4 Uhr the meeting (or proceedings) began (or opened)..., auch: the chair was taken ...

Sitzungs-bericht (⌣⌢...) m ㉒ report (or minutes pl.) of a meeting or of the proceedings; =periode f session of parliament, &c.; day fixed for a sitting or meeting, des Gerichtshofes: assize- (or court-)day; =saal m council- (or board-) room, parl. (floor of) the house.

Sitz-ventil (⌢...) n ㉒ mach. seat-valve; =wechsel m Turnerei: change of position.

Six F (⌢): meiner ~!, mein ~chen! on my word!, by Jove!, F by Jingo!

Sixtina (⌣⌢⌣) [1473-81 v. Papste Sixtus IV. erbaut] f ㊾ = Sixtinische (f. ds) Kapelle.

Sixtinisch (⌣⌢⌣) a. ⓡ: ~e Kapelle in Rom Sistine (or Sixtine) Chapel; ~e Madonna Sistine (or Sixtine) Madonna.

Sizilianer (⌣⌣(⌣)⌢⌣) m ㊻, ~in f ㊼, **sizilianisch** a. ⓡ Sicilian; hist. (1282) Sizilianische Vesper (Ermordung der Franzosen) Sicilian Vespers pl.

Sizili-en ♀ (⌣⌢(⌣)) [it. Sici'lia] npr/n. ㊵ (it. Insel) Sicily; ehm. Königreich beider ~ kingdom of the two Sicilies.

Skabiose ♀ (⌣(⌣)⌢⌣) [lt. Krätzen-(Heilkraut)] f ㊽ scabious (Scabio'sa).

Skala (⌢⌣) [it.] f ㊾(㊻) scale (= Stufenleiter u. ♪ = Tonleiter), ♪ auch: gamut.

Skalde [isld.: schelten] m ㊹ (altnordischer Sänger) scald, Scandinavian bard; **skaldisch** (⌢⌣) a. ⓡ scaldic.

Skalp ⸸ (⌢) m ㉔. (Schädelhaut) scalp.

Skalpell (⌣⌢) [lt.] n ㉔. surg. (Seziermesser) scalpel.

skalpieren ⸸ (⌣⌢⌣) v/a. ㊹ (der Kopfhaut berauben) to (deprive of one's) scalp.

Skalpier-messer (⌣⌢,⌢⌣) n ㉒ der Indianer: scalping-knife. [lock.]

Skalp-locke (⌢,⌣) f ㊻ der Indianer: scalp-

Skamandros ♀ (⌣⌣⌣) npr/m. ㉒ Alt.: der ~ (Flüßchen bei Troja) Scamander.

Skandal (⌣⌢) [grch.] m ⓓ. 1. = Ärgernis 1. — 2. ~ (Lärm) machen to make a (great) noise or disturbance, F to kick up a row; to cause a (great) riot.

Skandal-chronik (⌣⌢...) f ㊻, =geschichte f scandal, society-gossip.

skandalieren F (⌣⌣⌢⌣) v/n. (h.) ㊽ to pour out abuse (or invectives) upon a p.

skandalisieren (⌣⌣⌣⌢⌣) [fr.] I v/n. (h.) = skandalieren. — II sich ♀ v/refl. (Ärgernis nehmen) to be scandalized (or shocked) at (or by) a th., to take offence at a th.

Skandal-macher (⌣⌢,⌣⌢) m ㉒ rioter. **skandalös** (⌣⌣⌢) a.ⓡ(D 10) scandalous, offensive; (empörend) revolting, shocking.

skandal-süchtig (⌣⌢,⌣⌢) a. ⓡ fond of scandal or society-gossip.

skandieren (⌣⌢⌣) [lt.] v/a. ㊹: Verse ♀ (zergliedern) to scan verse.

Skandinavi-en ♀ (⌣⌣⌣⌢(⌣)) npr/n. ㉒a. (Schweden und Norwegen) Scandinavia; **Skandinavi-er**(in f ㊼) m ㊻ (⌣⌣⌣⌢⌣(⌣)), **skandinavisch** (⌣⌣⌣⌢⌣) a. ⓡ Scandinavian.

Skansion (⌣(⌣)⌢) [it., zu skandieren] f ㊻ scanning, scansion.

Skapulier (⌣⌣⌢) [lt. Schulterblatt:] n ⓓ. eccl. Kleidungsstück der Mönche: scapular.

Skarabäus ⚦ (⌣⌣⌢) [lt.; *grch. ka'rabos] m ㉗ ent. scarabæus, als käferförmiges Amulett der alten Ägypter, auch: scarab.

Skarifikator ⚇ (⌣⌣⌢⌣) [lt.] m ㊶ agr. (Reißpflug) scarifier.

Skat (⌢) [it.; *skartieren weglegen] m (n) ⓓc. a German card game.

Skelett (⌣⌢) [grch.] 1. n ⓓc. = Gerippe 1. — 2. f ㊻ = Skelettschrift.

skelett-artig (⌣⌢...) a. ⓡ = ♀förmig; =exerzieren ⚔ n skeleton-drill, ♀artig a. sk.-like; (dürr) reduced to a sk., F all (or nothing but) skin and bones.

skelettieren (⌣⌣⌢⌣) v/a. ㊹ (in ein Skelett umwandeln) to skeletonize.

Skelett-schrift ⚇ (⌣⌢,⌢) f ㊻ typ. (sehr schmale Schrift) skeleton-type. [doubt.]

Skepsis ⚦ (⌢⌣) [grch.] f, inv., phls., &c.]

Skeptik (⌢⌣) f ㊻ (Zweifelsucht) scepticism.

Skeptiker (⌢⌣⌣) [grch.] m ㊻ sceptic.

skeptisch (⌢⌣) [grch.] a. ⓡ sceptical.

Skeptizismus (⌣⌣⌢⌣) m ㊷ scepticism.

S. k. H. öst. abbr. = Seine kaiserliche Hoheit. [Hoheit.]

S. K(gl). H. abbr. = Seine Königliche

Ski (schi, ⌢) [norw., dän.] m ㊽, ⓓe. od. inv. (Schneeschuh) ski, (Norwegian) snow-shoe; =lauf m ski-ing.

Skink (⌢) [grch.; *afrik.] m ⓓb. zo. (Glanzschleiche) skink (Scincus).

Skizze (⌢⌣) [it. schizzo m] f ㊻ paint., &c. sketch; (hastig hingeworfene Zeichnung) auch: sketchy outline, rough draft or drawing, mit Bleistift: pencil sketch, pencilling, mit Tinte: pen-and-ink sketch; eine flüchtige ~ entwerfen to make a rapid (or hasty) sketch.

Skizzen-buch (⌢⌣,⌢) n ㉒ sketch-book. **skizzenhaft** (⌢⌣⌢) a. ⓡ, **skizzen-weise** (⌢⌣,⌢⌣) adv. (F a. a.) sketchy, in rough outlines.

skizzieren (⌣⌢⌣) [it.] v/a. ㊹ to sketch, to outline, to draw in the rough, paint. a. to adumbrate; flüchtig ♀ to dash off.

Skizzierer (⌣⌢⌣) [skizzieren] m ㉒ sketcher, draftsman.

Sklave (⌢⌣) [neu-grch. = Slawe] m ㊹, **Sklavin** f ㊼ (Unfreie[r]; ant. Freie) slave (a. fig.), thrall, bond(wo)man, weits. drudge; wie ein ~ arbeiten to slave, to drudge; zum ~n machen to enslave, to enthral; fig. ~ des Trunkes slave to drink or to the bottle.

Sklaven-arbeit (⌢⌣...) f ㉒ slave's work; drudgery; =aufseher m slave-driver; =befreiung f emancipation of slaves; =besitzer m sl.-owner; =dienst m slavery, thraldom, servitude; =emanzipation f = =befreiung; =halter m slaveholder; =handel m (treiben to carry on) slave-trade; =händler m sl.-trader, -dealer; =jagd f slave-hunting; =joch n (yoke of) bondage, thraldom; =krieg m, hist. servile war; =küste ♀ West-afrika: Slave Coast; =leben n sl.'s life; vgl. =dienst; =markt m sl.-market.

Sklaverei (⌣⌣⌢) f ㊻ = Sklaverei.

Sklaven-schiff ⚓ (⌢⌣...) n ㉒ (slave-) dhow, F slaver; =seele f, =sinn m slavish (or servile) mind; ehm. =staaten m/pl. Nord-amerikas: Slave States pl.; =stand m condition of a slave, slavery.

Sklaventum (⌢⌣⌣) n ㉔. = Sklaverei. **Sklaven-züchter** m ㉒ slave-breeder.

Sklaverei (⌣⌣⌢) f ㊻ slavery, thraldom, servitude, bondage, serfdom; (Gefangenschaft) captivity.

Sklavin (⌢⌣) f ㊼ f. Sklave.

sklavisch (⌢⌣) a. ⓡ slavish, servile, adv. auch: as a slave; like a drudge.

skontier/en ⚇ (⌣⌢) [it.] I v/a. ㊹ (ausgleichen) to balance (or settle) accounts. — II ~ n ㉓ und ♀/ung f ㊻ balancing (or settlement) of accounts.

Skonto ⚇ (⌢⌣) [it.] m, n ㊵ = Diskont. **Skontro** ⚇ (⌢⌣) [it.] n ㊵ (Abrechnung) clearing. [doch] scurvy.]

Skorbut (⌣⌢) [ndl.] m ⓓc. path. (Schar-] **skorbutisch** (⌣⌢⌣) a. ⓡ scorbutic.

Skorpion (⌣(⌣)⌢) [grch.] m ⓓd. zo. scorpion (a. her.) (Sco'rpio); ast. Scorpion; ~(s)-herz n ㉒ ast. Scorpion's Heart, Antares, a. α Scorpii; =spinne f, ent. scorpion-spider (Phala'ngium cancroi'des); =stich m sting of a scorpion.

Skorzonere ♀ (⌣⌣⌢⌣) [span. escorzone'ra] f ㊽ = Schwarzwurz(el) b.

Skribent (-⌢) [lt. Schreibender] m ㊷ writer, author; = Schriftsteller, b. s. = Stribler.

Skribler F (⌢⌣) [lt.] m ㉒, **~in** f ㊼ scribbler, indifferent writer, F quill-driver.

Skrofel (⌢⌣) [lt.] f ㊻ path.: ~n pl. scrofula, ⚕ king's evil; ♀artig (⌢...) a. ⓡ scrofulous; **~kranke(r)** s. [scrofulous.] scrofulous patient.

skrofulös (-⌢) [fr.] a. ⓡ (D 10) path.] **Skrupel** (⌢⌣) [lt.] m ⓓ. 2: a) n ⓓ. verm. v. 1 Gramm; b) m, fig. (Bedenklichkeit) scruple; sich keine ~ über et. m. not to scruple (or to have no scruples) about a th.

skrupulös (-⌢) a. ⓡ (D 10) scrupulous. **Skrutinium** (-⌢(⌣)⌣) [lt.] n ㉘ parl. (Prüfung der Stimmzettel) scrutiny, counting of voting-papers.

Skulptur (-⌢) [lt.] f ㊻ (Bildhauerei) sculpture; (Bildwerk) piece of sculpture.

Skupschtina (⌢⌣⌣) [serb.] f ㊾ (serbischer Landtag) Skupshtina, Skuptschina.

Zeichen (f. S. XVII): F familiär; P Volkssprache; ⸸ Gaunersprache; ⸜ selten; † alt (auch gestorben); * neu (auch geboren); ⸸ unrichtig;

[skurril] — 893 — [soeben]

skurril (⌣́⌣) [lt. *scurrī́lis*] a. ⑥⑥ (possenhaft) scurrilous, buffoonish.
Sly... s. Szy... [Slav, Slavonian.]
Slawe (⌣́⌣) [Slowene] m ④, **Slawin** f ④
slawisch (⌣́⌣) a. ⑥⑥ Slav(onian); die slawische Sprache, das Slawisch(e) n ⑰ the Slav(onian) language.
Slawismus (⌣⌣́⌣) [neul.-lt.] m ⑲ (slawische Spracheigenheit) Slav(onian) idiom.
Slawoni-en ♀ (⌣́⌣(⌣)⌣) npr/n. ㉓ z. (österreichisches Kronland) Slavonia.
Slawoni-er (⌣́⌣(⌣)⌣) m ㉒, **~in** f ④, **slawonisch** (-⌣́⌣) a. ⑥⑥ Slavonic, Slavonian.
Slowak (⌣́⌣) [slaw.] m ㉒, **~in** f ④, **Lisch** (-⌣́⌣) a. ⑥⑥ Slovak, Slovack.
Slowene (⌣⌣́⌣) [slaw.] m ④, **Slowenin** f ④, **slowenisch** a. ⑥⑥ Slovene.
sm ⚓ abbr. = Seemeile. [Majesty.]
S. M. abbr. = Seine Majestät His
Smaragd (⌣⌣́) [ahd., *grch.] m ①b. min. (Edelstein) emerald; **Len** (⌣⌣́⌣) a. ⑥⑥ (of) emerald; **2-farben** (-⌣́⌣⌣) a. ⑥⑥ emerald (-coloured), ⚡ smaragdine; **2-grün** a. u. n ㉒ emerald green.
Smirgel (⌣́⌣) 2c. s. Schmirgel 2c.
S. M. S. ⚓ abbr. = Seiner Majestät Schiff His Majesty's Ship. [carpet.]
Smyrna-teppich 🛍 (⌣́-⌣́⌣) m ㉒ Smyrna
s. o. abbr. = sieh(e) oben.
SO, öst. **SO.** abbr. = Südost.
so (⌣́) [ahd.: so] **I** adv. **1.** e-m „wie" antwortend: so, like that, in this (or that) manner or way; es ist mir so, als könnte ich fliegen I feel as though (or as if) I could fly; so spricht er thus he spoke. — **2.** (derart(ig) such; s. uff., usw.: **so ein** Mensch such a person, a p. of that kind; **so ein(er)** such a one; **so etwas** such a thing; so ist er nun einmal that's his way; s. einmal 4; so ist's! it is so!; that's how matters stand; dem ist nicht so that's not true or not the case; wenn dem so ist if that be the case or a fact; so seid ihr! that's like you!; so ist die Welt such is the world; wenn Sie es so nehmen (wollen) if you (like to) take it that way; so (et)was ist mir noch nie vorgekommen I never saw anything like it or of the sort; so geht's nicht it won't do (like that); so geht es, wenn // that's (always) the way (or case) when //; so mußte es kommen that was bound to happen; er spricht bald so, bald so he says first one thing, then another; **so oder so** wird es gehen it can be done in some way or other; so? (wirtlich) indeed?, (do) you (really) think so?; **ach so!** yes, of course!, oh, I see; **so recht!** just so!; **so so!** dear me!; vgl. soso, wieso; so, das reicht! how, that's enough! — **3.** ausrufend: er ist **so** (⌣́) reich! he is so (very) rich!; er hat so großen Hunger he is so (very) hungry; s. a. 7. — **4.** verstärkend, oft nicht übersetzt: ich habe so eine Ahnung, daß // I have some presentiment that //; wie ich mich so umsehe as I (happen to) look around me; das reicht nur so eben that only just suffices; it's barely enough; vgl. soeben; **so ziemlich** gut pretty good, fairly (or tolerably) well; das war **so recht** nach seinem Sinne that suited him exactly; Sie sagen das nur so you don't mean it or what you say. — **5.** ich bin so (ohnehin) schon müde I am very tired already or as it is; vgl. sowieso. — **6.** s. **soso**. — **7.** verstärkend: **a)** mit adv.: **so bald** so soon; komm(e) so bald als möglich come as soon as possible; er kam so bald nicht, wie // he did not come as soon as //; vgl. sobald; die Sache liegt mir **so fern**, daß // the matter is so foreign to me that //; vgl. sofern; ich bin **so gar** ein armer Mann I am such a very poor man; vgl. **so sehr** so much, to such an extent, in such a degree; stärker: so intensely; **so viel** so much; ich mache mir nicht so viel daraus I don't care that for it; vgl. 7 b u. soviel; nun sind wir **so weit** now here we are; so weit bin ich noch nicht I am not so far (advanced) yet; so weit geh(e)n (ob. es treiben) daß // to go so far as to //; er würde nicht so weit geh(e)n, es zu leugnen he would not go to the length of denying it; vgl. soweit; er hat **so wenig** gelernt, daß // he has learnt so little that // or too little to //; vgl. sowenig, **sowie**; du siehst **so wohl** aus you are looking so (or remarkably) well; vgl. sowohl (als auch); **b)** mit adj.: er ist nicht so dumm es zu glauben he is not so stupid as (or not silly enough) to believe it; die Sache ist **so gut wie** abgemacht ... is as good as settled; er war so gut wie vergessen he was almost (or all but) forgotten; so gut wie gar nichts next to nothing; **so viel Freunde** so many friends; so viel ist gewiß, (nämlich) daß // thus much (or one thing) is certain, namely that //; ich mag mir noch so viel Mühe geben whatever pains I (may) take; vgl. 7 a u. soviel; s. einmal 1; **c)** mit andern adv. zu cj. verbunden: **so gut als ich kann** to the best of my ability; er blieb **so lang(e)**, bis es aufhörte zu regnen he stayed until it ceased raining; vgl. solang(e); ich habe es dir **so oft** gesagt, daß // I have told you so often that //; vgl. sooft; er liest **so viel**, daß // he reads so much that //; vgl. soviel; **so wahr ich** lebe as true as I live or stand here; s. Gott 3 Schluß. — **8.** verallgemeinernd: **so** // auch however //; so reich er auch ist however rich he may be. — **9.** vor comp.: um **so** //, **als** // the //, as //; s. besser 1 am Ende; sie sind um so tiefer betrübt, als // they are all the more deeply grieved as or because //. — **10.** vergleichend: **so** // ob. **wie** // im ersten Gliede, **so** //, **wie** // ob. **als** // im zweiten Gliede der Vergleichung as //, as //; in the same degree as //, (so) //; so sanft wie eine Taube as gentle as a dove; so sehr sie ihn liebt, so sehr haßt sie uns in the same measure (or proportion. degree) as she loves him, (even so) she hates us; wie der Vater, so der Sohn like father like son. — **11.** bei unbestimmter Angabe vgl. **soundso**. — **12.** (folglich) er war ausgegangen — so war mein Gang vergebens ... so (or thus) my errand was useless; so wollen Sie nicht? so you don't want to?, then you won't? — **13. so daß** (-⌣́) ... cj. so (much) that ...; er ist krank, so daß er nicht kommen kann ... so that he is not able to come; er ist so schwach, daß er nicht gehen kann he is too feeble to walk; **so sehr, daß** // to such a degree that //; vgl. 7. — **14.** im Nachsatze: oft nicht zu übersetzen: da du müde bist, so will ich selbst hingehen as you are tired I will go myself; wenn das wahr ist. so hat er gelogen if that be true, then he has told a lie; kaum warst du fort, so kam er you were scarcely gone when (or you had no sooner gone than) he came; s. fehlen 6. — **II** rel. pron. inv. **15.** als Subjekt u. Objekt, meist in geh. Spr. ob. poet.: die Menschen. so auf Erden sind the people that are on this earth. — **III** cj. **16.** bsd. in Formeln = wenn: **so Gott will** if it please God. a. God willing, (It.) Deo volente (D. V.). ☞ Zssgn. s. sobald, sodann, soeben, sofern, sofort(ig), sogar, sogenannt, sogestalt, sogleich, sohin, solang(e), somit, sonach, sooft, soso, sotan, soundso, soviel, soweit, sowenig, sowie(so), wieso, sowohl, sozusagen.
so-bald (-⌣́) cj.: ⚓ (als) // as soon as //, a. the moment //, the instant //; in Briefen: ⚓ es Ihnen (nur irgend) möglich ist at your (very) earliest convenience; vgl. so 7 a.
Socke (⌣́⌣) [ahd.: sock; *lt. *soccus* m] f ④ (kurzer Strumpf) sock; fig. sich auf die ~u m. to make off, to take to one's heels.
Sockel (⌣́⌣) [fr.] m ㉒ arch. socle, basement: e-s Schornsteins 2c.: base, e-r Mauer: foot.
Sockel-gliederung (⌣́⌣...) f ㉒, **=sims** m base-moulding; **=platte** f base-table.
Socken-blume ♀ (⌣́⌣⌣) f ④ barrenwort, bishop's-hat (Epime´dium alpi´num).
Sod ⊕ (⌣́) [mhd.: sieden] m (n) ①(②)c. boiling(s pl.); bsd. Brauerei: (Wasser zum Brauen, Gebrauten) (water for) brewing.
Soda (⌣́⌣) [it.: *lt. *so'lida*] f ④ min. soda, chm. (kohlensaures Natron) sodium carbonate, carbonate of soda (Na_2CO_3).
Soda-asche (⌣́⌣...) f ④ soda-ash; **=fabrik** ⊕ f soda-works pl.; **=fabrikant** m soda-maker; **⚓haltig** a. ⑥⑥ containing soda, ⚡ sodaic; **=küpe** ⊕ f Färberei: sodavat; **=lauge** f soda-lye.
Sodalität (⌣⌣-⌣́) [lt.] f ④⑥ (Genossenschaft) sodality, partnership. [that.]
so-dann (-⌣́) adv. then, upon (or after)
Soda-salz (⌣́⌣...) n ㉒ (Natronsalz) soda-salt; **=seife** f soft soap. [to; s. fo **13.**]
so daß (-⌣́) cj. in such a way that or as
Soda-wasser (⌣́⌣...) n ㉒ soda-water; **=wasser-apparat** ⊕ m soda-fountain; **=wasser-bude** f soda-water stall.
Sod-brennen (⌣́⌣⌣) n ㉒ med. heartburn(ing), ⚡ pyrosis. [salt-works pl.]
Sode¹ (⌣́⌣) [: sieden] f ④ (Salzsiederei)
Sode² (⌣́⌣) [ndd.] f ④ (Rasenstück) sod.
Sodom ♀ (⌣́⌣) npr/n. ⓧa. bibl. Sodom; **~er** (⌣́⌣) m ㉒, mst **~it(in** f ④) m ㉒ (-⌣⌣́(⌣)) Sodomite; **~ie** (⌣⌣́) f ④⑥, **~iterei** (-⌣⌣-⌣́) f ④⑥ sodomy; **Litisch** (-⌣⌣́) a. ⑥⑥ sodomitic(al).
Sod-pumpe ⚓ (⌣́⌣⌣) f ㉒ bilge-pump.
so-eben (-⌣́⌣) adv. just now, a minute ago; er hat ⚓ gegessen he has just (this moment) dined; er ist ⚓ gekommen he has just come; vgl. so **4**.

♪ Musik; ⚡ Wissenschaft; ♀ Pflanze; ⊕ Geographie; ⊕ Technik; ⚒ Bergbau; ⚔ Militär; ⚓ Marine; 🛍 Handel; ✉ Post; 🚂 Eisenbahn

[Sofa] — 894 — [Soll-Bestand]

Sofa (¹-, a. ᵛ-)[nhd., türk.,*ar.] n († m) ᵇᵈ sofa. |-**kissen** n sofa-cushion.|
Sofa-ecke (ᵍ-...) f ⓶ corner of a sofa;
so-fern (-ᵛ) [mhd.] cj. (wenn) (in) so far as; ⓶ nur irgend möglich if by any chance possible; vgl. so 7a.
Soff¹ P(ᵛ) [soff²] m ⓒc. 1. drunkenness, F swilling, guzzling. — 2. (Trunk, guter Schluck) drink, good draught. — 3. mst contp. (Getränk) (inferior) beverage or liquor.   [saufen.|
soff² (ᵛ) ind., **söffe** (ᵛᵛ) subj. impf. von
Soffitte(n pl.)(ᵛᵛᵛ)[it.m] f ⓷ thea. (herabhangende Dekoration) flies, soffits pl.
so-fort (-ᵛ) adv. at once, on the spot, immediately, forthwith, directly, instantly, in an instant; **so-fortig** (-ᵛᵛ) a. ⓺ immediate, prompt. [the ship).|
Sog¹ ↧ (ᵛ) m ⓒc. (Kielwasser) wake (of
sog² (ᵛ) ind. impf. von saugen.
sog. abbr. = sogenannt.
so-gar (-ᵛ) adv. even; ⓶ die Steine möchten sich erbarmen the very stones ...; ja ⓶ // nay (even) //; vgl. so 7a.
söge (ᵛ-) subj. impf. v. saugen.
so-genannt(ᵛᵛᵛ) a. so-called; (sich fälschlich dafür ausgebend) would-be, self-styled, (fr.) soi-disant, sham.
so-gestalt (ᵛᵛᵛ) a. ⓺ so formed, of such a shape.
so-gleich (-ᵛ) adv. = sofort; vgl. gleich III.
so-hin (-ᵛ) adv. = somit.
Sohle¹ (ᵛ-; Hom. Sole) [ahd.: sole; *lt. sŏ'lĕa, sŏlum] f ⓸ 1. (Fuß- 2c.)~ sole of the foot, of a boot, &c. — 2. ~ (tiefster Teil) eines Ofens, Tunnels 2c.: bottom, ⚔ auch: level. — 3. ⊙ (Boden) floor; (Grundschwelle) ground-sill; Glasfabr.: (Untersatz der Schmelztiegel) bank; agr. ~ des Pfluges: sole, slade.
Sohle² (ᵛᵛ) f ⓸ ichth. = Scholle².
sohlen¹ (ᵛᵛ) v/a. ⓺ Stiefel 2c.: to sole.
sohlen² F prove. (ᵛᵛ) v/n. (h.) ⓺ = flunkern.
Sohlen-|**fleck** (ᵛᵛ...) [Sohle¹] m ⓶ Schuhmacherei: patch on the sole; **=gänger** m, zo. sole-walker, ⚘ plantigrade (animal); **=leder** ⊙ n Schuhmach.: sole-leather, leather for soles; **=lini-e** f horizontal line, level.   [timber.|
Sohl-holz ⊙ (ᵛ-ᵛ) [Sohle¹] n ⓶ sole-|
söhlig ⚔ (ᵛᵛ) [Sohle¹] a. ⓺ (wagerecht) horizontal, level.
Sohl-|**leder** (ᵛ-...) n ⓶ = Sohlenleder; **=platte** f, mach. sole- (or foundation-) plate; **=stein** m eines Hochofens: bottom- (or sole-)stone.
Sohn (ᵛ) [ahd.: son] m ⓒc. son; bibl. der verlorene ~ the prodigal son; des Menschen ~ the Son of Man.
Söhnchen (ᵛᵛ) n ⓶ (dim. von Sohn) 1. (dear) little son; F sonnie, sonny; mein ~! youngster! F Tommy! — 2. (verzogenes Kind) pet boy; vgl. Gold².
Sohnes-|**frau** (ᵛᵛ...) f ⓶ = Schwiegertochter; **=kind** n (Enkel[in]) grandchild; **=liebe** f filial love or affection. [tion.|
Sohnschaft (ᵛᵛ) f ⓺ sonship, jur. filia-|
Soiree (ßŏá-re') [fr. Abend(gesellschaft)] f ⓶ evening party, (fr.) soirée.
Soja (ᵛᵛ) [ostasiatisch] f ⓸, **~bohne** (ᵛᵛ...) f ⓶ Ost-J.: soy (Glyci'ne hi'spida); **~brühe** f soy.
Sokrates (ᵛᵛᵛ) npr/m. ⓖγ. (griech. Philosoph, 469 bis 399 vor Chr.) Socrates.

Sokratiker (-ᵛᵛᵛ) m ⓶ disciple of Socrates, auch: Socratic (philosopher).
sokratisch (-ᵛᵛ) a. ⓺ Socratic.
Solanaze-e(n pl.) ⚘ ᵋ (----ᵛ) [neu-lt.] f ⓷ (nachtschattenartige Pflanzen) solan(ac)eæ, solan(ac)eous plants pl.
so-lang(e) (-ᵛ(ᵛ) cj. as (or so) long as; ⓶ lebe as long as (or whilst) I am alive; vgl. so 7c.
Solanin ⚘ (-ᵛ¹) n ⓒc. chm. (Gift der Nachtschattengewächse) solanine (C₄₃H₆₉NO₁₆).
solarisieren (--ᵛ¹) [neu-lt.] v/a. n. v/n. (h.) ⓷ phot. (durch lange Belichtung schadhaft machen, werden) to solarize.
Solar-jahr (-"...) [lt. Sonnen..] n, ast. solar year; **=öl** n (deutsches Petroleum) solar oil.
Sola-wechsel (ᵛᵛ (ᵛ-...) [it. einzige] m ⓶ only bill (of exchange), sole bill; vgl. Prima-, Sekunda-wechsel.
Sol-bad (ᵛ-)n ⓶: a) saltwater (or brine-) bath; b) Badeort: saltwater springs pl.
solch (ᵛ) [ahd.: such; aus so-lich (Leiche)] demonstrative pron. u. a. ⓺ A2,3,B* such; ein ⓶er (od. ⓶ein)Mensch, ⓶ eine(r) such a one, such a person (aber: es gibt nur einen ⓶en Mann there is but one such man); ⓶e die // such as //; ⓶e guten Menschen such good people; ⓶e Leute pl. such people; auf ⓶e Weise in such a way, thus; als ⓶er as such, in that capacity; bibl. denn ⓶er ist das Himmelreich for of such is the kingdom of heaven (Matth. 19,14); ⓶e im Teilungssinne: er hat schon ⓶e (dergleichen) he has already some; ⓶e will er nicht he does not want (any of) that sort; adv. ein ⓶ (od. ⓶ ein) häßliches Kind so ugly a child, such a plain child.
solchen-falls (ᵛᵛᵛ) adv. in such a case, in that (or if that were the) case.
solcher (ᵛᵛ), **solche, solches** f. solch.
solcher=gestalt (ᵛᵛᵛᵛ)adv. in such a way or manner or form; ⓶lei (ᵛᵛ-) a., inv. of such a kind, such like; **=maßen** (ᵛᵛᵛ)adv. f. ...maßen; ⓶**weise** adv. in such a manner or way, in such wise.
Sold (ᵛ) [fr. solde f; *mlt. so'lidus] m ⓒb. (pl. ⓶) 1. a) ⚔ (Löhnung) soldier's pay (f. Halbsold); b) weitS. (Gehalt) salary, (Lohn) wages pl.; um ~ dienend hired mercenary (a. ⚔); in ~ nehmen to hire, to engage; im ~e einer ausländischen Macht stehen to be in the pay of a foreign power; e-m ~ zahlen to pay a p. — 2. fig. ~ der Minne reward (geh. Spr.: guerdon) of (true) love.
Soldat (ᵛ-ᵛ) [nhd. 16. sæc., *it. su Sold] m ⓶ (Militärperson); ~[in f ⓷] m der Heilsarmee) soldier (f. gemein 2 gegen Schluß); alter, gedienter ~ veteran; ~ werden to enter the army, to join the ranks, to enlist (F to go) as a soldier; Volkslied: wer will unter die ~en he that longs to be a soldier.
Soldaten-art ⚔ (ᵛᵛ...) f ⓶ soldier's manner; nach ~ in military fashion, as soldiers (are wont to) do; **=aushebung** f levy, conscription, recruiting; **=brauch** m soldierly habit or custom; vgl. -art; **=dienst** m military service; **=eid** m mil. oath; **=frau** f soldier's wife; **=geist** m martial spirit; **=gesindel** n military rabble, (ruffianly) gang of soldiers; vgl. Soldateska.

soldatenhaft (ᵛᵛᵛ) a. ⓺ soldier-like.
Soldaten-handwerk (ᵛᵛ...) n ⓶ profession of arms, F soldiering; vgl. **=stand**; **=kind** n soldier's child; **=kost**, fig. **=küche** f soldier's fare or food; **=leben** n soldier's (or military) life; **=lied** n soldier's song, martial air or tune; **=mütze** f foraging-cap; **=pferd** n trooper's horse; **=pflicht** f soldier's duty; **=rock** m soldier's coat or uniform; **=schenke** f (soldiers') canteen; **=stand** m soldier's profession, auch: soldiership; **=tracht** f military apparel or dress; **=volk** n: a) military nation, b) soldiers pl., soldiery; **=wesen** n military concerns, army-affairs pl., army-organization; **=wirt** m keeper (or steward) of a canteen, sutler; **=zucht** f military (or soldierly) discipline.
Soldateska (ᵛᵛᵛᵛ) [it.] f ⓸ b.s. undisciplined (gang of) soldiers, military rabble. [like, of a soldier, martial.|
soldatisch (ᵛᵛᵛ) a. ⓺ soldierly, soldier-|
Sold-buch ⚔ (ᵛᵛᵛ) n ⓶ soldier's small book or pocket-ledger.
Söldling (ᵛᵛ) [Sold] m ⓓ. = Söldner.
Söldner (ᵛᵛ) [mhd.] m ⓶ bsd. ehm. ⚔ mercenary (soldier), hireling; **~heer** ⚔ (ᵛᵛ...) n ⓶ army of mercenaries; **~truppen** f/pl. mercenary troops pl.
Sole (ᵛ-; Hom. Sohle) [mhd.: Salz] f ⓸ Saline: saltwater, brine.
Sol-ei (ᵛ-ᵛ) n ⓶ egg boiled in saltwater.
Solen-dampfpfanne ⊙ (ᵛ-...) f ⓶ brine-evaporator; **=leitung** f brine-conduit.
solenn (ᵛᵛ) [lt. söl(l)e'mnis] a. ⓺ (feierlich) solemn; **~ität** (ᵛᵛᵛᵛ) f ⓺ solemnity.
solfeggieren ♪ (ßᵛᵛᵛᴳᵛᵛ) [it.] I v/n. (h.) ⓷ to (sing) sol-fa. — II **~** n ⓶
Soli (ᵛᵛ) pl. von Solo.   [sol-fa.|
solid (ᵛᵛ) [it.] a. ⓺ 1. (fest und sicher) solid, firm(ly rooted or established), ⚔ sound, respectable, reliable, well established, solvent; ein ⓶es Haus a firm of good standing. — 2. (gesetzten Wesens) steady, steady-going, sterling, (anständig) decent.
Solidar-bürge (ᵛᵛᵛᵛ-) m ⓶, **=bürgschaft** f joint security or surety.
solidarisch, meist ⚔ (ᵛᵛᵛᵛ) [it.] a. ⓺ ⓶e (gemeinsame) Verbindlichkeit joint liability; adv. (einer für alle und alle für einen) conjointly, jointly and severally; **Solidarität** (ᵛᵛᵛᵛ) f ⓺ solidarity, joint liability.
Solidar-schuldner (ᵛᵛᵛᵛᵛ) m ⓶ (Gesamt-)schuldner; joint debtor.
Solidität (ᵛᵛᵛᵛ) [it.] f ⓺ (f. solide) 1. solidity, ⚔ soundness, respectability, reliableness, stability. — 2. steadiness, sterling character.
Solist ♪ (ᵛᵛᵛ) [it.] m ⓶ (ant. Chorist) soloist, solo singer, leading artiste.
Solitär (ᵛᵛᵛ)[fr. einsam] m ⓓ. (⚔) (einzeln gefaßter Diamant; a. Brettspiel mit Stiften ob. Kügelchen für eine Person) solitaire.
soll¹ (ᵛ) sg. pres. ind. von sollen.
Soll² (ᵛ) n ⓾ ob. inv.: a) strict order or injunction; b) ⚔ (ant. Kredit, Haben) (linke Seite des Hauptbuches) debit-side, debtor's side, Debit(ors pl.); ~ und Haben f. haben V; vgl. a. Debet.
Soll-Bestand ⚔ (ᵛ-...) m ⓶ calculated (or presumed) assets pl.; parl. ~ der

[Soll-Einnahme] — 895 — [Sonatine]

Flotte ⁊c.: desired (or required) strength ...; =Einnahme f supposed receipts pl.
sollen (☽) (ahd.: shall: Schuld) I v/n. (h.) ⊛ 1. Gebot: du sollst nicht stehlen thou shalt not steal; du sollst deinen Vater und deine Mutter ehren honour thy father and thy mother; ich soll reisen I am to travel; er soll kommen he shall come; er soll es nicht bekommen he shall not (F shan't) have it; nach verbs des Befehls: sagen Sie ihm, daß er kommen soll tell him to come or (that) he must come. — 2. Pflicht: wir tun nicht immer was wir (tun) 2 we don't always do what we ought to (do) or what we are (in duty) bound to do; was soll ich tun? what am I to do?; er hätte schreiben 2 (st.p.p. gesollt) he ought to have written; Sie sollten ihm doch gleich telegraphieren you had better telegraph to him at once; wo will er, daß wir hingeh(e)n 2? where does he wish us to go (to)? — 3. Nötigung, Zwang: sie sollte noch Schlimmeres erfahren she was (or had) to experience even worse things; das hat nicht sein 2 that was not to be. — 4. Zukunft: Sie 2 (es) sehen you shall (or will) see; man soll nicht einmal reden dürfen? are we not to be allowed even to speak?; die Stadt soll elektrisch beleuchtet w. it is intended (or proposed) to provide the town (or the town is to be illuminated) with electric light; das soll uns keine Sorgen machen that won't trouble us. — 5. Möglichkeit: wenn es regnen sollte if it should (come on to) rain; sollte er gestorben sein? may he be dead?; wenn Sie ihn sehen sollten if you should (happen) to see him; sollte ich dabei zugrunde gehen (even) though I should perish in the attempt; wie soll man da ernst bleiben? how can one remain serious? — 6. Wahrscheinlichkeit, Vermutung: man sollte glauben, daß // one would imagine that //; er muß Geld h., sollte ich meinen ... I should think; sollte man nach mir gefragt h.? have they really inquired after me?; sollte er sie wirklich verraten haben? is it possible that he has betrayed them?; soll das wirklich wahr sein? can that really be true? — 7. Gerücht: der König soll auf Reisen sein ... is said (or stated, reported) to be travelling, auch: ..., they say, is travelling; er soll schon längst tot sein he is believed (or supposed) to have been dead a long time. — 8. Herausforderung: nun soll einer noch kommen und mich anklagen // now let any one come to accuse me. — 9. Einräumung: nun, du sollst (meinetwegen) recht h.! well, you shall be right! — 10. mit erst und noch: so einer soll erst noch geboren w. such a one has yet to be born. — 11. ell.: a) was soll das (bedeuten)? what does that mean or signify?; was soll das alles? what's the meaning of it all?; b) was soll das (nützen)? of what use is that?, F what's the good of it?;
c) wem soll der Strauß (gehören)? for whom is the nosegay (intended)?; d) er soll nach Paris (reisen) he is to go to Paris; wohin soll ich (gehen)? where am I to go (to)?; der Brief soll auf die Post (getragen w.) ... must be posted; e) dich soll ja (dieser und jener holen)!, etwa: go and be hanged! — II ~ n ⊛ 12. duty, obligation. — 13. = Soll².
Söller (☽) [ahd.; *lt. solā'rium n] m ⊛ 1. = Altan. — 2. (Speicher) loft, top room, garret, storage-room.
Soll-posten ⊛ (☽⸍) m ⊛ = Debetposten.
Solmisation (˘˘-tz(⸍)¹) f ⊛ Solmisierung.
solmisier|en ♪ (˘˘́˘) [it.] I v/n. (h.) ⊛ to solmizate (= solfeggieren). — II ~ n ⊛ u. S/ung f ⊛ solmization.
solo¹ (˘́-) [it. allein] adv. alone, ♪ solo.
Solo² (~) m, n ⊛ 1. ♪ ⁊c. (a. ⊛) (Einzelvortrag, -spiel) solo. — 2. a) Lomber ⁊c.: ~! without taking!; b) Kartenspiel: solo.
Solo-geiger ♪ (˘́˘̄...) m ⊛ solo violinist; =gesang m solo.
solonisch (˘-́˘) [grch. Solon, 640—559 v. Chr., Gesetzgeber in Athen] a. ⊛ Solonic, ...ian; ~e Gesetze n/pl. Solon's laws pl.; 2e Weisheit Solonic wisdom.
Solo-sänger(in f) m ♪ (˘́˘̄...) ⊛ solo singer; =spieler(in f) m: a) ♪ soloist; b) Kartenspiel: solo player; =stimme ♪ f solo part; =stück n solo (auch ♪); =tanz m solo (dance), bisw.: (fr.) pas seul; =tänzer(in f) m, thea. solo (or first, leading) dancer.
Solözismus ⁊ (˘-́˘̆) [grch. Soloi ♀, St. in Zilizien] m ⊛ gr. (grober Sprachfehler) solecism.
Solper (˘-) [nbd. zigs. *Salzbrühe] m ⊛ = brine.
Sol-quelle (⸍...) f ⊛ saltwater well or spring; =rinne f brine-gutter, =salz n brine-salt.
Solstitial-punkt ⁊ (˘˘-tz(⸍)¹...) m ⊛ ast. solstitial point.
Solstitium ⁊ (˘˘-tz(⸍)˘) [lt.] n solstice (= Sonnenwende a).
solvent ⊛ (˘v⸍) [it.] a. ⊛ solvent, able to pay; (financially) sound; Solvenz (~) f ⊛ solvency, ability to pay.
Sol-wage ⊛ (⸍...) f ⊛ brine-prover or -gauge; =wanne f brine-bucket; =wasser n saltwater, brine.
so-mit (-⸍) adv. so, hence, therefore, consequently, thus.
Sommer (☽) [ahd.: summer] m ⊛ 1. summer; 2s, des ~s, im ~ in (or during) the summer, while the summer lasts; den ganzen ~ lang all (through) the summer. — 2. poet. = Jahr, z.B. sie zählt erst 16 ~ she has seen but sixteen summers; drei ~ sind vorbei three summers (or years) have flown; s. Schwalbe 1. — 3. fliegender ~ = Sommerfäden.
Sommer=abend (☽...) m ⊛ summer('s) evening; =anzug m summer-suit; =apfel m early apple; =aufenthalt m = =frische, =haus; =birne f early pear; =drehwurz ⚕ f species of lady's-tresses (Spira'nthes aesti'valis) gossamer (threads pl.); =fahr-plan m ⊛, ⁊c. summer time-table; =flecken m/pl., 2fleckig a. ⊛ = =sprossen, 2sprossig; =frische [nhd. 18. sae.] f (Erholungs-ort
für den Sommer) health-resort (for the summer); ~ in einem Orte nehmen to go to a health-resort (or spa) in the summer months; =frischler F m visitor (at a health-resort), holiday-maker, F tripper; =frucht f = =getreide; =gäste m/pl. in Bädern ⁊c.: visitors, holiday folk(s), summer guests pl.; =gerste f, agr. spring-barley; =getreide n, agr. summer-corn; =gewächs n summer-vegetable or -growth; =halbjahr n summery half of the year; =haus n country-house, summer-residence; =kartoffel f early potato; =kleidung f (light) summer clothing; =korn n = =getreide; 2lang a.: ein 2er Tag a long summer's day; =latte f, for. young sprig (or shoot) of a tree; =laube f = Gartenlaube; =levkoie f annual stock (Matthi'ola a'nnua).
sommerlich (☽) a. ⊛ summer-like, of summer, summery, ⁊ æstival; adv. auch: in summer-fashion.
Sommer=luft (☽...) f ⊛ summer(y) air; =monat m summer month; =morgen m summer's morning.
sommern, sömmern (☽) ⊛ a. I v/n. (h.), v/impers. 1. to be as in summer; es sommert it is becoming summer(y), summer is (drawing) near. — 2. der Baum sommert ... is putting on (new) wood. — II v/a. u. v/refl. 3. to summer; Betten 2 (sonnen) to air bedding in (or to expose it to) the sun. — 4. hort. einen Baum 2 (ausschneiteln) to prune ... — 5. agr. ein Feld 2 (mit Sommerfrucht bestellen) to sow ... with summer-seeds; Vieh 2 (den Sommer auf der Weide l.) to let cattle graze through the summer. — III ~ n ⊛ 6. s. Sommerung.
Sommer=nacht(s-traum m) f (☽...) ⊛ midsummer night('s dream, a. Titel e-s Lustspiels v. SH.); =pflanze f = =gewächs, auch: ⁊ æstival plant; =saat f, agr. spring-seeds pl.; =schlaf m, zo. mancher tropischen Tiere: ⁊ æstivation; =semester n summer-term or -session; =sprosse(n pl.) f freckle(s pl.), 2sprossig a. ⊛ freckled; =stoff m = =zeug.
Sommers=zeit s. Sommerzeit.
Sommer=tag (☽...) m ⊛ summer's day; =theater n open-air theatre.
Sommerung, Sö= (☽) f ⊛ (zu sommern I:) summery weather or warmth; (zu II:) summering, des Viehs: grazing of cattle during the summer months.
Sommer=weizen ⚕ (☽...) m ⊛ agr. summer-wheat (Tri'ticum aesti'vum); =wetter n, =witterung f summer(y) weather; =wohnung f = =haus; =wurz ⚕ f broom-rape (Oroba'nche); =zeit f summer time; =zeug n Schneiderei ⁊c.: light material (or cloth) for summer-wear, summer goods pl.
somnambul (☽⸍) [fr.] I a. ⊛: a) (nachtwandelnd) somnambulist(ic), walking in one's sleep; b) (mesmerisiert) mesmerized. — II ~e m ⊛, f ⊛ somnambulist, lady walking in her sleep.
Somnambulismus (˘˘˘˘) [lt.] m ⊛ somnambulism.
so-nach (-⸍ch) adv. = somit.
Sonate ♪ (˘⸍˘) [it.] f ⊛ sonata.
Sonatine ♪ (˘˘⸍˘) f ⊛ sonatina.

⊛ scientific; ⚕ botanical; ⊕ geography; ⊖ machinery; ✕ mining; ⚔ military; ⚓ marine; ⊛ commercial; ⊛ postal; ⊟ railway

[Sonde] — 896 — [Sonntagsentheiligung]

Sonde (⌣‿) [fr.] f ⊕ bſd. surg. probe; ſ a. Kugelſonde; mit der ~ unterſuchen to probe, to sound.

ſonder faſt † (⌣‿) [ahd.: (a)sunder] prp. mit acc. (bſd. noch poet. u. mſt vor Wörtchen ohne art.) without; ſ. ſondergleichen.

Sonder-abdruck (⌣‿…) m ⓬ separate impression; ⁀artig a. ⊕ peculiar; special; ⸗ausgabe f separate edition.

ſonderbar (⌣‿-) [mhd.] a. ⊕ (ungewöhnlich) singular, unusual; (eigentümlich) peculiar, singular, (befremdend) strange, curious, (ſeltſam) odd, queer, (einzig) unique; (brollig) droll; ein ⸗er Zufall a curious coincidence; ich finde es ⁀ von ihm, daß er geſpielt hat I think it strange of him to (or that he should) have played; es wurde ihm ⁀ zumute a strange feeling came over him.

ſonderbarer-weiſe(⌣‿⌣‿⌣) adv. singular to relate, strange to say; ⁀ iſt ſie hier curioſly enough she is here.

Sonderbarkeit (⌣‿⌣-) f ⊕ (ſ. ſonderbar): a) ohne pl. singularity; peculiarity; strangeness; oddity; b) mit pl. (etwas Sonderbares) singular (or strange, curious) thing or fact.

Sonder-beſtrebung(⌣‿…) f⊕, oft: particularism; ⸗bund m separate federation or league; ⸗bündler m separatist; ⸗bündelei, ⸗bündlerei f separatism; ⸗geſandtſchaft f special mission or embassy; ⸗geſetzgebung f special legislation; ⁀gleichen a. unequalled, matchless, peerless; vgl. ⸗gleichen.

Sonderheit (⌣‿-) f ⊕ = Beſonderheit; mſt adv.: in ⁀ particularly, especially.

Sonder-intereſſe (⌣‿⌣⌣) n ⓬ exclusive interest.

ſonderlich (⌣‿⌣) [ahd.] a. ⊕ (ungemein) extraordinary; (vorzüglich) excellent, superior; (beträchtlich) considerable, (hervorragend) distinguished, notable, remarkable; als adv. particularly, principally; (beſonders) (e)specially; oft negativ: es iſt nichts ⁀es daran there is nothing remarkable (or wonderful) about it; fein ⁀er Held no great hero; das iſt fein ⁀es Vergnügen that's no particular pleasure, it's not much of an amusement.

Sonderling (⌣‿⌣) m ⓪d. strange (or eccentric, singular) person or character, queer fellow, F oddity, rum chap.

ſondern¹(⌣‿)[mhd.; *ſonder] cj. meiſt nach e-r Negation: nicht er, ⁀ ſie hat es getan not he, but she has done it; nicht nur //, ⁀ auch // not only //, but also //.

ſondern²(⌣‿)[ahd.: sunder] I v/a. u. ſich ⁀ v/refl. ⓬a. to sunder, to set asunder, auswählend: to sift; (ſich) ⁀ (trennen) to separate (o.s.), to sever (o.s.). — II ~ n ⓬ ſ. Sonderung. [or privilege.)

Sonder-recht (⌣‿.) n ⓬ special right)

ſonders (⌣‿) adv. 1. ⊕ (beſonders) separately, apart. — 2. ſ. ſamt¹ I.

Sonder=ſtellung (⌣‿⌣) f ⓬ separate (or unique, exceptional) position.

Sonderung (⌣‿‿) f ⊕ sifting; separation, severance (vgl. Abſonderung).

Sonder-vermögen (⌣‿…) n ⓬ separate estate; ⸗zug m special (or extra) train.

ſondieren (⌣‿‿) [fr.] I v/a. u. v/n. (h.) ⓬: a) ⊥ to sound, to fathom (a. fig.);

fig. to approach cautiously; to feel one's way (towards); e-n ⁀ (aushorchen) to pump a p.; b) surg. to probe a wound. — II ~ n ⓬ ſ. Sondierung.

Sondier-inſtrument ⊥ (⌣⸗…) n ⓬ sounding-apparatus; ⸗ſtange f für Waſſer im Schiffsraume: sounding-rod.

Sondierung (⌣⌣‿) f ⊕ sounding, &c. (ſ. ſondieren I); ⁀s-verſuch (⌣⸗…) m ⓬ attempt to sound a th., fig. feeler.

Sonett (⌣‿) [it. sone′tto] n ⓬c. (Gedicht v. 14 Elſſilbern in beſtimmten Reimregeln) sonnet; ⁀en-dichter (⌣⌣⌣‿) m ⓬ (a. **Sonettiſt** (⌣⌣‿) m ⓬ sonnet-writer, sonneteer.

Sonn-abend (⌣‿-) [ahd.] m⊕d. Saturday; (des) ~s on Saturdays, on (F of) a S.

Sonne (⌣‿) [ahd.: sunʒ] f ⊕, poet. auch ⊕ sun; zur ~ gehörig solar; die ~ ſchien the sun shone, there was sunshine; Sprichw. es gibt nichts Neues unter der ~ there is no new thing (a. nothing new) under the sun; 's iſt nichts ſo fein geſponnen, es kommt doch an die ~n murder will out; the deepest secrets will come to light. [ſinnen.)

ſönne (⌣‿) 1. u. 3. Perſon subj. impf. v.)

ſonnen¹ (⌣‿) ⊕ I v/a. u. ſich ⁀ v/refl. 1 Betten ꝛc.: to expose … to the sun, to air …; chm., &c. auch: to insolate; ſich ⁀ to bask (in the sunshine). — 2. fig. ich ward geſonnt von der Liebe Glück love's happiness shone (or beamed) on me; ſich an (oder in) et. ⁀ (ergötzen) to (take) delight in a th. — II v/n. (h.) 3. von der Sonne: (ſcheinen) ſonnt the sun is shining, it is sunny. — III ~ n ⓬ 4. chm., &c. insolation.

Sonnen²=**anbetung** (⌣‿…) f ⊕ worship of the sun, ⚭ heliolatry; ⸗aufgang m: a) sunrise; ⚭ Oſten; ⸗auge n: a) poet. = Sonne; b) (leuchtendes Auge) bright sparkling eye; ⸗bad n sunbath, insolation; ⸗bahn f, ast. orbit of the sun, ſcheinbare: ⚭ ecliptic; ⸗ball m sun; ⁀beglänzt, ⁀beſchienen a. ⊕ lit up with sunshine, sunlit; ⸗beſchreibung f: ⚭ heliography; ⸗bild n picture of the sun; auch = ⸗ſpektrum; ⸗blick m: a) ray or glimpse, pl. oft: snatches of sunshine; b) fig. bright glance; ⸗blume ⁀ f (common) sunflower (Helia′nthus a′nnuus); ⸗brand m: a) (burning or scorching) heat of the sun; b) (Dunkelfärbung der Haut) tawny (or tanned) complexion; ⸗bruder P m tramp who sleeps in the open air (= Pennbruder); ⸗dach n sun-blind; vgl. ⸗zelt; ⸗durchmeſſer m diameter of the sun; ⸗fackel f, ast. luminous spot on the sun('s disk); ⸗ferne f (ant. =nähe): a) distance of the sun; b) ast. (größtmögliche Entfernung eines Planeten von der Sonne): ⚭ aphelion; ⸗fernrohr n solar telescope, helioscope; ⸗finſternis f solar eclipse, eclipse of the sun; ⸗fleck m sun-spot; ⸗förmig a. solar; ⸗glanz m splendour (or brilliancy) of the sun; fig. im ⁀e ſeiner Macht at the full height …; ⸗glut f blazing (or scorching) heat of the sun; ⸗gott m, myth. sun-god, Helios, Phœbus, Sol; ⁀haft (⌣‿‿) a. sunny (lustre, &c.), sunlike; bſd. fig. radiant, beaming; ⁀hell a.: as bright as sunshine;

fig. = ⁀klar; b) illuminated by the sun; ⸗hitze f heat of the sun, solar heat; ⸗höhe f, ast. sun's altitude; ⸗jahr n solar (or astronomical) year; ⸗käfer m, ⸗kälbchen n, ent. ladybird (Cocci′nella); ⁀klar a. fig. as clear as daylight, evident; et. ⁀ beweiſen to furnish a clear proof of a th., to prove a th. up to the hilt; ⸗kugel f globe of the sun, solar sphere; ⸗licht n sunlight; ⸗meſſer m, ast. heliometer; ⸗mikroſkop n solar microscope; ⸗nähe f (ant. =ferne): a) proximity of the sun; b) ast.: ⚭ perihelion; ⸗röschen ⁀ n sunflower (Helia′nthemum); ⸗roſſe n/pl. poet. sun-steeds pl.; ⸗ſcheibe f solar disk; ⸗ſchein m sunshine; es iſt (oder wir haben) ~ we are having sunshine or bright weather; ⸗ſchirm m sunshade; altmodiſcher, mit Franſen beſetzter auch: parasol; ⸗ſegel n = ⸗zelt; ⸗ſeite f (ant. Wetterſeite) sunny side or aspect, als Name, oft: Fairside; ⸗ſpektrum n, phys. solar spectrum; ⸗ſtand m, ast.: a) solstitial point; ⸗ſtäubchen n: a) a mote in a sunbeam; b) fig. (winzig Kleines) atom; ⸗ſtein m, min. sunstone; ⸗ſtich m, path. sunstroke, (Hitzſchlag) heat-stroke, biſw.: ⚭ siriasis; vom ~ getroffen werden to have a sunstroke; ⸗ſtillſtand m, ast.: ⚭ solstice; ⸗ſtrahl m sunbeam, ray of sunshine; ⸗ſyſtem n solar (or planetary) system; ⸗tag m sunny day, fig. day of happiness; ⸗tau ⁀ m sundew (Dro′sera); großer ~ round-leaved sundew (D. rotundifo′lia); ⸗tierchen n, zo. (Aufgußtierchen) sun-animalcule, ⚭ actinophrys; ⸗uhr f sun-dial; ⸗untergang m: a) sunset, sundown; b) ⚭ Weſten; ⸗verbrannt a. = ſonnverbrannt; ⸗weiſer m = ⸗zeiger; ⁀weit a. as far (distant) as the sun; ⸗weite f distance of the sun; ⸗welt f = ⸗ſyſtem; ⸗wende f: a) ast. solstice; b) ⚘ heliotrope, turnsol(e) (Heliotro′pium europæ′um); ⸗wendepunkt m solstitial point; ⁀wendig ⁀ a. heliotropic; ⁀e Wolfsmilch sunspurge (Eupho′rbia helioscopia); ⸗zeiger m, ast. needle (or hand) of a sundial; ⚭ gnomon; ⸗zeit f, ast. (ant. Sternzeit) solar time; ⸗zelt n ⁀ n awning.

ſonnicht ⁀, mſt **ſonnig** (⌣‿) [Sonne] a. ⊕ sunny (day, &c.); sunshiny; fig. bright, brilliant.

Sonntag (⌣‿) [ahd.: Sunday] m ⊕. Sunday, bſd. eccl. the Lord's Day, Sabbath; (des) ~s on Sundays, on (F of) a Sunday; es iſt ſein freier ~ it is his Sunday off or Sunday out; an Sonn- und Feſttagen on Sundays and holidays; Sprichw. es iſt nicht alle Tage ~ Sunday does not come every day.

ſonntägig (⌣‿⌣) a. ⊕ of Sunday.

ſonntäglich (⌣‿⌣) a. ⊕ 1. taking place on Sunday(s); adv. every Sunday. — 2. (wie am Sonntage) der Anzug Sunday dress or garment; ſich ⁀ (adv.) anziehen to put on one's Sunday clothes or F one's Sunday best.

Sonntags-arbeit (⌣⸗…) f ⊕ Sunday work or labour; ⸗entheiliger m Sabbath-breaker; ⸗entheiligung f, eccl. profanation (or desecration) of the

Zeichen (ſ. S. XVII): F familiär; P Volksſprache; Γ Gaunerſprache; ⁀ ſelten; † alt (auch geſtorben); * neu (auch geboren); ⁀⁀ unrichtig;

[Sonntagsessen] — 897 — [souffliren]

Lord's Day, breaking the Sabbath; =essen *n* Sunday dinner, =feier *f*, eccl. keeping (holy) the Lord's day; =gesicht *n*, *fig.* laughing (or cheerful) face; =heiligung *f* = =feier; strenge ~ Sabbatarianism; =jäger *m* amateur sportsman; =kind *n* child (or person) born on a Sunday; ein ~ sein to be born under a lucky star or with a silver spoon in one's mouth; =kleid *n* Sunday dress or garb or garment; ~er Sunday clothes *pl.*; =reiter *m* snobbish horseman (who rides out on Sundays); =ruhe *f* Sunday rest; =schule *f* Sunday-school; =staat *m* Sunday finery; =vergnügen *n* Sunday amusement.

sonn=verbrannt (˘–˘) *a.* ⓖ sun-burnt, tanned (by the sun).

sonor (˘⌣) [lt.] *a.* ⓖ = klangreich.

sonst (˘⌣) *en* (˘⌣) [ahd.; *so] I *adv.* 1. a) (anders) otherwise; b) mit *pronouns*: else; 2 etwas something else; 2 jemand (niemand) somebody (nobody) else; 2 nichts nothing else; 2 nichts als nothing but; 2 nirgends nowhere else; was 2? what else?; wer 2? who else?; 2 wer? anybody else?; wenn es 2 nichts ist if it be only that, if that's all; 2 befehlen (ober wünschen) Sie 2 noch etwas? can I get (or show) you anything else?, what is the next thing? — 2. (außerdem) besides, moreover, (im übrigen) in other respects, otherwise; (andernfalls) in the contrary case, (zu einer andern Zeit) (at) any other time; 2 einmal on some other occasion, some other day; (für gewöhnlich) ordinarily; wie 2 as usual. — 3. = ehemals. — II ~ *n*, *inv.* 4. das ~ (Einst) und das Jetzt the past and (the) present.

sonstig (˘⌣) *a.* ⓖ 1. (ander) other. — 2. (ehemalig) former, of former days.

sonst=wie (˘⌣) *adv.* in some other way; 2wo *adv.* elsewhere, somewhere else; 2woher *adv.* from elsewhere, from somewhere else; 2wohin = 2wo.

so=oft (˘⌣) *cj.* whenever, 2 du kommst as often as (or whenever, F every time) you come; 2 Sie wollen, 2 ihr wollt as often (or as many times) as you like; 2 ich auch klingeln mag however often I may ring, vgl. so 7c.

Soore F (⌣) *f* ⓖ (Beute): die ~ aus=ea.= machen (teilen) to divide the swag.

Sophie (˘f⌣) [grch.] npr/f. ⓖⓈ Sophia; ~n=kirche *f* ⓖ church of St. Sophia.

Sophisma ☉ (˘f⌣) [grch.] *n* ⓖ, Sophismus *m* ⓖ (Trugschluß) sophism.

Sophist (˘f⌣) [grch.] *m* ⓖ, ~in (˘f⌣) *f* ⓖ sophist; ~erei (˘f⌣) *f* ⓖ sophistry; ~ik (˘f⌣) *f* ⓖ art (or teaching) of the sophist(s); 2isch *a.* ⓖ (spitzfindig) sophistical.

sophokle=isch (˘f⌣) S (˘f⌣) [v. Sophokles, griechischer Tragiker, 496–406 vor Chr.] *a.* ⓖ Sophoclean, of Sophocles.

Sopran ♪ (˘⌣) [it. *sopra'no* höchste] *m* ⓖ d. soprano, treble ☉ = Diskant; ~ist(in (˘⌣) *m* ⓖ (˘˘˘⌣), ~=sänger(in *f*) *m* ⓖ soprano, auch: soprano singer, treble-singer, sopranist.

Sorbe¹ (⌣) [it. *sorba*] *f* ⓖ = Elsbeere.

Sorbe² (⌣) [slav.] *m* ⓖ, Sorbin f ⓖ (wendische[r] Bewohner zw. Elbe u. Saale) Sorb.

Sorbet(o) (˘⌣(˘)) [it., *ar.*] *n* ⓖ c.(Ⓢ) = Scherbett.

sorbisch (˘⌣) [Sorbe] *a.* ⓖ Völkerkunde: Sorbian, Sorbish.

Sordine ♪ (f...˘f⌣) [(˘˘) it. *sordi'no* m] *f* ⓖ = Dämpfer 2 ♪.

Sorge (˘⌣) [ahd..: sorrow] *f* ⓖ 1. care; (Kummer) grief, sorrow; (Unruhe) uneasiness, anxiety, concern, stärker: alarm; Kummer und ~(n) care and trouble; e-m ~ machen to cause a p. trouble or worry or anxiety; sich ~n u. um to concern o.s. about; mach' dir deshalb keine ~n you need not trouble yourself on that account, don't worry about that; außer ~n sein to be unconcerned; ~n verbannen, verjagen to dispel (or drive away) care(s). — 2. (Sorgfalt) care(ful attention, liebevolle: solicitude; das lassen Sie meine ~ sein (you may) leave that to me; ~ für et. tragen to take care of a th. (vgl. sorgen 2a); die ~ für et. übernehmen to take charge of a th., to undertake (the care of) a th.

sorgen (˘⌣) [ahd.: sorrow] I *v/n.* (h.) u. sich 2 *v/refl.* ⓖ 1 (in Sorge sein): *v/n.* to be uneasy or anxious or solicitous; (sich quälen) to worry; (fürchten) to be apprehensive; um (bibl. für) et. 2 to be anxious about a th. — 2. (Sorge für e-n, et. tragen): a) *v/n.* für e-n, et. 2 to take care of or to look after, to attend to a p., a th.; (zu et. Rat schaffen) to provide for a th.; für ihn ist gesorgt he is provided for; für j-s Bedürfnisse 2 to provide for a p.'s needs, (Nahrung besorgen) to cater for a p.; dafür werde ich 2 I will see to that; ich will dafür 2, daß es gepackt wird I will see it packed; lassen Sie mich nur für den Wagen 2 let me get (or see about) the carriage; dafür laß mich 2! that's my concern! (vgl. Sorge 2); b) *v/refl.*: sich um et. 2 to endeavour to obtain a th.; er hat sich sehr gesorgt he has been very anxious. — II ~ *n* ⓖ 3. = Sorge.

Sorgen=banner (˘⌣...), =brecher *m* ⓖ banisher of care, cup which drives away care; 2frei *a.* ⓖ free (or exempt) from care or trouble; lighthearted; =kind *n* child requiring great care, F handful; =last *f* load of care(s); 2los *a.* (ohne Sorgen) = 2frei; vgl. sorglos; =schwer *a.* weighed down with care or trouble; vgl. 2voll, =stuhl *m* arm-(or easy-)chair; 2voll *a.* full of care or anxiety or trouble, uneasy.

Sorgfalt (˘⌣) [ahd.] *f* ⓖ care(fulness), liebevolle: solicitude; (Aufmerksamkeit) attention, (Genauigkeit) exactness, accuracy, nicety; (Pünktlichkeit) precision; (Fleiß) application; (Gewissenhaftigkeit) scrupulousness, conscientiousness; große ~ auf et. verwenden to bestow great pains (up)on a th.; mit der allergrößten (od. aller möglichen) ~ with the utmost (or every possible) care, most carefully or scrupulously.

sorgfältig (˘⌣) *a.* ⓖ careful, heedful, attentive; exact, accurate, precise; conscientious, scrupulous, painstaking, bei einer Auswahl: particular; höchst 2 (*adv.*) gearbeitet most care-fully (or elaborately, conscientiously) worked; ~feit *f* ⓖ = Sorgfalt.

Sorghum ♀ (˘⌣) [neu=lt., *ind.*] *n* ⓖ: a) = Mohrenhirse; b) (chines. Zuckerrohr) sorg(ho) (Sorghum saccharatum).

sorglich (˘⌣) [ahd.] *a.* ⓖ 1. (sorgfältig) careful — 2. (sorgenvoll) full of care, anxious, solicitous. [solicitude.]

Sorglichkeit (˘⌣) *f* ⓖ (anxious) care,/ sorg=los (˘⌣) [mhd.] *a.* ⓖ (ohne Sorgfalt) without (a) care; (unbedacht) thoughtless, reckless; (gleichgültig) unconcerned, indifferent; (lässig) negligent, careless; =losigkeit *f* ⓖ thoughtlessness: unconcern; lightness of heart: (Fahrlässigkeit) negligence, carelessness; vgl. sorgenlos 2c.

sorgsam (˘⌣) [mhd.] *a.* ⓖ careful, painstaking, particular; solicitous, (vorsichtig) cautious, circumspect; ~feit (˘⌣) *f* ⓖ care(fulness); caution.

sorren ⚓ (˘⌣) *v/a.* Ⓢ (anknüpfen) to lash, to seize; die Hängematten (ein=)2 (aufrollen) to lash up the hammocks.

Sorring ⚓ (˘⌣) *f* ⓖ (Ⓢ) Art Bindsel: lashing, seizing.

Sorr=tau ⚓ (˘⌣) *n* ⓖ lashing, seizing.

Sorte (˘⌣) [mhd.: sort; *it. sorta*] *f* ⓖ sort, species; vgl. Gattung; ⓖ feinste ~ prime quality, choice(st) brand.

Sorten=rechnung (˘⌣...) *f* ⓖ, =zettel *m* ⓖ bill (or list) of specie.

sortierbar (˘⌣) *a.* ⓖ sortable.

Sortier=beamte(r) ⓖ (˘˘⌣˘) *m* ⓖ sorter.

sortier=en (˘⌣) [it. *assorti're*] I *v/a.* ⓖ to (as)sort, (ordnen) to put in order, to arrange; (auslesen) to pick (out), durch Sieben: to sift. — II ~ *n* ⓖ f. S/ung.

Sortierer (˘⌣) *m* ⓖ, ~in *f* ⓖ sorter.

Sortier=kasten ☉ (˘⌣˘) *m* ⓖ Papierfabr.: sorting-box or -chest. [ment.]

Sortierung (˘⌣) *f* ⓖ sorting, assort-/ Sortiment (˘⌣) [it. *assortime'nto m*] *n* ⓖ c. (Auswahl) assortment; (3f.=gehöriges, Satz) set; ~Pflanzen collection of plants; ~er ⓖ (˘⌣) *m* ⓖ = =buchhändler; Sortiments=buchhandel ⓖ (˘⌣...) *m* ⓖ retail book-trade; =buchhändler *m* (discount-)bookseller; =buchhandlung *f* bookseller's business or shop; =lager *n* bookseller's stock in hand.

so sehr (˘⌣) *adv.* u. *cj* f. so 7a, 10 u. 13.

so=so (˘⌣) *adv.* (nicht gut, nicht schlecht) so-so, mehr gbr.: tolerably good or well, F (pretty) middling; es steht damit 2 there is not much go about it, things are going on slowly; vgl. so 2 gegen Ende.

Soße (˘⌣) *f* ⓖ bsd. Tabakfabr.: = Sauce.

so=tan † (˘⌣) *a.* ⓖ (solch) such (like); unter 2en Umständen under these (aforesaid) circumstances.

Sotni=e ⚔ (˘⌣) [russ. Hundertschaft] *f* ⓖ (Abteilung Kosaken) sotnia.

sott (˘) *ind.*, sötte (˘⌣) *subj. impf. v.* sieden.

Sottise (˘⌣) [fr.] *f* ⓖ (Dummheit) foolish thing or remark; (Versehen) blunder.

Souffleur (su=, *a.* su=flö'r [fr.] *m* ⓖ, ~in *f* ⓖ prompter; =buch *n* ⓖ prompter's (or prompt-)book; ~kasten *m* (im engl. Theater unbekannt, weil hier der Souffleur hinter den Kulissen steht) prompter's box.

Souffleuse F (...flö=) *f* ⓖ = Souffleurin.

souffli=eren (su=, su=⌣) [fr. zuflüstern] *v/n.* (h.) u. *v/a.* ⓖ bsd. *thea.* e-m 2 to prompt a p.

[so-und-so] — 898 — [spanisch]

so-und-so (⁻ᵛ⁻ᴸ) **I** adv.: ≳ viel so much, a certain quantity (or amount, sum); 30 und ≳ viel Mark thirty odd shillings; den ≳ und so vielten such and such a day of the month. — **II** s. Herr ~ statt des Namens: Mr. So-and-so, mehr gebr.: F Mr.Thingumite,…y,auch Mr.What's-his-name. [n ⑳ (Abendbrot) supper.]

Souper (ſu-, a. ſu-pe') [fr.: *dtſch. Suppe]

soupieren (ſu-, a. ſu-ᴸᵛ) [fr.] v/n. (h.) ⑬ (zu Nacht speisen) to sup, mehr gbr.: to have (or eat) one's supper.

Soutache ⊕ (ſu-, a. ſu-tä'ſch⁵) [fr.] f ⑱, oft ˖˖ m ⑩ Näherei: (Borte, Litze) braid; mit ~ besetzen oder **soutachieren** (ſu-, a. ſu-tä-ſch⁻ᴸ) v/a. ⑬ to (edge with) braid.

Soutane (ſu-, a. ſu-ᴸᵛ) [fr. langer Priester-rock] f ⑱ Cath. eccl. soutane, cassock.

Souterrain (ſu-, a. ſu-ter-ä') [(˖˖) fr. m Gewölbe, Tunnel] n ⓪ (Kellergeschoß) basement of a house, underground story.

souverän (ſu-, a. ſu-w⁻ᴸ) [fr.] **I** a. ⑥⑥ sovereign, supreme. — **II** ~ m ⑳ d. (Herrſcher) sovereign, ruler.

Souveränität (ſu-, a. ſu-w⁻ᵛ⁻ᴸ) [fr.-lt.] f ⑯ (Herrſchaft) sovereignty, sovereign power; ~s-rechte ("...) n/pl. ⑬ rights pl. of sovereignty.

so-viel (-ᴸ) cj.: ≳ ich mich erinnern kann as far as I can remember; ≳ ich gehört habe from all that (or from what) I have heard; ≳ ich weiß as far as (or for aught) I know, to the best of my knowledge; nein, ≳ ich weiß not as far as I know; ≳ als (ſ. v. a.) the same as, equivalent to; vgl. so 7a, b, c.

so-weit (-ᴸ) = sofern; vgl. so 7au. weit 5.

so-wenig (-ᴸᵛ) adv. = eben ≳; vgl. so 7a.

so-wie (-ᴸ) cj. = sobald; vgl. so 10.

so-wie-so (ᴸ⁻ᴸᴸ) adv. (ohnehin; vgl. so 5) in either (or any) case; er wird ≳ ſein Ziel nicht erreichen he will not attain his end in any case or do what he may.

so-wohl (⁻ᴸ) cj. as well; ≳ // als auch both // and; not only // but also; ≳ die Dampfmaschine wie auch der Telegraph ſind moderne Erfindungen the steam-engine as well as the telegraph (or both the steam-engine and the telegraph) are…; vgl. so 7a.

Sozi F (ᴸᵛ) m ⑳ = Sozialdemokrat.

sozial (ᵛ(ᵛ)⁻ᴸ) [lt.] **I** a. ⑥⑥ (geſellſchaftlich) social. — **II** ~e(r) m ⑰ = Sozialiſt.

Sozial-demokrat (ᵛ(ᵛ)⁻...) m ⑳ social democrat, socialist; **~ie** f social democracy; **Liſch** a. ⑥⑥ socialist(ic).

Sozialismus (ᵛ(ᵛ)-ᴸᵛ) [lt.] m ㉗ socialism; ſ. Katheterſozialiſmus.

Sozialiſt (ᵛ(ᵛ)-ᴸ) [lt.] m ㊷ socialist; ehm. **~en-gesetz** n law against socialists; **~en-kongreß** m socialist congress; **~erei** (ᵛ(ᵛ)-ᵛᵛᴸ) f ⑯ socialistic doings pl.

sozialiſtiſch (ᵛ(ᵛ)-ᴸᵛ) a. ⑥⑥ socialist(ic).

Sozial-reform (ᵛ(ᵛ)⁻...) f ⑫ pol. social reform; **-revolutionär** m social revolutionist; **-wiſſenſchaft(lich)** a.) f (referring to) social science, auch: sociology (sociological).

Sozinianer (--(ᵛ)ᴸ) [Socinus 1539 bis 1604] m ⑳ eccl. hist. Socinian; **Sozinianiſmus** (--(ᵛ)⁻ᴸᵛ) m ㉗ Socinianism.

Soziolog ⚹ (ᵛ(ᵛ)⁻ᴸ) [lt.-grch.] m ⑫, **~e** ④ sociologist; **~ie** (-(ᵛ)⁻ᴸ) f ⑯ (Geſellſchaftslehre) sociology.

Sozius (-(ᵛ)⁻) [lt.] m ⑳ **1.** ⑬ (Teilhaber) partner. — **2.** (Mitgenoſſe) companion; F ein hübſcher ~ a nice fellow. — **3.** F = Sozialiſt, a. comrade. [as it were.]

so-zu-ſagen (ᴸ⁻⁻ᴸᵛ) adv. so to speak,

Spachtel (ᴸᵛ) m ⑳, f ⑱ = Spatel; typ. slice.

spack (ᵛ) a. ⑥⑥ **1.** ⊕ v. Holz: (leck) leaking. — **2.** (hinfällig) frail, infirm.

Spagat ſüdd. (⁻ᴸ) [it. spago] m ⑳ c. (Bindfaden) thread.

Spähe (ᴸᵛ) f ⑱ spying, watching.

spähen (ᴸᵛ) [ahd.: spy] ⑱ **I** v/n. (h.) to spy (about); (auf der Lauer ſein) to be on the look-out; ⚔ to scout; auf e-n, et. ≳ to watch for a p., a th. — **II** v/a. et. ≳ to look out for a th.; to espy a th.

Späher (ᴸᵛ) [ahd.] m ⑳, **~in** f ⑯ meiſt b.s. spy, prying person, prowler; weitS. look-out man (a. ⚔); ⚔ (Kundſchafter) scout; **~auge** ⚹ keen observing eye; **~blick** m prying glance.

Späherei (⁻ᵛᴸ) f ⑯ spying (system), prying, close watch(ing), der Polizei: espion(n)age, shadowing. [patrol.]

Späher-patrouille ⚔ (ᴸᵛ⁻...) f ⑱ scouting

Späh-glas (ᴸᵛᴸ) n ⑫ spy-glass.

Spahi ⚔ (⁻ᴸ) [fr., türk.: *perſ. Krieger] m ⑫ spahee, spahi.

Späh-ſchiff (ᴸᵛᴸ) ⚓ n ⑫ advice-boat.

Spake ⚓ (ᴸᵛ) [ndd. = hd. Speiche] f ⑱ capstan-bar, hand-spoke, des Steuerrades: wheel-spoke.

Spalier (ᵛ⁻ᴸ) [fr.; it. spallie'ra f] n ⑳ d. **1.** hort. (Lattengitter) trellis-(or lattice-)work, ⚹ espalier; Pflanzen am ~ ziehen to train … on trellis-work. — **2.** (v. Menſchen gebildete Gaſſe) lane, double row of people; ~ bilden to form a lane, to line the road, to draw up (or stand) in a (double) line.

Spalier-baum (ᵛ⁻ᴸ) m ⑲ tree trained on trellis-work, ⚹ espalier(-tree).

spalieren (ᵛ⁻ᴸᵛ) v/a. ⑬ **1.** eine Wand ⁊c. ≳ to cover … with trellis-work. ≳ **2.** Bäume ≳ to train … on trellis-work.

spalier-förmig (ᵛ⁻ᴸ...) a. ⑥⑥ like trellis-work, trellised; **-obſt** n ⑫ hort. wall-fruit; **-werk** n trellis-work.

Spalt (ᵛ) [ahd.: *ſpalten] m ⑳ b. **1.** split, fissure, crevice, rift; chink, gap, geol. crevasse; (Schlitz) slit, (Sprung) crack, in der Mauer a. cranny; (Ritz) tear, flaw; vgl. Ritz. — **2.** (abgeſpaltenes Stück Holz) chip (or splinter) of wood. [tomaceae pl.]

Spalt-algen ⚹ (ᵛ⁻ᴸᵛ) f/pl. ⑰ ⚹ dia-

spaltbar (ᵛ⁻) a. ⑥⑥ cleavable, easy to split or to chop, ⚹ fissi(b)le, scissi(b)le; **-keit** f ⑯ cleavability, ⚹ fissility, min. der Kriſtalle: cleavage.

Spalt-blume ⚹ (ᵛ⁻ᴸ) f ⑱ schizanthus.

Spalte (ᴸᵛ) [mhd.; *Spalt] f ⑱ **1.** = Spalt. — **2.** ⊕ typ. column of a page, &c.

spalten¹ (ᴸᵛ) [ahd.: ſpleißen] ⑱ (p.p. geſpalten, zu **II** a. geſpalten) **I** v/n. (ſn) **1.** to split; to slit; to crack. — **II** v/a. **2.** to split; to cleave (a. ⊕ v. Kristallen); Holz ⁊c. a. to chop, (reißen) to rend, to ſplit; (ſchlitzen) to slit; (in zwei Hälften teilen) to part (or divide) in two; fig. Haare ≳ to split hairs, to draw it fine; phys. einen Lichtſtrahl durch das Prisma in 7 Farben ≳ to decompose a ray of light; geſpalten, auch: fissured; mit gespaltenem Huf cloven-footed; mit ~ Schnabel ⚹ fissirostral. — **III** ſich ≳ v/refl. **3.** to split; to slit; von Kriſtallen: ſich (leicht) ≳ to cleave (easily); (Riſſe bekommen) to crack, von der Haut: to chap. — **4.** (ſich gabeln) to bifurcate, to branch out. — **5.** fig. (unter-ea. uneinig werden) to split up, to break up, to disintegrate, to separate. — **IV** ~n ⑬ = **6.** Spaltung 1.

ſpalten²-reich (ᴸᵛ⁻...) [Spalte pl.] a. ⑥⑥ cracked, fissured, v. Gletſchern ⁊c.: full of crevasses, crevassed; **-ſatz** ⊕ typ. setting up (type) in columns; **-weiſe** adv. in columns.

Spalter (ᴸᵛ) m ⑳ **1.** Perſon: splitter, slitter, cleaver. — **2.** ⊕ Werkzeug: cleaver, chopper.

Spalt-fläche (ᵛ⁻...) f ⑫ min. plane (or face) of cleavage; **-frucht** ⚹ f schizocarp; **-früchtig** ⚹ a. ⑥⑥ schizocarpic, …ous; **-füßig** a. zo. cloven-footed; fissiped, schizopod; **-füß(l)er** m/pl. zo. splitfeet, fissipeds, schizopods pl.; **-holz** n split wood, fire-wood.

ſpaltig (ᴸᵛ) a. ⑥⑥ **1.** with fissures or cracks; fissured, cracked. — **2.** (auch ſpältig) easy to split (or to cleave), ⚹ fissi(b)le. — **3.** in Zſſgn zu Zahlwörtern, zB. drei-≳ of (or in) three columns.

Spalt-keil ⊕ (ᵛ⁻...) m ⑳ wedge for cleaving; **-klinge** ⊕ f cleaving-knife, cleaver, bei Diamantſchneider: splitting-knife; **-latte** f split lath; **-los** a. ⑥⑥ fissureless, **-meſſer** ⊕ n, hort. grafting-knife; **-pfropfung** f, hort. slit- (or splice-)grafting; **-pilz** ⚹ m (ant. Sproßpilz): ⚹ fission-fungus, schizomycete; **-ring** m split ring.

Spaltung (ᴸᵛ) f ⑯ **1.** splitting; cleaving, &c. (ſ. spalten II), v. Holz: chopping; phys. decomposition of luminous rays. — **2.** cleavage, fissure, crack; fig. split, disintegration, disruption, durch Uneinigkeit: dissension, disunion, division; in der Kirche ⁊c.: schism; (Zweiteilung) bifurcation (auch von Schulklaſſen). [logie: fissiparism.)

Spalt-zeugung ⚹ (ᵛ⁻ᴸ) f zo. u. Bio-

Span¹ (ᴸ) [ahd.: spoon] m ⑳ c. **1.** splinter (or chip) of wood (f. Hobelſpäne); (Stückchen Holz) (small) stick of wood; (Dach-) shingle; fig. ſ. Gedankenſpäne; Sprichw. wo man Holz haut, da fallen Späne from chipping come chips. — **2.** ⚓ section of a ship. — **3.** provc. fig.: a) (Zwiſt) quarrel(ling), strife; Späne machen to make a fuss; b) (Geld) Späne h. to have (plenty of) money or F chips.

Span²-ferkel (ᴸ⁻ᵛᵛ) [ahd.: *spen Mutter-milch] n ⑫ sucking pig.

Spange (ᴸᵛ) [ahd.: spangle] f ⑱ an Büchern ⁊c.: clasp; (Schnalle) buckle.

Span²-grün (ᴸ⁻ᴸ) [mhd. spaniſch Grün] n ⑫ chm. verdigris (= Grünſpan); **-holz** ⊕ n match-wood.

Spani-en ⚹ (ᴸ(ᵛ)) npr/n. ㉓ Spain.

Spani-er (ᴸ(ᵛ)⁻) m ⑳, **~in** f ⑯ Spaniard, auch: Spanish lady or woman.

Spaniol ⚹ (ᵛ⁻ᴸ) [fr.] m ⑳d. Schnupftabak: Spanish snuff; **~e(r)** m ⑫(㊷) = Spanier.

ſpaniſch (ᴸᵛ) [ahd.] a. ⑥⑥ **1.** Spanish, of Spain; ſ. Fliege; Der Pfeffer ⚹ cayenne pepper (v. Ca'psicum a'nnuum); ſ. Rei-

Signs (see page XVII): F familiar; P vulgar; F flash; ⚹ rare; † obsolete (died); * new word (born); ˖˖ incorrect; ♪ music:

[spanisch-amerikanisch] — 899 — [Sparseide]

ter¹ 4, Rohr 3; ⊱e Schminke Spanish white or paint; ⚫ ⊱e Soda barilla; die ⊱e Sprache, das ~(e) n ⚙ the Spanish language, Spanish; ⊱er Stiefel (Folter-instrument) Spanish boot; ⊱e Wand folding-screen. — 2. fig. das kommt mir ⊱ (befremdend) vor that's all Greek (or double Dutch) to me, it seems strange to me.

spanisch-amerikanisch (⌣⌣...) a. ⚙ Spanish-American, a.: Hispano-American; =fliegen-pflaster n ⚙ blister; =gelb n (Auripigment) orpiment; =weiß ⚫ n (fein geschlämmter Kalt) Spanish white or paint.

Span¹-kasten (⌣⌣⌣) m ⚙ deal-box.
Spann¹ (⌣) [ndd.: spannen] m ⓗb. anat. des Fußes: instep, ⚳ acrotarsium.
spann² (⌣) ind. impf. v. spinnen.
Spann³-... (⌣...) [spann-en] s. Zssgn.
Spannadel ⊙ (⌣⌣) [Spann³-nadel] f ⚙ der Insektensammler setting-needle. [sinew.)
Spann²-ader ⊙ (⌣⌣) f ⚙ anat. (Sehne)
Spannagel ⊙ (⌣⌣) [Spann³-nagel] m ⚙e. brace-pin, Wagnerei: main pin, bolster-bolt. [new.)
spannagel-neu F (⌣⌣⌣⌣) a. ⚙ brand-
Spann²-balken ⊙ (⌣⌣) m ⚙ carp. girder.
spannbar (⌣⌣) a. ⚙ tensi(b)le.
Spann³-brett (⌣...) n ⚙ der Insektensammler: setting-board; =dienst m, hist. Feudalw.: corvée (or statute-labour) with teams.
Spanne (⌣⌣) [ahd.: span; *spannen] f ⚙ 1. (ausgespannte Hand als Längenmaß, etwa 21 cm) span; nach ~n messen to measure by spans. — 2. weit⊱. a) räumlich: short distance; b) zeitlich: short (or brief) space (or span) of time.
spannen (⌣⌣) [ahd.: span: spinnen] ⚙ I v/a. u. v/refl. 1. (sich) ⊱ to stretch, to bend; (straff ⊱, steif m.) to tighten, to brace; ein Pferd auf der Weide ⊱ (fesseln) to tie up (or to tether)...; et. eng, weit ⊱ to tighten, to loosen a th.; s. Bogen 3; ⊙ den Dampf ⊱ to increase the tension of steam; den Hahn (e-s Gewehres) ⊱ to cock the gun; jeden Nerv ⊱ to strain every nerve; ♪ eine Saite ⊱ to stretch (or tighten) a chord or string; s. Saite 2. — 2. mit prp. s. Folter, Joch 1; ⊙ Tuchmacher: in den Rahmen ⊱ to tenter; Schlosser: in den Schraubstock ⊱ to put in the vice, to hold (or clutch) with a vice; Pferde vor den Wagen, an die Deichsel ⊱ to put horses to (the carriage). — 3. der Rock spannt mich (ist zu eng) ... pinches me or is too tight for me; ⊱d tight. — 4. ♪ eine Oktave ⊱ können to (be able to) span (or reach) an octave. — 5. fig. j-s Erwartungen (Hoffnungen) hoch ⊱ to raise a p.'s expectations (hopes) to a high pitch; seine Forderungen zu hoch ⊱ to be exorbitant in one's demands or charges, to have too great (or lofty) pretensions; j-s Neugier aufs höchste ⊱ greatly to excite (or rouse, stimulate) a p.'s curiosity. — II v/n. (h.) 6. fig. dieser Roman spannt sehr ... is very exciting or fascinating; ⊱d exciting, fascinating, absorbing. — 7. von Kleidern: to be (too) tight, to fit (too) tightly. — 8. auf et. ⊱ (merken) to fix one's attention on a th.; vgl. gespannt. — III ~ n ⓘ 9. = Spannung 1.

spannen²-breit (⌣⌣...) [Spanne pl.], ⊱hoch, ⊱lang a. ⚙ a span wide, high, long; ⊱weise adv. by spans; =weite f ⚙ width of a span.
Spanner (⌣⌣) m ⚙ 1. von Personen: one who stretches or bends (a bow), s. Büchsenspanner. — 2. ent. (Falter aus der Spannraupe) geometrid (Geo'metra). — 3. anat. tensor (muscle). — 4. ⊙: a) Schlüssel für Fahrrad ⁊c.: spanner; b) ehm.: ~ einer Armbrust gaffle of a cross-bow; ⊱ Tuchmacherei: tenter.
...spänner (...⌣) in Zssgn mit Zahlwörtern, ⁊B. Ein-⊱ one-horse carriage.
Spann³-feder ⊙ (⌣...) f ⚙ tension-spring; =haken m tenter-hook.
...spännig (...⌣⌣) in Zssgn mit Zahlwörtern, ⁊B. zwei-⊱ with two horses; zwei-⊱er Wagen carriage-and-pair.
Spann³-joch ⚹ (⌣⌣) n ⚙ traverses pl.; =kette f drag(-chain); =kraft f elasticity, elastic force, phys. des Dampfes ⁊c.: tension, von Gasen: ⚳ expansibility, fig. energy, spring, des Geistes: buoyancy; med., physiol.: ⚳ tonic power, tonicity; =leiste ⊙ e-r Leiter: strutting-piece; =muskel m, anat. bender, ⚳ (ex)tensor; =nadel, =nagel s. Spannadel, Spannagel; =rahmen ⊙ m stretcher, Tuchfabr.: tenter-frame; =raupe f, ent. looper; =riegel ⊙ m, carp. footing-beam, binding-piece, tension-member, strutting-beam or -piece; =säge ⊙ f span- (or frame-)saw; =seil n tether; =stab n f Gurt I am Ende; =stange f tie-rod or -bolt, Bleicherei: tenter-bar; =stock m tenter; =strick m = =seil; =tau ⚓ n der Pioniere: shore-painter.
Spannung (⌣⌣) f ⚙ 1. (das Spannen) stretching, binding; tension (auch des Geistes). — 2. (Angespanntsein) tightness, strain (a. fig.); ⊙ einer Dampfmaschine: expansion; fig. (gespannte Aufmerksamkeit) close (or sustained) attention; (starke Neugier) lively (or eager) curiosity; (Bangen und Hangen) anxious suspense; e-n in ~ (er)halten to keep a p. in suspense; in großer ~ sein to be very anxious or in great suspense or on tenter-hooks; ~ zwischen Familien ⁊c. strained relationship, coolness. — 3. ⊙ ~ eines Gewölbebogens: span.
Spannungs-messer ⊙ (⌣...) m ⚙: a) Dampfm. indicator; b) elect. voltmeter; =steu(e)rung ⊙ f expansion-gear.
Spann³-weite (⌣...) f ⚙: a) arch. e-s Bogens: span; b) orn. der Flügel: expanse of wing, wing-spread; =wirbel ⊙ ♪ m am Klavier: tension-bar.
Spant ⚓ (⌣) [ndd.; *spannen] n ⚙b. (Schiffsrippe) rib of a (sea-going) vessel.
Spar¹-bank (⌣⌣) [spar-en] f ⚙ savings bank; =büchse f money-box; box to keep one's savings in; =deck ⚓ n spar-deck; =einlage f deposit in a savings bank; ⊱ savings-bank account.
sparen (⌣⌣) [ahd.: spare] I v/a. u. v/n. (h.) ⚙ 1. to spare, to be sparing (or), to husband one's resources; Geld ⁊c.: to save, to economize, to put (or lay) by; seine Kosten ⊱ to spare or (stint) no expense; sein Leben nicht ⊱ not to consider one's (own) life; weder Mühe noch Arbeit ⊱ to spare neither trouble nor toil, to exert o.s. to the utmost or uttermost; Sprichw. s. Rute 1 am Schluß; immer ⊱, immer darben ever spare ever bare. — 2. (aufschieben) to put off. — II ~ n ⓘ 3. (s. 1) saving, economizing, economy, stärker: parsimony, Sprichw. ~ bringt Haben a penny saved is a penny gained or earned.
Spar¹-endchen (⌣⌣⌣) n ⚙ end of a candle; (Leuchterknecht) save-all.
Sparer (⌣⌣) m ⚙ one who saves his money, &c., economical person, economizer.
Spargel ⚘ (⌣⌣) [mhd., It., *grch.] m ⚙ asparagus (Aspa'ragus officina'lis), P sparrow-grass; ~bau m growing (of) asparagus; ~beet n asparagus-bed.
Spar¹-geld (⌣⌣) n ⚙ = Sparpfennig.
Spargel-gewächs (⌣⌣⌣) n ⚙: ⚳ asparaginous plant; =kohl m Brokkoli; =messer n asparagus-knife; =pflanze f = Spargel; =pflanzung f, hort. asparagus-field or -plantation; =stecher m = =messer; =stoff m Asparagin; Kocht. =suppe f asparagus-soup; =zeit f asparagus-season.
Spar¹-herd (⌣⌣) m ⚙ (economical) kitchener or kitchen-range.
Spark ⚘ (⌣) [It.] m ⚛c. spurry (Spe'rgula).
Spar²-kalk (⌣⌣...) [:spar] ⊙ m ⚙ plaster; ¹kasse f savings bank; ~ der englischen Post post-office savings bank; Geld auf die ~ tun to put (or deposit) money in the savings bank; =kassen-buch n savings-bank book; =lampe f economical lamp.
spärlich (⌣⌣) (ahd.; *sparen] a. ⚙ (zerstreut) sparse, scattered; (kaum ausreichend) scant(y), barely sufficient, (in geringer Menge vorhanden) scarce; von Mahlzeiten: frugal (meal), slender (repast), meagre (fare), low (diet); adv. ⊱ bevölkert sparsely (or thinly) populated; ~keit f ⚙ sparseness; scant(i)ness, scarcity; frugality of a meal.
Spar¹-pfennig (⌣⌣⌣) m ⚙ savings, economies pl., money put by (in a savings bank); vgl. Notpfennig.
Sparren (⌣⌣) [ahd.: spar: sperren] m ⚙ ⊙ carp. (Quer-, Schräg-, Stiltz-balken) (Dach-)~ rafter, spar; her. chevron (so: ∧); F fig. einen ~ (zuviel) h. (verschroben im Kopfe sein) to be wrong in the upper story, to have a screw loose; to be cracked.
Sparren-fuß (⌣⌣...) m ⚙: =rafter-foot; =holz n timber (or wood) for rafters; =kopf m, arch. am Hauptgesims modillion; =nagel m rafter-nail; ⊱weise adv. rafterwise; =werk n rafters pl., rafter-work, des Daches: carcass-roofing.
sparrig ⚘ (⌣⌣) [Sparren] a. ⚙ squarrous, squarrose; etwas ⊱ squarrulose.
sparsam (⌣⌣) [ahd.; *sparen] a. ⚙ von Personen: economical, thrifty, (fond of) saving, stärker: parsimonious, ⊱ Leben sein to practise economy or thrift, to lead a frugal life; ⊱ mit et. umgehen to make spare of a th.; fig. ⊱ in der Rede ⁊c. chary of one's words, &c.
Sparsamkeit (⌣⌣⌣) f ⚙ economy, thrift (-iness), saving (or economical) turn of mind, kleinliche: parsimony; aus ~rücksichten for reasons of economy; a.: from economical motives. [thread.)
Spar¹-seide (⌣⌣⌣) f ⚙ fine silky)

⚳ scientific; ⚘ botanical; ⚜ geography; ⊙ machinery; ⚹ mining; ⚔ military; ⚓ marine; ⚫ commercial; ⚐ postal; ⌁ railway.

[Sparta-it]

Sparta-it ⚹ (⸗⸗) m ⓊC. min. (Art Kalkspat) spartaite.
Spartaner (⸗⸗⸗) [Sparta ♀ Hauptstadt von Lakonien] m ㉒, ~in f ㊼ Spartan;
spartanisch a. ⓊC Spartan, of the Spartans; hist. 2e (schwarze) Suppe Spartan (black) broth.
Sparter (⸗⸗) m ㉒ = Spartaner.
Spart-gras ⚹ (⸗,⸗) n ⓊA. esparto, alfa, alfa-grass (Stipa tenaci'ssima).
Spartiat (⸗(⸗)⸗) m ㊷ = Spartaner.
Spaß (⸗, südd. ⸗) [nhd.; *it. spasso] m ⓃA. südd. ⸗) [㊇a. (Zeitvertreib) amusement, pastime; (Lust) mirth, merriment; (Scherz) fun, joking, jesting; wir haben sehr viel ~ gehabt we (have) enjoyed ourselves immensely; das macht ihm großen ~ that greatly amuses him; immer ~ m. to be always cracking jokes, to be full of fun; es ist (wäre) ein Spaß, wenn // it is (would be) amusing (or a good joke) if //; das war nur ein ~ that was only (meant in) fun; das ist kein ~ it is no joke or no child's play; j-n ~ mit e-m treiben to joke a p., to make sport (or fun) of a p.; keinen ~ verstehen not to know how to take a joke; zum ~ as a joke, in jest, facetious(ly); nur zum ~ just for the fun of it, only for (a bit of) sport; ~ beiseite! (all) joking apart! [little joke.]
Späßchen (⸗⸗, südd. ⸗⸗) n (dim. v. Spaß)
spaßen (⸗⸗), südd. **spaßen** (⸗⸗) v/n. (h.) ⓐ to jest, to joke, to make fun (f. scherzen 1 u. 2); Sie 2 wohl! you are only joking!; damit ist nicht zu 2 that is no joking matter; er läßt nicht mit sich 2 he won't be played with, he is not to be trifled with.
Spaßerei (⸗⸗⸗) f ㊻ joking; vgl. Spaß.
spaßhaft (⸗⸗) a. ⓊC jocose (vgl. scherzhaft); ~igkeit f ㊻ = Scherzhaftigkeit.
spaßig, **spassig** (⸗⸗) a. ⓊC funny, droll.
Spaß-macher (⸗⸗) m ㉒ jester, joker; a. = Hanswurst; **-vogel** m merry person or soul; wag.
Spat¹ (⸗) [ahd.] m ⓊC.(⚒ ⑦)c. min. spar.
Spat² (⸗) [ahd.] m ㉒ vet. Krankheit im Sprunggelenk der Pferde: spavin.
spat³ † (⸗) [ahd.] adv. = spät.
spät (⸗) [ahd.] a. ⓊC (Dc) 1. late; früher oder 2er sooner or later; von früh bis 2 from morning till night; 2 aufstehen to get up late, to be a late riser; es ist (wird) 2 it is (is getting) late; wie 2 ist es? what time is it?; F what's the time? es ist schon 2 am Tage it is late in the day, the day is far spent; 2 in der Nacht nach Hause kommen to come home late at night; das kommt zu 2 that comes (or is)(too) late; ich (der Zug) kam 5 Minuten zu 2 I (the train) was five minutes late; die Uhr geht (um 5 Minuten) zu 2 ... loses (five minutes); wir werden 2er schon sehen we shall see by and by or later on; Sprichw. besser 2 als nie better late than never. — 2. attributiv: (2 eintretend, kommend ꝛc.) belated, coming (too) late; (vorgerückt) advanced; (hinterher geschehend) subsequent; (einer fernen Zeit angehörig) remote; in 2eren Jahren in after-years; in 2eren Zeiten at a later period, later on, (zukünftig) in the distant (or far-away) future.
Spät-apfel (⸗⸗⸗) m ㉒ late apple.
spät¹**-artig** (⸗⸗⸗) a. ⓊC min. sparry, spathose. [(or blooming) late.)
spät-blühend (⸗⸗⸗) a. ⓊC blossoming
Späte (⸗⸗) f ㊽ 1. lateness; late (or advanced) hour. — 2. late arrival.
Spat¹**-eisen-stein** (⸗⸗⸗⸗) m ㉒ min. sparry iron-ore (f. a. Flinz).
Spatel ⓞ (⸗⸗)[mhd.;*lt. spa'tula f] m ㉒, f ⑧ mst surg. u. pharm. spatula, slice, scoop; ⓞ spattle.
Spaten (⸗⸗) [ndb.: spade] m ㉓ agr. spade, zum Ründen der Rasenfläche: edging-iron or -tool; mit dem ~ umgraben to (turn up with a) spade; die Wissenschaft des ~s archæological excavation or research.
Spaten-kultur (⸗⸗⸗) f ⑨ agr. spade-husbandry or -culture; **-stich** m cut with a spade; den ersten ~ tun to cut the first sod.
später-hin (⸗⸗⸗) adv. later on.
spätestens (⸗⸗⸗) adv. at the latest.
Spät-frost (⸗⸗⸗) m ㉒ late frost; **-gotik** f, arch. modern Gothic (style).
spat¹**-haltig** (⸗⸗⸗) a. ⓊC = spatartig.
Spät-herbst (⸗⸗⸗) m ㉒ latter part of autumn (f. a. Altweibersommer a).
spatig¹ (⸗⸗) [Spat¹] a. ⓊC min. (spatartig, -haltig) spathose, spathic.
spatig² (⸗⸗) [Spat²] a. ⓊC vet. spavined.
Spatium (⸗⸗⸗(⸗)⸗) [lt.] n ㉘ bsd. ⓞ typ. (Zwischenraum) thin space, space-line; Spatien einsetzen to space. [autumn.)
Spät-jahr (⸗⸗⸗) n ㉒ end of the season,
spat²**-lahm** (⸗,⸗)[Spat²] a. ⓊC vet. spavined.
Spät-ling (⸗⸗) m ⓊD.: a) (ant. Frühling) calf, lamb, &c. born late in the year or in the season; b) late fruit.
Spät-obst (⸗⸗⸗) n ㉒ late fruit; **-reif** a. ⓊC backward (in ripening); tardy; **-reife**(n) f ㊻ backwardness (in ripening); **-sommer** m end (or latter part) of summer.
Spatz (⸗)[mhd.; *Sper(ling)] m ㉒(㉕a.), **Spätzin** (⸗⸗) f ㊼ orn. (cock, f hen) sparrow; fig. das pfeifen die ~en auf den Dächern, etwa: it is the talk of the town, every child knows it;
spatzen-haft (⸗⸗⸗) a. ⓊC as impudent as a sparrow.
spazieren (⸗⸗⸗) [mhd.; *(⸗⸗) it. spazia're schweifen (r-r passeggia're)] I v/n. (in) Ⓢ to walk about. — II ~ n ㉓ mst in Zssgn.
spazieren-fahren (⸗⸗⸗⸗) v/n. (in) Ⓢb** to take a (carriage-)drive, to go out for a drive, to ride out in a carriage, zu Wasser: to go out for a (F to have a) sail, to take a trip on the water; ~ n ㉓ driving, carriage-exercise, auf dem Rade: cycling, touring, im Automobil: motoring, zu Wasser: boating; ein Kind **2-führen** v/a. Ⓢ** to take ... (out) for a walk; **2-geh(e)n** v/n. (in) Ⓢ** to take (or to go for) a walk, to take walking-exercise or a stroll or a constitutional; to ramble (about); ~ n ㉓ walking (-exercise); pedestrianism; **2-reiten** v/n. (in) Ⓢb** to (take a) ride on horseback, F to have a ride.
Spazier-fahrt (⸗⸗⸗) f ㉒ carriage-drive, -ride, zu Wasser: row, sail, trip on the water; **-gang** m walk, ramble, stroll, gesundheitlicher: walking-exercise, constitutional; ~ aufs Land country-walk or -ramble; einen ~ machen to take a walk or a stroll or F a turn (round the town, &c.); **-gänger(in** f) m walker, rambler, stroller, pedestrian; **-platz** m place for walking, auch promenade; vgl. **-weg**; **-ritt** m ride (or outing) on horseback; **-stock** m, **-stöckchen** n walking-stick, cane; **-weg** m nice (road for a walk); footway.
Specht (⸗) [ahd. Spähter] m ⓊB. orn. wood-pecker (Picus); ~**-meise** (⸗⸗⸗) f ㊽ = Blauspecht.
Speck (⸗) [ahd.] m ⓊC. 1. ~ v. Schweine bacon, vom Walfische: blubber, von Menschen ꝛc.: fat; durchwachsener ~ streaky bacon; ~ ansetzen to grow fat or stout; mit ~ umwickeln to (dress in) lard. — 2. fig. ~ auf den Rippen h. to be fat or stout or in good condition, fig. (reich sein) to be well off; (F wie die Made) im ~ sitzen to be in clover, to be rolling in wealth, to live in luxury; Sprichw. f. Maus 3. — 3. ⓞ typ. (lohnende Arbeit) paying (or good) work, F fat.
speck-artig (⸗⸗⸗) a. ⓊC like bacon; **-bauch** m ㉒ = Schmerbauch; **-geschwulst** f, path. (⚒ lardaceous) tumour, ⚹ steatoma, lipoma; **-grieben** f/pl. gr(e)aves pl.; **-hals** m very fat neck; **-handel** m bacon-trade; **-händler** m dealer in bacon; **-haut** f: a) **-schwarte**; b) med. ~ des geronnenen Blutes: buffy coat. [(fett, glitschig) fatty, greasy.)
speckicht, **speckig** (⸗⸗) a. ⓊC bacon-like;
Speck-käfer (⸗⸗⸗) m ent. bacon- (or larder-)beetle (Derme'stes); **-krankheit** f, path. eines Organs: (Amyloid-entartung) fatty degeneracy; **-schnitte** f rasher (or slice) of bacon; **-schwarte** f rind of bacon; **-schwein** n fat pig; **-seite** f side (or flitch) of bacon; Sprichw. mit der Wurst nach der ~ werfen, etwa: to throw a sprat (in order) to catch a whale; **-stein** m, min. soap-stone, ⚹ steatite, chinesischer: agalmatolite.
spedieren ⓞ (⸗⸗⸗) [it. spedi're; * lt. expedi're] v/a. Ⓢ to forward, dispatch, expedite; to send off, zu Schiffe: to ship; F fig. ins Jenseits 2 to launch (or hurl) into eternity.
Spediteur ⓞ (⸗⸗⸗⸗) [it.=fr.] m ⓊD. forwarding (zu Wasser: shipping) agent, per Achse: carrier.
Spedition ⓞ (⸗=⸗(⸗)⸗)[it.spedizio'ne] f ㊻ forwarding (⚓ shipping-) agency, transmission (or carriage) of goods.
Speditions-bureau (⸗⸗⸗) n ㉒ forwarding-office; **-gebühren** f/pl. forwarding (or carrier's) charges pl.; **-geschäft** n forwarding-agency or -business (vgl. Spedition); ~e treiben, oft: to do business on commission; **-güter** n/pl. goods pl. (to be) forwarded through an agent; **-handel** ⚓ m carrying-trade; **-haus** n = **-geschäft**; **-kontor** n = **-bureau**; **-und Verladungsgeschäft** n forwarding and shipping agency.
Speer (⸗) [ahd.: spear] m ⓊC. spear, ⚔ lance, zum Werfen: javelin.
speer-ähnlich ⚔ (⸗⸗⸗), **förmig** a. ⓊC spear-shaped or -like, ⚹: ⚒ hastate;

Zeichen (f. S. XVII): F familiär; P Volkssprache; Γ Gaunersprache; ⚹ selten; † alt (auch gestorben); * neu (auch geboren); ⁑ unrichtig;

=**kampf** m ⊕ combat with spears or javelins; =**reiter** m lancer; **ſchaft** m shaft of a spear; =**ſtechen** ⊕ n Fiſcherei: spearing; =**ſtich** m stab (or thrust) with a spear, spear-wound; =**träger** m spearman, soldier armed with a spear.

Spei-becken (ᵘ·ᵛ·) n ⊕ spittoon.

Speiche (ᴸ·ᵛ) [ahd.: spoke] f ⊕ 1. ⊙ Wagenbau: spoke of a wheel; willſt du mit den Kinderhänden in des Schickſals ~n greifen? (Grillparzer) wilt thou with thy feeble hands try to stop the wheel of Fate? — 2. ⚕ anat. (äußerer Knochen am Vorderarm) spoke-bone, mehr gbr.: radius; zur ~ gehörig: ⚕ radial.

Speichel (ᴸ·ᵛ) [ahd.; *ſpeien] m ⊕ physiol., med. spittle, saliva, ausgeworfener: spit, aus dem Munde fließender: drivel, slaver; fig. f. lecken² 3. =**drüſe** (ᵘ·ᵛ···) f ⊕ anat. salivary gland; =**fluß** m, med. flow of saliva, salivation; den ~ haben to salivate; =**gang** m, anat. salivary fluid, duct; =**kur** f, med. (treatment by) salivation; **ᵒlecken** v/n. f. lecken² 3; =**lecker** m toady, flunkey, chm. a.: lickspittle; =**leckerei** f toadyism, flunkeyism, adulation.

ſpeicheln (ᴸ·ᵛ) v/n. (h.) ⊕a. (ſpucken) to spit; med. (viel Speichel abſondern) to give forth much saliva, ⚕ to salivate.

ſpeichen¹ ⊙ (ᴸ·ᵛ) v/a. ⊕: ein Rad ² to spoke a wheel, to furnish a wheel with spokes.

Speichen²=**hammer** ⊙ (ᵘ·ᵛ···) m ⊕ [Speiche] spoke-hammer; =**maß** n spoke-gauge; =**muskel** m, anat.: ⚕ radial muscle; =**rad** n spoked wheel, wheel with spokes; =**trieb-rad** n, mach. spider; =**zapfen** m thin (or sharp) end of a spoke.

Speicher ⊙ (ᴸ·ᵛ) [ahd.; *mlt. spica'rium n (lt. sp ̄ıcā Ähre)] m ⊕: a) für Getreide: granary, corn-loft; b) für Waren: warehouse, store-rooms, storage-place; auf den ~ bringen, a. **ſpeichern** v/a. ⊕a. to store (up); vgl. aufſpeichern.

Speicher-zelle ⊙ (ᵘ·ᵛ·ᵛ·) f ⊕ elect. accumulator (= Akkumulator).

ſpei-en (ᴸ·ᵛ) [ahd. spew] v/n. (h.) u. v/a. ⊕(§) physiol., &c. to spit, to expectorate; Blut ² to spit (or throw up) blood; weitS. (brechen) to vomit, to bring up; to spew; fig. f. Feuer ² am Schluß und Gift 3.

Spei-er (ᴸ·ᵛ) [ſpeien] m ⊕ spitter.

Spei-erei (ᵛ·ᴸ·) f ⊕ (much) spitting or expectorating. [(Sorbus dome'stica).]

Speierling (ᴸ·ᵛ) m ⊕d. service-tree]

Spei-gatt ⇓ (ᵘ·ᵛ) n ⊕ (rundes Loch zum Ablaufen des Waſſers) scupper (-hole).

Speik ⚕ (ᴸ) [mhd.; *lt. f. Spieke] m ⊕c.: echter ~ = Narde.

Speil (ᴸ) [ndd.] m ⊕c., =**e** (ᴸ·ᵛ) f ⊕, mſt.: ~**er** (ᴸ·ᵛ) m ⊕ (kleiner hölzerner Bratſpieß) (wooden) skewer; **ſpeile(r)n** v/a. ⊕(⊕a.) to skewer.

Spei-napf (ᵘ··) m ⊕ = =**becken**; =**röhre** ⊙ f discharge-pipe, an der Dachrinne: spout, mit Tierkopf: gargoyle.

Speis (ᴸ) ⊕ m ⊕a. Maurerei: = Speiſe 3.

Speiſe¹ (ᴸ·ᵛ) [ahd.; *lt. f. Speſe(n)] f ⊕ 1. food, weitS. nourishment, geistige: food for the mind; (Koſt) fare, diet, F grub; (Schwaren) victuals, provisions, seltener: viands pl.; (Gericht) dish, engS. = Mehlſpeiſe; ~ (oft: Speiſ') und Trank eating and drinking, meat and drink. 2. fig. ~ der Augen (Augenweide) s. th. to feast one's eyes upon, feast for the eyes. — 3. ⊕ Maurerei: mortar; metall. (Verbindung von Arſen mit Metallen) ⊺ speiss; (Glocken-)~ bell-metal.

Speiſe²=**amt** (ᵘ···) [ſpeiſen] n ⊕ an Höfen: steward's office; =**anſtalt** f = =**haus**; =**apparat** ⊙ m Dampfmaſch.: feeding-apparatus; ſelbſttätiger ~ self-acting (or automatic) feeder, feeding-regulator; =**brei** m, physiol. (Chymus) chyme; =**brett** n tray; =**fett** n Kochkunſt: fat (F goodness) for cooking; =**haus** n eating-house, restaurant; =**kabel** ⊙ n, elect. feeder-cable; =**kammer** f: a) =**ſchrank**; b) store-room for provisions; =**karte** f bill of fare, bei feineren Eſſen: menu; =**keller** m: a) cellar for provisions; b) underground restaurant; =**korb** m hamper, provision-basket; =**meiſter** m steward, bibl. governor of the feast.

ſpeiſen (ᴸ·ᵛ) [mhd.: *Speiſe] I ⊕⊕ 1. (eſſen): a) v/n. (h.) to eat, to (take a) meal, to take (or partake of) food; bſd. zu Mittag ² to dine, to have dinner, zu Abend od. z(u)r Nacht ² to sup, to have supper; auf dem Hauſe ² to dine out; an demſelben Tiſche ², bſd. ⚔ u. ⇓: to mess (together); in welchem Gaſthofe ² Sie? at which hotel do you take your meals or do you dine or board?; b) v/a.: etwas ² to eat (or partake of) s. th. — 2. v/a.: a) (mit Speiſe verſehen) e-n ² to feed (or board) a p.; (ernähren) to keep (or maintain) a p.; (bewirten) to entertain (or treat) a p.; fig. e-n mit leeren Hoffnungen ² to delude a p. (or to buoy a p. up) with vain hopes; b) ⊙ (mit Waſſer, Kohle ꝛc. verſehen) to feed; die Quellen ² die Stadt the springs supply (or provide) the town with water. — II ~ n ⊕ 3. ſ. Speiſung.

Speiſen-aufzug (ᵘ···) m ⊕ dinner-lift, plate-carrier; =**folge** f succession of courses, menu; =**zubereitung** f preparation of food.

Speiſe-öl (ᵘ···) n ⊕ salad-oil; =**opfer** n, bibl. meat-offering, offering of first fruits; =**pumpe** ⊙ f Dampfmaſch.: feed-pump or -engine; =**röhre** ⊙ f feed(ing)-pipe, supply-pipe, e-s Dampfkeſſels: stand-pipe, head-race; =**röhre** f: a) anat.: ⚕ œsophagus; b) ⊙ feed-pipe; =**ſaal** m dining-room, größerer: banqueting-hall; in Klöſtern: refectory; für Offiziere: mess-room; =**ſaft** m, physiol. = Chylus; =**ſchrank** m pantry, larder, meat-safe; =**tiſch** m dining-(room) table; =**vorrichtung** ⊙ f = =**apparat**; =**wagen** ⊕ m restaurant-car; =**wärmer** m hot-water plate; =**wirt** m keeper of an eating-house or of dining-rooms, restaurant-keeper; =**zettel** m = =**karte**; =**zimmer** n = =**ſaal**; =**zucker** m Koch-z.

Speis-kobalt (ᵘ·ᴸ·) m ⊕ min. arsenical cobalt, grey cobalt ore, ⊺ speiskobalt, smaltine, smaltite. [lus or concretion.)

Spei-ſtein (ᵘ·ᴸ·) m ⊕ med. salivary calcu-]

Speiſung (ᴸ·ᵛ) f ⊕ 1. (ſ. ſpeiſen 1) meal (-ing); dinner, supper. — 2. (ſ. ſpeiſen 2) feeding, board(ing); maintenance.

Speiſungs-wagen ⊕ (ᵘ·ᵛ·ᴸ·) m ⊕ für Kohlen, Waſſer ꝛc.: tender.

Spektakel (ᵛ·ᴸ·ᵛ) [lt. specta'culum n Schauſpiel] m (n) ⊕ 1. faſt † = Schauſpiel. — 2. F, mſt m (Lärm) noise, row.

Spektakel-macher (ᵛ·ᴸ·ᵛ·ᵛ·) m ⊕ noisy (or riotous) fellow.

ſpektakeln F (ᵛ·ᴸ·ᵛ) v/n. (h.) ⊕a. to make a noise or a hubbub, to kick up a row.

Spektakel-ſtück (ᵛ·ᴸ·ᵛ·) n ⊕ thea. sensational (auch: spectacular) piece.

ſpektral ⚕ (ᵛ·ᴸ) [lt.] a. ⊕ phys. (die Lichtquellen betr.) spectral; ~=**analyſe** (ᵛ·ᴸ·ᵛ·ᵛ·ᵛ·) f ⊕ spectral analysis.

Spektroſkop ⚕ (ᵛ·ᵛ·ᴸ) [lt.=grch.] n ⊕d. phys. (Apparat für Spektralanalyse) spectroscope.

Spektrum ⚕ (ᴸ·ᵛ) [lt.] n ⊕ ⊕⊕ (Erſcheinung) phys. Lichtſtrahlenbild) spectrum.

Spekulant ⚕ (ᵛ·ᴸ) [lt.] m ⊕, ~**in** f ⊕ speculator, an der Börſe, oft: operator.

Spekulation (ᵛ·ᵛ·tz(ᵛ·)ᴸ) [lt.] f ⊕: a) geiſtige, ⊕ geſchäftliche: speculation; ⊕ auch: venture; auf ~ F on spec; **ſpekulativ** (ᵛ·ᵛ·ᴸ·ᵛ) a. ⊕⊕ speculative (auch ⚕).

ſpekulieren (ᵛ·ᵛ·ᴸ·ᵛ) [lt.] v/n. (h.) ⊕: a) (grübeln) to speculate, ruminate, ponder; b) ⚕ (wagen) to speculate, venture; ſie ² auf die Erbſchaft they reckon (or have their eye) on the inheritance; auf das Fallen (Steigen) der Kurſe ² to speculate on the fall (on the rise).

Spelt ndd. (ᴸ) m ⊕b. = Spelz.

Spelunke (ᵛ·ᴸ·ᵛ) [lt., *grch.] f ⊕ (Schlupfwinkel) den; (gemeine Kneipe) low gin-shop or ale-house, F pot-house.

Spelz ⚕ (ᴸ) [ahd.; *lt. spelta f] m ⊕a. spelt (Tri'ticum spelta).

Spelze ⚕ (ᴸ·ᵛ) [mhd.; *Spelz] f ⊕ (Granne, Getreidehülſe) beard, ⚕ glume; **ſpelzig** a. ⊕ chaffy, ⚕ glumaceous.

Spende (ᴸ·ᵛ) [ahd. f. ſpenden] f ⊕ 1. (das Spenden) distribution of gifts or alms or food. — 2. (Gabe) gift, present, donation; (Almoſen) alms, charity; (milde Stiftung) endowment. — 3. Alt.: (Trankopfer) libation.

ſpenden (ᴸ·ᵛ) [ahd.: spend; *lt. expe'ndere] I v/a. ⊕ to give, to make a present of; (ausgeben) to spend; (austeilen) to distribute, dispense, dole out; das Abendmahl ² to administer the sacrament, Almoſen ² to bestow alms; reichlich ² to lavish. — II ~ n ⊕ ſ. Spendung.

Spender (ᴸ·ᵛ) m ⊕, ~**in** f ⊕ giver, donor; dispenser; weitS. (Wohltäter[in]) benefactor (f benefactress).

ſpendieren F (ᴸ·ᵛ·ᴸ) [it. (vgl. ſpenden)] v/a. u. v/n. (h.) ⊕ to give (or spend) lavishly; einem etwas ² to treat (F to stand) a p. to a th.

Spendier-hoſen (ᵛ·ᴸ·ᵛ·) f/pl. F co. die ~ anhaben to be liberally inclined.

Spendung (ᴸ·ᵛ) f ⊕ = Spende; eccl. ~ der Sakramente administration of the sacraments. [m ⊕ = Klempner.]

Spengler prov. (ᴸ·ᵛ) [mhd.; *Spange)]

Spenzer ⊺ (ᴸ·ᵛ) [engl.; *Lord Spencer, 1800] m ⊕ (kurze Jacke) spencer.

Sperber (ᴸ·ᵛ) [ahd. = Sper(lings)aar] m ⊕ orn. (Falken-art) sparrow-hawk (Acci'piter Nisus); ~=**baum** ⚕ m ⊕ = Eberſche; ~=**kraut** ⚕ n = Becherkraut.

Sperenzchen, Sperenzi-en F (ᵛ·ᴸ·ᵛ·) [dtſch (ſperren)=lt.] pl. inv. = Geſperre 1 b; m. ſie f-e ~! don't make a(ny) fuss!

Sperling (⌣⌣) [mhd.: sparrow + =ling] m ①d. orn.sparrow *(Passer dome'sticus)*; Sprichw. f. Dach 1 am Schluß u. Spatz. **sperlings=artig** (⌣⌣...) a. ⑥ orn. sparrow-like, ⚛ passerine; =**männchen** n ⑫ cock(-)sparrow; =**nest** n sparrow's nest; =**papagei** m, orn. passerine parrot *(Psitta'cula passeri'na)*; =**schrot** m, hunt. small shot; =**vogel** m; ⚛ passerine(bird); =**weibchen** n hen(-)sparrow; =**wurz** ⚘ f, =**zunge** ⚘ f sparrowwort *(Passeri'na)*. **Sperrad** (³·²) [Sperr=rad] n ②c. click-(or ratchet-)wheel (f. a. Gesperre 2b). **sperr=angelweit** F (⁸...) a. ⑥ = angelweit; =**baum** ⊕ m bar(rier), e-r Straße: turnpike, eines Hafens: boom; ²**beinig** a. straddle-legged; astride, straddling. **Sperre** (⌣⌣) [mhd.: sperren] f ⑧ 1. (das Sperren) closing (or shutting) of gates, &c., closure, einer Straße, eines Flusses: barring, des Verkehrs: block(ing), obstruction, stoppage, interruption, (Verbot) prohibition, ⚓ ↓ embargo; ↓ ⚔ (Blockade) blockade; in Fabriken: (Aussperrung der Arbeiter) lock-out; *parl.* die ~ anwenden to apply the closure or F co. the guillotine; die ~ verhängen über to closure. — 2. (et. das sperrt) = Sperrbaum; (Verrammlung) barricade; (Schlagbaum) toll-bar; (Riegel) bolt. — 3. f. Mund=, Tor=sperre.
sperren (⌣⌣) [ahd.: spar; *Sparren] ⑧ I v/a. 1. (aus=ea.=tun) to open wide, to put asunder; (aus=ea.=spreizen) to spread apart or out, to distend, die Beine: to straddle, to sprawl; ⊕ typ. ein Wort ² to space (out) a word. — 2. (hemmen, versperren) to bar (up), stop, interrupt, die Straße &c.: to block (up), to obstruct, durch Barrikaden: to barricade; (schließen) to close, to shut; (abschneiden) to intercept; ↓ ⚔ einen Hafen ² to lock (or trig) ... — 3. (durch Verbot hindern) to stop, prohibit, interdict; *parl.* e-e Debatte ² to closure a debate. — 4. mit Ortsbestimmung: e-n ins Gefängnis ² to put a p. in prison or in jail, to imprison a p.; e-n aus dem Hause ² to lock a p. out; to shut (or slam) the door in a p.'s face. — 5. e-n Pfarrer ² to suspend a clergyman's living. — II **sich** ⌣ v/refl. 6. (sich zur Wehr setzen) to offer resistance, to resist; *fig.* (sich sträuben) to object to, to refuse (et. zu tun doing a th.); aus Ziererei: to stand on ceremony, to make a fuss — 7. (sich spreizen) to spread o.s. out. — III ~ n ㉓ 8. = Sperrung 1.
Sperr=feder ⊕ (⁸...) f ⑫ mach. click-spring, Büchsenmach.: trigging-spring; =**fort** ⚔ n, frt. outer fort; =**geld** n fee for reopening the gates after closing time; =**gesetz** n prohibition, *eccl.* (f. sperren 5) law enacting the suspension of clerical livings; =**getriebe** ⊕ n = Gesperre 2b; =**glocke** f bell announcing the closing of the gates; =**gut** n, =**güter** n/pl. ⚓ bulky (or cumbersome) goods pl.; =**hahn** ⊕ m stop-cock; =**hafen** ⊕ m: a) catch, auch = =kegel; b) Schlosserei: = Dietrich¹; c) Gewehrschl.: ~ am Hahne: hook of the trigger; =**hebel** ⊕ m ratchet-lever; =**holz** ⊕ n wooden bar or wedge.

sperrig (⌣⌣) a. ⑥ 1. (aus=ea.=gesperrt) spread apart, wide open. — 2. (umfangreich) bulky, cumbersome, unwieldy (auch ⚓ von Gütern).
Sperr=kegel ⊕ (³...) m ⑫ mach. click, ratchet, trigger-pin; =**hafen** ⚓ a.; =**kette** f drag-chain, eines Hafens: chain of a harbour; =**klappe** f Orgelbau: organ-valve; =**klinke** ⊕ f = =kegel; =**klinkensteu(e)rung** f, mach.spring-catch; =**kraut** [+⸗ st. Speer=] ⚘ n: blaues ~ Jacob's-ladder *(Polemo'nium caeru'leum)*; =**rad** f. Sperrad; =**schrift** f, typ. spaced type; =**sitz** m, thea. stall, im Parkett: orchestra-stall; =**system** n prohibitive system.
Sperrung (⌣⌣) f ⑫ 1. (f. sperren 2) barring, stoppage; obstruction; interception; ↓ eines Hafens &c.: blockade; embargo; (f. sperren 3) prohibition. — 2. = Sperre 2.
Sperr=ventil ⊕ (³...) n ⑫ stop-valve; =**vorrichtung** ⊕ f catch(er), stop, stay; ²**weit** a. ⑥ = angelweit; =**zeug** ⊕ n der Schlosser: set of picklocks; =**zoll** ⚓ m prohibitory duty.
Spesen ⚓ (¹⌣) [mhd.; *it. spese f/pl.] pl. inv. (Kosten) charges, expenses pl. (incurred); unter Zurechnung Ihrer ~ including your expenses.
spesen=frei ⚓ (¹⌣...) a. ⑥ free of charge, (with) all expenses paid; =**nachnahme** f etwa: reimbursement of charges; =**rechnung** f bill of expenses (incurred); =**reiterei** F f running up (or piling on) the charges.
Spezerei ⚓ (-⌣⌣¹) [mhd.; *it. spezierie'] f ⑯ spices pl.; *en pl.* as Ware: grocery sg.; (Apothekerwaren) drugs pl. **Spezerei=handel** ⚓ (-⌣"...) m ⑫ grocer's (or grocery) trade; =**händler(in** f) m grocer; =**laden** m grocer's shop; =**waren** f/pl. grocery (goods pl.); =**warengeschäft** n, =**warenhandel** m grocer's (or grocery) business.
spezial (⌣(⌣)¹) [lt.] I a. ⑥ = speziell — II F ~ ⊕d.: a) m intimate (a. very special) friend; b) n glass of (spiced) wine.
Spezial=arzt (⌣(⌣)...) m ⑫ specialist; =**bericht** m special (or detailed) report; =**fach** n speciality, F special line.
Speziali=en (⌣(⌣)¹(⌣)) [lt.] n/pl. inv. details, (full) particulars pl.
Spezialisation (⌣(⌣)⌣tf(⌣)¹) [lt.] f ⑯ = spezialisieren II.
spezialisier=en (⌣(⌣)-⌣⌣¹) [lt.] I v/a. ⑱ (einzeln aufführen) to specialize, to specify. — II ~ n ㉓ u. S/ung f ⑯ specialization, specification.
Spezialist (⌣(⌣)⁻ˢ) m ⑫ specialist. **Spezialität** (⌣(⌣)⁻⌣¹) [lt.] f ⑯: a) Eigenheit, b) Hauptgeschäft: speciality, ⚓ auch special branch; ~**en=theater** (⌣(⌣)⁻⌣⌣"...) n ⑫ theatre of varieties, music-hall; vgl. Tingeltangel.
Spezial=karte (⌣(⌣)"...) f ⑫ special map; =**mittel** n specific remedy.
spezi=ell (⌣(⌣)⁸) [+⸗fr.] I a. ⑥ (besonder) special; ²e Angabe specification; et. ² (adv.) angeben to specify a th.; mein ²er Freund a particular (or special) friend of mine. — II ~**e(s)** n ⑰: bursch. (ich trinke) auf Ihr ~es, (ich komme Ihnen einen Schluck) aufs ~e (I drink) your health!

Spezi=es (¹(⌣)⌣) [lt.] f, inv. 1. (Art) species. — 2. *arith.* die vier ~ (Grundrechnungen) the four first rules pl. of arithmetic. [Dänemark: specie dollar.)
Spezi=es=taler (¹¹(⌣)⌣⌣¹) m ⑫ ehm. in) **Spezifikation** (⌣⌣¹-tf(⌣)¹) [lt.] f ⑯ specification, detailed account or statement. [med. specific (remedy).)
Spezifikum ⚛ (⌣⌣¹⌣⌣) [lt. Besonderes] n ⑳) **spezifisch** (⌣⌣ (⌣)¹) [lt.] a. ⑥ (eigentümlich) specific, *adv.* specifically; *phys.* ²es Gewicht specific gravity; ²e Wärme specific heat.
spezifizier=en (⌣⌣(⌣)-⌣⌣¹) [lt.] I v/a. ⑱ to specify, to particularize. — II ~ n ㉓ u. S/ung f ⑯ specification.
Spezimen (¹⌣⌣) [lt. spe'cimen] n ⑯ (Probe) specimen, sample.
Sphäre (ff⸗¹⌣) [grch. sphaira Kugel] f ⑧: a) *math.* (Kugel), *ast.* (Himmelskugel) sphere, globe, b)(Wirkungskreis) sphere (of action, &c.), range, province.
Sphären=harmonie (ff⸗¹⌣⌣...) f ⑫, =**klang** m, =**musik** f harmony (or music) of the spheres, celestial harmony.
sphärisch (ff⸗¹⌣) [grch.] a. ⑥ spherical. **Sphäro=id** ⚛ (ff⸗⌣¹) [grch.] n ②c. math. spheroid, oblate ellipsoid.
Sphen ⚛ (ff¹) [grch.] m ⊕d. min. sphene. **Sphinx** (ff¹) [grch. Würgende] grch. f ⑧, ägypt. m ①a. 1. myth. sphinx. — 2. ent. (Dämmerungsfalter) hawk-moth. **Sphragistik** ⚛ (ff⸗⌣¹) [grch.] f ⑯ = Siegelkunde. [zinc.)
Spiauter (⌣¹⌣) [ndl.] m ⑫ min. spelter,) **Spick=aal** (⁸·¹) [schwb. *spicka* räuchern] m ⑫ smoked eel.
spicken (⌣⌣) [v. Speck] v/a. ⑱ 1. Kocht.: to lard; (räuchern) to smoke; *fig.* seine Rede mit Zitaten ² to interlard (or interweave) one's speech with quotations or tags; einen Beutel mit Gold ² (füllen) to cram ... with (or full of) gold; gut gespickter Beutel well-lined purse; mit Nägeln gespickt studded with nails. — 2. F *fig.* e-n ² (bestechen) to bribe a p., bisw.: F to grease a p.'s palms. [goose; =**nadel** f larding-pin.)
Spick=gans (⁸...) f ⑫ Kocht. smoked) **spie** (¹) *ind.*, ²e (⌣) *subj. impf.* v. speien.
Spiegel (¹) [ahd.; *lt. spe'culum n] m ⑫ 1. looking-glass, auch glass, feinerer: mirror, zwischen zwei Fenstern: pierglass; *phys.* u. *med.* auch: ⊕ catopter, speculum, ⊕ reflector; sich im ~ besehen to look at o.s. in the glass; *fig.* glatt wie ein ~ as smooth as glass; das wird er nicht hinter den ~ stecken he won't make much boast of it; e-m einen ~ vorhalten to hold up a mirror to a p.; der ~ des Meeres the surface (or level) of the sea; der Ströme blauer ~ *(SCH.)* the azure surface of the rivers. — 2. *fig.* (Muster) model, pattern, paragon; ein ~ der Ehrlichkeit honesty itself; ein ~ der Höflichkeit the pink of politeness. — 3. ↓ = e-s Schiffes stern. — 4. *hunt.* der Rehe: escutcheon, white spot on the posterior. — 5. ⚔ der Scheibe: bull's-eye.
Spiegel=beleg (¹⌣...) m ⑫, =**belegung** f mirror-foil or -covering, quicksilvering (or tin-foiling) of a mirror; =**berg** npr/m. (Charakter in *SCH.*'s Drama

---

Signs (see page XVII): F familiar; P vulgar; ſ flash; ⚘ rare; † obsolete (died); * new word (born); ⧺ incorrect; ♩ music;

[Spiegelbild] — 903 — [Spielgenosse]

„Die Räuber"; danach frei: Sprichw. ~, ich kenne dich I know you of old, I know your little game; =bild n: a) image produced by a mirror; fig. treues ~ true reflexion or image; b) (Fata Morgana) mirage; ⚲blank a. ⊛ as smooth and bright as a mirror; =decke f, arch. mirrored ceiling. [ing.]
Spiegelei¹ (-◡⊥) f⊛ continued mirror-⌋
Spiegel=ei² (er pl.) (⊥◡...) n ⊠ Kocht. fried egg(s pl.); =eisen ⊛ n, metall. specular (cast-)iron, auch = =erz; =erz n, min. specular iron-ore; =fabrik ⊛ flooking-glass (manu)factory; =fabrikant m l.-glass manufacturer; =fechter m dissembler, prevaricator; =fechterei f: a) sham fight; b) öfter fig. (Blendwerk) dissimulation, feint; (Trug) deception, prevarication, humbug; =feld ⊛ n Tischlerei: (wooden) back of a mirror; =fenster n plate-glass window; =fernrohr n, ast.: ⚹ catoptric telescope, catopter, reflector; =fläche f: a) surface of a looking-glass; b) glassy (or perfectly smooth) surface; =folie ⊛ f s. Folie; =gießerei f = =fabrik; =glas (=fabrik f) n plate-glass (works pl.); ⚲glatt a. ⊛ (as) smooth (or polished) as a mirror; =glätte f perfect smoothness; =handel ⊛ m trade in mirrors; =händler(in f) m dealer in mirrors; =hütte f = =fabrik.
spiegelicht, ...ig (⊥◡◡) a. ⊛ (as) smooth as a glass, (glänzend) brilliant, lustrous.
Spiegel=karpfen (⊥◡...) m ⊠ ichth. mirror-carp (Cyprinus rex cyprinorum); =kasten ⊛ m: a) mirror-case; b) phys.: ⚹ catoptric chamber or box; =lampe f reflecting lamp; =lehre f, phys.: ⚹ catroptics; =macher m = =fabrikant; =metall ⊛ n, metall. specular metal; =mikroskop n reflecting microscope.
spiegeln (⊥◡) [mhd.; *Spiegel] ⊛a. I v/n. (h.) 1. to be as polished (or smooth) as a glass; weitS. to shine, to glitter, von Edelsteinen: to sparkle. — II v/a. 2. (zurückstrahlen) to reflect, to mirror; (im Spiegel besehen) to look at in the glass. — 3. (mit Spiegeln versehen) to provide with mirrors. — 4. Zuckerbäckerei: to ice a cake, &c. — III sich ◡ v/refl. 5. to be reflected, to reflect. — 6. to look at o.s. in a glass. — 7. fig. sich in et. ◡ (an et. ein Beispiel nehmen) to take an example by a th., to take s.th. for one's model or pattern. — IV ~ n ⊠ 8. s. Spiegelung.
Spiegel=pfeiler (⊥◡...) m ⊠ arch. pier; =rahmen m frame of a looking-glass; =saal m = =zimmer; =scheibe f pane of plate-glass; =schiff ⚓ n square-sterned vessel; =schleifer ⊛ m polisher of mirrors; =schrank m wardrobe (or cupboard) adorned with mirrors; =sextant ⚹ m, ast. reflecting sextant; =telegraph ⊛ m mirror; =teleskop n = =fernrohr; =tisch m, =tischchen n pier-table, im Schlafzimmer: toilet-table.
Spieg(e)lung (⊥(◡)◡) f ⊛ (s. spiegeln II) 1. reflexion. — 2. = Spiegelbild.
Spiegel=zimmer (⊥◡◡◡) n ⊠ room hung (or adorned) with mirrors (all round).
Spieke ⚲ (⊥◡) [it. spica Ähre] f ⚘ spike-lavender (Lavandula spica); aspic.

Spieker ⊛ ⚓ (⊥◡) [ndd.] m ⊠ (Nagel) large nail, spike.
spiekern (⊥◡) v/a. ⚓a. to spike.
Spiek=öl (⊥⊥) [Spieke] n ⊠ = Lavendel-öl.
Spiel [ahd.) n ⊠ 1. spell Schicht, Abwechselung] n ⊠c. 1. play(ing) (a. ♪), mit Karten, Ball, Regeln x. : game, im Freien: (outdoor) sport, zur Kurzweil: pastime, recreation; um Geld: gambling; ein ~chen m. to play (F to have) a (quiet) game; Fußball: im ~ on side; aus dem ~e (tot) out of play; Tennis: ~e gleich games all; wie steht das ~?, wie steh(e)n die ~e? what is the score? — 2. a) ♪ (Aufschlag) touch; (Technik) execution, (fr.) technique; (Manier) style; beim ~ der Harfen at the sound of the harps, aber abs. beim ~e in (or while) playing; ⚔ mit klingendem ~e with drums beating and trumpets sounding; b) thea.: 1. = Schauspiel; 2. (Darstellungsart) (style of) acting, F business; stummes ~ dumb show. — 3. mit prp., oft fig.: aufs ~ setzen (wagen) to risk, venture, hazard; auf dem ~e stehen to be at stake; lassen Sie mich aus dem ~e! leave me out of the question!; es ist Ehrgeiz dabei im ~e ambition is at the root (or bottom) of it; die Hand bei et. im ~e haben to be mixed up with a th. — 4. mit verbs, oft fig. ehrliches ~ fair play; e-m freies ~ l. to give a p. a free hand or full scope; s. gut 4; laßt genug sein des grausamen ~s (SCH.) make an end of this cruel sport; e-m gewonnen(es) ~ geben to declare (or acknowledge) o.s. beaten by a p.; gewonnen ~ haben to have won (or gained) one's point; leichtes ~ h. to have an easy task; s. leicht 2; der Satan hat sein ~ damit Satan (or Old Nick) has his finger in the pie; sein ~ mit et. treiben to make sport (or game) of a th.; das ~ verloren geben to give up the game as lost, to throw up the game or the sponge. — 5. fig. ein ~ (Spielball) der Winde sein to be a sport (or at the mercy) of the winds. — 6. ⊛ working of a machine, &c.; mach. ~ (Hub) des Treibkolbens play (or stroke) of the piston. — 7. zum Spielen Dienendes: pack of cards; (complete) set of chessmen, dominoes, nine-pins, &c. — 8. hunt. ~ (Schwanz) tail, des Fasans x. auch: pole.
Spiel=art (⊥◡...) f ⊠: a) manner of playing; vgl. =weise; b) ⚘, zo. (besondere Gattung, Abart) variety; =ball m: a) ball for playing; auch: cricket-, billiard-, golf- &c. ball; b) fig. s. Spiel 5; ein ~ in j-s Händen sein ... a p.'s tool or puppet; =bank f gam(bl)ing- (or roulette-) table. [for the stage, stageable.]
spielbar (⊥◡) a. ⊛ thea. fit (or suitable)⌋
Spiel=brett (⊥...) n ⊠ draught- (or chess-)board; =bruder m passionate gambler; =bude f gambling-booth.
Spielchen (⊥◡) n ⊠ (dim. von Spiel) (quiet) little game; s. Spiel 1.
Spiel=dose (⊥⊥◡) f ⊠ musical box.
Spiele (⊥◡) f ⊛ = Spule 1. [games all.)
Spiel=einstand (⊥◡⊥) m ⊠ Tennis:⌋
spielen (⊥◡) [ahd. s. Spiel] I v/n. (h.), v/refl. ⊛ 1. to play, ♪ ein Instrument ◡

to play an instrument; s. Geige, Klavier, Zither; ein Lied ◡ to play an air or a tune; vom Blatte ◡ to play at sight. — 2. thea. to perform; seine Rolle ◡ to act (fig. a. to play) one's part; s. Rolle 4; das Stück spielt in Venedig the scene (of action) is laid in Venice; heute wird nicht gespielt (there will be) no performance to-day, the theatre is closed to-day; fig.: et. ◡ (vorstellen wollen) to assume a part; den Angenehmen ◡ to do the amiable; den (großen) Herrn ◡ to play (or act) the (fine) gentleman. — 3. Karten, Schach, Würfel x. ◡ to play cards, chess, dice, &c; vgl. Ball, Billard 1, Blindekuh, Versteck 1; falsch ◡ to cheat at cards, &c.; hoch (niedrig) ◡ to play for high (low) stakes; so spielt man nicht that's not the game; wir beide ◡ zusammen we two are partners; gegen=ea. ◡ to be opponents (at a game); in der Lotterie ◡ to put in the lottery; beim dtsch. Billard: e-e Kugel ins Loch ◡ to pocket a ball; nur um die Ehre ◡, umsonst ◡ to play for love; um Geld ◡ to play for money, to gamble; die Partie um 1 ℳ ◡ to play a shilling a game; sich arm, sich um sein Vermögen ◡ to ruin o.s. with gambling; fig. mit einem unter einer Decke ◡ to play into a p.'s hands, to make common cause with a p.; ein gewagtes Spiel ◡ to play a bold (or hazardous) game. — 4. mit et. ob. e-m ◡ (sein Spiel treiben) to play (or trifle) with a th., a p.; to make sport of a th., a p.; er läßt nicht mit sich ◡ he is not to be trifled with; mit Worten ◡ to play on words, to pun; seinen Witz ◡ lassen to display (or show off) one's wit. — 5. v. Farben: das Band spielt ins Blaue ... has a bluish tint; ins Rote ◡ inclining to red; von Diamanten: in allen Farben ◡ to glitter (or sparkle) in all colours of the rainbow; von Fahnen x.: im Winde ◡ to flutter in the wind; ⚔ eine Mine ◡ l. to spring a mine. — 6. Ortsveränderung: e-m et. in die Hände ◡ to smuggle a th. into a p.'s hands; den Krieg nach Deutschland ◡ to carry the war into Germany; der Telegraph spielte nach allen Richtungen the telegraph flashed its messages in all directions; seine Augen über etwas ◡ (streifen) l. to pass a rapid glance over a th. — II ~ n ⊠ 7. = Spiel.
Spieler (⊥◡) m ⊠, ~in f⊛ player, Hasard: gambler, gamester; falscher ~ card-sharper; ♪ artist(e), professional; thea. actor, f actress (s. Schau=2).
Spielerei (-◡⊥) f ⊛ 1. play(ing) (Scherz) fun, sport, jesting, dallying, (Kinderei) toying, trifling (vgl. Spielwerk c). — 2. (Spielzeug) toy(s pl.); knickknack.
Spiel=ergebnis (⊥◡⊥◡) n ⊠ Fußball: score.
spielerig (⊥◡◡◡) a. ⊛ fond of playing or gambling; playful, frolicsome.
Spiel=feld (⊥...) n ⊠ Tennis: court, Kricket: cricket-field; =führer m Fußball: captain; =gehilfe m beim Roulett x.: croupier; =geld n money for playing; (Einsatz) stake, pool; =genosse m,

⚹ scientific; ⚘ botanical; ⚲ geography; ⊛ machinery; ⚒ mining; ⚔ military; ⚓ marine; ⊛ commercial; ⊛ postal; 🚂 railway.

[Spielgenossin] — 904 — [Spinnstubenerzählungen]

=genossin f playfellow, playmate; =gesellschaft f party of players, engS. card-party; =gleichstand m Tennis: games all; =glück n luck at cards, lucky chance; =grenze f Fußball: dead-ball line; =haus [ahd.] n, =hölle f gambling-house, -hell; =kamerad m playmate; =karte f playing-card; =kästchen n card-box; =kätzchen n playful kitten, fig. frolicsome girl; =klub m, =kränzchen n card-club; =leute pl.: a) pl. zu =mann; b) bsd. ⚔ drums and fifes, allg. bandsmen pl.; =mann [ahd.] m street-player, musician, engS. harpist, fiddler, Mittelalter: minstrel; =marke f counter, fish; =oper f (ant. Sprech=oper) grand opera; =partie f card-party, game of cards; =pfennig m = =marke; =platz m e-r Schule: playground; Tennis: ground; Kricket: field; ~ mit Anlagen recreation-ground(s pl.); =puppe f doll; =ratte f, a. =ratz(e f) m F person fond of playing or addicted to gambling; =raum m: a) room for moving; elbow-room; freien ~ haben to have full scope; b) ☉ ~ e-r Feder ꝛc.: free play; =regel f rule of the game; =rolle f Tennis: list; =sachen f/pl. = =zeug; =schuld f gambling-debt; =schule f school for infants, infant-school; kindergarten; =stand m Fußball: score; =stunde f play-hour or -time; =sucht f = =wut; =tag m play-day; ~e pl. provc. = Ferien; =teufel m: a) demon of gambling; b) passionate gambler; =tisch m card- (or gaming-, gambling-)table; =uhr f chiming watch or clock; =verderber m mar-feast; =vor n Tennis: advantage-game; Partie mit ~ advantage-set; =waren f/pl. = =zeug; =waren=handel ⊛ m toy-trade; =waren=händler m toy-merchant, toyman; =waren=handlung f toy-shop; =wart m Fußball: captain; =weise f manner (or style) of playing; =werk n: a) = =zeug; b) ☉ chime of a watch or clock; c) (leichte Aufgabe) easy thing, mere play(work) or trifle; =wut f passion for gambling; =zeug n playthings, toys pl.; (Kinderei) trifles, knickknacks pl.; =zeug=fabrik ☉ f toy-manufactory; =zeug=händler m toy-dealer; =zeug=kasten m box of toys; =zeug=laden m toy-shop; =zimmer n: a) play-room; b) card-room.
Spier(¹)[ndd.]m,n☉c.stalk,blade of grass.
Spierchen (¹⌣) n ㉓ 1. (Grasspitzchen) small blade of grass. — 2. fig. ein ⌒ (ein wenig) a little bit, a wee bit.
Spier-baum ♀ (¹⌣) m ㉒ = Speierling.
Spiere¹ ♀ (¹⌣) f ㊹ = Spiräe.
Spiere² ⚓ (¹⌣) [ndd.: spire] f㊽ (Sparren) spar, boom. [outrigger-torpedo.]
Spieren=torpedo ⚓ (⌣¹⌣¹⌣) m ㊷
Spierling ♀ (¹⌣) m ㊷ = Speierling.
Spier-staude ♀ (¹⌣) f ㊹ = Spiräe.
Spieß¹ (⌣) [ahd.] m ㉑a. 1. chm. ⚔ spear, pike; (Wurfgeschoß) javelin; fig. den ~ umkehren gegen, etwa: to turn the tables upon. — 2. † ⚔ (Spießträger) ☉ spearman. — 3. ⚙ typ. (beim Druck hochkommender Ausschluß) pick, black.
Spieß² (⌣) [ahd.] m ㉑a. 1. = Bratspieß; z.B. am ~e braten to roast

on a spit. — 2. ☉ Weberei: skewer. — 3. hunt. ~e pl. (zweispitziges Gehörn im 1. Jahre) first year's antlers pl.
Spieß²=bock (⁄⁄...) m ㉒ roebuck of the first head; =braten m joint roasted on the spit; =¹bürger m: a) ehm.: citizen armed with a pike; b) (alltäglicher ob. gewöhnlicher Mensch) narrow-minded (or slow, humdrum, commonplace) fellow; vgl. Philister; ²bürgerlich a. ⓖ narrow-minded, slow, humdrum, commonplace; vgl. philisterhaft; =bürgertum n = Philisterei; =²dreher m Küche: turnspit.
spießen (¹⌣) [mhd.; *Spieß¹ u.²] v.a. ㊉ to spear; to (put on a) spit; (durchbohren) to pierce, to transfix; auf die Gabel ☉ to stick on a fork; a. = pfählen 3; e-n Schmetterling auf das Brett ☉ to fix ... on the setting-board.   [bürger.)
Spießer¹ (¹⌣) [mhd.] m ㉒ P fig. = Spieß=
Spießer² (¹⌣) [mhd.; *spitz] m ㉒ hunt. (Spießhirsch) one-year-old buck.
spieß¹=förmig (⁄⁄...) a. ⓖ spear-shaped, ⚕ hastate; =gesell(e) m ㉒ urspr.: mate, companion, F pal, jetzt meist b.s. (Helfershelfer) accomplice; =²glanz m, min.: reiner ~ pure antimony; =glanz-butter f s. Butter 2; ⁰glanz=haltig a.: ⚕ antimoniferous; =glanz=oxyd n, =glanz=säure f = Antimon=oxyd, =säure; =glas n = =glanz; =glas=weiß ☉ n white precipitated oxide of antimony; =hirsch m = Spießer².
spießig (¹⌣) a. ⓖ 1. spear-shaped. — 2. ☉ Gerberei: badly tanned or dressed.
Spieß²=rute (⁄⁄...) f ㉑ ehm. ⚔: ~n laufen to run the gauntlet; =ruten=laufen n running the gauntlet; =¹träger m ehm. spearman, pikeman, vgl. Speerträger.
Spill ⚓ (⌣) [Spille] n ⓑ. (Ankerwinde) capstan; loses ~ Spanish windlass.
Spill=baum (⁄⁄...) m ㉒: a) ⚓ bar of the capstan; b) ♀ = Spindelbaum; =beting f windlass-bit.
Spille (¹⌣) [ahd.] f ㉑ 1. = Spindel. — 2. F (lange Zipfelmütze) nightcap.   [Dörnchen]m☉d. egg-plum.)
Spilling ♀ (¹⌣) [mhd.; *It. spi'nula]
Spill=kopf (⁄⁄...) m ㉒ ⚓ windlass-end, top of the capstan; =mage m relative on the female side; =spake ⚓ f capstan-bar.
Spinat ♀ (⌣¹) [fr., it., Pers.] m ㊺c. auch Kocht. spinach (Spina'cia olera'cea).
Spind (⌣) [ndd.] n, m ⑪⑬b., a. ~e (¹⌣) f ㊺ (Schrank) press. wardrobe.
Spindel (¹⌣) [ahd.: spindle; *spinnen] f ㊶ 1. spindle, distaff (a. fig.). — 2. anat. = Speiche 2. — 3. ☉: a) mach., mech. (Achse) axis, axle, Uhrm.: verge; (Wellbaum) arbor, shaft, beam; (Zapfen) peg, pin; ~ einer Drehbank: mandrel; ~ einer Schraube: worm; b) arch. ~ einer Treppe: newel; ~ e-r Mühle: pillar; c) Spinnerei: (Spule) bobbin. — 4. ein Stickmaß, s. XL.
Spindel=bank (⁄⁄...) f ㉒ bobbin-frame, flyer; =baum ♀ m spindle-tree, prick-timber, prickwood (Evo'nymus Europæ'us); =beine n/pl. long thin legs, F spider's legs pl.; ⁰beinig a. spindle-shanked or -legged; ⁰dünn, ⁰dürr a. ⓖ (as) thin as a lath, extremely slender; mit ⁰dünner Taille, oft: spindle- (or

wasp-)waisted; ⁰förmig a. spindle-shaped, ⚕, zo.: ⚕ fusiform; =holz ♀ n = Bergahorn; =macher m spindle-maker; =presse ☉ f press with worm-screw; =säule f, arch. spindle-shaped (or cylindrical) column; =schnecke f, zo. spindle-shell (Fusus); =treppe f, arch. spiral (or corkscrew, seltener: spindle-)staircase.   [spat) spindle.)
Spinell ⚘ (⌣¹)[lt.]m☉d. min (Art Kiesel=)
Spinett ♪ (⌣¹) [it. spine'tta f] n ☉c. ehm. (Art Klavier) spinet, virginals pl.
spinnbar (⌣'⌣) a. ⓖ fit for spinning, fit to be spun, textile.   [⚕c.: silk-gland.)
Spinn¹=drüse (⁎,¹⌣) f ㉑ der Seidenraupen
Spinne (¹⌣) [ahd.; *spinnen] f ㊸ zo. spider; fig. spiteful person; F pfui, ~! oh, horrid!, (how) nasty!
spinne=feind (⁎⌣¹) a. ⓖ nur prädikativ: einem ⌒ sein to be a p.'s bitterest (or sworn) enemy, to have a deep grudge against a p.
spinnen¹ (¹⌣) [ahd.: spin] v.a. und v/n. (h.) ㉔(b). 1. to spin; Sprichw. s. Sonne am Schluß; Tabak ☉ to twist ...; fig. e-n Gedanken weiter ☉ to follow up a thought or a thread; s. Seide am Schluß; Verrat ☉ to hatch treason, to (form a) plot. — 2. der Kreisel spinnt (dreht sich) the top is spinning round. — 3. die Katze spinnt ... purrs.
spinnen²=artig (⁎,¹⌣...) [Spinne] a. ⓖ spider-like, ⚕ arachnoid, araneous; ⁰beinig a. with spider-legs, a. spider-shanked; =füße m/pl. ⑥ spider's feet; =gewebe n = Spinngewebe; =kenner m ⚕ arachnologist; =kraut ♀ n = Graslilie; =krebs m spider-crab (Cancer ara'neus); =kunde f: ⚕ arachnology; =nest, =netz n = Spinngewebe; =tiere n/pl. zo.: ⚕ arachnid(ian)s, araneid(an)s pl.; =webe f = Spinngewebe.
Spinner (¹⌣) m ㉒ 1. a. ⁰in f ⑪ spinner. — 2. ent. (Falter, dessen Raupe sich in ein Gespinst verpuppt): ⚕ bombyx, bombycid.
Spinnerei (⌣⌣¹) f ㊹ 1. (art of) spinning, method of spinning. — 2. ☉ (Fabrik) spinning-mill or -works pl., seltener: spinnery.
Spinnerei=anlage (⌣⌣¹⌣⌣...) f ㉑ plant of a spinning-mill; =besitzer(in f) m owner of a spinning-mill.
Spinner=lohn (¹⌣⌣¹) m ㉒ spinner's wages pl., charge for spinning.
Spinne-web(e f) n = Spinngewebe.
Spinn¹=fäden (⁎,¹⌣...) [spinnen] m/pl. des Altweibersommers: gossamer, floating cobwebs pl.; =frau f woman who spins, spinner; =gefäß n, zo. spinner(et); =geschäft n spinning-trade; =²gewebe n [Spinne] cobweb, spider's toils pl. or web; =hanf m hemp for spinning; =haus n spin(ning)-house (ehm. auch Gefängnis für lose Dirnen); =hütte ☉ f für Seidenraupen: hut for cocooning silkworms; =⁰maschine ☉ f spinning-frame or -machine or -jenny; =meister m foreman at a spinning-mill; =rad n spinning-wheel; =rocken m distaff; =schule f school for spinning; =seide f silk for spinning; =stube f spinning-room; party of spinning women; =stuben-erzählungen f/pl., etwa: tales pl. of the fireside, nursery-tales pl.;

[Spinnwarze]

=warze f, zo. der Spinnen: spinning-wart; ⌇ arachnidial mammilla, arachnidium; =²web(e f, n) n [mhd.] = gewebe, =web(en)=haut f, anat. des Gehirns: ⌇ arachnoid; =werkzeug n spinning organ, ⌇ f. =warze; =¹wolle f wool for spinning.

Spinozismus ⌇ (-ᴗᴗ) [Spino'za, ndl. Philosoph 1632—77] m ㉗ Spinozism.

Spint prove. (ᴗ) [ahd.] m, n ㉒ b. (Fett)grease.

spintisieren F (ᴗᴗᴗ) [nhd. 16. sae.] v/n. (h.) ㉝ to meditate; (flügeln) to reason (with great subtlety), to sophisticate.

Spion (ᴗ¹) [nhd.; fr. espion; *dtsch Späher] m ㉔d., =in f ㊼ (Auskundschafter(in) spy, ⌅ m scout; f. Polizeispion.

Spionage (ᴗᴗ¹ᴗ) [fr. espionnage] f ㊽ =spying (system), espionage.

Spionen-riecherei (ᴗᴗ-ᴗᴗ¹) f ㊽ scenting (or excessive fear of) spies.

Spionentum (ᴗᴗ¹ᴗ) n ㉔d. = Spionage.

spionieren (ᴗᴗ¹ᴗ) [fr. espionner] I v/n. (h.) ㉝ (spähen) to spy (about), to act as spy, weitS. to pry (into people's affairs). — II ~ n ㉓, auch: **Spioniererei** (ᴗᴗ-ᴗ¹) f ㊽ spying (system), espionage.

Spiräe ♀ (-¹ᴗ) [lt.] f ㊽ spiræa.

spiral (-¹) [lt.] a. ㊺ (schraubenartig gewunden) spiral, ⌇ auch: ⌇ tortile.

Spirale (-¹ᴗ) [lt.] f ㊽ 1. bsd. math. spiral (line), ⌇ helix. — 2. arch. auch: volute; e-r Taschenuhr: spiral (spring).

Spiral-feder ⊙ (-"...) f ㊷ spiral (or helical) spring; =form f spirality; =förmig a. ㊻ (like a) spiral; =gefäß ♀ n spiral duct; =linie f = Spirale 1; =nebel m, ast.: ⌇ spiral nebula; =pumpe f spiral pump; =rad n spiral wheel.

Spirant (-¹) [lt.] m ㊷ (Hauchlaut) spirant.

Spiritismus ⌇ (-ᴗ¹ᴗ) [lt.] m ㉗ (Glaube an den Verkehr mit Geistern) spiritism.

Spiritist (-ᴗ¹) m ㊷, ⌅ isch a. ㊻ spiritist.

Spiritualismus ⌇ (-ᴗᴗ¹ᴗ) [lt.] m ㉗ phls. spiritualism, a. = Spiritismus.

Spiritualist (-ᴗᴗᴗ¹) m ㊷, ~in f ㊼ spiritualist; ⌅ isch a. ㊻ spiritualistic.

Spirituosen (-ᴗᴗ¹ᴗ) [lt.] pl. inv. (geistige Getränke) spirituous (or alcoholic) liquor(s pl.), spirits pl.

Spiritus (¹ᴗᴗ) [lt.] m, inv. od. ㉖ 1. spirit (of wine), alcohol, von normaler Stärke: proof-spirit. — 2. fig. spirit; (Feuer) fire, mettle. — 3. grch. gr. Spi'ritus asper (lenis) rough (smooth) breathing. — 4. Spi'ritus familia'ris (dienstbarer Geist) familiar spirit.

spiritus-artig (¹ᴗᴗ...) a. ㊻ alcoholic; =brennerei f ㊷ distillery (of spirits); =koch-maschine ⊙ f ætna, etna; =kraft-maschine/spirit-driven motor; =lampe f spirit-lamp; =wage f spirit-gauge, ⊙ alcohol(o)meter; (Nivellierwage) spirit-level. [hospital, infirmary.]

Spital (-¹) [mhd.; *lt. (Ho)spital] n ㉒ d./

Spital-fieber (-¹...) n hospital-fever; =schiff ↓ n hospital-ship.

Spittel (¹ᴗ) n (⚔ m) ㉒ = Spital.

spitz (¹) [ahd.; f. Spieß²] I a. ㊺ 1. (ant. stumpf) pointed (knife, &c.); ♀ u. min.: ⌇ acicular; (stechend) stinging, prickly; ⚵e Nase pointed nose; math. Der Winkel acute angle; ⚵ auslaufen to run to a point; ⚵ zulaufend tapering, ♀: ⌇ cuspidate(d). — 2. fig. (beißend, scharf)

biting, poignant, caustic, sarcastic; ⚵e Zunge sharp tongue; (zart) delicate, frail, von Kindern auch: peaky; F ich kann es nicht ⚵ kriegen (begreifen) I cannot make it out. — II **Spitz** m ㉔a. 3. Hunde-art: Pomeranian dog. — 4. F (leichter Rausch) tipsy state, tipsiness; einen (kleinen) ~ haben to be a bit on, to be slightly elevated.

Spitz-ahorn ♀ (¹...) m ㉒ = Lehne³; =amboß ⊙ m beaked anvil, bickern; =axt ⊙ ⚒ f pick(axe); =bart pointed whiskers pl. or beard; =berg ♀ m peak; =beutel m bag-filter; =blattern f/pl. path. chicken-pox; =bogen m (ant. Rundbogen) arch. pointed (or Gothic) arch, ogive; =bogen-stil m pointed (or Gothic) style (of architecture); =bohrer ⊙ m draw-point, scriber, (Zentrumbohrer) centre-bit; =bübchen n little rogue; =bube [nhd. 16. sae.] m, =bübin f: a) (Dieb[in]) thief, pickpocket; b) (Betrüger) villain, rogue, knave; c) liebkosend: (Schalk) rascal; =buben-bande f gang of thieves or rogues; =buben-gesicht n roguish (or hang-dog) face or look; =buben-sprache f thieves' language or F Latin; =buben-streich m, =büberei f (piece of) roguery, roguish trick; ⚵bübisch a. thievish; roguish, knavish.

Spitzchen (¹ᴗ) n ㉓: a) (dim. v. Spitze) small point, fine lace; b) (dim. von Spitz) small Pomeranian dog.

Spitze (¹ᴗ)[ahd.; *spitz] f ㊽ 1. point, (Zinke) spike, (spitzes Ende) point, pointed end; (äußerstes Ende) extremity, von Körperteilen auch: tip; ~ e-r Pfeife: mouthpiece; ~ e-s Berges: summit, top, peak; ~ e-s Turmes: spire, (Zinne) pinnacle. — 2. (hervorragendste Stelle) head; an der ~ stehen to be at the head, to act as leader; sich an die ~ einer Bewegung stellen to head a movement; an der ~ eines Unternehmens stehen to take the lead in an enterprise, to be at the head of an undertaking; die ~n der Behörden the administrative heads, the foremost (or leading) authorities pl.; die ~n der Gesellschaft the leaders (or F tiptops) of society. — 3. fig. einer Sache die ~ abbrechen to take the (sharp) edge off a th.; e-m die ~ bieten to make head (mit Erfolg: to hold one's own) against a p., to defy a p.; die Dinge auf die ~ (aufs äußerste) treiben to push things to extrem(iti)es or extreme lengths, to go too far. — 4. fig. (spitze Rede) pointed speech or allusion; F ~n austeilen to pass personal (or offensive) remarks. — 5. ⚔ (Kante) lace; Brabanter ~ Mechlin lace; geklöppelte ~ bone-lace; genähte ~ point-lace; sächsische ~ Dresden lace; ~ mit Netzgrund net-lace.

Spitzel (¹ᴗ) [nhd. 18. sae.;*öst.] m ㉒ = Polizeispion; ~tum (ᴗᴗ¹) n ㉔ : a) system of spies or informers, espionage; b) police-spies, informers pl.

spitzen (¹ᴗ) [spitz] v/a. u. v'refl. ㉚ 1. to point, einen Bleistift auch: to sharpen, eine Gänsefeder: to mend; ⊙ Stechnadeln ⚵ to put a point to ...; ♀ (fein) ge-

[spleißig]

spitzt: ⌇ cuspidate(d). — 2. v. Körperteilen: den Mund ⚵ to screw (or purse) up one's mouth; die Ohren (lauschend) ⚵ to prick up one's ears; sein Gesicht spitzt sich ... is growing long or thin. — 3. fig. seine Antwort ⚵ to give a pointed answer; das ist auf mich gespitzt that's meant (or intended) for me. — 4. F fig. sich auf etwas ⚵ (Hoffnung machen) to set one's hope (or heart) upon a th., to be confident of (the success of) a th.; auf et. gespitzt sein to be anxious (or longing, eager) to know (the result of) a th.

Spitzen-arbeit ⚒ (¹ᴗ...) [Spitze 5] f ㊷ lace-work; =band n lace-edging; =besatz m lace-trimming or -border(ing); =einsatz m l.-insertion, lace let in(to a dress, &c.); vgl. =streifen; =fabrikation f lace-making or -manufacture; =grund m Weberei: lace-ground, bobbin-net; =handel m lace-trade; =händler(in f) m lace-(wo)man, lace-merchant; =kleid n dress trimmed with lace; =klöppel m lace-bobbin, pl. a. bobbin-tools pl.; =klöppelei f lace-making; =klöppler(in f) m lace-maker; =kragen m l.-collar; =muster n l.-pattern; =stich m l.-stitch; =sticken n, =stickerei f l.-running; =sticker(in f) m lace-embroiderer, -runner; =streifen m l.-band; =tuch n lace-handkerchief; =werk n l.-arbeit; =wirker m lace-maker.

Spitz-feile ⊙ (¹...) f ㊷ taper-file; ⚵findig a. ㊻ subtle, cunning, crafty, in Kleinigkeiten: nice, captious, fault-finding; (verfänglich) sophistical; =findigkeit f subtleness, cunning, captiousness; (Verfänglichkeit) sophistry; =glas n conical wine-glass; =hacke f = =axt; =hammer ⊙ m, =haue f pick(-hammer); =hut m pointed hat.

spitzig (¹ᴗ) a. ㊻ (slightly) pointed, f. spitz I: ⚵ (adv.) auslaufend tapering. **Spitzigkeit** (¹ᴗᴗ) f ㊽ pointedness, sharpness; fig. (vgl. spitz 2 u. spitzig 4) poignancy, causticity, sarcasm.

Spitz-keimer ♀ (¹...) m (pl.) ㉒: ⌇ monocotyledon(s pl.); =klette ♀ f lesser burdock (Xa'nthium); ~ = common bur-weed (X. struma'rium); =kolumne f, typ. head-piece; =kopf m pointed (or long) head; ⚵köpfig a. ㊻ long-headed; =kugel ⚔ f conical bullet; =marke [Spitze] f (Überschrift) heading; =maul n pointed snout or mouth; =mäulchen F n von Kindern: button-mouth; =maus f, zo. shrew (-mouse) (Sorex ara'neus); =meißel ⊙ m pointed chisel; =name m nickname; ⚵nasig a. with a pointed nose; =pocken = =blattern; =reiter m = Vorreiter; =säule f, arch. pointed column, spire, ⚵ obelisk, pyramid; =turm m, arch. spire; =wegerich ♀ m rib-grass, rib-wort (Planta'go lanceola'ta); ⚵wink(e)lig a. math. acute-angled; =zahn m, anat. canine (or eye-)tooth.

Spleiße prove. (¹ᴗ) [mhd.] f ㊽ = Splitter.

spleißen ⊙ (¹ᴗ) [mhd. (ndd.): split] ㊿a. (㉙) I v/a. (spalten) to split, to cleave, metall. Kupfer ⚵ to refine ... — II v/n. (in) to split, to crack.

spleißig (¹ᴗ) a. ㊻ easy to split.

♪ Musik; ⌇ Wissenschaft; ♀ Pflanze; ♁ Geographie; ⊙ Technik; ⚒ Bergbau; ⚔ Militär; ↓ Marine; ⚓ Handel; ✉ Post; 🚂 Eisenbahn.

[splendid] — 906 — [Sprachbrief]

splendid F (⌣́) [lt.] a. ⓖ **1.** (freigebig) liberal; *typ.* Der Satz widely-spaced (or leaded) matter. — **2.** (prächtig) splendid, magnificent.

Splint (́) [ndd.: splint(er)] m ⓑb.: a) ⚘ ~ eines Baumes: sap-wood, ☞ alburnum; b) ⊕ forelock; ⚖-artig ⚘ a. ⓖ: ☞ alburnous; ~**bolzen** ⊕ m ⓺ forelock-bolt; ~**eisen** ⊕ n in Sägemaschinen: sapper; ~**holz** n = Splint a.

Spliß[1] (́) [splitz][2] m ⓐa. = Splitter.

spliß[2] (́) ind., **splisse** (́⌣) subj., **splissen**[1] pl. impf. von spleißen.

splissen[2] ⚓ (́⌣) [Spliß][1] **I** v/a. ⓐ: zwei Taue ⚖ (mit den Enden verflechten) to splice. — **II** ~ n ⓑ f. Splissung.

Spliß-hammer ⊕ (́...) m ⓺ splicing-hammer; **-horn** ⚓ n splicing-fid.

Splissung ⚓ (́⌣) f ⓺ splicing, splice, mit verjüngten Duchten: tapered splice.

Splitter (́⌣) [ndd.: splint(er): spleißen] m ⓑ splinter, shiver; (Bruchstück) fragment, eines Knochens: splintered bone, scale; *bibl.* der ~ in deines Bruders Auge the mote that is in thy brother's eye.

Splitter-bruch (́⌣...) m ⓺ *surg.* splintery fracture; **-holz** n splintered wood.

splitt(e)rig (́(⌣)́) a. ⓖ splintered, splintery; in fragments; ~**keit** f ⓺ splintered (or fragmentary) state.

Splitter-kohle (́⌣...⌣́) f ⓺ *min.* splint-(or slate-)coal.

splittern [f. Splitter] ⓐa. **I** v/a. to splinter, shatter, shiver; to reduce to shivers or fragments or pieces. — **II** v/n. (h. u. su) to splinter, to shiver (to pieces, stärker: to atoms).

splitter-nackt (́⌣...) a. ⓖ stark naked, without a bit of clothing on; -**netz** ⚓ n ⓺ Kriegsschiffe: splinter-netting; -**richten** v/a. ⓺⁕: to criticize (Bücher: to review) minutely and harshly; ~ n searching criticism; -**richter** m censorious critic, fault-finder; -**richterei** f = -richten.

splittrig (́⌣) a. ⓖ f. splitt(e)rig. [booty.]

Spoli-en (́⌣) [lt. Beute] pl. ⓺ spoils pl.

sponde-isch (́⌣) [grch.] a. ⓖ pros. spondaic; **Sponde-us** m ⓺ (Versfuß: - -) spondee.

spönne (́) subj. impf. v. spinnen.

Sponsali-en (⌣́⌣⌣) [lt.] pl. Verlobungsfeier) betrothal; **sponsieren** (⌣⌣́) [lt.] v/n. (h.) ⓺ (freien) to woo, to court, to pay one's addresses to.

spontan (⌣́) [lt.] a. ⓖ bsd. *physiol.* (freiwillig, von selbst) spontaneous; **Spontane-ität** (⌣⌣⌣⌣́) f ⓺ spontaneity.

Sponton (bsgl- ob. -tǭ') [fr. esponton] m ⓺ ehm. ⚔ (Halbpike als Paradewaffe der Offiziere) spontoon.

Sporaden ⚥ (⌣́⌣) [grch.] npr/f/pl. ⓺ (ant. Zyklades) (Gruppe von Inseln im Ägäischen Meere) Sporades pl.

sporadisch (⌣⌣́⌣) [grch.] a. ⓖ (zerstreut) sporadic, scattered; *adv.* sporadically.

Spore ☞ (⌣́⌣) [grch.] f ⓺ (Pilzkeim) spore.

Sporen[1] (⌣́⌣) [Spore] f pl. 1. v. Sporn; 2. v. Spore.

sporen[2] ☞ (⌣́⌣) v/n. (h.) ⓺ (trocknen) to dry (up); (schimmeln) to get mouldy.

sporen[3]-**bildend** ⚥ (⌣́...) [Spore] a. ⓖ forming spores; -**bildung** f ⓺ spore-formation; -**büchse** f der Farnkräuter: ☞ theca; -**frucht** f: ☞ sporocarp; -**kapsel** f: ☞ sporocyst; -**pflanze** f

= Afotyledone; -**schlacht** f, *hist.* (1302 und 1513) Battle of Spurs; -**stich** m (dig of a) spur; -**träger** m ☞ sporophore; -**zelle** ⚘ f spore-cell. [spurrier.]

Sporer ⊕ (⌣́) [mhd.] m ⓺ spur-maker,

sporig ☞ (⌣́) a. ⓖ = schimmelig.

Sporn (́) [ndh. (ahd.): spur] m ⓑb. (pl. mst Sporen) spur (a. v. Tieren u. *fig.*), e-s Kampfhahnes a. gaff; ⚘, *anat.*: ☞ calcar; *fig.* incentive, stimulus, impetus; die Sporen abschnallen (anlegen) to take off (to buckle on, put on) one's spurs; einem Pferde die Sporen geben to give a horse the spurs, to set spurs to (stärker: to dig one's spurs into) a horse; mit dem ~ verletzen to gall with the spur, to spur-gall; *fig.* sich die Sporen verdienen to win one's spurs, to make a name (for o.s.).

sporn-ähnlich (́...) a. like a spur, *anat.* calcarine; -**baldrian** m, -**blume** f ⚘ spur-flower, red valerian (*Centranthus ruber*).

spornen v/a. ⓖ **1.** to spur, to set spurs (or to give the spur) to; ein Pferd scharf ⚖ to dig (or plunge) one's spurs into a horse's sides; *fig.* to spur (on), vgl. anspornen I. — **2.** (mit Sporen versehen) to provide with spurs; sich ⚖ to put on spurs; gestiefelt und gespornt booted and spurred, fully equipped (for the road).

sporn-förmig (́...) a. ⓖ spur-shaped, ☞ calcariform; -**füße** m/pl. ⓺ *zo.* spurred (☞ calcariferous) feet pl.; -**leder** n spur-leather; -**rad** ⊕ n ⓺ spur-toothed wheel; -**rädchen** n (spur-)rowel; -**riemen** m strap of a spur, spur-strap; -**stätisch** a. man. restive; -**stich** m spur-gall; -**streichs** adv. at full gallop or speed, post-haste, on the spur of the moment; -**träger** m (leather) rest for the spurs.

Sport F (́) [engl.] m ⓐc. sport.

Sportel (⌣́) [ndh.; *it.* spo'rtula Gerichtssportel] f ⓺ n pl. ⓺ (Nebeneinkünfte) perquisites, F perks, pickings pl.; gerichtliche ~n legal costs pl.; ~**kasse** (́⌣⌣) f ⓺ fund of (or safe for) court-fees.

Sport-freund (́...) m ⓺ = -liebhaber; -**karren** m = -wagen.

sportlich (⌣́⌣) a. ⓖ relating to sport.

Sport-liebhaber (́...) m ⓺ sportsman, a. sporting man; -**neuigkeiten** f/pl. sporting-news sg.

Sports-mann F (́...) m ⓺ sportsman; -**mäßig** a. ⓖ sportsmanlike. [court-fees.]

sportulieren (⌣⌣́⌣) v/n. (h.) ⓺ to levy

Sport-wagen (́...) m ⓺ (zweirädriger Kinderwagen) mail-cart; -**welt** f sporting world; -**zeitschrift**, -**zeitung** f sporting-magazine, -paper.

Spott (́) [ahd.] m ⓑb. (o. pl.) **1.** (Scherz) jest(ing), höhnischer: mockery, scoffing, jeering, sneering, lauter: derision, verhüllter: irony, beißender: sarcasm, cutting (or caustic) remark(s pl.), witziger: satire; Hohn und ~ taunts and sneers, jeers and gibes pl.; Schande und ~ von et. haben to derive nothing but disgrace and ridicule from a th.; seinen ~ mit et. ob. treiben to make game (or sport) of a th., to turn a th. into ridicule; Sprichw.

f. Schaden[2] 4. — **2.** (Gegenstand des ~es) laughing-stock, ridiculous object.

Spott-benennung (́...) f ⓺ =-name; -**bild** n caricature; ⚖**billig** a. ⓖ ridiculously (or dirt-)cheap; -**dichter** m satirical poet, satirist; -**drossel** f, *orn.* mocking-bird (*Mimus polyglo'ttus*).

Spöttelei (⌣⌣́) [Spott] f ⓺ chaff(ing), banter, raillery, quizzing, gibe; sarcastic remark or words pl.

spötteln (⌣́⌣) [*dim.* von spotten] **I** v/n. (h.) ⓺a. to indulge in chaff or banter or gibes (über et. about a th.); to pass sarcastic (or ironical) remarks about a th. — **II** ~ n ⓺ = Spöttelei.

spotten (́) [ahd.] ⓺ **I** v/n. (h.) **1.** über e-n, et. ⚖ to mock (or scoff, jeer, laugh at a p., a th., schwächer: to ridicule (or deride) a p., a th., to turn a p., a th. into ridicule, to make game (or fun) of a p., a th. — **2.** *fig.* aller, jeder Beschreibung ⚖ to beggar (or defy) all description; aller Gefahr ⚖ to laugh all danger to scorn, to see no danger. — **II** v/a. u. v/refl. **3.** er läßt sich nicht (üblicher v/n.: nicht mit sich) ⚖ he is not to be trifled (or played) with; *bibl.* Gott läßt sich nicht ⚖ God is not mocked. — **III** ~ n ⓑ **4.** = Spott 1.

Spötter (⌣́) m ⓺, ~**in** f ⓺ mocker, scoffer, sarcastical person, *rel.* blasphemer; (Necker[in]) chaffer, quizzer.

Spötterei (⌣⌣́) f ⓺ continued scoffing or sneering or chaffing or quizzing; mockery; sarcasm.

Spott-gebot ⚖ (́...) n ⓺ ridiculous(ly low) offer; -**geburt** f/monstrosity; -**gedicht** n satirical poem, a squib; -**geist** m spirit of mockery; -**gelächter** n mocking (or scornful) laugh(ter); -**geld** n ridiculously small sum, vgl. -preis; um ein ~, a. for a mere song or trifle.

spöttisch (⌣́) a. ⓖ (f. Spott 1) mocking, scoffing, jeering, sneering, derisive; ironical; sarcastic, cutting, caustic, satirical; (geistreich) epigrammatical; (stolz höhnend) scornful; *adv.* a. with a mocking (or disdainful) air; (mit verhülltem Spott) ironically; sarcastically.

Spöttler (⌣́) m ⓺ sarcastic person.

Spott-lied (́...) n ⓺ satirical song; -**lust** f love of sarcasm or satire; ⚖**lustig** a. ⓖ fond of chaff or banter; sarcastic, satirical; -**name** m nickname; -**preis** ⚖ m preposterously (or ridiculously) low price or charge; vgl. -geld; -**rede** f mocking speech; -**schlecht** a. ⓖ execrable, vile; -**schrift** f satire, lampoon; -**sucht** f = -lust; ⚖**süchtig** a. = ⚖lustig; -**vers** m satirical verse; -**vogel** m: a) *orn.* icterine warbler (*Hypola'is icteri'na*); b) *fig.* mocker, quiz(zer), wag; ⚖**weise** adv. mockingly, derisively, in derision; in a sneering way; ⚖**wohlfeil** a. = ⚖billig.

sprach[1] (́) ind. impf. von sprechen.

Sprach[2]-**ähnlichkeit** (́...) [Sprache] f ⓺ analogy of language(s); -**armut** f poverty of a language or in speech; lack of words; -**art** f idiom; -**bau** m: a) structure of a language; b) grammatical structure; -**brief** m: englische

Signs (see page XVII): F familiar; P vulgar; ꜰ flash; ⚓ rare; † obsolete (died); * new word (born); ⁕ incorrect; ♪ music.

[**Sprachdenkmäler**] **— 907 —** [**spreizen**]

~e letters *pl.* for instruction in English; =**denkmäler** oder =**denkmale** *n/pl.* literary remains of a language.
Sprache (⌐ch~) [ahd.: sprechen] *f* ⑫ 1. (Sprachfähigkeit) speech, bsd. e-s Volkes 2c.: language, gewählter: tongue, gewisser Klassen oder Gewerbe: slang, e-s Werkes ob. Schriftstellers: style, diction; (Mundart) dialect; (Kauderwelsch) F lingo; alte und neuere (lebende und tote) ~n ancient and modern (living and dead) languages or tongues *pl.*; eine ~ beherrschen to know a language thoroughly; die ~ in seiner Gewalt haben to have a ready command (or a good flow) of language; er spricht viele ~n he speaks many languages, he is a polyglot; *fig.* ~ der Augen language of the eyes. — 2. (Sprachvermögen) (power of) speech; (Redeweise) mode of speaking or of utterance; parlance; (Vortrag) delivery, elocution; (Aussprache) pronunciation, articulation; accent; eine kühne ~ führen to use bold language or words; eine sanfte ~ haben to have a soft speech or voice. — 3. in Redensarten: frei mit der ~ herausgehen to speak out boldly; mit der ~ nicht recht heraus wollen to beat about the bush; et. zur ~ bringen to broach a subject, to open (or start) a discussion on s.th., *auch*: to mention a th.; zur ~ kommen to come under discussion, to become a topic (or subject, theme) of conversation.
Sprach=eigenheit (″ch…) *f* ⑫, =**eigentümlichkeit** *f* idiom; deutsche (französische, englische, lateinische) ~ Germanism (Gallicism, Anglicism, Latinism).
Sprachen=gewirr, =kampf, =karte, ⚗kundig, =studium, =verwirrung, =zwang (″ch~…) *s.* Sprach=…
Sprach=fähigkeit (″ch…) *f* ⑫ faculty (or power) of speech; linguistic gift or ability; =**fehler** *m* defect in (one's) speech; grammatical mistake or error; =**fertigkeit** *f* readiness (or fluency) of speech; F gift of the gab; =**forscher** *m* linguist, philologist; =**forschung** *f* linguistics, philology; vergleichende ~ comparative study of languages; =**führer** *m* colloquial guide (to a language); =**gebiet** *n* domain of a lang., district in which a lang. is spoken; =**gebrauch** *m* usage of a lang.; im gewöhnlichen ~ in colloquial (or every-day) language; =**gefühl** *n* linguistic feeling or instinct; ~ haben to understand the genius of a language; =**gelehrsamkeit** *f* = =**wissenschaft**; =**gelehrte(r)** *m* philologist; =**genie** *n* linguistic genius; =**gesetz** *n* rule of a lang., linguistic law; =**gewirr** *n* confusion of languages or tongues; =**grenze** *f* linguistic frontier.
…**sprachig** (…″ch~) *a.* ⑥: fremd⚗ (or relating to, in a foreign language.
Sprach=kampf (″ch…) *m* ⑫ struggle between two or more languages; =**karte** *f* linguistic map; =**kenner** *m*: ⚗ linguist; =**kenntnis** *f* knowledge of languages; ⚗**kundig** *a.* ⑥

rebend) speaking many languages, polyglot; =**lehre** *f* grammar; =**lehrer** *m* teacher (or professor) of languages.
sprachlich (⌐ch~) *a.* ⑥ of (or concerning) language, linguistic; grammatical.
sprach=los (″ch…) *a.* ⑥ speechless, (stumm) dumb; ⚗ w. to lose the power of speech; =**losigkeit** *f* ⑫ speechlessness, dumbness; =**meister** *m* = =**lehrer**; =**menger** *m* one who mixes (or interlards) his speech with foreign words; =**mengerei** *f* mixing the vernacular with foreign words; medley of tongues; =**neuerer** *m* neologist; =**neuerung** *f* neology; neologism; =**organ** *n* organ of speech; =**regel** *f* linguistic (or grammatical) rule; =**reiniger** *m* (linguistic) purist; =**reinigung** *f* purification of a language; =**reinigungs=sucht** *f* purism; =**richtig** *a.* grammatical(ly correct); =**richtigkeit** *f* grammatical correctness; =**rohr** *n* speaking-tube or -trumpet; =**schatz** *m* vocabulary of a language; =**schnitzer** F *m* grammatical blunder; =**studium** *n* study of languages, =**studien** *pl.* linguistic studies *pl.*; =**talent** *n* talent for (acquiring) languages; =**übung** *f* exercise in language or elocution; =**unterricht** *m* instruction in a lang. or in languages; englischen ~ erteilen to give lessons in English; =**verbesserer** *m* (=verbesserung *f*) reformer (reform) of a lang.; =**verderber(in** *f*) *m* spoiler (or corrupter) of a lang.; =**verein** *m* philological (or linguistic) society; ⚗**vergleichend** *a.* comparing (two or more languages); =**vergleichung** *f* comparative philology; =**vermögen** *n* power (or faculty) of speech or utterance; =**verwandtschaft** *f* relationship (or affinity) between languages; =**verwirrung** *f*: baby-lonische ~ confusion of tongues, F Babel of tongues, Tower of Babel; =**werkzeug** *n* organ of speech; ⚗**widrig** *a.* contrary to (the rules of) grammar; ungrammatical; =**widrigkeit** *f* ungrammatical structure, bad grammar; =**wissenschaft** *f* science of language, philology; =**wissenschaftlich** *a.* philological, linguistic; =**zwang** *m, pol.* compulsory use of a language.
sprang (⌐) *ind. impf. v.* springen.
spratzeln *ab.* (⌐~) [ahd.] *v/n.* (h.) ⓶ *a.* (knatternd spritzen, sprühen) to sp(l)utter, spit, spirt.
Sprech=apparat ⊕ (″…) *m* ⑫ beim Telegraphen 2c.: receiver; =**art** *f* = =**weise**.
sprechen (⌐~) [ahd.] ⓶ *a.* I *v/n.* (h.) 1. to speak; (sich unterhalten) to converse, to talk; (plaudern) to chat; es wird viel von ihm gesprochen he is much (being) spoken of or talked about; die ganze Stadt spricht davon it is the (general) talk of the town, it is in everybody's mouth; er läßt nicht mit sich ⚗ he won't listen to reason. — 2. *mit adv. u. prp.* ausführlich (ob. weitläufig) über et. ⚗ to discuss a matter at some length, to expatiate on a th.; *fig.* deutsch (deutlich) mit e-m ⚗, etwa: to speak plain English (or plainly) to a p., to give a p. a piece of one's

mind; (gebrochen) englisch ⚗ to speak (broken) English; frei ⚗: a) to speak openly; b) to speak extempore, to extemporize; viel ⚗ to talk a great deal; *fig.* die Bosheit spricht aus s-m Gesicht his malice is written in his face; Tatsachen, die für (wider) e-n ⚗ facts which tell (or argue) in favour of (against) a p.; über Politik mit e-m ⚗ to talk (about) politics with (or to) a p.; unter uns gesprochen between ourselves; von etwas anderem ⚗ to turn the subject; da wir (gerade) davon ⚗ as we are on the subject, by the by; man spricht davon, daß er abdanken will there is some talk of his intending to resign; vor Gericht ⚗ to plead (a cause). — II *v/a.* und *v/refl.* 3. to speak, utter, say; ein Gebet ⚗ to say a prayer; Recht ⚗, ein Urteil ⚗ to pronounce judgment, to pass a sentence; den Segen über e-n ⚗ to pronounce a blessing (or a benediction) upon a p.; die Neuigkeit spricht sich bald herum the news soon makes the round or spreads about. — 4. e-n zu ⚗ wünschen to ask to see a p.; er ist jetzt nicht zu ⚗ he cannot be seen now, *auch*: he is engaged; der Vater ist noch gar nicht gut auf Sie zu ⚗ (ist Ihnen noch böse) Father is still angry (or cross) with you; *drohend*: wir werden uns ⚗ we shall settle that presently. — 5. (durch e-n Spruch erklären) to declare, pronounce; frei⚗ to acquit; heilig⚗ to canonize; schuldig⚗ to find guilty, to sentence. — III ⚗d *p.pr. u. a.* ⓶ 6. = reden III; ⚗d ähnlich life-like; ein ⚗d ähnliches Bild a speaking likeness; ⚗de Ähnlichkeit striking resemblance.
Sprecher (⌐~) *m* ⓶, ~**in** *f* ⓶ 1. speaker. — 2. (Wortführer) spokesman; ~ der Geschworenen foreman of the jury.
Sprech=freiheit (″…) *f* ⑫ freedom of speech; =**gesang** *m* recitative; =**maschine** *f* talking machine, phonograph, gramophone; =**oper** *f* (*ant.* Spiel=oper) comic opera, operetta; =**schnitzer** *m* slip of the tongue; =**stelle** *f* Fernspr.: telephone call-office or -station; =**stunde** *f* hour at which a p. may be seen, ärztliche: consultation-hour; amtliche: office-hour; =**übungen** *f/pl.* conversational exercises *pl.*; =**unterricht** *m* instruction in speaking, lessons *pl.* in elocution or conversation; =**weise** *f* manner of speaking, (mode of) speech; (Ausdrucksweise) expression, language; =**zimmer** *n* parlour, e-s Arztes: consulting-room.
Sprehe nbd. (⌐~) *f* ⓶ *orn.* (Star) starling.
Spreiß=feder ⊕ (″…) *f* ⓶ Uhrm.: spring (in a clock) for checking the motion of a wheel, pendulum-spring; =**haken** *m* Köhlerei: hook for removing coals from a charcoal-kiln.
Spreit=decke (″⌐~) *f* ⑫ counterpane.
spreiten (⌐~) [ahd.: spreit] *v/a.* ⓶ (ausea.=breiten) to spread (out), to lay out.
Spreize ⊕ (⌐~) [spreizen 2] *f* ⓶ Bauwesen: (Stütze) prop, stay, strut, shore.
spreizen (⌐~) [ahd.: sprießen] *v/a.* u. sich ⚗ *v/refl.* ⑨⓪ (dritte Person des *pres. ind.*

⚗ scientific; ♀ botanical; ⚲ geography; ⊕ machinery; ⚒ mining; ⚔ military; ⚓ marine; ⬤ commercial; ✉ postal; ⚒ railway.

[Spreizenkopf] — 908 — [springfederig]

bisw. spreizt) 1. to spread asunder; die Finger 2 to spread out one's fingers; die Beine 2 to sprawl (or straddle) one's legs, to stand with one's legs wide apart; sich 2 to lie sprawling, fig. (sich breit m.) to put on fine airs, to ride the high horse; s. gespreizt. — 2. ein Gebäude 2 (stützen) to prop (or shore) up ...; mst fig. sich 2 (gegen etwas stemmen) to stand up (or strive) against a th., to resist a th.

Spreizen-kopf (⌣⌣⌣) m ㉒ carp. stay-head. [(-work or -operation).]

Spreng-arbeit ✕ (⌣⌣⌣) f ㉒ blasting

sprengbar (⌣-) a. ㊅ easy to blast or to blow up; explosive.

Spreng-bohrloch ⊕ (⌣...) n ㉒ = -loch; =**bombe** ✕ f explosive shell; =**büchse** f ehm. ✕, Minierkunst: petard.

Sprengel (⌣⌣) [mhd.] m ㉒ eccl. 1. (Sprengwedel) (holy-water) sprinkler, aspergillum. — 2. (Kirch-) ~ diocese; (Gemeinde) parish.

sprengen (⌣⌣) [ahd. = springen m.] I v/a. und v/n. (h. und s.) ㉘ 1. to burst open; (erbrechen) to force (open), to break open; (zersprengen) to burst asunder, to shatter, Felsen zc.: to blast; Löcher in einen Felsen 2 to blast holes into a rock; in die Luft 2 to blow up, to explode; Billard: e-n Ball 2 to spring a ball; ✕ ✕ eine Mine 2 to spring a mine; ⊕ Glaserei: Glas 2 to crack glass; fig. e-e Spielbank 2 to break a bank. — 2. Personen zc. aus-ea. 2 (treiben) to disperse, to scatter, e-e Versammlung: forcibly to dissolve; v. einzelnen: e-n nach e-m Orte hin 2 to drive up. to a place; sein Pferd über e-n Graben 2 to jump ... across a ditch. — 3. v/n. (su) (voranstürmen, bsd. von Reitern) to gallop (along), to ride (at) full speed, to run at full tilt; über e-n Graben 2 to take (or jump) a ditch; auf die Feinde (los) 2 to dash (or rush) at the enemy; daher-gesprengt kommen to come galloping (or dashing) along. — 4. v/n. (h.) u. v/a. Flüssigkeiten 2 (in Tropfen verbreiten) to sprinkle; im Garten (metonymisch: den Garten) 2 to water the garden; in den Straßen (v/a. die Straßen) 2 to water the streets; Wasser auf et. 2 to sprinkle water on a th.; v/impers. es hat nur gesprengt (vom Regen) we have had only a sprinkling (or a few drops) of rain. — 5. = sprenkeln. — II ~ n ㉓ 6. s. Sprengung.

Sprenger (⌣⌣) m ㉒ 1. (s. sprengen) a) one who bursts open, &c.; b) sprinkler. — 2. Billard: e-n machen to spring a ball.

Spreng-fabrikat ⊕ (⌣...) n ㉒ explosive; =**gelatine** f explosive (or blasting) gelatine, gelatinized nitroglycerine; =**geschoß** ✕ n explosive projectile, Kugel: expl. ball or bullet; =**gräber** ✕ m, frt. miner; =**granate** ✕ f (highly) explosive shell; =**grube** f, frt. mine; =**kanne** f watering-can; =**karren** m water-cart; =**kessel** m, eccl. holy-water pot or stock; =**kohle** ⊕ f Glaserei: cracking-coal; =**kraft** f explosive force; =**kugel** ✕ f bomb, shell; =**ladung**

✕ f, artill. explosive charge; =**loch** ✕ n blast-hole; =**loch-bohrer** ✕ m punch; =**maschine** f = Höllenmaschine; =**mittel** n explosive (substance or compound); =**öl** n, chm., &c. nitroglycerine; =**patrone** ✕ f expl. cartridge; =**pinsel** m der Maurer zc.: sprinkling-brush; =**pulver** ⊕ n blasting-powder; =**rakete** ✕ f explosive rocket; =**regen** m fine sprinkling rain, drizzle.

Sprengsel (⌣⌣) m, n ㉓ = Sprenkel 1.

Spreng-stoff (⌣...) m ㉒ explosive (matter); =**strebe** ⊕ f, carp. strutbrace; =**stück** ✕ n, artill. (Granatsplitter) splinter of a shell; =**trichter** m rose to a watering-can.

Sprengung (⌣⌣) f ㊻ (s. sprengen 1) bursting open, &c.; explosion; (s. sprengen 2) dispersal; forcible dissolution or disruption; (s. sprengen 3) gallop(ing), riding at full speed; (s. sprengen 4) sprinkling.

Spreng-wage (=**steife**) ⊕ (⌣...) f Wagenbau: splinter-bar (stay); =**wagen** m = -karren, auch: sprinkling-machine; =**wedel** m: a) eccl. = Sprengel 1; b) ⊕ der Schmiede: sprinkle; =**werk** ⊕ n: a) carp. (ant. Hängewerk) strut-frame, im Dach: strutted roof; b) explosives, &c. (s. -mittel); =**werks-brücke** ⊕ f strut-framed bridge; =**wirkung** f effect of blasting, explosive effect; =**zünder** ✕ m blasting-fuse; =**zylinder** ✕ m = Blasemaschine.

Sprenkel (⌣⌣) [ndd.: springe: springen] m ㉒ 1. Vogelfang: springe, snare, gin. — 2. [s. sprenkeln] (Tüpfel) speck(le), spot. — 3. provc. = Heuschrecke.

sprenk(e)licht ✕, mst **sprenk(e)lig** (⌣(⌣)⌣) a. ㊅ speckled, spotted.

sprenkeln (⌣⌣) [ndd.: sprinkle] v/a. ㉔ a. to speckle, to spot, mit Farbe auch: to plash; (marmorieren) bsd. Buchbind.: to marble; gesprenkeltes Papier splashpaper; grau gesprenkeltes Zeug pepper-and-salt material; vgl. gesprenkelt.

Spreu (⌣) [ahd.: spray] f ㊻ 1. agr. chaff; die Spreu vom Weizen sondern to sift (or separate) the chaff from the wheat. — 2. fig. (Wertloses) rubbish, trash; (Ausschuß) waste, refuse.

spreu-artig (⌣...) a. ㊅ chaffy, ⚔ pale(ace)ous; =**blättchen** ⚔ n: palea. [chaffy, ⚔: ⚔ paleaceous.]

spreuig (⌣⌣) a. ㊅ filled with chaff;

Spreu-kissen (⌣...) n ㉒ chaff-cushion; =**regen** m sprinkling (or drizzling) rain, F drizzle; =**sack** m chaff-bag, straw-bed; 2**tragend** ⚔ a. ㊅: ⚔ paleaceous. [sprechen]

sprich (⌣) imper., 2(s)t pres. ind. von

Sprich-wort (⌣...) [mhd.] n ㉒ proverb, (old) adage or saw, (sprichwörtliche Redensart) proverbial saying, household word; wie es im ~ heißt as the old adage has it, as the saying is or goes; zum ~ werden to pass into a proverb (or common) by-word; Sprichwörter dramatisch aufführen to act proverbs or charades; =**wörter-lexikon** n dictionary of proverbs; 2**wörtlich** a. ㊅ proverbial, 2 werden to become proverbial.

Spriegel ⊕ (⌣⌣) [mhd.] m ㉒ (schmale Schiene) narrow lath (bent into an arc); (Holzspan) splinter; zum Beröhren e-r Wand: reed-work (of a wall); am Wagen: cart-tilt holder.

sprießen (⌣⌣) [mhd.] sprout] I v/n. (h. und s.) ㉘ d. von Pflanzen: to sprout (forth), to shoot (up); (hervorkommen) to come (or spring) up, (ausschlagen) to bud, (keimen) to germ(inate); (gedeihlich wachsen) to thrive (a. fig.). — II v/a. ㊿ = sprießen II.

Spriet ↓ (⌣) [ndl.] n ㉔c. = Bugspriet.

Spring[1] ↓ (⌣) m ㉔c.: ~ des Decks (Steigung von vorn nach hinten) sheer (or spring) of the deck.

Spring[2]-**anker** ↓ (⌣...) [spring-en] m ㉒ small anchor, kedge; =**auf** m (Spielzeug) = Stehauf; =**ball** m india-rubber ball; =**beine** n/pl. ent.: ㉒ saltatorial legs pl.; =**bock** m, zo. spring-boc or -bok or -buck (Antilope eu'chore); =**brett** n spring-(or jumping-)board; =**brunnen** m (flowing) fountain; =**deckel** m einer Uhr: spring-lid. [horse.]

Springel (⌣⌣) m ㉒ Turnerei: vaulting-

springen (⌣⌣) [ahd.: spring] I v/n. (h. u. s.), v/a. u. v/refl. ㉗ 1. (ant. gehen) to leap, mit e-m Satze: to jump, to bound, mit Schwung: to vault, hüpfend: to skip, to frisk; auf e-n los 2 to spring at a p.; in die Bresche 2 to throw o.s. into (or to fill) the breach; ins Wasser 2 to jump into the water, mit dem Kopfe zuerst: to dive (into the water), to (take a) plunge; über eine Barriere 2 to take a fence; über e-n Graben 2 to jump over (or to clear) a ditch; zu e-m hin 2 to run up to a p.; kam gesprungen he came jumping (or running) along; ✕ über die Klinge l. to put to the sword; eine Mine l. to spring (or explode) a mine (a.fig.); fig. das springt (von selbst) in die Augen that is obvious or self-evident; F er muß 2 (abdanken) he must resign his post, F he has to go. — 2. von Quellen: to gush, to flow; vom Springbrunnen: to play; die Fontäne 2 l. to let the fountain play, to turn on the water (-works). — 3. mit Angabe der Wirkung: et. entzwei 2 to break (or crack) a th. by jumping on it; sich müde 2 to tire o.s. with jumping. — 4. (sich begatten) to copulate, v. Hengsten: to cover the mare. — 5. (sich plötzlich öffnen) to (spring) open suddenly; (bersten) to burst (asunder); (spalten) to split (s. aufspringen I); mir will fast der Kopf 2 my head feels ready to burst, I have a splitting headache; gesprungenes Glas cracked glass. — II ~ n ㉓ 6. leaping, geb. Spr.: saltation. — III 2**b** p.pr. u. a. ㊅ 7. leaping, &c. (s. I); 2**de Flamme** oft: lambent flames pl.; her. salient, saltant, ⚔ saltatory.

Springer (⌣⌣) m ㉒ 1. ~, ~**in** f ㊵ leaper, (good) jumper, vaulter. — 2. Schachfigur: knight.

Springerei (⌣⌣⌣) f ㊻ continual springing or jumping or skipping.

Spring[2]-**faden** ⚔ (⌣...) m ㉒: ⚔ elater; =**feder** ⊕ f elastic spring; 2**federig**

[Springfedermatratze] — 909 — [Sprühauge]

a. ⊕ elastic; =feder=matratze *f* spring-mattress; =flut ↓ *f* (*ant.* Nippflut) spring-tide; =fuß *m. zo.*: ↻ saltatory foot; =gurke ♃ *f* squirting cucumber (*Ecba'llium Elate'rium*); =hahn *m* cock in a poultry-yard; =hase *m, zo.* jumping-hare (*Pede'tes caffer*); =hengst *m* stallion; =ins=feld *m* ⊙*c.* young harunscarum, giddy young fellow; (wildes Mädchen) romp, tomboy; =käfer *m, ent.* leaping-beetle, spring-beetle, ↻ elater; =kraft *f* elastic force, elasticity, springiness; 2kräftig *a.* elastic, springy; =kraut ♃ *n* touch-me-not (*Impa'tiens*); =kunst *f* art of leaping or vaulting; =laus *f, ent.* jumping louse (*Psylla*); =luke ↓ *f* (cap-)scuttle; =maus *f, zo.* jerboa (*Dipus Aegy'ptius*); =prozession *f* dancing procession; =quell(e *f*) *m* spring, fountain, well; source; =röhre *f* jet-pipe; =schloß ⊙ *n* spring-lock, snap; =seil *n* skipping-rope; =spiel *n* jumping, leaping; =stange *f*, =stock *m* leaping-pole; =stunde *f* Schulsprache: hour (intervening) between two lessons; =tau ↓ *n* spring(-rope); =übungen *f/pl.* jumping-(or leaping-, vaulting-)exercises *pl.*; =wasser *n* in Wasserkünsten: flowing (or jet of) water; =welle *f* big tidal wave; =zeit *f*: a) Pferdezucht: coupling-time; b) ↓ period of spring-tides.

Sprit ♃ (²ˇ) *m* ⊙*c.* = Spiritus.
spritig (²ˇ) *a.* ⊕ spirituous, alcoholic.
Sprit=arbeit (³ˇ...)[sprit=en]/⊙: a) firemen's work; b) ⊙ Buchbinder *ꝛc.*: marbled work; =bad *n* shower-bath, douche; =bewurf ⊙ *m* rough-cast, plastering; =brett *n* splash-board; =büchse *f* Kinderspielzeug: wooden syringe, squirt-gun. Spritze (²ˇ) [mhd.] *f* ⊕ 1. a) kleine (Hand-*ꝛc.*) ~ squirt, syringe (vgl. Klistierspritze); *med.* ~, um Arzneien unter die Haut zu spritzen hypodermic syringe; (Feuer-) ~ hose, fire-engine; die ~ arbeiten l. to play with the hose, to work the engine; b) F *fig. bei der* ~ (auf dem Posten) sein to be at (F to stick to) one's post. — 2. (angespritzter Fleck) splash. — 3. F = Spritzfahrt.
spritzen¹ (²ˇ) [mhd.: spirt] ⊕ I *v/n.* (sn) von einer Feuchtigkeit: to spirt, vom Schmutze: to splash, von Schreibfedern *ꝛc.* auch: to sp(l)utter, von einem Wasserstrahl: to play, *v.* Walfisch *ꝛc.*: to spout; das Blut spritzte ihm ins Gesicht the blood spirted into his face. — II *v/a. u. v/n.* (h.): eine Flüssigkeit ⊙ to squirt ...; (besprengen) to sprinkle, to spirt, mit Schmutz: to splash, mit der Feuerspritze: to play with the hose upon, mit einer Handspritze: to squirt, to syringe, mit der Klistierspritze: to use the enema (f. be=spritzen); Öl in das Ohr ⊙ to inject oil into the ear. — III ~ *n* ⊕ (f. I u. II) spirting, &c.; der Feuerspritze: play(ing); *bid. med.* injection.
Spritzen²=haus (²ˇ...) [Spritze] *n* ⊕ fire-engine house, fire-station; =korps *n* f.-brigade; =ladung *f* hoseful, syringeful; =leute *pl.* firemen *pl.*; =macher *m* maker of fire-engines; =mann *m* fireman; =meister *m*: a) inspector of fire-engines; b) head-fireman; =rohr *n*, =röhre *f* pipe (or tube) of a fire-engine; =schlauch *m* hose (of a fire-engine).

Spritzer (²ˇ) *m* ⊕ 1. squirter, person that syringes. — 2. splash (= Spritze 2).
Spritz=fahrt F (³...) *f* ⊕ pleasure-trip, little outing, short excursion, drive into the country; =flakon mit Wohlriechendem: scent-squirt; =flasche *f, chm.* washing-bottle; =fleck *m* splash; =kanne *f* watering-pot; =kuchen *m* fritter; =leder an einem Wagen: splash-leather, mud-protector; =loch *n* eines Walfisches: spout(-hole), breathing-hole or -tube, ↻ spiracle; =malerei *f* = =arbeit; =mittel *n* injection; =nudeln *f/pl.* Kochk.: vermicelli; =regen *m* fine drizzling rain; =röhre *f*: a) =loch; b) tube of a syringe; =tour F *f* = =fahrt; =wasser *n* spray; =wurf ⊙ *m* = =bewurf; =wurm *m, zo.*: ↻ sipunculoid.
spröde (¹ˇ) [nhd. 16. sae.] I *a.* ⊕ 1. ⊕ (leicht brechend) brittle, *metall.* &c. auch: fragile, short; (kaltbrüchig) cold-short. — 2. (unbiegsam) unyielding, inflexible; vom Haar: rough, von der Haut: dry and hard, parched; (aufgesprungen) chapped. — 3. *fig. von Personen:* (cold and) reserved, difficult to approach; shy, retiring, *bsd.* von Mädchen: coy, prim, prudish, demure; ⊙ tun to be prudish or coy, to affect shyness. — II ~ *f* 4. ⊕ (⁂⁂ Mädchen) prim (or prudish) lady, prude. — 5. ⊕ = Sprödigkeit.
Spröde=tun (²·¹) *n* ⊕ prudishness, prudery, affected primness.
Spröd=glas=erz (¹·²·²) *n* ⊕ min. brittle silver-glance or -ore.
Sprödheit (¹·), mst Sprödigkeit (¹·−) *f* ⊕ (f. spröde) zu 1 u. 2: brittleness; unyieldingness; zu 3 *fig.*: reserve; shyness; coyness, primness, prudishness.
Sproß¹ (²) [ahd.: sprout; *sproß² *m* ⊕*a.* 1. ♃ shoot, sprout(ing bud), sprig, ↻ turio(n). — 2. (Nachkomme) scion, descendant, offspring.
sproß² (²) *ind. impf. v.* sprießen.
Sprößchen (²ˇ) *n* ⊕ (*dim.* von Sproß) young (or tender, tiny) shoot, little sprig or sprout (vgl. Schößling).
Sprosse¹ (²ˇ) [ahd.: sprossen] *f* ⊕ 1. ♃ = Sproß 1. — 2. [: sprießen] ⊙ (Querholz e-r Leiter) rung, rundle (a. von e-r Wagenleiter); ~ einer Treppenleiter: step.
Sprosse² (²ˇ) *m* ⊕ = Sproß¹.
sprosse (²ˇ) *subj. impf. v.* sprießen.
sproßte (²ˇ) *pl. ind. impf. v.* sprießen.
sprossen² (²ˇ) [nhd.: sprout] *v/n.* (h. u. sn) u. *v/a.* ⊕ = sprießen.
Sprossen³=bier (²ˇ...) [Sprosse] *n* ⊕ spruce-beer; =kohl ♃ *m* broccoli, (Rosenkohl) Brussels sprouts *pl.*; =tau *n* Tuchnerei: (knotted) climbing-rope; =tragend, =treibend ♃ *a.* ⊕: bearing buds, ↻ gemmiferous, proliferous.
Sprosser (²ˇ) *m* ⊕ *orn.* bastard nightingale (*Sy'lvia philome'la*).
Sprößling (²ˇ) *m* ⊙*d.* = Sproß.
Sproß=pilze ♃ (²·²ˇ) *m/pl.* ⊕ (*ant.* Spaltpilze) ↻ gemmiparous fungi.
Sprott (²) [ndd.] *m* ⊙*c.*, mst ~e (²ˇ) *f* ⊕ *ichth.* sprat (*Clu'pea sprattus*); (Kieler) ~en smoked (Kiel) sprats *pl.*

Sprotten=fang (²ˇ·²) *m* ⊕ sprat-catching; ein guter ~ a great haul of sprats.
Spruch (²ˇ) [mhd.: sprechen] *m* ⊙*c.* 1. (Urteil) sentence, judgment, der Geschworenen: verdict, finding, eines Orakels: (oracular) response; (Entscheidung) decision, des Richters: pronouncing the sentence; schiedsrichterlicher ~ (arbitrator's) award; e-n ~ fällen, tun to pronounce a sentence, to give a verdict; to make an award. — 2.(Ausspruch)pithy saying,short maxim, motto, aphorism; (Lehr-)~: ↻ apophthegm, dictum; ~ aus der Bibel passage of the Bible, scriptural quotation, scripture-text; Sprüche Salomonis Proverbs *pl.* (of Solomon).
spruch=artig (²ˇ...) *a.* ⊕ gnomic, aphoristic(ally expressed); =band *n* ⊕ (Inschriftenband auf Gemälden *ꝛc.*) banderol, *arch.* scroll; =behörde *f* court of arbitration; =buch *n* = =sammlung; =dichter *m* sentientious (or gnomic) poet; =dichtung *f* gnomic poetry.
Sprüchelchen (²ˇ...) *n* ⊕ = Sprüchlein.
spruch=fertig (²ˇ...) *a.* ⊕ = 2reif; =gedicht *n* ⊕ sentientious (or gnomic) poem.
spruchhaft (²ˇ...) *a.* sentientious.
Spruch=kollegium (²ˇ...·²(ˇ)·²) *n* ⊕ judges *pl.* in court delivering judgment.
Sprüchlein (²ˇ·) [Spruch, *dim.*] *n* ⊕ short motto or saying.
spruch=reich (²ˇ...) *a.* ⊕ sentientious, gnomic; 2reif *a.* ripe (or mature) for judgment; =reim *m* rhymed saying; =sammlung *f* collection of gnomes; 2weise *adv.* in the form of a pithy saying; sententiously, aphoristically; =weisheit *f* gnomic wisdom.
Spruch=wort (²ˇ...) *ꝛc.* I. Sprichwort *ꝛc.*
Sprudel (¹ˇ) [18. sae.: sprudeln] *m* ⊕: a) (das Sprudeln) bubbling, gush(ing); b) (sprudelnde Quelle) bubbling spring; Karlsbader ~ hot springs *pl.* (of or at) Karlsbad; c) *fig.* ~ von Worten (von Humor) overflow (or rich flow) of words (of humour).
Sprudel=bad (¹ˇ·²) *n* ⊕ shower-bath.
Sprud(e)ler (¹(ˇ)·) *m* ⊕, ~in *f* ⊕ voluble (or fast) talker, sp(l)utterer.
Sprudel=kopf (¹ˇ·²) *m* ⊕ impetuous (or blustering) person, hotspur.
sprudeln (¹ˇ) [obb.] ⊕ *a.* I *v/n.* 1. (sn) to bubble (or gush, flow) forth. — 2. (h.): a) von quellendem Wasser: to bubble, gush, flow; von Getränken: to effervesce; (plätschern) to (s)plash, von rinnendem Wasser *a.*: to murmur; der ⊙ Bach the purling brook; b) *fig. der Witz* sprudelt von f-n Lippen (oder als *v/a.* seine Lippen ⊙ Witze) he is bubbling over (or overflowing) with wit; in ⊙der Laune brimming over with good humour; c) (haftig reden) to sp(l)utter, to speak with great volubility or vehemence. — II *v/a.* 3. fattitiv zu I, z.B. Beleidigungen ⊙ to sputter forth insults. — III ~ *n* ⊕ 4. bubbling, &c. (f. I); *fig.* ~ des Geistes exuberance of spirits, overflow of wit.
Sprudel=quell(e *f*) (¹ˇ...) ⊕ = Sprudel b; =stein *m, min.* thermal tuff.
Sprüh=auge (²ˇ·²) *n* ⊕ bright (or sparkling) eye.

♪ Musik; ↻ Wissenschaft; ♃ Pflanze; ♁ Geographie; ⊙ Technik; ⚒ Bergbau; ⚔ Militär; ↓ Marine; ⊕ Handel; ⚘ Post; 🚂 Eisenbahn.

[sprühen] — 910 — [st.]

sprühen (*L*) [nhd.: spray: Spreu] *v/n.* (fn u. h.) und *v/a.* ⊕ **1. a)** to fly forth (with vehemence), zischend: to fizzle; vom Regen: to drizzle, von Funken auch: to scintillate; als *v/a.* to send forth, to shower; to emit (sparks, &c.), to sprinkle (drops of water, &c.); Feuer 2, auch: to spit fire; **b)** *fig.* to sparkle, to scintillate, to flash (fire); j-e Augen 2 Geist his eyes sparkle (or shine, flash) with intellect; 2der Witz brilliant wit. — **2.** *v/impers.* es sprüht it's drizzling, there is a sprinkling (or there are a few drops) of rain.

Sprüh=feuer (*"...*) *n* ⊕ bright(ly burning) fire; **=funken** *m/pl.* flying sparks *pl.*; **=regen** *m* drizzling (or sprinkling) rain, F drizzle, Scotch mist, ↓ (shower of) spray.

Sprung (*"*) [ahd.: *springen] *m* ⊕b. **1.** leap; (Satz, Aufsprung) jump, bound, auf das Pferd ꝛc. a. vault(ing); (Luft=)~caper, gambol(ling); (Abprall) rebound, ⚔ e-s Geschoßes ꝛc.: ricochet; im ~e (in) leaping or jumping; mit einem ~e at a bound; es ist nur ein ~ bis dahin it is only a stone's throw (or a few yards) from here; e-n ~ nach Hause m. to run home. — **2.** meist *fig.* Sprünge m. to jump, to frisk, *fig.* to be unruly or extravagant; keine großen Sprünge m. können to be unable to launch out; auf dem Sprunge sein od. stehen to be on the point of leaving or departure; wieder auf seine alten Sprünge (Gewohnheiten) kommen to return to (or fall into) one's old habits or ways; auf (oder hinter) j-s Sprünge (Schliche) kommen to find out a p.'s pranks; e-m auf die Sprünge helfen (fortbelfen) to put a p. in the right way; bisw.: to assist one's memory. — **3.** [springen 5] = Spalt 1.

Sprung=bein (*"...*) *n* ⊕ *anat.* anklebone, ⚔ astragalus, talus; **=bock** *m* Schafzucht: ram; **=brett** *n* diving plank; **=feder** *f* (scroll=)spring; **=feder=matratze** *f* spring-mattress; 2fertig *a.* ⊕ ready to spring; **=fischerei** *f* bait-fishing; **=gelenk** *n, anat.* ankle-joint.

sprunghaft (*"*) *a.* ⊕ *fig.* desultory; *adv.* by leaps and bounds.

Sprung=käfer (*"...*) *m* = Springkäfer; **=rahmen** *m* an e-r Bettstelle: frame of a spring-mattress; **=riemen** *m*: a) unten an der Hose: strap for keeping the trousers in position; b) = **=zügel**; **=schlag** *m* Tennis: half-volley; **=stoß** *m* Fußball: dropkick; e-n ~ m. to drop; **=tuch** *n* Feuerwehr: cloth used as life-saving apparatus; 2weise *adv.* (F a. a.) by leaps (and bounds), (unregelmäßig) by fits and starts; **=weite** *f* length of a leap, distance (to be) covered by a leap; **=zügel** *m, man.*, ⊕ Sattlerei: martingale.

Spucke P (*"...*) *f* ⊕ (Speichel) spittle, saliva; Sprichwort f. Geduld am Schluß.

spucken P (*"...*) [nhd.] *f* ⊕ (Speichel) spittle, und *v/a.* ⊕ to spit (a. v. Katzen), to expectorate; P *fig.* e-m auf den Kopf (ober Zopf) 2 to lead a p. a nice dance.

Spuck=kasten P (*"...*) *m* ⊕ = **=napf**; **=locken** F *f/pl.* P spit-curls, cowlicks *pl.*; **=napf** *m* spittoon.

Spuk (*L.* südd. *"*) [ndb.] *m* ⊕c. **1.** ghostly apparition or visitation, F auch: ℉ spook; (Gespenst) spectre, phantom, ghost; (Schreckbild) bogyman, bugbear; (toller Lärm) unearthly noise, hubbub, uproar, F deuce of a row. — **2.** *fig.* es ist ~ (et. Übernatürliches, Außergewöhnliches) dabei there is s.th. out of the common (or s.th. wrong) about it. — **3.** (dumme, fatale Geschichte) troublesome affair, bother.

spuken (*L*) [f. Spuk] *v/n.*(h.) ⊕ **1.** von Gespenstern: to walk, to appear, to haunt a place; *fig.* die Idee spukt noch immer bei ihm ... is still haunting (or pursuing) him. — **2.** *v/impers.* es spukt in dem Hause the house is haunted; *fig.* es spukt bei ihm im Oberstübchen oder in seinem Kopfe he is not right in his upper story, he is wrong in his head or F nut. — **3.** (lärmend) sein Wesen treiben) to make an unearthly noise, F to kick up an infernal row.

Spuk=geist (*"...*) *m* ⊕ (hob)goblin; spectre haunting a place; **=geschichte** *f* ghost-story.

spukhaft (*L*) *a.* ⊕ = gespenstisch.

Spul=back ⊕ (*"...*), **=bank** *f* ⊕ chest for bobbins, cuttee; **=draht** *m* spool-wire.

Spule (*L*) [ahd.: spool] *f* ⊕ **1.** (Gänsekiel) quill. — **2.** ⊕ ~ e-s Spinnrades: spool, bobbin; *elect.* coil, bobbin.

spulen ⊕ (*L*) *v/a.* ⊕: Garn, Seide 2 to wind on a spool or bobbin, to reel; (ab=)2 to unwind; (spinnen) to spin.

spülen (*L*) [ahd.] ⊕ I *v/n.* (h.) u. *v/a.*: a) *v/n.* (mit leichtem Wellenschlag netzen) gegen eine Mauer 2 to wash against a wall; b) *v/a.* die Wogen 2 das Ufer hohl ... hollow out (or undermine) the bank. — II *v/a.* mit persönlichem Subjekt: a) Geschirr 2 (reinigen) to wash crockery; Gläser 2 to rinse glasses; sich den Mund 2 to rinse one's mouth (out); b) ⊕ to wash, to cleanse (wool).

Spuler ⊕ (*L*) *m* ⊕ **1.** (auch ~**=in** *f* ⊕) Weberei: spooler, winder, reeler; (Ab=) ~ unwinder. — **2.** an der Nähmaschine: bobbin-holder, shuttle-winder.

Spüler (*L*) *m* ⊕, ~**=in** *f* ⊕ washer-up.

Spül=faß (*"...*) *n* ⊕ tub for rinsing, rinsing-tub, in der Küche: wash-up, pan for washing-up.

spul=förmig (*"...*) *a.* ⊕ bobbin-shaped.

Spül=frau (*"...*) *f* ⊕ washer (of dishes and plates), auch: scullery-maid; **=gefäß** *n* vessel for rinsing; vgl. **=faß**.

Spülicht (*L*) [nhd.] *n* ⊕d. dish-water or -wash, rinsings *pl.*; als Schweinefutter: hog-wash, swillings *pl.*

Spül=kammer (*"...*) *f* ⊕ für das Geschirr: scullery; **=lappen** *m* dish-cloth.

Spül=mädchen (*"...*) *n* ⊕ Spülerin.

Spül=magd (*"...*) *f* ⊕ = Spülfrau.

Spul=maschine ⊕ (*"...*) *f* ⊕ bobbin(-frame), spooling- (or reeling-)machine; zum Feinspinnen: jack-frame.

Spül=maschine (*"...*) *f* ⊕ rinsing-machine; **=napf** *m* Küche: slop-basin.

Spul=rad (*"...*) *n* ⊕ spooling-wheel; **=rädchen** *n* silk-reel; **=rohr** *n* bobbinreed.

Spül=stein (*"...*) *m* ⊕ sink; **=wasser** *n* water for washing up or rinsing; (Spülicht) dish-water, F slops *pl.*

Spul=wurm (*"...*) *m* ⊕ *zo.* maw-worm, ⚔ ascaris; **=würmer** *pl.*: ⚔ ascaridæ *pl.*

Spund (*"*) [mhd.; ndl.; *lt. puncta] *m (n)* ⊕c. ~**=zapfen** e-s Fasses: bung, bung-hole (= Spundloch); ⊕ (Zapfen) tap, faucet; (Pfropfen) plug, stopper.

Spund=austreiber ⊕ (*"...*) *m* ⊕ (Schlegel) bung-starter; **=bohrer** *m* tap-borer.

spunden, spünden (*L*) *v/a.* ⊕ **1.** ein Faß 2 to bung. — **2.** ⊕ *carp.* Bretter in ea. 2 (durch e-n Falz verbinden) to join ... by means of grooves.

Spünder (*L*) *m* ⊕ (f. spunden 1) man who bungs the casks; cellarman.

Spund=geld (*"...*) *n* ⊕ duty on (every cask of) alcoholic liquor; **=loch** *n* bung-hole; **=wand** *f* ⊕ Wasserbau: sheet-piling, pile-planking; **=zapfen** *m* f. Spund; **=zieher** *m* bung-pick or -drawer.

Spur (*L*) [ahd.: spüren] *f* ⊕ **1.** (zurückgelassener Eindruck) trace, trail, *hunt.*: scent, track, e-s Fußes: footprint, mark; e-s Schiffes: wake; (Gepräge) imprint, (Merkmal) mark; (Überbleibsel) remains *pl.*; einer Sache auf die ~ kommen to get a clue of a th., to trace a th.; j-s ~ folgen to tread in a p.'s footsteps. — **2.** *hunt.* trail, scent; die ~ des Wildes verfolgen to scent (or track) the game; von der ~ abbringen (abkommen) to throw (to get) off the scent or track. — **3.** mst negativ: keine ~ von et. not a trace (or sign, vestige) of a th; F keine ~ (nein) not a bit, not at all, no. — **4.** (Geleise) rut of a wheel, 🚂 permanent way, line.

Spur=breite (*"...*) *f* ⊕ = Spurweite.

spuren (*L*) *v/n.* (h.) ⊕ v. Wagen: to keep to (or to follow) the rut.

spüren (*L*) [ahd.: Spur] ⊕ I *v/n.* (h.), bisw. *v/a.* u. *v/refl. hunt.* u. *fig.* to scent, trace, track; to follow the track of; *fig.* nach e-m, et. 2 to go in quest (or to be on the track) of a p., a th. — II *v/a.* (empfinden) to feel; (wahrnehmen) to perceive, notice; ich kann nichts davon 2 I cannot discover (anything of) it.

Spürer (*L*) *m* ⊕ = Spürhund; ~**=ei** (*-L*) *f* ⊕ prying, der Polizei: espionage.

Spür=hund (*"...*) *m* ⊕: a) bloodhound, seltener: lime-hound, tufter; b) *fig.* prying fellow spy.

...spurig (*..."L*) [f. Spur] *a.* ⊕ in Zssgn, zB.: schmal2 narrow-gauge (railway).

Spür=kraft (*"...*) *f* ⊕ = Spürsinn.

spur=los (*"...*) *a.* ⊕ (n 10) trackless, without (leaving) a trace; *adv.* 2 verschwinden to vanish without leaving a trace (behind).

Spür=nase (*"...*) *f* ⊕ nose with a fine scent, F good (or fine) nose.

Spurre (*L*) *f* ⊕ umbelliferous jagged chickweed (*Holosteum umbella'tum*).

Spür=sinn (*"...*) *m* ⊕ sagacity.

Spur=weite 🚂 (*"...*) *f* ⊕ gauge.

sputen (*L*) [ndb.: speed] *v/refl.* ⊕ sich 2 (eilen) to make haste, to be quick; spute dich!, a. F look sharp!

Sputum ⚔ (*L*) [lt.] *n* ⊕ (Auswurf) expectoration.

sputzen ⚔ (*L*) *v/n.* (h.) ⊕ bsb. *bibl.* = speien.

Sr. *abbr.* = Seiner.

st (*"*) *int.* 'sh! hush!, seltener: (w)hist!

st. *abbr.* = statt.

Signs (see page XVII): F familiar; P vulgar; ℉ flash; ⚔ rare; † obsolete (died); * new word (born); ✱ incorrect; ♂ music.

[St] — 911 — [Stachel]

St abbr.=(fr.)Saint(heilig), z.B. St.-Denis. **St.** abbr. für: a) = Sankt, z.B. St. Peter (Petrus) Saint Peter; (Peterskirche) Saint Peter's (Church); b) = Stunde.

Staat (¹) [uhd.; *lt. status Stand] m ⓂC. 1. (politischer Körper) state; von ~s wegen for reasons of state; ♀ die Vereinigten ~en von Nordamerika the United States; vgl. Generalstaaten. — 2. (äußerer Aufwand) state, pomp; (Prunk) show, parade, (Pracht) splendour, (Putz) finery, F toggery, rig-out; im vollen ~ in full dress, F in full fig; großen ~ machen to make a (grand) display, to live in great (or fine) style; mit et. ~ machen to parade (F to show off) a th.; damit läßt sich nicht viel ~ machen there is not much to boast of (in that), F that's a poor show. **Staaten-beschreibung** (ᴵᴵ...) f ⓂⒸ political geography; **=bildung** f formation of states; **=bund** m confederacy (of states); **=geschichte** f history of states, political history; **=kunde** f political knowledge or science, politics; **=system** n political system.

staatlich (ᴵ ͜ᵛ) a. Ⓜ of (or belonging to, concerning) the state or the government, political, public; Ⓛ(adv.) unterstützte Industrie, Dampferlinie state-assisted (or subsidized) industry, steamer-line; ⓁⒺer-seits (ᴵᴵ ͜ᵛᴵ) adv. on the part of the state.

Staats-abgaben (ᴵᴵ...) f/pl. Ⓜ government taxes pl.; **=aktion** f state-proceedings pl.; **=amt** n public office, eines Beamten: civil-service appointment; **=angehörige(r)** s. subject (or citizen) of a state; **=angehörigkeit** f nationality; **=angelegenheit** f public matter, state-affair; **=anleihe** f gov.-loan; **=anwalt** m public prosecutor, solicitor for the crown; vgl. Kronanwalt; **=anwaltschaft** f public prosecutor's office; **=anzeiger** m official gazette or advertiser; **=archiv** n public archives or records pl.; **=ausgaben** f/pl. public expenditure; **=bahn** f state railway; **=bankrott** m national bankruptcy; **=beamte(r)** m civil-servant, state-official; officer of state; **=behörde** f public authorities pl.: government; **=bürger(in** f) m subject (or citizen) of state; Ⓛe**=bürgerlich** a. Ⓜ political; Ⓛe Rechte, auch: civic rights pl.; **=bürger-recht** n citizenship, franchise; **=degen** m dress-sword; **=diener** m civil-servant (s. a. Beamter); **=dienst** m civil-service, public service; im ~e, auch: in the service of the state; **=domänen** f/pl. public domains, crown-lands pl.; **=einkünfte** f/pl. public revenue sg.; **=eisenbahn** f = **=bahn**; **=gebäude** n: a) public building; b) political structure or edifice; c) splendid building; Ⓛe**gefährlich** a. dangerous (or pernicious) to the state; **=gefangene(r)** m state-prisoner; **=gefängnis** n state-prison; **=geheimnis** n state-secret; **=geschäft** n state-affair, government business; die ~e führen to carry on the government; **=gesetz** n law of the country or land; **=gewalt** f supreme power (of the state);

=grundgesetz n political constitution; **=gut** n public property; **=hämorrhoidarius** m old broken-down (or worn-out) official; **=haushalt** m administration of revenue; **=haushalts-etat**, **=haushalt-voranschlag** m budget, estimates of the public expenditure and revenue; **=hoheit** f sovereignty; **=kalender** m state- (or court-) calendar; **=kanzlei** f (**=kanzler** m) chancery (chancellor) of the state; **=kasse** f public exchequer, treasury; **=katholik** m Roman Catholic who recognizes the laws of the state; **=kirche** f established church; die englische ~ the Church of England; **=kleid** n robe of state, gala-dress; Ⓛe**klug** a. politic(al); **=klugheit** f political wisdom, statecraft; **=körper** m body politic, polity; **=kosten** pl.: auf ~ at public expense; **=kredit** m public credit; **=krippe** f, co. government post, state employment; **=kunde**, **=kunst** f political science or knowledge; statesmanship; **=kutsche** f state-coach; **=lehre** f = **=kunde**; **=mann** m statesman; Ⓛe**männisch** a. statesmanlike; **=maschine** f state-machinery, wheels of government; **=minister** m minister of state; a. = **=sekretär**; **=ministerium** n ministry (of a country); **=oberhaupt** n head of the state; sovereign, monarch; **=ökonomie** f political economy; **=ordnung** f political system; bsd. ehm: **=pächter** m farmer of taxes; **=papiere** n/pl. government-stock, public funds pl.; konsolidierte ~ consols pl.; **=prozeß** m state-trial; **=rat** m: a) coll. council of state, in Engl.: Privy Council; b) (Person) councillor of state, in Engl.: Privy Councillor; **=rätin** f wife of a councillor of state; **=recht** n political (or constitutional) law; Ⓛe**rechtlich** a. founded on (or relating to) constitutional law; **=regierung** f government (of the state), state administration; **=ruder** n, fig. helm of the state; **=säckel** m public purse; **=schatz** m public (e-s Reiches a. imperial) exchequer; **=schiff** n ship of state; das ~ lenken to be at the helm of the state; **=schriften** f/pl. state-papers pl.; **=schuld** f national (or public) debt, Ⓜ fundierte: consols pl.; **=schulden-tilgungs-kasse** f sinking-fund; **=schuld-schein** Ⓜ m treasury-bond; **=sekretär** m (in Engl.: verantwortlicher Minister, der staatliche Papiere unterzeichnet) secretary of state; **=sozialismus** m state-socialism; **=steuer** f government tax; **=streich** m [(fr.)] coup d'état; **=umwälzung** f political upheaval, revolution; **= und Reichs-angehörigkeit** f, etwa: imperial citizenship; **=unterhändler** m political agent, diplomatist; **=verbrechen** n (**=verbrecher** m) political crime (offender); **=verfassung** f political constitution; **=verrat** 2c. = Hochverrat 2c.; **=verwaltung** f administration of the state; (Regierung) government; **=wesen** n political organism, state, commonwealth; Ⓛe**widrig** a. subversive of (or hostile to) the state; **=wirren** f/pl. political disturbances

pl.; **=wirt** m pol. economist; **=wirtschaft** f pol. economy; **=wissenschaft(en** pl.) f pol. science; Ⓛe**wissenschaftlich** a. of (or relating to) pol. science; **=wohl** n public weal; **=zimmer** n state apartment; **=zuschuß** m government grant; durch =zuschüsse unterstützt state-aided, Ⓜ subsidized, bounty-fed.

Stab (¹, a.ᵛ) [ahd.: staff, stave] m ⓂC., 6. 1. staff, stick, rod, e-s Gitters: bar, e-s Schirmes: rib, im Vogelbauer: perch, des Taschenspielers: conjuror's (magic) wand; fig. seinen ~ weiter setzen to continue (or proceed on) one's journey; fig. s. brechen 1; mehr zum ~ Wehe als zum ~ Sanft greifen to prefer the rod to soft words, to apply rough measures rather than gentle means. — 2. Ⓖ 6. ehm. (1868—84) (Meter) metre. — 3. ⊕ metall. bar (of iron, &c.); (Blatt) sheet; (Stiel, Griff) handle; arch. (Leiste) fillet, ledge; (Rundstab, Ring um eine Säule) astragal, Ⓔ Böttcherei = Daube. — 4. ⚔ a) staff, staff-officers pl.; b) beim ~e († etatsmäßig) on the staff, von Soldaten 2c.: on the strength.

Stab-alge ♀ (ᴵᴵ ͜ᵛ) f ⌇ bacillaria. **Stäbchen** (ᴵ ͜ᵛ) n Ⓜ (dim. v. Stab) small staff or bar or wand; rod; **~bakteri-e** f Ⓜ: ⌇ rod-bacterium; Ⓛe**förmig** a. Ⓜ rod-shaped, ⌇ bacillary, bacilliform. **Stab-einguß** ⊕ (ᴵᴵ...) m Ⓜ ingot-mould; **=eisen** ⊕ n bar-iron, iron in bars. **Stäbel-erbsen** (ᴵ ͜ᵛ ͜ᵛ) f/pl. Ⓜ hort. peas pl. which climb on sticks. **stäbeln** (ᴵ ͜ᵛ) [Stab] V/a. Ⓜa. hort. to prop flowers, &c. with sticks, to train peas, beans, &c. on sticks. **stab-förmig** (ᴵᴵ...) a. Ⓜ staff-like, ⌇ rhabdoidal, bacilliform; Ⓛe**gereimt** a. pros. alliterat(iv)e, alliteral; **=gold** n Ⓜ gold in bars; **=halter** m mace-bearer, bsd. in Kirchen: verger; **=hammer** ⊕ m, metall. tilt(-hammer); **=hobel** ⊕ m, carp. rabbet-plane; **=holz** ⊕ n = Daubenholz.
...**stäbig** (...ᴵ ͜ᵛ) [Stab] a. Ⓜ in Zssgn, z.B. sieben-Ⓛe with seven bars.

stabil (ᵛᴵ) [lt.] a. Ⓜ bsd. mech. (feststehend) stable; **Stabilität** (ᵛ ͜ᵛᴵ) f Ⓜ stability. **Stab-körper** (ᴵᴵ...) m Ⓜ anat.: ⌇ bacillus; **=rechen-kunst** f: ⌇ rhabdology; **=reim** m. pros. alliteration.

Stabs-arzt ⚔ (ᴵᴵ ͜ᵛ) m Ⓜ surgeon-major. [tridium.] **Stab-schimmel** ♀ (ᴵᴵ ͜ᵛ) m Ⓜ: ⌇ bac-] **Stabs-offizier** (ᴵᴵ...) m Ⓜ staff- (or flag-) officer; **=quartier** n head-quarters pl.; **=schule** f staff-college; **=trompeter** m trumpet-major; **=veterinär*** m (= Oberroßarzt) Veterinary Surgeon-Major.

Stab-tierchen (ᴵᴵ...) n Ⓜ: ⌇ bacillus; **=träger** m =halter; **=wahrsagerei** f ⌇ rhabdomancy; Ⓛe**weise** † ⊕ adv.: Ⓛ verkaufen ... by the metre; **=wurz(-beifuß** m, **=männchen** n) f ♀ = Eberraute.

staccato ♪ (ᵛᴵ ͜ᵛ) [it. kurz abgestoßen] n, inv. u. adv. staccato; **~zeichen** n staccato-mark (• oder ı). [stechen.] **stach** (ᴵᶜʰ) ind. **stäche** (ᴵ ͜ᵛ) subj. impf. v.]
Stachel (ᴵᶜʰ ͜ᵛ) [ahd.: stechen, stichelen] m Ⓜ 1. (stechende Spitze) sting (auch v. Bienen, Skorpionen 2c.), sharp point, spike, von Pflanzen: prick(le), thorn, ⌇ acantha,

---

⌇ scientific; ♀ botanical; Ⓖ geography; ⊕ machinery; ⚒ mining; ⚔ military; ⚓ marine; Ⓜ commercial; ✉ postal; 🚂 railway.

[Stachelaloe] — 912 — [Stahl]

aculeus; ~ des Stachelschweins: quill, e-r Schnalle: tongue. e-s Sporns: prong; *anat.* (Grat) u. ?: spine. — 2. ~ zum Antreiben der Ochsen: goad; *fig.* (et. Anreizendes) stimulus, incentive, f. lecken³.

Stachel=aloe ?(⌂…) f ⊕ hedgehog-aloe (*A'loë echina'ta*); =**beere** f gooseberry; =**beer-spanner** m, *ent.* magpie-moth (*Abra'xas grossularia'ta*); =**beer-strauch** m gooseberry-bush (*Ribes grossula'ria*); =**beer-wein** m gooseberry-wine; =**bein** n, ?**beinig** a. ⊕ *zo.*: ⌂ acanthopod; =**draht** m barbed wire; =**draht-zaun** m barbed-wire fence (*auch* ⚔); =**flosse** f, *zo.*: ⌂ acantha; =**flosser** m, *ichth.* spiny-finned fish, ⌂ acanthoptere; ?**flossig** a. *ichth.* spiny-finned, ⌂ acanthopterygious, =**acanthodean; ?flügelig** a. *zo.*: ⌂ acanthopterous; ?**förmig** a. prick(le)-shaped, like a spike, ⌂ aculeiform; ?**früchtig** ? a. acanthocarpus; =**gewächs** n prickly plant; =**hals-band** n für Jagdhunde: prickly (or spiked) collar; =**häuter** m/pl. *zo.*: ⌂ echinodermata *pl.*; ?=**häutig** a.: ⌂ echinoderm*al*, …atous.
stach(e)licht ⚔, *mst* **stach(e)lig** (⌂⌂)(⌂) a. ⊕ 1. prickly, prickled, thorny; *zo.*, &c. spiny, spinous; (borstig) bristly; ⌂ acanthoid, …(ace)ous, aculeate(d), aculeous, ? *auch:* acanaceous. — 2. *fig.* stinging, poignant, caustic, sarcastic, biting, sharp.
stach(e)lig-gezähnt ? (⌂⌂(⌂)⌂⌂) a. ⊕: ⌂ spinoso-dentate.
Stachel-kraut ? (⌂⌂…) n ⊕ = Hauhechel; ?**los** a. ⊕ stingless, without prick(le)s; =**mohn** ? m prickly poppy, argemone (*Argemo'ne*).
stacheln (⌂⌂) v/a. ⊕a. 1. to provide with stings or pricks or sharp points, to spike. — 2. to sting, prick, prod; *fig.* (antreiben) to stimulate, rouse, urge (on), stärker: to goad, to egg on.
Stachel-rede (⌂⌂…) f ⊕ poignant or caustic, satirical speech; =**reden** *pl.* stinging (or sharp) words *pl.*; =**roche** m, *ichth.* thornback (*Raia clava'ta*); ?**rüsselig** a. ⊕: ⌂ acanthocephalous; =**same** ? m: ⌂ acanthospermum; =**schnecke** f, *zo.*: ⌂ murex; =**schwanz** m, *zo.* prickly tail; =**schwein** n, *zo.* porcupine (*Hystrix crista'ta*); =**stock** m prod; =**tierchen** n/pl. *zo.*: ⌂ acantharia; ?**tragend** a.: ⌂ acanthophorous; =**träger** m/pl. *zo.*: ⌂ aculeata.
stachlicht, …**ig** (⌂⌂) f. stach(e)licht, …ig.
Stadel obb. (⌂) [ahd.: stadile; *stehen] m ⊕(19) = Scheune, Schuppen, Stall.
Staden schwz. (⌂) [ahd.: staith; *stehen] m ⊕ (Ufer) bank, waterside.
Stadium (⌂(⌂)) [it., *grch.] n ⊕ 1. ~ (Stadion) Alt.: (Bahn zum Wettlauf) stadium, course. — 2. (Abschnitt in der Entwickelung) stage (a. *path.*); phase.
Stadt (⌂) [mhd. Stätte] f ⊕ (pl. ⌂, ⌂) (*ant.* Land 3) town; große ~ (a. ~ mit Kathedrale) city; die Heilige ~ (Jerusalem) the Holy City; in der ~ in the (in London: in) town; in der ~ erzogen town-bred; in die ~ geh(e)n to go into the (nach London: to) town; in unserer ~ within our walls; die ganze ~ weiß es the whole (or all the) town knows it.

Stadt-adel (⌂…) m ⊕ patrician stock, patricians *pl.*; =**amt** n: a) municipal office; b) das ~ the townhall; ?**artig** a. ⊕ town-like, urban; *auch:* townish; =**arzt** m physician of the town; =**bahn** f railway in a town, in London: metropolitan (or district-, circle-)railway; =**bann** m area of a town, township; =**bau-meister** m, *etwa:* architect appointed to supervise the construction of (public) buildings in the town, *auch:* town surveyor; =**behörde** f municipal authorities *pl.*, corporation; ?**bekannt** a. known all over the town; die Geschichte ist ~ … has made the round (or has been the talk) of the town; =**bewohner(in** f) m = Städter (=in); =**bezirk** m ward, urban district; =**bier** n beer brewed in the town; =**brief** m local letter; =**bürger** m burgher, der Londoner City ⚔c. *auch:* freeman; weitS. = Städter; =**bürger-recht** n municipal franchise, freedom of a city.
Städtchen (⌂⌂, ⚔ ⌂⌂) n ⊕ (*dim. v.* Stadt) small town(ship), mit Märkten: market-town; Sprichw. anders ~, anders Mädchen another sweetheart in every town.
Städte-bezwinger (⌂⌂…, ⚔ ⌂⌂…) m ⊕ vanquisher of cities; =**ordnung** f laws *pl.* regulating municipal government, in Engl.: Municipal Corporation Act.
Städter (⌂⌂, ⚔ ⌂⌂) [mhd., *Stadt] m ⊕, ~**in** f ⊕ towns(wo)man, inhabitant (or burgess) of a town, *pl. a.*: townsfolk, townspeople.
Städte-tag (⌂⌂…, ⚔ ⌂⌂…) m ⊕ meeting of delegates of cities or towns; =**wesen** n municipal concerns or affairs *pl.*
Stadt-gebiet (⌂…) n ⊕ township; =**gegend** f quarter of a town; =**gemeinde** f urban community; township, municipality (f. a. Gemeinde); =**gerechtigkeit** f municipal privileges *pl.*, ehm.: charter; =**gerede** n = Gespräch; =**gericht** n (*ant.* Landgericht) city-court; =**gespräch** n town-talk; zum ~ werden to become the talk of the town; =**graben** m town-moat; =**gut** n town-property; =**haus** n: a) (*ant.* Landhaus) town-house; b) = Rathaus.
städtisch (⌂⌂, ⚔ ⌂⌂) a. ⊕ of (or relating to) a town; (*ant.* ländlich) urban (population, &c.), town-like; ~e Kapelle town-band; ~es Leben, Wesen ⚔c. Stadt-leben, =**wesen** ⚔c. ~e Mode town-fashion; ~e Verwaltung municipal government.
Stadt-kämmerer (⌂…) m ⊕ treasurer of a town, der Londoner City: City Chamberlain; =**kind** n towns(wo)man; Berliner ~ Berliner; Londoner ~ Londoner, F cockney; =**klatsch** m town-gossip; =**klatsche** F f scandal-monger; =**kommandant** ⚔ m governor of a fortified town; =**kreis** m district formed by a town, in England: municipal borough; ?**kundig** a. ⊕: a) knowing the town; b) = Bekannt; =**leben** n town- (or city-)life; =**leute** *pl.* townsfolk, townspeople *pl.*; =**mauer** f town- (or city-)wall; =**miliz** f town- (or city-)militia, ehm. in Lo.: city train-bands *pl.*; =**musikant**, =**musikus** m town-musician; =**neuigkeit** f town- (or local-)news, weitS. =**klatsch**; =**obrigkeit** f municipal authorities *pl.*; =**ordnung** f by-laws *pl.* of a town; =**park** m park of a town; =**physikus** m medical officer of a town; =**polizei** f town- (or city-)police; =**post** f town- (or local)post; =**rat** m: a) *coll.* town-council, corporation, der City von Lo.: common council; b) town-councillor; =**recht** n municipal by-law(s *pl.*); =**reisende(r)** m town-traveller; =**schreiber(ei** f) m (office of the) town-clerk; =**schule** f municipal school; =**schulkommission** f education(al) committee (of a town council); =**schul-rat** m inspector of municipal schools; =**steuer** f town- (or borough-)rate; =**teil** m quarter; =**tor** n gate of a town, city-gate; =**väter** m/pl. co. (Bürgermeister und Stadtverordnete), *etwa:* city-fathers *pl.*; =**verordnete(r)** m town-councillor, Londoner City: Common Councilman; =**verordneten-versammlung** f town-council; =**verordneten-vorsteher** m chairman of the town-council; =**viertel** n quarter; =**vogtei** f town-jail; =**volk** n = Leute; =**wage** f public scales *pl.*; =**wappen** n coat of arms *pl.* of a town; city-arms; =**wesen** n municipal concerns, civic affairs *pl.*; =**wohnung** f town-house or -residence.
Stafette (⌂⌂) [it. (*dtsch. Stapfe)] f ⊕ (reitender Eilbote) mounted courier or express, *auch:* (fr.) estafette.
Staffage (⌂⌂G) [++ fr.: staffieren] f ⊕ paint. (Beiwerk) accessories, figures *pl.* (filling up the landscape).
Staffel (⌂⌂) [ahd.: staple; Stufe, stapfen] f ⊕ step; (Stufe) degree; ~ e-r Leiter rung.
Staffel-aufstellung ⚔ (⌂⌂⌂⌂) f ⊕ echelon (order). [*paint.* easel.]
Staffelei (⌂⌂⌂) [dtsch.-it.; *Staffel] f ⊕; **staffel-förmig** ⚔ (⌂⌂⌂) a. ⊕ forming (up in) echelons; =**gemälde** n ⊕ easel-picture or -piece; =**gesang** m, *eccl.* = Gradual(e).
staffeln (⌂⌂) v/a. ⊕a. to raise in steps, ⚔ to echelon; gestaffelt aufstellen to draw up in echelon (order).
Staffel-tarif ⚔ (⌂⌂…) m ⊕ sliding tariff or scale; ?**weise** ⚔ adv. (F a. a.) (forming) in echelon(s).
staffieren ⊕ (⌂⌂⌂) [ndl.; fr.; *Stoff] v/a. ⊕ 1. Hüte ⚔c.: to dress, trim; (fertigmachen) to finish; (schmücken) to decorate, adorn (vgl. ausstaffieren I). — 2. *paint.* (zur Füllung machen) to fill in figures, &c.
Staffierer ⊕ (⌂⌂⌂) m ⊕ 1. dresser, trimmer. — 2. = Staffiermaler.
Staffier-maler ⊕ (⌂⌂⌂…) m ⊕ decorative painter, (painter and) decorator; =**malerei** f decorative painting; =**naht** f Hutmacherei: garnish-seam.
Staffierung (⌂⌂⌂) f ⊕ trimming, decoration. [~ mainstay.]
Stag ⚓ (⌂) [dän.] n ⊕c. (⚔) stay; großes]
Stagnation (⌂-ts(⌂)⌂) [it.] f ⊕ (Stillstand, Stockung) stagnation, standstill.
stagnieren (⌂⌂⌂) v/n. (h.) ⊕ to stagnate, to be stagnant or at a standstill.
Stag-segel ⚓ (⌂⌂ (⌂…) n ⊕ stay-sail; =**talje** f (clew-)garnet.
stahl¹ (⌂) ind. impf. von stehlen.
Stahl² (⌂) [ahd.: steel] m ⊕(⚙)c. 1. ⊕ (entkohltes Eisen) steel (f. gerben 2); ~

Zeichen (f. S. XVII): F familiär; P Volkssprache; P Gaunersprache; ⚔ selten; † alt (auch gestorben); * neu (auch geboren); ⁺⁺ unrichtig;

[Stahlarbeit] — 913 — [Stammlehen]

härten to temper steel; ~ plätten to flatten steel; vgl. Bessemer=, Feuer=, Gußstahl; so hart wie ~ (as) hard as steel or flint, poet. (like) adamant. — 2. (Dolch, Schwert) dagger, sword; (Bolzen in Bügeleisen) (iron) heater; (Wetz=)~ steel for sharpening knives, &c. — 3. ● (Warenstempel) stamp (denoting the quality). — 4. ⊙c.⊕ [nbb.] (Muster, Probe) sample.

Stahl=arbeit(er m) f ⊙ (″...) ⊕ steelwork(er); ºartig a. ⊕ steel-like; =bad n: a) ⚥ chalybeate bath; b) (Badeort) iron (or ⚥ ferruginous) springs pl.; ºbepanzert a. steel-clad or -plated; =bereitung f manufacture of steel, steel-making; ºblau a. steel-blue or -coloured; =blech n (thin) steel plate; =bronze f steel-bronze; =brunnen m: ⚥ ferruginous (or chalybeate) spring; =draht m steel wire.

stähle(n¹ pl.) (ᴸ˘) subj. impf. v. stehlen.
stählen² (ᴸ˘) [Stahl] v/a. u. sich ² v/refl. ⊕ 1. ⊙ metall. (in Stahl verwandeln) to convert (or turn) into steel, ⚥ to acierate; (härten) to temper, to harden; Schmiede: (ver=)² to steel; von Klingen ꝛc.: gut gestählt well-tempered. — 2. fig. to steel, to harden; j-s Mut ², auch: to fortify (or brace up) a p.'s courage.
stählern (ᴸ˘) a. ⊕ (made of) steel; fig. like steel, like cast iron, hard; auch = stahlhart.

Stahl=erz (″...) n ⊕ min. steel-ore, ⚥ spathic iron(-ore); =fabrik f = =werf; =feder f: a) steel spring; b) (Schreibfeder) steel pen, nib; =federhalter m pen-holder; =frisch-feuer ⊙ n, metall. steel-finery; =gerben n tilting; =geschoß ⚔ n = =kugel; =geschütz ⚔ n cannon made of cast steel; ºgrau a. ⊕ grey as steel, auch: steel-grey; ºhaltig a. containing steel, ⚥ chalybeate; =hammer m: a) steel hammer; b) metall. st.-forge; ºhart a. (as) hard as steel; =härte f hardness of steel; =härtung f, metall. tempering of steel; =hütte f = =werf; =kette f steel chain; =kugel f steel ball or bullet; =luppe f lump of (malleable) steel; =ofen m, metall. st. (or cementing-)furnace; =panzer ⚔ u. ⚓ m steel armour; =platte f steel plate; =pulver n, med. ironpowder; =quelle f = =brunnen; =roß n (Fahrrad) poet. iron steed, steel horse; =schiene ⚚ f steel rail; =schmuck m st. jewellery; =schneider m steelcutter; =spiegel m st. mirror; =staub m st. filings pl.; =stecher m steel(plate) engraver, ⚥ siderographist; =stecherei, =stecherkunst f st.-engraving, ⚥ siderographic art; =stempel m = Stanze 2; =stich m steel-(plate) engraving, ⚥ siderographic print; =tropfen m/pl. med. steel-drops pl.; ºumgürtet a. poet. steel-girt; =walze f st. roller; =waren ● f/pl. st. goods pl. or ware, auch: cutlery, hardware; =wasser n ferruginous (or chalybeate) water; =werk ⊙ n steel-works pl. or -(manu)factory.

stak (ᴸ) ind. impf. von stecken².
Stake (ᴸ˘) [nbb.: Stecken¹] f ⊕ 1. ⊙ (Pfahl) stake, pile. — 2. ⚓ = Staken¹ 2.

stäke (ᴸ˘) subj. impf. von stecken².
Staken¹ (ᴸ˘) [nbb.: stake] m ⊕ 1. stake; (Stange) pole. — 2. ⚓ boathook, gaff, setter.
staken² ⚓ (ᴸ˘) I v/a. ⊕ to push with boat-hooks; (mit dem Bootshaken fassen) to gaff. — II v/n. F (ausschreiten) da stapft er hin there he comes stalking along.
Staket (˘ᴸ) [nbl.; it.; *Stecken] n ⊙c. (Einpfählung) palisade, stockade; (Lattenzaun) wooden railing or fence.
Stak=netz ⊙ (″...) n ⊕ (großes Sacknetz) stake-net; =netz-fischer m stake-netter.
Stalagmit, Stalaktit ⚥ (˘˘ᴸ) [grch.] m ⊙c.⊕ (empor-, herab-wachsender Tropfstein) stalagmite, stalactite.
Stall (ᴸ) [ahd.: stall: stellen] m ⊙b. 1. zum Einstellen von Vieh: stable (bsd. für Pferde), stall; für Hunde: kennel, für Kühe: cowshed, für Mietpferde: livery-stable, mews pl., für Schweine: pigsty; in den ~ stellen to (put into a) stable; Sprichw. s. Schaf 2. — 2. für andere Zwecke: (Schuppen) shed, für Holz: woodshed. — 3. F (erbärmliche Wohnung) miserable hole, auch: pigsty.
Stall=anzug (°˘) m ⊕ stable-clothes pl.
Stallaterne (˘˘˘) [Stall=laterne] f ⊕ stable-lantern.
Stall=besen (°...) m ⊕ stable-broom; =bürste f horse-brush; =decke f horsecloth or -rug; (Schabracke) caparison; =dienst m stable-work, ⚔ stable-duty; =dünger m stable-manure; =eimer m stable-pail.
stallen (ᴸ˘) ⊕ I v/a. 1. Vieh ² to stable (or stall) ..., weitS. to find room (or accommodation) for ... — II v/n. (h.) 2. von Pferden: to stand in a stable; (harnen) to stale, to (pass) urine. — 3. prove. von Personen: mit=ea. ² oder sich ² (sich vertragen) to agree; sie ² nicht mit=ea. they don't hit it off. — III ~ n ⊕ 4. stabling, &c. (s. I u. II).
Stall=fütterung (°...) f ⊕ agr. stallfeed(ing); =geld n für Pferde: stable- (or stabling-)money, (charge for the) keep of a horse; =halter m stablekeeper; =hof m stable-yard; =junge m stable-boy; =knecht m stable-man, ostler, groom; =laterne s. Stallaterne; =meister m e-s Fürsten: equerry, master of the horse; =miete f = =geld; =raum m stable-room, stabling; =tür(e) f stable-door.
Stallung (ᴸ˘) f ⊕ 1. = stallen III. — 2. (Stallraum) stabling; ~en pl. (meist in Hintergäßchen) mews pl.
Stambul ♀ (ᴸ˘) [türk.; *grch. eis tan pö'lin „in die Stadt" oder *(Konstantinopel] npr/n. ⊙α. Stamboul.
Stamin ● (˘ᴸ) n = Etamin.
Stamm (ᴸ) [ahd.: stem; *Stab] m ⊙c. 1. ♀ stem, einer Pflanze: stalk, e-s Baumes: trunk; eccl. ~ des Kreuzes tree of the cross; ● Holz auf dem ~ kaufen to buy standing timber or trees; Sprichw. s. Apfel. — 2. (Familie) family, house, in Schottland: clan; (Geschlecht) race, stock; (Nachkommenschaft) offspring, progeny; männlicher (weiblicher) ~ male (female) line; bibl. die zwölf Stämme Israels the twelve tribes of Israel; agr. schöner ~ Kühe fine breed of cows. — 3. (Grundlage): a) ~ der Kunden (Besucher) (stock of) regular customers (visitors), regulars pl.; vgl. =gast; b) (angelegtes Kapital) invested capital, principal. — 4. Spiel: a) (die nach dem Geben verbleibenden Karten) undealt pack of cards; b) (Einsatz) stake; c) en ~ Kegel schieben to play a game of skittles or ninepins. — 5. gram. ~ eines Wortes: stem. — 6. agr. (Bestand an Vieh) stock of cattle. — 7. ⚔ ~ eines Truppenteils: skeleton corps; vgl. Stammbataillon.
Stamm=aktie ● (°...) f ⊕ founder's (or original) share; =anteil m = =aktie; =bahn ⚚ f main (or principal) line; =bataillon ⚔ n in Engl. bleibender Stamm home battalion; =baum m genealogical tree; langer ~ (long) pedigree; =buch (=blatt) n (leaf of an) album; =buchstabe m, gram. radical letter; =buchvers m verse inscribed in an album; =burg f ancestral castle.
Stämmchen (ᴸ˘) n ⊕ (dim. v. Stamm) small trunk or stock.
stammeln (ᴸ˘) [ahd.: stammer: stumm] v/n. (h.) u. v/a. ⊕a. to stammer, bsd. path. to stutter; eine Entschuldigung ² to stammer (or splutter) forth an excuse; ²d adv. ⊕ with (or in) a faltering voice, with a stutter.
Stamm=eltern (°˘...) f/pl. ⊕ first parents, progenitors, (original) ancestors pl.
stammen (ᴸ˘) I v/n. (s.) ⊕ von Personen: to descend (or to derive one's origin) from; (herkommen) to originate (or spring, come) from; gram. das Wort stammt aus dem Griechischen ... is derived (or taken) from the Greek. — II ~ n ⊕ descent, derivation, origin.
Stamm=ende (°...) n ⊕ hort. stump (of a tree); =endung f gr. termination of the stem; =erbe m lineal descendant, (rightful) heir of a family.
Stammes=gefühl (°˘...) n ⊕ tribalism; =unterschied m racial (or tribal) difference or distinction.
Stamm=folge (°...) f ⊕ line of descent, genealogical order; =form f, gram. radical form; ºfrüchtig a. ⊕: ⚥ caulocarpic, ...ous; =gast m regular guest or customer, constant frequenter, (fr.) habitué; =gut n family estate, inherited property.
stammhaft (ᴸ˘) a. ⊕: a) = stämmig; b) gram. of the stem, radical.
Stamm=halter (°...) m ⊕ son and heir, first-born male descendant; =haus n: a) principal line; b) ● principal (or original) firm; =holz n standing timber, trunk- (or stub-)wood, logs pl. (of trees).
stämmig (ᴸ˘) [nbb.; *Stamm] a. ⊕ 1. von Bäumen: full-grown. — 2. fig. (stark) vigorous, robust, stout; (dick und gedrungen) well-set. F stumpy. — 3. in Essen, zB. dünn=² with a slender stem or trunk.
Stämmigkeit (ᴸ˘˘) f ⊕ fig. vigour, robustness, stoutness; F stumpiness.
Stamm=kapital ● (°...) n ⊕ original capital; =kneipe f (one's) favourite bar or (ale-)house or F pub; =land n mother-country; =lehen n fee-simple.

♪ Musik; ⚥ Wissenschaft; ♀ Pflanze; ♀ Geographie; ⊙ Technik; ⚒ Bergbau; ⚔ Militär; ⚓ Marine; ● Handel; ✉ Post; ⚚ Eisenbahn.

[Stammler] — 914 — [Standquartier]

Stammler (☞) [stammeln] *m* ②, **~in** *f* ⑳ stammerer, stammering (or stuttering) person.
Stamm-linie (☞...) *f* ②: a) principal (🜚 auch: main) or trunk-line; b) line of descent; **=liste** ✕, ↓ *f* = Musterrolle; **=lokal** *n* (one's favourite haunt, vgl. Kneipe; **=mutter** f. Stammmutter; **=prioritäts-aktie** ⚖ *f* preference-share; **=register** *n* = Geschlechts-register; **=rolle** ✕, ↓ *f* muster-roll; **=schloß** *n* = -burg; **=seidel** *n* in deutschen Wirtschaften: beer-mug reserved for a regular guest; **=silbe** *f*, *gram*. radical syllable; **=sitz** *m*: a) ancestral seat or estate or hall; b) e-s Volkes: original (or ancient) home; **=sprache** *f* original language; **=ständig** ⚹ *a*. ⓖ = stengel-ständig; **=tafel** *f* genealogical table; **=tisch** *m* eines Gasthofes: table reserved for regular guests. [ancestress.]
Stammutter (☞☞) [Stamm-mutter] *f* ㉑
Stamm-vater (☞...) *m* ② ancestor, progenitor; **=vermögen** *n* original property or capital or fund; ⚹**verwandt** *a*. ⓖ akin, kindred, cognate; **=verwandtschaft** *f* kinship (of race); *gram*. affinity; **=vokal** *m*, *gr*. radical vowel; **=volk** *n* primitive (von Ureingeborenen: aboriginal) race; ancestral stock; **=wappen** *n* family-arms *pl.*; **=wert** *m* jur. (Substanz) original value; **=wort** *n*, *gram*. stem, radical word.
Stampf-bau ⊕ (☞.¹) *m* ② = Pisébau.
Stampfe (☞) *f* ⑧ 1. ⊕ stamp(er), (Ramme) rammer, (Schlegel) beater, beetle, (Stößel) pestle; pounder. — 2. (Stutzglas) glass with a short thick stem.
stampfen (☞) [abd.: stamp] *v/a. u. v/n.* (h.) ⑧ 1. ⊕ a) mit dem Fuße (auf die Erde) ⚹ to stamp one's foot (on the ground), von Pferden: to paw (the ground), b) (fn) (schwer auftreten) to trample, to tramp along; c) ↓ von Schiffen: to pitch, to heave and set. — 2. meist ⊕ Erze ⚹ (pochen) to stamp (or pound, crush) ore; Kartoffeln ⚹ to mash potatoes; Korn ⚹ to bruise corn; Trauben ⚹ to crush grapes; im Mörser ⚹ to bray in a mortar; *metall*. (prägen, stanzen) to stamp. — 3. mit Angabe des Erfolges: die Erde fest ⚹ to batter (or ram) down ...; zerquetschend: klein ⚹ to crush, mash; zu Pulver ⚹ to pulverize; *fig*. aus dem Boden ⚹ to produce by magic, to conjure up; kann ich Armeen aus der Erde ⚹? (SCH.) can I call hosts by stamping on the ground?
Stampfer (☞) *m* ②, **~in** *f* ⑳ 1. von Lebewesen: a) (einer der et. klein stampft) stamper, rammer, pounder; b) (stampfendes Pferd) horse addicted to pawing (the ground), pawing horse. — 2. ⊕ (Werkzeug) = Stampfe. — 3. ↓ (stampfendes Schiff) pitching vessel.
Stampf-erde ⊕ (☞...) *f* ⓖ Bauwesen: stamped earth; **=gang** *m* Müllerei: crushing-mill.
stampfig (☞) *a*. ⓖ given to stamping, v. Pferden: addicted to pawing.
Stampf-maschine ⊕ (☞...) *f* ⓖ stamping-(or crushing-)machine; **=mühle** ⊕ *f*, ⊕ stamping- (or crushing-)mill, battery; **=see** ↓ *f* heavy sea washing

over the bow; **=stock** ↓ *m* am Bugspriet: martingale, dolphin-strike; **=stock-achterholer** ↓ *m* back-rope; **=trog** ⊕ *m* Papierfabr.: beating-trough; **=walze** *f*, *agr*. roller; **=werk** ✕ *n* = -mühle.
stand¹ (☞) ind. impf. von stehen.
Stand² (☞) [nhd.: stand; *stand¹] *m* ⓑ. 1. (das Stehen) standing, upright position (a. von Dingen). — 2. (Ort des Stehens) stand(ing-place), position; (Stelle des Aufbaus bei Rennen) start(ing-point); ~ e-s Krämers: pitch, stall, von Droschken: cab-stand; festen ~ fassen to take up a strong position, (firmly) to establish o.s.; seinen ~ an einem Orte haben to be posted in a place; f. standhalten; ~ der Preise level of prices; *ast*. ~ der Planeten: configuration. — 3. a) (Bestand) stock, oft in Zssgn, zB. er hat einen bedeutenden Fasanenstand he has a large stock of pheasants; b) (nach Zahlwort *pl., inv.*) vier ~ Betten four complete beds. — 4. (Zustand) state, (Beschaffenheit) condition, (Lage) situation, position; (Verbindung von Umständen) juncture; (Anordnung) arrangement; die Dinge auf den alten ~e lassen to leave things as they were, to let things go; mit einem einen harten ~ haben to have a great deal of trouble with a p.; e-n schweren ~ haben to have a hard struggle, to have much to contend with; gut im ~e (bei guter Gesundheit) sein to be in a good state of health; (vgl. 6) et. (gut) im ~e (in gutem ~e) erhalten to keep a th. in good condition or repair. — 5. (gesellschaftliche Stellung) social position, station (in life), (Beruf) vocation, (Rang) rank (of society), (Kaste) caste; f. heiraten II; ein Mann von (hohem) ~e a man of eminence or rank; Leute aus allen Ständen people of all classes; er ist seines ~es Jurist (Bäcker) ... a lawyer by profession (a baker by trade); f. geistlich 2; die höheren Stände the upper classes (or ranks) *pl*. of society; die gelehrten Stände the learned professions *pl*.; bibl. ehm. der dritte ~ (der Bürgerstand) the third estate, the Commons; die Stände *pl*. (Landesvertretung) the diet *sg*., the representatives of the people. — 6. in adverbialen Zssgn: f. außerstande, imstande, instand, zustande.
Standarte (☞☞) [mhd. 13. sae.; fr.; *it.] *f* ⑧ 1. standard, banner. — 2. *hunt*. (Schwanz des Fuchses) brush.
Standarten-junker (☞☞...) *m* ②, **=träger** *m* ✕ standard-bearer; **=stange** *f* shaft of the standard.
Stand²**-barometer** (☞...) *n* (*m*) ② stationary barometer; **=bild** *n* statue; **=bildkunst** *f* statuary (art); **=büchse** *f* rifle for target-shooting.
Ständchen (☞) [nhd. 17. sae.] *n* ② serenade; (Morgen)~ morning-music; e-m ein ~ bringen to serenade a p. [tub.)
Stande prov. (☞) *f* ⑧ (Faß, Butte) large)
Stände¹ (☞) *pl*. v. Stand (f. ds, bsd. 5).
stände² (☞) subj. impf. v. steh(e)n.
Ständer ⊕ (☞) [nhd.] *m* ② stand, für Hüte, Regenschirme ꝛc.: (hat-and-umbrella) stand; *arch*. (stehender Pfosten) (wooden)

post or pillar; (aufrechter Balken) upright; ~ (Fußgestell) e-r Säule: pedestal; *carp*. (Verbandstück) scantling (in a partition); *man*. ~ in der Mitte der Bahn: pillar.
Ständer-stock (☞...) *m* ② Bienenzucht: beehive on a post; **=werk** *n*, arch. stud-work.
Stände-saal (☞..¹) *m* ② für Abgeordnete: hall in which a diet meets.
Standes-abzeichen (☞...) *n* ② mark of one's rank; **=adel** *m* nobility by birth; **=amt** *n* registrar's (or registry-)office; **=beamte(r)** *m* registrar; **=ehe** *f* marriage for position; **=ehre** *f* professional honour; **=erhöhung** *f* elevation to a higher rank; **=gebühr** *f*: nach ~ in accordance with (or as befits) one's (social) position; ⚹**gemäß** *a*. ⓖ *u. adv.* suitable to (or in keeping with) one's (social) rank; ⚹ leben, auch: to live according to one's station; **=genosse** *m* one('s) equal in rank; auch: peer; **=herr** *m* mediatized prince or baron; **=herrschaft** *f* mediatized territory; ⚹**mäßig** *a*. = -gemäß; **=person** *f* p. of eminence or rank; **=register** *n* register of births, marriages, and deaths; **=rücksichten** *f/pl*. considerations *pl*. of rank; **=unterschied** *m* difference of rank, class-distinction; **=vorurteil** *n* social (or class-) prejudice; ⚹**widrig** *a*. derogatory to (or out of keeping with) one's rank or social position.
Stände¹**-tag** (☞...) *m* ②, **=versammlung** *f* meeting (or assembly) of a diet.
Stand²**-geld** (☞...) *n* ② = Budengeld; **=gericht** *n* (drumhead) court-martial.
standhaft *a*. ⓖ v. Personen: steady, steadfast; (nicht nachgebend) firm, unyielding, (beharrlich) persevering, constant, (entschlossen) resolute; (gleichmütig) stoical, indifferent, ⚹ (adv.) leugnen to deny flatly; sich ⚹ wehren to offer a stout resistance; **~igkeit** (☞☞-) *f* ⓖ steadiness, steadfastness; firmness, perseverance, constancy, (stoical) indifference, equanimity.
stand²**-halten** (☞...) *v/n*. ⓐ** (h.) (nicht weichen) to hold one's ground or one's own; to stand firm, to hold out, Sport: to stay; ⚖ ~ des Kurses steady rate of exchange.
ständig (☞) [nhd.; *Stand²] *a*. ⓖ = beständig; ⚹e Adresse permanent address; ⚖es Amt permanent post; ⚖es Einkommen fixed (or regular) income.
ständisch (☞) *a*. ⓖ = landständisch.
Stand²**-krämer** ⚖ (☞...) *m*, **~in** *f* ⑳ stall-keeper; **=lager** ✕ *n* = -quartier; **=linie** *f*, *surv*. base- (or station-)line; **=ort**, **=platz** *m*: a) stand, halting-place, station; ✕ garrison-town; b) ♃ Fundort: ⚶ habitat; **=pferd** *n* relay(-horse); **=punkt** *m*: a) point of view, *fig*. = Gesichtspunkt; seinen ~ ändern to shift one's ground, politisch: to change sides; das ist ein überwundener ~ that's an exploded idea, those are antiquated notions; b) (Punkt, auf dem et. steht) position, weitS. state, condition; *fig*. e-m f-n ~ klarmachen to give a p. a piece of one's mind; **=quartier** ✕ *n* fixed (or settled) quarters *pl*., für Feldtruppen: cantonment; sein ~ beim

Signs (see page XVII): F familiar; P vulgar; ꟻ flash; ⧹ rare; † obsolete (died); * new word (born); ⁓ incorrect; ♪ music.

Walde h. to be stationed (or posted) near the forest; =recht n summary justice, ⚔ im Kriege: martial law; ?rechtlich ⚔ a. ⊕ according to martial law; er wurde 2 erschossen he was shot by a sentence of court-martial; =rede f harangue, bfd. bei Wahlen: stump-speech; =redner m haranguer. stump-orator; =riß m, arch. Zeichenkunſt: elevation, upright; ſcheibe f der Schützen: fixed target; =uhr f timepiece; =viſier ⚔ n am Gewehre: block-sight; =wild n, das ſeinen Aufenthalt wenig ändert: game which keeps to the same haunts or grounds; =wind m steady breeze.
Stange (⌣) [ahd.] f ⊕ 1. pole, bar; rod (a. ⊕ mech.); ~ für Weinreben ꝛc.: stake, stick, für Hühner ꝛc.: roost, perch; ~ Eiſen rod (or bar) of iron; ~ Latwitzen, Pomade, Schwefel, Siegellack, Zimt: stick; Gerſtenzucker in ~n … in sticks; man. (Kinnketten=)~ curb-bit; ſ. Fahnen=, Hopfen=ſtange. — 2. fig. bei der (Sache) bleiben to keep (F to stick) to the point, im Handeln: to persevere; e-m die ~ halten: a) als Freund: to back (or support, countenance) a p.; b) als Gegner: to hold one's own against a p., to be a match for a p. — 3. hunt. ~ am Hirſchgeweih: branch, end. — 4. provc. (hohes Bierglas) tall beer-glass.
Stängelchen (⌣⌣) n ⊗ small bar or stick.
Stangen=barriere 🂠 (⌣⌣…) f ⊕ rod-barrier; =bier n beer (consumed in tall glasses; =bohne ♣ f climbing bean, runner (Phase'olus vulga'ris) — =bohrer ⊕ m (great) auger; =eiſen n: a) ⊕ rod-iron; b) hunt. (Fangeiſen) iron trap; ?förmig a. ⊕ in (the shape of) bars or rods; =gebiß n, man. = Kandare; Mundſtück eines =gebiſſes cannon-bit; =gerüſt n Bauw.: scaffolding (made) of poles; =gitter n grating; =holz n: a) young copsewood; b) arch. pole-timber; =kohle f, min. columnar anthracite; =kugel f cross-bar shot; =leiter f peg-ladder; =pferd n wheel- (or pole-, thill-)horse, wheeler; =pomade f cosmetic in sticks; =reiter ⚔ m, artill., &c. wheel-driver; =ſchwefel ⊕ m sticks (or rolls) pl. of sulphur; =ſeife ⊕ f bar-soap; =ſiegel=lack ⊕ m sticks pl. of sealing-wax; =ſpargel m Kochk.: asparagus served whole; =ſpringen n pole-leaping; =zaum m = =gebiß; =zaun m, agr. pole-fence (ſ. Geſtänge 1); =zirkel m beam-compasses pl.
Stank¹ ⌢ (⌣) [ahd.; *ſtank²] m ⊕c. 1. = Geſtank. — 2. = Stänkerei 2.
ſtank² (⌣) ind., ſtänke (⌣⌣) subj. impf. von ſtinken.
Stänker (⌣⌣) [Stank¹] m ⊗, 1 u. 3 a. ~in f ⊕ 1. stinking person, F stinker, stinkard. — 2. stinking tobacco or cheese. — 3. P: a) (Zwietrachtſtifter) brawler, quarreller; b) (Schnüffler) prying fellow, F Paul Pry.
Stänkerei (⌣⌣⌢) f ⊕ 1. stink, offensive (or obnoxious) smell. — 2. brawl, quarrel, row, unpleasant dispute.
Stänkerer (⌣⌣⌣) m ⊗ = Stänker.
ſtänk(e)rig (⌣(⌣)⌣) a. ⊕ stinking, feiner: malodorous, having (or giving off) an unpleasant (or offensive) smell.

ſtänkern (⌣⌣) v/n. (h.) ⊕a. 1. to give off a bad (or nasty) smell, F to stink. — 2. P: a) (Unfrieden ſtiften) to quarrel, to wrangle; b) (herumſchnüffeln) to pry about.
Stanniol ⊕ (⌣(⌣)⌣) [neu=lt. Zinn=] n ⊕d. (Zinnfolie) tinfoil.
Stanze (⌣⌣) [it. stanza] f ⊕ 1. pros. (Reimſtrophe) stanza. — 2. ⊕ metall., mint. (Stampfe) metal-stamp, die, punch; Kupferſtecherei: (Prägunterlage) matrix.
ſtanzen ⊕ (⌣⌣) [Stanze 2] v/a. ⊕ metall. Bleche 2 to stamp (or punch) …
Stanz=maſchine ⊕ (⌣⌣⌣⌣) [ſtanz=en] f ⊕ punching- (or slotting-)machine; auch = Stanze 2.
Stapel (⌣⌣) [ndd.: staple = hd. Staffel] m ⊗ 1. ⊕ (Stütze) support; (Gerüſt) scaffolding, platform, ⚓ für ein Schiff während des Bauens: stocks, slips pl.; auf dem ~ on the stocks; vom, von ~ geh(e)n to be launched (auch fig.); ein Schiff vom ~ laſſen to launch …; fig. eine Rede vom ~ laſſen to deliver …; neue Schiffe auf ~ legen to lay down new ships (on the stocks). — 2. ⚓ (Warenniederlage) staple, emporium, warehouse; (Haufe) pile, heap. — 3. ⊕ Spinnerei: = der Wolle ꝛc.: staple.
Stapel=gerechtigkeit (⌣⌣…) f ⊕ = =recht; =gut ⚓ n staple commodities or goods pl.; =handel m staple trade; =lauf ⚓ m launch(ing).
ſtapeln (⌣⌣) ⊕a. I v/a. = aufſtapeln. — II v/n. (ſn) F (einherſchreiten) to stalk (along), to strut (along), to stride, to take large strides.
Stapel=ort (⌣⌣…) m ⚓, =platz ⚓ m staple, emporium, mar(ke)t, (fr.) entrepôt; ehm. =recht ⚓ n staple-right.
Stapf ⌢ (⌣) [ahd.: step] m ⊗, ~e ⊕ (m ⊕), ~en m ⊕ = Fußſtapfe.
ſtapfen (⌣⌣) v/n. (h. u. ſn) to stamp (with one's feet).
Star¹ (⌣) [ahd.: starling] m ⊕c. ⊕ orn. starling (Sturnus vulga'ris).
Star² (⌣) [ndd.; *ſtarblind] m ⊕c. path. (Krankheit der Linſe des Auges, ehm. grauer ~) cataract; ſchwarzer ~ (Krankheit der Netzhaut), ⚗ amaurosis, bisw.: drop serene, (lt.) gutta sere'na; grüner ~: ⚗ glaucoma; e-m den ~ ſtechen to couch a patient's cataract; fig. to open a p.'s eyes. to undeceive a p.
Stär (⌣) [ndd.] m ⊕c. (Schafbock) ram.
ſtar²=artig (⌣…) a. ⊕ path. cataractous.
ſtarb (⌣) ind. impf. v. ſterben.
ſtar²=blind (⌣…) [ahd.; *ſtarren] a. ⊕ blind through a cataract; =blindheit f ⊕ blindness caused by a cataract.
Staren=kaſten (⌣⌣⌣⌣) m ⊕ = Starkaſten.
Star²=fleck (⌣…) m ⊕ vet. pearl-eye.
ſtark (⌣) [ahd.: stark] a. ⊕ (D 2, 7) 1. a) strong (auch gram.); (v. kräftigem Körperbau) robust, sturdy; (voll Tatkraft) vigorous; (mächtig) powerful; (heftig) violent, intens(iv)e; das Heer war 10000 Mann 2 … was ten thousand strong; Sprichw. ſ. Einigkeit; b) (beleibt) stout, corpulent, F big; 2 werden to grow stout; ſtärker w. to put on flesh, to increase in weight. — 2. mit nouns: 2e Brille strong (or powerful) glasses pl.; 2e Erkältung severe cold; 2er Eſſer large (or hearty) eater; 2er Froſt hard frost; 2es Ge=

dächtnis good (or tenacious) memory; 2er Geiſt strong mind; 2e Meile good mile; 2er Regenguß heavy shower; e-e 2e Stunde a good hour; in 2en Tagemärſchen by forced marches; F fig. das iſt 2er Tobak! that's (coming it) rather strong!; 2es Tuch stout cloth; ein 2er Wind a strong gust of wind; 2e Zigarre strong cigar. — 3. mit verbs: das iſt etwas 2! that's (rather) too much of a good thing!; adv.: es friert 2 it's freezing hard; zu 2 gebraten overdone; ⚓ 2 geſucht in great demand or request, of ready sale.
Stark¹=kaſten (⌣⌣⌣) m ⊕ box for starlings.
ſtark=beleibt (⌣⌣⌢) a. ⊕ = ſtark 1 b; ?beſetzt a. well filled or attended, vom Orcheſter: full.
Stärke (⌣⌣) [ahd.; *ſtarf] f ⊕ 1. strength, des Leibes auch: robustness, (Tatkraft) vigour, (Macht) power, (Heftigkeit) intensity; (ſtarke Seite) strong point, forte; (Beleibtheit) stoutness, corpulency, ⚔ volle ~ eines Regiments: establishment, full strength. — 2. ⚗ (Kraftmehl) starch.
ſtärke=artig ⚗ (⌣⌣…) a. ⊕ starchy, ⚗ amylaceous, amyloid; =blau n ⊕ blue starch; =fabrik f starch-factory; =fabrikant m starch-maker; =grad m (degree of) strength; =gummi, chm.: amylodextrine (ſ. auch Dextrin); ?haltig a. containing starch, ⚗ amylaceous; =händler m dealer in starch; =kleiſter m starch-paste; =mehl n starch-flour, fecula, ⚗ amylum; ?mehl=artig a. starchy, ⚗ amylaceous.
ſtärken (⌣⌣) [ahd.; *ſtark] I v/a. ⊕ 1. a. ſich 2 v/refl. (kräftigen) to strengthen, to invigorate, den Magen: to comfort, den Mut: to brace (up); ſich 2 to take refreshments; wieder 2 to restore; ⚕ strengthening, restorative, med. tonic. — 2. ⊕ Wäſche 2 to starch …, to stiffen … — II ~ n ⊕ 3. ſ. Stärkung.
Stärker (⌣⌣) m ⊕, ~in f ⊕ der Wäſche: (clear-)starcher. [sugar, ⚗ glucose.)
Stärke=zucker (⌣⌣⌣) m ⊕ ⊕, chm. starch-)
ſtark=formig (⌣…) a. ⊕ ſ. S. XXXIII; ?gläubig a. strong in (or of great) faith; ?glied(e)rig, ?knochig a. strong-limbed or -boned; ?leibig a. = ſtark 1 b; =leibigkeit f ⊕ stoutness, corpulency; =mut m (f) strength of mind, fortitude.
ſtar²=krank (⌣⌢) a. ⊕ path. suffering from (a) cataract, cataractous.
Stark=ſtrom ⚡ (⌣…) m ⊕ elect. strong current; =ſtrom=kabel n high-voltage (or high-tension)cable.
Stärkung (⌣⌣) f ⊕ 1. strengthening, invigoration. — 2. nur Stärkung: (Stärkungsmittel) refreshment, med. restorative; (Schnäpschen ꝛc.) drop of comfort, cordial, F pick-me-up.
ſtark=wirkend (⌣⌣⌣) a. ⊕ of powerful effect, (most) efficacious; von Mitteln auch: powerful, strong, drastic, potent.
Star¹=matz F (⌣…) m ⊕ starling; ein ~ ſchwatzen to talk like a parrot.
Star²=meſſer (⌣…) n ⊕, =nadel f, surg. cataract-knife, couching-needle; =operation f couching for (or operating on) a cataract.
Staroſt (⌣⌢) [ſlav.] m ⊕ (polniſcher Kreishauptmann) starost, Polish governor.

⚗ scientific; ♣ botanical; ⊕ geography; ⊕ machinery; ⚒ mining; ⚔ military; ⚓ marine; ⊛ commercial; ✉ postal; 🚂 railway.

[starr] — 916 — [Staubschwamm]

starr (⸗) [nhd.: stern: starren] a. ⑥
1. vom Blick: fixed, staring; im Tode glassy; e-n ⁓ (adv.) anblicken to stare at a p. — 2. (steif) stiff, vor Kälte: numb (with cold), benumbed; ⁓ werden to grow stiff, to stiffen; (unbeweglich) inflexible, rigid; fig. (unbeugsam) unbending, unflinching, stubborn. — 3. fig. ⁓ vor Entsetzen, Schrecken paralysed with fright, terror-stricken; ⁓ vor Erstaunen, Überraschung (struck) dumb with astonishment, flabbergasted, dumbfounded, thunderstruck.
Starre (⸗) f ⑯ = Starrheit.
starren¹ (⸗) [ahd.: stare] I v/n. (h.) ⑱: auf (ob. nach) et. ⁓ to stare at a th.; gedankenlos ⁓ to stare into vacancy.
— II ⁓ n ㉓ staring; fixed (or vacant) glance.
starren² (⸗) [mhd. starr w.] v/n. (h.) ⑱
1. = erstarren I; die Finger ⁓ mir vor Kälte my fingers are numb (or stiff) with cold. — 2. von etwas ⁓ (dicht besetzt sein) to be studded (or crowded) with, to bristle with; von Gold ⁓ to be covered with gold; von Schmutz ⁓ to be begrimed with dirt or filth, to be one mass of mud.
starr-gläubig (⸗⸗) a. ⑥ bigoted.
Starrheit (⸗-) f ⑯ (s. starr) fixedness (or glassiness) of the eye; stiffness (or numbness) of the limbs; inflexibility, rigidity; stubbornness, obstinacy.
Starr-kopf (⸗) m ⑫ stubborn head or person; ⁓köpfig a. ⑥ headstrong, stubborn, obstinate; ⁓köpfigkeit f stubbornness, obstinacy; ⁓krampf m, path. u. vet.: ⁊ tetanus; ⁓sinn m stubbornness; ⁓sinnig a. = ⁓köpfig; ⁓sucht f, path.: ⁊ catalepsy; ⁓süchtig a.: ⁊ cataleptic.
Star²-**stechen** (⸗⸗⸗) n ㉓ = ⁓operation.
Start ⁊ (⸗) [engl.: stürzen] m ⑫b. Rennsport: (Ablaufstelle) start.
starten ⁊ (⸗⸗) v/n. ⑲ (ablaufen) to start.
statarisch (⸗⸗⸗) [lt.] a. ⑥ Schule: ⁓e (ant. kursorische) Lektüre working slowly through (or careful reading of) an author. [gewichtslehre) statics.]
Statik (⸗⸗) [grch.] f ⑯ phys. &c. (Gleich-
Station (⸗tß(⸗)⸗) [lt.] f ⑯ 1. 🚉 station. (Haupt⁓) ⁓ terminus; (Halteplatz) halt, halting-place. — 2. (Kapelle) chapel, station. — 3. freie ⁓ (Kost u. Unterkunft) h. to have (free) board and lodging.
stationär (⸗tß(⸗)⸗⸗) [lt.] a. ⑥ (stillstehend) stationary.
stationieren (⸗tß(⸗)⸗⸗) [lt.] ⑲ I v/n. (n.): ⁓, stationiert sein (bsd. von Fuhrwerken) to be stationed. — II v/a. (aufstellen) to station.
Stations-**batterie** (⸗tß(⸗)⸗⸗⸗) f ⑫ tel. local (battery); ⁓gebäude ⛉ n station (-house); ⁓schiff ⚓ n stationary vessel; ⁓vorsteher 🚉 m station-master.
statiös (⸗tß(⸗)⸗) [lt.-fr.] a. ⑥ (D 10) (prachtvoll) magnificent, grand.
statisch ⊙ (⸗⸗) [grch.] a. ⑥ phys. static(al).
stätisch (⸗⸗) a. ⑥ von Pferden: restive.
Statist (⸗⸗) [grch.] m ⑭, ⁓in f ㊵ thea. (stumme Person) super(numerary), F dummy. [⸗⸗⸗) m ⑭ statistician.]
Statistik (⸗⸗⸗) [grch.] f ㊺ statistics; ⁓er
statistisch (⸗⸗⸗) [grch.] a. ⑥ statistical.

Stativ (⸗⸗f) [lt.] n ⑪ d. (Ständer, Stütze für Apparate) stand, support, holder. [⁓tate.]
Stätlein (⸗⸗) n ㉓ (dim. v. Staat) small ⸗
Statt¹ (⸗; Hom. Stadt) [ahd.: stead, *steh(e)n] f ⑯ 1. geh. Spr.= Stätte; gutes Wort findet (eine) gute ⁓ f. gut 4 an Schluß; f.a. anstatt, vonstatten, zustatten.
— 2. adv. in stehenden Verbindungen (meist klein geschrieben): f. statt-finden, ⁓geben, ⁓haben. — 3. **an Eides** ⁓ in lieu of an oath; f. Kind 1 am Ende; an meiner ⁓ = statt (f. das) meiner; an Zahlungs ⁓ instead of payment.
statt² [nhd.] (abbr. st.) als prp. mit gen. und cj. = anstatt; ⁓ dessen instead of that; ⁓ meiner in my place; instead of me, ⁓ daß er arbeitet instead of (his) working; ⁓ zu stricken sang sie instead of knitting she sang.
Stätte (⸗⸗) [nhd.; *Statt] f ⑯ place, room; (Wohnung) abode; heilige ⁓n holy places, auch sanctuaries pl.
statt¹-**finden** (⸗⸗⸗) [nhd.] v/n. ⑪**⁓haben; die Bitte ⁓ l., der Bitte **geben** v/n. (h.) ⑪c** to grant the petition, to give way; gebt nie dem tollen Wahn des Pöbels statt heed not the mad delusions of the mob; ⁓haben v/n. (h.) ⑪b** to take place, to come to pass; da hat das Schweigen besser statt then silence is the better course.
statthaft (⸗⸗⸗) [mhd.] a. ⑥ admissible; (erlaubt) permitted; (gültig) valid, (gesetzlich erlaubt) legal, lawful; ⁓igkeit (⸗⸗⸗⸗) f ㊺ admissibility; validity, lawfulness.
Statt¹-**halter** (⸗⸗⸗) m ⑫ (Stellvertreter) substitute; des Herrschers in e-r Provinz: governor; (Vizekönig) viceroy; ehm. ⁓halter von Holland: Stadholder; ⁓halterei f: a) (Amt) governorship; b) (Bezirk) government; ⁓halterin f governor's wife or spouse, in Indien &c. auch: vicereine; ⁓halterschaft f = ⁓halterei.
stattlich (⸗⸗) [ahd. (adv.)] a. ⑥ stately, (prächtig) magnificent, splendid; (würdevoll) portly; ⁓e Figur commanding (stärker: majestic) figure; eine ⁓e (bedeutende) Summe a considerable (or large) sum; ⁓ (adv.) ausgestattet luxuriously (or sumptuously) fitted up; **Stattlichkeit** (⸗⸗⸗) f ㊺ magnificence, stateliness, portliness, luxuriousness, sumptuousness.
Statu-**e** (⸗⸗⸗) [lt. stā'tŭä] f ㊺ (Bildsäule) statue. [statue.]
Statuette (⸗⸗⸗⸗) f ㊺ statuette, small ⸗
statuieren (⸗⸗⸗⸗) [lt.] v/a. ⑬ 1. (feststellen) to establish. — 2. (statthaben l.) a) (zugeben) to allow, to suffer; b) (anordnen) to arrange (s. Exempel 1).
Statur (⸗⸗⸗) [lt.] f ㊺ (Wuchs, Gestalt) figure, (Körperlänge) size, stature. height.
Status (⸗⸗) [lt.] m, inv. 1. ⊙ (Stand) state (of affairs); (Bilanz) balance-sheet. — 2. der ⁓quo. Status quo ante the actual state (of affairs).
Statut (⸗⸗) [lt.] n ㉓ jur. (Satzung) statute; (Regulativ) regulation.
statutarisch (⸗⸗⸗⸗) a. ⑥ (satzungsgemäß) statutory, according to statute.
Statuten-**buch** (⸗⸗⸗⸗) n ⑪ univ. &c. statute-book; ⁓gemäß, ⁓mäßig a. ⑥ = statutarisch; ⁓recht n statutory law; ⁓widrig a. contrary to statute.

Stau (⸗) [s. stauen] m ⑪c. nur in: ⁊ das Wasser ist im ⁓ (zw. Ebbe und Flut) the tide is turning; ⊙ Deichbau: das Wasser im ⁓ haben oder halten to dam up the water.
Staub (⸗) [ahd.: stieben] m ⑪c. dust; feiner ⁓, auch: fine powder; f. aufwirbeln 3; den ⁓ durch Sprengen dämpfen, legen to lay the dust; sich **aus** dem ⁓e (eilig davon) machen to (make one's) escape, F to make (or hurry) off. to bolt; **im** ⁓e kriechen to crouch (fig. a. to grovel) in the dust; fig. in den ⁓ treten, zerren, ziehen to drag through the mire or mud; orn. sich im ⁓e wälzen to roll in the dust, to pulverize; bibl. wieder **zu** ⁓ werden to return to dust; zu ⁓ zerfallen to crumble (in)to dust.
Staub-**abhalter** (⸗⸗⸗) m ⑫ dustguard; ⁓ähnlich, ⁓artig a. ⑥ like dust, powdery, pulverous; ⁓bach m. torrent forming clouds of spray in its descent; ⁓bad n shower-bath; von Vögeln: rolling in the dust; ⁓bedeckt a. covered with dust; ⁓besen m dust-broom; ⁓beutel ⚘ m: ⁊ anther; ⁓beutel-tragend ⚘ a.: ⁊ antheriferous; ⁓brille f coloured glasses pl. for the protection of the eyes, für Automobilisten: (pair of) goggles pl.
Stäubchen (⸗⸗) n ㉓ (dim. von Staub) small grain (or particle) of dust; ein bloßes ⁓ a mere atom.
stauben (⸗⸗) ⑱ v/n. (h. u. ſn) 1. (Staub abgeben) to give off dust; v/impers. es staubt it is dusty. — 2. (wie Staub fliegen) to fly like dust.
stäuben (⸗⸗) ⑱ I v/a. 1. Sand, Pulver auf et. ⁓ (streuen) to (strew with) sand. powder. — 2. die Feinde aus-ea. (=) ⁓ to scatter (or disperse)... — 3. (abstäuben) to (sweep away the) dust.
— II v/n. 4. = stauben.
Stäuber (⸗⸗) m ⑫: a) person who dusts; b) (Staublappen) duster.
stäubern (⸗⸗) v/a. ⑫a. to dust.
Staub-**erde** (⸗⸗⸗) f ⑫ dusty earth, dry mould; ⁓faden ⚘ m (Träger des Staubbeutels) filament; ⁓fäden tragend: ⁊ staminiferous; ⁓fleck m speck of dust; ⁓flocke f flue; ⁓geboren a.: a) baseborn; b) bsd. rel. of clay. mortal; ⁓gebor(e)ne(r) m f mortal (man), earthly creature; ⁓gefäß ⚘ n (Staubfäden und Staubbeutel): ⁊ stamen; ⁓hemd n blouse; ⁓hülle f, poet. human frame, tenement of clay.
staubig (⸗⸗) a. ⑥ dusty, covered with dust, powdery, ⁊ pulverulent; es ist ⁓ it is dusty; **Staubigkeit** f ㊺ dustiness, ⁊ pulverulence.
Staub-**kamm** (⸗⸗⸗) m ⑫ small-tooth comb; ⁓kittel m dust-coat, smock-frock; ⁓kohle f dusty (or small) coal; ⁓korn, ⁓körnchen n grain (or speck) of dust; ⁓lappen m duster; ⁓lawine f avalanche of dry snow. [⁓schwamm.]
Stäubling ⚘ (⸗⸗) m ⑪d. = Staub-⸗
Staub-**mantel** (⸗⸗⸗) m ⑫ dust-cloak; bisw. = Schmutzkittel; ⁓mehl n very fine flour. flour-dust; ⁓regen m fine drizzling rain, auch: Scotch mist; ⁓sammler m dust-collector; ⁓sand m very fine sand; ⁓schwamm ⚘ m puff-

Zeichen (f. S. XVII): F familiär; P Volkssprache; P̷ Gaunersprache; ⚶ selten; † alt (auch gestorben); * neu (auch geboren); ⁓⁓ unrichtig;

[Staubsieb] — 917 — [stecken]

ball (*Lycope'rdon bovi'sta*); =sieb *n* dust-sieve; =tee *m* tea-dust; =tuch *n* dusting-cloth, duster; =wedel *m* feather-broom, whisk, duster; =weg *m*: ⚒ pistil; =wirbel *m* whirling (columns *pl.* of) dust, in der Wüste: dust-storm; =wolke *f* dust-cloud, cloud of dust.

Stauche (¹ᶜʰᵥ) [ahd.: stook] *f* ⊕ *agr.* ~ (zum Trocknen aufgestellter Haufen) Hanf ꝛc. hemp, &c. put up in bundles for drying, stook of hemp, &c. — 2. = Muff³, Pulswärmer.

stauchen (ᴸᵛ) [ndd.] *v/a.* ⊕ 1. to toss (up), jog, jolt; sich den Arm (ver=)2 to sprain one's arm. — 2. ⊕ *agr.* den Hanf ꝛc. 2 to stook hemp, &c., to put up ... in bundles for drying; Schmiede: ein Eisenstück 2 to upset ...

Stauch=maschine ⊕ (ᴸᶜʰ-ᴗᴸ) *f* ⊕ Schmiede: upsetting-machine.

Stau=damm ⚓ (ᴸᵛ) *m* ⊕ coffer-dam.

Staude ♃ (ᴸᵛ) [ahd.] *f* ⊕ (small) shrub, bush, ⚘ suffrutescent plant.

stauden¹ ♃ (ᴸᵛ) [Staude] *v/n.* (h. u. sn) und sich 2 *v/refl.* ⊕ to develop (or grow) into a (small) shrub, to run into stalk, vom Salate: to form a head.

stauden²=artig ♃ (ᴸᵛ...) [Staude], =förmig *a.* ⊕ shrub-like, ⚘ suffrutescent, suffruticose; =gewächs *n* = Staude; =salat *m* = Kopfsalat.

staudig ♃ (ᴸᵛ) *a.* ⊕ = staudenartig.

stauen (ᴸᵛ) [ndd.; stow: steh(e)n] *v/a.* ⊕ 1. to stow (away) goods; ⚓ ein Schiff 2 (die Ladung verteilen und verpacken) to trim the ship or the hold, to stow (away) the cargo. — 2. ⊕ das Wasser 2 (anschwellen) to dam (or bank) up the water; *a. v/n.* (h.) u. *v/refl.*: das Wasser stauet (sich) ... is rising; das Eis staut sich ... is getting blocked or jammed.

Stauer ⚓ (ᴸᵛ) [stauen 1] *m* ⊕ stower of goods, stevedore.

Stau=holz ⚓ (ᴸᴸ) [stau=en] *n* ⊕ fathom-wood for stowing.

staunen (ᴸᵛ) [schwz.: (a)stound] I *v/n.* (h.) ⊕ to be astonished or surprised, to marvel (über *et.* at a th.), stärker: to be amazed at a th. — II ~ *n* ⊕ astonishment, amazement.

staunens=wert (ᴸᵛ...), =würdig *a.* ⊕ astonishing, amazing.

Staup=besen (ᴸᴸ) [Staupe¹] *m* ⊕ ehm. Strafwerkzeug: rod, scourge.

Staupe¹ (ᴸᵛ) [ndd.] *f* ⊕ ehm.: (public) flogging or whipping or scourging.

Staupe² (ᴸᵛ) [ndl. *stuip*] *f* ⊕ *path.* (Seuche) contagion, contagious disease.

Stäupe¹ u. ² ♃ (ᴸᵛ) *f* ⊕ = Staupe¹ u. ².

stäupen (ᴸᵛ) [ndd.] *v/a.* ⊕ ehm.: Verbrecher 2 to flog (or whip, scourge) offenders (publicly or in public).

Stau=raum ⚓ (ᴸᴸ) *m* ⊕ stowage; =schleuse *f* Wasserbau: retaining-sluice.

Stauung (ᴸᵛ) [stauen] *f* ⊕ 1. ⚓ stowing the cargo. — 2. ~ des Verkehrs stoppage of (or blocking) the traffic; ⊕ damming (up) the water.

Stau=wasser ⚓ (ᴸᴸ) *n* ⊕ back-water.

Stearin (ᵛᴸᴸ) [grch. *ste'ar* Talg] *n* ⊕d. *chm.* stearin(e) ($C_3H_5[C_{18}H_{35}O_2]_3$).

Stearin=kerze (ᵛᴸᴸ...) *f* ⊕, =licht *n* stearin(e)-candle, 🕯 composite candle; =sauer *a.* ⊕ stearic; =saures Salz

stearate; =säure *f. chm.* ⚒ stearic acid ($C_{18}H_{36}O_2$); =seife *f* stearin(e)-soap.

Stech=apfel ♃ (ᴸ...) *m* ⊕ thorn-apple (a. die Frucht). stramony (*Datu'ra Stramo'nium*); =apfel=säure *f, chm.* ⚒ daturine; =bahn *f*: a) chm. tilt-yard, lists *pl.*; b) *arch.* arcade; =baum ♃ *m* = Stech=eiche; =becken *n* für Bettlägerige: bed-pan; =beitel ⊕ *m. carp.* (ripping-)chisel; =bolzen ⚓ *m* reefing-earing; =dorn *m* Christ's-thorn (*Pali'urus austra'lis*); =eiche ♃ *f* = =palme; =eisen ⊕ *n* punch(eon), piercer, *metall.* tapping-bar.

stechen (ᴸᵛ) [ahd.: stitch] I *v a., v/n.* (mst h.) u. sich 2 *v/refl.* ⊕a. 1. (bohrend eindringen) (*ant.* hauen 3) (sich) 2 to prick (o.s.) with a pin, &c.; von Insekten ꝛc.: to sting, von Schlangen auch: to bite; Näherei: to stitch; mit einem spitzen Werkzeuge: to prod, ⊕ u. *surg.* to puncture; nach ein 2 to thrust at a p.; e-m den Degen durch den Leib 2 to run one's sword through a p.'s body); *fig. s.* hauen 3; *surg. s.* Star²; 2d stinging. pungent (smell); piercing (glance). — 2. mit Angabe der Wirkung: e-n tot ob. zu Tode 2 to stab a p. (to death); durch und durch 2 to run through (the body), to pierce, to transfix; Löcher in et. 2 to prick (or make) holes in a th., to perforate a th.; einem Löcher in die Ohren 2 to pierce a p.'s ears. — 3. (ritterlich mit Lanzen 2) to j(o)ust; e-n vom Pferde 2, aus dem Sattel 2 to unhorse a p.; nach dem Ringe 2 to run at tilts, to tilt. — 4. bsd. Schlächterei: ein Kalb 2 to kill a calf, ein Schwein 2 to kill (or stick) a pig. — 5. v. Empfindungen: es sticht mir (ob. mich) in der Milz I feel a pain (or a pricking) in my side; es sticht ihm (ihn) in der Seite he has a stitch in the side; grell in die Augen 2 to dazzle (or offend) the eye; die Sonne sticht (brennt heiß) ... is scorching or burning; *fig.* das stach ihm in die Augen that caught his eye, that struck him, (es gefiel ihm) it took his fancy; *s.* Hafer. — 6. F e-m eine Maulschelle, oft: eine 2 (auch stecken) to give a p. a box on the ear or a slap in the face. — 7. e-m *et.* 2 ob. stecken (heimlich mitteilen) to give a p. a quiet hint or a hint on the sly. — 8. Silben 2 (klauben) to split hairs, to quarrel about trifles; to be pedantic or punctilious. — 9. Wein (mit dem Stechheber) aus dem Fasse 2 to draw wine (with a siphon). — 10. ins Rote 2 to have a tinge of red or a reddish tinge. — 11. Kartenspiel: mit dem Könige den Buben 2 to beat (or take) the jack with the king; mit Trumpf 2 to (over)trump. — 12. ⊕ *agr.* Rasen 2 to cut (the) sods or turf; Spargel (Torf ꝛc.) 2 to cut asparagus (peat, &c.); am Gewehre: (das Stechschloß) 2 to pull the trigger; Gravierkunst: in Kupfer ob. Stahl 2 to engrave on ...; schreibt wie gestochen he writes like copperplate. — 13. ⚓ (in) in See 2 to stand for the offing. — II ~ *n* ⊕ 14. a) der Ritter: j(o)ust, tournament, tilt(ing); b) (Gravierkunst) (art of) engraving.

Stecher (ᴸᵛ) *m* ⊕ 1. Person: a) auf Turnieren: jouster, tilter; b) = Kupferstecher. — 2. Sache: a) ⊕ = Stecheisen; am Gewehre: hair-trigger; zum Untersuchen von Butter ꝛc.: scoop; b) (Augenglas) eye-glass; c) Orgelbau: mst. *pl.* ~ (*ant.* Abstrakten) sticker(s *pl.*).

Stecher=lohn (ᴸᵛ...) *m* ⊕ engraver's salary or fee; =schloß ⊕ *n* = Stechschloß.

Stech=fliege (ᴸᵛ...) *f* ⊕ *ent.* stinging fly; *vgl.* mücke; =gabel ⊕ *f* Fischerei: fish-spear; =ginster ♃ *m* furze, gorse (*Ulex europae'us*); =heber *m. phys.* (plunging) siphon; =kamm ⊕ *m* Nadler: pricking-comb; =kissen *n* (in Engl. unbekannt) pillow to carry a baby on; =mücke *f. ent.* gnat (*Culex*); (Moskito) mosquito; =nelke ♃ *f* rose campion (*Lychnis corona'ria*); =palme ♃ *f* holly (*Ilex Aquifo'lium*); ehm. =puppe *f* quintain; =ring *n* tilting-ring; =schloß ⊕ *n* an e-r Büchse: hair-trigger (lock); *s.* stechen 12; =spiel *n* tilt(ing), *vgl.* stechen II; =vieh *n* = Schlachtvieh.

Steck=amboß ⊕ (ᴸᵛ...) *m* ⊕ stake; =becken *n* = Stechbecken; =brief *m* warrant (for the apprehension of a p.); =brieflich *a.* ⊕, *adv.*: einen 2 verfolgen to take out a warrant against a p., *a.* to raise a hue and cry after a p.; er wird 2 verfolgt a warrant is out against him, *auch*: F he is wanted.

Stecken¹ (ᴸᵛ) [ahd.: stick: stecken²] *m* ⊕ (Spazierstock) walking-stick; (Stab) staff.

stecken² (ᴸᵛ) [ahd.: stick] I *v/n.* (h.) ⊕a. (*impf. stat. subj.* stäke; *pres.* † stick(f)t, *imper.* † stick) u. ⊕ 1. (sich befinden) to be (somewhere), to find o.s. (in a place); (befestigt sein) to be attached (or fixed) to a th., to stick in (or to) a th.; (festsitzen) to be firmly (im)planted or imbedded, to be stuck fast; 2 bleiben *s.* steckenbleiben; den Schlüssel 2 lassen to leave the key in the lock; das wird er nicht 2 (auf sich sitzen) lassen he won't leave that slur (or stain) on his character; voll von *et.* 2 to be full of a th. — 2. *fig.* er schreit, als ob er am Spieße stäke he screams as if he was going to be murdered; bis über die Ohren in Geschäften 2 to be right busy, to be over head and ears in work; *s.* Haut 2; was mag ihm nur im Kopfe 2? what can have taken possession of him?; *s.* Decke 2; zwischen Tür und Angel 2 to be in a (great) fix; e-n (in großer Not, Patsche) 2 lassen to leave a p. in the lurch. — 3. (verborgen sein) to be hidden away somewhere; immer zu Hause 2 to be (to sit or F stick) for ever at home; wo 2 Sie denn? where have you been (all this time)?, where did you get to?: in dem Kerl steckt etwas there is s.th. (or F some good stuff) in that fellow; *s.* dahinter. — 4. *v impers.* es steckt mir in allen Gliedern I feel it in all my limbs; hier steckt es mir there's s.th. wrong with me here; F da steckt's (das ist's) that's the point. there's the rub. — II *v/a.* ⊕ faktitiv zu I: 5. (wohin) 2 to stick (into a th.), to put (somewhere), (hineinstopfen) to stuff (or ram) in(to),

♪ Musik; ⚒ Wissenschaft; ♃ Pflanze; 🌍 Geographie; ⊕ Technik; ⚒ Bergbau; ⚔ Militär; ⚓ Marine; 🏛 Handel; ✉ Post; 🚂 Eisenbahn.

[**steckenbleiben**] — 918 — [**stehen**]

(einverleiben) to incorporate; **an den Spieß** ⸺ to (put on the) spit; to spear; **auf den Hut** ⸺ to stick (or put) on one's hat; **durch** et. hindurch ⸺ to pass (or slip) through a th.; das Haus **in** Brand ⸺ to set ... on fire; in=ea. ⸺ to fit (or fix) into each other; in die Erde ⸺ to put (or fix, plant) into the earth; ins Gefängnis (Kloster) ⸺ to shut up in prison (in a convent); Geld in ein Geschäft (hinein-) ⸺ to put ... into (or to sink ... in) a business; den Degen in die Scheide ⸺ to sheathe one's sword; in die Tasche (a. zu sich) ⸺ to (put in one's) pocket; **unter** die Soldaten ⸺ to put into the army, to make a soldier of; *fig.* f. Nase 2, Sack 6, Spiegel 1. — **6.** fest=⸺ to attach (or fix) with pins, &c.; los=⸺ to unfix, unfasten, unpin. — **7.** ohne Angabe des Wohin: a) *hort.* Erbsen ꝛc. ⸺ to plant peas, &c.; b) e-r Dame das Haar (ob. den Kopfputz) ⸺ to dress a lady's hair; c-e Haube ⸺ to dress (or make) a lady's cap or head-gear. — **8.** e-m ein Ziel ⸺ (festsetzen) to set a p. a certain task, to keep a p. in bounds. — **9.** = stechen 6 u. 7. — **III** *v/refl.* **10.** fich hinter e-n, et. ⸺ (verbergen) to ensconce o.s. (or take shelter) behind a p., a th. — **IV** ✶ ∿ *n* ⓔ **11.** ꝛB. *fig.* das ~ unter einer Decke secret understanding or conspiracy.

stecken²-bleiben (⸺ʋ,⸺ʋ) *v/n.* (fn.) ⓔ※※ to stick fast, to be stuck, to come to a standstill; im Dreck: to stick in the mud; in der Rede: to break down in one's speech; ~ *n* ⓔ sticking fast, standstill, in der Rede: break-down.

Stecken¹-**kraut** ⚥ (⸺ʋ...) *n* ⓔ giant fennel (*Fe'rula commu'nis*); =**pferd** für Kinder u. *fig.* hobby(-horse); (Liebhaberei) fad, fancy, amusement; =**streich** *m* cut with a stick; =**zaun** *m* fence made up of sticks.

Steck-erbsen (²...) *f/pl.* ⓔ *hort.* peas raised on sticks; =**kiffen** *n* = Stechkiffen; =**leuchter** *m* candlestick (to be) fastened in the wall. [slip, shoot.]

Steckling (⸺ʋ) *m* ⓔ *d. hort.* layer, cutting,

Steck-muschel (²...) *f* ⓔ *zo.:* ⚥ pinna; =**nadel** *f* pin, ganz schwarze: mourning-pin; Draht zu ~ *n* pin-wire; *fig.* es fehlt keine ~ daran there is not a particle of it missing; =**nadel-büchse** *f* pin-box; =**nadel-kiffen** *n* pincushion; =**nadel-kopf** *m* pin's head; =**nagel** *m* bolt, ✕ jig-pin; =**reis** *n* layer, cutting, slip; =**rübe** ⚥ *f* swede, Swedish turnip (*Bra'ssica Napus*); =**zirkel** ⊕ *m* compasses *pl.* with shifting points; =**zwiebel** ⊕ *f* bulb for planting.

Steg (¹) [ahd.: steigen] *m* ⓔ c. **1.** (Steig) path; alle Wege u. ~e kennen to know all the highways and by-ways of every road. — **2.** (schmale Brücke) narrow wooden bridge, aus Baumstämmen: tree-bridge, für Fußgänger: foot-bridge. — **3.** a) ♪ ~ der Violine ꝛc.: bridge; b) an Hosen: trousers-strap; *vgl.* Sprungriemen a. — **4.** ☉: a) *arch.* (Leistchen) fillet; ~ an Türen: panel-frame; b) *typ.* stick; ~e *pl.* furniture.

Steg-brücke (¹...) *f* ⓔ = Steg 2; =**fach** *n*, =**kasten** ⊕ *m*, *typ.* furniture-case.

Stegreif (¹¹) [ahd. (Auf-)steig-reif] *m* ⓔ c.: a) † = Steigbügel; b) *fig.* aus dem ~ (ohne Vorbereitung) extempore, impromptu; on the spur of the moment; aus dem ~ hersagen to extemporize.

Stegreif-dichter (¹¹...) *m* ⓔ, =**musiker**, =**redner** *m* improvisator(e); =**ritter** *m* highwayman. ehm. knight-robber.

Steh-auf(**chen** *n*) *m* (¹¹ᵛ) ⓔ Spielzeug: (cork)tumbler; =**bier-halle** (¹¹...) *f* bar.

steh(e)n (¹ᵛ) [ahd.: stay (stand): It. sta're] **I** *v/n.* (h. u. fn) u. *v/refl.* ⓔ **1.** to stand, to be upright or erect, to be on one's legs; ich kann kaum mehr ⸺ I can barely stand (on my legs). — **2.** mit Bestimmung des Ortes: da (hier) steht er there (here) he stands; da (in diesem Buche ꝛc.) steht's there it is (written), there you can read it; ea. gegenüber=⸺ to stand opposite (or to face) each other; *fig.* f. Kopf 2. — **3.** mit Bestimmung der Art und Weise: f. dahin=⸺; er steht uns fern he is a stranger to us; so viel steht fest, daß // so much is certain that //; das steht Ihnen frei you are quite free (or at liberty) to do so; gerade ⸺ to stand (or keep o.s.) upright; der Hafer steht gut oder schön the oats are in fine condition or look well; gut für e-n ⸺ to stand security (or bail) for a p.; die Tür steht offen ... stands (or is) open; das Geld steht sicher ... is well (or securely, safely) invested; die Sache steht so that's how the matter stands; still ⸺ to stand still, to stop (a. ☉ von Maschinen); meine Uhr steht (still) ... has stopped; er kann nicht still=⸺ he cannot keep quiet, he is restless or fidgety; *fig.* dabei steht mir der Verstand still that's beyond me; das wird ihm teuer zu ⸺ kommen he will have to pay dearly for that; wie er steht und geht just as he stands. — **4.** mit adjektivischem *part.:* fest begründet, gemauert ⸺ to be solidly based, constructed; die Pferde ⸺ (fertig) gesattelt ... are (ready) saddled; das steht geschrieben zu lesen so it is written, you can see it in black and white; in dem Buche steht nichts davon the book says nothing (or does not mention anything) about it; was steht (Neues) in der Zeitung? what news is there in the paper(s)?, what do the papers say?; *fig.* f. anschreiben 2. — **5.** als Bürge für e-n ⸺ to stand as (or to be) security for a p.; (als oder zu) Gevatter ⸺ f. Gevatter 1; einem Maler (als, zu) Modell ⸺ to stand (or serve as) model to an artist (vgl. 10 b); zu Gebot(e) ⸺ f. Gebot¹ 2; bsd. von Setzern: ⸺ (arbeiten) **bei** // to be in the employ of //. — **6.** *v/imp.* steht es gut oder schlecht mit ihm? are matters (going) well or ill with him?; es steht schlecht mit ihm he is in a bad way; wie steht's mit Ihrer Gesundheit? how are you (in health)?, how have you been?; wie steht es mit f-m Prozesse? how is his case getting on?; so steht's also? is that how matters stand?; vgl. Sache 5 am Schluß. —

7. von Kleidern ꝛc.: einem gut (schlecht) ⸺ to suit (or fit) a p. well (badly); e-m ausgezeichnet ⸺ to be most becoming to a p. — **8.** **sich** so und so ⸺: a) von der Bekanntschaft: wie ⸺ Sie (F sich) mit ea.? on what footing (or terms) are you?; F wir ⸺ uns nicht besonders we are not on the best of terms, we do not hit it off well; b) vom Einkommen, Gewinn: er steht sich auf (oder an) viertausend Mark he has an income of two hundred pounds, F he has (or earns, makes) two hundred a year; sich bei et. gut ⸺ to make a good profit on a th.; sie ⸺ sich nicht schlecht dabei they are no losers by it, F they don't do badly (at that). — **9.** mit *prp.:* **an**=ea. ⸺ to touch (one another); die Hütte stand am Meere ... stood by the sea-shore; an der Spitze von et. ⸺ to be at the head of a th., to take the lead in a th.; ⓔ die Aktien ⸺ **auf** 75 the shares are at 75; f. Brett 2; *gram.* der Dativ steht auf die Frage „wem" the dative answers the question: *to whom*; f. Fuß 7 gegen Ende; f. bestehen 6; auf e-r Liste ⸺ to figure (or appear) in a list; auf j-s Seite ⸺ to be on a p.'s side, to side (or hold) with a p.; das Barometer steht auf Regen ... points to (or indicates) rain; f. Kopf 3 und 8 (unter „auf"); es steht der Tod darauf it is a capital offence or a hanging-matter; es steht **bei** Ihnen (in Ihrer Macht) zu bleiben you are quite welcome (or at liberty) to stay; es steht nicht bei mir es zu tun it is not (with-) in my power to do it; ✕ bei der Garde ⸺ to serve in the Guards; **für** et. (gut. ob. ein-)⸺ to answer (or vouch) for a th., to guarantee a th.; sie ⸺ alle für **einen** Mann: a) they are all one; b) bei e-m Kampfe: they rise like one man; für allen Schaden ⸺ to make good all losses; ich mußte selbst für alles ⸺ (sorgen) I had to look after everything, everything devolved on me; f. **gegenüber**=; *gram.* das Objekt steht gewöhnlich **hinter** dem Subjekt the object usually comes (or is generally put) after the subject; **in** e-m Amte ⸺ to occupy a post, to be in an office; bei einem in Arbeit ⸺ to be in a p.'s employ; in Beziehung (ob. e-m Verhältnisse) zu e-m ⸺ to stand in a certain relationship to a p.; in Briefwechsel mit e-m ⸺ to be in correspondence with a p.; im zwölften Jahre ⸺ to be in one's twelfth year; ✕ im Lager (in Garnison) ⸺ to be in camp (in garrison); Tränen standen ihm in den Augen tears stood (or were) in his eyes; es steht (ganz) in Ihrer Macht it is a question (entirely) for you to decide, the matter rests (solely) with you; soweit es in meiner Macht steht as far as lies in my power or in me; in Verdacht ⸺ to be suspected; ich stehe nicht allein **mit** m-r Meinung I am not the only one that thinks so; **nach** etwas ⸺ = trachten; **neben**=ea. ⸺ to stand side by side; **über** (**unter**) e-m ⸺ to be above (below) a p., to be superior (inferior) to a p.; über=ea. ⸺ to range above each other;

Signs (see page XVII): F familiar; P vulgar; ꟼ flash; ∿ rare; † obsolete (died); * new word (born); ⁘ incorrect; ♪ music;

[stehenbleiben] — 919 — [steigen]

um e-n herum ℒ to stand around (or to surround) a p., to form a circle round a p.; es stand schlecht um ihn he was in a bad way or in a precarious position; **unter**: s. Pantoffel 2; unter den Waffen ℒ to be under arms; er steht mir immer **vor** Augen he is for ever present to my mind; ich stehe im Augenblicke **zu** Ihren Diensten I shall be at your service in a moment; s. Gebot¹ 2; e-m zur Seite ℒ to stand by a p.'s side, to assist a p.; zu eurem Vaterlande steht (haltet euch)! cling to your native land! — **10.** e-m ℒ: a) (ausharrend) to await a p.('s attack); b) beim Maler: to stand as (a) model. — **11.** *ell.* als v/a. s-n Mann ℒ to take one's stand, *fig.* to hold one's own; s. Rede 3, Schildwache b. — **12.** *hunt.* der Hund steht vor dem Hasen ... holds the hare. — **13.** v/refl.: a) sich müde ℒ to tire o.s. (out) with standing; b) v/imp. es steht sich (man steht) sicherer hier it is safer to stand here. — **14.** mit *inf.*: **a)** ohne „zu": ℒ bleiben s. steh(e)nbleiben; acht Pferde im Stalle ℒ haben to have (or keep) ... in one's stable; Geld bei e-m ℒ haben to have money standing with a p.; alles ℒ und liegen lassen to leave everything just as it stands; e-n ℒ lassen to leave a p. unnoticed; et. ℒ lassen to leave a th. as it is; eine Speise (ungegessen) ℒ lassen to leave a dish untouched; † das Wort sie sollen lassen stahn (*LU.*) none shall prevail against the Word of God; **b)** mit „zu": es steht zu erwarten, daß // it is to be expected that //. — **15.** ohne abhängige Verhältnisse: a) = still ℒ, zB.: das Blut zum ~ bringen to stanch the blood; b) (*ant.* fallen, umstürzen) to stand upright or erect; (bestehen) to exist; das Haus steht noch nicht lange ... has not been built long; solange die Welt steht as long as the world lasts; c) (nicht weichen) to stand one's ground, not to give way; d) *gram.* der Artikel steht vor Dingwörtern the article stands (or is used)...; e) (in der Schwebe sein) to balance; f) (im Amte sein) der Ort, wo er gestanden ... where he held his appointment. — **II** ~ *n* ㉓ **16.** standing; das ~ fällt ihm schwer he cannot stand long; im ~ schlafen to sleep while standing; Platz zum ~ standing-room; zum ~ bringen: a) to make (or cause to) stand; b) to bring to a standstill; to stop, to stay, to arrest (in its progress). — **III** stehend *p.pr.* u. *a.* ㊻ **17.** (*ant.* liegend) standing, zB. auf den Füßen ℒ standing on one's feet; (emporgerichtet) upright, erect; (senkrecht) vertical; ⊕ ℒe Welle upright shaft, spindle. — **18.** ℒen (u. ℒes) Fußes (sofort) on the spot, forthwith, at once, immediately. — **19.** ℒes (nicht fließendes, *ant.* lebendes) Wasser stagnant water. — **20.** (fest, unbeweglich) stationary, fixed, immovable; allein-ℒ isolated, lonely; ⊕ Färberei: ℒe Farbe fast colour; *typ.* ℒer Satz standing matter. — **21.** (immer wiederkehrend) periodical, regular; ℒer Ausdruck standing expression; ℒe Redens-art hackneyed (or stereotyped) phrase. — **22.** (ununterbrochen) continuous; ✕ ℒes Heer standing (or regular) army. — **IV** gestanden *p.p.* u. *a.* ㊻ **23.** ℒe Milch curdled milk; *obb.* ein ℒer (reifer) Mann a man of mature age.

steh(e)n-bleiben (⁽ᴸ⁾⁻ᴸ⁻) v/n. (sn) ⓽** to remain standing, *typ. v.* Sage: to stand, to remain in type; (einhalten) to stop (short, to make a stop); wo sind wir ℒ geblieben? where did we leave off or stop?; bei et. ℒ (sich damit begnügen) to confine o.s. to a th.; ~ n ㉓ = Stillstand.

Steher (ᴸ⁻) *m* ㉒ Rennsport: stayer.

Steh-kragen (⁻⁻¹⁻ᴸ⁻) *m* ㉒ stand-up collar.

stehlbar (ᴸ⁻) *a.* ㊻ stealable.

Steh-leiter (⁻⁻¹⁻ᴸ⁻) *f* ㉒ (pair of steps).

stehlen (ᴸ⁻) [*ahd.*: steal] **I** v/a., v/n. (h.) u. v/refl. ⓓ. **1.** to steal, *abs.* to thieve, (entwenden) to purloin, (mausen) to pilfer, F to prig, nick, crib, (wegnehmen) to remove, take, abstract, F to lift; Kinder, Weiber, Neger 2c. ℒ to kidnap children, women, negroes, &c.; einem et. ℒ to rob a p. of a th.; *bibl.* du sollst nicht ℒ thou shalt not steal. — **2.** *fig.* dem lieben Gott die Zeit ℒ to waste (or idle away) one's time; das kann mir gestohlen werden I don't care (a scrap) what becomes of it; der kann mir gestohlen werden he can go and be hanged; *g.s.* einem das Herz ℒ to captivate (or conquer) a p.'s heart; ich muß die Zeit förmlich dazu ℒ I have to make time for it somehow. — **3.** sich wohin ℒ (schleichen) to sneak to a place; er stahl sich aus dem Hause he stole (or slunk, sneaked) away from the house. — **II** ~ *n* ㉓ **4.** stealing, thieving, theft, aus Büchern: plagiarizing, plagiarism.

Stehler (ᴸ⁻) *m* ㉒ = Dieb; s. Hehler.

Stehl-sucht (⁻⁻¹⁻⁻⁻⁻) *f* ㊻: ⓐ cleptomania.

Steh-männchen (⁻⁻¹⁻ᴸ⁻) *n* ㉒ = Stehauf.

stehn (ᴸ) v/n. s. stehen.

Steh-platz (⁻⁻⁻¹⁻) *m* ㉒ standing-room; =pult *n* standing-desk; =seidel *f n* glass of beer emptied in standing (at the bar).

Stei(e)rer (ᴸ⁽⁻⁾⁻) *m* ㉒, **Steierin** *f* ㊵, **stei(e)risch** *a.* ㊻ Styrian.

Steier-mark ♀ (⁻⁻¹⁻ᴸ⁻) [Schloß Styra 12. *sae.*] *npr/f.* ㊻ Herzogtum: Styria; =märker(in *f*) *m* Styrian.

steif (¹) [*ndb.*: stiff] *a.* ㊻ **1.** stiff, *phys.,* &c. rigid, von Brei 2c.: (dick) thick, solid, (fest) fixed, firm, (unbiegsam) inflexible; von Gliedern des Körpers: (erstarrt) numb, benumbed, lifeless; ziemlich ℒ stiffish; vom Sitzen 2c. ℒ stiff with sitting, &c., von Rheumatismus 2c. set fast with rheumatism; *path.* ℒer Hals stiff neck; ℒer, schiefer Hals: ⓐ torticollis; ↓ ℒer Wind, ℒe Kühlte stiff breeze; ℒ machen to stiffen; ℒ werden to grow stiff or rigid (auch von Leichen, von Muskeln): to stiffen, to contract; ℒ werdend: ⓐ rigescent; *fig.* ermutigend: halten Sie die Ohren ℒ! keep up your pecker or your spirits!, never say die! — **2.** von der Wäsche: (gestärkt) stiff, (stiffly) starched; sehr ℒ, *a.* highly dressed (collar, linen, &c.). — **3.** von geistigen Getränken: ℒer (starker) Grog strong grog, stiff glass of grog. — **4.** a) (ungeschickt) awkward, heavy; F ℒer Bock oder Peter *co.* clumsy Dick; b) (gezwungen) strait-laced, starchy, F (as) stiff as buckram or a poker; (geziert) affected; (förmlich) formal, precise, punctilious, standing on ceremony; ℒe Verbeugung formal bow. — **5.** *fig.* ℒ u. fest behaupten to assert positively, to persist in saying; mit ℒem Mute with stubborn (or obstinate) courage.

Steife (ᴸ⁻) *f* ㊷ **1.** = Steifheit 2. — **2.** ⊕ a) (Stoff zum Steifmachen) Wäscherei: starch; Hutmacherei: dressing, stiffening; b) *carp.* &c. (Stütze) prop, support, stay, shore.

steifen¹ (ᴸ⁻) [steif] v/a. u. sich ℒ v/refl. ㊸ to stiffen, to make stiff; *fig.* sich auf et. ℒ und stemmen (et. fest behaupten) to insist (obstinately) on a th., to persist in (asserting a) thing.

steifen² (ᴸ⁻) [steif] v/a. ㊸: Wäsche ℒ to (clear-)starch ...; ⊕ e-n Hut ℒ to dress (or size, stiffen)...[*2c.*: dresser, stiffener.]

Steifer ⊕ (ᴸ⁻) [steifen²] *m* ㉒ Hutmacherei)

Steif-gaze ⓝ (⁻¹⁻...) *f* ㊷ foundation-muslin, grobe: foundation-net; =hals *m* (person, animal with a) stiff neck.

Steifheit (ᴸ⁻) *f* ㊻ **1.** (zu steif 1:) stiffness, rigidity, von Brei 2c.: thickness; einer Sache die ~ benehmen to make a th. limp. — **2.** *path.* ~ der Gelenke stiff(ness of the) joints, ⓐ anchylosis. — **3.** *fig.* (zu steif 4:) awkwardness, starchiness.

Steifigkeit (ᴸ⁻⁻) *f* ㊻ = Steifheit 2.

Steif-leinen (⁻¹⁻...) *n* ㊷ = =leinwand; ℒ *a.* ㊻ (of) buckram, F *fig. v.* Personen: stiff, starchy; s. steif 4 b; =leinwand ⓝ *f* buckram; =machen *n* stiffening, ⊕ von Zeug 2c. a. dressing; =ofen ⊕ *m* Hutmacherei: stove for dressing hats; =werden *n* stiffening, hardening; *engS. physiol.* erection; (Erstarren von Leichen) (it.) rigor mortis.

Steig¹ (¹) [*ahd.*: steigen] *m* ㉒c. (narrow or steep) path; (Fußpfad) foot-path; s. Bahnsteig, vgl. Steg 1.

Steig²-**bügel** ⊕ (⁻¹⁻ᴸ⁻)[*ndb.*: steigen] *m* ㉒: a) *man.* stirrup (s. Bügel 2); b) *anat.* im Ohre: ⓐ stapedial bone, stapes.

Steig-bügel-muskel (⁻⁻¹⁻⁻...) *m* ㉒ *anat.*: ⓐ stapedius; =riemen *m* = Bügelriemen; =trunk ㊻ stirrup-cup.

Steige¹ (ᴸ⁻) [*ahd.*: stile] *f* ㊷ **1.** narrow stairs *pl.* or staircase; pair of steps. — **2.** (abschüssiger Pfad) steep path. — **3.** (Stelle am Übersteigen in Zäunen 2c.) stile. — **4.** (Behältnis für Federvieh) coop for poultry, hen-roost.

Steige² (ᴸ⁻) ㊻ = Stiege (20 Stück).

Steige-... (⁻⁻...) in Zssgn = Steig=...

Steig²-**eisen** (⁻¹⁻ᴸ⁻) *n* ㉒: a) (Fußeisen zum Steigen) climbing-iron, crampo(o)n; b) = Steigbügel.

steigen (ᴸ⁻)[*ahd.*: † sty] **I** v/n. (sn u. h.) **1.** a) aufwärts: to ascend, mount, go up, climb (up), *mst v.* Dingen: to rise, *v.* Vögeln *a.* to soar; mit Leitern auf Mauern ℒ to scale the wall; b) abwärts: to descend, to go down. — **2.** das Thermometer, das Barometer steigt ... is rising; das Wasser steigt the water is rising, im Meere: the tide is coming in; e-n Drachen ℒ lassen to fly a kite; ⓑ die Kurse ℒ prices are (or the market

---

ⓐ scientific; ⑨ botanical; ♀ geography; ⊕ machinery; ⚒ mining; ✕ military; ↓ marine; ⓑ commercial; ⓝ postal; 🚂 railway.

[**Steiger**] — 920 — [**Steinkauz**]

is) going up or rising or improving or advancing; die Aktien find um ¼ gestiegen ... have risen ¼ or are ¼ better. — **3.** mit *prp.*: **anŜ Land** ⁂ to (come on) land, to go ashore; **auf daŜ Dach** ⁂ to climb on the roof, *fig.* f. **Dach 3** am Ende; **aufŜ Pferd** ⁂ to mount on horseback; **auf den Thron** ⁂ to ascend the throne; **auŜ** et. ⁂ to step forth from a th.; **durch daŜ (auŜ dem) Fenster** ⁂ to climb through (to get out at) the window; **inŜ (auŜ dem) Bett** ⁂ to go to (to get out of) bed; **daŜ Blut in den Kopf** ⁂ machen to cause gestion to the head; **über daŜ Gitter** ⁂ to get (or climb) over the fence; f. **Pferd**; *fig.* die Haare stiegen ihm **zu Berge** his hair stood on end; **zu Kopfe** ⁂d, oft: heady. — **4.** F (gehen) to walk, **wo** ⁂ Sie hin? where are you going to? — **5.** man. von Pferden: (fich bäumen) to rear. — **6.** burſch. das erſte Lied ſteigt we (shall now) sing the first song. — **II** ~ *n* ㉓ **7.** (In-die-Höhe-)~ ascent, rise, (Zunahme) increase, growth, (Fortſchritt) progress; das ~ und Fallen the rise and fall; **⚹**: ~ der Preiſe, Kurſe rise (or advance) in prices, ſtärker: boom; auf daŜ ~ der Kurſe ſpekulieren to buy for the rise, to bull the market. — Vgl. a. Steigung. — **III ⚹d** *p.pr. u. a.* ㊿ **8.** ascending, &c. (ſ. 1); mit ⚹dem Alter with increasing years or advancing age; im Verhältniŝ ⚹d rising proportionately; **⚹de** Richtung der Kurſe, Preiſe: upward tendency.

Steiger (¹‿) *m* ㉒ **1.** (a. **~in** *f* ㊼) person who ascends or descends, climber. — **2.** ⚒ foreman or headman, inspector, overseer) of miners.

Steigerer ⚹ (¹‿‿) *m* ㉒, **Steig(r)erin** f ㊼ one who sends (or forces) up prices or who booms the market, Börſe: bull.

ſteigern (¹‿) [ſteigen] ⚹a. **I** *v/a.* **1.** to raise, (vermehren) to increase, (verſchlimmern) to aggravate; (verſtärken) to strengthen, to enhance; den Mieter ⚹, e-n mit der Miete ⚹ to raise a tenant's (or lodger's) rent; **⚹** den Preiŝ einer Ware ⚹ to run (or send) up the price ...; Börſe: die Kurſe ⚹ to bull (or boom) the market. — **2.** Auction: to bid up (or outbid) other people. — **3.** gr. to compare. — **II** ſich ⚹ *v/refl.* **4.** to rise, to increase. — **III** ~ *n* ㉓ **5.** = Steigerung.

Steigerung (¹‿) *f* ㊻ (ſ. ſteigern I) raising, increase, aggravation, enhancement; *gr.* comparing, (formation of the degrees of) comparison; *rhet.* gradation, climax; **~Ŝ-grad** (‼...) *m* ㉒, **~Ŝ-ſtufe** f. gr. degree of comparison.

Steig²-rad ⊙ (‼...) *n* ㉒ einer Uhr: balance-wheel; **-riemen** *m* stirrup-leather or -strap; **-rohr** *n* e-r Pumpe: raising-tube, -main, *mach.* ascending (or ascension-) pipe, Gießerei ꝛc.: raising-pipe.

Steigung (¹‿) *f* ㊻ (Abhang) slope, incline, e-s Daches auch: pitch, gradient.

Steig²-zeug ⚒ (‼...) *n* ㉒ hoisting machinery.

ſteil (¹) [nhd.; *ſteigen] *a.* ㊿ steep (ascent, descent), precipitous (rock), bold (headland), sharp (incline), shelving (const.), sheer (cliff).

Steile (¹‿) *f* ㊻ **1.** = Steilheit. — **2.** (ſteiler Abhang) steep descent, precipice (ſ. Abgrund), ⚔ *frt.* escarpment, ⚓ sharp gradient, ⊕ steep incline.

Steilheit (¹‿) *f* ㊻ steepness, precipitousness, shelving nature of a coast.

Stein (¹) [ahd.: stone] *m* ⊙c. **1.** stone (a. Kern in Pflaumen ꝛc.), ⚭ lapis, (Fels) rock (a. *geol., min.*); (Geröll) shingle (ſ. Edel-, Kieſel-, Mühl-ſtein); *path.* ~ in der Blaſe ꝛc.: stone in the bladder, &c., ⚭ calculus; am ~ leiden to be troubled with the stone; **zu** ~ *m.,* **w.** to petrify; Alchimie: ~ der Weiſen (der Kupfer ꝛc. in Gold wandeln ſollte) philosopher's stone. — **2.** *fig.* ſ. Anſtoß 4, Bein 2; es fällt mir ein ~ vom Herzen that's a weight off my mind; er hat einen ~ auf dem Herzen his heart is weighed down (with grief) or heavily laden; e-m ~e (Hinderniſſe) in den Weg legen to put obstacles (or a stumbling-block) in a p.'s way; den erſten ~ auf e-n werfen (nach Joh. 8,7) to cast the first stone at a p.; das iſt ein Tropfen Waſſer **auf** einen heißen ~ (wirkungslos) that's (quite) inadequate or ineffectual; über Stock und ~ (eiligſt) laufen to run (or race) at full (or at the top of one's) speed; Sprichw. zwei harte ~e mahlen ſelten klein(e) od. rein(e) two hard (or strong) natures seldom agree well. — **3.** ⊙: *arch.* aus einem ~e beſtehendes Werk: ⚭ monolith, Uhrmach.: die Uhr geht auf 15 ~e(n) ... runs on fifteen jewels; Steinſchneidekunſt: (erhaben) geſchnittener ~ = Kamee; Beſchreibung geſchnittener ~e: ⚭ dactyliology. — **4.** Damenſpiel: man, piece; einen ~ aufdamen to crown a king; *fig.* ſ. Brett 5; Domino: domino; e-n ~ anſetzen to play (a domino). — **5.** ⚗ chm. nach Zeit und Ort verſchiedenes Gewicht: etwa: stone. — **6.** *path.* ſ. Blaſen-, Gallen-, Nieren-ſtein.

Stein-abdruck ⊙ (‼...) *m* ㉒ lithographic engraving or print; **-acker** *m, agr.* stony field; **-adler** *m, orn.* golden eagle (A'quila chrysa'etus); **⚹alt** *a.* ㊿ (as) old as the hills or as Methuselah; **-alter** *n* = -zeit; **-anbetung** *f* = -dienſt; **-arbeit** ⊙ *f* stone-work, masonry; **-arbeiter** *m* stone-mason or -polisher; **-art** *f* species of stone or rock, mineral; ⚹artig *a.* stone-like, stony, ⚭ lithoid; **-bach** *m* rocky stream; **-bank** *f*: a) stone bench; b) *geol.* stone-bed or -formation; **-bau** *m* st. building, druidiſches: cromlech; **-beſchreibung** *f* = -kunde; **-beſchwerden** *f/pl. path.:* ⚭ calculous disease; **-bild** *n* stone statue; **-bildung** *f, geol.* formation of stone, *path.:* ⚭ lithiasis; *path.* Lehre von der ~: ⚭ lithogeneſy; **-blatter** *f, path.* stone-pock; **-block** *m* block of stone; *geol.* erratiſcher ~ erratic boulder; **-bock** *m*: a) *zo.*: ibex (Capra ibex); b) *ast.* (Sternbild) Capricorn; **-boden** *m*: a) (ſteinige Erde) stony soil or ground; b) (mit Steinen belegter Fußboden) stone floor or pavement; **-bohrer** *m* ⚒ trepan; b) *zo.* (Bohrmuſchel) stone-borer, ⚭ pholas; ⊙ (Schnecke) rock-piercer (Terebe'lla); **-brech** ⚹ *m* (chm. Arzneimittel für den Stein 6) saxifrage (Saxi'fraga); drei-fingeriger ~ whitlow-grass (*S.* tridac'tyli'tes); knollentragender ~, körniger ~ granulated saxifrage, stone-break (saxi'fraga granula'ta); **-brecher** ⊙ *m* stone-breaker, in Steinbrüchen: quarry-man; **-brech-maſchine** ⊙ *f* stone-breaker, -crusher; **-bruch** *m* stone-pit, quarry; **-buche** *f* = Hagebuche (ſ. **buff**(e *f*) *m*), *ichth.* turbot (Rhombus ma'ximus).

Steinchen (¹‿‿) *n* ㉓ (*dim.* v. Stein) little stone, *geol.*: ⚭ lapillus; (Kieſel) pebble.

Stein-damm (‼...) *m* ㉒ in der See: stone jetty, kürzerer: groyne; **-dienſt** *m* worship of stones, ⚭ litholatry; **-droſſel** *f, orn.* rock-thrush (Monti'cola); **-druck** ⊙ *m*: a) lithography; b) (Abdruck) lithograph(ic print); **-drucker** *m* lithographer; **-druckerei** ⊙ *f* lithographic printing-office, lithographer's (work-)shop; **-druck-farbe** ⊙ *f* lithographic ink; **-eiche** ⚹ *f* holm-oak (Quercus Ilex); **-eppich** ⚹ *m*: a) bubo; **-erbarmen** *n*: *fig.* das iſt zum ~, etwa: that would melt a (heart of) stone.

ſteinern (¹‿) [nhd. für † ſteinen] *a.* ㊿ (of) stone, aus Steingut auch: (of) earthenware; der ~e Gaſt (in Mozarts Oper „Don Juan") the marble statue; *fig.* Des Herz heart (made) of flint or stone.

Stein-erzeugung (‼...) *f* = -bildung; **-eſel** *m* miller's ass; **-farn** *m* stone-fern (Ce'terach officina'rum); **-flachs** *m, min.* mineral flax, ⚭ asbestos; **-flechte** ⚹ *f* stone-rag (Parme'lia saxa'tilis); **-forelle** *f* = Bachforelle; **-förmig** *a.* ㊿ (shaped) like a stone; vgl. ⚹artig; **-frucht** ⚹ *f* stonefruit, ⚭ drupe; **-fuchs** *m, zo.* stone-fox (Canis lago'pus); **-galle** *f, vet.* wind-gall; **-garnele** *f, zo.* = Garnele; **-geräte** *n/pl.* stone (or flint) implements *pl.*; **-gerinne** ⊙ *n* = -rinne; **-geröll** *n* rubble, shingle; **-geſchirr** *n* = -gut; **-grab(denk)mal** *n* altes: dolmen, cromlech; **-grieß** *m* gravel; **-grube** ⊙ *f* = -bruch; **-grund** *m* stony ground, stone foundation; **-gut** ⚹ *n* ⊙ stoneware, earthenware; **⚹guten** P *a.* ㊿ of stoneware; **-gut-geſchirr** *n* crockery; **-gut-händler(in** *f*) *m* dealer in crockery; **-hammer** *m* stone hammer; **-händler** ⚹ *m* (der m. Edelſteinen handelt) dealer in precious stones; **⚹hart** *a.* (as) hard as stone, flint-like; **-härte** *f* hardness of stone; **-haue** ⊙ *f* stone-pick; **-hauer** *m* = -metz; **-hauſe(n)** *m* heap of stones, a. = -hügel; **-haus** *n* house built of stone, stone house; **-honig** *m* old crystallized honey; **-hügel** *m* stony hill or mount, in Schottland: cairn; **-huhn** *n, orn.* rock-partridge (Perdrix rubra).

ſteinicht (¹‿) *a.* ㊿ stone-like, stony.

ſteinig (¹‿) [ahd.] *a.* ㊿ stony, full of (or covered with) stones; rocky, flinty; *path.*: ⚭ calculous; ⚹ das Arabien Arabia Petræa, auch: Stony Arabia.

ſteinigen (¹‿‿) ⚹ **I** *v/a.* to throw (or cast) stones at ..., bſd. Alt.: to stone (to death). — **II** ~ *n* ㉓ = Steinigung.

Steinigung (¹‿) *f* ㊻ stoning.

Stein-karauſche (‼...) *f* ㊻ *ichth.* gibel (Cara'ssius gibe'lio); **-karre(n** *m*) *f* stone-cart; **-kauz** *m, orn.* little owl (Athe'ne

[Steinkenner] — 921 — [stellen]

no'ctua); =kenner m: ⚛ lithologist, mineralogist; =kenntnis f = =kunde; =kitt m lithocolla; =klee ⚘ m: echter ~ common melilot (Melilo'tus officina'lis), blauer ~ sweet melilot (M. caeru'lea); =klippe f cliff. reef; =klopfer m stone-breaker; =kluft f cleft (fissure, chink) in a rock; =kohle f (mineral) coal, coal from the pit, entschwefelte: coke.

Steinkohlen-bergwerk (ᴴᴸ...) n ⚒ coal-mine, -pit, colliery; =flöz n coal-bed, -seam; =gas n coal-gas; =gräber m coal-miner, collier; =grube f = =bergwerk; ₂haltig a. ⚒ carboniferous; =lager n = =flöz; =schacht m (shaft of a) coal-mine; =teer ⚒ m coal- (or gas-)tar; =teer-kampfer m = Naphthalin.

Stein-koralle (ᴸ...) f ⚛ stone-coral, ⚛ madrepore; ₂krank a. ⚕ path. suffering from stone, ⚛ calculous; ₂krankheit f stone, ⚛ calculus(-disease), lithiasis; =krug m stone jug; =krufe f stone bottle; =kruste f stone crust, coating of stone; =kugel ehm. ⚔ f stone shot; =kunde f lithology, mineralogy; =lager n layer of stones, stony foundation; =linde ⚘ f mock-privet (Philly'rea me'dia); =lorbeer ⚘ f m laurestine (Vibu'rnum Tinus); =marder m = Hausmarder; =mark n, min. stone-marrow; =mehl n stone-dust; =meißel ⚒ m stone-cutter's (or sculpturer's) chisel; =mergel m, min. stone-marl; =messer n: a) stone knife; b) surg. lithotome; =metz ⚒ m ⚒ stone-cutter, -dresser, -mason; vgl. =schneider; ehm. =mörser ⚔ m ⚒ artill. stone-mortar; =mörtel ⚒ m hard cement, concrete; =muschel f, zo.: ⚛ pholas; =nelke ⚘ f = Nelke (rauhe); =nuß f = Elfenbeinnuß; =obst ⚘ n = =frucht; =öl n petroleum, mineral (or rock-)oil; =operation f, surg.: ⚕ lithotomy; =pappe f strong pasteboard, zum Dachdecken: fire-proof pasteboard; (fr.) carton-pâte or -pierre; =pech n = Erd-pech; =pfeffer ⚘ m stonecrop (Sedum acre); =pflaster n stone pavement; =pilz ⚘ m edible boletus (Bole'tus edu'lis); =platte f stone slab, flagstone; =ramme f paving-beetle, rammer; =regen m shower (or hail) of stones; =reich (ᴴᴸ) n mineral kingdom; ₂ a. rich in stones, dagegen ₂reich f (ᴸᴴ) a. enormously rich, (as) rich as Crœsus; ₂ sein, a. to be rolling in wealth; =rinne ⚒ f stone drain; =säge ⚒ f stone- (or marble-)saw; =salz n, min. rock-salt, common salt; =salz-grube f rock-salt mine; =salz-lager n bed of rock-salt; =same(n) ⚘ m stoneseed, gromwell (Lithospe'rmum), echter ~ grey millet, pearl-plant (L. officina'le); =sammlung f collection of stones or minerals; =sand m gravel; =sarg m stone coffin, ⚛ sarcophagus; =schicht f (a. geol.) layer of stone(s); =schleifer ⚒ m polisher of stones; =schleuder f sling for throwing stones; ehm. =schloß n f. Gewehre: flint-lock; =schmätzer m, orn. fallow-finch or -chat (Saxi'cola oena'nthe); =schmerzen m/pl. path. pain(s pl.) arising from stone; =schneide-kunst f: a) ⚒ gem-carving; b) engraving on stone, ⚛ lithoglyptics;

=schneiden n: a) ⚒ cutting (of) stones; gem-carving; b) surg. = =schnitt b; =schneider ⚒ m lapidary; =schnitt m: a) ⚒ lapidary cut; Gravierkunst: lithoglyph; b) surg. operation for stone; lithotomy; =schrift f: a) inscription on stone; b) lapidary (style of) writing or character(s pl.); c) typ. Doric, Grotesque; =schutt m auf Chausseen broken flint or stones for making up the road, ballast; =schüttung ⚒ f ballasting (or making up) of a road. &c.; =schwalbe f = Mauerschwalbe; =setzer ⚒ m: a) (Pflasterer) paviour; b) Maurerei: stone-layer; =setzer-arbeit f paviour's work, paving; =stufe f stone step; =waffen f/pl. stone weapons pl.; =wahr-sagerei f: ⚛ lithomancy; =walze f stone(-)roller; =wälzer m, orn. turn-stone (Stre'psilas inte'rpres); =wand f: a) ⚒ arch. (ant. Fachwand) stone (or brick) wall; b) = Felswand; =ware f = =gut; =weg m paved road; =werk n: a) ⚒ stone-work, masonry; b) (Grottenwerk) rock-work, rockery; =wurf m (a. als Maß) (a) stone's throw; =wurz ⚘ f = Odermennig; =zeichnung ⚒ f lithographic design; =zeit f, geol. stone-age.

Steirer, steirisch (ᴸᵛ) f. Steierer, steierisch.

Steiß (ᴸ) [ahd.] m ⚒ a. backside. des Viehs: buttock. rump, einer gebratenen Gans ꝛc.: co. parson's nose.

Steiß-bein (ᴴ...) n ⚒ anat.: ⚛ coccyx; =drüse, =flosse f: ⚛ anal gland. fin; =fuß m, orn. grebe (Po'diceps); =geburt f, med.: ⚛ pelvic presentation.

Stele ⚛ (ᴸᵛ) [grch.] f ⚒ arch. (aufgerichtete Säule) stele, stela. [of sails.]

Stell ↓ (ᵛ) n ⚒ b. (Anzahl): ~ Segel set

Stelladen (ᴮᴸ) [Stell-laden] m ⚒ shutter.

Stellage F (ᵛᴸᴳᵛ) [dtsch.-fr.: *stellen] f ⚒ 1. = Gestell 1. — 2. (Vorrichtung) contrivance. — 3. ⚒ Börse: put and call.

stellbar (ᵛ) a. ⚒ capable of regulation, adjustable, movable; Stellbarkeit f ⚒ adjustableness, mo(va)bility.

Stell-bottich ⚒ (ᵛ...) m ⚒ = Gärbottich; =dich-ein n ⚒ meeting, appointment, (fr.) rendezvous; e-m ein ~ geben to make an appointment with a p.; Sport: meet; v. Liebenden auch: tryst; er kam nicht zum ~ he failed to keep his tryst; =dich-ein-platz m meeting-place, von Liebenden a. trysting-place.

Stelle (ᵛᵛ) [mhd.: stellen] f ⚒ 1. (Ort, Fleck) place, spot, wo j., et. steht: stand, zum Bauen: (building-)plot; schlechte ~ in der Kruste ꝛc.: fault, flaw; an Ort u. Stelle sein to be in the proper (or right, very) place, to be on the spot; nicht (recht) von (od. aus) der ~ kommen not to make (much) progress, to dawdle along; rührt euch nicht von der ~! don't stir or budge!; zur Stelle schaffen od. bringen to produce, ⚒ to deliver on the spot; zur ~ sein to be present. — 2. an ~ von in the place (or room) of; an die ~ von e-m, v. et. setzen to put in the place of a p., of a th.; to replace a p., a th.; to substitute for a p., a th.; an j-s ~ treten, kommen to step into a p.'s place, to supplant a p.; an seiner ~ in his case,

(anstatt seiner) in his stead; wenn ich an Ihrer ~ wäre if I were in your place or position, einfacher: if I were you; die ~ j-s vertreten to represent a p., to act on a p.'s behalf. — 3. (Anstellung) place, situation, post (vgl. Amt 1); (Beschäftigung) employment; f. bekleiden 2, einnehmen 5; e-e gute (bequeme) ~ haben to be in a good (snug, comfortable) berth or situation; offene ~ vacancy; sich zu e-r ~ melden to apply for a post or a vacancy. — 4. auf der ~ (sofort) on the spot, there and then; at once, immediately. — 5. in einem Schriftwerk ꝛc.: passage (a. ♪); angezogene ~ passage quoted or mentioned, quotation. — 6. arith. eine Zahl von sechs ~n (Ziffern) a number of six figures or digits or places; ein Dezimalbruch von zehn ~n a decimal (fraction) of ten places; vom Produkt drei (Dezimal-) ~n abschneiden to point off in the product three decimal places.

Stelle-... (ᵛ...) in Zssgn = Stellen-...

stellen¹ (ᵛ) [ahd.: Stall] I v/a., v/n. (h.) u. sich ₂ v/refl. ⚒ 1. (stch) ₂ to place (o.s.), to put (o.s.), to locate (o.s.), to station (o.s.); aufrecht ₂ to set (or put) up(right); wieder von neuem ₂ to put again, to reset; sich (nach dem Sitzen ꝛc.) ₂ to stand (up), to get up. — 2. mit prp. (oft fig.; vgl. a. setzen 3): an-₂ to put side by side; eine Leiter an die Wand ₂ to put a ladder against the wall; eine Tasse auf den Tisch ₂ to put a cup on the table; sich auf die Zehen ₂ to stand on tiptoe; er ist ganz auf sich gestellt he is entirely dependent on himself; seine Sache auf nichts ₂ to take no thought for the morrow. (bibl.) ₂ to be non-carish or reckless; ⚔ ein Geschütz auf ein Ziel ₂ to aim a gun; ⚒ es stellt sich auf 10 Mark it comes to ten shillings; in den Schuppen ₂ to put in a shed or under shelter; Pferde in den Stall ₂ to stable ...; fig. f. Abrede 2; etwas in j-s Belieben oder Ermessen ₂ to leave a th. to (or at) a p.'s discretion; in Frage, in Zweifel ₂ to question a th., to doubt a th. ⚒ ... die wir Ihnen in Rechnung ₂ w. ... which we will debit to your account; nach der Schnur ₂ to aline, to align; et. über (unter) et. anderes ₂ to esteem a th. above (below) s.th. else; vor Augen ₂ to present to the eye, to expose to view; zur Diskussion ₂ to open (or invite) a discussion upon ...; f. Rede 3; zur Schau ₂ to put on show, to exhibit. — 3. mit adjectives u. adverbs: die Sache stellt sich anders, als ich gedacht ... is different from what I thought; bereit ₂ to put in readiness; sich dahin ₂, sich dazwischen ₂ to interpose; die Füße einwärts ₂ to turn one's feet in; sich gegen n feindlich ₂ to take up a hostile attitude towards a p., engl. to oppose a p.; fest ₂ to establish; f. gegenüber ₂; gerade (schief) ₂ to put straight (awry); f. gleich ₂; gut ₂ to put in(to) a good position; gut (schlecht) gestellt in a good (wretched)

♪ Musik; ⚛ Wissenschaft; ⚘ Pflanze; ⚲ Geographie; ⚒ Technik; ⚒ Bergbau; ⚔ Militär; ↓ Marine; ⚒ Handel; ⚒ Post; ⚒ Eisenbahn.

[stellen] — 922 — [Stempelamt]

position or post, well (ill or badly) paid; der Preis stellt sich hoch (niedrig) ... is high (low); höher 2 to put up higher, to raise; von Preisen: sich höher 2 to rule higher; Champagner kalt 2 to keep champagne (in the) cool, to ice ch.; F fig. e-n kalt2 to leave a p. in the cold, to give a p. the cold shoulder, to send a p. to Coventry; e-n (sich) sicher 2 to secure a p. (o. s.); ich bin (aus Hause aus) so gestellt, daß ich es tun kann I am in such a position (or I am so placed) as to be able to do it, my means allow me to do it; sich vor et. 2 to secure o.s. against a th.; die Speisen warm 2 to keep the dishes (or the dinner) hot; e-n zufrieden2 to satisfy a p. — 4. sich 2 (für et. ausgeben) to pretend to, to put on an appearance of; er stellte sich krank he pretended (or feigned) to be ill, he shammed illness; sich taub 2 to turn a deaf ear to a p.'s request(s); er stellt sich nur so he is only shamming or pretending; sich unschuldig 2 to assume (or put on) an innocent air. — 5. (zum Stillsteh(e)n bringen, bsd. von lebenden Wesen): a) hunt. ein gehetztes Tier stellt sich ... stands at bay; e-n Hirsch 2 (aufspüren) to track a stag; ⚔ den Gegner 2 to bring the enemy to a stand, fig. to corner one's opponent; b) fig. e-n Verbrecher 2 to arrest a criminal. — 6. (zur Stelle schaffen) to produce, to supply; einen Bürgen, Bürgschaft 2 to give (or find) bail; f. Geisel; e-n Mann (ob. Stellvertreter) 2 to provide a substitute; seinen Mann 2 to be the right man for the post, F to be up to the mark; Sicherheit 2 to give security, e-m et. zur Verfügung 2 to put a th. at a p.'s disposal; Zeugen 2 to produce witnesses; ⚔ vor ein Kriegsgericht gestellt w. to be court-martialled or tried by court-martial, als v/refl.: sich 2 to present o.s.; sich dem Gerichte 2 to surrender to the court; sich der Polizei 2 to give o.s. up to the police; sich zum Kampfe 2 to accept battle, Turnier: to enter the lists. — 7. sich mit e-m (oder gegen e-n) nicht 2 (vertragen) können to be unable to agree (or hit it off) with a p.; (sich) mit e-m schlecht 2 to be on bad terms with a p. — 8. (an die rechte Stelle rücken): a) ⊕ to regulate; den Zeiger einer Uhr oder e-e Uhr 2 to regulate a watch; eine Uhr richtig 2 to put (or set) ... right; nach der Kirchenuhr ~ to set (right) by the church-clock; b) astrol. f. Horoskop; c) ⚔ ein Geschütz 2 to point (or lay, train) a gun; d) ⚓ die Segel nach dem Winde 2 to trim the sails to the wind. — 9. hunt. das Jagdzeug 2 (richten) to set the toils; Fallen, Garne ob. Netze 2 to set traps, snares; to spread nets; abs. den Hirsch 2 to trap the stag; vgl. 5a. — 10. fig. f. Bein 3 gegen Ende; e-m nach dem Leben 2 to attempt a p.'s life. — 11. (gehörig in Worte fassen) seine Worte in zierlicher Ordnung 2 to arrange (or put) one's words nicely or elegantly; f. Antrag 1; eine Frage 2 to put (or ask) ... — 12. (ordnend festsetzen) to fix; e-m eine Aufgabe 2 to set a p. a task; Bedingungen 2 to make conditions; einen Termin 2 to fix a (limited) time or a (certain) date; e-m ein Ziel 2 to set bounds to a p.; ✠ mäßige Preise 2 to charge moderate prices. — II ~ n ㉓ 13. f. 8: das 2 von Uhren regulation of (or regulating) watches and clocks. — 14. = Stellung 1.

Stellen²-gesuch (ˠ˰...) [Stelle] n ㊷ application for a post; **-jagd** f, **-jagen** n place-hunting; **-jäger** F m place-hunter; **-los** a. ⊕ out of employ(-ment) or work, without a situation or F a job, unemployed; die ~losen the unemployed pl.; **-sammlung** f aus Büchern: collection of passages or quotations; **-vermitt(e)lungs-bureau** n für Dienstboten ꝛc.: registry-office, employment-agency, für Arbeiter: labour-bureau, für Lehrer(innen) an höheren Schulen: scholastic agency; **-weise** adv. (F a. a.) in places, sporadically, here and there.

Stell-feder ⊕ (ˠ˰...) f ㊷ Uhrm.: stop-spring; **-garn** n Fischerei: stalker; **-geschäft** ⊕ n Börse: double option, put and call; **-haken** m adjusting clasp; **-hebel** m, elect. signalling-lever; **-holz** n movable support.

...stellig (...ˠ˰...) a. ⊕ in Zssgn mit Zahlwörtern, zB. fünf-2 of five figures or digits or places; f. mehrstellig.

Stell-jagd (ˠ˰...) f ㊷ = Stellenjagd; **-laden** m f. Stellladen; **-macher** ⊕ m cartwright, wheelwright; **-netz** ⊕ n Fischerei: fixed net; **-rad** ⊕ n Uhrm.: regulating-wheel; **-rechen** ⊕ m regulator; **-scheibe** ⊕ f der Uhr: rosette; **-schraube** ⊕ f, mech. regulating- (or adjusting-)screw; **-schütze** ⊕ f Wasserbau: regulating-sluice; **-spiegel** m movable mirror, cheval-glass.

Stellung (ˠ˰...) f ㊻ 1. (f. stellen, bsd. 1 u. 8) placing, putting, location; regulating, regulation; ~ von Zeugen: production ...; ⚔ ~ von Truppen: disposition ...; (Anordnung) arrangement (a. gr.). — 2. (Art, wie et., j. gestellt ist) position, (Anordnung) arrangement, disposition; (Körperhaltung) posture, attitude; (schickliche Haltung) deportment, eine ~ zu et. nehmen to define one's attitude (or position) regarding a th.; fenc. (Auslage) guard; Kommando: ~! attention! — 3. gesellschaftliche ~ (social) position or rank, station in life; er sucht eine bessere ~ he is looking out for a better post or situation or berth; in seiner ~ als Fürst (Gesandter) in his princely (ambassadorial) capacity; ihre ~ als Wirtin her character (or part) as a hostess. — 4. ⚔ (military or strategical) position, eine ~ einnehmen to take up a position, to post o.s.; seine ~ verteidigen to defend one's position, to hold one's ground; aus einer ~ vertreiben to dislodge; vorteilhafte ~ advantageous (or superior) position, vantage-ground; (sн) coign of vantage; seine ~ wechseln to shift one's ground, to move off.

Stellungs-befehl ⚔ (ˠ˰...) m ㊷ order to present o.s.; **-pflichtig** a. ⊕ bound to appear before the military authorities; of the right age for (or liable to) military (or army-)service.

stell-vertretend (ˠ˰...) a. ⊕ representative, vicarious; (ergänzend) supplementary, von Beamten, Geistlichen ꝛc.: acting (clergyman, consul, &c.), deputy (governor, &c.); **-vertreter(in** f) m ㊷ representative, delegate, eines Bischofs: surrogate, eines Geistlichen ꝛc.: (lt.) locum tenens; parl., &c. deputy; (Ersatzmann) substitute (vgl. Lückenbüßer); (Bevollmächtigte[r]) proxy (auch beim Abstimmen); **-vertreterschaft** f proxyship, **-vertretung** f representation, deputyship, substitution; ✠ in ~ by proxy, in (or per) procuration; **-wagen** m stage-coach, in Frankreich: diligence; **-zeiger** ⊕ m Uhrm.: pointer of the regulating-plate.

Stelz-bein (ˠ˰...) n ㊷ wooden leg, ⚔ co. auch: ammunition-leg; **-beinig** a.: a) with a wooden leg; b) with stiff legs; c) orn.: ⊗ grallatorial.

Stelze (ˠ˰) [ahd.: stilt: stolz] f ㊸ stilt; auf ~n geh(e)n, ~n laufen, 2n v/n. (s. u. fn) ⊕ to walk on stilts, fig. to be stilted or affected.

Stelzen-gang (ˠ˰...) m ㊷ walking on stilts; e-n ~ h. to stalk along; **-läufer** m: a) person that walks on stilts; b) orn. stilt-bird, -plover (Hima'ntopus); **-pflug** ⊕ m, agr. Belgian plough.

Stelz-fuß (ˠ˰...) m ㊷ = -bein; **-vögel** m/pl. orn.: ⊗ grallæ, grallatores pl.

Stemm-axt ⊕ (ˠ˰.ˠ) f ㊷ large (woodman's) axe.

Stemme (ˠ˰) f ㊸ stay, support.

Stemm-eisen ⊕ (ˠ˰...)(ˠ˰.ˠ.) n ㊷ (two-bevelled) chisel, driving- (or framing-) chisel.

Stemmmeißel ⊕ (ˠ˰...) [Stemm-meißel] m ㊷ caulking-chisel.

stemmen (ˠ˰) [ahd.: stem] v/a. u. sich 2 v/refl. ⊕ 1. to prop, to support; die Füße gegen e-n Felsen 2 to plant (or set, put) one's feet firmly against a rock; f. Seite 2 unter "in"; fig. f. steifen¹; sich gegen et. 2 to resist or oppose a th., to offer (strong or strenuous) opposition to a th. — 2. Wasser, einen Teich 2 (stauen) to dam up ... — 3. ⊕ (mit dem Stemmeisen (herstellen): Löcher 2) to chisel (out) holes.

Stemm-leder (ˠ˰...) n ㊷ Schuhm.: toe-cap, welt (-leather); **-meißel** f. Stemmmeißel; **-nadel** f Schuhm.: closing-needle.

Stempel (ˠ˰) [ndd., ndl.: stampfen] m ㊷ 1. ⊕ (Vorrichtung): a) stamp, Münze ꝛc.: die, (Locheisen) punch(eon), (Entwertungs-)~ defacing-stamp; b) (Stößel) stamper, pestle; einer Puppe ꝛc.: piston; ⚔ stemple, prop. — 2. (eingeprägtes Zeichen) stamp, mark, für das Datum: date-stamp (a. ⏱); Postistempel; ✠ auf Waren: trade-mark, brand; fig. es trägt den ~ der Unwahrheit it bears the stamp of untruth on the face of it. — 3. ❀ (weibl. Befruchtungsorgan) pistil, ⊗ gynæceum.

Stempel-abgabe (ˠ˰...) f ㊷ stamp-duty; **-amt** n stamp-office, inland-revenue office, in Lo. Somerset House;

Signs (see page XVII): F familiar; P vulgar; ꟿ flash; ꝯ rare; † obsolete (died); * new word (born); ∴ incorrect; ♪ music;

[Stempelbogen] — 923 — [Stereotypplatte]

=bogen *m* stamped sheet of paper; =bolzen ⊕ *m* starting-bolt; ²frei *a.* ⁶⁰ free from stamp-duty; =gebühr *f*, =geld *n* stamp-duty; =gesetz *n* st.-law; =hammer ⊕ *m* st.-hammer; ²los ⚲ *a.*: ⚲ agynary; =marke *f* (adhesive) stamp, für Wechsel: billstamp.
stempeln (⸺) *v/a.* ⑫a. **1.** a) (mit e-m Zeichen versehen) to mark, e-n Brief, e-e Urkunde ꝛc. ² (mit einem Stempel versehen) to stamp, to put (klebend auch: to stick) a stamp on; gestempelter Briefumschlag stamped envelope; b) statt der Unterschrift oder zur Beglaubigung, z. B. einer Quittung) to stamp; c) *fig.* e-n zum Schurken ² to stamp (or brand) a p. as a villain. — **2.** F *fig.* e-n ² (zu et. anleiten) to give a p. good instructions, to tutor a p., to prompt a p. to do a th.
Stempel-papier (⸺) *n* ⁶⁶ stamped paper; ²pflichtig *a.* ⁶⁰ subject to stamp-duty; =presse ⊕ *f* stamping-press; =schneide-kunst *f* stamp-cutting or -engraving, die-sinking; =schneider ⊕ *m* st.-cutter or -engraver, die-sinker; =steuer *f* = =abgabe; =steuer-hinterziehung *f* defraudation of the (inland) revenue; =taxe *f* = =gebühr; =träger ⚲ *m* gynophore, thecaphore; =wertzeichen *n* stamped form; =zeichen *n* = Stempel 2.
Stempler (⸺) *m* ⑫, ~**in** *f* ⁴⁷ stamper.
Stendel (⸺) *m* ⑫ =**kraut** (⸺) *n* ⓒc. orchis (= Knabenkraut).
Stenge ⚓ (⸺) [ndd.] *f* ⚓ topmast.
Stengel ⚲ (⸺) [ahd.: *Stange] *m* ⑫: a) e-r Pflanze: stalk, stem, ⚲ caulis, knolliger ~ bulb; langer, dünner ~ spindle; b) = Blatt-, Blumen-stiel.
stengel-artig ⚲ (⸺) *a.* ⁶⁰ stalk-like, stalky, ⚲ cauliform; =**blatt** *n* ⑫ stem-leaf, ⚲ caulinary leaf; ²**blütig** *a.*: ⚲ cauliflorous.
Stengelchen (⸺) *n* ㉓ (dim. v. Stengel) little (or short, thin, tiny) stalk or stem, ⚲ caulicule, caulicle.
Stengel-glas (⸺) *n* ⑫ glass with a stem; bisw.: wine-glass; ²**los** ⚲ *a.* ⁶⁰ stalkless, stemless, ⚲ acaulous; =**losigkeit** ⚲ *f* ⁴⁶: ⚲ acaulescence.
stengeln (⸺) *v/n.* (h. u. fn) ⑫a. to shoot (or grow) into a stalk or stem.
stengel-ständig ⚲ (⸺) *a.* ⁶⁰: ⚲ caulinar(y); ²**treibend** *a.* stemmed, ⚲ caulescent, cauliferous; ²**umfassend** *a.* stem-clasping, ⚲ amplexicaul.
Stenge-stag ⚓ (⸺) *n* ⚓ top(mast) stay; =**wanten** *f/pl.* ⚓ top(mast) rigging or shrouds *pl.*; =**winde-reep** *n* top-rope.
Stenogramm (⸺) [grch.] *n* ⓒd. (stenogr. Niederschrift) shorthand report or note.
Stenograph (⸺) [grch.] *m* ⁴² shorthand writer, seltener: stenographer; ~**ie** (⸺) *f* ⁴⁸ (Kurzschrift) stenography, shorthand; ²**ieren** (⸺) *v/a.* u. *v/n.* (h.) ⑬ to write (in) shorthand; ²**isch** (⸺) *a.* ⁶⁰ (of or in) shorthand, seltener: stenographic(al); ²**isch** auf-nehmen od. niederschreiben to take (or write) down in shorthand.
Stenotypist ⊕ (⸺) *m* ⑫ (~**in** *f* ⁴⁷ lady) shorthand type-writer.
Stentor-stimme (⸺) [Stentor, grch. Krieger vor Troja, dessen laute Stimme Homer rühmt] *f* ⑫ stentorian voice.

Stephan (⸺) *npr/m.* ⑮ (a. Bn.) Stephen; ~**i-e** (⸺) *npr/f.* (Bn.) ⑬⁸ Stephana; ~**it** (⸺) *m* ⓒc. min. stephanite; ~**skirche** (⸺) *f* ⑫ St. Stephen's church.
Stepp-decke (⸺) [steppen] *f* ⑫ quilted cover or covering, quilt.
Steppe (⸺) [russ.] *f* ⁴⁸ (baumlose Heide) steppe; treeless (Russian) plain.
steppen ⊕ (⸺) [ndd.] *v/a.* ⑱ to quilt; to (pad and) stitch.
Steppen-antilope (⸺) *f* zo. saiga (-antelope) (*Colus tata'ricus*); =**bewohner** *m* inhabitant of (the) steppes; =**fuchs** *m*, zo.: a) = Korsak; b) karagan (*Canis ka'ragan*); =**wolf** *m*, zo. coyote, prairie-wolf (*Canis latrans*).
Stepper ⊕ (⸺) [steppen] *m* ⑫ **1.** (~**in** *f* ⁴⁷) quilter. — **2.** der Nähmaschine: quilter.
Stepperei ⊕ (⸺) *f* ⁴⁶ quilting.
Stepp-faden ⊕ (⸺) *m* ⑫ stitching-thread; =**garn** *n* quilting-thread; =**nadel** *f* quilting-needle; =**naht** *f* = closing- (or quilting-)seam; =**ort** *m* Schuhmacherei: closing-awl; =**rock** *m* quilted coat or petticoat or dress; =**stich** ⊕ *m* backstitch.
Ster (⸺) [fr. *stère m*; *grch.] *n* (*m*) ⓒc. bsd. Holzmaß: (Kubikmeter) stere.
Ster.-A. *abbr.* = Stereotyp-ausgabe.
Sterbe-bett (⸺) *n* ⑫ death-bed, dying-bed; =**buch** *n* register of deaths; =**fall** *m* (case of) death, decease; =**fälle** deaths *pl.*; =**gebet** *n* prayer of (or for) a dying person; =**gedanken** *m/pl.* thoughts of death, funeral thoughts *pl.*; =**geld** *n* (von Sterbekassen ꝛc. ausgezahlt) payment made in case(s) of death; =**gesang** *m* funeral dirge or hymn or chant; =**gewand** *n* winding-sheet, shroud; =**glocke** *f* funeral (⚰ passing-) bell; =**haus** *n* house in which a death takes place, bibl. house of mourning; =**hemd** *n*: a) shirt in which a p. dies; b) = =**gewand**; =**jahr** *n* year of a p.'s death; =**kasse** *f* burial-fund or -club; =**kleid** *n* = =**gewand**; =**lager** *n* death-bed; =**lied** *n* = =**gesang**; =**liste** *f*: a) = =**buch**; b) table (or bill) of mortality; =**monat** *m* month in which a p. dies.
sterben (⸺) [ahd.: starve] **I** *v/n.* (fn) ⑱b. **1.** to die, feierlicher: to breathe one's last, to expire, give up the ghost, depart this life, pass away, F co. to kick the bucket, to hop the twig; furchtlos ² to die with fortitude, bsd. F to die game; er ist gestorben he has died, he is dead or F gone; als guter Christ ² to die (as) a good Christian; s. Fuchs 2. — **2.** mit *gen.*: s. Hunger 1. eines natürlichen Todes ² to die a natural death. — **3.** mit *prp.* u. *adv.*: **an** der Pest, am Schlage, am Zahnen ² to die of the plague, from apoplexy, through (or while) teething; **aus** Gram ² to die of grief; **darauf** will ich leben und ² nothing can shake my faith in this matter; **da-von** stirbt man nicht (leicht) that does not (easily) kill any one; **durch** e-n, j-s Hand ² to die by the hand of a p.; **den Tod für** das (ob. fürs) Vaterland ² to die (or to lay down one's life) for one's country; **über** seinen Plänen ² to die before the realization of one's

schemes; *fig.* **vor** Langerweile ² to be bored to death. — **II** ~ *n* ㉓ **4.** dying, death, feierlicher: decease; das große ~ the great plague; am ~ at the point of death; im (ob. ⚲ zum) ~ liegen to be dying or in a dying state or in the last agony; s. sterblich 2. — **III** 2d *p.pr.* u. *a.* ⁶⁶ **5.** dying, expiring, passing away, *fig.* auch: moribund, declining; kein ²des Wörtchen not a syllable (vgl. Sterbenswörtchen); der (die) ~**de** the dying (wo)man. — **IV ge-storben** *p.p.* u. *a.* ⁶⁶ (D9) **6.** (*abbr.* gest., †) dead, deceased; der, die kürzlich Gestorbene ⑰ the p. who lately died or passed away.
Sterbens-angst (⸺) *f* ⑫ fearful (or terrible) anguish; ²**bange** *a.* ⑬: mir ist ² I am in mortal fear or dread; ²**krank** *a.* dangerously ill, bibl. sick unto death; ²**lang-weilig** *a.* terribly dull or slow or tedious; =**mensch** *m*, =**seele** *f*: kein(e) ~ not a living creature or soul; =**wort**, =**wörtchen** *n*: er hat mir kein ~ gesagt he did not drop a word to me, he has not told me a syllable.
Sterbe-sakramente (⸺) *n/pl.* ⑫ *eccl.* last sacraments *pl.*, viaticum *sg.*; =**stunde** *f*, =**tag** *m* dying-hour, -day; hour, day of a p.'s death; =**zimmer** *n* death-chamber. — Vgl. auch Todes-...
sterblich (⸺) *a.* ⁶⁰ **1.** mortal (s. Hülle 2); die ~**en** mortal men or beings, mortals *pl.* — **2.** *fig.* ² (zum Sterben) verliebt sein to be desperately (or over head and ears) in love.
Sterblichkeit (⸺) *f* ⁴⁶ **1.** mortality. — **2.** *rel.* (irdische Welt) Gott hat ihn aus dieser ~ abgefordert ... has removed him from this earthly scene or called him from this world of ours.
Sterblichkeits-listen (⸺) *f/pl.* ⑫ tables *pl.* of mortality, Statistik: life-tables *pl.*; =**ziffer** *f* death-rate.
Sterbling (⸺) [: starveling] *m* ⓔd. child (or young animal) which dies soon after its birth; weakly (or sickly) creature.
Stereochemie (⸺) [grch.] *f* ⁴⁸ (Chemie fester Körper) stereochemistry.
Stereometrie ⚲ (⸺) [grch.] *f* ⁴⁸ *math.* (Geometrie des Raumes) solid geometry, seltener: stereometry; **stereometrisch** (⸺) *a.* ⁶⁰ relating to solids.
Stereoskop ⚲ (⸺) *n* ⓒc. *phys.* (Körpersehen) stereoscope; ~**bild** *n* ⑫ stereoscopic picture or view; ²**isch** (⸺) *a.* ⁶⁶ (körperlich erscheinend) stereoscopic(al).
stereotyp ⚲ (⸺) [grch.] *a.* ⁶⁰ *typ.* (unabänderlich) stereotyped (a. *fig.*).
Stereotyp-ausgabe (⸺) [grch.] *f* ⑫ Buchhandel: stereotype edition.
Stereotyp-druck (⸺) *m* ⑫ stereotype-printing, stereotype, stereotypography; =**drucker** *m* stereotyper, stereotypist; =**gießer** *m* stereotype-founder; =**gießerei** *f* stereotype-founding or -foundry.
Stereotypie ⊕ (⸺) *f* ⁴⁸ stereotypy.
stereotypieren ⊕ (⸺) *v/a.* ⑬ (Platten anfertigen) to stereotype; **stereotypisch** (⸺) *a.* ⁶⁰ stereotypical, stereotype(d).
Stereotyp-platte ⊕ (⸺) *f* ⑫ stereo(-type) plate, stereo.

⚲ scientific; ⚭ botanical; ♀ geography; ⊕ machinery; ⚒ mining; ⚔ military; ⚓ marine; ⚬ commercial; ⚮ postal; ▬ railway.

[steril] — 924 — [Steuerverweigerung]

steril ⚤ (⌣́⌣) [lt. steˈrilis] a. ⦿ (unfruchtbar) barren, unproductive, ⚹ sterile.
sterilisier|en ⚤ (⌣⌣⌣́⌣) [lt.] I v/a. ⑬ (enteimen) to sterilize. — II ~ n ㉓ und St ung f ㊻ sterilization.
Sterilität ⚤ (⌣⌣⌣⌣́) [lt.] f ㊻ (Unfruchtbarkeit) barrenness, unfruitfulness, sterility.
Sterke (⌣́⌣) [ndd.] f ㊽ (junge Kuh) heifer.
Sterlet (ʹ⌣⌣) [russ.] ⚤ n ⓐc. ichth. Art Stör: sterlet (Acipeˈnser Rutheˈnus).
Stern¹ (⌣́) [ahd.: star] m ⒠b. 1. star; mit ~en geschmückt, besät bespangled (or glittering, luminous) with stars, bestarred, poet. star-spangled; ~ des Auges: pupil; ~ (weißer Fleck) der Nägel: white; ☉ typ. (oft ~chen) asterisk (*); Branntweinbrennerei: Kognak mit drei ~en three-star brandy. — 2. fig. er hat weder Glück noch ~ luck is (or the fates are) against him; der Hoffnung letzte ~e the last gleam (or sign) of hope; es steht in den ~en geschrieben it is written in the stars.
Stern² ⇟ (⌣́) [engl.] m ⒠c. stern.
Stern¹-anbeter (⌣́⌣⌣) m ⦿ rel. starworshipper; -anbetung f = -dienst; -anis ⚹ m star- (or stellate) aniseed, Indian anise, badian (Illiˈcium aniˈsaˈtum); ²artig a. ⦿ starlike, astral; vgl. ²förmig; ²besät a. covered with stars, poet. star-sown; vgl. ²hell; ²beschreiber m: ⚤ astrographer; -beschreibung f: ⚤ astrography; -bild n. ast. constellation, des Tierkreises: sign of the zodiac; -blume f stellate flower, bsd. = Aster; vgl. -miere; ²blütige Gewächse stellates, madderworts pl. (Aspeˈrula, Gaˈlium, &c.).
Sternchen (⌣́⌣) n ㉓ (dim. v. Stern) little star, bisw. a. starlet; f. Stern¹ 1.
Stern¹-deuter (⌣́⌣⌣) m ⦿ astrologer; -deuterei, -deuterkunst f astrology; -deuterisch a. ⦿ astrological; -dienst m worship(ping) of stars, ⚤ astrolatry; -distel f star-thistle (Centaureˈa calciˈtrapa); -eidechse f, zo. stellion (Steˈlio).
Sternen-all (⌣́⌣⌣) n ⦿ stellar world; -bahn f orbit of stars; -banner m der U. S.: star-spangled banner, a. stars and stripes pl.; -bühne f (SCH.) poet., -decke, -feste f = -himmel; -gewölbe n starry vault (or canopy) of heaven; -glanz m lustre of stars; -heer m starry host or multitude; -himmel m starry sky; -licht n starlight; -schar f = -heer; -zelt n = -gewölbe.
stern¹-förmig (⌣́⌣) a. ⦿ star-shaped, ⚤ stellar, ⚹ stellate(d); (strahlig) radiate(d); -glas n ㊻ astronomical telescope; -gucker F m star-gazer; vgl. -seher; ²hagel|besoffen, -voll P a. blind (or dead) drunk; ²haufen m, ast. cluster of stars, der Milchstraße auch: ⚤ nebula; ²hell a. starlit, starbright, starry; -himmel m starry sky; -höhen-messer m = Astrolabium.
sternig (⌣́⌣) a. ⦿ starry.
Stern¹-jahr (⌣́⌣) n ⦿ ast. sidereal year; -kammer f (ehm. engl. Gerichtshof) Star Chamber; -karte f, ast. star-map, celestial chart; -kenner m astronomer; -kopf ⚹ m star-head (Scabioˈsa); -koralle f, zo. Polypengattung: ⚤ astræa; -kunde f astronomy; ²kundig a. versed in

astronomy; -kundige(r) m astronomer; -lehre f astronomy.
Sternlein (⌣́⌣) n ㉓ poet. = Sternchen.
Stern¹-los (⌣́⌣) a. ⦿ starless; -miere ⚹ f ⦿ starwort (Stellaˈria); großblütige ~ adder's-meat (St. holoˈstea); -moos ⚹ n marsh-moss (Mnium unduaˈtum); -nudeln f/pl. Kocht.. für Suppe: star-macaroni; -rad ☉ n Uhrm.: star-wheel; -rakete f star-shell; -register n catalogue of stars; -rohr n = -glas; -schanze ✶ f, frt. star-redoubt or -fort; -schnuppe f, a. -schuß m shooting (or falling) star; -schnuppenregen m shower (or fall) of meteors, meteoric shower or swarm; -seher m astronomer; vgl. -gucker; -seherei f astronomy, F star-gazing; -sucher m astronomical telescope, ⚤ astroscope; -tafel f astronomical table; -uhr f sidereal dial or clock; -wahrsagerei f astrology; -warte f (astronomical) observatory; -wissenschaft f astronomical science, astronomy; -zeit f (ant. Sonnenzeit) sidereal time.
Sterz (⌣́) [ahd.: †start] m ⒠a. 1. a) = Schwanz; b) = Steiß. — 2. a. ~e (⌣́⌣) f agr. (Handhabe am Pflug) plough-tail, -handle. ‖ (fortdauernd) continuous.
stet (⌣́) [ahd.: stehen] a. ⦿ steady, fixed;
Stete (⌣́⌣) f ㊻ = Stetigkeit.
Stethoskop ⚤ (⌣⌣⌣́) [grch.] n ⒠d. med. (Hörrohr z. Untersuchen der Brust ꝛc.) stethoscope.
stetig (⌣́⌣) [ahd.: steady] a. ⦿ continuous, continual; steady; (ununterbrochen) incessant; (ununterbrochen) uninterrupted; (beharrlich) constant; ~keit f ㊻ continuity; steadiness; constancy.
stets (⌣́) [mhd.; *stet] adv. always, (for) ever, at all times; (fortwährend) continually, constantly.
Steuer¹ ⇟ (⌣́⌣) [(mhd.) ndd.] n ㉒ (bei den Seeleuten meist „Ruder") helm, unter dem Wasser: rudder; (Ruderpinne) tiller; ~ an Backbord! port the helm!; das ~ führen to steer the vessel, to be at the helm (a. fig.); v. Schiff: gut auf das ~ lüstern to answer readily to the helm.
Steuer² (⌣́⌣) [ahd.] f ㊻ 1. impost, veranlagte: assessment, parlamentarisch bewilligte: grant, supply, staatlich auferlegte: (income-)tax, indirekte: duty; (städtische Umlage) (local or municipal) rate (vgl. Grundsteuer); die gesamten ~n, oft: rates and taxes pl.; f. ausschreiben 6 und eintreiben 3. — 2. (freiwilliger Beitrag) voluntary contribution or aid; fig. zur ~ der Wahrheit in the interest (or for the sake) of truth.
Steuer²-amt (⌣́⌣⌣) n ⒠: a) inland-revenue office; b) Behörde: board of assessment; -anschlag m assessment of taxes; -aufseher m surveyor of taxes.
steuerbar¹ ⇟ (⌣́⌣⌣) a. ⦿ von Schiffen: steerable, mehr gbr. manageable.
steuerbar² (⌣́⌣⌣) a. ⦿ taxable, assessable, ratable, auch = steuerpflichtig.
Steuerbarkeit¹ ⇟ (⌣́⌣⌣⌣) f ㊻ manageableness of a vessel, &c.
Steuerbarkeit² (⌣́⌣⌣⌣) f ㊻ taxability.
Steuer²-beamte(r) (⌣́⌣⌣⌣) m ⦿ revenue-officer, auch = Zollbeamte(r); -befreiung f exemption from taxes; -behörde f = -amt b; -bewilligungs-

recht n right of granting taxes or supply; -bezirk m tax-collector's district; -¹bord ⇟ (⌣⌣...) n (rechte Seite des Schiffes) starboard; -bord(s)-wache f starboard watch; -²buch n register of ratepayers (i. a. Kataster); -defraudation f defraudation of the revenue; -einnehmer, -erheber m tax-collector or -gatherer; -einschätzungs-kommission f commissioners pl. for the assessment of taxes; -¹ende ⇟ n stern, poop; -erhebung f collection of taxes; -erlaß m remission of taxes; -feder f. orn. rudder, ⚤ rectrix; -²frei a. ⦿ exempt from taxes, v. Waren: free of duty; -freiheit f immunity from taxes; -geld n amount of taxes; -gesetz n financebill; -hahn ☉ m, mach. valve-cock; -²kasse f tax-collector's office; -kollegium n board of inland-revenue; -kraft f capacity for paying taxes; -last f burden (or weight) of taxation; -mahnzettel m demand-note; -¹mann ⇟ m helmsman, steersman, man at the wheel, als Titel: mate; -manns-kunst f art of steering, navigation; -manns-maat m second mate.
steuern¹ (⌣́⌣) [ndd.: steer] I v/a. u. v/n. (h. u. fn) ⒠a. 1. ⇟: a) ein Schiff ⚤ to steer ..., to navigate ..., als Lotse: to pilot ...; b) v/n. vom Steuermann: to steer, vom Schiffe: to stand, to ply (nach Süden southward); das Schiff hat (er ist) nach London gesteuert the ship (he) was bound for London; vom Schiffe: gut (hart) ⚤ to answer the helm readily (with difficulty), to be easy (hard) of steerage. — 2. mit dat.: e-r Sache ⚤ (Einhalt tun) to check (or stop, repress) a th., vorbeugend: to prevent a th., abhelfend: to remedy a th — II ~ n ㉓ 3. f. Steu(e)rung.
steuern² (⌣́⌣) [ahd.] v/n. (h.) ⒠a. to pay taxes, freiwillig: to contribute (freely); vgl. beisteuern.
Steuer²-ordnung (⌣́⌣...) f ㊻ system of taxation; ²pflichtig a. ⦿ liable to pay taxes, v. Waren: dutiable; -pflichtige(r) s. = -zahler; -pflichtigkeit f liability to pay taxes; -quote f Zensus 1; -¹rad ⇟ n steering-wheel; -²rat m, etwa: councillor of the board of revenue; -register n = -buch; -rolle f tax-roll; -ruder n = Steuer¹; -²satz m rate of assessment; -schein m receipt for taxes paid; -stange ☉ f, mach. distributing-rod.
Steu(e)rung (⌣́(⌣)⌣) f ㊻ 1. steering, steerage, ☉ mach. distribution; fig. (Führung) direction. — 2. ☉ mach. valve-gear or -motion, distributing-regulator; Steuerung e-s Automobils: steering-gear or -wheel.
Steu(e)rungs-büchse ☉ (⌣́(⌣)⌣...) f ㊻ e-r Dampfmaschine: regulator-box; -hahn m distributing-cock; -hebel m distributing-lever; -mechanismus m reversing-gear; -stange f reversing-rod; -welle ⇟ f gearing-shaft.
Steuer²-verteilung (⌣́⌣⌣⌣) [f. Steuer² 1.] f ㊻ incidence of taxation; -verwaltung f administration of taxes; -verweigerung f refusal to pay taxes, parl. refusal to grant supply;

Zeichen (f. S. XVII): F familiär, P Volkssprache, Γ Gaunersprache, ⚹ selten, † alt (auch gestorben); * neu (auch geboren); ⁒ unrichtig;

[Steuervorrichtung] — 925 — [stiehl]

=**vorrichtung** ⊕ *f*, *mach.* steering apparatus or gear (f. auch Kataraft b); =²**wesen** *n* fiscal matters *pl.*, taxation; =**zahler** *m* tax-payer, rate-payer; =**zettel** *m*: a) = =schein; b) (vorher zugeschickter Zettel) tax-paper, tax-collector's notice; =**zuschlag** *m* increase of taxation, addition made (or penny added) to the income-tax; =**zylinder** ⊕ *m*, *mach.* valve-cylinder.

Steurung (⌣⌣) *f.* Steuerung.

Steven ↓ (⌣⌣) [ndd.: Stamm] *m* ㉓ (Vorder-)~ stem; f. Hintersteven.

StGB. *abbr.* = Strafgesetzbuch.

stibitzen F (-⌣⌣) [nhd. 18. sae.; burfch., F] *v*/*a*. u. *v*/*n*. (h.) ㊽ ㊾ to pilfer, filch, purloin, F to nick, sneak, pinch, F to make.

Stich¹ (⌣) [ahd.: stitch: stechen] *m* ㊉ *c*. (*pl.* nach Zahlen als Maß *inv.*) 1. sting of a bee, bite of a flea, prick of a pin (f. Dolch=, Nadel=, Spaten=stich); ⊕ und *surg.* auch: puncture; *fenc.* (Stoß) thrust; e-m e-n ~ beibringen to stab a p.; *fig.* das war ihm ein ~ durch die Seele that cut him to the quick. — 2. *fig.* (Anspielung) hit (F dig) at a p.; das ist ein ~ auf uns that's meant (or intended) for us. — 3. *fig.* in e-n ~ h.: a) von Betrunkenen: to be fuddled or tipsy; b) von Verrückten: F to have a screw loose, to be off one's chump or nut (vgl. Hieb 4). — 4. v. Farben: e-n ~ ins Blaue h. to have a bluish tinge; von säuerlichem Bier, Wein ꝛc.: e-n ~ h. to be turning (acid), to be sourish or sharp. — 5. Näherei: stitch; weite (enge) ~e *m*. to sew with wide (narrow) stitches; mit weiten ~en nähen to baste. — 6. ♣ = Tauschhandel. — 7. Kartenspiel: trick; e-n ~ m. to make a trick; Whist ꝛc.: feinen ~ m. to make a slam; das Spiel durch einen ~ retten to save a slam. — 8. *path.* shooting (or stinging) pain, twitch; ~ in der Seite stitch in the side. — 9. Gravierkunst: cut, engraving, engraved plate. — 10. Redensarten: ~ **halten** (fest ausdauern) to hold (good), to wear (or last) well; im ~(e) lassen to leave in the lurch, to forsake, Frau u. Kinder: to desert, ein Mädchen: to jilt,⎫

stich² (⌣) *imper. v.* stechen. [to throw over.⎭

Stich¹-blatt (⌣...) ⊕ *n* ㊷: a) des Degengefäßes: guard; b) *fig.* des Spottes: butt; c) Kartenspiel: winning (or trump-)card.

Stichel ⊕ (⌣⌣) [ahd.; *stechen] *m* ㉒ scorper, auch = Grab-stichel und =scheit.

Stichelei (⌣⌣⌣) [sticheln] *f* ㊶ 1. *co.* = Näherei. — 2. *fig.* taunt, sneer, gibe; (Neckerei) chaff, banter; quizzing, teasing.

stichel-haarig (⌣⌣⌣⌣) *a.* ㊻: mit Haar v. abstechenden Farben: rubican.

sticheln (⌣⌣) [nhd., *stechen] *v*/*n*. (h.) und *v*/*a*. ㉒ a. 1. *co.* = nähen. — 2. (Sticheleien führen) to make stinging (or sneering) remarks, to taunt a p., to sneer at a p.; (necken) to chaff, to tease.

Stichel-rede (⌣⌣⌣) *f* ㊸, =**wort** *n* = Stichelei 2.

Stich¹-entscheid (⌣...) *m* ㊷ des Präsidenten: chairman's casting-vote; ²**fest** *a.* ㊻ proof against sword-cuts, weitS. proof against danger; =**flamme** ⊕ *f* beim Löten fine jet; bei Feuersbrunst ꝛc.: sheet of fire, fiery tongue, blazing flame; ²**frei** *a.* invulnerable, proof against weapons; ²**haltig** *a.* standing the test, (dauernd) lasting, sound, solid; (glaubwürdig) plausible, (gültig) valid; =**haltigkeit** *f* soundness; plausibility, validity; =**herd** ⊕ *m* Gießerei: stoke- (or tapping-)hearth.

Stichler (⌣⌣) [sticheln 2] *m* ㉒, ~**in** *f* ㊽ person (fond of) taunting (or chaffing, quizzing) others, teaser.

Stichling (⌣⌣) *m* ㉓d. *ichth.* stickleback. tittlebat (*Gasteros'teus acules'tus*).

Stich¹-mal (⌣...) *n* ㊷ mark of (or scar left by) a stab; =**ofen** ⊕ *m, metall.* smelting- (or blast-)furnace; =**probe** ⊕ *metall.* assay taken at hazard; weitS. sample taken offhand, superficial test; =**säge** ⊕ *f* keyhole-saw. [v. stechen.⎫

stichst, sticht (⌣) 2., 3. Person *sg. pres. ind.*⎭

Stich¹-waffe (⌣...) *f* ㊷ weapon for thrusting or stabbing, foil; =**wahl** *f* second ballot; ²**weise** *adv.* by pricks or stitches; =**wort** *n*: a) stock-phrase, saying of the day; catch-word (auch ⊕ *typ.*); b) *thea.* (Merkwort) cue; das ~ überhören to miss one's cue; c) = Spitzname; =**wunde** *f* stab, thrust.

Stich²-älchen (⌣...) [sticken¹] *n* ㊷ *ent.* wheat-eel (*Tyle'nchus tri'tici*); =²**arbeit** [sticken²] ⊕ *f* embroidery; vgl. Stickerei; =**dunst** ♣ *m* choke-damp.

sticken¹ (⌣⌣) *v*/*n*. (fn) u. *v*/*a.* ㊿ = ersticken.

sticken² (⌣⌣) [ahd.: stitch: stechen] I *v*/*a.* ㊽ (mit feinen Stichen nähen) to embroider; schön gestickt, auch: beautifully worked (on canvas, cloth, &c.). — II ~ *n* ㉓ (f. I) embroidery.

Sticker (⌣⌣) *m* ㉒, ~**in** *f* ㊽ embroiderer.

Stickerei (⌣⌣⌣) *f* ㊶ (das Sticken u. Gestickte) embroidery, mit Wolle auf Kanevas: woolwork; weitS. fancy-needlework; ~**besatz** *m* ㊷ embroidered trimming.

Stick²-garn ㊵ (⌣...) *n* ㊷ embroidery-cotton; =¹**gas** *n* ehm. = =stoff; =²**gaze** ⊕ *f* canvas for wool-work; =**husten** *m* *path.* (Keuchhusten) whooping-cough.

stickig (⌣⌣) *a.* ㊻ suffocating, choking; stuffy (room, &c.), close (air, &c.).

Stick¹-luft (⌣...) *f* ㊷ close (or stuffy) air; =²**maschine** ⊕ *f* embroidering-machine; =**muster** *n* pattern for embroidering; =**nadel** *f*, =**rahmen** *m* embroidery-needle, -frame; =**seide** ⊕ *f* embroidery-silk; =¹**stoff** *m*, *chm.* = nitrogen (N); mit ~ verbinden to nitrogenize; ²**stoff-frei** *a.* ㊻ free from nitrogen, v. Stärke, Zucker ꝛc.: non-nitrogenous, amyloid; ²**stoff=haltig** *a.* nitrogenous (food, &c.); =**stoff=oxyd** *n* nitric oxide (NO); =**stoff=oxydul** *n* (Luftgas) nitrous oxide (N₂O); =**stoff-verbindung** *f* nitrogen-compound; =²**tuch** *n* (Muster zum Sticken) sampler; =**wolle** ⊕ *f* embroidery-wool; =**zeug** *n* requisites (F things) *pl.* for embroidering.

stieben (⌣) [ahd.: Staub] ㊻a. (㊾) I *v*/*n.* (h. u. fn) (stäuben) to give off (or to fly like) dust, weitS. to disperse, scatter; a. = sprühen 1 a. — II *v*/*a.* = stäuben 2.

Stief-bruder (⌣⌣) [ahd.: step...] *m* ㉓ stepbrother, half-brother.

Stiefel¹ (⌣⌣) [nhd.; it.; *lt. aestiva'le Sommer-(schuh)] *m* ㉒ (P.+㉖) 1. boot, hochschäftige ~ Wellington boots *pl.*; (f. Halbstiefel, Stulp[en]stiefel); in ~n und Sporen booted and spurred, f. spanisch 1. — 2. ~ e-r Tabakspfeife shank of a tobacco-pipe. — 3. *fig.* feinen (guten) ~ (guten Schritt) gehen to walk (at) a good pace. — 4. (Trinkgefäß, Trunk) einen guten ~ trinken to drink a good deal, F to be a great boozer; er kann e-n guten ~ vertragen he can stand a great deal (of liquoring).

Stiefel² (⌣⌣) [mhd. — ndd. Stiepel Stütze] *m* ㉒ = Pumpenstiefel.

Stiefel¹-absatz (⌣⌣...) *m* ㉒ heel of a boot, =**anzieher** *m* boot-pulls *pl.*; vgl. =**haken**, =**ausziehen** ⊕ = =knecht; =**band** *n* = =strippe; =**bürste** *f* blacking-brush.

Stiefelchen (⌣⌣⌣) *n* ㉓ (*dim. v.* Stiefel¹) small (or short) boot, *a. co.* bootikin.

Stiefel¹-dehner (⌣⌣...) *m* ㉒ = boot-stretcher; =**einsatz** *m* aus Kautschuk: elastic side-springs *pl.*

Stiefelette (-⌣⌣⌣) [dtsch.-fr.] *f* ㊸ (~ für Halbstiefel) 1. (Gamasche) gaiters *pl.* — 2. ~n *pl.* (Schnürstiefel) laced boots *pl.*

Stiefel¹-fabrikant (⌣⌣...) *m* ㉒ = Schuhmacher; ²**förmig** *a.* ㊻ boot-shaped; =**fuchs** F *m*: a) = =putzer; b) student's attendant, Fgyp; =**haken** *m* zum Stiefelanziehen boot-hook; =**knecht** *m* boot-jack; =**leisten** *m* = Leisten²; ehm. =**manschette** *f* ruffle of a boot.

stiefeln (⌣⌣) ㊻a. I F *v*/*n*. (h.) to walk with great strides, to stalk along; wo ~ Sie hin? where are you going (or off) to? — II *v*/*a.* (mit Stiefeln bekleiden) to boot, to provide with boots: gestiefelt f. Kater 1 und Spornen 2. — III sich ~ *v*/*refl.* (Stiefel anziehen) to put on (one's) boots.

Stiefel¹-putzer (⌣⌣...) *m* ㉒ shoeblack; (Hausknecht) boots; =**schaft** *m* (=**sohle** *f*) leg (sole) of a boot; =**strippe** *f* boot-strap; =**stulpe** *f* top of a boot, b.-top.

Stief-eltern (⌣⌣⌣) *pl.* ㉒ stepfather and stepmother.

Stiefel¹-wichse ⊕ (⌣⌣...) *f* ㊸ shoe-blacking, boot-polish; =**wichser** *m* shoeblack; =**zieher** *m* = =anzieher u. =knecht.

Stief-geschwister (⌣⌣⌣...) *m* *n*/*pl.* ㉒ stepbrothers and stepsisters, halfbrothers and half-sisters *pl.*; =**kind** *n* (auch *fig.*) stepchild; =**mutter** *f* stepmother, father's second wife; böse ~ cruel stepmother, *fig.* wicked mother; =**mütterchen** ♣ *n* heart's-ease, pansy (*Vi'ola tri'color*); ²**mütterlich** *a.* ㊻ stepmotherly; *fig.* ~ behandeln to treat cruelly, to neglect; =**schwester** *f* stepsister, half-sister (vgl. =bruder); =**sohn** *m* stepson; =**tochter** *f* stepdaughter; =**vater** *m* stepfather, mother's second husband; *fig.* er ist seinem Leibe kein ~ he does not stint himself anything; ²**väterlich** *a.* stepfatherly.

Stieg¹ (⌣) [= Steig] *m* ㉓c. steep path.

stieg² (⌣) *ind.* ²c¹ (⌣) *subj. impf. v.* steigen.

Stiege¹ (⌣⌣) [ahd.: stair; *steigen] *f* ㊸ staircase (= Treppe).

Stiege² (⌣⌣) [nhd.: sty] *f* ㊸ (20 Stück) score.

Stieglitz (⌣⌣) [nhd.; *tschech.] *m* ㉒a. (㊷) (Distelfint) goldfinch (*Fringi'lla cardue'lis*).

stiehl (⌣; *Hom.* Sti(e)l, ²ft, ²t (⌣) *imper.* 2. u. 3. Person *sg.* des *pres. ind.* von stehlen.

♪ Musik; ⚯ Wissenschaft; ♀ Pflanze; ♀ Geographie; ⊕ Technik; ⚒ Bergbau; ⚔ Militär; ⚓ Marine; ✋ Handel; ✉ Post; 🚂 Eisenbahn.

Stiel (´; *Hom.* stiehl, Stil) [ahd.; *lt. stīlus* „Stichel"] *m* ⓒc. **1.** (Handhabe) handle (or haft, helve) of a tool, &c., stick of a broom, stem of a pipe. — **2.** ♀ (Stengel) stalk, stem (auch einer gepflückten Blume u. Frucht); ~ der Blume: ☞ peduncle, pedicle, pedicel, des Blattes: ☞ petiole, zo., anat. ~(chen): ☞ pedic*le*, ...cel, ...cule; ⊝ shank; *carp.* puncheon, upright. — **3.** *fig.* den ~ umkehren to turn the tables upon a p.; mit Stumpf und ~ (vollständig) (with) root and branch; mit Stumpf und ~ ausrotten (utterly) to extirpate or eradicate or root out.

stiel-äugig (″...) *a.* ⓒ *zo.* stalk-eyed; **=blatt** ♀ n ⓒ: ☞ petiolate leaf; **♀blütig** ♀ *a.*: ☞ cauliflorous.

Stielchen (´) *n* ⓒ (*dim. v. Stiel*) little (or short) handle or stalk, ♀: ☞ petiolule (f. Stiel 2 zo., anat.).[*cus pedunculāta*].

Stiel=eiche (″.´.) *f* ⓒ common oak (*Quer-*)

stielen (´˘) **I** *v/a.* ⓒ **1.** to provide with a handle, to haft (or helve) an axe, &c. — **II** ge-stielt *p.p. u. a.* ⓒ **2.** (provided) with a handle. — **3.** ♀: ☞ pediculate, *v.* Blüten: ☞ pedunculate, *v.* Blättern: ☞ petiolate, petioled; *zo.* von Schneckenaugen: telescopic.

Stiel-ende ♀ (″.´.) *n* ⓒ e-s Blattes: base.

stielig (´˘) *a.* ⓒ: **a)** = stielen 3; **b)** in Zssgn, *z.B.* kurz=♀ with a short handle or stalk; *bisw. a. fig., z.B.* lang=♀ (f. ds).

Stiel-kloben ⊝ (″...) *m* ⓒ Schlosserei: tail-vice; **♀los** *a.* ⓒ stalkless, ☞ sessile; **♀rund** ♀ *a.* ⓒ *zo.*: ☞ terete.

stier[1] (´) [nhd.: starr] *a.* ⓒ vom Blicke: staring, fixed, glassy, (ausdruckslos) vacant; e-n ♀ (*adv.*) anblicken to stare (or to look vacantly) at a p.

Stier[2] (´) [ahd.: steer] *m* ⓒc. **1.** *zo.* u. *agr.* bull, steer; den ~ bei den Hörnern fassen to take the bull by the horns (a. *fig.*). — **2.** *ast.* Sternbild: ☞ Taurus.

stier²-artig (″.´.) *a.* ⓒ *zo.*: ☞ taurine.

stieren (´˘) [stier¹] *v/n.* (h.) = to stare, to look with a fixed (or vacant) gaze, to look vacant.

Stier²-fechter (″...) *m* ⓒ bull-fighter, berittener: toreador; **=gefecht** *n* bull-fight; **=gespann** *n* team (or span) of bullocks; **=hetze** *f* bull-baiting; **=kalb** *n* bull-calf; **=kämpfer** *m* = **=fechter**; **♀köpfig** *a.* with a bull's head; **=nacken** *m* bull-neck; **=opfer** *n* Alt.: ☞ tauroboliun; **=töter** *m* im spanisch. Stiergefecht: [matador.]

stieß (´) *ind. impf. v.* stoßen.

Stift[1] (´) [ahd.: Stab] *m* ⓒb. **1.** ⓒ peg, tag; (dünner Nagel ohne Kopf) tack; (Beschlag=) ~ ferrule, ferrel; (Bolzen) bolt, (Pflock) pin; mit e-m ~ festmachen to pin down; ~ am Phonographen, Telegraphen *z.*: style; *mach.* ~ (Zapfen) einer stehenden Welle pivot. ~ (Stumpf eines Zahnes) stump. — **3.** ~ zum Schreiben, Zeichnen: pencil, crayon, farbiger: crayon, pastel. — **4.** F *co.* (fl. Mensch) little fellow or dot, whipper-snapper, shrimp; (Junge) nipper, youngster.

Stift[2] (´) [nhd.: *stiften] *n* ⓒⓓc.: **a)** (wohltätige Stiftung) charitable foundation or endowment; home for the poor ⊝, for gentlefolk of limited means, &c.; ~ für adlige Damen *2c.* institution for ladies of rank, &c.; **b)** (Kloster) convent, monastery; (Bistum) bishopric; (Domkapitel) chapter (of a cathedral); (Seminar) seminary, training-college.

stiften (´˘) [ahd.: steif] **I** *v/a.* ⓓ **1. a)** (gründen) to found; (schaffen) to create, to originate, (hervorbringen) to produce; (einsetzen) to establish, to institute, to set on foot; eine Ehe ♀ to bring about a marriage, to act as match-maker; Freundschaft zwischen Menschen, Völkern ♀ to conciliate people, nations; Frieden ♀ to make (or establish) peace; Gutes ♀ to do good; Nutzen ♀ to be useful or of use; **b)** *et.* Schönes ♀ anstiften 1; F *iro.* da haben Sie was Schönes (an)gestiftet you have done a nice bit of business; Unfrieden ♀ to sow discord. — **2.** (gründen, besd. zu frommen Zwecken) to found, establish, endow; (vermachen) to bequeath. — **II** ~ *n* **3.** f. Stiftung. [originator.]

Stifter (´˘) *m* ⓓ, ~**in** *f* ⓓ founder;

Stift[1]-**farbe** (´...´) *f* ⓓ *paint.* pastel; **=halter** *m* crayon-holder.

stiftisch (´˘) [Stift²b] *a.* ⓓ of a chapter.

Stift[1]-**kreide** (³...´) *f* ⓓ *paint.* white chalk; **=malerei** *f* crayon-painting.

Stifts-amt (³...) [Stift²] *n* ⓓ canonicate; **=amtmann** *m* vidame; **=brief** *m* deed (or charter) of a foundation; **=dame**, **=frau** *f*, **=fräulein** *n* canoness; **=gebäude** *n* chapter-house; **=gemeinde** *f* congregation of a cathedral; **=gut** *n* capitular estate, endowment; **=hauptmann** *m* = =amtmann; **=haus** *n* = =gebäude; **=herr** *m* canon, prebendary; **=hütte** *f*, *bibl.* tabernacle; **=kanzler** *m* chancellor of a chapter; **=kirche** *f* collegiate church; (Hauptkirche e-s Bistums) cathedral; **=länderein** *f/pl.* chapterlands *pl.*; **=mäßig** *a.* ⓓ capitular; **=pfarrer** *m* incumbent of a collegiate church; **=pfründe** *f* canonry, canonship, prebend; **=schule** *f* cathedral- (or foundation-)school; **=versammlung** *f* meeting of a chapter.

Stiftung (´˘) *f* ⓓ **1.** (f. stiften I) foundation; creation; establishment. — **2.** (das Gegründete) (charitable) endowment or institution, milde ~ pious bequest.

Stiftungs-brief (³˘...) *m* ⓓ = Stifts-brief; **=fest** *n* anniversary of a foundation, commemoration- (or founder's) day; **=mäßig** *a.* ⓓ in accordance with (the conditions of) a foundation; **=tag** *m* = =fest; **=urkunde** *f* jur. deed of foundation. [drawing.]

Stift-zeichnung (³..´.) *f* ⓓ pastel

stigmatisieren (˘˘˘´) *v/a.* ⓓ (brandmarken) to stigmatize.

Stil (´; *Hom.* stiehl, Stiel) [nhd.: style; *lt.* (f. Stiel)] *m* ⓓc. **1.** style; alter, neuer ~ (Kalender) old, new style; nach dem eingeführten ~e (Brauche) according to established usage; in Schrift u. Kunst: style, manner; er schreibt einen angenehmen (schwerfälligen) ~ he writes (in) a pleasant (heavy) style; gekünstelter ~ mannerism; *arch.* im byzantinischen (gotischen *2c.*) ~ in the Byzantine (Gothic, &c.) style. — **2.** im großen ~e (auf großem Fuße) leben to live in great (or fine) style, F u. P to do it fat.

Stil-art (″.´) *f* ⓓ style.

Stilett (˘´) [*it.*; *dim. v. lt. stīlus*, f. Sti(e)l] *n* ⓓc. (fl. Dolch) stiletto, short pointed dagger. [highly finished.]

stil-gerecht (″..´) *a.* ⓓ correct in style,

stilisieren (˘˘´˘) [Stil] *v/a.* ⓓ: **a)** to pen, word, compose; *abs.* er kann gut ~ he writes well; schlecht stilisiert written in bad style, F badly put together; **b)** to touch up, to improve in style.

Stilist (˘´) *m* ⓓ accomplished (or elegant) writer, *auch:* stylist; ~**ik** *f* ⓓ theory of style, *a.* = Stillehre; **Stilisch** *a.* concerning style; in Stilischer Hinsicht as regards style.

still (´) [ahd.: still] **I** *a.* ⓓ **1.** (ohne Regung) still, calm, quiet, tranquil, placid, vom Wasser auch: without a ripple, stagnant (pool, &c.); (unbeweglich) motionless, (leblos) lifeless, inanimate, ♀ *a.* dull, flat; (leise) low, soft, noiseless; (schweigsam) silent, taciturn; (friedlich) peaceable, peaceful; *als int.:* ♀!, seid (ob. schweigt) ♀! silence!, hush!; ♀ davon! don't mention it!; F ♀ mal! do be quiet! — **2.** mit *nouns:* *eccl.* Der Freitag Good Friday; Des Gebet silent prayer; De Gegend quiet neighbourhood; ♥ Der Gesellschafter (ob. Associé) sleeping partner; ihr Des Glück their peace and happiness; De Hochzeit quiet (or private) wedding; De Liebe unavowed love; De Luft calm (or soft) air; *euph.* ein Der (toter) Mann sein to have found peace, to be dead (and buried); Der Mensch: **a)** calm and inoffensive person; **b)** silent person; *eccl.* De Messe low mass; De Mieter *m/pl.* quiet lodgers *pl.*; bei Der Nacht in the dead of night; ♀ der ~e (ober Große) Ozean the Pacific (Ocean); Der Schmerz dull pain; dem Den Trunk (P Soff) ergeben F given to drinking (or boozing) on the quiet or on the sly; Der Vorbehalt mental reservation; Der Vorwurf silent reproach; Der Wahnsinn (*ant.* Tobsucht) melancholy, melancholia; Des Wasser smooth water; Des Wetter calm weather, ♩ lull, calm; De Wohnung quiet lodging; De Zeit dull (or dead) season; bei Todesanzeigen: wir bitten um Des Beileid, etwa: no visits of condolence (desired); *Sprichw.* die Toten sind De Leute dead men tell no tales; De Wasser sind tief still waters run deep. — **3.** mit *verbs:* ♀ bekommen to (reduce to) silence; ♀ beten to pray in silence; ganz ♀ fortgeh(e)n to steal (or sneak) away; ♀ sein to be quiet; ♀ sein mit (ober von) et. to keep a th. snug; sich ♀ verhalten to keep still or quiet, not to stir; ♀ werden to grow calm or silent, vom Winde: to calm (or go, lull) down, to drop, to abate. — **II** *s.* ⓒ **4.** das ~e = Stille 1 und 3; im Den (unbemerkt) in silence; quietly, secretly, privately, *b. s.* underhand (vgl. Stille 3). — **5.** ein ~er a quiet person; die ~en *pl.* (Frommen) im Lande: the pious (F the goody-goody) people.

still-bleiben (³.´.) *v/n.* (fn) ⓓ** to remain (or keep) quiet, *engS.* to keep silence.

stille[1] F (´˘) bsd. wenn nichts folgt = still.

[Stille] — 927 — [stinken]

Stille² (⌣⌣)[ahd.] f ⊕ (f. still) 1. stillness, quiet(ness), tranquillity; (ant. Leidenschaft, Sturm) calm(ness), peace, lull; tiefe ~ profound (or dead) silence. — 2. = Stillstand. — 3. in der ~, in aller ~ silently, quietly, b. s. (heimlich) in an underhand way, F on the quiet, on the sly (vgl. still 4); in der ~ abziehen to slink (or steal, sneak) away.
Stilleben (⌣L⌣)[Still=leben] n ㉓: a) quiet (or retired life); b) paint. still-life.
Stillegung (⌣L⌣) [Still=legung] f ⊕ e-r Zeche ꝛc.: shutting down a mine, &c.
Stil=lehre (ᴜ̄·L⌣) f ⊕ (art of) composition.
stillen (⌣⌣) [ahd.; *still (ein)stellen] I v/a. ⊕ 1. (zum Stillstand bringen) to stop; Blutung 2 to stanch bleeding. — 2. (beruhigen, befriedigen) to still pain, to appease anger, hunger, to allay fear, to quench (one's) thirst, to quell an insurrection; nichts kann sein Sehnen 2 nothing can satisfy (or still) his longing. — 3. (schweigen m.) to silence, hush; den Sturm 2 to quiet (or calm) the storm. — 4. ein Kind 2 (säugen n.) to nurse (weniger fein: to suckle) a child. — II ~ n ㉓ 5. f. Stillung. — III 2d p.pr. u. a. ⊕ 6. Bed. des inf. — 7. med.
Stiller (⌣⌣) m ⊕ appeaser. [sedative.]
still=gestanden (⌣...) f. ⌣stch(e)n; ⌣halten (sich) ⊕a** to keep still; (einhalten) to (make a) stop, to pause, mit dem Wagen: to pull up; er kann den Mund nicht 2 he cannot hold his tongue; bisw. e-m 2 (e-n gewähren l.) to let a p. do as (s)he likes; ~ n ㉓ halt(ing), stoppage.
stilliegen (⌣L⌣) [still=liegen] v/n. (h.) ⊕** to lie quiet(ly), weit S. to keep quiet or still, v. Schiffen: to lie to; an e-m Orte unterwegs 2 to stop in a place; von den Geschäften, vom Handel: to be at a standstill, to lie dormant.
stil=los (ᴜ̄·L⌣) a. ⊕ without (or in bad) style.
still=schweigen (⌣...) v/n. (h.) ⊕** to be silent, to keep (or observe) silence (von et. about a th.); ~ n ㉓ silence; e-m ~ auferlegen to enjoin silence (or secrecy) on a p.; mit ~ übergeh(e)n to pass over in silence; f. beobachten 3; 2d a. ⊕, 2d(s) adv. silent(ly), in silence; 2d anerkannt tacitly understood, implied; 2sitzen v/n. (h.) ⊕** to sit quiet(ly), weit S. to remain inactive; nicht 2 können to be fidgety; =stand m ⊕ standstill, stop(page), fig. stagnation, lull (a. ⊕); (Stockung) deadlock, (Einstellung) suspension; (Untätigkeit) inaction; zum ~ bringen to stop machinery, &c., to shut down a factory, &c.; vgl. stillen 1; 2stch(e)n v/n. (h.) ⊕** to stand still (f. steh(e)n 3); bei et. nicht 2 not to stop at a th.; ⚔ 2gestanden! (stand at) attention!; die Geschäfte steh(e)n still business is dull or at a standstill; ~ n ㉓ =stand; 2d a. ⊕ at a standstill, stationary; vom Wasser u. fig. stagnant.
Stillung (⌣⌣) f ⊕ (f. stillen I) stanching of blood; appeasement; nursing a baby. [ing medicine, sedative.]
Stillungs=mittel (⌣L·⌣L⌣) n ㉓ med. calm-
still=vergnügt (⌣...) a. ⊕ quietly enjoying o.s., calm and serene; =wasser ↓ n ㉓ zwischen Ebbe u. Flut: slack tide.

stil=voll (ᴜ̄·L⌣) a. ⊕ stylish. in good style; (geschmackvoll) tasty.
Stimm=abgabe (⌣...) f ⊕ voting, vote; =band n, pl. =bänder anat. vocal cords or ligaments, ⚕ glottal ligaments pl.
stimmbar (⌣·) a. ⊕ 1. ♪ tunable. — 2. † = stimmberechtigt.
stimm=begabt (⌣...) a. ⊕ endowed with a good voice; 2berechtigt a. entitled to (a) vote; enfranchised; =berechtigung f ⊕ right of voting or to vote; f. =recht; =bruch m = =wechsel.
Stimmchen (⌣⌣) n ㉓ (dim. v. Stimme) thin (or little) voice.
Stimme (⌣⌣)[ahd.; †steven] f ⊕ 1. voice (f. dämpfen 2); f-e ~ abgeben to give one's opinion; pol. to vote; und was die innere ~ spricht (SCH.) and what the inner voice asserts or proclaims; f. laut, leise. — 2. ♪ ~ des Sängers: voice, in Bezug auf Klang a. organ; er ist nicht bei ~ he is not in good voice, F he's off song; (zu singende ob. zu spielende Musik u. Noten) part; die ~n austeilen to distribute the parts, to arrange the score; zweite ~ alto; (Orgelregister) stop. — 3. mst pol. vote (f. Sitz 1); e-m feine ~ geben to give a p. one's vote, to vote for a p.; die ~n sammeln to collect (the) votes, von Haus zu Haus: to go (round) canvassing.
stimmen¹ (⌣⌣)[ahd.] ⊕ I v/n.(h.).1.(in Einklang sein): a) ♪ to harmonize; to be in tune, to be tuned to the same pitch; b) fig. zu et. 2 to agree with (or correspond to) a th., to be in accord (or in keeping) with a th.; das stimmt that's all right (or alright); das stimmt nicht there's s.th. wrong. — 2. = abstimmen II. — II v/a. 3. ♪ ein Instrument 2 to tune ...; höher 2 to raise to a higher pitch; nach dem Klavier 2 to tune to the piano. — 4. fig. f-e Forderungen hoch 2 (spannen) to be exacting in one's demands; e-n gegen e-n (et.) 2 to prejudice a p. against a p. (a th.); e-n günstig 2 to put a p. in a favourable mood; e-n zu et. 2 to predispose a p. in favour of a th., to induce (or persuade) a p. to do a th.; gut gegen e-n gestimmt well-disposed towards a p.; e-n traurig 2 to make a p. sad, to depress a p.('s spirits); schlecht gestimmt ill-humoured, out of temper. — III ~ n ㉓ 5. f. Stimmung 1. — IV ~de(r) m f ⊕ 6. = Stimmgeber.
Stimmen=anzahl (⌣...) [Stimme pl.] f ⊕: er erhielt nicht die nötige ~ he did not obtain the requisite number of votes; =einh(elligk)eit f unanimity; mit ~ unanimously, auch: (It.) nem(ine) con(tradicente); =gewirr n confused din of voices; =gleichheit f even number (or equality, parity) of votes; =mehrheit (=minderheit) f majority (minority) of votes; =sammler m nach der Abstimmung: scrutator; vor der Wahl: canvasser; =teilung f splitting of votes; =verhältnis n proportion of votes; =zahl f = =anzahl.
Stimmer (⌣⌣) m ⊕ 1. (Klavier ꝛc.) ~ (piano-&c.) tuner. — 2. = Stimmhammer.
stimm=fähig (⌣...) a. ⊕ = 2berechtigt; =führer m ⊕: a) ♪ leader of a choir;

b) spokesman (or mouthpiece) of a party; =gabel ♪ f tuning-fork; =geber m voter; =gebung f = =abgabe.
stimmhaft (⌣·) a. ⊕ (ant. stimmlos) gr. u. Phonetik: Der Konsonant (Media) flat (or voiced) consonant, auch: voice.
Stimm=hammer ♪ (⌣...) m Instrumentenfabr.: tuning-hammer or -key; =holz, =hölzchen ♪ n = =stock.
...stimmig (...)(⌣·) [Stimme] a. ⊕, z.B. viel2 with many voices; ♪ vier2 for four voices, in four parts.
Stimmittel (⌣L·⌣) [Stimm=mittel] n/pl. ⊕ vocal power or resources pl. of a singer.
Stimm=lage ♪ (⌣·L⌣) f ⊕ pitch of the voice register.
stimmlich (⌣⌣) a. ⊕ relating to the voice; 2e Mittel bff. Stimmittel (f. ds).
Stimm=lippe (⌣...) f ⊕ anat. (der obere Teil des Kehlkopfes) vocal chord, *r-n ft. =band; =lippen=polyp m, path. polypus on the vocal chords; 2los a. ⊕ voiceless, mute, ⚕ aphonous, ...ic; gr. u. Phonetik (ant. stimmhaft): 2loser Konsonant (Tenuis) sharp (or voiceless) consonant, auch: breath; =losigkeit f voicelessness, ⚕ aphony; =mittel f. Stimmittel; =organ n, physiol. vocal organ; =pfeife ♪ f (zum Stimmen von Orgelpfeifen ꝛc.) tuning- (or pitch-)pipe; =recht n, pol. franchise; allgemeines ~ universal (or manhood-)suffrage; =ritze f, anat.: ⚕ glottis; =ritzen=deckel m: ⚕ epiglottis; =schlüssel ♪ m tuning-key; =stock ♪ m einer Geige: sound(ing)-post; =umfang ♪ m range of a voice.
Stimmung (⌣⌣) f ⊕ 1. ♪ (das Stimmen) tuning. — 2. (Art wie es gestimmt ist): a) ♪ pitch, key; ~ halten to keep in tune; b) fig. ~ des Gemüts frame of mind, mood, humour, temper, disposition; in der rechten ~ für et. in the right vein for a th.; in gehobener, gedrückter ~ buoyant, depressed; ~s=bild n ⊕ paint. picture in harmony with the time of day, the state of the weather, &c.; ~s=streik m Arbeiter: sympathy strike; 2s=voll a. ⊕ representing a certain frame of mind.
Stimm=vieh F (⌣...) n ⊕ contp., etwa: (unthinking) herd of voters, electoral mob; =wechsel m heranreifender Knaben: breaking of the voice; =zähler m, parl. teller; =zählung f counting of votes or ballot-papers; =zettel m voting-paper. [...la'ntia).]
Stimulans ⚕ (⌣·L⌣) [lt.] n (sg. inv., pl.)
stimulieren (⌣·L⌣) [lt.] v/a. ⊕ bsd. med. (reizen) to stimulate; Stimulus (⌣⌣) m ⊕ bsd. med. (Reizmittel) stimulant; fig. (Stachel) stimulus.
Stinkadores F co. (⌣·L⌣) [dtsch=span.; *stink-en] pl. inv. bad-smelling cigars, stinking weeds pl.
Stink=asant (⌣...) m ⊕ pharm. Art Harz: asafoetida; =baum ⚘ m stavewood (Stercu'lia fe'tida); =bock m stinking he-goat; =bombe f stinking bomb; =dachs m, zo. stinkard (Myda'us me'liceps).
stinken (⌣⌣) [ahd.: stink] I v/n. (h.) ⊕ ft 1. to stink, anständiger: to smell bad or nasty, to have an unpleasant smell or odour. — 2. fig. er stinkt vor Faulheit F he is as lazy as he is long or

⚛ scientific; ⚘ botanical; ⚲ geography; ⊕ machinery; ⚒ mining; ⚔ military; ↓ marine; ⊛ commercial; ✉ postal; 🚆 railway.

[stinkfaul] — 928 — [Stockschnupfen]

as Hall's dog; Sprichw. Eigenlob stinkt, fremdes Lob klingt self-praise is no recommendation. — II ~ n ② 3. = Gestank. — III 2d p.pr. u. a. ⑥⑥ 4. stinking. anständiger: fetid, malodorous. of unpleasant smell or odour; fig. 2de Lüge gross lie.

stink=faul (²⁻′) a. ⑥⑥ bone-lazy; =fliege (²...) f ② ent. stinking fly (Hemero'bius); =holz ⸗ n stinkwood, stinking-wood; ⚘ ceylonisches ~ olax of Ceylon (Olax Zeyla'nica).

stinkig (²⁻) a. ⑥⑥ = stinken III.

Stint=käfer (²...) m ② = Mistkäfer; =kalk m = =stein; chm. =kugel ⸗ f stinkball; =marder m = Iltis; =mergel m. min. bituminous marl; =nase f, path. (Rosengeschwür): ⸗ ozæna; =ratz m = Iltis; =schwamm ⸗ m stinkhorn (Phallus impudi'cus), =stein m. min. stinkstone, bituminous limestone; =tier n. zo. skunk (Mephi'tis mephi'tica); =topf ⸗ m stink-pot; =wiesel n = Iltis; =wild n fetid game. [Osme'rus).]

Stint (²⁻) [nbd. kurz] m ⓤb. ichth. smelt

Stipendiat(⸗⁻⸗⁻′) [lt.]m②exhibitioner, eines Stifts: foundationer.

Stipendi=en=fonds (-²⁻²...) [pl. v. Stipendium] m ② univ. scholarship fund.

Stipendium (⸗²⁻′) [lt.] n ② (Unterstützung für Schüler, Studierende, Künstler, Gelehrte) exhibition, scholarship.

Stipp=besuch F berlin. (²⁻⸗⁻ch) m ② flying visit, short call, look-in.

stippen (²⁻) [nbd.: steep] v/a. u. v/n.(h.) ⑧ (tunken) to dip, soak, steep.

stipulieren (⸗⸗⁻²⁻′) [lt.] v/a. ⑨ (festsetzen) to stipulate. [sg. pres. ind. v. sterben.]

stirb, 2st, 2t (²) imper., 2. u. 3. Person

Stirn (²) [ahd.] f ⑥⑥, a. =e (²⁻) f ⑱ 1. forehead, poet. brow (s. runzeln u. frech); dem Feinde die ~ bieten to face the enemy; dem Sturm, dem Unwetter (kühn) die ~ bieten to weather the storm; s. runzeln. — 2. arch. (Vorderseite) front(age), seltener: façade.

Stirn=ader (²...) f anat.: ⸗ frontal vein; =band n head-band, chm. als Kopfputz: frontlet; Alt.: fillet; =bein n, anat.: ⸗ frontal (bone); =binde f = =band; =blatt n metal ornament for the forehead; =blutader f, anat. frontal artery; =bogen ⊕ m, arch. frontal arch; =falte f wrinkle on the forehead; =fläche ⊕ f front(age), face; =haar n front hair; =höhle f, anat.: ⸗ frontal cavity. [a broad forehead.]

...stirnig (..."²⁻) a. ⑥⑥, z.B. breit2 with

Stirn=locke (²...) n ② arch. front-truss; =locke f curl on the forehead, forelock; bei Mädchen auch: F kiss-me-quick; =mauer ⊕ f, arch. front wall; =muskel m, anat.: ⸗ frontal muscle, zum Runzeln: ⸗ corrugator; =rad ⊕ n spur-wheel; =riemen m des Pferdegeschirrs: head-piece of the bridle; =runzeln n frown(ing); =seite f front(al side); ⊕ arch. face; =streifen m bei Pferden 2c.: =Blesse; =stück n front-piece, anat. central part of the coronal bone; ⊕ arch. (Vorderg iebel) frontispiece; =wand ⊕ f = =mauer.

Stoa (′⁻) [grch.] f ⑳ Alt.: stoa, porch.

stob(en¹ pl.) (¹⁻) ind., stöbe subj. impf. von stieben.

stoben² (¹⁻) [nbd., ndl.: Stube] v/a. ⑧⑤ Kocht.: (dämpfen) to stew (meat, fruit), to steam (potatoes, stive).

Stöber (⸗⁻) m ㉒ (a. ~=hund m ⑫) spaniel.

stöbern (⸗⁻) [nbd.: stieben] v/n. (h.) ⒶⒶ. 1. v/imp. es stöbert the snow is drifting; bei feinem Regen: it drizzles. — 2. (in allen Winkeln suchen) to hunt in every corner, to rummage (about).

Stöber=wetter (⸗⁻⸗⸗) n ② snow-drift, sleet(y weather), cold drizzling rain.

Stocher (²⁻) [nbd.: stechen] m ㉒ 1. = Zahnstocher. — 2. ⊕ (a. ~=eisen n ②) poker (= Schüreisen).

stochern (²⁻ch) [nbd.: stoke; *stechen] v/a. u. v/n. (h.) Ⓐa. 1. das Feuer 2 to poke (or stir up, rake) the fire; sich die Zähne 2 to pick one's teeth. — 2. auf e-n 2 = sticheln 2.

Stöchiometrie ⸗ (⸗ch⸗⸗⸗) [grch. Elementemessung] f ㊽ chm. (chemische Meßkunst) stoicheiometry.

Stock¹ (²) [ahd.: stock] m ⑦c. (vgl. 5, 9) 1. stick, (Stab) staff, (Spazier=)~ walking-stick; dünner ~cane, switch; (Rute) rod; (Knüttel) cudgel, (Billard=)~ cue; er muß am ~ geh(e)n he has to walk with (or to use) a stick; e=n mit dem ~ schlagen to beat a p. with a stick, to give a p. the stick. — 2. ⚘ (Pflanzen=) ~ trunk, stem. — 3. (einzelne Pflanze von Blumen= u. Topfgewächsen: pot-plant, stock, potted plant. — 4. (Baumstumpf) stump; fig. s. Block 3, Stein 2. — 5. ⊕b. fig. (Klotz) block (or log) of wood. — 6. ~ eines Zahnes: body ... — 7. = Stamm 3 bis 7. — 8. (Gebirgsmasse) chief stock (or central mass) of a mountain-range. — 9. m (n) ⑬b,6. (Geschoß, Stockwerk) story, floor, flat; das Haus ist 4 ~ hoch ob. hat 4 ~ ... is four stories high; im ersten ~ wohnen to live on the first floor; ein Haus von 3 ~(en) a three-storied house. — 10. (Fußblock als Folterinstrument) stocks pl.; in den ~ legen to put in the stocks. — 11. ⊕ Hutmacherei: block; einen Hut auf den ~ spannen to put a hat on the block; typ. = Klischee. — 12. (Bienen=)~ bee-hive.

Stock² ⚘ (²) [engl.] m ⓾ = Stammkapital, s. Stocks.

Stock¹=amboß (²...) m ⊕ der Kupferschmiede: round anvil; =amerikaner m thorough (or true, typical) American, F regular Yankee; =beil ⊕ n axe with (a) semi-circular edge; ⓞblind a. ⑥⑥ stone-blind, (as) blind as a bat or mole; =²börse f stock-exchange; =brite m true-born (F regular) Briton.

Stöckchen (²⁻) n ㉓ (dim. von Stock¹) little stick or cane, (Gerte) switch.

Stock¹=degen (²...) m ㉒ sword-cane or -stick; ⓞdumm (²⁻²⁻) a. ⑥⑥ thoroughly (or exceedingly) stupid, blockheaded; =dunkel a. = ⓞfinster; ⓞdürr a. exceedingly thin, emaciated, F all skin and bones; =eisen n, agr. drill.

stocken¹ (²⁻) [mhd.] ⑧Ⓘ v/n. (h. u. su) 1. a) to come to a standstill or deadlock, to stop (short), to discontinue, P to get stuck; (langsamer w.) to slacken, v. Flüssigkeiten: to cease to flow, to stagnate, vom Blute 2c.: to cease to circulate, vom Herzen 2c.: to cease to act, vom Gespräche: to flag, von der Stimme: to falter, ⚘ von Geschäften: to be slack or dull; 2d stagnant (water, trade, &c.); die Sache, das Unternehmen stockt the affair is at a standstill or dead-lock; die Unterhandlungen 2 the negotiations are suspended or hanging fire, there is a hitch; b) (gerinnen) to coagulate, to congeal, v. Blut u. Milch: to curdle. — 2. v/imp. es stockt mit der Sache the matter is not progressing, there is a hitch (somewhere). — 3. mit persönlichem Subjekt: im Reden 2 to break down (or F to stick) in the middle of a speech, to hesitate (or stammer) in speaking. — 4. (durch Feuchtigkeit verderben) to spoil through damp(ness) (schimmeln) to turn mouldy or fusty. — II ~ n ② 5. s. Stockung; ins ~ geraten to come to a standstill or deadlock or stop, vom Briefwechsel: to be broken off.

stocken² (²⁻) [Stock¹] v/a. u. v/refl. (mit einem Stocke versehen) a) to provide with a stick or stake; Reben 2 to prop ...; b) ⊕ ⓞ Tücher 2 (aufrollen) to roll ...

Stock¹=engländer (²...) m ⓾ thorough Englishman, F regular John Bull.

stöck(e)rig (²⁻) (⁻) [Stock¹] a. ⑥⑥ (as) lean as a rake, F all skin and bones.

Stock¹=fechten (²...) n ② fencing with sticks, single-stick practice; ⓞfinster a. ⑥⑥ pitch-dark; =fisch m: a) Fischerei u. ⚘: (getrockneter Kabeljau) stock-fish, dried cod; b) F fig. (Dummkopf) duffer, dunce; =fisch=fang m cod-fishing; =³fleck(en) [stocken¹ 4] m stain caused by damp(ness) or mould; =³flinte f cane-gun; =flöte f stick-flute; =franzose m true Frenchman; ⓞfremd a. quite (or utterly) strange; =geige f pocket-violin; =halter m cane- (mehr gbr.: umbrella-)stand; =händler m dealer (or trader) in sticks, cane-man; =haus n (Gefängnis) prison, jail.

stockig¹ (²⁻) [Stock¹] a. ⑥⑥ = stocksteif; fig. (hartnäckig) stubborn, stiff-necked, head-strong, self-willed, obstinate.

stockig² (²⁻) [stocken¹ 4] a. ⑥⑥ mouldy, fusty, musty, mildewed; es ist hier ~ the place is very close or fusty.

...stöckig (..."²⁻) a. ⑥⑥ in Zssg mit Zahlwörtern, z.B. drei2 (of or with) three stories, three stories high.

stöckisch (²⁻) a. ⑥⑥ = stockig¹.

Stock²=jobber ⚘ (²...) m ② dealer in (shares and) stocks, stock-jobber; =¹jude m thorough (or typical, F regular) Jew; =knopf m knob of a stick; =lack ⊕ vom Gummibaum: stick-lac; =²makler, =mäkler m stock-broker; =¹malve ⚘ f = =rose; =meister m jailer; =morchel ⚘ f eatable turban-top (Gyro'mitra escule'nta); =narr m thorough (or downright, regular) fool; =preuße m thorough Prussian; =prügel pl. cudgelling, thrashing; =rose ⚘ f hollyhock (Althæ'a ro'sea).

Stocks ⚘ (²) [engl.; s. Stock²] pl. inv. = Staatspapiere; ~=besitzer (²⁻⸗⸗) m ㉒ holder of stock(s), bondholder.

Stock²=schere ⊕ (²...) f⑱ bench-(or stock-) shears pl.; =schirm m umbrella (or sunshade) used as (a) walking-stick; =schläge m/pl. = =prügel; =³schnupfen

Zeichen (s. S. XVII): F familiär; P Volkssprache; Ⴒ Gaunersprache; ⸜ selten; † alt (auch gestorben); * neu (auch geboren); ++ unrichtig;

[stocken¹] m (cold causing) stoppage in the nose, F nosecough; **=ständer** m = =halter; ⚓stetf a. (as) stiff as a poker; ⚓still a. stock-still, motionless; ⚓taub a. stone-deaf, (as) deaf as a post; **=taube** f. orn. = Holztaube b.
Stockung (⌣⌣) f (stocken¹ I) 1. (coming a) standstill, stoppage; cessation, stagnation, in der Rede: hesitation; des Verkehrs: block, obstruction; ☿ dulness of trade. — 2. path. ~ des Blutes durch Überfüllung: congestion. ⚕ hyperæmia.
Stock-wache † (⌣…) f prison-guard; **=werk** n: a) = Stock 9; b) ⚒ stockwork; **=zahn** m = Backenzahn; **=zwinge** f ferrule to a stick, cane-ferrule.
Stoff (⌣) [nhd.: stuff; *it.] m ⓐb. 1. (gewebtes Zeug) (woven) material or stuff. — 2. allg.: (Materie) matter, substance, stuff; (Grund=, Ur=)~ element, chm., phys. einfacher = elementary body or component; fig. er ist aus anderem = gemacht he is differently made or constructed, he is cast in another mould. — 3. (Gegenstand) subject, eines Aufsatzes 2c. auch: subject-matter, theme; ~ zur Unterhaltung topic of (or food for) conversation; ~ zum Lachen laughing-matter, s. th. laughable or to laugh about; ~ zum Nachdenken s. th. to think about, matter for reflexion.
Stoffel, a. **Stöffel** (⌣⌣) [dim. v. Christoph] npr/m. ⓐⓑⓒ. 1. Christopher. — 2. fig.: a) (ungehobelter Kerl) uncouth fellow, booby; b) F (dummer Kerl) duffer, blockhead, dunce.
stoffen (⌣⌣)]Stoff] a. (made of) stuff.
stoff=haltig (⌣…) a. material, substantial; **=haltigkeit** f materiality, substantiality; **=lehre** f chemistry.
stofflich (⌣⌣) a. (u. adv.) material(ly).
stoff=los (⌣…) a.: a) phls. immaterial, incorporeal; b) void (of substance), poor, trashy; **=losigkeit** f phls. immateriality; **=mangel** m lack of substance or stuff, burch. lack of beer; **=name** m = =wort; ⚓reich a. rich in material, substantial; **=verwandtschaft** f material affinity; **=wechsel** m, physiol. change of matter, assimilation, ⚕ metabolism; **=wort** n concrete noun.
stöhle (⌣) subj. impf. von stehlen.
stöhnen (⌣) [nhd.] I v/n. (h.) to groan, to moan (über et. at a th.). — II ~ n groaning, groans pl., moaning.
Sto=iker ⚕ (⌣⌣⌣) [Stoa] m (urspr. Anhänger des grch. Philosophen Zeno, jetzt: standhafter Mensch) stoic; **sto=isch** (⌣⌣) a. stoic(al); **Sto=izismus** (-⌣⌣⌣) m stoicism.
Stola (⌣⌣) [it.] f, a. **Stole** f (weißes Kleidungsstück der Geistlichen 2c.) surplice, stole; (Kleidungsstück der Damen aus Federn, Pelz 2c.) stole, boa.
Stol=gebühren (⌣⌣⌣⌣) [Stola] f pl. eccl. surplice-fees pl.
Stoll=baum ⚒ (⌣⌣) [Stollen²] m tubbing-beam.
Stolle (⌣⌣) f = Stollen² 4 u. Stulle.
tollen¹ ⊕ (⌣⌣) v/a. Gerberei: ein Fell, eine Haut ⌣ to stretch a hide, to soften a skin.

Stollen² (⌣⌣) [ahd.; *stellen] m 1. (Pfosten) post, prop, standard. — 2. ⚒ (wagerechter Zugang zum Grubenbau) adit, gallery; blinder ~ blind level; ~ in Kohlengruben coal-drift. — 3. ⊕ (Eisgriff am Hufeisen) caulk(er). — 4. (länglicher Kuchen) loaf-shaped cake. — 5. in Kirchenliedern 2c.: pros. (Hälfte des Aufgesanges) one half of the introductory part of a hymn.
Stollen²-arbeit ⚒ (⌣⌣…) f, **=bau** m gallery-driving, construction of adits, heading; **=first** m, **firste** f head of an adit; **=schacht** m shaft of a gallery; **=wasser** n water flowing from an adit; ⚓weise adv. (F a. a.) in (form of) galleries. [gallery.]
Stöllner ⚒ (⌣⌣) m proprietor of a
Stoll=ort ⚒ (⌣…) m end of an adit.
Stolper (⌣⌣) [lautm.] m. **Stolperei** (⌣⌣⌣⌣) f stumbling.
Stolperer (⌣⌣⌣) m stumbler.
stolp(e)rig (⌣(⌣)⌣) a. (holperig) uneven.
stolpern (⌣⌣) [nhd.] v/n. (in und h.) ⓐa. to stumble, to trip (beide a. fig.); fig. ⌣ (einen Fehltritt tun) to make a slip or F a faux pas, to blunder, F to put one's foot in; über ein schweres Wort ⌣ to stumble over a difficult word.
stolz¹ (⌣) [ahd.: stout: Stelze] a. (D1,6) 1. proud (auf et. in a th.), (hochmütig) haughty, lofty, (eitel) vain; (wegwerfend) disdainful, supercilious, (anmaßend) arrogant; (ruhmredig) conceited, boastful; er kann ⌣ darauf sein that's s. th. for him to be proud of, it's a feather in his cap; gestern noch auf den Rossen yesterday still on prancing horses. — 2. fig. ein ⌣er (herrlicher) Tag a glorious (or remarkable, memorable) day.
Stolz² (⌣) m ⓐa. (o. pl.) (f. stolz) 1. pride (auf et. in a th.); haughtiness, loftiness, vanity; disdain, superciliousness, arrogance; conceit; seinen ~ in et. setzen to pride o.s. on a th., to take a pride in a th. — 2. (Gegenstand des ~es) object of pride; er ist der ~ seines Vaterlandes he is the glory (or pride) of his country.
stolzieren (⌣⌣⌣) [nhd.=it.] v/n. (in und h.) to walk proudly, to have a proud gait; to strut, flaunt, stalk, von Pferden: to prance; er kam daher stolziert he came strutting along.
Stopf=arznei (⌣…) f ⚕ med. binding (or astringent) medicine; **=buchse**, **=büchse** ⊕ f, mach. stuffing-box.
stopfen¹ (⌣⌣) [ahd.: stop; mlt.; *It. stuppa Werg] ⓐ I v/a. 1. (fest zu=pressen) to stuff, to squeeze hard; et. in einen Sack ⌣ to cram a th. into a sack; 2. oft meton.: a) (mit et. gehörig füllen) Kocht.: e-e Gans ⌣ to stuff a goose; Geflügel ⌣ (nudeln) to cram poultry; ⚓ ein Leck ⌣ to stop (up) a leak(age); ein Loch ⌣ to fill (or bung) up a hole; fig. den Leuten den Mund ⌣ to stop people's tongues or mouths or talk; vgl. Maul¹ 1; eine Pfeife ⌣ to fill a (tobacco-)pipe; gestopfte Pfeife pipe full of tobacco; Wurst ⌣ to make sausages, to fill sausage-skins; (sich) mit Speisen (voll) ⌣ to cram (or stuff, gorge) (o.s.) with food; der Saal war gestopft (gedrängt) voll the hall was crammed (full of people); b) (mit der Nadel ausbessern) Löcher in Kleidern ⌣ to patch up holes; Strümpfe ⌣ to darn (or mend) stockings; Weißwaren 2c. kunstvoll ⌣ to finedraw …; c) die Diarrhöe, die Leibesöffnung ⌣ to stop the diarrhœa; das Bluten ⌣: ⚕ styptic. — 3. ⚔ das Feuer ⌣ (einstellen) to stop firing; vgl. stoppen. — II v/n. (h.) 4. Eier, schwere Speisen 2c. ⌣ … are binding, …cause constipation or costiveness; ⌣d binding, constipating, ⚕ astringent. — III sich ⌣ v/refl. 5. a) f. 2a am Schluß; b) (sich zu=drängen) to collect at one point, to crowd together, v. Straßen: (versperrt w.) to be(come) blocked (up) or obstructed or congested. — IV ~n ⓐ 6. = Stopfung 1.
Stopfen² (⌣⌣) m (Stöpsel) stopper, aus Kork: cork; aus Holz 2c.: plug.
Stopfer (⌣⌣) m 1. a. **~in** f (stopfende Person): a) person who stuffs or crams; b) Näherei: darner, mender (vgl. Kunst=⌣). — 2. ⊕ = Stopfmaschine.
Stopf=garn (⌣…) n darning-cotton, -yarn; **=haar** n hair for stuffing chairs, &c.; **=lappen** m rag for stopping up chinks; **=maschine** f ⊕ stuffer; **=mittel** n = =arz(e)nei; **=nadel** f darning-needle; **=naht** f: a) darn, patch(ed place); b) feine: finedrawing; **=nudel** f/. Federvieh: flour-ball for stuffing poultry; **=stange** f: a) ⚔ boxing-pole; b) der Gießer: stopper.
Stopfung (⌣⌣) f 1. stuffing, cramming. — 2. der Stopfbüchsen: packing-tow.
Stopf=wachs (⌣…) n = Bienenharz; **=wasser** n (Widerstrom) stop-water; **=werg** ⚓ n oakum for caulking.
stopp! ⚓ (⌣) [imper. v. stoppen] (halt!) stop!
Stoppel (⌣⌣) [ndd.: stubble; *lt. sti'pŭla] f ⓐ 1. agr. stubble. — 2. a) ⌣ n pl. (Federkiele) young feathers pl. left in the skin of a plucked bird; b) (Bart=)~ bristly (or stubbly, scrubby) hair of the beard.
Stoppel=bart (⌣…) m = bristly (or scrubby) beard; **=butter** f (ant. Grasbutter) autumn butter; **=feder** f = Stoppel 2a, **=feld** n stubble-field; **=gans** f, orn. stubble-goose; **=gedicht** n patch-work poem, poem made up of scraps (of other poems); cento; **=korn** n corn grown on a stubble-field.
stoppeln (⌣⌣) v/a. u. v/n. (h.) ⓐa. (auf den Stoppeln nachlesen) to glean; fig. auf geistigem Gebiete a. to compile, to patch (together); (abschreiben) to plagiarize.
Stoppel=rechen (⌣…) m agr. stubble-rake; **=rübe** ♀ f late turnip; **=weide** f after-pannage, -pasture; **=werk** n Schrifttum: (literary) patch-work, compilation; auch = =gedicht. [(hemmen) to stop.]
stoppen ⚓ (⌣) [ndd.] v/a. u. v/n. (h.) ⓐ
Stopper ⚓ (⌣⌣) m (Tau=ende) stopper.
Stoppine ⚔ (⌣⌣) [it.] f artill. (Zündschnur) quick-match.
Stoppler (⌣⌣) m, **~in** f (f. stoppeln) gleaner; fig. compiler; plagiarist.
Stöpsel (⌣⌣) [ndd.; *stoppen] m 1. stopper, mit Schraubengewinde: screw-stopper, aus Kork: cork; vgl. Pfropf 1. — 2. fig. (kurze, dicke Person) stumpy (or podgy) p., F co. tub, dumpy little fellow.

♪ Musik; ⚕ Wissenschaft; ♀ Pflanze; ⚘ Geographie; ⊕ Technik; ⚒ Bergbau; ⚔ Militär; ⚓ Marine; ☿ Handel; ✉ Post; 🚂 Eisenbahn.

[stöpseln]

stöpseln (⌣⌣) v/a. ⊕a. to stopper, cork.
Stör¹ (⌣) [ahd.] m ⊕c. *ichth.* sturgeon (*Acipe'nser stu'rio*); vgl. Sterlet.
Stör² F (⌣) [: steerhingehen] f ⊕ (Arbeit v. Handwerkern im Hause der Kunden) auf die ~ geh(e)n, auf der ~ arbeiten to (do) work at a customer's house.
Storax (⌣⌣) [lt.; grch.; *sem̃t.] m ⊕⊕a. *pharm.* wohlriechendes Harz: storax; ~baum ⊕ m ⊕ storax-tree (*Styraxoffici'nalis*).
Storch (⌣) [ahd.: stork] m ⊕b., südd. ⊕ *orn.* stork (*Cico'nia*).
Storch=bein (⌣⌣) n ⊕: a) stork's leg; b) F *fig.* ~e spindle-legs *pl.*; ⊕**beinig** *a.* spindle-legged or -shanked.
Storch(en)=nest (⌣(⌣)⌣) n ⊕ stork's nest.
Störchin (⌣⌣) f ⊕ *orn.* female stork.
Störchling (⌣⌣) m ⊕d. young stork.
Storch=schnabel (⌣⌣⌣) m ⊕: a) stork's bill; b) ⚘ stork's-bill, cranesbill (*Gera'nium*); rundblätteriger ~ round-leaved cranesbill; c) *surg.* (lange Zange) cranesbill; d) ⊕ zum Vergrößern od. Verkleinern e-r Zeichnung: ⟲ pantograph.
stören (⌣⌣) [ahd.: stir] ⊕ **I** v/a. 1. (belästigen) to disturb, trouble, inconvenience; (aus der Ordnung, dem Gang bringen) to derange, to upset; (unterbrechen) to interrupt; Fußballspiel: to obstruct; den Frieden ~ to break the peace; j-s Ruhe, e-n in f-r Ruhe ~ to disturb a p.'s rest; ich hoffe, ich störe (Sie) nicht I trust I am not inconveniencing you, I hope I am not intruding or in the way; lassen Sie sich nicht von mir ~ don't let me disturb you, don't put yourself out for me. — **II** *prove.* v/n. (h.) 2. = stöbern 2. — **III** ~ n ⊕ 3. = Störung 1. — **IV** ⊕ *p.pr.* u. *a.* ⊕ 4. troublesome, annoying. — **V ge-stört** *p.p.* u. *a.* ⊕ 5. Bed. des *inf.*; z B. ⊕e Ruhe broken rest. — 6. mildernd für „verrückt": deranged, troubled in one's mind.
Stören=fried (⌣⌣⌣) [nhd.] m ⊕d. mar-peace, mischief-maker, intruder.
Störer (⌣⌣) m ⊕, ~**in** f ⊕ disturber, intruder, des Friedens: peace-breaker; ~**ei** (⌣⌣⌣) f ⊕ constant disturbance or interruption or intrusion.
stornieren (⌣⌣⌣) [it.] v/a. ⊕ to transfer from one account to another, to carry over.
Storr (⌣) [ahd. *storren* ragen] m ⊕, ~**en** (⌣⌣) m ⊕ (Baumstumpf) stump of a tree.
störrig (⌣⌣) [nhd.; *Storr(en)] *a.* ⊕ (halsstarrig) stubborn, headstrong, bsd. v. Kindern: unruly, wayward; (unlenksam) unmanageable, intractable, refractory, von Pferden auch: restive; **Störrigkeit** f ⊕ stubbornness, waywardness; refractoriness.
störrisch (⌣⌣) *a.* ⊕ = störrig.
Stör=stange (⌣⌣) [stören II] f ⊕, =**stock** m pole, stick for stirring.
Störung (⌣⌣) f ⊕ 1. disturbing, &c. (f. stören I). — 2. disturbance, trouble, inconvenience, upset, intrusion; (Unterbrechung) interruption (Unordnung) disarrangement, disorder; geistige ~ derangement, mental disorder; *phys.* ~ der Magnetnadel ꝛc.: perturbation.
Stoß (⌣) [ahd.; *stoßen] m ⊕c. 1. (das Stoßen) push(ing), thrust(ing), beim Schwimmen und Billard: stroke; Fußball: kick; ~ aufs Tor shoot; (Ruck) jerk; (Schlag) blow, in die Rippen: dig in the ribs, mit dem Fuße: kick, mit dem Kopfe: butt; ~ beim Erdbeben ꝛc.: concussion of the earth; ~ e-s Wagens: jolt(ing). eines Gewehres beim Abfeuern: recoil, kick, des Herzens: throb, pulsation; (Zs.-stoßen) collision, *mech.* impact; (Erschütterung) percussion; e-m e-n ~ versetzen to give a p. a push, to push a p.; das gab s-r Gesundheit einen empfindlichen ~ that seriously injured his health, it was a great shock to his constitution; Billard: e-n sicheren ~ h. to have a good stroke. — 2. *fenc.* thrust, lunge, pass; auf den ~ fechten to fence with foils; f. Hieb 1. — 3. ♪ ~ in ein Horn ꝛc.: blast, flourish; einen ~ in eine Trompete tun to blow on (or to sound) a trumpet. — 4. *fig.* das hat ihm e-n ~ (ins Herz) gegeben that has been a (great) blow to him; das wird ihm den letzten ~ geben that will give him the finishing stroke, it will be the end of him. — 5. (Haufen) pile, heap, von zf.=gestecken Papieren, Briefen: file, von Akten a. bundle. — 6. ⊕ (Stelle, wo etwas an=ea.=stößt) joint; Schneiderei: seam, hem. — 7. ⚒ (Eingang eines Stollens) stope. — 8. ⚔ *artill.* ~ (Bodenstück einer Kanone) breech.
Stoß=bewegung (⌣⌣...) f ⊕ propulsion; =**degen** m (ant. Haudegen) *fenc.* rapier, foil.
Stößel ⊕ (⌣⌣) m ⊕ beetle, rammer; {eines Mörsers: pestle.
stoßen (⌣⌣) [ahd.: lt. *tund-o*, (tu)tud-i] ⊕a. **I** v/a. 1. to push, mit einer Waffe ꝛc.: to thrust, mit dem Ellbogen: to (nudge with the) elbow, mit dem Fuße: to kick (auch im Fußballspiel), mit den Hörnern: to butt, von Stieren a. to gore, to toss; im Mörser ꝛc.: to pound, to bray; schnellend zu jerk, schlagend: to knock, to hit, schiebend: to shove, ea. ~ to jostle each other; Billard: den Ball ~ to play (a ball); ♩ eine Note ~ = abstoßen 2; gestoßener Zucker powdered sugar. — 2. mit *prp.* (oft *fig.*) e-n an die Wand ~ to push a p. against the wall; die Gläser aneinander ~ to touch glasses; Tischlerei, Näherei: an=ea. ~ to join (together), to put to; e-n mit der Nase auf et. ~ to put a th. very clearly before (or to) a p.; e-n aus dem Hause ~ to turn a p. out (of doors), F to kick a p. out; aus einem Verein ꝛc. ~ to expel (or exclude) from ...; e-m den Degen durch den Leib ~ to run one's sword through a p.('s body); e-n Pfahl in die Erde ~ to drive a stake into the ground; e-m den Dolch ins Herz ~ to stab a p. to the heart; e-m das Messer in die Brust ~ to thrust (or plunge) a knife in a p.'s breast; beim Billard: e-n Ball ins Loch ~ to send a ball into the pocket, to pocket (or make) a ball; e-n, et. über den Haufen ~ to knock (or push) a p., a th. down, to overturn a p., a th.; e-n von sich ~ to cast off (or repudiate, turn away) a p.; seine Frau ~ to divorce one's wife; sein Glück von sich ~ to fling (or thrust) away one's good fortune; e-n vom Throne ~ to dethrone a p.; e-n vor den Kopf ~ to affront (or offend) a p.; er ist wie vor den Kopf gestoßen ~ quite off his head. — 3. mit Angabe der Wirkung: die Erde fest ~ to batter (or ram) down the ground; et. klein ~ to pound a th., to break a th. into bits or small fragments, to crush a th.; zu Pulver ~ to pulverize, to reduce to powder; sich (*dat.*) den Fuß lahm (ein Loch in den Kopf) ~ to lame one's foot (to break one's head) by knocking it; ⊕ Tischlerei: mit dem Hobel glatt ~ to smooth with the plane. — **II** sich ~ v/refl. 4. sich an et. (*dat.* ob. *acc.*) ~: a) (anrennend) to knock (or run) against a th.; b) *fig.* (Anstoß nehmen) to be shocked (or to scruple) at a th.; c) v/imp. es stößt sich noch an einem Dinge one thing is still in the way. — **III** v/n. (h. und sn) 5. (h.) nach e-m, et. ~ to thrust at a p., a th.; von Raubvögeln: auf eine Taube ~ to pounce on ... — 6. (h. u. sn) mit den Füßen an den Tisch ~ to knock one's feet against ...; mit dem Kopfe gegen die Wand ~ to run one's head against ...; ⚓ ans Land ~ to touch bottom, to founder; ⚓ auf eine Klippe ~ to foul a reef, to dash against a rock; vom Lande ~ to push off the shore, to shove off, ⚓ to put to sea. — 7. auf einen, et. (durch Zufall) ~ to run against (or come across, stumble upon) a p., a th.; auf Hindernisse, Schwierigkeiten ~ to encounter (or meet with) obstacles, difficulties. — 8. (sn) bid. ⚔ zu et. ~ (sich begeben); zum Heere ~ to join the (main body of the) army. — 9. an etwas ~ (grenzen) to be adjoining (or close to, next door to) a th., to border on a th. — 10. ♪ ~ in die Trompete ~ to blow (or sound) the trumpet. — 11. *abs.* v. Bock, Stier: to butt, toss, v. Geschützen: to recoil, kick, v. Schiffen: to pitch, v. Wagen: to jolt (along), v. Winde: to blow in short gusts or puffs. — 12. Billard: das Queue stößt nicht gut the cue does not answer (well); wer stößt? who plays?, whose turn is it (to play)? — 13. *fenc.* (ant. hauen) to thrust, to lunge (out). — **IV** ~ n ⊕ 14. = Stoß 1, 2 u. 3.
Stößer (⌣⌣) [nhd.] m ⊕ 1. one who pushes or thrusts; ~ in einer Apotheke: chemist's boy or man who pounds the drugs, &c. — 2. ⊕ (Werkzeug) = Stößel. — 3. *hunt.* = Stoßvogel.
Stoßerei F (-⌣⌣) f ⊕ constant pushing or thrusting or jostling.
stöß(es)t (⌣) 2., **stößt** (⌣) 3. Person *sg.* *pres. ind.* von stoßen.
Stoß=fechten (⌣...) n ⊕ fencing with foils; =**gebet** n short and fervent prayer; =**heber** ⊕ m hydraulic ram; =**herd** ⊕ m. *metall.* percussion table.
stößig (⌣⌣) *a.* ⊕ v. Stier ꝛc.: given to (or fond of) butting or goring or tossing.
Stoß=kissen 🜚 (⌣...) n ⊕ buffer(-head), pad; =**klinge** f thrusting-blade; =**kraft** f impulsive force, impetus, *mech.* im-

[Stoßkraft]

Signs (see page XVII): F familiar; P vulgar; ꓝ flash; ⟋ rare; † obsolete (died); * new word (born); +⊦ incorrect; ♪ music.

[Stoßlappen] — 931 — [Strahlenbrechungslehre]

pact, (force of) percussion; =lappen ↓ m top-lining; =maschine ⊕ f keygroove engine; f. auch Bock 6; =naht f (feine Stopfnaht) finedrawing; =polster ⚔ n = =kissen; =rapier n, fenc. foil; =säge ⊕ f hand-saw; =scheibe ⊕ f bei Schraubenbolzen: washer-plate; =schnur f am Frauenrock: skirt-braid; =schwelle ⚔ f joint-sleeper; =seufzer m deep groan, auch: pious ejaculation; =vogel m bird of prey; engS. hawk; =waffe f weapon for thrusting; ⒉weise adv. (F a. a.) by jerks, by fits and starts; vgl. ruckweise; =wind ↓ m (sudden) squall, strong gust of wind; =zahn m von Tieren: tusk; =zeug ⊕ n Schriftgießerei: dressing-stick.

Stotterei (⌣⌣́) f ⊛ stuttering.
Stotterer (⌣⌣⌣) m ⊛, **Stotterin** f ⊛ stutterer, stammerer; (haftig Sprechende[r]) F sp(l)utterer. [mering.
stotterig (⌣⌣⌣) a. ⊛ stuttering, stam-)
stottern (⌣⌣) [ndd.: stutter: stoßen] I v/n. (h.) ⒜a. to stutter, to stammer (sprudelnd reden) F to sp(l)utter. — II ~ n ⊛ stuttering, stammering, als Naturfehler auch: impediment of speech.
stowen (⌣⌣⌣) v/a. ⊛ = stoben².
Str. abbr. = Straße.
stracks (⌣) [mhd.; *†strack a. gestreckt] adv. 1. räumlich: straight (away), direct. — 2. zeitlich: (sofort) straightway, directly.
Straf-änderung (⌣́…) f ⓬ jur. commutation of sentence; ⒉androhend a. ⊛ comminatory; =androhung f threat of punishment; Gericht: e-n unter ~ vorladen to subpœna a p.; =anstalt f house of correction; penitentiary; =antrag m sentence demanded by the public prosecutor; =arbeit f in Schulen: imposition; task to be done after school-hours; =arrest m: a) in Schulen: detention; b) ⚔ cell.
strafbar (⌣́⌣) a. ⊛ von Personen: liable to be punished; v. Handlungen: punishable (action), stärker: criminal (deed); (schuldig) culpable, guilty.
Strafbarkeit (⌣⌣́⌣) f ⊛ punishableness, criminality, culpability, guilt.
Straf-befehl (⌣́…) m ⓬ order to inflict a punishment or fine; =befugnis f right (or authority) to punish or fine; =bestimmung f paragraph (or article) in the penal code; =dienst m punishment- (or ⚔ ↑ fatigue-)duty.
Strafe (⌣⌣) [mhd.] f ⊛ punishment, zu zahlende: fine, penalty; jur. ~n, and pains and penalties pl.; körperliche ~ corporal punishment, zur Besserung: correction, als Züchtigung: chastisement; f. Prügelstrafe; bei ~ von // on pain of //; bei den gesetzmäßigen ~n on pain of being punished according to law; e-n bei ~ vorladen to subpœna a p.; f-e ~ abbüßen to undergo (or suffer) punishment, to pay one's penalty; seine ~ im Zuchthause absitzen F to do (one's) time; e-m eine ~ auferlegen to impose (or inflict) a punishment (or penalty) upon a p.; du wirst ~ bekommen you will be punished; die gebührende ~ erleiden to meet with condign (or the deserved) punishment; e-n in ~ nehmen to punish (or fine) a p.; in ~ verfallen to incur punishment or pains and penalties; to have to pay a fine.

strafen (⌣⌣) [mhd.] I v/a. ⊛ 1. to punish (züchtigen) to chastise, to correct; e-n an der Ehre ⒉ to disgrace (or degrade) a p.; e-n am Leben ⒉ to inflict capital punishment on a p., to sentence a p. to death; f. Leib 2; e-n mit Gefängnis ⒉ to send a p. to prison; e-n für ein Vergehen ⒉ to punish a p. for an offence; e-n um Geld ⒉ to fine a p.; biswl. v/refl. solche Fehler ⒉ sich (selbst) … bring about their own punishment, … meet with their due reward. — 2. fast †: e-n mit Worten ⒉ to reprove (or rebuke) a p.; f. Lüge. — II ~ n ⊛ 3. = Strafe. — III ⒉b p.pr. u. a. ⊛ 4. punishing, punitive, corrective, castigatory, jur.penal; ⒉der Blick reproachful glance.
Straf-engel (⌣́…) m ⓬ avenging angel; =erkenntnis n sentence, judgment; =erlaß m, =erlassung f remission of punishment; allgemeine(r) ~ f. politische ꝛc. Vergehen: amnesty; =exerzieren ⚔ n punishment-drill.
straff (⌣) [mhd., *ndd.] a. ⊛ (ant. schlaff) 1. tight, ↓ taut; v. Saiten ꝛc.: stretched; ⒉ (adv.) anliegen to fit tightly, to sit close; ⒉ anziehen, spannen to tighten, to pull tight(ly), ↓ to tauten; ↓ to stretch. — 2. fig. (streng) rigid, severe, austere, stern.
Straf-fall (⌣́…) m ⓬ jur. punishable offence; ⒉fällig a. ⊛ punishable, subject to a penalty or fine, culpable; =fälligkeit f punishableness, culpability.
straffen (⌣⌣) v/a. u. v/refl. (fich) ⒉ ⊛ to tighten, ↓ to tauten; to stretch.
straff=gespannt (⌣⌣) a. ⊛ stretched tightly, tight, ↓ taut; ⒉haarig a. ⊛ with bristly hair.
Straffheit (⌣⌣) f ⊛ (f. straff) 1. tightness, ↓ tautness; tension. — 2. fig. rigidity, severity, austerity.
straf=frei (⌣́…) a. ⊛ jur. ꝛc.: exempt from punishment; ⒉ ausgeh(e)n to go unpunished, to get off scot-free; =freiheit f exemption from punishment, impunity. [tension, ↓ tautening.
Straff=ziehen (⌣⌣⌣́) n ⓬ tightening,)
Straf=gebot (⌣́…) f ⓬ jur. inhibition accompanied by a threat of punishment; =gefangene(r) s. convict serving his (f her) time; =geld n penalty, fine; =gericht n tribunal; göttliches ~ divine judgment; ein ~ verhängen über to mete out justice to; =gerichtsbarkeit f criminal jurisdiction; =gerichtsordnung f (method of) procedure in criminal courts; =gesetz n penal law; =gesetzbuch n penal code; =gesetzgebung f penal (or criminal) legislation; =gewalt f = =befugnis; =kammer f criminal court; =kasse f office for collecting (or receiving) fines; =kodex m criminal (or penal) code; bsd. ehm. =kolonie f penal settlement, convict-establishment; =kompagnie ⚔ f company of refractory soldiers.
sträflich (⌣́⌣) [mhd.; *strafen] a. ⊛ 1. (strafbar) punishable; criminal. — 2. (strafend) punitive. — 3. F fig. (bsd. adv.) (ungeheuer) enormous(ly), awful(ly).

Sträflichkeit (⌣⌣́⌣) f ⊛ punishableness of an action; criminality of an offence.
Sträfling (⌣́⌣) m ⓭d. convict, F jailbird; ~s=jacke (⌣́…⌣⌣) f ⓬ convict's garb.
straf=los (⌣́…) a. ⊛, =losigkeit f ⊛ = =frei, =freiheit f; =mal n = =tor; =maß n measure (or amount) of punishment; =mittel n means of punishment; =porto n surcharge; =prediger(in f) m censorious preacher; moralist; =predigt f severe sermon or lecture; vgl. =rede; =prozeß m criminal proceedings pl. or case; =prozeß=ordnung f criminal procedure; =recht n. a) =befugnis; b) crim. jurisprudence or law; ⒉rechtlich a. criminal, penal; =rechts=lehrer m teacher (or professor) of criminal law; =rechts=pflege f crim. justice; =rede f (words pl. of) reprimand; vgl. =predigt; =richter m judge in a crim. court or for crim. cases, auch: crim. judge; =sache f crim. case; =stoß m Fußball: penalty-kick; =summe f penalty, (amount of) fine; =tat f = =fall; =tor n Fußball: penalty-goal; =urteil n sentence (for the punishment of a crime); über n ein ~ verhängen to sentence a p. to penal servitude, &c.; =verfahren n criminal procedure; =versetzung f transfer of an official by way of (disciplinary) punishment; =verwandlung f = =änderung; =vollstreckung, =vollziehung f, =vollzug m infliction of punishment, execution of a sentence; ⒉würdig a. deserving (of) punishment, auch = strafbar; =zeit f time (or period) of imprisonment; =zumessung f award of punishment.
Strahl (⌣́) [ahd.] m ⓭c. 1. ray, beam (vgl. Blitz=, Hoffnungs=strahl); ~en schießen to flash forth; ~en werfen to emit (or dart forth, cast forth) rays; ~en aussendend, werfend radiant, resplendent. — 2. (aus enger Öffnung hervorschießender ~ einer Flüssigkeit) jet, von springendem Wasser: waterspout. — 3. geom., Zeichenkunst: radius, straight line. — 4. vet. ~ (Erhöhung unten inmitten des Pferdehufes) frog of a horse's hoof. — 5. ⚔ schwz. P ~ (en pl.) (Kristalle) crystals pl. — 6. a) ♃ ~ (Blütenstielchen) einer Dolde spoke; ~ (Rand) einer Kompositenblüte: ⚔ involucre; b) zo. (Organ von Stachtieren) ⚔ spheromere, actinomere. [=Kamm.
Strähl südd. (⌣) [mhd.: strählen] m ⓭c.)
Strahl=ader (⌣́…) f ⓬ vet. vein in the frog of a horse's hoof; =blüte ♃ f radiate flower-head; =brenner ⊕ m für Gas: jet-burner.
strahlen (⌣́⌣) [mhd.; *Strahl] ⊛ I v/n. (h.) to radiate (a. fig.), weitS. to beam, shine; ⒉b radiant, resplendent; fig. vor Freude ⒉ to beam with delight. — II v/a. (⒉b verbreiten) to radiate forth. — III ~ n ⊛ f. Strahlung.
strählen bfd. südd. (⌣́) [ahd.; *Strähl] v/a. ⊛ to comb; vgl. striegeln.
strahlen=artig (⌣́…) a. ⊛ like beams, ♃ u. zo. radiate, radiatiform; actiniform, …oid; =blume ♃ f radiate (or stellate) flower; =blütige ♃ pl. asteraceæ pl.; ⒉brechend a. phys. refracting, …ive; =brechung f refraction; =brechungs=lehre f dioptrics;

⚔ scientific; ♃ botanical; ♁ geography; ⊕ machinery; ⚒ mining; ⚔ military; ↓ marine; ⊛ commercial; ✉ postal; 🚂 railway.

[Strahlenbrenner]

=brenner ⊕ m = Strahlbrenner;
=bündel n, phys. pencil of rays, cone of light, luminous brush; f. a. Büschel 3;
=büschel m, geom. system of radiating lines; ⁝förmig a. = ²artig; =glanz m(ir)radiance; =kranz m, =krone f glory, halo, nimbus, um Häupter der Heiligen: halo, a. aureole; ⁝los a. rayless; =meer n, fig. ocean of light; =messer m: ⌁ actinometer; =pilz ♀ m: ⌁ actinomyces; =werfen n irradiation. [radiate(d).]
strahlicht, mst strahlig (⌣´) a. ⊛ radiating,
Strahl=kies (″...) m ⊛ min. radiate iron-pyrites; =stein m, min.: ⌁ actinolite; =tiere n/pl. zo. (Echinodermen und Polypen): ⌁ actinoida, radiata.
Strahlung (⌣´) f ⊛ radiancy, radiation.
Strähne (⌣´) [ahd.: strand] f ⊛ (als Maß pl. inv.) 1. lock of hair, plait; (Teil einer Flechte, eines Seiles rc.) strand. — 2. ♃ ~ Garn rc. (a. als Maß) skein, hank.
...strähnig (...⌣´) a. ⊛ in Zssgn mit Zahlwörtern, zB.: drei=² of three strands, three-skeined.
Stramin ⊕ (⌣⌣´) [ndl.; *fr. étamine] m ⊛d. Weberei: canvas for needlework.
stramm (⌣´) [ndd.] a. ⊛ 1. = straff; typ. Farbe: stiff, hard. — 2. F fig. (ant. schlapp¹) ²er Bursche sturdy (F strapping) fellow; ²es Frauenzimmer, Mädel bouncing girl or lass, F bouncer, strapping wench; ²er Soldat smart soldier; ²e Zucht severe (or iron) discipline; F e-m die Hosen ² ziehen to dust a p.'s jacket.
Strammheit (⌣´) f ⊛ 1. = Straffheit. — 2. F fig. sturdiness; smartness (a. ⚔).
strampeln (⌣´) [ndd.] v/n. (h.) ⊛a. to move one's arms or legs about, to struggle, to fidget; mit den Füßen ² to kick; a. v/refl. mit Angabe der Wirkung: sich bloß ² (von einem im Bette Liegenden) to kick one's (bed-)clothes off.
Strand (⌣´) [ndd.: strand] m ⊛b. (Meeres-)shore, ⌁ strand, ⌁ flacher ~, a. beach; sandiger ~ sands pl.; am ~e weilen to stay at the seaside; ↓ auf den ~ laufen oder geraten to be stranded or beached or cast ashore, to run ashore.
Strand=batterie ⚔ (⌣´...) f ⊛ shore-battery; =bewohner m one living near the sea(-shore) or at the seaside, F seasider; =binse ♀ f seashore rush (Iuncus mari´timus); =eis n shore-ice.
stranden ↓ (⌣´) [ndd.] I v/n. (ſu u. h.) ⊛ von Schiffen, Walfischen rc.: to be stranded or beached, bef. von Schiffen: to run ashore, to be wrecked, to founder, to suffer shipwreck; gestrandet, auch: cast ashore. — II ~ n ⊛ = Strandung.
Strand=fischerei (⌣´...) f ⊛ fishing from the shore, shore-fishing; =gerechtigkeit f shore-rights pl.; =gut n, =güter ↓ n/pl. stranded goods pl., wreckage; schwimmendes ~ flotsam; =hafer ♀ m horsehair oats (E´lymus arena´rius); =herr m owner of a shore; =kohl ♀ m sea-kale (Crambe mari´tima); =korb m in Seebädern: wicker chair for (sitting by) the beach; =läufer m, orn. sandpiper, strand-runner (Tringa, Acto´dromas, &c.); =ordnung f regulations pl. respecting flotsam and jetsam; =räuber ↓ m wrecker; =recht n right of salvage;

=reiter m mounted coast-guard(sman); =richter m = Dispacheur; =schuhe m/pl. brown (leather) shoes, tan boots pl.
Strandung (⌣´) f ⊛ stranding, running ashore, shipwreck.
Strand=vögel (⌣´...) m/pl. ⊛ orn. beach-birds pl.; =vogt m wreck-master; =wache f coast-guard; =wächter m coast-guard(sman).
Strang (⌣´) [ahd.: string] m ⊛b. 1. cord (a. anat.); (Seil) rope; zum Anschirren von Zugtieren: trace; er wurde zum ~ verurteilt he was sentenced to be hanged, von Pferden: in die Stränge treten to kick over the traces (a. fig. f. 2). — 2. fig. alle Stränge anziehen to exert o.s. to the (or to do one's) utmost; wenn alle Stränge (ob. Stricke) reißen (im höchsten Notfalle) if the worst comes to the worst, if nothing avails; über die Stränge schlagen oder hauen (leichtfinnig leben) to kick over the traces, to overstep the mark, to run riot; sie ziehen alle an e-m ~e they are (all) pulling together or acting in unison. — 3. ⛧ (Geleise) track, rail.
Strang=scheide (⌣´...) f ⊛ trace-strap. =schläger m v. Pferden: horse given to kicking; =schlaufe ⊕ f trace-bearer.
strangulieren (⌣⌣⌣´) [it., *grch.] v/a. ⊛ to strangle (= erdrosseln).
Strapaze (⌣⌣´) [it. strapazzo m] f ⊛ fatigue, hardship, (wearying) toil, great exertion, auch: wear and tear.
strapazier/en (⌣⌣⌣´) [it.] v/a. und sich ² v/refl. 2. to fatigue, weary, harass; sich ² (anstrengen) to exert o.s., to fag; e-n Rock rc. ² (nicht schonen) to hack ..., to knock (or wear) out ...
Straß (⌣´) [Joseph Strasser 18. Jac., Erfinder] m (n) ⊕ ⊛a. (Glaspaste) strass.
Straße (⌣´) [ahd.: street; *lt. strata (via)] f ⊛ 1. ~ e-r Stadt, e-s Dorfes: street; (Fahr=, Land=) ~ road, highway; an der ~ (gelegen lying) by the wayside; auf der ~ in (Am. on) the street; auf offener ~ in a public thoroughfare; er liegt immer auf der ~ he is for ever knocking about the street(s); F auf die ~ werfen to turn out (of doors). Arbeiter rc.: to discharge, to sack; fig. die breitgetretene ~ des Herkommens the beaten (or well-worn) path of custom, auch: the old groove. — 2. (Schiffahrts-, Verkehrs-)weg route; engS. ♀ (Meer-enge) strait(s pl.); die ~ von Gibraltar the Straits pl. of G.; die ~ von Calais Strait(s) of Dover, the (English) Channel.
straß=ab (⌣´⌣) adv. down the street; ²auf (⌣´⌣) adv. up the street.
Straßen=anlage ⊕ (⌣´...) f ⊛ laying out (or making of) streets; vgl. =bau; =arbeiter m street-maker; paviour; =aufseher m surveyor of roads, road-surveyor; =bahn f tramway; =bahnlinie f tramway-line; =bahnwagen m tram(-or street-)car, elettrischer: electric car; =bau ⊕ m road-building or -making; vgl. =anlage; =bauer m constructor of roads, a. road-builder; =baumaterial n road-metal(ling); =beleuchtung f lighting (up) of streets; =bube m = =junge; =damm m: a) causeway; b) pavement; =dirne f street-

[Strauß]

walker; =ecke f street-corner; =eisenbahn f = =bahn; =feger m scavenger; vgl. Gassenkehrer; =gänger* m = Passant; =gesindel n mob of loafers or roughs; =handel m trade of street-vendors; =junge m street-boy; (Betteljunge) st.-arab; =kampf m fighting in the streets; =kehrer m, =kehr=maschine ⊕ f street-sweeper; =kot m mud in the road; =kreuzung f crossing (of the road); =laterne f street-lamp; =lokomotive f street-(or road-) locomotive; steam-roller; f. Lokomotive; =name m name of a street; =pflaster n pavement (of a street); =prediger m ranter; =raub m highway-robbery; =räuber m highwayman; =recht n right to use a thoroughfare or a (public) road; =reiniger m = =feger; =rufe m/pl. street-cries pl.; =sperrung f blocking of streets, obstruction of the traffic; =tür f street-door; =übergang m street-crossing; =verkäufer (=in f) m street-vendor; =verkehr m str.-traffic.
Stratagem (⌣⌣´), r-r: Strategem (⌣⌣´) [grch.] n ⊛d. (Kriegslift) stratagem; Stratege (⌣⌣´) m ⊛ strategist; Strategie (⌣⌣´) f ⊛ (Feldherrnkunst) strategy; Strategiker (⌣⌣´⌣) m ⊛ strategist; strategisch (⌣⌣´) a. ⊛ strategic(al).
sträuben (⌣´) [⌣´] ⊛ I v/a. 1. Haare, Federn ² to ruffle up; gesträubtes Gefieder ruffled plumage. — II sich ² v/refl. 2. vom Haare: to stand (up) on end, wie Borsten: to bristle up. — 3. sich gegen et. ² (stemmen) to struggle (F to kick) against a th., to oppose (or resist) a th.; sich heftig ² gegen to struggle hard against, to resist with might and main; soviel ich mich auch ² mochte in spite of my resistance or opposition; for all that I could do or say; die Feder sträubt sich, derartiges zu schildern ... refuses to describe such things. — III ~ n ⊛ 4. (f. 3) resistance, opposition; reluctance.
Straub=fuß (″...) m ⊛ orn. shaggy (or rough) foot; =huhn n fowl with ruffled feathers.
straubig, sträubig (⌣´) a. ⊛ 1. = struppig. — 2. refractory, rebellious.
Strauch (⌣´) [ahd.] m ⊛ ⊕c. shrub, bush, ♀: ⌁ arbuscle; fig. auf den ~ schlagen to beat about the bush.
strauch=artig ♀ (″...) a. ⊛ shrub-(or bush-)like, ⌁ arbuscular; =dieb m ⊛ (Buschklepper) footpad.
straucheln (⌣´) [mhd.: struggle] v/n. (ſu u. h.) ⊛a. to stumble, to trip (a. fig.); to make (fig. to take) a false step; nur fig. F to make a faux pas.
Strauch=holz (″...) n ⊛: a) underwood, brushwood; b) (Gesträuch) copse; =hopfen ♀ m wild hop (Hu´mulus lu´pulus).
strauchicht, mst ...ig (⌣´) a. ⊛ covered with shrubs (buschig), bushy, shrubby.
Straucher (⌣´) m ⊛ (f. straucheln) 1. (a. ~in f ⊛) stumbler. — 2. (Fehltritt) false step, blunder, (fr.) faux pas.
Strauch=werk (″...⌣) n ⊛ shrubbery; f. Strauchholz.
Strauß¹ (⌣´) [ahd.: ostrich; *grch.] m ⊛a. ⊛ orn. ~. a. F Vogel ~ ostrich a. bisw. camel-bird (Stru´thio came´lus)

Zeichen (f. S. XVII): F familiär; P Volkssprache; ⌐ Gaunersprache; ⟍ selten; † alt (auch gestorben); * neu (auch geboren); ⁜ unrichtig;

[**Strauß**] — **Strauß**² (´) [mhd.] *m* ⑦a. (hot) fight, combat, strife, tussle, feud.

Strauß³ (´) [nhd.] *m* ⑦a. 1.(Blumen=)~ nosegay, bouquet, bunch of flowers, einen ~ binden to make up a nosegay, to gather a bunch of flowers. — 2. *orn.* (Haube gewisser Vögel) crest. — 3.♀(Art Blütenstand): ⚭ thyrse, thyrsus.

Strauß³-binderin (´´‿‿) *f* ㊷flower-girl.

Sträußchen (´‿) *n* ㉓ (*dim. v.* Strauß³) small bunch of flowers, &c., fürs Knopfloch: button-hole.

Straußen¹**-ei** (´´‿...) *n* ㊷ ostrich-egg; **=feder** *f* ostrich-feather; **=¹magen** *m* alles vertragend: stomach of an ostrich, *mehr gbr.:* of a horse.

Strauß¹**-feder** (´´...) *f* ㊷ = Straußenfeder; **=²gras** ♀ *n:* ⚭ agrostis; **=händler(in)** *f m* florist that sells bouquets or button-holes.

Strazze ❀ (‿‿) [it.] *f* ㊽ = Kladde ❀.

Strebe ⊕ (´‿) *f* ㊽ *arch.* prop, support, shore, stay, eines Pfostens 2c.: spur; auch = **=band**, **=pfahl**.

Strebe-balken ⊕ (´´...) *m* ㊷ brace; vgl. Strebe; **=band** *n* strut, stretching-piece; **=bogen** *m* counterfort; arch of a vault; **=kraft** *f* force of expansion; tendency *towards* (or *away from*) a th.; **=mauer** *f* = =bogen.

streben (´‿) [mhd.: strive] I *v/n.* (h.) ⑧ 1. a) **nach** etwas ≗ to strive after (or for) a th.; (danach trachten) to aspire to (or to aim at) a th.; (Anspruch darauf erheben) to lay claim to a th.; vorwärts ≗ to press (or push) forward; b) bisw. *abs.* er strebt, er ringt he is striving, struggling; c) **gegen** (ob. **wider**) den Strom ≗ to oppose (or resist) the current, to try to stem the tide. — 2. v. Leblosem: to tend (or gravitate) *towards* a th.; nach dem Mittelpunkte ⸗de Kraft: ⚭ centripetal force. — II ~ *n* ㉓ 3. (f. I) striving *after* (or *for*) a th.; aspiration, aim, tendency; (Anstrengung) exertion, effort, endeavour; sein ~ (Ehrgeiz) geht dahin zu // it is his (great) ambition (or desire, aim, object) to //.

Strebe-pfahl (´´‿) *m* = **=pfeiler** strong post or pillar; spur, buttress.

Streber (´‿) *m* ㉓ pushing person, engS. ambitious official or officer; place-hunter; **~tum** (´‿) *n* ⓓ. striving (spirit), ambition, (lofty) aspiration; place-hunting.

Streb-katz(e) (´´‿(‿) *f* ㊷ Spiel, wobei jede Partei die andere an einem Seile zu sich hinüberzuziehen sucht: tug of war.

strebsam (´‿) *a.* ㊅ (eifrig) zealous, pushing, forceful; (fleißig) assiduous, industrious, (ehrgeizig) ambitious, go-ahead; **~keit** (´‿‿) *f* ㊻ zeal, F push; assiduity; ambition.

Streck-balken ⊕ (´´.‿) *m* ㉒ stay, brace; prop; vgl. Strebe.

streckbar (´‿) *a.* ㊅ capable of stretching or being stretched, extendible; (dehnbar) ductile, (hämmerbar) malleable; **Streckbarkeit** *f* extendibility; ductility, malleability.

Streck-bett (´´‿) *n* ㊷ orthopædic bed.

Strecke (´‿) [mhd.: *streck*en] *f* ㊺ 1. örtlich: tract (of land); extent (in length); eine gute ~ Weges a (good) long way, F a good stretch; eine ~ Weges zurücklegen to cover a long distance. — 2. *geom.* straight line. — 3. 🚂 (Bahnlinie) (section of a) line; horizontale ~ level track; ~fahren (*ant.* rangieren) to go along (or to use) the main line; die ~ freimachen to clear the line. — 4. ✕ gangway, gallery; schwellende ~ inclined drift; ~n treiben to drive. — 5. *hunt.* reihenweise geordnete Jagdbeute; game laid out in rows; das Wild zur ~ bringen to kill the game, (Beute machen) to make a bag.

Streck-eisen ⊕ (´´.‿) *n* ㊷ Gerberei: stretching-iron or -piece, stretcher.

strecken (´‿) [ahd.: stretch] I *v/a. u.* sich ≗ *v/refl.* ⑧ 1. a) zu Boden (auch hin- oder nieder=) ≗ to stretch on the ground, to lay low, to knock down or to the ground, mit einer Waffe: to fell (to the ground); b) sich zur Ruhe nieder= (oder hin=) ≗ to lie down to rest; sich bequem (hin=) ≗ to loll about; c) ✕ die Arme ≗ to stretch out one's arms; das Gewehr ob. die Waffen ≗ (niederlegen) to lay down (one's) arms, to surrender. — 2. (ausrecken): a) die Hände gen Himmel ≗ to raise (or lift) one's hands to(wards) heaven; die Glieder ≗, sich ≗ to stretch one's limbs, o.s.; alle vier(e) von sich ≗ to lie (or go) down full length; gestreckt daliegen to lie sprawling; die Zunge aus dem Munde ≗ to stretch (or put) out one's tongue; *fig.* f. Decke 2; b) von Pferden: sich im Laufe ≗ to run at full speed, to career along; im gestreckten Galopp at full speed or tilt, in full career, a. whip and spur; c) sich ≗ (wachsen) to grow. to shoot up. — 3. *meist* (dehnen) to stretch, flatten, extend, *metall. auch:* to laminate; mit dem Hammer ≗ to hammer out, mit der Walze: to roll (a. *metall.*), Glas 2c. ≗ auch: to spread ...; gestrecktes Glas broad (or spread) glass; Eisen ≗ to draw iron (in)to bars; glühendes Eisen läßt sich ≗ ... stretches (or flattens out) under the hammer. — II ~ *n* ㉓ 4. f. Streckung.

Strecken-arbeiter 🚂 (´´.‿...) *m* ㊷ workman on the line; **=betrieb** ✕ *m* driving; **=förderung** ✕ *f* underground hauling; **=geschwindigkeit** 🚂 *f* (ordinary) speed between any two stations; **=verkehr** 🚂 *m* local traffic; **=wärter** *m* linekeeper, signalman; **≗weise** *adv.* (F *a. 🚂*) by sections, in (some) parts, (to be found) here and there.

Strecker (´‿) *m* ㉓ 1. (f. strecken) one who stretches, &c., stretcher (*auch arch.* Mauerstein, der längs liegt). — 2. = Streckmuskel.

Streck-gut (´´...) *n* ㊷ Fischerei: young fry; **=lage** *f* Turnerei: stretched position; **=maschine** *f* Weberei: stretching-machine; **=muskel** *m*, *anat.* (*ant.* Beugemuskel) tightener, ⚭ (ex)tensor; **=rahmen** *m* stretching-frame; **=stütz** *f* Turnerei: resting on one's hands.

Streckung (´‿) *f* ㊻ (f. strecken I) stretching, &c.; ⊕ extension, *metall.* lamination, rolling.

[**streichen**] **Streck-walze** ⊕ (´´...) *f* ㊷ stretching-roll, flatter, drawing-roller, Spinnerei: drawing-machine; **=werk** *n*, *metall.* plate-rollers *pl.*, flatting-mill, *mint.* rolling-mill.

Streich (´) [mhd.: stroke: streichen] *m* ⓒ. 1. stroke, mit der Faust oder e-r Waffe: blow, mit der Hand: (gentle) tap, mit der Peitsche 2c.: lash (meist *pl.*), *bibl.*, &c. stripe (meist *pl.*); f. führen 7 am Schluß; e-m einen ~ versetzen to give a p. a blow; *fig.* auf einen ~ (auf einmal) at one blow, (SH.) at one fell swoop, F in one go; Sprichw. von einem ~e fällt keine Eiche, etwa: Rome was not built in a day. — 2. *fig.* (Handlung) action; (Unternehmen) stroke of business, (fr.) coup; dummer ~ silly action, stupid thing (to do); kluger ~ sensible action, piece of diplomacy, leichtsinniger ~ piece of folly, lose ~e pranks, F larks *pl.*; lustiger ~ piece of fun, mutwilliger ~ mischievous act, mad trick; schlechter ~ mean trick, base action; tolle ~e m. to indulge in mad freaks; er hat noch ganz andere ~e gemacht he has done worse things (than that); er hat wieder dumme ~e gemacht he has been at (or up to) his tricks again; e-m e-n ~ (Possen) spielen to play a p. a (nasty) trick.

Streich-blech (´´...) ✕ *n* ㊷ *artill.* der Lafette: locking-plate; **=bogen** ♪ *m* violin-bow; **=brett** *n* ⊕ u. ✕ lockingsheet, Tuchmacherei: smoothing-board; **=bürste** *f* Papierfabr.: gumming-brush; **=eisen** ⊕ *n* smoothing-iron, scraper, der Vergolder: paring-knife, der Nadler: rubber, Glasfabr.: sheet-iron blade.

streicheln (´‿) I *v/a.* ⓒa.: e-m die Wangen ≗ to stroke (or pat) a p.'s cheeks; bid. liebkosend: e-n ≗ to caress (or fondle) a p., berückend: to cajole (or wheedle round) a p. — II ~ *n* ㉓ stroking, caresses *pl.*, fondling, cajoling.

streichen (´‿) [ahd.: strike] ⓒ*aft.* I *v/n.* (h. u. fn) 1. (sich erstrecken, hinziehen) to extend, to run in a certain direction; von Norden nach Süden ≗ to run (or bear, trend) from north to south; ✕ zutage ≗ to crop out. — 2. (ziehen, wandern): a) von Personen: durch Feld und Wald ≗ to roam (or stroll) in field(s) and forest(s); an e-n, et. ≗ (anstreifen) to touch (or graze) a p., a th.; bisw. mit *acc.*: ein Menuett ≗ to dance ...; b) v. Vögeln: to fly, to take one's flight, to be on the wing; to migrate; die Elster strich zu Tale the magpie flew towards the valley; c) das Schiff streicht durch die Wellen ... is ploughing (or cleaving) the waves; der Wind strich durch den Forst ... swept through the forest; d) P einen ≗ (fahren) l. to pass wind. — 3. (nur h.): a) über et. hin ≗ to pass lightly (or gently) over a th.; e-m mit der Hand über das Gesicht ≗ to pass one's hand over a p.'s face; b) Fischzucht: (laichen) to spawn. — II *v/a.* 4. (der Oberfläche entlang bewegen) to pass along the surface; to stroke; sich die Haare ≗ to stroke (or arrange) one's hair; ein (Rasier=)Messer ≗ to set a razor; auf

♪ Musik; ⚭ Wissenschaft; ♀ Pflanze; ♆ Geographie; ⊕ Technik; ✕ Bergbau; ⚔ Militär; ⚓ Marine; ❀ Handel; ✉ Post; 🚂 Eisenbahn.

[**Streicher**] — 934 — [**Streithengst**]

e-n Wetzsteine ⟲ to whet, to grind; auf dem Wetzstahle ⟲ to sharpen on the steel; ein Zündholz an die Wand ⟲ to strike a match against the wall. — **5.** mit Angabe der Wirkung: f. ausstreichen 2; sich die Haare aus dem Gesichte ⟲ to push one's hair out of one's eyes; in die Höhe ⟲ to push back, to stroke up(wards) or back; Eisen mit dem Magnet ⟲ to magnetize iron; gestrichen voll brimful, full to overflowing. — **6.** ♪: a) die Geige mit dem Bogen ⟲ to (play with the) bow on the violin; den Baß ⟲ to play the bass; b) gestrichene Note note on the ledger line, note above (or below) the staff. — **7.** et. auf e-n Gegenstand ⟲ = schmieren 1, z.B. Butter auf Brot ⟲, Butterbrot ⟲ to spread butter on bread. — **8.** et. mit Farbe ⟲ = anstreichen 3; Warnung: frisch gestrichen! wet paint! — **9.** (sichtbare Striche m.) to mark. — **10.** = ausstreichen 1; von der Liste ⟲ to strike off the list; im Speisehaus: der Hasenbraten ist (auf der Speisekarte) gestrichen ... has been struck off, kürzer: ... is off; typ., &c. gestrich(e)ne Zeile line struck out, expunged line; f. Streichung. — **11.** e-n mit Geißeln, Ruten ⟲, a. abs. e-n ⟲ to scourge, to beat a p. — **12.** hunt. Lerchen ⟲ (mit Netzen fangen) to catch (sky)larks in nets. — **13.** ⊕ Spinnerei: Wolle ⟲ to card ...; Ziegelei: Ziegel ⟲ to make bricks or tiles. — **14.** ⚓: a) die Riemen ⟲ (rückwärts bewegen) to hold water, to back-water; streich überall! back all!, back astern!; b) die Flagge ⟲ (niederlassen) to strike the flag. — S. a. 2a. — **III** ~ n ㉓ **15.** (f. 1) extension; (Richtung) direction, trend. — **16.** (f. 2) roaming (or roving) life; migration (or passage) of birds. — **17.** ♪ (f. 6) bowing; play(ing). — **18.** = Streichung 1.

Streicher (⟂ ⌣) [mhd.] m ㉒ **1.** Person: a) one who strokes, &c. (f. streichen II); b) ⊕ oft = Anstreicher; c) meist i. Zssgn., f. Land-, Ziegel- (⁊c.)streicher. — **2.** Werkzeug: = Streicheisen.

Streich-feuer ⚔ (⟂ ⌣...) n ㉒ artill. flank (or enfilading) fire; **=feuerzeug** n match-box, box of matches; **=fisch** m, ichth. spawner; **=garn** ⊕ n Spinnerei: carded yarn; **=holz** n: a) = Hölzchen b) ⊕ der Töpfer ⁊c.: strike; **=hölzchen** n (friction-)match, lucifer(-match), zum Anzünden von Zigarren: fusee, schwedisches: safety-match; ein ~ anzünden to light (or strike) a match; **=holz-**, **=hölzchen-fabrik** f match-(manu)factory; **=holz-**, **=hölzchen-schachtel** f match- (or fusee-) box; **=instrument** ♪ n string- (or stringed, bow-)instrument; **=leder** n = **=riemen**; **=lini-e** ⚔ frt. flank; **=maß** ⊕ n mortise- (or marking-)gauge; **=messer** n: a) pharm. spatula; b) paint. palette-knife; **=musik** ♪ f music of string-instruments; **=netz** n zum Vogelfang: trammel; **=orchester** ♪ n string-band; **=quartett** ♪ n stringed quartet(te); **=riemen** m razor-strap, -strop; **=schiene** ⚔ f **=blech**; **=stein** m: a) (Prüfstein)

touchstone; b) (Wetzstein) hone; **=teich** m Fischzucht: spawning-, breeding-pond. **Streichung** (⟂ ⌣) f ㊻ (f. streichen) **1.** (Ausstreichen) striking (out), erasure, einer Stelle: suppression, typ. deletion. — **2.** (gestrichene Stelle) expunged (or suppressed, typ. deleted) passage.

Streich-vogel (⟂ ⌣...) m ㉒ = Zugvogel; **=werk** n: a) ⊕ Ölmühle: sweeper; b) ⚔ frt. bastion; **=wolle** f ⚙, ⊕ carding-wool; **=zeit** f season for the passage of birds, der Fische: spawning-time; **=zither** ♪ f zither (which is) played with a bow.

Streif (⟂) m ㉕. = Streifen¹.

Streif-band (⟂ ⌣...) n ㉓ wrapper; ⟿ unter ~ enclosed in a wrapper; **=blick** m random glance or look.

Streifchen (⟂ ⌣) n ㉓ (dim. von Streif(en)) thin stripe, narrow strip or band.

Streife (⟂ ⌣) f ㊻ = Streifzug.

Streifen¹ (⟂ ⌣) [mhd.: strip(e)] m ㉓ **1.** (langes schmales Stück) (narrow) strip(e), streak, strip of land, &c., slip of paper, &c., ⚬ stria; (Linie) line; ⊕ (Litze, Vorstoß) list; ~ (dünne Platte) Metall metal blade; arch., Ornamentif: band, fillet, fascia; Glasmacherei: ~ im Glase: vein, thread, im Spiegelglase: cloud. — **2.** ⊕ typ. (Fahne) proof-slip.

streifen² (⟂ ⌣) v/a. u. sich ⟲ v/refl. ⦻ (mit Streifen versehen) to stripe, to streak, ⚬ to striate; ⊕ eine Säule ⁊c. ⟲ to channel (or flute) ...; gestreift striped, streaky, ⚬: ⚬ striate(d).

streifen³ (⟂ ⌣) [mhd.: strip] ⦻ **I** v/a. u. v/n. (h.) **1.** (unmittelbar berühren) to scrape, to touch; et. ⟲, an et. ⟲ to graze (or skim) a th., to brush against a th. (über et. hingleiten) to glide (or slide) over a th.; fig. das streift an Wahnsinn that verges (or borders) on madness; Tennis: gestreift! let!, net! — **2.** (abziehen) einen Ring vom Finger ⟲ to pull (or take) a ring off one's finger; die Ärmel in die Höhe ⟲ to tuck up one's sleeves; das Laub von einem Zweige ⟲, meton.: den Zweig (ab-) ⟲ to strip a bough of its leaves, to strip the leaves off a bough. — **II** v/n. (h., bei Ortsveränderung: sn) **3.** (ziehen, wandern) to roam, rove, ramble, stroll; F to knock about (the country). — **4.** ⚔ to make inroads or incursions, to overrun a country; auf Kundschaft ⟲ to reconnoitre, to go scouting.

Streifen¹-farn ♣ (⟂ ⌣...) m ㉒ spleenwort (Asplenium); **⟲nervig** ♣ a. ㊻ with striate nervure; **⟲weise** adv. (F a.a.) in stripes.

Streifer (⟂ ⌣) m ㉒ rover, rambler.

Streiferei (⌣⌣⟂) f ㊻ roaming, ramble, excursion; ⚔ inroad; vgl. Streifzug.

Streif-hieb (⟂ ⌣⟂) m ㉒ grazing (or glancing) cut; vgl. Streifwunde.

streifig (⟂ ⌣) a. ㊺ striped, streaky.

Streif-jagd (⟂ ⌣...) f ㊻, **=jagen** n coursing, shooting-excursion; **=kolonne** f flying column; **=korps** ⚔ n reconnoitring (or scouting) party, ~ von Parteigängern party (or band) of partisans; **=licht** n, paint. accidental light(s pl.); fig. side-light; **=partei** f; **=korps**; **=ritt** m excursion on horseback; **=schar** (n pl.) ⚔ f irregular military (corps), corps of irregulars; **=schuß** m

grazing shot; **=wache** ⚔ f patrol; **⟲weise** adv. = streifenweise; **=wild** n, hunt. roving game (from another preserve); **=wunde** f slight (surface-)wound, (mere) scratch; **=zug** m (roving) expedition, incursion, invasion, raid.

Streik T (⟂) m ㉒c. (㊿) (Ausstand) strike, suspension of work, F turn-out.

Streik-bewegung (⟂ ⌣...) f ㊻ strike movement; **=brecher** m F blackleg, scab.

streiken (⟂ ⌣) v/n. (h.) ⦻ to strike, to stop work, to go on strike, F to come (or turn) out. [(work)man on strike.]

Streiker (⟂ ⌣) m ㉒ (Ausständiger) striker,]

Streik-kasse (⟂ ⌣...) f ㊻ strike-fund; **=posten** m picket; **=posten-stehen** n picketing (of strikers); **=unterstützung** f strike-pay.

Streit (⟂) [ahd.] m ㉒c. (pl. mst **=igkeiten**) (Zank) quarrel, wrangle; (Wortwechsel) dispute, argument, (lebhafte Besprechung) debate; (Erörterung) discussion, von Gelehrten: controversy; (Reibung, Kampf) conflict, strife, contention, fight; (Wettstreit) contest, competition; lärmender ~ brawl(ing), squabble, row; ~ um nichts quarrel about nothing, ~ vor Gericht litigation, lawsuit; ~ anfangen ⟲, geraten ⟲ unter „in"; mit einem im ~e liegen to be at variance (F at loggerheads) with a p.

Streit-axt (⟂ ⌣,⟂) f ㊻ battle-axe; die ~ begraben (wie ehm. die Indianer), fig. Frieden machen) to bury the hatchet.

streitbar (⟂ ⌣) a. ㊻ in fighting trim, able to carry arms; warlike, martial, (tapfer) valiant, brave.

Streitbarkeit (⟂ ⌣⌣) f ㊻ fitness for fighting; warlike (or martial) spirit.

streiten (⟂ ⌣) [ahd.] ⦻b. **I** v/n. (h.) **1.** to contend, mit Fäusten, Waffen: to fight, to (do) battle, mit Worten, Gründen: to dispute, argue, wrangle, bsd. vor Gericht: to litigate (über et. about a th.); darüber läßt sich ⟲ that's a matter of opinion or argument. — **2.** von Sachlichem: to be at variance with; der Umstand streitet (spricht) für uns ... tells (or speaks) in our favour; das streitet gegen die (gesunde) Vernunft that's contrary to reason, feiner: it militates against common sense. — **II** v/a. **3.** einen Kampf mit einem ⟲ (führen) to contend (or struggle) with a p. — **4.** (in Abrede stellen, leugnen) das will ich nicht ⟲ I won't deny (or dispute) it. — **III** sich ⟲ v/refl. **5.** sich mit einem um et. ⟲ to quarrel (or dispute) with a p. about a th.; f. Bart 4. — **IV** ~ n ㉓ **6.** = Streit. — **V** ⟲ b p.pr. und a. ㊻ **7.** contending; die ⟲e (ant. triumphierende) Kirche the Church Militant; die ⟲en Mächte the belligerent powers, the belligerents pl.; jur. die ⟲en Parteien the litigant parties, the litigants pl.

Streiter (⟂ ⌣) m ㉒, ~in f ㊼ combatant, fighter, warrior, mit Worten: disputant, (Vorkämpfer) champion.

Streiterei (⌣⌣⟂) f ㊻ (long) dispute.

Streit-fall (⟂ ⌣...) m ㊷, **=frage** f matter of dispute, (question at) issue; vgl. **=punkt**; **=hahn** m = Kampfhahn b; **=hammer** m, fig. brawler, squabbler; **=hammer** = **=kolben**; **=handel** m: a) quarrel, b) lawsuit; **=hengst** m = **=roß**.

Signs (see page XVII): F familiar; P vulgar; Ƒ flash; ⟍ rare; † obsolete (died); * new word (born); +⁺+ incorrect; ♪ music;

[ſtreitig] — 935 — [Striegel]

ſtreitig (⌣–)[ahd.] a. ⚛ 1. (ſtreitend) mit e-m über et. 2 ſein to dispute (or quarrel, squabble) with a p. about a th. — 2. (dem Streite unterworfen) disputed, in dispute, contested, ⚲ contestable; 2er Punkt point at issue; e-m et. 2 machen to dispute a p. a th.; e-m den Rang 2 machen to compete with a p., gerichtlich: die Sache ist noch 2 the matter is still pending or (lt.) sub judice.
Streitigkeit (⌣–) f ⚛ 1. bisw.: contestableness. — 2. = Streit, bſd. als pl. von Streit, z. B. ~en beilegen to arrange disputes or squabbles.
Streit-kolben (ʺ...) m ⚛ ehm. hurlbat, martel; (Keule) club, mace; =kräfte f/pl. military forces pl.; =luſt f love for fighting or wrangling, quarrelsome (or contentious) spirit or disposition; vgl. =ſucht; 2luſtig a. ⚛ fond of fighting or wrangling, quarrelsome, contentious, als Redner: argumentative; =macht f forces pl.; =punkt m point of controversy, disputed (or contentious) point; =roß n war-steed or -horse, charger; =ſache f: a) controversial matter; vgl. =fall; b) dispute; =ſatz m: 2 thesis; =ſchlichter m peacemaker, arbitrator; =ſchrift f polemical treatise or pamphlet; =ſucht f passion for fighting or disputing; quarrelsomeness, litigiousness; vgl. =luſt; 2ſüchtig a. fond of picking quarrels, quarrelsome; litigious, F litigating; =ſüchtige(r) s. quarrelsome person, F litigator; =übung f disputation, argument; =wagen m Alt.: war-chariot.
ſtremmen (⌣⌣) [ſtramm] v/n. (h.) ⚛ (beengen) to tighten.
ſtreng (⌣), a. 2e¹ (⌣⌣) [ahd.: strong] a. ⚛ 1. (ant. mild) severe, rigorous, stern; (hart) harsh, in Sitten: austere; (ſcharf, beſtimmt) strict, exact, von Regeln: stringent; adv. aufs, auf das ~ſte, 2ſtens most severely or sternly, in the most rigorous manner; 2 an et. feſthalten to adhere strictly to a th.; 2 auf et. halten to keep scrupulously to a th., to observe a th. to the letter; 2 gegen einen verfahren to deal harshly (or severely, sternly) with a p.; ⚔ j. Arreſt 2; 2er Feſttag strict holiday; 2er Kritiker uncompromising (or carping, censorious) critic; Sprichw. 2e Herren regieren nicht lange severe rulers have short reigns. — 2. (ant. gelinde) keen, sharp, vom Wetter: inclement; 2e Kälte severe (or intense, biting, bitter) cold; im 2ſten Winter in the depth of winter. — 3. (zuſ.-ziehend) bſd. vom Geſchmack: sharp, tart; (ſtark u. brennend) acrid; 2 (adv.) ſchmecken to have a sharp (or burning, pungent) taste.
Strenge² (⌣⌣) [ahd.: strength] f ⚛ 1. (ſ. ſtreng) severity, rigour, sternness; harshness, austerity, strictness; 2 der Witterung inclemency, der Kälte: intensity, des Geſchmacks: sharpness, tartness. — 2. path. = Harnſtrenge (ſ. Harnzwang).
ſtreng-flüſſig (⌣...) a. ⚛ chm. und ⊙ metall. difficult to fuse or to liquefy or of fusion, refractory; =flüſſigkeit f ⚛ refractoriness; 2genommen adv.

strictly speaking, taken literally; 2gläubig a. of the right faith, orthodox; =gläubige(r) s. true believer; =gläubigkeit f right (or orthodox) faith, orthodoxy. [(Astra'ntia).]
Strenze ⚘ (⌣⌣) [lt.] f ⚛ masterwort│
Streu (⌣) [mhd.: ſtreuen] f ⚛ für Vieh: litter, auch: strewing, für Menſchen: bed of straw, rough couch, F shake-down.
Streu-büchſe (ʺ⌣⌣) f ⚛ für Mehl: (flour-)dredger, dredging-box, für Pfeffer: pepper-box or -caster; für Sand: sand-box, für Zucker: sugar-caster.
ſtreuen (⌣⌣) [ahd.: strew: Stroh] I v/a. u. v/n. (h.) ⚛ 1. to strew; (ausbreiten) to spread (out); to scatter (broadcast), ſäend: to sow, fig. to disseminate; Blumen auf den Weg, meton.: den Weg mit Blumen 2 to strew (or sprinkle) flowers on the path or way; Pfeffer (Zucker) auf et. 2 to pepper (to sugar) a th. (all over); fig. ſ. Sand 2; die Götter 2 ihre Gaben auf ihn ... shower their gifts upon him. — 2. agr. Miſt 2 to spread manure; abs. den Kühen 2 to (make up) the litter for the cows; vom Getreide: 2 (Stroh liefern) to yield straw (for litters). — 3. ⚔, &c. v. Feuerwaffen: to spread. — II ~ n ⚛ 4. ſ. Streuung.
Streu-gabel (ʺ...) f ⚛ agr. stable-fork; =gold ⊙ n aventurine; =kuchen m seed-cake; =kügelchen n Homöopathie: ⚲ globule; =minen ⚓ f/pl. submarine mines pl.; =pulver n, med. powder for (strewing on) wounds, &c.; (Hexenmehl) lycopodium (powder); =ſand m writing-sand; =ſand-büchſe f sand-box.
Streuſel (⌣⌣) m, n ⚛ things pl. strewn, sprinkling(s pl.); ~kuchen (ʺ⌣⌣) m ⚛ seed-cake.
Streu-ſtroh (ʺ..¹) n ⚛ straw for litter.
Streuung (⌣⌣) f ⚛ strewing, &c. (ſ. ſtreuen I), agr. littering, fig. dissemination, ⚔, &c. v. Feuerwaffen: spread.
Streu-zeug (⌣...) n ⚛, =zucker m powdered sugar, ⚲ caster-sugar.
Strich¹ (⌣) [ahd.; *ſtrich²] m ⚛c. 1. ~ mit der Feder stroke with the pen; mit (od. in) einem ~(e) (hinter-ea. weg) at a stretch, at one stroke, without a break. — 2. (Linie) line (a. b. Tennis); (Streifen) strip(e), streak; e-n ~ unter et. machen: a) to underline a th.; b) fig. (et. abſchließen) to finish a th., er hat keinen ~ getan he has not done a stroke of work; ~ im Kerbholze notch, tally; e-n ~ durch et. machen to cross a th. out, to run one's pen through a th.; fig. das macht uns einen ~ durch die Rechnung that upsets all our plans or calculations; gram. = Komma, Binde=, Gedanken=ſtrich. — 3. (das Streichen): a) ein ~ mit der Bürſte (stroke with the) brush; ♪ drawing the bow (vgl. Bogenführung); paint. = Pinſelſtrich; b) ⚔ ~ einer Schicht, eines Ganges: direction, trend; c) ~ des Windes direction of the wind; ~ der Wolken flight of the clouds; hunt. ~ der Zugvögel: passage; ~ (Flug) zſ.-ſtreichender Vögel: flight; walk of snipe(s), covey of partridges; auf den ~ gehen to go out sniping or bird-catching; F fig.

von Mädchen: to walk the streets, von Männern: to go (or run) after the girls; d) F fig. einen auf dem ~e haben to have a grudge (or a spite) against a p. — 4. (kleines Längenmaß) millimetre. — 5. ~ (Zeugſtreif) an e-r Haube frill of a cap. — 6. (Strecke, Gegend) tract, region, (Bezirk) district; ⚓ ~ auf der See ocean-track; vom Schiffe: es hält den ~ she keeps her (right) course; ~ des Kompaſſes point of the compass; denſelben ~ mit e-m halten, ſegeln to steer the same course as a person. — 7. (Richtung der Faſern ꝛc.) grain; Sammet nach dem ~e (gegen den ~) bürſten to brush velvet the right (the wrong) way of the stuff; fig. es geht mir wider den ~ it goes against the grain, it is against my liking or inclination. — 8. ⚓ (Laichen) der Fiſche: spawning-time, (junge Brut) young fry. — 9. Ziegelei: ~ Ziegel batch of bricks made in one kiln.
ſtrich² (⌣) ind., 2e (⌣) subj. impf. v. ſtreichen.   [little stroke or dash.]
Strichelchen (⌣⌣⌣) n ⚛ (dim. v. Strich)│
ſtricheln (⌣⌣) v/a. ⚛ a. to mark with little lines or strokes, to dot, = ſchraffieren.
Strich¹-kraut ⚘ (⌣...) n ⚛: ⚲ datisca (Dati'sca cannabi'na); =punkt m semicolon (;); =regen m rain confined to a limited area, local shower; =ſchuß m band-hit; =vogel m, hunt. bird of passage; 2weiſe adv. (F a. a.): a) (mit Strichen) by means of strokes or lines; b) (in gewiſſen Gegenden) in certain tracts, here and there, by zones; c) v. Vögeln in flights or flocks; =zaun ⊙ m in Flüſſen: hurdled fence; =zeit f, hunt. season for the migration of birds.
Strick¹ (⌣) [ahd.] m ⚛b. 1. rope, bünnerer: line, cord; vgl. Strang 1 und 2; mit e-m ~ umwickeln to tie round with a rope, to cord (up). — 2. = Fallſtrick; hunt. = Fangleine. — 3. F fig. durchtriebener ~ scapegrace, young rogue or rascal; vgl. Galgenſtrick.
Strick²-arbeit (⌣⌣⌣) [ſtrick-en] f ⚛ knitting(-work).
ſtrickbar (⌣⌣) a. ⚛ knittable.
Strick²-beutel (⌣...) m ⚛ knitting-bag, reticule; =¹eiſen ⊙ n horseshoe with tarred padding.
ſtricken (⌣⌣) [ahd.; *Strick] v/a. ⚛ 1. e-n Strumpf ꝛc. 2 to knit ...; netzartig 2 to net. — 2. = ſchlingen¹.
Stricker (⌣⌣) m ⚛, ~in f ⚛ knitter.
Strickerei (⌣⌣⌣) f ⚛ knitting(-work).
Stricker-lohn (⌣⌣¹) m ⚛ fee (or money paid) for knitting.
Strick²-garn (⌣...) n ⚛ knitting-yarn or -cotton; =¹leiter f rope-ladder; =²maſche f mesh; =maſchine ⊙ f knitting-, stocking-machine; =muſter n pattern for knitting; =nadel f knitting-needle; =naht f knitted seam; =perle f bead (for knitting); =ſtrumpf m stocking which is being knitted; =zeug n things (or implements) pl. for knitting.
Striegel (⌣⌣) [ahd.; *lt. stri'gil's f] m ⚛ (oft ⊙): a) zum Putzen v. Pferden: curry- (or horse-)comb; b) für Menſchen: bath- (or bathing-)brush.

⚛ scientific; ⚘ botanical; ⚲ geography; ⊙ machinery; ⚒ mining; ⚔ military; ⚓ marine; ● commercial; ✉ postal; 🚂 railway.

[ſtriegeln] — 936 — [Strumpf]

ſtriegeln (´‿) v/a. ⓐa. 1. Pferde ♀ to curry(-comb) ...; (bürſten) to brush. — 2. fig.: a) (blant u. ſauber m.) to clean(se); b) (ſchinden) to handle roughly, to ill-use; (betritteln) to censure, F to slate.

Strieme (‿) [ahd.] f ⓐ u. m ④, ~n m ㉓1. stripe, streak, band (ſ. Streifen¹1). — 2. (blununterlaufener Wulſtſtreif in der Haut) wale, weal, mark (on the body) left by a whip or rod.

ſtriemig (´‿) a. ⓖ covered with wales; (ſtreiſig) striped, streaky, like a stripe.

ſtriezen F (´‿) [mhd.] v/n. (h.) ⓚ co. (mauſen) to pilfer.

ſtrikt (´) [lt. ſtreng] a. ⓖ strict; ♀(e) adv. strictly, in a strict sense of the word, accurately, (buchſtäblich) literally.

Striktur (‿´) [lt.] f ⓐ path. (Verengung der Harnröhre) stricture.

Strippe (‿) [ndd.] f ⓔ strap on trousers or boots; (Schnur) string.

ſtritt (´) ind. impf. von ſtreiten.

ſtrittig (‿´) [Stritt † m Streit] a. ⓖ = ſtreitig 2. [hair.]

ſtrob(e)lig (´(‿)´) a. ⓖ with dishevelled

Stroh (´) [ahd.: straw: ſtreuen] n ⓒc. straw, ſeltener: culm; (Dach-) ~ thatch; mit ~ ausſtopfen (überziehen) to stuff (to cover) with straw; mit ~ verſehen oder binden to (truss with) straw; fig. ſ. dreſchen 1.

Stroh-arbeit ⊕ (´...) f ⓑ straw-work; ♀artig a. ⓖ straw-like, ♌ stramineous; ♀band n straw band or tie (auch hort.); ♀bett n straw bed; vgl. ♀ſack; ♀blume f: a) (artificial) straw flower; b) ♀ = Immortelle; a. = Papierblume; ♀boden m straw-loft; ♀bund n truss of straw; ♀butter f winter-butter; ♀dach n thatched roof; ♀decke f: a) zum Pußen der Füße: straw mat; b) hort., &c. straw cover(ing); ♀decker ⊕ m thatcher.

ſtrohern (´‿) a. ⓖ: a) (made of) straw; (aus Stroh erbaut) straw-built; b) fig. (fade) insipid; (geiſtlos) dull, dry.

Stroh-farbe (´...) f ⓑ straw-colour; ♀farben, ♀farbig a. ⓖ straw-coloured; ♀feuer n straw-fire; fig. (passing) fit of passion, short-lived zeal, flickering ardour; ♀fiedel ♪ f straw-fiddle; ♀flaſche f bottle (or carboy) packed in straw; ♀flechter(in f) m straw-plaiter or -worker; ♀futter n: a) für Vieh: straw (as fodder); b) als Bekleidung: straw lining; ♀geflecht n st.-plaiting or -work; ♀gelb a. = ♀farben; ♀halm m straw; fig. nach einem ~ greifen to catch at a straw; ♀halme ziehen (loſen) to draw lots; ♀händler(in f) m dealer in straw; ♀haufen m heap of straw; ♀hut m straw hat or bonnet; ♀hütte f thatched hut or cottage.

ſtrohig (´‿) a. ⓖ strawy.

Stroh-kopf F (´...) m ⓑ empty-headed fellow; ♀lager n: a) layer of straw or thatch; b) = ♀bett; ♀mann m: a) (Figur von Stroh) man of straw (a. fig.); (Vogelſcheuche) scarecrow; b) Whiſt ꝛc.: dummy; ♀matte f straw mat(ting); ♀papier ⊛ n straw-paper; ♀pappe ⊛ f Papierfabr.: strawboard; ♀pfeife f reed; ♀puppe ⊕ = ♀mann i.; ♀ſack m straw mattress, palliasse; Fach, du gerechter ~! dear me!, good Gracious!; ♀ſchaub(e f) m zum

Dachdecken: straw-sheaf; ♀ſchneider m straw-chopper; ♀ſeil n straw-rope; vgl. ♀band; ♀ſtuhl m straw-bottomed chair; ♀teller m straw table-mat; ♀waren f/pl. straw goods pl.; ♀wein m straw-wine; ♀wieye f, ♀wiſch m: a) wisp of straw; b) als Warnungszeichen: firebrand; ♀witwe F f [nhd.] widow bewitched, grass-widow; ♀witwer F m widower for the time being; ich bin ~ my wife is away from home; ♀witwen- oder witwer-ſchaft f, -tum n, etwa: temporary absence (of husband or wife), F grass-widowhood.

Strolch (´) [nhd.: stroll] m ⓑb. tramp, loafer, a. = Lump 1; ♀en (´‿) v/n. (h. u. ſn) ⓘ = ſtreifen³ 3.

Strom (´) [ahd.: stream] m ⓒc. 1. (large) river; (et. Strömendes) stream, ſtärker: flood; (reißendes Gewäſſer) torrent; der Regen floß in Strömen ... poured (down) in torrents; fig. gegen (oder wider) den ~ ſchwimmen to swim against the tide. — 2. (Strömung im Meere) (ocean-) current; phys. elektriſcher ~ electric current; geſchloſſener ~ closed current or circuit; konſtanter (ununterbrochener) ~ constant (continuous) current; ~ erhalten to receive current; den ~ unterbrechen to break the current; den ~ umſchalten to switch off the current; Draht unter ~ live wire. — 3. meiſt fig.: a) (Menſchenmaſſe) (dense) crowd (or throng) of people; b) Ströme Blutes streams pl. of blood; ~ von Tränen flood of tears; ~ von Worten flow (or volume) of words.

ſtrom-ab(wärts) (´‿´(‿)) ↓ adv. downstream, down the river, auch: with the tide; ♀an (´‿) = ♀auf; ♀anker (´...) m kedge-anchor; ♀anwohner m one living by the riverside, auch: riverain dweller; ♀auf(wärts) (´‿´(‿)) ↓ adv. up-stream, up the river, auch: against the tide; ♀bett n Topographie: river-bed, bed (or channel) of a river; ♀brecher ⊕ m im Meere: groin.

ſtrömen (´‿) [nhd.; *Strom] I v/n. (h. u. ſn) ⓘ to stream; (fließen) to flow, gush, ſtärker: to pour (auch vom Regen) Tränen ſtrömen aus ſeinen Augen tears are trickling (or gushing) from his eyes; das Blut ſtrömte ihm nach dem Kopfe the blood rushed to his head; das Volk ſtrömt nach dem Schauſpielhauſe the people are flocking (or streaming, crowding) to the theatre. — II ~ n ㉓ = Strömung 1. [a river.]

Strom-enge (´‿´) f ⓑ narrows pl. of

Stromer P (´‿) m ㉒ [Γ 14. sae. = Kehlabſchneider] (Landſtreicher, Herumtreiber) tramp, loafer.

ſtromern F (´‿) [Stromer] v/n. (h.) ⓚa. to lead a tramp's life, to tramp it.

Strom-erzeuger (´...) m ㉒ elect.: ♌ rheomotor; ♀gebiet n river-basin; ♀gefälle n fall of a river, slope (or incline) of a river-bed; ♀karte f river-map or -chart; ♀kreis m, elect. circuit; ♀leiter m, elect.: ♌ rheophore.

Strömling (´‿) m ⓓ. ichth. small herring (in the Baltic).

Strom-meſſer (´...) m ㉒ elect. amperemeter; galvanometer; ♀meſſung

f, elect. galvanometry; ♀polizei f river-police; ♀quelle f, elect. source of current; ♀ſchiffer m waterman; master of a river-boat; ♀ſchnelle f rapid, shoot; ♀ſperre ↓ f boom; ♀ſtärke f, elect. power (or intensity) of a current; ♀ſtrecke f zwiſchen zwei Biegungen: reach.

Strömung (´‿) f ㊺ 1. (das Strömen) streaming, flowing, gush(ing). — 2. current, stream, flow, flood, drift, heftige: race, unter der Oberfläche: undercurrent; fig. revolutionäre ~ revolutionary movement.

Strom-unterbrecher (´...) m ㉒ elect. circuit-breaker, ♌ rheotome; ♀weiſe adv. in floods or torrents; ♀wender m, elect. commutator, current-reverser; ♀zeit, bſd. niederb. ♀tid f (FRITZ REUTER; vgl. Stromer) years (or time) of apprenticeship on a farm; ♀zuleitung f, elect., unterirdiſche: conduit.

Strontian T ♌ (‿´(‿)´) [~ ☿ ſchott. Ort] m (n)ⓑc. chm., a. ~erde f strontia (SrO); ſ. a. Zöleſtin; ♀it ♌ (‿´(‿)´) (kohlenſaurer ~) strontianite (SrCO₃).

Strontium ♌ (´(‿)(‿)´) n ⓑ chm. strontium (Sr); ♀chlorid n strontium chloride (SrCl₂); ♀oxyd n strontium oxide, strontia (= Strontian).

Strophe (´‿) [grch.] f ⓚ 1. thea. Alt. strophe. — 2. pros. (Versgebinde) stanza, auch ʃetzt: verse.

...strophig (...´‿) [Strophe] a. ⓖ in Zſſgn, 3b.: drei♀ of three stanzas.

ſtrophiſch (´‿) [grch.] a. ⓖ pros. strophic; arranged in stanzas.

Stropp (‿) [engl.] ↓ 1. ↓ m u. n (kurzes Tau o. Ende) strop. — 2. m F [ndd.] = Strick. d. i. Schlingel.

ſtroppen (´‿) v/a. ⊛ to strop.

Stroſſe ⚒ (´‿) [tſchech.] f ⓑ (Stufe) stope; Stroſſen-bau m ⓑ stoping.

ſtrotzen (´‿) [nhd.: strut] I v/n. (h.) ⓚ: von et. ♀ to be crammed full of a th., to be swelled up with s.th.; to abound in (or teem with) a th.; von Hochmut ♀ to be puffed up with pride; ♀d voll full to overflowing, crammed full; ♀d swelling, distended (udder, &c.); exuberant, turgescent; vor Geſundheit ♀d in the full enjoyment (or in the pink) of health. — II ~ n ㉓ exuberance, turgescence.

ſtrubb(e)lig (´(‿)‿) a. ⓖ = ſtrob(e)lig.

Strudel (´‿) [mhd.] m ㉒ 1. (Wirbel) whirlpool, eddy, vortex, swirling water; (Schnelle) rapid. — 2. fig. ~ der Geſchäfte pressure (or crush, rush) of business; ~ der Vergnügungen whirl of amusements, round of pleasure.

Strudel-kopf (´‿...) m ㉒ hot-headed (or impetuous) person; ♀köpfig, ♀köpfiſch a. ⓖ hot-headed. impetuous, fiery; auch: giddy, excitable.

ſtrudeln (´‿) I v/n. (h. u. ſn) ⓚa. 1. (ſich wirbelnd drehen) to whirl, swirl, eddy, boil; (ſprudeln, ſchäumen) to bubble, spout, froth, foam. — 2. fig. to be impetuous, to bluster, in der Rede: to sp(l)utter. — II ~ n ㉓ 3. whirl (-ing), eddy(ing); vgl. Strudel 1.

Struktur (‿´) [lt.] f ⓐ (Bau) structure.

Strumpf (´) [mhd.] m ⓒb. 1. (langer Frauen-♀) stocking, (kurzer Männer-♀)

Zeichen (ſ. S. XVII): F familiär; P Volksſprache; Γ Gaunerſprache; \ ſelten; † alt (auch geſtorben); * neu (auch geboren); ⁓+ unrichtig,

[Strumpfband] — 937 — [Studentenstreich]

ſock; ein Paar wollene Strümpfe anziehen to put on a pair of woollen stockings (ſ. anſtricken); ehm. (Fuß- und Bein-beklei̇dung) hose; F fig. e-m auf die Strümpfe helfen to render a p. assistance, to give a p. a lift; ſich auf die Strümpfe m. to make off, to get (or slip) away, F to hook it. — 2. ⊕ (Hülle an Glühlampen für Gas) mantle.

Strumpf-band (⁵...) n ㊅ garter; **-brett** ⊕ n stocking-stretcher; **-fabrik**(ant m) f stocking-manufactory (-manufacturer or -maker); **-flicker**(in f) m st.-mender; **-garn** ✿ n knitting-cotton; **-handel** m, **-händler**(in f) m **-waren-handel**, **-händler**(in); **-hoſe** f trousers and stockings pl. combined; ⁰**los** a. ㊅ stockingless; **-ſtricker**(in f) m st.-knitter; **-waren** ✿ f/pl. hosiery; **-waren-handel** m hosier's business; **-waren-händler**(in f) m hosier, haberdasher; **-weber** ⊕ m stockinger, frameknitter; **-weberei** f manufacture (or making) of stockings; **-wirker**(ei) = **-weber**(ei); **-wirker-garn** ✿ n stocking- (or hosiery-)yarn; **-wirker-ſtuhl** ⊕ m stocking-frame or -loom.

Strunk (⁵) [mhd.] m ⓑb. 1. (Pflanzenſtengel, zB. vom Kohl) stalk, stem. — 2. (Stamm e-s Baumes) trunk; (Stumpf) stump.

ſtrunkig ♀ (⁵) a. ㊅ stalky.

Strunſe(l), **Strunze**(l) (⁵) f ⓢ (Schmutz-weib) slut; alte ~ F old frump or geezer.

ſtruppiert (⁰⁵) [fr. estropié] a. ㊅ man. von Pferden: ⁰e Beine lame legs pl.

ſtruppicht, mſt **...ig** (⁵) [nhd.: ſträuben] a. ㊅ v. Haare: rough, dishevelled, unkempt; v. Barte: bristly, scrubby; neglected; **~keit** f ㊅ roughness, bristliness, scrubbiness.

Struw(w)**el-kopf** F (⁵...) [ſtrubb(e)lig, ſträuben], **-peter** m ㊅ (mit ungekämmten Haaren) person with unkempt hair, F mop-head; „Struw(w)elpeter", Titel eines Kinderbuches: shock-headed Peter.

Strychnin ⚗ (⁰⁵) [grch.] n ⓓd. chm. (heftiges Gift, Alkaloid der Brechnuß) strychnine ($C_{21}H_{22}N_2O_2$); **~ſäure** (⁰⁵-⁵) f ㊅ strychnic acid.

Stubbe (⁵) [: stub] f ㊺, mſt **~n** m ㉓ (Baumſtumpf) stump (of a tree).

Stübchen[1] provc. (⁵) [mlt. stopa] n ㉓ Flüſſigkeitsmaß, etwa: quart.

Stübchen[2] (⁵) n ㉓ (dim. von Stube) (cosy) little room or parlour, beim Schlafzimmer: boudoir; **~vermieten** (⁵...) n ㊅ (Kinderſpiel) puss-in-the-corner.

Stube (⁵) [ahd.: stove] f ㊺ (sitting-)room, apartment, parlour (vgl. Kammer 1); gute ~ = Putzſtube; eine ~ voll Menſchen a roomful of people.

Stuben-älteſte(r) (⁵...) m ㊅ (mſt ✕) senior of the room; **-arreſt** m (meiſt ✕) confinement to one's room; ~ haben to be confined to one's room, von Knaben ꝛc.: to be detained; **-aufſeher** m = **-älteſte**(r); **-burſche** m (student's) fellow-lodger; **-decke** f: a) floor-cloth; b) ceiling of a room; **-fliege** f, ent. common fly (*Musca domestica*); **-gefangene**(r) m person confined to his room; **-gelehrte**(r) m bookworm, savant without practical experience; **-genoſſe** m fellow-lodger; **-heizer** m one who attends to the fires;

-hocker m home-bird, stay-at-home; **-luft** f (impure) air of a room; close (or stuffy) air; **-mädchen** n housemaid, chambermaid; **-maler** m housepainter or -decorator; **-ofen** m stove; ⁰**rein** a. ㊅ v. Hunden u. Katzen: of clean habits, clean(ly); **-ſchlüſſel** m key of a room; **-ſitzer** m = **-hocker**; **-tür**(e) f door of a room; **-uhr** f timepiece; clock; **-vogel** m cage-bird.

Stüber (⁰⁵) [ndl. *stuyver*] m ㉓ ehm. Scheidemünze: stiver. [(ohne pl.) stucco.)

Stuck ⊕ (⁵) [it.; *dtſch Stück] m ⓑb.

Stück (⁵) [ahd.: steak: Stock] n ⑪ (P㉕④)b,6.(f.4) 1. piece, (Biſſen) morsel, (Bißchen) bit; (Teil) part, portion, (Bruchſtück) fragment; fliegendes ~ shiver, splinter; ♪ piece of music; thea. piece, play; ein ~ aufführen oder geben to act a play. — 2. aus einem ~e all of a piece; aus einem ~ beſtehen to be all one piece; ~ für ~ piece for piece, bit by bit; in ~e hauen to knock to pieces; in tauſend ~en a thousand bits, F all to smithereens; ❂ 10 Mark das ~ ... a piece, ... each. — 3. mit nouns: gutes ~ Arbeit good piece of work; ſchweres ~ Arbeit difficult task; ~ Brot (Butterbrot) piece (or slice) of bread (bread-and-butter); F ein ~ von einem Gelehrten a bit of a scholar, ein hübſches ~ (Sümmchen) Geld a good bit (or a nice sum) of money; ~ Land plot of land; ~ Raſen sod; ~ Tuch piece of cloth; ~ (Strecke) Weges (good) stretch, (long) distance; ein ~ Wein a butt of wine; ~ Zucker lump of sugar; bſd. in Zſſgn, zB.: Zweimark-⁵ two-shilling piece. — 4. meiſt inv. 20 ~ Vieh twenty head of cattle; wieviel Fiſche? acht ~ how many fish? eight; ſechs ~ von deinem Buche six copies of ...; P(ein) **~er** (ungefähr) zehn some (or about) ten. — 5. ~ e-r Zeitſchrift number; (Aufſatz) article; ~ aus e-r Rede extract (or passage) from a speech; ~ in einer Sammlung specimen; ❉ ~e pl. (Wertpapiere) stocks, securities pl. — 6. (Wert bildender Kunſt) work of art. — 7. (Tat) meiſt in Zſſgn, zB. Freundſchafts-⁵ act (or mark, proof) of friendship; oft = Streich 2; von (od. aus) freien ~en (aus eigenem Antriebe) of one's own accord, of one's own free will. — 8. (Vorfall) occurrence, event; (Sache, Umſtand) matter, circumstance, point; in allen ~en in all things; in allen ~en zuverläſſig reliable in every way or in every respect; in dieſem ~e in this (particular) instance; in vielen ~en in many points or respects; ſich große ~e einbilden to have high notions of o.s., to be very conceited; vgl. einbilden 2; große ~e auf e-n, et. halten to think a great deal of a p., a th. — 9. ✕ = Geſchütz, Kanone. [vgl. Stuff...]

Stuck-arbeit ⊕ (⁵-⁵) f ㊅ stucco-work;)

Stück-arbeit ⊕ (⁵...) f ㊅ piece-work, jobbing, work paid by the piece or the job; **-arbeiter**(in f) m pieceworker, F jobbing hand; **-butter** f = **Stückenbutter**.

Stückchen (⁵) n ㉓ (dim. von Stück) 1. small piece or morsel or bit; scrap;

verſchiedenartige ~ odds and ends pl. (of things); ~ Bindfaden small end of string; ~ Butter pat of butter; ein ~ Wegs a little way; er hat mir ein ~ (einen Streich) geſpielt he has played me a (nice) trick. — 2. thea. short piece or play; ♪ (popular) air, tune, snatch (of a song).

ſtückeln (⁵) I v/a. ⓢa. to cut (or chop) in pieces or bits; to mince; ⊕ = ausſtückeln. — II ~ n ㉓, **Stück**(e)**lung** f ㊺ chopping (up), mincing.

ſtücken (⁵) v/a. ⑱ 1. to piece (or put) together. — 2. = ſtückeln.

Stücken-butter ⊕ (⁵...) f ㊅ (ant. Faß-butter) butter in lumps; **-zucker** m lump-sugar. [(ſchlottern) to jolt, shake.)

ſtuckern F (⁵) v/n. (h.) ⓢa. von Wagen)

Stück-faß (⁵...) n ㊅ butt, large wine-cask; **-fracht** ⊕ f = -gut; **-gießer**(ei f) m ✝ = Kanonengießer(ei); **-gut** n: a) ✿ = -güter pl. goods in parcels or lots, auch: piece-goods pl.; b) ✝ ✕ = Kanonengut.

ſtückig (⁵) a. ㊅ 1. pieced (together), patched (up). — 2. in Zſſgn, zB. groß-⁵ in large pieces or lots or parcels.

Stück-kohlen ✿ (⁵...) f/pl. ㊅ cobbles pl.; **-meiſter** ✝ ✕ m. artill. (master) gunner; ↓ captain of turret; **-pforte** ↓ f port-hole; **-verkauf** ⊕ m retail-selling or -sale; **-verzeichnis** n specification, inventory; ⁰**weiſe** adv. (F a. a.) piece by piece; piecemeal, in pieces; ✿ (einzeln) by the piece; **-werk** n: a) piece-work; unſer Wiſſen iſt (nur) ~ ... oily patchwork; b) ⊕ = -arbeit; **-zahl** f number of pieces; **-zinſen** ❉ m/pl. interest sg. on shares; **-zucker** m f. Stückenzucker. [(philosophiae etc.).)

stud. (phil. etc.) abbr. = studiosus)

Studel ⊕ (⁰⁵) [mhd.] f ㊺ Waſſerbau: pile, post, pillar; **~bau** (⁰⁵-⁵) m ㊅ pile-work.

Student (⁰⁵) [mhd. 14/15. sae.; *lt.] m ㊷, **~in** f ㊺ student, univ. auch: collegian, undergraduate, nach Erwerbung des akademiſchen Grades: graduate (ein graduate, der noch weiter ſtudiert, heißt, bſd. Am., auch: postgraduate); ~ der Medizin medical student; ~ der Philoſophie in Deutſchland: student of philosophy, in England: graduate in arts; ~ der Rechte law-student; ~ der Theologie student of divinity, theological student; ~ in f lady (or woman, female) student, auch: girl (under)graduate.

Studenten-blume ♀ (⁰⁵...) f ㊅: a) French marigold (*Tagetes patula*); b) = Herzblatt a.

ſtudentenhaft (⁰⁵...) a. ㊅ = burſchikos.

Studenten-jahre (⁰⁵...) n/pl. ㊅ years (spent) at college, college-days pl.; **-kneipe** f room(s) set apart for convivial gatherings of (German) students; **-leben** n student's life, in England: college-life; **-mütze** f student's (in England: college-)cap.

Studentenſchaft (⁰⁵...) f ㊺ 1. (body of) students or collegians. — 2. = Studententum.

Studenten-ſprache (⁰⁵...) f ㊅ students' slang; **-ſtreich** m student's (in Engl. a. undergraduate's) trick.

♪ Muſik; ⚗ Wiſſenſchaft; ♀ Pflanze; ♁ Geographie; ⊕ Technik; ✕ Bergbau; ✕ Militär; ↓ Marine; ✝ Handel; ✉ Poſt; 🚂 Eiſenbahn.

[Studententum] — 938 — [stumpffein]

Studententum (ˇ˘˘-) n ⓓd. student's ways pl. or life or status.
Studenten=verbindung (ˇ˘˘...) f ㊼ students' Club or Association; =viertel n students' quarter. [Ende.]
Studentin (ˇ˘˘) f ㊼ f. Student am**studentisch** (ˇ˘˘) a. ㊏ = burschikos.
Studi-e (´(˘)˘) [it.] f ㊼ 1. (Übungsstück): a) eines Künstlers: study; b) eines Schriftstellers: sketch, essay. — 2. ~n pl. von Studium.
Studi-en=direktor (´´(˘)...) m ㊷, etwa: chairman of an educational council; =gang m course of studies; =genosse m fellow-student; ♀halber adv. for the purpose of study(ing) or attending lectures; =jahre n/pl. years pl. of study; a. college-days pl.; =kopf m, paint. head as (subject of) a study, study of a head; =lehrer m in Bayern: assistant master; =plan m syllabus; =rat m: a) coll. educational council; b) member of an educational council; =zeichnung f sketch, study; =zeit f hours pl. of study, time devoted to reading; a. = =jahre.
studieren (˘´˘) [mhd.; *It.] I v/n. (h.) u. v/a. ⓓ 1. etwas ♀ (geistig bearbeiten) to study a th., to apply o.s. to a th.; durch Lesen: to read up a th.; auf et. ♀ (sinnen) to reflect on a th., to think s.th. over; bisw. v/refl. mit Angabe der Wirkung, z.B. sich krank ♀ to make o.s. ill with reading. — 2. (die Hochschule besuchen) to go to college or to (the) university, to keep one's terms; um e-n Grad zu erlangen: to read for a degree; ♀ lassen to send to college; Mathematik ♀ to study (or read) mathematics; f. Medizin, Jura (ob. die Rechte) ♀ to study (or read) for the law; was studiert er? what is his branch of study or his speciality?; wo hat er studiert? which university has he been to? — II ~ n ③ 3. study(ing), reading. — III ~de(r) s. ㊲ 4. = Student(in). — IV studiert p.p. u. a. ㊿ 5. oft b.s. (erkünstelt) studied, affected, F put on. — 6. im aktiven Sinne: studierter Mann, Studierter university-man, one who has been to college, well-read man, (fine) scholar.
Studier=lampe (˘´´...) f ㊷ reading-lamp; =stube f study; =trieb m zeal for study(ing) or reading; =zimmer n study. [studio.)
Studio¹ (´(˘)-) [it.] n ㊳ (Künstlerwerkstatt)
Studio² F (´(˘)-) [it.] m ㊵, ~sus (-(˘)´˘) m ㊹ = Student; vgl. stud.
Studium (´(˘)˘) [it.] n ㊳ study, reading; seine Studien absolvieren to complete (or finish) one's studies, to go (or pass) through a university-course; j-n Studien eifrig obliegen to pursue one's studies assiduously or strenuously, to be a hard reader or a zealous student.
Stufe (´˘) [ahd.: Staffel] f ㊹ 1. ~ einer Treppe: step, einer Leiter: rung, vor der Haustür: door-step; fig. degree, grade, stage, standard; (Rang=)~ rank; auf gleicher ~ mit on a level (or par) with; höchste ~ der Ehren, des Glücks loftiest height, highest summit or pinnacle...;

~n in der Farbe shades, hues pl. — 2. gr. ~n der Vergleichung ob. Komparation degrees pl. of comparison; ♪ ~n der Töne intervals pl. — 3. ♘: a) notch, step cut in the rock; b) (erz-haltiges Stück) sample of ore.
stufen¹ (´˘) v/a. ㊻ to cut steps in(to).
stufen² (´˘) [nbb.] v/a. = stoben².
Stufen=alter (´´...) n/pl. ㊷ des Menschen: (the several) stages of human life; =artig a. ㊍ like steps; graduated; =bahn f ㊷ moving foot-way; =breite f, arch. width of stairs; =erz ♘ n pure ore; =folge f flight of steps; fig. gradation, gradual advance or progress; =förmig a. in (the) form of steps; vgl. ♀artig; =hauen n cutting (of) steps in ice, &c.; =jahr n, astrol. climacteric (year); =leiter f: a) step-ladder; b) fig. u. ♪ scale; ♀weise adv. (F u. a.) by steps or degrees, gradually, (it.) gradatim.
...stufig (...´˘) a. ㊍ in 3fgn, z.B.: viel=♀ with many steps or grades.
Stuhl (´) [ahd.: stool: stellen] m ⓒ. 1. chair; (Sessel) arm-chair, easy chair; (Schemel) footstool; ~ e-s Kontors (ohne Lehne) stool; geflochtener ~ wicker-chair; ~ eines Lehrers, Meisters: chair; der Apostolische, Heilige oder Römische ~ (Papst) the Holy (or Papal) See. — 2. fig. sich zwischen zwei Stühle setzen to fall (to the ground) between two stools; e-m den ~ vor die Tür setzen to turn a p. out (of doors), durch Entlassung: to send a p. away, to dismiss (or F sack) a p.; durch kühles Benehmen: to give a p. the cold shoulder, F to cut (or snub) a p. — 3. a) = Nachtstuhl, weits. zu ~e geh(e)n to go to the closet or to one's stool; b) = Stuhlgang. — 4. ⊙ Weberei: loom, frame.
Stuhl=bein (´´...) n ㊷ leg of a chair; =bezug m chair-covering.
Stühlchen (´˘) n ㊳ (dim. v. Stuhl) little chair, low stool; vgl. Kinderstuhl.
Stuhl=drang (´´...) m ㊷ urgent need of relieving one's bowels; =entleerung f relief of the bowels; =feier f, =fest n, eccl.: Petri ~ (18. Januar) St. Peter's Day; =flechter(in f) m one who makes (or bottoms) cane-chairs, caner of chairs; =gang m: a) visit (or going) to the closet, opening of the bowels; regelmäßigen ~ haben to go regularly to the closet, to have open bowels; b) (Exkremente) motion, med. stools, fæces pl., physiol.: ☞ fecal matter; =geld n, eccl. pew-rent; =gericht n secret tribunal; =gestell n frame of a chair; chm. =herr m justiciary; =kissen n chair-cushion; =lehne f back of a chair; =macher ⊙ m chair-maker; =richter m bjb. in Ungarn: presiding judge; =rohr n cane for (bottoming) chairs; =schlitten m hand-sledge; =sitz m bottom of a chair; =überzug m covering of a chair; =verhaltung f constipation; =vermieter(in f) m person that lets out chairs; =wagen m basket-carriage; =zwang m, path.: ☞ tenesmus. [stucco-worker.)
Stuffateur (˘˘´F'r) [fr.: Stuck] m ⓓ.f.)
Stuffatur (˘˘´) [it.] f ㊺ stucco-work.
Stuffo (´˘) [it.] m ㊵ = Stuck.

Stulle (´˘) [nbb.] f ㊸ slice of bread and butter; belegte: sandwich; ~n-büchse f ㊷ box for bread and butter.
Stulp, Stülp (´) [nbb.] m ⓑ. s.th. turned up; (Hutkrempe) (b)rim of a hat.
Stulpe, ♦ Stülpe (´˘) [nbb.] f ㊸ 1. = Stulp, bfd. an hohen Stiefeln: top. — 2. (Deckel, Stürze) pot-lid, metal cover.
stülpen (´˘) [Stulp(e)] v/a. ㊻ to turn (inside out); (zurückschlagen) to turn back or up; ein Butterbrot auf das andere ♀ to lay ... on the other; den Hut auf den Kopf ♀ to put one's hat on (one)
Stülpen=stiefel = Stulpstiefel. [side.)
Stülp=handschuhe (´´...) m/pl. ㊷ gauntlets, boxing- (or fencing-)gloves pl.; =hut m turned-up (or cocked) hat.
Stülp=nase (´´˘) f ㊷ turn(ed)-up nose, (fr.) nez retroussé, F u. P snub-nose.
Stülp=stiefel (´´˘) m/pl. ㊷ top-boots, turn-down boots pl.
stumm (´) [ahd.] a. ㊍ (unfähig zu sprechen) dumb; (sprachlos) mute, speechless, voiceless; (schweigend) silent, F mum; F ♀er Gehilfe (Künstler, der die Ehre für f-e Leistung e-m andern einräumt) ghost; ♀es Spiel dumb-show; f. Fisch 1 am Ende; ein ~er, eine ~e ㊲ a dumb person, thea., &c. a mute; gram. ♀es e, h silent (or mute) e, h.
Stummel (´˘) [ahd.] m ㊷ stump of an arm, a tree, &c., fag(-end) of a cigar, candle, &c.; ~affe m ㊷ zo. colobin (Co'lobus); ~pfeife f cutty(-pipe), short pipe.
Stummheit (´˘) f ㊺ dumbness, muteness, path.(Verlust der Stimme): ☞ aphony.
Stumm=laut (´´˘) m ㊷ = Muta.
Stümper (´˘) [nbb.: stumpf] m ㊷, ~in f ㊼ ignorant (or clumsy) person, F duffer; (Pfuscher[in]) botcher, bungler, blunderer, amateur; ~ei (˘˘´) f ㊸ bad work(manship); botching, bungling, amateurism, dilettantism; ♀haft (˘´˘), ♀=mäßig a. ㊏ clumsy, clumsily made; botched, bungled, amateurish.
stümpern (´˘) v/n. (h.) u. v/a. ㊺a. to work clumsily or badly; to botch, to bungle; auf einem Instrumente ♀ to strum on a piano, &c.
stumpf¹ (´) [ahd., f. Stumpf²] a. ㊍ 1. (ant. scharf) blunt, edgeless, ♀, geom., &c.: ☞ obtuse; ♀ machen to blunt. — 2. (ant. spitz) without a point, pointless; math. ♀er Kegel truncate(d) cone; ♀e Nase flat (or pug-)nose; fenc. ♀e Stoßrapiere buttoned foils pl.; typ. ♀ anfangen (enden, halten) to begin (end, make) even. — 3. fig.: a) (der Wirkung beraubt) worn out, used up; ♀ werden, a. to become shaky or weak, F to grow rusty; ♀ (adv.) gerittenes Pferd, oft: broken horse; b) vom Geiste, von den Sinnen: blunt, dull, (geschwächt) enfeebled; (unempfindlich) apathetic, callous, indifferent, (blöde) inert, dense; alt und ♀ old and infirm, broken down with (old) age.
Stumpf² (´) [ahd.: stump; *stumpf¹] m ⓑ. = Stummel; f. Stiel 3.
Stümpfchen (´˘) n ㊳ little stump, einer Kerze ꝛc.: short end.
stumpf¹=eckig (´´˘) a. ㊍ = ♀wink(e)lig.
Stumpf²=ende (´´...) n ㊵ blunted (or pointless) end; ♀¹fein a. ㊏ typ.: ♀e

Signs (see page XVII): F familiar; P vulgar; ґ flash; ⟋ rare; † obsolete (died); * new word (born); ⸭ incorrect; ♪ music;

[**Stumpffuß**] Linie obtuse (or blunt) rule; =**fuß** m club-(or clump-)foot.
Stumpfheit (⸗) f ⓺ (f. stumpf) bluntness, obtuseness, der Nase: flatness; geistige: dulness, denseness; callousness, indifference, apathy.
Stumpf¹=**näschen** (⸗...) n ⓶, =**nase** f pug-nose; ⸗**nasig** a. ⓺ pug-nosed; =²**schwanz** m bobtail; =¹**sinn** m dulness (of wit), (Blödsinn) idiocy; stupidity; ⸗**sinnig** a. dull(-witted), slow of apprehension; vgl. blödsinnig, stupid; =**werden** n growing blunt, losing the edge, fig. growing dull or stupid or indifferent; ⸗**wink(e)lig** a. obtuseangled (triangle); ⸗**zahn** m blunt tooth.
Stündchen (⸗) [Stunde, dim.] n ⓶ short hour; ein ~ verplaudern to have an hour's nice (or cosy) chat.
Stunde (⸗) [ahd.] f ⓺ 1. hour; von ~ zu ~ from hour to hour; in der elften ~ at the eleventh hour, at the last moment; von Stund' an oder ab from that very hour; zur ~ at this hour, at the present moment; (sogleich) immediately; ganze ~n lang for whole hours. — 2. (oft dim. Stündlein) = Todesstunde, zB. seine Stunde hat geschlagen oder ist gekommen his (last) hour has arrived or come. — 3. (Wegemaß, 3,75–4 Kilometer) zB. eine ~ (Wegs) von // an hour's walk (or journey) from //. — 4. (Unterricht) englische ~ English lesson; ~n geben to give lessons; ~n nehmen bei to take lessons of; Schule: ~ halten to give a(n hour's) lesson in class; 4 Mark für die ~ verlangen to ask four shillings a lesson. — 5. in Büchertiteln: ~n pl. der Andacht Hours of Devotion.
stünde (⸗) subj. impf. v. steh(e)n.
stunden (⸗) I v/a. ⓺: e-m eine Summe ~ to allow a p. time (or to grant a p. a respite) for payment. — II ~ n ⓶ f. Stundung.
Stunden=**geber** (⸗...) m ⓶ one who gives lessons, private teacher; =**gebet** n, eccl.: ⚛ horary prayer; =**geld** n fee paid for lessons; =**glas** ⚓ n hour-glass; =**glocke** f bell which sounds the hours; =**kreis** m, ast. hour-circle; ⸗**lang** a. ⓺ lasting (for) hours; adv. for hours (together), vgl. Stunde 1 am Ende; =**lohn** m an hour's wages pl.; =**marke** f ticket for a lesson; =**messer** m: ⚛ horometer; =**messung** f: ⚛ horometry; =**plan** m time-table, school-routine (vgl. Lehrplan); =**rad** ⚙ n e-r Uhr: hour-(or count-)wheel; =**rufer** m watchman (who calls the hours); =**säule** f mile-post; =**schlag** m striking of the hour(s); er kam mit dem ~e ... as the clock struck; mit dem ~e fünf at (or upon) the stroke of five; =**stein** m mile-stone; =**tafel** f ⚓, ast.: ⚛ gnomonic table; =**uhr** f clock which strikes the hours (only); ⸗**weise** adv. (F a. a.) by the hour; =**weiser** m = =**zeiger**; =**winkel** m, ast.: ⚛ horary angle; =**zeiger** ⚙ m einer Uhr: hour-hand.
stündig (⸗) [Stunde] a. ⓺ 1. of (or lasting) one hour, of an hour's duration, ⚛ horary. — 2. in Zssn

mit Zahlen, zB. drei=⚓ of three hours(' duration). [short hour; f. Stunde 2.)
Stündlein (⸗) n ⓶ (dim. v. Stunde))
stündlich (⸗) a. ⓺ 1. hourly, occurring (or repeated) every hour, adv. every hour. — 2. in Zssn mit Zahlen, zB.: zwei=⚓ (repeated) every two hours.
Stundung (⸗) f ⓺ grant of a respite (or short grace allowed) for payment; ~**s**=**frist** f ⓶ time (or grace) allowed for payment; ~**s**=**gesuch** n request for a respite.
stupend (⸜⸝) [It.] a. ⓺ (erstaunlich) stupendous, astounding.
stupid (⸜´) [It.] a. ⓺ (dumm, beschränkt) stupid, narrow-minded; ~**ität** (⸜⸝⸜´) f ⓺ stupidity, narrow-mindedness.
stürbe (⸝) subj. impf. v. sterben.
Sturm (⸝) [ahd.: storm: stören] m ⓸b. 1. (ant. Stille) storm, in geh. Spr.: tempest, ⚓ gale (of wind); heftiger ~ hurricane, cyclone, (Gewitter-)~ electric storm, thunderstorm; (jäher Windstoß) gust of wind; nur ⚓: (stürmisches Wetter) stormy (F dirty) weather; den ~ aushalten, bestehen to weather the storm, ⚓ vor Anker: to ride out a gale; es erhob sich ein ~ a storm arose; f. erregen I am Schluß und stillen 3; fig. ein ~ im Glase Wasser a storm in a tea-cup. — 2. (Ungestüm der Leidenschaft) gust (or burst of) passion, violence, stärker: fury; ~ und Drang storm and stress. — 3. F (Schwindel) giddiness; im ~e sein, einen ~ haben: a) (betrunken sein) to be tipsy; b) to be in a (violent) temper. — 4. (lärmender Andrang) commotion, tumult; noisy crowd. — 5. (Zeichen, Ruf) signal of alarm; ~ blasen to sound the alarm; ~ läuten to ring the alarm-bell. — 6. ⚔ (stürmender Angriff) assault, storming (a position); charge with the bayonet; einen ~ abschlagen to repel an assault, ~ laufen to make an assault; mit ~ nehmen to (take by) storm, to carry by assault or at the point of the bayonet.
Sturm=**angriff**, =**anlauf** ⚔ (⸝...) m ⓺² = Sturm 6; ehm. =**balken** ⚔ m, frt. herisson; =**band** n =**riemen**; =**banner** n =**fahne**; ehm. =**bock** ⚔ m battering-ram; =**brücke** ⚔ f bridge built for the purpose of an assault; =**dach** ⚔ n, frt.: a) röm. Alt.: tortoise, ⚔ testudo; b) jetzt: mantelet; =**egge** ⚔ f, frt. herse.
stürmen (⸝) [ahd.: storm] ⓼ I v/n. (h. u. sn) 1. (h.) der Wind stürmt ... howls or roars; das Wetter (od. **es**) stürmt it is stormy weather, F u. ⚓ it's blowing great guns; fig. in e-n mit Bitten ⚓ (bringen) to importune (or besiege) a p. with one's petitions, to beg hard of a p. — 2. (h.) bsb. ⚔ (im Sturm angreifen) to (make an) assault; to rush to the attack, to charge; mit 2der Hand erobern to take by storm, to carry by assault; auf seine Gesundheit los⚓ to ruin (or to be utterly regardless of) one's health; vgl. a. losstürmen. — 3. (sn) (ungestüm laufen) to rush (or tear) along, to dash (or hurry) forward; sie kamen in den Bahnhof gestürmt they came rushing (or storm-

ing) into the station; fig. (laut lärmen, toben) to storm. rage, rave, fume; durch das Haus ⚓ to storm the house down. — 4. mst v/imp. (h.) es stürmt (läutet Sturm) the alarm-bell (or tocsin) is ringing; vgl. auch 1. — **II** v/a. bfb. ⚔ 5. eine Festung 2c. ⚓ to storm .... (mit Sturm nehmen) to take (or carry) ... by storm or by an assault, to rush ...; mit Leitern ⚓ to scale, to escalade; eine Tür, ein Tor ⚓ to force ... (open); ehm. eccl. die Bilder ⚓ to break the images (of saints). — **III** ~ n ⓶ 6. (f. I u. II) raging of the storm; ⚔ storming, assault; rush; charge; vgl. Sturm 6. — **IV** 2d p.pr. u. a. ⓺ 7. in den Bed. des inf.; bfb. ⚔ die ~den the assailants, the stormers pl., a. = Sturmkolonne. — 8. fig. (ungestüm) impetuous, dashing; (heftig) violent.
Stürmer (⸝) m ⓶ 1. impetuous (or hot-tempered) man, blusterer, hotspur; Fußballspiel: forward. — 2. ⚔ = Sturmläufer, pl. a. = Sturmkolonne.
Sturmes=**brausen** (⸝...), =**tosen** n ⓶ howling (or roaring) of the storm.
Sturm=**fahne** ⚔ (⸝...) f ⓺ (vgl. Sturm 6) war-standard borne in front of a storming party; ⸗**fest** a. ⓺ tempest-proof; =**flagge** ⚓ f storm-flag; =**flut** f tide (or flood) raised by a storm; auch: stormy billows pl.; =**fock** ⚓ f storm-stay-sail; ⸗**frei** a. sheltered from the storm; =**geläute** n ringing the alarm-bell, sounding the tocsin; ⸗**gepeitscht** a. storm-swept; =**glocke** f alarm-bell, tocsin; ehm. =**haube** ⚔ f skullcap, steel cap, cusque, morion; =**hut** m: a) hat which protects against the storm: ⚓ south-wester; b) ⚔ =**haube**; c) ♃ aconite (Aconi'tum); echter ~ monk's-hood (A. Napel'lus); gelber ~ dog's-bane (A. Lycoc'tonum).
stürmisch (⸝)[mhd.]a.⓺:a) stormy, tempestuous; (vom Sturme gepeitscht) storm-swept, -tossed; das Meer ist ⚓ the sea is rough, the waves are running high; ⚓es Wetter stormy (⚓ dirty) weather; b) fig. (ungestüm) impetuous, passionate, boisterous; (heißblütig) hot-tempered; (tobend) uproarious, turbulent; mit ⚓em Beifall begrüßen to greet with tumultuous (or loud) applause; 2(adv.) bewegt passionately moved or agitated.
Sturm=**klüver** ⚓ (⸝...) m ⓶ storm-jib; =**kolonne** ⚔ f assaulting (or storming) party, a. forlorn hope; =**lauf** m: a) Turnen: storming-board; b) ⚔ (a. =**laufen** n) = Sturm 6; =**läufer** ⚔ m soldier taking part in an assault, stormer, weitS. assailer; pl. auch = =**kolonne**; =**läuten** n = =**geläute**; =**leiter** f: a) scaling-ladder; b) ⚓ rope-(ehm.: gallery-)ladder; =**lücke**⚔ f breach in a wall; =**marsch** ⚔ m charge (of a storming party), assault; a. = =**schritt**; =**möwe** f, orn. common gull (Larus canus); =**pfahl** ⚔ m palisade; =**riemen** m für eine Mütze: hat-guard, elastic for a hat or cap; =**säule** ⚙ f e-r Windmühle: central post; =**schritt** ⚔ m double quick march (or step); =**schwalbe** f, orn. stormy (or storm-)petrel (Procella'ria pela'gica); =**stangen** ⚙ f/pl. an der Kutsche:

[Sturmstimme] — 940 — [Subalternoffizier]

coach-joints pl.; =stimme ♪♩ f Orgel: bourdon stop; = und Drang-periode f der deutschen Literatur (1767—1781) Period of Storm and Stress; =vogel m, orn. petrel, ⚔ procellarian (Procella'ria); =warnung(s-signal n) f ↓ storm-signal; =wetter n stormy (or tempestuous) weather; =wind m storm, strong (or heavy) gale, hurricane.

Sturz (⸚) [ahd.: start] m ⓐa. 1. (heavy) fall, (sudden) downfall, tumble, ins Wasser: plunge, v. Pferde: F cropper; (f.-stürzen) crash, collapse, F smash (a. ⚓); (Umstoßen) overthrow, (Purzelbaum) somersault; fig. (Ungnade) disgrace; (Untergang) ruin; (Wasserfall) waterfall, cataract. — 2. (Ungestüm) impetuosity; ein Glas auf einen ~ austrinken to empty ... at one draught or gulp. — 3. ⚒ arch. (Kopfstück) eines Fensters, einer Tür: lintel, cap-piece, platband. — 4. ⚒, ⚒ (Ort, wo gestürzt wird, f. stürzen 5 am Ende) place for dumping (or grassing) ore or tailings, dumping-ground. — 5. ⚓ ~ e-r Kasse audit of accounts.

Sturz-acker (⸚...) m ⚒ field ploughed for the first time; =bach m torrent, rapid stream; =bad m plunge, showerbath; =becher m drinking-cup with a lid; =blech ⚒ n slab-plate; =brücke f = Fall-b.; =bügel man. m safety-stirrup.

Stürze (⸚) f ⚒ dish-cover; (Pfannendeckel) lid of a pan or pot; (Löschhütchen) extinguisher. [mel, Stumpf.]

Sturzel, Stürzel (⸚) m ⚒ = Stummstürzen (⸚) [ahd.: start] ⚒ I v/n. (fn) 1. to fall (heavily), to tumble, ins Wasser: to plunge into the water; vom Pferde: to fall off one's horse, kopfüber: to fall headlong, Sport: F to do a cropper; (umgestoßen w.) to be overthrown, to fall (or come) to the ground, fig. to come to grief. — II v/n. (fn) u. v/refl. 2. von Abgründen: to descend precipitously or perpendicularly. — 3. (sich rasch bewegen; das v/refl. hebt die Absicht hervor) (sich) ⚒ to rush forward; sich in j-s Arme ⚒ to fling (or throw) o.s. into a p.'s arms; er kam ins Haus gestürzt he came rushing into the house; Varus stürzte sich in sein Schwert ... fell upon his sword; sich ins Wasser stürzen: a) (sich ertränken) to drown o.s.; b) (tauchen) to plunge into the water, to dive; e-m zu Füßen ⚒ to throw o.s. at a p.'s feet; fig. sich in Ausschweifungen ⚒ to give o.s. over to (a life of) debauchery; sich blindlings in die Gefahr ⚒ to rush blindfolded into danger; sich in Kosten ⚒ to incur heavy expense(s); sich in Schulden ⚒ to plunge into debt; (wie) toll vorwärts ⚒ (stürmen) to urge on one's wild (or mad) career, to rush madly ahead. — III v/n. 4. faktitiv zu I: to make (or cause to) fall, to hurl, to throw (down), ins Elend: to plunge into misery, ins Verderben: to (bring to) ruin, to undo, vom Throne: to dethrone; abs. e-n Minister, ein Ministerium ⚒ to overthrow ..., to turn ... out (of office). — 5. (umkehren) to turn upside down; ein Behältnis =ausstürzen 1; e-n Krug ⚒ (leeren) to toss off ...; ⚒

e-n Karren ⚒ to shoot (or dip) a cart; e-e Ladung (Erzabfälle) ⚒ to dump a load (of tailings). — 6. einen Deckel über einen Topf ⚒ to put a lid on ...; ⚓ die Kasse ⚒ to count the cash, to audit the accounts, f. Sturz 5. — 7. agr. das Brachfeld ⚒ (aufbrechen) to break ..., to plough ... for the first time. — IV ~ n ⚒ 8. (heavy) fall, tumble, ⚓ von Kursen, Preisen auch: collapse; vgl. Sturz 1.

Sturz-furche (⸚...) f ⚒ agr. first ploughing, newly-ploughed furrow; =gut ⚓ ↓ n, =güter pl. goods laden in bulk; ein Schiff mit =gütern laden to load ... in bulk; =karren m tumbrel; =pflug ⚒ m, agr. fallow-plough; =see ↓ f heavy sea washing (or breaking) over the ship's deck; =stange ⚒ f, arch. lintel-bar; =weg m very steep pathorway; =welle (npl.) f breaker(spl.).

Stuß (⸚) [hebr.] m ⓐa. (Unsinn) nonsense, rubbish, F rot.

Stute (⸚) [ahd.: steed] f ⚒ mare.

Stuten[1] (⸚) m ⚒ (Weißbrot) white bread.

Stuten[2]-fohlen (⸚...) [Stute] n ⚒, =füllen n foal, filly; =milch f mare's milk; f. Kumys.

Stuterei (⸚⸚) f ⚒ stud (= Gestüt).

Stutz (⸚) [mhd.] m ⓐa. = Stoß; auf den ~ (plötzlich) suddenly, all of a sudden.

Stütz (⸚) m ⓐa. Turnerei, etwa: resting (on the parallel bars).

Stütz-ärmel (⸚⸚) m ⚒ short sleeve.

Stütz-balken ⚒ (⸚...) m ⚒ carp. supporting beam; joist; =band ⚒ n. carp. an e-m Balken: jamb.

Stutz-bart (⸚...) m ⚒ turned-up moustache; =bogen ⚒ m, arch. relieving arch; =büchse f bsd. ⚒ short rifle, carbine, ehm.: musketoon; =degen m short sword; =säbel.

Stütze (⸚⸚) [mhd.] = stud] f ⚒ 1. support, prop, (main-)stay (alle auch fig.); ⚒ arch., carp. (Balken, Pfosten) shore, stanchion, supporter, post; (Pfeiler) pillar, (fester Standpunkt) foothold, (firm) footing; (Stab) staff (a. fig.). — 2. ~ der Hausfrau lady's help; zur ~ der Hausfrau to help in the house.

stutzen[1] (⸚) [mhd.; *Stutz] ⚒ I v/a. 1. (kurz abschneiden) to cut short, to curtail (auch fig.); to crop ears, hair, &c., to dock a tail, to trim a beard, to clip wings, to prune (or lop) a tree, a hedge; ⚒ gestutzt ⚒ truncate. — 2. (richtig gestalten) to fashion, to shape; e-n zu et. (zurecht) ⚒ to trim (or dress, rig) a p. up for a th. — II v/n. (h.) 3. to start (back), to be startled, to stop short; bei (ob. über) et. ⚒ to be taken aback by a th.; (im Sprechen stocken) to hesitate (or falter) in one's speech; v. Pferden ꝛc.: sie ⚒ bei dem Geräusche they prick up their ears at the noise. — III ~ n ⚒ 4. (zu I:) curtailment, crop(ping). — 5. (zu II:) starting (back), hesitation.

Stutzen[2] (⸚) m ⚒ = Stutzbüchse.

stützen (⸚) [: stauen] I v/a. u. sich v/refl. ⚒ (f. Stütze) 1. to support, to prop (up), fig. auch: to back (up), to give support (or countenance) to, to be the main-stay of, to coun-

tenance; sich auf et. ⚒ to lean (or rest upon a th.; den (a. sich mit dem) Ellenbogen auf den Tisch ⚒ to rest one's elbow(s) on the table. — 2. (mit Stützen versehen) to provide with supports of props; ⚒ arch., carp. to shore (up) a wall, &c. — 3. fig. sich auf et. ⚒ (verlassen) to rely (or depend) on a th.; f-e Ansprüche ⚒ sich auf // rest (or are founded, are based) upon //; gestützt auf sein gutes Recht fortified by (or relying on) the justice of his cause. — II ~ n ⚒ 4. fig. giving support or countenance, &c. (i. I).

Stutzer (⸚) [mhd.; *stützen 2] m ⚒, ~in f ⚒ fop, beau, bsd. ehm.: dandy, buck, jetzt oft: F (dressed up) swell (auch f), masher; f fashionable lady, F girl (or lady) of the period; die Männer nachäffende ~in, jetzt oft: F co. new woman; stutzerhaft (⸚⸚), stutzermäßig a. ⚒ foppish, dandified, F doing the swell or the masher; stutzern v/n. (h.) ⚒a. to play the fop, F to do the swell.

Stutzertum (⸚⸚) n ⓐd. foppishness.

Stutz-flügel ♪♩ (⸚...) m ⚒ semi-grand (piano); =glas n low tumbler; =handschuh m mitten. [ping on one's hands.]

Stütz-hüpfen (⸚⸚) n ⚒ Turnerei: hop-f

stutzig (⸚⸚) [stutzen[1]] a. ⚒ startled, taken aback; (erstaunt) surprised, (verwirrt) perplexed; (verblüfft) F flabbergasted, flummuxed, ⚒ m. to startle, surprise, perplex, confuse; ⚒ w. to be startled; to be(come) confused or puzzled; Stutzigkeit f ⚒ surprise, perplexity, confusion.

Stutz-kopf (⸚...) m ⚒ (head with) hair cut short, F short crop; =lauf ⚒ m e-r Büchse: short rifled barrel.

Stütz-mauer ⚒ (⸚⸚...) f ⚒ Bauwesen: buttress, auch: retain-wall, am Fuße e-s Abhanges: breast-wall.

Stutz-nase (⸚...) f ⚒ snub-nose; =ohr n cropped ear; ⚒ohrig a. ⚒ crop-eared; =perücke f bobtail-wig.

Stütz-pfeiler (⸚⸚) m ⚒ prop, stay, pillar (auch fig.); =punkt m point of support; eines Hebels: fulcrum; keinen ~ haben to have no support.

Stutz-rohr (⸚...) n ⚒ = =büchse; =säbel m cutlass, hanger; =schwanz m docked tail, bobtail; auch: curtail-horse; ⚒schwänzig a. ⚒ bob-tailed; docked (horse); =uhr f timepiece.

Stütz-wechsel (⸚⸚⸚) m ⚒ Turnerei: changing over (of) hands.

stygisch (⸚⸚) [Styx, Fluß der Unterwelt] a. ⚒ Stygian. [styrol (C_8H_8).]

Styrol (⸚⸚) [grch.] n ⚒d. chm. (Storagol) f. u. abbr. = sieh(e) unten.

Suada (⸚⸚) [lt.] f. inv. 1. npr. myth. (Göttin der Überredung) Suada. — 2. ~ Suade f ⚒ (Überredungsgabe) power of persuasion, persuasive power or faculty; (Redefluß) fluency (or flow) of speech, volubility, F gift of the gab.

Suaheli (⸚⸚⸚) e-r Swahi'li) m, inv. (Volk Ostafrikas) Suaheli, Suahili; ihre Sprache: ~ n, inv. Suaheli.

sub (⸚) [lt.] prp. = unter.

sub-altern (⸚⸚⸚) I a. ⚒ (untergeordnet) subaltern. — II ~e(r) m ⚒, a. ~beamte(r) m ⚒ subordinate (or inferior) official; ~offizier m subaltern (officer).

Zeichen (f. S. XVII): F familiär; P Volkssprache; ⸚ Gaunersprache; ⸚ selten; † alt (auch gestorben); * neu (auch geboren); ⸚ unrichtig;

[Subdiakonus] — 941 — [sudelig]

Sub-diakon(us) (ˇˇᴗ(ᴗ)) [lt.] *m* ①d. ㊷ (⑭㉜) (Hilfs=prediger, =priester) subdeacon.
Subhastation (ˇᴗ-tʃ(ᴗ)ⁿ) [lt.] *f* ㊻ (Zwangs=versteigerung) forced sale; public auction; **subhastieren** (ˇᴗᴗᴗ) *v/a.* ⑬ to sell by public auction, to put up for sale.
Subjekt (ᴗˇ) [lt.] *n* ⓑd. **1** *gr.*, &c. subject. — **2.** F (Kerl) fellow; schlechtes ~ blackguard, villain, scoundrel.
subjektiv ⁊ (ˇ-ᴗˊ) [lt.] *a.* ⓺ *phls.* subjective; *gr.* ~(es Verbum) *n* ⓤb. neuter verb; ~ität (ᴗᴗ-ᴗˊ) *f* ㊻ *phls.* subjectivity.
subkutan (ˇᴗᴗⁿ) [lt. unter die Haut] *a.* ⓺ subcutaneous; ~**spritze** ⁊ (ˇᴗᴗˊˇᴗ) *f* ㊻ *med.* subcutaneous syringe.
sublim (ᴗˊ) [lt.] *a.* ⓺ (erhaben) sublime.
Sublimat (ᴗ-ˊ) *n* ⓤc. *chm.* (sublimiertes) sublimate; engS. = Ätzsublimat; ~**ion** (ᴗ--tʃ(ᴗ)ⁿ) *f* ㊻ *chm.* sublimation. [(verflüchtigen) to sublimate.]
sublimieren ⁊ (ᴗ-ˊ-ᴗ) [lt.] *v/a.* ⓭ *chm.*]
Sublimier=gefäß ⁊ (ᴗ-ˊ-ᴗᴗ) *n* ㊵ sublimating=vessel, sublimatory vessel; **=ofen** *m* sublimator.
Sublimierung (ᴗ-ˊᴗ) *f* ㊻ sublimation.
sub-lunarisch ⁊ (ˇ-ᴗˊ) [lt.] *a.* ⓺ (unter dem Monde befindlich, irdisch) sublunary.
submarin ⌁ (ˇᴗ-ᴗˊ) [spät=lt.] *a.* ⓺ (unterseeisch) submarine (boat, cable, &c.).
submiß (ᴗˊ) [lt.] *a.* ⓺ (D10) (unterwürfig) submissive.
Submission (ᴗᴗ(ᴗ)ⁿ) *f* ㊻: a) (Unterwerfung) submission, subjection; b) ⓡ u. *jur.* (Verdingung) contract (for public works).
Submissions=bedingungen (ᴗᴗᴗᴗᴗ) *f/pl.* ㊵ conditions on which a contract is undertaken or a tender is made; **=strich** *m* line drawn lengthwise from the foot of a document to the signature(s); **=weg** *m*: im ~e vergeben to entrust the execution of public works to one who has tendered for it.
Sub-ordination (ˇᴗ-ᴗ-tʃ(ᴗ)ⁿ) [lt.] *f* ㊻ subordination; **sub-ordinieren** (ˇᴗᴗᴗⁿ) *v/a.* ⓰ (unterordnen) to subordinate.
Subsellium (ᴗˇ(ᴗ)ᴗ) [lt.] *n* ㉘ (Schulbank) form, school=bench, (pupil's) desk.
Subsidi=en (ᴗˊ(ᴗ)ᴗ)[lt.] *pl.inv.*(Hilfsgelder) subsidies *pl.*; ⓡ bounty; durch ~ unterstützen to subsidize; ⓡ von ~ unterhalten bounty=fed (industry); subsidized (line of steamers, &c.).
Subsistenz (ᴗᴗˊ) [spät=lt.] *f* ㊻ (Unterhalt) subsistence; ~**los** (ˊ…) *a.* ⓺ without (any) means of subsistence; ~**mittel** *n/pl.* ㉓ means of subsistence.
Subskribent (ᴗᴗᴗˊ) [lt.] *m* ㊷ subscriber.
subskribieren (ᴗᴗᴗᴗⁿ) [lt.] *v/a.* ⑬: auf et. ~ (unterzeichnen) to subscribe to a th.
Subskription (ᴗᴗᴗtʃ(ᴗ)ⁿ) [lt.] *f* ㊻ subscription, ~**s-anzeige** ⓡ *f* ㊸ prospectus of a new company, publication, &c.; ~**s-ball** *m* subscription=ball; ~**s-liste** *f* subscription=list, list of subscriptions; ~**s-preis** *m* (price of) subscription; ~**s-schein** *m* receipt for a subscription.
Substantialität ⁊ (ᴗˇ(ᴗ)-tʃ(ᴗ)-ᴗˊ) *f* ㊻ (Wesenhaftigkeit) substantiality; **substantiell** (ᴗˇ(ᴗ)ˊ) *a.* ⓺ (wesenhaft) substantial.
Substantiv ⁊ (ᴗˇ-ᴗˊ) [lt.] *n* ⓤd., ~**um** (ᴗˊᴗᴗ) *n* ㊾ *gr.* (Hauptwort) noun, substantive; ᵉ**isch** (ᴗᴗˊᴗ) *a.* ⓺ substantival, *adv.* a. substantively, as a noun.

Substanz (ᴗˊ) [fr.] *f* ㊻ *phls.*, &c. (Stoff) substance, matter; stuff, material.
substituier=en (ᴗᴗᴗᴗⁿ) [lt.] **I** *v/a.* ⓭: e=n e=m ㊶, einer Sache eine andere ㊶ to substitute a p. for a p., a th. for a th. — **II** ~ *n* ㉓ u. ㉟**ung** *f* ㊻ substitution.
Substitut (ᴗᴗˊ) [lt.] *m* ㊷ *jur.* (Stellvertreter) substitute.
Substitutions=methode (ᴗᴗᴗᴗ(ᴗ)ˊ…) *f* ㊵ method of substitution; **=verfahren** ☉ *n* Zuckerfabrikation ⅔.: substitutional method or process.
Substrat ⁊ (ᴗˊ) [lt.] *n* ⓤc. (Grund=, Unterlage) substratum, basis.
subsumieren ⁊ (ᴗ-ᴗᴗⁿ) [lt.] *v/a.* ⓭ *phls.* (mitbegreifen) to subsume; weitS. to comprise in s.th. [sumption.]
Subsumtion ⁊ (ᴗᴗ-tʃ(ᴗ)ⁿ) [lt.] *f* ㊻ sub=]
Subtangente ⁊ (ˇᴗᴗ) [lt.] *f* ㊸ *math.* subtangent.
subtil (ᴗˊ) [lt.] *a.* ⓺ **1.** (zart, fein) subtile, delicate; fine(ly drawn); (spitzfindig) subtle. — **2.** *adv.* man muß mit ihm sehr ㊶ umgehen he has to be treated (or managed) with great caution or circumspection.
Subtrahend ⁊ (ᴗᴗˊ) [lt.] *m* ㊷ *arith.* (abzuziehende Zahl; *ant.* Minuend) subtrahend, value to be subtracted.
subtrahieren ⁊ (ᴗᴗᴗⁿ) [lt.] *v/a.* ⓭ *arith.* (abziehen) to subtract, to take away.
Subtraktion ⁊ (ᴗᴗ-tʃ(ᴗ)ⁿ) [spät=lt.] *f* ㊻ subtraction; ~**s-aufgabe** (ˊ…) *f* ㊸ subtraction sum; ~**s-methode** *f* method of subtraction.
subtropisch (ˇᴗˊ) *a.* ⓺ (an die Tropen grenzend) subtropical; semitropical.
Subvention (ᴗᴗtʃ(ᴗ)ⁿ) [spät=lt.] *f* ㊻ (Geldhilfe) subsidy (vgl. Subsidien).
subventionieren (ᴗᴗᴗ-ᴗᴗⁿ) [spät=lt.] *v/a.* ⓰ ((staatlich) unterstützen) to subsidize; subventionierte Dampferlinie subsidized (or state=aided) line of steamers.

Such=blatt (ˊ…) *n* ㊶ Questions and Answers *pl.*, Exchange and Mart; **=buch** *n* (Nachschlagewerk) book of reference.
Suche (ˊᴗ) [ahd.] *f* ㊸ search, *hunt.* tracking, scenting; auf der ~ nach in search (or quest) of, on the track of; auf die ~ gehen to go in search of a th., to go searching; auf der ~ sein to be on the look=out or F on the hunt. [probe.]
Such=eisen (ˊ…) *n* ㊷ der Wundärzte =]
suchen (ˊᴗ) [ahd.] ~**seek**: lt. *sagī're*: Sache] **I** *v/a.* und *v/n.* (h.) ⑱ **1.** et. ㊶ to seek for (or after) a th., stöbernd: to search (or hunt) for a th., forschend: to go in search (or quest) of a th., schauend: to look (out) for a th.; e=n Arbeiter &c. durch die Zeitungen ㊶ to advertise for …; ich habe was Sie ㊶ I have what you want or require; was hat er hier zu ㊶ (zu tun)? what business has he (to be) here? — **2.** mit *nouns*: Abenteuer ㊶ to go in quest of adventures; eine Ausflucht ㊶ to try to find an excuse; f. Handel 3; j-s Verderben ㊶ to seek (or plot) a p.'s ruin; das Weite ㊶ to run away, to beat a hasty retreat. — **3.** *mit prp. u. adv.*: et. **an** einem ㊶ to look for th. in a p.: das hätte ich **hinter** (oder **in**) Ihnen nicht gesucht (vermutet) I should not have thought (or could not have believed) that of

you; in allem et. ㊶ to be easily offended; seine (oder eine) Ehre in et. ㊶ (setzen) to glory in a th., to pride o.s. upon a th.: er sucht et. darin, jeden zu beleidigen he makes it a point to offend everybody; nach et. ㊶ (forschen) to inquire for (or after) a th.; nach Worten ㊶ (haschen) to be at a loss for words; was mag er nur darunter ㊶ (damit beabsichtigen)? what may he intend (or mean) by that? — **4.** mit Objektivsätzen: to seek (or try) to; sie ㊶ ihn zu überreden they try (or endeavour, seek) to persuade him. — **II** ~ *n* ㉓ **5.** search, quest; inquiry. — **III** ge=**sucht** *p.p.* und *a.* ⓺ **6.** sought for or after (s. I); Anzeige: gesucht (wird) eine Stelle &c. wanted a situation, &c.; das Gesuchte finden to find the thing wanted or required. — **7.** f. gesucht 2, 3.
Sucher (ˊᴗ) *m* ㉒, ~**in** *f* ㊼ **1.** person who seeks or searches, searcher after truth, &c. — **2.** *surg.* (Werkzeug) probe.
Such=glas (ˊ…) *n* ⓥ, **=rohr** *n*, *ast.* finder; **=hund** *m*, *hunt.* hound that tracks (or follows) the scent; **=ort**, **=schacht** ⚒ *m* prospecting=shaft.
Sucht (ˊᴗ) [ahd.] *siechen] *f* ㊻ (⑩) **1.** sickness, disease, complaint, meist mit *a.* oder in Zssgn, zB. fallende ~ Fallsucht; engS. (Entkräftung) debility, weak (or languishing) state. — **2.** [P: suchen] (krankhafte Begier) mania, passion, rage (nach et. for a th.); sie hat eine wahre ~, sich zu putzen she has quite a craze (or a perfect mania) for dress (=ing), she is madly fond of fine clothes; (krankhafte) ~ zu stehlen (Feuer anzulegen) ⁊ kleptomania (pyromania).
Such=tau ⌁ (ˊ…) *n* ⓥ **=** drag=rope.
süchtig (ˊᴗ) [Sucht] *a.* ⓺ **1.** a) suffering from a chronic malady; b) in Zssgn, zB. gelb~ suffering from jaundice. — **2.** zu Sucht 2 in Zssgn, zB. eifer~ (s. b).
Sud (ˊ) [mhd.: sieden] *m* ⓤc. seething, boiling; (Absud) decoction; a. = Brau~.
Süd (ˊ) [ndd.: south] *m* ⓤc., mit *art.* f. Süden (oft *abbr.* **S.**) south (*abbr.* S.).
Süd-afrika, **=amerika** ℚ (ˊ…) *npr* *n.* South Africa, South America.
Sudan ℚ (-ˊ, oft ˊ-ˊ) [*ar. pl.* die Schwarzen] *npr/m.* ⓡa: der ~ (Nord=afrika) the Soudan, der Krieg im ~ (gegen die Mahdisten, 1896—1898) the Soudan war.
sudanisch (-ˊᴗ) *a.* ⓺ Soudanese.
Süd=breite ℚ (ˊ…) *f* ㊸ south latitude; **°deutsch** *a.* ⓺ South German; **=deutschland** *npr/n.* South Germany.
Sudel (ˊᴗ) [mhd. Garkoch; *sieden] *m* ㉓ (Pfütze) puddle, pool, quagmire; weitS. (Dreckhaufen) heap of dirt or muck.
Sudel=arbeit (ˊ…) *f* ㊸ **=** Sudelei; **=bogen** ☉ *m*, *typ.* waste=sheet.
Sudelei (-ᴗˊ) *f* ㊻ **1.** = sudeln II. — **2.** (oberflächliche Arbeit) slop=work; (schlechtes Bild) daub, worthless painting; (Gekritzeltes) scribble, scrawl.
Sud(e)ler (ˊ(ᴗ)ᴗ) *m* ㉒, **Sudlerin** *f* ㊼ [(: sutler] **1.** = Sudel=koch, =köchin. — **2.** (Pfuscher, Schmierer) quack, botcher, dauber, sloven(ly worker); (Kritzler) scribbler, scrawler.
sudelhaft (ˊᴗᴗ), **sud(e)lig** (ˊ(ᴗ)ᴗ) *a.* ⓺ slovenly, unclean, nasty, F messy.

[Sudelkoch] — 942 — [Sumpfluchs]

Sudel-koch (ᴵᵛ...) m ②, **-köchin** f slovenly (or dirty) cook; **-magd** f, etwa: scullery-maid; **-maler** m dauber.

sudeln (ᴵᵛ) [mhd.: sieden] **I** v/n. (h.) u. v/a. ②a. 1. to work (or do) in a slovenly fashion; (manchen) to mess about (vgl. besudeln). — 2. (pfuschen) to botch, to bungle, malend: to daub, schreibend: to scribble, to scrawl. — **II** ~ n ② 3. (f. 1) slovenly work or workmanship or style, (f. 2) botching, bungling, daubing, scribbling.

Sudel-wäsche (ᴵᵛ...) f ②: a) linen got up in a slovenly style or fashion; b) dirty (or foul) linen.

Süden (ᴵᵛ) [f. Süd] m ㉓: im ~ der Stadt (to the) south of the town; der Wind weht von ~ the wind blows from (or is in) the south.

süd-französisch (ᴵᵛ...) a. ⑥⑥ South French; **-früchte** ⚥ f/pl. ⑫ southern fruit(s pl.), fruit(s pl.) from the south; **-grenze** f south(ern) frontier; **-kreuz** n, ast. (Sternbild in der Nähe des Südpols) Southern Cross; **-küste** f south(ern) coast; **-land** n southern country, a. = **-polarland**; **-länder(in** f) m inhabitant of a southern country, seltener: southerner.

Sudler (ᴵᵛ) m ② f. Sud(e)ler.

südlich (ᴵᵛ) a. ⑥⑥ south(ern), southerly, lying to(wards) the south, ⚕ meridional, austral, antarctic ♀ das ♀e Eismeer the Antarctic Ocean; ~es Kreuz = Südkreuz; ♀ von Spanien (to the) south of Spain; ♀st. am ♀sten south(er)most.

Süd-licht (ᴵᵛ...) n ⑫ phys. southern light, (lt.) aurora australis; **-ost(en)** m (abbr. S. O.) south-east (abbr. S. E.); **♀östlich** a. ⑥⑥ south-east (von // of //); **-pol** m south- (or antarctic) pole; **-polarland** n antarctic country or region; **-see** ⚥ npr/f. Pacific (Ocean), bsd. ehm.: South Sea; **-see-länder** ⚥ npr/n/pl. Australasia; **-seite** f south (or southern) aspect, south (or sunny) side; **-sonne** f noon; **-staaten** m/pl. southern states pl.; Krieg gegen die ~ der Union (1861—1865) War of Secession; ♀staatlich a. of (or belonging to) the southern states; **-süd-ost** m, ♀**süd-östlich** a. south-south-east; **-süd-west** (**-lich** a.) m south-south-west; ♀**wärts** adv. southward, to the south; **-west-afrika** ⚥ deutsche Kolonie: South West Africa; **-west(en)** m (abbr. S. W.) south-west (abbr. S. W.); **-wester** ⚓ m (Seemannshut) southwester, sou'wester; **-wester-sonne** ⚓ f three o'clock in the afternoon; ♀**westlich** a. south-west(ern); **-wind** m south wind, southerly breeze.

Sueven (ᴵᵛʷ) npr/pl. inv. röm. Alt.: (germanischer Volksstamm) Suevi pl. (= Schwaben). [ägyptische Stadt: Suez.]

Suez ♀ (ᴵᵛᵗˢ, auch: ᴵᵛ) npr/m, inv. **Suez-kanal** (ᴵᵛ...) m ⑫ zwischen dem Mittelländischen u. Roten Meere: Suez Canal.

Suff (ᵛ) [saufen] m ⑫⑦b: dem stillen ~ ergeben (fond of) tippling on the sly.

Suffet (ᵛᴵ) [lt. *phön.] m ⑫ Alt.: (hoher karthagischer Würdenträger) suffete.

süffig F (ᴵᵛ) [saufen] a. ⑥⑥ delicious, nice (or pleasant) to drink.

Suffix ⚕ (ᵛᴵ) [lt.] n ①a., gr. (angehängte Silbe) suffix.

Suffragan-bischof (ᵛᵛ⁻ᴵᵛ) [lt. Wahl-] m ⑫ eccl. (Weihbischof) suffragan (bishop).

suggerieren (ᵛᵛᴵᵛ) [lt.] v/a. ⑱ (bsd. einen Hypnotisierten beeinflussen) to suggest, abs. to influence a p.'s mind (or to direct a p.'s actions) by suggestions.

Suggestion (ᴵᵛ(ᵛ)ᴵᵛ) [lt.] f ⑭ Beeinflussung bsd. e-s Hypnotisierten) suggestion.

suhlen, sühlen (ᴵᵛ) v/n. (h.) u. sich ♀ v/refl. ⑱ hunt. to wallow in the mire.

Sühn-altar (ᴵᵛ·ᴵ) m ⑫ altar of expiation.

sühnbar (ᴵ⁻) a. ⑥⑥ expiable, atonable.

Sühnbarkeit (ᴵ⁻) f ⑭ possibility of expiating (or atoning for) an offence.

Sühn-bock (ᴵᵛ) m ⑫ bibl. u. fig. scapegoat. **-e** (ᴵᵛ) [mhd.] f ⑱ (Versöhnung) propitiation, reconciliation, (Buße u. Genugtuung) expiation, atonement.

sühnen (ᴵᵛ) [ahd.: versöhnen] **I** v/a. ⑱ et. ♀ (büßend gutmachen) to expiate a th., to atone for a th.; ♀d expiatory. — **II** ~ n ㉓ = Sühne.

Sühne-verfahren (ᴵᵛ...) n ⑫ proceedings for (the purpose of) conciliating contending parties; **-versuch** m attempt at reconciliation.

Sühn-geld (ᴵ...) n ⑫ bsd. ehm. fine paid for a murder, &c.; **-opfer** n rel. expiatory offering, propitiating sacrifice, bibl. und fig. atonement.

Sühnung (ᴵᵛ) f ⑭ = Sühne.

Suite (ᵛⁱᵗ'ᵛ) [fr.] f ⑭ 1. (Gefolge) suite, retinue, train. — 2. (Streich) trick.

Suitier (ᵛⁱᵗ-ᵗⁱ'ᵉ', a. schwi...) [fr.] m ⑫ dissipated (or fast) fellow; (toller Bursche) gay spark, giddy (young) fellow.

Sukkurs (ᵛᴵ) [lt.] m ①a., meist ⚔ (Verstärkung) succour, reinforcement.

Sukkursale ⚥ (ᵛ⁻ᴵ⁻ᵛ) [fr.] f ⑫ (Zweiggeschäft) branch of a business, branch office.

sukzedieren (ᵛ⁻ᴵ⁻ᵛ) [lt.] v/n. (fein) ⑱: e-m ♀ (nachfolgen) to succeed a p.

Sukzession (ᵛᵛ(ᵛ)ᴵ) [lt.] f ⑭ meist jur. succession; ♀**-berechtigt** (ᴵ...) a. ⑥⑥, ♀**-fähig** a. entitled to succession, capable of succeeding to an estate, &c.; **~s-krieg** m ⑫ war of succession.

sukzessiv (ᵛᵛ⁻ᴵᵛf) [lt.] a. ⑥⑥ (auf ea. folgend) successive; ♀e (ᵛ⁻ᴵᵛʷ) adv. successively, in succession.

Sulfat ⚥ (ᵛᴵ) [neu-lt. sulp(h)ur] n ⑫ chm. (schwefelsaures Salz) sulphate.

Sulfid ⚥ (ᵛᴵ) n ⑫ (Schwefelverbindung) sulphide. [SO₄) sulphion.]

Sulfion (ᵛ(ᵛ)ᴵ) n ⑫ chm. (Radikal

Sulfit ⚥ (ᵛᴵ) [lt.] m ⑫ chm. (schwefligsaures Salz) sulphite.

Sulfo-salz ⚥ (ᵛᵛᴵ...) n ⑫ chm. sulphosalt, sulphosel; **-säure** f (saure Schwefelverbindung) sulpho-acid.

Sultan (ᵛᴵ, mst ⁺⁺ ᵛ⁻) [ar.] m ⑫d., **~in** (ᵛᴵᵛ, ᵛᵛᴵ) f ⑭ (mohammedanischer Herrscher) sultan, f sultana, ...ess; **~at** (ᵛᵛᴵ) n ⑫c. sultanship, sultanate; country ruled by (or rank, reign, sway of) a sultan; **~ine** f (ᵛᵛᴵ) f ⑭ (Art Rosine) sultana (raisin).

Sultans-blume ⚥ (ᵛ⁻ᴵ...) f ⑫ sultan (-flower) (Centaurea moscha'ta); **-huhn** n; **-würde** f sultanship.

Sulze, Sülze (ᴵᵛ) [ahd.: *Salz] f ⑫ 1. brine. — 2. Kochkunst: (gallertartige Masse) jelly; (davon umschlossenes Fleisch) meat preserved in jelly; brawn.

sulzen, sülzen (ᴵᵛ) [Sulze, Sülze] v/a. ⑳ Kochkunst: to preserve (in jelly).

Sumach ⚥ (ᴵ⁻ch) [ar.] m ⑪d. sumac (-tree) (Rhus); chilenischer ~ (Rhus cau'stica); echter ~ = Gerberbaum; japanischer ~ red-lac (Rhus succeda'nea).

Summa (ᴵᵛ) [lt.] f ⑭ = Summe, meist nur adv.: in ~ (kurz) to sum up (briefly), in short, taking it all in all; ~ Summa'rum (Gesamtbetrag) sum total.

Summand (ᵛᴵ) [lt.] m ⑫ arith. term of a sum, (Posten) item.

summarisch (ᵛᴵᵛ) [lt.] a. ⑥⑥ (kurzgefaßt, rasch) summary; ♀ (adv.) vorgeh(e)n to take summary proceedings.

Sümmchen (ᴵᵛ) n ㉓ (dim. von Summe) small sum; nettes ~ round little sum (of money), F nice little pile.

Summe (ᴵᵛ) [mhd., *lt.] f ⑭ sum (auch math.) total; große ~ Geldes considerable sum (or large amount) of money; eine fehlende Summe ergänzen to make up a deficit or deficiency; höchste (niedrigste) ~ maximum (minimum).

summen¹ (ᴵᵛ) [mhd. lautm.] v/n. (h.) und v. a. ⑱ von Bienen ꝛc.: to buzz, v. Kreiseln ꝛc.: to hum; oder Laut a. droning sound; mir ♀ die Ohren my ears are buzzing or tingling; ein Liedchen ♀ ⑱ to hum a tune.

summen² (ᴵᵛ) [Summe] ⑱ = summieren.

Summ-episkopat (ᵛᵛᴵ⁻ᵛᵛᴵᵛ) [lt.] n (m) ⑪c.: ~ des Königs in der evangelischen Kirche: position as supreme head of the Protestant Church.

summieren (ᵛ⁻ᴵ⁻) [lt.] **I** v/a. u. v/refl. ⑱ to add (or sum) up, auch to cast (F to tot) up; sich ♀ to sum (or total) up, to run up. — **II** ~ n ㉓, **Summierung** f ⑭ addition, summing up, casting (F totting) up.

Sumpf (ᵛ) [ahd.: swamp] m ⑦b. swamp, bog; (sumpfiges Land) auch: marsh(y country), fen; einen ~ austrocknen to drain a marsh; im ~ stecken bleiben to stick in the mud; fig. ~ der Schändlichkeit den (or pool) of infamy; zo. in Sümpfen lebend: ⚕ stagnicolous, vgl. sumpfbewohnend.

sumpf-bewohnend (ᵛ...) a. ⑥⑥ living in marshes, ⚕ paludicole; **-bewohner** m ⑫ inhabitant of a fen-country; irischer ~. oft co. bog-lander, -trotter; **-dotter-blume** ⚥ f = Dotterblume.

sumpfen (ᵛ) v/n. (h.) ⑱ to be boggy; auch fig. (liederlich leben) to lead a dissolute (or fast) life.

Sümpfer ⊖ (ᵛ) [Sumpf] m ⑫ Ziegelei: workman kneading clay.

Sumpf-erz (ᵛ...) n ⑫ min. bog-iron ore; **-farn** ⚥ m marsh-fern (Aspi'dium thely'pteris); **-fieber** n. path. marsh-fever, malaria; **-garbe** ⚥ f ptarmica (Achille'a pta'rmica); **-gas** n. chm. (Metha'n) marsh-gas (CH₄); **-gegend** f swampy district; **-huhn** n: a) orn. moorhen (Rallus); b) F fig. (Wüstling, Säufer) debauchee, boozer, rake.

sumpficht, sumpfig (ᴵᵛ) a. ⑥⑥ swampy, marshy, boggy, ⚕ paludal, paludinous.

Sumpf-lache (ᵛ...) f ⑫ pool, quagmire; bsd. ehm. auch: slough; **-land** n marshy (or fen-)country, marshland; **-loch** n = -lache; **-luchs** m, zo. chaus

Signs (see page XVII): F familiar; P vulgar; ꝼ flash; ⚘ rare; † obsolete (died); * new word (born); ⁺⁺ incorrect; ♪ music;

[Sumpfmeise] — 943 — [süß]

(*Felis chaus*); =**meise** *f*, *orn.* marshtit (-mouse) (*Parus palu'stris*); =**moor** *n* moor, bog; =**parnassen-kraut** ⚕ *n* marsh-grass of Parnassus (*Parna'ssia palu'stris*); =**pflanze** ⚕ / plant thriving in marshy soil; =**porst** ⚕ *m* marsh-rosemary (*Ledum palu'stre*); =**schachtel-halm** ⚕ *m* tad-pipe (*Equise'tum limo'sum*); =**schildkröte** *f*, *zo.* mud-turtle (*Emys luta'ria*); =**schnepfe** *f* = Bekassine; =**viole** *f* = Schwanenblume; =**vogel** *m*, *orn.* wading bird, wader; =**wasser** *n* marshy (or boggy) water; =**weihe** *f*, *orn.* marsh-harrier (*Circus rufus*); =**wiese** *f* marshy (or swampy) meadow; =**zieft** ⚕ *m* marsh-woundwort, clown's all-heal (*Stachys palu'stris*).
Sums P (⁵) [mhd.] *m* ⓐa. (ohne *pl.*) buzzing (or humming) noise.
sumsen (⁵) *v/n.* (h.) ⓐ = summen¹.
Sund (⁵) [ndd.] *m* ⓑb. (Meerenge) strait (s *pl.*); ♀ = zw. Seeland u. Schweden: Sound.
Sunda-inseln ♀ (⁵-...) *f/pl.* ⓐ Sunda Islands *pl.*; =**straße** *f* zw. Sumatra u. Java: Sunda Strait.
Sünde (⁵) [ahd.: sin] *f* ⓐ sin, trespass (a. *rel.*); (Vergehen) offence, (Missetat) misdeed, (piece of) iniquity; (Übertretung) transgression, fault; *theol.* läßliche ~ venial offence; eine ~ begehen to commit an offence, vgl. sündigen; kleine ~n (s)light offences, F peccadilloes *pl.*; *fig.* es ist eine ~ (meist: Sünd') und Schande ober eine himmelschreiende ~ it is a sin and a shame or a wicked shame; ich hasse ihn wie die ~ I hate (or loathe) the very sight of him.
Sünden-bahn (⁵...) *f* ⓐ way of sin, sinful life; =**bock** *m*, *bibl.* scape-goat, *fig.* auch: one who suffers for (the wrongs of) others, F whipping-boy; =**erlaß** *m*, *eccl.* remission (or forgiveness) of sins, absolution (of sins); =**fall** *m* fall of man; ⁇**frei** *a.* ⓐ free from sin, guiltless; =**geld** *n*: a) ill-gotten money; b) = Heidengeld; =**knecht** *m* slave of sin, hardened sinner; =**knüppel** F *m*: alter ~ wicked old sinner; =**last** *f*, *rel.* burden of sin; =**leben** *n* life of sin, sinful existence; ein ~ führen to live in sin; ⁇**los** *a.* sinless (= sünd-los); =**losigkeit** *f* = Sünd-losigkeit; =**lust** *f* inclination to sin, pleasure derived from sin; =**maß** *n*: sein ~ war voll the measure of his iniquities was full; =**pfuhl** *m* pool of sin, den of iniquity; sich in einem ~e wälzen to wallow in sin; =**register** *n* register (or list, F budget) of sins; =**schuld** *f* guilt, (sum of) transgressions; =**tilger** *m*, *rel.* Redeemer, Saviour; =**tilgung** *f* blotting out of sin, propitiation; =**vergebung** *f* = =**erlaß**; ⁇**voll** *a.* full of sin or iniquity, sinful.
Sünder (⁵) [ahd.] *m* ⓐ, ~**in** *f* ⓐ 1. sinner, offender, transgressor; verstockter ~ hardened sinner. — 2. armer ~, arme ~in (dem peinlichen Gerichte Anheimfallende *r*) culprit, malefactor; criminal (lying under sentence of death or awaiting execution; vgl. Armesünder bei arm² 4.
Sünd-flut *2c.* s. Sintflut *2c.*
sündhaft (⁵) *a.* ⓐ von Taten: ⁇**igkeit** (⁵-) *f* ⓐ sinfulness, iniquity.

sündig (⁵) *a.* ⓐ 1. sinful, (schuldig) guilty, culpable; (zur Sünde geneigt) liable (or inclined) to sin, *theol.* bisw. peccant, peccable; wir sind nur ⁇ Menschen we are but poor (or miserable) sinners. — 2. = sündlich.
sündigen (⁵...) *v/n.* (h.) ⓐ to (commit a) sin, to trespass; was habe ich gesündigt? what wrong have I done?, in what (way) have I transgressed?; an ein*m* ⁇ to wrong a p.; **wider** Gott ⁇ to sin (or offend) against God.
Sündiger (⁵...) *m* ⓐ sinner.
Sündigkeit (⁵...) *f* ⓐ sinfulness.
sündlich (⁵) *a.* ⓐ von Taten: sinful, iniquitous; (unerlaubt) illicit, unlawful; (gottlos) impious; ~**keit** (⁵...) *f* ⓐ sinfulness, iniquity.
sünd-los (⁵...) *a.* ⓐ *rel.* sinless, bisw. impeccant, impeccable; ~**losigkeit** *f* ⓐ sinlessness, seltener: impeccancy.
Sunn-hanf ⚕ (⁵...) [ſft.] *m* ⓐ sunn (Bast von *Crotula'ria iu'ncea*).
Sunnit (⁵...) *m* ⓐ (e-r ber außer dem Koran die Sunna(h) anerkennt; *ant.* Schiit) Sunnite, believer in the Sunna(h).
super-fein (⁵-...) [nhd. 16. *sae.*] *a.* ⓐ superfine, very choice or select, a. A 1.
Super-intendent (⁵...) [lt.] *m* ⓐ, ~**in** *f* ⓐ *eccl.* bei Protestanten: superintendent (of churches and schools); ~**in** *f* sup.'s wife; ~**ur** (⁵...) *f* ⓐ superintendent's residence or post.
Superior (⁵...) [lt. Obere(r)] *m* ⓐ, ~**in** (⁵...) *f* ⓐ in Klöstern: (Father, f Lady) Superior. [legenheit) superiority.⁊
Superiorität (⁵...) [lt.] *f* ⓐ (Über-⁊
Superkargo (⁵...) ⚓ (⁵...) [span.] *m* ⓐ (Aufseher über die Ladung) supercargo.
super-klug F (⁵...) [nhd. 17. *sae.*] overwise, *iro.* too knowing, too clever (by half); ~**e**([r] *m*) *f* ⓐ wiseacre, prig.
Superlativ (⁵...) *m* ⓐd., ~**us** (⁵...) *m* ⓐ *gram.* superlative (degree); ⁇**isch** (⁵...) *a.* ⓐ (used) like a superlative.
Supernaturalismus (⁵...) [lt.] *m* ⓐ *theol.* supernaturalism.
Supernaturalist (⁵...) [lt.] *m* ⓐ *theol.* supernaturalist; ⁇**isch** *a.* ⓐ (übernatürlich) supernaturalist(ic).
Supernumerar (⁵...) *m* ⓐd., ~**ius** *m* ⓐ (überzähliger) supernumerary, F super; ~**iat** *n* ⓐc. supernumerary's post.
Super-oxyd ⚗ (⁵...) *n* ⓐc. *chm.* (höchstes Oxyd) superoxide, mehr gbr.: peroxide.
Superphosphat (⁵...) *n* ⓐc. *agr.*, *chm.* superphosphate (of lime).
Super-revision (⁵...*w*...)(-)(⁵) *f* ⓐ final revision; ⁇ *typ.* last proof, revise.
Supinum ⚗ (⁵...) [lt.] *n* ⓐ lt. *gram.* (z. B. factu(m) um zu machen) supine.
Süppchen (⁵...) *n* ⓐ small plate of soup or porridge; nice soup or broth.
Suppe (⁵) [fr.: soup; *nhd.: saufen]* f* ⓐ 1. soup, aus Hafermehl *2c.*: porridge; (Brühe) broth, vgl. Fleischbrühe; schwarze ~ der Spartaner: black broth; e-n auf einen Löffel ~ einladen to ask a p. to (a snack of) dinner or lunch; F rote ~ blood, Boxer-sl.: claret. — 2. *fig.* die ~ ausessen müssen to have to abide by the consequences; er hat es. in die ~ zu brocken he is well off, F he's in clover; he has a nice

little pile; s. einbrocken 2; das macht die ~ nicht fett s. fett 1; e-m die ~ versalzen to spoil a p.'s pleasure.
Suppen-anstalt (⁵...) *f* ⓐ soup-kitchen; =**fleisch** *n* meat to make soup of or with; boiled beef or mutton; =**freund** (in *f*) *m* one who is fond of soup; =**grieß** ⚕ *m* ground rice for soup; =**kaspar** *m* im deutschen Kinderbuche: the boy who would not eat soup and was reduced to a skeleton; =**klößchen** *n* small dumpling in the soup; =**kräuter** *n/pl.* potherbs *pl.*; =**löffel** *m*: a) (Eßlöffel) tablespoon; b) (zum Vorlegen) soup-ladle; =**marke** *f* für arme Leute: soup-ticket; =**napf** *m*, =**schüssel** *f* soup-tureen; =**schnittchen** *n* sippet; =**tafel** *f* condensed soup (in tablets); =**teller** *m* soup-plate; =**terrine** *f* = =**schüssel**; =**topf** *m* pot for making soup, stock-pot.
suppicht, mst **suppig** (⁵...) *a.* ⓐ soup- (or broth-)like, weitS. juicy, succulent.
Supplement (⁵...) [lt.] *n* ⓐc. (Ergänzung) supplement (auch *math.*).
Supplement-band (⁵...) *m* ⓐ supplementary volume; =**winkel** *m*, *math.* (Ergänzung zu 180 Grad) supplement.
supplieren (⁵...) [lt.] *v/a.* ⓐ (ergänzen) to supplement; to make up.
Supplik (⁵...) [lt.] *f* ⓐ (Bittschrift) petition.
Supplikant (⁵...) *m* ⓐ, ~**in** *f* ⓐ petitioner.
supplizieren (⁵...) [lt.] *v/n.* (h.) ⓐ: um et. ⁇ (ansuchen) to petition (or sue) for a th. [setzen) to suppose, to presume.⁊
supponieren (⁵...) [lt.] *v/a.* ⓐ (voraus-⁊
supra (⁵...) [lt.] *adv.* = oben 1.
Supremat (⁵...) [lt.] *m* ⓐc., *a.* ~**ie** (⁵...) *f* ⓐ (Oberherrschaft) supremacy.
Supremat-eid (⁵...) *m* ⓐ *eccl. hist.* oath of supremacy. [Wert. *sB.* V 5, V a) surd.⁊
Surde ⚗ (⁵...) *f* ⓐ *math.* (irrationaler⁊
Sure (⁵...) [ar.] *f* ⓐ (Kapitel des Korans) sura.
Surius F (⁵...) [dtsch.-lt.: *sauer*] *m* ⓐ co. sour wine. [buzz, whir, whiz.⁊
surren (⁵...) [nhd. lautm.] *v/n.* (h.) ⓐ to⁊
Surrogat (⁵...) [lt.] *n* ⓐc. (Ersatz) substitute; (Behelf) makeshift.
Susanna (-⁵...) ⓐ ⁇*a.*, **Susanne** (-⁵...) ⓐ ⁇*β. npr/f.* (Bn.) Susan. [Susie, Sukie.⁊
Süschen (⁵...) *npr/n.* ⓐ *a.* (*dim.v.* Susanne)⁊
Suse F (⁵...) *npr/f.* ⓐ*β.* = Susanne; *b.s.* (dumme Liese) silly goose.
suspendier|en (⁵...) [lt. aufhängen] **I** *v/a.* ⓐ (aufheben, zeitweilig vom Amte entheben) to suspend; (einstellen) auch: to stop, to hang up. — **II** ~**n** ⓐ u. S/**ung**, mst =**Suspension/** ⓐ suspension; stoppage.
Suspensorium (⁵...) [lt.] *n* ⓐ (Bruch- u. Trage-band) suspender, ... sor.
süß (⁵) [ahd.: sweet] *a.* ⓐ (D 10) 1. (*ant.* herb, sauer) sweet, (zucker-)⁇ like sugar, sugary; sugared, honeyed (beibe a. *fig.*), v. Worten a. suave; sich den Kaffee (well), ⁇ machen to sugar one's coffee (well); ⁇es (ungesäuertes) Brot unleavened bread; ⁇es Wasser fresh water; ⁇ (*adv.*) ruhen, der Ruhe genießen to have a good rest, to enjoy sweet repose. — 2. *fig.* (lieblich) lovely, sweet; (reizend) charming, attractive, winning; von Personen: (lieb, hold) dear, lovable. — 3. (schmeichelnd) flattering; ein ⁇er Herr, ein ⁇es Herrchen a (young) fop; F a namby-pamby (fellow); ⁇e Worte,

⚗ scientific; ⚘ botanical; ♀ geography; ⊕ machinery; ⚔ mining; ⚔ military; ⚓ marine; ⊛ commercial; ✉ postal; 🚂 railway

oft: wheedling words, F butter. — **II Süß** *n* [67] 4. ⚙ *typ.*, &c. F (noch nicht bezahlte Arbeit, *ant.* Sauer) fat.

Süß-apfel (‿...) *m* [62] sweet(ish) apple; **-brot** *n* unleavened bread; **-brötchen** *n* sweet biscuit.

Süßchen ↘ (´⏑) *n* [23] 1. (Süßigkeiten) sweets *pl.* — 2. darling, sweet one.

Süße (´⏑) [ahd.] *f* [48] sweetness.

süßeln F (´⏑) *v/n.* (h.) [92]a. to be rather (too) sweet; (süß reden) to talk sweetly.

süßen (´⏑) *v/a.* u. *v/n.* (h.) [90] to sweeten, *chm.*, *pharm.* auch to edulcorate.

Süß-gras ⚘ (‿...) *n* [62]: ⚗ glyceria; **-holz** *n*: a) ⚘ liquorice (*Glycyrrhi'za glabra*); b) *fig.* (übertriebene Artigkeiten) sweet phrases *pl.*; ~ raspeln to flirt, to talk soft nonsense or F soft solder or sawder, to do the la-de-da to the ladies; **-holz-raspler** F *m* flirt, masher; **-holz-saft** *m*, *pharm.* liquorice-juice; **-holz-wurzel** *f* liquorice-root.

Süßigkeit (´⏑-) *f* [46] 1. sweetness, in der Rede, Manier: suavity. — 2. (etwas Süßes) s.th. sweet or sugary, sweets *pl.*

Süß-kirsche (‿.´⏑) *f* [62] sweet cherry; (schwarze Herzkirsche) black-heart(cherry).

süßlich (´⏑) *a.* [66] sweetish; (widerlich) nauseous, v. Schmeicheleien &c.: fulsome.

Süßlichkeit (´⏑-) *f* [46] sweetishness.

Süß-liebchen (‿.´⏑) *n* [62] sweetheart, darling, F lady-love.

Süßling (´⏑) *m* [11]d. effeminate, F (namby-pamby) fellow; (Stutzer) fop.

Süß-mandel-öl ⚘ (‿...) *n* [62] oil of sweet almonds; **-maul** F *n* person fond of sweets or F with a sweet tooth; **-milch-käse** *m* cream-cheese; **∼sauer** *a.* [66] sour-sweet; **∼tönend** *a.* sweet-sounding; **-wasser** *n* fresh water; **-wasser-alge** ⚘ *f* (Faden-alge) conferva; **-wasser-fisch** *m* fresh-water fish; **-wasser-kalk** *m*, *min.* fresh-water limestone. [lehnsherr) suzerain.

Suzerän (-⏑´, -f⏑´) [fr.] *m* [11]d. (Ober-

Suzeränität (-⏑-⏑´, -f⏑-⏑´) [fr.-lt.] *f* [46] (Oberlehnsherrschaft) suzerainty.

s. v. a. *abbr.* = so viel als.

SW. *abbr.* = Südwest.

Sybarit (⏑⏑´) [Sy'baris ♀, Stadt in Unteritalien] *m* [42], **∼in** *f* [47] Alt.: Sybarite, *fig.* a. (Weichling) sensualist, voluptuary; **∼isch** (⏑⏑´⏑) *a.* [66] bsd. *fig.* sybaritic(al).

Syenit ⚗ (⏑-´) [Sye'ne ♀, ägypt. Stadt] *m* [11]c. *min.* syenite.

Sykomore ⚘ (-⏑´⏑) [grch.] *f* [48] sycamore (*Ficus syco'morus*).

Sykophant (-⏑f´) [grch.] *m* [42] (gemeiner Schmeichler, Angeber) sycophant.

sykophantisch (-⏑f´⏑) *a.* [66] sycophantic.

Syllabier-buch (´⏑‿.´) *n* [62] spelling-book, seltener: syllabary.

syllabieren ⚗ (´⏑‿⏑) [grch.] **I** *v/a.* u. *v/n.* (h.) [93] to divide into syllables, to spell. — **II** ~ *n* [23] u. **Syllabierung** *f* [46] syllabi(fi)cation. [syllabical.

syllabisch ⚗ (⏑´⏑) [grch.] *a.* [66] syllabic,

Syllabus (´⏑⏑) [lt., *grch.] *m*, *inv.* u. [58] (Verzeichnis, bsd. der kirchlich verbotenen Bücher) syllabus.

Syllogismus ⚗ (´⏑´⏑) [grch.] *m* [27] Logik: (Schlußsatz) syllogism.

syllogistisch (´⏑´⏑) *a.* [66] syllogistic(al).

Sylphe (´f⏑) [fr., *flt.] *m* [44], *f* [48], **Sylphide** (⏑f´⏑) *f* [48] (Luftgeist) sylph, *f* sylphid. [sylphine.

sylphenhaft (´f⏑⏑) *a.* [66] sylph-like, auch

Symbol (⏑´) [grch.] *n* [11]d. (Sinnbild) symbol. [symbolism.

Symbolik (⏑´⏑) *f* [46] bsd. *rel.* u. *theol.*

symbolisch (⏑´⏑) *a.* [66] (sinnbildlich) symbolical; ∼e Darstellung symbolization.

symbolisieren (´⏑‿⏑) **I** *v/a.* [93] to symbolize. — **II** ~ *n* [23] u. **Symbolisierung** *f* [46] symbolization.

Symmetrie (´⏑‿) [grch.] *f* [48] (Ebenmaß) symmetry.

symmetrisch (⏑´⏑) *a.* [66] (ebenmäßig, gleichmäßig) symmetric, symmetrical.

sympathetisch (´⏑‿⏑) *a.* [66] (gleichgestimmt, geheimnisvoll wirkend) sympathetic(al).

Sympathie (´⏑‿) [grch.] *f* [48] (Mitgefühl) sympathy, fellow-feeling.

sympathisch (⏑´⏑) [grch.] *a.* [66] (mitfühlend) sympathetic(al), sympathizing; congenial. [sympathize with a p.

sympathisieren (´⏑⏑‿⏑) *v/n.* (h.) [93] to

Symphonie ♪ (´f-‿) [grch.] *f* [48] (große Orchesterkomposition) symphony.

symphonisch (⏑f´⏑) *a.* [66] symphonic.

Symplegaden (´⏑-‿⏑) [grch.] *f/pl.* [48] *myth.* (zwei ehm. zs.-schlagende Felsen am Eintritt des Bosporus in das Schwarze Meer) Symplegades *pl.*

Symptom (⏑´) [grch.] *n* [11]d. *med.*, &c. (An-, Kenn-zeichen) symptom.

symptomatisch (´⏑-‿⏑) *a.* [66] symptomatic.

Synagoge (´⏑‿⏑) [grch.] *f* [48] synagogue.

Synalöphe ⚗ (´⏑‿f⏑) [grch.] *f* [48] *gram.* (Zs.-ziehung zweier Vokale, bsd. am Ende u. Anfang zweier Wörter) synalephe.

Synäresis ⚗ (⏑´⏑⏑) [grch.] *f* [50], **Synärese** (´⏑-‿⏑) *f* [48] *gram.* (Zs.-ziehung zweier Silben oder Vokale zu einer Silbe) synæresis.

Synchronismus ⚗ (´⏑r⏑´⏑) [grch.] *m* [27] (Gleichzeitigkeit) synchronism. [(-al).

synchronistisch (´⏑r⏑´⏑) *a.* [66] synchronic

Syndikat (´⏑‿) [lt., *grch.] *n* [11]c. (kaufmännische Genossenschaft) syndicate, F ring, pool, combine, trust.

Syndikus (´⏑⏑) [lt., *grch.] *m* [27][58] syndic.

Synedrion, ...um (⏑´⏑⏑) [grch.] *n* [28] Alt.: (hoher Rat zu Jerusalem) Sanhedrim.

Synesis ⚗ (´⏑⏑) [grch.] *f* [50] = Sinn 1; *gr. constru'ctio kata' sy'nesin* construction according to sense, ⚗ synesis.

Synizesis ⚗ (´⏑-tß‿⏑) [grch.] *f* [49] *gr.* (Zs.-ziehung v. 2 Vokalen zu 1 Silbe) synizesis.

Synkope ⚗ (´⏑-) [grch.] *f* [48] *gr.* (Ausfall e-s Inlautes), *med.* (Herzschlag), a. ♪ syncope.

synkopieren ⚗ (´⏑‿⏑) **I** *v/a.* [93] to syncopate. — **II** ~ *n* [23] u. **Synkopierung** *f* [46] syncopation.

Synkretiker ⚗ (⏑´⏑⏑) [grch.] *m* [22], **Synkretist** (´⏑-´) *m* [42] syncretist.

Synkretismus (´⏑-´⏑) *m* [27] (Streben, streitende Parteien zu vereinigen) syncretism.

Synod (⏑´) [grch.] *m* [11]c.: der Heilige ~ (Oberkirchenrat in Rußland) the Holy (Governing) Synod.

Synodal-beschluß (´⏑-‿...) *m* [62], **-ordnung** *f* synodal decision, order.

Synode (⏑´⏑) [grch.] *f* [48] (Kirchenversammlung) synod; **synodisch** ⚗ (⏑´⏑) *a.* [66] *ast.* (die Konjunktion eines Planeten oder Mondes betr.) synodic(al).

synonym (´⏑‿) [grch.] **I** *a.* [66] (sinnverwandt) synonymous. — **II** ~ *n* [11] ([25][59])d. synonymous word; vollständige ~e convertible (or equivalent) terms *pl.*

Synonymik (´⏑‿⏑) *f* [46] study of (als Buch: treatise on) synonyms, synonymy.

Synonymiker (´⏑‿⏑⏑) *m* [22] synonymist.

synonymisch (´⏑‿⏑) *a.* [66] synonymous.

Synoptiker (⏑´⏑⏑) [grch.] *m* [22] *theol.* synoptist; **synoptisch** (⏑´⏑) *a.* [66]: die ∼en Evangeli(st)en (Matthäus, Markus, Lukas) the synoptics *pl.*

syntaktisch (⏑´⏑) *a.* [66] *gram.* syntactical.

Syntax ⚗ (´⏑, a. ⏑´) [grch.] *f* [46] *gram.* (Satzlehre) syntax.

Synthese ⚗ (⏑´⏑) [grch.] *f* [48] (Zs.-fügung der Teile zum Ganzen) synthesis.

synthetisch ⚗ (⏑´⏑) *a.* [66] synthetic(al).

Syphilis (´f⏑⏑) [it.; *grch.] *f*, *inv.*, *path.* (Geschlechtskrankheit) syphilis, venereal disease; **Syphilitiker** (-f⏑´⏑⏑) *m* [22] syphilitic patient; **syphilitisch** (-f⏑´⏑) *a.* [66] syphilitic.

Syrakus ♀ (-⏑´) *npr/n. inv.* (alte Stadt auf Sizilien) Syracuse.

Syrakus(an)er (-⏑(-)´⏑) **I** *m* [22], **∼in** *f* [47] Syracusan, inhabitant of Syracuse. — **II** *a. inv.*, a. **syrakus(an)isch** *a.* [66] Syracusan, of Syracuse.

Syri-en ♀ (´(⏑)⏑) *npr/n.* [23]α. türk. Provinz in West-asien: Syria; **Syr(i-)er(in** *f* [47]) *m* [22] Syrian.

Syringe ⚘ (⏑´⏑) [grch.; *semit. (s. Sirach)] *f* [48] = Flieder.

syrisch (´⏑) *a.* [66] Syrian; die ∼e Sprache, das ~(e) *n* [67] the Syrian language, Syriac; **∼-chaldäisch** *a.* Syro-Chaldaic.

Syrte ♀ (´⏑) [grch. Sandbank] *f* [48] an der Nordküste Afrikas: syrtis.

System (⏑´) [grch.] *n* [11]d. 1. (Lehrgebäude) system; in ein ~ bringen, umwandeln to reduce to a system, to systematize. — 2. (Lehre) doctrine; (Schule) school.

Systematiker (⏑-´⏑⏑) *m* [22] systematizer, weitS. systematic person; **systematisch** (⏑-´⏑) *a.* [66] (geordnet, planmäßig) systematic(al); **system(at)isieren** (⏑-(-)⏑´⏑) *v/a.* [93] (in wissenschaftliche Ordnung bringen) to systematize.

s. Z. *abbr.* = seiner Zeit.

Szene (´⏑) [grch.] *f* [48] meist *thea.* scene; hinter der ~ (od. den ~n) behind the scenes (auch *fig.*); in ~ setzen to mount or stage a piece; weitS. to enact; **∼n-wechsel** *m* change (or shifting) of scenes.

Szenerie (-⏑´) *f* [48] *thea.* scenery.

szenisch (´⏑) *a.* [66] *thea.* scenic (effect, &c.); vgl. bühnenmäßig.

Szylla (´⏑) [lt.] *npr/f.* [59][49]β. [56][57]α. Alt.: Scylla; vgl. Charybdis.

Szythe (´⏑) *m* [44], **Szythin** *f* [47] Alt. Scythian; **Szythien** ♀ (´(⏑)⏑) *npr/n.* [23]α. Alt. Land: Scythia; **szythisch** (´⏑) *a.* [66] Völkerkunde: Scythian.

[T] — 945 — [Täfelung]

T, t (¹) *n, inv.* Buchstabe: T, t.
t, öft. *t abbr.* = Tonne.
T.A. *abbr.* = Taschenausgabe.
Tabagie † (⌣G¹) [fr.] *f* ⊕ smoking-room (in a coffee-shop or restaurant).
Tabak ⚥ (⌣⌣) [nhd. 1600; *indianisch] *m* ⊕d. **1.** tobacco (*Nicotia'na*), *pl.* ~e ⊕ (~sorten) sorts of tobacco; virginischer ~ common (or sweet-scented) tobacco (*N. Ta'bacum*); ~ kauen, rauchen to chew, to smoke tobacco; f. spinnen 1. — **2.** F *fig.* (P mst Tobak: ¹⌣) f. Anno; das ist starker ~ that's too strong, it's too much (of a good thing).
Tabak-bau (⌣⌣...) *m* ⊕ cultivation of tobacco; **=beize** ⊕ *f* tob.-juice; **=beutel** *m* f. Tabaks-b.; **=blatt** *n* tob.-leaf; **=bruder** F *m* inveterate smoker; **=dose** f f. Tabaks-d.; **=fabrik** *f* tob.-factory; **=fabrikant** *m* tob.-manufacturer; **=gesellschaft** *f* party of smokers; **=händler** *m* tob.-merchant, im kleinen: tobacconist; **=kauer** *n* tob.-chewer; **=laden** *m* tob.-shop; **=monopol** *n* tob.-monopoly; **=mühle** ⊕ *f* tob.-grater, für Schnupftabak: snuff-mill; **=pflanze** ⚥ *f* f. ~ 1; **=rauch** *m* tob.-smoke; **=rauchen** *n* smoking; **=raucher(in** *f*) *m* smoker.
Tabaks-beutel (⌣⌣⁻¹⌣) *m* ⊕ tobacco-pouch.
Tabak-schmaucher F (⌣⌣...) *m* ⊕ great smoker; **=schneide-maschine** ⊕ *f* tob.-cutter, tob.-cutting machine; **=schnupfer(in** *f*) *m* one who takes snuff, snuff-taker.
Tabaks-dose (⌣⌣...) *f* ⊕ für Schnupftabak: snuff-box; **=kollegium** *n: hist.* ~ des Königs Friedrich Wilhelm I. von Preußen tobacco-club, (fr.) tabagie; **=pfeife** *f* tob.-pipe; **=pfeifenstrauch** ⚥ *m* pipe-shrub or -vine (*Aristolochi'a Sipho*).
Tabak-spinner(in *f*)*m* (⌣⌣...) ⊕ tobacco-spinner or -dresser; **=spinnrad** ⊕ *n* tob.-wheel; **=steuer** *f* duty on tobacco; **=stube** *f* smoking-room; **=verschleiß** ⊕ öft. tob.-shop; **=verwaltung** *f* administration of the tobacco-monopoly.
tabellarisch (⌣⌣¹⌣) [it.] *a.* ⊕ tabular, tabulated, *adv.* in tabular form.
Tabelle (⌣⌣¹) [ahd.; *It.] *f* ⊕ (übersichtliches Verzeichnis) table(s *pl.*), index, schedule; in ~n anordnen ob. bringen to tabulate, to index; ⚥ n-förmig (⌣⌣...) *a.* ⊕ tabular; **=n-kopf** *m, typ.* heading; **=n-satz** *m, typ.* table-work.
Tabernakel (⌣⌣¹⌣) [It. *n*] *n* (*m*) ⊕ *rel., arch.* tabernacle.
Table d'hôte (tabl döt) [fr.] *f* ⊕ (Wirtstafel) table d'hôte, ordinary.
Tablett (⌣⌣¹) [fr.] *n* ⊕c. (Platte, Kaffee-, Tee- 2c. brett) tray, waiter, (silver) salver.
Tablette (⌣⌣¹) *f, pharm.* tablet.
tabu (¹⌣) [polynesisch] *a. inv.* ~ *n* ⊕ (auf den Südsee-inseln: et. Heiliges) taboo.
tabula (¹⌣⌣) [lt. Tafel] *f*: mit et. Tabula rasa machen (aufräumen) to make a clean sweep of a th., to do entirely away with a th.

Tabulatur ♪ (⌣⌣⁻¹) [It.] *f* ⊕ (ehm. Bezeichnung der Töne durch Buchstaben und Ziffern, Partiturtafel) tablature.
Tabulett (⌣⌣¹) [It.] *n* ⊕c. hawker's travelling-box, portable stand; **=kram** *m* ⊕ hawker's wares *pl.*; **=krämer** *m* hawker, pedlar; **=krämerei** *f* hawking, pedlar's trade.
Taburett (⌣⌣¹) [fr.] *n* ⊕c. (Sessel ohne Lehne) tabouret. [⊕ = Tachymeter.]
Tach(e)ometer ⚙ (⌣⊕(⌣)⌣⌣) [grch.] *n* (*m*)
Tachtel f. Dachtel.
Tachygraphie ⚙ (⌣⊕⌣f¹) [grch.] *f* ⊕ [Kunst der Geschwindschreibung] tachygraphy, shorthand.
Tachymeter ⚙ (⌣⊕⌣⌣⌣) [grch.] *n* (*m*) ⊕ (Geschwindigkeitsmesser) tachometer, speed-indicator.
Tachymetrie ⚙ (⌣⊕⌣⌣⌣⌣) *f* ⊕ tachometry.
T..., tacite-isch (⌣t⌣⁻¹⌣) [Tacitus, röm. Geschichtschreiber, geb. um 54, gest. nach 117] *a.* ⊕ of (or like) Tacitus.
Tadel (¹⌣) [nhd.] *m* ⊕ (*ant.* Lob) blame, seltener: reprehension; (Mißbilligung) reproof, (Vorwurf) reproach, rebuke, (Verweis) reprimand, F set-down, (Rüge) censure, Schule: bad mark; (scharfe Beurteilung) adverse criticism, seltener: animadversion upon; e-m einen scharfen ~ erteilen to give a p. a sharp reprimand; **ohne** ~ blameless, faultless; fr., *hist.* Ritter ohne Furcht und ~ (Bayard) knight without fear or reproach; über allen ~ erhaben beyond reproach, irreproachable, without a blemish.
Tadelei (−⌣¹) *f* ⊕ constant fault-finding or cavilling; (Nörgelei) nagging.
tadel-frei (¹⌣...) *a.* ⊕ = tadellos.
tadelhaft (¹⌣⌣) *a.* ⊕ reprehensible, deserving (of) blame, censurable, objectionable, faulty; **~igkeit** *f* (¹⌣⌣⌣-) ⊕ reprehensibleness, faultiness.
tadel-los (¹⌣...) *a.* ⊕ irreproachable, blameless, faultless, perfect; excellent, splendid; **=losigkeit** *f* ⊕ blamelessness, faultlessness; **=lust** = **=sucht**.
tadeln (¹⌣) [nhd. (LU.)] I *v/a.* ⊕a. to blame, ⟨ to reprehend; (mißbilligen) to disapprove of, to take exception to or at, auch: to reprove, (rügen) to censure, to rebuke; (bekritteln) to criticize, to animadvert (or reflect) upon; spitzfindig ⚦ to carp (or cavil) at; e-n wegen et. ⚦ to blame (or reprimand, reproach) a p. for a th., an allem et. zu ⚦ finden to find fault with (or to see a flaw in) everything; ⚦d censorious, reproachful, fault-finding. — II ~ *n* = Tadel.
tadelns-wert (¹⌣⌣...), ⚦ würdig *a.* ⊕ = tadelhaft, auch: calling for censure.
Tadel-sucht (¹⌣...) *f* ⊕ love of criticism or fault-finding, censoriousness, censorious spirit; ⚦ süchtig *a.* ⊕ fond of criticizing, censorious. [censure.]
Tadels-votum (¹⌣⌣⌣⌣)*n* ⊕ *parl.* vote of
Tadler (¹⌣) *m* ⊕, **~in** *f* ⊕ censurer, critic, fault-finder.

Tafel (¹⌣) [ahd.; *It. tă'bŭla*] *f* ⊕ **1.** table (*a. arch.*), zum Schreiben: tablet, für Anzeigen: board; (Schiefer=)~ slate, (Wand=)~ black board; (Platte) plate, von Blech: sheet, v. Stein: slab, v. Glas: pane; ~ Schokolade cake of chocolate; Alt.: ~ Gesetz der zwölf ~n Twelve-table law. — **2.** (langer Tisch) dinner-table, mit Essen besetzt: board; bei ~ at table, at (or during) dinner; festliche ~ festive board; freie ~ free board; große ~ bei Hofe 2c.: gala dinner, grand dinner-party; f. aufheben 5, besetzt 2; zur ~ eines Fürsten 2c. einladen oder heranziehen to invite to dinner; offene ~ halten to keep open table. — **3.** = Tabelle.
tafel-artig (¹⌣...) *a.* ⊕ = ⚦ förmig; **=aufsatz** *m* ⊕ centre-piece, fr. epergne; **=bai** *f*, **=berg** *m* am Kap der guten Hoffnung: Table Bay, Table Mountain; **=besteck** *n* (case with) knife, fork and spoon, f. a. Besteck 2; **=bier** *n* table-beer or -ale; **=blei** *n* ⊕ sheet-lead; **=bouillon** *f* Kocht.: (condensed) soup in tablets, desiccated soup; **=brot** *n* bread for the table; **=butter** *f* (best fresh) butter for the table.
Täfelchen (¹⌣⌣) *n* ⊕ (*dim.* von Tafel) (small) tablet, aus Schiefer: small slate.
Tafel-decken (¹⌣...) *n* ⊕ laying the table or the cloth; **=decker(in** *f*) one who lays the table; **=diamant** ⊕ *m* (flach geschliffener Diamant) table-diamond; **=diener** *m* boy (or lackey) waiting at table; **=ente** *f, orn.* dunbird, pochard (*Fuli'gula feri'na*); ⚦ förmig *a.* ⊕ tabular, *min., &c.*: ⚙ lamelliform; **=freuden** *f/pl.* pleasures of the table; **=freund(in** *f*) *m* lover of good eating and drinking; **=gedeck** *n:* a) set of table-linen; b) **=geschirr**; **=gelder** *n/pl.* allowance for board, für Offiziere: table-money *sg.*; **=gerät** *n* table-appointments or requisites *pl.*; **=geschirr** *n* dinner-service; **=glas** ⊕ *n* sheet-glass, geblasenes: crown-glass, (Spiegelglas) plate-glass.
Täfel-holz ⊕ (¹⌣⌣) *n* ⊕ woodwork.
Tafel-klavier (¹⌣...) *n* ⊕ square piano; **=land** ⚙ *n* table-land, plateau; **=musik** *f* music (played) during dinner time.
tafeln (¹⌣) *v/n.* (h.) ⊕a. to sit at table, to feast, to banquet; gern ⚦ to be fond of a good table or of good cheer or of good eating and drinking.
täfeln ⊕ (¹⌣) [Tafel] I *v/a.* ⊕a. join, einen Fußboden ⚦ to inlay (or board) ...; eine Wand ⚦ to wainscot ... — II ~ *n* = Täfelung 1.
Tafel-obst (¹⌣⌣) *n* ⊕ fruit for dessert; **=runde** *f, myth.* des Königs Artur: Round Table; **=scheibe** *f* pane of glass; **=schiefer** ⊕ *m* slate in leaves or slabs; **=spat** *m, min.* tabular spar; **=stein** *m:* a) = Schieferstift; b) ⊕ (flach geschliffener Edelstein) table-cut precious stone; **=stift** *m* slate pencil; **=tuch** ⊕ table-cloth.
Täf(e)lung (¹(⌣)⌣) *f* ⊕ **1.** (das Täfeln) boarding. — **2.** = Getäfel.

♪ Musik; ⚙ Wissenschaft; ⚥ Pflanze; ⊕ Geographie; ⊕ Technik; ✕ Bergbau; ⚔ Militär; ⚓ Marine; ⊕ Handel; ✉ Post; 🚂 Eisenbahn.

[Tafelwage] — 946 — [Takt]

Tafel=wage ☉ (⸚⸚...) f ⓖ weighing-machine or -table; **=wein** m = Tischwein.
Täfel=werk (⸚⸚⸚) n ⓖ (Dielung) flooring; (Wandverkleidung) wainscot(ing).
Tafel=zeug (⸚⸚⸚) n ⓖ table-linen.
Taf(fe)t ⚓ (⸚(⸚)) [it. *taffetà*; *pers.*] m ⓑd(b). (Art Seidenstoff) taffeta; **~band** n ⓖ taffeta ribbon; **2en** (⸚(⸚)⸚) a. ⓖ (made) of taffeta; **~kleid** n taffeta dress; **~papier** n satin paper.
Tag (⸚, ¹, pl. ⸚ᴸ) [ahd.: day] m ⓐⓒ. 1. (ant. Nacht) day, (Licht) daylight, (Luftraum) open air; der **~** nach (vor) der Schlacht the morrow (the eve) of the battle; der **~** des Herrn the Lord's Day. — 2. adverbial:
a) als gen. dieser **~**e: a) during the last few days, lately; b) (= nächster **~**e) one of these days, soon; heutigentags, heutigestags in our days, nowadays; eines (schönen) **~**(e)s one (fine) day, some day or other; einmal (zweimal) des **~**s once (twice) a day; b) als acc.: alle **~**e every day; den ganzen **~** (über) all day (long); ganze **~**e lang for whole days, vgl. tagelang; f. lang 3, hinter einander; einen **~** um den andern every alternate (or other) day; c) mit prp.: früh am **~**e early in the day; f. hell 2; am **~**e (ob. zutage) liegen to be evident or manifest to obvious or clear; auf seine alten **~**e in his old days or age; bei **~**e in the day-time; binnen acht **~**en within a week; f. acht¹ I; **~** für **~** day by day; in den **~** hinein at random, recklessly; ⚔ über **~**(e) overground; über acht **~**e a week hence, in a week; ⚔ unter **~**e underground; vor vierzehn **~**en a fortnight ago or since, f. Jahr 3 gegen Schluß; f. zutage, heutzutage; von **~** zu **~** from day to day.
— 3. mit verbs: an den **~** bringen (kommen) to bring (to come) to light; gute **~**e h. to have a good (or delightful) time (of it); an den **~** legen to lay bare, to exhibit, to disclose; es liegt zutage it is evident or manifest; sich e-n guten **~** m. to have a good day's enjoyment, F to make a (jolly) day of it; f. hell 2; es wird (heller) **~** the day is dawning or breaking; Sprichw. es kommt doch schließlich alles an den **~** everything comes to light at last; jeder **~** hat seine Plage each day brings its (own) trouble; f. Abend I am Schluß. — 4. mit adjectives: der festgesetzte **~** the appointed day; f. gut 1; der Jüngste **~** the Day of Judgment (auch bibl.), ⚔ Dooms-day.
Tag=arbeit (⸚...) f ⓖ day-work; **2aus** (⸚ᴸ) adv. f. 2ein; **=bau** m = Tagebau; **=blatt** f. Tageblatt; **2blind** a., path.: ⚕ nyctalopic; **~**(r) s.: ⚕ nyctalops; **=blindheit** f, path. day-blindness, ⚕ nyctalopy; **=bogen** m, ast. (ant. Nachtbogen) diurnal arc; **=dieb(in)** f. Tage=d.; **=dienst** m day- (or day's) service.
Tage=arbeit (⸚...) f ⓖ = Tag=a.; **=bau** ⚔ m (ant. Grubenarbeit) open work, work(ing) in the open; **=blatt** n daily paper or journal; **=buch** n diary, journal, ⚓ a. day-book; **=dieb(in)** f m (Müßiggänger[in]) idler, sluggard, F lazy-bones; **2dieben** v/n. (h.) ⚙ *** to idle away one's time; **=falter** m = Tagfalter.

=geld(er pl.) n (Diäten) daily fee or allowance. [day (of the week), daily.]
tag=ein (⸚ᴸ) adv. ⸚, 2aus adv. every
tage=lang (⸚...) adv. for days (together); **=lohn** m ⓖ day's (or daily) wages pl. or pay; **=löhner** m day-labourer, jobbing (or odd) man; **=löhnerei, =löhner=arbeit** f labourer's work, jobbing; **=löhnerin** f woman working by the day; für Hausreinigung ꝛc.: charwoman; **=löhnern** v/n. (h.) ⚙ₐ*** to work by the day, to do jobbing (work), v. Weibern: to go charring; **=marsch** m day's march.
tagen (⸚⸚) [ahd.: dawn] I v/n. (h.) ⓖ 1. der Morgen (oder v/imp. es) tagt the day is breaking, the day (or it) is dawning; es wird bald 2 it will soon be dawn(ing) or getting light; fig. es wird schrecklich 2! there will be a fearful awakening, some terrible things will come to light! — 2. [schwz.] (beraten) to sit in council, to deliberate (together), to hold a meeting. — II **~** n ⓷ 3. beim frühesten **~** in the early dawn (of day); vgl. Tagung.
Tage=reise (⸚⸚ᴸ⸚) f ⓖ day's journey.
Tages=anbruch (⸚⸚...) m ⓖ daybreak, break (or dawn) of day; **=angabe** f in Briefen ꝛc.: date; **=arbeit** f day's work; **=befehl** ⚔ m order of the day; **=bericht** m in Zeitungen ꝛc.: report of the day('s proceedings); **=billett** 🚂 n day-ticket; **=dienst** m day-service; **=ereignis** n (great) event of the day; **=fragen** f/pl. questions pl. of the day; **=geschichte** f history of the day or our own times; **=gespräch** n talk (or topic) of the day; **=grauen** n grey of the morning; vgl. =anbruch; **2hell** a. = tag=hell; **=helle** f brightness (stärker: glare) of day, bright daylight; **=kasse** f: a) thea. box- (or booking-)office; b) ⚓ (Einnahme des Tages) receipts (or takings) pl. of the day; **=korrespondenz** f daily (or day's) correspondence; vgl. **=post**; **=kurs** 💰 m current exchange, v. Aktien ꝛc.: quotation of the day; **=licht** n daylight; das **~** erblicken (scheuen) to see (to shun) daylight; an das **~** kommen to come to light, to become known or evident, to transpire; **=literatur** f literature of the day, current literature; **=neuigkeiten** f/pl. news of the day; **=ordnung** f, parl., &c. order of the day (a. fig.); das ist jetzt an der **~** that is now the order of the day or the fashion; zur **~** übergehen to proceed (or pass on) to the order of the day; **=politik** f politics of the day; **=post** f day's (or daily) mail; **=presse** f daily press; **=schrift=steller** m writer of the day; (Zeitungschreiber) writer for the press, journalist; **=stempel** m date-stamp; **=tafeln** f/pl., ast.: ⚕ ephemeris; **=zeit** f time of day, day-time; zu jeder **~** at every hour (or any time) of the day; bei früher (a. guter) **~** early in the day, at an early hour; **=zeitung** f daily paper, F daily. [work or task.]
Tage=werk (⸚⸚...) n ⓖ day's (or daily)
Tag=fahrt (⸚...) f ⓖ südd. = Termin; **=falter** m, ent. (day-)butterfly; **=gelder**

n/pl. = Tage=g.; **2hell** a. ⓖ (as) light (or clear) as day.
...tägig (..."ᴸ⸚) a. ⓖ in Zssgn mit Zahlen, zB. drei=2 (= drei Tage dauernd) of (or lasting) three days, three days'...
Tag=kreis (⸚ᴸ...) m ⓖ ast. diurnal circle.
täglich (⸚⸚) [ahd.] a. ⓖ 1. daily, every day('s), of daily occurrence, ⚓ diurnal (motion of the earth), bsd. med. quotidian (fever); adv. every day, daily, ⚓ a. per day; zweimal 2 twice a day; et. das 2 vorkommt an every-day occurrence. — 2. (alltäglich) commonplace, trite; seine 2en Kleider his ordinary (or every-day) clothes pl.
Tag=lilie ♀ (⸚ᴸ⸚(⸚)⸚) f ⓖ day-lily, ⚕ hemerocallis. [labourer.]
Tagner (⸚⸚) m ⓷, **~in** f ⓖ südd.: day=]
Tag=runde (⸚⸚⸚) f ⓖ daily round, ⚔ daily patrol.
tags (⸚) adv.: ⸚ d(a)rauf (on) the day after; 2 zuvor on the day previous.
Tag=satzung (⸚...) f ⓖ der Schweizer: diet, national assembly; **2schen** a. ⓖ shunning (or dreading) daylight (a. fig.); **=schicht** ⚒ f (Arbeit bei Tage) day-shift; **=schule** f = Externat; **=schüler** (**=in** f) m day-scholar. [during the day.]
tags=über (⸚ᴸ⸚) adv. in the day-time,]
tag=täglich (⸚ᴸ⸚⸚) a. ⓖ (occurring) daily, every day's; adv. every day.
Tag=und=nacht=gleiche (⸚⸚⸚⚙ᴸ⸚) f ⓖ ast.: ⚕ equinox.
Tagung (⸚⸚) [tagen] f ⓖ parl. session.
Tag=vogel (⸚...) m ⓖ = =falter; **=wache** ⚔ ⚓ f day-watch; 2weise adv. by the day.
Taifun (-ᴸ) [chin.] m ⓐd. (⓹) (Wirbelsturm, bsd. in Ostasien) typhoon.
Taille (täl-jᵉ) [fr.] ⓖ 1. a) waist; er faßte sie um die **~** he seized (or clasped) her round the waist, he put his arm round her waist; b) von Kleidern: (ant Rock) bodice. — 2. Kartenspiel: cutting and shuffling; **taillieren** (täl-jiᴸ⸚) v/n. (h.) ⓖ to cut and shuffle the cards.
Tajo ♀ (⸚ᴸ⸚) [span.] npr/m. ⓐa. der **~** (spanischer Fluß) the (river) Tagus.
Takel ⚓ (⸚ᴸ) [ndd.] n ⓖ tackle. [werk.]
Takelage ⚓ (⸚ᴸ⸚Gᵉ) [dtschfr.] f ⓼ = Takel=]
Takel=block ⚓ (⸚ᴸ...) m ⓖ tackle-block; **=boden** m rigging-loft; **=boots=mann** m rigging master.
Tak(e)ler ⚓ (⸚ᴸ(⸚)⸚) m ⓖ rigger.
Takel=garn (⸚⸚...) n ⓖ tarred twine; **=haken** m tackle-hook.
takeln (⸚ᴸ⸚) v/a. ⓖa. to rig a ship.
Tak(e)lung ⚓ (⸚ᴸ(⸚)⸚) f ⓼, **Takel=werk** (⸚⸚⸚) n ⓖ tackle, rigging, cordage.
Takt (⸚) [it.] m ⓐb. 1. ♪ time, measure; ⸚ Dreiviertel=2 measure of three crotchets, triple time; a. = =strich; mitten im **~** abbrechen to break off in the middle of a bar; den **~** angeben oder schlagen to beat time; **~** halten to keep (good) time, ⚓ beim Rudern: to keep stroke; e-n aus dem **~** e bringen to make a p. play (or sing) out of time, fig. to put a p. out, to disconcert a p.; aus dem **~** kommen to play (or sing) out of time; im **~** e marschieren to keep step (or time) in marching. — 2. fig. (Gefühl für das Geziemende) tact; feinen **~** h. to have (or use, exercise) great judgment or tact.

[Taktabteilung] — 947 — [Tann]

Takt=abteilung ♪ (⏑...) f ⊕ division of a bar; **=art** f time, measure; ⏑**fest** a. ⊕ keeping good time, fig. firm, strong-minded, consistent; **=festigkeit** f knack of keeping (good) time; fig. firmness, strength of mind, steadiness; **=führer** m conductor, leader, a. = **=schläger**; **=gefühl** n = Takt 2.

taktieren ♪ (⏑⏑) v/n. (h.) ⊕ to beat (the) time. [ductor's baton.]

Taktier=stab ♪ (⏑⏑...), **=stock** m ⊕ con-

Taktik ⚔ ⚓ (⏑⏑) [grch.] f ⊕ tactics (a. fig.); **Taktiker** (⏑⏑⏑) m ⊕ tactician; **taktisch** a. ⊕ tactical; **taktische Einheit** tactical unit.

takt=los (⏑...) a. ⊕ tactless, without tact, injudicious, indiscreet, v. Handlungen auch: ill-judged, **=losigkeit** f ⊕ tactlessness, want of tact, injudiciousness, als Handlung: ill-judged (or injudicious) action; ⏑**mäßig** a. well-timed or -measured, rhythmical; in Lem Schritte in measured steps; **=messer** m: ⚙ metronome; **=messung** f: ⚙ metronomy; **=note** f (ganze Note) semibreve; **=pause** f bar- (or semibreve) rest; **=schlag** m, **=schlagen** n beating time; **=schläger** m one who beats time; **=schritt** m measured (or regular) step; **=stock** m des Kapellmeisters conductor's baton; **=strich** m bar; ⏑**voll** a. full of (or endowed with) tact, judicious, discreet; Ler Mann man of tact; **=vorzeichnung** ♪ f time-signature.

Tal (⏑) [ahd.: dale (dell)] n ⊕c., poet. ⊕c. **1.** valley, poet. a. vale; kleines ~ dale, schluchtartiges: glen. — **2.** zu ~(e) [nhd.] down(ward); zu ~(e) (strom-abwärts) fahren to go downstream; f. Berg 2.

tal=(ab=)wärts (⏑⏑, ⏑⏑) adv. down the valley; down-hill or -stream.

Talar (⏑⏑) [it.] m ⊕d. (Amtskleid) (long) robe, barrister's, judge's, clergyman's (official) gown.

tal=aufwärts (⏑⏑⏑) adv. up the valley, uphill; ⏑**aus** (⏑⏑) adv. out of the valley; **=bahn** (⏑...) f ⊕ railway through (or crossing, traversing) a valley; **=bewohner** m inhabitant of a valley, auch: dalesman; **=brücke** f [valley, dale.] viaduct.

Tälchen (⏑⏑) n ⊕ (dim. von Tal) little

tal=ein (⏑⏑), ⏑**einwärts** (⏑⏑⏑) adv. into the valley; **=enge** (⏑⏑) f ⊕ narrow (part of a) valley; vgl. **=schlucht**.

Talent (⏑⏑) [fr., *grch.] n ⊕c. **1.** Alt. (Münze) talent; bibl. = Pfund 2. — **2.** fig. (Begabtheit) talent, (natural) gift, ability; (Fähigkeit) aptitude, capacity; ~ haben to be talented or (highly) gifted; er hat ~ für Musik... a talent (or a taste, a turn) for music (vgl. Gabe 3).

talentiert (⏑⏑⏑) a. ⊕ = talentvoll.

talent=los (⏑⏑...) a. ⊕ without talent(s) or ability, not gifted; ⏑**voll** a. talented, gifted, of great parts; richly endowed (by nature); (highly) accomplished.

Taler (⏑⏑) [nhd. 16. sae. böhm. *(Joachims)]thaler (Gulden)] m ⊕ **1.** ehm. (Silbermünze von 3 Mart) thaler, three-mark piece, weniger richtig: dollar. — **2.** F weiß. (Geld) das ist ein schöner ~ that's a nice sum of money.

Tal=fahrt (⏑⏑) f ⊕ down-journey, descent.

Talg (⏑) [nbd.] m ⊕b. tallow, suet.

talg=artig (⏑...) a. ⊕ tallowy, like tallow, ⏑**sebaceous**; **=baum** m ⊕ tallow-tree (Stilli'ngia sebi'fera); **=drüse(n** pl.) f, anat.: ⚙ sebaceous gland(s pl.).

talgen¹ (⏑⏑) ⊕ **I** v/n. (h.) **1.** Fleischerei: diese Ochsen ⚙ gut... yield much (or good) suet. — **2.** v. erkaltenden Speisen: to be(come) covered with grease. — **II** v/a. **3.** (schmieren) to grease (with tallow).

talgen² (⏑⏑) a. ⊕ (of or like) tallow.

talg=gebend (⏑...) a. ⊕ producing tallow, ⚙ sebiferous, sebiparous; **=grieben** f/pl. ⊕ greaves pl. (of suet).

talgicht (⏑⏑), mst ...**ig** (⏑⏑) a. ⊕ **1.** = talg=artig. — **2.** covered with tallow or suet.

Talg=licht (⏑⏑...) n ⊕ tallow- (gezogenes: dip-)candle; **=pfanne** f die man beim Verzinnen gebraucht: grease-pot.

Tal=grund (⏑⏑) m ⊕ bottom of a valley.

Talg=säure (⏑⏑...) f ⊕ chm.: ⚙ stearic acid; **=stoff** m, chm. stearine.

Tal=hang (⏑⏑) m ⊕ slope.

Talisman (⏑⏑⏑) [ar.; *grch. te'lesma] m ⊕d. (zauberhaftes Kleinod) talisman; (Geldstück) lucky piece or sixpence, piece for luck.

Talje ⚓ (⏑⏑; vgl. Taille) [nbd., *It.] f ⊕ tackle, ⊕ a. = Flaschenzug; ⏑**=reep** (⏑⏑) ⚓ (dünnes Tau) lanyard.

Talk (⏑) [fr., *ar.] m ⊕ b. min. talc, ⚙ talcum; gemeiner ~ common talc or soapstone; ⏑**=artig** (⏑...) a. ⊕ min. talcky, ⚙ talcose, ...ous, ...oid; ⏑**=erde** f = Magnesia, a. talcite, earthy talc.

Talk=kessel (⏑⏑, ⏑...) m ⊕ deep circular valley or gorge.

Talk=granit (⏑⏑⏑) m ⊕ min. talc-granite.

talkicht (⏑⏑), ...**ig** (⏑⏑) a. ⊕ = talfartig.

Talk=schiefer (⏑...) m ⊕ talc-schist, -slate, slate-talc, magnesian slate; **=spat** m (kohlensaure Magnesia) magnesite (MgCO₃).

Talmi=gold (⏑⏑⏑) [*(*) [Tallois in Paris] n ⊕ (⊕) (gold-ähnliche Bronzelegierung) talmi-gold, Abyssinian gold; fig. Talmi (Schein) (mere) sham, spurious article.

Talmud (⏑⏑) [hebr. Lehre] m ⊕d. (Satzungsbuch der Juden) Talmud; ⏑**isch** (⏑⏑) a. ⊕ Talmudic(al); ⏑**ist** (⏑⏑) m ⊕ Talmudist.

Talon ⊕ (⏑⏑') [fr.] m ⊕ (Leiste für Zinsscheine) bisw.: talon of coupons; (Erneuerungsschein) dividend-warrant.

Tal=schlucht (⏑...) f ⊕ glen, (deep) gorge-like valley; **=sohle** f bottom (or deepest part) of a valley; **=sperre** f dike (or wall) across a valley which bars (or regulates) a river; **=stern** ⚥ m masterwort (Astra'ntia); ⏑**wärts** adv. towards the valley, down(-hill); **=weg** m: a) road (leading) through a valley; b) mid-channel of a river-bed.

Tamarinde ⚘ (⏑⏑⏑) [it.; *ar. Dattel Indiens] f ⊕: a) tropische Schotenfrucht: tamarind; b) = **=baum**; ⏑**=baum** m ⊕ tamarind (-tree) (Tamari'ndus I'ndica).

Tamariske ⚘ (⏑⏑⏑) [it.] f ⊕ tamarisk (Ta'marix); deutsche ~ German tamarisk (Myrica'ria Germa'nica); französische ~ French (or common) tamarisk (T.Ga'llica).

Tambour (⏑būr) [fr., *ar.] m ⊕d. (⊕) **1.** mst ⚔: a) (Trommel) drum; b) (Trommelschläger) drummer. — **2.** ⊕ arch., mech., &c. tambour, drum.

Tambour=major ⚔ (⏑bur=⏑⏑) m ⊕ drum-major.

tamburieren ⊕ (⏑⏑⏑) [fr.] v/a. ⊕ (am Stickrahmen sticken) to tambour.

Tamburier=nadel ⊕ (⏑⏑⏑...) f ⊕ tambour-needle; **=rahmen** m tambour-frame; **=stich** m chain- (or lock-) stitch; **=sticker(in** f) m tambourer.

Tamburin (⏑⏑⏑) [it., *ar.] n ⊕d. (⊕) **1.** ♪ (Schellentrommel) tambourine. — **2.** ⊕ (Stickrahmen mit Walzen) tambour-frame.

Tamburin=schläger(in f) m ♪ (⏑⏑⏑...) ⊕ tambourine-player, player on the tambourine; ⊕ **=stich** m tambour-stitch; **=stickerei** f tambour-work.

Tamp ⚓ (⏑) [nbd.] m ⊕d. (kurzes Tauende) rope's end. [cotton wool).]

Tampon (ta-vg') [fr.] m ⊕ surg. plug (of **tamponieren** (⏑⏑⏑) [fr.] **I** v/a. ⊕ surg. (verstopfen) to tampon, plug. — **II** ~ n ⊕ tamponade, tamponage, plugging.

Tamtam (⏑⏑) [chin.] n (m) ⊕ **1.** (Hindutrommel) tom-tom. — **2.** ⚙ gong.

Tamule (⏑⏑) m ⊕, ...**lin** f ⊕ ostind. Volk: Tamil, Tamul; **tamulisch** a. ⊕ Tamil(ian), Tamul(ian).

Tand (⏑) [mhd.] m ⊕c. (o. pl.) (Kleinigkeiten) trifles pl., F petty (or trumpery) stuff; (Nippsachen) knickknacks, trinkets pl.; (Spielzeug) toys, baubles, playthings pl.; (Geschwätz) babble, tittle-tattle, prattle.

Tändelei (⏑⏑⏑) [nbd.] f ⊕ **1.** (Tändeln) dallying, trifling, toying, F fooling (about). — **2.** (Zaudern) dawdling, shilly-shallying. — **3.** (Liebelei) flirtation, F spooning, mashing.

tändelhaft, tänd(e)lig (⏑(⏑)⏑) a. ⊕ dallying, trifling, playful, full of fun; (leichtfertig) frivolous.

Tändel=kram (⏑⏑⏑) m ⊕ = Tand.

tändeln (⏑⏑) [nbd.] **I** v/n. (h.) ⊕ a. (lose spielen) to dally, trifle, play, F to fool about; (zaudern) to dawdle, to dilly-dally; (liebeln) to flirt. — **II** ~ n ⊕ = Tändelei, bsp. 1.

Tändel=schürze (⏑⏑⏑) f ⊕ einer Dame: ornamental silk apron, fancy-apron; **=werk** n = Tand.

Tändler (⏑⏑) m ⊕, ~**in** f ⊕ (f. tändeln I) trifler; dawdler.

Tang ⚘ (⏑) [dän.] m ⊕b. seaweed, seltener: tang(le), ⚙ fucus.

Tang=abdruck (⏑⏑⏑) m ⊕ geol.: ⚙ fucoid.

Tanganjika ♀ (⏑⏑⏑⏑) npr/m. ⊕α. See Zentral-afrikas: (Lake) Tanganyika.

Tang=asche (⏑⏑⏑) f ⊕ (reich an Kalisalzen und Jod) kelp, varec.

Tangente ⚙ (⏑⏑⏑) [it.] f ⊕ math. (Berührungslinie) tangent; ~**bussole** ⚓ f ⊕ tangent compass; ~**=viereck** n, geom. quadrilateral (im engl. Euklid: four-sided figure) formed by the tangents of a circle.

Tangential=bewegung ⚙ (⏑⏑⏑⏑⏑...) f mech. tangential (or centrifugal) movement; **=ebene** f tangential (or tangent-) plane; **=kraft** f tangential (or centrifugal) force.

Tanger ♀ (⏑⏑) [ar. Tandscha] npr/n. ⊕ Stadt in Marotto: Tangier.

tangieren (⏑⏑⏑) [it.] v/a. ⊕ to touch.

Tann¹ (⏑) [ahd.: Tanne] m ⊕b. large forest (of firs or pines).

⚙ scientific; ⚘ botanical; ♀ geography; ⊕ machinery; ⚒ mining; ⚔ military; ⚓ marine; ⊕ commercial; ✉ postal; 🚂 railway

[Tannapfel] — 948 — [Tarentiner]

Tann²-apfel (⌣‿⌣) [Tanne] m ⓺ = Tannenzapfen. [~ fir(-tree) (*Abies alba*).]
Tanne (⌣‿) [ahd.] f ⓸ (a. Weiß=, Edel=) [fir-tree (*Abies alba*).]
Tännel ¿ (⌣‿) n (m) ⓶ elatine (*Elati'ne*).
tannen, ~ **tännen** (⌣‿) a. ⓺ (made) of fir.
Tannen-apfel (⌣‿‿) m ⓶ = =zapfen; =artig a. ⓺ fir-like; =baum ¿ m fir(-tree) (*Abies*); =bohle f, =bord n, =brett n deal board; =gehölz n = =hain; =häher m, orn. nucifrage, nut-cracker (*Nuci'fraga caryocata'ctes*); =hain m fir-grove; =harz n resin (or rosin) from fir-trees; =harz=säure f, chm.: ⚗ abietic acid (C₃₀H₃₀O₂); =holz n fir-wood, deal; =meise f, orn. coal-mouse, cole-tit (*Parus ater*); =nadel f needle-leaf of a fir-tree, vgl. Nadel 2; =planke f deal plank; =wald m forest of fir-trees, a. fir-wood; =wedel ¿ m bottle-brush, mare's-tail (*Hippu'ris vulga'ris*); =zapfen m fir-cone. [of (young) firs.]
Tannicht, Tännicht (⌣‿) n ⓓc. nursery
tannig (⌣‿) a. ⓺ grown with firs.
Tannin (⌣´) [dtsch-lt.; *Tanne] n ⓓd. chm., a. ~=säure (⌣´‿́⌣) f ⓺ tannic acid, tannin (= Gerbsäure).
Tann-zapfen (⌣‿‿) m ⓶ = Tannen=z.
Tantal ⚗ (⌣‿) [Tantalus] n ⓓd. chm. (Metall) tantalum (Ta).
tantalig ⚗ (⌣´‿́) [Tantal] a. ⓺ chm.: ℞ Säure tantalous acid.
tantalisch (⌣´‿́) [Tantalus] a. ⓺ myth. u. fig. Tantalean, of Tantalus.
Tantalit (⌣‿´) m ⓓc. min. tantalite.
Tantal=lampe ⊙ (⌣‿...) f ⓶ elect. tantalum lamp; =säure f, chm. tantalic acid ('₃TaO₄).
Tantalus (⌣‿‿) npr/m. ⓺γ. myth. (phrygischer König, wegen Mitteilung der Göttergeheimnisse ewige Entbehrung leidend trotz köstlicher Genüsse vor Augen) Tantalus; ~=qual(en) f torments pl. of Tantalus, tantalization; e-m ~=qualen bereiten to tantalize a p.; ~=qualen/=leiden to be on thorns or tenter-hooks.
Tantchen, a. **Täntchen** (⌣‿) n ⓶ (dim. v. Tante) auntie, aunty.
Tante (⌣‿) [fr.] f ⓸⓺⓺ (ohne art. ⓹⓽) (mehr gebr. als Muhme) aunt.
Tanti-eme (tᾱ-tĭᵉ') [fr. *tantième*] m ⓸ royalty (= Gewinnanteil).
Tanz (´) [nhd. v. tanzen] m ⓸a. 1. dance, F hop (f. anführen 1, auffordern 1); zum ~ aufspielen to play dance-music, to strike up for a dance. — 2. fig. (Streit) quarrel, brawling; einen ~ (ob. ein Tänzchen) mit e-m wagen to try a fall with a p.; da ging der ~ (Lärm ꝛc.) los then the row began.
Tanz-abend (´‿‿) m ⓶ evening's dance.
tanzbar (´‿) a. ⓺ danceable.
Tanz-bär (´...) m ⓶ dancing bear; =bein n f. schwingen 1; =belustigung f merry dance; =boden m dancing- (or public ball-)room.
Tänzchen (⌣´‿) n ⓶ (dim. v. Tanz) (nice or quiet) dance, im Hause a. carpet-dance, auf dem Rasen: dancing on the lawn; fig. f. Tanz 2.
tänzeln (⌣´‿) v/n.(h.) ⓶a. to trip (or skip, frisk) along, Pferd a. to amble.
tanzen (´‿) [mhd.: dance; fr., it. (*ahd.*)] ⓽⓽ I v/n. (h., bei Ortsveränderung ſu) 1. to dance (a. v. Bären ꝛc.), F to hop, to toe and heel it; to spin (or whirl) round; auf dem Seile ⚬ to dance (or walk) on the rope; nach der Geige ⚬ to dance to the violin; fig. f. Pfeife 2; Sprichw. wer gerne tanzt, dem ist leicht geigen a willing person is easily led or soon pleased; f. aufspielen 1. — 2. das Schiff tanzt auf den Wellen ... is rocked on the waves; ein Kind auf den Knien ⚬ l. to dance a child on one's knees. — II v/a. u. v/refl. 3. Galopp, Walzer ꝛc. ⚬ to dance a gallop, a waltz, &c. — 4. mit Angabe des Erfolges: e-n zu Boden ⚬, über den Haufen ⚬ to knock a p. down in dancing; sich müde ⚬ to weary (or tire) o.s. with dancing. — 5. es tanzt sich gut hier it is nice dancing here; die Polka tanzt sich gut the polka is nice to dance. — III ~ n ⓶ 6. dancing.
Tänzer (⌣´‿) m ⓶, ~in f ⓸⓻ dancer (a. thea.); f-ſ ~(in) auf Bällen ꝛc. a p.'s partner.
Tanzerei (´‿‿´) f ⓺ continued (or mad, wild) dancing; **Tänzerei** f ⓺ faft nur in Zffgn, f. Seiltänzerei ꝛc.
tanzerlich, tänzerlich (⌣´‿‿) a. ⓺ es war mir gar nicht ⚬ (zumute) I felt no inclination (or I was not in the mood) for dancing, F I was not in a dancing mood or humour.
Tänzerschaft (⌣´‿‿) f ⓺ 1. (a. **Tänzertum** n ⓶d.) dancer's calling. — 2. coll. the dancers pl., thea. (corps de) ballet.
Tanz-fest (´...) n ⓶ = Ball²; =gefährte m, =gefährtin f partner at a dance; =gesellschaft f dancing-party, dance, die nur bis Mitternacht dauert: Cinderella dance; =karte f programme; =kneipe f low-class ball-room; =kränzchen n dancing-club; =kunst f art of dancing; =lehrer m dancing-master; =lehrerin f lady who teaches dancing, selten: d.-mistress; =lied n dancing-air or -tune; =lokal n = =boden; =lust f love for dancing; ⁰ =lustig a. fond of dancing; =meister m = =lehrer; =musik ♪ f dance-music; =paar n dancing couple; =pferd n prancing horse; =platz m open space for dancing; =saal m dancing-room; =schritt m d.-step; =schuh m d.-shoe, pump; =schule f d.-academy; =schüler(in) f m d.-pupil; =stunde f d.-lesson; =tour f figure (in square dances); =vergnügen n fun of (or pleasure derived from) dancing, a. = =belustigung; =wut f d.-mania.
Tapet (‿´) [it. *tappe'to* m Teppich, *grch.*] n ⓓc. nur noch in: et. aufs ~ (zur Sprache) bringen to bring a th. on the carpet or on the tapis, to broach a subject; aufs ~ kommen to come under (or to be brought up for) discussion, to become a topic of conversation.
Tapete (‿´‿) [pl. v. Tapet] f ⓸ 1. in Wolle ob. Seide gewirkte: tapestry, bisw.: arras. — 2. ⊙ papierene ~ paper hangings pl., wall-paper, paper (on the wall).
tapeten-artig ⊙ (‿´‿...) a. ⓺ like tapestry or wall-paper; =bahn ♀ f ⓺² width of paper; =borte f border(ing) of a wall-paper; =fabrik(ant m) f manufactory (manufacturer) of wall-paper; =händler(in f) m ♂ dealer in wall-paper; =leiste f edging of the (wall-)paper;

=macher(in f) m = =wirker(in); =papier n wall-paper; =stickerei f tapestry- (needle)work; =stuhl ⊙ m tapestry-loom; =tür(e) f door covered with paper; =weber(in f) m, =wirker(in f) m ⊙ tapestry-maker or -weaver.
Tapezier ⊙ (‿‿´) [it. *tappezzie're*] m ⓓd. 1. der Möbel polstert: upholsterer. — 2. der Zimmer mit Tapeten ausklebt: paper-hanger. [holstery; paper-hanging.]
Tapezier-arbeit ⊙ (‿‿´‿‿) f ⓺ up-
tapezieren, mſt ⊙ (‿‿´‿) [it.] I v/a. ⓺ to hang (or fit) with tapestry, mit Papier: to (hang with) paper; neu ⚬ to re-paper. — II ~ n ⓶ f. Tapezierung.
Tapezierer (‿‿´‿) m ⓶ = Tapezier; ~... (‿´‿...) in Zffgn = Tapezier=...
Tapezier-geschäft (‿‿´‿...) n ⓶ up-holstery- (or paper-hanger's) business; =spinnen fpl. tunnel-weavers pl. (*Territela'ria*). [rooms, walls, &c.]
Tapezierung (‿‿´‿) f ⓺ papering of
tapfer (´‿) [ahd.: dapper] a. ⓺ (D9) 1. im Kampfe: brave; (heldenmütig) valiant, valorous, heroic; (beherzt) courageous, plucky; (kühn) bold, daring, gallant; f. halten 8 am Ende; sich ⚬ (adv.) wehren to offer a stout resistance, to make a gallant stand. — 2. bfp. adv. = tüchtig, z.B. ⚬ marschieren to walk a good (F a tidy) pace; ⚬ drauf los! hit hard!, F go it!
Tapferkeit (´‿‿) f ⓺ bravery, valour; ✠ engl. Orden (mit Pension) für ~ Victoria Cross; ~=medaille (´‿...) f ⓶ medal (bestowed) for bravery.
Tapioka (‿(‿)´‿) [brasil.] f ⓺⓺ (Mehl aus den Wurzeln des Kassa'vastrauchs) tapioca.
Tapir ⚗ (´‿, bisw. a. ‿´) [brasil.] m ⓓd. ⓶ zo. tapir (*Ta'pirus*).
Tapisserie (‿‿‿´) [fr.] f ⓸ (Kanevasstickerei) tapestry-work, Berlin-wool work.
tapp¹ (´) [lautm.] int. tap!, pat!
Tapp² (´) m ⓓc. 1. tap. — 2. f. p. ~=zu, ~=ins-Mus (plumper Mensch) clumsy Jack, awkward fellow; (Bauer) clodhopper.
Tappe (´‿) [mhd.] f ⓸⓺ 1. paw, F (grobe Faust) heavy fist. — 2. = Fußtapfe.
tappeln F (´‿) v/n.(h.) ⓶a. (trippeln) to trip.
tappen (´‿) [mhd.; *tapp¹, Tapp(e)] v/n. (h. u. ſu) ⓸ 1. (plump schreiten) to walk (or tramp) clumsily or heavily. — 2. (taſten) to grope (F to poke) about (in the dark), F to fumble (about).
täppisch (´‿) [Tapp(e)] a. ⓺ clumsy, heavy, awkward, F fumble-fisted.
Taps (´) m ⓓa. = Tapp. [tap.]
Täpschen (⌣´‿) n ⓶ (dim. v. Taps) slight
tapſen (´‿) v/n. ⓺⁰ = tappen.
Tara ⓺ (´‿) [it., *ar.] f ⓺⓺ (Verpackungs-gewicht) tare, als Vergütung: deduction (made) for packages; verabredete ~ tare agreed upon.
Tarantel (‿´‿) [it.; *Tarent] f ⓸ ent. (Art giftige Spinne) tarantula (*Lyco'sa tara'ntula*); fig. wie von der ~ gestochen as if stung (by a gadfly), like one possessed, like mad. [tarantella.]
Tarantella (‿‿´‿) [it.] f ⓹⓺⓺ (it. Volkstanz)
Tara-rechnung (´‿...) f ⓶ tare-account; =vergütung f allowance for tare or packages.
Tarentiner (‿‿´‿) [Tare'nt(um) ♀, alte Hafenstadt Süd-italiens, jetzt Tara'nto] I m

---

Zeichen (f. S. XVII): F familiär; P Volkssprache; ⌐ Gaunerſprache; ↘ ſelten; † alt (auch gestorben); * neu (auch geboren); ↔ unrichtig;

[tarieren] — 949 — [tattern]

⊛, ~in *f* 🚂 Tarentine; inhabitant of (ancient) Tarentum, jetzt: of Taranto. — **II** *a. inv.* Tarentine; of Taranto.
tarieren (-ᴗ́-) [Tara] *v/a.* 💼 (die Tara in Anschlag bringen) to (allow for) tare.
Tarif ⊛ (ᴗ-́) [fr.; *ar. Bekanntmachung] *m* ⓦc. (Zolltafel) tariff, table of rates; 🚂 = Frachttarif, *a.* (Personen=)~ table of fares; laut (ob. nach) ~ as per tariff.
Tarif=ermäßigung ⊛ (ᴗ-́-ᴗᴗ) *f* 🔂 reduction of the tariff, 🚂 of the fare(s).
tarifieren (-ᴗ-́-) *v/a.* 💼 (im Tarif aufführen) to (put on the) tariff.
tarif=mäßig ⊛ (ᴗ-́...) *a.* 🄋 in accordance with the tariff; Arbeitersprch.: ⁀mäßige Löhne trade-union rates *pl.* (of pay); =satz *m* rate according to (the) tariff; =wesen *n* (system of) tariffs.
Tarlatan ⊛ (ᴗᴗ-, ⚘ ᴗᴗ-́) [indisch] *m* ⓦc. 🄋 (klar gewebter Musselin) tarlatan.
Tarn=kappe ⊛ (-ᴗ) *f* 🄋 [mhd.] magic hood, bisw.: tarn-cap (= Nebelkappe b).
Tarock (ᴗ-́) [it. *taro'cco* *m*] *n* (*m*) ⓦ (Kartenspiel) tarot(s *pl.*).
tarpejisch (ᴗ-́-) [lt.] *a.* 🄋: der ~e Fels auf dem röm. Kapitol: the Tarpeian Rock.
Tarsus ⚘ (ᴗ-́) [lt., *grch.] *m* ⓦ *anat.* (Fußwurzel) tarsus; *ent.* Tarsen *pl.* (Zehen der Insekten) tarsi *pl.*
Tartan ⁎ ⓦ (-ᴗ-) *m* ⓦ (buntgewürfeltes schottisches Zeug) tartan.
Tartane ⚓ (ᴗ-́-) [it.] *f* 🄋 (Küstenfahrzeug im Mittelmeere) tartan.
Tartar (ᴗ-́) ⚒ für Tatar ꝛc. (s. ds).
Tartaros, ...us (-ᴗᴗ) [grch.] *m* 🄋 *myth.* (Unterwelt, Reich der Schatten) Tartarus.
Tartsche (-ᴗ) [mhd.; fr. *targe*; (*dtsch. Zarge)] *f* 🄋 Mittelalter: target; ~n=träger *m* targeteer.
Täschchen (-ᴗ) *n* ⓩ (*dim. von* Tasche) small pocket or pouch or bag.
Tasche (-ᴗ) [ahd.; it.] *f* 🄋 **1.** pocket, bisw. a. fob; (Beutel) pouch, bag, für Geld: purse, der Pilger: scrip, der Bettler: wallet; ich muß ewig die Hand in der ~ haben I have for ever to put my hand in my pocket *or* to spend money; in die ~ stecken (to put into one's pocket; *fig.* e-n in die ~ stecken (können) to be far superior to a p.; aus j-s ~ leben to live at a p.'s expense. — **2.** = Schulmappe.
Täschel=kraut (-ᴗ-...) *n* 🄋 = Hirtentasche.
Taschen=ausgabe (-ᴗ-ᴗᴗ...) *f* 🄋 Buchhandel: pocket-edition; =buch *n* pocket- (or note-, memorandum-)book, als Jahrbuch: almanac, annual, als Führer: vademecum; =dieb *m* pickpocket, fein gekleideter: F swell mobsman; vor ~en wird gewarnt! beware of pickpockets!; =dieberei *f*, =diebstahl *m* picking pockets, pocket-picking; =format *n* Buchhandel: pocket-size; ⁀förmig *a.* 🄋 like a pocket, ⚘ bursiform; =geld *n* pocket-money; monatliches ~ monthly allowance; =kalender *m* p.-almanac, =kamm *m* p.-comb; =klappe *f* p.-flap, =kompaß *m* p.-compass; =krebs *m, zo.* common crab (*Cancer pagu'rus*); =macher *m* = Täschner; =messer *n* pocket- (or clasp-)knife; =muskel *m, zo.* der Beuteltiere: marsupial muscle; =pistol(e *f*) *n* pocket pistol; =spiegel *m* p.-glass; =spiel *n* juggling, conjur-

ing (tricks *pl.*); =spieler *m* juggler, conjurer; vgl. Gaukler; =spielerei, =spieler=kunst *f* jugglery, conjuring, legerdemain, sleight of hand; ⁀spiele(r)n *v/n.* (h.) 🄋 (🄋a.)* to do conjuring (tricks); =spieler=streich *m*, =stück *n* conjurer's (or conjuring) trick, F (clever) bit of legerdemain; =tuch *n* pocket-handkerchief, P wipe, F fogle, bandana; =uhr *f* watch, f. Nürnberger **II**; =wörterbuch *n* pocket-dictionary.
Taschner, Täschner südb. (-ᴗ) [Tasche] *m* 🄋 bagmaker; (Koffermacher) box- (or trunk-)maker.
Tasmani=er (ᴗ-́(ᴗ)ᴗ) [Tasma'nia ♀, austral. Insel, 1642 v. d. nbl. Seefahrer Tasman entdeckt] *m* 🄋, ~in *f* 🚂 Tasmanian.
Taß nordb. (ˊ) *m* 🄋a. *agr.* stack of sheaves; auch = Banse.
Täßchen (ˊᴗ) *n* ⓩ (*dim. von* Tasse) little (or small, tiny) cup.
Tasse (ˊᴗ) [fr., *ar.] *f* 🄋 cup, mit Untertasse: cup and saucer; größere (kleinere) ~ breakfast-cup (tea-cup); große (kleine) ~ Kaffee im Restaurant: large (small) cup of coffee; darf ich Ihnen noch eine ~ Tee einschenken? may I pour you out another cup of tea?; **Tassen=kopf** (-ᴗ-) *m* 🄋 = Obertasse.
Tastatur ♪ (ᴗᴗ-́) [it.] *f* 🄋 = Klaviatur.
tastbar (ˊ-) *a.* 🄋 palpable; tangible.
Taste ♪ (ˊᴗ) [it. *tasto*] *f* 🄋 key; weiße (schwarze) ~ der Klaviatur: white (black) note; auf den ~n hämmern to pound (or thump) on the keys.
tasten[1] (ˊᴗ)[mhd.: taste; *it.] ⊙ **I** *v/n.*(h.) **1.** = tappen **2.** — **2.** (fühlend prüfen) to feel one's way (a. *fig.*); to judge by one's touch; oder Versuch tentative trial or beginning. — **3.** nach et. 2 to stretch out one's hand(s) after (or for) a th. — **II** *v/a.* **4.** = antasten **1.** — **III** ~ *n* ⓩ **5.** touch; (Tappen) groping.
Tasten[2]**=bändiger** ♪ (ˊᴗ...) [Taste *pl.*] *m* 🄋 F co. (indifferent) pianist, one who thumps (on the piano); =brett, =lager *n* am Klavier ꝛc. keyboard; =hebel ⊙ *m*, *tel.* key-lever; =instrument *n* keyed instrument; =leiter *m* Klavier=üben: hand-guide; =stift *m* key-pin.
Taster (ˊᴗ) *m* 🄋 **1.** person who gropes about, F fumbler. — **2.** *ent.* (Fühler am Unterkiefer v. Insekten) palp (vgl. Fühlfaden). — **3.** *elect.* (Morse=)~ tapping-key, Morse sender. — **4.** ⊙ cal(l)ipers, cal(l)iper-compasses *pl.*
taster=artig (ˊᴗ...), =förmig *a.* 🄋 *ent.*: ⚘ palpiform; ⁀los *a. ent.* palpless; =zirkel *m* ⊙ = Taster **4.**
Tast=körperchen (ˊᴗ...) *n* ⓩ *anat.* touch-body, ⚘ tactile corpuscle; =organ, =werk=zeug *n* organ of touch; =sinn *m* sense of touch, feeling.
Tat[1] (ˊ) [ahd.: deed; **tat**[2] *f* 🄋(Handlung) action, einzelne: act, wichtige: deed, heldenmütige: exploit, geschichtl.: feat, große: achievement, performance; schlechte (verruchte) ~ foul (atrocious) deed or crime; auf (in, bei, über) der ~, auf frischer ~ ertappen to take in the very act, to catch red-handed; in der ~ (wirklich) in reality, in fact, indeed; er ließ die ~ dem Worte folgen he suited the action to the word; f. Rat **1.**

tat[2] (ˊ) *ind. impf.* von tun.
Tatar (ᴗ-́, oft ᴗ-́) [pers. *tátar*] *m* 🄋, ~in *f* 🚂 Tartar, r-r: Tatar; ~ei *npr/f.* 🄋 ♀ in Mittelasien: Ta(r)tary.
Tataren=horde (ᴗ-́ᴗ...) *f* 🄋 horde of Ta(r)tars; =nachricht *f* (seit dem Krimkriege: erlogener Bericht) mendacious (war-) news, false report; =tee *m* (geringe russ. Sorte Tee) brick-tea.
tatarisch (ᴗ-́-) *a.* 🄋 Ta(r)tar, Ta(r)tarian.
Tat=bestand (ˊ...) *m* 🄋 matter of fact, the real facts *r.-r.*: Tatar; (Sachlage) state of affairs; der objektive ~ the actual facts of the case; =beweis *m* proof founded on facts.
täte (-ᴗ) *subj. impf.* von tun.
taten[1] (ˊ-) *v/n.* 🄋 f. raten.
Taten[2]**=berg** (ˊ-...) *m* 🄋 (*SCH.*) pile of (glorious) deeds; =drang, =durst *m* eagerness to accomplish great feats; ⁀durstig, =gierig *a.* 🄋 eager to achieve noble deeds or exploits; ⁀los *a.* inactive, idle, indolent; ⁀reich, ⁀voll *a.* active (life, &c.); abounding in (great) achievements, eventful.
Täter (ˊᴗ) [Tat] *m* 🄋, ~in *f* 🚂 doer, bei Verbrechen: perpetrator of a crime, *abs.* evil-doer, culprit; (Urheber[in]) author(ess); ~schaft *f* 🄋 being the culprit; er leugnet die ~schaft nicht he does not deny having done it *or* doing it, gerichtlich: he pleads guilty.
Tat=handlung (ˊ-ᴗᴗ) *f* 🄋: a) outward act; b) (Gewalttat) deed of violence.
tätig (ˊ-) [ahd.; *Tat] *a.* 🄋 active, (up and) doing, (geschäftig) busy, astir; (tatsächlich) real, (wirksam) efficacious, working (well); als Arzt 2 sein to practise medicine, to follow the medical profession; in e-m Geschäfte 2 sein to be (employed or engaged) in a house of business; to work in an office.
Tätigkeit (ˊ-ᴗ-) *f* 🄋 activity, des Herzens ꝛc.: action; (Beschäftigung) occupation, (Beruf) profession, vocation; in voller ~ fully occupied, in full swing; in ~ setzen to put in(to) action or motion, to set going; außer ~ setzen to bring to a standstill; Beamte ꝛc.: to suspend, to ungear; ⊙ Maschinen: to throw out of gear or action; to ungear; ~s=form (ˊ-ᴗ-...) *f* 🄋 *gr.* active voice; ~s=trieb *m* eagerness to (do) work, active disposition; ~s=wort *n*, *gr.* verb.
Tat=kraft (ˊ...) *f* 🄋 energy, pluck; er hat keine ~ F he has no go (or push) in him; ⁀kräftig *a.* energetic; =kundig *a.* notorious; =kundigkeit *f* notoriety.
tätlich (ˊ-) *a.* 🄋 founded upon fact; bib. v. Begriffen: personal, violent; 2e Beleidigung assault (and battery); e-n 2 (*adv.*) mißhandeln to offer violence to a p., to commit an assault upon a p.; ~keit *f* (act of) violence, jur. assault (and battery).
tätowieren (ᴗᴗ-ᴗ, -ᴗ-́) [tahitisch] *v/a.* u. sich 2 *v/refl.* 🄋: (sich) 2 (den Körper durch eingestochene Punkte bemalen) to tattoo (o.s.).
Tat=sache (ˊ...) *f* 🄋 (matter of) fact; reality; ⁀sächlich *a* 🄋 founded (or based) on fact, actual, real, *adv.* a. in fact, in reality, f. a. faktisch.
Tatterich F (ˊᴗ...) [: dodder] *m* ⓦd. *path.* (Zittern, bsb. d. Hände) shakes *pl.* [shaky.]
tattern F (ˊᴗ) *v/n.*(h.) 🄋a. to dodder, to be ⌐

♪ Musik; ⚘ Wissenschaft; ♀ Pflanze; ♀ Geographie; ⊙ Technik; ✕ Bergbau; ⚔ Militär; ⚓ Marine; ⊛ Handel; ✉ Post; 🚂 Eisenbahn.

[tatuieren]

tatuieren ⚔ (⌣⌣⌣) = tätowieren.
Tatze (⌣) [mhd.] f ⊕: ~ e-s Bären ꝛc.: paw, claw, F co. v. Menschen: (heavy) fist; in j-s ~n in a p.'s clutches.
tatzen-förmig (⌣...) a. ⊕ paw-shaped, like a paw or claw; **-hieb** m ⊕ stroke with a paw.
Tau¹ (⌣) [ndd.: tow: ziehen] n ⓒc. (Seil) rope, dünneres: cord, ↓ cable, (Troſſe) hawser; f. aufſchießen 2, ausſtechen 6, Bucht 4.
Tau² (⌣) [ahd.: dew] m ⓒc. dew; es fällt ~ there is (a) dew falling.
taub (⌣) [ahd.: deaf: Duft] a. ⊕ 1. deaf, milder: hard of hearing; auf einem Ohre ⁑ deaf in (or of, on) one ear; ⁑ machen to deafen, to make deaf; ⁑ werden to grow (or become) deaf, to lose one's hearing; ein Tauber, (eine Taube) a deaf (wo)man, milder: a person who does not hear well. — 2. fig. ⁑ ſein bei (für, gegen, zu) j-s Bitten to turn a deaf ear to a p.'s entreaties; ⁑en Ohren predigen to preach to deaf ears or in the wilderness. — 3. (gefühllos) benumbed; without feeling, unfeeling, callous; die Hand iſt mir ⁑ my hand feels numb. — 4. fig. (unfruchtbar) barren, (leer) empty, void; ⁑es Ei addled egg; ⚔ ⁑er Gang barren load; ⁑es Geſtein: a) unproductive (or barren) rock; b) in e-m Gange (auch das **Taube**) dead lode, deads pl.; ⁑e Nuß hollow (or empty) nut.
Täubchen (⌣) [Taube dim.] n ⓒ 1. little pigeon or dove; unſchuldiges ~ F co. sucking dove. — 2. Koſewort: mein ~! my darling!, my love!, F (my) duckie!
Taube (⌣) [ahd.: dove] f ⊕ orn. pigeon, dove (Colu'mba), f. Hausttaube; verirrte ~ stray pigeon; fig. ſanft wie eine ~ (as) gentle as a dove; Sprichw. f. braten 3; Maul¹ 1 am Schluß; wo ~n ſind, fliegen ~n hin, etwa: nothing succeeds like success, bibl. to him that hath ſhall be given.
tauben-artig (⌣⌣...) a. ⊕ pigeon-, dove-like, ⚔ columbine; **-ausstellung** f ⊕ pi.-show; **-blume** ⚥ f: hohe ~ dove-plant (Peristeʹria elaʹta); **-ei** n pi.'s egg; **-einfalt** f dove-like simplicity.
tau²-benetzt (⌣⌣⌣) a. ⊕ = tau-feucht.
Tauben-falke (⌣...) m ⊕ orn. = Habicht; **-farbe** f dove-colour, bisw.: columbine; **⁑farbig** a. ⊕ dove-coloured; **-flug** m: a) pi.'s flight; b) coll. flight of pigeons.
taubenhaft (⌣⌣) a. ⊕ pigeon-(or dove-)like.
Tauben-hals-farbe (⌣⌣...) f ⊕ = -farbe; **-händler** m pi.-dealer; **-haus** n pi.-house, dovecot; **-kropf** m pi.'s crop; **-liebhaber** m pi.-fancier; **-paar** n couple (zſ.-gehöriges: pair) of pigeons; **-post** f correspondence carried on by means of carrier-pigeons; **-schießen** n pi.-shooting; **-schlag** m dovecot; F fig. house in which the servants often change; **-stößer** m, orn. = Habicht; **-züchter** m pigeon-breeder.
Tauber, Täuber (⌣) [mhd.: *Taube] m ⊕, **~ich** m ⓓd. cock-bird of pigeons, ſeltener: cock-pigeon.

— 950 —

Taub-feld ⚔ (⌣...) n ⊕ barren track; **-hafer** ⚥ m wild oats pl. (Aveʹna faʹtua).
Taubheit (⌣) f (ſ. taub) 1. deafness. — 2. (Gefühlloſigkeit) numbness. — 3. (Unfruchtbarkeit) barrenness of the soil; (Leere) emptiness.
Täubin (⌣) [Taube] f ⊕ female pigeon, auch: hen-pigeon. [(Agaʹricus).|
Täubling ⚥ (⌣) m ⓓd. Pilz: agaric
Taub-nessel ⚥ (⌣⌣) f ⊕ dead-nettle (Laʹmium); weiße ~ white dead-nettle (L. album).
Tau¹-brücke ↓ (⌣⌣⌣) f ⊕ rope-bridge.
taub-stumm (⌣...) a. ⊕ deaf and dumb; **~e([r]** m) f ⊕ a deaf and dumb person.
Taubstummen-alphabet (⌣⌣...) n ⊕ deaf-and-dumb alphabet; **-anstalt** f institution for the deaf and dumb; auch: deaf-and-dumb asylum; **-lehrer** m teacher of the deaf and dumb.
Taub-stummheit (⌣⌣-) f ⊕ deaf-and-dumbness.
Tauch-bad (⌣ch...) n ⊕ plunge-bath; **-batterie** ⊕ f, elect. plunge-battery.
tauchen (⌣⌣) [ahd.: duck] ⊕ I v/a. u. ſich ⁑ v/refl. 1. to dip, to duck; ſich ins Waſſer ⁑ to plunge (als Schwimmer: to dive) into the water. — II v/n. (h. u. ſn) 2. im Waſſer: to dive; die Sonne taucht ins Meer the sun dips (or sinks) into the ocean. — 3. (h.) bibl. mit der Hand (= die Hand) in eine Schüſſel ⁑ to dip into a dish. — 4. weit ſ. u. fig. ſ. auf-, ein-, unter-tauchen. III ~ n ⊕ 5. dipping, immersion.
Taucher (⌣ch⌣) [ahd.] m ⊕ 1. diver. — 2. orn. diver (Uriʹnator); vgl. Haubentaucher.
Taucher-anzug ⊕, ↓ (⌣⌣...) m ⊕ diving-dress; **-boot** n di.-boat; **-glocke** f di.-bell; **-helm** m di.-helmet; **-kolben** ⊕ m, mach. plunger; **-schiff** n diving-ship.
Tauch-käfer (⌣ch...) m ⊕ ent. diving-beetle (Dyʹticus); **-stange** ⊕ f b. Gerber: plunger.
tauen¹ ↓ (⌣) [Tau¹] v/a. ⊕: ein Schiff ⁑ (vorwärtsziehen) to tow a boat.
tauen² (⌣) [ahd.: thaw; *Tau²] ⊕ I v/n. (h. u. ſn) es taut it is thawing; der Schnee iſt von den Dächern getaut the snow has melted off the roofs. — II v/n. (h.): a) es taut (the) dew is falling, es hat ſtark getaut there has been a heavy dew; b) (von Tau befeuchtet ſein, glänzen) to be moist (or to glitter, sparkle) with dew. — III ~ n ⊕ (ſ. I) thaw; (ſ. II) (fall of) dew.
tauen³ ⊕ (⌣) v/a. ⊕ (weiß gerben) to taw.
Tau¹-ende (⌣⌣⌣) n ⊕ rope's end, pendant, tail (or end) of a cable.
Tauer (⌣) m ⊕ tawer of skins.
Tauf-akt (⌣...) m ⊕ eccl. christening-ceremony, (act of) baptism; **-becken** n baptismal (or christening-)font; **-buch** n parish-register.
Taufe (⌣) [ahd. ſ. taufen] f ⊕: a) eccl. baptism, v. jung. Kindern meiſt: christening, von Erwachſenen: adult baptism, immersion; ein Kind aus der ~ heben oder über die ~ halten to present a baby at the font, to stand godfather (or godmother) to a child; die ~ vornehmen to perform the christening-ceremony; b) = Taufschmaus.
taufen (⌣) [ahd.: dip: tief] ⊕ I v/a. ⊕ 1. a) meiſt eccl. to baptize, bſd. junge

[Taumellolch]

Kinder: to christen (auch von Glocken, Schiffen ꝛc.); ſie laſſen alle Jahre ⁑ they have a christening (or a new baby) every year; getaufte Juden converted Jews pl.; b) ↓ (hänſeln) to duck. — 2. F den Wein ⁑ (mit Waſſer verdünnen) to mix (or dilute) wine with water. — II ~ n ⊕ 3. = Taufe.
Täufer (⌣) [taufen] m ⊕ 1. one who christens or baptizes; Johannes der ~ John the Baptist. — 2. = Wiedertäufer.
tau-feucht (⌣-) a. ⊕ moist (or wet) with dew, bedewed, poet. dew-besprinkled or -bespangled, SH. dew-bedabbled.
Tauf-formel (⌣...) f ⊕ eccl. form of baptism; **-gebühr** f, **-geld** n christening fee; **-gelübde** n baptismal vow; **-gesinnte([r]** m) f ⊕ eccl. baptist; **-handlung** f = -akt; **-hemd** n = -kleid; **-kapelle** f in größeren Kirchen: baptistery; **-kind** n infant to be christened, a. = Pate 2; **-kissen** n pillow on which an infant (in Germany) is carried to the christening; **-kleid** n, **-mantel** m baptismal (or christening-)robe.
Täufling (⌣) m ⊕ eccl. infant (or baby, child) to be christened, candidate for baptism, dem Paten gegenüber: godchild.
Tauf-name (⌣...) m ⊕ Christian name; **-pate** m, f, **-patin** f = Pate 1; **-register** n = -buch. [bathed in dew.)
tau-frisch (⌣⌣) a. ⊕ fresh with dew,
Tauf-schein (⌣...) m ⊕ certificate of baptism; **-schmaus** m christening (-feast); **-stein** m, eccl. baptismal font; **-wasser** n water for christening, baptismal water; **-zeuge** m, **-zeugin** f = Pate 1, Gevatter 1; **-zeugnis** n = -schein.
taugen (⌣) [mhd.: Tugend, tüchtig] v/n. (h.) ⊕ to be good or fit or useful or of value, to answer (well), to serve a purpose; ſie ⁑ beide nicht viel they are neither of them worth (or F up to) much; nicht ⁑ (nichts oder zu nichts ⁑ to be worth (or good for) nothing, to be worthless or useless or of no use.
Tauge-nichts (⌣⌣-⌣) m ⓐa. ⊕ good-for-nothing (fellow), useless fellow, scape-grace, scamp.
tauglich (⌣) a. ⊕ good, fit, adapted, appropriate, available, serviceable (zu et. for a th.); able to do a th.; körperlich ⁑, v. Männern: able-bodied (a. ↓); v. Schiffen: (ſeefeſt) seaworthy; **Tauglichkeit** f ⊕ fitness, adaptedness.
Tau-haken ⊕, ↓ (⌣⌣⌣) m ⊕ cable-hook, chain-hook.
tauicht, mſt **tauig** (⌣) [Tau²] a. ⊕ dewy, covered (or moist, wet) with dew.
Tau¹-länge (⌣...) f ⊕ cable's length; **²-luft** f soft air, mild atmosphere.
Taumel (⌣) [mhd.: taumeln] m ⊕ wavering, reeling, (Schwindel) giddiness; (Rauſch) intoxication, inebriation; ſtärker: delirium; (Verzückung) frenzy, ecstasy; ~ der Gefühle exuberance of spirits. [inebriating cup.)
Taumel-becher (⌣⌣...) m ⊕ **-kelch** m ⊕
Taum(e)ler (⌣⌣) m ⊕ 1. one who reels. — 2. = Tummeltaube.
taum(e)lig (⌣⌣) a. ⊕ reeling, unsteady, staggering, tottering, giddy.
Taumel-kerbel ⚥ (⌣⌣...) m ⊕ hemlock-chervil (Chaerophyʹllum teʹmulum); **-lolch**

Signs (see page XVII): F familiar; P vulgar; ⚡ flash; ⚔ rare; † obsolete (died); * new word (born); ∴ incorrect; ♪ music;

[taumeln] — 951 — [Tee]

& m bearded darnel, cockle (*Lo'lium temule'ntum*).
taumeln (⌣́) [ahd.: tummeln] ②a. I *v/n.* (h. u. ſn) to reel, stagger, totter; (ſtürzen) to tumble; er iſt in das Zimmer getaumelt he staggered into ...; zu Boden ⁀ to fall reeling (von Dingen: to topple) to the ground; *fig.* er taumelt von dem unverhofften Glück the unhoped-for stroke of luck has turned his head or brain. — II ~ n ㉓ tottering (gait); ſ. Taumel.
Tau²-meſſer (⌣́⌣) m ㉒ *phys.:* ⚛ drosometer. [Taumeler, taumeln.]
Taumler (⌣́) m ㉒, **taumlig** a. ⑥⑥ ſ.⸗
Tau²-perle (⌣́) f ⑧ dewy pearl; =**punkt** m, *phys.* dew-point; =**regen** m, *etwa:* rain causing a thaw.
tauriſch (⌣́) [Tauris ⚓ Krim] a. ⑥⑥ Tauric.
Tauſch (⌣́) [nhd.] m ⓐa. exchange, ⚚ barter, truck; in ~ gegen ... in exchange for ...; e-n guten ~ machen to make a good exchange.
tauſchen (⌣́) [(mhd.) nhd.;*Tauſch*] I *v/a.* u. *v/n.* (h.) ⓠ to exchange (gegen for), P to swop, ⚚ (Tauſchhandel treiben) to barter, to truck; *eccl.* die Pfründe ⁀ to exchange livings; ich möchte nicht mit ihm ⁀ I would not change places with him or F be in his shoes; die Rolle mit e-m ⁀ to turn the tables upon a p. — II ~ n ㉓ = Tauſch.
täuſchen (⌣́) [mhd.: vertuſchen] I *v/a.*, *v/n.* (h.) u. ſich ⁀ *v/refl.* ⓠ: (ſich) ⁀ to deceive (o.s.); (hintergehen) to delude, to impose upon, to cozen; (prellen) to cheat, to trick, F to take in, to do; (irreführen) to mislead, (anführen) to mystify; das Äußere täuſcht (oft) appearances are (often) deceptive; wenn mich meine Augen nicht ⁀ if my eyes do not deceive me or play me false; darin ⁀ Sie ſich ſehr you are very much mistaken in that; ſich durch et. (leicht) ⁀ laſſen to be (easily) deluded (or ensnared) by a th.; in ſeinen Hoffnungen getäuſcht werden to be (or to see o.s.) disappointed or disillusioned or baffled; e-n um et. ⁀ (betrügen) to cheat (or trick) a p. out of a th. — II ~ n ㉓ ſ. Täuſchung, bſd. Artikel. — III ⁀d *p.pr.* u. *a.* ⑥⑥ (trügend) deceptive, delusive, illusory; ⁀de Ähnlichkeit striking resemblance; ſie ſind (ſich) ea. ⁀d (*adv.*) ähnlich they can easily be mistaken one for the other, they are like two peas in a pod; das iſt ⁀d nachgemacht oder ähnlich it's a perfect (or life-like) copy.
Tauſcher (⌣́) m ㉒, ~**in** f ㊽ one who exchanges or P swops, ⚚ barterer.
Täuſcher (⌣́) m ㉒, ~**in** f ㊽ deceiver, cheat(ing person); *vgl.* Roßtäuſcher.
Tauſcherei (⌣⌣́) f ㊻ deception, illusion.
Tauſch-geſchäft (⌣́...) n, =**handel** ⚚ m ㉒: a) (*ant.* Kaufhandel) barter(ing), truck(age); ~ treiben to barter, to truck; b) einzelnes ~ = Tauſch; =**händler** m barterer, trucker. [towing.]
Tau¹-ſchiffahrt ⚓ (⌣́⌣⌣) f ㊻ cable-]
tauſch-luſtig (⌣́⌣⌣) a. ⑥⑥ fond of exchanging or bartering.
Täuſchung (⌣́) f ㊻ 1. ⚘ (das Täuſchen) deceiving a p., practising deception

upon a p.; mystification of a p.; ~ zu einem angeblich frommen Zwecke pious fraud. — 2. (Getäuſchtwerden) deception (practised upon a p.), delusion, imposition; (Täuſchendes) makebelieve; optiſche ~ optical delusion; man gebe ſich darüber keiner ~ hin there must be no illusion (or mistake) about that.
Tauſch-vertrag (⌣́...) m ㉒ agreement (or treaty) by which an exchange is effected; ⁀**weiſe** *adv.* by way of exchange or barter or truck.
tauſend¹ (⌣́) [ahd.: thousand] *numer.* I *card. numb.* thousand; ⁀ Jahre a thousand years; ⁀ und aber=⁀ thousands upon thousands; nicht eine(r) unter ⁀ not one in a thousand; vor vielen ⁀ Jahren many thousand(s of) years ago; viel ⁀ Menſchen many thousands of people; in Flüchen ꝛc.: ⁀ (ſchock)ſchwerenot! hang it all!, damn it!; potz ⁀! goodness alive! — II ~ n ㉓ (die Zahl ~) thousand, ⚘ chiliad; ~ (1000 Stück) a thousand; zu ~en by (or in their) thousands; ⚚ vom ~ per thousand (F per thou.), a. pro mille; es geht in die ~e it runs into thousands.
Tauſend² (⌣́) [Daus²] m ⓐd. Ausruf: der ~ (noch einmal)!, ei der ~! dear me!, good gracious!, goodness alive!; *vgl.* potz tauſend.
tauſend¹=armig (⌣́...) *a.* ⑥⑥ with (or having) a thousand arms; =**blatt** ⚘ n ㉒ water milfoil (*Myriophy'llum*); =**eck** n, *math.:* ⚛ chiliagon.
Tauſender (⌣́⌣) m ㉒ 1. *arith.* (a) thousand. — 2. (die Ziffer 1000, M) (number) thousand.
tauſender-lei (⌣́⌣⌣) *a. inv.* (of) a thousand (different) kinds or species; wir ſprachen von ⁀ Dingen we spoke of a (hundred and a) thousand things.
tauſend¹=fach (⌣́...), =**fältig** *a.* ⑥⑥ thousandfold; in a thousand ways; =**fuß** m ⚘ *ent.* milliped, millepede; =**füß(l)er** m ㉒ *zo.:* ⚛ myriapod; =**gülden-kraut** ⚘ n centaury (*Erythrae'a*); echtes ~ common (or lesser) centaury (*E. Centau'rium*); ⁀**jährig** *a.* ⑥⑥ of a thousand years, a thousand years old; millenarian, millennial; ⁀es Reich Chriſti millennium; =**korn** ⚘ n = Bruchkraut; =**künſtler** ⚚ m one who knows many tricks; (Gaukler) co'njurer, juggler; ⁀**mal** *adv.* a thousand times; ⁀**malig** *a.* done (or repeated) a thousand times (over); ⁀**ſakerment** *int., etwa:* the deuce (take it all)!, damn (the lot)!; =**ſakramenter**, =**ſaſa** F m devil (*milder:* brick or trump) of a fellow; =**ſchön(chen** ㉓) ⚘ n ⓐd. (common) daisy (*Bellis pere'nnis*).
tauſendſt (⌣́) *ord.numb.* ⑥⑥ thousandth; *vgl.* hundertſt; ~**el** n ㉒, ⁀**el** *a. inv.* thousandth (part); ein ~el des Ganzen a thousandth part of the number; in Zſſgn *oft:* mill(i)..., z. B. ein ⁀el (¹⁄₁₀₀₀) Ster, Volt a millistere, millivolt; ⁀**ens** (⌣́⌣)*adv.* in the thousandth place.
tauſend¹=undeins ⚘ *a.* ⑥⑥ thousand and one; ein Märchen aus **⁀undeiner** Nacht one of the Arabian night-tales; ⁀**weiſe** *adv.* by thousands; ⁀**züngig** *a.* with a thousand tongues.

Tau¹-ſtopper ⚓ ⚓ (⌣́⌣) m ㉒ ring-rope, stopper.
Tautologie (⌣⌣⌣́) [grch.] f ㊽ (unnütze Wiederholung von Worten) tautology; **tautologiſch** (⌣⌣́⌣) *a.* ⑥⑥ tautological.
Tau²-tropfen (⌣́...) m ㉒ dew-drop; =**werk** n ropes *pl.*, cordage, tackle, *altes zerhacktes:* junk; =**wetter** n thaw, break in the weather; =**wind** m mild (westerly) breeze.
Tax¹ ⚘ (⌣́) m ⓐa. = Taxus.
Tax²... (⌣́...) [Taxe] ſ. taxfrei ꝛc.
Taxameter (⌣⌣́⌣) [⁺+. lt.=grch.] m ㉒ (Fahrpreis-anzeiger, Zeigerdroſchke) taximeter; ~**droſchke** f taximeter-cab, F taxicab.
Taxator (⌣́⌣) [lt.] m ㉟, ~**in** f ㊽ (Abſchätzer) taxer, valuer, appraiser; vereidigter ~ sworn assessor or valuer.
Taxe (⌣́) [lt.] f ㊽ 1. (Schätzung des Wertes) taxation, valuation. — 2. = Tax-ordnung. — 3. = Taxpreis. — 4. ⚚ (Abgabe, Steuer) tax, impost, rate.
tax²=frei (⌣́...) *a.* ⑥⑥ free from taxation; =**gebühr** f ㉒ appraiser's fee or charge.
taxieren (⌣⌣́) [lt.] I *v/a.* ⓠ 1. *ehm.* Brot, Fleiſch ꝛc. ⁀ to fix (or regulate) the price(s) of ..., *ehm.:* to assize ... — 2. (veranſchlagen) to value, to estimate, *mſt amtlich:* to appraise, tax, assess. — II ~ n ㉓ ſ. Taxierung.
Taxierer (⌣⌣́⌣) m ㉒ = Taxator.
Taxierung (⌣⌣́) f ㊻ (ſ. taxieren 2) valuation, estimate; appraisement, taxation, assessment.
Tax-ordnung (⌣́...) f ⑥⑥ (obrigkeitliche Feſtſetzung v. Preiſen) fixing (or regulation) of prices, assizement; =**preis** m price (or rate, charge) fixed (or allowed) by the authorities, *ehm.:* assize.
Taxus ⚘ (⌣́) [lt.] m, *inv.* = ~=baum.
Taxus-arten ⚘ (⌣́) f/pl. ⑥⑥ ⚛ taxaceae *pl.*; =**baum** m (Eibenbaum) (common) yew-tree (*Taxus bacca'ta*).
Tax=wert (⌣́...) m ㉒ appraised (or estimated) value. [*ci'ssus taze'tta*.]
Tazette ⚘ (⌣⌣́) [it.] f ㊽ tazetta (*Nar-*]
T-band (te"⌣) ⚓ ⚓ n ⓐ Schloſſerei: T-hinge.
Teak-baum, =**holz** ſ. Tiek...
Technik (⌣́⌣) [grch.] f ㊻ technical science, technics, technology; (Ausführung, Geſchid) workmanship, •execution, (technical) skill; (künſtleriſche Ausführung) technique; ~**er** (⌣́⌣) m ㉒ (technical) engineer, a. technicist; (techniſcher Leiter) working (or technical) manager; ~**um** (⌣́⌣) n ㉘㊾ technical school.
techniſch (⌣́⌣) [grch.] *a.* ⑥⑥ technical; ⁀e Ausdrücke, Einzelheiten, *oft:* technicalities *pl.*; ⁀e Hochſchule technical university. [(werbekunde) technology.]
Technologie ⚛ (⌣⌣⌣́) [grch.] f ㊽ (Ge-]
Techtelmechtel (⌣́⌣⌣) [jüd.] n ㉒ love-affair; (geheimes Einverſtändnis) secret understanding, intrigue.
Tecke (⌣́) [nhd.] f ㊽ *zo.* (Holzbock) tick (*Ixo'des*). [hund.]
Teckel (⌣́) [Dachs, *dim.*] m ㉒ = Dachs-]
Tede-um ♪ (— ⌣́⌣) [it.] n ㊿ Te Deum.
Tee (⌣́) [chineſ.] m ㉒ 1. tea; dünner (*ob. ſchwacher*) ~ weak (*nicht:* thin!) tea; ~ trinken to drink (or take) tea; er trinkt gern ſehr ſtarken ~ he likes his tea very strong or almost black; wir luden ſie zum ~ ein we invited her to

---
⚛ scientific; ⚘ botanical; ⚲ geography; ⊙ machinery; ⚒ mining; ⚔ military; ⚓ marine; ⚚ commercial; ✉ postal; 🚆 railway.

[teeartig] — 952 — [teilweise]

tea, we asked her to have (a cup of) tea with us. — 2. weit S. (Aufguß von Kräutern) infusion (of herbs), (herb-) tea. — 3. F im ~ (betrunken) sein to be drunk or in liquor; burſch.: ſich in ~ (Gunſt) ſetzen, F ~ reiten to curry favour.
Tee-artig (*"...*) a. ⑯ tea-like, ⚛ theiform; =**bau** m ⑫ tea-growing, cultivation of tea; =**baum** ⚘ m = =ſtrauch; =**blatt** n tea-leaf; =**brett** n tea-tray; =**büchſe** /tea-caddy; =**gebäck** == =kuchen; =**gerät**, =**geſchirr** n = =zeug; =**geſellſchaft** f tea(-party); =**händler** m tea-merchant; =**kanne** f tea-pot; =**käſtchen** n tea-caddy; =**keſſel** m: a) tea-kettle; b) F fig. (Dummkopf) blockhead; =**kind** F n Schulſprache: favourite; =**kiſte** ⚓ f tea-chest; =**klatſch** F m co. tea and scandal, tea-fight; =**kräuter** ⚘ n/pl. herbs pl. used for infusion(s); =**kuchen** m tea-cake; =**löffel** m tea-spoon; =**löffelvoll** m tea-spoonful; =**maſchine** f tea-urn; =**mütze** f zum Bedecken der Teekanne: tea-cozy.
Teer ⊙ (*¹*) [nbb.: tar] m (n) ⓐc. tar; mit ~ beſtreichen, beſchmieren to tar (over).
Teer-asphalt ⊙ (*"...*) m ⑫ artificial asphalt; ⚙**beſchmiert** a. ⑯ tarry, tarred; =**brenner** m tar-burner or boiler; =**brennerei** f tar-factory or -works pl.; =**büchſe**, =**bütte** f tar-box.
teeren ⊙ (*¹∨*) I v/a. ⑱ to (cover with) tar, ein Schiff: to (paint with) pitch. — II ~ n ⑱ tarring.
Teer-farben (*"...*) f/pl. ⑫ chm. aniline colours; =**farbſtoffe** m/pl. coal-tar (or aniline) dyes pl.; =**faß** ⊙ n tar-barrel; =**grube** f tar-pit; =**hütte** f = =brennerei.
teericht, teerig (*¹∨*) a. ⑯ tarry, tarred.
Teer-jacke (*"...*) f ⑫: a) tarred jacket; b) ⚓ [✠ P] fig. ⚓ (Matroſe) Jack Tar; =**keſſel** ⊙ m tar-kettle; =**öl** n tar-oil.
Tee-roſe ⚘ (*¹∨*) f ⑫ tea-rose (*Rosa I'ndica*).
Teer-pappe (*"...*) f ⑫ Dachbeckerei: tar-board; =**pinſel** m tar-brush or -link; =**quaſt** m pitch-mob; =**ſand** m viscous sand; =**ſchweler(ei** f) m = =brenner(ei); =**tonne** f = =faß; =**tuch** n tarpaulin(g).
Teerung (*¹∨*) f ⑯ tarring.
Teer-waſſer (*"...*) n ⑫ tar-water (a. med.); ⚙**Gasfabrik**: gas-water or -liquor; =**werg** m tarred oakum; =**ziſterne** f ⚙**Gasfabrik**: tar-cistern or -well.

Tee-ſieb (*"...*) n ⑫ tea-strainer; =**ſteuer** f duty on tea; =**ſtoff** m = Tein; =**ſtrauch** ⚘ m tea-plant or -shrub (*Thea chine'nsis*); =**taſſe** f tea-cup; =**tiſch** m tea-table; =**topf** m = =kanne; =**trinker(in** f) m tea-drinker; =**urne** f tea-urn; =**waſſer** n (boiling) water for (making) tea; =**zeug** n tea-things pl.
Tegel (*¹∨*) m ⑫ geol. sandy clay.
Tei-anker ⚓ (*¹∨*) [ſ. verteilen] m ⑫ (kleiner Bug-anker) small bower.
Teich (*¹*) [nbb.: ditch: Deich] m ⓐc. pond; (Behälter, Ziſterne) tank.
Teich-binſe ⚘ (*"...*) f ⑫ bulrush, ⚛ heleocharis; =**feder** ⚘ f = Bandgras; =**fiſch** m pond-fish; =**fiſcherei** f pond-fishing; =**gitter** n fence round a pond, pond-grating; =**karpfen** m, ichth. pond-carp (*Cypri'nus ca'rpio*); =**kolben** ⚘ f = reedmace (*Typha*); =**muſchel** f, zo. pond-mussel; =**rohr**, =**ſchilf** ⚘ n = Rohr 2;

=**roſe** ⚘ f water-lily (*Nuphar*); =**ſchnecke** f, zo. pond-snail, ⚛ limnæa.
Teig¹ (*¹*) [ahd.: dough] m ⓐc. Bäckerei: dough, paste; den ~ kneten to knead (or work) the dough.
teig² ſübb. (*¹*) a. ⑯ mellow.
Teig-affe F (*"...*) m ⑫ contp. (Bäcker) baker, F doughy; =**decke** f dough crust.
teigicht, teigig¹ (*¹∨*) a. ⑯ doughy, dough-like.
teigig² (*¹∨*) a. ⑯ = teig².
Teig-kneter (*"...*) m ⑫ dough-kneader; =**meſſer** n dough-knife; =**mulde** f kneading-trough; =**rädchen** n jagging-iron; =**rolle** f rolling-pin; =**ſcharre** f scraper; =**ſchneide-maſchine** ⊙ f doughing-machine.
Teil (*¹*) [ahd.: deal, dole] m (n) ⓐc. 1. part; (Abteilung) division, e-s Schriftwerkes: volume; edle ~e des Körpers: vital parts pl.; der größte (genauer: größere) ~ der Menſchen the greater part (or the majority) of mankind, most people; ein gut ~ von et. a good deal (F bit) of s.th.; beide ~e (Parteien) both parties or sides pl.; jur. der klagende (verklagte) ~ the plaintiff (defendant). — 2. mit Zahlwörtern: drei ~e (³/₄) von et. three parts (or quarters) pl. of a th.; zwei ~e (²/₃) two-thirds pl.; der vierte Teil von 60 the fourth part (or one-fourth) of sixty; oft verſchmelzend mit ~ (n), mſt abbr. in tonloſes ...**tel**, z.B. ein Dritt-⸺ oder Drittel one-third. — 3. meiſt n (Anteil) portion, share; gleiche ~e equal shares or halves pl.; er hat ſein ~ (bekommen) he has had his (full) share or his due; wenn er auch nicht viel ſpricht, ſo denkt er doch ſein ~ though he does not speak much he thinks all the more; F ich habe ihm ſein ~ gegeben (die Wahrheit geſagt) I gave him a piece of my mind; vgl. teilhaben, teilnehmen. — 4. adv. ich an meinem ~e, ich meinesteils, ich für mein(en) ~ I for my (own) part, I for one, as to me, as for me, as regards myself; um ein gut ~ reicher a good deal richer; zum ~ (abbr. z. T.) (nicht ganz) part(ial)ly; to some extent; zum ~, zum ~ // partly //, partly //; zum größten ~e for the greater part, in the main, (meiſtens) mostly; vgl. anderntels, einesteils, zuteil.
teilbar (*¹∨*) a. ⑯ divisible; bibl. math. (meßbar) commensurable; **~keit** f ⑯ divisibility; math. commensurableness.
Teil-begriff (*"...*) m ⑫ phls., gram. partial notion; =**beſitzer** m part-owner.
Teilchen (*¹∨*) n ⓐ (dim. von Teil) small part, particle; a. = Atom, Molekül.
teilen (*¹∨*) [ahd.: deal] I v/a. u. ſich ⚄ v/refl. ⑱ 1. to divide, in Grade: to graduate; (zerſtückeln) to dismember, (austeilen) to distribute, to portion (or parcel) out; (abſondern) to separate, to partition (off); auch = halbieren; den Unterſchied ⚄ to split the difference; von Straßen: ſich ⚄ to branch out; 12 läßt ſich durch 3 teilen twelve can be divided (or is divisible) by three; ſich in et. ⚄ to share a th. with s.o., zu zweien: to go halves. — 2. (teilhaben an, mitfühlen) et. mit e-m teilen to share a th. with a p.; e-s Freude ⚄ to rejoice

with a p.; e-s Gefühle ⚄ to enter into a p.'s feelings; e-s Kummer, Schmerz ⚄ to sympathize with a p. (in his grief), to feel for a p. — II ~ n 3. ſ. Teilung.
Teiler (*¹∨*) m ⑫ 1. a. **~in** f ⑯ one who divides, divider. — 2. arith. divisor; der größte gemeinſame ~ von zwei oder mehr Werten: the greatest common measure (abbr. g. c. m., G.C.M.).
teil-haben (*"...*) ⚄ v/n. ⑬b** (h.): an et. ⚄ to (have a)'share in a th., to partake of a th.; an Geſchäften: to have a share (or an interest) in a concern; ⚄ **b** a. ⑯ participating in, ⚂ participant of; =**haber(in** f) m ⑫ one who shares in, participator, ⚃ partner, joint (or co-)proprietor; ſtille(r) ~ sleeping partner; =**haberſchaft** ⚂ f partnership.
teilhaft (*¹∨*), mehr gebr. **~ig** (*¹∨*) a. ⑯: e-s Dinges ⚄ partaking of a th., participating in a th.; e-n einer Sache ⚄ m. to let a p. share (in) s.th.; e-r Sache ⚄ w. to partake of a th., to come in for (a share of) a th.
...teilig (*...¹∨*) [Teil] a. ⑯ in Zſgn: zehn~ in (or consisting of) ten parts.
Teil-kreis (*"...*) m ⑫ e-s Zahnrades: pitch-circle; =**maſchine** ⊙ f dividing-engine or -machine, ſ. =ſcheibe; =**nahme** f: a) participation in, bei Verbrechen: complicity; (Mitarbeiterſchaft) co-operation; b) (Mitempfindung) sympathy, (Mitleid) commiseration; ⚄**nahmlos** a. ⑯ without sympathy, indifferent, listless, callous; =**nahmloſigkeit** f indifference, listlessness, apathy; ⚄**nehmen** v/n. ⑬a** (h.): an et. ⚄ to participate in a th., to take part in a th., an einer Arbeit: to cooperate in a th., ſchriftſtelleriſch: to contribute to a work, an einem Plane 2c.: to be involved (or concerned) in a scheme, &c.; an e-m Spiel(e) ⚄ to join in a game; ⚄**nehmend** a. taking an interest in, (mitfühlend) sympathetic, sympathizing; =**nehmer(in** f) m = =haber(in); (Mitſchuldige[r]) accomplice.
teils (*¹*) [gen. von Teil] adv. partly; ⚄ in Geld, ⚄ in Gut partly in money, partly in kind; ⚄ zu Fuß, ⚄ zu Roß some on foot, some on horseback; ⚄ durch Spielen, ⚄ durch Trinken what with gambling, what with drinking. — ...**teils** in Zſgn ſ. Teil 4.
Teil-ſcheibe ⊙ (*"...*) f ⑫ zum Einteilen von Kreiſen: graduation-engine, graduator; =**ſtrecke** f section (or branch) of a (railway- or tramway-)line.
Teilung (*¹∨*) f ⑯ (ſ. teilen I) division, distribution; separation, partition, in Grade: graduation, in Stücke: dismemberment (of an empire, &c.), in Parzellen: parcelling out, v. Land: allotment.
Teilungs-artikel (*"...*) m ⑫ gram. partitive article; =**linie** f line of partition or demarcation, boundary-line; =**punkt** m point of division; =**recht** n right of partition; =**vertrag** m, pol. partition-treaty; =**zahl** f, arith. dividend; =**zeichen** n mark of division gr. (Bindeſtrich) hyphen.
teil-weiſe (*"...*) adv.: a) partly partially, in part; b) in parts; F

[Teilzahl] — 953 — [Teppichband]

a. partial; **zahl** *f* ⑫ quotient; **zahlung** *f* part-payment; instalment.
Te-in ⚗ (‑᷾) [neult.; *Tee] *n* ⓓ. *chm.* (Alkaloid im Tee) theine ($C_8H_{10}N_4O_2$).
Teint (tä) [fr.] *m* ⑪ (Gesichtsfarbe) complexion; e-n guten ~ haben, *a.* to have a good colour or a fine complexion.
T-Eisen ⊙ (‑᷾‑‿) *n* ㉓ T-iron.
Tektonik ⚗ (‑᷾) [grch.] *f* ㊻ tectonics.
tektonisch (‑᷾‿) *a.* ㊿ tectonic.
Tektur (‑᷾) [lt. Ded.] *f* ㊾ bsd. ⚔ (Deckblatt) circular (containing new instructions) printed on one side only.
Tele-funke(n)* (‑᷾‿‿) [grch.‑dtsch] *m* ⑫ wireless message, als Name e-r Gesellschaft: wireless telegraph company.
Telegramm ᵗ (‑‿᷾) [.+ grch. 1852] *n* ⓓ. (Drahtmeldung) telegram, telegraphic message, F wire; ein ~ aufgeben (absenden) to hand in (to send off) a telegram, F to wire.
Telegrammmarke (‑‿᷾‿) [Telegrammmarke] *f* ㊻ stamp for telegrams.
Telegramm-nachricht (‑‿᷾‿‿) *f* ⑫ = Drahtnachricht.   [telegraph.]
Telegraph (‑‿᷾) [fr. 1793; *grch.] *m* ⑫
Telegraphen-amt (‑‿᷾‿‿) *n* ⑫ telegraph-office; **beamte(r)** *m* = Telegraphist; **bote** *m* telegraph-messenger or ‑boy; **draht** *m* tel.-wire; **kabel** *n* tel.-cable; **leitung, linie** *f* tel.-line, line of telegraphs; **netz** *n* tel.-system; **stange** *f*, **strang** *m* tel.-pole, -wire; **wesen** *n* telegraphs, telegraphic concerns *pl.*
Telegraphie (‑‿‿᷾) *f* ㊽ (Fernschreibekunst) telegraphy; drahtlose ~ od. ~ ohne Draht wireless telegraphy; ✕ optische ~ visual signalling; ⚓ren *v/a.* ⚛ to telegraph, to wire; drahtlos ⚓ren to send a wireless message; **telegraphisch** (‑‿᷾‿) *a.* ㊿ telegraphic, *adv.* by telegraph, F by (⚛ per) wire.
Telegraphist (‑‿᷾) *m* ⑫, **~in** *f* ㊺ telegraph clerk or operator, telegraphist.
Telemach(os) (᷾‿‿, ‑᷾‿‿) *npr/m.* ⓒ. ⓓ(⑯)α. *grch. myth.* bsd. bei Homer: (Sohn des Odysseus) Telemachus.
Teleologie ⚗ (‑‿‿‿᷾) [grch.] *f* ㊽ *phls.* (Lehre von der Zweckmäßigkeit [der Weltordnung]) teleology; **teleologisch** (‑‿‿‿‿᷾) *a.* ㊿ teleological.
Telephon (‑‿᷾) [grch.] *n* ⓓ. (Fernsprecher) telephone; **~anschluß** *m* ⑫ telephonic connexion; ⚓ren (‑‿᷾‿) *v/a.* u. *v/n.* (h.) ⑭ to (communicate or call by) telephone; **~isch** (‑‿᷾‿) *a.* ㊿ telephonic (message. &c.); ⚒ *(adv.)* anfragen to inquire by telephone; **~istin** *f* telephone girl; **~kabel** *n* telephone cable; **~ruf** *m* telephone call; **~stelle** *f* telephone call-office.
Teleskop (‑‿᷾) [grch.] *n* ⓓ. *opt.* (Fernrohr) telescope; **~gasometer** ⊙ *n* ⑫ telescopic gasholder; ⚓isch (‑‿᷾‿) *a.* ㊿ telescopic; **~schnecke** *f, zo.* telescope-shell (*Trochus telescópium*).
Teller (᷾‿) [ndl.; *fr. *tailloir*] *m* ⑫ 1. plate, aus Holz: trencher (f. Präsentierteller). — 2. ⚗ *phys.* ~ e-r Luftpumpe table of an air-pump, *anat.* ~ der Hand palm of the hand; **-artig** *a.* ㊿ plate-like; **~brett** *n* ⑫ in Küchen: plate-rack; **-förmig** *a.* plate-shaped;

⚗ scutellate(d), hypocrateriform; **~korb** *m* plate-basket; **~lecker(ei)** *m* F = Schmarotzer(ei); **~ring** *m* napkin-ring; **~schneckentier** *n, zo.*: ⚗ planorbis; **~schrank** *m* sideboard, cupboard; **~tuch** *n*: a) (Serviette) (dinner-)napkin; b) zum Abwischen der Teller: tea-cloth; **~voll** *m* plateful; **~wärmer** *m* plate-warmer.
Tellur ⚗ (‑᷾) [lt. Erd-] *n* ⓓ. *chm.* (silberweißes, dem Schwefel ähnliches Element) tellurium (Te).
Tellur-blei ⚗ (‑᷾‿‿) *n* ⑫ *chm.* telluride of lead; **-erz** *n, min.* tellurium-ore.
tellurig ⚗ (‑᷾‿) [Tellur] *a.* ㊿ *chm.*: ⚒e Säure tellurous acid (H_2TeO_3).
tellurisch ⚗ (‑‿᷾) [lt.] *a.* ㊿ *geol.*, &c. (die Erde betr.) tellurian.
Tellurium ⚗ (‑‿᷾‿) *n* ㉘ 1. *chm.* = Tellur. — 2. (die Erdbewegungen im Sonnensysteme darstellende Vorrichtung) tellurion.
Tellur-oxyd ⚗ (‑᷾‿‿) *n* ⑫ *chm.* tellurous oxide; **⚒sauer** *a.* ㊿ telluric; ⚒saures Salz tellurate; **‑säure** *f* telluric acid (H_2TeO_4); **‑silber** *n* telluride of silver; **‑verbindung** *f* telluride; **‑wasserstoff** *m* telluret(t)ed hydrogen (H_2Te).
Tempel (᷾‿) [ahd.; *lt. *templum* n] *m* ⑫ 1. temple, *poet.* fane; (Heiligtum) sanctuary; F *fig.* e-n zum ~ hinauswerfen to turn a p. out (of doors). — 2. (Hasardspiel) game of chance. — 3. ⊙ Weberei: temple, weaver's stick.
Tempel-bau (᷾‿‿‿) *m* ⑫ building (or construction) of a temple; **‑diener** *m* officer of a temple, priest; **‑herr** *m* im Mittelalter: (Knight‑) Templar; **‑herrisch, -herrlich** *a.* ㊿ (Knights‑)Templars; **‑hof** *m:* a) Alt.: court of the temple; b) Mittelalter: residence of a Grand Master of the (Knights‑)Templars, auch: Temple.
tempeln (᷾‿) [Tempel 2] *v/n.* (h.) ⑫a. to gamble, to play games of chance.
Tempel-orden (᷾‿‿‿) *m* ⑫ (1118–1312) Order of the (Knights‑)Templars; **‑raub** *m* sacrilege; **‑räuberisch** *a.* ㊿ sacrilegious; **‑ritter** *m* = **‑herr**; **‑schänder** *m* desecrator of a temple.
Tempera-farbe (᷾‿‿‿) [it.] *f* ⑫ *paint.* distemper(‑colour); **‑malerei** *f* painting in distemper; **‑manier** *f:* in ~ malen to distemper.
Temperament (‑‿‿᷾) [lt.] *n* ⓒ. (Gemütsart) temperament; schlimmes (hitziges) ~ bad (hot) temper; **‑fehler** *m* defect of a p.'s temper; constitutional defect or fault; **⚒voll** *a.* high-spirited.
Temperanz-gesellschaft ᵗ (‑‿‿‿‿‿) [lt. Mäßigkeit] *f* ⑫ temperance-society.
Temperänzler (‑‿᷾‿) *m* ⑫ (Mäßigkeitler) abstemious person (vgl. Abstinenzler).
Temperatur (‑‿‿᷾) [lt.] *f* ㊻ 1. (Wärmestand) temperature; hohe, mittlere, niedere ~ high, mean, low temperature. — 2. ♪ (Abweichung von der Reinheit der Intervalle) temperament.
temperieren ♪ (‑‿‿᷾‿) [lt.] *v/a.* ⚛ am Klavier: to temper.
tempern (᷾‿) *v/a.* ⚛*a. metall.* (kühlen) to temper, to anneal, to cool down.
Templer (᷾‿) [Tempel] *m* ⑫ = **‑herr**; **~haus** *n* ⑫ Temple; **~orden** *m* Order of the (Knights‑)Templars.

Tempo (᷾‿) [nhd.; *it. Zeit(maß)] *n* ⓓ⑧ beim Fechten, Tanzen: time, measure (*a.* ♪), beim Reiten, Radfahren rc.: pace; ♪ ein anderes ~ annehmen, in anderem ~ spielen to change the time; im ~ in time; langsames (schnelles) ~ slow (quick) rate or pace or ♪ time; das ~ beschleunigen to increase the speed; in raschem ~ fahren to drive (or ride, go) at a good (or smart) pace or at great speed.
Temporali-en (‑‿‿᷾(‿)‿) [lt.] *pl.* ㉙ *eccl.* (Einkünfte der Geistlichen) temporal(itie)s *pl.*, (clergyman's) living; **~sperre** *f* sequestration of a (clerical or clergyman's) living.
temporär (‑‿᷾) [fr.; *lt.] *a.* ㊿ (vorübergehend) temporary, *adv.* temporarily, for the time (being), F *pro tempore.*
temporisieren (‑‿‿‿᷾‿) [fr.] **I** *v/n.* (h.) ⑫ (die Sache hinhalten) to temporize. — **II** ~ *n* ⑫ temporization.
Tempus (᷾‿) [lt. Zeit] *n* (*sg. inv., pl.* Te'mpora) tense of a verb.
Tenakel (‿᷾‿) [lt.] *n* ⑫ 1. *surg.* (beim Unterbinden v. Arterien gebrauchte krumme Nadel) tenaculum. — 2. (*a. m*) ⊙ *typ.* (zum Festhalten des Manuskripts) copy-holder.
Tendenz (‑‿᷾) [neu‑lt.] *f* ㊻ (Streben) tendency (nach et. hin towards a th.).
tendenziös (‑‿‿᷾)" *a.* ㊿(D 10) having a distinct tendency or purpose.
Tendenz-roman (‑‿᷾‿‿) *m* ⑫ (‑stück *n*) Schrifttum: novel (play) written for a (political, religious, &c.) purpose.
Tender ᵗ (᷾‿) [engl.] *m* ⑫ 1. ⚓ (Avisoboot) advice-boat. — 2. 🚂 tender of a locomotive; **~lokomotive, ~maschine** *f* tank-locomotive or ‑engine.
Teneriffa ⚲ (‑‿᷾‿) [span.] *npr/n.* ⓓα. (eine der Kanarischen Inseln) Teneriffe.
Tenne (᷾‿) [ahd.] *f* ㊽ bsd. *agr.* (Boden e-r Scheune) floor of a barn, thrashing-floor; **~n-patsche** *f*, **‑schlegel** *m* ⊙ beetle for making floors.
Tennis ᵗ (᷾‿) [engl.] *n, inv.* lawn-tennis; **~gesetze** (‿‿‿) *pl.* ㉙ laws of Lawn Tennis; **~schläger** *m* tennis bat; **~spiel** *n* game of tennis.
Tenor¹ (᷾‿) [lt.] *m* ㊿ (Inhalt) bsd. *jur.* teno(u)r or substance) of a document, &c.
Tenor² (‿᷾) [it.] *m* ⓓⓓ. 1. (Stimme zwischen Alt und Baß) tenor. — 2. = Tenorist.   [violin, alto-viola.
Tenor-geige ♪ (‿᷾‿‿) *f* ⑫ tenor)
Tenorist ♪ (‿‿᷾) *m* ⑫ tenor (singer), bisw. auch: tenorist.
Tenor-partie ♪ (‿᷾‿‿) *f* ⑫ tenor part; **‑sänger** *m* = Tenorist; **‑schlüssel** *m* tenor clef; **‑stimme** *f* tenor voice.
Tentamen (‑‿᷾‿) [lt.] *n* ⓓ (Vorprüfung) preliminary examination, auf englischen Universitäten auch: previous examination, little go.
Tenuis ⚗ (᷾‿) *f* (*sg. inv., pl.* Te'nues) *gr.* (Mitlauter k, p, t) tenuis.
Teppich (᷾‿) [ahd.; *it. f. Tapet] *m* ⓓ. carpet, im Schlafzimmer: bedroom carpet; (wollene Decke) rug, vor dem (engl.) Kamin: hearth-rug; Brüsseler ~ Brussels (carpet); mit e-m ~ bedeckt carpeted; mit ~en belegen to carpet.
Teppich-arbeit ⊙ (᷾‿‿‿) *f* ⑫ tapestry (‑work); **‑band** *n* carpet-binding;

♪ Musik; ⚗ Wissenschaft; ⚘ Pflanze; ⚲ Geographie; ⊙ Technik; ⚒ Bergbau; ✕ Militär; ⚓ Marine; ⓜ Handel; ✉ Post; 🚂 Eisenbahn.

[Teppichbeet] — 954 — [teuer]

=beet n, hort. c.-bed(ding); =drucker m c.-printer; =fabrikant m c.-maker; =händler m dealer in carpets, carpet-man; =macher m c.-maker; =stange f rod (or pole) on which carpets are beaten; =sticker m tapestry-weaver or -worker; =stift m carpet-tack; =weber, =wirker m carpet-weaver; =wirkerei f carpet-weaving or -manufacture; =zeug n carpeting.

Terebinthe ♀ (⌣‿⌣) [grch., *armen.] f ⑫ = Terpentinbaum.

Termin (⌣⌣́) [lt.] m ⑭d. 1. a) (festgesetzte Zeit) appointed time or day, auch: (fixed) term or date; den ~ einhalten to keep to one's time; b) ● (Frist) time allowed, delay (granted); respite; c) er ist die Miete noch für zwei ~e (Quartale) schuldig he owes two quarters' rent. — 2. Gericht: (Vorladung) summons; ich habe morgen ~ I am (summoned or ordered) to appear (in court) to-morrow.

Termin=geschäft ✱ (⌣⌣́...) n ⑫, =handel m time-bargain; =kalender m almanac giving the quarter-days, &c.

Terminologie ⚯ (⌣⌣⌣‿⌣) [lt.=grch.] f ⑫ (Kunstsprache) terminology, nomenclature; chemical, &c. notation; terminologisch (⌣⌣⌣⌣́⌣) a. ⑥ terminological.

Termin=tag (⌣⌣́⌣) m quarter-day.

Terminus (⌣́⌣⌣) [lt.] 1 npr/m. inv. röm. Alt.: (Grenzgott) Terminus. — II m ⑤ (Ausdruck) term, expression; Te'rmini te'chnici technical terms pl.

termin=weise (⌣⌣́...) adv. at fixed intervals or times; ♀ bezahlen to pay by instalments; zahlung f payment by instalments.

Termite (⌣⌣́⌣) [lt.] f ⑫ ent. (bfd. in den Tropen vorkommend) white ant, termite (Termes); ~n=bau, =hügel m ⑫ termitarium, termitary.

ternär ⚯ (⌣⌣́) a. ⑥ math. (von drei Veränderlichen abhängig) ternary.

Terne (⌣́⌣) [it. Drei...] f ⑭ (Treffer in e-r Zahlenlotterie) tern.

Terpentin ⊕ (⌣⌣⌣́) [neult.; *Terebinthe ♀] m ⑫d. (flüssiges, stark riechendes Harz d-r Nadelhölzer) turpentine; mit ~ tränken to terebinthinate; ♀=artig a. ⑥ turpentinic, terebinthine; ~=baum ♀ m ⑫ turpentine-tree, terebinth (Pista'cia terebi'nthus); ~=geist m ⊕ = ~öl; ~harz n: ⚯ abietine; ~öl n turpentine(-oil), auch: oil (or spirit) of turpentine, P turps pl.; ~öl=hydrat n hydrate of turpentine-oil; ~=pistazi-e ♀ f = ~=baum; ~=präparat n. med. terebinthinate; ~=spiritus m = ~öl.

Terra (⌣́⌣) [lt. u. it. Erde] f, inv.: a) Terra inco'gnita unkown land or region; fig. das ist ihm eine T. inc. that's Greek to him; b) ~ di Siena (⌣́⌣‿⌣) [it.] f, paint. (hellgelber Ocker) terra (di) Siena, sienna.

Terrain (⌣́) [fr.] n ⑭ (Gelände) ground, (fr.) terrain (f. kupieren 3); wellenförmiges ~ undulated (or rolling) country; (fr.) rideau; das ~ untersuchen to survey the country.

Terrain=kenntnis (⌣́...) f ⑫ local knowledge, topography; =schwierigkeit f difficult(y of the) country; =skizze

f topographical sketch; =verhältnisse n pl. conditions pl. of the ground; =wellen f/pl. undulations pl. of the ground.

Terrakotta, Terrakotte (⌣⌣́⌣) [it.] f ⑯, ⑱ Töpferei: terra cotta.

Terrarium ⚯ (⌣⌣́⌣⌣) [lt.] n ⑱ (Behälter für lebende Landtiere) terrarium.

Terrasse (⌣⌣́⌣) [fr.] f ⑫ a) (Erdstufe) terrace; b) (flaches Dach) flat roof; c) paint. (Vordergrund einer Landschaft) foreground.

terrassen=förmig (⌣⌣́⌣...) a. ⑥ in (form of) terraces, terrace-shaped; =gang m ⑫ terrace-walk; =land n country rising in terraces.

terrassieren (⌣⌣⌣́⌣) v/a. ⑫ to arrange in terraces, to terrace; ♂ die Böschung ♀ to step the side or bank.

terrestrisch (⌣⌣́⌣) [lt. irdisch] a. ⑥ ast. terrestrial. [tureen.]

Terrine (⌣⌣́⌣) [fr.] f ⑫ (Suppenschüssel))

Territorial=rechte (⌣⌣⌣⌣́...⌣) n pl. territorial rights pl.

Territorium (⌣⌣⌣⌣́⌣) [lt.] n ⑱ territory (a. U.S.: Gebiet, das noch nicht als Staat gilt).

terrorisieren (⌣⌣⌣⌣́⌣) [fr.] v/a. ⑫ (in Schrecken setzen) to terrorize; Terrorismus (⌣⌣⌣́⌣) [neu=lt.] m ⑫ (Schreckensherrschaft) terrorism; Terrorist (⌣⌣⌣́) m ⑫ terrorist; terroristisch (⌣⌣⌣́⌣) a. ⑥ terroristic, terrorizing.

Tertia (⌣́⌣⌣) [lt. dritte] f ⑲ 1. third highest form of a German secondary school, in England: fourth form. — 2. typ. (Schriftgattung von etwa 16 Punkten) two-line brevier. — 3. ♀ third of exchange. [Schulabschnitt) term.)

Tertial (⌣⌣́) [lt.] n ⑭d. (viermonatlicher)

Tertianer (⌣⌣́⌣) [lt.] m ⑫ Schule: pupil of the „Tertia".

Tertian=fieber (⌣⌣́...) [lt.] n ⑫ path. (dreitägiges Fieber) tertian fever or ague.

tertiär ⚯ (⌣⌣́) [lt.] a. ⑥ (zur dritten Ordnung gehörig) tertiary; ~ n ⑭d., ~=formation f, geol. tertiary formation or rock; ~=zeit f tertiary period.

Tertia=schrift (⌣́⌣⌣) f ⑫ = Tertia 2; =wechsel m = Tertia 3.

Terti-e (⌣́⌣⌣) [lt.] f ⑫ 1. Cath. eccl. (dritte Betstunde am frühen Morgen) t(i)erce. — 2. ast., &c. (1/60 Sekunde) one-sixtieth of a second.

Terz ♪ (⌣́) [lt.] f ⑫ 1. große (kleine) ~ major (minor) third. — 2. Kartenspiel: (Sequenz von drei Karten derselben Farbe) tierce. — 3. fenc. (Brust außen) tierce.

Terz=dezime ♪ (⌣́...) f ⑫ thirteenth.

Terzen=lauf (⌣́⌣...) m ⑫ run of thirds.

Terzerol (⌣⌣́) [it.] n ⑭d. pocket-pistol.

Terzeron(e) (⌣⌣́⌣) [span.] m ⑫ ⑭ (Mischling von Weißen und Mestizen od. Mulatten) quadroon. [trio.)

Terzett ♪ (⌣́) [it. Drei=] n ⑭c. terzetto,)

Terz=hieb (⌣́...) m ⑫ fenc. = Terz 3.

Terzine (⌣⌣́⌣) f ⑫ [it. terzina] f ⑫ (Art Strophe) terza-rima.

Teschen (⌣́⌣, oft ⌣⌣́) [Teschen ♀, öst. St.] n ⑭d. gun of small bore.

Tessin ♀ (⌣́) [lt. Tici'nus] npr/m. ⓂA. (schweizerischer Fluß u. Kanton) Ticino.

Test ⚯ (⌣́) [lt.] m ⑫b. 1. metall. (Treibscherben, Kapelle z. Abtreiben) test, cupel. — 2. (chm. v. Beamten in England zu leistender Eid auf die Glaubensartikel der Staatskirche)

test; Test=akte f ⑫ (1673—1826 bestehendes englisches Gesetz, das Nicht-anglikaner vom Staatsdienste ausschloß) test-act.

Testament (⌣⌣́) [lt.] n ⑭c. 1. jur. will, feierlicher: last will and testament; jur. mündliches ~ nuncupatory (or ...ive) will; ein ~ m. to make one's will; ohne ~ sterben to die without (leaving) a will, to die intestate (f. Anhang 2 u. bedenken 2). — 2. theol.: Altes (Neues) ~ Old (New) Testament.

testamentarisch (⌣⌣⌣⌣́⌣), testamentlich (⌣⌣⌣́⌣) a. ⑥ meist jur. testamentary, adv. by will; ♀ hinterlassen to will (away), to leave in one's will.

Testaments=erbe (⌣⌣́...) m ⑫, =erbin f jur. testamentary heir(ess f); =(er)öffnung f opening of the will; =nachtrag, =zusatz m codicil to a will; =vollstrecker(in f) m executor (f executrix); ♀=weise adv. by will.

Testator (⌣⌣́⌣) [lt.] m ⑫, Testatrix (⌣⌣́⌣) f (sg. inv., pl. Testatri'zes) jur. (Erblasser[in]) testator, f testatrix.

Test=eid (⌣́...) m ⑫ = Test 2.

Testier=bogen (⌣⌣́...) m ⑫ auf deutschen Hochschulen: blank form for a certificate of attendance at university-lectures.

testieren (⌣⌣́⌣) [lt.] v/a. u. v/n. (h.) ⑫ 1. to make a will; to dispose of property, &c. by will. — 2. (bezeugen) to testify; (bescheinigen) to certify, to attest.

Testierer (⌣⌣́⌣) m ⑫, ~in f ⑪ 1. = Testator. — 2. professor who certifies a student's attendance.

Testimonium (⌣⌣⌣́⌣⌣) [lt.] n ⑲⑳ (Zeugnis) testimony, testimonial; Testimo'nium morum certificate of good conduct; Testimo'nium paupertatis f. Armutszeugnis.

Tete ⚔ (⌣́) [fr.] f ⑯ -r Marschkolonne: head of a marching column; ~=à=tete (⌣́⌣⌣) [fr.] n, inv. tête-à-tête, meeting of lovers. geh. Spr. tryst.

Tetrachord ♪ (⌣⌣́) [grch.] m u. n ⑭c. (4saitige Leier; 4 Töne e-r Quarte) tetrachord.

Tetradynamia ⚯ ♀ (⌣⌣⌣‿⌣) [grch.] f ⑲ (15. Klasse nach Linné) tetradynamia; tetradynamisch a. ⑥ (viermächtig: mit vier längeren u. zwei kürzeren Staubgefäßen) tetradynamian.

Tetra=eder ⚯ (⌣⌣́⌣) [grch.] n ⑫ math. (Vierflach) tetrahedron; tetra-edrisch a. ⑥ (vierflächig) tetrahedral.

Tetrarch (⌣́) [grch.] m ⑫ Alt.: (Vierfürst) tetrarch; ~ie (⌣⌣́) f ⑫ tetrarchy.

Tetrathion=säure (⌣⌣⌣́⌣...) f ⑫ tetrathionic acid ($H_2S_4O_6$).

teuer (⌣́⌣) [ahd.: dear] a. ⑥ (D 9) 1. (ant. billig 2) dear, costly, expensive; et. ♀ (adv.) bezahlen to pay dearly for a th. ; 2. (ver)kaufen to buy (to sell) dear(ly) or at a high price; wie ♀ ist das? how much (is it)? wie ♀ ist dieses Zimmer? how much do you want (or ask) for fürzer: how much is this room?; ● teurer Kaffee high-priced coffee; die Wolle ist ♀ wool stands high; Tee ist teurer als Kakao tea is dearer than cocoa; fig. hoch und ♀ schwören to swear solemnly, to take a solemn oath; das wird ihm ♀ zu stehen kommen he will have to pay

Signs (see page XVII): F familiar; P vulgar; ⌐ flash; ╲ rare; † obsolete (died); * new word (born); ✕ incorrect; ♪ music;

dear(ly) for it; sein Leben 2 verkaufen to sell one's life dearly. — 2. (Mangel leidend) es war im Lande 2 ober teure Zeit there was a famine in the land; (knapp) scarce; da war guter Rat 2 there we were, and did not know what to do; it was a difficult position (to be in). — 3. (lieb) dear, precious, cherished, beloved; alles, was uns 2 ist all that is dear to us, all that we cherish or love.

Teu(e)rung (ʹ‿◡) ꝛc. s. Teurung ꝛc.
Teufe ⚒ (ʹ‿) [ahd.] f ⑱ (Tiefe) depth.
Teufel (ʹ‿) [ahd.: devil;* grch. *diá'bolos* m ① 1. devil; (böser Geist) demon, fiend; der ~, a. the Evil one, F Old Nick, Old Blazes, Old Gooseberry, Old Scratch, the Old Gentleman (himself); v. Menschen: der arme ~ the poor devil or rogue. — 2. (oft *fig.*) in (mst F) Redewendungen: pfui ~! it's a great (F a damned) shame!; Tod u. ~!, der ~!, zum ~ noch einmal! F the deuce!, damned (or what a) nuisance!, hang (or drat) it! s. besessen II; er fragt den ~ danach he does not care a straw (or F a hang) about it; es geht alles zum ~ everything is going to the dogs; er hat den ~ im Leibe ob. im Nacken the devil's in him; der ~ ist los hell is loose; s. holen I; er muß des ~s sein he must have Old Nick in him, he must be mad; da soll ja gleich der ~ (dreinschlagen)! confound (or damn) it (all)!; weiß der ~, da sind sie wieder! the deuce (or damn it), there they are again!; weiß der ~, was ihn dazu getrieben hat goodness knows what has driven him to it; in des ~s Küche geraten, kommen to get into an awful scrape or mess; das müßte mit dem ~ zugehen the devil must be in (or mixed up with) it; zum ~ mit ihm! let him go to hell or to Jericho!; scher dich zum ~! go to hell!, milder: go to Bath!; zum ~ (weg) sein to be gone or lost; was zum ~ macht er da? what the dickens (or deuce) is he doing there?; Sprichw. s. malen 2; was zum ~ soll das alles bedeuten? what the devil (or deuce) does it all mean?

Teufel=austreibung (ʹ‿◡‿◡) f ⑫ exorcizing the devil, *bibl.* casting out devils.

Teufelchen (ʹ‿◡) n ㉓ (*dim.* von Teufel) little (or young) devil, imp, *bisw.*: devilkin; kartesianisches ~ Cartesian devil or diver; bottle-imp. [trick(ery).

Teufelei (‿‿ʹ) f ㊻ devilry, devilish)

teufel=mäßig (ʹ‿‿◡) *a.* ⑯ = teuflisch.

Teufels=abbiß ♀ (ʹ‿‿...) m ② devil's-bit (*Succi'sa prate'nsis*); =anbeter m =verehrer; =balg F m (böses Kind) young demon, imp, F pickle; =bann m exorcism; =banner, =beschwörer m exorcist; =beschwörung f = =bann; =braten m (schlechter Mensch) villain, scamp, blackguard; =brücke npr/f. Devil's Bridge; =brut f set of imps, infernal crew; =dienst m devil-worship, ⚗ demonolatry; =dreck m, *pharm.* (Gummiharz aus der Wurzel von *Fe'rula asa f(o)e'tida*) asafoetida; =junge =kerl m devil (lobend: brick or trump)

of a boy, of a fellow; =kind n: a) imp, young devil, *vgl.* =balg; b) *rel.* =kinder *pl.* children of Satan or Hell; =kirsche ♀ f = Belladonna; =klaue f: a) ♀ = Bärlapp; b) ⚗ (Windehafen) sling-dog; =krabbe f, *zo.* spider-crab (*Maia*); =kunst f devilry, black art, witchcraft; =lärm m infernal noise, F devilish (or devil of a) row; =mäßig *a.* ⑯ devilish, like Old Nick (blitzschnell) like lightning; =spaß, =spuk m ⑫ devilish frolic, *co.* devilment; =streich m devilish (or diabolical) trick; =verehrer m devil-worshipper; =weib n she-devil, devil of a woman; =werk n devilish work, stärker: fiendish action; =wesen n, =zeug n devilry, devilish trickery; =zwirn ♀ m box-thorn (*Ly'cium ba'rbarum*).

teufen ⚒ (ʹ‿) *v/a.* ⑱ = tiefen.

teuflisch (ʹ‿) *a.* ⑯ devilish, diabolical.

Teukr(i=)er (ʹ‿◡)◡ m ㉒, ~in f ㊼ grch. Alt.: (Trojaner[in]) Teucrian, Trojan.

Teurung (ʹ‿) f ㊻ dearness (or scarcity) of provisions, dearth; (Hungersnot) famine; ~s=zulage (ʹ‿◡‿...) f ⑫ increase of salary on account of the high price of provisions.

Teutone (‿ʹ‿) m ㊹, ...nin f ㊼ (Germane, ...nin, Deutsche[r]) Teuton; **teutonisch** (‿ʹ‿) *a.* ⑯ Teutonic, German(ic).

Text (ʹ) [mhd.; *fr. lt.*] m ⓐ a. 1. ~ e-s Werkes: original (text); (Schrift) Bibelspruch) text; (Druck) letterpress; ♪ ~ zu einem Liede: words *pl.*, zu einer Oper: book; *jur.* ~ einer Urkunde context (or tenor, substance) of a deed. — 2. *fig.* aus dem ~e kommen to lose the thread (of one's discourse), to be put out, to break down (in the middle of a speech); s. lesen 4; (nur) weiter im ~e! go on!, proceed! — 3. f ㊺ (o. *pl.*) ⊕ *typ.* (Schrift von 20 Punkten) paragon-type.

Text=abbildung (ʹ‿...) f ⑫ illustration accompanying the text or letterpress; =ausgabe f edition of the text only; =berichtigung f emendation of the text; =buch n, *thea.* book of words; =fälscher m interpolator; =fälschung f =gemäß ⓖ textual, in conformity with the text.

Textil=industrie ⊕ (‿ʹ‿...) [lt. *=Spinn...*] f ⑫ textile industry; =ware(n *pl.*) f textile fabrics or goods *pl.*

Text=kritik (ʹ‿...) f ⑫ textual criticism; =mäßig *a.* ⑯ = =gemäß; =schrift f ⊕ *typ.* = Text 3.

Textur (‿ʹ) [lt.] f ㊺ (Gewebe) texture.

Text=verdrehung (ʹ‿‿ʹ‿) f ⑫ straining a text.

T.F. *abbr.* = Taschenformat.

T=förmig (ʹ‿◡) *a.* ⑯ T-shaped; *anat.* T-förmiger Knochen tau-bone. [deus.

Thaddäus (‿ʹ‿) [hebr.] npr/m. ⑯ γ. Thad=)

Thalia (‿ʹ‿) [lt., *grch.] npr/f. ⑯ β. ⓢ α. *myth.* (Muse des Lustspiels) Thalia.

Thallium ⚗ (ʹ(‿)◡) [grch.] n ⑬ *chm.* thallium (Tl).

Thallium=oxyd ⚗ (ʹ‿...) n ⑫ thallium trioxide (Tl₂O₃); =oxydul n thallium monoxide (Tl₂O).

Thallophyten ♀ (‿‿ʹ‿) [grch.] *pl.* (Lagerpflanzen) thallogens, thallophytes.

Than (ʹ) [schott.] m ⑨ d.⑯ (ehm. hoher schottischer Adliger) thane.

Thaumaturg ⚗ (‿‿ʹ) [grch.] m ⑫ (Wundertäter) thaumaturge, thaumaturgist.

Theater (‿ʹ‿) [grch. „Schau"bühne] n ㉒ 1. (Schauspielhaus) theatre, playhouse; (Bühne) stage; (Vorstellung) theatrical performance, play; im ~ sein to be at the theatre; ins ~ gehen to go to (öfters: to frequent) the theatre, to go to see a play; zum ~ gehen (Schauspieler[in] w.) to go on the stage; heute ist kein ~ there is (or will be) no performance to-day. — 2. anatomisches ~ anatomical theatre.

Theater=bericht (‿ʹ‿...) m ⑫ theatrical news; =besuch m, =besucher(in f) m theatre-going, -goer; =billett n ticket for the theatre; =coup m stage-trick; =dichter m writer for the stage, dramatic author, playwright; =direktor m manager of a theatre; =effekt m stage-effect; =gerät n stage-properties *pl.*; =kasse f ticket- (or box-)office; =leben n theatrical life or profession; =loge f box at a theatre; =maler m scene-painter; =mantel m opera-cloak; =meister m stage-manager; =stück n (theatrical) play or piece; =vorstellung f theatrical performance; =wesen n theatrical concerns, theatricals *pl.*; =zeitung f dramatic paper; =zensur f (in England vom Lord Chamberlain als Sittenrichter ausgeübt) censorship of stage-plays; =zettel m play-bill.

Theatiner (‿‿ʹ‿) [it. (Bischof Cajetan von) Theate (Papst Paul IV.) 1524] m ㉒, =in f ㊼, *a.* ~=mönch m =nonne f, *Cath. eccl.* Theatin(e) monk, f nun.

theatralisch (‿‿ʹ‿) [Theater] *a.* ⑯ theatrical, stage-like, auch stag(e)y; *adv.* in theatrical fashion or style, with a theatrical pose.

Thebaner (‿ʹ‿) m ㉒, ~in f ㊼, **thebanisch** *a.* ⑯ Alt.: Theban, of Thebes.

Theben ⚥ (ʹ‿) npr/n. ⑬ α. Alt.: (Stadt: a) in Böotien, b) in Ägypten) Thebes.

thebisch (ʹ‿) *a.* ⑯ Theban, Thebaic.

The=ismus ⚗ (‿ʹ‿◡) [grch.] m ㉗ (Gottesglaube) theism; **The=ist** (‿ʹ) m ㉒ theist; **the=istisch** (‿ʹ‿◡) *a.* ⑯ theistic(al).

Thekla (ʹ‿) npr/f. ⑯ β. ⓢ α. Thecla.

Thema (ʹ‿) [grch. Satz] n ㉘ ⑯ (Gegenstand der Besprechung ꝛc.) theme (a. ♪), eines Gespräches: topic, eines Aufsatzes: subject.

thematisch ♪ (‿ʹ‿) *a.* ⑯ thematic.

Themis (ʹ‿) [grch.] npr/f. *inv.*, *myth.* (Göttin der Gerechtigkeit) Themis.

Themse ♀ (ʹ‿) npr/f. ⑱: die ~ (engl. Fluß) the (river) Thames.

Theobromin=säure ⚗ (‿‿ʹ‿‿ʹ‿) f ㊺ *chm.* theobromic acid ($C_{64}H_{128}O_2$).

Theodorich (‿ʹ‿◡) npr/m. ⑮ Theodoric.

Theodizee (‿‿◡ʹ) [lt., *grch.] f ㊺ (Rechtfertigung Gottes) theodicy.

Theodolit (‿‿◡ʹ) [?] m ⓐc. (‿‿ʹ) *surv.* (Meßwerkzeug) theodolite.

Theodor (ʹ‿◡) [grch. Gottesgeschenk] npr/m. (Vn.) ⑮ ⑯ α. Theodore; ~a (‿ʹ‿) npr/f. ⑯ β. ⓢ α. (Vn.) Theodora.

Theogonie (‿‿‿ʹ) [grch.] f ㊸ *myth.* (Lehre von der Abstammung der Götter) theogonyr

Theokrat (‿‿ʹ) [grch.] m ⑫ (Mitglied eine Theokratie) theocrat; =ie (‿‿‿ʹ) f ㊸ (Gottes-Priester-herrschaft, Priesterreich) theocracy. =isch (‿‿ʹ‿) *a.* ⑯ theocratic(al).

⚗ scientific; ♀ botanical; ♁ geography; ⊕ machinery; ⚒ mining; ⚔ military; ⚓ marine; ⚖ commercial; ✉ postal; 🚂 railway.

Theokrit, ~os (⸗⸗⸗, ⸗⸗⸗) npr/m. ⑮ ⑯α. (grch. Bukoliker 3. sae. v. Chr.) Theocritus.

Theolog, ~e (⸗⸗⸗) [grch.] m ㊷, ㊶, ~in f ㊾ (Gottesgelehrte[r]) theologian, divine, als Student: student of divinity, auch theological student; ~ie (⸗⸗⸗) f ㊽ theology, divinity (s. Doktor 1, Student); Lisch (⸗⸗⸗) a. ㊻ theological.

Theophil (⸗⸗⸗) [grch.] npr/m. ⑮㊹c. Theophilus.

Theorem ⚯ (⸗⸗⸗) [grch.] n ①d. math. (Lehrsatz) theorem, proposition (of Euclid).

Theoretiker (⸗⸗⸗) [grch. Anschauer] m ㉒ (ant. Praktiker) theorist, contp. faddist.

theoretisch (⸗⸗⸗) a. ㊻ (ant. praktisch) theoretical; speculative; adv. auch: in theory. [Praxis] theory; f. grau.

Theorie (⸗⸗⸗) [grch. Anschauung] f ㊽ (ant.f.

Theosoph ⚯ (⸗⸗⸗) [grch.] m ㊷ (Gottesweiser) theosophist; ~ie (⸗⸗⸗) f ㊽ (Erkenntnis göttl. Dinge durch Eingebung) theosophy; Lisch (⸗⸗⸗) a. ㊻ theosophic(al).

Therapeut ⚯ (⸗⸗⸗) [grch. Diener, Wärter] m ㊷ therap(eut)ist; ~ik ⚯ (⸗⸗⸗) [grch.] f ㊽ = Therapie; Lisch (⸗⸗⸗) a. ㊻ therapeutic(al).

Therapie ⚯ (⸗⸗⸗) [grch.] f ㊽ med. (Heilkunde) therapeutics.

Thereschen (⸗⸗⸗) n ㉓a. Terry, Tess.

Therese (⸗⸗⸗) npr/f. ㊹β, feierlicher: **Theresia** (⸗⸗⸗) f ㊻㊱a. (Vn.) Theresa.

Theriak (⸗⸗⸗) [grch. gegen „Tier" biß] m ①d. ㊶ pharm. ehm.: (Gegengift) theriac(a).

Thermal-quelle (⸗⸗⸗) [grch. the'rmē Wärme] f ㊷ (a. **Therme** (⸗⸗) f ㊷) thermal (or hot) spring or spa.

Thermen (⸗⸗⸗) [grch.] f/pl. ㊽ (Bäder) thermal waters pl. [thermochemistry.]

Thermo-chemie ⚯ (⸗⸗⸗⸗) [grch.] f ㊽.

thermo-elektrisch ⚯ (⸗⸗⸗⸗) [grch.] a. ㊻ thermo-electric(al).

Thermo-elektrizität ⚯ (⸗⸗⸗⸗) [grch.] f ㊻ phys. thermo-electricity.

Thermometer (⸗⸗⸗) [grch.] n (m) ㉒ phys. (Wärmemesser) thermometer (s. Celsius, Réaumur), selbstregistrierender: ⚯ thermometrograph; s. Kugel 1; der ~ steht drei Grad unter Null the thermometer stands at (or is, registers) three degrees below zero.

thermometrisch (~⸗) a. ㊻ thermometric(al).

Thermopylen ⚯ (⸗⸗⸗⸗) npr/f/pl. inv. Alt.: (Engpaß in Lokris, den Leo'nidas gegen die Perser verteidigte) the Thermopylæ pl.

Thermostatik ⚯ (⸗⸗⸗⸗) [grch.] f ㊽ (Lehre vom Gleichgewichte der Wärme) thermostatics.

Thesaurus (-⸗-) [lt.; *grch. Schatz] m ㊹㊻ (Wortschatz) thesaurus, vocabulary.

These (⸗⸗) [grch. Satz] f ㊽, **Thesis** f ㊾: a) (zu beweisender Satz); b) pros., &c. (Senkung des Tones; ant. Arsis): thesis.

Thesmophori-en (⸗⸗⸗⸗) [grch.] pl. inv. Alt.: (in Athen zu Ehren der Demeter gefeiertes Fest) Thesmophoria.

Thesmothet (⸗⸗⸗) [grch. Gesetzgeber] m ㊷ Alt., in Athen: thesmothete.

Thespis-karren (⸗⸗⸗⸗) [Thespis, ältester attischer Schauspieldichter im 6. sae. v. Chr.) m ㊷: am ~ ziehen to be a strolling actor.

Thessali-en ⚥ (⸗⸗⸗) npr/n. ㉓a. nordöstl. Landschaft Griechenlands: Thessaly.

Thessali-er (⸗⸗⸗) m ㉒, ~in f ㊾, **thessalisch** (⸗⸗⸗) a. ㊻ Thessalian.

Thessalonich (⸗⸗⸗) npr/n. ㉔a. Alt.: (Stadt in Mazedonien; jetzt: Saloniк[i]) Thessalonica; ~er (in f ㊾) m ㉒ (⸗⸗⸗⸗⸗) Thessalonian; bibl. Brief des Paulus an die ~er Epistle to the Thessalonians.

The-urg ⚯ (⸗⸗) [grch.] m ㊷ (Wundertäter) theurgist; ~ie (-⸗-) f ㊽ theurgy.

Thio-schwefelsäure ⚯ (⸗-...) [grch. theion Schwefel] f ㊽ chm. (unterschweflige Säure, f. bs) thiosulphuric acid ($H_2S_2O_3$).

Thomas (⸗⸗) npr/m. inv. od. ㊷γ (Vn.) Thomas, Tom; ungläubiger ~ unbelieving person, unbeliever, sceptic.

Thomas-christ(en pl.) (⸗⸗⸗⸗) m ㊷ an der Malabarküste, Ostindien: Thomæan(s), Thomean(s), Thomite(s).

Thor-erde (⸗⸗⸗) f ㊷ min. thorinic (or thori[n]um) oxide, thoria.

Thorit ⚯ (-⸗) m ①c. min. (kieselsaure Thorerde) thorite.

Thorium ⚯ (⸗⸗⸗) n ㊳ chm. (Metall) thori(n)um (Th.); ~oxyd (⸗⸗⸗⸗) n ㊷ = Thorerde.

Thrazi-en ⚥ (⸗⸗⸗) od. **Thraki-en** (⸗⸗⸗) npr/n. ㉓α. Thracia; **Thrazi-er** (⸗⸗⸗⸗) od. **Thraker** (⸗⸗) m ㉒, ~in f ㊾, **thrazisch** (⸗⸗⸗) od. **thrakisch** (⸗⸗⸗) a. ㊻ Thracian.

Thron (⸗) [fr., *grch.] m ⑪ (fast † ㉕)c. throne; den ~ besteigen to ascend (or mount, fig. a. to come to) the throne; auf den ~ erheben to raise to the throne; vom ~e stoßen to dethrone; rel. vor dem ~e Gottes before the throne (or in the presence of) God.

Thron-besteigung (⸗⸗...) f ㊷ accession to the throne; -bewerber m one who aspires to the throne, pretender (to the crown); -bewerbung f laying claim to the throne, pretendership.

thronen (⸗⸗) v/n. (h.) ㊽ to sit on a throne, to be seated on the throne (a. fig.), to be enthroned.

Thron-entsagung (⸗⸗...) f ㊷ abdication; -erbe m, -erbin f heir(ess f) to the throne, heir(ess f) apparent or presumptive; -erledigung f vacancy of the throne, demise (of the sovereign); -folge(r m) f succession (successor) to the throne or crown; -himmel m canopy, dais; -raub (-räuber) m usurpation (usurper of the thr.; -rede f speech from the thr., parl. King's (or Queen's) Speech; -saal m throne-room, presence-chamber; -wechsel m change of sovereigns or rulers.

thucydide-isch (---⸗⸗) [Thucy'dides, grch. Geschichtschreiber etwa 460 bis 400 vor Chr.] a. ㊻ Thucydidean, of Thucydides.

Thuja ⚥ (⸗⸗) [neu=lt.] f ㊽ (Lebensbaum) thuya, a. (lt.) arbor vitæ (Thuja); vgl. auch Lebensbaum b.

Thun (⸗) [grch.] m ⑪c. ichth., meist **Thunfisch** m tunny (Thynnus).

Thüringen ⚥ (⸗⸗⸗) npr/n. ㉓α. deutsche Landschaft: Thuringia.

Thüringer (⸗⸗⸗) m ㉒ u. a. inv., ~in f ㊾, **thüringisch** a. ㊻ Thuringian.

Thymian ⚥ (⸗(⸗)-) [ahd.; *grch.] m ①d. thyme (Thymus vulga'ris).

Thymian-öl (⸗(⸗)-⸗) n ㊷ pharm. oil of thyme.

Thyrsos, mst ~us ⚯ (⸗⸗) [grch.] m ㊷㊻, auch ~stab m Alt.: (mit Efeu u. Weinlaub bekränzter Bacchusstab) thyrsus.

Tiara, a. **Tiare** (⸗⸗⸗) [pers.] f ㊽: a) Alt.: (Art Turban, bsd. der Perser) tiara; b) jetzt: (päpstliche Krone) tiara, triple crown.

Tiber[1] ⚥ (⸗⸗⸗) [lt.] npr/f. inv. (oft m ㊷) die ~ (Fluß, an dem Rom liegt) the Tiber.

Tiber[2] (⸗⸗), ~ius (⸗⸗⸗⸗) npr/m. ⑪c. ⑯γ (röm. Kaiser, 14—37 n. Chr.) Tiberius.

Tibetaner (-⸗⸗⸗) m ㉒, ~in f ㊾, **tibetisch** (⸗⸗⸗) a. ㊻ T(h)ibetan [Tibet, Hochland in Asien].

tick[1] (⸗) int. (lautm.) tick; ~ tack tick-tack; ~ tack geh(e)n, von Uhren: to tick, vom Herzen: to (go) pit-a-pat.

Tick[2] (⸗) m ⑪c. 1. (Berührung) (slight) tap. — 2. fig. einen ~ haben (eingebildet sein) to be conceited, (wunderlich sein) to be strange or eccentric.

ticken (⸗⸗) [lautm.] ㊽ I v/n. (h.) to tick. — II v/a. to tap, to touch with the tip of one's finger.

ticktack (⸗⸗), ~ n ㊳ f. tick[1]; ~en (⸗⸗⸗) v/n. (h.) ㊽ von Uhren: to (go) tick.

tief (⸗) [ahd.: deep] I a. ㊻ 1. deep, nur abstract: profound (secret, knowledge, &c.); (niedrig) low (valley, &c.); der Schnee ist zwei Fuß ~ ... two feet high; im ~sten Elend in utter (or abject, extreme) misery; in ~en Gedanken deep in thought(s); ~es Geheimnis profound secret; des Herzens ~ste Gründe pl. the deepmost (or deepest) recesses of the heart; ~ere Lage, Stellung lower (abstract: inferior) position; in ~em Schlafe fest (stärker: dead) asleep; aus ~ster Seele from the depth of one's heart; vom Teller soup-plate; Sprichw. f. still 2. — 2. meist adv. (oft fig.): sich ~ beugen to make a low bow, fig. to stoop low; das läßt ~ blicken that affords one a deep insight, that tells its own tale, now I (begin to) see, a. it's an eye-opener; den Hut ~ in die Augen drücken to pull one's hat over one's eyes; ~ eingewurzelt deep-rooted; ~ empfunden deep-felt; ~ liegende (vgl. Liegend) Augen eyes deeply imbedded in the sockets, auch: sunken eyes; ~ seufzen to draw a deep sigh; ~ in Schulden stecken to be deep(ly) in debt or deeply involved; ~ im Walde, im ~en Walde in the depth (or heart) of the forest; ~ trauern, in ~ster Trauer sein: a) to be deeply afflicted; b) (schwarz gehen) to be in the deepest mourning, ⚓ das Schiff geht drei Meter ~ ... draws ten feet of water; aufs ~ste beklagen to deplore most deeply, to be sore afflicted (or grieved) at. — 3. ♪ von Tönen: deep; ~e Stimme deep (a. bass) voice; einen Ton ~er singen, spielen to go down a note; ein Instrument ~er stimmen to lower the pitch of ... — 4. (weit vorgerückt) deep, far advanced; ~ im Gehölze deep in the wood; in ~er Nacht at (or in the) dead of night; im ~(st)en Winter in the (very) depth of winter. — II **Tief** n ㊳c. 5. (Wasser von e-r gewissen Tiefe) (very) deep water.

Tief-auf(an-)schlag (⸗⸗...) m ㊷ Tennisspiel: ~ (mit Drehung) underhand-(twist-)service; ~äugig a. ㊻ hollow-eyed; =bau m: a) ⛏, Straßenbau 2c.: (ant. Hochbau) underground workings pl. or structure; b) ⚒ deep level or work-

[tiefbetrübt] — 957 — [Tinte]

ing; betrübt a. deeply grieved; bewegt a. deeply moved or agitated; blau a. dark blue; blick m searching (fig. a. penetrating) glance; penetration; blickend a. keen-sighted; bohrer ☉ m squarer; denkend a. deep-thinking, penetration; denker m deep (or profound) thinker; druck m, typ. intaglio.

Tiefe (ˇ) f ㊸ 1. depth (a. ⚔ v. Truppenaufstellungen); von der Stimme ꝛc.: deepness; nur abstrakt: profundity, profoundness; ohne ~ shallow, fig. auch: superficial. — 2. (etwas Tiefes) deep (place), (Grube) pit; (Abgrund) abyss; aus dem ~ des Herzens from the bottom (or depth) of one's heart; ↓ ~ e-s Untersegels: drop, des Grundes: sounding (s pl.).

Tief=ebene (ˑˑ) f ㊷ low plain, lowland.

tiefen (ˑˇ) v/a. und v/n. (h.) ㊳ 1. to deepen, to hollow out. — 2. ↓ (loten) to sound, to cast the lead.

Tiefen=messer (ˑˑ...) m ㊷ sea-gauge, ⚓ bathometer; =messung f (taking a) sounding. [the level, levelling down.]

Tiefer=legung ☉ (ˑˑˑˇ) f ㊷ lowering

tief=ernst (ˑˑ...) a. ㊻ very solemn; =gang ↓ m ㊷ ship's draught; =gehend a. profound, ↓ v. Schiffen: deep-drawing; greifend a. far-reaching, radical (change, &c.); grün a. deep (or dark) green; gründig a. deep; hammer m Klempnerei: hollowing- (or chasing-) hammer; =lade=linie ↓ (deep)load-line; =land n lowland(s pl.); liegend a. (lying) low (auch ☿); deep-seated, von Augen: deep-set; =lot ↓ n deep-sea lead; =lotleine ↓ f deep-sea line; =pflug ☉ m, agr. subsoil-plough; schäftig ☉ a. Weberei: of low warp; gewebt basse-lisse; =see f deep(est part of the) sea; =see=forschung f deep-sea research; =see=kabel n deep-sea cable; =see=reich n Zoogeographie: ⚓ Bassalia; =sinn m deep thought, thoughtfulness, profoundness (of mind); (Schwermut) melancholy; sinnig a.: a) deep-thinking, thoughtful, profound; b) (schwermütig) melancholic; =sinnigkeit f = =sinn; =stimme f deep (or bass) voice; stimmig a. deep-voiced or -mouthed; =ton m, pros., &c. (ant. Hochton) secondary accent or stress; tonig a. low-toned; tönend a. deep-sounding, with a deep (or hollow) sound.

Tiegel (ˑˇ) [: tile; It.; *grch.: Ziegel] m ㊷ 1. Küche: saucepan. — 2. chm. ☉ metall. ~ zum Schmelzen: crucible, melting-pot. [or melting-pot.]

Tiegelchen (ˑˑˇ) n ㊷ small crucible

Tiegel=druck(presse) f m ㊷ (ˑˑˑˇ...) ☉ typ. platen-press; =guß m crucible-smelting; =guß=stahl m crucible-steel; =ofen m crucible-furnace.

Tiek=baum (ˑˑ...) [indisch] m ㊷ teak (-tree) (Tecto'n(i)a grandis); =holz n bsd. zum Schiffsbau: teak(-wood).

Tiene (ˑˇ) [fr., It.] f ㊸ small tub.

Tier (ˇ) [ahd.: deer] n ⓒc. 1. a) (ant. Pflanze, Mineral) animal; vierfüßiges (zweibeiniges) ~ quadruped (biped); b) (ant. Mensch) beast, mit Hervorhebung des Viehischen: brute; von wilden ~en zerrissen torn by wild (or savage) beasts; c) weitS. (Geschöpf) creature; (Wesen) (living) being, ⚓ zoon. — 2. engS. (Reit=)~ F mount; biSw. (Maul=)~ mule; hunt. (Hirschkuh) doe, deer. — 3. F von Personen: a) (ungeschlachter Mensch) beast, brute (of a fellow); b) großes ~ (wichtige Person) big (or great) gun or swell or pot; c) ein gutes ~ a kind soul.

tier=ähnlich (ˑˑ...) a. ㊻ like an animal, beast-like, ⚓ zooid; =anbeter m worshipper of beasts, ⚓ zoolater; =anbetung f worship of animals, ⚓ zoolatry, zootheism; =art f species of animals; =arznei f medicine for animals or cattle; =arznei=kunde, =kunst f veterinary surgery or science; arzneilich a. veterinary; =arzneischule f veterinary college; =arzt m veterinary surgeon; ärztlich a. veterinary; e Hochschule vet. academy; =bändiger m tamer (or trainer) of animals; =beschreiber m: ⚓ zoographer, ...ist; =beschreibung f: ⚓ zoography, =buch n book on animals, zoological treatise, engS. ehm.: bestiary; =bude f wild-beast show, (small) menagerie; =chemie f animal chemistry, ⚓ zoochemistry.

Tierchen (ˑˑ) n ㉓ (dim. von Tier) little (or tiny) animal or beast or creature, schott. beastie; mikroskopisches: ⚓ animalcule; Sprichw. s. Pläsierchen.

Tier=epos (ˑˑ...) n ㊷ beast-epic; =fabel f fable on animals; =fresser m: ⚓ zoophagan; =freund(in f) m friend to (or lover of) animals, ⚓ zoophilist; =garten m: a) (Gehege für Wild) preserve, park; b) zoological gardens pl.; =gefecht n fight between (wild) beasts; =gemälde n stück, =geographie f: ⚓ zoogeography; =geschichte f: a) story about animals; b) zoology; =haus n menagerie; =heil=kunde f veterinary science, ⚓ zootherapy.

Tierheit (ˑˇ) f ㊶: a) (Wesen der Tiere) animality; b) (Roheit) bestiality, brutality. [beasts, chase.]

Tier=hetze (ˑˑˇ) f ㊷ hunting (of) wild

tierisch (ˑˇ) a. ㊻ 1. (ant. pflanzlich) animal, of animals. — 2. von Menschen: (viehisch) bestial, brutal, like a beast.

Tier=kampf (ˑˑ...) m ㊷ =gefecht; =kenner m = =kundige(r); =kreis m, ast. zodiac; =kunde f zoology; =kundige(r) s. zoologist; =leben n animal life.

Tierlein (ˑˑ) n ㉓ = Tierchen.

Tier=magnetismus (ˑˑ...) m ㊷ animal magnetism; ⚓ zoomagnetism; =maler (=in f) m (=malerei f) painter (painting) of animals; =natur f animality; =pflanze f: ⚓ zoophyte; =pflanzenkunde f: ⚓ zoophytology; =quäler m tormentor of animals; =quälerei f cruelty (shown) to animals; =reich n (ant. Pflanzen=, Mineral=reich) animal kingdom; reich a. rich in animals; =sage f, etwa: legend (or ancient tale) about animals or beasts; vgl. =epos; =schau f show of animals; =schutzverein m society for the prevention of cruelty to animals; =sprache f language of beasts; =stück n painting of animals; =versteinerung f: ⚓ zoolite; =wärter

m keeper of animals or of a menagerie; welt f animal world; =wesen n: a) (Tier) animal; b) (tierisches Wesen) animality.

Tiger (ˑˇ) [mhd.; lt.; grch.: *perj.] m ㊷, in f ㊵ zo. tiger, f tigress (Felis tigris); f. Königstiger; fig. ein wahrer ~ a bloodthirsty person, a person with a tiger's (or of tigerish) disposition.

tiger=artig (ˑˑ...) a. ㊻ tiger-like, (blutdürftig) tigerish; =decke f ㊷, =fell n, tiger's skin; fleckig a. spotted like a tiger; =haut f = =fell; =herz n tiger's heart; =hund m Dalmatian dog; =katze f, zo. margay (Felis tigri'na); =lili=e ♀ f tiger-flower (Tigri'dia pavo'nia), chinesische: tiger-lily (Li'lium tigri'num).

tigern (ˑˇ) v/a. ㊳a. to speckle; s. getigert.

Tiger=schlange (ˑˑ...) f ㊷ zo. spotted rock-snake (Python molu'rus); =schnecke f, zo. tiger-shell or -cowry (Cypra'ea tigris); =tier n = Tiger; =weibchen n tigress; =wolf m, zo. spotted hyena (Hyae'na macula'ta).

Tilde (ˑˇ) [span.] f ㊸ 1. (Wiederholungszeichen) sign of repetition (~). — 2. span. gram. (Zeichen über dem n wie in señor) tilde.

tilgbar (ˑˇ) a. ㊻ destructible, extinguishable, redeemable; ~keit (ˑˑˑ) f ㊵ destructibility, redeemableness.

tilgen (ˑˇ) [ahd.] I v/a. ㊳ (vernichten) to destroy, annihilate, cancel, (auslöschen) to extinguish; (verwischen) to wipe (or blot) out; to efface, erase, expunge, obliterate; vom Erdboden ~ to sweep off the face of the earth; (streichen) to strike (out), ☉ typ. to delete; (ausrotten) to eradicate, to extirpate; to discharge (or pay off, clear off) debts or liabilities, to redeem a bond, &c.; e-e alte Schuld ~, auch: to wipe off an old score. — II ~ n ㊷ s. Tilgung.

Tilger (ˑˇ) m ㊷ one who annihilates, &c. (f. tilgen I); (Zerstörer) destroyer.

Tilgung (ˑˇ) f ㊶ (f. tilgen) destruction, annihilation; effacement, erasure, expunction, ☉ typ. deletion, discharge of debts, paying (or clearing) off liabilities, redemption or amortization of bonds, &c.

Tilgungs=fonds (ˑˑ...) m ㊷, =kasse f ㊸ sinking-fund; =schein ⚒ m bill of amortization, certificate of redemption; =zeichen n, typ. dele (✠).

Till (ˇ) npr. m. ⓒc. ㊹ f. Eulenspiegel.

Timokratie ⚓ (-ˑˑˇ) [grch.] f ㊹ (Herrschaft der Besitzenden) timocracy.

timokratisch (-ˑˑˇ) a. ㊻ timocratic(al).

Timotheos, mst ....us (ˑˑˑ) [grch.] npr/m. ⓒ⒁c. (a. Bn.) Timothy.

Timothy=gras ♀ (ˑˑˑ...) n ㊷ timothy-grass (Phleum prate'nse).

Tingeltangel (ˑˑˑˇ) m (n) ㊷ music-hall, variety-theatre or -entertainment.

Tinkal ⚒ (ˑˇ) [malaiisch] m ㊹ min. (roher, natürlicher Borax) tincal, crude borax.

Tinktur (ˑˇ) [lt.] f ㊶: a) (Färbung), b) (Auszug aus Pflanzenstoffen) tincture.

Tinte (ˑˇ) [ahd.; * lt. tincta gefärbt] f ㊸ 1. ink (for writing); unauslöschliche ~ indelible (or marking-) ink; mit ~ beflecken, beschmieren to (smear with) ink, to blot (with ink); fig. einen in die ~ (Patsche) bringen, führen to get a p. into trouble; in die ~ kommen ob. geraten

to get (o.s.) into a scrape or a (sad) pickle; in der ~ sein oder sitzen to be in a pretty mess or plight; P~ gesoffen haben (verdreht sein) to be mad, P to be off one's chump or nut. — 2. *paint.* (Färbung) tint, tincture.

Tinten=fabrikant ⊙ (ᵈ⌣...) *m* ⑫ inkmaker; =faß *n* inkstand; =fisch *m*, *zo.* (Sepia) cuttlefish; =flasche *f* ink-bottle; =fleck *m* ink-blot, stain of ink; =holz (=baum *m*) *n* ♀ ink-wood (*Hype'late panicula'ta*); =klecks *m* = =fleck; =kleckser *m* quill-driver, F ink-slinger or -spiller; =nuß ♀ *f* = Myrobalane; =pulver *n* inkpowder; ♀schwarz *a.* ⑯ (as) black as ink; bsd. ehm. =stecher *m* inkhorn; =stein *m, min.* ink-stone; =stift *m* inkpencil; =strich *m* line drawn (or made) with ink; =wischer *m* pen-wiper.

tintig (ᵈ⌣) *a.* ⑯ 1. inky, like ink; der Wein schmeckt ♀ (*adv.*) the wine has an inky taste. — 2. blotted with ink.

Tinto=wein ⊙ (ᵈ⌣|) *m* ⑫ (dunkelroter span. Wein) tinto; tent(-wine).

tipp! (ᴶ) [lautm.]: tipp, tapp! pit-a-pat.

Tippel (ᵈ⌣) [ndd.] *m* (*n*) ⑫ = Tüpfel.

tippeln (ᵈ⌣) ⊙ *a.* I *v/a.* = tüpfeln. — II F *v n.* (jn) sto walk on tiptoe(s).

tippen (ᵈ⌣) [ndd.] *v/a. u. v/n.* (h.) ⑱ to touch lightly or gently, to tap.

Tirade (-¹ᵛ) [fr.] *f* ⑱ bsd. *thea.* (lange Rede eines Schauspielers) tirade; weitS. wearying (or dull, humdrum) speech.

Tirailleur ⚔ (-räī-jōʻr) [fr.] *m* ⑥d.(⑫) skirmisher; ~s *pl. a.* flanking party.

tirailliren ⚔ (-räī-jīʻᵛ) *v/n.* (h.) ⑬ (plänkeln) to skirmish, to fight in extended (or distended, loose) order.

tirili (⁻¹ᵛ) [lautm.] **I** *int.* ♪!, etwa: tara-la! — II ~ ♪ *n* ⓾ der Lerche tirra-lirra; note of the skylark.

tirilieren (-ᵛ¹ᵛ) *v/n.* (h.) ⑬ von der Lerche: to warble, to carol. [(the) Tyrol.)

Tirol (-¹) *npr/n.* ⑯*a.* (öst. Kronland)

Tiroler (-¹⌣) *m*, **Tirolerin** *f* ⑬, **tirol(er)isch** *a.* ⑯ Tyrolese.

tiron(ian)isch (-(-⌣)¹) [Tiro (Freigelaffener des Cicero, Erfinder e-r it. Kurzschrift)] *a.* ⑯ röm.Alt.: Le Noten *pl.* Tironian notes *pl.*

Tisane (-¹ᵛ) [grch.] *f* ⑱ bsd. ehm. (Arzneitrant) tisane, ptisan.

Tisch (ᴶ) [ahd.: dish, desk; lt.; *grch. (Diskus = Platte)] *m* ⑩*a.* 1. table (f. abdecken 1 u. decken 2); am grünen (Rats=)~e at the council-board; *rel. f.* Herr 2 am Ende; *parl.* auf den ~ des Hauses niederlegen to lay on the table of the house, *a.* to table; *fig.* reinen ~ machen to make a clean sweep (of it), to settle (up) accounts. — 2. (Kost) board; (Mahlzeit) meal; am ~e at table, at dinner; e-n guten ~ führen to keep a good table; s. frei 6; Scheidung (ob. Trennung) von ~ und Bett separation from bed and board, mehr gbr.: judicial separation; vor (nach) ~e before (after) a meal; zu ~e bitten oder laden to invite (or ask) to dinner or supper; zu ~e gehen, sich zu ~e setzen to sit down to a meal or to dinner or to supper. — 3. *fig.* = Tischgesellschaft; der ganze ~ geriet in Aufregung the whole (or all the people at the) table became excited.

Tisch=aufsatz (ᵈ⌣...) *m* ⑫ = Aufsatz 2; =bein *n* leg of a table; =besen *m* crumb-brush; =besteck *n* cover; knife, fork and spoon; =bier *n* table-beer; =blatt *n* top (z. Einlegen: leaf) of a table.

Tischchen (ᵈ⌣) *n* ㉓ little table.

Tisch=dame (ᵈ⌣...) *f* ⑫ lady taken in to dinner; vgl. Herr u. =nachbar(in); =decke *f* table-cloth or -cover.

tischen ↘ (⌣) *v/n.* (h.) ⑬ 1. to lay the table. — 2. to be (or sit) at table.

Tisch=gabel (ᵈ⌣...) *f* ⑫ fork; =gänger(in *f*) *m* boarder; =gast *m* guest (invited to dinner or supper); =gebet *n* grace (vor od. nach dem Essen before or after meat); das ~ sprechen to say grace, nach dem Essen: to return thanks; =geld *n* (fee paid for) board; =genoß, =genosse *m*, =genossin *f* = =nachbar(in); fellow-boarder; bisw.: messmate; =geschirr *n* things used for the table; table-requisites *pl.*; =gesellschaft *f* (company invited to a) dinner-party, ⚔ mess, vgl. Tisch 3; =gespräch *n* table-talk; =glocke *f*: a) dinner-bell; b) gong or (hand-)bell on the table; =herr *m* gentleman taking a lady in to dinner; vgl. =dame; =karte *f* menu; =kasten *m* drawer of a table; =klappe *f* leaf (or flap) of a table; =klopfen *n* Geisterseherei: table- (or spirit-)rapping; =korb *m* plate-basket; =lade *f* table-drawer.

Tischlein (ᵈ⌣) *n* ㉓ = Tischchen; das ~ deck' dich im Märchen, etwa: the magic table which at a moment's notice appears laden with rich viands. [cabinet-maker.)

Tischler ⊙ (ᵈ⌣) *m* ⑫ joiner (Kunst=)~

Tischler=arbeit ⊙ (ᵈ⌣...) *f* ⑫ joiner's work, joinery, feinere: cabinet-work; =bank *f* joiner's bench.

Tischlerei ⊙ (ᵈ⌣¹¹) *f* ⑯ 1. joinery, joiner's (or cabinet-maker's) craft or trade or art. — 2. joiner's workshop.

Tischler=geselle (ᵈ⌣...) *m* ⑫ journeyman joiner; =handwerk *n*, =kunst *f* = Tischlerei 1; =leim *m* strong glue; =meister *m* master joiner.

tischlern ⊙ (ᵈ⌣) *v/n.* (h.) ⑬*a.* to do joiner's (or cabinet-maker's) work.

Tischler=werkstatt (ᵈ⌣...) *f* ⑫, =werkstelle *f* joiner's workshop; =werkzeug *n* joiner's tool(s *pl.*).

Tisch=matte (ᵈ⌣...) *f* ⑫ table-mat; =messer *n* table-knife; =nachbar(in *f*) *m* neighbour at table; =ordnung *f* order in which the guests take their seats at table; =platte *f* = =blatt; =rede *f* after-dinner speech, toast; =rücken *n* Geisterseherei: table-moving, -turning; =segen *m* = =gebet; =trunk *m* beverage for the table; =tuch *n* tablecloth; =wein *m* (ordinary) table- (or dinner-) wine, light wine; =zeit *f* dinner-time; =zeug *n* table-linen.

Titan [grch.] **I** (⁻¹ᵛ) *npr/m.* ⑥⑯*a.* *myth.* (Sonnengott) Titan. — **II** (-¹) *m* ⑫, *a.* ~e (-¹⌣) ⑭ *myth.* bsd. in *m pl.* ~en (die Götter bekämpfendes Riesengeschlecht) Titans. — **III** ⚛ (-¹) *n* ⑩d. *chm.* titanium (Ti).

Titan=eisen=erz ⚛ (-¹¹¹...) [Titan III] *n* ⑫ *min.* titaniferous iron-ore.

titanenhaft (-¹⌣⌣) *a.* ⑯ = titanisch.

Titanen=kampf (-¹¹... ⌣ᴶ) *m* ⑫ *myth.* battle of Titans, ⚛ Titanomachy.

Titan=erz (-¹¹...) *n* ⑫ *min.* rutile; ♀haltig *a.* ⑯ titaniferous. [Titanesque.)

titanisch (-¹ᵛ) *a.* ⑯ Titanic, Titanian,

Titanium ⚛ (-¹(ᵛ)¹) *n* ⑬ = Titan III.

Titan=metall (-¹¹...) *n* ⑫ = Titan III; ♀sauer *a.* ⑯ *chm.* titanic; ♀saures Salz titanate; =säure=anhydrid *n* titanic anhydride (TiO₂).

Titel (¹ᵛ) [ahd.: * lt. *tiʻtulus*] *m* ⑫ **1.** title, F co. handle to one's name; vgl. Rechts= titel); der ~ Graf oder eines Grafen the title (of) count; bloßer ~ mere (or empty) title; einen ~ haben to have (or bear) a title; sich einen ~ beilegen to assume a title. — 2. (Überschrift, Rubrit) head(ing); Buch mit aufgedrucktem ~ lettered book; ⚖ jur. (jetzt Abschnitt) section, title.

Titel=auflage (¹ᵛ...), =ausgabe *f* ⑫ Buchhandel: edition with merely the title changed; =bild *n* frontispiece: =bildchen *n* = =vignette; =blatt *n* title-page; =bogen *m*, *typ.* title-sheet, *pl. auch:* oddments *pl.*, preliminary matter *sg.*; =jagd *f*, *fig.* hunting after titles; =kopf *m* e-s Artikels: heading, head-line; =kupfer *n* (engraved) frontispiece; ♀los *a.* ⑯ without a title; =narr *m* person madly fond of titles; =rolle *f*, *thea.* title-rôle; =sucht *f* mania for titles; ♀süchtig *a.* fond of titles; =vignette ⊙ *f*, *typ.* vignette in the title; =wesen *n* (system of bestowing) titles *pl.*

titrieren ⚛ (-¹ᵛ) [fr.] *v/a. u. v/n.* (h.) ⑬ *chm.* (durch die Maß-analyse den Gehalt einer Flüssigkeit bestimmen) to titrate.

Titrier=methode ⚛ (-¹¹...¹ᵛ) *f* ⑱ *chm.* titration(-method). [prince.)

Titular=fürst (ᵛ¹ᵛ...) [lt.] *m* ⑫ titular)

Titulatur (ᵛ¹ᵛ) [lt.] *f* ⑯ titles *pl.*

titulieren (ᵛ¹ᵛ) [lt.] *v/a.* ⑬ (betiteln, anreden als) to (call by a) title, to style: e-n Herzog ♀ to give a p. the title of duke, to address a p. as duke, to call a p. duke. [short frizzled hair.)

Titus=kopf (¹ᵛ...ᴶ) F *m* ⑫ (head with))

Tivoli (¹ᵛ⌣) [~ ♀, it. St. (ehm. Tibur)] *n* ⑯: a) (Vergnügungsort) tivoli, place of amusement; b) ~(spiel) bagatelle.

Tjost (ᴶ) [fr.] *f* ⑯ Turnier; j(o)ust.

Tl. *abbr.* = Teil.

Toast ⟋ (tōst) [engl.: urspr. „geröstete" Brotschnitte, dann auch Trinkspruch] *m* ⑩*a.* toast; e-n ~ auf e-n ausbringen to propose (or drink) a p.'s health, to toast a p.; **toasten** (tō'=stᵛ) *v/n.* (h.) ⑬ to give a toast, to drink a friend's [health.)

Tobak P (⁻¹ᵛ) *m* ⑩d. f. Tabak 2.)

toben (⁻¹ᵛ) [ahd.] **I** *v/n.* (h.) ⑱ **1.** von Menschen: to rave, to rage, to (fret and) fume, von Sturm und Wellen: to roar; (zornig schreien) to vociferate, to bawl out, to make an uproar; (lärmend spielen) to romp (about), to frolic; (poltern) to be noisy or uproarious. — **II** ~ *n* ㉓ 2. raving, &c. (i. I); fury. — **III** ♀d *p.pr. u. a.* ⑯ 3. in den Bed. des *inf.* — 4. enraged, furious, (rasend) frantic; (stürmisch) tempestuous, (ungestüm) boisterous, blustering.

Tobias (-¹ᵛ) [hebr.] *npr/m.* ⑯*a.* Tobias, Toby; *bibl.* das apokryphische Buch ~ ob. Tobiä the book of Tobit.

Signs (see page XVII): F familiar; P vulgar; ⟋ flash; ↘ rare; † obsolete (died); * new word (born); ⁺⁺ incorrect; ♪ music;

[Tobsucht] — 959 — [tollen]

Tob=sucht (ʺ...) f *path.* raving madness, frenzy; ⸗süchtig a. ⓰ raving mad, frantic, seized with frenzy.

Tochter (ʺchtr) [ahd.: daughter] f ⓴ daughter; ~ des Hauses, oft: young lady (of the house); F co. höhere Töchter young ladies pl. (who are) still at school; f. Fräulein. [establishment.]

Tochter=anstalt (ʺchtrʹ...) f ⓱ branch-⎦

Töchterchen (⌣⌣) n ⓻ little daughter; ihr einziges ~, a. their only little girl.

Tochter=kind (ʺchtr...) n ⓱ daughter's child, grandchild; ⸗kirche f filial church; ⸗land n colony.

töchterlich (⌣⌣) a. ⓰ daughterly, of (or like) a daughter.

Tochter=liebe (ʺchtrʹ...) f ⓱ daughter's love; ⸗mann m ⓻ Schwiegersohn.

Töchter=schule (⌣⌣ʹ...) [schwz. (*fr.*)] f ⓱ young ladies' school; höhere ~ high school for girls.

Tochter=sprache (ʺchtrʹ...) f ⓱ derivative language; ⸗staat m, ⸗stadt f colony.

tockieren (⌣⌣ʹ⌣) [it.] v/n. (h.) ⓷ *paint.* (mit kecken Strichen ausführen) to paint with (a few) bold touches (of the brush).

Tod (¹) [ahd.: death] m ⓶c. (pl. ⌣, dafür oft Todesfälle) 1. (ant. Leben) death, feierlicher: decease, departure from life, last journey, von hohen Personen auch: demise; f. Kind 2; den ~ in den Wellen finden to find a watery grave; sich den ~ holen to kill o.s. with hard toil, &c.; dem ~e nahe at death's door; dem ~e kühn ins Auge schauen to face (or meet) death boldly; es (er) wird mein ~ sein it (he) will be the death of me; ich will des ~es sein, wenn // I will fall down dead if //; e-s schönen ~es sterben to die a beautiful death, to have (or come to) a beautiful end; f. natürlich. — 2. Sprichw. des e-n ~ ist des andern Brot one man's misfortune is other man's fortune, what is good for one is bad for the other; umsonst ist (nur) der ~ everything costs money; f. Kraut 3. — 3. mit *prp.* (oft *fig.*); Kampf auf ~ und Leben mortal combat; auf Leben 2; sich auf den ~ erkälten to catch one's death of cold; auf den ~ krank dangerously ill, hovering between life and death, vgl. todkrank; (bis) auf den ~ verwundet mortally wounded; er ist uns (bis) in den ~ verhaßt ob. zuwider we hate (or loathe) him like sin or poison, milder: we heartily dislike him; treu bis in den ~ faithful unto death; mit dem ~e abgehen to die, to pass away, auch: to depart this life; e-n vom ~e erretten to save a p. from death or destruction; sich zu ~e arbeiten, schinden to work (or slave) o.s. to death; sich zu ~e ärgern to worry (or fret) o.s. to death; f. bluten II, grämen u. hetzen 3; sich zu ~e hungern to be starved, to starve o.s. (to death); sich zu ~e lachen to die with laughing; einen zu ~e quälen to worry a p. to death; zum ~e betrübt mortally grieved; zum ~e verurteilt sentenced to death.

tod=ähnlich (ʺ...) a. ⓰ death-like; ⸗bang a. frightened to death, mortally afraid; vgl. todesbang; ⸗blaß, ⸗bleich (f. a. toten...) deadly pale; ⸗bringend a. inflicting death; deadly (climate, &c.), fatal (disease), mortal (grief).

Todes=ahnung (ʺ...) f ⓱ presentiment of death; ⸗angst f: a) agony (of death); b) *fig.* in einer wahren ~ sein, in ängsten schweben to be in mortal dread; ⸗anzeige f announcement of a p.'s death, bei der Behörde: notification (or notice) of death; a. = Nekrolog; ⸗art f manner of death; ⸗bang a. ⓰ in mortal fear; vgl. todbang; ⸗blaß, ⸗bleich a. deadly pale, (as) pale as a ghost; ⸗blässe f deadly paleness; ⸗block m (des Schafotts) fatal block; ⸗botschaft f, ⸗engel m message, angel of death; ⸗fackel f funeral torch; ⸗fall m (case of) death, decease; ⸗fälle deaths, ⚔ oft: casualties pl.; ⸗furcht f fear of death; ⸗gedanke m thought of death; sich ~ machen to meditate on death; ⸗gefahr f peril of losing one's life; in ~ schweben, a. to be in imminent danger or in danger of one's life; einen aus ~ retten to save a p.'s life; ⸗hauch m deadly breath; ⸗jahr n year of a p.'s death; ⸗kampf m: a) eines Sterbenden: death-struggle, throes pl. of death, last agony; b) ⚔ (todbringender Kampf) mortal combat; ⸗kandidat F m dying person; ⸗keim m germ (or seeds pl.) of death; ⸗not f pressing danger, great peril or jeopardy; in ⸗nöten struggling with death, in one's last agony; ⸗pein, qual f pangs pl. of death; ⸗pfeil m fatal arrow; ⸗röcheln n death-rattles pl.; ⸗schlaf m sleep of the dead; *fig.* death-like sleep; ⸗schrecken m: a) fear of death; b) *fig.* mortal dread or fear; ⸗schweiß m cold sweat of death; ⸗stille f. Toten...; ⸗stoß m death-blow, finishing stroke; ⸗strafe f capital punishment; bei ~ on pain of death; die ~ erleiden to suffer the death-penalty; ⸗streich m = ⸗stoß; ⸗stunde f hour of death, last (or fatal) hour; ⸗tag m: a) day of death; b) anniversary of a p.'s death; ⸗ursache f cause of (one's) death; ⸗urteil n sentence of death; death-sentence, -warrant; ein ~ fällen, vollstrecken to pronounce, to carry out a sentence of death; ⸗verachtung f contempt (or defiance) of death; ⸗verbrechen n capital crime; ⸗wunde f mortal (or fatal) wound; ⸗würdig a. deserving (of) death.

tod=feind (ʺ...) a. ⓰ prädikativ: e-m ~ sein to be a p.'s deadly (or sworn) enemy.

Tod=feind(in f) m (ʺ...) ⓺ deadly (or mortal) enemy or foe; ⸗feindschaft f mortal enmity; ⸗krank a. ⓰ hopelessly ill, *bibl.* sick unto death.

tödlich (⌣⌣) [ahd.:*Tod*] a. ⓰ deadly; (verhängnisvoll) fatal (stroke, &c.), mortal (wound, &c.); (mörderisch) murderous, bsd. von Giften: ⚔ lethiferous; e-n ⌣ (adv.) hassen to have a deadly hatred against a p.; **Tödlichkeit** f ⓰ deadliness; ~ einer Wunde &c.: serious (stärker: fatal, hopeless) nature ...

tod=matt, ⸗müde (ʺ...) a. ⓰ tired (or harassed) to death, worn (F fagged) out; ⸗sünde f ⓶ *theol.* deadly (or mortal) sin; ⸗still a. ~ = totenstill; ⸗wund a. mortally wounded.

Töffel (⌣⌣) npr/m. ⓶⓺ = Stoffel.

Toga (¹⌣) [it.] f ⓳ ⓰ Alt. (Gewand der römischen Bürger) toga; in der ~ toga(t)ed.

Togo (¹⌣) [afrik.] npr/n. ⓶a. dtsche Kolonie: Togoland.

Tohuwabohu (⌣⌣¹⌣) [hebr. wüst u. leer] n, *bibl.* (1. Mose 1, 2) (Wirrwarr) tohu bohu, chaos, confusion, hubbub.

Toilette (toaʹ⌣) [fr.] f ⓱ 1. (Putztisch) toilet-(or dressing-)table; (Putz) dress, a. toilet; ~ machen to dress; in großer ~ in full dress, in evening dress, F co. in full fig. — 2. (Abort) lavatory.

Toiletten=gegenstände (toaʹ⌣⌣...) m/pl. ⓶ articles pl. of dress or toilet; ⸗kasten m, ⸗kästchen n dressing-case; ⸗schwamm m, ⸗seife f toilet-sponge, -soap; ⸗spiegel m toilet-glass, großer schwingender: cheval-glass; ⸗tisch m dressing-(or toilet-)table; ⸗zimmer n (ladies') dressing-room.

Tokai-er (⌣⌣, P mst ⌣ʹ⌣) [Tókaj ⓺, ungar. St.] m ⓶, a. ~wein m Tokay (wine).

Tokio ⓺ (¹⌣⌣) npr/n. ⓶a. Hauptstadt von Japan: Tokio, Tokyo.

Töle F (¹⌣) f ⓳ (Köter) cur.

Toledaner (⌣⌣ʹ⌣) [Toléʹdo ⓺, span. Stadt] a. *inv.:* ~ Klinge Toledo (blade).

tolerant (⌣⌣ʹ) [it.] a. ⓰ (duldsam) (gegen towards, to); **Toleranz** f ⓰(Duldsamkeit) tolerance, toleration; **tolerieren** (⌣⌣ʹ⌣) v/a. ⓷ (dulden) to tolerate.

toll[1] (¹) [ahd.: dull] I a. ⓰ 1. (unsinnig) nonsensical, senseless, foolish; (rasend) raving, mad, frantic, infuriated, wild; (ungereimt) absurd, strange, odd, extravagant; (spaßhaft) droll, comical; ⸗er Einfall, Streich mad freak, trick; ⸗er Hund mad (or rabid) dog; ⸗er Lärm frightful noise, Fu. P infernal row; ⸗e Wirtschaft loose (or disorderly) state of affairs; es ging sehr ⸗ her there was a great uproar; das ist doch zu ⸗ that's too bad; das ⸗ste dabei ist // the funniest (or most ludicrous) part of it is //; das wird noch ⸗er kommen the worst is to come (or in store) yet; ⸗ machen to drive mad, to madden; e-m den Kopf (durch Lärm &c.) ganz ⸗ machen to make a p.'s head split with noise, &c.; ⸗ werden to go (raving) mad, to feel distracted; *fig.* über et. ⸗ werden to be(come) enraged at a th.; je ⸗er, desto besser the madder the merrier. — 2. eng S. ⸗ und voll (betrunken) F dead (or blind, roaring) drunk; wie ⸗ laufen to run like mad. — II ~e(r)s. 3. person who is raving (mad); mad person; madman. f madwoman; lunatic.

toll[2]..., **Toll**[2]... (⌣...) [tollen[2]] f. Zsgn.

Toll[1]**-beere** ⚘ (⌣ʹ⌣) f ⓸ = ⸗kirsche.

Tolle (⌣⌣) [: Dolde] f ⓸ 1. *orn.* (Federbusch) tuft, crest. — 2. von Personen: (Haarschopf) top-knot, (hoher Kopfputz) raised (or puffed) head-dress. — 3. (Krause) frill. [(or goffering-)iron.]

Toll[2]**=eisen** ⓸ (⌣ʹ⌣) n ⓶ crimping-⎦

tollen[1] (⌣⌣) [toll] v/n. (h. u. sn) ⓷ ⓰ to be boisterous or rollicking, to frolic,

---
⚕ scientific; ❦ botanical; ⚲ geography; ⊕ machinery; ⚒ mining; ⚔ military; ⚓ marine; ✉ commercial; ✆ postal; 🚂 railway.

[tollen] — 960 — [Topfbrett]

to romp (about), F to kick up a row; durch die Straßen ~ to rush (or romp) like mad through the streets.

tollen² (⌣) [Tolle] v/a. ⊕ 1. Wäsche ~ (fälteln) to crimp (or goffer) linen. — 2. das Haar ~ (träufeln) to frizzle (or crimp) the hair.

Toll¹=haus (⌣...) n ⓔ = Irrenanstalt; =häusler m madman, maniac, lunatic.

Tollheit (⌣–) f (f. toll) 1. madness, frenzy; fury, rage. — 2. (toller Streich) mad trick, piece of folly.

Toll¹=kirsche (⌣...) f ⓔ deadly nightshade; =kopf m mad brain or person, madcap; ²köpfig a. ⓔ mad, harebrained; hot-headed; =korn ⚥ n: a) = Lolch; b) =körner pl. (Früchte vom Stechapfel) seeds of the thorn-apple; =kraut ⚥ n: a) = Kirsche; b) = Stechapfel; ²kühn a. foolhardy, rash; =kühnheit f foolhardiness, rashness; =sucht f = Tollheit 1; =wut f raving (madness), von Hunden ꝛc.: ⚕ rabies, (Wasserscheu) ⚕ hydrophobia, von Menschen: frenzy. [Tölpel 1.]

Tolpatsch (⌣–) [madj. Breitfuß] m ⓐa. =

Tölpel (⌣–) [ndd. Dörper Dörfler] m ⓔ 1. (ungeschlachter Mensch) awkward (or clumsy) fellow, booby, lout, dolt; (Bauernflegel) duffer, clodhopper, country bumpkin, (Dummkopf) blockhead, duffer. — 2. orn. ~ gannet (Sula); gemeiner ~ common gannet, channel-goose (S. bassa'na).

Tölpelei (⌣⌣–) f ⓔ awkwardness; clumsiness, doltishness; boorish manners pl.

tölpelhaft (⌣⌣–) a. ⓔ awkward, clumsy, loutish, doltish; ill-bred; ~igkeit f ⓔ awkwardness in manners, &c., loutishness, ill-breeding; vgl. Tölpelei.

tölpeln (⌣–) v/n. (h. u. sn) ⓔ a. to be clumsy (or loutish) in one's manners.

tölpisch (⌣–) a. ⓔ = tölpelhaft.

Tolu=balsam (–⌣–) m ⓔ tolu-balsam, balsam of Tolu (aus Myro'xylontolui'ferum).

Tomate ⚥ (⌣–⌣) [merif.] f ⓔ (Liebesapfel) tomato; ~n=sauce f ⓔ tomato sauce.

Tombak (⌣–) [it., *malai.] m (n) ⓓ. (Legierung v. Kupfer u. Zink) tombac, ...k, pinchbeck; ²en (⌣–⌣) a. ⓔ (of) tombac.

Ton¹ (–) [nhd. (ahd.)] m ⓔ c. clay, potter's earth, feuerfester: fire-clay.

Ton² (–) [lt., *grch.] m ⓓ c. 1. tone, einzelner musikalischer: note; (Schall, Laut) sound; (Art zu sprechen) strain; keinen ~ hervorbringen not to utter (or emit) a sound; fig. er wagt keinen ~ zu reden he dare not utter a word or open his mouth; einen andern ~ anschlagen, aus einem andern ~e reden to change one's tone or note; in einem hohen ~e reden to speak in a lofty tone or strain, F to ride the high horse; in schroffem ~ in a rough tone, abruptly; in spöttischem ~e in a jeering tone, sneeringly. — 2. fig. tone, fashion, es ist jetzt feiner ~ (od. gehört zum feinen ~e) it is now the right thing or the fashion; f. angeben 1. — 3. ♪ (Klangfarbe) timbre, (Ton=art) key; ~ halten to keep in tune. — 4. gr. (Betonung) (tonic) accent. — 5. print. tone, shade, tint.

Ton²=abstand (–⌣–) m ⓔ interval; ²angebend a. ⓔ setting the fashion, leading; =angeber(in f) m leader of the fashion(able world) or of society; =arbeiter m worker in clay; =art (Erd-art:) kind of clay; ²art f nature of a sound, engS. ♪ key, pitch (f. Dur, Moll²); bsd. fig. in allen ~en in all keys; in every possible strain or tune; ²artig a. clayey, claylike, ⚕ argillaceous; =bach ⊕ m Zucker=fabr.: clay-trough; ²beschaffenheit ♪ f tonality; =bild n musical picture or tableau; symphony; =bildung f formation of sound; ²boden m clayey soil, clay-ground; =brei ⊕ m Töpferei: clay-pulp; =brenn=ofen ⊕ m clay-kiln; ²dämpfer m f. Dämpfer 2; ²dichter m =setzer; =dichtung f musical composition; =eisen=stein m, min. clay iron-ore, ⚕ argillaceous iron-stone.

tonen (–⌣) [Ton¹] v/a. ⓔ (mit Ton bestreichen) to cover with clay.

tönen (–⌣) [mhd.; *Ton²] v/n. (h.) u. v/a. ⓔ to sound; (klingen) to ring; (widerhallen) to resound; (Töne hören lassen) to utter (or emit, give forth) sounds; hell 2d sonorous.

Ton¹=erde (–⌣...) f ⓔ min.: ⚕ argillaceous earth, chm. alumina, aluminium oxide (Al_2O_3), schwefelsaure ~: ⚕ aluminium sulphate ($Al_2[SO_4]_3$); ²erde=haltig a.: alumin(ifer)ous; =erde=hydrat n, chm.: ⚕ aluminium hydroxide, hydrate of alumina ($H_2Al_2O_4$); =erde=metall n ⚕ aluminium; =erde=salz n, =erde=verbindung f: ⚕ aluminate.

tönern (–⌣) [Ton¹] a. ⓔ 1. (made) of clay, earthen; f. Koloß. — 2. clayey, ⚕ argillaceous, argilliferous, ⚕ argillous.

Ton²=fall (–⌣...) m ⓔ pros., &c. cadence, modulation; =farbe f, phys. timbre, ²figur f clay figure; ²folge f succession of sounds; ♪ diatonic scale; tune, melody; =führung f modulation; ²gefäß n earthen(-ware) vessel; =gefäß=malerei f: ⚕ ceramography; ²gemälde n = =bild; ²geschirr n pottery(-ware); ²gesetz n law of sound, ♪ tonal law; ²grube f clay-pit; ²halle f concert-room; ²haltig a. clayey, ⚕ argilliferous; ²höhe ♪ f pitch of a note. [npr/m. ⓔ Tony.)

Toni (–⌣) [Anton(ie)] npr/f. ⓔ (subd. a.)

tonicht, tonig (⌣–) a. ⓔ = tönern 2.

Tonika ♪ (–⌣⌣) [it.] f ⓔ (Grundton) tonic.

tonisch (–⌣) [grch.] a. ⓔ physiol., &c. (die Spannkraft erhöhend) tonic.

Tonka=baum (–⌣...) m ⓔ [südamer.] m coumarou (Di'pterix odora'ta); =bohne f tonka-bean; =kampfer m = Kumarin.

Ton²=kunst (–⌣...) f ⓔ (art of) music, musical art; gr.: phonics; =künstler(in f) m musician; ²lage f, =lager (in f) m musician; clay-bed or -course; ²lehre f, phys.: ⚕ acoustics, phonics; =leiter ♪ f scale, gamut; die ~ spielen to play the scales; ²los a. ⓔ: a) (klanglos) toneless; (ohne Stimme) ⚕ aphonous; b) gr. (unbetont) unaccented, without stress; =malerei ♪ f tone-painting, music imitative of natural sounds; =maß n pros., &c. measure, time, metrical quantity; ²mergel m clay-marl, ⚕ argillo-calcite; ²messer m, phys.: ⚕ tonometer, monochord; =messung f measurement of sounds, ⚕ tonometry; ²mühle ⊕ f clay-mill; ²²nachahmend a. ⓔ: ⚕ onomatopoetic; =nach-ahmung f ⓔ: onomatopœia.

Tönnchen (–⌣) n ⓔ (dim. v. Tonne) small cask or barrel, keg.

Tonne (–⌣) [ahd. ton; *fr.] f ⓔ 1. (großes Faß) tun, butt, kleineres: cask, barrel; puncheon. — 2. Maß (abbr. t): a) ⚖ (= 1000 Kilogramm) weight of a thousand kilograms or about 2205 pounds Avd.; b) ⚓ (Schiffs=)~ ton of shipping; vgl. a. Registertonne; c) ⚓ (Seezeichen) buoy. — 3. F fig. very stout person, (regular) tub or butt.

Tonnen=butter ⚥ (–⌣...) f ⓔ butter in tubs; ²förmig a. ⓔ barrel-shaped; tubby; ²gehalt ⚓ m ship's tonnage or burden; =geld n tonnage; =gewölbe n, arch. barrel- (or tunnel-) vault; =ladung, =last f, =maß n ⚓ tonnage; =reif(en) m hoop (of a barrel); ²weise adv. (F a. a.) (taken) by (or in) tuns or barrels or casks.

Ton²=papier ⊕ (–⌣...) n ⓔ phot. toned paper; ²pfeife f clay pipe; =pfropf ⊕ m, metall. clay plug; =platte f, typ. toned (or tinted) plate, tint-block; ²röhre f earthenware tube; =sandstein m, min.: ⚕ argillaceous sandstone; =schicht f, geol. clay-bank; =schiefer m, min.: ⚕ argillaceous schist or slate, argillite; =schneide ⊕ f clay-cutter, potter's saw; =seife ⊕ f aluminous soap; ²setzer m musical composer; =setz-kunst, =setzung f musical composition; =silbe f accented (or tonic) syllable; =spiel n music, musical entertainment, concert; =stück n musical piece; =stufe f pitch of a note.

Tonsur (–⌣) [lt.] f ⓔ (geschorene Platte der Geistlichen) tonsure, shaven crown.

tonsuriert (⌣–⌣) a. ⓔ v. Mönchen ꝛc.: tonsured, with a shaven crown.

Tonsur=träger (–⌣...) m ⓔ tonsured (or shaven) priest or monk.

Ton²=umfang ♪ (–⌣...) m ⓔ der Stimme ꝛc.: compass, range; =veränderung f change of tone or accent; =verhältnis n relation of sounds, rhythm; ²waren f/pl. earthenware (goods pl.); vgl. =geschirr; =waren=fabrik(ation) f (making of) pottery; ²werkzeug n musical instrument; =zeichen n: a) ♪ note; b) gr. accent; ²zubereiter ⊕ m Ziegelei: clay-maker or -man.   [topaz.]

Topas (–⌣) [mhd., *grch.] m ⓐa. min.=

Topf [mhd.: tief] m ⓓ b. 1. pot, eiserner zum Kochen: (iron) sauce-pan, irdener: earthen(ware) vessel or pan, (Krug) jar; f. papinisch; Pflanzen in den ~ setzen to pot ...; Redensarten: in alle Töpfe gucken to poke one's nose into everything; alles in einen ~ werfen to throw everything into the same pot, fig. to treat everything (or all) alike; Sprichwort: gesprungene Töpfe halten am längsten creaking hinges last (or hold) the longest. — 2. provc. (Kreisel) top.

Topf=binder ⊕ (–⌣...) m ⓔ workman who mends crockery (with wires); =blume f = =pflanze; =brett n pot-board, für Blumentöpfe: shelf for flower-pots.

Zeichen (f. S. XVII): F familiär; P Volkssprache; F Gaunersprache; ⚹ selten; † alt (auch gestorben); * neu (auch geboren); ⚐ unrichtig;

[Töpfchen] — 961 — [tot]

Töpfchen (⌣⌢) n ⓘ (dim. v. Topf) 1. small pot or mug or jar; ~ Bier pint of beer. — 2. = Nachtgeschirr.
Topf=deckel (⌣⌣⌢) m ⓘ lid (or cover) of a pot, saucepan-lid.
Töpfer ⓘ (⌣⌢) m ⓘ potter. [pottery.]
Töpfer=arbeit (⌣⌣⌢⌣) f ⓘ potter's work,
Töpferei (⌣⌣⌣⌢) f ⓘ 1. potter's trade, als Kunst: ceramic art. — 2. = Töpferwerkstatt. — 3. = Töpferware.
Töpfer=erde (⌣⌣⌢…) f ⓘ potter's earth or clay; **=gesell** m journeyman potter; **=gut** n = =ware; **=handwerk** n potter's trade; **=kunst** f ceramic (or potter's) art; **=meister** m master potter.
töpfern¹ ⓘ (⌣⌣⌢) v/n. (h.) ⓘ a. to make pottery, to do potter's work.
töpfern² (⌣⌣⌢) a. ⓘ made of (potter's) clay.
Töpfer=säge ⓘ (⌣⌣⌢…) f ⓘ potter's saw; **=scheibe** f potter's wheel; **=ton** m potter's clay; **=ware** f potter's ware, pottery, crockery; **=werk=statt, =stätte** f potter's workshop; **=zeug** n = =ware.
Topf=fabrik ⓘ (⌣⌢ …) f ⓘ pottery; **=flicker** m mender of pots and pans; **=form** f mould for pots; **=glasur** f potter's varnish; **=gucker** F m man who is fond of pottering about the kitchen, weitS. meddlesome person; **=haken, =henkel** m pot-hook, -handle; **=lecker** F m: a) one who licks the dishes and plates; ~ lick-pot; b) greedy person; **=markt** m market (or fair) for crockery; **=pflanze** f, hort. potted plant, flower growing in a pot; **=scherbe** f (piece of a) broken pot, † potsherd; **=ständer** m flower-stand; **=stein** m, min. potstone; **=stürze** f = =deckel.
Topik ⓘ (⌣⌢) f ⓘ phls. (Methode der Auffindung von Beweisgründen) topics.
topisch (⌣⌢) [grch.] a. ⓘ bsd. med. (örtlich) topical (affection, &c.); local.
Topograph ⓘ (⌣⌣⌢) [grch.] m ⓘ (Ortsbeschreiber) topographer; **~ie** (⌣⌣⌣⌢) f ⓘ topography; **=isch** (⌣⌣⌢⌣) a. ⓘ topographical.
topp¹ ⓘ [fr.] int. ⓘ! that's a bargain!, agreed!, be it so!, all right!, alright!
Topp² ↓ (⌢) [ndd., engl. Zopf] m ⓘ d. ⓘ (oberes Ende aller aufrechtstehenden Hölzer) top, head (s. lenzen). [top-timbers pl.]
Topp=auflanger ↓ (⌣⌣⌣⌢…) m/pl.
Töppel (⌣⌢) [ndd.] m ⓘ (Federbusch) tuft of feathers; **~ente** (⌣⌣⌣⌢) f ⓘ orn. tufted duck. [(eine) (topping-)lift.]
Topp(e)nant ↓ (⌣⌣⌢) [Topp²] ↓
Topp²=laterne (⌢⌣⌣⌢) f ⓘ top-light; **=mast** m topmast; **=reep** n guy; **=segel** n topsail.
Tor¹ (⌢) [ahd.: door: Tür] n ⓘ c. gate (s. eisern, ⓘ), (infahrt) gateway; ehm.: (Stadt=, Zoll=) ~ bar; vor das ~ gehen to (take a) walk outside the (city-)gates or the town; ⓘ vor den ~en stehen to be at the gates; Fußballspiel: goal; ein ~ gewinnen, zählen to score a goal; fig. s. öffnen I.
Tor² (⌢) [mhd.: Dusel, dösig] m ⓘ, **Törin** f ⓘ fool(ish person), simpleton; f a. foolish (or silly) woman or girl.
Tor¹=angel (⌢ …) f ⓘ gate-hinge; **=artig** a. ⓘ like a gate; **=ball=spiel** n = Kricket; **=baum** m bar of a gate; ehm. **=einnehmer** m receiver of tolls or excise, tollman at the gate.

Tores=schluß (⌣⌣⌢) s. Torschluß.
Torf (⌢) [ndd.: turf] m ⓘ b. Brennstoff: peat, ↘ turf; ~ graben od. stechen to cut peat.
Tor¹=fahrt (⌢⌢) f ⓘ = Torweg.
torf=artig (⌢…) a. ⓘ peat-like, peaty; **=asche** f ⓘ peat-ashes pl.; **=bagger** ⓘ m peat-drag; **=beere** ⓘ f = Moosbeere; **=boden** m peat-soil.
torfen (⌣⌢) v/a. ⓘ: agr. einen Acker ⓘ to manure ... with turfy mould.
Torf=erde (⌢…) f ⓘ min. peaty earth or mould; **=feuer** n peat-fire; **=feuerung** f: a) firing (or heating) with peat; b) peat-fuel; **=gas** n peat-gas; **=geschmack** m v. Whisky ⓘ: peaty flavour; **=gräber** m peat-cutter or -digger; **=gräberei** f: a) cutting (of peat); b) = =grube; **=grube** f peat-pit; **=händler** m peatman; **=kohle** f peat-charcoal, carbonized peat; **=lager** n: a) = =moor; b) ⓘ peat-store or -shed; **=land** n peat-land. [gate.]
Tor¹=flügel (⌢⌢…) m ⓘ gate-wing of a
Torf=moor (⌢…) n ⓘ peat-bed or -bog, auch: turf-moss, turfy bog, turbary; **=moos** ⓘ n peat-moss (Sphagnum cymbifo'lium); **=preß=maschine** ⓘ f peat-machine; **=sode** ⓘ f peat (in brick-shape); **=spaten** m peat-spade; **=staub** m = =erde; **=stechen** n peat-cutting or digging; **=stecher** m = =gräber; **=stich** m = =stechen; auch: turbary.
Tor¹=geld (⌢…) n ⓘ gate-money paid after the gates are shut; **=glocke** f gate-bell; vgl. Sperrglocke; **=halle** f. arch. porch.
Torheit (⌢⌣) [mhd.; *Tor²] f ⓘ 1. foolishness, folly, (Einfalt) simple-mindedness, silliness; Sprichw. s. Alter² 2. — 2. foolish act, piece of folly. [porter.]
Tor¹=hüter (⌢⌣⌣) m ⓘ gate-keeper,
töricht (⌣⌢) [mhd.] a. ⓘ foolish (s. Jungfrau b); (einfältig) simple-minded, silly; adv. er hat sich sehr ⓘ benommen to acted like a thorough fool, he has made a great fool (or ass) of himself; **~er=weise** adv. like a fool, in a silly
Törin (⌢⌣) f ⓘ s. Tor². [manner.]
Torkel F (⌣⌢) [ahd., *lt.] m ⓘ: a) f. südd. = Kelter; b) fig. = Sau 6.
torkeln F (⌣⌢) v/n. (h. u. ſn) ⓘ a. von Betrunkenen: to reel, F to be off one's legs; vgl. taumeln.
Tornister (⌣⌣⌢) [madj.; *grch. (Kanister)] m ⓘ: a) ⓘ (soldier's) knapsack; b) für Schüler: (schoolboy's) satchel, school-bag.
Torpeder ↓ ⓘ (⌣⌣⌢) [Torpedo] m ⓘ torped(o)ist, torpedo-gunner; **torpedieren** (⌣⌢⌣⌢) v/a. ⓘ to attack with torpedoes, to torpedo.
Torpedo (⌣⌣⌢) [lt.] m ⓘ 1. ichth. = Zitterroche. — 2. ↓ unterseeische Kriegsmaschine: torpedo; s. Fischtorpedo; durch ~ beschädigen to torpedo.
Torpedo=abteilung ↓ (⌣⌣⌣⌢…) f ⓘ torpedo-boat division; **=boot** m torp.-boat; **=boot=zerstörer** m = =zerstörer; **=fänger** m torpedo-catcher; **=netz** n torp.-net(ting); **=stange** f torp.-boom; **=sucher** m torpedo-detector or -finder; **=zerstörer** m torpedo-destroyer.
Tor¹=pförtchen (⌢…) n ⓘ wicket; **=pfosten** m Fußballspiel: goal-post.

Torricellisch (⌣⌣⌢⌣) [⌣⌣⌢⌣] [Torricelli, it. Physiker, 1608–47] a. ⓘ phys. ~e Leere, Röhre Torricellian vacuum, tube.
Tor¹=schließer (⌢…) m ⓘ = =hüter; **=schluß** m closing (or barring) of the gate(s); **=schlüssel** m key of a gate; ehm. **=schreiber** m = =einnehmer.
Torsion ⓘ (⌣⌣⌢) [lt.] f ⓘ (Drehung, Windung) torsion, twisting, wrenching; **~s=elektrometer** n (m) ⓘ torsion-electrometer; **~s=wage** f s. Coulomb; **~s=winkel** m angle of torsion.
Torso (⌣⌢) [it.] m ⓘ Bildhauerei: (Rumpf einer Bildsäule) torso.
Tor¹=sperre (⌢…) f ⓘ = Torschluß; ehm. **=steuer** = Akzise; **=stoß** m Fußballspiel: goal-kick.
Tort F (⌢) [ndd.; *fr.] m ⓘ c. (pl. ↘) wrong, injury, nur jur. tort; e-m einen (a. etwas zum) ~ (Ärger) antun to do a th. to vex (or spite) a p., to serve a p. a nasty trick.
Törtchen (⌢⌣) n ⓘ (dim. von Torte) Kuchenbäckerei: tartlet.
Torte (⌣⌢) [mhd.: tart; fr. tarte; *it.] f ⓘ Kuchenbäckerei: (iced) cake, fancy-cake, (Frucht=)~ tart.
Torten=bäcker (⌣⌣⌢…) m ⓘ pastry-cook; fancy-baker; **=form** f ⓘ Kuchenbäckerei: cake-mould; **=rolle** f = Kuchenrädchen; **=teig** m dough (or paste) for fancy-cakes, puff-paste.
Tortur (⌣⌢) [lt.] f ⓘ (Folter) torture, rack; e-n auf die ~ spannen to torture (or rack) a p.; weitS. to torment a p.
Tor¹=wache ⓘ (⌢…) f ⓘ guard(-house) at the gate; **=wächter** m ⓘ Fußball: goal-keeper; **=wart** m in Ballspielen: wicket-keeper; **=wärter** m = =hüter; **=wärter=häuschen** n gate-keeper's (or porter's) lodge; **=weg** m gateway, für Wagen: carriage-way, überwölbter: archway; **=zoll** m gate-money, toll paid at the gate; excise.
tosen (⌣⌢) [ahd.] I v/n. (h. u. ſn) ⓘ bsd. vom Winde ⓘ.: to roar, howl, storm, rage; weitS. to be uproarious or noisy; to clash, crash. — II **~** n ⓘ = Getöse.
Toskana ⓘ (⌣⌣⌢) npr/n. ⓘ a. ehm. it. Großherzogtum: Tuscany; **Toskaner(in** f ⓘ) m ⓘ, **toskanisch** a. ⓘ Tuscan.
tot (⌢) [ahd.: dead] I a. ⓘ 1. (gestorben) dead (and gone), feierlicher: deceased, defunct; (leblos) lifeless, inanimate (a. fig.); (öde) dreary, desolate; (glanzlos) dead, dull; Fußball: out of play; Tennis: not up! — 2. mit nouns: med. ~es Fleisch proud flesh; jur. Tote Hand (Stiftung auf ewige Zeiten) mortmain, a. dead-hand; (die Kirche als Besitzerin) the Church as owner of inalienable estate; ⓘ ~es Kapital dead (or unemployed) capital or stock; ⓘ das Tote Meer the Dead Sea; ~er Ort dead-alive place; ⓘ ~er Punkt einer Kurbel: dead point; Sport: ~es (unentschiedenes) Rennen dead heat; ~e Sprachen f/pl. dead languages pl.; ↓ ~es (niedrigstes) Wasser dead neap; bsd. ehm.: ~es Werk (Oberschiff) dead-works pl.; ~er Winkel dead angle; ⓘ ~e Zeit dead season. — 3. mit verbs s. totarbeiten ⓘ., totjagen ⓘ., liegen ⓘ am Ende; sich ⓘ stellen to pretend to be

♪ Musik; ⓘ Wissenschaft; ⓘ Pflanze; ⓘ Geographie; ⓘ Technik; ⚒ Bergbau; ⚔ Militär; ↓ Marine; ⓘ Handel; ⓘ Post; ⓘ Eisenbahn.

[total] — 962 — [trachten]

dead. — II s. ⊙ 4. **Totes**, das Tote (the) dead (or lifeless) thing or object; geol. das rote Tote ob. das **Tot-liegende** (the) lower new red sandstone.

total(-́) [mlt.] a.⊙ (gänzlich) total, entire; adv. totally, altogether, quite.

Total-ansicht (-"...) f ⊙ general view or survey; =**betrag** m total (amount or sum), sum total; =**eindruck** m general impression, auch: (fr.) tout ensemble; =**finsternis** f, ast. total eclipse of the sun or moon.

Totalisator (-‿‿́‿) [engl.=lt.] m ⊙ Rennsport: (Wettapparat) totalizer.

Totalität (-‿‿́) [fr.=lt.] f ⊙ (Gesamtheit) totality; (Gesamtzahl) total number.

Total-summe (-́‿‿‿) f ⊙ = =betrag.

tot-arbeiten (́‿‿́‿) ⊙**: v/refl. sich ⊆ to work o.s. to death; =**bleiben** v/n. (ʃu) ⊙** to be killed (on the spot); ⚔ to remain on the battle-field.

Tote (́‿) m, f ⊙ dead person; (Leiche) corpse; der, die ~ the deceased, the departed; pl. die ~n the dead.

töten (́‿) [ahd.] *tot] I v/a. und sich ⊆ v/refl. ⊙ to kill, slay, destroy; to cause the death of, gewaltsam: to put to death, durch Ersticken: to smother, to suffocate, mit Gift: to poison; (morden) to murder, P to do for; (hinrichten) to execute; bibl. du sollst nicht ⊆ thou shalt not kill; sich ⊆ to kill o.s., to lay hands on o.s., to put an end to one's life, to commit suicide; fig. Farben ⊆ to deaden (or soften down) colours; das Fleisch ⊆ to mortify the flesh; med. einen Nerv ⊆ to kill a nerve. — II ~ n ⊙ = **Tötung**; das ~ der Singvögel ist verboten it is prohibited to kill singing-birds, the destruction of singing-birds is unlawful or contrary to law.

Toten-acker ⚰ ('...) m ⊙ = Gottesacker; =**ähnlich** a. ⊙ deathlike; =**amt** n, eccl. burial-service, musikalisches: requiem; vgl. =messe; =**bahre** f bier; =**beschwörer** m necromancer; =**bett** n death-bed; =**blaß** a. deadly (or ghastly) pale, (as) pale as death; =**blässe** f deadly (or ghastly), cadaverous pallor; =**bleich** a. = =blaß; =**buch** n register of deaths; =**eule** f = Kauz 1 b; =**farbe** f livid colour; vgl. =blässe; =**farbig** a. livid, F cadaverous-looking; =**feier** f obsequies pl.; =**fest** n, eccl. festival in commemoration of the dead; =**flagge** ⚓ f flag (hoisted) at half-mast; =**fleck** m livid spot (on a dead body); =**gebeine** n/pl. dead men's bones pl.; =**gebet** n prayer for the dead; =**geläut(e)** n tolling of the funeral bell; knell; =**geleit** n funeral procession; e-m das ~ geben to attend (or go to) a p.'s funeral, to pay a p. one's last respects; =**gerippe** n (dead man's) skeleton; =**geruch** m cadaverous smell; =**gerüst** n catafalque; =**gesang** m funeral chant, eccl. a. (it.) De Profundis; =**glocke** f funeral bell, death-knell; =**gräber** m: a) grave-digger; sexton; b) zo. (Käfer) burying-beetle (Necro'phorus); =**gräberei** f grave-digging; =**gruft** f sepulchre, tomb.

totenhaft (́‿‿) a.⊙ deathlike; (leichenhaft) cadaverous; ⚰e Stille = Totenstille.

Toten-hand ("...) f ⊙ hand of a dead person; fig. hand of death; hand as cold as death; =**haus** n = Leichenhaus; =**hemd** n shroud, winding-sheet; =**hügel** m (alte Grabstätte) barrow; =**kalt** a. (as) cold as death; =**kasse** f burial-fund; =**klage** f bewailing (or lamenting) the dead; =**kopf** m: a) death's head; b) a. =**kopfschwärmer** m, ent. (Achero'ntia a'tropos) death's-head moth; c) chm. = Kolkothar; =**köpfchen** n, zo. saimiri (Ca'llithrix sciu'rea); =**krampf** m, path.: ☤ tetanus; =**krone** f funeral wreath; =**lied** n funeral song, dirge; =**liste** f list of the dead, obituary, a. = Sterbeliste; =**mahl** n = Leichenmahl; =**marsch** ♪ m funeral march; =**maske** f plaster mask; =**messe** f, eccl. mass for the dead; vgl. =amt; =**opfer** n Alt.: sacrifice offered to the Manes; =**register** n = =buch; =**reich** n realm of the dead or the shades, Hades; =**richter** m judge of the dead; =**schau(er** m) f = Leichenschau(er); =**schein** m certificate of death; =**schild** n, her. hatchment; =**schlaf**, =**schlummer** m = Todesschlaf; =**stadt** f city of the dead, necropolis; =**starre** f rigidity of death, (lt.) rigor mortis; =**still** a. ⊙ (as) still as death; =**stille** f stillness of death, dead(ly) (or deathlike) silence; =**tanz** m Kunst: death-dance, dance of death, auch: dance macabre; =**träger** m = Leichenträger; =**uhr** f, ent. (im Holze lebender Käfer) death-watch or =tick (Ano'bium pe'rtinax); =**urne** f funeral (or sepulchral) urn; =**verbrennung** f cremation (of the dead); =**wache** f watching by a dead body, bsd. in Irland: wake; =**wagen** m hearse.

Toter (́‿) m ⊙ f. Tote. [Mörder.]

Töter ⚔ (́‿) m ⊙ = Totschläger,]

tot-geboren ("...) a. ⊙ still-born; =**geburt** f⊙ still-born child; =**geglaubt** a. believed (or supposed) to be dead; =**holz** n dead wood; =**jagen** v/a. ⊙**: ein Pferd ⊆ to ride (or drive) ... to death; =**kriegen** F v/a. ⊙**: nicht ⊆ zu kriegen (⊙) = unverwüstlich; =**lachen** v/refl. ⊙** sich ⊆ to split one's sides with laughing; ~ n: es ist zum ~ it would make a donkey laugh; Posse zum ~ screaming farce; =**liegend(e)**s Kapital dead capital; =**liegende(s)** n ⊙ f. tot am Schluß; =**machen** v/a. ⊙** to kill; fig. eine Sache ⊆ to suppress (or hush up) a th.; das macht einen auch nicht tot that won't kill anybody; =**schämen** v/refl. ⊙**: sich ⊆ to be thoroughly ashamed (of oneself); =**schießen** v/a. ⊙(e)t** f. schießen 1 v/refl. sich ⊆ to shoot o.s., to blow out one's brains; ~ n ⊙ killing with shots or bullets, F fig. es ist zum ~ it is more than one can endure; =**schlagen** v/a. ⊙ b** to put to death, to kill, to slay; =**schläger** m: a) homicide, one guilty of manslaughter; b) (Stod mit Bleiknopf) life-preserver; =**schweigen** v/a. ⊙** f. schweigen II; =**segeln** v/a.

⚓a**: ein Schiff ⊆ to outsail...; =**stechen** n: a) des kranken Viehs killing, slaughtering; b) (Mord) stabbing (with a knife); =**treten** v/a. ⊙d** to kick to death, to kill by kicking.

Tötung (-‿) f ⊙ putting to death, &c. (f. töten I); (Totschlag) homicide; fahrlässige ~ e-s Menschen manslaughter; fig. mortification of the flesh.

Tour(túr) [fr. m] f ⊙ 1. (Umdrehung; Wendung) turn; (Ausflug) tour, trip, excursion, ⚲ (Besuch auswärtiger Kunden) business round or tour (for the purpose of looking up customers); (Droschkenfahrt) journey; (Kehr beim Tanz, Spiel) figure, set; außer der ~ (Reihe) out of one's turn. — 2. (falsche Haare) false wig or hair.

Touren-maschine ⊙ (tu"...) f ⊙, =**rad** n Radsport: roadster (for tourists); =**zahl** f number of turns or revolutions; =**zähler** m, mach. speed-indicator.

Tourist ꜝ (tu') m ⊙ (Vergnügungsreisender) tourist, excursionist, F tripper; ~en**klub** (-‿‿) m ⊙ tourist-club; =**isch** (tu'‿‿) a. ⊙ of (or concerning) tourists.

Tournee (tur) [fr.] f ⊙(⊙) (Künstlerreise) touring, travelling, F starring.

tournieren (tur'‿‿) [fr. wenden] v/a. ⊙ Kartenspiel: to turn up (a card).

Toxikologie ⚕ (‿‿‿‿̋) [grch.] f ⊙ (Giftkunde) toxicology.

Trab (ā) [ndd.] m ⊙b.: a) man. trot; im ~e at a trot; ~ gehen, reiten to trot; sein Pferd in leichten ~ setzen to put ... at an easy trot; b) fig. dich werde ich auf den ~ bringen wait, I'll make you trot or run; vgl. bringen 8 unter „auf".

Trabant (‿ā́) [(P: traben) türf., *perſ.] m ⊙: a) ehm. (Leibwächter) halberdier, life-guardsman; b) ast. (Nebenplanet, Mond): satellite.

traben (́‿)[ndd.] I v/n. (h. u. ſu) ⊙ bsd. von Pferden u. F v. Menschen: to trot (along); f. hochtrabend; hoch ⊙des Pferd high-stepper; ⊆ lassen to (put to a or at a) trot. — II ~ n ⊙ trot(ting).

Traber (́‿) m ⊙ man. trotter, trotting horse; ~**klub** (-‿‿) m ⊙ bsd. Am. trotting club; ~**sport** m, Am. trotting sport.

Trab-gänger (́‿‿) m ⊙ trotter; =**reiten** n trotting; =**rennbahn** f bsd. Am. trotting-course; =**rennen** n bsd. Am. trotting-match.

Tracheotomie ⚕ (‿‿‿‿̋) [grch.] f ⊙ surg. (Luftröhrenschnitt) tracheotomy.

Tracht (ä́) [mhd.: draught; *tragen] f ⊙ 1. (Art sich zu kleiden) style of dressing, fashion; (Kleidung) dress, costume, habiliment, garb, apparel, clothing. — 2. (soviel man tragen kann) load, charge; ~ Wasser (full) supply of water; ⚓ ~ eines Schiffes: shipment, cargo; fig. ~ Schläge good beating, sound thrashing. — 3. junger Hunde, Katzen: litter of puppies, of kittens. — 4. ⊙ arch. ~ (Tragfähigkeit) eines Balkens, Bogens: bearing(-capacity).

trachten (́‿) [ahd.; *lt. tracta're] I v/n. (h.) ⊙: nach et. ⊆ to strive for (or after) a th., to aspire to a th. (f. dichten² 1); sie ⊆ danach, uns zu befreien they endeavour (or are making an effort) to rescue us; sie ⊆ nur danach, Geld zu

---

Signs (see page XVII): F familiar; P vulgar; ⌐ flash; ⟍ rare; † obsolete (died); * new word (born); ∹+ incorrect; ♪ music;

[**trächtig**] — 963 — [**trainieren**]

verdienen their sole object (or only aim) is to make money; e-m nach dem Leben ⁎ to have a design upon (or to attempt, to seek) a p.'s life. — II ~ n ㉓ (f. I) striving, aspiration; endeavour, effort; (Ziel) aim; f. dichten² 4; all sein Sinnen, all sein ~ all his thoughts and desires pl., all his scheming and striving.
trächtig (⸺) [Tracht] a. ㊅ von weiblichen Säugetieren: (big) with young, pregnant; ⁎e Kuh cow with calf; ⁎e Stute mare in (or with) foal; **~keit** (⸺) f ㊺ pregnancy; gestation (a. Zeit der ~).
Trachyt (⸺ᴸ) [grch. Rauh-] m ⓒc. geogn. vulkanische Felsart: trachyte.
trachytisch ⸺ (⸺ᴵᴵ) a. ㊅ trachytic.
Tradition (-⸺(ᵛ)ᴸ) [lt.] f ㊺ (überlieferung) tradition.
traditionell (-⸺(ᵛ)⸺) [fr.] a. ㊅ traditional.
traf (ᴸ) ind., **träfe** (ᴸ⸺) subj. impf. von treffen. [Laden] (tobacco-)shop.]
Trafik ⊕ öft. (⸺ᴸ) [it.] m ⓜ, f ㊺ ([Tabak-])
Traft ↓ (ᴸ) f ㊺ (großes Floß) large raft.
Trag-altar (⸺⸺ᴸ) m ㉒ portative (or portable) altar.
Tragant (⸺ᴸ) [grch. Bocks-] m ⓒc. ♃ tragacanth, milk-vetch (Astra'galus).
Tragant-gummi ❀ (⸺⸺) n ㉒ (gum) tragacanth (von Astra'galus verus); **-staude** f, **-strauch** m ♃ = Tragant; **-stoff** m, chm.: ☌ bassorin.
Trag-bahre (⸺⸺) f ㊺ stretcher, litter, **-balken** ⊕ m, carp. beam (serving as support), girder, transom, **-band** n: a) = Hosenträger; surg. suspender; b) ⊕ arch., carp. strap, brace.
tragbar (ᴸ⸺) a. ㊅ 1. portable, easy to carry; (stützbar) supportable; (als Kleid tauglich) wearable, fit to wear; noch ⁎ (anständig) still decent, respectable. — 2. (fruchttragend) fruit-bearing, fruitful, fertile, productive.
Tragbarkeit (ᴸ⸺-) f ㊺ 1. portableness, portability; v. Kleidern: fitness for wear; respectability. — 2. (Fruchtbarkeit) fruitfulness, fertility, productiveness.
Trag-baum (⸺⸺) m ㉒: a) **-bäume** pl. einer Sänfte: carrying-poles pl.; b) ⊕ Papierfabr.: arbor; Wagnerei: shaft of a carriage, arch. bearing-bar; **-bett** n portable bed, vgl. -bahre; **-beutel** m, surg. suspender; **-binde** f sling; **-bogen** ⊕ m, arch. supporting-arch.
Trage (ᴸᵛ) f ㊺ = Bahre 1; (Tragejoch) yoke.
Trage-... (ᴸᴵᴵ⸺) in Zssgn f. Trag-...
träge (ᴸᵛ) [ahd.] a. ㊅ (lässig) lazy, indolent, remiss; (faul) inactive, slothful; (schläfrig) sleepy, drowsy; (langsam) slow; (schwerfällig) heavy, sluggish, dull; (zögernd) tardy; (ohne Leben) inert (auch phys., path.).
tragen (ᴸᵛ) [ahd.: draw] ⓢb. I v/a. 1. to carry; (befördern) to convey, Leichtes: to take (along); (ertragen) to bear, to endure; (hervorbringen) to bear, yield, produce, bring forth; als Kleid zc. ⁎ to wear; (stützen) to support, to uphold; leicht zu ⁎ easy to carry or to bear, fig. bearable, tolerable; auf die Post ⁎ to take (Schreiben:) to carry to the post-office; fig. f. Achsel 2 und Hand 4 unter „auf". — 2. mit Angabe des Erfolges: die Stiefel schief ⁎ to wear one's boots down on one side. — 3. mit nouns: den Arm in der Schlinge ⁎ to wear one's arm in a sling; ⁎ bedenken 6, Haut 2; die Kosten ⁎ to bear the expense, to pay the costs; f. Lehen 1, Leid² 3, Mantel 1, Nase 2, Rechnung 5; Samen ⁎ to bear seed(s); die Schuld an et. ⁎ to be the cause of a th.; f. Sorge 2; die Verantwortung für et. ⁎ to bear the reponsibility for a th.; Verlangen nach et. ⁎ to have a longing (or long) for a th.; Zinsen ⁎ to bear (or yield) interest; das Kapital trägt fünf Prozent (Zinsen)... bears (or brings in) five per cent. (interest). — II v/n. (h.) 4. to carry loads; an et. schwer zu ⁎ h. to be heavily laden (or burdened) with a th.; der Baum trägt ... bears (fruit); der Baum trägt nicht ... does not bear, ... is not firm. — 5. ⚔ artill. das Geschütz trägt vier Kilometer weit the gun has a range of (or carries, ranges) two-and-half miles. — III v/refl. 6. F bisw. sich nach Hause ⁎ to proceed homewards, to go home. — 7. sich mit et. (herum-) ⁎ to lug (or drag) a th. about, fig. (sich damit beschäftigen) to be (pre)occupied with a th.; (darauf sinnen) to meditate a th., to brood over a th., to harbour (or entertain) an idea; man trägt sich mit dem Gerücht the rumour is going about, the report is spreading; sie ⁎ sich mit der Hoffnung, daß // they cherish the hope that //, they live in hopes that //. — 8. mit Angabe der Wirkung: sich müde ⁎ to tire o.s. with carrying. — 9. sich so und so ⁎: a) in der Haltung: to have a certain deportment or carriage; b) in der Kleidung: sich anständig ⁎ to go about decently dressed; sich sauber ⁎ to dress neatly. — 10. von Kleidungsstücken, Stoffen: sich gut ⁎ to wear well, to last (well); dieses Tuch trägt sich leicht fadenscheinig ... soon wears (or goes) threadbare; v. Lasten: der Korb trägt sich unbequem the basket is uncomfortable to carry. — IV ~ n ㉓ 11.(f.I) carriage, conveyance; (Haltung) deportment; das ~ v. Waffen ist verboten the carrying of (fire-)arms is prohibited. — V ge-tragen p.p. u. a. ㊅ (D9) 12. in den Bed. des inf. —
13. v. Kleidern worn (or second-hand) clothes pl., abgelegte: left-off clothes pl.; ♪ ⁎e Töne sustained notes pl.
Träger (ᴸᵛ) m ㉒ (f. tragen) 1. (a. ~in f ㊺) carrier, bearer, von Lasten auch: porter, eines Mantels, einer Krone zc.: wearer; der ~ eines großen Namens the holder (or bearer) of a great name. — 2. a) = Dienstmann; b) = Hausierer. — 3. anat. (oberster Halswirbel:) ⚹ atlas, first cervical vertebra; zo. (Stiel) ⚹ peduncle. — 4. ⊕ arch. bearer, girder, beam; (Pfeiler) pillar, (Stütze) prop, support.
Träger-brücke ⊕ (⸺ᴵᴵ⸺) f ㊺ girder-bridge; **-lohn** m carriage, carrier's fee, porterage; **-muskel** m, anat.: **-schwelle** ⊕ f einer Fachwand: breast-summer.
trag-fähig (ᴵᴵ⸺) a. ㊅ capable of bearing or carrying or producing; ↓ = lastig; **-fähigkeit** f ㊺: a) agr. des Bodens: productiveness; b) ⊕ capacity of bearing, vgl. -kraft; c) ↓ e-s Schiffes: carrying capacity, tonnage; **-feder** ⊕ f bsd. 🚂 bearing-spring; **-hebel** ⊕ m, mech. lever of the second kind.
Trägheit (ᴸ-) f ㊺ (f. träge) laziness, indolence, remissness, sloth(fulness); sluggishness, inertness, phys. inertia; physiol. natürliche ~ phlegm.
Trägheits-gesetz (ᴵᴵ...) n ㉒ (=**kraft** f) phys. law (force) of inertia; **-moment** n, phys. moment(um) of inertia, (lt.) vis inertiæ. [n = -joch.]
Trag-himmel (ᴵᴵ...) m ㉒ canopy; **-holz**
Tragik (ᴸᵛ) [grch.] f ㊺ tragic art or poetry; (Traurigkeit) sadness, mournfulness. [b) = Tragöde.]
Tragiker (ᴸᵛᵛ) m ㉒: a) tragic poet;
tragi-komisch (ᴸᵛ-ᴵᴵ) [grch.] a. ㊅ tragicomic(al). [u. ㊸ tragicomedy.]
Tragi-komödie (ᴸᵛ-ᴵᴵ(ᵛ)⸺) [grch.] f ㊺
tragisch (ᴸᵛ) [grch.] a. ㊅ tragic(al); ⁎e Muse tragic muse; fig. ⁎e Begebenheit tragical (or sad, mournful, lamentable, unfortunate) event; ⁎ (adv.) enden to end tragically, to take a sad end; F Sie müssen das nicht gleich (so) ⁎ nehmen you must not take that (so) seriously or take too gloomy a view of it.
Trag-joch (ᴵᴵ...) n ㉒ zum Tragen von Eimern zc.: yoke; **-kissen** n = Stechkissen; **-kleidchen** n für Kinder: long clothes pl.; **-knospe** f, hort. bearing-bud; **-korb** m portable basket, crate, hamper; **-kraft** f bearing-power or -capacity; **-lohn** m porterage, carriage; **-mantel** m baby's long cloak; **-mulde** ⊕ f für Maurer zc.: hod.
Tragöde (ᵛᴸᵛ) [grch.] m ⓜ, **Tragödin** (ᵛᴸᵛ-) f ㊺ tragic actor (f actress), tragedian. [Trauerspiel] ㊸ tragedy.]
Tragödi-e (ᵛᴸᵛ(ᵛ)⸺) [grch. „Bocksgesang";
Tragödien-dichter (ᴸ⸺...) m ㉒, **-schreiber** m tragic poet or author; **-spieler**(in f) m = Tragöde zc.
Trag-pfeiler ⊕ (ᴵᴵ...) m ㉒ arch. (supporting) pillar; **-pfosten** ⊕ m post serving as a support; **-platz** m zc. Flüssen, Eisenbahnen zc.: portage; **-reis** n, hort. bearing bough; **-riem(en)** m strap, einer Kutsche: main brace; **-sattel** m pack-saddle; **-seil** ⊕ n einer Hängebrücke: iron rope of a suspension-bridge; **-sessel** m sedan-chair; **-stein** m = Kragstein; **-stempel** ⊕ m, mint. bearing-beam (f. a. Bühnloch); **-stuhl** m = -sessel; **-stütze** f prop, support.
Tragung (ᴸᵛ) f ㊺ = tragen IV; jur. zur ~ der Kosten verurteilt w. to be mulcted in (or to have to pay) the costs.
Trag-vermögen ⊕ (ᴵᴵ...) n ㉒ einer Brücke: carrying-power, transverse strength; **-weite** f einer Schußwaffe, der Stimme zc.: range of a gun, of the voice, &c., fig. (Bedeutung) bearing, import(ance); **-zeit** f der Tiere: (period of) gestation.
Traille (trä'l-je; Hom. Tralje) [fr.] f ㊺ (Fähre, fliegende Brücke) ferry.
Train ⚔ (trä) [fr.] m ⓾ army service corps, transport section of the train.
trainieren (trä⸺ᴸ) [fr.] I v/a. ⊕ Sport: (zum Üben, Boxen, Wettreiten zc. vorbereiten) to train. — II ~ n ㉓ training.

⚹ scientific; ♃ botanical; ⚹ geography; ⊕ machinery; ⚔ mining; ⚔ military; ↓ marine; ● commercial; ✉ postal; 🚂 railway.

[Trainkolonne] — 964 — [transportabel]

Train-kolonne ⚔ (tra"...) f ⑫ transport column; **-soldat** m wagoner; **-wagen** m wagon belonging to a military column train; **-wesen** n army service, (everything relating to) military transport.

Trajan (-¹) npr. m. ⑮ (röm. Kaiser, 98 bis 117) Trajan; **~s-säule** (-"¹·¹) f ⑫ in Rom Trajan's Column.

Trajekt (-²) [lt.] m ⑪b.: a) (Überfahrt) crossing, passage; b)/([Eisenbahn-]Fähre) (railway-)ferry. [jectory.

Trajektori-e ⚔ (-·¹(·)) f ㊽ math. tra-

Trakehner (·¹·¹) [Trakehnen ♀, Dorf in Ostpreußen] m ⑫ horse from the royal stud of Trakehnen.

Trakt (²) [lt.] m ⑪b. (Strecke) tract.

Traktament (·²·²) [lt.] n ⑪c. 1. (Bewirtung) entertainment, treat. — 2. ehm. ⚔ (Löhnung) soldier's pay.

Traktat (·¹·²) [lt.] m(n) ⑪c.: a) (Abhandlung) treatise, rel. tract; b) (Vertrag) treaty.

Traktätchen (·¹·¹) n ⑳ (religious) tract.

traktieren (·²·¹) [lt.] I v/a. u. v/n. (h.) ⑱ 1. (behandeln) to treat. — 2. (bewirten) to entertain, F to give a treat to. — II **Traktierung** f ㊻ 3. entertainment.

Tralje ⦿ (²·¹) [: Hom. Traille) [ndl.; *fr. treille] f ㊽ bar of a grate, grate-bar.

tralla (·²) int. ²! trolly!, als Kehrreim auch: derry-down!

trallalla(lala! (·¹(·)²) int. tol-de-rol.

trällern (¹·¹) [lautm.] v/a. u. v/n. (h.) ⑫a.: ein Lied ² to hum a tune, bisw. to roll out a song; vgl. trillern.

Tram-bahn ㊀ (²·¹) f ⑫ = Tramway.

Trampel F (·¹) m ⑫ (㊶) (ungeschickte Person) awkward (or heavy, clumsy) p.

trampeln (·¹) [ndd.] v n. (h.) ⑫a. to trample, to stamp the ground; (plump gehen) to have a clumsy gait, to trudge (along); auf et. ² to trample (or stamp) on a th., to trample s.th. under foot; mit den Füßen ² to stamp one's feet.

Trampel-tier (·¹·¹) [P aus Dromedar] n ⑫: a) zo. two-humped (or Bactrian) camel (Camelus bactriánus); b) F = Trampel.

Trampolin (·¹·¹) [it.] n. m ⑪d.. ⚔ (·²·¹) f ㊽ (Sprungbrett für Kunstsprünge) spring-board for high jumping.

Trampolin-sprung (·¹·¹·¹) m ⑫ high jump from the spring-board.

Tram-seide ⦿ (·¹·¹) f ㊽ (Einschlagseide) tram; **-wagen** m tram-car; elektrischer: electric car; **-way** ㊀ m ⑩, f ㊽ tramway, auch: tram-line, tramroad.

Tran (¹) [ndd. trahn, train(-oil)] m ⑪b. train-(or fish-)oil; weitS. (Speck der Wale 2c.) blubber; P fig. im ~ (betrunken) sein to be the worse for drink, to be in liquor, to be well on.

Trän-auge (¹·¹·¹) n ⑫ path. weeping (or watering) eye, ⚔ lachrymation.

Tran-brenner ⦿ (·¹·²) m ⑫ boiler of train-oil, blubber-boiler; **-brennerei** f = **-siederei**. [trench.

Tranchee ⚔ (tra-ichée) [fr.] f ㊽ (Laufgraben)

Tranchee-arbeiter (·¹·¹·¹) m ⑫ trencher.

Tranchier-brett (trǎsch·¹·¹·¹) n ⑫ trencher.

tranchieren (trǎsch·¹·¹) [: trench; *fr.] v/a. ⑱ einen Braten, eine Gans 2c. ² (vorschneiden) to carve (or cut up) joint of meat, a goose. &c.

Tranchier-messer (trǎsch·¹·¹·¹) n ⑫ (Messer zum Vorschneiden) carving-knife.

Träne (¹·¹) [ahd. pl. Tropfen] f ㊽ tear; f. ausbrechen 6; fig. in ~n schwimmen od. zerfließen to be bathed in tears; unter ~n amid tears; zu ~u gerührt werden to be moved to (or to melt into) tears; ~n vergießen to shed tears, to cry, geh. Spr.: to weep.

tränen (¹·¹) I v/n. (h.) ㊸ to run (with tears); die Augen ² ihm (vom Schnupfen, Rauch 2c.) his eyes are (or look) watery; mit ²den Augen with tearful eyes. — II ~ n ㉓ = Tränenfluß.

Tränen-auge (¹·¹·¹) n ⑫ = Tränauge; **-bach** m flood (or flow) of tears; **-bein** n. anat. lachrymal bone; **-benetzt** a. ㊻ moist with tears, tearful; **-drüse** f. anat. lachrymal gland; **-feucht** a. ㊻ moist (or bedewed) with tears; **-feuchtigkeit** f. physiol. lachrymal fluid; **-fistel** f, path. lachrymal fistula; **-fluß** m, path.: ⚔ epiphora, dacryoma; **-flut** f = **-bach**; **-förmig** a.: ⚔ lac(h)rymiform, ...æ-...; **-gang** m, anat. lachrymal duct; **-gefäß** n: a) lachrymal vessel; b) = **-krug**; **-geschwür** n, path. im inneren Augenwinkel: ⚔ ægilops; **-gras** ⚔ ⚔ coix; **-höhle** f der Hirsche: lachrymal sinus, larmier; **-kanal** m, anat. lac. canal; **-krug** m Alt.: ⚔ lachrymatory; **-leer**, **-los** a. tearless, without a tear; **-quell** m, **-quelle** f source of tears; **-reich** a. tearful, bathed in tears, lachrymose; **-sack** m, anat.: ⚔ lachrymal sac, ~ der Hirsche = **-höhle**; **-schwer** a. heavy with tears; **-stein** m, path.: ⚔ lachrymal calculus, dacryolite; **-urne** f = **-krug**; **-voll** a. = **-reich**; (beklagenswert) deplorable.

tranicht\ mit tranig = **tranig** (¹·¹) a. ㊻ (smelling or tasting) like train-oil. weitS. oily.

tränicht, mit **tränig** (¹·¹) a. ㊻ tearful.

trank¹ (²) ind. impf. von trinken.

Trank² (²) [mhd.: drench; *trank¹] m ⑪b. 1. drink, beverage, für Schweine: swill; Speise und ~ meat and drink. — 2. med., oft dim. Tränkchen (¹·¹) n ㉓ (medical) draught, potion; (Arznei) physic, (Absud) decoction, (Aufguß) infusion.

Tränkchen (¹·¹) n ㉓ f. Trant.

Tränke¹ (¹·¹) [ahd.] f ㊽ 1. watering (of) cattle. — 2. watering-place for cattle, für Pferde: horsepond; zur ~ führen to water cattle.

tränke², ²n¹ pl. (¹·¹) subj. impf. v. trinken.

tränken² (¹·¹) [ahd.: drench] I v/a. ㊸ 1. e-n ² to give a p. s.th. to drink. to still (or allay, quench) a p.'s thirst, to refresh a p. with a (cooling) draught; das Vieh ² to water ...; der Regen hat die Felder getränkt ... has watered the fields. — 2. (durchnässen) to drench; (einweichen) to steep, to soak, ⊙ to impregnate (wood, &c.), mit Kreosot: to creosote, mit Kupfersalzlösung: to copperize, mit Öl: to soak in oil; chm., &c. (sättigen) to saturate; fig. to imbue; mit Blut getränkt steeped in (or reeking with) blood or gore. — II ~ n ㉓ 3. stilling a p.'s thirst, (f. I) ; ⊙ impregnation; chm.. &c. saturation.

Tränk-faß (²·¹) n ⑫ = Tränktrog.

Tränklein (¹·¹) n ㉓ = Tränkchen.

Trank-opfer (²·¹) n ⑫ rel.. bibl. Alt.: drink-offering, libation; **-rinne** f fürs Vieh: wooden box for watering cattle.

Tränk-rinne (²·¹·¹) f ㊺ wooden gutter of a watering-trough.

Trank-steuer (²·¹·¹) f ㊺ excise (or duty) on alcoholic liquor. [ing-trough.

Tränk-trog (²·¹) m ⑫ für Vieh: water-

Tränkung (¹·¹) f ㊻ (f. tränken²) quenching a p.'s thirst; watering cattle; chm. saturation. [blubber-lamp.

Tran-lampe (²·¹·¹) f ㊽ train-oil (or)

trans-alpinisch (·¹·¹·¹) [lt.] a. ㊻ transalpine; **-atlantisch** (·¹·¹·¹) a. ㊻ transatlantic; ²er Dampfer. a. Atlantic steamer or steam-boat or liner.

Transch F (²) m ⑪a. (Vorwurf) reproof, reproach; einem e-n ~ machen to give a p. a (good) scolding. F to blow a p. up.

transchieren (·¹·¹·¹) öst., bayr. = tranchieren.

Transept (·¹·¹) [lt. trans-sept-] m (n) ⑪b. arch. (Querschiff) transept.

Transformator ⊙ (·¹·¹·¹) [lt.] m ㉛ elect. (Apparat) transformer. converter.

Tran-sieder (²·¹·¹) m (·) **-brenner**; **-siederei** f train-oil factory, place where blubber is boiled.

Transit (·¹·¹) m (·) [lt. tra'nsitus] m ⑪c. (㊶) transit (= Durchfuhr 2).

Transit-güter ⚔ (·¹·¹·¹) n/pl. ⑫ transit-goods pl.; **-handel** m transit-trade.

transitieren ⚔ (·¹·¹·¹) v/n. (h.) ⑱ to be in transit, to pass through.

transitiv (·¹·¹·¹) [lt.] a. ㊻ gr. (zielend): ²es Zeitwort. a. ~(um) (·¹·¹·¹·¹) n ⑪d. (㊾) transitive verb. [warehouse.

Transit-lager ⚔ (·¹·¹·¹) n ⑫ bonded

transitorisch (·¹·¹·¹) [lt.] a. ㊻ (vorübergehend) transitory, transient, fleeting, (quickly) passing. [Durchgangs-...

Transit-verkehr (·¹·¹·¹) m ⑫, **-zoll** m =

Trans-kaukasi-en ♀ (·²-¹(·)) npr/n. ²a. russische Provinz: Transcaucasia.

trans-leithanisch ♀ (·²·¹·¹) a. ㊻ (ant. zisleithanisch) Transleithan.

Translokation ⚔ (·¹-iß·²") f ㊺ (Versetzung) translocation: removal (a. in Schulen)

translozieren (·¹·¹tß·¹·¹) [lt.] v/a. ⑱ (versetzen) to translocate, to remove (from one place to another); to shift.

Transmission (·¹·¹(·)²) [lt.] f ㊺ (Übermittlung) transmission (of forces, &c.), ⊙ mach. a. belt-gearing; **~s-apparat** (²...) m ⑫ tel. transmitter.

Transp. abbr. = Transport 2.

transparent (·¹·¹·²) [lt.] I a. ㊻ (durchscheinend) transparent. — II ~ n ⑪c. (durchscheinendes Bild) transparency.

Tran-speck (²·¹·¹) m ⑫ blubber.

Transpiration (·¹·¹-iß(·)") [lt.] f ㊺ perspiration; **transpirieren** (·¹·¹") [lt.] I v/n. (h.) ⑱ (schwitzen) to perspire. — II ~ n ㉓ perspiration.

transponier-en (·¹·¹") [lt.] I v/a. ⑱ bfd. ♪ (umsetzen) to transpose. — II ~ n ㉓ u. **T/ung** f ㊻ transposition.

Transport (·¹·²) [fr.] m ⑪c. 1. (Beförderung) transport, conveyance, carriage, in Karren: cartage, zu Schiff: shipment. — 2. ⚔ (Übertragung in Rechnungsbüchern 2c.) (carrying) forward, (carried) over; (Übertrag) amount carried (or brought) forward; per ~ carried forward.

transportabel (·¹·¹·¹·²) a. ㊻ transportable.

Zeichen (f. S. XVII): F familiär; P Volkssprache; P Gaunersprache; \ selten; † alt (auch gestorben); * neu (auch geboren); ⁒ unrichtig;

Transporteur (⌣⌣ᵇ'r) [⸺ fr. Beförderer] m
ü d.(⑳)1. transporter, remover, carrier.
— 2. math. (Winkelmesser) protractor.
transport-fähig (⌣ᴸ⌣) a. ⑥, **transportierbar** (⌣⌢⌣) a. ⑥ (fortschaffbar) transportable, fit (or ready) for conveyance or removal.
transportieren (⌣⌣⌣) [fr.] v/a. ⑳ 1. to transport, convey, carry, in Karren: to cart, zu Schiffe: to ship; (fortschaffen) to remove. — 2. ⊕ in Rechnungsbüchern: to carry (or bring) forward.
Transport-kosten (⌣ᵇ...) pl. ⑫ = **preise**; **-makler** m forwarding agent; **-mittel** n means of conveyance or transport; **-preise** m/pl. charges pl. for transport, carriage; **-schiff** ↓ n transport(-vessel); **-wagen** m removing van.
Transvaal ♀ (⌣f⌣) npr/n. ⑳a. englische Kolonie in Süd-Afrika: the Transvaal.
transversal (⌣w⌣⌢) [lt. quer] a. ⑥ (querdurchgehend) transversal, transverse; **~e** (⌣w⌣⌢) f ⑱ math. transversal line.
Transversal-schwingung (⌣w⌣ᴸ,⌣) f ⑫ phys. transversal vibration.
transzendent ⚔ (⌣⌢) [lt.], **⸗al** (⌣⌣⌢) a. ⑥ phls., &c. (die Begriffe übersteigend) transcendental, beyond conception.
Trapez (⌣⌢) [grch. Tisch] n ⑳a. 1. ⚔ geom. (ungleichseitiges Viereck mit zwei parallelen Seiten) trapezoid. — 2. Turnerei: (Hängereck zum Schwingen) trapeze. — **⸗förmig** (⌣⌢...) a. ⑥: ⚔ trapeziform, trapezoid; **~fünftler** m ⑫ Zirkus ꝛc.: trapezist.
Trapezo-eder ⚔ (⌣⌣⌣⌣) [grch.] n ⑫ math. (Vierundzwanzigflach) trapezohedron.
Trapezo-id ⚔ (⌣⌣⌣⌢) [grch.] n ⑫c. geom. (ungleichseitiges Viereck ohne parallele Seiten) trapezium, vgl. Trapez 1.
Trapezunt ♀ (⌣⌣⌢) npr/n. ⑳a. Stadt in Kleinasien: Trebizond, Alt.: Trapezunt.
trapp¹ (⌣) [lautm.] I int. ⚬ ⚬ ⚬!, etwa: pit-a-pat! — II **Trapp** m ⑬b. patter (or pattering) of feet; das Trapptrapp der Hufe the clattering of hoofs. [trap.)
Trapp² (⌣) m ⑬b.min. (schwarzer Porphyr)
Trappe¹ (⌣) [mhd.] f ⑱, m ⑭ orn. bustard (Otis tarda).
Trappe² (⌣⌣) [ndd.] f ⑱ 1. (Spur) footprint, track. — 2. (Falle) trap.
trappeln (⌣⌣) [trappen] v/n. (h.) ⑳a. to patter, stamp, trot; to scud along.
trappen (⌣⌣) [: trampen] v/n. (h. u. ſu) ⑱ to tread heavily, to trample, to trudge along. [Pelzjäger] trapper.)
Trapper (⌣⌣) m ⑫ (⑥) (nordamerikanischer
Trappist (⌣⌢) (La Trappe), ehm. Abtei in Frankreich, erstes Kloster der ~en) m ⑫ Trappist, **~en-orden** (⌣⌣⌣⌣) m ⑫ order of Trappists or of La Trappe.
Trapp-porphyr (⌣⌣⌣) [Trapp-porphyr] m ⑫ min. porphyritic trap, ⚔ melaphyre.
trara (⌣⌢) [lautm.]: ⚬! ta(ra)ntara!
Traß (⌣) [ndbl.; *it. terra'zzo] m ⑬a. min. (vulkanische Schlacke aus der Gegend von Koblenz, a. als Mörtel benutzt) trass, terrace.
Trassant ⊕ (⌣⌢) [it.] m ⑫: ~ (Aussteller) eines Wechsels: drawer.
Trassat ⊕ (⌣⌢) [⦁] m ⑫: ~ (Bezogener) drawee.
Trasse ⊕ (⌣⌣) [fr. trace] f ⑱ (abgesteckte Linie) alinement, trace.
trassieren¹ (⌣⌣⌣) [fr. tracer] v/a. ⑳ Straßenbauwesen, 🜛, &c. (e-e Trasse ziehen, abstecken, vorzeichnen) to trace, to mark out.

trassieren² ⊕ (⌣⌣⌣) [it. trassa're] v/a. u. v/n. (h.) ⑱ (e-e Tratte, e-n Wechsel ziehen) ⚬ auf // to draw (a bill) on //; ſ. Saldo; trassierter Wechsel draft.
trat (⌣) ind., **träte** (⌣⌣) subj. impf. v. treten.
Tratsch (⌣) m ⑬a. nur in: Klatsch und ~ tittle-tattle, idle gossip.
tratschen, trätschen (⌣⌣) v/n. (h.) u. v/a. ⑬ (schwatzen) to jabber, chat(ter), gossip.
Tratte ⊕ (⌣⌣) [it. Zug] f ⑱ (gezogener, trassierter Wechsel) draft, bill of exchange.
Trau-altar (⌣⌢⌣⌢) [trau-en 3] m ⑫ marriage-altar.
Traube (⌣⌣) [ahd.] f ⑱: a) (Wein-) ~ bunch of grapes; ~n pflücken to gather grapes; bibl. kann man auch ~n lesen von den Dornen? (Matth. 7,16) do men gather grapes of thorns? Sprichw. die ~n ſind ſauer (ſagte der Fuchs, weil er ſie nicht bekommen konnte) the grapes are sour (said the fox, because he could not reach them); b) ♀ cluster, ⚔ raceme.
Trauben-abfall (⌣⌢...) m ⑫ husks pl. of grapes; **⸗ähnlich** a. ⑥, **⸗artig** a. grape-like, in clusters, ⚔ racemose, ...ous; vgl. ⸗förmig; **⸗blut** n grape-juice; **⸗blüte** ♀ f vine-blossom; **⸗blütig** a.: ⚔ racemose, racemed; **⸗förmig** a.: ⚔ aciniform, acinose, min. staphyline, botryoid, vgl. ⸗ähnlich; **⸗geländer** n trellis-work for grape-vines; **⸗haut** f. anat. des Auges: ⚔ uveous coat of the eye, (lt.) tunica uvea; **⸗kamm** m grape-stalk; **⸗kern** m grape-stone; **⸗krankheit** f grape- (or vine-)disease; **⸗kur** f. med. grape-cure; **⸗lese** f gathering in of grapes, vintage; **⸗most** m = Most 1; **⸗quetsche** ⊕ f grape-crusher; **⸗reich** a. abounding in grapes; **⸗rosinen** f pl. raisins pl. in bunches; **⸗saft** m grape-juice; **⸗säure** f, chm.: ⚔ racemic acid ($C_4H_6O_6$); **⸗schimmel** ♀ m: ⚔ botrytis; **⸗sieb** n grape-funnel; **⸗stein**, min.: ⚔ botryolite; **⸗steinbrech** ♀ m aizoon-like saxifrage (Saxi'fraga Aizo'on): **⸗tragend** a. ⑥ bearing grapes. **⸗racemiferous**; **⸗zeit** f vintage; **⸗zucker** m grape-sugar, chm.: ⚔ dextrose, dextroglucose ($C_6H_{12}O_6$).
traubig (⌣⌣) a. ⑥ 1. clustered. — 2. laden with (or bearing) grapes.
trauen (⌣⌣) [ahd.: trow: treu] ⑱ I v/n. (h.), v/a. u. ſich ⚬ v/refl. 1. a) auf e-n, et. ⚬ to trust (or confide) in a p... a th.; (ſich darauf verlaſſen) to rely (or depend) on a th., to place confidence in a p., a th.; b) e-m, einer Sache ⚬ (Glauben ſchenken) to believe in a p., a th.; e-m unbedingt ⚬ to put implicit confidence in a p.; e-m, einer Sache nicht ⚬ to distrust a p., a th.; er wollte ſ-n Augen nicht ⚬ he would not believe his eyes; wir ⚬ ihm nicht über den Weg, um die Ecke we do not trust him out of sight, we trust him no further than we (can) see him; fig. ſ. Friede 3; Sprichwort: dem Glück iſt nicht zu ⚬ fortune is fickle; trau, schau, wem proved and tried, in him confide. — 2. als v/refl. = getrauen. — II v/a. 3. die Gatten ⚬ to unite ... in wedlock or matrimony, to marry; ſich ⚬ laſſen to be (or get) married, to marry, F

co. to get spliced. — III ~ n ⑳ 4. ſ. Trauung, bibl. Artikel.
Trauer (⌣⌣) [mhd. vgl. trauern, traurig] f ⑱ 1. (Kummer) sorrow, grief, affliction; ~ um e-n Verſtorbenen mourning for a departed one. — 2. (~kleidung) mourning (-garb), e-r Witwe: widow's weeds pl.: tiefe ~ deep mourning; Halb-~ half-mourning; ~ haben to be in mourning; ~ an-(ab-)legen to go into (out of) mourning.
Trauer-anzeige (⌣⌢...) f ⑫ announcement of a death; vgl. ⸗brief; **⸗anzug** m = ⸗kleid; **⸗behang** m black hangings pl.; **⸗binde** f um den Arm, Hut: mourning-band; vgl. ⸗flor; **⸗birke** ♀ f weeping (or drooping) birch (Be'tula pe'ndula); **⸗botschaft** f mournful tidings, message of a p.'s death; **⸗brief** m mournful letter; (gedruckte Todes-anzeige) mourning-card; **⸗esche** ♀ f weeping-ash (Fra'xinus excel'sior pe'ndula); **⸗fahne** f black flag; **⸗fall** m mournful (or sad) event; death (in a family); **⸗farbe** f mourning-colour; **⸗flor** m crape, lang herabhängender: weeper; vgl. ⸗binde; **⸗gedicht** n mournful poem, elegy; **⸗gefolge** n funeral procession; **⸗geläut(e)** n tolling of the bells at a funeral; **⸗geleit** n = ⸗gefolge; **⸗gepränge** n funeral pomp; **⸗gerüst** n catafalque; **⸗gesang** m mourning-song, funeral chant or dirge; **⸗geschichte**, **⸗gestalt** f mournful (or sad) (hi)story, figure; **⸗gewand** n mourning (-garb); **⸗gottesdienst** m funeral service; **⸗haus** n house (full) of mourning; **⸗jahr** n year of mourning, sad year; **⸗kapelle** f memorial chapel, mortuary chamber; **⸗kleid** n, **⸗kleidung** f mourning(-dress); ſ. Trauer 2; **⸗kloß** F m burſch. humdrum fellow, stick; **⸗kutsche** f mourning-coach.
Trau-erlaubnis (⌣⌢...) f = Trauschein b.
Trauer-mahl (⌣⌢...) n ⑫ funeral repast; **⸗mantel** m: a) mourning-cloak; b) ent. (Schmetterling) Camberwell beauty (Vane'ssa anti'opa); c) ♀ lady's-mantle (Alchemi'lla vulga'ris); **⸗marsch** ♪ m funeral march, dead march; **⸗musik** ♪ f funeral music.
trau-ern (⌣⌢) [ahd.: drowse] I v/n. (h.) ⑳a. 1. to mourn for a p.; to grieve (or fret) over (or about) a th.; to be plunged into (deep) sorrow; um e-n ~ to lament a p.'s loss; die ⚬den Verwandten the afflicted (or sorrowing, grief-stricken) relations pl. — 2. äußerlich ⚬ to be in (or wear) mourning (um e-n for a p.). — II ~ n ⑳ 3. mourning, grief, sorrow(ing).
Trauer-nachricht (⌣⌢...) f ⑫ = ⸗botschaft; **⸗nadel** f mourning-pin; **⸗ordnung** f regulations pl. about mourning (to be observed at court); **⸗papier** n black-edged (note-)paper; **⸗post** f = ⸗botschaft; **⸗rand** m black edge; **⸗rede** f funeral oration; **⸗ring**, **⸗schleier** m mourning-ring, -veil; **⸗spiel** n tragedy; **⸗spiel-dichter** m tragic poet, writer of tragedies; **⸗stück** n, etwa: touching piece or play; **⸗tag** m day of mourning; **⸗taube** f, orn. Am.

♪ Muſik; ⚔ Wiſſenſchaft; ♀ Pflanze; ⊕ Geographie; ⊙ Technik; ⚒ Bergbau; ⚔ Militär; ↓ Marine; ⊕ Handel; ⚫ Poſt; 🜛 Eiſenbahn.

Carolina (or mourning) dove (*Zenaidu'ra caroline'nsis*); =**tuch** n black cloth; ≈**voll** a. ⓖ mournful, doleful, melancholy, sad; =**wagen** m mourning-coach; =**weide** ⚥ f weeping (or drooping) willow (*Salix babylo'nica*); =**zeit** f time of mourning; =**zug** m funeral procession. — Vgl. Sterbe=, Leichen=...
Trauf-bad (″...) n ⓑ shower-bath; =**dach** n über e-r Türe ꝛc.: weather-mould.
Traufe (ᴸᵛ) [ahd.: triefen] f ⓑ: a) (Tropfenfall) water dripping from the roof; Sprichw. f. Regen; b) (Dachrinne) gutter.
träufeln (ᴸᵛ) [träufen] ⓑa. I v/n. (h. und fn) to drip, to drop, to fall in drops; (riefeln) to trickle; von Kerzen: to gutter. — II v/a. to drip, to let down in drops; fig. Balfam auf ein wundes Herz ≈ to pour balm on a sore heart. — III ~ n ⓒ dripping. trickling; drops falling.
traufen v/n. (h. u. fn) und **träufen** v/a. (ᴸᵛ) ⓑ [ahd.: triefen m.] = träufeln.
Trauf-faß (″...) n ⓑ water-butt; =**rinne** ⊙ f gutter; =**röhre** ⊙ f gutter-pipe, arch. auch drip-nose; =**stein** m dripstone, in Küchen ꝛc.: sink; =**wasser** n dripping (or trickling) water; (Regenwasser) rain-water; (Rinnsal) rill (of water); (Bächlein) streamlet.
Trau-gebühr (″...) f ⓑ, =**geld** n marriage-fee; =**handlung** f marriage-ceremony, (Hochzeit) wedding.
traulich (ᴸᵛ) [trauen 1] a. ⓖ confidential, intimate; (ungezwungen) familiar; (herzlich) cordial; (anheimelnd) homely, cosy, snug, (behaglich) comfortable; ~**keit** f ⓖ intimacy; familiarity, cordiality; cosiness, snugness, comfort(ableness).
Traum (ᴸ) [ahd.: dream; *trügen] m ⓞc. 1. dream, eines Wachenden: reverie, day-dream; quälender ~ (Alp) nightmare; weitS. (Halbschlummer) somnole(sce)nt state; im Reich der Träume in dreamland; ich habe einen schönen ~ gehabt I have had (or dreamt) a beautiful dream; Träume treffen selten ein dreams seldom come true; er spricht (wie) im ≈ he speaks as though he were dreaming; Sprichw. f. Schaum 2. — 2. fig. (Einbildung) fancy(-picture), imagination; ich habe auch (od. bloß) nicht im ≈e nicht (od. bloß: nicht im ≈e) daran gedacht oder es mir einfallen lassen I never dreamt (or thought) of such a th., it never (even) entered my thoughts or head, it never occurred to me.
Traum-ausleger (″...) m ⓑ = =**deuter**; =**bild** n apparition in a dream, vision. phantom, picture of fancy; =**buch** n dream-book, book on dreams: =**deuter** (=in f) m interpreter of dreams. ◊ oneirocritic, oneiroscopist: =**deuterei**, =**deutung** f interpretation of dreams, ◊ oneirocritics, oneiroscopy.
träumen (ᴸᵛ) [ahd.: dream] I v n. (h.) und v/a. ⓑ to dream; wachend ≈ to be in a dreamy (or somnolent) state; lebhaft (schwer, süß) ≈ to have lively (heavy, sweet) dreams; ich träumte (oder v/impers. es träumte mir oder mir träumte), daß ich fiele I dreamt (that) I was falling; mir hat et. Wunderbares geträumt I dreamt of a

wonderful dream; fig. das hätte ich mir nie ≈ lassen I should never have dreamt of such a thing or entertained such a thought; vgl. Traum 2. — II ~ n ⓒ dream(ing), dreamy (or somnolescent) state; fig. reverie.
Träumer (ᴸᵛ) m ⓦ, ~**in** f ⓕ dreamer, fig. a. visionary, dreamy (or absent-minded) person; ~**ei** (-ᵥᴸ) f ⓕ dreaming, fig. reverie, fancy, vision, (Nachbrüten) brooding, (deep) meditation, musing, F brown study: **Lisch** (ᴸᵛᵛ) a. ⓖ dreamy, (fond of) brooding, fig. chimerical, visionary; **Lischer Mensch = ~**; **Lisches Wesen** dreaminess.
Traum-gebilde (″...) n ⓑ, =**gesicht** n, =**gestalt** f = =**bild**; =**gott** m. myth. god of dreams; Morpheus.
traumhaft (ᴸᵛ) a. ⓖ dreamlike.
Traum-leben (″...) n ⓑ dream-life; er führt nur ein ~ he lives in dreams or in a cloud; =**spiel** n phantasmagoria; ≈**verloren** a. ⓖ, ≈**versunken** a. lost in dreams or reveries; =**warnung** f warning (given) in a dream; =**welt** f world (or realm) of dreams or visions or fancy; dreamland.
traun (ᴸ) [nhd. in Treuen] int. truly!, indeed!, foorsooth!, aye!
Trau-rede (″...) f clergyman's address to the bridal pair; =**register** n register of marriages.
traurig (ᴸᵛ) [ahd.: dreary; *trauern] a. ⓖ sad (über an); (betrübt) grieved, sorrowful, doleful, (schwermütig) melancholy, gloomy, (niedergeschlagen) depressed, cast down, dejected; (unheilvoll) dismal, woeful; (elend) wretched; (öde) dreary; der Anblick sorry (or sad, deplorable) sight; das ≈e bei der Sache ist // the sad part (or the pity) of it is //; **Traurigkeit** f ⓖ sadness; grief, sorrow, melancholy, gloom. depression, dejection.
Trau-ring (″...) m ⓑ wedding-ring; =**schein** m: a) marriage-certificate; b) (Trau-erlaubnisschein) marriage-license.
traut (ᴸ) [ahd.] a. ⓖ dear, beloved, stärker: dearly beloved; (innig vertraut) intimate; a. = traulich.
Trau-ung (ᴸᵛ) f ⓕ (f. trauen 3) marriage-ceremony or -service; (Hochzeit) wedding, nuptial feast; ~**s-tag** m ⓑ day of marriage; wedding-day.
Trau-zeuge (″ᴸᵛ) m ⓑ witness to a marriage, engS... bsd. in der engl. Kirche: person who gives the bride away.
traven ↓ (ᴸᵛᵛ) v/a. ⓚ: eine Ladung ≈ (durch Schrauben zs.-pressen) to steeve ...
Travestie (≈ᵛᵛᴸ) [it.] f ⓕ (entsteuende Nachahmung, vgl. Parodie) travesty, burlesque, F take-off; **Lren** (≈ᵛᵛᴸᵛ) v/a. ⓕ to travesty, burlesque, F to take off.
Treber (ᴸᵛ) [ahd.], a. ~**n** f pl. (Rückstand von Trauben ꝛc.) husks pl. of grapes, &c., von Malz: draff, brewer's grains pl.
Treber-wein (″ᵥᴸ) m ⓑ = Tresterwein.
trecken ↓ (ᴸᵛ) [ndd.: track] v/a. ⓕ: ein Fahrzeug ≈ to tow...; to drag...
Treck-schuit ↓ (″ᴸᵛ) f ⓑ (holl. Kanalboot) trekschuyt; =**seil** n towing-rope or -line; =**weg** n tow(ing)-path.
Treff¹ (ᴸ) [treffen] m ⓑb. blow: fig. (schlagende Bemerkung) (good) hit.

Treff² (ᴸ) [fr. *trèfle*] n ⓓ (schwarze Farbe im Kartenspiel) clubs pl. (= Kreuz 7).
Treff-fähigkeit ⚥ (″ᴸ~) [Treff¹-fähigkeit] f ⓕ art. hitting power, effectiveness (of cannon). [=**bube** m knave of clubs.]
Treff²**-as** (″...) n ⓑ ace of clubs;]
treffen (ᴸᵛ) [ahd.] I v/a., v/n. (h.) u. sich v refl. ⓑa. (impf. traf) 1. to hit, (wirken) to take effect, to tell; bfd. schießend: die Scheibe ≈ to hit (or strike) the target; das Ziel ≈ to hit the goal. to make (or score) a bull's-eye; meist fig. to hit the mark; das Ziel nicht ≈ to miss the mark (auch fig.). nur fig. to miss one's aim; der Schuß hat (nicht) getroffen the shot has (not) gone home or has (not) taken effect; von Schützen: (immer) gut ≈ to be a good (stärker: a dead) shot or an excellent marksman; getroffen! (a) hit!; vom Blitze getroffen struck by lightning; Sprichw. nicht alle Kugeln ≈ not every bullet finds its billet. — 2. fig. sich getroffen fühlen to feel hurt (by a p.'s remarks), das trifft Sie that's aimed at you; f. Nagel 1; ihn traf das Los the lot fell upon him; die Reihe trifft dich it's your turn; vom Schlage getroffen werden to have an apoplectic stroke or seizure, to be struck (or seized) with apoplexy; wen trifft die Schuld? who is at fault?, who is to blame?; der Vorwurf trifft ihn the reproach is cast (or levelled) at him, the blame rests upon him; Sprichw. wer sich getroffen fühlt, nehme sich bei der Nase, etwa: let him whom the cap fits wear it. — 3 paint. &c. to strike off the features of a p.; sein Bild ist gut getroffen it (or his portrait) is a good likeness of him or is life-like; bin ich gut getroffen? is it (or the picture, photo) like me? — 4. ♪ von Sängern: to strike (or hit, pitch) the right note. — 5. (richtig finden) to find the thing wanted; Sie haben es getroffen you have hit the right thing; getroffen! that's just it!, there you are right!; es (un)glücklich ≈ to come at the right (wrong) time or season. — 6. ~n (a. auf e-n) ≈ (e-m begegnen) to light on (or to fall in with) a p., to meet (or run against) a p.; ich habe ihn in seiner Wohnung nicht getroffen I did not find him at home; da trifft er ja Bekannte he will certainly be among friends there; der Brief wird ihn nicht mehr ≈ ... will not reach him in time; sich (oder ea.) ≈ to meet (one another). — 7. das trifft (stimmt)! that's just the thing (wanted)!; wie sich das trifft! how fortunate (that is)!; wie es sich (gerade) trifft just as it may happen. as occasion requires. — 8. (ins Werk setzen) f. Anstalt 1, Auswahl 1; Vorkehrungen für et. ≈ to make provision(s) (or preparations) for a th., Vorsichtsmaßregeln ≈ to take precautions. — II ~ n ⓒ 9. hitting, &c. (f. I). — 10. ⚔ (Kampf) combat, (Gefecht) fight, engagement, action, (Schlacht) battle; es kam zum ~ it came (or led) to an engagement or a

---

Signs (see page XVII): **F** familiar; **P** vulgar; ┌ flash; ╲ rare; † obsolete (died); * new word (born); ⁒ incorrect; ♪ music;

[Treffer] — 967 — [Trema]

(pitched) battle; ein ~ liefern to give battle, to fight a battle, auch: to strike a blow. — 11. a. ⚓ (Linie der Schlachtordnung) division engaged in battle, battle-line; vorderes ~ front line, van(guard); mittleres ~ centre (of the battle); hinteres ~ rearguard.— III ⚓ p.pr. u. a. ⚙ 12. to the purpose, to the point; (genau) exact; (schlagend) striking; (klar, entscheidend) clear, decisive; (angemessen) suitable; ⚓de Bemerkung pertinent remark; das ⚓de Wort the right word, the appropriate (or proper) term.

Treffer (⚓) m ⚙ 1. (Person): a) (guter Schütze) good shot; b) (guter Maler) clever portrait-painter. — 2. (Sache): a) = Treffschuß; b) (Gewinnlos) prize; c) thea. (Zugstück) great hit or success, F draw; fig. (Zutreffendes) lucky hit or chance; einen guten ~ machen ober haben to make a lucky find or hit.

Treff¹-**fähigkeit** (⚓...) f ⚙ s. Treffähigfeit; ²**könig** m king of clubs.

trefflich (⚓) a. ⚙ excellent, (ausgesucht) exquisite, choice; ⚓! very good!, first-rate!, capital!, F (that's) fine!; ~**keit** f ⚙ excellency; exquisitenes, choiceness; first-rate quality.

Treff¹-**schuß** (⚓...) m ⚙ good shot, shot that goes home, hit, bull's-eye; ²**sicher** a. ⚙ accurate(ly aimed); ⚔ ⚓ ⚓es Feuer accurate firing; =**sicherheit** f im Schießen dead certainty (of aim) in shooting, accuracy of aim.

Treib-**achse** ⚓ (⚓...) f ⚙ driving-axle; =**anker** ⚓ m driving-anchor; =**apparat** m propeller, propelling apparatus.

Treibe-**beet** (⚓...) n ⚙ hort. hot-bed.

Treib-**eis** (⚓...) n ⚙ floating (or drift-)ice.

treiben (⚓) [ahd.: drive] ⚙ I v/a. 1. to drive; (in Bewegung setzen) to put in motion, to set going; der Fluß treibt Eis ... carries ice; Fußball: to dribble; e-e Herde ⚓ to tend a herd or a flock; e-n Kreisel ⚓ to spin (or whip) a top; das Pulver treibt die Kugel ... propels the bullet or ball; einen Nagel ⚓ to drive in a nail; hunt. das Wild ⚓ to beat up the game; ⚓ eine Maschine ⚓ (in Gang halten) to drive (or work) a machine; ⚓de Kraft motor force, motive power. — 2. mit prp. (oft fig.): Kühe **auf** die Weide ⚓ to drive ... to the pasture, to take ... to graze; et. **aufs Äußerste**, auf den Gipfel, auf die Spitze ⚓ to push a th. to extremes; e-n **aus** dem Besitz e-r Sache, aus f-m Gut ob. Hause ⚓ to eject (or evict) a p.; e-n aus dem Lande ⚓ to expel (or banish) a p. from the country; **in** die Enge ⚓ to press hard; vgl. Enge 2; e-n ins Elend, ins Exil ⚓ to drive a p. into exile, to exile a p.; den Feind in die Flucht ⚓ to put ... to flight, to rout ...; e-m das Blut, die Röte ins Gesicht ⚓ to send the blood to a p.'s face, to make a p. blush; die Preise in die Höhe ⚓ to send (or force) up prices; bei Versteigerungen: in die Höhe ⚓ to bid up; **über** das Ziel hinaus (zu weit) ⚓ to push too far, to overshoot the mark, **von**=ea. ⚓ to scatter, to separate; e-n vom Amte ⚓ to drive a p. out of office; vom Wunsche getrieben zu // actuated (or impelled) by a desire to //; e-n **zu** et. ⚓ to urge (or egg) a p. on to do a th., to incite (or stimulate) a p. to do a th.; die Leute zur Arbeit ⚓ to drive the men to their work; e-m das Haar zu Berge ⚓ to make a p.'s hair stand on end; e-n zur Eile ⚓ to hurry (or F drive) a p., bfd. Am. to hustle a p.; f. Paar I; e-n zur Verzweiflung ⚓ to drive a p. (in)to despair. — 3. mit adv.: e-e Sache **so** weit als möglich ⚓ to push a matter as far as possible; so weit möchte ich es doch nicht ⚓ I should not like to go so far; **vorwärts** ⚓ to drive (or push) forward, to urge on; als v/impers. **es** treibt mich fort something drives me from hence, I feel that I must leave. — 4. med. diese Arznei treibt den Schweiß (aus dem Körper) ... produces (or promotes) perspiration; biswl. abs. der Wein treibt (sehr) wine acts as a (strong) diuretic. — 5. von Pflanzen: a) Blüten, Früchte ⚓ to shoot (or sprout) forth ..., Knospen, Zweige a. to put forth ...; b) hort. faktitiv: Pflanzen in Mistbeeten ic. ⚓ to force plants in hot-beds, &c.— 6. = auftreiben 4. — 7. (üben, betreiben): a) to practise, exercise, pursue; was ⚓ sie für ein Gewerbe ober Handwerk? what trade do they carry on or belong to?, what is their trade?; Musik, Sprachen ic. ⚓ to study (or cultivate) ...; ⚓ Trigonometrie they are working (F grinding) at ...; b) in bestimmten Verbindungen: Aufwand ⚓ to live in sumptuous (or great) style; Kindereien ⚓ to do childish things; Kurzweil ⚓ to indulge in sport or fun, to amuse o.s.; Mutwillen, Possen ⚓ to carry on one's pranks or F larks; er läßt keinen Unsinn mit sich ⚓ he won't stand any nonsense, he won't be played with; sein Wesen ⚓ to be full of life or fun or mischief; es gar zu arg ⚓, es toll ⚓ to outstep the mark, to exceed all bounds, to go too far; f. bunt 4; Sprichw. wie man's treibt, so geht's as you make your bed, so you must lie on it; man treibt's solange es geht there is an end to everything. — 8. ⚓ Böttcherei: einen Reifen ans Faß ⚓ to hoop a cask; Gerberei: die Häute ⚓ (schwellen) to soak ...; Bäckerei, Kochf.: den Teig ⚓ (ausrollen) to roll the dough; Metall-arbeit: ein Metallstück ⚓ (austiefen) to emboss, mit dem Meißel: to chase; getriebene Arbeit embossed (or chased) work; metall. (ab=)⚓ to refine, to cupel. — 9. ⚒ Erze ⚓ to extract ore; Strecken ⚓ to drive galleries. — II v/n. (h., bei Ortsveränderung sn) **10.** = v/a. ohne Objekt, zB. 4 und 5. — 11. (sich bewegen): a) to drift, to be driven, to be carried along by the wind or waves or by some irresistible force; warum treibt sich das Volk so? (q.) why are the people rushing along so?; im Wasser ⚓ to drift, to float; sich ⚓ lassen to float on the water; b) ⚓ das Schiff treibt ... is drifting; ans Land ⚓ to be cast (or washed) ashore; auf einen Felsen ⚓ to foul a rock, to be driven (or cast) on a reef; auf den Sand ⚓ to run aground; vor Anker ⚓ to drag the anchor; c) der Schnee treibt (in Flocken) ... is drifting (in flakes); d) das Bier treibt (gärt) aus dem Faß ... is overflowing the vat; der Saft treibt (steigt) ... is rising; e) die Knospen ⚓ ... are springing forth. — III ~ n ⚙ 12. (f. I u. II); ~ der Herde tending of the flock; ~ der Blätter, des Laubes shooting forth (or budding, sprouting) of leaves or foliage; ⚓ metall. cupellation; ⚒ extraction of ore. — 13. (Geschäftigkeit) bustle, stir, life; activity, (Verkehr) traffic; sein Tun u. ~ all his doings and dealings pl., his whole (line of) conduct; das ~ der Welt the ways (and doings) of the world; ein wüstes ~ disorderly goings-on, riotous scenes pl. — 14. hunt. (Treibjagd) battue.

Treiber (⚓) m ⚙, 1 u. 2 a. ~**in** f ⚙ 1. one who drives, &c. (f. treiben I), driver. — 2. a) ~ v. Vieh: drover; b) hunt. ~ des Wildes: beater; c) (unbarmherziger Dränger) oppressor, der Arbeit: taskmaster, F nigger-driver, Am. hustler; d) (f. der zu et. antreibt, die Triebfeder ist) main spring (F life and soul) of a concern; e) ⚓ (Arbeiter am Maschinengetriebe) driver. — 3. ⚓ mach. (Getriebe) driving gear, driver, propeller; pinion; Weberei: Schnur des ~s pecking-cord.

Treiberei (⚓) f ⚙ driving (vgl. treiben 12 u. Getreibe), biswl. = Hetzerei.

Treib-**hammer** (⚓...) m ⚙ chasing-hammer; =**haus** n, hort. hot-house, conservatory; =**haus**-**früchte** f/pl. hot-house (or forced) fruit; =**haus**=**gewächs** n, =**pflanze** f hot-house plant; =**herd** m, metall. refining-hearth, cupelling-furnace; =**holz** n: a) drift-wood; b) typ. shooting-stick; =**jagd** f, =**jagen** n battue; =**kasten** m, hort. hot-bed; =**kraft** f, phys. moving (or motor, motive) force or power; vgl. Triebkraft; =**ofen** m = =herd; =**prozeß** m, metall. refining, cupellation; =**punzen** m chasing-chisel; =**rad** n, mach. driving (or fly-)wheel, e-r Uhr: pinion; =**reis** n e-s jungen Baumes: sprout, sprig; =**riemen** m, mach. driving band or belt, (endless) strap; =**sand** m = Flugsand; =**scherben** m = Kapelle²; =**schnur** f, mach. lathe-band, driving cord; =**stange** ⚓ f, mach. connecting rod, Weberei: driving bar, working beam; =**welle** f e-r Maschine: main (or driving) shaft; =**werk** n, mach. driving-gear.

Treidel ⚓ (⚓) m Flußschiffahrt: (Schlepptau) tow-line, towing-rope.

Treidelei (⚓) f ⚙ towing.

Treid(**e**)**ler** ⚓ (⚓) m ⚙ (Schleppschiffer) tower, tracker.

treideln ⚓ (⚓) [ndb.: trail] I v/a. ⚓ a. Fluß-, Kanal-schiffe ⚓ to tow (along) ... — II ~ n ⚙ towing, trackage.

Treidel=**pfad** m, =**steig** m, =**weg** (⚓...) m ⚙ am Fluß-, Kanal-ufer: towing-path.

Trema (⚓) [grch.] n ⚙ ⚙ gr. (Trennpunkte", zB. in Aleuten) diaeresis.

⚓ scientific; ⚓ botanical; ⚓ geography; ⚓ machinery; ⚒ mining; ⚔ military; ⚓ marine; ⚓ commercial; ⚓ postal; ⚓ railway.

[Tremse] — 968 — [treten]

Tremse ? (⌣⌣) [ndd.] f ⊕ = Kornblume.
Tremulant ♪ (⌣⌣⌣) m ㊷ (Bezug der Orgel) tremor, tremolo-stop.
tremulieren ♪ (⌣⌣⌣⌣) v/n. (h.) ㊾ to shake, to quaver, to sing tremolo.
trendeln (⌣⌣) v/n. (h.) ㊷a. to dawdle.
trennbar (⌣⌣)a.㊿separable, ↘severable; divisible; **~keit** f ㊻ separableness, ...ility; divisibleness, ...ility.
trennen (⌣⌣) [ahd.] I v/a. u. **sich** ⦵ v/refl. ⑧ 1. (sich) ⦵ to separate, part, sever, (loslösen) to detach; (sondern) to (put a)sunder, Zs.=gehöriges: to disconnect, to disjoin; (vereinigen) to disunite; (auflösen) to dissolve, eine Naht: to rip up, to undo; (teilen) to divide; Eheleute ⦵ to separate (or divorce) husband and wife, ein Pärchen Vögel: to separate, to put apart; sie leben getrennt von=ea. they live apart from each other, they are separated. — 2. sich ⦵, auch: to part (company), von Eheleuten: to separate, ⊗ v.Handelsgenossen: to dissolve partnership; von Wegen: to branch off; wo sich die Wege ⦵ at the parting of the ways. — II ~ n ㉓ 3. s. Trennung.
Trenn=messer (⌣⌣...) n ㉒ ripping-knife or -tool, ripper; **=punkte** m/pl. = Trema; **=scherbe** ⊕ f Töpferei: parting-shard; **=schicht** ⊕ f, tel. separator.
Trennung (⌣⌣) f ㊻ (s. trennen I) separation, severance, partition; disconnexion, disunion; dissolution; division; die ~ von Freunden the parting of friends; s. Tisch 2.
Trennungs=flächen (⌣⌣...) f/pl. ㊷ der Kristalle: planes pl. of cleavage; **=partikel** f, gr. disjunctive particle; **=schmerz** m pain of parting (friends); **=stunde** f parting-hour; **=zeichen** n, gram., typ.: a) (Divis) hyphen; b) (Trema) diæresis.
Trense (⌣⌣) [ndd., ndl., span.?] f ⊕ man. (ant. Kanda're) snaffle, bridoon.
trensen (⌣⌣) v/a. ㊾: ein Tau, Stag ⦵ (mit Hanf ausfüllen) to worm...
Trensen=gebiß (⌣⌣⌣) n ㊷ man. snafflebit.   [surg. = Schädelbohrer.⌉
Trepan ⚕ (⌣⌣) [grch. try'panon] m ⊕d.⌋
Trepang (⌣⌣) [malaiisch] m ⊕d. ㊷ zo. (eßbare Seegurke) trepang (Holothu'ria edu'lis).
trepanieren ⚕ (⌣⌣⌣⌣) [Trepan] v/a. ⑧ surg. einen ⦵ (j=s Schädel anbohren) to trepan a p.; **Trepanier(end)er** m trepanner. [(Schädelbohrer) trephine.⌉
Trepanier=säge ⚕ (⌣⌣⌣⌣) f ㊷ surg.⌋
trepp=ab (⌣⌣) adv. (coming) downstairs; **trepp=auf** (⌣⌣) (going) upstairs.
Treppe (⌣⌣) [ndd.] f ⊕ arch. staircase, (flight of) stairs, ↓ ladder; halsbrechende ~ break-neck staircase; steinerne ~ vor dem Hause: (stone) steps pl.; sich windende ~ winding staircase, geheime ~ private staircase; oberes (unteres) Ende der ~ top (foot) of the stairs; eine ~ (zwei ~n) hoch wohnen to live on the first (on the second) floor; eine ~ höher up another flight of stairs, on the next floor; die ~ hinabgehen (hinaufgehen) to go downstairs (upstairs); die ~ hinunterfallen (hinunterrollen) to fall (or roll) down the stairs; e=n die ~ hinunterwerfen to throw a p. downstairs; fig. beim Haarschneiden: e=m ~n schneiden to chop (or jag) a p.'s hair.

Treppen=absatz (⌣⌣...) m ㊷ arch. landing, resting-place; **=bau** m construction of a staircase; **=baum** m spindle of a winding staircase; **=flucht** f flight of stairs; **=flur** m landing (-place) of a staircase; ⦵**förmig** a. ㊿ in the form of a staircase; ⦵: ⚘ scalariform; **=gefäße** ⚘ n/pl. scalariform vessels pl.; **=geländer** n railing, balustrade, banister(s pl.); **=haus** n well of a staircase; **=läufer** m stair-carpet; **=läufer=stange** f stair-rod; **=spindel** f= **=baum**; **=stein** m vor der Haustüre: stone step; **=stufe** f step of a staircase; **=turm** m turret with a winding staircase; **=wange** ⊕ f, carp. notch-board.
Tresor (⌣⌣) [fr.] m ⊕d. ㊿ (Schatzkammer) treasury; **~=schein** m (⌣⌣⌣) m treasury-bill or -note.
Trespe ? (⌣⌣) f ㊸ brome-grass (Bromus); weiche ~ soft brome-grass (Br. mollis).
Tresse (⌣⌣) [fr.] f ㊸ (gold or silver) lace, auch: galloon, eines Unteroffiziers etwa: (sergeant's) stripes pl. (in Engl. am Ärmel getragene Litzen); ⚔ wenn er seine ~n hat od. bekommt when he gets his stripes, when he becomes a (corporal or a) sergeant; mit ~n besetzt gallooned; **~n=hut** (⌣⌣...) m ㊷, **~n=rock** m gallooned hat, laced coat.
tressieren ⊕ (⌣⌣⌣) [fr.] v/a.: Haare ⦵ (flechten) to plait hair; **Tressierer** m ㊷ plaiter (of hair).
Trester (⌣⌣) [ahd.] pl. ㊷ husks (or skins) pl. of pressed grapes, &c. (= Treber): **~=kuchen** m ㊷ grape-cake; **~=wein** m wine made from the pressed skins of grapes.
Tret=butte (⌣⌣) f ㊷ für die zu kelternden Trauben, bsd. ehm.: treading-vat.
treten (⌣⌣) [ahd.: tread] ⑧ I v/n. (h. u. sn) 1. (h.) to tread, to put (or set) one's foot on the ground, ausschlagend: to kick; daneben= (oder fehl=) ⦵ to miss one's footing, leise ⦵ to walk (or step) softly or gently, fig. to (be a) sneak. — 2. (in) (sich fortbewegen) to (take a) step; (vorrücken) to advance; (sich hinstellen) to stand (up); (hinübergehen) to pass, to cross. — 3. mit prp. an das Fenster ⦵ to step (or go) to the window; ans Licht ⦵: a) von Personen: to step into the light; b) von Sachen: to come to light; thea. an die Rampe ⦵ to come forward, to appear before the footlights; an die Spitze ⦵ to place o.s. at the head of an army, a movement, &c.; to take the lead; an j=s Stelle ⦵ to take a p.'s place or post; gr. die Endung tritt an den Stamm the termination is affixed (or joined, appended) to the stem; auf et. ⦵ to step (or tread) on a th.; e=m auf den Fuß ⦵ to tread (or stamp) on a p.'s foot, heimlicherweise: to kick a p. under the table, to give a p. a sly hint; e=m auf die Hacken ⦵ to tread on a p.'s heels; auf die Rednerbühne ⦵ to step on the platform; auf die Seite ⦵ to step (or stand) aside; fig. auf j=s Seite ⦵ to go over to (or to take) a p.'s side, to side with a p.; ⚔ auf der Stelle ⦵ (ohne zu marschieren) to mark time; e=m auf die Zehe ⦵ to tread on a p.'s toes; aus dem Dienste ⦵ to leave (or quit) service; der Fluß ist aus den Ufern getreten ... has overflowed its banks; in et. ⦵ to step into a th.; ins Dasein ⦵ to come (or spring) into existence, to arise; in den Ehestand ⦵ to enter matrimony or married life; s. Fußtapfe; der Schweiß trat ihm ins Gesicht the perspiration rose to his face; in ein Haus ⦵ to step into a house, to enter a house; ins Leben ⦵ to come into existence, to make one's appearance; s. Mittel[2] 3; in den Priesterstand ⦵ to take holy orders; ⚔ s. Reihe 1; in die Schranken ⦵ to enter the lists; mit e=m in Unterhandlung ⦵ to enter into negotiations with a p.; mit e=m in Verbindung ⦵ to become connected with a p.; e=m in den Weg ⦵ to stand in (or block, obstruct) a p.'s way, fig. auch: to thwart (or balk) a p.; in Wirksamkeit ⦵ to take effect, to come into force; ⚔ s. Gewehr; ast. die Sonne tritt in das Zeichen des Löwen ... enters (the sign of) Leo; über die Ufer ⦵ to overflow (or flood) the banks; e=m unter die Augen ⦵ to face a p.; vgl. Auge 5; ich bin mitten unter euch getreten I have come (or dropt) into your midst; vor e=n (hin=) ⦵ to appear before a p.; ein Wölkchen trat vor den Mond a little cloud passed over (or flitted across) the moon; fig. s. Riß 3; ihr Bild trat ihm vor die Seele her image rose up in his mind; zu e=m ⦵ to step (or walk) up to a p.; zutage ⦵ to come (or rise) to the surface, ⚒ s. zutage ⦵. — 4. mit advs. beiseite ⦵ to step aside; ⦵ dazwischen ⦵: wenn nichts dazwischentritt if nothing happens in the meantime; ⦵ Sie dorthin! go over there!; ⦵ Sie herauf! come up!, step up here!; näher ⦵ to draw nearer; ⦵ Sie näher! step this way!, step in!; fig. e=m zu nahe ⦵ to affront (or offend) a p., to hurt a p.'s feelings; einer Frage näher ⦵ to consider a question carefully, to look (more) closely into a th. — II v.a. 5. to tread (or trample) on; mit Füßen (oder unter die Füße) ⦵ to tread (or trample) under foot; to kick; fig. sein Glück mit Füßen ⦵ to spurn one's good fortune, to be blind to one's (own) interest; s. Balg 2, Pflaster 2 am Ende; Takt ⦵ to beat time with one's foot; Wasser ⦵ (schwimmend) to tread water; einen Weg ⦵ (wandeln) to follow a road or a path. — 6. barfüßes: fig. e=n ⦵ (bsd. an Zahlen mahnen) to press a p. for payment, F to dun a p. — 7. von männlichen Vögeln, bei der Begattung: to tread (the hen, &c.). — 8. meist ⊕ (bearbeiten) to work with one's feet, die Nähmaschine, die Pedale einer Orgel ꝛc. auch: to treadle; Töpferei: den Ton ⦵ to tread the clay. — 9. mit Angabe der Wirkung: et. entzwei ⦵ to break a th. (in two) by treading on it; sich (dat.) einen Dorn in den Fuß ⦵ to run a thorn into one's foot; seine Schuhe schief ⦵

Zeichen (s. S. XVII): F familiär; P Volkssprache; ⌐ Gaunersprache; ↘ selten; † alt (auch gestorben); * neu (auch geboren); ⁓ unrichtig;

[Treter] — 969 — [Trifolium]

to run (or wear) one's boots down on one side; in den Staub 2, zu Boden 2 to crush under foot; ein Tier tot 2 to kill ... by stamping on it. — III~ n ᠉e treading (on), &c. (f. I u. II).
Treter (¹⁻) m ᠉ one who treads, &c. (f. treten), treader; vgl. Balgentreter.
Tret=faß ⊕ (ᵘ⁻...) n ᠉, **=kufe** f = =butte; **=mühle** ⊕ f, mech. treadmill (auch als Strafwerkzeug); **=presse** ⊕ f tread-press; **=rad** ⊕ n tread-wheel; **=schemel** ⊕ m am Webstuhl 2c.: treadle; **=schlitten** m ᠉ Rennwolf; **=vogel** m burſch. (ungestüm mahnender Gläubiger) dun, unpatient creditor; **=zuber** m = =butte.

treu (¹) [ahd.: true: trauen] a. ⊕ faithful, true to, (ergeben) loyal to, devoted to; (aufrichtig, bieder) sincere, honest; (bewährt) reliable, trusty, trustworthy; (der Wahrheit gemäß) truthful; 2e Freunde stanch friends pl.; 2es Gedächtnis faithful (or retentive, tenacious) memory; eine 2e Seele a good (or kind) soul; f-n Grundsätzen 2 bleiben to remain true (or to adhere stanchly) to one's principles; f-m Vorsatz 2 bleiben to stick to one's purpose; Briefſchluß: Ihr 2 ergebener) Yours faithfully ⊕.

Treu²(¹) f ⊕ = Treue, ₃B.: a) bekräftigend: auf meine ~!, (bei) meiner ~! on my soul!, ſeltener: by (or upon) my faith!, iriſch 2c.: faith!; b) f. Glaube 1 am Ende; üb' immer ~ und Redlichkeit! be ever faithful and upright!

Treu=bruch (ᵘ⁻...) m ᠉ breach of faith; (Meineid) perjury; (Verrat) treason, disloyalty, perfidy; **=brüchig** a. ⊕ faithless; disloyal, perfidious.

Treu=e(¹⁻)[ahd.;*treu] f ⊕ (pl.~) faithfulness (auch fig. einer Schilderung. Übersetzung 2c.), nur v. Perſonen: fidelity; (Ergebenheit) loyalty (or stanchness, attachment) to; ~ im Halten e-r Zuſage: (good) faith; ~ des Gedächtnisses retentiveness (or tenacity) of a p.'s memory; puniſche ~ (Treuloſigkeit) Punic faith; die ~ brechen to break faith or one's word; dem Könige ~ ſchwören to swear allegiance to the King.

treu=ergeben (ᵘ⁻...), **=gehorsam**, **=gesinnt** a. ⊕ loyal(ly attached) to; **=hänber** m ⊕ (Testamentsvollstrecker) executor (of a will); a. = Depositar; **=herzig** a. true-hearted; (offen) candid, frank; (unbefangen) ingenuous, simple-minded; **=herzigkeit** f ⊕ true-heartedness; candour; simplicity of mind.

treulich (¹⁻) a. ⊕ = treu; adv.: faithfully, truly, loyally; sincerely, honestly, stanchly; (gewiſſenhaft) conscientiously, scrupulously; (der Wahrheit gemäß) truthfully.

Treu=liebchen (ᵘ⁻...) n ᠉ true-love, sweetheart; **=los** a. ⊕ faithless, perfidious; (verräteriſch) treacherous, false (to one's professions); **=losigkeit** f ⊕ faithlessness, perfidy; (Verrat) treachery, als Handlung: treason(able act), treacherous (or disloyal) deed.

Triangel (¹⁻⁻) [lt. tria'ngulum n Dreieck] m ᠉ ♩, geom., a. triangle, als Schlaginstrument a. cymbal; **Triangler** ♩ m ᠉ triangle-(or cymbal-)player.

triangulär ⊘ (ᵛᵛᵛ¹) [lt.] a. ⊕ (dreieckig) triangular. [gulation.]
Triangulation ⊘ (ᵛᵛᵛ⁻tß(ᵛ)¹) f ⊕ trian-
triangulieren ⊘ (ᵛᵛᵛ¹ᵛ) [lt.] surv. I v/a. ⊕ (in Dreiecke zerlegen) to triangulate, to survey with the aid of trigonometry. — II ~ n ᠉ u. **Triangulierung** f ⊕ triangulation.
Triari-er⅋(ᵛ¹⁻(ᵛ)ᵛ)[lt.] m/pl. ᠉ röm. Alt.: (Kerntruppen im 3. Treffen) triarians pl.
Trias ⊘ (¹ᵛ) [grch.] f, inv. 1. (Dreiheit) triad. — 2. geol. trias.
Trias=formation (ᵘ⁻...) f ᠉, **=gebirge** n trias(sic) formation.
Tribachys ⊘ (¹ᵛᵛ) [grch.] m, inv. pros. (Versfuß ᵛᵛᵛ¹) tribrach(ys).
tribulieren (ᵛ⁻¹ᵛ) [lt.] I v/a. ⊕ (quälen, plagen) to vex, torme'nt, harass. — II ~ n ᠉ u. **Tribulierung** f ⊕ vexation, to'rment; tribulation.
Tribun (ᵛ¹) [lt.] ⊕d. bſd. Alt. (Beamter, Offizier): tribune.
Tribunal (ᵛ⁻¹) [lt.] n ⊕d. (Gerichtshof) tribunal, court of justice, law-court.
Tribunat (ᵛ⁻¹)[lt.] n ⊕c. Alt.: (Amt[szeit eines Tribuns) tribuneship, tribunate.
Tribüne (ᵛ¹ᵛ) [fr.] f ⊕: a) (Rednerbühne) (speaker's) platform; b) (Gerüst für Zuschauer) stand (for spectators), platform.
tribuniziſch (ᵛ⁻¹⁻) [Tribun] a. ⊕ Alt. tribunitial, tribunicial.
Tribus (¹ᵛ) [lt.] f, inv. röm. Alt.: (politische Volksabteilung) tribe.
Tribut¹ (ᵛ¹) [lt.] m ⊕c. (Zins, Abgabe) tribute (auch fig.); e-m einen ~ auferlegen to impose (or lay) a tribute on a p.; ~ bezahlen (od. entrichten) müſſen to be obliged to pay tribute.
tributär (ᵛ⁻¹) [fr.] a. ⊕ = tributpflichtig.
tribut¹**=frei** (ᵛ¹⁻...) [Tribut] a. ⊕ exempt from (paying) tribute; **=komitien** [Tribus] n/pl. ᠉ röm. Alt.: (Volksversammlung) (lt.) comitia tributa; ²**=pflichtig** a. tributary; **=zahlung** f payment of tribute.
Trichine ⊘ (ᵛ¹ᵛ) [grch.] f ⊕ zo. trichina (Trichi'na spira'lis); **~n=krankheit** f ⊕ = Trichinose.
trichinig, ...iſch (ᵛ¹⁻), **trichinös** (ᵛᵛ¹) a. ⊕ von Schweinefleiſch 2c.: trichinous.
Trichinose⊘(ᵛᵛ¹⁻)f⊕path. trichinosis.
Trichter (¹ᵛ) [ahd.; *ult. tracta'rius] m ᠉ funnel, anat.: ⊘ infundibulum; ⊕ Müllerei: (mill-)hopper; (Öffnung e-s Bulkans) crater (f. Nürnberger II) durch einen ~ gießen to pour through a funnel.
trichter=förmig (ᵛᵛᵛᵛ) a. ⊕ funnel-shaped, ♀ u. zo.: ⊘ infundibular, ...ate, ...iform.
trichtern (ᵛᵛ) v/a. ᠉a. to pour (or pass) through a funnel.
Trichter=öffnung (ᵛᵛ...) f ⊕ e-s Bulkans: crater; **=stativ** n, chm. funnel-stand; **=winde** ♀ f: ⊘ ipomœa, purpurrote: morning-glory (Ipomœ'a purpu'rea).
Trick ⊘ (¹) [engl.] m, n ⊕d. ⊕ 6. Whist: (Stich) trick. [trick-track.]
Tricktrack (ᵛᵛ) [fr.] n ⑤ backgammon.
Trident ⊘ (ᵛ¹) [lt.] npr/n. ⑤ α. (Stadt in Welſchtirol, mſt Trient) Trent; **~iner**, ²**iniſch** (⁻¹ᵛ⁻) a.⊕Tridentine, of Trent; hist. eccl.~iniſches Konzil, **~inum** (⁻¹ᵛ⁻) n ⑤ (1545—63) Council of Trent.

Trieb¹ (¹) [mhd.; *trieb², treiben] m ⊕c. 1. driving, drift(ing); ♀ (Keimkraft) germinative power; (Hervorgetriebenes) young shoot, sprout. — 2. (Kraft, mit der et. fortgetrieben wird) driving (or propelling, acting) force; momentum, movement; (force of) impulsion, impulsive force. — 3. (innere Regung, Antrieb) impulse, impetus; (Neigung) inclination, bent, zum Böſen: propensity, evil turn of mind; natürlicher ~ instinct; ſinnlicher ~ sensual appetite or passion or desire; er hat keinen ~ zum Studieren ... no taste (or liking, inclination) for study or for books. — 4. (Herde) drove, herd.
trieb² (¹) ind., **triebe** (¹ᵛ) subj. impf. v. treiben.
Triebel ⊘ (¹ᵛ) [mhd.] m ᠉ Töpferei: turning-staff; typ. = Treibholz b; Böttcherei; driver; mach. = Kurbel.
trieb¹**=fähig** (ᵘ⁻...)a.⊕capable of growth; **=feder** f ⊕ (elastic) spring, fig. main spring, (central) motive; **=feile** ⊕ f Uhrm.: pinion-file; **=kraft** f propelling force, motive power. ♀ vegetative power, growth; **=maß** ⊕ n Uhrm.: pinion gauge; **=rad** ⊕ n. mach. = Treibrad; **=recht** n right of pasture; **=rolle** ⊕ f, mach. driving pulley; **=sand** m drifting sand(s pl.); vgl. Flugsand; **=stahl=draht** ⊕ m Uhrm.: pinion-wire; **=stange** f, mach. connecting rod, driver; **=welle** ⊕ f driving shaft; **=werk** n, mach. driving gear, mechanism; machinery, works pl. of a machine; **=zeug** ⊕ n, mach. (driving) gear, gearing. — Vgl. a. Treib=.
Trief=auge (ᵘ⁻...) m ᠉ blear-eye, watery eye; ²**äugig** a. ⊕ blear-eyed.
triefen (¹ᵛ) [ahd.: Traufe, Tropfen] I v/n. (h. u. ſn) n. v/a. ⊕d ſt ob. ⊕ 1. = träufe(l)n; der Schweiß troff ihm von der Stirn, seine Stirne troff von Schweiß the perspiration was dripping from (or running down) his forehead, his forehead was wet with perspiration; 2d dripping (with wet, with perspiration). — 2. path. to discharge a fluid; die Augen 2 ihm his eyes are running or watering. — II ~ n ᠉ 3. = träufeln III.
triefig (¹ᵛ) a. ⊕ dripping, trickling, running; (led) leaking.
Trief=nase (ᵘ⁻...) f ⊕ running nose; ²**naſig** a. ⊕ with a running nose, a. snivelling; ²**naß** a. dripping wet, wet through; vgl. a. pudelnaß.
Tri=ennium (ᵛᵛ(ᵛ)ᵛ) [lt.] n ᠉ triennial period, space of three years; akademiſches ~ three years' university-course.
Tri-ent ♀ (ᵛᵛ) npr/n. f. Trident.
Trier ♀ (¹ᵛ) [Treviri] npr/n. ⊕α. alte Stadt an der Moſel: Treves.
Tri-erarch (ᵛ⁻¹) [grch.] m ᠉ Alt. Befehlshaber ob. Ausrüſter e-r Triere) trierarch.
Tri-ere (ᵛ¹ᵛ) f ⊕ = Trireme.
Trie=st (ᵛ¹) npr/n. ⊕α. ♀ öft. Hafenstadt an ⊙ Adriatiſchen Meere: Triest(e); **~(in)er** (in f ⊕) m ᠉ inhabitant of Triest(e).
triezen (¹ᵛ) v/a. ⊕ to vex.
triff, **=ſt**, **=t** (¹) imper., 2. und 3. Perſon des pres. ind. von treffen.
Trifolium (ᵛ¹(ᵛ)ᵛ) [lt.] n ᠉ = Dreiblatt.

♩ Muſik; ⊘ Wiſſenſchaft; ♀ Pflanze; ⊕ Geographie; ⊕ Technik; ⚒ Bergbau; ⚔ Militär; ⚓ Marine; ⚖ Handel; ✉ Poſt; 🚂 Eiſenbahn.

[**Trift**] — 970 — [**Triumphator**]

Trift (ˇ) [mhd.: drift; *treiben] f ⓐ (f. 2 u. 3) **1.** a) = Triftgerechtigkeit; b) road (or passage) for the cattle; c) (Weideplatz) pastur(ag)e, common; d) (Herde) ~ Ochsen drove (or herd) of oxen. — **2.** (auch m ⓦb.) = Drift² 1. — **3.** ↓ (a. n ⓦb.) f. Drift² 2. [grain.]
Trifte (ˇˇ) f ⓐ (Kornschober) stacked
Trift-geld (ˇ...) n ⓑ fee for the use of pasture-land, ehm.: faldage; **=gerechtigkeit** f right of pasturage.
triftig¹ ↓ (ˇˇ) [triften treiben] a. ⓐ (im Wasser treibend) drifting, adrift; ² sein (vom Anker) to drag.
triftig² (ˇˇ) [mhd., *treffen] a. ⓐ (wohlbegründet) well founded or established; valid (reason, &c.); (bündig) conclusive, clinching (argument, &c.); (überzeugend) convincing, cogent (proof, &c.); (glaubwürdig) plausible (argument, &c.); (gewichtig) weighty (reason, &c.); er tat es aus ²en Gründen he did it from excellent motives or for weighty reasons.
Triftigkeit (ˇˇ-) f ⓐ (f. triftig²) validity; conclusiveness, cogency; plausibility, plausibleness; weightiness.
Trift-strömung (ˇ...) f ⓐ drift-current.
Trigeminus (ˇˇˇ) [lt.] m, inv., anat. (dreifacher Gesichtsnerv) trigeminal nerve.
Triglyph ⚘ (ˇˇ) [grch.] m ⓦd., ~e (-ˇˇ) f ⓐ = Dreischlitz.
Trigonometrie ⚘ (ˇˇˇˇ) [grch.] f ⓐ math. (Dreiecksberechnung) trigonometry; **trigonometrisch** (ˇˇˇˇ) a. ⓐ trigonometrical (formula, function, &c.).
Trikolore (ˇˇˇˇ) [fr. dreifarbig(e Flagge)] f ⓐ three-coloured flag, (fr.) tricolore.
Trikot (ˇtō') [fr. tricot m] m (n) ⓐ, etwa: stockin(g)et, (fr.) tricot; **~beinkleider** n/pl. ⓐ der Akrobaten ꝛc.: tights, fleischfarbene a. fleshings pl.
Triller ♪ (ˇˇ) [lt. trillo] m ⓐ trill; **trillern** v/n. (h.) u. v/a. ⓐa. to trill, quaver, shake, von der Lerche: to warble; als v/a. auch: to sing (or adorn, vary) with trills or shakes.
Trillion (ˇˇˇ) [lt.] f ⓐ math. (= 1 000 000 × 1 000 000 × 1 000 000) trillion.
Trilogie ⚘ (ˇˇˇ) [grch.] f ⓐ (drei ein Ganzes bildende Dramen) trilogy.
Trimester (ˇˇˇ) [lt. dreimonatlich] n ⓐ three months' time or term.
Trimeter (ˇˇˇ) [grch.] m ⓐ pros. (sechsfüßiger Vers) trimeter; **trimetrisch** (ˇˇˇ) a. ⓐ trimetric(al), trimeter.
Trine (ˇˇ) I npr/f. ⓐ⚭β. (dim. von Katharina) Kate. — II f ⓐ fig. (dumme Weibsperson) silly goose or wench.
Trinitari-er (-ˇˇ(ˇ)ˇ) [lt.] m ⓐ Cath. eccl. Trinitarian. [keit) trinity.)
Trinität (-ˇˇ) [lt.] f ⓐ theol. (Dreieinig-)
Trinitatis (-ˇˇˇ) [lt. gen. von tri'nitas: Dreieinigkeit] nur in: Sonntag ~ (erster Sonntag nach Pfingsten) Trinity Sunday.
Trinitro-zellulose ⚘ (ˇˇˇˇˇˇˇ) f ⓐ chm. = Schießbaumwolle.
trinkbar (ˇˇ) a. ⓐ drinkable, fit (or nice) to drink, seltener: potable; der Wein ist nicht ² ... is undrinkable, ... is unfit to drink; **~keit** f ⓐ: a) drinkableness; b) (Grad der Reife) des Weines, Branntweins ꝛc.: matured state or stage.
Trink-becher (ˇˇˇˇ) m ⓐ drinking-cup, (Pokal) goblet.

trinken (ˇˇ) [ahd.: drink] I v/a., v/n. (h.) v/refl. ⓞ ft **1.** a) to drink; weit ⓢ., auch arzneilich: to take; f. Bescheid 4; (zu sich nehmen) to imbibe; Luft ꝛc. ² (einsaugen) to inhale ..., to draw in ...; aus der Flasche ² to drink from the bottle; eine Flasche Wein mit e-m ² to empty (or F crack) a bottle of wine with a p.; b) eng²· von Säufern: to be fond of the bottle. — **2.** Redensarten: was ² Sie? what do you drink or take?, F what's your drink or your liquor?; ich trinke Wein, Bier, Kaffee ꝛc. I drink or take ...; was wollen Sie ²?, oft: what will you have (to drink)?; gern eins ² to be given to drinking, to be fond of one's glass or F of a drop; to be a tippler or F booser; der Wein läßt sich (gut) ² ... is (very) drinkable or nice to drink; F co. ... goes down nicely; auf j-s Gesundheit ² to drink a p.'s health. — **3.** mit Angabe der Wirkung: sich arm (krank) ² to drink o.s. poor (ill); sich (dat.) e-n Haarbeutel, e-n Rausch ² to get tipsy or drunk or F boozed; sich voll ² to drink one's fill or too much or to excess; ein Glas leer ² to drink up (or to empty) a glass. — **II** ~ n ⓑ **4.** (f. I) drinking; imbibing; gewohnheitsmäßiges ² tippling; (Völlerei) hard drinking, drunkenness; der Wein reizt zum ~ ... entices one to drink; er kann das ~ nicht l. he is addicted to drink (-ing), he is an inveterate drunkard or tippler, F he's an old boozer.
Trinker (ˇˇ) m ⓐ, **~in** f ⓐ drinker, b.s. = Säufer(in); **~asyl** n ⓐ, **~heilanstalt** f home (or asylum) for inebriates or drunkards.
Trinkerei (ˇˇˇˇ) f ⓐ habitual drinking.
Trink-gefäß (ˇ...) n ⓐ drinking-vessel; **=gelage** n drinking-bout, carousal; **=geld** n gratuity to servants, waiters, &c., auch: fee, F tip; e-m ein ~ geben to fee (F to tip) a p.; **=genoß** m bottle-friend, F fellow-tippler or -boozer; **=geschirr** n = =becher, =gefäß, =glas, =schale; **=gesellschaft** f people who drink together, F party of tipplers, boozing lot; **=glas** n drinking-glass, tumbler; **=halle** f: a) in Bädern: pump-room; b) = =stube; **=horn** n drinking-horn; **=lied** n drinking-song; **=napf** m am Vogelbauer: drinking-fountain; **=schale** f shallow cup; die volle ~, auch die flowing bowl; **=spruch** m = Toast; **=stube** f tap-room, (private) bar, auf Bahnhöfen: refreshment-room; **=szene** f orgy; **=wasser** n drinking-water.
Trinom (ˇˇ) [grch.] n ⓦd. math. (dreigliederige Größe) trinomium, trinomial value; ²isch (-ˇˇ) a. ⓐ trinomial.
Trio ♪ (ˇˇ) [it.] n ⓐ (dreistimmiges Tonstück) trio.
Triole ♪ (ˇˇˇ) [it.] f ⓐ triplet, triole.
Triolett (ˇˇˇ) [fr., it.] n ⓐc. pros. (achtzeiliges Ringelgedicht) triolet.
Trio-walzwerk ⊕ (ˇˇˇˇ) n ⓐ metall. trio-rollers pl.
Tripel-allianz (ˇˇ...) [fr. triple dreifach] f ⓐ (Dreibund) triple alliance.
Tripel² ⊕ (ˇˇ) [Tripolis] m ⓐ, auch **~erde** f ⓐ (mineralisches Polierrmittel) tripoli powder, (englische Erde) rottenstone.

tripeln ⊕ (ˇˇ) [Tripel²] v/a. ⓐa. (polieren) to polish with tripoli powder.
Tripel-takt (ˇˇ...) m ⓐ triple time or measure, a. triplex.
Triphan ⚘ (ˇf-) m ⓦc. min. triphane.
Triphthong ⚘ (ˇˇf) [grch.] m ⓦb. ⓐ gr. (Dreilaut) triphthong.
triplieren (ˇˇˇˇ) [fr.] v/a. ⓐ (verdreifachen) to triple, to treble; Billard: to strike the cushion twice with the ball.
Triplit ⚘ (ˇˇ) m ⓦc. min. (phosphorsaures Mangan- und Eisen-oxybul) triplite.
Tripmadam ♀ (ˇˇˇˇ) [fr.] f ⓐ (gelber Mauerpfeffer) trip-madam (Sedum refle'xum).
Tripolis ♀ (ˇˇˇ) npr/n. inv. (Staat und Stadt in Nord-afrika) Tripoli; **Tripolitaner(in** f ⓐ), m ⓐ, **tripolitanisch** a. ⓐ Tripolitan.
Tripp ⚘ (ˇ) m ⓦc. ⓐ mock-velvet.
trippeln (ˇˇ) [udd. lautm.] v/n. (h. u. su) ⓐa. to trip, to make (or walk with) short steps; da kommt sie hergetrippelt there she comes tripping along.
Tripper (ˇˇ) [udd.: tropfen] m ⓐ path. (Geschlechtskrankheit) gonorrhœa, F clap.
Tripp-sam(me)t (ˇˇˇˇ) m ⓐ = Tripp.
Triptychon ⚘ (ˇˇˇˇ) [grch.] n ⓑ ⓐ eccl. (Altargemälde in 3 Teilen) triptych(on).
Trireme ↓ (ˇˇˇ) [grch.] f ⓐ Alt.: (dreirudriges Schiff) trireme.
trist (ˇ) [fr.] a. ⓐ (traurig, elend) sad, miserable, wretched.
Trithion-säure (ˇˇˇˇˇ) f ⓐ chm.: ⚘ trithionic acid $(H_2S_3O_6)$.
Triton (ˇˇ) [grch.] m ⓐ myth. (Meergott) Triton; **~en-gruppe** f ⓐ sculp. group of Tritons; **~s-horn** n, zo. (große Muschel) Triton's-horn. [v. treten.)
tritt¹ (ˇ) imper. u. 3. Person sg. pres. ind.)
Tritt² (ˇ) [mhd.; *tritt] m ⓦb. **1.** (das Treten) tread(ing), in regelmäßiger Folge: footfall, footing, ⊕ einer Maschine: treadling; (Schritt) step, pace; (Stoß mit dem Fuße) kick; e-m einen ~ geben oder versetzen to give a p. a kick; e-m ~e geben to kick a p.; e-n sicheren ~ h. to be sure-footed; Sicherheit des ~es sureness of foot, sure-footedness; mit schweren ~en with a heavy tread or gait; ✕ ~ halten to keep pace; im ~! (keep) time!; ohne ~! at ease!; ~ wechseln! change over!; f. Schritt 1. — **2.** (Spur der Schritte) trace, track, footstep. — **3.** meist ⊕: a) ~ e-s Spinnrades ꝛc.: treadle, am Fahrrade: pedal, am Wagen: carriage-step, am Kutschbock: footboard; b) (Blumengestell) flower-stand; c) footstool (= Fußbank); d) (erhöhtes Gestell am Fenster) step before (or leading up to) a window, estrade; e) = Trittleiter.
Tritt²-brett (ˇ...) n ⓐ = Tritt 3a; **=harfe** ♪ f pedal-harp; **=leiter** f pair of steps; **=rad** n ⊕ Spinn. spinning-wheel with a treadle.
trittst (ˇ) 2. Person sg. pres. ind. v. treten.
Tritt-stufe (ˇ...) f ⓐ tread of a step, am Wagen: carriage-step; **=wechsel** ✕ m change of step, changing over.
Triumph (ˇˇf) [lt.] m ⓦb. Alt.: (Siegesfeier) triumph (a. fig.); im ~ triumphantly; victoriously, as victor(s).
Triumphator (ˇˇˇˇ) [lt.] m ⓐ triumphant victor, conquering hero.

Signs (see page XVII): F familiar; P vulgar; F flash; ↘ rare; † obsolete (died); * new word (born); ⸫ incorrect; ♪ music;

[Triumphbogen] — 971 — [trompeten]

Triumph-bogen (⸗ˢf...) m ⓖ triumphal arch; **=gesang** m triumphal song.
triumphieren (⸗ᵛⁱᴸᵛ) [it.] v/n. (h.) Ⓑ Alt. u. fig. (siegen, frohlocken) to triumph; eccl. die Öde (ant. die streitende) Kirche (die Seligen) the Church triumphant.
Triumph-marsch (⸗ˢf...) m ⓖ triumphal march; **=wagen** m tr. chariot or car; **=zug** m tr. procession.
Triumvir (⸗ᵛw⸗) [it.] m Ⓖ Alt.: triumvir.
Triumvirat (⸗ᵛw⸗ᵘ) [it.] n ⑪c. (Dreiherrschaft) triumvirate.
trivial (⸗w(⸗)ᴸ) [lt. tri'vium „Dreiweg", öffentliche Straße] a.⑥ (abgedroschen) trivial, stale, trite, commonplace, hackneyed.
Trivialität (⸗w(⸗)⸗ᴸ) f ⑯ triviality, staleness, triteness.
Troas ♀ (ᴸᵛ) [grch.] npr/n. inv. Alt.: Landschaft in Klein-asien: the Troad.
trochä-isch ⚔ (⸗ᴸⁱ) a.⑥ trochaic; 2e Verse trochaic lines, a.: trochaics pl.
Trochä-us ⚔ (⸗ᴸᵛ) [grch.] m ㉗ pros. (Versfuß: -⸌) trochee.
trocken (⸗ᵛ) [ahd.: dry] I a. ⑥ (D 9) 1. dry, von Holz ꝛc. auch well-seasoned; (dürr) parched, arid; fig. (langweilig) tedious, dull; höchst 2 (as) dry as a bone, fig. (bsd. von Schriften) a.: (as) dry as dust; s. Ohr 3 unter „hinter". — 2. mit nouns: s. Faden 2, Fuß 2; 2es Futter für Vieh: fodder; 2er Mensch prosy fellow, F dry stick; e-n Gast mit leerem Munde (od. 2) sitzen l. to offer no refreshments to a guest; 2er Wechsel bill drawn on o.s. — 3. mit verbs: s. 2-legen; 2 w. to become dry, to dry up; s. 2-wohnen. — II 4. das ~e dry part or ground or land; auf dem 2en sein od. sitzen ⇓ to be high and dry, fig. to be hard up (for money); im 2en sein od. sitzen to be under cover, fig. (wohlhabend sein) to be in clover; s. Schäfchen 1.
Trocken-apparat ⊕ (⸗ᵛ...) m ⓖ dryingapparatus, chm. desiccator; vgl. **=kasten**; **=boden** m drying-loft or -floor; vgl. **=schuppen**; **=brett** n drying-board; **=dock** ⇓ n dry-dock; **=element** n, elect. dry cell; **=farbe** ⊕ f pencil-colour; **=fäule** f dry rot; **=firnis** ⊕ m drying varnish; **=futter** n, agr. des Viehes: provender; **=fütterung** f dry feeding; **=gehäuse**, **=gestell** n drying-case, -frame; **=gewicht** ⊕ n net weight; **=haus** n drying-house.
Trockenheit (⸗ᵛ) f ⑯ dryness (a. fig.); (gänzliche Dürre) aridity, aridness, infolge von Regenmangel: drought; fig. (Langweiligkeit) dulness, prosiness.
Trocken-kammer ⊕ (⸗ᵛ...) f ⓖ dryingchamber; **=kasten** m, chm., &c. dryingstand; **legen** v/a. ⓧ** to dry up, Land: to drain; **=legung** f von Land: draining, drainage; **=leine** f für Wäsche: drying-line; **=mittel** n siccative; **=obst** n dried (or dry) fruit; **=ofen** m dryingstove or -kiln; **=öl** n (Leinöl) drying oil, drier; **=platte** f, phot. dry plate; **=platz** m für Wäsche: drying-ground or -yard; **=rahmen** m bsd. für Tuch: tenter; **=raum** m —, **=schuppen**, **=schuppen** m drying-room, -shed; **=tuch** n: a) bisw. = Handtuch; b) in Pulverfabr.: dryingcloth; **=verfahren** n dry process or way; **2wohnen** v/a. ⓧ** ein Haus 2 to inhabit a new house which has not

had time to dry; **=wohner(in** f) m first tenant of a newly-built house; **=zylinder** m drying-cylinder.
trockne (⸗) [ahd.] f ⑯ 1. = Trockenheit. — 2. (festes Land) dry land, (it.) terra firma.
trocknen (⸗ᵛ) [mhd.; *trocken] ⓑ. I v/n. (sn) to (become) dry, durch die Hitze: to be parched. — II v/a. (trocken m.) to (make) dry; (trockenlegen) to lay out to dry, Land: to drain; durch Abwischen 2 to wipe dry, durch Aufbewahrung: to season, durch Aufhängen: to hang out to dry, Malz 2 to (kiln-)dry (auf d. Welsboden: to air-dry) malt; Wäsche ꝛc. fertig 2 to air; 2des Mittel (de)siccative; getrocknete Feigen dried figs pl. — III ~ n ㉓ u. **Trocknung** f ⑯ drying (process), desiccation.
Troddel (⸗ᵛ) [mhd.] f ⑱ tassel, tuft; **~mütze** (⸗ᵛ⸌) f ⑯ cap (adorned or provided) with a tassel.
Trödel (ᴸᵛ) [mhd.] m ㉒ 1. secondhand furniture or articles pl., weitS. (old) lumber or rubbish; F der ganze ~ F the whole concern or show or lot. — 2. burschikos: (tolles Durcheinander) hubbub, uproar; (Spaß) (piece of) fun, fine sport, F (jolly) lark or spree.
Trödel-bude (ᴸᵛ⸗) f ⑯ old-clothes shop, marine-store(s pl.).
Trödelei (⸗ᵛᴸ) f ⑯ 1. dawdling, loitering. — 2. ⓑ trade in second-hand goods, old-clothes trade.
Trödel-frau (ᴸᵛ...) f ⑯ woman dealing in second-hand clothes or goods; **=geschäft** n, **=handel** m trade in old clothes or second-hand furniture; **=hans** m = Trödler 1; **=kram** m = Trödel 1; **=laden** m second-hand (furniture-)shop, old-clothes shop; **=mann** m = Trödler 2; **=markt** [mhd.] m old-clothes market, rag-fair.
trödeln (ᴸᵛ) [: trendeln] I v/n. (h.) ⓑa. 1. (sich langsam bewegen) to dawdle loiter, crawl along. — 2. ⓑ (mit Trödel handeln) to deal in second-hand goods. 3. burschikos: (s. Trödel 2) to carry on fine fun or sport, F to lark about. — II ~ n ㉓ 4. = Trödelei 1.
Trödel-ware ⓑ (ᴸᵛ...) f ⓖ second-hand goods pl.; **=weib** n = **=frau**.
Trödler (ᴸᵛ) m ㉒. **~in** f ⑰ (s. trödeln) 1. dawdler, a. slow coach, snail. — 2. ⓑ dealer in second-hand clothes or goods, old-clothesman, second-hand dealer.
Tro-er (ᴸᵛ) m ㉒, **~in** f ⑰ = Trojaner.
troff (ˡ) ind., **tröffe** (ˡᵛ) subj. impf. v. triefen.
trog (ᴸ) ind. impf. v. trügen.
Trog² (ᴸ, ˡ; pl.ᴸᵛ) [ahd.: trough] m Ⓒc. trough, ⊕ zum Tragen von Mörtel und Steinen: (bricklayer's) hod; **~batterie** ⊕ f, phys. trough-battery.
tröge (ᴸᵛ) subj. impf. von trügen.
Troglodyt ⚔ (⸗⸗ᴸ) [grch.] m ⓖ (Höhlenbewohner[in]) troglodyte. [(Mactra).
Trog²-muschel (ᴸ⸗ᵛ) f ⓖ zo. trough-shell
Troikart (ᴸᵛ) [fr.] m Ⓒc. ⓖ = Trokar.
tro-isch (ᴸᵛ) a. ⑥ = trojanisch.
Troja ♀ (ᴸᵛ) npr/n. Ⓓa. (gen. a. Trojens) Alt.: Hauptstadt von Troas ⓓa. Troy, **~ner** (-in f ⑰) m ㉒, **nisch** a. ⑥ Trojan; der ~nische Krieg the Trojan War.

Trokar ⚔ (ᵛᴸ) [fr. trocart] m ⑪d. Ⓓ surg. u. vet. (dreischneidiges Instrument) trocar.
trokieren ⓑ (⸗ᴸᵛ) [fr. troquer] v/n. (h.) Ⓑ (Tauschhandel treiben) to (carry on) truck.
Troll-blume ♀ (ᴸᵛ⸗) f ⓖ globe-flower (Tro'llius [Europae'us]).
trollen (⸗ᵛ) [mhd.: troll: trotte(l)n] ⓑ I v/n. (sn) to troll, to trot (or F toddle) along. — II F **sich** 2 v/refl. to be off, F to toddle (or walk) off, to make o.s. scarce, to take French leave.
Troll-wagen ⊕ (⸗ᴸᵛ) m ⓖ (Rollwagen) trolley. [spout.
Trombe (⸗ᵛ) [it.] f ⑯ (Wasserhose) water-
Trommel (⸗ᵛ) [mhd.: drum; *fr., it.] f ⓖ 1. ♪ drum; vgl. Schellentrommel; die ~ rühren od. schlagen to beat the drum; mit ~n und Trompeten with drums beating and trumpets sounding. — 2. ⊕ (hohler Zylinder) drum, am Kran, Steuerrad ꝛc.: barrel, an e-r Baggermaschine: tumbler; vgl. Kaffeetrommel. — 3. anat.: ⚔ tympanum.
Trommel-baß ♪ (⸗ᵛ⸗) m ⓖ drum-bass.
Trommelei (⸗ᵛᴸ) f ⑯ (constant or much) drumming or beating of drums.
Trommel-fell (⸗ᵛ...) n ⓖ: a) ♪ drumhead, drum-skin; b) anat. drum of the ear, ⚔ (membrane of the) tympan(um); **=fell-erschütternd** a. ⑥ ear-splitting, deafening; **=fisch** m, ichth. drum-fish (Labrus cromis); **=gehäuse** n = **=sarg**; **=höhle** f, anat. drum of the ear, ⚔ tympan(um); **=kasten** m = **=sarg**; **=klöppel** m = **=stock**; **=kranz** ⊕ m beim Schachtbau: drum-curb.
trommeln (⸗ᵛ) ⓑa. I v/n. (h.) 1. ♪ u. ♪ to (beat the) drum; v/imp. es trommelt the drums are beating. — 2. von ähnlichen Tönen: mit den Fingern auf dem Tische 2 to beat a (or F the devil's) tattoo on the table; mit den Füßen vor Ungeduld ꝛc. they are stamping their feet ...; auf dem Klavier 2 to strum on the piano; P ich lasse nicht auf mir 2 I won't be played with. — II v/a. 3. e-n Marsch 2 to strike up a march (on the drum), a. to drum a march; fig. s. pfeifen 4. — 4. mit Angabe der Wirkung: e-n aus dem Schlafe 2 to awaken (or rouse) a p. with the sound of drums or with drumming.
Trommel-rad ⊕ (⸗ᵛ...) n ⓖ drumwheel; **=sarg** m drum-case; **=schlag** m beat of the drum; **=schlag** mit ~ with drums beating; bei gedämpftem ~e with muffled drums; **=schläger** m drummer; **=schlegel** m = **=stock**; **=sieb** ⊕ n drumsieve, rotary screen; **=signal** n drumcall; **=stock** m drum-stick; **=sucht** f, path.: ⚔ tympanitis; **=wirbel** m ♪, ♪ roll of the drum.
Trommete † (⸗ᴸᵛ) f ⑯ poet. = Trompete.
Trommler ♪ (⸗ᵛ) m ㉒ drummer.
Trompete (⸗ᴸᵛ) [mhd., *fr., it.] f ⓖ 1. ♪ trumpet; auf der ~ blasen, in die ~ stoßen to sound (or blow) the trumpet (a. fig.). — 2. anat. eustachische ~ Eustachian tube (vgl. eustachisch); fallopische ~n Fallopian drums pl.
trompeten (⸗ᴸᵛ) ⓑ (p.p. trompe'tet) I v/n. (h.) 1. ♪ to (sound the) trumpet; v/imp. es hat trompetet the trumpet has (been) sounded or has rung forth. —

⚔ scientific; ♀ botanical; ♃ geography · ⊕ machinery; ⚒ mining; ⚔ military; ⇓ marine; ⓑ commercial; ✉ postal; 🚂 railway.

[Trompetenbaum] — 972 — [Trotzerin]

II v/a 2. e-n Marsch 2 to play a march on the trumpet. — 3. mit Angabe der Wirkung: aus dem Schlafe 2 to rouse with the sound of trumpets. — III ~ n 4. sound of a trumpet, flourish (or blowing, sounding) of trumpets.
Trompeten=baum ♃ (⌣'⌣...) m ⑫ snakewood (Teco'ma ra'dicans); =**bläser** m trumpeter; =**geschmetter** n flourish (or blare) of trumpets; =**register** n e-r Orgel: trumpet-stop; =**schall** m sound of trumpets; unter ~ bekannt=m. to trumpet forth; =**schnecke** f. zo. trumpet-shell (Triton); =**signal** n trumpet-call or =signal, zum Satteln und Aufsitzen: boot and saddle; =**stoß** m trumpet-blast; =**stück(chen)** n tune (to be played) on the trumpet; piece set for trumpets; =**tusch** m flourish of a trumpet; =**zug** m = =register. — Vgl. Trompeter=... [bugler.]
Trompeter ⚥ ♪ (⌣⌣) m ⚔ trumpeter,/
Trompeter=muskel (⌣⌣⌣...) m ⑫ anat. trumpeter's muscle; =**pferd** ⚥ n trumpeter's horse; =**stückchen** n air played on the trumpet; trumpeter's flourish; =**tisch** m (Nebentischchen) little side-table for menials or children.
Trope (⌣⌣) [grch.] I m ⑭ (f ⑱) rhet. (bildliche Redeweise) trope. metaphor. — II ~n pl. inv. ast._ ♀ tropics pl.
Tropen=fieber (⌣'⌣...) n ⑫ path. tropical fever; =**gegend** f (heiße Zone nördl. und südl. vom Äquator) tropical region; =**klima** n tropical climate; =**koller** m, path. (fit of) frenzy (or madness) produced by a tropical climate. a. tropical frenzy; =**pflanze** f tropical plant; =**welt** f tropical world; in der ~, auch: in the tropics.
Tropf (⸮) [mhd.: tropfen] m ⓓ (einfältiger Mensch) simpleton. dunce, duffer, gudgeon, F u.P juggins; armseliger ~ miserable wretch; armer ~ poor wretch, f poor woman, dim. poor little thing. [douche.]
Tropf=bad (⸮⸮) n ⑫ shower-bath, (fr.)/
tropfbar (⌣⌣) a. ⑯ (a. ⚔=**flüssig**) liquid; 2=**flüssiger Körper** liquid. fluid; ~**keit** f ⑯ liquidity, mehr gbr.: liquid state.
Tropf=brett ⚔ (⸮⸮) n ⑫ droppingboard, Zuckerfabr.: drainer.
Tröpfchen (⌣⌣) n ⑳ 1. (dim. v. Tropfen) little drop, seltener: droplet. — 2. (dim. von Tropf) = (armer) Tropf.
tröpfeln (⌣⌣) [mhd.: dribble] ⓒ a. I v/n. (h. u. sn) to drip, to trickle, to fall (down) in drops; to form drops; von e-r Decke ꝛc. (herab=)2 to drip down from ...; vom Regen: es tröpfelt there are a few drops falling. vgl. tropfen² I. — II v/a. to let trickle, to let fall in drops, von Arzneien ꝛc.: to dispense (or add) in drops; (einträufeln) to instil.
Tropfen¹ (⌣⌣) [ahd.] m ⑳ drop of water, &c., bead of perspiration; ein paar ~ Regen a few drops (or F spots) of rain; F einen ~ (Schnaps ꝛc.) nehmen to have (or take) a drop (of s.th.).
tropfen² (⌣⌣) [ahd.- dro(o)p] ⑱ I v n. (h. u. sn) to drip, to trickle; es tropft (a few drops (or F spots) are falling, a. we are having a few drops (or a sprinkling) of rain, F it's only dripping. — II v/a. = tröpfeln II.

Tropfen=fall (⌣⌣...) m ⑫ drip(ping); vgl. Traufe a; ♀**förmig** a. ⑯ (shaped) like a drop, ♃ guttiform; =**messer** o m. chm.. &c. drop-meter; =**weise** adv. (F a. a.) (taken) by drops; ♀ **trinken** to drink (or take) by sips. to sip; =**zähler** m. pharm. dropping-bottle or -tube.
Tropf=flasche (⌣...) f ⑫ pharm. dropping-bottle; =**glas** n drop-glass; ♀**naß** a. ⑯ = triefnaß; =**pfanne** f für flüssiges Fett: dripping-pan; =**stein** m, min.: a) herabhängender: ♃ stalactite; b) emvorwachsender: ♃ stalagmite; ♀**stein=artig** a.: ♃ stalactiform; =**stein=bildung** f: ♃ stalactitic formation; =**stein=höhle** f stalactite cave(rn); =**trichter** m dropping-funnel; =**wein** m drippings pl. from a wine-cask.
Tropha-e (⌣'⌣) [grch.] f ⑱ (Siegeszeichen) trophy; ~n des Krieges ꝛc. spoils pl.
Tropik=vogel (⌣'⌣..) m ⑫ orn. tropicbird. star- (or wig-)tail (Pha'ethon).
tropisch (⌣⌣) [grch.] a. ⑯ 1. ♀ tropical; fast 2 subtropical, semi-tropical. — 2. rhet. (biblich. übertragen) tropical, metaphorical, figurative.
Tropus (⌣⌣) m ⑳ = Trope I.
Troß (ⱷ) [fr. trousse] m ⓐ. 1. ⚔ heavy baggage, nebst Leuten u. Wagen: baggagetrain; (Nachzügler) camp-followers. F hangers-on pl. — 2. fig. (Bande) gang, set; (Haufe beschwerlicher Dinge) heap of cumbersome things; lumber. trash.
Troß² (⸮) f ⑯ (n ⓐ.) = Trosse.
Troß=bube ⚔ (⸮⸮⸮) m ⑫ = =junge.
Trosse ⚓ (⸮⸮) [ndd.] f ⑱ (Kabeltau) hawser; stählerne ~ steel-hawser, wire-rope.
Troß=junge ⚔ (⸮⸮) m ⑫, =**knecht** m boy (or man) that looks after the baggage, chm.: baggager; =**pferd** n. =**wagen** m baggage-horse, -cart.
Trost (⸮) [ahd.] m ⓑ (o. pl.) 1. consolation, (Beruhigung) comfort, solace. relief, in Worten ausgedrückt ꝛc.: soothing words pl.; es gereicht mir zum ~e. daß // es gewährt mir ~ daß // it is a comfort (or a relief) to me (to think) that /; ~ schöpfen aus // to draw consolation from //, to derive comfort from //; e-m ~ zusprechen to speak words of comfort to a p. — 2. F nicht recht (od. nicht wohl) bei ~e (bei Sinnen) sein not to be in one's right senses or mind.
trostbar (⸮⸮) a. ⑯ consoling.
tröstbar (⸮⸮) a. ⑯ consolable.
trost=bedürftig (⸮...) a. ⑯ in want (or need) of (words of) comfort, needing consolation; =**brief** m ⑫ consolatory letter or epistle; letter of condolence; ♀**bringend** = ♀**reich**; =**bringer** m comforter; one who soothes (or allays) grief.
trösten (⸮⸮) [ahd.: Trost] I v/a. (h) ♀2 v/refl. ⑪ 1. to console, to (give) comfort, to solace (wegen et. about a th.. concerning a th.): sich damit 2. daß // to console o.s. with the fact that //; (aufheitern) to cheer up; sich mit eitlen Hoffnungen 2 to buoy o.s. up with vain hopes; ♀Sie sich (nur)! be comforted!. take comfort!; don't be disheartened!, don't worry!; sie sind nicht zu ♀ they are inconsolable, they

won't be comforted. — 2. sich einer Sache (gen.) ♀ (zufrieden geben) to put up with (or to acquiesce in) a th. — II ~ n ⓩ 3. = Tröstung.
Tröster (⸮⸮) [ahd.] m ⑫ 1. ~**in** f ⑰ comforter; du bist ein schlechter ~ you are one of Job's comforters; theol. der ~ (der Heilige Geist) the Comforter. — 2. F: a) (urspr. wohl Gebetbuch, dann: alter Schmöker) old (or second-hand) book; b) iro. (Stock z. Prügeln) rod, cane.
tröstlich (⸮⸮) a. ⑯ consoling. consolatory, comforting; (aufheiternd, wohltuend) cheering. pleasing. pleasant.
trost=los (⸮"...) a. ⑯ disconsolate. stärker: inconsolable, despairing; (freudlos) cheerless; =**losigkeit** f ⑯ disconsolate state, despair; =**rede** f ⑫ consolatory (or comforting) speech or words pl.; ♀**reich** a. comforting. consoling, consolatory; soothing, cheering; =**schreiben** n. =**schrift** f consolatory letter; =**sprecher** m comforter; =**spruch** m comforting sentence.
Tröstung (⸮⸮) f ⑯ 1. ⚔ (das Trösten). ꝛ.: mit sanfter ~ with sweet words of comfort, with soothing speech. — 2. (Tröst. bsd. im pl. für den fehlenden pl. von Trost) consolation. comfort.
Trost=wort (⸮"...) n ⑫ word of comfort.
Trott (⸮) [it. *dtsch.] m ⓑ. trot; leichter ~ jog-trot; im ~ reiten to trot.
Trotte (⸮⸮) [ahd.] ⚔ *treten f ⑫ (Kelter) wine-press. [(Dummkopf) blockhead.)
Trottel F (⸮⸮) m ⑳ (Blödsinnige[r]) idiot;/
trotteln (⸮⸮) v/n. (sn) ⓐ a. to trudge along.
trotten (⸮⸮) v/n. (h. u. sn) ⓐ to trot.
Trottoir (tro-tā'r) [fr.] n ⓓ.(⑫) asphalt, stone. &c. pavement. Am. side-walk (= Bürgersteig).
Trotz¹ (⸮) [mhd.] m ⓐ. (o. pl.) defiance; (Halsstarrigkeit) stubbornness, obstinacy; (Widerspenstigkeit) refractoriness, waywardness; (Hochmut) haughty bearing; (Unverschämtheit) insolence; aus reinem ~ out of sheer spite. purely to spite a p.; zum ~e j-s. e-m zum ~(e) in defiance (or in spite) of a p.; dem (heftigen) Winde zum ~ in the teeth of the wind or gale; e-m ~ bieten (a. trotzbieten) to defy (or bid defiance to) a p.; dem Sturme ~ bieten to weather (or face) the storm.
trotz² (⸮) [mhd.: *Trotz¹] I prp. mit gen. u. dat. 1. (ungeachtet) despite (of), notwithstanding: in spite (or in defiance) of; ♀**dem**. ♀ alledem (und alledem) for all that, nevertheless, all the same. — 2. ♀ e-m (mit e-m um die Wette) as well (or as much) as a p.; er spielte 2 e-m Künstler ... like (or better than) an(y) artist. — II cj. 3. 2. mehr gbr. ♀**dem** (⸮⸮) although; granted that /; ♀**dem** (daß) er reich ist (even) though he be (or is) rich. despite his being rich or his wealth.
trotzen (⸮⸮) [mhd.] v/n. (h.) ⑩ 1. e-m ♀ to defy a p.. to bid a p. defiance; aller Gefahr ♀ to brave all danger; auf et. ♀ (pochen) to boast of a th.. to glory (or pride o.s.) in a th.. to presume upon a th. — 2. F (schmollen) to sulk, to be in the sulks; to mope.
Trotzer (⸮⸮) m ⑫, ~**in** f ⑰ defiant (or haughty, insolent) person.

Zeichen (s. S. XVII): F familiär; P Volkssprache; /̄ Gaunersprache; \ selten; † alt (auch gestorben); * neu (auch geboren); ⚕ unrichtig;

[trotzig] — 973 — [Trunkelbeere]

trotzig (⌣̇) [mhd.] *a.* ⑯ defiant, haughty, insolent, (anmaßend) arrogant; (eigensinnig) obstinate, (widerspenstig) refractory, wayward; 2e Haltung defiant attitude; mit 2em Mute with daring courage, with intrepid valour; e-n 2 ansehen to look at a p. disdainfully; 2lich *adv.* defiantly; daringly.

Trotz-kopf (⌣̇...) *m* ⑫ headstrong (or stubborn) person; **-köpfchen** *n* obstinate (or wayward) little thing; 2**köpfig** *a.* ⑯ headstrong, stubborn, obstinate; **-köpfigkeit** *f* stubbornness, obstinacy; **-maul** F *n* sulky person; **-wort** *n* word of defiance, defiant remark, (Herausforderung) challenge.

Troubadour (trū-ba-dū'r) [fr.] *m* ⓓ.⑤ (Minnesänger im Mittelalter) troubadour.

trüb (⌣̇). 2e (⌣̇) [ahd.: trüeben] *a.* ⑯ (ant. klar, heiter, hell) von Flüssigkeiten 2c.: turbid, troubled, muddy; thick; vom Wetter: gloomy, dark, dreary, overcast, lowering, murky; von der Stimmung: downcast, dejected, mournful, doleful, sad; von Edelsteinen 2c.: clouded, cloudy; (undurchsichtig) opaque, (matt, glanzlos) dull, tarnished; 2e Gedanken gloomy thoughts *pl.*; die Lampe brennt 2 (*adv.*) ... burns dimly, gives a dim light; 2 machen, werden (von Metallen 2c.) to tarnish; *fig.* es sieht 2 damit aus things are looking dark or desperate; i. fischen 2. [sighted.\ **trüb-äugig** (⌣̇⌣̇) *a.* ⑯ dim-eyed or\ **trübe**¹ (⌣̇) *a.* ⑯ i. trüb.

Trübe² (⌣̇) [ahd.] *f* ⑱ = Trübheit.

Trubel (⌣̇) [fr. *trouble*] *m* ㉒ turmoil, disturbance, Fhubbub; (Verwirrung) bustle, confusion, F upset; (Aufregung) excitement, commotion, (Lärm) uproar, F row.

trüben (⌣̇) [ahd.] *v.a.* und **sich 2** *v/refl.*, bisw. a. *v.n.* (h.) ⑰ § **1.** (trübe machen) to make turbid or muddy, to trouble, (umrühren) to stir up; (dunkel machen) to darken, to obscure; durch Wolken: to cloud; der Himmel trübt sich the sky is (becoming) overcast or F looks lowery; von Flüssigkeiten: sich 2 to become turbid or thick (a. *path.* vom Harn); *fig.* er sieht aus, als ob er kein Wässerchen 2 könnte he looks the picture of innocence or as if butter would not melt in his mouth. — **2.** (glanzlos machen) to make dull or dim; to dull, to tarnish. — **3.** (düster, traurig machen) to make gloomy or sad or dismal, to cast a gloom over, to sadden, (stören) to disturb, to upset; (verderben) to spoil; nichts trübt ihr Glück nothing dims (or casts a shadow on) their happiness; sich 2 to grow gloomy or dismal.

Trübheit (⌣̇⌣̇) *f* ⑯ (i. trüb) turbidness; gloom(iness), dreariness, cloudiness; opaqueness, dulness, dimness (des Wetters) dull weather, overcast (or dark) sky.

Trübsal (⌣̇⌣̇) [ahd.] *f* ⑱ (n ⓓ.) (deep) affliction, (great) trouble; (Not) distress, misery, (Drangsal) tribulation, bsd. *rel.* cross, trial; F *fig.* ~ blasen: a) (traurig sein) to mope, to be downcast or miserable; auch: to sing small; b) (im Elend sein) to be in (great) misery, F to be low down (in the world).

trübselig (⌣̇⌣̇) *a.* ⑯ [Trübsal + -ig] troubled; doleful, dismal, sad; (jammervoll) wretched, piteous, pitiful; in 2er Stimmung, oft: in the dumps; **~keit** *f* dolefulness, sadness; wretchedness.

Trüb-sinn (⌣̇...) *m* ⑫ melancholy, sadness, gloom; dejected mood, low -spirits *pl.*; 2**sinnig** *a.* ⑯ melancholy, sad, gloomy; dejected, low-spirited; **-sinnigkeit** *f* ⑯ = -sinn.

Trübung (⌣̇⌣̇) *f* ⑯ troubling, &c. (i. trüben); (trüber Zustand) turbid state, turbidity, v. Spiegeln 2c.: cloudiness.

Truchseß (⌣̇ch⌣̇) [ahd. (⌣̇ P = *dapifer*)] *m* ⑫ (ⓓa.) (ehm. Hofbeamter), jetzt etwa: Lord High Steward (of the Household), ehm.: dapifer.

Trudchen (⌣̇⌣̇) *npr n.* ㉓ z. (dim. von Gertrud) little Gertrude, F Gertie, Trudy.

Trudel (⌣̇) **I** *m* ㊵ (Dirne) loose (or fast) girl. — **II** F *f* ⑱ (kleines dickes Weib) dumpy (or stumpy) little woman.

trudeln F (⌣̇) *v/n.* (in) und *v.a.* ㉒a. to trundle, to roll.

Trüffel ♀ (⌣̇) [fr. *trufle* (↘ it. *truffe*)] *f* ⑱: echte oder eßbare ~ truffle (*Tuber cibarium*); deutsche ~ white truffle of Germany (*Choiromyces albus*); französische ~ French truffle (*Tuber melanosporum*).

Trüffel-boden (⌣̇...) *m* ⑫ truffle-soil; **-brut** *f* young truffles *pl.*; **-hund** *m* truffle-dog; **-jagd** *f* truffle-hunting, search(ing) for truffles; **-lager** *m* truffle-ground or -plot.

trüffeln (⌣̇) *v/a.* ㉒a. to season (or flavour) with truffles.

Trüffel-sucher (⌣̇⌣̇...) *m* ⑫ trufflehunter; **-zucht** *f* cultivation (or growing) of truffles.

Trug¹ (⌣̇) [mhd.: trügen] *m* ⓓc. (*pl.* ↘) deception, bsd. der Sinne: delusion, illusion; (Betrug) fraud, imposture, imposition (i. Lug¹).

trug² (⌣̇) *ind. impf.* von tragen.

Trug¹-bild (⌣̇...) *n* ⑫ airy vision, delusive picture, phantom; phantasmagoria; **-dolde** ♀ *f*: ↗ cyme.

trüge(n¹ *pl.*) (⌣̇⌣̇) *subj. impf. v.* tragen.

trügen² (⌣̇⌣̇) [+ (ahd.) triegen] **I** *v/a.*, *v/n.* (h.) und **sich 2** *v/refl.* ⓓd.: (sich) 2 to deceive (o.s.); to delude (o.s.); wenn mich meine Augen nicht 2 if my eyes do not deceive (or mislead) me; *v/n.* to prove fallacious, von Personen: to be deceitful; nicht 2 können (unfehlbar sein) to be infallible; Sprichw. der Schein trügt appearances are deceptive. — **II** ~ *n* ㉓: das Lügen und ~ lying and deceiving, falsehood and fraud.

trug¹-erfüllt (⌣̇⌣̇...) *a.* ⑯ full of deception, deceitful, artful.

trügerisch (⌣̇⌣̇⌣̇) *a.* ⑯ deceitful, deceptive, delusive, fallacious (vgl. betrügerisch); (verfänglich) captious, von Schlüssen: sophistical.

Trug¹-gebilde (⌣̇⌣̇...) *n* ㉓ **-gestalt** *f* (mocking) phantom; **-gewebe** *n* tissue of lies or falsehood; **-grund** *m* specious (or fallacious) argument, sophism.

trüglich (⌣̇⌣̇) *a.* ⑯ = trügerisch; **~keit** (⌣̇⌣̇)*f*⑯ deceitfulness, fallaciousness.

Trug-los (⌣̇...) *a.* ⑯ guileless, artless, unsophisticated; **-schluß** *m* ⑫ false conclusion, fallacy, *log.*: ↗ paralogism; 2**voll** *a.* deceptive, delusive; **-werk** *n* deception, fraud, delusion.

Truhe (⌣̇) (↗: Trog) *f* ⑱ trunk, chest, für Kleider auch: press.

Truhen-macher (⌣̇⌣̇⌣̇...) *m* ⑫ trunkmaker. [Dirne) troll.\ **Trulle** *provc.* (⌣̇) [Trudel] *f* ⑱ (lose\ **Trum** ⚔ (⌣̇) *m* ⑫ (Nebenpalatte) leader. **Trumeau** (trü-mō') [fr.] *m* (↘ n) ⓓ (*pl. a.* ~x) (Pfeilerspiegel) pier-glass.

Trumm (⌣̇) [ahd.: thrum] *m. n.* ⓓb. **1.** end (-piece); (Stumpf) stump; (Bruchstück) fragment. — **2.** ⊕ Weberei: (Saum an der Leinwand) thrum.

Trümmer (⌣̇⌣̇) [*pl. v.* Trumm] *n/pl.* (a. *sg.*; *f* ⑱, ↘ *n* ㉓) (Schutt) wreckage, ruins, (fr.) debris *pl.*; rubbish, (überbleibsel, Bruchstücke) remains, fragments *pl.*; zu ~n (oder in ~) gehen to fall (or tumble) to pieces; mein *fig.* to go to wreck and ruin; in ~ legen to lay in ruins; zu ~n schlagen to break (or smash, batter) to pieces, to wreck.

trümmer-artig (⌣̇⌣̇...) *a.* ⑯ in (or like) ruins, decayed, crumbling to pieces; fragmentary; 2**besät** *a.* covered with wreckage, strewn with debris; **-gestein** *n. min.*, *geol.* fragments of rock, rubble, ↗ breccia, conglomerate. [-artig. \ **trümmerhaft** (⌣̇⌣̇...) *a.* ⑯ = trümmer-\ **Trümmer-haufe(n)** (⌣̇⌣̇...) *m* ⑫ heap of ruins; 2**weise** *adv.* in fragments.

Trumpf (⌣̇) [(⌣̇) fr. *triomphe*] *m* ⓓb. **1.** Kartenspiel: trump(-card); was ist ~? what are trumps?; Schüppen ist ~ spades are trumps; (e-n) ~ ausspielen to lead (or play) trumps; Herz zum ~ machen to make hearts trumps, durch Umschlagen: to turn up hearts. — **2.** *fig.* der Reichtum ist ~ (das Höchste) wealth ranks foremost or is everything; j-e Trümpfe ausspielen (Vorteile benutzen) to use every advantage; einen ~ (ein derbes Wort) d(a)raufsetzen to give a smart answer, to make a stinging reply; den letzten ~ (aus)spielen to use one's last shift, *a.* to play (out) one's last trump(-card). [knave of trumps.\ **Trumpf-bube** (⌣̇⌣̇...) *m* ⑫ Kartenspiel:\ **trumpfen** (⌣̇⌣̇) *v.n.* (h.), *v/a.* ⑱ Kartenspiel: to play trumps, to trump; höher 2 to over-trump (*fig.* i. abtrumpfen 2); *fig.* auf etwas 2 (stolz sein) to pride (or pique, plume) o.s. on a th.; (darauf bestehen) to insist on a th.

Trumpf-farbe (⌣̇...) *f* Kartenspiel: trump(-suit); **-karte** *f* trump-card.

Trum-säge ⊕ (⌣̇⌣̇) *f* ⑱ *carp.* cross-cut\ **trundeln** P (⌣̇⌣̇) nordd. = trudeln. [saw.\ **Trunk** (⌣̇) [ahd.: trinkan] *m* ⓓb.**1.** draught, stärker: gulp; einen (tiefen) ~ tun to take a (deep or copious or good) draught; auf einen ~ at one draught. — **2.** (gewohnheitsmäßiges Trinken) drink (-ing), drunkenness, F boozing; dem ~ ergeben addicted (or given) to drink, of intemperate habits, F fond of one's drops; sich dem ~e ergeben to take to drink(ing) or to the bottle or F to boozing. — **3.** (Trinkgelage) drinkingbout. — **4.** (Getränk) drink, beverage; (alcoholic) liquor, F booze; vgl. Trank 2.

Trunkel-beere (⌣̇⌣̇⌣̇) *f* ⑱ bog whortleberry (*Vaccinium uliginosum*).

♩ Musik; ⚛ Wissenschaft; ⚘ Pflanze; ♁ Geographie; ⊕ Technik; ⚒ Bergbau; ⚔ Militär; ⚓ Marine; ⚖ Handel; ✉ Post; ⚒ Eisenbahn.

[trunken] — 974 — [Tugend]

trunken (⌣‿) [ahd.: drunk(en); *trinken] a. ⓖ (D 9) (ant. nüchtern) drunk, intoxicated, tipsy, fig. a. inebriate(d) (or elated) with; ℒ vor Freude exuberant with joy. [ard, tippler, F boozer.∫
Trunkenbold (⌣‿) [mhd.] m ⓖc. drunk-
Trunkenheit (⌣‿) f ⓰ drunkenness, intoxicated (or drunken, tipsy) state, fig. intoxication, inebriation.
Trunk-sucht (‵...) f ⓰ mania for drinking or tippling; ⚕ dipsomania; ⸗süchtig a. ⓖ given to drink(ing); ~e(r) s. ⓰ drunkard, ⚕ dipsomaniac.
Trupp (‵) [fr. troupe f] m ⓖ (ⓖc.) 1. troop, band, gang. — 2. hunt. = Rudel.
Trüppchen (⌣‿) n ⓰ (dim. von Trupp u. Truppe) small troop (or band).
Truppe (⌣‿) [fr. troupe] f ⓰ = Trupp 1, bfd.: a) (Gesellschaft von Schauspielern ꝛc.) troupe, travelling (or touring) company; b) ⚔ body of soldiers; ~n troops, (military) forces pl.
Truppen-aushebung ⚔ (⌣‿...) f ⓰ levy (-ing) (or raising) of troops; ⸗bewegungen f/pl. military movements or evolutions pl.; ⸗einschiffung f embarkation of troops; ⸗gattung f branch, a. arm of the service; ⸗körper m = ⸗korps, corps, body of troops; ⸗musterung f muster of troops, parade, vgl. ⸗schau; ⸗nachschub m reinforcement(s pl.); ⸗schau f (military) review; ⸗teil m = ⸗korps; ⸗transportschiff ⚓ n troop-ship, F trooper; ⸗übungs-platz m manœuvring-ground (for troops).
trupp-weise (⌣⌣‿) adv. (F a. a.) in troops or bands or gangs or flocks. [(Lota).∫
Trüsche (⌣‿) f ⓖ ichth. lote, burbot.∫
Trut-hahn (‶...) [lautm.] m ⓖ turkeycock (Melea'gris); junger ⸗ turkey-poult; rot wie ein ~ (as) red as a turkey-cock; ⸗henne f turkey-hen; ⸗hühner n/pl. turkey-fowls.
Trutz (‵) [mhd.] m ⓖa. 1. = Trotz; allen Gewalten zum ~ sich erhalten (a.) bravely to defy powers low and high. — 2. zu Schutz und ⸗ defensive(ly) and offensive(ly); Schutz- und ~bündnis n defensive and offensive
trutzen (⌣‿) ꝛc. = trotzen ꝛc. [alliance.∫
Trutz⸗lied (‵...) n ⓖ defiant song; ⸗waffen f/pl. offensive arms, weapons pl. for attack.
Tsad-see ♀ (‵‿) [afrik.] npr/m. ⓖ im Innern Nord-afrikas: Lake Tchad or Chad.
tschaha, tschahi (⌣‿) int. etwa: falderal!
Tschako ⚔ (⌣‿) [madj.] m ⓖ militärische Kopfbedeckung: shako.
Tscheche (⌣‿) n ⓖ, **Tschechin** f ⓖ, **tschechisch** a. ⓖ [slaw.] Czech; die tschechische Sprache, das Tschechisch(e) n ⓖ (der slawische Dialekt Böhmens) the Czech language, Czech.
Tscherkesse (⌣‿) n ⓖ, ...ssin f ⓖ, **tscherkessisch** a. ⓖ Circassian (= Zirkassier(in).
Tscherokese (⌣‿‿) [indian.] npr/m. ⓖ Cherokee (Indian). [pfeife) chibouk.∫
Tschibuk (‿‿) [türk.] m ⓖ (türkische Wasser-
T⸗Schiene ⊙ ♦ (t⸗‵‿) f ⓖ T-rail.
Tschifu ♀ (⌣‿) [chin.] npr/n. ⓖa. Seehafen: Chefoo.
Tschuktschen (⌣‿) m/pl. ⓖ (Volk Sibiriens) Tchuktches, Tchuktchis pl. [T-sill.∫
T⸗Schwelle ⊙ (t⸗‵‿) f ⓖ einer Zugrampe:

Tsetse-fliege (‵⌣⌣‿) f ⓖ ent. (in Süd-afrika) tsetse(-fly) (Glossi'na mo'rsitans).
Tuba ♪ (‵‿) [it.] f ⓖ (tiefstes Blasinstrument) tuba.
Tubalka-in (‿⌣‵) npr/m. ⓖⓖa. bibl. (1. Mos. 4,22) Tubal-Cain.
Tuben (‵‿) pl. von Tuba und Tubus.
Tuberkel ♀ (‿‵) [it.] f ⓖ (‿ m ⓖ) anat., zo., path. (Knötchen in Lungen ꝛc.) tubercle.
tuberkel-artig (‿‵⌣...) a. ⓖ tubercular, ...ous; ⸗bildung f ⓖ tubercul(iz)ation; ⸗krank a. tuberculous; ⸗krankheit f tuberculosis (= Tuberkulose).
Tuberkulin ⚕ (‿⌣‿‵) [it.] n ⓖd. med. (Kochsche Lymphe) tuberculin.
tuberkulös ⚕ (‿⌣‿‵) a. ⓖ (D 10) path. tuberculous, ...ose.
Tuberkulose ⚕ (‿⌣‿‵‿) f ⓖ tuberculosis, tubercular disease or consumption.
Tuberose ♀ (‿⌣‵‿) [it.] f ⓖ tuberose (Polya'nthes tubero'sa).
Tubus (‵‿) [it. Röhre] m ⓖⓖ tube, bfd. = Fernrohr.
Tuch (‵) [ahd.] n ⓖ ⓖc. 1. cloth, weitS. stuff, fabric, material (for clothing); ~ weben to weave or manufacture, make) cloth; feines (gewalktes, schweres) ~ fine (milled, heavy or stout) cloth; in der Wolle gefärbtes ~ cloth dyed in the grain or ingrain. — 2. pl. ⸗e, weniger richtig Tücher, nach Zahlwörtern inv. (Stücke Tuch) pieces of cloth; ~e (Tucharten) cloths pl. — 3. hunt. (Jagd-)Tücher toils pl. — 4. pl. Tücher: a) (Hals-..., Kopf-... ꝛc.) ~ (hand)kerchief; (Umschlage-)~ shawl, wrap, dickes, wollenes: muffler, comforter; f. die Bssgn, z.B. Hand-, Taschentuch; b) ~ zum Abwischen: duster, rubber; c) ⚓ = Segel. — 5. F zweierlei ~ soldiers, red coats pl., the army.
tuch-artig (‵ch...) a. ⓖ cloth-like; ⸗baum ⊙ m ⓖ (Tuchbereiter); ⸗bereiter m Tuchfabrikation: cloth-dresser.
Tüchelchen (‵⌣⌣) n ⓖ (dim. von Tuch) little piece of cloth, engS. small neckerchief or handkerchief.
tuchen (‵ch‿) a. ⓖ (made) of cloth.
Tuch⸗fabrik (‵ch...) f ⓖ cloth-(manu-)factory or -mill; ⸗fabrikant m cloth-manufacturer, clothier; ⸗fabrikation f cloth-manufacture; ⸗falter m cloth-lapper; ⸗färber m cloth-dyer; ⸗geschäft ✰ n = ⸗handel, ⸗handlung; ⸗halle f, etwa: cloth-workers' (or drapers') hall; ⸗handel m cloth-trade; ⸗händler m cl.-merchant, weitS. (woollen-)draper; ⸗handlung f, ⸗laden m clothier's (or woollen-draper's) shop; ⸗kleid n cloth dress; ⸗kratze f card (for cloth); ⸗kräusler m friezer; ⸗lager n cloth-warehouse; ⸗lappen m cloth rag; ⸗macher(in f) m cl.-worker or -maker or -weaver; ⸗macher-innung f company of cloth-workers; ⸗macherei f (art of) cloth-making or -weaving; ⸗manufaktur f = ⸗fabrik(ation); ⸗nadel f (Schmucknadel für Halstücher ꝛc.) breast- (or shawl-)pin; ⸗nopper m = ⸗scherer; ⸗presse f cloth-press; ⸗rahmen m cl.-frame, tenter; ⸗rasch m serge; ⸗rauher(in f) m carder; ⸗rauh-maschine f cl.-dressing machine; ⸗rest m remnant of cloth; ⸗rock m cloth

coat; ⸗schere f cl.-shears pl.; ⸗scherer m cl.-shearer; napper; ⸗schrot n = ⸗streifen; ⸗stopfer(in) s. finedrawer; ⸗streifen m list (of cloth); Schuhe aus ~ list-shoes pl.
tüchtig (⌣‿) [mhd.] a. doughty; *taugen] a. ⓖ fit, fitted, qualified, suitable (zu et. for a th.); (fähig) (cap)able, efficient; (derb, kräftig) strong, vigorous, robust; (gesund) sound, hearty; (geschickt) skilled, clever, smart; (vortrefflich) excellent (s. gehörig 4); in et. ℒ sein to be proficient in a th.; thoroughly to know (or understand) a th.; er ist ℒ in der Mathematik he is clever (or gifted, good) in mathematics; zu et. ℒ sein to be qualified (or fit, suited) for a th.; zu nichts ℒ good for nothing, useless; sich ℒ (adv.) plagen to work well or with a vengeance; ℒer Arbeiter good (stärker: splendid) worker or workman; ℒe Leistungen pl. excellent work sg., capital performances pl.; ℒer Schüler smart (or clever, hard-working) pupil; ℒ (adv.) schwitzen to perspire profusely.
Tüchtigkeit (⌣‿‿) f ⓖ (f. tüchtig) fitness, qualification, (cap)ability, capacity, efficiency, vigour; soundness, cleverness, smartness, excellency, proficiency, thoroughness; ~ zu et. fitness (or suitability) for a th.
Tuch-walker ⊙ (‵ch...) m ⓖ fuller; ⸗waren ✰ f/pl. cloths, cloth goods pl.; ⸗wäscher m cloth-cleanser; ⸗weber m = ⸗macher; ⸗weberei f = ⸗macherei.
tuck[1] (‵) [lautm.] int. ⹁! ⹁! (Lockruf für Hühner) chuck!, chuck!
Tuck[2] (‵) [mhd. Stoß] m ⓖc. = Tücke.
Tücke (⌣‿) [mhd. pl. v. Tuck] f ⓖ malice, spite; malicious craft or cunning, (hinterlistiger Streich) underhand (or mischievous, F nasty) trick; fig. ~ des Schicksals whims pl. of fortune.
tucken (⌣‿) v/n. (h.) ⓖ (glucken) to cluck.
tückisch (⌣‿), F **tücksch** (‵) a. ⓖ malicious, spiteful, crafty, cunning, underhand, von Pferden ꝛc.: vicious; ℒe Krankheit malignant disease; auf einen ℒ sein to have a spite (or a grudge) against a p.
Tuder, Tüder prov. (‵‿) [ndd.] m ⓖ (Spannstrick für weidendes Vieh) tether.
Tu-erei (‿⌣‵) [tun] f ⓖ idle doings pl.
Tuff ⚕ (‵) [it. tufo] m ⓖc. min. (poröser Stein) (calcareous) tuff, auch ⸗ tufa.
tuff-artig (‵...) a. ⓖ min. tufaceous; ⸗kalk m ⓖ calcareous tufa, tufaceous limestone, ⸗kegel m, geol. um die Öffnung e-s Vulkans: tuff-cone; ⸗stein m = Tuff.
Tüftelei F (⌣⌣‵) f ⓖ very precise (or punctilious) way of acting; (Spitzfindigkeit) subtlety, hair-splitting.
tüft(e)lig (⌣(⌣)‿) a. ⓖ most precise, very fussy.
tüfteln (⌣‿) [mhd.] v/n. (h.) ⓖa. to do things very precisely or F just so, to be very fussy.
Tugend (‵‿) [ahd.; *taugen] f ⓖ virtue; er hat keine einzige ~ he has not a single good quality; Sprichw.: die ~ findet ihren Lohn in sich selbst virtue is its own reward; aus der Not (⸗wendigkeit) eine ~ machen to make a virtue of necessity; f. Jugend 2.

Signs (see page XVII): F familiar; P vulgar; F flash; ⹁ rare; † obsolete (died); * new word (born); ‡‡ incorrect; ♪ music

[Tugendbild] — 975 — [tun]

Tugend=bild (⁻ᵕ...) n ⊛ model (or pattern, stärker: paragon) of virtue; **=bold** F m self-righteous p., sham moralist; **=bund** m, hist. (Geheimbund in Deutschland, 1808-1816), etwa: League of Virtue.

tugendhaft (⁻ᵕᵕ) a. ⊛ virtuous; **~igkeit** (⁻ᵕᵕᵕ) f ⊛ virtuousness, virtue.

Tugend=held(in f) m (⁻ᵕ...) ⊛ rigid moralist; vgl. =bold; **=lehre** f moral philosophy, morals, ethics; **=lehrer** m moralist; **=pfad** m path of virtue; **=reich** a. ⊛ rich in virtues, most virtuous; **=richter** m moralist.

tugendsam jetzt † (⁻ᵕ-) a. ⊛ virtuous.

Tugend=spiegel (⁻ᵕ-ᵕ) m ⊛ = =bild.

Tuileri-en (tü-ᵕ⁻) [fr.] f/pl. inv. die ~ (ehm. Palast in Paris) (Palace of) the Tuileries pl.

Tukan (-⁻) [brasil.] m ⊛d. orn. (Pfefferfresser) toucan, pepper-bird, preacher-bird (*Rhampha'stus*).

Tula-metall ⊛ (⁻ᵕᵕ) [Tula ♀, russ. St.] n ⊛ (Silber, Kupfer, Blei und Schwefel) Tula-metal.

tulich ꝛc. (⁻ᵕ) a. ⊛ s. tunlich ꝛc.

Tüll ⊛ (⁻) [Tulle ♀, fr. St.] m ⊛d. (⊛) tulle; (Baumwoll=)~ bobbin-net; (Wasch=) ~ net.

Tülle ⊛ (⁻ᵕ) [mhd.] f ⊛ (Hals eines Rohres) spout, nozzle; socket.

Tüll=fabrikant ⊛ (⁻ᵕ...) m ⊛ tulle-maker or -manufacturer, manufacturer of net(-lace); **=gardine** f lace-curtain; **=macher**(in f) m ⊛ tulle-worker or -weaver, maker of net(-lace); **=spitze** f point-net, net-lace.

Tulpe (⁻ᵕ) [it. *tulipa*] f ⊛ 1. ♀ tulip (*Tu'lipa*); wilde ~ wild tulip (*T. silve'stris*); Name von Schnecken und Muscheln: tulip (*Fasciola'ria, &c.*). — 2. (Art Bierglas) tulip-shaped pint-glass.

tulpen=artig ♀ (ᵕ-ᵕ...) a. ⊛ tulip-like; **=baum** ⊛ m ♀ tulip-tree (*Liliode'ndron tulipi'fera*); **=beet** n bed of tulips; **=flor** m bloom(ing) of tulips; reicher ~ (rich) profusion of tulips; **=lieb-haber** m = =züchter; **=narr** m tulipomaniac; **=narrheit** f tulipomania; **=zucht** f, hort. tulip-growing, cultivation of tulips; **=züchter** m tulip-fancier, a. tulipist; **=zwiebel** ♀ f tulip-bulb.

...tum (...⁻) [:...dom] n, m ⊛d. Anhängesilbe, dient zur Bildung von s. aus nouns, verbs u. adjectives, z.B.: Königtum n kingdom zu König; Wachstum n growth zu wachsen; Eigentum n property zu eigen; Reichtum m riches zu reich.

tumm(e)lig (⁻(ᵕ)ᵕ) a. ⊛ = taum(e)lig.

tummeln (⁻ᵕ) [ahd.: taumeln] ⊛a.
I v/a. to turn in a circle, to wheel (round), weits. to put in motion, to set going; (antreiben) to drive, to stir, F to keep on the move; ein Pferd ~ to work (or exercise) ... (well). —
II sich ~ v/refl. to bestir o.s., to move (or bustle) about, F to keep on the go or move; (sich beeilen) to hurry (along), to make haste, to speed (or race, run, rush) along, bei der Arbeit: to buckle to; tummelt euch! be quick!, look sharp!, F u. P buck up!

Tummel=platz (⁻ᵕ...) m ⊛ a) für Pferde: riding-school; b) ♀ Ringen ꝛc. wrestling-place, (Spielplatz) playground; (Kampf-) platz) lists pl., arena; battle-ground, scene of action; c) bsd. ⚓ (Sammelplatz) rendezvous; **=taube** f = Tümmler.

Tummler (⁻ᵕ) m ⊛ 1. (Rosse=)~ rider who exercises a horse. — 2. zo. meist **Tümmler**: a) orn. tumbler(-pigeon) (*Colu'mba li'via gyra'trix*); b) Art Delphin: porpoise, dolphin. — 3. ⊛ Weberei: warp-staff.   [nant) pool, puddle.

Tümpel (⁻ᵕ)[ndd.: dimple] m ⊛ (stag-|

Tumult (ᵕ⁻) [it.] m ⊛b.(Getümmel) tumult, disturbance, uproar, row;(Aufruhr)riot.

Tumultuant (ᵕᵕᵕ⁻) m ⊛ rioter.

tumultuarisch (ᵕᵕᵕ⁻ᵕ) a. ⊛ (lärmend) tumultuous, uproarious, riotous.

tumultuieren (ᵕᵕᵕ⁻ᵕ) v/n.(h.) ⊛ to raise a tumult or disturbance, to (cause a) riot; F to kick up a row or shindy.

tumult=voll (ᵕ⁻,f.) a. = tumultuarisch.

tun (⁻) [ahd: do] I v/a., v/n. (h.), bisw. v/refl. ⊛ to do, to make, (ausführen) to perform, to effect; (ant. leiden) to act.
1. mit neutralem pron. ob. a. als Objekt: ich habe es getan I have done it; er kann nichts Besseres ~ he cannot do (anything) better; das können Sie ~ (auch) lassen you may do or not do it (just as you like), you may (either) do it or leave it (just as you please); das ist so gut wie getan it's as good as done; das läßt sich (nicht) ~ that's (not) practicable or feasible; das will getan sein that wants doing, it requires care or skill; das Seinige ~ to do one's best or utmost; was läßt sich da ~? what's to be done?; was man auch ~ mag whatever one may do; was soll ich ~? what am I to do?; ~ Sie was wollen! do as you like!; please yourself!; des Guten zu viel ~ to go too far; vgl. gut 11 gegen Ende und Leid² 1; e-m et. zuliebe ~ to do a th. to please a p.; e-m et. zum Possen ~ to do a th. to spite a p. — 2. mit nouns als Objekt in stehenden Verbindungen: s. Abbitte, Abbruch 4, Bescheid 4; eine Bitte ~ to make a request; eine Bitte an e-n ~ to beg of (förmlicher: to petition) a p.; tiefe Blicke in et. ~ to look well (or to gain a deep insight) into a th.; s. Buße 1; einen Eid(schwur) ~ to take an oath; s. Einspruch, erwähnen II, Fall¹ 1, Fürbitte a, Fußfall, Gefalle(n), Genüge 2, Griff 1 u. 4; e-m Gutes ~ to act kindly to a p., to confer (or bestow) a benefit upon a p.; s. Liebe 3; e-m Schaden ~ to do a p. injury or harm; einen Schluck,Zug ~ to take a draught; s. Schritt 3; seine Schuldigkeit ~ to do one's duty; s. Schuß 3; einen Spruch ~ to pronounce judgment; e-n Sprung ~ to (take a) leap; e-m unrecht ~ to do a p. wrong, to inflict an injustice upon a p.; s. Verzicht, Vorschub 2; Wunder ~ to do wonders. — 3. mit a. u. adv. (so und so berühren): das tut einem wohl that does one good; s. gemutigt, gleichtun, gütlich 2, fundtun, leid¹, not 6c. nötig 2. — 4. a) (arbeiten) nichts ~ to do nothing, to idle away one's time; (viel) zu ~ haben to find (or to have) plenty to do, to be (very) busy; alle Hände voll zu ~ h. to have one's hands full; ich habe et. anderes zu ~ I have other business (to attend to) or F other fish to fry; es ist viel zu ~ there is a great deal to do or to be done; ⊛ haben Sie viel zu ~? are you very busy?, are you doing much (business)?; b) (handeln) Sie haben recht getan, daß Sie gekommen sind you have done right (or acted wisely) in coming; nichts ~ als trinken to do nothing but drink; sie ~ nichts als schreien, a. they are for ever bawling; e-m wohl ~ to do good (or to be kind) to a p.; Sprichw.: tue recht und scheue niemand do right and fear no one; was Gott tut, das ist wohlgetan God's works are good works; c) (wirken) Wasser tut es nicht water won't do it or is not sufficient(ly strong); es täte gut, wenn // it would do good if //. — 5. mit abhängigem inf.: a) e-m et. zu wissen (kund) ~ to give notice of a th. to a p., to inform a p. of a th.; b) pleonastisch (impf. ind. oft: tät): laufen ~ sie schon, aber // they do run, but //; verwöhnen ~ sie mich wahrhaftig nicht they are not spoiling me; indeed, they are not; ich tät das Reisen wählen I did go on my travels. — 6. (sich [ver]stellen): a) sie ~ (taten) so, als ob sie uns nicht sähen they pretend(ed) not to see us; ~ Sie, als wenn Sie zu Hause wären! make yourself (von mehreren: yourselves) quite at home!; b) meist mit prädikativem a.: betrübt ~ to sham grief, to assume a sorrowful air or look; s. dicktun, bes. Artikel; fromm ~ to play the saint; ~ groß-tun, bsd. Artikel; mit einer Dame schön ~ to flirt with ...; spröde ~ to be prudish or squeamish; er tut nur so he only pretends or shams; ~ Sie doch nicht so! don't sham (F put on) so!, don't make so much fuss! — 7. mit Ortsangabe: tut das Brot dorthin! put (or lay) ... (down) there!; sie tat es auf den Schrank she put (or placed) it on the cupboard; et. aus dem Sack (heraus=, fort=, weg=)~ to take (or pull) a th. out of the sack; et. beiseite ~ to put a th. aside; et. in die Tasche ~ to put a th. into one's pocket; e-n in die Schule ~ to send a p. to school; et. von sich ~ to remove (or get rid of) a th.; s. hintun. — 8. mit sachlichem Subjekt: viel (wenig) ~ (bedeuten) to matter (or signify) much (little), to be of great (small) consequence; (das) tut nichts that's of no consequence; eine Entschuldigung zurückweisend: don't mention it, it does not matter; was tut das (dir)? what does it matter (to you)? — 9. e-m et. ~ (zuleide ~): was hat er dir getan? what (harm) has he done to you?; warum hat er uns das getan? why has he done (or wrought) us such wrong?; das tut ihm nichts that does not (F won't) hurt him. — 10. etwas dazu od. zur Sache (diese Förderndes) ~ to put one's hand to a th. or one's shoulder to the wheel; ich kann nichts dazu ~ I can do nothing in the matter; was läßt sich (dabei) ~?

⚕ scientific; ♀ botanical; ⊕ geography; ⊛ machinery; ⚒ mining; ⚔ military; ⚓ marine; ⊛ commercial; ⊛ postal; 🚂 railway.

[Tünche] — 976 — [türmen]

what can be done (in it)? — **11.** du wirst es mit ihm zu 2 (zu schaffen) bekommen you will have to deal with him or F have him down on you; er wird es mit der Polizei zu 2 bekommen he will have trouble with the police; (nichts) mit e-m zu 2 h. to have (no) business (or dealings) with a man; jetzt haben wir mit=ea. zu 2 now we may settle our business; das hat mit dem Früheren nichts zu 2 that's in no way connected with what preceded; ich will mit ihm, der Sache nichts mehr zu 2 h. I will have nothing more to do with him, with it. — **12.** a) es (oder die Sache) ist damit getan (fertig) that finishes it, there the matter ends; damit ist es noch nicht getan that won't do yet; b) es ist mir sehr darum zu 2 (kommt mir darauf an) it is of great consequence to me, I attach great importance to it; es ist ihm nur um das Geld zu 2 he only cares (or troubles) about the money; es war ihnen um nichts anderes zu 2 als // they had no other object in view but //. — **13.** ein vorangegangenes v. vertretend, mst mit es oder das: er kocht besser, als sie es je getan he cooks better than she ever did; wer soll spielen, wenn du es nicht tust! who is to play if you don't! — **14.** v/refl. das tut sich auch so it can be done that way. — **II Tun** n 23 **15.** doing(s pl.), dealing(s pl.); proceeding(s pl.); (Aufführung) conduct, behaviour, (Benehmen) way of acting; s. lassen IV; Sprichw. Sagen und Tun ist zweierlei saying and doing (or performing) are two (different) things.

Tünche (⸗⸗) [ahd.; *lt. tu′nica] f 🌐 **1.** ⊙ Maurerei: a) (Anstrich mit Kalk- oder Erdfarben) lime-wash(ing), whitewash (-ing); b) = Tünchfarbe. — **2.** fig. (äußerer Anstrich) (outside) varnish.

tünchen ⊙ (⸗⸗) [ahd. s. Tünche] v/a. 🌐 Bauwesen: to lime-wash, mit Leimfarbe: to distemper, colour; (weißen) to whitewash; (mit Putz bewerfen) to parget.

Tüncher (⸗⸗) m 22 whitewasher; (Anstreicher) (house-)painter.

Tüncherei (⸗⸗) f 46 = Tünche 1a.

Tünch-farbe ⊙ (⸗...) f 62 lime-wash, colouring, weiße: whitewash; =pinsel m brush for colouring or whitewashing; =schicht f coat(ing) of whitewash; =werk n colouring; whitewash(ing).

Tung-ste(i)n (⸗⸗) m 3c. min. tungsten; ~säure f 46 chm. = Wolframsäure.

Tunguse (⸗⸗⸗) m 4. **Tungusin** f 46 Nomade in Ostsibirien: Tungus(ian).

tungusisch (⸗) a. 46 Tungusic, ...lär:

Tu-nicht-gut (⸗⸗⸗) m 3c. (pl. a. ~ inv.) ne'er-do-well (s. a. Taugenichts).

Tunika (⸗⸗⸗) [lt.] f 46 (5) röm. Alt. (Untergewand) tunic.

Tunke (⸗⸗) [tunken] f 46 **1.** Kocht.: sauce; (Fleischsaft) gravy. — **2.** ⊙ (das Eintunken) dipping.

tunken (⸗⸗) [ahd.] v a. 88 to dip, (einweichen) to steep, to soak.

Tunk-näpfchen (⸗...) n 62, =schale f sauce-boat, gravy-dish.

tu(n)lich (⸗⸗) [nhd.] a. 66 feasible, (ausführbar) practicable; (möglich) possible; (angemessen) expedient, opportune, convenient, suitable.

Tu(n)lichkeit (⸗⸗⸗) f 46 feasibility, practicability; expediency; um die ~ zu beweisen, auch: to prove that it is feasible or that it can be done.

Tunnel ⚐ (⸗⸗) m 30, a. 22 (unterirdischer gemauerter Gang unter e-r Straße rc.) tunnel, subway; s. bohren 1.

Tunnel-anlage (⸗⸗...) f 62 ⊙ u. 🚇 construction of tunnels, tunnel-making, tunnelling; =bahn 🚇 f (Untergrundbahn in Lo. rc.) tube; =bau m = =anlage.

tunnel(is)ieren (⸗⸗(⸗)⸗⸗) v/n. (h.) u. v/a. 88 to drive (or cut) a tunnel, to tunnel.

Tupf (⸗) [nhd.] m @b. dot, spot.

Tupf-bällchen ⊙ (⸗...) n 62, =ballen m, typ. printer's ball, dabber.

Tüpfchen (⸗⸗) n 23 dim. v. Tupf(en).

Tüpfel (⸗⸗)[nhd. a: dapple: dim. zu Tupf] m, n 22 point, dot, tittle; (kleiner Fleck) little spot or speck; dim. das **~chen** auf dem i the dot on the i; fig. etwas bis aufs ~chen (kleinste) wissen to know the minutest details of a th.

Tüpfel-farn ⚐ (⸗⸗⸗) m 62 polypody (Polypo′dium). |speckled, full of spots.|

tüpf(e)lig (⸗⸗) a. 66 = tüpfeln II, a.|

tüpfeln (⸗⸗) I v/a. 22a. (pünktlen) to dot; to punctuate. — **II ge-tüpfelt** p.p. u. a. 66 dotted, spotted, marked with.

Tupfen¹ (⸗⸗) m 23 = Tupf. [spots.]

tupfen² (⸗⸗)[ahd.:dab]v.a.88 **1.** (a. **tüpfen**) to touch lightly (with the tip of one's finger); eine Wunde mit einem Läppchen 2 to dab ... with a linen rag. — **2.** (mit farbigen Flecken versehen) to spot, to mark with spots or specks. — **3.** ⊙ = tüpfeln 2.

Tür (⸗) [ahd.: door] f 46 **1.** ~ eines Hauses, Zimmers rc.: door, eines Wagens: carriage-door; oft = Haustür; vor der ~ outside (the door); s. aufmachen 1, begleiten 2, öffnen I; fig. sich nach der ~ umsehen to try to escape; einem die ~ weisen ob. zeigen to show a p. the door; die ~ hinter e-m zumachen to shut the door behind (or after) a p.; s. Nase 3 am Ende. — **2.** fig. s. Angel¹ 1, fallen 4, kehren¹, öffnen I, Stuhl 2; vor der ~ sein (bevorstehen) to be (near or close) at hand, to be fast approaching or coming on. — **3.** F ein paar ~en (Häuser) von hier a few doors from here.

Tür-angel (⸗⸗⸗⸗) f 46 door-hinge.

Turani-er (⸗⸗(⸗)⸗) m 22. ~in f 46, **turanisch** (⸗⸗⸗) a. 66 Turanian.

Turban (⸗⸗) [ar. dulband] m 3d. (5) turban; e-n ~ tragend turbaned.

Tür-band (⸗⸗⸗) n 62 iron work of a door.

Turban-tuch (⸗⸗⸗⸗) n 62 turban-cloth.

Tür-beschläge ⊙ (⸗⸗⸗⸗⸗) m pl. 22 mountings pl. of a door.

Turbine (⸗⸗⸗) [lt.] f 46 mach. turbine, horizontal water-wheel; ~ndampfer ↓ m 22 turbine steamer.

Türchen (⸗⸗) n 23 (dim. von Tür) door, in größerem Sinne: wicket.

Türe (⸗⸗) f 46 = Tür.

Tür-einfassung ⊙ (⸗⸗⸗⸗) f 62 door-case; vgl. =rahmen; =falze f door-folding; =feder f door-spring; =feld n panel of

a door, d.-panel; =fenster n window in a door, über der Tür: fan-light; =flucht f space for a door to swing in; =flügel m leaf of a (folding-)door; =füllung f door-panel; =gerüst n = =rahmen; =gewände n d.-jamb; =gewicht n (das die Tür zuschlägt) weight attached to a d.; =griff m d.-handle, knob of a door; =hammer m knocker; =hüter(in f) m doorkeeper('s wife), Am. ob. co. (It.) janitor, f janitress; vgl. Türsteher.

Türke (⸗⸗) m 44, **Türkin** f 46 [it. turco] Turk(ish woman f); ehm. der ~ (Herrscher der ~n) the Grand Turk.

Türkei ⚐ (⸗⸗) [it. Turchi′a] npr/f. 46 die ~ Turkey. the Turkish empire.

Türken-bund (⸗⸗...) m 62 turban; =bund-lilie ⚐ f Turk's-cap, martagon(-lily) (Li′lium Ma′rtagon); =glaube m Mohammedan faith; =krieg m war with (or against) the Turks; =säbel m (Turkish) scimitar; =sattel m Turkish saddle.

Türkentum (⸗⸗⸗) n ⚐d. **1.** Turkish manners or ways pl.; auch = Türkenglaube. — **2.** (all) the Turks pl., the Moslem world.

Türken-zug (⸗⸗⸗) m 62 hist. expedition against the Turks.

Turkestan (⸗⸗⸗) = Turkistan.

Tür-kette (⸗⸗⸗) f 46 chain of a door.

Türkis (⸗⸗) [it. türkisch] m @a. min. (meist hellblauer Stein) turquoise.

türkisch (⸗⸗) a. 66 Turkish; 🚇 2e Erde Turkey earth; 2e Teppiche Turkey carpets pl.; ⚐ 2er Weizen (Mais) maize, Indian corn.

türkisch-ägyptisch (⸗⸗...) a. 66 Turco-Egyptian; =blau n 66 Turkey-blue; =rot n Turkey-red; =rot-färberei ⊙ f Turkey-red dyeing.

Turkistan ⚐ (⸗⸗⸗, weniger richtig ⸗⸗⸗) npr. 30 Land in Inner-asien: Turkestan.

Tür-klinke (⸗⸗⸗) f 46 door-latch; =klopfer m knocker (of a door).

Turkmene (⸗⸗⸗) m 44, **Turkmenin** f 46 Turcoman: **Turkmenen-land** n ⚐ in Inner-asien: Turcomania.

Turko ⚔ (⸗⸗) m 30 (fr. Soldat aus Algerien) Turco.

Tür-kontakt (⸗⸗⸗) m 22 elect. electric (burglar-)alarm.

Turm (⸗) [mhd.: tower; *fr.] m @b. **1.** tower (auch fig. et Startes, Gewaltiges; s. Babel), e-r Burg: keep; (Kirch=) steeple; ↓ (Kommando=)~ e-s Kriegsschiffes conning tower; drehbarer ~ revolving turret. — **2.** (Gefängnis) prison, jail, (Kerker) dungeon. — **3.** Schach: castle, rook.

Turmalin ⚐ (⸗⸗⸗) m @d. min. turmaline: roter: rubellite; schwarzer: schorl.

turm-artig (⸗⸗⸗) a. 66 tower-like.

Tür-matte (⸗⸗⸗) f 46 door-mat.

Turm-bau (⸗⸗) m 22 building (or construction) of a tower.

Türmchen (⸗⸗) n 23 (dim. v. Turm) arch. little tower, turret, (Turmspitze) spire.

Turm-drehmaschine (⸗⸗⸗⸗⸗⸗) f 62 turret-revolving engine.

türmen (⸗⸗) [Turm] 88 **I** v a. to pile (or raise) up (to the sky). — **II** v/n. (h.) u. sich 2 v/refl. to (stand like a) tower, to rise to a lofty height or

---

Zeichen (s. S. XVII): F familiär; P Volkssprache; ⸗ Gaunersprache; ⸗ selten; † alt (auch gestorben); * neu (auch geboren); ⸗ unrichtig;

[Türmer] — 977 — [Tyrus]

eminence. — **III ge-türmt** *p.p. u. a.* ⊕ towered, turreted; (gebäuft) piled up, heaped up, in a heap, in heaps.
Türmer (⌣⌣) *m* ㉒ keeper (or warder, watchman) of a tower or keep.
Turm-fahne (⌣'⌣⌣) *f* ㊷ vane; **=falk(e)** *m. orn.* krestel (*Falco tinnu'nculus*); **förmig** *a.* ⊕ tower- (or steeple-)like; **=geschütz** ⚔ ↓ *n* turret-gun; **hoch** *a.* (as) high as a tower, steeple-high, *fig.* very high or lofty; **=hüter** *m*: a) keeper (or warder) of a tower; b) jailer.
...türmig (...'⌣⌣) [Turm] *a.* ⊕: zwei= with two towers or steeples.
Turm-knopf (⌣'⌣⌣) *m* ㊷ knob on (the top of) a steeple; pommel of a steeple; **=schiff** ↓ *n* turret-ship. ehm. monitor; **=schwalbe** *f.* **=segler** *m. orn.* (black) swift (*Cypselus apus*); **=spitze** *f* top of a steeple; *auch:* spire; **=uhr** *f* turret-clock. an einer Kirche: church-clock; **=verlies** *n* dungeon. ehm. einer Burg: keep; **=wächter** *m.* **=wart** *m* = Türmer; **=zinne** *f* battlement of a tower.
Tür-nagel ("⌣⌣) *m* ㊷ door-nail.
Turn-anstalt (⌣'⌣⌣) *f* ㊷ school for gymnastics; *vgl.* **=halle**.
turnen (⌣⌣) [nhd. (*JAHN*) aus turnieren] **I** *v/n.* (h.) ⊛ to do (or practise) gymnastics, to go through (a course of) gymnastic exercises. — **II ∼** *n* ㉓ gymnastics, gymnastic exercises *pl.*, für Mädchen: callisthenics; (Kampfspiele) athletic games or sports *pl.*, gymnastic display.
Turner (⌣⌣) *m* ㉒, **∼in** *f* ㊼ gymnast, *oft:* lady gymnast; **∼ei** (⌣⌣'⌣) *f* ㊻ = turnen II; **=isch** (⌣⌣) *a.* ㊿ gymnastic(al). weitS. athletic; **∼schaft** *f* ㊻ body (or society) of gymnasts.
Turn-fahrt (⌣'⌣⌣) *f* ㊷ march (or excursion) of gymnasts; **=fest** *n* gymnastic fête or display, in Engl. oft: athletic sports *pl.*; **=gerät** *n* gymnastic apparatus; **=halle** *f* gymnasium, gymnastic hall.
Turnier ehm. (⌣'⌣) [mhd.; *fr. tournoi*] *n* ⑲d. tournament, tourney, bsd. z. Übung: tilting, j(o)usting.
Turnier-bahn (⌣'⌣'⌣) *f* ㊷ tilt-yard; **=dank** *m* prize (awarded) in a tournament.
turnieren (⌣'⌣) [mhd.; *fr. tourner*] *v/n.* (h.) ⑬ to tilt, to j(o)ust, to hold (or to take part in) a tournament.
Turnier-fähig (⌣'⌣⌣) *a.* ㊿ qualified for (admission to) a tournament; **=helm** *m* ㊷ j(o)usting-helmet; **=lanze** *f* tilting-lance; **mäßig** *a.* ㊿ according to the rules of tilting; **=pferd** *n* j(o)uster; **=platz** *m* tilting-place; lists *pl.*; *vgl.* **=bahn**; **=rennen** *n* tilting (match); **=rüstung** *f* tilting-armour; **=schild** *m* tilting-shield; **=schranken** *f/pl.* lists *pl.*
Turn-kleidung (⌣'⌣⌣) *f* ㊷ gymnast's dress; **=kunst** *f* gymnastics. für Mädchen: callisthenics; **=lehrer(in** *f*) *m* teacher (or instructor) of gymnastics or callisthenics; **=platz** *m* open-air gymnasium, athletic grounds *pl.*;

=riege *f* squad of gymnasts; **=saal** *m* gymnasium (= =halle); **=stunde** *f* lesson in gymnastics; **=übung** *f* gymnastic (or athletic) exercise; **=unterricht** *m* instruction in gymnastics.
Turnüre (⌣'⌣) [*fr. tournure*] *f* ㊷ **1.** (gewandtes Benehmen) elegant (or F society) manners *pl.*, F good form. — **2.** (Kleiderwulst) dress-improver, bustle.
Turnus (⌣⌣) [mlt.] *m* ⑯ (Reihenfolge) turn, rotation; weitS. succession.
Turn-vater (⌣'⌣⌣) *m* ㊷ (Friedrich Ludwig Jahn) Founder of (German) gymnastics; **=verein** *m* gymnastic society or club; **=wart** *m* leading gymnast, leader of a squad; **=wesen** *n* gymnastics, weitS. athletics; **=zeug** *n* = **=gerät** u. **=kleidung**.
Tür-pfosten (⌣'⌣⌣) *m* ㊷ door-post; **=platte** *f* finger-plate; **=rahmen** *m* door-frame, frame of a door; **=riegel** *m* bolt, ring of a door; **=ritz(e)** *f* *m* chink (or crack) in a door; **=schelle** *f* house-bell; **=schild** *n* mit Namen: door-plate, aus Messing: brass plate; **=schließer** *m* doorkeeper. *vgl.* **=hüter**; **=schloß** *n.* **=schlüssel** *m* lock, key of a door; **=schnäpper** 🚂 *m* an Güterwagen: doorpin; **=schwelle** *f* threshold (of a door), door-sill; **=steher** *m* porter. in Gerichten &c.: usher; *vgl.* **=hüter**; **=stock** *m* post of a door. ⚔ prop. stanchion, upright; **=stück** *n* painting over a door; **=sturz** *m* door-lintel or -head.
Turtel-taube (⌣'⌣⌣) [ahd.. *lt.*] *f* ㊷ (turtle-)dove (*Turtur*); junge ∼, *dim.* **=täubchen** *n* young (turtle-)dove.
Tür-verkleidung ⊙ (⌣'⌣⌣⌣) *f* ㊷ door-dressings *pl.*; **=vorhang** *m* door-curtain; **=wächter,** **=wärter** *m* = **=hüter**.
Tusch¹ ♪ (⌣) [bayr. "Stoß"] *m* ⑬a. flourish of trumpets; einen ∼ blasen to sound a flourish (of trumpets).
Tusch² (⌣) [*fr. touche(r)* berühre(n)] *m* ⑬a. burschikos: (slight) affront provoking a (challenge to a) duel.
tusch³ (⌣) *int.* ∼! (=ft!(b) ftill!) tush!, hush!
Tusch⁴=**blau** (⌣'⌣) *n* ㊷ water-colour blue.
Tusche (⌣⌣) [tuschen¹] *f* ㊻: (schwarze od. chinesische) ∼ Indian ink, China-ink; Stück ∼ cake of Indian ink.
tuscheln F (⌣⌣) [tuschen²] *v/n.* (h.) u. v/a. ㊼a. to whisper (softly).
tuschen¹ (⌣⌣) [(≠+) *fr. toucher*] *v/a.* u. v/n. (h.) ⑪ *paint.* to draw (or outline, sketch) in Indian ink; to wash; getuschte Zeichnung = Tuschzeichnung.
tuschen², *a.* **tüschen** (⌣⌣) [tusch³] *v/a.* ㊶ (beschwichtigen) to hush, to quiet, e-n Aufruhr ♀ to quell (or suppress) a rising, to smother a rebellion;
Tusch-farbe (⌣'⌣⌣) *f* ㊷ water-colour.
tuschieren (⌣'⌣) [*fr.; f. Tusch²*] *v/a.* ㊶ **1.** (berühren) to touch. — **2.** burschikos: (beleidigen) to affront, to insult.
Tusch⁴=**kasten** (⌣'⌣⌣) *m* ㊷ paint- (or colour-) box; **=manier** *f* aquatint(a); **=napf** *m* saucer (for painting); **=pinsel** *m* ink-brush; **=zeichnung** *f* sketch in Indian ink, China-ink drawing.

Tütchen (⌣⌣) *n* ㉓ dim. von Tüte (f. ds).
∼=dreher, **∼=krämer** *m* ㊷ small shopkeeper or tradesman, retail dealer.
Tute (⌣⌣) *f* ㊻ **1.** ∼ = Tuthorn. — **2.** = Tüte.
Tüte (⌣⌣) *f* ㊻ paper-bag, gedrehte: screw.
Tutel (⌣⌣) [lt.] *f* ㊻ *jur.* guardianship.
tuten F (⌣⌣) [lautm.] *v/n.* (h.) u. v/a. ⑧⑨ to tootle on a horn or trumpet.
Tüten-fabrikation ⊙ (⌣'⌣⌣) *f* ㊷ manufacture of paper bags. [horn.]
Tut-horn ("⌣⌣) *n* ②c. watchman's (long)
Tüttel (⌣⌣) [nbd.] *m* (*n*) ㊷, **∼chen** (⌣⌣) *n* little dot, tittle, jot; *fig.* kein ∼chen not the least bit, not a scrap, not a jot.
Typ bid. ↓ (⌣) *m* ⑬c. = Typus.
Type ⊙ (⌣⌣) [*fr., *grch.*] *f* ㊽ *typ.* type (for printing), printing-letter.
Typen-druck ⊙ (⌣'⌣⌣) *m* ㊷ type- (or letter-) printing; **=druck-telegraph** *m, tel.* printing- (or type-setting) telegraph; **haft** (⌣⌣) *a.* ㊿ = typisch; **=hebel** *m* der Schreibmaschine: type-lever; **=metall** *n* type-metal; **=rad** *n* am Hughes-apparat: type-wheel; **=setzmaschine** *f* type-setting machine.
typhös (-⌣⌣) [grch.] *a.* ㊿ (D 10) *path.* (typhusartig) typhoid, typhous.
Typhus ♂ (⌣⌣) [grch.] *m* ⑯ ㊷ *path.*: a) (der meist epidemisch auftretende Fleck=2) typhus, camp- (or hospital-)fever, ⚔ petechial fever; b) (der meist endemisch auftretende Unterleibs=2, früher meist: Nervenfieber) typhoid fever.
typhus-artig ("⌣'⌣⌣) *a.* ㊿ *path.* typhoid, typhous; **=fieber** *n* ㊷ = Typhus; **=kranke(r)** *s.* patient suffering from typhus or typhoid fever.
typisch (⌣⌣) [grch.] *a.* ㊿ typical.
Typograph ⊙ (-⌣⌣) [grch.] *m* ㊷ (Schriftsetzer) typographer, F typo; **∼ie** (-⌣⌣'⌣) *f* ㊸ typography; **=isch** (-⌣⌣'⌣) *a.* ㊿ typographical.
Typus (⌣⌣) [grch.] *m* ⑰ (Vorbild) type.
Tyrann (-⌣) [grch. Alleinherrscher] *m* ㊷ **1.** Alt.: tyrant, king, zB. Ödipus ∼us oder der ∼ King Œdipus. — **2.** *fig.* (Gewaltherrscher) tyrant, despot.
Tyrannei (-⌣⌣') [grch.] *f* ㊻ tyranny.
Tyrannen-herrschaft (-⌣'⌣⌣) *f* ㊷ tyrant's rule, tyranny; **=joch** *n* tyrant's yoke, yoke of despotism; **=laune** *f* tyrant's whim or caprice; **=mord** *m* murder of a tyrant, tyrannicide.
tyrannisch (-⌣⌣) [grch.] *a.* ㊿ tyrannical, despotic; (herrschsüchtig) domineering;
tyrannisieren (-⌣⌣'⌣) *v/a.* ⑬ to tyrannize (over), to domineer over, *abs.* to rule tyrannically, to act the tyrant or the despot.
Tyri-er (⌣'⌣) [Tyrus] *m* ㉒, **∼in** *f* ㊼. **tyrisch** (⌣⌣) *a.* ㊿ Tyrian, of Tyre.
tyrrhenisch ♀ (⌣⌣⌣) *a.* ㊿ Alt.: (etruskisch) Tyrrhenian; ∼es Meer Tyrrhenian Sea.
tyrtä-isch (⌣'⌣⌣) [Tyrtä'us, grch. Kriegslieder-dichter 7. sae. vor Chr.] *a.* ㊿ Tyrtæan, of Tyrtæus.
Tyrus ♀ (⌣⌣) npr/n. inv., Alt.: (Hauptstadt Phöniziens) Tyre.

U

U, u (¹) *n, inv.* Buchstabe: U, u; *fig.* e-m ein X für ein U machen [x = 10 für v = 5 anschreiben] to deceive (or cheat, swindle) a p.
U *chm.* Symbol für Uranium.
u. *abbr.* = und and.
u. a. *abbr.* = und andere(s), unter anderm, unter andern among others or other things, among the rest.
u. ä. *abbr.* = und ähnliche(s) and the like, and such like.
u. a. m. *abbr.* = und andere(s) mehr and others besides.
U. A. w. g. *abbr.* = Um Antwort wird gebeten (s. Antwort 1).
übel¹ (¹⁻) [ahd.: evil: über] *a.* (D9) 1. evil, bad, *comp.* worse, *adv.* ill, badly, *comp.* worse; aus 2 ärger w. to go from bad to worse; j-s übles Aussehen a p.'s sickly look or appearance; übler Laune sein ... in a bad (or cross) humour; einem einen üblen Streich spielen to do a p. an ill turn, to play (or serve) a p. a nasty trick; von übler Vorbedeutung foreboding evil, inauspicious. — 2. mit *verbs*: 2 angebracht ill-timed, out of place, out of season; f. ankommen 3, anschreiben 2; et. 2 aufnehmen to take a th. amiss; f. auslegen 2; 2 aussehen to look ill; es sieht 2 mit ihm aus he is in a bad way; sich 2 befinden to be in ill (or bad, poor) health; es ist ihm 2 bekommen he had to suffer (or to pay) for it, gesundheitlich: it did not agree with him; 2 beraten ill-advised; 2 von einem denken to think ill of a p.; f. deuten 5, ergehen 5, übelgesinnt, mitspielen; f. übelnehmen; 2 riechen (schmecken) to have an unpleasant smell (taste), to smell (to taste) nasty; 2 daran sein to be badly off; mir ist 2 I feel sick or unwell; auf einen 2 zu sprechen sein to have nothing good to say of a p.; f. übeltun; dabei kann einem 2 werden it could (or is enough to) make one sick; f. übelwollen. — 3. wohl oder übel (ob gern oder ungern) whether willing or not (willing). — 4. mit *neg.*: nicht 2 not bad, moderately (or pretty, tolerably) good; das Pferd ist (oder gefällt mir) nicht 2 I don't dislike ..., F ... is not half bad; das wäre nicht 2 it would not be bad or amiss, I should not mind it; das klingt nicht übel that sounds pretty good or favourable; kein übler Bissen not a bad (or rather a nice) morsel; nicht 2 Lust zu et. haben to have a great mind (or to be more than half inclined) to do a th.; er ist kein übler Mensch he is not a bad sort (of fellow). — 5. als *s/n.*: e-m Übles gönnen oder 2(:)wollen to wish a p. ill, to be pleased at a p.'s misfortune(s); Übles von e-m reden to talk badly (or ill) of a p.. F to run a p. down; er hat mir viel Übles getan he has done me great harm or injury; es ist vom ~ it is based on evil.

Übel² (¹⁻) [ahd.: *übel¹] *n* evil, ill; (Leiden) complaint; malady; *bibl.* erlöse uns von dem ~ deliver us from evil.

Übel¹-befinden (²⁻...) *n* indisposition, engS. sickly feeling; 2gelaunt *a.* ill-humoured, in bad humour; ill-tempered, in bad (or out of) temper; cross, sulky; =gelauntheit *f* ill (or cross) humour or temper, sulkiness; 2gesinnt *a.* evil-minded.

Übelkeit (¹⁻⁻) *f* sickly feeling, sickliness, nausea, qualmishness; ~ empfinden to feel sick(ly) or qualmish.

Übel¹-klang (²⁻...) *m* discordance, dissonance (auch *fig.*); 2klingend *a.* ill-sounding, discordant; 2laut(end *a.*) *m* = klang; 2klingend; 2nehmen *v a.* Ga** to take a th. amiss; et. nicht 2 to take a th. in good part; 2nehm(er)isch *a.* easily offended; (empfindlich) sensitive, touchy; 2riechend *a.* having a bad (or nasty) smell, malodorous, vom Atem: foul; =sein *n*: a) =befinden; b) = Übelkeit; =stand *m* evil, inconvenience, drawback; abuse; =tat *f* misdeed, offence; =täter(in *f*) *m* evil-doer, offender; =tun *n* wrongdoing; 2wollen *v/a.* **; e-m 2 to bear (or have) a grudge against a p.; =wollen *n* ill-will, spite; 2wollend *a.* ill-disposed, spiteful.

üben (¹⁻) [ahd.] I *v/a.* u. sich 2 *v/refl.* 1. to exercise (one's limbs or faculties, a horse, &c.), to practise (drawing, cycling, music, the piano, the violin, &c.), to drill (recruits, &c.); (gebrauchen) to use, to give play to; (sich) auf dem Klavier *2c.* 2 to practise (or to play exercises) on ..., auch: to practise (on) ...; sich im Fechten, Schwimmen 2 to practise fencing, swimming. — 2. mit *nouns*: f. Barmherzigkeit, Betrug; Gastlichkeit an e-m 2 to show hospitality to a p.; Geduld 2 to exercise one's patience; Gerechtigkeit gegen e-n 2 to do justice to a p.; Gewalt 2 to use force or violence, to exert one's authority; eine Kunst 2 to cultivate an art; Milde, Nachsicht gegen e-n 2 to show clemency, leniency to a p.; to deal kindly, leniently with a p.; Rache an e-m 2 to wreak one's vengeance (or to take revenge) on a p.; die Rechtspflege 2 to administer justice or the law; f. Treu² am Ende. — II ~ *n* 3. exercise, practice, vgl. Übung, bsp. Artikel. — III ge-übt *p.p.* u. *a.* 4. practised, in (full) practice; (geschickt) skilled; clever at a th.; (erfahren) experienced (or versed) in a th.

über (¹⁻) [ahd.: over: auf] (*ant.* unter) I *prp.* mit *dat.* u. *acc.* (F Zs-ziehungen: 2m = 2 dem, 2n = 2 den, 2s = 2 das) 1. örtlich *dat.* auf die Frage wo, mit *acc.* auf die Frage wohin: above, over; 2 dem Wasser above the water; 2 das Wasser across the water; 2 et. fort, hinweg across a th.; den Schuh 2 den Leisten schlagen to put the shoe upon the last. — 2. Ausdehnung, a. Beschirmung bezeichnend: f. Herz 1 unter „über" und gewinnen 5 am Ende; 2 e-n Gewalt (oder Macht) haben to have (great) power over a p.; sie kann (oder vermag) viel 2 ihn she has great influence over him; 2 ein Volk herrschen to rule over (or govern) a nation; f. Lippe am Schluß; es schwebt ein Dunkel 2 der Sache there is a mystery hanging over the affair; 2 e-n, et. setzen to place over a p., a th.; 2 e-m, stehen to be above a p., a th., bsd. *fig. a.* to be superior to a p., a th. — 3. Weiterhinausgehen, auch Vorzug bezeichnend: f. gehen 10 unter „über"; Gott 2 alles lieben to love God above (or beyond) all things; das geht mir 2 alles andere I put (or esteem) it above everything else; f. Begriff 1 u. 2 u. Berg 2; 2 Berlin nach Hamburg reisen to go via (or by) Berlin to Hamburg; 2 die besten Jahre hinaus sein to be past one's prime, to have seen one's best days; ↓ 2 Bord fallen (werfen) to fall (to throw) overboard; 2 eine Brücke gehen to go across (or to cross) a bridge; 2 die Dreißiger hinaus sein to be over (or on the wrong side of) thirty; 2 alles Erwarten beyond (all) expectation; der Übergang 2 den Fluß crossing (or the passage across) the river; 2 Gebühr more than was due or right; 2 einen Graben setzen, springen to leap over (Sport: to take) a ditch; f. Grenze gegen Ende; 2 das Knie herabreichen to reach below the knee; f. Kraft 2; 2 alle (od. 2 die) Maßen schön exceedingly (or indescribably) beautiful; 2 Meer, 2 See across the sea; 2 sein Verdienst more than he deserved beyond his desert; er wohnt 2 (jenseits) der Straße he lives across the road; 2 das Ziel hinaus schießen to overshoot the mark; Sprichw. f. gehe 10 unter „über". Für bis 2 f. bis 2 am Ende. — 4. ein Mehr bezeichnend: a) (und noch dazu) 2 dies = überdies Häufungen: Fehler 2 Fehler fault upon faults; Geld 2 Geld more and more money; einmal 2 das andere time after time; over and over again; b) (mehr als) upwards of; 100 Mark more than five pounds; das Dorf ist 2 8 Kilometer entfernt the village is more than five miles off or distant. — 5. mit *dat.* ein Beweilen, bisw. daneben den Grund bezeichnend: 2 der Arbeit sein to be (busy) at one's work; 2 den Büchern sitzen or hocken to be poring (or sweating) over one's books; 2 dem Essen during dinner; 2 einem Glase Bier over a glass of beer; 2 dem Lärm et. über-

[über=...] — 979 — [überbrücken]

hören not to hear a th. for (or on account of) the noise; ≳ dem Dichter den Menschen vergessen to forget the man in the poet; ≳ dem Spiele die Geschäfte versäumen to neglect one's business over (or for the sake of) play(ing); mit substantiviertem inf., z.B. ≳ dem Lesen while reading; ≳ dem Zanken during the quarrel. — 6. meist mit acc. (wegen, in betreff von): meine Ansicht ≳ ihn, die Sache my opinion about (or concerning, respecting) him, the matter; ≳ den Verlust ist er sehr betrübt, bekümmert he is very grieved at (or greatly grieves over) the loss; s. freuen II, klagen 1, lachen¹ 1; ≳ et. sprechen to speak about (or of) a th. or on a subject; s. grau 1; sie weint ≳ euer Elend she weeps over (or sheds tears at) your misery, she cries to see you so wretched; als Buchtitel: ≳ die Sitten der Römer on Roman customs. — 7. elliptisch als int.: Fluch (komme) ≳ dich! a curse upon you!; Wehe (rufe ich) ≳ die Mörder! woe to the murderers!; o ≳ die Jugend! oh, (the folly of) youth! — 8. zeitlich: a) heute ≳ acht Tage this day week; zehn Minuten ≳ elf ten minutes past eleven; ≳ ein Jahr a twelvemonth hence, in a year's time; ≳s Jahr next (or in the coming) year; vgl. Jahr 3, bsd. gegen Ende; ≳ kurz oder lang sooner or later; b) ≳ Nacht overnight; Sprichw. guter Rat kommt oft ≳ Nacht night is the mother of counsel; c) hinter einem s. der Zeit im acc. oder gen.: den Tag über=≳, auch tag=≳ all day (long); during the day, in the day-time; die ganze Zeit ≳ all the time, F all along. — II adv. 9. über und über (vollständig) thoroughly, entirely, completely; ≳ und ≳ naß wet to the skin, thoroughly drenched; sie ist ≳ und ≳ rot geworden she blushed up to her ears or eyes; ≳ und ≳ voll full to overflowing, brimful. — 10. a) = gegenüber (s. ds 1); b) F = vorüber, z.B. das Fieber ist ≳ ... is gone, ... has disappeared; c) F e-m in et. ≳ (über=legen) sein to surpass (or beat) a p. in a th.; er ist dir (weit) ≳ you are no match for him; F ich habe die Sache ≳, mir ist die Sache ≳ (überdrüssig) I am tired (or sick) of the matter. — 11. in Zssgn mit voranstehendem s., z.B. kopf=≳ head foremost; mit adv. s. dar=≳, her=≳, hin=≳, gerade=≳ ꝛc.

=ber=... (ᴗᴗ... ob. ᴗᴗ...) Vorsilbe in Zssgn mit verbs und adjectives: I mit verbs (ᴗᴗ...) immer trennbar (**) 1. (hinüber): ≳fahren to drive (or ferry) across, to cross. — 2. (darüber): ≳ziehen to pull over. — II in sogenannten echten Zssgn mit v. (ᴗᴗ... nebentonig) immer untrennbar (*) 3. (mehr als genug): ≳füttern to overfeed. — 4. (bedeckend): ≳schatten to overshadow. — 5. (wiederholend): ≳malen to touch up. — 6. mit v/n., welches dadurch v/a. wird: ≳schreiten to pass over; to exceed, to transgress. — 7. (siegend): ≳treffen to excel, to surpass. — 8. (sich ausbreitend):

≳schauen to survey. — 9. (hingebend): ≳liefern to deliver. — 10. (oberflächlich): ≳lesen to glance over. — 11. (auslassen): ≳sehen to overlook. — 12. bisw. mit e-m von e-m n/pr. abgeleiteten v. = übertreffen, z.B. Schiller ≳schillern, etwa: to out-Schiller Schiller (vgl. SH. to out-herod Herod). — III mit s. 13. (hinübergehen) ~fahrt f crossing, passage. — 14. (Bedeckung) ~rock m overcoat. — 15. (Rest) ~bleibsel n remainder, remnant. — 16. (Ausbreitung) ~blick m survey. — 17. (Hingeben) ~gabe f surrender. — 18. chm. (höchste Verbindung) ~chlorsäure f perchloric acid. — 19. von v. abgeleitet: ~schreitung f passage (across); transgression. — IV mit a. 20. einen hohen Grad bezeichnend: ≳groß exceedingly (or uncommonly) large; (much) too big. — V zur Bildung von adv. 21. ≳all everywhere; ≳dies moreover. [over.⌋
über-ackern (ᴗᴗᴗ) v/a. ⓐ** to plough⌉
über-all (ᴗᴗ, ᴗᴗ) [ahd.] adv. everywhere, in every place, in all places, F co. all over the shop; das findet man ≳, oft: you find that wherever you (may) go; ≳ gegenwärtig ubiquitous, rel. von Gott: omnipresent; Kanzleistil = schlechterdings; ~ m, inv.= Hans ~ one who is here and there and everywhere, auch: Paul Pry; ≳=her adv. from all sides or quarters; ≳=hin adv. everywhere, to every part or place, in all directions.
über-ängstlich (ᴗᴗᴗ) a. ⓐ over-anxious; ≳anstrengen (ᴗᴗᴗ) v/a. u. sich ≳ v/refl. ⓐ* (sich) to over-exert (o.s.), to overwork (o.s.); ~ n und =anstrengung f ㉓ over-exertion; ≳antworten (ᴗᴗᴗ) v/a. ⓐ* to surrender; (ausliefern) to deliver up, ausländische Verbrecher: to extradite; ~ n ㉓ und =antwortung f ㊻ surrender; delivery, extradition; =arbeit (ᴗᴗᴗ) f ㊻ overtime; ≳arbeiten I v/a. u. sich ≳ v/refl. ⓐ* = ≳anstrengen; er hat sich übera"rbeitet he has overexerted himself; ich bin übera"rbeitet I am overworked; II (ᴗᴗᴗ und ᴗᴗᴗ) v/a. ⓐ* u. ⓐ** (noch einmal bearbeiten) to do (over) again, to touch up, Schriften: to revise, Kunstwerke ꝛc. ≳ (vollendend) to give the finishing touch(es) to ..., to finish ...; er hat zwei Stunden ü"bergearbeitet (über die gew. Zeit hinaus) he has done two hours of overtime; ~ n ㉓ und =arbeitung f ㊻ touching up, revision, finish(ing touches pl.); =ärmel (ᴗᴗᴗ) m ㉒ oversleeve; ≳aus (ᴗᴗᴗ) adv. extremely, exceedingly; (übermäßig) excessively, uncommonly, egregiously, beyond measure; =bau (ᴗᴗᴗ) m ⓒc. (pl. a. =bauten) (vorragender Bau) projecting part (or story) of a building; (der obere Bau) superstructure; upper part of a building; ≳bauen (ᴗᴗᴗ) ⓐ* v/a. u. v/refl. to raise (a structure) above s.th.; to build over (an estate, a plot), sich ≳ to build too much; to ruin o.s. with building, to put too much money into bricks and mortar; (ᴗᴗᴗ) v/a. u. v/n. (h.) (über et. anderes bauen) to build over, to raise above; (höher

bauen) to raise, to add another story to; (über die Grenze bauen) to build beyond the boundary(-line); ~ n ㉓ u. =bauung f ㊻ raising (a structure), &c; addition of another story; ≳behalten (ᴗᴗᴗ) v/a. ⓐa*/*: seinen Mantel ≳ to keep one's cloak on; (übrig behalten) to have left, to keep over; =bein (ᴗᴗᴗ) n ⓒc.: a) path. node, am Knochen: ⚕ exostosis, an Sehnen: ⚕ ganglion; b) vet. (Knochen des Pferdefußes hinter dem Schienbein) splint; =bett (ᴗᴗᴗ) n ⓒc. = Deckbett; ≳beugen ⓐ***. ≳biegen ⑦a** (ᴗᴗᴗ) v/a. u. v/refl. to bend over; sich ≳ auch: to lean over or forward; ⚘ ü"bergebogen drooping, nodding, ⚘ declinate; ≳bieten (ᴗᴗᴗ) v/a. u. v/n. (h.) ⑦a**: er bietet noch zwei Mark über (mehr) he bids two shillings more; (ᴗᴗᴗ) v/a. u. v/refl. ⑦a*: et. ≳ to bid over s.th.; to bid too much for s.th.; e-n ≳ to outbid a p.; sich ≳ to bid too much; fig. (übertreffen) to surpass, excel, outdo, outstrip, beat; sie überbo"ten sich in Höflichkeiten they vied with (auch: they tried to outdo) each other in politeness; ≳bilden (ᴗᴗᴗ) v/a. ⓐ* to over-educate; überbi"ldet too highly educated, too refined; ~ n ㉓ u. =bildung f ㊻ over-education; over-refinement; =binde (ᴗᴗᴗ) f ㊻ surg. outer bandage; ≳binden v/a. (ᴗᴗᴗ) ⑦** to tie (or bind, wrap) over; (ᴗᴗᴗ) ⑦*: e-e Wunde mit leinenen Lappen ≳ to tie (or bind, wrap) up a wound in linen rags; ≳blatten ⓞ (ᴗᴗᴗ) v/a. ⓐ* carp. join. to rebate; ≳blättern v/a. ⓐa* (ᴗᴗᴗ) eine Stelle ≳ to skip a passage; ⓐa*(*) ein Buch ≳ (flüchtig lesen) to glance (or run) through ..., to skim ...; ≳bleiben v/n. (s.n.) ⓒ** (ᴗᴗᴗ) to remain (over), to be left; (ᴗᴗᴗ) ⓐ** meist im p.p. ≳bliebensurviving, remaining; die bliebenen the survivors pl.; =bleibsel (ᴗᴗᴗ) n (m) ㉒ leavings pl.; (Rest) remainder, remnant; remains pl.; (Trümmer) ruins, (fr.) debris pl.; (Reliquie) relic; (Rückstand) residue; =blick (ᴗᴗᴗ) m ⓒc. general view, survey, hastiger: hasty (or cursory) glance; kurzer ~ (Abriß) epitome, brief summary or sketch; zs=fassender ~ comprehensive (or complete) survey, ⚕ synopsis; mit raschem ~ begabt gifted with a quick eye; ≳blicken (ᴗᴗᴗ) v/a. ⓐ* to survey, to take in at a glance; ≳blieben (ᴗᴗᴗ) s. ≳bleiben; ≳blühen ∖ (ᴗᴗᴗ) ⓐ* v/a. to cover with blossom(s); sich ≳ v/refl. to blo(ss)om too profusely; ≳breiten ∖ v/a. (ᴗᴗᴗ) ⓐ* to spread a cover over; (ᴗᴗᴗ) ⓐ* den Tisch mit e-r Decke ≳ to cover the table (over) with a cloth; =brettl (ᴗᴗᴗ) n ㉒ variety theatre or entertainment; ≳bringen (ᴗᴗᴗ) ⓐ*: e-m et. ≳ to take (or bring, carry, convey, deliver, transmit) a th. to a p.; feierlich: to present a th. to a p.; ~ n ㉓ =bringung (ᴗᴗᴗ); =bringer (ᴗᴗᴗ) m ㉒, ~in f ⓐ bearer (of a letter, a message, &c.), carrier; =bringung f ㊻ carriage (bsd. ⓐ), delivery, transmission; presentation; ≳brücken (ᴗᴗᴗ) v/a. ⓐ* to bridge over, to throw (or build) a bridge

⚕ scientific; ⚘ botanical; ⚲ geography; ⊕ machinery; ⚒ mining; ⚔ military; ⚓ marine; ⚖ commercial; ✉ postal; 🚆 railway.

[Überbrückung] — 980 — [Überfluß]

across, to span a river; ~ n ㉓ und =brückung f ㊻ bridging (over); ⸗bunt (ᴗ́ᴗ) a. ⓺ too gay or F loud; ⸗bürden (ᴗ́ᴗ) v/a. ⓼* to overburden, to overload, durch Arbeit auch: to overwork, to overtask; ⸗bür"det overburdened; ~ n ㉓ und ⸗bürdung f ㊻ overburdening, &c., auch: excessive work or task; ⸗chlor=sauer ⸗ (ᴗ́-ᴗᴗ) a. ⓺ chm. perchloric; ⸗es Salz perchlorate; =chlor=säure(ᴗ́-ᴗᴗ) f ㊻ perchloric acid (HClO₄); ⸗dach (ᴗ́ᴗ) n ⓶c. = Schutzdach b; ⸗dachen (ᴗ́ᴗᴗ) v/a. ⓼* to cover with a roof, to roof (in); ⸗dacht (ᴗ́-ᴗcht) p.p. und a. ⓺ s. ⸗denken; =dachung (ᴗ́ᴗᴗ) f ㊻ roofing; ⸗das (ᴗ́ᴗ) adv. = ⸗dies; ⸗dauern (ᴗ́ᴗᴗ) v/a. ⓶a* to outlast; a. = überleben; =decke (ᴗ́ᴗ) f ㊻ outer (or additional) covering; (Bedbett) coverlet; =decken v/a. (ᴗ́ᴗ)⓼*: et. ᴗ to spread s.th. over a th.; (ᴗᴗ́) ⓼*: et. mit et. ᴗ to cover a th. over with s.th.; arch. mit einem Gewölbe ᴗ to vault (over); =deckung f ㊻ cover(ing); ⸗dem ᴗᴗ́ (ᴗᴗ́) adv. = überdies; ⸗denken (ᴗᴗ́ᴗ) v/a. ⓼* to think over, to revolve in one's mind, to reflect (or meditate) on, to consider; wohl überda'cht well-considered, well-weighed; ~ n ㉓ reflexion, meditation; ⸗dies (ᴗᴗ́) adv. in addition to that; moreover, besides, further; a.: what is more, //; ⸗drehen (ᴗᴗ́ᴗ) v/a. ⓼* to overwind a watch, to hamper a lock; =druck ⊕ (ᴗ́ᴗ) m ⓶c. typ. (Zuschußbogen) supernumerary sheet; (Umbruck) transfer; ⸗ ~ auf Postmarken surcharge; mach., elect., &c. over-pressure, excessive pressure or strain or tension; ⸗drucken ⊕ (ᴗ́ᴗᴗ) v/a. ⓼** typ. to transfer; =druß (ᴗ́ᴗ) [mhb.] m ⓶c. weariness (of mind); (Ekel) disgust; (übersättigung) repletion, satiety; et. (bis) zum ~ hören (müssen) to be sick (or tired) of hearing a th., to have to hear a th. ad nauseam; ⸗drüssig (ᴗ́ᴗᴗ) a. ⓺ weary (or sick, tired) of; disgusted at or with; replete (bisw.: satiate(d) with, F u. P fed up with; ⸗düngen (ᴗᴗ́ᴗ) v/a. ⓼* agr. to (over-)manure; ⸗eck(s) (ᴗ́ᴗ) adv. = über Ecke (s. Ecke 2), auch diagonally; =eifer (ᴗ́ᴗᴗ) m ⓶ overgreat zeal; ⸗eifrig (ᴗ́ᴗᴗ) a. ⓺ too eager, too zealous; (zu dienstfertig) (too) officious; ⸗eile (ᴗ́ᴗ) f ㊽ overgreat hurry; ⸗eilen (ᴗᴗ́ᴗ) v/a. u. v/refl. ⓼* ⸗ = ⸗holen (zu sehr drängen) to hurry on too much, to press forward (too fast), to precipitate, die Arbeit: to scamp; sich ᴗ to act (too) hastily or precipitately or rashly, to be in too great a hurry; ᴗ Sie sich nicht! there is no hurry!, take your time!; ⸗eilt (ᴗᴗ́) p.p. u. a. ⓺ (too) hasty, precipitate, rash; (unbedacht) reckless, inconsiderate; (voreilig) premature; ~ n ㉓ = ⸗eilung; in ⸗eilter Weise, ⸗eilter-weise adv. hurriedly, in a flutter; =eilung f ㊻ hastiness, precipitancy, rashness; recklessness, inconsiderateness; bei der Arbeit: scamping (or slurring, rushing) one's work.

über-ein (ᴗᴗ́) adv. conformably; (mitea. stimmend) in agreement, in accord. über-ein-ander (ᴗᴗᴗ́ᴗ) adv. one above (or atop of) the other, over (or above) one another; ~fallen (ᴗᴗ́-ᴗᴗ) n ㉓ ⸗ superincumbence; ᴗ=greifen v/n.(h.) ⓺bft** to overlap (each other); ~ n ㉓ overlapping; ᴗ=legen v/a. ⓼** to lay one on the top of another, in Haufen: to pile up; ~=liegen n ㉓ superposition; ᴗ=liegend p.pr. u. a. ⓺ super(im)posed, superincumbent, (arranged) in layers; die Arme ᴗ=schlagen v/a. ⓺b** to fold one's arms; mit ᴗ=geschlagenen Armen with folded arms, with his (her) arms folded; die Beine ᴗ=schlagen to cross (or to double up, F to cock up) one's legs, to put one leg over the other; ~=setzen n ㉓ superposition.

über-ein-kommen (ᴗᴗ́ᴗᴗ) v/n. (ſn) ⓺**: a) to be conformable to; b) über et. ᴗ to agree on (or about) a th., to come to an understanding about (or concerning) a th.; abs. wir sind ᴗgekommen we have come to an agreement; ~ n ㉓, =kunft f ㊿ agreement, mit den Gläubigern x.: arrangement; (Vergleich) settlement, compromise; laut ~ mit // according to the agreement made with //; ⸗stimmen v/n. (h.) ⓼**: a) persönlich: mit e-m ᴗ to agree (or concur) with a p. on a th., to share a p.'s opinion about a th.; ich stimme mit Ihnen überein I am (quite) of your opinion; ich stimme mit ihnen nicht überein I do not agree (or hold) with them, I differ with (or from) them; sachlich: to harmonize (or to tally, to be in keeping) with a th.; to correspond to a th.; gr. mit einem Worte im Geschlechte und in der Zahl ᴗ to agree ... in gender and number; ⸗stimmend a. ⓺ conformable, harmonious, corresponding; (folgerichtig) consistent; =stimmung f agreement, conformity; harmony; consistency; (Einklang) concord; (Eintracht) unity; in ~ mit in concert with; in ~ bringen mit // to bring in(to) unison (or to make agree) with //; die Einnahme mit der Ausgabe in ~ bringen to make the receipts cover (or tally with) the expense(s); ⸗treffen v/n. (ſn) ⓺a** to coincide (or agree, correspond, tally) with, F to be on all fours with.

über-eisen¹ (ᴗᴗ́-ᴗ) n ㉓ man. für hinfende Pferde: beak; ⸗eisen² (ᴗᴗ́ᴗ) v/a. ⓼* to cover with ice; bſd. p.p. überreist frozen over; ⸗essen ⓼* (ᴗᴗ́ᴗ), sich ᴗ v/refl. to overeat o.s., to eat immoderately, to gormandize, F to stuff (or cram) o.s.; er hat sich überge"ssen, a. he has overloaded his stomach; (ᴗᴗᴗ́) ⓼** v/a. sich (dat.) eine Speise ᴗ to sicken o.s. of a certain dish (by partaking too freely of it); ⸗fahren [mhd.] (ᴗᴗ́ᴗ) ⓺b** v/n. (ſn) to pass over, to cross (over) in a coach, by boat, &c., to ferry over, to drive (or sail) across; ~ v/n. (ſn) to convey (or drive) across, to take (or ferry, row) over; (ᴗᴗᴗ́) ⓺b* v/a. e-n mit dem Wagen x. ᴗ to run (or drive) over a p.; das Kind ist ᴗ worden the child was run over (by

a carriage or cart); Flüsse x. ᴗ to cross ..., mit dem Dampfer (Segelſchffe): to steam (to sail) across ...; die Tafel mit dem Schwamme ᴗ to pass the sponge over the slate; =fahren-werden n ㉓: die Gefahr des ~s the danger of being run over; =fahrt (ᴗ́ᴗ) f ㊻ passage across a bridge, &c.; crossing (or ferrying over) a river, &c.; ~s-geld n ferryman's fee, a. passage, ferriage; ~s-ort m, ~s-stelle f ferry-station, ferry; =fall (ᴗ́ᴗ) m ⓶c. sudden attack or assault; surprise; ⨯ in ein Land: inroad, incursion, invasion, raid; ⊕ Wasserbau: (Wehr, Abfluß eines Deiches) overfall-weir; ⸗fallen (ᴗᴗ́ᴗ) ⓺a* v/a. to fall (stärker: to pounce or rush) upon, to attack suddenly, to surprise; ein Land ᴗ to make an inroad into ..., to invade ..., to raid ...; fig. die Nacht hat uns ᴗ night overtook us; Schrecken überfiel ihn he was seized with terror or terror-stricken; ↓ vom Sturm ᴗ w. to be caught in a storm or gale; (ᴗ́ᴗᴗ) ⓺a** v/n. (ſn) to fall over (the side), to topple over, to tumble sideways; ⸗fällig ⌾ u. ↓ (ᴗᴗ́ᴗ) a. ⓺ (zur fälligen Zeit nicht eingetroffen) overdue; ⸗feilen ⊕ (ᴗᴗ́ᴗ) v/a. ⓼* to pass the file over, fig. to touch up; ⸗fein (ᴗᴗ́) a. ⓺ superfine, fig. over-refined (auch ⊕), too elegant, too smart; von Reden, Gründen x.: subtle; vom Geschmack: fastidious, dainty; ⸗firnissen (ᴗᴗ́ᴗᴗ) v/a. ⓼* to varnish over, to coat with varnish; ⸗flechten v/a. (ᴗᴗ́ᴗ) ⓺b** (über die Flasche) Stroh ᴗ u. (ᴗᴗᴗ́) ⓺b** die Flasche mit Stroh ᴗ to cover the bottle with plaited straw or wicker work; überflochtene Flasche wicker-bottle; ⸗fleißig (ᴗᴗ́ᴗᴗ) a. ⓺ over-diligent; ⸗fliegen (ᴗᴗ́ᴗᴗ) ⓺a** v/n. (ſn) to fly over or across; (ᴗᴗᴗ́) ⓺a* v/a. to cross (or pass) in flying; eine Zeitung x. mit den Augen ᴗ to glance at (or over) ...; ich habe die Seite überflo"gen I skimmed the page; (überziehen) ihr Antlitz überflo"g ein roter Schein a ruddy light spread over (or flushed) her countenance; ⸗fließen (ᴗᴗ́ᴗᴗ) ⓺d**, poet. ob. † (ᴗᴗᴗ́) ⓺d* v/n. (ſn) to flow (or run) over, to overflow, bſd. von Flüssen: to overflow the banks; die Milch ist ü"bergeflossen the milk ran (or flowed) over; fig. von et. ᴗ to brim over with (or to abound in) a th.; vor Freude ᴗb exultant with joy; ~ (ᴗᴗ́-ᴗ) n ㉓ overflow(ing); zum ~ voll full to overflowing, brimful (ᴗᴗᴗ́) ⓺d* v/a. (überschwemmen) to flood, swamp, inundate; die überflo"ſſenen Felder the flooded fields; ⸗floren (ᴗᴗ́ᴗ) v/a. ⓼* to cover with crape; ⸗flügeln (ᴗᴗ́ᴗ)v/a. ⓶a*: ⨯ den Feind ᴗ to outflank the enemy; fig. e-n ᴗ to surpass (or excel, outdo, outstrip) a p., geh. Spr.: to soar above a p.; =fluß (ᴗ́ᴗ) [mhd.] m ⓶a. abundance, (mehr als genug) superfluity, ⌾ a. glut; (Fülle) plenty, profusion; (Reichtum) wealth, an Worten: redundancy; (üppiges Wuchern) exuberance; im ...ſſe (in großem ...ſſe) da (vorhanden) ſein

Zeichen (ſ. S. XVII): F familiär; P Volksſprache; Γ Gaunerſprache; ⸗ ſelten; † alt (auch geſtorben); * neu (auch geboren); ⁒ unrichtig;

[überflüssig] — 981 — [überhandnehmen]

to be (super)abundant or plentiful; ~ an et. h. to abound in a th.; ~ an Geld h. to have plenty (or to be flush) of money, F to have money galore or heaps of money; ❀ ~ an Waren surplus of goods; ²flüssig (ᴵᴵ‿ᴗ) [mhd.] a. ⑥: a) (unnötig) superfluous, useless; (unnütz) redundant, ² m. to supersede; b) (überreichlich) (super)abundant, plentiful; ~keit f ㊺ superfluousness; ²fluten (ᴵ‿ᴗᴗ) ⑬a* to overflow, inundate, flood; ~ n ㉓ u. flutung f ㊻ overflow, inundation, flood(ing); ²fordern (ᴵ‿ᴗᴗ) v/a. u. v/n. (h.) ㉒a* n ² to overcharge a p., to ask too much of a p.; ~ n ㉓ u. forderung f ㊺ excessive (or exorbitant) charge or demand; =fracht ❀, 🚂 (ᴵᴵ‿ᴗt) f ㊻ overfreight, overweight, excess (of) freight or luggage; ²frachten (ᴵ‿ᴗᴗ) ᶜʰᵗv/a. ㉘* to overfreight, to load too heavily; ²fressen (ᴵ‿ᴗᴗ) ㉗* v/refl. unb (ᴵ‿ᴗᴗ) ㉗** v/a. von Tieren u. P derb von Menschen = ²essen; ²frieren (ᴵ‿ᴗᴗ) v/n. (fn) ⑯c* to freeze over; ²frösteln (ᴵ‿ᴗᴗ) v/a. ㉒a* to chill; =fuhr (ᴵᴵ‿ᴵ) ⑥ (Fähre) ferry; ²führen (ᴵᴵ‿ᴵ‿ᴗ) ㉘** v/a. to lead across; to convey, transfer, transport; ⊕ mach. den Treibriemen ² to shift the belt; (ᴵ‿ᴗᴗ) ㉘* v/a. durch Gründe: to convince of a th.; e-n eines Verbrechens ² to convict a p. of a crime; e-r Schuld überfü"hrt w. to be found guilty (of a charge); ~ n ㉓ u. führung f ㊻ transfer, von Gefangenen auch: transportation; convincing proof, conviction; =fülle (ᴵᴵ‿ᴗ) ᴗᴗ f ㊸ repletion, superabundance, redundance; profusion, exuberance; ²füllen (ᴵ‿ᴗᴗ) ㉘** v/a.: in ein anderes Gefäß ² to pour from one vessel into another; (ᴵ‿ᴗᴗ) ㉘* v/a. u. v/refl. to overfill, to cram (full), mit Speisen a..: to surfeit, mit Menschen: to overcrowd; ❀ den Markt: to overstock, to glut; von Straßen: mit Wagen, Karren überfü"llt choked (or blocked) with carriages, carts; sich mit Speisen ² to gorge o.s., to overload one's stomach; ~ n ㉓ und füllung f ㊺ overfilling, &c.; cramming, surfeit(ing), des Magens a..: repletion, glut(ting); ²füttern (ᴵ‿ᴗᴗ) v/a. ㉒a* to overfeed, to feed too richly or too well; =gabe (ᴵᴵ‿ᴵ) f ㊸: ~ von Briefen, Waren ꝛc. delivery, eines Besitztums auch: actual transfer; ⚔ ~ e-r Festung: surrender, durch Vertrag: capitulation; eine Festung zur ~ auffordern to summon a fortress to surrender; die ~ verweigern to refuse to surrender. Über-gang (ᴵᴵ‿ᴵ) m ⑦c. 1. crossing a bridge, &c.; ~ über die Alpen crossing (or passage across) the Alps; ⚔ ~ zum Feinde going over to the enemy; hier ist fein ~! no crossing (allowed)! — 2. ~ (Wechsel) von et. zu et. transition (or change) from a th. to a th.; stufenweiser (unmerklicher) ~ gradual (imperceptible) transition; paint. Übergänge vom Licht zum Schatten shades pl.; parl. ~ zur Tagesordnung passing (on) to the order of the day. ²bergangs-bestimmung (ᴵᴵ‿ᴗ...) f ㊷ regulation made for a time of

transition; =gebirge n, =kalk m, geol. transition rocks pl., limestone; =punkt m crossing, 🚂 über e-e Straße: level crossing; =scheibe 🚂 f traversing-table; =stil m transition style; =widerstand m, elect. contact resistance; =zeit f transition period; =zustand m state of transition, transitionary state.
über-gar (ᴵᴵ‿ᴵ) a. ⑥ too much done or boiled; ⊕ metall. ²es Kupfer overrefined copper; ²er Stahl burnt steel; ²gären (ᴵ‿ᴗᴗ) v/n. (h.) ⑯a.㉘** to overflow during fermentation; ²geben (ᴵᴵ‿ᴵ‿ᴗ) ㉒c** v/a.: (zum überdecken geben) to (put a) wrap round; (ᴵ‿ᴗᴗ) v/a. u. v/refl. ㉒c*: e-m et. ² to give (or yield) up a th. to a p., to surrender a th. to a p.; (liefern) to deliver (up); (anvertrauen) to give in charge of, to commit to the care of, to consign (or entrust) to; den Flammen ² to consign (or give over) to the flames; e-e Sache den Gerichten ² to take a matter before the law-courts; e-e Bahn ꝛc. dem Verkehr ² to open ... for traffic; ⚔ e-e Festung ² to surrender a fortress; sich ² (erbrechen) to vomit, to be sick, to bring up one's food; sich ² wollen to retch, to heave; ~ n ㉓ = =gabe; =gebot ⚖ jur. (ᴵᴵ‿ᴵ) ⓜc. (höheres Gebot bei e-r Versteigerung) higher (or better) bid, advance (on a previous offer), F going (one) better; ²gebührlich (ᴵ‿ᴗᴗ) a. supererogatory; =gebung f ㊻ = =gabe; ²geh(e)n (ᴵ‿ᴗᴗ)(ᴗ) ㉗** v/n. (fn) to go (or pass) over to; jur. a. to devolve on, meist fig. to pass on to; zu et. ² (vornehmen) to proceed to a th.; (sich in et. verwandeln) to change (or turn, ausarten: to degenerate) into a th.; das Geschäft ist in andere Hände ü"bergegangen the business has passed into other (or has changed) hands; in Fäulniß ² to decay, to putrefy, F to go (or turn) bad; ⚔ zum Feinde ² to go over (or desert) to the enemy; zur Gegenpartei ² to change sides, F pol. to rat; zu e-r anderen Religion ² to change one's religion; parl. zur Tagesordnung ² to pass on to the order of the day; von Flüssigkeiten und deren Behältnis =²fließen; fig. die Augen gingen ihm über tears came into his eyes, his eyes (were) filled with tears; Sprichw. s. Herz 1 am Ende; ~ n ㉓ = Übergang; ~ von Truppen desertion, defection (beide auch fig.); (ᴵ‿ᴗ)(ᴗ) ㉘* v/a.: etwas ² (unbeachtet lassen) to pass over (or by) a th., to omit a th., beim Lesen: to skip a th.; (übersehen) to overlook, not to notice; e-n in f-m Rechte ꝛc. ² to leave a p. out; mit Stillschweigen ² to pass over in silence; er ist übergangen worden he has been passed over; ein Feld ² (besichtigen) to inspect a field; eine Rechnung ꝛc. ² to glance (F to run) over ...; ⊕ et. ² (auf der Oberfläche bearbeiten) to work along the surface of a th.; v/refl. sich ² (zu viel gehen) to overexert o.s. in walking, to walk too much; ~ n ㉓ u. =gehung f ㊻ passing over, omission; rhet.: ☞ pretermission;

allgemeine(s) absichtliche(s) ~ mit Stillschweigen, oft: conspiracy of silence; ²gelehrt (ᴵ‿ᴗᴗ) a. ⑥ over-learned; ²genug (ᴵ‿ᴗᴗ) adv. more than enough, enough and to spare, too much; =gewalt (ᴵ‿ᴗᴗ) f ㊺ predominant (or paramount, supreme) power, supremacy; =gewicht (ᴵ‿ᴗᴗ) n ⑨c. over-weight, excess of weight; fig. preponderance, predominance, ascendancy, superiority; (Herrschaft) sway, dominion; das ~ h. to predominate over; e-m das ~ geben, verleihen to turn the scales (or to decide a matter) in favour of a p.; ²gießen (ᴵ‿ᴗᴗ) ⑯d** v/a. to pour over, aus Versehen: to spill (in pouring out); in ein anderes Gefäß ² to pour into another vessel, chm.: ☞ to transfuse; ~ n ㉓ transfusion; (ᴵ‿ᴗᴗ) ⑯d* to cover with a fluid; fig. mit Licht ² to bathe in light; mit Wasser ² to pour water on; mit Zucker ² to ice (or candy) over; von Schweiß wie übergo"ssen sein to be in a bath of perspiration; fig. es übergo"ß sie purpurrot she turned (F burst) scarlet; she blushed (up to her ears); mit Schamröte übergo"ssen suffused with blushes, F blushing all over; ²gipsen (ᴵ‿ᴗᴗ) ⓐ ㊲ to plaster (over), to parget; ²gittern (ᴵ‿ᴗᴗ) v/a. ㉒a* to cover with lattice-work or with a grating; opt.: to divide into squares, ☞ to cover with a retic(u)le; ²glasen (ᴵ‿ᴗᴗ) v/a. ㊲* to glaze over; ²glücklich (ᴵ‿ᴗᴗ) a. ⑥ overjoyed, extremely happy; Sie machen mich ², oft: you make me the happiest of mortals; ²golden (ᴵ‿ᴗᴗ) v/a. ㉘* to gild over, auch: fig. to gild on the surface; ²grasen (ᴵ‿ᴗᴗ) v/a. u. sich ² v/refl. ㊲*: (sich) ² to cover (to become covered) with grass; ²greifen (ᴵ‿ᴗᴗ) v/n. (h.) ⑯bt** to overlap, fig. = eingreifen 3 u. 4; (ᴵ‿ᴗᴗ) ⑯bt*: sich die Hand ² to sprain one's hand (in grasping or clutching); ~ n ㉓, auch =griff (ᴵ‿ᴗᴗ) m ⓐc. = eingreifen II; ²groß (ᴵ‿ᴵ) a. ⑥ (by far) too great; (riesenhaft) monstrous, colossal, enormous, immense, huge, vast, gigantic; ²grünen (ᴵ‿ᴗᴗ) v/a. ㉘* to cover with verdure; =guß (ᴵ‿ᴵ) m ⑧a. covering (or crust) formed by a melted substance, bsd. v. Zucker: icing, candy(ing); ²gut (ᴵ‿ᴵ) a. ⑥ too good, adv. too well; ❀ superfine; ²haben (ᴵ‿ᴗᴗ) v/a. ⓑ**: e-n Rock ² to have a coat on; F (übrig h.) to have left or remaining; F fig. (überdrüssig sein) to have enough of, to be tired of; ²halten (ᴵ‿ᴗᴗ) v/a. ㉒a** to hold over; =hand f † = Oberhand.
Über-hand-nahme f ㊸ (ᴵ‿ᴗᴵ..., ᴵ‿ᴗᴗ..) rapid growth or increase; extensive spread; ²nehmen v/n.㉒a** to become too plentiful or too numerous, to grow rapidly or apace, to gain ground; (sich verbreiten) to spread (far and wide), to become prevalent; (sich vermehren) to multiply; das Feuer nimmt überhand the fire is spreading or gaining ground; die Heuschrecken haben ²genommen the locusts have increased rapidly; ~ n ㉓ = =nahme.

Musik; ☞ Wissenschaft; ♀ Pflanze; ♆ Geographie; ⊕ Technik; ⚒ Bergbau; ⚔ Militär; ⚓ Marine; ❀ Handel; ✉ Post; 🚂 Eisenbahn.

[Überhang] — 982 — [überlaufen]

Über-hang (‒‿‿) m ⓞc. = ₌hangen n; (et. überhangendes) s.th. hanging over or impending or jutting forth, arch. auch: salient part; (Vorhang) curtain; ₂hangen (‒‿‿‿) v/n. (h.) ⓰b** to hang over, to impend; bjd. arch. (jchief jtehen) to lean over, to incline; (vorragen) to project, to jut (or stand) forth or out; ₂de Augenbrauen projecting eyebrows pl., in geh. Spr. auch: beetling brows pl.; ~ n ㉓ hanging over; arch. incline, projection; ₂hängen (‒‿‿‿) ⓰** v/a. to hang over; einen Mantel ₂ to wrap o.s. in a cloak; eine Flinte ₂ to sling a gun round one's shoulder; F ⟂ v/n. (h.) = ₂hangen; typ. ₂de (r-r ₂hangende) Buchſtaben kerned letters pl.; (‒‿‿‿) ⓰** (hängend überdecken) to hang over; ₂hä"ngt mit // cloaked in //; ₂harſchen (‒‿‿‿) v/a. ⓰* to cover with a crust, to encrust; ₂haſten (‒‿‿‿) v/a. ⓰* to hurry over a th.; to do a th. too hurriedly or hastily; ₂hauchen (‒‿‿‿ch) v/a. ⓰* to breathe upon; von Pflaumen ꝛc.: von Duft ₂hau"ch with a bloom upon them; ₂häufen (‒‿‿‿) v/a. ⓰* to (over)load, to overburden; (faſt erdrücken) to overwhelm; mit Höflichkeiten, Komplimenten ₂ to overwhelm with civilities, compliments; e-n mit Wohltaten ₂ to heap benefits upon a p., to overwhelm a p. with kindness; mit Arbeit ₂hän"ft over head and ears in work, very busy; ~ n ㉓ u. ₌häufung f ⓯ (over)loading, &c.; overwhelming load of business, &c.; accumulation of work, &c.; ₂haupt (‒‿) [mhd. jämtlich (Haupt = Stück Vieh)] adv. on the whole, generally (speaking), altogether; (ſchließlich) after all; ₂ nicht not at all; wenn ₂ if at all; wenn's Ihnen ₂ Ernſt iſt if you really mean business, if you are in real earnest; ₂heben ⟂ (‒‿‿‿) ⓰b** v/a. to lift over; (‒‿‿‿) ⓹(⑦)b* v/a. u. v/refl. (frei m. von) to exempt (or free, excuse) from; e-n einer Mühe ₂ to save a p. the trouble; einer Aufgabe, Mühe, Sorge überhoben ſein to be relieved from a task, to be spared the trouble, the worry; ſich ₂ (durch Heben verletzen) to injure (or rupture) o.s. with lifting a heavy load; ſich e-r Sache (gen.) ₂ (zu ſehr rühmen) to be too proud of a th., to pride o.s. too much on a th.; ohne mich ₂ zu wollen without boasting, abs. ſich ₂ to be overweeningly proud, to presume too much; ~ n ㉓ u. ₌hebung f ⓯ exemption from; overweening pride, great (or haughty) presumption or assumption or conceit; (Eitelkeit) vanity; ₂heiß (‒‿) a. ⓰ too hot, overheated; ₂heizen (‒‿‿‿) v/a. ⓰* to overheat (the flues, a room, &c.); ₌hemdchen (‒‿‿‿) n shirt-front, F dicky; ₂her (‒‿) from all sides or quarters; ₂hin (‒‿‿) everywhere, to every place, in all directions; ₂ adv. (oberflächlich) on the surface, superficially; ₂hitzen (‒‿‿‿): ſich ₂ v/refl. ⓰* to overheat o.s.; ₌hitzung f ⓯ overheating; ₂hobeln (‒‿‿‿) v/a. ⓰a* to plane over; ₂hoch (‒‿‿) a. ⓰ extremely (or too) high or lofty;

₂höhen (‒‿‿‿) v/a. ⓰* bjd. ⚔ to tower over, to command; ₂holen v/a. (‒‿‿‿) ⓰**: e-n ₂ to fetch a p. over (in a boat); hol' über! ferryman ahoy!; et. ₂ to haul a th. over; ⚓ die Segel ₂ (umlegen) to shift the sails; (‒‿‿‿) ⓰*: e-n ₂ (hinter ſich zurücklaſſen) to outstrip (or outrun, distance) a p., to get ahead of a p.; Tennis: to pass; ₂hören (‒‿‿‿) [mhd.] v/a. ⓰*: et. ₂ (nicht hören) not to hear (or catch) a th., abſichtlich: not to listen to a th.; ich habe die letzten Worte überhö"rt I missed the last words; (anhörend prüfen) e-n ₂, e-m ſeine Aufgabe ₂ to hear a p. (say or repeat) his lesson; ~ n ㉓, ₂B.: ~ e-r Lektion hearing a (pupil's) lesson; ſich ein Lied, eine Oper ü"bergehört h. to be sick of hearing a song, an opera; ₌hoſe (‒‿‿‿) f ⓯ overalls pl.; ₂hüpfen ⟂ (‒‿‿‿) ⓰** v/n. (in) to jump (or skip) over; (‒‿‿‿) ⓰* v/a.: et. ₂ to skip a th.; (auslaſſen) to leave out; ₂irdiſch (‒‿‿‿) a. ⓰ (raised) above the earth; (überweltlich) supermundane, (übernatürlich) supernatural, unearthly; (geiſtig) spiritual; (himmliſch) celestial, heavenly; ₂jagen (‒‿‿‿) v/a. ⓰*: et. ₂ to precipitate (or rush) a th.; ein Pferd ₂ (zu ſehr anſtrengen) to founder (or override, overwork) a horse; ₂jährig (‒‿‿‿) a. ⓰: a) more than a year old; b) (veraltet) superannuated, too old; ₌jod-ſäure f, chm. periodic acid (HJO$_4$, 2H$_2$O); ₂kalken (‒‿‿‿) v/a. ⓰* to chalk over; to parget, to plaster; ₂kippen (‒‿‿‿) ⓰** v/n. (in) to topple over; v/a. to tip (or tilt) over, to upset, to overthrow; ₂kitten ⊙ (‒‿‿‿) v/a. ⓰* to cement (or putty) over; ₂kleben v/a. (‒‿‿‿) ⓰** to paste paper, &c. over; (‒‿‿‿) ⓰*: ein Brett mit einem Blatt Papier ₂ to paste (or glue) ... over with a sheet of paper; ₌kleid (‒‿‿) n ⓞc. upper (or outer) garb or garment or vestment; ₂kleiden (‒‿‿‿) v/a. ⓰*: et. mit et. ₂ to clothe s.th. in s.th.; ₂kleiſtern v/a. (‒‿‿‿) ⓰a** u. (‒‿‿‿) ⓰a* to paste over (with size); ₂klettern (‒‿‿‿) ⓰a**, ₂klimmen v/n. (in) to climb over; (‒‿‿‿) ⓹a.⓰* v/a.: das Gebirge ₂ to cross the mountains; ₂klug (‒‿‿) a. ⓰ mſt iro. overwise, too clever (by half), too knowing, priggish; ₂er Menſch wiseacre; ₌klugheit f ⓯ priggishness; ₂knüpfen (‒‿‿‿) v/a. ⓰*** to button over; ₂kochen (‒‿‿‿ch) v/n. (in) ⓰** to boil over, fig. a. to boil with rage over, to fret and fume, to be in a passion; ₂kommen (‒‿‿‿) v/a. ⓰*** = hinüberkommen; (‒‿‿‿) ⓰* (bekommen) to receive, obtain, get; (in ſeine Gewalt bekommen) to seize, grasp; mit ſachlichem Subjekt = befallen 1; v/n. (h.): e-m ₂ v. Geld ꝛc.: to come (or fall) to a p., v. Überlieferungen ꝛc.: to come down to a p.: wir haben es von den Vorfahren ₂ it has come down to us from our forefathers; es hat ihn Ekel ₂ he began to feel sick; ₂köten (‒‿‿‿) vet. ſich ₂ v/refl. ⓰* to dislocate the fetlock-joint; ₌kötung f ⓯ vet. dislocation of the fetlock-joint; ₌kraft f ⓾ excess (or abundance) of strength;

₌kräftig (‒‿‿‿) a. ⓰ too strong or powerful; overbearing; ₂kritzeln (‒‿‿‿) v/a. ⓰a* to scribble (all) over; ₂kugeln F (‒‿‿‿): ſich ₂ v/refl. ⓰a* to turn head over heels, to topple (or roll) over, to go sprawling; ₂künſteln (‒‿‿‿) v/a. ⓰a* to do with too much art or affectation; ₂laden (‒‿‿‿) ⓰bⶠv/a. to shift a cargo; (‒‿‿‿) ⓰bⶠv/a. u. v/refl. to overload a cart, &c.; to overfreight a ship; ſich ₂ to overburden o.s.; ſich (dat.) den Magen ₂ to overload one's stomach, to overeat o.s.; ₂ p.p. u. a. Kunſtſtil ꝛc.: overdone, too profuse, mit Zieraten: gorgeous, florid, too (highly) ornate; ~ n ㉓ u. ₌ladung f ⓯ overloading, &c., elect. overcharge, des Magens auch: surfeit(ing), repletion; im Kunſtſtil: (a. ₌ladenheit (‒‿‿‿) f ⓯) etwa: profuseness of style, of ornaments, &c.; ₌land-(eiſen)bahn 🚂 (‒‿‿‿...) f ⓬ transcontinental railway, overland route; ₌land-poſt f engliſch-indiſche: overland mail; ₌land-telegraph overland telegraph; ₂lang (‒‿‿) a. ⓰ too long; ₂langen ⟂ (‒‿‿‿) v/a. ⓰** to hand over, to pass (over); ₂laſſen (‒‿‿‿) ⓰a**: e-n ₂ to let a p. cross over, (übriglaſſen) to leave over; (‒‿‿‿) ⓰a* v/a. (im Beſitze l.) to leave in possession; (abtreten) to yield (up), cede, resign, surrender, (übermachen) to make over, (übertragen) to transfer; (verlaſſen) to relinquish, to abandon; e-n ſ-m Schickſal ₂ to leave a p. to his fate; es iſt ihm ₂, was er tun will he is at (full) liberty to act as he pleases, a. the matter is left in his hands or to his discretion; überlaßt das mir! leave that to me!; ſich ſelbſt ₂ ſein to be left to one's own resources or devices; den Wellen ₂ (left) at the mercy of the waves; ſich ₂ v/refl.: ſich dem Kummer ₂ to give way to grief; ſich dem Vergnügen ₂ to give o.s. up to pleasure, to plunge into dissipation; ~ n ㉓ u. ₌laſſung f ⓯ leaving (in possession); yielding (up), cession, transfer; relinquishment; ₌laſt (‒‿‿) f ⓯ overweight; (Läſtiges) great trouble, burden or bother; ₂laſten (‒‿‿‿) v/a. ⓰* to overload, fig. to overburden, to encumber; ₂laſtig ⚓ (‒‿‿‿) a. ⓰ v. Schiffen: overloaded, overfreighted; ₂läſtig (‒‿‿‿) a. ⓰ most troublesome or burdensome or bothersome; ₂laufen (‒‿‿‿) ⓰a** v/a. e-n ₂ to run over a p.; v/n. (in): a) v. Flüſſigkeiten: to run (or flow) over, to overflow, von Kochendem: to boil over, typ. v. Zeilen: to run over; das Waſſer iſt ü"bergelaufen the water overflowed or boiled over; die Augen laufen ihm über his eyes are filled (or wet) with tears, he is all in tears; f. Galle¹ 2 gegen Ende; b) (übergehen) to go over to, zum Feinde auch: to desert (oft ⚔); ~ n ₂ running over; zum ~ voll full to overflowing, brimful; ⚔ zum Feinde: desertion; (‒‿‿‿) ⓰a* (ſich verbreiten über) to run (or spread) over; gewaltſam, ve wüſtend: to overrun, to infest; beläſtigen: to importune, pester, besiege; (überſchwemmen) to inundate; er (der Arzt) wird von Patienten rein ₂ he is regularly

---

Signs (see page XVII): F familiar; P vulgar; ſ flash; ⟂ rare; † obsolete (died); * new word (born); ++ incorrect; ♪ music

besieged (or eagerly sought after) by patients; es überlief ihn ein kalter Schauder a cold shudder came over him; es überlief mich (eis)kalt a cold shiver came over me, cold shivers ran down my back; et. mit den Augen 2 to glance (or run) over s.th.; (überholen) to outrun, to outstrip (or beat) in running; sich 2 v/refl. (durch Laufen abmatten) to fatigue (or exhaust) o.s. with running; =läufer (‒‿‒‿) m 22: a) ⚔ deserter, runaway; b) pol. turncoat; c) rel. renegade; 2laut (‒‿‒/) a. 66 too loud or noisy; clamorous; 2leben (‒‿‒‿) v/a. u. v/refl. 88*: e-n, et. 2 to survive (or outlive) a p., a th.; er hat sie alle überle"bt he has lived longer than any of them; das wird er nicht 2 that will be the death of him; sich 2 to outlive o.s., to be no more o.s.; das hat sich überle"bt that's out of date or out of fashion, it has had its day; ~ n 23 survival; ~de([r] m) f 67 survivor; =lebsel (‒‿‒‿) n 22 = Überrest; =lebensgroß (‒‿‒/) a. 66 above life-size; 2legen¹ (‒‿‒‿) v/a. 88** to lay over or upon; zum Prügeln: to flog (or whip) on one's knee, &c.; (‒‿‒/‿) 88* v/a.: mit Brettern x. 2 to overlay (or cover) with ...; (überlasten) to overload; fig. (erwägen) to turn over (or to revolve) in one's mind, to think over, consider, reflect upon; mit e-m et. 2 to deliberate (or consult) with a p. about a th.; ich will es mir 2 I will think (or turn) it over; alles wohl überle"gt (ob. wenn man es genau überle"gt) considering all things, taking everything into account; sich et. zweimal 2 to think (or look) twice before doing a th.; das will wohl überlegt sein that requires careful consideration; ~ n 23 s. =legung; 2legen² (‒‿‒‿) [nhd.] a. 66 superior to; du bist ihm an Verstand 2 you are his superior (or you surpass him) in intellect; mit 2er Miene with a superior air; =legenheit (‒‿‒‿‿) f 46 superiority (über e-n over a p.), superior power or strength, pre-eminence; (Übergewicht) preponderance; 2legsam (‒‿‒/) a. 66 thoughtful; =legung (‒‿‒‿) f 46 consideration, reflexion; deliberation; bei nochmaliger ~ on second consideration or thoughts; mit ~ deliberately; mit ~ verübtes Verbrechen premeditated crime; ohne ~ thoughtlessly, inconsiderately; =legungs-kraft (‒‿‒‿‿/) f 40 power of reflexion, thinking power, (sound) judgment; 2leiten (‒‿‒‿) 88** v/a. (hinüberführen) med. Blut 2 to transfuse ..., v/n. (h.) to lead over to; (einen Übergang bilden) to form a transition; ~ n 23 u. =leitung f 46 transition, transfusion; 2lernen (‒‿‒‿‿ u. ‿‒‿‿) 88*(*): seine Lektion 2 to go over (or learn) one's lesson again; 2lesen (‒‿‒‿) 8a* v/a. (a. ‒‿‒‿88**): e-n Brief 2 to read (or glance, run) over ..., to peruse ... (in haste); (beim Lesen übersehen) to skip in reading; sich 2 2 refl. to read too much; sich ein Buch 2 to be sick of reading a book; 2liefern (‒‿‒‿) v/a. 2a*: e-m einen

Brief x. 2 to deliver (or give up) ... to a p.; a. = übergeben; (weiter verbreiten) to spread abroad, to circulate; der Nachwelt 2 to hand down (or transmit) to posterity; überliefert traditional; ~ n 23 = =lieferung a; =lieferung f 46: a) delivery, transmission, b) (Fortpflanzen einer Kunde) tradition; 2liegen (‒‿‒‿) v/n. (h.) 24** to lie over (time); ⚓ 2 lassen to allow (to be) on demurrage; =liege-tage; =liege-tage m/pl., =zeit f ⚓ days of demurrage, additional lay-days pl.; 2listen (‒‿‒‿) v/a 88*: e-n 2 to outwit (or overreach) a p.; (betrügen) to dupe, cheat, deceive, defraud; ~ n 23, =listung f 46 outwitting; cheat(ing), deception, fraud (practised on).

überm F (‒/) = über dem.

über-machen (‒‿‒/‿) 8* v/a.: e-m et. 2 to make over (or transmit, forward, convey) a th. to a p.; ⚓ Geld durch Wechsel x. 2 to remit money; übermachte Summe remittance, (‒‿‒‿‿) 88** v/a.: to put on or over; =macht (‒/‒‿/cht) f 40 mst ⚔ superior(ity of) forces pl.; weits. superior (or excessive) power, predominance; der ~ die Spitze bieten to face (or fight against) great odds; der ~ weichen to yield before superior numbers; 2mächtig (‒‿‒‿‿) a. 66 of superior power; too mighty or powerful; paramount; =machung (‒‿‒/‿) f 46 making over, transmission, v. Geld x.: remittance; 2malen (‒‿‒‿) 88** v/a. to paint over or out; (‒‿‒/‿) 88* v/a.: ein Bild mit e-m andern 2 to cover one painting with another; (färben, anstreichen) to colour, to paint; ein fertiges Bild 2 (nachbessern) to touch up ...; 2mangan-sauer (‒‿‒‿‿) a. chm. permanganic; übermangansaures Salz permanganate; =mangan-säure f 46 permanganic acid (II Mn O₄); 2mannen (‒‿‒‿) v/a. 88* to overpower, overwhelm, overcome, master, subdue; vom Schlaf überma"nnt overcome by drowsiness, succumbing to sleep; =mannung f 46 overpowering, getting the better of; =maß (‒‿‒/) [nhd.] n ⚓a. overflowing (or brimful) measure; fig. profusion, excess, im Essen: gluttony, im Trinken: intemperance, in Genüssen: debauchery, licentiousness; ~ von Freude, oft: unbounded joy; im ~(e) excessively; bis zum ~e to excess, to a fault; ⚓ zum ~e versehen mit ... overstocked (vom Markte a. glutted) with ...; 2mäßig (‒‿‒‿) a. 66 unmeasured, immoderate; profuse, (übertrieben) excessive, exorbitant, (äußerst) extreme, (ungeheuer) monstrous, enormous, adv. oft: beyond measure. to excess, out of proportion; 2 arbeiten to work too hard; 2 groß enormous, unwieldy, huge; =mäßigkeit f 46 immoderateness, excess; 2masten ↓ (‒‿‒‿) v/a. 88** to overmast; 2mauern ⊙ (‒‿‒‿) v/a. ⚓a* to wall in, to enclose in walls; 2meistern (‒‿‒‿) v/a. ⚓a* = bemeistern; =mensch (‒/‒‿) m ⚓ superman, exalted being. person of supernatural qualities; 2menschlich (‒‿‒‿‿) a. 66 superhuman,

more than human; (übernatürlich) supernatural; 2messen (‒‿‒‿) ⚓** v/a. to measure too abundantly; aus einem Sack in den andern 2 to fill from one sack into another; (‒‿‒/‿) ⚓* v/a. u. v/refl. to measure on the surface; (bis ans Ende überblicken) to take in at a glance; sich 2 to make a mistake in measuring; 2mitteln (‒‿‒‿) v/a. ⚓a* to transmit, to deliver; =mitt(e)lung ⚔ f 46 von Befehlen: transmission, delivery, Meldungen: transmission, delivery; 2morgen (‒‿‒‿) adv. the day after tomorrow; 2d a. 66: der 2de Tag the day after tomorrow; 2müden (‒‿‒‿) v/a. u. v/refl. ⚓** (sich) 2 to overfatigue (o.s.), to overtire (o.s.); übermü"det overtired, F deadbeat, knocked up; =müdung f 46 overfatigue; (große Ermüdung) great weariness; =mut (‒/‒‿/) m ⚓c. (übergroße Lustigkeit) high spirits pl., unrestrained mirth; (Mutwille) wantonness; (Vermessenheit) impertinence, F sauciness; (Anmaßung) arrogance, insolence, F cockiness; (Hochmut) haughtiness, pride; (Überhebung) presumption, F uppishness; bisw. (übermütiger Mensch) insolent (or impertinent, F saucy) fellow; 2mütig (‒‿‒‿) [ahd.] a. 66 (s. =mut) in high spirits, exceedingly merry, wanton; impertinent, insolent, F saucy; arrogant, insolent, F cocky; haughty, very proud, presumptuous, F uppish; 2nachten (‒‿‒‿‿) ⚓* v/n. (h.) to pass (or stay, spend) the night, to get a night's shelter or lodging; wo haben Sie überna"chtet? where did you stay (for) the night?; v/a.: e-n 2 to harbour (or accommodate) a p. for the night, to give a p. a night's shelter or lodging; 2nächtig (‒‿‒‿‿) a. 66 lasting all night; having watched (or stayed up) all night, weary with (a night's) watching; 2 aussehen to look as if one had not slept (or had sat up) all night, F to look seedy; =nachtung (‒‿‒‿‿) f 46 spending the night, finding a night's shelter; 2nähen (‒‿‒‿) v/a. ⚓** to sew over; (‒‿‒/‿) ⚓* to fasten (or cover) with stitches; =nahme (‒‿‒‿) f 48 (s. übernehmen) taking (or entering into) possession of, einer Arbeit: taking in hand, undertaking, e-r Erbschaft: coming into, von etwas Anvertrautem: taking charge of, v. Waren: acceptance; nach ~ eines Amtes after entering upon an office. über-nahme, Über-nahms-bedingungen (‒‿‒‿(‿)...) f/pl. 62 conditions pl. of acceptance; =liste f consigner's list of prices; (Inventar) inventory. über-narben v/n. (fn) ⚓* von Wunden: to form a skin or scar or crust; 2natürlich (‒‿‒‿‿) a. 66 supernatural; (wunderbar) miraculous; 2nehmen (‒‿‒‿) ⚓a** v/a. to take across; e-n Mantel 2 (über sich decken) to wrap o.s. in a cloak; Kartenspiel: e-n Stich 2 to make a trick with a higher trump; (‒‿‒/‿) v/a. u. v/refl. ⚓a* (in Besitz nehmen) to take possession of; (auf sich nehmen) to take upon o.s., eine Arbeit, ein Geschäft: to take in hand,

[Übernehmer] — 984 — [überschlagen]

to undertake; (in Empfang nehmen) to accept, Geld: to receive, Anvertrautes: to take charge of, ein Amt: to enter upon; er hat die Führung überno"mmen he has taken the lead; das Kommando von et. 2 to take (the) command of a th.; die Verantwortlichkeit für et. 2 to assume the responsibility for a th.; von Gefühlen: es überna"hm ihn die Angst he was seized with fear; e-n 2 (zu viel von ihm fordern) to overcharge a p.; sich in et. 2 (das Maß überschreiten) to overdo a th., to carry a th. to excess; im Essen und Trinken: to eat and drink too much, to indulge too freely; (sich überanstrengen) to overexert o.s.; (zu viel auf sich nehmen) to undertake too much; =nehmer (⌣—⌣⌣) m ㉒ one who takes possession (or charge) of, eines Baues ꝛc.: contractor; =normalklasse(n pl.) f ㊽ Tennis: class(es) above scratch; =ordnen (⌣—⌣⌣) v/a. ㉒b** to place (or range) above; =oxyd (⌣—⌣) n ㉓ c. chm. = Super=oxyd; =oxydierung (⌣—⌣⌣⌣) f ㊻ chm.: ⚛ hyperoxygenation; =pflanzen (⌣—⌣⌣) v/a. ㊾* nach e-m anderen Orte: to transplant; (⌣—⌣) ㊾* (bedecken) to plant with; =pflanzung f ㊻ transplantation; =pflügen (⌣—⌣⌣) v/a. ㊽* to plough over; =pichen (⌣—⌣⌣) v/a. ㊽* to (cover with) pitch; =pinseln (⌣—⌣⌣) ㉒a**, (⌣—⌣⌣) ㉒a* v/a. to paint (or daub, plash, splash) over with a brush; =polstern (⌣—⌣⌣) v/a. ㉒a* to upholster; =polt ⊙ (⌣—⌣) a. ㊻ metall. vom Kupfer: (zu jung) overpoled; =produktion (⌣—⌣⌣(*)⌣) f ㊻ overproduction; =quer (⌣—⌣) adv. crossways, crosswise, athwart; =queren (⌣—⌣⌣) v/a. ㊽* to go across, to cross; sie überquerte die Straße she crossed the road; =ragen (⌣—⌣⌣) v/n. (h.) ㊽** (überhangen) to overhang, impend, (hervorstehen) to project; (⌣—⌣⌣) v/a. ㊽* to overtop, to tower above, to overlook, bsd. fig. to surpass, ⚔ frt. to command; (bekrönen) to crown; =ranken (⌣—⌣⌣) v/a. ㊽* to cover with tendrils; =raschen (⌣—⌣⌣) v/a. ㊽* to (take by) surprise, to take aback or unawares; e-n unvorbereitet 2 to come upon a p. unawares, F to catch a p. on the hop; vom Gewitter überra"scht caught in the storm; 2d surprising, astonishing, amazing; ganz 2d schnell surprisingly quick, with astonishing speed; er war ganz überra"scht davon he was quite surprised (or astonished) at it; ~ n ㉓ und =raschung f ㊻ surprise; =rechnen (⌣—⌣⌣) v/a. ㊽b* to reckon (or count) over, to calculate, eine Aufstellung, Rechnung: to run (or glance) over, to examine; (auch ⌣—⌣⌣, ㊽b**) (flüchtig durchrechnen) to cast up; ~ n ㉓ u. =rechnung f ㊻ (hasty or superficial) calculation, examination of bills &c.; =reden (⌣—⌣⌣) v/a. u. sich 2 v/refl. ㊽* to talk over, to persuade (or prevail upon) a p. to do a th.; sich zu et. 2 lassen to be talked into a th., durch Gründe: to be prevailed upon to do a th.; 2d persuasive, convincing; ~ n ㉓ und =redung f ㊻ persuasion; =gabe (⌣—⌣…) f ㉒ gift of persuasion;

=s=kraft f power of persuasion, persuasive force of power; =s=kunst f art of persuasion; =reich (⌣—⌣) a. ㊻ extremely rich, abounding in wealth; 2 an // abounding in //; overflowing (or teeming) with //; =reichen (⌣—⌣⌣) v/a. ㊽*: e-m et. 2 to hand a th. (over) to a p., to present (or pass) a th. to a p.; er ließ sich die Bittschrift 2 he had the petition presented to him; ~ n ㉓ f. =reichung f; =reichlich (⌣—⌣⌣) a. ㊻ superabundant; adv. a. in profusion, very richly; =reichung (⌣—⌣⌣) f ㊻ presentation; =reif (⌣—⌣) a. ㊻ overripe, too ripe; =reife (⌣—⌣⌣) f ㊻ overripeness; =reifen¹ (⌣—⌣) [reif] ㊽* v/a. to make too ripe; v/n. (sn.) to grow overripe or too ripe; =reifen² (⌣—⌣⌣) [Reif³] v/a. ㊽* to cover with hoarfrost; =rei"ft hoary, ⚚: ⚛ pruinous; =reiten (⌣—⌣⌣) ㊽b* v/a. ⌣—⌣ ㊽b*) to ride over, to knock down in riding; ↘ v/n. (sn) to ride across; er ist ü"bergeritten he rode across; (⌣—⌣⌣) ㊽b* v/a. er hat das Kind überri"tten he rode over the child; 2 (überholen) to outride a p., mehr gbr.: to overtake a p. on horseback; ein Pferd (erschöpfen) to overwork (or founder) …; =reiz (⌣—⌣) m ⓐa. overexcitement; powerful stimulation or stimulant; =reizen (⌣—⌣⌣) v/a. ㊾* to overexcite, to irritate (or stimulate) to excess; =rei"zt von den Nerven ꝛc.: overwrought; ~ n ㉓ u. =reizung, auch =reiztheit (⌣—⌣) f ㊻ overexcitement, excessive irritation or stimulation; =rennen v/a. ⌣—⌣⌣ u. ⌣—⌣⌣ ㊽b**: e-n 2 to run over a p.; (⌣—⌣⌣) ㊽b* = überlaufen; =rest (⌣—⌣) m ⓐb. remainder, von Tuch ꝛc.: remnant; ~e eines Gebäudes: ruins pl.; von Heiligen: relics pl.; von Speisen: broken victuals pl. or food; chm. residue; geol. getrümmerte ~e pl.: ⚛ detritus; =rhein ♀ (⌣—⌣) südb. npr. ⓦc.: der ~ the country beyond the Rhine; =rheinisch (⌣—⌣⌣) a. ㊻ from (or of) yonder side of the Rhine, transrhenane; =rieseln (⌣—⌣⌣) v/a. ㉒a* to irrigate; =ries(e)lung f ㊻ irrigation; =rock (⌣—⌣) m ⓒ c. der Männer: a) (gentleman's) frock-coat (a. ⚔); b) = Überzieher; der Frauen: skirt; =rumpeln (⌣—⌣⌣) v/a. ㉒a* bsd. ⚔ den Feind: to attack unexpectedly, to surprise, e-e Festung: to carry by surprise; sie wurden überru"mpelt, sie ließen sich 2 they were taken by surprise, they were caught napping; fig. = =raschen; ~ n ㉓ u. =rump(e)lung f ㊻ unexpected (or sudden) attack, surprise.

übers F (⌣—) = über das.

über=säen (⌣—⌣⌣) v/a. ㊽* to sow over with; von Sternen übersä"t bespangled with stars; =salzen (⌣—⌣⌣) v/a. ㊾* to oversalt, to salt too much or to excess; =satt (⌣—⌣) a. ㊻ oversatiated, mehr gbr.: glutted, surfeited, cloyed; =sättigen (⌣—⌣⌣) v/a. und v/refl. ㊽* to surfeit, to cram with food; sich 2 to eat to excess, to gormandize; fig. übersä"ttigt von // sick and tired of //; chm. to oversaturate; ⊙ mach. übersä"ttigter

Dampf surcharged (or overheated) steam; =sättigung f ㊻ surfeit, auch: fulness,repletion;chm.oversaturation; =säuern (⌣—⌣⌣) v/a. ㉒a* to make too sour or too acid; den Magen 2 to produce acidity in (or of) the stomach; =schallen (⌣—⌣⌣) v/a. ㊽* to sound above, to be louder than, to drown a voice; =scharf (⌣—⌣) a. ㊻ too sharp; =schatten (⌣—⌣⌣) v/a. ㊽* to overshadow, to cast a shadow over; fig. to put in the shade, to eclipse; =schätzen (⌣—⌣⌣) v/a. u. sich 2 v/refl. ㊾* (sich) to overestimate (o.s.), to overvalue (o.s.), to overrate (o.s.), to think too highly of (o.s.); j-s Eigenschaften 2. auch: to have too good (or too high) an opinion of a p.; e-n b. d. Steuereinschätzung 2 to overassess a p., to assess a p. too highly; ~ n ㉓ u. =schätzung f ㊻ overestimation, overvaluation, bei der Steuereinschätzung: overassessment; ~ seiner selbst: presumption, conceit; =schau (⌣—⌣) ㊻ survey; =schauen (⌣—⌣⌣) v/a. ㊽* to look over; to survey; der Hügel 2schau"t den Fluß … overlooks (or commands a view of) the river; =schäumen (⌣—⌣⌣) v/n. (sn) ㊽* to froth over, to brim over with foam; =schicht, meist ⚒ (⌣—⌣) f ㊻ extra shift; vgl. =stunde; =schicken (⌣—⌣⌣) v/a. ㊽* =senden; =schießen (⌣—⌣⌣) ⓒ(e)ft* v/n. (sn) (durch Übeneigen stürzen) to fall (or shoot) forward, Sport: to go a cropper; ⚓ der 2de Ballast the shifting ballast; (überfließen) to overflow; (überschüssig sein) to be in excess; die 2de Summe the surplus (amount), the balance (left); (⌣—⌣⌣) ⓒ(e)ft* v/a. u. v/refl. (hinwegeilen über) to shoot (or hurry) across; das Ziel 2 to overshoot the mark; (im Fluge überholen) to fly faster than, to be swifter than; sich 2 to turn (or throw) somersaults; =schiffen (⌣—⌣⌣) ㊽* v/n. (sn) to sail across, to cross in a boat; nach England 2 to cross over to …; v/a. (auch ⌣—⌣⌣, ㊽*) to ship over, to carry (or convey) across (the water); e-e Meerenge 2 to cross …; =schlafen (⌣—⌣⌣) ㊻a* v/a.: eine Zeit 2 to sleep over a certain time; sich 2 v/refl. to oversleep o.s.; =schlag (⌣—⌣) [nhd.] m ⓒ c.: ~ (Ausschlag) der Wage turn of the scales; Turnerei: somersault; arith., &c. (annähernde Berechnung) rough (or approximate) calculation or estimate; einen ~ m. to make a rough calculation, auch: to form (or frame) a rough estimate; med. (äußerliches Heilmittel) poultice; =schlagen (⌣—⌣⌣) [mhd.] ㊽b** v/n. (sn) to pass rapidly over; die elektrischen Funken schlagen über … flash (or dart) across; (überkippen) to topple over, to tumble, to lose one's balance; v. d. Stimme: to break, von der Magschale: to incline, to drop; hinten=2 to fall backwards; in et. anderes=2 (übergehen) to turn (or change) rapidly (or suddenly) into s. th. else; v/a. ein Tuch (zur Bedeckung) 2 to put (or throw) a cloth over; feuchte Lappen ꝛc.: to apply, to put on; im p.p. bisw. ㊽b*:

Zeichen (s. S. XVII): F familiär; P Volkssprache; ⚑ Gaunersprache; ↘ selten; † alt (auch gestorben); * neu (auch geboren); ‡ unrichtig;

[Überschlagsdecke] — 985 — [Übersichtszeichnung]

(faltend zf.=legen) to fold (up); die Beine ⸗ to cross one's legs; mit ü"bergeschlagenen Beinen with crossed legs, cross-legged; (‗◡◡‗) ⑱* v/n. (jn) = beschlagen II; (lauwarm w.) to grow lukewarm; Waſſer ꝛc. ⸗ I. to take the chill off …; v/a. fig. ſein bloßer Wink überſchlä"gt die Wagſchale … turns the scales; (auslaſſen, bſd. im Leſen) to pass over, to skip, omit, leave out; (bedecken) to cover (over); die Koſten ⸗ (ungefähr berechnen) to calculate roughly …, to compute …; to make a rough estimate of …; ſich ⸗ v/refl. (hintenüberfallen) to fall backwards; Turnerei: to throw a somersault. =ſchlag(s)=decke (‗◡‗ …) f ⑫ rug, für Pferde: horse-cloth; =ſchlag(s)=kragen m: leinener ~ turn-down collar; =ſchlag(s)=rechnung / rough calculation or estimate; ⸗ſchleichen (‗◡‗◡) v/a. ⑩a* = beſchleichen I; ⸗ſchleiern (‗◡‗◡) v/a. ⑫a* to (cover with a) veil, fig. a. to wrap in mystery; ⸗ſchmelzen ⊕ (‗◡‗◡) v/a. ⑨* (f. ſchmelzen II) to enamel; ⸗ſchmieren (‗◡‗◡ u. ‗◡‗) v/a. ⑱* u. ⑱** to (be)smear (or rub over) with a th.; ⸗ſchnappen (‗◡‗◡) v/n. (jn u. h.) ⑱** to snap, to slip (over), mit der Stimme: to sing falsetto, F fig. to go mad; er iſt ü"bergeſchnappt (verrückt) he is cracked or crazy or F dotty; ⸗ſchneien (‗◡‗◡) v/a. ⑱* to cover with snow; überſchneit blocked up (or obstructed) with snow; ⸗ſchnei"te Pfade snowed-up paths pl.; ⸗ſchreiben (‗◡‗◡) ⑱** v/a. to write over; (auch ‗◡‗◡, ⑱*) (ſchreibend übertragen) to transcribe; bſd. ✠ am Schluſſe der Seite: to carry over; (‗◡‗◡) ⑱* v/a. = beſchreiben 1; (mit einer Aufſchrift verſehen) to superscribe, inscribe, head, einen Brief: to address, to write the address on, to direct; ✠ (bezeichnen) to label, to mark; ⸗ſchreien (‗◡‗◡) ⑱* v/a.: e-n, j-s Stimme ⸗ to make a p.('s voice) inaudible by one's shouting; ſich ⸗ v/refl. (zu ſtark ſchreien) to (over)strain (or overtax) one's voice or vocal organs; ⸗ſchreiten (‗◡‗◡) ⑱b* v/n. (jn) to step over; du biſt ü"bergeſchritten you have stepped across; (‗◡‗◡) ⑱b* v/a. to go beyond, e-n Bach ꝛc.: to cross, mit e-m Schritte: to step across; du haſt die Grenze überſchri"tten you have crossed the boundary, you are over (or across) the frontier; fig. ein Geſetz ⸗ to transgress (or infringe) a law; die Grenze des Schicklichen (nicht) ⸗ to overstep (to keep within) the bounds of decency; alles Maß ⸗ to overstep the mark; das überſchrei"tet alles Maß that exceeds all bounds, F that's going too far; ✠ ſein Konto (oder Guthaben) ⸗ to overdraw one's account; ~ n ㉓ u. ⸗ſchreitung f ㊻ crossing; fig. transgression, infraction, excess; =ſchrift (‗◡‗) f ㊻ = Aufſchrift; auch: inscription; (Titel) title; =ſchuh (‗◡‗) m ⑩c. etwa: shoe worn over a boot; ~e pl. (Gummiſchuhe) india-rubber shoes, goloshes, galoshes pl.; =ſchuh=fabrikant m ㊷ maker of goloshes; ⸗ſchuldet (‗◡‗◡)

a. ⑥ involved in (or encumbered with) debt, deeply involved; Les Eigentum encumbered property; =ſchuldung (‗◡‗◡) f ㊻ jur. heavy indebtedness; =ſchuß (‗◡‗) m ⑧a. what is over; surplus(age), ⓧ auch: balance. ⸗ſchüſſig [nhd.; * ⸗ſchießen] a. ⑥ left over, exceeding the sum required; Les Geld surplus (funds pl.), balance (left); ⸗ſchütten (‗◡‗◡) ⑱** v/a. to pour over, durch Verſehen: to spill; (‗◡‗) ⑱* v/a.: mit et. ⸗ to cover (or strew) with a th.; ⊙ eine Straße mit Steinſchlag ⸗ to metal a road; fig. e-n mit et. ⸗ (überhäufen) to overwhelm (or load) a p. with s. th., to lavish (or shower) a th. upon a p.; ⸗ſchwang (‗◡‗) m ⑦c. superabundance, exuberance, ⸗ſchwanken (‗◡‗◡) v/n. (h.) ⑱** etwa: to lose one's balance, v. Flüſſigkeiten: to be spilled, to run over, to over-flow; ⸗ſchwappen (‗◡‗◡) v/n. (jn) ⑱** vom Waſſer im Eimer ꝛc.: to splash over; ⸗ſchwemmen (‗◡‗◡) v/a. ⑱* to overflow, ſtärker: to flood, inundate, deluge; (unter Waſſer tauchen) to submerge; fig. ✠ den Markt mit einer Ware ⸗ to overstock the market…; ~ n ㉓ und ⸗ſchwemmung f ㊻ flood(ing), inundation; submersion, overflow (of water); ⸗ſchwemmungs=gefahr f ㊻ danger of inundation; ⸗ſchwenglich (‗◡‗◡) [nhd.; *⸗ſchwang] a. ⑥ superabundant, excessive; (übertrieben) extravagant, im Ausdruck der Gefühle: exuberant, high-flown, gushing; (unendlich) infinite, (unermeßlich) immense, boundless; (unerſchöpflich) inexhaustible; mit Ler Luſt with rapturous (or wild) delight; =ſchwenglichkeit f ㊻ superabundance; extravagance, exuberance; boundlessness; im Ausdruck: high-flown style, gush; ⸗ſchwer (‗◡‗) a. ⑥ too weighty, too heavy, fig. exceedingly difficult; ⸗ſchwimmen (‗◡‗◡) v/a. (h.) ⑫a(b)** to swim over or across; ⸗ſee (‗◡‗) adv. u. ~ n, inv.: ⸗ (ob. nach ~) geh(e)n to cross the ocean, to go across the sea; ⸗ſeeiſch (‗◡‗◡) a. ⑥ transoceanic (steamer), transmarine (cable), oversea (route); Le Länder countries pl. across (or beyond) the sea(s); Les Telegramm cablegram; ⸗ſegeln ↓ (‗◡‗◡) ⑫a** v/n. (jn) to sail over or across; (‗◡‗◡) ⑫a* v/a.: ein Schiff ⸗ to run down …, (im Segeln darauf ſtoßen) to foul …, (in den Grund ſegeln) to sink …, (ſegelnd überholen) to outsail, to overtake in sailing; ⸗ſeh=bar (‗◡‗‗) a. ⑥ in full view, observable; visible (or to be seen) at a glance; ⸗ſehen (‗◡‗◡) ⑫a** v/n. (h.) to look over; v/refl. ſich ein Stück (thea.) ü"berſehen h. to be sick of seeing a piece; (‗◡‗◡) ⑫a* v/a. to look over, to overlook, to survey, to see (or take in) at a glance; das Ergebnis läßt ſich noch nicht ⸗ the result cannot yet be foreseen or ascertained; (den Blick ſchweifen l. über) to (cast a) glance over; ſich eine Lektion noch einmal ⸗ (meiſt: ‗◡‗◡) to look once more over …; (hinwegſehen über) to overlook, not to notice, mit Abſicht: to take no notice of, Fehler ⸗

to connive at; ſie wurden ⸗ they were taken no notice of; ſolche Kleinigkeiten werden leicht ⸗ such trifles easily escape notice; ~ n ㉓ overlooking, &c.; (Verſehen) oversight, mistake; abſichtliches ~ von Fehlern: connivance; ⸗ſein ‧ (‗◡‗) v/n. ⑩a** (übrig ſein) to be (left) over; (vorüber ſein) to be a thing of the past; das iſt mir über (ich bin es überdrüſſig) I am (sick and) tired of it; F ſie iſt ihm über(legen) she is above (or superior to) him, she outshines him; ⸗ſelig (‗◡‗◡) a. ⑥ most happy, full of bliss or joy, overjoyed; ⸗ſenden v/a. (‗◡‗◡) ⑫a** to send across; (‗◡‗◡) ⑫a* to send to, to forward (or transmit, dispatch) to; ✠ to consign to, Geld: to remit to; ~ n ㉓ f. ⸗ſendung; ⸗ſender (‗◡‗◡) m ㉒ bſd. ✠ consigner, von Geld: remitter; ⸗ſendung (‗◡‗◡) f ㊻ sending; ✠ consignment, remittance; ⸗ſetzbar (‗◡‗‗) a. ⑥ translatable; nicht ⸗ untranslatable; ⸗ſetzen (‗◡‗◡) ⑫* v/n. (jn) to cross (over), to jump (or leap) over, über ein Waſſer: to cross (over); du ſetz(eſ)t auf einer Fähre über you ferry over or across; er iſt auf einer Fähre ü"bergeſetzt he crossed over in a ferry; (‗◡‗◡) ⑫* v/a. (in eine Sprache übertragen) to translate from one language into another; (verdolmetſchen) to interpret; buchſtäblich ⸗ to render word for word, to translate literally; falſch ⸗ to mistranslate, to misinterpret; ins Franzöſiſche ꝛc. ⸗, oft: to turn into French, &c.; du überſe"tz(eſ)t ganz richtig your translation is quite correct; ich habe ſchon viel überſe"tzt I have done many translations; (übermäßig beſetzen) to overstock (or overcrowd) with, ⊙ den Hochofen ꝛc.: to overcharge; ~ n ㉓ f. ⸗ſetzung; ⸗ſetzer(in f ㊻) m ㉒ translator; (Dolmetſcher) interpreter; =ſetzung f ㊻ translation, bſd. in die Mutterſprache auch: version; falſche ~ misrendering, misinterpretation; getreue ~ faithful rendering, correct interpretation.
Über=ſetzungs=aufgabe (‗◡‗ …) f ⑫ translation (exercise); =fehler m mistake of the translator or (made) in translating; =kunſt f art of translating; =recht n right of translation.
Über=ſicht (‗◡‗) f ㊻ view, survey; (Fernſicht) perspective; (Auffaſſungsgabe) power of apprehension, intellectual grasp, mental (range of) vision; (kurzgefaßte Darſtellung) short (or concise) account, (rapid) sketch, summary, eines größeren Werkes a.: ㉗ synopsis, epitome; (Auszug) extract, in tabellariſcher Form: ㉗ synoptical tables pl.; ⸗ſichtig (‗◡‗◡) a. ⑥ long-sighted; =ſichtigkeit f ㊻ long-sightedness; ⸗ſichtlich (‗◡‗◡) a. ⑥ easy to survey (vgl. überſehbar: (klar gefaßt) clearly (or lucidly) arranged or expressed or put; well-digested; perspicuous; in der Darſtellung lucid exposition, comprehensive view; =ſichtlichkeit f ㊻ clearness (of arrangement), lucidity (of style); perspicuity.
Über=ſichts=karte (‗◡‗ …) f ㉒ outline-map; ⸗plan m general plan; ⸗ſkizze f general sketch or draft; ⸗tafel f: ㉗ synoptical table; ⸗zeichnung f = ⸗ſkizze.

♪ Muſik; ⚜ Wiſſenſchaft; ♀ Pflanze; ☿ Geographie; ⊕ Technik; ⚒ Bergbau; ⚔ Militär; ↓ Marine; ✠ Handel; ✉ Poſt; 🚂 Eiſenbahn.

[übersiedeln] — 986 — [Übertragung]

über=siedeln (‒‿‿‿) ⓐa**, ⤬ (‿‿‿‿) ⓐa* v/n. (ſn): nach Amerika ꝛc. ⚹ to emigrate to ...; (ausziehen) to remove (to new quarters), to shift (one's residence); v/a. to transplant, to remove; ~ n ㉓ und =ſied(e)lung f ㊻ emigration, e-s Volkes ꝛc.: transmigration; (Auszug) removal; ⚹ſilbern ⊕ (‿‿‿‿) v/a. ⓐa* to silver over, to plate (with silver); ⚹ſinnlich (‿‿‿‿) a. ⓰ supersensual; (ſtofflos) immaterial, transcendental, metaphysical, abstract; (übernatürlich) supernatural; ⚹ſinnlichkeit f ㊻ immateriality, transcendentalism, abstractness; ⚹ſommern (‿‿‿‿) ⓐa* v/n. (h.): an einem Orte ⚹ to spend the summer at a place; v/a.: Vieh ⚹ to keep cattle during the summer; ⚹ſpannen (‿‿‿‿) ⓐ** v/a. to span (or stretch) over; (‿‿‿‿) ⓐ* v/a.: mit e-m Teppich ⚹ to cover over with a carpet, to carpet; (mit ausgeſtreckter Hand meſſen) to span; (zu ſtark ſpannen) to overstretch, to overstrain; (zu hoch ſpannen) to exaggerate; ⓜ mach. ben Dampf: to surcharge, to overheat; fig. den Geiſt ⚹ to overexcite the mind; ~ n ㉓ = ⚹ſpannung; ⚹ſpannt p.p. und a. ⓰ overstrained, fig. overexcited, v. Geiſte auch: overwrought; (übertrieben) exaggerated, im Ausbrude: gushing; (ungereimt, toll) extravagant, eccentric, queer; (verrückt) crazy, cracked; ⚹e An-ſichten eccentric opinions, mad ideas pl.; ⚹ſpanntheit (‿‿‿-) f ㊻ overwrought state (of mind); exaggeration; extra-vagance, eccentricity, craziness; ⚹ſpannung f ㊻ overstraining, exces-sive tension, overexcitement; ⚹ſpinnen ⊕ (‿‿‿‿) v/a. ⓐa* to spin over, mit Seide to gimp; überſpo"nnene Saite spun music-string; ⚹ſpringen (‿‿‿‿) ⊕n** v/n. (ſn) to leap over, to jump across, von elektriſchen Funken: to flash (or dart) across; fig. von einem Gegenſtande zum andern ⚹ to flit from one sub-ject to another; path.: a) von einer Sehne: to start; b) v. e-r Krankheit: auf andere Teile ⚹ to shift to other parts, to break out in fresh places; (‿‿‿‿) ⊕* v/a. u. v/refl. e-n Graben: to leap (or jump) over or across...; (überſchlagen) to skip, miss, omit; das Fieber über-ſpri"ngt einen Tag ... intermits for a day; fig. e-n im Amte ⚹ to be put over the head of a p.; ſich ⚹ (im Springen übernehmen) to hurt o.s. in leaping; ⚹ſprudeln (‿‿‿‿ u. ‿‿‿‿) v/n. (ſn u. h.) ⓐa*(*) to bubble over; fig. von Freude ⚹ to be brimful of delight; ⚹der Witz overflowing (or sparkling, brilliant) wit; ⚹ſtändig (‿‿‿‿) a. ⓰ having stood too long, spoiling from age; stale, flat; ⚹es Holz overseasoned wood; ⚹ſtechen (‿‿‿‿) ⓐa** u. (‿‿‿‿) ⓐa* v/n. (h.) u. v/a. Karten: to play a higher card, to beat, mit Trumpf: to overtrump; ⚹ſteh(e)n (‿‿‿‿(‿)) v/n. (h.) ⓐ** to stand above or over; (hervorragen) to jut out, project, impend; (ſtehen bleiben) to stand over; die Wäſche ſteht über ... remains in the tubs (for a day or two); (‿‿‿‿(‿)) ⓐ* v/a.(beſtehen) to overcome, to surmount;

to weather (⤓ to ride out) a storm; (er-tragen) to endure, to stand; eine Krank-heit glücklich ⚹ to get over (or through) an illness; die von ihnen überſta"ndene Mühſal the hardships pl. endured by them, the trouble (which) they have gone through; ⚹ſteigbar (‿‿‿‿) a. ⓰ surmountable; ⚹ſteigen (‿‿‿‿) ⓑ** v/n. (ſn) to climb (or mount) over; er iſt ü"bergeſtiegen he climbed over; v. Gewäſſern: to overflow (the banks); (‿‿‿‿) ⓑ* v/a. u. v/refl.: Berge ⚹ to cross (over) ...; er hat die Felſen überſtie"gen he scrambled over the rocks; fig. e-e Schwierigkeit ⚹ to over-come (or surmount) ...; das überſtei"gt alle Begriffe that passes (or exceeds) all comprehension; (höher ſteigen als) to rise above, to excel; ſich ⚹ (ſteigend überanſtrengen) to overexert o.s. in climbing, (ſich verirren) to lose one's way in climbing; ⚹ſteigern (‿‿‿‿) v/a. ⓐa*: den Preis der Lebensmittel ⚹ to force up ..., to raise ... exorbitantly; e-n ⚹ to outbid a p., to bid higher than a p.; ⚹ſteiglich (‿‿‿‿) a. ⓰ = ⚹ſteigbar; =ſtich (‿‿‿‿) m ⓒc. Kartenſpiel: higher (or better) card; ⚹ſtimmen (‿‿‿‿) v/a. ⓐ** ♪ am Klavier ꝛc.: to tune too high or above concert-pitch; e-e Partei ⚹ to outvote ..., to defeat ... by a majority of votes; ⚹ſtolz (‿‿‿‿) a. ⓰ overproud; ⚹ſtrahlen (‿‿‿‿) v/a. ⓐ* to shine upon, to outshine, to surpass in lustre, to eclipse; ⚹ſtrecken (‿‿‿‿) v/a. ⓐ*: ⚹ſtre"ckte (gefälſchte) Weine adulterated (F doctored) wines pl.; ⚹ſtreichen (‿‿‿‿) v/a. ⓐa** to spread over; (‿‿‿‿) ⓐa*: mit et. ⚹ to smear (or rub, paint) over with a th.; mit Firnis ⚹ to varnish; mit Pech ⚹ to (cover with) pitch; ⚹ſtreifen v/a. (‿‿‿‿) ⓐa** to draw (or pull) over; (‿‿‿‿) ⓐa* to stripe, to colour with stripes; ⚹ſtreuen v/a. (‿‿‿‿) ⓐa** to strew (or sprinkle) over; (‿‿‿‿) ⓐa* (beſtreuen) to strew with; ⚹ſtricken (‿‿‿‿) v/a. ⓐa* to knit over; ⚹ſtrömen (‿‿‿‿) ⓐa** v/n. (ſn) to over-flow, to flow (or run) over; der Fluß iſt ü"bergeſtrömt the river has over-flowed (its banks); fig. ihr Herz ſtrömt über vor Freude her heart exults with joy; ſein Mund ſtrömt über von ihrem Lobe he praises her in most glowing terms, he is loud in her praise; (‿‿‿‿) ⓐa* v/a. to overflow; das Waſſer hat die Felder überſtrö"mt the water has flooded (or submerged) the fields; ~ n ㉓ u. ⚹ſtrömung f ㊻ overflow, flood(ing), inundation; =ſtrömungs=röhre ⊕ f overflow-pipe; ⚹ſtrumpf (‿‿‿‿) m ⓒb. outer stocking; ⚹ſtudieren (‿‿‿‿) ⓐ*: ſich ⚹ v/refl. to study too hard or too much, to overtax one's brain with reading; ü"berſtudiert too learned, too bookish; v/a. (raſch durch-ſtudieren) to study (up) in haste; ⚹ſtül-pen (‿‿‿‿) v/a. ⓐa** to tilt (or cover, F whip) over; =ſtunde (‿‿‿‿) f ⓐ extra hour or lesson; bſd. ⊕ typ. "u (auch Überſtunden-arbeit) machen to do (or work, make) overtime; ⚹ſtürzen (‿‿‿‿) ⓑ** = überſtülpen; v/n (ſn) (überkippen)

to topple over; nach hinten ⚹ to fall backwards; (‿‿‿‿) ⓑ* v/a. u. v/refl.: mit et. ⚹ to cover over with a th.: einen Kochtopf ⚹ to put a lid on a saucepan; fig. et. ⚹ (zu haſtig ausführen) to hurry (or rush, precipitate) a th.; überſtü"rztprecipitate, rash, headlong; ſich ⚹ to act too hurriedly or pre-cipitately or rashly, to go ahead too fast, to run helter-skelter; ⚹ Sie ſich nicht!, oft: don't be rash, F don't flurry yourself!; ~ n ㉓ u. =ſtürzung f ㊻ precipitancy, hurried (or rash) proceeding; nur keine ~! don't hurry!, there is no hurry!, F go it gently!; ⚹ſüß (‿‿‿‿) a. ⓰ oversweet; ⚹täfeln ⊕ (‿‿‿‿) v/a. ⓐa* to board, to plank; to wainscot; ⚹takelt ⤓ (‿‿‿‿) a. ⓰ oversparred; ⚹täuben (‿‿‿‿) v/a. ⓐa* to deafen, auch = überſchallen; ⚹teuer (‿‿‿‿) a. ⓰ overdear, too dear, too expensive, exorbitant; ⚹teuern (‿‿‿‿) v/a. ⓐa* (verteuern) to raise too much in price; einen ⚹ (überfordern) to overcharge a p.; ~ n ㉓ u. =teu(e)rung f ㊻ (great) raising of prices; exorbi-tant charge; ⚹tölpeln (‿‿‿‿) v/a. ⓐa* to impose upon; j. a. betölpeln; =töl-p(e)lung f ㊻ imposition; ⚹tönen (‿‿‿‿) v/a. ⓐa* to sound above, to drown a sound; =trag ⓜ (‿‿‿‿, ‿‿‿‿) m ⓒc.: auf die andere Seite: carrying over; (übertragener Poſten) sum brought for-ward or carried over, transferred account; ⚹tragbar (‿‿‿‿) a. ⓰ trans-ferable, auch = ⚹ſetzbar; path. v. Krank-heiten: infectious, catching; ⚹tragbar-keit f ㊻ transferableness; path. in-fectiousness; ⚹tragen (‿‿‿‿) ⓑb** v/a.: a) ein Kleib ⚹ to wear ... over (another); b) to carry over; in ein anderes Buch ⚹ to enter in another book, to transcribe; ⓜ auf die nächſte Seite ⚹ to carry over or forward; in das Haupt-buch ⚹ to enter in the ledger; (‿‿‿‿) ⓑb* v/a. u. v/refl. c) (hinübertragen) to carry (or convey) across; et. auf e-n ⚹ to transfer (or convey, make over, assign) a th. to a p. (a. jur.); das ihm ⚹e Amt the office to which he has been appointed; e-m die Beſorgung von et. ⚹ to charge (or entrust, com-mission) a p. with a th.; e-m eine Ehre, Würde ⚹ to confer ... upon a p.; auf j-s Namen ⚹ to register in a p.'s name; ⊕ mach. eine Bewegung, eine Kraft ⚹ to transmit ...; path. eine Krankheit ⚹ to spread, convey (or transmit, carry, communicate) a disease; d) aus e-r Sprache in die andere ⚹ (überſetzen) to translate; ins Engliſche ⚹ to render (or turn) into English; fig. ⚹e Be-deutung figurative (or metaphorical) meaning; e) ſich ⚹ v/refl.: a) (zu ſchwere Laſten tragen) to carry too heavy loads; β) von Krankheiten: to be infectious or contagious or catching; die Peſt über-trä"gt ſich auf Ratten ꝛc. the plague is transmitted (or attacks) rats, &c.; ~ n ㉓ = ⚹tragung a; =trager (‿‿‿‿) m ㉒: a) (Überſetzer) translator; b) (der einen Wechſel abtritt) endorser; c) ⊕ tel. relay, repeater; =tragung f ㊻: a) (zu ⚹tragen c) carrying (or car-

Signs (see page XVII): F familiar; P vulgar; F flash; ⤬ rare; † obsolete (died); * new word (born); ‡ incorrect; ♪ music.

riage) across; transfer, conveyance, assignment; transcription; ⚙ *mach.*, *phys.* transmission of a force; (Übersetzung) translation, rendering; (zu c) transmission or spread(ing) of a disease, (Ansteckung) infection; b) *rhet.* (bildlicher Ausdruck) figure of speech, metaphor(ical expression).

Über-tragungs-apparat (′◡″◡…) *m* [62] *tel.* transmitter, relay; **-schraube** ⚙ *f* translating-screw; **-station** *f*, *tel.* relay-station or -office; **-urkunde** *f* *jur.* deed of conveyance.

über-treffbar (′◡″-) *a.* [66] surpassable; **≗treffen** (′◡″◡) *v/a.* [73]a*: e-n an (od. in) et. ≗ to surpass (or excel) a p. in a th.; einen weit ≗ to eclipse a p., F to beat a p. hollow; er wird nur von wenigen im Schießen übertro″ffen there are but few who can beat (or outdo, match) him in shooting; **≗treiben** (″◡′◡) [81]** *v/a.* to drive over or across; er hat das Vieh ü″bergetrieben (über den Bach ɪc.) he drove the cattle across; *v/n.* (sn) (überfließen) to overflow; (′◡″◡) [81]* *v/a.*: das Vieh ≗ (überanstrengen) to overdrive …, abstrakt: (zu weit gehen mit) to overdo, to carry to excess; erzählend (a. ohne Objekt): to exaggerate, magnify, overdraw, F to pile (it) on; er hat stark übertrie″ben he gave an exaggerated account or a highly coloured view; vgl. ≗trieben *p.p.*; ~ *n* [23] = -treibung; **-treiber** (′◡″◡) *m* [22] exaggerator, (Prahler) braggart; **-treibung** *f* [46] excess; exaggeration; extravagance; **≗treten** (″◡′◡) [82]d** *v/n.* (sn): a) to step over, von Flüssen: to overflow (the banks); b) zu j-s Partei (od. zu e-m) ≗ to go over (or secede) to (or to join) a p.('s party); zu einer anderen Partei (Religion) ≗ to change sides (one's religion); zum Katholizismus ≗ to turn (or to become a) Roman Catholic; er ist zu ihnen ü″bergetreten he has gone over to them; *v/a.* Stiefel ≗ (schief laufen) to tread (or run) down … on one side; (′◡″◡) [82]d* *v/a.* u. **sich** ≗ *v/refl.*: sich (*dat.*) den Fuß ≗, sich (*acc.*) ≗ to sprain one's foot or ankle; *fig.* (vgl. ≗schreiten *fig.*) to transgress, to exceed; (nicht beobachten) to trespass (or offend) against the commandments, &c., to infringe or break a law, a rule, to violate s.th. sacred; ein Gebot ≗ to act contrary to (or in contravention of) an order, a decree; er hat das Gesetz ≗ he has transgressed (or broken) the law; ~ *n* [23] = -tretung; **-treter** (′◡″◡) *m* [22], **~in** *f* [47] transgressor; trespasser, offender; law-breaker; **-tretung** *f* [46] transgression, trespass(ing), infringement, violation; sich einer ~ schuldig m. to transgress, to trespass, to commit an offence (against the law); **-tretungs-fall** (′◡″◡-″) *m*: im ~(e) in case of transgression or contravention; **≗trieben** *p.p.* u. *a.* [66] (D 9) overdone, excessive, exaggerated, overdrawn; von Ansichten ɪc.: extravagant (notion, &c.), extreme (view), von Kosten: exorbitant (charge, price); aus übertrieb(e)nem Eifer from excess of zeal, from overzeal; **~heit** *f* [46] excessiveness, von Ansichten auch: extremeness; **-trift** (″◡″) *f* [46] right of way for cattle; **-tritt** (″◡″) *m* [11]c. (s. ≗treten) going over to, secession to, bsd.: change of religion, conversion; **≗trumpfen** (″◡″◡) [88]** u. (′◡″◡) [88]* *v/a.* Kartenspiel: to overtrump, *fig.* a. to defeat, durch List: to outwit, F to beast; **≗tünchen** ⚙ (′◡″◡) *v/a.* [88]* Bauwesen: to whitewash; *bibl.* wie die übertü″nchten Gräber (Matth. 23,27) like unto whited sepulchres; *fig.* to gloss (or polish) over, to varnish, to deck out; Europens übertü″nchte Höflichkeit (SEUME) Europe's sham (or counterfeit) politeness; **-verdienst** (″◡f◡′) *m* [11]d. extra profit or gain or F money; **≗versichern** ❀ (″◡f◡″◡) *v/a.* [92]a*/* to over-insure; **-versicherung** *f* [46] over-insurance; **≗völkern** (′◡f″◡) *v/a.* [92]a* to overpeople; ≗vö″lkert overpopulated, overcrowded; **-völkerung** *f* [46] surplus (or excess) population; **≗voll** (″◡f″) *a.* [66] overfull, too full, a. F chock-full, von Gefäßen: brimful, vom Theater ɪc.: overcrowded; **≗vorteilen** (′◡f″-◡) [nhd.] *v/a.* [88]* to overreach, to impose upon, to take advantage of, F to best, take in sell; die von ihm übervo″rteilten Leute the people defrauded (or F taken in) by him; ~ *n* [23] und **-vorteilung** *f* [46] overreaching, imposition, F sell, take-in; **≗wachen** (′◡″ch◡) [88]* *v/a.* to watch over, superintend, supervise; scharf ≗ to watch narrowly, to keep a strict eye upon; **sich** ≗ *v/refl.* to wear o.s. out (or to overtire o.s.) with watching or sitting up; ~ *n* [23] s. -wachung; **≗wachsen** (″◡″ß◡) [85]b** *v/n.* (sn) to grow over; (′◡″ß◡) [85]b* *v/a.* u. *v/n.* (sn) (bewachsen) to overgrow; mit Laub ≗ *p.p.* clad in foliage; ↘ *v/a.* (wachsend überragen) to outgrow, to grow beyond; **sich** ≗ *v/refl.* (zu stark wachsen) to grow too fast, von Kindern auch: sie ≗ sich they outgrow their strength; **-wachung** *f* [46] superintendence, supervision, control; **≗wallen** (″◡″◡ und ′◡″◡) *v/n.* (sn) [88]*(*) to boil (or gush, run) over (vgl. überfließen); *fig.* heftig ≗ to be seething (or boiling) with passion; **≗wältigen** (′◡″◡◡) [nhd.] *v/a.* [88]* to overwhelm, overpower, overcome; (besiegen) to defeat, to vanquish, (unterwürfig machen) to subdue; vom Schlafe überwä″ltigt overcome with sleep; ≗des Schauspiel imposing scene; ~ *n* [23] u. **-wältigung** *f* [46] overwhelming, &c.; **≗weg** ↘ (′◡″) *adv.*: ≗ geh(e)n to cross (or go across) the road; **≗weise** (″◡′◡) *a.* [66] overwise; **≗weisen** (′◡″◡) *v/a.* [81]*: einem et. ≗ to make over (or assign) a th. to a p.; *jur.* dem Geschwornengericht überwie″sen committed for trial (at the assizes); einen eines Irrtums, einer Schuld ≗ to bring home an error, a fault to a p.; ~ *n* [23] u. **-weisung** *f* [46] making over, assignment, durch Urkunde: conveyance; **≗weißen** ⚙ (′◡″◡, ″◡′◡) *v/a.* [88]*(*) to whiten over, (tünchen) to whitewash; **≗wendlich** ⚙ (′◡″◡) *a.* [66] u. *adv.* Näherei: ≗e Naht overcast (or whip-stitch) seam; **≗wendlings** nähen to whip (down); **≗werfen** (″◡″◡) [73]b** *v/a.* to throw over or across; e-n Mantel ≗ to put (F to whip) on a cloak; (′◡″◡) [73]b* *v/a.* u. **sich** ≗ *v/refl.* = bewerfen; e-n ≗ (über den Haufen werfen) to knock a p. over; ↘ e-n ≗ (im Werfen übertreffen) to beat (or outdo) a p. in throwing; sich ≗ (sich überschlagen) to fall backwards; *fig.* sich mit e-m ≗ (entzweien) to fall out with a p., to quarrel with a p.; **≗wichtig** (″◡″◡) *a.* [66] of excessive weight, too heavy, ✉ overweight; *fig.* most (or extremely) important; **≗wickeln** (′◡″◡) *v/a.* [92]a* = bewickeln; **≗wiegen** (′◡″◡) *v/a.* [76]c*: etwas ≗ to weigh a th. down, to outweigh a th.; a. ohne Objekt (oft: ″◡′◡, [76]c**) (den Ausschlag geben) to prevail, preponderate, predominate; ≗d (′◡″◡) predominant, paramount; mit ≗der Mehrheit by an overwhelming (or a crushing) majority; **≗winden** (″◡″◡) [71]** ↘ *v/a.* to wind over or round; (′◡″◡) [ahd.] [71]* *v/a.* u. *v/refl.* (bewickeln) to wrap round; to overcome, vanquish, conquer, subdue, Hindernisse, Schwierigkeiten: to surmount, to get over; *fig.* s. Standpunkt a; Sprichw. Geduld überwi″ndet alles patience conquers all things; **sich** selbst ≗ to carry a victory over o.s.; sich ≗, etwas zu tun to prevail upon o.s. to do a th.; ~ *n* [23] s. -windung; **-winder** (′◡″◡) *m* [22] vanquisher, conqueror, victor; **≗windlich** (′◡″◡) *a.* [66] conquerable, surmountable; **-windung** *f* [46] overcoming, &c.; die ~ des Feindes, eines Heeres: the victory (or triumph) over …; (*abs.* ohne *gen.*) = Selbstüberwindung, zB. es gehört viel ~ dazu, um // it requires great self-restraint or self-control to //; das hat mir ~ gekostet it cost me an effort, I did it with great reluctance or much against my liking; **≗wintern** (′◡″◡) [92]a* *v/n.* (h.): an einem Orte ≗ to (spend the) winter at a place, bsd. von Tieren: ⚗ to hibernate; (den Winter überdauern) to last through the winter; *v/a.* to (keep through the) winter, to hibernate; ~ *n* [23] u. **-winterung** *f* [46]: ⚗ hibernation; **≗wo** ↘ *adv.* wherever; **≗wölben** (′◡″◡) *v/a.* [88]* *arch.* to (cover with a) vault, to vault over, to over-arch; überwö″lbt vaulted, arched; **≗wölken** (′◡″◡): **sich** ≗ *v/refl.* [88]* to assume a cloudy appearance; überwö″lkt cloudy, overcast; der Himmel überwö″lkt sich, a. F it's coming over lowery; **≗wuchern** (″◡″ch◡) [92]a** und (′◡″◡) [92]a* *v/n.* (sn) to grow luxuriantly or profusely; (′◡″◡) [92]a* *v/a.* to cover with luxuriant (or rank) growth, to overrun, erstickend: to choke up; **-wurf** (″◡″) *m* [7]c. (loses Gewand) loose outer garment, loose gown, tunic, covering for the shoulders, für Kinder: overall; **-zahl** (″◡′) *f* [46] surplus (number); (Übermacht) superior number(s) or ⚔ forces *pl.*, numerical superiority, odds *pl.*; **≗zählen** (′◡″◡) [88]* *v/a.*: ich habe das Geld zweimal überzä″hlt I have counted … twice

[**überzählig**] — 988 — [**Uhrgehänge**]

over; ~ sich 2 v/refl. to miscount, to make a mistake in counting; °**zählig** (⌣‿⌣) [nhd.] a. ⊕ supernumerary, odd; ~es Geld money (or change) left over, surplus (amount), odd pounds or shillings pl.; ~e Person bsd. von Angestellten und Schauspielern: supernumerary, F super; =**zähligkeit** f ⊕ bisw.: supernumerariness; =**zahn** (⌣‿⌣) m ⊙c. anat. projecting tooth; °**zeichnen** v/a. (⌣‿⌣) ⊕b** to draw over; (⌣‿⌣) ⊕b* ⊕ eine Anleihe 2 to oversubscribe a loan; =**zeichnung** f ⊕ oversubscription; °**zeugen** (⌣‿⌣‿) [mhd.] v/a. u. v/refl. ⊕* to convince, to persuade; schwer zu 2 difficult to convince, hard of belief; ich bin fest überzeu"gt davon I am firmly convinced of it, I firmly believe (in) it; sich 2 to convince (or satisfy) o.s.; sich mit eigenen Augen von et. 2 to make sure of a th. by seeing it with one's own eyes; man überzeu"ge sich selbst! go and judge for yourself!; 2d p.pr. und a. ⊕ convincing; (beweisend) conclusive, clinching; ~ n ⓘ u. =**zeugung** f ⊕ persuasion; (fester Glaube) conviction; (Grundsätze) principles pl.; gegen seine bessere ~ handeln to act contrary to one's convictions; ich bin der festen ~, daß // I feel thoroughly convinced (or confident) that //, it is my firm belief that //. **überzeugungs=kraft**(⌣...) f ⊕ persuasive power; °**treu** a. ⊕ true to one's convictions, stanch in one's principles; =**treue** f depth of one's conviction, stanch adherence to one's principles. **über=ziehen** (⌣⌣⌣) ⊕b** v/a.: a) (hinüberziehen) to pull (or draw) to the other side; b) (seitwärts ziehen) to pull aside; c) to pull (or put) over; d) e-m eins (oder einen Hieb) mit dem Stocke 2 to give a p. a cut with the stick; v/n. (jn) e) to move (or pass) over or to the other side; f) (übersiedeln) to (re)move (to other quarters); in eine neue Wohnung 2 to go (or shift) into new apartments or a new house; (⌣‿⌣) ⊕b* v/a. und sich 2 v/refl. g) mit sachlichem Subjekte: et. 2 to cover a th.; der Himmel überzie"ht sich mit Wolken the clouds are gathering (in the sky), auch: it looks (F it's coming over) lowery; h) mit persönlichem Subjekte, faktitiv: to cover (or coat, overlay) a th. with a th., ein Bett (mit Leinen) 2 to put clean sheets on a bed, to change the bed-linen; ein frisch überzo"g(e)nes Bett a bed with clean sheets (and pillow-cases); mst ⊕: mit Fett, Schmiere, Rost 2 to grease, to rub (over), mit Gips: to plaster, mit Tapete: to paper (over), mit Zucker: to sugar (over), to ice; ein Land mit Heeresmacht, mit Krieg 2 to invade (or overrun) a country (with armed forces); =**zieher** (⌣‿⌣) [nhd.] m ⊕ overcoat, top-coat, für den Sommer: summer overcoat, dust-coat, wasserdichter: waterproof (coat); =**zieh=hose** (⌣‿⌣...) f ⊕ overalls pl.; =**zieh=jacke** f jacket (to be) worn over a dress, outside (or loose) jacket; °**zinken** ⊕ (⌣‿⌣) v/a. ⊕* to zinc over, to line (or coat) with zinc; °**zinnen**

(⌣‿⌣) v/a. ⊕* to tin (over), to overlay with tin; °**zuckern** (⌣‿⌣) v/a. ⊕a* to sugar (over), Früchte: to candy, Kuchen ꝛc.: to ice; fig. to sugar over, to make less bitter; eine (bittere) Pille 2 to gild over a pill. to sweeten a bitter draught; =**zug** (⌣‿⌣) m ⊙c. [°ziehen f] removal (to new quarters); [°ziehen h] covering; coat(ing) (of varnish &c.); ⊕ galvanischer ~ electro-coating; ♀ flaumartiger, seidenartiger ~ fluff, down; min. crust, ⸫ incrustation; ~ eines Bettkissens: pillow-case, med. der Zunge: fur; =**zugs=papier** n paper for covering furniture, carpets, &c.; °**zwerch** (⌣‿⌣) a. ⊕ awry, bsp. gbr. als adv. across, aslant, slantwise, crosswise, athwart.

üblich (⌣‿) [nhd.: *üb-en-lich] a. ⊕ usual, customary, accustomed, wonted; in vogue; (herkömmlich) conventional; von Redensarten: much used, in (general) use; common (expression); von Sitten: prevailing (custom); der ~e Sinn eines Wortes: the accepted meaning...; nicht mehr 2 out of use, disused, antiquated. **üblichkeit** (⌣‿‿) f ⊕ customariness; widely spread use; prevalence. **übrig** (⌣‿) [mhd.; *über-ig] a. ⊕ 1. prädikativ: (left) over; 2 **behalten** oder 2 **haben** to have over or left or to spare; fig. sie haben nicht viel für ihn 2 they don't think much of him; 2 **sein** to be left (over); vgl. bleiben 5. — 2. attributiv: remaining; spare (time, &c.); odd (pence, &c.); mein ~es Geld my other (or the rest of my) money, my spare cash. — 3. F (übel angebracht): inopportune, uncalled for; Ihre Reden sind 2 your remarks are out of place. — 4. s.: a) die (alle) ~en (all) those who are left (over), (all) the others, (all) the rest (of them); b) das ~e the remainder, the remnant, ⸫ the residue; ein ~es (über das Nötige) tun to do more than (is) required or than (the) needful, to strain a point, to make a special effort; im ~en übrigens. [remain (over).] **übrig=bleiben** (⌣‿‿‿) v/n. (jn) ⊕** to **übrigens** (⌣‿‿) adv. as for the rest, after all; (außerdem) moreover, besides; (indessen) however. [over or behind.] **übrig=lassen** (⌣‿‿‿) v/a. ⊕a** to leave **Übung** (⌣‿) f ⊕ 1. (das Üben) exercising; (Ausüben) practice; (Gewohnheit) use, custom; ~ auf dem Klavier ꝛc. practising (or playing exercises) on the piano, &c.; alltägliche ~ daily routine or use or experience; Sprichwort f. Meister 3. — 2. mit prp.: aus der ~ kommen (sein) to get (to be) out of practice; außer (Gebrauch) sein to be out of use or fashion; in der ~ bleiben, sich in der ~ erhalten to keep o.s. in practice, F to keep one's hand in. — 3. (et. das zum Üben dient) exercise, ♪ auch: study. — 4. ⚔ manœuvre, drill(ing), training. **Übungs=aufgabe** (⌣‿...) f ⊕ exercise; =**geschwader** ⚓ n manœuvring squadron; =**lager** ⚔ n training - camp; =**marsch** ⚔ m practice in marching; =**platz** m practice- (⚔ drill-)ground;

=**spiel** n gymnastic exercise; pl. auch: athletic sports pl.; =**stück** n exercise; =**zeit** f time for practising or drilling or exercises. [(mehr).]

u. dgl. (m.) abbr. = und dergleichen U-**Eisen** ⊕ (⌣‿) n ⓘ U-shaped iron. **Ufer** (⌣‿) [nhd.] n ⓘ (Rand e-s Gewässers) water's edge, e-s fließenden: bank, e-s größeren: shore, e-s Meeres: beach, coast (vgl. Gestade, Küste, Strand); ans ~ gehen to go ashore; am ~ eines Flusses gelegen (lying) by the riverside, a. riverain; sich aus sicheres ~ retten to reach the safe shore. **Ufer=bahn** (⌣‿...) f ⊕ railway skirting the riverside or the shore; =**bau** m embankment; =**bau=kunst** f art of building embankments; =**bewohner**(in f) m one who dwells by the bank or riverside, geb. Svr. riparian dweller; =**bezirk** m riparian district; =**damm** m quay; =**land** n shoreland; °**los** a. ⊕ without banks or shores, shoreless, fig. boundless; eine ~e Politik an adventurous policy; =**lose** Pläne ill-considered (or airy, F wild) schemes pl.; =**schutzbauten** pl.: a) am Flusse: embankment sg.; -b) am Meere: dikes, sea-walls pl.; =**schwalbe** f, orn. bank-swallow, sand-martin (Co'tyle ripa'ria); =**seite** f bank, e-s Flusses auch: riverside.

uff! (⌣) int. ugh!   [Gallery.]
Uffizi=en (⌣‿(⌣)⌣) pl. in Florenz: Uffizi] **ugrisch** (⌣‿) a. ⊕ Ethnologie: (Lappen, Finnen, Ungarn betreffend) Ugrian.   [ugh!]
uh! (⌣) int. staunend: oh!, erschreckt:
Uhlane (‿⌣‿) m ④ = Ulan.
Uhle (⌣‿) f ⊕ nordd. = Eule 4.
Uhr (⌣, Hom. Ur) [nhd. 16. sae.: *lt. hora] f ⊕ 1. nur in sg., zur Angabe der Tagesstunde: hour (of the day), o'clock; es ist ein (neun) ~ it's one (nine) o'clock; es ist zwölf ~ ... twelve o'clock; mittags auch: ... noon, mitternachts auch: ... midnight; halb drei (~) half-past two (o'clock); was (ob. wie-viel) ist die ~?, wieviel ~ ist's? what is the time?, auch: what does the clock say?, fast † what o'clock is it?; der um 5⁰⁰ (2⁴⁰) abfahrende (ob. ankommende) Zug, Postwagen the five o'clock (the two-forty) train, mailcoach. — 2. (Zeitmesser): a) kleinere ~, F ticker, ohne Schlüssel aufzuziehende: keyless watch; b) größere ~, clock; vgl. Stutz=, Taschen=, Turm=, Wand=uhr; f. ablaufen 6, aufziehen 4; eine ~ in Gang bringen to set a clock or watch) going; eine ~ stellen nach // to regulate (or set) a watch (or clock) by //; fig. ein Mann nach der ~ a man punctual to his time; wie nach der ~ like (or as if regulated by) clock-work. **Uhr=band** (⌣‿...) n ⓘ watch-cord or guard; =**deckel** m outer case of a watch. **Uhren=fabrik** ⊕ (⌣‿‿...) f ⊕ watch-manufactory; =**fabrikant** m (=**fabrikation** f) watch-and-clock maker (making); =**handel** m trade in watches and clocks; =**richter**, =**steller** m regulator of watches and clocks, clock-setter. **Uhr=feder** ⊕ (⌣‿...) f ⊕ watch-spring; =**futteral** n watch-case; =**gehänge** n

Zeichen (f. S. XVII): F familiär; P Volkssprache; Γ Gaunersprache; ~ selten; † alt (auch gestorben); * neu (auch geboren); ++ unrichtig;

[Uhrgehäuse] — 989 — [umackern]

watch-trinkets pl., einzelnes a. charm; =gehäuse n w.-case; =gestell n w.-stand; =getriebe n pinion of a watch; =gewicht n weight of a clock; =glas n watch-glass; =glocke f glass shade over a clock; =haken m watch-hook; =halter m watch-stand; =tapfel f w.-case; =kasten m clock-case; =kette f watch-chain or -guard; =macher m watch-maker, clockmaker; macherei, macherkunst f watchmaking, clockmaking. ⚕ horology; =schlag m strike of a clock; =schlüssel m watch-key; key of a clock; =tasche f watch-pocket; fob; =werk n works pl. (or mechanism) of a watch, clock-work. movement of a clock: =zeiger m hand of a watch or clock. [eagle-owl (strix bubo).]
Uhu (⌣-) [nhd. lautm.] m ⓢe.(ⓢ) orn.
Ukas (⌣⌣) [russ. ⌣⌣ Befehl] m ⓢa. (a. inv.) ukase, decree of the Tsar.
Ukelei (⌣⌣⌣) [poln.] m ⓢd.ⓢ ichth. alburn, bleak (Albu'rnus lu'cidus).
Ulan ⚔ (-⌣) [nhd. 1808; poln.; *tatar.] m ⓢ₂, a. ~e ⓢ₄ uhlan, lancer.
Ulanka ⚔ (-⌣⌣) f ⓢ₅ lancer's uniform.
Ulema (⌣⌣⌣) [ar.] m ⓢ₁ coll. (Gesamtheit der türk. Rechts- u. Gottes-gelehrten) ulema.
Ulfe ♀ (⌣⌣) f ⓢ₅ (Alge) ribbon-laver (Ulva).
Ulfilas (⌣⌣⌣) [Wölfl(ein)] npr/m. ⓢ₆γ. (Gotenbischof, Bibelübersetzer, 311—381) Ulphilas.
Ulk F (⌣) [erst nhd.] m ⓢb. burschikos: (jolly) fun, F spree, skylarking.
ulken (⌣⌣) v/n. (h.) ⓢ₈ to have (jolly) fun, F to lark (about).
Ulkerei (⌣⌣⌣) f ⓢ₁ skylarking.
ulkig (⌣⌣) a. ⓢ₀ frolicsome.
Ulme ♀ (⌣⌣) [nhd.; *lt. ulmus] f ⓢ₃ elm(-tree) (Ulmus); ⚭n (⌣⌣) a. ⓢ₀ of elm (-wood); ⚭n=artig (⌣⌣...) a. ⓢ₀; ⚕ ulmaceous; ~n=baum m = Ulme; ~n=pflanzung f nursery of young elm-trees; ~n=wäldchen n elm-grove.
Ulrich (⌣⌣) [ahd. Erbherr] npr/m. ⓢ₆ⓢα. (Bn.) Ulric; F co. den heiligen ~ anrufen (sich erbrechen) to be sick, to vomit.
Ulrike (⌣⌣) npr/f. ⓢ₄ⓢ₃. (Bn.) Ulrica.
Ultimatum (⌣⌣⌣) [neu-lt.] n ⓢ₃ⓢ pol. ⚔ (letzte Forderung) ultimatum.
Ultimo ⚖ (⌣⌣) [it. letzt] m ⓢ₃ⓢ₈ u. ultimo adv. last day of the month; ⚖ des laufenden Monats: at the end of this month; ⚖ August (at the) end of August.
Ultimo=liquidation (⌣⌣⌣ ...) f ⓢ₂, =regulierung f settlement at the end of the month, monthly settlement.
Ultra (⌣⌣) [it.] m ⓢ₀ extremist, a. ultra.
ultra=liberal (⌣⌣...) a. ⓢ₀ ultra-liberal; =linke f ⓢ₂ extreme left; =mari'n a ⓢd. Malerei: (Lasurblau) ultra-marine; ⚖monta'n a., =montane(r) m ⓢ₇ (der jenseit der Berge, der Alpen, b. h. in Rom, f n Stützpunkt sucht) ultramontane; =montanismus m ⓢ₂ ultramontanism.
Ulysses (-⌣⌣) npr/m. ⓢ₆γ. Ulysses.
um (⌣) [ahd.: grch. amphi] I prp. mit acc. 1. ursp. örtlich: um, auch: um ... herum (im Kreise oder wie im Kreise) (a)round; about; sich um et. (herum)drehen to turn (or revolve) round a th.; alles dreht sich um ihn everything turns (or depends) on him; um ein Haus (herum) gehen to walk (or to take a turn) round a house; er ist immer um sie he is always about (or near, with) her; e-m um den Hals fallen to fall on (or round) a p.'s neck; er weiß nicht, wie mir ums Herz ist ... how I feel (in my own heart); um sich schlagen to lay about one; nur zeitlich: about, near, towards, genauer: at; um die sechste Stunde about (or near) the sixth hour; in bestimmterem Sinne: um elf Uhr at eleven o'clock; begründend, erstrebend: for, on account of; f. ängstigen I, bemühen II, beneiden, bewerben I, bitten 1 u. 2, freien 1; sich um et. grämen to grieve for a th., to worry about a th.; e-n um seinen Freimut lieben to like a p. for his openness; ich habe um die Sache geschrieben I have written for it; es ist schade um das Geld it's a pity for the money (spent); vgl. schade². — 2. um e-r Sache. j-s willen od. wegen mit zwischengeschobenem gen., den Beweggrund angebend: for the sake of ..., on the score of ..., on the plea of ...; alles um des lieben Friedens willen tun to do anything for peace' sake or for peace and quietness; um Gottes (um des Himmels) willen erbarmt euch! for God's (or Heaven's) sake have pity! (f. meinetwillen, deinetwillen). — 3. mit allgem. Beziehung: about; es sieht übel um ihn aus he is in a bad way; wie steht es um die Sache? how does the matter stand?, how are things progressing?; um et. wissen to know about (or concerning) a th.; es ist eine ernste Sache um das Heiraten it is a serious matter to get married; es ist etwas Schönes um die Liebe there is something beautiful in (or about) love; vgl. umeinander. — 4. den Lohn, Preis bezeichnend: for; um Lohn arbeiten to work for wages; um bares Geld kaufen to buy for (ready) cash; f. Preis¹ 1; das täte ich um alles in der Welt nicht I would not do it for anything in (or for all) the world; um nichts for nothing; vgl. umsonst; um ein bedeutendes od. erkleckliches for a considerable amount; bibl. Aug' um Auge an eye for an eye. — 5. einen Unterschied, Abstand bz.: f. Haar 4; um ein bedeutendes geringer considerably (or a great deal) less; um die Hälfte vergrößern to increase by one-half; um zwei Jahre älter als // two years older than //; um einen Kopf größer sein als // to be a head taller (or taller by a head) than //; sich um zehn Mark verrechnen to be ten shillings out (in one's calculation); um desto (oder um so viel) ärmer so much the poorer; um so besser! all (or so much) the better!; um so mehr verdient sie es she deserves it all the more; um wie viel mehr ist er zu beklagen how much more is he to be pitied; um so weniger al the less; um so weniger müssen Sie hingehen you have all the more reason not to go there. — 6. einen Verlust bz.: f. betrügen, bringen 8 unter „um" und geschehen 5; um et. kommen to lose s.th.; durch Betrug: to be done out of a th.; f. Leben¹ 2 am Ende und Hals 3 gegen Ende; e-n um 40 Mark strafen to fine a p. (or to mulct a p. in) two pounds. — 7. Aufeinanderfolge (mit artikel- und flexionslosem s. vor und nach um oder mit ein und der andere) bz.: ausgesendet wird Bot' um Bote oder ein Bote um den andern messenger upon messenger, one messenger after another is dispatched; Tag um Tag day after (or by) day; e-n Tag um den andern every other (or each alternate) day. — II cj. 8. je mehr er hat, um desto (ob. um so) mehr will er haben the more he has, the more he wants (to have). — 9. um zu ... (inf.) in order to ... (inf.); um Ihnen zu zeigen, daß // (in order) to show you that //; um mich ganz klar auszudrücken to express myself quite clearly, to be quite clear; er hat nicht genug um zu leben he has not enough to live upon; nach „zu" mit a.: er ist zu klug, um seinen Ärger zu verraten he is too shrewd to betray his vexation. — III adv. 10. f. kehren² 1, linksum, rechtsum; um so mehr (weniger) all the more (less), vgl. so 9. — 11. um und um round about; (von allen Seiten) on all-sides, (from) everywhere; (ganz und gar) entirely; et. um und um kehren oder wühlen to turn a th. over and over; wenn es um und um kommt when all is told, after all (that can be said). — 12. ell.: um mit dem Baume (haut ihn um)! down with the tree!; f. links 1. — 13. umsein: a) räumlich: über Wien zu reisen ist um (ein Umweg) it is a long way round (to travel) by Vienna; der Weg ist weit um it's a very roundabout way; b) zeitlich: um (abgelaufen) sein to be up or over or gone; als das Jahr um war when the year had expired or passed; meine Zeit ist um my time is up.
um=... (⌣... und ⌣⌣⌣) Vorsilbe in Zssgn mit verbs I (⌣...") mit dem Ton auf dem Grundworte, immer untrennbar (*), zur Bildung von transitiven verbs dienend, bz. 1. im Kreise um e-n, et. herum: die Soldaten umstanden (⌣⌣⌣) den Feldherrn the soldiers stood (or gathered) round the general; eine Insel umsegeln (⌣⌣⌣) to sail round an island; sich im Bogen bewegend: ein Dorf umgeh(e)n (⌣⌣(⌣)) to go round (or avoid) a village. II (⌣...) mit dem Ton auf der Vorsilbe. immer trennbar (**) 2. um et. herum: umbehalten (⌣⌣⌣) to keep round one; im Kreise drehen: den Kopf umdrehen (⌣⌣⌣) to turn one's head round. — 3. hier-(hin) und dort(hin): umirren (⌣⌣⌣) to wander to and fro, to roam about. — 4. vorbei, vorüber, von der Zeit: umlaufen (⌣⌣⌣) to go by, to come round. — 5. zu Boden, nieder: umfallen (⌣⌣⌣) to fall down. — 6. anders, neu: umbilden (⌣⌣⌣) to transform. — 7. aus einem Gefäß in ein anderes: umfüllen (⌣⌣⌣) to pour from one vessel into another.
um=ackern (⌣⌣⌣) v/a. ⓢa** agr.: a) den Boden ⓢ to turn up the soil with the plough; b) einen Strauch ⓢ (beim Ackern umwerfen) to knock down ... with the plough; c) P (umwühlen) to

♪ Musik; ⚕ Wissenschaft; ♀ Pflanze; ⚲ Geographie; ⊕ Technik; ⚒ Bergbau; ⚔ Militär; ⚓ Marine; ⚖ Handel; ✉ Post; 🚂 Eisenbahn

[umändern] — 990 — [umfassen]

turn over (and over), to stir up, to ransack; ²ändern (ᵟᵛᵛ) v/a. ᵂa** to change (completely or thoroughly), to alter; (verwandeln) to transform; ~ n ²³ und =änderung f ⁴⁶ (complete or thorough) change, alteration, transformation; ²arbeiten (ᵟᵛᵛ) v/a. ⁶⁹** to work over (again), Schriften: to rewrite, to revise; gänzlich ² to recast, to remodel; agr. den Boden: to turn up, a. = ²ackern, ²graben; ~ n ²³ u. =arbeitung f ⁴⁶ recast(ing), remodelling, einer Schrift: revision; ²armen (ᵟᵛᵛ) v/a. und sich ² v/recip. ⁸⁸*: (sich) ² to embrace or hug (each other); sie uma"rmte ihn, a. she clasped him in her arms or to her bosom; ~ n ²³ und =armung f ⁴⁶ embrace, hug; =bau (⁸¹) m ⓒc. rebuilding, reconstruction; alterations pl. made in a house; (pl. meist ~ten) (neues Gebäude) new (or remodelled, renovated) building or premises pl.; ²bauen (ᵟᵛᵛ) ⁸⁸* v/a. to surround (or hem in) with buildings or walls, to wall in; rings umbau"t hemmed (or shut) in by houses or walls; (ᵟᵛᵛ) ⁸⁸** v/a. to build anew, rebuild, reconstruct; to make alterations in; das Schloß ist u"mgebaut the castle has been rebuilt; ²behalten (ᵟᵛᵛ) v/a. ⁸⁸*/* to keep round one, f-n Mantel: to keep on.
Umber¹ (ᵟᵛ) [Umbra] m ²² f. Umber=erde.
Umber² (ᵟᵛ) [It. umbra] m ²² ichth. f. Umberfisch. [=²fisch m umber.]
Umber¹=erde (ᵟᵛ...) f ⁴² umber, umbra;]
um=beschreiben (ᵛᵛᵛ) v/a. ⁸⁸/* math. bsd. im p.p.: u"mbeschriebener Kreis circle described about a triangle, &c.; ²betten (ᵟᵛᵛ) v/a. ⁶⁹** to put into a new (or fresh) bed; ²biegen (ᵟᵛᵛ) u. sich ² v/refl. ⓦa**: (sich) ² to bend (over), to turn down or back, to double (down); die Blätter e=s Buches an der Ecke ² to dog's-ear (or turn down) the leaves of a book; ²bilden (ᵟᵛᵛ) v/a. ⁶⁹** to transform, remodel, recast, to cast in(to) a new mould, bessernd: to reform; ~ n ²³ und =bildung f ⁴² transformation, remodelling, recast(ing), reform(ing); =bildner (ᵟᵛᵛ) m ²² transformer, (Verbesserer) reformer; ²binden v/a. (ᵟᵛᵛ) ⓦ** to tie (or bind) round; (sich) ein Tuch ² to tie a cloth round (one's) throat); sich e-e Schürze ² to put (or tie) on an apron; er hat sich e-e Reisedecke u"mgebunden he tied (or wrapt) a travelling rug round him; ein Buch ꝛc. (neu binden) to rebind ..., to bind ... afresh;(ᵟᵛᵛ)⁹*: mit et. ² to tie (or wrap) round with a th.; umbu"nden tied (or wrapt) round; ²blasen v/a. (ᵟᵛᵛ) ⁸⁶a** to blow down; (ᵟᵛᵛ) ⁸⁶a*: von den Winden ² tossed about by the wind, exposed to every gust of wind; ²blättern (ᵟᵛᵛ) v/a. u. v/n. (h.) ⓦa** to turn over the leaves (of a book); =blick (ᵟᵛᵛ) m ⓒc. look (or glance) around; (Aussicht) (panoramic) view; (Rückblick) glancing (or looking, turning) back; fig. retrospect; =blicken (ᵟᵛᵛ) v/n. (h.) u. sich ² v/refl. ⁸⁸** to look (or glance) round; (sich) nach et. ² to look (round) for a th.; ²blühen (ᵟᵛᵛ) v/a. ⁸⁸* to wreathe in (or surround with) flowers.
Umbra (ᵟᵛ) [It.: *Umbrien ♀] f, inv., min. u. paint. (brauner Farbstoff) umber.
um=brassen ↓ (ᵟᵛᵛ) v/a. ⁹⁰** to brace about or at the other side; ²brausen (ᵟᵛᵛ) v/a. ⁹⁰** to roar (a)round; von Stürmen umbrau"st amid (or exposed to) howling storms; =brechen (ᵟᵛᵛ) ⓦa** v/a. ² a) to break down; der Zaun ist u"mgebrochen the fence has broken (or come) down; b) agr. to break (up) the soil; c) ⊙ (ᵟᵛᵛ) ⓦa* typ. (den Satz zu Seiten bilden) to make up (into pages), to page, beim Korrigieren: to overrun; der Satz wird vom Schriftsetzer umbro"chen the matter is made up by the compositor; (ᵟᵛᵛ) ⓦa** v/n. (fn) to break down, to be weighed down.
Umbri=en ♀ (ᵟᵛᵛ) [It.] npr/n. ²³ Alt. Landschaft in Mittel=italien: Umbria; Umbri=er(in f ⁴⁷) m ²² Umbrian.
um=bringen (ᵟᵛᵛ) v/a. u. v/refl. ⁹** to put to death; to slay, kill, murder, destroy; (ersticken) to smother, (würgen) to strangle; meuchlings: to assassinate; sich (selbst) ² to kill (or destroy) o.s., to put an end to (or to take) one's (own) life, to lay hands upon o.s., to make away with o.s.; to commit suicide.
umbrisch (ᵟᵛ) a. ⁶⁶ röm. Alt.: Umbrian.
Um=bruch ⊙ (ᵟᵛᵛ) m ⓒc. agr. newly broken (up) soil; ⚒ break (in a drive or gallery); typ. paging, making-up; ²dämmen ⊙ (ᵟᵛᵛ) ⁸⁸** to pave afresh; (ᵟᵛᵛ) ⁸⁸* to embank, to surround (or protect) with a dike; ²decken v/a. (ᵟᵛᵛ) ⁸⁸** to cover (or put) all (a)round; (anders od. neu decken) den Tisch ² to lay the table differently or afresh; ² ein Dach ² to retile (or reslate) a roof; (ᵟᵛᵛ) ⁸⁸* to cover (or protect) the shoulders, &c.; ²destillieren (ᵟᵛᵛ¹) v/a. ⁸⁸** chm., &c. to distil afresh, Branntwein: to rectify; ²deuten (ᵟᵛ¹) v/a. ⁸⁸** to interpret anew, to give a fresh interpretation to; ²dichten (ᵟᵛᵛ) v/a. ⁸⁸** to cast in(to) a new (poetic) mould, einfacher: to recast poetry, to compose a poem afresh; ²drängen (ᵟᵛᵛ) v/a. ⁸⁸* to crowd (or flock, swarm, throng) around; ²drehen (ᵟᵛ¹) v/a. und sich ² v/refl. ⁸⁸**: (sich) ² to turn (or twirl) round or about, to twist round; to turn the reverse way, ↓ to reverse; sich auf dem Absatz ² to turn on one's heel; sich im Grabe ² to turn round in one's grave; sich um seine Angel ² to turn on an axis, to revolve, to rotate, im Fluge: to whirl (or spin) round; e-m Huhn(e) den Hals ² to wring a fowl's neck; fig. den Spieß ² to turn the tables upon a p.; f. Hand 2 Ende; ~ n ²³ f. =drehung; =dreher (ᵟᵛ¹) m ²² one who turns (or twirls) round, &c. (f. ²drehen); =drehung f ⁴⁶ turning round or about; turn, rotation, revolution; whirl (-ing); math. a.: ⚇ circumvolution.
Umdrehungs=achse (ᵟᵛᵛ...) f ⁶² axis of rotation or revolution; =bewegung f ⁴⁶ rotatory motion or movement; revolution; =ellipsoid n, math.: ⚇ ellipsoid of revolution; =geschwindigkeit f velocity of rotation; =zähler m counter.
Um=druck ⊙ (ᵟᵛᵛ) m ⓒc. typ. reprint, re-impression; ²drucken ⊙ (ᵟᵛᵛ) v/a. ⁸⁸** typ. to reprint; ~ n ²³ = Umdruck. =druck=verfahren n ²³ metallography; ²duften (ᵟᵛᵛ) v/a. ⁶⁹* to wrap (or clothe) in perfume or fragrance, to waft fragrant odours round; to scent; ²dunkeln (ᵟᵛᵛ), ²düstern (ᵟᵛᵛ) v/a. ⓦa* to wrap (or clothe) in darkness, to cast a gloom over; ²einander (ᵟᵛᵛ) adv. round (or for, at, &c.) each other; ²fächeln (ᵟᵛᵛ) v/a. ⓦa* to fan (from all sides); ²fahen †, noch poet. (ᵟᵛᵛ) v/a. ⁸⁸* = umfangen; ²fahren (ᵟᵛᵛ) v/n. (h. u. fn) a): sich ² v/refl. to drive a long way round or a roundabout way; b) (umherschweifen) to wander (or roam) about; v a. e-n ² to drive over a p., to run over a p. (with a carriage); u"mgefahren run over (by a carriage); (ᵟᵛᵛ) ⓢb*: die Stadt ² to drive (or cycle, motor) round the town; ↓ to sail (or steam) round, to circumnavigate an island, to double a cape; er hat die Südspitze zweimal ² he sailed twice round the most southerly point; ²fahrt (ᵟᵛ¹) f ⁴⁶ driving round (in a carriage, &c.); tour, amtliche: circuit; e-e ~ halten um (od. in) to make the round of, to drive round a town, &c.; =fahrung f ⁴⁶ driving round, circumnavigation; =fall (ᵟᵛᵛ) m ⓒc. = =fallen n; ²fallen (ᵟᵛᵛ) v/n. (fn) ⓢ⁶a** to fall (or tumble) down, to drop; von einem Wagen.. to be upset; vom Vieh (crepieren) to die (on the spot); fig. (versagen) to fail (to appear); ~ n ²³ fall, tumble; upset; zum ~ müde ready to drop, dead tired; =fang (ᵟᵛᵛ) m ⓒc.: a) (umschließende Grenze) circumference (a. math.), ⚇ periphery, perimeter; ⊙ ~ e-s Baumes ꝛc. a. girth, width; Schneiderei: ~ des Körpers width round the chest; zehn Meter im ~ h. to be eleven yards round; b) (Ausdehnung) extent, size, bsd. fig. compass, range; von großem ~ of large dimensions or size; spacious; (Bereich) sphere, domain; c) (Geräumigkeit) capacity; körperlicher ~ volume, bulk, math. solid contents pl.; d) ♪ ~ e-r Singstimme od. e-s Instruments: diapason, a. range, volume; ²fangen (ᵟᵛᵛ) v/a. ⓢb* to embrace, to clasp (round), to encircle; (umgeben) to surround, to enclose, ⚔ den Feind: to envelop, to hem in (on all sides); ~ n ²³ embrace, &c., ⚔ envelopment; ²fänglich (ᵟᵛᵛ), ²fangreich (ᵟᵛ=¹) a. ⁶⁶ extensive, förperlich: voluminous, bulky; (geräumig) spacious, wide; ²färben ⊙ (ᵟᵛᵛ) v/a. ⁸⁸* to dye all around; (ᵟᵛᵛ) ⁸⁸** (anders färben) to dye another colour; ²fassen A (ᵟᵛᵛ) ⁹⁰* v/a. mit der Hand: to span, mit den Armen: to embrace, to clasp (round), mit den Blicken: to take in (at a glance); (einschließen) to encompass, (einhegen) to enclose; ⚔ den Feind ² to envelop (or hem in) the enemy; fig. (in sich schließen) to include, comprehend, comprise; hierin ist alles umfa"ßt this includes every-

Signs (see page XVII): ǂ familiar; P vulgar; ꟼ flash; ⟍ rare; † obsolete (died); * new word (born); ⁒ incorrect; ♪ music;

[Umfassung] — 991 — [umgürten]

thing; 2d comprehensive; (geräumig) extensive, capacious, wide, 2de Ansichten broad (or large) views pl.; 2de Maßregeln, Vorbereitungen treffen zu take ample precautions, to make large preparations; ♀ den Stengel 2d: ⚹ amplexicaul; ~ n ㉓ spanning, embrace, &c.; ✕ envelopment (of troops); B (ᛌᛌ) ⑳** v/a. Edelsteine: to reset, einen Ring: to remount; er hat die Brillanten u"mgefaßt he has reset the brilliants u"mfassung (ᛌᛌ) f ㊻: a) spanning, &c., ✕ envelopment of the enemy (s. umfassen); b) (Einfriedigung) enclosure; fence; ~s=mauer / ⑫ enclosure-wall, outer (or exterior) wall; ⁰flattern (ᛌᛌ) v/a. ⑭a* to flutter (or hover) around; F fig. e-n ⚹ to dangle around (or to hang on to) a p.; ⁰flechten v/a. (ᛌᛌ) ⑲b** to plait (or braid) again or afresh or in a different style; (ᛌᛌ) ⑲*: mit et. ⚹ to plait (or weave) round with a th.; umflo"chtene Flasche wickerbottle; ⁰fliegen (ᛌᛌ) v/a. ⑭a* to fly (a)round; to avoid in flying; (ᛌᛌ) (fn) ⑭a** (fliegend einen Umweg machen) to fly a roundabout way; ⁰fließen (ᛌᛌ) v/a. ⑭d* to flow (a)round; to encircle (or encompass) with waves, &c.; ⁰floren (ᛌᛌ) v/a. ⑭** to wrap (or wind) round with (or to veil in) crape; fig. den Blick ⚹ to dim the sight; ⁰fluten (ᛌᛌ) v/a. ⑭* to flow (a)round, to encompass with waves; ⁰formen (ᛌᛌ) v/a. ⑭** u. ~ n ㉓ =⁰bilden; =⁰former (ᛌᛌ) m ㉒ elect. continuous current transformer, rotary converter; =⁰formung f ㊻ =⁰bildung; =⁰frage (ᛌᛌ) f ㊻ inquiry all around; bei weiterer ~ on further inquiries (being made) in the neighbourhood, ~ halten (auch) ⁰fragen (ᛌᛌ) v/n. (h.) ⑧ (↷ ⑧b)**) to inquire all around or in every quarter, to gather information (everywhere), to ask everybody; ⁰fried(ig)en (ᛌᛌ)(⌄) v/a. ⑧(⑧)* u. ⁰fried(ig)ung f ㊻ = einfriedigen; ⁰führen (ᛌᛌ) v/a. ⑭** (Umwege führen) to lead a roundabout way; ⁰füllen (ᛌᛌ) v/a. ⑭** to fill (or pour) from one vessel into another, to transfuse; ~ n ㉓, =⁰füllung f ㊻ transfusion.
Um=gang (ᛌᛌ) m ⓪c. 1. arch. circular gallery or passage, gallery round a building. — 2. going (the) round, round; feierlicher ~ procession; e-n ~ halten: a) to take a turn round; b) to hold (or go in) a procession; ~ (Drehung) e-s Rades 2c.: turn, revolution, rotation. — 3. ~ (Verkehr) mit intercourse with; (genaue Bekanntschaft) intimate acquaintance; (Verhältnis) relation(ship); mit e-m ~ haben oder pflegen to have (or hold) intercourse with a p., to associate with a p.; sie haben keinen ~ mit=ea. they don't visit (each other) or associate (with each other); durch vielen ~, oft: by mixing much with people; fleischlicher (od. geschlechtlicher) ~ sexual (verblümt: intimate, jur. criminal) intercourse; coll. circle of friends or acquaintances; (good, bad) companionship; sie haben wenig ~ they keep (or see) little company, they have few friends.

um=gänglich (ᛌᛌ) a. ㊻ sociable, companionable, genial; pleasant, affable; sie sind sehr ⚹ they are very pleasant company; ~keit (ᛌᛌ-) f ㊻ sociability, geniality, affability.
Um=gangs=formen (ᛌᛌ...) f/pl. forms pl. of (social) intercourse; strenge ~, a. etiquette; =sprache f colloquial (or every day) language, speech of every day life, familiar talk; die englische ~ conversational (or colloquial) English.
um=garnen (ᛌᛌ) v/a. ⑧* to ensnare (a. fig.); to encircle with nets; ⁰gaukeln (ᛌᛌ) v/a. ⑭a* to flit (or frolic, play, gambol) around; ⁰gehen A (ᛌᛌ) ⑭c* v/a. u. sich ⚹ v/refl.: (sich) to surround (o.s. with); (einschließen) to enclose, encompass, hem in, environ, mit einer Mauer: to wall in, mit einem Zaune: to fence in; (rings) von Eis ⚹ ice-bound, vgl. ⁰schließen; von Schwierigkeiten ⚹ beset with difficulties; (rings) von Land ⚹ p.p. landlocked; B (ᛌᛌ) ⑭c** v/a.: e-m seinen Mantel ⚹ to put a cloak round a p.; =gebung (ᛌᛌ) f ㊻ surroundings, surrounding objects pl.; persons pl. around (or about) one, those near (or with) a p.; er hat schlechte ~ he keeps bad company; auch ==gegend; =gegend (ᛌᛌ) f ㊻ surrounding country, country around, neighbourhood, vicinity, einer Stadt auch: environs pl.
um=geh(e)n (ᛌᛌ) ⑭** I v/n. (fn) 1. von Rädern: (sich drehen) to go (or turn, spin) round; to make a rotation or revolution; fig. = herumgehen 2c. — 2. um et. geh(e)n = herumgeh(e)n a. — 3. der Reihe nach ⚹ (lassen) to come alternately or by rotation (to take a th. in turns); 2d (wechselnd) alternate(ly); in turn(s); 2d (ob. mit 2der Post) antworten to answer by return of post, to reply by the next mail. — 4. = umhergeh(e)n. — 5. (als Geist spuken) to walk, to haunt a place; auch v/imp. (h.) es geht in dem Schlosse um the castle is haunted. — 6. (in Umlauf sein) to circulate; es geht ein Gerücht um, daß // it is rumoured (or reported) that //. — 7. (e-n Umweg m.) auch v/refl. sich ⚹ to go a roundabout way; wir sind (ob. haben uns) eine gute Strecke u"mgegangen we have gone a long distance out of our way. — 8. mit e-m ⚹ (verkehren) to have intercourse (or to associate) with a p.; gern mit e-m ⚹ to be fond of a p.'s company; er weiß mit Menschen u"mzugeh(e)n he knows how to deal with people, a. he knows (or is a man of) the world; Sprichw. sage mir, mit wem du u"mgehst, und ich will dir sagen, wer du bist tell me the company you keep, and I will tell you who you are. — 9. mit et. ⚹ (sich beschäftigen) to deal with a th.; mit et. u"mzugeh(e)n (ans Ziel zu gelangen) wissen to know how to manage (or handle) a th.; mit e-m Gedanken ⚹ to contemplate a th.; mit einem Plane ⚹ to have a plan, to be hatching a scheme, to entertain a project; damit ⚹, sich zu verheiraten to think of (stärker: to be bent on) marrying; to contemplate

marriage. — 10. mit et., mit e-m gut (schlecht) ⚹ (verfahren) to treat (or use) a p. well (ill); nachsichtig mit e-m ⚹ to deal leniently with a p.; sparsam mit et. ⚹ to be sparing of a th. — II (ᛌᛌ)(⌄) ⑭* v/a. 11. einen Garten 2c. ⚹ to take a turn round ...; die Grenze ⚹ (besichtigen) to beat the bounds. — 12. ✕ den Feind ⚹ to turn the enemy's flank, to get to the rear of the enemy('s position). — 13. et. im Bogen ⚹ to take a circuitous route round a th.; fig. (vermeiden) to avoid, elude, shun; wenn wir es ⚹ können if we can help it or keep out of it. — III ~ n ㉓ u. Um=gehung (ᛌᛌ) f ㊻ 14. ~ des Feindes envelopment of the foe, turning the enemy's flank. — 15. (Vermeidung) elusion, evasion.
um=gekehrt (ᛌᛌ) p.p. u. a. ㊻ in den Bed. des inf. umkehren; mit 2er Hand with the back of one's hand; Schlag mit 2er Hand back-handed blow; 2e Ordnung inversion; in 2er Ordnung in the reverse order, inversely; 2e Seite: a) e-r Münze: reverse; b) e-s Tuches: wrong side; c) fig. opposite side or view; in 2em Verhältnisse steh(e)n zu // to be in the inverse ratio of //; ⚹ (gerade das Gegenteil)! it's just the other way, (round)!, (it's) quite the contrary!; das ~e the reverse, the contrary, the opposite; adv. contrariwise, inversely, reversely; er behauptet ⚹, daß // he asserts on the contrary that.
um=gestalten (ᛌᛌ) v/a. u. v/refl. ⑭*/*: et. ⚹ to alter the shape of a th., to transform (or metamorphose) a th.; bessernd: to reform (or reorganize) a th.; sich ⚹ to be(come) transformed; ~ n ㉓ und =gestaltung f ㊻ transformation, metamorphosis; reform; reorganization; ⁰gießen A (ᛌᛌ) v/a. ⑭d** to pour from one vessel into another, to transfuse; ⊙ Glocken 2c.: to refound, recast, new-cast; ~ n ㉓ transfusion; B (ᛌᛌ) ⑭d** to surround with a fluid; von Äther 2c. umgo"ssen circumfused with (or enveloped in) ...; ~ n ㉓ circumfusion; ⁰gittern (ᛌᛌ) v/a. ⑭a* to surround with a grating or railing, to rail in; ⁰glänzen (ᛌᛌ) v/a. ⑭* to surround with splendour or lustre; ⁰graben A (ᛌᛌ) ⑭b** v/a. to dig up a field, &c., to break up the soil (with a spade); tief ⚹ to trench-plough, mit dem Untergrundpflug: to subsoil; einen Baum ⚹ (grabend umstürzen) to uproot a tree in digging; ~ n ㉓ f. =grabung; B (ᛌᛌ) ⑭b** v/a. to dig (or throw) up the earth round a tree, &c.; =grabung f ㊻ digging up, &c.; spade-work or =labour; ⁰grenzen (ᛌᛌ) v/a. ⑭* to form a boundary (a)round; to encircle, limit, circumscribe; (einhegen) to fence (or rail) in; (umschließen) to enclose; ~ n ㉓ u. =grenzung f ㊻ (forming a) boundary (around); limitation, circumscription; enclosure; ⁰gürten v/a. (ᛌᛌ) ⑭** to gird (round), ein Schwert ⚹ to buckle on; er hat das Schwert u"mgegürtet he buckled on his sword; ⑭*: seine Lenden ⚹ to gird (up) one's loins; um=

⚹ scientific; ♀ botanical; ⊕ geography; ⊕ machinery; ✕ mining; ✕ military; ⚓ marine; ⚹ commercial; ✉ postal; 🚃 railway.

gü"rtet mit dem Schwert girt with his sword; ~ n ② und =gürtung f ㊻ girding; =guß (ᴵᴸ) m ⑨a. (f. umgießen) transfusion; ⊖ refounding, recast, recasting, new-casting; ⁜haben F (ᴶᴸ∪) v/a. ⑩b** to have round one, to be wrapped (or wrapt) up in; einen Mantel ≈ to have a cloak on; ⁜hacken (ᴶᴸ∪)⑧** v/a. bſp. agr. to turn (or break) up with the hoe; (fällen) to hew (or cut) down with an axe, &c., to fell a tree, &c.; (ᴶᴸ∪) ⑧* v/a. to work round with a hoe; ⁜halfen (ᴶᴸ∪) v/a. ⑨*: e-n ≈ to fall round a p.'s neck; to embrace (or hug) a p.; ~ n u. =halſung f ㊻ embracing, embrace, hug(ging); =hang (ᴶᴸ) [mhd.] m ⑦c. (Vorhang) curtain; s.th. to hang over or to cover one's shoulders with; für Damen: opera-cloak, loose wrap; (Mäntelchen) cape; ⁜hängen v/a. (ᴶᴸ∪) ⑧* (hängend umgeben) to hang round (mit with); (ᴶᴸ∪) ⑧**: einen Mantel ≈ to throw ... round one's shoulders, to put on ...; (anders hängen) to hang afresh or in a different way; =häng(e)tuch (ᴶᴸ∪)·ᴸ·ch) n ⑨c. wrap, shawl; ⁜hauen (ᴶᴸ∪) v/a. ⑨c** to cut down; f. a. umhacken.

um-her (ᴶᴸ)[mhd.] adv. round about, all around, (nach allen Seiten) on all sides, f. rings; (in verschiedenen Richtungen) in various directions; this way and that, hither and thither, here and there; (aufs Geratewohl) at random.

☞ um-her-... in Zssgn vgl. herum-...

um-her-blicken (ᴶᴸ...) v/n. ⑧** (h.) to look about (one); ~ n ② looking about, glancing around; ⁜fahren ⑧b** v/n. (ſn) to drive (or ride) about in a carriage, auf d. Fahrrade: to cycle about, im Automobil: to go motoring; v/a. to take (or drive) about in a carriage; ~ n ② carriage-drive, cycling-tour, motoring; ⁜fechten F v/n. (h.) ⑩b**: mit den Händen ≈ to gesticulate; ⁜flattern v/n. (h.) ⑨a** to flutter to and fro or here and there; ⁜fliegen v/n. (ſn) ⑩a** to fly about; ⁜führen v/a. ⑧** to act as guide to, in d. Stadt: to take (or show) about (the town); ⁜gaffen v/n. ⑧** to stand gaping, to stare about one; ⁜geh(e)n v/n. (ſn) ⑨** to walk about, müßig: to lounge (or loaf, saunter) about; ⁜irren v/n. (ſn) ⑧** to wander (or roam) about; ⁜irrend p.pr. u. a. ㊻ wandering, roaming, roving; ⁜laufen v/n. (ſn) ⑨aſt** to run (or ramble) about; ~ n running about, rambles pl.; ⁜liegen v/n. (h.) ⑨** = herumliegen; ⁜lungern v/n. (h. u. ſn) ⑨a** to lounge (or loaf) about; ⁜reiſen v/n. (ſn) ⑨** to travel about; in der Welt ≈ to go (F knock) about the world; ~ n ② travelling about, a.touring, excursion; ⁜reiten v/n. (h.) ⑨b** to ride (or go) about on horseback; ⁜schleichen v/n. (ſn) ⑨aſt** to sneak (or creep, slink) about; ⁜schlendern v/n. (ſn) ⑨a** to stroll (or lounge, saunter) about; ⁜schweifen v/n. (ſn) ⑧** to roam (or ramble) about, to lead a roving life; ſeine Blicke ≈ laſſen to let one's eyes wander freely; ⁜ſitzen v/n. (h.)

⑨**: a) to sit about; b) to be settled about the neighbourhood; ⁜ſpringen v/n. (ſn) ⑩n** to jump (or skip) about; ⁜ſteh(e)n v/n. (h.) ⑨** = herumſtehen; ⁜ſtreichen v/n. (ſn) ⑨a** to roam (or loaf) about; ⁜ſtreifen v/n. (h. und ſn) ⑧** to tramp about; ~ n ② tramp(ing); ſich ⁜treiben v/refl. ⑨** to wander (or F knock) about; ⁜trippeln v/n. (h.) ⑨a**: immer ≈ to be constantly on the move; ⁜wandern v/n. (ſn) ⑨a** to wander about; ⁜werfen v/a. ⑨b** to throw (or fling) about; ſich im Bette ≈ to toss about in bed; ⁜ziehen v/n. (ſn) ⑩b** to wander about; to move from place to place; ⁉ itinerant, strolling.

um-hin (ᴶᴸ) adv.: nicht ≈ können et. zu tun to have no choice but to do a th.; ich kann nicht ≈, es zu ſagen I cannot help (or forbear or refrain from) saying so, I cannot do otherwise but (mſt: I feel bound to or I am obliged to) mention it.

Um-hülle (ᴶᴸ∪) f ㊻ lady's wrap, s. th. to cover the shoulders; ⁜hüllen (ᴶᴸ∪) v/a. ⑧* to wrap up (or envelop) in s.th., mit Schleier: to veil; (bedecken) to cover with s.th.; (bekleiden) to clothe in s.th., to dress; ⊖ to case, to protect; ~ n ② = =hüllung a; =hüllung f ㊻: a) wrapping (up), &c.; b) wrap(per), veil; cover(ing); ⊖ casing, case, jacket, eines Kabels ꝛc.: sheath, coating; ⁜jauchzen (ᴶᴸ∪ch㎊) v/a. ⑨* to cheer from all sides, to surround amid jubilant shouts; =kehr (ᴶᴸ) f ㊻ turning back, return, fig. (Bekehrung) conversion; mending (one's way), turning over a new leaf; =kehrbar (ᴶᴸ∪) a. ㊻ convertible, (umdrehbar) reversible; =kehrbarkeit f ㊻ convertibility, reversibility; ⁜kehren (ᴶᴸ∪) ⑧** v/n. (ſn) to turn back, to return, auf demſelben Wege: to return the same way, to retrace one's steps; fig. (ſich bekehren) to reform, to mend (one's ways), to amend one's life, to turn over a new leaf; v/a. to turn round or about or over, to reverse, von innen nach außen: to turn one's pockets, &c. inside out; ≈, F a. um und um (das Oberſte zu unterſt) kehren to turn upside down or topsy-turvy, to overturn, to invert, fig. (umſtürzen) to overthrow, subvert, revolutionize; den Braten ≈ to turn (over) the joint; math. e-n Bruch ≈ to invert a fraction, fig. wie man eine Hand umkehrt in the turn of a hand; vgl. Hand 2 gegen Ende; das ganze Haus ≈ to turn the house upside down; den Karren ≈ to tip the cart over; gram. die Reihenfolge der Wörter ≈ to invert the order of words; log. e-n Satz ≈ to convert a proposition; f. Schuh 2, Spieß 1; elect. den Strom ≈ to reverse the current; ſich ≈ v/refl. to turn round; ſich im Bette ≈ to turn over in (one's) bed; fig. das Herz im Leibe (oder alles) kehrt ſich in einem um it makes one's heart ache, it's a sickening (or revolting) sight; von einem Verſtorbenen: im Grabe kehrte er ſich um, wenn // he would turn in his grave if //; vgl. ⁜gekehrt; ~n u. =kehrung f ㊻ = =kehr; turning round, &c., fig. overthrow, subversion; math., gram.

inversion, log. conversion; elect. (des Stromes) reversal; ⁜kippen (ᴶᴸ∪) ⑧** v/n. (ſn) to tilt (or topple) over, to overturn, von Schiffen: to capsize, von Wagen: to upset; v/a. to overturn, to upset; ⁜klaftern (ᴶᴸ∪) v/a. ⑨a* to encompass; vgl. ⁜faſſen; ⁜klammern (ᴶᴸ∪) v/a. ⑨a* to cling round or to, to clasp (in one's arms), to entwine, to embrace, to hug; ⁜klappen (ᴶᴸ∪) v/n. (ſn) ⑧** to drop (down), to collapse; ⁜kleiden A (ᴶᴸ∪) ⑧** v/a. und v/refl.: e-n ≈ to dress a p. anew, to change a p.'s clothes; ſich ≈ to change one's dress, to put on other clothes or fresh garments; er hat ſich m' gekleidet he has changed his clothes; ~ n ② change of clothes; B (ᴶᴸ∪) ⑧* v/a. to clothe, cover, envelop; fig. to invest (or adorn, surround) with new charms, &c.; ſchwarz umklei"det draped in black; ~ ≈ u. =kleidung f ㊻ clothing; investment, adornment; ⁜knicken (ᴶᴸ∪) ⑧** v/n. (ſn) to snap and sink to the ground; v/a. to bend in two, to snap (or break) off; ⁜kommen (ᴶᴸ∪) v/n. (ſn) ⑧** to perish with fright, &c., to die of hunger, &c.; (unterliegen) to succumb to heat and fatigue; durchs Schwert ≈ to perish by the sword; in der Schlacht ≈ to perish (or fall) in battle; man möchte vor Hitze ≈ the heat is enough to kill one; fig. vor Lang(er)weile ≈ to be bored to death; von Sachen: (verloren gehen) to get lost; (verderben) to spoil; ⁜kränzen (ᴶᴸ∪) v/a. ⑨* to wreathe, to festoon, to entwine (or adorn, crown) with wreaths or garlands; =kreis (ᴶᴸ) m ⑨a. circle, circuit; weitS. = Umfang a u. b; im Umkreiſe von acht Kilometern for five miles round; ⁜kreiſen (ᴶᴸ∪) v/a. ⑨* to circle round or about, to turn (or wheel) round, von Planeten: to revolve (or rotate, move) round the sun; ~ n ② und =kreiſung f ㊻ circular movement round, &c.; ⁜krempe(l)n (ᴶᴸ∪) v/a. ⑧(⑨a)** to turn over at the edge, to tuck up; fig. to change thoroughly or radically; ⁜laden (ᴶᴸ∪) v/a. ⑨bſt**: e-n Wagen ≈ to unload and reload a van; Waren ≈ to shift goods from one wagon (or truck) to another, ⚓ to tran(s)ship goods; ~ n ② u. =ladung f ㊻ unloading and reloading; shifting, ⚓ tran(s)shipment; =lage (ᴶᴸ) f ㊻ assessment of taxes; ſtädtiſche ~n (Abgaben) local rates pl.; ⁜lagern (ᴶᴸ∪) v/a. ⑨a** to surround closely, to hem in; fig. e-n umla"gert halten to besiege (or beset) a p.; (ᴶᴸ∪) ⑨a** v/a. u. ſich ≈ v/refl. to change one's couch or one's sleeping-apartment; =lauf (ᴶᴸ) m ⑦c.: a) (Kreisbewegung) circular motion; ~ des Blutes circulation of the blood, aſt., &c. revolution, mach. rotation; b) (dauernde Bewegung) circulation; des Geldes: currency; in ~ bringen od. ſetzen to put into circulation, to circulate, ein Gerücht auch: to spread (about), ein Wort: to obtain currency for; in ~, im ~e ſein to circulate

(freely), von Neuigkeiten auch: to go the round (of the town), to be bruited about; ₌lauf-bewegung (⁸ᴸ⁄…) f ⁶² rotatory movement, rotation; ₂laufen (⁸ᴸ⁄) ⁶⁹ast** v/a.: e-n ₂ to run a p. down, to knock a p. down in running; (⁸ᴸᴸ, ⁶⁹ast*) to run round a th.; v/n. (ſn) a) (ſich im Kreiſe drehen) to turn (or whirl) round, um eine Achſe: to spin round, revolve, rotate; b) (ſich fortdauernd bewegen) vom Blute, Säfte ꝛc.: to circulate, von Gerüchten auch: to spread (or go) about; von der Zeit: (ablaufen) to expire, F to run out; wir ſind (od. haben uns) zwei (deutſche) Meilen u"mgelaufen we have gone nine (English) miles out of our way; ~ n ㉓ = Umlauf; ₌lauf(s)₌kapital ♆ (⁸ᴸ⁄…) n ⁶² working capital; ₌lauf(s)₌ſchreiben n circular (letter); ₌laufs₌zeit f time (or period) of revolution or rotation; ₌laut (⁸ᴸ⁄) m ⑪c. gram.: a) (Umlaut von a, o, u in ä, ö, ü) modification of a (German) vowel, mutation, auch: 7 umlaut; b) (der Laut ſelbſt) modified vowel; ₂lauten (⁸ᴸ⁄) ⁶⁹** gram. v/n. (h.): viele Plurale auf …er lauten um (zB. Land, pl. Länder) … modify, … are modified, … undergo mutation; v/a. den Vokal ₂ to modify …; ₌leg(e)₌kragen (ᵁᴸ(ᵛ)…) m lay-down (or turn-down) collar; ₂legen A (⁸ᴸ⁄) ⁶⁸* v/a. to lay round (mit with); B (⁸ᴸ⁄) ⁶⁸* v/a. u. ſich ₂ v/refl. to lay (or put) round; e-n Verband ₂ to apply a bandage; (zum Liegen bringen) to lay down; das Korn: to beat down, to lay; einen Kragen ꝛc.: to turn down; (anders legen) to lay (or place) cards, &c. differently; to relay a floor, a pavement; von einer Spitze: ſich ₂ to bend over, to blunt; ⚓ das Schiff ₂ (wenden) to lay a ship on her side, to careen; lavierend: to tack about; die Segel ₂ to shift the sails; vom Schiffe: ſich ₂ to careen (over); vom Winde: ſich ₂ to veer (round); ⚔ Truppen ₂ = ₂quartieren; die Koſten auf die Teilnehmer ₂ to apportion the costs among …; ~ n ㉓ u. ₌legung f ⁴⁶ laying round; application of a bandage; ⚓ careening; tacking about; ₂leiten (⁸ᴸ⁄) v/a. ⁶⁹** to lead (or conduct) in a different direction; to turn off (vgl. ableiten); ₂lenken (⁸ᴸ⁄) v/a. ⁶⁸** v/n. (h. und ſn) ⁶⁸** to turn round or back; fig. abs. to change one's opinion or one's mind; ₂lernen (⁸ᴸ⁄) v/a. und v/n. (h.) ⁶⁹** to learn anew or afresh; ₂leuchten (⁸ᴸ⁄) ⁶⁹* to surround (ſeltener: to circumfuse) with light; (beleuchten) to shed light on; ₂liegen (⁸ᴸ⁄) v/n. (h.) ⁴** to lie (a)round, to be situated around, meiſt als p.pr. ₂d surrounding, circumjacent, neighbouring; ₂de Gegend country (a)round, surroundings, environs pl.; ₌mantelung ⊕ (⁸ᴸ⁄…) für Keſſel ꝛc.: jacket, casing; ₂mauern (⁸ᴸ⁄) ⁶⁹a* to surround (or fortify) with walls, to wall in or round; ⁶⁹a** (anders mauern) to change the walls (or masonry) of; ₂modeln (⁸ᴸ⁄)⁶⁹a** to remodel; ₌mod(e)lung

f ⁴⁶ remodelling; ₂münzen (⁸ᴸ⁄) v/a. ⁶⁹a**u. ~ n ㉓, münzung f ⁴⁶ = ₂prägen; ₂nachten (⁸ᴸ⁄chi⁄) v/a. u. v/refl. ⁶⁹* to wrap (or shroud) in darkness; vom Geiſte: ſich ₂ to become deranged; ₂na"chtet wrapt in darkness, benighted; ſein ₂na"chteter Geiſt his clouded intellect, his deranged mind; ₌nachtung f ⁴⁶ benighted state; mental derangement; ₂nähen v/a. (⁸ᴸ⁄) ⁶⁹* to sew all round; (ſäumen nch) to hem; (⁸ᴸ⁄) ⁶⁹** to sew (or stitch) anew or afresh; ₂nebeln (⁸ᴸ⁄) v/a. ⁶⁹a* to wrap (or envelop) in mist or fog, to cloud; fig. to (be)fog, to obfuscate; ₂ne"belt befogged; ₂nehmen (⁸ᴸ⁄) v/a. ⁶⁹a** to take (or put) round one, e-n Mantel: to put on; ₂packen (⁸ᴸ⁄) v/a. ⁶⁸** to pack afresh or over again; abs. (den Koffer) ₂ to repack one's trunk; ₌packung f ⁴⁶ fresh packing, repacking; ₂panzern (⁸ᴸ⁄) v/a. ⁶⁹a* to cover with (a coat of) mail (vgl. panzern); mit Stahl umpa"nzert, a. sheathed in steel, steel-clad; ₌panzerung f ⁴⁶ coat of mail; armour (a. ⚓); ₂pfählen (⁸ᴸ⁄) v/a. ⁶⁹* to surround (or fence round) with a paling or with stakes, to palisade (auch ⚔); ₂pflanzen v/a. A (⁸ᴸ⁄) ⁶⁸** hort. to replant; (anderswohin pflanzen) to transplant; u"mgepflanzt transplanted; (aus den Töpfen herausnehmen) to unpot; ~ n ㉓ = ₌pflanzung; B (⁸ᴸ⁄) ⁶⁸* mit Bäumen ꝛc. ₂ to plant round with …; umpfla"nzt mit surrounded with (trees, &c.); ₌pflanzung f ⁴⁶ replanting; t ansplantation; ₂pflaſtern v/a. (⁸ᴸ⁄) ⁶⁹a** to pave afresh, to repave; (⁸ᴸ⁄) ⁶⁹a* to pave all round a house, &c.; ₂pflügen (⁸ᴸ⁄) v/a. ⁶⁹b** agr. to plough up, to break up with a plough; (⁸ᴸ⁄) v/a. ⁶⁸* (mit einer Furche umziehen) to plough a furrow around; ₂planken (⁸ᴸ⁄) v/a. ⁶⁸* to enclose (or encase) in planks; ₂prägen (⁸ᴸ⁄) v/a. ⁶⁹a*: die Münzen ₂ to recoin (or new-coin) money; ~ n ㉓ und ₌prägung f ⁴⁶ recoinage; ₂purzeln (⁸ᴸ⁄) v/n. (ſn) ⁶⁹a** to topple over; ₂quartieren (⁸ᵛᴸ⁄) v/a. ⁶⁹* to remove to fresh quarters; ⚔ Truppen ₂, auch: to shift troops (into other quarters); ₌quartierung f ⁴⁶ removal (or moving) to other quarters; ₂rahmen (⁸ᴸᴸ⁄) v/a. ⁶⁸* to (put into a) frame; to form a frame round; ₂rändern (⁸ᴸ⁄) v/a. ⁶⁹a* to border or edge (mit with), to put a border round; ₂ranken (⁸ᴸ⁄) v/a. ⁶⁸*: a) clasp with tendrils, to entwine; von Efeu umra"nkt ivy-clad; b) fig. to clasp (round), to cling to; ₂rauſchen (⁸ᴸ⁄) ⁶¹* to roar (a)round, von (den) Wellen umra"uſcht encircled (or surrounded) by roaring waves; ₂rechnen ♆ (⁸ᴸ⁄) v/a. ⁶⁹b** (umwechſeln) to change; Papiergeld in Gold ₂ to convert paper money into gold; Taler in Mark ₂ to reduce thalers to marks; ~ n ㉓ und ₌rechnung f ⁴⁶ conversion, reduction; ₌rechnungs-tabelle f ⁶² tables pl. of exchange; ₂reiſen (⁸ᴸ⁄) ⁶⁰* v/a. to travel (or tour) round, to take a trip round;

(⁸ᴸ⁄) ⁶⁰*** v/n. (ſn) to travel by a circuitous route, to make a roundabout journey; weit ₂ to go far out of one's way; ₂reißen A (⁸ᴸ⁄) ⁶⁰a** v/a. to pull down, ein Haus ꝛc. auch: to break down, demolish, wreck; vom Winde: to blow down; u"mgeriſſen pulled down, vom Winde: blown down; ~ n ㉓ pulling down, demolition, wreckage; B (⁸ᴸ⁄) ⁶⁰a* v/a. (in Umriſſen zeichnen) to outline, to make a (rough) sketch of; umri"ſſen roughly sketched; ₂reiten A (⁸ᴸ⁄) ⁶⁰b* v/a. to ride round, e-n Bezirk auch: to travel round (von Richtern ꝛc. bſd. ehm.: to go the circuit) on horseback; B (⁸ᴸ⁄) ⁶⁰b** v/n. (ſn) to ride a roundabout way; v/a. ein Kind ꝛc. ₂ to ride over …; to knock down … while riding on horseback; vgl. niederreiten; ₂rennen (⁸ᴸ⁄) v/a. u. v/n. (ſn) ⁶⁰b** = ₂laufen; er hat das Kind u"mgerannt he ran over the child, (⁸ᴸ⁄) ⁶⁰b*: er hat die Strecke umra"nnt he completed the distance round; ₂ringeln (⁸ᴸ⁄) v/a. ⁶⁹a* to describe circles round; to coil round; ₂ringen (⁸ᴸ⁄) v/a. ⁶⁹* to encircle, to encompass; (dicht umgeben) to enclose, to surround, ⚔ a. to invest; (umzingeln) to hem in, to beset on all sides; ₌riß (⁸ᴸ⁄) m ⑪a. paint., &c. outline, (fr.) contour; fließende, leicht hingeworfene ₌riſſe light sketches pl.; ₌riſſe des Geſichts outline of the face; im ~ entwerfen to outline, sketch, a. skeletonize; fig. in kräftigen ₌riſſen ſchildern, zeichnen to sketch in bold outlines; ₂riſſen (⁸ᴸ⁄) p.p. ſ. ₂reißen B; ₌riß-(land)karte f ⁶² skeleton-map; ₌riß-zeichnung f sketch; ₌ritt (⁸ᴸ⁄) m ⑪c. (Umzug zu Pferde) cavalcade; [₂reiten] (riding) round (e-s Richters ꝛc.: circuit) on horseback; ₂rühren (⁸ᴸ⁄) v/a. ⁶⁹** to stir round or up; ⊕ metall. im Flammofen ₂ to puddle, to rake; auch = polen; ₂rütteln (⁸ᴸ⁄) v/a. ⁶⁹a** to shake up. ums (⁸) (⁄) = um das, bisw. = um des, zB.: ₂ Himmels willen! for Heaven's sake! um-ſägen (⁸ᴸ⁄) v/a. ⁶⁸**: einen Baum ₂ to saw down a tree; ₂ſatteln (⁸ᴸ⁄) ⁶⁹a* v/a.: ein Pferd ₂ to resaddle …; v/n. (h.) fig. to change one's (or to leap into a new) saddle; F fig. (Beruf ꝛc. wechſeln) to change one's vocation or profession or trade; pol. to change sides, F to rat; ~ n ㉓ u. ₌ſattelung f ⁴⁶ (ſ. ſatteln) change of saddle; F fig. change of profession; pol. change of (or changing) sides, desertion (of party), F ratting; ₌ſatz (⁸⁄) m ⑪a. exchange; bſd. ♆ turnover, business (done); (Abſatz) sale (effected); (Einnahme) returns, receipts pl.; es fand ein großer ~ in Weizen ꝛc. ſtatt large amounts of wheat, &c. changed hands; ₌ſatz-betrag ♆ m amount of turnover or of business done; ₌ſatz-kapital n working capital; ₂ſäumen (⁸ᴸ⁄) v/a. ⁶⁸** to hem (round); ₂ſauſen (⁸ᴸ⁄) v/n. ⁶⁰* to whiz (or whistle) around; ₂ſchaffen (⁸ᴸ⁄) v/a. ⁶⁹a** to transform; (neu erzeugen) to create anew, to regenerate; a. = ₂bilden; ~ n ㉓ und

♪ Muſik; ⚗ Wiſſenſchaft; ♣ Pflanze; ♁ Geographie; ⊕ Technik; ⚒ Bergbau; ⚔ Militär; ⚓ Marine; ♆ Handel; ✉ Poſt; 🚂 Eiſenbahn.

[Umschaffung] — 994 — [umsehen]

=schaffung f ⑯ transformation; regeneration; =schalten ⊙ (⌐⌐) v/a. ⑧** elect. to switch, commute, reverse, change the current; ~ n ㉓ =schaltung; =schalter ⊙ (⌐⌐) m ㉒ elect. (pole-changing) switch, commutator; =schalter-brett n ㉒ tel. switchboard; =schaltung f ⑯ switching, commutation; =schaltungs-taste f ㉒ reversing-key; =schanzen ⚔ (⌐⌐) v/a. ⑨* to intrench, to circumvallate; ~ n ㉓ und =schanzung f ⑯ intrenchment, circumvallation; =schanzungs-linie f ㉒ line of circumvallation; =scharren (⌐⌐) v/a. ⑧** to scratch (or scrape, dig) up; =schatten (⌐⌐) v/a. ⑨* to shade on all sides, to cast a shadow around; =schau (⌐⌐) f ⑯ looking round; ~ halten to look round or about, ⚔ to scout, to reconnoitre, nach etwas: to look out (or to be on the look-out) for a th.; =schauen (⌐⌐) v/n. (h.) u. sich ⌐ v/refl. to look round; to spy about; vgl. =sehen; =schaufeln (⌐⌐) v/a. ⑫a**: Korn ⨯c. ⌐ to turn (over) ... with a shovel; =schichten (⌐⌐) v/a. ⑨** to pile afresh; =schichtig (⌐⌐) a. ⑯ u. adv. in layers; fig. (abwechselnd) alternately, in turns; =schienen (⌐⌐) v/a. ⑧* to put fresh bands (or hoops) of iron around; =schießen (⌐⌐) ⑯c(e)s t* v/a.: a) ⚔ to shoot down; b) ⊕ typ. to impose columns anew; v/n. (in) ↓ der Wind schießt um ... is veering round or shifting or chopping about; =schiffbar ↓ (⌐⌐) a. ⑯ circumnavigable; =schiffen ↓ A (⌐⌐) ⑧* v/a. to circumnavigate, to sail (or steam) round; ein Vorgebirge ⌐ to double a cape; ~ n ㉓ und =schiffung f ⑯ circumnavigation; B (⌐⌐) v/a. Waren ⨯c.: (umladen) to tran(s)ship; =schlag (⌐⌐, ⌐⌐) m ⓒc.: a) (plötzlicher Wechsel) sudden change, turn; fig. revulsion, revolution, upheaval, des Glücks: reverse (of fortune), des Wetters: change of the weather, atmospheric change; b) an der Kleidung: = Aufschlag 3; (Kragen) collar; (Umhüllung) wrap(per), cover(ing), für Briefe: envelope; ⌐ unter ~ senden to send under cover; c) med. poultice, von Brei ⨯c.: cataplasm; (Bähung) fomentation; Umschläge m. um // to apply poultices to //, to poultice //; d) (Falte) fold, tuck, (umgebogener Rand) turned-down edge.

Umschlag-bohrer ⊙ (⌐⌐...) m ㉒ centre-bit, spike-gimlet; =deckel m cover of a book; =eisen n f. Eisenblech hatchet-stake.

Umschlage-kragen m ㉒ turn-down collar.

um-schlagen A (⌐⌐) ⑯b** I v/n. (in) 1. to topple over, to fall down (with vehemence), to overbalance o.s., von Wagen ⨯c.: to be overturned or upset. ↓ v. Booten: to capsize. — 2. (plötzlich anders w.): a) to change suddenly, vom Winde: to shift, to veer (round), vom Wetter: to break up; das Wetter ist umgeschlagen there is a break-up (or a sudden change) in the weather; b) von Bier, Wein ⨯c.: to turn (sour), von Speisen ⨯c.: to turn (F to go) bad; c) von der Stimme: to break; d) die Krankheit ⨯c. schlägt um ... is taking

a (new) turn, ... has come to a turning-point or crisis. — 3. in et. ⌐ (übergehen) to turn (zum Schlechten: to degenerate) into s.th.; zum Guten ⌐ to take a good (or favourable) turn. — II v/a. 4. (umwerfen) to knock (or beat, throw) down. — 5. (herumlegen) to lay (or put) round; Kompressen, nasse Lappen ⌐ to apply poultices, wet rags; Reifen ⌐ to put hoops round, to bind with hoops; ein Tuch ⌐ to wrap (or tie) a cloth round, to wrap (up) in a shawl. — 6. (umbiegen) to bend (at the edge); die Ärmel ⌐ to turn (or tuck) up ...; e-e Karte ⌐ to turn up ...; e-n Kragen ⌐ to turn down ...; die Seiten eines Buches ⌐ (wenden) to turn over the leaves of a book. — 7. (anders schlagen) to recast, Münzen: to recoin. — III ~ n ㉓ 8. toppling over, &c. (f. I); upset; sudden change; e-r Krankheit ⨯c.: turning-point, crisis (vgl. Umschlag a). — 9. knocking down, &c. (f. II); application of a poultice, &c. — B (⌐⌐) v.a. ⑯b*10. typ. (umwenden) to turn over...

Umschlag(e)-papier (⌐⌐..., ⌐⌐...) n ㉒ wrapping-paper; =faum m turned-in seam; =tuch n wrap, shawl.

um-schleichen (⌐⌐) ⑯aft* v/a. to sneak (or prowl) (a)round; (⌐⌐) ⑯aft** v/n. (in) to sneak (or prowl) about; =schleiern (⌐⌐) ⑫a* to cover with (or to wrap in) a veil, to veil; =schließen (⌐⌐) v/n. (h.) ⑯d* to surround, to encompass, (einschließen) to enclose; mit den Armen ⌐ to clasp in one's arms, to hug; ⚔ e-e Festung ⌐ to invest ..., belagernd: to besiege or beleaguer ...; ~ n ㉓ und =schließung f ⑯ (f. ⌐schließen) enclosure; ⚔ investment; siege; =schlingen (⌐⌐) ⑯ft**: sie hat sich (dat.) das Tuch umgeschlungen she wrapt the cloth round her; (⌐⌐) v/a. u. sich ⌐ v/recip. ⑯ft* to clasp (or cling) round, to twine round or about; to entangle (a. fig.); sich (ea.) ⌐ to embrace, to hug (closely); sich ea. umschlungen halten to be locked in each other's arms; er hielt sie fest umschlungen he held her tightly in his embrace or grasp, he clutched her tightly; seid umschlungen, Millionen (SCH.) with one embrace I greet you, millions; ~ n ㉓ und =schlingung f ⑯ clasping round, &c.; embrace, (close) hug; =schmeißen P F (⌐⌐) v/a. u. v/n. (in) ⑯a*** derb = ⌐werfen; =schmelzen (⌐⌐) ⑯b** to melt again, ⊙ to refound, to recast; =schmieden v/a. (⌐⌐) ⑨** to forge anew, reforge, weld afresh; (⌐⌐) ⑧* to forge (or weld) (a)round; =schnallen (⌐⌐) v/a. ⑧** den Degen ⌐ to buckle on one's sword; =schnüren v/a. (⌐⌐) ⑧** to lace (or strap, cord) in a different way; (⌐⌐) ⑧* to lace, strap, cord; =schränken (⌐⌐) v/a. ⑧* to put barriers around, to fence in, fig. to restrict; =schreiben A (⌐⌐) ⑨** v/a.: a) to write differently, einen Brief: to write again, to rewrite; umgeschrieben rewritten; b) (übertragen) to transcribe, in ein anderes Alphabet: to

transliterate; jur.: auf e-n ⌐ to transfer (or convey) to a p. (by a deed of document); c) geom. to circumscribe about a circle; to describe a circle round a triangle, &c.; d) ~ n ㉓ = =schreibung A, B (⌐⌐); =schreiben ⌐ (⌐⌐) ⑧*: e) (mit einer Umschrift versehen) to put an inscription round; f) (durch Worte erklären) to paraphrase, to express by circumlocution; ⌐b periphrastic; ~ n ㉓ = =schreibung ⌐; =schreiben A (⌐⌐) f ⑯ (f. ⌐schreiben A) transcription, transliteration; jur. transfer; B (⌐⌐) (f. ⌐schreiben B) paraphrase, circumlocution; =schrieben (⌐⌐) [p.p. v. =schreiben] a. ⑯ (D⑨) geom. circumscribed; =schrift (⌐⌐) f ⑯ circular inscription, auf e-r Münze: legend, transcription; vgl. ⌐schreiben; =schütteln (⌐⌐) v/a. ⑨a** to shake (or toss) up or about; =schütten (⌐⌐) ⑨** a) to upset a glass; to spill a liquid; (umwerfen) to overturn; (in ein anderes Gefäß gießen) to transfuse, to pour into another vessel; b) (⌐) to cover a. th. up with earth, &c., to pour (or heap) sand, &c. over (or on) a th.; =schwärmen (⌐⌐) ⑨** to swarm (or buzz, flit) round; von Anbetern umschwärmt surrounded by a crowd of adorers; ⚔ den Feind ⌐, auch: to harass ..., to hover round ...; =schweben (⌐⌐) v.a. ⑧* to float (or flit, hover) round; =schweif (⌐⌐) m ⓒc. roundabout way, im Reden: circumlocution; (Abschweifung) digression; feine ~e m. to use plain language or words, not to mince the matter; lange ~e machen to make a long rigmarole (of it), to digress, to ramble; ohne ~(e) without (much) ado or fuss, straight(a)way, point-blank; =schwenken (⌐⌐) v/n. (h.) ⑧** to wheel round (bsd. ⚔); bisw. a. = ⌐satteln F fig.; =schwirren (⌐⌐) v/a. ⑧* to whiz (or buzz) around; =schwung (⌐⌐) m ⓒc. (Umdrehung) rotation, revolution, Turnerei: swing (or turn) round the bar, &c.; fig. (plötzliche Änderung) sudden (or rapid) change or turn or reaction, im Glücke oft: vicissitude (vgl. ⌐schlag a); es trat ein ~ in der öffentlichen Meinung ein there was a veering round of public opinion; =segeln ↓ (⌐⌐) ⑨** v/a.: ein Schiff ⌐ to run foul of a ship in sailing; vgl. =übersegeln; v/n. (in) (e-n Umweg m.) to sail a roundabout way; (⌐⌐) ⑫a* to sail round; to circumnavigate, to double a cape; ~ n ㉓ u. =seg(e)lung f ⑯ circumnavigation; =sehen (⌐⌐) v/a.: sich ⌐ v/refl., bisw. a. v/n. (h.) ⑫a** to look round or back; to turn one's head (round); ohne sich u"-zusehen without (a moment's) hesitation; fig. eh' man sich u"-msieht od. im ⌐ in the twinkling of an eye, F in a jiffy, before you can say Jack Robinson; to take a survey, F to have a look round; ⚔ († sich orientieren) sich an einem Orte ⌐ to look about a place; sich in der Stadt ⌐ to take a turn (or a walk) round the town; er hat sich viel in der Welt umgesehen he has seen a good bit (or a good deal) of the world; sich nach e-m, et. (suchend) ⌐

Signs (see page XVII): F familiar; P vulgar; ℱ flash; ⌐ rare; † obsolete (died); * new word (born); ‡ incorrect; ♪ music.

[umsein] — 995 — [umstoßen]

to look out (or to be on the look-out) for a p., a th.; F *fig.* er soll sich anderswo 2 he must find s.th. elsewhere; da kann er sich lange 2 he may wait a long while; ~ n ⊕: ein ~ taking a look (or glance) round; 2sein *v/n.* (sn) ⓜa**: f. um 13; 2seitig *a.* on the other (or opposite) side or page, overleaf; 2setzbar *a.* convertible; in bares Geld 2 realizable, marketable, saleable; =setzbarkeit *f* convertibility; saleability, saleableness; 2setzen A *v/a.* u. sich 2 *v/refl.* ⓜ**: a) to set (or put) (a)round; b) (anderswohin setzen) to place (or put) elsewhere, to transpose, Bäume ꝛc.: to transplant; ein Musikstück in eine andere Tonart 2 to transpose (weitS. to re-arrange) a piece of music; ⊕ *typ.* to set up afresh, to recompose; c) (umwandeln) to transform; sich 2 in // to be converted (or turned) into //, to turn into //; d) ⊛ to sell, to dispose of; in bares Geld 2 to turn (or convert) into cash, to realize; es ward nur wenig umgesetzt there was but a small turnover or little business doing; *v/n.* (h.) der Wind setzt um the wind is shifting (vgl. 2schlagen); ~ n ⊕ f. =setzung; B (besetzen mit) *v/a.* ⓜ* to surround (with); mit Perlen und Edelsteinen umse"tzt set round with pearls and precious stones (a.), =setzung *f* (f. b) transposition (a. ♪), transplantation; ⚓ ~ der Gezeiten turn of the tides; =sich-greifen *n* ⊕ eines Feuers, einer Krankheit ꝛc.: spread(ing), progress (made by //); (Wachstum) growth; (Fortpflanzung) propagation (vgl. Überhandnahme); =sicht *f* ⊕: a) view (all) round, panorama; b) *fig.* circumspection; (Vorsicht) caution, prudence; (Vorsorge) foresight, far-sightedness; (Takt) discretion; (Behutsamkeit) wariness; mit ~ handeln to act cautiously or circumspectly or warily; 2sichtig *a.* (f. =sicht b, ant. kurzsichtig) b) circumspect, cautious, prudent; far-sighted; discreet; wary; 2 (adv.) handeln to act cautiously, to use discretion; ~keit *f* =sicht b; 2sinken *v/n.* (sn) ⓜ* to sink down; vor Müdigkeit 2 to drop down with fatigue; ohnmächtig 2 to fall (or sink) down in a faint or in a swoon; 2so-mehr f. um 5 u. 8; 2sonst [mhd.; vgl. sonst] *adv.* for nothing, gratis, gratuitously, F for the mere asking, for love, ⊛ free of charge; 2 arbeiten to work without pay; halb 2 kaufen to buy for almost nothing or for a mere song; Sprichw. 2 ist der Tod nothing for nothing; everything costs money; (vergebens) in vain, to no purpose; unsere Anstrengungen waren 2 our efforts proved useless or were unavailing; drohend: das soll er nicht 2 getan haben! he shall pay for that!; er hat das nicht 2 (ohne Grund) getan he had some reason (or design) in doing it; 2soweniger f. um 5; 2spannen *v/a.* ⓜ**: die Saiten 2 to change the strings of an instrument; die Pferde ꝛc. metonymisch: den Wagen 2 to change

horses; ⓜ* to span round; (umfassen) to span, encompass, encircle; einen Ort mit Netzen 2 to spread (one's) nets round a place; 2spielen *v/a.* ⓜ** to play round; ein Lächeln umspielt seinen Mund a smile is hovering (or flickering, fluttering) round his mouth; 2spinnen *v/a.* ⓜa* to spin (all) round; to entangle (or ensnare) in one's weft or net (auch *fig.*); 2springen A ⓜü** *v/a.* to overthrow in jumping; *v/n.* (sn) (oft *fig.*); mit e-m 2 (wie die Katze mit der Maus) to deal (arbitrarily) with a p., to treat a p. (unceremoniously or roughly); damit werde ich bald 2 I shall soon manage (or settle) that; er weiß mit ihnen u"mzuspringen (umzugehen) he knows how to handle (or to deal with) them; Wind: (sich plötzlich ändern) to veer (round), to chop about; B ⓜü* *v/a.*: e-n 2 to jump (or skip, dance) round a p.; 2spülen *v/a.* ⓜ* Wellen: to wash (round), *poet.* to lave.

Um-stand [mhd.] *m* ⓘc. 1. circumstance; das kommt auf die Umstände an it all depends (on circumstances); alle Umstände auseinandersetzen to give (or go into, furnish) full particulars or details; unter allen Umständen under any circumstances, in any case, anyhow; ein mildernder ~ a redeeming feature; *jur.* f. erschweren 2 u. mildern; unter keinen Umständen not on any account, by no manner of means; unter solchen (od. so bewandten) Umständen in these circumstances, as matters stand; der ~, daß er arm ist // (the fact of) his being poor //. — 2. Umstände *pl.* (Lage, Verhältnisse) position, condition, state (of affairs); in guten (beschränkten) Umständen sein to be in good (in straitened) circumstances, to be well (badly) off; von Frauen: in andern (od. gesegneten, interessanten) Umständen sein to be in the family way, to be pregnant or (fr.) enceinte. — 3. Umstände (Förmlichkeiten) ceremonies, formalities *pl.*; große Umstände m. to raise great difficulties; machen Sie unseretwegen feine Umstände don't put yourself out on our account; ohne Umstände without (much) ado, summarily; das hat ihm viel Umstände (Beschwerlichkeiten) gemacht that has caused him a great deal of trouble or inconvenience; nicht viel Umstände (Aufhebens) m. to make no great fuss or bother. — 4. *gr.* adverb, adverbial phrase or clause. umstände-halber *adv.* owing to (particular) circumstances.

um-ständlich *a.* ⊕ 1. circumstantial, in detail, detailed, minute. — 2. (weitläufig) involving ceremonies or formalities; prolix, diffuse; (beschwerlich) troublesome, bothersome; das wäre sehr 2 zu tun that would be a great trouble or bother; 2 (adv.) erzählen to tell with full particulars, to give a detailed (or full, minute) account of, to particularize. — 3. ~ von Personen: ceremonious, precise, fussy, slow.

Um-ständlichkeit *f* (f. umständlich) 1. circumstantiality; minuteness. — 2. ceremoniousness, formality; (Verdruß) trouble, bother. — 3. ~ fussiness.

Um-stands-bestimmung (...) *f* ⊕ adverbial modification; =brot, =brötchen *n* sandwich; =kommissarius, =krämer F *m* ceremonious (or fussy) p., pedant(ic fellow); slow coach; =satz *m* adverbial sentence or clause; =wort *n* adverb.

um-stechen *v/a.* ⓜa** *agr.* den Boden 2 turn (or break) up … with a fork; ⚒ Kupferstecherei: e-e Platte 2 to re-engrave a plate; 2stecken *v/a.* ⓜ* to stick (or fasten, pin) all (a)round with; j-s Kopfputz 2 to re-arrange a p.'s head-dress or head-gear; 2steh(e)n A ⓜ" ⓜ* *v/a.* to stand (a)round; von der Menge umsta"nden surrounded (or encircled) by the crowd; B ⓜ" *v/n.* (h.): a) *mst* im *p.pr.* 2stehend von Menschen: die 2en Personen, die ~en the people standing around, the bystanders *pl.*; b) von Geschriebenem ꝛc.: auf der 2en Seite, im 2en (öfter 2 *adv.*) on the other side, on the following (or opposite) page, ⊛ wie 2 as stated (or booked) overleaf; c) von Getränken: (verderben) to grow stale, F to go flat; von Tieren. (krepieren) to fall, to die; =steig(e)-billett *n*, =steig(e)-karte *f* ⊕ bei Straßenbahnen ꝛc.: through-ticket, correspondence-ticket; 2steigen ⊞ *v/n.* (sn) ⓜ** (in andere Wagen steigen) to change carriages; nach Berlin 2! (all) change for Berlin!; müssen wir hier 2? have we to change here; 2stellen A ⓜ** *v/a.* (andersstellen) to place (or arrange) differently; *gr.* Wörter ꝛc.: to transpose, to invert; to put in inverted (or different) order, to transpose; ~ n ⊕ f. =stellung; B ⓜ** *v/a.* (umgeben) to surround with; (einschließen) to enclose, encompass, hem in; *typ.* = 2A; =stellung *f* ⊕ transposition, inversion, *math. a.* permutation; 2stempeln *v/a.* ⓜa** to restamp, to stamp again or afresh; *fig.* = 2stimmen; 2steuern ⓜ" ⓜa* *v/a.*: a) ⚓ to steer round; weitS. to evade, to steer clear of; b) ⊕ ⓜ** *v/a.*: e-n elektrischen Strom ꝛc. 2 to reverse …; =steu(e)rung *f* ⊕ (f. 2steuern b) reversal, reversing action; 2stimmen ⓜ" ⓜa** ♪ to tune again or to another pitch; *fig.* e-n 2 to alter a p.'s opinion, to bring a p. round (to one's own way of thinking), to take a p. over; zu j-s Gunsten 2 to incline in favour of a p.; er läßt sich nicht leicht 2 he does not easily give way, he is difficult to move or to convince; =stimmung *f* change of opinion, revulsion of feeling; 2stoßen ⓜ" *v/a.* ⓜa**: a) to push (or knock) down; to overthrow, overturn, upset (a. *fig.*); b) *fig.* to annul or cancel or invalidate or make void an agreement, &c.; to set aside or upset a will, a treaty, &c.; to abolish (or abrogate) a custom, a law, &c.; ein Erkenntnis 2 to quash (or reverse) a sentence; einen Kauf 2 to undo

a bargain; ~ n ⓔ f. =ſtoßung; ⟨ſtößlich⟩ (ˢᴸ◡) a. ⓐ easy to overthrow or to upset, easily cancelled or set aside, fig. annullable, reversible; =ſtoßung (ˢᴸ◡) f ⓐ overthrowing, &c. (f. ⟨ſtoßen a⟩), overthrow; fig. annulment, cancelling, e-s Urteils: reversal; ⟨ſtrahlen⟩ (ˢᴸ◡) v/a. ⓑ* to beam on from all sides, to enwrap in rays; ⟨ſtricken⟩ v/a. (ˢᴸ◡) ⓑ** to enclose in network, mit Drahtgeflecht: to wire round; fig. to ensnare, to entangle, to draw into one's net; (ˢᴸ◡) ⓑ** to (undo and) knit afresh; ⟨ſtrömen⟩ (ˢᴸ◡) v/a. ⓑ* to stream (or flow) round, von Wellen a..: to lash round, to wash; ⟨ſtülpen⟩ v/a. (ˢᴸ◡) ⓑ⁸* to tilt (or turn, tip) over; to overturn; (ˢᴸ◡) ⓑ* typ. to turn crosswise, to tumble; =ſturz (ˢˢ) m ⓐ a. overthrow, subversion (a. fig.), einer Mauer ꝛc.: fall, crash; bſd. fig. downfall; (Umwälzung) revolution, upheaval, der ſtaatlichen Ordnung: anarchy; (Zerſtörung) destruction, ruin; auf ~ hinzielend subversive, anarchical; =ſturzbeſtrebungen, =ideen, =lehren f/pl. subversive (or revolutionary, anarchical) tendencies, ideas, doctrines pl.; ⟨ſtürzen⟩ (ˢᴸ◡) ⓞ** v/n. (ſn) to fall down, to fall (or come) to the ground; to tumble, to topple over; von einem Wagen ꝛc.: to be upset; v/a. to turn (or tip) over, to upset, (umwerfen) to overthrow, overturn, pull down, fig. to subvert, (zerſtören) to destroy, to demolish; ~ n ⓔ f. =ſtürzung; =ſtürzler (ˢᴸ◡) m ⓑ revolutionist; ſtärker: anarchist; ⟨ſtürzleriſch⟩ a. ⓐ revolutionary, anarchical; =ſturzmann m ⓑ revolutionist, anarchist; =ſturzpartei f ⓐ revolutionary (ſtärker: anarchical) party; =ſtürzung f ⓐ = Umſturz; ⟨ſummen⟩ (ˢᴸ◡) v/a. ⓑ* to buzz round; ⟨tanzen⟩ (ˢᴸ◡) v/a. to dance round; (ˢᴸ◡) ⓞ** to overthrow (or to knock down or over, to upset) in dancing; ⟨taufen⟩ (ˢᴸ◡) v/a. ⓑ* eccl. ⓐ to rebaptize; to rechristen (a. fig.); fig. e-n, et. ⓐ to give a p., a th. a new name; =taufung (ˢᴸ) m ⓐ a. exchange, ⓑ barter, bartering, (von Waren gegen Arbeit) truck; F u. P swop; ⟨tauſchen⟩ (ˢᴸ◡) v/a. ⓞ** to (ex)change (F u. P to swop) for; ⓑ to barter for; to truck; ⟨toben⟩ (ˢᴸ◡) v/a. ⓑ* to rage (or rave, storm) round; ⟨tönen⟩ (ˢᴸ◡) v/a. ⓑ* to encompass with (musical) sounds; ⟨toſen⟩ (ˢᴸ◡) v/a. ⓑ* to roar round; ⟨treiben⟩ (ˢᴸ◡) ⓞ** to drive (or chaſe) round; ein Rad ꝛc. ⓐ to turn (or ſpin) round, to revolve; =trieb (ˢᴸ) m ⓑc. (circular) movement; =triebſtillen) activity; ~e pl. machinations, manœuvres, stratagems pl.; heimliche ~e ſecret plots or intrigues pl.; =trunk m ⓞc.: e-n ⓐ halten to have a drink all round; ⟨tun⟩ (ˢᴸ) ⓞ** v/a.: e-n Mantel ⓐ to put on ...; ſich ⓐ v/refl.: ſich nach et. ⓐ (umſehen) to look out (or about) for a th., to try (or seek) for a th.; ſich bei Leuten nach et. ⓐ (erkundigen) to inquire (or to make inquiries) of people about (or concerning) s.th.; ⟨wachſen⟩ (ˢᴵᵗᵍ◡) v/a. ⓑb* to grow

round, to overgrow, to entwine; ⟨währen⟩ (ˢᴸ◡) v/a. ⓑ** to enclose; =währung f ⓐ enclosure; ~smauer f ⓑ surrounding wall; ⟨wallen⟩ (ˢᴸ◡) v/a. ⓑ* ✕ frt. to circumvallate; (wallend umgeben) to float (a)round; =wallung ✕ f ⓐ circumvallation; ⟨wälzen⟩ (ˢᴸ◡) v/a. u. v/refl. ⓞ** to roll round or over; (umſtürzen) to overthrow, fig. to subvert, revolutionize; ſich ⓐ to whirl round, to revolve; ~ n ⓔ u. =wälzung f ⓐ rolling round, um die Achſe: rotation; pol. revolution(ary change); e-e ~ hervorbringen in // to revolutionize //; ⟨wandeln⟩ (ˢᴸ◡) ⓑa* v/a.: ⓐd des Theaters Rund walking round the amphitheatre; (ˢᴸ◡) v/a. u. v/refl. ⓑa** (verwandeln) to change, convert, transform, er iſt wie u"mgewandelt he is quite altered or different, he has turned over a new leaf; ſich ⓐ to change, to be (or become) converted or transformed, physiol. to be(come) assimilated; ~ n ⓔ u. wand(e)lung f ⓐ change, conversion, transformation; ~sprozeß m: ⓜ metamorphosis; ⟨wandern⟩ (ˢᴸ◡) ⓑa** v/a. to walk (or travel, wander) round; ⟨weben⟩ v/a. (ˢᴸ◡) ⓑb ⓑ** to weave afresh or again; (ˢᴸ◡) ⓑb** to weave round, to make a weft (or web) round; fig. von alten Sagen umwo"ben adorned with ancient myths, woven round with legendary lore; ⟨wechſeln⟩ (ˢᴸᵗᵍ◡) ⓑa** v/n. (h.) = abwechſeln; v/a. to exchange (for), Geld: to change; ~ n ⓔ u. =wechſ(e)lung f ⓐ alternate use; (Tauſch) exchange; changing money; =weg (ˢᴸ) m ⓞc. roundabout (or circuitous) route or way, (fr.) détour; fig. oft: crooked way; ~e machen to go out of one's way; fig. auf ~en oft: by a sideway, indirectly; auf ~en erfahren to hear by the way or through a side-channel; ohne ~e straight to the point, straightforward(ly); ⟨wehen⟩ v a. (ˢᴸ◡) ⓑ** to blow down; (ˢᴸ◡) ⓑ* to blow (all) round, to fan (with breezes); ⟨wenden⟩ (ˢᴸ◡) ⓑa** v/a.: a) to turn round or about, ein Blatt: to turn over; auch = ⟨kehren⟩; mit u"mgewandter Hand with the back of one's hand, auch: backhanded(ly); bitte u"mzuwenden!, wenden Sie gefälligſt um! (abbr. W. S. g. u.) please turn over! (abbr. P. T. O.); b) fig. der Jammer wendet mir das Herz um ... makes my heart ache; ſich ⓐ v/refl.: to turn round or back, vom Winde: to veer (round); v/n. (h. u. ſn) = ⟨kehren⟩; =wendung f ⓐ turn (-ing); reversal; ⟨werben⟩ (ˢᴸ◡) v/a. ⓑb* to court, to woo; ſie war viel umwo"rben she was much courted, she had many admirers or suitors; ⟨werfen⟩ (ˢᴸ◡) ⓑb** v/a. to overthrow, overturn, knock down, den Wagen: to upset, e-n Mantel ꝛc. ⓐ to throw ... round one('s shoulders), to put on ...; agr. die Erde mit dem Pfluge ⓐ to turn up ... with the plough; v/n. (h. u. ſn) biSw. mit dem Wagen ⓐ to be overturned; ⚓ von Fahrzeugen: to capsize; fig. meiſt co. to come to grief, to break down; ⚑ to go bankrupt, to

fail (in business), F u. P to go smash; ⟨werten⟩ (ˢᴸ◡) v/a. ⓑ** to value afresh, to revalue; =wertung f ⓐ: ~ aller Werte (NIETZSCHE) revaluation of all values; ⟨wickeln⟩ (ˢᴸ◡) ⓑa** to wrap round, einen Strick: to cord; (anders wickeln) to wrap differently; (ˢᴸ◡) ⓑa* mit et. ⓐ to wrap (or wind) round with s.th., to envelop in s.th.; ⟨winden⟩ v/a. (ˢᴸ◡) ⓞ* to wind round with, mit Tüchern ꝛc. ⓐ to swathe; to entwine; j-s Stirn mit Lorbeer ⓐ to crown a p.'s forehead with laurel; (ˢᴸ◡) ⓞ** to wind (or twine) round; ⟨wirbeln⟩ (ˢᴸ◡) ⓑa* to whirl (or swirl) round, to envelop in dust or smoke; ⟨wittern⟩ v/a. ⓑa* poet. to float (a)round, to breathe round; Zauberhauch, der euern Zug umwi"ttert (G.) magic breeze which wafts around your throng; ⟨wogen⟩ (ˢᴸᵘ◡) v/a. ⓑ* to flow round; ⟨wohnen⟩ (ˢᴸ◡) v/a. ⓑ to dwell (a)round; ⓐd (ˢᴸ◡) p.pr. u. a. ⓐ: die ⓐden Leute, die ~den (auch =wohner (ˢᴸ◡) m/pl. ⓑ) the neighbouring folk, the people (living) around; ⟨wölken⟩ (ˢᴸ◡) v/a. u. v/refl. ⓑ** vom Himmel: ſich ⓐ to assume a cloudy appearance, to look overcast; fig. der Gram umwo"lkte ſeine Stirn clouds of grief had gathered on his brow; ⟨wühlen⟩ ⓑ** v/a. to root up, to uproot (vgl. aufwühlen); weitS. to ransack, to pull about; (ˢᴸ◡) ⓑ* v/a. to rummage all round; ⟨zäunen⟩ (ˢᴸ◡) v/a. ⓑ* to enclose with a hedge or fence, to fence in, hedge in, hedge round with; ⟨zäunung⟩ (ˢᴸ◡) f ⓐ enclosure, hedge, fence; ~snetze n/pl. Tennis: stop-nets pl.; ⟨zeichnen⟩ (ˢᴸ◡) ⓑb** Waren ⓐ to mark ... differently; ein Bild ⓐ to draw ... (over) again; (ˢᴸ◡) ⓑb* to adorn with drawings all round; ⟨ziehen⟩ (ˢᴸ◡) ⓑb** v/n. (ſn) to remove (to other quarters or another house), to change one's apartments; ich bin u"mgezogen I have gone to new apartments or changed my address; von Dienſtboten ꝛc.: to go into a new situation; v/a. und v/refl.: a) Schuhe ꝛc. ⓐ to put on fresh ...; b) ſich ⓐ to change one's clothes or linen; ich habe mich u"mgezogen I have changed my (or put on other) clothes; ~ n ⓔ = =zug; (ˢᴸ◡) ⓑb* v/a. ⟨~ ⟨ziehen⟩; mit Vorhängen ꝛc. ⓐ to hang round with ..., to put ... round, mit ſachlichem Subjekt: to cover all round, to surround; vom Himmel: der Himmel hat ſich umzo"gen the sky is overcast, it has come over lowery; ſich ⓐ = ſich ⟨wölken⟩; ⟨zingeln⟩ ⓑa* biS. ✕ to hem in, to encircle, to cut off on all sides; vgl. ⟨ringen⟩; =zug (ˢᴸ, ˢᴸ) m ⓞd. removal, change of residence or apartments, eines Dienſtboten: change of situation or service; j-s ~ beſorgen to move a p.; (feierlicher Aufzug) procession, zu Pferde: cavalcade; ~sgelde (ˢᴸ...) ⓑ allowance for removal ⓐshalber adv. owing to removal; ~skoſten pl. cost of removal; ~stag m ; ~stermin m day or time appointed (or fixed) for removal.

Zeichen (ſ. S. XVII): F familiär; P Volksſprache; ⌐ Gaunerſprache; ⟨ ſelten; † alt (auch geſtorben); * neu (auch geboren); ‡ unrichtig

un-... (⏑..., bisw. ⏑...) [ahd.: un-] Vorsilbe in Zssgn mit *adjectives*, bsd. mit *verbal adjectives* auf bar und lich, mit *adverbs, p.pr.* u. *nouns*, bezeichnet: **1.** Nichtvorhandensein, Mangel: un-ähnlich *a.* unlike, dissimilar; un-befriedigend *a.* unsatisfactory; Un-freiheit *f* want of freedom. — **2.** Gegenteil, Ungehörigkeit: un-gar *a.* half cooked, underdone; Un-glück *n* misfortune; un-glücklich *a.* unfortunate; un-höflich *a.* discourteous, uncivil; Un-höflichkeit *f* incivility; un-schwer *a.* not difficult, *adv.* without difficulty; Un-sinn *m* nonsense. — **3.** et. das Maß überschreitendes: Un-menge *f* immense number; un-zählig *a.* innumerable, very numerous.

☞ Bemerkung: Bei allen *nouns* rückt der Hauptton auf die Vorsilbe, z.B.: Un-mensch (⏓⏑), ebenso bei den *adjectives*, die nicht auf bar, lich, sam endigen, bsd. wenn das Wort auch ohne un als *ant.* vorkommt, z.B. un-befriedigt (⏓⏑⏑). bei manchen *verbal adjectives* auf bar, lich auf die Stammsilbe des Zeitworts, z.B. un-aussprechlich (⏑⏓⏑⏑); bei manchen ist Doppelbetonung, je nachdem die Verneinung oder die Grundbedeutung des Zeitworts hervorgehoben werden soll, z.B. un-zweifelhaft (⏓⏑⏑ u. ⏑⏑⏓). Auch sonst wechselt der Ton, je nachdem die ursprüngliche Bedeutung der Stammsilbe noch empfunden wird oder nicht. So unterscheidet man z.B. un-bedacht (⏑⏓) u. un-bedacht (⏓⏑).

un-abänderlich (⏑⏑⏓⏑⏑, ⏓⏑⏑⏑⏑) *a.* ⓖⓑ unalterable, unchangeable, immutable; (unwiderruflich) irrevocable; (ewig dauernd) eternal; **~keit** (⏑⏑⏓⏑⏑⏑) *f* ⓖⓐ unalterableness, unchangeableness, immutability; irrevocableness; **₂ab-gefertigt** (⏑⏓⏑⏑⏑) *a.* ⓖⓑ undispatched; **₂abgemacht** (⏑⏓⏑⏑⏑ht) *a.* ⓖⓑ not disposed of; not settled (a. ⓥ); **₂abhängig** (⏑⏓⏑⏑) *a.* ⓖⓑ independent of; unconnected with; *gram.* oft: absolute; ₂ (*adv.*) von independently of, irrespective(ly) of, without any reference to; apart from; *eccl., pol.* **~e** *pl.* ⓖⓟ Independents *pl.*; **=abhängigkeit** (⏑⏓⏑⏑⏑) *f* ⓖⓐ independence; **~s-erklärung** *f, hist.* (*U.S.*, 4. Juli 1776) Declaration of Independence; **~s-krieg** *m* war of (or struggle for) independence; **~s-sinn** *m* independent spirit; **₂abkömmlich** (⏑⏓⏑⏑) *a.* ⓖⓑ v. Personen: indispensable; not to be spared; required in one's place or at one's post; **~keit** *f* indispensableness; **₂abläßig, ₂abläßlich** (⏑⏓⏑⏑) *a.* ⓖⓑ incessant, uninterrupted, continual; ₂ (*adv.*) bemüht sein, etwas zu erreichen to be unremitting (or untiring, unwearying) in one's efforts towards accomplishing a th.; etwas ₂ tun to keep (or go on) doing a th.; **₂ablösbar** (⏑⏓⏑⏑), **₂löslich** (⏑⏓⏑⏑) *a.* ⓖⓑ undetachable; meist ⓥ von Hypotheken, Anleihen ⓚ.: irredeemable (mortgage), perpetual (loan); ₂e Anleihe consolidated fund; **₂absehbar** (⏑⏓⏑⏑), **₂absehlich** (⏑⏓⏑⏑) *a.* ⓖⓑ extending beyond the field of vision; unbounded, immense, immeasurable; in ₂e Ferne gerückt removed out of sight, *fig.* adjourned *sine die*, put off to the Greek calends; ₂e Folgen incalculable effects *pl.*; **=absehbarkeit** (⏑⏓⏑⏑⏑) *f* ⓖⓐ immensity, immeasurableness; boundlessness; **₂absetzbar** (⏑⏓⏑⏑) *a.* ⓖⓑ von Richtern ⓚ.: (**~keit** *f* ⓖⓐ) irremovable (-ness); **₂absichtlich** (⏑⏓⏑⏑) *a.* ⓖⓑ unintentional, unpremeditated; (zufällig) accidental; *adv.* auch: without set purpose, involuntarily; **~keit** *f* ⓖⓐ unpremeditatedness, involuntariness; **₂abweisbar** (⏑⏓⏑⏑), **₂abweislich** (⏑⏓⏑⏑) *a.* ⓖⓑ not to be refused; (dringend) pressing, urgent; (gebieterisch) imperative, peremptory; (vgl. unvermeidlich) **~keit** *f* ⓖⓐ urgency, urgent necessity; **₂abwendbar** (⏑⏓⏑⏑) *a.* ⓖⓑ inevitable; (vom Verhängnis bestimmt) fated; allotted (by fate); **~keit** *f* ⓖⓐ inevitableness; **₂achtsam** (⏑⏓⏑⏑)ht-) *a.* ⓖⓑ inattentive; (nachlässig) careless, heedless, thoughtless, negligent; (zerstreut) distracted, absent-minded; (leichtfertig) easy-going; *adv.* auch: inadvertently; **~keit** (⏑⏓⏑⏑⏑+) *f* ⓖⓐ inattention; carelessness, heedlessness, thoughtlessness, negligence; distraction, absent-mindedness; aus (reiner) **~keit** through (sheer) inadvertence or carelessness; **₂ad(e)lig** (⏑⏑⏓(⏑)⏑) *a.* ⓖⓑ not of noble birth, not titled, without noble rank, meist: plebeian; (unedel) ignoble; ein **~er** a commoner (auch *pol.*); **₂ähnlich** (⏑⏓⏑) *a.* ⓖⓑ unlike, not like, dissimilar; **~keit** *f* ⓖⓐ unlikeness, dissimilarity, von Personen oft: bearing no resemblance to a p., to each other, &c.; **₂anfechtbar** (⏑⏓⏑⏑) *a.* ⓖⓑ incontestable, indisputable; (unverwerflich) unexceptionable; **~keit** *f* ⓖⓐ incontestableness; **₂angebaut** (⏑⏓⏑⏑) *a.* ⓖⓑ uncultivated, untilled, lying waste; **₂angebracht** (⏑⏓⏑⏑) *a.* ⓖⓑ out of place; **₂angefochten** (⏑⏓⏑⏑) *a.* ⓖⓑ not contested, undisputed; (unbestritten) uncontradicted, uncontroverted; (unbelästigt) unmolested, undisturbed; laßt mich ₂! leave me at rest!, let me alone!, let me be!; **₂angekleidet** (⏑⏓⏑⏑⏑) *a.* ⓖⓑ undressed, not dressed (vgl. unbekleidet); in (one's) deshabille or morning-gown; **₂angemeldet** (⏑⏓⏑⏑⏑) *a.* ⓖⓑ unannounced, *adv.* without being (previously) announced; ⓥ unadvised, ₂ kommen to come without previous announcement or notice; **₂angemessen** (⏑⏓⏑⏑) *a.* ⓖⓑ inadequate, unsuitable, unfit; (außer Verhältnis) disproportionate, incongruous, incommensurate; (unschicklich) improper, unbecoming (vgl. Unpassend); **~heit** *f* ⓖⓐ inadequacy, unsuitableness; incongruity; impropriety; **₂angenehm** (⏑⏓⏑⏑) *a.* ⓖⓑ unpleasant, disagreeable, von Geschmack: unpalatable, unsavoury; (verdrießlich) annoying, troublesome, unwelcome; f. berühren 3; in ₂er Lage in an awkward plight, F in a nasty fix; ₂er Mensch rough (or ugly) customer, uncouth fellow; wenn es Ihnen nicht ₂ ist if you are agreeable to it, if you don't object (to it) or mind it; wäre es ihm ₂, wenn //? would he mind (or not like) it if //?; **₂angerührt** (⏑⏓⏑⏑) *a.* ⓖⓑ untouched, intact, *adv.* without having been touched; **₂angesehen** (⏑⏓⏑⏑⏑) *a.* ⓖⓑ (ohne Ansehen) disregarded, little considered, not eminent, not much thought of; (ungesehen) unseen, Kanzleistil: *prp.* mit *gen.* od. *acc.* (ohne Rücksicht auf) irrespective of; **₂angetastet** (⏑⏓⏑⏑⏑) *a.* ⓖⓑ ungerührt; **₂angreifbar** (⏑⏓⏑⏑) *a.* ⓖⓑ unassailable; **~keit** *f* ⓖⓐ unassailableness, unassailability; **₂an-nehmbar** (⏑⏓⏑⏑) *a.* ⓖⓑ (**~keit** *f* ⓖⓐ) inacceptable(ness); **=an-nehmlichkeit** (⏑⏓⏑⏑⏑) *f* ⓖⓐ mit *pl.*: unpleasantness, (Übelstand) inconvenience, drawback; (Ärger) vexation, annoyance; wir wollen Ihnen keine **~en** bereiten we don't want to cause you any unpleasantness or bother; sich **~en** zuziehen to bring trouble upon o.s., mehr gbr. to get (o.s.) into trouble or hot water; mit *pl.*: disagreeableness; **₂ansehnlich** (⏑⏓⏑⏑) *a.* ⓖⓑ: a) of mean appearance, mean-looking, uncomely; (häßlich) plain(-looking), homely; (winzig) diminutive; b) inconsiderable, insignificant; **~keit** *f* ⓖⓐ: a) mean(ness of) appearance, plainness, homeliness; b) inconsiderableness; **₂anständig** (⏑⏓⏑⏑) *a.* ⓖⓑ: a) meist vom Betragen: unbecoming, unseemly, improper; für Männer: ungentlemanly, für Frauen: unladylike; stärker: indecent, indecorous, immodest; (verletzend) shocking; b) von Personen: illmannered, ill-behaved (vgl. ₂gezogen); **~keit** (⏑⏓⏑⏑⏑) *f* ⓖⓐ: a) unbecomingness, unseemliness, impropriety; indecency; b) unmannerliness; **₂anstößig** (⏑⏓⏑⏑) *a.* ⓖⓑ inoffensive, unobjectionable, harmless; **₂antastbar** (⏑⏓⏑⏑) *a.* ⓖⓑ not to be touched; (unverletzlich) inviolable; **~keit** *f* ⓖⓐ inviolability; **₂anwendbar** (⏑⏓⏑⏑) *a.* ⓖⓑ inapplicable; (ungeeignet) ill-adapted, unadapted; unsuitable; **~keit** *f* ⓖⓐ inapplicability; unadaptedness; **₂appetitlich** (⏑⏓⏑⏑⏑) *a.* ⓖⓑ not appetizing, unsavoury, unpalatable, uninviting, stärker: disgusting, loathsome; **=art** (⏑⏓) *f* ⓖⓐ: a) ohne *pl.*: (ungehörige Aufführung) unmannerly (or improper) conduct, ill (or rude) behaviour, ill breeding, rudeness, v. Kindern a.: naughtiness, v. Pferden: vice, viciousness; b) mit *pl.*: (Verstoß gegen die Lebensart) unmannerly (or naughty, mischievous) trick, rude action; (üble Gewohnheit) bad (or vicious) habit; *m* ⓐⓒ. (unartige Person) naughty boy, mischievous (or saucy) boy, troublesome (or rude) fellow; F pickle, (young) Turk; **₂artig** (⏑⏓⏑) *a.* ⓖⓑ ill-behaved, ill-bred, ill-mannered, saucy; naughty (child), mischievous (boy), troublesome (fellow), vicious (horse); zu Kindern: seid nicht so ₂! don't be so naughty or so troublesome!,(do) behave yourselves!; (unhöflich) discourteous, uncivil, impolite, disobliging; (grob) rude, gegen Frauen: ungallant; **~keit** (⏑⏓⏑⏑) *f* ⓖⓐ = Unart a; **₂artikuliert** (⏑⏑⏑⏓⏑) *a.* ⓖⓑ *gram.* inarticulate; (undeutlich) indistinct; **₂ästhetisch** (⏑⏓⏑⏑) *a.* ⓖⓑ not æsthetical, mehr gbr.: offensive, coarse; (garstig) nasty; (ekelhaft) nauseous, disgusting.

Unau (⸺) m ⓔ zo. (zweifingeriges Faultier) unau (Cho'topus dida'ctylus).
un-auffindbar (⸺⸺) a. ⓕ not to be found (anywhere), undiscoverable; ≗**aufgefordert** (⸺⸺) a. ⓕ unasked, unbidden; adv. (aus eigenem Antriebe) of one's own accord, spontaneously; ≗**aufgeklärt** (⸺⸺) a. ⓕ: a) von Geheimnissen ꝛc.: unsolved, unexplained; b) von Personen: unenlightened, unschooled; ≗**aufgelöst** (⸺⸺) a. ⓕ undissolved; ≗**aufgeschlossen** (⸺⸺) a. ⓕ not unlocked, not opened (yet); 2es Gebiet unexploited (or undeveloped) country; ≗**aufgeschnitten** (⸺⸺) a. ⓕ not cut open (yet); unused (book); ≗**aufhaltbar**, ≗**aufhaltsam** (⸺⸺) a. ⓕ not to be stopped; irresistible; in dem Laufe in one continuous course, in full career; **~keit** f ⓕ irresistibleness; ≗**aufhörlich** (⸺⸺) a. ⓕ incessant, constant, continuous, unceasing; (endlos) never ending, endless, interminable, perpetual; adv. oft: without intermission, without ceasing or stopping; (immer) for ever; **~keit** f ⓕ continuousness; endlessness; ≗**auflösbar** (⸺⸺), ≗**auflöslich** (⸺⸺) a. ⓕ indissoluble (tie, &c.); insoluble (a. math., chm.); von Nebelflecken ꝛc.: irresolvable; von Geheimnissen ꝛc.: inexplicable, unfathomable; **~keit** f ⓕ in(dis)solubility; ≗**aufmerksam** (⸺⸺) a. ⓕ inattentive; (zerstreut) distracted, absent-minded, F wool-gathering; **~keit** f ⓕ inattentiveness, inattention, want of attention; ≗**aufrichtig** (⸺⸺) a. ⓕ insincere; **~keit** f ⓕ insincerity, lack of sincerity; ≗**aufschieb-bar** (⸺⸺), ≗**aufschieblich** (⸺⸺) a. ⓕ not to be put off, brooking no delay; (dringend) pressing, urgent; ≗**aufschieb-barkeit** (⸺⸺)f ⓕ urgency; ≗**ausbleiblich** (⸺⸺) a. ⓕ unfailing; bound to happen; (unvermeidlich) inevitable, (gewiß) certain, sure (to come); **~keit** f ⓕ inevitableness, certainty; ≗**ausdehnbar** (⸺⸺) a. ⓕ incapable of extension; phys., &c.: ≈ indiffusible, inextensible, inexpansible, non-expansible: inductile; ≗**ausführbar** (⸺⸺) a. ⓕ incapable of execution; (untunlich) impracticable, unworkable, unfeasible, (unmöglich) impossible; **~keit** f ⓕ impracticability, unfeasibleness; ≗**ausgebacken** (⸺⸺) a. ⓕ Bäckerei: slack-baked, not (quite) baked enough; ≗**ausgebildet** (⸺⸺) a. ⓕ not (fully) formed or developed, ♃ u. zo. rudimentary; geistig: uncultivated, uncultured, ✶ untrained, raw (recruit); ≗**ausgeführt** (⸺⸺) a. ⓕ not carried out, not executed, unachieved, unaccomplished, unperformed; Kunst ꝛc.: unfinished; ≗**ausgefüllt** (⸺⸺) a. ⓕ not filled up, von Scheinen, Wechseln ꝛc.: (in) blank; ≗**ausgemacht** (⸺⸺) a. ⓕ not settled, undecided; (ungewiß) uncertain (matter), open (question); (fraglich) questionable (gain); ≗**ausgesetzt** (⸺⸺) a. ⓕ uninterrupted, incessant; (beständig) constant, continual, perpetual; 2e Tätigkeit restless activity; adv. a. without interruption or intermission or rest;

≗**auslöschbar** (⸺⸺), ≗**auslöschlich** (⸺⸺) a. ⓕ vom Feuer ꝛc.: inextinguishable, vom Durst ꝛc.: unquenchable, quenchless, von Tinte: indelible, v. e-r Schrift: ineffaceable; fig. lasting (impression); deeply engraved (in one's memory), indelibly impressed (on one's mind); **~keit** f ⓕ unquenchableness, indelibility; ≗**ausrottbar** (⸺⸺) a. ⓕ ineradicable, von Tieren: not exterminable; ≗**aussprechbar** (⸺⸺) a. ⓕ unpronounceable, F co. jaw-breaking; ≗**aussprechlich** (⸺⸺) a. ⓕ (durch Worte nicht ausdrückbar) inexpressible, ineffable, unutterable, unspeakable (horror, &c.); (unbeschreiblich) indescribable (joy, &c.); verblümt: die ~en (Hosen) unmentionables, inexpressibles pl.; **~keit** f ⓕ inexpressibleness, ineffability; ≗**ausstehlich** (⸺⸺) a. ⓕ unbearable, insufferable, intolerable, unpleasant; (verhaßt) odious, hateful; er ist ihr ≈ she cannot bear the (or she hates the very) sight of him; **~keit** f ⓕ intolerableness, odiousness; ≗**austilgbar** (⸺⸺) a. ⓕ ineradicable, a. = ≗auslöschbar; ≗**ausweichbar** (⸺⸺), ≗**ausweichlich** (⸺⸺) a. ⓕ unavoidable; ≗**band** F (⸺⸺) m ⓗ ⓖ c. unruly (or unmanageable, ungovernable, wayward) person or child; vgl. ≗art; ≗**bändig** (⸺⸺) a. ⓕ unruly, unmanageable, intractable, ungovernable, uncontrollable, wayward; F (ungeheuer) excessive, bsd. adv. 2 viel Geld great (F awful, tremendous) lot of money; 2 dumm extremely (F awfully) stupid; **~keit** (⸺⸺) f ⓕ unruliness, unmanageableness, intractability; ≗**barmherzig** (⸺⸺) a. ⓕ unmerciful, merciless, pitiless, ruthless, (hart) harsh, hard, (grausam) cruel, barbarous; **~keit** f ⓕ unmercifulness, mercilessness, harshness, cruelty; ≗**bärtig** (⸺⸺) a. ⓕ beardless, whiskerless (a. zo.); **~keit** f ⓕ beardlessness; ≗**beabsichtigt** (⸺⸺) a. ⓕ unintentional (vgl. ≗absichtlich); ≗**beachtet** (⸺⸺) a. ⓕ unnoticed, unobserved, unheeded, disregarded; (nicht gewürdigt) unappreciated; 2 l. leave unnoticed, to ignore, (vernachlässigen) to neglect; ≗**beanstandet** (⸺⸺) a. ⓕ not objected to, unopposed, von Wahlen auch: uncontested; et. 2 lassen to let a th. take its course; ≗**beantwortet** (⸺⸺) a. ⓕ unanswered; e-n Brief 2 l. to leave ... unanswered, not to answer ...; ≗**beantwortlich** (⸺⸺) a. ⓕ unanswerable, which cannot be answered; ≗**bearbeitet** (⸺⸺) a. ⓕ: a) Kunst u. Schrifttum: der Gegenstand subject which has not been dealt with or treated; b) von Rohstoffen: raw, crude, unwrought, in the native state; v. Häuten: untanned, raw, green; ≗**beaufsichtigt** (⸺⸺) a. ⓕ without supervision, uncontrolled; ≗**bebaubar** (⸺⸺) a. ⓕ agr. unfit for cultivation; ≗**bebaut** (⸺⸺) a. ⓕ agr. uncultivated, untilled, fallow (field); (ohne Gebäude) not built upon, vacant (plot); ≗**bedacht**[1] (⸺⸺) a. ⓕ roofless, without a roof;

≗**bedacht**[2] (⸺⸺), ≗**bedächtig** (⸺⸺), ≗**bedachtsam** (⸺⸺) a. ⓕ inconsiderate, thoughtless, heedless, in der Rede: indiscreet; ≗**bedacht(sam)erweise** inadvertently, rashly, heedlessly, without thinking; ≗**bedachtsamkeit** (⸺⸺) f ⓕ inconsiderateness, thoughtlessness; indiscretion; aus ~ through inadvertency; ≗**bedeckt** (⸺⸺) a. ⓕ uncovered; (ohne Dach) roofless; (bloß) bare; mit dem Haupte bareheaded; ≗**bedenklich** (⸺⸺) a. ⓕ von Dingen: requiring no (previous) consideration, unobjectionable, harmless, unquestioning; v. Personen: unscrupulous; adv. without hesitation or scruple; ≗**bedeutend** (⸺⸺) a. ⓕ insignificant; (ohne Wichtigkeit) unimportant, inconsiderable, immaterial, trifling; (gering) petty, paltry, trivial, (nichtig) frivolous; 2e Stellung inferior position, F back-seat; ≗**bedeutenheit** (⸺⸺) f ⓕ insignificance, paltriness, frivolousness; ≗**bedingt** (⸺⸺) a. ⓕ unconditional, unqualified, unquestioning; (unbeschränkt) unlimited, unbounded, absolute; implicit (trust, &c.); adv. auch: without reserve, on any condition, in any case, under any circumstances; ≗**be-eidigt** (⸺⸺) a. ⓕ not sworn (in), unsworn; ≗**beeinflußt** a. ⓕ uninfluenced; ≗**beeinträchtigt** (⸺⸺) a. ⓕ unprejudiced, uninjured, unimpaired (von by); ≗**beendigt** (⸺⸺) a. ⓕ unfinished, not completed, incomplete; ≗**be-erbt** (⸺⸺) a. ⓕ without heirs or issue; ≗**be-erdigt** (⸺⸺) a. ⓕ unburied, uninterred; without a burial; ≗**befähigt** (⸺⸺) a. ⓕ incompetent, not qualified for, weit.S. unfit for; vgl. unbegabt; ≗**befahrbar** (⸺⸺) a. ⓕ impassable, ⚓ not navigable; ≗**befahren** ⚓ (⸺⸺) a. ⓕ never previously navigated or crossed; 2(es) Volk (ungeübte Matrosen) inexperienced mariners, F fresh (or green) hands, landlubbers pl.; ≗**befangen** (⸺⸺) a. ⓕ (vorurteilsfrei) unprejudiced, unbiassed; (nicht beteiligt) unconcerned, disinterested, (unparteiisch) impartial, (sorglos) unconcerned, F easy-going, nonchalant; (natürlich) natural, unaffected; (offen u. ehrlich) ingenuous, unsophisticated, (freimütig) candid, open, frank, outspoken; **~heit** (⸺⸺) f ⓕ (f. ≗befangen) freedom from prejudice; unconcern, disinterestedness, impartiality, F nonchalance; unaffectedness; ingenuousness, candour, frankness; ≗**befestigt** (⸺⸺) a. ⓕ unfortified, open (town, &c.), defenceless (shore, &c.); ≗**befiedert** (⸺⸺) a. ⓕ featherless, unfeathered (vgl. ≗geflügelt); unfledged; ≗**befleckt** (⸺⸺) a. ⓕ unsullied, stainless, spotless, fig. a. impolluted, undefiled, unblemished; immaculate; rel. 2e Empfängnis Mariä immaculate conception of the Virgin; **~heit** f ⓕ stainlessness, spotlessness, immaculateness; ≗**befördert** (⸺⸺) a. ⓕ v. Briefen ꝛc.: not forwarded, not dispatched, not transmitted; von Personen: not promoted; ≗**befriedigend** (⸺⸺) a. ⓕ

Signs (see page XVII): F familiar; P vulgar; ꟼ flash; ⌇ rare; † obsolete (died); * new word (born); ⁒ incorrect; ♪ music;

[unbefriedigt] — 999 — [unbeschäftigt]

unsatisfactory; (nicht hinreichend) insufficient; 2befriedigt (⌣–⌣) a. ⑥ unsatisfied, (unzufrieden) dissatisfied, discontent; (enttäuscht) disappointed, (ungesättigt) not satisfied, unappeased; es hat ihn 2 gelassen it did not come up to his expectations; ~heit f ⑥ dissatisfaction, discontent; disappointment; 2befugt (⌣–⌣) a. ⑥ unauthorized; incompetent, having no right (or permission) to; 2es Betreten e-s Grundstücks ꝛc.: trespassing; bsd. jur.: ~e trespassers pl.; adv. 2erweise without authority or permission; (dem Gesetz zuwider) unlawfully; =befugt-heit (⌣–⌣-) f ⑥ being unauthorized, incompetency; 2begabt (⌣–⌣) a. ⑥ not gifted, not talented, untalented; without ability or cleverness; ~heit f ⑥ lack of talent; 2begeben ⚥ (⌣–⌣) a. ⑥ undisposed of, unsold, still on hand; 2begleitet (⌣–⌣) a. ⑥ unaccompanied, unattended; without retinue or attendants; (allein) alone, solitary; 2begraben (⌣–⌣) a. ⑥ unburied; 2begreiflich (⌣–⌣) a. ⑥ incomprehensible, inconceivable; (unverständlich) unintelligible, (unerklärlich) inexplicable, mysterious; ~keit f ⑥ incomprehensibleness, inconceivableness; (Geheimnis) mystery, mysterious (or strange) affair; 2begrenzbar (⌣–⌣-) a. ⑥ illimitable; 2begrenzt (⌣–⌣) a. ⑥ unlimited, unbounded, boundless; ~heit f ⑥ boundlessness; 2begriffen (⌣–⌣) a. ⑥ uncomprehended; 2begründet (⌣–⌣) a. ⑥ unfounded, baseless, groundless; ~heit f ⑥ baselessness, groundlessness; 2begütert (⌣–⌣) a. ⑥ without estates, having no (real or landed) property, weitS. without substance or means; 2behaart (⌣–⌣) a. ⑥ hairless, denuded of hair. ⚥ und zo. smooth, ⚥ glabrous; vom menschlichen Kopfe auch: bald; 2e Stelle oft: bare place; zo. mit 2em Schwanze: ⚥ nudicaudate; =behagen (⌣–⌣) n ㉓ = Mißbehagen; 2behaglich (⌣–⌣) a. ⑥ uncomfortable, prädikativ a. ill at ease; sich 2 fühlen, auch: to feel uneasy, not to feel at home, F to be out of sorts; ~keit f ⑥ uncomfortableness, discomfort, uneasiness; 2behauen (⌣–⌣) a. ⑥ unhewn, uncut, von Bauholz a.: unsquared, unframed, undressed; vgl. berinden; 2behelligt (⌣–⌣) a. ⑥ unmolested, undisturbed, adv. a. in peace and comfort; e-n 2 lassen to leave a p. unmolested or F alone; 2beherzigt (⌣–⌣) a. ⑥: et. 2 lassen not to take a th. to heart, to disregard a th., to leave a th. unheeded; 2behilflich (⌣–⌣) a. ⑥ deprived of the use of one's limbs, helpless, weitS. = 2beholfen; ~keit f ⑥ = =beholfenheit; 2behindert (⌣–⌣) a. ⑥ unhindered, unhampered, unimpeded, unfettered, unclogged, adv. auch: without restraint; 2beholfen (⌣–⌣) a. ⑥ not handy; (plump) awkward, clumsy; (schwerfällig) heavy, unwieldy, ungainly; (verlegen) embarrassed; ~heit f ⑥ awkwardness, clumsiness; heaviness, unwieldiness;

2behülflich (⌣–⌣) ꝛc. s. 2behilflich ꝛc.; 2behütet (⌣–⌣) a. ⑥ unguarded; 2behutsam (⌣–⌣) a. ⑥ unwary, (unvorsichtig) incautious, improvident, careless, a. = 2bedacht(sam); adv. without caution or circumspection; ~keit f ⑥ unwariness, want of caution, improvidence; 2be-irrt (⌣–⌣) a. ⑥ unswerving (vgl. 2erschrocken); 2 (adv.) vorangehen to go straight ahead; 2bekannt (⌣–⌣) a. ⑥ passivisch: (nicht gekannt) unknown to, not known to; das ist mir 2 I am not aware of it; es ist Ihnen gewiß nicht 2, daß // you surely cannot be ignorant of the fact that //; er wagt sich nicht gern auf ein ihm 2es Gebiet he does not like to venture upon unfamiliar ground; er ist mir 2 I do not know him, he is a stranger to me; von Personen: (ruhmlos) obscure; ein ~er (Fremder) a stranger; die schöne ~e the fair stranger; math. 2e Größe unknown quantity; die ~e the unknown; attivisch: mit et. 2 sein to be ignorant of (or unacquainted with) a th.; ich bin hier (ganz) 2 I am (quite) a stranger here; 2bekannter=weise (⌣–⌣–⌣) adv. without knowing (or being known to) a p.; auch: though unknown, though a stranger; 2bekannt-heit (⌣–⌣) f ⑥ being unknown; obscurity; auch = =bekanntschaft; =bekanntschaft (⌣–⌣) f ⑥ ignorance of, unacquaintance with; 2bekehrbar (⌣–⌣-) a. ⑥ inconvertible; 2bekehrt (⌣–⌣) a. ⑥ unconverted; 2beklagt (⌣–⌣) a. ⑥ unlamented; 2bekleidet (⌣–⌣) a. ⑥ unclothed, undressed, unapparelled; without clothing; 2bekümmert (⌣–⌣) a. ⑥ careless, unconcerned, F noncarish (um about); reckless of; (gleichgültig) indifferent about or to; sei nur ganz 2! don't be uneasy!, don't alarm yourself!; ~heit f ⑥ carelessness, unconcern(edness); indifference; 2beladen (⌣–⌣) a. ⑥ unloaded, unladen, empty; ⚓ without cargo; 2belästigt (⌣–⌣) a. ⑥ unmolested; 2belaubt (⌣–⌣) a. ⑥ without foliage or leaves, leafless; bare; 2belebt (⌣–⌣) a. ⑥ lifeless, inanimate, dead, dull, slack (alle auch fig. und ⚥); nur von Personen: apathetic; vgl. 2besucht; ~heit f ⑥ lifelessness, deadness, dulness, apathy; 2beleckt (⌣–⌣) a. ⑥ unlicked; fig. von der Kultur 2 without any trace (or F suspicion) of culture, untouched by civilization; unpolished, ill-bred, uncivilized, uncultured; 2belesen (⌣–⌣) a. ⑥ not well-read; unlearned, unlettered, illiterate; ~heit f ⑥ want of reading or learning; illiteracy; 2beliebt (⌣–⌣) a. ⑥ not much liked by, stärker: not in favour with, disliked by; beim Volke 2 unpopular (with the people); ~heit f ⑥ unpopularity; seine ~heit war groß, auch: he was very little liked; 2belohnt (⌣–⌣) a. ⑥ unrewarded, unrecompensed; 2bemannt ⚓ (⌣–⌣) a. ⑥ unmanned; 2bemerkbar (⌣–⌣) a. ⑥ imperceptible, indiscernible, not noticeable, not observable; 2bemerkt (⌣–⌣) a. ⑥ unnoticed, unperceived,

unobserved, unheeded; adv. without being noticed or observed or seen; (verstohlen) stealthily, by stealth; 2bemittelt (⌣–⌣) a. ⑥ without means or money or funds, not wealthy; F hard up (for cash), co. impecunious; ~heit f ⑥ lack of means; impecuniosity; 2benannt (⌣–⌣) a. ⑥ nameless; arith. 2e Zahl abstract number; 2benommen (⌣–⌣) a. ⑥ not prohibited; permitted, allowed; es ist (oder bleibt) Ihnen 2, zu // you are (quite) at liberty to //; you need not be afraid to //; 2benutzt (⌣–⌣) a. ⑥ unused, not in use, unemployed, v. Kapitalien: uninvested, lying idle; das wird er nicht 2 l. he is sure to avail himself (or to take advantage) of it, he won't let the opportunity slip (by); 2beobachtet (⌣–⌣) a. ⑥ unobserved, et. 2 l. to pay no attention to a th.; 2bequem (⌣–⌣) a. ⑥ uncomfortable, (ungelegen) inconvenient, inopportune, (lästig) troublesome, irksome, burdensome, (unangenehm) disagreeable; ~lichkeit (⌣–⌣-) f ⑥ discomfort; inconvenience; 2berechenbar (⌣–⌣-, ⌣–⌣-) a. ⑥ incalculable, von Personen oft: tricky, uncertain; not to be reckoned (or depended) upon, unreliable; ~keit f ⑥ incalculability; 2berechtigt (⌣–⌣) a. ⑥ unauthorized, (unzulässig) illegitimate; (unbegründet) unfounded, adv. (auch 2erweise) without authorization or authority; 2beredt (⌣–⌣) a. ⑥ not (very) eloquent; 2berichtigt (⌣–⌣) a. ⑥ uncorrected; die Rechnung ist noch 2 ... is not yet settled, ... remains unpaid; 2beritten (⌣–⌣) a.: a) vom Reiter: unmounted; without a mount; b) vom Pferde: (nicht zugeritten) not broken in; 2berücksichtigt (⌣–⌣) a. ⑥ unconsidered, not taken into account; disregarded; 2 lassen not to take into consideration, to pay no regard (or heed) to, to make no allowance for; 2berufen (⌣–⌣) a. ⑥ uncalled for, (unaufgefordert) unbidden; adv. without being asked; (ohne Berechtigung) unauthorized; (als Eindringling) intruding, officious, adv. intrusively, as an interloper; sich 2 in et. mengen to intermeddle with a th.; abergläubischer Ausruf: 2 u. unbeschrien! may no evil befall us!, Heaven shield us (from harm)!; 2berühmt (⌣–⌣) a. ⑥ not famous, inglorious, unrenowned, unknown to fame; (verborgen) obscure; ~heit f ⑥ obscurity; 2berührt (⌣–⌣) a. ⑥ untouched, intact, von Speisen auch: untasted; virgin (soil, forest, &c.); (ungerührt) unmoved; auch = 2erwahrt; 2beschadet (⌣–⌣) a. ⑥ prp. mit gen. without prejudice (or detriment) to, without detracting from; (vorbehaltlich) save; 2 Ihrer Forderung without prejudice to (or quite apart from) your claim; 2beschädigt (⌣–⌣) a. ⑥ unhurt, uninjured, unharmed, not damaged, safe and sound, in geh. Spr.: unscathed; ⚥ in good (or sound, perfect) condition; ganz 2 a. (as) sound as a bell, F (as) right as a trivet; 2beschäftigt (⌣–⌣) a. ⑥ unemployed, out of work;

⚥ scientific; ⚘ botanical; ⚱ geography; ⊕ machinery; ⚒ mining; ⚔ military; ⚓ marine; ⊛ commercial; ⊛ postal; 🜨 railway.

[Unbeschäftigtheit] — 1000 — [unbewölkt]

disengaged, at leisure; =beschäftigtheit f ⓐ lack (or being out) of employment or work; leisure; ⚘bescheiden (ᵇᵘ¹ᵛ) a. ⓐ immodest, (anmaßend) arrogant, overbearing, presumptuous; (ungezogen) impertinent, insolent, rude, F cheeky; (anspruchsvoll) exacting; Ⴎe Forderung unreasonable (or exorbitant) claim; ~heit f ⓐ lack of modesty, arrogance, presumption; impertinence, insolence, rudeness, F cheek; ⚘bescheinigt (ᵇᵘ¹ᵛ) a. ⓐ uncertified; ⚘beschlagen (ᵇᵘ¹ᵛ) a. ⓐ von Pferden: (ohne Hufeisen) unshod; F fig. in einem Fache Ⴎ (unbewandert) unskilled (or not versed, not at home) in a th., unfamiliar with a th.; ⚘beschnitten (ᵇᵘ¹ᵛ) a. ⓐ uncircumcised; von Münzen: unclipped, von Büchern: uncut, v. Bäumen ꝛc.: unlopped, untrimmed; Ⴎer Rand des Papiers: outside edge; ⚘bescholten (ᵇᵘ¹ᵛ) a. ⓐ blameless (conduct), irreproachable (life), unblemished (character), unsullied (name); jur.: er ist noch Ⴎ he has never been punished, he has honourable (or excellent) antecedents or a stainless record; ~heit f ⓐ blamelessness, irreproachableness, stainlessness (of character); integrity; ⚘beschränkt (ᵇᵘᵛ, ᵇᵘᵛ) a. ⓐ unlimited, unbounded, boundless, unrestricted, unstinted (praise, &c.); (unbedingt) absolute; ⚘ Gesellschaft mit Ⴎer Haftbarkeit (abbr. G. m. u. H.) joint-stock company [☞ jede engl. Aktiengesellschaft o. die Bezeichnung Limited, abbr. Ltd., ist = G. m. u. H.]; Ⴎe Macht absolute (or arbitrary) power; ~heit f ⓐ unboundedness; absoluteness; ⚘beschreiblich (ᵇᵘᵛ) a. ⓐ indescribable, inexpressible, defying (or beyond) all description; adv. oft: (außerordentlich) extremely, exceedingly; ein Ⴎer Wirrwarr an indescribable confusion, a tumult beggaring all description; ~heit f ⓐ indescribable nature or grandeur; ⚘beschrieben (ᵇᵘᵛ) a. ⓐ von Papier: not written upon, blank; (wovon keine Beschreibung gemacht ist) undescribed; ⚘beschri-en (ᵇᵘᵛ) a. ⓐ f. beruſen; ⚘beschuht (ᵇᵘᵛ) a. ⓐ unshod; ⚘beschützt (ᵇᵘᵛ) a. ⓐ unprotected, unguarded, defenceless. ✕ auch: exposed; ⚘beschwert (ᵇᵘᵛ) a. ⓐ = behelligt u. ⚘behindert; auch: unburdened, unencumbered, vom Gewissen: light, easy, clear, free; ⚘beseelt (ᵇᵘᵛ) a. ⓐ without a soul, soulless; (leblos) lifeless, inanimate; ~heit f ⓐ lack of (a) soul; lifelessness; ⚘besehen (ᵇᵘ¹ᵛ) a. ⓐ, a. Ⴎ(s) adv. not (adv. without being) previously seen or examined, uninspected, as it is; without looking at it; et. Ⴎ kaufen to buy a pig in a poke; ⚘besetzt (ᵇᵘᵛ) a. ⓐ unoccupied, vacant (post, &c.); vgl. frei 4; (ohne Besatz) not trimmed, without trimming, plain (dress, &c.); ⚘besiegbar (ᵇᵘᶥ⁻, ᵇᵘᵛᵛ), ⚘besieglich (ᵇᵘᵛᵛ) a. ⓐ invincible, unconquerable, irresistible; ~heit f ⓐ invincibility, invincible (or unconquerable) strength; ⚘besiegt (ᵇᵘᵛ) a. ⓐ unconquered,

never vanquished, unsubdued; ⚘besoldet (ᵇᵘᵛ) a. ⓐ unsalaried, unpaid; von einer Stelle auch: without a salary (attaching to it); honorary (post); ⚘besonnen (ᵇᵘᵛ) a. ⓐ ill-considered, ill-advised; thoughtless, heedless, F giddy; in der Rede: indiscreet, (unklug) imprudent, (voreilig) rash, hasty; ~heit f ⓐ thoughtlessness, heedlessness, F giddiness; indiscretion; imprudence, rashness, hastiness; ⚘besorgt (ᵇᵘᵛ) a. ⓐ unconcerned, careless, ſtärker: light-hearted, happy-go-lucky; ſei(e)n Sie deshalb Ⴎ! make your mind easy (or don't worry) about that!; (nicht ausgeführt) not executed, von Aufträgen: not attended to; ~heit f ⓐ unconcern(edness), ſtärker: light-heartedness; ⚘bestand (ᵇᵘᵛ) m Ⴎc. instability, unsteadiness, (Veränderlichkeit) changeableness; ⚘beständig (ᵇᵘᵛ) a. ⓐ unstable, unsteady, inconstant, vom Wetter: unsettled; (veränderlich) changeable, variable, (ſchwankend) vacillating, fickle, wavering; ~heit f ⓐ instability, inconstancy, des Wetters: unsettled state; (Wankelmut) vacillation, fickleness, levity; vgl. =bestand; ⚘bestätigt (ᵇᵘᵛ, ᵇᵘᵛ) a. ⓐ unconfirmed (rumour, &c.), uncorroborated (statement, &c.); ⚘bestechbar (ᵇᵘᵛ⁻), ⚘bestechlich (ᵇᵘᵛ) a. ⓐ incorruptible, unbribable; =bestechlichkeit f ⓐ incorruptibility, incorruptibleness; weitS. integrity (of character). (thorough) honesty; ⚘besteigbar (ᵇᵘᵛ⁻) a. ⓐ not (fit) to be ascended or mounted, inaccessible; ~heit f ⓐ inaccessibility; ⚘bestellbar (ᵇᵘᵛ⁻) a. ⓐ not deliverable, ⚘ auf Briefen: not known; Ⴎer Brief dead letter; agr. unfit for cultivation or the plough, not arable; ~keit (ᵇᵘᵛ⁻) f ⓐ impossibility of delivering a letter, &c., ⚘ a. deadness of a letter, &c.; agr. unfitness for cultivation; ⚘bestellt (ᵇᵘᵛ) a. ⓐ not ordered, not bespoke(n); von Briefen ꝛc.: not delivered; agr. uncultivated, untilled; ⚘besteuert (ᵇᵘᵛ) a. ⓐ untaxed, exempt from taxes; ⚘bestimmbar (ᵇᵘᵛ⁻) a. ⓐ indeterminable, undefinable, weitS. vague; ~keit f ⓐ undefinableness, vagueness; ⚘bestimmt (ᵇᵘᵛ) a. ⓐ undetermined, undefined; indefinite (a. gr.); (unentſchieden) undecided, (undeutlich) indistinct, vague, hazy, (verworren) confused; (unſicher) uncertain; Ⴎer Ausdruck vague expression, ambiguous term; math. Ⴎe Gleichung indeterminate equation; auf Ⴎe Zeit vertagen to put off indefinitely, Verſammlungen ꝛc.: to adjourn sine die; ~heit f ⓐ indeterminateness, indefiniteness, indecision, vagueness, haziness; uncertainty; ⚘bestochen (ᵇᵘᵛ) a. ⓐ uncorrupted, incorrupt, unbribed; (ehrbar) upright; ⚘bestraft (ᵇᵘᵛ) a. ⓐ unpunished; Ⴎ bleiben to go unpunished; jur. = ⚘bescholten; ⚘bestreitbar (ᵇᵘᵛ⁻) a. ⓐ incontestable, indisputable, incontrovertible, unquestionable; ~keit f ⓐ incontestability; incontrovertibleness, unquestionableness; ab-

solute certainty; ⚘bestritten (ᵇᵘᵛ) a. ⓐ uncontested, uncontroverted, undisputed, unquestioned, adv. indisputably; ⚘besucht (ᵇᵘ¹ᶜʰᵗ) a. ⓐ not (much) visited, unfrequented; ſtärker: deserted, avoided (by travellers); (einſam) lonely; ⚘beteiligt (ᵇᵘᵛ) a. ⓐ: bei et. Ⴎ not participating (or sharing, interested) in a th.; Ⴎ ſein bei to have no part (or share) in a th., bei Handlungen: to be no party to a th.; ~e ⓐ, oft: disinterested parties, outsiders pl.; ⚘betont (ᵇᵘᵛ) a. ⓐ unaccented, without (an) accent, unstressed, ⚘ atonic; ⚘beträchtlich (ᵇᵘᵛ) a. ⓐ inconsiderable, trifling, insignificant; ~keit f ⓐ inconsiderableness, trifling nature or character; ⚘betrauert (ᵇᵘᵛ) a. ⓐ unmourned (for), unlamented; ⚘betretbar (ᵇᵘᵛ⁻) a. ⓐ inaccessible; ⚘betreten (ᵇᵘᵛ) a. ⓐ untrodden (path), unbeaten (track); ⚘beugſam (ᵇᵘᵛ) a. ⓐ unbending, unbendable, inflexible, (nachgiebig) unyielding, (halsſtarrig) stubborn, obstinate; ſein Ⴎer Sinn b.s. his stubborn mind, g.s. his indomitable pluck; ~keit f ⓐ inflexibility, unyieldingness; stubbornness, obstinacy; ⚘bewacht (ᵇᵘᵛᶜʰᵗ) a. ⓐ not watched over, unwatched, unguarded, uncontrolled; defenceless; fig. Ⴎer Augenblick unguarded (or weak) moment; ⚘bewaffnet (ᵇᵘᵛ) a. ⓐ unarmed, defenceless, Ⴎ: ⚘ inerm(ous); mit Ⴎem Auge with the naked (or unaided) eye; ⚘bewaldet (ᵇᵘᵛ) a. ⓐ unwooded, von Bergen auch: bare; ⚘bewandert (ᵇᵘ⁻ᵛ) a. ⓐ not versed in, not conversant with, unacquainted (or unfamiliar) with, unskilled in; ⚘beweglich (ᵇᵘᵛ) a. ⓐ immovable, motionless; (ſeſtgemacht) fixed; eccl. Ⴎe Feſte set feasts pl.; jur.: Ⴎes Gut real estate or property; Ⴎe Güter oder Sachen immovables pl.; Ⴎ ſteh(e)n bleiben to remain fixed on the spot; fig (empfindungslos) impassive, unfeeling, callous, (unbeuglich) inflexible; ~keit (ᵇᵘᵛ⁻) f ⓐ (ſ. ⚘beweglich) immovableness, immobility; impassiveness; inflexibility; ⚘bewegt (ᵇᵘᵛ) a. ⓐ unmoved (a. fig.); ⚘bewehrt (ᵇᵘᵛ) a. ⓐ unarmed, defenceless; ~heit f ⓐ defencelessness; ⚘beweibt (ᵇᵘᵛ) a. ⓐ wifeless; unwedded, unmarried, single; ~heit f ⓐ unmarried state; engS. bachelorhood; ⚘beweint (ᵇᵘᵛ) a. ⓐ unwept (for), unlamented, undeplored; ⚘beweisbar (ᵇᵘᵛ⁻), ⚘beweislich (ᵇᵘᵛᵛ) a. ⓐ not provable, admitting no proof, indemonstrable; ~keit f ⓐ impossibility of s.th. being proved. ⚘ indemonstrability; ⚘bewiesen (ᵇᵘ⁻ᵛ) a. ⓐ unproved, bſd. ſchottiſch: unproven, not proven (a. jur.); ⚘bewohnbar (ᵇᵘᵛ⁻) a. ⓐ uninhabitable; ~keit f ⓐ uninhabitableness; ⚘bewohnt (ᵇᵘᵛ) a. ⓐ uninhabited, von e-m Hauſe auch: unoccupied, untenanted, vacated; (veröbet) deserted, desolate, lonely; ~heit f ⓐ uninhabited (or unoccupied) state; desertedness; ⚘bewölkt (ᵇᵘᵛ) a. ⓐ unclouded, cloudless, (klar) serene,

Zeichen (ſ. S. XVII): F familiär; P Volkssprache; Γ Gaunerſprache; ⚘ ſelten; † alt (auch geſtorben); * neu (auch geboren); ⁺⁺ unrichtig;

[unbewußt] — 1001 — [uneben]

clear, bright; 2bewußt (˘◡◡) a. ⓖ
passivisch (nicht bekannt): unknown; das ist
mir 2 I know nothing about it; das
geschah mir ganz 2 (adv.) that happened
quite without my knowledge or unbeknown to me, aktivisch (nicht wissend):
a) sich (dat.) einer Sache 2 sein to be
unconscious (or ignorant, unaware)
of a th., to be unacquainted with a
th.; b) (unwillkürlich) involuntary; (instinktmäßig) instinctive; et. ganz 2 tun
to do a th. quite mechanically or
instinctively; das ~e ⓖ bes. in: Philosophie des ~en (philosophisches Werk von
E. v. Hartmann) philosophy of the unconscious; 2bezahlbar (˘◡‼‒) a. ⓖ not
to be bought (or got) for money; fig.
(höchst kostbar) inestimable, invaluable,
priceless; das ist 2 F that's rich or
very good; 2bezahlt (˘◡‼) a. ⓖ unpaid, von Rechnungen auch: not (yet)
settled, von Forderungen: outstanding;
2bezähmbar (˘◡‼‒) a. ⓖ untamable,
bes. von Menschen u. geistigen Eigenschaften:
indomitable, unconquerable; 2bezeugt (˘◡‼) a. ⓖ unattested, unwitnessed; 2bezogen (˘◡‼◡) a. ⓖ (s.
beziehen): a) von e-m Hause: uninhabited,
untenanted; b) von e-m Kissen: without
a case, vom Bette: without sheets;
c) ♪ von e-r Geige 2c.: without strings,
unstringed; 2bezweifelbar (˘◡‼◡‒) a.
ⓖ indubitable, not to be doubted;
2bezweifelt (˘◡‼◡) a. ⓖ undoubted,
certain (vgl. 2bestritten); 2bezwingbar
(˘◡‼‒), 2bezwinglich (˘◡‼◡) a. invincible, unconquerable, v. Festungen:
impregnable, von Hindernissen: unsurmountable, von Mute 2c.: indomitable;
~keit f ⓖ invincibility, impregnability; 2bezwungen (˘◡‼◡) a. ⓖ unconquered, unsubdued, never vanquished;
2biblisch (˘‼◡) a. ⓖ not biblical, unscriptural, contrary to Holy Writ;
2biegsam (˘‼‒) a. ⓖ unbending, unbendable, inflexible, not pliant; (steif)
rigid, stiff (vgl. 2beugsam); ~keit f ⓖ
unbendingness, inflexibility; rigidity, rigour, stiffness; =bild (˘‼) n ⓑⓒ.
(Karte ohne Bild) blank card; =bilde(n
pl.) [uhd.] f ⓒ, sg. = Unbill (f. ds.)
die ihm zuteil gewordenen od. zugefügten
Unbilden the injustice meted out to
him, the wrongs inflicted on him,
his wrongs or injuries pl.; Unbilden pl.
des Wetters inclemency (or roughness)
of the weather; 2bildsam (˘‼‒) a. ⓖ
not easy to form or to mould, von
Menschen auch: not easy to educate,
difficult to teach, indocile; 2e Sprache
inflexible language; =bildung (˘‼◡) f ⓒ
lack of education, want of culture, stärker: illiteracy; =bill (˘‼) f (pl. f. =bilde) iniquity; (Ungerechtigkeit) injustice, wrong;
(Unglimpf) injury, insult; 2billig (˘‼◡)
a. ⓖ inequitable, unfair, unjust; (unvernünftig) unreasonable; ~e(s) n ⓖ, z.B.
~es erträgt kein edles Herz (SCH.) no generous heart endures inflicted wrong;
=billigkeit (˘‼◡‒) f ⓒ (s. 2billig) o. pl.:
unfairness, injustice; unreasonableness; mit pl.: unfair (or unjust) action,
act of injustice; 2blutig (˘‼◡) a. ⓖ
bloodless (victory, &c.); not sullied

(or stained) with blood; adv. without
bloodshed; 2botmäßig (˘‼‒) a. ⓖ insubordinate, rebellious; ~keit f ⓖ
insubordination; 2brauchbar (˘‼ch‒)
a. ⓖ useless, of no use, unserviceable,
unavailable, good (or fit) for nothing;
von Personen auch: incompetent, unfit,
good-for-nothing; ↓ von Schiffen: unseaworthy; ⚔ u. ↓ (dienstunfähig) disabled; ein Geschütz 2 machen to dismount (or disable) a gun; ~keit f ⓖ
uselessness, unserviceableness, incompetency, ineptitude, incapacity,
unfitness; ↓ e-s Schiffes: unseaworthiness; brauchbar=machung (˘‼ch‒◡) f
ⓖ: ~ e-s Dinges rendering a th. useless; ⚔
eines Geschützes dismounting (or disabling) a gun; 2brüderlich (˘‼◡◡) a.
ⓖ unbrotherly, seltener: unfraternal;
~keit f ⓖ unbrotherly spirit or conduct, lack of brotherly affection;
2bürgerlich (˘‼◡◡) a. ⓖ not citizenlike, unworthy of a (good or loyal)
citizen; 2bußfertig (˘‼◡◡) a. ⓖ impenitent, unrepenting, unrepentant;
2er Sünder, a. hardened sinner; von
Verbrechern: 2 (adv.) sterben to die
game; ~keit f ⓖ impenitence, unrepenting spirit; =christ (˘t‒) m ⓖ
unchristian person; (Ungläubiger) infidel, unbeliever; (Heide) heathen;
2christlich (˘t◡) a. ⓖ unchristian(like);
=christlichkeit f ⓖ unchristian conduct
or spirit, bisw. auch: unchristianness.
und (˘) [ahd.: and] (abbr. u.; &) cj.
1. and; 2 so weiter (abbr. usw.) and
so on, and so forth (abbr. &c. = (lt.)
et cetera); verstärkend: durch 2 durch
thoroughly; f. fort 2, für II. nach 5; bei
comp.: immer größer 2 größer greater
and greater; verteilend (vor Zahlen):
zwei 2 zwei two at a time, two and
two, beschreibend: an dem 2 dem Orte
in such and such a place (vgl. der 3).
— 2. ell.: a) erwartungsvoll: und
(was geschah weiter)? and after that?,
what then?; b) iro. ich 2 Einfluß
haben! to think that I should have
influence!, F me, and influence! (vgl.
der 3). — 3. mit cj. u. adv.: 2 auch
dann noch and even then; 2 dabei
noch der Regen and with it …, und
… besides or as well; 2 damit gute
Nacht! and after that, good night!;
mit Verneinungen: kein Brot 2 kein Geld
h. to have neither bread nor money;
2 er auch nicht nor he either; er
schreibt nicht 2 ich auch nicht he does
not write, neither (or nor) do I; vgl.
zwar 1. — 4. durch koordinierte Sätze ein
abhängiges Verhältnis ausdrückend: laufe
hin 2 sage es ihm (es ihm zu sagen) run
and tell him; er kam 2 holte mich ab
he came to fetch me; sei so gut 2
schreibe ihm (ihm zu schreiben) (will you)
be so kind as to (mehr gbr.: will you
kindly) write to him.
Un-dank (˘‒) m ⓑⓒ. ingratitude, ungratefulness; Sprichw. s. Lohn 1;
2dankbar (˘‒‒) a. ⓖ ungrateful (gegen
e-n to a p., für et. for a th.); 2e Aufgabe thankless (or unthankful) task;
sich 2 erweisen to prove (or show o.s.)
ungrateful; ~e(r) m f ⓖ ungrateful

person, a. ingrate; ~keit f ⓖ ingratitude, ungratefulness; unthankfulness of a task, &c.; 2datiert (˘◡‒) a. ⓖ
undated, bearing no date, without
date; 2definierbar (˘‒‒‒) a. ⓖ log.
undefinable; ~keit f ⓖ undefinableness; 2dehnbar (˘‼‒) 2c. = 2ausdehnbar 2c.; 2deklinierbar (˘‒◡‒) a. ⓖ gr.
indeclinable; ~keit f ⓖ indeclinableness; 2denkbar (˘‼◡) a. ⓖ incomprehensible, unimaginable, phls. unthinkable; (unbegreiflich) inconceivable;
eine Besserung ist 2 an improvement
is not to be thought of or is out of
the question; ~keit f ⓖ incomprehensibleness, phls. unthinkableness,
inconceivableness; 2denklich (˘‼◡) a.
ⓖ out of mind, (längst vergangen) long
past; seit 2er Zeit from time immemorial, (from) time out of mind, for
ages; 2deutlich (˘‼◡) a. ⓖ indistinct;
(verworren) confused, (unbestimmt) hazy,
vague, (trübe) dim, (dunkel) obscure;
(schwer zu verstehen) difficult to understand, v. Lauten 2c. inarticulate, von
der Schrift: difficult to decipher, illegible; 2es Bild hazy (or blurred)
image; ~keit f ⓖ indistinctness,
vagueness; dimness, obscurity;
2deutsch (˘‼) a. ⓖ not German, contrary to German ideas or ways or
habits, v. Redewendungen auch: unidiomatic; 2dicht (˘‼) a. ⓖ not tight
(-ly closed), letting in air or water,
unretentive, ↓ leaky; 2 sein to leak;
2dichterisch (˘‼◡◡) a. ⓖ unpoetical;
=dichtheit (˘‼), =dichtigkeit (˘‼◡) f ⓖ
leakiness; 2dienlich (˘‼◡) a. ⓖ unserviceable, useless, (ungeeignet) unsuitable, inexpedient, unadapted;
~keit f ⓖ unserviceableness, uselessness, unsuitableness; 2dienstfertig
(˘‼◡‒) a. ⓖ disobliging, disinclined to
serve (people); ~keit f ⓖ disoblingingness; =ding (˘‼) n ⓑⓒ. non-existent
matter, non-existence, nonentity
(a. phls.); (etwas Widersinniges) absurdity,
nonsense; 2diszipliniert (˘‒◡‒‒) a. ⓖ
bes. ⚔ undisciplined, untrained, raw
(recruits, &c.); 2dramatisch (˘‒‼◡) a.
undramatic(al); 2duldsam (˘‼‒) a. ⓖ
intolerant; (hart) harsh; adv. a. with
intolerance; ~keit f ⓖ intolerance;
harshness; 2durchdacht (˘◡‼cht) a. ⓖ ill-considered, v. Entwürfen a.: raw, immature; 2durchdringlich (˘◡‼◡) a. ⓖ impenetrable (a. fig.), bes. für Flüssigkeiten: impermeable, (unergründlich) inscrutable; ~keit f ⓖ impenetrableness, impermeability, inscrutableness; 2durchforscht (˘◡‼) a. ⓖ unexplored; 2durchführbar (˘◡‼‒) a. ⓖ
unaccomplishable, impracticable, unfeasible; 2durchlässig (˘◡‼◡) a. ⓖ
impermeable to water, &c.; 2durchsichtig (˘◡‼◡) a. ⓖ not transparent;
impervious to light, opaque; ~keit f
ⓖ opaqueness, opacity; 2eben (˘‼◡)
a. ⓖ uneven, not level, not uniform;
(rauh) rough (road, &c.), rugged
(ground), (hügelig) hilly, broken
(country), rolling (prairie); fig. (ungelegen) inconvenient, unsuitable, bes.
mit Verneinung: nicht 2 not amiss, not

♪ Musik; ⚛ Wissenschaft; ⚘ Pflanze; ⚲ Geographie; ⚙ Technik; ⚒ Bergbau; ⚔ Militär; ↓ Marine; ⚖ Handel; ✉ Post; ⛋ Eisenbahn.

[unebenbürtig] — 1002 — [unerkenntlich]

half bad, fairly good, *adv.* tolerably (or fairly) well; ꝛebenbürtig (ˈ-ˌ-ˌ) *a.* ⓖ of inferior birth or parentage or descent; *fig.* inferior; =ebenheit (ˈ-ˌ-) *f* ⓐ unevenness, roughness, ruggedness; =ebenmaß (ˈ-ˌ-) *n* ⓤa. want of symmetry or proportion; ꝛebenmäßig (ˈ-ˌ-ˌ-) *a.* ⓖ unsymmetrical, disproportionate; ꝛecht (ˈ-) *a.* ⓖ not genuine, spurious (document, &c.); (nachgemacht) counterfeit, sham, false, imitation (jewellery, &c.), (künstlich hergestellt) artificial (teeth, &c.), (verfälscht) adulterated; (unrechtmäßig) illegitimate; ꝛe Farben fading (or fugitive) colours *pl.*, auch: colours that won't wash; *arith.* Der Bruch (z.B. 9/7) improper fraction; ꝛe Waren adulterated goods *pl.*; ~keit *f* ⓐ spuriousness; artificialness; ꝛedel (ˈ-ˌ-) *a.* ⓖ ignoble; (gemein) mean, vulgar; ꝛe Metalle base metals *pl.*; ꝛegal (ˈ-ˌ) *a.* ⓖ = ꝛebenmäßig; ꝛehelich (ˈ-ˌ-) *a.* ⓖ illegitimate (birth, &c.), illicit (relationship, &c.); *v.* Kindern: born out of wedlock, illegitimate, natural; ~keit *f* ⓐ illegitimacy; ꝛehrbar (ˈ-ˌ) *a.* ⓖ unbecoming, stärker: indecent, disgraceful; ~keit *f* ⓐ unbecomingness, indecency; =ehre (ˈ-ˌ) *f* ⓑ dishonour, discredit; e-m ~ m., zur ~ gereichen to reflect discredit upon a p., to disgrace a p.; ꝛehrenhaft (ˈ-ˌ-) *a.* ⓖ dishonourable, discreditable, disgraceful; ꝛehr-erbietig (ˈ-ˌ-ˌ-) *a.* ⓖ disrespectful, gegen Eltern ꝛc.: undutiful, *rel.* &c. irreverent; sich ~ gegen e-n betragen to behave disrespectfully to a p.; ~keit *f* ⓐ disrespect(fulness), undutifulness, irreverence; ꝛehrlich (ˈ-ˌ-) *a.* ⓖ dishonest, vgl. ꝛehrenhaft; (ohne Treu und Glauben) not straightforward; faithless, underhand, false; (schändlich) infamous, disgraced; Fußball: foul; ~keit *f* ⓐ dishonesty; bad faith; infamy, disgrace; ꝛeigen-nützig (ˈ-ˌ-ˌ-) *a.* ⓖ disinterested, unselfish; (edelmütig) noble-hearted; ~keit *f* ⓐ disinterestedness, unselfishness; ꝛeigentlich (ˈ-ˌ-) *a.* ⓖ not literal, not in the proper sense of the word, weitS. figurative; ꝛeinbringlich (ˈ-ˌ-ˌ-) *a.* ⓖ irrecoverable, irretrievable (loss); ꝛeingebunden ⊕ (ˈ-ˌ-ˌ-) Buchbinderei: unbound; (noch roh) in sheets; ꝛeingedenk (ˈ-ˌ-ˌ) *a.* ⓖ unmindful of, regardless of, forgetful of; ꝛeingeladen (ˈ-ˌ-ˌ-) *a.* ⓖ uninvited, unasked, *adv.* without being invited; ꝛeingesalzen (ˈ-ˌ-ˌ-) *a.* ⓖ not salted, not pickled (with salt); ꝛeingeschränkt (ˈ-ˌ-ˌ) *a.* ⓖ unrestricted; ꝛeingeweiht (ˈ-ˌ-ˌ) *a.* ⓖ uninitiated; die ~en the uninitiated, the outside public, outsiders *pl.*; ꝛeinig (ˈ-ˌ-) *a.* ⓖ disunited, discordant, disagreeing; ꝛ sein to disagree, to differ, to be at variance, *vgl.* uneins; ꝛ w. mit // to fall out (or quarrel) with //; ~keit *f* ⓐ disunion, discord, disagreement; (Spaltung) division, split, (Mißhelligkeit) dissension; in ~keit mit e-m leben not to hit it off with a p.; ꝛein-nehmbar, meist ⚔ (ˈ-ˌ-ˌ-) *a.* ⓖ impregnable, weitS. safe from

all assaults; ꝛeins (ˈ-) *adv.* = ꝛeinig, z.B. mit sich selbst noch ꝛ sein to be wavering or vacillating, to be in two minds about a th.; ꝛeinträglich (ˈ-ˌ-ˌ) *a.* ⓖ unprofitable, not lucrative; ꝛelastisch (ˈ-ˌ-) *a.* ⓖ unelastic, inelastic; ꝛempfänglich (ˈ-ˌ-ˌ) *a.* ⓖ insusceptible (für of), für Eindrücke: unimpressionable; ~keit *f* ⓐ insusceptibility; ꝛempfindlich (ˈ-ˌ-ˌ) *a.* ⓖ insensible, not sensitive, unfeeling (gegen towards, to); (stumpf) apathetic, callous; (kalt) cold, (gleichgültig) indifferent to, proof against; (standhaft) stoical, stolid; für Liebe ꝛc. ꝛ inaccessible to love, &c.; ꝛ gegen Kälte ꝛc. inured to cold, &c.; ꝛ gegen Schläge, Unglück ꝛc. hardened against blows, misfortune, &c.; *v.* Körperteilen: numb, benumbed, without feeling, *med.*: ⚕ anæsthetic, durch betäubende Mittel: narcotized; ꝛ machen to (be)numb, *med.*: ⚕ to anæsthetize, to narcotize; ~keit *f* ⓐ (f. ꝛempfindlich) insensibility, apathy; coldness, indifference; numbness, *med.*: ⚕ anæsthesia; ~ erzeugend(es Mittel) ⚕ anæsthetic, narcotic; ꝛempfunden (ˈ-ˌ-ˌ) *a.* ⓖ unfelt; ꝛendlich (ˈ-ˌ-) *a.* ⓖ infinite (auch *math.*, bezeichnet durch ∞); endless, without end, interminable; (unermeßlich) immense; ꝛ groß infinite, boundless; ꝛ große Anzahl countless multitude, F no end of; ꝛ klein infinitesimal *math.* ꝛe Reihe infinite series; ins ꝛe to infinity, (lt.) *ad infinitum*; das geht ins ꝛe there is no end to (or of) it; ꝛ(e)mal an infinite number (F no end) of times; ~keit *f* ⓐ infinity, infinite space, endlessness; immensity; ꝛenglisch (ˈ-ˌ-) *a.* ⓖ un-English, contrary to English notions or ways or manners; ꝛentbehrlich (ˈ-ˌ-ˌ) *a.* ⓖ indispensable, (durchaus notwendig) absolutely necessary or requisite, urgently needed (zu for); ~keit *f* ⓐ indispensableness, absolute necessity; ꝛentdeckt (ˈ-ˌ-) *a.* ⓖ undiscovered; ꝛentgeltlich (ˈ-ˌ-ˌ) *a.* ⓖ gratuitous, *adv.* auch: gratis, for nothing, free of charge; ~keit *f* ⓐ gratuitousness; ꝛenthaltsam (ˈ-ˌ-ˌ) *a.* ⓖ incontinent, intemperate; ~keit *f* ⓐ incontinence, intemperance; ꝛentmutigt (ˈ-ˌ-ˌ) *a.* ⓖ not discouraged, undaunted, *adv.* without losing courage or heart, without flagging; ꝛentschieden (ˈ-ˌ-ˌ) *a.* ⓖ undecided, undetermined; (zweifelhaft) doubtful, dubious, uncertain; (noch schwebend) pending, F hanging fire; Fußball, Kricket ꝛc.: drawn; ꝛe Frage open question; ꝛes Rennen dead heat; ꝛes Spiel, ꝛe Schlacht drawn game, battle; ~keit *f* ⓐ indecision; uncertainty; ꝛentschlossen (ˈ-ˌ-ˌ) *a.* ⓖ irresolute; ich bin noch ꝛ I am still undecided or wavering or hesitating, I am in two minds (or I have not made up my mind) about it; ~keit *f* ⓐ irresoluteness, irresolution, indecision; ꝛentschuldbar (ˈ-ˌ-ˌ) *a.* ⓖ inexcusable, unpardonable; ꝛentwegbar (ˈ-ˌ-ˌ), ꝛentwegt * (ˈ-ˌ)[schwz. unverrückbar] *a.* ⓖ

oft co. unswerving, unflinching; firm, steadfast, constant, immutable of purpose; ꝛentwickelt (ˈ-ˌ-ˌ) *a.* ⓖ undeveloped; not unfolded; ꝛ u. zo. abortive, embryo(nic); ꝛer Zustand undeveloped (or embryo) state; ~heit *f* ⓐ undeveloped state; ꝛentwirrbar (ˈ-ˌ-ˌ) *a.* ⓖ inextricable; ~keit *f* ⓐ inextricableness; ꝛentzifferbar (ˈ-ˌ-ˌ-) *a.* ⓖ undecipherable; ꝛentzündbar (ˈ-ˌ-ˌ) *a.* ⓖ uninflamable, incombustible; ꝛerachtet (ˈ-ˌ-ˌ) *prp.* ⓖ geachtet; ꝛerbaulich (ˈ-ˌ-ˌ) *a.* ⓖ unedifying; ꝛerbaut (ˈ-ˌ) *a.* ⓖ unedified; ꝛerbeten (ˈ-ˌ-) *a.* ⓖ unasked for, unbidden, unrequested; unwelcome; ꝛerbittlich (ˈ-ˌ-ˌ) *a.* ⓖ inexorable, unrelenting, relentless; (streng) stern, harsh, (unbeugsam) inflexible, (erbarmungslos) pitiless; ~keit *f* ⓐ inexorableness, sternness, inflexibility; ꝛerbrochen (ˈ-ˌ-ˌ) *a.* ⓖ von einem Schlosse, Briefe ꝛc.: not broken open, intact; v. e-r Tür a. not forced open; ꝛerfahren (ˈ-ˌ-ˌ) *a.* ⓖ inexpert, inexperienced (in in), new (to), F raw (a. ⚔), green; ~e(r) *s.* ⓔ novice, F greenhorn; ~heit *f* ⓐ inexperience, F rawness; ꝛerfindlich (ˈ-ˌ-ˌ) *a.* ⓖ not to be found, undiscoverable; (unverständlich) incomprehensible; ꝛerforschbar (ˈ-ˌ-ˌ) *a.* ⓖ inexplorable; ꝛerforschlich (ˈ-ˌ-ˌ) *a.* ⓖ impenetrable, inscrutable, (geheimnisvoll) mysterious; ~keit *f* ⓐ inscrutableness; ꝛerforscht (ˈ-ˌ-) *a.* ⓖ unexplored; (verborgen) occult, hidden (from the eye); ꝛerfreulich (ˈ-ˌ-ˌ) *a.* ⓖ not pleasing, not gratifying; (unangenehm) unpleasant, unsatisfactory; (verdrießlich) disagreeable, annoying, vexatious; ~keit *f* ⓐ unpleasantness; ꝛerfüllbar (ˈ-ˌ-ˌ) *a.* ⓖ which cannot be fulfilled or redeemed or performed, von Hoffnungen ꝛc.: unrealizable; ꝛerfüllt (ˈ-ˌ) *a.* ⓖ unfulfilled, (unausgeführt) unachieved, unaccomplished, unperformed; ꝛ bleiben a) v. Erwartungen: not to be realized, to be disappointed; b) v. Gelübden u. Versprechungen: not to be redeemed or to be broken; c) v. Weissagungen: not to come true, to prove false; ꝛergiebig (ˈ-ˌ-ˌ) *a.* ⓖ unproductive, (unfruchtbar) barren, sterile; ~keit *f* ⓐ unproductiveness, barrenness, sterility; ꝛergründlich (ˈ-ˌ-ˌ) *a.* ⓖ unfathomable; (bodenlos) bottomless, abysmal; (erforschlich) impenetrable; ~keit *f* ⓐ unfathomableness; ꝛerheblich (ˈ-ˌ-ˌ) *a.* ⓖ insignificant, irrelevant, inconsiderable; (gering) slight, trifling; ~keit *f* ⓐ insignificance, irrelevancy, slightness; ꝛerhört (ˈ-ˌ) *a.* ⓖ unheard of, unprecedented, (empörend) shocking, (übermäßig) excessive; ✱ ꝛe Preise fabulous (or exorbitant) prices *pl.*; (nicht gewährt) not granted, not acceded to; ꝛ bleiben to find no hearing; ꝛ l. to turn a deaf ear to; ꝛerkannt (ˈ-ˌ-) *a.* ⓖ unrecognized, unknown, *adv.* oft: incognito; ꝛerkennbar (ˈ-ˌ-ˌ) *a.* ⓖ unrecognizable, undiscernible; ꝛerkenntlich (ˈ-ˌ-ˌ) *a.* ⓖ forgetful of

Signs (see page XVII): F familiar; P vulgar; ꟻ flash; ⟍ rare; † obsolete (died); * new word (born); ⁒ incorrect; ♪ music;

[Unerkenntlichkeit] — 1003 — [Unfrieden]

kindness(es) shown to one, stärker: ungrateful; **erkenntlichkeit** f ⑯ ingratitude; ⚥**erklärbar**(⌣⌢⌣⌣), ⚥**erklärlich** (⌣⌢⌣⌣) a. ⑯ inexplicable, unaccountable, undefinable; (rätselhaft) perplexing, puzzling; **erklärbarkeit**, **erklärlichkeit** f ⑯ inexplicableness; ⚥**erläßlich** (⌣⌢⌣⌣) a. ⑯ irremissible, not to be let off (vgl. ⚥**entbehrlich**); ⚥**erlaubt** (⌣⌢⌣) a. ⑯ unpermitted, not allowed; (ungesetzlich) unlawful, illegal, illicit, (verboten) prohibited, (verstohlen) clandestine; ⚥**erledigt** (⌣⌢⌣) a. ⑯ unsettled, not disposed of; von Geschäften: undispatched, von Pflichten: undischarged; ⚥**ermeßlich** (⌣⌢⌣⌣) a. ⑯ immeasurable, immense, (unbegrenzbar) unlimited, illimitable, boundless, (unendlich) infinite; (ungeheuer) enormous, vast, huge, untold (wealth, &c.); ~**keit** f ⑯ immeasurableness, immensity, immense size; boundlessness; vastness; ⚥**ermittelt** (⌣⌢⌣⌣) a. ⑯ unascertained, undiscovered, not found out; ⚥**ermüdet** (⌣⌢⌣⌣) a. ⑯ unwearied; ⚥**ermüdlich** (⌣⌢⌣⌣) a. ⑯ indefatigable, untiring, (unablässig) unflagging; ~**keit** f ⑯ indefatigableness; ⚥**eröffnet** (⌣⌢⌣⌣) a. ⑯ unopened, v. Briefen ꝛc. auch: not broken open; ⚥**erörtert** (⌣⌢⌣⌣) a. ⑯ undiscussed; ⚥**erprobt** (⌣⌢⌣) a. ⑯ untried, not tested, unproved, von Erzen ꝛc.: unassayed; ⚥**erquicklich** (⌣⌢⌣⌣) a. ⑯ uncomfortable, unpleasant, unedifying, stärker: annoying, vexatious; ~**keit** f ⑯ uncomfortableness, unpleasantness; ⚥**erreichbar** (⌣⌢⌣⌣) a. ⑯ out of (one's) reach, bsd. fig. unattainable, (unzugänglich) inaccessible, F co. not get-at-able; ~**keit** f ⑯ unattainableness; inaccessibility; ⚥**erreicht** (⌣⌢⌣) a. ⑯ unattained, (unvergleichlich) unequalled, unrivalled, unparalleled, unmatched, Sport: bisher ⚥e Leistung record performance; ⚥**ersättlich** (⌣⌢⌣⌣) a. ⑯ insatiable (a. fig.), (heißhungrig) voracious, ravenous, (gierig) greedy, gluttonous; ~**keit** f ⑯ insatiability; voracity, greed(iness); ⚥**erschaffen** (⌣⌢⌣⌣) a. ⑯ uncreated; ⚥**erschöpflich** (⌣⌢⌣⌣) a. ⑯ inexhaustible, never failing; ~**keit** f ⑯ inexhaustibleness; ⚥**erschöpft** (⌣⌢⌣) a. ⑯ unexhausted; ⚥**erschrocken** (⌣⌢⌣⌣) a. ⑯ intrepid, undaunted, dauntless, fearless, daring; unflinching; ~**heit** f ⑯ intrepidity, dauntlessness, fearlessness, daring; ⚥**erschütterlich** (⌣⌢⌣⌣) a. ⑯ unshakable; (sich nicht beirren lassen) imperturbable, unswerving, unflinching, steadfast, (fest) firm, immovable, unmoved (vgl. **unerschrocken**); ~**keit** f ⑯ imperturbability, firmness; ⚥**erschüttert** (⌣⌢⌣⌣) a. ⑯ unshaken (a. fig.); unmoved, unflinching; ⚥**erschwinglich** (⌣⌢⌣⌣) a. ⑯ beyond one's means or power; ⚥e Kosten enormous costs pl.; ⚥e Preise exorbitant (or immoderate, prohibitive) prices pl.; ⚥**ersetzbar** (⌣⌢⌣⌣), ⚥**ersetzlich** (⌣⌢⌣⌣) a. ⑯ person who (or thing which) cannot be replaced or substituted; bsd. von Verlusten: irretrievable, irreparable, irrecoverable; ⚥**ersprießlich** (⌣⌢⌣⌣) a.

⑯ unprofitable, unproductive, stärker: fruitless; ⚥**ersteiglich** (⌣⌢⌣⌣) a. ⑯ unscalable, inaccessible (vgl. ⚥**besteigbar**); ⚥**erträglich** (⌣⌢⌣⌣) a. ⑯ unbearable, intolerable, insupportable, insufferable; past endurance; ⚥e Hitze ꝛc. auch: overpowering heat, &c.; ~**keit** f ⑯ unbearableness, intolerableness; ⚥**erwachsen** (⌣⌢⌣⌣) a. ⑯ not fullgrown, under age; not fully developed; ⚥**erwähnt** (⌣⌢⌣) a. ⑯ unmentioned; et. ⚥ lassen to make no mention of a th., not to mention a th.; to pass a th. over (in silence); ⚥**erwartet** (⌣⌢⌣⌣) a. ⑯ unexpected, unlooked for, (unvorhergesehen) unforeseen; (plötzlich) sudden; adv. oft: all of a sudden, (unversehens) unawares; ⚥**erweichbar** (⌣⌢⌣⌣), ⚥**erweichlich** (⌣⌢⌣⌣) a. ⑯ which cannot be softened; (zähe) tough; fig. = ⚥**beugsam**; ⚥**erweislich** (⌣⌢⌣⌣) a. ⑯ = **unbeweisbar**; ⚥**erwidert** (⌣⌢⌣⌣) a. ⑯ v. Briefen ꝛc.: unanswered, von Liebe(sdiensten): unrequited, unreturned, (unvergolten) unrepaid; ⚥**erwiesen** (⌣⌢⌣⌣) a. ⑯ not proved; s. a. ⚥**bewiesen**; ⚥**erwogen** (⌣⌢⌣⌣) a. ⑯ unconsidered; ⚥**erwünscht** (⌣⌢⌣) a. ⑯ undesired, undesirable, unwished for, unwelcome; out of season: das kam ihm sehr ⚥ (adv.) it came as a great blow to him; ⚥**erzählbar** (⌣⌢⌣⌣) a. ⑯ not (fit) to be related, unfit for narration; ⚥**erzogen** (⌣⌢⌣) a. ⑯ not brought up (well), uneducated, b.s. ill-bred; ⚥**explodierbar** (⌣⌢⌣⌣) a. ⑯ non-explosive, inexplosive; ⚥**fähig** (⌣⌣) a. ⑯ incapable of (doing) a th., unable (or incompetent) to do a th.; unfit (or not qualified) for a th.; e-n ⚥ zu et. ⚥ machen to disable (or disqualify, incapacitate) a p. for a th.; ⚥ zu zahlen insolvent; ~**keit** f ⑯ incapacity, inability, incompetency; unfitness; disability (a. jur.); ⚥**fahrbar** (⌣⌣) a. ⑯ von Wegen: impassable, impracticable, ⚓ not navigable; ⚥**fall** (⌣⌣) m ⓒc. accident, mishap, mischance, stärker: misfortune, disaster, catastrophe; e-n ⚥ h. to meet with an accident; es ist ihnen ein schwerer ⚥ zugestoßen they have met with (or had) a severe accident; =**fallverhütung** f prevention of accidents. **Unfallversicherung** (⌣⌣⌣⌣⌣⌣) f ⑫ insurance against accidents; ~s-**gesellschaft** (⌣...) f ⑫ accident-insurance company; ~s-**gesetz** n accident-insurance bill, in Engl.: Workmen's Compensation Act; ~s-**kasse** f von Arbeitervereinen: provident fund.

un-faßbar (⌣⌣⌣), ⚥**faßlich** (⌣⌣) a. ⑯ unseizable; difficult to grasp (a. fig.); weitS. incomprehensible (= ⚥**begreiflich**); ⚥**fehlbar** (⌣⌣) a. ⑯ unfailing, unerring, von Heilmitteln: safe, reliable; (untrüglich, nie irrend) infallible (auch eccl. vom Papste); er wird ⚥ (adv.) kommen he will come without fail, he is sure to come; ~**keit** f ⑯ infallibility; ⚥**fein** (⌣⌣) a. ⑯ unrefined, indelicate, unmannerly; (roh, unhöflich) impolite; Fußballspiel: unfair; coarse; ~**heit** (⌣⌣) f ⑯ lack of refinement,

unmannerliness; coarseness; ⚥**fern** (⌣⌣) adv. not far off, near (at hand); als prp. mit gen., dat. und mit von: not far from, near, in the vicinity (or neighbourhood) of; ⚥**fertig** (⌣⌣⌣) a. ⑯ unfinished; unready; fig. immature; ~**keit** f ⑯ unfinished state; unreadiness; ⚥**findbar** (⌣⌣⌣) a. ⑯ unfindable, not to be found; =**flat** (⌣⌣) [mhd.] m ⓒc. filth, dirt, nasty (F beastly) mess or muck; (Zoten) smut; a. = =**flater**; =**flater** (⌣⌣⌣) m ⑫ filthy (or dirty, nasty, lewd, smutty) fellow; ~**ei** (⌣⌣⌢) f ⑯ filth(y stuff), filthiness, F beastliness; smut; ⚥**flätig** (⌣⌣⌣) [mhd.] a. ⑯ filthy, dirty, nasty, F beastly, messy; (sottig) smutty, lewd, obscene; ~**keit** f ⑯ filth(iness), nastiness, F beastliness; lewdness, obscenity; =**fleiß** (⌣⌣) m ⓒa. want of application or diligence; (Lässigkeit) indolence, laziness, idleness; ⚥**fleißig** (⌣⌣⌣) a. ⑯ indolent, lazy, idle; without application; ⚥**folge-richtig** (⌣⌣⌣⌣⌣) a. ⑯ illogical (= **folgewidrig**); ⚥**folgsam** (⌣⌣⌣) a. ⑯ disobedient, von Kindern auch: wayward; ~**keit** f ⑯ disobedience, waywardness; =**form** (⌣⌣) f ⑯ (Mißgestalt) deformity; ⚥**förmig** (⌣⌣⌣) a. ⑯ deformed, misshapen, shapeless; (nicht im rechten Verhältnis stehend) out of shape, disproportionate; (ungeschlacht) monstrous, enormous; ~**keit** f ⑯ deformity, shapelessness; disproportion; monstrosity; ⚥**förmlich** (⌣⌣⌣) a. ⑯ rude, (unkünstlerisch) inartistic, (ungehobelt) unpolished, (unfein) unrefined; ⚥**frankiert** (⌣⌣⌣) a. ⑯ unpaid (for), not prepaid, ehm.: unfranked; adv. without prepayment, without paying the postage; ⚥**französisch** (⌣⌣⌣) a. ⑯ contrary to French ideas or manners, foreign to the French; adv. in bad (or broken) French; ⚥**frei** (⌣⌣) a. ⑯ not free; (nicht freigelassen) not freed, not emancipated; (geknechtet) serving, servile; ~**er** ⑥ bond(s)man, serf; ⚥**freigebig** (⌣⌣⌣) a. ⑯ illiberal, parsimonious; (knickerig, close, mean, niggardly; ~**keit** f ⑯ illiberality, parsimony; =**freiheit** (⌣⌣⌢) f ⑯ want of liberty or freedom; (Knechtschaft) bondage, serfdom, in Engl. ehm.: villeinage; fig. constraint, narrow compass; ⚥**freiwillig** (⌣⌣⌣⌣) a. ⑯ involuntary, compulsory; (widerwillig) unwilling; physiol. reflex (action, &c.); ⚥**freundlich** (⌣⌣⌣) a. ⑯ unfriendly, unamiable, unkind; (ungefällig) disobliging; (barsch) ungracious, discourteous, rude, rough, offhandish; (übel gelaunt) sullen, sulky, (grämlich) morose, gruff, (finster) gloomy; pol. ⚥er Akt unfriendly act; ⚥es Wetter dull (stärker: disagreeable, rough, inclement) weather; ⚥e Wohnung cheerless habitation; e-m ⚥ (adv.) begegnen to treat a p. with discourtesy, to be rude to a p.; ~**keit** f ⑯ unfriendliness, ungraciousness, rudeness, sullenness, sulkiness; des Wetters: dulness, inclemency, e-r Wohnung: cheerlessness; ⚥**freundschaftlich** (⌣⌣⌣⌣) a. ⑯ not amicably inclined towards a p.; unfriendly; =**friede(n)** (⌣⌣) m (⌣⌣) disturbed condition,

🜚 scientific; ♀ botanical; ♁ geography; ⊕ machinery; ⚒ mining; ⚔ military; ⚓ marine; ● commercial; ✉ postal; 🚂 railway.

[unfriedlich] — 1004 — [ungefügig]

(Uneinigkeit) discord, disunion, (Zwist) dissension, strife, quarrel, F sparring; (Mißhelligkeit) misunderstanding, F tiff; Sprichw. s. Friede 1; ⁰friedlich (ˢᴸ) a. ⁶⁶ unpeaceable, not peaceably inclined; discordant, dissentient, stärker: quarrelsome; ~keit f ⁴⁶ unpeaceableness, quarrelsomeness; ⁰fruchtbar (ˢᴸ–) a. ⁶⁶ unfruitful, barren (a. fig. vom Geiste); (keine Frucht bringend) sterile; (keinen Nutzen gewährend) unproductive, unprofitable; poor (land, &c.); fig. (urspr. bibl.) auf ⁰en Boden fallen to fall upon stony ground, not to take root, v. Ermahnungen a. to make no impression upon a p.; ~keit f ⁴⁶ barrenness, sterility; unproductiveness; ⁼fug (ˢᴸ) m ⓊⒸ. (Unrecht) wrong, offence; jur.: grober ~ gross misdemeanour; leichter ~ light offence; (ungebührliches Treiben) nuisance, disorder(ly conduct); excess, mischief, jur. disturbance of the peace; (ärgerlicher Auftritt) scandal(ous proceeding); ~ treiben to be up to mischief or to one's tricks, to be a nuisance (to the neighbourhood); ⁰fügsam (ˢᴸ–) a. ⁶⁶ unaccommodating, unyielding, stärker: refractory, intractable; ~keit f ⁴⁶ refractoriness, intractability; ⁰fühlbar (ˢᴸ–) a. ⁶⁶ intangible, impalpable; (unbemerkbar) imperceptible; ⁰fundiert (ˢᴸ) a. ⁶⁶ von Staatsschulden: unfunded, unconsolidated, floating; ⁰fürstlich (ˢᴸ) a. ⁶⁶ unprincely, not worthy of (or unbecoming to) a prince.

...ung (...ˢ)[abb.: ...ing] f ⁴⁶ Anhängesilbe (suffix) dient: 1. zur Bildung von abstrakten s/f. aus transitiven oder reflexiven, selten intransitiven Zeitwörtern und hat: a) die Bedeutung des substantivierten Infinitivs, kann jedoch nicht abs. gebraucht werden wie dieser, z.B. entdecken to discover, das Entdecken und die Entdeckung Amerikas the discovery of America; aber nur: sein Hang zum Entdecken his taste for discovery; b) die Bedeutung des aus der Tätigkeit des Zeitworts Hervorgegangenen, z.B. zeichnen to draw, die Zeichnung the drawing. — 2. zur Bildung von Sammelwörtern aus Ding- und Eigenschafts-wörtern, z.B. Holz wood, Holzung f wooded land; fest strong, Festung f fortress.

un=galant (ˢᴸ) a. ⁶⁶ ungallant, discourteous (or disobliging) to ladies; ⁰gangbar (ˢᴸ–) a. ⁶⁶ v. Wegen: impassable (or unfit) for pedestrians, (wenig betreten) little used; (ungewöhnlich) ⁰es Wort unusual (or rare) word; ※ von Münzen (außer Kurs): not current; von Waren: unsaleable, unmarketable; ~keit f ⁴⁶ unsaleableness; ⁰gar¹ (ˢᴸ) a. ⁶⁶ not sufficiently boiled or cooked, underdone, (half) raw.
Ungar² (ˢ–) [Hunnen-(g)war hunnischer Mann] m ⓶, ~in f ⓶ Hungarian; ⁰isch (ˢ––) a. ⁶⁶ Hungarian; die ⁰e Sprache, das ⁰(e) n ⓺ the Hungarian language, Hungarian; ~=land n ⓺₂ = Ungarn.
Ungarn ⓆⓀ. nprⓃ. ⓈⒶ. Hungary.
Ungar=wein (ˢ–ᴸ) m ⓺₂ Hungarian wine.
un=gastlich (ˢᴸ) a. ⁶⁶ (~keit f ⁴⁶) inhospitable(ness); ⁰geachtet (ˢᴸ–⁶ᵗ¹) a. ⁶⁶ not esteemed, not respected, disregarded; prp. (mit gen. vor= od. nach= stehend) regardless of; notwithstanding, despite (of), stärker: in spite of; vgl. dessen=2; ⁰ F-r Fehler liebe ich ihn doch with all his faults I love him still; cj. though, although, seltener: albeit; ⁰geahndet (ˢᴸ) a. ⁶⁶ unpunished (vgl. ungerächt), adv. with impunity; ⁰geahnt (ˢᴸ) a. ⁶⁶ not anticipated, unsuspected, never dreamt (or thought) of; (unerwartet, ungehofft) unlooked for, unexpected, unhoped for.
ungeb. abbr. = ungebunden.
un=gebahnt (ˢᴸ) a. ⁶⁶ untrodden (path), unbeaten (track); ⁰gebändigt (ˢᴸ–) a. ⁶⁶ untamed, uncurbed, unsubdued, fig. auch: unbroken; ⁰gebärdig a. ⁶⁶ unmannerly, rude; troublesome, unruly, refractory; (unartig) naughty; ⁰gebessert (ˢᴸ–) a. ⁶⁶ unmended, unimproved, unreformed, unreclaimed; ⁰gebeten (ˢᴸ–) a. ⁶⁶ unasked, unsolicited, (uneingeladen) uninvited, unbidden; ⁰er Gast intruder; (Schmarotzer) sponger; adv. without being asked, (freiwillig) of one's own accord; ⁰gebeugt (ˢᴸ) a. ⁶⁶ unbent, uncurbed; ~keit f ⁴⁶ uncurbed spirit; ⁰gebeutelt ⊙ (ˢᴸ) a. ⁶⁶ Müllerei: unbolted (flour, meal); ⁰gebildet (ˢᴸ–) a. ⁶⁶ uneducated, im Benehmen: unpolished, ill-bred; ungentlemanly, unladylike; (ohne Schulbildung) untaught, unlettered, illiterate; (unzivilisiert) uncivilized, primitive, stärker: barbarous; die ⁰e Menge the ignorant masses pl.; ⁰ge= bleicht ⊙ (ˢᴸ) a. ⁶⁶ unbleached; ⁰geboren (ˢᴸ–) a. ⁶⁶ unborn; ⁰gebrannt (ˢᴸ) a. ⁶⁶ unburnt, von Backsteinen: unbaked; F co. ⁰e Asche (Stock) good stick, cudgel, (Prügel) cudgelling; ⊙ ⁰er Ziegel unburnt (or air-dried) brick; ⁰gebräuchlich (ˢᴸ–) a. ⁶⁶ not customary; obsolete; (ungewöhnlich) unusual, uncommon; ⁰ w. to fall into disuse, to go out of use, to grow obsolete; ~keit f ⁴⁶ obsoleteness; ⁰gebraucht (ˢᴸcht) a. ⁶⁶ unused, not worn, quite new, fresh (from the shop); ⁰gebrochen (ˢᴸ–ch) a. ⁶⁶ unbroken, fig. auch: undejected; opt. v. Lichtstrahlen: unrefracted; ⁼gebühr (ˢᴸ) f ⁴⁶ indecency, impropriety, a. jur. misdemeanour; (Ungerechtigkeit) injustice; (Mißbrauch) abuse, excess; zur ~ excess, improperly, unduly, unfairly; ⁰end, ⁰lich (ˢᴸ–) a. ⁶⁶ undue, adv. unduly, (ungerecht) unjust, unfair; (unschicklich) unbecoming, unseemly, unmannerly, rude, stärker: indecent, (ungehörig) improper; ~lichkeit f ⁴⁶ unseemliness, indecency, impropriety, v. Handlungen: unseemly (or improper) action; vgl. =gebühr; ⁰gebunden (ˢᴸ–) a. ⁶⁶ unbound, untied; v. Büchern: ⁰ = Leingebunden; ⁰e Rede, de Schreibart = Prosa; fig. (frei) free, unrestrained, b.s. (ausschweifend) dissolute, loose, debauched, licentious; ein ⁰es Leben a free and easy (b.s. a wild and reckless) life; ~heit f ⁴⁶ freedom, unrestraint, free and easy manner or way; b.s. dissoluteness, looseness, licentiousness; ⁰gedeckt (ˢᴸ–, ˢᴸ) a. ⁶⁶ un-

covered; der Tisch ist noch ⁰ the cloth (or table) has not been laid (yet); (ohne Schutz) unprotected, unsheltered, defenceless, unsupported; ※ (ohne Deckung) uncovered; ⁰gedeihlich (ˢᴸ–) a. ⁶⁶ not thriving; unprofitable, unremunerative; von Nahrungsmitteln: unwholesome, vom Klima: unhealthy; ⁰gedruckt (ˢᴸ–) a. ⁶⁶ unprinted, not (yet) in print, in manuscript, (nicht veröffentlicht) unpublished; ⁼geduld (ˢᴸ) f ⁴⁶ impatience; vor ~ brennen zu // to burn with a desire to //, to be most eager or anxious to //; F von Kindern: impatient child, F fidget; ⁰geduldig (ˢᴸ–) a. ⁶⁶ impatient; (unruhig) fidgety, bsd. v. Kindern a.: peevish; ⁰ w. to grow impatient, to lose patience; ⁰ (adv.) erwarten to await anxiously; ⁰ge=ehrt (ˢᴸ) a. ⁶⁶ unhonoured, unrespected; adv. without honour; ⁰ge=eignet (ˢᴸ–) a. ⁶⁶ unsuitable, unfit, inappropriate (zu et. for a th.); ~keit f ⁴⁶ unsuitableness, unfitness, inappropriateness.
un=gefähr (ˢᴸ)[mhd.:*ohn-gefähr] I adv. about, near(ly); (annähernd geltend) approximately; ⁰ zwanzig Mark a pound or so; ⁰ vierzehn Tage a fortnight or thereabouts; er sagte ⁰ dasselbe wie // he spoke (much) to the same effect as //. — II ⟟ a. ⁶⁶ (zufällig) casual; (annähernd richtig) approximate (value, &c.), rough (calculation, &c.). — III ~ n ⓺ (Zufall) accident, chance, casualty; von ⁰ accidentally, by chance, casually; ich traf ihn ganz von ⁰ it was quite by accident (that) I met him, I happened (by mere chance) to meet him.
un=gefährdet (ˢᴸ–) a. ⁶⁶ not endangered, not imperilled, not jeopardized; not in danger, safe, well secured; ⁰fährlich (ˢᴸ–) a. ⁶⁶ not dangerous, not risky, not hazardous; (unschädlich) harmless, innocuous; ⁰gefällig (ˢᴸ–) a. ⁶⁶ disobliging, discourteous, rude, unkind, unaccommodating; (kein Gefallen erregend) displeasing, unpleasant, ungraceful; ~keit (ˢᴸ–) f ⁴⁶ disobliging spirit or nature, discourtesy, rudeness, unkindness; unpleasantness, lack of grace(fulness); ⁰gefälscht (ˢᴸ–) a. ⁶⁶ unadulterated, (echt) genuine, sterling; (rein) pure; ⁰gefärbt (ˢᴸ–) a. ⁶⁶ uncoloured, undyed; (farblos) colourless; ⁰e Seide raw silk; fig. (ungeschminkt) unvarnished, true; ⁰gefaßt (ˢᴸ) a. ⁶⁶ von Juwelen: not set; ⁰ge= fesselt (ˢᴸ–) a. ⁶⁶ unfettered, unchained, fig. auch: unrestrained, untrammelled, free from (all) restraint; ⁰gefiedert (ˢᴸ–) a. = ⁰befiedert; ⁰ge= fleckt (ˢᴸ–) a. ⁶⁶ unspotted; ⁰geflügelt (ˢᴸ–) a. ⁶⁶ wingless, without wings, ¶ u. zo.: ↯ apterous; ⁰e Insekten aptera(ns) pl.; ⁰gefragt (ˢᴸ–) a. ⁶⁶ unasked, adv. without being asked or questioned; ⁰gefrierbar (ˢᴸ––) a. ⁶⁶ not freezable, phys.: ↯ uncongealable; ⁰gefrühstückt F (ˢᴸ–) a. ⁶⁶ co. (ohne Frühstück) without (having had) a breakfast; ⁰gefüge, ⁰gefügig (ˢᴸ–) a. ⁶⁶ unwieldy, fig. unyielding, unmanage-

Zeichen (s. S. XVII): F familiär; P Volkssprache; ⌐ Gaunersprache; ⍀ selten; † alt (auch gestorben); * neu (auch geboren); ⁺⁺ unrichtig;

[ungefüttert] — 1005 — [ungeordnet]

able, intractable; (eigenſinnig) stubborn; ⸗gefüttert (⏑⏑⏑) a. ⚭ von Tieren, F co. von Menſchen: unfed, with an empty stomach; v. Kleidern: not lined; ⸗gegerbt ⊙ (⏑⏑⏑) a. ⚭ untanned, raw, vom Leder auch: undressed; ⸗gegeſſen (⏑⏑⏑) a. ⚭ uneaten; Faktiviſch: without having eaten (anything), dinnerless, with an empty stomach; ⸗gegliedert (⏑⏑⏑) a. ⚭ ⚥ u. zo. unjointed, without joints, ⚕ inarticulate; ⸗gegoren (⏑⏑⏑) a. ⚭ unfermented; ⸗gegründet (⏑⏑⏑) a. ⚭ unfounded, groundless, (eingebildet) imaginary, false; ⸗gehalten (⏑⏑⏑) a. ⚭ not held, not fulfilled; fig. (unwillig) indignant, (ärgerlich) angry, vexed, mortified; auf e-n ⸗ ſein to be indignant (or cross, displeased) with a p.; über et. ⸗ ſein to be angry (or annoyed) about a th.; ⸗geheißen (⏑⏑⏑) a. ⚭ unbidden, not ordered, (eigenwillig) voluntary, adv. of one's own accord, spontaneously; ⸗geheizt (⏑⏑⏑) a. ⚭ unheated, von e-m Zimmer: without a fire; ⸗gehemmt (⏑⏑⏑) a. ⚭ unhampered, unhindered, unrestrained, unfettered, unchecked, adv. without hindrance or restraint; freely; ⸗geheuchelt (⏑⏑⏑⏑) a. ⚭ unfeigned, not shammed; (aufrichtig) sincere, candid; ⸗geheuer (⏑⏑⏑) [ahd.] a. ⚭ (D9) monstrous, prodigious; (rieſig, groß) enormous, colossal, F thundering, thumping, whacking; (unermeßlich) immense, vast; (erſtaunlich) astonishing; (erſchrecklich) awful, dreadful; ein ungeheurer Zudrang a tremendous crush; die 2ſten Miſſetaten the most appalling crimes pl.; ⸗ (adv.) billig exceedingly cheap; ⸗ lachen to laugh uproariously or tremendously; das ⸗e ⚭ the vastness of a th.; das Ungeheure iſt geſchehen the dreadful deed has been enacted, the tragic event has come to pass; ⸗ (⏑⏑⏑) [ahd.] n ㉒ monster, prodigy, monstrous creature; ⸗geheuerlich (⏑⏑⏑⏑, ⏑⏑⏑⏑) a. ⚭ monstrous, prodigious; ⸗keit f ㊻ monstrosity; enormity of a crime, &c.; ⸗keiten atrocities pl.; ⸗gehindert (⏑⏑⏑⏑) a. ⚭ = ungehemmt; ⸗gehobelt (⏑⏑⏑⏑) a. ⚭ unplaned; fig. unpolished, unrefined, coarse, rustic; ⸗gehofft (⏑⏑⏑) a. ⚭ unhoped for; ⸗gehopft (⏑⏑⏑) a. ⚭ without hops; ⸗gehörig (⏑⏑⏑) [mhd.] a. ⚭ undue; (unſchicklich) unbecoming, unseemly, improper, (unpaſſend) unsuitable, not meet; Fußball: foul, unfair; ſich ⸗ (adv.) benehmen to behave improperly, to misbehave o.s.; ⸗keit f ㊻ unbecomingness, impropriety; unsuitableness; (Regelwidrigkeit) licence, liberty; ⸗gehorſam (⏑⏑⏑) a. ⚭ disobedient, ⚔ insubordinate; e-m ⸗ ſein to disobey a p.; ⸗ m ⓪d. disobedience (gegen das Geſetz to the law), gerichtlich: contumacy, default, ⚔ insubordination; ⸗s⸗verfahren ⚔ n jur. procedure for contempt of court; ſ. a. Kontumaz; ⸗gehört (⏑⏑⏑) a. ⚭ unheard; ⸗gehudelt F (⏑⏑⏑⏑) a. ⚭ undisturbed, unmolested; laſſen Sie mich ⸗! let me alone!, don't worry (or bother) me!; ⸗geiſtlich (⏑⏑⏑) a. ⚭ unspiritual; (weltlich) worldly, secular, temporal, profane; (nicht zu den Geiſtlichen gehörig) lay, unclerical; (eines Geiſtlichen unwürdig) not becoming (or not befitting) a clergyman; ⸗gekämmt (⏑⏑⏑) a. ⚭ uncombed, unkempt, with unkempt hair, ⊙ von der Wolle: not carded; ⸗gekannt (⏑⏑⏑) a. ⚭ unknown to; ⸗gekocht (⏑⏑⏑) a. ⚭ unboiled, raw; ⸗gekränkt (⏑⏑⏑) a. ⚭ not mortified, uninjured, unharmed, unhurt; adv. without injury, in peace; ⸗gekrönt (⏑⏑⏑) a. ⚭ uncrowned; ⸗gekünſtelt (⏑⏑⏑⏑) a. ⚭ unaffected; (ungeſucht) unstudied, (einfach) simple, artless, unsophisticated, (natürlich) natural; (wahr) true, genuine; ⸗heit f ㊻ unaffectedness; simplicity, artlessness; ⸗geladen (⏑⏑⏑) a. ⚭ von Schußwaffen: not loaded, (uneingeladen) uninvited; = ⸗beladen; ⸗geläufig (⏑⏑⏑) a. ⚭ not fluent; (nicht vertraut) unfamiliar; es iſt mir ⸗ I am not acquainted with (F not well up in) it; I have not learnt (F got) the knack of it (yet); ⸗geläutert (⏑⏑⏑⏑) a. ⚭ unclarified, unrefined, not purified; raw (spirits, &c.); ⸗geld F (⏑⏑) n ⓒc. (o. pl.): a) immense sum (F no end, awful lot) of money; b) prov. (Steuer) tax, auf Nahrungsmittel ꝛc.: duty, accise; ⸗geleckt (⏑⏑⏑) a. ⚭ unlicked; fig. Der Bär (ungehobelter Menſch) unpolished fellow, F unlicked cub, regular bear; ⸗gelegen (⏑⏑⏑) a. ⚭ inopportune, inconvenient, out of place; ill-timed, unseasonable; adv. at the wrong time or season; das kommt mir recht ⸗ it comes at a very inconvenient (or awkward) time, I find it very awkward; ⸗heit f ㊻ inopportuneness, inconvenience; unseasonableness; (Unannehmlichkeit) trouble, unpleasantness, annoyance; e-m (große) ⸗en bereiten to give a p. (a great deal of) trouble; ſich ⸗en machen to put o.s. to much inconvenience; ⸗gelegt (⏑⏑⏑) a. ⚭ unlaid (a. von Eiern); fig. ⸗e Eier undecided matters, ill-matured plans pl. (vgl. Ei 2); ⸗gelehrig (⏑⏑⏑⏑) a. ⚭ unteachable, indocile, (ſchwer von Begriff) slow (of comprehension); ⸗keit f ㊻ unteachableness, indocility, slowness; ⸗gelehrt (⏑⏑⏑) a. ⚭ unlearned, ſtärker: unlettered, illiterate, untaught, unschooled. (unwiſſend) ignorant; ⸗heit f ㊻ want of learning, illiteracy; ignorance; ⸗geleimt (⏑⏑⏑) a. ⚭ unglued, v. Papier: unsized; ⸗gelenk(ig) (⏑⏑⏑(⏑)) a. ⚭ not supple, not pliant (enough), (ſteif) stiff; fig. (linkiſch, ungeſchickt) awkward, clumsy; ⸗gelenkigkeit (⏑⏑⏑(⏑)⸗) f want of suppleness or pliancy, stiffness; awkwardness, clumsiness; ⸗geleſen (⏑⏑⏑) a. ⚭ unread; ⸗gelöſcht (⏑⏑⏑) a. ⚭ unquenched; ⸗er Kalk unslaked lime (vgl. a. Kalk); ⸗gelöſt (⏑⏑⏑) a. ⚭ unsolved; eine noch ⸗e Frage a question yet to be solved or settled; ⸗gelüftet (⏑⏑⏑⏑) a. ⚭ unaired; ⸗gemach (⏑⏑) n ⓒc. discomfort; (Entbehrung) privation; (Mühſal) trouble, hardship, toil, fatigue; (Trübſal) affliction, adversity, das von ihm erduldete ⸗ the hardships endured by him; ſich dem ⸗ der Witterung ausſetzen to face the inclemency of the weather; ⸗gemächlich (⏑⏑⏑⏑) a. ⚭ uncomfortable, inconvenient, unpleasant; (mühſelig) toilsome, troublesome; ⸗keit f ㊻ uncomfortableness, discomfort, inconvenience; ⸗gemein (⏑⏑⏑, ⏑⏑⏑) a ⚭ uncommon, rare; (außergewöhnlich) extraordinary; (erſtaunlich) wonderful; oft als adv. e-n hohen Grad bezeichnend: ⸗ flach exceedingly (or singularly, marvellously, F uncommonly) flat; ⸗ groß enormous, ⸗ bewegt, gerührt deeply (or profoundly) moved, touched; ⸗ viel plenty of, F no end of; ⸗gemeldet (⏑⏑⏑⏑) a. ⚭ unreported; (unangemeldet) unannounced; ⸗gemengt (⏑⏑⏑) a. ⚭ = ⸗gemiſcht; ⸗gemeſſen (⏑⏑⏑) a. ⚭ unmeasured; (unbeſchränkt) unlimited; (unermeßlich) immense, boundless, infinite; (kein Maß haltend) immoderate, excessive; ins ⸗e geh(e)n to come to an immense amount; ⸗gemiſcht (⏑⏑⏑) a. ⚭ unmixed, unmingled, von Metallen ꝛc.: unalloyed; (rein) pure; ⸗gemünzt (⏑⏑⏑) a. ⚭ uncoined; ⸗es Gold, Silber gold, silver in bars; bullion; ⸗gemuſtert ⊙ (⏑⏑⏑⏑) a. ⚭ von Zeugen: unfigured, plain; ⸗gemütlich (⏑⏑⏑⏑) a. ⚭ von Orten u. Dingen: comfortless, cheerless, uncomfortable; von Perſonen: unsociable, uncompanionable, ſtärker: disagreeable; ⸗keit f ㊻ comfortlessness, discomfort; unsociableness; ⸗genannt (⏑⏑⏑) a. ⚭ unnamed, anonymous; (ohne Namen) nameless; ⸗genau (⏑⏑⏑) a. ⚭ inexact, inaccurate, (unrichtig) incorrect; ⸗ (adv.) paſſend fitting loosely; ⸗heit, bſſ. ⸗igkeit f ㊻ inaccuracy; ⸗geneigt (⏑⏑⏑) a. ⚭: e-m ⸗ disaffected (or ill-disposed, unfriendly) towards a p.; (mit wenig Hang zu et.) disinclined (or unwilling, not disposed) to do a th., having no inclination for a th.; ⸗heit (⏑⏑⏑⸗) f ㊻ disaffection (or ill-will) towards a p.; disinclination (or unwillingness) to do a th.; ⸗geniert (⏑G⏑⏑) a. ⚭ unceremonious, free and easy (vgl. ⸗gezwungen); ⸗heit f ㊻ unceremoniousness, free and easy way; ⸗genießbar (⏑⏑⏑⏑) a. ⚭ unfit to eat or to drink, unfit for consumption; uneatable, undrinkable; (unſchmackhaft) unpalatable, nasty; weitS. (ſchal) stale, insipid; F von Perſonen oft: = ⸗ausſtehlich; ⸗keit f ㊻ unpalatableness; weitS. staleness, unpleasantness; ⸗genötigt (⏑⏑⏑⏑) a. ⚭ uncompelled, unconstrained, adv. without being forced, without compulsion; ⸗genügend (⏑⏑⏑⏑) a. ⚭ insufficient, (knapp) scanty; ⚓ ⸸ bemannt undermanned; ⸗genügſam (⏑⏑⏑⏑) a. ⚭ not easily satisfied, (unerſättlich) insatiable, greedy; (habſüchtig) grasping; ⸗keit f ㊻ insatiability, greed(iness); grasping spirit; ⸗genützt (⏑⏑⏑) a. ⚭ = benutzt; ⸗geöffnet (⏑⏑⏑⏑) a. ⚭ unopened; ⸗geordnet (⏑⏑⏑⏑) a. ⚭ unarranged, unregulated; without order, in disorder;

♪ Muſik; ⚛ Wiſſenſchaft; ⚘ Pflanze; ⚭ Geographie; ⊙ Technik; ⚒ Bergbau; ⚔ Militär; ⚓ Marine; ⚖ Handel; ✉ Poſt; ⛢ Eiſenbahn.

[ungepaart] — [ungetadelt]

²gepaart (⁓⌣¹) a. ⓰ unpaired, von Vögeln ꝛc.: unmated; ²gepflegt (⁓⌣¹, ⁓¹) a. ⓰ untended, uncared for, neglected; ²gepflügt (⁓⌣¹) a. ⓰ unploughed; ²geprägt (⁓⌣¹) a. ⓰ = ²gemünzt; ²geprüft (⁓⌣¹) a. ⓰ not examined, (unerprobt) untried, untested; (nicht revidiert) unaudited; ²er Lehrer uncertificated teacher; ²geputzt (⁓⌣¹) a. ⓰ unclean(sed). von Lampen: untrimmed, von Stiefeln: not cleaned, unpolished, von Personen: unadorned, plainly dressed; ²gerächt (⁓¹) a. ⓰ unavenged, seltener: unresented; et. ² lassen to take no revenge for a th., to leave a th. (or to let a th. go) unpunished; ²gerade (⁓⌣) a. ⓰ not straight, uneven (surface, &c.); arith. a. ²gerad-zählig (⁓⌣,¹) a. ⓰ (durch 2 nicht ohne Rest teilbar) odd (number); ²geraten (⁓⌣¹) a. ⓰ (ungestalt) misshapen; (ohne Erfolg) miscarried, unsuccessful; bsd. von Kindern: ill-bred, spoilt, mischievous, unruly, troublesome; (nicht erraten) not guessed, unsolved; ²gerechnet (⁓⌣¹) a. ⓰ uncounted, (nicht einbegriffen) not included; adv. without counting or including or taking into account; die Reisekosten ² not reckoning (or apart from) the travelling expenses; ²gerecht (⁓¹) a. ⓰ unjust, unfair; ²gerechtfertigt (⁓⌣⌣¹) a. ⓰ unjustified, unwarranted; ²gerechtigkeit (⁓⌣⌣¹) f ⓭ injustice, unfairness; eine ~ begehen to commit an (act of) injustice, to act unfairly; ²geregelt (⁓⌣¹) a. ⓰ not (or ill-) regulated; ein ²es Leben führen to lead a disorderly (or an irregular) life; ²gereimt (⁓¹) a. ⓰ pros. rhymeless; ²e Verse pl. blank verse; fig. (unstimmig) absurd, preposterous; ²es Zeug reden to talk nonsense or rubbish; ~heit (⁓¹-) f ⓭ pros. rhymelessnes; fig. absurdity.

un-gern (⁓¹) adv. (s. gern; comp. ⌕ ²er) unwillingly, reluctantly. against one's inclination; er sieht es ² he does not like (or he is sorry, stärker: he is grieved) to see it; gern oder ² whether willing or not, seltener: willy-nilly.

un-gerochen (⁓⌣⌣¹) a. ob. poet. = ²gerächt; ²gerufen (⁓⌣¹) a. ⓰ uncalled, unbidden, adv. without being called; ²gerügt (⁓¹) a. ⓰ uncensured, unreproved, unblamed; ich kann nicht ² lassen, daß // I cannot omit censuring that //; ²gerührt (⁓¹) a. ⓰ fig. (ohne Rührung) unmoved, untouched, unaffected; ²gerupft (⁓¹) a. ⓰ unplucked; fig. ² davonkommen to get off without being robbed or fleeced, to come off scot-free; ²gerüstet (⁓⌣¹) a. ⓰ unprepared; ²gesagt (⁓¹) a. ⓰ unsaid; ² lassen to leave unmentioned, not to utter (a word of); das will ich ² (sein) lassen I won't speak of it or mention it; ²gesalzen (⁓⌣¹) a. ⓰ unsalted, von Fischen ꝛc. auch: fresh; fig. insipid, dull; ²e Witze pointless (or stale) jokes pl.; ²gesattelt (⁓⌣¹) a. ⓰ unsaddled; auf ²em Pferde reiten to ride (a horse) bare-backed or without a saddle; ²gesättigt (⁓⌣¹) a. ⓰ unsat(iat)ed, mehr gbr.: not satisfied;

chm. not saturated; ²e (alkalische) Salze basic (or alkaline) salts pl.; ²gesäubert (⁓⌣¹) a. ⓰ unclean(sed); ²gesäuert (⁓⌣¹) a. ⓰ von Broten: unleavened, ⚕ azymous; ²gesäumt (⁓¹) a. ⓰ (ohne Saum) unhemmed; (ohne Säumen) immediate, adv. oft: without delay or hesitation, at once, there and then, forthwith; er soll ² kommen he shall come immediately or this minute; ²geschaffen (⁓⌣¹) a. ⓰ uncreated; ²geschält (⁓¹) a. ⓰ unpeeled; ²geschehen (⁓⌣¹) a. ⓰ undone; ² machen to undo; man kann das nicht ² m. that cannot be undone; ²gescheut (⁓¹) adv. (ohne Scheu) without fear, fearlessly, undauntedly, boldly; ²geschichtlich (⁓⌣¹) a. unhistorical, not based on history, without historical foundation; ²geschick¹ n ⓓc. (o. pl.) lack of skill, awkwardness, clumsiness; F m (ungeschickte Person) awkward person, F clumsy Jack; Sprichw. s. ²geschickt; ²geschicklichkeit (⁓⌣⌣¹) f ⓭ körperliche: clumsiness, geistige: incapacity, ineptitude, (Unerfahrenheit) inexperience; ²geschickt (⁓⌣¹) a. ⓰ awkward, clumsy (auch von Dingen); nur von Personen: unskilled, unskilful, geistig: without ability or capacity for a th.; ²er Mensch clumsy fellow, bungler; er hat's ² (adv.) angefangen he has gone the wrong way to work; Sprichw. ² (auch Ungeschick) läßt grüßen! you are (or I am) clumsy!, iro. how clever you are or I am!; ~heit f ⓭ unskilfulness; vgl. Ungeschick; ²geschlacht (⁓⌣¹) [ahd.] a. ⓰ (rauh, roh) uncouth, rude, rough, coarse, clownish, boorish, (ungesittet) uncivilized, barbarous, (täppisch) clumsy; ~heit f ⓭ uncouthness, rudeness, coarseness, clownishness; clumsiness; ²geschliffen (⁓⌣¹) a. ⓰ von Messern: not sharpened, blunt; (nicht poliert) unpolished; v. Edelsteinen: uncut, rough; fig. (unhöflich) uncivil, impolite, (grob) rude, rustic; ~heit f ⓭ want of polish; incivility, impoliteness, rudeness; ²geschmälert (⁓⌣¹) a. ⓰ undiminished, unimpaired, unabated, uncurtailed; (ganz) whole; ²geschmeidig (⁓⌣¹) a. ⓰ not supple, not pliant, inflexible; fig. auch: unaccommodating, unyielding; ~keit f ⓭ want of suppleness or pliancy; inflexibility, unaccommodating (or unyielding) nature or spirit; ²geschminkt (⁓⌣¹) a. ⓰ unpainted, not painted, not rouged; fig. unvarnished (account), unadorned (truth), plain (facts); ²geschmückt (⁓¹) a. ⓰ unadorned, without ornament(s), plain, bare; ²geschoren a. ⓰ (⁓⌣¹) unshorn, unshaven; ²er Sam(me)t uncut velvet; (⁓⌣¹) fig. unmolested; laßt mich ²! let me alone!, don't bother (or worry) me!; ²geschult (⁓¹) a. ⓰ unschooled; ²geschützt (⁓¹) a. ⓰ unprotected, unshielded, gegen Wind und Wetter: unsheltered, without shelter; uncovered; ²geschwächt (⁓¹) a. ⓰ unweakened; ²e Tatkraft unimpaired (or unabated) energy; ⚕ mit ²en

Mitteln with undiminished resources or means, without reduction of capital; ²geschwänzt (⁓⌣¹) a. ⓰ tailless, without a tail, ⚕ acaudal, acaudate; ²geschworen (⁓⌣¹) a. ⓰ unsworn; ich glaube es dir ² I take your plain word for it, I readily believe what you say; ²gesehen (⁓⌣¹) a. ⓰ unseen, unnoticed; et. ² kaufen to buy a pig in a poke; ²gesellig (⁓⌣¹) a. ⓰ unsociable, uncompanionable, auch: shy, retired; ~keit f ⓭ unsociableness, shyness; ²gesetzlich (⁓⌣¹) a. ⓰ unlawful, illegal, illicit; auch: irregular (proceeding); ~keit f ⓭ unlawfulness, illegality; ²gesetzmäßig (⁓⌣⌣¹) a. ⓰ contrary to law, auch = ²gesetzlich; ²gesittet (⁓⌣¹) a. ⓰ unmannerly, rude, unpolished, ill-bred, boorish, weitS. uncivilized, ~heit f ⓭ rudeness, ill-breeding, weitS. lack of culture; ²gesondert (⁓⌣¹) a. ⓰ not separate(d), not severed; vgl. ²getrennt; ²gesprächig (⁓⌣¹), a. ²et (⁓⌣¹) a. ⓰ taciturn, silent; ²gestalt (⁓¹) a. ⓰ deformed, ill-shaped, misshapen; ~(et)heit (⁓⌣(⌣)¹-) f ⓭ deformity, bad shape or figure, misshapenness; ²gestärkt (⁓¹) a. ⓰ not strengthened; von der Wäsche ꝛc.: unstarched; ²gestempelt (⁓⌣¹) a. ⓰ unstamped; ²gestielt (⁓¹) a. ⓰ ⚕ stalkless, stemless, ⚕ acaulous, von Blättern: sessile; von Hammer ꝛc.: without a handle; ²gestillt (⁓¹) a. ⓰ unstilled (pain, &c.), unappeased (hunger, &c.), unslaked or unquenched (thirst), unstanched (blood); ²gestört (⁓¹) a. ⓰ undisturbed, untroubled, peaceable; (ruhig, glatt) unruffled, smooth, calm, (ununterbrochen) uninterrupted; einen ²en Fortgang nehmen to proceed smoothly; die Vorstellung ging ² (adv.) voran the performance went on without a hitch; ~heit f ⓭ undisturbed (or peaceable, calm) state, tranquillity; ²gestraft (⁓¹) a. ⓰ unpunished, adv. with impunity; s. hingehen; ~heit f ⓭ impunity; ²gestüm (⁓¹) [ahd.: stumm] a. ⓰ impetuous, boisterous, turbulent, (heftig) violent, furious, vom Wetter ꝛc. auch: blustering, stormy; (tobend) tumultuous, (hitzig) hot-headed; ~ m u. n ⓓd. impetuosity, boisterousness, turbulence, violence; ~ des Sturmes fury of the gale; ~ des Wetters stress of weather; mit ~ impetuously, boisterously; ²gesucht (⁓⌣cht) a. ⓰ unsought (for); fig. unaffected, artless, not studied, (natürlich) natural, simple; ~heit f ⓭ unaffectedness, artlessness, simplicity; ²gesund (⁓⌣) a. ⓰ unhealthy, sickly, nur von Menschen: in ill (or in a poor state of) health; von Stoffen, Verhältnissen ꝛc.: unsound; (der Gesundheit schädlich) injurious (or detrimental) to health, von der Luft, von Orten ꝛc.: unwholesome, unhealthy, insalubrious, insanitary; Sprichw. s. allzuviel; ~heit (⁓⌣-) f ⓭ unhealthiness, sickliness, ill health; unsoundness; unwholesomeness, insalubrity; ²getadelt (⁓⌣¹) a. ⓰ un-

---

Signs (see page XVII): F familiar; P vulgar; F̸ flash; ⌕ rare; † obsolete (died); * new word (born); ++ incorrect; ♪ music;

[ungetan] — 1007 — [Unglücksmensch]

blamed, unreproved, uncensured; ⸗getan (⸗⸗) a. ⓖ undone; et. 2 lassen to leave a th. undone or unperformed; ⸗getauft (⸗⸗) a. ⓖ unchristened, unbaptized. F vom Weine ꝛc.: undiluted; ⸗geteilt (⸗⸗) a. ⓖ undivided, (ganz) entire; (einfach) simple; (einstimmig) unanimous; ~heit f ⓖ undividedness; ⸗getrennt (⸗⸗) a. ⓖ unseparated, unsevered; (ungeschieden) unparted; ⸗getreu (⸗⸗) a. ⓖ unfaithful (vgl. 2treu); ⸗getröstet (⸗⸗) a. ⓖ uncomforted, disconsolate; ⸗getrübt (⸗⸗) a. ⓖ untroubled, undimmed, clear, von Metall ꝛc.: untarnished; (wolkenlos) unclouded, cloudless; 2es Glück serene (or perfect) happiness; ~heit f ⓖ untroubled state; cloudlessness; serenity; ⸗getüm (⸗⸗) [nhd. zu ⸗tum] n ⓓd. monster, monstrous creature, prodigy; 2(lich) a. ⓖ monstrous; ⸗geübt (⸗⸗) a. ⓖ unpractised, unexercised; untrained, undrilled (a. ⚔); 2e Arbeiter inexperienced (F green) hands pl.; ⚔ 2e Rekruten raw recruits pl.; ~heit f ⓖ want of practice or exercise; inexperience; ⸗gewandt (⸗⸗) a. ⓖ unskilled, unskilful; ~heit f ⓖ lack of skill, unskilfulness; ⸗gewarnt (⸗⸗) a. ⓖ unwarned; ⸗gewaschen (⸗⸗) a. ⓖ unwashed; (schmutzig) dirty, unclean; ⓞ 2e Wolle wool in the grease or in the yolk; (⸗⸗) fig. (lästerlich) abusive; ein 2es Maul a foul (or slanderous) tongue; (unsinnig) absurd; 2es Zeug reden to talk rubbish or stuff and nonsense; ⸗geweiht (⸗⸗) a. ⓖ unconsecrated; ⸗gewiegt (⸗⸗) a. ⓖ: ich werde 2 schlafen I shall sleep without being rocked; ⸗gewiß (⸗⸗) [ahd.] a. ⓖ uncertain; (zweifelhaft) doubtful, dubious, (unbestimmt) undecided, vague, (unsicher) precarious; (noch fraglich) questionable, problematic(al); (gewagt) hazardous; aufs ungewisse at random, on speculation; im ungewissen bleiben, lassen to leave in uncertainty or in the dark; sich ins Ungewisse wagen to take a leap in the dark, to plunge (wildly); ⸗gewißheit (⸗⸗-) f ⓖ uncertainty, doubt(fulness), precariousness; e-n in ~ lassen to keep a p. in suspense; in ~ sein to be (kept) in suspense; in angstvoller ~ in terrible (or anxious, agonizing) suspense, on the rack, on tenter-hooks; ⸗gewitter (⸗⸗⸗) [mhd.] n ⓶ (violent) storm, thunderstorm (vgl. Gewitter); ⸗gewöhnlich (⸗⸗⸗) a. ⓖ uncommon, unusual, stärker: extraordinary, singular, strange; (neu) novel; (ungebräuchlich) unaccustomed, unwonted; in Heiratsanzeigen: auf diesem nicht mehr 2en Wege in this no longer unusual manner, in this now customary way; 2 (adv.) rauhes Wetter uncommonly (or exceptionally) rough weather; ~heit f ⓖ uncommonness, unusualness, singularity, strangeness; novelty; ⸗gewohnt (⸗⸗) a. ⓖ von Personen: unaccustomed to, unused to; v. Dingen: unwonted, unusual; ~heit f

strangeness, novelty; ⸗gewürzt (⸗⸗) a. ⓖ unseasoned; ⸗gezählt (⸗⸗) a. ⓖ uncounted, unnumbered, untold; (zahllos) numberless, countless; (in Bausch und Bogen) in the lump; ⸗gezähmt (⸗⸗) a. ⓖ untamed, fig. auch: uncurbed (spirit), unbridled (passion); ⸗gezäumt (⸗⸗) a. ⓖ unbridled; ⸗gezeichnet (⸗⸗) a. ⓖ unmarked; ⸗geziefer (⸗⸗) [mhd.: Zifer] n ⓶ vermin, weitS. noxious insects or animals pl.; voll ~ verminous, full of vermin; ⸗geziemend (⸗⸗) a. ⓖ unseemly, unbecoming, stärker: improper, indecent, insolent; (frech) impudent, saucy, F cheeky; ⸗gezogen (⸗⸗⸗) a. ⓖ vulg. ill-bred, unmannerly, ill-mannered, rude, bsd. von Kindern: naughty; vgl. ⸗geziemend; ⓞ von Gewehren: unrifled; ~heit (⸗⸗⸗-) f ⓖ ill-breeding, unmannerliness, rudeness, naughtiness, impudence, als Handlung: rude action, in Worten: insolent expression, impertinence; ⸗gezügelt (⸗⸗⸗) a. ⓖ unbridled; ⸗gezwungen (⸗⸗⸗) a. ⓖ unconstrained, not forced; voluntary; et. 2 tun to do a th. spontaneously or of one's own free will; (natürlich) unaffected, natural, vom Benehmen, Stil ꝛc.: easy (and unaffected), graceful; ~heit (⸗⸗⸗-) f ⓖ unconstraint; unaffectedness, ease, gracefulness; ⸗giftig ꝛc. f. ⸗gültig ꝛc.; ⸗glaube (⸗⸗) m ⓶ incredulity; =glaubig (⸗⸗) a. ⓖ meist rel. unbelieving. weitS. irreligion, impiety; ⸗gläubig (⸗⸗) a. ⓖ incredulous, disbelieving; meist rel. unbelieving, weitS. irreligious, impious; (nicht christlich) infidel; (an allem zweifelnd) sceptical; s. Thomas; ~e(r) s. unbeliever; infidel; sceptic; ~keit f ⓖ = ⸗glaube, auch: sceptism; ⸗glaublich (⸗⸗) a. ⓖ incredible, beyond (or past all) belief; 2 (adv.) stark stronger than one would believe or credit, marvellously strong; es geht ins, grenzt ans ~e it is almost incredible, one would hardly believe (or credit) it; ~keit f ⓖ incredibility; ⸗glaub-würdig (⸗⸗⸗) a. ⓖ unworthy of belief or credit; untrustworthy (source, person, &c.), unreliable (witness, news, &c.); (nicht beglaubigt) unauthenticated (document, &c.); ~keit f untrustworthiness; ⸗gleich (⸗⸗) a. ⓖ unequal, (verschieden) different from, (unähnlich) unlike, dissimilar; (unverhältnismäßig) disproportionate, out of proportion with, inconsistent with; (uneben) uneven; (schwankend) varying, vacillating, wavering, vom Wetter ꝛc.: changeable, med. v. Puls oft: irregular, ⚕ intercurrent; von 2er Gemütsart of an unequal (or a changeable, fickle, whimsical) temper(ament); ⧫ von 2er Güte varying (or not uniform) in quality; adv. vor comp. (bei weitem) (by) far; (unvergleichlich) incomparably; 2 schöner much (or a great deal) handsomer, far more beautiful. un-gleich-artig (⸗⸗⸗) a. ⓖ dissimilar, different, ⚛ heterogeneous; (nicht zusagend) uncongenial; =artigkeit f hetero-

geneousness; ⸗farbig a. variegated, ⚛ heterochromous; ⸗fiederig ♃ a.: ⚛ imparipinnate; ⸗förmig a. not uniform, unequal, ⚛ difform; (ohne Symmetrie) unsymmetrical; (unregelmäßig) irregular; ⸗förmigkeit f want of uniformity or symmetry; irregularity. Un-gleichheit (⸗⸗) f ⓖ (s. ungleich) inequality; unlikeness, dissimilarity, disparity; disproportion; unevenness, variation, changeableness, irregularity. un-gleich-mäßig (⸗⸗...) a. ⓖ unsymmetrical, disproportionate; ⸗mäßigkeit f ⓶ want of symmetry (= ⸗förmigkeit); a. disproportion; ⸗namig a. of different names, ⚛ heteronymous; math. v. Brüchen: of different denominations; phys. 2e Pole unlike (or opposite) poles pl.; ⸗seitig a. with (or of) unequal sides; math. 2es Dreieck ⚛ scalene triangle; ⸗silbig a. gr.: ⚛ imparisyllabic; ⸗teilig a. chm.: ⚛ anisomeric; zo., ♃, chm.: ⚛ heteromerous. Un-glimpf (⸗⸗) m ⓶b. ungentle (or unfair) dealing; (Härte) harshness, (Beschimpfung) insult, affront, (Unrecht) injury, wrong; 2lich (⸗⸗) a. ⓖ ungentle, unfair; harsh; insulting; e-n 2lich behandeln to deal harshly with (F to be hard on) a p. Un-glück (⸗⸗) n ⓦc. (pl. ⸗, dafür oft: ~s-fälle) misfortune, mischance, mishap, im Spiele ꝛc.: ill (or b..) luck, fortgesetztes: run of ill luck; vgl. Mißgeschick; (Unfall) accident (a. 🚂); (schwerer Unglücksfall) calamity, disaster, F hard luck, hard lines pl.; (Schicksalsschlag) reverse; (Elend) distress; zum ~ unfortunately, unluckily; (schweres) ~ h. to be (very) unlucky; von schwerem ~ heimgesucht visited by grave misfortunes, F hard hit; Sprichw. kein ~ so groß, es ist ein Glück dabei it's an ill wind that blows nobody any good, there is a silver lining to every (dark) cloud; ein ~ kommt selten allein it never rains but it pours. un-glücklich (⸗⸗) a. ⓖ unfortunate, unlucky, stärker: disastrous or ill-fated or ill-starred (enterprise, &c.); (elend) miserable, wretched; 2e Ehe unhappy marriage, 2 (adv.) enden to end in disaster; to fail, F to turn out a failure; sich 2 fühlen to feel unhappy or wretched or miserable; 2 lieben to be crossed in love; 2 spielen to be unlucky (at play, at cards, &c.); 2erweise adv. unfortunately, unluckily, through ill luck, by mischance. Un-glücks-bote (⸗⸗...) m ⓶ bearer of ill tidings; ⸗botschaft f evil (or ill) tidings pl.; (schlimme Nachricht) bad news. un-glückselig (⸗⸗) a. ⓖ unfortunate, bsd. von Personen: (most) unhappy or wretched or miserable, nur v. Dingen: disastrous, calamitous; ~keit f ⓖ unhappiness, wretchedness, misery. Un-glücks-fall (⸗⸗...) m ⓶ stroke of ill luck, misfortune, disaster; (Unfall) accident, casualty; ⸗gefährte, ⸗genoß m fellow-sufferer, companion in misfortune; ⸗jahr n disastrous year; ⸗kind n, ⸗mensch m unfortunate person,

[Unglücksprophet] — 1008 — [Unkenntnis]

F unlucky wight or chap, auch: child of sorrow; =prophet(in f) m prophet(ess f) of evil; =rabe m, etwa: evil-boding raven, F croaker; =stunde f, =tag m fatal (or ill-starred) hour, day; =vogel m: a) bird of ill omen; b) F person who brings ill luck (to others); vgl. =rabe; =zeichen n evil omen, ehm.: prodigy.

Un=gnade (ˊ‿ˊ‿) f ⑱ disgrace; (Ungunst) disfavour; bei e-m in ~ fallen, sich j-s ~ zuziehen to incur a p.'s displeasure, to fall into disgrace with a p., to incur a p.'s displeasure, F to get into a p.'s bad books; s. a. Gnade 2; 2gnädig (ˊ‿ˊ‿) a. ⑯ ungracious; weitS. (übellaunig) ill-humoured, out of temper (auf e-n with a p.); Der Bescheid unfavourable reply; et. 2 (adv.) aufnehmen to take a th. amiss, to take offence at a th.; 2göttlich (ˊ‿‿) a. ⑯ not divine, not of God('s essence or nature); ungodlike, unlike (or unworthy of) a god(dess); 2grammatisch (‿‿‿) a. ungrammatic, contrary to (the rules of) grammar; =grund ⸗ (ˊ‿) m ⓒc. fig. = Grundlosigkeit b; 2gründlich (ˊ‿‿) a. ⑯ without foundation; (oberflächlich) superficial, shallow; adv. (only) on the surface; ~keit (ˊ‿‿) f ⑯ superficiality, shallowness; 2gültig (ˊ‿‿) a. ⑯ invalid, (null and) void; von Fahrkarten ꝛc.: not available; von Münzen: not current; base, bad; Tennis: let; bsd. jur. für 2 erklären, 2 machen to invalidate, to annul, abolish, rescind, cancel; pol. eine Wahl für 2 erklären to declare an election void; durch Verjährung 2 werden to fall into desuetude; ⊛ ein Versicherungsschein wird durch falsche Angaben 2 (gemacht) a policy is voided by false statements; ~keit (ˊ‿‿) f ⑯ invalidity, nullity; v. Fahrkarten ꝛc.: unavailableness; bsd. jur. =keits=erklärung f invalidation, nullification; Klage auf =keits=erklärung der Ehe nullity suit; ~=machen n invalidation; ~werden n nullification, extinction; =gunst (ˊ‿) f ⑩ (s. Gunst) disfavour, des Wetters: inclemency; bei e-m in ~ stehen, etwa: to be in a p.'s black books; zu=ungunsten von // to the disadvantage (or detriment) of //; der Prozeß fiel zu f-n ~en aus the lawsuit was decided in his disfavour or went against him; das spricht zu seinen ~en that tells against him, it does not speak (or it's not) in his favour; 2günstig (ˊ‿‿) a., ⑯ unfavourable (news, &c.), unpropitious or inauspicious (sign, &c.); disadvantageous (bargain, &c.), contrary (wind); im 2sten Falle in the worst case, if the worst comes to the worst; e-m 2 sein to be ill-disposed or unfavourably inclined towards a p.; 2gut (ˊ‿) a. ⑯: (nicht) für 2 (übel) nehmen to take amiss (in good part); nehmen Sie es nicht für 2, wenn // don't think it unkind if //; nichts für 2! no offence!, I mean(t) no harm!, no harm (was) meant!, 2gütig (ˊ‿‿) a. ⑯ unkind; etwas 2 (adv.) aufnehmen to take a th. in an unfriendly (or in a wrong) spirit; 2haltbar (ˊ‿‿)

a. ⑯ not durable, not lasting, not solid; flimsy; von Versprechungen ꝛc.: incapable of fulfilment or performance, von Gründen ꝛc.: untenable; ~keit (ˊ‿‿) f ⑯ want of durability or solidity; untenableness; 2har=monisch (ˊ‿‿) a. bsd. ♪ unharmonious, stärker: discordant, harsh.

Un=heil (ˊ‿) n ⓒc. evil, harm, trouble.
un=heilbar (ˊ‿‿) a. ⑯ incurable, past recovery or remedy; von Dingen auch: irreparable, irremediable; ~keit f ⑯ incurableness; irreparableness.
unheil=bringend (ˊ‿...) a. ⑯ fatal, pernicious (für e-n to a p.); 2drohend a. ill-boding, ominous, portentous.
un=heilig (ˊ‿‿) a. ⑯ unholy, unhallowed, (ungeweiht) unconsecrated, profane; (weltlich) worldly; (gottlos) ungodly, impious; ~keit f ⑯ unholiness, profanity; impiousness.
unheil=schwanger (ˊ‿...) a. ⑯ fraught with disaster, big with ruin; =stifter m ⑫ mischief-maker; 2verkündend a. portentous, ominous; 2voll a. = =bringend, a. disastrous, unfortunate, unlucky, calamitous, baneful.
un=heimlich (ˊ‿‿) a. ⑯ dismal (place, &c.), sinister (look, &c.), gruesome or weird (affair, &c.); ihm wurde 2 zumute he began to feel uneasy or alarmed; F 2 (adv.) viel Menschen an immense number of people, a tremendous crush or crowd; 2heizbar (ˊ‿‿) a. ⑯ that cannot be heated; 2höflich (ˊ‿‿) a. ⑯ uncivil, impolite, discourteous; (unfreundlich) disobliging, von Worten, Reden ꝛc.: uncomplimentary, rude, disrespectful; ~keit f ⑯ uncivility, impoliteness, discourtesy; disobliging way, rudeness; 2hold (ˊ‿) a. ⑯ ungraceful; (ungnädig, unfreundlich) ungracious, unkind, without affection for; (übelwollend) ill disposed towards, hostile to; ~(in f ㊸) m ⓒc. (häßliches Geschöpf) ill-favoured person, stärker: monster; (bösswillige Person) mischievous person, stärker: fiend, dragon; (Dämon) demon, evil spirit; f (Hexe) witch, hag, scorceress; 2hörbar (ˊ‿‿) a. ⑯ inaudible; ~keit f ⑯ inaudibleness.
unieren (‿ˊ‿) [neu=lt.] v/a. ⑬ (vereinigen) to unite; to make one, to bring together; uniert p. p. united; Unierte m/pl. ⑰ members pl. of the Union.
Uniform (‿ˊ‿) [lt.] f ㊻ bsd. ⚔ (Dienstkleidung) uniform; in voller ~ in full uniform or regimentals, F co. in full fig; in kleiner (oder Interims=)~ in undress; nicht in ~ in plain (or in civilian's) clothes, ⚔ in mufti.
uniformieren (‿‿ˊ‿) [lt.] v/a. ⑬ 1. mst ⚔ to dress (or put) in uniform(s), weitS. to clothe (uniformly). — 2. (einheitlich m.) to render (or make) uniform.
Uniformierung (‿‿ˊ‿) f ⑯ 1. (das Uniformieren) mst ⚔ dressing in (or supply of) uniforms. — 2. uniforms pl. worn by soldiers, &c.
Uniformität (‿‿‿ˊ) [lt.] f ㊻ (Gleichförmigkeit) uniformity, evenness.
Unikum (ˊ‿‿) [lt. einziges] n ⓼ ⓿ unique thing; Buchhandel: single (or only) copy of a book.

un=interessant (ˊ‿‿‿) a. ⑯ uninteresting, devoid of interest; 2interessiert (ˊ‿‿‿) a. ⑯ not interested; (uneigennützig) disinterested; ~heit f ⑯ lack of interest; disinterestedness.
Union (‿ˊ) [lt.] f ㊻ (Vereinigung, Bund) union; ~ist (‿‿ˊ) m ⑫ unionist; v. s. Unionist; 2istisch a. unionist.
unisono ♪ (‿ˊ‿, a. ‿‿ˊ‿) [it.] adv. (einstimmig) in unison.
Unitari=er (‿‿ˊ(‿)‿) [neu=lt.] m ⑫ rel. (i. der Gott als eine Person anbetet; ant. Trinitarier) Unitarian.
universal (‿‿‿ˊ) [lt.] a. ⑯ (allgemein) universal; ~erbe (ˊ...) m ⑫, ~erbin f sole heir (f heiress), jur. a. residuary legatee; ~genie F n all-round man; ~geschichte f universal history; ~ität (‿‿‿‿ˊ) [lt.] f ⑯ universality; ~mittel n universal remedy, panacea; ~schrauben=schlüssel ⊛ m universal screw-wrench.
universell (‿‿‿ˊ) a. ⑯ = universal.
Universität (‿‿‿‿ˊ) [lt.] f ㊻ (Hochschule) university; die ~ Oxford Oxford University, the University of Oxford; die ~ beziehen to go to the university or to college; auf der ~ sein to pursue a course of university=studies, in England meist: to be at college, to keep one's terms; vgl. beziehen 1; er hat(te) eben die ~ verlassen he is (was) fresh from college.
Universitäts=diener (‿‿‿‿ˊ...) m ⑫ in England: proctor's man or servant or F bulldog; =druckerei f University Press; =freund m college-friend, fellow-student or =collegian; =gebäude n university(-building), college-building; =leben n university-life, in England: college-life; =lehrer m lecturer (in the university), in Engl. auch: college-tutor, F don; =professor m university professor; =richter m etwa: university judge, in England: proctor; =studien n/pl. university studies pl., reading at college; =unterricht m, =wesen n university (or collegiate, higher) teaching; =zeit f time (or years pl.) spent at the university, in Engl. college-years pl. [universe.]
Universum (‿‿ˊ‿) [lt.] n ⑳ (Weltall) un=jagdbar (ˊ‿‿) a. ⑯ hunt. not fit for the hunt, unfit for the chase; 2kanonisch (‿ˊ‿‿) a. eccl. (nicht als Richtschnur dienend) uncanonical; 2kauf=männisch (‿ˊ‿‿) a. ⑯ uncommercial, unbusinesslike.
Unke (ˊ‿) [ahd. lautm.] f ㊻: a) zo. orange-speckled toad (Bombina'tor i'gneus); F fig. voll wie eine ~ (as) drunk as a fiddler or a lord; b) fig. = Stuben=hocker. [toads.]
Unken=gesang (ˊ‿‿‿) m ⑫ croaking of un=kennbar (ˊ‿‿), 2kenntlich (ˊ‿‿) a. ⑯ unrecognizable, indiscernible; f-e Handschrift, Stimme ꝛc. 2 m. to disguise ...; ~keit f ⑯ indiscernibleness, durch Verhüllung ꝛc.: disguise, durch Entstellung: disfigurement; bis zur ~ entstellt past recognition; =kenntnis (ˊ‿‿) f ⑱ unacquaintance with, ignorance of; e-n in ~ erhalten über // to keep a p. in the dark about //.

Zeichen (s. S. XVII): F familiär; P Volkssprache; ſ Gaunersprache; ⸲ selten; † alt (auch gestorben); * neu (auch geboren); ⁎ unrichtig;

[Unkenruf] — 1009 — [unmusikalisch]

Unken=ruf (⁵⌣⁻¹) m ㊷ *fig.* croaking.
un=keusch (⁸¹) *a.* ㊿ unchaste, impure; lewd, lascivious; ² leben to lead an impure life; ~heit *f* ㊻ unchastity, impurity; lewdness, lasciviousness; ²kindlich (⁸⌣⌣) *a.* ㊿ unchildlike, gegen die Eltern: unfilial, undutiful; (widerspenstig) froward, wayward; (frühreif) precocious. forward; ~keit *f* ㊻ unchildlike nature. unfilial conduct, undutifulness, frowardness; precociousness, precocity. forwardness; ²kirchlich (⁸⌣⌣) *a.* ㊿ not ecclesiastical, unclerical. stärker: anticlerical. (weltlich) worldly, secular; ~keit *f* ㊻ anticlerical tendency; worldliness; ²klar (⁸¹) *a.* ㊿: a) not clear; (trübe) vom Wasser ꝛc.: turbid, muddy, in geh. Spr.: troubled; (nebelig) misty, hazy, foggy; (undeutlich) dim, indistinct, vague, confused; (unverständlich) unintelligible, F muddled; (dunkel) dark, obscure, von der Schreibart: abstruse; im ²en sein über et. to be in the dark (or in uncertainty, F in a fog) about a th.; b) ⚓ von Tauen ꝛc.: unclear, foul; ²er Anker anchor which has fouled; ² laufen von to run foul of; ~heit *f* ㊻ want of clearness; haziness; indistinctness, vagueness, confusion; darkness (or obscurity) of meaning, abstruseness of style; ²klug (⁸¹) *a.* ㊿ injudicious, imprudent; (nicht schlau) impolitic; (töricht) unwise, foolish, stupid; das war ² (*adv.*) gehandelt that was acting unwisely or rashly, it was a piece of folly; ~heit *f* ㊻ imprudence; unwisdom, foolishness; als Handlung: piece of folly, stupid (or foolish) act(ion); ²kollegial(isch) *a.* unlike (or unworthy of) a colleague; ²königlich (⁸¹⌣⌣) *a.* ㊿ unkingly, unkinglike; antiroyal; ²konstitutionell (⌣⌣—tẛ⌣)⁻⁵) *a.* ㊿ unconstitutional; ²kontrollierbar (⌣⌣⌣⁻) *a.* ㊿ uncontrollable; ²körperlich (⁸⌣⌣) *a.* ㊿ incorporeal, immaterial, (körperlos) bodiless; ~keit *f* ㊻ incorporeality, immateriality; =kosten [nhd.] (⁸⌣) *pl. inv.* cost(s *pl.*) (vgl. Kosten); e-n in große ~ stürzen to put a p. to great expense; sich in ~ stürzen to go to great expense; ❋ nach Abzug aller ~ (all) charges paid, deducting expenses; ²kräftig (⁸⌣⌣) *a.* ㊿ infirm, feeble, von Speisen: not strengthening; low (diet) ꝛc.; (unwirksam) ineffectual (remedy. &c.); =kraut (⁸¹) [ahd.] *n* ②c. weed. *coll.* weeds *pl.*; bibl. *bibl.* ~ unter den Weizen säen to sow tares among the wheat. *fig.* von Personen: useless person, ne'er-do-well; Sprichw. ~ vergeht nicht ill weeds grow apace; ²kriegerisch (⁸¹⌣⌣) *a.* ㊿ unwarlike; ²kultiviert (⌣⌣—w¹) *a.* ㊿ uncultivated. von Menschen auch: uncultured, uncivilized, unpolished, unmannerly, uncouth; =kultur (⁸⌣¹) *f* ㊻ want of culture or civilization; ²kündbar ❋ (⁵⁵—) *a.* ㊿ unredeemable, consolidated; ~keit *f* ㊻ unredeemableness; =kunde (⁸⌣⌣) *f* ㊸ lack of knowledge (vgl. Unkenntnis); ²kundig (⁸⌣⌣) *a.* ㊿: einer Sache (*gen.*) ² unacquainted (or not conversant) with a th., ignorant of a th.; er ist des Deutschen ² he is not acquainted with (or he knows no, he has no knowledge of) German; des Weges ² not knowing one's way; ²künstlerisch (⁸⌣⌣⌣) *a.* ㊿ inartistic; =land (⁸⌣) *n* ②c. *agr.* untilled land; ²längst (⁸⁵) [mhd.] *adv.* lately, of late, not long ago; (neulich) recently, (only) the other day; ²lauter (⁸¹⌣) *a.* ㊿ (D 9) impure, unclean; sordid, mean; (unedel) ignoble; (eigennützig) interested; ²er Wettbewerb unfair competition; ~keit *f* ㊻ impurity; meanness; interestedness; ²leidlich (⁸⌣¹) *a.* ㊿ insufferable, intolerable; er ist ihr ² she cannot bear him, F she can't bear the sight of him; ~keit *f* ㊻ intolerableness; ²lenkbar, ²lenksam (⁸⁵—) *a.* ㊿ ungovernable, unmanageable, unruly, intractable; ~keit *f* ㊻ unruliness, intractableness; ²lesbar (⁸⁵—) *a.* ㊿ illegible, stärker: undecipherable; ~keit *f* ㊻ illegibility; ²leugbar (⁵⁻¹) *a.* ㊿ undeniable; (unbestreitbar) incontestable. indisputable; (offenbar) obvious, evident, manifest; ~keit *f* ㊻ undeniableness, obviousness; ²lieb (⁸¹) *a.* ㊿ unpleasant, displeasing; fast nur als Prädikat: es ist mir ², das zu hören I am not at all pleased (or I am sorry or loath) to hear it; ²liebenswürdig (⁸¹⌣⌣) *a.* ㊿ unamiable, unkind; ²lieblich (⁸⌣⌣) *a.* ㊿ unpleasing, unlovely. vom Geschmack: unsavoury; ²liebsam (⁸¹⌣) *a.* ㊿ unpleasant, disagreeable; ~keit *f* ㊻ unpleasantness; ²löblich (⁸⌣⌣) *a.* ㊿ not praiseworthy, deserving no praise; ²logisch (⁸¹⌣) *a.* ㊿ *phls.* illogical; ²lösbar (⁸¹⁻). ²löslich (⁸⌣⌣) *a.* ㊿ in(dis)soluble, in(dis-)solvable. von Aufgaben auch: not admitting (of) solution, von Knoten: inextricable; ~keit *f* ㊻ in(dis)solubility; ²löschbar (⁸⁵—) *a.* ㊿ inextinguishable, unquenchable; =lust (⁸⁵) *f* ⑩ displeasure, (Unbehagen) discomfort; (Abneigung) disinclination, dislike; (Überdruß) disgust, aversion, repugnance; ~ zum Essen want of appetite; ²lustig (⁸⌣⌣) *a.* ㊿ cheerless, sad, dreary; (grämlich) morose; (abgeneigt) disinclined, reluctant; (Unlust erregend) not pleasurable, displeasing; ²malerisch (⁸⌣⌣) *a.* ㊿ not picturesque; ²manierlich (⁸⌣⌣) *a.* ㊿ unmannerly, ill-behaved, uncouth; ~keit *f* unmannerliness, ill behaviour; ²männlich (⁸⌣⌣) *a.* ㊿ unmanly; (weibisch) effeminate; ~keit *f* ㊻ unmanliness, effeminacy; =masse (⁸⌣⌣) *f* ㊸ vast quantity, immense number; eine ~ Geld F no end of (auch: heaps, piles, loads *pl.*) of money; ²maßgeblich (⁸¹¹⌣⌣) *a.* ㊿ unauthoritative; open to correction; *adv.* oft: with due deference, without presumption, with diffidence; nach m-r ²en Meinung in my humble opinion; ²mäßig (⁸⌣¹) *a.* ㊿ immoderate, im Trinken ꝛc.: intemperate; (übertrieben) excessive, (ausschweifend) dissolute, licentious, extravagant; ~keit *f* ㊻ immoderation, intemperance; extravagance; ²melodisch (⁸⌣¹⌣) *a.* ㊿ unmelodious; =menge (⁸⌣) *f* ㊸ immense number or quantity; =mensch (⁸⁵) *m* ㊷ inhuman being, brutal (or ferocious) person, monster, fiend, savage; F co. ich will kein ~ sein I won't refuse, I won't be unsociable; ²menschlich (⁸⌣⌣) *a.* ㊿ inhuman, brutal, ferocious, savage; barbarous, atrocious; (übermenschlich) superhuman; ²e (gewaltige) Kraft prodigious (or mighty, gigantic, enormous) strength; verstärkend: F sich ² (sehr) freuen to be immensely delighted; ~keit *f* ㊻ inhumanity, brutality, als Tat: inhuman (or savage) deed, atrocious (or fiendish) act, atrocity; ²merkbar (⁸⁵—), ²merklich (⁸⌣⌣) *a.* ㊿ imperceptible, not noticeable; unobservable; ~keit *f* ㊻ imperceptibleness; ²meßbar (⁸⁵—) *a.* ㊿ immeasurable, *bib. math.* incommensurable; ~keit *f* ㊻ immeasurableness, incommensurableness; ²methodisch (⁸⌣¹⌣) *a.* ㊿ unmethodical, without method; ²militärisch (⁸⌣¹⌣⌣) *a.* ㊿ unmilitary, unsoldierlike; ²mitteilbar (⁸⁵—) *a.* ㊿ incommunicable; unfit for publication; ²mitteilsam (⁸¹—) *a.* ㊿ incommunicative. reserved; (schweigsam) taciturn, close; ~keit *f* ㊻ incommunicativeness, reserve; taciturnity, closeness; ²mittelbar (⁸⌣⌣—) *a.* ㊿ immediate: direct; ²er Grund direct (or proximate) cause; *hist.* ²e Reichsstände *pl.* immediate States of the Empire; ² nach meiner Abreise immediately (or directly) after my departure; ² vor ihr Ankunft just before (or only a moment previous to) his arrival; ~keit *f* ㊻ immediateness; directness; ²möbliert (⁸⁻¹) *a.* ㊿ unfurnished; ²modern (⁸⌣⌣), ²modisch (⁸⌣⌣) *a.* ㊿ unfashionable, old-fashioned, out of date; ²möglich (⁸⌣⌣, ⁸¹⌣) *a.* ㊿ impossible (of performance), *adv.* mst: not possibly; ganz oder schlechterdings, rein (F platterdings) ² quite out of the question; fast ² next to (or well-nigh) impossible; ich kann es ² tun I cannot possibly do it; das läßt sich ² tun, erreichen that cannot (possibly) be done; it is unfeasible, unattainable; ~es leisten to do impossible (or wonderful) things; sich in der guten Gesellschaft ² m. to lose caste; Sprichw. ~es kann man von niemand verlangen we must not expect impossibilities; ~keit *f* ㊻ impossibility; das wäre eine (oder ein Ding der) ~keit that would be a matter of impossibility or an impossible matter or thing; ²monarchisch (⁸⌣⌣) *a.* ㊿ not monarchical, contrary to monarchy or to the monarchical principle; ²moralisch (⁸⌣¹⌣) *a.* ㊿ immoral; ²motiviert (⁸⁻w¹) *a.* ㊿ without (any) motive, not founded on any motive; ²mündig (⁸⌣⌣) *a.* ㊿ *jur.* under age, not of age; ²er *s.* minor; ²es Kind child of tender age, (young) infant or babe; ~keit *f* (⁸⌣⌣—) *f* ㊻ *jur.* minority; tender age, infancy; ²musikalisch (⁸—⌣¹⌣) *a.* ㊿ unmusical (sound, &c.), von Personen: not musical,

without a taste (or an ear) for music; =mut (˘⊥) 2c. m Ꮯc. f. Mißmut 2c.; 2mütterlich (˘⊥˘˘) a. ⊛ unmotherly; 2nach-ahmbar (˘-˘⊥˘), 2nach-ahmlich (˘-˘⊥˘) a. ⊛ inimitable; ~keit f ⊛ inimitability; 2nachgiebig (˘⊥˘˘) a. ⊛ unyielding, unaccommodating, unbending, uncompromising, inflexible; (unerbittlich) unrelenting; ~keit f ⊛ unyieldingness, inflexibility; 2nachsichtig, 2nachsichtlich (˘-˘˘) a. ⊛ without indulgence; unrelenting, pitiless; (streng) strict, stern, severe, hard, harsh; 2nahbar (˘⊥˘) a. ⊛ unapproachable; ~keit f ⊛ unapproachableness, inaccessibility; haughty reserve; ~natur a. ⊛ unnaturalness, anomaly, stärker: monstrosity; 2natürlich (˘⊥˘˘) a. ⊛ unnatural, contrary to (the laws of) nature, anomalous; (scheußlich) monstrous; (geziert) affected, (gezwungen) forced; ~keit f ⊛ unnaturalness, monstrousness; affectation; 2nennbar (˘⊥˘) a. ⊛ not to be named, unutterable, unmentionable; 2nötig (˘⊥˘), ˘⊥˘) a. ⊛ unnecessary, needless; (überflüssig) superfluous (vgl. unnütz); 2er-weise adv. unnecessarily, needlessly, (all) for nothing; 2nütz (˘˘) a. ⊛ useless, unprofitable, good for nothing; of no use to; F u. P no good to; v. Kindern: = 2artig; bibl. den Namen des Herrn 2(lich) (im Munde) führen to take the name of the Lord in vain; 2es Geschwätz idle talk, twaddle; 2es Zeug trash, rubbish; sich 2 m. to make o.s. obnoxious, to be too forward; e-m 2e Worte m. to abuse a p.; 2nützlich † (˘⊥˘) a. ⊛ = 2nütz; 2ordentlich (˘⊥˘˘) a. ⊛ von Personen 2c.: disorderly, untidy, careless, negligent; vom Lebenswandel 2c.: irregular, loose, fast; von Orten u. Dingen a.: without order, confused, muddled; vom Anzuge 2c.: slovenly; ⚔ 2e Flucht headlong flight, rout; 2 umherliegen to lie littered about or F higgledy-piggledy, to litter up the place; ~keit f ⊛ disorderliness, untidiness, want of order; irregularity; slovenliness; =ordnung (˘˘˘) f ⊛ disorder; (Verwirrung) confusion, tumult, muddle, F mess; irregularity; wilde ~ anarchy, ⚔ rout; in ~, oft: at sixes and sevens; in ~ bringen to throw into disorder or confusion, to put out of order; to disarrange, embroil, disturb, das Haar 2c.: to tangle, eine Maschine: to throw out of gear; in ~ geraten, kommen to be thrown into disorder or confusion, to get out of order; in ~ sein to be in a muddle, von e-r Stube 2c.: to be (all) upset or in a litter or F in a mess; 2organisch (˘⊥˘˘) a. ⊛ inorganic; 2orthographisch (˘˘˘⊥˘) a. ⊛ not orthographical, wrongly spelt, misspelt; 2 (adv.) schreiben to make spelling mistakes (in writing), to spell badly; 2paar (˘⊥) a. ⊛ = 2gerade; 2ig (˘˘) (nicht gepaart) not paired, not one of a pair, von einzelnen Handschuhen 2c.: odd; anat. von Muskeln, Adern 2c.: ⚔ azygous; ⚔ 2 gefiedert: ⚔ imparipinnate; ~igkeit (˘˘˘) f ⊛ oddness;

bisw.: imparity; =paar-zeher ⚔ m ⚔ zo. perissodactyl; 2parlamentarisch (˘˘˘˘⊥˘) a. ⊛ unparliamentary; 2partei-isch (˘˘⊥˘) a. ⊛ impartial, unbiassed (opinion), evenhanded (justice); (unbeteiligt, unbefangen) disinterested, unprejudiced, unwarped (judgment); 2 (adv.) behandeln to deal fairly with; ~(e)r) m ⚔ = Schiedsrichter; =parteilichkeit f ⊛ impartiality; disinterestedness; fairness, fair play; 2paß (˘˘) a. prädikativ = 2päßlich; 2passend (˘˘˘) a. ⊛ unfit; (ungeeignet) unsuitable; (unschicklich) inconvenient, improper, unseemly; (schlecht angebracht) misplaced, out of place, odd, (ungelegen) inopportune; (unzeitig) unseasonable, untimely; sie benahm sich sehr 2 (adv.) she behaved in an unbecoming (or unladylike) way; 2passierbar (˘˘⊥˘) a. ⊛ impassable, unfit to cross, von Flüssen auch: unfordable; 2päßlich (˘˘) a. ⊛ indisposed, unwell, ailing, poorly F out of sorts; ~keit (˘˘-) f ⊛ indisposition, poor; (state of) health, (slight) ailment; 2patriotisch (˘˘⊥˘) a. ⊛ unpatriotic; 2persönlich (˘⊥˘) a. ⊛ gr. und phls. impersonal; ~keit f ⊛ impersonality; 2philosophisch (˘˘⊥˘˘) a. ⊛ unphilosophical, unlike a philosopher; 2po-etisch (˘˘⊥˘) a. ⊛ unpoetical; 2politisch (˘⊥˘) a. ⊛ unpolitical; (unklug) impolitic, undiplomatical; 2populär (˘˘⊥) a. ⊛ unpopular; =popularität (˘˘˘˘⊥) f ⊛ unpopularity; 2praktisch (˘˘˘) a. ⊛ not practical; (nicht ausführbar) impracticable, unfeasible, unworkable; 2produktiv (˘˘⊥) a. ⊛ unproductive; ~ität (˘˘-˘⊥) f ⊛ unproductiveness; 2proportioniert (˘˘-˘˘(˘)˘⊥) a. ⊛ disproportionate; 2pünktlich (˘˘˘) a. ⊛ unpunctual; irregular; ~keit f ⊛ unpunctuality; irregularity; 2qualifizierbar (˘-˘˘⊥-) a. ⊛ unqualifiable; 2rasiert (˘˘⊥) a. ⊛ unshaven, adv. without having shaved (o.s.); =rast (˘˘) f ⊛ (Ruhelosigkeit) restlessness; m ⚔a. (ruheloses Kind) restless (or fidgety) child; =rat (˘⊥) [ahd.] m ⚔c. (ohne pl.) dirt, rubbish, F muck, mess; (Abfälle) refuse, garbage, vom Schlachthause: offal; (Kehricht) sweepings pl.; (Müll) dust; (Kot) human excrements pl.; fig. ~ merken oder wittern to notice s.th. wrong or awry, to get wind of s.th. amiss; to smell a rat; 2rationell (˘˘˘(˘)˘⊥) a. ⊛ (nicht der Vernunft gemäß) irrational; =rat-kehrer m ⚔ scavenger; 2rätlich (˘⊥˘), 2ratsam (˘⊥˘) a. ⊛ inadvisable; (unzeitig) inopportune, inexpedient; 2recht (˘˘) a. ⊛ not right, wrong; (ungerecht) unjust, unfair, (unrichtig) incorrect; (ungeeignet) improper; f. ankommen 3; et. 2 (adv.) auslegen to misinterpret a th., to misconstrue a th.; er hat 2 daran getan it was wrong of him (to do it); in 2e (ob. in die Zen) Hände fallen to fall into the wrong hands, to be delivered to the wrong address; in die 2e Kehle kommen to go (down) the wrong way; 2e Seite v. Tuch 2c. wrong side; zur 2en Zeit at the

wrong time or season, out of season; Sprichw. f. gedeihen 1; der, die ~e the wrong (wo)man; f. geraten 2 unter „an"; an den ~en kommen to come to the wrong man, F to get into the wrong box, to catch a Tartar; ~ n ⚔b. wrong, injustice, jur. tort; (Schädigung) injury, prejudice; mit, zu ~wrong(ful)ly, unjustly; ein ~ begeh(e)n to commit an injustice; es ist ihm 2 (ob. ein ~) geschehen he has been wronged, he has suffered an injustice; 2 haben, 2 (ob. im ~) sein to be wrong. stärker: to be in the wrong; e-m 2 geben to disagree with a p.; e-m 2 tun to do a p. wrong or an injustice, to wrong a p.; Sprichw. besser 2 leiden als 2 tun better suffer ill than do ill; 2rechtlich (˘˘˘) a. ⊛ wrongful, unjust, rel. unrighteous; (ungesetzlich) unlawful; ~keit f ⊛ wrong, wrongfulness, injustice, unrighteousness; unlawfulness; 2rechtmäßig (˘˘˘⊥˘) a. ⊛ unlawful, illegal; illegitimate (heir, &c.); (er Besitz usurpation; 2er Besitzer usurper; 2er-weise adv. unlawfully; ~keit f ⊛ unlawfulness, illegality; illegitimacy; 2redlich (˘˘˘) a. ⊛ dishonest, dishonourable, unfair; underhand; ~keit f ⊛ dishonesty, improbity; (Handlung) unfair dealing; 2re-ell ⚔ (˘-˘) a. ⊛ (unzuverlässig) unsound, unreliable, F shady; 2regelmäßig (˘⊥˘˘˘) a. ⊛ irregular; (v. Gewöhnlichen abweichend) out of the common, abnormal, anomalous; jur. informal; 2 (adv.) leben to lead an irregular life; ⚔ mit 2er Blüte: ⚔ anomaliflorous; mit 2 stehenden Blättern: ⚔ anomophyllous; ~keit f ⊛ irregularity, anomaly; 2reif (˘⊥) a. ⊛ unripe, von Früchten auch: green; fig. immature, abortive; ill-considered or crude (scheme, &c.); raw (youth, &c.); =reife (˘⊥˘) f ⊛, =reifheit (˘⊥-) f ⊛ unripeness; fig. immaturity, crudeness, crudity; rawness; 2rein (˘⊥) a. ⊛ unclean; impure (a. sittlich), vitiated (air, &c.), tainted (atmosphere, &c.), muddy (water, &c.), foul (abode, &c.); 2er Diamant, Edelstein flawy (or clouded) diamond, gem; 2er Stil incorrect (or inelegant) style; ♪ 2er Ton discord; typ. 2 (gedruckt) rough(ly printed); ich habe es erst im ~en (ins ~e) geschrieben I have made a rough copy of it, I jotted it down; =reinheit (˘⊥-) f ⊛ uncleanness; impure (or vitiated) state, impurity, foulness; =reinigkeit (˘⊥-) f ⊛ = Unreinheit; (etwas Unreines) s.th. unclean; (Schmutz) dirt, filth, (Müll) dust; 2reinlich (˘⊥˘) a. ⊛ uncleanly; dirty, filthy; ~keit f ⊛ uncleanliness; 2rentabel ⚔ a. ⊛ not paying, unremunerative (business, &c.); 2republikanisch (˘-˘˘⊥˘) a. ⊛ not republican, anti-republican; 2rettbar (˘⊥-) a. ⊛ past saving or praying for, beyond help or recovery; 2 verloren irretrievably lost, irrecoverable, von Menschen: ruined, in a hopeless condition; ~keit f ⊛ irrecoverableness, hopeless state; 2richtig (˘⊥˘) a. ⊛ not right, wrong, incorrect; (irrig)

Signs (see page XVII): F familiar; P vulgar; F flash; ⟍ rare; † obsolete (died); * new word (born); ⁺⁺ incorrect; ♪ music;

erroneous; (falsch) false, v. Maß u. Gewicht: unjust; (fehlerhaft) faulty, (ungenau) inaccurate; die Uhr geht ≈ ... does not keep correct time, F does not go right; ≈richtiger=weise adv. erroneously, by mistake, mistakenly; ~keit f ⑯ incorrectness; error; fault(iness), inaccuracy; ≈ritterlich (⌣⌣⌣) a. unknightly, unchivalrous; ~keit f ⑯ unchivalrous conduct or action.

Un-ruh (⌣¹) f ⑯ Uhrm.: (das die Bewegung regelnde Schwungrad) balance (of a watch or clock); ~=deckel ⊕ (⌣¹⌣⌣) m ⑫ balance-lid.

Un-ruhe (⌣¹⌣) f ⑱ 1. unrest, restlessness, disquiet(ude); (Bewegung) commotion; (Gemütsbewegung) emotion, (Aufregung) agitation, excitement, nervöse: fidgetiness; (Besorgnis) alarm, anxiety, uneasiness, (Verlegenheit) trouble, embarrassment; (Störung der öffentlichen Ruhe) disturbance; (Auflauf) riot; in großer ~ sein to be very anxious or ill at ease. — 2. F (rastlose Person) restless p., fidgety fellow, F fidget.

un-ruhig (⌣¹⌣) a. ⑯ (s. Unruhe 1) restless, disquieted; in commotion; excited, fidgety; alarmed, uneasy (über about); troubled, disturbed, (lärmsüchtig) turbulent, riotous; ≈es Pferd restive horse; ⌄ ≈e See rough sea, heavy swell; ≈e Zeiten stirring (or unsettled) times pl.; eine ≈ (adv.) verbrachte Nacht a restless night.

un-rühmlich (⌣¹⌣) a. ⑯ inglorious; ~keit f ⑯ ingloriousness.

Un-ruh-scheibe ⊕ (⌣¹...) f ⑫ Uhrm.: balance-ring; =stifter m one who stirs up trouble, disturber of the peace, agitator; ≈voll a. ⑯ restless, unsettled; full of trouble, troublous (times, &c.).

un-rund (⌣¹) a. ⑯: not round, not true; ≈e Räder wheels pl. out of centre.

uns (⌣) [ahd.: us: lt. nos] dat. u. acc. pl. von ich: to us, us; ein Freund von ≈ a friend of ours; geben Sie ≈ eine Flasche Wein give us a bottle of wine; er gehört zu ≈ he is one of our party or of us; grüße ihn von ≈! remember us to him!; zurückbezüglich: wir retten ≈ (selbst) we save ourselves; wir freuen ≈ we rejoice; unter ≈ between ourselves; wir sehen ≈ (einander) nie we never see each other; wir trafen ≈ we met.

un-sagbar (⌣¹⌣), ≈säglich (⌣¹⌣) [ahd.] a. ⑯ unspeakable, ineffable, unutterable; ≈sanft (⌣¹) a. ⑯ not soft, ungentle; harsh (words. &c.), rough (treatment,&c.); ≈sauber (⌣¹⌣), =sauberkeit = unrein, Unreinheit; ≈säuberlich (⌣¹⌣) a. ⑯ unclean, uncleanly; adv. ≈ (hart) mit e-m verfahren to deal roughly (or harshly) with a p.; ≈schabhaft (⌣¹⌣) a.⑯ undamaged, uninjured, intact;ingood condition,sound,whole; ≈schädlich (⌣¹⌣) a. ⑯ uninjurious, harmless, innocent, innocuous (plant, &c.); ≈ m. to render harmless; to neutralize (a poison, &c.); ~keit f ⑯ harmlessness; ≈schädlich-machung f ⑯ rendering a th. harmless or innocuous; neutralization; ≈schätzbar (⌣¹⌣) a. ⑯ inestimable, invaluable,

priceless; ~keit f ⑯ inestimableness; ≈scheinbar (⌣¹⌣) a. ⑯ insignificant (-looking); (schlicht) unpretending, plain, homely; (nicht grell) subdued; (glanzlos) dull; ≈ w. to grow dull, to tarnish; ~keit f ⑯ insignificance; plainness, homeliness; lack of lustre; ≈schicklich (⌣¹⌣) a. ⑯ = ≈anständig a; ~keit f ⑯ = ≈anständigkeit a; ≈schiffbar (⌣¹⌣) a. ⑯ not navigable; =schlitt (⌣¹) [ahd.] n (⌣ m) ⑯c. (Talg) tallow, suet; (Fett) grease; =kerze f tallow candle; ≈schlüssig (⌣¹⌣) a. ⑯ irresolute, undecided; (schwankend) vacillating, wavering, (zaudernd) hesitating; (verlegen) embarrassed, perplexed, puzzled; ~keit f ⑯ irresolution; vacillation, hesitation; embarrassment; ≈schmackhaft (⌣¹⌣) a. ⑯ unsavoury, unpalatable, (schal) stale, flat, tasteless, insipid; ~igkeit f ⑯ unsavouriness, unpalatableness, staleness, tastelessness, insipidity; ≈schmelzbar (⌣¹⌣) a.⑯ unfit to (s)melt, chm. &c. infusible, incapable of fusion; ~keit f ⑯ infusibility; ≈schmiedbar ⊕ (⌣¹⌣) a. ⑯ not forgeable, not malleable, unfit for forging; ~keit f ⑯; ≈schön (⌣¹) a. ⑯ not beautiful, unhandsome, unlovely; plain, ugly, homely; fig. not handsome, not fair; ≈ (adv.) handeln to act unfairly, to do a mean thing; =schuld (⌣¹) f ⑯ innocence; (Reinheit) purity (of heart, of mind); (Keuschheit) chastity; ursp. bibl. ich wasche meine Hände in ~ I wash my hands of it; er sagte das in aller ~ (des Herzens) ... quite innocently, without any design; F co. (unschuldige Person) innocent (or unsophisticated) person; die Kleine ~ the innocent little girl; s. Land 3; ≈schuldig (⌣¹⌣) a. ⑯ innocent, (ohne Schuld) guiltless, blameless; (harmlos) harmless, inoffensive, (rein) pure; (ohne Falsch) candid, ingenuous; (jungfräulich) virgin; für ≈ erklären to declare innocent, to acquit; ≈er-weise adv. innocently, in an innocent way, not (or without) meaning any harm; ≈schuldsvoll a. ⑯ innocent; ≈schwer (⌣¹) a. ⑯ meist als Prädikat od. adv. not difficult, easy; et. ≈ erraten to guess a th. without difficulty, to have no difficulty in guessing a th.; =segen (⌣¹⌣) m ㉓ lack of prosperity, ill success, adversity, misfortune, failure, stärker: (Fluch) curse; er hat nichts als ~ he has (or gets) nothing but disappointments or ill luck; ≈selbständig (⌣¹⌣⌣) a. ⑯ dependent (on others), unable to do (or to act) for o.s.; fig. irresolute, leaning on others; ~keit f ⑯ dependence (on others); ≈selig (⌣¹⌣) [mhd.] a. ⑯ unblessed, unhappy, unfortunate, (verhängnisvoll) fatal, tragical; dieser ≈e Hang this accursed propensity, ~keit f ⑯ fatality; accursedness.

unser (⌣⌣)[ahd.;*uns] I pers. pron. (gen.v. wir pl.) ⑯ C, D9 of us; erbarme dich ≈ (++ ≈er) take pity (feierlich: have mercy) upon us; es waren ≈ (++ ≈er) vier there were four of us. — II a. u. possessive

pron. m u. n, uns(e)re f u. pl. our; Vater ≈ (od. ~ Vater) Our Father; prädikativ: der Hund, das Pferd ist ≈ ... ours. — III possessive pron.: a) uns(e)rer, uns(e)re, uns(e)res ⑯ A2; b) mit dem def. art. der (die, das) Uns(e)re oder Uns(e)rige ⑯ ours; die Uns(e)r(ig)[e]n our people or party; das Uns(e)r(ig)e our own; our share; our duty.

unser-einer ⑯ A2, ≈eins inv. (⌣¹(⌣)) one of our sort, one of us, such as we. uns(e)rer-seits (⌣(⌣)⌣) adv. on our side, on (or for) our part, as for (or as to) ourselves.

unser(e)s-gleichen (⌣⌣(⌣)⌣) pron. inv. people like us, F (people of) our sort. uns(e)res-teils (⌣(⌣)⌣¹) adv. = uns(e)rerseits. uns(e)rig (⌣¹(⌣)) s. unser III. [seits.] uns(e)r-seits (⌣⌣⌣¹) adv. = uns(e)rerseits. unsers-gleichen (⌣⌣⌣⌣⌣)f.uns(e)resgleichen. unsert-halben (⌣⌣...), ≈wegen, (um) ≈willen adv. for our sakes, on our behalf, because (or on account) of us, for (the sake of) us.

un-sicher (⌣¹⌣) a.⑯ (D9) unsafe, insecure (vgl. ungewiß); das Leben ist ≈ life is uncertain; ≈es Dasein precarious existence, ≈es Gedächtnis weak (or treacherous) memory; mit ≈er Hand with an unsteady (or a shaky) hand; die Landstraßen ≈ m. to infest the roads; F co. er macht die Gegend ≈ he haunts (F is all over) the place; ~keit f ⑯ unsafeness, insecurity, uncertainty, precariousness; ≈sichtbar (⌣¹⌣) a. ⑯ invisible, imperceptible, F co. ≈ w., sich ≈ m. to vanish, to make o.s. scarce; phys. ≈e Wärmestrahlen obscure (or dark) rays pl.; das ≈e the invisible (world); ≈er-weise adv. without being seen; ~keit f ⑯ invisibility; ≈sichtig (⌣¹⌣) a. ⑯ v. der Luft: (trüb) hazy; ≈singbar (⌣¹⌣) a. ⑯ unsingable; =sinn (⌣¹) [mhd.] m ⑯c. nonsense, (Unverstand) unreasonableness, (Ungereimtheit) absurdity, F bosh, trash, (Narrheit) folly, madness; das ist barer ~ that's stuff and nonsense, it's a pack of rubbish; ~ reden to talk nonsense or twaddle; ~ treiben to indulge in jokes or F larks; to play the fool; ≈sinnig (⌣¹⌣) a. ⑯ nonsensical; unreasonable, irrational, absurd; foolish, mad, insane; eine ≈e Mode a senseless (or mad) fashion; ≈ (adv.) verliebt sein in // to be madly in love with //; ~keit f ⑯ irrationality, absurdity, foolishness; als Handlung: foolish (or irrational) doing, absurd action, vgl. Unsinn; ≈sinnlich (⌣¹⌣) a. ⑯ not sensual, not material, phls. auch: transcendental; =sitte (⌣¹⌣) f ⑯ bad (or mischievous, wicked) habit or custom; (Mißbrauch) abuse; ≈sittlich (⌣¹⌣) a. ⑯ immoral; (ohne feste Grundsätze) unprincipled, licentious; (ohne Scham und Anstand) indecent; ~keit f ⑯ immorality; indecency; als Handlung: immoral (or indecent) act(ion); ≈soldatisch ⚔ (⌣¹⌣⌣) a. ⑯ unsoldierlike; ≈solid (⌣¹⌣) a. ⑯ not solid, fig. vom Charakter: loose, dissipated; ≈es Haus: a) ⚙ unreliable (or F shaky, shady) firm; b) F

⚙ scientific; ♄ botanical; ⊕ geography; ⊕ machinery; ⚒ mining; ⚔ military; ⚓ marine; ⚙ commercial; ✉ postal; 🚂 railway.

[unsorgfältig] *fig.* fast (or loose, rackety) fellow; ≎sorgfältig (߸߸߸), ≎sorgsam (߸߸-) *a.* ⑯ careless, F non-carish.

unsre (߸߸) f. unser.

unsrer≠seits f. unsererseits.

unsres=gleichen, ≎teils f. unser(e)s=[gleichen.]

unsrige f. unser III. [statesmanlike.]

un=staatsmännisch (߸߸߸) *a.* ⑯ un-

un=statthaft (߸߸߸) *a.* ⑯ not (to be) allowed, inadmissible; (verboten) forbidden, prohibited, illicit, unlawful; (nicht ausreichend) insufficient; (ungeeignet) unsuitable, ~igkeit *f* ⑯ inadmissibleness; illicitness; insufficiency; unsuitableness; ≎sterblich (߸߸߸) *a.* ⑯ immortal; ≎ machen to immortalize; F *co.* sich ≎ (*adv.*) blamieren to make o.s. awfully ridiculous; ~keit*f* ⑯ immortality; =stern (߸߸) *m* ⑪*c.* unlucky star; (Unglück) disaster; adversity; (Mißgeschick) misfortune, ill luck; seinem ~ erliegen to succumb to an adverse fate; es waltet ein ~ über ihm fate is (dead) against him, *auch:* he was born under an unlucky star; ≎stet (߸߸) *a.* ⑯ unsteady, (rastlos) restless, (wandelbar) fickle, unstable, inconstant; (umherirrend) unsettled, roving, wandering; ≎ (*adv.*) umherschweifen to wander aimlessly about, to have no fixed abode; (nicht fest) not firm, F shaky, wobbling; mit ≎em Blick a) with a furtive glance; b) with a vacant look; (wechselvoll, oft unterbrochen) fitful, intermittent; ≎stetig (߸߸߸) *a.* ⑯ = ≎stet; *math.* ≎e Größe discrete quantity or value; ~keit *f* ⑯ unsteadiness, restlessness, fickleness, instability, inconstancy; unsettled state; aimlessness; ≎stillbar (߸߸߸-) *a.* ⑯ that cannot be stilled; unappeasable, unquenchable; ≎störbar (߸߸-) *a.* ⑯ undisturbable, imperturbable; fixed; ≎sträflich (߸߸߸) *a.*⑯undeserving of punishment; (nicht schuldig) not culpable, inculpable; (untadelhaft) irreproachable, (unbescholten) blameless; ~keit *f* ⑯ inculpableness, irreproachableness; blamelessness; ≎streitig (߸߸߸) *a.* ⑯ incontestable, indisputable, *adv. oft:* unquestionably, without doubt, undoubtedly; ≎studiert (߸߸߸) *a.* ⑯ *v.* Dingen, Handlungen: unstudied; (aus dem Stegreif) extemporaneous; (unbeabsichtigt) unpremeditated, (ungekünstelt, natürlich) unaffected, natural; von Personen: unlearned, unread, unlettered, uneducated, stärker: illiterate; ≎sühnbar (߸߸߸) *a.* ⑯ unatonable, inexpiable; (unverföhnlich) irreconcilable; =summe (߸߸߸) *f* ㊸ immense sum, enormous amount, F awful lot of money, &c.; ≎symmetrisch (߸߸߸߸) *a.* ⑯ (ungleichmäßig) unsymmetrical; ≎systematisch *a.* ⑯ (*u. adv.*) unsystematic(-ally); ≎tadelhaft (߸߸߸߸)*a.*⑯irreproachable, blameless, unimpeachable, irreprehensible, faultless; ~igkeit *f* ⑯ irreproachableness; blamelessness; ≎tad(e)lig (߸߸߸߸) *a.* ⑯ = ≎tadelhaft; =tat (߸߸) *f* ㊻ misdeed, atrocious (or monstrous) crime; ≎tätig (߸߸߸) *a.* ⑯ inactive, (müßig) idle, indolent, (unbeschäftigt) unemployed, out of work or em-

ployment; ~keit*f*⑯inaction, inactivity; idleness, indolence; want (or lack) of employment; (Muße) leisure; ≎tauglich (߸߸߸) *a.* ⑯ unfit(ted), unsuitable, unserviceable (für for); useless, F (of) no use (für to); ※ *u.* ⚓ zum Dienste disabled, ⚓ von Schiffen: inefficient, unseaworthy; ⚓ *m.* to disqualify, to incapacitate; ※*u.*⚓ die (zum Dienst) ~en inefficients *pl.*; ~keit *f* ⑯ unfitness, unsuitableness; uselessness; disqualification; ⚓inefficiency (*auch* ※), unseaworthiness; ≎teilbar (߸-) *a.* ⑯ indivisible; ~keit *f* ⑯ indivisibility; ≎teilhaft(ig) (߸߸߸) *a.* ⑯ e-r Sache (*gen.*) ≎ having no share (or not participating) in a th., not partaking of a th.

unten (߸߸) [ahd.: unter] I *adv.* (*ant.* oben) **1.** below; (unter etwas) beneath, underneath; im Hause oft: downstairs; ich habe ≎ (im Erdgeschosse) ein Zimmer I have a room on the ground-floor; ≎ liegen: a) to lie underneath or below; b) F *bisw.* (unterliegen) to be (or get) worsted; sich(e)≎(*abbr.*f.u.) see below, see at the foot of the page. — **2.** mit *prp. u. adv.*: ≎ am Hügel at the foot of the hill; ≎ durch down through; F ≎ durch sein to be ruined or done for or despised; ≎ im Fasse at the bottom of the cask; ≎ im Lande in the plain, in the valley; ≎ hinaus out below; dort ≎ down there; hier ≎ down here; nach ≎ downwards; von oben bis ≎ from top to bottom; von ≎ auf from (deep) below; von ≎ auf dienen to serve from the ranks; weiter ≎ further (or lower) down. — **II** ~ *n* ≎ **3.** das ~ the part below or beneath, the lower part. **unten=an** (߸߸߸…) *adv.* at the lower end, at the bottom; ≎aus *adv.* out below; ≎benannt *a.* undernamed, named below, under-mentioned, in Akten *2c.*: (as) hereunder, in Büchern: (to be found) at the foot of the page; (von) ≎her *adv.* from below; (nach) ≎hin *adv.* down below; ≎stehend = ≎benannt.

unter (߸߸) [ahd.: under] I *prp.* mit *dat.* und *acc.* **1.** (*ant.* über) mit *dat.* auf die Frage wo, mit *acc.* auf die Frage wohin: under(neath), below, beneath; ≎ dem Bette, ≎ das Bett under(neath) or beneath …, ≎ dem Bette hervor from under …; f. Arm¹ 2; ≎ „Arm" (im Wörterbuche) lesen wir // under the heading of „Arm" we read //; f. Auge 3; was versteht man ≎ diesem Ausdrucke? what is meant by that expression?; f. bringen 8 „unter", Decke 2; ≎ dem Gesetze stehen to be under (or subject to) the law; ♀ ≎ dem zehnten Grade nördlicher (südlicher) Breite (ten) degrees north (south) latitude; ≎ Hand 4 "unter", Himmel 2, Hut¹ 1; ≎ dem Meeresspiegel below sea-level or the level of the sea; in Zeitungen: ≎ dem Strich among miscellaneous items (in the lower part of the paper); f. Schein 2, Schloß 1; ≎ Segel gehen to put to sea; f. Siegel; ⚔ ≎ Tage below ground, underground; ≎ (dem) Wasser schwimmen to swim under water; ≎ Wasser setzen to set

under water, to flood; ≎ Wasser stehen to be under water; ≎ Wasser tauchen to immerse, to plunge (into water). als *v/n.* von Schwimmern: to dive. — **2.** begleitend, obwaltend, *bisw.* zeitlich: ≎ dieser Bedingung on this condition; ≎ jeder Bedingung upon any terms, unconditionally; ≎ dem heutigen Datum oder † Dato (dated) this day; ≎ dem Befehle von Moltke under the command (or leadership) of …; ≎ dem Donner der Kanonen amid the roar(ing) of cannon: ≎ Glockengeläute amid ringing of bells; ≎ der Predigt during the sermon; ≎ Tränen amid tears; f. Umstand 1; ≎ dem Vorwande, daß …, under the pretext that //, pretending that //. — **3.** e-n geringeren Grad, Rang, Wert bezeichnend: ich kann es Ihnen nicht ≎ 60 Mark geben I cannot let you have it for (or at) less than £ 3; etwas ≎ sich h. to be in command (or charge) of s.th.; er ist (oder steht) ≎ mir he is below me, he is inferior to me (in rank); ≎ dem Gefrierpunkt, ≎ Null below freezing-point, below zero; f. Kanone 1, Kritik, heiraten II und Nachtwächter. — **4.** einbegreifend, einschließend: ≎ den vielen war keiner der Klügste ≎ allen the wisest of all; f. andere II gegen Ende und bleiben 4 am Schluß; nicht einer ≎ hundert not one in a hundred; wenn's ≎ die Leute kommt // if it gets wind //; sich ≎ die Leute mischen to mix with the people; f. Mensch 2; ≎ (die) Räuber geraten to fall among (or into the hands of) brigands; ≎ die Soldaten gehen to join the ranks, to go into the army, (sich anwerben l.) to enlist; ≎ uns (in unserem Kreise) among ourselves, in our circle. — **II** *adv. bisw. ell.* **5.** die Sonne ist ≎(gegangen) … is down or has set. — **III** *a.* ⑯ (*sup.* ≎st. f. 7) **6.** low(er), inferior; ≎e Kinnlade undermandible, lower jaw; die ≎en Klassen e-r Schule the lower (or junior) forms; die ≎en Stände the lower classes (of society); ☉ der ≎e Mühlstein the nether millstone. — **7.** ≎st *sup.* lowest; nethermost; (lezt) last; die ≎sten Volksschichten the lowest strata of society, (die gänzlich Verarmten, Versunkenen) the submerged tenth; zu ≎st in the lowest part, undermost, nethermost, quite low down, last of all, at the bottom of the class, &c.; zu ≎st gesetzt w. to be placed at (or sent to) the bottom of the class. — **8.** *s.* die ≎en inferiors, subordinates *pl.*; der ≎ste in der Klasse the last boy (of all); die ≎sten *pl.* the lowest of the low, the refuse *sg.* of society; das ≎ste the lowest part, the foot, the base; das ≎ste zu oberst kehren to turn everything upside down or topsy-turvy, *auch:* to upset everything.— **IV** ~ *m* ㉙ **9.** Karte: knave.

unter=… (߸߸…,߸߸…,…) Vorsilbe in Zssgn mit *verbs*, *adjectives* und *nouns*: I mit *verbs*: a) (߸߸…) immer trennbar (**); ≎ducken (߸߸߸) ⑯** to duck (under);

Zeichen (f. S. XVII): F familiär; P Volkssprache; ┌ Gaunersprache; ╲ selten; † alt (auch gestorben); * neu (auch geboren); ++ unrichtig;

[Unterabteilung] — 1013 — [untergeben]

b) mit dem Tone auf dem Grundworte, immer unrennbar (*): ⌂handeln (ʊ‿‿) ⓐa* to negotiate. ⌂nehmen (ʊ‿‿) ⓐa* to undertake. — II Unter=..., unter=... (ʊ...) mit s. und a. (ant. Ober=...). ʒB. =aufseher m subinspector; =bauch m: ⁊ hypogastrium; =gericht n inferior (or lower) court; =kleid n undergarment; =lippe f nether (or under-)lip; ⌂würfig a. submissive, meek. (knechtisch) servile. Unter=abteilung (ʊ‿‿‿) f ⓯ subdivision, (auch ⁊ und zo.). einer Wissenschaft, eines Geschäfts ꝛc.: branch, department; =admiral ↓ (ʊ‿‿‿) m Ⓒc. vice-admiral; =amt (ʊ‿) n ⓐa. subordinate (or inferior) office; =arm (ʊ‿) m Ⓑc. anat. forearm; =ärmel (ʊ‿‿) m ⓴ undersleeve; =art (ʊ‿) f ⓯ sub-species; =arzt (ʊ‿) m ⓐa. junior surgeon, physician's (or doctor's) assistant; ⚔ surgeon-major's assistant; =aufseher (ʊ‿‿‿) m ⓴ sub-inspector. auch: junior inspector; =balken ⊙ (ʊ‿‿) m ⓫ arch. lower beam or joist; architrave; =bau ⊙ (ʊ‿) m Ⓒc. (pl. mit =ten) arch. substructure; (Grundmauer) foundation (-wall), basement; ⛃ groundwork; ↓ ~ für Stapelklötze groundways pl.; =bauch (ʊ‿‿) m Ⓒc. anat. lower belly, ⁊ lower abdominal region, hypogastrium; ⌂bauen ⊙ v/a. (ʊ‿‿) Ⓑ** to build below or underneath; (ʊ‿‿) Ⓑ* arch.: ein Gebäude ⌂ to build a substructure (or to lay a foundation) for...; =baum ⊙ (ʊ‿) m Ⓒc. Weberei: (Tuchbaum) weaver's cloth-beam; Wagenbau: pole of a carriage, shafts pl. of a cart; =beamte(r) (ʊ‿‿) m ⓰ subordinate (or inferior, lower) official or functionary. F understrapper; =befehlshaber ⚔ (ʊ‿‿‿) m ⓴ second (officer) in command; =behörde (ʊ‿‿) f ⓯ inferior authorities pl. or board; =bein (ʊ‿) n Ⓒc. lower (part of the) leg; =beinkleid (ʊ‿‿) n Ⓒc. = Unterhose; =bett (ʊ‿) n Ⓒc. under-bedding; =bibliothekar (ʊ‿‿‿) m ⓴ sublibrarian, deputy-librarian; =bilanz ⚖ (ʊ‿‿) f ⓯ deficit, deficiency, shortness; ⌂binden (ʊ‿‿) Ⓑ** v/a. to tie (or bind) underneath, to bandage below; wir haben ein Tuch u"ntergebunden we tied a cloth underneath; (ʊ‿‿) Ⓑ* v/a. surg. (zf. binden) to tie up an artery, ꝛc.; die Amme hat die Nabelschnur unterbu"nden the nurse has tied (up) the umbilical cord; fig. e-m die Lebensadern ⌂ to drain (or sap) a p.'s life(-blood) or vitals pl.: ~ n ⓦ und =bindung f ⓯ surg. ligature; =bischof (ʊ‿‿) m Ⓒc. suffragan (bishop); =blatt (ʊ‿) n Ⓒc. lower leaf, underleaf. ⊙ foil. von Zigarren: filler; ⌂bleiben (ʊ‿‿) v/n. (fn) Ⓑ** to be left undone, to be omitted, not to take place; (aufhören) to cease, to be discontinued; das muß in Zukunft ⌂ that must be stopped (or not occur again) in the future; es ist eine kleine Weile unterblie"ben it did not happen for a little while; ~ n ⓦ omission; cessation, discontinuance; =boden (ʊ‿‿) m ⓦ(ⓩ) underfloor; e-s Knopfes ꝛc.:

bottom part, base; =bogen ⊙ (ʊ‿‿) m ⓦ(ⓩ) arch. subarch; =bootsmann ↓ (ʊ‿‿) m Ⓒc. boatswain's mate; ⌂brechen (ʊ‿‿) v/a. Ⓐa* to interrupt; to cut short (a speech, &c.). to break (silence, &c.); (nicht fortsetzen) to discontinue. stop, suspend; (stören) to disturb, to upset; (abschneiden) to intercept, to cut off, elect. to switch off; elect. den Strom ⌂ to break (an electric) circuit; sich ⌂ to stop short; ~ n ⓦ ʃ. =brechung, =brecher (ʊ‿‿) m (auch ⊙ des elektrischen Stromes) interrupter; =brechung (ʊ‿‿) f ⓯ interruption; break; discontinuance, stop, suspension; disturbance, interception; ohne ~ without intermission, without a pause or break; ⌂breiten v/a. (ʊ‿‿) Ⓑ**; et. ⌂ to spread s.th. underneath; die u"ntergebreitete Decke the rug spread (or tucked) underneath; (ʊ‿‿) Ⓑ* Kanzleistil: (vorlegen) to submit for examination or approval, to lay before; die unterbrei"tete Schrift the submitted document; ⌂bringen (ʊ‿‿) v/a. Ⓖ** to put (or stow) away in safety, to find accommodation for, to give shelter to, in einer Wohnung: to lodge, to provide quarters for, in einer Stelle: to find (or get) a post (or a situation) for; Pferde ⌂ to stable ...; ⚖ Waren ⌂ to sell ..., to dispose of ...; Kapital: to find employment for; to place, put out, invest; Wechsel ⌂ to negotiate bills; =bringung f ⓯ finding accommodation (or employment, a situation) for; ⊙ placing, investment; ⌂brochen p.p. von ⌂brechen und ⌂ interrupted; cut off; physiol. unterbrochene Lebenstätigkeit suspended animation; =bromig ⁊ (ʊ‿‿) a. ⓰ chm. hypobromous; =bruch (ʊ‿‿) m Ⓒc. = =brechung; =chlorig ⁊ (ʊ‿‿) a. chm. hypochlorous; ⌂c Säure hypochlorous acid (HClO); ⌂chlorig-sauer a. ⓰ chm. hypochlorous; ⌂chlorigsaures Salz hypochlorite; =deck ↓ (ʊ‿‿) n Ⓒc. lower deck; =decke (ʊ‿‿) f ⓯ undercover; ⌂der-hand (ʊ‿‿‿) adv. (= im stillen, heimlich) on the sly, secretly, (verstohlen) in an underhand way; ⌂des (ʊ‿) adv. u. cj. in the meantime, meanwhile; ⌂drücken (ʊ‿‿) Ⓑ** v/a. to press down, to push under (water); (ʊ‿‿) Ⓑ* v/a. to repress (a sigh, &c.); (bedrücken) to oppress; (am Erscheinen hindern) to suppress, to nip in the bud; (ersticken) to stifle; (vertuschen) to hush up; (im Zaum halten) to restrain, to check, to keep (with)in bound(s); einen Aufstand ⌂ to put down (or quell. crush) a rebellion; die Unterdrü"ckten pl. ⓰ the oppressed; ~ n ⓦ ʃ. ⌂drückung; =drücker (ʊ‿‿) m ⓴, ~in f ⓯ oppressor; one who suppresses, &c.; ʃ. ⌂drücken; =drückung f ⓯ repression; oppression; suppression; ⌂ducken (ʊ‿‿) v a. u. sich ⌂ v/refl. Ⓑ** to duck (under). untere (ʊ‿‿) a. ⓰ ʃ. unter III. unter-ein-ander adv. I (ʊ‿‿‿) 1. between (or with) each other, one with the other; (gegenseitig) each other, one

another; mutually, reciprocally. — 2. in Verbindung mit verbs (= durcheinander). ʒB. ⌂liegen to lie higgledy-piggledy or in (a heap of) confusion, to be at sixes and sevens or F in a muddle or in a jumble; ⌂mengen, ⌂werfen to mix (F to muddle or jumble) up. to put topsy-turvy. — II (ʊ‿‿‿) one beneath (or underneath) the other. Unter=einteilung (ʊ‿‿‿) f ⓯ subdivision; =erdgeschoß (ʊ‿‿‿) n Ⓒa. underground story, basement (floor); ⌂fahren (ʊ‿‿) Ⓑb* v/a. u. v/n. (fn). den Wagen ⌂, abs. ⌂ to put up one's carriage; (ʊ‿‿‿) Ⓑb* v/a.: a) ⊙ Bauwesen: ein Haus ⌂ (mit Grundmauern versehen) to underpin ...; b) ⚒ die Erze ⌂ to drive right under a lode; =faktor (ʊ‿‿, ‿‿‿) m ⓪ typ. second foreman (or clicker) of printers; ⌂fangen (ʊ‿‿) v/refl.: sich einer Sache (gen.) Ⓑb*: ⌂ to attempt a th., kühn wagend: (boldly) to venture (or hazard, risk, dare) a th.; er hat sich ⌂ sie zu kritisieren he has presumed (or was bold enough) to criticize them; ~ n ⓦ (bold) attempt or venture, (risky or daring) enterprise or undertaking or scheme; ⌂fassen (ʊ‿‿) v/a. Ⓑ** ⌂ to seize (or grasp) from underneath. (stützen) to support, to uphold; e-n ⌂ (unter den Arm fassen) to take a p.'s arm; sich ⌂ v/recip. to walk arm in arm; =feldherr (ʊ‿‿) m ⓵ (general who is) second in command (of an army); ⌂fertigen ⚖ (ʊ‿‿) v/a. Ⓑ** to sign; der Unterfe"rtigte ⓰ the undersigned; =fläche (ʊ‿‿) f ⓯ lower (surface; base; ⌂flechten v/a. (ʊ‿‿) Ⓑ** : et. ⌂ to entwine (or intertwine) a th.; (ʊ‿‿‿) Ⓑb* mit et. ⌂ to intertwine (or interlace) with a th.; =förster (ʊ‿‿‿) m ⓴ under-ranger; =franken ⚐ (ʊ‿‿) npr n. ⓦ α. Lower Franconia; ⌂führen (ʊ‿‿‿) v/a. Ⓑ** : eine Straße ist u"ntergeführt (unter eine andere) a subway has been built; (ʊ‿‿‿) Ⓑb* die Straße wird (durch einen Tunnel ꝛc.) unterfü"hrt the road is (being) tunnelled, a tunnel is (being) driven under the road; =führer (ʊ‿‿) m ⓴ second in command; =führung (ʊ‿‿) f ⓯ ⛃ subway; =fuß (ʊ‿) m ⓐa. lower part of the foot; =futter (ʊ‿‿) m ⓴ inner (or inside) lining; ⌂füttern v/a. (ʊ‿‿) Ⓑa** to put silk as lining underneath or as inner lining; (ʊ‿‿‿) Ⓑa* to line (underneath); =gang (ʊ‿‿) m Ⓒc. going down, sinking; der Sonne, des Mondes, der Gestirne ꝛc.: setting; (das Zugrundegehen) ruin, loss, e-s Schiffes: shipwreck. e-s Geschäfts ꝛc.: failure, collapse; (Zerstörtwerden) destruction, (Sturz) fall, crash, (Verfall) decay, (Aussterben) extinction. ~ der Welt, oft: end of the world; ⌂gärig ⊙ (ʊ‿‿) a. ⓰ Brauerei: Les Bier beer fermented from below; =gärung (ʊ‿‿) f ⓯ fermentation from below, sedimentary fermentation; =gattung (ʊ‿‿) f ⓯ subordinate species or kind; (Unter-art) subspecies; =gebäude (ʊ‿‿‿) n ⓴ lower (part of a) building; substructure; ⌂geben

♩ Musik; ⁊ Wissenschaft; ⚘ Pflanze; ⚱ Geographie; ⊙ Technik; ⚒ Bergbau; ⚔ Militär; ↓ Marine; ⚖ Handel; ✉ Post; ⛃ Eisenbahn.

[Untergebener] — 1014 — [unterländisch]

(ᵕ‿ᵕ) ⓢc** v/a. to lay under; (ᵕ‿ᵕ) ⓢc* v/a. to place under, to submit to; to commit to a p.'s care, to put under a p.'s control; (ᵕ‿ᵕ) p.p. u. a. ⓯ u.=gebene(r) s. ⓰ subordinate, inferior, subaltern, dependent; e-m ⁓ zu to be (placed) under a p.('s care), to be under a p.'s command; ⁓gebenheit (ᵕ‿ᵕ) f ⓰ subordination, inferiority, dependency; ⁓geh(e)n (ᵕ‿ᵕ) v/n. (jn) ⓰**: a) (versinken) to go down or under, to sink, to be(come) submerged, von Schiffen auch: to founder, to be wrecked, von Gestirnen: to set, to sink below the horizon; (verschlungen werden) to be swallowed up (or engulfed) by the waves, a flood, &c.; (vernichtet w.) to perish, to be destroyed, v. Tiergattungen, Völkern ꝛc. a.: to become extinct, to cease to exist, von der Welt: to come to an end; das u"ntergegangene Schiff the foundered (or wrecked) vessel; die U"ntergegangenen pl. those who perished, the engulfed, the extinct; die ⁓de Sonne the setting sun; b) (Raum h.) der Heuwagen ꝛc. ging nicht unter (den Schuppen ꝛc.) ... would not go underneath; ⁓ n ⓩ = ⁓gang; ⁓gehölz (ᵕ‿ᵕ) n ⓐa. = ⁓holz; ⁓geordnet (ᵕ‿ᵕ) a. ⓰ p.p. von ⁓ordnen; subordinate, inferior; von der Bedeutung of secondary importance; ⁓e Rolle minor part; ⁓e(r) s. ⓰ subordinate, junior (officer); ⁓gericht (ᵕ‿ᵕ) n ⓐc. lower (or inferior) (law-)court; ⁓gerichtsbarkeit (ᵕ‿ᵕ) f ⓰ inferior jurisdiction; ⁓geschoben (ᵕ‿ᵕ) a. ⓰ supposititious (child, &c.); (gefälscht) interpolated (passage, &c.), forged, spurious, counterfeit; ⁓geschoß (ᵕ‿ᵕ) n ⓐa. arch. ground-floor; ⁓gestell ⊙ (ᵕ‿ᵕ) n ⓐc.: a) Wagenbau: ⁓ e-s Vorderwagens: under-carriage; b) (lower part of a) stand; c) arch. substructure; ⁓gewand (ᵕ‿ᵕ) n ⓐc. under-garment; lower garment; ⁓gewehr öst. ⚔ (ᵕ‿ᵕ) n ⓐc. side-arms pl.; ⁓gewicht ⓰ (ᵕ‿ᵕ) n ⓐc. short(ness of) weight, underweight; ⁓glied (ᵕ‿ᵕ) n ⓐc. lower limb, log. minor term; ⁓graben: a) (ᵕ‿ᵕ) ⓢb** v/a. to cover by digging, agr. to dig in (manure, &c.); b) (ᵕ‿ᵕ) ⓢh* v/a. to undermine, to sap (beide auch fig.); (unterhöhlen) to hollow out; fig. auch: to destroy, to (bring to) ruin; das Fieber hat ihm die Gesundheit ⁓ ... has shattered (or ruined, undermined) his health; ⁓ n ⓩ u. ⁓grabung f ⓰ undermining, &c. (f. b); destruction, subversion; ⁓grad (ᵕ‿ᵕ) m ⓒ. inferior grade or degree; ⁓grund (ᵕ‿ᵕ) n ⓒ. agr. subsoil; paint., typ. (back-)ground; ⁓grund=bahn 🚇 f ⓲ underground railway; ⁓grund=pflug m. agr. subsoil-plough; ⁓haben F (ᵕ‿ᵕ) v/a. ⓐb**: ein Kleidungsstück ⁓ to wear ... underneath; (besiegt h.) to have conquered or overcome or got under or worsted; ⁓halb (ᵕ‿ᵕ) adv. u. prp. mit gen. (ant. oberhalb) below, at the lower end of; der Baum steht ⁓ der Mühle ... lower down than the mill, ... beyond the mill; ⁓halt m ⓒ. sustenance, support, maintenance, für das Leben

auch: livelihood; seinen ⁓ h. to have sufficient to live on; (sich ernähren) to make a living; ⁓halten: a) (ᵕ‿ᵕ) ⓢa** v/a. to hold under(neath); die u"ntergehaltene Hand the hand held underneath; b) (ᵕ‿ᵕ) ⓢa* v/a. und v/refl. to entertain; (unterstützen) to support, maintain, keep; (beschäftigen) to occupy, ergötzlich: to amuse; die von ihm unterha"ltene Familie the family supported by him; sich ⁓ to amuse o.s., reden: to converse with, to talk to; sie haben sich gut ⁓ they (greatly) enjoyed themselves, they had an enjoyable time; ⁓ n ⓩ u. ⁓haltung f ⓰ (f. b) entertainment; support, maintenance, keep; conversation, talk, chat; Unterhaltung bei Tische table-talk; Gegenstand der Unterhaltung topic of (or food for) conversation.

Unterhaltungs=blatt (ᵕ‿ᵕ) n ⓲ journal for general (or light) reading; ⁓gabe f conversational gift or powers; ⁓kosten pl. cost of maintenance (a. für Gebäude ꝛc.), für eine Person auch: keep; ⁓kunst f art of conversation; ⁓lektüre f light (or easy) reading; ⁓pflichtig a. = alimentations=pfl.; ⁓stück n (dramatic or musical) entertainment; ⁓ton m conversational tone; ⁓weise adv. by way of conversation, conversationally.

unter=handeln (ᵕ‿ᵕ) v/n. (h.), bisw. v/a. ⓢa** to negotiate (about) a treaty, a loan, &c., to be in treaty (or to treat) with a p. about a th., to transact s.th. with a p.; mit Eingeborenen ꝛc. ⁓ to (hold a) palaver with natives, &c.; meist ⚔ ⁓ to (hold a) parley with the enemy; ⁓ n ⓩ f. ⁓handlung, bsd. Artikel; ⁓händler (ᵕ‿ᵕ) m ⓩ. ⁓in f ⓰ negotiator, mediator (f bisw.: mediatress, mediatrix), agent, oft: contp. go-between, ⚔ commissioner for negotiating a truce, &c.; 💰 (Makler) broker, commission-agent; ⁓ verbeten! no agents need apply!, only principals dealt with!; ⁓handlung (ᵕ‿ᵕ) f ⓰ (f. ⁓handeln) negotiation, mediation, (Verhandlung) transaction; ⚔ parley; sich in ⁓(en) einlassen, in ⁓(en) treten to enter into negotiations, ⁓ pflegen (mit with); ⁓en führen, in ⁓ stehen mit // to conduct (or carry on) negotiations with //; ⁓=kunst f art of negotiation, in Staatssachen ꝛc.: (art of) diplomacy, diplomatic craft; ⁓hauen (ᵕ‿ᵕ) ⓢc* v/n. 🔨 to extract ore from the lower surface of the lode; v/a. P (unterzeichnen) to sign; ⁓haus (ᵕ‿ᵕ) n ⓐa. lower part of a house or building; pol. das englische ⁓ the House of Commons, the Lower House; ⁓haut (ᵕ‿ᵕ) f ⓰ underskin; ⁓haut=gewebe ⚕ n eines Blattes ꝛc.; ⚕ hypoderm(a); ⁓haut=zellgewebe n, anat.: ⚕ hypodermic cellular tissue; ⁓hemd (ᵕ‿ᵕ) n ⓐc. undershirt; ⁓hof (ᵕ‿ᵕ) m ⓒ. lower (part of a) court or yard, inner yard, für Geflügel: poultry-yard; ⁓hofmeister (ᵕ‿ᵕ) m ⓰ subtutor to a prince, &c.; ⁓höhlen (ᵕ‿ᵕ) v/a. ⓢb** to hollow out (from underneath), to undermine, to dig (or excavate) under, to tunnel; ⁓holz (ᵕ‿ᵕ) n ⓐa. for. underwood, undergrowth, brush-

wood, copse, coppice; ⁓hose(n pl.) (ᵕ‿ᵕ) f ⓰ drawers pl. (meist für Frauen), pants pl. (meist für Männer); ⁓irdisch (ᵕ‿ᵕ) a. ⓰: a) subterranean, ...eous; underground (railway, &c.); der Gang tunnel, unter Bahnhöfen u. Straßen: subway; f. Katakomben: die Kapelle od. Kirche, oft: crypt; der Weg subway (a. 🚇); b) myth. of the nether world, infernal; das ⁓e Reich the lower (or infernal) regions pl., Hades; die ⁓en pl. the infernal gods; ⁓itali=en ♀ (ᵕ‿ᵕ) npr. n ⓩa. (Süditalien) Lower Italy; ⁓jacke (ᵕ‿ᵕ) f ⓰ undervest, guernsey; woll(e)ne ⁓ flannel vest; ⁓jochen (ᵕ‿ᵕ) v/a. ⓢb**: ein Volk ⁓ to subdue (or subjugate) ..., to reduce ... to submission; (zu(m) Sklaven m.) to enslave, in geh. Spr. to enthral; ⁓ n ⓩ u. ⁓jochung (ᵕ‿ᵕ) f ⓰ subjugation; enslavement; ⁓kellner (ᵕ‿ᵕ) m ⓩ (under-)waiter; ⁓kiefer (ᵕ‿ᵕ) m ⓩ anat. (untere Kinnbacke) lower jaw, underjaw, ⚕ inferior maxilla; ⁓kiel ⚓ (ᵕ‿ᵕ) m ⓩ. lower keel; ⁓kinn (ᵕ‿ᵕ) n ⓒ. bisw. für Doppelkinn: double chin; ⁓klasse (ᵕ‿ᵕ) f ⓰ lower class, in Schulen auch: lower (or junior) form; ⁓kleid (ᵕ‿ᵕ) n ⓐc. under-garment, lower garment; ⁓r pl. underclothing, underwear sg.; ⁓koch (ᵕ‿ᵕ) m ⓒ. cook's assistant, undercook, ⚓ cook's mate; ⁓kommen (ᵕ‿ᵕ): a) v/n. (sn) ⓢa** to get under shelter, to find a place of refuge; (Aufnahme finden) to find accommodation or a lodging; wo sind Sie u"ntergekommen? where did you find accommodation?, where did you put up?; (eine Stelle finden) to find a situation or a berth, to get employment; b) ⁓ n ⓩ (place of) shelter, accommodation, lodging, situation, berth, employment; ein ⁓ finden = ⁓ a; ⁓könig (ᵕ‿ᵕ) m ⓐd., ⁓in f ⓰ viceroy, f vicereine; ⁓körper (ᵕ‿ᵕ) m ⓩ lower part (or limbs pl.) of the body; ⁓fötig (ᵕ‿ᵕ) nordd. a. ⓰ festering inwardly or under the surface, F fig. rotten in the core; ⁓e Geschichte nasty (F rotten) business; ⁓kriechen (ᵕ‿ᵕ) v/n. (sn) ⓢc**dst to creep (or crawl) under; ⁓ sucht ein Plätzchen, wo er ⁓ kann he is looking for a place where he could hide; ⁓kriegen F (ᵕ‿ᵕ) v/a. ⓢb** to get the better of, to subdue, overpower, put down; (besiegen) to conquer, vanquish; ⁓kunft (ᵕ‿ᵕ) f ⓾ = ⁓kommen b; ⁓kunfts=hütte f bsd. in den Alpen: refuge for travellers; ⁓kunfts=lose(r)s. = Obdachlose(r); ⁓lage (ᵕ‿ᵕ) f ⓰ s.th. laid (or put, placed) under(neath) s.th. else (to support it), beim Schreiben: s.th. to rest one's arm upon; blotting-pad; ⁓ (Untergrund) subsoil, geol., a. substratum; (unterste Schicht) lowest (or bottom) layer; (Unterfutter) lining; mech. ⁓ eines Hebels fulcrum of a lever, bsp. von ⚕: ⚕ hypomochlion, ⊙ a. ⁓lager n ⓩ (⚒ ⓳) basis, base, bottom, bsd. arch. foundation; (Bühne) platform; mach. (Stütze) support, stay, prop; stand, bearer; ⁓land (ᵕ‿ᵕ) n ⓒ. lowland, low country; ⁓länder (ᵕ‿ᵕ) m ⓩ lowlander; ⁓ländisch (ᵕ‿ᵕ) a. ⓰ of

Signs (see page XVII): F familiar; P vulgar; ⸗ dash; ⟍ rare; † obsolete (died); * new word (born); ⟋ incorrect; ♪ music;

[Unterlaß] — 1015 — [Unterrichtsfach]

(or lying in) the low country; ⸗laß (⁸⁻³) m, nur gbr. in: ohne ~ without intermission or stoppage or pause, incessantly, unremittingly; ⸗lassen (⁸⁻⁻⁻) ⓐa* v/a. (ant. begehen 3) to omit or neglect doing a th., aus Schonung: to forbear doing a th.; (sich enthalten) to abstain from doing a th.; er soll das ⸗ he shall leave that alone or discontinue it, F he can drop that; ⸗ Sie nicht zu schreiben don't fail to write, write without fail; ich werde nichts ⸗, mich ihm gefällig zu zeigen I shall do everything in my power (or my very best) to please him; ~ n ㉓ f. Unterlassung, (⁸⁻⁻⁻) ⓐa** v/a.: einen ⸗ to allow a p. to take (or to give a p.) shelter, to let a p. come in, to harbour a p.; ⸗lassung f ㊻ omission, non-performance, neglect, oversight, failure, jur. default; ⸗lassungs-fall (⁸⁻⁻⁻...)m ㉒ case of omission or neglect or oversight; ⸗lassungs-sünde f, rel. sin of omission; ⸗last ↓ (⁻⁻ᵘ) f ㊻ ballast; ⸗lauf (⁸⁻ᵘ) m ⓓc.: ~ e-s Flusses: lower course of a river; ⸗laufen (⁸⁻⁻⁻) ⓐa* v/n. (fn) to run for shelter; mit ⸗ to run (or slip) in with others; es können leicht Fehler (mit) ⸗ mistakes can easily creep in; es sind in den Akt einige Fehler mit u"ntergelaufen a few errors have crept into the deed, (⁸⁻ᵘᵘ) ⓐa* v n. (fn) (auf der Oberfläche, bsd. der Haut, durchscheinen lassen) to show on the surface, to suffuse, vom Blute auch: ↓ to extravasate; mit Blut ⸗ (p.p.) suffused with blood, bsd. von den Augen: blood-shot; med. von Blut ⸗er Fleck: ↓ ecchymosis; ~ n ㉓ =laufung; ⸗läufer (⁸⁻⁻⁻)m ㉒ (Eindringling) intruder, interloper, F bore; ⸗laufung f ㊻ suffusion; ⸗leder (⁸⁻ᵘ) n ㉓ underleather, ⊙ Schuhmacherei: leather for soles; ⸗lee-segel ↓ (⁸⁻⁻⁻) n ㉒ (viereckiges Beisegel) lower studding-sail.

unter-legen¹ v a. A (⁸⁻⁻⁻) ⓐ** to lay (or put) under(neath); e-m Huhne Eier zum Brüten ⸗ to put eggs under a hen (to be hatched by her); typ. Zeilen, Wörter im Satz ⸗ to justify; einem Kinde frische Windeln ⸗ to put clean napkins on a baby; e-r Melodie Worte ⸗ to put new (or to adapt) words to an air; e-r Stelle ꝛc. e-n neuen Sinn ⸗ to attach a new meaning to ..., to read a new meaning into ..., to put a new construction on ...; das u"ntergelegte Holz the wood placed underneath; Pferde ⸗ (auf e-r Zwischenstation bereithalten) to keep (ready) a relay of horses; B (⁻⁻⁻⁻) ⓐ**: et. mit et. ⸗ to raise s.th. with s.th.; mit Staniol unterle"gtes Glas glass lined with tin foil; ⸗² (⁻⁻⁻⁻) p.p. v. ⸗liegen. Unter=lehrer (⁸⁻⁻⁻) m ㉒ assistant (master), oft: contp. usher.
Unter=leib (⁸⁻⁻¹) m ⓓc. anat. abdomen, ↓ hypogastrium; zum ~ gehörig: abdominal, ↓ hypogastric; ⸗leibchen (⁸⁻⁻⁻) n ㉓ (Mieder) corset.
Unter=leibs-gegend (⁸⁻⁻⁻...) f ㊷ anat. abdominal region; ⸗krankheit f, ⸗leiden n, path. abdominal complaint; ⸗typhus m, path. typhoid (or enteric) fever.

Unter-leutnant † ↓ (⁸⁻⁻⁻) m ㊿ second lieutenant, Am. under-lieutenant; ⸗liegen A (⁻⁻⁻⁻) ⓐ* v/n. (fn) to succumb, to be overthrown or defeated or overcome, to be (or get) worsted; e-r Last ⸗ to sink under a load; das unterliegt keinem Zweifel it admits of no doubt, it cannot be doubted; er ist unterle"gen he succumbed, he had to yield; B (⁻⁻⁻⁻) ⓐ** v/n. (h.) to lie underneath, to serve as basis, to form a foundation, et hat u"ntergelegen it lay underneath; ⸗lippe (⁸⁻⁻⁻) f ㊻ underlip (a. ♪ einer Orgelpfeife), nether lip.
unterm F (⁻⁻) = unter dem.
unter-malen: a) (⁸⁻⁻⁻) ⓐ*: f-n Namen ꝛc. ⸗ to paint ... underneath; b) (⁻⁻⁻⁻) v/a., paint.: ein Bild ⸗ (die Grundfarben auftragen) to lay on the ground-colour, to put on the first (layer of) colour; (obenhin entwerfen) to sketch hastily; ~ n ㉓ u. ⸗malung f ㊻ (f. b) laying on the ground-colour(s), auch: grounding; ⸗mauern (⁻⁻⁻⁻) v/a. ⓐ**(*) Bauwesen: to build a foundation to or a wall under, to underpin; ⸗mengen (⁸⁻⁻⁻) ⓐ** v/a.: etwas ⸗ to intermix (or intermingle) s.th.; (⁻⁻⁻⁻) ⓐ*: et. mit et. ⸗ to mix (up) s.th. with s.th.; Wein mit Wasser ⸗ to water one's wine; ~ n ㉓ u. ⸗mengung f ㊻ intermixture; ⸗mieter m ㉒ lodger; ⸗minieren (⁻⁻⁻⁻) v/a. ⓐ* to undermine, f. a. ⊙graben b; ⸗mischen v/a. (⁻⁻⁻⁻) ⓐ** u. ⓐ* = ⸗mengen; ⸗mühlstein ⊙ (⁸⁻⁻⁻)m ⓓc. = Bodenstein.
untern F (⁻⁻) = unter den.
unter-nehmen (⁻⁻⁻⁻) v/a. ⓐa* to undertake, to take upon o.s.; (versuchen) to attempt; et. ⸗ (sich auf et. einlassen) to venture upon (or engage in) a th., to hazard (or risk) a th.; eine Reise ⸗ to undertake a journey, to go travelling; zu vielerlei auf einmal ⸗ to have too many irons in the fire; ~ n ㉓ f. =nehmung; ⸗d p.pr. und a. ⓖ enterprising, pushing; venturesome, bold, daring; ♦ speculative; ⸗nehmer (⁻⁻⁻⁻) m ㉒, ~in f ㊷ person undertaking a th. or engaged in an enterprise, von Bauten ꝛc.: contractor, builder; ⊕ (Arbeitgeber) employer; ♦ Ring von ~n ring, trust, syndicate, pool; ⸗nehmertum (⁻⁻⁻⁻) n ㉔d. people of enterprise, enterprising persons, speculators; Baufach: builders pl., ♦ capitalism; ⸗nehmung f ㊻ undertaking, enterprise; (Versuch) attempt; gemeinschaftliche ~ joint enterprise; kühne ~ bold venture, ♦ risky speculation, plunge.
Unter-nehmungs-geist (⁻⁻⁻⁻...) m ㊷ spirit of enterprise, speculative spirit; ⸗lustig a. ⓖ full of enterprise; vgl. unternehmend.
Unter-offizier (⁸⁻⁻⁻) m ⓓc. ⚔ non-commissioned officer, corporal, sergeant, ↓ petty officer; ~, der Rekruten einexerziert drill-sergeant; ~e u. Gemeine pl. rank and file; ~⸗schule (⁻⁻⁻²...) f ㊷ school for non-commissioned officers; ~s-dienstuer (⁻⁻⁻...) m ㉒ soldier doing (or on) corporal's duty; ~-tresse f, in England: sergeant's stripes pl.; vgl. Tresse.

unter=ordnen (⁸⁻⁻⁻) v/a. u. sich ⸗ v/refl. ⓖb**: (sich) ⸗ to subordinate (o.s.); ⸗ordnung f ㊻: a) subordination; ⚖ jur.: Vergeh(en) gegen die ~ disciplinary offence; b) (untergeordnete Stellung) subordinate (or inferior) position; c) = ⸗abteilung; ⸗pacht (⁸⁻⁻⁻) f ㊻ subtenancy; ⸗pächter m ㉒, ~in f ㊷ subtenant; ⸗pfand (⁸⁻⁻⁻) n ⓓc. = Pfand 1 u. 2; et. als ~ besitzen to hold a th. as security; ⸗pfändlich (⁸⁻⁻⁻) a. ㊻ u. adv. (serving) as security, jur. hypothecary; ⸗pfarre (⁸⁻⁻⁻) f ㊻ curacy; ⸗pfarrer (⁸⁻⁻⁻) m ㉒ curate; ⸗pflasterbahn f ㊻ underground railway; ⸗pflügen (⁸⁻⁻⁻) v/a. ⓐ** agr. to plough in, to underfurrow; Samen ⸗ to sow underfurrow; ⸗phosphorig ↑ (⁻⁻⁻⁻) a. ⓖ chm.: ⸗e Säure hypophosphorous acid (H_3PO_2), ⸗saures Salz hypophosphite; ⸗phosphorsauer ↑ (⁻⁻⁻⁻...) a. ⓖ hypophosphoric, ⸗es Salz hypophosphate; ⸗phosphorsäure f ㊷ hypophosphoric acid ($H_4P_2O_6$); ⸗prima (⁻⁻⁻⁻) f ㊻ lower division of the highest form of a German secondary school, in Engl. etwa: lower sixth; ⸗primaner (⁸⁻⁻⁻) m ㉒ scholar of an „Unterprima"; ⸗quartiermeister ⚔ (⁻⁻⁻⁻) m ㉒ quartermaster-sergeant; ⸗reden (⁻⁻⁻⁻) v/refl. ⓖ*: sich mit e-m ⸗ to converse (feierlicher: to commune or discourse) with a p., beratend: to confer with a p.; ~ n ㉓ u. ⸗redung f ㊻ conversation, discourse, conference; ⸗rhein ♀ (⁸⁻⁻¹) npr/m. ⓓc.: der ~ Lower Rhine; ⸗rheinisch (⁸⁻⁻⁻) a. ㊻ of (or belonging to) the Lower Rhine.
Unter-richt (⁸⁻⁻¹) m ⓤb. (Ausbildung) education, training; (Lehren) teaching, instruction (given or received), bsd. an einzelne: tuition, in Klassen: class-teaching, in Schulen: schooling, stundenweise: lesson, mündlich: oral lesson; (Vortrag) lecture, lecturing; f. erteilen I am Ende; er gibt guten ~ he is a good (or efficient) teacher; französischen ~ nehmen bei // to take lessons in French (or French lessons) of or from //; in Schulen: den ~ stören to disturb the class; den ~ in e-r Klasse übernehmen to take a class.
unter-richten (⁸⁻⁻⁻) v/a. und v/refl. ⓖ* 1. e-n in et. ⸗ to instruct a p. in s.th..., to teach (or show) a p. a th., F to coach (up) a p. in a subject, gehörig u. gründlich: to drill a th. into a p. — 2. e-n von (ob. über) et. ⸗ (benachrichtigen) to inform (or apprise, advise) a p. of a th., to acquaint a p. with a th., ⚔ to report a th. to a p.; sich von et. ⸗ to make o.s. acquainted with a th.; e-n fortlaufend (von et.) ⸗ to keep a p. well posted up (in a th.); über oder von et. wohl unterri"chtet sein to be well informed about (or fully aware) of a th.
Unter-richter (⁸⁻⁻⁻) m ㉒ inferior (or junior, puisne) judge.
Unter-richts-anstalt (⁸⁻⁻⁻...) f ㊷ educational establishment; ⸗brief (e pl.) m etwa: correspondence-lesson(s pl.) in English, &c.. a. epistolary method of teaching French, &c.; ⸗fach n branch of instruction, educational subject;

↓ scientific; ♀ botanical; ♁ geography; ⊕ machinery; ⚒ mining; ⚔ military; ⚓ marine; ♦ commercial; ✉ postal; 🚂 railway.

[Unterrichtsgesetz] — 1016 — [unterstehen]

=gesetz n, etwa: law regulating public instruction, bsd. als Vorlage a. school-bill, für die engl. Volksschulen: new code; =kommission f, etwa: board of education; =lokal n class-room; =methode f method of teaching (or of instruction in) languages, &c., educational method; =minister m minister of public instruction, in England: President of the Board of Education; =ministerium ministry of public instruction, in England seit 1900 Board of Education; =stunde f hour of instruction, lesson; =system n system of instruction; =verwaltung f administration of public instruction or of schools; =weise f manner (or method) of teaching; =werk n educational work or publication, für Schulen: school-book; =wesen n (matters pl. concerning) public instruction; scholastic affairs pl.; =zweig m =fach.
Unter-richtung (⌣⌣⌣⌣) f ⑮ instruction.
Unter=rinde ♀ (⌣⌣⌣) f ⑮ lower bark; =rippe (⌣⌣⌣) f ⑮ lower rib; =rippengegend (⌣⌣⌣…) f ♋ anat.: ♋ hypochondriac region; =rock (⌣⌣⌣) m ①c, (ant. Oberrock) der Frauen: petticoat; (Rock des Kleides) skirt; =roßarzt † ⚔ (⌣⌣⌣) m ①a. = Unterveterinär.
unters F (⌣⌣) = unter das.
unter-sagen (⌣⌣⌣⌣) v/a. ⑱*: einem et. 2 to forbid a p. doing a th. or to do a th., amtlich: to prohibit (or interdict) a p. (from) doing a th.; der Arzt untersagte ihm das Rauchen von Zigarren oder Zigarren zu rauchen the doctor would not allow him to smoke cigars; ~ n ㉓ und Untersagung f ⑮ prohibition, interdiction.
Unter=salpetersäure ♋ (⌣⌣⌣⌣…) f ㉖ chm.: hyponitric acid, jetzt mst nitrogen tetroxide (NO₂ oder N₂O₄); =satz (⌣⌣⌣) m ①a.: a) basis, base; (Stütze) support, stay; (Gestell) stand; trestle; ~ für einen Blumentopf saucer for a flower-pot; arch. (Fußgestell) pedestal; chm., metall. ~ für Schmelztiegel crucible-stand; b) log. (ant. Obersatz) b) minor (proposition); =schale (⌣⌣⌣) f ⑮ einer Tasse: saucer; =schätzen (⌣⌣⌣⌣) v/a. ⑲* to undervalue, to make (too) light of; (herabsetzen) to depreciate; ~ n ㉓ u. =schätzung f ⑮ depreciation; =scheidbar (⌣⌣⌣⌣) a. ⑯ distinguishable, discernible; =scheiden (⌣⌣⌣⌣) v/a. und v/refl. ⑳* to distinguish, scharfsinnig: to discern, to discriminate (between), wissenschaftlich: to differentiate, nach bestimmten Merkmalen: to specialize; es ist schwer, sie zu 2 it is difficult to tell one from the other or to tell which is which; sich 2 to differ from; 2d p.pr. und a. ⑯ in den Beb. des inf.; distinctive; (charakteristisch) characteristic; path.: ♋ diagnostic; ~ n ㉓ u. =scheidung f ⑮ distinction, discernment, discrimination, differentiation, vgl. Unterschied.
Unter-scheidungs=begriff (⌣⌣⌣⌣…) m ㉒ log. specific difference; =gabe, =kraft f (power of) discernment; =merkmal n mark of distinction; vgl. =zeichen; =vermögen n = =gabe; =zeichen n distinctive mark, phls. criterion, path.:

diagnostic sign; =zoll ⚙ m differential duty; =zug m distinctive (or characteristic) trait or feature.
Unter=schenkel (⌣⌣⌣⌣) m ㉒ (auch anat.) shank; =schicht (⌣⌣⌣) f ⑮ geol. lower layer or stratum, substratum; 2schieben (⌣⌣⌣⌣) ⑩c** v/a. to push (or shove) under(neath); (⌣⌣⌣⌣) ⑩c** v/a. (an die Stelle von et. setzen) to substitute, to put in the place of; e-m et. 2 to foist (or father) a th. on a p.; in eine Schrift einen Satz ꝛc. 2 to interpolate … in a text; Worten einen falschen Sinn 2 to put a wrong construction upon …, to misconstrue …; ein Testament 2 to forge a will vgl. 2geschoben, bsd. Art.); ~ n ㉓ u. =schiebung f ⑮ substitution; interpolation; wrong construction, misconstruction; =schied (⌣⌣⌣) [ahd.] m ⑩c. difference; (Unterscheidung) distinction; feiner ~ nice distinction; nur ein geringer ~ only a shade of difference; e-n ~ machen zwischen // to discriminate (or differentiate) between //; das macht wenig ~ that matters little; es macht keinen ~ it's all (or it comes to) the same (thing), it makes no (or not the slightest) difference; was ist (denn) der ~? what's the difference or F the odds?; ohne ~ indiscriminately; ohne ~ des Alters irrespective of age; zum ~e von // in contradistinction to //; 2schieden (⌣⌣⌣⌣) p.p. von 2schieben und a. ⑯ distinct, different, diverse; bisw. = mehrere, z.B. 2e Sachen divers (or various) matters pl.; 2schiedlich (⌣⌣⌣⌣) a. ⑯ distinct; 2schiedslos (⌣⌣⌣⌣) adv. indiscriminately, without distinction or exception; 2schlächtig ⊙ (⌣⌣⌣⌣) a. ⑯ Mühlenbau: undershot (mill, wheel); =schlag ⊙ (⌣⌣⌣) m ①c. typ. blank line at the end of a page; 2schlagen (⌣⌣⌣⌣) ⑤b** v/a.: die Arme 2 to cross one's arms; e-m ein Bein 2 (stellen) to trip a p. up; mit u⁻ntergeschlagenen Beinen with crossed legs; (⌣⌣⌣⌣) ⑤b** v/a.: Gelder 2 (betrüglich für sich behalten) to embezzle money, a. abs. to defalcate; Briefe 2 (auffangen) to intercept …; ein Testament 2 to suppress …; er hat den Brief unterschla"gen he has intercepted the letter; ~ n ㉓ und =schlagung f ⑮ embezzlement (vgl. =schleif); interception; suppression; =schleif (⌣⌣⌣) [nhd.] m ⑩c. (Betrug) fraud, grober: defraudation, embezzlement, defalcation, malversation; (Veruntreuung öffentlicher Gelder) jur. peculation; e-n ~ begehen to commit a fraud, to defraud; =schlupf m ①⑩c. (place of) shelter, refuge (vgl. =kommen); 2schlupfen, 2schlüpfen (⌣⌣⌣⌣) v/n. (fn) ⑱*** to seek (or find) shelter or a hiding-place; 2schnitten (⌣⌣⌣) p.p. von 2schneiden u. a. ⑯ typ. undercut (letter); arch. intersected (ornament); 2schreiben (⌣⌣⌣⌣) ⑤b** v/a. to write underneath; (⌣⌣⌣⌣) ⑤b** v/a. und v/refl.: e-n Brief ꝛc. 2 to sign …, eine Urkunde ꝛc. 2 to put (or affix) one's signature to …, to put one's name to …, beipflichtend 2 to subscribe to (a donation, a loan, &c.); das möchte ich nicht 2 (bil-

ligen) I do not approve of that; unterschrieben und untersiegelt signed and sealed; ~ n ㉓ = =schreibung; =schreiber m ㉒: a) (⌣⌣⌣⌣) one who signs (or subscribes) to, subscriber; b) (⌣⌣⌣⌣) underclerk; =schreibung f ⑮ (putting one's) signature to; subscription; =schrift (⌣⌣⌣) f ⑮: (Namens=) signature, bsd. durch Zeichen: sign manual; beipflichtende ~ auf Listen ꝛc.: subscription; laut m-r (eigenen) ~ witness my hand; mit e-r ~ versehen to sign; =schule (⌣⌣⌣) f ⑮ primary school; 2schwefelsauer ♋ (⌣⌣⌣⌣⌣) a. ⑯ chm.: des Salz dithionate; 2schweflig ♋ (⌣⌣⌣⌣) a. ⑯ chm. 2e Säure: † hyposulphurous acid, jetzt thiosulphuric acid, vgl. Thioschwefelsäure; =schwelle ⊙ (⌣⌣⌣) f ⑮ Bauwesen: window-sill, ground-sill, sill of a door-frame; 🚂 sleeper, subsill; =see-boot ⚓ (⌣⌣⌣⌣) n ⑩c. submarine boat; 2see-isch ⚓ (⌣⌣⌣⌣) a. ⑯ submarine; =segel (⌣⌣⌣) n ㉒ lower sail; =segel-geh(e)n ⚓ (⌣⌣⌣⌣⌣) n ㉓ getting under sail; =seite (⌣⌣⌣) f ⑮ underside, lower side; =sekretär (⌣⌣⌣⌣) m ⑩c. under-secretary (auch e-s Kabinettsministers); =sekunda (⌣⌣⌣⌣) f ⑮ lower second (class) of a German secondary school, in Engl.: lower fifth; =sekundaner (⌣⌣⌣⌣⌣) m ㉒ scholar of an „=sekunda"; 2setzen v/a. (⌣⌣⌣⌣) ⑨** to put under(neath); seinen Namen 2 to affix one's name or signature; der u"ntergesetzte Eimer the pail (that was) placed underneath; (⌣⌣⌣⌣) ⑨* (stützen) to support; (mischen) to mix; =setzer (⌣⌣⌣⌣) m ㉒ für Blumentöpfe u. dgl.: stand; support; 2setzt (⌣⌣⌣) a. ⑯ (gedrungen) short and stout, squat, square-built, thick-set, contp. dumpy, stumpy; (gemischt mit et.) mixed; ~heit (⌣⌣⌣⌣) f ⑮ shortness (of stature), squat(ti)ness, stumpiness; =siegeln (⌣⌣⌣⌣) v/a. ⑫a* to put (or affix, set) one's seal to; 2sinken (⌣⌣⌣⌣) v/n. (fn) ⑩fi** to sink (under), to be submerged, to go down; 2spülen (⌣⌣⌣⌣) v/a. ⑱* vom Wasser: to hollow out, to wash away (from below).
unterst (⌣⌣) f. unter 7 u. 8.
Unter=staatssekretär (⌣⌣⌣⌣⌣⌣) m ⑩c. pol. under-secretary of state; =stadt (⌣⌣⌣) f ⑩ lower (part of the) town or city; =stallmeister (⌣⌣⌣⌣⌣) m ㉒ etwa: deputy-equerry, (junior) master of the horse or the stud; =stand (⌣⌣⌣) m ⑩c. shelter, cover; 2ständig ♀ (⌣⌣⌣⌣) a. ⑯ inferior, ♋ hypogynous; 2stands-los a. ⑯ without a shelter, homeless; =statthalter (⌣⌣⌣⌣⌣) m ㉒ pol. lieutenant-governor, deputy-governor; 2stecken (⌣⌣⌣⌣) ⑱** v/a. to put (or stick) in from below, to push underneath; (einverleiben) to put in among (others), to incorporate, ⚔ a. to draft into a regiment, (⌣⌣⌣⌣) ⑱* v/a.: mit et. 2 to fix (or fasten, pin with s.th. from below; 2steh(e)n (⌣⌣⌣⌣) ⑨** (fn) to stand below; to come (or be) under; er hat u"ntergestanden he stood below, bei Regenwetter: he stood up (during the shower); (⌣⌣⌣⌣) ⑨* v/n. (h.): (unterstellt sein) er 2sta"nd e-m strengen Herrn he had a strict

Zeichen (s. S. XVII): F familiär; P Volkssprache; F̄ Gaunersprache; ⚘ selten; † alt (auch gestorben); * neu (auch geboren); ⁺⁺ unrichtig;

[unterstellen] — 1017 — [Unterzahn]

master over him, he served under a severe master; v/refl. sich 2 (vermessen) to venture (or hazard) to; to make bold to (inf.); das würde ich mich nicht 2 I would not dare do it, I should not attempt (or be bold enough) to do it; er hat sich untersta"nden, uns zu drohen he had the impudence (F the cheek) to threaten us; 2stellen (ˊ˘˘ˋ) ⑱* v/a. u. v/refl.: einen Wagen ꝛc. 2 to place (or put) ... under (cover or shelter); sich 2 to stand up (under s.th.) during a shower. &c., to seek shelter from the rain, &c.; (˘˘˘ˋ) ⑱* u. (ˊ˘˘ˋ) ⑱** v/a. to place (or put) under; fig. e-m et. 2 (zuschieben) to impute a th. to a p.; solche Dinge sind uns untersteˊllt worden such things have been attributed to us; e-m untersteˊllt (untergeben) sein to be (placed) under a p.; =stellung (ˊ˘˘ˋ) f ㊻ imputation; =steuermann ⚓ (˘˘˘ˊ) m ②c. (pl. ...leute) second mate; 2streichen (ˊ˘˘ˋ) v/a. ⑱aſt*: ein Wort 2 to underline ..., to underscore ...; 2streuen (ˊ˘˘ˋ) v/a. ⑱** to strew (or sprinkle) among or under (-neath); Pferden Stroh 2 ㊻ to litter horses; =strömung (ˊ˘˘ˋ) f ㊻ undercurrent; =stufe (ˊ˘˘ˋ) f ㊽ lower (or inferior) step or degree or grade; 2stützen (ˊ˘˘ˋ) v/a. ⑱* (mit einer Stütze versehen) to support, to prop (up), durch Balken auch: to shore up, durch Strebepfeiler: to buttress; helfend: to aid, to assist, ⚔ to reinforce, Fußball: to back up; in der Not: to succour, to relieve; bestärkend: to support, to back up; beistimmend: to second a proposal, &c.; bekräftigend: to bear out the truth of s.th., to corroborate a statement, &c.; befürwortend: to advocate, begünstigend: to favour, countenance, patronize; staatlich durch Geldmittel 2 to subsidize; staatlich untersu"tzt subsidized (by government), v. Schulen 2c.: state-aided; f. Rat 1; (˘˘˘ˋ) ⑳: er hatte die Hand u"ntergestützt he had supported it with his hand; ~ n ㉓ u. =stützung f ㊻ (vgl. 2stützen) support; aid, assistance, reinforcement (a. ⚔), succour, relief; countenance, patronage; subsidy. Unter-stützungs-anstalt (ˊ˘˘˘...) f ㊷ charitable institution; 2bedürftig a. ㊅ in need of assistance or help, auch: indigent; =fonds m relief-fund; =gesuch n application for relief; =kasse f benevolent fund; =mauer ⚓ f retain- (or bearing-)wall; =trupp ⚔ m auxiliary force, reinforcements pl.; =verein m friendly (or benevolent) society; =wohnsitz m residence (or domicile) which gives a claim to relief. unter-suchen (˘˘ˊ˘) v/a. ⑱** to inquire (or search, look) into; (prüfen) to examine, genau: to scrutinize, to sift (to the bottom), to go thoroughly into, chm. to analyse; vgl. prüfen 1; (erforschen) to explore; ⚓ mit dem Senkblei 2 to sound; surg. eine Wunde mit der Sonde 2 to probe ...; gerichtlich: einen Fall 2 to make a judicial inquiry (or to inquire) into a case. weit2. to try (or hear) a case, vom Leichen-

beschauer: to hold an inquest (on a case); die untersu"chten Fälle the investigated cases pl., the cases (which have been) gone into; ~ n ㉓ f. Untersuchung; =sucher (ˊ˘˘˘ch) m ㉒, ~in f ㊼ inquirer, searcher; examiner; explorer; investigator; =suchung (˘˘ˊ˘) f ㊻ (f. 2suchen) inquiry into, (re)search into; examination, scrutiny; investigation; chemische ~ analysis; gerichtliche ~ judicial inquiry, trial.
Unter-suchungs-akten (˘˘ˊ˘...) f pl. ㊷ documents pl. relating to a case under trial, bei einer Leichenschau: (minutes of) proceedings at an inquest; =ausschuß m committee (or commission) of inquiry; =gefangene(r) s. prisoner upon trial or to be tried; =gericht n court of inquiry; =haft f imprisonment (or detention) on remand; =kammer f chamber of inquiry; =kommission f = =ausschuß; =richter m examining magistrate; =station ⊕ f, tel. testing-station.
unter-tan (˘˘ˊ) [ahd. p.p. v. 2tun] I a. ㊅ nur prädikativ: e-m 2 subject to a p., dependent on a p.; sich (dat.) e-n, et. 2 m. to subdue (or conquer) a p., a th. — II ~ m ㊱c., ~in f ㊼ subject of a prince. a state, &c.; seine ˜en his subjects, his people pl.; seine treuen ˜en oft: his faithful lieges pl.
Unter-tanen-eid (˘˘ˊ˘) m ㉒ oath of allegiance; =pflicht f allegiance; =treue f loyalty of a subject; =verhältnis n relation(ship) of a subject to his sovereign; =verstand F m: beschränkter ~ limited understanding of the common herd.
unter-tänig (˘˘ˊ˘) a. ㊅ = untertan I, a. submissive, in Briefen ꝛc.: 2ſter Diener your very (humble and) obedient servant; ich bitte 2ſt I beg most humbly; dies alles iſt mir 2 (sch.) all these my sceptre sways: I am lord over all I survey; ~keit (˘˘ˊ˘) f ㊻ state of a subject; (Demut) submissiveness, humility, humble ways pl. or spirit; =tasse (˘˘ˊˋ) f ㊽ saucer; 2tauchen (ˊ˘˘ˋ) ⑱**: a) v/n. (h. u. ſn) to dive; to plunge, submerge, duck, dip; ₵ u"ntergetaucht submerged, submersed, b) v/a. to plunge, submerge, duck, dip, immerse; ~ n ㉓ nur zu a: diving; zu a. u. b: plunge, submersion, ducking, dip(ping), immersion; =teil (ˊ˘ˋ) m, n ㊱c. lower (or inferior) part, base, bottom; =teller ⊕ m plate to stand s.th. upon; vgl. =tasse; =tertia (ˊ˘˘˘tz) f ㊽ lower third (form) of a German secondary school. in Engl. etwa: lower fourth; =tertianer (ˊ˘˘˘tz(˘)˘) m ㉒ scholar of the ,,Untertertia"; =tor (ˊ˘ˋ) n ㊱c. lower gate; 2treten (ˊ˘˘ˋ) ⑳d** v/n. (ſn) to step under (-neath); (Zuflucht suchen) to seek shelter, beim Regen: to stand up; ⑳d* v/a. to tread (or trample, kick) down; 2tun v/a. ⑲** to put under (-neath); 2tunneln ₵ (ˊ˘˘ˋ) ⑳a* to drive a tunnel under, to tunnel; =verdeck ⚓ (˘˘ˊˋ) n ㊱c. f. =deck; =vermieter (˘˘ˊ˘ˋ) m ㉒ one who sublets

a house, &c., underletter, jur. sublessor; =verwalter (˘˘ˊ˘ˋ) m ㉒ under-steward, under-bailiff, sub-manager; =veterinär ⚔ (˘˘w˘ˊ) m assistant veterinary surgeon; =vormund (ˊ˘˘ˋ) m ①③c. under-guardian; auch = Mitvormund; 2wachsen ⚔ (˘˘ˊ˘ˋ) ⑯* with an undergrowth; mit Fett 2 streaky (meat, &c.), surg. v. Wunden: mit wildem Fleisch 2 rank with proud flesh; =wald (ˊ˘ˋ) m ②c. underwood; =wanten ⚓ (ˊ˘˘ˋ) f pl. ㊽ lower shrouds pl.; 2wärts (ˊ˘ˋ) adv. downwards; underneath, beneath, (down) below; 2waschen (ˊ˘˘ˋ) v/a. ⑯b* to wash away from below, to underwash; to undermine; =wasser (ˊ˘˘ˋ) n ㉒ (o. pl.) lower (or deeper) part of the water; =wasser-bau ⊕ (ˊ˘˘˘ˋ) m subaqueous works pl.; =wasser-boot ⚓ m submarine boat; =wasser-lancier-apparat ⚓ m für Torpedos: submarine (or underwater) tube; =wasser-leitung f, tel. subaquatic wire or cable; 2wegs (˘˘ˊˋ) [mhd.] adv. on the way. on the road, ⚔ on the march; immer 2 always on the move; fig. 2 bleiben not to take place. to remain in abeyance; et. 2 l. to leave a thing undone; 2weilen (˘˘ˊ˘) adv. now and again; 2weisen (˘˘ˊ˘ˋ) v/a. ⑲* to instruct a p. in s.th., to teach (or show) a p. s.th.; ~ n ㉓ u. =weisung f ㊻ instruction (auch ⚔), teaching; =welt (ˊ˘ˋ) f ㊻ myth. nether world, lower (or infernal) regions pl.; (Erde) earth, auch: sublunary world; 2werfen (˘˘ˊˋ) ⑲l* v/a. u./refl. to subject to (a trial, &c.); (untertan ꝛc.) to subdue (vgl. 2jochen); (bändigen) to curb, to overcome; sich 2 to submit (or surrender) to, to yield (or resign o.s.) to; to acquiesce in; ~ n ㉓ und =werfung f ㊻ subjection (unter et. to a th.); submission (or surrender) to, resignation to, acquiescence in; 2wertig (˘˘ˊˋ) a. ㊅ below (the full) value, depreciated; =weste (˘˘ˊˋ) f ㊽ undervest, under-waistcoat; =wind (˘˘ˊˋ) m ①c. undercurrent of air. wind (blowing) near the surface of the earth or the sea; 2winden faſt ‡ (˘˘ˊˋ) v/refl. ⑰*: sich einer Sache (gen.) 2 (unterfangen) to hazard a th., to venture (upon) a th.; =wind-gebläse ⊕ n under-grate blower; 2wölben (˘˘ˊˋ) v/a. ⑱* to (build a) vault below. ⚔ to casemate; 2worfen p.p. v. 2werfen und a. ㊅ in den Bed. des inf.: die von Napoleon 2en Länder the countries conquered by (or subject to) Napoleon; die ˜en the conquered pl.; e-r Sache 2 sein to be subject (or liable, exposed) to a th.; =wuchs (˘˘ˊˋ) m ②a. undergrowth; 2wühlen (˘˘ˊˋ) v/a. ⑱* to grub up; (unterböten) to undermine; 2würfig (˘˘ˊˋ, ˘˘˘ˋ) a. ㊅ subject. submissive, (ehrerbietig) obsequious; (demütig) humble. meek, (knechtisch) servile. slavish, (kriechend) crawling, cringing, truckling; sich (dat.) e-n 2 m. to reduce a p. to subjection, to make a p. submit or surrender; ~keit f ㊻ submissiveness, obsequiousness, meekness, servility; =zahn (˘˘ˊˋ) m ㊱c. lower

♪ Musik; ⚛ Wissenschaft; ❦ Pflanze; ♆ Geographie; ⊕ Technik; ⚒ Bergbau; ⚔ Militär; ⚓ Marine; ❀ Handel; ✉ Post; 🚆 Eisenbahn.

[unterzeichnen] — 1018 — [unverdient]

tooth; ≈zeichnen (⌣⌣⌣) ⓑ** v/a. to draw underneath; (⌣⌣⌣) ⓑ* v/a. to sign (vgl. unterschreiben); einen Vertrag endgültig 2 to ratify a treaty; ♣ Versicherungspolicen ꝛc.: to underwrite policies, &c.; ich Unterzeichnete(r) ⓖ I the undersigned; ~ n 23 f. ≈zeichnung; ≈zeichner (⌣⌣⌣) m 22 = ≈schreiber a, ⚜ auch: underwriter; ≈zeichnung f ⓖ (affixing one's) signature, eines Vertrages: ratification; ≈zeug (⌣⌣) n ⓒ c. underwear, underclothing; ≈ziehen v/a. (⌣⌣⌣) ⓑb** to draw (or pull) under, to put under cover; Futter 2 to put a lining into, to insert a lining; Kleidungsstücke: to put on under(neath) other clothes; ⓧ Bauwesen: e-e Schwelle 2 to lay (or fix) a sill under(neath); der u"ntergezogene Balken the beam fixed (or attached) beneath; (⌣⌣⌣) ⓑb* v/a.: et. mit et. 2 to put (or fix, paste) s.th. underneath a th.; v/refl. sich einer Sache (dat.) 2 to take a th. upon o.s., to undertake a th.; er hat sich einer Operation unterzo"gen (unterworfen) he has submitted to (or undergone) an operation.

un-tief (⌣⌣) a. ⓖ not deep, shallow, low; **≈tiefe** (⌣⌣) f ⓖ o. pl.: want of depth, shallowness; mit pl.: a) ⚓ (seichte Stelle) shallow (place), shoal, bank; (Sandbank) sands; b) (unergründliche Tiefe) immense (or bottomless) depth, abyss, chasm, poet. unfathomable deep; **≈tier** (⌣⌣) n ⓒ c. monster (auch fig.), savage (or monstrous) beast; **≈tilgbar** (⌣⌣⌣) a. ⓖ (unauslöschbar) inextinguishable, indelible; von Schulden: not payable, von Anleihen: irredeemable; **≈trennbar** (⌣⌣⌣) a. ⓖ inseparable from; **~keit** f ⓖ inseparableness; **≈treu** (⌣⌣) a. ⓖ unfaithful, stärker: faithless (gegen to); (verräterisch) treacherous, (treulos) perfidious, gegen seinen Herrn: disloyal to; e-n seiner Pflicht 2 m. to turn (or divert) a p. from the path of duty; e-r Sache 2 w. to desert a cause, pol. to rat; j-n Schwüren 2 w. to break one's oaths; **≈treue** (⌣⌣) f ⓖ unfaithfulness, faithlessness, infidelity; treachery, perfidy, disloyalty; ~ im Amte breach of trust; ~ in der Liebe inconstancy, fickleness; Sprichw. ~ schlägt ihren eigenen Herrn treachery comes home to the traitor; **≈trinkbar** (⌣⌣⌣) a. ⓖ undrinkable, not fit to drink; **≈tröstbar** (⌣⌣), **≈tröstlich** (⌣⌣⌣) a. ⓖ inconsolable, disconsolate; **≈tröstlichkeit** f ⓖ disconsolate state; **≈trüglich** (⌣⌣⌣) a. ⓖ unerring, infallible, von Sachen: unmistakable, certain, sure; **~keit** f ⓖ infallibility, certainty; **≈tüchtig** (⌣⌣) a. ⓖ unfit(ted), not qualified, useless (für for); abs. auch: incapable, ⚔ disabled; **~keit** f ⓖ unfitness, incapacity; **≈tugend** (⌣⌣) f ⓖ vice, fault; (üble Gewohnheit) bad (or vicious, evil) habit; **≈tu(n)lich** (⌣⌣⌣) a. ⓖ not feasible, impracticable; (unmöglich) impossible; **~keit** f ⓖ impracticableness, bisw.: infeasibleness, impossibility; **≈überlegt** (⌣⌣⌣) a. ⓖ = ≈bedacht²; **~keit** f ⓖ = ≈bedachtsamkeit;

≈überschreitbar (⌣⌣⌣) a. ⓖ not (fit) to be crossed, bsd. fig. insurmountable; ≈übersehbar (⌣⌣⌣) a. ⓖ extending beyond (one's) range of sight; boundless, immense, vast; **~keit** f ⓖ boundlessness, vastness; ≈übersetzbar (⌣⌣⌣) ꝛc. impossibility of translating a word, &c.; ≈übersteigbar (⌣⌣⌣), ≈übersteiglich (⌣⌣⌣) a. ⓖ insurmountable (auch fig.), nur fig. insuperable (obstacle); ≈übertragbar (⌣⌣⌣) a. ⓖ not transferable, jur. v. Eigentum: unassignable, ♣ v. Wertpapieren: not negotiable, ⓧ von Kräften: intransmissible; ≈übertrefflich (⌣⌣⌣), ≈übertrefflich (⌣⌣⌣) a. unsurpassable, unrivalled, unequalled, matchless, peerless; (unvergleichlich) incomparable; ≈übertroffen (⌣⌣⌣) a. ⓖ unsurpassed, unexcelled, unmatched; er steht als Dichter 2 da as a poet he stands foremost or takes the highest rank; ≈überwindlich (⌣⌣⌣) a. ⓖ unconquerable, invincible, indomitable, von Schwierigkeiten: insurmountable, insuperable. ⚔ v. Festungen: impregnable; **≈überwindlichkeit** f ⓖ unconquerableness, invincibleness; ≈überwunden (⌣⌣⌣) a. unconquered, unvanquished, unsubdued, (ungebändigt) uncurbed; ≈umgänglich (⌣⌣⌣) a. ⓖ unsociable, (unerläßlich) indispensable; 2 (adv.) notwendig absolutely necessary or needed; quite unavoidable; **~keit** (⌣⌣⌣) f ⓖ unsociableness, (⌣⌣⌣ -erläßlichkeit) indispensableness, absolute necessity; ≈umschränkt (⌣⌣⌣) a. ⓖ = ≈beschränkt; von der Gewalt auch: sovereign, stärker: despotic, arbitrary; 2 befehlen to have absolute power or command; **~keit** f ⓖ = ≈beschränktheit, v. d. Gewalt auch: (absolute) sovereignty, despotic power; ≈umstößlich (⌣⌣⌣) a. ⓖ that cannot be overthrown, unsubvertible, (unwiderlegbar) irrefragable, irrefutable; (unbestreitbar) incontestable; (unwiderruflich) irrevocable; **~keit** f ⓖ irrefragableness, incontestableness; irrevocableness; ≈umwunden (⌣⌣⌣) a. ⓖ open, frank, candid, outspoken; (rückhaltlos) unreserved; (derb) blunt, plain; 2es Geständnis, oft: full (or free and open) confession; adv. auch: in plain words or English; (rückhaltlos) without reserve, point-blank, to one's face; **~heit** f ⓖ openness, frankness, candour, outspokenness; ≈unterbrochen (⌣⌣⌣) a. ⓖ uninterrupted, v. e-r Reise ꝛc.: unbroken, (fortlaufend) continuous, (unaufhörlich) incessant, unceasing, (unablässig) unremitting; elect. 2er Strom continuous current; adv. auch: without interruption or break or intermission; 2 4 Wochen lang for four weeks running or in succession, ≈unterscheidbar (⌣⌣⌣⌣) a. ⓖ undistinguishable, indiscernible; ≈unterschrieben (⌣⌣⌣) a. unsigned; ≈untersucht (⌣⌣⌣) a. ⓖ uninvestigated; ich will es 2 lassen, ob // I will not inquire (or examine) whether //; ≈unterzeichnet (⌣⌣⌣) a. ⓖ unsigned, von Geldbeträgen: unsubscribed; ≈väterlich (⌣⌣⌣) a. ⓖ un-

fatherly; adv. in an unfatherly way; ≈ver-altet (⌣⌣⌣) a. ⓖ not obsolete; ≈ver-änderlich (⌣⌣⌣) a. ⓖ unchangeable, unalterable; (unwandelbar) immutable, constant, gram. invariable; (unverderblich) incorruptible; **~keit** f ⓖ unchangeableness, immutability, constancy, incorruptibleness; ≈ver-ändert (⌣⌣⌣) a. ⓖ unchanged, unaltered; the same as before; et. 2 l. to leave a th. (just) as it was; ≈ver-antwortlich (⌣⌣⌣⌣) a. ⓖ von Personen: irresponsible, not answerable (for one's actions); (⌣⌣⌣⌣) (unverzeihlich) inexcusable; **~keit** f ⓖ (⌣⌣⌣⌣) ~ e-r Person irresponsibility; (⌣⌣⌣⌣) ~ e-r Sache inexcusableness; ≈ver-arbeitet (⌣⌣⌣⌣) a. ⓖ ⓧ unwrought, not worked up, von Stoffen, Zeugen: not made up, (roh) raw, in the native state; fig. von Ideen ꝛc.: undigested, crude; ≈ver-äußerlich (⌣⌣⌣⌣) a. ⓖ jur. ꝛc. inalienable, vom engl. Grundbesitz: entailed; **~keit** f ⓖ inalienability; ≈verbesserlich (⌣⌣⌣) a. ⓖ von Personen: incorrigible, irreclaimable; confirmed (liar, &c.), inveterate (drunkard, &c.); von Dingen: unmendable, (vortrefflich, vollkommen) unexceptional, faultless; **~keit** f ⓖ incorrigibleness; faultlessness; ≈verbessert (⌣⌣⌣, ⌣⌣⌣) a. ⓖ unimproved, unreformed, v. Sachen: unmended; ≈verbindlich (⌣⌣⌣) a. ⓖ not obligatory, not compulsory, not binding; (unfreundlich) disobliging, unkind, (unhöflich) discourteous, impolite, uncivil; **~keit** f ⓖ non-obligation; disobligingness, unkindness; ≈verblümt (⌣⌣⌣) a. ⓖ not figurative; (einfach) plain, simple; er sagte es ihm 2 (gerade heraus) he told him plainly or point-blank or (straight) to his face; ≈verborgen (⌣⌣⌣) a. ⓖ unconcealed, not hidden; ≈verboten (⌣⌣⌣) a. ⓖ unforbidden, unprohibited; ≈verbrennbar (⌣⌣⌣), ≈verbrennlich (⌣⌣⌣) a. ⓖ incombustible, (feuerfest) fire-proof; **~keit** f ⓖ incombustibleness; ≈verbrieft (⌣⌣⌣) a. ⓖ unchartered, not guaranteed by charter; ≈verbrüchlich (⌣⌣⌣) a. ⓖ never to be broken; inviolable; mit 2er Treue with unswerving loyalty; **~keit** f ⓖ inviolableness; ≈verbunden (⌣⌣⌣) a. ⓖ unconnected with, uncombined with; (nicht verpflichtet) not obliged, not bound (to), without obligation, adv. apart from; ≈verbürgt (⌣⌣⌣) a. ⓖ unwarranted, not vouched for; von Nachrichten: unconfirmed, unauthenticated; ≈verdächtig (⌣⌣⌣) a. ⓖ unsuspected, above suspicion; trustworthy; **~keit** f ⓖ trustworthiness; ≈verdaulich (⌣⌣⌣) a. ⓖ indigestible; fig. auch: crude; **~keit** f ⓖ indigestibleness, als Magenbeschwerde: indigestion; fig. crudeness, crudity; ≈verdaut (⌣⌣⌣) a. ⓖ undigested; ≈verderblich (⌣⌣⌣) a. ⓖ not easily spoilt, not subject to decay, bsd. fig. incorruptible; **~keit** f ⓖ incorruptibility; ≈verderbt (⌣⌣⌣) = ≈verdorben; ≈verdient (⌣⌣⌣) a. ⓖ undeserved, unmerited, v. Geld: un-

---

Signs (see page XVII): F familiar; P vulgar; ⌐ flash; ╲ rare; † obsolete (died); * new word (born); ‡ incorrect; ♪ music;

[unverdorben] — 1019 — [Unverstand]

earned; (ungerecht) unjust; Ler=maßen, Ler=weise adv. undeservedly, unjustly; without deserving it; ᚽverdorben (♪↓⌣) a. ⊛ unspoilt, unimpaired, not vitiated, von Fleisch, Luft ⁊c.: untainted, fresh; bsd. fig. incorrupt; (gesund) sound, wholesome; (rein) pure, spotless; sittlich: uncorrupted, not depraved, innocent. (unbescholten) unblemished; ~heit f ⊛ unspoilt state, incorruptness; soundness; innocence. unblemished state; ᚽverdrossen (♪↓⌣) a. ⊛ unwearied, (unermüdlich) untiring, indefatigable, (beharrlich) persevering, assiduous, plodding, (geduldig) patient; ⁊c. 2 (adv.) tun to do a th. cheerfully or without grumbling or complaining; ~heit f ⊛ indefatigableness; assiduity; cheerfulness (of spirit); ᚽver=ehelicht (♪↓⌣) a. ⊛ unmarried, unwedded, single; Le Dame spinster lady; gerichtlich: die ~e N. Miss N.; ᚽver=eidet, ᚽver=eidigt (♪↓⌣) a. ⊛ unsworn, not sworn (in); ᚽver=einbar (♪↓⌣) a. ⊛ incompatible. irreconcilable, inconsistent (mit with); (widersprechend) contradictory to; ~feit f ⊛ incompatibility, inconsistency; ᚽverfälscht (♪↓⌣) a. ⊛ unadulterated; (echt) genuine. real; (lauter) pure; fig. von der Gesinnung ⁊c.: candid, true; ~heit f ⊛ genuineness; ᚽverfänglich (♪↓⌣) a. ⊛ not captious, harmless (question, &c.); (arglos) undesigning; ~feit f ⊛ harmlessness; ᚽverfroren (♪↓⌣) a. ⊛ not frozen, not destroyed (or touched) by frost, not frost-bitten; F fig. [corr. aus ndd. unverféren nicht erschreckt] unabashed; (höchst gelassen) imperturbable. very cool; (unverschämt) impudent. F cheeky: er rauchte 2 (adv.) weiter he continued smoking most unconcernedly; ~heit f ⊛ imperturbability. coolness; impudence. effrontery, F cheek; ᚽverführt (♪↓⌣) a. ⊛ unseduced, undebauched; ᚽvergänglich (♪↓⌣) a. ⊛ imperishable; (dauernd) everlasting, perpetual; (unsterblich) immortal; ~feit f ⊛ imperishableness; immortality; ᚽvergessen (♪↓⌣) a. ⊛ unforgotten; ᚽvergesslich (♪↓⌣) a. ⊛ never to be forgotten, ever memorable; indelibly impressed on one's memory; das wird mir 2 bleiben I shall never forget it; ᚽvergleichbar (♪↓⌣), ᚽvergleichlich (♪↓⌣) a. ⊛ incomparable. matchless, unparalleled; (einzig) unique; (alles übertreffend) (most) eminent (scholar, &c.), peerless (orator, writer, &c.), transcendental (genius. &c.); =vergleichlichkeit f ⊛ incomparableness. matchlessness; ᚽvergolten (♪↓⌣) a. ⊛ unrewarded, . unrecompensed. unrequited; ᚽverhältnis=mäßig (♪↓⌣⌣) a. ⊛ disproportionate, out of proportion; (übermäßig) excessive; 2 (adv.) groß great beyond measure or comparison; ~feit f ⊛ disproportion. want of proportion; ᚽverheiratet (♪↓⌣⌣) a. ⊛ unmarried (vgl. unverehelicht); ᚽverhofft (♪↓⌣) a. ⊛ unhoped for; (unerwartet) unexpected. (unvorhergesehen) unforeseen; Le Ein=

nahme, Erbschaft windfall; Sprichw. 2 kommt oft it's always the unexpected that happens; ᚽverhohlen (♪↓⌣) a. ⊛ unconcealed, undisguised, unreserved; adv. (offen) openly, avowedly, without reserve or concealment; ᚽverhüllt (♪↓⌣) a. ⊛ unveiled. unconcealed; (nackt) naked, bare; ᚽverjähr=bar (♪↓⌣⌣) a. ⊛ jur. imprescribable. imprescriptible; ~feit f ⊛ imprescriptibility; ᚽverjährt (♪↓⌣) a. ⊛ not (grown) obsolete, still in force; ᚽver=käuflich (♪↓⌣⌣) a. ⊛ unsaleable. unmarketable; (hanging) on hand; Le Ware, ⁊c.: dead stock. ~feit f ⊛ unsaleableness, unmarketableness; ᚽverkauft (♪↓⌣) a. ⊛ unsold; ᚽverkenn=bar (♪↓⌣⌣) a. ⊛ unmistakable. easy to recognize. stärker: evident; ᚽver=kümmert (♪↓⌣⌣) a. ⊛ not stunted; (unbeschränkt) unstinted; ᚽverkürzt (♪↓⌣) a. ⊛ uncurtailed, unabated; fig. (unverletzt) intact; ᚽverletzbar (♪↓⌣⌣), ~feit f ⊛ invulnerable. (unantastbar) inviolable; (heilig) sacred; ~feit f ⊛ invulnerability; inviolability; sacredness, sanctity; ᚽver=letzt (♪↓⌣) a. ⊛ unhurt, uninjured. not violated; (wohlbehalten) safe and sound; (unversehrt) intact. ⊛ not damaged; ᚽverlierbar (♪↓⌣⌣) a. ⊛ that cannot get lost. never lost; in safe keeping; ᚽverloren (♪↓⌣) a. ⊛ not lost, well preserved. safe; ᚽver=löschlich (♪↓⌣⌣) a. ⊛ inextinguishable. unquenchable; ᚽvermählt (♪↓⌣) a. ⊛ unmarried; ᚽvermeidbar (♪↓⌣⌣), ᚽver=meidlich (♪↓⌣⌣) a. ⊛ unavoidable. inevitable. stärker: fated. fatal; sich in das ~e fügen. schicken to resign o.s. to the inevitable; ~feit f ⊛ unavoidableness. inevitableness; ᚽvermengt (♪↓⌣) a. ⊛ unmixed, unmingled; ᚽvermerkt (♪↓⌣) a. ⊛ unperceived, unnoticed. unobserved, adv. without being perceived. unawares; ᚽver=mietet (♪↓⌣⌣) a. ⊛ unlet, untenanted, v. Häusern auch: vacant. empty; ᚽver=mindert (♪↓⌣⌣) a. ⊛ undiminished. unabated, (ganz) entire; ᚽvermischbar (♪↓⌣⌣) a. ⊛ unmixable; bisw. auch: immiscible; ᚽvermischt (♪↓⌣) a. ⊛ unmixed, bsd. fig. unalloyed; (unverfälscht) unadulterated; Le Rasse pure breed; ᚽvermittelt (♪↓⌣⌣) a. ⊛ without intermediate stage. (plötzlich) sudden; =ver=mögen (♪↓⌣) n ⊛ inability, disability, impotence; Le zu zahlen insolvency; ᚽvermögend (♪↓⌣) a. ⊛ a) mit inf.: Le etwas zu tun unable to do a th.. incapable of doing a th.; b) abs. powerless, (kraftlos) impotent; (mittellos) without funds, penniless. destitute, impecunious; =vermögen=heit (♪↓⌣⌣) f ⊛ incapacity. impotence; (Not) destitution; =vermögens=fall m: im ~e in case of insolvency; ᚽver=mutet (♪↓⌣) a. ⊛ unsuspected. never thought of; (unerwartet) unexpected; (unvorhergesehen) unforeseen, unlooked(-) for; 2 (adv.) geschehen to happen unexpectedly, to come as a surprise; ᚽvernehmbar (♪↓⌣⌣), ᚽvernehmlich (♪↓⌣⌣) a. ⊛ inaudible, unintelligible;

indistinct; ~feit f ⊛ inaudibleness, indistinctness; ᚽvernunft (♪↓⌣) f ⊛ lack of reason, unreasonableness, irrationality; das ist die höhere ~ that's the height of folly or absurdity; ᚽvernünftig (♪↓⌣⌣) a. ⊛ (ohne Vernunft) devoid of reason; Le Wesen irrational beings pl.; Le Tiere (wild) brutes pl.; so handelt nur ein ~er no person in his senses (or no rational being) would act like that; (wider die Vernunft) contrary to reason, unreasonable, irrational. absurd; ᚽveröffentlicht (♪↓⌣⌣) a. ⊛ unpublished; ᚽverpackt (♪↓⌣) a. ⊛ unpacked, loose(ly packed); ↓ 2 verladen to stow in bulk; ᚽverrichtet (♪↓⌣⌣) a. ⊛ unperformed, not carried out; Ler Sache, Ler=dinge without effecting (genauer: without having effected) one's purpose or object. with empty hands, unsuccessfully (s. ab=ziehen II am Ende); ᚽverrückbar (♪↓⌣⌣) a. ⊛ immovable. jur. Les Inventar=stück fixture; ᚽverrückt (♪↓⌣) a. ⊛ unmoved; (fest) (solidly) fixed, firm; 2 ansehen to gaze steadily at; ᚽver=schämt (♪↓⌣) a. ⊛ shameless, impudent. brazen-faced; (ted) pert, audacious, as bold as brass; (frech) insolent. F saucy. cheeky; 2 lügen to tell barefaced lies; Sie sind ein ~er!. F ~ läßt grüßen! you are an impertinent fellow!. F you have some cheek (about you)!; ~heit f ⊛ shamelessness, impudence; insolence, impertinence. effrontery, F sauce. cheek; sich mit ~ durchhelfen to face (F to cheek) it out; ᚽverschließbar (♪↓⌣⌣) a. ⊛ that cannot be locked or shut, a. unlockable; ᚽverschnitten (♪↓⌣) a. ⊛ uncut, von Bäumen: not pruned, untrimmed; von Tieren: entire; ᚽverschuldet (♪↓⌣) a. ⊛ undeserved, unmerited; Ler=maßen. Ler=weise adv. undeservedly, innocently; (ohne Schulden) not (deep) in debt, not (much) indebted, without (great) liabilities, von Gütern: unencumbered; ᚽverschwiegen (♪↓⌣) a. ⊛ indiscreet; ~heit f ⊛ indiscretion; ᚽversehen (♪↓⌣) ⚘ ⊛ unforeseen; 2S adv. in an unforeseen manner, unexpectedly. unawares; e-m (⚔ dem Feinde) 2S e-n Vorsprung abgewinnen to steal a march upon a p. (⚔ the enemy); ⚔ 2S überfallen to make an unexpected attack upon. to surprise; ᚽversehr=bar (♪↓⌣⌣) ⁊c. = ᚽverletzbar ⁊c.; ᚽver=sehrt (♪↓⌣) = ᚽverletzt; ᚽversichert (♪↓⌣) a. ⊛ uninsured; ᚽversiegbar (♪↓⌣⌣), ᚽversieglich (♪↓⌣⌣) a. ⊛ inexhaustible; (ewig dauernd) everlasting, perennial; ᚽversiegelt (♪↓⌣) a. ⊛ unsealed, not sealed, without a seal; ᚽversöhnlich (♪↓⌣⌣) a. ⊛ irreconcilable. stärker: implacable, unforgiving, uncompromising; ~feit f ⊛ irreconcilableness, implacability; ᚽversöhnt (♪↓⌣) a. ⊛ unreconciled, unappeased; ᚽversorgt (♪↓⌣) a. ⊛ unprovided for; without means (of subsistence); =verstand (♪↓⌣) m ⊙c. want of (common) sense or judgment, lack of understanding or intelligence; (Unklugheit) imprudence; (Torheit) folly,

⚛ scientific; ⚘ botanical; ⚚ geography; ⊕ machinery; ⚒ mining; ⚔ military; ⚓ marine; ⚙ commercial; ✉ postal; 🚂 railway.

[unverstanden] — 1020 — [unwillig]

unwisdom; (Dummheit) stupidity; ²ver=
ſtanden (ᵇᶠᵛᴗ) a. ⑯ not understood, (verkannt) misunderstood; ²ver=
ſtändig (ᵇᶠᵛᴗ) a. ⑯ not sensible,
lacking (in) good sense, injudicious;
(unklug) imprudent; (töricht) foolish,
unwise; ²verſtändlich (ᵇᶠᵛᴗ) a. ⑯ unintelligible, incomprehensible, von
Schriften ꝛc. a. abstruse; (undeutlich) indistinct, vague; die Sache iſt mir ganz
² I cannot make head or tail of the
affair; ~keit f ⑯ unintelligibleness,
incomprehensibility; ²verſtellt (ᵇᶠᵛᴗ)
a. ⑯ undissembled, unfeigned; ²ver=
ſteuert ⊛ (ᵇᶠᵛᴗ) a. ⑯ for which no
duty has been paid, duty unpaid; ²
im Zollhauſ in bond; (vgl. verzollt);
²verſucht (ᵇᶠᵛᴗcht) a. ⑯ untried, un-
attempted; er hat nichts ² gelaſſen he
has tried everything, fig. he has not
left a stone unturned; ²vertauſchbar
(ᵇᶠᵛ–) a. ⑯ unexchangeable, ⊛ von
Papiergeld: inconvertible; ²verteidigt
(ᵇᶠᵛᴗ) a. ⑯ undefended, unguarded,
unprotected; ²vertilgbar (ᵇᶠᵛ–) a. ⑯
indelible, ineradicable; ~keit f ⑯ indelibility; ²verträglich (ᵇᶠᵛᴗ) a. ⑯
v. Perſonen: unconciliating; (ungeſellig)
unsociable; (ſtreitſüchtig) quarrelsome;
(reizbar) irritable; von Dingen: = ²ver=
einbar, bſd.: incompatible with; ~keit
(ᵇᶠᵛᴗ–) f ⑯ unconciliating spirit;
unsociableness; quarrelsomeness;
incompatibility; ²verwahrt (ᵇᶠᵛ–)
a. ⑯ unguarded; ²verwandt (ᵇᶠᵛᴗ)
a. ⑯ unmoved, unturned, fixed, adv.
without turning aside, unflinchingly, steadily, fixedly; ſeine Blicke ²
auf et. richten to rivet (or fix) one's
eyes upon a th.; ¹en Blick(es) ² without
taking off one's eyes, with a steady
gaze; (nicht verwandt) not related (mit
to), von Sachen: incongruous; ²verwehrt
(ᵇᶠᵛᴗ) a. ⑯ not forbidden. unprohibited;
permitted; es iſt Ihnen ² zu reden you
are at (full) liberty to speak; ²ver=
weigerlich (ᵇᶠᵛᴗ–) a. ⑯ that cannot be
refused or denied; ²verweilt (ᵇᶠᵛ–) adv.
without delay, directly, immediately,
at once, forthwith; ²verwelklich
(ᵇᶠᵛᴗ) a. ⑯ unfading, imperishable;
ever green; (ewig jung) for ever
young; ~keit f ⑯ imperishableness;
eternal youth; ²verwelkt (ᵇᶠᵛᴗ) a. ⑯
unfaded, unwithered, (still) fresh;
²verwerflich (ᵇᶠᵛᴗ) a. ⑯ unobjectionable, unexceptionable, irrefragable; ~keit f ⑯ unexceptionable-
ness, irrefragableness; ²verweslich
(ᵇᶠᵛᴗ) a. ⑯ incorruptible, undecay-
ing, bisw. auch: imputrescible; ~keit
f ⑯ incorruptibility; ²verwindbar
(ᵇᶠᵛ–) a. ⑯ von Verluſten: irreparable;
²verwiſchbar (ᵇᶠᵛ–) a. ⑯ that cannot
be wiped out; ineffaceable. Indelible; ²verwundbar (ᵇᶠᵛᴗ) a. ⑯ invulnerable; ~keit f ⑯ invulnerable-
ness; ²verwüſtlich (ᵇᶠᵛᴗ) a. ⑯ indestructible, von Zeug. which cannot
be worn out, lasting for ever; fig.
evergreen, (as) hard as a nail; vom
Humor: imperturbable; ~keit f ⑯
indestructibleness; ²verzagt (ᵇᶠᵛ–) a.
⑯ undismayed, undaunted, intrepid;

adv. auch: pluckily, resolutely; ſei ²!
(pluck up) courage!; never say die!;
~heit f ⑯ undauntedness, intrepidity;
pluck; ²verzeihlich (ᵇᶠᵛᴗ) a. ⑯ unpardonable, inexcusable; ~keit f ⑯
unpardonableness, inexcusableness;
²verzinsbar (ᵇᶠᵛᴗ)~. ²verzinslich (ᵇᶠᵛᴗ)
a. ⑯ bearing (or yielding) no interest; ²es Darlehen free loan; ²ver=
zollt ⊛ (ᵇᶠᵛᴗ) a. ⑯ ²verſteuert, auch:
unentered; (im Zollverſchluß) in bond;
²verzüglich (ᵇᶠᵛᴗ) a. ⑯ immediate,
instant, prompt; adv. = ²verweilt;
²vollendet (ᵇᶠᵛᴗ) a. ⑯ unfinished,
uncompleted, et. ² laſſen to leave a
th. half finished or in a raw state;
²vollkommen (ᵇᶠᵛᴗ) a. ⑯ imperfect,
(mangelhaft) defective; (gebrechlich) frail;
~heit f ⑯ imperfection, defectiveness; frailty; ²vollſtändig (keit f ⑯)
(ᵇᶠᵛᴗ(–)) a. ⑯ incomplete(ness); vgl.
unvollendet, unvollkommen; ²voll=
zählig (ᵇᶠᵛᴗ) a. ⑯ below the full number or complement. incomplete; ~keit
f ⑯ incompleteness; ²vor-ausſehbar
(ᵇᶠ–ᴗᴗ) a. ⑯ that cannot be foreseen,
hidden in the future; ²vorbereitet
(ᵇᶠ–ᴗᴗ) a. ⑯ unprepared, extempore
(sermon, speech), offhand; adv. without preparation or previous notice;
² predigen, ſprechen to extemporize;
²vordenklich (ᵇᶠ–ᴗ) a. ⑯ immemorial,
vgl. ²denklich; ²vorgreiflich (ᵇᶠ–ᴗ) a.
⑯ Kanzleiſpr.: meines ²en Dafürhaltens
etwa: without wishing to prejudice
you, in my humble opinion; ²vorher=
geſehen (ᵇᶠ–ᴗᴗ) a. ⑯ unforeseen, unexpected; das kam ganz ² (adv.) that
came as a great surprise or like a
bolt from the blue; ²vorſätzlich (ᵇᶠ–ᴗ)
a. ⑯ unpremeditated, undesigned, involuntary; adv. a. unintentionally;
²vorſichtig (ᵇᶠ–ᴗ) a. ⑯ improvident;
incautious, careless, heedless; (über=
legt) ill-considered (action, &c.); (unklug)
imprudent; ~keit f ⑯ improvidence,
incautiousness. carelessness; imprudence; aus ~keit, oft: by mistake,
inadvertently; ²vorteilhaft (ᵇᶠᵛᴗ) a.
⑯ disadvantageous. unprofitable, unremunerative; ²wägbar (ᵇᶠ–) a. ⑯
phys.: ♁ imponderable; ~keit f ⑯: ♁
imponderability; ²wählbar (ᵇᶠᵛᴗ) a. ⑯
ineligible; ~keit f ⑯ ineligibleness;
²wahr (ᵇᶠᴗ) a. ⑯ untrue, false; (lügen=
haft) mendacious, (erdichtet) fabulous,
fictitious; v. Perſonen: (living) under
false appearances; (heuchleriſch) hypocritical, double-faced; ²wahrhaft, mſt
²ig (ᵇᶠᴗᴗ) a. ⑯ untruthful, lying;
(unzuverläſſig) unreliable; ~igkeit (ᵇᶠ–ᴗᴗ)
f ⑯ untruthfulness, unreliableness;
=wahrheit (ᵇᶠᴗ–) f ⑯ ohne pl.: untruthfulness, ſtärker. mendacity, (Unwirklich=
keit) unreality; mit pl.: (etwas Unwahres)
untruth, falsehood, false (or untruthful) statement; lie, F fib, story; er
hat uns wiſſentlich die ~ geſagt he
told us a deliberate falsehood;
²wahrnehmbar (ᵇᶠ–ᴗᴗ) a. ⑯ imperceptible, not noticeable; ²wahr=
ſcheinlich (ᵇᶠ–ᴗᴗ) a. ⑯ improbable, unlikely; es iſt höchſt ², daß ſie ein=
willigt she is most unlikely (or not

at all likely) to consent; ~keit f
⑯ improbability, unlikeliness;
²wandelbar (ᵇᶠᵛᴗ–) a. ⑯ immutable,
unchangeable, unalterable; bisw.
gram. indeclinable; ~keit f ⑯ immutability, unchangeableness; auch
gram. indeclinableness; ²wegſam
(ᵇᶠ–) a. ⑯ impassable, pathless; ~
keit f ⑯ impassableness; =weib (ᵇᶠ–)
n ④c. monstrous (or terrible) woman,
virago, F she-dragon; ²weiblich (ᵇᶠᴗ)
a. ⑯ unwomanly, unfeminine; ²
(adv.) handeln to act in an unwomanly manner; ~keit f ⑯ unwomanly (or unfeminine) character;
or manner; ²weigerlich (ᵇᶠᵛᴗᴗ) a. ⑯
unresisting; ²er Gehorſam blind (or
unquestioning) obedience; adv. unhesitatingly; ²weiſe (ᵇᶠᴗᴗ), ²weislich
(ᵇᶠᴗᴗ) a. ⑯ unwise, imprudent, foolish; adv. unwisely, without wisdom;
²weit (ᵇᶠ–) adv., auch prp. mit gen. =
²fern; ²wert (ᵇᶠ–) a. ⑯ unworthy
of s.th., not worth s.th.; ↘ (wertlos)
worthless, of little (or no) value;
~ m ⑫c. unworthiness, worthlessness; low value; (Unbedeutenheit)
futility; =weſen (ᵇᶠᴗᴗ) n ㉓ = ²fug; (un=
geſtaltes Weſen) monster; ²weſentlich
(ᵇᶠᴗᴗ) a. ⑯ unessential, (nebenſächlich)
accessory, accidental; ²e Dinge unimportant matters, non-essentials pl.;
~keit f ⑯ accessoriness, unimportance, non-essentiality; =wetter
(ᵇᶠᴗᴗ) n ㉒ rough (or unpleasant, inclement, bad, stormy, ↓ dirty,
foul) weather; (Windſtoß) squall; (Ge=
witter) thunderstorm; das drohende ~
the gathering storm; ²wichtig (ᵇᶠᴗᴗ)
a. ⑯ unimportant, insignificant,
inconsiderable, trifling; ~keit f
⑯ unimportance, insignificance;
²widerlegbar (ᵇᶠ–ᴗ–), ²widerleglich
(ᵇᶠ–ᴗᴗ) a. ⑯ that cannot be dis-
proved; incontrovertible, irrefutable, irrefragable; ~keit (ᵇᶠ–ᴗᴗ) f ⑯
irrefutableness; ²widerruflich (ᵇᶠ–ᴗᴗ)
a. ⑯ bſd. jur. irrevocable, indefeas-
ible, irreversible; ~keit f ⑯ irrevocableness, indefeasibleness; ²wider=
ſprechlich (ᵇᶠ–ᴗᴗ) a. ⑯ incontestable,
adv. a. without contradiction; ~keit
f ⑯ incontestableness; ²widerſtch=
lich (ᵇᶠ–ᴗᴗ) a. ⑯ irresistible; ſich ²
(adv.) hingezogen fühlen zu // to feel
o.s. irresistibly (or magically,
magnetically) attracted by //; ~keit
f ⑯ irresistibility, irresistible force;
²wiederbringlich (ᵇᶠ–ᴗᴗ) a. ⑯ irrecoverable, irretrievable, irreparable, irreclaimable; past recovery
or redemption; ~keit f ⑯ irrecoverableness, irreparableness; ²wille
(ᵇᶠᴗ) m ㉗(23) indignation, displeasure; (Ärger) vexation, annoyance; (Zorn) wrath, anger; allge=
meinen ~ erregen to scandalize (or
vex) everybody; ²willfährig (ᵇᶠᴗᴗ)
a. ⑯ uncomplying. disobliging; ~keit
f ⑯ non-compliance, disobligingness; ²willig (ᵇᶠᴗᴗ) a. ⑯ indignant
at, displeased with, angry about a th.
or with a p.; das machte ihn ſehr ²
that greatly vexed (or annoyed) him,

Zeichen (ſ. S. XVII): F familiär; P Volksſprache; Γ Gauneſprache; ↘ ſelten; † alt (auch geſtorben); * neu (auch geboren); ⁺⁺ unrichtig;

[unwillkommen] — 1021 — [unzweifelhaft]

(widerstrebend) unwilling (or reluctant, loath) to do a th.; ℒwillkommen (⏑⏓⏑⏑) a. ⓖ unwelcome, unbidden; (lästig) troublesome; (unangenehm) unpleasant, disagreeable; er kam ihnen sehr ℒ he came to them as a very unwelcome visitor; ℒwillkürlich (⏓⏑⏑⏑) a. ⓖ involuntary, instinctive, mechanical; (unbeabsichtigt) unintended; et. ℒ (adv.) tun to do a th. mechanically or automatically or unintentionally; ~keit f ⓐ involuntariness, instinctiveness; ℒwirklich (⏓⏑⏑) a. ⓖ unreal; ~keit f ⓐ unreality; ℒwirksam (⏓⏑) a. ⓖ inefficacious, ineffectual, inefficient; inoperative, ℒ m., oft.: to render abortive, to neutralize, (vereiteln) to frustrate; ~keit f ⓐ inefficacy, inefficiency; ℒwirsch (⏓⏑) [mhd.] a. ⓖ cross, peevish, testy; (unfreundlich) morose, surly, (barsch) rude, uncouth, offhandish; ~heit f ⓐ peevishness, moroseness, rudeness; ℒwirtbar (⏓⏑-), ℒwirtlich (⏓⏑⏑) a. ⓖ inhospitable; fig. von Orten: desolate, dreary, deserted; =wirtlich= keit f ⓐ inhospitableness; ℒwirtsam (⏓⏑) a. ⓖ = ℒwirtlich; ℒwirtschaftlich (⏓⏑⏑⏑) a. ⓖ unthrifty, not economical; (verschwenderisch) wasteful, extravagant; ~keit f ⓐ unthriftiness, want of economy; extravagance; ℒwissend (⏓⏑⏑) a. ⓖ: a) (ohne Kenntnisse) ignorant, unlettered; ℒer Mensch uneducated (or illiterate) person, F ignoramus, dunce, noodle; b) (in Unkenntnis) ignorant of, not cognizant of, without knowledge of, ill informed of; adv. ℒer= weise unknowingly, unwittingly, without knowing (it), unconsciously; =wissenheit (⏓⏑⏑-) f ⓐ ignorance, lack of knowledge or information, illiteracy; =wissenheits=fehler m fault (or error) due to (sheer) ignorance; ℒwissenschaftlich (⏓⏑⏑⏑⏑) a. ⓖ unscientific; (erfahrungsgemäß) empirical; adv. unscientifically; ~keit f ⓐ want of scientific method, unscientific (or empirical) ways pl.; ℒwissentlich (⏓⏑⏑⏑) a. ⓖ not knowing = unwissend b, bsd. adv.; ℒwohl (⏓⏑) a. not well, unwell, indisposed, F seedy, off colour; mst. prädikativ: (mir ist ℒ) ich bin ℒ, ich fühle mich ℒ I feel unwell or queer or poorly, I don't feel well or F up to much, I am out of sorts; sie ist fast immer ℒ she is nearly always ailing or suffering or on the sick-list; =wohl=sein (⏓⏑-) n ⓒ being unwell, indisposition, ill health, poor state of health; ℒwohn= lich (⏓⏑) a. ⓖ uninhabitable; (unbehaglich) uncomfortable, cheerless; ℒwürdig (⏓⏑) a. ⓖ unworthy of; das ist seiner ℒ that is beneath him, it's below his dignity or F infra dig. (lt. dignitatem); ~keit f ⓐ unworthiness; want of dignity; ℒzahl (⏓⏑) f ⓐ immense number of, numberless host of, F legion (or no end) of; ℒzahlbar (⏓⏑-) a. ⓖ not payable, ⓟ von Wechseln: (nicht fällig) not (yet) due; ℒzählbar (⏓⏑-), ℒzählig (⏓⏑⏑) a. ⓖ innumerable, numberless, countless;

(nicht zu berechnen) incalculable; ~keit f ⓐ innumerableness; ℒzählige=mal adv. times out of number, F ever so many times; ℒzähmbar (⏓⏑-) a. ⓖ untamable, indomitable, difficult to curb; fierce; ~keit f ⓐ untamable (or indomitable) nature; fierceness of a tiger, &c.; ℒzart (⏓⏑) a. ⓖ indelicate, not tender, not gentle (enough); rough, rude, coarse; =zart= heit f ⓐ indelicacy, want of tenderness or gentleness or refinement; roughness. [(kleines Gewicht) ounce.
Unze¹ (⏓⏑) [ahd.; *lt. u'ncia ¹⁄₁₂ (ℝ)] f ⓐ⁸
Unze² (⏓⏑) (fr. once, it. lonza) f ⓐ zo. (Raubtier aus dem Katzengeschlechte) ounce.
Un=zeit (⏓⏑) f ⓐ unseasonable (or wrong, ill-chosen) time; zur ~ unseasonably, out of season, at the wrong time, inopportunely; (vorzeitig) prematurely; ℒzeitgemäß (⏓⏑⏑-) a. ⓖ = ℒzeitig a; adv. =ℒ zur Unzeit (s. das); ℒzeitig (⏓⏑⏑) a. ⓖ: a) (zur Unzeit erfolgend) untimely, unseasonable, ill-timed, (unpassend) inopportune; (unreif) unripe, bsd. fig. immature; (vorzeitig) premature, abortive; ℒe Geburt premature birth, miscarriage, abortion; ~keit (⏓⏑-) f ⓐ untimeliness, unseasonableness, inopportuneness; prematureness.
unzen=weise (⏓⏑⏑⏑) adv. by the ounce.
un=zerbrechlich (⏓⏑⏑⏑⏑) a. ⓖ unbreakable, not fragile, ⓖ u. z infrangible; ~keit f ⓐ unbreakableness; ℒzerleg= bar (⏓⏑⏑⏑-) a. ⓖ bsd. chm. indecomposable, auch: elementary, simple; ℒzer= reißbar (⏓⏑⏑⏑-), ℒzerreißlich (⏓⏑⏑⏑⏑) a. ⓖ untearable; ℒzersetzbar (⏓⏑⏑⏑-) a. ⓖ = ℒzerlegbar; ℒzerstörbar (⏓⏑⏑⏑-), ℒzerstörlich (⏓⏑⏑⏑⏑) a. ⓖ indestructible, (unvergänglich) imperishable; =zerstör= barkeit f ⓐ indestructibleness; =zer= stört (⏓⏑⏑-) a. ⓖ undestroyed; ℒzer= teilbar (⏓⏑⏑⏑-) a. ⓖ indivisible; ~keit f ⓐ indivisibleness; ℒzerteilt (⏓⏑⏑-) a. ⓖ undivided; ℒzertrennbar (⏓⏑⏑⏑-), ℒzertrennlich (⏓⏑⏑⏑⏑) a. ⓖ inseparable, indissoluble; (innewohnend) inherent; (angeboren) innate; ~e inseparables, orn. love-birds pl.; ~keit f ⓐ inseparableness, indissolubility, inherency; =zeug (⏓⏑) n ⓒ. ohne pl. trash, (bad) stuff, rubbish.
Unzial=buchstabe z (⏑⏓(⏑)ⁿ⁾⁾ᴴ ⏑⏑-⏑) [lt.] m ⓑ typ., &c. uncial letter.
un=ziemend, ℒziemlich (⏓⏑⏑) a. ⓖ unseemly, unbecoming, improper; =ziemlichkeit f ⓐ unseemliness, unbecomingness; ℒzier (⏓⏑) f ⓐ, =ziersde (⏓⏑⏑) f ⓐ uncomeliness, ungracefulness; e-m zur ~ gereichen to be unbecoming (or a disfigurement) to a p., to disfigure a p.; ℒzierlich (⏓⏑⏑) a. ⓖ uncomely, ungraceful, inelegant, unsightly; ~keit f ⓐ inelegance, vgl. =zier; ℒzivilisierbar (⏓⏑⏑⏑-⏑⏑-) a. ⓖ incapable of civilization or culture; ℒzivilisiert (⏓⏑⏑-⏑⏑-) a. ⓖ uncivilized, primitive, rude, barbarous; =zucht (⏓⏑) [mhd.] f ⓐ (pl. ℒ) unchastity, lewdness, lechery; (Hurerei) prostitution, harlotry, bsd. bibl. fornication; ~ treiben to lead a lecherous (or an unchaste) life;

züchtig (⏓⏑) [nhd.] a. ⓖ unchaste, immodest, lascivious, lewd, lecherous; (schamlos, schmutzig) obscene, smutty; ℒe Schriften pl. pornographic literature; pornography; ~keit f ⓐ lecherousness, obscenity; vgl. =zucht; ℒzu= frieden (⏓⏑-⏑) a. ⓖ dissatisfied with, dauernd: discontented with; die ~en the discontented (ones), pol. a. the malcontents pl.; Sprichw. der ~e hat nie genug grumblers are never satisfied; ~heit f ⓐ dissatisfaction, discontent(edness), F spirit of grumbling; ℒzugänglich (⏓⏑⏑⏑) a. ⓖ inaccessible, unapproachable, impervious (für to); (ungesellig) unsociable, not genial or affable; der Schmeichelei (dat.) ℒ proof against flattery; ~keit f ⓐ inaccessibility; ℒzukömmlich a. ⓖ unsuitable, unfit; ~keit f ⓐ unfitness; ℒzulänglich (⏓⏑⏑⏑) a. ⓖ insufficient, inadequate; ℒe Vorräte pl. short supply sg.; ~keit f ⓐ insufficiency, inadequacy; shortness; ℒzulässig (⏓⏑⏑⏑) a. ⓖ inadmissible; ~keit f ⓐ inadmissibility; ℒzünftig (⏓⏑⏑) a. ⓖ not belonging to (or not connected with) any guild or corporate society; weitS. unprofessional; ℒzurechnungs= fähig (⏓⏑⏑-⏑⏑-) a. ⓖ (morally) not responsible or irresponsible (for one's actions), unfit to undertake any responsibility; (blödsinnig) imbecile, jur. (lt.) non compos (mentis); die Leidenschaft macht ihn ℒ passion makes him unfit for reasoning; ~keit f ⓐ incapacity for responsible action, (moral) irresponsibility; imbecility; ℒzureichend (⏓⏑⏑-⏑) a. ⓖ insufficient; ℒzusammenhängend (⏓⏑-⏑⏑-⏑) a. ⓖ unconnected, disconnected, incoherent, disjointed, detached; ℒe Bemerkun= gen desultory (or digressive) remarks pl.; ℒzuständig (⏓⏑-⏑⏑) a. ⓖ jur. incompetent; ~keit (⏓⏑-⏑⏑-) f ⓐ incompetence; ℒzuträglich (⏓⏑-⏑⏑) a. ⓖ not agreeable, inconvenient; (nachteilig) disadvantageous, prejudicial; (ungesund) unwholesome; ~keit f ⓐ inconvenience; unwholesomeness; ℒzutreffend (⏓⏑-⏑⏑) a. ⓖ inconclusive; ℒzuverlässig (⏓⏑-⏑-⏑⏑) a. ⓖ untrustworthy, unreliable, not to be trusted, vom Gedächtnis auch: treacherous; (unsicher) uncertain, unsafe, precarious; (zweifelhaft) doubtful; (unpünktlich) unpunctual; (ungenau) inaccurate, inexact; ⓟ ℒe Firma shaky firm; ~keit f ⓐ untrustworthiness, unreliableness, uncertainty, precariousness, inaccuracy; ⓟ shakiness; ℒzweck= mäßig (⏓⏑⏑-⏑⏑) a. ⓖ not to the (or not answering its) purpose, unsuitable, inappropriate, inexpedient; ~keit f ⓐ unsuitableness, inexpediency; ℒzweideutig (⏓⏑⏑-⏑⏑) a. ⓖ unequivocal, unambiguous, plain, simple; ~keit f ⓐ unequivocalness, plainness; =zweifelhaft (⏓⏑⏑-⏑) a. ⓖ not to be doubted, undoubted, indubitable; adv. doubtless(ly), without (stärker: beyond all) doubt, unquestionably; das ist ℒ wahr that's, no doubt, true; there can be no doubt about the matter or

♪ Musik; ⚗ Wissenschaft; ⚘ Pflanze; 🜨 Geographie; ☉ Technik; ⚒ Bergbau; ⚔ Militär; ⚓ Marine; ⚖ Handel; ✉ Post; 🚂 Eisenbahn.

[Unzweifelhaftigkeit] — 1022 — [Urlaubsgesuch]

the truth of it; **Zweifelhaftigkeit** f ④ indubitableness; dead certainty.
Upas ⚥ (⌣⌣) [malai. Gift] n, inv. upas (tree) (Anti'aris toxica'ria).
üppig (⌣⌣) [ahd.: über, übel] a. ⑥ vom Pflanzenwuchs ꝛc.: (wuchernd) luxuriant; (in Fülle gedeihend) exuberant; (reichlich) plentiful; (wollüstig) sensual, voluptuous, lascivious; ꝛes Mahl sumptuous (or plenteous, rich) repast; ꝛes Unkraut rank weed(s pl.); ꝛe Weiden, Wiesen rich pastures, meadows pl.; ꝛer Wuchs v. Frauen full(y) developed figure or bust; **Üppigkeit** f ④ luxury, luxuriancy; exuberance; plenty, sensuality, voluptuousness; sumptuousness, richness; rankness.
Ur (⌣; Hom. Uhr) [ahd.] m ⓒc. Auerochs.
Ur-..., ur-... (⌣...) [ahd.] untrennbare Vorsilbe in Zssgn mit nouns und adjectives, bz. 1. den ersten Anfang, das Freisein von Fremdem, z.B.: ~**anfang** m first beginning, prime origin; ~**bedeutung** f original (or primal) meaning; ~**begriff** m primitive notion; ~**bild** n: ⚥ prototype, archetype; ~**enkel** m great-grandson; ~**wald** m primeval (or virgin) forest. — 2. mit a. einen hohen Grad, z.B. ꝛalt a. extremely old, very ancient. — 3. bisw. = der Vorsilbe er~, z.B. Urlaub m leave, furlough.
Urach (⌣⌣) npr/n. ⓒc. ⑥ bsd. F wilder ~ savage (or brutal) fellow.
Ur-ahn (⌣⌣) [mhd.] m ⓒc., ~**e** (⌣⌣) f ⑧; -ahn-herr m, -ahn-frau f great-grandfather, f great-grandmother; ancestor, f ancestress.
Ural ⚥ (⌣⌣) npr/m. ⓒ④α. russ. Fluß u. Gebirge: der ~ the Ural (or Oural) river or mountains pl.; **⚥isch** (⌣⌣⌣) a. ⑥ Uralian; ~**it** ⚥ (⌣⌣) [neu-lt.] m ⓒc. (Art Hornblende) uralite.
ur-alt (⌣⌣) [ahd.] a. ⑥ extremely old, v. Personen auch: very aged or ancient, von vergangenen Dingen: very primeval, F as old as the hills; seit ꝛen Zeiten from time(s) immemorial (vgl. alt² 4 und altehrwürdig).
Uran ⚥ (⌣⌣) [grch.] n ⓓd. chm. uranium (U).
Ur-anfang (⌣⌣⌣) m ⓒc. first beginning, prime origin; **ur-anfänglich** (⌣⌣⌣⌣) a. ⑥ original, primordial, primeval, primal.
Uran-gelb ⊕ (⌣⌣...) n ⑫ uranium-yellow; ~**glimmer** m, min. uranite, uran-mica. [der Himmelskunde) Urania.⌋
Urania ⌣ (⌣⌣⌣) npr/f. ⓒ⑯α. myth. (Muse
Ur-anlage (⌣⌣⌣) f ⑱ 1. original design or foundation or plant. — 2. original disposition or talent.
Uran-ocker (⌣⌣⌣) m ⑫ min. uranochre; ~**oxyd** ⊕ n, chm. Glasflüsse grüngelb färbend: uranic oxide (UO₃); ~**oxydul** n Glasflüsse schwarz färbend: uranous oxide (UO₂); **⚥sauer** a. ⑥ chm.: ⚥ uranic; **⚥saures Salz** uranate.
Uranus (⌣⌣⌣) m ⓒ⑯γ. myth. (Himmelsgott, Vater des Kronos) u. ast. (Planet) Uranus.
Ur-aufführung (⌣⌣⌣⌣) f ⑲ thea. ~ eines Bühnenstücks original performance of a stage-play or an opera.
Uräus-schlange (⌣⌣⌣⌣) f ⑫ zo. (ägypt. Giftschlange, Sinnbild des ägyptischen Königtums) uræus.

Urban¹ (⌣⌣) [lt.] npr/m. ⓒ⑯α. (bsd. Name v. Päpsten) Urban.
urban² (⌣⌣) [lt.] a. ⑥ (leutselig) affable, courteous, polite, auch: urbane; ~**ität** (⌣⌣⌣⌣) f ④ courtesy, urbanity.
Urbar¹ (⌣⌣) [mhd. Ertrag] n ⓓd. = ~ium.
ur-bar² (⌣⌣) [mhd.; *Urbar¹] a. ⑥ agr. vom Acker: cultivated, tilled; (pflügbar) arable; ꝛ m. to reclaim a bog, &c., to clear the land (for tillage), to bring virgin soil under cultivation.
Urbar¹-buch (⌣⌣⌣⌣) n ⑫, **Urbarium** (⌣⌣⌣⌣) [dtsch-lt.] n ⑱ = Grundbuch.
Urbar²-machen (⌣⌣...) n ㉓, **-machung** f ⑱ clearance of the land, (preparing for) cultivation.
Ur-bedeutung (⌣⌣⌣⌣) f ⑯ original meaning or import or signification; ⚥**beginn** (⌣⌣⌣) m ⓒc. = anfang; ⚥**begriff** (⌣⌣⌣) m ⓒc. primitive notion, einer Wissenschaft: rudiments, elements pl.; ⚥**bestand-teil** (⌣⌣⌣⌣) m ⓒc. primitive constituent or component; ⚥**bewohner** (⌣⌣⌣⌣) m/pl. ② original inhabitants; natives, native tribes, aborigines, ⚥ autochthones pl.; ⚥**bild** (⌣⌣) n ⓓc. original (type), ⚥ prototype, archetype; **vollkommenes** ~ perfect model, (fr.) beau-ideal; **⚥bildlich** (⌣⌣⌣⌣) ⑥ original, primal, ⚥ prototyp(ic)al; (vollkommen gut) ideal, absolutely perfect; **christ** (⌣⌣⌣) m ⑫ primitive Christian; ⚥**christentum** (⌣⌣⌣⌣) n ⓓd. primitive or early Christianity; ⚥**deutsch** (⌣⌣⌣) a. ⑥ thoroughly German (vgl. ferndeutsch); ⚥**eigen** (⌣⌣⌣) a. ⑥ quite original, innate (eigenartig) most peculiar, very odd, very queer; ⚥**eigenheit** (⌣⌣⌣), ⚥**eigentümlichkeit** (⌣⌣⌣⌣⌣) f ④ originality, peculiarity; ⚥**einwohner** (⌣⌣⌣⌣) m/pl. ② = bewohner, geh. Spr.: native dwellers of the soil; ⚥**elter-mutter** (⌣⌣⌣...) f ㉑ great-great-grandmother; ⚥**eltern** (⌣⌣⌣) pl. inv. unsere ~ our first parents or ancestors pl.; ⚥**elter-vater** m ⑲ great-great-grandfather; ⚥**enkel** (⌣⌣⌣) m ⑫, ~**in** f ㉑ great-grandchild, bsd. m great-grandson, f great-granddaughter; ⚥**evangelium** (⌣⌣⌣⌣⌣, a. ⌣⌣...) n ⑱ original gospel; ⚥**farbe** (⌣⌣⌣) f ⑱ primary colour; ⚥**fehde** (⌣⌣⌣) [mhd.] f ⑱ im Mittelalter: oath of peace, solemn oath to abstain from revenge or feuds; ⚥**fels** (⌣⌣⌣) f ⑫ primitive (or primary) rock; **⚥fidel** F (⌣⌣⌣) a. ⑥ burschikos: very jolly, as merry as a grig; ⚥**form** (⌣⌣⌣) f ⑯ original (or primal) form or shape (vgl. ⚥bild); ⚥**gebirge** (⌣⌣⌣⌣) n ② geol. primitive (or primary) mountains or rocks pl.; ⚥**geist** (⌣⌣) m ⓓb. innate spirit; **⚥gemütlich** (⌣⌣⌣⌣) a. ⑥ extremely comfortable or snug; vgl. gemütlich; ⚥**geschichte** (⌣⌣⌣⌣) f ⑱ earliest (or dawn of) history; ⚥**gestalt** (⌣⌣⌣) f ⑱ original (or primal) shape (vgl. ⚥bild); ⚥**gestein** (⌣⌣⌣) n ⓓc. = ⚥fels; ⚥**gneis** (⌣⌣⌣) m ⓓa. min. primitive gneiss.
Ur-groß-eltern (⌣⌣⌣⌣) pl. great-grandparents pl.; ⚥**mutter** f great-grandmother; ⚥**vater** m great-grandfather.
Ur-grund (⌣⌣) m ⓒc. primitive (or first, original, primal) cause.

Ur-heber (⌣⌣⌣) [mhd. urhab Anfang] m ⑫, ~**in** f ㉑ author(ess f), originator, (Gründer[in]) founder, f foundress, (Schöpfer) creator; a. = Anstifter(in); er ist der ~ davon he has set it afoot, he is at the bottom of it (all); ~**recht** n ⑫ copyright; ~**schaft** f ⑯ (⌣⌣⌣), ~**tum** (⌣⌣⌣) n ⓓd. authorship.
Ur-heimat (⌣⌣⌣) f ⑯ original home.
Urian (⌣⌣⌣) m ⓓd.⑰ (ungenannte Person) der Herr ~ Mr. What's-his-name or What-d'ye-call-him Meister ~ (unwillkommener Gast) unwelcome guest, bore, auch: = Teufel.
Urias (⌣⌣⌣) [hebr.] npr/m. ⓒγ. (bibl.: Gemahl der Bathseba) Uriah; ~**brief** m fig. der den Überbringer ins Verderben stürzt: treacherous (or perfidious) letter.
Urin (⌣⌣) [lt.] m ⓓd. urine (= Harn); ⚥**untersuchung** des ~s: ⚥ ur(in)oscopy, **⚥ieren** (⌣⌣⌣⌣) v/n. (h.) ⑧ = harnen.
Ur-kanton (⌣⌣⌣, ⌣⌣ᵍ⌣) m ⓒc. hist. original canton of Switzerland; ⚥**keim** (⌣⌣) m ⓒc. primitive germ; ⚥**kirche** (⌣⌣⌣) f ⑱ primitive church; ⚥**komisch** (⌣⌣⌣) a. ⑥ extremely comical or humorous or funny, most amusing; ⚥**kraft** (⌣⌣) f ⑩ original strength or power or force; moving principle; ⚥**kräftig** (⌣⌣⌣) a. ⑥ exceedingly strong or powerful; ⚥**kunde** (⌣⌣⌣) [ahd.] f ⑱ meist jur.: 1. deed, document, legal instrument, muniment, bsd. pl. auch: rolls; als Belag: record, title(-deed); voucher; (Freibrief) charter. — 2. (Beglaubigung) evidence; zu Urkund dessen in witness whereof.
Ur-kunden-abschreiber (⌣⌣⌣...) m ⑫ jur. engrosser; ⚥**bewahrer** m keeper of the records, am engl. High Court of Chancery: Master of the Rolls; ⚥**beweis** m documentary evidence or proof; ⚥**buch** n roll-book, register, e-r Kirche ꝛc. auch: cartulary; ⚥**fälscher** m (⚥**fälschung** f) forger (forging) of documents; ⚥**forscher** m = ⚥**kenner**; ⚥**gewölbe** (⚥**haus**) n vault (house) in which records are kept, record-office, archives pl.; ⚥**kenner** m expert (or person well versed) in diplomatics; diplomatic; ⚥**kenntnis**, ⚥**lehre** f diplomatics; ⚥**sammler** m collector of records; ⚥**sammlung** f collection of documents, archives pl., a. = ⚥buch; ⚥**schrank** m chest to keep records in, safe for deeds and documents; ⚥**wissenschaft** f = ⚥kenntnis.
ur-kundlich (⌣⌣⌣) a. ⑥ documentary, ...al; (auf Akten beruhend) founded on documents, authentic; (archivalisch) archival; ⚥ (adv.) beweisen to prove by documents, to authenticate; ⚥ dessen habe ich ... in witness whereof ...
Ur-laub (⌣⌣) [ahd.: erlauben] m ⓒc. leave (of absence), bsd. ⚔ furlough; krankheitshalber: sick-leave; auf ~ gehen to take one's holiday, ⚔ to go on furlough; auf ~ sein to have (or spend) one's holiday, ⚔ to be on furlough; ~ nehmen to take (or get) a holiday or (⚔) one's furlough; **Ur-lauber** ⚔ (⌣⌣⌣) m ⑫ (Beurlaubter) soldier on furlough.
Ur-laubs-gesuch (⌣⌣⌣...) n ⑫ application for a holiday or for leave of ab-

Signs (see page XVII): F familiar; P vulgar; ꟾ flash; ⌇ rare; † obsolete (died); * new word (born); ‡ incorrect; ♪ music;

[Urlaubskarte] — 1023 — [Uzerei]

sence or ⚓ for furlough: =karte f, =schein m, etwa: certificate of leave.
Ur=laut (‴⌣) m ①c. primitive sound; =mensch (‴⌣) m ㊷: a) (the) first man; b) 🌱 (ureigener Mensch) original (person); =mutter (‴⌣) f ㉑ first mother; ~ des Menschengeschlechtes (Eva) Eve.
Urne (⌣⌣) [lt.] f ㊽ 1. (Gefäß) urn; f. Totenurne. — 2. 🌿 Moosfrucht: urn, ⚛ theca; ⌂n=artig (⌣⌣...), ⌂n=förmig a. ㊌ urnal, urn-shaped, like an urn; ~n=kammer f chamber of urns, röm. Altertum: ⚛ columbarium. [= Päderast.]
Urning (⌣⌣) [(Venus) Urania] m ⓓd.]
Ur=ochs (‴⌣) m ㊷ = Auerochs.
Uroskopie ⚛ (⌣⌣⌣‴) [grch.] f ㊺ med. (Harnuntersuchung) uroscopy.
ur=plötzlich (‴⌣) a. ㊌ very sudden, adv. all of a sudden, all at once, at a moment's notice; =quell (‴⌣) m ①c. original source or fountain, fountain-head; fig. origin, primary source; fig. ~ aller Freude well-spring of (all) joy.
Ur=sache (‴⌣ch) [mhd.] f ㊽ (first) cause; (Grund) reason, ground, (Beweggrund) motive; Anlaß occasion, (Vorwand) pretext; letzte ~ ultimate cause; aus welcher ~?, aus was für (einer) ~? for what cause or reason?, from what motive?, what for?, why?; er hat wenig ~ dazu he has little cause for; er beklagte sich, und nicht ohne ~ ... and he was right (in doing so), kürzer: and well he might; keine ~!: a) (zum Danken) don't mention (it)!; b) (sich zu entschuldigen) don't apologize!; man hat ~ zu glauben, daß // there is (some or much) reason to believe that //; Sprichw. keine Wirkung ohne ~ no effect without cause; kleine ~n (haben oft) große Wirkungen great things often spring from trifling causes or small beginnings; ⌂sachlich, ⌂sächlich (‴⌣) a. ㊌ causal, gr. causative; =sächlichkeit f ㊺ causality.
Ur=sage (‴⌣) f ㊽ ancient tradition; =satz (‴⌣) m ①a. axiom(atic truth); =schrift (‴⌣) f ㊺ primitive writing; jur. original (copy or text), (Konzept) first draft, minute, (eigene Handschrift des Verfassers) autograph; ⌂schriftlich (‴⌣) a. ㊌ autograph(ic); =sitz (‴⌣) m ㊁a. = Stammsitz; =sprache (‴⌣) f ㊽a. primitive language or speech; bisw. (Sprache e-r Urschrift) original language.
Ur=sprung (‴⌣) [mhd.] m ①c. (Quelle) source, fountain, spring; fig. origin, first commencement; (Grund-ursache) foundation, primal cause; seinen ~ h. (oder nehmen) von // to originate in //, to descend (or emanate, come) from //; ⌂ englischen (deutschen) ~s made in England (in Germany), English-made (German-made); ⌂sprünglich (‴⌣) a. ㊌ original, primitive, primary, primal; ⚛ primordial; adv. auch: in the beginning, at first; ⌂ aus Deutschland stammen to be of German origin or descent; =sprünglichkeit f ㊺ originality, primitiveness. Ur=sprungs=land ⚓ (‴⌣...) n ㉒ country of origin, country where goods are produced or manufactured or come from; =zeugnis n certificate of origin.

Ur=stamm (‴⌣) m ①c. original stock or breed, bes. von Menschen: primitive race or tribe; aboriginal (or native) tribe; =stand (‴⌣) m ①c. primitive state; =stoff (‴⌣) m ①c. primary (⚛ primordial) matter or substance, principle, chm., &c. element; =stoff=lehre f, phls., &c. atomic theory, ⚛ atomism; =stoff=teilchen n atom, molecule, elect. ion.
Ursulinerin (⌣⌣‴⌣) f ㊼, Ursuliner=nonne f ㊷ eccl. Ursuline nun.
Ur=teil (‴⌣) [mhd. Erteilung] n ①c. 1. ~ des Richters: judgment, sentence, decision, d. Geschworenen: verdict, e-s Schiedsrichters: award; früheres maßgebendes ~ precedent; das ~ der Geschworenen lautet auf schuldig the verdict of the jury is (or the jury return a verdict of) guilty; e-m das ~ sprechen to sentence a p.: sich selbst (durch Geständnisse ꝛc.) sein ~ sprechen to implicate o.s.; sich dem ~ unterwerfen to submit to a sentence. — 2. (Ansicht) opinion; ein ~ über et. abgeben oder fällen to give (or pass, pronounce) an opinion (or to sit in judgment) upon a th.; ein gutes (oder richtiges) ~ haben to judge correctly, to be a good judge; selbst ein ~ haben to judge for o.s., to have a mind of one's own; meinem ~e nach in my opinion or judgment, as far as I can judge; nach dem ~e der Welt in the eyes of the world. — 3. phls. (Satz) proposition.
ur=teilen (‴⌣) v/n. (h.) ㊱*,* jur. to deliver (or pass, pronounce) sentence on, to give judgment on; (entscheiden) to decide, to determine; weitS. to judge of; to give one's opinion on or about; darüber kann er nicht 2 he is no judge (in these matters); nach seinen Reden (oder seiner Sprache nach) zu 2 judging (or to judge) from his own words.
Ur=teils=eröffnung (‴⌣...) f ㊺ publication (or pronouncement) of a judgment or decree; ⌂fähig a. ㊌ competent to judge or to pronounce an opinion, judicious; =fähigkeit f = =kraft; =fällung f passing a sentence; =kraft f (power of) judgment; (Unterscheidungskraft) discernment, discrimination; ⌂los a. ㊌ without judgment (of one's own), (unverständig) injudicious; =spruch m sentence, judgment, von Geschworenen: verdict, von Schiedsrichtern: award; =vermögen n = =kraft; =vollstreckung f carrying out (or execution of) a sentence.
Urtel (⌣⌣) n ㉒ poet. = Urteil.
Ur=text (‴⌣) m ①a. original (text); =tier (‴⌣) n ①c. zo.: ⚛ protozoon, bsd. pl. ~e od. =tierchen (‴⌣) ㉓ (mikroskopische Wassertierchen): ⚛ protozoa.
urtümlich (⌣‴⌣) a. ㊌ (ursprünglich) original.
Ur=typus (‴⌣) m ㊳ = Urbild.
ur=ur=alt (‴⌣...) a. ㊌ very, very old, von Personen auch: of very advanced age; =eltern pl. ㊷ progenitors, ancestors pl.; =enkel m great-great-grandchild, auch: m great-great-grandson, f great-great-granddaughter; =großmutter f great-great-grandmother; =großvater m great-great-grandfather.

Ur=vater (‴⌣) m ⑲ first progenitor or parent; ⌂väterlich (‴⌣) a. ㊌ ancestral; =väter=zeit (‴⌣) f ㊲ olden times pl., days pl. of yore or of old; =vergangenheit (‴⌣) f ㊺ remote ages, prehistoric times pl.; =vernunft (‴⌣) f ㊺ supreme reason; =versammlung (‴⌣) f ㊺ general meeting of voters; ⌂verwandt (‴⌣) a. ㊌ Sprache ꝛc. cognate, of kindred origin; =volk (‴⌣) ㉒b. aborigines pl., primitive people; =vorfahr (‴⌣) m ㊷ (㉕d.) first ancestor; =wahl (‴⌣) f ㊺ election by the general body of voters; =wähler (‴⌣) m ㉒ elector (or voter) possessing the general (or lower) franchise.
Ur=wähler=liste (‴⌣...) f ㊷ general register of (primary) voters; =versammlung f meeting of the general body of electors or voters.
Ur=wald (‴⌣) m ②c. primeval (or virgin) forest; =welt (‴⌣) f ㊺ primeval world; ⌂weltlich (‴⌣) a. ㊌ primeval; ⌂e Tiere, auch: antediluvian animals pl.; =wesen (‴⌣) n ㉓ primitive (or first) being; (fundamental) principle, originality; =wort (‴⌣) n ①c. gram. primitive word; ⌂wüchsig (‴⌣ch) a. ㊌ original, native, natural; fig. (derb) blunt, rough; =heit f ㊺ originality; =zeit (‴⌣) f ㊺ primeval age or period, hoary (or remote) antiquity; =zeugung (‴⌣) f ㊺ spontaneous generation; =zustand (‴⌣) m ①c. primitive state, ⚛ primordial condition; ⌂zuständlich (‴⌣) a. ㊌ primitive, ⚛ primordial; =zweck (‴⌣) m ①c. first (or original, prime) object, chief purpose.
Usance (ü=sa̅'=ß⌣) [fr.] f ㊽ bsd. 💼 usage, custom (= Brauch), z.B. nach ~, a. ⌂n=mäßig a. ㊌ u. adv. according to custom, in the usual (or customary) way.
usf. abbr. = und so fort.
Uso (‴⌣) [it. Gebrauch] m ㊳ (Wechselzeit) time which a bill has to run.
Uso=wechsel (‴⌣...) m ㊷ bill at usance.
Usurpation (⌣⌣⌣ts(⌣)‴) [lt.] f ㊺ (gewaltsame Anmaßung, Besitz=ergreifung) usurpation.
Usurpator (⌣⌣‴⌣) [lt.] m ㉛ usurper.
usurpatorisch (⌣⌣‴⌣) a. ㊌ usurping.
usurpieren (⌣⌣‴⌣) [lt.] v/a. ㊱ to usurp.
Usus (‴⌣) [lt.] m, inv. jur. = Verkehrssitte.
usw. abbr. = und so weiter.
Utensili=en (⌣⌣‴(⌣)) [it.] pl. inv. (Gerätschaften) utensils, implements, contrivances pl. [mutter.]
Uterus ⚛ (⌣⌣⌣) [it.] m ㊳㊱ = Gebär=]
Utilitari=er (⌣⌣⌣‴(⌣)) [lt.] m ㉒, utilitarisch (⌣⌣⌣‴) a. ㊌ utilitarian.
Utilitarismus (⌣⌣⌣⌣‴) [lt.] m ㉗ (Richtung auf das Nützliche) utilitarianism.
Utopie † (⌣‴) [grch.] f ㊽ Utopian scheme or notion (s. Hirngespinst).
Utopi=en (⌣‴(⌣)) [grch. Thomas More, 1516] npr n. ㉓ α. Utopia, dreamland.
utopisch (⌣‴⌣) a. ㊌ Utopian. [dreamer.]
Utopist (⌣‴⌣) m ㊷ Utopian, (political)]
Utraquist (⌣⌣‴) [neu=lt.] m ㊷ eccl. (das Abendmahl in beiderlei Gestalt beanspruchender husitischer Settierer) Utraquist.
uzen F u. prov. (‴⌣) [nhd.] I v/a. ㊱ (foppen) to chaff, tease, mock, quiz, rile. — II ~ n ㉓ teasing, mockery.
Uzerei (⌣⌣‴) f ㊺ chaffing, quizzing.

V

V, v (fau) *n*, *inv.* Buchstabe: V. v.
v. *abbr.* = von, vom of.
v. = vide, vidi.
V. *abbr.* = Vers verse.
V. *abbr.* auf Eisenbahnfahrplänen = vormittags (Zeit von 12 Uhr nachts bis 12 Uhr mittags) A. M. (= ante meridiem).
V abbr. = vertatur.
Vademekum (w‿́‿) [lt. geh mit mir] *n* ⑤³ (Reiseführer) vademecum, guide-book.
vadimonisch ♀ (w‿‿́‿) *a.* ⑥⁶ Alt.: der ~e See (in Etrurien) Lake Vadimo.
vag (w‿́) [lt.] *a.* ⑥⁶ (unbestimmt) vague.
Vagabund (w‿‿́) [lt.] *m* ㊷, ~**in** *f* ㊸ (Landstreicher[in]) vagabond, tramp.
Vagabunden=leben (w‿‿́‿‿) *n* ⑥² tramp's (or vagrant, roving) life.
vagabundenhaft (w‿‿́‿‿) *a.* ⑥⁶ like a tramp, vagrant, roving.
Vagabundentum (w‿‿́‿) *n* ②d.: a) vagrant life, vagrancy, vagabondage; b) *coll.* (all) vagabonds *pl.*
vag(abund)ieren (w‿‿‿́, w‿‿́) *v/n.* (h. u. jn) ⑨³ (ein Leben als Vagabund[in] führen, to lead a vagrant (or roving) life, to tramp (or rove) about, F to tramp it.
Vagant (w‿́) [lt.] *m* ㊷ Mittelalter: (fahrender Schüler) strolling scholar.
Vagheit (w‿́‿) [vag] *f* ㊸ vagueness.
vakant (w‿́) [lt.] *a.* ⑥⁶ (erledigt) vacant; vacated; (unbesetzt) unoccupied.
Vakanz (w‿́) [lt.] *f* ㊸ **1.** (Erledigung e-r Stelle) vacancy. — **2.** (Ferien) vacation.
vakat (w‿́) [lt. er 2c. fehlt] *inv.* in Verzeichnissen: wanting; von Ämtern: (unbesetzt) vacant; ~ ⑤ *typ.* (unbedrucktes Blatt) white (or blank) page.
Vakuum ♀ (w‿́‿) [lt.] *n* ⑤⁹ *phys.* (luftleerer Raum) vacuum.
Vakuum=bremse 🚂 (‿‿́‿...) *f* ㊸ vacuum-brake; =**meter** *n* (m) vacuum-gauge or =indicator; =**pfanne** ⊙ *f* Papierfabr.: vacuum-pan; =**pumpe** ⊙ *f* an Dampfmaschinen: vacuum-pump.
vakzinieren (w‿‿‿́) [neut-lt.; *lt. vacca* Kuh] *v/a.* ⑨³ to vaccinate (= impfen 2).
Vale (w‿́‿) [lt. leb' wohl!] *int.* farewell!
Valentin (w‿‿‿) *npr/m.* ⊙⁴ *a.* ~**e** (w‿‿́‿) *f* ⑨⁴⑧③ (Bn.) Valentine; =**tag** (‿́‿) *m* ⑥² (14. Februar, an welchem Tage in England junge Leute neckische Liebesbotschaften u. Liebesgedichte austauschen) (St.) Valentine's Day.
Valenz ♀ (w‿́) [lt.] *f* ㊸ = Wertigkeit.
Valerian (w‿‿(‿)‿́) *npr/m.*, ~**us** ⑮ ⑯ α. Alt.: (bfp. röm. Kaiser, 253—260) Valerian.
Valet (w‿́) [lt. *vale'te* lebet wohl!] *n* ⑤⁰ (Abschied) farewell, valediction.
Valet=sagen (w‿‿́...) *n* ⑥² farewell- (or leave-)taking, bidding good-bye. F send-off; =**schmaus** *m* farewell-dinner.
validieren ♀ (w‿‿‿́) [lt.] *v/a.* ⑨³ (gültig machen, sein) to render (or be) valid; ⑤ lassen gegen // to set off against //.
Valuta ♀ (w‿‿́‿) [lt.] *f* ㊸ (Wert) value; (Gegenwert) equivalent; (Währung) (monetary) standard; feste ~ (Normalpreis) fixed rate; ~**notierung** (‿‿́...) *f* ㊸ quotation of the exchange.
valutieren ♀ (w‿‿‿́) *v/a.* ⑨³ to value.

Valvation (w‿‿-tß(‿)‿́) [lt.] *f* ㊸ (Schätzung, bfb. Münzwertung) valuation; ~**s=tabelle** (‿́...) *f* ㊸ *mint.* valuation-table.
Vampir (w‿́-) [ferb.; *grch. Empu'sa*] *m* ⓓd.: a) zo. (Art Fledermaus) vampire (*Phyllo'stoma spectrum*); b) *fig.* (Blutsauger) vampire. blood-sucker: ⑤=**artig**, ⑥**ifch** *a.* ⑥⁶ vampiric.
Vanadin ♀ (‿‿́) [neut-lt.] *n* ⓓd *chm.* (seltenes Metall) vanadium (v).
Vanadin=bleierz (‿‿́...) *n* ⑥² *min.* vanadinite; =**säure** *f. chm.* vanadic acid ($H_3 VO_4$); =**säure=anhydrid** *n* vanadium pentoxide (V_2O_5).
Vandale (w‿‿́‿) *m* ㊹, **Vandalin** *f* ㊼ *hist.* Vandal, *fig.* (Zerstörer von Kunstwerken) vandal.
vandalisch (w‿‿́‿) *a.* ⑥⁶ *hist.* Vandalic. *fig.* vandalic, like a vandal.
Vandalismus (w‿‿‿́) [neut-lt] *m* ㉗ (rohe Zerstörungswut) vandalism.
Vandiemens=land ♀ (‿‿́‿‿‿́) [van Diemen, holl. Gouverneur von Ost-J., 17. sae.] *npr/n.* ⓓα. (Insel) ~ ehm.: Van Diemen's Land, jetzt Tasmania.
Vanille ♀ (w‿‿́li‿) [fr.;*span. Schötchen*] *f* ㊸ (Pflanze und Schote) vanilla; ~**krankheit** (‿́...) *f* ⑥² *path.* vanillism; ~**n=pflanze** ♀ *f* vanilla-(plant) (*Vani'lla aroma'tica*); ~(**n**)=**schokolade** *f* vanilla-chocolate; ~**n=schote** ♀ *f* vanilla-bean.
Vanillin ♀ (w‿‿́) [neut-lt.] *n* ⓤc. *chm.* (Alkaloid der Banille) vanillin(e) ($C_8 H_8 O_3$).
Varia (w‿́(‿)‿) [lt. verschiedene Dinge] *pl. inv.*, meist ohne *art.* divers (or miscellaneous, sundry) matters, sundries *pl.*
variabel (w‿‿(‿)‿́) [lt.] *a.* ⑥⁶ (D9) variable (= veränderlich).
Variante (w‿‿(‿)́‿) [lt.] *f* ㊸ (verschiedene Lesart) variant, different reading.
Variation (w‿‿(‿)-tß(‿)‿́) [lt.] *f* ㊸ ♪, *ast., math.* variation; ⑤**=fähig** (‿́...) *a.* ⑥⁶ variable; ~**s=fähigkeit** *f* ㊸ variability; ~**s=karte** *f. phys.* Magnetismus: variation-chart; ~**s=rechnung** *f. math.* calculus of variations / variety.
Vari-etät (w‿‿(‿)‿́) [lt.] *f* ㊸ (Abart).
vari-ieren (w‿‿(‿)‿́) [lt.] *v/n.* (h.) u. *v/a.* ⑨³ (wechseln) to vary, to take in turn(s); ♪ to play variations (on an air).
Varinas ♀ (w‿‿́, r-r w‿‿́) ⑤ Stadt in Venezuela *m, inv.*, ~**knaster**, ~**tabak** (‿́...) *m* ⑥² varinas.
Variol(o-id)en ♀ (w‿‿‿(‿)‿́, w‿(‿)‿́) [neut-lt.] *f/pl.. path.* (durch Impfung gemilderte Pocken) varioloids *pl.*
Varus=schlacht (w‿́‿-‿‿t) *f* ㊸ [Varus, von den Deutschen unter Hermann im Teutoburger Walde 9 nach Chr. besiegter röm. Feldherr] *hist.* defeat of (the Romans under) Varus. / ㊵ (Lehnsmann) vassal.|
Vasall (w‿́) [mhd.. fr., *flt.*] *m* ㊷, ~**in** **Vasallen=dienst** (w‿‿́...) *m* ⑥² vassalage, feudal service; =**eid** *m*, =**huldigung** *f* vassal's oath (of allegiance); =**pflicht** *f* duty of a vassal. vassal's fealty.
Vasallenschaft (w‿‿‿́) *f* ㊸ **1.** vassalage. — **2.** *coll.* (all) the vassals *pl.*

Vasallen=staat (w‿‿‿́...) *m* ⑥² tributary state; =**treue** *f* loyalty of a vassal.
Vasallentum (w‿‿‿́‿) *n* ②d. = Vasallenschaft.
Vase (w‿́‿) [fr.] *f* ㊸ (Ziergefäß, bfd. für ⑤ Blumen 2c.) vase.
Vaselin (w‿‿́) [neu-lt.] *n* ⓓd., *a.* ~**e** (w‿‿́‿) *f* ㊸ (reinstes Kunstfett) vaseline.
vasen=förmig (w‿́‿...) *a.* ⑥⁶ vase-shaped, ♀: ✡ vasculiform; =**lampe** *f* vase-lamp.
Vaskulose ♀ (w‿‿‿́‿) [neut-lt.] *f* ㊸ *chm.* Pflanzenstoff: vasculose ($C_{36} H_{20} O_{16}$).
Vater (‿́) [*ahd.*: father: lt. *päter*] *m* ⑨, ⑥⑤ (o. *art.* bisw. F *dat.* u. *acc.* ~**n**) father. (male) parent, geh. Spr. (Sport von Rennpferden 2c.) sire (vgl. Alte 1, heilig 1); *rel.* Gott der ~ God the Father; unser himmlischer ~ our Father in Heaven; der ~ der Lüge (Satan) the Father of lies; F *co.* die Väter der Stadt the city-fathers *pl. thea.* die Rollen der edlen Väter parts of noble (F heavy) fathers; röm. Alt.: die versammelten Väter *pl.* the Conscript Fathers *pl.*, the Senate *sg.*; *fig.* zu f-n Vätern versammelt werden (sterben) to be gathered to one's fathers.
Vater=bruder (‿́...) *m* ⑥² f. Vaters=b.
Väterchen (‿́‿) *n* ㉓ (*dim.* von Vater): a) dear father or dad, pa(pa), daddy; altes ~ little old man; b) *co.* = Zar.
Vater=freuden (‿́...) *f/pl.* ⑥² paternal joys *pl.*, =**haus** *n* father's house, pat. roof; =**herz** *n* pat. heart; =**land** *n* native land, (native) country, home country, bfp. mit Bezug auf Deutschland: Fatherland; fein zweites ~ his adopted country; ⑤**ländisch** *a.* ⑥⁶ relating to one's country, native; ⑤e Lieder, Sitten patriotic songs, national customs *pl.*; =**lands=freund(in** *f*) *m* patriot; =**lands=liebe** *f* love for one's country, patriotism; ⑤**land(s)=liebend** *a.* patriotic; =**lands=verteidiger** *m* defender of the country, soldier.
väterlich (‿́‿‿) *a.* ⑥⁶ fatherly, *adv.* in a fatherly manner, like a father; (dem Vater eigen) paternal; von ⑤er Seite, ⑤er=**seits** by (or on) the father's side.
vater=los (‿́...) *a.* ⑥⁶ fatherless; =**losigkeit** *f* ㊸ fatherlessness, orphaned state; =**mord** *m* parricide; =**mörder** *m*: a) parricide; b) ehm. F Herrenhalstragen: (old-fashioned) stand-up (F stick-up) collar; ⑤**mörderisch** *a.* parricidal; =**name(n)** *m* father's name, (Geschlechtsname) patronymic; =**pflicht** *f* father's duty.
Vaters=bruder (‿́...) *m* ⑥² father's brother, paternal uncle; =**brudersohn** *m.* =**bruder=tochter** *f* first cousin by the father's side.
Vaterschaft (‿́‿‿) *f* ㊸ paternity, fatherhood; =**s=klage** (‿́...) *f* ㊸ *jur.* paternity suit, affiliation case.
Vater=schwester (‿́...) *f* ㊸ f. Vaters=...; =**segen** *m* father's blessing.
Väter=sitte (‿́‿‿) *f* ⑥² manners (o. customs) *pl.* of our (fore)fathers.

Zeichen (f. S. XVII): F familiär; P Volkssprache; ſ Gaunersprache; ✳ selten; † alt (auch gestorben); * neu (auch geboren); ⸭ unrichtig,

[Vatersschwester] — 1025 — [verabscheuen]

Vaters-schwester (ĭ⁻ʯ...) f ⑫ father's sister, aunt by the father's side; ₌schwester-sohn m, ₌schwester-tochter f first cousin by the father's side.

Vater-stadt (ĭ⁻ʯ...) f ⑫ native town or city; ₌stelle f: bei e-m ~ vertreten to act as (or to be like) a father to a p.; ₌teil n patrimony; ⚥ u. mutter-los a. without (either) father or mother, orphan(ed); ₌unser n ⑫ Lord's Prayer; ein ~ beten to say the Lord's Prayer.

Vatikan (w⁻ʯ¹) [lt.] m ⑪d. (sehr großer päpstlicher Palast in Rom) Vatican; ₌isch a. ⑯ of the Vatican.

v. Chr. (G.) abbr. = vor Christo (vor Christi Geburt) B. C. (= before Christ).

Vedette ⚔ (w⁻¹ʯ) [it.] f ⑬ vedette, mounted guard.

Vegetabili-en (w⁻ʯ⁻¹(⌣)⁻) [lt.] pl. inv. (Pflanzen) vegetables, F greens pl.; **vegetabilisch** (w⁻ʯ⁻¹ʯ) a. ⑯ vegetable (growth, &c.); der Balsam: ⚘ oleoresin.

Vegetarianer ⚥ (w⁻ʯ⁻(⌣)¹ʯ), **vegetarianisch** (w⁻ʯ⁻(⌣)⁻ʯ) [engl. 1842] *neu-lt. (lt. vě'gětus gewedt)* † = **Vegetarier** ⚥ (w⁻ʯ⁻¹ʯ) m ⑫, ~in f ⑰ (s. der kein Fleisch ißt) vegetarian; **vegetarisch** a. ⑯ vegetarian (food, restaurant, &c.), **Vegetarismus** (w⁻ʯ⁻¹ʯ) m ㉗ vegetarianism.

Vegetation (w⁻ʯ⁻tʃ(⌣)¹) [lt.] f ㊻ (Pflanzenwuchs) vegetation; **vegetativ** (w⁻ʯ⁻⁻¹f) a. ⑯ vegetative (ant. animalisch); **vegetieren** (w⁻ʯ⁻¹ʯ) v/a. ⑬ to vegetate, fig. auch: merely to exist, to lead a bare existence, to live on (in a miserable way). [= Heftigkeit).)

Vehemenz (w⁻ʯ⁻¹ʯ) [lt.] f ㊻ vehemence)

Vehikel (w⁻ʯ⁻¹) [lt. vehi'culum Fahrzeug] n ㉓: a) vehicle, conveyance; b) pharm. ⚘ (Lösungsmittel) solvent.

Veilchen ⚘ (ĭ¹⁻) [mhd.; *lt. vi'ola + disch dim. ₌chen] n ㉓: (wohlriechendes) ~ (sweet) violet (Vi'ola [odora'ta]). ₌blau (ĭ¹ʯ...) a. ⑯ violet (blue); purple blue; Le Augen eyes pl. of a violet blue; ₌duft m ⑫ scent (or perfume, fragrance) of violets; ⚥farben violet-coloured, ⚘ ianthine; ₌fresser m, prove. (Geck) fop, F masher; ₌geruch m =duft; ₌schnecke f, zo. violet-shell or -snail (Ia'nthina); ₌stein m, min.: ⚘ iolite; ₌stock ⚘ m violet-plant; ₌strauß m bunch of violets; ₌wurzel f: a) ⚘ root of violets; b) ⚘ n. pharm. orris-root (bfd. von Iris florenti'na).

Veit (ĭ¹) [lt.] npr/m. ⑪ Guy, Vitus.

Veits-bohne (ĭ¹ʯ...) f ⚘ kidney-bean (Phase'olus vulga'ris); ₌tag m (15. Juni) St. Vitus'(s) Day; ₌tanz (St. Veit wurde dagegen angerufen) m, path. St. Vitus'(s) dance, ⚘ chorea.

Vejenter (w⁻ʯ¹ʯ) [Veji ⚥, uralte Stadt in Etrurien] m ⑫, ~in f ⑰ röm. Alt.: Veian, inhabitant of Veii. [radius vector.)

Vektor ⚘ (w¹ʯ) [lt.] m ⑪ geom. (Radius)~)

Velin ⚘, ⚘ (w⁻¹, w⁻¹) [fr.] n ⑪d. vellum; ~papier n ⑫ vellum-paper, (wire-wove) paper.

Velit ⚔ (w⁻¹) [lt. ve'lites pl. v. veles] m ⑫ röm. Alt.: (Plänkler) velite.

Velle-ität ⚘ (w⁻ʯ⁻¹) [fr.] f ㊻ (schwankendes Wollen) vacillation, ⚘ velleity.

Velo (w⁻¹) [=Velo(ziped)] n ㉚ cycle.

Velodrom * (w⁻ʯ¹) [lt. = grch.] m ⑪d. (Radfahrer-übungsbahn) cycling-track or -course, cycling-school, school (or course) for cyclists.

Velo-sport (w¹⁻ʯ) m ⑫ cycling (sport).

Velours (w⁻¹u⁻ʯ) [fr.] m ㉝ (Samt) velvet.

Velociped (w⁻ʯtʃ⁻¹) [neu-lt.] n ⑪c. cycle, F machine, wheel; chm.: velocipede (vgl. Fahrrad); ~ist (w⁻⁻tʃ⁻¹ʯ) m ⑫, ~istin f ⑰ ₌ Radfahrer(in).

Velt(e)lin ⚥ (i⁻ʯ⁻¹ʯ) npr/n. ㉙a. (nord-ital. Tal) Valtel(l)ine, Valtelina.

Velten (ĭ¹ʯ) npr/m. ㉙a. [dim. v. Valentin] Sanft ~ Saint Valentine; potz ~! good gracious!. goodness alive!

Vende-er (wa¹⁻¹) /Vendée ⚥, fr. Departement der Westküste] m ⑫, ~in f ⑰ Vendean.

Vendetta (w⁻ʯ⁻¹) [it.] f ㊾ ₌ Blutrache.

Vene ⚘ (w⁻¹) [lt.] f ㊻ (Ader) vein; Lehre von den ~n: ⚘ phlebology.

Venedig ⚥ (w⁻ʯ¹) npr n. ㉙a. (nord-ital. St., ehm. Republik) Venice.

Venen-blut (w⁻ʯ...) n ⑫ venous blood; ₌entzündung f, path. inflammation of the veins, ⚘ phlebitis; ₌erweiterung f, path. ⚘ varicosity; ₌puls m, path. venous pulse.

Venerie (w⁻ʯ¹) [fr.] f ㊸ path. venereal disease (=Lustseuche); **venerisch** (w⁻ʯ¹ʯ) a. ⑯ venereal (= syphilitisch).

Veneter (w⁻ʯ¹) m/pl. ⑫ Alt.: Volk in Nord-italien u. Bretagne: Veneti pl.

Veneti-en (w⁻ʯ⁻¹tʃ(⌣)⁻) npr/n. ㉓a. Alt.: nord-östliche Landschaft Italiens: Venetia, später: (the republic of) Venice.

Venezianer (w⁻ʯ⁻tʃ⁻¹ʯ) m ⑫, ~in f ⑰, **venezianisch** a. ⑯ Venetian, of Venice; **Venezianisch-rot** n ⑰ min. (roter Oker) Venetian red. [Venezuelan.)

Venezolaner (w⁻ʯ⁻¹ʯ) [Venezuela] m ⑫)

Venezuela ⚥ (w⁻ʯ⁻¹ʯ) [Klein-Venedig] npr/n. ㉙a. Staat in Süd-amerika: Venezuela; **venezuelisch** a. ⑯ Venezuelan.

venös ⚘ (w⁻¹) [lt.] a. ⑯ (D 10) (aderig, aderreich) venous.

Ventil (w⁻¹) [mlt. Wind-] n ⑪d. anat., ⚘, ⊙ (Klappe) valve, ♪ piston, stop; ⊙ mach. =Luftklappe, a.: air-regulator.

Ventilation (w⁻ʯ⁻tʃ(⌣)¹) [lt.] f ㊻ (Lüftung) ventilation; airing of rooms. **Ventilations-maschine** ⚘ ⚙ (w⁻ʯ⁻tʃ(⌣)¹...) f air-machine; ₌rädchen n in e-r Fensterscheibe: whirligig-ventilator. [ator.)

Ventilator ⊙ (w⁻ʯ⁻¹) [lt.] m ⑪ ventil-)

ventilieren ⊙ (w⁻ʯ⁻¹) [lt.] I v/a. ⑬ 1. e-n Raum ⚘ (lüften) to ventilate (or air) ... — 2. fig. eine Frage ⚘ (erörtern) to discuss (or thrash out) a question. — II ~ n ㉓ 3. ventilation, fig. discussion.

Ventil-klappe ⊙ (w⁻ʯ¹...) f ⑫ flap-, leaf-valve; ₌sitz m valve-seat; ₌steu(e)rung f valve-gear; ₌stütze f valve-guard.

Ventrikel ⚘ (w⁻¹) [lt.] m ⑪ anat. (Herzkammer) ventricle (of the heart).

Venus (w⁻¹) [lt.] npr/f. inv. a) myth. (Göttin der sinnlichen Liebe, fig. schönes Weib) Venus; b) ast. (Planet) Venus, morning- (or evening-)star; ⚥ ₌ Fliegenfalle.

Venus-berg (w⁻ʯ...) m ⑫ anat. (lt.) mons Veneris; ₌blüten f/pl. path. (venerischer Ausschlag) Venus's-blossoms pl., (syphilitic) pimples (or eruption) in the face; ₌dienst m worship of Venus; ₌durchgang m, ast. transit of (the planet) Venus; ₌fliegenfalle ⚘ f = Fliegenfalle, ₌gürtel m: (Gürtel der Venus, fig. weiblicher Liebreiz) girdle of Venus, cestus; ₌haar ⚘ n Venus's-hair, (golden) maiden-hair (Adia'ntum capi'llus Ve'neris).

venushaft (w⁻ʯ...) a. ⑯ like a Venus.

venusinisch (w⁻ʯ⁻¹ʯ) [Venu'sia ⚥ in Apulien, Vaterstadt des Horaz] a. ⑯ Venusian.

Venus-muschel (w⁻ʯ...) f ⑫ zo. Venus's-shell, venus, clam (Venus mercena'ria); ₌priesterin f priestess of Venus; fig. (öffentliche Dirne) prostitute.

ver-..., Ver-... (f⁻ʯ...) [ahd.: for-; vgl. forget: vergessen, forlorn: verloren] Vorsilbe in Zssgn mit verbs u. daraus abgeleiteten nouns u. adjectives. immer untrennbar (*), bz.: 1. Erschöpfung, zB. das Mehl verbacken to use up all the flour in baking. — 2. Irrtum, Versehen, zB. verdrehen to turn the wrong way; die Karten vergeben to misdeal the cards. — 3. Bedeckung, Wegräumung, zB. verhängen to cover over; verbergen to hide. — 4. Anwendung, zB. die Zeit verplaudern to talk (or chat) away the time. — 5. ein Aufhören, zB. verbrausen to cease fermenting. — 6. Sterben, zB. verdursten to perish with thirst. — 7. Gegenteil, Abwesenheit dessen, was das einfache v. besagt, zB. verachten not to esteem, to despise; auch sonstige Abweichung von der ursprünglichen Bed. des einfachen v., zB. verbieten to forbid; vergeben, verzeihen to forgive. — 8. Stärkung der ursprünglichen Bed., zB. vermehren to multiply; verwickeln to entangle. — 9. mit a., oft im comp., bildet es verbs, die eine Umwandlung bezeichnen, edel noble, veredeln to ennoble, größer greater, vergrößern to enlarge, to aggrandize.

ver-abfolg/en (f⁻ʯ⁻¹ʯ) I v/a. u. v/n. (h.) ⑬*: eine Kiste an e-n ⚘ to remit (or deliver, consign, hand over) ... to a p.; e-m etwas ⚘ lassen to let a p. have a th. — II ~ n ㉓ und B/ung f ㊻ delivery, consignment.

ver-abred/en (f⁻ʯ⁻¹ʯ) I v/a. u. v/refl. ⑬*: et. ⚘ to agree upon (or plan) a th., Tag u. Stunde: to fix upon; jur. (abmachen) to stipulate; sich mit e-m ⚘ to make an arrangement (or appointment) with a p., to come to an agreement with a p.; zur verabredeten Zeit at the appointed time; vorher verabredet preconcerted. — II ~ n ㉓ f. B/ung.

ver-abredeter-maßen (f⁻ʯ⁻⁻⁻¹ʯ) adv. as agreed upon, according to (a previous) agreement or arrangement.

Ver-abredung (f⁻ʯ⁻¹) f ㊻ agreement, stipulation, arrangement, appointment; frühere ~ previous engagement.

ver-abreichen (~) v/a. ⑬* to hand (over), to tender, Arzneien ꝛc.: to dispense; e-m et. ⚘ to give a p s.th. due to him; e-m eine Ohrfeige ⚘ to give (F to land) a p. a box on the ear, to box a p.'s ears.

ver-absäumen (f⁻ʯ⁻¹) v/a. ⑬* to neglect; to shirk; (unterlassen) to omit, to leave undone; (vergessen) to forget, overlook.

ver-abscheuen (f⁻ʯ⁻¹) I v/a. ⑬* to detest, to abhor, to abominate, to hold in abhorrence, mit Ekel: to loathe; sie ⚘

[Verabscheuung] — 1026 — [verärgert]

alles Gemeine anything vulgar is their aversion or abomination. — II ~ n 23 f. Verabscheuung.
Ver-abscheuung f 46 (f~ঊ~) detestation, abhorrence, loathing; ≗s-wert (f~ঊ~...), ≗würdig a. 66 detestable, abominable, loathsome, execrable.
ver-abschied/en (f~ঊ~) 68* I v/a. to dismiss, to discharge, stärker: to send away, F to sack, to give a p. his (f her) congé; mit Ruhegehalt ≗ to pension off; ⚔ Truppen ≗ (auflösen) to disband troops; parl. ein Gesetz ≗ to pass a bill. — II v/refl. sich von (oder bei) e-m ≗ to take leave of a p., to bid a p. farewell, to say good-bye to a p. — III ~ n 23 und B/ung f 46 dismissal, discharge; leave-taking, (bidding or taking) farewell.
ver-achten (f~ঊchtv~) I v/a. 68* to despise, stärker: to scorn, to hold in contempt, to look down upon, ↘ to contemn; (geringschätzen) to disdain, den Tod: to brave; nicht zu ≗(d) not to be despised, F not to be sneezed at, not half (or not a quarter) bad; (well) worth having. — II ~ n 23 f. Verachtung.
Ver-ächter (f~ঊ~) m 22, ~in f 47 despiser, scorner, scornful person; (Verkleinerer) belittler, detractor. [octuple.]
ver-achtfachen (f~ঊchtv~chy) v/a. 68* to
ver-ächtlich (f~ঊ~) a. 66 1. (verachtend) scornful, contemptuous, disdainful; ≗ (adv.) behandeln to treat with scorn or contempt, to look down upon, auch to snub. — 2. (verachtungswert) despicable, contemptible; (verworfen) abject, vile, base, mean.
Ver-ächtlichkeit (f~ঊ~) f (f. verächtlich) 1. scornfulness. — 2. despicableness, contemptibleness; abjectness.
Ver-achtung (f~ঊchtv~) f 46 scorn, contempt; disdain; mit ~ behandeln to treat contemptuously or with scorn.
ver-achtungs=wert (≗...), ≗würdig a. f. verächtlich 2; =würdigkeit f = Verächtlichkeit 2. [ilate, to make similar.)
ver-ähnlichen (f~ঊ~) v/a. 68* to assim-
ver-akkordieren (f~ঊ~) v/a. 68*: et. mit e-m ≗ to (make a) contract (or to arrange terms) with a p. about a th.
ver-akzisen (f~ঊ~) v/a. 68*: et. ≗ to pay excise (or duty) on a th.
ver-allgemeinern (f~ঊঊ~) I v/a. 92a* to generalize. — II ~ n 23 und Ver-allgemeinerung f 46 generalization.
ver-alten (f~ঊ~) I v/n. (fn) 68* to grow old or obsolete or stale, to go out of use or date; ≗d obsolescent; veraltet obsolete, out of use or date, antiquated, old-fashioned, von Worten auch: archaic; veralteter Ausdruck archaism; (verjährt) superannuated. — II ~ n 23 obsolescence; superannuation.
Veranda T (w≗ঊ) [ind.] f 46⑤ arch. (Vordach e-s Hauses) veranda.
ver-änderlich (f~ঊ~) a. 66 variable (auch math.), changeable, mutable; (unbeständig) inconstant, unstable, unsteady, Wetter 2c. auch: unsettled; (wankelmütig) vacillating; (schwankend) fluctuating; ~keit f 46 variability, changeableness, mutability; inconstancy, instability, unsteadiness, vacillation; fluctuation.

ver-ändern (f~ঊ~) 92a. I v/a. = ändern; (abwechseln) to vary; (verwandeln) to transform; die Szene ≗ to shift the scene. — II sich ≗ v/refl. to change (for the better, for the worse), to alter, to vary; vorteilhaft: to improve, to better o.s., to find a better place; nachteilig: to deteriorate, bsd. ❋ to fall off (in quality); P (in einen andern Dienst treten) to change one's place, to take another situation; (sich verheiraten) to get married.
Ver-änderung (f~ঊ~) f 46 change, alteration, variation, teilweise: modification, vollständige: sweeping (or radical) change; (Verwandlung) transformation, ⚹ metamorphosis; (Schwankung) fluctuation (f. erleiden 1); er liebt die ~ he is fond of change or of chopping and changing (about); ~ der Stimme bei Jünglingen: breaking of the voice; ≗s-halber adv. for (the sake of) a change.
ver-ankern (f~ঊ~) v/a. 92a* 1. ⊕ Bauwesen 2c.: Mauern ≗ to grapple ..., to fasten ... with grappling-irons; ein Gewölbe, einen Ofen ≗ to bind a vault, a furnace. — 2. ⚓ to anchor, to moor (fast).
ver-anlagen (f~ঊ~) I v/a. 68* 1. Steuern ≗ to assess taxes. — 2. (einrichten) to establish, to organize. — 3. fig. er ist nicht dazu veranlagt he is not cut out (or suited) for it; gut veranlagter Mensch talented (stärker: highly gifted) person. — II ~ n 23 und Ver-anlagung f 46 4. (f. 1) assessment of taxes; (f. 3) talent(s pl.), giftedness.
ver-anlassen (f~ঊ~) I v/a. 68* to occasion, give rise to, bring about or on; (hervorrufen) to provoke, call forth; (anstiften) to instigate; (verursachen) to cause; e-n zu et. ≗ to induce (F to get) a p. to do a th., verlockend: to tempt (or allure) a p. to do a th.; e-n zu dem Glauben ≗, daß // to make a p. think that //, to lead a p. to suppose that //, to drive a p. to the conclusion that //. — II ~ n 23 f. Veranlassung.
Ver-anlasser (~) m 22, ~in f 47 one who occasions a th., author; instigator.
Ver-anlassung (f~ঊ~) f 46 occasion, cause (zu et. of a th.); (Beweggrund) inducement, motive, (Antrieb) impulse; auf meine ~ at my instigation, stärker: by my orders; ~ zu et. geben to give rise to a th.
ver-annehmlichen (f~ঊ-ঊঊ) v/a. 68* to render agreeable or pleasant.
ver-anschaulichen (f~ঊ-ঊঊ) v/a. 68* to afford a view of, to make clear, to render palpable, to be illustrative (or to furnish an illustration) of, auch anschaulich (f. bs) machen.
Ver-anschaulichung (~) f 46 illustration, demonstration; auch: object-lesson; zur ~ e-r Sache dienen to illustrate (or throw light on) a subject, to serve as (an) object-lesson; ~s-apparat m 22 apparatus for (purposes of) illustration; ~s-mittel n/pl. Schule: illustrative objects (for object-lessons) pl.
ver-anschlag/en (f~ঊ-ঊ) I v/a. 68* to estimate, appraise, value (auf at); Bauwesen: to make an estimate of; et. zu hoch (zu gering) ≗ to overrate (to underrate) a th.; annähernd veranschlagt roughly estimated, on an approximate calculation. — II ~ n 23 u. B/ung f 46 estimate, valuation.
ver-anstalt/en (f~ঊ-ঊ) I v/a. 68* to arrange, to bring about, (bewerkstelligen) to contrive, manage; (Vorbereitungen m. zu) to prepare; ein Fest 2c.: to organize, to get up. — II ~ n 23 f. B/ung.
Ver-anstalter (f~ঊ-ঊঊ) m 22, ~in f 47 contriver; organizer; (Bewirtender) host, founder of the feast.
Ver-anstaltung (f~ঊ-ঊঊ) f 46 arrangement; preparation; organization, management; ~en m. (ob. treffen) für to make arrangements (or to prepare) for.
ver-antworten (f~ঊ-ঊঊ) 68* I v/a. to answer (or account) for; to take upon o.s.; er hat es zu ≗ he is responsible (for it), the responsibility rests upon him; das will ich schon ≗! I will see to that!, leave that to me! — II sich ≗ v/refl.: sich wegen et. bei e-m ≗ (verteidigen) to justify (or vindicate, defend) one's doings before a p. — III ~ n 23 f. Verantwortung.
ver-antwortlich (f~ঊ-ঊঊ) a. 66 1. answerable for, responsible for; (rechenschaftspflichtig) accountable for; gegenseitig ≗ mutually responsible or bound; e-n für et. ≗ m. to hold (or make) a p. responsible for a th. — 2. von Sachen: (gerechtfertigt) justifiable.
Ver-antwortlichkeit (f~ঊ-ঊঊঊ-) f 46 responsibility, accountability, gegenseitige: solidarity; pol. ~ des Ministeriums ministerial responsibility (f. laden² 1).
Ver-antwortung (f~ঊ-ঊঊ) f 46 answering (or accounting) for; auf Ihre ~ on your responsibility, at your peril or risk; tun Sie es auf meine ~ I'll be answerable (if you will do it). — 2. (Rechtfertigung) justification, vindication.
ver-antwortungs=los (f~ঊ-ঊঊ...) a. 66 without (or free from) responsibility, irresponsible; =rede, =schrift f 62 jur. defence; ≗voll a. 66 responsible.
ver-arbeiten (f~ঊ-ঊঊ) I v/a. 68* 1. ⊕ (als Stoff verwenden, verbrauchen) to use (up) in working, to work up, to consume; Stoffe, die sich leicht ≗ lassen materials (which are) easy to work or easily worked (up). — 2. (gestalten) to mould in working, to work (zu into), to manufacture; verarbeitetes Metall wrought metal. — 3. physiol. die Speisen ≗ to digest the food. — 4. fig. im Gemüte ≗ to elaborate, to ponder (or think) out. — 5. F fig. e-n ≗ (geißeln, bsd. in Zeitschriften) to criticize a p. severely, F to pitch into a p., to slate a p., to pick holes in a p. — II ~ n 23 u. **Ver-arbeitung** f 46 6. working up, consumption of materials, manufacture; digestion of food; fig. elaboration.
ver-argen (f~ঊ~) v/a. 68*: e-m et. ≗ to find fault with a p. for a th., to take a th. amiss of a p.; wir ≗ es Ihnen (gar) nicht we don't think any the worse of you for (doing) it; das kann ihm niemand ≗ no one can blame (or reproach) him for it.
ver-ärgert (f~ঊ~) a. 66 full of vexation; ≗ aussehen to look vexed or annoyed or sullen.

Signs (see page XVII): F familiar; P vulgar; F flash; ↘ rare; † obsolete (died); * new word (born); ⁺⁺ incorrect; ♪ music.

[verarmen] — 1027 — [verbinden]

ver-armen (⌣⌣⌣) ⓑ* I v/n. (ſn) to grow poor, to become impoverished or reduced to poverty; (betteларm w.) to become a pauper. — II v/a. (arm m.) to impoverish, ſtärfer: to pauperize, to reduce to beggary. — III ~ n ㉓ u. **Ver-armung** f ㊻ impoverishment, pauperization, pauperism; beggary.

ver-äſteln (⌣⌣⌣) I v/a. u. ſich ⌢ v/refl. ⓐ*: (ſich) ⌢ to branch out, to ramify; ver-äſtelt: ⚯ ramulous. — II ~ n ㉓ u. **Ver-äſt(e)lung** f ㊻ ramification.

Veratrin ⚯ (w—ᴸ) [lt. Vera'trum album ⚘ weiße Nieswurz] n ⓓd. chm. veratrine; **~ſäure** f ㉒ veratric acid ($C_9H_{10}O_4$).

ver-auktionier/en (⌣⌣-tg(⌣)-ᴸ⌣) v/a. ⓑ. **B/ung** f ㊻ = verſteigern, Verſteigerung.

ver-ausgab/en (⌣⌣ᴸ-) I v/a. ⓑ* to expend or spend on or for, to pay (away) for. — II ſich ⌢ v/refl. to run short (or out) of money. — III ~ n ㉓ u. **B/ung** f ㊻ expenditure.

ver-äußerlich (⌣⌣⌣⌣) a. ㊻ alienable.

ver-äußer/n (⌣⌣ᴸ) I v/a. ⓐ* to alienate; (verkaufen) to dispose of, to sell. — II ~ n ㉓ u. **B/ung** f ㊻ alienation; sale.

Verb (wᵛ) n ㉕d. = Verbum.

ver-backen (⌣⌣⌣) ⓑb* I v/a. to make bread of; täglich einen Sack Mehl ⌢ to use up in baking one sack of flour a day; Mehl zu Brot ⌢ to turn (or convert) ... into bread. — II v/a. u. v/n. (ſn) (ſchlecht backen, backend mißraten) to spoil in baking; das Brot iſt ⌢ ... badly baked, ... spoilt.

Verbal=adjektiv (wᵛᴸ...) n ㊷ gr. verbal adjective; **=injurie** f jur. insult(ing words pl.), | vide with) libel. | vide with) ballast.

ver-ballaſten ⌄ (⌣⌣⌣⌣) v/a. ⓑ* to (pro-)

ver-ballhorn/en (⌣⌣⌣⌣)[ſ. Ballhorniſieren] v/a. ⓑ* to mend (or correct) in a clumsy (or bungling) way, to make sham improvements in, to make worse instead of better; Schriften: to Bowdlerize; **B/ung** f ㊻ clumsy correction, literary botching, Bowdlerization.

Verbal=note (wᵛᴸᴸ) f ㊷ Diplomatie: verbal note or communication.

Ver-band (⌣ᵛ) m ⓓb. 1. (Verbindung) union, geſellſchaftlicher ~, a. association, society; vgl. Berufsgenoſſenſchaft; ~ von Radfahrern cycling club. — 2. surg. dressing, bandaging; ligature, ⚯ fasciation. — 3. ⊖ Bauweſen: ~ im Mauerwerk ꝛc., binding, assemblage.

Ver-band=apparat (⌣ᵛ...) m ㊷ surg. appliance(s pl.) for dressing wounds; **=holz** ⊖ n, carp. framing-timber; **=kaſten** m, surg. surgeon's dressing-case; **=läppchen** m compress; **=platz** ⚔ m place where wounds are dressed.

Ver-bands=kaſſe (⌣ᵛ...) f ㊷ funds pl. of a society or union; **=mitglied** n member of an association or a society, typ. society-hand.

Ver-band=ſtück ⊖ (⌣ᵛ...) n ㊷ carp. framing-piece; **=zeug** n, surg. rolls pl. of bandage, things used for dressing wounds.

ver-bannen (⌣⌣⌣) ⓑ* I v/a. to banish, pol. to exile, Alt. a.: to ostracize; (ächten) to outlaw, to proscribe; (vertreiben) to expel; fig. Sorgen ꝛc. ⌢ to banish (or dispel) ... — II **Ver-bann=**

te(r) s. ㊷ exile; outlaw, (Ausgeſtoßener) outcast. — III ~ n ㉓ f. Verbannung.

Ver-bannung (⌣⌣ᴸ) f ㊻ banishment, exile, ostracism; outlawry, proscription; expulsion; in der ~ leben to live in (or as an) exile; weitS. to be an outlaw; **~s=ort** m ㊷ (place of) exile.

ver-barg (⌣ᴸ) ind., **verbärge** ↙ (⌣⌣ᴸ) subj. impf. v. verbergen.

ver-barrikadieren (⌣⌣⌣⌣ᴸ⌣) v/a. ⓑ to barricade or obstruct a street, &c., to block (or bar) up an entrance, &c.; ſich ⌢ to barricade (or entrench) o.s.

ver-bat (⌣ᴸ) ind., **ver-bäte** (⌣⌣ᴸ) subj. impf. v. verbitten.

ver-bau/en (⌣⌣ᴸ) ⓑ* I v/a. 1. to obstruct (or block up) with buildings or walls, to build up; e-m Hauſe das Licht ob. die Ausſicht ⌢ to obstruct (or to wall up) the view (or lights) of a house. — 2. (ausgeben, verwenden) 1000 Mark ⌢ to spend £ 50 in building; viel Holz ⌢ to use up ... in building. — 3. (falſch bauen) to build badly, to misconstruct, to spoil in building. — II ſich ⌢ v/refl. 4.: a) v. Baumeiſter: to blunder in building; b) v. Bauherrn: to lavish one's money in building. — 5. ⚒ die Zeche verbaut ſich (bedt die Koſten) the mine is paying its way. — II ~ n ㉓ 6. ſ. B/ung.

ver-bauern (⌣⌣ᴸ) v/n. (ſn) ⓐ* to adopt rustic (or boorish) manners, to grow into a rustic, F to become countrified.

Ver-bauung (⌣⌣ᴸ) f ㊻ (f. 1) obstruction of the view or lights; (f. 3) faulty (or wrong, defective) construction.

ver-beißen (⌣⌣ᴸ) ⓐ* I v/a. (die Zähne zſ.=beißend unterdrücken) to suppress (by an effort), to stifle, choke, restrain; fig. ſeinen Ärger ⌢ to swallow one's anger; ſich das Lachen ⌢ to bite one's lips (so as not to burst out laughing); wir konnten uns das Lachen nicht ⌢ we could not help (or refrain from) laughing. — II ſich ⌢ v/refl. bſd. von Jagdhunden: to lock one's teeth in biting; fig. von Perſonen: ſich in et. ⌢ to be mad after (or hot on) a th. — III **ver-biſſen** ſ. bſd. Artikel.

Verbene ⚘ (wᵛᴸ) [lt.] f ㉒ = Eiſenkraut.

ver-berg/en (⌣⌣ᴸ) I v/a. u. ſich ⌢ v/refl. ⓓb(a)*: (ſich) ⌢ to conceal (o.s.), bſd. aus Vorſicht ob. ſpielend: to hide (o.s.); ſich ⌢, auch: to be (or keep) in hiding; (dem Auge entziehen) to keep out of sight; (verheimlichen) to hush up (vgl. verdecken); ſich vor e-m ⌢ to hide from a p.; ſich vor aller Augen ⌢ to shun (or avoid, eschew) all eyes or glances. — II ~ n ㉓ u. **B/ung** f ㊻ concealment, hiding. — III **ver-borgen** p.p. u. a. ㊻ (D 9) concealed, hidden, out of sight; (geheim) secret, von Schriften ꝛc.: occult; (heimlich, unerlaubt) clandestine, furtive; (ruhmlos) obscure, verborgen (wirkend) latent (a. phys.); ⚘ verborgene Befruchtung: ⚯ cryptogamy; zo. mit verborgenem Kopfe: ⚯ cryptocephalous; im verborgenen ſecret, secretly; im verborgenen lauern, liegen to lurk, to lie in wait or in ambush.

Ver-beſſerer (⌣⌣⌣) m ㊷, **Ver-beſſe(re)rin** f ㊷ (a)mender; von Fehlern: corrector; (Umgeſtalter[in]) reformer.

ver-beſſerlich (⌣⌣⌣) a. ㊻ (a)mendable, corrigible; reformable, improvable.

ver-beſſer/n (⌣⌣ᴸ) I v/a. u. v/refl. ⓐa* 1. to (make) better, to ameliorate, ſittlich, geiſtig: to improve; (berichtigen) to correct, amend, rectify, (vervollkommnen) to perfect; (umgeſtalten) to reform, to remodel, (nachbeſſern) to touch up; verbeſſerte Auflage revised (and improved) edition. — 2. ſich ⌢ to grow better, to improve, beim Sprechen: to correct o.s., in ſeinen Umſtänden: to better o.s., in ſeinem Betragen: to mend (one's ways), to turn over a new leaf; to reform. — II ~ n ㉓ 3. ſ. Verbeſſerung. — III ⌢d p.pr. u. a. ㊻ 4. Bed. des inf. — 5. corrective, reformatory.

Ver-beſſerung (⌣⌣⌣) f ㊻ change for the better, amelioration, emendation; correction, rectification, improvement; reform(ation).

Ver-beſſerungs=antrag (⌣⌣⌣...) m ㊷ parl., &c. amendment; **=bedürftig** a. ㊻ needing (or with room for) improvement; **=fähig** a. capable (or susceptible) of improvement or reform; vgl. verbeſſerlich. | Verbeſſerer ꝛc.)

Ver-beßrer, Ver-beßrung (⌣⌣⌣) ꝛc. ſ.)

ver-beten (⌣⌣⌣) p.p. von verbitten.

ver-beugen (⌣⌣⌣) I ſich ⌢ v/refl. ⓑ* to (make a) bow, to make an obeisance, to do reverence (vor e-m to a p.). — II ~ n ㉓ u. **Ver-beugung** f ㊻ bow, obeisance, reverence.

ver-biegen (⌣⌣ᴸ) I v/a. u. v/refl. ⓐaſt* to bend (or twist) the wrong way; (aus der Form bringen) to put out of shape, to distort, (krümmen) to curve; ſich ⌢ to get bent or twisted, vom Holze: (ſich werfen) to get warped, to warp. — II ~ n ㉓ u. **Ver-biegung** f ㊻ wrong bend or twist; warp(ing).

ver-bieten (⌣⌣ᴸ) [ahd. forbid] I v/a. ⓐa* to forbid, amtlich: to prohibit; (unterſagen) to interdict; die Herausgabe e-r Flugſchrift ꝛc. ⌢ to suppress a pamphlet, &c.; Cath. eccl. ein Buch ⌢ to put ... on the index; Rauchen (iſt hier) verboten! no smoking allowed!; das Spucken iſt hier verboten! do not spit!, you are requested not to spit (on the floor). — II ~ n ㉓ = Verbot.

ver-bild/en (⌣⌣⌣) [ahd.] I v/a.ⓑ* u. ſich ⌢ v/refl. 1. to give a wrong shape to, fig. to pervert; (ſich) ⌢ to form in a wrong way; (entſtellen) to malform, deform, disfigure. — 2. (falſch erziehen) to miseducate. — II ~ n ㉓ u. **B/ung** f ㊻ 3. (giving a) wrong shape, fig. perversion; (Entſtellung) malformation, deformity, disfigurement. — 4. miseducation, wrong (or bad, faulty) training; ill-breeding.

ver-bildlich/en (⌣⌣⌣⌣) v/a. ⓐa* to represent pictorially or emblematically or figuratively; to symbolize, to typify; **B/ung** f ㊻ symbolization.

ver-billig/en (⌣⌣⌣) I v/a. ⓑ* to cheapen, to reduce (or lower) in price. — II **B/ung** f ㊻ reduction in price.

ver-binden (⌣⌣⌣) [ahd.] I v/a. u. ſich ⌢ v/refl. ⓓ* 1. (vereinigen) to unite, chm., &c. to combine, mit Quecksilber: to amalgamate (a. fig.); (verschmelzen) to

⓸ scientific; ⚘ botanical; ⚱ geography; ⊖ machinery; ⚒ mining; ⚔ military; ⚓ marine; ⬤ commercial; ✉ postal; ⛟ railway.

[Verbinder] — 1028 — [verblüffen]

coalesce; (an-ea.schließen) to join (together), enger: to knit (or link) together, zu einem Bunde: to ally, durch die Ehe: to join in wedlock, Getrenntes: to connect, Zf.-gehöriges: to assort, to associate; elect., tel. mit der Erde 2 to (put to) earth; zu einer Schleife 2 to loop; sich 2 mit // to form a connexion (or an alliance) with //, to join //, to make common cause with//, chm. to combine with//, als Geschäftsteilhaber: to go into partnership with //, in der Ehe: to marry //, to wed //; das Nützliche mit dem Angenehmen 2 to combine business with pleasure; durch das Band der Ehe verbunden joined in wedlock, united in marriage, married, wedded; mit einiger Gefahr, mit e-m gewissen Risiko verbunden attended with (or involving) a certain amount of danger or risk; es sind damit viele Vorteile verbunden it combines (or offers) many advantages; die damit verbundenen Verhältnisse the surrounding (or concomitant) circumstances pl.; chm. mit Sauerstoff (Wasserstoff) verbunden oxidized (hydrogenized, hydric); Fernspr. 2 Sie mich mit N.! put me on to N.!; 2b connecting, connective; log. (zf.-setzend) synthetical; elect. die Pole 2b interpolar. — 2. e-n zu et. 2 (verpflichten) to oblige a p. to do a th.; ich bin Ihnen sehr (zu Dank) verbunden I am very much obliged (or greatly indebted) to you; sich zu et. 2 to undertake (to do) a th. — 3. (bindend verschließen) to bind (or tie) up, Wunden auch: to dress, to bandage (up); e-m die Augen 2 to blindfold a p.; bibl. dem Ochsen das Maul 2 to muzzle the ox. — 4. ⊕ Buchbinderei: (falsch binden) to misbind, to bind wrongly or in the wrong order. — II ~ n 23 5. uniting, &c. (f. 1); binding (or tying) up (f. 3); surg. das ~ von Wunden the dressing (or bandaging) of wounds. — 6. f. Verbindung. [(of wounds).]
Ver-binder (f~v~) m 22 surg. dresser]
ver-bindlich (f~v~) a. 66 1. (verpflichtend) binding (agreement, treaty, &c.), obligatory, compulsory; durch Höflichkeit: obliging, courteous; e-m seinen Dank sagen, 2st (adv.) danken to return (or render) a p. one's heartiest thanks, to thank a p. most sincerely; e-m viel ~es sagen to say many complimentary things (or to pay many compliments) to a p. — 2. (verpflichtet) (in duty) bound, obliged; sich 2 m. zu // to bind (or engage, pledge) o.s. to //.
Ver-bindlichkeit (f~v~) f 46 (f. verbindlich) 1. binding force of agreements, treaties, &c.,compulsoriness; obligingness, courtesy; (Gefälligkeit) favour, kindness. — 2. obligation, liability, f. nachkommen; ⊕ ohne ~ without (any) liability or a(ny) guarantee.
Ver-bindung (f~v~) f 46 1. = verbinden 5. — 2. union, combination (á. chm.); mst chm. u. fig amalgamation; ~ (Verschmelzung) von Farben blending of colours; mst pol. coalition, alliance; in ~ mit // in conjunction (or unison)

with //, jointly (or together) with //. — 3. a) (Gesellschaft) society, association; eheliche ~ marriage (contract), match, matrimonial tie or alliance; geschäftliche ~en business connexions or friends pl.; (Studenten-)~ students' association or club; b) ~ (Verkettung) von Umständen juncture; c) chm. chemische ~ (Vereinigung mehrerer Elemente) chemical composition; d) ⊕ ~ der Hölzer: assemblage; (Balkenband) brace. — 4. (Verkehr) communication; 🚂 railway-communication or -connexion; ⚔ die ~en abschneiden to cut off the enemy's communications; ~ halten mit to keep in touch (or contact) with; nach mehreren Orten die ~ vermitteln to connect several places. — 5. (Beziehung) relation(ship), connexion; mit etwas in ~ stehen to be connected with a th; mit e-m in ~ stehen to be in touch (or contact) with a p.; in brieflicher ~ stehen mit // to carry on (or keep) up a correspondence with //, to correspond with //; in ~ treten mit // to form a connexion (or enter into correspondence) with //.
Ver-bindungs-bahn 🚂 (f~v~...) f 62 junction-line; =gang m, arch. connecting passage, (Bogengang) archway; =geleise 🚂 n junction-rail; =glied n connecting link; =kanal m channel of communication or intercourse; =linie f line of communication; =los a. without communication or connexion; =mittel n means of communication; =rohr n, =röhre f ⊕ connecting pipe or tube, conduit(-pipe); =stange ⊕ f, mach. connecting rod; 🚂 e-r Weiche: switch-rod; =strich m hyphen; =stück ⊕ n Bauw. &c.: tie, brace, joint; =treppe f communicating staircase; =verhältnis n, chm. proportion of combining atoms or molecules, combining proportion; =weg ⚔ m line of communication; =wort n, gr.: a) für Subj. u. Präd.: copula; b) für Sätze: conjunction; =zeichen n = =strich.
ver-birg([f]t) (f~v~) imper. (pres.) v. verbergen. [subst. impf. v. verbeißen.]
ver-biß(f~v~)ind., ver-bisse(n¹ pl.) (f~v~)]
ver-bissen² (f~v~)[p.p. v. verbeißen] a. 66 (D9) fig. very sullen or sour-tempered, crabbed, morose; ~heit (f~v~-) f 46 sullenness, sour(ed) temper, crabbedness, moroseness.
ver-bitten (f~v~) v/a. 4* to deprecate; sich (dat.) et. von e-m 2 to desire a p. not to do a th., stärker: to insist on a p. not doing a th.; sich Besuche, Briefe &c. 2 to decline ...; warnend: das 2 wir uns (für die od. in Zukunft)! we cannot allow (or tolerate) that (in the future)!
ver-bittern (f~v~) [mhd.] 2a* I v/a. meist fig. to embitter, to fill with bitterness; e-m das Leben 2, oft: to worry a p.'s life out. II v/n. (sn) u. sich 2 v/refl. (bitter w. in der Stimmung) to grow sour-tempered or sullen.—III Ver-bitterung (f~v~) f 46: ~ des Gemüts bitterness of heart,sour(ness of) temper,sullenness.
ver-blasen (f~v~) v/a. 6n* 1 fortblasen: to blow away. 2. ⊕ Glasfabr.: (Glasmasse verwenden) die Glasmasse ist

schon 2 the glass has all been used up (for blowing). — 3. paint. die Farben 2 (schwach auftragen) to dilute the colours (in painting).
ver-blassen (f~v~) v/n. (sn) 90* = verbleichen, von Stoffen u. Farben: to fade, to discolour, von Farben auch: F to fly; verblaßter Druck faded type; in geh. Spr. er ist verblaßt he has passed away, he is dead.
ver-blättern (f~v~) v/a. 2a*: eine Stelle im Buche 2 to lose a place in turning over the leaves of a book.
ver-bläuen (f~v~; Hom. verbleuen) v/n. (sn) 88* (blau w.) to turn blue.
Ver-bleib (f~¹) m ⓜc. place where a th. has been left or has got to; ich weiß nichts über den ~ der Ringe I don't know anything about the whereabouts (or I have no clue as to what has become) of the rings.
ver-bleiben (f~¹) [mhd.] I v/n.(sn) 61* 1 to be left, to remain (permanently), to continue (in the same condition); (verweilen) to stay, to abide; bei seiner Meinung 2 to persist in (F to stick to) one's opinion; lassen wir es dabei 2 let us leave things as they are, let the matter rest there; oft als Briefschluß: wir 2 hochachtungsvoll // we remain respectfully //; believe us respectfully (to be) //. — II ~ n 23 2. hier ist m-s ~s nicht I cannot stay here (any longer); dauerndes, längeres ~ an einem Orte permanent stay or residence. — 3. dabei muß es sein ~ haben matters will (or must) rest there. — 4. = Verbleib.
ver-bleichen(f~¹)[ahd.] I v/n.(sn) ⓜaft*̸ 1. to grow (or turn) pale or wan or livid, to blanch, v. Farben: to fade, to pale, F to fly; das verblichene Rot ihrer Wangen the faded (or departed) ruddiness of her cheeks. — 2. poet. des Todes 2 to expire, to pass away; der(die) Verblichene 60 the deceased.—II~n 23(f.1) growing pale, &c., als Bleichsucht.
ver-bleien ⊕ (f~v~) v/a. 88* to (cover with) lead, to fill with lead.
ver-blenden (f~v~) [mhd.] I v/a. 69* 1. to blind, to dazzle, durch äußeren Schimmer: to delude, infatuate; e-n über et. 2 to mislead a p. with regard to a th.; durch sein Glück verblendet dazzled (or deluded) by his good fortune; verblendete Liebe blind (or unreasoning) love. — 2. (verdecken) to cover up; ⊕ arch. to face with bricks, masonry, &c. — II ~ n 23 3. f. Verblendung.
Ver-blender(f~v~)m 22,Ver-blend-klinker, =stein (f~v~) ⊕ m brick (or stone) for facing.
Ver-blendung (f~v~) f 46 1. (zu verblenden 1:) blinding, dazzling, delusion, infatuation. — 2. (zu 2:) ⊕ arch. facing.
ver-bleuen F (f~v~; Hom. verbläuen) v/a. 88* = verprügeln.
ver-blich(en) (f~v~), ver-blieb(en) (f~¹) impf. (p.p.) v. verbleichen, verbleiben.
ver-blies (f~¹) impf. v. verblasen.
ver-blinden (f~v~) 88* I v/a.= verblenden. — II v/n. (sn) to grow blind.
ver-blüffer (f~v~) [ndd.: bluff] v/a. 88* to dumbfound, stupefy, bewilder; to put out (of countenance), F to flab-

[Verblüfftheit] — 1029 — [Verbürgung]

bergast, to flummux; verblüfft dastehen to stand (like) dumbfounded, to stagger; sie war ganz verblüfft she was quite thunderstruck or taken aback.

Ver-blüfft-heit (f⌣-) f ⑭, **Ver-blüffung** (f⌣⌣) f ⑭ dumbfoundedness, stupefaction, bewilderment.

ver-blühen (f⌣⌣)[ahd.] I v/n.(h. u. fn) ⑱*: a)(h.) to cease blooming or blossoming or flowering; b) (fn) (welfen) to fade, to wither; verblüht ⚥ deflowered, ☞ deflorate; fig. Schönheit verblüht bald good looks soon fade or depart, beauty lasts but a day; sie ist verblüht she is passée or a faded beauty. — II ~ n fading, mst fig. deflorescence.

ver-blümen (f⌣⌣) v/a. ⑱* to smother with flowers; to disguise, meist fig. et. 2 to make covert allusions to a th.; verblümt figurative, allegorical; s. ausdrücken 4 am Ende und Blume 3.

ver-bluten (f⌣⌣) [mhd.] I v/n. (fn) u. sich 2 v/refl. ⑱* to bleed to death, to shed one's life-blood; (aufhören zu bluten) to cease bleeding; fig. die Sache hat sich verblutet (ist vergessen) the matter has died a natural death or has blown over. — II ~ n ㉓ u. **Ver-blutung** f ⑭ bleeding to death, a. = Blutfluß.

ver-boden/en ⊕ (f⌣⌣) v/a. ⓑ*: ein Faß 2 to bottom ...; B/ung f ⑭ bottoming.

ver-bog(en)(f⌣¹(⌣))impf. (p.p.)v.verbiegen.

ver-bohlen ⊕ (f⌣⌣) v/a. ⑱* to plank, to board (up), to line with planks.

ver-bohren ⊕ (f⌣⌣) v/a. ⑱* 1. carp. (durch [Bohrlöcher u.] Holznägel verbinden) to fasten with wooden pins, to pin. — 2. (a. v/refl. sich 2) eine Röhre ꝛc. 2 (falsch bohren) to bore badly or wrongly; F fig. sich in et. 2, auf et. verbohrt sein to be madly bent (F to be gone) on a th.; v. Personen: verbohrt wrong in the head, crazy, cracked, cranky.

ver-bollwerken × (f⌣⌣⌣) v/a. ⑱* to fortify (with bulwarks), weitS. to block up, to barricade.

ver-borgen[1] (f⌣⌣) v/a. ⑱* = borgen 2.

ver-borgen[2] (f⌣⌣) s. verbergen III; Lerweise adv. in secret, secretly, clandestinely, (verstohlen) stealthily, on the sly; ~heit f ⑭ concealment, hiddenness; secrecy, occultness; obscurity; (Zurückgezogenheit) retirement, seclusion.

Ver-bot[1] (f⌣¹) [mhd.] n ⓐc. (s. verbieten I) prohibition; interdiction; suppression of a book; jur. inhibition of legal proceedings; das von den Behörden erlassene 2 the prohibition issued (or published) by the authorities.

ver-bot[2] (f⌣¹) impf. v. verbieten.

ver-boten (f⌣⌣) [p.p. v. verbieten] a. ⑭: Ler Eingang! no admission!

ver-brach (f⌣ch) impf. v. verbrechen.

ver-bracht (f⌣cht) p.p., Le impf. von verbringen.

ver-bräm/en (f⌣⌣) [mhd.] I v/a. ⑱* to border, edge, trim, mit Pelz: to (trim with) fur. — II ~ n ㉓, B/ung f ⑭ bordering), trimming, weitS. adornment.

ver-brannt (f⌣⌣) p.p. v. verbrennen.

ver-braten (f⌣⌣)⑱a* I v/a. 1. viel Butter ꝛc. 2 to use (up) ... in roasting or frying — 2. (schlecht braten) to spoil in roasting. — II v/a. 3. (fn) to be spoilt in roasting.

Ver-brauch (f⌣ch) m ⓐc. consumption; übermäßiger ~ waste, extravagance.

ver-brauchen(f⌣ch)v/a. ⑱* to use (up), to consume; stärker: to waste; (abnutzen) to wear out, (erschöpfen) to exhaust; verbrauchte Kleider cast-off clothes pl.

Ver-brauchs-artikel ⊕ (f⌣⌣ch...) m ⑫, =gegenstand m article of consumption; =steuer f duty on articles of consumption, (Akzise) excise.

ver-brauen (f⌣⌣) v/a. ⑱*: Malz, Hopfen ꝛc. 2 to use up ... in brewing.

ver-brausen (f⌣⌣) v/n. (h. u. fn) ⑨* to cease fermenting, fig. meist von jungen Leuten: to calm (or sober, settle) down.

ver-brechen (f⌣⌣) [ahd.] I v/a.⑬a*: et. 2 to commit an offence; was habe ich verbrochen? what (wrong or harm) have I done?; F co. er hat einen Roman verbrochen he has ventured on (writing) or F has perpetrated a novel. — II ~ n ㉓ offence, delinquency, stärker: crime, misdeed, jur. felony; (gewaltsamer Eingriff) trespass, stärker: outrage.

Ver-brecher (⌣) m ⑫, ~in f ⑰ offender, delinquent, stärker: criminal, evildoer, malefactor, jur. felon (vgl. Frevler); ~gesicht n ⑫ = ~physiognomie.

ver-brecherisch (f⌣⌣) a. ⑭ criminal, jur. felonious; das ⓒ einer Tat: the criminality of an action.

Ver-brecher-karren (f⌣⌣...) m ⑫ ehm. tumbrel; =kneipe f public house frequented by criminals; =kolonie f convict-colony or -establishment, penal settlement; =laufbahn f, =leben n criminal career, life of crime; =physiognomie f criminal's face, hangdog look.

ver-breit/en (f⌣⌣) I v/a. u. sich 2 v/refl. ⑱* 1. (sich) 2 to spread, diffuse, disperse; (fortpflanzen) to propagate; (aussäen) to disseminate; (ausdehnen) to extend; Nachrichten ꝛc. 2 to spread (about) ..., to circulate ...; es hat sich ein Gerücht verbreitet, daß // a rumour has been set afloat that //; the report goes that //, it is being reported that //; weitverbreitet wide-spread; über die ganze Welt verbreitet world-wide. — 2. sich über et. 2 (aussprechen) to expatiate (or enlarge) on s.th. — II ~ n ㉓ 3. = B/ung.

Ver-breiter (f⌣⌣) m ⑫ u. ~in f ⑰ one who spreads or diffuses, propagator.

ver-breiter/n (⌣) v/a. ⑫a* to widen (out), to broaden; B/ung f ⑭ widening.

Ver-breitung (f⌣⌣) f⑭ spread(ing), diffusion; propagation; dissemination; extension; circulation; geographische ~ v. Pflanzen ꝛc. geographical distribution.

ver-brennbar (f⌣⌣) a. ⑭ combustible; ~keit f ⑭ combustibleness.

ver-brennen (f⌣⌣) [mhd.] ⓑb* I v/n. (fn) 1. to burn (away), to be(come) consumed by fire, to perish in the flames, v. lebenden Wesen a. to be burnt to death. — II v/a. u. v/refl. 2. to burn (up); (versengen) to singe, to scorch; sich (dat.) die Finger 2 to burn one's fingers (a. fig.); von der Sonne verbrannt sunburnt, tanned; verbrannte Stelle burn; sich 2 to burn o.s., to be burnt; F path. to catch the disease. — 3. (brennend aufbrauchen) to burn up, to consume. — III ~ n ㉓ 4. s. Verbrennung.

ver-brennlich (f⌣⌣) ꝛc. s. verbrennbar ꝛc.

Ver-brennung (f⌣⌣) f ⑭ burning, combustion, der Toten: cremation, als Todesstrafe: death by fire; (Entzündung) ignition, ☞ deflagration; ~s-ofen (⌣...) m ⑫ für Abfälle: destructor; für Leichen: crematory furnace, crematorium; ~s-prozeß m process of combustion, für Leichen: cremation.

ver-brief/en (f⌣⌣) I v/a. ⑱* 1. to recognize (or acknowledge, confirm) in a document, to secure by charter; verbriefte Rechte chartered (or vested) rights pl. — 2. (verpfänden) to pledge, mortgage. — II B/ung f ⑭ 3. recognition (or confirmation) by charter.

ver-briet (f⌣¹) impf. v. verbraten.

ver-bringen (f⌣⌣) v/a. ⑰* to spend (or pass) away one's time, &c., to squander (or F run through) one's money, &c.

ver-brochen (f⌣⌣) p.p. v. verbrechen.

Ver-bruch (f⌣ch) m ⓐc. (Vergehen) offence; vgl. verbrechen II.

ver-brüder/n (f⌣⌣)⑫a* I v/a. to unite like brothers. — II v/refl. sich mit e-m 2 to fraternize (or to form a close friendship) with a p. — III ~ n ㉓ u. B/ung f ⑭ fraternization, brotherly affection, (forming a) brotherhood.

Ver-brüderungs-fest (f⌣⌣⌣⌣,⌣) n ⑫ feast of brotherhood.

ver-brühen (f⌣⌣) v/a. u. sich 2 v/refl. ⑱* (sich) 2 to scald (o.s.); **ver-brüht** (f⌣¹) a. ⑭ scalded; Le Stelle der Haut scald.

ver-buchen (f⌣⌣) v/a. ⑱* to book.

ver-buhlen (f⌣⌣) v/a. ⑱* to spend on paramours or in debauchery.

ver-buhlt (f⌣¹) p.p. u. a. ⑭ amorous(ly inclined), stärker: lecherous, (liederlich) debauched, fast; ~heit (f⌣¹-) f ⑭ amorousness, stärker: lecherousness; debauchery, fast life.

Verbum (w⌣¹) [lt.] n ⑱ gram. (Zeitwort) verb; ~ finitum (regierendes Zeitwort) finite verb.

ver-bummeln (f⌣⌣)⑫a* I v/a. 1. Geld 2 to squander ...; seine Zeit 2 to waste (or idle away) ... — 2. (versäumen, vergessen) to neglect, to forget. — II v/n. (fn) 3. to be(come) ruined by idleness, to fall into idle ways; verbummelt (given to) idling, fond of loafing about, stärker: dissolute, rakish.

ver-bunden (f⌣⌣) p.p. v. verbinden.

ver-bünden (f⌣⌣) [mhd.] ⑱* I v/a. to confederate, to unite (in a league), to ally; die verbündeten Heere the allied armies pl. — II sich 2 v/refl. to form (or enter into) a confederacy or an alliance; Verbündete ⑰ confederates, bsd. von Staaten: allies pl.

Ver-bund-maschine* ⊕ (f⌣⌣,⌣⌣) f ⑫ compound steam-engine.

Ver-bündung (f⌣⌣) f ⑭ alliance.

ver-bürg/en (f⌣⌣) [mhd.] I v/a. u. v/refl. ⑱*: et., sich für et. 2 to warrant (or guarantee) a th., to stand security for a th.; (dafür einstehen) to answer (or vouch) for a th., to back up a th.; sich für e-n bei Gericht 2 to stand bail for a p.; wohl verbürgt well-founded (report), authentic (news). — II ~ n ㉓ u. B/ung f ⑭ warrant(ing), guarantee (-ing); standing security or bail.

[verbüßen] — 1030 — [Verdichtungsapparat]

ver-büß/en (f⌣⌣) v/a. ⊕*: et. ⁀ to suffer the consequences of a th., to pay the penalty for a th. (vgl. abbüßen); nach v/ter Strafzeit after serving one's time.

Ver-dacht (f⌣cht) [mhd.: verdenken] m⊕b. suspicion; (Mißtrauen) distrust; e-n in ~ bringen to throw (or cast) suspicion upon a p., to make a p. suspected; e-n wegen einer Sache in ~ haben to suspect a p. of a th.; keinen ~ hegend, ohne ~ zu hegen unsuspecting(ly); in ~ kommen to incur (or excite) suspicion; wegen einer Sache im ~ stehen to be suspected of a th.

ver-dächtig (f⌣⌣) a. ⊕ suspicious, suspected, arousing suspicion; (nicht zu trauen) not to be trusted, untrustworthy, F fishy; (zweifelhaft) doubtful, equivocal; ⁀ m. = ⁀en; eines Mordes ⁀ suspected (or under suspicion) of (having committed a) murder.

ver-dächtig/en (f⌣⌣⌣) I v/a. und v/refl. ⊕* to cause to be suspected, to cast suspicion upon, weitS. to cast the blame on; bisw. sich ⁀ to render o.s. suspicious, vor Gericht: to inculpate o.s. — II ~ n ⁀ = ⁀ung. [ness.]

Ver-dächtigkeit (f⌣⌣-) f ⊕ suspicious-

Ver-dächtigung (f⌣⌣⌣) f ⊕ casting suspicion (or the blame) on a p.; making insinuations against a p., throwing out hints about a p.

Ver-dachts-grund (f⌣⌣cht...) m ⊕ cause (or ground) of suspicion; =moment n suspicious fact or appearance.

ver-dammen (f⌣⌣) [ahd.: damn; *lt.] I v/a. ⊕* 1. to condemn, zur Höllenstrafe: to damn; (verwerfen) to reject (a. bibl.); ich will verdammt sein, wenn // F u. P I'll be damned (or hanged) if //; vgl. verfluchen u. verurteilen. — II ~ n ⁀ 2. f. Verdammung. — III ver-dammt p.p. u. a. ⊕ 3. in den Bed. des inf. — 4. (verwünscht) F cursed; ein verdammter Schuft a damned (or deuced, P bloody) scoundrel; er ist verdammt schlau ... devilishly (F deucedly) artful; ich mache mir verdammt wenig daraus I don't care a jot or a straw; Fluch: verdammt! damn it (all)!; milder: confound it!, hang it!

ver-dammens-wert (f⌣⌣⌣.⌣) **ver-dammlich** (f⌣⌣) a. ⊕ condemnable, stärker: damnable.

Ver-dammnis (f⌣⌣) f ⊕ bibl. damnation, (everlasting) perdition or doom.

Ver-dammung (f⌣⌣) f ⊕ (f. verdammen) condemnation, damnation.

Ver-dammungs-spruch (f⌣⌣⌣...) m ⊕, =urteil n sentence (of condemnation), geh. Spr.: doom; ⁀wert, ⁀würdig a. ⊕ = verdammenswert.

ver-dampf-bar (f⌣⌣-) a. ⊕ vaporizable; (flüchtig) volatile.

ver-dampf/en (f⌣⌣) ⊕* I v/n. (fn) 1. to evaporate, to rise as vapour, to vaporize. — II v/a. 2. to (cause to) evaporate. — 3. F viel Tabak ⁀ to smoke away ... — III ~ n ⁀ u. B/ung f ⊕ 4. evaporation, vaporization.

ver-danken (f⌣⌣) [mhd.] v/a. ⊕* = danken 5; wir ⁀ ihm viel we owe him a great deal or a great debt of gratitude.

ver-darb (f⌣⌣) ind. impf. von verderben.

ver-dauen (f⌣⌣) [ahd.: thaw] I v/a. u. v/refl. ⊕* to digest (a. fig.); diese Speisen ⁀ sich leicht ⁀.. are easily digested or very digestible. — II ~ n ⁀ = B/ung.

ver-daulich (f⌣⌣) a. ⊕ digestible; leicht ⁀, auch: easy (or light) of digestion; schwer ⁀ hard to digest, indigestible; ~keit f ⊕ digestibleness.

Ver-dauung (f⌣⌣) f ⊕ digestion.

Ver-dauungs-beschwerde (f⌣⌣⌣...) f ⊕ (fit of) indigestion; =geschäft n process of digestion; =kanal m alimentary canal or duct; =kraft f digestive power; ⁀los a. ⊕ dyspeptic; =losigkeit f indigestion, dyspepsia; =mittel n remedy for (improving) the digestion, ⁀ peptic; =organ n digestive organ; =saft m gastric juice; =schwäche f weak digestion, dyspepsia; =stoff m, chm.: ⁀ pepsin; =störung f = =beschwerde, mit Gallenfieber: bilious attack; =system n, physiol. digestive system; =werkzeug n digestive organ.

Ver-deck (f⌣⌣) [ndd.] n ⊕c. 1. ⊕ Wagnerei: ⁀ eines Wagens: roof ..., hood ... (vgl. Plane). — 2. ⇓ deck; auf dem ⁀ on deck, on board (ship); auf das ⁀ geh(e)n to go on deck.

ver-deck/en (f⌣⌣) [mhd.] v/a. ⊕* to cover (up), das Gesicht, & e-e Stellung auch: to mask; (einhüllen) to wrap up; (verschleiern) to veil; (bemänteln) to cloak, to palliate; (nicht merken l.) to dissemble (vgl. verbergen); verdeckte Treppe blind staircase; & verdeckt aufstellen to place (or put) under cover or in a sheltered position; & frt. verdeckte Batterie masked battery; verdeckter Weg covert way.

Ver-deck-leder ⊕ (f⌣⌣...) n ⊕ Wagenbau: leather hood of a carriage; =sitz m auf einem Omnibus ⁊c. seat on the top (or outside) of an omnibus, &c.

ver-deckter-weise (f⌣⌣⌣...) adv. under cover; in veiled language.

Ver-deck-wagen (f⌣⌣...) m ⊕ coach with a hood (to it); ⁀zelt ⇓ n awning.

ver-denken (f⌣⌣) [ahd.] ⊕* = verargen.

Ver-derb (f⌣⌣) m⊕b. ruin(ation), destruction, waste, decay; deterioration.

ver-derb/en (f⌣⌣) [mhd.: darben] ⊕b* (als v/a. auch ⊕*) I v/n. (fn) 1. to spoil, to get spoiled or damaged, (an Güte abnehmen) to deteriorate, (verfallen) to decay, to (go to) waste; (verfaulen, vermodern) to rot, to moulder; (zugrunde gehen) to perish, to come to grief, to go to rack and ruin, v. Personen auch: to die; (längst) gestorben und verdorben dead and gone (long ago). — 2. fig. an ihm ist ein Schauspieler verdorben he would have made a good actor, he was cut out for an actor. — II v/a. 3. (f. I) to spoil, to damage; (verschlechtern) to deteriorate, (zugrunde richten) to ruin, undo, destroy, sittlich: to demoralize, pervert, corrupt, deprave, debauch; sich (dat.) die Augen ⁀ to ruin (or spoil) one's eyes or sight; e-m die Freude, die Lust ⁀ to spoil (or mar) a p.'s pleasure; e-m die Lust an et. ⁀ to set a p. against a th.; f. Magen am Ende; Sprichw. f. Beispiel am Ende. — 4. es mit e-m ⁀ to lose a p.'s favour or friendship, to incur a p.'s displeasure; to fall out (or to quarrel) with a p.; ich will es mit ihm nicht ⁀ I want to keep in with him or to keep on the right side of him; er will es mit keinem ⁀ he tries to please everybody. — III ~ n ⁀ 5. (f. 1) spoiling; deterioration; decay, waste; (f. 3) perversion, corruption. — 6. (Untergang) ruin(ation), destruction, bsd. rel. perdition; das bedeutet ~ für ihn that means (or spells) ruin to him; e-n ins ~ stürzen to ruin (or undo) a p.; sich ins ~ stürzen to rush (headlong) into destruction or perdition; Weg zum ~ road to ruin. — 7. **ver-derbt**, meist demoralized, perverse, corrupt, corrupted; (lasterhaft) depraved, debauched, vicious. — IV **ver-dorben** p.p. u. a. ⊕ (D9) 8. a) Bed. des inf.; ⁀es Fleisch tainted meat; ⁀e Luft vitiated air; ⁀es Wasser stale (or putrid) water; b) (verwesend, faulend) decaying, rotting, decomposing, putrescent; c) dazu ist er ⁀ he is not fit(ted) (or cut out) for it; that's not in his line.

ver-derben-bringend (f⌣⌣...) a. ⊕ ruinous, destructive, fatal; ⁀schwanger a. ⊕ big with ruin, mehr gebräuchlich: portentous, ominous.

Ver-derber (f⌣⌣) m ⊕, ~in f ⊕ spoiler; destroyer; perverter, corrupter of morals, &c.; ⁀ der Freude, oft mar-feast.

ver-derblich (f⌣⌣) a. ⊕ (leicht verderbend) easily spoiled or damaged, corruptible (body, &c.), perishable (goods, &c.); (verhängnisvoll) fatal to; (gefährlich) dangerous to; (unglückbringend) unfortunate for, pernicious to; (zerstörend) ruinous to, destructive to; das könnte ihnen leicht ⁀ w. that could easily lead to their ruin or prove fatal to them; ~keit f ⊕ corruptibility, perishableness, perishable nature; perniciousness; ruinousness, destructiveness.

Ver-derbnis (f⌣⌣) f ⊕ (n ⊕) = verderben 5; sittliche ~, a. (moral) depravity.

ver-derbt (f⌣⌣) f. verderben 7; ~heit (f⌣⌣-) f ⊕ perversity, corruptness; depravity, vice; decadence.

ver-deutlich/en (f⌣⌣⌣) I v/a. ⊕* to make (or render) plain or clear or intelligible, to elucidate. — II ~ n ⁀ u. B/ung f ⊕ clearing up, elucidation.

ver-deutsch/en (f⌣⌣⌣) I v/a. ⊕* to render (or translate) into German, weitS. (deutsch m.) to Germanize. — II ~ n ⁀ u. B/ung f ⊕ translation into German, weitS. Germanization.

ver-dichtbar (f⌣⌣-) a. ⊕ condensable, (zf.-drückbar) compressible; ~keit (⌣⌣-) f ⊕ condensability, compressibility.

ver-dicht/en (f⌣⌣) [dicht] I v/a. und v/refl. ⊕* phys., chm., &c. to condense, durch Druck: to compress, bsd. Gase: to solidify; sich ⁀ to become condensed or concentrated or solid (vgl. verdicken I). — II ~ n ⁀ f. Verdichtung.

Ver-dichter ⊕ (f⌣⌣) m ⊕ mach., &c. condenser, condensing apparatus.

Ver-dichtung (f⌣⌣) f ⊕ condensation, durch Druck: compression; concentration; solidification of gases, &c.; ~s-apparat

---

Signs (see page XVII): F familiar; P vulgar; Γ flash; \ rare; † obsolete (died); * new word (born); ⁒ incorrect; ♪ music;

[Verdichtungszisterne] — 1031 — [verdrücken]

⊕ (⏑‿⏑...) m ㉒ = Verdichter; ~s-zisterne f condensing cistern.

ver-dick/en (⏑‿⏑) **I** v/a. u. sich ² v/refl. ⑧*: (sich) ² to thicken, bsd. von Flüssigkeiten a. to turn into jelly, bsd. ⚗ to incrassate, to inspissate; (eingekocht) to boil down; (geronnen m.) to clot, ⚗ to coagulate (vgl. verdichten I). — **II** ~ n ㉓ und **B/ung** f ㊻ thickening, bsd. ⚗ incrassation, inspissation; Verdickung der Haut callosity; **B/ungs-mittel** n ㉒ incrassative.

ver-bielen ⊕ (⏑‿⏑) v/a. ⑱ = dielen.

ver-dienen (⏑‿⏑) [ahd.] **I** v/a. ⑱* **1.** Geld ² to earn — by; et. ² an to make money out of a p., out of (or by) a th.; f. Brot 3; hier und da ein bißchen (Geld) ² to pick up a few shillings (or pence) now and again; einen Haufen Geld ² to coin money, F to make heaps of money; er hat sich ein Vermögen verdient he has made his fortune or F his pile; fig. man verdient dabei nicht das Salz zur Suppe there is not much to be made by that, it brings in next to nothing. — **2.** to merit (v. Strafen &c.: to deserve) a th.; das habe ich von Ihnen nicht verdient I have not deserved that from you; sich um das Vaterland verdient m. to deserve well of one's country; f. Dank 6. — **3.** bisw. v/refl. sich um e-n, et. ² (in verdienstlicher Weise bemühen) to deserve well of a p., a th.; attribisch: ein verdienter Mann a man of merit, a deserving man; e-e (wohl) verdiente Strafe a well-deserved (or a condign) punishment. — **II** ~ n ㉓ **4.** earning money; Sprichw. ~ ist besser als Sparen earning is better than saving.

Ver-dienst (⏑‿⏑) [mhd.] ⒜ a. **1.** m (verdientes Geld, Erwerb) money earned, earnings pl., (Lohn) wages pl.; (Gewinn) gain, profit; das ist mein ganzer ~ dabei that's all I make (or get) by it; Sprichw. keine Mühe, kein ~ no pains no gains. — **2.** n (Geleistetes) merit, bsd. b.s. desert; seine ~e um die Stadt his services to (or his efforts on behalf of) the town; es ist vorzüglich sein ~, daß // it is especially due to him that //; sich das ~ einer Sache zuschreiben to claim (or take) the credit for a th.; nach ~ deservedly, duly; man wird ihn nach ~ behandeln he will get his deserts or his due; nicht ohne ~ not undeserving; ein Mann von vielen ~en a man of great merit or worth or deserts; Sprichw. f. Krone 2; das ~ wird selten belohnt merit (or virtue) seldom meets with its reward.

Ver-dienst-adel (⏑‿⏑...) m ㉒ title of nobility (in Engl.: peerage) attained by merit; =kreuz n (=medaille f) cross (medal) for distinguished services (rendered) to the country.

ver-dienstlich (⏑‿⏑) a. ㊻ meritorious, deserving, worthy (of reward); **~keit** f ㊻ merit(oriousness).

ver-dienst-los (⏑‿⏑...) a. ㊻: a) without merit, undeserving; b) von Personen: earning nothing; von Geschäften: unprofitable; **=losigkeit** f ㉒: a) undeservingness; b) want of (profitable) employment; **=orden** m order of merit; **=voll** a. = verdienstlich.

ver-dient (⏑‿⏑) &c. f. verdienen 3; **Ler-maßen, =weise** (⏑‿⏑‿⏑) adv. deservedly, according to (one's) merit or deserts.

Ver-dikt ㋉ (w‿⏑, w‿⏑) [lt. vere dictum, Wahrspruch] n ⒞c. jur. verdict.

Ver-ding (⏑‿⏑) m ⒝b. **1.** letting out on hire. — **2.** giving out (or contracting for) work; (Vertrag darüber) contract; im ~ by contract; in ~ nehmen to undertake by contract, to contract for.

ver-ding/en (⏑‿⏑) [ahd.] **I** v/a. u. sich ² v/refl. ⑩st* (p.p. a. verdingt): a) Sachen: to let out on hire; b) Personen: seinen Sohn als Diener bei e-m ² to put ... to service with a p.; sich ² bei // to bind o.s. as apprentice, &c. to //, als Diener, Magd: to go into service, to take a servant's situation or place (bei e-m with a p.); sich als Knecht ² to go as a farm-servant or -hand; c) Arbeiten ² to put (or give) out work by contract; einen Bau &c. ² to contract for the construction of a house, &c. — **II** ~ n ㉓ = **B/ung** 1.

Ver-dinger (⏑‿⏑) m ㉒, **~in** f ㊻ one who keeps a registry-office.

Ver-dingung (⏑‿⏑) f ㊻ **1.** letting out on hire, &c. (f. verdingen I). — **2.** contract, agreement; **~s-wesen** n ㉒ contracting (for work), contract-work. [verderben.]

ver-dirb([f]t) (⏑‿⏑) imper. (pres. ind.) v./

ver-dolmetschen (⏑‿⏑‿⏑) = dolmetschen.

ver-donnern (⏑‿⏑) v/a. ⑱a* **1.** = andonnern; verdonnert thunderstruck, dumbfounded, adv. F provc. verdonnert flink tremendously quick; verdonnert viel Geld an awful lot of money. — **2.** F (verurteilen) to sentence; to condemn.

ver-doppeln (⏑‿⏑) **I** v/a. u. sich ² v/refl. ⑫a* to double, gr., &c. a. to reduplicate; den Eifer ² to redouble one's zeal; s-e Schritte ² to quicken one's pace; ²d reduplicative; mit verdoppelter Anstrengung with redoubled (or increased) exertions. — **II** ~ n ㉓ u. **Ver-dopp(e)lung** f ㊻ doubling, reduplication; von Konsonanten a.: ⚗ gemination. [f ㊻ = Verderbtheit.]

ver-dorben (⏑‿⏑) f. verderben IV; **~heit**/

ver-dorren (⏑‿⏑) [mhd.] ⑧* **I** v/n. (fn) to dry up, to wither (away), to be parched; die verdorrten Halme (or dried) blades pl. — **II** v/a. to dry up, wither, parch.

ver-drängen (⏑‿⏑) **I** v/a. ⑧* to push aside or away, to displace, to remove, ⚔ to dislodge the enemy; e-n Nebenbuhler ² to supplant a rival; e-n aus s-m Besitz ² to dispossess (or eject) a p.; ein durch die Maschinen verdrängtes Handwerk a craft displaced (or superseded) by machinery. — **II** ~ n ㉓ u. **Ver-drängung** f ㊻ displacement, removal; dispossession.

ver-drehen (⏑‿⏑) **I** v/a. u. v/refl. ⑧* **1.** to distort, to twist (the wrong way), gewaltsam: to wrench; sich ² to become twisted; (dat.) den Arm &c. ² to sprain (or dislocate) one's arm, &c.; die Augen ² to roll (about) one's eyes; das Gesicht ² to make grimaces; ein Schloß ² to spoil a lock by turning the key the wrong way. — **2.** fig. (verkehrt auslegen) to distort, to twist the meaning of, to put a false construction on, to misinterpret, (falsch darstellen) to misrepresent; e-m den Kopf ² to turn a p.'s head or brain; das Recht ² to pervert (the course of) justice. — **II** ~ n ㉓ **3.** = Verdrehung.

ver-dreht (⏑‿⏑) p.p. u. ⓶ **1.** Bed. des inf. — **2.** (verrückt) crazy, cracked; fig. ²er Kopf queer head; ²e Pläne mad (or absurd, preposterous) plans pl.

Ver-dreht-heit (⏑‿⏑...) f ㊻ distortedness; craziness; queerness, absurdity.

Ver-drehung (⏑‿⏑) f ㊻ distortion (auch fig.); fig. misinterpretation, misrepresentation, perversion; von Tatsachen, der Wahrheit: prevarication.

ver-drei-fach/en (⏑‿⏑‿⏑) **I** v/a. und sich ² v/refl. ⑧* to treble, to triple. — **II** ~ n ㉓ u. **B/ung** f ㊻ triplication.

ver-drießen (⏑‿⏑) [mhd.: threat(en); lt. tru'dere] v/a. ⑩d* **1.** mit sächlichem Subjekt: e-n ² to vex (or annoy, grieve, trouble) a p., auch = ärgern 1; es hat ihn verdrossen, daß Sie nicht kamen he felt vexed at your not coming, he was put out because you did not come. — **2.** ich lasse mich et. nicht ² I won't be discouraged by a th.; sich keine Mühe und Kosten ² lassen to spare (or grudge) neither trouble nor expense; sie läßt sich nichts ² she spares (or grudges) no pains, she has an indomitable energy.

ver-drießlich (⏑‿⏑) [mhd.] a. ㊻ **1.** (voll Ärger) vexed, annoyed, grieved, cross (über et. at a th., about a th.); (schlecht gelaunt) ill-humoured, out of temper, peevish, sulky; ² sein to be vexed, to feel annoyed, to be out of temper or in the sulks; ² w. to become vexed, to turn cross, to grow ill-tempered. — **2.** (Ärger erregend) vexatious, annoying, troublesome, irksome; (widerwärtig) untoward; ²e Geschichte tiresome (or bothersome, unpleasant, unfortunate) affair.

Ver-drießlichkeit (⏑‿⏑...) f ㊻ **1.** crossness, ill humour or temper, sullen mood, peevishness, sulkiness, moroseness. — **2.** vexatiousness, troublesomeness, irksomeness; e-m ~en bereiten to cause a p. annoyance or vexation or unpleasantness or bother.

ver-droß (⏑‿⏑) ind. impf. v. verdrießen.

ver-drossen (⏑‿⏑) p.p. von verdrießen u. a. ㊻ (D9) **1.** als p.p. Bed. des inf. — **2.** = verdrießlich 1; weitS. (unlustig) unwilling, reluctant, loath; (faul) lazy, adv. auch: half-heartedly, listlessly, with a bad grace.

Ver-drossenheit (⏑‿⏑‿⏑) f ㊻ = Verdrießlichkeit 1; weitS. (Unlust) unwillingness, reluctance, loathness; half-heartedness.

ver-drucken (⏑‿⏑) v/a. ⑧* typ. **1.** misprint; (an e-e falsche Stelle bringen) to transpose. — **2.** viel Papier ² (verbrauchen) to use up (or to waste) ... in printing.

ver-drücken (⏑‿⏑) v/a. ⑧* **1.** to crush, ein Kleidungsstück a. to crumple, tumble, crease. — **2.** fig. F (aufessen) to devour, to polish off.

⚗ scientific; ♃ botanical; ⚱ geography; ⊕ machinery; ⚒ mining; ⚔ military; ⚓ marine; ⚫ commercial; ✉ postal; 🚂 railway.

[Verdruß] — 1032 — [vereinsamen]

Ver-druß (f⸗̆) [mhd.] m ⑧ a. 1. annoyance, trouble, a. = Ärger; (Kummer) grief, worry; (Unzufriedenheit) discontent; (Unwille) indignation, (Ekel) disgust; e-m ~ m. to vex (or annoy, irritate) a p., et. mit ~ tun to do a th. with reluctance or with a bad grace; e-m et. zum ~ tun to do a th. to spite (or in defiance of) a p. — 2. (et. Verdrießliches) unpleasantness, bother (some affair). — 3. F einen ~ (Buckel) haben to be hunchbacked.

ver-duft/en (f⸗̆̆) I v/n. (sn) und sich ~ v/refl. 1. to evaporate. — 2. F fig. von Personen: to vanish, to take French leave, F to take o.s. off, bsd. Am. to skedaddle; verdufte! make yourself scarce!, be off! — II ~ n ㉓ und B/ung f ㊻ 3. evaporation.

ver-dumm/en (f⸗̆̆) [mhd.] ⑧* I v/n. (sn) to grow stupid or silly. — II v/a. to make stupid, to blunt the intellect(s) of; (viehisch m.) to brutalize; verdummt besotted; bereft of intellect. III ~ n ㉓ u. B/ung f ㊻ brutalization; B/ungs-system n ㉒ obscurantism.

ver-dumpfen (f⸗̆̆) ⑧* v/n. (sn): a) vom Tone: to grow dull or hollow; b) (abstumpfen, gefühllos w.) to grow callous or indifferent or blunt; c) (muffig w.) to grow musty or stuffy.

ver-dungen (f⸗̆̆) p.p. von verdingen.

ver-dunkeln (f⸗̆̆) [mhd.] I v/a. u. sich ~ v/refl. ⑧a* 1. to darken, durch Wolken: to cloud, fig. to (render) obscure, to obfuscate; sich ~ to darken, to grow dark(er) or dim or dusky; Farben ~ to deepen ...; Himmelskörper: to eclipse (auch fig.). — 2. fig. (übertreffen) to put in the shade, to outshine, to eclipse, F to take the shine out of. — II ~ n ㉓ u. Ver-dunk(e)lung f ㊻ 3. darkening, &c. (s. I); obscuration, obfuscation; eclipse of a celestial object.

ver-dünnbar (f⸗̆̆) a. ㊻ capable of being thinned or diluted, &c. (s. verdünnen); dilutable; phys. von luftartigen Körpern: ⇄ rarefiable; ~keit f ㊻ dilutableness, rarefiableness.

ver-dünn/en (f⸗̆̆) I v/a. u. sich ~ v/refl. ⑧* to (make) thin, ⊕ durch Hobeln: to plane down; mst fig. to attenuate, Flüssigkeiten: to weaken, dilute, mit Wasser: to mix with) water; Farben: to temper, wash, Gase: to rarefy ⊕ (sich) allmählich ~ (zuspitzen) to taper off; chm. eine verdünnte Lösung a dilute(d) (or weak) solution. — II ~ n ㉓ u. B/ung f ㊻ thinning, attenuation, dilution, rarefaction.

ver-dunstbar (f⸗̆̆) a. ㊻ evaporable, phys. ⇄ vaporizable.

ver-dunsten (f⸗̆̆) v/n. (sn) ⑧* to evaporate, to pass off as vapour.

ver-dünsten (⸗) v/a. ⑧* bsd. chm. to (cause to) evaporate, to turn into vapour, ⇄ to vaporize, volatilize.

Ver-dunstung, -dünstung (⸗) f ㊻ evaporation, ⇄ vaporization, volatilization; ~s-... = Ausdünstungs-... [derben.]

ver-bürbe (f⸗̆̆) subj. impf. v. ver=]

ver-durst/en (f⸗̆̆) I v/n. (sn) ⑧* to die with thirst; ~d auch: parched (with thirst); sie sind fast verhungert und verdurstet they almost perished with hunger and thirst. — II ~ n ㉓, B/ung f ㊻ death (caused) by thirst.

ver-düstern (f⸗̆ ̆) ⑧a* = verdunkeln 1, a. to cast a gloom over; die verdüsterte Landschaft the clouded landscape.

ver-dutzen (f⸗̆̆) [mhd.] ⑧* = verblüffen.

ver-dutzt (f⸗̆̆) a. ㊻ taken aback, embarrassed, disconcerted; ~ m. to put out of countenance; to startle, bewilder, puzzle; ~ aussehen to look aghast or dumbfounded or stupefied or puzzled; ~heit (f⸗̆̆) f ㊻, Ver-dutzung f ㊻ = Verblüfftheit.

ver-edeln (f⸗̆̆) [mhd. (ant.) entarten] I v/a. u. v/refl. ⑧a* 1. (edler m.) to ennoble. — 2. (heben) to improve, raise, durch Zucht: to cultivate, breed (cattle, &c.); (läutern) to purify, to refine; (vervollkommnen) to perfect, to bring to (greater) perfection; ♀ hort. Bäume: to graft; veredelnd wirken auf to ennoble, elevate, ameliorate; sich ~ to improve, to grow (or become) (more) perfect. — II ~ n ㉓ u. Ver-ed(e)lung f ㊻ 3. improvement, cultivation, purification, refinement, des Geistes a.: culture.

ver-eh(e)lich/en (f⸗̆(̆)⸗̆) I v/a. u. v/refl. ⑧* to give (away) in marriage; sich ~ to marry, to get married, to enter matrimony; Karoline G., verehelichte R. Caroline G., by marriage (or afterwards) Mrs. R. — II ~ n ㉓ u. B/ung f ㊻ marriage.

ver-ehren (f⸗̆̆) [mhd.] I v/a. ⑧* 1. to respect, stärker: to venerate, revere, ein göttliches Wesen: to worship, to adore (auch fig.), ein geliebtes Wesen: to admire; verehrter Herr! (dear) Sir! (fast nie: Honoured Sir!); verehrter Herr Professor! (my) dear Professor! — 2. e-m et. ~ (schenken) to make a p. a pre'sent of s.th., to prese'nt a p. with s.th. — II ~ n ㉓ 3. s. Verehrung.

Ver-ehrer (f⸗̆̆) m ㉒, ~in f ㊼ reverer, worshipper, votary, adorer; (Anbeter) admirer; (Anhänger) partisan, adherent.

ver-ehrlich (⸗) a. ㊻ honoured, estimable, bsd. brieflich: Ihr ~es Schreiben your esteemed lines pl., ⚘ a. your favour.

Ver-ehrung (f⸗̆̆) f ㊻ (s. verehren I) veneration, reverence, worship(ping), adoration (of saints, &c.); e-s geliebten Wesens: admiration; ~ der Natur (=kräfte) nature-worship; ~s-voll a. ㊻ reverent, ~s-wert, ~würdig a. ㊻ venerable, stärker: adorable, Höflichkeitsausdruck: worshipful, estimable, esteemed, respected.

ver-eid(ig)/en (f⸗̆(̆)⸗̆) [mhd.] I v/a. ⑧* (⑧*) to administer an oath to, Beamte auch: to swear in; ⚔ Truppen ~ in Deutschland ꝛc.: to swear troops to their colour(s); vereidet, vereidigt bound by (an) oath, sworn in. — II ~ n ㉓ und B/ung f ㊻ swearing-in.

Ver-ein (f⸗̆) m ⑫c. 1. abstrakt: union; (Bund) alliance, confederation, ⚖ syndicate, (Genossenschaft) co-operative association; im ~ mit meinen Freunden in conjunction (or conjointly) with my friends. — 2. association, society, club; (Gewerk=)~ der Arbeiter trade union, auch: trades-union.

ver-einbar (f⸗̆̆) a. ㊻ combinable; (verträglich mit) compatible with, consistent with; (in Einklang mit) reconcilable with, harmonizing with; ~ sein mit to harmonize (or tally) with.

ver-einbaren (f⸗̆̆) [mhd.] I v/a. u. v refl. ⑧* et. ~, sich über et. ~ to come to an understanding (or agreement, arrangement) about a th., to agree upon a th. — II ~ n ㉓ f. Vereinbarung.

Ver-einbarkeit (f⸗̆̆⸗) f ㊻ compatibility, consistency; reconcilableness.

ver-einbarter=maßen (f⸗̆⸗̆⸗̆̆) adv. as agreed upon, as arranged.

Ver-einbarung (f⸗̆̆⸗) f ㊻ agreement, arrangement.

ver-einen (f⸗̆̆) = vereinigen.

ver-einfach/en (f⸗̆̆⸗̆) I v/a. ⑧* to simplify; ~d simplificative. — II ~ n ㉓ u. B/ung f ㊻ simplification.

ver-ein(ig)en (f⸗̆(̆)⸗̆) [mhd.] I v/a. u. sich ~ v/refl. ⑧* to unite; (verbinden) to combine, to join, durch Schmelzen: to fuse (together); (zs.-bringen) to assemble, to collect, in e-n Brennpunkt: to focus; (zs.-passen) to fit together, Farben ꝛc.: to blend; (in Übereinstimmung setzen) to reconcile with, to make agree (or to bring in agreement) with; (einverleiben) to incorporate with; (sich) auf einen Punkt ~ to concentrate; sich zu demselben Zwecke ~ to combine for one common object or purpose, to pull together; ⚓ sich ~ to effect a junction; ⚥ von Flüssen ꝛc.: sich ~ to meet, to unite; die beiden Dinge lassen sich nicht mit-ea. ~ ... are not consistent (or compatible, in accord) with each other; ... cannot be reconciled (with one another); sich wieder ~ to re-unite, ⚔ to rally. — II ver-ein(ig)t p.p. und a. ㊻ united; die Vereinigten Staaten (von Nord-amerika) the United States (of North America); mit vereinten Kräften with combined efforts, with united strength; vereintes Handeln oder Vorgeh(e)n concerted (or joint) action; zu e-r Körperschaft vereinigt corporate.

Ver-einigung (f⸗̆̆⸗̆) f ㊻ 1. union, combination, junction; von Flüssen: juncture, confluence; (Verbindung) alliance, coalition, confederacy; (Zusammenkunft) assembly, meeting; (Übereinstimmung) agreement, accord; (Verschmelzung) fusion, bsd. fig. amalgamation. — 2. = Verein 2.

Ver-einigungs=balken (f⸗̆̆⸗̆...) m ㉒ Bauwesen: ~ für Stichbalken: assembling-piece; =fähig a. ㊻ capable of uniting or harmonizing; =mittel n means of (effecting a) union; tie, (connecting) link; =ort m place of assembly; =punkt m juncture, rallying-point, common centre, phys. focus, fig. a. point of agreement; bsd. ⚔ rendezvous; =recht n Vereins- und Versammlungs-recht; =stelle f, anat.: ⇄commissure. [~ zu take..., to receive...]

ver-ein-nahmen (f⸗̆̆⸗̆) v/a. ⑧*: Geld ꝛc.]

Ver-eins=abend (f⸗̆̆⸗̆) m ㉒ club-night; evening on which a society meets.

ver-ein-sam/en (f⸗̆̆⸗̆) ⑧* I v/n. u. sich ~ v/refl.: (sich) ~ to isolate (o.s.); sich ~,

---

Zeichen (f. S. XVII): F familiär; P Volkssprache; Ƒ Gaunersprache; ⸜ selten; † alt (auch gestorben); * neu (auch geboren); ⁓ unrichtig.

[Vereinsamung] — 1033 — [verfangen]

a. to shut o.s. off (from the world); sich vereinsamt fühlen to feel solitary or lonely. — II v/n. (jn) to become isolated, to remain solitary. — III ~ n 23 u. B ung f 46 isolation; loneliness.

Ver-eins-gebiet (f~ᵘ...) n 42 states pl. belonging to the German custom-union or Zollverein; =gesetz n law on (the right of forming) associations; =haus n, =lokal n club-house; =kasse f exchequer (or funds pl.) of a club or society; =taler m thaler of the German custom-union; = und Versammlungs-recht n right of combination and assembly, right to combine and to meet; =vermögen n property of a society, capital of a co-operative association; =wesen n matters pl. relating to clubs and societies, der Arbeiter a. unionism.

Ver-eint-blütler ⚘ (f~ᵘ⁻ᴸᵛ) m 22 (Kompositen) composite (flower).

ver-einzeln (f~ᴸᵛ) I v/a. u. sich ⁂ v/refl. 2a*: (sich) ⁂ to isolate (o.s.), to detach (o.s.), to separate (o.s.), to sever (o.s.); (zerstückeln) to dismember; (einzeln behandeln) to treat singly, to individualize; (einzeln bezeichnen) to specify; vereinzelt single, solitary; vereinzelte Fälle isolated cases pl.; vereinzelt auftretend sporadic (a. v. Krankheiten), occurring now and again. — II ~ n 23 u. B/ung f 46 isolation, separation, severance; dismemberment; specification.

ver-eisen (f~ᴸᵛ) [Eis] v/n. (h.) 9⁸* to be converted (or to turn) into ice; geol. vereist ⁂ glaciated.

ver-eiteln (f~ᴸᵛ) [mhd.] I v/a. 2a* to frustrate (or baffle, balk, thwart) a p.'s designs; (zunichte machen) to shatter (or disappoint) a p.'s hopes, to defeat (or discomfit) a p.'s schemes. — II ~ n 23 u. **Ver-eit(e)lung** f 46 frustration; defeat, discomfiture.

ver-eiter/n (f~ᴸᵛ) I v/n. (jn) u. sich ⁂ v/refl. 2a* to fester, suppurate. — II ~ n 23 und B/ung f 46 suppuration.

ver-ekeln (f~ᴸᵛ) v/a. 2a*: e-m et. ⁂ to render a th. loathsome to a p., to disgust a p. with s.th.

ver-elenden (f~ᴸ⁻ᴸᵛ) 9⁸* v/n. (jn) to sink very low; verelendet very low (in the world), in misery; pauperized.

ver-enden (f~ᴸᵛ) [mhd.] v/n. (h. u. jn) 9⁸* bsd. hunt. vom Wilde: to succumb, perish, die; vom Rindvieh auch: to fall.

ver-enge(r)n (f~ᴸᵛ) I v/a. und sich ⁂ v/refl. 9⁸*(2a*) to narrow (down), to make (to grow) narrower, to straiten; (zs.-ziehen) to contract; (zs.-schnüren) to tighten, ⚕ to constrict; 9b: ⚕ constrictive. — II ~ n 23 und **Ver-eng(er)ung** (f~ᴸᵛ) f 46 narrowing, contraction; anat. ~-s-Kanals ⁊c.; ⚕ coarctation, der Gefäße: obliteration; path. ~ der Harnröhre stricture of the urethra.

ver-erb/en (f~ᴸᵛ) [mhd.] 9⁸* I v/a. e-m (od. auf e-n) ⁂ to bequeath to a p., to leave (as a legacy) to a p., to will to a p., als unveräußerliches Erblehen: to entail upon a p.; fig. to transmit a disease, to hand down a tradition, &c.; vererbt hereditary. — II v/n. (jn) und sich ⁂ v/refl.: (sich) auf e-n ⁂ to devolve

upon a p., to fall to a p., v. Krankheit ⁊c.: to be transmitted to a p ; abs. to be hereditary, to run in the family, to be in the blood. — III ~ n 23 = B/ung.

ver-erblich (f~ᴸᵛ) a. 46 transmissible (by will, &c.); physiol. hereditary.

Ver-erbung (f~ᴸᵛ) f 46 bequeathing, bequest, leaving (as a legacy, &c.), (hereditary) transmission, v. entfernten Ahnen: atavism, physiol. heredity; ~-s-fähigkeit (f~ᴸᵛ...) f 46 ability (or right) to bequeath or to leave (by will) or to will away; ~-s-theorie f, physiol., &c. doctrine of heredity.

ver-erzen (f~ᴸᵛ, a. f~ᴸᵛ) 9⁸* min., geol. I v/n. (jn) und sich ⁂ v/refl. to turn to (or to change into) ore. — II v/a. to mineralize. — III ~ n 23 und **Ver-erzung** f 46 mineralization.

ver-ewigen (f~ᴸᵛ) [mhd.] I v/a. 9⁸* to perpetuate; (unsterblich m.) to immortalize. — II ~ n 23 f. Verewigung. — III verewigt p.p. u. a. 46 rel. gone to one's eternal home or rest; (verstorben) deceased, late, lamented, departed, dead, at rest; der, die Verewigte 67 the deceased, the lamented one. — IV **Ver-ewigung** f 46 perpetuation, immortalization.

ver-fachen ⊙ (f~ᴸᵛ chy) v/a. 9⁸* carp., &c. to provide (or fit, frame) with timber-work, to timber.

ver-fahren (f~ᴸᵛ) [mhd.] 9⁸b* I v/n. (jn u. h.). 1. to proceed, to set (or go) to work; mit Nachsicht (Strenge) ⁂ to act leniently (severely); mit e-m, et, schlecht ⁂ to deal with (or to treat) a p., a th. badly; mit et. vorsichtig ⁂ to handle (or use) a th. carefully or cautiously; jur.: sie sind strafrechtlich gegen ihn ⁂ they took criminal proceedings against him, they prosecuted him. — II v/a. 2. (fahrend ausgeben) to spend on vehicles or in driving; ⚓ Waren ⁊c. ⁂ (fortschaffen) to convey (or carry, transport) ... — 3. die Wege ⁂ to spoil the roads. — 4. et. ⁂ (verwirren) to embroil a th., to muddle (up) a th., to make a muddle of a th.; fig. der Karren der verfahrene matter, geh. Spr. the tangled skein, the imbroglio; die Sache ist gründlich ⁂ the matter is hopelessly entangled or in a hopeless confusion or tangle, F it's a regular muddle. — 5. ⛏ seine Schicht ⁂ to work one's stint. — III sich ⁂ v/refl. 6. to lose (or mistake) one's way in driving; fig. to blunder (grossly), (sich in eine verwickelte Lage bringen) to implicate (or entangle) o.s., F to get muddled or into a muddle. — IV ~ n 23 7. proceeding, procedure, chm., &c. process, treatment; (Art und Weise) method, manner; (Leitung einer Sache) management, conduct; ehrliches (hinterlistiges) ~ honest (underhand) dealing or policy; jur. (mündliches) ~ oral procedure. — 8. ⚓ **Ver-fahrung** f 46 (f. 2) conveyance (or carriage, transmission, transport) of goods.

Ver-fahrungs-art (f~ᵘ...), =weise f 42 mode of procedure, method, vgl. verfahren 7; =lehre f: ⚕ methodology.

Ver-fall (f~ᴸᵛ) m 7b. 1. (state of) decay, ruin, von Gebäuden ⁊c.: dilapidation; (Einsturz) downfall, fall, collapse, crumbling; (Vernichtung) destruction, ruin; (Abnahme) decline; (Ausartung) degeneracy, deterioration, (Verderbnis) corruption, (Auflösung) dissolution; der Sitten: (moral) depravity; in ~ geraten oder kommen = verfallen 1; im ~ sein to be going down or on the down grade or on the decline. — 2. ⚓ (Fälligkeit von Wechseln) maturity; bei ~ when due, at the expiration of the time. — 3. (Verwirktsein): a) von Rechten: forfeiture; b) von Ansprüchen: lapse; c) von Pfandverschreibungen: foreclosure.

ver-fallen (f~ᴸᵛ) [mhd.] 9a* I v/n. (jn) 1. to (fall into) decay, to come to ruin or to grief; v. Gebäuden: to go (or get) out of repair; (einstürzen) to fall (down); (abnehmen) to decline; (ausarten) to degenerate, deteriorate, e-m traurigen Lose ⁂ to meet with a sad fate; 2b decadent; ⁂es Gebäude dilapidated (or tumble-down) premises pl. — 2. mit prp. auf et. ⁂ (od. kommen) to bethink o.s. of a th., durch Glück: to hit upon a th.; auf den wäre ich nicht ⁂ I should never have thought of him; in die alten Fehler ⁂ to slip back into one's old ways; in eine Geldstrafe ⁂ to be mulcted in a fine, to be fined; in eine Krankheit ⁂ to be seized with (an) illness, to fall ill; in eine Strafe ⁂ to incur a penalty. — 3. mit sachlichem Subjekt: einem ⁂ (anheimfallen) to fall to a p.('s share), to devolve upon a p.; von einem Lehen ⁊c.: to lapse; wieder ⁂ to relapse; ⁂e Güter confiscated estates pl., jur. auch escheated (real) estate or property sg.; ⁂es Pfand forfeited pledge. — 4. ⚓ (fällig w.. sein) to be(come) due; (ablaufen) to expire, to elapse; der am 1. Oktober ⁂e Coupon the coupon (which falls) due on October 1ˢᵗ (= the first). — II ~ n 23 5. = Verfall.

Ver-fall-frist (f~ᴸᵛ...) f 42 maturity; =tag m day (or date) of maturity, day on which a bill falls due; =zeit f time of payment; bis zur ~ until maturity, till due.

ver-fälschbar (f~) a. 46 falsifiable, von Waren: subject to adulteration, liable to be adulterated or tampered with.

ver-fälsch/en (f~ᴸᵛ) [mhd.] I v/a. 9⁸* to falsify, Waren ⁊c. to adulterate, to tamper with ...; Münzen ⁂ to debase (or counterfeit) coin; eine Stelle in e-r Schrift ⁂ to interpolate a passage ...; Urkunden, Handschrift ⁊c. ⁂ to forge ...; Wein ⁂ F to doctor ...; verfälscht adulterated, v. Münzen: debased, base, counterfeit. — II ~ n 23 f. B/ung.

Ver-fälscher (f~ᴸᵛ) m 22, ~in f 67 falsifier; adulterator; counterfeiter; interpolator, forger.

Ver-fälschung (f~ᴸᵛ) f 46 (f. verfälschen I) falsification; adulteration; interpolation, forgery; ~-s-mittel (f~ᴸᵛ...) n 22 adulterant, base admixture.

ver-fangen (f~ᴸᵛ) [mhd. (mhd.)] 9b* I sich ⁂ v/refl. to be (or get) caught

♪ Musik; ⚕ Wissenschaft; ⚘ Pflanze; ♁ Geographie; ⊙ Technik; ⛏ Bergbau; ⚔ Militär; ⚓ Marine; ⚖ Handel; ✉ Post; 🚂 Eisenbahn.

[verfänglich] — 1034 — [Verfluß]

or entangled; der Wind hat sich im Schornstein 2 ... has lodged in the chimney; von Personen und Tieren: sich 2 (schwer atmen) to be short (or out) of breath. — II v/n. (h.) mit sachlichem Subjekt: (frommen, nützen) to take effect, to operate, to tell (bei on); bei ihm will nichts 2 nothing seems to avail with him, it's all thrown away on him.

ver-fänglich (⸏⸍⸏⸍) a. ⓖ captious, catching, ensnaring, enticing, insidious; **~keit** f ⓖ captiousness, insidiousness.

ver-färben (⸏⸍⸏⸍) ⓖ* I v/a. to use (or spoil) in dyeing, to discolour. — II v/refl. u. v/n. (h.) (sich) 2 to change (or lose) colour; to turn pale, to fade. — III ~ n ⓖ u. **Ver-färbung** f ⓖ (f. I) discoloration; (f. II) change (or loss) of colour, fading.

ver-fassen (⸏⸍⸏⸍) [mhd.] I v/a. ⓖ* 1. e-e Abhandlung 2c. 2 to compose ..., einen Brief 2c.: to pen, ein Buch 2c.: to write, eine Urkunde: to draw up, to draft; ein von ihm verfaßtes Gedicht a poem composed by him or of his (own) composing. — 2. ⸌ einen Edelstein 2 (schlecht fassen) to set (or mount) ... badly. — II ~ n ⓖ 3. f. Verfassung.

Ver-fasser (⸏⸍⸏⸍) m ⓖ, **~in** f ⓖ author (-ess f), writer, e-s Wörterbuches: lexicographer, parl. u. jur.: draftsman; **~korrektur** f ⓖ typ. author's proof; **~schaft** f ⓖ authorship.

Ver-fassung (⸏⸍⸏⸍) f ⓖ 1. state (or condition) of a th., des Gemütes: disposition, frame of mind; (Lage) position, situation; üble ~ (wretched or sore) plight. — 2. (Staatsgrundgesetz) constitution, organic law (or form of government) of a country; städtische ~ municipal constitution; die ~ betreffend constitutional.

Ver-fassungs-bruch (⸏⸍⸏⸍...) m ⓖ violation (or breach) of the constitution; **=eid** m oath taken on the faithful observance of the constitution; **=feind** m anticonstitutionalist; **=freund** m constitutionalist; **=gegner** = **=feind**; **=los** a. ⓖ without a constitution; **=mäßig** a. constitutional, constituted (authority, &c.); **=mäßigkeit** f constitutionality; **=partei** f constitutional party; **=treu** a. loyal to the constitution; **=urkunde** f constitution(al charter); **=widrig** a. anticonstitutional, unconstitutional; **=widrigkeit** f unconstitutionality, unconstitutionalness, weitS. illegality.

ver-faulbar (⸏⸍⸏⸍) a. ⓖ liable to decay or to rot, corruptible, ⚛ putrescible.

ver-faulen (⸏⸍⸏⸍) [mhd.] ⓖ* = faulen.

ver-faulenzen (⸏⸍⸏⸍) v/a. ⓖ*: die Zeit 2 to idle away one's time.

ver-fecht/en (⸏⸍⸏⸍) [mhd.] I v/a. ⓖb* to fight (or contend) for a th.; to defend (or uphold) one's right, (stoutly) to assert (or maintain) one's opinion, to advocate (or plead for) a cause. — II ~ n ⓖ f. B/ung.

Ver-fechter (⸏⸍⸏⸍) m ⓖ, **~in** f ⓖ defender; advocate (or champion) of a cause. **[tion; advocacy.]**

Ver-fechtung (⸏⸍⸏⸍) f ⓖ defence, assertion.

ver-fehlen (⸏⸍⸏⸍) [mhd.] ⓖ* I v/a. to miss one's aim, a train, &c.; f. Beruf 2; ea. 2 to miss each other, not to meet (at an appointed place); kein Wort (von ihm) verfehlt den Eindruck not one word (of his) misses the mark, every word (of his) tells or goes home; den Weg 2 to lose (or mistake) one's way; das wird nicht 2, Aufsehen zu machen it will not fail to cause a stir; ihr dürft nicht 2 hinzugehen be sure to (mehr gbr.: and) go there; verfehlt unsuccessful (attempt), unsuitable (method); miscarried (plan), wrong (course); verfehlte Sache failure. — II sich 2 v/recip. to miss each other, not to meet; sie haben sich verfehlt, auch: they failed to meet. — III **Ver-fehlung** f ⓖ jur. failure.

ver-feinden (⸏⸍⸏⸍) I v/a. u. v/refl. ⓖ*: Personen mit ea. 2 to set people against each other or by the ears; sich mit e-m 2 to make an enemy of a p., to fall out with a p.; stark ob. gründlich (mit=ea.) verfeindet bitterly hostile or opposed (to each other), at daggers drawn. — II ~ n ⓖ u. **Ver-feindung** f ⓖ making enemies (or an enemy) of; hostile feeling (created in).

ver-feiner/n (⸏⸍⸏⸍) I v/a. u. v/refl. ⓖa* to refine; (glätten) to polish; (verbessern) to improve; (läutern) to purify (sämtlich a. fig.); sich 2 to grow (more) refined, von Menschen auch: to become more civilized; to improve; to be (or become) purified. — II ~ n ⓖ und **B/ung** f ⓖ refinement; polish(ing); improvement; purification.

ver-femen (⸏⸍⸏⸍) [mhd.] *Feme] v/a. ⓖ* to outlaw; F fig. to send to Coventry.

ver-fertigen (⸏⸍⸏⸍) [mhd.] I v/a. ⓖ* to make, to manufacture, hastig: to knock up; Arzneien 2 to prepare ..., Maschinen 2c.: to construct, e-e Schrift: to compose; hastig verfertigt: a) von Waren: blown together; b) von Briefen, Gedichten 2c.: dashed off. — II ~ n ⓖ f. Verfertigung.

Ver-fertiger (⸏⸍⸏⸍) m ⓖ, **~in** f ⓖ maker, manufacturer, constructor.

Ver-fertigung (⸏⸍) f ⓖ making, manufacture; preparation, construction.

ver-fett/en (⸏⸍⸏⸍) I sich 2 v/refl. ⓖ* to turn to fat. — II ~ n ⓖ u. B/ung f ⓖ fatty degeneracy, ⚛ adiposis.

ver-feuern (⸏⸍⸏⸍) v/a. ⓖa* 1. viel Holz 2 to burn up ... — 2. viel Pulver 2 to fire (or blaze) away ...; to waste ...

ver-fiel (⸏⸍⸏⸍) impf. v. verfallen.

ver-filzen (⸏⸍⸏⸍) v/a. und v/refl. ⓖ* to (cover with) felt, das Haar: to mat; sich 2 to get matted or entangled.

ver-fing (⸏⸍) impf. v. verfangen.

ver-finster/n (⸏⸍⸏⸍) I v/a. u. sich 2 v/refl. ⓖa* to make dark or gloomy (vgl. verdunkeln 1). — II ~ n ⓖ u. B/ung f ⓖ = verdunkeln II; ~ des Geistes mental darkness or gloom.

ver-firsten ⊕ (⸏⸍⸏⸍) v/a. ⓖ* Dachdeckerei: ein Dach 2 to ridge (or to put a ridge to) a roof or a house.

ver-fitzen (⸏⸍⸏⸍) v/a. ⓖ* to (en)tangle; sich 2 v/refl. ⓖ to get entangled.

ver-flach/en (⸏⸍⸏⸍) (⸏⸍⸏⸍) I v/n. (h) u. sich 2 v/refl. ⓖ* to grow flat or shallow (a. fig.), to flatten, to become level. — II v/a. (a. **ver-flächen**) to make flat or shallow, to flatten (down), to (make) level. — III B/ung f ⓖ flattening, levelling, der Geister: intellectual decline.

ver-flackern (⸏⸍⸏⸍) v/n. (sn) ⓖa* to flicker (away), to go out with a flicker.

ver-flauen ⚓ (⸏⸍⸏⸍) v/n. (sn) ⓖ* von den Geschäften 2c.: to grow dull or flat or slack, to slacken, to droop, to give way; verflaute Kurse a drooping market, receding prices pl.

ver-flecht/en (⸏⸍⸏⸍) I v/a. u. sich 2 v/refl. ⓖb* 1. (sich) 2 to interlace, interweave, intertwine; fig. e-n in eine Angelegenheit 2 to entangle (or implicate, involve) a p. in s.th. — 2. to use up (or to spoil) in plaiting. — II ~ n u. B/ung f ⓖ 3. (f. I) interlacing, &c.; fig. entanglement, implication; ~ von Umständen combination of circumstances, (strange) coincidence.

ver-flieg/en (⸏⸍⸏⸍) [mhd.] ⓖafst* I v/n. (sn) to fly off or away or out of sight, fig. to vanish; Zeit: to pass rapidly, to fly; (sich verflüchtigen) to evaporate, bsd. chm. to volatilize; verflogene Tauben stray pigeons pl. — II sich 2 v/refl. to lose (or get scattered) in flying.

ver-fließen (⸏⸍⸏⸍) [mhd.] v/n. (sn) ⓖd* 1. to flow off or away, v. Fluten: to subside, v. der Zeit: to elapse, to glide (or slip) by, to expire; im verflossenen Jahre in the past year, last year; in verflossenen Jahren in former (or past) years; F co. der verflossene Minister the ex-minister. — 2. (verschwimmen) to dissolve, to vanish; von Farben: in=ea. 2 to run into each other; to mix.

ver-flixt F (⸏⸍) a. ⓖ = verflucht 3.

ver-flocht(en) (⸏⸍⸏⸍(⸏⸍)), **ver-flog(en)** (⸏⸍(⸏⸍)), **verstoß(en)** (⸏⸍⸏⸍), **verflossen** (⸏⸍⸏⸍) impf. u. p.p. v. ver-flechten, -fliegen, -fließen.

ver-flößen (⸏⸍⸏⸍) v/a. ⓖ*: Holz 2 to carry ... on rafts, to float ...

ver-fluchen (⸏⸍⸏⸍) [ahd.] I v/a. ⓖ* 1. to curse, to call down curses upon, to damn; (in den Kirchenbann tun) to anathematize; (verwünschen) to execrate. — II **ver-flucht** (⸏⸍⸏t) p.p. u. a. ⓖ 2. cursed, accursed, execrable. — 3. F (in Flüchen und lebhaften Ausdrücken) damned, confounded, F deuced, blessed; das ist seine verfluchte Schuldigkeit it is his bounden (F his damned) duty; als int. verflucht! damn (or confound) it!, botheration (take it)!; es ist verflucht (adv.) kalt it is devilishly (or fearfully) cold; sie ist 2 geizig she is dreadfully (or fearfully) mean; et. verflucht Unangenehmes an awful nuisance. — III ~ n ⓖ 4. f. Verfluchung.

ver-fluchens-wert (⸏⸍⸏⸍...) a. ⓖ, **=würdig** a. execrable, damnable.

ver-flüchtig/en (⸏⸍⸏⸍) I v/a. und v/refl. ⓖ* 1. to (cause to) evaporate, bsd. chm. to volatilize; sich 2 f. verfliegen. — 2. F fig. sich 2 to make o.s. scarce. — II ~ n ⓖ u. B/ung f ⓖ 3. evaporation, bsd. chm. volatilization, subtilization.

Ver-fluchung (⸏⸍⸏⸍) f ⓖ (f. verfluchen I) cursing, damning; anathema(tization); execration, malediction.

Ver-fluß fast † (⸏⸍) [verfließen] m ⓖ lapse; nach ~ eines Zeitraumes after (or at) the expiration of a (fixed) period.

Signs (see page XVII): F familiar; P vulgar; ⸌ flash; ⸌ rare; † obsolete (died); * new word (born); ⸌ incorrect; ♪ music;

[verflüssigen] — 1035 — [vergeben]

ver-flüssig/en (⌣‿⌣⌣) *phys.* **I** *v/a.* u. sich 2 *v/refl.* ⊛* to liquefy. — **II** ~ *n* 23 u. B/ung *f* 46 liquefaction. [fechten.]
ver-focht(en) (⌣‿⌣t(⌣)) *impf. (p.p.) v. ver=*
Ver-folg (⌣‿) *m* ⓐb. continuation; course, progress; im ~ m-s Schreibens in pursuance (or confirmation) of my (previous) letter.
ver-folgbar (⌣‿‿) *a.* 46 easy to pursue, pursuable, gerichtlich: suable.
ver-folgen (⌣‿⌣) [mhd.] **I** *v/a.* ⊛* **1.** to pursue, ungerecht, grausam: to persecute, hart, lebhaft: to press hard, to follow on the heels of, unablässig: to hunt after, to track, to dog, gerichtlich: to prosecute; f. steckbrieflich; ⚔ den fliehenden Feind 2 to pursue (or press) the flying foe; hunt. einen Hasen mit der Meute 2 to course a hare; ⚓ ein Schiff (scharf) 2 to give chase to ..., to chase ... — **2.** *fig.* eine Laufbahn, Spur ꝛc. 2 to follow up..., to pursue ...; ⚓ einen Kurs 2 to hold on one's course; seine Pläne 2 to prosecute one's plans, to push (forward) one's schemes; eine Sache mit Eifer 2 to push on a matter; sein Vorhaben bis ans Ende 2 to carry one's project (successfully) through; seinen Weg (ruhig) 2 to go (quietly) on one's way; weiter 2 to continue; to adhere to one's purpose, &c. — **II** ~ *n* 23 **3.** f. Verfolgung.
Ver-folger (⌣‿⌣) *m* ⓐ, ~in *f* 45 pursuer, v. Tieren u. Verbrechern: a. tracker; grausamer ~ persecutor, *f* a. persecutrix.
Ver-folgung (‿‿) *f* 46 (zu verfolgen 1:) pursuit; persecution, prosecution; chase; (zu 2:) pursuance; continuance.
Ver-folgungs=feuer ⚔ (⌣‿⌣...) *n* 42 fire of the pursuing army; =geist *m*, =sucht *f* spirit of persecution; =süchtig *a.* 46 bent on persecution; =wahn(sinn) *m* persecution mania.
ver-frachten ⚓ und ⚓ (⌣‿⌣t(⌣)) **I** *v/a.* ⊛* **1.** e-n Wagen ⚓ (vermieten) to let ... out on hire, ein Schiff ⚓ to charter. — **2.** Waren ꝛc. 2 = frachten. — **3.** (die Fracht bezahlen für) to pay for the carriage (or shipment, transport) of. — **II** ~ *n* 23 **4.** f. Verfrachtung.
Ver-frachter ⚓ und ⚓ (⌣‿⌣t(⌣)) *m* ⓐ consigner, shipper, freighter.
Ver-frachtung (‿‿) *f* 46 (f. verfrachten I) chartering; von Waren: consignment, shipment, freighting.
ver-fressen F P derb (⌣‿⌣) *v/a.* ⊛* to eat up; 2 *p.p.* (gefräßig) voracious.
ver-frieren (⌣‿⌣) *v/n.* (fn) ⓐc* to freeze; F ein verfrorener (für Kälte empfindlicher) Mensch a *p.* sensitive to cold, F a chilly mortal; f. a. erfrieren.
ver-frühen (⌣‿⌣) **I** *v/a.* ⊛* to do before the (proper) time, to anticipate; die Nachricht ist verfrüht ... is premature. — **II** ~ *n* 23 u. **Ver-frühung** *f* 46 anticipation; prematureness.
ver-fügbar (⌣‿‿) *a.* 46 at a p.'s disposal or command, selten: disposable, mehr gbr.: available; ~keit *f* 46 availability.
ver-fügen (⌣‿⌣) ⊛* **I** *v/a.* etwas 2 to arrange a th.; (vorschreiben) to prescribe, to order, (entscheiden) to decide; (anordnen) to decree, feierlicher: to ordain; das Gesetz verfügt, daß // the law provides (or enacts) that //. — **II** *v/n.* (h.): über e-n, et. 2 to dispose of a *p.*, a th.; Sie dürfen über mich 2 I am at your disposal or command; ich kann (nicht) frei über meine Zeit 2 I am (not) master of my time, my time is (not) my own; letztwillig über et. 2 to leave a th. by will, to will a th. (away). — **III** *v/refl.* sich wohin 2 (begeben) to betake o.s. (or to proceed, repair) to a place, to start for a place.
ver-füglich (⌣‿⌣) *a.* 46 = verfügbar.
Ver-fügung (⌣‿‿) *f* 46 (f. verfügen) zu **I**: arrangement; order, decree; gesetzliche ~ enactment; ~en über et. treffen to make provisions for a th., to give orders for a th. (to be done); zu **II**: disposal, disposition; e-m immerfort zur ~ sich(e)n to be at a p.'s beck and call; einem zur ~ stellen to place at a p.'s disposal or command.
ver-fuhr (⌣‿) *ind. impf. v. verfahren.*
ver-führbar (⌣‿‿) *a.* 46 **1.** capable of conveyance, ⚓ transportable. — **2.** corruptible, bsd. v. Mädchen: seducible. [fahren.]
ver-führe(n¹ *pl.*) (⌣‿⌣) *subj. impf. v. ver=*
ver-führen² (⌣‿⌣) [mhd.] **I** *v/a.* ⊛* **1.** Waren ꝛc. auf der Achse, zu Schiffe ꝛc. 2 to convey (or carry, transport) ..., außer Landes: to export ... — **2.** (irreführen) to lead astray, misguide, mislead, misdirect (sämtlich a. *fig.*). — **3.** nur *fig.* (verlocken) to entice, to tempt; (verleiten) to corrupt, to debauch, bsd. ein Mädchen: to seduce; Zeugen ꝛc.: to suborn; einen zu etwas 2 to induce (or tempt, prevail upon) a *p.* to do a th., to talk a *p.* into a th. — **4.** bisw. = vollführen, bsd. im Übermaße, z.B. einen großen Lärm 2 to make a dreadful noise, F to kick up a great shindy or row. — **II** ~ *n* 23 **5.** f. Verführung.
Ver-führer (⌣‿⌣) *m* ⓐ, ~in *f* 45 (f. verführen) corrupter (of morals), tempter, debaucher, seducer.
ver-führerisch (⌣‿⌣) *a.* 46 seducing; (verlockend) tempting, seductive, alluring, enticing, captivating, fascinating; (in Versuchung führend) tempting, bsd. *rel.* leading into temptation.
Ver-führung (⌣‿‿) *f* 46 (f. verführen 1) conveyance, carriage; (f. verführen 3) (moral) corruption, seduction. von Zeugen ꝛc.: subornation.
Ver-führungs=kunst (⌣‿⌣...) *f* 42 art of seduction; =künste, oft: fascinating (or winning) ways *pl.*; =mittel *n* means of seduction, (Bestechung) bribe(ry).
ver-füllen (⌣‿⌣) *v/a.* ⊛*: den Wein 2: a) aus einem Fasse ꝛc. in ein anderes: to pour ... from one cask, &c. into another; b) in ein falsches Faß: to fill (or pour, put) ... into a wrong cask.
ver-fumfei-en P (⌣‿⌣) *v/a.* ⊛* (vergeuden) to squander.
ver-fünf-fachen (⌣‿⌣ch) *v/a.* ⊛* to increase fivefold, to quintuple.
ver-füttern (⌣‿⌣) *v/a.* ⊛a* **1.** (futternd verbrauchen) to use up as fodder or provender. — **2.** (überfüttern) to overfeed; ein Kind 2, a. to cram ... with food, to give ... (over)rich food.
ver-gaben (⌣‿⌣) *v/a.* ⊛* (verschenken) to give away (as a present or in presents).

ver-gaffen (⌣‿⌣) [mhd.] *v/refl.* ⊛*: sich in e-n, et. 2 to fall in love (F to be smitten) with a *p.*, a th., to become enamoured of (or infatuated with) a *p.*, a th.
ver-gähnen (⌣‿‿) *v/a.* ⊛* to spend one's time in yawning, to yawn away the time.
ver-gällen (⌣‿⌣) [mhd.; *Galle*] *v/a.* ⊛* **1.** e-m et. 2 (verbittern) to set a *p.* against a th.; sich das Leben 2 to embitter one's life, to make one's life (or o.s.) miserable, to mar one's own joy; die ganze Welt ist mir vergällt (v., Faust) life's pleasures all to me are gall. — **2.** * (denaturieren) to make undrinkable.
ver-galoppieren (⌣‿⌣⌣): sich 2 *v/refl.* ⊛* to blunder by overgreat haste or by overhaste, to act (too) rashly.
ver-galt (⌣‿) *ind. impf. v. vergelten.*
ver-gangen (⌣‿⌣) *p.p.* u. *a.* 46 (D9) in den Bed. *des inf.* vergehen, bsd. von der Zeit: gone by, past; 2e Zeiten, auch: bygone days *pl.*; im 2en Jahre during the past year, last year; laß das ~e 2 sein (G.) let bygones be bygones.
Ver-gangenheit (⌣‿⌣‿) *f* 46 past (times or things *pl.*), *gr.* past tense, preterit(e).
ver-gänglich (⌣‿⌣) [mhd.] *a.* 46 transitory, transient, evanescent, fleeting, (flüchtig) fugitive; (schnell zugrunde gehend) perishable; alles Irdische ist 2 all earthly things (will) perish or pass away; ~keit (⌣‿⌣‿) *f* 46 transitoriness, evanescence; perishableness; (Unbeständigkeit) instability, (Hinfälligkeit) frailty.
ver-ganten südd. (⌣‿⌣) [Gant] *v/a.* ⊛* to put up for auction (= versteigern).
ver-gären (⌣‿⌣) ⚛a ⊛* = ausgären.
ver-gasen (⌣‿⌣) **I** *v/a.* ⊛* (in Gas verwandeln) to gasify. — **II** ~ *n* 23 f. Vergasung.
ver-gaß (⌣‿) *ind. impf.* von vergessen.
Ver-gasung (⌣‿‿) *f* 46 gasification.
ver-gatter/n (⌣‿⌣) [mhd.] **I** *v/a.* ⊛a* et. 2 to enclose a th. with a grating (vgl. vergittern). — **II** ~ *n* 23 und B/ung *f* 46 ⚔ (beating of drums as) signal to assemble or to rendezvous.
ver-geb-bar (⌣‿‿) *a.* 46 pardonable.
ver-geben (⌣‿⌣) [ahd.: forgive] **I** *v/a.* und *v/refl.* ⊛c* **1.** to give away to, to confer on; sich 2 to give away too much, to ruin o.s. by giving (vgl. a. 4); ein Amt, eine Stelle 2 to bestow ... on; die Stelle ist noch nicht 2 ... is still vacant; die Hand s-r Tochter 2, seine Tochter 2 to give one's daughter in marriage; ihre Hand ist schon 2 she is engaged (to be married); ⚓ die Lieferung von Schienen 2 to give away the contract for (the supply of) rails; die Pfarre wird vom Bischof 2 ... is in the gift of the bishop; eine Pfründe zu 2 haben to have the patronage of a benefice; ich habe den nächsten Tanz schon 2 I am already engaged (or bespoke) for the next dance. — **2.** sein Recht 2 (hingeben) to yield up one's right(s); e-m von f-m Rechte et. 2 (verkürzen) to give (some of) a p.'s rights away, to prejudice (or to derogate from) a p.'s rights; seiner Ehre oder Würde oder sich nichts 2 to guard jealously over (or not to forget) one's honour or dignity. — **3.** einem et. 2 (verzeihen) to pardon (or forgive) a *p.*

⚛ scientific; ❦ botanical; ⚱ geography; ⊕ machinery; ⚒ mining; ⚔ military; ⚓ marine; ⊛ commercial; ✉ postal; 🚂 railway.

s.th., to condone a p.'s fault; *rel.* Gott wird ihm die Sünde 2 God will pardon his sin; es soll dir 2 sein you shall be forgiven. — 4. Spiel: (falsch geben) die Karten 2, sich 2 to misdeal; es ist 2 it's a misdeal. — II *p.p. u. a.* ⓐ 5. Bed. des *inf.* — 6. ↘ als reines *a.* = vergebung. — III ~ n 23 *u.* 7. f. Vergebung.

Ver-gebens (f̌ʋ́ʋ) [mhd.] *adv. u. prädikatives a.* in vain, to no purpose, of no avail, F (of) no use; er redet 2 he is wasting his words or breath; sich 2 abmühen to have one's trouble for nothing, to labour (or toil) in vain.

Ver-geber (f̌ʋ́ʋ) *m* 22 giver, donor.

ver-geblich (f̌ʋ́ʋ) [urspr. vergeben(d)lich] *a.* ⓐ vain, fruitless, unavailing, futile; (überflüssig) superfluous; (unnötig) needless; 2e Angst needless fear; 2er Gang useless errand, wild goose-chase; sich (*dat.*) 2e Mühe m. to labour in vain, to lose one's labour; *als adv.* = vergebens; **~keit** *f* ⓐ vanity, fruitlessness; needlessness, uselessness.

Ver-gebung (f̌ʋ́ʋ) *f* ⓐ (f. vergeben 1) gift, bestowal, *eccl.* einer Pfründe, auch collation; (f. vergeben 3) pardon(ing), forgiving, forgiveness, *rel.* remission of sins; als Höflichkeitsausdruck: (ich bitte) um ~! I beg your pardon!, pardon me!, (pray) excuse me!

ver-gegenwärtig/en (f̌ʋ́ʋʋ) *I v./a.* ⓐ* (vividly) to represent to, to bring home to, to describe graphically to; sich (*dat.*) et. 2 to picture a th. (to o.s.), to conjure a th. up in one's mind, to realize (or grasp) a th., ↗ to visualize a th. — II ~ n 23 *und* B/ung *f* ⓐ (vivid) representation; graphic description, realization, ↗ visualization.

ver-geh(e)n (f̌ʋ́(ʋ)) [mhd.] ⓐ* *I v./n.* (jn) 1. v. d. Zeit: to pass (away), to glide by, to slip (away), to elapse; die Jahre 2 rasch the years roll by rapidly; im vergangenen Monat in the past month; in längst vergangenen Zeiten in days long gone by, in remote ages; *vgl.* vergangen. — 2. (hinfließen) to pine away, to droop; (verschwinden) to disappear, to vanish; (aufhören) to cease, to end; (sich verlieren) to subside, to abate; (umkommen) to perish, to die; (hinschmelzen) to melt away; Sprichw. f. Unkraut; **vor** Angst 2 to be in mortal dread; vor Gram 2 to pine away, to fret one's heart out; vor Ungeduld (fast) 2 to be (almost) dying with impatience. — 3. mit persönlichem Dativ: ihm verging Hören und Sehen, *etwa*: his sight and hearing (von Ohnmächtigen: his senses) failed him; mir ist alle Lust vergangen I have lost all inclination (or desire) for it; sich (den Gedanken an) et. 2 lassen to give up all thoughts of a th. — **II** sich 2 *v./refl.* 4. (das Recht verletzen) to commit an offence, to trespass; sich gegen das Gesetz 2 to offend (or transgress) against (*or* to infringe) the law; sich gegen (oder wider) e-n 2 to offend (or insult) a p., tätlich: to assault a p. — **III** ~ n 23 5. ohne *pl.* (f. 1) das ~ der Jahre the flight (or lapse) of years; (f. 2) disappearance. — 6. mit *pl.* (f. 4),

bisw. auch **Ver-gehung** *f* ⓐ offence, trespass(ing); transgression; *jur. auch* misdemeanour.

ver-geistig/en (f̌ʋ́ʋʋ) 'I *v./a.* ⓐ* to spiritualize, intellectualize; *chm.* eine Flüssigkeit ~ to alcoholize … — **II** ~ n 23 *und* B/ung *f* ⓐ spiritualization.

ver-geltbar (f̌ʋ́ʋ-) *a.* ⓐ remunerable.

ver-gelten (f̌ʋ́ʋ) [ahd.] *I v./a.* ⓐ*: e-m et. 2 to repay (*a.* to requite) a th. to a p.; es ist ihm vergolten worden it has come home to him; e-m einen Dienst 2c. 2 to remunerate a p. for …; Böses mit Gutem 2 to return good for evil; Gleiches mit Gleichem 2 to give tit for tat, to pay back in the same coin, to retaliate upon a p.; Gott vergelte es Ihnen! God bless you for it! — **II** ~ n 23 f. Vergeltung.

Ver-gelter (f̌ʋ́ʋ) *m* 22, **~in** *f* ⓐ one who repays, &c.; (f. vergelten) (Rächer[in]) avenger, vindicator.

Ver-geltung (f̌ʋ́ʋ) *f* ⓐ requital, return; als Feind: retaliation, reprisal.

Ver-geltungs-recht (f̌ʋ́ʋ…) *n* ⓑ right of retaliation or reprisal; **-tag** *m* day of retribution; **-zoll** *m* retaliation duty.

ver-gesellschaft/en (f̌ʋ́ʋʋʋ) *I v./a.* ⓐ*: ⓑ (sich) 2 to associate, to unite with. — **II** ~ n 23 *u.* B/ung *f* ⓐ association, union.

ver-geßbar (f̌ʋ́ʋ-) *a.* ⓐ that can be forgotten; easily (or soon) forgotten.

ver-gessen (f̌ʋ́ʋ) [ahd.: forget] ⓐ* *I v./a.* et. (öft. a. an ob. auf et.) 2 to forget; (versäumen) to overlook; (auslassen) to omit, to leave out; e-n etwas 2 m. to make a p. forget s.th., to put a th. out of a p.'s mind or head; ich habe ganz 2, wie er redet I quite forget how he talks; sie 2 darüber Essen und Trinken (they are so busy that) they forget their eating and drinking over it; Rosen auf den Weg gestreut und des Harms 2! (HÖLTY) scatter roses on your path, and forget your trouble!; 2 Sie nicht zu kommen! be sure and come!; längst 2 long forgotten, buried in oblivion, effaced from people's memories; das ist vergeben und 2 that's forgiven and forgotten. — **II** sich 2 *v./refl.*: a) von Personen: to forget o.s. (so weit zu f/) so far as to *f*); b) von Dingen: to be forgotten, to slip one's memory. — **III** ~ n 23 forgetting, oblivion.

Ver-gessenheit (f̌ʋ́ʋʋ-) *f* ⓐ 1. oblivion; der ~ anheimgeben to consign to oblivion, *poet.* to drown in Lethe; in ~ bringen to bury in oblivion; der ~ anheimfallen, in ~ geraten to fall (or sink) into oblivion, to be forgotten, to drop from people's memories or minds. — 2. ↘ = Vergeßlichkeit.

ver-geßlich (f̌ʋ́ʋ) [mhd.] *a.* ⓐ 1. v. Personen: forgetful, easily forgetting, oblivious, of weak (or with a bad) memory. — 2. v. Dingen: easily forgotten (= vergeßbar); **~keit** (f̌ʋ́ʋ-) *f* ⓐ forgetfulness, obliviousness, weak(ness of) memory.

ver-geuden (f̌ʋ́ʋ) [mhd.] *I v./a.* ⓐ* to squander (away), dissipate, lavish; (wegwerfen) to throw (or fling) away; (verschwenden) to waste time, money, &c.,

allmählich: to fritter away, wie ein Narr: to fool away; (durchbringen) F to run through a fortune, to make ducks and drakes of one's money. — **II** ~ n 23 f. Vergeudung.

Ver-geuder (f̌ʋ́ʋ) *m* 22, **~in** *f* ⓐ squanderer, spendthrift, wastrel.

Ver-geudung (f̌ʋ́ʋ) *f* ⓐ squandering, dissipation; waste(fulness).

ver-gewaltigen (f̌ʋ́ʋʋʋ) [mhd.] *I v./a.* ⓐ*: e-n to offer violence to a p., to use force with a p.; *jur.*: ein Mädchen 2 to commit a rape (or an assault) on a girl, to ravish a maiden. — **II** ~ n 23 f. Vergewaltigung. [ravisher.)

Ver-gewaltiger (~) *m* 22 oppressor,

Ver-gewaltigung (~) *f* ⓐ violence (offered), force (used); oppression; rape.

ver-gewisser/n (f̌ʋ́ʋʋ) [mhd.] *I v./a.u.v./refl.* ⓐ* 1. et. 2 to ascertain a th. — 2. e-n e-r Sache (*gen.*) 2, e-n über et. 2 to assure (or convince) a p. of a th.; sich e-r Sache 2 to make sure of a th. — **II** ~ n 23 *u.* B/ung, *wißrung* *f* ⓐ 3. ascertaining, …ment; assurance.

ver-gieß/en (f̌ʋ́ʋ) [ahd.] ⓐd* *I v./a.* 1. Blut, Tränen 2 to shed blood, tears; heiße Tränen 2. auch: to weep bitterly or bitter tears; die um ihn vergossenen Tränen the tears shed for (or over) him. — 2. (verschütten) to spill water, milk, &c. — 3. ⓞ: a) *metall.*: (gießend verderben, aufbrauchen) to spoil (or use up) in casting; b) Bauwesen: (befestigen) Klammern mit Blei 2 to fix clamps with molten lead. — **II** sich 2 *v./refl.* ⓞ 4. (abfließen) to drain off. — 5. (schlecht gießen) to cast badly. — **III** ~ n 23 *u.* B/ung 23 shedding; spilling; effusion.

ver-giften (f̌ʋ́ʋ) [mhd.] *I v./a. u. v./refl.* ⓐ* 1. to poison (*a. fig.*); sich 2, auch: to take poison. — 2. (giftig m.) to make poisonous, to envenom, *fig. a.* to taint, vitiate. — **II** ~ n 23. f. Vergiftung.

Ver-gifter (~) *m* 22, **~in** *f* ⓐ poisoner.

Ver-giftung (~) *f* ⓐ poisoning.

Vergil (w…) *npr./m.* ⓑ ⓐ*a.* = Virgil.

ver-gilben (f̌ʋ́ʋ) [mhd.] *v./n.* (jn) ⓐ* to turn yellow.

ver-gilt (f̌ʋ́ʋ) *imper. v.* vergelten.

ver-ging (f̌ʋ́ʋ) *ind. imperf. v.* vergehen.

ver-giß (f̌ʋ́ʋ) *imper.*, **ver-gissest** (f̌ʋ́ʋ-) 2. Person, **ver-gißt** 2. u. 3. Person *sing.* des *pres. ind. von* vergessen.

Ver-gißmeinnicht (f̌ʋ́ʋ-) [mhd.] *n* ⓑ c. (*a. inv.*) forget-me-not (*Myoso'tis*); echtes ~ true forget-me-not (*M. palu'stris*).

ver-gittern (f̌ʋ́ʋ) *I v./a.* ⓐa* to enclose with trellis-work or lattice-work or a grating, mit Drahtgitter 2 to wire in; vergittert latticed. — **II** ~ n 23 und **Ver-gitterung** *f* ⓐ (enclosing with) trellis-work or lattice-work, grating.

ver-glasbar ⓞ (f̌ʋ́ʋ-) *a.* ⓐ vitrifiable, vitrescible; **~keit** *f* ⓐ vitrifiability.

ver-glasen ⓞ (f̌ʋ́ʋ) ⓐ* *I v./n.* (jn) u. sich 2 *v./refl.* to become (or to turn to) glass, to vitrify. — **II** *v./a.* to vitrify, ein Fenster: to glaze, to provide with panes; verglaster Backstein clinker. — **III** ~ n 23 und **Ver-glasung** *f* ⓐ vitrification; glazing, putting in (of) panes; **Verglasung** (Glaswert) eines Gebäudes glass-work, windows *pl.*

Zeichen (f. S. XVII): F familiär; P Volkssprache; ϝ Gaunersprache; ↘ selten; † alt (auch gestorben); * neu (auch geboren); ⚹ unrichtig;

[Vergleich] — 1037 — [vergrößern]

Ver-gleich (f⌣́) m ⓒc. 1. (gütliche Beilegung e-s Streites) (amicable) arrangement; agreement, accommodation, mit Gläubigern ꝛc. auch: composition; (Ausgleich) compromise, settlement, (Vertrag) contract, convention; einen ~ schließen to come to an arrangement or to an understanding or to terms; Sprichw. f. mager 2. — 2. (Vergleichung) comparison; einen ~ anstellen to draw a parallel; einen ~ aushalten (können) mit // to bear comparison with //; das ist nichts im ~ mit od. zu // that's nothing in comparison (or if compared) with //; F kein ~ damit! not a patch on it!

ver-gleichbar (f⌣́⌣) a. ⓖ comparable; ~keit f ⓖ comparableness.

ver-gleichen (f⌣́⌣) [mhd.] I v/a. u. v/refl. ⓖb* 1. (gleichen) to equalize, to make even. — 2. fig. (ins Gleichgewicht bringen) to adjust differences, disputes; (versöhnen) to conciliate disputants; sich mit e-m ⌣ to come to an agreement (or understanding) with a p.; sie haben sich gütlich verglichen they have made an amicable arrangement. — 3. etwas mit etwas anderem ⌣ (prüfend zf.-halten) to compare with or to, to liken to, to draw a parallel between, Abschriften mit dem Original: to collate; sie lassen sich nicht mit=ea. ⌣ they are not to be compared; niemand läßt sich mit ihm ⌣ he is incomparable, there is no one like him, he has not his equal; ⌣d(e Grammatik) comparative (grammar). — II ~ n ㉓ 4. s. Vergleichung.

ver-gleichlich (f⌣́⌣) a. ⓖ = vergleichbar.

ver-gleichs-mäßig (f⌣̋…) a. ⓖ conventional, agreed upon, fixed by contract; =mittel n ⓖ means of (bringing about a) reconciliation; =termin m day of settlement; =verfahren n, bsd. ⌣ arbitration; =versuch m attempt at conciliation; attempted settlement; ⌣weise adv. (a.) by way of agreement.

Ver-gleichung (f⌣́⌣) f ⓖ (s. vergleichen 1) equalization; (s. vergleichen 2) adjustment; (s. vergleichen 3) comparison, parallel; collation of manuscripts.

Ver-gleichungs-gabe (f⌣́⌣…) f ⓖ gift (Phrenologie: bump) of comparison; =grad m, gr. degree of comparison; erster (zweiter, dritter) ~ positive (comparative, superlative) degree; =punkt m point of comparison or agreement; =satz m, gr. comparative clause; =stufe f = =grad; =vermögen n comparative faculty, vgl. =gabe; ⌣weise adv. by way of comparison, comparatively speaking.

ver-gletschern (f⌣́⌣) ⓖa* geol. I v/n. (sn) u. v/a. to turn to glaciers, bisw. ⌣ to glaciate. — II ~ n ⓖ Vergletscherung f ⓖ formation of glaciers, ⌣ glaci(eriz)ation. [gleichen.)

ver-glich(en) (f⌣́(⌣)) impf. (p.p.) von ver=)

ver-glimmen (f⌣́⌣) v/n. (sn) und sich ⌣ v/refl. ⓖa* to cease glimmering or burning, ⌣ to go out (gradually), vom Feuer auch: to drop out, to die away; ⌣de Asche dying embers pl.

ver-glomm (f⌣́) impf., ⌣en (f⌣́⌣) p.p. von verglimmen.

ver-glühen (f⌣́⌣) ⓖ* I v/n. (sn) 1. to cease glowing, (sich abkühlen) to cool down (by degrees). — 2. (glühend vergehen) to be consumed (or perish) by fire. — II v/a. 3. ⓣ Porzellan ⌣ (brennen) to fire porcelain.

ver-gnügen¹ (f⌣́⌣) [mhd.: genug] v/a. ⓖ* to gratify, amuse, divert; sich ⌣ v/refl. to enjoy (or amuse) o.s.; to (take a) delight in; vergnügt s. ds.

Ver-gnügen² (f⌣́⌣) [⌣] n ㉓ pleasure; (Zerstreuung) distraction, amusement; (Scherz) fun; (Genuß) enjoyment, (Befriedigung) gratification; ~ an et. finden to (take a) delight in a th.; wir hatten viel ⌣ we had great fun, we greatly enjoyed ourselves; es wird mir ⌣ m. zu kommen it will give me pleasure (or I shall be delighted) to come; et. mit ⌣ tun to do a th. with pleasure or gladly; et. zum ~ tun to do a th. for pleasure or for (an) amusement; ⌣shalber adv. for pleasure, as an amusement, for fun.

ver-gnüglich (f⌣́⌣) a. ⓖ 1. von Personen: pleased, content(ed). — 2. von Dingen: pleasurable, delightful, enjoyable; (angenehm) pleasing, pleasant; ~keit (f⌣́⌣) f ⓖ 1. contentedness. — 2. delightfulness, pleasantness.

ver-gnügt (f⌣́) p.p. v. vergnügen u. a. ⓖ = froh 1 u. 2; ⌣ aussehen to look pleased; höchst ⌣ über // delighted (or overjoyed) at //, greatly pleased with //.

Ver-gnügung (f⌣́⌣) f ⓖ pleasure, pleasuring; im Freien: (outdoor) sport(s pl.); pastime, recreation; auf ~en ausgehen to go out pleasuring, F to go galivanting, to shake a loose leg.

Ver-gnügungs-fahrt (f⌣́⌣…) f ⓖ = =reise; ⌣halber adv. for amusement, for the sake of enjoyment; =kommissar m in Badeorten: official appointed to provide amusement(s) for the visitors; =kommission f etwa: entertainment committee; =lokal n, =ort m place of amusement; holiday-resort; =reise f pleasure- (or holiday-)trip, outing, excursion, größere: tour; =reisende(r) s. excursionist, holiday-maker, tourist, F tripper; =sucht f (inordinate) love of pleasure or amusement; ⌣süchtig a. pleasure-seeking, (exceedingly) fond of pleasure, bent on enjoyment; ⌣süchtiger Mensch, oft: pleasure-hunter or =seeker; =zug m excursion-train.

Ver-golde-grund (f⌣́⌣…) m ⓖ gilding-size, aus Eiweiß u. Wassersize-water; =kunst f (art of) gilding; =leim m gilder's size.

ver-golden (f⌣́⌣) [mhd.] I v/a. ⓖ* to gild (over) (a. fig.); galvanisch ⌣ to electro-gild; vergoldet gilt. — II ~ n ㉓ = Vergoldung.

Ver-golde-pinsel ⓣ (⌣…) m ⓖ, =presse f gilding-brush, =press.

Ver-golder ⓣ (⌣) m ⓖ, ~in f ⓖ gilder.

Ver-golder-… (⌣…) = Vergolde=…

Ver-golde-stempel (f⌣́⌣,⌣) m ⓖ gilding-tool, Buchbinderei: pallet.

Ver-goldung (f⌣́⌣) f ⓖ gilding; galvanische ~ electro-gilding; nasse (trockene) ~ water- (leaf-)gilding.

ver-gölte (f⌣́⌣) subj. impf., **ver-golten** p.p. von vergelten.

ver-gönnen (f⌣́⌣) [mhd.] v/a. ⓖ* to permit, to give permission for; to allow (or grant) a p. a th.; es war(d) mir nicht vergönnt, ihn zu sehen I was not granted the pleasure (or privilege) of seeing him.

ver-goß (f⌣́) ind., **ver-gösse** (f⌣́⌣) subj. impf., **ver-gossen** (f⌣́⌣) p.p. v. vergießen.

Ver-götterer (f⌣́⌣) m ⓖ worshipper, von Götzenbildern: idolater.

ver-götter n (f⌣́⌣) I v/a. ⓖa* to deify; fig. (wie e-n Gott verehren) to idolize, to make an idol of, to worship; ⌣d idolatrous. — II ~ n ⓖ und V ung f ⓖ deification, apotheosis; idolizing, idolatry, worship(ping).

ver-graben (f⌣́⌣) [mhd.] I v/a. u. v/refl. ⓖb* = begraben, mit dem Nebensinne des Heimlichen: to hide (or conceal) in the ground; s. Pfund 2; unter s-n Büchern ⌣ buried among his books; sich ⌣: a) von Tieren, bsd. Kaninchen: to burrow; b) ⚔ to intrench o.s. (in earthworks). — II ~ n ㉓ u. **Ver-grabung** f ⓖ burying, interment.

ver-gräm(e)l)n (f⌣́⌣) ⓖ (ⓖa)* I v/a. 1. sein Leben ⌣ to pass (or spend) … in grief. — 2. e-n ⌣ to make a p. sad; vergrämt care-worn, grief-stricken, woebegone. — II sich ⌣ v/refl. 3. to pine away (in grief), to (live in) sorrow, F to worry (or fret) one's life out.

ver-grasen (f⌣́⌣) v/n. (sn) ⓖ* to be(come) covered (or grown over) with grass.

ver-greifen (f⌣́⌣) [mhd] ⓖb* I v/a. 1. (falsch greifen) to seize wrongly or by mistake; ♪ die Saite (ob. den Ton) ⌣ to touch a wrong note. — 2. ⌣ eine Ware ⌣ (rasch aufkaufen) to buy … up quickly; das Buch (die Auflage) ist (auch v/refl. hat sich) vergriffen the book, the edition is exhausted or out of print; der Vorrat ist vergriffen (the whole) stock is sold or gone or exhausted; schnell vergriffene Ware goods which sell rapidly or go off like steam. — II sich ⌣ v/refl. 3. (fehlgreifen) to (make a) mistake in seizing. — 4. sich an e-m, etwas ⌣ to lay (violent) hands on a p., a th., to seize a p., a th. by main force; an den Gesetzen: to violate (or infringe) the law, an heiligen Dingen: to desecrate (or profane) a sanctuary, &c., an einer Kasse: to embezzle (or purloin) money, to rob a safe. — III ~ n ㉓, meist **Ver-greifung** f ⓖ 5. violent seizure of, violation (or desecration) of; an Geldern: embezzlement, robbery, peculation. [greifen.)

ver-griff(en) (f⌣́(⌣)) impf. (p.p.) v. ver=)

ver-gröber n (f⌣́⌣) ⓖa* I v/a. to make coarse(r) or rude(r) or gross. — II sich ⌣ v/refl. to grow coarse(r); V ung f ⓖ making (or growing) coarse.

Ver-größ(e)rer (f⌣́⌣) m ⓖ magnifier.

ver-größer n (f⌣́⌣) I v/a. u. v/refl. ⓖa* to enlarge, bsd. fig. to aggrandize; (vermehren) to increase, enhance, raise, augment, durch Vergrößerungsgläser u. fig. beim Erzählen: to magnify, (übertreiben) to exaggerate; (schlimmer m.) to aggravate; opt. stark ⌣de Gläser powerful glasses or magnifiers pl.; sich ⌣ to increase (in size or bulk), to grow

♪ Musik; ⚙ Wissenschaft; ⚘ Pflanze; ⚱ Geographie; ⊙ Technik; ⚒ Bergbau; ⚔ Militär; ⚓ Marine; ⊛ Handel; ✉ Post; 🚂 Eisenbahn.

[Vergrößerung] — 1038 — [verharschen]

(larger), to expand; in vergrößertem Maßstabe on an enlarged scale. — II ~ n ㉓ u. Ver-größerung (f⌣⌣⌣) f ㊻ enlargement; increase, augmentation, exaggeration.

Ver-größerungs-glas (f⌣⌣⌣...) n ㉒ opt. magnifying glass, microscope; =kamera f, phot. enlarging (or magnifying) camera; =kraft f magnifying power; =laterne f magic lantern; =linse f magnifying (or convex) lens; =messer m an Fernrohren ⌒ auxometer, dynameter; =spiegel m concave mirror; =verfahren n enlarging process; =wort n, gr.: ⌒ augmentative.

ver-grub (f⌣⌣) ind. impf. v. vergraben.

ver-grübeln (f⌣⌣⌣) v/a. ㊻* to waste time, &c. in brooding or ruminating.

ver-grünen (f⌣⌣⌣) v/n. (fn) ㊻* 1. to lose the green colour, to fade — 2. ↯ v. Blumenblättern (grün w.) to turn green.

ver-gucken (f⌣⌣⌣): sich ⌒ v/refl. ㊻* = sich versehen 7 u. vergaffen..

ver-gülden (f⌣⌣⌣) v/a. ㊻* altertümlich od. poet. = vergolden.

Ver-gunst (f⌣⌣) f, inv. permission; mit ~ with your (kind) permission or leave.

ver-günstig/en (f⌣⌣⌣⌣) v/a. ㊻* to grant, permit; B/ung (f⌣⌣⌣⌣) f ㊻ (special) permission or favour or privilege; ↯ abatement, allowance, (Abzug) deduction.

ver-güten (f⌣⌣⌣) I v/a. ㊻*: e-m et. ⌒ to make a th. good to a p.; (Ersatz bieten für) to make amends (or to compensate) for, to make up (a loss); (zurückerstatten) to restore, to refund; e-m die Auslagen, die Kosten ⌒ to reimburse (or indemnify) a p. — II ~ n ㉓ u. Ver-gütung f ㊻ making amends for, compensation, reimbursement, indemnification, allowance.

Ver-hack (f⌣⌣) m (n) ⓦb. = Verhau.

ver-hacken (f⌣⌣⌣) v/a. ㊻* to hack.

Ver-haft (f⌣⌣) m ⓦb. = Haft II; in ~ nehmen to arrest, F to collar.

ver-haften (f⌣⌣⌣) [Haft] I v/a. ㊻*: e-n ⌒ to arrest (or apprehend) a p., to take a p. in charge or into custody; e-n ⌒ I. to give a p. in charge; der Verhaftete the p. given in charge, the prisoner. — II ~ n ㉓ u. Ver-haftung f ㊻ arrest, apprehension, attachment, eines Verfolgten: capture.

Ver-haft(ung)s-befehl (f⌣⌣⌣...) m㉒ jur. warrant of apprehension, writ of attachment or capias, writ to apprehend the body; einen ~ gegen e-n erlassen to issue a warrant for a p.'s apprehension or attachment; e-n ~ vollziehen to serve a writ upon a p.

ver-hageln (f⌣⌣⌣) I v/n. (fn) ㊺* to be damaged (or spoiled) by hail(stones); fig. f. Peterselle. — II ~ n ㉓ u. Ver-hag(e)lung f ㊻ = Hagelschaden.

ver-häkeln (f⌣⌣⌣) v/a. ㊻* 1. to join (or fasten) with little hooks. — 2. Seide ic. ⌒ to use up ... in crochet-work.

ver-half (f⌣⌣) ind. impf. v. verhelfen.

ver-hallen (f⌣⌣⌣) v/n. (fn) ㊻* von Tönen: to die away; ♪ sanft ⌒d lingering, (it.) smorzando, smorzato; fig. sein Ruhm ist verhallt his fame is extinct.

Ver-halt (f⌣⌣) m ⓦb. state of affairs; der (Sach)~ ist the facts are these.

ver-halten (f⌣⌣) [mhd.] ⓐa* I v/a. 1. to retain; (unterbrücken) to suppress; den Atem ⌒ to hold in one's breath; sich das Lachen ⌒ to keep (or restrain o.s.) from laughing; den Urin ⌒ to keep back (or stop) one's urine; sich den Zorn ⌒ to suppress (or check, control) one's anger; mit 2em Atem with bated breath; sein schlecht 2er Zorn his pent-up wrath. — II sich ⌒ v/refl. 2. von Dingen: a) (stattfinden) to be (in a certain condition or position); die Tatsachen ⌒ sich anders the facts are different; wissen Sie, wie sich die Sache (oder wie es sich damit) verhält? ... how the matter stands or how things are (going on)?; wenn es sich so verhält if such be the case or the (actual) state of affairs; b) vergleichend: sich zu et. ⌒ to bear a (certain) proportion (or relationship) to a th.; math. A verhält sich zu B wie C zu D A is to B as C is to D; sich umgekehrt ⌒ zu // to be in inverse ratio to //. — 3. von Personen: (sich benehmen) to behave, to conduct o.s.; sich neutral (passiv) ⌒ to maintain a neutral (a passive) attitude; sich ruhig ⌒ to keep quiet; ich weiß nicht, wie ich mich dabei ⌒ soll ... how (I am) to act in this matter; Kinder, verhaltet euch brav! children, behave yourselves or be good! — III ~ n ㉓ 4. (f. 1) retention, restraint, suppression. — 5. das ~ (Benehmen) behaviour, conduct, demeanour; attitude; way (or manner, mode) of acting; (Verfahren) procedure; chm. das ~ e-r Säure ic. gegen the effect (or reaction) ... upon.

Ver-hältnis (f⌣⌣⌣) n ㉗ 1. meist persönlich: a) relation(ship), connexion; in freundschaftlichem ~ mit (ob. zu) e-m stehen to keep up a friendly intercourse (or to be on friendly terms) with a p.; f. gespannt 3 am Ende; b) F = Liebschaft, Liebste. — 2. mst sachlich: (~mäßigkeit) proportion, math. ratio, rate; im ~ zu in proportion to; (when) compared with; im (nicht im) ~ stehend (dis)proportionate, in (out of) proportion (mit-ea. with each other); und alles übrige im ~ (dem entsprechend) and everything else accordingly or in keeping or in proportion; math. gerades ~ direct ratio; in quadratischem ~ in duplicate proportion or ratio; im umgekehrten ~ in inverse proportion or ratio; klimatische ...sse climatic conditions pl. — 3. meist pl. (Lage) situation; (Lebensstellung) position; (Vermögenszustand) circumstances, means pl.; in angenehmen ...ssen in easy (or good) circumstances; f. beschränken IV; über seine ...sse beyond one's income; unter solchen ...ssen under these circumstances, such being the case or the state of affairs.

Ver-hältnis-anteil (f⌣⌣⌣...) m ㉒ (proportionate) share, quota, ↯ dividend; =anzeiger m, math. exponent; ⌒los a. ㊻ without relation(ship); disproportionate, (begläglich) relative; adv. auch: in proportion, comparatively speaking, ↯ pro rata; =mäßigkeit f proportion(ateness); =regel f, arith. rule of proportion, rule of three; ⌒widrig a. disproportionate, out of proportion; =wort n preposition; =zahl f, math. proportional number.

Ver-haltung (f⌣⌣⌣) f ㊻ = verhalten III.

Ver-haltungs-art (f⌣⌣⌣...) [vgl. verhalten 5] f ㊻ (line of) conduct, (kind of) behaviour; =befehl m instruction, direction; =maßregel(n pl.) f instructions, orders pl.

ver-handeln (f⌣⌣⌣) [mhd.] ⓐa* I v/n. (h.) u. v/a. 1. über et. ⌒ to negotiate (or discuss, transact) a th., to deliberate upon a th.; to treat about peace, &c.; to parley (a. ⚔); (lebhaft erörtern) to debate (upon), to argue; jur. gerichtlich ⌒ to plead (before a court). — II v/a. 2. b.s. (Handel treiben mit) to traffic (or deal) in. — 3. (durch den Handel verlieren) to lose in trade; er hat sein Vermögen verhandelt he has lost all his money in trading or speculating. — III ~ n ㉓ u. Ver-handlung f ㊻ 4. negotiation, discussion, transaction, deliberation, parley (a. ⚔); debate (auch parl.); vor Gericht: pleading, weitS. proceeding, trial, hearing.

Ver-handlungs-buch (f⌣⌣⌣...) n ㉒ bei Berichten, Notaren ic.: minute-book; =führer ⚔ jur. m recorder, clerk of sessions; =saal m e-s Gerichts: session-court or -hall; =termin m day (or date) appointed for the hearing of a case.

ver-hängen (f⌣⌣⌣) [mhd.] v/a. ㊻(ⓦb.) 1. to hang, to cover over (with a cloth or a curtain); to veil; mit schwarzem Tuch verhängt hung with black cloth, draped in black. — 2. to hang badly. — 3. e-m Pferde die Zügel ⌒ (schießen l.) to give ... the reins; mit verhängtem Zügel at full speed or gallop. — 4. et. (übles) über e-n ⌒ (beschließen) to decree a th. against a p.; eine Strafe über e-n ⌒ to inflict a punishment (or a penalty) on a p.; die Todesstrafe über e-n ⌒ to sentence a p. to death, to pronounce the death-sentence upon a p.; ⚔ den Belagerungszustand über eine Stadt ⌒ to proclaim martial law in a town, to declare a town in a state of siege; das von Gott Verhängte God's ordinances pl.. what the Lord has decreed.

Ver-hängnis (f⌣⌣⌣) n ㉗ (das über e-n Verhängte) fate, destiny, rel. heavenly decree; schlimmes ~ doom; vgl. Geschick 3.

Ver-hängnis-glaube (f⌣⌣⌣...) m ⓦ fatalism; ⌒gläubig a. ㊻ fatalistic; =gläubige(r) s. fatalist; ⌒voll a. fateful, fatal; (unselig) disastrous, unfortunate.

ver-härmen (f⌣⌣⌣) v/a. u. sich ⌒ v/refl. ㊻* to pine away (with grief).

ver-harren (f⌣⌣⌣) [mhd.] I v/n. (h. u. fn) ㊻* (verbleiben) to abide, remain, (beharren) to persevere; auf seinen Ansichten ⌒ to persist in one's opinions; in Briefen: ich verharre Ihr ergebener I remain your obedient servant or yours sincerely. — II ~ n ㉓ u. Ver-harrung f ㊻ perseverance; persistency.

ver-harsch/en (f⌣⌣⌣) ㊻* I v/n. (fn) to form a crust or a scar, ⌒ to cicatrize; v. Wunden auch: to close. — II v/a. to

Signs (see page XVII): F familiar; P vulgar; ℱ flash; \ rare; † obsolete (died); * new word (born); ⁒ incorrect; ♪ music;

[Verharschung] — 1039 — [verhundertfältigen]

heal up, ⚕ to cicatrize. — III ~ n ⓝ u. B/ung f ⓜ: ⚕ cicatrization.

ver-härten (⌣⌣́) [mhd.] ⓑ* I v/n. (ſn), a. **ver-harten** u. ſich **ver-härten** v/refl. to harden, to grow hard or obdurate, to indurate (alle a. fig.); ſich gegen et. ⌣ to harden (or steel) one's heart against; verhärtet hardened to. obdurate, callous. — II v/a. to harden, to make hard(er), to indurate (alle a. fig.); med. den Leib ⌣ to constipate (the bowels). — III ~ n ⓝ = Verhärtung 1.

Ver-härtung (⌣) f ⓜ 1. hardening, obduracy, induration. — 2. path.: a) Leib: ⚕ constipation; b) Haut: callosity.

ver-harzen (⌣⌣́) ⓑ* I v/n. (ſn) u. ſich ⌣ v/refl. to turn to resin or rosin, to become resinous, ⚕ to resinify. — II to cover (or to close up) with resin or rosin. — III ~ n ⓝ u. Ver-harzung f ⓜ: ⚕ resinification.

ver-haspeln (⌣⌣́) I v/a. u. ſich ⌣ v/refl. ⓑa* to tangle in reeling off; fig. ſich ⌣ beim Reden: to become embarrassed or perplexed, to get muddled; vgl. verwickeln. — II ~ n ⓝ u. Ver-haſp(e)-lung f ⓜ: entanglement.

ver-haßt (⌣⌣́) [ahd.] a. ⓜ (much) hated, odious; das iſt mir ⌣ it's hateful to me, I hate it; ſich ⌣ m. bei ⸗ to make o.s. obnoxious to // or unpopular with //.

ver-hätſcheln (⌣⌣́⌣) I v/a. ⓑa*: ein Kind ꝛc. ⌣ to (over-)indulge (or coddle, cosset, pamper, spoil) ...; ein verhätſcheltes Kind a pampered (or spoilt) child. — II ~ n ⓝ u. Ver-hätſch(e)lung f ⓜ (over-)indulgence shown to.

Ver-hau (⌣⌣́) m ⓒc. bſd. ✕ frt. abat(t)is, barricade formed of trunks and branches of trees.

ver-hauchen (⌣⌣́⌣) v/a. ⓑ* to exhale; vgl. aushauchen.

ver-hauen (⌣⌣́) [ahd.] v/a. u. ſich ⌣ v/refl. ⓒc. ⓑ* 1. to injure by knocking or cutting; F einen ⌣: a) prügelnd: to knock a p. about; b) fechtend: to hack (or cut) a p. about, to gash a p.'s face. — 2. = zerhauen. — 3. (hauend auſbrauchen oder verderben) to chop up, to use up (or to spoil) in cutting. — 4. ⌣, ſich ⌣ (ſchlecht hauen) to cut badly; fenc. ſich ⌣ to lay o.s. open to an attack, to expose o.s.; fig. ſich im Reden ⌣ (Blößen geben) to blunder in speaking, to talk at random. — 5. e-m den Weg ⌣ (verſperren) to bar (or barricade, obstruct) a p.'s way.

ver-heben (⌣⌣́) v/a. u. ſich ⌣ v/refl. ⓑ (⑦)b*: ſich (dat.) den Arm ⌣ to sprain one's arm in lifting (a heavy load); ſich ⌣ to injure o.s. in lifting.

ver-heddern F (⌣⌣́⌣) v/a. ⓑa* to entangle; ſich ⌣ v/refl. to get entangled.

ver-heeren (⌣⌣́) [ahd.: harry] I v/a. ⓑ*: ein Land ꝛc. ⌣ to lay waste ..., to devastate ..., to ravage ..., (öde m.) to desolate ...; mit Feuer und Schwert ⌣ to ravage (or lay waste) with fire and sword; ⌣d destructive; e-e vom Feuer verheerte Stadt a town ravaged (or destroyed, consumed) by fire. — II ~ n ⓝ ſ. Verheerung.

Ver-heerer (⌣⌣́) m ⓐ, ~in f ⓜ devastator, ravager; destroyer.

Ver-heerung (⌣⌣́⌣) f ⓜ devastation, ravaging; desolation; ~ anrichten unter // to make (or spread, work) havoc among //, to devastate ...

ver-heften (⌣⌣́) v/a. ⓑ* 1. surg. eine Wunde ⌣ to sew up ... — 2. viel Garn ⌣ to use up ... in stitching. — 3. (falſch heften) to stitch in wrong order, to transpose the sheets of a book.

ver-hehlen (⌣⌣́) [ahd.] I v/a. ⓑ* 1. to conceal, dissemble. — II ~ n ⓝ u. Ver-hehlung f ⓜ 2. = Hehlerei; auch: dissimulation; underhand work. — III ver-hohlen p.p. u. bſd. a. ⓒ 3. Bed. des inf. — 4. v. Gemüt: (heimlich, verſteckt) deep and cunning, artful, underhand.

ver-heilen (⌣⌣́) I v/n. (ſn) ⓑ*: v. Wunden: to heal (or close) up. — II ~ n ⓝ u. Ver-heilung f ⓜ healing (process).

ver-heimlich/en (⌣⌣́⌣) I v/a. ⓑ*: e-m et. ⌣ to keep a th. secret (or dark, back) from a p., to conceal a th. from a p., to keep a p. in ignorance of a th.; ſchweigend ⌣ to hush up, to keep quiet; (bemänteln) to disguise, to dissemble. — II ~ n ⓝ u. Ver-B/ung f ⓜ concealment; dissimulation.

ver-heiraten (⌣⌣́⌣) [mhd.] ⓑ* I v/a.: e-e Tochter ⌣ to give ... away in marriage (an e-n to a p.), to marry (F to get) off ...; ihre verheiratete Tochter her married daughter; F fig. ſie ſind ja nicht verheiratet they are not wedded (or tied) to each other. — II ſich ⌣ v/refl. to get married, to marry, a. to settle down (in life), to enter the matrimonial state, geh. Spr. to wed; ſich glücklich ⌣ to make a good match; ſich wieder ⌣ to marry again, to remarry. — III ~ n ⓝ u. Ver-heiratung f ⓜ marriage; vor ihrer ~ previous to her marriage, before she (got) married.

ver-heißen (⌣⌣́) [mhd.] I v/a. ⓑd* (p.p. ⌣) to (hold out) a promise. — II ~ n ⓝ u. Ver-heißung f ⓜ promise; bibl. das Land der ~ the Land of Promise, the Promised Land.

ver-heißungs-voll (⌣⌣⌣,⌣́) a. ⓜ u. adv. full of promise, promising, adv. in a promising way or tone.

ver-helfen (⌣⌣́) [mhd.] v/n. (h.) ⓑb*: e-m zu et. ⌣ to help a p. to (procure) a th., to assist a p. in obtaining (or getting) a th.; e-m zu ſ-m Rechte ⌣ to see that a p. gets his rights or that a p. is righted, to see a p. righted.

ver-henkert F (⌣⌣́) a. ⓜ damned, devilish, cursed, F deuced, confounded.

ver-herrlichen (⌣⌣́⌣) I v/a. ⓑ* to glorify, (ſchmücken) to adorn; in Liedern verherrlicht famed in song. — II ~ n ⓝ ſ. Verherrlichung.

Ver-herrlicher (⌣⌣́⌣) m ⓐ glorifier.

Ver-herrlichung (~) f ⓜ glorification.

ver-hetzen (⌣⌣́) [mhd.] I v/a. ⓑ* to goad on (vgl. aufhetzen I). — II ~ n ⓝ u. Ver-hetzung f ⓜ = Aufhetzerei.

Ver-heu(e)rer ⚓ (⌣⌣́(⌣)⌣) m ⓐ freighter, charterer.

ver-heuern ⚓ (⌣⌣́⌣) v/a. ⓑa*: ein Schiff ⌣ to freight ..., to charter ...

ver-hexen (⌣⌣́) v/a. ⓑ* to bewitch.

ver-hieb, -hielt, -hieß (⌣⌣́) ind. impf. v. ver-hauen, -halten, -heißen.

ver-himmel/n (⌣⌣́⌣) v/a. ⓑa* I v/a. to deify. — II v/n. (ſn) (in ſeligem Gefühle ſchweben) to go into (or to be in) raptures; verhimmelt ſein, auch: to be in the seventh heaven (of delight) or in Elysium or in ecstasy, to be enraptured. — III ~ n ⓝ u. B/ung f ⓜ deification, apotheosis.

ver-hindern (⌣⌣́⌣) [mhd.] I v/a. ⓑ* = hindern I. — II ~ n ⓝ ſ. Verhinderung.

Ver-hinderung (⌣⌣⌣́) f ⓜ prevention; hindering; vgl. Hindernis; im ~s-falle in case I (you, &c.) should be prevented (from coming or attending).

ver-hob(en) (⌣⌣́(⌣)) impf. (p.p.) v. verheben.

ver-hochdeutſchen (⌣⌣́⌣⌣) v/a. ⓑ* to express in (or render into) High German.

ver-hoffen (⌣⌣́) v/n. (h.) ⓑ* † = hoffen; noch jetzt gbr.: wider alles ~ contrary to all expectation(s).

ver-hohlen (⌣⌣́⌣) p.p. ſ. verhehlen III.

ver-höhnen (⌣⌣́⌣) [mhd.] I v/a. ⓑ* to mock, to jeer (or sneer) at, (auspfeifen) to hoot at; (lächerlich m.) to deride, to (turn into) ridicule, to laugh at, to make fun of; (necken) to chaff, to tease, (foppen) to quiz; die Vernunft ꝛc. ⌣ to run counter to ..., to fly in the face of ... — II ~ n ⓝ ſ. Verhöhnung.

Ver-höhner (⌣⌣́⌣) m ⓐ, ~in f ⓜ mocker.

Ver-höhnung (~) f ⓜ mockery; derision.

ver-höckern (⌣⌣́⌣) v/a. ⓑa* to (sell in) retail, bisw.: to huckster.

Ver-hol-boje ⚓ (⌣⌣́⌣⌣) f ⓑ tow-buoy.

ver-holen ⚓ (⌣⌣́⌣) v/a. ⓑ*: ein Schiff ⌣ (ſchleppen) to take in) to tow.

Ver-holer ⚓ (⌣⌣́⌣) m ⓑ (Schlepper) towboat, als Dampfer: steam-tug.

ver-holfen (⌣⌣́⌣) p.p. von verhelfen.

Ver-hol-tau ⚓ (⌣⌣́,⌣) n tow-line.

ver-holzen (⌣⌣́⌣) I v/n. (ſn) ⓑ* to turn (in)to wood, ⚕ to lignify. — II F v/a. (prügeln) to cudgel, beat, thrash.

Ver-hör (⌣⌣́) n ⓑ jur. examination of a prisoner or defendant, weitS. trial, hearing; ins ~ bringen to put on one's trial, to bring up for examination, to interrogate, to question; ins ~ nehmen to cross-examine.

ver-hören (⌣⌣́⌣) [mhd.] I v/a. ⓑ* 1. bſd. jur.: e-n Angeklagten ⌣ to (cross-)examine ..., to interrogate ... (über et. on a th.). — 2. die Schüler(innen) ⌣, den Schüler(inne)n ihre Lektion ⌣ to hear the (lessons of the) pupils, to hear the boys' (girls') lessons. — 3. ſich ⌣ v/refl. (falſch hören) to hear wrong(ly), misunderstand, misapprehend. — II ~ n ⓝ u. Ver-hörung f ⓜ 4. jur. (cross-)examination.

ver-hub ⚓ (⌣⌣́) ind. impf. v. verheben.

ver-hülfe (⌣⌣́⌣) subj. impf. v. verhelfen.

ver-hüll/en (⌣⌣́⌣) [mhd.] I v/a. u. ſich ⌣ v/refl. ⓑ* to cover (over), to veil, to wrap (or muffle) up; (bemänteln) to cloak, die Wahrheit: to disguise; in ⌣en (ob. verhüllten) Worten in veiled language; euphemistically; verhüllt disguised, ✕ (maſkiert) masked. — II ~ n ⓝ u. Ver-hüllung f ⓜ cover, covering, veil(ing); disguise.

ver-hundert-fachen (⌣⌣́⌣⌣), ⌣fältigen (⌣⌣́⌣⌣) v/a. u. ſich ⌣ v/refl. ⓑ* to increase a hundredfold, to centuple.

⚕ scientific; ⚘ botanical; ⚲ geography; ⊕ machinery; ⚒ mining; ✕ military; ⚓ marine; ● commercial; ✉ postal; ⛓ railway.

[verhungern] — 1040 — [Verkehrsmittel]

ver-hungern (f̃ˇˇ) I v/n. ®a* to die of hunger or starvation, to starve; 2 I. to starve, to famish; verhungert aussehen to look famished or (half-)starved or emaciated. — II ~ n ® u. Verhung(e)rung f ® starvation.

ver-hunzen F (f̃ˇˇ) [Hund] v/a. ®* to spoil through lack of skill, to botch, to bungle (up).

ver-huren (f̃ˇ´) v/a. ®* to spend on harlots or gay women or in debauchery; verhurt debauched.

ver-hüten (f̃ˇ´) [mhd.] I v/a. ®*: ein Unglück 2 to prevent (or ward off) a misfortune, to avert an accident; (davor bewahren) to preserve from a calamity; das verhüte Gott! God (or Heaven) forbid!; 2d prevent(at)ive, preservative, med.: ⌑ prophylactic. — II ~ n ® f. Verhütung.

ver-hütten ⚒ (f̃ˇˇ) v/a. ®*: Erz 2 to work (off) ...; das verhüttete Erz the ore treated or dealt with.

Ver-hütung (f̃ˇ´) f ® prevention, med.: ⌑ prophylaxis.

Ver-hütungs-maßregel (f̃ˇˇ...) f ® preventive measure; =mittel n preventive, preservative, ⌑ prophylactic.

Verifikation (w–ˇˇ–tẑ(ˇ)´) [it.] f ® (Beurkundung) verification.

verifizier/en (w´ˇˇˇ´) [it.] I v/a. ® (beurkunden) to verify. — II ~ n ® u. ℬ/ung f ® verification.

ver-innerlich/en (f̃ˇˇˇˇ) I v/a. ®* to intensify. — II ~ n ® u. ℬ/ung f ® intensification.

ver-innigen (f̃ˇˇˇ) v/a ®* to intensify; to make more intimate.

ver-irren(f̃ˇˇ) [mhd.] I v/a. (ſu) u. ſich 2 v/refl. ®* to err, stray, go astray; to lose o.s. or one's way; beſ. fig. to swerve from the right path; verirrtes Schaf stray(ing) (or wandering, rel. auch: misguided) sheep; verirrte Kugel stray bullet. — II ~ n ® u. Ver-irrung f ® erring, erratic (or wrong) course; straying, wandering; fig. aberration of judgment, &c.; jugendliche Verirrung youthful error or mistake.

ver-jag/en (f̃ˇ´) [ahd.] I v/a. ®* to drive (or chase) away, to expel, × (in die Flucht schlagen) to put to flight, von einem Posten ꝛc.: to dislodge. — II ~ n ® u. ℬ/ung f ® driving away, expulsion, × auch: dislodgement.

ver-jährbar (f̃ˇ´–) a. ® jur. prescriptible; =keit f ® prescriptibility.

ver-jähren (f̃ˇ´) [mhd.] I v/n. (ſu) ®* mſt jur. 1. to increase with age; verjährt venerable, (eingewurzelt) deep-rooted; verjährte (auf langem Befitz geſtützte) Rechte prescriptive rights pl. — 2. auch ſich 2 v/refl. (im Laufe der Jahre ſich abſchwächen, ſich verlieren) to grow obsolete, to be(come) superannuated, to be(come) cancelled by the statute of limitation; verjährte Forderung (Schuld) superannuated claim [nach dem statute of limitation läßt ſich eine Geldſchuld nach Verlauf v. 6 Jahren nicht mehr vor Gericht geltend machen]. — II ~ n ® u. Ver-jährung f ® 3. prescription; superannuation.

Ver-jährungs-friſt (f̃ˇˇ...) f ® term (or period) of limitation; =geſetz n statute of limitation.

ver-jammern (f̃ˇˇ) v/a. ®a* to spend in wailing or in lamentations.

ver-jauchen (f̃´chˇ) I v/n. (ſu) ®* path. vom Blute, von Säften: to turn to sanies. — II ~ n ® u. Ver-jauchung f ®: ⌑ sanious (or ichorous) ulceration.

ver-jubeln (f̃ˇˇ) v/a. ®a* 1. ſ-e Zeit 2 to spend ... in merriment or jubilation. — 2. ſein Geld 2 to spend ... freely; to lavish ... [juden II.)

ver-jüdeln (f̃ˇ´) v/n. (ſu) ®a* = ver-ſ

ver-juden (f̃ˇˇ) ®* I v/a. to turn (or convert) into a Jew, to Judaize. — II v/n. (ſu) to become (or turn) a Jew, to Judaize; to adopt Jewish habits.

ver-jüngen (f̃ˇˇ) I v/a.u. v/refl. ®*1. to make young (again), to rejuvenate; to restore to youth; ſich 2 (auffriſchen) to renovate, to become young (again), to grow juvenile. — 2. Zeichenkunſt: (in kleinerem Maßſtabe darſtellen) to reduce (to a smaller scale); im verjüngten Maßſtabe on a reduced (or smaller) scale; arch. ſich 2 (ſpitz auslaufen) to taper off. — II ~ n ® u. Ver-jüngung (f̃ˇˇ) f ® 3. (ſ. 1) juvenescence, renovation; (ſ. 2) reduction; arch. tapering off, (gradual) diminution.

Ver-jüngungs-kunſt (f̃ˇˇˇ...) f ® art of restoring (to) youth; =maßſtab m reduced scale. [merriment.)

ver-juxen F (f̃ˇˇ) v/a. ®* to spend in)

ver-kalben (f̃ˇˇ) v/n. (h.) ®* von Kühen: to calve before the time; fig. to miscarry, to prove abortive. [calcinable.)

ver-kalkbar (f̃ˇ–) a. ® chm., metall.)

ver-kalken (f̃ˇˇ) ®* I v/n. (ſu) u. ſich 2 v/refl. to become chalk(ed) or chalky, to calcify. — II v/a. to turn into chalk, chm., metall. to calcine.

ver-kalkulieren F (f̃ˇˇˇ´): ſich 2 v/refl. ®* to miscalculate.

Ver-kalkung (f̃ˇˇ) f ® physiol. calcification; chm., metall. calcination.

ver-kam (f̃ˇ´) ind. impf. v. verkommen.

ver-kannt (f̃ˇˇ) p.p., 2e (f̃ˇˇ) ind. impf. v. verkennen; ~heit (f̃ˇ–) f ® being misunderstood.

ver-kapp/en (f̃ˇˇ) ®* I ® v/a.: e-e Mauer 2 to cope ... — II v/a. u. v/refl. (verhüllen) to muffle up, disguise; ſich 2 to (put on a) mask, to disguise o.s., als Schriftſteller ꝛc. to write under an assumed name; ein verkappter Prieſter a priest in disguise. — III ~ n ® u. ℬ/ung f ® making, disguise; mummery.

ver-kapſel/n (f̃ˇˇ) I v/refl. ®a* zo. ſich 2: ⌑ to encyst. — II ~ n ® u. ℬ/ung f ®: ⌑ encystation, encystment.

ver-karſten (f̃ˇˇ) v/n. (ſu) ®* to become (a bare and) barren land.

ver-käſen (f̃ˇ´) I v/n. (ſu) ®* to turn into cheese. — II Ver-käſung (f̃ˇ´) f ® path.: ⌑ caseation.

Ver-kauf (f̃ˇ´) m ®c. (ant. Kauf) sale; zum 2 on sale, zum 2 ausſtellen to put up (or expose, offer) for sale.

ver-kaufen (f̃ˇˇ´) [mhd.] I v/a. u. v/refl. ®*1. to sell, Waren ꝛc. auch to dispose of, ● to clear (off), bisw. : to vend; ſ. klein 8; mit Verluſt 2 to sell at a loss or at a sacrifice; billiger als ein anderer 2 to undersell a p.; zu 2 ſein to be for sale or for disposal; ſ. teuer 1;

fig. verraten und verkauft thoroughly deceived, F sold; ſich (leicht, langſam) 2 to sell (readily, slowly); die Ware verkauft ſich ſchwer ... is difficult to sell or to get rid of, ... is not easily disposed of; der Diamant läßt ſich nicht 2 the diamond is not saleable or finds no sale or hangs on hand. — 2. ſich 2 (einen ſchlechten Kauf tun) to make a bad bargain; Sprichw. an guter Ware verkauft man ſich nie a good article is never dear. — II ~ n ® 3. selling, ● clearing; vgl. Verkauf.

Ver-käufer (ˇ–) m ®, ~in f ® seller, dealer in, im kleinen: retailer, retail dealer, im Laden: sales(wo)man; shopman, f shopwoman, shopgirl; beſ. jur. vendor.

ver-käuflich (f̃ˇ´–) a. ® 1. to be sold, for sale; saleable, marketable, vendible; leicht 2 easy to sell, commanding a ready sale or market; fig. (feil, beſtechlich) venal, mercenary. — 2. adv. (durch Verkauf) by (way of) sale.

Ver-käuflichkeit (f̃ˇ´–) f ® saleableness, marketableness; fig. venality.

Ver-kaufs-bedingung ● (f̃ˇˇ...) f ® condition of sale; =buch n sales-book, day-journal; =bude f, =lokal n stall, shop, für Auktionen: sale(s)-room, auction-room; =preis m selling-price, market-value; =recht n right to sell; =ſtelle f place of sale.

Ver-kehr (f̃ˇ´) m ®c. 1. traffic, auf der Straße: street-traffic; (Geſchäft) business; (Handel) trade, commerce; (freundſchaftliche Beziehung) (social or friendly) intercourse; den ~ mit e-m abbrechen to drop a p.'s acquaintance, to break (off all connexion) with a p.; ~ mit e-m h., im ~ mit e-m ſteh(e)n to be on friendly terms (or to keep in touch) with a p.; in ~ mit e-m treten to enter into friendly intercourse (or relations) with a p., ſchriftl. to enter into or open a correspondence with a p.; ſchriftlicher ~ correspondence; ● Börſe: bei Eröffnung des ~s at the opening of the market. — 2. ⚒, ® communication between places; eine Bahn dem ~ (Betrieb) übergeben to open a railway-line (to traffic).

ver-kehren (f̃ˇ´–) [mhd.] ®* I v/n.(h.) 1. to go and come; Gaſthof, in dem viel(e) Fremde 2 ... much frequented by strangers. — 2. mit e-m 2 to have intercourse (or to associate) with a p.; bei e-m 2 to visit (or to be a frequent visitor at) a p.'s house. — II v/a. und v/refl. 3. (aus der gehörigen Richtung bringen) to turn the wrong way; (umkehren) to turn upside down; to invert, reverse, fig. to pervert. — 4. (verwandeln) to transform, convert; ſich in et. 2 to change (or to be turned) into a th.

Ver-kehrs-ader (f̃ˇ´...) f ® thoroughfare, (chief) artery (of a town); =anſchwellung f (great) inflation (or increase) of traffic; =bericht ⚒ m traffic-returns pl.; =erleichterungen f/pl. new facilities pl. for traffic; =freiheit f freedom of trade, free (or unfettered) trade; =gebiet n area traversed by a railway, &c.; =mittel n means of communication; (Fuhrwert) vehicle, conveyance; (Geld)

[Verkehrsordnung] — 1041 — [verkochen]

currency, coin (age); **=ordnung** *f* traffic-regulations *pl.*; **=sitte** ⚓ *f* (Usus) usage (or rule) of trade; **=stockung, =störung** *f* interruption of traffic, block, 🚂 auch break-down; **=straße** *f* trade-route, highroad of commerce; **=wesen** *n* traffic, 🚂 service (of trains).

ver-kehrt (ˇ-ˇ) [*p.p. v.* verkehren] *a.* ⑯ turned the wrong way. inverted, reversed, wry, *fig.* perverted; 2e Seite wrong side; eine 2e Welt the world turned upside down or gone wrong; *fig.* (unsinnig) absurd, preposterous; ein 2er (eigensinniger) Mensch a wrong-headed fellow; et. 2 (*adv.*) anfangen to start a th. at the wrong end, to go the wrong way to work; 2 anziehen to put on awry or upside down; ⚘ 2 herzförmig: ⚯ obcordate.

Ver-kehrt-heit (ˇ-ˇ-) *f* ⑯ perversity; absurdity; als Handlung: absurd or preposterous) action, perverse deed.

Ver-kehrung (ˇ-ˇ-) *f* ⑯ (s. verkehren II) reversal, perversion; ~ der Tatsachen misstatement of the facts.

ver-keilen (ˇ-ˇ-) ⑧* I *v/a.* 1.⊕ to wedge (tightly), to tighten with wedges. — 2. F burschikos: (verkaufen) to sell. — 3. P = prügeln. — II sich 2 *v/refl.* 4. F bursch. (sich verlieben) to be smitten with.

ver-kennbar (ˇ-ˇ-) *a.* ⑯ easily mistaken or misunderstood.

ver-kennen (ˇ-ˇ-) I *v/a.* ⑯ b*: e-n 2 to fail to recognize a p.; to mistake a p., to take a p. for somebody else; et. 2 to misconstrue (or misjudge) a th.; wir 2 die Schwierigkeit nicht we are (not un)aware of ...; er wird von allen verkannt he is misunderstood by everybody; verkanntes Genie, verkannter Mensch, Verkannte(r) ⑰ misunderstood person, F queer (or odd) fellow. — II ~ *n* 23 u. **Ver-kennung** *f* ⑯ misconstruction of a th.

ver-ketteln (ˇ-ˇ-) *v/a.* ⑫a* to fix (or attach) with a little chain.

ver-ketten (ˇ-ˇ-) I *v/a.* ⑧* to chain (or link) together, *fig.* to concatenate. — II ~ *n* 23 u. **Ver-kettung** *f* ⑯ *fig.* enchainment. concatenation of facts. &c.

ver-ketzer/n (ˇ-ˇ-) I *v/a.* ⑫a* 1. to charge with heresy. to treat (or brand) as a heretic. — 2. *fig.* to brand, to stigmatize; to decry. — II ~ *n* 23 u. 3/ung *f* ⑯ 3. charge of heresy.

ver-kieseln (ˇ-ˇ-) I *v/a. u. v/n.* (jn) ⑫a* *geol.*: ⚯ to silicify; ⊕, *chm.* verkieselt silicated. — II ~ *n* 23 u. **Ver-kieselung** *f* ⑯: ⚯ silicification.

ver-kirchlichen (ˇ-ˇ-) *v/a.* ⑧*: Schulen ꝛc. 2 to put ... under ecclesiastical (or clerical) government or rule.

ver-kitten ⊕ (ˇ-ˇ-) [Kitt] I *v/a.* ⑧* to (join with) cement, to (fasten with) putty, *bib. chm.* to lute. — II ~ *n* 23 und **Ver-kittung** *f* ⑯ cementing, cementation, *bib. chm.* lutation.

ver-klagen (ˇ-ˇ-) I *v a.* ⑧* *jur.* to sue, to take legal proceedings against. to bring (or enter) an action against; weitS. = anklagen 1. — II ~ *n* 23 = IV. — III Ver-klagte(r) *m)* ⑰ defendant, accused — IV. **Ver-klagung** *f* ⑯ taking legal proceedings against;

weitS. = Anklage 4, auch: (making a) charge against. [to grow stiff or numb.)

ver-klammen nordd. (ˇ-ˇ-) *v/n.* (jn) ⑧*

v. klammern (ˇ-ˇ-) *v/a.* ⑫a* to fasten with clamps or cramp-irons, to grapple; *typ.* to brace.

ver-klang (ˇ-ˇ-) *ind. impf. v.* verklingen.

ver-klären (ˇ-ˇ-) *v/a.* und *v/refl.* ⑧* to shed a flood of light upon, to transfigure (a. *bibl.*), to glorify; sich 2 to be(come) transfigured; *fig.* ein verklärtes Aussehen h. to look beaming (with delight) or radiant, to have a serene (or bright) countenance.

Ver-klarung ⚓ (ˇ-ˇ-) [ndl.] *f* ⑯ seaprotest, ship's (or extended) protest.

Ver-klärung (⚯) *f* ⑯ transfiguration (auch *bibl.*), glorification.

ver-klatsch/en (ˇ-ˇ-) I *v/a.* ⑨* 1. e-n 2 to talk against a p., to defame (or backbite) a p. — 2. Stunden 2 to waste ... in gossip(ing), to prattle away ... II 3/ung *f* ⑯ 3. defamation.

ver-klausel/n (ˇ-ˇ-) ⑫a*, **ver-klausulier/en** (ˇ-ˇ-ˇ-) ⑬* I *v/a.* to guard (or ensure) by clauses, to make a special provision about, to stipulate; verklauselt, verklausuliert specially provided (for) or stipulated, bisweilen: clausular. — II 3/ung *f* ⑯ special proviso (or provision) made. stipulation.

ver-kleben (ˇ-ˇ-) I *v/a.* ⑧* to stick (or paste) together, mit Leim: to glue (together), mit Pflaster: to plaster over, to apply a plaster to. — II ~ *n* 23 u. **Ver-klebung** *f* ⑯ sticking or pasting, gluing together, &c. (s. I); ⚯ agglutination.

ver-kleck/en (ˇ-ˇ-) *v a.* ⑩* to waste (or spill) in scribbling or daubing; to (daub with) ink, to smudge.

ver-kleiben (ˇ-ˇ-) ꝛc. = verkleben ꝛc.

ver-kleid/en (ˇ-ˇ-) I *v/a. u. sich 2 v/refl.* ⑧* 1. (sich) ⊖ to disguise (o.s.); to (put on a) mask; als Bettler verkleidet dressed up as a beggar; *thea.* sich 2 als ‖ to make up as ‖ — 2. ⊖ (verdecken) to case (or line) with wood, &c., *arch.* to face; mit Planken 2 to board; mit Täfelwerk 2 to wainscot; ⚒ einen Schacht durch Holzwände 2 to timber ... — II ~ *n* 23 u. **Ver-kleidung** *f* ⑯ 3. (s. I) disguising. disguise, mummery, *thea.* make-up; (s. 2) ⊖ casing, lining, facing: boarding, planking, wainscoting; ⚒ timbering.

Ver-klein(e)rer (ˇ-ˇ(ˇ)-) *m* 22': ~ fremden Verdienstes ꝛc.: belittler, detractor.

ver-kleinern (ˇ-ˇ-) I *v/a.* ⑫a* 1. to make small(er). to reduce in size; (vermindern) to diminish, to lessen; (verengern) to narrow down; *arith.* einen Bruch 2 to reduce ...; Zeichenkunst: = verjüngen 2; 2⊖ diminutive (bib. *gram.*). — 2. *fig. et.* 2 (herabsetzen) to belittle a th., to derogate (or detract) from a th., verleumden: to cry (or F run) down a p.; j-s Verdienste 2 to disparage a p.'s merit; den Wert von et. 2 to depreciate a th. — II ~ *n* 23 und **Ver-kleinerung** *f* ⑯ 3. (s. 1) reduction, diminution; (s. 2) belittlement, derogation. detraction, disparagement, depreciation.

Ver-kleinerungs-glas (ˇ-ˇ-ˇ-ˇ-) *n* ⑫ *opt.* diminishing glass, concave lens; **=maßstab** *m* Zeichnen: scale of reduction; **=silbe** *f*, **=suffix** *n* ⑯ *gr.* diminutive syllable or suffix; **=süchtig** *a.* ⑯ detractory, slanderous; **=wort** *n, gr.* diminutive.

ver-kleistern (ˇ-ˇ-) *v/a.* ⑫a* to paste together; ⚫ *fig.* (bemänteln) to cloak.

ver-klingen (ˇ-ˇ-) *v/n.* (jn) Öst* von Tönen: to die away; *fig.* to become extinct, to die out, to fade away.

ver-klommen (ˇ-ˇ-) [*p.p. v.* †verklimmen] *a.* ⑯ (D9) numb, stiff = verklammt.

ver-klopfen F. meist **ver-kloppen** P (ˇ-ˇ-) *v/a.* ⑧* (verkaufen) to sell to get rid of, to dispose of.

ver-klungen (ˇ-ˇ-) *p.p. von* verklingen.

ver-knallen (ˇ-ˇ-) *v/a.* ⑧*: Pulver 2 to waste (one's) powder.

ver-kneifen (ˇ-ˇ-) *v/a.* ⑩b* to pinch; F sich (*dat.*) et. 2 to deny o.s. a th., to forego (or to dispense with, to do without) a th.

ver-kneipen F (ˇ-ˇ-) *v.a.* ⑧* to spend one's money, &c. in public-houses or on drink or F in boozing; auch: to guzzle away.

ver-kniffen (ˇ-ˇ-) *p.p. von* verkneifen.

ver-knittern (ˇ-ˇ-) *v/a.* ⑫a* to crumple (up), to crease, to ruffle.

ver-knöchern (ˇ-ˇ-) ⑫a* I *v/n.* (jn) to turn bone. ossify; *fig.* to harden (in one's opinions), to grow pedantic or narrow-minded or F crusty. — II *v a.* bib. *physiol.* to ossify; *fig.* verknöcherter Mensch pedant(ic fellow), P co. fossil. — III ~ *n* 23 u. **Ver-knöcherung** *f* ⑯ bib. *physiol.* ossification: *fig.* hardening (in one's opinions), F co. fossilizing. fossilism.

ver-knorpel/n (ˇ-ˇ-) I *v/n.* (jn) und sich 2 *v refl.* ⑫a* *physiol. u. path.* to turn to cartilage or gristle. — II ~ *n* 23 u. 3/ung *f* ⑯ ⚯ cartilaginification.

ver-knoten (ˇ-ˇ-) *v/a.* ⑧* to (tie into a) knot. to entangle. *fig.* to knit together. — II F [Knote] *v/n.* (jn) to become a cad.

ver-knüpf/en (ˇ-ˇ-) I *v a. u. v/refl.* ⑧* 1. = verbinden 1; 2⊖ connective; mit großen Kosten verknüpft involving (or entailing) a large expense. very costly; mit Schwierigkeiten verknüpft attended (or beset) with difficulties; mit gewissen Übelständen verknüpft subject to certain drawbacks; eng verknüpft mit ‖ closely associated (or connected) with ‖, bound up with ‖; *phls.* logisch verknüpft logically arranged or connected. in logical sequence. — 2. to (tie into a) knot (= verknoten). — II ~ *n* 23 u. 3/ung *f* ⑯ 3. (s. 1) connexion (vgl. Verbindung 2); eine seltsame ~ v. Umständen: a strange coincidence or concurrence; (s. 2) knotting (together), entanglement.

ver-knurren F (ˇ-ˇ-) ⑧* I *v/refl.* sich 2 to wrangle, ⚓ to keep bickering and biting; sich mit e-m 2 to fall out (or to quarrel) with a p. — II *v/a.* = einsperren und verurteilen.

ver-kochen (ˇ-ˇ-) ⑧* I *v/n.* (jn) 1. to be spoiled in cooking. — 2. (kochend verfliegen) to boil away, to evaporate; *fig.* sein Zorn verkocht bald his anger

♪ Musik; ⚯ Wissenschaft; ⚘ Pflanze; ⚘ Geographie; ⊕ Technik; ⚒ Bergbau; ⚔ Militär; ⚓ Marine; ⚖ Handel; ✉ Post; 🚂 Eisenbahn.

[verfohlen] — 1042 — [verlangen]

soon blows over or soon subsides. — II v/a. 3. to use up in cooking, to boil away. — 4. to boil too much or too long, to boil to rags or to nothing.
ver-kohl/en[1] (⌣⌢⌣) [Kohle] ⊛* I v/n. (ſn) to turn to coal, to get charred, chm. to be(come) converted into carbon; die v/ten Reſte the charred (or carbonized) remains pl. — II v/a. (zu Kohle machen) to burn to coal, to char, chm.: ⚬ to carbonize. — III ~ n ㉓ und V/ung f ㊻ charring, ⚬ carbonization.
ver-kohlen[2] (⌣⌢⌣) [Kohl] v/a. ⊛* F u. burſch. to hoax, to impose upon.
ver-koken ⊙ (⌣⌢⌣) v/a. u. ſich ⚪ v/refl. ⊛* to (burn to) coke.
ver-kommen (⌣⌢⌣) v/n. (ſn) ⊛* to go to (wreck and) ruin, to (fall into) decay, von Perſonen: to come down in the world, F to go to the bad (vgl. ver-kümmern I); ⚪ p.p. ruined, decayed, ſittlich: degenerate, demoralized, depraved; **~heit** f ㊻ degeneracy, demoralization, depravity.
ver-koppeln (⌣⌢⌣) I v/a. ⓺a* to couple, to join (or tie) together. — II Ver-kopp(e)lung f ㊻ coupling.
ver-korken (⌣⌢⌣) v/a. ⊛* to cork (up).
ver-korkſen P (⌣⌢⌣) v/a. ⓺0* = verpfuſchen.
ver-körper/n (⌣⌢⌣) I v/a. u. v/refl. ⓺a* to embody; (als Perſon darſtellen) to personify; (in Fleiſch und Blut verwandeln) to incarnate; ſich ⚪ to become embodied. — II ~ n ㉓ und V/ung f ㊻ embodiment; personification; incarnation. [to feed.]
ver-köſtigen (⌣⌢⌣) v/a. ⊛* to board;]
ver-krachen F ⊛ (⌣⌢⌣) v/n. (ſn) ⊛* to become bankrupt; verkracht bankrupt, F gone to smash, P broke.
ver-kramen (⌣⌢⌣) v/a. ⊛* (räumend verlegen) to mislay, to disarrange.
ver-krampf/en (⌣⌢⌣) v/a. ⊛* to cramp; mit v/ten Fäuſten with clenched fists.
ver-kriechen (⌣⌢⌣): ſich ⚪ v/refl. ⓺dſt* to creep into a nook or hiding-place or hole; ſich in das Bett ⚪ to creep into bed; fig. ſich vor jedermann ⚪ to shun everybody('s presence); fig. ſich vor (oder gegen) et., e-m ⚪ haben zurücktreten) müſſen to be no match for a th., a p.; er muß ſich vor ... ⚪ he cannot hold the candle to ..., he is not to be compared with ..., he's not a patch on ...
ver-kritzeln (⌣⌢⌣) v/a. ⓺a* to waste (or spoil) in scribbling. [verkriechen.]
ver-kroch(en) (⌣⌢⌣) impf. (p.p.) von]
Ver-kröpfung ⊙ (⌣⌢⌣) f ㊻ arch. am Dachfenſter: shoulder-piece.
ver-krümeln F (⌣⌢⌣) v/a., v/n. (ſn) und ſich ⚪ v/refl. ⓺a* to fritter away; fig. ſein Geld ⚪, a. to squander ...; ſich ⚪ (vertieren) to dwindle (or crumble) away.
ver-krümm/en (⌣⌢⌣) v/a. ⊛* to make crooked, to curve, to bend; ſich ⚪ v/refl. to grow crooked, to become bent or deformed; verkrümmt crooked, bent, out of shape, misshapen. — II ~ n ㉓ und V/ung f ㊻ crookedness, curvature of the spine, &c.
ver-krüppeln (⌣⌢⌣) ⓺a* I v/n. (ſn) von Pflanzen und Perſonen: to be(come) stunted in one's growth. — II v/a. (zum Krüppel machen) to cripple, to

maim; verkrüppelt, auch: deformed. — III ~ n ㉓ und **Ver-krüpp(e)lung** f ㊻ crippling, maiming; deformity; malformation, stunted growth.
ver-kruſten (⌣⌢⌣) I v/n. (ſn) und ſich ⚪ v/refl. ⊛ to form a crust, to become incrusted. — II ~ n ㉓ und **Ver-kruſtung** f ㊻ incrustation.
ver-kühlen öſt. (⌣⌢⌣): ſich ⚪ I v/refl. ⊛* to cool down, v. Perſonen: to catch a cold. — II **Ver-kühlung** f ㊻ = Erkältung.
ver-kümmer/n (⌣⌢⌣) ⓺a* I v/n. (ſn) von Pflanzen uſw.: to be stunted in (one's) growth; (kümmernd vergehen) to languish, to pine (or wear) away, von Perſonen auch: to be consumed with grief (vgl. verkommen); ⚪ laſſen to leave to perish; ♀ u. zo. verkümmert stunted, dwarfed, ⚬ abortive. — II v/a. (ſtörend ſchmälern) to curtail (or encroach upon) a p.'s rights, &c.; j-s Freude ⚪ to spoil a p.'s pleasure; j-s Leben ⚪ to embitter a p.'s existence. — III ~ n ㉓ u. V/ung f ㊻ (ſ. I) stunted growth; pining away, sickly state, ⚬ a. atrophy, ♀ a. etiolation. (ſ. II) curtailment; embitterment.
ver-künden (⌣⌢⌣) ⊛* geh. Spr., ſonſt:
ver-kündigen (⌣⌢⌣) ⊛* ㉔a* I v/a. (ſn) to announce; (kundtun) to make known, circulate, spread about, öffentlich: to publish, promulgate, proclaim, laut: to trumpet (or blazon) forth; im voraus: to predict, to prophesy; das Evangelium ⚪ to propagate (or preach) the gospel; ein Urteil ⚪ to pronounce sentence; ſeine Miene verkündet nichts Gutes his look (fore)bodes nothing good; Schlimmes ⚪ presaging evil, ominous, portentous. — II ~ n ㉓ ſ. Verkündigung.
Ver-künd(ig)er (⌣⌢⌣) m ㉒, **~in** f ㊵ announcer, bearer of news, oft: harbinger of evil, &c.; (Bote) messenger; (j. der öffentlich bekanntmacht) proclaimer, herald, ⚆ promulgator.
Ver-künd(ig)ung (⌣⌢⌣) f ㊻ announcement, publication, promulgation, proclamation; (Vorherſagung) prediction; eccl. Mariä Verkündigung Annunciation-Day, Lady-day.
ver-künſteln (⌣⌢⌣) I v/a. ⓺a* to spoil by too much art(ifice), to over-refine. — II ~ n ㉓, **Ver-künſtelung** f ㊻ over-refinement; vgl. Künſtelei.
ver-kupfern ⊙ (⌣⌢⌣) v/a. ⓺a* to copper, to coat (or line, plate, sheathe) with copper, typ. to copperface.
ver-kuppeln (⌣⌢⌣) I v/a. ⓺a* = kuppeln[1] I. — II ~ n ㉓, **Ver-kupp(e)lung** f ㊻ = Kuppelei u. Kupplung.
ver-kürz/en (⌣⌢⌣) I v/a. und v/refl. ⓺0* 1. to cut short, to shorten, paint. to foreshorten; (abkürzen) to abridge; (vermindern) to diminish, to lessen, (ſtuzen) to curtail, (beſchränken) to retrench, to stint; e-m den Lohn ⚪, e-n an ſ-m Lohn ⚪ to cut down (or dock) a p.'s wages; e-m (ſich) die Zeit ⚪ to beguile a p.'s (to while away one's) time; ſich ⚪ to grow short(er); to shorten; von Muskeln ꝛc.: to become contracted, to contract. gram. in der Mitte ⚪: ⚬ to syncopate; die bei

einer Erbſchaft Verkürzten heirs who do not get their full (or fair) share. — 2. = ſchmälern 2; bisw. abs. e-n ⚪ to wrong a p. — II ~ n ㉓ und V/ung f ㊻ 3. shortening; abridgment; diminution, curtailment, retrenchment; gram. e-s Wortes: contraction, in der Mitte: ⚬ syncope.
ver-lachen (⌣⌢⌣) v/a. ⊛* to laugh at, to deride, to (turn into) ridicule.
ver-laden (⌣⌢⌣) I v/a. ⊛ bſ.*: ⚆ Waren ꝛc. ⚪ to load (or lade) ..., ⚓ to ship (or freight) ..., 🚂 auch: to consign, to forward. — II ~ n ㉓ = Verladung.
Ver-lader (⌣⌢⌣) m ㉒ loader, 🚂 consignor; ⚓ shipping-agent.
Ver-ladung (⌣⌢⌣) f ㊻ loading, ⚓ shipping (a cargo), shipment, 🚂 consignment, forwarding.
Ver-ladungs-kommis (⌣⌢⌣...) m ㉒ shipping-clerk; **=koſten** f charges pl. for l(o)ading, ⚓ shipping-expenses pl.; **=platz** m place of shipment; **=ſchein** m bill of lading (B./L.).
Ver-lag (⌣⌢⌣) m ⑦(①)c. 1. (Mittel für den Geſchäftsbetrieb) funds pl. (or capital stock) of a business; Verläge pl. (Auslagen) money laid out, outlay. — 2. Buchhandel: a) publication of a book; den ~ eines Buches übernehmen, ein Buch in ~ nehmen to undertake the publication of a book, to publish a book; dies Buch erſcheint im ~ von L. ... is published by L.; b) coll. publications pl., works published by a firm; c) = ~s-buchhandlung.
Ver-lags-artikel ⊛ (⌣⌢⌣...) m ㉒ publication; **=bücher** n/pl. books pl. published, **=buch-handel** m publishing (or publisher's) business or trade; **=buch-händler** m publisher; **=buch-handlung** f firm of publishers; **=geſchäft** n = buchhandel; **=katalog** m publisher's catalogue; **=koſten** pl. publishing expenses pl.; **=recht** n copyright; ⚪rechtlich a. ㊅㊅: Ausgabe copyright edition; **=tätigkeit** f publisher's career, activity of a publishing firm; **=werk** n publication, published work. [lame.]
ver-lahmen (⌣⌢⌣) v/n. (ſn) ⊛* to grow]
ver-langen (⌣⌢⌣) ⊛* I v/n. u. v/imp. (h.) 1. nach et. ⚪ to have a great desire (or longing, wish) for a th., ſehnſüchtig: to long for a th., to hanker (or crave) after (or for) a th.; nach et. Verlorenem ⚪ to regret the loss of a th.; nach einem Arzte ⚪ to wish to see (or to consult) a doctor. — 2. es verlangt mich zu erfahren I very much desire to hear, I am anxious to know. — II v/a. 3. = fordern 1; z.B. ſie ⚪ das nicht von uns they do not expect that of us; was ⚪ Sie von ihm? what do they want (or require) of him?; wieviel ⚪ ſie? how much do they want or ask (for)?; das iſt zu viel verlangt that's asking too much. 4. die Arbeit verlangt (erfordert) Geduld ... requires patience. — III ~ n ㉓ 5. desire, longing, wish; ein (heftiges) ~ nach et. tragen, oft: to have a (great) longing (or craving, hankering for (or after) a th., auf

Signs (see page XVII): F familiar; P vulgar; ⌐ flash; ⚆ rare; † obsolete (died); * new word (born); ⁒ incorrect; ♪ music;

[verlängern] — 1043 — [Verlegenheit]

j-s ~ at a p.'s desire or request; ⊕ auf ~ zahlen to pay on demand; auf ~ rückzahlbar (re)payable at call. — 6. = Forderung 1.

ver-länger/n (f´⌣⌣) I v/a. ⊕a* 1. to lengthen, to elongate, to add (a piece) to, to eke out, math. to produce a line, &c. — 2. (ausdehnen) to extend; (fortsetzen) to continue, zeitlich auch: to prolong (a. ⊛), to protract, ⊛ Wechsel: to renew. — 3. v/refl. sich ⚥ to grow longer, to lengthen, to extend. — II ~ n ⓘ 4. = B/ung 1.

Ver-längerung (f´⌣⌣) f ⓘ 1.(f.verlängern I)lengthening, elongation, math. production; prolongation (jur. ⊛ v. Wechseln), protraction; ~ einer Zahlungsfrist extension of the time of payment, respite (granted). — 2. (Zusatz) additional piece; (Fortsetzung) continuation; (Fortsatz) process.

Ver-längerungs-gurt ⊕ (f´⌣⌣...) m ⓘ Sattlerei: lengthening-strap; =stück n lengthening-piece; ⚒ ~ eines Erdbohrers lengthening-joint (or -rod) of an earth-borer.

ver-langsamen (f´⌣⌣) I v/a. ⊕* to slacken, retard, delay; ⊕ e-n Betrieb ec.: to slow down. — II ~ n ⓘ

Ver-langsamung f ⓘ slackening (down); retardation, delay(ing).

ver-langter-maßen (f´⌣⌣...II.) adv. as demanded, by demand, as desired.

ver-läppern F (f´⌣⌣) v/a. ⊕a* to fritter (or trifle) away, to spend (or waste) on trifles, F to fribble away; sich ⚥ v/refl. to dribble (or melt) away, to go by driblets or by degrees.

ver-larv/en (f´⌣⌣) I v/a. und sich ⚥ v/refl. ⊕*: (sich) ⚥ to (put on a) mask, to disguise (o.s.); v/t masked, ent. in the larva state, ⛿ larvate(d), ⛿ personate. — II ~ n ⓘ und B/ung f ⓘ masking, masquerade, mummery, disguise; ent. (entering the) larva state.

ver-las (f´⌣) ind. impf. v. verlesen.

ver-laschen (f´⌣⌣) v/a. ⊕* ⚒ to fish; verlaschter Stoß fish-joint.

ver-läse (f´⌣) subj. impf. v. verlesen.

Ver-laß (f´⌣) m ⓘa. — Zuverlässigkeit; es ist kein ~ auf ihn there is no reliance to be placed on him, he cannot be trusted or relied upon.

ver-lassen (f´⌣⌣) ⊕a* I v/a. to leave, gänzlich: to quit; (im Stich lassen) to leave in the lurch, to abandon, to forsake, böswillig: to desert, to run away from, unfreiwillig: to relinquish; (räumen) to vacate; sie verläßt nie das Haus she never moves (or budges) from the house; der Gedanke hat mich nie ⚥ that thought has never left me or has always haunted me; seine Kraft, sein Mut verließ ihn ... failed him. — II v/refl. sich auf e-n ⚥ to rely (or depend) upon a p., voll Zuversicht: to trust a p., to place confidence in a p.; sich wegen et. auf e-n ⚥ to depend upon (or look to) a p. for a th.; Sie können sich darauf ⚥, daß // you may rest assured (or confident) that //. — III p.p. u. a. ⓘ (im Stich gelassen) abandoned, forsaken, deserted, (hilflos) forlorn, (mittellos)destitute; (allein)

quite alone, lonely, solitary; (nicht mehr bewohnt) derelict, (öde) desert(ed); die Elenden und ~en pl. the wretched and forlorn. — IV ~ n ⓘ (f. I und III) leaving; abandonment, desertion, relinquishment, dereliction.

Ver-laffenheit (f´⌣⌣~) f ⓘ (f. verlassen III) abandoned (or deserted) state, forlorn (or destitute) condition, destitution; loneliness.

Ver-laffenschaft (f´⌣⌣) f ⓘ jur. = Hinterlaffenschaft.

ver-läffig, ver-läßlich (f´⌣⌣) a. ⓘ (zuverlässig) reliable, trustworthy.

Ver-laffung (f´⌣⌣) f ⓘ = verlassen IV.

ver-lästern (f´⌣⌣) ⊕a* = lästern.

ver-latten ⊕ (f´⌣⌣) v/a. ⊕* = belatten.

Ver-laub (f´⌣) m ⓘc. in höflicher Rede: mit ~ by your leave, with your (kind) permission.

Ver-lauf (f´⌣) m ⓘc. 1. von der Zeit: expiration; flight of time; im ~ einiger Tage in the course of a few days; nach ~ von drei Jahren after (a lapse of) three years; im ~ der Zeit in process of time. — 2. von sich entwickelnden Dingen: progress; der natürliche ~ der Dinge the natural course (or issue) of events; von Krankheiten ec.: einen schlimmen ~ nehmen to take a bad turn, von Krankheiten: to end fatally; weiterer ~ sequel.

ver-laufen (f´⌣⌣) ⊕a* I v/refl., v/n. (sn) 1. sich ⚥ to run the wrong way, to lose one's way. — 2. Billard: mein Ball hat sich ⚥ my ball has gone astray. — 3. (a. v/n.) v. e-r Menge: (sich zerstreuen) to disperse, to be scattered (to the four winds); eine sich ⚥e Herde a roving (or scattered) herd. — 4. (a. v/n.) v. Gewässern: to flow away or off, to subside, to fall; vom Terrain: (sich allmählich senken) to form a gentle incline or slope; von der Zeit: to expire, elapse, pass (away). — 5. paint. (v. Farben) sich in ⚥ea. (abstufend) to blend (imperceptibly), to shade off (by degrees). — 6. (mst v/n.) (soundso) ⚥ (den ob. den Verlauf nehmen) to pass (or come) off, to take a certain course; wie ist die Sache ⚥? how did the affair go off?, how did it all end or turn out? — II v/a. 7. (durch Laufen vertreiben, verbauen) to dispel (or cure, digest, work off) by running; sich (dat.) Kopfschmerzen ⚥ to walk off one's headache, to cure one's headache by walking. — 8. e-m den Weg ⚥ (abschwimmen) to block (or obstruct) a p.'s way (in running), to run a p.'s way. — III ⚥ p.p. und a. ⓘ (D9) 9. Bed. des inf. — 10. (flüchtig) fugitive; (sich umhertreibend) vagrant, homeless, forlorn, wandering, F on the tramp; ⚥er Hund stray dog; ⚥es Vieh stray (or roving, runaway) cattle. — IV ~ n ⓘ 11. (f. I) dispersal of a crowd; subsidence of water; expiration (or lapse) of time. [hazard.]

Ver-läufer (f´⌣⌣) m ⓘ Billard: losing]

ver-lautbaren (f´⌣⌣~) ⊕* I v/a. to make known, to divulge, to report. — II v/n. (h., a. sn) = verlauten.

ver-lauten (f´⌣) v/n. (h., a. sn) ⊕* to become known, to be bruited (or spread) about, to transpire, to get wind; et. ⚥ I. to let out a th., to blab a th. out; wie verlautet as announced, by all accounts, according to what people say.

ver-leben (f´⌣⌣) I v/a. ⊕* 1. to live through; den Sommer ec. auf dem Lande ⚥ (zubringen) to spend ... in the country; sie haben schöne Tage verlebt they have spent (some) happy days, F they had a glorious (or fine) time (of it). — 2. (durch Lebensgenuß aufbrauchen) to use up (or wear out) with fast (or riotous) living. — II ver-lebt p.p. u. a. ⓘ 3. (entschwunden) past, spent. — 4. (erschöpft) used up, worn (F played) out, durch Alter: decrepit.

ver-ledern (f´⌣⌣) v/a. ⊕a* 1. ⊕ to (line with) leather. — 2. F fig. e-n ⚥ (verhauen) to give a p. a (good) leathering or thrashing.

ver-legen¹ (f´⌣⌣) ⊕* I v/a. 1. a) räumlich: to shift (or transfer) to a place, (auch ⚒ von Truppen); sein Geschäft nach Köln ⚥ to remove one's business to Cologne; den Schauplatz e-r Erzählung in die Schweiz ⚥ to lay (or locate) the scene ... in Switzerland; den Schwerpunkt anderswohin ⚥ to shift (or move) the centre of gravity to another point; ⊕ Bausteine ec. ⚥ (legen) to set; auf die hohe Kante ⚥ to set up edgeways; b) zeitlich: to postpone, to defer, auf e-n andern Tag: to put off; die Sitzung auf e-n späteren Tag ⚥ to adjourn the meeting. — 2. (falsch hinlegen) to mislay, to misplace; to put in the wrong place. — 3. e-m den Weg, die Straße ⚥ (versperren) to bar(ricade or block, obstruct) a p.'s way. — 4. ⊛: a) (mit dem Nötigen versehen) e-n Markt ec. mit Waren ⚥ to supply (or stock, feed) ... with goods; b) Buchhandel: ein Werk ⚥ to publish (or bring out) ..., to undertake the publication of ... — II v/refl. 5. sich auf et. ⚥ (sich et. angelegen sein I.) to apply (or devote) o.s. to a th., stärker: to put one's heart and soul into a th.; sich aufs Hebräische ⚥ to take up (F to go in for) Hebrew. — III ~ n ⓘ 6. f. Verlegung.

ver-legen² (f´⌣⌣) [mhd. p.p. von verliegen] a. ⓘa(D9) 1. ⊛ spoiled (or ruined) through lying, (beschädigt) damaged, (abgestanden) stale, flat, ⚥e Waren damaged (or unsaleable) goods pl. — 2. (befangen) embarrassed, perplexed, puzzled, confused; ⚥ machen s. Verlegenheit 1; um et. (Fehlendes) ⚥ sein to be at a loss for a th.; um Geld ⚥ sein to be hard up (or F pinched) for money, to be financially embarrassed; er ist nie um eine Antwort ⚥ he is never at a loss for an answer, he has always a reply ready.

Ver-legenheit (f´⌣⌣~) f ⓘ (f. verlegen² 2) 1. embarrassment, perplexity, puzzle, dilemma; (Verwirrung) confusion; (Gezwungenheit) constraint; e-n in ⚥ setzen (verlegen m.) to embarrass (or perplex, puzzle, F nonplus) a p. — 2. e-m ⚥en (Unannehmlichkeiten) bereiten to give

⚗ scientific; ⚘ botanical; ⚥ geography; ⊕ machinery; ⚒ mining; ⚔ military; ⚓ marine; ⚛ commercial; ✉ postal; 🚂 railway.

[Verleger] — 1044 — [verloben]

a p. trouble, to cause a p. embarrassment; f. helfen 3 unter „aus"; e-n aus der ~ ziehen to extricate a p. from a perplexing position; f. kommen 10 unter „in"; in ~ (Not) sein to be in distress or F in a fix, in a scrape, in a hobble, in Geldsachen: to be in financial difficulties or straits.

Ver-leger ● (f-ʲ-) m ㉒ Buchhandel: ~ e-s Werkes publisher; f. Verlagsbuchhändler.

Ver-legung (f-ʲ-) f ㊻ (f. verlegen¹ 1) räumlich: shift(ing), transfer, removal; zeitlich: postponement, putting off, adjournment; (f. verlegen⁴ 4 b) publishing, publication of books.

ver-leiden (f-ʲ-) v/a. ⓼*: e-m et. ² to disgust a p. with a th., to give a p. a dislike for a th., to set a p. against a th.; e-m seine Freude ² to spoil (or mar) a p.'s pleasure; der Ort ist ihm verleidet he has taken a dislike to the place, he is sick (and tired) of the place.

ver-leihbar (f-ʲ-) a. ⓺ loanable.

ver-leihen (f-ʲ-) I v/a. ⓼* 1. to lend (out), to loan; sie hat es an e-n verliehen she lent it to somebody; (vermieten) to let out. — 2. Lehnwesen: e-m ein Gut, eine Abtei ²c. (als Lehen geben) to invest (or enfeoff) a p. with ... — 3. (gewähren) Ämter, Titel ²c. ² to confer ..., to bestow ...; eccl. eine Pfründe ² to collate ...; Rechte ² to grant (or concede, vouchsafe) ...; möge Gott ihm Kraft u. Gesundheit ²! may God bless (or endow) him with ... or grant him ...; die ihm verliehenen Gaben the talents (that) he is endowed with or possessed of; weit-s. seinen Gefühlen Ausdruck ² to give utterance (or lend expression) to one's feelings. — II ~ n ㉓ 4. = Ⅴung.

Ver-leiher (f-ʲ-) m ㉒, ~in f ㊼ 1. lender. — 2. (f. verleihen 3) one who confers, conferrer, bestower. eccl. einer Pfründe: collator, auch: patron; jur. grantor.

Ver-leihung (~) f ㊻ (f. verleihen I) lending (or letting) out; investiture; bestowal; grant; endowment; eccl. einer Pfründe: collation.

ver-leiten (f-ʲ-) I v/a. ⓼* = verführen 2 u. 3; er verleitete sie zu dem Glauben, daß // he led them to believe that //; sich ² lassen zu to be betrayed (or talked) into; er ließ sich von ihnen dazu ² he was led away (or astray) by them, they set him on to it. — II ~ n ㉓ = Ⅴleitung. [führer(in).)

Ver-leiter (f-ʲ-) m ㉒, ~in f ㊼ = Ⅴer-

Ver-leitung (f-ʲ-) f ㊻ misguidance, misleading (a. fig.); nur fig. corruption, seduction, temptation.

ver-lernen (f-ʲ-) v/a. ⓼* 1. et. ² to unlearn a th., to forget (or lose) s.th. (that one has learnt or acquired); das Tanzen ² to forget how to dance. — 2. (lernend verbringen) to spend one's time in learning or study.

ver-lesen (f-ʲ-) I v/a. u. v/refl. ⓼a* 1. (laut lesen) to read aloud; die Namen ² to call over the names, Schule und ⚔: to call the roll. — 2. (falsch lesen) to read wrong(ly), to misread; sich ² to make a mistake in reading. —

3. bsd. p.p. ² (aufs Lesen versessen) madly (or passionately) fond of reading. — 4. Kaffee ²c. ² (auslesen) to pick (out), to select. — II ~ n ㉓ und **Ver-lesung** f ㊻ 5. (f. 1) reading aloud, der Namen: roll-call (auch Schule und ⚔); (f. 2) mistake (made) in reading.

ver-letzbar (f-ʲ-) a. ⓺ vulnerable, easily (or liable to be) injured or damaged; (empfindlich) sensitive, delicate; (gebrechlich) frail, fragile; **~keit** f ㊻ vulnerability, sensitiveness, frailty.

ver-letzen (f-ʲ-) [mhd.] I v/a. u. v/refl. ⓼* to injure, to damage (vgl. beschädigen 1); (verwunden) to hurt, to wound, (ritzen) to scratch; (beleidigen) to offend, stärker: to outrage; (verstoßen gegen) to infringe a rule, to fail in one's duty; sich ² to injure o.s., to hurt o.s.; er hat sich leicht am Fuße verletzt he has slightly injured (or hurt) his foot; geistig: leicht verletzt easily offended, sensitive, F touchy; den Anstand ² to offend against the rules(!) of decency, to shock people's feelings; j-s Ehre ² to violate (or to encroach on) a p.'s honour; j-s Interessen ² (schädigen) to prejudice a p.('s interest), to wrong a p.; ²de Bemerkung offensive (or cutting, insulting, scathing, stinging) remark. — II ~ n ㉓ u. **Ver-letzung** f ㊻ (f. I) injury, damage; hurt, wound(ing); offence, outrage; infringement, infraction; shock; violation; wrong, wronging; e-e leichte (schwere) ~ davontragen to sustain a slight (severe) injury; ~ der Pflicht, des Vertrauens breach of duty, of confidence.

ver-leugnen (f-ʲ-) I v/a. u. v/refl. ⓼b* 1. f-n Herrn ²c. ² to deny ... ein Kind ²c.: to disown, to disavow; (zuwider handeln) to act contrary to, to renounce one's principles, &c.; Kartensp.: Farbe ² not to follow suit, to revoke; sich (selbst) ² to practise self-denial; sie ließ sich für Besucher ² she was not at home to any visitor, she would not be seen by anybody; solche Fehler ² sich nicht leicht ² it is not easy to hide. — 2. sich vor e-m ² 1. to deny o.s. to a p. — II ~ n ㉓ 3. f. Verleugnung.

Ver-leugner (f-ʲ-) m ㉒ one who denies, disowns, &c. (f. verleugnen I).

Ver-leugnung (~) f ㊻ denial, disavowal; renunciation; Kartenspiel: revoking.

ver-leumden (f-ʲ-) [mhd.: *Leumund] I v/a. ⓼* to slander, to calumniate; (verschreien) to defame, to decry, to bring into bad repute, (anschwärzen) to backbite, to traduce, bisw. a. to asperse; (verkleinern) to belittle, to detract from. — II ~ n ㉓ i. Ⅴung.

Ver-leumder (f-ʲ-) m ㉒, ~in f ㊼ slanderer, calumniator; defamer, backbiter, traducer; detractor, libeller.

ver-leumderisch (f-ʲ-) a. ⓺ slanderous, calumniatory, calumnious; defamatory, backbiting, libellous.

Ver-leumdung (f-ʲ-) f ㊻ slander(ing), calumny; defamation, backbiting, aspersion, detraction; **~s-prozeß** m ㉒ action for defamation of character, mehr gbr.: action for libel.

ver-lieben (f-ʲ-) v/refl. ⓼*: sich ² in e-n to fall in love with a p., to take a fancy (or a liking) to a p.; sich leicht ²d amorous(ly inclined), easily falling in love, a. soft-hearted.

ver-liebt (f-ʲ-) p.p. u. a. ⓺ in love with, enamoured (or fond) of, F sweet on, gone on; närrisch in e-n ² sein to be smitten (stärker: infatuated, madly in love) with a p.; ²e Augen m. to cast amorous glances (or to make sheep's eyes) at a p.; **~e([r])** m f ㊻ lover, a. love-sick swain or youth; **~heit** (f-ʲ-) f ㊻ being in love; amorous disposition, amorousness.

ver-liederlichen (f-ʲ-) ⓼* I v/a. to squander, to dissipate, to waste in dissipation or fast living. — II v/n. (in) von Personen: = verkommen.

ver-liegen (f-ʲ-) ⓼* I v/a.: die Zeit ² to spend (or waste) ... in lying or resting. — II v/n. (in) to get spoiled (or ruined) with lying (too long). — III sich ² v/refl. = ² II. v. Personen a. to lose all activity. [leihen.)

ver-lieh(en) (f-ʲ-(~)) impf. (p.p.) von ver-

ver-lierbar (f-ʲ-) a. ⓺ (that can be) easily lost; bisw.: amissible.

ver-lieren (f-ʲ-) [ahd.: forlorn, lose: los] ⓼c* I v/a. 1. to lose; Äste, Blätter, Zähne ²c. auch: to shed ..., to cast ...; f. Gesicht 1, Kopf 2, Lust 1, Mut 1; wir haben keinen Augenblick zu ² we have not a moment to spare or to lose. — 2. mit prp. u. adv.: viel an e-m ² to lose much (or a great friend) in a p.; viel an e-n ² to lose much in dealing (or playing) with a p.; viel bei e-m ² greatly to lose (or sink) in a p.'s estimation; ● er hat viel dabei verloren he has lost (F dropt) a good deal over it, auch: he is greatly out of pocket (through it); wir wollen kein Wort darüber ² we won't waste any words over (or on) it. — II sich ² v/refl. 3. to be (or get) lost, (auf Abwege geraten) to lose o.s.; (verschwinden) to vanish, to disappear; sich unter der Menge ² to be lost in the crowd. — 4. v. e-r Menge: (sich verlaufen) to disperse; v. Farben: to fade (away), F to fly; v. Schmerzen ²c.: (nachlassen) to subside, pass away, wear off; von Sagen ²c.: sich in das graue Altertum ² to be lost in the mist of ages, to date back into remote antiquity. — III p.p. 5. f. ver-loren.

Ver-lierer (f-ʲ-) m ㉒, ~in f ㊼ loser.

Ver-lier-spiel (f-ʲ-L) n losing game.

Ver-lies, † **Ver-ließ¹** (f-ʲ-) [nhd.: Verlust = fr. oubliette] n ⓐ. (unterirdisches Gefängnis) dungeon, keep.

ver-ließ² (~) ind. impf. v. verlassen.

ver-loben (f-ʲ-) [mhd.: (ge)loben] I v/a. und sich ² v/refl. ⓼*: e-m seine Tochter ² to betroth (or promise) ... to a p.; sich ² mit to become engaged to; verlobter Bräutigam (verlobte Braut) oder der (die) Verlobte ㊽ the betrothed, the affianced, the (girl's) fiancé, (man's) fiancée; das verlobte Paar die (beiden) Verlobten the engaged couple; ihr Verlobter, seine Verlobte her, his intended (husband, wife)

Zeichen (f. S. XVII): F familiär; P Volkssprache; Γ Gaunersprache; ⸍ selten; † alt (auch gestorben); * neu (auch geboren); ⁺⁺ unrichtig;

[**Verlöbnis**] — [**Vermerk**]

her fiancé, his fiancée. — II ~ ㉓ s. Verlobung.
Ver-löbnis (f⌣⌣́) n ⑰ († f⑱)= Verlobung.
Ver-lobte(r) (f⌣⌣́) s. f. verloben I.
Ver-lobung (f⌣⌣́) f ㊻ betrothal, engagement (to be married); eine ~ aufheben ob. rückgängig m. to break off an engagement.
Ver-lobungs-anzeige (f⌣⌣⌣...) f ㊻ (public) announcement of a betrothal or an engagement; =feier f, =fest n (in England unbekannt) (festivities pl. in) celebration of a betrothal; =ring m engagement-ring, F engaged ring.
ver-locken (f⌣⌣́) I v/a. ⑱* to entice, to allure; to tempt (away) (vgl. verführen 2 u. 3). — II ~ n ㉓, meist **Ver-lockung** f ㊻ enticement, allurement; temptation.
ver-logen (f⌣⌣́) [mhd. p.p. von † verlügen] a. ㊻ fond of (or given to) lying, mendacious; ~**heit** f ㊻ lying disposition, mendacity.
ver-lohnen (f⌣⌣́) v/imp. ⑱*: es verlohnt die (ob. sich der) Mühe it is worth the trouble, it is worth while; es verlohnt sich nicht (der Mühe) it is not worth troubling about, the game is not worth the candle, F it does not pay (for the trouble). [von verlieren.]
ver-lor (f⌣́) ind., **ver-löre** subj. impf.
ver-loren (f⌣⌣́) p.p. von verlieren u. a. ⑱ (D 9) 1. lost; in Gedanken ⌣ lost (or absorbed) in thought; (verirrt) forlorn, (a)stray; ⌣e (vergebliche) Arbeit, Mühe labour lost, fruitless effort; das ~e Paradies von Milton: Paradise Lost; ⚔ ⌣er Posten forlorn hope; ⌣er Schuß random (or stray, F wild) shot; f. Sohn; fig. f. Hopfen; Sprichw. Ehre ⌣, alles verloren give a dog a bad name, and (you may as well) hang him; f. Kaiser. — 2. mit verbs: für ⌣ achten, ⌣ geben to give up as (or for) lost; das Spiel ⌣ geben to throw up the game (as lost); ⌣ geh(e)n to get (or be) lost, von Briefen ꝛc. auch: to miscarry; an ihm ist ein Diplomat ⌣ gegangen he was cut out (or F made) for a diplomat(ist), he ought to have been a diplomat (vgl. verderben 2); ~**geh(e)n** n v. Briefen ꝛc.: loss, being lost, miscarriage.
Ver-lorenheit (f⌣⌣́) f ㊻ lost (or forlorn) condition, auch: forlornness.
ver-löschbar (f⌣-) a. ㊻ extinguishable.
ver-löschen (f⌣⌣́) [mhd.] I v/n. (fn) ⓢb(⑪)*, -† = erlöschen I, meist fig. to become extinct. — II v/a. ⑨* ⓚ Geschriebenes ⌣ (verwischen) to efface..., to obliterate... — III ~ n ㉓ und **Ver-löschung** f ㊻ extinction; effacement.
ver-losen (f⌣⌣́) I v/a. ⑨*: et. ⌣ to dispose of a th. by lots or in a lottery, to (put in a) raffle; weit⌣. (an einzelne verteilen) to allot. — II ~ n ㉓ und **Ver-losung** f ㊻ lottery, raffle; bfd. ⓔ allotment.
Ver-losungs-geschäft (⌣...) n ㉒ lottery-business (in England unbekannt).
ver-löten ⊕ (f⌣⌣́) v/a. ⑨*: eine Blechkiste ꝛc. to solder (up)...
ver-lotter/n (f⌣⌣́) ⑫* I v/a. to squander in debauchery, to waste in riotous living, f-e Zeit: to dawdle (or fritter

away. — II v/n. (sein) von Personen: to lose one's energy and self-respect; bfd. v. Dingen: to go to rack and ruin; verlotterter Mensch dissolute (or dissipated or rackety) fellow; ⓑ/ung f ㊻ waste; dissipation, depravity.
ver-lud (f⌣́) ind. impf. v. verladen.
ver-ludern (f⌣⌣́) = verlottern.
ver-lumpen (f⌣⌣́) v/n. (fn) u. v/a. ⑱* 1. v/n. v. Kleidungsstücken: to go to rags; als v/a.: seine Kleider ⌣ to wear one's clothes to rags; verlumpt ragged, F out at elbow; verlumpter Mensch ragamuffin, tatterdemalion. — 2. v/n. v. Personen: to be(come) reduced to beggary.
Ver-lust (f⌣́) [ahd.: lost] m ⓐa. ⓚ dem Feinde ~e beibringen to inflict losses (or punishment) on the enemy; ⚔ schwere ~e erleiden to suffer heavy (or severe) losses; die erlittenen ~e the (list of) casualties pl.; (ant. Gewinn) loss sustained, ⊕ von Gas, Dampf ꝛc.: escape, leakage; (erlittener Schaden) damage suffered; detriment, prejudice; (Abgang) waste; (Schlappe) defeat; (Entziehung) privation; ~ der Krone forfeiture of the crown; f. verkaufen 1.
ver-lust-bringend (f⌣⌣⌣) a. ㊻ causing (or involving) a loss, detrimental, prejudicial.
ver-lustieren faft † (f⌣⌣́): sich ⌣ v/refl. ⑱* to enjoy o.s., to have plenty of fun.
ver-lustig (f⌣⌣́) a. (nur als Prädikat gbr.) losing; einer Sache (gen.) ⌣ geh(e)n, ⌣ werden, sich einer Sache ⌣ machen to incur (or suffer) the loss of a th.., to lose, v. Rechten ꝛc.: to forfeit, to be(come) deprived of; e-r Sache ⌣ sein to have lost (or suffered the loss of) a th.
Ver-lust-liste ⚔ (f⌣⌣́...) f ㉒ list of casualties; ⌣**reich** a. ㊻ suffering (or involving) great losses; =**und Gewinn-konto** ⓑ n profit-and-loss account.
ver-machen (f⌣⌣́) v/a. ⑱*: e-m et. ⌣ to bequeath (or will, leave) a th. to a p.
Ver-mächtnis (f⌣⌣́) n ⑰ († f⑱) 1. will. — 2. (das Vermachte) bequest, legacy.
Ver-mächtnis-erbe (⌣...) m ㉒ jur. legatee; =**geber** m legator; =**nehmer(in** f) m legatee; vgl. Legatar.
ver-mahlen (f⌣⌣́) v/a. ⑱* (p.p. ⌣) 1. Weizen ⌣ to grind ... (to flour). — 2. to grind badly.
ver-mählen (f⌣⌣́) [mhd.: (Ge)mahl] ⑱* I v/a. bfd. von Standespersonen: to give away in marriage, to unite in wedlock; vermählt mit married to, feierlicher: wedded to. — II v/refl. sich ⌣ mit to marry, to get married to, feierlicher: to join in matrimony, to wed; die Vermählten pl. the bridal couple.
Ver-mählung (f⌣⌣́) f ㊻ marriage; wedding, nuptials pl.
Ver-mählungs-feier (⌣...) f ㉒, =**fest** n = Hochzeit; =**tag** m day of the wedding; wedding-day.
ver-mahn/en (f⌣⌣́) v/a. ⑱* to admonish. — II ~ n ㉓ und ⓑ/**ung** f ㊻ admonition, exhortation.
ver-maledei/en (f⌣⌣⌣⌣) [mhd.; *lt. maledi'cere*] v/a. to curse, to execrate; vermaledeiter Kerl! confounded (or damned, F deuced) fellow! — II ⓑ/**ung** f ㊻ execration.

ver-mannig-fachen (f⌣⌣⌣⌣), =**fältigen** (...⌣⌣⌣) v/a. ⑱* to diversify, to vary.
ver-manschen (f⌣⌣́) v/a. ⑨* Getränke: to doctor (up).
ver-maß (f⌣́) ind. impf. v. vermessen.
ver-mauern (f⌣⌣́) I v/a. ⑨a* 1. to use up in building walls. — 2. to wall up or in, to enclose with walls, bfd. ehm.: (lebendig) ⌣ to immure. — II ~ n ㉓ u. **Ver-mau(e)rung** f ㊻ 3. walling in or up, ehm.: immurement.
ver-mehrbar (f⌣-) a. ㊻ capable of increase or enlargement; multipliable.
ver-mehren (f⌣⌣́) I v/a. u. sich ⌣ v/refl. ⑱*: (sich) ⌣ to increase, to augment, an Zahl: to multiply; (vergrößern) to enlarge, to add to; (fortpflanzen) to propagate; von Tieren: sich rasch ⌣ to breed rapidly; zo. sich durch Teilung ⌣: ⌣ fissiparous; ⓑ vermehrte u. verbesserte Auflage enlarged and revised edition. — II ~ n ㉓ f. Vermehrung.
Ver-mehrer (f⌣⌣́) m ㉓. ~**in** f ㊼ multiplier, durch Fortpflanzung: propagator.
Ver-mehrung (f⌣⌣́) f ㊻ increase, augmentation, multiplying, multiplication; enlargement; growth; propagation; ♀, zo. ~ durch spontane Teilung: ⌣ fissiparous generation.
Ver-mehrungs-organe (f⌣⌣⌣...) n/pl. ㉒ organs pl. of propagation; =**zahl** f, math. multiplier, factor; =**zeug** ⊕ n, mach. multiplying gear.
ver-meidbar (f⌣-) a. ㊻ avoidable, easy to avoid or to evade or to shun.
ver-meiden (f⌣⌣́) I v/a. ⑨* to avoid, geschickt: to elude, evade, escape, sorgfältig: to give a wide berth to, ängstlich: to shun, ⚓ und fig. to steer clear of, aus Abneigung: to shirk; es läßt sich nicht ⌣ it is unavoidable, it cannot be helped; die vermiedene Gefahr the danger shunned or eluded. — II ~ n ㉓ und **Ver-meidung** f ㊻ avoidance, evasion; bei ~ unserer Ungnade on pain of (incurring) our displeasure.
ver-meinen (f⌣⌣́) v/a. ⑱* to believe, suppose, imagine (vgl. meinen 1).
ver-meintlich (f⌣⌣́) a. ㊻ = angeblich.
ver-melden faft † (f⌣⌣́) v/a. ⑱*: e-m et. ⌣ to notify a th. to a p. (vgl. melden 1 u. 3); mit Ehren oder Respekt zu ⌣ with (all) due deference to you; es ist mir vermeldet worden, daß / I have been (duly) informed that //.
ver-meng/en (f⌣⌣́) I v/a. u. sich ⌣ v/refl. ⑱* = mengen I; (verwechseln) to confuse; (bunt) vermengt promiscuous; fig. in eine Sache vermengt involved (or entangled) in a matter, mixed up with an affair. — II ~ n ㉓ u. ⓑ/**ung** f ㊻ mixing (or muddling) up, mixture; confusion; entanglement.
ver-menschlich/en (f⌣⌣⌣) I v/a. ⑱* to represent in (a) human form or shape, to make a human being of, Barbaren, Wilde: to humanize, to civilize; Götter ꝛc.: ⌣ to anthropomorphize. — II ~ n ㉓ u. ⓑ/**ung** f ㊻ (f. I) humanization, ⌣ anthropomorphosis, anthropomorphism.
Ver-merk (f⌣́) m ⓑb. note, notice, remark, entry.

♪ Musik; ⌇ Wissenschaft; ⚘ Pflanze; ⚲ Geographie; ⊕ Technik; ⚒ Bergbau; ⚔ Militär; ⚓ Marine; ⓑ Handel; ⓟ Post; 🚆 Eisenbahn.

ver-merken (͞ ͜ ͝) v/a. ⑱* 1. ⟋ = bemerken. — 2. gut (übel) ⚌ (auslegen) to take in good part (to take amiss).
ver-meßbar (ͬ ͜ ͝) a. ⑯ measurable.
ver-messen (ͬ ͜ ͝) ⑱* I v/a. 1. = messen I. — II sich ⚌ v/refl. 2. (falsch messen) to measure inaccurately. — 3. (sich allzu kühn zu et. anheischig machen) sich e-r Tat (gen.) ⚌, sich ⚌, et. zu tun oder daß man etwas tun will to make bold (or to venture) to do (or to perform) a th., to dare a (perilous) deed, laut prahlend: boastfully to promise the achievement of s.th. (audacious); sich hoch und teuer ⚌, et. zu tun to make a solemn promise to accomplish a th.; sich zu hoch ⚌ to be too rash, to be over-confident. — III ⚌ p.p. u. a. ⑯ 4. bold, venturesome, daring, audacious, fool-hardy, rash; (anmaßend) presumptuous, overweening; (frech) insolent, impudent. — IV ~ n ㉓ 5. = Vermessung u. Vermessenheit.
Ver-messenheit (ͬ ͜ ͝ ͞) [vermessen III] f ⑯ boldness, daring (spirit), audaciousness, audacity, foolhardiness, rashness; presumption, overweeningness; insolence. [boldly, audaciously.]
ver-messentlich (ͬ ͜ ͝ ͞)[vermessen 4] adv.
Ver-messung (ͬ ͜ ͝) f ⑯ measurement, des Landes: survey(ing).
Ver-messungs-arbeit (ͫ ...) f ⑫ survey, surveying; **-beamte(r)** f m surveyor, surveying officer; **-kunst** f art of surveying, ⚏ geodesy. [meiden.]
ver-mied(en) (ͬ ͜ ͜ ͝) impf. (p.p.) v. ver-
ver-mieten (ͬ ͜ ͝) ⑱* I v/a. 1. to let (out); Häuser ꝛc. auf eine Reihe von Jahren ⚌ to let ... on lease; Möbel ꝛc. ⚌ to let ... on hire; Pferde und Wagen ⚌ to job ...; Anzeige: Haus und Stall zu ⚌ house and stable to (be) let; zwei Zimmer zu ⚌ two rooms to let. — II sich ⚌ v/refl. 2. = sich verdingen. — 3. gute Häuser ⚌ sich leicht oder lassen sich leicht ⚌ ... (are) easily let. — III ~ n ㉓ 4. f. Vermietung.
Ver-mieter (ͬ ͜ ͝) m ㉒, ~in f ㊼ (f. vermieten I) one who lets houses, apartments, &c., jur. lessor, von Pferden und Wagen: jobber; (Häuseragent) house-agent. [&c. (f. vermieten I).]
Ver-mietung (ͬ ͜ ͝) f ⑯ letting (out),
Ver-mietungs-bureau (ͫ ...) n ㉓: a) house- (or estate-)agent's office; b) registry-office for servants; **-zettel** m bill for letting a house, a room, &c.
ver-mindern (ͬ ͜ ͝) I v/a. u. sich ⚌ v/refl. ⑱a* 1. = mindern I. — 2. (einschränken) to retrench; (schwächen) to enfeeble, (beeinträchtigen) to impair; um die Hälfte, ein Drittel ⚌ to reduce by one-half, one-third; sich ⚌ (von Preisen) to go down, to fall, von Leidenschaften, Schmerzen ꝛc. to subside, abate, calm down. — II ~ n ㉓ und **Verminderung** f ⑯ 3. = mindern II; von Ausgaben: retrenchment, v. Preisen: fall.
ver-mischbar (ͬ ͜ ͝) a. ⑯ mixable.
ver-mischen (ͬ ͜ ͝) I v/a. u. sich ⚌ v/refl. ⑱* 1. = mengen I; mit Wasser ⚌, oft: to dilute (with water), to water; Rassen (von Tieren) ⚌ (kreuzen) to interbreed ..., to cross ...; ⚏ Metalle mit-

ea. ⚌ (legieren) to alloy ...; sich leicht ⚌ lassen to blend (or amalgamate) well. — 2. sich mit e-m Weibe (fleischlich) ⚌ to have carnal (or sexual) intercourse (or to cohabit) with a woman. — II ~ n ㉓ 3. f. Vermischung. — III **ver-mischt** p.p. u. a. ⑯ 4. mixed; promiscuous; in Zeitungen ꝛc.: vermischte Nachrichten, Vermischtes miscellaneous news or items pl.; vermischte Schriften miscellanies pl.
Ver-mischung (ͬ ͜ ͝) f ⑯ (inter)mixing, mixture, v. Metallen: alloy(ing), mit Quecksilber: amalgamation, v. Rassen: crossing; fleischliche Vermischung carnal (or sexual) intercourse, cohabitation.
ver-missen (ͬ ͜ ͝) [ahd.] I v/a. ⑱* to miss; (den Verlust einer Sache, Person beklagen) to deplore the loss (or absence) of a th. or a p.; er wird sehr vermißt he is greatly missed, als guter Gesellschafter ꝛc. auch: his loss is keenly felt or much regretted, he leaves a great gap or blank; die Vermißten the missing (ones) pl. (a. ⚔). — II ~ n ㉓ und **Ver-missung** f ⑯ missing; deploring (or regretting) the loss of; schmerzliches Vermissen keen regret.
ver-mitteln (ͬ ͜ ͝) I v/a. ⑱a* to mediate, to act as intermediary in; to intervene (or interpose, intercede) in; to settle (or adjust, arrange) a difference or a dispute, &c.; to bring about a truce, a reconciliation, &c.; to convene a meeting; to negotiate peace or ⚜ a loan; to conciliate (or reconcile) conflicting notions or strong contrasts; ⚌d eintreten to intervene (or interpose, intercede) in s.th. — II ~ n ㉓ f. Vermittelung.
ver-mittels, a. **ver-mittelst** (ͬ ͜ ͝) prp. mit gen. = mittels.
Ver-mitt(e)lung (ͬ ͜ ͜ ͝) f ⑯ mediation, intervention, interposition, intercession; (Beilegung) settlement, adjustment, arrangement; (Versöhnung) (re-)conciliation; durch j-s ~, a. through a p.'s instrumentality or agency or good offices.
Ver-mitt(e)lungs-anstalt (ͫ ...) f ⑫ agency-business; **-bureau** n für Dienstboten ꝛc.: registry-office; **-versuch** m attempted settlement, attempt at reconciliation; **-vorschlag** m proposal for the adjustment of a dispute, &c.
Ver-mittler (ͬ ͜ ͝) m ㉒, ~in f ㊼ mediator (f a. mediatrix), intermediary; intercessor; bsd. ⚜ agent, middleman; bsd. b. s. go-between; match-maker.
ver-möbeln (ͬ ͜ ͝) v/a. ⑱a* F fig. 1. ⚌ (losschlagen) to dispose (or to get rid) of a th., to turn s.th. into money or cash. — 2. a) = durchprügeln; b) (schelten, herunter machen) to scold, to lecture.
ver-mocht (ͬ ͜ ͝) p.p. von vermögen.
ver-moder/n (ͬ ͜ ͝) I v/n. (sn) ⑱a* = modern¹ I, a. to fall to dust; v. Toten: längst vermodert long dead and gone. — II ~ n ㉓, B/ung f ⑯ = modern¹ II.
ver-möge (ͬ ͜ ͝) [mhd.] prp. (mit gen.) by virtue of (one's office, &c.), by dint of (hard work, &c.); (gemäß) in conformity with, according to; (infolge von) in consequence of; (nach Maßgabe von) on the strength of.

ver-mögen (ͬ ͜ ͝) [ahd.] I v/a. ⑱* 1. a) mit zu u. inf. to be able to do a th., to have it in one's power (or to be in a position) to do a th.; sie vermag es nicht zu verhindern she cannot (or has no power to) prevent it; b) mit pron. als Objekt: alles über einen ⚌ to have great influence over a p.; ich vermag das nicht I cannot do it; wenn er es über sich vermag if he can prevail upon (or can bring) himself to do it. — 2. e-n zu et. ⚌ (bestimmen, bewegen) to induce (or to prevail upon) a p. to do a th. — II ~ [mhd.] n ㉓ 3. (das Können) (cap)ability, capacity, faculty; (Macht) power; was nur in m-m ~ steht all that lies in my power. — 4. (Hab und Gut) fortune, wealth, riches pl., property; sich ein ~ erwerben to make (or acquire) a fortune; vier Millionen im ~ haben to possess ..., auch: to be worth ... — III ⚌d p.pr. und a. ⑯ 5. able to do a th., capable of doing a th.; viel ⚌d powerful, influential. — 6. (wohlhabend) well-to-do, wealthy, opulent; ⚌de Dame lady of (large) means, lady of fortune; ⚌der Mann man of money or wealth; die ~den pl. the well-to-do, the plutocracy.
Ver-mögenheit (ͬ ͜ ͝ -) f ⑯ (Fähigkeit) (cap)ability, faculty.
Ver-mögens-abschätzung (ͬ ͞ ...) f ⑫; **-aufnahme** f valuation of property; **-bestand** m amount of property, jur. estate; assets pl. of a bankrupt, &c.; **-bilanz** f balance; **-los** a. ⑯ without means or a fortune; stärker: penniless, impecunious; **-losigkeit** f want of means; ⚌rechtlich a. referring to the rights of property. adv. in pecuniary matters; **-steuer** f property-tax; **-stücke** n/pl. effects; **-umstände** m/pl., **-verhältnisse** n/pl. pecuniary circumstances, means pl.; in guten ~n in easy circumstances, in a good position; **-verwaltung** f jur. administration of an estate, trusteeship.
ver-möglich südd. (ͬ ͜ ͝) a. ⑯ well-to-do, wealthy; **-keit** f ⑯ wealth.
ver-morschen (ͬ ͜ ͝) v/n. (sn) ⑱* to moulder; vermorschtes Holz rotten wood.
ver-muckern F (ͬ ͜ ͝) v/n. (sn) ⑱a* to grow sanctimonious, F to turn saintly to join the goody-goody people.
ver-mummen (ͬ ͜ ͝) [: mum] I v/a. u. sich ⚌ v/refl. ⑱* to muffle up, bsd. = verlarven I; der, die Vermummte the mask(ed person); Vermummte pl. persons in disguise or fancy-dress masqueraders, bsd. ehm. mummers. — II ~ n ㉓ u. **Ver-mummung** f ⑯ mummery; disguise, masquerade.
ver-muten (ͬ ͜ ͝) [ndd.] I v/a. ⑱* (voraussetzen) to suppose, to presume, auf Geratewohl: to conjecture, (erraten) to guess; (sich einbilden) to fancy, to imagine, (argwöhnen) to surmise, to suspect; ich vermute, er ist schon hier oder daß er schon hier ist I imagine (or have an idea) (that) he is already here; niemand hatte et. davon vermutet nobody had any suspicion (or idea, F inkling) of such a thing. — II ~ n ㉓ f. Vermutung.

ver-mutlich (⏑−⏑) a. ⓺ supposed, presumable; (wahrscheinlich) probable, likely.
Ver-mutung (⏑−⏑) f ⓐ supposition, presumption, conjecture, guess; bloße ~ mere surmise; gegen (ob. wider) alle ~ contrary to all expectation; das brachte ihn auf die ~ it raised in him the idea or the suspicion.
ver-nachlässig/en (⏑−⏑⏑⏑) I v/a. u. sich ⏑ v/refl. ⓑ*: (sich) ⏑ to neglect (o.s.), to bestow little care on (o.s.); (geringschätzen) to slight. — II ~ n ⏑ u. B/ung f ⓐ neglect(ing), negligence; careless treatment; slight(ing).
ver-nageln, mst ⊕ (⏑−⏑) v/a. ⓑa* 1. (mit Holznägeln versehen) to peg. — 2. (mit Nägeln verschließen, verderben) to nail up a door, &c.; to injure a horse in shoeing, ⚔ to spike a cannon, F fig. (im Kopfe) vernagelt sein to be very stupid or dull or dense or blockheaded.
ver-nähen (⏑−⏑) v/a. ⓑ* 1. viel Zwirn ꝛc. ⏑ to use up … in sewing. — 2. (zunähen) ⏑ to sew up, to fasten with stitches.
ver-nahm (⏑−⏑) ind. impf. v. vernehmen.
ver-narben (⏑−⏑⏑) ⓑ* I v/n. (in) u. sich ⏑ v/refl. to cicatrize, to (form a) scar; (zuheilen) to heal, to close up. — II ~ n ⏑ u. **Ver-narbung** ⓐ cicatrization.
ver-narren (⏑−⏑⏑) v/refl. ⓑ*: sich in einen, et. ⏑ = vergaffen; sie hat sich in ihn vernarrt she is smitten (or infatuated, madly in love) with him, F u. P she's gone on him.
Ver-narrt-heit (⏑−⏑−) f ⓐ foolish (or mad) love, infatuation.
ver-naschen (⏑−⏑⏑) v/a. ⓐ¹* to spend (or waste) on dainties or sweets.
ver-nehmbar (⏑−⏑) a. ⓺ perceptible; (hörbar) audible, within ear-shot.
ver-nehm/en (⏑−⏑) [ahd. ganz nehmen] ⓑa* I v/a. 1. (gewahr werden) to perceive, to become aware of; (erfahren) to learn, to understand; (hören) to hear. — 2. jur. = verhören 1. — II sich ⏑ v/refl. 3. sich aus et. ⏑ (es begreifen) to understand (or comprehend) a th.. to see a th. clearly; ich kann mich nicht daraus ⏑ I cannot fathom it, F I can't make head or tail of it. — 4. sich mit einem ⏑ (verständigen) to come to an agreement (or understanding) with a p. — III ~ n ⏑ 5. (f. 1) perceiving, perception; dem ~ nach from what I (or we) hear or gather or understand, by (or according to) all accounts; gutem ~ nach ist sie krank I am told (or have it) on the best authority that she is ill. — 6. (f. 2) jur. = Verhör. — 7. (f. 4) = Einverständnis.
ver-nehmlich (⏑−⏑⏑) a. ⓺ = vernehmbar; (verständlich) intelligible, distinct, clear; ~keit f ⓐ perceptibility; audibility; intelligibleness; distinctness.
Ver-nehmung (⏑−⏑) f ⓐ = Verhör.
ver-neigen (⏑−⏑) I sich ⏑ v/refl. ⓑ* to (make a) bow, von Damen: to (drop a) curtsy (vor e-m to a p.). — II ~ n ⏑ und **Ver-neigung** f ⓐ bow, curtsy.
ver-neinbar (⏑−⏑) a. ⓺ deniable.
ver-neinen (⏑−⏑) I v/a. ⓑ* to answer in the negative; (leugnen) to deny, to disavow; von allen Geistern, die ⏑ (G.. Faust), etwa: of all the spirits of

negation or contradiction; das will ich nicht ⏑ I won't gainsay that. — II ~ n ⏑ f. Verneinung. — III ⏑d p.pr. u. a. ⓺ negative (reply, &c.), log. u. gr. a.: ⚛ privative; eine ⏑de Antwort geben to answer in the negative.
Ver-neiner (⏑−⏑) m ⏑, ~in f ⓐ one who denies, &c. (f. verneinen I).
Ver-neinung (⏑−⏑) f ⓐ (f. verneinen I) negation; denial, disavowal.
Ver-neinungs-fall (⏑−⏑⏑−) m ⓐ nur gbr. in: im ~e in case of a negative reply, should the answer be in the negative; **=partikel** f, gr. negative particle; **=satz** m. gr. negative sentence; **=wort** n, gr. negative.
ver-nichtbar (⏑−⏑−) a. ⓺ annihilable, destructible, exterminable.
ver-nichten (⏑−⏑) [mhd.] I v/a. ⓑ* to annihilate, to reduce to nought; (für null und nichtig erklären) to declare null and void, to nullify, annul, cancel; (widerrufen) to revoke; (abschaffen) to abolish; (zerstören) to destroy, to demolish, ⚔ to destroy by fire, to burn (down); (ausrotten) to exterminate, extirpate, (zerschmettern) to crush, Hoffnungen auch: to defeat, foil, (umstoßen) to overthrow; in der Knospe vernichtet nipped in the bud (a. fig.); sein vernichtetes Glück his wrecked fortune, his ruined happiness. — II ~ n ⏑ f. Vernichtung. — III ⏑d p.pr. u. a. ⓺ annihilating; destructive.
Ver-nichter (⏑−⏑) m ⏑, ~in f ⓐ annihilator; destroyer; exterminator.
Ver-nichtung (⏑−⏑) f ⓐ (f. vernichten I) annihilation; annulment; destruction, demolition; extermination, extirpation, overthrow.
Ver-nichtungs-kampf (⏑−⏑⏑−) m ⓐ war of extermination, war to the knife, auch: deadly struggle.
ver-nickeln (⏑−⏑⏑) I v/a. ⓑa* to (plate with) nickel. — II ~ n ⏑ u. **Ver-nick(e)lung** f ⓐ nickel-plating, nickeling, nickelization.
ver-nieten ⊕ (⏑−⏑) I v/a. ⓑ* to rivet; (nietend verbinden) to clinch. — II ~ n ⏑ f. Vernietung.
Ver-nieter ⊕ (⏑−⏑) m ⏑ riveter.
Ver-nietung ⊕ (⏑−⏑) f ⓐ riveting, rivet-work, clinching.
ver-nimm (⏑−⏑) imper., ⏑(f)t pres., **vernommen** (⏑−⏑) p.p. von vernehmen.
Ver-nunft (⏑−⏑) [ahd.: vernehmen] f, inv. (ohne pl.) reason; (Begriffsvermögen) (power of) understanding, intellect; intelligence; (Urteilsfähigkeit) judgment, discernment; (gesunder Menschenverstand) common (or good) sense, shrewdness; es ist der ~ gemäß, daß // it is rational, it stands to reason that //; es ist der ~ zuwider, daß // it is irrational (or contrary to reason) that //; e-n zur ~ bringen to bring a p. to his senses.
ver-nunft-begabt (⏑−⏑⏑−) a. ⓺ endowed with reason, rational, sensible; **=begriff** m ⓑ idea; **=beweis** m proof founded on reason, ⚛ ratiocination; **=ehe** f =heirat.
Ver-nünftelei (⏑−⏑⏑⏑) f ⓐ over-subtle (or sophistical) reasoning, sophistry.

ver-nünfteln (⏑−⏑⏑) [Vernunft] I v/n. (h.) ⓐa* to reason (or argue) too subtly or nicely. — II ~ n ⏑ = Vernünftelei.
ver-nunft-gemäß (⏑−⏑...) a. ⓺ conformable to reason, reasonable, rational; ⏑ denken to rationalize; **=gemäßheit** f ⓐ reasonableness; rationality; **=glaube** m rational belief, rationalism; **=gläubige(r)** s. rationalist; **=grund** m argument founded on reason, **=heirat** f prudent (or sensible) marriage.
ver-nünftig (⏑−⏑) [mhd.] a. ⓺ rational (being, &c.); (folgerichtig) logical, (auf Vernunft gegründet) reasonable; (verständig) sensible, judicious; v. Kindern: (artig) well-behaved; v. a. (adv.) handeln to act wisely or sensibly; ⏑er-weise adv. in all reason; from a rational point of view, rationally speaking; ~keit f ⓐ rationality; reasonableness; (good) sense, wisdom.
Ver-nunft-lehre (⏑−⏑−⏑) f ⓑ science of reasoning, logic; philosophy.
Ver-nünftler (⏑−⏑⏑) m ⏑ subtle reasoner, sophist; argumentative person.
ver-nunft-los (⏑−⏑...) a. ⓺ (de)void of reason or sense, unreasonable, irrational, senseless; **=losigkeit** f ⓑ unreasonableness, irrationality; **=mäßig(keit f)** a. = gemäß(heit); **=recht** n law of reason; **=religion** f natural (or rational) religion; **=schluß** m reasoning, ⚛ ratiocination, schulgerechter syllogism; **=wahrheit** f truth based on reason(ing); **=wesen** n rational being; ⏑widrig a. contrary to reason, unreasonable, irrational; **=widrigkeit** f unreasonableness, irrationality; **=wissenschaft** f logic.
ver-öden (⏑−⏑) ⓑ* I v/n. (in) to become deserted or desolate. — II v/a. to lay waste, to make desolate, (verheeren) to devastate, (entvölkern) to depopulate. — III ~ n ⏑ u. **Ver-ödung** f ⓐ desolation, devastation; depopulation; Börse: Veröden des Verkehrs stagnation (or flatness) of the market.
ver-öffentlich/en (⏑−⏑⏑⏑⏑) I v/a. ⓑ* to make public(ly known); to publish (auch ein Buch ꝛc.); durch Anzeigen: to announce (publicly), to advertise; ein Gesetz ⏑ to promulgate a law. — II ~ n ⏑ u. B/ung f ⓐ publication; (public) announcement; promulgation of laws.
Veronese (w−⏑−⏑) ⏑ero'na ⚥, alte St. Norditaliens) m ⓐ, ...fin f ⓐ, ...fer a. inv.
veronesisch a. ⓺ Veronese, of Verona.
Veronika (w−⏑⏑⏑) ⓐ I npr/f. Heilige: Veronica. — II ⚘ (Ehrenpreis) veronica.
ver-ordnen (⏑−⏑⏑) I v/a. ⓑb* to order; (festsetzen) to establish, to institute, jur. to decree, to enact; vom Arzte: e-m et. ⏑ to prescribe a th. for a p.; e-n zum Richter ꝛc. ⏑ (einsetzen) to appoint (or nominate) a p. as a judge, &c. — II ~ n ⏑ f. Verordnung.
Ver-ordner (⏑−⏑⏑) m ⏑, ~in f ⓐ one who orders or decrees or prescribes.
Ver-ordnete(r) (⏑−⏑⏑⏑) m ⓑ delegate, commissioner; f. Stadtverordnete(r).
Ver-ordnung (⏑−⏑⏑) f ⓐ (f. verordnen I) order, institution, jur. decree, enactment, edict, ärztliche: prescription; (Einsetzung) appointment of a judge, &c.

⚛ scientific; ⚘ botanical; ⚥ geography; ⊕ machinery; ⚒ mining; ⚔ military; ⚓ marine; ⚛ commercial; ✉ postal; 🚂 railway.

[Verordnungsblatt] — 1048 — [verraten]

Ver-ordnungs-blatt (⌣⌣⌣…) n ⓶ official gazette; **⸗mäßig** a. ⓺ according to an order or an edict or a prescription, by order; as enacted.

ver-pachtbar (⌣⌣⌣⌣-) a. ⓺ leasable.

ver-pacht/en (⌣⌣⌣) I v/a. ⓺⁹*to (let on) lease, Güter a. to farm out, e-e Jagd ꝛc.: to let out. — II ~ n ⓶ f. B/ung.

Ver-pachter (⌣⌣⌣), **Ver-pächter** (⌣⌣⌣) m ⓶, **~in** f ⓸⁷ lessor.

Ver-pachtung (⌣⌣⌣t⌣) f ⓸⁶ letting on lease, leasing.

ver-packen (⌣⌣⌣) I v/a. ⓺⁸* 1. (einpacken) to pack (up); in Papier, Matten ꝛc. ⚑ to wrap up in paper, matting, &c. — 2. (verkehrt packen) to pack (up) the wrong way. — II ~ n ⓶ 3. f. Verpackung.

Ver-packer (⌣⌣⌣) m ⓶ packer.

Ver-packung (⌣⌣⌣) f ⓺ packing (up), in Fässer: casking, ↓ stowage of cargo; innere ~ inner lining; ⊕ mach. ~ (Liderung) e-r Stopfbüchse leathering, packing-tow.

Ver-packungs-art (⌣⌣⌣…) f ⓶ manner of packing; **⸗gewicht** ⚑ n (Tara) tare; **⸗leinwand** f pack-cloth, sackcloth.

ver-palisadier/en (⌣⌣⌣⌣ꞌ⌣) v/a. ⓺³* to palisade; B/ung f ⓺ palisading.

ver-pan(t)schen (⌣⌣⌣) v/a. ⓺¹*: Wein ⚑ to adulterate, F to doctor (up) …

ver-panzern (⌣⌣⌣) v/a. ⓺²a* = panzern.

ver-päppeln (⌣⌣⌣) v/a. ⓺²a*: ein Kind ⚑ (verhätscheln) to pamper (or coddle) …

ver-passen (⌣⌣⌣) v/a. ⓺¹*: et. ⚑ to let slip an opportunity; den Zug ⚑ to miss (or lose) …; ⚏ den Regen unter e-m Baume ꝛc. ⚑ to stand up for the rain under a tree, &c.

ver-peilen ↓ (⌣⌣⌣) v/a. ⓺⁸* to sound.

ver-pesten (⌣⌣⌣) I v/a. ⓺⁹* to fill with a pestilential disease or odour; (anstecken) to infect, to taint; (vergiften) to poison; ⚑d, a. pestilential, pestiferous. — II ~ n ⓶ u. Ver-pestung f ⓺ infection, taint(ing).

ver-pfählen (⌣⌣⌣) v/a. ⓺⁸* to palisade (a. ⚔ frt.); to pale (in), to enclose (or protect) with stakes; ⊕ Bauwesen: to support on (or to strengthen with) piles.

ver-pfänden (⌣⌣⌣) [mhd.] I v/a. ⓺⁹* to (put in) pawn, to (give as a) pledge, F co. to put up the spout; jur.: mittels Urkunde ⚑ to mortgage, to hypothecate; fig. to engage; sein Wort ⚑ to plight one's faith. — II ~ n ⓶ 3, **Ver-pfändung** f ⓺ pawning, pledging; jur. mortgaging, hypothecation.

ver-pfeffern (⌣⌣⌣) v/a. ⓺²a* to pepper too much, to spoil by peppering.

ver-pflanzbar (⌣⌣⌣) a. ⓺⁶ transplantable.

ver-pflanzen (⌣⌣⌣) I v/a. ⓺⁰* agr. to transplant (a. fig.); hort. Blumen ⚑ to pot (or bed) out … — II ~ n ⓶ und **Ver-pflanzung** f ⓺ transplantation.

ver-pflegen (⌣⌣⌣) I v/a. ⓺⁸* 1. to tend, Kranke: to nurse, Kinder ꝛc.: to take care of, to mind, to look after; die in der Anstalt Verpflegten the persons provided for in the asylum. — 2. (speisen) to feed, to provide with food; (beköstigen) to board, to maintain; ⚔ an Bord ⚑ to provision or victual … — II ~ n ⓶ u. **Ver-pflegung** (⌣⌣⌣) f ⓺ 3. tending, nursing; jur. (Alimentierung)

maintenance; ⚔ eines Heeres: provisioning, victualling, commissariat; med. die vorgeschriebene ~ the prescribed diet; vgl. Naturalverpflegung.

Ver-pflegungs-amt (⌣⌣⌣…) n ⓶: a) ⚔ = Proviantamt; b) office of the guardians of the poor; **⸗anstalt** f für Arme: charitable institution; für Kranke: hospital; **⸗entschädigung** f allowance for board and lodging; **⸗gelder, ⸗kosten** pl. cost(s pl.) of maintenance, (charge for) board and lodging, für die getrennte Frau: alimony; **⸗haus** n für Kranke: infirmary; vgl. ⸗anstalt; **⸗wesen** n: a) ⚔ = Proviantw.; b) relief (or maintenance) of the poor; **⸗zuschuß** ⚔ m supply.

ver-pflichten (⌣⌣⌣) v/a. u. v/refl. ⓺⁸* 1. e-n zu et. ⚑ to oblige (or bind) a p. to do a th.; zu etwas verpflichtet (in duty) bound to do a th.; sich gegen e-n zu et. ⚑ to pledge (or bind) o.s. to do a th. for a p.; e-n zu Dank ⚑ to put a p. under an obligation; e-m zu Dank verpflichtet sein, a. to be beholden (or indebted) to a p.; Rennsport: der von ihnen verpflichtete Jockey the jockey engaged by them. — 2. e-n eidlich ⚑ to bind a p. by (or to make a p. swear) an oath.

Ver-pflichtung (⌣⌣⌣) f ⓺ 1. (das Verpflichten) obliging, &c. (f. verpflichten 1). — 2. obligation; (Pflicht) duty, (Obliegenheit) liability; jur. gemeinsame ~ joint liability; ~en eingehen to enter into an engagement, to undertake a responsibility; ~en gegen e-n h. to be (or feel) under an obligation to a p.; seinen ~en nachkommen to meet (or discharge) one's liabilities.

ver-pflöcken ⊕ (⌣⌣⌣) v/a. ⓺⁸* to peg (or plug, pin) up.

ver-pfuschen (⌣⌣⌣) v/a. ⓺¹* to bungle, to botch, to spoil (by careless work), F to make a hash (or a mess) of, bsd. v. Künstlern: to murder; verpfuschte Arbeit scamped (or botched) work.

ver-pichen (⌣⌣⌣) [Pech] v/a. ⓺⁸* 1. ⊕ to (coat with) pitch, to close up with pitch. — 2. auf et. verpicht sein to be bent (or intent) upon a th., vgl. erpicht.

ver-plappern (⌣⌣⌣), **ver-plaudern** (⌣⌣⌣) ⓺²a* I v/a. 1. die Zeit ⚑ to prattle (F to mag) away the time, to waste one's time in gossip(ing). — 2. to neglect over gossiping. — II sich ⚑ v/refl. 3. (sich verraten) to blab out a secret, F to let the cat out of the bag, to give o.s. away. — 4. so verplaudert sich die Zeit so (or how soon) the time slips by when you are gossiping.

ver-plempern F (⌣⌣⌣) [ndd.] ⓺²a* I v/a. to spend foolishly, to waste, to lavish; to fritter (F to fribble) away one's money. — II sich ⚑ = sich verlieben.

ver-pönen (⌣ꞌ⌣⌣) [lt. poena Strafe] v/a. ⓺⁸* to put (or lay) a penalty on, to interdict; verpönt forbidden, prohibited.

ver-posamentieren P bursch. (⌣⌣⌣⌣ꞌ⌣) v/a. ⓺³* (durchbringen) to squander, to spend foolishly, vgl. verplempern.

ver-prassen (⌣⌣⌣) v/a. ⓺⁰*: sein Vermögen ⚑ to waste (or squander) one's fortune in revelry or feasting.

ver-preußen (⌣ꞌ⌣⌣) v/a. ⓺⁰* to Prussianize.

ver-proviantieren ⚔ (⌣⌣⌣⌣ꞌ⌣⌣) ⓺³* ꝛc. = proviantieren ꝛc.

ver-prügeln (⌣⌣⌣) v/a. ⓺²a*: e-n ⚑ to thrash a p., to give a p. a (good) hiding.

ver-puffen (⌣⌣⌣) ⓺⁸* I v/n. (sn) to puff away, chm. to detonate, to decrepitate, F to go off (with a bang), mit Flamme: to fulminate; fig. to vanish. — II v/a. to (cause to) detonate, to decrepitate; fig. to make away with; das verpuffte Pulver the wasted powder. — III sich ⚑ v/refl. to use up all one's powder, fig. to spend every farthing. — IV ~ n ⓶ u. **Ver-puffung** f ⓺ detonation, decrepitation, loud explosion, fulmination.

ver-pulvern (⌣⌣⌣) v/a. ⓺²a* to pulverize; F fig. = verplempern I.

ver-pumpen F (⌣⌣⌣) v/a. ⓺²a* to lend, to give on credit or F on tick.

ver-puppen (⌣⌣⌣) I sich ⚑ v/refl. ⓺⁸* ent. to change (or turn) into a chrysalis or pupa, ⚏ to pupate. — II ~ n ⓶ u. **Ver-puppung** f ⓺ change into the chrysalis (or pupa) state, ⚏ pupation.

ver-pusten (⌣⌣⌣): sich ⚑ v/refl. ⓺⁸* to recover one's breath.

Ver-putz ⊕ (⌣⌣) m ⓶ a. = Putz 2.

ver-putzen (⌣⌣⌣) v/a. ⓺⁰* 1. F sein Geld ⚑ to squander … — 2. P (ganz aufessen) to polish off a goose, a ham, &c. 3. ⊕ = abputzen 2.

ver-quacksalbern (⌣⌣⌣⌣) v/a. ⓺²a* to spend on (quack) medicines.

ver-qualmen (⌣⌣⌣) ⓺⁸* I v/n. (sn) to dissolve in smoke. — II v/a. to puff away (as smoke); F (für Tabak ausgeben) to spend on smoking or tobacco.

ver-quellen (⌣⌣⌣) v/n. (sn) Tb* 1. to flow away. — 2. ⊕ von Holz ꝛc.: (durch Feuchtigkeit anschwellen) to warp, to get warped; verquollen warped.

ver-quer (⌣⌣ꞌ) adv. = quer 2.

ver-quicken (⌣⌣⌣) [nhd. Ꙛ: Quecksilber] I v/a. u. sich ⚑ v/refl. ⓺⁸* chm. (sich) ⚑ to amalgamate, to mix, weitS. to combine; fig. mit et. verquickt (intimately) mixed up with a th. — II ~ n ⓶ u. **Ver-quickung** f ⓺ amalgamation, combination; mixture.

ver-quisten F prov. (⌣⌣⌣) v/a. ⓺⁸* (durchbringen) to squander, to waste.

ver-quollen (⌣⌣⌣) p.p. von verquellen: sein ⚑es Gesicht his bloated face.

ver-ramme(l)n (⌣⌣⌣) v/a. ⓺⁸(²a)* to barricade, to block (up).

Ver-ramm(e)lung, Ver-rammung f ⓺ barricading. [bei: verschleudern

ver-ramschen ⚔ (⌣⌣⌣) v/a. ⓺¹* Buchhan-

ver-rann (⌣⌣ꞌ) ind. impf. v. verrinnen.

ver-rannt (⌣⌣ꞌ) p.p. v. verrennen u. a. fig. (eigensinnig) stubborn; (eingenommen) prejudiced; in et. ⚑ sein to be stuck fast in a th.; **~heit** f ⓺ stubbornness.

Ver-rat (⌣⌣ꞌ) m ⓶c. (o. pl.) treason (vgl. Verräterei); einen ~ an e-m begehen to act as a traitor to a p.; **to betray** a p.

ver-raten (⌣⌣ꞌ) [ahd.] v/a. u. v/refl. ⓺⁶a* 1. to betray, F u. F to peach (or split) upon (f. verkaufen 1); (preisgeben) to deliver up; (offenbaren) to disclose, reveal, divulge, blab out, F to let out; ihr dürft nichts ⚑! you must not tell tales!; sich ⚑ to betray (im-

Zeichen (f. S. XVII): F familiär; P Volkssprache; F̄ Gaunersprache; ⚏ selten; † alt (auch gestorben); * neu (auch geboren); ‡‡ unrichtig.

[Verräter] — 1049 — [Versalzung]

reden: to commit o.s., F to give o.s. away; daß von ihr ℒ Geheimnis the secret unfolded (or divulged) by her. — 2. fig. (hindeuten auf) to denote; sein Benehmen verrät den feinen Mann his manners show (or bespeak, prove) him a gentleman; diese Worte ℒ großen Scharfsinn ... argue (or show, betoken, indicate) great sagacity.

Ver-räter (f⌣⌣) m 22, ~in f 47 betrayer of a secret, &c., an einer Sache, einer Person: traitor (f auch: traitress) to a cause, to one's king, &c.; (Angeber[in]) informer, spy; **~ei** (f⌣⌣″) f 46 treason (-able conduct), treachery; perfidious act; **ℒisch** (f⌣⌣) a. 66 treacherous; (treulos) perfidious, disloyal, faithless, false, in politischen Dingen: treasonable (action, &c.), seltener: traitorous.

ver-rauchen (f⌣⌣) 88* I v/n. (in) 1. to rise up as smoke; (verdampfen) to evaporate. — 2. die Suppe ℒ (abkühlen) lassen to let the soup cool down; fig. seinen Zorn ℒ l. to cool down in one's anger. — II v/a. 3. (aufrauchen) to spend on tobacco or in smoking.

ver-räuchern (f⌣⌣) v/a. 2a* 1. viel Weihrauch ꝛc. ℒ to burn up ... — 2. ein Zimmer ℒ to fill ... with smoke.

ver-rauschen (f⌣⌣) v/n. (in) 90* to rush away; (rauschend verschwinden) to hurry past (like a rushing stream), to rush past, von der Zeit: to slip by, to pass away (pleasantly).

ver-rechnen (f⌣⌣) 92b* I v a. to reckon up, to put to account. — II sich ℒ v refl. to miscalculate, to be out in one's reckoning (beide a. fig.), to make a mistake in one's calculation or account(s); fig. a. to meet with (a) disappointment. — III ~ n 23 u. **Ver-rechnung** f 46 (s. I) reckoning up, (putting to) account; (s. II) miscalculation, wrong calculation; mistake (in accounts); fig. disappointment.

ver-recken P (f⌣⌣) [mhd.] v/n. (in) 88* von Tieren (contp. a. von Menschen) to drop (or fall) down dead, to perish (by the roadside), F to croak.

ver-reden (f⌣⌣) I v'a. et. ℒ to forswear (or abjure) a th., solemnly to renounce a th.; ich will es nicht ℒ I won't say nay to it. — II v/n. (h.), üblicher: sich ℒ v/refl. (sagen was man nicht sagen wollte) to blunder (or to commit o.s.) in speaking; (sich verraten) to betray o.s., F to let the cat out of the bag; prov. (sich entschuldigen) to plead excuses.

ver-regnen (f⌣⌣) v/a. 92b* to spoil by rain (y weather); ein verregneter Sonntag a Sunday spoilt by (constant) rain, auch: a dripping Sunday.

ver-reiben (f⌣⌣) 89* I v/a. 1. to grind well. — 2. to use up in grinding.

ver-reisen (f⌣⌣) 90* I v/n. (in) to go (or start) on a journey or on a tour or on one's travels; to start, leave, depart; oft ℒ to travel (F to knock about) a good deal; seit wann sind sie verreist? how long have they been travelling or away (from home)?; er ist in Geschäften verreist he is away (or has left) on business. — II v/a. Geld, Zeit ℒ to spend ... in travelling.

ver-renken (f⌣⌣) I v a. 88*: e-n Arm ꝛc. ℒ (verstauchen) to sprain ..., ⟋ to luxate ..., (ausrenken) to put ... out of joint, to dislocate ...; er hat sich (dat.) den Fuß verrenkt he has sprained his foot; verrenkt sprained, dislocated. — II ~ n 23 und **Ver-renkung** f 46 sprain(ing), dislocation.

ver-rennen (f⌣⌣) 96b* I v/a.: e-m et. ℒ (verserren) to bar (or block) a p.'s way to a th. — II sich ℒ v/refl. (falsch laufen) to run the wrong way; fig. to get stuck in one's argument, &c.; s. verrannt.

ver-richten (f⌣⌣) I v/a. 89* to perform, to do, (ausführen) to execute, accomplish, achieve, (erfüllen) to fulfil; (sich einer Pflicht entledigen) to acquit o.s. of (or to discharge) a duty; s. Gebet 1, Geschäft 5 u. Notdurft. — II ~ n 23 = Verrichtung.

Ver-richtung (f⌣⌣) f 46 performance, execution, accomplishment, achievement, fulfilment; discharge; ~ mit der Hand manipulation; ~ eines körperlichen Organs ꝛc.: function, tägliche ~en every-day business, daily routine or duties or work. [reiben.]

ver-rieb(en) (f⌣(⌣)) impf. (p.p.) v. ver-

ver-riechen (f⌣⌣) v/n. (in) u. sich ℒ v/refl. 79c* v. e-r Blume ꝛc.: to lose its smell.

ver-rief (f⌣ʹ) ind. impf. v. verrufen.

ver-riegeln (f⌣⌣) v/a. 92a* to (bar and) bolt up; weit 3. fig. to close.

ver-riet (f⌣ʹ) ind. impf. v. verraten.

ver-ringern (f⌣⌣) I v/a. u. v/refl. 92a*: (sich) ℒ to diminish, lessen, decrease; die Münzen ℒ (geringhaltiger prägen) to depreciate the coinage. — II ~ n 23, **Ver-ringerung** f 46 diminution, decrease.

ver-rinnen (f⌣⌣) v/n. (in) 92b(a)* to run off, fig. von der Zeit: to elapse, to pass away (quickly), to flit by.

ver-roch(en) (f⌣⌣(⌣)) impf. (p.p.) v. verriechen. [wildern ꝛc.]

ver-roh/en (f⌣⌣), **ℬ/ung** f 46 = ver-

ver-rönne (f⌣⌣) subj. impf. v. verrinnen.

ver-ronnen (f⌣⌣) p.p. v. verrinnen.

ver-rosten (f⌣⌣) v/n. (in) 88* to grow (or get) rusty or dull, to rust (alle a. fig.), chm. to oxidize; verrostet rusty (a. fig.).

ver-rotten (f⌣⌣)[ndd.: rot] I v/n. (in) 88* to rot, putrefy. — II **ver-rottet** p.p. u. a. 66 fig. ℒe Ansichten obsolete (or antiquated) notions, exploded ideas pl.

ver-rucht (f⌣⌣ɥt) [mhd.] a. 66 nefarious, infamous, villainous; heinous (crime, &c.), atrocious (deed, &c.); (gottlos) ungodly, godless, impious, wicked, stärker: sacrilegious (act, &c.); der Mensch villain; ℒe Tat atrocity; der ~este von allen the most infamous (or execrable) of all; **Ver-rucht-heit** f 46 nefariousness, infamy, atrociousness; impiety, wickedness.

ver-rückbar (f⌣⌣) a. 66 movable.

ver-rücken (f⌣⌣) I v/a. 88* 1. to (re)move, shift; to displace; fig. e-m den Kopf ℒ to turn a p.'s head or brain. — 2. in Unordnung bringen) to derange, bsd. fig. to disturb. — II ~ n 23, s. Verrückung.

ver-rückt (f⌣⌣) p.p. u. a. 66 1. in den Bed. des inf.; ℒe Uhr watch (which is) out of order. — 2. (geistesirre) (mentally) deranged, distracted, insane, crazy, mad, out of one's mind, F cracked, off one's head or chump or nut; (unvernünftig) senseless, foolish; rein ℒ quite crazy, F clean gone; sie machen mich ℒ they drive me mad; schreien wie ℒ to shout like mad; **Verrückte(r)** s. 67 lunatic, (Tolle[r]) mad(wo)man, maniac; **~heit** (f⌣-) f 46 mental derangement, insanity, craziness, madness; lunacy; als Handlung: mad (or foolish) act(ion).

Ver-rückung (f⌣⌣) f 46 (s. verrücken I) displacement; derangement.

Ver-ruf (f⌣ʹ) m ꝛc. ill name, ill (or bad) repute; in ~ bringen to bring (into) discredit, to bring into disrepute, to cry down; in ~ erklären ob. tun (aus einer Gesellschaft bannen) to taboo, to send to Coventry, to boycott, (ausstoßen) to cast out; in ~ sein (kommen) to be in (to fall into) disrepute or ill odour (bei e-m with a p.).

ver-rufen (f⌣⌣) I v/a. 96b* 1. = berufen 4. — 2. (außer Kurs setzen) to depreciate ℒ, to withdraw ... from circulation. — 3. fig. (beschimpfen) to decry, to cry down, to give a bad name to. — II p.p. u. a. 66 (D9) 4. in ill (or bad) repute or odour, ill-reputed, ill-famed; (berüchtigt) notorious, disreputable.

Vers (f. a. f.) [ahd.*lt. versus] m Wa. verse (a. bibl.), Verse pl. auch: (lines of) poetry; (Strophe) stanza, seltener: strophe; Verse schreiben to make (or write) poetry, to versify; fig. er kann sich keinen ~ darauf (Begriff davon) machen he cannot make head or tail of it.

ver-sagen (f⌣⌣) 88* I v/a. 1. (verweigern) to refuse; den Dienst ℒ to be (found) wanting, to break down; die Beine ℒ mir den Dienst my legs sink down under me or won't carry me; das ihr versagte Glück the good fortune denied (or not granted) to her; sich (dat.) et. ℒ to deny o.s. a th., to forego a th.; ich mußte es mir ℒ I had to go (or do) without it. — 2. (anderen vorher gewähren) previously to grant (or promise) to others; anderwärts (z. B. zum Essen) versagt sein to have another (or a previous) engagement; die Stelle ist bereits versagt the vacancy is already filled up, the appointment has been made; auf dem Balle: ich bin versagt I am (already) engaged. — II v/n. (in) 3. mit unpersönlichem Subjekt: — den Dienst ℒ (s. I), von Gewehren: (nicht losgehen) to miss fire, not to go off. — III ~ n 23 u. **Ver-sagung** f 46 4. (s. I) refusal; denial; die ~ ihrer Hand the previous promise of her hand, a. her previous engagement.

ver-sah (f⌣ʹ) ind. impf. v. versehen.

Vers-akzent (f⌣⌣⌣) m 29 metrical accent. **Versal** (w⌣ʹ) [neu=lt.] m 29d. **~buchstabe** (w⌣ʹ...) m 52 typ. capital letter, abbr. cap.; **~satz** m capitalizing, capitalization.

ver-salzen (f⌣⌣) I v/a. 90* (p.p. ℒ) to salt too much, to oversalt; fig. e-m eine Freude ℒ to spoil (or mar) a p.'s pleasure. — II ~ n 23 u. **Ver-salzung** f 46 oversalting.

♪ Musik; ⚗ Wissenschaft; ⚘ Pflanze; ⚱ Geographie; ⊕ Technik; ⚒ Bergbau; ⚔ Militär; ⚓ Marine; ⊛ Handel; ✉ Post; 🚂 Eisenbahn.

[versammeln] — 1050 — [verschiedengeformt]

ver-sammeln (⌣⌣⌣) I v/a. u. v refl. ⚔a* to assemble, convoke, convene; to call together; ⚔ versprengte Truppen ⚑ to rally (or gather) scattered troops; sich ⚑ to assemble, meet, gather; bibl. zu seinen Vätern versammelt werden to be gathered to one's fathers. — II ∼ n ㉓ = Versammlung 1.

Ver-sammlung (⌣⌣⌣) f ㊻ 1. (das Versammeln) assembling, convocation, convening. — 2. (die Versammelten) assembly, meeting, gathering; in der Kirche: congregation; (Zuhörerschaft) audience; wissenschaftliche ꝛc.: conference, politische ꝛc.: congress, ⚔ rendezvous.

Ver-sammlungs-form(ation) (⌣⌣⌣) f ㊻ rendezvous; =haus n house of meeting, club, assembly-rooms pl.; =ort, =platz m meeting-place, bsd. ⚔ rallying-point, rendezvous; =recht n right of assembling or of public meeting or of holding (public) meetings; =saal m hall for meetings, assembly-rooms pl., englischer Studenten in ihrem College: common room; =tag m day of meeting; =zeit f time of meeting; =zimmer n, etwa: drawing-room, in Gasthöfen: general room; thea. für die Schauspieler: green-room.

Ver-sand ⚛ (⌣⌣) [versenden] m ①b. dispatch, ins Ausland: export(ation).

Ver-sand-artikel ⚛ (⌣⌣⌣...) m ㉒ article of exportation, pl. oft: exports; ⚑ bereit a. ㊺ ready for dispatch or export (-ation); =bier n beer for exportation.

ver-sanden (⌣⌣⌣) ⊛* v/n. (ſn) und sich ⚑ v/refl. to be (or get) choked (or filled) up with sand, to silt (up). [business.

Ver-sand-geschäft ⚛ (⌣⌣⌣⌣) n ㊷ export-]

ver-sandt (⌣⌣) p.p. v. versenden. [harbour.]

Ver-sandung (⌣⌣⌣) f ㊻ silting (up) of a]

Vers-art (⌣⌣) f ㊷ kind of verse, metre.

Ver-satz (⌣⌣) m ⑦a. 1. (Versetzen) pawning, pledging; (das Versetzte) pledge(d article); et. in ∼ geben to pawn (or pledge) a th. — 2. ⚒ (Kohlengruß und Geröll) gobbing, refuse of a coal-pit.

Ver-satz-amt (⌣⌣⌣...) n ㊷ pawnbroker's shop, F u. P my uncle's; =kopf ⊙ m e-r Drehbank: eccentric chuck; =stück n. thea. set piece, pl. auch: movable scenery sg.

ver-sauen F (⌣⌣) v/a. ⊛* to soil, to dirty, F to mess (or muck) up.

ver-sauern (⌣⌣⌣) ⚔a* I v/n. (fig. geistig stumpf w.) to grow sour or acid; fig. F to get seedy. — II v/a. (r:v. **ver-säuern**) to make (too) sour or acid, ⚗ to acidify; fig. = verbittern I.

ver-saufen P (⌣⌣⌣) I v/a. ⊛* : Geld ⚑ to spend ... on drink or F booze; fig. seinen Verstand ⚑ to muddle one's brain with drink(ing) or tippling. — II **ver-soffen** p.p. u. a. ㊺ (D⁹) (dem Saufen ergeben) given to drink(ing), fond of tippling, given to boozing; versoffenes Gesicht drunkard's (besotted) face; versoffener Mensch drunken fellow, drunkard, tippler, F boozer.

ver-säumen (⌣⌣⌣) ⊛* I v/a. 1. to let a th. slip; to miss a lesson, an opportunity, a train, &c.; to neglect (or shirk, slight) a duty, &c.; to throw away a chance of; nichts ⚑ to leave nothing undone; absichtlich die Schule ⚑ to play (the) truant, ⚔ den Appell ⚑ to absent o.s. (from the roll-call); er darf nicht ⚑ zu schreiben he must not omit (or fail, forget) to write; die versäumte Gelegenheit the missed opportunity or chance; das von ihm Versäumte that which he omitted (or forgot) to do, the things pl. neglected by him. — 2. F e-n ⚑ (aufhalten) to delay (or detain) a p. — II sich ⚑ v/refl. 3. (sich vernachlässigen) to neglect o.s. — 4. (zu spät kommen) to come (or be) too late. — III ∼ n ㉓ 5. f. Versäumnis.

Ver-säumnis (⌣⌣⌣) f ⑱, n ⑰ 1. = Versäumung; vgl. Pflicht-⚑, Schul-⚑. — 2. (versäumte Zeit) loss of time; delay.

Ver-säumnis-liste (⌣⌣⌣...) f ㊷ list of absentees or of absence; =urteil n = Kontumaz-urteil.

Ver-säumung (⌣⌣⌣) f ㊻ (f. versäumen I) missing an opportunity, &c., neglect of duty, &c.; omission. [versification.]

Vers-bau (⌣.¹) m ⓶ metrical structure,]

ver-schachern (⌣⌣⌣) v/a. ⚔a* to barter (or chaffer) away, to hawk about.

ver-schaffen (⌣⌣⌣) I v/a. ⊛* : e-m et. ⚑ to procure (or supply) a th. for a p. or a p. a th.; to provide (or furnish) a p. with a th., F to get a th. for a p.; sich et. zu ⚑ suchen to try to get a th., F to be after a th.; f. Achtung 2; sich (dat.) Gehör ⚑ to obtain a hearing, to make o.s. heard; sich (dat.) Geld ⚑ to raise money; sich selbst Recht ⚑ to obtain justice or redress, stärker: to take the law into one's own hands. — II ∼ n u. **Ver-schaffung** f ㊻ procuring, supply(ing), &c. (f. I).

ver-schäfern (⌣⌣⌣) v/a. ⚔a* to spend in frolicking or play, to dally away.

ver-schalen¹ (⌣⌣⌣) v/a. ⊛* ⊙ = beschalen 1 u. 2; ⚒ einen Stollen ⚑ to timber an adit.

ver-schalen² (⌣⌣⌣) v/n. (ſn) ⊛* (schal werden) to grow stale or flat.

ver-schallen (⌣⌣⌣) I v/n. (ſn) 1. ⊛* (verhallen) to die away; die Lieder sind verschallt the songs have died away or are no longer heard. — 2. ⓑ* fig. (in Vergessenheit geraten) to sink (or fall) into oblivion. — II **ver-schollen** p.p. u. a. ㊺ (D⁹) 3. missing, (long) forgotten; lost; er ist längst ⚑ he has not been heard of for a long time; a. M went away long ago, and has never been heard of since; jur. für ⚑ erklären to declare dead in the eyes of the law.

Verschalung (⌣⌣⌣) f ㊻ planking.

ver-schämt (⌣⌣) [mhd.] a. ㊺ ashamed (of o.s.), bashful, shamefaced, (verlegen) confused; (blöde) timid; ⚑e Arme pl. poor (but respectable) folk who are ashamed to beg; ⚑ tun to put on a bashful air; ∼heit f ㊻ bashfulness, shamefacedness; confusion; timidity; ∼tun (⌣⌣¹) n ㊷ feigned bashfulness, simpering, prudishness.

ver-schandeln F (⌣⌣⌣) v/a. ⚔a* to spoil.

ver-schanzen ⚔ (⌣⌣⌣) I v/a. und v/refl. ⊛* frt. ein Lager ⚑ to entrench (or fortify) ...; sich ⚑ to entrench o.s.; sich ⚑ hinter ⚑ to take shelter behind ... — II ∼ n ㉓ und **Ver-schanzung** f ㊻ entrenchment, fortification.

ver-schärfen (⌣⌣⌣) v/a. ⊛*: j-s Strafe ⚑ to inflict a severer punishment on a p., to raise a p.'s penalties or fines.

ver-scharren (⌣⌣⌣) ⊛* ꝛc. = einscharren ꝛc.

ver-schäumen (⌣⌣⌣) ⊛* I v/a. to (turn into) froth. — II v/n. (ſn) to dissolve in(to) foam, to fly off as foam, to turn into froth.

ver-scheiden (⌣⌣⌣) [mhd.] I v/n. (ſn) ⓝ* to expire, to pass away, to die; der Verschied(e)ne ⓖ the deceased. — II ∼ n ㉓ death, decease; im ∼ liegen to be dying or on the point of death.

ver-schenken (⌣⌣⌣) I v/a. ⊛* 1. to give away, to make a present of. — 2. Getränke ⚑ (ausschenken) to retail ... II ∼ n ㉓, **Ver-schenkung** f ㊻ giving away, present(ation), donation.

ver-scherzen (⌣⌣⌣) v/a. ⊛* 1. den Tag ꝛc. ⚑ to trifle away ... — 2. (durch Unbedacht, Leichtsinn verlieren) to lose by one's folly, to fool (or fling) away; sein Glück ⚑ to spurn one's good fortune, to throw (or fling) one's good chances (or one's opportunities) away.

ver-scheuchen (⌣⌣⌣) v/a. ⊛* to drive (or scare, frighten, chase) away; to dispel; fig. die Sorgen ⚑ to banish care.

ver-schicken (⌣⌣⌣) I v/a. ⊛* to send away, dispatch, forward. — II ∼ n ㉓ und **Ver-schickung** f ㊻ sending away, dispatch(ing), forwarding.

ver-schieben (⌣⌣⌣) I v/a. u. v/refl. ⓒ* 1. to shift, to move out of its (former) place; to remove, displace, dislodge; ⛊ e-n Zug ⚑ to shunt; sich ⚑ to get out of (one's) place; (in Unordnung bringen) to disarrange; math. verschob(e)nes (schiefwinkliges) Viereck lozenge (-shaped quadrangle). — 2. = aufschieben 2. — II ∼ n ㉓ und **Ver-schiebung** f ㊻ 3. shifting; removal; disarrangement. — 4. = aufschieben II.

ver-schieden¹ (⌣⌣⌣) [ndd.] a. ㊺ (A 2, 3, D9) 1. different from, differing from; (unähnlich) dissimilar, unlike, diverse; (sich deutlich unterscheidend) distinct from; (abwechselnd) varied; himmelweit ⚑ as different as chalk from cheese; ⚑ m. to diversify; ⚑ sein to differ. — 2. ⚑e (mancherlei) Arten divers (or separate, several, sundry, various) kinds pl.; zu ⚑en Malen at different times, on various occasions; von ⚑ster Größe of all sizes, of every (possible) size; ⊛ ⚑e Artikel sundries pl. — 3. ⚑es (manches) sundry matters pl.; ∼es (Dinge der Art) different things pl.; F fig. da hört doch ⚑es auf that's too much of a good thing, that's too bad.

ver-schieden² (⌣⌣⌣) p.p. v. verscheiden.

ver-schieden-artig (⌣⌣⌣...) a. ㊺ of a different kind or species or character, ⚗ heterogeneous; (ea. entgegengesetzt) opposite; (mannigfaltig) diversified, varied; **-artigkeit** f ㊻ difference in kind, ⚗ heterogeneity; variety.

ver-schiedenerlei (⌣⌣⌣⌣) a. inv. various (or sundry) kinds of, divers, several.

ver-schieden-farbig (⌣⌣⌣...) a. ㊺ of different colours, (bunt) variegated, particoloured, motley, ⊙ mottled (soap, &c.); ⚑förmig, ⚑geformt a. of different form or shape(s), ⚗ heteromorphic.

Signs (see page XVII): F familiar; P vulgar; ⚑ flash; ⚔ rare; † obsolete (died); * new word (born); ⧻ incorrect; ♪ music;

[Verschiedenheit] — 1051 — [verschlichen]

Ver-schiedenheit (ᴗ‿ᴗ‐) f ⓦ difference; (Mangel an Übereinstimmung) diversity, disparity; (Mannigfaltigk. unter ea.) variety; (Unähnlichkeit) unlikeness; ~ der Meinungen = Meinungsverschiedenheit.

ver-schiedentlich (ᴗ‿ᴗ‿) a. ⓦ bsf. adv. zu „verschieden": a) different(ly); b) in different (or sundry) ways; (mehr als einmal) at different times, more than once.

ver-schienen (ᴗ‿ᴗ) v/a. ⓦ* = schienen².

ver-schießen (ᴗ‿ᴗ) ⓦc(ef)t* I v/a. 1. mit Schußwaffen: to shoot off, to discharge (a. Pfeile ꝛc.); bsf. zwecklos: sein Pulver unnütz ⓠ to waste one's powder; (verbrauchen) sein Pulver, f-e Munition ⓠ, a. v/refl. sich ⓠ to use up (or exhaust) one's (stock of) ammunition, a. to run out (or short) of shot and powder; fig. er hat sein Pulver verschossen a) he has no resources left; b) he is impotent or worn out. — 2. bsf. v/refl. sich ⓠ (fehlschießen) to miss one's aim (in shooting). — 3. paint.: Farben ⓠ (abstufen) to shade off ... — 4. ⓞ typ. die Kolumnen ⓠ (falsch ausschießen) to impose ... in a wrong way. — II sich ⓠ v/refl. 5. f. 1 u. 2. — 6. F fig. sich in e-n ⓠ (verlieben) to fall desperately in love with a p.; in e-n verschossen sein to be smitten with a p. — III 7. v/a. (in) von Farben: (verbleichen) to fade, F to fly; von Stoffen ꝛc.: (sich entfärben) to lose colour; verschossen, a. faded, discoloured. — IV ~ n ⓦ 8. (f. 1) keine Munition mehr zum ~ no ammunition left; (f. 7) fading of colours, discoloration.

ver-schiffbar ↓ (ᴗ‿ᴗ‐) a. ⓦ capable of being shipped, fit to be sent by water.

ver-schiffen ↓ (ᴗ‿ᴗ) I v/a. ⓦ* to ship, to carry by (ship's) bottom, to send by water or across the ocean, ins Ausland ꝛc. to export; (verladen) to freight. — II ~ n ⓦ, **Ver-schiffung** f ⓦ shipping, shipment, carriage, export(ation).

Ver-schiffungs-agent („...‿) m ⓦ shipping-agent; -spesen pl. shipping charges.

ver-schimmel/n (ᴗ‿ᴗ) v/n. (in) ⓦa* to grow (F to go, to get) mouldy or musty; ⓑ/ung f ⓦ mouldiness.

ver-schimpf(ier)en (ᴗ‿ᴗ, ᴗ‿ᴗ‿) v/a. ⓦ ⓦ* to disfigure, (entstellen) to deface.

Ver-schiß P (ᴗ‿ᴗ) m ⓦa. bursch. = Verruf.

ver-schlacken (ᴗ‿ᴗ) I v/a. (in) und sich ⓠ v/refl. ⓦ* to be reduced to (or turned into) dross or slag or scoria. — II ~ n ⓦ u. **Ver-schlackung** f ⓦ scorification.

ver-schlafen (ᴗ‿ᴗ) [mhd.] I v/a. ⓦa* 1. den Vormittag ⓠ to sleep away the morning; die ⓠen Stunden the hours pl. spent in sleep. — 2. ich habe die Zeit (ob. v/refl. mich) ⓠ (verspätet) I have overslept myself, I slept too long. — 3. et. ⓠ (schlafend verlieren, vertreiben) to sleep away one's senses, &c., to sleep off one's fatigue, &c.; (schlafend vergessen) to forget in one's sleep. — II p.p. u. a. ⓦ (D9) 4. in den Bedeutungen v. 2. — 5. (schläfrig, schlaftrunken) sleepy, drowsy, overcome with sleep; mit ⓠen Augen with sleepy eyes.   [drowsiness.]

Ver-schlafenheit (ᴗ‿ᴗ‐) f ⓦ sleepiness,

Ver-schlag (ᴗ‿ᴗ) m ⓞc. partition, compartment; (abgeschloffener Raum) locker, closet; (Kämmerchen) box-room, boudoir.

ver-schlagen (ᴗ‿ᴗ) ⓦb* I v/a. 1. ⓞ mit Brettern ⓠ to board up; (abteilen) to partition off; mit Nägeln ⓠ to nail up. — 2. (verwenden, verbrauchen) viel Nägel ⓠ to use up (a good) many nails; reines Gold zu Blattgold ⓠ to beat pure gold into gold leaf. — 3. (durch Schlagen verderben) to spoil by beating or striking; ⚒ die Eifen ⓠ to blunt the tools in hewing or working. — 4. aufgeschlagene Stelle im Buche, das Buch ⓠ to lose one's place in a book. — 5. (schlagend verlieren, von der Bahn abbringen) e-n Ball ⓠ to strike a ball beyond bounds or off the field, to lose a ball; ⚓ ein Schiff von der Fahrt ⓠ to drive a ship off her course; vom Sturme ⓠ (p.p.) cast adrift by the storm, storm-tossed. — 6. sich (dat.) et. ⓠ (etwas durch eigene Schuld einbüßen) to lose a th. through one's own fault or indiscretion; sie hat sich eine gute Partie ⓠ she has missed a good match. — II v/n. (in u. h.) 7. (in) heiße (lu. bsf. falte) Getränke ⓠ (lauich w.) lassen to make ... tepid or lukewarm; to take the chill off cold water, &c. — 8. (in) ⚓ durch den Sturm verschlagen wir nach Norwegen the storm drove us to(wards) Norway. — 9. (h.) mit sachlichem Subjekt, mst verneinend ob. fragend: es verschlägt (bedeutet) nichts it does not matter or signify, it makes no difference or F odds, it's quite indifferent; was verschlägt das? what does it matter?, F what's the odds?; nichts will bei ihm ⓠ nothing is of any avail with him, it's all lost on him. — III sich ⓠ v/refl. 10. hunt. v. Schuß to go astray. — IV ⓠ p.p. u. a. ⓦ (D9) 11. in den Beb. des inf. — 12. [mhd.] (schlau) sly, cunning, artful, crafty, astute, designing, F deep.

Ver-schlagenheit (ᴗ‿ᴗ‐) f ⓦ slyness, cunning, artfulness, craft(iness), astuteness, F depth.

ver-schlammen (ᴗ‿ᴗ) v/n. (in) ⓦ* to silt up, to get choked (or filled) up with mud; verschlammter Fluß silted river.

ver-schlämmen (ᴗ‿ᴗ; Hom. verschlemmen) v/a. ⓦ* to fill (or stop) with mud; sich ⓠ v/refl. = verschlammen.

ver-schlang (ᴗ‿ᴗ) ind. impf. v. verschlingen.

ver-schlechter/n (ᴗ‿ᴗ‿) I v/a. und v/refl. ⓦa* to make worse, a. to worsen; to deteriorate, impair, debase; sich ⓠ to grow worse; to deteriorate, to degenerate; v. Waren ꝛc.: to fall off in quality (vgl. verschlimmern I). — II ~ n ⓦ, ⓑ/ung f ⓦ change for the worse, deterioration, debasement, degeneracy.

ver-schleichen (ᴗ‿ᴗ) I v/n. (in) ⓦa* von der Zeit: to pass slowly, to creep along. — II v/a. fich ⓠ (davonschleichen) to slink away.

ver-schleiern (ᴗ‿ᴗ‿) v/a. ⓦa* to veil (a. fig.); (verhüllen) to throw a veil over, to wrap in mystery; sich ⓠ v/refl. to veil o.s. or one's face, to put on a veil; **Ver-schlei(e)rung** f ⓦ veiling.

ver-schleifen¹ (ᴗ‿ᴗ) I v/a. ⓦb* 1. = abschleifen I. — 2. (schleifend verderben) to spoil (or ruin) in grinding. — II ~ n ⓦ 3. = Abschleifung.

ver-schleifen² ♪ (ᴗ‿ᴗ) v/a. ⓦ*: Töne ⓠ to slur notes.

ver-schleimen (ᴗ‿ᴗ) ⓦ* I v/a. 1. to obstruct (or to stop up) a passage with phlegm or mucus; path. verschleimt sein to suffer from (stärker: to be choked with) phlegm; verschleimte Zunge furred tongue. — 2. ⚒ ein Gewehr ⓠ to foul ... — II v/n. (in) u. sich ⓠ v/refl. 3. to become obstructed (or blocked) with phlegm or mucous matter; (sich verstopfen) to get stopped up. — 4. ⚒ vom Gewehr ꝛc.: to (become) foul. — III ~ n ⓦ und **Ver-schleimung** f ⓦ 5. (f. I u. II) obstruction caused by phlegm; path. furring of the tongue; ⚒ fouling of a gun.

Ver-schleiß ⚒ südd. (ᴗ‿ᴗ) [nhd.] m ⓦa. (sale by) retail, retail trade.

ver-schleißen¹ (ᴗ‿ᴗ) [mhd.] v/n. (in) und sich ⓠ v/refl. ⓦa* to get used up or worn out, als v/a. faktitiv: to use up, to wear out; halb verschliffene Kleider half worn-out (or threadbare) clothes pl.

ver-schleißen² ⚒ südd. (ᴗ‿ᴗ) v/a. ⓦ*: Waren ⓠ to sell ... by retail, to retail ...

ver-schlemmen (ᴗ‿ᴗ) v/a. ⓦ*: sein Geld ⓠ to squander one's money on good eating and drinking, to waste one's substance in guzzling and gormandizing; die Zeit ⓠ to spend one's time in feasting or revelry.

ver-schlendern (ᴗ‿ᴗ‿) v/a. ⓦa* to idle lounge, saunter away one's time, &c.

ver-schleppen (ᴗ‿ᴗ) I v/a. ⓦ* 1. et. ⓠ to take a th. to a wrong place, to misplace (or mislay) a th.; eine Krankheit irgendwohin ⓠ to carry (the seeds of) a disease to a place, to spread a contagious malady (or an epidemic) in a place; (heimlich mit fortnehmen) to carry off with fraudulent intent; to pilfer, to purloin. — 2. (in die Länge ziehen) to postpone, delay, put off; auch v/refl. sich ⓠ to suffer delay; to drag on, F to hang fire. — II ~ n u. **Ver-schleppung** f ⓦ 3. (f. 1) misplacement; spread(ing) of a disease; (f. 2) postponement, delay; (Aufschub) procrastination; parl. (Verhinderung der Beschlußfassung) obstruction.

Ver-schleppungs-politik („...‿) f parl. obstructionism.

Ver-schleuderer (ᴗ‿ᴗ‿) m ⓦ spendthrift, squanderer, wasteful person.

ver-schleudern (ᴗ‿ᴗ‿) I v/a. ⓦa* 1. e-n Stein ꝛc. ⓠ to hurl (or fling) ... (with a sling). — 2. fig. (leichtsinnig hingeben) to spend freely; to squander, lavish, waste; sein Geld ⓠ, auch: to throw (or fritter) away ...; sein Vermögen ⓠ to make ducks and drakes of one's fortune. — 3. ✱ die Ware ⓠ (losschlagen) to sell off ... below cost-price or at a loss, auch: to give away ... — II ~ n ⓦ und **Ver-schleuderung** f ⓦ 4. (f. 2) squandering, waste; (f. 3) selling under (or below) cost-price.

ver-schlich(en) (ᴗ‿ᴗ(‿)) impf. (p.p.) v. verschleichen.

⚛ scientific; ⚘ botanical; ⚱ geography; ⚙ machinery; ⚒ mining; ⚔ military; ⚓ marine; ✱ commercial; ✉ postal; 🜢 railway.

[verschlief] — 1052 — [verschonen]

ver-schlief (ˇ‿¹) *ind. impf. v.* verschlafen.
ver-schließbar (ˇ‿¹‑) *a.* ⓺ capable of being shut or closed or locked or bolted; (provided) with lock and key.
ver-schließen (ˇ‿¹‿) [mhd.] *I v/a. u. v/refl.* ⓓⓐ* **1.** to shut, to close, mit e-m Schlüssel: to lock (up); die Türen fest 2 to bolt and bar the doors; im Schrank verschlossen locked up in the cupboard, kept under lock and key; verschloßener Brief sealed letter; *fig.* sein Herz gegen et. 2 to harden (or steel) one's heart against a th., to show no sympathy for a th.; er hat sein Herz gegen ihr Flehen verschloßen he turned a deaf ear to their supplications; sich einer Sache 2 to pay no heed (or to shut one's eyes) to a th.; sich in sich selbst 2 to be wrapt up in o.s., to seclude o.s. from everybody; ein Geheimnis in sich 2 to keep a secret locked up in one's bosom. — **2.** = einschließen 2; in einen Schrank 2 to lock up in a cupboard. — II **Ver-schließung** *f* ⓺ **3.** (f. I) shutting, &c. — III **verschloßen** *p.p. u. a.* ⓺ (D9) **4.** Bed. des *inf.* — **5.** von Personen: uncommunicative, self-contained, close, (too) reserved, F buttoned up; (schweigsam) taciturn.
ver-schliff(en) (ˇ‿¹(‿)) *impf. (p.p.) v.* verschleifen. [verballhornen.]
ver-schlimmbessern (ˇ‿¹‿‿) *v/a.* ⓓⓐ*
ver-schlimmer/n (ˇ‿¹‿) *I v/a., v/n.* (fn) *u. v/refl.* ⓓⓐ* **1.** = verschlechtern I; sittlich 2 to deprave, debauch, demoralize. — **2.** (erschweren) to aggravate. — II ~ *n* ⓶, *B/ung f* ⓺ **3.** = verschlechtern II; (Erschwerung) aggravation.
ver-schlingen¹ (ˇ‿¹‿) ⓓⓕ* *v/a.* (gierig schlucken) to gulp down (auch Getränke); (fressen) to eat greedily, to devour, F to gobble up; er verschlang hastig sein Frühstück he hastily swallowed (down) his breakfast; das Meer hat sie verschlungen ... engulfed (or swallowed) them; er sieht aus, als wollte er einen 2 he looks as if he would eat (or devour) one; *fig.* das wird viel Geld 2 that will cost a mint of money.
ver-schlingen² (ˇ‿¹‿) *I v/a. u. v/refl.* ⓓⓕ* (in-ea.-schlingen) (sich) 2 to interlace, intertwine, entangle, twist, *v/refl.* auch: to become interlaced, &c.; verschlungen, a. tortuous, complicated, v. Pfaden: meandering, winding. — II ~ *n* ⓶ = Verschlingung.
Ver-schlinger (ˇ‿¹‿) *m* ⓶ devourer, great eater, gormandizer.
Ver-schlingung¹ (ˇ‿¹‿) *f* ⓺ (f. verschlingen¹) gulping down, &c.; ~² (f. verschlingen²) interlacing, entanglement; complication; intricacy, maze.
ver-schliß (ˇ‿¹) *ind. impf.*, **ver-schlißen** (ˇ‿¹‿) *p.p. v.* verschleißen¹.
ver-schloßen (ˇ‿¹‿) *p.p. von* verschließen (f. ds, bsp. III); **~heit** *f* ⓺ being closed, *fig.* closeness, v. Personen a. reserve.
ver-schlucken (ˇ‿¹‿) ⓓⓐ* *I v/a.* **1.** to swallow (vgl. verschlingen I), (einsaugen) to imbibe, to draw in; die Erde verschluckt das Wasser ... absorbs the water; F *fig.* das ist schwer zu 2 (glauben) that's difficult to swallow, F it won't go down (with me). — **2.** die Wörter 2 (undeutlich aussprechen) to swallow (or clip, mumble) one's words. — II sich 2 (falsch schlucken), F auch sich **verschluckern** **3.** to let a th. go down the wrong way; ich habe mich verschluckt something has gone (down) the wrong way.
ver-schlummern (ˇ‿¹‿) *v/a.* ⓓⓐ* to spend in slumbering, to sleep away.
ver-schlungen (ˇ‿¹‿) *p.p. v.* verschlingen.
Ver-schluß (ˇ‿¹) *m* ⓺a. **1.** (das Verschließen) shutting (or locking) up. — **2.** (Vorrichtung) contrivance for shutting; (Schloß) lock; ⚔ ~ e-s Hinterladers breech(-action); *phot.* shutter; et. unter ~ h. to keep a th. under lock and key, ⚓ to keep a th. in bond. ⚓ aus dem Verschlusse (des Zollamtes) nehmen to take out of bond. — **3.** (verschlossener Raum) locker, cupboard.
Ver-schluß-kopf ⚔ (ˇ‿¹...) *m* ⓶ movable breech; **=laut** *m* Phonetik: explosive (sound) (= Muta); **=stück** ⓸ *n* plug, an Hinterladern: breech-block; **=vorrichtung** ⓸ *f* locking-apparatus.
ver-schmachten (ˇ‿¹‿) ⓓⓐ* *I v/n.* (fn) to languish, to pine away; (schwach, ohnmächtig w.) to faint; vor Durst 2 to be parched with thirst; vor Hitze 2 to perish with (the) heat. — II ↘ *v/a.* sein Leben 2 to drag on a miserable life, to linger on, to pine away. — III ~ *n* ⓶ und **Ver-schmachtung** *f* ⓺ languishing; lingering death caused by thirst or hunger, &c.
ver-schmähen (ˇ‿¹‿) [mhd.] *I v/a.* to disdain, scorn, spurn, reject, a. = verachten; sie 2 die Arbeit they refuse to work; die Verschmähte ⓺ (Frau, Geliebte) the forsaken (or deserted) wife, the jilted sweetheart or girl, the cast-off paramour. — II ~ *n* ⓶ und **Ver-schmähung** *f* ⓺ disdain, scorn, rejection; refusal; (Verachtung) contempt.
ver-schmauchen (ˇ‿¹‿) *v/a.* ⓓⓐ* to consume in smoking; to spend on tobacco.
ver-schmausen (ˇ‿¹‿) *v/a.* ⓺* to spend on good fare, to lavish (or spend) in feasting or banqueting or revelry.
ver-schmelz/en (ˇ‿¹‿) *I v/a.* ⓺ (ⓓb)* (verbrauchen) to consume (or use up) in (s)melting; mit od. in et. 2 to (s)melt (or fuse) with a th.; Farben 2 to blend colours; *fig.* die Betriebe sind mit-ea. verschmolzen worden the works have been amalgamated. — II *v/n.* (fn) ⓓⓐ* to melt (away); (flüssig w.) to liquefy; (sich auflösen) to (dis)solve; *fig.* to merge (or melt) into each other, to coalesce. — III ~ *n* ⓶, *B/ung f* ⓺ (s)melting, fusion, liquefaction, v. Farben *c*.: blending; graduation; *fig.* amalgamation, coalescence.
ver-schmerzen (ˇ‿¹‿) *v/a.* ⓺* et. 2 to get over the loss of a th., to forget a th.: er hat es noch immer nicht verschmerzt it is still rankling in his breast.
ver-schmieren (ˇ‿¹‿) *v/a.* ⓺* **1.** to smear over; (verstopfen) to stop up (mit Lehm with clay), chm. to lute. — **2.** to use up in smearing or greasing, Papier 2 to waste in scribbling or scrawling, Tinte: to spill. — **3.** Metall verschmiert die Feile ... clogs up (or fills) the file.

ver-schmitzt (ˇ‿¹) *a.* ⓺, **~heit** *f* ⓺ durchtrieben 2c.
ver-schmolz(en) (ˇ‿¹(‿)) *impf. (p.p.) von* verschmelzen.
ver-schmoren (ˇ‿¹‿) ⓺* *I v/n.* (fn) a) Kochkunst: to boil to rags; das Gemüse war verschmort ... was too much boiled; b) *fig.* (vor Hitze vergehen) to be parched, to parch, to be suffocated with (the) heat. — II *v/a.* Kochkunst: viel Butter 2c. 2 to use up ... in cooking.
ver-schmutzen (ˇ‿¹‿) *v/a.* ⓺* to soil.
ver-schnappen (ˇ‿¹‿): *v/refl.* ⓺* sich 2 (übereilt reden) to put one's foot in (by an ill-considered remark), to blurt out (a th.), to betray o.s. (by a slip of the tongue), oft: to commit o.s.
ver-schnapsen (ˇ‿¹‿) *v/a.* ⓺* to spend on spirits or liquor. [away.]
ver-schnarchen (ˇ‿¹‿) *v/a.* ⓺* to snore
ver-schnauben ⓓc ⓺*, **ver-schnaufen** ⓺* (ˇ‿¹‿) *v/n.* (fn) u. sich 2 *v/refl.* to recover one's breath, to breathe again, to get one's second wind; ein Pferd 2 I. to breathe (or wind) a horse.
ver-schneiden (ˇ‿¹‿) *I v/a.* ⓺c* **1.** to cut away, to clip (short), to prune (closely). — **2.** (verderben) to spoil in cutting or in the cut, ein Kleidungsstück: to cut badly — **3.** (verbrauchen) to cut up. — **4.** (kastrieren) to castrate ...., *vet.* to geld ...., F to doctor ..., verschnittenes Tier (bsb. Pferd) gelding. — **5.** Wein 2 (verfälschen) to adulterate ..., F to doctor ... — II ~ *n* ⓶
Ver-schneidung *f* ⓺ **6.** (f. 1) cutting away, clipping; (f. 4) castration, *vet.* gelding of stallions, &c.; (f. 5) adulteration, F doctoring.
ver-schneien (ˇ‿¹‿) *v/n.* (fn) u. *v/a.* ⓺* to get covered (or blocked, obstructed) with snow; von Menschen, Tieren, Wegen, Zügen 2c.: verschneite snowed up, snow-bound, buried in (or blocked up with) snow. [chips *pl.* (of wood).]
Ver-schnitt¹ (ˇ‿¹) ⓸ *m* ⓶b. carp., &c.
ver-schnitt²(en) (ˇ‿¹(‿)) *impf. (p.p.) v.* verschneiden. **~(e)r** *m* ⓺ eunuch.
ver-schnörkelt (ˇ‿¹‿) *a.* ⓺ adorned (or ornamented) with flourishes.
ver-schnupfen (ˇ‿¹‿) *v/a.* ⓺* **1.** [schnupfen] to spend on snuff. — **2.** [Schnupfen] das nasse Wetter verschnupft leicht ... is apt to give one a cold; bsd. gbr. im *p.p.* verschnupft sein to have a cold (in the head); *fig.* das verschnupft (verdrießt) ihn that vexes (or annoys, nettles) him; er ist verschnupft he feels vexed or nettled or offended.
ver-schnüren (ˇ‿¹‿) *v/a.* ⓺* **1.** to provide with laces, to lace (up). — **2.** ein Paket 2 (binden) to tie up a parcel.
ver-schob(en) (ˇ‿¹(‿)) *impf. (p.p.) von* verschieben. [schallen.]
ver-scholl(en) (ˇ‿¹(‿)) *impf. (p.p.) v.* verschallen.
Ver-schollenheit (ˇ‿¹‿-) *f* ⓺ prolonged absence; **~s-erklärung**(⊥) *f* ⓺ declaring a missing p. after being advertised for, but not discovered legally dead.
ver-schon/en (ˇ‿¹‿) *I v/a.* ⓺* **1.** e-n ∕ j-s, einer Sache *gen.* 2 to spare (or forbear with) a p., a th.; verschont bleiben to be spared, von einer Krankheit 2c.: to remain immune. — **2.** e-n mit et. 2 (nicht behelligen) to exempt (or excuse

Zeichen (f. S. XVII): F familiär; P Volkssprache; Γ Gaunersprache; ↘ selten; † alt (auch gestorben); * neu (auch geboren); ++ unrichtig;

[verſchönen] — 1053 — [verſchwitzen]

a p. from a th.; to let a p. off a th.; ² Sie mich damit! don't trouble (or worry) me with it!, auch: (you might) spare me that! — II ~ n 23 3. = Ⅎſung.
ver-ſchönen (⌣⌣́) v/a. ⓼⓼ to embellish; ſich ² v/refl. to grow beautiful.
Ver-ſchönerer (⌣⌣́⌣) m ㉒ embellisher. der Damen: F beauty-doctor.
ver-ſchönern (⌣⌣́⌣) I v/a. u. v/refl. ㉒a* to embellish, beautify, adorn; ſich ² to grow (more) beautiful, to improve in looks or appearance; die Stadt hat ſich ſehr verſchönert the town has (been) much improved. — II ~ n 23 u. **Verſchönerung** f ㊻ embellishment, adornment, improvement.
Ver-ſchönerungs-verein (⌣⌣́⌣⌣⌣́) m ㊲ society for the improvement of (urban) scenery or paths, parks, &c.
Ver-ſchonung (⌣⌣́⌣) f ㊻ sparing, forbearance; (Nichtbehelligung) exemption.
ver-ſchoſſen (⌣⌣́) p.p. von verſchießen (ſ. b., bſp. 6 u. 7); **~heit** f ㊻ 1. von Farben: faded state. — 2. von Verliebten: mad passion for a p., infatuation instilled by a p.
ver-ſchränken (⌣⌣́) v/a. ⓼⓼*; die Arme ² to fold (or cross) one's arms, &c.; Balken ² to joggle beams, typ. to bond; auch = ſchränken 2; mit verſchränkten Armen with folded arms.
ver-ſchrauben (⌣⌣́) v/a. ⓻ⓒ⓼* to screw (on); (zu ſtark ſchrauben) to overscrew; (falſch ſchrauben) to screw (on) the wrong way; ſ. verſchroben, bſb. Artikel.
ver-ſchreiben (⌣⌣́) I v/a. u. v/refl. ⓼* 1. to use (up) in writing; zwei Stunden ² to spend ... in writing. — 2. (falſch ſchreiben) to write incorrectly, biſw. to miswrite; ſich ² to make a mistake in writing. — 3. Arbeiter ꝛc. ² (kommen l.) to send for ... Waren ꝛc. ² to order ... (by letter). — 4. med. e-m Patienten eine Arznei (ob. metonymiſch: ein Rezept) ² to prescribe (medicine) for a patient. — 5. jur. ꝛc. e-m et. (durch Urkunde verſprechen oder zuſichern) to assign (or transfer, make over) a th. to a p. (by a deed or a legal document); v/refl. ſich e-m ² to give one's bond (or note of hand) to a p.; ſich dem Teufel ² to sell o.s. (or one's soul) to the devil. — II ~ n 23 6. (ſ. 1) using up (of) ink. ꝛc. — 7.**Ver-ſchreibung** f (ſ. 3) written order; (ſ. 4) prescribing, (Rezept) prescription; (ſ. 5) assignment, transfer, bond, note of hand.
ver-ſchreien (⌣⌣́) I v/a. ⓼*; e-n. et. ² to decry (or to cry down) a p., weit² to defame (F to run down) a p.; verſchrien (held) in ill repute. — II ~ n 23 u. **Ver-ſchreiung** f ㊻ defamation.
ver-ſchrieb(en) (⌣⌣́⌣) impf. (p.p.) v. verſchreiben.
ver-ſchrie(n) (⌣⌣́) impf. (p.p.) v. verſchreien.
ver-ſchroben (⌣⌣́) [mhd.] a.⑥⑥(D9) 1. p.p. von verſchrauben: fig. (verworren) confused, entangled, intricate. — 2. fig. (geiſtig) ² wrong-headed, queer, odd, perverse; (überſpannt) eccentric.
Ver-ſchrobenheit (⌣⌣́⌣) f ㊻ mit fig. 1. confusion, intricacy. — 2. wrong-headedness, queerness, oddity, perversity; eccentricity.

ver-ſchroten (⌣⌣́⌣) v/a. ⓼⓼* = ſchroten 1.
ver-ſchrumpfen (⌣⌣́⌣) ⓼⓼* I v/n. (ſn) (einſchrumpfen) to shrink, to shrivel (up); agr. vom Getreide (brandig w.) to get mildewed or blighted. — II v/a. fatitiv: ² (cause to) shrink, durch Hitze: to frizzle up, to parch (up).
ver-ſchüchtern (⌣⌣́⌣) v/a. ㉒a* to intimidate, to frighten, F to bully.
ver-ſchulden (⌣⌣́) ⓼⓼* I v/a. 1. ² (mit Schulden beladen) to load with (or involve in) debt; noch gbr. p.p. verſchuldet (deeply) indebted or in debt. von Gütern: encumbered. — 2. e-m verſchuldet (verpflichtet) ſein to be under an obligation to a p., to be indebted to a p. — 3. meiſt mit ſachlichem pron. als Objekt: (Schuld tragen an) to be guilty of a th.; ² to cause mischief, &c., to commit an offence, to do s.th. wrong; er hat's verſchuldet he is the cause (or the instigator) of it; ſie haben ihr Unglück ſelbſt verſchuldet they have brought their misfortune upon themselves; was hat er verſchuldet? what (wrong) has he done? — 4.(Schlimmes verdienen) to deserve punishment for a th.; er hat es an uns verſchuldet he has had (or has met with) his due for his conduct to us. — II (bſb. bibl.) ſich ² v/refl. 5. = ſich verſündigen. III ~ n u. **Ver-ſchuldung** f ㊻ 6. (ſ. 1) indebtedness, encumbrance; (Schuld) guilt, offence, fault, (Urſache) cause; ohne mein ~ without my fault, without (or not through) any fault of mine.
ver-ſchuldeter-maßen (⌣⌣́⌣⌣) adv. in proportion to one's offence or indebtedness, deservedly; (ſchuldigermaßen) as in duty bound, duly.
ver-ſchütten (⌣⌣́) v/a. ⓼⓼* 1. Waſſer ꝛc. ² to spill ...; fig. ² = verderben 4. — 2. (verdecken) to cover up; (vergraben) to bury; (ausfüllen) to fill up.
ver-ſchwägern (⌣⌣́⌣) I v/a. und ſich ² v/refl. ㉒a*: ſich ² to become related by marriage; er iſt mit ihnen verſchwägert he has married into their family. — II **Ⅎung** f ㊻ relationship by marriage.
ver-ſchwand (⌣⌣́) ind. impf. v. verſchwinden.
ver-ſchwär|en (⌣⌣́) I v/n. (ſn) ㉒a* to fester, ulcerate. — II ~ n 23 ſ. Ⅎung.
ver-ſchwärmen (⌣⌣́⌣) I v/n. (h.) von Bienen: to cease swarming. — II v/a. die ganze Nacht ² to spend the night in revelry, F to make a night of it.
Ver-ſchwärung (⌣⌣́⌣) f ㊻ ulceration.
ver-ſchwärzen (⌣⌣́⌣) v/a. ⓼⓼* fig. = anſchwärzen I.
ver-ſchwatzen, ver-ſchwätzen (⌣⌣́⌣) ⓽* I v/a. 1. ein Stündchen ꝛc. ² to spend ... in chatting or gossiping. — 2. et. ² = ausplaudern I. — 3. e-n ² (verleumden) to backbite (or slander) a p. — II ſich ² v/refl. 4. = verreden II. — 5. f. (ſich ſchwatzend verſäumen) to let the time slip (by) in gossiping.
ver-ſchweigen (⌣⌣́) I v/a. ⓼⓼* 1. et. ² to keep a th. secret or close or Fsnug; (mit Stillſchweigen übergehen) to pass over in silence, ſtärker: to suppress; (verheimlichen) to conceal from a p.; verſchwiegen bleiben to remain a secret;

et. verſchwiegen halten to keep a th. snug or dark. — II ~ n 23 u. **Ver-ſchweigung** f ㊻ 2. (ſ. I) keeping secret; suppression; concealment; reticence observed with regard to a th. — III **ver-ſchwiegen** p.p. u. a. ⑥⑥(D9) 3. Bed. des inf. — 4. (ſchweigſam) silent, reticent, taciturn, close; (zurückhaltend) reserved, discreet. [praſſen.]
ver-ſchwelgen (⌣⌣́) v/a. ⓼⓼* =]
ver-ſchwellen (⌣⌣́) v/n. (ſn) ⑥b* to swell out; to close (up) in swelling.
ver-ſchwenden (⌣⌣́) [mhd.] I v/a. ⓼⓼* = vergeuden I; verſchwendete Mühe useless trouble, lost labour, labour lost. — II ~ n 23 ſ. Verſchwendung.
Ver-ſchwender (⌣⌣́⌣) m ㉒, **~in** f ㊼ squanderer, spendthrift; wasteful (or extravagant) p.; geh. Spr.: prodigal.
ver-ſchwenderiſch (⌣⌣́⌣) a. ⓻ⓐ lavish, wasteful, too liberal, extravagant; profuse; (prachtliebend) sumptuous; ² (adv.) mit et. umgehen to be lavish (or open-handed) with a th., to lavish a th., to spend a th. freely or lavishly; geh. Spr.: to be prodigal of a th.
Ver-ſchwendung (⌣⌣́⌣) f ㊻ dissipation, lavishness; waste (of money), wastefulness; extravagance, prodigality.
ver-ſchwieg(en) (⌣⌣́⌣) impf. (p.p.) von verſchweigen.
Ver-ſchwiegenheit (⌣⌣́⌣⌣) f ㊻ reticence, closeness, discretion; unter dem Siegel der ~ under the seal of secrecy.
ver-ſchwielen (⌣⌣́) v/n. (ſn) ⓼⓼ von der Haut: to grow horny or callous.
ver-ſchwiemelt F (⌣⌣́⌣) a. ⓺⓺ worn out with dissipation, F seedy, washed out.
ver-ſchwimmen (⌣⌣́) I v/n. (ſn) ㉒a(b)* to dissolve, to fade (or melt) away, to vanish; (unbemerkl. w.) to grow hazy or indistinct; in-ea. ² (verſchmelzen) to merge (or melt) into one another. v. Farben: to blend. — II **ver-ſchwommen** p.p. u. a. ⑥⑥(D9) hazy, indistinct, vague.
ver-ſchwinden (⌣⌣́) I v/n. (ſn) ⑦⓽* to disappear, to vanish, to be lost to sight; (vergehen) to pass away, to dissolve; (verblaſſen) to fade away; von Perſonen: (ausreißen) to decamp, F to disappear from the scene, to make o.s. scarce; ² neben, vor to sink into insignificance by the side of; ² laſſen to put out of the way, zauberhaft: to spirit away; ²d klein infinitesimal. — II ~ n 23 disappearance, loss, med. einer Geſchwulſt ꝛc.: ⁊ delitescence.
Ver-ſchwinde-punkt (⌣⌣́⌣⌣) m ㉒ Perſpektive: vanishing point.
ver-ſchwiſtern (⌣⌣́⌣) I v/a. u. v/refl. ㉒a* ſich ² to form a sisterly alliance, fig. to become closely united or allied; verſchwiſtert ſein ... (like) brother(s) and sister(s); verſchwiſterte Seelen congenial (or kindred) souls pl. — II ~ n 23 und **Ver-ſchwiſterung** f ㊻ sisterly (or brotherly) union, fig. close union or alliance.
ver-ſchwitzen (⌣⌣́) ⓼⓼* I v/n. u. ſich ² v/refl. 1. (ſich) ² to pass off as perspiration or sweat. — II v/a. 2. to sweat off or out (of one's body). — 3. (ſchwitzend verderben) to spoil a coat, &c. by perspiring. — 4. F co. (vergeſſen)

to forget; ich habe mein Französisch ganz verschwitzt I have quite lost my knowledge of French, my French has grown very rusty. [schwellen.

ver-schwoll(en) (f⌣´(⌣) *impf.* (*p.p.*) v. ver-

ver-schwommen (f⌣´⌣) s. verschwimmen II.

Ver-schwommenheit (f⌣´⌣-) *f* [46] haziness, indistinctness, vagueness.

ver-schwor(en) (f⌣´(⌣) *impf.* (*p.p.*) von verschwören und verschwären.

ver-schwören (f⌣´⌣) [Wb]* **I sich** ∼ *v/refl.* 1. to conspire (with others), to form a conspiracy, to (hatch a) plot; sie haben sich zu seinem Untergang verschworen they plotted his ruin. — 2. to swear solemnly; sich hoch und teuer ∼ zu // to pledge o.s. by a solemn oath to // (*inf.*). — **II** *v/a.* 3. (verwünschen) to curse. — 4. (schwören, etc. zu unterlassen) to forswear, to abjure, to renounce by an oath; das Trinken ∼ to take the pledge (to abstain from alcoholic liquor), to renounce drinking. — **III** ∼ *n* [23] 5. = Verschwörung. — **IV Ver-schwor(e)ne(r)** *m*) *f* [67] 6. conspirator, plotter.

Ver-schwörer (f⌣´⌣) *m* [22] conspirator, plotter, person involved in a plot.

Ver-schwörung (f⌣´⌣) *f* [46] 1. conspiracy, plot; eine ∼ anzetteln to hatch (or form) a plot. — 2. (s. verschwören 2) solemn oath; (s. verschwören 4) abjuration, renunciation.

ver-schwunden (f⌣´⌣) *p.p.* v. verschwinden.

ver-schwüre (f⌣´⌣) *subj. impf.* von verschwören.

ver-sechs-fachen (f⌣´⌣⌣) *v/a.* [B]* to increase sixfold, to sextuple.

ver-sehen (f⌣´⌣) [Sa]* **I** *v/a.* 1. (a. *v/refl.*) e-n (sich) mit et. ∼ (versorgen) to provide (or furnish, supply) a p. (o.s.) with a th., ⊙ eine Maschine: to feed with s.th.; mit Hausgerät ∼ to furnish; mit Lebensmitteln ∼ to store (or supply) with provisions, to victual; reichlich mit Mitteln ∼ sein to have ample (or plenty of) means, to be flush of money; e-n (sich) mit dem Nötigen ∼ to stock (or equip) a p. (o.s.) with necessaries, to keep a p. supplied with all that he requires; mit einem Saume ∼ to hem; das Schriftstück war mit seiner Unterschrift ∼ the document bore his signature. — 2. jur.: mit Vollmacht ∼ to invest with full power(s); ✱ wohl ∼es Lager well-assorted stock; mit dem Akzept ∼ to accept, to honour; einen Wechsel mit dem Giro ∼ to endorse a bill. — 3. *eccl.* e-n (mit den Sterbesakramenten) ∼ to administer the last sacrament to a p. — 4. et. ∼ (besorgen) to attend to a th.; to conduct (or manage, administer) a th.; j-s Amt od. Dienst ∼ to do duty for a p., to discharge a p.'s duties, to fill a p.'s place; die Küche, den Stall &c. ∼ to look after …; eine Pfarre für einen andern ∼ to take charge of a parish; die Wirtschaft ∼ to keep house, to look after the household. — 5. meist mit sächlichem *pronoun*: (unachtsam tun) etwas ∼ to mistake a th., to err (or blunder) in a th.; (übersehen) to overlook; er hat es bei ihr ∼ he has incurred her displeasure, he is in her black (or bad) books. — **II sich** ∼ *v/refl.* 6. s. 1. — 7. sich ∼ (einen Irrtum begehen) to make a mistake, to commit an error, to err; Sprichw. ∼ ist auch verspielt, etwa: a miss is as good as a mile. — 8. sich eines Dinges zu e-m ∼ (es sicher von ihm erwarten) to look to a p. for a th.; ehe man sich's versieht in the twinkling of an eye, F before you can say Jack Robinson; ich hatte mich dessen nicht ∼ I had not expected (or was not prepared for) such a th. — **III** ∼ *n* [23] 9. oversight; mistake, error, blunder, im Schreiben, Sprechen: slip of the pen, of the tongue; aus ∼, **ver-sehentlich** (f⌣´⌣⌣) *adv.* through inadvertence, inadvertently; by (a) mistake.

ver-sehren (f⌣´⌣) [mhd.: sear] *v/a.* [B]* to hurt, injure; (beschädigen) to damage.

ver-seichten (f⌣´⌣) [B]* **I** *v/n.* (sn) v. Gewässern &c.: to grow shallow. — **II** *v/a.* to make shallow or superficial.

ver-seifen (f⌣´⌣) [B]* **I** *v/a.* u. *v/n.* (sn) to turn to soap, *chm.*, &c.: ⚗ to saponify. — **II** ∼ *n* [23] u. **Ver-seifung** *f* [46]: ⚗ saponification. [saponifier.

Ver-seifungs-mittel ⊙ (f⌣´⌣⌣⌣) *n* [62]

ver-seilen ⊙ (f⌣´⌣) *v/a.* [B]* to (twist into a) strand; verseilter Drahtstrang stranded wire. [stranding-machine.

Ver-seilungs-maschine ⊙ (f⌣´⌣⌣⌣) *f* [62]

Vers-einschnitt (f´⌣⌣) *m* [62] = Zäsur.

ver-sendbar (f⌣´-) *a.* [66] transportable.

ver-senden (f⌣´⌣) **I** *v/a.* [Ba]* to send away or off (vgl. absenden), ins Ausland: to export, zu Schiffe: to ship; ✱ die von uns versandten Waren *pl.* the goods dispatched (or shipped) by us. — **II** ∼ *n* [23] = Versendung.

Ver-sender (f⌣´⌣) *m* [22] sender, ✱ consignor, exporter, shipper (of goods).

Ver-sendung (f⌣´⌣) *f* [46] consignment, dispatch; export(ation), shipment.

Ver-sendungs-art (f⌣´⌣…) *f* [62] mode of transmission; **-artikel** ⊙ *m* article of export(ation); **-gebühren** *f/pl.*, **-kosten** *pl.* charges for conveyance.

ver-sengen (f⌣´⌣) *v/a.* [B]* (*v/refl.* **sich**) ∼ to singe, stärker: to scorch or burn (o.s.); von der Sonne versengt scorched (or burnt) by the sun.

ver-senk/en (f⌣´⌣) **I** *v/a.* u. *v/refl.* [B]* 1. to (cause to) sink; einen Sarg ∼ (hinablassen) to lower …, to let down …; ein Schiff ∼ to sink, to submerge, durch Anbohren: to scuttle, durch starke Wellen: to swamp. — 2. *fig.* **sich** ∼ to plunge into (deep) meditation; tief in Gedanken versenkt deeply absorbed in thought. — **II** ∼ *n* [23] 3. = V/ung 1.

Ver-senkung (f⌣´⌣) *f* [46] 1. sinking, submersion. — 2. *thea.* trap; (Falltür) trap-door.

ver-sessen (f⌣´⌣) [*p.p.* v. versitzen] *a.* [66] (D9) auf et. ∼ (erpicht) sein to be bent on (doing) a th., to be madly in love with (or enamoured of) a th., to be (madly) hankering after a th.; **∼heit** *f* [46] mad love for a th.

Ver-setz-amt (f⌣´⌣) *n* [62] = Leihhaus.

ver-setzbar (f⌣´-) *a.* [66] removable, *gr.*, &c. transposable; im Leihhause: pawnable.

ver-setzen (f⌣´⌣) **I** *v/a.* und **sich** ∼ *v/refl.* [B]* 1. (falsch setzen) to misplace, to put in a wrong place; *typ.* Wörter ∼ to transpose words. — 2. (an eine andere Stelle setzen): to displace, remove, shift, *math.*: ⚗ to permute; Bäume ∼ to transplant …, Buchstaben: to transpose; Beamte, ⚔ Offiziere: to transfer …., *eccl.* Bischöfe: to translate …; Redewendungen mit *prp.*: e-n **in** Angst oder Schrecken ∼ to frighten (or alarm) a p.; e-n in Anklagezustand ∼ to put a p. on his trial; Schüler in eine höhere Klasse ∼ to (re)move … (in)to a higher form, to promote …; in üble Laune ∼ to put in(to) a bad humour, to put out; das versetzt mich in die Notwendigkeit zu reden that places me under the necessity of speaking, it compels me to speak; in den Ruhestand ∼ to pension off; als *v/refl.*: ∼ Sie sich in meine Lage place (or imagine) yourself in my position; ∼ wir uns in jene Zeiten let us go (or hark) back to those times, let us retrace (or reconstruct) that period; **unter** die Götter ∼ to enrol (or rank) among the Gods, to deify. — 3. (als Pfand weggeben) to pledge, to (put in) pawn, F to put up the spout, to pop. — 4. (vermischen) to mix, *chm.* to combine, Metalle: to alloy. — 5. (versperren) den Eingang mit Steinen ∼ to bar (or block) the entrance with …; das versetzte mir den Atem, die Luft that took my breath away; als *v/refl.*: die Blähungen ∼ sich in den Gedärmen the wind settles (or the gases collect) in the bowels; versetzte Blähungen *pl.* flatulency *sg.* — 6. e-m einen Hieb, Schlag, e-m eins ∼ to give (F to deal) a p. a blow or a knock; e-m e-n Stoß ∼ to give a p. a push. — 7. (erwidern) to reply, answer, retort. — **II** ∼ *n* [23] 8. s. Versetzung.

Ver-setz-schiene 🚂 (f⌣…) *f* [62] switch (-rail); **-stücke** *n/pl. thea.* movable scenery, scenery that can be shifted.

Ver-setzung (f⌣´⌣) *f* [46] (s. versetzen 1) misplacement, mislocation; (s. versetzen 2) displacement, removal, *math.*: ⚗ permutation; von Buchstaben &c.: transposition, ⚗ metathesis; von Beamten: transfer, *eccl.* von Bischöfen: translation; von Schülern: removal, remove, promotion; ⚔ seine ∼ erhalten to get a shift; *med.* ∼ e-r Krankheit: ⚗ metastasis; (s. versetzen 3) im Leihhause: pawning; (s. versetzen 4) mixture, *chm.* combination.

Ver-setzungs-arbeit (f⌣´⌣…) *f* [62] Schule: test-paper set previous to the remove; **-examen** *n* = -prüfung; ∼**fähig** *a.* [66] fit to be removed; **-konferenz** *f* meeting of class-teachers for the purpose of arranging the remove or the promotion of pupils; **-prüfung** *f* examination held previous to remove or for the purpose of placing pupils; **-regel** *f*, *arith.* rule of alligation; **-schreiben** *n* an Gesandte &c.: letter of recall; **-tag** *m* day on which the new class-lists are published; **-zeichen** ♪ *n* sign of transposition.

[verseuchen] — 1055 — [verspickern]

ver-seuchen (f‿‿) ⊕* I v/a. med. to infect. — II v/n. (in) to become infected. — III ~ n 23 u. **Ver-seuchung** f 46 infection, (spreading) contagion.
ver-seufzen (f‿‿) v/a. 90* to spend in sighing or groaning, to sigh away.
Vers-fuß (f‿‿) m 62 metrical foot.
ver-sicherbar (f‿‿) a. 6 insurable
Ver-sicherer ⊕, ↓ (f‿‿) m 22 insurer, bsd. für Schiffe ꝛc.: underwriter.
ver-sichern (f‿‿) I v/a. u. sich 2 v/refl. 9a* 1. (sich) 2 to assure (o.s.); seien Sie meines Eifers versichert you may rest assured of my zeal; (beteuern) to protest, (bezeugen) to assert; eidlich (oder an Eides Statt) 2 to affirm. — 2. ⊕ (sich) 2 to insure (o.s.) against fire, &c.; sein Leben 2 to insure one's life, to take out a life-policy; Versicherte(r) s. person insured, a. policy-holder. — 3. e-n e-r Sache (gen.) 2 to assure (or convince) a p. of a th.; sich e-r Sache 2 to make sure (or certain) of a th., to lay (or seize) hold of a th., geistig: to ascertain a th.; sich j-s 2 to secure a p. — II ~ n 23 u.
Ver-sicherung (f‿‿) f 46 4. (s. 1) assurance; protestation, assertion; affirmation; (s. 2) ⊕ gegen Feuer ꝛc., insurance, des Lebens a.: (life-) assurance; eine ~ erlischt a policy lapses or becomes void or is voided.
Ver-sicherungs-agent (f‿‿‿) m 62 insurance-agent; =anstalt f insur.-office; =antrag m application (made) to an insurance-office; =betrag m amount (or sum) insured; =bureau n = =anstalt; =gebühr f = =prämi-e; =gericht ↓ n maritime court; =gesellschaft f insurance-company; =gesetz n law relating to insurance; =kontor n = =anstalt; =makler, =mäkler m insurance-broker; =police f = =schein; =prämi-e f premium of insurance, insurance-money; =schein m policy (of insurance); =summe f = =betrag; =wesen n insurance-matters pl.
ver-sichtbaren (f‿‿) v/a. ⊕* to make visible or manifest. [away.}
ver-sickern (f‿‿) v/n. (in) 9a* to ooze
ver-siechen (f‿‿) v/n.(in) ⊕* to languish, pine away, droop; (kränfeln) to be sickly.
ver-sieden (f‿‿) v/n. (in) u. v/a. ⊙e ⊕* to boil away, to evaporate in boiling.
ver-siegbar (f‿⊥) a. 6 v Bächen, Quellen: liable to run dry, easily drying up.
ver-siegeln (f‿‿) I v/a. 9a* to seal up a letter, &c.; gerichtlich 2 to put under seal, to affix seals to. — II ~ n 23 u.
Ver-sieg(e)lung f 46 sealing; putting under seal.
ver-sieg/en (f‿‿) [ahd.] I v/n. (in) ⊕* to run dry, to dry up, weits. to get exhausted, to come to an end; nie 2de Quelle perennial stream, inexhaustible source. — II ~ n 23, B/ung f 46 running dry, failure.
Versifex F (w‿‿) [lt.] m 9a. (Versemacher) versifier, (inferior) poet. [tion.}
Versifikation (w‿‿-ts(‿)⊥) f 46 versifica-
versifizieren (w‿‿⊥) [lt.] I v/a. 9 to versify, to turn into verse. — II v/n. to write poetry. — III ~ n 23, B/ung f 46 versification, writing poetry.

ver-silber/n (f‿‿) I v/a. 9a* 1. to silver (over), to plate; ⊙ ⊕ galvanisch versilberte Waren pl. electro-plate(d goods). — 2. ⊕ (zu Gelde machen) to turn into money, to realize; Aktien 2 to sell (or to dispose of) shares. — II ~ n 23 und B/ung f 46 3. silvering, ⊙ galvanische B/ung electro-silvering, galvanic plating; ⊕ conversion into money, realization; sale.
ver-simpeln F (f‿‿) v/n. (in) 9a* to lose one's mental power(s), to grow silly or underwitted, to become an idiot.
ver-singen (f‿‿) ⊕t* I v/a.: seine Zeit 2 to spend ... in singing. — II v/n. (h.), a. v/refl. sich 2 to sing wrong (or false) notes, to sing out of tune.
ver-sinken (f‿‿) I v/n. (in) ⊕t* to sink (down), to go to the bottom, (verschlungen werden) to be swallowed up, to become submerged; in einen Abgrund 2 to become engulfed; fig. in Gedanken versunken lost (or absorbed, buried, wrapt) in thought; im Laster (im Sumpfe des Lasters) 2 to plunge into vice; im Laster versunken steeped in vice, a. depraved; vgl. versumpfen fig. — II ~ n 23 ⊕ submersion; die Wege waren zum ~ the roads were bottomless or like a swamp.
ver-sinnbild(lich)en (f‿‿(‿)‿) v/a. ⊕(8)* to symbolize, to allegorize.
ver-sinnlich/en (f‿‿‿) ⊕* I v/a. 1. to render perceptible or tangible; to illustrate. — 2. (sinnlich machen) to make sensual. — II v/n. (in) und sich 2 v/refl. 3. to grow sensual. — III ~ n 23 u. B/ung f 46 4. illustration.
Version (w‿(‿)⊥) [lt.] f 46 version.
ver-sittlichen (f‿‿‿) v/a. ⊕* to improve the morals of, to raise the moral tone of, to civilize.
ver-sitzen (f‿‿) ⊕* I v/a.: die Zeit 2 to spend one's time in sitting, to sit out the time. — II sich 2 v/refl. to lose the use of one's limbs by sitting too much, to lead a sedentary life; to pore over (the) books. — III p.p. s. versessen, bsd. Artikel.
Vers-kunst (f‿⊥) f 46 (art of) versification, poetic art; =künstler m = =macher; =lehre f prosody; =machen n versification; =macher m versifier, verse-maker; poet; =maß n metre, (poetic) measure; dem ~ entsprechend, auf das ~ bezüglich metrical; s. verstoßen I; =messung f scanning, scansion, ♒ metrics.
Verso (w‿-) [lt.] n 53 (Rückseite eines Blattes) verso. [saufen.}
ver-soff/en (f‿‿(‿)) impf. (p.p.) v. ver-
Ver-soffenheit (f‿‿‿-) f 46 drunkenness.
ver-sohlen 2 (f‿‿) v/a. ⊕* Schuhmach.: Stiefel 2 [wieder] besohlen) to (re)sole ...; F fig. e-m die Haut (oder das Fell), auch e-n 2 (durchprügeln) to thrash a p., F to tan a p.'s hide, to give a p. a good hiding.
ver-söhnbar (f‿⊥-) a. 6 reconcilable, appeasable.
ver-söhnen (f‿‿) [mhd.: Sühne] I v/a. und v/refl. ⊕* to reconcile (or conciliate) with or to; bsd. rel. den Himmel 2 to propitiate Heaven; sich 2 to become reconciled; sich mit e-m 2, auch:

F to make it up with a p.; 2d conciliatory; rel. expiatory, propitiatory. — II ~ n 23 = Versöhnung.
Ver-söhner (f‿‿) m 22, ~in f 46 reconciliator; propitiator; mediator (f a. mediatrix); (Friedensstifter[in]) peace-maker.
ver-söhnlich (f‿‿-) a. 6 easy to conciliate or reconcile, rel. propitiable; forgiving; conciliatory (conduct, &c.); ~keit f 46 forgivingness; conciliatory spirit or attitude.
Ver-söhnung (f‿‿) f 46 (re)conciliation; bib. rel. propitiation; atonement.
Ver-söhnungs-fest (f‿‿‿...) n 62: a) day of reconciliation; b) rel. ~ der Juden day of atonement (= langer Tag); =opfer n: a) (Handlung) expiatory sacrifice: b) (Opfertier) expiatory victim; =politik f conciliatory (or peace-) policy; =tag m = =fest; =tod m, rel. expiatory death of Christ.
ver-sorg/en (f‿‿) I v/a. u. v/refl. ⊕* 1. = versehen 1. — 2. e-n 2 (sicherstellen) to provide (or to make provision) for a p.; seine Kinder sind versorgt his children are settled (in life); sie ist gut versorgt she is well provided for, she has an ample income or allowance. — II ~ n 23, s. B/ung 1.
Ver-sorger (~) m 22, ~in f 46 one who provides or supplies; supporter, fig. main-stay; e-r Familie a. bread-winner.
Ver-sorgung (f‿‿) f 46 1. (das Versorgen) providing for, (making) provision for; maintenance of; ✕ ~ mit Lebensmitteln (re)victualling, provisioning, supply. — 2. (das Versorgtsein) settlement, settled income; (Brotstelle) (good) place, situation, berth.
Ver-sorgungs-anspruch (f‿‿...) m claim to maintenance (or employment) after many years' service; =anstalt f home for invalids or aged people, alms-house; weits. (Armenhaus) workhouse; 2berechtigt a. 6 entitled to maintenance; =bureau n, etwa: employment-agency, -bureau; =haus n = =anstalt.
ver-sparen (f‿‿) v/a. ⊕* 1. (aufsparen) to save, to put by (for a rainy day). — 2. auf eine andere Zeit 2 to spare for another occasion or time; (aufschieben) to defer, to put off.
ver-späten (f‿‿) I v/a. und v/refl. ⊕* to make late, (aufhalten) to delay, to retard; sich 2 to be (or come) too late, to be late, to be behind (one's) time, ✚ u. ↓ a. to be overdue; verspätet too late, belated, overdue. — II ~ n 23 u.
Ver-spätung f 46 delay, retardation; lateness; der Zug ꝛc. hat eine Stunde ~ ... is an hour late or overdue.
ver-speisen (f‿‿) v/a. 9* to eat up, to consume, F to polish off.
ver-spekulieren (f‿‿‿) v/refl. ⊕* sich 2 to make a bad speculation; alles 2 to lose everything in speculating, to ruin o.s. by speculation.
ver-sperren (f‿‿) I v/a. ⊕* = sperren 2; e-m die Aussicht 2 to obstruct a p.'s view; e-m den Weg 2 to bar (or block) a p.'s way. — II ~ n 23 u. **Ver-sperrung** f 46 barring, barricading, obstruction, e-s Hafens ꝛc.: blockade.
ver-spickern ↓ (f‿‿) v/a. 9a* to spike.

⚗ scientific; ⚘ botanical; ⚲ geography; ⊕ machinery; ✕ mining; ✕ military; ↓ marine; ⊕ commercial; ✉ postal; 🚂 railway.

[verspielen] — 1056 — [verstäuben]

ver-spiel/en (ˇ‿ˊ) I v/a. ⊛* 1. to lose in gambling or in playing or at cards, to gamble away; viel ² to lose heavily (at cards), to come off a heavy loser; ihr habt (es) verspielt you have lost (the game). — 2. den Abend ꝛc. ² to spend ... in playing or gambling. — II ~ n ㉓ = B/ung.
Ver-spieler (ˇ‿ˊ) m ㉒ loser, F victim.
Ver-spielung (ˍ) f ㊻ losing the game, losing at cards, &c.
ver-spiller n (ˇ‿‿) v/n. (fn) ㉒ª* von Pflanzen: = verkümmern I; B/ung f ㊻ ² = verkümmern III.
ver-spinnen (ˇ‿‿) ㉒ª* I v/a. allen Flachs ² to use up all the flax in spinning. — II sich ² v/refl. = einspinnen II.
ver-splittern (ˇ‿‿) v/a. ㉒ª* 1. Zeit und Geld ² to squander ..., to fritter away. — 2. biѕw. = zersplittern.
ver-sponnen (ˇ‿‿) p.p. von verspinnen.
ver-spotten (ˇ‿‿) I v/a. ⊛* to mock (at), to scoff (or sneer) at; to make fun (or a mockery) of, to turn (into) ridicule; (necken) to tease, chaff, quiz; (verhöhnen) to jeer (or hoot) at. — II ~ n ㉓ = Verspottung.
Ver-spotter (ˇ‿‿) m ㉒. ~in f ㊼ mocker, scoffer; teaser.
Ver-spottung (ˇ‿‿) f ㊻ mocking, mockery, scoffing; teasing, chaff, chaffing, quizzing; jeering.
ver-sprach (ˇ‿ˊ) ind. impf. v. versprechen.
ver-sprech/en (ˇ‿‿) ㉒ª* I v/a. 1. to promise; er hat es versprochen, auch: he has given his promise or pledged his word (that he will do it); er hat ihr die Ehe versprochen he promised to marry her, he made her a promise of marriage; f. golden ²; wir ² uns nicht viel davon we don't think it very promising, we set no great hopes on it; viel ²d very promising, very hopeful; das Versprochene the thing(s) promised. — II sich ² v/refl. 2. = verloben I. — 3. (sich beim Sprechen irren) to make a mistake in speaking; ich habe mich (er hat sich ꝛc.) versprochen, a. it was a slip of the tongue on my (his, &c.) part. — III ~ n ㉓ u. B/ung f ㊻ 4. (f. I) promise; e-m ein ~ abnehmen to draw (or exact) a promise from a p.; vgl. abnehmen 3 u. erfüllen 2, (f. II) = Verlobung.
ver-sprengen (ˇ‿‿) I v/a. ⊛* to disperse (or scatter) a multitude; ⚔ versprengte Truppen pl. isolated (or detached) body of troops; Billard: einen Ball ² to knock ... off the board. — II ~ n ㉓ u. **Ver-sprengung** f ㊻ dispersal; ⚔ isolation.
ver-springen (ˇ‿‿) v/a. ⓓfi* I sich (dat.) den Fuß ² to sprain (or hurt) one's foot in jumping or leaping or springing. — II sich ² v/refl. to run too far, to go astray.
ver-spritzen (ˇ‿‿) ⁹⁰* I v/a. to spill; to squirt (out); sein Blut für das Vaterland ² to shed one's blood for one's country; das verspritzte Blut the spilt (or spilled) blood. — II v/refl., ⚓ von Wellen: sich am Felsen ² to dash (wildly) against the rock.
ver-sprochen (ˇ‿ˊ) p.p. v. versprechen.

ver-sproch(e)ner-maßen (ˇ‿ᶜʰ(ˇ)‿ˊ‿) adv. as promised, in the way promised.
ver-sprungen (ˇ‿‿) p.p. von verspringen.
ver-spunden (ˇ‿‿), **ver-spünden** (ˇ‿‿) v/a. ⊛* to bung (up) (= spunden, spünden).
ver-spüren (ˇ‿ˊ) v/a. ⊛* = spüren II.
ver-staatlich/en (ˇ‿‿) I v/a. ⊛* to turn into state-property, to put under the care (or control) of the state; to take over railways, telegraphs, &c.; Kirchenschulen: to secularize, das Land: ² to nationalize. — II ~ n ㉓ u. B/ung f ㊻ (f. I) absorption (or acquisition) by the state; secularization; ~ des Grundeigentums nationalization of the land.
ver-stählen ⚔ ⊕ (ˇ‿ˊ) ⊛* ꝛc. = stählen² ꝛc.
ver-stampfen (ˇ‿‿) v/a. ⊛* to stamp, to crush (by stamping), to pound.
Ver-stand¹ (ˇ‿ˊ) [mhd.] m ⓒc. (o. pl.) 1. (Denkkraft) understanding, mental power(s pl.); (Geist) mind, wit; (Erkenntnis) intellect, intelligence, (Auffassung) comprehension, grasp, (Urteilsfähigkeit) judgment, discernment; (Scharfsinn) sagacity, shrewdness; gesunder ~ sound understanding, good (or common) sense; ein klarer ~ a clear brain or head; mit ~ reden to talk sensibly; da steht mir der ~ still I cannot comprehend (or fathom) it, that's past my comprehension, F it's too much for me, it's beyond me; man muß f-n (F sein bißchen) ~ zusammennehmen one has to collect (all) one's thoughts, F you must have all your wits about you. — 2. mit prp.: der Kranke blieb bei ~e the patient retained his mental faculties; er ist nicht bei ~(e) he is not in his right senses, he is out of his mind; das geht über meinen ~ it passes my understanding, that's beyond me; zu ~e kommen to come into (or attain) the full possession of one's reason or faculties; Sprichw. ~ kommt (erst) mit den Jahren wisdom comes with age, auch: you cannot put old heads on young shoulders. — 3. ~ (Bedeutung) sense, meaning (or acceptation) of a word, &c.
ver-stand²(en) impf. (p.p.) v. verstehen.
Ver-standes-begriff (ˇ‿‿...) m ㊷ phls. (abstract) idea; =gabe f gift of intellect; =kasten F m, co. (Kopf) knowledge- (or brain-)box; =kraft f intellectual power (or faculty); =mäßig a. ⓐ) reasonable; b) intellectual; =mensch m: a) p. endowed with intellect. a. intellectual(ist): b) b.s. matter-of-fact (or unimaginative), non-sentimental, prosy p.; =schärfe f keenness of mind, (mental) acumen, F cuteness; =schwäche f mental weakness, weak-mindedness. stärker: imbecility; =tätigkeit f activity of the brain or mind; =welt f intellectual world; =wesen n intelligent (or sensible) being.
ver-ständig (ˇ‿‿) a. ㊻ intelligent; (vernünftig) reasonable, sensible, shrewd; (vorsichtig) cautious, prudent, wise; (richtig urteilend) judicious; ²es Alter sensible age, years pl. of discretion; ²er Mann man of sense, man of (sound) judgment; ² (adv.) reden to talk sense or sensibly.

ver-ständigen (ˇ‿‿) I v/a. und sich ² v/refl. ⊛* 1. e-n von et. ² to inform (or advise) a p. of a th.; to acquaint a p. with a th.; einen über et. ² (aufklären) to explain a th. to a p. — 2. sich mit e-m ² to come to an understanding (or agreement, arrangement) with a p.; to arrange (or settle) with a p. — II ~ n ㉓ = 3. f. Verständigung.
Ver-ständigkeit (ˇ‿‿ˍ) f ㊻ sensibleness, good sense, shrewdness, prudence.
Ver-ständigung (ˇ‿‿) f ㊻ (f. verständigen 1) explanation; (f. verständigen 2) (mutual) understanding, agreement, (amicable) arrangement; ~s-mittel (ˇ...) n ㊷ means of making each other understand.
ver-ständlich (ˇ‿‿) a. ㊻ intelligible, comprehensible; (klar) clear, perspicuous, lucid; (faßlich) easy to understand or to comprehend; schwer ² difficult to grasp, abstruse; sich ² (adv.) ausdrücken to express o.s. clearly; sich ² machen to make o.s. understood; e-m et. ² machen to make a p. understand a th.; ~keit (ˇ‿‿ˍ) f ㊻ intelligibleness; clearness (of expression), perspicuity, lucidity.
Ver-ständnis (ˇ‿‿) n ㉗ comprehension, understanding; ~ für etwas haben to show appreciation for a th., to be fully alive to a th.; er hat kein ~ dafür he does not comprehend it, he cannot grasp it, thea. szenisches ~ h. to understand scenic effects.
ver-ständnis-innig (ˇ...) a. ㊻ of deep meaning; ein ²er Blick a glance of mutual understanding or secret meaning, a. a knowing glance; ²los a. incapable of comprehending or grasping; devoid of understanding; =losigkeit f ㊷ lack of comprehension; ²voll a. intelligent; ein ²es Lächeln an appreciative smile; adv. e-m ² zunicken to give a p. a knowing wink.
ver-stänkern (ˇ‿‿) v/a. ㉒ª* to fill with stench(es) or unpleasant odour(s).
ver-stärken (ˇ‿‿) I v/a. u. v/refl. ⊛* to strengthen, to fortify, Töne, Gefühle ꝛc. to intensify; sich ² to grow stronger; (vermehren) to increase (or augment) in number, bſp. ⚔ auch: to reinforce; (dicker machen) to enlarge; (ärger machen) to aggravate; Farben ² to deepen (or enrich) ...; die Stimme ² to raise one's voice; chm. e-e Säure ꝛc. ² to concentrate an acid. &c.; ♪ Töne ² to swell notes. — II ~ n ㉓, **Ver-stärkung** f ㊻ (f. I) strengthening; reinforcement (auch ⚔); enlargement; aggravation; chm. concentration.
Ver-stärkungs-flasche (ˇ‿‿...) f ㊷ elect Leyden jar; =truppen f/pl. reinforcements pl., support sg.; =wort n. gr. augmentative (word).
ver-statt/en (ˇ‿‿) I v/a. ⊛* = gestatten, vergönnen. — II B ung f ㊻ permission.
ver-stauben (ˇ‿ˊ) ⊛* I v/n. (fn) u. sich ² v/refl. to become (or get) dusty, to be(come) covered with dust; (wie Staub verfliegen) to fly away like (or in the shape of) dust. — II ± st. verstäuben.
ver-stäuben (ˇ‿ˊ) I v/a. ⊛* to cover with dust; to reduce to dust or to

Zeichen (ſ. S. XVII): F familiär; P Volkssprache; Γ Gaunersprache; ↘ selten; † alt (auch gestorben); * neu (auch geboren); ⁺⁺ unrichtig.

fine powder, to pulverize. — II ~ n ㉓ = Verstäubung.

Ver-stäuber ☉ (ⁱ‿ᵛ) m ㉒ spray-diffuser or -instrument, sprayer.

Ver-stäubung (ⁱ‿ᵛ) f ㊻ pulverization; ~ś-apparat m ㉒ = Verstäuber.

ver-stauch/en (ⁱ‿ᵛ) [ndd.] **I** v/a. ⊛* surg.: to sprain, to put out (of joint); sich den Fuß ⁓ to sprain one's foot; vgl. verrenken I. — **II** ~ n ㉓ u. ᵛ/ung f ㊻ sprain(ing), ⁊ luxation.

ver-stechen (ⁱ‿ᵛ) v/a. ⊛a* **1.** Näherei: ein Loch ꝛc. ⁓ (stopfen) to darn … — **2.** Lanzen (im Turnier) ⁓ (brechen) to break … — **3.** Kartenspiel: seine Trümpfe ⁓ to use up (or to play all) one's trumps.

Ver-steck (ⁱ‿ᵛ) n ⑰b. **1.** o. pl. (Verstecken) concealment; Spiel: ~ spielen to play (at) hide-and-seek. — **2.** mit pl. (Ort) hiding- (a. lurking-)place, place of concealment, retreat; (Winkel) nook, (safe) corner; (Ritz) cranny; ⚔ (Hinterhalt) ambush, ambuscade.

ver-stecken (ⁱ‿ᵛ) **I** v/a. und v/refl. ⊛* **1.** = verbergen I; (geheimhalten) to secrete from a p.; sich versteckt halten to keep in hiding, F to lie low; sich im Gebüsch versteckt halten to hide up (or ensconce o.s.) in the bushes. — **2.** fig. sich vor e-m ⁓ müssen (hinter e-m zurückstehen) to be unable to complete (or cope) with a p., to be no match for a p. — **II** ~ n ㉓ **3.** = Versteck 1. — **III** p.p. **4.** f. versteckt.

Ver-steck-spiel(en) (ⁱ‿ᵛ‿ᵛ(ᵛ)) n ㉒ playing (at) hide-and-seek.

ver-steckt (ⁱ‿ᵛ) [p.p. v. verstecken] a. ㊺ **1.** hidden, concealed; ⁓e Anspielungen (Vorwürfe) veiled (or covert) hints (reproaches) pl.; b.s. es ist etwas ~es und Listiges in s-m Gesicht there is s.th. underhand and artful in his face. — **2.** ⁓er Mensch close (or reserved, b.s. sly, underhand person, F sly-boots. sly-fox.

Ver-steckt-heit (ⁱ‿ᵛ-) f ㊻ (f. versteckt 2) closeness. reserve, b.s. underhand ways pl., slyness, cunning.

ver-steh(e)n (ⁱ‿ᵛ)n (ⁱ‿ᵛ) ⊛a* **I** v/a. **1.** to understand, (begreifen) to comprehend, to grasp, F to twig, schwächer: to apprehend. (sich vorstellen) to conceive, realize, imagine; verstehen Sie (mich)?, a. verstanden? do (or did) you understand?; ich konnte das letzte Wort nicht ⁓ I could not catch (hold of) the last word; e-m ⁓ zu geben to give a p. s.th. to understand. to intimate (or hint, suggest) a th. to a p.; man hat mir ausdrücklich zu ⁓ gegeben, daß // I have been expressly given to understand (or explicitly told) that //. — **2.** Redensarten: aufs halbe Wort ⁓ to be quick of understanding, a. to see things at a glance; aus dem Grunde ⁓ to know thoroughly; was ist darunter verstanden? what is meant (or implied) by it? ⁓ Sie, was er damit sagen will? do you see what he is driving at?; (fein) Deutsch ⁓ to know (no) German; et. Botanik, Griechisch ꝛc. falsch ⁓ to misunderstand (or mis-

construe) a p.('s words); ⁓ Sie mich recht! don't misunderstand (or misapprehend) me!; ich verstehe die Sache nicht I cannot make it out, F I don't see it; f. Rummel 4, Spaß; et. unrecht ⁓ to misunderstand (or misconstrue) a th., to put a wrong construction on a th.; wohl verstanden it is (or let it be) understood; er versteht es zu erfinden he knows how to invent; ein wenig verstandener Geist a mind but little understood. — **II** sich ⁓ v/refl. **3. a)** sich mit e-m ⁓ to have an understanding with a p., to play into a p.'s hands; **b)** das versteht sich von selbst oder bisw. F am Rande that's understood or a matter of course; **c)** sich auf etwas ⁓ to understand (or know) a th. (thoroughly). to be at home in (or F a good hand at) a th.; sich zu et. ⁓ (bequemen) to accede (or agree, consent) to a th., to acquiesce in a th.; er wollte sich nicht dazu ⁓ he would not condescend to do it. — **III** ~ n ㉓ **4.** understanding; intellectual (or mental) faculty; vgl. Verstand.

ver-steifen (ⁱ‿ᵛ) **I** sich ⁓ v/refl. Börse: (von Preisen: fester werden) to stiffen, to harden. — **II Ver-steifung** f ㊻: ~ von Geldsätzen stiffening (or hardening of monetary rates.

ver-steigen (ⁱ‿ᵛ): sich ⁓ v/refl. ⓐ* to climb (or mount) too high, to lose o.s. among the lofty heights of a mountain; fig. so hoch habe ich mich nie verstiegen I (have) never aspired to (or as high as) that; er verstieg sich zur Behauptung he went (or ventured) so far as to assert. he had the audacity to maintain; Dichter ⁓ sich oft zu hoch poets often soar too high or take too high a flight; er hat sich zu weit verstiegen: **a)** he roamed too far; **b)** he aimed too high; verstiegen (hoch gespannt) high-flown; (überspannt) eccentric.

Ver-steigerer (ⁱ‿ᵛᵛ) m ㉒ auctioneer.

ver-steigern (ⁱ‿ᵛ) **I** v/a. ⓐa* to sell by auction, to put up for sale, to bring (or put) to the hammer. F to knock down (to the highest bidder). — **II** ~ n ㉓ und **Ver-steigerung** f ㊻ auction; public sale.

ver-steinern (ⁱ‿ᵛ) ⓐa* **I** v/a. to petrify; ⁓d: ⁊ petrescent: versteinert petrified, fossilized: versteinerte Frucht. ⁊ lithocarp. — **II** v n. (ſn) u. sich ⁓ v/refl. to become petrified, to petrify.

Ver-steinerung (ⁱ‿ᵛᵛ) f ㊻: (das Versteinern) petrification, fossilization, petrescence; (Versteinertes) petrifaction, (versteinerte Pflanze ꝛc.) auch: fossil (plant, &c.), (versteinertes Tier) petrified animal, ⁊ zoolite; ⁓ś-fähig ("...") a. ⊛ ⁊ petrifiable; ~ś-kunde f ㉒ science of fossils, ⁊ palæontology.

ver-stellbar (ⁱ‿ᵛᵛ) a. ㊺ adjustable, movable; ~keit f ㊻ mo(va)bility.

ver-stellen (ⁱ‿ᵛ) ⊛* **I** v/a. **1.** to (re-)move, to shift; (verkehrt stellen) to misplace; man hat mir alle Bücher verstellt all my books have been disarranged or put in wrong places. **2.** (versperren) e-n Weg ⁓ to bar (or block, obstruct) … — **3.** ⚔ = entstellen. —

4. (unkenntlich m., verleiden) to disfigure, disguise, durch Täuschung: to dissemble one's voice, handwriting, &c.; verstellt pretented (kindness, &c.); sham (love, &c.). — **II** sich ⁓ v/refl. **5.** (f. 4) to disguise o.s.; sich gegen ein ⁓ to act the hypocrite to(wards) a p., to appear in false colours before a p.; (die Wahrheit verbergen) to dissemble, feign, sham, F to put it on; sich gut ⁓ to act (one's part) well; to be a good actor (f actress). — **III** ~ n ㉓ u. **Ver-stellung** f ㊻ **6.** (f. 1) removal; disarrangement; (f. 2) obstruction; (f. 4 u. II) disguise; dissimulation; hypocrisy; sham; (Erdichtung) fiction.

Ver-stellungs-kunst ("...") f ㉒ art of dissimulation or shamming; hypocrisy.

ver-sterben (ⁱ‿ᵛ) v/n. (ſn) ⓑ* = sterben I; p.p. verstorben f. bsh. Artikel.

ver-steuern (ⁱ‿ᵛ) **I** v/a. ⓐa*: et. ⁓ to pay duty (für Spiritus ꝛc. auch: excise) on a th.; 🏛 Waren versteuert senden to send … duty-paid. — **II** ~ n ㉓ und **Ver-steu(e)rung** f ㊻ payment of (or paying) duty on (or for) a th.

ver-stieben (ⁱ‿ᵛ) v/n. (ſn) ⓑa* to fly away like dust, to be scattered (to the winds, F to go to atoms. [steigen.]

ver-stieg(en) (ⁱ‿ᵛ(ᵛ)) impf. (p.p.) v. versteigen.

ver-stimmen (ⁱ‿ᵛ) v/a. u. v/refl. ⊛* **1.** ♪ ein Instrument ⁓ to put … out of tune; verstimmt out of tune, von Klavieren a. too low; bisw. sich ⁓ to get out of tune. — **2.** fig. e-n ⁓ to put a p. out (of humour); verstimmt in a bad humour or temper; depressed, dejected. low spirited; put out, upset.

Ver-stimmt-heit (ⁱ‿ᵛ-), **Ver-stimmung** (ⁱ‿ᵛ-) f ㊻ **1.** ♪ being out of tune. — **2.** fig. ill-humour; depression (a. 🌑), dejectedness. dejected mood. [ben.]

ver-stob(en) (ⁱ‿ᵛ(ᵛ)) impf. (p.p.) v. verstie-

ver-stocht(en) (ⁱ‿ᵛ(ᵛ)) p.p. v. verstechen.

ver-stocken (ⁱ‿ᵛ) ⊛* **I** v/n. (ſn) **1.** = stocken¹ 4. — **II** v n. (ſn) u. sich ⁓ v/refl. **2.** (im Bösen beharren) to get hardened or obdurate, to grow callous. — **III** v/a. (f. 2) **3.** to harden, to make obdurate or callous; theol. verstocktes Herz impenitent heart; verstockter Sünder hardened (theol. unrepenting, unreclaimed) sinner. — **IV** ~ n ㉓ **4.** growing mouldy or musty.

Ver-stockt-heit (ⁱ‿ᵛ-), **Ver-stockung** (ⁱ‿ᵛ-) f ㊻ hardness of heart, obduracy, callousness; theol. impenitence.

ver-stohlen (ⁱ‿ᵛ)[verstehlen † = stehlen] a.㊺ **1.** ⚔ (diebisch) thievish. — **2.** stealthy, furtive; (heimlich) secret, clandestine, surreptitious, underhand; ⁓er Blick furtive (or sly) glance. — **3.** adv. ⁓er-maßen. ⁓weise (ⁱ‿ᵛᵛᵛ...) adv. stealthily, &c., a. F on the sly.

ver-stopfen (ⁱ‿ᵛ) v/a. und v/refl. ⊛* **1.** to stop (or plug) up, with einem Kork: to cork up, mit einem Spund: to bung up; eine Leitungsröhre, einen Kanal ꝛc.: to choke up, to obstruct; sich ⁓ to become choked or obstructed or F bunged up. — **2.** med. to constipate, to make costive; ⁓d constipating, binding; verstopft constipated, auf die Dauer: costive. — **II** ~ n ㉓ und **Ver-**

♪ Musik; ⁊ Wissenschaft; ♀ Pflanze; 🌐 Geographie; ☉ Technik; ⚒ Bergbau; ⚔ Militär; ⚓ Marine; 🏛 Handel; ✉ Post; 🚂 Eisenbahn.

ver-stöpfung f 🔹 (f. 1) stopping, stoppage; obstruction; (f. 2) med. ~ der Gefäße: ⚕ obliteration, des Leibes: constipation, hardness of the bowels, costiveness; die ~ aufhebend, lösend easing the bowels, aperient, purgative; an ~ leiden to be costive.

ver-stöpseln (f‿‿) v/a. 🔹a* to cork.

ver-storben (f‿‿) p.p. v. versterben (f. bs) u. a. 🔹(D9) deceased, defunct (beide a. jur.); längst ≈ dead and gone; m-e ≈e Mutter my late (F a. my poor) mother; 🔹 der, die ~e the deceased (p.); die ~en the dead, bſd. rel. the departed (spirits) pl.; ≈ als Zeitungsrubrik: Deaths pl.

ver-stören (f‿‿) v/a. 🔹* 1. to disturb, interfere with. — 2. e-n ≈ (außer sich bringen) to upset (or bewilder, trouble, agitate) a p.; verstört, a. disconcerted; ein verstörtes Gesicht haben, ganz verstört aussehen to have a wild look or a weird expression, to look bewildered or strange or distracted. — 3. ⤫ Diebe ≈ (verjagen) to expel ...

Ver-stört-heit (f‿⊥) f 🔹 bewildered (or troubled, agitated, wild) look.

Ver-stoß (f‿⊥) m 🔹a. offence against, breach of; (Fehler) mistake, error, fault; (fr.) faux pas; ~ gegen e-e Regel infraction of a rule; e-n ~ gegen et. m. to offend against a th., to violate a th.

ver-stoßen (f‿‿) 🔹a* I v/n. (h.) 1. gegen et. ≈ to offend against (or violate) a th., to act (or be) contrary to the rules of courtesy, &c., to commit (or be) a breach of etiquette; gegen die Wahrheit ≈ to run counter to the truth; gegen das Versmaß ≈d not in keeping with the metre, ⚕ antimetrical. — II v/a. 2. (von sich stoßen) to reject, to cast out, to repudiate; to divorce (or put away) one's wife, to cast off (or disown) a son, &c.; aus dem Hause 2c.: to eject, to turn (or put) out, aus e-r Gesellschaft: to expel. — III ~ n 🔹 und **Ver-stoßung** f 🔹 3. (f. 1) = Verstoß. — 4. (f. 2) rejection, repudiation; divorce, disownment; ejection, expulsion.

ver-streichen (f‿‿) 🔹a* I v/n. (ſu) von der Zeit: to pass away, slip by, elapse; die Frist ist verstrichen the appointed time has expired; 3 Jahre sind verstrichen seit // ... have gone by (or flown) since //. — II v/a. (verschmieren) to stop (or close, fill) up gaps, chinks, &c.; die Fugen ≈ to flush the joints; mit Gips ≈ to plaster; Ritzen ≈ to stop (or fill) up cracks; viel Butter 2c. ≈ (aufbrauchen) to use up ... in spreading. — III ~ n 🔹 und **Ver-streichung** f 🔹 (f. I) lapse of time; expiration; (f. II) stopping up, &c.

ver-streuen (f‿‿) I v/a. 🔹* 1. (hierhin u. dorthin streuen) to strew here and there; mehr gbr.: to disperse, to scatter, (in Unordnung bringen) to litter (F to mess) up; weithin verstreut scattered far and wide; geol. verstreute Felsblöcke erratic blocks pl. — 2. (zur Streu verbrauchen) to use up as litter. — II ~ n 🔹, **Ver-streuung** f 🔹 (f. 1) strewing; (f. 2) dispersal.

ver-stricheln (f‿‿) I v/a. 🔹a* Gravierkunst: to impaste. — II ~ n 🔹 und **Ver-strichelung** f 🔹 impastation.

ver-strich(en) impf. (p.p.) v. verstreichen.

ver-stricken (f‿‿) [stricken 1] I v/a. und v/refl. 🔹* 1. to use up (or spend) in knitting. — 2. fig. to ensnare, (bestrich) to entangle; sich ≈ to get entangled in a th. — II ~ n 🔹 u. **Ver-strickung** f 🔹 3. entanglement.

ver-studieren (f‿‿‿⊥‿) v/a. 🔹* to ruin one's health through studying, to spend time, money on one's (university) education or studies; verstudiert worn out with (hard) study.

ver-stümmeln (f‿‿‿) [mhd.] I v/a. und v/refl. 🔹a* to mutilate, to maim; (abstumpfen) to truncate; (verkrüppeln) to cripple; gr., rhet. to cut down; eine verstümmelte Rede, Stelle a curtailed speech, passage. — II ~ n 🔹 und **Ver-stümmelung** f 🔹 mutilation, truncation; curtailment; von Kunstwerken oft: vandalism.

ver-stummen (f‿‿‿) I v/n. (ſu) 🔹* to grow (or to be struck) dumb, to become speechless or silent, vor Erstaunen: to be dumbfounded; ≈ m. to (reduce to) silence; alles war verstummt all was hushed in silence. — II ~ n 🔹 f. Verstummung.

Ver-stümmler (f‿‿‿) m 🔹, ~in f 🔹 mutilator, v. Kunstwerken: vandal.

Ver-stummung (f‿‿‿) f 🔹 loss of (one's) speech or voice, med.: ⚕ aphony.

ver-stünde (f‿‿) subj. impf. v. verstehen.

ver-stutzen (f‿‿) v/a. 🔹* = stutzen 1.

Ver-such (f‿⊥) m 🔹c. trial, für wissenschaftliche 2c. Zwecke: experiment; Fußball: try; (Probe) test; (Unternehmen) attempt; (Anstrengung) effort; ~e anstellen to make experiments, to experimentalize; einen ~ mit e-m, et. m. to give a p., a th. a trial; to try a p., a th.; to put a p., a th. to the test; ~(s)bohren ⤫ n 🔹 experimental boring, exploratory work.

ver-suchen (f‿‿) I v/a. u. v/refl. 🔹* 1. to try (an on), Schwieriges: to attempt (zu ... to mit inf.); (auf die Probe stellen) to (put to the) test; (prüfen, kosten) to taste; es mit e-m ≈ to give a p. a trial, to put a p. to the test; sein Glück, sein Heil ≈ to try one's luck, to seek one's fortune; alles ≈, um zu // to make every (possible) effort (or to do one's utmost) in order to //; der Kranke versuchte aufzustehen the invalid made an effort (or attempt) to get up; et zu erlangen ≈ to try for a th.; sich an et. ≈ to try one's hand at a th.; sich auf allen Gebieten ≈ to try everything. — 2. er hat sich (ethischer dat.) viel versucht, er hat sich (acc.) in der Welt versucht he has seen (a good deal of) the world. — 3. e-n ≈ (zu verlocken suchen) to tempt (away) a p., (to try to) entice a p., to lead a p. into temptation. — II ~ n 🔹 4. = Versuch.

Ver-sucher (f‿⊥‿) m 🔹, ~in f 🔹 tempter (bſd. bibl. = Teufel), f temptress; (Verführer[in]) seducer, seductive (or fascinating) person.

Ver-suchs-kaninchen (f‿‿‿...) f 🔹 med., &c. rabbit used for vivisection (purposes); =methode f experimental (or tentative) method; =person f, med., &c. person experimented upon, subject (treated); =schießen ⚔ n trial gun (or artillery) practice, gunnery test; =station f station for (scientific) experiments; ≈weise adv. (F a. a.) by way of (a) trial or (an) experiment; 🔹 ≈ nehmen to accept (or take) on approval.

Ver-suchung (f‿⊥‿) f 🔹 temptation, enticement; in ~ führen: a) rel. to lead into temptation; b) to tempt away; in ~ kommen: a) rel. to be led into temptation; b) to be tempted to //.

ver-sudeln (f‿‿‿) v/a. 🔹* to bedaub, besmear, soil, F to mess up.

ver-sumpf/en (f‿‿‿) I v/n. (ſu) 🔹* 1. to become marshy or boggy or swampy; versumpftes Land boggy (or swampy) country, fens pl. — 2. fig. to sink into (the slough of) corruption or depravity, F to go to the bad. — II ~ n 🔹 u. **Ver-sumpfung** f 🔹 3. conversion into a swamp, swampy condition.

ver-sündig/en (f‿‿‿) I sich ≈ v/refl. 🔹* to sin (an e-m, etwas against a p., a th.), to trespass, transgress; sich an e-m ≈, a. to wrong a p. — II ~ n 🔹 u. **Ver-sündigung** f 🔹 🔹 sinning, trespass(ing), transgression, offence (an e-m against a p.); wrong inflicted on a p.

ver-sungen (f‿‿‿) p.p. von versingen.

ver-sunken (f‿‿‿) p.p. v. versinken; ~heit f 🔹 bſd. fig. decline, degradation; sittliche: depravity, demoralization.

ver-süßen (f‿‿‿) I v/a. und v/refl. 🔹* to sweeten, mit Zucker: to sugar; chm.: ⚗ to edulcorate; (zu süß m.) to make too sweet or too sugary; sich ≈ to become sweet(er). — II ~ n 🔹 und **Ver-süßung** f 🔹 sweetening, ⚗ edulcoration.

vers-weise (f⊥...) adv. verse by verse; =zeichen n 🔹 typ. verse.

vert. abbr. = vertatur.

Ver-täfelung ⊕ (f‿‿⊥‿) f 🔹 wainscot-[ing.]

ver-tagen (f‿‿) I v/a. u. v/refl. 🔹* 1. to adjourn a meeting, &c., to prorogue parliament; sich ≈ to adjourn. — 2. 🔹 vertagter (fällig gewordener) Wechsel bill which has run out or is due. — II ~ n 🔹 u. **Ver-tagung** f 🔹 3. (f. 1) adjournment, prorogation.

ver-tan (f‿⊥) p.p. von vertun.

ver-tändeln (f‿‿‿) v/a. 🔹a*: die Zeit ≈ to trifle (or idle) away one's time; ſu Geld ≈ to fribble away one's money.

ver-tanzen (f‿‿‿) v/a. 🔹*: die Nacht ≈ to spend (or pass) the night in dancing; e-n Kummer 2c. ≈ to dance off one's grief, &c.

ver-tat (f‿⊥) ind. impf. v. vertun.

vertatur (w‿⊥‿) [lt. es (das Blatt) werde umgewendet] meist abbr. P. T. O. (= please turn over).

ver-täuen ⚓ (f‿‿‿) v/a. 🔹* = verteien.

ver-taumeln (f‿‿‿) v/a. 🔹a* to spend in a whirl of excitement.

ver-tauschbar (f‿‿⊥) a. 🔹 exchangeable; math. (versetzbar) permutable; ~keit f 🔹 exchangeability, permutableness.

ver-tauschen (f‿‿‿) I v/a. 🔹* 1. et. gegen (für, mit, um) et. ≈ to exchange s.th. for a th.; Plätze ≈ to (ex-)change places; 🔹 Waren ≈ to barter goods. — 2. math. oft: to substitute

---

Signs (see page XVII): F familiar; P vulgar; F flash; ⤫ rare; † obsolete (died); * new word (born); ⁺⁺ incorrect; ♪ music;

to permut(at)e. — 3. = verwechseln. — II ~ n 23 und **Ver-tauschung** f 40 4. (f. 1) exchange; (Austausch) interchange; (f. 2) substitution; permutation.

ver-tausend-fachen (f˘ᴗᴗ˘ᴗ), ˘fältigen (....ᴗᴗᴗ) v/a. 88* to increase a thousandfold.

verte (wᴗ˘-) [lt. wende um!] = vertatur.

ver-teidigen (f˘ᴗᴗ) [† Teidig = Tageding] jur. u. × I v/a. und v/refl. 88* to defend one's life, &c., to uphold (or support) truth, &c., to advocate (or plead) a cause, to stand up for (or to vindicate) one's right, to maintain a proposition; sich 2 (beschützen) to protect o.s., to take care of o.s.; sich 2 (rechtfertigen) to justify o.s.; × sich heldenmütig 2 to offer a heroic resistance. — II ~ n 23 f. Verteidigung.

Ver-teidiger (f˘ᴗᴗᴗ) m 22, ~in f 40 defender, upholder, supporter, advocate, jur. counsel for the defendant or prisoner; Fußball: back(s pl.).

Ver-teidigung (f˘ᴗᴗᴗ) f 40 (f. verteidigen I) defence, support(ing), advocacy, vindication, plea(ding), maintenance; protection; justification; zur ~ dienend defensive; × sich auf die ~ beschränken to keep on the defensive.

Ver-teidigungs-anstalten (f˘ᴗᴗᴗ...) f/pl. 42 preparations pl. for defence; =bündnis n defensive alliance; =grund m plea for the defence, ground on which to base (or to found) a defence; =krieg m defensive war; =lini-e f line of defence; =los a. defenceless, unarmed; =maßregeln f/pl. defensive measures; =mittel n means of defence; =rede f =s Advokaten: defence, plea(ding); weitS. apology; =schrift f apologetic pamphlet, jur. written defence; =stand × m: e-e Festung ꝛc. in ~ setzen to put ... in(to) a state of defence; =stellung f defensive position; =waffe f defensive weapon, weapon of defence; =weise f mode of defence; 2weise adv. by way of defence; 2 verfahren to act on the defensive; =werke × n/pl. defensive works; =zustand m state of defence.

-**er-teien** ↓ (f˘ᴗᴗ) v/a. 88*: ein Boot 2 to moor ...

-**er-teilbar** (f˘ᴗ-) a. 66 distributable, easy to distribute or to share.

-**er-teilen** (f˘ᴗᴗ) I v/a. und v/refl. 88* to distribute, to parcel out (unter among), an die dazu Berechtigten: to apportion to or among, to allot to; (unter sich teilen) to share; (teilen) to divide; Farben 2 to spread colours; milde Gaben 2 to dispense charity (among the poor); thea. die Rollen 2 to assign the parts; Steuern 2 to assess Taxes; sich auf viele 2 to (have to) be divided among many; path. e-e Geschwulst verteilt sich ... is dissolving, .. disappears. — II n 23 f. Verteilung.

-**er-teiler** (f˘ᴗᴗ) m 22, ~in f 40 distributer; ~scheibe f tel. distributor.

-**er-teilung** (f˘ᴗᴗ) f 40 distribution, apportionment, allotment; assessment of taxes; (Einteilung) division; =ue ~ repartition; paint. richtige ~ on Licht und Schatten right apportionment of light and shade; × ~ in die Quartiere quartering; thea. ~ der Rollen, oft: casting (or cast of) the characters of a play; ~s-reservoir n 42 Wasserleitung: distributing-reservoir.

ver-teuen ↓ (f˘ᴗ) v/a. 88* = verteien.

ver-teuern (f˘ᴗᴗ) I v/a. 92a* to make dear(er), to raise in price, to enhance the value of. — II n 23, **Verteu(e)rung** f 40 raising the price(s) of.

ver-teufelt (f˘ᴗᴗ) a. 66 bsd. in Flüchen: devilish, deuced, infernal; Les Geschäft confounded business; Ler Kerl devil of a fellow; adv. ein 2 feines Mädel an uncommonly fine (or awfully smart) girl; 2 klug marvellously shrewd; es war 2 heiß it was terribly (F infernally, deucedly) hot.

Ver-teurung (f˘ᴗᴗ) f 40 f. Verteuerung.

ver-tiefen (f˘ᴗᴗ) I v/a. und v/refl. 88* 1. to deepen, to make deeper; to sink a well, &c.; (austiefen) to hollow out, Bildhauerei: to chisel out; vertieft (adv.) geschnitten deeply engraved or incised, ⚘ diaglyphic. — 2. sich 2 to deepen, to grow deeper or (more) hollow; sich in et. (geistig) 2 to plunge into a th.; sich in Gedanken 2 to become absorbed (or engrossed, wrapt) in thought; in Studien vertieft deeply engaged in study. — II ~ n 23 3. = Vertiefung 1.

Ver-tieft-sein (f˘ᴗ-) n 23 preoccupation.

Ver-tiefung (f˘ᴗᴗ) f 40 1. deepening, hollowing; durch Graben: excavation. — 2. hollow, cavity, (Falz) groove, notch, in der Mauer: recess, niche.

ver-tieren (f˘ᴗᴗ) 88* I v/n. (ſn) to grow brutal, to become brutalized. — II v/a. to brutalize. — III ~ n 23 u. **Ver-tierung** f 40 brutalization.

vertikal (wᴗᴗ˘!) [lt.] a. 66 = senkrecht; ~linie f 42 vertical line; ~projektion f Zeichenkunst: orthographic projection; ~schnitt m vertical section.

Vertiko (wᴗᴗ-) [~w, Berliner Fabrikant] m (n) 50 (feines Schränkchen, Zierschrank) elegant cabinet.

ver-tilgbar (f˘ᴗ-) a. 66 exterminable, eradicable; (verwischbar) effaceable.

ver-tilgen (f˘ᴗᴗ) I v/a. 88* to exterminate; (ausrotten) to extirpate, eradicate, uproot; (zerstören) to destroy; (vernichten) to annihilate, to crush; (auslöschen) to extinguish, to efface; F co. (auffessen) to polish off a goose, &c.; (austrinken) to discuss a bottle of wine. — II ~ n 23 = Vertilgung.

Ver-tilger (f˘ᴗᴗ) m 22, ~in f 40 exterminator, extirpator; destroyer.

Ver-tilgung (f˘ᴗᴗ) f 40 extermination, extirpation, eradication, destruction.

Ver-tilgungs-krieg (f˘ᴗ-ᴗ!) m 62 war of extermination, war to the knife.

ver-tonen ↓ (f˘ᴗᴗ) 88* (in Musik setzen, komponieren) to set to music, to compose.

ver-tönen (f˘ᴗᴗ) v/n. (ſn) 88* = verklingen.

ver-trackt (f˘ᴗᴗ) [mhd. verwirrt] a. 66 1. von Personen: a) körperlich: distorted; b) geistig: strange (in one's manner), eccentric, odd, queer. — 2. v. Dingen: (verwickelt) intricate; auch = fatal.

Ver-trag (f˘ᴗ˘) [mhd.] m ⊙c. agreement, schriftlicher: contract, zwischen Staaten: treaty; bindender ~ compact; (Übereinkunft) agreement, convention, ⚪ composition, settlement; × ~ behufs Übergabe capitulation; e-n ~ abschließen to make a contract, to conclude a treaty, to come to an agreement, ⚪ to strike a bargain.

ver-tragen (f˘ᴗᴗ) [ahd.] 85b* I v/a., bisw. a. v/n. (h.) (f. 5) 1. to carry away; (verlegen) to mislay. — 2. Kleider 2 (verbrauchen) to wear out ... — 3. (ertragen) to bear, endure, tolerate, Schmerzliches: to suffer, Verluste: to sustain; f. Puff 2 3; können Sie die See(reisen) gut 2? are you a good sailor?; er kann viel Wein 2 he can stand a good deal of wine. — 4. ∿: a) Personen (mit=ea.) 2 (aussöhnen) to conciliate ..., to make peace between ...; b) = schlichten 1 fig. — 5. ∿ (e-n Vertrag schließen mit) to treat with. — II v/refl. 6. sich mit e-m (wieder) 2 to settle one's differences with a p., to make it up (again) with a p. — 7. sich (gut, schlecht) mit=ea. 2 to agree (well, ill) together, to get on (well, ill) together; sie können sich nicht mit=ea. 2 they do not hit it off well, they are not made for each other; sich wie Hund und Katze 2 to lead a cat-and-dog life. — 8. Sachen: (mit=ea. vereinbar sein) to agree (together); to be consistent (or compatible) with; to tally with; Grün und Blau 2 sich nicht green and blue don't blend (or don't go) well together.

ver-traglich (f˘ᴗᴗ) a. 66 u. adv. (dem Vertrage nach) (stipulated) by contract, agreed upon; 2 zu et. verpflichtet sein to be bound by contract to do a th.

ver-träglich (f˘ᴗᴗ) a. 66 1. (ant. zänkisch) von Personen: conciliatory; (umgänglich) sociable, genial; (gutmütig) good-natured, easy-going, accommodating, yielding; (friedfertig) peaceable. — 2. von Sachen: compatible, consistent.

Ver-träglichkeit (~-) f 40 1. conciliatory nature; sociability, geniality; easy-going disposition; peaceableness. — 2. compatibility, consistency.

Ver-trags-artikel (f˘ᴗ...) m 62 article of agreement; =bruch m breach of contract.

ver-trag-schließend (f˘ᴗ...) a. 66: Le Teile contracting parties pl.; ~e(r) m f ⚪, =schließer m 22 contractor, jur. u. pol. contracting party.

ver-trags-mäßig (f˘ᴗ...) a. 66 u. adv. in accordance with an agreement, stipulated, agreed upon, adv. according to (⚪ as per) agreement; =mäßigkeit f conformity with an agreement; =recht n: a) right of concluding treaties; b) treaty-right; =urkunde f deed embodying an agreement, indenture; =strafe f jur. =Konventionalstrafe; 2widrig a. contrary to an agreement or a contract; =widrigkeit f contravention to an agreement or a contract.

ver-trällern (f˘ᴗᴗ) v/a. 92a* to spend time in trilling or singing or humming.

ver-trank (f˘ᴗ) ind. impf. v. vertrinken.

ver-trat (f˘ᴗ) ind. impf. v. vertreten.

[vertrauen] — 1060 — [verübeln]

ver-trauen¹ (⌣⌣) ⓺* **I** v/n. (h.): e-m ⌣, auf e-n, et. ⌣ to (put one's) trust in a p., a th.; to put (or place) confidence in a p., a th.; (e-m unbedingt trauen) to confide in a p.; (sich verlassen auf) to put one's reliance (or to rely) upon; * ⌣, daß // (sich darauf verlassen, daß) to be confident that //; rel. auf Gott ⌣ putting one's trust in God, confiding in the Lord; zu sehr auf sich (selbst) ⌣ too self-reliant, overconfident. — **II** v/a. und v/refl.: e-m et., sich e-m ⌣ = anvertrauen.

Ber-trauen² (⌣⌣) n ㉓ trust; ~ auf oder in e-n, ~ zu e-m h. to trust a p., to have confidence (or faith) in a p.; im ~ auf Ihre Nachsicht trusting to (or relying on) your indulgence; e-m et. (ganz) im ~ sagen oder offenbaren to tell a p. a th. (quite) confidentially or privately or in (strict) confidence, to confide a th. to a p.; e-m sein ~ schenken to put one's trust in a p., to place confidence in a p.; ganz im ~ gesagt strictly confidential or private; ins ~ ziehen to take into confidence, to make a confident of.

Ber-trauens=amt (⌣²⌣...) n ㉒ confidential post; **=mann** m reliable man, confidant; **=mißbrauch** m abuse of a p.'s confidence; **=person** f person who can be trusted or confided in; (Vertraute) confidante; **=posten** m position (or office) of trust. vgl. =amt; **=sache** f confidential matter; ⌣selig, ⌣voll a. ⓺ full of confidence, confiding, easily trusting; **=seligkeit** f blind confidence; **=stellung** f position of trust; **=votum** n vote of confidence; ⌣würdig a. trustworthy, worthy of confidence; **=würdigkeit** f trustworthiness.

ver-trauern (⌣⌣) ⓶a* **I** v/a.: sein Leben ⌣ to pass ... mournfully or sorrowfully or in mourning. — **II** sich ⌣ v/refl. to pine away, to languish.

ver-traulich (⌣⌣) a. ⓺ 1. = vertrauensselig. — 2. (traulich verkehrend) intimate, familiar; er tut sehr ⌣ he is very affable or friendly or F nice. — 3. ⌣e Mitteilung confidential (or private, friendly) communication. F sly hint.

Ber-traulichkeit (⌣⌣⌣) f ⓺ (vertraulich) 1. confidence. — 2. intimacy, familiarity; affability; sich gewisse ~en herausnehmen to take certain liberties. — 3. confidentiality; privacy.

ver-träumen (⌣⌣) v/a. ⓺* to spend in dreams or reveries, to dream away; sein Glück ⌣ (verscherzen) to miss one's chance (or opportunity) while dreaming; die verträumte Zeit the time wasted in (idle) reveries; eine verträumte Natur a dreamy nature.

ver-traut (⌣⌣) **I** a. ⓺ 1. (eng befreundet) intimate, familiar; mit e-m ⌣ sein, auf dem Fuße ⌣ mit e-m stehen to be intimate (or on terms of intimacy) with a p., F to be hand and glove with a p.; ein sehr ⌣er Freund a very intimate (or special) friend. — 2. mit et. ⌣ (genau bekannt) sein to be intimately acquainted with a th., to be conversant with (or versed in) a th.; sich mit et. ⌣ m. to make o.s. conversant with a th., to familiarize o.s. with a th., to master a th., durch Studium: to make a thorough study of a th. — **II** = e(r) s. ⓺ 3. confidant(e f), confidential (or intimate) friend, stärker: bosom-friend; j-e ~en his intimates, his daily companions pl.

Ber-traut-heit (⌣⌣⌣) f ⓺ 1. intimacy, familiarity. — 2. ~ mit et. intimate acquaintance (or familiarity) with (or knowledge of) a th.

ver-treiben (⌣⌣) **I** v/a. ⓺¹* 1. to drive (or chase) away, to expel; (auseinander-treiben) to disperse, to scatter; sich (dat.) die Grillen ⌣ to dispel care or grief; med. e-e Krankheit ⌣ to cure a disease, to remove a complaint; sich (dat.) die Zeit mit et. ⌣ to beguile (or while away) one's time with a th. — 2. mit prp. e-n aus seinem Besitztum ⌣ to dispossess a p., gerichtlich: to evict (or eject) a p.; e-n aus dem Lande ⌣ to banish (or exile) a p., (ächten) to outlaw; e-n aus einem Orte ⌣ to eject a p. from a place, to oust a p.; e-n aus seiner Wohnung ⌣ to turn a p. out of house and home; ✠ den Feind aus e-r Stellung ⌣ to dislodge (or expel) the enemy; Gewalt mit Gewalt ⌣ to repel force by force; e-n von seinem Platze ⌣ to turn a p. out of a place, to oust a p.; von Haus und Hof vertriebener Pächter evicted farmer. — 3. ⌣ Waren ⌣ (absetzen) to dispose of goods, to clear (one's) stock, to retail commodities. — 4. paint. Farben ⌣ (abstufen) to soften colours, to tone (or shade) down tints. — **II** ~ n ㉓ 5. = Vertreibung. — **III** Ver-triebene(r) s. ⓺ 6. exile, outlaw; fugitive.

Ber-treib-pinsel ⊙ (⌣⁻·⌣) m ㉒ paint. softener.

Ber-treibung (⌣⌣⌣) f ⓺ (s. vertreiben I) expulsion; dispossession; ejection; ✠ dislodgment; ⌣ = Vertrieb; paint. softening of colours.

ver-tretbar (⌣⌣⌣) a. ⓺ capable of being substituted or replaced.

ver-treten (⌣⌣) **I** v/a. und v/refl. ⓶d* 1. sich (dat.) den Fuß ⌣ to sprain one's foot (in treading). — 2. sich (dat.) die Beine ⌣ (durch Gehen wieder gelenkig m.) to walk the stiffness out of (F to stretch) one's legs. — 3. (tretend zerstören) to tread (or trample) under foot, to crush in treading. — 4. e-m den Weg ⌣ (versperren) to bar (or block) a p.'s way or passage. — 5. a) die Stelle j-s ⌣, e-n ⌣ to take a p.'s place, to replace a p.; f. Vaterstelle: b) ⌣ auf dem Markte nicht ⌣ (zu finden) sein not to be found in the market. — 6. e-n, j-s Sache ⌣ (verteidigen) to plead (or advocate, uphold, support) a p.'s cause; to intercede on behalf of a p., to act as a p.'s agent or legal adviser, to look after a p.'s interest; (für e-n auftreten) to represent a p., to act (or appear) for (or on behalf of) a p.; parl. e-n Wahlbezirk ⌣ to sit for a borough or county; die von ihm ⌣e Wählerschaft his constituency. — **II** ~ n ㉓ 7. = Vertretung 1.

Ber-treter (⌣⌣⌣) m ㉒, ~in f ㊵ 1. = Stellvertreter. — 2. (Fürsprecher) advocate, intercessor; ~ des Volkes representative of the people; ✠ representative (of a firm), agent, factor.

Ber-treterschaft (⌣⌣⌣) f ⓺ body of representatives, representative body.

Ber-tretung (⌣⌣⌣) f ⓺ 1. (zu vertreten 1:) spraining one's foot; (zu 2:) stretching one's legs; (zu 5, a. 6:) replacement; advocacy, intercession; representation; die ~ des beurlaubten N. übernimmt Herr P. Mr. P. undertakes duty for Mr. N. who is on leave; in ~ des // in the place of //; as representative of //. — 2. ✠ (Agentur) agency.

Ber-tretungs=kosten (⌣⌣⌣...) pl. ⓶ expenses pl. of (or accruing from) representation; ⌣weise adv. (F a. a. ⓺) as (a) representative, a. vicariously.

Ber-trieb¹ ✠ (⌣⌣) m ⓶c. sale (or clearance) of goods or stock. [vertreiben.]

ver-trieb²(en) (⌣⌣(⌣)) impf. (p.p.) v.f

Ber-triebs=gesellschaft (⌣⁻²...) f trading company; ⌣recht n Buchhandel: copyright.

ver-trinken (⌣⌣) v/a. ⓶i* to spend in drinking or on drink, to drink away; die Nacht ⌣ to go on drinking (or carousing, F boozing) all night.

ver-trocknen (⌣⌣⌣) v/n. (sn) ⓶b* to dry up, to be(come) parched (up), hort. a. to wither, to shrivel up; das vertrocknete Laub the dry foliage. poet. the sear leaf; ⌣ung f ⓺ drying up.

ver-trödeln (⌣⌣⌣) v/a. ⓶a* 1. die Zeit 2c. ⌣ to dawdle (or idle, fritter, F muddle, fribble) away... — 2. (trödelnd verkaufen) to hawk about, to sell as a street-vendor or hawker.

ver-trösten (⌣⌣⌣) **I** v/a. u. v/refl. ⓶* 1. e-n ⌣ to comfort (or console) a p. — 2. e-n auf et. ⌣ to hold out hopes (for the future) to a p., to feed a p. with hope or promises; von e-m Tage zum anderen ⌣ to put off from one day to the next. — **II** ~ n ㉓ u. Ber-tröstung f ⓺ 3. holding out hopes; empty promise(s pl.).

ver-trug (⌣⌣) ind. impf. v. vertragen.

ver-trumpfen (⌣⌣⌣) v/a. ⓺* Spiel: alle seine Trümpfe od. sich ⌣ v/refl. to play (out) all one's trumps.

ver-trunken (⌣⌣⌣) p.p. von vertrinken.

Ber-tuer (⌣⌣) m ㉒, ~in f ㊵ waster, spendthrift. [⓺ extravagant.]

ver-tuerisch (⌣⌣⌣), **ver-tulich** (⌣⌣⌣) a.f

ver-tun (⌣⌣) ⓺⁵* **I** v/n. (h.) to do one's duty. — **II** v/a. (verschwenden) to lavish, squander, waste; (verbrauchen) to use up; er hat wenig zu ⌣ he has little to spare; er hat alles vertan he has spent everything, he has run through all his property.

ver-tuschen (⌣⌣⌣) [mhd.] **I** v/a. ⓺¹* **ver-tuscheln** ⓶a*) to hush up, to keep snug or dark; (bemänteln) to disguise, (beschönigen) to gloss over, to palliate, (nicht ruchbar werden l.) to suppress; vertuschte Sache hushed-up affair, s.th kept dark, suppressed fact. — **II** ~ n ㉓ u. **Ber-tusch(e)lung** f ⓺ hushing up; palliation, suppression.

ver-übeln (⌣⌣⌣) v/a. ⓶a* e-m et. ⌣ to blame a p. for a th.; s. verargen.

Zeichen (s. S. XVII): F familiär; P Volkssprache; ⌐ Gaunersprache; ⌣ selten; † alt (auch gestorben); * neu (auch geboren); ⌣ unrichtig

[verüben] — 1061 — [verwalten]

ver-üb|en (ⁱ⁻ᶻ⁻) I v a. ⊛*: ein Verbrechen ⁓ to commit (jur. a. to perpetrate) …; Gewalttaten ⁓ to practise deeds of violence; Grausamkeiten an e-m ⁓ to use (or to act with) cruelty towards a p.; die von ihm verübten Streiche the tricks *pl.* played by him. — II ~ n ㉓ = V/ung.
Ver-über(…) m ㉒, **~in** f ㊷: e-s Verbrechens perpetrator of a crime.
Ver-übung (…) f ㊻ committing an offence; commission, perpetration.
ver-un-edeln (ⁱ⁻ᶻ⁻⁻) v a. (u. sich ⁓ v/refl.) ㉒a*: (sich) ⁓ to make (or become) ignoble, to debase (o.s.).
ver-un-ehren (ⁱ⁻ᶻ⁻) I v/a. ⊛* to dishonour, disgrace, discredit, disparage. — II ~ n ㉓ u. **Ver-un-ehrung** f ㊻ dishonour(ing), disparagement.
ver-un-einig|en (ⁱ⁻ᶻ⁻⁻) I v/a. u. v/refl. ⊛* to disunite; sich ⁓ to disagree, to fall out (vgl. entzweien I u. II). — II ~ n ㉓ u. **V/ung** f ㊻ disuniting, (sowing) discord; disunion; disagreement.
ver-un-glimpf|en (ⁱ⁻ᶻ⁻⁻) I v/a. ⊛* = verunehren, auch: to detract from, to revile, to vilify, F to run down, to drag into the mire, to pick holes in; (verleumden) to slander, backbite, defame, calumniate, durch eine Schmähschrift: to libel. — II ~ n ㉓ f. V/ung.
Ver-un-glimpfer (ⁱ⁻ᶻ⁻⁻) m ㉒ reviler, slanderer, defamer, calumniator.
Ver-un-glimpfung (…) f ㊻ disparagement; vilification; slander(ing), defamation, calumniation, libel(ling).
ver-un-glück|en (ⁱ⁻ᶻ⁻⁻) I v/n. (ſn) ⊛*: 1. to meet with an accident, to come to grief; (zugrunde gehen) to perish; V/te(r) s. ⑥ victim; ⚓ das Schiff ist v/t… was wrecked or lost; die V/ten the victims *pl.*, the killed and injured, those who perished. — 2. (mißglücken) to miscarry, fail; v/ter Versuch abortive attempt. — II ~ n ㉓ u. V/ung f ㊻ 3. accidental death or loss; casualty. — 4. miscarriage, failure, ill success.
ver-un-heiligen (ⁱ⁻ᶻ⁻⁻) I v/a. ⊛* to desecrate a holy shrine, &c. — II ~ n ㉓ u. **Ver-un-heiligung** f ㊻ desecration.
ver-un-reinig|en (ⁱ⁻ᶻ⁻⁻) I v/a. u. v/refl. ⊛* to soil, to dirty, fig. to defile; sich ⁓, auch: to begrime (or bespatter) o.s.; die Luft ⁓ to vitiate (or contaminate, infect) …; Wasser ꝛc. ⁓ to pollute …; Aufschrift: dieser Ort darf nicht v/t werden! commit no nuisance!, auch: decency forbids! — II ~ n ㉓, V/ung f ㊻ soiling, fig. defilement; vitiation, contamination, infection; pollution.
ver-un-stalten (ⁱ⁻ᶻ⁻⁻) I v/a. ⊛* to disfigure, deform, deface, to put out of shape, to spoil (the look of). — II ~ n ㉓ u. **Ver-un-staltung** f ㊻ disfigurement, defacement.
ver-un-treuen (ⁱ⁻ᶻ⁻) I v/a. ⊛* to administer unfaithfully, anvertrautes Gut: to embezzle, to misappropriate, jur. auch: to peculate. — II ~ n ㉓ = Veruntreuung. ǀdefaulter, jur. peculator.ǀ
Ver-un-treuer (ⁱ⁻ᶻ⁻) m ㉒ embezzler,ǀ
Ver-un-treuung (ⁱ⁻ᶻ⁻⁻) f ㊻ embezzlement, misappropriation, jur. auch: peculation, malversation; ⁓ öffentlicher Gelder defalcation.

ver-un-zieren (ⁱ⁻ᶻ⁻⁻) v a. ⊛* = verunstalten, a. to mar; (verderben) to spoil.
ver-ursach|en (ⁱ⁻ᶻ⁻⁻) I v/a. ⊛* to cause; (Anlaß geben zu) to occasion, to give rise to; (hervorbringen) to produce, (hervorrufen) to call forth; Kosten ⁓ to involve (or entail) expense; e-m schwere Kosten ⁓ to put a p. to heavy expense. — II ~ n ㉓ = V/ung.
Ver-ursacher (ⁱ⁻ᶻ⁻⁻) m ㉒ originator, prime mover, author; instigator.
Ver-ursachung (…) f ㊻ occasion(ing).
ver-urteil|en (ⁱ⁻ᶻ⁻⁻) I v/a. ⊛* to sentence (vgl. verdammen), zu einer Geldbuße: to fine, zum Tode: to pass a sentence of death (or a death-sentence) upon; zum Tode verurteilt sentenced to death, lying under a sentence of death, bib. ehm. cast for death. — II ~ n ㉓ = Verurteilung.
Ver-urteilte(r) (ⁱ⁻ᶻ⁻⁻) s. ㊲ condemned person; convict(ed criminal).
Ver-urteilung (ⁱ⁻ᶻ⁻⁻) f ㊻ condemnation, durch Geschworene: verdict, zum Tode: (passing a) death-sentence upon a p.
ver-viel=fachen (ⁱ⁻ᶠⁱ⁻⁻⁻). ⁓fältigen (ⁱ⁻ᶠᵘ⁻⁻) I v/a. u. v/refl. ⊛* (sich) ⁓ to multiply, (nachbilden) to reproduce, to copy. — II ~ n ㉓ ſ. Vervielfältigung.
Ver-vielfältiger ⊙ (ⁱ⁻ᶠᵘ⁻⁻) m ㉒ mech. multiplying gear, multiplier.
Ver-vielfältigung (ⁱ⁻ᶠᵘ⁻⁻) f ㊻ multiplication; ~s=glas n ㉕ opt. multiplying glass, ⌀ polyscope, polyoptron; ~s=recht n right of reproduction.
ver-vierfachen (ⁱ⁻ᶠⁱ⁻⁻⁻) v/a. ⊛* to quadruple, to multiply by four.
ver-vollkommn|en (ⁱ⁻ᶠᵒ⁻⁻⁻) I v/a. u. sich ⁓ v/refl. ㉒b*: (sich) ⁓ to perfect (o.s.); vgl. verbessern. — II ~ n ㉓ = V/ung.
Ver-vollkommner (…) m ㉒ one who perfects, perfecter, ⊙ a.: finisher.
Ver-vollkommnung (…) f ㊻ perfection; improvement; ⁓s=fähig (″…) a. ㊻ capable (or susceptible) of perfection, perfectible; ~s=fähigkeit f ㊷: ⌀ perfectibility.
ver-vollständigen (ⁱ⁻ᶠᵒ⁻⁻⁻) I v/a. ⊛* to (make) complete, to supplement, ⚔ auch: to bring up to the full number or total; ⚔ das Lager wieder ⁓ to replenish one's stock, a.: to take (fresh) stock. — II ~ n ㉓ u. **Ver-vollständigung** f ㊻ completion.
ver-wachen (ⁱ⁻ᶻ⁻⁻) v/a. ⊛*: die Nacht ⁓ to (keep) watch through the night, to sit up all night.
ver-wachs|en (ⁱ⁻ᶻ⁻⁻) ⊛b* I v/a. 1. ⌀ Kleidungsstücke ⁓ to outgrow garments, to grow out of clothes; eine Narbe ⁓ to lose a scar through (or in) growing. — II sich ⁓ v/refl. ⊛*. (überwachsen) to become overgrown with s.th. — 3. sich zu et. ⁓ to grow into s.th. — III v/n. (ſn) 4. (wachsend sich ausfüllen) to coalesce, to fill up (in growing); die Wunde verwächst the wound is healing (up) or closing. — 5. (wachsend sich verbinden) to grow together; (sich verschlingen) to interlace; dicht ⁓ ⚘ p.p. v. Blüten: ⌀ synanthous; mit den Blättern: ⌀ gamophyllous, symphyllous; mit den Kelchblättern: ⌀ gamosepalous; mit den Staubbeuteln: ⌀ synantherous, syngenesian; orn. mit den Zehen: ⌀ syngenesious. — 6. (fehlerhaft wachsen) to grow out of shape, to become deformed; von Personen: (buckelig werden) to grow hunchbacked; ⁓ p.p. deformed; hunchbacked, (krumm) crooked. — IV ~ n ㉓ 7. = Verwachsung.
Ver-wachsenheit (ⁱ⁻ᶻ⁻⁻) f ㊻, **Ver-wachsen-sein** (ⁱ⁻ᶻ⁻⁻) n ㉓ 1. cohesion, e-r Wunde: cicatrization. — 2. d. Körpers deformity, crooked form or shape.
Ver-wachsung (ⁱ⁻ᶻ⁻⁻) f ㊻ (ſ. verwachsen 1) outgrowing; (ſ. verwachsen 4) coalescence, e-r Wunde: healing (up), closing, ⌀ cicatrization.
Ver-wahr (ⁱ⁻ᶻ⁻) n ꝛc. = Verwahrung.
ver-wahr|en (ⁱ⁻ᶻ⁻) I v/a. u. v/refl. ⊛* 1. et. ⁓ to keep a th. (in safe custody), to guard a th.; (ſicher unterbringen) to put in(to) a safe place; mit einem Schloß ⁓ to put under lock and key; mit Schlössern und Riegeln ⁓ to lock and bolt (up); e-m et. zu ⁓ geben to give a th. in a p.'s charge, to entrust a th. to a p.('s custody), to deposit a th. with a p.; ⚘ gut verwahrt well packed; et. das sich gut ⁓ läßt s.th. that keeps well or is easily preserved. — 2. gegen (oder vor) et. ⁓ to keep from s.th., to preserve (or secure) against a th. — 3. sich gegen et. ⁓ to take precautions against a th., to provide against (or for) a th., bib. jur. to protest against a th. — II ~ n ㉓ 4. = Verwahrung.
Ver-wahrer (ⁱ⁻ᶻ⁻) m ㉒, **~in** f ㊷ keeper, guardian, custodian, von anvertrautem Gute: depositary, person in charge.
ver-wahrlos|en (ⁱ⁻ᶻ⁻⁻) [mhd.] ⊛* I v/a. to (spoil by) neglect; verwahrlost, auch: uncared for, abandoned; v/te Kinder neglected children, a.: waifs and strays *pl.* — II v/n. (ſn) to waste (or spoil) through neglect or inattention. — III ~ n ㉓ u. V/ung f ㊻ neglect(ing); careless (or negligent) treatment of.
Ver-wahrung (ⁱ⁻ᶻ⁻) f ㊻ 1. (zu verwahren 1:) keeping, guard, guarding; custody. — 2. (zu 2:) preservation; et. in ⁓ nehmen to take charge (or care) of a th.; e-n in ⁓ nehmen to take a p. into custody, to put a p. in(to) jail. — 3. (zu 3:) jur.: ⁓ einlegen gegen to (enter a) protest against.
Ver-wahrungs=mittel (ⁱ⁻ᶻ⁻⁻…) n ㉕ preservative; jur. protest, =ort m depot, für Möbel ꝛc.: repository.
ver-waisen (ⁱ⁻ᶻ⁻⁻, Hom. verweisen) ⊛* I v/n. (ſn) to become an orphan, to lose one's parents; verwaist orphan (-ed), bereft of parents; fig. destitute, deserted. — II v/a. to orphan, to deprive of father and mother. — III ~ n ㉓ und **Ver-waisung** (auch **Verwaist-heit**) f ㊻ orphanhood, mehr gebr.: orphaned state; fig. destitution.
ver-walt|en (ⁱ⁻ᶻ⁻) I v/a. ⊛* 1. to administer, manage, supervise, superintend; schlecht ⁓ to mismanage; ⚖ Vermögen ⁓ to act as trustee to a p.'s property or estate; ⁓d administrative, bſd. ⚖ managerial. — 2. (leiten) to guide, to govern; (führen, handhaben)

♪ Muſik; ⌀ Wiſſenſchaft; ⚘ Pflanze; ⚱ Geographie; ⊙ Technik; ⚒ Bergbau; ⚔ Militär; ⚓ Marine; ⚖ Handel; ✉ Poſt; 🚂 Eiſenbahn.

[Verwalter] — 1062 — [Verweis]

to conduct; (in Händen h.) to hold; ein Amt ♎ to discharge (or to attend to) the duties of an office, to fill (or hold) a situation; die Regierung ♎ to carry on the government. — II ~ *n* ㉓ 3. = Verwaltung 1.

Ver-walter (f͜u͜) *m* ㉒, **~in** *f* ㊼ administrator (*f* a. administratrix). c-r Konkursmasse auch: trustee, assignee; eines Geschäfts ʓc.: manager (*f* auch: manageress); eines Landgutes: steward (*f* steward's wife; dagegen stewardess mit ↓), bailiff.

Ver-waltung (f͜u͜v) *f* ㊻ 1. (f. verwalten I) administration, management, supervision; discharge of (official) duties; (oberste Leitung) direction (or conduct) of affairs. — 2. Behörde: (managing) board, (guiding) authorities *pl.*; jur. und ♣ trustees *pl.*; (Regierung) government, ministry, executive.

Ver-waltungs-ausschuß (f͜u͜v...) *m* ㉒ managing (or working) committee, board of directors or governors; **=be=amte(r)** *m* administrative officer, public functionary; **=behörde** *f* board of management, staatliche: (heads of the) administration; **=bezirk** *m* administrative district; jurisdiction; **=dienst** *m* civil service; **=fach** *n* (administrative or public) department; **=jahr** *n* year of administration or management; **=kosten** *pl.* expenses *pl.* of (or attaching to the) administration or management; **=rat** *m*: a) coll. = =ausschuß; b) als Person: bsd. ♣ (managing) director, jur. a. trustee; **=weg** *m*: auf dem ~e administratively; **=weise** *f* mode (or method) of administration; **=wesen** *n* (public) administration; **=zweig** *m* branch (or department) of the administration; vgl. =fach.

ver-wandelbar (f͜u͜v.) *a.* ㊻ transformable, mehr gbr.: commutable, convertible, changeable; **~keit** *f* ㊻ commutability, convertibility.

ver-wandeln (f͜u͜v) I *v/a. u. v/refl.* ㉒ᵃ* to transform (a. *math.*), to transfigure, F co. to transmogrify, in et. ♎ to convert (or turn) into s.th., bsd. *myth. u. path.* to metamorphose; **sich ♎** to change; sich in et. ♎ to be(come) transformed (or converted) into s.th., to change into a th.; in einen Aschenhaufen ♎ to reduce to ashes or cinders; in Geld ♎ to turn in(to) money, to realize; in Staub ♎ to turn to dust; to reduce to powder, to pulverize; jur.: eine Strafe in eine andere ♎ to commute a punishment; das in Wasser verwandelte Eis the ice turned into water. — II ~ *n* ㉓ u. **Ver-wandlung** *f* ㊻ transformation, transfiguration; conversion (auch ♣ von Staatspapieren), ⟋ metamorphosis; change, commutation, reduction; *thea.* auf der Bühne: shifting of scenes; *eccl.* ~ von Brot und Wein in den Leib und das Blut Christi transubstantiation.

Ver-wandlungs-künstler (ʓ...) *m* quick-change (or lightning-change) artist(e).

ver-wandt¹ (f͜u͜v) *p.p. von verwenden*.

ver-wandt² (f͜u͜v) [mhd.] I *a.* ㊻ 1. (a)kin, related; mit e-m durch Heirat ♎ sein to be connected with (or allied to) a p. by marriage; wie find Sie mit ihm ♎? how are you related to him?; wir sind nahe (weitläufig) ♎ we are near (distant) relatives or relations. — 2. *fig.* (ähnlich) kindred, similar; (gleichartig); ⟋ homogeneous; Le Begriffe cognate ideas *pl.*; Malerei u. Dichtkunst sind mit=ea. ♎ ... are closely associated (or allied) with each other; Le Seelen congenial (or kindred) souls *pl.* — 3. (mit einem, et. verbunden) attached to a p.. a th. (by common ties). — II **~e([r]** *m*) *f* ㊺ (*f* ⟋ **Ver-wandtin** *f*⁴⁷) 4. relative, relation; kinsman, *f* kinswoman; die nächsten ~en *pl.* the nearest relations, *jur.* the next of kin. [visit from relatives.]

Ver-wandten-besuch (f͜u͜v.⟋ch) *m* ㉒

Ver-wandtschaft (f͜u͜v) *f* ㊻ 1. (das Verwandtsein) kinship, relationship; (Abstammung) parentage; *fig.* analogy, congeniality; chemische ʓc. ~ chemical, &c. affinity; ~ von Begriffen connexion (or association) of ideas. — 2. (Gesamtheit v. Verwandten) all the relatives or relations, the whole kith and kin, F the whole kit (of them); zur ~ gehören to be (or form) one of the family; **♎lich** (f͜u͜v͜v) *a.* ㊻ kinsmanlike, kindred; customary among relatives; *adv.* like relations or kinsfolk.

Ver-wandtschafts-grad (ʓ...) *m* ㉒ degree of kinship or relationship or affinity; **=tafel** *f, chm.* table of affinities.

Ver-wandt-sein (f͜u͜v⁻¹) *n* ㉓ kinship, relationship; f. Verwandtschaft 1.

ver-warf (f͜u͜v) *ind. impf. v. verwerfen.*

ver-warnen (f͜u͜v) I *v/a.* ㊻* to warn, im voraus: to forewarn, ermahnend: to admonish, strafend: to reprimand; Fußball: to caution. — II ~ *n* ㉓, meist: **Ver-warnung** *f* ㊻ warning, admonition, reprimand; caution.

ver-waschen (f͜u͜v) I *v a.* ㊺b* 1. viel Seife ♎ (verbrauchen) to use (up) ... in washing. — 2. Flecke ♎ (wegwaschen) to wash out ..., to remove ... by washing. — 3. *paint.* die Farben ♎ to wash ... — II *p.p. u. a.* ㊻ 4. in den Bed. des *inf.* — 5. (verschwommen) hazy, vague; (ausgeblaßt) faded, discoloured, pale, F washed out (a. *fig.*).

Ver-waschenheit (f͜u͜v.) *f* ㊻ vagueness (of outline); discoloured state; *fig.* indecision (of character), F flabbiness.

ver-wässern (f͜u͜v) ㉒ᵃ I *v/a.* to water (or dilute) too much, to spoil (or weaken) by watering; *fig.* (traft= und geistlos m.) to enfeeble, to make insipid; (weit ausspinnen) to spin (or spread) out; verwässerte Geschichte long drawn-out story. — II *v/n.* (in) to grow watery, *fig.* to become weak or insipid. — III **Ver-wässerung** *f* ㊻ watering, dilution (a. *fig.*); weakening; spinning out, extension.

ver-weben (f͜u͜¹) I *v/a.* ㊺b*㊷* 1. Baumwolle, Garn ʓc. ♎ (verarbeiten) to use (up) ... in weaving. — 2. von Spinnen: to cover over with cobwebs. — 3. *a. v/refl.* (in=ea.=weben) (sich) ♎ to interweave, to interlace; mit et. innig verwebt ob. verwoben sein to be closely interwoven with a th. — II ~ *n* ㉓ u. **Ver-webung** *f* ㊻ 4. interweaving; intertexture.

ver-wechselbar (f͜u͜v͜fch~) *a.* ㊻ interchangeable; (umkehrbar) convertible.

ver-wechseln (f͜u͜v͜fch) I *v/a.* ㉒ᵃ* 1. et. mit et. anderem ♎ to mistake a th. for s.th. else, to confound (or mix up) one thing with another; wir haben unsere Hüte verwechselt we exchanged our hats; Spiel: Verwechselt=ea.=Bäumchen spielen to play Puss-in-the-corner. — 2. ♣ Geld ♎ (eintauschen) to change ... — II ~ *n* ㉓ u. **Ver-wechs[e]lung** *f* ㊻ 3. confusion; exchange; (Irrtum) mistake; fie sehen sich zum Verwechseln ähnlich they might easily be (mis)taken one for the other, there is a marvellous likeness between them, they are like two peas in a pod.

ver-wegen (f͜u͜v) [mhd.] *a.* ㊻(D9) rash, foolhardy; (kühn) bold, daring, (keck) audacious, insolent, (waghalsig) hazardous, risky, venturesome; **~heit** *f* ㊻ rashness, foolhardiness, temerity; (Kühnheit) boldness, daring; (Keckheit) audacity, insolence; **♎lich** (f͜u͜v͜v) *adv.* boldly, daringly, F in a devil-may-care sort of way.

ver-wehen (f͜u͜v)㊺* I *v/a.* 1. vom Winde: to blow (or drive) away the clouds, the dust. ♎: (zerstreuen) to scatter; ↓ vom Sturm verweht driven off the right course, storm-tossed. — 2. (wehend verwischen) der Wind hat die Spur, den Weg mit Schnee verweht ... has covered the road with (drifted) snow. — II *v/n.* (in) 3. to be blown away; (sich zerstreuen) to disperse, to scatter.

ver-wehren (f͜u͜v) I *v/a.* ㊺*: e-m et. ♎ to prevent (or restrain) a p. from doing a th.; (verbieten) to forbid a p. to do a th., to prohibit a p. from doing a th.; sie verwehrten ihm den Eintritt they would not allow him to enter. — II ~ *n* ㉓ prevention; prohibition.

ver-weichlich-en (f͜u͜v) I *v/a. u. v/refl.* ㊻* to weaken, to soften, to make delicate; sich ♎ to grow effeminate or delicate; verweichlicht effeminate, delicate. — II ~ *n* ㉓ u. **B/ung** *f* ㊻ weakening, &c. (f. I); effeminacy.

ver-weiger/n (f͜u͜v) I *v/a.* ㉒ᵃ* to refuse or deny (e-m et. a p. a th.); vgl. abschlagen 7. — II ~ *n* ㉓ = B/ung.

Ver-weigerung *f* ㊻ refusal, denial; im **~s=fall** in case of refusal.

ver-weilen (f͜u͜v) ㊻* I *v/n.* (h.) und bisw. **sich ♎** *v/refl.* to stay, abide, linger, gewählter: to sojourn; längere Zeit: to reside; bei et. ♎ to dwell on a th. — II *v/a.* in geh. Spr.: e-n ♎ to stop a p. — III ~ *n* ㉓ stay; sojourn.

ver-wein/en (f͜u͜v) *v/a.* ㊺* 1. Tränen ♎ to shed ... — 2. Stunden ♎ to spend ... in weeping. — 3. seinen Kummer ♎ to ease ... by weeping. — 4. fiche Augen ♎ to ruin ... by weeping, F to cry out; *v/te* Augen eyes *pl.* red (or swoln, swollen) with tears, tearful eyes *pl.*

Ver-weis (f͜u͜¹) [mhd.] *m* ㉒ᵃ. reprimand, reproof, F set-down, blowing-up, wigging; e-m wegen et. einen ~ geben to reprimand (or reprove) a p. for s.th.

Signs (see page XVII): F familiar; P vulgar; ℱ flash; ⟋ rare; † obsolete (died); * new word (born); ⟋⟋ incorrect; ♪ music;

[verweisen] — 1063 — [Verwirkung]

ver-weisen[1] (f⌣́⌣; *Hom.* verwaisen) [ahd.] *v/a.* ⓡ*: e-m et. ⁀ to reprimand a p. for a th., mit Vorwürfen: to reproach (or upbraid) a p. with a th., to cast a th. in a p.'s teeth; e-n zur Ordnung ⁀ to call a p. to order.

ver-weisen[2] (f⌣́⌣) [mhd.] I *v/a.* ⓡ* 1. e-n an e-n, et. ⁀ to refer a p. to a p., a th.; e-n vor das Schwurgericht ⁀ to commit a p. for trial at the assizes. — 2. e-n auf eine Insel ꝛc. ⁀ to relegate a p. to ...; e-n aus dem Lande (oder des Landes) ⁀ to banish (or exile) a p.; er ist verwiesen worden: a) v. e-m Schüler: he has been expelled (from school); b) v. e-m Studenten: he has been rusticated or sent down (from college); ein Verwiesener ⓥ one who has been banished or expelled, exile. — II ~ n ⓥ u. **Ber-weisung** *f* ⓥ 3. (f. 1) reference to a p., a th.; (f. 2) relegation; banishment, exile, aus der Schule: expulsion, von der Universität: rustication.

ver-welken (f⌣́⌣) *v/n.* ⓡ* to fade away, to wither, to lose one's freshness, von Blumen auch: to droop; verwelkte Schönheit faded beauty.

ver-weltlich/en (f⌣́⌣) ⓡ* I *v/a.* 1. to make worldly. — 2. Klöster ꝛc. ⁀ to secularize... — II *v/n.* (jn) 3. to grow (or turn) worldly. — III ~ n ⓥ u. *B/ung f* ⓥ 4. secularization.

ver-wendbar (f⌣́⌣) *a.* ⓥ available for; zu et. ⁀ applicable to a th.; ~keit *f* ⓥ availableness; applicability.

ver-wenden (f⌣́⌣) ⓡa* I *v/a.* 1. (abwenden) to turn away; bsd. mit *neg.* er verwandte kein Auge von ihr he kept his eyes (or his gaze) steadily fixed upon her. — 2. ⚔ (auf die Gegenseite wenden) to turn over or about; mit der verwendeten (oder verwandten) Hand with the back of one's hand. — 3. (gebrauchen) e-n ob. et. zu et. ⁀ to employ (or use) a p. or a th. for s.th., to apply a p. or a th. to s.th.; (ausgeben, aufwenden) to spend, expend, lay out, Kapital: to invest; nützlich ⁀ to utilize; Geld zu falschen Zwecken, zum eigenen Nutzen ⁀ to misappropriate money; Sorgfalt auf et. ⁀ to bestow care upon s.th.; Zeit auf et. ⁀ to devote (or appropriate, give) time to a th.; seine Zeit zu et. ⁀ to fill up one's time with a th., to spend one's time on a th. — II *v/refl.* 4. sich für e-n ⁀ (bewerben) to use one's influence (or interest) on behalf of a p. (bei e-m with a p.); to intercede for (or on behalf of) a p. — III ~ n ⓥ u. **Ber-wendung** *f* ⓥ 5. (f. 3) employment, application; expenditure, investment; utilization; bestowal; appropriation; keine (rechte) ~ für et. h. to have no (proper) use for a th.; (f. II) intercession.

ver-werfen (f⌣́⌣) I *v/a. u.* sich ⁀ *v/refl.* ⓡb* 1. a) to throw about, to scatter (about), to disperse; b) (an e-e falsche Stelle bringen) to throw (or put) in(to) a wrong place, to misplace; sich ⁀ to make a mistake in throwing, to throw wrong, beim Kartenspiele: to play the wrong card; c) vom Holze: sich ⁀ (sich krumm ziehen) to get warped. — 2. (durch Werfen verbrauchen) to use up in throwing. — 3. (wegwerfen) to cast (or throw) away, als untauglich: to reject, to condemn. — 4. (von sich weisen) to spurn, to repudiate; to object to; (mißbilligen) to disapprove, to disallow; jur. eine Klage ⁀ to dismiss a case, to nonsuit the plaintiff; Geschworene ꝛc. als parteiisch ⁀ to challenge a jury, &c.; ein Urteil ⁀ to quash a verdict; *parl.* die verworfene Vorlage the rejected bill. — 5. *rel.* von Gott: e-n ⁀ (verdammen) to cast out a p. — 6. von Tieren: to miscarry. — II ~ n ⓥ 7. = Verwerfung.

ver-werflich (f⌣́⌣) *a.* ⓥ objectionable; (tadelnswert) reprehensible; (schlecht) bad, wicked, stärker: abominable, detestable; ~keit *f* ⓥ objectionableness; reprehensibility; badness, detestableness.

Ber-werfung (f⌣́⌣) *f* ⓥ (f. verwerfen 3) rejection, condemnation, (f. verwerfen 4) repudiation, disapproval; jur. dismissal of a case, challenging a jury, quashing a verdict.

ver-wertbar (f⌣́⌣) *a.* ⓥ realizable.

ver-werten (f⌣́⌣) I *v/a.* ⓡ*: et. ⁀ to turn a th. to account, to utilize a th., Papiere ꝛc. ⁀ (versilbern) to convert (or turn) stock, &c. into money or cash, to realize (or sell) shares, &c.; sich gut ⁀ I. to be most useful or adaptable, F to come in handy, ⓢ to fetch (or command) a good price. — II ~ n ⓥ u. **Ber-wertung** *f* ⓥ utilization; ⓢ realization, sale; ich habe keine ~ dafür I cannot turn it to any account, I have no use for it.

ver-wesen[1] (f⌣́⌣) I *v/n.* (jn) ⓡ* ursprünglich: to cease to exist; engS. (durch Fäulnis vergehen) to putrefy, decay, rot; to decompose, to go into (a state of) decay, to turn to dust; (absterben) to perish; ⁀d, halb verwest putrefying, putrescent, half rotten. — II ~ n ⓥ f. Verwesung[1].

ver-wesen[2] (f⌣́⌣) [mhd.] I *v/a.* ⓡ* = verwalten; bsd. stellvertretend: j-s Amt ⁀ to do duty for (or to perform the official duties of) another person, a. to act as (a p.'s) substitute; das Land, Reich ⁀ to act as regent. — II ~ n ⓥ f. Verwesung[2].

Ber-weser (f⌣́⌣) *m* ⓥ. bisw. ~in *f* ⓥ administrator (*f* bisw. administratrix); (Stellvertreter[in]) substitute; ~(in) e-s Landes regent; ~ einer Pfarre (lt.) locum tenens.

ver-weslich (f⌣́⌣) *a.* ⓥ liable to putrefy or to decay, perishable; corruptible; ~keit *f* ⓥ perishableness, perishable nature of a th.; corruptibility.

Ber-wesung[1] (f⌣́⌣) *f* ⓥ putrefaction, decay; decomposition, corruption; in der ~ begriffen in a state of putrefaction or decay.

Ber-wesung[2] (f⌣́⌣) *f* ⓥ administration.

Ber-wesungs-prozeß ("...) *m* ⓥ process of decomposition or decay or putrefaction.

ver-wetten (f⌣́⌣) *v/a.* ⓡ* 1. to spend time, money, &c. in betting; to wager, to stake. — 2. to lose money in betting or by a wager.

ver-wettern (f⌣́⌣) I *v/a.* ⓡa* 1. = verfluchen, bsd. gbr. im *p.p.* II **ver-wettert** *p.p. u. a.* ⓥ 2. (verdammt, verflucht) damned, confounded, F deuced. — 3. (v. Wetter zerstört) weather-beaten.

ver-wichen (f⌣́⌣) [verweichen] *a.* ⓥ (D9) past (times, &c.), last (year, &c.), bygone (days, &c.); in jüngst⁀er Zeit latterly, these last (few) months or weeks.

ver-wichsen (f⌣́⌣) *v/a.* ⓡ* 1. to spend on (boot-)blacking. — 2. F = verjubeln 2. — 3. F = durchprügeln.

ver-wickeln (f⌣́⌣) I *v/a. u. v/refl.* ⓡa* 1. von Garn ꝛc.: to (en)tangle; sich ⁀ to get entangled. — 2. *fig.* eine Sache ⁀ (verwirren) to entangle (or involve) a matter, eine verwickelte Sache a complicated (or intricate) affair; e-n in et. ⁀, e-n mit et. ⁀ to implicate (or involve) a p. in a th., *b.s.* to draw (or drag) a p. into a th.; sich in et. ⁀ to become implicated (or concerned) in s.th., F to get mixed up with (or in) a th.; sich in seinen eigenen Worten ⁀ to be caught in one's own words. — II ~ n ⓥ u. **Ber-wick(e)lung** *f* ⓥ 3. (f. I) entanglement; implication. — 4. nur Verwickelung: (Verwickeltsein) complication, complexity, intricacy; (Verwirrung) imbroglio, confusion, tangle; ~ im Drama ꝛc. plot, knot, intrigue; (et. Verwickeltes) entangled (or complicated) affair.

ver-wiegen (f⌣́⌣) *v/a.* ⓡc* to weigh out.

ver-wiesen (f⌣́⌣) *p.p.* v. verweisen.

ver-wildern (f⌣́⌣) I *v/n.* (jn) *u. v/refl.* ⓡa* to grow wild or savage, von Pflanzen a. to run to seed or to waste, von Personen a. to grow brutish or brutal, von Kindern: to run wild, to grow unmanageable; von Feldern: ⁀ l. to leave uncultivated. — II ~ n ⓥ = Verwilderung. — III **ver-wildert** *p.p. u. a.* ⓥ wild, savage, fierce, barbarous, brutal(ized); (unbändig) intractable, unruly, unmanageable; (ungepflegt) uncultivated; vom Haar und Bart: untrimmed, rough.

Ber-wilderung (f⌣́⌣) *f* ⓥ growing (or running) wild; von Personen auch: brutalization; von Feldern ꝛc.: wild (or uncultivated, untilled) state.

ver-willigen ⚔ (f⌣́⌣) *v/a.* ⓡ* = bewilligen I.

ver-winden (f⌣́⌣) *v/a.* ⓡ* et. ⁀ (überwinden) to get the better of a th., to overcome a th.; ich kann es nicht ⁀ I cannot get over it or reconcile myself to it.

ver-wirken (f⌣́⌣) *v/a.* ⓡ* 1. a) (einbüßen) to suffer (the loss of); sein Leben ⁀ to forfeit one's fief; Leben und Gut ⁀ to lose...; er hat das Leben verwirkt he has forfeited his life; b) e-e Strafe ⁀ (als Buße verdienen) to incur a punishment. — 2. (verarbeiten) to work up, knetend: to knead (thoroughly). — II ~ n ⓥ 3. = Verwirkung.

ver-wirklich/en (f⌣́⌣) I *v/a. u. v/refl.* ⓡ* to realize, to materialize, sich nicht ⁀, oft: to prove delusive or a delusion. — II ~ n ⓥ u. *B/ung f* ⓥ realization, materialization, (Verkörperung) embodiment. [forfeiture; loss.]

Ber-wirkung (f⌣́⌣) *f* ⓥ (f. verwirken 1a)

⚜ scientific; ❦ botanical; ⚘ geography; ⊕ machinery; ⚒ mining; ⚔ military; ⚓ marine; ⚕ commercial; ✉ postal; 🚂 railway.

ver-wirren (ˌˈ) [mhd.] **I** v/a. u. v/refl. ⊕* (p.p. auch: verworren) **1.** Garn ɛc.: to (en)tangle, weitS. (in Unordnung bringen) to disarrange, e-m die Frisur ⚪ to tumble a p.'s head-dress; sich ⚪ to get entangled. — **2.** fig. e-n ⚪, verwirrt m. to flurry (or puzzle, perplex, confuse) a p.; das hat ihn (a. das hat ihm den Kopf) verwirrt that turned (or F muddled) his brain or his head; sich im Reden ⚪ to lose the thread, to be put out, F to get muddled. — **II** ~ n ㉓ **3.** = Verwirrung. — **III** ver-worren, ver-wirrt p.p. u. a. ⑥ **4.** entangled; confused; verwirrten Geistes troubled in one's mind; distracted, bewildered, perplexed. **5.** nur verworren (einen Zustand bezeichnend): intricate, geistig: crazy; seine verworrenen Gedanken, Vorstellungen his confused (or hazy, vague, F muddled) ideas, conceptions pl.

Ver-wirrung (ˌˈ) f ㊻ **1.** entanglement, disarrangement. — **2.** (Verwirrtsein) confusion, disorder, des Geistes: distraction, bewilderment, perplexity; in ~ geraten to be thrown into confusion or disorder, geistig: to be(come) perplexed. to show o.s. embarrassed or bewildered.

ver-wirtschaften (ˌˌˌ) v/a. ⑨* to squander through bad management, to waste (in a household), to run through, to spend (lavishly).

ver-wischbar (ˌˌˌ) a. ⑥ easily wiped (or blotted) out, effaceable.

ver-wischen (ˌˌ) **I** v/a. u. v/refl. ⊕* **1.** to wipe (or blot) out; to efface, to obliterate (beide a. fig.); aus dem Gedächtnis verwischt blotted out (or erased) from the memory; sich ⚪ to become effaced, to vanish; von Zeichnungen ɛc.: verwischt blurred. — **2.** Pastellmalerei: (mit dem Wischer behandeln) to (rub down with the) stump. — **II** ~ n ㉓ u. **Ver-wischung** f ㊻ **3.** effacement, obliteration; v. Zeichnungen ɛc.: blurring.

ver-witter/n (ˌˌ) [mhd.: wither] a* **I** v/n. (ſn) to decay (or disintegrate, crumble away) through atmospheric action or through being exposed to the air; (in Staub zerfallen) to crumble into dust, to moulder; von Mauern, Kristallen ɛc.: (sich beschlagen) to effloresce; verwittert (durch den Einfluß des Wetters zerfallen) weather-worn. — **II** v/a. to decompose. — **III** ~ n ㉓ u. **B/ung** f ㊻ decay, disintegration; efflorescence; decomposition.

ver-witwen (ˌˌ) ⊕* **I** v/n. (ſn) v. Frauen (Männern): to become (or to be left) a widow(er). — **II** v/a. to make a widow of, meist im p.p.: verwitwet widowed; von fürstlichen Witwen: verwitwete Kaiserin (Königin, Herzogin) Empress (Queen, Duchess) Dowager. — **III** ~ n ㉓ u. **Ver-witwung** f ㊻ widowed estate, widowhood. [weben.]

ver-wob(en) (ˌˌ(ˌ)) impf. (p.p.) von ver-

ver-wogen¹ (ˌˌˌ) p.p. von verwägen, bzb. = verwegen, und von verwiegen.

ver-wogen² (ˌˌˌ) v/n. (ſn) ⊕* von Wellen: to flow away, von Tönen: to die away = verhallen.

ver-wohnen (ˌˌ) v/a. ⊕*: ein Haus ⚪ to spoil (or ruin) ... in occupying it.

ver-wöhn/en (ˌˌ) **I** v/a. u. v/refl. ⊕* **1.** to pamper, coddle, Kinder ɛc. a. to spoil, to bring up in luxurious habits or ways; e-n im Essen ⚪ to make a p. fastidious or dainty; verwöhnte Person pampered (or fastidious) p., coddle, molly. — **2.** sich ⚪ to pamper (F to coddle) o.s., to (over-)indulge o.s., to acquire (or contract) luxurious habits. — **II** ~ n ㉓ **3.** = B/ung **1.**

Ver-wöhnung (ˌˌ) f ㊻ **1.** pampering, &c. (ſ. I). — **2.** (auch **Ver-wöhnt-heit** (ˌˌˌ-) f ㊻) luxury, luxurious habits pl., im Essen: fastidiousness, daintiness.

ver-worfen (ˌˌ) p.p. von verwerfen und a. ⑥ (D 9) **1.** Beb. des inf. — **2.** (ausgestoßen) cast out, cast off, abject, abandoned; (lasterhaft) depraved, profligate, irreclaimable, (niederträchtig) base, vile, infamous, ein ~er ⑦ a reprobate, a profligate, a villain; ~heit f ㊻ abjectness; depravity, baseness, infamy; profligacy, villainy.

ver-worren (ˌˌ) [: worse] p.p. ſ. verwirren III; ~heit f ㊻ confused (or disorderly, geistig: distracted) state.

ver-wundbar (ˌˌ-) a. ⑥ vulnerable, easily wounded or hurt (a. fig.); (empfindlich) sensitive, F touchy; ⚪e Stelle sore place, weak point, foible, geb. Spr. u. poet. a. heel of Achilles.

Ver-wundbarkeit f ㊻ vulnerability.

ver-wunden¹ (ˌˌ) **I** v/a. u. v/refl. ⊕* **1.** to wound, hurt, injure (ſämtlich a. fig.). — **2.** ſich an e-m Messer ɛc. ⚪ to cut (or gash) o.s. with ... — **II** ~ n ㉓ = Verwundung.

ver-wunden² (ˌˌ) p.p. von verwinden.

ver-wunderlich (ˌˌ) a. ⑥ astonishing, wonderful; (befremdlich) strange, odd; wenig ⚪ little to be wondered at.

ver-wundern (ˌˌ) ⊕a* **I** v/a. e-n ⚪ to astonish (ſtärker: to amaze) a p.; a. = überraschen; das ist nicht zu ⚪ that's not to be wondered at, it's no wonder. — **II** sich ⚪ v/refl. to be astonished (or surprised) at, to wonder (or marvel) at. — **III** ~ n ㉓ und **Ver-wunderung** f ㊻ astonishment, amazement, surprise, wonder(ment); in die größte ~ setzen to fill with the greatest amazement, to startle; das ist zum ~ that's astonishing or (most) remarkable, a. you astonish me.

Ver-wunderungs-ausruf (ˌˌ-) m ㉒ cry (or scream) of surprise; ⚪voll a. ⑥ full of astonishment or surprise; amazed.

Ver-wundung (ˌˌ) f ㊻ **1.** wounding, &c. (ſ. verwunden I). — **2.** wound, hurt, injury; tödliche ~ fatal wound.

ver-wünschen (ˌˌ) **I** v/a. ⊕* (zu 1: p.p. a. verwunschen) **1.** (verzaubern) to enchant, to bewitch, to cast a spell on or over; F co. eine verwunschene Prinzessin an enchanted princess. — **2.** (verfluchen) to curse, to execrate; das verwünschte Geld the cursed (F deuced, confounded, blessed) money; verwünscht! F hang it (all)!, confounded!, damn it!, milder: bless me!; bisweilen F einen hohen Grad bezeichnend, zB.: verwünscht gescheit awfully (or deucedly) clever. — **II** ~ n ㉓ und **Ver-wünschung** f ㊻ **3.** (ſ.1) enchantment, spell, (ſ.2) cursing, curse, execration, malediction; ~en gegen e-n ausstoßen to hurl curses (or imprecations) at a p.

ver-würzen (ˌˌ) v/a. ⑨* **1.** eine Speise ⚪ (zu stark würzen) to spice (or season) ... too much. — **2.** (der Würze berauben) to deprive of all piquancy or flavour.

ver-wüsten (ˌˌ) v/a. ⊕* to lay waste, to devastate (= verheeren); das Land war weit und breit verwüstet the country far and wide was a scene of desolation, or was made a wilderness.

Ver-wüster (ˌˌ) m ㉒ devastator, (Zerstörer) destroyer.

Ver-wüstung (ˌˌ) f ㊻ devastation; die von den Soldaten angerichteten ~en the ravages made (or the havoc wrought) by the soldiers.

ver-zagen (ˌˌ) v/n. (h.) ⊕* to grow despondent, to despond, to lose courage or heart, to give way; (verzweifeln) to despair (an et. of a th.); nicht ⚪ to bear up well.

ver-zagt (ˌˌ) [p.p. v. verzagen] a. ⊕* despondent, discouraged, dispirited, disheartened, dejected; (kleinmütig) pusillanimous; (furchtsam) timid, nervous, faint-hearted; nur nicht ⚪ don't despair!, F never say die!: ⚪ machen to discourage, dishearten, intimidate; ⚪ werden = verzagen; ~heit (ˌˌ-) f ㊻ despondency, despair, dejectedness; pusillanimity, timidity, nervousness, faint-heartedness.

ver-zählen (ˌˌ): ſich ⚪ v/refl. ⊕* to make a mistake in counting or enumerating, to make a wrong calculation, to count wrong.

ver-zahnen ⊕ (ˌˌ) **I** v/a. und v/refl. ⊕* ein Rad ⚪ (mit eingreifenden Zähnen versehen) to tooth ..., to cog ..., to put cogs on ...; carp. einen Balken ɛc. ⚪ to notch (or joggle, indent) ...; sich in ea. ⚪ to catch on (by means of cogs). — **II** ~ n ㉓ = Verzahnung 1.

Ver-zahnung ⊕ (ˌˌ) f ㊻ **1.** cogging; indentation. — **2.** a) Maurerei: toothwork; b) mach. (Zahnradgetriebe) toothed wheelwork; tönische ~ bevelled gearing; c) carp. joggle-joining, joggling.

ver-zapfen (ˌˌ) **I** v/a. ⊕* **1.** Getränke ⚪ to have ... on tap, mehr gbr.: to sell (or have) ... on draught, to retail ...; F fig. es wird nichts verzapft (du bekommst nichts) you will get nothing; co. Meidinger ⚪ to make stale (or bad) jokes, F to serve (or dish) up old chestnuts; das heute verzapfte Bier the beer on tap to-day. — **2.** ⊙ carp. (mit Zapfen verbinden) to (join by) mortise. — **II** ~ n ㉓ u. **Ver-zapfung** f ㊻ **3.** (ſ.1) retailing of beer, &c.; (ſ.2) mortising.

ver-zappeln (ˌˌ) v/n. (ſn), ſich ⚪ v/refl. ⊕a* to exhaust o.s. (or to wear o.s. out) with struggling or wriggling or tossing about, fig. to fidget (about).

ver-zärteln (ˌˌ) **I** v/a. ⊕a* = verweichlichen; (verwöhnen) to pamper, pet, coddle; verzärtelt, auch: effeminate, delicate, verzärtelte Person pampered p., F (molly-) coddle, lobloly. — **II** ~ n ㉓ und **Ver-zärtelung** f ㊻ pampering; over-indulgence.

Zeichen (ſ. S. XVII): F familiär; P Volkssprache; ſ Gaunersprache; ⚪ selten; † alt (auch gestorben); * neu (auch geboren); ⚪ unrichtig.

[verzaubern] — 1065 — [verzücken]

ver-zaubern (ˊ‿‿) I v/a. 2a* 1. (behexen) to bewitch. — 2. (durch Zauber verwandeln) to change by magic or sorcery, to enchant; in e-n Baum verzaubert transformed (or turned) by some magic spell into a tree. — II ~ n 23. u. **Ver-zauberung** f 46 3. magic (schwächer: marvellous) change or transformation, enchantment.

ver-zäun|en (ˊ‿‿) I v/a. 8* to hedge (or fence) in, to enclose with a fence. — II B/ung f 46 fencing; (Zaun, Einfriedigung) fence, enclosure.

ver-zechen (ˊ‿‿) v/a. 8* to spend money, time in drinking or F boozing.

ver-zehnfachen (ˊ‿‿) v/a. u. v/refl. 8*: (sich) 2 to increase tenfold, to decuple. [tithe(s) for.]

ver-zehnten (ˊ‿‿) v/a. 8* to pay]

ver-zehrbar (ˊ‿ˊ-) a. 66 consumable.

ver-zehren (ˊ‿‿) 8* I v/a. to consume; (aufessen) to eat up, (verschlingen) to devour; (in sich aufnehmen) to absorb; (durchbringen) to waste; 2de Leidenschaft burning (or ardent, consuming, fierce, fiery) passion; das vom Feuer verzehrte Schloß the castle (which was) consumed (or destroyed, gutted) by fire. — II sich 2 v/refl. to waste away; fig. von Personen auch: to pine away with grief, &c. — III ~ n 23 = Verzehrung.

Ver-zehrer (ˊ‿‿) m 22. ~in f 40 consumer; devourer. [waste.]

Ver-zehrung (ˊ‿‿) f 46 consumption:]

ver-zeichn|en (ˊ‿‿) I v/a. 2b* 1. ein Bild 2 to misdraw ..., mehr gbr.: to draw ... badly; auch v/refl. sich 2 to make a mistake in drawing, to draw incorrectly. — 2. (aufzeichnen) to note (or write) down, amtlich, geschichtlich: to record, einzeln: to specify, inventarisch: to make an inventory of, to catalogue; (eine Liste machen von) to register, to list; auf e-r Liste verzeichnet sein to figure on ...; ⚓ zu den verzeichneten Kursen at the prices quoted (or mentioned. — II ~ n 23. 3. = B/ung.

Ver-zeichnis (ˊ‿‿) n 17 record; genaueres: specification, von Möbeln, Waren ꝛc.: inventory, catalogue; bsd. von Namen: list, amtliches ꝛc.: register; (Steuerregister ꝛc.) roll; typ. ~ von Druckfehlern (list of) errata or misprints; ~ des Inhalts table of contents, am Schluffe eines Buches: index; ⚓ ~ versandter Waren: invoice; ~ von Warenpreisen list of prices.

Ver-zeichnung (ˊ‿‿) f 46 (s. verzeichnen 1) bad (or incorrect) drawing; (s. verzeichnen 2) noting down, &c.; specification, inventory.

ver-zeihen (ˊ‿‿) [mhd.] I v/a. 81* mſt.: to pardon, e-m et. a. p. a th.); (vergeben) to forgive, to condone; (entschuldigen) to excuse; e-m einen Fehler 2 (hingehen lassen) to pass over (or overlook) a p.'s fault; nicht zu 2 unpardonable, inexcusable; eccl. e-m die Sünden 2 to remit a p.'s sins; als Höflichkeitsformel: 2 Sie!, Sie (werden) 2! pardon me!, I beg your pardon!; excuse me!; das ist ihm nie verziehen worden he has been never forgiven that. — II ~ n 23 = Verzeihung.

ver-zeihlich (ˊ‿‿) a. 66 pardonable; (zu entschuldigen) excusable; eccl. 2e Sünde venial sin; ~feit f 46 excusableness, veniality; lightness of an offence.

Ver-zeihung (ˊ‿‿) f 46 pardon(ing); forgiving, forgiveness, condonement; eccl. remission of sins; e-n um ~ bitten to beg a p.'s pardon.

ver-zerren (ˊ‿‿) I v/a. und v/refl. 8* to distort; sich 2 to become distorted or twisted; das Gesicht (or Mund) 2 to make a wry face (mouth). — II ~ n 23 = Verzerrung.

ver-zerrt (ˊ‿) a. 66 distorted; (im Bilde) 2 darstellen to caricature.

Ver-zerrt-heit (ˊ‿-), **Ver-zerrung** (ˊ‿‿) f 46 distortion, contortion, des Gesichts: (making a) wry face; grimace; (Krampf) convulsion.

ver-zetteln (ˊ‿‿) I v/a. u. v/refl. 2a* (zerstreuen) to scatter; (verkrümeln) to fritter away; (vergeuden) to squander, to waste (little by little); sich 2 to get scattered. — II **Ver-zett(e)lung** f 46 (gradual) waste.

Ver-zicht (ˊ‿) m 2b. renunciation; (Abtretung) resignation, cession, abandonment (or relinquishment) of a claim; ~ leisten (⚓ tun) = verzichten.

ver-zichten (ˊ‿‿) I v/n. (h.) 8*: auf et. 2 to renounce a th.; (abtreten) to resign, yield up, cede, jur. auch: to disclaim, abandon; to waive a claim to; ich mußte auf das Vergnügen 2 I had to forego (or to deny myself) that pleasure. — II ~ n 23 = Verzicht.

Ver-zicht-leistung (ˊ‿-‿) f 42 renunciation, disclaimer, abandonment.

ver-zieh(en¹) (ˊ‿(‿)) impf.(p.p.)v.verzeihen.

ver-ziehen² (ˊ‿‿) I v/a., v/refl. u. v/n. (ſn) 8b* 1. to distort; (zuſammenziehen) to contract; vom Holze: ſich 2 (werfen) to get warped; bisw. auch v/a. faktitiv: Krämpfe verzogen ſein Geſicht convulsions distorted (or disfigured) his face; öfter mit perſönlichem Subjekt: den Mund 2 to draw (or pucker up, screw up) one's mouth; den Mund zum Lachen 2 to put on a forced (or sickly) smile. — 2. Kinder 2 (schlecht erziehen) to spoil ...; verzogenes Kind a. ill-bred child. — 3. im Brettſpiel: sich 2 to make a wrong move. — 4. (fort-, weg-ziehen: a) von Perſonen: to (re-)move, to change one's residence or address; in die Stadt 2 to go to live in the town; bisw. ſich 2 to withdraw, vanish, disappear; b) von Sachen: 2 von Dünsten ꝛc.: to dissolve; von einer Geschwulst: to go away, to subside; von Wolken: to pass over, to clear away, to disperse. — 5. v/refl. v/n. (ſäumen, zögern) to tarry, to delay; (ſich in die Länge ziehen) to drag on; (verweilen) to dwell, abide, stay. — II ~ n 23. 6. = Verziehung.

Ver-ziehung (ˊ‿‿) f 46 (s. verziehen 1) distortion; contraction; (s. verziehen 2) spoiling, ill-breeding; (s. verziehen 4) removal, change of residence; (s. verziehen 5) delay.

ver-zieren (ˊ‿‿) I v/a. 8* 1. to adorn, ornament, Größeres: to decorate; (verſchönern) to embellish, a. to beautify; durch Besatz: to trim; 2d decorative, ornamental. — 2. ein Buch mit Bildern (Kupfern) 2 to illustrate ... (with engravings); ♪ verzierter Kontrapunkt figurate counterpoint. — II ~ n 23. 3. = Verzierung 1.

Ver-zierer (ˊ‿‿) m 22, ~in f 40 decorator, von Kleidern, Hüten ꝛc.: trimmer.

Ver-zierung (ˊ‿‿) f 46 1. adornment, ornamentation, decoration; (Verſchönerung) embellishment. — 2. (Verzierendes) ornament, decoration, am Kleide ꝛc.: trimming; arch. ornamental (or decorative) work; (durchbrochene Arbeit) tracery; ♪ musikalische ~en flourishes, variations pl. of an air, &c.

ver-zimmern ⊙ ⚒ (ˊ‿‿) v/a. 2a* to timber, mit Brettern: to plank, to board; ⚓ ein Schiff 2 (ausbessern) to repair, to refit (with timber-work).

ver-zinken ⊙ (ˊ‿‿) I v/a. 8* to (coat with) zinc, auch to zinkify. — II ~ n 23 = Verzinkung.

Ver-zinker ⊙ (ˊ‿‿) m 22 zinc-worker.

Ver-zinkung ⊙ (ˊ‿‿) f 46 zinkification.

ver-zinnen ⊙ (ˊ‿‿) I v/a. 8* to (coat with) tin; verzinntes Eisenblech tinned iron(-plate), galvanized sheet-iron, F auch: tin. — II ~ n 23 = Verzinnung. [ing-iron.]

Ver-zinn-kolben ⊙ (ˊ‿-‿) m 22 solder-]

Ver-zinnung (ˊ‿‿) f 46 tinning (over); tin coating or casing or lining.

ver-zinsbar (ˊ‿-) a. 66 = verzinslich.

ver-zinsen (ˊ‿‿) 8* I v/a.: et. 2 to pay interest on a th.; mit 4 Prozent verzinst bearing four per cent. interest. — II sich 2 v/refl. to yield (or to bear, to bring in) interest (zu 5% at the rate of 5 per cent.). — III ~ n 23 = Verzinsung.

ver-zinslich (ˊ‿‿) a. 66 bearing (or paying, yielding, bringing in) interest; 2e Papiere pl. interest-bearing stock sg. or bonds or shares pl.

Ver-zinsung (ˊ‿‿) f 46 paying (or yielding, bearing) interest.

ver-zog(en) (ˊ‿(‿)) impf.(p.p.) v. verziehen.

ver-zögern (ˊ‿‿) 2a* I v/a. to delay, to retard; (aufſchieben) to put off, postpone, defer; (vertagen) to adjourn; (in die Länge ziehen) to protract. — II sich 2 to be delayed; (auf ſich warten laſſen) to be long (or slow) in coming, to hang fire. — III ~ n 23 u. **Ver-zögerung** f 46 delay, retardation, postponement; adjournment.

ver-zollbar (ˊ‿-) a. 66 subject to duty, dutiable, excisable.

ver-zoll|en ⚓ (ˊ‿‿) I v/a. 8* to pay duty (or excise) on; ⚓ to clear goods. — II ~ n 23 u. B/ung f 46 payment of duty or excise; ⚓ clearance.

ver-zotteln (ˊ‿‿) v/a. 2a* (in Unordnung bringen) to disarrange; (zerſtreuen) to scatter (about), to strew (or throw) about, (hier u. da liegen l.) to leave about.

ver-zucken (ˊ‿‿) I v/a. 8* to twist, to convulse. — II v/n. (in) to cease throbbing, to pass away, to die. — III ~ n 23 = Verzuckung.

ver-zücken (ˊ‿‿) I v/a. 8* to enrapture, entrance; verzückt auch: in raptures, in ecstasy. — II ~ n 23 = Verzückung.

♪ Muſik; ⚛ Wiſſenſchaft; ⚘ Pflanze; ⚥ Geographie; ⊙ Technik; ⚒ Bergbau; ⚔ Militär; ⚓ Marine; ⚕ Handel; ⚖ Post; ⚐ Eisenbahn.

ver-zuckern (ⁿ˘‿˘) v/a. Ⓑa* Kochk., Bäckerei ꝛc.: to sugar over, Früchte: to candy, Kuchen: to ice. [last throbs pl.]
Ver-zuckung (ⁿ˘‿˘) f ㊻ convulsion.
Ver-zückung (ⁿ˘‿˘) f ㊻ rapture, ecstasy.
Ver-zug (ⁿ˘˘, ⁿ˘⌣) [verziehen 5] m Ⓒc. delay; ohne ~ without delay, forthwith, there and then; es ist Gefahr im ~(e) (Aufschub ist gefährlich) delays are dangerous; P ⁓⁓ (Gefahr ist im Anzuge) there is danger threatening or ahead; die Sache leidet keinen ~ the matter does (or will) not brook delay or must not be delayed; ⚥ ~s-zinsen pl. interest payable on account of deferred (or belated) payment. [(lint).]
ver-zupfen (ⁿ˘⌣˘) v/a. Ⓑ* to ravel out
ver-zweifeln (ⁿ˘⌣˘) I v/n. (h. u. ſn) Ⓑa* to despair (an et. of a th.); abs. to be desperate or in despair (vgl. verzagen). — II ~ n ㉓ = Verzweif(e)lung, es ist zum ~, oft: it's enough to drive one (in)to despair, it makes one (feel) desperate. — III **ver-zweifelt** p.p. u. a. ㊻ despairing, desperate; (hoffnungslos) hopeless; der Kampf desperate (or life-and-death) struggle; auch für verdammt: cursed, F confounded; ⚥ langweilig dreadfully (or terribly) dull.
Ver-zweif(e)lung (ⁿ˘⌣(˘)˘) f ㊻ despair; e-n in (ob. zur) ~ bringen to drive a p. (in)to despair; aus reiner ~ from (or out of) sheer desperation; in ~ geraten to (fall or sink into) despair, to grow desperate.
Ver-zweif(e)lungs-mut (ⁿ˘ⁿ(˘)˘…) m ㊻ courage of despair; ⚥voll a. ㊻ full of despair, despairing, desperate.
ver-zweigen (ⁿ˘⌣˘) I v/refl. Ⓑ*: sich ⚥ to ramify (auch fig.), to branch out, to form branches; **verzweigt** branched, ⚶ ramose, ramous. — II ~ n ㉓ und **Ver-zweigung** f ㊻ ramification.
ver-zwergen (ⁿ˘⌣˘) v/n. (ſn) Ⓑ* to become dwarfed or stunted; **verzwergt** dwarfish, dwarfed, stunted (in one's growth), undersized.
ver-zwicken (ⁿ˘⌣˘) I v/a. Ⓑ* 1. agr. Weinstöcke ꝛc. ⚥ to clip (the suckers off) …, to prune. — 2. ⊙ Schiffszimmerei: Nägel ⚥ to bend (or blunt) the points of nails. — 3. fig. etwas ⚥ (verwickeln) to confuse (verdrehen) to twist, to distort. — II **ver-zwickt** p.p. u. a. ㊻ 4. Bed. des inf. — 5. (i. 3) confused, intricate; (seltsam) strange, odd, quaint; (schwierig) puzzling, difficult.
Ver-zwickt-heit (ⁿ˘⌣˘) f ㊻ intricacy, strangeness, oddity, quaintness.
Vesikatorium ⚶ (w-⌣⁄(˘)˘) [lt.] n ㉘ med. (Blasenpflaster) vesicatory, blister.
Vesper (ⁿ˘⌣) [ahd. *lt.] f ㊻ 1. eccl. vespers pl., evening-service; bisw. fig. = Abend. — 2. hist. Sizilianische ~ (Ermordung der Franzosen auf Sizilien 1282) Sicilian Vespers pl.
Vesper-brot (ⁿ˘⌣…) n ㊵ afternoon-tea; supper; ⚥gesang m evening-hymn; ⚥glocke f, ⚥läuten n evening-bell.
vespern (ⁿ˘⌣) [Vesper] v/n. (h.) Ⓑa. to take afternoon-tea, to have supper.
Vesper-prediger (ⁿ˘⌣…) m ㊷, **⚥predigt** f afternoon-preacher, -sermon; **⚥stunde**

⚥**zeit** f: a) vesper-hour; b) evening, poet. eventide.
Vesta (w-˘) npr/f. ㊸. Ⓑa. röm. myth. (Göttin des Herdes), ast. Planetoide: Vesta.
Vestalin (w-⌣-) f ㊼, **Vesta-priesterin** (w-˘…) f röm. Alt.: Vestal (virgin), priestess of Vesta.
Vestibül (w-˘⌣) [fr.] n Ⓒd. vestibule.
Vesuv ♁ (w-⌣ ſ) npr/m. Ⓑa. feuerspeiender Berg bei Neapel: der ~ (Mount) Vesuvius.
vesuvisch (w-⌣˘ⁿ˘ſ˘) a. ㊻ Vesuvian, of (Mount) Vesuvius.
Veteran ⚥ (w-⌣⁄) [lt.] m ㊷ (⑲d.) (ausgedienter Soldat) veteran (soldier).
Veteranen-schaft (w-⌣⌣˘) f ㊻: a) position of a veteran; b) coll. (all the) veterans; **⚥verein** m league of vet.
Veterinär ⚥ (w-⌣⌣⁄) [fr.; *lt. vete′rī′na n/pl. Zugvieh (*vĕho, vect-)] n Ⓑd. (Roßarzt) veterinary surgeon, a. F abbr. vet.
Veterinär-akademie ⚥ ("…) f ㊺ (Tierarzneischule) academy for veterinary surgeons; **⚥arzt** m (Roßarzt) veterinary surgeon; **⚥schule** f = ⚥akademie.
Veto (w-˘) [lt. ich verbiete] n ⑪ (Einspruch) veto; unbedingtes ~ absolute veto; ein ~ gegen et. einlegen to veto a th.
Vettel (ⁿ˘⌣) [mlt.; *lt. ve′tula Alte] f ㊸ (dirty) old woman or hag or witch, F old crock or jade (vgl. Schachtel²).
Vetter (ⁿ˘⌣) [ahd.: Vater] m ㉖ (㊹) (male) cousin; **⚥e** f hierzu: Base¹; **leibliche ⚥n** (Geschwisterkinder) first cousins pl.; **⚥n zweiten Grades** second cousins pl.
vetterlich (ⁿ˘⌣˘) a. ㊻ cousin-like.
vettern (ⁿ˘⌣) v/a. Ⓑa. to treat (or address) as a cousin or as cousins.
Vetter(n)-gunst (ⁿ˘⌣…) f ㊺ favour shown to cousins and other relations, pol. nepotism; **⚥straße** F f: die ~ ziehen to visit (and sponge on) one's cousins.
Vetterschaft (ⁿ˘⌣˘) f ㊻: a) (Verwandtschaft) cousinship, …hood; relationship (of cousins); b) coll. (all the) cousins pl.
Vetter-wirtschaft (ⁿ˘⌣˘) f ㊻ = ⚥gunst.
Vetturin (w-⌣) [it.] m Ⓑd. **~o** (Lohnkutscher) vetturino; hackney-coachman.
Vetver-wurzel ♃ (w˘w-˘⌣˘) f ㊷ (Wurzel von Andropo′gon murica′tus) vetiver, cuscus-root. [(vexatious.)]
vexatorisch (w-⌣⁄˘ ſ) a. ㊻ (belästigend)
Vexier-becher (w-⌣⁄…, ⚿ſ˘…) m ㊷ Taschenspielkunst: conjuring (or Tantalus) cup; **⚥dose** f magic box.
vexieren (w-⌣⁄, ſ w-⌣⁄) [lt.] I v/a. ㊻ = foppen, a. to puzzle, mystify. — II ~ n ㉓ (a. Vexiererei (w-⌣⌣-⁄, ⚿ſ-⌣⁄) f ㊻ hoaxing, teasing, quizzing.
Vexier-glas ⊙ (w-⌣ⁿ…, ⚿ſ-⌣ⁿ…) n ㊵ anaclastic glass; **⚥gurke** ♃ f (Springgurke) squirting cucumber (Ecba′llium officina′le); **⚥ring** m puzzle-ring; **⚥schloß** ⊙ n Schlosserei: combination-lock; **⚥spiegel** m magic (or distorting) mirror; **⚥spiel** n Chinese puzzle; **⚥stück** n puzzle, puzzling (or conjurer's) trick, weitS. mystification, hoax; **⚥uhr** f clock-puzzle. [cf. or cp.]
vgl. abbr. = vergleiche compare (abbr.)
Via (w-⌣˘) [lt.] I f/sg. inv. röm. Alt. = Straße, zB. ~ A′ppia via Appia, Appian road. — II via adv. vor Städtenamen: (auf dem Wege) über, zB. via Hamburg via (or by way of) Hamburg.

Viadukt ♁ (w-⌣⌣) [lt.] m ⑭b. (Überbrückung) viaduct.
Viatikum (w-⌣⌣˘) [lt.] n ㊾ 1. (Reisepfennig) money for travelling, (lt.) viaticum. — 2. Cath.eccl. (Abendmahl für Sterbende) extreme unction.
Vibration (w-⌣-tſ(˘)⁄) [lt.] f ㊻ phys. &c. (Schwingung) vibration.
vibrieren (w-⌣⁄) [lt.] v/n. (h.) ㊻ (Schwingungen m.) to vibrate; ⚥d vibrating, vibratory, von der Stimme: tremulous.
Vibrione ⚶ (w-⌣-˘) [lt.] f ㊻ zo. (Zittertierchen) vibrio(n). [vice versa.]
vice versa (w-ⁿſ˘ w-⁄) [lt.] (umgekehrt)
Vicomte (w-⁄˘) [fr.] m ㊶, **⚥sse** f ㊸ (Adelsstufe, in England zw. earl u. baron[ess f]) viscount(ess f).
Vidi (w-⁄) [lt. vidi ich habe gesehen] n, inv. u. ㊵ vidimus; mit dem Vidi versehen = vidimieren.
Vidimatum (w-⌣-⁄˘) [neu=lt.] n ㊵ u. ㊾ (pl. a. …te) (mit Vidi versehenes Schriftstück) authenticated copy (of a document).
vidimier/en (w-⌣-⁄) [lt. vi′dimus wir haben gesehen] I v/a. ㊻ to attest the correctness of (a document), to legalize, to authenticate. — II ~ n ㉓, B/ung f ㊻ legalization, authentication.
Vieh (f-⁄) [ahd.: fee; lt. pĕcus] n Ⓒc. 1. (vierfüßige Nutztiere, bsd. Horn- und Klauen- ~) cattle; f. Rindvieh, hüten 1; zehn Stück ~ ten head of cattle; großes und kleines ~ big and small cattle; bsd. auf Gütern: live stock; Menschen und ~ men and beasts pl.; cattle stets als pl., zB.: das ~ ist auf der Weide the cattle are on the pasture; das ~ grast the cattle are grazing. — 2. (unvernünftiges Tier, auch verächtlich v. Menschen: (stupid) beast, brute; zum ~ m. (w.) to brutalize (to become brutalized).
Vieh-arz(e)nei (f-⁄…) f ㊷ ꝛc. = Tierarz(e)nei ꝛc.; **⚥arzt** m = Tierarzt; **⚥ausstellung** f cattle-show; **⚥besitzer** m owner of cattle or live stock; **⚥bremse** f = Rinderbremse; **⚥dieb** m cattle-stealer; **⚥dumm** a. ㊻ brutish; **⚥futter** n food (or fodder, F feed) for cattle; **⚥handel** m ca.-trade; **⚥händler** m ca.-dealer; **⚥herde** f herd (or drove) of ca.; **⚥hirt** m herdsman, Am. cowboy; **⚥hirtin** f woman who tends cattle, a. herdswoman; **⚥hof** m: a) yard for cattle, stock-yard; b) cattle-run, weitS. farmyard. [brutish.]
viehisch (f-⁄˘) a. ㊻ bestial, beastly,
Vieh-knecht (f-⁄…) m ㊷ cattle-breeder's (or farmer's) man; **⚥magd** f servant-girl attending to the cattle; dairymaid; **⚥markt** m cattle-market or -fair; **⚥mäßig** a. ㊻ = viehisch; **⚥mast** f: a) fattening of cattle; b) (das Futter) mast (or food) for ca.; **⚥mäster(in f)** m ca.-fattener; **⚥schaden** m: a) loss of cattle; b) damage done by cattle; **⚥schau** f ca.-show; **⚥schwemme** f pond (or stream) for watering cattle; **⚥seuche** f cattle-plague, ⚶ epizooty; **⚥sperre** f prohibition to import cattle; **⚥stall** m cattle-shed, stall (or shed, stand) for cattle; **⚥stamm** m breed of cattle; **⚥stand** m auf einem Gute: stock of cattle, live stock; **⚥sterbe(n n)** f = ⚥seuche; **⚥treiber** m (cattle-)drover; **⚥trift** f:

[Viehwagen] — 1067 — [viellöcherig]

a) right of pasture; b) pastur(age) (for cattle), grazing-ground; =wagen m cattle-truck or -van or -wagon; =weide f pasture-land; =weider m. Am. rancher; =zoll m duty on (live) cattle; =zucht f cattle-breeding, raising of cattle, stock-farming; =züchter m cattle-breeder, stock-farmer.

viel (f¹; Hom. fiel) [ahd. voll] a. ⑥ (A 2, 3†) u. adv. (comp. mehr, sup. meist, s. die als bjd. Artikel) (ant. ein¹, wenig) 1. much, pl. many: **a)** mit s.: 2(e) Freunde many friends; 2e and(e)re (Personen) many others (other persons) pl.; durch 2en Fleiß by dint of great industry; 2 Gutes tun to do a great deal of good; Sprichw. s. Geschrei 2 u. Lärm 1; **b)** adv. vor comp.: er hat 2 mehr (ᵘ ᴸ) als du he has much (or a great deal) more than you, vgl. vielmehr (ᴸ ᴸ); er ist 2 (od. um 2es) größer als ich he is much (or a good deal) taller than I; s. essen 1, halten 2; **c)** substantivisch: 2e sagen many (people) say; das will 2 sagen that means (or which is saying) a great deal; **d)** mit v.: er hat 2(es) erlebt he has seen (or gone through) a great deal, auch: he has had many adventures; er hat 2 gelesen he has read a great deal, he is well read; es fehlt 2 (daran), daß // it is far from true (or from being the case) that //; iro. ich frage 2 danach!, ich kümmere mich 2 darum! what do I care!, I don't care a bit or a straw; s. fragen 1 gegen Ende; im pl.: es kamen ihrer (sehr) 2e (a great) many of them came; s. auserwählt; nicht 2es (vielerlei). sondern 2 (u. non multa, sed multum) not many things, but much; ohne ihn würde ich 2es nicht wissen ... I should be ignorant of many things; **in 2em** in many things or matters, in many respects; **mit 2em** with much; er ist mit 2em nicht einverstanden he does not agree with a great many things; um 2(es) by much (s. oben b); um 2es besser far (or much, a great deal) better, better by far; Sprichw. s. allzuviel, auskommen 6. — **2.** mit definite article od. possessive adjective: das 2e Geld the (great) amount of money, so much money; trotz seines 2en Geldes with (or despite) all his money; die 2en Menschen, welche das tun the great number (or multitude) of persons (or the many people) who do so; seine 2en Geschäfte his numerous transactions, the great amount of business (which) he has on hand; er ist einer von den 2en, die // he is one of the many who //. — **3.** mit näherer Bestimmung: **ein bißchen 2, etwas 2, ein wenig 2** rather too much, more than enough; **ebenso 2** just as much; **gleich 2** (just) as much; beide haben gleich 2 both have the same (amount of property); vgl. gleichviel; **nicht 2** not much, hardly any; es hätte nicht 2 gefehlt, so hätte er // within an ace (or a little more and) he would have //; s. los² 2; **recht** 2(e), **sehr** 2(e) very much (many), plenty of; sehr 2e Menschen a very large number (or crowd) of people, a great many persons; so 2(ᵘ ᴸ) tun, daß // to do so much that //, vgl. soviel (ᴸ ᴸ) cj.; so 2e so many, s. so 7; so 2e Male (od. soviel mal) als nötig as many times (or as often) as required; soundso 2 a certain quantity; soundso 2e such and such a number of; der soundso 2te Teil such and such a part or fraction; s. noch² 3; **wie 2, wie** 2(e): **a)** fragend: how much (many)?; **b)** ausrufend: see how many!, what a number!, F what a lot!; s. Uhr 1; verallgemeinernd: **wie 2** man auch lernen mag however much one (or you) may learn, however great (or extensive) your knowledge may be; wie 2e Kinder sie auch haben mag whatever may be the number of her children, a. F however many children she may have; **ziemlich 2** pretty much, a good deal (of); ziemlich 2e a good many, a fair (or goodly) number (of); Zahlen: 2(e) hundert many hundreds (of).

viel=ährig a. (fᵘ...) a. ⑥ many-eared, ⚭ polystachous; 2armig a. with (or having) many arms; 2artig a. manifold, varied, multifarious; 2ästig ⚭ a. with many branches, branched, ⚭ ramous, ramose; 2äugig a. many-eyed, ⚭ polyommatous; 2bändig a. (consisting) of many volumes; 2bedeutend a.: a) most significant, full of (or fraught with) meaning; b) having many meanings or significations; 2beinig a. many-legged, with many legs; 2beschäftigt a. much occupied, very busy, von Advokaten, Ärzten 2c. auch: much sought after, greatly in vogue; 2besprochen a. much spoken (or talked) of; 2besucht a. much (or greatly) frequented; 2blätt(e)rig ⚭ a. many-leaved, ⚭ polyphyllous, n. Blumenkronen: ⚭ polypetalous; mit 2blätterigem Kelch polysepalous; 2blumig, 2blütig ⚭ a. many-flowered, multiflorous; =brüderig ⚭ a. polyadelphian; 2deutig a. of various meanings, ambiguous, (doppeldeutig) b.s. equivocal; =deutigkeit f ⑫ ambiguity; =eck n. math.: a) polygon; b) (räumliche Figur) polyhedron; 2eckig a. with many corners; math. multangular, polygonal, vgl. 2wink(e)lig; =eckmessung f, math. polygonometry; =ehe f (auch ⚭ u. zo.) polygamy; 2ehig a., ⚭ u. zo. polygamous; 2erfahren a. of great experience, very experienced.

vieler=lei (f–ᴸᴸ, fᴸ⸺) inv. **I** a. of many sorts or kinds, manifold; 2 Dinge a great variety of things. — **II ~** n great variety (or selection) of things.

Viel=esser (fᵘ...) n ⑫ = esserei; =esser m great eater, glutton; =esserei f gluttony; path. (Wolfshunger) ⚭ polyphagia; 2fach a. ⑥: **a)** of many (or divers) kinds, manifold, multifarious, m. u. ⊕ (vervielfacht) multiple; b) (wiederholt) multiplied; adv. often, frequently; das **~e** ⑪ einer Größe, e-s Wertes the multiple of a quantity; 2fächerig a. with many compartments or partitions, ⚭ multilocular, multiseptate; =fachheit f = =fältigkeit; =fach=umschalter m, elect. multiple switchboard; 2fältig a.: a) = 2fach; b) (reichlich) abundant; =fältigkeit f diversity, variety, multifariousness; multiplicity; frequency; =farbig a. many-coloured, variegated, ⚭ polychromatic; =farbigkeit f variety of colour(s), ⚭ polychromy; 2fingerig a. with many fingers, ⚭ polydactylous; =flach n = =eck b; 2flächig a., math. polyhedral, …ous; =flächner m = =eck b; 2flüg(e)lig a. with many wings, ⚭ polypterous; 2förmig a. of many forms, multiform, ⚭ polymorphous; =förmigkeit f variety of form; multiformity, ⚭ polymorphism; =fraß m: a) gluttonous (or greedy, voracious) animal; von Personen: glutton, P greedyguts, greedy hog; b) [(P,+.) schwb. Fjällfräs] zo. glutton (Gulo borea'lis); amerikanischer ~ wolverene, wolverine (Gulo luscus); =fresser 2c. = esser 2c.; 2füßig a. with many feet, ⚭ polypod; 2gattig a.: ⚭ polyandric; =gebräuchlich a. much (or frequently) used, in common use; 2geliebt a. well-beloved, dearly beloved; 2genannt a. often named, frequently mentioned; (berühmt) distinguished, famous; 2geprüft a. much tried; 2gereist a. having travelled much; ein 2er Mann a travelled man, besser: a great traveller; 2geschäftig a. much occupied, very (or exceedingly) busy; 2gestaltig a. of many shapes; vgl. =förmig; 2glied(e)rig a. having (or provided with) many limbs; bsd. zo. many-jointed, ⚭ multiarticulate; math. polynomial; math. 2gliedrige Größe multinomium, polynome; =götterei f polytheism; 2gradig a. of many degrees; =griff(e)lig a. ⚭ polystylous.

Viel=heit (fᴸ–) f ⑯ multiplicity, plurality; (Menge) great number or quantity or amount, multitude.

Viel=herrschaft (fᵘ...) f ⑫ government by many, ⚭ polyarchy, polycracy; vgl. Pöbelherrschaft; =hufer m/pl., zo.: ⚭ multungulate quadrupeds, multungulates pl.; 2hufig a. ⑯ multungulate; 2jährig a. of many years(' duration), of long standing; 2er Freund very old friend; 2e Freundschaft friendship of many years' standing; 2kantig a. many-cornered, multangular; 2kapselig ⚭ a. multicapsular; 2kernig ⚭ a. with many pips or stones; 2klappig a..zo. many-valved, ⚭ multivalvular; vgl. 2schalig; 2knotig a. with many knots; ⚭: ⚭ multinodal, polygonate; 2köpfig a. many-headed, ⚭ polycephalous; 2körnig ⚭ a. with many grains, ⚭ polyspermal; 2lappig ⚭ a. multilobate, …ed, …ular; 2leicht (f–ᴸ) [uhd. sehr leicht] adv. perhaps; (zufällig) perchance, peradventure; Sie haben 2 recht you may (possibly) be right; sollte es 2 Regen geben, so fahren wir should there be rain …, should it happen (or come on) to rain …; =liebchen (f–ᴸᴸ) n dearly-beloved one, darling, sweetheart; guten Morgen, ~…! (good morning,) ⚭ philippina (a. philippine. philopœna, fillipeen)!; 2löch(e)rig (fᵘ...) a. with many holes.

⚭ scientific; ⚭ botanical; ⚭ geography; ⊕ machinery; ⚒ mining; ⚔ military; ⚓ marine; ⚭ commercial; ⚭ postal; ⚭ railway.

[vielmalig] — 1068 — [vierte]

perforated; ²malig a. often repeated. reiterated; (häufig) frequent; ²mal(s) adv. many times, often, frequently; ich danke Ihnen ² I thank you very much, many (seltener much) thanks (to you); =männerei f: ⚔ polyandry; ²männig ⚘ a.: ⚔ polyandrian, ...ous; ²mehr adv. vgl. viel 1; (im Gegenteil) on the contrary; rather; ²namig a. of (or with) many names, ⚔ multinomial, polyonymous; ²nervig a. many-nerved, ⚔ multicostate; ²paarig ⚘ a. multijugate. ...ous; =regiererei F f. etwa: officialdom, ⚔ polyarchy; ²reihig a. (arranged) in many rows, ⚔ multiserial. ...ate; ²sagend a. (most) telling. (highly) suggestive, expressive; (umfassend) comprehensive; (bedeutungsvoll) significant; ²saitig ⚘ a. many-stringed, ⚔ polychord, ²samig ⚘ a. with many seeds, ⚔ polyspermous; ²säulig a. arch. many-columned. ⚔ polystyle; ²schalig a. ⚘ u. zo. multivalve; ²schotig ⚘ a. multisiliquous; ²schreibend a. writing much, von Schriftstellern: prolific. voluminous; =schreiber m: a) one who writes much; author of many books, prolific writer, b. s. scribbler; b) ⊕ polygraph; =schreiberei f writing much, ⚔ polygraphy, b.s. mania for writing. (endless) scribbling; ²seitig a.: a) many-sided (auch fig.); math. polygonal: b) fig. von Personen: versatile; vom Wissen: extensive. comprehensive; ²er (a. ² veranlagter) Mann, oft: all-round man, man of varied acquirements; =seitigkeit f, bjw. fig. many-sidedness. versatility; von Kenntnissen: comprehensiveness; ²silbig a. gram. polysyllabic; ²es Wort polysyllable; =silbigkeit f polysyllab(ic)ism; ²spaltig ⚘ a. multifid(ous); ²spitzig a. with many points; zo. von Backenzähnen: ⚔ multicuspid; ²sprachig a. in many languages; ²e Bibel polyglot bible; =sprecher m great talker. loquacious person; ²steng(e)lig ⚘ a. with many stems, ⚔ multicauline; ²stimmig a. many-voiced, ⚔ polyphonic; ♪ ²er Satz counterpoint; ²streifig ⚘ a.: ⚔ multistriate; ²stufig a. with many steps or grades; =tätigkeit f many-sided activity; ²teilig a. of many parts, multipartite; ⚘ von Blättern: ⚔ polytomous; math. multinomial, =teiligkeit. -teilung ⚘ f: ⚔ polytomy; ²tönig a. (composed of many sounds, multisonous; =tuer m busybody. meddler; =tuerei f officiousness, bustling (about); ²umfassend a. comprehensive. extensive, vast; ²umworben a. much wooed. eagerly competed for; ²verheißend a. = ²versprechend; ²vermögend a. very powerful. bisw. multipotent; ²versprechend a. most promising; =weiberei f polygamy; ²weibig ⚘ a. polygynous. ...ian; ²winkel(e)lig a. with many angles; vgl. ²eckig; =wissen n extensive (or encyclopædic) knowledge, gelehrtes; erudition; ²wissend a. knowing much, rich in knowledge; =wisser m person of extensive knowledge, polyhistor, great

scholar, F co. walking dictionary; =wisserei f knowledge (or smattering) of many things. ⚔ polymathy; ²züngig a. many-tongued; fig. = ²sprachig.
vier (f¹) [ahd.: four: lt. quatuor] numer. I card. numb. (ohne s. P auch. ²e) 1. four; je ² und ² four each time, by fours; um halb ² at half past three; ² und zwanzig (a. als ein Wort gschr.) twenty-four, a. four-and-twenty; sie waren zu ² there were four of them; wir sind unser ²(e) we are four, there are four of us; Tennis: ² Spiele zu, zu ² four games all; Spiel zu ²en four-handed game. — 2. i. Auge 3; mit ² Pferden (ob. mit ²en, F ²e lang) fahren to drive four-in-hand; in seinen ² Wänden ob. Pfählen within one's four walls, at home; ² Wochen. oft: a month; auf allen ²en gehen to walk on all fours; alle ²e von sich strecken to lie (at one's) full length; ⚘ zu je ²en vorhanden: ⚔ quaternary. — II (die Zahl) ~ f ⑯ 3. (number) four.
vier-armig (f"...) a. ⑯ four-armed, with four arms; ²beinig a. four-legged: i. ²füßig; =blatt n ⑫: a) ⚘ four-leaved trefoil (Paris quadrifo'lia); b) arch. quarterfoil (= =paß); c) Kartenspiel: sequence of four cards; ²blät-t(e)rig ⚘ a. four-leaved, ⚔ quadriphyllous, von der Blumenkrone: ⚔ tetrapetalous; vom Kelch: ⚔ tetraphyllous, =bund m. =bündnis n quadruple alliance; ²dimensional ⚔ a. having four dimensions; =draht ⊕ m (Art Zeug) of four threads, four-threaded.
Viere (f¹⚘) f ⑧ = vier II.
Vier-eck (f"...) n ⑫: a) math. four-sided figure. quadrangle. quadrilateral (figure); rechtwinkliges ~ rectangle, oblong; verschobenes ~ rhomb(us); b) ⚓ square; (Festungs-) ~ quadrilateral; ²eckig a. ⑯ four-cornered, geom.. &c. quadrangular; ² machen to square.
vieren (f¹⚘; Hom. fieren) v'a. ⑧⁺ I to square; her. ein Wappenschild ² (in vier Felder teilen) to quarter a coat-of-arms. — II ge-viert p.p. u. a. ⑯ quartered.
Vierer (f¹⚘) m ⑫ 1. everything marked with 4. — 2. ⚔ soldier of the fourth regiment. — 3. = Quadrille.
vierer-lei (f¹⚘) a.. inv. of four kinds or sorts, four (different or distinct) kinds (or sorts) of: auf ² Art in four different ways.
vier-fach (f"...) a. ⑯ fourfold. quadruple; um das ²e vermehren to quadruple; ²fäch(e)rig ⚘ a. four-celled, ⚔ quadrilocular; ²fältig a. = ²fach; =felder-wirtschaft f ⑫ ob. ²feldrige Wirtschaft four-course system, (farming with a) rotation of crops; ²fing(e)rig a. with four fingers. ⚔ quadridigitate; =flach n. math. tetrahedron; ²flächig a. tetrahedral; ²flüg(e)lig a. four-winged, ⚔ tetrapterous; =fürst m. hist. tetrarch; =fürstentum n tetrarchy; =füßer m. zo. quadruped; ²füßig a. four-footed. von Versen: (consisting of) four feet; ²es Tier = =füßer; ²er Vers in Daktylen tetrameter; =füßler m = =füßer; =gesang ♪ m song (or singing) in four

voices, quartet(te); =gespann n. team of four horses, Mtt.: four-horse chariot, (It.) quadriga; auch: = =spänner; ²gestrichen ♪ a. von Noten: four-tailed; ²glied(e)rig a. with four limbs or parts; math. ²e Größe quadrinomial; =händer m. zo. (Affe): ⚔ quadrumane, pl. a. quadrumana; ²händig a.: a) with four hands, zo. quadrumanous; ²es Tier = =händer: b) ♪ ²es Stück four-handed piece, mehr gbr.: ² (adv.) spielen to play a duet; =herr(scher) m Mtt.: tetrarch; =herrschaft f tetrarchate. ...y; ²hörnig a. with four horns. ⚔ quadricorn; ²hundert numer.. a. four hundred; ²hundertste(r) a. u. s. four-hundredth; =hundertstel n (² a.) four-hundredth (part); ²jährig a. of four years. four years old. quadrennial; ein ²es Kind a four-year-old child; ²jährlich a. every (or once in) four years. quadrennial; ²kantig a. four-edged; ²kapselig ⚘ a. quadricapsular; ²kappig ⚘ a. von Staubbeuteln: quadrivalvular, ...e; ²lappig ⚘ a. quadrilob(at)ed.
Vierling (f¹⚘) m ⑧ 1. (¼ Pfund) quarter of a pound. — 2. ²e pl. four children (or young) at a birth.
vier-mal (f¹...) adv. four times; ²malig a. ⑯ occurring four times; ²männ(er)ig ⚘ a. (mit vier Staubgefäßen): ⚔ tetrandrian, ...ous; =paß m ⑫ arch. qua(r)terfoil, quatrefoil. cross-quarters pl.; =pfünder ⚔ m. artill. four-pounder; ²pfündig. of (or weighing) four pounds; ²räd(e)rig a. four-wheeled; ²e Droschke four-wheeler. F growler; ²reihig ⚘ a. four-rowed, in four rows, quadrifarious, quadriserial; =ruderer m four-oared boat. Mtt.: boat with four benches of oars(men), quadrireme; ²ruderig a. four-oared; ²saitig ♪ a. four-stringed; Mtt.: ²e Leier tetrachord; ²samig ⚘ a. tetraspermous; ²schrötig [ndd.] a. square-built, (kräftig gebaut) robust, F strapping; ²er Mensch F strapper, whacker; ²seitig a. four-sided, quadrilateral (a. math.); ²e Figur = =eck a; ²silbig a. gram. of four syllables, quadrisyllabic; ²sitzig a. with four seats, von Wagen a. carrying four persons; =spänner m carriage with (or drawn by) four horses, carriage and four; =vier-in-hand; ²spännig a. drawn by four horses; ²er Wagen = =spänner; ² (adv.) fahren to drive (with) four horses or in a carriage and four, to drive four-in-hand; ²spitzig a. with four points, von Zähnen: quadricuspidate; ²stimmig ♪ a. for four voices; ²es Stück quartet(te); ²stöckig a. four stories high; ²stündig. a. of (or lasting) four hours. ²viert (f¹) adv.: wir sind zu ² there are four of us, we are (a party of) four.
vier-tägig (f¹...) a. ⑯ of four days, four days old; ²es Fieber quartan fever; =tausend numer.. a. four thousand.
vierte (f¹⚘) ord. numb. ⑯ (the) fourth; der ² Stand the fourth estate; Heinrich der ². (gschr.: IV.) Henry the Fourth (gschr.: IV); ²es Kapitel fourth chapter, chapter the fourth; Datum: der ²

[viertehalb] — 1069 — [Viper]

(am 2n) Januar (4. Januar) (on) the fourth of January, Jan. the fourth (gidjr.: January 4th, in Briefen oft: 4 Jan.); im 2n Stock on the fourth floor. [half. **vierte-halb** (f″ ʊ ˘) a. (3½) three and a **Vier-teil** (f″...) n ② (vgl. a. Dritteil) = Viertel; ⁀**teilen** (f″ ᴗ ˘, bisw. f⁰ ᴗ ˘) v/a. ⊛*₊*: ehm. einen Verbrecher ⁀ (in vier Teile zerteilen) to (draw and) quarter ...; ⁀**teilig** a. ⓖⓖ in (or consisting of) four parts, ⚚ quadripartite.

Viertel (f⁰ ᴗ, ˘ f⁰ ᴗ) [mhd. vier+Teil] I n ② fourth (part); quarter (a. einer Stadt); das erste (letzte) ⁓ des Mondes: the first (last) quarter..; drei ⁓ (auf) fünf (Uhr) a quarter to five; ein ⁓ nach vier od. ein ⁓ (auf) fünf a quarter past four; es hat ein ⁓ geschlagen it has struck the first quarter. — II ⁂ a., inv.: eine ⁂ (¹/₄) Elle one-quarter of a yard; drei ⁂(³/₄) Stunden three-quarters of an hour. **Viertel-bogen** (f⁰ ᴗ...) m ② quarter of a sheet; =**elle** f quarter of a yard or an ell; =**hundert** n quarter of a hundred, twenty-five; =**jahr** n quarter (of the year), three months pl.; drei =**jahre** nine months pl.; =**jahr-hundert** n quarter of a century, twenty-five years pl.; =**jährig** a. ⓖⓖ of (or lasting) three months; =**jähr-lich** a. quarterly, adv. every quarter, every three months; =**jahrs-gehalt** n (m) quarter's (or quarterly) salary; =**jahrs-geld** n quarterly allowance or pay; =**jahrs-schrift** f quarterly (review or magazine); =**jahrs-tag** m quarter-day; =**kreis** m, geom. quadrant; =**meile** f quarter of a mile.

vierteln (f⁰ ᴗ) ⓖⓖ a. I v/a. to divide in four; to quarter (a. her.). — II v/n. (h.) ⛶: to strike the quarters.

Viertel-note ♩ (f⁰ ᴗ...) f ⓖⓖ crotchet; =**pause** ♪ f crotchet-rest; =**pfund** n quarter of a pound (= ¹/₄ ℔); =**pfündig** a. ⓖⓖ weighing a quarter of a pound.

Viertels-... (f⁰ ᴗ...) f. Viertel-...

Viertel-schwenkung ⚔ (f⁰ ᴗ...) f ⓖⓖ quarter-wheel; =**strich** ↓ m am Kompaß: quarter-point (2° 48′ 45″); =**stunde** f quarter of an hour, fifteen minutes pl.; drei ⁓n three-quarters of an hour; vgl. Viertel II; =**stündig** a. ⓖⓖ lasting a quarter of an hour; =**takt** ♪ m fourth of a bar; =**ton** ♪ m quarter of a tone; fourth; =**tonne** f quarter of a ton (in Engl. = 5 cwts.); =(**s**=)**wendung** f ⚔ u. e-r Treppe: quarter-wheel.

viertens (f⁰ ᴗ, a. f⁰ ᴗ) adv. fourthly (4thly), in the fourth (4th) place.

Vier-undsechziger(=**format**)(f⁰ ᴗᴗᴗ...) n ② typ., &c. sixtyfour-mo (abbr. 64mo); =**und-sechzigstel** n ② Bruchzahl: sixty-fourth (part); =**undsechzigstel-note** ♪ f semi-demi-semiquaver, quadruple quaver; =**undzwanzig-flach** n, =**flächner** m, math. tetrakishexahedron, trapezohedron.

Vierung (f⁰ ᴗ) f ⓖⓖ 1. math. squaring; ⁓ des Zirkels quadrature of the circle. — 2. = geviert II. — 3. arch. (Kreuzfeld e-r Kirche) intersection of the nave. [central cupola.)

Vierungs-kuppel (f⁰ ᴗᴗ ᴗ) f ⓖⓖ arch.)

Vierviertel-pause ♪ (f⁰ ᴗ...) f ⓖⓖ semi-breve rest, =**takt** ♪ m common time.

Bier-waldstätter See ⚢ (f⁰ ᴗᴗ ᴗ ˘) m ㉝ (Schweiz) Lake of the Four Forest Cantons, mehr gbr.: Lake of Lucerne.

vier-weibig ⚢ (f″...) a. ⓖⓖ tetragynian. ...ous; ⁀**wink**(**e**)**lig** a. four-cornered. geom. quadrangular; =**zahl** f ⓖⓖ Lotto ꝛc. quaternary number; =**zählig** a. ⓖⓖ quaternary; =**zähnig** a. with four teeth, ⚢: ⚚ quadridentate; =**zehig** a. zo. four-toed, ⚚ tetradactylous.

vierzehn (f⁰ ᴗ, ˘ f⁰ ᴗ) [ahd.: fourteen] I card. numb., inv. fourteen; ⁂ Tage (zwei Wochen) (a) fortnight; heute in ⁂ Tagen oder über ⁂ Tage this day fort-night, a fortnight hence; heute vor ⁂ Tagen a fortnight ago or since. — II (die Zahl) ⁓ f ⓖⓖ (number) fourteen.

Vierzehner (f⁰ ᴗ ᴗ) m ② 1. everything marked with 14. — 2. ⚔ soldier of the fourteenth (14th) regiment.

vierzehn-fach (f⁰ ᴗ...) a. ⓖⓖ fourteen-fold; ⁀**jährig** a. fourteen years old; ⁀**lötig** a. weighing (or of) seven ounces; ⁀**tägig** a. lasting a fortnight, fortnightly; ⁀er Urlaub a fortnight's (or two weeks') leave or ⚓ furlough.

vierzehnte (f⁰ ᴗ, ˘ f⁰ ᴗ) ord. numb. fourteenth; Ludwig der ⁓ (gidfr.: XIV.) Louis the Fourteenth (gidfr.: XIV.) Datum: der ⁓ (den, am ⁓n) März (on) the fourteenth of March, March the fourteenth, March 14th, in Briefen oft: 14 March; ⁓l n ②, 21 a. inv. fourteenth (part); ⁀**ns** adv. fourteenthly (14thly), in the fourteenth (14th) place.

vier-zeilig (f″...) a. ⓖⓖ four-lined, of four lines; pros. ⁂es Gedicht, ⁂e Strophe quatrain; ⁀**zellig** a. having four cells, ⚢: ⚚ quadrilocular.

vierzig (f⁰ ᴗ, ˘ f⁰ ᴗ) [ahd.: forty] numer. I card. numb. forty; im Alter von ⁂ Jahren at the age of forty; zwischen ⁂ u. fünfzig Jahren in the forties, on the shady (or wrong) side of forty. — II (die Zahl) ⁓ f ⓖⓖ (number) forty (40).

Vierziger (f⁰ ᴗ ᴗ) I m ② 1. (⁓in f ㊷) person forty (and more) years old, person between forty and fifty (years of age). — 2. ⚔ soldier of the fortieth regiment. — II ⁂ a., inv. 3. die ⁂ Jahre (Zeitrechnung und Lebensalter) the forties pl. [old.)

vierzig-jährig (f⁰ ᴗ...) a. ⓖⓖ forty years) **vierzigste** (f⁰ ᴗ ᴗ) ord. numb. fortieth; ⁓l n ②, 21 a. inv. fortieth (part); ⁀**ns** adv. in the fortieth (40th) place.

vierzig-tägig (f⁰ ᴗ ᴗ) a. ⓖⓖ of (or lasting) forty days; ⁂e Fastenzeit forty days' fast, vor Ostern: Lent.

Vigili-e (w ᴗ ᴗ(ᴗ) ᴗ) [lt.] f ㊷ 1. Cath. eccl. (heiliger Abend vor Fasten) vigil; ⁓n pl. (nächtliche Andacht) vigils pl. — 2. röm. Alt.: (einer der vier Teile der Nacht) watch.

Vignette (wĭn-jĕ't-ᵊ) [fr.] f ㊷ typ. (Verzierung) vignette, typ. a. cut.

Bigogne (wĭ-gŏ'n-jᵊ) [fr., *span.] f ㊷: a) zo. = Vikunja; ⁀**wolle**; ⁀**tier** n ㊷ = Vikunja; ⁀**tuch** ⚢ n vicugna-cloth; ⁓**wolle** ⚢ f vicugna(-wool).

Vikar (w ᴗ ᴗ) [lt.] m ② d. (Stellvertreter e-s höheren Geistlichen) substitute (or locum tenens) of a prelate, vicegerent; (Gehilfe des Pfarrers) curate; weitS. = Stellvertreter; ⁓**iat** (w ᴗ ᴗ(ᴗ) ᴗ) n ② c. Amt eines Stellvertreters oder Verwesers) office of locum tenens; vicegerency; weitS. vicarious (or temporary) employment.

vikariieren (w ᴗ ᴗ(ᴗ) ᴗ) v/n. (h.): für e-n ⁂ (j-s Stelle vertreten) to officiate as a p.'s deputy or substitute; to act vicariously for a p. [ⓖⓖ a. Victor.)

Viktor (w..., P a. f⁰ ᴗ) [lt. Sieger] npr/m.)

Viktoria (w..., P a. f⁰ ᴗ(ᴗ) ᴗ) [lt.] I f ㊷ victory (=Sieg); ⁓ schießen to celebrate an event with booming (of) guns. — II npr/f. ㊷ ⓐ (auch Vn.): a) myth. Victory; b) ⁓, Königin v. England Victoria, Queen of England 1837–1901.

Viktoria-chaise (w ᴗ ᴗ ᴗ) f ㊷ victoria; ⁀**rufen** n shouts pl. of victory; ⁀**schießen** n firing of guns in celebration of a victory; vgl. Freudenschießen.

Viktuali-en (w..., P a. f⁰ ᴗ(ᴗ) ᴗ) [lt.] pl. inv. (Lebensmittel) victuals, provisions, eatables pl.; food, F grub; ⁓**händler** m ② provision-dealer or -merchant.

Vikunja (wĭ-kŭ'n-jä) [span.] n ㊶ zo. Südamerika: (Kameltsjchaf) vicu(g)na, vicuña (Auche'nia vicu'nna).

Villa (w ᴗ ᴗ) [it.] f ㊷ (Landfitz, Landhaus) villa, country-house or -residence; (halb-)freistehende ⁓ (semi-)detached villa, vorstädtische ⁓ suburban villa.

Villeggiatur (wᴗᴗᴗᴗgā-ᴗ) [it.] f ㊷ (ländlicher Aufenthalt) stay (or holiday, residence) in the country; rural life, ruralizing.

Villen-bewohner (wᴗ ᴗ...) m pl. ② people living (or residing) in villas, coll. auch F villadom; ⁀**viertel** n suburb consisting (chiefly) of villas.

vindizieren (wᴗᴗᴗᴗ) [lt.] v/a. ㉛ (in Anspruch nehmen) to claim, to lay claim to, jur. a. to vindicate.

Vinzenz (wᴗᴗ) [lt.] npr/m. 35γ. Vincent.

Viola ♪ (ᴗᴗ ᴗ) [it.] f ㊷ viol(a); vgl. Bratsche. [2. ⚢ = Veilchen.]

Viole (wᴗ ᴗ ᴗ) [it.] f ㊷ 1. ♪ = Viola. —)

violett (wᴗᴗᴗ) [fr.] I a. ⓖⓖ violet; (dunkel) ⁂ purple (blue); vgl. veilchenblau. — II ⁓ n ②c. violet (colour or hue).

violett-blau (wᴗᴗᴗ ᴗ) a. ⓖⓖ violet blue.

violetten (wᴗᴗᴗ) a. ⓖⓖ = violett I.

Violin-block ♪ (w ᴗ ᴗ...) m ② fiddle-block; =**bogen** ♪ m violin-bow, F fiddle-stick.

Violine ♪ (wᴗᴗᴗ ᴗ) [it.] f ㊷ (Geige) violin, fiddle; die erste (zweite) ⁓ spielen: a) to play the first (second) violin, to lead; b) fig. to play (or be) first (second) fiddle.

Violinist ♪ (wᴗᴗᴗᴗ) m ②, ⁓in f ㊷ (Violinspieler[in]) = Geiger(in).

Violin-kasten (wᴗᴗᴗ...) m ② violin-case; =**saite** f violin-string, F fiddle-string; =**schlüssel** ♪ m treble-clef; =**schule** f exercises (or studies) pl. for the violin; =**spiel** n playing (on) the violin; =**spieler** m = Geiger; =**stimme** f part for the violin, violin-part; =**virtuose** m. =**virtuosin** f celebrated (or world-famed) violin-player, famous violinist. — Vgl. auch Geigen...

Violoncell, ⁓**o** ♪ (wᴗᴗᴗᴗtfd̄[-](·) [it.] n ②d., ㊿(58) (violon)cello; ⁓**ist** (wᴗᴗᴗᴗtfd̄st) m ② (violon)cello-player, cellist.

Viper (wᴗ ᴗ) [ahd.; *lt. vivi'para lebendig(e Junge) gebärend] f ㊷ zo. (Otter) gemeine ⁓ (common) viper or adder (Vipe'ri-na

♪ Musik; ⚚ Wissenschaft; ⚢ Pflanze; ⚢ Geographie; ⓖ Technik; ⚒ Bergbau; ⚔ Militär; ↓ Marine; ⬢ Handel; ⎈ Post; 🚂 Eisenbahn.

oder Vi'pera); ~=biß m [52] bite (or sting) of a viper or an adder.

Virgil (w⏑–) npr/m. [S][G]α., **~ius** (w⏑–(⏑)⏑) [36]γ. Alt.: (bsd. der römische Dichter Publius Vergilius Maro, 70—19 vor Chr.) Virgil; ~ianisch (w⏑-(⏑)–⏑), bss. ~isch (w⏑–⏑) a. [66] Virgilian, of Virgil.

Virginia (w⏑–(⏑)⏑) [lt. die Jungfräuliche] 1. npr. f [S][49]β. [S][G]α. röm. Alt.: (a. Vn.) Virginia. — 2. a) n [51] = Virginien; b) f [56] (Zigarre) Virginia cigar.

Virginia=tabak ✱ (w⏑–(⏑)⏑...) m [52] Virginia. [der U.S.) Virginia.

Virgini-en ♀ (w⏑–(⏑)⏑) npr/n. [23]α. (e-r

Virgini-er (w⏑–(⏑)⏑) m [22], **~in** f [47], **virginisch** (w⏑–⏑) a. [66] Virginian, of Virginia; ✱virginisch. Tabakvirginia.

Viril=stimme (w⏑–...) [lt. männlich] f [52] pol. single (or individual) vote.

virtuell (w⏑⏑–) [fr.] a. [66] (der Möglichkeit nach vorhanden) virtual.

virtuos (w⏑⏑–) [it.] I a. [66] (D10) (kunstfertig) (highly) skilled, artistic; masterly. — II m [42], **Virtuose** (w⏑⏑–⏑) m [44], **Virtuosin** f [47] (Künstler[in] von großem Ruf) virtuoso, mehr gbr.: far-famed (or eminent) artist, (musical) star, great master; **virtuosenhaft** (w⏑⏑–⏑) a. [66] highly artistic (style, &c.); **Virtuosenschaft** f [46], **Virtuosentum** (w⏑⏑–⏑-) n [D]d., **Virtuosität** f [46] (hohe Kunstfertigkeit) virtuosoship, mehr gbr.: professional (or consummate) skill, artistic perfection, masterly style or play.

Visa (w–⏑) [pl. v. Visum] n [23] (amtliche Beglaubigung) visa, official endorsement.

vis-à-vis (wi-sâ-wi') [fr.] adv. (gegenüber) opposite; **Visavis** n [S] s.th. opposite; person sitting (or living) opposite.

Visier (w..., P a. f⏑–) [nhd. (mhd.); *fr., it.] n [U]d. 1. ~ am Helme: visor. — 2. ⚔ an Gewehr- u. Geschützrohren: sight, aim, am Grabbogen: sight-hole. — 3. = Diopter.

Visier=ebene ⚔ (⌣...) [visieren] f [52] plain of direction; **=einrichtung** f contrivance for taking aim.

visieren (w..., P a. f⏑–⏑) [fr.] [53] I v/a. 1. e-n Paß ~ to visé (or endorse) ... — 2. ⚙ (abgleichen) to adjust; Hohlmaße ~ (eichen) to gauge. — II v/n. (h.) 3. nach et. ~ (zielen) to (take) aim at a th. — III ~ n [23] 4. = Visierung.

Visierer ⚙ (⌣) m [22] gauger.

Visier=gebühr (w..., P a. f⏑–...) f [52], **=geld** n, surv. gauger's fee; **=instrument** n diopter; **=kimme** ⚔ f notch on the top of the tangent-scale; **=kompaß** m surveyor's compass; **=korn** ⚔ n sight, aim; **=lineal** n dioptric rule; **=linie** ⚔ f line of sight; **=maß** ⚙ n standard measure; **=punkt** ⚔ m, artill. point of sight; **=scheibe** f, surv. vane; **=stab**, **=stock** ⚙ m gauging-rod or -rule.

Visierung (w..., P a. f⏑–⏑) f [46] (s. visieren 1) visé(ing), endorsement of a passport; (s. 2) adjustment; gauging.

Visier=winkel ⚔, ⚙ (w..., P a. f⏑–⏑...) m [52] angle of sight, visual angle.

Vision (w⏑(⏑)–) [lt.] f [46] = Gesicht 4.

Visionär (w⏑(⏑)⏑–) [fr.] m [U]d., **visionenhaft** (w⏑(⏑)–⏑⏑) a. [66] visionary.

Visitation (w..., P a. f⏑⏑-tß(⏑)–) [lt.] f [46]: a) (Durchsuchung) search; b) (Besichtigung) (visit of) inspection, seltener: visitation.

Visitator (w..., P a. f⏑–⏑) [lt.] m [31] (Untersuchender, Durchsuchender) searcher, inspector; (Zollbeamter) custom-house (or excise-)officer.

Visite (w..., P a. f⏑–⏑) [fr.] f [48] (Besuch) visit; kurze ~ (short) call, flying visit.

Visiten=karte (⌣...) f [52] (visiting-)card; seine ~ abgeben to leave one's card; **=karten=papier** ⚙ n enamelled paper; **=karten=täschchen** n oder **=tasche** f card-case; **=tag** m visiting-day; (regelmäßiger Empfangstag) at-home (day).

Visitier=eisen ⚔ (w..., P a. f⏑⏑–⏑...) n [52] artill. searcher.

visitieren (w⏑⏑–⏑) [lt.] I v/a. [53]: e-n Koffer &c. ~ (durchsuchen) to search ...; (prüfend besichtigen) to inspect, to examine. — II ~ n [23] u. **Visitierung** f [46] = Visitation. [sight; s. prima vista.

Vista ✱ u. ♪ (w–⏑) [it.] f [56]: a vista at

Visum (w–⏑) [lt.] n [S][D] = Visa.

vital (w–) [lt.] a. [66] (z. Leben gehörig) vital.

Vitalität (w--⏑–) [neu=lt.] f [46] (Lebensfähigkeit) vitality, vital force or power.

Vitrine (w⏑–⏑) [fr.] f [48] (Glasschaukasten) glass show-case.

Vitriol (w..., P a. f⏑⏑–) [fr.] m, n [U]d. chm. (schwefelsaures Metallsalz) vitriol; blauer ~ s. Kupfer=~; grüner ~ s. Eisen=~; weißer ~ (schwefelsaures Zink) white vitriol, sulphate of zinc ($ZnSO_4$).

vitriol=artig (⌣...) a. [66]: ⚗ vitriolic; **=erz** n [52] vitriolic ore; **=fabrik** f vitriol-works pl. or -house; **~haltig** a. vitriolated; **=hütte** f = =fabrik. [haltig.

vitriolig (w..., P a. f⏑⏑–⏑) a. [66] = vitriol=

Vitriol=öl (w..., P a. f⏑–...) n, **=säure** f (Schwefelsäure) oil of vitriol, ⚗ sulphuric acid; **=siederei** f, **=werk** n = =fabrik.

vivant (w–w⏑) [lt. sie mögen leben!] zB. ~ die Gäste! three cheers for the guests!

vivat (w–w⏑, P f–f⏑) [lt.] = er (sie) lebe hoch (s. hoch 6), zB. ~ der Kaiser! long live the Emperor!; ~ n [51] cheer; shout raised to greet (or acclaim, cheer) a p.

Vivisektion ⚗ (w-w⏑⏑tß(⏑)–) [lt.] f [46] (Zergliederung lebender Tiere) vivisection;

Vivisektor (w-w⏑–⏑) m [31] vivisectionist, vivisector.

Vize=admiral (f..., w⏑–...) [lt. vice an Stelle] m [52] vice-admiral; **=feldwebel** ⚔ m, etwa: vice-sergeant-major; **=kanzler** m vice-chancellor; **=könig** m viceroy, für Irland auch: Lord Lieutenant; **=königin** f vicereine; **=königswürde** f, **=königtum** n viceregal dignity, viceroyalty; **=konsul** m vice-consul; **=präsident** m vice-president; deputy-chairman; **=statthalter** m deputy-governor; **=wirt** m landlord's (or landlady's) agent or deputy who deals with tenants, &c. [parish-road.

Vizinal=straße (w⏑tß⏑–...) f [52], **=weg** m

Viztum ehm. (f–) [mhd.; *mlt. vicedo'minus] m [U]d. eccl. (Verweser geistlicher Güter) vidame, vicegerent.

v. J. = vorigen Jahres of last year.

Vlies (f–) [mhd.: fleece: Flaus] n [U]a. fleece, grch. myth. das Goldene (von den Argonauten unter Jason in Kolchis erbeutete) ~ the golden fleece.

Vlissingen ♀ (f⏑⏑) npr/n. [23]α. (holländischer Seehafen) Flushing.

vm. abbr. = vormittags.

v. M. = vorigen Monats of last month; am 15. v. M. on the 15th ult. (= ultimo).

v. o. abbr. = von oben.

Vogel (f–⏑) [ahd.: fowl] m [19] 1. bird, ehm. u. bibl. fowl; bibl. die Vögel unter dem Himmel (Gen. 1, 26) the fowl of the air [in dem neueren Sinne von „Huhn" nimmt fowl das Zeichen der Mehrzahl: 2 gebratene Hühner two roast fowls]; vor dem Namen eines Vogels nicht zu übersetzen, zB. der ~ Strauß the ostrich. — 2. hunt. fliegender ~ bird on the wing; hölzerner ~ zum Vogelschießen provc. popinjay, shaw-fowl; (Falke) falcon, hawk. — 3. fig. u. Sprichw.: arger, durchtriebener ~ sly bird; s. locker 2 am Ende u. lose 3; lustiger ~ gay spark, jolly fellow; er hat den ~ abgeschossen he has carried off the prize or the palm; der ~ ist ausgeflogen (der Mensch ist entschlüpft) the bird has flown; einen ~ (Sparren) h. to be cracked or crazy, to have a bee in one's bonnet; die Vögel, welche zu früh singen, frißt die Katze don't sing till you are out of the wood, don't crow too early; bsd. v. Kindern: early ripe, early rotten; es ist ihm so wohl, wie dem ~ im Hanfsamen he's as happy as a bird, (er ist reich) he's in clover; s. fressen 3.

Vogel=art (f–⏑...) f [52] species of birds; **~artig** a. [66] bird-like; **=auge** n: a) bird's eye, eye of a bird; b) ⚘ bird's-eye (Pri'mula farino'sa); **=bauer** m (n) bird-cage, größerer: aviary; **=beer=baum** ⚘ m = Eberesche, a. rowan(-tree); **=beere** ⚘ f: a) Frucht: berry of the mountain-ash, a. rowan(-berry); b) = Eberesche; **=beize** f, hunt. falconry, hawking.

Vögelchen (f–⏑⏑) n [23] (dim. von Vogel) little bird, birdie, Kinderspr.: dicky-bird; fig. ich hab' ein ~ davon singen hören a little bird (has) told me.

Vogel=darm (f–⏑...) m [52] gut of a bird; **=deuter** m = =schauer; **=deuterei** f = =schau a; **=dünger** m guano; **=dunst** m small shot (= Dunst 3); **=ei** n bird's egg.

Vög(e)lein (f–(⏑)-) n [23] = Vögelchen.

Vog(e)ler (f–(⏑)⏑) m [22] = Vogelfänger.

Vogel=fang (f–⏑...) m [52] bird-catching, mit Klappnetzen: bird-baiting; **=fänger** m bird-catcher, bsd. ehm.: fowler; **=flinte** f, hunt. fowling- (or birding-)piece; **=flöte** f bird-call, ♪ kleine ~ zuf(f)olo; **=flug** m flight of birds, ✈ aviation; **=frei** a. outlawed; für ~ erklären to outlaw, to proscribe; **=fuß** m: a) bird's foot or claw; b) ⚘ bird's-foot (Orni'thopus); **=futter** n food for birds; (Samen) bird-seed; **=garn** n net for bird-catching; (Schlinge) snare; **=gesang** m singing (or song, warbling) of birds; **=gezwitscher** n warbling (or chirping) of birds; **=handel** m bird-trade; **=händler** m bird-seller or -fancier, dealer in birds; **=haus** n aviary; **=hecke** f breeding-cage; **=herd** m fowling-floor, decoy (for birds); **=käfig** m bird-cage; **=kenner** m ornithologist; **=kirsch=baum** m, **=kirsche** f ⚘ a) = Süßkirsche (Prunus a'vium); b) = Eberesche; **=klaue** f bird's claw, talon; **=knöterich** ⚘ m knot-grass (Poly'gonum avicula'ria);

[Vogelkopf] — 1071 — [Volksmann]

=kopf ⚥ m sparrowwort (*Passeri'na*); =kraut ⚥ n = Hühnerdarm b; =kunde f ornithology; =kundige(r) s. ornithologist, F birdman; =laus f, ent. bird-louse (*Liothe'um*); =laus=fliege f, ent. bird-fly (*Ornithomy'ia avicula'ria*); ⚲leicht a. (as) light as a bird; =leier f = =orgel; =leim m bird-lime; =männchen n male bird, a. cock-bird; =miere ⚥ f chickweed (*Stella'ria me'dia*); =milch ⚥ f star-of-Bethlehem (*Ornitho'galum*); =mist m bird-dung, 🜨 guano; =napf m, =näpfchen n trough in a bird-cage; =nest n: a) bird's nest; Ausnehmen von ~en bird-nesting; 🜨 eßbares ~ aus Ostindien eatable bird's nest; b) ⚥ (Orchidee) bird's-nest (*Neo'ttia nidus avis*); =netz n, hunt. bird-net; vgl. =garn; =orgel 🎵 f bird-organ; =paar n pair of birds; =perspektive f bird's-eye view; aus der ~ entworfener Plan bird's-eye sketch; =pfeife f bird-call; =schar f flight (or flock) of birds; =schau f: a) Alt.: observation of birds, ornithoscopy, bisw. = auspice; oft = =wahrsagerei; b) = =perspektive; =schauer m Alt.: auspex; oft = =wahrsager; =scheuche f scarecrow, *fig.* von häßlich gekleideten Menschen: F right, guy; =schießen n shooting-match; =schnabel m bill (or beak) of a bird, bird's beak; =schrot m = =dunst; =schutz(=verein) m (society for the protection of birds; =spinne f, ent. bird-catching spider, bird-spider (*Avicula'ria*); =stange f: a) perch, roost; b) = Leimrute; c) beim =schießen: *prov.* pole for a popinjay or shaw-fowl; ⚲stellen: a) v/n. (h.) 🜨*₊* to go bird-catching; b) =stellen n bird-catching (= =fang); =steller m = =fänger; *auch:* decoyman; =strich m flight (or migration) of birds of passage; =wahrsager m Alt.: augur; =wahrsagerei f ornithomancy, Alt.: augury; =weibchen n female (bird), v. kleineren Vögeln: hen-bird; =weid f = =beize; =welt f feathered world; =wicke ⚥ f bird's-tares (*Vi'cia Cracca*); =zucht f breeding of birds; =züchter m bird-breeder or -fancier; =zunge f: a) bird's tongue; b) ⚥ bird's-tongue (*bsd. Ornithoglo'ssum*).

Vogesen (w⸮⸮) [✛ aus lt. *Vo'segus* = Wasgenwald; *Basken] npr/pl. inv. die ~ (südlicher Teil des west-oberrhein. Gebirges) the Vosges (Mountains) pl.; vogesisch a. 🜨 of the Vosges.
Vöglein (f⸮) n ㉓ = Vögelchen.
Vogler (f⸮) m ㉑ f. Vog(e)ler.
Vogt *fast* † (f⸮) [ahd.; *lt. *advoca'tus*] m Ob.: (Amtmann) bailiff, justiciary, warden; (Schirmherr) protector, patron; (Richter) judge, magistrate; (Aufseher) overseer; (Verwalter) administrator, e-s Gutes ꝛc.: steward; (Feldhüter) keeper; *bsd. gbr. in Zssgn, s. zB. Armen=, Burg=, Haus=, Schloß-vogt.
Vogtei (f⸮) f 🜨 1. (f. Vogt) bailiwick; district (or domain) administered by a bailiff or governor, &c.; office (or jurisdiction, residence) of a steward, &c. — 2. 🜨 (Gefängnis) jail, prison.
vogteilich (f⸮L) a. 🜨 relating (or belonging) to the office of a „Vogt".

Vokabel (w⸮L⸮) [lt. *voca'bulum*] f 🜨 in Schulen: (Wort, bsd. e-r fremden zu erlernenden Sprache) word especially of a foreign language, bisw. a. vocable; ~buch n 🜨 vocabulary, word-book; ~lernen n learning words (by rote), committing words to memory.
Vokabular(ium) (w⸮⸮L⸮(⸮)⸮) [lt.] n 🜨d. (㉘) vocabulary, collection of words.
Vokal (w⸮L) [lt.] I m 🜨d. gr. (Selbstlauter; *ant.* Konsonant) vowel. — II 🜨 a. 🜨 (auf die Stimme bezüglich) vocal, relating to the voice.
Vokal=anlaut (w⸮L⸮) m 🜨 gr. u. Phonetik: initial vowel; =auslaut m terminal (or final) vowel; mit ~ ending in a v.
vokalisch (w⸮L⸮) [lt.] a. 🜨 gr. (ant. konsonantisch) of (or relating to) vowels; der Auslaut vowel-ending, vgl. Vokalauslaut.
vokalisier/en (w⸮⸮L⸮) 🜨 I v/a. (stimmhaft m.) to vocalize. — II v/n. (h.) 🎵 (solfeggieren) to sol-fa. — III ~ n ㉓ und ⸮ung f 🜨 vocalization; 🎵 sol-fa.
Vokalismus (w⸮⸮L⸮) m ㉗ gr. vocalism, system of vowels, vowel-system.
Vokal=musik 🎵 (w⸮L⸮) m 🜨 vocal music; =punkt m in der hebr., ꝛc. Schrift: vocal point, vowel dot; =satz m musical phrase; =steigerung f guna.
Vokativ (w⸮⸮L⸮f) [lt.] m 🜨d., ~us (w⸮⸮L⸮w⸮) m 🜨 [lt.] 1. gr. (Ruffall) vocative (case). — 2. F nur ~us m 🜨🜨 (Schalk) sly (or artful, sharp) fellow, sly fox.
vol. *abbr.* = Volumen volume. [flounce.)
Volant (w⸮Ig⸮) [fr.] m 🜨 (loser Besatz)
Volk (f⸮) [ahd.- folk] n 🜨b. 1. people *pl.*, das gemeine ~ the common folk or people, the populace, the lower classes *pl.*; die große (*ob.* breite) Masse des ~es the multitude, the million, the (broad) masses *pl.*; im Munde des ~es popularly (or vulgarly) speaking; viel ~(s) a great multitude (of people) Sprichw. des ~es Stimme ist Gottes Stimme the voice of the people is the voice of God. — 2. (die Bewohner eines Landes) people *sg. ob. pl.*, nation; ein ganzes ~ betreffend national. — 3. (Klasse von Leuten) class (or set) of people; race; das kleine ~ little people or folk(s), the children *pl.*; ungezogenes ~ ill-bred people *pl.*, F a rude lot; es war viel feines ~ da there were many elegant people (or fine folk) present, there was a smart set of people there. — 4. a) ⚔ (Kriegs=)=troops, forces, men *pl.*; b) ⚓ (Schiffs=)=(ship's) crew; c) *prov.* (Gesinde, Dienstboten) establishment (of servants), people employed in a household. — 5. von Tieren: troop, herd, flock, von Vögeln: flight, von Bienen: swarm; *hunt.* zwei ~ *ob.* Völker Rebhühner two covies of partridges. [peopled.)
volk=arm (f⸮⸮L) a. 🜨 thinly (or sparsely))
Völkchen (f⸮) n ㉔ (*dim. von* Volk) small nation; (Stamm) tribe, clan; das junge ~ the young folk, the little ones *pl.*; e. lustig ~ a merry set or crew or F lot.
Völker=beschreibung (f⸮⸮⸮) f 🜨: 🜚 ethnography; =friede(n) m peace between nations, international (stärker: universal) peace; =krieg m war between two or more nations; =kunde f,

=lehre f: 🜚 ethnology; =psychologie f: 🜚 ethnopsychology; =recht n law of nations, international law; ⚲recht-lich a. relating to the law of nations; founded on international law, a. international.
Völkerschaft (f⸮⸮⸮) [Volk] f 🜨 nation(-ality), people; (Stamm) tribe; tribesmen *pl.*; ⚲lich (f⸮⸮⸮) a. 🜨 national.
Völker=schlacht (f⸮⸮⸮) f 🜨 (bei Leipzig, 1813) *etwa:* great battle, Battle of the Nations; =straße f highway of nations; =verkehr m international traffic or intercourse; =wand(e)rung f (great) migration of people.
völkisch (f⸮⸮) [Volk] a. 🜨 national.
volk=leer (f⸮⸮L) a. 🜨 deserted.
Völklein (f⸮⸮) n ㉔ = Völkchen.
volkreich (f⸮⸮L) a. 🜨 densely (*or* thickly) peopled, populous.
Volks=aberglaube (f⸮⸮⸮) m 🜨 popular superstition; =abstimmung f (general) vote of the people, *pol.* plebiscitum; =angelegenheit f national affair; =anwalt m people's spokesman or tribune; =aufruhr, =aufstand m popular (*or* general) rising, insurrection of the people; =aufwiegler m agitator, *pol.* demagogue; =ausdruck m popular expression; =ausgabe f pop. edition; =bank 🜨 f people's bank; ⚲beliebt a. 🜨 popular; =belustigung f popular amusement; =beschluß m, *pol.* plebiscitum; =bewaffnung f arming of the people; =bewegung f popular (or national) movement; a. = =aufruhr; =bibliothek f people's (free) library; =bildung f instruction of the people, national education, education of the masses; =buch n book for the million, popular book; =charakter m national character; =dichter m (ant. Kunstdichter) popular (or national) poet, *auch:* poet sprung from the people; =dichtung f (ant. Kunstdichtung) pop. (or nat.) poetry; =epos n pop. (or nat.) epic; =erziehung f = =bildung; =etymologie f popular etymology; =feind m enemy of the people; ⚲feindlich a. hostile (or opposed) to the people; =fest n: a) popular fête; b) national fête or festival or holiday; =freund m friend of the people; ⚲freundlich a. friendly to the people, popular; =führer m leader of the people, *b.s.* demagogue; =geist m national (or public) spirit; =gewühl n throng (or crowd) of people; =glaube m: a) popular belief; b) (Religion) national creed; =glück n national welfare; =gunst f popularity; =haufe(n) m crowd of people, mob, multitude; =heer n army recruited from the people; =herrschaft f government by the people, democratic rule, democracy; =hochschul=wesen n, *etwa:* university extension; =justiz f, *etwa:* lynch-law; =klasse f class of the people; =krieg m national war; =küche f soup-kitchen for the poor (folk); =kunde f folklore; vgl. Völkerkunde; =leben n life of the (common) people, national life; =lehrer m teacher of the people; =lied n popular (or national) song; =mann m man after the people's

⚗ scientific; ⚘ botanical; ⚱ geography; ⚙ machinery; ⚒ mining; ⚔ military; ⚓ marine; 🜨 commercial; ✉ postal; 🚂 railway.

[Volksmärchen] — 1072 — [Vollbürger]

heart, popular man; =märchen n pop. (fairy-)tale or myth; =maſſe f = menge; 2mäßig a. popular; =mäßigkeit f popularity; =meinung f public opinion or feeling; =melodie f popular air or tune; =menge f crowd (of people), multitude; l.s. mob; =name m name of a people; =poeſie f = dichtung; =redner m popular speaker; =ſache f national affair; =ſchicht f social layer or rank; =ſchlag m race (or stock) of people; =ſchrift f book for the people or the million; =ſchrift-ſteller(in f) m pop. author(ess) or writer; =ſchule f clementary (ethm.: national) school; =ſchul-lehrer(in f) m elementary teacher; =ſchul- lehrer- ſeminar n training-college for elementary teachers; =ſchul-weſen n elementary (school-)teaching, (system of) national education; =ſeele f inner mind of a nation; =ſitte f national custom; =ſouveränität f sovereignty (or self-government) of the people; =ſprache f language of the people, popular (or vernacular) speech; eccl. vulgar tongue; =ſtamm m race (of people), tribe; =ſtimme f voice of the people, public voice; =ſtimmung f public feeling; =ſtück n, thea. popular piece; =ton m popular tone; =tracht f national dress; =tribun m tribune of the people. Volkstum (fʰ-) [nhd.] n ② d. nationality. volkstümlich (fʰ-~) a. ⓺ (im Volke wurzelnd) popular; (dem Volkstum gemäß) national. Volkstümlichkeit (fʰ-~) f ⓺ 1.(o. pl.) conformity with the national character; (Beliebtheit beim Volke) popularity. — 2. national characteristic or trait. — 3. ~en pl. popular tales or sayings pl. Volks-unterricht (fʰ ...) m ⓺ public instruction; vgl. =bildung; =verſammlung f popular assembly, public meeting; =vertreter m representative of the people, deputy; =vertretung f: a) representation of the people; b) coll. representatives (pl.) of the people, national assembly, parliament; =weiſe f popular air; =wille m popular will, will of the people; =wirt m political economist; =wirtſchaft f political economy; 2wirtſchaftlich a. relating to political economy; =wirtſchafts-lehre f (science of) political economy; =wohlſtand m national wealth; =zahl f (number of the) population; =zähler m statistician, census-officer; =zählung f census (of the people); eine ~ halten to take a census; =zeitung f people's journal or (news)paper.

voll (fʰ) [ahd.: full] a. ⓺ (oft: voller inv., wenn es prädikativ vor nouns ohne Artikel ſteht, ſ. bſ. 1b u. 3) (ant. leer) 1. a) full; von et. 2 ſein to be full of (or filled with) a th.; ein Glas 2 Wein a glass (full) of wine; das Glas iſt ganz 2 the glass is brimful; der volle Mond the full moon; der Mond iſt voll we have full moon; ſeltener: the moon is (at the) full; b) nur als Prädikat: ſie ſind Ler Hoffnung they are full of (or filled with) hope; der Boden liegt Ler Schnitzel the floor is littered (up) with shavings; ſie iſt Ler Liſt she is full of cunning; c) mit vorausgehendem s. in Maßbeſtimmungen: ein Arm2 Holz an armful of wood; ein Beutel 2 Gold a bagful of gold; eine Hand2; den Kopf 2(er) Gedanken h. to be full of (or deep in) thoughts; ein Löffel2 Arznei a spoonful of medicine; ſ. Mund2; ⊢ er hat die Hoſen 2 oder ſich die Hoſen 2 gemacht his breeches are in a mess, he has messed (or dirtied) his breeches; er hat die Taſche(n) 2 Geld he has a (or his) pocket(s) full of money, he is well-stocked with cash; d) nur als Attribut: in Ler Arbeit fully employed or occupied. v. Maſchinen ꝛc.: in full working (order); 2e Börſe full (or well-lined, well-filled) purse; ⊥ Fahrt mit Ler Dampfkraft full-power run; in Lem Ernſte in good (or sober) earnest; ſ. Hals 3, Hand 1; aus Lem Herzen from the bottom of one's heart, (most) heartily; es iſt ein 2es Jahrhundert ſeit // it is fully a century since //; ſ. Kehle 1; mit Ler Kraft with full force, with might and main; ſ. Ladung 1 2 am Ende, vollaufen, Recht 2 1, Rüſtung 2, Segel 1; im 2ſten Sinne des Wortes in the fullest sense of the word; in Lem Trabe at full trot or speed. — 2. von runden Körperformen: well filled out, im Geſichte: full in the face; ſ. a. vollbäckig; (fleiſchig) fleshy, F crumby; (beleibt) stout, corpulent, plump. — 3. bſd. von beſuchten Räumen: (angefüllt) full (of people); übermäßig 2, zum Erdrücken 2 overcrowded, crowded to excess or to suffocation; crammed (full); war es 2 im Theater? was the theatre full or well filled?; der Saal war ganz 2(er) Leute the hall was crowded (with people) or crammed full; es war dort gar zu 2 the place was overflowing with people; in Gaſthöfen ꝛc.: bei uns iſt alles 2 (beſetzt) we are full up; ⊥ Schaffner! — der Wagen iſt 2! Guard! — the carriage is full (up)!, there is no room! — 4. (vollſtändig) complete; 2 und ganz full and entire; ein Les Jahr a whole year, a full twelvemonth; es iſt Le zehn Jahre her ... quite ten years ago; ſ. Maß 2; die Le Summe the entire sum, the total amount; die Le Wahrheit the full (or plain, whole) truth; ⊢ ich kann das Geld nicht für 2 annehmen I cannot accept the coin at its full value(vgl. a. 7); die Aktien ſind 2 (adv.) eingezahlt the shares are fully paid up. — 5. (ſatt) full (of meat and drink), satiated, ſtärker: replete (with food), crammed; (betrunken) drunk, tipsy, F boozed. — 6. mit verbs: 2 bezahlen to pay in full; 2 (fr)eſſen: ſich recht 2 freſſen to eat one's fill, to fill one's belly, ſtärker: to gorge o.s., to gormandize; 2 füllen, 2 gießen, 2 packen, 2 ſchenken to fill (up); 2 machen to make full, to fill (up); (vervollſtändigen) to complete; F e-n 2 (betrunken) m. to make a p. drunk; ſich 2 (ſchmutzig) m. to dirty (or mess) o.s.; eine Summe 2 m. to make up a sum or an amount; um das Unglück 2 zu m. to crown all; ſich den Kopf mit Wiſſen 2 pfropfen to cram one's head with knowledge; e-m den Buckel 2 ſchlagen to give a p. a good beating or thrashing; ſ. ſchlagen 4 am Ende; die Uhr hat 2 geſchlagen ... has struck the (full) hour; einen Bogen 2 ſchmieren to scribble a sheet of paper all over; e-m die Ohren 2 ſchreien (ſchwatzen) to deafen a p. with shouting (to din into a p.'s ears); e-n 2 ſpritzen to splash a p. all over, to bespatter a p.; 2 ſtopfen to stuff, to cram; ſich mit Eſſen 2 ſtopfen to stuff (o.s.), to gorge o.s.; ſich 2 trinken to drink one's fill, to drink immoderately or to excess; 2 von et. werden to become filled (or replete) with a th., trinkend: to get drunk on a th. — 7. für 2 nehmen, rechnen to take at the full (or nominal) value; nicht für 2 gelten not to be thought much of, not to be taken seriously. — 8. als s. (auch klein geſchr.): im Vollen (in der Fülle) leben to live in (the lap of) luxury, to be in clover; ins 2e greifen, aus dem Len ſchöpfen to have plenty to do with, to have ample means or plenty of money to spend.

...voll (...ʰ-fʰ) [: ...ful] a. ⓺ z. B.: ſorgen 2 sorrowful; vgl. auch voll 1 c.

voll-ährig (fʰ-...) a. ⓺ agr. with full ears; =aktie ⚹ f ㊷ fully paid-up share; 2 auf (fʰ..) adv. in abundance, abundantly, in plenty; 2 zu tun haben to have plenty to do, ⚹ to have plenty of orders on hand.

vollaufen (fʰ-~) [voll-laufen] v/n. ㊹** to be filled to overflowing. [sonorous.

vollautend (fʰ-~) [voll-lautend] a. ⓺

voll-bäckig (fʰ-...) a. ⓺ full-faced or -cheeked, bſd. v. Kindern: chubby (-faced); =bad n ⓶ complete bath, mit Tauchen: plunge(-bath), F dip; =bahn ⚹ f (ant. Nebenbahn) principal (or main) line; =bart m full beard; =bauer m (ant. Halbbauer) peasant-proprietor; 2 berechtigt a. fully entitled or qualified; =beſitz m full (or complete) possession; =bild n in Zeitſchriften ꝛc.: full-page illustration; =blut ↑ n, man. (ant. Halbblut) thoroughbred (horse); =bluthengſt m thoroughbred stallion; 2 blütig a. full-blooded; med.: ⚕ plethoric; =blütigkeit f richness of blood; med. repletion, ⚕ plethora.

voll-bringen (fʰ∠-) I v/a. ㊹* to accomplish, (zu Ende führen) to achieve, to consummate (vgl. vollenden); (ausführen) to carry out or through, to execute, eine Pflicht: to perform, ein Verbrechen: to perpetrate; nach vollbrachter Tat after accomplishing the task, when the deed was done; bibl. (Joh. 19. 30) es iſt vollbracht it is finished. — II ~ n ㉓ = Vollbringung.

Voll-bringer (fʰ∠-) m ㉒, ~in f ㊵ accomplisher, achiever; performer, perpetrator (vgl. Vollender).

Voll-bringung (fʰ∠-) f ㊻ accomplishment, achievement, consummation; performance, perpetration.

voll-brüſtig (fʰ-...) a. ⓺ full-breasted or -bosomed; =bürger m ㉒(ant. Halbbürger)

Zeichen (ſ. S. XVII): F familiär; P Volksſprache; ⚸ Gaunerſprache; ⚊ ſelten; † alt (auch geſtorben); * neu (auch geboren); ++ unrichtig.

[vollbürtig] — 1073 — [voltairisch]

citizen possessing the full franchise, burgess; ≈bürtig a. von Geschwistern: born of the same parents; ≈bürtigkeit f descent from the same parents; ≈busig a. ⊙ full-bosomed, with a full bust; ≈dampf ⊙ m full(-pressure) steam; ≈druck ⊙ m full pressure.

vollleibig (⌣‿⌣) [voll-leibig] a. ⊙ (beleibt) corpulent; ~keit f ⊙ corpulence.

voll-enden (⌣‿⌣) I v/a. ⊛* 1. (fertig m.) to finish. (absichtlich) to terminate, to bring to a close; (vollständig m.) to complete, (vollkommen m.) to perfect (vgl. vollbringen I). — II ~ n ⌑ a. 2. = Vollendung. — III voll-endet p.p. u. a. ⊙ 3. in den Bed. des inf. — 4. (vollkommen) perfect, consummate (art, &c.); Der Künstler, a. thorough artist; ⊙ hoch ≈ highly finished, of perfect finish, of first-rate workmanship;

Voll-ender (⌣‿⌣) m ⌑ finisher; one who completes a th. (vgl. Vollbringer).

vollends (⌣‿⌣) adv. 1. wholly, entirely, altogether; das wird ihn ≈ zugrunde richten that will complete his ruin or utterly ruin him. — 2. (außerdem noch) besides, moreover; to crown all.

Voll-endung (⌣‿⌣) f ⊙ 1. (s. vollenden I) finishing, termination, completion, perfecting (vgl. Vollbringung); paint., &c. (giving the) finishing touches. — 2.(Vollkommenheit) perfection. [von voll.]

voller (⌣‿) I = voll (s. ds). — II comp.f

Völlerei (⌣‿⌣ⁿ) f ⊙ immoderate eating and drinking; (Trunkenheit) drunkenness, intemperance; debauchery.

voll-fressen (⌣‿⌣) ⊛** s. voll 6.

voll-führen (⌣‿⌣) I v/a. ⊛* = ausführen 5. — II ~ n ⌑ und Voll-führung f ⊙ = Ausführung fig.

voll-füllen (⌣‿⌣) ⊛** s.voll 6; ≈gebaut a. ⊙ Schiff: broad-bottomed; ≈gefühl n ⊙ full consciousness, fulness of heart; in ~ seiner Würde fully conscious of his dignity; ≈gehalt m bes. e-r Münze full value; ≈gehaltig a. of full value, von Münzen auch: = ≈haltig; ≈genuß m full enjoyment; ≈gepfropft, ≈gerammt, ≈gerüttelt, ≈gestopft a. crammed (full); der Saal war ≈ (von Menschen) the hall was packed or crowded (with people) or full to overflowing; ≈gewalt f full (or absolute, unlimited) power; ≈gewicht ⊛ n full weight; ≈gießen s. voll 6; ≈gültig a. of full value, (perfectly) valid, unexceptionable (references, &c.); conclusive (evidence, &c.); ≈gültigkeit f full (or genuine) value, sterling quality, (perfect) validity; ≈gymnasium n (ant. Progymnasium) classical school of the first rank with the full complement of nine classes; ≈haarig a. quite hairy or shaggy, ⊙ v. Tuch: with a rich nap; ≈haltig a. bes. von Münzen: of good alloy, standard (coinage).

Vollheit (⌣‿) f ⊙ fulness, completeness; plenitude (of power, &c.).

Voll-hering (⌣‿⌣) m ⊙ full herring.

völlig (⌣‿) [voll] a. ⊙ 1. full; (ganz) whole, entire, adv. wholly, entirely, altogether; (vollständig) complete. adv. auch: downright, quite, ≈e Gewißheit absolute (or dead) certainty; ≈e Ruhe perfect calm; Cath. eccl. Der Ablaß plenary indulgence; ≈ (adv.) hergestellt thoroughly (or entirely) restored; ≈ überzeugt fully (or thoroughly) convinced; ≈ (adv.) wach wide awake, thoroughly roused. — 2. = vollkommen 2.

voll-inhaltlich (⌣‿...) a. ⊙ complete, adv. all round; ≈jährig a. jur. (majoren) of (full) age; ≈jährigkeit f ⊙ majority; ≈kantig ⊙ a. full-squared (timber); ≈klang ♪ m full chord.

voll-kommen (⌣‿⌣) a. (⌣⌣‿) [mhd.] a. ⊙ 1. perfect, (völlig ausgebildet) accomplished, (vollendet) consummate; (gründlich) thorough; (unbedingt) absolute (vgl. (vollständig). ≈ m. to perfect, to consummate. — 2. F von Kleidern: (reichlich weit) ample, amply large (or wide) enough; ~heit (⌣‿⌣-) f ⊙ perfection, consummateness; thoroughness.

voll-körnig (⌣‿...) a. ⊙ full-grained; ≈kraft f ⊙ full vigour or energy; in der ~ der Jahre in the prime of life; ≈kräftig a. vigorous, energetic; chm. ≈kugel & f artill. great (or round) shot; ≈machen ⊛** s. voll 6; ≈macht f ⊙: a) full power(s) or authority; unbedingte ~ full discretion, (fr.) carte blanche; e-m ~ geben, et. zu tun to authorize a p. to do a th.; b) gerichtlich: power of attorney; ≈macht-geber(in f) m jur. mandator; ≈macht-haber, ≈träger m, jur. mandatary, ⊛ proxy; ≈matrose ⚓ m able-bodied seaman (abbr. A.B.S.); ≈milch f (ant. Magermilch) unskimmed (or rich) milk; ≈mond m full moon; wir haben (denn es ist) ≈ we are having (or it is) full moon, vgl. voll 1; ≈monds-gesicht n face like a full moon, full round face; ≈packen u. ≈pfropfen ⊛** s. voll 6; ≈saftig a. full of juice, juicy, succulent, von Bäumen: full of sap; med. von Personen (mit ≈säftig): replete, vgl. ≈blütig; ≈saftigkeit f juiciness, succulence, richness in sap; med. (meist ≈säftigkeit) repletion, vgl. ≈blütigkeit; ≈schenken ⊛** s. voll 6; ≈schiff ⚓ n (voll getakeltes Schiff) full-rigged ship; ≈schlagen ⊛** u. ≈schmieren ⊛** s. voll 6; ≈sein n fulness, vom Essen: repletion, vom Trinken: drunkenness, drunken state; ≈spritzen ⊛** s. voll 6.

voll-ständig (⌣‿⌣) a. ⊙ complete, (ganz) whole, entire, adv. wholly, quite, altogether; (voll) full, plenary (power, &c.); ≈e Finsternis total eclipse; ≈e Niederlage utter (or crushing) signal defeat (vgl. vollkommen 1); ≈ machen to complete; um das Unglück ≈ zu machen to crown (or finish) it all, to make matters (still) worse; von Wagen: ≈ (adv.) besetzt quite full, full up; von Personen: ≈ im unklaren quite puzzled or fogged, F utterly at sea, all abroad.

Voll-ständigkeit (⌣‿⌣-) f ⊙ (s. vollständig) completeness, entireness, entirety; fulness; (Unversehrtheit) integrity; Buchhandel: die ~ des Werkes wird verbürgt the work is warranted (or guaranteed) complete.

voll-stimmig ♪ (⌣‿⌣) a. ⊙ full-voiced, von Instrumenten: full-toned; ~keit f ⊙ full tone; (complete) harmony.

voll-stopfen (⌣‿⌣) v/a. ⊛** s. voll 6.

voll-streckbar (⌣‿⌣-) a. ⊙ jur. admitting (or allowing) of execution; ~keit f ⊙ possibility of being carried out.

voll-strecken (⌣‿⌣) I v/a. ⊛* to execute, to carry (or put) into effect, to carry out; ein Todesurteil ≈ to execute (or carry out) a death-sentence; ≈d executive (power, &c.), jur. a. executory. — II ~ n ⌑ = Vollstreckung.

Voll-strecker (⌣‿⌣) m ⌑ one who executes, &c. (s. vollstrecken); vgl. Testaments≈; ~s Todesurteils executioner.

Voll-streckung (⌣‿⌣) f ⊙ execution.

Voll-streckungs-befehl (‿...) m ⌑ jur. execution-warrant, writ of execution.

voll-tönend (⌣‿...), ≈tönig a. ⊙ full-toned, sonorous, v. d. Stimme: of rich tone, rich in tone; rhet. von Sätzen: well-rounded (period); ≈treffer m ⊙ ⚔ artill. well-aimed shot; ≈trinken s. voll 6; ≈versammlung f plenary meeting; ≈wangig a. = ≈bäckig; ≈werden s. voll 6; ≈wertig a. fully worth the money, of high quality; ≈wichtig a. of full weight, fig. weighty, momentous; ≈wichtigkeit f full weight, fig. weightiness; ≈zählig a. full-grown, fully grown, ⊙ (numerically) complete, bib. & in full muster; ≈e Versammlung full assembly, parl. full house; ≈ machen to complete; ⚔ ein Bataillon ≈ m. to raise a battalion to its full strength; ≈zähligkeit f (numerical) completeness, full complement or muster; fulness; ≈zähligmachung f ⊙ completion.

voll-ziehen (⌣‿⌣) I v/a. u. sich ≈ v/refl. ⊛6* 1. = vollbringen I, vollstrecken I; die Ehe ≈ to consummate a marriage; sich ≈ to be accomplished (or consummated), to take place; ≈de Gewalt executive power; ihre vollzogene eheliche Verbindung zeigen an ..., meist unter der Zeitungsrubrik "Marriages" nur die beiden Namen. — 2. jur. ein Aktenstück ≈ to execute (or sign) a deed; einen Vertrag ≈ to ratify a treaty. — II ~ n ⌑ 3. = Vollziehung.

Voll-zieher (-) m ⌑, ~in f ⊙ jur. executor. f executrix.

Voll-ziehung (-) f ⊙ consummation of a marriage; execution of a deed; ratification of a treaty.

Voll-ziehungs-beamter (‿...) m ⌑ executory officer; (Gerichtsvollzieher) officer of the court, (court-)bailiff; ≈befehl m writ of execution; ≈ziehen s. voll 6.

voll-zog(en) (⌣‿⌣) impf. (p.p.) v. voll-Voll-zug (⌣‿) m ⊙c. = Vollziehung.

Volontär (w‿t⌣²) [fr.] m ⊙d. (⊛): a) ≈ (Freiwilliger) volunteer; b) ⊙ (unbezahlter Handlungsgehilfe) unsalaried (or unpaid) clerk, in gewissen Geschäften, auf Gütern ꝛc. auch: improver.

Bolster (w‿) m ⌑, ~in f ⊙ röm. Alt.: Volscian, pl. ≈ (Volk in Mittel-italien), auch: Volsci; volskisch a. ⊙ Volscian.

Bolt ⊙ (w‿) [Volta, it. Physiker, † 1827] n ⊙b,6. elect. (elektrische Maßeinheit: Einheit der elektrischen Spannung) volt.

voltairisch (w‿tä‿⌣), meist voltairesch (w‿tä‿risch) [Voltaire, fr. Schriftsteller, 1694 bis 1778] a. ⊙ Voltairean, Voltairian.

♪ Musik; ⚗ Wissenschaft; ♣ Pflanze; ⌂ Geographie; ⊙ Technik; ⚒ Bergbau; ⚔ Militär; ⚓ Marine; ⊛ Handel; ⚘ Post; 🚂 Eisenbahn.

volta-isch (wˇ-~) [f. **Volt**] *a.* ⊛ Voltaic, of Volta; *phys.* Der Bogen Voltaic arc; Le Säule Voltaic pile.
Volta=meter ⊙ (wˇ⊥⌣) *n* (*m*) ⊛6. *elect.* (Messer der Stromstärke) voltameter.
Volt=ampere † (wˇ…) *n* ⑫ *elect.* volt-ampere, ampere-volt (= Watt); **=coulomb** † *n* (Einheit der Arbeit) volt-coulomb, joule (= Joule).
Volte (wˇ⌣) [fr., it.] *f* ⊛: a) *man.* (Kreisritt); b) *fenc.* (Seitenhieb): volt.
Voltigeur (wˇ⌣) [fr.] *m* ⓐd. ⊛) a) ehm. ✕ (leichter Infanterist) voltigeur; light-infantry soldier; b) (Luftspringer) vaulter. [(Luftsprünge *m.*) to vault.]
voltigieren (wˇ⌣⌣) [fr.] *v/n.* (h.) ⊛ **Voltigier=kunst** (wˇ⌣G″…) *f* ⊛ art of vaulting; **=pferd** *n*: hölzernes ~ wooden vaulting-horse.
Volt=meter ⊙ (wˇ⊥⌣) *n* (*m*) ⊛6. *elect.* u. ⊛ (Spannungsmesser) volt-meter.
Volubilität (wˇ⌣⌣⊥) [neu=lt.] *f* ⊛ (Beweglichkeit, bsd. der Zunge) volubility.
Volum △ (wˇ⊥) *n* ⓐd. ~ Volumen a.
Volumen (wˇ⌣⊥⌣) [lt.] *n* ⊛③ (a) Rauminhalt, Umfang; b) *typ.* Band) volume; **~messung** *f* ⊛: △ volumenometry.
Volum=gesetz △ (wˇ⊥…) *n* ⊛ *phys.* (Gay Lussac's) law of (gaseous) volumes; **=gewicht** *n* weight of volume.
voluminös (wˇ⌣⊥⌣) [fr.] *a.*⊛(D10) (umfangreich) voluminous, bulky, bsd. von Werken: compendious. [of volume or bulk.]
Volum=zunahme (wˇ⊥⌣…) *f* ⊛ increase **Volute** (wˇ⊥⌣) [lt.] *f* ⊛ *arch.* volute, **vom** (fˇ) = von dem. [scroll.]
Vom=blatt=spielen ♪ (fˇ⊥⌣) *n* ⊛ playing at (first) sight, (it.) prima vista.
vomieren (wˇ⌣⌣) [lt.] *v/n.* (h.) ⊛ *med.* (sich [er]brechen) to vomit; **Vomitiv** (wˇ⌣⊥f) *n* ⓐd. (Brechmittel) vomitive, emetic.
von (fˇ) [ahd.] *prp.* m. *dat.* (statt: von dem oft: vom) (*ant.* bis) **1.** örtlich: from; f. Herz 1 unter „**von**"; der von London kommende Zug the down train; er kam von Schweden he came from Sweden; nimm das vom Tische (weg) take that (away) from (or take it off) the table. — **2.** für den Genitiv: a) f. Haus 1, König von Preußen king of Prussia; Zinsen von Zinsen compound interest; ein Freund von mir a friend of mine; b) als partitiver Genitiv: f. hundert II; einer von vielen one out of many; eins von den Kindern one of the children; oft nach Superlativen: f. best 3; das Schlimmste von allem the worst of it all. — **3.** beim Passiv: by; er wird von allen geliebt he is loved by all; von Gottes Gnaden (eingesetzt) by the grace of God; von ihm sind diese Werke (verfaßt) these works are (or were written) by him; gedruckt und verlegt von // printed and published by //; ein Gemälde von Turner a painting by Turner. — **4.** a) den Stoff bezeichnend: der Tisch ist von Eisen ... is (made) of iron; sein Bart ist nicht von Flachse (R.) his beard is not flaxen; von Holz bauen to build (out) of wood; b) den Gegenstand des Gespräches bz.: f. of, about, concerning, respecting, (up)on; f. reden 2 am Ende und sagen 5; von wem sprechen Sie? von ihnen of whom are you speaking? of them; das Buch, von dem ich rede ... of (or about) which I am speaking, ... which I am speaking of or about; der Mann, von dem man behauptet, daß er alles weiß ... of whom they assert that he knows all, ... who is reported (or said) to know all; c) Eigenschaft bz.: ein Kind von drei Jahren a child three years old or of age, a three-year-old child; klein von Gestalt small of stature, of small size; ein Engel von einem Mädchen an angel of a girl; ein Dichter von urwüchsiger Kraft a poet of original power; d) Abel bz.: Herr (Baron) von Lavalette Baron L.; auch als *s.*: das Von the (German, &c.) prefix (or mark) of nobility; f. Habenichts; e) Datum bz.: sein Brief vom 1. dieses Monats his letter of the first instant. — **5.** von seiten: wir haben Gutes von ihm empfangen we have received (or met with) kindness at his hands; f. erhalten 3, grüßen 1 und hören 1; das wäre grausam von Ihnen that would be cruel of you or on your part; das war ein dummer Streich von ihm that was a silly thing of him to do. — **6.** mit verbs: f. abnehmen 1; vom Original abschreiben to copy from the original; f. abziehen 4 u. 5, borgen 1, bringen 8 unter „**von**"; von e-m geh(e)n to leave (or desert) a p.; f. vonstatten; ich hörte es von ihnen I heard it from them, I was told (so) by them; f. kaufen 1; von Sinnen kommen to lose one's head, F to go off one's chump; f. leben 2 2; von der Arbeit ruhen to rest from one's labour; sich von seiner Frau scheiden l. to get a separation (or a divorce) from one's wife; getrennt von seinen Freunden separated (or cut off) from his friends; was wollen Sie von mir? what do you want of me? — **7.** mit folgendem *adv.* ob. folgender *prp.*: von heute **an** from this day forth, from to-day; f. jetzt 3; von seiner Quelle **an** from its source; von Grund **aus** f. Grund 2; von den Alpen **bis** zum Meere from the Alps to the sea; ich spielte von 3 bis 5 (Uhr) I played from three to (or till) five (o'clock); von oben bis unten from top to bottom; von **außen** from (or on) the outside; von **da**, von **dort** from there, (from) thence; von alters **her** f. Alter 3; von der Kanzel **herab** from the pulpit; f. hier 1; von **hinten** from behind, from the back; von **innen** from (or on) the inside; von **vorn** bis hinten from front to back, ↓ von Stamm zu Stamm; von **Westen** nach Osten from west to east; von Fall **zu** Fall (taking each case) singly, as the case arises; von Zeit zu Zeit from time to time; f. wannen; von Rechts **wegen** by right(s).
von-ein-ander (fˇ-⌣⌣) *adv.* = auseinander; 2 gehen to part, to separate.
von-nöten (fˇ⌣⊥) f. Not 6 gegen Ende.
von-statten (fˇ⌣⊥) [Statt!] *l.* 2 (vorwärts) geh(e)n to go on well, to progress; (gedeihen) to succeed, prosper, thrive.

vor (fˇ) [ahd.: for(e): für] I *prp.* mit *dat.* auf die Frage „**wo**?", mit *acc.* auf die Frage „**wohin**?" **1.** zeitlich: a) (*ant.* nach) before, previous to, ere; f. Alter 3; vor Christi Geburt (*abbr. v.* Chr. [G.]) before Christ (*abbr.* B. C.); f. Empfang 2; der Tag vor dem Feste the day previous (or antecedent, prior) to the fête, the eve of the festival; f. gehören 2 unter „**vor**", Hand 4 gegen Ende u. vorderhand; ein Viertel vor zehn a quarter to ten; vor der Zeit: a) before the time, prematurely; b) (vorher) beforehand, previously; vor Zeiten in ancient times, long ago; b) (sowohl lange her): vor acht (vierzehn) Tagen a week (fortnight) ago or since; vor einigen Tagen a few days back, the other day; f. Jahr 3, kurz 3, lang 3. — **2.** örtlich (*ant.* hinter) before, in front of; f. abnehmen 1, Anker 1, Auge 2 (am Ende) und 3; (dicht) vor dem Feinde in full view of the enemy; f. gehören 2 unter „**vor**"; vor Gott in the presence of God; f. Kopf 8 am Ende; e-m e-e Kugel vor den Kopf schießen to send a bullet through a p.'s head; f. Nase 3 am Schluß; den See vor sich h. to be opposite (or to face) the lake; vor dem Tore outside the gate; e-n vor die Tür werfen to turn a p. out (of doors); (gerade) vor uns (just) ahead of us; vor f-m Untergange stehen to be on the verge (or brink) of ruin; das Subjekt steht vor dem (ober: stellt man vor das) Zeitwort ... comes before (or precedes) the verb. — **3.** Vorzug bezeichnend: before, in preference to; vor allem, vor allen Dingen above all; Gnade vor (bisw. für) Recht ergehen lassen to temper justice with mercy; den Vorrang vor e-m h. to take precedence of a p.; Sprichw. f. Gewalt 3 am Ende. — **4.** Rücksichtnahme, Gefühle bz.: Abneigung vor e-m h. to have an aversion for (or to) a p.; f. Abscheu 1, Achtung 2; sich vor et. in acht nehmen, hüten to beware of a th., to be on one's guard against a th.; fliehen vor to flee (or escape) from; Furcht vor fear of; sich fürchten vor to be afraid of; ich habe keine Geheimnisse vor Ihnen I keep no secrets from you; vor e-m schützen to protect against (or from) a p.; vor dem Winde geschützt sheltered from the wind; sein Herz vor etwas verschließen to shut one's heart to (or against) a th.; sich vor e-m verstecken to hide (or conceal o.s.) from a p.; Schutz vor dem Winde shelter from the wind. — **5.** a) Hindernis bz.: er konnte vor Aufregung nicht sprechen he could not speak for (or with) excitement; f. Baum 2; b) Ursache bz.: from, for, with, through, by; f. Freude am Ende; vor Hunger, Kummer sterben to die of hunger, of grief; f. Kälte, Müdigkeit; er heulte vor Wut he howled with rage. — **6.** fast † = für, z.B. Schritt vor Schritt step for step.
II **Vor** *n, inv.* **7.** das Vor und Nach the (or what comes) before and after. —

Signs (see page XVII): F familiar; P vulgar; ☞ flash; ⟋ rare; † obsolete (died); * new word (born); ⧺ incorrect; ♪ music.

III *adv.* 8. a) meist † = vorher; noch gbr. in: nach wie vor now (or then) as before; vgl. nach 5 am Ende; b) *ell.* vor! (tretet vor!) (step) forward!; ⚔ Offiziere 2! officers to the front!

vor-..., **Vor-...** (f"...) Vorsilbe in Zssgn I mit *verbs*, die immer trennbar (**) sind: 1. in der Bed. von „vor 1": etwas ₂halten *v/a.* to hold s.th. before or in front (of). — 2. (voraus, vorher): ₂bedenken *v/a.* to think over beforehand. — 3. (in Gegenwart von): Freunden etwas ₂erzählen to relate s.th. before (or in presence of) friends; e-m et. ₂spielen to play s.th. to a p. — 4. (zur Anleitung von): e-m et. ₂zeichnen to show a p. how to draw a th. — 5. (hervortretend): dieses Gefühl herrschte vor that feeling predominated *or* prevailed. — II mit *nouns* 6. (ant. Hinter-...): ~garten *m* front garden. — 7. (ant. Nach-...): ~sommer *m* early summer. — III mit *adjectives*, bsd. mit von *npr.* gebildeten: 8. ₂adam(it)isch pre-adam(it)ic, ₂christlich ante- (or pre-)Christian.

vor-ab (f-ˇ) *adv.* (vor allem) above all (things), before everything else, first of all; (besonders) especially.

Vor-abend (f"...) *m* ⓒc. evening before s.th.; am ~ großer Ereignisse on the eve of great events; ₂**adam(it)isch** *a.* ⓒ *f.* vor-... III; ₂**ahnen** *v/a.* ⓒ**: et. ₂ to have a foreboding (or presentiment) of a th., schwächer: to anticipate a th.; ₂d prophetic; ~ *n* ⓒ und ₂**ahnung** *f* ⓒ foreboding, presentiment, von Bösem: misgiving; **-alpen** ♀ *f/pl.* ⓒ Lower Alps, spurs of the Alps.

vor-an (f-ˇ) *adv.* before; at the head, in front (of the others); nur 2! (go) on!, move on!, (push) ahead!.

vor-an-eilen (f-ˢ...) *v/n.* (sn) ⓒ** to hurry on (before); ₂**geh(e)n** *v/n.* (sn) ⓒ** to go before or ahead or in advance, to (take the lead, to walk at the head (of a procession); e-m ₂ to march (or walk) in front of a p., to precede a p.; e-m mit gutem Beispiele ₂ to set a p. a good example; ₂**kommen** *v/n.* (sn) ⓒ** to advance, to progress; ₂**laufen** *v/n.* (sn) ⓒ**, ₂**rasen** *v/n.* (sn) ⓒ** to run on before; ₂**leuchten** *v/n.* (h.) ⓒ** to hold a light before, to shine in front of; ₂**machen** *v/n.* ⓒ** to hasten; mach voran! hurry on!, be quick!, F look sharp!; ₂**reiten** *v/n.* (sn) ⓒ b** to ride in advance, to gallop along; ₂**schicken** *v/a.* ⓒ** to send on before.

Vor-anschlag (f"...) *m* ⓒc. preliminary (or rough) calculation, (previous) estimate; *parl.* budget; ₂**anstalt** *f* ⓒ: a) previous arrangement; preparation, preliminary (step); b) preparatory establishment.

vor-an-stellen (f-ˢ...) *v/a.* ⓒ** to place in front (of); ₂**stürmen** *v/n.* (sn) ⓒ** to rush forward or ahead, to gallop on.

Vor-anzeige (f"...) *f* ⓒ previous (or preliminary) announcement or advice or notice; **-arbeit** *f* ⓒ preliminary (or preparatory) work or labour; bei Schriftwerken: preliminary studies *pl.*;

₂**arbeiten** ⓒ** *v/n.* (h.): e-m ₂ to work in advance of a p.; *v/a.* e-m (et.) ₂ to prepare a p.'s work, to pave (or smooth) the way for a p.; et. ₂ (vor der eigentlichen Arbeit) to get a piece of work ready; **-arbeiter** *m* ⓒ head worker, in Fabriken ꝛc.: leading hand or operator; (Werkmeister) foreman (of a workshop); **-arm** *m* ⓒc. *anat.* forearm; **-ärmel** *m* ⓒ false sleeve; ₂**auf** (f-ˡ) *adv.* = voran.

vor-aus (f-ˡ) *adv.* örtlich: before; der Bote eilte ₂ ... was (hurrying on) in advance; e-m ₂ sein to have the start of a p.; als Vorzug: et. vor e-m ₂ haben to have an advantage over a p., to excel a p. in s.th.; zeitlich: ₂, im (oder zum) ₂ (f"ˡ) (vorher) beforehand, in advance, previously, (vorzeitig) by anticipation, before the time; im ₂ abgemacht, verabredet preconcerted; im ₂ ersonnen, geplant premeditated; im ₂ geneigt *u.* || predisposed to ||; in Briefen: mit bestem Dank im voraus thanking you beforehand.

vor-aus-bedenken (f-"...) *v/a.* ⓒ*/* to think over beforehand; ₂**bedingen** *v/a.* ⓒ*/* to stipulate in advance, sich et. ₂ to reserve a th. to o.s.; **-bedingung** *f* = Vorbedingung; ₂**bestellen** *v/a.* ⓒ*/* to order beforehand, to bespeak in advance (a. = abonnieren); ~ *n* = ₂bestellung; **-besteller** *m* ⓒ one who orders beforehand, a. = Abonnent; **-bestellung** *f* order given beforehand; vgl. Abonnement; ₂**bestimmen** *v/a.* ⓒ*/* to predetermine; **-bestimmung** *f, theol.* predetermination, predestination; ₂**bewerten** ⓒ *v/a.* ⓒ*/* to discount; der vielfach ₂bewertete Ernteberich the largely discounted harvest-report; ₂**bezahlen** *v/a.* ⓒ*/* to pay in advance, to prepay; ~ *n*, **-bezahlung** *f* ⓒ payment in advance, prepayment; ₂**datieren** *v/a.* ⓒ** to foredate, to antedate; ₂**empfangen** *v/a.* ⓒ b*/* to receive in advance; ₂**empfinden** *v/n.* (h.) ⓒ*/* to have a presentiment, to perceive beforehand; ₂**fahren** *v/a.* ⓒ** to send (by carriage, &c.) in advance; *v/n.* (sn) to drive (or cycle, sail, &c.) in advance; ₂**geh(e)n** *v/n.* (sn) ⓒ** to go before or in advance, to lead the way; dem Zuge gingen Trommler voraus drummers walked in front of (or preceded) the procession; im ₂**gehen**den (weiter oben) in the previous; chapter(s) or passage(s), above; ₂**laufen** *v/n.* (sn)** (sn) to run in advance; **-nahme** *f* ⓒ anticipation (auch jur.); ₂**nehmen** ⓒ a** to take beforehand, to anticipate; ₂**reisen** ⓒ**, ₂**reiten** ⓒ b** *v/n.* (sn) to travel, to ride in advance; **-sage** *f* ⓒ prediction; ₂**sagen** *v/a.* ⓒ** to foretell, to predict; (wahrsagen) to prophesy; ₂**schicken** *v/a.* ⓒ** to send in advance; dies ₂geschickt, gehen wir zur Sache über after these preliminary remarks ...; ₂**sehen** *v/a.* ⓒa** to foresee; ₂**sein** *v/n.* (sn) ⓒa** to be ahead (or in advance) of others; ₂**setzen** *v/a.* ⓒ** to (pre)suppose; (annehmen) to assume;

(vermuten) to presume; et. als bekannt ₂ to take (the knowledge of) a th. for granted; ₂**gesetzt, daß** // supposing (or provided) that //; **-setzung** *f* ⓒ supposition; (Annahme) assumption, ₇ hypothesis; ₂**sicht** *f* ⓒ: a) (Vorhersehen) foresight, (Vorbedacht) forethought; b) (Aussicht) prospect; in der frohen ~, daß er gewinnen wird in the joyful anticipation of his winning; ₂**sichtlich** *a.* ⓒ to be foreseen or anticipated, presumable, prospective; *a.* = wahrscheinlich; ₂**wissen** *v/a.* ⓒ*/* to know beforehand; ~ *n* ⓒ foreknowledge, prescience; ₂**zahlen** *v/a.* ⓒ** = ₂bezahlen.

Vor-bande (f"...) *f* ⓒ Billard: der Ball muß ~ h. the ball must first touch the cushion; **-bau** *m* ⓒc. *arch.* front building or structure, eines Ladens: front; (Vorhalle) porch, portico, entrance-hall; ₂**bauen** *v/a.* ⓒ**: a) to build in front of; (vorspringend bauen) to build out; b) *fig.* einer Sache (*dat.*) ₂ (verhütend vorbeugen) to take precautions (or to guard) against a th.; to (try to) obviate (or prevent, preclude) a th.; kluge Leute bauen vor the wise provide for the future or for (all) emergencies; ~ *n* ⓒ und **-bauung** *f* ⓒ (f. b) *fig.* precaution; prevention, preventive measure, provision for the future; **-bedacht** *m* ⓒc. forethought, premeditation; mit ~ deliberately, purposely, on purpose, *jur.* bei Verbrechen: with malice aforethought or prepense; ohne ~ unintentionally; ₂**bedächtig** *a.* ⓒ considerate, cautious; *adv.* = mit Vorbedacht (f. ds); ₂**bedenken** *v/a.* ⓒ*/* to think over (or consider) beforehand, vorbedacht, auch: premeditated (crime), wilful (murder); ₂**bedeuten** *v/a.* ⓒ*/* to forebode, portend, prognosticate, presage; **-bedeutung** *f* ⓒ foreboding, omen, portent, prognostic(ation), gute: good augury, favourable sign or symptom; ₂**bedingen** *v/a.* ⓒ*/* to stipulate beforehand; ~ *n* ⓒ und **-bedingung** *f* ⓒ previous stipulation, preliminary condition; **-begriff** *m* ⓒc. preliminary notion or conception, preconception; **-behalt** *m* ⓒc. reservation, reserve(d right); *jur.* stiller ~ mental reservation; mit ~ m-r Rechte without prejudice to my rights; ohne ~ without (any) restriction, unconditionally; unter dem (gewöhnlichen) ~ with the (usual) proviso or reservation; unter ~ aller Rechte all rights reserved; ₂**behalten** *v/a.* ⓒa*/*: eine Maske, Schürze ꝛc. ₂ to keep ... on; e-m et. ₂ (für e-n et. wahren) to keep or reserve, save) a th. for a p.; sich Rechte ꝛc. ₂ to reserve ... to o.s.; ~ *n* ⓒ = Vorbehalt; ₂**behaltlich**, ₂**behältlich** *prp.* mit *gen.* with a reservation (or proviso or restriction) as to; ₂ seiner Zustimmung subject to (or provided he gives) his consent; **-behaltung** *f* ⓒ = Vorbehalt.

vor-bei (f-ˡ) *adv.* 1. örtlich: (in passing) by; mit *verbs* der Bewegung meist: to pass, zB. an, neben, vor et. ₂**gehen** ꝛc.

to pass by (the side of) a th.; s. vor=bei=... — 2. zeitlich: (weg, verschwunden) past, over; es ist zehn (Uhr) ~ it is past (F gone) ten (o'clock); es ist mit ihm ~ (zu Ende) it is all over (or up) with him, he is done for; he is lost or ruined; die Zeit ist ~ the time is past or gone; Sprichw. ~ ist ~ bygones are bygones. — 3. *ell.* b. Scheibenschießen: drei Schüsse ~! missed three times!

vorbei=eilen (f-″...) *v/n.* (sn) [88]**: (an et.) ~ to hurry past a th., to pass a th. hurriedly; ~**fahren** *v/n.* (sn) [Sb]** to drive (or sail, &c.) past; ~**fliegen** *v/n.* (sn) [70a]** to fly past; ~**fließen** *v/n.* (sn) [70d]** to flow by or past; ~**führen** *v/a.* [88]** to lead past; ~**geh(e)n** *v/n.* [94]** (sn): an et. ~ to go (or pass) by a th.; ~ *n* [23] passing; **im** ~ in passing; (beim Reden) by the way; ~**jagen** *v/n.* (sn) [88]** to gallop past, von einer Schar: to sweep by; ~**kommen** *v/n.* (sn) [84]** to pass (by); ~**können** *v/n.* (h.) [98]* to be able to pass or to get past; ~**lassen** *v/a.* [Sa]** to let pass, F to let by; ~**laufen** *v/n.* (sn) [Saft]** to run past; ~**marsch** ⚔ *m* march past, defile; ~**marschieren** *v/n.* (sn) [93]** to march past, ⚔ to defile; ~**müssen** *v/n.* (h.) [98]** to be obliged to pass; ~**reiten** *v/n.* (sn) [80b]** to ride past; ~**schießen** *v/n.* [76c(ef)t]**: a) (sn) to shoot (or rush) by; b) (h.) (schießend das Ziel verfehlen) to miss the mark or the bull's-eye; ~**schlagen** *v/n.* (h.) [Sb]** to miss in striking; ~**sein** *v/n.* (sn) [Wa]** s. vorbei 2; ~**stoßen** *v/n.* (h.) [Sa]** to miss in thrusting; ~**werfen** *v/n.* (h.) [70b]** to miss in throwing; ~**ziehen** *v/n.* (sn) [70b]** to pass (in a body); auch = ~marschieren.

vor=bekommen (f-″...) *v/a.* [84]*/*: das Kind bekam eine Schürze vor... had a pinafore put on; (hervorholen) ich kann es nicht ~ I cannot get it out; Spiel: ich habe 10 Points von ihm ~ he gave me ten points (to start with); ~**bemeldet** ↘ *a.* [66] = vorbenannt; ~**bemerkung** *f* [46] preliminary (or introductory) remark, introduction, zu e-m Gesetze &c.: preamble; ~**benannt** *a.* [66] aforesaid, aforementioned; ~**beraten** *v/n.* (h.) [Sa]*/* to consult (or deliberate) beforehand (über et. about a th.); ~**beratung** *f* [46] preliminary consultation; ~**bereiten** *v/a.* und **sich** ~ *v/refl.* [89]*/*: (sich) ~ to prepare (o.s.); e-n **für** et. ~ (empfänglich m.) to dispose a p. for a th.; sich **auf** etwas, **zu** et. ~ to get (or make) ready for a th., to make preparations (or arrangements) for a th., durch Leibesübungen &c.: to train for a th.; sich zu einer Prüfung ~ to prepare (or read) for an examination; ~d preparatory, preliminary; auf etwas vorbereitet sein to be prepared (or ready) for a th.; ~ *n* [23] u. ~**bereitung** *f* [46] preparation; predisposition; training; ~en (Zurüstungen) zu e-r Reise treffen od. m. to make arrangements for travelling.

Vor=bereitungs=anstalt (f″⌣⌣...) *f* [62] preparatory establishment or school; training-college for teachers, &c.; für Prüfungskandidaten: (Army) coaching establishment; ~**kenntnisse** *f/pl.* elementary knowledge; ~**klasse** *f* preparatory class; ~**maßregel** *f* preliminary measure; ~**schule** *f* preparatory school; ~**stunde** *f* elementary lesson; ~**unterricht** *m* preparatory teaching, elementary instruction.

Vor=berge ♀ (f″...) *m/pl.* [U]c. spurs *pl.* of a mountain-range; vgl. Voralpen; ~**bericht** *m* [U]c. preliminary report, zu einem Gesetze &c.: preamble, preface; ~**besagt** *a.* [66] aforementioned; ~**ermaßen** *adv.* as previously stated or mentioned; ~**bescheid** *m* [U]c. meist jur. preliminary discussion or debate; ~**bestraft** *a.* [66] jur. previously convicted; ~**bestrafung** *f* [46] previous conviction; ~**beten** *v/n.* (h.) u. *v/a.* [89]**: e-m ein Gebet &c. ~ to say (or pronounce, recite) a prayer, &c. before a p.; bei Tische ~ to say grace; in der Kirche ~ to lead in prayer; das Vaterunser ~ to repeat the Lord's prayer; ~**beter** *m* [22] *rel.* (bsd. bei den Juden) one who leads in prayer; ~**beugen** [88]** *v/a.* to bend forward; *v/n.* (h.) einem Übel &c. ~ = vorbauen b; ~d preventive, precautionary, *med.*: ⚕ prophylactic; *v/refl.* **sich** ~ to bend (or lean) forward; ~ *n* [23] u. ~**beugung** *f* [46] bending forward; beim ~ des Körpers in leaning forward; prevention, *med.*: ⚕ prophylaxis; ~**beugungs=maßregel** *f*, ~**mittel** *n* preventive measure, preservative, *med.* prophylactic (remedy); ~**bild** *n* [4]c. (Muster) model, pattern, standard, (Beispiel) example; (Urbild) (proto)type, original; (vorbedeutendes Bild) symbol, emblem; ~**bilden** *v/a.* [89]**: a) (darstellen) to represent, in Umrissen: to shadow forth, als Urbild: to typify, b) durch Unterricht: to impart the rudiments to; gut vorgebildet well grounded; ~ *n* [23] = Vorbildung; ~**bildlich** *a.* [66] figurative, representative, typical, symbolic(al), emblematic(al) (für of); ~**keit** *f* [46] figurativeness; typicalness; ~**bildung** *f* [46] (s. vorbilden a) representation, typification; (s. vorbilden b) grounding, preparatory teaching; (Vorbereitung) preparation; allgemeine ~ general education or knowledge (required for a professional training); ~**bildungs=anstalt**, ~**schule** *f* [62] preparatory establishment or school; junior forms *pl.* of a college; ~**binden** *v/a.* [71]** to tie in front of; eine Schürze ~ to tie (or put) on an apron; Buchbinderei: dem Buche das Inhaltsverzeichnis ~ to bind the table of contents in the front part of the book; to tie first; e-m et. ~ to tie a th. in presence of a p.; *provc.* F sich e-n ~ to reprimand a p., to give a p. a good talking-to; ~**blasen** ♪ *v/a.* [Sa]**: e-m et. auf dem Horn ~ to blow (or play) s.th. to a p. (or a p. s.th.) on the horn; ~**bohren** *v/a.* und *v/n.* (h.) [88]** ⚙ to (bore) open with a gimlet or an auger; ⚒ to open up by boring; ~**bohrer** ⚙ *m* [22] first bit, auger; ~**börse** 💰 *f* [48] etwa: dealing (in the street) previous to official hours; ~**bote** [ahd.] *m* [44] forerunner, *fig.* precursor, harbinger (of glad news, &c.), herald; (Vorzeichen) early (or previous) sign, *path.* preliminary symptom.

Vor=bram=brasse ⚓ (f″⌣...) *f* [62] foretopgallant brace; ~**segel** *n* foretopgallant sail; ~**stenge** *f* foretopgallant mast.

vor=brechen (f″...) *v/n.* (sn) [70a]**: aus e-m Hinterhalt ~ to sally forth from an ambush; ~**bringen** *v/a.* [97]**: a) = hervorbringen; b) (aussprechen) to utter, say, express, (behaupten) to assert, to maintain; (zur Sprache bringen) to put forward, to bring forward or on the carpet, to broach a subject; (vorlegen) to produce; (vorschlagen) to propose; (anführen) to allege, to quote, zur Entschuldigung: to plead (in one's defence); eine Klage ~ to make a complaint, gerichtlich: to prefer a charge; er konnte kein Wort ~ he could not utter (or say) a word; ~ *n* [23] (s. b) utterance; assertion; proposal, allegation; ~**buchstabieren** *v/a.* [93]**: e-m einen Namen &c. ~ to spell (out) ... before (or for, to) a p.; ~**bühne** *f* [48] *thea.* front (part) of the stage; Alt. proscenium; ~**burg** *f* [46] (Gebäude außerhalb der Burgmauer) outbuildings (or outer works) *pl.* of a castle; (Burg, die einer andern als Schirm dient) castle (or fort) protecting another castle or fort; ~**christlich** *a.* [66] ante- (or pre-)Christian; ~**dach** *n* [2]c. projecting roof, (Schutzdach) penthouse; ~**datieren** *v/a.* [93]**: e-n Brief &c. ~ to antedate; ~**deck** ⚓ fore-deck; ~**dem** (f⌣⌣) *adv.* formerly = ehemals; ~**demonstrieren** (f″...) *v/a.* [93]** to demonstrate to, to explain to.

Vorder=achse 🚂 (f⌣...) *f* [62] leading axle; ~**ansicht** *f* front view; ~**arm** *m* forearm; ~**asien** ♀ *n* Anterior Asia, oft: the Near East; ~**blatt** *n*: a) Schlächterei: fore-quarter of a sheep, &c.; vgl. ~bug; b) ⚙ *typ.* frontispiece; ~**brust** *f* front part of the chest; ~**bug** *m* Schlächterei: shoulder(-blade) of mutton or veal; ~**bühne** *f*, *thea.* front part of the stage; ~**deck** ⚓ *n* forepart of the deck.

vordere (f⌣⌣⌣) [ahd.: further: fürder] *a.* [66] (*ant.* hintere) in the front (rank), front(al), von Körperteilen: anterior.

Vorder=eck (f⌣⌣...) *n* [62] beim Kegelspiel: front skittle; ~**eisen** ⚙ *n* Hufschmiede: front (or fore-) shoe of a horse; ~**ende** *n* fore-end; ~**fassade**, ~**front** *f*, *arch.* front(age), bisw.: forefront; ~**fläche** *f* front (or anterior) surface; ~**flagge** ⚓ *f* flag of the bowsprit; ~**fleck** ⚙ *m* Schuhmach.: fore-end of the sole; ~**fuß** *m*: a) forefoot; b) front part (or forepart) of the foot; ~**garten** *m* front garden; ~**gebäude** *n* front (part of a) building; ~**gestell** ⚙ *n* eines Wagens: fore-frame of a coach, fore-carriage; ~**giebel** *m*, *arch.* front gable, frontispiece; ~**glied** *n*: a) *zo.* front (or anterior) limb; b) *arith.* ~ eines Verhältnisses antecedent of a proportion; *log.* antecedent, auch = ~satz b; c) ⚔ front rank; ~**grund** *m* foreground; in den ~ stellen to put in the foreground or front (rank), to place foremost, to throw into relief; *fig.* to

[Vorderhaar]

consider first; in den ~ treten to come to the front, von e-r Angelegenheit, Frage: to crop up; =haar n front hair; =hand¹ (f~ೲ) f: a) anat. forepart of the hand, ⚕ metacarpus; b) man. fore-hand; c) Kartenspiel: lead.
vor-der-hand² (f~ೲ) adv. for the present, for a while; as yet, just now.
Vorder-haupt (f~...) n ⑫ anat. anterior part of the head, ⚕ sinciput, auch = Stirn; =haus n front (part of a) house; =hof m fore-court; =indien ⚕ npr/n. India (proper), a. Hindustan; =kastell ↓ n forecastle; =kopf m = =haupt; =lader ⚔ m (ant. Hinterlader) muzzle-loader, muzzle-loading gun; =lauf m: a) hunt. =läufe fore-legs pl.; b) ⊙ Büchsenmach.: fore-end of the barrel; =leder ⊙ n Schuhmach.: front (part) of the boot, toe-cap; =leib m fr. part of the body, ent. thorax; =leute m/pl.(vgl. auch =mann) men in the front rank (auch ⚔); =loge f, thea. front box; =luke ↓ f fore-hatchway; =mann m: a) ⚓ previous endorser of a bill; b) ⚔ = in der Rotte: front-rank man, leader of a file; ↓ next ahead; ~ und Hintermann front and rear rank; c) ich habe noch zehn männer ... ten (men) ahead of me, als Beamter ೫c. auch: ... ten seniors; =mast ↓ m foremast; =mauer f, arch. front wall; =perron m front platform of a tram-car; =pferd n leading horse, leader; =rad n fore-wheel, e-s Fahrrades a.: steering-wheel; =rast ⚔ f half-cock; =raum ↓ m eines Schiffes: forehold; =reihe f front rank; =rhein ⚕ N.-Schweiz: Fore Rhine, Vorder-Rhein; =rücken m, ent.: ⚕ pronotum; =ruhe f = =rast; =satz m: a) gram.: ⚕ protasis; b) log. major (proposition); =schiff ↓ n fore-body of a ship; =seite f: a) arch. front(age), front side, (fr.) façade; b) e-r Münze: obverse; =sitz m im Wagen: fr. seat.
vorderst (f~ೲ) sup. v. vorder; das ~e zuhinterst kehren to put the reverse (or wrong) side in (the) front; vgl. zuvorderst; der ²e (vorgerückteste) the foremost, the first, the headmost, the most advanced; ²e Seite front(age).
Vorder=steven ↓ (f~...) m ⑫ e-s Schiffes: stem; =stube f front room; =stück n fr. piece; =teil m, n front part, forepart; ↓ e-s Schiffes: prow; =tor n front gate; =treffen ⚔ n front (line), advanced body of an army, (Vortrab) van(guard); =tür(e) f front door; =viertel n beim Schlachtvieh: fore-quarter; =wagen m fore-carriage, ⚔ artill. (Protze) limber; =wand f front wall; =zahn m front tooth, tooth in the front; =zimmer m fr. room.
vor=drängen (f~...) v/a. und v/refl. ⑱** to press (or push, thrust, urge) forward; sich ²e, F ²drängeln ⑱a** to press (or push, crowd) forward; to intrude; sich ²o obtrusive pushing, forward; ²drängen v/n. (jn) ⑪fi** to push on, to advance mst fig. to make (gewaltsam: to force) one's way, to make headway, to go (or push) ahead; to gain ground (a. ⚔), ~ n ㉓ advance, progress; ²dringlich a. ⑯ pushing (forward), forward; (zudringlich) intrusive, obtrusive; =druck¹ ⊙

m ⑫c. beim Keltern: new wine of the first pressing, first runnings pl. (ant. Nachlauf); =druck² m ⑫c. typ. (das zuerst Gedruckte) first (or rough) impression or proof; ²drucken ⊙ v/a. ⑱** typ. to print in front of a book, an article, &c.; ²drücken v/a. ⑱** to press (or push) forward, to push on, to force; ²du-deln v/a. ⑫a**: e-m et. ²e to sing (or play) a th. in a humdrum tone to a p., weitS. to bore a p. with a long tale; =ebbe ↓ f ⑱ beginning of the ebb-tide; setting-in of low tide (or low water, receding (or ebbing) of the tide; ²eilen v/n. (jn) ⑱** to advance rapidly, (vorauseilen) to hurry on before or in advance; einem ²e to outrun a p., to leave a p. behind, to get before (or ahead of) a p.; ⊙ mach. den Schieber, das Schubventil ²e laffen to cushion the piston; ²eilig a. ⑯ overhasty, rash, precipitate, (verfrüht) premature; bsd. Am. previous; (früh-reif) precocious; (unüberlegt) ill-considered; adv. auch: in too great a hurry, (too) hastily, too soon; ~keit f ⑯ overgreat haste, rashness, precipitateness, precipitancy; ²einander adv. before (or in front of) each other; ²eingenommen a. ⑯ prepossessed, prejudiced, biassed (für et. in favour of a th.; gegen et. against a th.); ~heit f⑯ prepossession. prejudice, bias; =eltern pl., inv. forefathers. jur. ancestors, progenitors, F co. forebears pl.; ²empfin-den v/a. ⑪*/* to perceive (or feel) beforehand, to have a presentiment of; ~ n ㉓ u. =empfindung f ⑯ presentiment, premonition; ²enthalten v a. ⑯a*/*: e-m et. ²e to withhold a th. from a p., to keep a th. back from a p.; ~ n ㉓ und =enthaltung f ⑯ withholding, detention; =entscheidung f ⑯ jur. precedent, previous judgment; =erinnerung f ⑯ previous warning, premonition; (einleitende Bemerkung) prefatory (or introductory) remark; preface; =erklärung f ⑯ preliminary declaration, introductory remark; =ernte f ⑯ first harvest or crop; ²erst (f~ೲ) adv. (zuvor) previously; (vor allem) first of all, before everything else; (vorläufig) for the present, for the time being; ²erwählen v/a. ⑱*/* to choose (or elect) beforehand. to pre-elect; rel. to predestinate; ²er-wähnt a. ⑯ beforementioned, previously mentioned or quoted, aforenamed, aforesaid, auch: aforementioned; =erzählen v/a. ⑱*/*: e-m et. ²e to relate a th. to a p.; ²essen v/a. ⑱*/*: einem et. ²e to eat s.th. in presence of a p.; ~ n ㉓ Kochkunst: (Gericht vor dem Hauptessen) introductory course, first dish; ²fabeln v/a. ⑫a**: e-m et. ²e to tell a p. tales (or fibs) about a th.; =fahr [mhd.] m ⑫(⑳d.) (mst im pl.; ant. Nachfahr) progenitor; mein ~ (e-r meiner Voreltern) one of my ancestors or forefathers; f. a. Voreltern; ²fahren v/n. (jn) ⑱b**: bei e-m zum Besuche ²e to drive (in a carriage) up to a p.'s door, to stop (or pull up) one's carriage at a p.'s house; den Wagen (vor die Tür) ²e laffen

[vorführen]

to order the carriage (to drive up) to the door; e-m ²e: a) (fahrend voraneilen) to drive (or cycle, motor) in advance of a p.; b) (in den Weg kommen) der Wagen fuhr uns vor ... blocked (or obstructed) our way; =fall m ⑫c.: a) occurrence, incident, (Begebenheit) event; (Fall) case, (Zs.-treffen von Umständen) juncture; unangenehmer ~ misadventure; b) path. (Hervortreten eines Organs) dropping of the womb, &c., ⚕ prolapsus, procidence; ⊙ Uhrmacherei: ~ am Schlagwerke e-r Uhr: detent; ²fallen v/n. (jn) ⑯a**: a) to occur, to happen, unvermutet: to come to pass; er tat, als wenn nichts vorgefallen wäre he behaved (or went on) as if nothing had happened; was ist Neues vorgefallen? what news is there?; et. kürzlich Vorgefallenes a recent incident or occurrence, s.th. that happened lately or recently; b) (nach vorn fallen) to fall forward. path.: ⚕ to prolapse; ²b: ⚕ procident; ~ n ㉓ = Vorfall, ²fallen-heit f ⑯ occurrence; =fall-klöbchen ⊙ n ⑫ Uhrmach.: detent-pin; ²fassen v/a. ⑯** ◊ to preconceive, bsd. gbr. im p.p.: vorgefaßte Meinung preconceived opinion, preconception; (Vorurteil) prejudice; ²fechten v/n. (h.) ⑯b**: e-m ²e to show a p. how to fence, to give a p. a lesson in fencing; =fechter m ㉒: ²e auf dem Fechtboden: assistant fencing-master; (Vorkämpfer) champion; =feier f ⑱ prelude to (or first part of) a fête; (Vorabend eines Festes) eve of a festival or fête; =fenster n ㉒ arch. outside window; ²finden ⑪** (f. finden) v/a. to find (on one's arrival); (begegnen) to meet with, to light upon; alles von ihnen Vorgefundene everything found by them, all their findings pl.; sich ²e v/refl. to be (found) somewhere, to be there, to be in existence; ²findlich a. ⑯ to be found in a place; ²fliegen v/n. (jn) ⑯a** to fly forth or forward; (vorausfliegen) to fly in front of, to outfly, to outstrip (in flying); =flöße f ⑱ right to float first; ²flunkern v/a. ⑫a**: e-m et. ²e to tell a p. tales or fibs (or stories); =flut ↓ f ⑱ coming-in (of the) tide, rise of the tide; ²fordern v/a. ⑫a** to cite, to summon (vgl. vorladen); ~ n ㉓ u. =forderung f ⑱ citation, summons; =frage f. ⑱ preliminary (or previous) question; parl. die ~ stellen to move the previous question; ²fragen v/n. (h.) ⑱(+,⑮b)**: bei e-m ²e, ob // to call on a p. to make inquiry (or to inquire) if //; =freude f ⑱ anticipated joy, pleasure enjoyed beforehand; vgl. Vorgenuß; =frucht f, agr. u. fig. early crop or fruit; ²fühlen v/a. ⑱**: et. ²e to have a presentiment of s.th., to anticipate s.th.; ²führen v/a. ⑱** to lead forward or forth, to bring (or take) to the front, ein Pferd ೫c.: to trot out; zur Schau, Prüfung ²e to present; jur.: dem Richter ²e to bring up (or take) before the judge, Zeugen ²e to produce witnesses (in court); der vorgeführte Verbrecher the criminal appearing in court; ~ n ⓛ

♪ Musik; ⚕ Wissenschaft; ❦ Pflanze; ⚘ Geographie; ⊙ Technik; ⚒ Bergbau; ⚔ Militär; ↓ Marine; ⚜ Handel; ✉ Post; 🚂 Eisenbahn.

[Vorführung] — 1078 — [vorher]

und =führung f 🕮 presentation; production of witnesses; =führungsbefehl m ⚔ jur. warrant to appear (in court); =gabe f 🕮 Spiel, Sport ꝛc.: points given (or odds allowed) to weaker competitors; a. start; =gabe-rennen n 🕮 handicap (race); =gabe-spiel n Tennis: handicap; =gang m Ⓓc.: a) (das Vorausgehen) precedence; einem den ~ lassen to give precedence to a p.; (Frühersein, Vorzug) priority; b) (früherer ähnlicher Fall) precedent; (Beispiel) example, (Muster) model; c) (Verfahren) proceeding(s pl.), transaction; d) = Vorfall; e) thea. act (= Akt); =gänger m 🕮, ~in f 🕮 one preceding or coming before, im Amte ꝛc.: predecessor; ⚲gängig a. 🕮 foregoing, preceding (= vorläufig); =gangs-recht n 🕮 right of priority or precedence; =garn ⊙ n Spinnerei: roving; =garten m 🕮 front garden; ⚲gaukeln v/a. 🕮a*: e-m et. ⚲ to conjure a th. up before a p.'s eyes, to deceive a p. by trickery, to buoy a p. up with vain hopes; das uns vorgegaukelte Abenteuer the adventure (that) we were made to believe or that was so plausibly told us; =gebäude n 🕮 front (part of a) building; ⚲geben v/a. 🕮c**: a) einem et. ⚲ (e-n Vorsprung gewähren) to give a p. an advantage, im Billard ꝛc.: to give (or allow) a p. points, bei Rennen: drei Meter ⚲ to give a start of three yards; b) (in der Rede vorbringen) to put forth, to allege, zur Entschuldigung: to plead, als Vorwand: to use as pretext; Erdichtetes ⚲ to feign, pretend, sham; sie gab vor eine Millionärin zu sein she pretended (or professed) to be a millionairess; ~ n 🕮 (f. b) allegation, plea, pretext, pretence, sham, make-believe, nachdrückliches ~: profession; =gebirge n 🕮 promontory (= Kap 1); ♀ Grünes ~ (West-afrika) Cape Verd(e); a. =Vorberge; ⚲geblich a. 🕮 pretended, so-called, ostensible; (untergeschoben) supposed, make-believe, would-be; (geheuchelt) sham (illness, &c.); adv. as alleged; vgl. angeblich; ⚲gedacht a. = vorerwähnt; ⚲gefaßt f. vorfassen; =gefecht ⚔ n Ⓓc. skirmish (or engagement) between advanced posts; =gefühl n Ⓓc. presentiment; banges ~ (anxious) foreboding, misgiving; ⚲geh(e)n v/n. (ſu) 🕮**: a) die Uhr geht vor ... is (too) fast; die Uhr geht täglich 5 Minuten vor ... gains five minutes a day; b) (vor e-m hergehen) to walk (or march, trot) in front of a p.; (vorausgehen) to go first, to (take the) lead, bitte, geh(e)n Sie vor! please lead the way!; c) (vorwärtsgehen) to go on or forward; ⚔ auf den Feind ⚲ to march on ..., to advance against ...; d) mit et. sachte ꝛc. ⚲ (verfahren) to proceed gently, &c. with a th.; schärfer oder strenger ⚲ to act (or deal) more severely; geh(t) nicht weiter vor damit! don't proceed (or take any further steps) in the matter!; e) meist arch. (vorragen) to project; f) = vorfallen a; er weiß nicht, was hier vorgeht ... what is going on here, F... the goings-on

here; was ist mit ihm vorgegangen? what (change) has taken place with him?; während dies noch vorging whilst this was happening, in the meanwhile; g) mit dat.: e-m ⚲ to precede a p.; h) (den Vorrang vor e-m haben) to have the precedence of a p.; diese Arbeit geht jeder andern vor ... has the preference of (or precedes) all the rest; i) e-m als Muster ⚲ to serve a p. as pattern or model; ~ n 🕮 (f. c) (Vormarsch) forward march, advance; (f. d) (Handeln) procedure; (Verfahren) proceeding(s pl.); gemeinschaftliches ~ concerted action, combined movement (auch ⚔), (f. h) (Vorrang) precedence; ⚲geigen ♪ v/a. 🕮**: einem ein Stück ⚲ to play a p. a tune on the violin; =gelege ⊙ n 🕮 Maschinenwesen: connecting (or intermediate) gear or gearing, communicator; typ. steam-fixture; =gemach n Ⓓc. antechamber; ⚲gemeldet ⚲, ⚲genannt a. 🕮 aforementioned; vgl. vorerwähnt; =genuß m 🕮a. previous (or anticipated) enjoyment, vgl. Vorfreude; =gericht n Ⓓc. first dish; =gesang m Ⓓc. introductory song or chant; =geschichte f 🕮 prehistoric times pl.; previous history, history of a preceding period, e-r Person: antecedents pl.; ⚲geschichtlich a. 🕮 prehistoric(al); =(ge)schmack m Ⓓc. foretaste; =gesetzte(r) s. 🕮 (ant. Untergebene[r]) superior, senior (officer, &c.); (Vorsteher) principal, chief; =gespinst ⊙ n Ⓓb. Spinnerei: roving; feines, grobes ~ fine, coarse roving; ⚲gestern adv. the day before yesterday; ⚲ abend on the evening before last; ⚲gestrig a. 🕮 of (or happening) the day before yesterday; ⚲getan (p.p. von vortun); f. nachbedenken Sprichw.; =giebel m 🕮 arch. front gable(-end); ⚲glänzen v/n. (h.) 🕮** to shine forth; fig. einem ⚲ to be a shining (or a brilliant) example to a p.; ⚲greifen v/n. (h.) 🕮b**: a) zeitlich: mit et. ⚲ to anticipate a th.; einem ⚲ (zuvorkommen) to forestall a p.; einer Frage ⚲ to prejudge a question; e-m in seinen Rechten ⚲ to encroach on a p.'s rights; ⚲d anticipatory; b) örtlich: mit dem rechten Arme ⚲ to stretch out one's right arm; ~ n 🕮 = Greifung; =greifung f 🕮 (f. Greifen a.) anticipation; encroachment; =griff m Ⓓc. =greifung; ⚲haben v/a. 🕮b**: a) eine Schürze ꝛc. ⚲ to have ... on, to wear ...; b) et. ⚲ (sich damit beschäftigen) to be engaged in (or busy with) a th., to be at (or about) a th.; e-n ⚲ (vornehmen) to call a p. to account or to book, to take a p. to task, to handle a p. severely or roughly, F to pitch into a p.; ich habe ihn schon vorgehabt (ausgefragt) ... already questioned (or examined) him, (ausgescholten) ... already scolded (or reprimanded) him; c) (im Sinne haben) to have in view, to intend, purpose, design; Böses ⚲ to have evil designs; er hat es gut mit Ihnen vor he has good intentions (or he means well) towards you; große Dinge mit e-m ⚲ to have great

schemes with regard to a p.; er hat vor, nach Italien zu reisen he intends to go (kürzer: he is going) to Italy; was habt ihr heute vor? what are your plans (or intentions) for to-day?; what are you going to do with yourselves to-day; ~ n 🕮 (f. c) intention, purpose, design, plan, scheme; er mußte von f-m ~ ablassen, abstehen he had to desist from his purpose or to abandon his scheme; =hafen m 🕮 outer port; =halle f 🕮 arch. ~ e-s Hauses: vestibule, (entrance-)hall, parl., thea., &c. lobby; (Säulenhalle) portico, porch, vor e-m grch. Tempel: ⚲ propylæum; fig. e-r Wissenschaft: rudiments, elements, first steps pl.; =halt m Ⓓc. (Vorwurf) reproach; (Vorstellung) remonstrance, expostulation; representation; ⚲halten 🕮a** v/a.: a) to hold before a p. or a th.; e-m eine Büchse ⚲ to hold a rifle to a p.'s head or chest; b) e-m et. ⚲ (vorwerfen) to reproach (or twit, upbraid) a p. with a th., to remonstrate (or expostulate) with a p. about a th.; das wird mir beständig vorgehalten that is constantly being thrown in my face or rammed down my throat; v/n. (h.) (dauern, lange halten) to hold out; von Stoffen ꝛc.: to wear well, von Mitteln ꝛc.: to last, vom Essen, oft: F to stick to one's ribs; Fleisch hält besser vor ... is more substantial; ~ n 🕮 u. =haltung f 🕮 (f. b) reproach, remonstrance; =hand f 🕮 = Vorderhand; Kartenspiel, Whist ꝛc.: elder hand; wer hat die ~ (wer spielt aus)? whose lead is it?; Tennis: (mit) ~ (gespielt) fore-hand; ⚲handen (f-♂) a. 🕮 at hand, 🕮 on hand, in stock; (bestehend) existing, extant; (gegenwärtig) present, ready; (vorliegend) actual; ⚲ sein to exist; reichlich ⚲ sein to abound, to be abundant or in abundance; (sich vorfinden) to be (met with); es ist nichts mehr davon ⚲ there's none of it left, 🕮 we are out of it; =handen-sein (f-♂) n 🕮 (being in) existence; presence; =hang (f^n ...) m Ⓓc. curtain; bibl. veil of the tabernacle; thea. ~ für Zwischenakte: drop-scene, act-drop; den ~ aufziehen (niederlassen) to pull up (to let down or pull down) the blind, thea. to raise (to drop) the curtain; der ~ geht auf (fällt) the curtain rises (drops); ⚲hangen v/n. (ſu) 🕮b** to hang before, to be suspended in front; (vorragen) to jut out, to project; ⚲hängen v/a. 🕮** (f. hängen) to hang before, to suspend in front; ein Schloß ⚲ to put (or fix) a padlock to; =häng(e)schloß n 🕮 padlock; =haupt n Ⓓc. = Vorderhaupt; (Stirn) forehead; =haut f 🕮 anat. foreskin, ⚲ prepuce; =hautverengerung f, path.: ⚲ phimosis; =hemdchen n 🕮, =hemd(e) n 🕮b.(🕮) shirt-front, F dicky; ehm. ~ für Frauen chemisette; =hemd-knopf m stud.

vor-her (f-≀, f-⸺) adv. 1. before(hand), in advance, previously; (früher) formerly; am Abend ⚲ on the preceding (or previous) evening, (on) the night before. — 2. = voraus.

Signs (see page IX): F familiar; P vulgar; F flash; ⚲ rare; † obsolete (died); * new word (born); ++ incorrect; ♪ music;

[vorherbedenken] — 1079 — [vorlaufen]

vorher=bedenken (f-"..., f"-...) v/a. ⊕*/* to reflect (or consider) beforehand; ≈**bestimmen** v/a. ⊕*/* to determine (or settle) beforehand, to predetermine, *theol.* to predestinate, to preordain; =**bestimmung** f. *theol.* predestination; =**bestimmungs=lehre** f doctrine of predestination. [first part of autumn.]
Vor=herbst (f"⌣) m ⓑb. early autumn,
Vorher=dasein (f—"..., f"-...) n ⊕ preexistence; ≈**empfinden** v/a. ⊕*/* = vorempfinden; =**erkennen** v/a. ⊕b*/* to recognize (or know) beforehand; ≈**geh(e)n** v/n. (fn) ⊕** : einer Sache ≈ to precede a th.; ≈**gehend** preceding, anterior, antecedent, preliminary (e-r Sache to a th.); aus dem ~en folgt it follows from previous remarks or from what has already been stated; im ≈en ist gesagt worden, daß // it has been previously mentioned that //; ≈**geschehen** v/n. (fn) ⊕a*/* to take place before(hand).
vor=herig (f"⌣, f"⌣) a. ⊕: a) preceding, previous; b) (wie früher) former.
vorher=merken (f"⌣⌣) v/a. ⊕** to notice (or observe) beforehand.
vor=herrschen (f"⌣) I v/n. (h.) ⊕** to predominate, to prevail; ≈d predominant, prevalent. — II ~ n ⊕ predominance, prevalence.
vorher=sagen (f"⌣⌣) v/a.⊕**: a) (f—"⌣⌣) = voraussagen; b) vorher (früher) sagen (f"—⌣⌣) to say previously; =**sagung** f/⊕ prediction; ≈**sehen** v/a. ⊕a** to foresee; es war vorherzusehen it was to be foreseen or anticipated; =**sehung** f ⊕ prophetic vision; anticipation; =**verkünd(ig)en** v/a. ⊕(⊕)*/* to announce beforehand, to predict; =**verkündigung** f/⊕ prediction, prophecy; =**wissen** v/a. ⊕** to know beforehand.

vor=heucheln (f"...) v/a. ⊕a**: e-m et. ≈ to pretend (or sham) s.th. before (or to) a p.; e-m Freundschaft ≈ to feign (or pretend) friendship for a p.; ≈**heulen** v/a.⊕**: e-m et. ≈ to howl or cry, yell out s.th. before (or to) a p.; e-m sein Unglück ≈c. ≈ to tell a p. in a howling (or crying, whining) tone of one's misfortune(s), &c.; =**himmel** m ⊕ entrance to (or foretaste of) heaven or paradise; ≈**hin** (f—⌣, bisw. f⌣) adv. (vor turzem) quite recently, a little while ago; (eben erst) just now, a minute ago; ≈**hinein** öft. (f"—⌣) adv.: im ≈ in advance; ≈**historisch** (f"—...) a. ⊕ prehistoric(al), previous to historical times; =**hof** m ⓒc. front yard or court, forecourt; auch =**halle**; *anat.* ~ des Herzens: ⟨⟩ auricle (= Vorkammer); ~ des Ohres: ⟨⟩ vestibule; ≈**holen** ↓ v/a. ⊕**: die Schoten ≈ to haul the sheets home; =**hölle** f ⊕ forecourt of hell, limbo, (Fegefeuer) purgatory; ≈**homerisch** a. ⊕ pre-Homeric; ≈**hören** v/a. ⊕**: (heraushören) man hört ihn e Stimme unter allen vor you can hear ... above all the rest; =**hut** f ⊕: a) *agr.* right of first pasturage or grazing; b) ⨯ e-s Heeres: advanced guard.

vorig (f"⌣) a. ⊕ former, preceding; bfp. (letztvergangen) past, last, z.B. ≈es Jahr, ≈en Jahres (abbr. **v. J.**) last year, of last year; ⦿ Ihr Geehrtes vom 15. ≈en Monats (abbr. **v. M.**) your favour of the 15th ultimo (abbr. **ult.**); im ≈en (früher Gesagten) in the previous chapter(s), above.

Vor=instanz (f"...) f ⊕ *jur.* lower court; =**jahr** n ⓓc. preceding year; * (voriges Jahr) last year; ≈**jährig** a. ⊕ of last year; ⦿ ≈e Waren last year's goods; ≈**jammern** v/a.⊕a**: e-m et. ≈ to wail (or lament) about a th. in a p.'s presence or before a p.; =**kammer** f ⊕ antechamber, anteroom, *anat.* ~ des Herzens; ⟨⟩ auricle (of the heart); ≈**kämpfen** v/n. (h.) ⊕** to fight in the front rank (of the battle); =**kämpfer** m ⊕ one who fights in the front rank; *fig.* champion; ≈**kauen** v/a. ⊕**: einem Kinde ≈c. et. ≈ to chew a th. for ...; *fig.* man muß ihm alles ≈ one has to explain to him (or he has to be told) things over and over again; =**kauf** m ⓒc. *jur.* right of first purchase, pre-emption; ⦿ (Aufkaufen) forestalling, dealing in futures; ≈**kaufen** ⦿ v/a. ⊕** to buy up beforehand, to forestall; =**käufer** ⦿ m ⊕, ~**in** f forestaller, dealer in futures; =**kaufs=recht** n ⊕ right of preemption or refusal; das ~ auf et. haben to have the refusal of a th.; =**kehr** f ⊕ = =kehrung; ~ treffen = Vorkehrungen treffen; =**kehren** v/a. ⊕** to put outside; =**kehrung** f ⊕ provision, precaution(ary measure); ~en treffen für to make (one's) arrangements for; die nötigen ~en treffen to make the necessary provision, to take the required steps or measures; =**kenntnis** f ⊕ preliminary (or previous) knowledge; gute ≈kenntnisse in e-m Fache besitzen to be thoroughly acquainted with the rudiments (or elements) of a branch, to be well grounded in a subject; =**kette** f ⊕ von Bergen: lower(or secondary) chain, (Ausläufer) spur; =**kirche** f ⊕ *arch.* porch of a church; ≈**klassisch** a. ⊕ anterior (or prior) to the classical period, pre-classic; ≈**klimpern** v/a. ⊕a**: e-m et. ≈ to strum a p. a tune; ≈**klingen** v/n. (h.) ⊕fi** to sound beforehand; (vor den Ohren klingen) to fall on the ear; (vorherrschend klingen) to sound above (or louder than) the rest, to predominate; ≈**kommen** v/n. (fn) ⊕**: a) = hervorkommen; b) (sich finden) to be found, to be met (with); Platin kommt wenig vor platinum is of rare occurrence or is rarely met with; c) von Sachen: bei Gericht ≈c. ≈ (zur Verhandlung kommen) to come up for discussion, to be argued (in court); d) (sich ereignen) to occur, to happen, to take place; (sich darbieten) to turn up, to offer; ≈**denfalls**, bei ≈der Gelegenheit should the case arise, if the occasion offers (itself), when the opportunity presents itself; so etwas ist noch nie vorgekommen such a thing never happened before; solche Gaunerei ist mir noch nie vorgekommen I never met (or heard of) such roguery; e) (erscheinen) to seem, to appear; das kam mir sehr komisch vor that struck (or impressed) me as very curious, I thought it rather strange; f. spanisch 2; ich weiß nicht, wie Sie mir heute ≈ I don't know what to make of you to-day; etwas nie Vorgekommenes s.th. never known before, an unprecedented case; f) e-m ≈ (zuvorkommen) to come sooner (or earlier) than another person, to get the start of a p.; g) ⌣ bei e-m ≈ = bei e-m vorsprechen; h) ~ n ⊕ = Vorfall 2, ∮ ~ v. Pflanzen: ⟨⟩ habitat ...; *min.* ~ von Kupfer ≈c. presence ..., occurrence ...; ⦿ von Wechseln: bei ~ on presentation; =**kommenheit** f ⊕, =**kommnis** n ⊕ s.th. that happens, occurrence (vgl. Vorfall a); ≈**können** v/n. (h.) ⊕** to be able to advance or to get to the front; =**korrektur** ⊕ f ⊕ *typ.* first (or rough)proof; =**kost** f ⊕ (Vorgericht) first course; weit.S. provisions, victuals *pl.*; ≈**kosten** v/a. ⊕**: e-m et. ≈ to taste a th. in presence of a p.; =**kost=händler** (in f) m ⊕ provision-dealer or -merchant; =**kost=handlung** f provision-warehouse; ≈**kriechen** v/n. (fn) ⊕fi**a. ⨯ v.b. Infanterie b. Angriff: to creep forward, to advance stealthily or by stealth; =**laden** v/a. ⊕b** (f. laden³): gerichtlich ≈ (vorfordern) to cite, to summon, to serve a notice upon, bei Strafe: to subpœna; der Vorgeladene the p. summoned (to appear in court); ~ n f. Vorladung; =**lader** m ⊕ summoner; =**lade=schein** m, =**ladung** f ⊕ *jur.* summons, citation, mit Strafandrohung: subpœna; e-r ~ Folge leisten to obey (or to appear in response to) a summons; ~s=**befehl** m, ~s=**schreiben** n writ, bisw. letter citatory; =**lage** f ⊕ (Verlängerungsstück) piece put (or added) on, eking-piece; (et. zur Beratung Vorgelegtes) proposal, matter (or subject) brought forward for discussion; *parl.* (Gesetzes=)~ bill (submitted to parliament), legislative proposal; (Schreib=, Zeichen=)~ = Vorlegeblatt; *chm.* = Rezipient, auch: adapter; *metall.* nozzle of a zinc-furnace; =**lager** ⨯ n ⊕ head of a camp; ≈**lagern** v/a. ⊕a** to extend in front of; ≈**lassen** v/a. ⊕**: e-m et. ≈ to stammer out (or mumble) a th. to a p.; =**land** n ⊕ (f. Land) foreland; ehm. die österreichischen ~e (im jetzigen Baden) SCH. the Swabian provinces of Austria; ≈**längst** ⌣ (f—⌣, f"⌣) adv. long ago, long since, (in days of yore) (f"...) v/a. ⊕a** (f. lassen) (vorkommen lassen) to allow to come before, to give the precedence to, beim Start: to allow a p. to get the start of one; beim Laufen: to allow a p. to pass one; (in j-s Gegenwart kommen lassen) e-n ≈ to admit a p. (into one's presence); vorgelassen werden to be shown (or ushered) in; ~ n ⊕ und =**lassung** f ⊕ admission, admittance; =**lauf** m ⓒc. beim Rennen: start; Fußball: den ~ verbieten to disallow the charge; ⊕ Branntweinbrennerei: first runnings *pl.*, first (lot of) spirits distilled; ≈**laufen** v/n. (fn) ⊕fi** to run before or in advance; Fußball:

⟨⟩ scientific; ♀ botanical; ♁ geography; ⊙ machinery; ⨯ mining; ⨯ military; ⚓ marine; ⦿ commercial; ✉ postal; 🚂 railway.

[Vorläufer] — 1080 — [Vornamen]

to charge; e-m 2 to outrun a p.; to overtake (or catch up) a p., to get ahead of a p.; =läufer m ② (a. ~in f ㊼) = =bote; ♀ ~ pl. eines Gebirges spurs pl. of a mountain-chain; 2läufig a. ㊅ precursory, previous; (der Hauptsache vorangehend) preliminary, introductory; (einstweilig) provisional; adv. for the present or moment, for the time (being), in the meanwhile, F in the interim, (It.) pro tem(pore); ♀ 2 ausverkauft, nicht mehr zu bekommen temporarily (or just now) sold out, no more to be had; gerichtlich: 2 freigesetzt provisionally released; =laut a. ㊅ mst hunt. overloud, too noisy; (naseweis) pert, forward; (dünkelhaft) conceited, (übermütig) impertinent, saucy, F cheeky; 2es Wesen pertness, forwardness, F cheek; =leben n ㉓ (früheres Dasein) former (or previous) life, (Vorgeschichte, Vergangenheit) antecedents pl.; 2legbar a. ㊅ presentable.

Vor-lege=blatt (fᵘᴸ⌣...) n ㊻ für Zeichnen od. Schönschreiben: drawing-(or writing-) copy; =gabel f carving-fork; =kelle f für Fisch: fish-slice; =löffel m: a) für Suppe: soup-ladle; b) für Sauce: gravy-spoon, large table-spoon; =messer n für Braten ꝛc.: carving-knife.

vor-legen (fᵘᴸ⌣) I v/a. und v/refl. ㊽** 1. to lay (or put, place) before or in front; frische Pferde 2 to put fresh horses to (the coach); ein Schloß 2 to put on a padlock; sich 2 to lean forward. — 2. e-m et. 2: a) zur Ansicht: to exhibit (or display) a th. before a p., to show a p. a th.; b) zur Begutachtung: to submit (or propose) a th. to a p.; c) zur Beantwortung: e-m e-e Frage 2 to propound (or address, put) a question to a p. — 3. e-m bei Tische et. 2 to help a p. to s.th., to serve a p. with s.th.; e-m zweimal Geflügel 2 to give a p. two helpings of poultry. — 4. (nach vorn legen) et. weiter 2 to push a th. further to the front. — II ~ n ㉓ 5. = Vorlegung.

Vor-leger (fᵘᴸ⌣) m ㉒ 1. bei Tische: one who helps the meat, the vegetables, &c.; (Vorschneider) carver. — 2. (Bett=) ~ bedside rug or carpet.

Vor-lege=schloß (fᵘᴸ⌣...) n ㊻ padlock.

Vor-legung (fᵘᴸ⌣) f ㊻ (s. vorlegen 1) laying before, &c.; (s. 2) exhibition, display; submission, proposal.

vor-lehnen (fᵘ...): sich 2 v/refl. ㊽** to lean (or bend) forward; =leiern v/a. ㊷a**: e-m et. 2 to play a p. a humdrum tune (as on a barrel-organ), fig. to din (or drum) a th. into a p.'s ears; =lesbar a. ㊅ fit to be read aloud; =lese f ㊽ in Weinbergen: beginning of the vintage; preliminary (or early) vintage (f. 2lesen b); 2lesen v/a. ㊷a**: a) to read aloud (to others or to an audience); e-m et. 2 to read a th. (out) to a p.; er läßt sich die Briefe 2 he has his letters read (out) to him; b) abs. (im Weinberge Vorlese halten) to gather the first (ripe) grapes, to hold an early vintage; c) ~ n ㉓ (s.a.) reading aloud; f. =lesung b; =lese=pult n (m)

reader's (or lecturer's) desk; =leser m ㉒, ~in f ㊼ reader; (i. der eine Vorlesung hält) lecturer; =lesung f ㊻: a) = vorlesen c; b) (Vortrag) öffentliche ~ lecture. univ. university- (or academic) lecture; ~en halten über Logik ꝛc. to deliver a course of lectures (or to lecture) on logic, &c.; ~en hören to attend (a course of) lectures; 2letzt a. ㊅ last but one, gr. penultimate; 2e Silbe last syllable but one, penult(ima); 2leuchten v/n. (h.) ㊽**: e-m 2 to carry a light before a p., to hold a candle to a p.; fig. to shine forth (from the rest), to outshine (all) others; e-m als Beispiel 2 to set a brilliant example to a p.; 2lieb (f⁻ᴸ) adv. = fürlieb; =liebe (fᵘ...) f ㊽ predilection; preference; eine ~ haben für // to have a (special) liking (or a partiality) for //, to be partial to //, to be fond of //; 2liegen v/n. (h.) ㊹** to lie in front, to be placed (or situated) before; e-m 2 (vor Augen liegen) to be under consideration or discussion; es liegt heute nichts vor there is nothing that calls for discussion to-day; ♀ Ihr Geehrtes vom 8. d. M. liegt uns vor your favour of the 8th inst. has come to hand or is in our possession; (dasein): es lag eine Täuschung vor there was some deception (about it); 2d p.pr. u. a. ㊅ (augenblicklich 2d) present, actual; der 2de Fall the case before us or in question; ⚓ 2de Werke pl. = Vorwerk b; 2lügen v/a. ㊷d**: e-m et. 2 to tell a p. lies or falsehoods or F crammers.

vorm. (¹) = vor dem.

vorm. abbr.: a) = vormals; b) = vormittags.

vor-machen (fᵘ...) v/a. ㊽**: ein Brett ꝛc. 2 to put (or place, fix) ... before; eine Schürze 2 to put an apron on; e-m et. 2: a) als Muster: to show a p. how to do a th.; b) zur Täuschung: to impose upon a p., to trick (or deceive, mystify) a p.; f. Dunst 2; =magen m ㉓(㉙) zo. = Blättermagen; 2mähen v/n. (h.) ㊽** agr. to mow first; e-m 2 to show (or teach) a p. how to mow; 2malen v/a. ㊽**: e-m et. 2 to paint s.th. before a p., bsd. fig. to depict (or sketch out) a th. to a p.; e-m et. schön 2 to give a p. a most glowing description (or account) of a th.; 2malig a. ㊅, 2mals adv. = ehemalig, ehemals; =mann m ②c. ♀ auf Wechseln, bisw. a. ⚔ = Vordermann, Spiel: player coming before another; Whist ꝛc. oft: elder hand; ⊙ bisw. = =arbeiter; =mars ↓ m ㉓a, f ㊻ foretop; =marsch ⚔ m ⑦a. advance; 2marschieren ⚔ v/n. (fn) ㊽** to advance (on the march).

Vor-mars=fall ↓ (fᵘᴸ...) n ㉒ foretopsail halyard; =segel n foretopsail; =stenge f foretopmast.

vor-märzlich (fᵘᴸ...) a. ㊅ hist. Deutschland: (happening) previous to the revolution of March 1848; =mast ↓ m ㉓b. = Fockᴅ; =mauer f ㊻ outer (or front) wall; bisw. fig. (Schutzwehr) bulwark; 2merken v/a. ㊽** to mark, to note (or jot) down, bsd. ♀ to make a note

of; ~ n ㉓ u. =merkung f ㊻ (making a) note; 2messen v/a. ㊽**: e-m et. 2 to measure a th. before (or out to) a p.; =mittag (fᵘᴸ⌣) m ②c. forenoon, morning (hours pl.); des ~s = vormittags; gestern 2 yesterday (in the) morning; 2mittägig (fᵘᴸ⌣⌣) a. ㊅ of (or in) the forenoon, antemeridian; 2mittags (fᵘᴸ⌣) adv. in the forenoon, (It.) ante meridiem (abbr. a. m.).

Vor-mittags=besuch (fᵘᴸ⌣...) m② morning call; =gottesdienst m, =kirche f, =predigt f. eccl. morning service, sermon; =schule f morning school; =stunde f, =unterricht m morning hour. Schule: morning lesson; =wache ↓ f forenoon watch; =zeit f morning time.

Vor-mitter=nacht (fᵘᴸ⌣...) f ㊾ (the) time before midnight; **vor-mitternächtlich** a. ㊅ (happening) before midnight.

Vor-mund (fᵘᴸ...) [ahd.] m ②ᶜ., =münderin f ㊼ jur. guardian, trustee; =munds-bestellung f ㊻ appointment of a guardian or trustee; =mundschaft f ㊻ jur. guardianship, trusteeship; auch: tutelage; unter ~ stehen (stellen) to be placed (to place) under the care of a guardian or trustee; 2mundschaftlich a. of (or relating to) a guardian(ship) or trustee(ship), a. tutelar(y), pupillary.

Vor-mundschafts=amt (fᵘᴸ⌣...) n ㉒, =behörde f court for the protection of wards, in Engl.: Court of Chancery; =gelder n/pl. property of a ward, trust-money; =gericht n court for the protection of wards, in Engl.: Court of Chancery; =ordnung f (statutory) law relating to guardianship; =rechnung f account rendered of a ward's estate or of trust-money; =wesen n matters pl. relating to guardianship.

vor-müssen (fᵘᴸ⌣) v/n. (h.) ㊽** to be obliged to come (or move) forward, to have to appear (on the scene or thea. before the curtain).

vorn (fᵘ) [ahd.], auch 2e (fᵘ⌣) I adv. (ant. hinten) 1. in front, in the forepart; 2 heraus wohnen to live in the front (of the house), to have (the) front rooms; 2 eintreten to walk in at (or to enter by) the front door; 2 im Buche on the front page (or at the beginning of the book); 2 und hinten before and behind, ↓ fore and aft; fig. 2 und hinten sein to be here, there, and everywhere; vgl. hinten am Ende. — 2. nach prp.: nach 2 fallen to fall forward, to topple over; Zimmer nach 2 hinaus room in the front (of the house), front room; von 2(e): a) (im Angesichte) in the face; b) (neu anfangend) von 2 anfangen to begin at the beginning; c) (wieder, von neuem) anew, afresh, ♪ da capo; (wieder) von 2 anfangen to begin all over again, to start (all) afresh; f. von 7 gegen Ende. — II ~ , inv. 3. das ~ und hinten (both) front and back.

vor-nageln (fᵘ...) v/a. ㊽a** to nail before or in front; =nahme [vornehmen] f ㊻ taking a th. in hand, undertaking a th.; =name m ㊲, ~ n m ㊲ first name, röm. Altertum: praenomen; (Taufname) Christian name.

Zeichen (s. S. XVII): F familiär; P Volkssprache; ⸍ Gaunersprache; ⸌ selten; † alt (auch gestorben); * neu (auch geboren); ⁂ unrichtig;

[vornan] — 1081 — [vorrücken]

vorn-an (f⌣) *adv.* in front; ⁂ sitzen to sit in the front (row or rank).
vorne (f⌣) f. vorn.
vorne=hin (f⌣.ᵉ) *adv.* to the front.
vor-nehm (f¹–.) [mhd.] *a.* ⑯ **1.** nur im sup.: capital, principal; bibl. das ⁂ste und größte Gebot the first and greatest commandment. — **2.** (den höheren Ständen angehörig) **a)** von Personen: aristocratic, of high (or gentle) rank or birth, (most) genteel; (stattlich) stately; f. Dame 1; ⁂e Haltung dignified bearing; die ⁂en Leute, die ~en pl. people of rank or quality or (high) position; die ~sten in e-r Stadt the foremost (or first, leading, chief) people in a town; die ⁂e Welt the world of fashion, a.: the upper ten, high life; den ~en spielen to play the fine gentleman, F to do the grand or the swell; ⁂ tun to put on great (or fine) airs, F to do it fat, to do it thick, to swell it; ⁂ und gering, ~e und Geringe (both) high and low, (both) gentle and simple; **b)** v. Sachen: elegant, fashionable, stylish; ein ⁂es Äußere haben to have a distinguished (or genteel) air or appearance; ⁂ (adv.) gekleidet elegantly dressed, stylishly apparelled.

vor-nehmen (f¹¹–.) I v/a. ⑳a** **1.** to take before one; eine Schürze ⁂ to put on ... — **2.** (sich mit e-m, et. beschäftigen) e-n, et. ⁂ to take up a p., a th.; to deal with a p., a th.; Veränderungen ⁂ to make changes; F e-n ⁂ (anpacken) to tackle a p., to call a p. to book; (heruntermachen) to scold or rebuke, reprimand a p. — **3.** et. ⁂ (beginnen) to undertake (or engage in) a th., to take a th. in hand; wieder ⁂ to resume. — **4.** sich (dat.) et. ⁂ to purpose (or design) doing a th. — II ~ n ㉓ **5.** (f. 3) undertaking; (f. 4) purpose, design.

Vor-nehmheit (f¹¹–.) f ㊺ high rank, distinction, gentle birth, gentility; im Äußeren: genteel (or distinguished) appearance; ⁂nehmlich *adv.* chiefly, pre-eminently, principally, particularly; (vor allem) above all, first and foremost; =nehmtuerei f ㊺, =nehmtun n ㉓ putting on fine (or superior) airs, assuming an air of superiority. F doing the grand or the swell.

vor-neig/en (f¹¹–.) I v/a. u. sich ⁂ v/refl. ㉖** **1.** (sich) ⁂ to bend (or lean) forward, to incline; sich grüßend ⁂ to bow. — II ~ n ㉓ u. ⁂ung f ㊺ **2.** (f. 1) bending forward. — **3.** fig. (vorgefaßte Neigung) (marked) inclination, predilection.

vorn(e)=weg (f¹(⌣).ᵉ) *adv.* from the first, to start (or begin) with.
vorn=herein (f¹.⌣˔ˌ) *adv.*: von ⁂ from the very beginning, at the outset, from the first; (o. weiteres) as a matter of course; ⁂hinein *adv.* in by the front; ⁂über *adv.* head foremost; den Kopf ⁂ beugen ob. neigen to bend one's head forward; ⁂weg f. vorneweg.
Vor-oberleesegel ⚓ (f¹¹⌣⋅̣ʟ⌣) n ㉖ foretopmast studding-sail.
Vor-ort (f¹¹–.) m ⑫c. bis 1848 in der Schweiz: (Zürich, Luzern, Bern) ⁂ vorort, seat of the executive, central place for the executive of an association, &c.; ~e pl. (Ortschaften um e-e Stadt herum) suburbs (or outlying districts) pl. of a town; =verkehr m ㉓ suburban traffic; =ortzug m suburban train; =parlament n ⑫c. preliminary meeting of parliament; ⁂pfeifen v/a. ⑳b**: e-m et. ⁂ to whistle s.th. to a p.; ⁂plappern v/a. ㉒a**: ⁂plaudern; =platz m ⑦a. place (or square) in front of a house, &c.; (Treppenabsatz) landing; vgl. =halle u. =hof; ⁂plaudern v/a. ㉒a**: e-m et. ⁂ to prattle (or chat) to a p. about s.th.; b.s. e-m et. Erdichtetes ⁂ to (try to) make a p. believe some fictitious tale; =pommern ♀ npr/n. ㉓α. (Pommern westl. der Oder) Hither Pomerania.

Vor-posten ⚔ (f¹–⌣) m ㉓ outpost, advanced post or guard; auf ~ on outpost-duty; ~ ausstellen to throw out pickets; ~=dienst m ㉖ duty of outposts, outpost-duty, picketing; ~=gefecht n skirmish(ing) between advanced guards; ~=kette f chain of outposts or pickets; ~=linie f outpost-chain, picket-line.

vor=prahlen (f¹¹–.) v/a. ㉖**: e-m (von) et. ⁂ to boast (or brag) of a th. to (or before) a p.; ⁂predigen v/a. ㉖**: e-m et. ⁂ to preach to (or to sermonize) a p. about a th.; belehrend, einschärfend: to inculcate (F to drive) a th. into a p.; ⁂prüfen v/a. ㉖** to examine (or test) beforehand; ~ n ㉓ u. =prüfung f ㊺ preliminary (or previous) examination, in Cambridge auch: little go, in Oxford: smalls pl.; ⁂ragen ꝛc. = hervorragen ꝛc.; =rang m ⑫c. precedence, priority, pre-eminence; den ~ vor e-m h. to take precedence of a p., to rank before a p.; =rat m ⑫c. stock (in hand), store, storage, (vollständige Sammlung) assortment; (Tripartes) reserve(-fund); ~ an Lebensmitteln (supply of) provisions pl.; sich einen ~ von etwas anlegen, et. im ~ anschaffen to lay in a store of s.th.; mit ~ (oder Vorräten) überhäuft overstocked, ⚓ vom Markt: glutted; ⚓ ~ Lager stock on hand; in ~ halten to keep in stock; unser ~ von Bändern ist erschöpft our stock of ribbons is exhausted or has dwindled away, we are (sold) out of ribbons; ⁂rätig *a.* ⑯ in stock, in store, stored up, ⚓ on hand; et. ⁂ haben (halten) to have (to keep) a th. in stock; der Artikel ist nicht mehr ⁂ ... is sold out, we are out of ...; ⁂ bei allen Buchhändlern to be had of all booksellers.

Vor-rats-achse ⚔ (f¹¹–.) f ㉘ spare axle-tree; =boden m loft, für Getreide: corn-loft; =haus n storehouse; (Lagerhaus) warehouse; =kammer f storeroom; (Speisekammer) larder; =kasten m, typ. fount-case; =rad ⊕ n spare wheel; =schrank m, =spind n pantry, cupboard, für Fleisch: meat-safe; vgl. =kammer; =verzeichnis n inventory; =wagen ⚔ m tender; ⚔ artill. store-wagon; =zimmer n store-room.

vor=rechnen (f¹¹–.) v/a. ㉒b**: e-m et. ⁂ to calculate (or cast up) s.th. in presence of a p.; to enumerate (or reckon up) a th. to a p.; ich kann Ihnen leicht ⁂, was dabei gewonnen wird I can easily show you what is gained by it; =recht n ⑫c. privilege, special (or exclusive) right, höherer Art: prerogative; (älteres Recht) prior right, priority; ⁂recken v/a. ㉖** to stretch forth, den Hals: to crane (forward); =rede f ㊺ introductory speech, prefatory remark; (Einleitung zu e-m Gesetze ꝛc.) preamble; ~ zu einem Buche: preface; mit einer ~ versehen to preface, to write a preface to; ⁂reden v/a. ㉖**: e-m et. ⁂ (redend vorspiegeln) to tell a p. a th. in a plausible way, to make a p. believe s.th.; sich et. ⁂ l. to be led away (or taken in) by a p.'s plausible tale, F to swallow a th. (wholesale); was er uns vorgeredet hat the tales he has told us; =redner m ㉒ one who spoke before, previous (or last) speaker; parl. mein (geehrter) ~ the honourable member who spoke last, the last speaker; ⁂reiben v/a. ㉖** to grind (or pound, pulverize) beforehand; =reiber m ㉒ catch (or patent lock) of a window, chest or case; ⁂reif *a.* ⑯ premature, v. Kindern: precocious; =reigen, =reihen m ㉓ opening of the ball, lead in a dance; den ~ haben to lead a dance; ⁂reißen ⊕ (f¹¹–.) v/a. ㉒a** (den ersten Umriß m.) to make a first sketch of; eine Linie ⁂ (vorzeichnen) to draw, to trace; carp. Holz ⁂ to trace (or scribe) wood; ⁂reiten ㉖b** v/n. (sn): e-m (e-m Wagen) ⁂ to ride before (or in advance of) a p. (a carriage); e-m ⁂ (e-n reitend überholen) to overtake a p. on horseback; e-m ⁂ (zeigen, wie man reitet) to show (or teach) a p. how to ride; v/a. ein Pferd ⁂ (vorführen) to trot out ..., to put ... through his paces; F fig. e-m et. ⁂ (prahlend vorführen) to parade a th. before a p., to make a show (or a boast) of a th. to a p.; =reiter m ㉒ (vorreitender Diener) outrider, mounted courier; (auf einem Vorderpferde sitzender Reitknecht) postilion; ⁂rennen v/n. (sn) ㉖b** to run forward or in advance; e-m ⁂ to outrun a p., to beat a p. in a foot-race; ⁂richten v/a. ㉖**: a) = ⁂rücken; b) (vollständig herrichten) to prepare (well), to fit up (thoroughly), to get (quite) ready or in order; ⊕ Stoffe ⁂ (zubereiten) to dress ...; ~ n ㉓ u. ⁂richtung f ㊺: c) (f. b) preparing, &c.; ~en zu einer Reise ꝛc.: preparations (or arrangements) pl. for ...; d) ⊕ nur =richtung: (zwecm. Einrichtung) (suitable) contrivance, device, mechanism, pl. a.: appliances; e-e sinnreiche ~ an ingenious device, a clever artifice; selbsttätige ~ self-acting (or automatic) mechanism; ⁂riß [vorreißen] m ⑫a. first sketch, rough draft or outline; =ritt m ⑫c. riding before; ⁂rücken v/a. ㉖**: a) to push (or move) forward, eine Uhr: to put on; b) = ⁂halten b; v/n. (sn) to advance, to go ahead, to push on; die Arbeit rückt vor the work is progressing or making headway; ⚔ Truppen ⁂ l. to push (or move) ... forward; in vorgerücktem Alter at an advanced age; die Erntearbeiten sind weit vorgerückt the harvest operations

[vorrufen] — [vorschütten]

are far advanced or fast progressing; ~ n 🜨 advance, progress, forward move; ℔rufen v/a. 🜨b** to call forth, gerichtlich: to summon; ℔rüften v/a. 🜨** = vorrichten b.

vors (f²) = vor das.

Vor-faal (f"...) m 🜨c. arch. (Vorzimmer) ante-room, entrance-room or [-hall, parl., &c. lobby; (Wartesaal) waiting-room, bei vornehmen Personen: antechamber; ℔fagen v/a. 🜨**: a) = voraussagen; b) e-m ℔ to say a th. before a p., to recite a th. to a p.; e-m allerlei Schönes ℔ (vorgauteln) to tell a p. many pretty things or tales, to pay a p. many nice compliments; c) e-m et. ℔ (einblasen, zuflüstern) to whisper a th. to a p., abs. to prompt a p.; =fager m 🞅 prompter; =fänger m 🞅, ~in f 🞅 bsd. eccl. precentor, singing-man, chanter; (Chordirektor) leader of the chorus, in Kirchen: leader of the choir; =fatz m 🜨a: a) anything set before a th.; 🜨 typ. ~ eines Buches: paste-down; b) (Vorhaben) design, intention, purpose, (Entschluß) resolution, resolve; mit ~ designedly, purposely, intentionally, on purpose, (mit Vorbedacht) with premeditation, deliberately, wilfully; die von ihm gefaßten Vorsätze the resolutions (which) he had formed, what he had resolved upon; Sprichw. der Weg zur Hölle ist mit guten Vorsätzen gepflastert the road to hell is paved with good intentions; ℔fätzlich [Vorsatz] a. 🜨 intentional, deliberate; adv. a.: purposely, on purpose, with premeditation, jur. with malice prepense or aforethought; =fchult-widerftand m 🜨 elect. series resistance; =fchanze ℔ f 🜨 frt. outwork, redoubt; =fchein m 🜨c. appearance; zum ~ bringen to bring to light, to produce; zum ~ kommen to appear, to come to light, to crop (or come) up, to make one's appearance, to see day-light; mit et. zum ~ kommen to come out with a th.; wieder zum ~ kommen to reappear, F to pop up afresh; =fchicht f 🜨 geol. first layer or bed or stratum; ℔fchicken v/a. 🜨** to send forward or in advance; bei e-m ℔ to send a messenger (round) to a p.('s house); 🞅 Truppen ℔ (rücken l.) to send on (or push forward) ..., to dispatch ... to the front; ℔fchieben v/a. 🜨c** to push (or shove) forward (f. Riegel 1); 🞅 Tirailleurs ℔ to throw out skirmishers; zu weit vorgeschoben too far forward, too much in advance; 🞅 vorgeschobene Forts, Stellung advanced forts pl., position; vorgeschobene Truppen troops pl. ahead (or in advance) of the main body, vanguard; e-n (als Deckung) ℔ to put forward (or to shield o.s. behind) a(nother) person; fig. et. ℔ (als Vorwand gebraucht) to use a th. as pretext; vorgeschobene Person, oft: man of straw, dummy; =fchieber 🜨 m 🞅 (Riegel) slide-bolt; (Aufziehfenster) sash-window; =fchießen 🜨c(ef)t**: a) v/n. (h.): mit e-m Schießgewehre e-m ℔ to shoot in presence of a p., bsd. to show a p. how to shoot; b) (zu) to shoot (or dart, rush) forth; v/a. c) 🜨 e-n Riegel ℔ to shoot a bolt; (f. d.) e-m eine Summe Geld ℔ to advance (or lend) a p. a sum of money; ich will das Geld ℔ I will advance (or provide, supply, find) ...; e) ~ n 🜨 (f. d.) advance (or loan) of money; =fchlag (f"·℔) m 🜨c: a) previous (or first) stroke or blow; b) (Antrag) proposal, proposition, parl. motion; ein ~ zur Güte a friendly proposal, an amicable offer or suggestion; e-n ~ annehmen to agree to a proposal; f. eingehen ℔; c) 🜨 amount put on the price to be afterwards deducted (as discount); d) grace-note, beat, (it.) appoggiatura; e) gr. initial (weak) element of a sound; durch ~ eines „e" by prefixing an 'e'; pros. ~ e-r Silbe: 🜨 anacrusis; f) 🜨: a) Buchbinderei: ~ an der Heftlade: templet; b) Uhrmacherei: warning; c) Maurerei: first coat(ing); ℔fchlagen 🜨b** v/a.: a) e-m et. ℔ to propose (or suggest) s.th. to a p.; parl. et. ℔ to move s.th.; der ~ de the mover of a resolution, &c.; b) e-n ℔: zu e-m Amte: to propose a p. for a post; eccl. zu e-r Pfründe: to present a p. to a living; der Vorgeschlagene the presentee; pol. zu einer Wahl: to nominate a p. for an election; der Vorgeschlagene the nominee; c) (vorn anfügen) to put on before; gr. e-e Silbe ℔ (vorsetzen) to prefix a syllable; d) 🜨 (e-n Preis fordern, wovon man sich et. abhandeln läßt) (at first) to ask more for an article than one means to take for it; auf eine Ware 3 Mark ℔ to put (F to clap) three shillings on (to) the price of an article; wir schlagen nie vor we never overcharge our customers; e) 🎵 einem den Takt ℔ to beat time to a p.; v/n. (zu): f) to have the first stroke, Fußball: to knock on; g) von der Waage: to kick, to weigh down; ~ n 🜨 (f. a) proposal; (f. b) presentation; nomination; (f. d) das ~ ist nicht meine Art I am not accustomed to ask more than (what) I mean to take, auch: I have fixed prices. **vor-fchlag(s)-fähig** (f"·℔...) a. 🜨 presentable; =lifte f 🜨 list of candidates proposed for an appointment; =note 🎵 f = Vorschlag d; =recht n zu e-r Stelle 2c.: right of presentation or nomination, parl. u. eccl. a.: patronage; =filbe f, pros.: 🜨 anacrusis.

Vor-fchmack (f"...) m 🜨c. foretaste; ~ Vorgeschmack; ℔fchmecken 🜨** v/n. (h.) von einem Gewürz 2c.: to taste (the) strongest, to predominate; v/a. den Pfeffer 2c. ℔ to taste ... more than anything else; =fchneide-brett n 🜨 für Brot 2c.: trencher; =fchneide-messer n carving-knife, carver; ℔fchneiden v/a. 🜨c** : Braten, Geflügel 2c. ℔ to carve; (vor andern schneiden) to carve before other people; e-m Gesichter ℔ to make grimaces (or faces) at a p.; =fchneider m 🞅 carver; ℔fchnell a. 🜨 = zeitig; ℔fchrauben v/a. 🜨c** to screw on to, to screw on in front; ℔fchreiben v/a. 🜨**: et. vor etwas ℔ to write s.th. before s.th.; e-m als Muster et. ℔ to set a copy for a p.; e-m als Verhaltungs-maßregel et. ℔ to prescribe (or dictate) a th. to a p., to order (or command) a p. to do a th.; ich lasse mir nichts ℔ I won't be ordered about or dictated to; die von der Natur uns vorgeschriebenen Lebensregeln the rules of life which nature has laid down for us; in der vorgeschriebenen Ordnung in the appointed (or prescribed) order; ℔fchreien v/a. 🜨**: e-m et. ℔ to shout a th. to a p., to bawl (or yell, scream, din) a th. into a p.'s ear(s); ℔fchreiten v/n. (zu) 🜨b**: a) = fortschreiten; die Arbeit ist weit vorgeschritten ... is far advanced, F... is very forward; b) e-m ℔ to step (or walk) in front (or in advance) of a p., to outstep a p.; =fchrift f writing-copy, copy-slip; (Vorgeschriebenes, Verordnetes) prescription (a. med.); precept, rule; (Auftrag) order, command, (Verhaltungsbefehl) direction, instruction; (Bestimmungen) regulations pl.; nach ℔ according to prescription or rule, as prescribed or ordered; med. pharm. nach ~ zu nehmen to be taken as directed; =fchriften-buch n in Schulen: copy-book; ℔fchrifts-mäßig a. 🜨 u. adv. according to prescription or directions or regulations, (as) prescribed, (as) appointed; in due form; 🞅 Der Degen regulation sword; ℔fchrifts-widrig a. contrary to regulations, against the rules; =fchub (f"·℔) m 🜨c. Kegelspiel: first throw; den ~ haben to throw first, to be the first to play; (Unterstützung) furtherance, assistance, support; e-m ~ leisten (od. tun) to assist (or support, back up) a p., to forward a p.'s interest; e-r Sache ~ leisten to push on a matter, to favour (or countenance, forward) a th.; =fchub-bewegung 🜨 (f"·℔...) f mach. feed-action or -motion; =fchuh (f"...) m 🜨c. Schuhmacherei: ~ e-s Stiefels: forepart, toe-cap; (Oberleder) upper leather, vamp; ein Paar ~e a pair of new front(ing)s; ℔fchuhen 🜨 v/a. 🜨**: Stiefel ℔ to new-front ..., to new-foot ..., to refoot ..., to put new feet to ...; =fchule (f 🜨...): a) preparatory school, eines Gymnasiums 2c.: junior school or forms pl.; b) fig. (Einleitung zu etwas) introduction to grammar, geology, &c.; als Titel oft: Elementary Course, Primer, First Steps pl.; =fchüler m 🜨 pupil of (or boy at) a preparatory school or class.

Vor-fchuß (f"·℔) m 🜨: a) (Geld) ~ advance of money, money (or cash) advanced (auf Wertpapiere 2c.: on securities, &c.); (Darlehen) loan; um 100 Mark im ~ sein to have (received) five pounds in advance; Vorschüsse leisten oder tun to advance (or loan) money; b) (erster Schuß) first shot; Sie haben den ~ you shoot (or fire) first; ~-bewilligung f 🜨 grant of an advance; ~-kaffe f loan-fund; ~-verein m loan-society; vgl. Darlehnsgesellschaft; ℔-weife adv. (F a. a.) as an advance, by way of a loan; ~-zahlung f payment in advance, money advanced. **vor-fchütten** (f"...) v/a. 🜨** to pour out to; dem Vieh Futter ℔ to throw fodder

---

Signs (see page XVII): F familiar; P vulgar; F̃ flash; 🞂 rare; † obsolete (died); * new word (born); ⁺⁺ incorrect; 🎵 music;

[vorschützen]

before (or to give food to) the cattle; ⊕ Dämme 2 to throw (or put) up dikes, to erect (or construct) dikes; 2schützen v/a ⊛**: a) et. 2 to use a th. as (a) pretext or a screen, to take shelter (or ensconce o.s.) behind a th., to plead s.th. (as an excuse); er schützte Krankheit vor he pleaded (b.s. shammed) illness, he pretended to be ill, ⚔ & b.s. he malingered; b) fig. = vorgeben; ~ n ⓘ u. =schützung f ⓙ (using a) pretext, pleading, plea; (leere Vorspiegelung) hollow pretence; =schwarm m ⓑb. Bienenzucht: first (or virgin) swarm; 2schwatzen v/a. ⊛**: e-m etwas 2 = 2plaudern; 2schweben v/n. (h., bisw. ſn) ⊛**: e-m 2 to float (or hover) before a p.; das schwebt mir deutlich vor that is distinctly present to my mind; es schwebt mir nur noch dunkel vor I have now only a dim (or faint) recollection (or notion) of it (left); 2schwefeln F v/a. ⊛**: e-m et. 2 to tell a p. a pack of lies (about s.th.); 2schwimmen v/n. (ſn) ⓐa(b)** to swim before; e-m 2 to overtake (or outmatch) a p. in swimming; 2schwindeln v/a. ⊛a**: e-m et. 2 to humbug (or delude) a p. about (or in) s.th.; =segel ⚓ n ⓒ: ~ pl. (Segel vorn am Fockmast) head-sails, foresails pl.; 2segeln ⚓ v/n. (ſn) ⓐa** to sail before or in advance; e-m Schiffe 2 (es überholen) to outsail a vessel; 2sehen ⓐa**: a) = voraussehen; b) et. 2 (im voraus erwägen, besorgen) to consider a th. beforehand, to provide (or arrange) for a th.; der Fall ist im Gesetze nicht vorgesehen that case has not been provided for by (or in) law; ſich 2 v/refl. (ſich hüten) to be on one's guard, to be cautious, to take care or heed; als Ausruf: vorgesehen! look out!, beware!, attention!, mind (where you are going)!; ſich mit et. 2 to provide o.s. with s.th., to lay in a stock (or store) of s.th.; =sehung f ⓙ providence; die göttliche ~ Divine (or God's) Providence; vor der ~ verordnet providential; 2sein v/n. ⓐa**: e-m 2 to be before (or in advance of) a p.; jur.: 2 (verhandelt w.) to be under consideration (of the court); was ist jetzt vor? what (case) is on now?; die Sache ist schon vorgewesen the case has already been tried or heard; da sei Gott vor! God (or Heaven) forbid!; =setz-blatt n 2-es Buches: fly-leaf; =setzblech n iron plate to (be) put before an opening, especially before the firehole of a furnace; 2setzen v/a. ⊛**: a) (vorwärts setzen) to put forward; b) (vor etwas setzen) to set (or put, place) before (or in front of) a th.; Brettspiel: einen Stein (als Schutz) 2 to cover one piece with another; ♪ e-r Note ein Kreuz 2 to put a sharp before a note, to mark a note with a sharp; gr. e-e Silbe 2 to prefix a syllable; c) e-m etwas (zu Genießendes) 2 to set s.th. (to eat or to drink) before a p.; was darf ich Ihnen 2? what may I offer you (in the way of eating or drinking)?; man kann das Fleisch niemand (od. keinem)

— 1083 —

2 the meat is not fit for the table or for consumption; d) ſich (dat.) einen Zweck 2 to resolve (or determine) to do a th.; er hat ſich's feſt vorgesetzt he has thoroughly made up his mind to (do) it, he is bent upon doing it; e) e-n e-r Sache, e-m Amte 2 to place a p. at the head of ...; e-n e-m anderen 2 to set (or put) a p. over another p.; ihre vorgesetzte Behörde their superiors pl., the authorities (or powers) above them; ſ. Vorgesetzte(r), bſd. Artikel: ⚔ e-m Gegenstande etwas 2 (vorziehen) to prefer a th. to a th.; ~ n ⓘ = =setzung f ⓙ; =setzer m ⓒ s.th. to set before a th.; screen; (Ofen=)~ fender, fire-screen; ⊕ Gießerei: gate-shutter.

Vor-setz-fenſter (f"...) n ⓒ outside window; =gitter n grating; =laden m shutter; =papier n Buchbind.: fly-leaf; =ſilbe f, gr. prefix(ed syllable); =ſtück n, thea. shifting scene, flat.

Vor-setzung (f"...) f ⓙ putting forward or before, &c. (ſ. vorſetzen); ♪ a. ~=zeichen n ⓒ = Vorsetzzeichen.

Vor-setz-zeichen ♪ (f"...) n ⓒ: a) allgemein: (Bezeichnung der Tonart) signature; b) (Kreuz) sharp; c) (vorgesetztes b) flat.

Vor-ſich-hin-lächeln (f"...) n ⓒ smiling to o.s.; =sprechen n talking to o.s.

Vor-ſicht (f"...) f ⓙ (pl. ⚔, mehr gbr. Vorſichtsmaßregeln): a) (Vorausſicht) foresight; b) (Behutſamkeit) circumspection, caution, prudence; (Zurückhaltung) discretion; Maßregel der ~ (act of) precaution; mit ~ zu Werke gehen to go cautiously to work, to act prudently; als Ausruf: ~! take care!, beware!, mind (what's coming), look out!; als Auffſchrift: ~! with care! Sprichw. ~ ist die Mutter der Weisheit prevention is better than cure; ~ ist beſſer als Nachſicht caution is the mother of wisdom; 2ſichtig a. ⓖⓖ (ſ. Vorſicht) b) circumspect, cautious, prudent, discreet; (ſorgſam) careful; (behutſam) wary, in der Rede: guarded; (für die Zukunft ſorgend) provident; 2e Worte guarded words pl.; ſei(b) 2! be on your guard!; ſehr 2 handeln to act very cautiously, to use every precaution; ~keit ⚔ f ⓙ = =ſicht b.

vorſichts-halber (f"...) adv. (as) a (or by way of) precaution; =maßregel f ⓙ precaution(ary measure); ~n treffen to take (the necessary) precautions.

Vor-ſilbe (f"...) f ⓙ gr. prefix; 2ſingen v/a. ⓐ⊛** to sing before a p.. to sing to a company; (zum Zwecke des Nachſingens) to lead the singing, the choir; to intone a hymn, &c.; =ſinger m ⓒ = =ſänger; 2ſintflutlich a. ⓖⓖ antediluvian (auch fig.) existing before the flood; =ſitz m ⓒa. presidency, chair, chairmanship; den ~ führen oder haben to preside (over a meeting, &c.), to be in the chair; den ~ übernehmen to take the chair; 2ſitzen v/n. (h.) ⊛** to preside; e-m 2 (den Vorrang vor ihm h.) to sit above (or before) a p.; =ſitzende(r) m u. f ⓕ, a. =ſitzer m ⓒ president, chairman; f lady president, bisw.: chairwoman; =ſommer m ⓒ early (part of) summer; =ſorge f ⓙ foresight, timely

[Vorſput]

care or provision, early attention; ~ tragen (oder treffen), daß et. geschieht to take care (or make provision) that a th. is done; 2ſorgen v/n. (h.) ⊛** to provide (beforehand). to take (early) precautions, to adopt precautionary measures; Sprichw. vorgesorgt iſt halb getan well begun is half done, auch: a stitch in time saves nine; 2ſorglich a. ⓖⓖ provident, careful, adv. by way (or as a matter) of precaution; ~keit f ⓙ carefulness; =spann m ⓒc. relay, change of horses; fresh (or additional) horses pl.; =spanndienst m (compulsory) supply of relays; 2spannen v/a. ⊛** ein Seil, Tuch ꝛc.: to span (or stretch) ... before or in front of; Pferde 2 to put (fresh) horses to (a carriage); =spann-maschine 🜲 f ⓒ additional engine; =spann-pferd n fresh (or additional) horse; =speise * f ⓙ = Entrée 3; 2ſpiegeln v/a. ⓐa**: e-m et. 2 to show a p. a th. in a bright mirror or in a brilliant light or in dazzling colours; fig. to give a p. a highly coloured (or a rosy) view of a th.; abs. to delude (or deceive) a p. by a fine show; die ihr vorgeſpiegelten Hoffnungen the false hopes (that were) held out to her or dangled before her eyes; ~ n ⓘ und =ſpieg(e)lung f ⓙ fig. highly coloured view; delusive (or dazzling, deceptive) account or view; delusion, (hollow) pretence, sham, mockery; =spiel n ⓒc.: a) ♪: α) prelude (auch fig.); β) jetzt oft für Ouvertüre: overture; b) thea. introductory piece or play; einaktiges ~, oft: F curtain-raiser; 2spielen v/a. ⊛** to prelude; e-m et. 2 to play s.th. to (or before) a p.; =spinn-krempel ⊕ m ⓒ rover; =spinnmaschine ⊕ f roving-frame or -machine or -mill, auch: slubber, slubbingmachine; zweite ~ dandy-rover; =sprache f ⓙ intercession (= Fürsprache); 2sprechen ⓐa** v/a.: e-m et. 2 to pronounce a word before a p., bſd. ~ to show (or teach) a p. how to pronounce a word; e-m 2, was er ſagen ſoll to tell a p. what to say, to prompt a p.; v/n. (h., bisw. ſn): bei e-m 2 to call (F to look in) at a p.'s house, to call on a p., to pay a p. a short (or flying) visit; 2sprengen v/n. (ſn) ⊛** to gallop on before or in advance; 2springen v/n. (h. u. ſn) ⊛** (ſn) to leap before, to spring forward; e-m 2: a) to show a p. how to jump; b) to outdo a p. in leaping; fig. (hervortreten) bſd. arch. to jut forth or out, to project; 2d prominent (part), salient (angle, feature); 2des Fenster bay-window; =sprung m ⓒc. (vorspringender Teil) bſd. arch. projecting (or salient) part, projection, prominence, bisw.: ajutment; ~ e-s Felsens (projecting) ledge of a rock; arch. (vorspringende Verzierung) moulding, (Kranzgesims) cornice; e-n ~ bilden = 2springen fig.; (Vorteil beim Laufen ꝛc.) start, advantage; den ~ vor e-m gewinnen (haben) to get (to have) the start of a p.; =spuk m ⓒc. ghostly warning;

⚛ scientific; ⚘ botanical; 🜨 geography; ⊕ machinery; ⚒ mining; ⚔ military; ⚓ marine; ● commercial; ✉ postal; 🜲 railway.

[vorspuken] — 1084 — [Vortrag]

portent, omen; =**spuken** v/n. (h.) ⊕*** to serve as a portent or as an omen; =**stadt** f ⑩ suburb, outskirts pl. of a town; =**städter** m ㉒, ~**in** f ㊼ inhabitant of a suburb, auch: suburban dweller or resident; =**städtisch** a. ⑥⑥ suburban; =**stag-segel** ↓ n ㉒ fore-staysail; =**stand** m ⑦c.: a) coll. board of directors, governing body, managing committee; b) ein einzelner: director, governor; ✪ chief (or head, principal) of a firm; ~**schaft** f ㊻ position of a director or governor, directorate (a. ✪).
Vor-stands-mitglied (f"ᵁ...) n ㉒ director, member of a governing body or a managing committee; =**sitzung** f meeting of a board of directors; =**wahl** f election of the board or of the (managing) committee or of the directors (auch ✪). [forelock.]
Vor-stech-eisen ⊕ (f"ᵁˌᴸ⁻) n ㉒ Schlosserei: ∫
vor-stechen (f"ᵁ⌣) ⊕a** v/n. (h.) (hervorstechen) to be prominent or conspicuous, to predominate; v/a. ⊕ (Löcher vorbohren) to prick (or bore) out holes.
Vor-stecher ⊕ (⌣) m ㉒ punch(eon).
Vor-steck-ärmel (f"ᵁ...) m ㉒, etwa: sleeve-protector, sleeve to protect (or cover) the sleeve of the dress; =**blume** f flower for the dress; buttonhole.
vor-stecken (f"ᵁ⌣) v/a. ⊕*** to stick (or pin, fasten) before; sie hat sich eine Brosche vorgesteckt she wears a brooch in front of her dress; den Kopf ⁁ to put one's head forward; fig. = vorsetzen d; das vorgesteckte Ziel the appointed goal.
Vor-stecker (⌣) m ㉒ s.th. stuck on (or into) as fastener, (Stift) peg; ⊕: a) = Vorsteckslinse; b) am Pfluge: cheek-pin.
Vor-steck-lätzchen (f"ᵁ...) n ㉒ für kleine Kinder: pinafore; =**linse** ⊕ f am Wagenrad: linch-pin; =**nadel** f breast- (or scarf-) pin; =**nagel** ⊕ m pin, cotter, am Pfluge: forelock, cheek-pin; =**pflock** =**stift** ⊕ m Uhrmacherei: stud.
vor-steh(e)n (f"ᵁ⌣) v/n. (h. südd. a. sn) ⊕*** 1. = hervorstehen; (hervorragen) to jut out, to project. — 2. (ant. nachstehen): a) der Reihenfolge nach: to stand (or come) before, to precede; das ~ be the foregoing (or above) remarks pl.; im ⁁dem, im ⁁den in the preceding parts (of the book), above; b) im Range: to rank before. — 3. einer Sache ⁁: a) beaufsichtigend: to superintend (or conduct, direct) an affair; dem Hause ⁁ to manage the house(hold), to keep house, ✪ to represent the firm; b) verwaltend: to govern, to preside over; e-m Amte ⁁ to fill an office, to hold an appointment.
Vor-steher (f"ᵁ⌣) m ㉒, ~**in** f ㊼ superintendent, director, manager, (Oberhaupt) chief, head, (Verwalter) administrator (f... trix), e-s Gefängnisses, e-s Museums, der Münze ꝛc., warden; ~ e-r Schule head master (f head mistress), principal of a school; ~**amt** n ㉒ office of a director or manager, auch: managerial post; directorate, management; ~**drüse** f, anat.: ♂ prostate gland; ~**schaft** f ㊻ = Vorsteheramt.
Vor-steh-hund (f"ᵁ...) m ㉒, hunt.: a) kurzhaariger: pointer; b) langhaariger: setter.

vor-stellbar (f"...) a. ⑥⑥ presentable, representable, (denkbar) imaginable, conceivable; =**stellen** v/a. und v/refl. ⑥⑥**: a) (sich) e-m ⁁ to introduce (o.s.) to a p.; ich erlaube mir, Ihnen vorzustellen I beg to introduce myself to you; sich e-m ⁁ 1. to be (or get) introduced (bei Hofe ꝛc.: to be presented) to a p.; b) (vorrücken) to put (or place) forward; eine Uhr ⁁ to put on a watch or a clock; c) (vor et. hinstellen) to put before (or in front of) a th.; sich (schützend) ⁁ to place o.s. in front of, to cover (with one's body); d) e-m et. ⁁: α) (anschaulich darstellen) to represent (or point out) a th. to a p.; β) (zur Entscheidung vorstellen) to lay (or put) a th. before a p.; γ) (vor die Seele führen) to urge a th. on a p.; to remonstrate with a p. about a th.; e) sich (dat.) et. (in Gedanken) ⁁ to picture a th. to o.s., to imagine (or conceive, fancy) a th., als wirklich: to realize a th.; stellen Sie sich eine solche Lage vor! just think of such a position!; et., das man sich nicht ⁁ kann s.th. inconceivable; f) thea. u. weitS.: e-e Person (od. Rolle) ⁁ to play (or act, perform) a part, to represent (or personate) a character; et. ⁁, was man nicht ist to pose (or set up) as s.th. or somebody; wenig ⁁ to be insignificant or of no consequence or of mean appearance; (bedeuten) to signify; was soll das ⁁? what is the meaning (or purport) of that? ~ n ㉓ f. Vorstellung. =**stellig** a. ⑥⑥: ~ e-m et. ⁁ (anschaulich) machen to make a th. clear to a p., to explain (or delineate, describe) a th. to a p.; bei e-r Behörde ⁁ werden (eine Eingabe m.) to present (or send in) a petition to the authorities, to memorialize a (local) board; =**stellung** f ㊻ (⁁stellen) (zu a:) introduction, presentation, (zu e:) representation, wegen e-s Unrechts: remonstrance; (zu e:) conception, (Begriff) notion, idea, (Bild) image; das geht über alle ~(en) that's inconceivable; ich habe keine ~ davon I have not the least notion (or idea) of it; sich (dat.) eine ~ m. von // to form an idea of //; (zu f:) thea. performance, representation; keine ~! the theatre will be closed to-day!; ✕ review.
Vor-stellungs-fähigkeit (f"ᵁ...) f, =**kraft** f imaginative faculty or power, power of conception; =**recht** n right of presentation or nomination; =**vermögen** n = =fähigkeit; =**weise** f manner of picturing a th. to o.s.; weitS. mode of conception or thought.
Vor-stenge ↓ (f"...) f ㊽ foretop mast, =**stenge-wanten** f/pl. ㉒ foretopmast shrouds pl.; =**steven** ↓ m ㉓ (Schiffsschnabel) ship's stem; =**stich** m ⑦c. Schneiderei: running stitch; =**stopfen** v/a. ⑥⑥** to stuff in front: to cram in; =**stoß** m ⑦c. pushing forward; ✕ a. (sudden) attack or advance; =**stoßball** ✕ rush; einen ⁁ machen to rush, ✕ to push forward, to forge ahead, to make a dash; ⊕ (Vorragung) salient (or projecting) part; (Ansatzstück)

cking-piece; (Randschnur) edging, braid; metall. eiserner ~ (Kondensator) (sheet-)iron condenser; =**stoßen** ⊕a** v/a. to push (or thrust) forward; einen Saum ⁁ to edge; v/n. (sn) Fußball: to rush; ✕ von Truppen: a) to push forward, to advance; b) (heftig angreifen) to make a sudden (or concentrated) attack; (h.) (vorragen) to project, to protrude. F to poke out; =**strecken** v/a. ⑥⑥**: a) to stretch (or thrust) forward. to put forth, to protrude; den Kopf ⁁ to put (or bend) one's head forward; die Zunge ⁁ to put out one's tongue; b) e-m Geld ⁁ (vorschießen) to advance (or lend) a p. money; ~ n ㉓ u. =**streckung** f ㊻ (f. a.) protrusion; (f. b) advance, loan; =**streuen** v/a. ⑥⑥** to strew before, to scatter in front; den Hühnern Korn ⁁ to throw corn to the fowls; =**strich** m ⑦c. stroke before a word or a letter; =**stricken** v a. ⑥⑥** to knit on to; einen Strumpf ⁁ to refoot a stocking; =**stube** f ㊽ front room; anteroom; =**stück** m ⑦c. front piece or part: thea. = Vorspiel b; =**studien** n/pl. ㉒ preliminary studies pl.; ~ ꝛu et. m. to read (or study) up a subject; =**stufe** f ㊽: a) first step; b) = Vorschule a; =**stürzen** v/n. (sn) ⑨⑥** to rush (or dash) forward or to the front; =**suche** f ㊽ preliminary search; =**suchen** v/a. ⑥⑥** to search out; unter et. ⁁, auch: F to rummage out of ...; vgl. hervorsuchen; =**sündflutlich** vorsintflutlich; =**tanzen** ⑨⑥** v/a.: e-m e-n Walzer ⁁ to dance ... before a p.; v/n. (h.) to lead off the dance; =**tänzer** m ㉒, ~**in** f ㊼ leader of a dance; first (or leading) dancer.
Vor-teil (f"ᴸ⁻: in Vor- und Nach-teil jedoch: f"ᴸ ⌣ "ʰᴸ⁻) m ⑦c. advantage (a. beim Tennis), benefit; (Gewinn) gain, profit; ~ bringen to yield a profit, to be profitable or advantageous; ~ von et. h. to benefit (or profit) by a th.; er hat den ~, der ⁁ ist auf seiner Seite the odds are in his favour; man muß jeden ⁁ mitnehmen every little helps, all is grist (that comes) to our mill; es ist zu seinem ~e it is to his interest, f. sehen 3 unter „auf"; ~ aus et. ziehen to derive advantage from a th., to turn a th. to account; ⁁ (Kunstgriff) knack.
vor-teil-bringend (f"⁻⌣⌣) = vorteilhaft.
vor-teilhaft (f"⌣⌣) a. ⑥⑥ advantageous (für to); (nutzbringend) profitable, lucrative, remunerative; ⁁e Gelegenheit favourable opportunity; das ~este wäre // the most profitable thing to do would be //; adv. auch: with advantage or profit; aufs ⁁este most advantageously, to the best advantage; ✪ a. at the best price.
vor-teil-suchend (f"⌣⁻ᴸ⁻⌣) seeking one's (own) advantage, self-seeking.
Vor-trab ✠ ✕ (f"...) m ⑦c. van(guard); advanced column(s pl.); =**traben** v/n. (sn) ⑧⑧ to trot on before or to ride in advance; =**trag** m ⑦c.: a) (das Vortragen) reciting; report(ing); den ~ haber to be (or to act as) spokesman; von Ministern: ~ beim Könige h. to (make)

Zeichen (f. S. XVII): F familiär; P Volkssprache; Γ Gaunersprache; ⁁ selten; † alt (auch gestorben); * neu (auch geboren); ⁺⁺ unrichtig.

[vortragen]

report to the king, mehr gbr.: to be in personal attendance on the king; b) (Art des Vortragens) mode of reciting or lecturing; delivery, elocution; ♪ e-n schönen ~ h. to have a fine delivery; c) (mündlicher ob. schriftlicher Bericht) report; (Auseinandersetzung) exposition; (Abhandlung) discourse; rednerischer ~ recital (auch fig.); Vorträge halten to deliver (or give) lectures, to lecture (über et. on s.th.); d) 💰 (f. vortragen); ~ auf neue Rechnung balance of an account carried forward; ≈tragen v/a. ⑤ᵇ**: a) e-m et. ≈ (vorantragen) to bear (or carry) a th. before (or in front of) a p.; b) (hersagen) to recite a poem, &c.; (Vorlesung halten über) to lecture on; (berichten) to report on; seine Ansicht ≈ to give (or express) one's opinion; eine Bitte ≈ to solicit a favour; ≈der Rat councillor who has to (make a) report; ♪ Musikstücke ≈ to play (off) ...., größere: to recite (or perform, execute) ...; mit Gefühl ≈ to throw feeling into one's play, to play with feeling; eine Arie ≈ to sing an air or a song; c) (vgl. Vortrag d) den Saldo auf neue Rechnung ≈ to carry forward the balance.

Vor-trags-art (ï⁻ᵘ...) f ⑫ = Vortrag b; **=kunst** f art of reciting or lecturing or delivery; **=meister** m master of elocution; **=weise** f = Vortrag b.

vor=trefflich (ï⁻ᵘᵛ... bisw. a. ï⁻ᵘᵛ) a. ⑥ excellent, exquisite; (very) superior, first-rate; (hervorragend) eminent, distinguished; (vollkommen) perfect; ≈er Mensch capital (F a brick of a) fellow; ≈e Geschichte famous (old) story; Ausruf: ≈! very good!, well done!; ≈ spielen to play beautifully; **~keit** f ⑯ excellency; (great) superiority, superior (or first-rate) quality, eminence; ≈treiben (ï⁻ᵘ...) v/a. ⑨** to drive before or on; ⚒ Minierkunst ꝛc.: eine Galerie ≈ to drive (or construct) a gallery; **=treppe** f ⑱ = Freitreppe; ≈treten v/n. (ſn) ⑧ᵈ**: a) (f. treten) to step before or forward, to come forward, to stand forth; fig. mit et. was nicht ≈ wollen to be chary of telling a th., to hold back with a th.; b) = hervortreten; c) ↯ e-m ≈ to march (or walk) in front of a p.; ≈trinken v/a. ⑪** to drink before a p. or first; bsd. (ihm zutrinken) to drink a p.'s health, to pledge a p.; **=tritt** m ⓒc. step forward or in advance; (Vorrang) precedence; den ~ vor e-m haben to take precedence of a p.; unter ~ von // preceded by //; **=trupp** ⚔ m ⓑⓒ. front detachment, picket, outpost; **=en** f/pl. troops pl. (forming part) of the vanguard; **=tuch** n ⓒc. neckerchief worn in front (of the dress); **=tür(e)** f ⑯ ⑱ outer door, first entrance; ≈turnen v/n. (h.) ⑧** ᵘ to lead (or teach) a squad of gymnasts; **=turner** m ㉒ leader of a squad (or section) of gymnasts; ≈üben v/a. ⑧** to practise (or exercise) beforehand or previously; ~ n ㉓ = Vorübung.

or-über (ï⁻ᵘ...) adv. (vorbei): a) örtlich: past, over, by, along; b) zeitlich: past,

— 1085 —

gone, over; der Regen ist ≈ ... is over. ... has ceased, ... has stopped F ... has held up; sein Ruhm war schnell ≈ ... had soon faded or vanished.

vor-über=fliegen (ï⁻ᵘᵛ...) v/n. (ſn) ⑦⑥ᵃ** to fly past; ≈geh(e)n v/n. (ſn) ⑨** örtlich und zeitlich: to go by, to pass; (vergehen) to pass away, to slip (by); eine Gelegenheit ≈ l. to let an opportunity slip, to miss a chance; ~ n ㉓ passing, passage; ≈gehend a. ⑥: a) örtlich: passing; die ~en ⑰ the passers-by pl.; b) zeitlich: (quickly) passing, transitory, transient, stärker: ephemeral; (flüchtig) fugitive, fleeting, evanescent; (zeitweilig) temporary; sich ≈ an einem Orte aufhalten to make a short stay at a place; ≈können v/n. (h.) ⑱** to be able to pass by; ≈kutschieren F v/n. (ſn) ⑬** to drive past in a coach; ≈sausen v/n. (ſn) ⑨⁰** to whiz past; die an uns ≈den Automobile the motor-cars rushing (or flying) past us; ≈schießen v/n. ⑬(e)f** = vorbeischießen a; ≈segeln v/n. (ſn) ⑫ᵃ** to sail past; ≈ziehen v/n. (ſn) ⑦ᵇ** to march past; das ≈de Gewitter the passing storm.

Vor-übung (ï⁻ᵘ...) f ⑯ previous (or preliminary) practice or exercise; auch: preparatory exercise; **=untersuchung** f ⑯ jur. preliminary examination or inquiry or trial; **=urteil** n ⓒc. prejudice; weitS. (vorgefaßte Meinung) preconceived opinion or notion, prepossession; f. befangen 2.

vor-urteils-frei (ï⁻ᵘᵛ...) a. ⑥, **=los** a. free from prejudice or bias, unprejudiced, unbiassed, open-minded; **=freiheit** f, **=losigkeit** f ⑯ freedom from prejudice or bias; open-mindedness; **=voll** a. full of prejudice(s); prejudiced, biassed.

Vor=vater (ï⁻ᵘ...) m ⑲ = Ahr; **=väter** pl. = Eltern; **=verfahren** n ㉓ jur. preliminary procedure or trial; **=vergangenheit** f ⑯ gram. past perfect, pluperfect; von Personen: antecedents pl.; **=verhör** n ⓒc. jur. preliminary examination; **=verkauf** m ⓒc. ♣ advance sale; thea., &c. booking (or bespeaking) beforehand or in advance; **=versammlung** f ⑯ previous (or preliminary) meeting; **=vordern** m/pl. ㉒ ancestors pl.; ≈vor-gestern adv. three days ago or since; ≈vorig a. ⑥ last but one; **vor=letzt** a. ⑥ last but two; gram. ㉗ antepenultimate (syllable); **=wachs** n ⓐ. bee-glue; **=wacht** ⚔ f ⑯ advanced guard; ≈wagen v/refl. ⑧**: sich ≈ to venture forth, to advance boldly; ≈wägen v/a. ⑦ᵃ⑧** to weigh before; **=wahl** f ⑯ preliminary election; nomination; **=wall** m ⓒc. frt. outer (or exterior) rampart, sillon; ≈walten v/n. (h.) ⑨**: a) to prevail, to predominate; b) = obwalten 2; **=walzen** ⊕ f/pl. ⑱ metall. preparing-rolls pl.; **=wand** m ⓒc. pretext; (Ausflucht) subterfuge, pretence; (Entschuldigung) excuse, plea; (Deckmantel) cloak; (Anstrich) colour; auf diesen ~ hin on this pretext; unter dem ~, daß //, on the plea that //, pleading that //.

[Vorwind]

vor-wärts (ï⁻ᵘ... ↯ ï⁻ᵘ) [: forward] adv. forward, onward; ≈ u. rückwärts vor- und rück-wärts forward and backward; to and fro; als Zuruf: ≈! (go or push) on!, go ahead!, an den Kutscher ꝛc.: go!, start!, von seiten der Polizisten zur Volksmenge: move on!; in Verbindung mit verbs, oft zu einem Worte verbunden: sich ≈ bewegen to move forward, to push on; ≈ eilen to hurry (or press) on; ≈ gehen to go (or move) on, to proceed; es will nicht mit ihm ≈ gehen he does not get on (well); e-m (sich) ≈ helfen to help a p. (o.s.) along or forward, fig. to advance a p.'s interest; ≈ kommen to get on, advance, progress, fig. to make headway or one's way (in the world); Sprichw. langsam kommt man auch vorwärts slow and steady wins the race; ≈ streben to push (or go) ahead or forward; ≈ strebend pushing (ahead), F go-ahead; **~beuge** f Turnerei: bending forward; ≈geh(e)n v/n. (ſn) ⑨** (sich verbessern) das Geschäft ist ≈gegangen the business has improved; **~kommen, ~schreiten** n ㉓ advance, progress; improvement.

vor=weg (ï⁻ᵘ...) adv. before(hand); mit der Zunge ≈ sein to be forward with one's tongue, to let one's tongue go too freely, to have a loose tongue; (vor der gehörigen Zeit) in advance, before the time; **~leistung** 💰 f ⑫ payment in advance, instalment; **~nahme** f ⑱ anticipation; ≈nehmen v/a. ⑦ᵃ** to take beforehand, to anticipate.

Vor=wein (ï⁻ᵘ...) m ⓒc. unpressed wine; ≈weinen v/a. ⑧**: e-m et. ≈ to (set up a) cry before a p.; ≈weisen v/a. ⑨**: e-m et. ≈ to produce (or exhibit) a th. before a p., to show a p. a th.; ~ n ㉓ und **=weisung** f ⑯ production, exhibition, show; **=welt** f ⑯: a) (ant. Nachwelt) past times, former ages pl.: vgl. Vorzeit; b) (Vorfahren) forefathers pl.; c) (Urwelt) prehistoric world or age; ≈weltlich a. ⑥ = urweltlich; ≈wenden v/a. ⑨ᵃ** = ≈schützen; ≈werfen v/a. ⑨ᵇ**: a) to throw before; Fußball: to throw forward; dem Vieh Futter ≈ to throw food to the cattle; b) fig. e-m et. ≈ (zum Vorwurfe machen) to cast a th. in a p.'s teeth, to reproach (or tax, upbraid, twit) a p. with a th.. F u. P: to throw a th. at a p.; man wirft ihm Habsucht vor he is charged (or taxed) with avarice; sie haben einander nichts vorzuwerfen they can't find fault with each other, they are equally bad, (the) one is as bad as the other, F there is six of one, and half a dozen of the other; ich habe mir nichts vorzuwerfen I have nothing to reproach myself with; **=werk** ⓒc. a) farm (adjacent to the manor) b) ⚔ outwork, ~e einer Festung: advanced forts pl.; ≈wiegen ⑦ᶜ** v/n. (h.) to prevail, preponderate, predominate; ≈d p.pr. predominant, prevalent; v a. e-m et. ≈ (vorwägen) to weigh a th. out to a p.; ≈wimmern, ≈winseln v/a. ⑧**: e-m etwas ≈ to whine before a p.; **=wind**

♪ Musik; ⚗ Wissenschaft; ⚘ Pflanze; 🌍 Geographie; ⊕ Technik; ⚒ Bergbau; ⚔ Militär; ⚓ Marine; 💰 Handel; 📮 Post; 🚂 Eisenbahn.

[Vorwinter] — 1086 — [Wache]

↓ m ⦿c. head-wind; =winter m ㉒ commencement of winter; early winter; =wissen n ㉓ foreknowledge, previous knowledge, prescience; es geschah mit meinem ~ it was done with my (full) knowledge (and consent), I knew of its being done; ohne mein (sein) ~ without my (his) knowledge, unbeknown to me (to him); ohne ~ ihrer Mutter without her mother knowing (of) it; =wiß m ⦿a. (prying) curiosity, inquisitiveness, forwardness; (sucht sich einzumischen) meddlesomeness, interfering spirit, impertinence; Sprichw. was deines Amtes nicht ist, da lasse deinen ~ do not meddle in things that do not concern you, in älterer Form: meddle not with what you have nothing to do withal; F (vorwitzige Person) prying (or inquisitive) person, Paul Pry; ≈witzig a. ⓖ (fond of) prying, inquisitive, forward; meddlesome, (fond of) meddling; =wort m ⦿c. preface to a book; gram. ⦿c. preposition; =wurf m ⦿c. reproach, reproof; (Tadel) blame; es gereicht ihm zum ~e it is a reproach (or a discredit) to him, it casts a slur upon him; es wird ihm zum ~ gemacht, daß er sie beschützt hat he is blamed (or found fault with) for having shielded them; j. ≈werfen b u. treffen 2; (Gegenstand der Verhandlung) subject (of treatment); matter to be treated or to be dealt with; artist's study, in der Kunst auch: motive.

vor-wurfs-frei (f^u...) a. ⓖ free from reproach, irreproachable, blameless, unimpeachable; ≈voll a. reproachful.

vor-zählen (f^u...) v/a. ⦿**: e-m et. 2 to count over (or enumerate) a th. to a p.; ~ n ㉓ u. =zählung f ⓖ enumeration; =zahn m ⦿c. (Raffzahn) bucktooth; ≈zaubern v/a. ⦿a**: e-m et. 2 to conjure up a th. before a p.; fig. to delude a p. with a th.; =zeichen n ㉓ previous indication, premonitory sign or symptom; f. Omen; (vorgesetztes Zeichen): a) math. sign; b) ♪ signature, (Versetzungszeichen) accidental; =zeichnen v/a. ⦿b**: a) e-m Schüler et. 2 to draw (or sketch) s.th. for a pupil, (to copy from); b) (zeichnen vor die Augen stellen) to design, delineate, sketch (out); c) et. als Richtschnur Dienendes: to mark (or chalk, trace) out, zur Stickerei ⦿.: to draw as a pattern; d) ♪ (mit Vorzeichen versehen) to prefix sharps (or flats) to, to put the signature(s) to; ~ n ㉓ = =zeichnung: =zeichner m ㉒, ~in f ㊵ designer, delineator; tracer; =zeichnung f ⓖ: a) a drawing for a pupil, ⦿c. (f. ≈zeichnen a); b) (Vorgezeichnetes) drawing-copy, design; model; Stickerei ⦿.: pattern; ≈zeigen v/a. ⦿** to show forth, to expose to view, to produce, to exhibit; ⦿ e-n Wechsel 2 to present a bill (of exchange); Fahrkarten 2! please show tickets!, (all) tickets, please!; ~ n ㉓ = =zeigung; =zeiger ⦿ m ㉒: ~ dieses bearer of this (bill of exchange); =zeigung f ⓖ showing forth, producing, exhibition; ⦿ presentation of a bill; =zeit f ⓖ (remote) antiquity; olden (or ancient) times pl., days of yore, bygone days pl.; die graue(ste) ~ hoary antiquity, a. the dawn of history; ≈zeiten (f^u...) adv. once upon a time, in olden times, in days of yore; formerly; ≈zeitig (f^u...) a. untimely (death, &c.); (verfrüht) premature (birth, &c.); ≈zeitlich [Vorzeit] a. ⓖ ancient, belonging to past times; ≈ziehbar a. ⓖ preferable; ≈ziehen v/a. ⦿b**: a) v/a. (hervorziehen) to draw forth; × die Artillerie 2 to put the artillery (further) to the front, b) 2 vor (vor et. hinziehen) to draw in front of; c) fig. (den Vorzug geben) to prefer s.th. to a th., to give the preference to s.th. over a th.; ich ziehe das Weiße dem Roten vor I prefer white to red, I like white better than red; ich möchte 2 u. warten I would rather wait; sie hat es vorgezogen zu schweigen she preferred (or chose, elected) to remain silent; v/n. (in) d) × to march in front; e) to move to the front; =zimmer n ㉒ anteroom, antechamber; thea., &c. oft: lobby; =zug (f^u...) m ⦿c.: a) preference; (Vorrang) precedence, (Vorrecht) privilege; (Vorzüglichkeit) excellency, (Überlegenheit) superiority; (Verdienst) merit; f. ≈ziehen c; die vielen Vorzüge des neuen Verfahrens the many advantages (or excellent points) of the new method; den ~ vor e-m h. to be preferred to a p., to have the advantage over a p., to excel a p.; b) ⛴ train sent in advance of the principal train, a pilot-train; ≈züglich (f^u...) a. ⓖ preferable, superior, (ausgezeichnet) excellent, (auserlesen) choice, select; ganz 2 exquisite: first-class, first-rate, F A 1; das 2ste Backwerk the most delicious pastry; die 2sten Gerichte the daintiest (or most appetizing) dishes pl.; × ein 2es Regiment a picked (F a crack) regiment; der, die, das ~ste the most excellent; the first, best, foremost; der 2ste (hauptsächlichste) Teil the principal part; adv. = vornehmlich; =züglichkeit f ⓖ excellence, excellency, choiceness, pre-eminence; superior, or excellent, first-rate, high-class quality.

Vor-zugs-aktien (f^u...) ⦿ f pl. ⓖ² preference-shares pl.; =behandlung f preferential treatment; =preis m exceptional (or special) price, preferential rate; =recht n privilege, prerogative; =tage ⦿ m/pl. days pl. of grace or respite; =tarif f preferential tariff; ≈weise adv. (F a. a.) preferably, by preference, pre-eminently, especially, chiefly.

votieren (w-^L...) [neu-lt.] v/n. (h.) u. v.a. ⓖ² (abstimmen, durch Abstimmung beschließen) to vote; die ~den the voters pl.

Votiv-bild (w-^u...) n ⦿², =gemälde n votive (or commemorative) picture; =kirche f votive church (= Dankeskirche); =tafel f votive tablet.

Botum (w-^v-) [lt.] n ㉘ ⦿² a) = Gutachten; b) pol. (Stimme) vote, suffrage.

v. R. w. abbr. = von Rechts wegen.

v. u. abbr. = von unten.

vulgär (w-^L) [fr.] a. ⓖ (gewöhnlich, alltäglich) vulgar, (gemein) common; ~=sprache f vulgar language, auch = Volkssprache.

Vulgata (w-^v-) [lt.] f, inv. (lat. Bibelübersetzung von Hieronymus) Vulgate.

vulgo (w-^v-) [lt. Ablativ v. vulgus Pöbel] adv. = gemeinhin.

Bulkan (w-^v-) [lt.] I npr/m. ⦿⦿⦿a. myth. (Gott des Feuers u. der Schmiede) Vulcan. — II m ⦿c. (feuerspeiender Berg) volcano. — III (P w-^v-) ⊕ ↓ name of a shipbuilding yard near Stettin.

vulkanisch (w-^L) a. ⓖ volcanic.

vulkanisier|en ⊕ (w-^v-^L) I v/a. ⦿: Kautschuk 2 (mit Schwefel verbinden) to vulcanize ... — II ~ n ㉓ u. Bung f ⓖ vulcanization.

Bulkanismus ⦿ (w-^v-) m ㉗ geol. (vulkanische Tätigkeit) volcanism.

Bulkanist (w-^v-) m ㊷ (j. der die Tätigkeit des Feuers für das Wesentliche bei der Erdbildung hält) volcanist.

v. w. o. = verhandelt wie oben.

𝔚

W, w (^L) n, inv. Buchstabe: W, w.
W.! abbr. = Wenden! (= vertatur, verte); vgl. W. S. g. u.
W, öft. W. abbr. = West(en).
W chm. Symbol für Wolfram.
Waadt (^L) [fr. Vaud (*dtsch Wald)]: die ~ npr/f. inv., ~=land ⦿ (^u) n ⦿c. (schwz. Kanton) (Pays de) Vaud; ~=länder(in f ㊵) m ㉒, ≈ländisch a. ⓖ Vaudois.
wabb(e)lig prov. (^v(v)v) [ndb.] a. ⓖ wabbling, flabby.

wabbeln prov. (^v-) [ndb.] v/n. v/imp. ⦿a. to wabble, to quake; es wabbelt mir I feel queer or F funny.
Wabe (^L) (ahd.: weben: ndb. Waffel) f ㊵, \~n m ㉓ Bienenzucht: honey-comb.
waben-artig (^u-...) a. ⓖ: ⊘ faveolate, alveolar; 2e Zelle: ⊘ faveolus; =honig ⦿ honey in the comb.
wach (sch) [nhd. 17. sae.; *wachen] a. ⓖ awake, astir; (lebendig, munter) brisk, alive, wide awake; 2er Traum daydream; 2 bleiben, erhalten to keep awake; 2 werden to awake, to wake up; in 2em Zustand in a wakeful (or sleepless) state.
Wach=bett (sch...) n ⦿²: a) bed of a nurse or a p. watching through the night; b) × öft. = Wachtbett; =dienst × öft. = Wachtdienst.
Wache (sch) (ahd.: wachen) f ⊘ 1. meist × (mit der Nebenform Wacht) guard, ⦿B.: a) (Wachtdienst) ~ haben oder tun, auf

---

Signs (see page XVII): F familiar; P vulgar; ꟻ flash; ↘ rare; † obsolete (died); * new word (born); ++ incorrect; ♪ music;

[wachen] — 1087 — [Wacke]

sein to be on guard, am fürstlichen Hofe: to be in waiting; ~ steh(e)n to stand sentry; auf ~ ziehen, die ~ beziehen to mount guard; von der ~ (ab)ziehen to come off duty, to be relieved; b) (Wachtmannschaft) coll.(men on) guard; Aufziehen der ~ mounting guard, guard-mounting; ~ (')raus! turn out, guard!; f. Feldwache; c) (Wachtlokal) guard-room;(Polizei)~police-station. — 2. ~ halten (auf der Lauer sein) to (be on the) watch, to keep a sharp look-out for a th.; ↓ (vierstündiger Dienst auf Deck) four hours' watch.

wachen (ˇ) [ahd.: wake, watch: wecken] I v/n. (h.) ⑱ 1. to be awake; (noch auf sein) to be astir, to be (still) up; bei e-m ⁂ to sit up with a p. (during the night). — 2. (achthaben) to watch (über e-n, poet. a. e-m over). — 3. ↓ (über dem Wasser hervorragen) to be out of the water; eine Ankerboje wacht the buoy is floating in sight. — II ~ n ㉓ 4. wakefulness; watching.

wach(e)-stehend ⚔ (ˇ) a. ⑯ doing (or on) sentry-duty.

Wach-frau (ˇ...) f ⑫ nurse; ⸗habend ⚔ ⨁ ⁊c. = wachthabend ⁊c.; ⸗mann m öst. = Schutzmann.

Wacholder (ˇˇ) [ahd. (P⸗): Holder] -der = tree]m㉓1. ⚘ juniper(-tree)(Iuni'perus). — 2. = Wacholderbranntwein.

Wacholder-baum ⚘ (ˇˇ...) m ⑫ = Wacholder 1; ⸗beere ⚘ f juniper-berry; ⸗branntwein m gin; vgl. Genever; ⸗busch m juniper-bush, -shrub; ⸗drossel f. orn. = Kram(met)svogel; ⸗harz ⚘ n German sandarach; ⸗holz n juniper-wood; ⸗holz-öl n, chm. essential oil of juniper-wood; ⸗öl n, pharm. &c. juniper-oil; ⸗strauch m = Wacholder 1.

Wachs¹... (ˇ...) [wachs-en¹] f. Zssgn.

Wachs² (ˇ) [ahd.: wax: wichsen] n ⑫a. wax, vgl. Bienenwachs; mit ~ be-streichen, überziehen to beeswax, to coat with wax; mit ~ überzogen coated with wax, ⸙ cerated; ~ er-zeugend: ⸙ ceriferous. [in wax.)

Wachs²-abdruck (...) m ⑫ impression

wachsam (ˇ...) a. ⑯ watchful, stärker: vigilant; (auf der Hut) on the alert, wide awake, on one's guard; ein ⁂es Auge auf e-n, et. haben to watch (or to keep a sharp eye) upon a p., a th.; ⁂ auf (ob. über) et. sein to keep watch over a th., F to have one's eye upon a th.; von Hunden: (sehr) ⁂ sein to keep good watch. [stärker: vigilance.)

Wachsamkeit (ˇ...) f ⑱ watchfulness,

wachs²-artig (ˇ...) a. ⑯ wax-like, waxy; ⸗bild n waxen image; ⸗bild-nerei f modelling in wax, ⸙ ceroplastics; ⸗bleich a. like wax, (as) pale as death; ⸗bleiche(rei) ⊕ f wax-bleaching; ⸗blume f: a) wax flower; b) ⚘ honeywort (Ceri'nthe minor); ⸗boh-ner m floor-polisher; ⸗¹bottich ⊕ m Alaunfabr.: roching-cask.

wachsen¹ (ˇ) [ahd.: wax] ⑱ b(e)st I v/n. (sn) 1. to grow, von Pflanzen: to come (or shoot, spring) up; (keimen) to sprout (a. ⨁ vom Malz); (gedeihen) to thrive; (zunehmen) to increase, vom Monde: to wax, v. Wasser: to rise, von einem Werke:

(fortschreiten) to advance, (sich ausdehnen) to extend, to expand; sich den Bart ⁂ lassen to grow whiskers or a beard; fig. und Sprichw. f. Baum 2, Gras 2, grau 1, Kamm 3, Schnabel 2. — 2. mit prp. an Weisheit ⁂ to grow in wisdom; fig. er (das) ist ihm ans Herz gewachsen he (it) is nearest to his heart; aus den Kleidern ⁂ to grow out of (or to out-grow) one's clothes; in die Breite ⁂ to grow broad or in width, auch: to widen (out); in die Höhe ⁂ to grow tall, to shoot up; sehr ins Holz, ins Kraut ⁂ to run to wood, to leaf; einem über den Kopf ⁂ to outgrow a p., fig. to gain the ascendancy over a p., to get the upper hand of a p. — II v/refl. 3. sich fest ⁂ to take firm root. — III ~ n ㉓ 4. growing, growth, in-crease; rise of the water, expansion of trade, &c.; der Mond ist im ~ ... is waxing or on the increase; ⊕ ~ des Alauns, Salpeters crystallization of alum, nitre. — IV ⸘ p.pr. und a. ⑯ 5. growing, increasing, on the in-crease, vom Monde oft: waxing. —
V ge-wachsen p.p. u. a. ⑯ (D 9) 6. in den Bed. des inf.; vom Körper: gut ⁂ well-made; von Pflanzen ⁊c.: krumm ⁂ of crooked growth. — 7. fig. e-m (nicht) ⁂ sein to be a (no) match for a p.; einer Aufgabe (nicht) ⁂ sein to be (un)equal to a task.

wachsen², **wächsen** (ˇ⸗) [Wachs²] v/a. ⑯ to coat with or treat with) wax.

wächsern (ˇˇ) [Wachs²] a. ⑯ (of) wax, waxen; fig. einem eine ⁂e Nase drehen to lead a p. by the nose, to impose upon (or humbug) a p. [ind. v. wachsen¹.)

wächs(es)t (ˇˇ, ˇˇ) 2. Person sg. pres.

Wachs²-farbe (ˇ...) f ⑫ colour of wax; ⸗farbig a. ⑯ wax-coloured; ⸗figur f wax figure; ⸗figuren-kabinett n wax-works pl.; ⸗form f wax mould; ⸗gelb a. = ⸗farbig; ⸗händler(in f) m dealer in wax; ⸗haut f, orn. am Schnabel der Raubvögel &c.: ⸙ cere; ⸗haut-artig a. ⸙ cerous; ⸗kerz-chen n zum Anstreichen: wax match or vesta, auch: vesta-light or -match; ⸗kerze f wax candle or light; ⸗leinen n, ⸗leinwand f oil-cloth; ⸗licht n wax candle; ⸗¹machen n (letzte Kristallisation des Alauns) roching; ⸗malerei f en-caustic (or wax-)painting; ⸗maske f wax mask; ⸗modell n wax model or mould; ⸗modellierer m moulder in wax; ⸗modellier-kunst f: ⸙ cero-plastics; ⸗myrte ⚘ f wax-myrtle (Myri'ca ceri'fera). [mann.)

Wach-soldat ⚔ (ˇ...) m öst. = Wacht-

Wachs²-palme ⚘ (ˇ...) f ⑫ wax-palm (Coperni'cia ceri'fera); ⸗papier n wax-paper; ⸗perle f wax bead or pearl; ⸗puppe f wax doll; ⸗röhrchen n = ⸗sonde; ⸗salbe f, pharm. cerate; ⸗scheibe ⚘ f cake of wax; ⸗schmelze ⊕ f melting-house for wax; ⸗sonde f, surg. bougie; ⸗stock m (roll of) wax taper; ⸗stock-büchse f, ⸗stock-leuchter m, ⸗stock-schere f taper-holder or -stand; ⸗streichholz n = ⸗kerzchen; ⸗tafel f: a) cake of bees' wax, wax tablet; b) = Honigwabe; ⸗taf(fe)t ⊕ m oil-skin;

wach-stehend (ˇ...) f. wachestehend.

Wach-stube (ˇ...) öst. = Wachtstube.

Wachs²-tuch ⊕ (ˇ...) n ⑫ oil-cloth; ⸗tuch-papier n oil-cloth paper.

Wachstum (ˇ...) n ⑫d. 1. = wachsen¹ III; Kinder, Bäume ⁊c. im ~ aufhalten to stunt ... in their growth, to check the growth of ...; das ~ in Anschlag bringen to allow for growth; über-mäßiges ~ overgrowth. — 2. ~ der Pflanzen: vegetable growth, vegeta-tion; üppiges ~ rank growth. — 3. vom Weine ⁊c.: = Gewächs.

wachs²-weich (ˇ...) a. ⑯ (soft) like wax; ⸗zieher ⊕ m wax-chandler; ⸗ziehe-rei f manufacture of wax-candles; ⸗zündholz n = ⸗kerzchen.

Wacht (ˇ) [ahd.] f ⑱ guard, ↓ watch; vgl. Wache 1a und b; die ~ am Rhein (Titel eines Liedes) Watch on the Rhine.

Wacht-bett ⚔ (ˇ...) n ⑫ (soldier's) camp-bed; ⸗boot ↓ n guard-boat; vgl. ⸗schiff; ⸗dienst m (guard-)duty.

Wachtel (ˇ...) [ahd.] f ⑱ 1. orn. quail (Te'trao cotur'nix); die ~ schlägt the quail is calling. — 2. F = Ohrfeige.

Wachtel-falk(e) (ˇ...) m ⑫ = Würg-falk(e); ⸗fang m quail-catching; ⸗garn n quail-net; ⸗hund m (Hunderasse) spaniel; ⸗hündchen n king Charles's(s) dog; ⸗hündin f spaniel bitch; ⸗könig m, orn. corn-crake, land-rail (Crex prate'nsis); ⸗netz n = ⸗garn; ⸗pfeife f quail-call or -pipe; ⸗ruf, ⸗schlag m call of the quail; ⸗streichen n, ⸗strich m: a) = ⸗zug; b) = quail-catching; ⸗weizen ⚘ m = Kuhweizen; ⸗zeit f season for quails; ⸗zug m migration (or flight, passage) of quails.

Wächter (ˇˇ) [mhd.; *Wacht] m ⑫, ~in f ⑱ guard(ian), warder, attendant, nur m auch: watchman, keeper; ↓ ~ im Mast-korbe: look-out man.

Wächter-geld (ˇˇ...) n ⑫ watchman's, &c. fee or pay; ⸗häuschen n watch-man's hut, ⸙ watch-box; ⸗kontroll-uhr ⊕ f time-detector; elektro-magnetische ~ electro-magnetic watch-clock; ⸗lohn m = ⸗geld; ⸗ruf m watchman's call.

Wacht-feuer (ˇ...) n ⑫ watch- (or bivouac-)fire; ⸗frei a. ⑯ exempt from (guard-)duty; ⸗glas ↓ n watch- (or hour-)glass; ⸗habend a. (being) on duty; ⸗haus n guard-house, ↓ binnacle; ⸗kommandant m commander of the guard; ⸗leute pl. v. ⸗mann; ⸗loch F n für Arrestanten: (night-)cell, black hole; ⸗lokal n f. Wache 1c; ⸗mann m man on guard or ↓ on watch; ⸗mannschaft f (men on) guard, picket; ↓ (men on) watch; ⸗mantel m sen-tinel's cloak; ⸗meister m sergeant-major of cavalry and field-artillery; ⸗offizier m officer of the guard; ⸗parade f (parade of soldiers on) mounting guard, guard-mounting; ⸗posten m: a) post; b) = Schild-wache; ⸗pritsche f guard-bed; ⸗schiff n zur Aufsicht im Hafen guard-ship, revenue-cutter; ⸗stube f guard-room; ⸗turm m watch-tower; ⸗türmchen n = watch-turret, outlook. [trapp-tuff.)

Wacke (ˇ⸗) [mhd.] f ⑱ min.: ⸙ ⁑ wacke,

⸙ scientific; ⚘ botanical; ⌘ geography; ⊕ machinery; ⚒ mining; ⚔ military; ↓ marine; ⑯ commercial; ✉ postal; ⛘ railway.

[Wackelgelenk] — 1088 — [Wagenlauf]

Wackel=gelenk (⌣‿⌣) n ② anat.: ⚋ amphiarthrosis.
wack(e)lig (⌣(⌣)) a. ⑥⑥ shaky, tottering, von alten Möbeln ꝛc. auch: rickety; Der Wagen jolting (or F crazy old) coach; *pg.* die Sache steht auf Den Füßen die affair is in rather a shaky (or precarious, tottering) condition.
Wackel=kopf (⌣‿...) m ② shaky (or nodding) head; ⚋**köpfig** a. ⑥⑥ with a shaky head.
wackeln (⌣⌣) [mhd.: wag(g)le] ②a. I v/n. 1. (h.) to shake, von Zähnen: to be loose; (wanken) to rock, (taumeln) to totter, reel, stagger; Dd (schlotterig) gehen to waddle (or slouch) along; mit dem Kopfe 2 to shake one's head, to nod; ein Oder Alter a doddering old man; v/imp. es wackelt mit seiner Gesundheit his health is very shaky or precarious. — 2. (jn) er ist die Straße hinaufgewackelt he tottered (F toddled) up the street; da kamen zwei Betrunkene gewackelt two drunken men came reeling (or stumbling) along. — II ~ n ② 3. (s. I) shaking of the head, &c; looseness of teeth; tottering (gait).
wacker (⌣⌣) [ahd.: wachen] a. ⑥⑥ (D9) 1. good, honest (= brav 1 u. 2). — 2. F *adv.* well, thoroughly (= gehörig 4).
Wackler (⌣⌣) m ②, ~in f ④ totterer.
wacklig (⌣⌣) a. ⑥ s. wack(e)lig.
Wade (⌣‿) [ahd.] f ⑧ calf (of the leg).
Waden=bein (⌣‿...) n ② anat. splintbone, ⚋ fibula; =**bein=muskel** m: ⚋ peroneal muscle; =**krampf** m, *path.* cramp in the (calf of the) leg; =**nerv** m, *anat.*: ⚋ peroneal nerve; =**strumpf** m long stocking (covering the calf).
Waffe (⌣‿) [ahd.: weapon] f ⑧ weapon; ~n arms *pl.*; in ~n in arms; das Volk in ~n the people in arms; gegen eine Welt in ~n † [SH. H. IV, I, 5, 1] against the world in arms; e-m die ~n abnehmen to disarm a p.; f. greifen 6 am Ende, strecken 1 am Ende; ~n tragen to carry arms; blanke ~ (ant. Feuer~) side-arm.
Waffel (⌣‿) [ndd.: wafer: Wabe] f ⑧ kleinere: wafer, größere: gofer.
Waffel=decke (⌣‿...) f ② honeycomb-quilt; =**eisen** n gofering-iron.
Waffen (⌣⌣) n ② altertümlich: = Waffe.
Waffen=arbeit ☼ (⌣‿...) f ② (business of) war; =**bruder** m brother (or companion) in arms; =**brüderschaft** f ② brotherhood (or companionship) in arms; =**dienst** m military service; =**fabrik** f (manu)factory of arms; =**fabrikant** ◯ ⓜ manufacturer of arms; ⚋**fähig** a. able to bear arms; =**gang** m passage at arms; =**gattung** f kind of arms; bei welcher ~ dient er? to what arm (of the service) does he belong?; =**gefährte** m = ~bruder; =**geklirr** n clash(ing) of arms; =**gerüst**, =**gestell** n stand for arms; =**getöse** n din of arms or battle; =**gewalt** f force of arms, armed force; =**glück** n: das ~ versuchen to appeal to arms, to trust in the fortune of war; =**händler** m armourer; =**handwerk** n profession of arms; =**haus** n armoury, arsenal; =**herold** m king-at-arms; =**klang** m = =geklirr; ⚋**los** a. unarmed, defenceless; =**platz** m place of arms; =**rock** ☼

m: a) *ehm.*: coat-of-arms; b) *jetzt*: tunic; =**ruhe** f cessation (or suspension) of hostilities; =**ruhm** m military glory; =**rüstung** f armour; =**saal** m armoury; =**schau** f review; *schott. ehm.*: † wapenshaw; =**schein** m license for carrying arms; =**schmied** ◯ m armourer; =**schmiede** f armourer's workshop; =**schmiede=arbeit**, =**kunst** f armourer's trade or art; =**schmuck** m warlike accoutrement, F co. war-paint; im vollen ~ in full armour; =**stillstand** m armistice, truce; *vgl.* =ruhe; =**tanz** m war-dance, *fig.* war; =**tat** f warlike deed, military feat; =**tragen** n carrying of arms; das ~ ist verboten it is prohibited to carry arms; ⚋**tragend** a. carrying (or bearing) arms; =**träger** m armour-bearer; (Schildknappe) esquire; =**übung** f military exercise; =**wache** f Rittertum: knight's watch with his arms; ⚋**weise** *adv.* (F a. a.) according to the arm of the service (which troops belong to); =**wirkung** f effect of arms.
waffnen (⌣⌣) [ahd.: Waffe] ②b. I v/a. u. v/refl. to arm; sich 2 to arm o.s. with a sword, &c., to take up arms, geb. Spr.: to buckle on one's (shield and) armour; sich gegen et. 2 to guard against a th.; sich mit Geduld 2 to possess one's soul in patience; mit gewappneter Hand with armed forces, by force of arms. — II ~ n ② armament.
wäg=bar (⌣‿) a. ⑥⑥ *phys.*: ⚋ ponderable; ~**keit** f ⑥: ⚋ ponderability.
Wage (⌣‿) [ahd.] f ⑧ 1. a) balance (s. Ausschlag 4); pair of scales, beam and scales, größere: weighing-machine, mit Laufgewicht: steelyard; chemische ~ chemical (or analytical) balance; b) *ast.* Libra. — 2. (Gleichgewicht) balance, equipoise, ⚋ equilibrium; in der ~ halten to equipoise, to keep in balance; ea. die ~ halten to counterpoise (or counterbalance) each other. — 3. ◯ = Bleiwage.
Wäge=... (⌣‿...) in Zssgn s. Wag(e)=...
Wage=balken (⌣‿...) m ② (scale-)beam, lever of a balance; =**geld** (auch **Wägegeld**) n weighing-fee; =**hals** m daring (or foolhardy) person; *vgl.* =mut; ⚋**halsig** a. ꝛc. s. waghalsig ꝛc.; =**haus** n weighing-house, public scales *pl.*
Wägelchen (⌣⌣), **Wägelein** (⌣‿) n ② (dim. von Wagen) little carriage, F trap, für Kinder: perambulator, mail-cart (s. Kinderwagen).
Wage=macher (⌣‿...) m ② maker of scales; =**meister** m keeper of the public scales; =**mut** m: a) (kühner Mut) daring (courage); b) *poet.* (kühner Geselle) (bold) adventurer.
wagen[1] (⌣‿) [mhd.: Wage] I v/a. und v/refl. ⑧ to venture, to hazard; (der Gefahr aussetzen) to jeopardize, to stake (one's life, &c.); (sich getrauen zu tun) to dare (*impf.* dared; *mehr gbr.* aber *weniger richtig*: durst; *mehr gbr.*, aber weniger richtig: dared); (versuchen) to attempt; et. 2, auch: to risk (or chance) a th.; wir 2 es nicht we dare not do it; alles 2 to risk (or chance) everything; er hat es gewagt he has taken the risk or his chance; ich will's 2

I will take my chance, I'll chance it; es mit e-m 2 to try a fall (or take up a quarrel) with a p., to stand up to a p.; zu viel 2 to venture (or presume) too far; sie 2 nicht, uns zu belästigen they have not the courage (or pluck) to molest us, they dare not interfere with us; sich an et. 2 to venture upon a task; sie 2 sich nicht aus dem Hause they do not venture out of doors; sich in den Wald 2 to venture (forth) into the forest; sich unter die Leute 2 to venture (to go) out; Sprichw. frisch gewagt ist halb gewonnen fortune favours the brave, well begun is half done; s. gewinnen 1 gegen Ende. — II ~ n ② 2. venturesome deed, (ad)venture; (Kühnheit) daring, boldness. — III **gewagt** *p.p.* u. a. ⑥⑥ 3. Beb. des *inf.* — 4. (gefährlich) venturesome, adventurous, hazardous, risky, (kühn) daring (deed, &c.), bold (enterprise, &c.).
Wagen[2] (⌣‿) [ahd.] m wain: (be)wegen] m ②③ 1. carriage, elektrischer: car (beide auch 🚋), weitS. vehicle, conveyance; (Kutsche) coach, leichterer Art: dog-cart, gig; s. Automobil, Droschke; für schwere Fracht: wagon, 🚋 auch: truck, für Möbel ꝛc.: (furniture-)van, für umherziehende Künstler ꝛc.: caravan, (Karren) cart; ein ~ voll a vanful, a wagon-load; s. anspannen 3, fahren 3 u. 4, halten 10; 🚋 ~ erster, zweiter Klasse first-class, second-class carriage; *vgl.* Güter-, Salon-, Schlaf-wagen. — 2. *fig.* s. Pferd 2. u. fünfte 2. — 3. *ast.* der ~ (der Große Bär) Charles's(s) Wain.
wägen (⌣‿) [ahd.: weigh: (be)wegen] ②a. ⑧ in geh. Spr.: to weigh (a. *fig.*), to poise, to balance; *fig.* = erwägen; Sprichw. erst 2, dann wagen, etwa: first think. then act; look before you leap.
Wagen[2]=**abteil(ung** f) m (⌣‿...) ② 🚋 s. Abteil; =**achse** f axle-tree; =**bau** m coach-building; =**bauer** m coach-maker; (Wagner) cartwright; =**baum** ◯ m Stellmacherei: carriage-pole; =**bauwerkstätte** ◯ f coach-builder's shop or yard; =**beschläge** m/*pl.* metal fittings (of a carriage); =**büchse** f Radbüchse; =**burg** ☼ f Alt.: barricade formed by chariots, jetzt in Süd=afrika: laager; =**decke** f = Plane; =**deichsel** f carriage-pole, shaft of a cart.
Wag(e)ner (⌣(⌣)) m ② s. Wagner.
Wagen[2]=**fabrikant** (⌣‿...) m ② coach-maker; =**fenster** n carriage-window; =**führer** m driver, wagoner, Alt.: charioteer; =**gedränge** n block (or dense mass) of carriages; =**geleise** n = Geleise 1 u. 2; =**gerassel** n rattling of carriages; =**geschirr** n harness(ing); =**gestell** ◯ n carriage-frame; *vgl.* =kasten; =**gestirn** n = Wagen[2] 3; =**haus** n coach-house; =**kämpfer** m Alt.: warrior fighting from a chariot, =**kappe** f hood of a carriage; =**kasten** m body of a carriage; =**kette** f drag-chain = Hemmkette; =**klasse** 🚋 f class of a carriage; Fahrkarte dritter ~ third-class ticket; =**knecht** m carter, driver; =**korb** m hamper; =**ladung**, =**last** f wagon-(or cart-)load; =**lauf** 🚋 m train-

Zeichen (s. S. XVII): F familiär; P Volkssprache; ⌐ Gaunersprache; ⚲ selten; † alt (auch gestorben); * neu (auch geboren); ‡‡ unrichtig;

[Wagenleiter] service, service of trains; =leiter f cart-rack, wagon-ladder; ~n pl. rails of a cart; =lenker m = =führer c =macher m: a) cart-maker; vgl. =bauer; b) [Wage] maker of scales; =meister m: a) = Geschirrmeister; b) 🚂 wagon-master; c) ⚔ baggage-master; =park m: a) ⚔ park, train of wagons; b) 🚂 rolling-stock; =pferd n carriage- (or cart-)horse; =rad n carriage- (or cart-)wheel; =radkranz m tire (or tyre) of a carriage; =remise f = =schuppen; =rennen n Alt. chariot-race; =schere f s. Schere 3; =schlag m carriage-door; =schmiere f cart-grease; =schuppen m: a) coach-house; b) shed for carts or wagons; =sitz m seat in a carriage; =sperre ⊕ f drag-chain; =sport m coaching; =spur f = Radspur; =straße f carriage-road; =streiter m = =kämpfer; =tritt m carr.-step; =verkehr m carr.-traffic; =wechsel 🚂 m change of carriages; =winde ⊕ f lifting-jack, draw-beam, mit Zahnstange: rack-jack; =zug 🚂 m train of carriages).
Wager (⌣⌢) m ⓶ one who ventures, daring person, dare-devil, bold spirit.
Wäger (⌣⌢) m ⓶, ~in f ⓸ weigher.
wag(e)recht (⌣(⌣)⌢) a. ⓺ horizontal, level; =stück ⊕ f. Wagstück.
Wage=zünglein ⊕ (⌣⌢⌣⌢) n ⓺ needle of the balance.
Waggon 🚂 (⌣ɡɑ̃) [fr.] m ⓼ (⌢d.) railway-carriage, Am. car, offener: truck; ⒉ weise adv. (F a. a.) by truck-loads.
Wag=hals (⌣⌢...) m ⓺ f. Wagehals; ⒉halsig a. ⓺ daring, foolhardy, venturesome; =halsigkeit f daring, foolhardiness.
Wagner ⊕ (⌣⌢) [ahd.; *Wagen²] m ⓶ wheelwright, cartwright.
Wagner=arbeit ⊕ (⌣⌢⌣⌢) f ⓺ wheelwright's work.
Wagnerianer (–⌣(⌣)⌢⌢) [Richard Wagner, Komponist. 1813–1883] m ⓶, ~in f ⓸ admirer of Wagner (music), Wagnerite.
Wagnis (⌣⌢) n ⓵⓲ (f ⓲) 1. hazard, risk, chance. — 2. (et. Gewagtes) bold venture, hazardous (or risky) enterprise.
wag-recht (⌣,⌢) f. wagerecht.
Wag-schale (⌣⌢...) f ⓺ scale (of the balance); die ~ sinken machen to kick the beam; fig. seine Worte auf die ~ legen to weigh one's words; =stück n daring feat, hazardous enterprise.
Wägung (⌣⌢) f ⓺ weighing.
Wahl(⌣) [ahd.: wählen] f ⓺ 1. choice, sorgfältige: selection, pol. election, poll (-ing), parl. return of a member; ~ durch Kugeln oder Stimmzettel: ballot; f. eng 3; städtische: municipal election; eine ~ (für) ungültig erklären to declare an election void, to invalidate an el.; to unseat a member of parliament; ~ zwischen zwei Dingen alternative; auf ~ begründet elective; auf ~en bezüglich electoral; f. eigen 1 und frei 2. — 2. mit verbs: j-s ~ et. anheimstellen to leave a th. to a p.'s choice; Sie haben die ~ (you may) take (or have) your choice; e-m die ~ lassen to let a p. take his choice, to give a p. the option between two or more things; seine ~ treffen to make one's selection, to choose; eine gute ~ treffen to make a good choice; zur ~ vorschlagen to nominate (or propose) as candidate (for an election); Sprichw. ~ macht Qual the larger the choice, the greater the puzzle; choosing is irksome.
Wahl=abt (⌣...) m ⓶ elective abbot; =akt m election, poll; =akten f/pl. election-returns pl.; =amt n elective office; =aufruf m electoral manifesto.
wählbar (⌣⌢) a. ⓺ eligible; nicht ⒉ ineligible; ~keit f ⓸ eligibleness.
Wahl=bedingung (⌣...) f ⓺ condition attaching to an election; =beeinflussung f influencing (of) voters, electoral corruption; ⒉berechtigt a. ⓺ entitled to (a) vote, enfranchised; =berechtigung f = =recht; =bericht m return; =bewegung f electioneering; =bezirk m electoral district, in Städten: ward; ehm.: bühne f, parl. hustings.
wählen (⌣⌢) [ahd.: wollen] I v/a. ⓷ 1. to choose; (auslesen) to pick (out), to select, pol. to elect (durch Stimmenmehrheit) by a majority of votes); to poll for; ⒉ Sie! take your choice!; gut, schlecht ⒉ to make a good, a bad choice; sich einen Wohnsitz ⒉ to choose (or fix upon) a (place of) residence; ins Parlament, zum Abgeordneten ⒉ to return to parliament, to elect as member of parliament; zum Könige ⒉ to elect (as) king; zum Vorsitzenden ⒉ to vote into the chair; parl. die Gesamtheit der ~den the constituency. — II ~ n ⓵ 2. = Wahl 1. — III ge=wählt p.p. und a. ⓺ 3. in den Bed. des inf. — 4. (auserlesen) choice, picked (workmen, &c.), gewählte Gesellschaft select company.
Wähler (⌣⌢) m ⓶, ~in f ⓸ pol. elector, voter, im Verhältnis: a) zum Wahlflecken: burgess. b) zum Abgeordneten: constituent; ~bestechung (⌣⌢⌣⌢) f ⓺ bribery at an election, weitS. corrupt electoral practices pl.
Wählerei (⌣–⌢) f ⓺ 1. pol. electioneering. — 2. ihn verdrießt eure lange ~ he is vexed at your being so long in choosing or selecting.
Wahl=ergebnis (⌣⌣⌢⌣) n ⓶ returns pl., result of the poll or an election.
wählerisch (⌣⌢⌣) a. ⓺ particular (in one's choice), nice (in one's habits), very exact; im Essen: fastidious, dainty; (zimperlich) prim, squeamish, prudish. [voters; vgl. Wahlliste.\
Wähler=liste (⌣⌢⌣⌢) f ⓺ register of/
Wählerschaft (⌣⌢⌣) f ⓺ 1. franchise. — 2. body of voters, electoral body, parl. constituency, constituents pl.
Wähler=versammlung (⌣⌢=⌣⌢⌣) f ⓺ meeting of (registered) voters.
wahl=fähig (⌣...) a. ⓺: a) = ⒉berechtigt; b) passivisch: eligible; =fähigkeit f ⓺: a) electoral right; b) passivisch: = =rechtb; ⒉frei* a. (fakultativ) optional; =fürst m: a) elective prince; b) = Kurfürst; =gesetz n electoral law, law regulating election, in Engl. a. Franchise Act; =kaiser m elective emperor; =kampf m electoral contest; =kapitulation f ehm. imperial capitulation; =kommissar m returning officer; =körperschaft f electoral body; =kreis m = =bezirk; =kugel f ballot; =liste f electoral register; vgl. Wählerliste; =lokal n = =ort; =mann m in Preußen u. delegate chosen for the election of a deputy; =männer=wahl f election of delegates (f. =mann); =ort, =platz m (Hom. Walplatz) place of election; polling-place; =programm n election (eering-)programme, a. platform; =prüfung f examination of the returns, verification of the poll, scrutiny; =recht n: a) aktives: right to vote, electoral franchise or qualification, allgemeines: universal suffrage; b) passives: eligibleness of a candidate for election; =rede f election- (F stump-)speech; =register n register of voters; =reich n elective empire or kingdom; =spruch m device, motto; =stimme f vote, suffrage; =tag m day of election, day of the poll, polling-day; =umtriebe m/pl. electioneering practices pl.; =urne f ballot-box; =versammlung f meeting of voters, electoral assembly; ⒉verwandt a. having an affinity (to), congenial; =verwandtschaft f: a) chm. ⚗ elective affinity; b) fig. congeniality; =vorgänge m/pl. proceedings at an election, election incidents pl.; =zelle f polling-booth; =zensus m property-qualification; =zettel m voting-paper; =zeuge m teller, scrutineer; =zimmer n room in which an election is held, für die Papstwahl: conclave.
Wahn¹ (⌣) [ahd.: wähnen] m ⓼c. (pl. ~) erroneous (or delusive) idea, vain imagining, false opinion, (Einbildung) fancy; (Verblendung) delusion, illusion, eines Geisteskranken: hallucination; (Torheit) folly, (Wahnsinn) madness, craze; eitler ~ chimera; von einem ~ befangen labouring under a delusion.
wahn²(⌣) [ahd.] a. ⓺ wanting (= leer).
Wahn¹=bild (⌣...) n ⓶ delusive image or notion; phantom, vision.
wähnen (⌣⌢) [ahd.: ween; = Wahn¹] I v/a. u. v/n. (h.) ⓼ (sich einbilden) to fancy, to imagine; (sich in Täuschung wiegen) to be under a delusion that; (meinen) to think (or believe) erroneously or mistakenly or wrongly; (dafür halten) to presume, to suppose; to have an idea that. — II ~ n ⓵ fancy(ing), vain imagining, delusion; erroneous (or mistaken) belief; (mere) supposition.
Wahn¹=glaube (⌣...) m ⓶ erroneous (or false, mistaken) belief; (Aberglaube) superstition; =²kante ⊕ f, carp. bad level, blunt edge; ⒉kantig ⊕ a. ⓺ carp. (stumpfkantig) blunt-edged; =²korn n empty ear of corn; =²sinn (⌣⌢) [erst nhd.] m ⓼c: a) path. insanity, lunacy; stiller ~ melancholy, madness; fig. es wäre reiner ~, das zu tun it would be sheer madness (or craziness) to do so; tobender ~ raving madness; b) (geistige Störung oder Aufregung) delirium; dichterischer ~ poetic frenzy; bis zum ~ lieben to love to distraction, to be madly fond of //; ⒉sinnig (⌣⌣⌣) a. ⓺ path. insane, deranged, out of one's mind; (verrückt) mad, crazy, F cracked, dotty, off one's chump, bsd. schott. daft; ⒉ machen

[**Wahnsinniger**] — 1090 — [**Wal-...**]

to drive mad; 2 w. to go mad, to go out of one's mind; *fig.* es ist zum ~ werden it is enough to drive one mad; =**sinnige([r]** *m* *f* ⑥ insane person, lunatic, madman, *f* madwoman; (von Sinnen) distracted, beside o.s., seltener: demented; =**witz** (ᴵᴵ‿) [ahd.] *m* ⑪ a. lack of reason, senselessness; weitS. = **Wahnsinn**; **Qwitzig** (ᴵᴵ‿‿) *a.* ⑥ senseless, absurd, *a.* = wahnsinnig.

wahr(¹; *Hom.* war) [ahd.: lt. *vē′r-us*] *a.* ⑥ 1. true, *adv.* truly; (echt, wirklich) genuine, real; (eigentlich) proper; v. Personen: (wahrhaft) truthful, veracious; (aufrichtig) sincere, frank, open; das ~e daran ist // the truth of it is //; das ~e mit dem Falschen verwechseln to mistake falsehood for truth. — 2. mit *nouns*: die 2e Bedeutung einer Sache the true meaning (or inwardness) of a th.; es ist ein 2es Glück it is really most fortunate; s. Jakob II; es ist kein 2es Wort oder nichts ~es daran there is not a word of truth in it; *ast.* der 2e Gesichtskreis the true (or astronomical, celestial, real) horizon. — 3. mit *verbs*: er will es nicht 2 haben he does (or will) not admit it; et. 2 machen to make a th. come true; er hat das Sprichwort 2 gemacht he has proved the truth of the adage; sein Wort 2 machen to make good one's word; 2 **reden**, 2 **sprechen** to speak (or tell) the truth; 2 **werden** to come (or prove) true. — 4 fragend: a) allgemein: **nicht** 2? is it not true?, don't you think so?; (vgl. gelt¹); b) nach einem Bejahungssätze: nicht 2, er ist zurückgekehrt? he has returned, has he not?; c) nach einem Verneinungssätze: nicht 2, er weiß es nicht? he does not know it, does he? — 5. in Beteuerungen: das muß 2 sein! upon my word!; 2 und wahrhaftig! in truth!, really and truly!, geh. Spr.: forsooth!; so 2 ich ein ehrlicher Mann bin! upon my word of honour!; so 2 ich lebe!, so 2 ein Gott lebt! as true (or as sure) as I live!, by my soul, feierlich: as true as there is a God in Heaven!; so 2 mir Gott helfe! feierlich: so help me God!, mehr gbr.: by Heaven!

Währ-... (ᴵᴵ‿...) s. Wer-...

.wahren (ᴸ‿) [ahd.] *v/a.* u. *v/refl.* ⑧ = bewahren 1; einen vor et. 2 to preserve a p. from a th.; sich gegen et. 2 to (be on one's) guard against a th.

währen (ᴸ‿) [ahd.: Wesen] I *v/n.* (h.) ⑧ to last, *bibl.* auch: to endure; (fortfahren zu sein) to continue, to hold out; ewig 2 to last for ever, never to die or to perish; es währte nicht lange, so brach der Krieg aus it was not long before the war broke out; es kann noch lange 2, ehe (oder bis) er kommt it may be (or last) a long while before (or until) he comes, he may be a long time coming; Sprichw. was lange währt, wird gut good work takes (a long) time; s. ehrlich 2 am Ende; ewig 2 eternal, everlasting, never ending. — II 2d *p.pr.* u. *a.* ⑥: in 2der Arbeit during the work;

ewig 2d everlasting; als *prp.* u. *cj.*, s. bsd. während.

während (ᴸ‿) [nhd. *p.pr.* v. währen] I *prp.* mit *gen.* (bisw. mit *dat.*): during; 2dessen (2dem) (in the) meanwhile; 2 eines Jahres for (the space of) a twelvemonth; 2 der Nacht during (or in the course of, kürzer: in) the night; 2 der Regierung der Königin Viktoria in (or during) the reign of Queen Victoria; 2 der Untersuchung pending the inquiry. — II *cj.* (bisw. 2 daß) (solange als) as long as: a) zeitlich: while, whilst; 2 sie abreiste, kam ich an whilst she was leaving (or just as she left) I arrived; 2 sie las, weinte sie while (she was) reading she cried; b) gegensätzlich: er wurde gefaßt, 2 sein Gefährte entkam he was seized whereas (or whilst) his companion escaped.

wahrhaft (ᴸ‿) [ahd.] *a.* ⑥ = wahr 1.
wahrhaftig *a.* ⑥ 1. (ᴸ‿‿) = wahr 1. — 2. (‿ᴸ‿) als Beteuerung: 2! in truth!; seltener: forsooth!; (traun) surely!; in der Tat) really!; vgl. wahrlich; 2? is it true?, do you mean it?; ~**keit** (ᴸ‿‿) *f* ⑥ truthfulness, veracity; sincerity.

Wahrheit (ᴸ‿) [ahd.] *f* ⑥ (das Wahrsein und mit *pl.* wahrer Ausspruch; *ant.* Erdichtung): truth (s. Körnchen); (Wirklichkeit) reality, (Tatsache) fact; in ~ in truth, in fact; der ~ gemäß true, truthful, *adv.* truly; die volle ~ the whole truth; 2 bleiben 4 unter „bei"; e-m derb die ~ sagen to give a p. a piece (or a bit) of one's mind; man hat ihm rund heraus die ~ gesagt he has been told the plain truth; um die ~ zu sagen to tell the truth, ehm.: to say sooth; die ~ sprechen to speak the truth; er will die ganze ~ wissen he wants to get to the bottom of it (all), he means to sift the matter thoroughly; Sprichw. s. Kind 3 am Schluß; im Wein ist ~ wine has no secrets, (lt.) in vino veritas.

Wahrheits-eifer (ᴸ‿...) *m* ② zeal(ous regard) for the truth; =**forscher** *m* inquirer (or seeker) after truth; 2**gemäß**, 2**getreu** *a.* ⑥ true, truthful, veracious, *adv.* truly, in accordance with the true facts; =**liebe** *f* love of truth, veracity; 2**liebend** *a.* truthful, veracious; =**sinn** *m* = =liebe.

wahrlich (ᴸ‿, ‿ᴸ) [mhd.] *int.* 2! indeed!, to be sure!, (most) certainly!, (most) assuredly! as true as I live!; vgl. wahrhaftig 2; *bibl.* 2, 2, ich sage euch verily, verily, I say unto you.

wahr-nehmbar (ᴸᴸ‿) *a.* ⑥ perceivable, mehr gbr.: perceptible, observable, noticeable, (sichtbar) visible; nicht 2 imperceptible; ~**keit** *f* perceptibility.
wahr-nehmen (ᴸᴸ‿) [ahd.] I *v/a.* ⑧ a**: et. 2 to perceive (or notice, observe, see) a th.; to become aware of a th.; (achten auf) to heed, to pay attention to; eine Gelegenheit 2 to seize an opportunity; j-s Vorteil 2 to look after a p.'s interest. — II **Wahr-nehmung** *f* ⑥ perception, observation; paying attention to; looking after; **Wahr-nehmungs-vermögen** *n* ⑫ perceptive faculty, power(s *pl.*) of observation; bsd. phls. auch perceptivity.

Wahr-sage-kunst (ᴸᴸ‿‿) *f* ⑫ art of soothsaying or fortune-telling.
wahr-sagen (ᴸᴸ‿) [ndd.] I *v/a.* u. *v/n.* (h.) ⑧*** (**) to prophesy, aus Karten ꝛc.: to tell people's fortunes, aus d. Sternen: to read (in) the stars; vgl. voraussagen. — II ~ n ② = Wahrsagung.
Wahr-sager (ᴸᴸ‿) *m* ②, ~**in** *f* ⑥ soothsayer, fortune-teller; prophet(ess *f*); Alt.: aus dem Fluge der Vögel: augur, aus dem Getröse der Opfertiere: haruspex; ~**ei** (ᴸ‿‿ᴸ) *f* ⑥ = Wahrsagung, divination; ~ aus den Gestirnen: astrology, Alt.: aus dem Fluge der Vögel: augury, durch Geisterbeschwörung: necromancy; 2**isch** (ᴸᴸ‿‿) *a.* ⑥ soothsaying, telling people's fortunes; prophetic.
Wahr-sagung (ᴸᴸ‿) *f* ⑥ prophesying, soothsaying, fortune-telling; Alt.: vaticination; vgl. Wahrsagerei.
wahr-scheinlich (ᴸᴸ‿, ᴸᴸ‿) *a.* ⑥ likely, probable; plausible; es ist sehr (nicht) 2, daß er gewinnt there is every (no) chance of his winning, he is most (not) likely to win; er wird 2 (*adv.*) kommen he will probably (or he is likely to) come; ~**keit** *f* ⑥ likelihood, probability; plausibility; aller ~ nach in all probability, in all likelihood, most probably; ~**keits-rechnung** *f* ⑫ *math.* theory of probabilities.
Wahr-spruch (ᴸᴸ‿‿) *m* ⑫ der Geschworenen verdict of a jury.
Währung (ᴸ‿) [mhd.: Gewähr] *f* ⑥ 1. (Münzfuß) standard (of coinage); s. Doppelwährung. — 2. (Geltung) importance; von echter ~ of sterling value or quality, truly genuine.
Wahr-zeichen (ᴸᴸ‿) [mhd.] *n* ② a) distinctive mark or sign; token; b) (Vorzeichen) premonitory sign, omen; symptom; c) ⚒ specimen of ore (taken from a lode).

Waiblinger (ᴸ‿‿) [Waiblingen ⚐, württembergische Stadt] *m* ② *hist.* (Anhänger des Kaisers in Italien; *ant.* Welfe), **waiblingisch** *a.* ⑥ Ghibelline.
Waid⚐ (ᴸ; *Hom.* Weid) [ahd.: woad] *m* ⚒. (Färber~) woad, pastel (*I′satis tincto′ria*).
Waid-bau (ᴸ‿...) *m* ⑫ cultivation of woad; =**blau** ⚒ *n* woaded blue; =**färber** *m* woad-dyer; =**kuchen** ⊙ *m* woad-ball or -cake; =**küpe** ⊙ *f* woad vat; =**mühle** *f* woad-mill.

Waise (ᴸ‿; *Hom.* Weise) [ahd.: Witwe] *f* ⑥ (von einem Knaben bisw. auch ~ *m* ⑭) orphan (child); unmündige ~ ward; zur ~ machen to orphan.
Waisen-anstalt (ᴸ‿...) *f* ⑫, =**haus** *n* orphan-asylum; =**kind** *n* = Waise; =**knabe** *m* orphan boy; F *fig.* er ist der reine ~ gegen ihn he is a fool to (or not a patch on) him; =**mädchen** *n* orphan girl; =**mutter** *f* matron of an orphan-asylum; =**stand** *m* orphanhood; =**vater** *m* male superintendent of an orphan-asylum. [the ice.)

Wake *prov.* (ᴸ‿) [ndd.] *f* ⑱ hole cut in)
Wal¹ (ᴸ) [ahd.: whale] *m* ⑫ *c.* zo. whale (= Walfisch); ~**e** (= Waltiere) *pl.*: a) allgemein (Fischfängetiere): ⚯ cetacea; b) (Walfische) ⚯ balaenidae.
Wal²-... (ᴸ‿...) [ahd. Schlachtfeld: lt. *vulnus* Wunde] s. Walfeld ꝛc.

Signs (see page XVII)· F familiar; P vulgar; ⸙ flash; ⚊ rare; † obsolete (died); * new word (born); +'+ incorrect; ♪ music;

Wal³... (⸺...) [welsche] f. Walnuß.
Walache (⸺ch⸺) [Welscher, d. i. Italiener] m ⊕, **Walachin** f ⊕ Wallachian (f. a. Wallach); **Walachei** f ⊕ (⸺ch⸺) f ⊕ (Donaufürstentum, Teil von Rumänien) die ~ Wallachia; **walachisch** (⸺ch⸺) a. ⊕ Wallachian. [*ova'ta*).]
Walch ⚚ (⸹) m ⊕b. ægilops (*Ae'gilops*
Wald (⸹) [ahd.: wold, wood] m ⊕b. 1. (*ant.* Feld) wood, größerer: forest; (Hain) grove; hochstämmiger ~ timberforest; junger ~ (Baumschule) nursery, ⚚, zo u. poet. in Wäldern lebend, wachsend sylvan, ⚚ nemorose; Sprichw. f. Baum 2; wie man in den ~ ruft, so schallt's heraus the answer is suited to the question; as you give so you receive. — 2. *fig.* ein ~ (Wulst) von Haaren a good (or thick) head of hair; ein ~ von Masten a forest of masts; ehm. Buchtitel: Wälder collected poems *pl.*
Waldai-gebirge ⚲ (⸺⸺...) *n*, **-höhen** *f/pl.*, **-plateau** *n* (russ. Bergland, Quellgebiet der Wolga) Valdai Hills *pl.*
Wald-ameise (⸹...) f zo. wood-ant, red ant (*Formi'ca rufa*); **-anemone** ⚚ f wood-anemone (*Anemo'ne nemoro'sa*); ⚚**-artig** a. ⊕ sylvan, forestine; **-aufseher** m ranger; ⚚**-aus** (⸹...) *adv.* out of the forest or wood; **-bach** m forest-stream; **-bau** m fo.-culture; *vgl.* pflege; **-baum** m fo.-tree; **-baum-schule** f nursery of fo.-trees; ⚚**-bedeckt** *a.* (well) wooded, covered with forests; **-beere** ⚚ f = Heidelbeere; ⚚**-bekränzt** *a.* adorned with forests; **-bereiter** m = -reiter; **-bewohner(in** *f*) m inhabitant of a forest, *pl.* a. forest-folk; **-biene** *f,* ent. wild bee; **-blume** *f* flower of the woods; **-brand** m fire in a wood, größerer: conflagration of a forest; **-bruder** m (Einsiedler) hermit living in a wood.
Wäldchen (⸺) *n* ⊕ (dim. von Wald) little wood, grove; (Gebüsch) bush(es *pl.*), shrubbery; (Dickicht) thicket.
wald-ein (⸹,⸹) *adv.* into (or towards) the forest or wood; ⚚**-einsamkeit** (⸹...) *f* ⊕ sylvan solitude, als Ort: woodland retreat. [Waldemar, Voldemar.]
Waldemar (⸺⸺) *npr/m.* ⊕⊕ *a.* (⚚n.)
Waldenser (⸺⸺) [Petrus Waldus, Kaufmann in Lyon, Stifter der start verfolgten Waldenser Sekte, 1170] m ⊕ **~in** *f* ⊕ *hist.* bsd. in ~ Südfrankreich: adherent of Waldo. bsd. *pl.* Waldenses; **waldensisch** *a.* ⊕ Waldensian, (fr.) Vaudois.
Wald-erdbeere ⚚ (⸺⸺⸺) *f* ⊕ wood-strawberry (*Fraga'ria vesca*).
Waldes-dunkel (⸹...) *n* ⊕ forest-gloom; **-grün** *n* verdure of the woods; **-kühle** *f* coolness of the forest; **-saum** m fringe (or skirts *pl.*) of a forest; am ~ entlang gehen to skirt the forest; **-stille** *f* stillness (or dead silence) of the forest.
Wald-eule (⸹...) *f* ⊕ = Kauz 1 a; **-frevel** *m* offence against forest-laws; **-gebirge** *n* range of wooded mountains; **-gegend** *f* woodland, wooded (or woody) country; **-gehege** *n* preserve(d wood); **-geier** *m* = Bussard; **-geist** *m* sylvan spirit, faun, satyr; **-gerste** ⚚ *f* wood-barley (*Ho'rdeum silva'ticum*); **-geschrei** *n* hunting-cry; **-glöckchen**, **-glöcklein** ⚚ *n* blue-bell

(*Campa'nula rotundifo'lia*); **-gott** *m,* myth. sylvan god; *vgl.* -geist; **-gottheit** *f* sylvan deity; **-göttin** *f* sylvan goddess; *vgl.* -nymphe; **-grün** *n* ⚚ Waldes-; **-hase** *m* hunt. woodland hare; **-honig** *m* wild honey; **-horn** ♪ *n* bugle(-horn), French horn; **-hornbläser**, **-hornist** *m* bugler, bugle-man; **-hüter** *m* keeper of a forest.
waldig (⸺) *a.* ⊕ wooded, woody; *poet.* an ⸺er Stelle amid sylvan surroundings, in the woodland.
Wald-kapelle (⸹...) *f* ⊕ chapel in a forest; **-kauz** *m* = Kauz 1 a; **-kirsche** *f* wild cherry; **-kultur** *f* = pflege; **-land** *n* woodland, forest-land; **-landschaft** *f* woodland (or forest) scenery; **-läufer** *m* ranger, forester.
Wäldlein (⸹⸺) *n* ⊕ = Wäldchen.
Wald-lerche (⸹...) *f* ⊕ orn. woodlark (*Alau'da arbo'rea*); **-leute** *pl.*: a) forest-folk; b) ⊕ Schweiz: inhabitants of the Four (old Swiss) Cantons (f. -stätte); **-mann** *m:* a) woodman; b) = -geist; **-männchen** *n* forest-sprite, hobgoblin, imp; **-mast** *f* = Eichelmast; **-maus** *f* = Feldmaus; **-meister** *m:* a) = -hüter; b) ⚚ woodruff (*Aspe'rula*); bsd. wohlriechender ~ (*Asp. odora'ta*); **-mensch** *m:* a) wild man (of woods); b) zo. = Orang-Utan; **-nessel** ⚚ *f* = -ziest; **-nymphe** *f* nymph of the woods, dryad; **-ordnung** *f* forest-laws or -regulations *pl.*; **-pfad** *m* fo.-path; **-pflanzen** *f/pl.* fo.-plants; **-pflege** *f* forestry, ⚚ sylviculture, *vgl.* -bau; **-rauch** *m:* a) = Herauch: b) ⚚ = Bisamkraut; **-rebe** ⚚ *f* lady's-bower, clematis (*Cle'matis*); **-recht** *n:* a) forest-laws *pl.*; b) rights and privileges *pl.* of the owner of a forest; ⚚**-reich** *a.* rich in forests, well-wooded, woody; **-reiter** *m* mounted wood-ranger or forester; **-revier** *n* = -gegend; **-sänger** *m* (Singvogel) forest-songster; **-schaden** *m* damage done in a forest; **-schau** *f* inspection of a forest; **-schloß** *n* castle in a forest; **-schnepfe** *f,* orn. wood-cock (*Sco'topax rusti'cola*); **-schrat** *m* f. Schrat; **-stadt** *f* town situated in a forest; **-stätte** *pl.*: ⚚ Schweiz: die vier ~ (Uri, Schwyz, Unterwalden [Luzern]) the Four (old Swiss) Cantons *pl.*; *vgl.* Vierwaldstätter See; **-streu** *f* litter consisting of dry leaves, &c. collected in the forest; **-strom** *m* forest-stream, torrent passing through a wood; **-teufel** *m:* a) = -geist; b) zo. = Mandrill; c) Kinderspielzeug: pasteboard rattle; ⚚**-umkränzt** *a.* = -bekränzt; *poet.* wood-embosomed, forest-clad.
Waldung (⸺⸺) *f* ⊕ woodland, woods *pl.*; wooded (or well-timbered) country or district or grounds *pl.*
Wald-vergißmeinnicht ⚚ (⸹...) *n* ⊕ wood scorpion-grass (*Myoso'tis silva'tica*); **-vogel** *m* bird of the forest, wood-bird; **-wärter** *m* = -hüter; ⚚**-wärts** *adv.* towards the wood; **-weg** *m* forest-road, road through a wood; **-weide** *f* forest-pasture; **-wiese** *f* fo.-glade; **-wiesel** *n, zo.* = Frett²; **-wirtschaft** *f* = -pflege; **-wolle** ⚚ *f* pine-needle wool; **-wollöl** ⚚ *n* pine-needle oil; **-zeichen** *n, for.* mark on forest-

trees, blaze; **-ziest** ⚚ *m* hedge-nettle (*Stachys silva'tica*). — *Vgl. auch* Forst-...
walen ⚓ (⸹) *v/n.* (h.) ⊕: a) vom Schiffe, das keine Fahrt hat: to have no steerage-way; b) von der Magnetnadel, die ihren Magnetismus verloren hat: to vacillate.
Wales (welß) [engl. = Welsch] *npr/n. inv.* (Landschaft in West-england, früheres Fürstentum, mit keltischer Sprache) Wales, der Prinz von ~ the Prince of Wales, f. Neusüdwales; *dazu:* Waliser.
Wal²-feld †*od. poet.* (⸹,⸹) *n* ⊕ battle-field.
Wal¹-fisch (⸹,⸹) [ahd. f. Wal¹] *m* ⊕ zo. whale (*Balae'na*); junger ~ whale-calf; ⚚**-fisch-artig** *a.* ⊕ ⚚ cetaceous; **-fisch-fahrer** *m* (Schiff) whaler; **-fisch-fang** *m* whale-catching or -fishing; auf den ~ geh(e)n to go whaling; **-fisch-fänger** *m* whaler, whale-fisher; **-fisch-laus** *f. zo.* whale-louse (*Cy'amus Ceti*); **-fisch-speck** *m* (whale-)blubber; **-fisch-tran** *m* whale- (or train-)oil; **-fisch-weibchen** *n* whale-cow.
wälgern *prove.* (⸺⸺) *v/a.* a. (glatt rollen) to roll (down), to smooth by rolling.
Wälg-holz (⸹,⸹) *n* Bäckerei: rolling-pin.
Walhalla (⸺⸺) [isländ.*Wal²*] *f.* a. **Walhall** (⸺) *m* ⊕ **1.** *myth.* (Himmel der Germanen) Walhalla, Valhalla. — **2.** (Ehrenhalle) Memorial Hall; bsd. die von Ludwig I. von Bayern bei Regensburg errichtete: German Pantheon.
Waliser (⸺⸺) [Wales] **I** *m* ⊕, **~in** *f* ⊕ Welshman, *f* Welshwoman; die ~ the Welsh (people) *pl.* — **II** ⚚ *a. inv.* (auch **walisisch** ⊕) Welsh, of Wales, *a.* Cymric, Kymric. — *Vgl.* Walliser.
Walk-bürste (⸹...) *f* ⊕ felting-brush.
Walke (⸺) *f* ⊕ **1.** = walken II; die letzte ~ geben to give the last fulling. — **2.** = Walk-hammer, -mühle.
walken (⸺) [ahd.: walk] **I** *v a.* ⊕ **1.** ⊕ Tuchmacherei ꝛc.: to full, to mill. — **2.** F *fig.* = prügeln. — **II** ~ *n* ⊕ *fig.* fulling, milling of cloth, &c.
Walker ⊕ (⸺⸺) *m* ⊕ Tuchfabrikation: fuller, dresser of cloth.
Walk-erde (⸹,⸹) *f* ⊕ fuller's earth.
Walkerei ⊕ (⸺⸺) *f* ⊕: a) = walken II; b) fullery (= Walkmühle).
Walker-erde ⊕ (⸹...) *f* ⊕ = Walk-erde; **-lohn** *m* fuller's fee; **-roche** *m, ichth.* fuller (*Ra'ia fullo'nica*); **-ton** *m* = Walk-erde.
Walk-haare ⊕ (⸹...) *n pl.* ⊕ fulling-hair; **-hammer** *m* fulling-hammer or -pestle or -wood; **-kessel** *m* = -trog; **-mühle** *f* fulling-mill, bisw.: fullery; **-müller** *m* = Walker; **-stätte** *f* der Hutmacher ꝛc.: battery; **-tafel** *f* Hutmacherei: table for felting; **-ton** *m* = -erde; **-trog** *m* fulling-trough. [*myth.* Valkyr(ia).]
Walküre (⸺⸺) [isländ.*Wal²*] *f* ⊕ german.
Walk-werk (⸹,⸹) *n* ⊕ = Walkmühle.
Wall¹ (⸹) [mhd.: wall; *lt. vallum n*] *m* ⊕b. **1.** ⚔ *frt.* rampart(a. *fig.* u. als Spaziergang). — **2.** (Einfriedigung) enclosure; (Damm) dike, dam, embankment; (erhöhtes Erdreich) mound of earth; ⚓ (Küste) shore, coast; *vgl.* Legerwall.
Wall² (⸹) [wallen²] *m* ⊕b. (Wallen einer Flüssigkeit) bubbling (or boiling) up.
Wall³ (⸹) [ndd.] *n* ⊕b, 6. Maß im Heringshandel (80—84 Stück), etwa: fourscore.
Wall¹-absatz ⚔ (⸹,⸹) *m* ⊕ *frt.* berm(e).

[**Wallach**]

Wallach(ˇ-ch)[**Walache**] m ⑪c. ⑫ (verschnittener Hengst) castrated horse, gelding.
wallachen (ˇ-ch) [**Wallach**] v/a. ⑧: vet. einen Hengst 2 (verschneiden) to castrate (or geld) a stallion.
Wallafette ⚔ (ˇ-ˇ-ˇ) [**Wall-lafette**] f ⑫ standing-bed of a rampart-gun.
Wall²-anker ⚓ (ˇ...) m ⑫ shore-anchor; =**arbeit** ⚔ f throwing up ramparts, rampart-work; =**arbeiter** m trencher, navvy working at (the) ramparts; =**böschung** f rampart-slope; =**bruch** m breach in a rampart; ehm. =**büchse** f rampart-gun.
wallen¹ (ˇˇ) [ahd.] I v/n. (ſn u. h.) ⑧ to wander, to travel; (pilgern) to go on (or make) a pilgrimage. — II ~ n ㉓ travelling; pilgrimage.
wallen² (ˇˇ) [ahd.: well: Welle] I v/n. (ſn u. h.) ⑧ beim Kochen: 1. to bubble (or boil) up, gelinde: to simmer, vom Blute in den Adern: to boil; (ſich in Wellen bewegen) to undulate, von der See: to be running high; fig. (ſich aufregen) to be (-come) agitated or excited, vgl. aufwallen 1 u. 2. — 2. (flattern, wehen) to float, to flutter, to stream in the wind, to wave; 2des Gewand flowing gown; 2des Haar waving hair; 2der Rauch curling smoke. — II ~ n ㉓ undulation (a. phys.); bubbling up, ebullition; effervescence; vgl. Wallung.
wällen (ˇˇ) [wallen m.] v/a. ⑧ Kochkunſt: to (let) boil; (gelinde kochen l.) to (let) simmer; gewällte Kartoffeln boiled potatoes pl. [fahrer(in).]
Waller (ˇˇ) m ㉒, =**in** f ⑰ bisw. = Wall-ʃ
wall²-fahren (ˇ...) [wallen¹] v/n. (ſn) ⑧*ˣ* to go on a pilgrimage; =**fahrer(in** f) m ⑫ pilgrim, ehm. auch: palmer; =**fahrt** [mhd.] f pilgrimage; ²**fahrten** v/n. (ſn) ⑧*ˣ* = ²fahren; =**fahrtsort** m place of pilgrimage, holy shrine; =¹**gang** ⚔ m terre-plein of a rampart; =**geſchütz** n rampart-gun; =**graben** m ditch of a rampart; =**gräber** m = =arbeiter.
Wallis ♀ (ˇˇ) [Welſch] npr/n. inv. (Kanton in der Schweiz) Valais.
Walliſer (ˇ-ˇ) [**Wallis**] I m ㉒, ~**in** f ⑰ a. inv. (a. **walliſiſch** a. ⑯) Valaisan, of Valais. — Vgl. Waliſer.
Wall¹-keller ⚔ (ˇ...) m ⑫ frt. casemate; =**lafette** f ʃ. Wallafette; =**meiſter** m inspector of ramparts.
Wallone (ˇ-ˇ) m ⑭, **Wallonin** f ⑰ (e-m fr. redenden Volksſtamme in Belgien Angebörige[r]), **walloniſch** a. ⑯ Walloon.
Wall¹-ſchild (ˇ...) m ⑫ ⚔ ravelin; =**ſtraße** f rampart-road.
Wallung (ˇˇ) f ⑰ 1. boiling up; (Aufbrauſen) ebullition, effervescence. — 2. (wallende Bewegung) undulation; (Aufregung) agitation, emotion, excitement, flutter; in ~ bringen to excite, to flutter; in ~ geraten to fly in(to) a passion; in ~ ſein: a) vom Blute: to be boiling, to be up; b) vom Pulſe: to be high, to throb.
Walm ⊙ (ˇ) [: wallen, wölben] m ⑪b. arch. hip-side of a roof; ~=**dach** ⊙ (ˇ-ch) n ⑫ hipped roof, hip-roof.
walmen ⊙ (ˇˇ) v/a. ⑧ arch.: ein Dach 2 to slope a roof.

Wal²-nuß ♀ (ˇ...) [ndd.] f ⑫ (a. welſche Nuß) (large) walnut; =**nuß-baum** ♀ m walnut-tree (Iuglans regia); weißer nordamerikaniſcher ~ hickory (Carya alba); =**nuß-ſchale** f walnut-shell, grüne äußere: outer shell (or husk) of a walnut.
Wal²-platz † ob. poet. (ˇˇ) m = =feld.
Walpurgis (ˇ-ˇ) [ahd.: *walten+Burg] npr/f. inv. (biſ. Abtiſſin zu Heidenheim im 8. sae.) Walpurgis; ~=**nacht** f ⑫ (vom 30. April zum 1. Mai mit e-m Hexenſabbat auf dem Blocksberge) Walpurgis Night, St. Walpurgis, Witches' Sabbath.
Wal¹-rat (ˇ...) m, n ⑫ pharm. u. ⊙: ⚗ spermaceti; =**rat-fett** n ʃ. Cetin; =**roß** n [dän.] zo. walrus (Trichechus rosmarus).
wälſch (ˇ) ꝛc. ʃ. welſch ꝛc. [= Walfeld.]
Wal²-ſtatt poet. (ˇˇ) f (sg. ⑯, pl. =ſtätten)]
walten (ˇˇ) [ahd.: wield] I v/n. (h.) u. v/a. ⑱: a) abs. to rule, govern, sway; to hold the reins of government (ſ. ſchalten I); im Hauſe (im Lande) 2 to rule (or manage) the house (the land); Gnade 2 l. to act with clemency, to show mercy; den lieben Gott 2 l. to leave everything to God, to trust in Providence; b) mit abhängigem Kaſus, mſt mit gen.: ſeines Amtes 2 to discharge (or attend to) one's duties; formelhaft: des (ob. das) walte Gott! (may) God grant it!, may it please Heaven!, auch: amen!; c) über et. 2 to superintend a th., to attend to a th.; Gott läßt ſ-e Gnade über den (ob. acc. die) Guten und Böſen 2 God bestows his mercy on the good and the wicked. — II ~ n ㉓ rule, government, sway; management; rel. Gottes ~ God's ordinances or ways pl.
Walter¹ (ˇ) (ˇˇ) [walten] m ㉒ = Verwalter. [(a. Vn.) Walter.]
Walter² (ˇ) (ˇˇ) [Walthari] npr/m. ⑳a.ʃ
Walz-blech ⊙ (ˇ...) n ⑫ rolled plate; =**blei** n sheet-lead.
Walze (ˇˇ) [ahd.: walzen] f ⑱ 1. cylinder (a. math.), ⊙ (Garten-, Straßen- ꝛc.) ~ roller; ~ in einer Drehorgel ꝛc. barrel. — 2. P ʄ (o. pl.) (Wanderſchaft) tramp.
Walz-eiſen ⊙ (ˇ-ˇ) n ⑫ rolled (or malleable) iron.
walzen (ˇˇ) v/a. 1. ⊙ (mit e-r Walze bearbeiten) to roll out, to flatten (out) with a roller; Bäckerei: den Teig 2 to roll the dough; metall. Blei ꝛc. 2 to mill ..., Eiſen 2 to roll (or laminate) ...; zu Blech 2 to roll into sheets, to laminate; gewalztes Eiſen rolled iron. — II v/n. (h.) 2. a) (dance a) waltz; ~**de**(r) s. waltzer; b) 2de (vom Gut getrennt verkäufliche) Grundſtücke lands to be sold apart from the estate. — 3. P ʄ v/n. (ſn) to (go on the) tramp.
wälzen (ˇˇ) [ahd.: Welle] ⑱ I v/a. to roll, to turn about, ſchwere Bücher ꝛc. to thumb; fig. die Schuld auf e-n 2 to lay (or put) the blame upon a p.'s shoulders; eine Schuld von ſich 2 to exculpate (or clear) o.s. — II ſich 2 v/refl. to roll (o.s. over); ſich in ſ-m Blute 2 to lie in a pool of blood, to be bathed in blood; ſich im Kote 2 to wallow in the mire or mud; ſich ſchlaflos im Bette 2 to toss from side to side; fig. er wälzt ſich vor Lachen he is splitting with laughter. — III ~ n ㉓ rolling, &c. (ʃ. I u. II); das iſt zum ~ that's most laughable, F it's enough to make a cat laugh.
Walzen-apparat ⊙ (ˇ-ˇ...) [Walze] m ⑫ = =geſtell; =**bürſte** f revolving brush; =**druck** m, typ. cylinder-printing; =**druck-maſchine** f cylinder-printing machine; =**form** f cylindrical form or shape; ²**förmig** a. cylindrical, cylindriform; =**geſtell** n Färberei: rolling-frame, typ. roller-frame; =**kaliber** n groove, caliber, calibre; =**keſſel** m cylindrical boiler; =**mange** f Weberei: calender.
Walzer (ˇˇ) m ㉒ (Tanz u. Muſik) ʄ waltz.
Wälzer F (ˇˇ) m ㉒ (dickleibiger Band) stout (or heavy) volume, unwieldy book.
Walz-holz ⊙ (ˇ...) n ⑫ Bäckerei ꝛc.: rolling-pin; =**hütte** f = =werk a; =**maſchine** f rolling-machine or -mill; =**prozeß** m process of rolling, lamination; =**werk** n: a) rolling- (or flatting-)mill or -works pl.; b) laminating-rollers pl.; a. = =maſchine. — Vgl. Walzen=...
Wamme (ˇˇ) [mhd.: womb] f ⑱ 1. Kürſchnerei: belly part of a skin. — 2. F (Wanſt) paunch, belly. — 3. vet. ~ am Halſe des Rindes: dewlap; mit ~ behaftet dewlapped.
Wams (ˇ) [mhd.; alt-fr.; *dtſch Wamme] n (⟨ m) ⑨a. jacket, ehm. a. doublet, jerkin; vgl. Jacke 1. [jacket.]
Wämschen (ˇˇ) n ⑭ little (or short)]
wamſen F (ˇˇ) v/a. ⑨: e-n (durch=)2 to give a p. a sound (or good) thrashing.
Wand¹ (ˇ) [ahd.; *wand²] f ⑫ 1. ~ eines bewohnten Raumes: wall of a room, &c.; hölzerne (Scheide=) ~ partition; ſpaniſche ~ folding-screen; fig. u. Sprichw. e-n an (ob. gegen) die ~ drücken to press (or push) a p. hard; ſ. Horcher, Kopf 8 unter „mit", malen 2, Narrenhände; die Wände haben Ohren walls have ears; leeren Wänden predigen to talk to deaf ears or to empty chairs. — 2. (Seitenfläche eines Gefäßes ꝛc.) side of a vessel, shaft, &c., panel of a coach, &c., vgl. Wange. — 3. anat. ~ des Magens ꝛc. coat (or lining) of the stomach, &c. — 4. typ. Wände pl. einer Preſſe cheeks of a press. — 5. (Felſen=)~ rocky wall.
wand² (ˇ) ind. impf. von winden.
Wand¹-anſtrich (ˇ...) m ⑫ painting of a wall; =**arm** m für Gas ꝛc.: bracket; =**bank** f bench placed against the wall; =**bein** n, anat.: ⚗ parietal bone; =**bewurf** ⊙ m = Putz 2.
Wandel (ˇˇ) [ahd.: wenden] m ⑫ 1. (Wechſel) change, alteration; ~ ſchaffen in et. to bring about (or effect) a change in s. th.; es iſt ein großer ~ mit ihm vorgegangen a great change has come over him. — 2. (Art des Verhaltens) conduct, behaviour; habits pl.; mode of life. — 3. = Verkehr 1; Handel und ~ trade and traffic, ʃ. Handel 5 am Ende. [arcade.]
Wandel-bahn (ˇˇ-ˇ) f ⑫ covered walk,]
wandelbar (ˇˇˇ) a. ⑯ 1. = veränderlich. — 2. (gebrechlich) fragile, frail; (vergänglich) perishable, transient. [lichkeit.]
Wandelbarkeit (ˇˇ-ˇ-) f ⑯ = Veränder=]

[**Wandelbarkeit**]

Wandel=bilder (⸺...) n/pl. ⓶ dissolving views pl.; **=gang** m, parl. lobby.
wandelhaft (⸺) a. ⓺ = veränderlich.
wandeln (⸺) [ahd.: winden, wand²] ⓶ a. **I** v/n. (ſn) (wandern) to wander, walk, travel; er iſt (ob. kam) dieſes Weges gewandelt he came along this way; rel. den Weg der Gerechtigkeit (vor dem Herrn) ⸺ to walk in the way(s) of righteousness (in the way[s] of the Lord). — **II** v/a. u. v/refl. geh. Spr. = (ſich) ver⸺. — **III** ~ n ⓶ f. Wandlung.
wandel=los (⸺...) a. ⓺ unchangeable, geh.Spr.: immutable; **=ſtern** m ⓶ planet; **=turm** ⚔ m ehm. movable tower.
Wand(e)lung (⸺) f ⓺ f. Wandlung.
Wandel=wand (⸺) f ⓶ thea. shifting (or movable) scene.
Wander=blöcke (⸺...) m/pl. ⓶ geol. erratic blocks pl.; **=buch** n für Handwerksburſchen: travelling journeyman's book (in England unbekannt); **=bühne** f stage of strolling players; **=burſch(e)** m travelling (or itinerant) journeyman.
Wand(e)rer (⸺) m ⓶. **Wand(r)erin** ⓺ wanderer, pedestrian; (Touriſt) tourist, excursionist; (Waller) pilgrim.
Wander=falk(e) (⸺...) m ⓶ orn. gamehawk, passenger-falcon, peregrine (falcon) (Falco peregri'nus); **=herde** f wandering (or migratory) herd or flock; **=heuſchrecke** f. zo. migratory locust (Pachy'tylus migrato'rius); **=jahre** n/pl. journeyman's, &c. years pl. of travelling; Wilhelm Meiſters ~ (G.) Wilhelm Meister's years of travel; **=lager** ⚔ n itinerant vendor's stock, der Zigeuner ꝛc.: caravan; **=leben** n roving (or migratory) life; **=lehrer** m itinerant teacher; touring lecturer; **=lied** n traveller's song; **=luſt** f desire to travel or to see the world; f. Reiſeluſt; **=luſtig** a. fond of a roving life.
wandern (⸺) [mhd.: wander] **I** v/n. (ſn) ⓶a. to wander, to travel (on foot), to walk, to go; f. aus=, ein=ꝛc.; ſeines Weges ⸺ to go (or proceed on) one's way; aus der Heimat ⸺ to leave one's native land, to emigrate; ins Gefängnis ⸺ to go to prison; mit einem durchs Leben ⸺, etwa: to tread the path of life together; ſeine Uhr iſt aufs Leihhaus gewandert ... has gone to the pawnshop, F co. ... is up the spout; ohne „wohin": (von der Stelle rücken) die Dünen ⸺ ... are shifting or moving; ſich müde ⸺ to tire o.s. with walking. — **II** ~ n ⓶ = Wanderung 1. — **III** 2d p.pr. u. a. ⓺ wandering, travelling; itinerant (artist, &c.), strolling (player), nomadic (tribe); geol. &c. erratic, bſd. zo. migratory.
Wander=niere (⸺...) f ⓶ (auch wandernde Niere) path. movable kidney; **=prediger** m itinerant preacher; ranter; **=ratte** f, zo. brown (or Norway) rat, surmulot (Mus decuma'nus); **=raupe** f, zo. processionary caterpillar.
Wanderſchaft (⸺) f ⓶ travelling, travels pl., journey; auf die ~ gehen to go travelling or on one's travels; auf ~ ſein to be travelling or F knocking about, to be on a tour, F co. to be on the tramp.

Wanders=mann (⸺) m ⓶c. (pl. Wandersleute) man travelling on foot, bſd. geh. Spr. auch: wayfarer; vgl. Wanderer.
Wander=ſtab (⸺...) m ⓶ (walking-)staff; den ~ ergreifen, zum ~ greifen to set out on one's travels; **=ſteine** m/pl. = **=blöcke**; **=taube** f, orn. passengerpigeon (Ectopi'stes migrato'rius); **=tiere** n/pl. zo. migratory animals pl.; **=trieb** m roving (or restless) spirit.
Wand(e)rung (⸺) f ⓺ 1. wandering, &c.(f.wandern I), zo., physiol., &c.migration. — 2. (Fußreiſe) (pedestrian) tour or journey, walking-tour, in die Fremde: travels (abroad), foreign travels pl.; (Ausflug) excursion, trip, outing.
Wander=vögel (⸺...) m/pl. ⓶ orn. birds of passage; **=volk** n nomadic people or tribe; **=zeit** f = **=jahre**.
wand¹=feſt (⸺...) a. ⓺ fixed to the wall; **=gemälde** n ⓶ paint. mural painting, fresco; **=getäfel** ⊕ n wainscoting; **=haken** m hook in the wall; vgl. Kleiderhaken. | thin walls or sides.
...wandig ("...) (⸺), z. B.: dünn⸺ with/
Wand¹=kalender (⸺...) m ⓶ almanac to be hung up on the wall, a. wall-almanac; (Abreißkalender) block-almanac; **=karte** f school-room map; **=kraut** ⚘ f = Glaskraut a.; **=laus** f ⚘ Wanze.
Wandler (⸺) [wandeln] m ⓶ poet. one who wanders (or strays, strolls, saunters, rambles) about; rambler.
Wand¹=leuchter (⸺...) m ⓶ candlestick attached (or bracket fastened) to the wall, für Gas: gas-bracket.
Wandlung (⸺) [wandeln] f ⓺ (complete or thorough) change, transformation, ⚘ metamorphosis; (Verkleidung) disguise; theol. (Verwandlung der Hoſtie beim Abendmahl) transubstantiation.
Wand¹=malerei (⸺...) f ⓶ Kunſt: mural (or fresco=)painting; **=pfeiler** m pillar inserted in a wall, pilaster (on a wall).
Wandrer(in f) m f. Wand(e)rer ꝛc.
Wandrung (⸺) f ⓺ f. Wand(e)rung.
Wand¹=ſäule (⸺...) f ⓶ arch. wall-pillar; **=ſchirm** m folding-screen; **=ſchrank** m cupboard; **=ſpaltig** ⚘ a.: ⚘ septicidal; **=ſpiegel** m mirror adorning a wall; pier-glass; **=tafel** f in Schulen black board.
wandte (⸺) ind. impf. v. wenden.
Wand¹=teller (⸺...) m ⓶ decorative plate; **=teppich** m tapestry, hangings pl.; **=uhr** f (hall- or kitchen-)clock (hanging on the wall).
Wandung (⸺) f ⓺ wall, partition.
Wand¹=verkleidung ⊕ (⸺...) f ⓶ wainscoting; **=vertiefung** f. arch. niche.
Wange (⸺) [ahd.] f ⓺ 1. bſd. poet. (Backe) cheek; die Scham rötete ihre ~n she blushed for shame, a. shame crimsoned her face or coloured her cheeks. — 2. arch. ~ e-r Treppe: string- (or bridge-)board. — 3. ⚒ f. Schale¹ 4. — 4. ⊕ oft = Wand 2; ~n e-r Preſſe cheeks pl. of a press; ~e-s Schornſteins withe of a chimney; ~n eines Schraubſtocks cheeks pl. of a vice.
Wangen=bein (⸺...) n ⓶ anat. cheekbone, malar bone, ⚘ zygoma; **=brett** n = Wange 2; **=grübchen** n dimple in the cheek; **=naht** f, anat. ⚘ zygomatic suture.

Wankel=mut (⸺...) m ⓶ inconstancy, fickleness, vacillation; **=mütig** a. ⓺ inconstant, fickle, vacillating, wavering, irresolute; **=mütigkeit** f = **=mut**; **=rede** f wavering speech.
wanken (⸺) [ahd.: wackeln] **I** v/n. (h. u. ſn) ⓶ = ſchwanken I; nicht ⸺ und nicht weichen, weder weichen noch ⸺ not to flinch or budge, not to yield or swerve, to stand as firm as a rock; ⚔ den Feind ⸺ m., ⸺ ins ~ bringen to shake (ſtärker: to shatter) the enemy's ranks. — **II** ~ n ⓶ = Schwankung. — **III** 2d p.pr. u. a. ⓺ = ſchwanken III; nie 2d unflinching, unswerving; ſein 2der Mut his faltering (or failing) courage; den Feind 2d m., zum ⸺ bringen to shake the enemy's ranks.
wann (⸺) [ahd.: when: wenn] **I** adv. 1. ⸺? when?; ſeit ⸺ iſt er hier? since what time (or how long) has he been here? — 2. dann und ⸺ now and then, now and again, from time to time. — **II** cj. 3. ⸺ es ſei, ⸺ es wolle whenever (or whatever time) it may be; ich weiß, ⸺ ſie kommt ... when (or at what time, at what hour) she may (or will) come.
Wanne (⸺) [ahd.; *lt. vannus] f ⓺ 1. ⓶ agr. winnowing-fan = (Getreide=) ſchwinge). — 2. (muldenförmiges Gefäß) tub, coop, zum Baden: bath; chm. f. pneumatiſch. — 3. = Waſchwanne.
wannen¹ (⸺) adv. des Ortes, meiſt pleonaſtiſch: von ⸺ (from) whence, from what place.
Wannen²=bad (⸺...) [Wanne] n ⓶ (warm) bath in a tub, F tubbing; **=weher** [ahd.] m = Turmfalke.
Wanſt (⸺) [ahd.] m ⓵b. zo. u. F zo. von Menſchen: belly, paunch. F periphery; fetter ~ F fat guts pl.; **~=ſtecher** (⸺...) m ⓶ surg. u. vet. trocar.
Want ⚓ (⸺) [ndd.] f ⓶ mſt im pl. ~en (Taue zum Feſthalten von Maſten und Stangen nach den Seiten hin) shrouds (of the mast); große ~en main shrouds pl.; die ~en ſtraff anziehen to tauten the shrouds; Tau zu ~en shroud-rope.
Want=klampe ⚓ (⸺...) f ⓶ shroud-cleat; **=ſchlag** m (geſchlagenes Tauwerk) shroud-laid rope; **=ſtopper** m shroud-stopper.
Wanze (⸺) [mhd. 13. sae. Wand(lau)s] f ⓺ zo. bug (vgl. Bett=~); Familie der ~n: ⚘ rhynchota; ~n und Flöhe, oft: F co. (eig. ♠) flats and sharps pl.
Wanzen=biß (⸺...) m ⓶ bite of a bug, bug-bite; **=brut** f brood of bugs; **=geruch** m smell of bugs; **=kraut** ⚘ f = ſtinkendes ~ bug-bane or =wort (Cimici'fuga fe'tida); **=mittel** n remedy for bugs, vgl. =tod; **=neſt** n nest of (or place infested with) bugs; **=ſame** ⚘ m tickseed (Corispe'rmum); **=tod** m bugdestroyer, weiß. = Inſektenpulver.
wanzig (⸺) a. ⓺ buggy, full (or smelling) of bugs, infested with bugs.
Wapiti (⸺) [indianiſch] m ⓶, auch **~=hirſch** m, zo. wapiti (Cervus canade'nsis).
Wappen (⸺) [(mhd.) ndd.: Waffe] n ⓶ her. escutcheon, coat-of-arms, armorial bearings pl., im Siegel ꝛc.: crest; ein ~ auf et. malen to emblazon a th.; in ſein ~ aufnehmen to quarter in one's shield; ein ~ führen to bear

♪ Muſik; ⚛ Wiſſenſchaft; ⚘ Pflanze; ⌬ Geographie; ⊕ Technik; ⚒ Bergbau; ⚔ Militär; ⚓ Marine; ☿ Handel; ✉ Poſt; 🚂 Eiſenbahn.

a coat-of-arms; mit seinem ~ siegeln to seal with one's crest.

Wappen=amt (ᵍ...) n ⑫ herald's office; **=ausleger** m = kundige(r); **=auslegung** f = kunde; **=balken** m fesse; ²berechtigt a. ⑥ entitled to armorial bearings or to bear a coat-of-arms; **=bild** n figure in a coat-of-arms; heraldic figure; **=buch** n book on armoury or heraldry, armorial (book); vgl. Adelsbuch; **=erklärung** f = kunde; **=feld** n field of an escutcheon, quarter; **=halter** m supporter; **=herold** m = könig; **=kenner** m = kundige(r); **=könig** m King-at(of)-Arms; **=kunde** f armoury, heraldry, blazonry; **=kundige(r)** m expert in heraldry, armorist; **=kunst** f heraldic art; **=maler** m (em)blazoner, heraldic painter; **=malerei** f (em-)blazonry, heraldic painting; **=mantel** m, her. mantling; **=schild** m (n), **=schildchen** n armorial bearings pl., (e)scutcheon, blazon; **=schmuck** m emblazonment, emblazonry; **=schneider** m heraldic engraver; **=spruch** m heraldic motto or device; **=steuer** f in Engl.: license for armorial bearings; **=tierchen** n, ent. tortoise-rotifer (Brachi'onus); **=zierde** f (heraldic) accompaniment(s pl.).

wappnen (ᵍ) v/a. ⑥b. = waffnen.

war (¹; Hom. wahr) [ahd.: was, were], **warb** (¹), **ward** (¹) poet. 1. u. 3. Person sg. ind. impf. v. sein¹, werben, werden.

Wardein (ᵛ¹) [mhd.; *warten] m ⑫c. = Münzwardein; **wardieren** (ᵛ¹ᵛ) [dtsch-It.] v/a. ⑬ (Münzen prüfen) to assay coin, weitS. (abschätzen) to value.

Ware ⑨ (¹ᵛ) [ndd.: ware] f ⑬ ware, commodity, article (of commerce); ~n goods pl., merchandise; baumwollene, seidene, wollene ~n cotton, silk, woollen goods or fabrics; cottons, silks, wools pl.; irdene ~ crockery; s. kurz 1 ⑨; schlechte ~ worthless goods, trash(y articles pl.); sofort lieferbare ~ spot-goods, spots pl.; schwer verkäufliche ~ unsaleable goods pl., drug in the market; verbotene ~ contraband goods pl.; fig. das ist teure ~ that's an expensive affair or a luxury; s. verkaufen 1 u. 2; Sprichw. s. loben 1.

wäre (¹ᵛ) subj. impf. von sein¹.

waren¹ (¹ᵛ) pl. ind. impf. v. sein¹.

Waren²=absender ⑨ (¹ᵛ...) m ⑫ consigner, ...or, shipper, exporter; vgl. Spediteur; **=adreß=zettel** m label for goods, auch docket; **=angabe=schein, =zettel** m bill of entry; **=ausfuhr** f exportation of goods, export(-trade); **=ballen** m bale of goods; **=bedarf** m requirement of goods, demand; **=bestand** m stock (of goods) on hand; **=bestellungs=buch** n order-book; **=beziehen** m importer (of goods); **=einfuhr** f import(ation of goods); **=einsender** m consigner ..., ...or; **=empfänger** m consignee; **=etikette** f label for (marking) goods; **=geschäft** n transaction in goods; **=gewölbe** n vault for storing goods, storehouse; **=haus** n warehouse, stores pl.; **=haus=dieb(in** f) m (female) shop-thief; **=kenntnis** f = kunde; **=konto** n goods-account; **=kunde** f knowledge of mercantile wares or articles, als Buchtitel: Commercial Dictionary; **=lager** n stock (or assortment) of goods; vgl. Lager 6, Kramladen; **=lieferant** m purveyor, contractor; **=makler** m commission-agent, broker; **=niederlage** f warehouse, storage-house; **=partie** f parcel of goods, lot; **=preis** m price of goods; (market-)quotation; **=probe** f: a) sample (of goods); b) examination (or sampling) of goods; **=rechnung** f invoice; s. Faktur; **=rest** m remnant of goods; **=sendung** f consignment of goods; **=stempel** m trademark; **=steuer** f duty charged (or paid) on merchandise; **=tausch** m barter; **=verkaufs=buch** n book of sales; **=versender** m = absender; **=verzeichnis** n list of goods; **=vorrat** m = bestand; **=zeichner** m marker of goods; **=zoll** m (custom-house) duty payable (or levied) on goods.

warf (ᵍ) ind. impf. von werfen.

warm (ᵍ) [ahd.: warm] a. ⑥ (comp. wärmer, sup. wärmst) (ant. kalt) 1. warm; es ist ² it is warm; mir ist ² I am warm; paint., &c. Der Farbenton warm colour; ein ²es Nest a snug (or cozy) corner; mit Den Worten warmly, with fiery words; ich möchte et. ~es essen I should like s.th. warm to eat or a hot dinner (or supper). — 2. mit verbs: sich ² arbeiten to get heated with work(ing); ² auftragen to serve up hot; ² baden to take a warm bath; sich ² gehen to get warm (stärker: to heat one's blood) by walking; (sich) ² halten to keep (o.s.) warm; F fig. den muß man ² halten he must be kept in good humour; ² machen to make warm, to heat; e-m den Kopf ² m. to make a p. angry, to provoke (or rouse) a. p.; die Sonne scheint ² the sun is warm; ² sitzen to sit in a warm place, fig. to be in clover; ² stellen to put to warm; in der Küche: to put on the fire or in the oven; ² werden to get hot or heated, fig. auch: to warm to (or with) one's subject, im Streite: to grow passionate; ² w. für et. to grow enthusiastic about a th.; ² nicht ², nicht kalt neither hot nor cold, lukewarm, auch: neither one thing nor the other; Sprichw. s. Eisen² 1.

Wärm=apparat ⊕ (ᵍᵛ¹) m ⑫ heating-apparatus.

Warm=bad (ᵍ...) n ⑫ warm bath; a. = **=brunnen**; **=bier** n hot ale; **=blütig** a. ⑥ zo. warm-blooded, ✠ hæmatothermal; **=brunnen** m thermal (or hot) springs, hot wells pl.

Wärme (ᵍᵛ) [ahd.;*warm] f ⑧ warmth, seltener: warmness; phys., &c. heat, ✠ caloric (s. binden 11); die ~ betreffend: ✠ thermal; ~ durchlassend: ✠ transcalent; ~ erzeugend: ✠ calorific, calorifiant; physiol. tierische ~ animal heat; fig. sich mit ~ einer Person annehmen to make strenuous efforts on behalf of a p.; mit ~ für eine Sache sprechen to advocate a cause with great warmth (of feeling).

Wärme=ausstrahlung (ᵍᵛ...) f ⑫ phys. radiation of heat; **=einheit** f unit of heat, ✠ calory, calorie; **=elektrisch** ꝛc. f. thermo=elektrisch ꝛc.; **=entwicklungs=vermögen** n tierisch. Körper: ✠ caloricity; **=erzeugend** a. ⑥ producing heat, calorifacient, calorifiant; **=erzeugung** f production of heat, ✠ calorification; **=grad** m degree of heat; hoher, niedriger ~ high, low temperature; **=halle** f bsd. für Obdachlose: shelter (or hall) with a fire for poor people; **=kapazität** f capacity for heat, ✠ caloric capacity; **=kraft=lehre** f: thermo-dynamics; **=lehre** f theory of heat; ²leitend a. conducting heat; **=leiter** m conductor of heat; **=maß** n temperature; **=menge** f quantity (or amount) of heat; **=messer** m, phys.: calorimeter, thermometer; **=messung** f: ✠ calorimetry.

wärmen (ᵍᵛ) [ahd.] I v/a. u. v/refl. ⑱ to warm, to heat; sich (dat.) die Füße ² to warm one's feet; sich ² to warm o.s., F to have a warm, am Feuer: to warm o.s. by the fire, in der Sonne: to bask in the sun. — II ~ n ⑳ = Wärmung.

Wärme=quelle (ᵍᵛᵛ) f ⑫ source of heat. **Wärmer** (ᵍᵛ) m ⑫ warmer, bsd. = Warmhalter und Wärmflasche.

Wärme=spektrum (ᵍᵛ...) n ⑫ phys. heat-spectrum, ✠ thermal spectrum; **=stoff** m: ✠ caloric; **=strahl** m ray of heat, ✠ calorific ray; **=verlust** m loss of heat; **=zeiger** m: ✠ thermoscope.

Wärm=flasche (ᵍᵛ) f ⑫ für Bett, Füße ꝛc.: hot-water bottle; vgl. =pfanne.

Warm=halter (ᵍ...) m ⑫: a) für Teller ꝛc. plate-warmer; b) für die Teekanne: teacozy; **=haus** n = Treibhaus; ²herzig a. ⑥ warm-hearted.

Wärm=kruke (ᵍᵛ¹ᵛ) f ⑫ = flasche. **Warm=luft=heizung** ⊕ (ᵍ·ᵍ·¹ᵛ) f ⑫ heating with hot-air pipes. **Warm=ofen** (ᵍ...) m ⑫ stove; **=pfanne** f warming- (or bed-)pan; **=rohr** n heating- (or hot-water, hot-air) pipe; **=saal** m = Wärmehalle; **=stein** m warming-stone, hot brick, foot-warmer; **=stube** f warming-chamber or -room, calefactory. [wärmen), ✠ calefaction.}

Wärmung (ᵍᵛ) f ⑯ warming, &c. (s. **Wärm=wasser=heizung** ⊕ (ᵍ·ᵛ·¹ᵛ) f ⑫ heating with hot-water pipes. **Wärm=zimmer** n = stube.

Warn=eidechse (ᵍ·¹ᵛ·ᵗʸ) f ⑫ zo. monitor. **warnen** (ᵍᵛ) [ahd.: warn: wahren] I v/a. ⑱: e-n vor et. ² to warn a p. of a th., to caution a p. against a th.; vorher ² to forewarn; sich nicht ² l. to heed no warning; Aufschrift: vor Taschendieben wird gewarnt! beware of pickpockets! — II ~ n ⑳ = Warnung.

Warner (ᵍᵛ) m ⑫, ~in f ⑰ warner, monitor, f bisw. monitress.

Warn=glocke (ᵍ...) f ⑫ signal- (or warning) bell; **=ruf** m warning call. **Warnung** (ᵍᵛ) f ⑯ warning, caution; (Wink) hint; (vorherige Erinnerung) premonition; lassen Sie sich das zur ~ dienen let that be a warning (or a lesson) to you.

Warnungs=anzeige (ᵍᵛ...) f ⑫ public warning; **=tafel** f notice-board.

warpen ⚓ (ᵍᵛ) v/a. ⑱: ein Schiff ² (am Seile fortziehen) to warp ...

[Warschau] — 1095 — [Wäsche]

Warschau ♀ (ˇ-) npr/n. ⚲ a. (Hauptstadt v. Russ.-Polen) Warsaw. [inv. Varsovian.)
Warschauer (ˇ-ˇ-) m ⚏, ~in f ⚐, 2 a.,|
warst (ˊ) sg., **wart**¹ pl. 2. Person ind. impf. v. sein¹.
Wart² fast † od. poet. (ˊ) [ahd.: ward] m ⚇… = Hüter (vgl. Schrift-, Turn-2).
Warte¹ (ˇ-) [ahd.: ward: warten] f ⚐ look-out; (hoher Turm) watch-tower, ehm. ⚔ barbican; ast., &c. observatory.
Warte²-**frau** (ˇ-ˇ…)[warten]f ⚁ female attendant, nurse; =**geld** n: a) fee for attendance; b) ⚔ half-pay; auf ~ setzen to put on half-pay.
warten (ˇ-) [ahd.: ward] I v/n. (h.) und v/a. ⚏ 1. to wait; (bleiben) to stay; warte mal!, wart' doch ein wenig! just wait a bit or a second!; drohend: wart', wenn ich dich erwische! let me (or wait till I) catch you!; auf e-n 2, ehm. e-s 2 to wait for a p.; auf eine (bessere) Gelegenheit 2 to wait for a (better) chance, to bide one's opportunity; er läßt immer auf sich 2 he is always behind time, he is never in time; er ließ nicht lange auf sich 2 he was not long in coming; mit dem Essen auf e-n 2 to wait dinner (or supper) for a p.; warte, bis er kommt wait until he comes; **worauf** 2 wir? what are we waiting for?; iro. da können sie lange 2, da können sie 2, bis sie schwarz werden they may wait till doomsday or till they are sick and tired of it. — 2. = pflegen I, zB. e-n 2, bisw. e-s 2 to wait upon a p., to nurse a p.; j-s Amtes 2 to attend to one's duties; Kinder 2 to mind children; die Pferde 2 to groom the horses; iro. e-m auf den Dienst 2 od. passen to watch a p.'s doings very closely or narrowly. — II ~ n ⚏ (i. l) 3. ich bin des ~s müde I am tired (or weary, sick) of waiting.
Wärter (ˇ-) m ⚏, ~in f ⚐ 1. keeper, attendant (vgl. Wächter); ~in female attendant, für Kinder, Kranke ꝛc.: nurse. — 2. 🚂 = Bahnwärter. [häuschen.
Wärter-**haus** (ˇ-ˇ-) n ⚇ = Bahnwärter-
Warte²-**saal** (ˇ-ˇ-) m ⚐ = waiting-room; =**schule** f infant-school, nursery (for babies); =**zeit** ⚔ f = Liegezeit; =**zimmer** n eines Arztes, der Post ꝛc. = waiting-room. [heim-2 homeward.
…wärts (…ˊ) als Suffix für adv. dienend, zB.]
Wart²-**turm** (ˇ-ˇ-) m ⚐ watch-tower.
Wartung (ˇ-) f ⚁ (s. warten 2) attendance; care taken of; sie haben schlechte ~ they are badly looked after; ~ e-s Kranken nursing of a patient, der Blumen: cultivation, der Kinder ꝛc. Haustiere: minding, der Pferde: grooming.
warum (-ˊ) [ahd.] adv. u. cj. 1. 2? why?, wherefore?, for what reason? on what account?; 2 denn? why so?; 2 ist sie so traurig? what is she so sad for or about?; ich weiß, 2 sie lachen why you are (or the reason for your) laughing; das ist der Grund, 2 er das Zweirad kauft that is the reason for his buying (or that's why he buys) the bicycle; elliptisch: 2 ich will wissen, 2 I want to know (the reason) why; negativ: 2 nicht? why not?; 2 nicht

gar! you don't say so!, certainly not!, &c. (s. gar 4 am Ende); 2 bin ich nicht reich? oh, if I were only rich!, would I were rich!; das ~ und Weshalb the why and the wherefore. — 2. = um was, richtiger: worum, s. ds.
Wär-**wolf** (ˊ-ˊ-) m ⚇ = Werwolf.
Wärzchen (ˇ-) n ⚏ (dim. von Warze) little wart, ⚛ papilla; mit ~ bedeckt: ⚛ verruculose.
Warze (ˇ-, a. ˊ-) [ahd.: wart] f ⚐ 1. path. (Haut-auswuchs) wart (auch ⚛ u. ent.), ⚛ verruca. — 2. (Brust-)~ nipple, ⚛ papilla, mammilla; (Saug-) ~ e-s Tieres: teat, dug.
warzen-**artig** (ˇ-ˇ…), =**förmig** a. ⚏ wart-like, ⚛ verrucous, …ose, papillary, …ate, …ose, …iform; anat. a.: ⚛ mastoid; =**fortsatz** m ⚏ anat. des Schläfenbeins: ⚛ mastoid (process); =**hütchen** n nipple-cap; =**kürbis** ⚛ m squash-gourd or -melon (Cucurbita verrucosa); =**melone** ⚛ f cantaloup; =**mittel** n remedy against (or cure for) warts; =**muskel** m, anat. des Herzens: papillary muscle; =**ring** m, anat.: ⚛ areola (of the nipple); =**schlange** f zo. wart-snake (Acrochordus); =**schwein** n, zo. wart-hog (Phacochoerus); =**stein** m, geol. (fossiler Seeigelstachel) wart-stone, ⚛ mammillary stalagmite.
warzig (ˇ-) a. ⚏ warty, full of (or covered with) warts (vgl. warzenartig).
was (ˊ) [ahd.: what: lt. quod] I interr. pron. 1. als Subjekt u. als Prädikats-nominativ: 2 beliebt? what is your pleasure?; 2 führt Sie her? what brings you here?; 2 geschah? what happened?; 2 ist (od. fehlt) Ihnen denn? what is the matter with you?, what ails you?; 2 ist das? what is it?, what's that?; 2 ist Ihr Vater? what is your father (by trade or by profession)?; 2 kann da sein? what does it matter? — 2. als Objekt vor v/a.: 2 bekommen Sie?: a) zum Kunden in e-m Geschäfte: what do you require?; what shall (or can) I show you?; b) zum Kellner im Wirtshause: how much is my account?, F what's to pay?; 2 hilft's? of what use is it?, F what's the good of it?, what good can it do?; 2 machst du da? what are you doing there?; 2 Sie sagen! you don't say so!; vgl. sagen 5 am Ende u. schaden¹ 2; 2 (soll ich) tun? what am I to do? — 3. mit int. und adv. und nach prp.: s. ach I; 2 dann? what then?; 2 denn? what (did you say)?, what is it?, höflicher: I beg your pardon!; 2 weiter? what more?, what further?; als int.: 2, schon wieder! what, again!; mit 2, von 2 (mehr gbr. womit, wovon)? with what, of what? — 4. = wieviel, zB.: 2 kostet der Spiegel? how much (or what) does … cost?; F 2 ist die Uhr? what's the time?; 2 da nicht alles zu sehen war! how much (F what a lot) there was to be seen! — 5. im Ausruf: 2 wir gelacht! how (much) we laughed!; 2 wir nicht alles gesehen haben! what have we not seen!; 2 der Junge doch reitet! how well the boy rides!; 2 das

für ein lästiger Mensch ist! what a bore that fellow is! — 6. **was für** (indeklinabel vor s.): 2 für eine Person ist sie? what kind (or sort) of person is she?; 2 ist das für ein Lärm? what noise is that?; 2 für Bücher? what (kind of) books?; 2 für schlechtes Zeug! what miserable stuff! — II relative pron. 7. als Subjekt, Prädikatsnominativ und Objekt: ich weiß, 2 Sie in Erstaunen setzt … what astonishes you; Sie sehen, 2 wir sind … what we are (like); das zeigt, 2 für ein Mensch er ist that shows what kind of fellow he is; 2 noch mehr (noch schlimmer) ist (and) what is more (worse); 2 mich betrifft as for me, as regards myself; alles, 2 er weiß all (that) he knows; das, 2 Sie sagen what (or that which) you are saying; er bat mich zu schreiben, 2 ich auch tat he asked me to write, which I did or and I did (so). — 8. verallgemeinernd: 2 es koste, 2 es wolle (let it) cost what it may, whatever the expense may be; ich lief, 2 ich (nur) konnte I ran as fast as I could or as my legs would carry me; 2 er auch immer tut whatever he may do, no matter what he does; 2 für Hilfsmittel ein Staat auch haben mag whatever resources a state may have; s. immer 6. — III F 9. = etwas: 2 Neues s.th. new; zB. iro. das ist (auch) recht 2 od. 2 Rechts! that's not much, surely!, auch: you call that much?; das ist 2 anderes that's (quite) another thing, F that's another pair of breeches; so 2 hat man nie gesehen!, so 2 lebt nicht! such a thing has never been seen or heard of; F well, I never!; auch als s/n. inv.: ein unbekanntes Was an unknown something. — IV F 10. = warum; 2 braucht er zu lügen? why need he tell lies?, F what must (or does) he tell lies for?
Wasch-**anstalt** (ˇ…) f ⚁ = Wäscherei 2; =**apparat** m washing-apparatus or -machine, typ. washing-trough; =**balje** f = **bütte**; =**bank** f washing-bench, bench for washing; =**bär** m, zo. racoon, Am. coon (Procyon lotor); =**becken** n washing- (or hand-)basin. [beutel ꝛc.
Wäsch-**beutel** (ˇ…) m ⚏ = Wäsche-]
Wasch-**blau** ⚔ (ˇ…) n ⚏ washing-blue, bluing; =**bleuel** ⊙ m washing-beetle; =**bock** m washing-stool or -horse; =**bottich** m washing-vat; =**brett** n washing-board; =**bühne** ⚓ f buddling-dish; =**bürste** ⊙ f, typ. cleaning brush; =**bütte** f wash(ing)-tub.
Wäsche (ˇ-) f ⚐ 1. a) (Waschen von Leinenzeug) wash(ing); große ~ great (annual, &c.) wash; in die ~ geben oder schicken to put (or send) out to wash, to have washed; in der ~ sein to be in the wash; freien Tisch und freie ~ h. to have free board and washing; b) ⚒ metall. washing of ore, buddling. — 2. (zu waschendes oder gewaschenes Zeug) linen, clothes pl.; (Leib-)~ body-linen, underlinen, underwear; reine (oder frische) ~ clean (or fresh) linen; ant. schmutzige (oder schwarze) ~ dirty (or foul) linen, dirty

⚛ scientific; ⚛ botanical; ♀ geography; ⊙ machinery; ⚒ mining; ⚔ military; ⚓ marine; ⚲ commercial; ⚙ postal; 🚂 railway.

[Wäschebeutel] — 1096 — [Wasserdichtigkeit]

clothes pl.; frische ~ anziehen to put on clean linen; schmutzige ~ ausziehen to take off one's dirty clothes. — 3. Ort: wash-house; place for washing ore, &c., ⚒ metall. auch: dressing-floor. ⚒ linen, dirty-clothes bag. **Wäsche-beutel** (⌣⌣⌣) m bag for dirty **wasch-echt** (⌣⌣) a. 🌐 that washes well, washable, dyed in the grain, von Farben auch: fast, fig. genuine, thorough. **Wäsche-geschäft** 🌐 (⌣⌣...) n 🌐 ready-made underlinen warehouse; **-kammer** f linen-cupboard; **-kasten** m, **-kiste** f linen-chest; **-klammer** f clothes-peg; **-mange** f mangle.

waschen (⌣⌣) [ahd.: wash: Wasser] I v/a., v/refl. u. v/n. (h.) 🌐b. 1. to wash; fie ⚒ sich (dat.) das Gesicht they are washing their faces; für e-n ⚒ to wash for a p., to take in a p.'s washing; abs. wir ⚒ heute to-day (or this) is our washing-day; ⚒ metall. Erze ⚒ to wash ore, to buddle; typ. die Formen ⚒ to wash up; ⚒ lassen to get washed; außer dem Hause ⚒ l. to put (or send) out one's washing; sich ⚒ to wash (o.s.), F to have a wash; vgl. sich 1; von Zeugen: sich ⚒ l. to wash (well), to stand washing. — 2. fig. u. Sprichw. die Gurgel ⚒ to wet one's whistle; f. Hand 2 (gegen Ende) u. 3, Kopf 2 am Schluß und Mohr[1] 1 b; F fig. das hat sich gewaschen (ist vortrefflich) that's capital or proper or first-rate. — 3. F = klatschen 3. — II ~ n 🌐 4. = Waschung.

Wäscher (⌣⌣) m 🌐, **~in** f 🌐 washer, jetzt bsd. ~in (Frau, die schmutzige Wäsche wäscht) washerwoman, feiner: laundress. **Wäscherei** (⌣⌣⌣) f 🌐 1. = Waschung. — 2. (Anstalt zur Wäsche) washhouse, laundry; ⚒ metall. place for buddling, dressing-floor. — 3. F fig. (Gewäsche) gossip(ing), auch: washerwoman's talk. **Wäscher-lohn** (⌣⌣...) m 🌐 fee (or charge) for washing. [n mangling.) **Wäsche-rolle** (⌣⌣...) f 🌐 mangle; **-rollen** f **Wasch-erz** ⚒ (⌣⌣) n 🌐 buddled ore. **Wäsche-schrank** (⌣⌣...) m 🌐 linen-press; **-trocken-ständer** m clothes-horse, horse for drying (or airing) linen; **-zeichnerin** f marker of linen. **Wasch-fahne** F (⌣...) f 🌐 (cheap cotton) dress that can be washed; **-farbe** f. paint. mit wässerigem Bindemittel: gouache; **-faß** n = **-bütte**; **-frau** f washerwoman, feiner: laundress; **-geld** n washing-money, charge for washing; **-gelegenheit** f washing-accommodation; **-gerät**, **-geschirr** n: a) utensils pl. for washing; b) für den Waschtisch: toilet-set; **-gold** 🌐 n gold obtained by washing; **-hammer** m Tuchfabr.: wash-stock; **-handschuhe** m/pl. gloves pl. that can be washed; **-haus** n wash-house, laundry; **-kessel** m copper for washing (or boiling) linen; **-kleid** n dress that can be washed; **-korb** m washing (or clothes-)basket; **-küche** f: a) (zum Spülen) scullery; b) = **-haus**; **-kufe** f wash(ing)-tub; **-lappen** m: a) dish-cloth; b) F fig. (Mensch ohne Willenskraft) etwa: weakling, person of weak character or mind, F milk-

sop, molly; **-leder** n wash-leather, shammy (leather); 🌐Ledern a. (of) shammy; 🌐Lederne Handschuhe wash-leather gloves pl.; **-leine** f clothes-line; **-magd** f laundry-maid; **-maschine** 🌐 f washing-machine, washer, dolly; **-maul** F n = **-weib** b; **-mittel** n, pharm. lotion; **-napf** m = **-becken**; **-platz** m place for washing; **-raum** m in Bahnhöfen &c.: lavatory; **-schüssel** f = **-becken**; **-schwamm** m sponge (for washing); **-seife** f washing-soap, a. plain (or yellow) soap; **-stein** m in Küchen: sink (for washing up); **-tag** m washing-day; **-tisch** m, **-toilette** f wash-stand; **-topf** m washing-vessel; **-trog** 🌐 m trough for washing, washing-trough, ⚒ zum Erzschlämmen: standing-buddle, zum Goldwaschen: cradle; **-trommel** 🌐 f Papierfabrik ⁊c.: wash-cylinder, washing-cylinder or -drum, Gerberei: tub-wheel.

Waschung (⌣⌣) f 🌐 washing of linen, &c.; bsd. rel. ablution; med. lotion; ⚒ metall. washing of ore, buddling. **Wasch-wanne** (⌣⌣⌣) f 🌐 wash-tub. **Wäsche-waren** ⚒ (⌣⌣⌣) f/pl. 🌐 linen goods pl., underclothing. **Wasch-wasser** (⌣...) n 🌐: a) water for washing (up); b) F fig. von dünnen Getränken: reines ~ mere slops pl.; c) pharm. wash, lotion; **-weib** n: a) = **-frau**; b) F fig. gossip, scandal-monger, a. (regular old) washer-woman (auch von Männern); **-wolle** 🌐 f washed wool; **-zettel** m washing-list or -bill; **-zeug** n = **-gerät**; **-zimmer** n = Toilettenzimmer; **-zuber** m = **-bütte**.

Wasen prov. (⌣⌣) [ahd.] m 🌐 1. = Rasen. — 2. = Faschine. [Abdecker(ei).} **Wasen-meister(ei)** f (⌣⌣...) (⌣⌣) m 🌐 =} **Wasgau** 🌐 (⌣) [Basken] npr/m (n) 🌐c., auch **Wasgen-wald** (⌣⌣) m 🌐c. (südlicher Teil des westoberrheinischen Gebirges) the Vosges (Mountains) pl.

Wasser (⌣⌣) [ahd.: water] n 🌐 (für 1 b u. c auch 🌐) 1. a) als Getränk: water; bei ~ und Brot sitzen to be put on bread and water; v. Stiefeln: ~ ziehen to let in water; c) (zubereitete Flüssigkeit) gebranntes ~ distilled water, (alcoholic) liquor, spirit(s); kohlensäurehaltiges ~ carbonic water; f. Kölnisch; wohlriechendes ~ scent, perfume; d) chm. water (H₂O), ⚗ aqua; mit ~ verbinden: ⚗ to hydrate; Verbindung mit ~: ⚗ hydrate; hartes (weiches) ~ hard (soft) water; mit ~ verdünnen (to dilute with) water; e) fig. zu ~ (zunichte) m. to bring to nought; to wreck, ruin, frustrate; f. Mühle 2, reichen II gegen Ende und Brunnen 4; wie ~ like water, in abundance; er spricht französisch wie ~ (fließend) he speaks French fluently or with fluency; zu ~ (nichts) w. to fall to the ground, to come to nought or to grief. — 2. (ant. Land) (piece of) water; fließendes (stehendes) ~ running (stagnant) water; salziges (süßes) ~ salt (fresh) water; auf das ~ bezüglich, auf (ob. in) dem ~ lebend aquatic; ⚗ aus dem ~ erzeugt generated by water, ⚗ undigenous; über

das große ~ (nach Amerika ⁊c.) fahren to cross the water or the ocean; fig. sich mit Not über(m) ~ (flott) erhalten to keep one's head barely above water; unter ~ setzen to submerge, to flood, stärker: to inundate; vom ~ eingeschlossen water-bound; zu ~ und zu Lande by land and by water; zu ~ reisen to go by water; Sprichw.: bis dahin wird noch viel ~ ins Meer fließen that will be many a long day (to come) yet; f. Balken 1 und still 2 am Schluß. — 3. 🌐: a) (Grad der Klarheit) von Diamanten und Perlen: lustre; vom reinsten ~ of the purest water; b) (wellenförmiges Aussehen) von gewohnten Stoffen: ein schönes ~ h. to be finely watered. — 4. (flüssige Bestandteile des Körpers): a) (Urin) sein ~ lassen oder abschlagen to make water; med. das ~ beschauen to examine the urine; b) meist fig. der Mund steht (ob. läuft) ihm voll ~, das ~ läuft ihm im Munde zusammen it makes his mouth water; c) (Tränen) tears pl.; d) (Schweiß) perspiration, sweat; das ~ lief mir vom Leibe herunter I was in a bath of perspiration.

Wasser-ablaß (⌣⌣...) m 🌐, **-ableitung** f 🌐 draining (off the water), drainage; **-abort*** m water-closet; **-abschlag** m letting off water, discharge of water; **-ampfer** ♀ m water-dock (Rumex aqua'ticus); **-amsel** f, orn. water-ouzel (Cinclus aqua'ticus); 🌐arm a. 🌐 scantily supplied with water, stärker: water-less, von Wüsten: arid; **-armut** f scarcity of water, in Städten u. a. water-famine; **-arzt** m hydropathic doctor, hydropathist; **-auge** n, path. watery eye, ⚗ hydrophthalmia; **-bad** n water-bath (auch chm.); **-bau** 🌐 m hydraulic structure, meist pl. **-bauten** building operations under water; **-bau-kunst** f hydraulic architecture or engineering; **-bau-meister** ob. **-techniker** m hydraulic architect or engineer; **-becken** n basin; vgl. Bassin; **-behälter** m reservoir (for water), a. cistern, tank, e-r Dampfmasch.: well, e-s Kochherdes: boiler; ⚒ **-water-house**; ⚒be**-schädigt** a. damaged by water; **-beschreibung** f hydrography; **-bett** n für Kranke: water-bed; **-bewohner** m = **-tier**; **-bindend*** a. hydraulic; **-blase** f bubble, path.: ⚗ vesicle, pustule; **-blattern** f/pl. = **-pocken** (⌣⌣); **-blau**: a) a. marine-(or sea-)blue; b) n 🌐 Färberei: water-blue; **-blei** n, min.: a) = Graphit, b) (Molybdänglanz) molybdenite; **-blume** ♀ f aquatic flower; **-bombe** ⚒ f, artill. water-shell; **-brei** m Kocht. watery paste or pap; **-bruch** m, path.: ⚗ hydrocele.

Wässerchen (⌣⌣) [Wasser, dim.] n 🌐 small stream or pond or pool, streamlet, rivulet; fig. er trübt kein ~ he would (or does) not hurt a fly, he does no harm (to a soul).

Wasser-damm 🌐 (⌣⌣...) m 🌐 dike, dam; **-dampf** m aqueous vapour, steam; 🌐dicht a. 🌐 water-proof, ⚓ von Schiffen ⁊c.: water-tight; ⚒er Stoff, ⚒es Zeug waterproof; ⚒er Mantel mackintosh; **-dichte**, **-dichtheit**, **-dichtigkeit** f wa.-proof (or ⚓ wa.-tight) quality; ⚓ im-

---

Zeichen (f. S. XVII): F familiär; P Volkssprache; ⸙ Gaunersprache; 🌐 selten; † alt (auch gestorben); * neu (auch geboren); ⁊ unrichtig.

[Wasserdoktor] — 1097 — [Wassersäugetier]

permeability; =doktor m: a) = arzt; b) (Quacksalber) quack; =dost(en) ♃ m hemp-agrimony (*Eupato'rium canna'binum*); =druck m. mech.: ⚙ hydrostatic pressure; =druck-lehre f: ⚙ hydrodynamics; =dunst m watery (or aqueous) vapour; =eidechse ⚭ = wasserhaft; =eimer m water-pail; =faden ♃ m hairweed, river-weed (*Confe'rva bomby'cina*); aus =fäden gebildete schwimmende Masse wa.-flannel; eine ~ machen ♧ f trip on the water, im Ruderboote: row, im Segelschiffe: sail; =fall m f. Fall¹ 2; =fang m, etwa: water-butt, cistern; =farbe f: a) colour (of the) water; b) Malerei: wa.-colour; in ~n malen to paint in wa.-colours; =farben-malerei f wa.-colour painting, painting in wa.-colours; =faß n water-butt or -tub; ♃fest a. ♃dicht; =feuerwerk n fireworks pl. (let off) on the water; =fläche f expanse (or sheet) of water; =flasche f water-bottle; =floh m, ent. water-flea (*Da'phnia pulex*); =flut f (watery) flood, stärker: inundation, deluge; =fracht f carriage by water, freight (on board); ♃frei a. free from water, chm.: ⚙ anhydrous; Der Alkohol absolute(ly pure) alcohol; Le Säure 2c.: ⚙ anhydride; =freund(in f) m friend (or lover) of (the) water; =frosch m, zo. wa.-frog (*Rana escule'nta*); =furche f wa.-furrow; =galle f wa.-gall; =gallig a. full of puddles or pools; =gang m: a) aqueduct, canal; b) ↓ zum Abfließen des Wassers: waterway; =garn ♃ n watertwist; =gebläse ⊙ n, metall. hydrostatic blast; =gefahr f danger (arising) from water or inundation(s); =gefäß n water-cask; irdenes ~ wa.-jar; vgl. =krug; =geflügel n wa.-fowl; =gehalt m amount (or percentage) of water contained in s th.; =geist m water-sprite; ♃gerade a. = recht a.; =gerechtigkeit f = recht b; =gesetzgebung f legislation relating to rivers, canals, &c.; =geusen m pl., hist. Gueux of the Sea; =gewächs ♃ n aquatic plant; =glas n: a) tumbler; b) chm. wa.-glass, soluble glass, ⚗ potassium silicate; ♃gleich a.: a) watery, aqueous; b) = recht a; =gleiche f: a) horizontal (or level) surface; b) = wage; =gott m watergod, Alt. Neptune; =göttin f watergoddess, Alt. Thetis; =graben m wa.-ditch, ⚔ frt. moat, agr. wa.-trench, drain; =grube f cistern; =guß m: a) sink; (Speiröhre) spout; b) heavy downpour (or fall) of rain.
wasserhaft (⚭) a. ⊕ aqueous, physiol. auch: serous (blood, &c.).
Wasser-hahn ⊙ (⚭...) m ⊕ mech. watertap; =hahnenfuß ♃ m water-crowfoot (*Ranu'nculus aqua'tilis*); ♃haltig a. ⊕ containing water, watery, aqueous, chm. hydrated; ♃hart a. Töpferei: dried in the air, air-dried, impermeable to water; =hebe-maschine ⊙ f hydraulic engine; =heil-anstalt f, med. hydropathic establishment, F hydro; =heil-kunde f, =heil-methode f cold-water cure, ⚙ hydropathy, hydrotherapeutics; =heizung f heating with hot-water pipes; ♃hell a. (as) clear as water; =hose ↓ f waterspout; =huhn n, orn. (bald) coot (*Fu'lica*); =hund m, hunt. water-dog or -spaniel.
wässericht ⚭, mst **wässerig** (⚭) a. ⊕ watery, full of water, auch = wasserhaft; fig. insipid (style, &c.), vapid (speech, &c.), flabby (joke, &c.), dull (reading, &c.); Des Getränk watery (or weak) beverage, F washy (or sloppy) stuff, vom Tee: water bewitched; vgl. dünn 3; De Lösung aqueous solution; De Schreibart milk-and-water style; ♃ machen to water, to dilute; fig. einem den Mund ♃ machen (nach et.) to make a p.'s mouth water (for a th.).
Wässerigkeit (⚭) f ⊕ wateriness; physiol. serosity; v. Getränken: weakness, F washiness, sloppiness; fig. v. Stil 2c.: insipidity, dulness, flabbiness.
Wasser-jagd (⚭...) f ⊕, jagen n, hunt. shooting (of) aquatic birds; =jungfer f: a) myth. naiad, nymph; b) ent. = Libelle 2; =käfer m, ent. water-beetle (*Dy'ticus, &c.*); =kanne f water-jug, ewer; =kante f = Waterkant; =karren m wa.-cart; =karte f hydrographic(al) chart; =kasten m, mach. feeding-cistern; =kegel ⊙ m Wasserbau: water-obelisk; =kessel m kettle, größerer: copper, mach., &c. boiler; =kissen n: a) für Kranke: water-cushion; b) (Pflanzendecke auf stehenden Gewässern) vegetable mass floating on a pond or lake; =kitt m hydraulic cement; =klee ⚭ m marsh- (or water-)trefoil, bogbean (*Menya'nthes trifolia'ta*); =klosett n water-closet (W.-C.); =kopf m, path. (person with) water on the brain, ⚙ hydrocephalus; ♃kopf-artig a. ⊕: ⚙ hydrocephaloid, ...ous; =korso m regatta; =kraft f water-power; =kraft-lehre f, mech.: ⚙ hydrodynamics; =kraft-maschine ⊙ f, mach. water-power engine; =kraft-motor ⊙ m hydromotor; =kresse ♃ f = Brunnenkresse; =krug m water-jug, pitcher; =kunde f, phys.: ⚙ hydrology; =kundige(r) m hydrologist; =kunst f: a) = werk (Springbrunnen); b) ⊙ ⊕ mach. hydraulic engine; =kur f, med. wa.-cure, hydropathic cure or treatment; =lache f pool of water; =lauf m wa.-course; drain (for letting off water); =läufer m, ent. water-measurer or -tick (*Hydro'metra*); ♃leer a. without water, dried (or parched) up; =leitung f: in Hause: wa.-supply or -system; eine ~ in Hause anlegen to have the water laid on; et. in die ~ gießen to pour a th. down the sink; b) ⊙ Wasserbau: water-conduit, aqueduct; =leitungs-anlage f laying down water-pipes; =leitungs-röhre f water- (or conduit-)pipe; =lili-e ♃ f: a) = Schwertlilie; b) (Seerose) waterlily (*Nymphae'a*); =lini-e ↓ u. ⊙ f wa.-line, high-water mark, für Frachtschiffe: load-line; =linse ♃ f duck-weed or -meat (*Lemna*); =loch n: a) hole full of water; b) (Senkgrube) cesspool, sink; =losung ⚒ f von Gruben: drainage; =malerei f = farbenmalerei; =mangel m scarcity (or lack) of water, in Städten auch: water-famine; (Dürre) drought; =mann m: a) water-bearer or -carrier; b) ast. (Sternbild) Aquarius; **marke** f: a) wa.-mark, Brückenbau 2c.: high-water-mark; b) ⊙ Papierfabr. = zeichen; =maschine ⊙ f hydraulic engine; =maß n gauge; =masse f body (or volume) of water, fließende: flow of water; =melone ♃ f water-melon (*Citru'llus vulga'ris*); =menge f quantity of water; =messer ⊙ m water-meter, hydrometer; =meß-kunst f hydrometry; =milbe f, zo. water-mite (*Hydra'chna*); =minze ♃ f wa.-mint (*Mentha aqua'tica*); =molch m, zo. wa.-newt (*Triton palu'stris*); =mörtel ⊙ m wa.-cement, hydraulic (or Roman) cement; =motte f, ent. caddis-fly (*Phryga'nea*); =mühle ⊙ f water-mill; =müller m owner of a water-mill.
wässern (⚭) va. I v/n. (h.) 1. to discharge water, bsd. ihm ♃ die Augen his eyes are watering or watery or full of water; mir wässert der Mund danach it makes my mouth water. — II v/a. 2. = bewässern I. — 3. = einwässern; Gerberei: Häute ♃ to steep (or soak) ... — 4. Wein 2c. ♃ to water (or dilute) ...; chm. gewässert: ⚙ hydrated, hydrous. — 5. ⊙ Zeuge ♃ (wetten) to water (or cloud, tabby, wave) ... — III ~ n ⊕ = Wässerung.
Wasser-nix (⚭...) m ⊕, **nixe** ♃ f water-nixy, nixie; =not f scarcity of water; vgl. Wassersnot!; ♃nötig ⚔ a. ⊕ flooded with water; =nuß ♃ f: indische ~ Singhara-nut, auch water-caltrop or -nut (Frucht von *Trapa natans bispino'sa*); =nymphe f wa.-nymph, naiad; =opal m, min. aqueous opal, ⚙ adularia; =orgel ♪ (chm.) f wa.-organ; =partie f = fahrt; =paß: a) = wasserwage; =paß-recht a. level with the (surface of the) water, horizontal; b) ~ m level (of the water); =perle f imitation pearl; =pest ♃ f: canadische ~ water-weed, ⚙ anacharis (*Elo'dea Canade'nsis*); =pfahl ⊙ m Bauwesen: pile in the water; =pfeffer ♃ m wa.-pepper, smartweed (*Poly'gonum Hydro'piper*); =pflanze ♃ f water-plant or -weed, aquatic plant; =pocken f pl. path. chickenpox, ⚙ varicella, =polack [18. sae., bsd. seit 1848] m, =polackin f F Pole in Upper Silesia; =probe f (chm.: Gottes-urteil) water-ordeal; =pumpe f water-pump; =quelle f fountain, (fresh-water)spring; =rabe m = Kormoran (=scharbe); =rad ⊙ n water- (Seegnersches: reaction) wheel; horizontales ~ horizontal wa.-wheel, turbine; =ralle f, orn. water-rail, common rail (*Rallus aqua'ticus*); =ratte f: a) zo. wa.-rat (*Arvi'cola amphi'bius*); b) F fig. alte ~ (erfahrener Seemann) old sea-dog or salt; ♃recht a: a) horizontal, level; b) ~ n laws pl. relating to water; ♃reich: a) a. abounding in water, well watered; b) ~ n watery kingdom; =rinne f: a) water-channel; b) arch. gutter, gully; =röhre f water-pipe; =rose ♃ f = Seerose; =röste ⊙ f des Flachses: water-retting; =rübe f, hort. (weiße Rübe) turnip (*Bra'ssica rapa*); =rutschbahn f (water-)shoot; =sack m e-r Tabakspfeife: heel, knob; =säugetier

[Wassersäule] — 1098 — [Weberknecht]

n. zo. aquatic mammal, (Walltier) & cetacean; =säule *f* column of water; =säulen-maschine ⊙ *f* water-pressure engine; =schacht ⚒ *m* draining-shaft; =schaden *m* damage caused by water or floods; =schaufel ⊙ *f* Wasserbau. floated wheel; =scheide ♀ *f* watershed. *auch:* parting-line of the waters; =schenkel ⊙ *m*, *arch.* weather-rail; =scheu *a.* afraid of water; b) ~ *f* fear (or dread) of water. *path.* hydrophobia; =schierling ♀ *m f.* Schierling b; =schlange *f:* a) *zo.* wa.-snake, hydra; b) *ast.* Hydra; =schlauch *m:* a) (water-)hose; b) ♃ bladder-wort (*Utricula'ria*); =schlund *m. etwa:* watery gulf, abyss of water; =schnecke *f. zo.* wa.-snail; *vgl.* Teichschnecke; =schnepfe *f. orn.* = Bekassine; =schöpf-maschine ⊙ *f* water-scooping machine; =schöpf-rad ⊙ *n* wheel for drawing up water. pot-wheel; =schraube ⊙ *f* hydraulic (or Archimedean) screw; =schwalbe ⊙ *f* Ufer-schwalbe; =schwärmer ⊙ *m* Feuerwerk. water-rocket; =schwein *n* water-hog (*Hydrochoe'rus capyba'ra*), brasilisches ~ Tapir; =schwert ⊙ *f* wa.-flag, yellow iris (*Iris pseuda'corus*); =seite *f* side facing the water. waterside; =semmel *f* kind of (French) roll; =scorpion *m, ent.* wa.-scorpion (*Nepa*). Wassers-not (⊙...) *f* (Überschwemmung. *f.* Wassernot!) distress caused by floods. Wasser-speier (⊙...) *m* ⊙ *arch.* gargoyle; =spiegel *m* (reflecting) surface of the water; =spinne *f. ent.* water-spider (*Argyro'neta aqua'tica*); =spinn-maschine ⊙ *f von* Arkwright: wa.-frame; =spitz-maus *f. zo.* wa.-shrew (*Cro'ssopus fo'diens*); =sport *m* aquatic sport, aquatics; =spritze *f* wa.-engine; =sprudel *m* bubbling spring or fountain; =stag ⚓ *n* bobstay; =stand *m* height (or level) of the water; =ständer *m* water-tub; =stands-anzeiger *m.* =messer *m* ⊙ water-gauge; =standslini-e *f* wa.-level or -line; =station *f* watering-station; =staub *m* spray; =stern ♀ *m* water-starwort (*Calli'triche verna'lis*); =stern-gras ♀ *n* wa.-stargrass (*Scho'llera grami'nea*); =stiefel *m/pl.* waterproof (fishing- or hunting-)boots *pl.;* =stoff *m, chm.* hydrogen (H); mit ~ verbinden ⊙ to hydrogenate; =stoff-flamme *f* hydrogen flame; =stoff-gas *n* hydrogen gas; =stoff-haltig *a.:* ⊙ hydrogenated, ...ized, ...ous; =stoff-säure *f* (⊗. Chlorwasserstoff II Cl) hydracid; =stoff-super-oxyd *n* hydrogen peroxide (O₂H₂); =stoff-verbindung *f* hydride; =strahl *m* jet of water, *von* springendem Wasser: wa.-spout; =straße *f* wa.-highway, navigable river; =strecke *f* wa.-course, expanse of water, *bei einem Strome auch:* reach; =streif(en) *m:* a) watery streak; b) *von* Brot: doughy streak; =strom *m* stream (or flow) of water; =strudel *m* whirlpool; =sturz *m* =fall; (Stromschnelle) rapid, shoot, chute; =sucht *f, path.* dropsy; =süchtig *a.* dropsical; =suppe *f* wa.-gruel, watery soup; =teilchen *n, phys.:* ⊙ aqueous particle, molecule of water; =tier *n* aquatic animal; =tonne *f* wa.-butt or

-cask; ⚓ *a.* = Boje; =topf *m* wa.-pot or -jug; =tor ⊙ *n* Wasserbau: flood- (or water-)gate; =tracht ⚓ *f eines Schiffes:* ship's draught of water; =träger *m* wa.-carrier; =transport ⚒ *m* wa.-carriage, transport (or carriage) by water; =treibend *a. med.* = harntreibend; =trense ♀ Sattlerei: watering-bit; =treten *n* treading water; =treter *m* one who treads water; =triebwerk ⚒ *n* hydraulic machine; =trinker *m* wa.-drinker. (geistigen Getränken Entsagender) total abstainer, teetotaler; =trog *m* water-trough; =tropfen *m* drop of water; =turm *m* Wasserleitung: tower with reservoir for water; =uhr *f* bsd. chm. water-clock, *a.:* ⚓ clepsydra; =umschlag *m* cold-water compress or dressing. Wässerung (⊙...) *f* watering, (Berieselung) irrigation; ~s-graben (⊙...) *m* ⊙ *agr.* ditch for irrigation. Wasser-verdrängung ⚓ (⊙...) *f* ⊙ displacement; =vergoldung *f* water-gilding; =verschluß *m* hydraulic lute or cement; =versorgungs-gesellschaft *f* water-company; =vögel *m pl. orn.* water-fowls, aquatic birds *pl.;* =vorrat *m* stock (or supply) of water; =wage ⊙ *f:* a) *surv.* water-level; b) *phys.* hydrostatic level; =wägung *f:* a) levelling; b) *phys.* hydrostatic operation; =wanze *f. ent.* water-bug (Familie *Ne'pidae, &c.*); =weg *m* waterway, auf dem ~e (*ant. zu Lande*) by water; =wegerich ♀ *m* wa.-plantain (*Ali'sma planta'go*); =wehr ⊙ *n* Wasserbau. weir, wear; =weide ♀ *f* = Korbweide; =welt *f, etwa:* aquatic (or oceanic) -world; =werk ⊙ *n. c-s Stadt* ⚒: water works *pl.* of a town. central station for the supply of water; *a.* =kunst b; =wirbel *m* whirlpool, eddy; =woge *f* large (sea-)wave, billow; =wüste *f* watery waste; =wut *f* mania for water; =zeichen *n* Papierfabr.: wa.-mark; =zins *m* water-rate; =zuleitungsrohr *n* water-pipe. wäßricht, ...ig (⊙...) *a.* ⊙. Wäßrung (⊙...) *f* ⊙ = wässericht, ...ig. Wässerung. Wat † (⊙) [ahd.: weed] *f* ⊙ (Gewand) garment. [drag- (or sweep-)net.] Wate ⊙ (⊙) *f* ⊙ Fischerei: (Zuggarn) waten (⊙) [ahd.: wade] *v/n.* (h. u. ſn) ⊙: im Wasser, Schlamm *rc.* ⊙ to wade in (or through) water. mud, &c.; durch einen Bach, Fluß *rc.* ⊙ to wade through a stream, river, &c. Water-kant *f* (⊙...) [nbdt.. nld.] *f* ⊙ (Ufer, Küste) water's edge. bank, shore. watsch(e)lig (⊙...) *a.* ⊙ waddling, toddling, shambling; unsteady (gait). watscheln (⊙...) *a. ⊙.) v/n.* (h. u. ſn) ⊙ *a.* to waddle (along), to toddle (along). Watt¹ ⊙ (⊙) [James ~ npr/m. (Vervollkommner der Dampfmaschine, 1736—1819)] *n* ⊙ *6. elect.* (Maßeinheit der electr. Leistung) watt; *vgl.* Amperevolt u. Voltampere. Watt² ⚓ (⊙) [nbdt.] *n (m)* ⊙ *c.* ~e¹ (⊙...) *f* ⊙ (Untiefe) low beach which is under water at high tide, *oft im pl.* ~e(n) (bſd. in der Nordsee) sand-banks. Watte² (⊙...) [nhd.] *f* ⊙ wadding, bſd. *med.* cotton-wool; mit ~ füttern = wattieren.

watten¹-artig (⊙...) *a.* ⊙ like wadding; =fabrikant *m* = =macher; =²fahrer *m* flat boat for the shallows; =fischerei *f* fishing in the shoals, =¹macher *m* maker of wadding, wadding-maker; =²meer *n* shallows *pl.* in the ocean, shoals *pl.,* sea-bottom (which becomes) visible at low tide; =¹rock *m* wadded petticoat. wattieren (⊙⊙) [Watte²] *v/a.* ⊙ to wad, to line (or stuff) with wadding; to pad. Wattierer (⊙⊙) *m* ⊙ padder. Wattierung (⊙⊙) *f* ⊙ padding. watt(i)sch ⊙ (⊙) [Watt¹] *a.* ⊙ *mach.* of Watt; ~es Parallelogramm Watt's parallelogram. parallel motion. Watt¹-messer ⊙ (⊙...) *m* ⊙ *elect.* wattmeter; =stunde *f* watt-hour. Wat-vogel (⊙ˡ⊙) [waten] *m* ⊙ *orn.* wader, wading bird. [bow-wow.] wau (⊙) [das Hundegebell nachahmend] *int.*] Wau² ♀ (⊙) [ndl.. *lt.] m ⊙ c.* dyer's-weed, weld, wold (*Rese'da lute'ola*). wauwau (⊙⊙) I *int.* = wau¹. — II ~ *m ⊙* ⊙. ⊙ Kindersprache: dog(gie), bow-wow; b) *fig.* bugbear, bogy. WB. *abbr.* = Wörterbuch. web-bar (⊙⊙...) *a.* ⊙ textile. Webe (⊙) [: web] *f* ⊙ 1. = Gewebe, eng. ⊙. (Stück Leinwand) web, piece of linen. — 2. = Spinngewebe. Webe-art (⊙...) *f* ⊙ mode of weaving; =baum *m* = Weberbaum; =faser *f* textile fibre; =gewerbe *n* textile industry; =kunst *f* art of weaving; =leine ⚓ *f* der Wanten: ratlin(e); =maschine ⊙ *f* power-loom. weben (⊙) [ahd.: weave] I ⊙ ⊙ ⊙ *v/a.* 1. ⊙ to weave cloth, &c., to work tapestry. &c.; damastartig ⊙ to damask; gewebte Strümpfe woven stockings *pl.;* *fig.* ſie (die Frauen) flechten und ⊙ himmlische Rosen ins irdische Leben (SCH.) with roses grown in Eden's bowers they intertwine this life of ours; *poet.* was die Parzen ⊙ what's woven by the Fates. — II ⊙ 2. *v/n.* (h.) to be engaged in weaving; *zo.* ⊙ ⊙: ⚓ telarian; *fig.* (ſich regen und bewegen) to stir, to move; ſie leben und ⊙ darin their minds (or energies) are absorbed in it; ſ. leben² 7. — 3. *bisw. v/a.* fakultiv zu ⊙: to stir, to set astir. — III ~ *n* ⊙ 4. (ſ. I) weaving; *vgl.* Weberei. — 5. (ſ. II) ihr Leben und ~ their whole life and thought, all their doings and movements *pl.* Weber (⊙⊙) *m* ⊙, ~in *f* ⊙ weaver. Weber-arbeit (⊙⊙...) *f* ⊙ weaver's work; =blatt *n* weaver's reed, slay; =baum ⊙ *m* weaver's beam, cloth-beam; =distel ♀ *f* fuller's-teazel or -thistle (*Di'psacus fullo'num*). Weberei (⊙⊙...) *f* ⊙ 1. (Weben) weaving, weaver's trade. — 2. (Gewobenes) woven material. texture. tissue. — 3. (Gebäude) weaving-mill. Weber-einschlag (⊙⊙...) *m* ⊙, =eintrag *m* weft, woof; =gesell(e) *m* journeyman weaver; =handwerk *n* weaver's trade; =kamm *m* = =blatt; =karde ♀ *f* = =distel; =knecht *m:* a) = =gesell(e); b) *zo.* (Afterspinne) shepherd-spider, *auch:* daddy-long-legs (*Phala'ngium*)

Signs (see page XVII): F familiar; P vulgar; ꟾ flash; ⚹ rare; † obsolete (died); * new word (born); ⁺⁺ incorrect; ♪ music;

=knoten ⊕ m weaver's knot or slip; =kunst f weaver's art or craft; =lade ⊕ f batten; =meister m master weaver; =nest n Tuchmach.: flaw in the cloth; =schere f weaver's shears pl.; =schiffchen n (weaver's) shuttle; =schlichte f = Schlichte 2; =schule f = Webschule; =schütze f = schiffchen; =spule f (weaver's) bobbin, (winding-) spool; =tritt m treadle of a loom; =vogel m, orn. weaver-bird, palm-bird (Plo'céus); =zettel ⊕ m warp.

Web=schiffchen ⊕ (″...) n ⊕ = Weberschiffchen; =schule f school for weavers; =stuhl m weaving-loom; =waren ⊕ f/pl. textile (or woven) goods pl.; =waren-handel m textile trade.

Wechsel (″tsch) [ahd.: weichen] m ⊕ (in 1 pl. meist ~fälle) 1. (Veränderung) change, mit regelmäßiger Wiederkehr: turn, alternation, rotation (of crops), succession (of seasons); (Übergang) transition; (Schwankung) fluctuation; (~fall des Lebens) vicissitude, schlimmer: reverse; ~ der Mondgestalten phases pl. of the moon. — 2. (Tausch) exchange, von Geldsorten auch: change; ~ der Pferde relay of horses; ~ der Ringe (als Zeichen der Verbindung) exchange of rings. — 3. ⊕ (Anweisung auf einen Geldbetrag) bill (of exchange) (über 400 Mark for twenty pounds); s. Akzept, akzeptieren, ausstellen 4, begeben 6, girieren, Giro, honorieren 3, protestieren; ~ auf Sicht bill payable at sight; ~ auf kurze Sicht, kurzer ~ short bill; eigener (od. trockener) ~ bill drawn on o.s.; gezogener (oder trassierter) ~ draft (auf zwei Monate Ziel at two months); auf das Ausland gezogener ~ (Devise) foreign bill or draft; offener ~ blank cheque; letter of credit. — 4. burschlos: student's monthly, quarterly, &c. allowance from home. — 5. hunt. (Weg des Hochwildes) usual route taken by big game. — 6. ⊕ joint; (Verbindungsröhre) joint-pipe.

Wechsel=agent ⊕ (″tsch...) m ⊕ billbroker; =agio n exchange; =akzept n acceptance of a bill; =armig a. ⊕ Turnerei: with alternate arms; =balg m changeling, (Mißgeburt) false conception; (Ungeheuer) monster; (ungezogenes Kind) little demon, young Turk; =bank ⊕ f discount-house.

wechselbar (″tsch...) a. ⊕ changeable, exchangeable; convertible.

Wechsel=begriff (″tsch...) m ⊕ reciprocal notion, auch: convertible term; =bewegung f reciprocal movement or motion; =beziehung f mutual relation(ship), correlation; =bezüglich a. ⊕ correlative; =brief m = Wechsel 3; =buch n bill book; =bürge m one who stands surety for (the payment of) a bill; =bürgschaft f surety for the payment of a bill; =chor ♪ m antiphony; =courtage f bill-brokerage; =diskontierer m bill-discounter.

Wechselei (″tsch...) f ⊕ chopping and changing, constant changes pl.

wechsel=fähig ⊕ (″tsch~...) a. ⊕ able (or authorized) to draw bills (of exchange); =fähigkeit f ⊕ right to draw (and endorse) bills; =fall m:

a) alternate case; b) =fälle pl. (s. Wechsel 1) des Lebens: vicissitudes (or ups and downs) pl. of life; =fälscher m, =fälschung f forger, forging of bills; =farbe f changeable (or iridescent) colour; ⊕farbig a. changing colour, iridescent; =fieber n, path. intermittent fever, ague; =folge f alternation; =forderung ⊕ f claim based on a bill of exchange; =frist f time allowed for the payment of a bill, days of grace, usance; =gebrauch m usance; =gebühr f discount on bills; =geld n: a) (Bankvaluta) bank-money; b) (kleine Münze) small coin, change; =gesang ♪ m alternating (or amoebæan) song, ☌ amoebæum, eccl. antiphony; vgl. Rundgesang; =geschäft ⊕ n: a) banking-business or transaction; b) (Ort) bill-broker's business, discount-house; =gespräch n dialogue, auch: colloquy; =gläubiger ⊕ m holder of a bill, vgl. =inhaber; =glück n fickle fortune; =handel ⊕ m bill-brokerage; =händler m bill-broker, discounter of bills; =handlung f = =geschäft b; =haus n discount-house; =inhaber m bearer (or holder) of a bill; =klage f action (or suit) arising out of a bill (of exchange); =kläger m plaintiff in a suit relating to a bill; =konto n bill-account; =kopier-buch n =buch; =kredit m credit for bills; =kurs m rate of exchange; =kurs-berechnung f arbitration of exchange; =kurs-vergleicher m arbitragist; =makler m bill-(or exchange-)broker.

wechseln (″tsch) [ahd.] I v/n. (h. u. sn) n. v/a. ☌a. 1. to change; et. 2, mit et. 2 (et. anderes an die Stelle setzen) to substitute (or supplant) a th.; (austauschen) to exchange, to interchange; den Eigentümer 2 to change hands; die Farbe 2 to change colour; Geld 2 to change money; e-m eine Goldmünze 2 to give a p. change for a gold coin; seine Kleider 2 to change one's clothes; s. Kugel 2; s-n Wohnort 2 to change one's residence, to shift one's quarters; (harte) Worte mit einem 2 to bandy (rude or insulting) words with a p.; die Zähne 2 to shed one's teeth. — 2. v/n. u. v/refl. to change, to vary; mit et. (sich) 2 (an die Stelle von et. treten) to take the place of a th., to supplant a th.; mit e-m 2 to change places with a p.; fortwährend 2 to be for ever chopping and changing; ☌d alternat(iv)e. — 3. ⊕ to do banking(-business). — 4. hunt. vom Hochwilde: to change its haunts. — 5. ⚔ die Wetter 2 (es herrscht ein guter Luftzug) there is a good current (or draught) of air. — II ~ n ⊕ 6. = Wechsel 1 u. 2; dies ewige ~ der Dienstboten, Wohnung ꝛc.: this (constant) chopping and changing (about).

Wechsel=nehmer (″tsch~...) m ⊕ taker (or buyer) of a bill; =note ♪ ⊕ appog(g)iatura, pl. ...e; =ordnung ⊕ f regulations (or laws) pl. relating to (bills of) exchange; =pari n par of exchange; =platz m place of exch.;

=protest m jur. protest in case of non-payment of a bill; =provision f = =courtage; =rechnung f account connected with (bills of) exch.; =recht n = =ordnung, auch: law of exchange; =rede f = =gespräch; =reime m/pl. alternate rhymes pl.; =reiten F n = =reiterei; =reiter f m bill-jobber; =reiterei F f bill-jobbing, co. kite-flying; =schritt m Tanzkunst: change of step; =schuld f debt founded on bills (of exchange); ⊕seitig a. ⊕ = gegenseitig b; =seitigkeit f = Gegenseitigkeit; =sendung ⊕ f remittance of bills of exchange; =sensal m = =makler; ⊕ständig a. alternate; =stempel m bill-stamp; =streit m conflict; =strom m, elect. alternating (or alternate) current; dreiphasiger ~ three-phase alternating current; =strom-lampe f alternating-current lamp; =strom-maschine f alternator, alternating-current machine; =strommotor m alternating-current motor; =tag m, med. critical day; =tierchen n/pl. (mikroskopische Tierchen von wechselnder Gestalt) amoebæ pl.; =verhältnis n reciprocal relation(ship): =verjährung f jur. prescription of a bill of exchange; =voll a. subject to frequent changes, varied; (ereignisvoll) eventful; ⊕weise adv. (Fa.a.) by (or in) turns, alternately; (gegenseitig) mutually, reciprocally; =wild n, hunt. game frequently changing its haunts; =winkel m/pl., math. alternate angles pl.; =wirkung f reciprocal (or mutual) effect or action; =wirtschaft f, agr. rotation of crops; =wucher ⊕ m usurious discounting of bills; =zustand m reciprocity.

Wechsler ⊕ (″tsch) m ⊕ money-changer („Bantier" und „Geldwechsler" in England durchaus verschieden!).

Wechsler=laden ⊕ (″~/...) m ⊕ money-changer's office or shop, weitS. (private) banking-business.

Wechslung (″tsch) f ⊕ = wechseln II.

Weck f ⊕ ⊕c., ~e (″) f ⊕. ~en¹ (″) m ⊕ (French) roll; small loaf of finest wheaten bread.

wecken² (″) [ahd.: wake: wachen] I v/a. ⊕: ~c-n 2 to (a)waken (⊥+, aber viel gbr.: to wake) a p., to rouse a p. (out of his sleep), des Morgens: to call a p. in the morning, durch Schellen: to ring a p. up; j-s Mut wieder 2 to put new courage into a p. — II ~ n ⊕ ⚔ rouse.

Wecker (″) m ⊕ 1. (auch ~in f ⊕) awakener, one who rouses a p. (out of his sleep) or calls him in the morning or rings him up. — 2. = Weckuhr. — 3. ⊕ elect. am Fernsprecher ꝛc.: electric bell, alarm-bell, mit Selbstunterbrechung: trembling bell; den ~ einschalten to put a bell in circuit; das Tönen der ~ the ringing of the alarm-bells.

Wecker=batterie (″~...) ⊕ f ⊕ elect. ringing-battery; =knopf ⊕ m, elect. bell-push; =uhr f = Weck-uhr; =vorrichtung f, =werk n (works pl. of an) alarum.

Weck=glocke (″...) f ⊕ alarum-bell; =ruf m, =trommel f ⚔ ⊥ = Reveille; =uhr f alarum(-clock), ⚔ alarm-clock.

Weda ☌ (⊥~) [ifd.] m ⊕⊕ (heiliges Buch der Brahmanen) Veda.

☌ scientific; ♀ botanical; ⚲ geography; ⊕ machinery; ⚒ mining; ⚔ military; ⚓ marine; ⊕ commercial; ⊕ postal; 🚂 railway.

[Wedel] — 1100 — [wegdrängen]

Wedel (⌣) [ahd.; *wehen] m ⚥ 1. zum Fächeln: fan, zum Stäuben: whisk; vgl. Staubwedel. — 2. = Sprengwedel b. — 3. hunt. (Schwanz bei Dam-, Elen- u. Rotwildes) tail, brush. — 4. ♀ (blattartiges Organ bei Farnkräutern ꝛc.): ⚥ frond, ~ pl. coll.: ⚥ frondage.

Wedel-bürste (⌣⌣...) f ⚥ zum Stäuben: whisk, feather-brush; **⸗förmig** a. ⊙ fan-shaped, ⚥ flabelliform.

wedeln (⌣) [mhd.; *Wedel] I v/n. (h.) u. v/a. ⚥a. 1. den (ob. mit dem Fächer) ⚥ to fan the air; mit Angabe der Wirkung: e-m die Fliegen vom Leibe ⚥ to fan the flies off a p. — 2. bſd. v. Hunde: mit dem Schwanze ⚥ to wag (with) one's tail, ſtärker: to wriggle one's tail about; fig. (hündiſch kriechen) to fawn upon a p., to cringe (or crouch) before a p.; v. Pferde: mit dem Schweife ⚥ to whisk (or flap) with its tail. — II ~ n ⚥ 3. (ſ. 1) fanning; (ſ. 2) wagging (with) one's tail.

weder (⌣) [ahd.: whether] cj. ⚥ ∥ noch ∥ neither ∥ nor ∥; ⚥ er noch ſie iſt (ob. ſind) gekommen neither he nor she has (have come faſch!) come; ich ſah ⚥ ihn noch ſie I saw neither him nor her, I did not see either him or her; bin ⚥ Fräulein, ⚥ ſchön (a.) I'm neither a lady, nor am I fair.

wediſch (⌣) [Weda] a. ⊙ Ved(ant)ic.

Weg¹ (⌣) [ahd.: way: lt. via] m ⚥c. 1. way, course, path, track; (Straße) road, street(vgl. Chauſſee); (Verbindungsſtraße) route, kürzere: (short) cut; (Durchgang) passage (auch anat., &c.), unter der Straße: subway, bedeckter: covert way; (Gang) walk, kürzerer: (short) turn; halber ~, Mitte des ~es halfway, midway; der nächſte ~ the nearest way, the shortest cut; ſ. betreten 3 u. gangbar 3; Auſſchrift: hier geht kein ~! no thoroughfare (here!); Sprichw. ſ. Rom. — 2. mit verbs mſt als Objekt: ſ. bahnen; einen falſchen ~ betreten to take a wrong route or turn; ſ. Mittel² 1 am Ende; ſ-n ruhigen ~ fortgehen to go (or walk) quietly along; ~e gehen (als Bote) to run errands; den kürzeſten ~ gehen to take the shortest cut (possible); ſ. Fleiſch 1; fig. das hat gute ~e (es geht gut damit) all is going on well, things are in a fair way (of success); es hat damit gute ~e there is no hurry, (das kommt noch lange nicht) it is a long way off, F it won't come (off) yet; e-m den ~ weiſen to show a p. the way; e-m die ~e weiſen (ihn gehen heißen) to send a p. away or F packing, flying. — 3. als gen. (vgl. ...wegs): ein tüchtiges Stück ~es a good distance or step; eine Stunde ~es an hour's walk or drive or ride or journey; desſelben (oder e-s) ~es mit e-m gehen to go the same way (or to follow the same route) as a(nother) p.; geht eures ~es! go your way!, get along!; be off!; er kam des ~es (gegangen) he came walking (or marching) along; woher des ~es? where are you coming (or hailing) from?; wohin des ~es? where are you going (to) or F off to?, geh. Spr. whither are you bending your steps or steering your course?; fig. laſſen Sie ihn ſ-r Wege gehen! let him go or be!, leave him alone!; adv. aller ~e, alle ~e = alle(r)wege, allerwegen. — 4. nach prp.: am ~e by the road(side); auf dem ganzen ~e all (along) the way; ſich auf den ~ begeben ob. machen to set out (on one's way or journey), ſ. bringen 8 unter „auf"; e-m et. auf den ~ geben to give a p. s.th. to take with him on his journey; auf dem ~e der Beſſerung ſein to be on the way to (or in a fair way of) recovery; die Sache iſt auf gutem ~e the matter is progressing (well); auf gütlichem ~e in a friendly way, amicably; auf halbem ~e ſtehen bleiben to stop half-way (a. fig.); e-m auf halbem ~e entgegengehen to meet a p. half-way (a. fig.); auf rechtem ~e ſein to be on the right path; Glück auf den ~! I wish you a good (or safe) journey!; chm. auf naſſem ~e by moist (or humid) process; aus dem ~e gehen to make way (or room) for a p., to stand aside while a p. passes; e-m aus dem ~e gehen to go out of a p.'s way, to avoid (or shun) a p.; das liegt aus (ob. außer) meinem ~e (fern) it lies out of my way, fig. it is not in my line; ſ. räumen 1; **bei** ~e ſein to be up (and doing); gut bei ~e (beiwege, mehr gbr. zuwege) ſein to be well or in good health; **in**: bſd. jur. im ~e Rechtens in a legal way, by law; im ~e einer Polizeiverordnung by way (or by means) of a police regulation; e-m (hindernd) im ~(e) ſteh(e)n ob. ſein to be in a p.'s way or fight; Fußball: to obstruct; ſich ſelbſt im ~(e) ſteh(e)n to stand in one's own light, to act against (or contrary to) one's own interest; e-m in den ~ laufen ob. kommen to run in(to) a p.'s way; e-m Hinderniſſe in den ~ legen to lay (or place, throw) obstacles in(to) a p.'s way; to thwart a p.'s plans; in die ~e leiten (vorbereiten, unternehmen) to pave the way for, to bring about, to start; e-m nicht **über** den ~ trauen not to trust a p. (any further than one can see him); **von** ~en ſ. wegen 2; **vom** ~e abkommen to miss (or lose) one's way, to stray from the right path; **zu** ~e ſ. zuwege.

weg² (⸍) [mhd. (in den) Weg¹] I adv. 1. away; (weit) far (off); ell. mit weggelaſſenem v. der Bewegung: ſie ſind ⚥ they are gone; wir wollen ⚥!, oft: let us go!, we must be off!; meine Uhr iſt ⚥ ... is gone or lost; ⚥!, ⚥, marſch! away with you!, bisw. get you gone!; ⚥ mit dir! go!, be off!; ⚥ damit! take it away!; ⚥ iſt er! he is off!; das Buch iſt ⚥ ... is gone or lost; der Reiz iſt ⚥ the charm has departed; ⚥ wie der Blitz off like a shot; das Haus liegt weit ⚥ von der Straße ... lies far back (or removed) from the street. — 2. ganz ⚥ (außer ſich) ſein to be quite beside o.s. with joy, &c., to be smitten with love, &c. — 3. über et. ⚥ (hinaus) ſein to be beyond a th.. to have passed a th. — 4. d(a)runter ⚥ ſein (für nichts gelten) to be thought nothing of, to be low down (in people's esteem); in Verbindung mit anderen verbs, ſ. weg²⸗..., Weg²⸗... — 5. nach prp.: hinter⸗ea. ⚥ one after another, in (rapid) succession; in einem ⚥ continually, F at one stretch or go; ſ. Leber; Hände ⚥! hands off!; Kopf ⚥! head(s) back!, look out for your head(s)!; ⚥ mit den Grillen und Sorgen! banish (or away with) gloomy thoughts and cares!; ⚥ mit den Komplimenten! save (or spare) your compliments!; ⚥ mit dir, Satan! avaunt, Satan! — II **weg²⸗**...(⸍...) 6. in Verbindung mit verbs, immer trennbar (**), u. in Zſſgn mit verbal nouns u. adjectives bz. Trennung, Entfernung.

...weg³ (...⸍) adv. zB. dreiſt⚥ boldly; frei⚥ ⚼ u. Turnerei: forward, march!

weg²⸗arbeiten (⸍...) v/a. ⊙** to work off, to remove by working; ⚥**ätzen** v/a. ⊙** mſt surg. to corrode, surg. to remove with caustics or by cauterizing, auch: to burn off.

Weg¹⸗bahner (⸍⌣) m ⚥ path-maker, fig. pioneer, Sport: pace-maker.

weg²⸗begeben (⸍...) v/refl. ⊙c*/*: ſich ⚥ to go away, to absent o.s.; to depart, withdraw, set out; ⚥**beißen** v/a. ⊙a**: a) to drive off by (or with) biting; b) F fig. e-n⚥ to cut a p. out, to push a p. aside, to take a p.'s place; ⚥**beizen** v/a. ⊙** = ⚥ätzen; ⚥**bekommen** F v/a. ⊙⁴*/*: a) (wegſchaffen) to get off, to remove; b) (zuſtande bringen) to accomplish; c) (verſtehen, lernen) to learn the knack of, F to catch hold of; d) eins ⚥ to get a knock or a blow; to catch a disease; ⚥**berufen** v/a. ⊙b*/* to call away; ⚥**beten** v/a. ⊙** to exorcize; ⚥**blaſen** v/a. ⊙a** to blow off or away, to puff away; ſie ſind wie ⚥geblaſen they have (mysteriously) disappeared or vanished; ⚥**bleiben** v/n. (ſn) ⊙**: a) to stay (or keep) away; bleiben Sie ja nicht weg! be sure (or don't fail) to come!; er bleibt nicht lange weg he was not away for long; b) (ausgelaſſen w.) to be omitted; hier iſt ein Wort ⚥geblieben, auch: a word has dropt out; F bleiben Sie davon weg! don't meddle with it!; ⚥**blicken** v/n. (h.) ⊙** to look another way, to take one's eyes off a th.; ⚥**brauchen** v/n. (h.) ⊙** bſd. mit neg.: er braucht noch nicht weg he need not go yet; ⚥**brechen** v/a. ⊙a**: a) to break (or pull) off; b) med. to vomit, to bring up one's food; ⚥**brennen** ⊙b**: a) v/a. to burn down, to destroy by fire, surg. = ⚥ätzen; b) v/n. (ſn) to be burnt down, to burn down; ⚥**bringen** v/a. ⊙⁷**: a) Sachen: to carry (or take) away, to remove, to convey; ich kann den Flecken nicht ⚥ I cannot get the stain out; b) Perſonen: to take away, to get out of the way; er iſt nicht wegzubringen he won't move or budge; ⸗**bringung** f ⊙ von Sachen: carriage, conveyance; ⚥**bügeln** v/a. ⊙a** to remove by ironing; ⚥**denken** v/a. ⊙⁷** to imagine as absent or as not being there; ſich ⚥ v/refl. to fancy o.s. away; ⚥**drängen** v/a. ⊙** to push away or aside; fig. to supplant, F

[wegdrücken] — 1101 — [Wegnahme]

to cut out; ⸗drücken v/a. ⊛** to remove by pressing or squeezing; ⸗dürfen v/n. (h.) ⊛** to be allowed to go (or F get) away; ich darf nicht weg I may (or must) not leave.

Wege=amt (⸗ͧ…) n ② surveyor's office; ⸗aufſeher m surveyor (or overseer) of the roads or highways; ⸗bau ⊕ m road-making; ⸗bau-amt n board of roads; ⸗bau-meiſter m constructor (or builder) of roads; ⸗beſſrung f ob. ⸗beſſerung road-mending; ⸗breite f = Wegerich; ⸗dorn ⚘ m buckthorn, waythorn (Rhamnus); ⸗enge ⚔ f (narrow) defile; ⸗geld n turnpike-toll; ⸗geld-einnehmer m turnpike-man; ⸗haſpel f an Fußſteigen: turnstile.

weg²=eilen (⸗ͧ…) v/n. (ſn) ⊛** to hasten (or hurry) away; über et. ⚔: a) to cross a th. rapidly; b) fig. to take a cursory (or hasty) glance at a th., to skim a th.; ~ n ㉓ hasty (or hurried) departure; ⸗ekeln F v/a. ⚔a** to drive away (by uncivil conduct or unfriendly remarks).

Wege=lag(e)rer (⸗ͧ…) m ② highwayman, brigand, ſeltener: waylayer; ⸗lagern v/n. (h.) ⚔a**.* to waylay travellers (on the road); ⸗lagerung f brigandage (on the highway); ⸗los ⚔ ⊛ without roads, pathless; ⸗macher m road-maker; ⸗meſſer ⊕ m: ⚒ hodometer, für Droſchken ꝛc.: taximeter.

wegen (⸗ͧ) [nhd. aus von Wegen] prp. mit vors oder nachgeſetztem gen., biswꝛ. auch mit dat. 1. on account of, because (or by reason) of, for the sake of; ſ. meinet ꝛc.; der Freundſchaft ⚔ for friendship's sake. — 2. (in Anbetracht) in consideration of; (in betreff) with regard (or reference) to; regarding, respecting, (infolge) in consequence of, owing to; von ⚔ mit eingeſchobenem gen.: von ⚔ (ſeitens) j-s on a p.'s part; ſ. Amt 2; von Polizei ⚔ by order of the police, according to police-regulations; ſ. Recht² ⚔ am Ende und Staat; von Todes ⚔ owing to a p.'s death.

Weger ⊕ u. ⚓ (⸗ͧ) m ㉒ (Planke) plank.

Wege=recht (⸗ͧ⸗ͧ) n ②: a) right of way or passage, a. way-leave; b) regulations pl. concerning highways.

Wegerich ⚘ (⸗ͧͧ) [ahd.] m ⊕d. plantain (Planta'go); großer ~ waybread (Pl. maior); lanzettblätteriger ~ rib-grass, ribwort (Pl. lanceola'ta); mittlerer ~ lamb's-tongue (Pl. me'dia).

Wege=ſäule (⸗ͧ⸗ͧ) f ②: a) = Weg-weiſer; b) milestone.

weg²=eſſen (⸗ͧ…) v/a. ⊛**: a) to eat up quickly or greedily, to devour; b) F co. e-n ſcheidenden Freund ꝛc.: to give a p. a farewell-dinner or a send-off.

Wege=ſtein (⸗ͧ…) m ② road-stone; ⸗ſtrecke f = Wegſtrecke; ⸗ſtunde f ſ. Wegſtunde; ⸗tritt ⚘ m = Wegerich; ⸗überführung ⛙ f, ⸗übergang ⛙ m, ⸗unterführung, ⸗wart(e) f, ⸗zehrung f ſ. Weg-überführung, ⸗übergang uſw.; ⸗zoll m = Wegegeld.

weg²=fahren (⸗ͧ…) ⊕b**: a) v/n. (ſn) to drive away or off (in a carriage); to leave by boat; to set sail, to sail (away); to start on a cycle, &c., to depart; über et. ⚔ to drive (or cycle, ⚓ sail, steam) over a th.; mit der Hand über et. ⚔ to pass one's hand over a th.; b) v/a. Laſten ⚔ to remove (or take away) in a carriage or cart or boat, to cart (or carry) off; Perſonen: to take away in a carriage; ⸗fall m ⑦c. (Aufhören) cessation; (Unterdrückung) suppression; (Abſchaffung) abolition; in ~ bringen to suppress, to abolish; in ~ kommen = ⸗fallen b; ⸗fallen v/n. (ſn) ⊛a**: a) to fall away or off; b) to cease; to be suppressed or abolished; ⸗fangen v/a. ⊛b** to catch (beforehand), to capture, to snatch away; ⸗fegen v/a. ⊛** to sweep away, to whisk off; ⸗feilen v/a. ⊛** to file off; ⸗fiſchen v/a. ⊛**: a) to fish (beforehand); b) fig. to net, to carry off; e-m et. ⚔ to snatch a th. (away) from a p.; ⸗fliegen v/n. (ſn) ⊛a** to fly away; über et. ⚔ to fly over (or across) a th.; ~ n ㉓ flight, departure; beim ~ on flying away; ⸗fließen v/n. (ſn) ⊛d** to flow away; ⸗laſſen to drain off; ⸗freſſen v/a. ⊛** to eat up greedily, to devour; ⸗führen v/a. ⊛** to lead (or take) away, Gefangene: to march off, to transport; bſd. Güter: to convey; ⸗gabeln v/a. ⚔a** = ⸗fiſchen b; ⸗gang m going away, departure from a place; beim ~ on (or while) leaving; beim ~ aus der Kirche in coming out of church; ⸗geben v/a. ⊛c**: a) et. ⚔ to give a th. away, ⊛ to dispose of a th., to sell a th.; b) ſeinen Sohn ꝛc. von Hauſe ⚔ to send … to a boarding-school; ⸗geh(e)n ⊛**: a) v/n. (ſn) to go away, to depart; ſie gingen einer nach dem andern ſtill weg they dropped off (F took their exit) one after another; in der Eile ⚔ to leave hurriedly, to hurry (or scamper) away; v/impers. es geht jetzt weg we are now leaving; e-n ⚔ heißen to bid a p. be off; über et. (leicht) ⚔ to pass a th. (lightly) over; b) ~ n = ⸗gang; ⸗gewöhnen v/a. ⊛*/*u./v/refl.: e-n von e-m Orte ⚔ to accustom a p. to stay away from a place; ſich von et. ⚔ to wean o.s. from a th.; ⸗gießen v/a. ⊕d** to pour away; ⸗gleiten v/n. (ſn) ⊛b** to glide (or slip) away; ⸗haben v/a. ⊕b**: a) et. ⚔ to have received (one's share of) a th.; er möchte ihn (es) gern ⚔ he would like to get rid of him (of it); b) et. ⚔ (gut verſtehen) to understand (F to twig) a th., to have a th. at one's fingers' ends or a thorough knowledge of it; er hatte es ſchnell weg he quickly saw through it; ⸗halten v/a. ⊕a** to keep away or off or at a distance; den Kopf ⚔ to turn one's head away; ⸗hängen v/a. ⊛** to hang away or elsewhere; ⸗haſchen v/a. ⊕** to snatch away; ⸗hauchen v/a. ⊛** to blow (gently) away, to breathe away; ⸗hauen v/a. ⊛c**to hew away, to cut off; ⸗heben v/a. ⊛(⑦)b** to lift (and carry) away; ſich ⚔ v/refl. to take o.s. off (= hinwegheben); bſd. in Beſchwörungen: hebe dich weg! be gone!, avaunt!; ⸗helfen v/n. (h.) ⊛b**: e-m ⚔ to help a p. get away or to escape, to assist a p. in getting away, to aid a p. in his flight; ⸗hinken v/n. (ſn) ⊛** to limp away; ⸗holen v/a. ⊛** to fetch (or take) away, to carry off; ⸗humpeln ⚔a** = ⸗hinken; ⸗hüpfen v/n. (ſn) ⊛** to skip (or hop) away; über etwas ⚔ to skip over a th. (auch fig.); ⸗huſchen v/n. (ſn) ⊛** to slip (or flit) away, F to slide off; ⸗jagen v/a. ⊛** to drive (or chase, turn) away; to expel from school, &c.; v/n. (ſn) to gallop off; ⚔ mit Schimpf und Schande ⚔ to drum out of the regiment; ⸗kapern v/a. ⚔a** to snatch away, ⚓ ein Schiff: to capture (as a prize); (abfangen) to intercept; ⸗kehren v/a. ⊛**: a) to sweep away, to brush off; b) das Geſicht ⚔ (abwenden) to turn one's face away; ⸗kommen ⚔** v/n. (ſn): a) früh von Hauſe ⚔ to leave (one's) home at an early hour or age; macht, daß ihr ⚔kommt! be off! go away! P take your hook!; ich mache, daß ich ⚔komme! F I am (or shall be) off (now)!; engS. (entkommen) to get (or slip) away or off, to escape; b) (verlegt, verſetzt werden) der Ring iſt mir ⚔gekommen I have lost or mislaid …; der Beamte kommt nächſtens weg … will soon be shifted or moved; c) über et. (Schwieriges) ⚔ to get over a difficulty; d) = davonkommen; e) bei et. gut, ſchlecht ⚔ to come (or get) off well, badly over a th.; ⸗können v/n. (h.) ⊛** to be able to get away; ich kann nicht weg, a. I cannot leave home; er kann des Geſchäfts halber nicht weg he is detained in business; ⸗kratzen v/a. ⊛** to scratch off or out; ⸗kriechen v/n. ⊕ſ* (ſn) ⊛** to crawl (or creep) away; ⸗kriegen b) = ⸗bringen; ⸗küſſen v/a. ⊛** to kiss away; ⸗laſſen ⊛a**: a) e-n ⚔ to let a p. depart, to allow a p. to go or to leave; (freilaſſen) to release, to set free; b) et. ⚔ (auslaſſen) to leave out, to omit; ~ n ㉓ und ⸗laſſung f ⓰ omission; ⸗laufen v/n. (ſn) ⚔ſt** to run away or off; to hurry away, to take to one's heels. F to decamp; ⸗legen v/a. ⊛** to lay (or put) aside; ⸗leihen v/a. ⊛** to lend out; ⸗leiten v/a. ⊛** (ableiten) to turn aside; ⸗leugnen v/a.⊛b** to deny (flatly), to disavow; ⸗locken v/a. ⊛** to entice (or lure) away; ⸗machen ⊛**: a) v/a. to remove, to take off; Flecken: to take out; b) ſich ⚔ v/refl. (fortgehen) to go (or run) away, F to make (or get) off, to make o.s. scarce, to make tracks; ⸗marſch m marching off, departure; ⸗marſchieren v/n. (ſn) ⊛** to march away or off; ⸗mögen v/n. (h.) ⊛** to like (or feel inclined) to leave or to go away; ⸗müſſen v/n. (h.) ⊛** von Perſonen: to be obliged to leave; er muß weg he must go or be off; fig. he will have to die; von Sachen: es muß weg it must be put away; ⸗nahme f ⓰ taking a th. away, removal of a th., ⚔ ⚓ capture; (Entwendung) abstraction; (Beſchlag) seizure,

[wegnehmen] — 1102 — [Wegzoll]

confiscation, ⚓ auf Schiffe: embargo; ≈nehmen ⓐa** v/a. to take away (with one), ⚔ ⚓ to capture; (entwenden) to abstract; (mit Beschlag belegen) to seize (upon), to confiscate, to put an embargo on; e-n von der Schule 2c. ≈ to take a p. (away or to remove a p.) from school, &c.; von seiner Stelle ≈ to displace, to remove; Terpentinöl nimmt Fettflecken weg turpentine oil takes out (or removes) grease-spots; die Hand ≈ to take off one's hand; Platz, Raum ≈ to take up room or space, to be in the way; ⚓ einen Posten ≈ to withdraw a post; ~ n 23, ≈nehmung f ㊻ removal (= ≈nahme); ≈packen ⓐ8** v/a. to pack (or put, stow) away; b) F sich ≈ v/refl. F to pack off, to take o.s. off, to make o.s. scarce, to hook it; ≈peitschen ⓐ9**, ≈prügeln ⓐ2a** v/a. to drive off with whips, with cudgels; ≈putzen v/a. ⓐ0**: a) to remove with cleaning, to rub off; b) F (entwenden) to abstract; ≈radieren v/a. ⓐ8** to erase; ≈raffen v/a. ⓐ8** to snatch away; to carry (or sweep) off (auch von Krankheiten); ≈räumen ⓐ8** v/a. to clear (or pack) away, to put out of the way; bsd. fig. ein Hindernis ≈ to remove an obstacle; ~ n 23 u. ≈räumung f ㊻ clearance, removal; ≈reise f ⓬ departure; ≈reisen v/n. (sn) ⓐ0** to depart, to leave, to start (on a journey); ≈reißen v/a. ⓐ0a** to tear (or pull, snatch) away, Häuser 2c.: to pull down, to demolish, vom Sturme: to carry off; ≈reiten v/n. (sn) ⓐ0b** to ride away, to leave (or start, depart) on horseback; ≈rennen v/n. (sn) ⓐ5b** to run away or off; ≈rollen v/a. u. v/n. (sn) ⓐ8** to roll away; ~ n 23 eines Fasses, Wagens 2c.: rolling away; ≈rücken ⓐ8** v/a. den Tisch 2c.: to push away, to (re)move; v/n. (sn) to move away, to withdraw; ≈rudern ⓐ2a** v/a. den Kahn: to push off (from shore); v/n. (sn) to row away, to push off (in a boat); ≈rufen v/a. ⓐ0b** to call a p. away; vom Schauplatz seiner Tätigkeit durch den Tod weggerufen werden to be summoned away by death from the scene of one's activity.

...wegs (..."¹) adv. ¿B. halb≈ halfway; unter≈ on the way, on the road. weg²-sägen (⁸⚓⚓) v/a. ⓐ8** to saw off. wegsam (⁸—) a. ㊻ passable, accessible. weg²-schaben (⁸...) v/a. ⓐ8** to scrape off; ≈schaffbar a. ㊻ removable, transportable, transferable; ≈schaffen v/a. ⓐ8**: a) to clear away, to remove (= ≈bringen a); auf Wagen: to cart away; b) (wegräumen) to clear away, to move out of the way; (beseitigen) to push aside, to rid o.s. of; Hindernisse, Schwierigkeiten ≈ to remove (or smooth away) obstacles, difficulties; ⚙ math. e-e Unbekannte aus e-r Gleichung ≈ to eliminate an unknown; ~ n 23 u. ≈schaffung f ㊻ removal, cartage; math.: ⚙ elimination; ≈scharren v/a. ⓐ8** to rake away; ≈schenken v/a. ⓐ8** to give away (as a present); ≈scheren v/a. ⓐa(ⓐ8)**

to shear, to shave (or clip) off; F sich ≈ v/refl. ⓐ8** F to take o.s. off, to make o.s. scarce, to toddle (or be) off; ≈scheuchen v/a. ⓐ8** to scare (or frighten) away; ≈schicken v/a. ⓐ8**: Briefe: to send off or away; to dispatch; Diener ≈: a) = ≈ausschicken, b) = entlassen; ≈schieben v/a. ⓐc** u. v/n. (h.) to push (or F shove) away or out of the way; ≈schießen v/a. ⓐc(et)t** to shoot off or away; v/n. (sn) to dart off, to shoot (or rush) off; ≈schiffen v/n. (sn) ⓐ8** to leave by boat; ≈schlagen v/a. ⓐb** to beat (or knock) off; ≈schleichen v/n. (sn) u. sich ≈ v/refl. ⓐa8** to sneak (or slink, steal) away, to take French leave; ≈schleppen v/a. ⓐ8** to drag (or pull) away; ≈schleudern v/a. ⓐ2a** to fling away, to hurl; ≈schließen v/a. ⓐd** to lock up, to put (away) under lock and key; ≈schlüpfen v/n. (sn) ⓐ8** to slip (or sneak) away; ≈schmeißen F v/a. ⓐ9a** to throw (or fling) away; ≈schnabulieren F v/a. ⓐ3** to pilfer; ≈schnappen v/a. ⓐ8** to snatch away, fig. to snap up; ≈schneiden v/a. ⓐ0c** to cut away or off, hort. to lop off, surg. to amputate a limb, aus einem Körperteile: to excise; ~ n 23 cutting away, surg.: ⚙ amputation, excision; ≈schnellen v/a. ⓐ8** to jerk away; ≈schrecken v/a. ⓐ8** to frighten away; ≈schreiten v/n. (sn) ⓐ0b**: über et. ≈ to stride across a th.; ≈schwemmen v/a. ⓐ8** to wash away; von den Wellen ≈geschwemmt carried away (or off) by the waves; ≈schwimmen v/n. ⓐa(b)** (sn) to swim away; ≈segeln ⚓ v/n. (sn) ⓐ2a** to sail away, to set sail for a place; ≈sehen v/n. (h.) ⓐa**: a) to look away or off; vgl. ≈blicken; b) über et. ≈ to shut one's eyes to a th.; sich ≈sehnen v/refl. ⓐ8** to wish o.s. away. to long to get away; ≈sein v/n. (sn) ⓐa** s. weg² I; er ist lange ≈gewesen he has been away (or absent) a long time; ≈senden v/a. ⓐa** to send away or off; ≈sengen v/a. ⓐ8** to singe off; ≈setzen v/a. ⓐ0**: a) v/a. to put away, to set aside; b) v/n. (sn) über einen Graben 2c. ≈ to jump over ..., to dart across ..., zu Pferde: to take ..., to clear ...; c) sich über et. ≈ ≈ sich hinwegsetzen; ≈sickern v/n. ⓐ2a** to ooze away; ≈sollen v/n. (h.) ⓐ8** = ≈müssen; ≈sprengen v/a. ⓐ8** to burst (or blow) off; v/n. (sn) to gallop off; ≈springen v/n. (sn) ⓐn** to jump (or leap) away or off; ≈spülen v/a. ⓐ8** vom Wasser: to wash away, das Ufer: to encroach upon; ≈stechen v/a. ⓐa** to remove with s.th. pointed; ≈stecken v/a. ⓐ8** to put away or aside; (verbergen) to hide (away); ≈stehlen v/a. ⓐd** to steal, purloin, filch; sich ≈ v/refl. to steal (or sneak) away; ≈stellen v/a. ⓐ8** to put away or out of the way, zurück: to put back; ≈sterben v/n. (sn) ⓐb** to die off; ≈stoßen v/a. ⓐ8** to push away or aside, im Gedränge: to hustle; mit dem Fuße: to kick aside.

Weg¹-strecke (⁻⚓⚓) f ⓬ length of (the) way; (Entfernung) distance. weg²-streichen (⁸⚓⚓) v/a. ⓐa**: a) to stroke aside, die Haare auch: to smooth away; b) = ausstreichen 1. Weg¹-stunde (⁻⚓⚓) f ⓬ league. weg²-stürmen (⁸...) v/n. (sn) ⓐ8**, ≈stürzen v/n. (sn) ⓐ0** to rush away, to dart off. to leave hurriedly; ≈taumeln v/n. (sn) ⓐa** to stagger away; ≈traben v/n. (sn) ⓐ8** to trot (or jog) off or away; ≈tragen v/a. ⓐb** to carry away or off; ≈treiben v/a. u. v/n. (sn) ⓐl** (vertreiben) to drive out or away or off; v/n. (sn): mit dem Strome ≈ to drift (away) with the tide or current; ≈treten v/n. (sn) ⓐ2d**: a) to step aside; b) ⚔ to break the ranks; ≈trinken v/a. ⓐi** to drink off or up; ≈tun v/a. ⓐ5** to put (or push) away or aside; tu[e] die Finger weg! take your fingers off!; (verwahren) to put (or hide) in a safe place.

Weg¹-überführung ⛧ (⁻⚓...) f ⓬ viaduct, overbridge; ≈übergang ⛧ m culvert; ≈unterführung f subway, underbridge. weg²-wälzen (⁸...) v/a. ⓐ8** to roll away; ≈wandern v/n. (sn) ⓐ2a** to wander away, to migrate. Weg¹-wart(e) ♀ (⁻⚓⚓) m (f) ⓬ wild succory or chicory (Cicho'rium i'ntybus). weg²-wehen (⁸...) v/a. ⓐ8** to blow away; ≈weisen v/a. ⓐ8** to turn a p. away (from one's door), to show a p. the door. Weg¹-weiser (⁻⚓⚓) m: a) (mit f = ≈in) guide; b) (Armsäule an Landstraßen 2c.) sign- (or finger-)post; (Reisebuch) traveller's guide-book or vademecum. weg²-wenden (⁸...) v/a. ⓐa** to turn away or off, to avert; ≈werfen: a) v/a. ⓐb** to throw away (auch Karten im Spiel), als unbrauchbar: to cast off, to reject; (verschwenden) to squander, to lavish; das Geld ist (so gut wie) ≈geworfen the money is thrown away or (as good as) wasted; b) sich ≈ v/refl. to debase (or degrade) o.s.; sich an e-n ≈ to throw o.s. away upon a p.; c) ≈d p.pr. u. a. ㊻: α) in den Reden inf.; β) (verächtlich) disdainful, adv. auch: with disdain; ~ n 23 u. ≈werfung f ㊻ (f. a) throwing away, rejection; (f. b) debasement; (f. c) disdain; ≈wischen v/a. ⓐ1** to wipe away or off; to efface; ≈wollen v/n. (h.) ⓐ9**: a) to wish to leave or to depart; er will nicht weg he refuses to go; b) s. weg² 1; ≈wünschen v/a. u. sich ≈ v/refl. ⓐ8** to wish a p., a th. away; ich wünsche ihn weg I wish he would go; sich ≈ = sich ≈sehnen; ≈zaubern v/a. ⓐ2a** to conjure (or charm, spirit) away; wie ≈gezaubert flown as if by magic, dissolved in thin air. Weg¹-zehrung (⁻⚓⚓) f ⓬ travelling expenses pl., (lt.) viaticum. weg²-zerren (⁸...) v/a. ⓐ8** to drag (or pull) away; ≈ziehen ⓐb** v/a. to draw (or drag) away; v/n. (sn) to depart, to leave, (ausziehen) to (re)move; v. Truppen: to march away, v. Vögeln 2c.: to migrate; vgl. auswandern; ~ n 23 = ≈zug. Weg¹-zoll (⁻⚓⚓) m ⓬ = Wegegeld.

Signs (see page XVII): F familiar; P vulgar; F flash; ⚓ rare; † obsolete (died); * new word (born); ++ incorrect; ♪ music;

[Wegzug]

Weg²-zug (⸗⸗) m ② departure; removal; (Wanderung) migration, emigration.

weh¹ (⸗) [ahd.: woe: lt. vae] **I** int. 1. ?!, o ?!, auch **wehe** (⸗⸗) (Schmerz bezeichnend): a) absolut: alas!, oh dear!; b) ach und 2 schreien to lament, to (groan and) wail; c) drohend: 2 ihm! woe betide him! — II a. ⑥⑥, auch: 2. attributiv: painful; südd. ein 2er Finger a sore finger. — 3. prädikativ oder adv.: a) mit „sein" u. „werden": mir ist 2(e), es ist mir 2 zumute, zu Sinn oder ums Herz I feel sick (or sore) at heart, poet. woe is me; mir wird übel und 2 ums Herz I begin to feel very qualmish or very queer or F very bad; b) mit „tun" — e-m 2(e) tun to give (or cause) a p. pain, to pain a p.; das tut e-m in den Ohren 2 that grates (or jars) upon one's ears; sich 2 tun to hurt o.s.; der Kopf tut mir 2 my head aches; das tut mir im Innersten (oder in der Seele) 2 that pains (or grieves) me to the heart; v. e-m Toten: ihm tut kein Zahn mehr 2 his troubles are (all) over or at an end, he is at rest; es tut mir 2 zu sehen ‖ it pains (or sickens) me to see ‖.

Weh² (⸗) [ahd.: *weh¹] n ⓒ. (pl. a. ~en, f. 3b) **1.** (der Ausruf „weh") cry of woe; mit Ach und ~ with lamentations and groans (vgl. weh 1b). — **2.** (etwas schmerzlich Empfundenes) woe, pain, pang; f. Wonne; (Kummer) grief; (Unglück) misfortune; sein Wohl und ~ liegt mir am Herzen his weal and woe are (mehr gbr.: his interest is) nearest to my heart. — **3.** (Schmerz): a) mit näherer Bestimmung: b) Kopf=, Zahn=2 headache, toothache; b) path. = wehe¹ II.

wehe¹ (⸗⸗) **I** int., a., adv. = weh. — **II** ~ f ⑱, mst ~n pl.: path. e-r Wöchnerin: labour-pains, birth-throes pl.; ~n haben to have labour-pains, to be in (child-)labour or in travail.

Wehe² (⸗⸗) [wehen¹] f ⑱ = Schneewehe.

wehen¹ (⸗⸗) [ahd.: Wind] ⑱** **I** v/n. (h.) v. Winde: to blow, waft; (im Winde flattern) to flutter (or flap) in the wind, to wave; es wehte kein Lüftchen there was not a breath (of wind) stirring; es weht ein starker Wind there is a strong gale (of wind blowing), the wind is high; da wehet Gottes Odem (GEIBEL) there wafts the breath of God. — **II** v/a. (wehend tragen) to blow (or waft) along; (treiben) to drift.

Wehen² (⸗⸗) pl. f. wehe¹ II.

Weh-frau (⸗⸗…) f ② = Hebamme; =gefühl n feeling of sadness; =gesang n plaintive song; =geschrei n woeful cries or screams pl.; =klage f lamentation, (loud) wailing; 2klagen v/n. (h.) ⑱*⁎* to lament, to wail, to groan and moan; =mut f woefulness, (sweet) melancholy, (tender) sadness or grief; 2mütig a. ⑥⑥ woeful, sorrowful, doleful; 2mutsvoll a. full of (sweet) melancholy or tender sadness; =mutter f = Hebamme. [boil. ulcer.]

Wehne prov. (⸗⸗) [ndd.: wen] f ⑱ (Beule).]

Wehr¹ (⸗) [ahd.: wehren] f ⑯ (auch n ⓒ. f. 2) **1.** defence, (Widerstand) resistance; sich zur ~ setzen to stand on one's defence, to defend o.s., to offer resistance, v. Wilde ꝛc. auch: to stand at bay. — **2.** (bisw. n) (ursprünglich Schutzwaffe, dann Waffe überhaupt) weapon (of defence); mit ~ und Waffen fully armed, fully equipped (for battle); vgl. Schutzwehr. — **3.** (bewaffnete Schar) body of armed men, guard, troops pl.

Wehr² ⓞ (⸗) [mhd.: weir: wehren] n ⓒ. dike, dam; Wasserbau: (Abdämmung zum Stauen des Wassers) weir.

Wehr¹-anstalten (⸗⸗…) f pl. ② preparations pl. for defence.

wehrbar (⸗⸗) a. ⑥⑥ = wehrhaft.

Wehr²-bau ⓞ (″…) m ②, pl. =bauten = Wehr²; **=baum** m bar(rier); **=bezirk** m military district; **=damm** ⚓ m e-s Hafens: mole.

wehren (⸗⸗) [ahd.] ⑱ **I** sich 2 v/refl.: a) to defend o.s.; (Widerstand leisten) to offer (or make) resistance, to resist; sich mit aller Macht, aus Leibeskräften, mit Hand und Fuß 2 to resist with all one's might, auch: to fight tooth and nail; b) mit gen.: sich i-s Lebens, Leibes, seiner Haut 2 to defend o.s. to the utmost or to the last, to fight for one's life; sich e-r Sache mutig 2 to resist a th. manfully, to offer courageous opposition to a th. — **II** v/a. u. v/n. (h.): et. 2 (hindern) to prevent (or obviate, check) a th.; e-m Angriffe 2 to repel an attack; (abwenden) to avert; dem Feuer 2 to arrest (or check) the progress of fire or the flames; e-m et. 2 to keep (or prohibit, restrain, stop) a p. from doing a th.; (ihm et. verbieten) to forbid a p. to do a th.; wer will es 2 (verwehren)? who will prevent it?

Wehr¹-gehenk ⚔ (″…) n ⑱ shoulder- (or sword-)belt; **=geld** n f. Wergeld; **=gesetz** n law relating to military service. parl. auch: army-bill; **=gestell** n: a) guard; b) ⚔ stand for arms.

wehrhaft (⸗⸗) a. ⑥⑥ able to defend (or protect) o.s. or to bear arms; (mannbar) able-bodied, manful, valiant, F full of fight; 2 m. to arm; ~igkeit f ⑯ ability to defend o.s. or to bear arms, auch: defensive capacity, fighting-power; weits. (Mut) valour.

Wehr¹-kraft (″…) f ② defensive (or armed) force; 2los a. ⑥⑥ defenceless, unarmed, unprotected; ?: in ermous; 2 m. to disarm; =losigkeit f defencelessness; =losmachung f disarmament; =macht f defensive force; =mann m warrior, soldier, engS. man of the reserve or militia; =mannschaft f body of soldiers, engS. (army-)reserve, militia; =ordnung f regulations pl. concerning military service; =pflicht ⚔ f obligation (or liability) to serve in the army; allgemeine ~ universal military service; 2pflichtig a. bound (or liable) to serve in the army; =stand m (ant. Lehr= und Nähr=stand) military profession, profession of arms; coll. the military, the army; (all) soldiers pl.; =verfassung ⚔ f military organization; =vorlage f, parl. army-bill; =wolf m ⁺⁺ = Werwolf; =zahn m des Ebers ꝛc.: tusk.

Weh-stand (⸗⸗) m ② sad (or sorrowful) condition.

Weib (⸗) [ahd.: wife] n ④c. **1.** (ant. Mann) woman, female; böses ~ vixen, termagant; schönes ~ handsome woman, beautiful (or lovely) creature; die ~er womankind, the (fair) sex. — **2.** (Gattin) wife, spouse, co. better half; e-m f-e Tochter zum ~ geben to give a p. … in marriage; zum ~e nehmen to take for a wife, to marry, to wed.

Weibchen (⸗⸗) n ② (dim. von Weib) **1.** little woman or wife, wifie. — **2.** zo. allgemein: female, v. Vögeln: hen.

We(i)bel (⸗⸗) [ahd.] m ② (bsd. schweizerisch) usher of the court, vgl. Feldwebel.

Weiber-art (″…) f ② women's way(s pl.) or manner(s pl.); **=feind** m womanhater, ⚕ misogynist; **=feindschaft** f: a) ⚕ feind: hatred of (or for) women, ⚕ misogyny; b) (Feindschaft zw. Weibern) enmity between women; **=geklatsch** ⓒ n women's gossip or prattle; **=gelüst(e)** n woman's longing or passion(ate desire); **=geschrei** n crying (or screaming) of women; **=geschwätz** n, **=gewäsch(e)** F n = =geklatsch; **=gunst** f favour of women; Sprichw. ~ ist wie Aprilwetter a woman's favour is as fickle as the weather in April.

weiberhaft (⸗⸗) a. ⑥⑥: a) g.s. womanlike, like a woman, womanly, feminine; b) b.s. (weibisch) womanish, unmanly, effeminate.

Weiber-haß (″…) m ② = =feindschaft; **=hasser** m = =feind; **=held** m lady-killer, (gay) Lothario; **=herrschaft** f rule of women, feminism, ⚕ gynarchy, F co. petticoat-government; **=kenntnis** f knowledge of women or the fair sex; **=kleid** n woman's dress; **=knecht** m ladies' man; **=kram** m women's knickknacks or paraphernalia or things pl.; **=krankheit** f women's disease or malady or complaint; **=laune** f woman's fancy or caprice; **=leh(e)n** n Kunkellehen; **=liebe** f: a) woman's love; b) love for women, bisw.: ⚕ philogyny; **=list** f women's cunning or artfulness; **=männig** a. ⑥⑥ = gynandrian; **=narr** m amorous fool, one who is mad after women, F one who runs after every petticoat; **=raub** m abduction (or rape) of women; **=rechtlerin** f woman pleading women's right(s), feminist, pol. suffragette; **=regiment** n = =herrschaft; **=rock** m woman's dress or gown; (Unterrock) petticoat; **=rolle** f, thea. female part; 2scheu a. shy (or afraid) of women; **=sommer** m = Altweibersommer; **=staat** m women's finery; pol. state ruled by women; **=stimme** f female or woman's (or womanish) voice; hohe (tiefe) ~ soprano (contralto); 2toll a. womanmad, mad after women; **=tracht** f woman's apparel; **=volk** n womankind, F womenfolk; women pl.; the fair (or gentle, weaker) sex; **=zwinger** m = Harem.

…weibig ♀ (…⸗⸗) a. ⑥⑥ nur mit vorangehender Zahl, z.B. drei2 with three pistils, ⚕ trigynous, trigynous.

[…weibig]

⚕ scientific; ♀ botanical; ⚘ geography; ⓞ machinery; ⛏ mining; ⚔ military; ⚓ marine; ⊕ commercial; ✉ postal; 🚂 railway

[weibisch] — 1104 — [Weidengeflecht]

weibisch(⌣) a. ⓖ womanish, unmanly; (weichlich) effeminate; sich ⁓ (adv.) benehmen to behave like a woman; ⁓ werden to grow effeminate.

weiblich(⌣) [mhd.] a. ⓖ (ant. männlich) 1. feminine (auch gr.); zo., &c. female (f. Geschlecht 2 u. 3); (Frauen gezierend) womanly; pol. ⁓es Stimmrecht women's (right to) vote, female suffrage; Anhängerin des ⁓en Stimmrecht(e)s woman suffragist, (fr.) suffragette; das ewig ⁓e the eternal(ly) feminine, true womanliness; die Hexen in Macbeth haben wenig ⁓es an sich … have little that is feminine (or womanly) about them. — 2. = weibisch. — 3. pros. Der (zweisilbiger) Reim feminine (or female, double) rhyme.

Weiblichkeit(⌣-) n ⓖ woman's character or nature or frailty; feminine grace or qualities pl.; womanly conduct, womanliness, bisw.: feminality.

Weibling ⌇ (⌣) m ⓓd. effeminate fellow. F milksop, mollycoddle.

Weibs-bild (⌣⌢) n ⓖ (big) woman, (strong) female, contp. wench; schlechtes ⁓ F low huzzy, baggage, P bitch; schmutziges ⁓ slut.

Weibsen P (⌣) n ⓖ = Weibsbild.

Weibs-leute (⌣…) pl. ⓖ women, females pl. (f. a. Weibervolk); **-person** f, **-stück** n = -bild; **-volk** n = Weibervolk.

weich[1] (¹) [ahd.: weich; weichen] a. ⓖ (ant. hart u. fest) 1. soft, mild; (mürbe) mellow, vgl. breiweich; (zart) tender, delicate; (geschmeidig) supple, pliant, yielding; (schwach) weak (vgl. weichlich); sich ⁓ anfühlend soft to the touch, von dichten Wollstoffen ꝛc. auch: fluffy; ⁓ m. to make soft or tender, to soften; ⁓ w. to grow soft or tender, to soften. — 2. ⁓e, ⁓ gekochte oder gesottene Eier gently (or soft, lightly) boiled eggs, a. soft eggs pl.; Eier ⁓ kochen to boil eggs gently or soft; Fleisch ⁓ kochen to boil meat until (it is) tender; ⁓es (wenig Kalk enthaltendes Fluß-, Regen-) Wasser soft water; ♪ ⁓e Tonart minor key; ⁓e Töne soft (or sweet, melodious) notes pl.; ⊕ metall. ⁓es Eisen soft (or pure) iron; Stahl ⁓ m. to soften (durch Entkohlung: to decarbonize) steel. — 3. fig. in Bezug aufs Gemüt, Herz: soft, tender, delicate, sensitive; ⁓es Gemüt, Herz gentle disposition, sympathetic heart; ⁓ (adv.) gestimmt in a gentle mood; ihm wird ganz ⁓ ums Herz he feels deeply moved or affected, his heart is melting.

Weich[2]**-bild** (⌣⌢) [ahd.; *lt. vicus] n ⓞc. (Stadtgebiet) precincts (or environs) pl. of a town; municipal area or district.

Weich[1]**-blei** (⌢…) n ⓖ metall. soft (or refined) lead; **-bottich** m = -faß.

Weiche[1] 🜨 (⌣) [weichen] f ⓖ siding, shunt(ing[-place]), turn-out (place), switch; selbsttätige ⁓ self-acting (or automatic) switch, a. spring-switch.

Weiche[2] (⌣) [weich] f ⓖ 1. [ahd.] softness, soft (or weak) part (vgl. Weichheit). — 2. [mhd.] anat. meist ⁓n pl. (knochenlose Stelle zw. Rippen u. Lenden) groin, side.

weichen[1] (⌣) [ahd.: weich] I ⓖ v/a. u. v/n. (h. u. ſn) 1. to soften. — II ⓖaft. v/n. (ſn, bisw. h.) 2. (nachgeben) to yield, to give (or make) way, nur fig. to give in; (sich entfernen) to withdraw, to go away; (sich zurückziehen) to retire, ↖ to (effect a) retreat, to beat a (hasty) retreat; (v. der Stelle rücken) to move, to change one's position, to shift; f. wanken I; ⊛ Börse: die Kurse ⁓ prices are dropping or declining or on the downgrade; (all the) stocks and shares are going down. — 3. mit prp.: aus den Fugen ⁓ to come undone or unglued; e-m nicht von der Seite ⁓ not to budge from a p.'s side, F to hang on to a p.; von der Stelle ⁓ to shift (or change) one's position; nicht von der Stelle ⁓ not to budge (or move) an inch; nie vom Pfade der Tugend ⁓ never (once) to forsake the path of virtue; ↓ von der Küste ⁓ to make for the offing. — 4. ⊛ (im Preise fallen) to decline, to (have a) fall, to go down, to recede. — III ~ n ⓖ 5. (f. I) — Erweichung. — 6. (f. II) yielding, &c.; e-n zum ⁓ bringen to make a p. yield, ↖ den Feind: to cause the enemy's ranks to waver, to drive the enemy back; ⊛ die Kurse kommen ins ⁓, sind im ⁓ prices are giving way or easing off or receding; vgl. 2 am Ende.

Weichen[2]**-bedienung** 🜨 (⌣…) [Weiche¹] f ⓖ management of switches; vgl. -stellung; **-bock** m switch-box; **-bruch** [Weiche²] m, path.: ⚕ inguinal rupture; **-gegend** f, anat. groin, ⚕ inguinal region; **-hebel** m switch-lever; **-hebelapparat** m switch-stand; **-schiene** f siding-(or slide-, switch-)rail; **-signal** n switch-signal; **-steller** m pointsman, switchman, switcher; **-stellung** f shifting of the points, switch-turning, switching; vgl. -bedienung; **-stellwerk** n central switch-stand or switch-work; **-vorrichtung** f switcher-gear; **-wärter** m = -steller; **-wechsel** m = -stellung; **-zunge** f switch-tongue.

Weich[1]**-faß** ⊙ (⌢…) n ⓖ Brauerei ꝛc.: steeping-cistern or -trough or -tub or -vat; **-flosser** m/pl. ichth.: ⚕ malacopterygians pl.; **-fresser** m, orn. insect-eating (⚕ insectivorous) bird; ⁓gekocht, ⁓gesotten a. ⓖ f. weich 2; ⁓gestimmt a. in a gentle (or yielding) mood; ⁓haarig a. soft-haired.

Weichheit(⌣-) f ⓖ softness, v. Obst: mellowness, v. Fleisch ꝛc.: tenderness; fig. v. Gemüt, Herz, a.: gentleness, tenderness; (Schwäche) weakness.

weich[1]**-herzig** (⌢…) a. ⓖ soft-(or tender-)hearted; **-herzigkeit** f ⓖ soft-(or tender-)heartedness; ⁓hufig a. bsd. v. Pferden: with soft (or tender) hoofs; **-käse** m cream-cheese; **-kübel** ⊙ m = -faß.

weichlich(⌣) a. ⓖ too soft or tender; (schlaff) limp, flabby, flaccid, fig. (weibisch) effeminate; (lässig) indolent; (schwächlich) weakly, von Kindern auch: F peaky, vom Stil ꝛc. auch: emasculate, tame, insipid, paint. der Pinselstrich delicate blending of colours; ⁓ (adv.) aufgezogen delicately brought up; **-keit** f ⓖ (overgreat) softness or tenderness, limpness, flabbiness; effeminacy; weakly nature, weakness.

Weichling(⌣) m ⓓd.: a) weakling, weakly (or delicate, effeminate) man, F molly (coddle); b) ⦿ (Wollstifling) voluptuary. **Weich**[1]**-machen** (⌢…) n ⓖ softening; ⁓mäulig a. ⓖ von Pferden: tender-mouthed; ⁓mütig(keit f) a. = ⁓herzig (-keit); ⁓schalig a. with soft shells or skins, soft-shelled, von Früchten: soft-skinned; **-schiene** f = Weichenschiene.

Weichsel[1] (⌣tʃ) f ⓖ ♀ (in die Ostsee fließender Strom) the Vistula.

Weichsel[2] (⌣tʃ) f [mhd., *lit. wyszna kirsche] f ⓖ = Weichselkirsche.

Weichsel-gegend (⌢tʃ…) f ⓖ basin (or banks pl.) of the (river) Vistula; **-holz** n ⓖ mahaleb wood; **-kirsch-baum** ♀ m mahaleb (Prunus Ma'haleb); **-kirsche** ♀ f mahaleb- (or perfumed) cherry; **-rohr** n cherry-wood tube for pipes; **-zopf** [poln. wieszczyce] m. path. elf-lock, Polish plait, ⚕ plica (polonica).

Weich[1]**-tier** (⌢…) n ⓖ zo. mollusk, Anatomie der ⁓e: ⚕ malacotomy; **-tierkenner** m: ⚕ malacologist; **-wanze** f, ent. plant-bug, ⚕ capsid; **-wasser** n water for steeping or soaking; **-werden** n softening, v. Fleisch: growing tender; fig. relenting. ⌊(-ing).⌋

Weid[1] (¹; Hom. Waid ♀) f. inv. hunt⌋ **weidbar** (¹-) a. ⓖ pasturable.

Weide[1] ♀ (⌣) [ahd.: withy] f ⓖ willow (-tree) (Salix); graue ⁓ grey willow, water-willow or -sallow (S. cine'rea), purpurblütige ⁓ purple willow (S. pur'pu'rea); vgl. Korb-, Sal-, Trauer-weide.

Weide[2] (⌣) [ahd.] f ⓖ 1. pasture (-ground), pasturage; (Gemeindeland) common; die Herde auf die ⁓ treiben to drive (or take) the herd to pasture, to graze (or tend) the flock. — 2. (Nahrung) food, fig. auch nutriment, (Augenweide) delight, feast.

Weide[2]**-acker** (⌢…) m ⓖ field serving for pastur(ag)e; **-geld** n fee (paid) for grazing cattle or for the right of pasture; **-land** n pasture-land, grazing-ground. ⌊or osier; willow, osier.⌋ **weiden**[1] ♀ (⌣) a. ⓖ (made) of willow⌋ **weiden**[2] (⌣) [ahd.] I v/n. (h.), v/a. und v/refl. ⓖ 1. vom Vieh, v/n. und sich ⁓ to (go to) pasture, to go to grass, to graze, to feed. — 2. v/a. (auf die Weide führen) to lead cattle to pasture, to tend a flock, to turn (or put) cows, horses, &c. out to grass. — 3. fig. (ergötzen) to delight; seine Augen, Blicke an et. ⁓ to feast one's eyes on a th., boshaft: to gloat over a th. — II ~ n ⓖ 4. pastur(ag)e, grazing.

weiden[3]**-artig** ♀ (⌢…) [Weide¹] a. ⓖ willow-like, willowy, …ish, osier-like, ⚕ salicaceous; **-asche** f ⓖ willow-ashes pl.; **-bach** m stream fringed (or edged) with willows; **-band** n rope of willow-twigs, withe; **-bast** m, hort. bast (or inner bark) of willows; **-bastgeflecht** n zu Hütten: willow-sheets pl.; **-baum** ♀ = Weide¹; **-bitter** n, chem. salicin(e) ($C_{13}H_{18}O_7$); **-blatt** n wi.-leaf; **-blattkäfer** m, ent. wi.-beetle (Chryso-me'la vitelli'na); **-bohrer** m, ent. goat-moth (Cossus lignipe'rda); **-busch** m wi.-bush; **-gebüsch**, **-gehölz** n wi.-plot or -ground or -plantation; **-geflecht** n

[Weidengerte] — 1105 — [Wein]

wicker-work; =gerte f osier switch; =holz n willow-wood; =holz-bohrer m = =bohrer; =kätzchen n wi.-catkin; =korb m wicker basket; =kranz m willow-crown or wreath; =pflanzung f = =gebüsch; =röschen ⚥ n willow-herb (Epilo'bium); schmalblätteriges ~ French willow (Ep. angustifo'lium); zottiges ~ codlings-and-cream (Ep. hirsu'tum); =rute f = =gerte; =staude f willow-bush or -shrub.
Weide²-**nutzung** (˝˘) f ⊕ pasturage.
Weiden³=**wespe** (˝...) f ⊕ ent. willow-sawfly; =zweig m willow-twig.
Weide²-**platz** (˝...) m ⊕ pasture-ground; =recht n right of pasture.
Weiderich ⚥ (˘˘)[mhd.] m ⊕d.: a) willow-weed (Lythrum); b) = Weidenröschen.
Weide²=**vieh** (˝...) n ⊕ grazing cattle; ⚥**wund** a. ⊕ = weidwund.
weid=**gerecht** (˝...) a. ⊕ hunt. = jagd-gerecht; =**gesell**(**e**) ⚥ m ⊕ fellow-huntsman. =**gesell**(**e**) [willow-plot.]
Weidicht (˘˘) [ahd.; *Weide¹] n ⊕c.
weidlich (˘˘)[mhd.; *Weid] a. ⊕ 1. (frisch) lively; (rüstig) hardy, lusty. — 2. ⊕ adv. (gehörig) thoroughly, greatly, well, F with a vengeance; ⚥ schmausen to dine sumptuously, F to have a good feed.
Weidling ⚥ (˘˘) m ⊕d. = Champignon.
Weid=**mann** (˝˘) [mhd.] m ⊕c. hunts-man, hunter, sportsman. F co. Nimrod.
weid=**männisch** (˘˘˘) a. ⊕ huntsmanlike, sportsmanlike, adv. like a hunter.
Weidmann(**s**)=**kunst** (˝˘...) f ⊕ = Jagd 2; =**sprache** f hunting-terms pl., language of the chase or the hunting-field.
Weid=**messer** (˝˘) n ⊕ hunting-knife, hanger; vgl. Hirschfänger.
Weidner† (˘˘) [mhd.] m ⊕ = Weidmann.
Weid=**sack** (˝...) m ⊕ = Jagdtasche; =**spruch** m: a) hunter's maxim or motto; b) favourite saying; =**werk** n: a) chase, hunt(ing), huntsmanship; dem ~ obliegen to go hunting or shooting; b) (Wild) game; ⚥**wund** a. ⊕ vom Wilde: wounded (or injured) in the bowels.
Weife ⊕ (˘)[mhd.] f ⊕ (Haspel) reel; **weifen** v/a. u. v/n. (h.) ⊕ to reel yarn.
weigern (˘˘)[ahd.: (Ge)weih] ⊕ a. I v/a.: e-m et. ⚥ to refuse a p. a th. (= ver-weigern). — II v/refl. sich ⚥ et. zu tun to refuse (or decline) to do a th., stärker: to rebel (or kick) against a th. — III ~ n ⊕ u. **Weigerung** f ⊕ refusal; hartnäckige Weigerung point-blank refusal; stubborn resistance, firm (or determined, stout) opposition.
Weigerungs=**fall** (˘˘˘˘) m ⊕: im ~(e) in case of refusal, ⊕ in case of non-acceptance of a bill. [(Falco milvus).]
Weih¹ (˘) [ahd.] m ⊕ (⊕c.) orn. kite
Weih²=**altar** (˝...) [weih-en] m ⊕ eccl. consecrated (or holy) altar; =**becken** n holy-water font or stone or stock, aspersorium; =**bild** n sacred image; =**bischof** m suffragan (bishop).
Weihe¹ (˘˘) m ⊕, f ⊕ = Weih¹.
Weihe² (˘˘) [ahd.: weihen] f ⊕ 1. con-secration (a. eccl.), einer Kirche: dedi-cation, eines Priesters: ordination; die ~(n) empfangen to be(come) ordained, to take holy orders. — 2. fig. (hohe, heilige Kraft) (divine) inspiration; poet's sacred fire; (Salbung) unction, pathos.

— 3. (Einweihung, Einführung) initia-tion, inauguration.
weihen(˘˘)[ahd.] I v/a. u. sich ⚥ v/refl. ⊕ 1. to consecrate, eine Kirche ⚥c.: to de-dicate, einen Geistlichen: to ordain, Brot, Wasser ⚥c. zum Gottesdienste: to bless; dem Dienste Gottes ⚥ to dedicate to the service of God; sich ⚥ I. to take (or receive) holy orders. — 2. fig. (mit hoher, heiliger Kraft erfüllen) to fill with a sacred fire or strength, (heiligen) to hallow, to sanctify; (widmen) to de-vote; sein Leben der Wissenschaft ⚥ to give up (or devote) one's life to scientific pursuits. — II ~ n ⊕ 3. f. Weihe⁷ 1. — III **ge**=**weiht** p.p. u. a. ⊕ 4. Bed. des inf.; den Göttern ⚥ sacred (or dedicated, consecrated) to the gods. — 5. dem Tode, dem Untergange ⚥ doomed to death, to destruction.
Weiher¹ [ahd.; *lt. viva'rium n] m ⊕ (small) pond, (Fischteich) fish-pond.
Weihe²=**rede** (˘˘...) f ⊕ solemn speech; =**stunde** f sacred (or solemn) hour; =**voll** a. ⊕ solemn; pathetic.
Weih²=**gabe** (˝...) f ⊕ = =geschenk; =**gelübde** n sacred (or solemn) vow; =**geschenk** n oblation, consecrated (or votive) gift or offering; =**kessel** m = =becken.
Weih=**nacht** (˝˘) [mhd. weih † a. = heilig], ~**en** [dat.] pl.: a) f ⊕ (~ en ⊕ 23) (Fest der Geburt Christi, 25. Dezember) Christmas (oft abbr. Xmas); vgl. Weih-nachtsfest; b) ~(en) m = =gabe.
weih=**nachtlich**(˘˘ ˘˘) a. ⊕ (of or relating to) Christmas, F Christmassy.
Weih=**nachts**=**abend**(˝˘ ˘chts...)m⊕Christ-mas-eve, Christmas Eve; =**baum** m Chr.-tree; =**feier** f, =**fest** n celebration of Christmas, Chr.-festivities pl., eccl. auch: Feast of Christ's nativity; =**gabe** f, =**geschenk** n Chr.-present, für die Dienstboten ⚥c.: Chr.-box; =**kind** n the child Jesus; =**lied** n Chr.-carol; =**mann** m (old) Father Christmas, als Freund der Kinder: Santa Claus; =**markt** m Chr.-fair; =**messe** f. eccl. Chr.-matins pl.; =**rose** ⚥ f Chr.-rose (Helle'borus niger); =**sänger** m/pl. waits; =**tag** m Christmas Day, zweiter: Boxing Day; =**zeit** f Christmas-time or -tide, Yule-tide.
Weih=**rauch** (˝˘) [ahd.] m ⊕c. (o. pl.) 1.(Harz) frankincense, incense.— 2.fig. (schmeichelndes Lob) incense, flattery, adulation, fulsome praise; e-m ~ streuen oder opfern to flatter a p., ⚥ to laud (or praise) a p. to the skies, F to give a p. (plenty of) butter.
Weih=**rauch**=**büchse** (˝˘ ˘...) f ⊕ incense-box; =**dampf** m fumes pl. of incense.
weih=**räuchern** (˝˘˘) v/n. (h.) ⊕ a*⚥*: e-m ⚥ to cense a p., fig. to flatter (F to butter up) a p.
Weih=**rauch**=**faß** (˝˘ ˘ch...) n ⊕ Cath.eccl. censer, ⚥ thurible; =**faß**=**träger** m, eccl.: ⚥ thurifer; =**harz** n, pharm.: indisches ~ olibanum; =**körner** n/pl. grains pl. of (frank)incense; =**strauch** m thuriferous shrub, bjb. Boswe'llia glabra.
Weih²=**tafel** (˝˘˘) f ⊕ votive tablet.
Weihung (˘˘) f ⊕ = Weihe² 1, 3B. ~ der Hostie ⚥c.: consecration of the host, &c.
Weih²=**wasser** (˝˘˘) n ⊕ eccl. consecrated (or holy) water; =**wasser**=**becken** n, =**kessel**

m = =becken; =**wedel** m holy-water sprinkle, aspergillum, asperge.
weil (˘)[mhd. while; *dieweil (Weile)] cj. 1. den Grund bezeichnend: because, schwächer: since, as; (insofern) in as much as; ⚥ nun doch, ⚥ nun einmal considering (or seeing) that; nicht ⚥ not that; er kam nicht, ⚥ sein Sohn krank war ... because his son was ill, auch: ... because (or on account) of (or owing to) his son's illness; oft durch Partizipialkonstruktion zu übersetzen: a) bei gleichem Subjekte: sie fürchtete sich, ⚥ sie allein war being alone she felt afraid, auch: she felt afraid because (or on account) of her being alone; b) bei verschiedenem Subjekte: wir wurden ängstlich, ⚥ er nicht schrieb we grew anxious because (or on ac-count) of his not writing; ⚥ dem nun so ist, kann ich ihm nicht helfen now this being the case, I cannot assist him. — 2. fast †, noch poet., die Dauer bz.: whilst, while, as long as; freut euch des Lebens, weil noch das Lämp-chen glüht (USTERI) make the best of your life while its lamp is aglow; das Eisen schmieden, ⚥ es noch warm ist to strike the iron while it is hot.
weil. abbr. = weiland.
weiland (˘˘) [ahd.: whilom] adv. once (upon a time), formerly, of old, of yore, poet. auch: whilom.
Weilchen (˘˘) n ⊕ dim. von Weile; wart' ein ~ wait a little while or F a bit.
Weile (˘˘) [ahd. while] f ⊕ 1. while, short space of time; eine ganze (ge-raume, gute ob. lange) ~ a (good) long while or time; eine kleine, kurze ~, ein Weilchen (for) a short time, for a (little) while; über eine kleine ~ (with)in a short time, before (or ere) long, later on; damit hat es gute ~ (keine Eile) there is no hurry (about it), it will all come in good time; Zeit und ~ mit et. verlieren to waste one's time over a th.; Sprichw. s. Ding 4; adv. f. mittler⚥; bei nächtlicher ~ at night-time, during the night. — 2. (Muße) leisure; Sprichw. eile mit ~ (the) more haste, (the) less (or worse) speed.
weilen (˘˘) [ahd. while] v/n. (h.) ⊕ ⊕ to stay (on), seltener: to abide; (säumen) to tarry, linger, loiter; wo mag er nur ⚥? where can he be now?, I wonder where he may be (all this while); seine Blicke weilten auf dem Bilde his eyes (or glances) rested on the picture.
Weiler (˘˘) [ahd.; *lt. villa're n] m ⊕ hamlet, small village or parish.
Weimuts=**kiefer**⊥(˘˘˘˘)[Lord Weymouth] f ⊕ ⚥ Weymouth pine (Pinus strobus).
Wein¹ (˘) [ahd.: wine; *lt. vinum n] m ⊕c. 1. wine (f. Faß 1); roter, weißer ~ = Rotwein, Weißwein; er hat die besten ~e, oft: he has one of the best cellars (of wine); fig. s. ein-schenken. — 2. weitS. (geistiges Getränk gebrauert) ~ = Branntwein; f. Apfel-wein ⚥c. — 3. ~(rebe) vine; wilder ~ Virginia creeper (Ampelo'psis hedera'cea); ~ bauen, pflanzen to cultivate the vine, to grow wine. — 4. (Trauben) den ~ lesen to gather (in) the grapes or the vintage, ~ keltern to press the grapes.

♪ Musik; ⚛ Wissenschaft; ⚥ Pflanze; ⚥ Geographie; ⊕ Technik; ✕ Bergbau; ⚔ Militär; ⚓ Marine; ⊕ Handel; ✉ Post; 🚂 Eisenbahn.

[Wein=...] — 1106 — [Weise]

Wein²=... (ᵘ...) [wein-en] f. Weinkrampf ꝛc.
wein¹=ähnlich (ᵘ...) a. ⊕ winy, vinaceous; **=apfel** m ⊕ wine-apple; **=arm** a. producing (but) little wine, lacking wine; **=bau** m cultivation of the vine, vine-culture, wine-growing, viticulture; **=bauer** m wine-grower, viticulturist; **=becher** m wine-cup, größer: goblet; **=beere** f grape; **=beer-hülse** f skin of grapes; **=beer-kern** m grape-stone; **=beer-saft** m grape-juice; ⁀**befränzt** a. vine-clad; **=bereitung** f making of wine; **=berg** m vineyard, bibl. der ~ des Herrn the vineyard of the Lord; **=bergs-besitzer** m owner of vineyards or a vineyard; **=bergs-schnecke** f s. Schnecke 1 a; **=bergs-schutz** m keeper of (the) vineyards; ⁀**bewachsen** a. overgrown with vines; **=blatt** n vine-leaf; **=blatt-laus** f, ent. vine-fretter, ☞ phylloxera; **=blume** f perfume (or aroma) of wine, vgl. Blume 2 a; **=blüte** f vine-blossom, Zeit der ~ flowering (season) of the vine; **=bohrer** m, ent. vine-borer (Prionus laticollis); **=butte** f kind of hod for carrying the grapes, (Kufe) wine-coop; **=drossel** f, orn. redwing (Turdus iliacus).

weinen (ᴸᵛ) [ahd.: whine: weh(e)] **I** v/n. (h.), v/a. und v/refl. ⊛ to weep, to cry, to shed tears; (schluchzen) to sob, F to snivel; um e-n ≥ to bewail a p.(‛s loss); vor Freude ≥ to weep for joy; Krokodilstränen ≥ to shed crocodile('s) tears; sich tot ob. zu Tode ≥ to cry o.s. to death; sich (acc.) blind, sich (dat.) die Augen aus dem Kopfe ≥ to cry one's eyes out; ≥d weeping, crying, in tears, auch: lachrymose, ein ~der a p. shedding (or in) tears.
— **II** ~ n ⊗ weeping, &c. (f. I); e-n zum ~ bringen to move a p. to tears, to make a p. cry.

Weinerei (-ᵛᵢ) f ⊕ = Geweine.
weinerlich (ᴸᵛ) a. ⊕: mir ist, wird ≥ (zumute) I feel in a crying mood, I feel inclined to weep; ≥es Lustspiel lachrymose comedy; in ≥em Tone in a whining (or whimpering, F snivelling) tone; ≥es Wesen, a. **~keit** f ⊕ crying mood, tearful nature; whining (or lachrymose) tone.

Wein¹=ernte (ᵘ...) f ⊕ vintage; ⁀**erzeugend** a. ⊕ wine-producing, **=essig** m vinegar made from wine; **=farbe** f winy colour, colour of wine; **=farben**, ⁀**farbig** a. wine-coloured, vinaceous; **=faß** n: a) w.-cask or -butt; b) (starker Trinker) w.-bibber; **=flasche** f w.-bottle; für die Tasche: wine-flask; **=fleck** m stain from wine; **=fuhre** f load of wine (-casks); **=garten** m vineyard; **=gärtner** m vine-dresser; **=gärung** f fermentation of wine, chm. vinous ferm.; **=gegend** f wine-growing district or country; wine-country; **=gehalt** m vinous quality, vinosity; **=geist** m spirit(s) of wine, alcohol; ⁀**geisthaltig** a. spirituous, alcoholic; **=geistmesser** m: ☞ alcohol(o)meter; **=gelag(e)** n wine-party; **=gelände** n vine-clad hill; **=geländer** n trellis for (training) vines; **=geruch** m bouquet (or flavour) of wine; **=geschäft** n wine-

merchant's business; **=geschmack** m winy taste: **=glas** wine-glass; vgl. Römer²; **=gott** m god of wine, Bacchus; ⁀**grün** a. v. Fässern: seasoned by (or for) wine; **=hacke** f hoe (used) for vine-yards.
weinhaft (ᴸᵛ) a. ⊕ = weinicht.
wein¹=haltig (ᵘ...) a. ⊕ vinous; **=handel** m ⊕ wine-trade; **=händler** m w.-merchant, bsd. ehm.: vintner; **=handlung** f: a) w.-shop, auch: bodega; b) = =geschäft; **=haus** n w.-vaults pl.; auch Handlung a; **=heber** ⊕ m siphon for drawing (off) wine; **=hefe** f dregs (or lees) pl. of wine; **=honig** m: ☞ œnomel; **=hügel** m vine-clad hill, vineyard (situated on a hill); **=hülse** f skin of grapes.

weinicht, ...**ig** (ᴸᵛ) a. ⊕ (tasting or smelling) like wine, of a winy flavour or taste; winy, vinous; weiniger Auszug vinous tincture or extract.

Wein¹=jahr (ᵘ...) n ⊗ (good, bad) wine-year; **=kalt(e)schale** f, etwa: cold wine-soup; **=kanne** f w.-can or -jug; **=karaffe** f w.-decanter; **=karte** f wine-card, price-list of wines; **=kauf** m buying (or purchase) of wine; **=keller** m wine-cellar or -vaults pl.; **=kelter** ⊕ f w.-press; **=kenner** m connoisseur (or good judge) of wine; **=kneipe** f w.-shop; feinere = =stube; **=koster** m w.-taster; **=²krampf** m crying-fit, convulsive (or hysterical) sobbing; **=¹krankheit** f vine-disease; **=kranz** m garland of vine-leaves; **=krug** m wine-jug, tankard; **=kufe** f wine-tub; **=küfer**, **=küper** m w.-cooper; **=kühler** m w.-cooler; **=lage** f position of a vineyard; **=lager** n: a) stock (or store) of wine(s); vgl. =keller; b) (Gestell im Keller) support for wine-casks; **=land** n w.-country; vgl. =gegend; Frankreich ist das erste ~ der Welt ... the greatest w.-producer in the world; **=laub** n foliage of a vine, vine-leaves pl.; **=laube** f vine-arbour or -bower; **=laubstab** m Alt.: staff twined round with vine-leaves, des Bacchus: thyrsus; **=laune** f merry humour produced by wine(-drinking); **=lese** f vintage; zur ~ gehörig vindemial; **=leser(in** f) m vintager, grape-picker; **=lieb-haber** m lover of wine; **=lied** n wine-song; **=maß** n wine-measure; **=meister** m: a) steward of the vineyards; b) head butler; **=messer** a) m = =wage; b) n vine-dresser's pruning-knife; **=met** m, pharm. vinous hydromel; **=monat** m wine-month, October; **=most** m must; **=mutter** f = =hefe; **=niederlage** f = =lager a; **=palme** ♀ f toddy-palm (bsd. Caryota); **=pan(t)scher** m adulterator of wine, one who doctors wine; **=pfahl** m = Rebpfahl; **=presse** f w.-press; **=probe** f: a) tasting of wine; b) sample of wine; **=ranke** f tendril of a vine, vine-branch; **=rausch** m intoxication caused by wine; **=rebe** f: a) ♀ (grape-)vine (Vitis); edle ~ cultivated vine (V. vinifera); b) (Rebenstock) stem of a vine, als Spazierstock: vine-cane; ⁀**reben-artig** ♀ a.: ☞ sarmentaceous; **=rebenzucht** f = =bau; **=rechnung** f wine-bill; ⁀**reich** a. abounding in

wine or vines; **=reisende(r)** m wine-traveller, traveller for a w.-business; **=rose** f eglantine, sweet-briar, -brier (Rosa rubiginosa); ⁀**rot** a. claret-(or ruby-)coloured; **=sauce** f w.-sauce; ⁀**sauer** a. vinous, ☞ chm. tartaric: ≥es Salz tartrate; ≥es Antimonylfalium = Brechweinstein; s. a. Seignettesalz u. =stein; ⁀**säuerlich** a. like sourish wine, weiß. slightly tart; **=säufer** m wine-bibber, bottle-man; **=säure** f: a) acidity of wine; b) u. chm. tartaric acid ($C_2H_6O_6$); **=schank** m: a) retail(ing) of wine; b) = =schenke; **=schank-recht** n wine-license; **=schenk** m keeper of a wine-shop; **=schenke** f w.-shop or -house; **=schlauch** m: a) w.-skin; b) F fig. w.-bibber, guzzler; **=schmierer** m = =pan(t)scher; **=schöne** ⊕ f gelatine for fining wines; **=schröter** m wine-merchant's cellarman or drayman; **=schuld** f debt for wine; **=schwärmer** m, ent.: großer ~ larger vine hawk-moth (Sphinx Elpenor); kleiner ~ lesser vine hawkmoth (S. porcellus); ⁀**selig** a. elevated with wine(-drinking); **=sorten** f/pl. different kinds of wine or grapes; **=spalier** n trellis-work for training vines; **=stein** m (saures weinsaures Kali) tartar, ☞ chm. hydrogen potassium tartrate ($KC_4H_5O_6$); gereinigter ~, auch: **=stein-rahm** m cream of tartar, (lt.) cremor tartari; ⁀**steinartig** a. ☞ tartar(e)ous; **=stein-bildung** f: ☞ tartarization; ⁀**stein-sauer** a. = ⁀sauer chm.; **=stein-säure** ☞ f = =säure b; **=stock** m = =rebe; **=stube** f wine-room at a hotel or public house, auch: w.-shades pl.; **=suppe** f w.-soup; ⁀**tragend** a. w.-producing; **=traube** f bunch of grapes; **=trauben-kur** f grape-cure; **=treber**, **=trester** pl. = Trester; ⁀**trunken** a. drunk with wine; **=und-Speise-wirt** m restaurant-keeper with wine-license; **=verfälscher** m = =pan(t)scher; **=vorrat** m store (or stock) of wine; **=wachs** m growth of wine, guten ~ h. to produce good (or plenty of) wine; **=wage** f wine-gauge, ☞ vinometer, œnometer; **=wetter** n weather favourable for wine-growing; **=wirt (=schaft** f) m = =schenk(e); **=zeche** f wine-score or -bill, ehm. **=zeichen** n tavern-sign, bush; **=zoll** m duty on wine; **=zucht** f = =bau; ⁀**züchter** m = =bauer. **weiß¹**... s. Essen Machen, Sagen, ...tum. **weiß²** (ᴸ; Hom. weiß), **weise¹** imper. v. weisen.
weise² (ᴸᵛ; Hom. Waise) [ahd: wise: wissen] **I** a. ⊕ wise, (lebensklug) prudent, shrewd, F knowing; ≥ Frau = Hebamme, a. = Kartenschlägerin. — **II** ~ ([r] m) f ⊕: ein ~r (der ~) a (the) sage, a (the) wise man; die sieben ~n Griechenlands the seven wise men of Greece; bibl. die drei ~n aus dem Morgenlande the three Kings (or wise men) of the East, the three Magi pl.; s. Stein 1.

Weise³ (ᴸᵛ) [ahd: wise] f ⊛ **1.** manner (vgl. Art¹ 1, das oft mit ~ verbunden wird); (Gewohnheit) habit, custom; (Gebrauch) us(ag)e, (Mode) fashion; gram. mood; ♪ = Melodie; Wort und ~ words pl. and music. — **2.** mit prp.: auf die eine ob. andere ~ in one way or (an)other;

Signs (see page XVII): F familiar; P vulgar; ꟾ flash; ⸜ rare; † obsolete (died); * new word (born); ∴ incorrect; ♪ music.

[...weife] — 1107 — [weit]

auf jede (ober alle) ~ in every way, in any case; auf feine ~ in no wise, by no means; auf folche ~ in such a way, auf welche (ob. was für eine) ~? in what manner or way?, how?; in feiner ~ in no way, not in any way; jeder nach feiner ~ each (one) after his own fashion; machen Sie es nach Ihrer ~ do it (in) your own way.

...weife (..."²ᴸ⸜) adv. (z.B. F⸍⸍+ₐ. 66): a) mit adj.: gewohnter² in the accustomed way; gleicher² likewise; verſteckter² in an underhand way or manner; weitere ſtehen unter den betr. adjectives oder als beſondere Titelköpfe; b) mit nouns, z.B. haufen² in heaps.

Weiſel (ᴸ⸜) [mhd.; *weifen] m 22 ent. (Bienenkönigin) queen-bee.

weifen (ᴸ⸜) [ahd. weiſ¹ (wiſſend) machen] I v/a, v/n. (h.) u. v/refl. 80 1. e-m et. ~ to show a p. s.th. (= zeigen); iro. e-m die Tür (oder die Wege) ~ to show a p. the door; einem die Zähne ~ to show a p. one's teeth, to defy a p. — 2. e-n irgendwohin ~ to direct (or show) a p. to some place. — 3. mit prp.: e-n an e-n ~ to address (or refer) a p. to a p.; man wieſ ihn an den Bürgermeiſter he was referred to the mayor; der Zeiger (metonymiſch: die Uhr) weiſt auf 12 the hand points to twelve; mit den Finger, mit Fingern auf e-n ~ (ob. zeigen) to point (one's fingers) at a p.; e-n aus der Schule, der Stadt ~ (verweiſen) to expel a p. from school, from the town; aus dem Lande ~ to exile; ⚔ Soldaten ins Quartier ~ to billet (or quarter) soldiers; et. von der Hand, von ſich ~ to refuse (or decline, reject) a th. — 4. ~ verweiſen¹, z.B. er will ſich nicht ~ laſſen he won't listen to reason, he won't be taught. — 5. ſ. zurechtweiſen. — II ~ n 23 6. ſ. Weiſung. — III gewiefen p.p. u. a. 66 (D9) 7. in den Bed. des inf. = 8. (feſt, beſtimmt) definite, certain.

Weiſe(r¹) (ᴸ⸜) m 67 ſ. weiſe² II.

Weiſer² (ᴸ⸜) [mhd.: weiſen] m 22 1. ⸜ one who shows or points, pointer, indicator; oft in Zſſgn, z.B. Wegweiſer. — 2. ⊕ (Uhrzeiger) hand (of a clock).

Weisheit (ᴸ⸜) [mhd.; *weiſe] f 46 wisdom; (Klugheit) prudence, shrewdness, discretion; (Wiſſen) knowledge; mit ſ-r ~ zu Ende ſein to be at one's wits' end; Sprichw.: ~ iſt beſſer als Stärke wisdom (or discretion) is better than strength; ſ. freſſen 3.

Weisheits=dünkel (⸜"...) m 62 learned conceit, priggishness; =kram m display (or store) of wisdom, learned stuff or rubbish; =lehre f philosophy; =lehrer m philosopher; =ſpruch m wise sentence, aphorism; =voll a. 66 full of wisdom or learning; =zahn m wisdom-tooth; ſeine =zähne bekommen to cut (or get) one's wisdom-teeth.

weislich (ᴸ⸜) adv. wisely, prudently, shrewdly, discreetly, with prudence.

weis¹=machen ("⸜ᴸ⸜ʒʋ) [ahd.] v/a. 68** e-m et. ~ to make a p. believe a th.; (einem et. vorſpiegeln) to palm a th. off on a p.; das machen Sie andern weis! tell that to the marines!, F I can't

swallow that!; laſſen Sie ſich nichts ~! don't be imposed upon or taken in!

weiß¹ (ᴸ; Hom. weiſ) [ahd.: white] I a. 66 (D6,10) 1. white; her. (ſilberfarbig) argent; ſ. Bohne¹ 2, Fluſs 3; ♀ das ~e Meer the White Sea; eccl. der ~e Sonntag the first Sunday after Easter, auch: Low Sunday; ♀ ~e Ware linen, (linen-) draper's goods pl.; ~e Wäſche clean linen; vgl. kreide=~, ſchnee=~, ſilber=~. — 2. mit verbs: ſ. brennen 9 b; ~ gerben to taw; ~ machen (~en) to make white, to whiten; ~ nähen to do white (needle-)work; fig. einen ~ waſchen to whitewash (or exculpate, excuse) a p. — II s. 67 3. ~e([r] m) f (ant. Farbige(r) white (wo)man, engſ. Caucasian, Aryan, bei den Indianern: paleface; die ~en the white (or Caucasian) races, the whites pl. — 4. 66. berl. F eine ~e a glass of pale Berlin beer. — 5. das ~e: a) im Auge: the white of the eye, path. auf der Hornhaut: 𝛼 the albugo, the leucoma, b) im Ei: the white of the egg, auch: the glair, 𝛼 the albumen, c) in der Scheibe: the bull's-eye. — 6. das ~ the white (colour); etwas ſchwarz auf ~ haben ſ. ſchwarz 4; ~ (Schminke) auflegen to put on white paint; in ~ gekleidet (dressed) in white. [wiſſen.]

weiß² (ᴸ) 1. u. 3. Perſon sg. pres. ind. von/

weiß=ſagen (ᴸⁿ⸜ᴸ⸜) [ahd.] v/a. 68**: a) = wahrſagen, bſd.: to predict, foretell, prophesy; Alt.: to vaticinate; b) mit ſachlichem Subjekt: to presage, to forebode; =ſagend a. 66 predictive, mehr gbr.: prophetic; =ſager(in f 47) m 2 = Wahrſager(in); =ſagung f 46 prediction, prophecy; Alt.: vaticination.

Weiß¹=anſtreichen ("...) n 69 painting white; (Tünchen) whitewashing; =armig a. 66 white-armed; =backen a.: ~es Brot = ~brot; =bäcker m = ~brot-bäcker; =bart m (man with a) white beard; =bärtig a. wh.-bearded; =bier n pale Berlin beer; =bier=ſtube ober =wirtſchaft f bar for (the consumption of) pale Berlin beer; =binder ⊕ m pargeter; =birke ♀ f common white birch (Betula alba); =blätt(e)rig a. 66 white-leaved; =blau a. whitish (or pale) blue; =blech ⊕ n tinned sheet-iron, tin-plate, white metal, auch: tin; =blech=waren ⊕ f/pl. tin(ned iron) ware, auch: tin(ned) goods pl.; =bleiche ⊕ f cotton-bleaching; =blei=erz ⊕ n white lead-ore; cerus(s)ite; =blütig a., med.: 𝛼 leucemic; =blütigkeit f leucemia; =brot n white (wheaten) bread; =brot=bäcker m baker who makes white (wheaten) bread; =buch n in der deutſchen Regierung: White Book; =buche ♀ f (Hagebuche) hornbeam (Carpi´nus Be´tulus); ♀buſig a. white-bosomed; =dorn m = Hagedorn; Frucht des ~ ſhaw.

Weiße (ᴸ⸜) f: a) 67 ſ. weiß¹ II; b) ~ whiteness, white colour.

weißen (ᴸ⸜) I v/a. und v/n. (ſn) 90 to whiten, blanch; (Tünchen) to whitewash. — II ~ n 23 whitening, &c. (ſ. I).

Weiße(r¹) (ᴸ⸜) m 67 ſ. weiß¹ 3.

Weißer² ⊕ (ᴸ⸜) [weißen] m 67 whitener; (Tüncher) whitewasher;

weiß¹=farbig ("...) a. 66 white-coloured, blanched; =fichte ♀ f 62 = Pechtanne; =fiſch m. ichth. whiting, dace (Arten von Gadus, Leuci´scus. &c.), kleinerer in England viel gegeſſener: whitebait; ♀fleckig a. white-spotted; =fuchs m: a) zo. white fox (Vulpes alba); b) (Pferd) light sorrel horse; ♀füßig a. white-footed; ♀gar ⊕ a. Gerberei: tawed (skin, &c.); ſ. a. alaungar; ♀gekleidet a. dressed in white; ♀gelb a. light (or pale) yellow; flaxen; =gerben ⊕ v/a. 66** to taw; =gerber m tawer; =gerberei f tawer's trade or workshop; ♀glühend ⊕ a. white-hot, incandescent; =glühhitze f white heat, incandescence; =gold n platinum; ♀grau a. whitish (or light) grey; =gülden=erz, =güldig=erz n, min. white silver-ore; ♀haarig a. white-haired; ♀halſig a. white-necked; ♀händig a. white-handed; =kohl ♀ m (common) white cabbage (Brassica olera´cea capita´ta); =kopf m (p. with a) white head; ♀köpfig a. white-headed or -haired; =kram m.prov. = =warengeſchäft; =kraut n = =kohl; =kupfer n white tombac, a. = Neuſilber.

weißlich (ᴸ⸜) a. 66 whitish; albescent, canescent; (gebleicht) bleached, blanched.

Weißling (ᴸ⸜) m ⊕d. 1. ichth. = Weißfiſch. — 2. ent. (Schmetterling): 𝛼 pieris.

Weiß¹=mehl ("...) n 69 fine wheaten flour; =näh(t)erei f plain needlework, plain work; =näh(t)erin f seamstress who does plain work; =pappel ♀ f = Silberpappel; =pinſel [weißen] ⊕ m whitewasher's brush; ehm. =ruſsland ♀ npr/n. White Russia; ♀ſcheckig a. 66 white-speckled; ♀ſeiden a. of wh. silk; ♀ſieden ⊕ v/a. 76 ⓔ**: Silber, Stecknadeln ~ to whiten ..., to blanch ...; =ſieder m blancher; =ſpießglanz=erz n, min. antimony-bloom; =ſud=keſſel ⊕ m blanching-boiler or -copper; =tanne ♀ f fir (ſ. Tanne); =waren ⊕ f linen goods pl.; =baumwollene ~ white cotton goods pl.; =waren=geſchäft n linen-warehouse; =waren=händler(in f) m linendraper, jetzt mſt: draper; =wein m white wine; =werden ⊕ n blanching, 𝛼 albication, der Haare ꝛc.: turning wh.; =wurz ♀ f (Polygona´tum) ſ. Salomonsſiegel; =zeug n (household- or house-)linen.

Weistum (ᴸ⸜) [mhd.: wisdom] n ⊕d. ehm. jur. (früherer Urteilsſpruch) precedent.

Weiſung (ᴸ⸜) f 46 showing, indication, direction; (Befehl) order, instruction; ~(en) des Auftraggebers instructions pl. of (or given by) the client.

weit (ᴸ) [ahd.: wide] I a. 66 (D1,6) und adv. 1. (Ausdehnung bezeichnend; ant. eng) wide, spacious, extensive, ample, capacious; (breit) broad; (unmäßig) comprehensive; (unermeßlich) immense, vast, bſd. von Kleidern: zu ~ ſein to be too wide or too full or too loose; ~ (adv.) ausgeſchnitten low(-necked); die ~e Welt the wide (wide) world; in die ~e Welt gehen ob. ziehen to go out into the world; fig. ein ~es Gewiſſen an elastic conscience; ein ~es Gewiſſen haben auch: to have no scruples, to be unscrupulous; die Augen ~ aufmachen to open one's eyes wide; die

𝛼 scientific; ♀ botanical; ♀ geography; ⊕ machinery; ⚒ mining; ⚔ military; ⚓ marine; ● commercial; ✉ postal; 🚂 railway.

[weit] — 1108 — [weitläuf(t)ig

Tür stand 2 offen ... was wide open; *fig.* alle Herzen wurden 2 ... expanded; im Leften Sinne des Wortes in the widest (or most comprehensive) sense of the word. — 2. Längenrichtung bz., auch zeitlich: a) (*ant.* nah) far (off), distant, remote. a long (or great) way off; einen 2en Umweg machen to go a long way round; ein 2er Weg a long way; die Zeit ift nicht mehr 2 ... is not far off, ... is drawing near; b) *adv.* 2 und breit far and wide, far and near; 2 weg far away; so 2 thus far, up to that point; wie 2 wollen Sie uns begleiten? how far do you wish to accompany us?; zwei Meilen 2 two miles off; ganze Meilen 2 some miles away or off, *vgl.* meilen2; *fig.* die Tränen waren mir nicht 2 I was very near (or not far off) crying. — 3. Abstand bezeichnend: s. entfernt 1 und Feld 2; *vgl.* fehlen 3; wir haben noch 2 bis in die Stadt we are still a good distance from the town; es ist nicht mehr 2 von hier it is but a little way from here. — 4. mit *verbs*, meist *fig.*: es 2 bringen to get on (in the world); die Verzweiflung kann e-n so 2 bringen, daß man // despair can drive one so far as to // (*inf.*); das geht zu 2 that's going too far; man ging so 2, ihn zu schimpfen they went so far as to abuse him; ich gehe so 2 zu behaupten, daß // I would venture (so far as) to assert that //; *vgl.* gehen 9 a unter „weit"; ⊙ *typ.* die Zeilen, den Satz 2 halten to drive out the matter of the composition; 2 kommen to get far; es ist 2 mit ihm gekommen he is far gone. he is low down (in the world); ist es so 2 mit dir gekommen? have you come to that? *Sprichw.* mit der Zeit kommt man auch 2 time and patience conquer all things; s. reichen 1; 2 (vorgerückt) sein to be far advanced; so 2 ist es noch nicht, die Sache ist noch nicht so 2 it has not come to that yet; wenn Sie so 2 (fertig) sind when you are ready; wie 2 ist er mit der Arbeit? how far has he advanced (or got on) with his work?; er ist oft sehr 2 weg (mit seinen Gedanken) he is often very absent-minded; es zu 2 treiben to exceed all bounds, to go too far. — 5. mit *adv.*: a) 2her: er ist nicht 2her (stammt aus der Nähe) he comes from near by, he is not a stranger; das ist nicht 2 her (nichts wert) that's not (worth) much; 2 über einen Punkt hinweg sein to be far beyond (or long past) a (certain) point; b) (in)foweit in so far as; so 2 ist es mir gelungen er ist so (or thus) far I have succeeded; er ist so2 genesen, daß er gehen kann he has sufficiently recovered to be able to walk; so 2 Sie es für gut finden as far as you approve of it; er mag so 2 recht haben, aber // he may be right so far, but //; *vgl.* reichen 1; so 2 ich zurückdenken kann as far (back) as I can remember; ich weiß, inwieweit (od. bis wieweit) ich ihm trauen kann ... how far (or up to what point) I may trust him. — 6. zur Steigerung des *comp.* u. *sup.*: ein 2 größerer

Abstand a far greater distance; 2 (auch: Laus) der größte by far the greatest, the biggest by a long way; auch mit *verbs* der Vergleichung: e-n 2 übertreffen, einem 2 überlegen sein to excel a p. by far. — II ~ *n* ⊙c. 7. ⚓ (Schiffsweite) (greatest) width of a ship. — III das ~e *s/n.* ⊙ 8. a) (weite Ferne) das ~e suchen to take to one's heels, to decamp, to abscond, F to hook it; b) das geht ins ~e (Unglaubliche) that's beyond all bounds. — 9. *adv.* (meist klein geschrieben): bei 2em by far; bei 2em besser far (or much, a great deal) better; bei 2em nicht by a long way; bei 2em nicht vollständig far from complete; bei 2em nicht so nett not nearly so nice; von 2em from a distance, from afar.
weit-ab (⎵⎴) *adv.* far away, a long way from here; 2äftig (⎴⎵...) *a.* ⊙ with wide branches; 2aus (⎵⎴) *adv.* by far; 2ausgebreitet (⎴⎵...) *a.* wide-spread; 2ausfehen *a.* s. aussehen 7; 2berühmt *a.* far famed; 2bewundert *a.* much admired; 2blickend *a.* far-sighted.
Weite (⎵⎵) I *f* ⊙ 1. (Ausdehnung) width, spaciousness, extent; amplitude (*ast.* u. *math.*); ~ e-s Gefäßes: capaciousness, e-s Kleides auch: fulness, e-r Röhre: diameter, eines Schraubengangs: pitch, e-r Schußwaffe: bore; *fig.* eines Begriffes: comprehensiveness; ~ des Blicks breadth of view. — 2. ⊙ (large) space, room; ~ im Lichten inside width. — 3. (Ferne) distance, remoteness; in die ~ ziehen to take one's travels abroad, to go on a far journey. — II *n* s. weit III.
weiten (⎵⎴) ⊙ *v/a.* u. *v/refl.* sich 2 to widen, expand, *v.* Schuhen ꝛc. *a.* to stretch.
weiter (⎵⎵) *comp. v.* weit 1. a) *abs.* wider, &c.; more distant; b) mit *a.* oder *adv.*, meist: farther, further, z.B.: 2 entfernt farther off, further removed; am weitesten zurück hindmost. — 2. Fortsetzung bz. — 2 lesen ꝛc. to continue reading, &c.; 2!, nur 2! go on!, proceed!; nicht 2! stop!, not a step farther!; Ausflüchte dulden wir nicht 2 we won't allow any further evasions or excuses; hören Sie 2! listen to what follows!, hear the rest!; 2 niemand, niemand 2 nobody (or no one) else; 2 nichts?, wenn's 2 nichts ist if it's nothing more than that, if that is all; nichts 2 davon! not (or let me not hear) another word about it!; und 2? what then?; anything more?; was 2? what else?, what more?; was ist denn da 2? what harm is there in that?, what does it matter?, what of that?; 2 habe ich nichts zu sagen I have nothing more (or further) to say; 2 hast du keine Schmerzen? (Mozart, Don Juan) have you any further troubles?, is that all you want?; 2 hat es keinen Zweck it has no further (or other) object; und so 2 (*abbr.* usw.) and so forth, and so on, etcetera (*abbr.* &c.). — 3. mit *verbs*: 2 bringen to further, to promote; das bringt mich nicht 2 that does not help me on; e-n Schüler 2 bringen to

get (or push) ... on; 2 führen to carry on, to continue; 2 geben to pass on (to the next); ich kann 2 geh(e)n als du I can walk further (or a longer distance) than you; *vgl.* 2-geh(e)n; e-m 2 helfen to help a p. along; 2 kommen to advance, progress. make headway; nicht 2 können: a) im Sprechen: to break down, to stop short; b) beim Gehen: to be unable to proceed; 2 sagen to retell. to repeat; 2 schicken to (send) forward; 2 treiben to drive (or push) on; 2 wandern. 2 ziehen to go on walking or marching. to continue one's journey or march. — 4. als attributives *a.* further, additional, z.B. alle 2en Forderungen all further claims *pl.*; ohne 2en Aufschub without further delay; in 2en Kreisen in wide(r) circles, widely; ohne 2e Umstände without further (or more) ado, unceremoniously. — 5. als *s/n.*: das ~e ⊙ what follows, the remainder; das ~e morgen the rest (or further details) to-morrow; bis auf 2es (vorläufig) until further notice, for the present; ohne 2es without (further) ado, forthwith; des 2en darlegen to state fully or in detail, to particularize; davon belehrt uns die Geschichte eines (oder des) 2en history gives us full (or exact, circumstantial) information about that.
weiter=befördern ❋ (⎴⎵...) *v/a.* ⊙*a*※※ to forward (on); =beförderung *f* ⊙ u. ❋ forwarding on, (further) dispatch. (re)transmission; =bildung *f* (further) development; =fort *adv.* farther off or on; =führung *f* continuation, e-r Bahn ꝛc.: extension; 2geh(e)n (fortfahren) *v/a.* ⊙*a*※※ to continue, (vorangehen) to go on, to proceed, *vgl.* weiter 3; 2hin *adv.* further (or farther) on or ahead; =marsch *m* continuation of a march. weitern (⎵⎴) *v/a.* und sich 2 *v/refl.* ⊙*a.* = erweitern.
Weiter=reise (⎴⎵...) *f* ⊙ continuation of a journey; auf der ~ in continuing one's journey, while continuing (or during the rest of) one's travels; =schreiten *n* progressive advance; =sendung *f* = beförderung; =umsichgreifen *n* (further) spread.
Weiterung (⎵⎴) *f* ⊙, bsd. ~en *pl.* difficulties, (unnecessary) formalities *pl.*; (Verwicklungen) complications *pl.*
Weiter=ziehen (⎴⎵...)=marsch, =reise.
weit-gehend (⎴⎵...) *a.* ⊙ that goes far, far extending, vast; =gereiste(r) *m* *f* ⊙ great traveller, one who has travelled much; 2greifend *a.* far-reaching, extensive; 2her *adv.* from afar; s. a. weit 5; 2hergeholt *a.* far-fetched; 2hin, 2hinaus *adv.* far away, in the distance; 2läuf(t)ig *a.*: a) distant, (zerstreut) scattered, *v.* Dörfern ꝛc.: straggling, *adv.* far (removed) from each other; 2 verwandt distantly related; 2er Verwandter distant relative; b) (von großem Umfange) wide, extensive, roomy, spacious, stärker: vast; c) (ausführlich, *ant.* gedrängt) detailed, cir-

Zeichen (s. S. XVII): F familiär; P Volkssprache; ⌐ Gaunersprache; ⟋ selten; † alt (auch gestorben); * neu (auch geboren); ⁎ unrichtig

cumstantial, *adv.* with full particulars, at great length; (sehr genau) minute; (zu ausgedehnt) diffuse, prolix, verbose, long-winded, *adv.* in a round-about way; die Sache ist sehr ~ (umständlich) it's a very complicated (or intricate) matter; ~ über et. reden, sich ~ über et. ausbreiten, auslassen to expatiate upon a th.; -**läuf(t)igkeit** *f* (s. ~läuf(t)ig): a) straggling character of a village, &c.; b) width, spaciousness, stärker: vastness; c) circumstantiality; diffuseness, prolixity, intricacy; ~en machen to make difficulties; ~**maschig** *a.* with wide meshes; ~**reichend** *a.* far reaching; ~**schichtig** *a.* with layers wide apart; mst *fig.* (weit ausgedehnt) vast, extensive; -**schichtigkeit** *f* [62] vast extent; ~**schweifig** *a.* = ~läuf(t)ig b und c, auch: circuitous; (langweilig) tedious; -**schweifigkeit** *f* diffuseness, prolixity; tediousness; (Wortschwall) verbosity; ~**sichtig** *a.*: a) *med.* (*ant.* kurzsichtig) long-sighted; b) *fig.* (in die Zukunft schauend) far-sighted, far-seeing; -**sichtigkeit** *f*: a) (*ant.* Kurzsichtigkeit) long-sightedness, ⚗ presbyopia; b) *fig.* far-sightedness, perspicacity; -**sprung** *m* Turnerei: long jump; ~**spurig** *a.* = breitspurig; ~**tragend** *a.* carrying far or to a great distance; von Schußwaffen ꝛc.: of long range; ~**umfassend** *a.* extensive, vast, comprehensive.

Weitung (´˘) *f* [46] (s. weiten) widening, expansion; (Weite) width; (Umfang) circumference, girth.

weit-verbreitet (″...) *a.* [66] widely spread or circulated, prevalent; ~**verzweigt** *a.* widely ramified; ~**vorstehend** *a.* far projecting, salient; -**winkel** ⚙ *m* [62] *phot.* wide-angle lens.

Weizen (´˘) [ahd.: wheat] *m* [23] **1.** *agr.* wheat, F oft: corn; *fig.* mein (sein ꝛc.) ~ blüht my (his, &c.) chances are good or improving, I am (he is, &c.) in luck's way or in clover. — 2. ⚘: a) gemeiner ~ common wheat (*Tri'ticum*); b) englischer ~ English (or duck-bill) wheat (*Tr. tu'rgidum*); polnischer ~ Polish wheat (*Tr. polo'nicum*); c) türkischer ~ = Mais.

Weizen-acker (″˘...) *m* [62] wheat-field; ~**artig** *a.* [66] wh.-like, ⚗ frumentaceous; -**bau** *m*, *agr.* wh.-growing, cultivation of wheat; -**boden** *m* soil adapted for wh.-growing; -**brand** (-**pilz**) ⚘ *m* collarbags (*Ustila'go se'getum*); -**brot** *n* wheaten bread; -**ernte** *f* wheat-harvest or -crop; -**graupen** *f/pl.* hulled wheat; -**grieß** *m* grits *pl.* of wheat; -**land** *n* wheatland; vgl. -boden; -**mehl** *n* wheaten flour; -**mücke** *f*, *ent.* wheat-midge or -fly (*Diplo'sis tri'tici*); -**sortier-sieb** ⚙ *n* wheat-riddle; -**stroh** *n* wheat-straw, wheaten straw.

welch (´) [ahd.: which; *wie-lich] *pron.* 1. *interr. pron.* u. *a.* [66] A 2, 3†, B*: a) in enger Verbindung mit *nouns*: which, what, zB. ~er Mann (~e Frau)? which (or what) (wo)man?; b) durch das *v.* sein vom *s.* getrennt, immer: ~es, zB. ~es ist dein Name? what is your name?; ~es sind Ihre Schwestern? which are your sisters?; c) als Ausruf: ~er (oder ~ ein) Erfolg! what a success!; ~ Wunder! what a wonderful thing!, how wonderful!; ~e guten Leute! what good people!; d) mit folgendem od. zu ergänzendem partitivem *gen.*, zB. ~e dieser (oder von diesen) Damen? which of these ladies?; ~er von beiden? which of the two? — 2. *relative pron.* u. *a.* (aber *gen. sg. m* u. *n*: dessen, *f* deren; *gen. pl.* deren; auch sonst bss. der III); **a)** *nom.* u. *acc. m* u. *f*, *sg.* u. *pl.* who (*acc.* whom), which, that (s. derjenige): der Mann, ~er es behauptet the man who (or that) asserts it; das Kind, ~es weinte the child which (or that) cried; die Hühner, ~e legen the fowls which (or that) lay; seine Mutter, ~e gestern ankam his mother who [nicht that, weil that sich nicht auf einen beschränkten Begriff oder Eigennamen beziehen kann!] arrived yesterday; der Soldat (der Baum), ~en ich sah the soldier (the tree) whom (which) I saw (F u. P auch ohne whom, which!); zuweilen umgestellt: 100 Mark, ~e Summe Sie einliegend finden five pounds which sum you will find enclosed; der Bauer und der Jäger, ~ **letzterer** eine gute Flinte besaß the peasant and the huntsman the latter of whom possessed a good gun; im *acc.* oft nach *prp.*: die Leute (die Briefe), durch ~e ich es erfuhr the people (the letters) from whom (from which) I gleaned it; **b)** *gen.* dessen, deren whose, of which; der Mann, dessen Frau // the man whose wife //; die Frau, deren Mann // the woman whose husband //; die Hüte, deren Bänder // the hats of which the bands // or the bands of which //; **c)** *dat.* to whom, to which; die Dame, ~er (a. der) ich schrieb ... to whom I wrote; die Kugeln, ~en (a. denen) er entging ... from which he escaped; der Ort, in ~em er geboren ist the place in which (weniger genau: where) he was born; bei indirekter Frage: niemand weiß, in welcher Stadt Homer geboren wurde ... in which (or what) city Homer was born. — **3.** *indef. pron.*: a) ~ **auch immer**, mit folgendem *verb*: who(so)ever, which(so)ever; what(so)ever; ~es auch immer ihre Ansprüche sein mögen whatever their claims may be; ~e(r) von ihnen es auch sein mag whichever of them it may be; b) im Teilungssinne: hast du Zucker? ich habe ~en have you any sugar? I have some; es kamen ~e von ihnen some (or several, a few) of them came; c) irgend~e *pl.* s. irgend 1.

welcher-art (″˘...) *adv.* in what way or manner; ~**gestalt** *adv.* in what form or manner, by what means, how; (demzufolge) in consequence of which; ~**lei** *a.*, *inv.* of what kind; what?; ~ (Art) auch seine Waren sein mögen whatever the quality of his goods may be; *bibl.* mit ~ Maß ihr messet, wird euch gemessen werden (Matth. 7,2) with what measure ye mete, it shall be measured to you again; ~**weise** *adv.* in what way or manner.

Welf [ahd.: whelp] *m* [11]b., *n* [4]b. *hunt.* [whelp, cub.]

Welfe (´˘) *m* [44], *f* **Welfin** [47] (ehm. Anhänger des Papstes, *ant.* Waiblinger; jetzt Anhänger der ehm. Königsfamilie v. Hannover) Guelph.

welfen (´˘) *v/n.* (h.) [88] *hunt.* to cub.

Welfen-fonds (″˘-fõ) *m* [62] Guelph Fund, (former) property of the Guelphs.

Welfentum (´˘-) *n* [2]c. party(-spirit) of the Guelphs; **welfisch** (´˘) *a.* [66] Guelph, Guelphic, of the Guelphs.

welk (´) [ahd.] *a.* [66] **1.** (*ant.* frisch) v. Pflanzen ꝛc.: withered, faded (beide auch *fig.*); (runzlig) wrinkled; (schlaff) limp, flabby, flaccid; (siech) languishing, sickly; ~ machen, ~ werden, s. welken II u. I. — **2.** (gedörrt) parched, shrivelled (face, &c.), dried (fruit, &c.), dried up.

welken (´˘) **I** *v/n.* (sn) to wither, to fade (away), to dry (up). — **II** *v/a.* (welk m.) to fade, parch, dry (up).

Welkheit (´-) *f* [46] withered state; limpness, flabbiness, flaccidity.

Well-bank ⚙ (″...) *f* [62] potter's lathe; -**baum** *m* axle-tree (of a water-wheel); arbor, shaft; -**blech** *n* corrugated sheet-iron; -**daumen** *m*, *mach.* cog, arm of an arbor, lifter-cog.

Welle (´˘) [ahd.: well] *f* [48] **1.** a) ~ auf dem Wasser: wave, stärkere: billow, (Sturz-)~ breaker (vgl. Brandung); sein Grab in den ~n finden to find a watery grave; die ~n geh(e)n hoch the waves are running high, there is a heavy sea on; ~n schlagen to form (or to rise in) waves, *phys.*, &c.: ⚗ to undulate; vgl. schlagen 3 gegen Ende; von den ~n geschleudert wave-tossed; b) *poet.* = Wasser; c) *phys.*, &c. v. der Luft ꝛc.: ⚗ undulation. — **2.** Turnerei: (kreisförmige Bewegung ums Reck) circling (or turning, revolution) round the horizontal bar, F grinder; vgl. Arm-, Knie-~. — **3.** ⚙ *mach.* (um s-e Achse sich bewegender Zylinder) axle(-tree), arbor, shaft (vgl. Walze 1); dünne, stehende ~ spindle; s. Rad 1. — **4.** (Reisigbündel) fagot, bundle of brushwood; ~n m. to tie up fagots.

wellen (´˘: wällen) [ahd.: wallen[2]] *v/a.* [88] Kochk. ꝛc.: to let boil or wallop; gewelltes Haar wavy hair; ⚙ gewelltes Blech corrugated sheet-iron.

wellen-artig (″˘...) *a.* [66] = ~förmig; ~**atmend** *a. poet.* (G.) bathing in the waves; -**bad** *n* [62] bathe in the open river or sea, F dip in the waves; -**berg** *m*: a) elevation of a wave; b) mountainous wave; -**bewegung** *f* undulatory motion, undulation; -**binden** *n* fagot-making; -**binder** *m* fagot-maker; -**brecher** ⚙ *m* am Seestrande: breakwater; ~**förmig** *a.* wave-like, wavy, bsd. *phys.*, &c.: ⚗ undulating, undulatory; ~e Bewegung = -bewegung; ~es Land undulated country, rolling plain; ~**gekräusel** *n* rippling of the waves; -**kamm** *m* crest (or ridge) of a wave; -**länge** *f*, *phys.*, &c. length of an undulation; -**lehre** *f*, *phys.*: ⚗ undulatory theory; -**lini-e** *f*

Wellenschlag] waving (or wavy) line, *typ.* waved rule: **=schlag** *m* beating (or dashing) of the waves, (regular) succession of waves; kurzer ~ choppy waves *pl.* or sea; **schwingung** *f. phys.*: ↻ undulation; **=tal** *n* depression between two waves; **=telegraphie*** *f* (drahtlose Telegraphie) wireless telegraphy; **=theorie** *f* = **=lehre**; **=transmission** ⊙ *f* shafting.

Weller ⊙ (~) *m* ⚒ Bausach: cylinder of clay round laths; loam and straw.

wellern ⊙ (~) va. **I** *v/a.* to build with (or of) loam and straw. — **II** *v n.* (h.) to build mud-walls.

Well=fleisch (~...) *n* ⌂ Kochkunst: boiled breast of pork; **=grund** ↓ *m* aus Triebsand: shifting ground.

wellig (~) *a.* ⚇ wavy (a. vom Haare), waving, ↻ undulated.

Well=rad (~...) *n* ② wheel and axle; **=sand** ↓ *m* shifting sand.

Wellung (~) *f* ⚇ waviness, waving; *phys., &c.*: ↻ undulation.

Well=zapfen ⊙ (~) *m* ② pivot.

Wels [mhd.: Wal¹] *m* ⓐa. *ichth.* sheat-fish, silure (*silu'rus*).

welsch (~) [flt.] *a.* ⚇ **1.** (fremdländisch) foreign, alien, outlandish; (romanisch) Romance, *a.* = französisch, italienisch; die 2e Schweiz French Switzerland; (walisisch) Welsh; **~e([r]** *m*) *f* ⓐ Frenchman, Italian, weits. foreigner. — **2.** in bestimmten Verbindungen: 2e Bohne ⚑ haricot bean, 2er Hahn, 2es Huhn = Trut=hahn, =henne; 2es Korn = Mais; 2e Nuß large walnut.

welschen (~) *v/n.* (h.) ⚑ to speak French or Italian, to speak with a French (or an Italian) accent; (fremdartig sprechen) to jabber, to talk gibberish or double Dutch.

Welsch=kohl (~...) *m* ⚒, **=kraut** ⚑ savoy (= Wirsing); **=korn** *n* = Mais; **=land** *n* bsd. im Mittelalter = Italien, bisw. Frankreich; **=tirol** *npr/n.* Italian Tyrol.

Welschtum (~-) *n* ②d. foreign (or French, Italian) manners or customs, outlandish ways *pl*.

Welt (~) [ahd.: world] *f* ⚇ **1.** world; die Alte (Neue) ~ the Old (New) World; (Erdkugel) globe; (Weltall) universe; die ganze ~ the whole world; (alle Leute) all the world, everybody; f. vornehm 2; auf der ganzen ~ all over the world, all the world over; *rel.* diese böse ~ this wicked world (of ours); in Ausrufen: Himmel und die ~!, poz (alle) ~! good gracious!, stärker: good Heavens! — **2.** mit *prp.*: auf die ~ kommen, das Licht der ~ erblicken to come into the world, to be born; er tut auf Gottes ~ nichts he does absolutely nothing, he's not doing a stroke of work; e-n **aus** der ~ bringen (schaffen oder räumen) to put a p. out of the way, to kill a p., F to do for a p.; so geht's **in** der ~, das ist der ~ Lauf oder der Lauf der ~ that's the way of the world; was in aller ~ dachten Sie? what on earth were you thinking of?; eine Reise **um** die ~ m. to travel (or to take a trip) round the world or globe; um alles in der ~ nicht not for anything in the world; **zur** ~ bringen to bring into the world. — **3.** *fig.* (Lebensart) viel ~ h. to be well-bred or gentlemanly (/lady-like).

Welt=achse (~...) *f* ② axis of the world or earth; **=all** *n* universe; **=alter** *n* age, period (in the world's history), ↻ cosmic period; **=angeln** *f pl.* poles of the world; **=anschauung**, **=ansicht** *f* (general) view of the world or of life; **=auge** *n*: a) (eye of) Providence; b) bsd. *poet.* (the) Sun; God; **=ausstellung** *f* international exhibition; **=ball** *m* globe; **=bau** *m*: a) structure of the world, ↻ cosmic system; b) universe; **=begebenheit** *f* important event (in the world's history); **⌀bekannt** *a.* ⚇ known all over the world, known to everybody, *b.s.* notorious; **⌀berühmt** *a.* world-renowned, of world-wide fame; **=berühmtheit** *f* world-wide fame or reputation; **=beschreiber** *m*: ↻ cosmographer; **=beschreibung** *f* cosmography; **=bezwinger** *m* conqueror of the world; **=bildung** *f*: a) cosmogony; b) good breeding of a man (or a woman) of the world; **=blatt** *n* newspaper with a world-wide circulation; **=brand** *m* universal conflagration; **=bühne** *f* (great) stage of the world; **=bummler** *m* F co. globe-trotter; **=bürger(in** *f*) *m* citizen(ess *f*) (or denizen) of the world, auch: cosmopolite; F ein kleiner ~ ist angekommen a little stranger has arrived, a child has come into the world or to town; **⌀bürgerlich** *a.* cosmopolitan; **=bürgersinn** *m*, **=bürgertum** *n* cosmopolitanism; **=dame** *f* woman of the world, lady of fashion; **=diener** *m* worldling; **=ehre** *f* worldly honour; **=eitelkeit** *f* worldly vanity, *rel.* auch worldliness.

Welten=all (~...) *n* ② = Weltall; **=bildung** *f*: ↻ cosmogony; **=lehre** *f*: ↻ cosmology; **=meer** *n* infinity of world; **=staub** *m* cosmic dust.

welt=entrückt(~...) *a.* ⚇ detached (or isolated) from the world; **=entstehung** *f* ② formation (or origin) of the world; **=entstehungs=lehre** *f*: ↻ cosmogony.

Welten=zeugung (~...) *f* ② (HAECKEL) creation of (new) worlds.

Welt=ereignis (~...) *n* ② important historical event; **⌀erfahren** *a.* ⚇ experienced (or versed) in the ways of the world, *rel.* worldly wise; **=erfahrung** *f* experience (or routine) in worldly affairs, *rel.* worldly wisdom; **=erlösend** *a.* world-redeeming; **=eroberer** *m* conqueror of the world; **⌀erschütternd** *a.* world-shaking, shaking the world('s foundations); **=firma** *f* = **=geschäft**; **=fremd** *a.* secluded from the world; **=friede** *m* universal peace; **=gebäude** *n* = **=bau**; **=gebieter** *m* ruler of the world; **=gegend** *f* region of the w., quarter of the globe; **=geist** *m*, *rel.* worldly spirit or mind; **=geistliche(r)** *m* (*ant.* Klostergeistlicher) secular priest; **=geistlichkeit** *f* secular clergy; **=gericht** *n*: a) last judgment, doomsday (= Jüngstes Gericht); b) judgment of humanity; **=geschäft** *n* business of world-wide fame; **=geschichte** *f* world's (or universal) history; **⌀geschichtlich** *a.* of (or relating to) universal history; most important (event, &c.); **=gesetz** *n* universal law; **⌀gewandt** *a.* = **=erfahren**; **=gewandtheit** *f* = **=erfahrung**; **=gürtel** *m* zone; **=handel** ⚑ *m* world's commerce, international trade; **=händel** *m/pl.* public affairs; **=herrschaft** *f* empire of the world; **=karte** *f* /map (or chart) of the w.; **=kenntnis** *f* knowledge of the w.; (keine) ~ haben to be (un)acquainted with the ways of the w.; **=kind** *n*, *rel.* child of this w., worldling, worldly-minded person; **⌀klug** *a.* worldly wise, politic; **=klugheit** *f* worldly wisdom; f. a. **=erfahrung**; **=körper** *m* celestial (or heavenly) body; **=kreis** *m* = Welt; **=kugel** *f* celestial globe, orb; **=kunde** *f*: a) ↻ cosmology; b) = **=kenntnis**; **⌀kundig** *a.* knowing the (ways of the) world; **=lage** *f* condition of international (or the world's) affairs, general political situation; **=lauf** *m* course of the world; das ist der ~ such is the way of the w., auch: such is life; **=leben** *n*: a) *rel.* worldly life; b) political life; ↻ cosmic life; **=lehre** *f*: ↻ cosmology.

weltlich (~) *a.* ⚇ of the world, mundane, bsd. *rel.* worldly; (zeitlich) temporal, (*ant.* geistlich) secular, *a.* lay, civil, (*ant.* heilig) profane; 2e Güter temporal possessions, temporalities *pl.*; geistliche Güter ꝛc. 2 machen to secularize...; die 2e Macht the secular arm; *rel.* 2 gesinnt worldly-minded; am ~en hangen to be attached to the world or to worldly things.

Weltlichkeit (~-) *f* ⚇ (f. weltlich) **1.** (o. *pl.*) worldliness; secularity; profanity. — **2.** (mit *pl.*) (weltliche Macht) temporal power; ~en (weltliche Rechte ꝛc.) secular rights *pl.* [Güter ꝛc.: secularization.]

Weltlich=machung (~...) *f* ⚇ geistlicher **Welt=licht** (~...) *n* ② light of the world, (Sonne) sun; bsd. *fig.* luminary, star.

Weltling (~) *m* ②d. worldling; weits. auch = Weltmann.

Welt=literatur (~...) *f* ② universal literature; **=lust** *f* worldly (or earthly) pleasure; **=macht** *f* world- (or first-class) power; **=mann** *m* man of the world; (well-bred) gentleman; **⌀männisch** *a.* ⚇ well-bred, gentlemanly; **=markt** ⚑ *m* (the) world's market, international trade; (Stapelplatz) emporium; **=meer** *n* ocean; **=mensch** *m* worldling; **⌀müde** *a.* weary of the world; **=ordnung** *f* system of the w., ↻ cosmic system; natural laws *pl.*; die jetzige ~ the world as it is (constituted) to-day; die sittliche ~ the (eternal) moral law; **=post** ⚑ *f* international post; **=post=karte** *f* Postal-Union post-card; **=post=verein** *m* Postal-Union; **=priester** *m. eccl.* secular priest; **=raum** *m* universal space; **=reich** *n*, etwa: world-embracing empire; **⌀scheu** *a.* shunning social intercourse, misanthropic(al); **=schmerz** F *m* world-woe, mehr gw.: weariness of life, spleen; an ~ leidend world-weary; **=schmerzler(in** *f*) *m*

Signs (see page XVII): F familiar; P vulgar; F flash; \ rare; † obsolete (died); * new word (born); ⧺ incorrect; ♪ music;

[Weltschöpfer] — 1111 — [wenn]

pessimist; =schöpfer m Creator (of the world); =seele f world-pervading spirit, soul of the universe; =sinn m worldly mind, worldliness; =sprache f universal language; =stadt f city (or capital) of the first rank, great (imperial) city; Lo. oft: metropolis; =städtisch a. of (or relating to) a great (imperial) city, von Lo. oft: metropolitan; =stellung f position in the world; =strich m region of the globe, part of the world, geh. Spr.: clime; =system n astronomical system; =teil ⚥ m quarter of the globe; (Festland) continent; umsegler m (umsegelung f) circumnavigator (circumnavigation) of the world; =umspannend a. world-embracing; =untergang m end of the world; ⚥verachtend a. cynical; =verachtung f cynicism; =verkehr m international or world's traffic; =verlassenheit f isolation from the world; ⚥verloren a. ⊚ lost to (or cat off from) the world; =weise(r) m philosopher; =weisheit f philosophy; =wunder n Mt.: die sieben ~ the seven wonders of the world.

wem (¹) [ahd.: whom] dat. von wer: to whom?; ~ gehört das Haus? to whom does the house belong?, whose house is it?; von ⁓? of (or from) whom?; zu ⁓ spricht er? to whom is he speaking?; ich weiß, mit ⁓ er ritt I know with whom he rode, I know what person he was riding with.

Wem=fall (ᴵᴵ⁓) m ⊚ gr. = Dativ.

wen (¹) [ahd.: whom] acc. von wer: ⁓ sehen Sie? whom do you see?; ⁓ man auch wählen mag whomsoever they may elect; mit prp., zB. an ⁓? to whom?; für ⁓? for whom?

Wende¹ (⁓ᴸ) m ⊕, Wendin f ⊕ (von slawischem Volkstum) Wend.

Wende² (⁓ᴸ) [ahd.: wenden] f ⊕ 1. turn (-ing) (vgl. Wendung); (Stelle, wo et. sich wendet) turning(-point), s. Sonnen=⁓; (Biegung) bend. — 2. (Änderung) change; (neuer Zeitraum) new epoch or era.

Wende=hals(vogel) (⁓ᴸ...) m ⊕ orn. wry-neck, tongue-bird (Iynx torqui'lla); =kreis m ast., ⚥ tropic (des Krebses: of Cancer, des Steinbocks: of Capricorn); zw. den =kreisen liegend intertropical.

Wendel=baum ⊕ (⁓ᴸ...) m ⊕ = Welle 3; =steig m steep and winding path; =treppe f: a) arch. winding staircase or stairs pl., hohle: well- (or newel-)staircase; b) zo. (Schnecke) staircase-shell, Twentletrap (Scala'ria).

wenden (⁓ᴸ) [ahd.: wend: winden] I v/a. u. sich ⁓ v.refl., bisw. a. v/n. (h.) ⊚a. 1. (sich) ⁓ to turn (about or round); sich anderswohin ⁓ to turn in a different direction; s. drehen 2, bsd. am Ende; sich ⁓ (ändern) to undergo a) change, to take a new turn; das Heu rc. ⁓ to turn over ...; ein Kleid rc. ⁓ to turn (about) ...; ein gewendeter Rock a coat that has been turned; ⊛ mit ⁓der (umgehender) Post by return of post; fig. j-s Herz oder Sinn ⁓ to work upon (or influence) a p.'s heart or mind, to alter a p.'s opinion; s. Blatt 9 gegen Ende u. Rücken 2 gegen Ende. — 2. bisw.

= ab², zB. Schlimmes ⁓ to avert (or prevent) evil; fein Auge von e-m ⁓ not to take one's eyes off a p. —
3. ⚓ ein Schiff ⁓ to veer (or bring) round. — 4. mit prp.: sich an e-n (um Hilfe) ⁓ to apply (stärker: to appeal) to a p. (for assistance), to make application to a p.; viel Geld an et. ⁓ to spend (or lavish) much money on (or over) a th.; seine Kräfte, seine Zeit auf et. ⁓ to devote one's strength, one's time to a th.; sein ganzes Vermögen auf et. ⁓ to spend one's whole fortune on a th.; F et. auf sich ⁓ to spend some money on o.s., F to treat o.s. to a th.; die Augen auf et. ⁓ to cast one's eyes on (or a glance at) a th.; sich gegen et. ⁓ to turn towards (or against) to a th.; sich von et. ⁓ to turn away from a th.; sich (zum Guten) ⁓ to take a good turn, to turn out for the best, von Personen: to turn over a new leaf. — II ~ n ⊚ 5. s. Wendung. — III p.p. 6. s. ge-wandt.

Wende=pflug ⊕ (⁓ᴸ...) m ⊕ swivel- (or side-hill) plough; =punkt m: a) turning-point, fig. critical point or moment, crisis; sie stehen au einem wichtigen ~(e) they are at the parting of ways; b) ast.: ⚲ solstitial point; =rohr ⊕ n e-r Feuerspritze: movable tube; =schemel m am Wagen: rider, riding-bed.

wendisch (⁓ᴸ) [Wende] a. Völkerkunde: Wendish, Wendic, of the Wends.

Wendung (⁓ᴸ) f ⊚ 1. (das Wenden) turning, turn, ⚔ auch: facing (about), wheeling round; ~en machen to wheel round; ⚓ veering, tacking, als Übung: evolution; bei Krankheiten rc.: crisis, critical stage, im Trauerspiele rc.: catastrophe, weits. = Wendepunkt; bei dieser ~ der Dinge at this juncture; ~ zum Besseren, zum Schlimmeren change for the better, for the worse, auch: favourable, unfavourable turn. — 2. mit verbs: e-r Sache eine andere ~ geben to give a th. a new turn, auch: to put a new face on things; eine andere ~ nehmen to take a new turn or shape. — 3. sprachliche ~ phrase, saying, idiom(atical expression); ~ im Satze turn in a sentence. — 4. sinuosity (= Windung).

Wen=fall (ᴵᴵ⁓) m ⊚ gr. = Akkusativ.

wenig (⁓ᴸ) [ahd. kümmerlich, elend): wee] 1. a. ⊚ A 2, 3 † little, comp. less, sup. am 2sten least; sein 2es Geld the little money (that) he has, auch: his few pounds or shillings; ⁓ Gutes little good; es ist ⁓ Hoffnung (vorhanden) there is (but) little hope; 2e gute Menschen (a) few good people; unsere 2e (geringe) Hoffnung what small hope we have; ein ⁓ Wasser (or) a little water; mit 2(en) Worten in a few words; nicht ⁓ and(e)re a good many others; nur 2e Schritte only a few steps; vgl. nur 3; die 2en Male, daß // the few times that or when //. — 2. s. 2e few; 2e glauben few (people) believe; die 2en, welche // the few who //; einige 2e some few; nicht 2e not a few; so 2e so few, such a small number; so 2(e) auch however

little (few); Sprichw. ⁓ aber gut little and good; viele ~ machen ein Viel many a little make a mickle; es fehlte ⁓. so wäre er ertrunken he was very near being drowned; das 2e, was er hat the little (that) he is possessed of, auch: what little he has; die 2en, welche übrigblieben the few that were left; dieses 2e this small amount or property; um ein 2(es) besser a trifle (or a shade) better; so ⁓ (ᴵᴵ ᴸ⁓) so little, such a small quantity; er ist so 2 arm, daß er vielmehr // he is so far from (being) poor that, on the contrary //; vgl. (eben)sowenig; zu ⁓ (ᴵᴵ ᴸ⁓) too little; vgl. zu2 (ᴵᴸ⁓); zwei Mark 2. to two shillings short. — 3. adv. ihm ist ⁓ zu trauen he is not much to be trusted, he's not very reliable; ein 2 (ᴵᴸ⁓) a little, somewhat; ein 2 schneller a little, somewhat (or a trifle) faster. — 4. im comp.: fünf 2er drei five less (math. minus three; das kostet nicht 2er als (volle, ganze) 200 Franken that costs no less than eight pounds; nicht 2er als acht Mann no(t) fewer than eight men; er ist nichts 2er als reich he is anything but rich; nichts=destoweniger nevertheless, all the same; um so 2er darf er kommen so much the less ought he to come; um so 2er als // all the less since //; 2er werden to diminish, to decrease. — 5. im sup. der 2ste Schaden the least damage; die 2ste Sorge the least (or slightest) grief; die 2sten (Menschen) the fewest people, the smallest number of persons; es ist das 2ste, was Sie tun sollten that's the least you can do, you could do no less (than that); am 2sten least (of all), the least; 2stens adv., zum 2sten at the (very) least; er muß 2stens 4000 Mark verloren haben he must have lost at least (F to put it mildly, to put it at a low figure) two hundred pounds.

Wenigkeit (ᴵᴸ⁓) f ⊚ 1. o. pl.: littleness, smallness; (geringes Maß) small quantity; (geringe Zahl) small number, fewness, paucity. — 2. mit pl.: (Kleinigkeit) trifle. — 3. meine (eigene) ~ (höflich: ich): Fritz und meine ~ ... and my unworthy (or insignificant) self, F co. ... and my little self, ... and yours truly.

Wenigft=... (ᴵᴸ⁓) m = Mindest=...

wenigstens (ᴸ⁓) adv. s. wenig 5.

wenn (⁵) [mhd.: when: wann] I cj. 1. zeitlich: when (vgl. wann); (sooft als) whenever; (solange als) as long as; ⁓ man reich ist, hat man Freunde whilst you are rich you have friends; ⁓ er da ist, wollen wir anfangen as soon as he is there we will begin; ⁓ man ihn hört, sollte man glauben, daß // to hear him speak one would think that //; ⁓ die Stunde naht // when (or as soon as) the hour approaches //. — 2. (bedingend, einräumend) oft mit einem impf. subj. oder plup. subj., um die Annahme und Folgerung als unmöglich darzustellen: if, in case; (zugegeben) granted (that); (vorausgesetzt) provided (that); ⁓ man ihn erwischt, wird er bestraft (werden)

⚲ scientific; ⚘ botanical; ⚥ geography; ⊕ machinery; ⚒ mining; ⚔ military; ⚓ marine; ⊚ commercial; ✉ postal; 🚂 railway.

[wenngleich] — 1112 — [werden]

if he is (feiner: be) caught he will be punished; 2 er hier wäre if he were here; 2 er telegraphieren sollte if he should telegraph, were he to wire; 2 er es nicht weiß, kann er es nicht ausplaudern if he does not know it he cannot let it out; 2 er es wüßte, würde er es mir sagen if he knew he would tell me; 2 ich das gewußt hätte, wäre ich gekommen if I had (ohne cj.: had I) known that ...; 2 er nicht gewesen wäre, würde ich reich sein if it had not been for him (or had it not been for him, kürzer: but for him) I should be rich; es soll mich freuen, 2 ich erfahre, daß // I shall be pleased to hear that //; es ist nicht gut, 2 man zu viel schläft it is not good to sleep too much; 2 ich Ihnen die Wahrheit sagen soll // (if I am) to tell you the truth //; allemal oder jedesmal 2 er // whenever (F each time) he //. — 3. mit anderen Redeteilen: als (ob. wie) 2 as if, as though; nicht als 2 das nicht häufig vorkäme not as if that did not frequently occur; es ist, als 2 er uns nie gesehen hätte one would think that he had never seen us; 2 aber but if; 2 anders s. anders 3; außer 2 except when or if, unless; (und) 2 auch, 2 gleich (al)though, granted (that); 2 er auch (oder 2 gleich er) König ist // though he (may) be king //; 2 er auch noch so jung ist // he be (ob. though he be) ever so young //; 2 er sich auch auf den Kopf stellt though he may try his utmost, despite anything that he may do; 2 doch if only, if indeed; 2 es doch nur geschehen wäre I only wish it were already done; 2 einmal when (or if) once; 2 etwa if by chance, though perchance; selbst 2. und 2 granted (or suppose) that; selbst 2 ich es könnte // even if I could do it //; Sie müssen es kaufen, und 2 es noch so teuer wäre ... though it be (or if it were) ever so dear; 2 man doch einmal sterben muß // since (or as) we have to die some day //; 2 nicht if not, unless; 2 er kein (oder nicht ein) Narr ist if he is not (or unless he be) a fool; 2 nicht ... so doch // if not ... yet //; 2 nicht heute, so doch morgen if not to-day then (surely) to-morrow; 2 nichts dazwischen kommt if nothing (or unless s.th.) unforeseen should happen; 2 nur provided (that); man schaudert, 2 man nur daran denkt one shudders only to think (or at the mere thought) of it; 2 nur im geringsten if only in the slightest degree; though (it be) ever so little; 2 schon (häufig getrennt): 2 er schon nicht viel gelernt hat // though he has not (or may not have) learnt much //; schon 2 man ihn nur hört, möchte man lachen only to hear him ...; 2 schon, denn schon if (it is to be done) at all, then (let us do it) thoroughly; selbst 2. und 2 s. weiter oben. — II das ~ inv. 4. the if; Sprichw. s. aber III; wenn das ~ nicht wäre, etwa: if ifs and ans were pots and pans.

wenn=gleich (2·ᵘ) cj. s. wenn 3.
Wenzel (2·) [slaw.] I npr/m. 2a. Wenceslaus. — II m 22 Figur in dtsch. Karten: knave (= Bube).
wer¹ (2, a. ᵕ) [ahd.: who: lt. quis] pron. (gen. wessen, wes, dat. wem, acc. wen) 1. interr. pron. in direkter und indirekter Frage: who, 2. 2 ist da? who is there? 2 da? who goes there?; von bestimmten Personen: which, 2B. 2 von ihnen ist es? which of them is it?; allgemeiner: 2 kann denn das sein? whoever can it be?; ich weiß nicht, 2 gerufen hat I don't know who has called; 2 anders?, 2 sonst? who else?, what other person(s)? — 2. interr. a. fast nur im gen.: wes Geistes ist er (sie)? what kind of person (or F genius) is he (she)? — 3. relative pron. = derjenige, welcher; diejenige, welche; 2 den Becher kann wieder zeigen, er mag ihn behalten (sch.) he that can show me the cup again may claim it as his own; Sprichw. s. fühlen 5, kommen 1 u. lügen 2; 2 will, der kann where there is a will there is a way; 2 nur immer anybody who or that. — 4. indef. pron.: a) = jemand, 2B. 2, der's tun will, der komme if any one would like to do it, let him (f her) come; ich höre wen rufen I hear somebody call; 2 auch immer anybody who; 2 es auch sei who(so)ever it may be; b) den Wunsch bz.: 2 das lassen könnte if one could only leave it alone; c) Bedingung bz.: 2 ein Narr wäre // a fool were he who //.
Wer²... (2..) [ahd.: lt. vir Mann] nur in Zssgn, s. Wergeld.   [whirl.]
Werbe¹ (2·) [: Wirbel] f 22 (Strudel)
Werbe²=bureau 2 (2·...) [werben] n recruiting-office or depot; =geld n, etwa: earnest paid on enlistment, in England: King's shilling; =liste f list of recruits.
werben (2·) [ahd.] I v/n. (h.) u. v/a. Vb. 1. um e-n, et. 2 = bewerben 1. — 2. nach et. (2B. Lob, hohem Preise 2c.) 2 (trachten) to strive after, to aspire to a th. — 3. e-n zu et. 2 (anwerben) to engage a p. for s.th., bfd. 2 zum Kriegsdienste, Soldatenstande 2 to enlist, to enrol, in größerer Zahl: to raise, levy, beat up, durch Gewalt u. List. bfd. ehm.: to press, to crimp (a p. ↓); abs. für eine Sache 2 to make propaganda for a th., to agitate for a cause; um Stimmen 2 to canvass for votes. — II ~ n 4. = Werbung.
Werbe²=offizier 2 (2·...) m 22 in England 2c.: recruiting officer; =platz m recruiting-place or -depot.
Werber (2·) m 22 1. (Freier) wooer, suitor. — 2. 2 recruiting-officer or -sergeant, ehm.: crimp.
Werber=handwerk 2 (2·.2·) n 22 recruiting, ehm.: crimping.
Werbe²=trommel 2 (2·.2·) f 22: die 2 rühren to beat up (for) recruits.
Werbung (2·) f 22: a) e-s Freiers: courting, wooing, courtship; b) pol., &c. eines Stimmensammlers: canvassing; c) nach Ruhm 2c.: striving after, aspiring

to (s. werben 2); d) 2 v. Rekruten: enlistment, enrolment, levy(ing), &c. (s. 3).
Wer=da(=ruf 2 (2·.(2·)) [s. wer¹] n 23 the sentinel's (or sentry's) call.
Werde=gang (2·2·) m 22 process of formation, 2 genesis, (Wachstum) growth.
werden (2·, a. ᵕ) [ahd.: † worth] I v/n. (sn) 2c. 1. to become, allmählich: to grow; (entstehen) to arise, originate; to be born or created; to come into existence; bald wird Friede 2 there will be (or we shall have) peace soon; s. Licht 1 am Ende; alle Tage, die Gott 2 läßt every day (that) God gives (us); man weiß nicht, was noch 2 mag there is no knowing what may yet happen; Sprichw. was nicht ist, kann noch 2 what is not may yet be, mehr gbr.: we never know what may happen. — 2. mst F (sich gestalten, entwickeln) der Kranke wird wieder (genest) ... is recovering, ... is getting on; die Sache wird (kommt zustande) the matter is progressing or maturing; es wird (ja) schon it will be all right, all will come right (in the end); ungeduldig: nun, wird's (bald)? now then, how long will you be?; do make haste! — 3. mit aus: aus ihm wird nichts he will never be anything (in the world); was soll aus dir 2? what is to become of you?; was wird aus ihm? what is he going to be or to do?; s. aus 3 u. daraus. Sprichw. s. Kind 3 und nichts 5. — 4. e-m wird et. (zuteil) a person receives (or obtains) s.th. (as his share); vgl. zuteil; was wird mir dafür? what shall I receive (or get) for it?; Recht soll euch 2 justice shall be done to you, you shall receive (or get) your due; so gut ist es (solch Glück ist) mir niemals geworden such good luck has never fallen to my share, I have never been so fortunate; was ist ihm zum Lohne geworden? what did he receive as (a reward)?; ihm ward Ehre und Glück honour and happiness were (or fell to) his portion; e-m zu eigen 2 to fall to a p.'s share; ❋ Ihr Wertes vom 9. d. M. ist mir erst heute geworden your favour (or communication) of the 9th inst. has come to hand only to-day. — 5. mit s. als Prädikat: a) Beruf, Religion 2c. bz.: Arzt 2 to become a doctor, to adopt (or enter) the medical profession; ein Christ 2 to become a Christian, to embrace the Christian religion; Kaufmann 2 to become a commercial man; to go into business; er ist Oberst geworden he has been promoted to colonel, a. he has received his colonelcy or his regiment; s. Soldat; b) adv. und im gen.: 2 andere 2 gegen Ende u. froh 3; man möchte des Teufels 2 it's enough to drive one crazy. — 6. mit a. und adv. ad(e)lig 2 to receive a title of nobility, in Engl.: to be raised to the peerage, to be made a lord; alt 2 to grow old; ärger 2 to grow worse; s. bekannt 3 am Ende und 4; blind 2 to become (or go) blind, to lose one's sight; böse 2 to grow

Zeichen (s. S. XVII): F familiär; P Volkssprache; ſ Gaunersprache; ↘ selten; † alt (auch gestorben); * neu (auch geboren); +× unrichtig;

[Werder] — 1113 — [Werf]

(or F get) angry; der Rauch wurde immer dichter ... grew more and more dense; f. einig¹; enger 2 to grow narrower, to contract; ernst 2 to become (more) serious; f. fertig 3 u. 4; gelinde 2 to grow gentle or mild; f. gerecht 2; geringer 2 to grow less, to diminish; gesund 2 to recover; f. gewahr, groß 1; es wird noch alles gut 2 all will be (or come) right (in the end); f. a. gut 3 am Ende; f. hell 2; katholisch 2 to become a (or to turn) Roman Catholic; f. flug 2, krank 1; kürzer 2 to grow shorter, to shorten; lang 2 to grow long, to lengthen; f. a. lang 3 gegen Ende; die Tage 2 länger ... are getting longer; f. los 3 am Schluß; sauer, schimmelig 2 to turn (F to go) sour, mouldy; selten 2 to grow scarce or obsolete; das Wetter ist warm geworden the weather has become (or turned) warm or mild; wie wird die Ernte? how is the harvest progressing? — 7. mit es als Subjekt: es muß anders 2 there must be a change; es wird jetzt sehr früh dunkel it now gets (or is) dark very early, the days are drawing in; es wird morgen jährig it will be a year to-morrow; es wird kalt it is getting cold; es wird Krieg 2 there will be (or we shall have) war; es ist Mode geworden, daß // it has become the fashion to // (inf.); es wird Nacht (the) night is setting in; vgl. Nacht; es wird nötig zu // it is becoming necessary to //; f. Tag 3; es wird Zeit, daß wir aufbrechen it will now be time for us to start; wie wird es mit deiner Reise? what has been arranged as regards your travels?, what about your travelling? — 8. mit hinzutretendem Dativ: f. Angst II; mir wird (oder es wird mir) leicht ums Herz I feel relieved or a great relief, I feel a burden taken off my mind; mir wird übel I (begin to) feel sick or ill or F queer, bad; du kannst denken, wie mir zumute wurde you may imagine how (or what) I felt; wie ward mir! how (strange) I felt! — 9. mit zu: zu et. 2 to be changed (or converted, turned) into a th.; f. Beute 1 2; zum Gelächter der Leute 2 to become (or be made) the laughing-stock of the people; zu nichts 2 to be reduced to nothing; to come to nought; f. Sprichwort; zu Staube 2 to fall (or turn) to dust; der Schnee wird zu Wasser 2 ... is turning to water, ... is melting; vgl. Wasser 1e. — II als Hilfszeitwort: 10. a) zur Bildung des *future* und *conditional*: wir 2 fahren we shall (or are going to) drive; ich werde es ihm (gleich) sagen I will (or shall) tell him (directly); er würde es mir gesagt h. (= er hätte es mir gesagt) he would have told me (of it); b) F *future* statt des *present*: wo werde ich nur den Schlüssel h.? where may I have left the key?; das wird wohl kaum wahr sein that's hardly (or that could scarcely be) true; c) fragend: wer wird sich denn vor einem Kinde fürchten?

who would be afraid of a child?; es wird ihm doch nichts zugestoßen sein? I trust (or hope) nothing has happened to him; d) *ell.* drohend: wart! euch werd' ich (kommen. die Streiche wehren)! wait, I'll give it you or you shall get it!; e) mit *p.p.* zur Bildung des Passivs, wobei statt „geworden" in der Schriftsprache „worden" gilt: das Schloß wird (noch immer) gebaut the castle is being built; Erdbeeren 2 im Sommer gegessen strawberries are eaten in summer; ihm wurden zwei Pferde erschossen he had two horses killed; es wurde viel gelacht, gezecht there was a good deal of laughing, carousing; er ist viel von ihnen gequält worden he has been tormented by them a great deal; es ist uns gesagt, mitgeteilt worden, daß // we have been told, informed that //; f. von 3. III ~ *n* 11. becoming, growing, growth; (Ursprung) origin; (Entstehung) rise, birth. *s* genesis; (Bildung) formation; (Entwicklung) development; noch im ~ sein to be still growing or nascent or developing or in one's infancy. — IV 2d *p.pr.* u. *a.* 12. in den Bed. des *inf*. — 13. in one's infancy, nascent. *s* embryonic.

Werder (*s*) [mhd.: Wert³] *m* small river-island, small plot (of land) surrounded by water; holm, islet.

Werde=zeit (*s..·*) *f* period of growth, time of development.

Wer=fall (*s..*) *m* *gr.* = Nominativ.

werfen (*s*) [ahd.] I *v.a.*, *v/n.* (h.) u. *v refl.* 1. to throw, F to shy, P to chuck. mst *fig.* to cast; (schleudern) to fling, hurl, pitch, *v.* Geschossen *a.* to project; den Ball 2 to throw the ball; vgl. 5; Blasen 2 to form (or throw up) bubbles; das Los 2 to cast a lot (über et. for a th.); das Lot 2 to heave the lead, to take soundings; Schatten 2 to cast a shadow, tüftelnen: to give shade; Strahlen 2 to dart forth beams, to beam forth. — 2. mit *prp.* (oft *fig.*): e-m Steine **an** den Kopf 2 to throw stones at a p.'s head; die Augen (den Blick) **auf** et. 2 to cast one's eyes on (one's glances at) a th.; die Sorge warf ihn aufs Krankenlager worry made him ill, he was stricken down with grief; aufs Papier 2 to jot down on paper; sich auf e-n 2 to throw o.s. upon a p., to rush at a p.; sich aufs Pferd 2 to leap into the saddle; sich auf ein Studium 2 to take up (or to apply o.s. to) a study (with great earnestness or zeal); e-n **aus** dem Hause 2 to turn a p. out (of doors); den Feind aus e-r starken Stellung 2 to dislodge (or drive) the enemy from a strong position; **durch**=ea. 2 to jumble (or muddle) up; **in** die Höhe 2 to toss (or throw) up; e-n ins Gefängnis 2 to cast (or throw, put) a p. into prison or jail; f. Flinte; Bomben in die Stadt 2 to throw shells into the town, to shell the town; Truppen in eine Festung 2 to send (a body of) troops into a fortress, to garrison a

fortress; sich in die Brust 2 f. Brust 2; sich ins Zeug 2 to put one's shoulders to the wheel, to set to (with might and main); alles in einen Topf 2 to treat everybody (or everything) alike; Steine **nach** e-m 2 to throw (or fling, F shy) stones at a p.; **über** den Haufen 2 to overthrow, to overturn; vgl. Haufe 2; Güter über Bord 2 to throw (or cast) ... overboard; einen Mantel **um** (auch über) die Schultern 2 to throw a cloak over one's shoulders; mit Beleidigungen um sich 2 to insult everybody; mit Geld um sich 2 to throw one's money away, to spend one's money lavishly; mit lateinischen Brocken um sich 2 to make lavish use of Latin tags, to air one's Latin (on all occasions); **unter**=ea.=2 to jumble, to mix up; et. **von** sich 2 to throw a th. away, to cast a th. off; e-m et. **vor** die Füße 2 to throw (P to chuck) a th. (contemptuously) at a p.; jdm **zu** Füßen 2 to throw o.s. at a p.'s feet. — 3. mit Angabe der Wirkung: e-n mit Steinen tot 2 to stone a p. to death; e-m ein Loch in den Kopf 2 to break a p.'s head with a stone; sich müde 2 to tire o.s. with throwing or with playing skittles. — 4. *abs.* von Tieren: 2 (Junge gebären) to bring forth young, to drop. von der Kuh oft: to calve, von der Stute: to foal, vom Raubtiere: to cub, vom Schweine: to litter, to farrow. — 5. Spiel: Kegel 2 to throw skittles, to play (at) skittles; Kartenspiel: das Spiel 2 (aufgeben) to throw down the cards; Würfelspiel: Sie 2 zuerst you throw first; ich habe vier geworfen I have made four; Lawntennis: mit dem Ball zuerst (anschlagen) to serve. — 6. v. Holze 2c.: sich 2 (krumm ziehen) to warp, to get warped. — II ~ *n* 7. throwing, &c. (f. I), throw, von Geschossen: projection.

Werft¹ (*s*) [mhd.] (ahd. warf)] *m* (Kette e-s Gewebes) warp.

Werft² (*s*) [ndl.] *f*, *n* (*s*), *a.* ~e (*s*) *f* wharf, (Schiffsbauhof) ship-wright's (or ship-building) yard, dockyard.

Werft²=aufseher (*s...*) *m*, =besitzer *m* wharfinger; =division *f* der engl. Marine: technical and administrative division (engineers, engine-room artificers, stokers, mechanics, carpenters); =geld *n* wharfage.

Werg (*s*) [ahd.: wirken] *n* tow; (gezupftes altes Tauwerk) oakum; geteertes ~ black oakum; ~ zupfen, ausziehen to pick oakum. [für Totschlag] wergild.)

Wer²=geld (*s..*) [mhd.] *n* (ehm. Geldbuße)

Werk (*s*) [ahd.: work: grch. *érgon*] *n* 1. (Arbeit) work: (Verrichtung) (manual) labour; performance; (Unternehmung) enterprise; (Handlung) action; (Erzeugnis) production; ~e *pl.* der Barmherzigkeit ob. Liebe works of charity, charitable acts or deeds *pl.*; das ist nicht mein ~ (meine Art) that's not my way (of dealing with things); Sprichw. f. loben 1 am Schluß. — 2. mit *prp.*: **ans** ~ geh(e)n, Hand ans ~ legen, sich ans ~ begeben ob. machen to set to work;

♪ Musik; ⚗ Wissenschaft; ⚘ Pflanze; ♀ Geographie; ⊕ Technik; ⚒ Bergbau; ⚔ Militär; ⚓ Marine; ⊛ Handel; ✉ Post; 🚂 Eisenbahn.

[Werkbank] — 1114 — [Wesen]

es ist et. (Großes) im ~e there is s.th. (important) on foot or in the wind; die Sache ist schon im ~e the matter is already preparing or in hand; ins ~ setzen to set on foot, to set going; to bring about; (zu) rasch zu ~e geh(e)n to go to work (too) hastily or hurriedly; auf die (un)rechte Art zu ~e gehen to go the right (wrong) way to work; vorsichtig zu ~e geh(e)n to proceed cautiously, to feel one's way; Sprichw. tut nach meinen Worten und nicht nach meinen ~en do according to my words and not (according to) my deeds. — 3. ⊙ (et. kunstvoll zs.-gesetztes) mechanism: works pl. of a watch, clock, &c.; gearing of a machine; vgl. Räderwerk. — 4. (zum Betriebe dienende Anstalt) works pl.: (Fabrik) (manu)factory; bsd. in Zssgn, s. Berg-, Hütten-. — 5. ⊙ metall. raw (or workable) lead; Münze: alloy. — 6. typ. gedrucktes ~ (printed) work, book, zum Nachschlagen: work (or book) of reference; Schillers sämtliche ~e Schiller's complete works pl. — 7. ℳ. Festungs-: offenes, vorgeschobenes ~ open, advanced work.

Werk-bank ⊙ (⁻...) f ⑫ work(ing)-bench; =blei n crude lead; vgl. Werk 5; =brett n ℨ. Zuschneiden: cutting-board.

Werkchen (⁻⌣) n ㉓ (dim. von Werk) mst typ. small work, miniature work. (it.) opusculum (auch ♪).

Werk-druck ⊙ (⁻...) m ⑫ typ. book-printing; =druckerei f. typ. book-house.

Werkel-tag (⁻⌣,⌣) ꝛc. = Werktag ꝛc.

Werk-führer (⁻...) m ⑫ foreman; =heilig a ⑱ sanctimonious; =heilige(r) s. sanctimonious person, hypocrite; =heiligkeit f sanctimoniousness, hypocrisy; =hof m (building-, &c.)yard; =holz n timber; =holz-käfer m, ent. death-watch (Ano'bium stria'tum); =leute (pl. von dem ungbr.-mann) workmen, F hands pl.; =loch ⊙ n, mach. manhole; =meister m workmaster, mehr gbr.: foreman; =meisterin f workmistress, mehr gbr.: forewoman; =probe ⊙ f Gießerei: specimen of the cast (metal); =satz m, typ. book-work; =schrift f. typ. book-face; =seide f floss-silk; =statt, =stätte, =stelle f workshop, e-s Künstlers: studio; =stein m Bauwesen: freestone, quarry-stone; =stellig a. nur in 2 m. - bewerkstelligen; =stube f working-room; =stuhl ⊙ m Weberei: loom; =tag m working- (or week-)day; =täglich a. u. adv. of (or on) all working- (or week-)days; =tags adv. on week-days; =tagsrock m every-day coat; =tätig a. operative, efficacious; =tätigkeit f operativeness, efficaciousness; =tisch m work(ing-)table; =zeug n: a) (working-)tool, instrument; implement of husbandry, &c.; fig. e-n zu ſ-m ~e m. to make a tool (or a puppet) of a p.; b) (die Lebenstätigkeit erhaltender Teil eines Körpers) organ; =zeugkasten m tool-chest or -box, chest (or box) of tools; =zeug-maschine ⊙ f engine- (or machine-)tool; =zeug-tasche f e-s Arbeiters: tool-bag, e-s Arztes: bag for surgical instruments, e-s Radlers: wallet for tools; =zink n, chm., metall. raw zinc.

Wermut ℥ (⁻,a.⌣) [ahd.: wormwood] m @c. wormwood (Artemi'sia Absi'nthium); fig. (et. Bitteres) bitterness, gall.

Wermut-baum ℥ (⁻...) m ⑫ tree-wormwood (Artemi'sia arbo'rea); =becher m fig. cup of bitterness; den ~ leeren to drain (or empty) the cup (of bitterness) to its dregs.

werpen ↓ (⁻⌣) [ndd.] v/n.(h.) ⑧ (den Wurfanker ausjagen) to warp; a. — warpen.

Werre südd. (⁻⌣) f ⑧ = Maulwurfsgrille.

Werst (⁻) [russ. wirsta'] f ⑯. (1,0668 km) verst (= about 1170 yards).

wert¹ (⁻) [ahd.: worth] a. ⑯ 1. a) mit acc. zur wirklichen Preisbestimmung: worth, of the value of; das Pferd ist (seine) 100 Taler 2 ... is worth (its) fifteen pounds; das ist keinen roten Heller, keinen Schuß Pulver 2 that's not worth a farthing or a sou or powder and shot; das ist Geld 2 that's worth some money, fig. von einer köstlichen Geschichte auch: it's a capital story, F that's rich; vom Vermögen: er ist 100 000 Mark 2 he is worth (or he has, he possesses) £ 5000; b) in allgemeinen Redensarten: nichts 2 sein to be worthless; das ist nicht viel 2 that's not worth much; einer ist so viel 2 als der andere one is as good as the other, they are much of a muchness; das ist schon viel 2 that's a great point gained or a distinct advantage. a. it's a step in the right direction; ebensoviel 2 wie equivalent (or tantamount) to; weniger 2 less valuable; das Buch ist 2, daß man es liest the book deserves to be read or is worth reading; er ist nicht 2, daß man von ihm spricht he is not worth talking about. — 2. 2 (würdig) sein, meist mit gen. to be worthy of, to deserve; er ist dessen (od. es) nicht 2 he is not deserving of it; s. Ehre 2 gegen Ende; Mühe und Rede 1 gegen Ende; Sprichw. s. Dienst 1 am Schluß, eigen 1 gegen Ende u. Arbeiter 1; oft zs.-geschoben mit dem gen., ℨ.B. achtens-, achtungs-2 worthy of esteem. — 3. (lieb, teuer) dear; (geehrt) honoured; (achtbar) estimable, esteemed; er ist uns lieb und 2 we love and esteem him; als höflicher Ausdruck: wie ist Ihr 2er Name? may I ask (or what may be) your name?; Ihr 2es Schreiben (oft: Ihr ~es) your esteemed lines, ♥ your favour, auch einfach: your letter.

Wert² (⁻) [ahd.: worth; *wert¹] m ⓪b.: a) (Geltung) value, worth (s. Gehalt 2); (Verdienst) merit; (gute Eigenschaft) good quality, virtue; math. fester ~ fixed quantity; größter (kleinster) ~ einer veränderlichen Größe: maximum (minimum) value ...; ⊙ Börse: russische, italienische ~e Russian, Italian stocks, auch: Russians, Italians pl.; b) Redewendungen: e-m Dinge großen (geringen) ~ beilegen to set great (little or no great) store by a th.; das hat nur wenig ~ that's of little value or use; großen (geringen) ~ auf etwas legen to attach great (little) value (or importance) to a th.; to lay great (little) stress on a th.; s. gleich 1 unter "sein".

Wert³ (⁻) [ahd.] m (n) ⓪b. islet (=Werder).

wert-achten (⁻...) v/a. ⑧** to esteem, appreciate, respect; to have (a great) regard for; =achtung f ⑫ =schätzung; =angabe ♥ f declaration (or statement) of value, declared value; beim Zoll: entry (made); =bestimmung f valuation, appraisement, taxation; =brief ♥ m letter containing valuables, money-letter. [value, to appraise; vgl. be2. **werten** (⁻⌣) [ahd.] v/a. ⑧ (abschätzen) to

Wert-ersatz (⁻...) m ⑧ equivalent; compensation; =geber ♥ m giver of a bill; =geschätzt a. ⑯ valued. (highly) esteemed ⑧ a** = 2achten; =herabsetzung f depreciation.

...wertig (...⁻⌣) in Zssgn mit a. und Zahlwörtern s. drei-, gleich-, minder-, zwei-2.

Wertigkeit (⁻⌣) f ⑯ bsb. chm. ⑳ quantivalence of atoms; atomicity.

wert²-los (⁻...) a. ⑯ worthless, valueless; (unbedeutend) trifling, trashy; (nutzlos) useless, futile; =losigkeit f ⑯ worthlessness, uselessness, futility; =messer m ⑫: der ~ für ... the standard (of value) for ...; =paket ♥ n (registered) parcel with valuables; =papier ♥ n security, bond, scrip; Papiere 2; =sachen f/pl. valuables pl.; =schätzen ⑧** v/a. =2achten; =schätzung f esteem for, appreciation of, respect (or regard) for; =sendung f consignment of valuables; (Geldsendung) remittance; =verringerung f depreciation (or decrease) of value; =versicherung ♥ f: a) insurance of the value; b) value insured; 2voll a. valuable, precious; =zeichen n: a) (Papiergeld) paper money; b) (Marke) stamp; =zoll ♥ m ad valorem duty.

Wer²-wolf (⁻,⌣) [mhd.] m ⑫ (Mensch in Wolfsgestalt) myth. u. Sage: werwolf, wolfman.

wes (⁻), [ahd.: whose] † od. poet. — wessen; Sprichw. s. Herz 1 am Schluß.

Wesen (⁻⌣) [ahd.: was] n ㉓ 1. (Dasein, Sein) existence, being; (das wahre Sein) essence; phls. ㉗ entity; (Wirklichkeit) reality, substance; (innere Eigenschaft) intrinsic property or virtue; das gehört zum ~ der Sache that's the (very) essence of the thing, that's (part of) its nature. — 2. (Art u. Weise des Seins) mode of existence; (Zustand) condition; (Anstand, Haltung) manners f.; demeanour, conduct; (Eigentümlichkeit) peculiarity, character, nature; s. angenehm 1; gesetztes ~ quiet (or sedate) manner; gezwungenes ~ affected air, stiff manner; vornehmes ~ superior (or condescending) air; genteel ways pl. — 3. (Tätigkeit, Geschäft) sein ~ treiben to be active or F on the move or on the go, v. e-m Gespenst ꝛc.: to haunt a place; vgl. treiben 7. — 4. viel ~s (Aufhebens) m. to make a great deal of fuss, to be very fussy; ohne viel ~s (Umstände) zu m. without much ceremony, very unceremoniously. — 5. (einzelnes) das Höchste ~ (Gott) the Supreme Being; lebendes ~ living being, creature; kein lebendes ~ not a living soul or creature. — 6. (größeres Ganze) concern, body, organization, establishment. von Verwaltungszweigen: service, department; das gemeine ~

Signs (see page XVII): F familiar; P vulgar; ℱ flash; ↘ rare; † obsolete (died); * new word (born); ++ incorrect; ♪ music;

[**Weseneinheit**] — 1115 — [**wetterleuchten**]

the Commonwealth, auch: the common weal; bsd. in Zssgn, zB. das Finanz-≈ financial affairs or matters pl.; vgl. Haus=, Heim=, Kriegs=, Post=, Proviant=≈.
Wesen=einheit (⌣‑...) f ⊕ theol.: ⚛ consubstantiality; ≈gleich a. ⊕ identical, ⚛ consubstantial; =gleichheit f, phls. complete identity.
wesenhaft (⌣‑) a. ⊕ really existing; substantial; ~igkeit f ⊕ real existence.
Wesen=lehre (⌣‑...) f ⊕ phls.: ⚛ ontology; ≈los a. ⊕ unsubstantial, incorporeal, unreal; =losigkeit f ⊕ unsubstantialness, incorporeality, unreality; =reich n, etwa: living world.
Wesens=... (⌣‑...) in Zssgn f. Wesen=...
wesentlich (⌣‑) [mhd.] a. ⊕ 1. ohne comp. = wesenhaft. — 2. (zum inneren Wesen gehörend) essential, substantial, (den Grund bildend) fundamental, (höchst wichtig) highly important; material, vital; ≈er Bestandteil essential component, principal ingredient; ≈er Inhalt e-s Buches ꝛc. (main) substance; ≈e Teile integral (or constituent) parts pl.; ein ≈er Vorteil a real (or positive) advantage; das ~e the essential part (of a th.), the gist (of the matter); im ≈en essentially, substantially; ~keit f ⊕: a) (o. pl.) essentiality; b) (mit pl.) essential (or important) matter.
Wes=fall (⌣‑) m ⊕ = Genitiv.
wes=falls (⌣‑) adv. in which case, and in that case, if that be the case.
wes=halb (⌣⌢) adv.: a) fragend: why?, wherefore?, for what reason?, what for?; b) relativ: and on that account; ≈ ich telegraphieren mußte ... and therefore, I had to telegraph; F so I had to wire.
Wesir (‑⌣) [türk.; *ar. Stütze] m ⊕d. (Minister e-s Sultans ꝛc.) vizier; ~at (‑‑⌣) n ⊕c. vizierate, viziership.
Wesleyaner (⌣lĕ‑ā‑⌣) [Wesley, Gründer der Methodistensekte, † 1791] m ⊕, ~in f ⊕, **wesleyanisch** a. ⊕ Wesleyan.
Wespe (⌣‑) [ahd.: wasp: lt. vespa] f ⊕ ent. wasp (Vespa).
wespen=ähnlich (⌣‑...) a. ⊕ wasp-like, waspish; =bussard m ⊕ orn. honey-buzzard (Pernis apivorus); =königin f queen wasp; =nest n wasps' (or hornets') nest; in ein ~ stechen od. stören to stir up (or disturb) a wasps' nest, meist fig. to raise a nest of hornets about one's ears; =schwarm m swarm (or flight) of wasps; =stich m sting of a wasp, wasp's sting; =taille f e‑r Dame: wasp (auch: F co. spider's) waist.
wessen (⌣‑) [wes] gen. von wer (f. ds) und von was: 1. interrogative: ≈ Schwert hat ihn erschlagen? whose sword has slain him?; ≈ klagt man ihn an? what is he accused of?; besitzanzeigend: ≈ ist der Mantel? whose is the cloak?, to whom does the cloak belong? — 2. relative: das ist alles, ≈ er mich anklagt ... (which) he accuses me of.
West (⌣) [f. Westen] m ⊕d. (abbr. W.) 1. o. pl. ⚓, ast., ⚲ west (f. Westen); ~ gegen Nord (Süd) west by north (south). — 2. mit pl. = Westwind.
West=afrika ⚲ (⌣‑...), =asien npr/n. ⊕α. West (or Western) Africa, Asia.

Westchen (⌣‑) n ⊕ (dim. v. Weste) small (or short) waistcoat or vest.
West=deutschland (⌣‑) npr/n. ⊕α. West of Germany.
Weste (⌣‑) [(‑+) fr.] f ⊕ waistcoat, bsd. in der Schneidersprache: vest.
Westen¹ (⌣‑) [ahd.: west] m ⊕ (abbr. W.) West (abbr. W.), Occident; nach ~, gegen ~ westward, towards (the) west.
West=end(e) (⌣‑⌣) n ⊕ West End.
Westen²=futter (⌣‑...) n [Weste] ⊕ Schneiderei: waistcoat-lining; =knopf m, =tasche f waistcoat-button, -pocket.
Wester=hemd prov. (⌣‑⌣) n ⊕ (Tauffleid) christening-robe. | **Western Europe**.
West=europa (⌣‑⌣) npr/n. ⊕α.
Westfale (⌣‑) [fahl] m ⊕, **Westfälin** f ⊕ Westphalian; **Westfalen** ⚲ npr/n. ⊕α. (preußische Provinz) Westphalia.
westfälisch (⌣‑) a. ⊕ Westphalian; ~er Friede (1648) Peace of Westphalia.
West=friesland ⚲ (⌣‑...) npr/n. ⊕ West Friesland, West(ern) Frisia; =gote m. =gotin f. hist. Visigoth; ≈gotisch a. ⊕ Visigothic; =indien ⚲ npr/n. ⊕ West India, the West Indies pl.; ≈indisch a. ⊕ West Indian; =küste f west(ern) coast.
westlich (⌣‑) a. ⊕ west(ern), westerly, occidental; ≈ von ... westward of ...
West=mächte (⌣‑...) f/pl. ⊕ pol. Western Powers pl.; =minster=abtei f (alter Dom in Süd-London) Westminster Abbey; =nord=west m West-North-West; =preuße m. =preußin f West Prussian; =preußen ⚲ npr/n. West Prussia; ≈römisch a. hist.: ≈es Reich Western (or Occidental) Empire; =seite f west(ern) side; =süd=west m West-South-West; ≈wärts adv. westward; =wind m west(erly) wind.
weswegen (⌣‑) = weshalb.
wett (⌣) [mhd.; *Wette] a. ⊕ nur prädikativ: even, equal, F quits; ≈ sein to be quits with a p.; f. wettmachen.
Wett=apparat (⌣‑...) m ⊕ = Totalisator; =bewerb m ⊕ (Konkurrenz) competition; f. unlauterer; in ~ treten to enter into competition with; =bewerber m competitor, rival; =buch n book for entering bets, betting book; =bureau n etwa: betting-room, bookmaker's stand or booth (ein eigentliches ~ ist in England gesetzlich verboten).
Wette (⌣‑) [ahd.: wed.: lt. vadimo'nium] f ⊕ 1. wager, bet; eine ~ eingehen to (lay) a wager, to (make) a bet; eine (sehr) ungleiche ~ eingehen gegen // to lay (heavy) odds against //; was gilt die ~? what will you bet? — 2. adv. um die ~, in die ~ (mit-ea. wetteifernd) vying with each other, emulating each other; um die ~ fahren, laufen, schwimmen ꝛc. to race each other, auch to race for a wager; sie bemühten sich um die ~, ihn zu trösten they vied with each other in their endeavour (einfacher: they each and all did their best) to comfort him.
Wett=eifer (⌣‑...) m ⊕ fig. (spirit of) emulation, rivalry; (Mitbewerbung) competition; =eiferer m (Mitbewerb[er]in) (female) rival; ≈eifern v/n. (h.) ⊕a≈ to vie (or compete, cope) with a p., to

emulate a p., to try to outdo a p.; ≈eifernd emoulous, competitive.
wetten (⌣‑) [Wette] I v/n. (h.) und v/a. ⊕ to (lay) a wager, to (make) a bet; (um) eine Mark ≈, daß // to bet (or lay) a shilling that //; darauf ≈, daß // to lay a wager that //; ich wette zehn gegen eins, daß // I lay ten to one that //; es läßt sich hundert gegen eins ≈, daß // the chances are (or F it is) hundred to one that //; ich wette so hoch Sie wollen I'll bet you what (-ever) you like or any amount; es wurde hoch gewettet the bets ran to high figures; Klub für ~de betting-club (in Engl. verboten!); Spiel: ich wette auf Kopf (Schrift) I guess heads (tails); fig. ich wette, daß Sie es nicht können I defy you to do it, F I bet you can't do it; so haben wir nicht gewettet (so gilt es nicht) that's not what we agreed upon. — II ~ n ⊕ wagering, betting.
Wetter¹ (⌣‑) [wetten] m ⊕ one who bets or wagers; betting man, bookmaker, F u. P bookie.
Wetter² (⌣‑) [ahd.: weather] n ⊕ 1. weather, auch: atmospheric conditions pl., condition of the sky (f. freundlich 2 am Ende und unfreundlich); es war schönes ~ the weather was fine or beautiful, it was a fine day; was ist jetzt für ~? how is the weather now?, F what kind of a day is it?; ich glaube, es wird schönes ~ I believe it will turn out a fine day or it will be fine; f. erlauben 1 u. Wind 1. — 2. a) = Gewitter; b) = Blitz; c) F fig. nun geht das ~ (der Spektafel) los now the row is coming; d) in Flüchen: alle ~!, Donner und ~!, ~ noch eins! confound it!, bewundernd: dear me!, you don't say so! — 3. ⚒ (Luft in den Gruben) air (in underground workings), ventilation; böses ~ choke-damp; die Grube hat böse ~ the mine is badly ventilated; schlagende ~ = Grubengas a.
Wetter=anzeiger (⌣‑...) m ⊕ weather-signal; =beobachter m meteorologist; =beobachtung f meteorological observation; =bericht m meteorological report; =bube F m devil of a boy; =dach n penthouse, open shed; =fahne f vane, weathercock (a. fig.); =fahrschaft ⚒ f air-shaft; ≈fest a. ⊕ weather-proof, von Menschen a.: inured to all weathers; =führung ⚒ f ventilation (of the mine); =glas n weather-glass, barometer; =hahn m weathercock; fig. er ist ein ~ he is a turncoat or time-server; =häuschen n (Wetterwechsel anzeigend) weather-box; =hexe f F co. devil of a girl; =junge F m = =bube; =karte f meteorological chart; =kenner m weather expert, meteorologist; ≈flüchtig a. for. split by frost; =kunde f meteorology; ≈kundig a. weather-wise; =lage f state of the weather; ≈launisch a. = ≈wendisch; =läuten n ringing of bells during a storm; =leitung ⚒ f air-hole; ≈leuchten v/n., bsd. v/impers. (h.) ⊕**: es ≈leuchtet there is (or we are having) sheet-lightning; ~ [mhd. (P)] n sheet- (⚔ summer-)lightning

---

⚛ scientific; ⚘ botanical; ⚲ geography; ⊕ machinery; ⚒ mining; ⚔ military; ⚓ marine; ⊛ commercial; ✉ postal; 🚂 railway.

[**Wetterloch**] (*ant.* (forked) lightning: Blitz); =**loch** *n*, *etwa*: quarter from which the bad weather comes; =**lotte** ⚒ / zur Entfernung der Luft: air-escape; =**maschine** ⚒ *f* ventilator of a mine.
wettern (⌢) ②*a*. I *v/n*. (h. u. ſn): a) *bſd. v/impers.* es wettert it is stormy, we are having a thunderstorm; b) (fluchen) to curse, to swear, to storm (the house down). — II ~ *n* ㉓: a) stormy weather; b) cursing, swearing.
Wetter-prognoſe (⌢...) *f* ⑫ weather forecast; =**prophet** *m* weather-prophet; =**prophezeiung** *f* (making) forecasts *pl.* of the weather; =**ſchacht** ⚒ *m* air-shaft; =**ſchaden** *m* damage caused by stormy weather; =**ſcheide** *f* line at which thunder-clouds separate; meteorological limit; =**ſchenkel** *m, arch.* weather-board; =**ſchirm** *m* screen protecting from the weather; penthouse, portico; =**ſchlag** *m* clap of thunder; =**ſeite** *f* (*ant.* Sonnenseite) weather-side; =**ſtange** *f* = Blitzableiter; =**ſtein** *m, geol.*: ⚒ belemnite; =**ſtrahl** *m* = Blitzſtrahl; =**ſtrecke** ⚒ *f* air-head, intermediate air-shaft; =**ſturm** *m* storm(y weather); =**tür** ⚒ *f* trap-door, air-gate; =**trommel** ⚒ *f* centrifugal ventilator; =**verſorgung** ⚒ *f* system of ventilation; =**vorhang** *m* awning; =**vorherſage** / weather forecast; =**warte** *f* meteorological observatory; =**wechſel** *m*: a) change of the weather; b) ⚒ underground ventilation, current of air; ⚒**windiſch** *a.* fickle, capricious; (as) changeable as the weather; =**wolken** *f|pl.* stormy clouds, thunder-clouds *pl.*; =**zeichen** *n* sign of (approaching) bad weather, auf Wetterhalten: weather symbol; =**zeiger** *m* weather-indicator or -gauge; =**ziegel** ⊙ *m* weather-tile.
Wett-fahren (⌢...) *n* ㉒, =**fahrt** *f*: a) zu Lande: driving-competition (vgl. Trabrennen), der Radler: cycling-race; Alt.: cariot-race; b) zu Waſſer: boat-race, yachting-race, regatta; =**fliegen** *n* flying-match; =**geſang** *m* singing-match; =**kampf** *m* contest, match, trial of strength, von Boxern: prize-fight; Alt.: agonism; *vgl.* =**ſtreit**; =**kämpfer** *m, etwa*: prize-fighter, pugilist; Alt.: agonist; =**lauf** *m* running-match, foot-race; ⚒**laufen** *v/n.* (ſn) ⓐa**: to run a race or a match; ~ *n* =lauf; =**läufer** *m* one who runs in a (foot-)race; fast runner; ⚒**machen** *v/a.* ⓐ** to square (up) an account, &c.; ſeine Verluſte ⚒ to make good (or recover) one's losses; ⚒**rennen** *v/n.* (ſn) ⓐb**: to run (or take part) in a race; ~ *n* ㉓ (horse-)race, *auch*: races *pl.*.. mit Hinderniſſen: steeple-chase; =**renner** *m* (Rennpferd) race-horse, *auch*: runner; =**rudern** *n* boat-race, rowing-match; =**ſpiel** *n* Fußball, Tennis ꝛc.: match; =**ſtreit** *m* emulation; *vgl.* =**eifer**; von Läufern, Schwimmern ꝛc.: match, race; vgl. =**kampf**; ſich mit e-m in einen ~ einlaſſen to enter the lists with a p., to enter into competition (or to compete) with a p.
Wetturnen [Wett-turnen] (⌢...) *n* ㉓ gymnastic exhibition.

wetzen (⌢) [ahd.: whet] ⑩ I *v/a.* to whet, grind, sharpen; *fig.* den Geiſt od. Verſtand ⚒ to sharpen one's wits. — II *v/n.* (h.): mit dem Dolche an den Wänden ⚒ to scrape the walls with the dagger.
Wetz-ſchiefer ⊙ (⌢...) *m* ⑫ *min.* razor-stone, whet(stone)-slate, hone-slate; =**ſtahl** *m* steel for sharpening knives, der Schlächter: butcher's steel; =**ſtein** *m* whetstone, für Senſen ꝛc.: hone; *vgl.* Schleifſtein.
Wewelings, Wewelinnen ♉ (⌢... ⌢⌢⌢) [nbd.] *pl.* ratlines *pl.*
Whig ⓣ (h)wig, *a. w*⌢) *m* ⑩ *pol.* Whig; =**whiggiſtiſch** (⌢⌢⌢; *f.* Whig) *a.* ⑥⑥ Whig, of the Whig party.
Whig-partei ((h)w⌢⌢⌢, *auch* w⌢⌢⌢) *f* ⑫ Whig party, *auch*: old Liberal school.
Whisky ⓣ (h)wi-ſti⌢. *a. w*⌢) *m* ⑩㉓ (Kornbranntwein) whisky.
Whiſt ⓣ (h)wiſt. *a. w*⌢) *n* ⓦb.㉞) Kartenſpiel; whist; mit e-m ~ ſpielen to play whist with a p.; wollen Sie e-e Partie ~ *m.*? will you take a hand at whist?
Whiſt-karten (⌢...) *f pl.* ⑫ whist-cards *pl.*; =**partie** *f* whist-party; =**ſpieler**(**in** *f*) *m* whist-player.
wibbeln (⌢⌢) *v/n.* (h.) ⓦa.: es fribbelt und wibbelt weiter (*FONTANE*) things crawl and wriggle on and on.
wich (⌢) *ind. impf.* von weichen[1] II.
Wichs F (⌢t) [nhd. 18. ſae.: wichſen] *m* ⓦa. burſchitoſ.: gala; in vollem ~ in full dress, F in full fig; ſich in ~ ſetzen od. werfen to put on one's best (toggery), to dress (or F tog) up for the occasion, to smarten (or get) o.s. up.
Wichs-bürſte ⚒ (⌢tſ⌢⌢) *f* ⑫ blacking- (or polishing-)brush.
Wichſe (⌢tſ⌢⌢) *f* ⑱ 1. für Schuhe: blacking. — 2. ⚒ = Bartwichſe; ⊙ (Polier-wachs) polishing-wax, wax for polishing. — 3. F *fig.* (Prügel) flogging, hiding, thrashing.
wichſen[1] (⌢tſ⌢⌢) [ahd.: *Wachs] *v/a.* ⑩ 1. Schuhzeug ꝛc. ⚒ to black (or polish) ..., F to shine (up) ... — 2. einen Faden ⚒ (wachſen) to wax ...; den Fußboden ⚒ to polish ... — 3. F (Wichſe 3) = prügeln.
wichſen[2] F (⌢tſ⌢⌢) [Wichs] *v/a.* ⑩ *bſd. im p.p.* gewichſt dressed up (to the knocker), F togged out, looking smart.
Wichſer (⌢tſ⌢⌢) *m* ⑫ polisher, shoeblack.
Wichs-glanz (⌢tſ⌢⌢) *m* ⑫ polish.
Wichſier (~ſiʹ) [dtſch (wichſen)⌢] -fr.) *m* ⑩ burſch. student's attendant. in Cambridge: F gyp, in Oxford: scout.
Wichs-lappen ⊙ (⌢tſ⌢⌢) *m* ⑫ rag for blacking leather; =**ſtiefel** *m'pl.* boots that require blacking.
Wicht (⌢) [ahd.: wight] *m* ⑪④b. 1. wight; (Geſchöpf) creature; armer, elender ~ poor, miserable fellow or wretch; vgl. Böſewicht; grober ~ rough customer. — 2. kleiner ~ F mannikin, (Junge) urchin, F little chap, nipper; (kleines Kind) little child. F chit.
Wichtchen (⌢⌢⌢) *n* ㉔ *dim. v.* Wicht (ſ. ds 2).
Wichtel-männchen (⌢⌢⌢⌢) [mhd.] *n* ㉔ (hob)goblin. imp.
wichtig (⌢⌢) [nhd. aus gewichtig] *a.* ⑥⑥ 1. weighty. — 2. *fig.* important, momentous; (erheblich) considerable,

material; (weſentlich) essential; (folgenreich) consequential; höchſt ⚒ of great importance or consequence; etwas ⌢es s.th. important, s.th. of consequence: ⚒ tun, ſich ⚒ *m.*, es ⚒ h. to assume (or put on) an air of importance.
Wichtigkeit (⌢⌢⌢) *f* ⑯ (ſ. wichtig) weightiness, importance; (Bedeutſamkeit) significance; ohne ~ of no importance or account or consequence, unimportant; Sache von großer ~ matter of (great) consequence.
Wichtig-macher (⌢⌢⌢...). =**tuer** *m* ⑫ consequential (or pompous) person; =**macherei**, =**tuerei** *f* consequential (or pompous) manner or air, pomposity.
Wichtlein (⌢⌢⌢) *n* ㉔ *dim. v.* Wicht (ſ. dſ 2).
Wicke ⚘ (⌢⌢) [ahd., *lt. vīcia*] *f* ⑱ vetch (*vīcia*), kleine ~ early vetch (*v. lathyroīdes*); F *fig.* in die ~n (zugrunde) geh(e)n to be ruined, to go down (in the world). F to go to pot or to the dogs.
Wickel (⌢⌢) [ahd.] *m* ㉒ 1. (et. Gewickeltes) s.th. rolled up, roll; ⊙ =gewickelter Docht) roll of wick; (Füllung e-r Zigarre) filler of a cigar; ⚘ (Form des Blütenſtandes): ⚒ cincinnus. — 2. (et. zum Aufwickeln Dienendes) winder; (Garn ⚒, *a.* Haar- u. Locken-⚒). — 3. *auch* F (*pl.* ⌢n) = Wickelzeug. — 4. = Perücke, Haar; F *fig.* beim ~ kriegen (seize by the) collar, to catch (or seize) hold of.
Wickel-band (⌢⌢⌢...) *n* ㉓ roller, für Säuglinge: swaddling-band; =**bär** *m* Kinkaju; =**binde** *f, surg.* roll-bandage; =**blatt** *n* = Einlage 3; =**draht** *m* (thin) binding wire; =**frau** *f* (monthly) nurse; =**kind**(**lein**) *n* child in swaddling-clothes, *mehr gbr.*: baby in long clothes; =**maſchine** ⊙ *f* Spinnerei. zum Knäuelwickeln: ball-winding machine.
wickeln (⌢⌢) [mhd.] *v/a.* u. *v/refl.* ⓦa. 1. (ſich) um et. (herum) ⚒ to wind (o.s.) round a th., to coil (o.s.) round a th.: *fig.* man kann ihn um den Finger ⚒ you can twist (or turn) him round your little finger. — 2. mit *prp.* auf e-e Rolle ⚒ to wind on a reel; Zſ.-gewickeltes aus-ea.⚒ to untwist ..., to unroll ...; *fig.* ſich aus e-r Sache ⚒ to get (o.s.) out of a scrape, to extricate o.s. from s.th.; einen Gegenſtand in et. ⚒ to wrap a th. up in s.th.: zu einem (od. in ein) Knäuel ⚒ to roll into a ball; ſich die Haare zu (oder in) Locken ⚒ to curl up one's hair, to put one's hair in curling-papers. — 3. in bloßem Objekt: die Haare, Locken ⚒ to curl (up) the hair; ein Kind ⚒ to wrap up ...; ein Knäuel, Paket ⚒ to make up ...; ⊙ Seide ⚒ to wind ...; Zigaretten, Zigarren ⚒ to make ...; F *fig.* ſchief gewickelt ſ. ſchief 3.
Wickel-puppe (⌢⌢⌢...) *f* ⑱ doll in long clothes, baby doll; =**ranke** ⚘ *f* tendril, ⚒ cirrus; =**raupe** *f, ent.*: ⚒ tortricid caterpillar; =**ſchlange** *f, zo.*: ⚒ tortricid; =**ſchwanz** *m. zo.* prehensile tail; =**tuch** *n* wrapper; baby's roller or napkin; =**zeug** *f.* Säuglinge: swaddling-clothes, *mehr gbr.*: baby long clothes *pl.*
wicken-artig ⚘ (⌢⌢⌢...) [Wicke] *a.* vetch-like; =**futter** *n, agr.* oats and vetches *pl.*; =**ſtroh** *n* vetch-straw.

Zeichen (ſ. S. XVII): F familiär; P Volksſprache; Ƒ Gaunerſprache; ⧵ ſelten; † alt (auch geſtorben); * neu (auch geboren); ⁑ unrichtig.

[Wickler] — 1117 — [Widerspruch]

Wickler (⌣‿) m ㉒ **1.** (a. ~**in** f ㊼) one who winds (or rolls, wraps) up, curler of hair, &c., = Spuler 1. — **2.** ent.: ↗ tortricid; a. = Blattwickler.

Widder (⌣‿) [ahd.: wether] m ㉒: a) (Schafbock, ant. Schaf) ram, P tup; b) ast. (Sternbild) Aries; c) Mil.: (Belagerungswerkzeug) battering-ram; d) ⚓ ~-schiff.

Widderchen (⌣‿⌣) n ㉓ ent. = Widderschwärmer. [**-kopf** m ram's head.]
Widder-fell (⌣‿) n ㊷ ram's skin;
Widderlein (⌣‿⌣) n ㉓ = Widderschwärmer.
Widder-schiff ⚓ (⌣‿) n ㉓ ram; **-schwärmer** m, ent. burnet-fly or -moth (Zygæna).

wider (⌣‿; Hom. wieder) [ahd.: with]
I prp. mit acc. **1.** (gegen) against, in opposition to, contrary to; ☉ Willen against one's inclination, reluctantly; ☉ meinen Willen against my wish, in defiance of me, in spite of me (vgl. gegen 2); für und ☉ for and against, auch: pro and con; oft als s.: das Für und (das) ~ the reasons for and against, the pros and cons pl. — **II** adv. **2.** hin und ☉ (meist wieder) (every) now and then, now and again. — **3.** im Sinne der Vergeltung: (oft wieder) in return for, in exchange for.

Wider-..., **wider-...** (⌣‿..., ‿⌣...) Vorsilbe in Zssgn mit nouns u. adjectives = gegen=...; in Verbindung mit verbs, nicht trennbar (*) und mit betontem Grundworte, bz. Entgegenstreben, Feindliches, Erwiderung, Wechselseitigkeit. zB. ☉streiten (⌣‿⌣) v. to act in opposition to.

wider-bellen F (⌣‿⌣) v/n. (h.) ㊽** to reply sharply or gruffly or rudely;
-beller m ㉒, **~in** f ㊼ disagreeable (or cantankerous) person; ☉**bellig** a. ㊺ cantankerous; **-christ** (⌣‿‿) m ㉒. ㊷ Antichrist; ☉**christlich** (⌣‿‿) a. ㊺ antichristian, opposed to Christianity;
-druck (⌣‿) m ㉒. a) = Gegendruck; b) ⊙ Kupferstecherei: counter-proof; vgl. Wiederdruck; ☉**fahren** (⌣‿⌣) v/n. (fn) ㊻** to happen, to occur; mir ist viel Gutes von ihnen ☉ I have received great kindness at their hands; das kann ihm auch ☉ the same may happen to him, he may meet with the same fate; was ist ihm ☉? what has befallen him?; e-m Gerechtigkeit ob. Recht ☉ l. to mete out justice to a p.;
☉**haarig** (⌣‿...) a. ㊺ cross-grained; fig. stubborn, refractory, rebellious;
~keit f ㊻ stubbornness, refractoriness, rebellious spirit; **-häkchen** ⊙ n ㉓ (dim. v. Widerhaken) bes. Fischerei: small barb; **-haken** n ㉒ barbed hook, an Pfeilen, Angeln 2c.: barb, seltener: beard; an der Gabeldeichsel: shaft-hook; mit einem ~ versehen (auch **widerhakig** a. ㊺) provided with barbed hooks, barbed; **-hall** m ㉒. reverberation, oft: echo, responsive sound, phys. reflexion of sound, ♪ a.: repercussion, resonance; e-n ~ im Herzen finden to be re-echoed (or to meet with a response) in the heart; ☉**hallen** v/n. (h.) (⌣‿⌣) ㊽*, mst (‿⌣‿) ㊽** to resound, to be (re-)echoed, to (re-)echo (a. fig.); **-halt** (⌣‿...) m ㉒. s.th. to lean against; support, prop;
☉**haltig** a. ㊺ offering resistance, v.

Speisen: substantial, solid, rich; nourishing, nutritious; **-kette** ⊙ f ㊻ an der Deichsel eines Wagens: pole-chain;
-klage f ㊻ jur. counter-plea; **-lager** ⊙ n ㉒ arch. abutment; (Gegenpfeiler) counterfort; ☉**legbar** (‿⌣‿) a. ㊺ refutable, confutable, refragable; **~keit** f ㊻ refutability; ☉**legen** (‿⌣‿) v/a. ㊽* to refute, confute, disprove; schlimme Nachreden durch sein Leben ☉ to live down evil reports; ein Satz, der sich nicht ☉ läßt an irrefutable proposition; ~ n ㉓ **-legung**; ☉**leglich** (‿⌣‿) a. . ☉legbar; **-legung** f ㊻ refutation, confutation.

widerlich (⌣‿⌣) a. ㊺ repugnant, (abstoßend) repulsive, (ekelhaft) disgusting, loathsome (disease, &c.), offensive (smell), nauseous (flavour), unsavoury (food); fulsome (praise); ☉ süß sickly sweet, of a sickly taste.

Widerlichkeit (⌣‿⌣‿) f ㊻ repulsiveness; loathsomeness, offensiveness, v. Speisen 2c.: nauseousness, unsavouriness.

widern (⌣‿) [mhd. entgegen sein] v/n. (h.) ㊽** 2a.: et. widert mir, es widert mir vor et. s.th. is repugnant (or loathsome, disgusting) to me, s.th. makes me heave or feel sick; vgl. anekeln; f. an☉. er☉.

wider-natürlich (‿⌣‿⌣) 2c. = unnatürlich 2c.; **-part** [mhd.] m ㉒. (auch f ㊻): a) = Gegenpart; b) einem ~ halten to make (or to act in) opposition to a p., to oppose (or thwart) a p.; Spiel: den ~ machen to be on the opposite side, to play against a p.; **-prall** m ㉒. = Gegenprall; ☉**raten** (‿⌣‿) v a. ㊻a*: e-m et. ☉ (abraten) to dissuade a p. from a th., to talk (or reason) a p. out of a th.; ☉**rechtlich** (‿⌣‿...) a. ㊺ contrary to law, unlawful, illegal; (unbillig) unfair, wrong; adv. auch: in defiance of the law; sich etwas ☉ aneignen to usurp a th.; **~keit** f ㊻ unlawfulness, illegality; **-rede** (⌣‿⌣) f ㊻ contradiction, objection; ohne ~ without contradiction, (unzweifelhaft) unquestionably, vgl. Widerspruch;
☉**reden** (‿⌣‿) ㊽* u. (⌣‿⌣) ㊽** v/n. (h.) = ☉sprechen; **-rist** (⌣‿) m ㉒ [: withers, wrist] m ⓐb. vet. am Pferdehalse: (erhabene Stelle zw. Hals u. Rücken) withers pl.; mit hohem ~ versehen high-withered; **-ruf** (⌣‿) m ⓐb. revocation, recantation, retractation, disavowal, einer Behauptung 2c.: withdrawal, einer Bestellung 2c.: counter-mand(ing); jur. disclaimer; ~ tun, oft: to recant, to retract, to withdraw (a statement, &c.); ☉**rufbar** (‿⌣‿) a. ㊺ = widerruflich; ☉**rufen** (‿⌣‿) v/a. ㊻b* to revoke an order, to recant an opinion, a doctrine, to retract or withdraw one's words, to disavow an assertion; eine Bestellung ☉ to countermand an order; ein Gesetz ☉ to repeal a law; ein Urteil ☉ to quash a sentence; ~ n ㉓ **-ruf**; ☉**ruflich** a. ㊺ revocable, retractable; **~keit** f ㊻ revocableness; **-rufung** f ㊻ = ruf;
-sacher (⌣‿⌣) [ahd.] m ㉒, **~in** f ㊼ adversary, antagonist, opponent, (Feind) enemy, foe, bibl. der ~ Satan;
-schall (⌣‿) m ⓐb. (also Echo) echo;
☉**schallen** (‿⌣‿⌣) ㊻a*(*) v/a. to reverberate, (re-)echo; **-schein** (⌣‿) m ⓐb. reflexion,

☉**scheinen** (‿⌣‿⌣) v/n. (h.) ㊽** to reflect, to emit (or give off) reflected light;
-schlag m ⓐb. (Gegenschlag) Rückprall: return-stroke, rebound; ☉ (a. **wieder**-) **schlagen** (‿⌣‿⌣) v/a. ㊻b*: e-n ☉ to strike a p. back; ☉**setzen** (‿⌣‿⌣) v/refl. ㊾*: sich e-m, sich e-m Dinge ☉ to resist (or oppose) a p., a th. ☉ to offer opposition to a p., a th.; sich einer Meinung 2c. ☉ to combat ..., to fight against ...; sich dem Gesetze ☉ to disobey the law; ☉**setzlich** a. ㊺ refractory, gegen Vorgesetzte: insubordinate, (ungehorsam) disobedient; **~keit** f ㊻ refractoriness, insubordination, disobedience; **-setzung** f ㊻ resistance, opposition; **-sinn** (⌣‿) m ⓐb. contrary (or wrong) sense, (Unsinn) nonsense, absurdity, F bosh; (Widerspruch) (spirit of) contradiction; paradox; ☉**sinnig** (‿⌣‿) a. ㊺ contrary to common sense or to the ordinary rules, inconsistent, contradictory, abnormal, paradoxical; (unsinnig) nonsensical, absurd, preposterous;
~keit f ㊻ inconsistency, nonsensicalness, absurdity, preposterousness;
☉**spenstig** [mhd.; *Span 3a] a. ㊺ refractory, (halsstarrig) obstinate, stubborn, (unlenksam) intractable, unmanageable, F obstreperous; bes. von Kindern: wayward, froward, unruly; (aufsässig) rebellious, (ungehorsam) disobedient, insubordinate, F und P contra'ry, von Pferden: restive; ☉ sein gegen et., a. to rebel (or F kick) against a th.; **~e(r)** s. ㊷ refractory, &c. person; Der ☉en Zähmung (Lustspiel von SH.) The Taming of the Shrew;
-spenstigkeit f ㊻ refractoriness, obstinacy, stubbornness, unmanageableness, F obstreperousness; waywardness, unruliness; rebelliousness, disobedience, insubordination;
☉**spiegeln** (‿⌣‿⌣) v/a. u. v/refl. ㊻a** to reflect, bes. fig. a. to mirror; sich ☉ to be reflected, to reflect o.s.; **-spiel** (⌣‿) n ⓐb. = Gegenspiel u. Gegenteil; ☉**sprechen** (‿⌣‿⌣) v/n. (h.) u. v/a. ⓐa*: einem ☉ to contradict (or gainsay) a p., einer Behauptung ☉ to contest (or deny) an assertion; (sich dagegen verwahren) to protest (or F kick) against a th.; dem wurde von allen Seiten widersprochen it was opposed on all sides, it raised general opposition; diese Sätze ☉ sich these propositions are contradictory (in terms) or inconsistent; er hat sich widersprochen he has made contradictory statements, he contradicted himself; mit sachlichem Subjekte: das widerspricht meinem Gefühle that's repugnant to my feelings; ~ n ㊷ contradiction; vgl. -spruch; ☉d p.p. und a. ㊺: a) in den Bed. des inf.; b) contradictory, inconsistent; conflicting (news, &c.); **-sprecher** m ㉒ contradicter, person who contradicts (everything); **-spruch** (⌣‿) m ⓐb. contradiction, gainsaying; (Gegensatz) opposition; (Meinungsverschiedenheit) disagreement; **-spruch**: conflict (of opinions); bei solchem ~ der Ansichten with such a clashing of opinions; auf heftigen ~ bei e-m stoßen, starken ~

[Widerspruchsgeist] — 1118 — [wie]

bei e-m finden to meet with violent opposition (or stout resistance) at the hands of a p.; im ~e stehen mit // to be contradictory to //, to be inconsistent (or at variance) with //; im ~ (stehend) mit incompatible with, not in keeping with; vgl. =rede; =spruchs-geist m spirit of contradiction.

Wider-stand (⌣‿) m ①c. resistance (a. ⚔, mech., phys., &c.), opposition to; ~ leisten to offer resistance, vgl. ②stehen a; elect. ~ ausschalten to switch out (or off) resistances; ~ einschalten to insert resistances; Einheit des ~es unit of resistance, vgl. Ohm³.

widerstands-fähig (‿‿…) a. ⑥ able to offer resistance; =fähigkeit f ⑫ capacity of resistance; =kraft f power of resistance; ²los a. offering no resistance, not resisting; =moment n, mech. momentum of resistance; =rolle ⊖ f, tel. bobbin of resistance, resistance-coil; =rollenkasten m res.-box.

wider-steh(e)n (⌣‿‿‿) [: withstand] v/n. (h.) ⑭*: a) to resist, to offer resistance to, to make opposition to; to set one's face against; to strive (or stand up or F kick) against; der Versuchung (nicht) ² to withstand (to yield to) temptation; b) mit sachlichem Subjekt: (zuwider sein) to be repugnant to; fette Speisen ² mir … disagree (or do not agree) with me; stärker: … make me heave, F … won't remain (or stay) on my stomach; =stoß (‿‿‿) m ①a. (counter)shock; vgl. Gegenstoß; ² (auch **wieder**=)stoßen (‿‿‿) v/a. ⑭a** to push (or thrust) back; ²strahlen (‿‿‿) ⑭** = abstrahlen; ²streben (‿‿‿) v/n. (h.) ⑭*: e-m, dem Willen j-s ² to oppose (or resist) a p.('s wish) (vgl. ²stehen a); et. widerstrebt mir s.th. is repugnant to me; ~ n ㉓ opposition, resistance; mit ~ with reluctance, reluctantly; ohne ~ readily, with a good grace or will; =streit (‿‿‿) m ①c. (o. pl.) antagonism, opposition; contest; ~ der Meinungen conflict (or difference) of opinions; ²streiten (‿‿‿) v/n.(h.)⑭b*: einem Dinge ² to be contrary (or opposed) to a th., to run counter to a th., to clash with a th., to militate against a th.; ²d, auch: antagonistic, conflicting; vgl. wider=; =strom (‿‿‿) m ①c. countercurrent, backwater (beide a. ⚓); =ton § [mhd.] m ①c. haircap-moss (Poly'trichum commu'ne); ²wärtig (‿‿‿) [ahd.] a. ⑥a) = widerlich; b) (verdrießlich) vexatious, disagreeable, unpleasant, F tiresome: eine ²e Geschichte a bothersome (stärker: a hateful, a disgusting) business; ~keit f ⑥ a) o. pl. = Widerlichkeit; a. vexatiousness; bothersomeness; b) mit pl. (etwas Widerwärtiges) vexation, disagreeable (F tiresome) affair, F nuisance; (Plackerei) bother, worry, tribulation; (widriger Zufall) untoward event, unfortunate incident; (Schicksalsschlag) reverse (of fortune), disaster, calamity; =wille, ~n (‿‿‿) m ㉗, ㉓ repugnance; (Ekel) disgust, loathing, abhorrence; (Abneigung) dislike, aversion, antipathy; (Haß) hatred, (deep) grudge, ill-will; mit (großem) ~n

(most) reluctantly, (much) against one's inclination or liking, a. with a bad grace; mit ~n erfüllen to (fill with) disgust, to sicken; ~n erregend distasteful; (Unlust) disinclination, unwillingness; ²willig a. ⑥ reluctant, unwilling, adv. auch: against one's own wish or will or heart; =wind ⚓ m ①c. = Gegenwind.

widmen (‿‿) [ahd.; *Wittum] v/a. und v/refl. ⑭b. 1. e-m ² (zueignen) to dedicate (or inscribe) a book, &c. to a p. — 2. = weihen 2, z.B. sein Leben der Geschichtsforschung ² to give up one's life to historical research; seine Zeit e-m, e-r Sache ² to devote one's time to a p., to a th.; Schwesterliebe widmet Euch dies Herz (sch.) my heart a sister's love vouchsafeth thee; sich e-r Sache ganz (oder mit voller Seele) ² to devote o.s. entirely (or to give one's whole mind) to a th., to bestow great (or the fullest) attention on a th.

Widmer (‿‿) m ㉒ dedicator. [book, &c.] **Widmung** (‿‿) f ⑯ dedication of a **Widmungs-exemplar** (‿‿‿…) n ⑫ dedication-copy; =schrift f dedication.

widrig (‿‿) [wider] a. ⑥ 1. contrary; adverse (wind, fate, &c.); (unglücklich) unfortunate, untoward (event, &c.); (zuwider) obnoxious; (feindlich) hostile; ²e Umstände adverse circumstances pl. — 2. = widerlich und widerwärtig. **widrigen-falls** (‿‿‿, ‿‿‿) adv. in the contrary (or reverse) case; failing which; jur. in default whereof.

Widrigkeit (‿‿‿) f ⑥ 1. = Widerwärtigkeit. — 2. (Widerlichkeit) repulsiveness. **wie** (¹) [ahd.] I adv., als cj. gbr. 1. in direkten und indirekten Fragen: a) ²? how?; in what way?; ² denn anders? how could it be otherwise?, of course!; ²so denn? how is that?, seltener: how so?; vgl. wieso; b) mit a. und adv.: ² alt sind Sie? how old are you?, what is your age?; ² breit ist das Zimmer? what is the width of (or how wide is) the room?; ² lange sind Sie hier? how long have you been here?; ² lange waren Sie dort? how long did you stay there?; ² oben (w. o.) as above, as previously mentioned; ² spät ist es? what's the time?, F what does the clock say?; ² stark war die Gesellschaft? how many were there at the party?; ² weit ist er? how far has he got?; ² weit ist es nach //? how far is it to //?; c) mit verbs: s. befinden 3; ² (beliebt)?, ² sagten Sie? what did you say?, feiner: I beg your pardon?; ² gefällt es Ihnen in Berlin? how do you like Berlin?; s. gehen 9 gegen Ende; ² kam es, daß //? how came (or was) it that //?; ich weiß nicht, ² er es meint … what he means by it; ² nennt man's? what is it called?; Frage des Verkäufers im Laden zc.: ² ist es heute mit Kaffee? do you require (or are you in want of) any coffee to-day?; s. stehen 6, ell. ² (wäre es), wenn er gar nicht käme? how if he were not to come at all?; ² aber, wenn er krank ist? but what (do you say) if he is ill?; auch: but suppose he is ill! — 2. in Ausrufen:

² froh war ich! how pleased I was!; ² leicht läßt man sich täuschen! how easily one can be deceived!; ² mancher how many a one; o, ² oft! oh, how often!; oh, how many times!; aber eingeschoben: sie hatte, ² oft, dort gestanden she had stood there so many times; ² sehr hat er sich getäuscht! how much he was deceived!; ² siehst du aus! how ill (or strange) you look!; vgl. wieviel; ² ward mir da! how (strange) I felt!; F ell. als Antwort: singt er schön? — und wie (schön)! oder: aber wie! does he sing well? — F rather!, or he does (sing well)! — 3. in Vergleichen: a) (s. als 4) sanft wie ein Lamm (as) gentle as a lamb; er sah aus wie ein Bettler he looked like a beggar; er schien wie vom Blitz getroffen he seemed as if (or as though) struck by lightning; er schrie wie toll he shouted like mad; ein Mann wie er a man like him or of his sort, F one of his kidney; wenn ich wie du wäre if I were in your place; ein solcher Held wie er such a hero as he; manche Leute, wie zum Beispiel (abbr. z. B.) mein Bruder // many people like my brother. for instance, //; b) s. gleichwie; so … wie, wie … so s. so 10; so gut wie s. so 7b; eins ist so gut wie das andere one is as good as the other, F it's all the same (thing); c) wie nach comp. = als 5. — 4. in vergleichenden Nebensätzen: a) (in der Art, wie) so wie ich bin such as I am, just as I stand; wie man mir gesagt hat as (or from what) I have been told; wie es recht und billig ist as is right and proper, (just) as it should be; wie die Sachen jetzt stehen as matters now stand; wie weiß, wie das gekommen ist … how it has come about; er ist noch hier, wie ich sehe I see he is still here; das war, wie Sie sich denken können, für uns eine Freude that was, as you may imagine, a pleasure for (or to) us; Sprichw. wie du mir, so ich dir as you do to me, I do to you, auch: tit for tat; b) (in dem Maße wie) das Geschick ist Ihnen günstig, wie es mich verfolgt fate favours you in the same measure as it pursues me; c) mit vorgestelltem a.: verwegen wie der Schmuggler ist, wird er sicher schießen the smuggler, like the dare-devil he is, will be sure to shoot; d) erklärend: Carlos, wie er sich nannte, … as he called himself. — 5. zeitlich = als 3, z.B. wie ich so vorbei kam just as I was passing by. — 6. wie … auch zur Verallgemeinerung, meist einräumend: wie schlau sie auch waren oder sein mochten however cunning they were or might be, with (or despite) all their cunning; wie schwer es mir auch ankommt however hard it may be for me; wie dem auch sei however that may be, be that as it may; wie sehr er auch zu bemitleiden ist much as he is to be pitied; wie auch immer s. immer 6; bisw. ohne auch: (und) wie sie alle heißen mögen whatever their names may be. — 7. fast = daß: er sagte uns, wie er bedaure, daß //

[Wiebel] — 1119 — [wiedererkennen]

told us how sorry he felt that ‖. — 11 s/n. inv. 8. das Wie und das Warum the why and the wherefore; Sprichw. auf das Wie kommt es an it all depends on how (or the way) it is done. **Wiebel** (´‿) m ❷ ent. (Kornwurm) weevil. **Wiede** obd. (´‿) f ❸ (Weidenrute zum Binden) withe, willow twig. **Wiedehopf** (´‿‿) [ahd.: wood u. hop] m ❸❹ ib. orn. hoopoo, hoopoe (*Upupa*). **wieder** (´‿; *Hom*. wider) [= wider] adv. 1. (nochmals) again, anew, afresh, once more; wie, schon 2! what, again (at it)!; es sind 2 drei Wochen vergangen another three weeks have elapsed; s. hin 5. — 2. in Verbindung mit vielen Ausdrücken, bsd. verbs, zB. 2 aufstehen to rise again; da bin ich 2 here I am again; 2 ins Leben rufen to revive, to bring to life again; 2 neu machen to restore; Speisen ꝛc. 2 von sich geben to bring up one's food, &c. again; 2 zu sich kommen to recover; vgl. die Zssgn mit Wieder-... — 3. = wider II, zB. e-n 2 grüßen to return a p.'s bow or ꝛc salute. — 4. = wiederum.

Wieder-a"bdruck ⊙ (´‿..., a.´‿...) m ⓒc. typ. reimpression, reprint; **2a"bdrucken** v/a. ⓒ** to reprint; **2a"bgeben** v/a. ⓒe** to return to, to give back; **2a"b-reisen** v/n. (su) ⓒ** to depart (or leave) again, mehr gbr.: to start afresh; **2a"bsagen** v/a. ⓒ** to countermand; **2a"bschreiben** v/a. ⓒ** to recopy; **2a"bsenden** v/a. ⓒa** to redispatch; **2a"bteilen** v/a. ⓒ** to subdivide; **2a"btreten** v/a. ⓒd** to retrocede; **-a"btretung** f ⓒ** retrocession; **2a"n-fachen** v/a. ⓒ** to rekindle, to set alight again; **-a"nfang** m ⓒc. fresh beginning, recommencement; ~ des Schulunterrichts reopening of school; **2a"nfangen** v/a. u. v/n. (h.) ⓒb** to begin afresh or anew, to recommence, to resume; **2a"ngeh(e)n** v/n. (su) ⓒ** to begin afresh; die Schule geht heute wieder an school reopens to-day; **2a"nheften** v/a. ⓒ** to reattach; **2a"nknüpfen** v/a. ⓒ** to renew an acquaintance, &c.; **-a"nknüpfung** f ⓒ renewal of friendship, &c.; **2a"nlegen** v/a. ⓒ** to relay, to re-establish, Geld: to reinvest; **-a"nlegung** f ⓒ re-establishment, v. Geld: reinvestment; **2a"nmachen** v/a. ⓒ** to fasten (or tie) again, Feuer: to rekindle, to relight; **-a"nnahme** f ⓒ readoption; **2a"nnehmen** v/a. ⓒa** to reassume, reaccept, readopt; **2a"nregen** v/a. ⓒ** to raise afresh, to revive; **2a"n-schaffen** v/a. ⓒ** to procure again; **2a"nstellen** v/a. ⓒ** to reappoint, to reinstall; **-a"nstellung** f ⓒ reappointment, reinstallation; **2a"ntreten** v/a. ⓒd** to resume a journey, &c.; **2a"n-wachsen** v/n. (su) ⓒb** to grow afresh; **2a"nwenden** v/a. ⓒa** to reapply; **2a"nziehen** v/a. ⓒb** : a) to attract again; b) Kleider: to put on again or afresh; ~ n ❷ und **-a"n-ziehung** f ⓒ phys. (nach der Abstoßung) reattraction; **2a"nzünden** v/a. ⓒ** to rekindle; **-a"ufbau** m ⓒc. rebuilding, reconstruction; **2a"ufbauen** v/a. ⓒ**

to rebuild, to reconstruct; **2a"f-blühen** v/n. (su) ⓒ** to flourish again, to blossom afresh; ~ n ❷ der Wissenschaften: revival of learning; **2a"f-ersteh(e)n** v/* ꝛc. = auferstehen ꝛc.; **2a"f-erwecken** v/a. ⓒ*/* vom Tode: to raise (from the dead), to resuscitate, a. u. resurrect; **2a"f-finden** v/a. ⓒ** to find again, to recover s.th. lost; **-au"f-findung** f ⓒ recovery; **2a"f-forsten** v/a. ⓒ** to re(af)forest; **-a"f-forstung** f ⓒ re(af)forestation; **2a"f-frischen** v/a. ⓒ** to refreshen, to revive; **2a"f-führen** v/a. ⓒ** thea. to play again, to reproduce (on the stage); **-au"f-führung** f ⓒ reproduction of a play, &c.; **2a"f-geh(e)n** v/n. (su) ⓒ** to reopen, to open afresh; **2a"fheben** v/a. ⓒ(⑦)b** (rückgängig m.) to abrogate, annul, rescind; **2a"f-kommen** v/n. (su) ⓒ** to rise again, von Kranken: to recover; ~ n ❷ recovery; **2a"fleben** v/n. (su) ⓒ** to show new (signs of) life, to come to life again, to revive; ~ n ❷ revival; **2a"flegen** v/a. ⓒ** to put (or lay) on again, ein Buch: to reissue, to republish; **2a"fmachen** v/a. ⓒ** to reopen; **-au"fnahme** f ⓒ einer Verhandlung &c.: resumption; **2a"fnehmen** v/a. ⓒa** : eine Arbeit ꝛc. 2 to resume ...; **2a"frichten** v/a. ⓒ** to set up again, to raise again; to re-erect; ~ n ❷ u. **-au"f-richtung** f ⓒ re-erection; **2a"fsteh(e)n** v/n. (su) ⓒ** to rise (up) again; ~ n ❷ vom Krankenbette ꝛc.: recovery; **2a"ftreten** v/n. (su) ⓒd** to reappear on the stage, &c.; ~ n ❷ reappearance; **2a"ftun** v/a. ⓒ** to reopen, to throw open again; **2a"f-wachen** v/n. (su) ⓒ** to (a)wake again; **2a"fwärmen** v/a. ⓒ** to warm up again; **2a"fsprechen** v/n. (su) ⓒa** to break out afresh; **-au"sbruch** m ⓒc. breaking out again, fresh outbreak, path. und fig. a. recrudescence, ꝛc. renewal of hostilities; **-au"sfuhr** f ⓒ re-exportation; **2a"sführen** v/a. ⓒ** to re-export; **2a"sgraben** v/a. ⓒb** to dig up again, Tote: to disinter, to exhume; ~ n ❷ u. **-au"sgrabung** f ⓒ disinterment, exhumation; **-au"s-söhnung** f ⓒ reconciliation.

Wieder-beginn (´‿...) m ❷ fresh beginning, recommencement; reopening of school, &c., ꝛc of hostilities, &c.; **2bekehren** v/a. ⓒ** to reconvert; **2bekommen** v/a. ⓒ*/* to get back, to recover; **2beleben** v/a. ⓒ**/* to recall (or restore) to life, to reanimate, revive, resuscitate; **-belebung** f ⓒ reanimation; ~s-mittel n ❷ means of restoring life, restorative; ~s-versuch m attempt to restore (a p. to) life; **2berufen** v/a. ⓒb*/* to recall, ein Parlament: to reconvene; **2besetzen** v/a. ⓒ*/* : ein Land 2 to reoccupy ..., mit Ansiedlern: to recolonize, einen Teich mit Fischen, ein Gehege mit Fasanen ꝛc.: to restock ...; e-n Lehrstuhl 2 to fill a vacant (professorial) chair; **-besetzung** f ⓒ reoccupation; **sich 2besinnen** v/refl. to reflect again; (wieder zur Besinnung kommen) to recover

one's consciousness; **-besitz-ergreifung** f ⓒ taking fresh possession of, reseizure, reoccupation; **2besohlen** ⊙ a. ⓒ** Schuhmacherei: to resole; **-betretungs-fall** m ⓒc. jur. im ~ if caught (in the act) again, in case of a second offence; **2bevölkern** v/a. ⓒa*/* to repeople; **2bezahlen** v/a. ⓒ*/* to repay; e-m Auslagen 2 to reimburse a p. for ...; **-bezahlung** f ⓒ repayment; reimbursement; **2bringen** v/a. ⓒ** to bring back, (zurückgeben) to restore, return; ~ n ❷ restoration, restitution; **-druck** m ⓒc. typ. (Neudruck) reprint. **wieder-ei"nbringen** (´‿..., a.´‿...) v/a. ⓒ** : e-n Verlust 2 to make up (for) a deficiency, to retrieve (or recoup, repair) a loss; **2ei"nführen** v/a. ⓒ** to reintroduce, einen Gebrauch ꝛc.: to re-establish, Waren: to reimport; **-ei"nführung** f ⓒ reintroduction, re-establishment, ꝛc reimportation; **2ei"ngeh(e)n** v/n. (su) ⓒ** ꝛc von Geldern: to come in again; **2ei"nkassieren** ⊛ v/a. ⓒ** to take again (in cash); **2ei"nlenken** v/n. (h.) ⓒ** = einlenken I; **2ei"nlösen** v/a. ⓒ** : Verpfändetes 2 to redeem ..., to take ... out of pawn; **-ei"nlösung** f ⓒ redemption; **-ei"nnahme** ꝛc f ⓒ recapture of a fortress, &c.; **2ei"nnehmen** v/a. ⓒa** to recapture, to retake; dieselbe Stellung 2 to resume one's former position; **2ei"npacken** v/a. ⓒ** to pack up again; **2ei"nrenken** v/a. ⓒ** = einrenken I; **2ei"nrichten** v/a. ⓒ** to rearrange, to reorganize, sein Haus 2: to fit up again, to refurnish; surg. Glieder 2 to reset ...; **-ei"nrichtung** f ⓒ rearrangement, reorganization; surg. resetting of limbs; **2ei"nschiffen** ⚓ v/a. ⓒ** to re-embark; **-ei"n-schiffung** f ⓒ re-embarkation; **2ei"n-schlafen** v/n. (su) ⓒ** to fall asleep again, to go to sleep again; fig. die Sache ist wiedereingeschlafen the matter has (been) dropt again; **2ei"nschließen** v/a. ⓒd** to lock up again; **2ei"nsetzen** v/a. ⓒ** to reinstate, to reinstall, in frühere Rechte: to rehabilitate, einen Herrscher: to restore to the throne; **-ei"nsetzung** f ⓒ reinstatement, reinstallation, rehabilitation, restoration (to the throne); ~ in den vorigen Zustand: a) jur. restitution; b) ꝛc postliminium; **2ei"ntreten** v/n. (su) ⓒd** : a) von Personen: to re-enter, ꝛc to re-enlist, to rejoin the ranks or the army; b) von Ereignissen: to happen again, to recur; ~ n ❷ u. **-ei"ntritt** m ⓒc. re-entrance, re-enlistment; v. Vorfällen: recurrence; **2ei"nziehen** ⓒb v/a.: seine Gelder 2 to get in ...; v/n. (su) to move in again. **wieder-ergänzen** (´‿...) v/a. ⓒ*/* to supplement afresh, auch. to redintegrate; **2erhalten** ⓒa*/* = erlangen; **2erinnern** v/a. u. v/refl. ⓒa*/* : sich 2 to recollect, to remember, to recall to (one's) memory; **-erinnerung** f ⓒ recollection, remembrance, reminiscence; **2erkennen** v/a. und v/rpr. ⓒb*/* (sich ob. ea.) to recognize each other, to know one another again; leicht

─────────────────────
⚔ scientific; ❦ botanical; ⚱ geography; ⊕ machinery; ⚒ mining; ⚔ military; ⚓ marine; ⊛ commercial; ✉ postal; 🚂 railway.

[Wiedererkennung] — 1120 — [wiegen]

wiederzuerkennen(d) easy to recognize, recognizable; nicht wiederzuerkennen(d) unrecognizable; =erkennung f ⑯ recognition; ꝛerlangen v/a. ⑱**/* to recover, to get back; =erlangung f ⑯ recovery; ꝛerobern v/a. ㉒a**/* to reconquer, recapture, retake; =eroberung f ⑯ reconquest, recapture; ꝛeröffnen v.a. ⑳b**/* to reopen; ꝛerreichen v/a. ⑱**/* to reattain; ꝛerscheinen v/n. (fn) ⑱*/* to reappear; ein Buch ⁓ lassen to republish ...; =erscheinung f ⑯ reappearance; ꝛersetzen ⑱**/*; v/a. to restore s.th. lost; to make up a p.'s loss; to repay a loan, &c.; e-m die Kosten ꝛerstatten to refund (or reimburse) a p.('s expenses); =ersetzung. =erstattung f ⑯ restoration, restitution, repayment; v. Ausgaben: reimbursement; ꝛerwachen v/n. (fn) ⑱**/* to (a)wake again; ꝛerwählen v/a. ⑱**/* to re-elect; =erwählung f ⑯ re-election; ꝛerwecken v/a. ⑱**/* vom Tode: to revive, to resuscitate, F to resurrect; ꝛerzählen v/a. ⑱**/* to retell, (was man von einem zweiten gehört hat, einem dritten usw. erzählen) to tell again, to repeat, an viele: to spread about; ꝛerzeugen v/a. ⑱**/* to reproduce, to regenerate; ⓶d reproductive; =erzeugung f ⑯ reproduction, regeneration; ꝛfangen v/a. ⑱b**/* to recatch, to catch again, to recapture; ꝛfinden v/a. ⑰**/* to find (or meet) again, Verlorenes: to recover; ⁓ n ㉓ recovery; ꝛflo"ttmachen ↓ v/a. ⑱**/* to refloat a stranded ship, a wreck; ꝛfordern v/a. ㉒a**/* to ask back, to redemand; ꝛfüllen v/a. ⑱**/* to refill; =gabe f ⑯ return, restitution, im Bilde: reproduction, durch Übersetzung: rendering, translation; =gebären v/a. ⑯f*/* theol. to regenerate; ꝛgeboren werden to be born anew or again; ꝛgeben v/a. ⑱c**: a) (zurückgeben) to give back, to return; e-m seine Ehre, Gesundheit ⁓ to restore a p.'s honour, health; b) (übersetzen) to render, to translate; ⁓ n ㉓ = =gabe; =geburt f ⑯ theol. regeneration (in the spirit), new (spiritual) birth, rebirth, conversion; ꝛgenesen v/n. (fn) ⑳b**/* to recover (from illness); =genesung f ⑯ recovery. convalescence; ꝛgewinnen v/a. ㉒a(b)**/* to regain, recover; nicht wiederzugewinnen(d) irretrievable; ꝛgrüßen v/a. u. v/n. (h.) ⑱**/* to return a bow or ⚔ a salute, to bow (⚔ to salute) in return; ꝛgu"tmachen v/a. ⑱** to make good, to repair a loss &c.; to make amends for, to compensate for; =gu"twerden v/n. (fn) ⑳c**: a) v. Wunden: to heal again; b) F v. Freunden: to become friendly (or good friends) again, to make it up again; ꝛhaben v/a. ⑳b**/* to have back (again); =hall ꝛc. f. Widerhall ꝛc. wieder=hera"bsteigen(¹⁰⁻⁻⁻, a.**⁻⁻⁻) v/n. ⑱** (fn) to come down again, to redescend; =herau"sgabe f ⑯ restitution, return, von Büchern: reissue, republication; =herau"sgeben ⑱c**: Genommenes: to give back, to disgorge;

Bücher: to reissue, to republish; ꝛhe"rstellbar a. ⑯ mendable, med. curable; ꝛhe"rstellen v/a. ⑱** = herstellen b; v. e-m Kranken: er ist ganz ꝛhe"rgestellt he has quite recovered (from his illness), he is quite restored (to health); =he"rsteller(in f) m restorer; =he"rstellung f ⑯ = Herstellung; eines Kranken: recovery; ⁓s-mittel n ⓮ restorative; ⁓s-zeichen ♪ n (h) natural; ꝛhervo"rbringen v/a. ⑰**/* to reproduce; =hervo"rbringung f ⑯ reproduction; ꝛhervo"rsuchen v/a. ⑱** to bring out of a hiding-place; ꝛhinau"fsteigen v/n. (fn) ⑱** to reascend, remount; ꝛhinei"ngeh(e)n v/a. (fn) ⑭** to re-enter; ꝛhi"ngeh(e)n v/n. (fn) ⑭** to return to the same place).

wieder=holen A (¹⁻⁻⁻⁻) ⑱** v/a. u. v/refl. to repeat; (noch einmal tun) to reiterate; (erneuern) to renew, (wieder sagen) to recapitulate; seine Gründe kurz ⁓ to sum up one's arguments; diese Dinge ⁓ sich oft ... frequently recur, ... are of frequent occurrence; er ꝛholt sich gern he is fond of saying the same thing over and over again, von einem Künstler od. Schriftsteller: he (often) repeats himself; die Geschichte läßt sich nicht ⁓ ... does not bear retelling, B (¹⁻⁻⁻) v/a. ⑱** (zurückholen) to fetch (or bring) back; er hat es ꝛgeholt he has fetched (or brought) it back; ꝛholentlich adv. repeatedly, again and again, over and over again, on more than one occasion; ꝛholt p.p. u. a. ⑯ repeated; adv. ⓶, zu ꝛen Malen = ꝛholentlich; =holung f ⑯ repetition, reiteration, recapitulation; recurrence; überflüssige ⁓ tautology; ⁓s-fall m ⑫: im ⁓s-falle in case of repetition, should it occur again; ⁓s-zeichen ♪ n repeat. wieder=käuen (¹⁻⁻⁻⁻) v/n. (h.) u. v/a. ⑱**(⑱**): a) zo. to chew the cud; to ruminate; b) F fig. (fortwährend wiederholen) to repeat (or to keep saying) over and over again, abs. to be for ever harping upon the same string; =käuer m ㉒: a) zo. ruminant; b) F fig. one who keeps telling the same (old) tales; =kauf m ⑫ repurchase; ꝛkauf, ꝛkaufen v/a. ⑱**/* to repurchase; =käufer m ㉒ repurchaser; =kehr f ⑯ return (= Rückkehr); (wiederholtes Vorkommen) recurrence, in regelmäßigen Zwischenräumen: periodical occurrence or appearance; ꝛkehren v/n. (fn) ⑱** to return, to come back; von Dingen: (sich wiederholen) to repeat itself, to recur; ⓶d repeatedly happening; immer wiederkehrend constantly recurring, happening again and again; math. ⓶de Reihe recurring series; ꝛkommen v/n. (fn) ⑭** to come back, to return to one's home; ꝛkriegen v/a. ⑱** to get back; =kunft f ⑩ coming back, return; theol. die ⁓ des Herrn the second advent of the Lord; ꝛmachen v/a. ⑱** to repair; =nahme f ⑯ recapture; ꝛnehmen v/a. ㉒a** to retake, to recapture (beide auch ⚔); ꝛrufen v/a. ⑱b** to call back; ꝛsagen v/a. ⑱** to repeat, to say (over) again, to retell, (bekanntmachen) to publish, to divulge; ꝛsammeln v/a. ㉒a** to

reassemble, ⚔ auch: to rally scattered troops; ꝛschaffen v/a. ⑱** und ㉒a** to create (or make) again; to restore; =schall ꝛc. = Widerhall ꝛc. = schein m. ꝛscheinen v/n. (h.) ⑥¹**/* f. Widerschein, widerscheinen; ꝛschelten ꝛc. ꝛschimpfen ꝛc. ꝛschicken v/a. ⑱** to return; ꝛschießen v/a. ⑳c(ej)** to shoot back; ꝛschimpfen v/a. u. v/n. (h.) ⑱** to abuse in return; =schlag m (zurückgegebener Schlag) return-stroke; ꝛschlagen v/a. ⑱b** to strike a p. back; ꝛschlimmer=werden v/n. (fn) ⑳c** to grow worse; ⁓ n ㉓ einer Krankheit: relapse; ꝛsehen v/a. ㉒a** to see again, e-e Person auch: to meet again; ⁓ n ㉓ meeting again; auf ⁓! till we meet again, I hope soon to see you again, (fr.) au revoir, kürzer: till next time; ꝛstoßen v/a. ㉒a** = widerstoßen; ꝛsuchen v/a. ⑱** to seek (again); =taufe f eccl. rebaptizing, second baptism; ꝛtaufen v/a. ⑱** to rebaptize; =täufer m ㉒ anabaptist; ꝛtönen v/a. ⑱** = widerhallen; ꝛtun v/a. ⑤** to do in return; ꝛum adv. again, anew, afresh; (andrerseits) on the other hand; (dagegen) in return; diese ⁓ these in their turn; ꝛu"mkehren v/n. (fn) ⑱** to return, to retrace one's steps; ꝛvereinigen v/a. ⑱**/* to reunite, (versöhnen) to reconcile; =vereinigung f ⑯ reunion, reconciliation; ꝛvergelten ⑬e** ꝛc. = vergelten ꝛc.; ꝛverheiraten v/a. u. v/refl. (sich) ⓶ ⑯**/* to remarry; =verheiratung f ⑯ remarriage; =verjüngung f ⑯ making (or growing) young again, rejuvenescence, second youth; =verkauf m ⑩ c. resale, im kleinen: retail (trade); =verkäufer(in f) m reseller; retailer, retail dealer; ꝛvermieten v/a. ⑱**/*: a) to relet; b) (aftervermieten) to sublet, to underlet; ꝛversöhnen ⑱**/* ꝛc. = versöhnen ꝛc.; ꝛwachsen v/n. (fn) ⑳b** to grow again; =wahl f ⑯ re-election; ꝛwählbar a. re-eligible; =wählbarkeit f re-eligibleness; ꝛwählen v/a. ⑱** to re-elect; ꝛzahlen v/a. ⑱** to pay back. wieder=zu"lassen (¹⁻⁻..., a.**⁻⁻⁻...) v/a. ㉒a** to readmit; =zu"lassung f ⑯ readmission; =zu"nahme f ⑯ fresh increase, new growth; ꝛzurü"ckfordern v/a. ㉒a** to ask back again, to redemand; ꝛzu"stellen v/a. ⑱** to restore (to the owner), to return a th. to a p.

wie=fern (¹⁸) vgl. inwiefern, inwieweit.

Wiege (¹⁻⁻) [ahd.: wägen] f ⑯ 1. cradle (auch oft fig.), korbartige: bassinet; fig. von der ⁓ bis zur Bahre from the cradle to the grave, from birth to (bibl.) unto) death; das ist ihm nicht an seiner ⁓ gesungen worden no one could have foretold him that at his birth. — 2. = Wiegemesser.

Wiege=brett ⓾ (¹⁻⁻...) n ⑫ choppingboard; =frau f woman that rocks the cradle, (a baby's) nurse; =maschine f chopping-machine; =messer n: a) Küche: chopping-knife; b) ⓾ Kupferstecherei: graving-tool.

wiegen¹ (¹⁻⁻) [: wägen] v/a. ⑳ c. I v/a. (wägen, das Gewicht bestimmen) to weigh, to put on the scales. — II v/n. (h.)

Zeichen (f. S. XVII): F familiär; P Volkssprache; ℐ Gaunersprache; ⚔ selten; † alt (auch gestorben); * neu (auch geboren); ⁺⁺ unrichtig;

[wiegen] — 1121 — [Wildhaut]

(ein Gewicht b..: to weigh two pounds. &c.. to have a weight of a ton, &c.; *fig.* schwerwiegende Gründe weighty (or highly important) reasons *pl.*; *vgl.* gewogen.
wiegen² (´‿) [Wiege] **I** *v/a.* und *v/refl.* ⊕ 1. (leicht schaukeln) to rock a cradle: in (den) Schlaf ℒ to rock to sleep; ein Kind auf dem Schoße, in den Armen ℒ to nurse a baby; sich ℒ to sway to and fro; sich auf einem Beine ℒ to balance (or poise) o.s. on one leg; ein ℒer Gang a rolling gait; *fig.* sich in Sicherheit ℒ to lull o.s. in security. — 2. Kocht.: (zerkleinern) to chop (with a chopping-knife). — **II ge-wiegt** *p.p. u. a.* ⊕ 3. smart, clever; in et. sehr ℒ sein to be well versed (or very skilled) in a th., F to be well up in a th.
Wiegen³-druck ("‿‿) [Wiege] *m* ⊕ *typ.* (alter Druck des 15. *sæc.*) ⫻ incunabulum; **=fest** *n* = **=Geburtstag**; **=kind** *n* child (or infant) in the cradle; **=korb** *m* basket-cradle; **= Korbwiege**; **=lied** *n* lullaby, *fr.* berceuse; **=pferd** *n* rocking-horse = **Schaukelpferd**; **=stuhl** *m* rocking-chair (= **Schaukelstuhl**).
Wieger (´‿) [wiegen¹] *m* ⫻ weigher.
Wieg-messer ("‿‿) *s.* **Wiegenmesser**.
wiehern (´‿) [*laut.*] *v/n.* (h.) *u. v a.* ⊕ 1. vom Pferde: to neigh. — 2. (laut lachen) to burst out laughing: ℒdes Gelächter horse-laugh. — 3. (laut schreien) to shout (or scream) aloud, to yell, to howl. [Meeresbucht] creek.]
Wiek ↓ (´) [*ndd.*]: wick *f* ⊕ (kleine)
Wiefe *prov.* (´‿) [*ndd.*: wick] *f* ⊕ *surg.* (Rolle Scharpie) piece of lint, tent; eine ℒ in eine Wunde legen to tent a wound.
Wiener (´‿) [Wien ⚘ Hauptstadt Österreichs an der Donau] **I** *m* ⊕ ~in *f* ⊕ inhabitant of Vienna, Viennese. — **II** *a. inv.* of Vienna, Viennese. [Vienna.]
wienerisch (´‿‿) *a.* ⊕ Viennese. off]
Wiepe *prov.* (´‿) [*ndd.*: wipe] *f* ⊕ ⫻
wie's (´) = wie es. [Strohwisch.]
wies¹ (´) *ind. impf.* von weisen.
Wies²-baum ⊙ *prov.* ("‿) *m* ⊙ *agr.* hay-pole (= **Heubaum**); *s.* bäumen **I**.
wiese¹ (´‿) *subj. impf. v.* weisen.
Wiese² (´‿) [*ahd.*; ✝ woosy] *f* ⊕ meadow, auch: (green) field, *poet.* mead, (Au) lea.
Wiesel (´‿) [*ahd.* weasel] *n* (*m*) ⫻ zo. weasel (*Puto'rius vulga'ris*); ℒ=artig ("‿‿) *a.* ⊕ weasel-like or -shaped, ⫻ musteline; ~fell *n* ⊕ weasel skin.
wiesen-artig ("‿‿) *a.* ⊕ meadow-like, meadowy; **=bach** *m* ⊕ brook flowing across a meadow; **=bärenklau** ⊙ *m, f* cow-parsnip, hogweed (*Hera-cle'um Spondy'lium*); **=bau** *m, agr.* cultivation (or irrigation) of meadows; **=bauer** ⫻ **=bewässerer** *m* meadower; **=blume** *f* meadow-flower; **=erz** *n. min.* (Rasen-eisenstein) meadow-ore; **=feld** *n* grass-land; **=flachs** *m* purging-flax (*Linum cathar'ticum*); **=gras** *n* meadow-grass; **=grün** *n* verdure of meadows; **=grund** *m* meadow-land; **=klee** *m* ⫻ clover growing in meadows; roter ~ common purple trefoil (*Trifo'lium praten'se*); **=knarre** *f. orn.* corn-crake = **Wachtelkönig**; **=knopf** *m* (großer) great burnet (*Sanguisor'ba officina'lis*); **=kresse** ⚘ *f* = **Schaumkraut**; **=kümmel** ⚘ *m* (common)

caraway (*Carum car'vi*); **=lein** ⚘ *n* = **=flachs**; **=lerche** *f. orn.* meadow-pipit (*Anthus praten'sis*); **=pfad** *m* path across a meadow; **=pflanze** *f* meadow-plant; **=pieper** *m* = **=lerche**; **=plan** *m* (plain covered with) meadow-land; **=quelle** *f* spring flowing from a meadow; **=raute** *f* meadow-rue (*Thalic'trum*); gelbe ~ fenrue, false rhubarb (*Th. flavum*); **=safran** ⚘ *m* = **Herbstzeitlose**; **=salbei** ⚘ *m. f* me.-sage (*Sal'via praten'sis*); **=scharrer** *m* = **Wachtelkönig**; **=schaumkraut** ⚘ *n* lady's-smock, cuckoo-flower (*Carda'mine praten'sis*); **=tal** *n* valley (clothed) with meadows; green vale or valley; **=teppich** *m* velvet-like meadow, grassy carpet; **=wachs** *m* growth of a meadow, grass-crop; F Anno ~ long, long ago: in days of yore or of old.
wie-so (-´) **?** ℒ weißt du das? how is it you know that?; *vgl.* wie I a.
Wies²-wachs (´‿‿‿⁽⁽⁾) *m* ⊕ = **Wiesenwachs**.
wieten *ndd.* (´‿) *v/a.* ⊕ *hort.* to weed.
wie-viel (-´) 1. a) how much?, *pl.* wie viele how many?; ℒ (od. wie viele) Herren waren es? how many gentlemen were there?; ℒ ist das wert? how much is it worth?, what is its value?; ℒmal? how many times?; *s.* Uhr 1; b) in Ausrufen: ℒ billiger wäre es — how much cheaper it would be!; um ℒ mehr ist das jetzt der Fall! how much more ...! — 2. als *s.* das ~ the quantity, the number: der, die, das ℒ(f)te ℒ ? what number?, which?; den ℒ(f)ten haben wir heute? what day of the month is it?; zum ℒ(f)ten Male? how many times (does this make)?
wie-weit (-´) inwieweit; *vgl.* wie 1 b.
wie-wohl (-´) *cj.* ⊕ obgleich; die einzige ℒ beste Belohnung the only, though the best recompense. [Seeheld] Viking.]
Wiking (´‿) [Wiek] *m* ⊕ (≙) d. (altnordischer)
wild (´) [*ahd.* wild] **I** *a.* ⊕ 1. wild: (roh, unbändig; *ant.* gesittet) savage (tribe, &c.), barbarous or uncivilized (people, &c.); (grimmig) fierce (look, &c.), ferocious (beast, &c.), brutal (fellow, &c.); (blutdürstig) bloodthirsty, truculent, (unbändig) unruly, (wütend) furious, enraged; (lärmend) turbulent; (ungebildet) uncultured, unpolished, uncouth; (unangebaut) uncultivated. — 2. mit *nouns*: ℒer Boden virgin soil; *s.* Ehe; *path.* ℒes Fleisch proud flesh, ℒe Flucht headlong flight, rout; ℒe Gegend wild (or rugged) country; ℒes Gestein dead rock; ℒes Haar dishevelled (or unkempt) hair; ℒe Jagd wild chase, *fig.* noisy set (of people); *s.* Jäger 1; ℒes Leben wild (or disorderly, dissolute) life; ℒes Mädchen tomboy, romp; *fig.* ℒer Mann bogey; ℒer Obstbaum wild tree; ℒes Pferd intractable (or ungovernable) horse; ℒer Reis wild rice (*Ziza'nia aqua'tica*); ℒ ℒer Spinat wild spinach (*Cheno-po'dium bonus Henri'cus*); ℒes Volk savage tribe. — 3. mit *verbs*: ℒ blicken to have a wild (or strange) look; ℒ m. to enrage, to exasperate, F to make wild, ein Pferd ℒc. to make shy; seid nicht so ℒ! don't be so noisy!; alles

lag ℒ umher things were (lying about) in a most disorderly state; ℒ wachsen to grow wild or in a wild state; ℒ wachsend (*ant.* gesät) of wild (or spontaneous) growth, self-sown; ℒ w. to turn wild or savage; (in Wut geraten) to become furious. — **II ~e([r]** *m*) *f* ⊕ 4. der ℒe, ein ℒer the (a) savage. — 5.: a) in Schulen: one who passes the final examination at a „Gymnasium" or „Realgymnasium" without having gone through the usual school-course; b) *univ.* student that belongs to no club or association; c) *parl.* deputy that is not attached to any particular party, independent member (of parliament). — 6. das ℒe in seinem Aussehen *&c.* his wild look, &c. — **III** ~ *n* b. (*pl.* ℒ) 7. (Tier als Gegenstand der Jagd): a) *coll.* game, hohes (kleines) ~ big (small) game, mit ~ gut besetzt well stocked (with game); b) (einzelnes Tier) head of game, (Reh) deer; rotes (mein Rot-) ~ red deer; ein Rudel ~ a herd (or flock) of deer; c) Kochkunst: venison.
Wild-acker (´‿‿) *m* ⊕ tilled field in a park; **=bad** *n* (natürliches warmes Quellbad) thermal spring-bath, natural mineral-water baths *pl.*; **=bahn** *f*: a) = **Jagdbezirk**; b) *hunt.* (Weg für Wild u. Jäger in einem Jagdbezirk) lane through a hunting-field or preserve; **=bann** *m. hunt.* exclusive right of chase; **=braten** *m* Kocht.: roast venison; **=bret** *n* [*mhd.*: Braten] a) game; b) Kochkunst: venison; **=bret-artig** *a.* ⊕ gamy (flavour, &c.); **=bret-braten** *m* = **=braten**; **=bret-händler** *m* game-dealer; **=dieb** *m* poacher; **=dieben** *v n.* (h.) ⊕ ‼ to poach; **=dieberei** *f* poaching.
Wilde (´‿) **I** *f* ⊕ 1. (o. *pl.*) = **Wildheit**. — 2. = **Wildnis**. — **II** 3. ⊕ *s.* wild **II**.
Wild-ente (´‿‿) *f* ⊕ *orn. hunt.* common wild duck.
wildenzen (´‿‿‿) *v n.* (h.) ⊕ to (have a) taste of venison. F to taste gamy.
Wilde(r) (´‿) *m* ⊕ *s.* wild **II**.
Wilderei (´‿‿) *f* ⊕ poaching.
Wilderer (´‿‿) *m* ⫻ = **Wilddieb**.
wildern (´‿) *v n.* (h.) ⊕ *a.* 1. to be rather wild or of a wild character, *v.* Pflanzen *&c.*: to revert to the wild state. — 2. = **wilddieben**.
Wild-esel (´‿‿) *m* ⊕ zo. wild ass (*Equus o'nager*); **=fang** [*mhd.*] *m*: a) trapping of game; b) captured (and tamed) horse or hawk; c) *fig.* unruly (or frolicsome) creature, romp, wild youth, (ausgelassenes Mädchen) tomboy, *biew. a.* hoiden; **=fleisch** *n* Kocht.: venison; **=fremd** *a.* ⊕ quite strange or unknown; er ist uns ℒ he is an utter stranger to us; unter ℒen Leuten among perfect strangers; **=garten** *m.* = **=gehege** *n* (game-)preserve, game-cover, park (stocked with game); (**=geruch**) = **=geschmack** *m* gamy (smell) taste, (odour) taste of venison; *vgl.* Hautgout; **=graf** *m alter Titel*: Wildgrave, Waldgrave; **=grube** *f* pitfall for (catching) game; **=hafer** ⚘ *m* = **Flughafer**; **=haut** *f*: a) deerskin; b) ⊕ ℒe häute American hides *pl.*.

[Wildheit] — 1122 — [Wimpelstock]

Wildheit (ˇ-) f ⓰ 1. ohne pl.: (Wildsein) wildness. wild nature; savageness. barbarity. savage (or barbarous) state; fierceness, ferocity, truculency; unruliness; e-r Landschaft: ruggedness. — 2. mit pl.: (wildes Handeln) (act of) savagery, atrocity, ferocious deed.
Wild-heuer (ˇ...) m ⓶ schwz. one who mows grass on the mountain-slopes; **=hüter** m game-keeper; **=kalb** n fawn; **=katze** f wild cat (Felis catus); **=leder** ⓪ n deerskin, buckskin; **ˈledern** a. ⓰ ⒠e Handschuhe buckskin gloves pl.
Wildling (ˇ⌣) m ⓭ 1. hort. wild tree or stock. des Holzapfelbaums: crab-stock. — 2. animal in its wild state. — 3. von Personen: rude (or uncouth, unpolished) fellow, barbarian, ruffian; (Wilde[r]) savage, man in a wild state.
wild-los (ˇ...) a. ⓰ gameless; **=meister** m ⓶ ranger; vgl. **=hüter**.
Wildnis (ˇ⌣) f ⓲ 1. wilderness, wilds pl., (Wüste) desert; fig. (Unordnung) wild disorder; confusion, chaos. — 2. (Zustand der Freiheit) wild (or savage) state.
Wild=obst (ˇ...) n ⓶ wild-grown fruit; **=park** m = garten; **=pret** n = brett; **=recht** n, hunt. bsd. der Hunde: quarry; **ˈreich** a. ⓰ abounding in game; **=ruf** m, hunt. (huntsman's) call; **=schaden** m damage caused by game; **=schur** f [poln.] fur-coat with the hair turned outside; **=schütz(e)** m (milder für dieb) poacher; **=schwein** n wild boar or sow (Sus scrofa); **=schwein(s)=jagd** f boarhunt(ing), in Ostindien. pig-sticking; **=schweins-kopf** m boar's head; **=sohl-leder** n buckskin; **=spur** f scent (of the game), track; **=stand** m stock of game; **ˈwachsend** ♣ a. (ant. gesät) growing wild, auch: wild-growing; **=wasser** n = Sturzbach; **=werk** ⧹ n game; **=zaun** m fence (or paling) of a preserve or park.
wildzen (ˇ⌣) v/n. (h.) ⓽⓪ = wildenzen.
Wilhelm (ˇ-) npr/m. ⓯⓰ a. William, auch: Willie, F Bill. [mina, Minnie.)
Wilhelmine (ˇ⌣⌣) npr/f. ⓯⓮⓷ Wilhel-)
will 1. u. 3. Person sg. pres. ind. v. wollen.
Wille (ˇ⌣) [ahd.: willi = wollen] m ⓱, auch ~n m ⓙ 1. will (auch im Vaterunser, f. Himmel 1), bsd. phls. volition; Sprichwort f. Himmelreich. — 2. a) mit a.: beim besten ~n despite one's best intentions; böser ~ ill-will, malice; es war dein eigener ~ it was your own wish, you wished it yourself; freier ~ free will, phls. auch: free agency; guter ~ good (or kind) intention; letzter ~ last wishes pl., (Testament) last will and testament; b) mit verbs: f. durchsetzen 2; Ihr ~ soll geschehen, oft: you(r instruction shall be obeyed; er will seinen ~n haben he wants (to have) his own way; wenn es Ihr ~ ist if you wish (or desire) it. zu Hochgestellten: if such be your pleasure; e-m seinen ~n tun to do as a p. wishes, to carry out a p.'s orders or commands; im gen.: Ins sein zu // to be willing (or ready) to // (inf.); c) mit prp.: aus freiem ~n of one's own accord, willingly, voluntarily; gegen (od. wider) meinen ~n against my will, contrary to my wish(es); et. gegen

seinen ~n tun to do a th. reluctantly or unwillingly or against one's inclination: mit ~n: α) on purpose, expressly; β) mit (freiem) ~n of one's own accord, spontaneously; mit j-s Wissen und ~n with a p.'s knowledge and consent; nach j-s ~n in accordance with a p.'s wishes; wenn es nach meinem ~n ginge if I could have my way (or if I had anything to say) in the matter; ohne meinen ~n without my consent or wish; um ... In als prp. f. um 2: wider ~n unwillingly, against one's inclination; f. o. gegen; einem zu ~n fein to be willing to serve (or oblige, please) a p.
Willen¹ (ˇ⌣) m 23 = Wille.
willen² (ˇ⌣) [Wille]: um ... f. um 2.
willen³ ✝ (ˇ⌣) v/a. ⓰, dazu: gewillt (f. ds).
willen los (ˇ⌣...) a. ⓰ without a will of one's own; (schwach) weak(-minded); (unentschlossen) irresolute. undecided. shilly-shally(ing); **ˈlosigkeit** f ⓰ want (or lack) of will, weakness (of purpose). irresoluteness. indecision.
willens (ˇ⌣): ~ sein f. Wille 2b.
Willens-akt (ˇ⌣. .) m ⓶ act of volition; **=änd(e)rung** f change of mind; **=äußerung** f expression of one's will, wish uttered; **=bestimmung** f decision. in einem Testamente: testamentary disposition; **=erklärung** f jur. manifestation of will; **=festigkeit** f firmness of purpose, (strong) determination; **=freiheit** f freedom of (the) will, free will; **=kraft** f force of will, power of volition, strength of mind; **=meinung** f expression of a wish or desire; **=stärke** f = kraft; **=vermögen** n (faculty of) volition; vgl. kraft.
willentlich (ˇ⌣⌣) a. ⓰ wilful, intentional, adv. a.: purposely, designedly.
willfahren (⌣ˇ⌣, ˇ⌣⌣) [spät-mhd.] ⓶* oder *.* I v/n. (h.): einem in etwas ~ to gratify (or grant) a p.'s wish(es), schwächer: to please (or humour) a p. in s.th.; der Bitte j-s ~ to accede to (or comply with) a p.'s request, to grant a p.'s suit, to acquiesce in a p.'s demand(s); man hat seinem Gesuch gewillfahrt his petition has been granted, what he asked for was conceded. — II ~ n 23 f. Willfahrung.
willfährig (ˇ⌣⌣, ˇ⌣⌣) a. ⓰ ready to oblige; (gefällig) obliging, complaisant; (willig) willing; (fügsam) accommodating, easy-going, yielding; b.s. obsequious, adv. a.: with a good grace.
Willfährigkeit (ˇ⌣⌣) f ⓰ readiness to oblige, obligingness, complaisance; willingness; b.s. obsequiousness.
Willfahrung (⌣ˇ⌣) f ⓰ gratification of a p.'s wish(es); compliance with a p.'s request.
willig (ˇ⌣) [ahd.] a. ⓰ willing, (bereitwillig) ready, (folgsam) docile, tractable, manageable, von Pferden ꝛc. auch: gentle; sich zu et. ~ finden f. to show o.s. willing (or readily disposed) to do a th.; et. ~ (oder mit Lem Herzen) tun to do a th. willingly or with a good heart or with a good cheer; der Geist ist willig, aber das Fleisch ist schwach the spirit is willing, but the flesh is weak. ⓢ ⒠e Käufer (ob. Neh-

mer) finden to meet with ready purchasers, to be eagerly bought (up), to sell readily; Börse: Geld ist ~er money is easier or more abundant.
willigen (ˇ⌣⌣) v/n. (h.) ⓯⓳: in et. ~ to consent (or accede, assent, agree) to a th., to comply with a th.
Willigkeit (ˇ⌣⌣) f ⓰ (f. willig) willingness, readiness; (Eifer) zeal, zest.
Willkomm (ˇ⌣. ⌣ˇ) [mhd.: welcome] m ⓶d. 1. = willkommen II. — 2. ~(=becher) cup of welcome.
willkommen (⌣⌣ˇ⌣) I a. ⓰ (D⓽) welcome; (angenehm) agreeable; acceptable; (gelegen) seasonable, opportune; e-n ~ heißen to welcome a p., to bid a p. (or to give a p. a) welcome; seien Sie mir (uns) ~! be welcome!, I am (we are) happy to see you!; das ist mir höchst ~ that comes most opportunely or just in the nick of time. — II ~ n (m) 23 welcome; (freundlicher Empfang) kind reception or greeting.
Willkomm(s)=becher (ˇ⌣...) m f. Willkomm 2; **=mahl** n dinner in honour of a p.'s home-coming; **=trunk** m drinking the health of a new comer, cup of welcome; vgl. Willkomm 2.
Willkür (ˇ-) [mhd.] f ⓰ (o. pl.) free will; (freie Wahl) free choice; (eigenmächtige Handlungsweise) arbitrary action, high-handed proceeding; (unbeschränkte Macht) arbitrary (or unlimited) power; nach ~ at will, F to the top of one's bent, (lt.) ad lib(itum); handeln Sie nach Ihrer ~, ich lasse das in Ihre ~ gestellt I leave that to you(r discretion), F (you may) please yourself about it, do as you like about it; er ist ihrer ~ preisgegeben he is (lying) at their mercy, he is in their power.
Willkür-herrschaft (ˇ-...) f arbitrary (or despotic) rule, despotism; **=herrscher** m absolute (or despotic) ruler, despot.
willkürlich (ˇ⌣⌣, ⌣ˇ⌣⌣) a. ⓰ arbitrary, despotic; absolute (power, &c.).
Willkürlichkeit (ˇ⌣⌣⌣) f ⓰ 1. (o. pl.) arbitrariness, despotic character. — 2. (mit pl.) arbitrary act or proceeding.
Willkür-verfahren (ˇ-⌣...) n ⓶ arbitrary (or high-handed) proceeding.
wimmeln (ˇ⌣) [(mhd.) ndd.] v/n. (h., bei Ortsveränderung zu) ⓶a. 1. to swarm; gewimmelt kommen to come in swarms or crowds; es wimmelt v. Ameisen ꝛc. the place is alive with ants, &c. — 2. (großen Überfluß haben an) to abound in, to teem with; (stark angefüllt sein) to be crammed (or crowded) with.
Wimmerer (ˇ⌣⌣) m ⓶ whimperer; whining (F snivelling) person.
Wimmer=holz (ˇ⌣. f (ˇ⌣) n ⓶, etwa: fiddle (with a twangy sound).
wimmern (ˇ⌣⌣) [mhd.] v/n. (h.) ⓶a. to whimper, whine, moan (über et. about a th.); vgl. winseln.
Wimpel ⚓ (ˇ⌣) [ahd.: wimple; *Wind-pallium] m ⓶ pennant, streamer; den ~ aufhissen to hoist the pennant; fig. eine Flotte von 20 ~n a fleet of twenty ships or pennants; **=fall** n ⓶ pennant-halyard; **=gast** m sailor who attends to the pennants; **=stange** f, **=stock** m staff for a pennant.

Signs (see page XVII): F familiar; P vulgar; ʄ flash; ⧹ rare; † obsolete (died); * new word (born); ✢ incorrect; ♩ music;

[Wimper] — 1123 — [Windsturm]

Wimper (⌣) [ahd. (sich) win(bende) Braue] f ⊕ 1. anat. eyelash. — 2. ⚘, anat., zo. ~n pl.: ⚔ cilia, f. wimpern II.
wimper-artig (⌣...) a. ⊕ (gewimpert) ⚔ ciliate(d); ⚘förmig a.: ⚔ cili(i)form; =fortsätze m/pl. ⊕: ⚔ ciliary processes pl.; =härchen n/pl.: ⚔ cilia pl.; =kiemen f pl. ichth. ciliated gills; =muskel m, anat. ciliated muscle.
wimpern (⌣) I v/n. (h.) ⚘a. to twinkle (with the eyes), to wink. — II ge-wimpert p.p. u. a. ⊕ ⚔ ciliate(d). [cili(i)ferous, ciliate(d).
wimper-tragend(⌣...) a.⊕anat., zo.: ⚔
Wind (⌣) [ahd.: wind: lt. vent-us: wehen] m ⊕b. 1. wind, gelinder: breeze, lieblicher, sanfter: zephyr, schärfer: searching (or piercing) wind, stärker: high wind, gale; s. stark 2 u. wehen I; ⚓ günstiger ~ fair wind; guten ~ h. to have the wind in one's favour; steifer ~ stiff breeze or gale; stürmischer ~ hurricane, storm; den ~ im Rücken h. to have the wind at one's back; vor dem ~e segeln to run before the wind; ~ u. Wetter dienend wind and weather permitting; durch ~ und Wetter behindert wind-and-weather bound; s. abkneifen, segeln 1. — 2. fig. F es ist alles ~ F it's all humbug or gas or puff; s. Mantel 1; ~ machen (prahlen) to brag, to boast; (faseln) to talk rubbish or twaddle, F to gas; in den ~ reden to preach to deaf ears or to the winds, to speak in vain; et. in den ~ schlagen (unbeachtet l.) to pay no heed to a th., to disregard a th.; Sprichw. wer ~ säet, wird Sturm ernten he that sows the wind will reap the whirlwind; fig. das wird seinen Namen schnell in alle ~e tragen that will soon spread his name abroad. — 3. hunt. (Geruchssinn der Tiere) scent; fig. ~ (Kunde) von et. bekommen to get to hear of a th., F to get the scent (or an inkling) of a th. — 4. med. (Blähung) wind; ~e pl. flatulency; e-n ~ l. to break wind.
Wind-ball (⌣...) m ⊕ ball filled with air, (small) air-balloon; =beschreibung f biswl.: ⚔ anemography; =beutel m: a) bag filled with air; b) F fig. windy (or F gasy) fellow, auch: windbag, F gas-bag; (Großsprecher) braggart, auch: humbug; c) Kuchenbäckerei: cream-puff, puff-pastry; =beutelei F swaggering, bragging, vapouring, puff, F gas(ing), wind; (Aufschneiderei) humbug, blarney; ⚘beuteln F v/n.(h.) ⚘a*.* ⚘* to (boast and) brag, to humbug; =blatter f = =pocke; =blume ⚘ ⚘ = Anemone; =bruch m: a) for. windfall(en trees pl.), damage caused by a storm; b) path.: ⚔ pneumatocele; ⚘brüchig a. ⊕ for. windfallen (branch, tree, &c.); =büchse f airgun, ~ wind-gun; =drehung f change (or shifting) of the wind; ⚘dürr a.: a) dried in the air, air-dried; b) F fig. emaciated; vgl. spindeldürr.
Winde (⌣) [ahd.: *winden] f ⊕ 1. ⚘ bindweed (*Convo'lvulus*). — 2. ⊕ Werkzeug: a) ⚘ Garnwinde; b) zum Heben u. Herablassen v. schweren Lasten: windlass, winch, (hand-)jack, crane; liegende ~ whim; stehende ~ capstan.

Winde-baum ⊕ (⌣...) m ⊕ mech. crabbar; =haken m sling-dog.
Wind-ei (⌣...) n ⊕ wind-egg.
Windel (⌣...) [⚔ *winden*] f ⊕ swaddling-clothes, mehr gbr.: long clothes pl., einfacherer Art: baby's napkin; noch in den ~n liegen to be (a baby) in long clothes.
Windel-band (⌣...) n ⊕ swathing-band; =bohrer ⊕ m wimble, centre-bit; =kind n infant in long clothes.
windeln(⌣)v/a.⚘a. to swaddle, swathe.
windel-weich (⌣...) a. ⊕ quite soft or limp; e-n ⚘ schlagen, etwa: to beat (or pound) a p. to a jelly or a pulp.
winden[1] (⌣) [Wind] v/n. (h.) ⊕ 1. mst v/imp. es windet it is windy, the wind is blowing, there is a (high) wind. — 2. hunt. vom Jagdhunde und Wilde: to take the scent.
winden[2] (⌣) [ahd.: wind: wenden] ⚔ I v/a. 1. to wind; to twist, to twirl (round); Garn auf die Winde ⚘ to wind yarn on the reel, to reel yarn; Garn von der Weife (ab-) ⚘ to unwind (or reel) yarn; Kränze ⚘ to make (or bind) flowers, &c. into wreaths or garlands. — 2. e-m et. aus den Händen ⚘ to wrest (or wrench) a th. from a p.'s hands. — 3. ⊕ et. (vermittelst e-r Winde) in die Höhe ⚘ to wind up a th., to hoist (or lift, raise) a th. with a windlass or crane. — II sich ⚘ v/refl. 4. to wind (o.s.), vom Wurm ⚘.: to wriggle, to turn; der Efeu windet sich um die Bäume ivy winds (or climbs) round trees; Schlangen, Taue ⚘. ⚘ sich um et. ... coil round a th.; sich vor Schmerzen ⚘ to writhe with pain; s. drehen 1, krümmen 2 u. 3. — 5. ein Bach windet (schlängelt) sich durch das Tal a stream winds (or meanders) through the valley; sich durch eine dichte Menschenmasse ⚘ to squeeze (or force) one's way through a dense crowd. — III ~ n ⊕ 6. winding, twisting; torsion; trotz allem Krümmen u. ~ with all his (or their, &c.) grovelling and crawling, weits. despite the most strenuous (stärker: desperate) efforts. — Vgl. auch Windung. — IV ⚘d p.pr. u. a. ⊕ 7. ⚘ sich ⚘d: winding, tortuous; ⚘de Täler sinuous valleys pl. — V ge-wunden p.p. u. a. ⊕ (D9) 8. wound, twisted; tortuous, spiral.
winden-artig (⌣...) [Winde 1] a. ⊕ convolvulaceous; =gewächse n/pl. ⊕: ⚔ convolvulaceæ pl.; =schwärmer m, ent. convolvulus hawk-moth (*Sphinx convo'lvuli*).
Winde-seil (⌣...) n ⊕ rope of a capstan.
Windes-eile, =geschwindigkeit (⌣...) f ⊕ velocity of the wind; mit Windes-eile with lightning-speed.
Wind-fackel (⌣...) f torch which can burn in (spite of) the wind; =fahne f vane, vgl. Wetterfahne; =fall m, for. windfall; =fang m: a) ⊕ ventilator, ⚘ a. air-trap; b) ⊕ metall. vent-hole; c) arch. (Vorbau der Haustür) porch, portico; d) weits. windy (or draughty) place; =fege ⊕ f = Fegemaschine; ⚘frei a. ⊕ sheltered from the wind, ⚓ under the lee of the shore; =galle f.

vet. windgall; =geschwulst f, path.: ⚔ emphysema; =gott m, myth. god of the winds, Æolus; =hafer ⚘ m bastard (or wild) oats (*Ave'na fa'tua*); =harfe ⚘♪ f Æolsharfe; =hauch m breath (or puff) of wind; =hose f w.-spout; =hund [ahd. wint] m: a) zo. (englischer: glatthaariger) greyhound, (schottischer: rauhhaariger) deer-hound; b) F fig. = Windbeutel.
windig (⌣) I a. ⊕ windy, breezy; exposed to the wind; es ist ⚘ it is windy or F blowy, the wind is blowing, there is a (high) wind; fig. von Personen: giddy, F gasy; vgl. luftig 3. — II ~ m ⚘d. e vt. (Falter) = Winden-schwärmer; ⚘keit f ⊕ windiness, airiness; fig. giddiness, F gasiness.
Wind-instrument ♪ (⌣...) n ⊕ wind-instrument; =kappe f cowl of a chimney; =karte ⚓ f pilot's (wind-) chart; =kessel ⊕ m, mach. air-chamber or -vessel; =klappe f ⊕ eines Blasebalgs: air-valve; =kolik f, path. windy colic, a. wind-colic; =kunde f: ⚔ anemology; =lade f: a) ⚒ ventilator; b) ⊕ Orgel-bau: wind-chest of an organ; =licht n candle protected by a shade; =loch n: a) = Wetterloch; b) metall. vent-hole; =lotte ⚒ f air-channel; =macher m: a) ⊕ in e-m Zimmer: ventilator; b) F = beutel; =macherei f = =beutelei; =maschine ⊕ f: a) ventilator; b) metall. air-compartment; =messer m, phys.: a) wind-gauge, anemograph, anemometer, anemo-dynamometer; ⚓ Manometer; =messung f, phys. anemometry; =mühle ⊕ f windmill; =mühlen-flügel m sail of a windmill; =müller m owner of a windmill; =ofen ⊕ m, metall. wind-furnace; =orgel ♪ f musical anemometer; =pocke f, path. pustule produced by chicken-pox; ~n pl. chicken-pox sg.; =rad n ventilator(-wheel), fan-blower; =rad-welle ⊕ f wind-shaft; =rohr n, metall. blast-pipe; =röhre ⊕ f Orgelbau: windpipe; =röschen ⚘ n = Anemone; =rose ⚓ f rhumb- (or compass-)card; nach allen Richtungen der ~ in all quarters of the globe, in every direction.
Winds-braut (⌣...) [ahd. P aus Windsprüt] f ⊕ strong gust of wind, great gale, hurricane, auch = Wirbelwind.
Wind-schacht ⚒ (⌣...) m ⊕ air-shaft or -course; =schaden m damage caused by a gale or a storm; ⚘schief a. ⊕ warped, all on one side; ⚘ werden to warp; =schiffer m = Luftschiffer; =schirm m screen against the wind; =schlauch m bag filled with air; ⚘schnell a. (as) quick as lightning, (as) swift as an arrow; =seite f windy side, ⚓ des Schiffes: weather-side; gegen die ~ to windward; =spiel n [uspr. (ahd. wint)] (Italian) greyhound; ⚘still a. calm, becalmed; =stille ⚓ f calm, lull (after the storm); becalmed (poet. Halcyon) sea; =stock ⊕ m Hydraulik: windpipe; =stoß m blast (or gust) of wind, stärker: squall; =strecke ⚒ f air-head; =streich-holz n = Zündhölzchen; =strich ⚓ m point of the compass, rhumb; =strom m, =strömung f current of air; =sturm m (strong) gale (of wind), storm,

[Windsucht] — 1124 — [Wintervorrat]

squall, hurricane; =sucht f, path.: ⚕ tympanitis; ²süchtig a. ⚕ tympanitic; =tür ⚓ f wind-gate.
Windung (ˊ˘) f ㊻ 1. = winden² II. – 2. (sich windende Linie) sinuous line, sinuosity, ⚲, phys., &c. torsion; zo. einer Schlange: coil, einer Muschel: whorl; mit ~en versehen winding (round), sinuous; ⚕ voluted. — 3. ⊕ ~ einer Schraube: worm of a screw.
Wind=vierung ↓ (ˊ˘...) f ㊷ quarter of a ship; ²wärts ↓ adv. windward; =wehe f snow-drift; =zeiger m, phys.: ⚕ anemoscope; =zug m: a) (Luftzug) current of air, draught; b) air-hole; vgl. =loch b; =zünd=hölzchen n fusee, lucifer (match).
Winfried (ˊ...) npr. ⑲ Winfred, Winfrid.
Wingert südd. (ˊ˘) [ahd. Weingarten] m ⑪c. (Weinberg) vineyard.
Wink (ˊ) [ahd.: winken] m ⑪b. 1. mit den Augen: wink(ing), mit der Hand: beckoning; fig. hint; (Rat) suggestion, advice; (Zeichen) sign; sie müssen ihn auf den ~ bedienen they have to be at his beck and call; e-m mit den Augen (mit dem Kopfe) einen ~ geben to give a p. a wink (a nod); e-m einen guten ~ geben to give (or drop) a p. a broad hint, F to give a p. the straight tip; f. winken 1; den ~ verstehen to take the hint. — 2. in einem ~ (Augenblick) in a twinkle, F in a jiffy.
Winkel (ˊ˘) [ahd.: Wange] m ㉒ 1. math., &c angle; bsd. arch. in den ~ bringen, auf den ~ prüfen to square. — 2. ⊕ = ~hafen, =maß. — 3. (stilles Plätzchen) (snug) corner. (quiet) nook; (Versteck) hiding-place; in allen ~n und Ecken in every nook and corner; die verborgensten ~ des Herzens the deepest recesses (or folds) of the heart; im entlegensten ~ Deutschlands in the remotest corner (or part) of Germany.
Winkel=advokat (ˊ˘...) m ㊷, etwa: lawyer('s clerk) who practises without possessing the full qualifications, bsd. hum.: pettifogger, F hedge-lawyer; =band ⊕ n. carp., &c. angle-iron; =bandstück n. carp. angle-tie piece; =blatt, =blättchen n small local paper or F sheet; =bogen m, math. arc of an angle; =bohrer ⊕ m (boring) angle-brace; =börse ⚲ f, etwa: outside broker's business, F bucket-shop; =börsen=spekulant m, etwa: ⁓ one who speculates at a bucket-shop; =dach ⊕ n, arch. square roof; =drucker m, etwa: small unknown printer; =druckerei f small obscure printing-office; =ehe f clandestine marriage; =eisen ⊕ n: a) (eisernes =maß) iron square or rule; b) (Eckeisen) iron clamp or cramp (bent at right angles), knee-iron, a. H- (or L-, T-)iron; ²förmig a. ㊶ angular; =funktion f, math. circular (or angular) function; =gasse f slum, obscure street or lane, auch = Sackgasse; =geschwindigkeit f, mech. circular velocity; =haken ⊕ m: a) carp., &c. = =maß, angle-piece; b) typ. composing-stick, mit Keilverschluß: Grover-stick, mit Schraubenverschluß: screw-stick; =hobel ⊕ m angle-plane; =holz ↓ n angle-staff.

wink(e)licht, wink(e)lig (ˊ(˘)˘) a. ㊶ 1. angular, cornered; weitS. (kniefőrmig gebogen) bent at right angles, auch: L- (or T-)shaped; winklige Straße winding (or crooked) street. — 2. in Bfgn -angled, f. recht=, spitz=, stumpf=².
Winkel=klammer ⊕ (ˊ˘...) f ㊷ = =eisen b; =klotz m angle-block; =kneipe f = =schenke; =konsulent m = =advokat; =makler ⚲ m outside broker; =maß n, carp., &c. (carpenter's) square, rule, (Maurerkelle) angle-float; =maß=instrument n Astronomie: circular instrument; =messer m, math., &c. Instrument: protractor, goniometer, angle-meter; =meßkunst, =messung f measurement of angles, ⚲ goniometry; =naht f, anat. an der Hirnschale: ⚕ lambdoid(al) suture; =poet m obscure poet or rhymster, poetaster; =presse f =druckerei; ²recht a. ㊶ at right angles, square; vgl. rechtwink(e)lig; =scheibe f, math.: ⚕ astrolabe; =schenke f, etwa: obscure (roadside) inn; unlicensed beer-shop; =schreiber, =schriftsteller m obscure (hum. a. Grubstreet-)writer; =schule f small adventure-school, ehm. auch: hedge-school; =spiegel ⊕ m, surv. optical square; =spiel ⚲ m puss-in-the-corner; ²ständig ⚲ a. = achselständig; =stange f, tel. angle-pole; =streichmaß n, join. scribing-block; =treppe f private staircase; =zug m, mst =züge m/pl. dodges, shifts, subterfuges, cunning devices, artful tricks pl.; =züge machen to prevaricate, to shuffle, to use trickery; ²zügig a. shuffling, tortuous.
winken (ˊ˘) [ahd.: wink: wanken] v/n. (h.) u. v/a. ㊸ 1. mit den Augen (blinzeln) to wink one's eyes; e-m mit den Augen ² to give a p. a wink, to wink one's eyes at a p.; e-m mit der Hand ² to beckon a p., to wave one's hand to a p.; e-m mit dem Taschentuch ² to wave one's handkerchief to a p.; er winkte mir, ich solle herankommen ob. heranzukommen he beckoned me to come up (to him); F co. e-m mit dem Laternenpfahl ob. Zaunpfahl ob. Scheunentor ² (ob. einen Wink geben) to give a p. a broad hint, to make a p. clearly understand; Sprichw. man braucht (ihm zc.) nicht mit dem Zaunpfahl zu winken a nod is as good as a wink. — 2. abs. to make a sign; er braucht nur zu ², so geschieht es his very nod is obeyed, his word is law. — 3. als v/a.: e-m Stillschweigen ² to make a sign to a p. to be silent; mit Angabe des Erfolges: e-n beiseite, näher ² to beckon (to) a p. aside, to come nearer.
winklicht, ...ig (ˊ˘) f. wink(e)licht, ...ig.
Winkel=affe (ˊ˘ˊ˘) m ㊷ zo. weeper, capuchin (Cebus capuci'na).
Winselei (˘˘ˊ) f ㊶ = Gewimmer.
Wins(e)ler (ˊ˘˘) m ㉓ whining person, ⚞ whiner, moaner, F sniveller.
winselig (ˊ˘˘) a. ㊶ whining, moaning, v. Kindern a. puling, F snivel(l)ing.
winseln (ˊ˘) [mhd.: whine] v/n. (h.) ㊸a. to whine, whimper, moan, wail, von Kindern auch: to pule; e-m die Ohren voll ², etwa: to pour out one's complaints (or troubles) to a p.

Winsel=stimme (ˊ˘ˊ˘) f ㊷ whining (or moaning) voice.
Winsler (ˊ˘) m ㉓ f. Wins(e)ler.
Winter (ˊ˘) (ahd. winter „weiße" Zeit) m ㉒ winter; im ~, des ~s in winter. in the winter-time; mitten im ~ in the depth of winter, a. in mid-winter; den ~ verbringen (to pass the) winter, bsb. zo.: ⚕ to hibernate.
Winter=abend (ˊ˘...) m ㉒ winter-evening; =anzug m winter-dress or -garment or -clothes; =apfel m wi.-apple; =aufenthalt m wi.-abode; =bedarf ⚲ m wi.-demand or -stock; =beere ⚲ f winterberry (Prinos, Nordamerika); =birne f winter-pear; =brache f, agr. winter-fallow; =fahr=plan m winter time-table; =feldzug m wi.-campaign; =fenster n outer window; =frucht f, agr. winter-crop; =futter n, agr. wi.-fodder; =garten m wi.-garden; =gerste f, agr. wi.-barley; =getreide n wi.-corn, autumn-sown corn; =gewächs n wi.-plant; =grün ⚲ n: a) winter-green (Pi'rola); b) (Zimmergrün) periwinkle (Vinca), doldiges ~ Am. pipsissewa (Chimo'phila umbella'ta); =haar n, zo. winter-coat or -fur; =hafen ↓ m harbour for the winter; =hafer m, agr. winter-oats pl.
winterhaft (ˊ˘˘) a. ㊶ = winterlich.
Winter=haus (ˊ˘...) n ㊷ winter-house, hort. hothouse; =holz n wood for the winter; =kälte f cold of winter; =kleidung f = =anzug; =könig m: a) orn. = Zaunkönig; b) hist. (Friedrich V. v. d. Pfalz, 1619–20 König v. Böhmen), etwa: king for one winter; =korn n = =getreide; =kresse ⚲ f = Barben=kraut; =lager n: a) ⚔ winter-camp; b) ⚲ wi.-stock; =landschaft f wi.-scenery; =levkoje ⚲ f f. Levkoie.
winterlich (ˊ˘˘) a. ㊶ winter-like, of winter, wint(e)ry, seltener: winterly, ⚕ hibernal. ⚞ hiemal; adv. as in winter, in wintry fashion.
Winter=märchen (ˊ˘...) n ㊷ fairy-tale for winter-evenings; das ~ (sh.) the Winter's Tale; ²mäßig a. ㊶ = winterlich; =morgen m winter-morning.
wintern (ˊ˘) ㊷a. I v/n. (h.) v/imp. es wintert it is (getting) winter or wintry, we are now in (the midst of) winter. — II v/a. to (keep through the) winter, ⚕ to hibernate. — III ~ n ㉓ = Winterung 1.
Winter=nacht (ˊ˘...) f ㊷ winter-night; =obst n winter-fruit; =quartier ⚔ n winter-quarters pl.; die ~e beziehen to take up one's winter-quarters.
winters (ˊ˘) adv. = des Winters.
Winter=saat (ˊ˘...) f ㊷ agr.: a) sowing of winter-corn; b) winter-crop(s pl.); =schlaf m, zo. winter-sleep, hibernation; =schläfer m, zo. hibernating animal; =seite f north(ern) side; =sturm m wintry storm or gale; =überzieher m winter-overcoat.
Winterung (ˊ˘˘) f ㊷ 1. (f. wintern II) wintry weather; (f. wintern II) wintering, ⚕ hibernation. — 2. place for keeping winter-stores, hort. (Treibhaus) hothouse, conservatory.
Winter=vergnügen (ˊ˘...) n ㊷ amusement for the winter; =vorrat m win-

Zeichen (f. S. XVII): F familiär; P Volkssprache; Γ Gaunersprache; ⚞ selten; † alt (auch gestorben); * neu (auch geboren); ⚆⚆ unrichtig.

[Winterweizen] — 1125 — [wirksam]

ter-stock or -stores or -provisions *pl.*; **=weizen** *m, agr.* winter-wheat; **=wetter** *n* wintry weather; **=wohnung** *f* winter-residence; **=zeit** *f* wi.-time or -season or -months *pl.*

Winzer (♩‿) [ahd.:*lt.vi'nitor*:Wein] *m* ㉒. **~in** *f* ㊼ 1. (Weinbauer) vine-dresser; wine-grower, owner of a vineyard. — 2. (Traubenleser[in]) vintager, gatherer of grapes, grape-gatherer, -picker.

Winzer=fest (♩‿...) *n* ㉒ vintage; **=lied** *n* song of grape-pickers; **=messer** ⊙ *n* vine-knife, vine-dresser's knife.

winzig (♩‿) [mhd.; *wenig] *a.* ㊅㊅ very small; diminutive (stature, &c.), minute (particle, &c.), puny (child, &c.); (geringfügig) petty; (klein u. zierlich) tiny, F wimmeny-pimmeny; (sehr dürftig) very poor or scanty; ᴅer Betrag trifling sum, paltry amount; ᴅes Männchen (little) mannikin, hop-o'-my-thumb; ᴅes Stückchen wee little bit.

Winzigkeit (♩‿..) *f* ㊻ diminutive size or stature, diminutiveness, minuteness.

Wipfel (♩‿) [ahd.: wippen] *m* ㉒ top of a tree, tree-top. ┃with a top.┃ **wipf(e)licht, ...ig** (♩‿‿) *a.* ㊅㊅ (crowned) **wipfeln** (♩‿) ㊚a. I *v/n.* (h.) *v/refl.* (sich) ᴅ to tower, to rise aloft, to stand very high. — II *v/a.* ᴅ kappen 2.

wipp! (') *int.* ᴅ! quick!

Wippchen F (♩‿) [Wippe] *n/pl.* ㉓ tricks, dodges *pl.*; (Flunkerei) fibs, F flams *pl.*; (Winkelzüge) subterfuges *pl.*

Wippe (♩‿) [ndd.] *f* ㊸ 1. = Kippe 1; auf ᴅer ᴅ stehen to stand atilt. — 2. (Vorrichtung zum Schaukeln) seesaw, rocking-board. — 3. = Wippgalgen. — 4. = Peitsche. — 5. Kippe und ᴅ = Kipperei. — 6. Turnerei: (wiegende Bewegung oder Schwingung) balancing. — 7. ⊙: a) ᴅ (Hebebalken einer Zugbrücke) bascule, plier, swipe-beam; b) *tel.* tumbler-switch; c) Nadlerei: heading-machine, header.

wippeln (♩‿) ㊚a. = wippen I u. II.

wippen (♩‿) [ndd.; whip] ㊇ I *v/n.* (h.) 1. to balance (o.s.); to rock, to seesaw, to swing up and down; die Knaben ᴅ sich ob. ca. the boys are playing seesaw; eine ᴅde Bachstelze a restless wagtail; auch als *v/refl.* der Storch wippt (sich) erst mit den Flügeln ... first flaps his wings. — II *v/a.* u. *v/recip.* 2. e-n ᴅ (schaukeln) to rock (or seesaw) a p.; e-n ᴅ (zu Fall bringen) to upset a p. — 3. ⚔ ehm. e-n ᴅ (auf dem Wippgalgen) ᴅ to strappado a p. — 4. f. kippen 2. — III ~ *n* ㉓ 5. balancing, &c. (f. wippen I); f. a. kippen 2 II.

Wippen=bohrer ⊙ (♩‿‿) *m* ㉒ lever-drill. ┃㊺ f. Kipperei 1.┃

Wipper (♩‿) *m* ㉒ f. Kipper; **~ei** (♩‿‿) *f*

Wipp=galgen ⚔ (♩‿‿) *m* ㉒ strappado.

wir (') [ahd.: we] *personal pron. pl.* v. ich ㊅㊅ A1(3) we; ᴅ alle we all, all of us; ᴅ beide both of us; wir Deutsche(n) we Germans; ᴅ drei we three, the three of us; ᴅ Engländer we English (folk); ᴅ selbst we ourselves; ᴅ Verlassene we forsaken ones; ᴅ find es it is we, it is P it's us; ᴅ, die ᴅ nicht rauchen // we who do not smoke //; f. Gnade 1.

wirb (') *imper.* von werben.

Wirbel (♩‿) [ahd.: whirl: werben] *m* ㉒ 1. (kreisende Drehung) whirl, twirl, rotation, gyration; sich im ~ drehen to whirl (or reel) round. — 2. (Rauch=) ~ wreath(s) (or curl) of smoke; (Wasser=)~ eddy, größerer: whirlpool, vortex. — 3. (Schwindel) giddiness, dizziness, ʒ⃞ vertigo; vgl. Taumel. — 4. (Scheitel) crown (or top) of the head, *anat.*: vertex; vom ~ bis zur Zehe from top to toe, from head to foot. — 5. ♪: a) (Triller) trill(ing), warbling of birds; b) ~ auf der Trommel roll of the drum; ⚔ einschlagen to roll (a drum). — 6. *anat.* (Knochen des Rückgrats) ʒ⃞ vertebra; zum (Rücken=)~ gehörig: ʒ⃞ vertebral. — 7. ⊙ contrivance for turning; swivel, lever; ~ e-r Drehbank collar of a lathe; Weberei: sheave of a spinning-wheel; ~ an Fenstern bolt (or button, fastener) of a window; ♪ ~ zum Spannen von Saiten peg of a violin, &c.

Wirbel=bein (♩‿..) *n* ㉒ *anat.*: vertebra; **=block** ↓ *m* swivel-block; **=borste** *f*, **=dost** *m* ⚘ basil-weed (*Clinopo'dium vulga're*); **=förmig** *a.* ㊅㊅ a) spindle-shaped, whirling; b) *anat.* ʒ⃞ vertebral; c) ⚘: ʒ⃞ verticillate **=gelenk** *n*: a) ⊙ swivel-joint; b) *anat.*: ʒ⃞ vertebral articulation.

wirbelhaft (♩‿‿) *a.* ㊅㊅ = wirb(e)lig.

Wirbel=haken ↓ (♩‿‿) *m* ㉒ swivel-hook.

wirb(e)licht, wirb(e)lig (♩‿‿) *a.* ㊅㊅ 1. whirlende, whirly, rotatory; bisw. = schwindelig. — 2. (ungestüm) impetuous. — 3. von Haaren: (im Wirbel gewachsen) on the crown (or top) of the head.

Wirbel=kasten ♪ (♩‿..) *m* ㉒ der Violine: hollow of the neck; **=knochen** *m* = =bein; **=los** *a.* ㊅㊅ zo. spineless, ʒ⃞ invertebrate; ᴅlose Tiere invertebrates *pl.*

wirbeln (♩‿) [ahd.: whirl] I *v/n.* (h.); bei Ortsveränderung (n) u. *v/refl., v/a.* ㊚a. 1. (sich) ᴅ to whirl, to turn (or twist, twirl, spin) round, vom Schnee: to drift, vom Wasser: to eddy, to swirl; *fig.* mir wirbelt der Kopf my head is in a whirl; vgl. schwindeln 1.; die Lerche wirbelt (ihr Lied) the skylark is warbling (its song) or carolling (forth) its note; ♪ auf der Trommel ᴅ to roll (a drum), to beat a roll. — II ~ *n* ㉓ 3. whirling, &c. (f. 1); warbling of a bird; ♪ roll of a drum.

Wirbel=säule (♩‿..) *f* ㊻ *anat.* vertebral column, spine, ʒ⃞ rachis; **=schlagader** *f, anat.*: ʒ⃞ vertebral (artery); **=sturm** *m* cyclone, tornado; **=sucht** *f, path.* giddiness, vertigo; **=tier** *n, zo.* vertebrate animal, *a.* vertebrate; **=tierchen** *n/pl.* = Rädertiere; **=trommel** ♪ *f* flat drum; **=wind** *m* whirl-wind, tornado; **=zentrum** *n* centre of rotation or gyration.

wirblicht, ...ig (♩‿‿) *a.* ㊅㊅ f. wirbelicht, ...ig.

wirbst, wirbt (') *pres. ind.* von werben.

wird (') 3. Person *sg. pres. ind. v.* werden.

wirf, 2t, 2t (') *imper.*, 2. u. 3. Person des *sg. pres. ind. v.* werfen. ┃kneading-trough.┃

Wirk=bank ⊙ (♩‿) *f* ㉒, **=brett** n Bäckerei:

wirken (♩‿) [ahd.: work: Werk] I *v/n.* (h.) u. *v/a.* ⑧ 1. to (be at) work, to (take) effect, to operate; (hervorbringen) to produce, to bring about; Gutes ᴅ to do good; Wunder ᴅ to work wonders; *abs.* die Arznei hat gewirkt ... has taken effect; bei diesen Leuten wirkt nichts nothing has any effect with (or all is lost on) these people; beruhigend ᴅ to have a quieting (or soothing) effect; dahin ᴅ, daß et. geschieht to labour (or strive) hard so that s.th. (may) be done. — 2 mit *prp.*: **an** e-r Schule (als Lehrer) ᴅ to teach (or to be a master) at a school; **auf** e-n, et. ᴅ to act (or operate) on a p., a th.; to affect a p., a th.; nachteilig auf et. ᴅ to have a prejudicial effect upon a th., auf j-s Gesundheit: to tell on a p.'s health; **für** e-n ᴅ to work hard (or to exert o.s.) for a p.; **gegen**=ea. ᴅ to counteract each other. — 3. ⊙: a) Weberei: to work at the loom, to weave; gewirkt woven; b) Bäckerei: den Teig ᴅ (kneten) to knead the dough; c) Hufschmiede: den Huf ᴅ to pare a horse's hoof; d) Saline: Salz ᴅ to boil salt. — II ~ *n* ㉓ 4. working, &c. (f. 1); labour(ing); activity; (Anstrengung) exertion, effort, endeavour; f. Wirkung. — III ᴅd *p.pr.* und *a.* ㊅㊅ 5. acting, operating, operative, effectual, efficacious, telling. *phls.* causative; stark ᴅd highly effective, very telling, powerful, drastic.

Wirker (♩‿) *m* ㉒ 1. worker, one who works. — 2. ⊙: a) Weberei: weaver; vgl. Strumpfwirker; b) Bäckerei: kneader; c) = Salzwirker.

Wirkerei ⊙ (♩‿‿) *f* ㊻ Weberei: weaving, working at the loom; oft in Zssg. f. Strumpf-, Salz-wirkerei.

wirklich (♩‿) *a.* ㊅㊅ 1. real; (tatsächlich) actual, material, substantial (gain, &c.), positive (fact, &c.); (wahrhaft) veritable, true (character, &c.); (echt) genuine, sterling (gold, &c.); ᴅ machen to realize; ᴅ werden to become real(ized); ⚔ ᴅe Stärke eines Truppenkörpers: effective strength ...; ⚓ ᴅer Vorrat visible supply, stock on hand; in Titeln: ᴅer Geheimer Rat. etwa: acting privy counsellor. — 2. *adv.* oft: really, truly, in fact; haben Sie das ᴅ gesagt? did you really (or actually, positively) say that?; ᴅ? indeed?, is that a fact?, is that so?, are you sure?; ich weiß ᴅ nicht, ob // I am not quite sure (or altogether certain) whether //.

Wirklichkeit (♩‿‿) *f* ㊻ (*ant.* Schein) 1. *o. pl.*: reality, real existence or life; actuality, positiveness; truth; in ᴅ in reality, in fact, really; in die ᴅ übersetzen, zur ᴅ. to realize, materialize. — 2. mit *pl.*: (et. Wirkliches) real fact, positive case; (real) substance.

Wirk=meister ⊙ (♩‿..) *m* ㉒ Weberei: master weaver; **=messer** *n* der Hufschmiede: farrier's paring-knife.

wirksam (♩‿) *a.* ㊅㊅ (wirkend) active, operative; (Wirkung hervorbringend) effective, effectual, efficacious, powerful (remedy, &c.); bfd. v. Personen: efficient; ᴅ sein to produce (the desired) effect; ᴅ gegen acting against, v. Arzneien ꝛc. auch: good for.

♪ Musik; ʒ⃞ Wissenschaft; ⚘ Pflanze; 🏆 Geographie; ⊙ Technik; ⚒ Bergbau; ⚔ Militär; ↓ Marine; ⊕ Handel; ✉ Post; 🚂 Eisenbahn.

[**Wirksamkeit**]

Wirksamkeit (⌣-) f ⓰ activity (of a person, &c.), operation (of the law, &c.); agency; effectiveness, efficaciousness, efficacy, efficiency; (wirkende Kraft) virtue, *chm.* strength; außer ~ setzen: a) ⊕ *mach.* to throw out of gear; b) *jur.* to suspend a law; in ~ sein: a) to be at (one's) work; b) von Gesetzen: to be in force or operation; in ~ treten: a) to enter on one's duties; b) von Gesetzen: to come into force or operation, to take effect.

Wirk-tafel ⊕ (⌣...) f ⓰, **=tisch** m Bäckerei: kneading-table.

Wirkung (⌣) f ⓰ 1. = wirken II, z.B. eine ~ auf e-n ausüben to act (or operate) upon a p. — 2. (et. Bewirktes) effect, result; (Eindruck) impression; (Folge) consequence; ~ h., seine ~ tun to work (well), to take effect, to be effective, von Geschützen: to do (great) execution; seine ~ h., ohne ~ bleiben to be (or prove) ineffectual, to have (or produce) no effect, to make no impression on a p., a th.; Sprichw. keine ~ ohne Ursache no smoke without a fire.

Wirkungs-art (⌣..) f ⓰ mode of acting or operation; **=kraft** f active force; efficiency, efficacy, virtue; **=kreis** m sphere of action; province, domain, F line; ⚔ ~ eines Geschützes effective range of a gun; ⓺los a. ⓰ without effect or result; ineffectual; **=losigkeit** f ineffectualness, inefficacy; ⓺voll a. having (good) effect, effective, efficacious, a. telling; **=weite** f, *elect.* striking distance. [goods *pl.*]

Wirk-waren ⊛ (⌣.⌣) f/pl. ⓰ woven ⏋

wirr (⌣) [nhd.; *wirren²] a. ⓰ confused, in confusion, (en)tangled, in a tangle; disorderly; ⓺ durch-einander at sixes and sevens, pell-mell, F higgledy-piggledy; ⓺es Durcheinander (heap of) confusion, chaotic disorder; vgl. Wirrwarr; ⓺e Haare = Wirrhaar; ⓺ im Kopfe wrong in the head, F muddle-headed.

Wirr-bund (⌣.⌣) n ⓰ *agr.* bundle of (short) straw.

Wirre (⌣) [ahd.: war] f ⓰ 1. confusion, disorder, *fig.* chaos, F muddle; (Irrgang) maze, labyrinth. — 2. ~n¹ *pl.* (Zwist und Hader) squabbles, troubles, F ructions, rows *pl.*; (Verwicklungen) complications *pl.*

wirren² (⌣) [ahd.] I v/a. und v/refl. ⓰ et. durch- (auch in- ob. unter-) ea. ⓺ to (en)tangle a th. (vgl. verwirren 1); sich in-ea. ⓺ to become entangled; et. aus-ea. ⓺ to disentangle a th. — II ~ n ⓰ s. Wirrung.

Wirr-garn (⌣...) n ⓰ (en)tangled yarn; **=haar** n unkempt (or rough, ruffled) hair; **=kopf** m: a) head (or person) with ruffled hair, F mophead; b) (wirrer Geist) confused head or brain, crazy (or F muddle-headed) fellow; ⓺köpfig a. ⓰ confused, crazy, F muddle-headed.

Wirrnis (⌣) f ⓰, **Wirrsal** (⌣-) n ⓓ confusion, disorder, imbroglio.

Wirr-seide ⊕ (⌣...) f ⓰ (en)tangled (threads of) silk; **=stroh** n, *agr.* short straw.

Wirrung (⌣) f ⓰ entanglement; *fig.* embroilment; vgl. Wirre.

Wirr-warr (⌣.⌣) m ⓹⓪ confusion, medley, *fig.* chaos, F muddle. jumble; (verworrener Lärm) confused noise, (great) hubbub, hurly-burly, F row, shindy.

Wirsing(=kohl) ⚘ (⌣(-⌣) [it.] m ⓓⓓ. savoy (*Bra'ssica olera'cea sabau'da oder bulla'ta*).

wirst (⌣) 2. Person *sg. pres. ind. v.* werden.

Wirt (⌣) [ahd. (Auf-)wartender) m ⓰b., **~in** f ⓰ 1. (Hauswirt[in]) master (mistress, lady) of the house; (Hausbesitzer[in]) landlord (landlady), owner of the house. — 2. (der Gäste hat) host(ess f), vgl. Gastgeber; den ~ (die ~in) machen to play (or act) the host(ess), to do the honours to the guests, to receive the company. — 3. (Gastwirt[in]) host(ess), landlord (landlady) of a hotel, &c., hotel-keeper, F co. mine host(ess); e-r Schenke: innkeeper, publican; bar-keeper; vgl. Kaffee- und Speise-wirt; Sprichwort: die Rechnung ohne den ~ machen to reckon without one's host; *auch:* to count one's chickens before they are hatched. — 4. (e-r, der möblierte Zimmer vermietet) landlord (landlady), lodging-house keeper. — 5. (e-r, der die Haushaltung führt) good, bad, &c. housekeeper; ein guter (schlechter) ~ sein to be a good (bad) manager, to manage (a house) well (badly).

wirtbar (⌣-) a. ⓰ von Orten: a) (bewohnbar) habitable; b) (gastlich) hospitable.

Wirtel (⌣) [mhd.] m ⓶ 1. ⊕ (Nuß der Handspindel) whorl. — 2. ⚘ (Quirl) whirl, whorl. ⌒ verticil.

wirtel-förmig (⌣.⌣.), **wirt(e)lig** ⚘ (⌣(⌣)⌣) a. ⓰ whorled, ⌒ verticillate(d).

wirtlich (⌣) a. ⓰ 1. (sparsam) thrifty, economical, sparing. — 2. = wirtbar.

Wirtlichkeit (⌣⌣-) f ⓰ 1. thrift(iness), economy, economical (or careful) management. — 2. hospitality; eines Hauses: habitable state; comfort to be found in a house.

Wirtschaft (⌣⌣) [ahd.] f ⓰ 1. ([häusliche] Verwaltung) housekeeping, (domestic) management; die ~ besorgen, führen to keep house, to attend to the housekeeping; die ~ gut verstehen to be a good manager (of a household). — 2. a) (Hauswesen) household, (domestic) establishment; b) = Gastwirtschaft; oft auch für Restauration; z.B. Bahnhofs-~ refreshment-room or -bar at a railway-station; c) = Landwirtschaft b. — 3. F (lärmendes Treiben) goings-on, doings *pl.*, bustle, hubbub, F to-do; er macht immer soviel ~ he is always so fussy or so noisy, he is for ever kicking up a row; das war eine tolle ~ that was a mad proceeding, there was a fearful hubbub or riot.

wirtschaften (⌣⌣) I v/n. (h.) ⓰ 1. to keep house, to conduct (or manage) a household; auf einem Gute (als Eigentümer oder Verwalter) ⓺ to manage (or carry on) a farm; gut ⓺ to manage well; mit dem eigenen Vermögen geschickt ⓺ to administer one's fortune cleverly or ably; sparsam ⓺ to practise economy, to be thrifty, to

[**Wischer**]

husband one's resources. — 2. to keep a public-house or a hotel. — 3. (wüst lärmen) to make a great riot or row, F to kick up a rare shindy; bfs. arg, toll ⓺ (hausen) to cause great devastation, to make sad havoc; (plündern) to pillage. — II ~ n ⓰ 4. management of household or farm; administration of a fortune, &c.

Wirtschafter (⌣⌣⌣) m ⓶, **~in** f ⓰ 1. housekeeper, manager(ess f); auf einem Landgute: steward, bailiff; (Einkäufer[in]) caterer, f bisw.: cateress. — 2. ein guter ~ sein to be a good manager, to manage well.

wirtschaftlich (⌣⌣⌣) a. ⓰ 1. relating to domestic matters; ⓺es Gebäude = Wirtschaftsgebäude; ⓺e Kenntnisse *pl.* knowledge of domestic (or political) economy. — 2. (haushälterisch) thrifty, careful, economical; (ordentlich) steady; *adv.* a. with economy, with a sparing (or careful) hand.

Wirtschaftlichkeit (⌣⌣⌣-) f ⓰ thrift, thriftiness, carefulness, economy.

Wirtschafts-amt (⌣⌣...) n ⓶ management of an estate; **=aufseher** m = Wirtschafter 1; **=beamte(r)** m steward (or bailiff) of an estate, agent of a land-owner; **=betrieb** m management of a household or farm; **=buch** n housekeeper's (or housekeeping-)book; **=gebäude** n: a) *agr.* farm-buildings, outhouses *pl.*; b) (Haus, Bureau des Wirtschafters) steward's house or office; **=geld** n housekeeping-money; **=gerät** n household-utensils *pl.*; **=hof** m farmyard; **=inspektor** m = =beamte(r); **=kenntnisse** f/pl. knowledge of farming; **=krise**, **=krisis** f economic crisis; **=kunst** f (art of) husbandry; **=politik** f political economy. auch: economics; **=verwalter** m = =beamte(r).

Wirts-frau (⌣...) f ⓰ landlady, hostess (= Wirtin); **=haus** n public(-)house, F pub, ale-house (vgl. Schenke); immer im =hause liegen ob. sitzen to be for ever (drinking) at the pub or bar; **=haus-leben** n life in public-houses and hotels; **=haus-tisch** m ordinary; **=junge** m pot-boy; **=leute** *pl.* landlord and landlady, host and hostess; **=stube** f (private) parlour of a public-house; **=tafel** f, **=tisch** m ordinary, (fr.) table d'hôte.

Wisch (⌣) [ahd.: whisk] m ⓓa. 1. rubber; vgl. Wischlappen; (Stroh-) ~ whisk, wisp of straw. 2. *contp.* (Fetzen Papier) piece of paper, F rag, beschriebener: badly written manuscript or copy, bedruckter: miserable print or publication, badly printed bill.

wischen (⌣) [ahd.] ⓹⓪ I v/a. 1. to wipe (with a cloth), to rub off gently, to (dab with a) sponge; sich die Augen, den Mund ⓺ to wipe one's eyes, one's mouth. — 2. Zeichenkunst ⌜.: (mit dem Wischer behandeln) to stump a drawing. — II v/n. (sn) 3. (entschlüpfen) to slip away; vorbei ⓺ (huschen) to whisk (or slip, glide, flit) by.

Wischer (⌣⌣) m ⓶ 1. one who wipes. — 2. Zeichenkunst ⌜.: (kleine Papierrolle zum Wischen) stump; mit dem ~

Signs (see page XVII): F familiar; P vulgar; ℱ flash; ⟋ rare; † obsolete (died); * new word (born); ⟋+ incorrect; ♪ music;

[**Wischerstange**] — [**Wittenberger**]

behandeln to stump. — **3.** ⊕ Gießerei: mop with iron handle; ⚔ artill. (zum Reinigen des Geschützrohrs) sponge, cleaning-rod. — **4.** F fig. (Verweis) reprimand, F wigging, wipe-down.
Wischer-stange ⚔ (ˇ-ˇ) f ⚙ sponge-staff; **überzug** m sponge-cap.
Wisch-gold ⊙ (ˇˇ) n ⚙ gold-leaf. [waſch.]
Wischiwaschi F (ˇ-ˇ-ˇ) n (m) 𝔐 = **Wisch=**
Wisch-kolben ⚔ (ˇ...) m ⚙ artill. sponging-rod; **=lappen** m cloth (or rag) for wiping or cleaning, für Küchengeſchirr: dish- (or tea-)cloth, für Fußböden: house-flannel, zum Stäuben: duster.
Wischnu (ˇ-) [ſitt. Durchdringer] npr m 𝔐 (indiſche Gottheit) Vishnu; **=anbeter** (ˇ-...) m ⚙ worshipper of Vishnu.
Wisch-wasch F (ˇ-ˇ) m 𝔚a. (Geſchwätz) chit-chat, tittle-tattle, gabble.
Wisent (ˇ-) [ahd.] m 𝔚e. zo. (European) bison, ure-ox, aurochs (Bos primigē nius).
Wismut (ˇ-) [nhd.] n (m) 𝔚e. chm., min. bismuth (Bi).
wismut-artig (ˇ-...) a. ⚙ ⚗ bismuthal; **=butter** f ⚗, **=chlorid** n, chm. bismuth trichloride (BiCl₃). [with bismuth.]
wismuten ⊙ (ˇ-ˇ) v. a. ⚙ to solder(y)
Wismut erz ⚒ (ˇ-ˇ) n ⚙ bismuth-ore; **=haltig** a. ⚙ containing bismuth, ⚗ bismuthal, bismuthiferous; **=ocker** m, min. (gediegenes Wismutoxyd) bismuth-ochre, bismite; **=oxyd** n, chm. bismuth trioxide (Bi₂O₃); **=ſauer** a. bismuthic; **=ſaures Salz** bismuthate; **=ſäure anhydrid** n bismuth pentoxide (Bi₂O₅).
Wispel † (ˇ-ˇ) m 𝔐 Maß: = 24 Scheffel (13hl).
wispeln [ahd.], **wispern** (ˇ-ˇ) [nhd.: whisper] **I** v/n. (h.) 𝔚a. to whisper, to talk softly, vom Winde auch: to breathe softly; e-m et. ins Ohr ⚪ to whisper s.th. into a p.'s ears. — **II** ~ n ⚙ whisper(ing), des Windes auch: soft breath or murmur(ing), sough.
wißbar (ˇ-) a. ⚙ knowable.
Wiß-begier(de) (ˇ-...) f ⚙ desire (or craving, longing) for knowledge; (Neugier) curiosity, inquisitiveness; **=begierig** a. ⚙ desirous of knowing, eager to learn, craving for (or after) knowledge, (neugierig) curious, inquisitive. — Vgl. a. Wiſſens=...
wissen (ˇ-ˇ) [ahd.: wit (wis): lt. vidēre] **I** v. a. ⚙ **1.** to know, to have a knowledge of; to be aware of; (verſtehen) to understand; er will alles immer besser ⚪ he fancies (that) he knows (everything) better than anybody (else); wir ⚪ es aus guter Quelle we have it from a good source or on good authority; mit inf. u. Nebenſätzen: zu leben ⚪ to know how to live; er weiß zu reden he can talk; f. helfen **5**; sie wußten ihn zu bereden they managed to talk him over; er weiß was er zu tun hat he knows what he has to do; Sprichw. f. heiß **2** u. Barthel. — **2.** mit s. u. pron. als Objekt: a) f. Bescheid **3**; e-m für et. Dank ⚪ to feel grateful (or indebted) to a p. for a th.; f. Rat **4**; b) wir ⚪ ihn geborgen we know him (to be) safe: c) sie ⚪ nichts davon they know nothing of it, they are quite in the dark about it; wir ⚪ kein Sterbenswörtchen davon we don't know a syllable about it; F weißt du was, wir wollen radeln I'll tell you what (to do), we'll cycle. — **3.** mit adv. weder aus noch ein ⚪ not to know which way to turn; et. genau ⚪ to be thoroughly (or intimately) acquainted with a th.; f. gewiß **1** am Ende; nicht ⚪ not to know, to be ignorant (or unaware) of; ich wüßte nicht, nicht daß (od. ſoviel) ich wüßte not that I know of, not that I am aware of; ſoviel ich weiß as far as (or for aught) I know, to the best of my knowledge; wie du weißt, wie Sie ⚪ as you know, as you are aware; er ist krank, wie Sie ⚪ he is ill you know; wir ⚪ ſehr wohl, daß / we are fully aware that /; woher ⚪ Sie das? where did you hear (or learn) that?, who has told you so? — **4.** mit prp.: an allem et. ⚪ (tadeln) to find a fault (or pick holes) in everything; et. auf (od. gegen) einen ⚪ to know s.th. against a p.; aus Erfahrung ⚪ to know from experience; über (od. von) et. ⚪ to know about a th.; von (od. um) et. ⚪ to know of (or about) a th., to be aware of a th.; er weiß von keiner Sorge he does not know what (a) care is, auch: he knows (or has) no care; sie will von ihm nichts ⚪ she wants to have nothing to do with him; davon will er nichts ⚪ he does not want to hear of it, stärker: he is dead against it. — **5.** als inf. von anderen verbs abhängig: et. zu ⚪ bekommen to come to hear of a th.; einen et. ⚪ lassen, einem et. zu ⚪ tun to let a p. know a th., to notify (or announce) a th. to a p..; to notify (or acquaint) a p. of a th.; f. kundtun: wenn Sie es doch ⚪ wollen if you particularly want to know, if you must be told; et. von e-m getan ⚪ wollen to wish a th. to be done by a p.; man will ⚪, daß // it is asserted (or rumoured) that //. — **6.** Redensarten: a) mit anderen verbs: ich möchte wohl ⚪, ob // I should like to know whether //, auch: F I wonder if //; b) mit neg.: man kann nicht ⚪, ob // there is no knowing whether (or if) //; er weiß nicht, was er will he does not know his own mind; nicht mehr ⚪, was man tun soll not to know what to do or what to be about; nicht ⚪, wie man beſchert iſt (verdutzt ſein) to be perplexed or F flummuxed; ich weiß die Zeit nicht, wann (od. daß) ich ihn geſehen habe I don't remember the time when I last saw him. — **7.** bei Ausrufen, Fragen und Beteuerungen: das mag Gott ⚪! Heaven (or God) knows!; Gott weiß, wie viele dort waren! goodness knows how many there were!; was weiß ich? how do (or can) I know?; er ist reich, weiß Gott! ... Heaven knows!; das weiß die liebe Zeit! F goodness only knows!; als Einleitung für et. Unerwartetes: weißt du was?, ⚪ Sie was? (do) you know what? vgl. oben 2c am Schluß; zur Bezeichnung eines hohen Grades: dann wäre ich jetzt wer weiß wo I should now be who (or F goodness) knows where. — **II** ~ s/n. ⚙ **8.** knowledge; ohne mein ~ without my knowledge, unbeknown to me; mit ~ und Willen deliberately, intentionally, on purpose; er hat es mit ~ und Willen seiner Eltern getan he did so with the knowledge and consent of his parents; f. Wille **2c** unter mit; meines ~s to the best of my knowledge; meines ~s ist er nicht hier so far as I know (or am aware), he is not here; f. Gewissen. — **9.** (Kenntnisse, store of) knowledge, learning, all that one knows; oberflächliches ~ superficial knowledge or acquaintance, smattering; tiefes ~, bſd. von Büchern: deep scholarship, erudition; mit seinem ~ ist es nicht weit her his knowledge is not very extensive or F not up to much; er besitzt ein tiefes (ein vielseitiges) ~ he is a deep (an all-round) scholar. — **III** ⚪d p.p. und a. ⚙ **10.** knowing; (eingeweiht) initiated into; um (oder von) etwas ⚪ cognizant (or aware) of a th.
Wissenschaft (ˇ-ˇ-ˇ) f ⚙ **1.** scientific pursuit or study, bſd. von naturwiſſenſchaftlich-mathematiſchen Dingen: (natural) science; die schönen ~en polite learning or literature, (fr.) the belles lettres, schöne ~en und klaſſiſche Sprachen, oft: humanities pl. — **2.** (Wissen) knowledge; (Gelehrsamkeit) scholarship, erudition. — **3.** (Kunde) intelligence.
Wissenschaft(l)er (ˇ-ˇ-ˇ) m ⚙ scientific man, man of learning, deep (or fine, great) scholar; (Natur=)~ scientist, man (or student) of science.
wissenschaftlich (ˇ-ˇ-ˇ) a. ⚙ scientific, adv. scientifically; (planmäßig) methodical, systematical; (vernunftgemäß) rational; eine ⚪e Bildung haben to be thoroughly schooled or educated, to be a good (or ripe) scholar; ⚪ (adv.) gebildet learned, of scholarly attainments; **~keit** f ⚙ scientific character or nature, scholarly method.
Wissenschafts-drang (ˇ-ˇ-ˇ...) m ⚙, **=durst** m = Wissensdrang; **=lehre** f, phls. etwa: theory (or doctrine) of learning; **=**⚪ philosophy.
Wissens-drang (ˇ-ˇ-ˇ) m ⚙, **=durst** m, **=trieb** m eager desire for learning, thirsting after (or thirst for) knowledge; vgl. Wißbegier(de); ⚪**wert**, ⚪**würdig** a. ⚙ worth knowing or learning, (merkwürdig) interesting, curious; **=würdigkeit** f, etwa: interesting nature of a subject; (Merkwürdigkeit) remarkable (or interesting) fact; **=zweig** m branch of knowledge, department of learning.
wissentlich (ˇ-ˇ-ˇ) [wissend] a. ⚙ knowing, conscious, (abſichtlich) deliberate, b. s. wilful; adv. knowingly, seltener: wittingly, (abſichtlich) deliberately, on purpose, b. s. wilfully.
Wisser (ˇ-ˇ) m ⚙ one that knows; bſd. in Zſſgn b.s.: f. Halb=, Mit=, Viel=wisser.
wist (ˇ) int. (links) = hott a. [= Witwe.]
Witfrau (ˇ-ˇ), **Witib** † (ˇ-) [ahd.] f ⚙, ⚙
Wittelsbacher (ˇˇ-ˇ) [Wittelsbach ⚙, bayr. Schloß] a. inv. of Wittelsbach, auch: member of the Wittelsbach dynasty.
Wittenberger (ˇ-ˇ-ˇ) [Wi'ttenberg ⚙, preuß. St.] m ⚙ u. a. inv. native of Wittenberg.

⚔ scientific; ⚘ botanical; ⚙ geography; ⊕ machinery; ⚒ mining; ⚔ military; ⚓ marine; ⚙ commercial; ✉ postal; 🚂 railway.

[wittern] — 1128 — [Wochenlöhner]

wittern (ˇ) [mhd.; *Wetter] **I** v/n. (h.), v/a. und v/refl. ⓐa. **1.** ↘ es wittert so und so it is such or such weather. — **2.** = wettern I. — **3.** hunt., &c.: a) nach et. 2 (spüren) to follow the scent of a th.; b) etwas 2 (spüren wahrnehmen) to scent (or smell) a th., weit S. to perceive (or notice) a th., to get wind (or an inkling) of a th.; c) fig. er wittert überall nur Verrat he suspects (nothing but) treason everywhere; Unrat 2 to notice that there is s.th. in the wind or s.th. wrong, F to smell a rat. — II ~ n ⓖ **4.** scenting, &c. (f. 3).
Witterung (ˇ) f ⓖ **1.** [wittern 1 u. 2]: a) (Beschaffenheit der Luft, des Wetters) atmospheric (or meteorological) conditions pl., state of the atmosphere, weather; bei günstiger ~ if the weather permits; bei jeder ~ in all weathers; rauhe ~ inclement (or rough) weather or atmosphere; b) ⚔ state (or quality) of the air in the underground workings. — **2.** [wittern 3] bsd. hunt.: a) (Geruchssinn) scent of the hounds, &c.; b) (Geruch des Wildes ꝛc.) scent, trail, fig. ~ von et. bekommen to get wind (or an inkling) of a th.
Witterungs=anzeichen (ˇ…) n ⓖ sign of the (coming) weather; **=beobachter** m = =forscher; **=bericht** m meteorological report; **=einflüsse** m/pl., **=einwirkung** f influence of the weather; **=forscher** m meteorologist; **=kunde** f, **=lehre** f meteorology; **=umschlag** m = =wechsel; **=verhältnisse** n/pl. atmospheric (or meteorological) conditions pl., weit S. temperature; **=wechsel** m atmospheric change.
Wittib (ˇ) öft. = Witib.
Wittum (ˇ-) [ahd.: wedding] n (a. m) ⓓd. jointure, dowry, widow's estate.
Witu ♀ (¹-)npr/n. ⓖ α. afrikan. Reich: Vitu.
Witwe (ˇ) [ahd.: widow] f ⓖ **1.** widow; bsd. jur. relict; ~ von Stande dowager, ₃B. Königin~ queen dowager; zur ~ gemacht widowed. — **2.** orn. (Art Hänfling) whidah-bird or -bunting or -finch (Vi'dua).
Witwen=gehalt (ˇ…) n ⓖ, **=geld** n widow's pension or allowance; **=haube** f widow's cap; **=jahr** n (widow's) year of deep mourning; **=kasse** f widow's fund.
Witwenschaft (ˇ) f ⓖ widowhood.
Witwen=schleier (ˇ…) m ⓖ widow's veil or weeds pl.; **=sitz** m widow's estate or seat, **=stand** m widowhood.
Witwentum (ˇ-) n ⓓd. = Witwenschaft.
Witwen=verbrennung (ˇ…) f ⓖ suttee; **=verpflegungs=anstalt** f widows' home.
Witwer (ˇ) m ⓖ widower; **~leben** n ⓖ, **=stand** m life, condition of a widower.
Witz (ˇ) [ahd.: wit: wissen] m ⓐa. **1.** (o. pl.) als Eigenschaft des Geistes: wit, von Reden ꝛc. auch: wittiness; vgl. Mutterwitz; von raschem ~ quick-witted; scharfer ~ keen (or biting) wit; f. schlagfertig b u. sprudeln 2 b; viel ~ h. to have much (or a fine) wit, to be very witty; mit wenig ~ und viel Behagen (G., Faust) with little wit and great conceit. — **2.** als einzelne Kundgebung: witticism, witty remark, joke, (Wortspiel) pun,

(Spaß) jest; alter ~ stale (or stereotype[d]) joke; vgl. Meidinger; beißender ~ sarcasm; (faule) ~e m. ob. reißen to make (or crack) (bad) jokes; das ist (oder darin liegt) ja eben der (ganze) ~: a) bisw.: that's the whole fun of it; b) (darin liegt die Schwierigkeit) that's just the thing or the point, that's where it lies; stehender ~ standing joke. — **3.** burschikos: (et. Lustiges) fun, merriment, joke, F lark, ~ = Schabernack, bisw. = Tanzvergnügen.
Witz=blatt (ˇ…) n ⓖ comic journal or paper, als Name auch: Fun; **=bold** m ⓒc. witty fellow, a. wit, punster, F jokist.
Witzelei (ˇ…ˋ) f ⓖ **1.** ohne pl.: (trying to make) fun, continuous joking or punning. — **2.** mit pl.: (witzelnde Äußerung) jocose (or facetious) remark, poor (or indifferent) joke, (Wortspiel) pun, quibble, play on the word.
witzeln (ˇ) v/n. (h.) ⓐa. to make (or crack) indifferent jokes, to make a poor display of wit, mit Wortspielen: to pun, to quibble; über e-n 2 to make fun of (F to poke fun at) a p., to joke at a p.('s expense).
Witz(es)=funken (ˇ(ˇ)ˇ) m ⓖ flash (or sally) of wit, brilliant joke.
witzig (ˇ) [ahd.] a. ⓖ witty; (scherzend) droll, facetious; weit. nicht von Sachen: funny; (sinnreich) ingenious; (beißend) biting, sarcastic; 2e Antwort (witty) repartee, smart reply; 2er Einfall bright idea, brilliant sally or remark; 2er Kopf wit(ty fellow).
witzigen (ˇ) **I** v/a. ⓖ to make wise(r); e-n 2, auch: to sharpen a p.'s wit; gewitzigt w. to learn wisdom or a lesson; to grow wise(r) by experience. — **II Witzigung** f ⓖ teaching (or learning) by experience. [be witty or funny.⌋
Witz=jäger (ˇ…ˋ) m ⓖ one who tries to⌉
Witzler ⓖⓖ, **Witzling** ⓓd. (ˇ…) m poor joker, indifferent punster, would-be wit.
witz=los (ˇ…) a. ⓖ without wit; (schal) stale, dull, poor; 2reich a. full of wit or jokes, witty; **=reißer** m ⓖ = =bold; 2sprühend a. of sparkling (or brilliant) wit, overflowing with wit; **=wort** n = Witz 2.
Wladimir (ˇˊˇ, oft ˊˇ ˊˇ) npr/m. ⓖⓖ α. Vladimir, Wladimir. [Wladislav.⌋
Wladislaw (ˇ…) npr/m. ⓖⓖ α. Vladislas,⌉
Wladiwostok ♀ (ˇˇˇ) [russ.] npr/n. (Seestadt in Hinterasien) Vladivostok.
wo (¹) [ahd.: where] **I** adv. **1.** örtlich: a) fragend: where?; wo ist er? where (or in what place) is he?; wo ist er durchgekommen? what place did he pass through?; wo mag er denn nur sein? where on earth can he be?; b) relativ: hier ist es, wo ich wohne it is here where (or that) I live; das Haus, wo (= in welchem) ich lebe the house where (richtiger: in which) I live; er ging nach England, (als) wo große Freiheit ist … where there is great liberty; es gibt kein Land, wo er nicht gewesen ist … (that) he has not been to, … but (what) he has been to; ich weiß nicht, wo er jetzt ist … where he is (just) now, … his present whereabouts; der Ort, von wo ich komme the place where I come from

or whence (or from which) I am coming; wo … her, wo … hin f. woher, wohin; c) unbestimmt: somewhere; wo er auch sein mag wherever he may be; f. woanders; d) substantiviert: es kommt auf das Wo an all depends on the locality or Fon where it is (to be). — **2.** zeitlich, relativ: in einer Zeit, wo man nicht an ihn dachte at a time when he was not thought of; im Februar, wo die Vögel sich paaren in February when the birds are pairing. — **3.** provc.: a) = wie, zB. wo werd' ich so dumm sein? do you think me so stupid?; b) ach wo! (denkt nicht dran) not I!, nothing of the kind!, (I) shan't think of it! — **II** cj. **4.** = wenn, zB. wo ich nicht irre if I am not (or unless I be) mistaken; drohend: wo du das noch einmal sagst! (if) you dare say that again!, never you repeat those words!; wo möglich if possible, if feasible, if (or provided) it can be done; vgl. womöglich.
w. o. abbr. = wie oben. [elsewhere.⌋
wo=anders (-ˇˇ) adv. somewhere else,⌉
wo=… vor Vokalen: **wor=…** (ˊ…, der Hauptton liegt meist auf dem folgenden Worte), verschmelzend mit prp. oder adv., bildet fragende u. relative adverbs u. conjunctions entsprechend dem fragenden „was", dem relativen „was", dem auf Sachliches bezüglichen „welche(r), welches" oder dem unbestimmten „irgend etwas".
wob (¹) ind. u. **wöbe** (¹ˇ) subj. impf. v. weben.
wo=bei (-¹) a) fragend: near what place?, a.: near where?; 2 ist er stehen geblieben? where did he stop?) b) relativ: whereat, whereby; at (or by, during) which; 2 mir einfällt, daß // (a fact) which reminds me that //; 2 es sein Bewenden hatte and there the matter rested (for the time being).
Woche (ˇˇ) [ahd.: week] f ⓖ **1.** week (f. heilig 1 am Ende); in drei ~n, heute über drei ~n three weeks hence, in (genauer: this day) three weeks; vor sechs ~n six weeks ago or since; einmal die ~ once a week; (den Dienst für) die ~ h. to be on duty (during the week); er hat die ~ it's his week. — **2.** fig. (Kindbett) in (den) ~n (ursprünglich: Sechs=Zn) sein, die ~n halten to be in childbed, to lie in; sie wird bald in die ~n kommen she will soon be confined, she is near her time, her confinement is at hand; mit einem Sohne in die ~n kommen to be delivered of a son; zu früh in die ~n kommen to have a premature confinement or a miscarriage.
Wochen=ausweis (ˇˇ…) = **=bericht** m ⓖ weekly report or return; **=besuch** m visit to a woman in childbed; **=bett** n childbed; in das ~ kommen to be confined, bsd. ehm. auch to be brought to bed; **=blatt** n weekly journal or paper; **=einnahme** f weekly receipts pl.; **=geld** n weekly money or allowance; vgl. =lohn; **=gesell(e)** m journeyman engaged by the week; **=kind** n newborn infant or child; **=kleid** n every-day dress or garment; 2**lang** adv. (auch: ganze Wochen lang) for whole weeks (together), for weeks; **=lohn** m (n) weekly wages pl. or pay; **=löhner**

Zeichen (f. S. XVII): F familiär, P Volkssprache, Γ Gaunersprache, ↘ selten; † alt (auch gestorben); * neu (auch geboren); ++ unrichtig;

[Wochenprediger] — 1129 — [Wohlgefallen]

m labourer (who is) paid by the week; =prediger m (=predigt f) week-day preacher (sermon); =schrift f weekly publication or print; =stube f lying-in room; =suppe f soup for a woman in childbed; =tag m weekday, day of the week; ²tags adv. on weekdays.
wöchentlich (²⌣) [Woche] a. ⓖ weekly, univ., eccl., &c. a.: hebdomadal, ...ary | adv. auch: every week; by the week; zweimal ² twice a week.
Wochen-übersicht (²⌣...) f ⓒ Kocht. F co. (Pastete od. Ragout aus Fleischresten) resurrection-pie; ²weise adv. (F a. a.) by the week, weekly; =zettel m weekly bill. thea., &c. auch: bill for the week.
...wochig (..."chy), ...wöchig (..."⌣): letzt-² of last week, last week's; mehr-² lasting (for) several weeks.
Wöchnerin (⌣⌣) f ㊼ woman (or lady) lately confined or in childbed, ehm. auch: lying-in woman; Hospital für ~nen lying-in hospital. [Rocken¹).]
Wocken (⌣) f [ndd.] m ㉓ distaff (=|
Wodan (¹⌣) [ahd.] npr/m. ⓢⓨα. (o. pl.) (nordische Gottheit) Woden, Wodan, Odin.
wo-durch (-¹): a) whereby?, by what means?; b) relativ: by (means of) which, through which; ²fern (-⌣) cj. provided (that), in case (that); ² nicht (außer wenn) except if, unless; ²für (-¹): a) for what?, what for?; ² ist das gut? what is that good for?; ² halten Sie mich? what do you take me for?; b) relativ: for which; es ist nicht das, ² sie kämpften that's not what they fought for; et., ² ich kein Geld ausgebe s.th. (that) I spend no money for or on; einräumend: ² es auch stehen mag whatever it may be meant for.
wog (¹) ind. impf. von wägen u. wiegen¹.
Woge (¹⌣) [ahd.: (be)wegen] f ⓑ billow, huge wave; brandende ~n surging waves, breakers pl. (vgl. Welle).
wo-gegen (-¹⌣): a) against what?; b) relativ: against which, tauschend: in return for which; cj. whereas.
wogen (¹⌣) I v/n. (h. u. su) ⓢ vom Meere: to surge, schwellend: to heave, von Kornähren zc.: to wave (to and fro); es wogt das Meer the sea is rough or stormy or tempestuous, there is a (heavy) swell on; hin u. her ² to roll to and fro, to fluctuate; das ²de Meer the surging (or tempestuous) sea; die ²de Menschenmasse the heaving multitude, the moving masses of people. — II ~ n ㉓ surging, rolling of the waves, heave of the sea; fig. fluctuation.
Wogen=getöse (²⌣...) [Woge] n ㉒ tumult (or roaring) of waves; =gürtel m (SCH.) belt of waves, encircling flood; ²weise adv. in huge waves.
wogig (¹⌣) a. ⓖ billowy, surging; wavy; von der See auch: rough, tempestuous.
wo-her (-¹): a) whence?, from what place?; ² stammt er (auch: wo stammt er her)? where does he come from?, what countryman is he?; ² weiß er das? how does he know that?. from what source(s) had he heard it?; b) relativ: ² er auch kommen mag (auch: wo er auch herkommen mag) wherever he may come from; ²hin (-¹): a) whither?,

where (to)?, to what place?; ² gehst du (auch: wo gehst du hin)? where are you going (to)?; gr. diese Präposition regiert den Akkusativ auf die Frage: ²? this preposition governs the accusative in response to (or when answering) the question: whither?; b) relativ: der Ort, ² ich ziehe (auch: wo ich hinziehe) the place (where) I am moving to, richtiger: the place to which I am moving; ² er auch segeln mag wherever he may sail to; ²hina"b: a) down where?; b) relativ: down (or beneath) which; ²hinau"s fragend: which way?, in what direction?; ²hinge"gen cj. whereas; while, whilst; ²hi"nter: a) behind what?; b) relativ: behind which.
wohl (¹) [ahd.: well: wollen] I a. ⓖ 1. well, comp. ²er better, sup. am ²sten best (in health, &c.): a) nur adv. (als comp. besser, sup. best) ² bekomm's (Ihnen)! I trust it may do you good!, iro. much good may it do you!; leben Sie ²! good bye!, farewell!, fare ye well!; (ich) wünsche (Ihnen), ² zu schlafen I wish you a good night's rest; ² sein f. 2; er ist ² auf he is quite well; es ist den Fröschen am wohlsten, wenn sie im Wasser sind frogs are never so happy as when they are in the water; es war ihm ² zu Mute he felt in good spirits; sich's ² sein lassen to take one's ease, to enjoy o.s.; ² tun (vgl. ²tun); es tut mir ², wenn // it does me good (or it pleases me) when //; s. tun 4 b; b) oft mit p.p., zB. ² berechnet well computed; c) mit so: er so ² wie dein Bruder he as well as ..., both he and ...; vgl. sowohl; d) bsd. als Ausruf: ²! (nun geht's) well then!, now then!; ja²! certainly!, to be sure!, of course!; ² oder übel (mag er wollen oder nicht) whether he likes it or not; willy, nilly; ² oder übel, er muß uns folgen ... whether he likes it or not ..., come what may ...; e) vermutend: es sind ² drei Jahre, daß // it must be (or I should say it's) about three years since //; er kommt ² heute I suppose he will come to-day; das ist ² nicht möglich that's scarcely (or hardly) possible; f) einräumend: das mag ² sein that may well (or possibly) be, F (it's) most likely; ich weiß sehr ², daß // I am fully (or clearly, perfectly) aware that //; wenn nicht heute, so doch ² morgen if not to-day, then perhaps to-morrow; das wird ² ganz richtig sein I dare say that's quite true; g) in Wünschen: s. mögen 3 am Ende. — 2. (in guter Gesundheit) ² sein to be well, to be in (or to enjoy, to have) good health; ich bin nicht ² I am not well, F I am out of sorts; er ist wieder ganz ² he is quite well again, he has quite recovered; die Reise wird ihn wieder ² machen ... will make him well again, ... will restore him or his health; wieder ² w. to get ² well again, F to be picking up (one's strength) again. — 3. als int. mit dat. der Person = Heil (ant. weh), zB. ² dem, der // happy he who //; o, ² dem

hochbeglückten Haus (a.) oh, blessed is the prosperous house; ² ihm, daß er entkam lucky he to have escaped. — 4. nach ob ...: a) in Fragen: ob er ² noch am Leben ist? I wonder whether (or if) he is still alive; b) obwohl cj. bisw. auch getrennt durch ein personal pron., zB. ob er ² krank ist // although he is ill //. — II ~ [ahd.: weal] n ⓒ c. (o. pl.) 5. well-being. welfare, prosperity; (Glück) happiness; (Vorteil) advantage; das allgemeine ~, oft: the common weal, the good of the commonwealth; auf Ihr ~! (to) your health! s. Weh² 2.
wohl-achtbar (¹⌣...) a. ⓖ (ehm. als Titulatur) worshipful; ²an (-¹) adv.: a) boldly; b) meist als int.: well then!, come (or go) on!, F go it!; ² (es sei denn! all right!; ²angebracht a. well-timed, (most) opportune, seasonable; ²anständig a. = anständig; ~keit f ⓒ = Anstand 1; ²auf (¹") int. = ²an b; =bedacht a.: m mit ~ after mature consideration; b) ², auch: ²bedächtig a. well-considered, deliberate; =befinden n well-being, bsd.: (good) health; ²befugt a. fully competent, well qualified; ²begabt a. fairly (stärker: highly) gifted; ²begründet a. well-founded; ²begütert a. with (or possessing) good means; =behagen n (feeling of) ease and comfort; ²behalten a. safe and sound, in good condition or health; ²bekannt a. well-known, b.s. notorious; ²belaubt a., etwa: with good (or rich) foliage; ²beleibt a. = beleibt; ~heit f = Beleibtheit; ²beritten a. well-mounted; ²bestallt a. duly installed or appointed; ²bewandert a. well-versed in. intimately acquainted with; =edel(=geboren) a. (ehm. als Titulatur), etwa: of gentle birth. high and noble; ehm. ²ehrwürden f (Titel für Geistliche) Ew. (Euer) ~ Reverend Sir; ²ehrwürdig a. ehm. reverend; ²erfahren a. (thoroughly) experienced; =ergeh(e)n n well-being. welfare, prosperity; ²erzogen a. well-bred; =fahrt f welfare; =fahrts-ausschuß m committee of public safety; ²feil [mhd.] a. cheap (F u. P auch als adv.), adv. auch: at a low (or reasonable, moderate) rate (s. billig 2); am ²sten kaufen ... at the lowest rate or in the cheapest market; hier ist (oder kann man) ² leben living is cheap here; Ⓒ ²er als die anderen verkaufen to undersell the others; fig. ²en Kaufs davonkommen to get off cheaply or easily; ~heit f cheapness, reasonableness (of price); =ferlei ² n [Wohl für allerlei] = Wohlverleih; ²geartet a. well-behaved or -conducted; ²gebärdig a. well-mannered; ²gebaut a. von Personen: well-made or -shaped; ²gebildet a. well-formed, finely-shaped; (schön) handsome; =geboren [mhd.] a. (veralteter Titel für Bürgerliche) a) auf dem Briefumschlage: Herrn A. Bossert ~ A. B. Esq. (nicht: Mr. A. B. Esq.!); b) sonst meist nicht zu übersetzen, zB. ~er Herr! (Dear) Sir; =gefallen n liking; nach Ihrem ~ at your pleasure; sein

♩ Musik; ⚙ Wissenschaft; ⚘ Pflanze; ⚲ Geographie; ⊕ Technik; ⚒ Bergbau; ⚔ Militär; ⚓ Marine; ⚖ Handel; ✉ Post; 🚂 Eisenbahn.

[wohlgefällig] — 1130 — [Wolf]

~ an etwas finden oder haben to take a pleasure in s.th.; *bibl.* mein Sohn, an dem ich mein ~ habe my beloved Son in whom I am well pleased; sich in ~ auflösen: a) to turn out satisfactorily; b) *b.s.* to end in smoke, to come to nothing; ˚gefällig *a.* pleasant, agreeable; eine 2e Miene machen to put on a self-complacent air; et. 2 (*adv.*) aufnehmen to receive a th. graciously, to take a th. in good part; ˚gefühl *n* feeling of comfort, pleasant (or agreeable) sensation; ˚gegliedert *a.* well-arranged; ˚gehärtet ⊙ *a.* well-tempered; ˚gelitten *a.* much liked, very popular; ˚gemeint *a.* well-meant or -intended; 2er Rat friendly advice; ˚gemut *a.* cheerful, cheery, of good cheer; recht 2 aussehen to look hale and hearty; ˚genährt *a.* well-fed, stout; sleek, plump; ˚geneigt *a.* well-disposed, kind(ly inclined); ˚geruch *m* perfume, pleasant odour, (sweet) scent; (Duft) aroma; ˚geschmack *m* pleasant (or agreeable) taste or flavour; ˚gesetzt *a.*: mit 2en Worten with well-chosen words, ˚gesinnt *a.* = gutgesinnt; ˚gesittet *a.* well-mannered or -bred; ˚gestalt *f* fine (or handsome) shape or form; ˚gestalt(et) *a.* = gebaut u. 2e bildet; ˚getan *a.* well-done; ˚getroffen *a.* von Bildnissen: speaking or striking (likeness); like the original; ˚gewogen *a.* well-inclined; ˚gewogenheit *f* good-will, favour; affection; ˚habend *a.* wealthy, well-to-do, opulent, meist prädikativ: well-off; ˚habenheit *f* wealth, opulence; ˚häbig *a.* very comfortable, in easy circumstances; **wohlig** (2~) *a.* ⑯ 1. (feeling) at one's ease, comfortable, snug. — 2. delicious, pleasant; 2e Stille delightful calm. **Wohl=klang** (″...) *m* ⑫ melodious sound, harmony, melody; *rhet.* u. *gram.* bisw. euphony; ˚klingend *a.* ⑯ melodious, sweet-sounding, bisw. euphonious, ...ic; ˚laut *m* = ˚klang; ˚leben *n* good (or luxurious, rich) living, life of pleasure or luxury, gay life; (Schmauserei) good cheer, revelling, feasting; ˚löblich *a.* = löblich; ˚meinend *a.* well-meaning; friendly; ˚reden(heit *f*) *n* eloquence; ˚reden(heit *a.* well-spoken, eloquent; ˚riechend *a.* of pleasant odour, fragrant; (durchduftet) scented, perfumed; ˚riechend(s) *n* = Parfüm; ˚schmeckend *a.* of pleasant taste, savoury, palatable, relishing, appetizing; ˚sein *n* good health; auf Ihr ~ (I drink to your (good) health!; a. = ˚ergehen; ˚stand *m* well-being, welfare; (Reichtum) wealth, (large) fortune; ˚tat [ahd.] *f*: a) good (or kind) action; e-m ~en erweisen to bestow benefits on a p.; b) (etwas Wohltuendes) s.th. pleasant or comforting; ein kaltes Bad ist heute eine wahre ~ ... is a real treat (or luxury) to-day; F das ist e-e wahre ~ (ein großes Glück) that's a real blessing; ˚täter(in *f*) *m* benefactor, benefactress; ˚tätig *a.*: a) doing good, beneficent; (mildtätig) charitable; b) (heilbringend) beneficial, salutary,

wholesome; ˚tätigkeit *f* beneficence, benevolence; (Mildtätigkeit) charitableness; ~s=anstalt *f* benevolent (or charitable) institution, charity; ~s=fest *n* charity fête; ~s=verein *m* benevolent society; ˚tuend *a.* doing good, beneficent; beneficial, pleasant; 2e Wärme comforting (or delicious) warmth; ˚tun *v/n.* (h.) ⑮**: a) (gut handeln) to do good (to others), to dispense charity or favours; ~ bringt Zinsen a good action yields good fruit; e-m 2 (Gutes erweisen) to benefit (or comfort) a p., e-m wohl tun (Freude m.) to give pleasure to a p.; der Ausflug hat ihr sehr wohlgetan she has derived great benefit (or pleasure) from her trip; das tut e-m wohl it does one good; ˚überlegt *a.* well-considered; ˚unterrichtet *a.* well-informed, well-advised; ˚verdient *a.* well-merited or -deserved; condign (punishment, &c.); 2er Mann man of (great) merit; 2ermaßen *adv.* deservedly; ˚verhalten *n* good conduct; ˚verleih ⚤ *m* [(P): Wolf] = Arnika 1, auch leopard's-bane; ˚versorgt *a.* well provided for; ˚verstanden! you must understand!, don't misunderstand!, auch: you know! ˚verwahrt *a.* well guarded, well taken care of; ˚weislich *adv.* very wisely or prudently; ˚wollen: a) *v/n.* (h.) ⑨**: e-m 2 to be kindly disposed to(wards) a p., to wish a p. well, to favour a p.; b) ~ *n* good-will, kind feeling or disposition; 2d *p.pr.* u. *a.* kind(ly disposed); benevolent; ˚ziemend *a.* becoming, seemly.
wohnbar (1~) *a.* ⑯ habitable; ~keit *f* ⑯ habitable state or condition.
wohnen (2~) [ahd.: won : Wonne] I *v/n.* (h.) ⑱ to live in a place, feiner: to dwell in a house, &c., to reside; im Logis: to lodge, to be in lodgings, möbliert: in furnished apartments; er wohnt bei uns he is living (or staying) with us; s. Land 3; wissen Sie, wo er wohnt? ... where he lives or F *co.* hangs out?; ... his (present) address?; *fig.* so wahr ein Gott im Himmel wohnt as true as there is a God in heaven; die Hoffnung wohnt in seinem Herzen hope lingers in his heart, his heart is full of hope; *v/refl.* es wohnt sich dort sehr angenehm (sehr teuer) it is a very nice (very expensive) place to live in. — II ~ *n* ⑬ living, &c. in a place (s. I), residing, residence. — III s. Wohnung.
Wohn=gebäude (″...) *n* ⑫ = ˚haus; ˚gelegenheit *f* = Wohnung 2.
wohnhaft (2~) *a.* ⑯ living, feiner: dwelling, residing, resident, bsd. *jur.* domiciled; sich irgendwo 2 niederlassen to take up one's (fixed) abode (or to go to live) at a place, to settle down somewhere.
Wohn=haus (″...) *n* ⑫ dwelling- (or living-)house, habitation, *jur.* auch habilimend, stattliches: mansion.
wohnlich (2~) *a.* ⑯ habitable; (bequem) comfortable, convenient, snug, cosy; ~keit *f* ⑯ habitableness; comfort (-ableness), convenience, cosiness.

Wohn=ort (″...) *m* ⑫ dwelling-place, place of residence, bsd. *jur.* auch domicile; ˚sitz *m* (fixed) abode, residence, vornehmer: mansion, (country-)seat; er hat s-n ~ am See aufgeschlagen he has settled down (or he resides, lives, geb. Spr.: he dwells) by the lake; ˚stätte *f* = ˚ort; ˚stube *f* sitting- (or living-)room, parlour.
Wohnung (2~) *f* ⑯ 1. dwelling, habitation, bsd. *jur.* domicile, tenement, auch = Wohnsitz; s. aufschlagen 5 u. frei 6; *bibl.* in meines Vaters Haus sind viele ~en (Joh. 14,2) in my Father's house are many mansions. — 2. (bewohnbare Zimmer mit Zubehör) apartments, lodgings, (set of or suite of) rooms, F diggings *pl.*, feinerer Art: chambers *pl.*; (möbliertes Stockwert) (furnished) flat.
Wohnungs=anzeiger (″...) *m* ⑫ Buch: directory, auch court-guide; ˚entschädigung *f* = ˚geldzuschuß; ˚frage *f* question of residence or apartments, *pol.* housing question; ˚geld=zuschuß *m* für Beamte rc.: allowance for rent or lodging; ˚mangel *m*, ˚not *f* scarcity of (available) dwelling-houses or lodgings; ˚suche *f*: auf der ˚sein to go house-hunting, to look about for lodgings; ˚veränderung *f* = ˚wechsel; ˚vermieter(in *f*) *m* p. letting apartments, lodging-house keeper; ˚wechsel *m* change of residence or apartments, removal.
Wohn=zimmer (″...) *n* ⑫ = Wohnstube.
Woilach (2~) [russ. Filz] *m* ⑭(⑫) horse-rug (in several folds), thick blanket.
Woiwod (2~,-r-,2~) [slaw. waſiwo´ba Kriegs=führer] *m* ⑫, *a.* ~e (-2~) *m* ⑭ voivode, waywode; ~at (-2~) *n* ⑫c., ˚schaft (-2~) *f* ⑯ voivodeship, waywodeship.
Wölb(e)=dach ⚤(2~...) *n* ⑫ vaulted roof.
wölben (2~) [ahd.] I *v/a.* u. *v/refl.* ⑬ Bauw. 1. (rund erhaben vortreten l.) to vault, to arch; einen Bogen 2 to spring an arch; einen Weg rc. to raise (or swell out) in the centre, to barrel. — 2. sich 2 to form a vault, to (form an) arch. — II ~ *n* ⑬ 3. constructing (or construction of) a vault, vaulting; s. Wölbung. — III gewölbt *p.pr.* u. *a.* ⑯, bisw. **wölbend** *p.pr.* ⑯ 4. vaulted, arched; Straßenbau rc. barrelled; (rund erhaben) convex; gewölbter Gang arched passage; mit hoher, gewölbter Brust deep-chested.
Wölb(e)=stärke ⊙ (2~...) *f* ⑫ strength (or thickness) of the vault(ing); ˚stein *m* archstone, (fr.) voussoir; (Schlußstein) keystone.
Wölbung (2~) *f* ⑯ 1. = Gewölbe. — 2. (gewölbte Form) curvature, convexity; innere ~ am Fuß einer Glasflasche: kick; ~ des Gaumens roof of the mouth.
Wolf (2~) [ahd.: wolf] *m* ⓓc 1. *zo.* wolf (*Canis lupus*); **Wölfin** *f* ④ she-wolf; hungrig wie ein ~ (as) hungry as a wolf or a hunter; ein Rudel Wölfe a pack of wolves; Spiel: ~ und Schaf fox and geese; *fig.* ~ in Schafskleidern wolf in sheep's clothing; Sprichw.: mit den Wölfen muß man heulen when you are at Rome you must do as Rome does or as the Romans do; der ~ in der Fabel ob. wenn man vom ~ spricht.

Signs (see page XVII): F familiar; P vulgar; ⚡ flash; ↘ rare; † obsolete (died); * new word (born); ∴ incorrect; ♩ music.

[**Wölfchen**] — 1131 — [**wollen**]

so ist er nicht weit talk of the devil, and his imps appear, feiner: talk of celestials, and the angels appear. — — 2. *path.* (wunde Stelle vom langen Reiten ⅇc.) sore caused by friction or chafing, auch: gall; sich e-n ~ reiten ob. gehen to chafe one's skin (or to get sore) in riding or walking. F co. to lose leather. — 3. ☉ = Rammbär; *metall.* (Eisen, das im Ofen festsitzt) devil; Spinnerei: (Reiß-)~ willow-machine.

Wölfchen (⌣⌣) *n* ㉓ (*dim. von* Wolf) little (or young) wolf, wolf's cub, bisw.: wolfkin. [willow.]

wolfen ☉ (⌣) *v/a.* ⑧ Spinnerei: to]

Wölfin (⌣⌣) *f* ㊼ von Wolf (s. bs 1).

wölfisch (⌣⌣) *a.* ⑥⑥ wolfish, like a wolf.

Wolfram ⚵ (⌣⌣) *n* ㊿ *min., chm.* (Metall) † wolfram(ium), tungsten (w); ²-**haltig** a. ⑥⑥ tungsteniferous; ~-**metall** *n* ㉖ metallic tungsten; ~-**oker** *m* tungstic ochre, tungstite; ²-**sauer** *a.* wolframic; ²-**saures** Salz tungstate, wolframate; ~-**säure** *f* tungstic (or wolframic) acid (H_2WO_4).

Wolfs-art (²...) *f* ㉒: a) *zo.* species of wolf; b) wolf's (or wolfish) nature; -**balg** ⚹ *m* wolf's skin; -**bohne** ⚵ *f* = Lupine; -**brut** *f* (pack of) young wolves; -**eisen** *n*: a) *hunt.* wolf-trap, ehm.: caltrop; b) *metall.* (gefrischtes Eisenstück) bloom(-iron); -**falle** *f, hunt.* trap for wolves, auch = **eisen** a; -**garn** *n* net for catching wolves; -**gebiß** *n, man.* kind of sharp bit; -**geheul** *n* wolf's howl, howling of wolves; -**gesicht** *n* wolfish face or visage; -**grube** *f*: a) *hunt.* wolf-trap; b) ⚷ etwa: pitfall; -**hetze** *f, hunt.* wolf-baiting; -**hund** *m* wolf-dog, auch = Spitz 3; -**hunger** *m* = Heißhunger; auch ~ haben, oft: F to have a wolf in one's inside; -**jagd** *f* wolf-hunting; -**jäger** *m* one who hunts wolves, auch: wolfer; -**kirsche** ⚵ *f* = Tollkirsche; -**lager** *n, hunt.* wolf's lair or haunt; -**luchs** *m* = Luchs 1; -**magen** *m* wolf's stomach, *fig.* wolfish (or ravenous) appetite; -**milch** ⚵ *f* spurge, milk-weed (*Euphorbia*); ²-**milchartig** *a.*; ⚵ euphorbiaceous; -**pelz** *m* wolf's fur; -**rachen** *m* wolf's jaw(s *pl.*); -**schlucht** *f* wolves' glen; -**sucht** *f. path.* Art Wahnsinn; ⚷ lycanthropy; -**zahn** *m* eines Pferdes: wolf-tooth.

Wolga ⊕ (⌣⌣) [russ. Große] *npr/f.* ⑥⑥α. die ~ (russ. Strom) the Volga.

Wolhyni-en ⊕ (⌣¹⌣⌣) *npr/n.* ㉓α. westrussisches Gouvernement: Volhynia.

Wölkchen (⌣⌣) *n* ㉓ (*dim.von* Wolke) little cloud, bisw.: cloudlet, *path.* (Nebelfleck im Auge) white speck, ⚷ nebula.

Wolke (⌣⌣) [ahd. welkin] *f* ⑧ 1. cloud; f. Schäfchen 3 u. Regen-, Staub-wolfe; mit ~n bedeckt clouded, cloudy; *fig.* wie aus den ~n gefallen quite taken aback, vgl. fallen 4; Alt.: die ~n (Lustspiel v. Aristophanes) the Clouds *pl.* — 2. (et. den ~n Ähnliches): a) in Edelsteinen: flaw; b) ~ von Heuschrecken cloud (or swarm) of locusts; c) *fig.* (et. das den Geist trübt, umnebelt) s.th. which clouds (or darkens) the intellect.

wolken (nur v/n.), sonst: **wölken** (⌣⌣) *v/a., v/n.* (h.) u. *v/refl.* ⑧ vom Himmel: (sich)

2 to (begin to) look overcast, F to look (or come over) lowery; vgl. überwölfen.

Wolken-achat (²...) *m* ⑫ *min.* clouded agate; ²-**an** *adv.* up to the clouds; ²-**artig** *a.* ⑥⑥ cloud-like, (looking) like clouds; -**bruch** *m* torrential rain, F violent downpour (of rain).

wolkenhaft (⌣⌣⌣) *a.* ⑥⑥ = wolkig.

Wolken-himmel (²...) *m* ⑫ clouded (or overcast, lowering) sky; cloudy region, poet. welkin; ²**hoch** a. ⑥⑥ as high as the clouds, vgl. himmelhoch a; -**kratzer** *m* sky-scraper (= Himmelskratzer; -**kuckucksheim** *n* (nebelhaftes Land von Aristophanes: Nephelococcygia; ²-**leer** ²-**los** *a.* cloudless, unclouded; (klar) serene; -**losigkeit** *f* cloudlessness; -**maschine** *f, thea.* cloud-apparatus; -**saum** *m* edge (or border) of a cloud; -**schicht** *f* bank (or stratum, mass, heap) of clouds; -**schieber** F *m*: a) = Kulissenschieber; b) (Mütze mit geradeausstehendem Schirm, z.B. der Automobilfahrer) cap with a straight peak; -**soffitten** *f/pl. thea.* sky-pieces *pl.*; -**wand** *f* = -**schicht**; -**zug** *m* passage (of flight, travelling) of the clouds.

wolkicht ⚹, mst **wolkig** (⌣⌣) *a.* ⑥⑥ cloudy, clouded; vgl. wolkenartig.

Woll-abgang ☉ (²...) *m* ⑫ refuse of wool, wool-waste; -**arbeit** *f* wool-work; -**arbeiter(in** *f*) *m* wool-dresser or -picker; ²-**artig** *a.* ⑥⑥ woolly; -**ausfuhr** *f* export(ation) of wool; -**ausstäubmaschine** *f* wool-duster; -**ball** *m, vet.* im Tiermagen: wool-ball; -**baum** *m*: a) silk-cotton tree (*Bombax*); b) bentang-tree (*Eriodendron*); -**bereiter(in** *f*) *m* wool-dresser; -**blume** ⚵ *f* = Königskerze; -**börse** ⚼ *f* wool-exchange; -**brecher** ⊕ *m* Spinnerei: devilling-machine; -**decke** *f* wool(len) rug, blanket.

Wolle (⌣⌣) [ahd.: wool] *f* ⑱ 1. ⚳ wool; ungewaschene ~ wool in the yolk, wool in grease; (Bließ) fleece of a sheep; f. färben 1. — 2. *fig. u. Sprichw.*: f. Geschrei 2; in der ~ (weich und warm) sitzen to live in luxury or affluence, F to be in clover; ~ lassen müssen to burn one's fingers, to come off badly, (betrogen w.) to be (F to get) fleeced. — 3. (Flaum) down (auch ⚹), *hunt.* ~ (Haar) e-s Hasen ⅇc.: hair, coat of a hare, &c.

wollen¹ (⌣⌣) [Wolle] *a.* ⑥⑥(D9) woollen, made of wool; 2e Strümpfe, a. worsted stockings *pl.*; f. Decke 1, Jacke 1.

wollen² (⌣⌣) [ahd. = will] **I** *v/a. u. v/n.* (h.) ⑲ 1. (bereit sein) to be willing, (wünschen) to wish, fast feierlich: to will; (beabsichtigen) to intend (or purpose) doing a th.; (verlangen) to demand, to request; f. durchaus 2 am Ende, eben¹ 4 u. lieb 3; ich will, daß dies geschehe I will have it done; ich will es I wish it (to be done), dagegen: ich will es (nicht) tun I will (will not or won't) do it; er will durchaus, daß wir sie empfangen he insists on our receiving them; er wollte es he would have it; er könnte, wenn er wollte he could if he would; er hat nicht zahlen 2 he would not pay, he did not want (or he de-

clined) to pay; was 2 Sie von mir? what do you want of me?; *rel.* Gott will es God wills it, f. Gott 3 gegen Ende; drohend: das will ich mal sehen I should like to see that done; mit leblosem Subjekt: der Baum will fetten Boden ... requires a rich soil; die Feder will nicht schreiben ... won't write; Sprichw. was du nicht willst, daß man dir tu', das füg' auch keinem andern zu do unto others as you would (that) others do unto you, kürzer: do (by others) as you would be done by. — 2. a) hoffend: ich will mich gern geirrt h. I trust (or wish) I may be mistaken; b) einräumend: ich will mich geirrt h. I admit that I (have) made a mistake; c) in Wunschsätzen: das wolle Gott! would to (mehr gbr.: may it please) God!; das wolle Gott nicht! God (or Heaven) forbid!; ich wollte (möchte) gern kommen I would gladly come; Anzeige: nähere Erkundigungen wolle man einholen bei // for further particulars apply to //; d) in Bedingungssätzen: wollte es einer untersuchen if anyone were to examine it. — 3. e-m wohl 2 = wohlwollen. — 4. *ell.* mit ausgelassenem *inf.*: er wollte nach Italien (reisen) he wanted to go (or travel) to Italy; was will er damit (sagen)? what does he mean by it?; dem sei, wie ihm wolle! be that as it may; f. mögen 1 a; wie gern ich auch wollte however much I should like (to do) it; drohend: wart, ich will dich (schon) (packen)! wait, I'll be after you!; let me catch you! — 5. a) = müssen, in negativen Sätzen: = dürfen: das will flugs ausgeführt sein it has to be done prudently; b) = dem Hilfszeitwort „werden": wir 2 sehen we shall (F we'll) see; was das nur werden will? I wonder what that's going to be; c) = sollen: wie wollt' es euch zu Ohren kommen? how could you have heard it?; damit will nichts gesagt sein that does not imply (or mean) anything; d) = können: ich wollte es malen I could paint it. — 6. *pleonastisch oder mildernd*: das will ich wohl meinen I should think so, indeed; ich will das gern glauben I willingly believe it; das wollte ihm wohl gefallen that pleased him very much; mir will scheinen, daß // it would seem to me that //; das will etwas (nichts) sagen, bedeuten oder heißen that means (or signifies) s.th. (nothing); there is some (no) meaning in that. — 7. bei zweifelhaften Aussagen und Vorspiegelungen: a) er will es selbst gesehen haben he says (or asserts) that he has seen it himself; b) ich will es nicht gehört h. I shall (F I'll) pretend not to have heard it; ich will nichts gesagt haben let it appear as if I had said nothing. — 8. mit einem zu ergänzenden *inf.* der Bewegung: (zu) hoch hinaus 2 to have ambitious plans, to soar too high; das will mir nicht (recht) in den Kopf, in den Sinn I won't (or can't) believe that, that's more than I can fathom; die Sache will nicht vorwärts the matter is not making headway

---

⚷ scientific; ⚵ botanical; ⊕ geography; ⊕ machinery; ⚒ mining; ⚔ military; ⚓ marine; ⚘ commercial; ⚙ postal; 🚂 railway.

or not progressing; zu wem ~ Sie? who is it (that) you want to go to? — **II** ~ *n* 23 9. (*ant.* Tat) wish, will, willingness, intention, purpose, *phls.* volition; das ~ für die Tat nehmen to take the will for the deed. — **III ~d** *p.pr.* u. *a.* 66 10. willing, ready; nicht ~d unwilling; dem ~den wird viel aufgebürdet a willing horse has to do double work. — **IV ge-wollt** *p.p.* u. *a.* 66 11. intended, desired; das von ihm Gewollte what he wished (for), the object of his desire.

Wollen³-atlas ✱ (⏑...) [Wolle] *m* 62 worsted satin; **-fabrik** *f* woollen-cloth (manu)factory; **-fabrikant** *m* woollen-cloth manufacturer; **-garn** *n* = Wollgarn; **-musselin** *m* woollenet(t)e; **-sam(me)t** *m* plush, worsted velvet; **-stoff** *m* wool(len) material; **-träger** *m, zo.* wool-bearing (*♂* laniferous) animal; **~-waren** ✱ *f/pl.* woollen goods *pl.*; **-weber** *m* weaver of woollen materials, worsted-manufacturer; **-zeug** *n* woollen cloth *or* material.

Woll-färber ⊙ (⏑...) *m* 62 wool-dyer; **-färberei** *f* wool-dyeing; **-fett** *n* yolk, wool-oil; **-garn** *n* woollen yarn, worsted; **-geschäft** ✱ *n* wool-business; **-gras** ⚘ *n* cotton-grass (*Erio'phorum*); **-großhändler** ✱ *m* wool-stapler; **-haar** *n*: a) (einzelnes Haar) wool-hair; b) (wolliges Haar) woolly hair; **-handel** ✱ *m* wool-trade; **-händler** *m* wool-merchant *or* -dealer, dealer in wool; **-hemd** *n* woollen shirt.

wollig (⏑⏑) *a.* 66 1. (auch **wollicht**) woolly, (feeling) like wool, vom Tuche auch: nappy. — 2. (Wolle tragend) wool-bearing; ⚘ und *zo.*: *♂* lanate(d), laniferous, lanuginous, ...ose.

Woll-industrie (⏑...) *f* 62 woollen industry; **-kamm** ⊙ *m* wool- (*or* carding-) comb; **-kämmer(in** *f*) *m* wool-comber; **-kämmerei** s. Kämmerei²; **-kämmmaschine** *f* wool-combing machine; **-kratze** *f* w.-card, carding-tool; **-kratzmaschine, -krempel-maschine** *f* carding-machine; **-locken** s. Wollocken; **-makler** ✱ *m* wool-broker; **-markt** ✱ *m* wool-market, wool-staple, Lo., &c.: wool-sale; **-maus** *f, zo.* biscacha, chinchilla (*Chinchi'lla lani'gera*); **-messe** *f* wool-fair.

Wollocken ⊙ (⏑⏑⏑) [Woll-locken] *f/pl.* wool-locks.

Woll-produzent ✱ (⏑...) *m* 62 wool-grower; ~**reich** *a.* 66 rich in wool, very woolly; **-reinigungs-maschine** ⊙ *f* wool-picker *or* -cleaner; **-reißer** *m* w.-carder; **-sack** *m* wool-bag, wool-pack, als Sitz des Lordkanzlers im Oberhause: woolsack; **-same** ⚘ *m* woolly seed; **-schere, -schur** *f* = Schafschere, -schur; **-sortieren** *n* sorting of wool, a. w.-breaking; **-sortierer** *m* wool-sorter *or* -picker; **-spinner** *m* wool-spinner; **-spinnerei** *f* w.-spinning (factory); **-staub** *m* Papierfabr.: w.-flocks *pl.*; **-stickerei** *f* auf Kanevas: wool-work; **-tapete** ✱ *f* flock-paper; ~**tragend** *a.* wool-bearing.

Wollust (⏑⏑) [mhd. wolluft] *f* 69 **1.** ↘ great pleasure *or* delight. — **2.** *b.s.* (sinnliche Lust) sensual pleasure, sensuality, voluptuousness, lust; (Geilheit) lewdness, lasciviousness, (Ausschweifung) debauchery; ~**-atmend** (⏑⏑-⏑⏑) *a.* 66 breathing voluptuousness.

wollüstig (⏑⏑⏑) *a.* 66 (s. Wollust 2) (highly) sensual, voluptuous, lustful; (geil) lascivious, lewd; rank, ruttish.

Wollüstling (⏑⏑⏑) *m* ⓦd. (highly) sensual person, sensualist, stärker: voluptuary; (ausschweifender Mensch) debauched person, libertine, F rake.

Woll-vieh (⏑...) *n* 62 Viehzucht: wool-beast; **-waren** ✱ *f/pl.* woollen articles *or* goods *pl.*; **-waren-händler** *m* woollen-draper; **-wäsche(rei)** *f* wool-washing, washing of wool; **-züchter** *m* wool-breeder; **-zupfer** *m* wool-picker.

wo-mit (-⏑): a) with what?, by what means?; ~ beschäftigt er sich? what does he occupy himself with?, what does he do with himself (all day)?, how does he spend his time?; s. dienen 3; b) relativ: wherewith, with (*or* by) which; et., ~ ich nicht einverstanden bin s.th. (that) I do not agree with; et., ~ man Aufsehen erregen kann s.th. to create a sensation with: ✱ ~ sich unser Konto ausgleicht which settles our account; ~**möglich** (-⏑⏑) *adv.* (vielleicht) perhaps, possibly; ~**nach** (-⏑): a) after what?; b) relativ: whereafter, whereupon, after which; ~**neben** (-⏑⏑) relativ: near (*or* by the side of) which.

Wonne (⏑⏑) [ahd.] *f* 69 great joy, delight; bliss; (großes Vergnügen) great pleasure, glee; (Entzückung) rapture, ecstasy; in ~ aufgelöst, schwimmend dissolved in ecstasies, filled with (stärker: swimming in) delight, enraptured; in ~ und (in) Weh in joy and (in) sorrow.

wonne-bebend (⏑⏑..) *a.* 66 trembling (*or* quivering) with delight; ~**berauscht** *a.* = ~trunken; **-gefühl** *n* 62 feeling of bliss *or* joy, delicious sensation; **-leben** *n* delightful life; ~**leer**, ~**los** *a.* joyless, void of happiness; **-monat** *m* [ahd. Wonne † = Wiese, Weide], **-mond** *m* month of May.

wonnesam (⏑⏑-) *a.* 66 = wonnig.

Wonne-schauer (⏑⏑..) *m* 62 thrill of delight; **-taumel** *m* ecstasy (of delight), rapture; **-tränen** *f/pl.* tears *pl.* of joy; ~**trunken** *a.* 66 intoxicated (*or* overbrimming) with joy, mehr gbr.: in raptures, enraptured; ~**voll** *a.* = wonnesam.

wonnig(lich) (⏑⏑(⏑)) *a.* 66 delightful, delicious; blissful; pleasurable.

Wootz † ⊙ (wū'tß) [ind. *ukku* Stahl] *m* ⓦa. u. *inv.*, auch: **~-stahl** *m* 62 (ausgezeichneter indischer Gußstahl) wootz, Indian cast steel.

woran (-⏑): a) ~ denkt er nur? what on earth is he thinking of *or* about?; ~ erkennen Sie ihn? what do you know (*or* recognize) him by?; b) relativ: das Buch, ~ ich arbeite ... at which I am working; ich weiß, ~ es liegt ... what is the cause of it; c) unbestimmt: du mußt doch ~ (an etwas) gedacht h. you must have been thinking of something.

worauf (-⏑): a) upon what?; ~ sinnt er? what is he meditating on?; b) relativ: whereupon, upon which; zeitlich: ~ alle flohen whereupon all fled.

woraus (-⏑): a) out of what?, from what?; b) relativ: out of which, from which, whence; der Brunnen, ~ er das Wasser schöpft the well where (*or* that *or* which) he draws the water from.

worden (⏑⏑) *p.p.* von werden, meist beim passiven Perfekt gbr. (= geworden).

worein (-⏑) (entsprechend dem in mit dem *acc.*): a) into what?; ~ mischen Sie sich? what are you meddling with?; b) relativ: into which.

Worfel ⊙ (⏑⏑) *f* 48 *agr.* = Wurfschaufel; **worfeln** [ndd.; = werfen] *v.a.* 92a. to winnow (*or* fan) the corn; **Worfler** *m* 22 winnower, fanner of corn.

Worf-maschine, -schaufel *f* 69 s. Wurf-...

worin (-⏑) (entsprechend dem in mit dem *dat.*): a) in what?; b) relativ: wherein, in which.

Wort (⏑) [ahd.: word] *n* ⓤb. (zu 1: ⓓb.) **1.** mst. word, Bd. ~, *pl.* **Wörter** (ohne Bezug auf den Zs.-hang) (single *or* detached) word; (Ausdruck) term, expression; neu(gebildet)es ~ neologism; sämtliche Wörter einer Sprache the whole vocabulary *sg.* of a language; s. Sinn 2; Sprichw. s. Mann 1 am Ende. — **2.** *pl.* **Worte** (das Ausgesprochene; *ant.* Gedanken) (connected) words *pl.*: **a)** meist mit *adjectives*: in angemessenen ~en in appropriate words *or* language; s. dürr 3; ein ~ gibt das andere one word leads to another; man konnte sein eigen(es) ~ nicht hören you could not hear your own voice; s. geflügelt; genug der ~e enough has been said, that's enough, say no more; s. gut 3 u. 4; kein ~ mehr! not another word!; leere ~e idle words *pl.*; s. abspeisen 2, dies waren seine letzten ~e those were his last words; **nur ein paar** ~e only a word or two; **es ist kein wahres** ~ daran there isn't a word (*or* grain) of truth in it, that's a pure invention; **b)** mit *verbs*: s. abwägen 3; sein ~ brechen (nicht halten) to break one's word; das ~ ergreifen to begin to speak, *parl.* to address the House; das ~ erhalten s. erhalten 3; e-m das ~ erteilen to give a p. permission to speak; ein ~ fallen lassen to drop a word, to let out a th.; s. fallen 11; das ~ führen to be the spokesman, das große ~ führen: a) to lead the conversation; b) to talk big; *parl.* das ~ haben to be in possession (*or* to have the ear) of the House; et. nicht ~ h. (zugestehen) wollen not to own (up) a th.; to deny a th., er will es nicht ~ h., daß // he won't admit that //; (sein) ~ (Versprechen) halten to keep one's word; einige ~e hinwerfen to throw out a few suggestions, to make a casual remark; (viel) ~e machen to talk too much, F to spin (*or* make) a long yarn; um nicht viel ~e zu machen to cut a long tale short, to put it in a very few words; s. mitreden; einer Sache (fürsprechend) das ~ reden to speak in favour of a th., to speak up for a th.; s. wechseln 1; **c)** mit *prp.*: **aufs** ~ gehorchen to obey to the letter; s. achten II; auf Ihre ~e hin on the strength (*or* in consequence) of your remarks; **bei** diesen ~en at these words; e-n beim ~(e) nehmen to take a p. by his word; ~

[Wortableiter]

für ~. von ~ zu ~ word for word, (lt.) verbatim; 30 Mark, in ~en dreißig Mark .... in words (🖋 in full letters) thirty shillings; f. Ehre 4 am Ende; er brach in die folgenden ~e aus he uttered (or spoke) the following words; f. kleiden 3; mit einem ~e in a word. briefly speaking. in short; et. den ~en nach verstehen to take a th. in its literal sense; *parl.* **ums** ~ bitten to ask (for) permission to speak; wenn ich ums ~ bitten darf if I may be allowed to say a word (or two); ein Mann von ~ sein to be as good as (auch: to be a man of) one's word; ich konnte nicht zu ~e kommen I could not put (or get) in a word edgeways; d) Gottes ~: a) (Bibel) the Word of God. Holy Writ; b) F co. = Pastor. — 3. *nur im sg.*: a) *rel.* das ~ (das Schaffende) the Word; b) (Spruch) saying; (Sprichwort) proverb, adage; c) das ~ (die Auflösung des Rätsels) the solution, the right word. — 4. ♪ *nur im pl.*: die ~e (der Text) zu einem Liede; the words *pl.* (*ant.* Weise, Melodie).

Wort=ableiter (~ ...) *m* 🖋 etymologist; **=ableitung** *f* derivation of words. etymology; **=ähnlichkeit** *f* affinity (or similarity) of words; **=akzent** *m* verbal accent; **=arm** *a.* 🖋 poor in words; **=armut** *f* poverty of words; **=art** *f* kind of word; *gram.* (Redeteil) part of speech; **=aufwand** *m* = =fülle; **=bau** *m* structure of words; **=biegung** *f*, *gram.* (grammatical) inflexion; **=biegungs=lehre** *f*, *gram.* accidence; **=brüchig** *a.* false to one's word; 2 werden to break one's word; *vgl.* eidbrüchig; **~keit** *f* perfidiousness with regard to promises made, *jur. bfd. e-e* Liebhabers: breach of promise.

Wörtchen (~) *n* 🖋 (*dim. von* Wort) little (or short, insignificant) word; *gram.* unabänderliches ~: 🖋 particle.

Wort=endung (~, ~) *f* 🖋 *gram.* ending (or termination) of a word.

Wörter=bildung (~...) *f* 🖋 formation of words; **=buch** *n*: a) (alphabetisches Wörterverzeichnis mit Erklärungen) dictionary (*vgl.* Lexikon); deutsch=englisches ~ German-English dictionary; ~ zur Erklärung minder bekannter Wörter in einem Schriftsteller 2c., oft: glossary; *vgl.* Aussprache2; b) (Wörterverzeichnis ohne Erklärungen) vocabulary; **=buch=** **=bücher=** **schreiber** *m* author of a dictionary or of dictionaries. 🖋 lexicographer.

Wort=erklärung (~, ~) *f* 🖋 (*ant.* Sach=erklärung) verbal definition.

Wörter=verzeichnis (~, ~) *n* 🖋 list of words; *vgl.* Wörterbuch.

Wort=fassung (~...) *f* 🖋 = Wortlaut; **=fechter** *m* stickler (for words); **=fechterei** *f* wrangling (or haggling) about words. 🖋 dialectics; *vgl.* =klauberei; **=folge** *f* order of words; **=forschung** *f* etymological research, 🖋 etymology; **=fügung** *f*, *gr.* arrangement (of words) in a sentence; **=fügungs=lehre** *f*: 🖋 syntax; **=führer(in)** *f* *m* speaker, *nur m* spokesman; **=fülle** *f* abundance of words; **=gedächtnis** *n* verbal memory; **=gefecht** *n* dispute

about words; **=geklingel** *n* jingle of words, sonorous phrases *pl.*; **=gemälde** *n* word-picture; **=gepränge** *n* pomp of words. bombast; **=geschichte** *f* history of a word; **=getreu** *a.* 🖋 literal. *adv.* auch: to the letter; **=gläubig** *a.* believing every word. 🖋 orthodox; **=habend** *a.* being spokesman. *parl.* in possession of the House; (vorsitzend) presiding; **=held** *m* = Prahlhans; **=kampf** *m* = =gefecht; **=karg** *a.* sparing of words, taciturn, laconic; 2er Mann man of few words; **~heit** *f* taciturnity, laconism; **=klauber** *m* hair-splitter, quibbler, pedant. 🖋 logomachist; **=klauberei** *f* catching at words. hair-splitting. quibbling. 🖋 logomachy; **=kram** *m* (idle) display of words. verbiage; **=krämer** *m. etwa:* pompous speaker. phrasemonger; **=krieg** *m. fig.* war of words. wordy contest; **=kritik** *f* verbal criticism; **=künstelei** *f* affectation in style. affected (or stilted) language; **=laut** *m* wording (or text) of a document. &c.

Wörtlein (~) *n* 🖋 = Wörtchen.

wörtlich (~) [mhd.; *Wort] *a.* 🖋 1. verbal. *adv.* a. (lt.) literal. *adv.* a. (lt.) literatim; (fich dem Wort= laute eng anschließend) literal. *adv.* a. (lt.) literatim; et. zu 2 nehmen to take a th. too literally or in too literal a sense; a. Wortsinn. — 2. *ohne comp.* (*ant.* tätlich); 2e Beleidigung verbal injury or insult.

Wörtlichkeit (~, ~) *f* 🖋 einer Übersetzung: literalness, a. closeness, faithfulness.

Wort=macher F (~...) *m* 🖋 big talker; **=macherei** F 🖋 big (or idle) talk; verbosity; **=mangel** *m* = =armut; **=rätsel** *n* enigma, 🖋 logograph; **=register** *n* (index of words); **=reich** *a.* 🖋 : a) rich in words; b) (voll Wortschwall) wordy, verbose; **=schatz** *m* stock of words. des Volkes: (common) vocabulary of the people; **=schwall** *m.* **=schwulst** *m* profusion (or rich flow, stärker: torrent) of words. F (long) rigmarole; bombast, verbosity; **=sinn** *m* meaning of a word; (wörtlicher Sinn) literal sense; **=spiel** *n* play upon words, pun, quibble, 🖋 paragram; **=spieler(in)** *s.* punster, **=stamm** *m* stem of a word; **=stellung** *f* = =fügung; **=streit** *m*: a) = =gefecht; b) (Streit mit Worten) squabble, wrangling; **=tarif** *m.* *taxe* *f.* *tel.* scale of prices varying with the number of words (telegraphed); *auch*: word-tariff or =rate; **=verderber** *m* = Sprachverderber; **=verdreher** *m* word-twister. distorter of words; **=verdrehung** *f* twisting (or distortion) of words; **=versetzung** *f* transposition (or shifting) of words; im Satze auch: inversion; **=verstand** *m* literal sense; **=verwechs(e)lung** *f*: a) confusion (F mixing=up) of words or terms; b) *gram.* = Metonymie, **=verzeichnis** *n* list of words, *auch* = =register, **=vorrat** *m* = =schatz; **=wechsel** *m* exchange of words, discussion; (Streit) altercation. dispute; e-n ~ *h.* mit ... to have a quarrel (F some words) with //; in heftigen ~ geraten to come to high words; **=witz** *m* = =spiel;

[Wucherer]

=zeichen *n*: 🖋 logogram; **=zerteilung** *f*, *gram.* 🖋 tmesis.

worüber (~) : a) 2 klagt er? what is he complaining of?; 2 weinen sie? what are they crying about?; b) *relativ*: whereof, whereat; over (or at, about, &c.) which; et. 2 ich ärgerlich war s.th. at which I felt vexed; et. 2 sie sich streiten s.th. (that) they quarrel about; die Mauer, 2 (= über die) er gesprungen ist the wall (that) he jumped over.

worum (~) : a) what for?, about what?; b) *relativ*: for (or about) which.

worunter (~) : a) under (or beneath) what?; b) *relativ*: under (or among) which; die Pflanzen, 2 diese gehören ... among (or to) which these may be classed.

wo=selbst (~) *relativ*: where, in which.

wo=von (~) : a) of what?; 2 sprechen sie? what are they talking about?; b) *relativ*: whereof. of which; das, 2 sie leben what (or that which) they live upon.

wo=vor (~): a) before (or of. from) what?; b) *relativ*: das, 2 er sich am meisten fürchtet what (or that which) he is most afraid of.

wo=wider (~) = wogegen.

wo=zu (~): a) for what (purpose)?; das? what is that for?, F what's the good of that?; 2 das Geld? why that money?; b) *relativ*: whereto, for which; et. 2 viel Mut gehört s.th. that requires great courage; 2 noch kommt // to which must be added //; c) unbestimmt: das muß 2 bestimmt sein that must be intended for something.

wo=zwischen (~) between which.

Wrack ♪ (~) [*ndd.*] *n* 🖋 1. cast-off, cast aside; 2es Holz waste wood; 2 werden to become a wreck, to be wrecked. — II ~ *n a. b.* (N) 2. a) (Trümmer eines Schiffes) wreck (or wreckage, debris) of a stranded ship; b) (altes morsches Schiff) crazy old craft. F old wreck. — 3. *a.* **Wrak(ing)** (~) *f* 🖋 (Abtrift) drift. leeway. [gut, =recht.

Wrack=gut ♪ (~...), **=recht** *n* 🖋 = Strand=

wricken ♪ (~) [*ndd.*: wriggle] *v/n.* (h.) *u. v.a.* 🖋 ein Boot 2 (mit 1 Ruder v. hinten fortbewegen) to scull. to paddle astern.

Wricker ♪ (~) *m* 🖋 sculler.

wringen (~) [*ndd.*: wring] *v/a.* Wäsche 2 (ausringen) to wring (out) ...

Wring=maschine ⊙ (~, ~) *f* 🖋 wringing=machine. (clothes=)wringer. [rübe *a.*

Wruke ♪ *prov.* (~) [*ndd.*] *f* 🖋 = Kohl=

W. S. g. u.! *abbr.* = Wenden Sie gefälligst um! P.T.O. (please turn over).

Wucher (~, ~) [*ahd.*: wach(f)en] *m* 🖋 1. *b. s.* usury, usurious (or exorbitant) interest; ~ treiben to practise usury, to carry on usurious (or extortionate) practices. — 2. *bisw.*: (Zinsertrag) interest (borne or yielded); eine Wohltat mit ~ vergelten to repay ... with (double) interest or with usury.

Wucher=blume (~, ~) *f* 🖋 ox-eye daisy (*Chrysa'nthemum leuca'nthemum*).

Wucherei (~, ~) *f* 🖋 usury, usurious (or extortionate) practice(s *pl.*) or dealing.

Wucherer (~, ~) *m* 🖋, **Wuch(r)erin** *f* 🖋 usurer; money-lender.

[**Wuchergerste**] — 1134 — [**Wundergeschichte**]

Wucher-gerste f =Pfauen-g.; **-geschäft** n usurious business; **-gesetz** n law regulating usury, usury-law.
wucherhaft a usurious.
Wucher-handel m usurious trade.
wucherisch a usurious.‖trade.∫
Wucher-jude m usurious Jew.
wuchern I v/n. (h.) 1. a) bsd. von Gewächsen: to grow rankly or luxuriantly to luxuriate, seltener: to pullulate; b) path vom Fleische in Wunden: to form proud flesh; c) fig. (sich rasch ausbreiten) to spread rapidly, to be rampant. — 2. (reichen Ertrag bringen) to bring in large profits; sein Geld ⁓ l. to put out one's money at usurious (rates of) interest. — 3. (Wucher treiben) to practise usury: mit dem Gelde ⁓ to lend out one's money at exorbitant (or usurious) rates of interest, mit s-n Talenten ⁓ to make the best (or the most) of one's (natural) gifts or talents. — II ⁓ n 4. (f 1) rank (or luxuriant) growth; rapid spread, (f. 3) usury. usurious practice(s pl) or trade.
Wucher-pflanze f =rank weed or growth; **-prozent** n: zu ⁓en at an exorbitant rate of interest; **-zins** m usurious (rate of) interest.
Wuchs¹ m 1. von Gewächsen ⁊c. (Wachstum) growth; (Entwickelung) development; (In-die-Höhe-Schießen) shooting-up. — 2. (Gestalt e-r Person) shape, F build. make; (Höhe) stature, height, size. [von Mädchen.]
Wuchs² ind., **wüchse** subj. impf.∫
Wucht f 1. weight, pressure, burden; (Schwere) heaviness, mech. momentum; mit großer ⁓ with great force or impetus. — 2. ⊙ (Stützpunkt e-s Hebels) fulcrum.
wuchten I v/n. (h.) to weigh heavy or heavily, to press heavily. — II ⊙ v/a. to raise (or lift up) ..., to prize up ... [mittels e-s Hebebaumes bewegen]
wuchtig a. weighty, heavy.
wühlen I v/n. (h.) 1. to root (or turn) up the ground; von Tieren: to burrow; nach Würmern ⁓ to dig for worms. — 2. in e-m Haufen ⁓ to rake up a heap (of things); in Schubladen ⁊c. ⁓ to rummage in ..., to ransack ..., to turn ... upside down; sich (dat.) in den Haaren ⁓ to run one's hand(s) through one's hair; fig. im Gelde ⁓ to be rolling in wealth. F to be made of money; der Schmerz wühlt mir in den Eingeweiden ... is raging (or gnawing) in my bowels; in einer Wunde ⁓ to (rip) open an old sore, to touch a delicate point. — 3. fig. (die Gemüter aufrühren) to agitate; to carry on a (political) campaign or propaganda, durch Reden: to make stirring speeches, to use inflammatory language, bei Wahlen: F to be on the stump; es wurde nach allen Seiten hin gewühlt a widespread agitation was carried on. — 4. vom Wasser: to form hollows or channels, to undermine the ground. — II v/refl. 5. mit Angabe der Wirkung: sich in die Erde ⁓ to burrow (down) into the earth. — III ⁓ n 6. rooting up the ground, burrowing. digging, raking.
Wühler m 1. zo. ⁓ pl. burrowing animals pl. — 2. fig. mst pol. b.s. (s. wühlen 3) (political) agitator or wirepuller. demago⁓, (Wahlredner) stump-orator
Wühlerei f 1. constant digging or burrowing or rummaging. — 2. (s. wühlen 3) (political) agitation, demagogic(al) intrigues or manœuvres pl.. demagogism; (Wahlreden) stumporatory [demagogic(al).∫
wühlerisch a. agitating.....ive.∫
Wühl-huber F (⁓..) m b.s. =**Wühler** 2; **-maus** f zo. vole, ⁓arvicoline (Arvicola).
Wulst [ahd.: wale] m b., f 1. roll, zum Ausstopfen: pad(ding), hinten am Kleide: dress-improver, bustle; (Bausch) bunch. puff. anat.. zo.: ⁓ torus; ⁓ von Haaren: a) im Genick chignon. b) über der Stirn: fringe. — 2. arch.: ⁓ torus, am ionischen Kapitell: coussinet.
wulst-artig a. roll-shaped. like padding, bunched up.
wulsten I v/n. (in) u. v/refl. (sich) ⁓ to form a bunch, to be bunched up. — II v.a. to bunch (or puff) up.
wulst-förmig a. = ⁓artig; **-haar** n zo., etwa: hair rolled up in a bunch.
wulstig a. padded (aufgedunsen) puffed up, tumid. zo.: ⁓ torous. torose.
Wulst-lippe f F blubber-lip.
wund [ahd., f. **Wunde**] a. sore, chafed, ⁓ excoriated. v. Reiten: saddle-sore; (verwundet) wounded; sich die Füße ⁓ gehen, laufen to make one's feet sore with walking, running; vgl. laufen 2; sich ⁓ liegen to become (F to get) bed-sore; ⁓ reiben to rub open, chafe, gall; ⁓ geriebene Stelle sore, raw place; sich die Hände ⁓ ringen to wring one's hands (in despair); e-n ⁓ schlagen to beat a p. black and blue; fig. Der Punkt sore (or delicate, weak) point, (Charakterschwäche) foible.
Wund-arz(e)nei-kunst f surgery; **-arz(e)neilich** a. surgical; **-arz(e)nei-schule** f school for surgery; **-arzt** m surgeon, F co. saw-bones; **-ärztlich** a. surgical; **-balsam** m, pharm. balm for wounds, ⁓ vulnerary balsam.
Wunde f [ahd.: wound] f wound(ed part); (Verletzung) injury, hurt; eiternde (offene) ⁓ running (open) sore; klaffende ⁓ gash; leichte (leichter) ⁓ slight (severe) injury; s. aufreißen 2; ⁓n heilend healing (wounds), ⁓ vulnerary. s. schlagen 3; er starb an s-n ⁓n, er erlag s-n ⁓n he died of his wounds, he succumbed to his injuries; s. verbinden 3.
Wund-eisen n surgeon's probe.
wunden-frei a. free from wounds, not wounded, unhurt, uninjured, (a. poet.) unscathed; **-mal** n = Wundmal.
Wunder [ahd.: wonder] n 1. (et. durch überirdische Kräfte Hervorgerufenes) miracle, s.th. miraculous or supernatural; (ganz Außerordentliches) marvel, marvellous sight or event, prodigy, wonderful (or extraordinary, strange) thing or being, s.th. wonderful, (seltene, merkwürdige Erscheinung) phenomenon, s.th. phenomenal; (et. über allen Vergleich Erhabenes) paragon (of beauty), s.th. unparalleled or matchless; ein ⁓ der Weisheit a prodigy of wisdom; s. Weltwunder; es grenzt an ein ⁓ it borders on the miraculous or supernatural; ⁓ schreien to cry marvel upon marvel; er hat ⁓ getan he has done wonders; ⁓ tun, ⁓ wirken to work miracles; o ⁓! how wonderful!, how marvellous!; Zeichen und ⁓ signs and wonders pl. (a. bibl.). — 2. (Gefühl staunender Neugier) (feeling of) wonder, wonderment, amazement; es nimmt mich ⁓, daß // I wonder that //, I am astonished (or surprised) that //. — 3. (et. Staunen Erregendes): a) es ist kein ⁓, daß // it's no wonder that //, it's not to be wondered at that //; b) ⁓s (der Seltenheit) halber for curiosity's sake; was ⁓. wenn // it's not to be wondered at if //, what is there astonishing if //; er bildet sich ⁓ (meist: ⁓s) was darauf ein he is wonderfully proud of it; ich dachte ⁓ (auch: ⁓s), was es wäre I expected to see (or I thought it was) s.th. wonderful; er denkt ob. glaubt ⁓ (auch: ⁓s) was er tut he thinks (or fancies) that he is doing s.th. wonderfully clever or s.th. quite extraordinary; sein blaues ⁓ sehen, hören, erleben to be (thoroughly) amazed or astounded; vgl. blau 2 am Schluß; c) mach' mir nicht so viel ⁓! don't make so much fuss about it!
wunder-alt a. wonderfully old; **-apfel** m = Balsamapfel.
wunderbar a. 1. wonderful, geb. Svr.: (merkwürdig) wondrous, marvellous. phenomenal, prodigious, (erstaunlich) amazing, astonishing, astounding; ⁓ (adv.) flug wonderfully shrewd, remarkably wise; das ⁓e an ihm ist // what is so marvellous in him is //. — 2. (übernatürlich) miraculous, supernatural, (zauberhaft) magic, bewitching, fairy-like. — 3. (sonderbar) singular, strange, peculiar; (ungewöhnlich) extraordinary, out of the common.
wunderbarer-weise adv. singularly; strange to say or to relate.
Wunderbarkeit f 1. (ohne pl.) wonderfulness; miraculousness. — 2. (mit pl.) wonder(ful thing); s.th. wonderful or miraculous or strange.
wunderbarlich a. = wunderbar.
Wunder-bau m 1. wonderful (or marvellous) structure; **-baum** m: a) wonderful tree; b) = unechte Akazie; c) = Rizinus; **-baum-öl** n castor-oil; **-bild** n a) wonderful picture; b) eccl. miraculous (or miracle-working) image; **-blume** f marvel of Peru (Mirabilis); **-brunnen** m miraculous well; **-ding** n wonderful (or marvellous) thing, wonder, marvel; ⁓e von e-m erzählen to tell wonderful things (or tales) about a p.; **-doktor** m quack (doctor); **-erde** f, min. (farbige Tonart) stone-marrow. ⁓ lithomarge; **-erklärung** f explanation of miracles; **-geschichte** f: a) marvellous story; (Märchen) fairy-tale. (Gespenstergeschichte) ghost-

Signs (see page XVII): F familiar; P vulgar; ꟼ flash; ⸗ rare; † obsolete (died); * new word (born); ⁺⁺ incorrect; ♪ music;

story; b) *eccl.* history of miracles; =geſchöpf *n* marvellous creature, prodigy; =glaube *m*: a) belief in miracles; b) faith that works miracles; ⸗groß *a.* ⚛ of (a) prodigious size or height, colossal; ⚖hold *a.* wonderfully sweet, most charming, very lovely; =horn *n* enchanted horn; des Knaben ~ (deutſche Liederſammlung von v. Arnim und Brentano) The Boy's Magic Horn; ⚖hübſch *a.* wonderfully pretty, exceedingly fine or beautiful; =kind *n* wonder(ful) child, öſter: youthful prodigy; =kur *f* miraculous cure; =lampe *f* magic lamp; =land *n* land of wonders, wonderland; wonderful country; =laterne *f* magic lantern; =lehre *f*: ⚛ thaumatology.

wunderlich (⚛⚐) *a.* ⚛ singular; (ſeltſam) strange, eccentric, F funny; (ſonderbar) peculiar, curious, odd, queer, F rum; (ſchwer zu befriedigen) difficult to please, fanciful, crotchety, fastidious; (ungeſellig) unsociable; e-n Kauz 2: he has had 2 (*adv.*) ergangen he has had (or met with) a strange adventure; ~keit *f* ⚛ singularity; strangeness, eccentricity; oddity; fastidiousness.

wunder=lieblich (⚛⚐...) *a.* ⚛ = ⚖hold; =mädchen *n* ⚛ wonderful girl, marvellous maid; =mann *m*: a) wonderful man; b) miracle-worker; =märchen *n* wonderful story or fairy-tale; =mär(e) *f* marvellous report or tale; ⚖mild *a.* wonderfully gentle, auch wondrous kind; =mittel *n* wonderful remedy, (Univerſalmittel) panacea.

wundern (⚛⚐) [ahd. wonder] ⚛a. I *v/n.* (h.) u. *v/a.*: a) das wundert mich that astonishes (or surprises) me, I wonder at that; mich wundert ſehr, daß // I am amazed (or quite surprised) that //; es wundert uns gar nicht, daß // we are not in the least surprised that //; es ſollte mich ⚛, wenn // I should be astonished if //; es ſoll mich doch ⚛ (ich möchte wiſſen), ob // I wonder (or should like to know) whether (or if) //. — II ſich ⚛ *v/refl.* to wonder, to be (or feel) astonished or surprised or amazed (über et. at a th.); ich wundere mich zu hören, daß // I am surprised (or amazed) to hear that //, I hear with surprise (or amazement) that //.

wunder=nehmen (⚛⚐...) *v/a.* ⚛a**: e-n ⚛ to astonish a p.; vgl. Wunder 2. =palaſt *m* ⚛ fairy-palace; =quell *m*, =quelle *f* miraculous spring or fountain; ⚖reich¹ *a.* ⚛: a) full of wonders or marvels; b) marvellously rich; =reich² *n* = =land; =ring *m* magic (or enchanted) ring; =ſalz *n*: a) miraculous salt; b) *chm.* = Glauberſalz.

wunderſam (⚛⚐) *a.* ⚛ = wunderbar.

wunder=ſchön (⚛⚐...) *a.* ⚛ exceedingly beautiful, exquisite, auch wondrous fair; vgl. ⚖hold; ⚖ſelten *a.* exceedingly rare; =ſpiegel *m* ⚛ magic mirror; =ſtab *m* magic wand; =ſucht *f* mania (or craze) for miracles, (passionate) love for the miraculous; =tat *f*: a) miraculous act or deed, miracle; b) wonderful feat; =täter(in *f*) *m* miracle-worker, ⚛ thaumaturgus, ...iſt, ...e; ⚖täteriſch *a.* performing

miracles, ⚛ thaumaturgic(al); ⚖tätig *a.* working wonders, miraculous; ~keit *f*: a) miraculous virtue; b) miracle-working, ⚛ thaumaturgy; =tier *n* prodigious animal, monster; F co. von Menſchen: prodigy; ⚖voll *a.* wonderful, marvellous, geh. Spr.: wondrous; =welt *f* world of wonders, enchanted world; vgl. =land; =werk *n*: a) marvellous work; b) miracle; =zeichen *n* miraculous sign, portent, supernatural incident.

Wund=fieber (⚛⚐...) *n* ⚛ *surg.* fever caused by a wound; ⚖gedrückt *a.* ⚛ chafed, galled; ⚖gelaufen *a.* foot-sore; ⚖gerieben *a.* chafed, sore through; Wundheit (⚛⚐) *f* ⚛ soreness. [rubbing.⎫

Wund=klee (⚛⚐...) *m* ⚛: ⚛ anthyllis, echter ~ kidney-vetch (*Anthy'llis vulnera'ria*); =kraut ⚛ *n* vulnerary herb or plant; =liegen *n* eines Kranken: (being) bedsore; vgl. =ſein; =mal *n* mark left by a wound, (Narbe) scar; *eccl.* ~e *pl.* Chriſti ꝛc.: stigmata *pl.* of Christ. &c.; =mittel *n* remedy (or cure) for wounds, ⚛ vulnerary, traumatic; =pflaſter *n*, *pharm.* plaster for wounds; =röhrchen *n. surg.*: cannula; =ſalbe *f, pharm.* salve (or ointment) for wounds; =ſchere *f, surg.* probe-scissors *pl.*; =ſchorf *m, surg.* scab (forming on a wound); =ſein *n* soreness, ⚛ excoriation; =waſſer *n, pharm.* lotion for wounds, ⚛ vulnerary water; =werden *n* becoming (F getting) sore or chafed.

Wune *obb.* (⚛⚐) *f* ⚛ Fiſcherei: hole cut in(to) the ice for the purposes of fishing.

Wunſch (⚛⚐) [ahd.: wish] *m* ⚛a. 1. wish (nach et. for a th.); (Verlangen) desire for, belonging for or after; auf j-s ~ at a p.'s desire or request; gegen j-s ~ against (or contrary to) a p.'s wish; nach ~ according to one's (heart's) desire, as one wishes; ihm geht alles nach ~ things are going on smoothly (or swimmingly) with him, he succeeds in everything; ſ. fromm 2; e-n ~ äußern, tun to express a desire, to utter a wish; j-s ~ gewähren to grant a p.'s request; *gr.* e-n ~ ausdrückend; ⚛ optative. — 2. (Gegenſtand e-s ~es) thing wished for; die Reiſe war ſchon lange ihr ~ ... had been her (great) wish (or ambition) for a long time.

wünſchbar (⚛⚐) *a.* ⚛ 1. desirable. — 2. that may be wished for.

Wünſchel=hut (⚛⚐...) *m* ⚛, =hütlein *n* im Märchen: wishing-cap, magic hood; =rute *f* divining-rod, magic wand, zum Aufſuchen v. Waſſer ꝛc.: dowsing-rod; mit der ~ Quellen ſuchen to dowse.

wünſchen (⚛⚐) [ahd.: wish] I *v/a.* ⚛ 1. to wish for; (begehren) to desire, ſehnſüchtig: to long (or yearn) for; (verlangen) to request; ich wünſche mir et. mehr Ruhe I should like (ſtärker: I am anxious to get) a little more rest. — 2. mit nouns: ich wünſche Ihnen gute Beſſerung I trust you may soon be better; e-m Glück ⚛ to wish a p. joy or good luck; e-m et. Glück ⚛ to congratulate a p. on s.th.; ſ. glücklich I; wir ⚛ ihm den glücklichſten Erfolg we wish him the greatest success;

ſ. Morgen 2, Ruhe 2 am Schluß, ruhen 1 am Schluß, ſchlafen 1 gegen Ende. — 3. in Redensarten: ſich an j-s Stelle ⚛ to wish o.s. in a p.'s place; das läßt viel zu ⚛ übrig this leaves much to be desired; ⚛ Sie ſonſt noch etwas? do you wish (⚛ im Laden: can I show you) anything else?; meiſt iro. ⚛ Sie noch was? (is there) anything else you would like?; mit Sägen: ich wünſche, ich wäre ſchon dort I wish I was (or were) there now; ich wünſchte (möchte) nicht, daß ſie es merkte I should not wish (or like) her to notice it. — II ~ *n* ⚛ 4. wish, wishing; desire, longing.

wünſchens=wert (⚛⚐...), ⚖würdig *a.* ⚛ desirable, biſ. v. Perſonen a.: eligible; es wäre mir ⚛ wert zu wiſſen I should like (or I very much wish) to know; et. Wünſchenswertes oft: a (great) desideratum; =würdigkeit *f* desirability.

Wunſch=erfüllung (⚛⚐...) *f* ⚛ fulfilment (or realization) of a p.'s wish(es); =form *f, gr.* optative form; ⚖weiſe *adv.* in the form (or by way) of a wish; =weiſe *f, gr.* optative mood; =zettel *m* list of what one would like at Christmas, &c.

wupp! (⚛⚐) [lautm.] *int.* there goes!, ho!, hallo!; (wie der Wind) like winking.

Wuppdich F (⚛⚐) *m* ⚛ (*a. inv.*): mit e-m ~ in a twinkle or twinkling, F in a jiffy.

würbe (⚛⚐) *subj. impf. v.* werben. [werden.⎫

wurde *ind.*, würde¹ (⚛⚐) *subj. impf. v.*

Würde² (⚛⚐) [ahd.: worth: wert] *f* ⚛ 1. dignity; (Hoheit und Adel) noble bearing or demeanour; ich halte es unter meiner ~ I think it beneath me or F infra dig. (= lt. dignitatem), auch: I would not stoop to it; ſ-r ~ et. vergeben to set aside one's dignity, to stoop too low; vgl. vergeben 2 am Schluß. — 2. (Amt, Ehrenſtelle) office, post (of honour); akademiſche ~ academical (or university-)degree; in Amt und ~n in a lucrative post or position; zu den höchſten ~n gelangen to attain the highest honours; Sprichw. ~n ſind Bürden great honours are great burdens. — 3. (innerer Wert) intrinsic value, virtue; unter aller ~ beneath contempt, vgl. 1.

würde=los (⚛⚐) *a.* ⚛ undignified.

Würden=träger (⚛⚐...) *m* ⚛ dignitary, high official, F big gun.

würde=voll (⚛⚐) *a.* ⚛ full of dignity; dignified, of noble bearing; majestic.

würdig (⚛⚐) [ahd.: worthy] *a.* ⚛ 1. mit *gen.*: er iſt deſſen nicht ⚛ he is not worthy (or deserving) of it; e-r beſſeren Sache ⚛ worthy of a better cause; ſie iſt ⚛, e-s Fürſten Gattin zu ſein she is worthy of being (or she deserves to be) a prince's consort. — 2. *abs.* (well-)deserved; (ehrwürdig) respectable, estimable; ⚛es Paar worthy couple; (würdevoll) dignified.

würdigen (⚛⚐) I *v/a.* ⚛ 1. e-n e-r Sache (*gen.*) ⚛ to deem a p. worthy of a th.; ſie wollte mich keines Blickes (Wortes) ⚛ she would not deign (or condescend) to look at (to speak to) me. — 2. *fig.* to appreciate, to estimate; er weiß es richtig zu ⚛ he attaches the

[Würdigkeit] — 1136 — [Würmerspeise]

right value (or importance) to it, he fully appreciates it; fähig et. zu 2 appreciative. — II ~ n 3. f. Würdigung.
Würdigkeit (*ᛒ*) f ⑯ worthiness; (Wert) worth; (Verdienst) merit; (würdiges Aussehen) dignified look or appearance.
würdiglich (*ᛒ*) adv. = würdig.
Würdigung (*ᛒ*) f ⑯ (f. würdigen 2) appreciation, estimation; valuation.
Wurf (*ᛒ*) [ahd.: werfen] m ⓓ b. 1. a) throw (of dice, &c.), cast (of the net, &c.), mech. projection; den ersten ~ h. to throw first; fig. alles auf einen ~ setzen to risk (or stake) all on the cast of a die, auch: to put all one's eggs into one basket; fig. wenn der große ~ gelungen, eines Freundes Freund zu sein (SCH.) he that reached the highest goal to be a friend unto a friend; einen ~ tun to throw, to have a fling at a th., F to shy; einen guten ~ tun to throw well, fig. (es glücklich treffen) to make a lucky hit, F to strike oil; b) (Entwurf, Skizze) draft, sketch; der erste ~ the first outline; c) ~ des Gewandes fall (or arrangement) of the drapery. — 2. F e-m in den ~ kommen, laufen, setzen (eigentlich von aufstoßender Jagdbeute) to come suddenly across a p., F to run against a p. — 3. (das Geworfene) (number of) things thrown; von Tieren: (die geworfenen Jungen) litter, brood, nest of young (ones).
Wurf-angel ⊕ (*ᛒ*) f ⑫ fishing-line attached to a rod; **-anker** ↓ m kedge (-anchor); **-ankertau** n stream-cable; **-bewegung** f. mech. motion of projectiles; **-blei** ↓ n (sounding-)lead.
würfe (*ᛒ*) subj. impf. von werfen.
Würfel (*ᛒ*) f ⊕ = Wurfschaufel.
Würfel (*ᛒ*) [ahd.: werfen] m ㉒ 1. zum Spiel: die, pl. dice; f. falsch 3; ~ spielen to play (at) dice; f. fallen 1 gegen Ende. — 2. math., &c. cube, ⌂ hexahedron; f. Kubus; Brot c. in ~ schneiden to cut ... in(to) square pieces or F in squares.
würfel-artig (*ᛒ*) a. ⑯ = Oförmig; **-becher** m Spiel: dice-box; **-bein** n, anat.: ⌂ cuboid bone; **-brett** n draught-board; **-bude** f auf Jahrmärkten: booth for dice-playing; **-erz** n, min. (arsenikfaures Eisen) cube-ore, native arsenate of iron; **-fall** m cast of the die or dice, number of points thrown; **-form** f cubic form; Oförmig a. cubiform, cubic(al); **-fuß** m cubic foot.
würf(e)licht.mft ...ig(*ᛒ*)a.⑯ 1.(gewürfelt) checkered, arch. tesselated. — 2. like a die, math. cubic(al), ⌂ hexahedral.
Würfel-inhalt (*ᛒ*...) m ⑯ math. volume of a cube, cubic (or solid) contents pl.; **-kapitell** n. arch. cubiform capital; **-kohle** f, coll. small coal; cobbles, nuts pl.; **-muster** ⊕ n checkered pattern, auch: checks pl. [feln.
wurfeln ⊕ (*ᛒ*) v/a. ⑫a., agr. = wor-
würfeln (*ᛒ*) ⑫a. I v/n. (h.) 1. to play (at) dice; um etwas 2 to throw (dice) for s.th. — II v/a. 2. to cut into square pieces. — 3. von Zeugen: to check(er). — 4. Sachen durch-ea.- 2 to throw things into confusion,

to put things higgledy-piggledy; durch-ea.-gewürfelt jumbled up. — III ~ n ㉓ 5. (f. 1) dice-playing. — IV ge-würfelt p.p. u. a. ⑯ 6. f. bfd. Art.; ⊕ gewürfelte Zeuge checks pl.
Würfel-salpeter (*ᛒ*...) m ⑫ min. (falpetersaures Natron) cubic nitre; **-spat** m, min.: ⌂ cube-spar, anhydrite, anhydrous sulphate of lime; **-spiel** n dice-playing, game of dice, playing (or gambling) with dice; **-spieler** m dice-player; **-zahl** f cubic number, cube; **-zeolith** m f. Chabasit; **-zucker** ⊕ m cube-sugar; **-zuckerschneidemaschine** f cube-sugar machine.
Wurf-erde (*ᛒ*...) f ⑫ earth thrown up; **-geschoß** ⚔ n missile, projectile; **-gestell** ⚔ n frame for firing rockets; **-hafen** ↓ m grappling-iron or -hook; **-kraft** f, mech. force of projection, projectile (v. Pulver: propelling) force.
Wurfler ⊕ (*ᛒ*) m ⑫ = Worfler.
Würfler (*ᛒ*) m ⑫ dice-player.
würflicht...**ig** (*ᛒ*) a. ⑯ f. würfelicht 2c.
Wurf-linie (*ᛒ*...) f ⑫ mech. line (or curve) of projection; **-maschine** f: a) ⊕ agr. (auch Worfmaschine) winnowing-machine; ⊕ projecting-engine, ⚔ Alt.: catapult, ballista; **-netz** n casting- (or drag-)net; **-pfeil** m dart; **-riemen** m Falknerei: leash; **-sämaschine** ⊕ f, agr. broadcast sower; **-schaufel** (auch Worfschaufel) f, agr. winnowing-shovel; **-scheibe** f quoit, Altertum: discus; **-scheiben-spiel** n quoits pl.; **-schlinge** f = Lasso; **-speer, -spieß** ⚔ m javelin; **-stein** m Spiel: stone for throwing; **-weise** adv. by way of throwing or hurling; **-weite** ⚔ f. artill. range (of projection); **-zeug** n contrivance for throwing.
Würg(e)band (*ᛒ*...) n ㉓ arch. clip; **-birne** f choking pear. [rota-rubber.]
Würgel-maschine⊕(*ᛒ*ᛒ*)f②Spinnerei:
würgeln (*ᛒ*) v/a. ⑫a. to flatten out with a roller, (walzen) to roll.
Würgel-walze (*ᛒ*ᛒ*) f ⑫ Walzwerk: upper cylinder of a flattening-mill.
würgen (*ᛒ*) [ahd.: worry] ⑱ I v/n. (h.) u. sich 2 v/refl. 1. a) to choke, to feel choked, beim Brechen: to retch; er würgt (sich) an dem Bissen, der Bissen würgt ihm im Halse the morsel chokes him or has stuck (fast) in his throat; b) (auch v/a.) faktitiv: to cause n p... &c. to choke, to produce a choking sensation; et. hinunter 2 to swallow a th. with a great effort, F to get a th. down one's throat; c) fig. an e-r Arbeit 2 to slave away at (or to sweat over) a task. — II v/a. 2. e-n 2 (am Halse packen) to seize a p. by the throat. — 3. (erdrosseln) to strangle, to throttle; weits. to massacre, (ausrotten) to exterminate, slay, destroy. — 4. ⊕ Raketen 2c. (mit einer Schnur fest umschlingen) to choke ... — III ~ n ㉓ 5. f. Würgung.
Würg-engel (*ᛒ*ᛒ*) m ⑫ bibl. destroying angel, destroyer.
Würger (*ᛒ*) m ⑫ 1. (auch: ~in f ⑯) strangler, throttler, garrotter, weits. exterminator, slayer, destroyer; (Mörder) murderer, cut-throat. —

2. orn. shrike, butcher-bird (La'nius); (Raub-)~ great (or grey) shrike (L. excu'bitor); rotköpfiger ~ wood-shrike, woodchat (Enneo'ctonus rufus); rotrückiger ~ = Dorndreher — 3. ⌂ (Sommerwurz) broom-rape (Oroba'nche).
Würgerei (*ᛒ*...) f ⑯ = Würgung.
würgerisch (*ᛒ*) a. ⑯ choking; weits. destructive, murderous.
Würg-falk(e) (*ᛒ*...) m ⑫ lanner(et) (Falco lania'rius); **-holz, -knebel** m ⊕ Brückenbau: packing-stick; **-leine, -schnur** ⊕ f Feuerwerkerei: choking-line, choker; **-schwert** n, ⚔ m sword of destruction, murderous steel.
Würgung (*ᛒ*) f ⑯ 1. (f. würgen 1) choking, retching; f. hängen 5. — 2. (f. würgen 3) strangling, strangulation; massacre, extermination.
Wurm (*ᛒ*) [ahd.: worm] m (P n) ⓓ (poet. a.⑦)b. 1. worm, Sprichw. f. krümmen 2; (Made) maggot, grub; (kriechendes Tier) reptile; voller Würmer full of worms, ⌂ vermiculate; von Würmern zerfressen worm-eaten; fig. (Krebsschäden, Kummer) canker; der nagende ~ des Gewissens the (gnawing) pangs pl. of conscience; f. Nase 3 unter "aus". — 2. bisw. (Schlange) serpent, vgl. Lindwurm; fig. das war der Kopf des ~es that was the chief danger, auch: he was at the head of it all. — 3. fig. (kleines, jämmerliches Geschöpf) poor little wretch, helpless creature or child; (mere) chick or chit or dot; nordd. P oft n: du armes ~ (oder Würmchen)! poor little thing or mite! — 4. fig. (Grille) crotchet, freak; e-n ~ h., Würmer (Schrullen) im Kopfe h. to have a bee in one's bonnet, to be cracked or crazy, F to be off one's chump. — 5. (Krankheit) ~ am Finger whitlow. — 6. vet.: a) (Rotz in den Lymphdrüsen eines Pferdes) farcy; b) (Toll-)~ (Sehnenband unter der Hundszunge) worm.
wurm-abtreibend (*ᛒ*...) a. ⑯ med. acting against worms, ⌂ (ant)helminthic, helminthagogic; ‿es Mittel = ‿arz(e)nei; **-ähnlich, -artig** a. worm-like, ⌂ vermicular, helminthoid; **-arz(e)nei** f ⑫ medicine (or remedy) against (or for) worms, ⌂ vermifuge, (ant)helminthic; **-beifuß** ⚘ m: santonica (Artemi'sia contra); **-bewegung** f worm-like (or vermicular) motion.
Würmchen (*ᛒ*) n ㉔ (dim. von Wurm) 1. little (or tiny) worm, bisw. vermuling, ⌂ vermicule. — 2. fig. f. Wurm 3.
wurmen (*ᛒ*) v/n. (h.) ⑱ 1. (wurmstichig w.) to become worm-eaten. — 2. mit persönlichem Subjekt: (F auch: **wurmisieren** ‿‿‿ ⑬) to worry, to brood (over things). — 3. das wurmt in m-m Innern (verdrießt mich) I feel (inwardly) vexed (or annoyed) about it; mit persf. acc.: das wurmt mich (das vexes or annoys, worries) me. — 4. et. wurmt mir (erregt Grimmen) im Magen s.th. gripes (or pinches) me in the stomach, F I have the gripes.
würmer-erzeugend (*ᛒ*...) a. ⑯ worm-producing, ⌂ vermiparous; **fressend** a. worm-eating, ⌂ vermivorous; **-speise** f ⑫ food (F roast meat) for worms.

Zeichen (f. S. XVII): F familiär; P Volkssprache; ℾ Gaunersprache; ⸢ selten; † alt (auch gestorben); * neu (auch geboren); ⸢⸣ unrichtig;

Wurm=essenz (ˊ...) *f* Ⓔ = =arz(e)nei; =**fieber** *n, path.* fever caused by worms, auch: worm-fever; ²**förmig** *a.* Ⓜ *zo.*, &c. worm-shaped, ⚗ vermicul*ar*, ...ate; =**fraß** ⚙ *m* worm-eaten place, damage done by worms; ²**fräßig** *a.* worm-eaten.

wurmig (ˊˇ) *a.* Ⓜ **1.** wormy, maggoty; full of worms or maggots; worm-eaten; ⚗ vermicul*ose*, ...ous, ...ate. — **2.** *fig.* (verdrießlich) vexed, annoyed, F maggoty, sour-tempered.

wurmisieren F (ˇˇˊˇ) *v/n.* (h.) Ⓦ f. wurmen 2.

Wurm=kolben (ˊ...) *m* Ⓔ ⚙ *chm.* worm; ²**krank** *a. path.* suffering from worms; =**krankheit** *f*: ⚗ vermination, helminthiasis, oft a. worms *pl.*; =**kraut** ⚘ *n* = Rainfarn; natterkopfartiges ~ = =salat; =**kuchen** *m, pharm.* worm-cake or -tablet; =**kunde** *f*: ⚗ helminthology; =**larve** *f* worm-larva; =**loch** *n* hole made by worms; vgl. =stich; =**mehl** *n* dust from worm-eaten wood; =**mittel** *n, med.* cure for worms; vgl. =arz(e)nei; =**nudeln** *f/pl.* Kochkunst: vermicelli; =**plätzchen** *n* = =kuchen; =**pulver** *n* worm-powder; =**rinde** *f, pharm.* worm-bark; =**rinden=baum** ⚘ *m* cabbage-tree (*Andi'ra*); =**röhre** *f, zo.* worm-shell (*Se'rpula*); =**salat** ⚘ *m* bristly ox-tongue (*Helmi'nthia echioi'des*); =**same(n)** *m, pharm.* (getrocknete Knospen verschiedener Beifuß-arten) wormseed, ⚗ semencine, santonica; =**samen=bitter** *n, chm.*: ⚗ santonin(e) ($C_{15}H_{18}O_3$); =**stich** *m* worm-hole; ²**stichig** *a.* Ⓜ w.-eaten, ⚗ vermiculate; ~**keit** *f* w.-eaten state, seltener: w.-eatenness; =**tod** ⚘ *m* = Wermut; ²**treibend** *a.* = ²abtreibend.

Wurscht (ˊ), **wurschtig** (ˊˇ) f. Wurst, wurstig.

Wurst (ˊ) [ahd.] *f* Ⓦ **1.** sausage, aus Schweinefleisch: pork-sausage, aus Rindfleisch: beef-sausage (f. Blut=, Brat=, Leber=, Zervelat=wurst). — **2.** *fig.* ~ wider ~ measure for measure, tit for tat; Sprichw. f. Speckseite; burschikos: das ist mir ~ oder Wurscht (gleichgültig) that's all the same to me, F that doesn't trouble (or worry) me. — **3.** ⚔ Minierkunst: (Zünd=, Pulver=)~ pudding, (fr.) saucisson. — **4.** = Wulst 1.

Würstchen (ˊˇ) *n* Ⓦ (*dim.* von Wurst) small sausage, (small) saveloy; Wiener ~ (small) Vienna sausage.

Wurst=darm (ˊ˗ˊ) *m* Ⓔ Schlächterei: (pig's) gut for sausages.

wursteln (ˊˇ) Ⓐ a., **wursten** (ˊˇ) Ⓜ **I** *v/n.* (h.) to make sausages or black-puddings; F *fig.* es wird weiter gewurstelt we go on at the same old trot. — **II** *v/a.* to shape like a sausage. — **III** ~ *n* Ⓦ = Wurstfabrikation.

Wurster (ˊˇ) *m* Ⓦ südd. = Wurstmacher.

Wurst=fabrikation (ˊ...) *f* Ⓔ sausage-manufacture or -making; =**fett** *n* sa.-fat; =**fleisch** *n* sa.-meat; =**gift** *n* poison (contained) in bad sausages, *chm.*: ⚗ allantotoxicon; =**hack=maschine** ⚙ *f* sausage-cutter or -machine; =**händler(in** *f)* *m* person that sells sausages; (Schweinemetzger) pork-butcher; =**haut** *f* skin of a sausage; =**horn** ⚙ *n* Schlächterei: funnel (or filler) for sausage-making.

wurstig (ˊˇ) *a.* Ⓜ **1.** = wulstig. — **2.** F (gleichgültig) (quite) indifferent, callous, F non-carish; **Wurstigkeit** *f* Ⓦ (total) indifference, callousness, F non-carishness.

Wurst=kessel (ˊ...) *m* Ⓔ: a) copper (or boiler) for sausage-making; b) F *fig.* jetzt sitze ich im ~ now I am in a nice fix or F mess; =**kraut** *n* herb for seasoning sausages; bfd. ⚘ = Majoran; =**lippe** *f* (dicke Lippe) blubber-lip; =**macher** *m* sausage-maker, pork-butcher; =**maul** F *n* (mouth with) blubber-lips *pl.*; thick-lipped person; ²**mäulig** F *a.* with blubber-lips, thick-lipped; =**stopf=maschine** ⚙ *f* sausage-machine or -stuffer; =**suppe** *f* black-pudding broth; =**vergiftung** *f, path.* sausage-poisoning; =**wagen** ⚔ *m* ehm. *artill.* ammunition-waggon with padded seat; =**zipfel** *m* (thin) end of a sausage.

Württemberg ♀ (ˊˇˊ) [Wirtenberg, Burg bei Cannstatt] *npr/n.* Ⓜ α. Kingdom of Württemberg or Wurtemberg, ehm. auch: Wirtemberg.

Württemberger (ˊˇˊˇ) **I** *m* Ⓦ, ~**in** *f* Ⓦ inhabitant of Württemberg. — **II** *a. inv.*, **württembergisch** *a.* Ⓜ of W.

Wurz † ob. *provc.* (ˊ) [ahd.] *f* Ⓦ = Wurzel.

Würz=duft (ˊ˗ˊ) *m* Ⓔ aroma(tic odour), perfume, scent, fragrance.

Würze (ˊˇ) [ahd.: wort] *f* Ⓦ **1.** a) = Gewürz; b) (Würzen, würzige Zutat) seasoning, flavouring; *fig.* (scharfer, würziger Geschmack) spicy (or sharp, hot, pungent) taste. — **2.** ⚙ Brauerei: (aus Malz und Hopfen bereitete Flüssigkeit) (brewer's) wort, malt liquor.

Wurzel (ˊˇ) [ahd.; *Wurz + wale] *f* Ⓦ **1.** root (a. ⚘, *anat.*, *gr.*, *math.*, &c.); (Zahn=)~, a. fang, e-s alten Zahnes: stump; gelbe ~ = Mohrrübe; mit der ~ ausreißen od. ausrotten to pull up by the root(s), to root up, *fig.* to eradicate; ~ fassen to take root; f. schlagen 3 am Ende; zur ~ gehörig radical; *fig.* hier (im Vaterlande) sind die starken ~n deiner Kraft (*SCH.*) here rests the solid basis of your strength; *math.* eine ~ ausziehen to extract a root. — **2.** *anat.*, *zo.* ~ des Fußes: ⚗ tarsus.

wurzel=artig (ˊ...) *a.* Ⓜ root-like, ⚗ radiciform; =**ausziehen** *n* Ⓔ *math.* extraction of roots, ⚗ evolution; =**auszieher** *m* (Zange des Zahnarztes) forceps for extracting stumps; =**ballen** *m* (conglomerate of) tangled roots *pl.*; =**bäume** ⚘ *m/pl.* rhizophora *pl.*; =**bildung** ⚘ *f* radication; =**blatt** ⚘ *n* radical leaf; =**blüt(l)er** ⚘ *m*: ⚗ rhizanth, *pl.* a. rhizantheæ; =**buchstabe** *m, gr.* radical letter.

Würzelchen (ˊˇˇ) *n* Ⓦ (*dim.* v. Wurzel) small (or tiny) root, rootlet, radicle.

Wurzel=exponent (ˊ...) *m* Ⓔ *math.* radical index; =**faser** ⚘ *f* fibre (or thread) of a root; rootlet; ²**förmig** *a.* Ⓜ = ²artig; ²**fressend** *a. zo.*: ⚗ rhizophagous; ²**früchtig** ⚘ *a.*: ⚗ rhizocarp*ous*, ...ic; =**früchtler** ⚘ *m* rhizocarp; =**füß(l)er** *m, zo.* (mikroskopisches Wassertierchen): ⚗ rhizopod, *pl.* a. rhizopoda; =**gemüse** *n* (dish of) eatable roots *pl.*; =**gewächs** ⚘ *n* plant with eatable root(s); =**gewächse** *agr.* (weiße Rüben, Runkelrüben &c.) root-crops *pl.*; =**größe** *f, math.* radical quantity, surd.

wurzelhaft (ˊˇˇ) *a.* Ⓜ *gram.* radical.

wurz(e)lig (ˊ(ˇ)ˇ) *a.* Ⓜ: a) = wurzelartig; b) full of (or knotted with) roots.

Wurzel=keim ⚘ (ˊˇ...) *m* Ⓔ radicle; =**knollen** ⚘ *m* tuber, bulb; =**knoten** ⚘ *m* knot (⚗ node) of a root; ²**los** ⚘ *a.* Ⓜ without a root, von Schmarotzern: ⚗ arrhiz*al*, ...ous; =**münder** *m, zo.*: ⚗ rhizostome; ²**mündig** *a.* rhizostomatous.

wurzeln (ˊˇ) *v/n.* (h. u. sn) u. *v/refl.* Ⓐ a. to take (or strike) root, to send out (its) roots; in et. ² to be (fast) rooted in a th.; **sich** fest ² to strike deep root, to become firmly rooted; fest gewurzelt deep-rooted, firmly rooted.

Wurzel=pilz ⚘ (ˊˇ...) *m* Ⓔ: ⚗ rhizomorph; *pl.* a. rhizomorpha; =**ranke** *f*, =**reis** *n* = =schoß; =**schneide=maschine** *f*, =**schneider** *m* ⚙ *agr.* Zuckerfabr.: root-breaker or cutter; =**schoß**, =**schößling**, =**sprosse** *m* ⚘, *agr.*, *hort.* sucker, runner, tiller, ⚗ stolon; ²**sprossend** ⚘ *a.* Ⓜ sending out suckers, ⚗ stoloniferous; =**stand** ⚘ *m* radication; ²**ständig** ⚘ *a.* radical; =**stock** ⚘ *m* root-stock, rhizoma; *zo.* e-s Polypen: ⚗ rhizocaul; ²**tragend** ⚘ *a.*: ⚗ rhizophorous; ²**treibend** ⚘ *a.* sending forth roots, ⚗ radicant; =**trüffel** ⚘ *f*: ⚗ rhizopogon; =**werk** ⚘ *n* (tangled or interlaced) roots *pl.*; =**wort** *n, gram.* radical word, mehr gbr.: stem; =**zahl** *f, math.* root of a number; vgl. =größe; =**zeichen** *n, math.* radical sign (√).

würzen (ˊˇ) [ahd.: Würze] *v/a.* Ⓜ: a) Kochkunst: to spice (a. *fig.*), to season; stark gewürzt highly seasoned, a. very hot or spicy, *fig.* very piquant; b) (duftig machen) to perfume, to scent; to fill with aroma, auch: to aromatize.

Würz=fleisch (ˊ...) *n* Ⓔ Kochk. spiced meat, auch = Ragout; =**geruch** *m* odour of spices, a. = =duft.

würzhaft, **würzig** (ˊˇ) *a.* Ⓜ spicy, well-seasoned, *fig.* piquant; (duftend) aromatic, fragrant; ² machen = würzen; das Würzige e-s Gerichts the spiciness (or spicy flavour) of a dish.

Würz=kräuter (ˊ˗ˇ) *n/pl.* Ⓔ aromatic [herbs.]

Würzling (ˊˇ) *m* Ⓜ d. = Wurzelranke.

würz=los (ˊ...) *a.* Ⓜ not spiced, not seasoned; (schal) flat, insipid; =**stoff** *m* Ⓔ Kochk.: seasoning, spice, condiment.

Würzung (ˊˇ) [würzen] *f* Ⓦ seasoning.

Würz=wein (ˊ.ˊ) *m* Ⓔ spiced (or mulled) wine. *med.* ehm.: ⚗ hippocras.

wusch[1] (ˊ) *int.* = husch 1. [v. waschen.]

wusch[2] (ˊ) *ind.*, **wüsche** (ˊˇ) *subj. impf.*

wußte *ind.*, **wüßte** (ˊˇ) *subj. impf.* v. wissen.

Wust (ˊ) [mhd.; *wüst] *m* Ⓜ b. **1.** confused (or tangled) heap or mass, confusion, chaos, F mess; gelehrter ~ learned lumber. — **2.** (et. Ekelerregendes) s.th. disgusting or loathsome; (Unrat) rubbish, lumber, refuse, dirt.

wüst (ˊ) [ahd.: waste] *a.* Ⓜ **1.** waste (ground, &c.), de'sert or desolate (region, &c.), dese'rted (place, &c.); (unbebaut) uncultivated (land); (unbewohnt) uninhabited (region); von Feldern: ² liegen to (lie) waste; ⚔ ² legen to lay waste, to devastate; ♀ das ~e Arabien desert Arabia, (lt.) Arabia deserta. —

[Wüste] — 1138 — [Yuffa]

2. (wirr) confused, (en)tangled; der Kopf ist mir 2 vom vielen Schreiben my head feels quite dizzy (or F muddled) from (or with) so much writing; bibl. die Erde war 2 und leer (1. Mos. 1 u. 2) the earth was without form and void. — 3. bsd. oberd. (garstig) ugly, (widerwärtig) repulsive, disgusting; (schlimm) wicked, villainous, vile; (roh) rude; der Lärm deafening noise, fearful hubbub or racket; ein 2es Leben führen to lead a disorderly (or dissolute, riotous, wild) life.

Wüste (⌣⌣) [ahd.; *wüst] f ⑱ (Öde) waste (land), desert, desolate region, wilderness; (Wasser∼) watery waste; bibl. Prediger in der ∼ one who crieth in the wilderness.

wüsten (⌣⌣) [mhd.] v/n. (h.) ⑨ (wüst wirtschaften) to act (or live) wastefully; mit dem Gelde 2 to waste (or squander, throw away) one's money.

Wüsten-bewohner (⌣⌣⌣⌣⌣) m ⑫ inhabitant (geh. Spr. dweller) of the desert. **Wüstenei** (−⌣⌣) f ⑯ desert, wilderness. **Wüsten-könig** (⌣⌣...) m ⑫ king of the desert; ∼luchs m, zo. = Karakal; ∼sand m sand(s) of the desert; ∼schiff n, fig. (Kamel) ship of the desert; ∼sohn m son of the desert.

Wüst-heit (⌣−) f ⑯ 1. deserted state, desolate state. — 2. (Ausschweifung) dissoluteness, wild life. — 3. (Bosheit) wickedness, villainy; (Roheit) brutality.

Wüstling (⌣⌣) m ⑬d. dissolute (or debauched) fellow, rake, libertine.

Wut (⌣) [ahd.: † wood] f ⑩ (ohne pl.) 1. (heftige Erregung) (great) rage, fury, enraged state, passion; (heftiger Zorn) violent wrath or anger; (Aufwallung) fit of bad temper, F wax; (Wahnsinn) madness, frenzy; (Hunds∼) rabies; seine ∼ an e-m auslassen to vent one's passion (or rage) upon a p.; e-n in ∼ bringen to make a p. furious or F wild, to enrage (or exasperate) a p.; in ∼ geraten to fly into a passion, to grow furious, F to get into a temper; f. schäumen fig. — 2. (heftige Neigung) mania, craze; ∼ zu malen, zu schreiben mania (or passion) for painting, for writing.

Wut-anfall (⌣⌣⌣) m ⑫ fit of rage or temper or passion, geh. Spr.: paroxysm of fury; ∼anfälle, oft: F tantrums pl.

wüten (⌣⌣) [ahd.; *Wut] I v/n. (h.) ⑨ to (be in a) rage, to be enraged or furious or in a fury or F in a wax, stärker: to rave (like a madman), to be mad with rage; vom Sturme etc.: to rage, to sweep along, to howl furiously, von der Pest etc.: to rage, to work havoc or destruction; gegen sein eigenes Fleisch und Blut 2 to rage against one's own flesh and blood. — II ∼ n ㉓ (fit of) rage, (outburst of) fury; das ∼ einer Krankheit, oft: the great prevalence (or rapid spread) ... — III 2b p.pr. und a. ⑯ raging, enraged, furious, mad with rage, frantic, F in a wax, von Hunden etc.: rabid; Volksaberglaube: 2des Heer [corr. aus Wodans Heer] wild hunt or chase, a. Arthur's chase; e-n 2den Hunger haben to have a ravenous appetite, to be ravenous; einen 2d machen to enrage (or infuriate) a p.; 2d werden = in Wut (f. ds) geraten.

wut-entbrannt (⌣⌣⌣) a. ⑯ inflamed with rage, infuriated, enraged.

Wüter (⌣⌣) m ⑫ enraged (or furious, mad, savage) person, F terror.

wut-erfüllt (⌣⌣⌣) a. ⑯ filled (F wild) with rage, furious, enraged.

Wüterich (⌣⌣⌣) [mhd.] m ⑬d. cruel (or ruthless, bloodthirsty, truculent) person, savage (or ferocious) fellow; (blutdürstiger Tyrann) cruel tyrant; ... entgegnet ihm finster der ∼ (SCH.) ... the despot savagely replied.

Wut-geschrei (⌣⌣⌣) n ⑫ cry (or howl, yell) of rage or fury.

wütig (⌣⌣) a. ⑯ = wüten III.

wutsch (⌣) [lautm.] int. = husch¹.

wut-schäumend (⌣⌣...) a. ⑯, 2schnaubend a. breathing rage, mehr gbr.: infuriated, mad (or foaming) with rage, in a towering passion; 2voll a. =wuterfüllt.

WB. abbr. = Wörterverzeichnis.
Wwe. abbr. = Witwe.

X

X, x (⌣) n, inv. Buchstabe X, x; fig. f. U; sich ein X für ein U machen lassen to (allow o.s. to) be bamboozled or F taken in. **x** math. (unbekannte Größe) x, the unknown (quantity); die Stadt X (deren Namen man nicht nennen will) the town (of) X or N.

Xanthen, Xanthin (⌣⌣) [grch.] n ⑬d. chm. im Blut etc.: xanthine ($C_5H_4N_4O_2$).

Xanthippe (⌣⌣⌣) npr/f. ⑨⑭⑬. Alt.: (Frau des Sokrates) Xanthippe; fig. (zänkisches Weib) (Kamel) termagant, scold, Tartar, ehm. (SH., &c.): shrew.

xanthogen-sauer (⌣ ⌣⌣⌣⌣...) a. ⑯ xanthic; 2saures Salz xanthate; ∼säure f ⑫ xanthic acid.

Xaver (⌣⌣) npr/m. ⑨⑭α. Xavier.

X-Beine (⌣...) n/pl. ⑫ turned-in (or knock-kneed) legs pl., auch F knock-knees pl.; 2beinig a. ⑯ knock-kneed, bow-legged; 2beliebig a. f. beliebig.

Xeni-e (⌣⌣⌣) [grch. xė'nia Gastrecht, Gastgeschenke; auch der Titel des 13. Buches von Martial] f ⑫, etwa: epigram.

Xeni-en-dichter (⌣⌣⌣...) m ⑫, etwa: epigrammatist; ∼streit m deutsche Literatur: controversy raised by the „Xenien" of Goethe and Schiller.

Xenophontisch (⌣⌣⌣⌣) [Xe'nophon, bsd. der grch. Feldherr und Schriftsteller, ungefähr 430—354 vor Chr.] a. ⑯ of Xenophon.

x-mal F (⌣⌣) adv. (ever so) many times F; f. ich habe es ihm 2 gesagt I have told him (I don't know how) many times, a.: I have impressed it on him over and over again; f. xte.

Xr. abbr. für Kreuzer (f. ds 1).

X-Strahlen (⌣⌣⌣) m/pl. ⑫ (Röntgenstrahlen) X-rays, Röntgen-(or Rontgen-)rays pl.

xte (⌣⌣⌣) a. ⑯ math.: die 2 Potenz the xth power; auf die 2 Potenz erheben to raise to the xth power or the power of x; zum 2n Male F for the hundredth (or thousandth) time.

Xylograph ⌣ (⌣⌣⌣) [grch.] m ⑫ woodcarver; f. a. Holzschneider; ∼ie (⌣⌣⌣⌣) f ⑱ wood-carving; f. a. Holzschneidekunst; 2ieren ⌣ (⌣⌣⌣⌣) v/n. (h.) ⑨ to carve in (or engrave on) wood; 2isch (⌣⌣⌣⌣) a. ⑯ xylographic.

Xylol ⌣ (⌣⌣) [grch.] n ⑬d. chm. (Art Benzin) xylol (C_8H_{10}). [xylophone.]

Xylophon ♪ (⌣⌣⌣) [grch.] n ⑬d.

Xyloplastik ⌣ (⌣⌣⌣⌣) [grch.] f ⑯ (Holzschnitzerei) wood-carving or -engraving.

Y

Y, y (⌣⌣, f. Ypsilon) n, inv. Buchstabe Y, y. **Y** ent., auch Ypsiloneule f (Schmetterling) Y-moth (No'ctua gamma).

Y chm. Symbol für Yttrium.

y math. (zweite unbekannte Größe) y.

Yacht [engl.] f. Jacht.

Yak (⌣) [tibet.] m ⑭ zo. = Grunzochs.

Yams-wurzel ⌣ (⌣⌣⌣) [port., *afrik.] f ⑫ yam (Dioscore'a villo'sa oder Bata'tas).

Yankee ⓣ (jä'nß-ti) m ⑩, ∼in f ⑯ Yankee (gentleman), f Yankee lady; weitS. North American.

yankeehaft (⌣⌣⌣) a. ⑯ Yankee-like, a.: F yankeefied.

Yankeetum (⌣⌣⌣) n ⑬c. Yankeedom, Yankees pl.

Ypsilon (meist ü'p-ßi-lön, r-r ⌣⌣⌣) [grch.] n ⑪ Greek name of the letter y (υ); ⬛ ein ∼ bildendes Geleise n/pl. Y-track.

Ypsilon-eule (⌣...) f ⑫ = Y; ∼knorpel m, anat. (Darm- und Sitzbein vereinigend) Y-cartilage.

Ysop ⌣ (⌣⌣) [mhd., grch., *hebr.] m ⑫ hyssop (Hysso'pus officina'lis).

Ytter-erde ⌣ (ü"⌣...) [Yttrium] f ⑫ chm., min. yttria (Y_2O_3); 2haltig a. ⑯ yttrious, yttric, yttriferous; ∼spat m xenotime, phosphate of yttrium.

Yttrium ⌣ (ü"⌣⌣) [Ytterby ⊕, schwb. Ort] n ⑬ chm. (seltenes Metall, Grundlage der Yttererde) yttrium.

Yttrium-oxyd (⌣⌣⌣⌣) n ⑫ = Yttererde.
Yttro-tantalit ⌣ (ü"-⌣⌣⌣) m ⑫ min. yttrotantalite.

Yuffa ⌣ (j⌣⌣) [indian.] f ⑰ (Palmlilie) yucca.

Signs (see page XVII): F familiar; P vulgar; ꟼ flash; ⧹ rare; † obsolete (died); * new word (born); ⧺ incorrect; ♪ music;

Z

Z, z (᷄) *n, inv.* Buchstabe Z, z; von A bis Z from beginning to end, vgl. A 2.
Z. *abbr.* = Zahl, Zeile.
z. *abbr.* = zu, zum, zur.
Zacharias (⌣ʧ⌣⌣)[grch.;*hebr. Sacharja] *npr.m.* ⑥γ. (bjb. *bibl.*) Zechariah, Zachary, F Koseform auch: Zach.
Zachäus (⌣ʧ⌣) *npr.m.* ⑥γ. (bjb. *bibl.*) Zacheus; **~öl** ⊕ *n* ⑫ oil of Bohemian olives.
Zäckchen (⌣⌣) *n* ㉓ (*dim.* von Zacke[n]) small prong or tooth or dent, an Spitzen: purl, ~ *pl.* an Frauenkleidern: scalloped (or scolloped) work. an Papierverzierungen ꝛc.: pinking.
Zacke (⌣⌣) *f* ⑧ [(mhd.) nbd.: tack] **1.** (spitz Hervorragendes) pointed (or jagged) part, e-s Felsens: jag, auf Mauern ꝛc.: spike, e-r Gabel ꝛc.: prong, tine, an Kristallen ꝛc.: point; (Zahn) tooth of a saw, &c.; dent; *mech.* cog of a wheel; (Eis-)~(n) icicle; vgl. Kerbe. — **2.** ~n *pl.* (Spitzen am Rande e-s Kleides ꝛc.) scalloping, scolloping; lace-border, purled edge or edging, an Papier ꝛc.: pinking. — **3.** ♀: ⌒ crenature. — **4.** ⊕ *metall.* plate.
Zack-eisen ⊕ *n* ⑫ toothing-iron.
Zackel-(schaf-)wolle ⊕ (⌣⌣⌣⌣) *f* ⑫ refuse (of) wool.
Zacken[1] (⌣⌣) *m* ㉓ = Zacke.
zacken[2] (⌣⌣) ⊕ **I** *v/a.* to furnish with points, to point; to jag, (in)dent, notch, Kleidersäume: to scallop, to scollop. — **II** sich ~ *v/refl.* to be jagged or dented or notched. — **III** ge-zackt *p.p. u. a.* ⑥ = zackig.
Zacken-blatt ♀ (⌣⌣...) *n* ⑫: ⌒ serrate (or dentate) leaf; **=fels** *m* rock with sharp points, crag(gy cliff); ♀**förmig** *a.* ⑥ notched, jagged; vgl. zackig; **=haupt** *n* e-s Berges: jagged (or craggy) mountain-peak; **=holz** *n* branched wood, wood of branches; **=kreuz** *n* square (or Maltese) cross (✠); **=lini-e** *f* notched (or zigzag) line, ⌒ *n.* serration, dent(icul)ation; **=schnitt** *m* indentation; **=walze** ⊕ *f* dented roller; **=werk** *n* indented (or notched) work, auch =Zacke 1; **=wolle** *f* = Zackelwolle. [zanten) to squabble.]
zackieren F (⌣⌣⌣) *v/n.* (h.) ⑬ (sich)
zackicht[2], mst **zackig** (⌣⌣) *a.* ⑥ notched, (in)dented, jagged, (äftig) branched, (gezähnelt) toothed, ⌒ (bjb. ♀ *u.* zo.) serrate(d), dentate(d), *v.* Blättern ꝛc.: crenate; von Kleidersäumen: scalloped, scolloped, von Verzierungen: pinked; ~ machen to jag; das ~e jaggedness.
zag (⌣, auch: ⌣) [ahd.] *a.* ⑥ = zaghaft.
Zagel *provc.* (⌣⌣) *m* ㉒ tail (= Schwanz).
zagen (⌣⌣) [ahd.] **I** *v/n.* (h.) ⑱ to lack (in) courage, to be faint-hearted or timid or nervous or afraid or F funky; zittern und ~ to be shivering and shaking, ~ to be tremulous (with fear), F *u.* P to be in a blue funk. — **II** ~ *n* lack of courage, timidity, nervousness, fear, (Zaudern) hesita-

tion; mit Zittern und ~ trembling (or tremulous) with fear, shaking in one's shoes, with great trepidation.
zaghaft (⌣⌣) [zag] *a.* ⑥ (*ant.* herzhaft) faint-hearted, timid, nervous, afraid, F funky; (blöde) shy; (kleinmütig) despondent, pusillanimous; (unentschlossen) wavering, vacillating, F shaky, wabbling; *adv. auch:* with trepidation; ~ machen to intimidate; **~ig-keit** (⌣⌣⌣) *f* ㊻ faint-heartedness, timidity, nervousness, shyness; despondency; pusillanimity; wavering, vacillation; trepidation.
zäh (⌣), ⌒ e[1] (⌣) [ahd.: tough] *a.* ⑥ tough, tenacious (beide auch *fig.*), schwächer: toughish; (sehnig) sinewy, (lederartig) leathery; (kleberig) viscous, sticky, gluey, clammy, ⌒ glutinous, (schleimig) slimy, ⌒ mucous; ~es Fleisch tough meat; ein ~es Leben haben to be very tough, to be tenacious of life; ⊕ ~es Metall ductile metal; ~ werden to toughen, vom Weine ꝛc.: to thicken, to inspissate; (zf.-kleben) to stick together, to cohere.
Zähe[2] (⌣⌣) *f* ⑧, **Zäh(igk)eit** (⌣⌣⌣⌣) *f* ㊻ (f. zäh) toughness, tenacity; viscosity, stickiness, clamminess, ⌒ glutinousness, sliminess, ⌒ mucousness, mucosity; **Zähigkeits-messer** ⊕ *m* ⑫ visco(si)meter.
Zahl[1] (⌣) [ahd.: tale] *f* ㊻ number; (Ziffer) figure, cipher (f. benennen III, ganz 1 am Ende, unbenannt); Spiel, Sport: ~ der gemachten Points score; Jäger a large field; die größere (kleinere) ~ the majority (minority); auf ~en bezüglich numerical; um die ~ vollzumachen (als Lückenbüßer) to make up the (full) number or complement.
Zahl[1]**-adverb(ium)** (⌣...) *n* ⑫ *gram.* (z.B. „zehnmal") numeral adverb; **=amt** [zahl-en] *n* pay-office, treasury.
Zähl-apparat (⌣⌣⌣⌣) *m* ⑫: a) ⊕ Maschinen ꝛc.: counter; b) für Ein- oder Austretende: turnstile.
zahlbar ⑫ (⌣⌣) *a.* ⑥ payable; ~ bei Sicht (bei Verfall) payable at sight (when due); ~ machen to make payable, Wechsel auch: to domicil(iat)e; ~ werden to fall (or become) due.
zählbar (⌣⌣) *a.* ⑥ countable, computable, seltener: numerable.
Zahlbarkeit ⑫ (⌣⌣⌣) *f* ㊻ solvency.
Zähl-brett (⌣⌣) *n* ⑫ counting-board.
Zahl[1]**-buchstabe** (⌣⌣⌣⌣) *m* ⑫ numeral letter, (bjb. römisches Zahlzeichen) Roman numeral. [registering turnstile.]
Zähl-drehkreuz (⌣⌣⌣⌣) *n* ⑫ self-
zahlen (⌣⌣) [ahd.; Zahl 1] **I** *v/a., v/n.* (h.) ⑱ to pay, F to stump up; (nicht) imstande sein zu ~ to be (un)able to pay, to be (in)solvent; (abtragen) to pay off, to discharge, to settle, F to square; ich zahlte im Laden nur die Hälfte I paid (or was charged) at the

shop only half-price; in Gasthäusern: Kellner, ~! waiter, the bill (or my account), please!; die ihm zu ㉞e Summe the sum to be paid to him, the amount payable (or due) to him; ein nicht ㉞er Schuldner, nicht ㉞er a defaulter. — **II** ~ *n* ㉓ payment; wenn's zum ~ kommt when it comes to paying or settling up.
zählen (⌣⌣) [ahd.: tell] **I** *v/a., v/n.*(h.), *v/refl.* ⑱ **1.** to count money, &c., to number, bei Spielen: *parl.*, &c. to tell the votes, Tennis: to score, die Bevölkerung, ein Heer ꝛc.: to take the census of; (rechnen) to reckon, compute, calculate; *fig.* f. drei 2; sie ~ mich zu f-n Freunden they count (or reckon, include) me among his friends. — **2.** (betragen, sich belaufen auf) to amount to, to come to; das Bataillon zählt etwa 1000 Mann the battalion counts (or numbers) about a thousand men. — **3.** auf e-n ~ = rechnen 3. — **II** ~ *n* ㉓ **4.** f. Zählung.
Zahlen-bruch (⌣...) *m* ⑫ numerical fraction; **=folge** *f* num. order; **=größe** *f* num. quantity; number; **=kunst**, **=lehre** *f* theory of numbers; (Rechenkunst) arithmetic; **=lotterie** *f*, **=lotto** *n* lottery (with numbers), lotto; **=mensch** *m* man of figures, F calculating-machine; **=reihe** *f* series of numbers; **=schloß** ⊕ *n* letter-lock, secret (or Bramah) lock; **=schreiben** *n* numeration; **=sinn** *m* taste (or talent) for figures or calculation; **=system** *n*, *math.* system (or scale) of notation; vgl. Zählmethode; **=teilung** *f* division; **=verhältnis** *n* numerical proportion; **=wert** *m* numerical value.
Zahler (⌣⌣) *m* ㉒, **~in** *f* ㊻ payer; er ist ein säumiger ~er he is slow (or dilatory) in his payments; ein schlechter ~ one who pays badly, bisw.: F a bad paymaster.
Zähler (⌣⌣) *m* ㉒ **1.** (*a.* **~in** *f* ㊻) one who counts, *parl.* teller; beim Billard ꝛc.: marker; ~ der Bevölkerung ꝛc.: census-officer, enumerator. — **2.** ⊕ = Zählapparat. — **3.** *math.* (z.B. 4 in ⁴⁄₅; *ant.* Nenner) numerator. — **4.** *fig.* (*ant.* Null) die Fürsten waren die ~, die Völker die Nullen the princes alone counted, the nations were mere ciphers. [teller or scrutineer.]
Zähler-amt (⌣⌣⌣) *n* ⑫ *parl.* office of
Zahl[2]**-fähig** (⌣...) *a.* ⑥ able to pay, solvent; **=figur** *f* ⑫ = =zeichen; **=größe** *f* numerical quantity or value; **=hammer** *f* = =amt.
Zähl-karte (⌣⌣⌣) *f* ⑫ form (or schedule) used for (the purposes of) a census.
Zahl[2]**-kasse** (⌣...) *f* ⑫ = =amt; **=kellner** *m* in Gasthäusern ꝛc.: head-waiter who receipts the bills; ⌒[1]**los** *a.* ⑥ numberless, innumerable, countless, infinite; ⌒lose Menge infinity; **=losigkeit** *f* numberlessness, innumerableness.
Zähl-maschine ⊕ (⌣⌣⌣⌣) *f* ⑫ numbering machine, automatic counter.

⚛ scientific; ♀ botanical; ♁ geography; ⊕ machinery; ⚒ mining; ⚔ military; ⚓ marine; ⓒ commercial; ⓟ postal; 🚂 railway.

[Zahlmeister] — 1140 — [Zahnwurm]

Zahl²meister (″ˊ‿) m ㉒ paymaster (a. ⚔), ↓ purser; (Schatzmstr.) treasurer; (Kassier) cashier; ⚔ ~ der Kompagnie: paymaster-sergeant; **~amt** n ㉒ paymastership (a. ⚔), ↓ pursership; treasurership.
Zähl=methode (″‿ˊ‿) f ㊷ method of counting or numeration, math. numerical system, arithmetical notation. **Zahl²=muschel** (″...) f ㉒ = Kauri; **=¹ord nung** f order of numbers; **=²perlen** f/pl. (round) pearls pl. (used for counting); **=pfennig** m counter; **²¹reich** a. ㊽ numerous; **=²stelle** f place where payments are made; pay-office, in Banken ꝛc.: (pay-)counter; **=tag** m pay-day, settling-day; **=tisch** ob. **Zähl=tisch** m paying-desk, counter.
Zahlung (‿ˊ‿) f ㊽ 1. (das Zahlen und die gezahlte Summe) payment; f. einstellen 3 am Ende, leisten 2 am Ende; als Unterschrift: ~ erhalten paid, (payment) received. — 2. ~ (Tilgung) e-r Schuld clearance (or discharge, liquidation, settlement) of a debt; jur. ♆ an ~³ Statt in lieu of) payment.
Zählung (‿ˊ‿) f ㊽ counting, numeration; census of a population, &c.; (Auf=²) enumeration; (Berechnung) computation, calculation; ~ der Stimmzettel bei einer Wahl: scrutiny of the ballot-box.
Zahlungs=adresse ⊙ (″‿...) f ㉒ domicile of a draft (= Domizil); **=anweisung** f order for the payment of money, draft, cheque, ♆ für einen Gewinnanteil: dividend-warrant, ⚓ post-office order (P.O.O.), telegraphische: telegraphic money-order; **=aufschub** m delay of payment; **=befehl** jur. m order to pay or for payment, gerichtlich: writ of execution; **=einstellung** f suspension of payment, insolvency; **=erleichterungen** f/pl. facilities pl. for payment; **=ermächtigung** ⊙ f warrant (for payment); **²fähig** a. ㊽ able to pay, solvent; **=fähigkeit** f ability to pay, solvency. [schedule.]
Zahlungs=formular (″‿‿ˊ) n ㉒ census
Zahlungs=frist (″‿ˊ) f ㉒ time allowed for payment; grace, respite.
Zahlungs=kommission (″‿‿(‿)ˊ) f ㉒ commission appointed to take (or organize) a census.
Zahlungs=mittel (″‿...) n ㉒ means of payment; gesetzliches ~ legal tender or coin; **=schein** m: a) (Quittung) receipt; b) = =befehl; **=termin** m date (or day) of payment, ♆ bei Wechseln auch: day of maturity; vgl. =frist; **²unfähig** a. ㊽ insolvent; **=unfähigkeit** f insolvency; **=verbindlichkeit** f liability to pay; **=vermögen** n = =fähigkeit; **=wert** m numerical value.
Zahl¹=wert (″...) m ㉒ numerical value; **=wort** n, gr. numeral (adjective); number; **=zeichen** n numeral sign or character, arithmetical symbol; figure, cipher.
zahm (ˊ) [ahd.: tame] a. ㊻ 1. von Tieren ꝛc.: tame, domesticated; (gezähmt, nicht mehr wild) tamed, not wild; von Personen: (gefügig) tractable, docile, (sanft) gentle, (friedlich) peaceable (und zu machen) tame; ♉ w. to grow tame or gentle. — 2. von Gewächsen: cultivated, not in the wild (or natural) state.

zähmbar (ˊ‿) a. ㊽ von Tieren: tamable, weits. tractable; **~keit** f ㊽ tamability.
zähmen (ˊ‿) [ahd.: tame] I v/a. ㊻ 1. ein Tier: to tame (a. fig.), to domesticate, ein Pferd: to break in (a. fig.); (abrichten) to train. — 2. fig. (bändigen) to curb, subdue, overcome, Leidenschaften: to bridle, check, restrain, control, master; a. v/refl. sich ♉ to check (or curb) o.s. or one's passion; er muß sich ♉ lernen he must learn (how) to control himself. — II ~ n ㉓ 3. = Zähmung. [Zirkus ꝛc. auch: trainer.]
Zähmer (ˊ‿) m ㉒ tamer, für den Sport,)
Zahmheit (ˊ‿) f ㊽ tameness, tame (or domesticated) state; fig. gentleness.
Zähmung (ˊ‿) f ㊻ der Tiere: taming, domestication, fig. check(ing), curb, curbing, restraint (put upon).
Zahn (ˊ) [ahd.: tooth: lt. dent-: grch. odont-] m ⓪c. 1. tooth, v. Hunden, Wölfen: fang, von Ebern: tusk; f. falsch 2 am Ende und faul 1; kleiner ~ = Zähnchen; künstliche Zähne (set of) artificial teeth pl.; zu den Zähnen gehörig dental; fig. der ~ der Zeit the ravages of time; mit verbs: f. ausziehen 2, blecken; Zähne bekommen to get (or cut) one's teeth; gute Zähne haben to have a good set of teeth; fig. e-m auf den ~ fühlen to feel a p.'s pulse; vgl. fühlen 6; Haare auf den Zähnen haben to have plenty of pluck; vgl. Haar 3; e-m et. aus den Zähnen reißen to snatch a th. from a p.'s grip or grasp; f. weisen 1; f. weh¹ 3b. — 2. = Zacke(n), tooth, e-s Kammrades: cog; mit Zähnen versehen to teeth, to cog; Zähne des Weberblatts: dents pl.; ⚔ (Bajonetthülse) cog on the ring of a bayonet.
zahn=arm (ˊ...) a. ㊽ with (or having) few teeth, ⚕ edentate; **=arz(e)nei** f ㉒ = =mittel; **=arz(e)nei=kunde**, **=kunst** f = =heilkunde; **=arzt** m (surgeon-)dentist, dental surgeon; **=ausnehmen**, **=ausziehen** n pulling out (or extraction) of teeth, tooth-drawing; **=aus schlag** m der Kinder: tooth-rash; **=bein** n dentine; **=bildung** f formation (or growth) of teeth, dentition; **=bohrer** m, surg. tooth- (or nerve-)drill; **=brasse** f, ichth. dentex; **=brecher** m tooth-drawer; **=buchstabe** m, gram. dental (letter); **=bürste** f tooth-brush.
Zähnchen (ˊ‿) n ㉓ (dim. v. Zahn) little (or tiny) tooth, bisw.: toothlet, ⚕ u. ⊙ denticle, zo. einer Muschel: dentile.
Zähne=fletschen, **=gefletsch** (ˊ‿...) n von Negern ꝛc.: showing one's (white) teeth, F sporting one's ivory.
Zahn=eisen (ˊ‿ˊ‿) n ㉒ = Zahnzange.
Zähne=klappern (ˊ‿...) n ㉒ chattering of teeth; **=knirschen** n grinding (bibl. gnashing) of teeth.
zähneln (ˊ‿) v/a. ⚒a. to indent; gezähnelt ⊙ u. ⚕ denticulate(d), dentilated.
zahnen (ˊ‿) I v/n. (h.) ㊻ von Kindern: to cut one's teeth, to be teething. — II ~ n ㉓ cutting of teeth, teething, dentition. — III bff. **zähne(l)n** ⊙ v/a. (㋄a.) (mit Zähnen versehen) to tooth, to indent, Räder: to cog. — IV **ge-zahnt**, **ge-zähnt** p.p. u. a. ㊽ toothed; vgl.

zackig ⚡, &c.: ⚕ dentate(d), buchtig: dentate-sinuate, fein: denticulate(d), sägeförmig: dentate-serrate.
Zahn=fach (ˊ...) n ㉒ = =höhle; **=fäule** f, path. caries (or rotting) of teeth; **=fieber** n, path. der Säuglinge: teething-fever; **=fistel** f, path. fistula in the gums; **=fleisch** n. anat. gums pl.; **=fleisch-geschwulst** f swelling of the gums, ⚕ epulis; **=fleisch=geschwür** n = =geschwür; **²förmig** a. ㊽ tooth-shaped, dentiform, odontoid; **=füllung** f filling (of a tooth); **=geschwür** n, path. gumboil, abscess in the gums, ⚕ parulis; **=heil=kunde** f dental surgery, (surgical) dentistry; **=hobel** ⊙ m tooth(ing)-plane; **=höhle** f, anat. socket of a tooth, ⚕ alveolus, ...e.
zahnig (ˊ‿) a. ㊽ 1. provided with teeth, toothed; in Zssgn scharf² with sharp teeth. — 2. a. **zähnig** in Zssgn, zB. zwei² bidental, bidentate(d).
Zahn=kitt ⊙ (ˊ...) m ㉒ Zahnheilkunde: stopping (or cement) for the teeth; **=künstler** m dentist (who makes artificial teeth); **=lehre** f: ⚕ odontology; **²los** a. ㊽ toothless, ⚕ edental, ...ulous, ent. edentate; **²loses Mütterchen** toothless old woman, F co. old Mother Gum(s); **=losigkeit** f toothlessness, ⚕ edentation; **=lücke** f gap between (the) teeth; **=lücker** m/pl. zo.: ⚕ edentals, edentata pl.; **²lückig** a. gap-toothed; **=meißel** ⊙ m dentist's scraper; **=mittel** n remedy (or cure) for (the) toothache; **=nerv** m, anat. nerve of a tooth; **=operation** f dental operation; **=pasta** f tooth-paste; **=pulver** n tooth-powder, dentifrice; **=rad** ⊙ n cogged (or toothed) wheel, cog ... ſeel, einer Uhr auch: dented wheel; ~ ⚙ ⚔ Sperrklinke ratchet and pawl; **=rad=bahn** f cog-wheel railway or line; **=räder werk** n tooth-gearing; **=reihe** f row (als Gebiß: set) of teeth; **=reißen** n (violent) toothache; **=röhrchen** n, anat. dental canal; **=säckchen** n, physiol. tooth-sac; **=schlüssel** ⊙ m zum Zahnziehen: (dentist's) tooth-key; **=schmelz** m, anat. enamel of a tooth, ⚕ encaustum; **=schmerz** m toothache, ⚕ odontalgy, odontalgia; ~en h. to have the toothache; **=schnäbler** m, orn.: ⚕ dentiroster; **=schnecke** f, zo. tooth-shell (Denta'lium); **=schnitt** ⊙ m denticulation, arch. dentil, denticle; **=stange** ⊙ f, mach. rack, 🚆 cog-rail; **=stangen-getriebe** n rack-and-pinion; **=stein** n, arch. toothing-stone; **=stocher** m toothpick; **=stocher=behälter** m toothpick-case; **=stummel**, **=stumpf** m stump (or snag) of a tooth; **=substanz** f = =bein; **=technik** f science of dentistry, manufacture of artificial teeth; **=tinktur** f tincture for the teeth; vgl. =wasser; = **und Lippen=buchstabe** m, gr. dentilabial (letter).
Zahnung (ˊ‿) f ㊽ toothing, cogs pl.
Zahn=wasser (ˊ...) n ㉒ tooth-wash, lotion for the teeth; **=wechsel** m shedding of teeth, second dentition; **=weh** n = =schmerz; **=wurz** f toothwort (Plumba'go); **=werk** ⊙ n tooth- (or rack-)work; **=wurm** m, path.: ⚕ caries (of

Zeichen (s. S. XVII): F familiär; P Volkssprache; Ր Gaunersprache; ⚘ selten; † alt (auch gestorben); * neu (auch geboren); ++ unrichtig;

[Zahnwurzel] — 1141 — [Zartsinnigkeit]

the teeth); =wurzel f root (or fang) of a tooth; =zange ⊕ f dentist's forceps, tooth-drawer. [tear.)
Bähre † (⁻ᴗ) [ahd.: tear] f ⊕ poet.)
Bain ⊕ (¹) [ahd.: tine] m ⑪c. metall. gegoffener, gewalzter oder gefchmiedeter ~ ingot, bar (of metal), bfd. von Gold auch: wedge; ~ fchmieden to forge the bars.
Baine (⁻ᴗ) [Bain] f ⊕ (Flechtwerk, Korb) wicker-work, basket.
Bain-eifen ⊕ (⁻...) n ⑫ metall., Schmiede: iron in bars, rod-iron; =eifen-fchneidehammer m =werk n slitting-mill.
zainen ⊕ (⁻ᴗ) v/a. ⑧⑧ metall. to cast into ingots, to forge into bars.
Zainer ⊕ (⁻ᴗ) m ㉒ master smith.
Bain-filber ⊕ (⁻⁻ᴗ) n ⑫ silver in bars or ingots, bar-silver.
zambonifch (ᴗ⁻ᴗ) [Bamboni, it. Phyfiker] a. ⑯ elect. ℒe Säule Zamboni's dry pile.
Bampel ⊕ (ᴗ⁻) [engl. sample] m ⑫ Weberei: loom for (making) figured material, simple; ~hafen m ⑫ simple-hook; ~ftuhl m simple-loom.
Bander (ᴗ⁻) [ndl.] m ⑫ ichth. = Sander.
Banella ⊕ (ᴗᴗ⁻) n ⑩ (Art Satin) sateen.
Bange (⁻ᴗ) [ahd.: tongs] f ⊕ 1. größere: (pair of) tongs pl., flache: (pair of) pliers pl., kleinere: (pair of) pincers pl.; (Haar-)~ (pair of) tweezers pl.; vgl. Beißzange; surg. ~ des Zahnarztes 2c.: forceps; vgl. Geburtszange. — 2. zo. (zangenartiger Körperteil): ⚕ forcipate(d) claw or jaw; (Kauwerkzeug der Infekten): ⚕ mandible. — 3. ⊕ metall. (Stahlpaket) faggot of steel.
Bängelchen (⁻ᴗᴗ) n ㉓ (dim. von Bange) (pair of) small pincers or nippers.
Bänge(l)=hammer ⊕ (⁻ᴗ...) m ⑫ shingling-hammer; =horn n, zo. der Spinnen: ⚕ chelicer(a); =mafchine ⊕ f shingling-machine; =walzen f/pl. shingling-rolls pl.
zangen=artig (⁻ᴗᴗ...) a. ⑯ = ²förmig; =entbindung f ⑫ surg. delivery with instruments; ²förmig a. formed like tongs, ⚕ forcipated; =geburt f = =entbindung f, fig. desperate task; =ring ⊕ m ring of sliding tongs; =fchanze f, =werk n ⚔ frt. tenail(le).
Bank (⁽) [ahd. 15. sae.: zanken] m ⒪b. (pl.ˆ) quarrel, dispute, ftärker: altercation, mit lautem Lärm: squabble, brawl(ing), row (vgl. Streit); Hader und ~, oft: bickering and biting; immer ~ und Streit h. to be for ever sparring or nagging or squabbling.
Bank=apfel (⁻ᴗᴗ) m ㊉ myth. (Apfel der Eris) und weitS. apple of discord. auch: bone of contention.
zanken (⁻ᴗ) [mhd.] I v/n. (h.) und fich ℒ v/recip. ⑱: mit e-m ℒ to quarrel (or wrangle) with a p.; fich ℒ to (have a) quarrel, ftärker: to altercate, mit lautem Lärm: to squabble, to brawl, to (have a) row; fie ℒ fich unaufhörlich they are for ever sparring; fich über nichts, um des Kaifers Bart ℒ to quarrel about nothing or about trifles. — II ~ n ㉓ = Zank.
Bänker (⁻ᴗ) m ㉒, ~in f ㊼ wrangler, brawler, quarrelsome (or litigating) person, F nagger; vgl. Zankteufel.
Bankerei, Zänkerei (ᴗᴗ⁻) f ㊻ = Gezänk.

Bank=geift (⁻...) m ⑫ quarrelsome spirit; =gier f = =fucht.
zankhaft, zänkifch (⁻ᴗ) a. ⑯ quarrelsome, contentious, gerichtlich: litigating, (ewig habernd) nagging, cantankerous.
Bank=luft (⁻...) f ⑫ = =fucht; =ftifter m, etwa: mischief-maker; =fucht f quarrelsomeness, contentiousness, quarrelsome (or litigating) disposition or character; ²füchtig a. ⑯ quarrelsome, contentious, litigating, fond of brawling; =teufel m brawler, wrangler, litigating person; (zänkifches Weib) auch: termagant, dragon, nagging woman.
Banzibar f. Sanfibar.
Zapf=bier (⁻...) n ⑫ Schantwirtfchaft: beer from the tap or cask or wood.
Zäpfchen (⁻ᴗ) n ㉓ (dim. von Zapfen) 1. little peg or plug. — 2. anat. (Verlängerung des Gaumenfegels): ⚕ uvula.
Zäpfchen=drüfen (⁻ᴗ...) f/pl. ⚕ uvular glands pl.; =entzündung f, path. inflammation of the uvula, ⚕ staphylitis; =fchnitt m. surg.: ⚕ staphylotomy; Inftrument zum ~: ⚕ staphylotome.
zapfen¹ (⁻ᴗ) [mhd.; *Zapfen²] v/a. ⑧⑧ to tap (or broach) a cask, &c.; Bier ℒ to draw beer from the tap or cask; surg. Wafferfüchtige ℒ to tap dropsical patients.
Zapfen² (⁻ᴗ) [ahd.: tap: Zipfel] m ㉓ 1. (hölzerner Pfropfen) plug, e-s Faffes: bung, spigot, faucet, spile; (Faßhahn) tap; Bier vom ~ fchenken to draw beer from the tap; fig. ein voller ~ a drunken fellow, one who has had enough (to drink), a drunkard. — 2. ⊕ (Pflock, Stift) plug, peg, (wooden) pin; carp. tenon, f. Rute; (Dreh-, Kurbel-) ~ an der Türangel, e-r Welle 2c.: trunnion, pivot, liegender: gudgeon. — 3. anat. = Zäpfchen; ♃ (Frucht der Nadelhölzer) cone of pines, firs, &c., f. Tannenzapfen; vgl. Eiszapfen.
zapfen²=ähnlich (⁻ᴗ⁻ᴗ...) ²artig a. ⑯ shaped like a plug, ⚕ strobiliform; =bäume ⚕ m/pl. ⑫ cone-bearing trees, ⚕ conifers pl.; =bohrer m tap- (or tenon-)borer, ⚒ artill. pin-drill, der Uhrmacher: pivot-drill; =feile f pivot-file; ²förmig a. ⑯ = ²ähnlich; =frühtig ℒ a. = ²tragend; =lager n, mech. rest, socket, e-r Türangel 2c.: pan, mach. bearing, pillow, footstep, e-r Dampfmafchine: plumber-block; =lager=metall n antifriction metal; =loch n: a) am Faffe: bung- (or tap-)hole; b) carp., &c. pivot-hole, mortise; =loch=bohrer m counter-gauge; =loch=mafchine f mortising-machine; =nadel f pivot-pin; =nagel m mortise-bolt; =palmen ♃ f/pl. cycads (Cyca'deae); =rad m mortise-wheel; =fäge f tenon-saw; =fchneid=mafchine f tenoner, tenoning-machine; =ftreich [im 30 jährigen Kriege Streich auf den Bierfaßzapfen bei Beginn der Polizeiftunde] ⚔ m tattoo, retreat; den ~ fchlagen to beat a tattoo; =ftreich=maß n mortise-gauge; ²tragend ♃ a. cone-bearing, ⚕ coniferous; =träger ♃ m/pl.: ⚕ conifers pl.
Zapfer (⁻ᴗ) m ㉒ Wirtshaus: one who draws beer, &c. from the tap, tapster.
Zapf=kellner (⁻ᴗ...) m ㉒ tapster.

Zapf=röhre ⊕ (⁻ᴗ⁻ᴗ) f ⑫ tapping-pipe.
Zapp(e)ler(in f) m (ᴗ)(ᴗ)(ᴗ) m ㉒, f ㊼ fidgety (or restless) person or child.
Zappel=fritze F (⁻ᴗ⁻ᴗ) m ⑫ fidgety boy.
zapp(e)licht, ...ig (ᴗ)(ᴗ)(ᴗ) a. ⑯ fidgety, restless. [mann.)
Zappel=mann (⁻ᴗ⁻) m ㉒ = Hampel=)
zappeln (⁻ᴗ) [ahd.] v/n. (h.) ⑫a. to move convulsively or impetuously, to jerk, to sprawl (or kick, toss) about, bfd. v. Kindern: to fidget (about), to be restless; im Waffer, Sumpfe 2c. ℒ to flounder (about); mit Händen und Füßen ℒ to struggle with (one's) hands and feet; mit den Beinen ℒ to kick about; fig. e-n ℒ (fich abängftigen) laffen to keep a p. in suspense or in a state of alarm, to tantalize a p.
Zappler, zapplicht, ...ig f. Zapp(e)ler 2c.
Zar (⁻) [ruff. von *Cäfar (Kaifer)] m ㊷ (⑪d.), ~in f ㊼ Tsar, f Tsarina, =en=palaft m ⊕ palace of the Tsar(s).
Zarewitfch (⁻ᴗᴗ) [ruff. Sohn des Zaren] m ⑪a ⑯ (ruff. Thronfolger) Tsarevitch; vgl. Cäfarewitfch.
Zarewna (⁻ᴗᴗ) [ruff. Tochter des Zaren] f ㊶ Frau des Zarewitfch: Tsarevna.
Zarge ⊕ (⁻ᴗ) [ahd.: target] f ⊕ border, edging, edge; (Rand) rim; (Rahmen) frame, case; carp. (Zwinge) cramp.
Zarg(e)=zieher ⊕ m Böttcherei: turrel.
zarifch (⁻ᴗ) [Zar] a. ⑯ Tsarish.
zart (¹) [ahd.] a. ⑯ (D5,6) 1. (ant. zäh, feft, ftarf) tender (meat, fig. conscience, heart, &c.), delicate (blossom, child, health, &c.), von der Gefundheit auch: frail, weak; (zerbrechlich) fragile. — 2. (ant. grob, dick) fine, slender, thin, slim; (fanft) soft (skin, &c.), von Farben: subdued (colour), pale (green, &c.); paint., sculp. ℒer Ton mellow tone; ein ℒes Wefen a delicate creature; fig. ℒer (leifer) Wink, Verweis gentle hint, reminder.
Zärtelei (⁻ᴗ⁻) f ㊻ affected (or affectation) of tenderness or sensitiveness.
zart=fühlend (⁻...) ²fühlig a. ⑯ with (or of) fine (or delicate) feelings, tender(-hearted); ²füßig a. tender-footed; =gefühl n ⑫ delicacy of feeling; ²glied(e)rig a. with delicate limbs.
Zartheit (⁻⁻) f ㊻ (f. zart) tenderness, delicacy, frailty, weakness, fragile nature; softness (a. von Farben); fig. auch: gentleness; paint. nachgeahmte ~ des lebenden Fleisches, biSw.: (it.) morbidezza.
zärtlich (⁻ᴗ, a. ⁻ᴗ) [zart] a. ⑯ 1. tender (in one's ways or feelings); (liebevoll) fond, affectionate; (verliebt) amorous, in love; ℒ (adv.) lieben to love fondly or dearly, to be devoted to; ℒ tun to affect tenderness or fondness. — 2. ⚘ (empfindlich) sensitive; (zart) delicate.
Zärtlichkeit (⁻ᴗ⁻) f ㊻ (f. zärtlich 1) 1. (o. pl.) tenderness; fondness, affection; (Verliebtheit) amorousness. — 2. (mit pl.) affectionate (or loving) action, pl. ~en, auch: fond (or sweet, tender, gentle, loving) words, caresses pl.
Zärtling (⁻ᴗ) m ⑪d. delicate (or effeminate) person, milksop, F coddle
zart=rofa (⁻⁻ᴗ) a. ⑯ pale pink; ²finnig a. = ²fühlend; auch: considerate (for others); =finn(igkeit f) m ⑫ = =gefühl.

♪ Mufit; ⚕ Wiffenfchaft; ♃ Pflanze; ⚱ Geographie; ⊕ Technik; ⚒ Bergbau; ⚔ Militär; ⚓ Marine; ⊛ Handel; ✉ Poft; 🚆 Eifenbahn.

[Zasel] — 1142 — [zechen]

Zasel ♀ (‿́‿) m ㉒ (Blütenkätzchen) catkin.
Zaser (‿́‿) [nhd.] f ⊛ = Faser; **~blume** ♀ f ⊛ fig-marigold (*Mesembrya'nthemum*).
Bäserchen (‿́‿) n ㉓ *dim.* tiny fibre.
zaserig (‿́‿) a. ⊛ fibrous.
Bäsium ♂ (tś‿́‿) [lt. blaugrau] n ⊛ *chm.* (1860 entdecktes seltenes Leichtmetall) caesium (Cs); **~hydroxyd** n ⊛ caesium hydroxide (CsHO).
Zaspel ♀ (‿‿) [nhd.] f ⊛ = Strähne 2.
Bäsur ♂ (‿́‿) [lt.] f ⊛ *pros.* (Verseinschnitt) caesura, cesura; weitS. break. rest; auf die ~ bezüglich caesural.
Zauber (‿́‿) [ahd.: tiver „Mennig f. Runen"] m ㉒ 1. ~(-formel, -mittel) charm, spell; (das Zaubern) enchantment, magic. conjuring; (zauberische Wirkung) magic effect; wie durch ~ as if by magic; vom ~ gebannt spell-bound; den ~ lösen to dissolve the charm, to break the spell. — 2. F der ganze ~ (Plunder) the whole concern or F kit, shoot, all the (blessed) lot; f. faul 2 gegen Ende.
Zauber-apparat (‿́‿‿) m ㉒ juggler's apparatus; **=becher** m magic cup; **=bild** n magic image, talisman; *fig.* charming creature, F charmer; **=blick** m enticing (or fascinating) glance; **=brunnen** m magic well or fountain; **=buch** n conjuring-book; **=doktor** m der Neger ꝛc.: witch-doctor, medicine-man.
Zauberei (‿‿́‿) f ⊛ magic (art), sorcery, witchcraft, witchery; (schwarze Kunst) black art; (Geisterbannung) ♂ necromancy; (Taschenspielerei) conjuring, juggling, sleight-of-hand. legerdemain; *fig.* charm, (Bezauberung) enchantment, fascination.
Zaub(e)rer (‿́‿‿) m ㉒, **Zauberin** f ㊼ magician, sorcerer. f sorceress; wizard; vgl. Hexe; (Geisterbanner) necromancer; (Taschenspieler) conjurer, juggler, sleight-of-hand man; *fig.* (bezaubernde Person) enchanting person, nur f enchantress, charmer.
Zauber-flöte (‿́‿‿) f ⊛ magic flute; **=formel** f magic formula; auch: charm, spell; **=gehenk** n amulet; **=gürtel** m magic girdle.
zauberhaft (‿́‿) a. ⊛ = zauberisch.
Zauber-insel (‿́‿‿) f ⊛ enchanted isle.
zaub(e)risch (‿́‿‿) a. ⊛ (acting by) magic, enchanting (beide a. *fig.*), (feenhaft) fairy-like, mst *fig.* (reizend) charming, fascinating; (wunderbar) wonderful, stärker: miraculous; *adv.* magically; ~ wirken to have a magic effect, to work (as if) by magic, to act miraculously.
Zauber-kasten (‿́‿‿) m ㉒ conjuring-box; **=kraft** f magic virtue or power; **=kräftig** a. magic. **=kunst** f: a) witchcraft, magic, sorcery; b) Künste conjuring tricks *pl.*, juggling, **=künstler** m conjurer, juggler, illusionist; **=land** n: a) enchanted land; b) fairyland; **=laterne** f magic lantern; **=lehrling** m magician's apprentice; **=macht** f = **=kraft**; **=märchen** n fairy-tale; **=mittel** n magic contrivance or agency, charm, spell.
zaubern (‿́‿) ⊛a. I v/n. (h.) to practise magic or witchcraft. to use charms or spells; bsd. *fig.* 2 können to do things by magic. — II v/a. to do by magic; to cast a spell on, mit Angabe der Wirkung: e-n jung 2 to make a p. young (again) by magic (art); e-m das Geld aus dem Beutel 2 to conjure ... out of a p.'s purse, to draw (or remove, take) ... out of a p.'s pocket by magic. — III ~ n ㉓ (practising) magic or sorcery, vgl. Zauberei.
Zauber-posse (‿‿́‿) f ⊛ *thea.* pantomime; **=reich:** a) n realm of fairies; vgl. =land; b) a. ⊛ full of enchantment; **=ring** m magic ring; **=rute** f = **=stab**; **=schlaf** m enchanted sleep; **=schlag** m magic stroke; **=schloß** n enchanted castle; **=schrift** f magic writing; **=segen** m = **=spruch**; **=siegel** n magic seal; **=spiegel** m magic mirror; **=spiegelung** f, *phys.* mirage; **=spruch** m magic words *pl.*; charm, spell, incantation; **=stab** m magic wand, **=stück(chen)** n conjuring trick; **=teppich** m Märchen: magic carpet; **=trank** m magic potion; (Liebestrank) philter; **=werk** n = Zauberei; **=wesen** n: a) magic, sorcery; b) charming creature, F charmer; **=wort** n magic word; **=worte** *pl.* spell *sg.*; **=zeichen** n magic sign.
Zaubrer(in), zaubrisch (‿́‿‿) f. Zaub(e)r...
Zauberei (‿‿́‿) f ⊛ wavering, hesitation.
Zaud(e)rer (‿́‿‿) m ㉒, **Zauderin** f one who is fond of putting off things, wavering (or dilatory, irresolute, shilly-shallying) person; dawdler, loiterer. (f. die bessere Zeiten abwartet) temporizer; röm. Altertum: Fabius der ~ Fabius Cunctator.
zauderhaft (‿́‿) a. ⊛ dilatory, tarrying, hesitating; (unschlüssig) wavering, irresolute; (langsam) tardy, slow, dawdling; *adv.* with hesitation; **~igkeit** f ⊛ dilatoriness, dawdling (disposition), hesitancy; (Unschlüssigkeit) irresoluteness, (Langsamkeit) slowness, tardiness.
zaudern (‿́‿) [nhd.] I v/n. (h.) ⊛a. to waver, tarry, hang back; mit et. 2, 2 et. zu tun to delay (doing) a th., to hesitate (before) doing a th.; abs. (günstigere Zeit abwartend) to temporize; 2⊛ wavering, hesitating, shilly-shallying. — II ~ n ㉓ wavering; hesitation; temporizing, temporization.
Zauderer(in f) m (‿‿́‿) f. Zaud(e)rer ꝛc.
Zaum (‿́) [ahd.: ziehen] m ⊙c. 1. man. bridle, rein; ein Pferd ꝛc. gut im ~e halten to keep a tight rein on (or a tight hand over) ..., to keep ... well in hand. — 2. *fig.* seine Begierden, Leidenschaften ꝛc. im ~e halten to bridle (or curb. check, repress, restrain, subdue) ..., to keep ... under (control); f-e Zunge im ~e halten to keep one's tongue in check or in order.
zäumen (‿́‿) v/a. ⊛ 1. ein Pferd ꝛc. 2 to bridle ..., to put the reins (or the bit) on ... — 2. *bibl.* = zähmen.
Zaum-geld (‿́‿) n ㉒: ~ (das der Käufer dem Stallknecht für den Zaum gibt) bridle-money, mehr gbr.: purchaser's tip to the ostler or groom; **=los** a. ⊛ without a bridle. *fig.* unbridled; 2**recht** a. von Reittieren: accustomed to the bridle; **=schnalle** ⊙ f bridle-buckle; **=zeug** n e-s Pferdes: head-harness or -gear.

Zaun (‿́) [ahd.: town] m ⊙c. (wooden) fence; (Gitter) railing; geflochtener ~ wicker(ed) (or wattled) fence; lebendiger ~ living (or quickset) hedge; Fischerei = Fischzaun; *fig.* (Scheidewand) partition; mit einem ~e umgeben to fence (or hedge) in, to enclose; *fig.* Sprichw.: et., e-e Gelegenheit vom ~e brechen (das erste beste hervorbringen) to drag s.th. in (by the head and shoulders), to seize (upon) the first (or earliest) opportunity for doing (or uttering) a th.; f. brechen 10 am Ende; das ist nicht hinter dem ~ zu finden that's not a very common thing, F you can't pick it off hedges; hinterm ~ (auf der Wanderschaft) sterben to die in a ditch or by the roadside.
zaun-dürr (‿́‿) a. ⊛ (as) thin as a lath.
zäunen (‿́‿) [Zaun] v/a. ⊛ to fence in.
Zaun-gast (‿́‿) m ㉒ F co. one who looks over the hedge or looks on without paying, looker-on; weitS. intruder; **=könig** [ahd.] m, *orn.* wren (*Troglo'dytes pa'rvulus*); **=latte** ⊙ f picket; **=lilie** ♀ f spiderwort (*Anthe'ricum lili'ago*); **=lücke** f gap in a fence; **=macher** m, *agr.* hedger, hedge-maker; **=pfahl** ⊙ m fence-pale or -rail, hedge-stake or -pole; f. winken 1; **=rebe** ♀ f = wilder Wein. f. Wein 3; **=rübe** ♀ f bryony (*Bryo'nia*); rote ~ red-berried bryony (*B. dio'ica*); weiße ~ white bryony (*B. alba*); **=wicke** ♀ f vetch, wild vetch (*Vi'cia se'pium*); **=winde** ♀ f bearbind. bindweed (*Convo'lvulus se'pium*).
zausen (‿́‿) [ahd.: tease. touse] v/a. u. sich 2 v/recip. ⊛ to tug, to pull (or drag. haul) about, F to tousle; (zerrupfen) to pick to pieces, auch = zupfen; sie haben sich tüchtig gezaust they (have) pulled each other about nicely.
z.B. *abbr.* = zum Beispiel. [half-pay.|
z.D. ✕ *abbr.* = zur Disposition; onf|
z.E. *abbr.* = zum Exempel (= z.B.)
Zebaoth (‿‿́‿) [hebr. ‿‿́‿] m/pl. *inv. bibl.* der Herr ~ God Sabaoth, mehr gbr.: the Lord of Hosts.
Zebedäus (‿‿́‿) npr/m. ⊛γ. *bibl.* (Vater der Apostel Jakobus und Johannes) Zebedee.
Zebra (‿́‿) [afrik.] n ⊛ zo. zebra (*Equus zebra*); 2**artig** (‿́‿‿) a. ⊛ like a zebra, zebrine, 2**-a.** gestreift zebra; **~pflanze** ♀ f ⊛ zebra-plant (*Mara'nta zebri'na*).
Zebu (‿́‿) [ind. Kuh] m ⊛ zo. (indischer Buckelochs) zebu, Indian bull (*Bos taurus i'ndicus*).
Zech-bruder (‿́‿‿) m ㉒ boon-companion; (Säufer) tippler, toper, F boozer.
Zeche (‿́‿) [nhd.] f ⊛ 1. (Wirtshausrechnung) score, reckoning; a p.'s share or scot; die ~ bezahlen to pay the bill, to pay for all, F to stand treat (all round), *fig.* to pay the piper; seine ~ bezahlen to pay one's score or due; was macht meine ~? what does my bill (or account) come to? — 2. (Gasterei) banquet, b.s. (Trinkgelage) drinking-bout. F booze. — 3. (Zunft) guild, corporation. — 4. ✕ (Bergwerk) mine; (Bergwerksgesellschaft) mining-company.
zechen (‿́‿) [ahd.: take] I v/a. u. v/n. (h.) ⊛ 1. to drink (copiously or freely or hard), to carouse, guzzle, tipple, F to booze,

---

Signs (see page XVII): F familiar; P vulgar; ✶ flash; ✵ rare; † obsolete (died); ✱ new word (born); ⨯⨯ incorrect; ♪ music;

[Zechenbesitzer] — 1143 — [Zehrwurz]

to lush up (= kneipen² I). — 2. (ein Gelage halten) to (give a) banquet. — II ~ n ㉓ 3. (hard) drinking, carousal, F boozing.
Zechen-besitzer⚒(ˊ˘…) m ㉑ mine-owner; **=haus** n mine-house; **=holz** n timber in a mine; **=schreiber** m clerk of a mine.
Zecher (ˊ˘) m ㉒, **~in** f ㊼ (hard) drinker, tippler, toper, F boozer; person fond of the bottle.
Zecherei (˘ˊ˘") f ㊻ = Gezeche.
zech-frei (ˊ…) a. ㊇ scot-free, free of expense; e-n ⁓ halten to pay for a p.'s drink, to treat a p.; **=gast** m ㉒ guest (or customer) at an ale-house or a pub; **=gelage** n drinking-bout, carousal; **=genoß** m drinking- (or boon-)companion, bottle-friend; **=gesellschaft** f drinking-party.
Zechine (˘ˊ˘) f [it. 1280 von (*ar.) La Zecca „Münzhaus" v. Venedig] f ㊽ (ehm. it. Gold-münze, im Werte von etwa 9 Mark) sequin(o).
Zech-preller (ˊ…) m ㊽ im Wirtshause: one who gets away without paying for his drink; **=prellerei** f sneaking away from a bar or public-house without paying one's score; **=schuld** f debt for drink or liquor; **=stein** m, min. Permian limestone, a. ꝉ zech-stein; **=stein-formation** f, geol. Permian formation. [vgl. Fanchonzect.]
Zeck (ˊ) m ⓑ. (playing at) catching;
Zecke (ˊ) f [mhd.: tick] f ㊽ ent.
Zeck-spiel (ˊ…) n ㊼ = Zeck. [tick (Ixo'des).]
Zedent (˘ˊ) [lt.] m ㊷, **~in** f ㊼ (Ab-tretender) ♂ u. jur. transferrer, assignor.
Zeder ♀ (ˊ˘) [ahd., lt., *grch.] f ㊽ 1. cedar (Pinus cedrus); ⁓ vom Libanon c. of Lebanon (Cedrus Li'bani). — 2. europäische ⁓ (Lärche) larch(-tree or -fir) (Larix europae'a). — 3. rote virginische ⁓ red cedar (Iuni'perus Virginia'na).
Zeder-baum ("…) m ㉑, **=fichte** f ♀ = Zeder; **=kiefer** ♀ f = Zirbel.
zedern (ˊ˘) [Zeder] a. ㊇ (made of) cedar; cedrine.
Zedern-harz ("˘ˊ) n ㊺ cedar-gum, cedrium. [(Cedre'la odora'ta).]
Zeder-tanne ♀ ("˘ˊ˘) f ㊷ cedrela
zedierbar (˘ˊ…) a. ㊇ transferable.
zedieren (˘ˊ˘) [lt.] v/a. ㊲ u. jur. (ab-treten) to cede (or assign, transfer, make over) to a p.
Zedrach ♀ (ˊ˘ch) [ar.] m ⓓ. glatter ⁓ bead-tree (Me'lia aze'darach).
Zedrat (˘ˊ) [neut.] n ㉖. (verzuckerte Schale unreifer Zitronen) candid lemon-peel.
Zeh (ˊ) [ahd.: toe] m ⓒ. ㊷, **~e** (ˊ˘) f ㊽ anat. toe; große (kleine) ⁓e big (little) toe; auf den ⁓en gehen (stehen) to walk (to stand) on tiptoe; s. Wirbel 4.
zehen (ˊ˘) ꝛc. s. zehn.
Zehen-gang ("˘ˊ) m ㊶ walking on the toes or on tiptoe; **=gänger** m, zo.: ♉ digitigrade; **=spitze** f tip (or point) of a toe, auf den =spitzen stehend stand-ing on tiptoe; **=strecker** m, anat.: ♉ extensor of the toes.
zehent (ˊ˘) I ord. numb. s. zehnte. — II ~: a) n ⓒ. = Fahrzeh(e)nt; b) m ㊷. ~e [ahd.] m ㊹ = Zehnte.
zehenten (ˊ˘˘) v/a. = zehnten.
Zehen-tier ("˘ˊ…) n ㊻ = =gänger; **=ver-wachsung** f, surg.: ♉ dactylion.

…**zehig** (…"ˊ˘) [Zeh(e)] a. ㊇: fünf⁓ with (or having) five toes.
zehn (ˊ) [ahd.: ten: lt. decem: grch. deka], wenn nichts folgt, P a. ⓒe (ˊ˘) numer.
I card. numb. ten; Anzahl von ⁓, F Stücker ⁓ half a score, about ten, F tenner; s. Gebot 1; von der Uhr: es ist halb zehn it is half past nine; Zeit-raum von ⁓ Jahren decade; ⁓ mit ⁓ Staubfäden: ♉ decandrian; Klasse der Pflanzen mit ⁓ Staubfäden: ♉ decan-dria. — II (die Zahl) **Zehn** f ㊻ (number) ten (10, X); Kartenspiel: eine (Schippen) ⁓ a ten (of spades).
zehn-blätterig ♀ ("…) a. ㊇: ♉ deca-phyllous; **=eck** n ㊷ geom. ten-sided figure, decagon; ⁓eckig a. ㊇ ten-sided, geom. decagonal; **=ender** m, hunt. stag of ten antlers, auch: ten-tiner.
Zehner (ˊ˘) m ㉒ 1. s.th. consisting of ten parts or marked with a ten. — 2. arith. ⁓ und Einer tens and units pl. — 3. = Zehnkreuzer-, Zehnpfennig-stück. — 4. Kartenspiel: the ten. — 5. member of a council of ten. — 6. von jungen Leuten: in den ⁓n stehen to be in one's teens.
zehnerlei (ˊ˘˘) a. inv. of ten (different) kinds or sorts. [of tens.]
Zehner-reihe ("˘ˊ˘) f ㊻ arith. column
zehn-fach ("…) a. ㊇, **=fältig** a. tenfold, ♉ decuple; das =fache ten times the number or amount; **=flach** n, **=flächner** m ㊷ f. Dekaeder; ⁓füßig ♀ a. with ten feet; zo.: ♉ decapodal; **=füß(l)er** m/pl. zo. (Krebse): ♉ decapoda pl.; **=herr** m member of a council of ten, römisches Alt.: decemvir; **=herrschaft** f decemvirate; ⁓jährig a. of ten years, ten years old or of age; ein ⁓jähriges Kind a ten-year-old child; ⁓jährlich a. hap-pening every ten years, decennial; ehm. **=kreuzer-stück** n in Österreich: ten-kreuzer piece, twopence halfpenny; ⁓lappig ♀ a. ten-lobed; ⁓lötig a. of five ounces; ⁓mal adv. ten times; ⁓malig a. occurring ten times; ⁓männ(er)ig ♀ a.: ♉ decandrian; **=markstück** n ten-mark piece, (German) half sovereign; **=pfennig-stück** n ten-pfennig piece, (German) penny; **=pfünder** ⚔ m, artill. ten-pounder; ⁓punktig a. with ten points or spots, zo.: ♉ decempunctate; **=säulig** ♀ a. arch. decastyle; ⁓silbig a. gram. of ten syllables; decasyllabic; **=stem-p(e)lig** ♀ a.: ♉ decagynian.
Zehnt (ˊ) m = Zehnte.
Zehnt-ablösung ("˘ˊ˘) f ㊷ com-mutation of tithes.
zehn-tausend ("…) card. numb. ten thousand; ⁓tausendste a. ㊇ ord. numb. ten-thousandth.
zehnte [ahd.] I ord. numb. ㊇ (the) tenth, der ⁓ (10.) Mai May the tenth (May 10th), tenth of May; ⁓s Kapitel chapter the tenth (chapter X). — II **Zehnte** m ㊹ bsd. ehm. (Zehntel des Ertrages als Abgabe) tithe; den ⁓n an die Kirche entrichten to pay tithe to the church. — III ~[r] m ㊷: der ⁓ the tenth; das weiß der ⁓ nicht not one in ten knows it.
zehn-teilig ("˘ˊ˘) a. ㊇ of (or in) ten parts.

Zehntel (ˊ˘) n ㉓ u. ⓒ a. inv. tenth (part); fünf ⁓ machen ein halb five-tenths ($^5/_{10}$) make (or are equal to) one-half ($^1/_2$).
Zehntel-meter ("˘˘ˊ˘) n (m) deci-meter, decimetre; s. Dezimeter.
zehnten (ˊ˘) v/a. ㊾ besonders ehm. 1. to levy tithe on, to tithe. — 2. to pay tithe(s) to the clergy, &c.
zehntens (ˊ˘) adv. (oft gschr. 10.) tenthly (10thly), in the tenth place.
zehnt-frei (ˊ…) a. ㊇ free (or exempt) from tithe; **=herr** m ㊷ tithe-owner; **=land** n land subject to tithe; ⁓pflichtig a. subject to (the payment of) tithe, tithable; **=rechnung** f, arith. decimal calculation; **=recht** n right to levy tithe.
zehn-weib(er)ig ♀ (ˊ…) a. ㊇ (mit 10 Pistillen): ♉ decagynian; ⁓zeilig a. of ten lines, ten-lined; ⁓zöllig ㊹ bisw. decastich.
zehren (ˊ˘) [ahd.: zerren] ㊺ I v/n. (h.) 1. to take nourishment or food, to eat and drink; an et. ⁓ to live (or feast) on a th. (a. fig.); an e-m Schinken ⁓ to eat (or dine) off a ham; fig. an schönen Erinnerungen ⁓ to feast on happy memories of the past; auf j-s Kosten ⁓ to live at somebody's expense; aus fremdem Beutel ⁓ to live at other people's expense, to live on others; bei einem Wirte ⁓ to spend money at a hotel or restaurant; von j-n Zinsen ⁓ to live on one's interest. — 2. fig. (zerstörend nagen) to gnaw at, to consume, to undermine (a p.'s health or strength); der Kummer zehrt an ihrem Herzen grief is eating into her heart. — 3. abs. (am Körper) ⁓ to waste the body; der Wein, Tee ꝛc. zehrt … does not nourish, … gives no nourish-ment, … makes thin; die Seeluft, das Baden zehrt sea-air, bathing gives an appetite. — 4. (h. u. sn) (abnehmen) to be(come) reduced, to shrink; von Personen: (mager werden) to grow thin, to be wasting or falling away, to lose flesh. — II v/refl. 5. fig. der Kum-mer zehrte (fraß) sich bis tief in sein Ge-müt grief rankled deep in his mind. — III ⓓd p.pr. u. a. ㊇ 6. eating and drinking, &c. (s. I); path. (abzehrend) consumptive, wasting (away); ⁓des Fieber hectic fever.
Zehr-fieber ("…) n ㊻ path. hectic fever; ⁓frei a. ㊇ with free board; **=geld** n, **=pfennig** m money for provisions, (Reisegeld) travelling-expense(s pl.).
Zehrung (ˊ˘) f ㊻ 1. (das Zehren) con-sumption of food, &c., im Gasthause: ex-penses pl. incurred at a hotel or an inn; s. Zeche; freie ⁓ h. to have free board. — 2. (das zehrende Schwinden) (loss through) shrinkage, waste; path. bisw. = Abzehrung. — 3. (Mund-vorrat) provisions, victuals pl. — 4. eccl. letzte oder heilige (Weg=)⁓ extreme unction, (lt.) viaticum.
Zehrungs-kosten ("˘ˊ…) pl. ㊷ expense(s pl.) for food or board, für Dienstboten: board-wages pl., für e-e Reise: travel-ling expenses pl., **=steuer** f duty on articles of food.
Zehr-wurz ♀ ("˘ˊ) f ㊷ cuckoo-pint, wake-robin (Arum macula'tum).

♉ scientific; ♀ botanical; ♁ geography; ⚙ machinery; ⚒ mining; ⚔ military; ⚓ marine; ⬤ commercial; ✉ postal; 🚂 railway.

[Zeichen] — 1144 — [Zeit]

Zeichen¹ (⌣́) [ahd.: token] n 23 1. token, sign, fernhin wahrnehmbares, verabredetes: signal, aushängendes: sign-board; (Wert-) ~ mark, aufgestempeltes: stamp (a. ⚕), eingebranntes: brand (auch ⚕); vgl. Fabrikzeichen; (Anzeichen) indication, med., &c. auch symptom; (Abzeichen) badge, pl. a. insignia; (Beweis) proof, evidence; er hielt das für ein glückliches od. günstiges ~ he deemed that a happy omen or augury; zum ~ seiner Liebe in token of his love, as a token of his affection; zum ~, daß // as a proof that //; eccl. ~ des Kreuzes sign of the cross; ~ und Wunder signs and wonders pl.; thea. das ~ zum Heben des Vorhangs geben to ring up the curtain. — 2. ast. = Himmelszeichen; Astrologie: unter einem glücklichen ~ geboren sein to be born under a lucky star; das gilt mir für ein gutes ~ I deem that a happy omen, that augurs (or promises) well. — 3. (Merkmal eines Gewerbes): welches ~s ist er? what is his trade?, of what trade is he?; er war seines ~s ein Schneider he was a tailor by trade.

Zeichen²**-brett** (⌣⌣...) [zeichnen] n 23 drawing-board; **=buch** n drawing- (or sketch-)book; **=deuter** m interpreter of (heavenly) signs, alt.: augur; (Sterndeuter) astrologer; **=deuterei, =deutung** f interpretation of (heavenly) signs; (Sterndeuterei) astrology; **=erklärung** f in Büchern, auf Landkarten ꝛc.: key to the signs used; **=²feder** f drawing-pen; **=¹garn** n. ⊕ n thread for marking, marking-thread; **=geber** m, tel. communicator; **=heft** n drawing-book; **=klasse** f drawing-class; **=kreide** f drawing-chalk, crayon; **=kunst** f art of drawing or sketching; **=¹lehre** f: ⚇ sematology; **=²lehrer** m drawing-master; **=mappe** f drawing-portfolio; **=papier** n drawing-paper, ⊕ auch: designing-paper; **=pult** n drawing-desk; **=saal** m in Schulen: class-room for drawing, ⊕ in Fabriken: drawing-office; **=schrift** f hieroglyphics pl.; **=schule** f drawing- (or art-)school, school of design; **=setzung** f, gram. punctuation; **=sprache** f language of signs, chm. chemical notation; (Geheimschrift) cipher, tel. code; **=²stift** m crayon, pencil; **=stunde** f drawing-lesson; **=talent** n talent for drawing; **=¹telegraph** m semaphore; **=tinte** ⊕ f für Wäsche ꝛc.: marking-ink; **=²tisch** m drawing-table; **=unterricht** m drawing-lessons pl.; **=vorlage** f dr.-copy.

zeichnen (⌣́) [ahd.: *Zeichen] I v/a., v/n. (h.) u. v/refl. ⚇b. 1. to draw, to delineate, Muster ꝛc.: to design; flüchtig: to sketch, to outline; nach dem Modell, nach der Natur ⌣ to draw from models, from life; ⌣de Künste graphic arts pl. — 2. (mit e-m Zeichen versehen) to mark linen, a passage in a book, &c., to brand cattle, &c.; von Hunden ꝛc.: schön gezeichnet beautifully marked. — 3. eine Schrift ⌣, seinen Namen unter eine Schrift ⌣ to sign a document (f. unterzeichnen); als Briefschluß: und zeichne (mich) hochachtungsvoll ergeben(st) // I remain (seltener

I have the honour to be) Yours respectfully /; zu einem Denkmale 100 Mark ⌣ to subscribe five pounds towards (the erection of) a monument; ⚕ auf eine Anleihe ⌣ to subscribe to a loan; Aktien ⌣ to subscribe for shares, to take (up) shares (by subscription). — II ~ n 23 4. f. Zeichnung 1.
Zeichner (⌣⌣) m 23, **=in** f 47 1. drawer, draftsman, designer. — 2. ⚕ ~ einer Anleihe ꝛc. subscriber to a loan. &c.
Zeichnerei (⌣⌣⌣) f 46 indifferent (or bad) drawing or designing or sketching.
Zeichnung (⌣⌣) f 46 1. drawing, delineation, sketching, designing, v. Umrissen: outlining; (f. zeichnen 3) signing, subscription to a loan, &c. — 2. (gezeichnetes Bild) drawing, draft, sketch, design, f. Grundriß a und Muster 2. — 3. (Kennzeichen) mark(ing). — 4. (Unterschrift) signature, (gezeichnete Summe) sum subscribed towards a charity, &c., ⚕ subscription to a loan, &c.; eine Anleihe zur ~ auflegen to issue a loan, to offer a loan for (public) subscription.
Zeichnungs-stelle (⌣⌣⌣⌣) f 22 appointed place for subscription.

Zeidel-bär (⌣⌣...) [alt-flow.] m 22 = Honigbär; **=baum** m tree with hives of wild bees; **=heide** [mhd.] f heath used for the rearing of bees; **=meister** m bee-master, vgl. Zeidler.
zeideln ⟋ (⌣⌣) v/a. u. v/n. (h.) ⚇a.: (die Bienen) ⌣ to cut the honeycombs.
Zeidler (⌣⌣) [ahd., *flaw.] m 22 bee-keeper or -master, hiver.

zeigbar (⌣́) a. 46 presentable.
Zeigefinger (⌣⌣⌣) m 22 forefinger, index; ~**muskel** m anat.: ⚇ indicator (muscle).
zeigen (⌣́) [ahd.: teach] I v/a., v/refl. u. v/n. (h.) ⚇ 1. (sich) ⌣ to show (o.s.); (deuten auf) to point out, point at, indicate; (an den Tag legen) to display, (kundtun) to manifest, publish, (zur Schau stellen) to exhibit; (darlegen) to unfold; (beweisen) to prove, betoken, demonstrate, to give evidence of; die Pläne, die mir gezeigt worden sind ... which I have been shown or allowed to see; ich will ihnen ⌣, was ich kann (was ich bin) I'll show them (or let them see) what I can do (what I am made of); ich zeigte ihr den Weg nach dem Dorfe I showed her the way (or I directed her to) the village; seine Handlungen ⌣, daß er ein Ehrenmann ist his actions prove him to be a man of honour or bespeak him an honourable man. — 2. als v/refl.: (erscheinen) to appear, to make one's appearance, to come forward; (zum Vorschein kommen) to come to light or on the scene, to crop up; (sich offenbaren) to become evident or manifest; er darf sich nicht ⌣ (blicken lassen) he dare not show his face; er will sich ⌣ he wants to show off or to make a mark; darin zeigt er sich wieder (als) recht unvernünftig in that he proves himself again (to be) very unreasonable; sich mutig ⌣ to show pluck or fight; es wird sich bald ⌣, ob it will soon be(come) evident (or be seen) whether //, we shall soon see if /;

es zeigt sich jetzt, daß / it is now shown (or evident, manifest) that //, it now turns out (or appears) that /; es zeigte sich bald, daß er ein rechter Gauner war he soon turned out to be a regular scamp. — 3. nur v/n.: die Magnetnadel zeigt nach Norden... points to the north; das Thermometer zeigt 20 Grad ... shows (or /registers) twenty degrees. — II ~ n 23 4. showing, &c. (f. I); indication; display.
Zeiger (⌣⌣) m 23 1. one that shows or exhibits, seltener: demonstrator. — 2. ⊙ index, indicator, e-r Uhr: hand, e-r Sonnenuhr: pin, dial-hand, gnomon; e-s Barometers ꝛc.: pointer, am Kompasse: needle. — 3. = Zeigefinger. — 4. math. index.
Zeiger-apparat (⌣⌣...) m 22 tel. single-needle instrument; **=barometer** n (m), phys. wheel-barometer; **=lini-e** f einer Sonnenuhr: substyle, substylar line; **=telegraph** ⊙ m dial- (or single-needle) telegraph; **=uhr** f Uhrm.: clock which points the hours without striking; **=wage** f mit rechtwinkligem Hebelarm: bent-lever balance; **=werk** n e-r Uhr: dial-train or -work, hour-train.
Zeige-tisch (⌣⌣⌣) m 22 table on which s.th. is exhibited, show-table.
zeihen (⌣́) [ahd.: grch. deíknymi] v/a.: einen e-r Lüge ⌣ to accuse a p. of a lie, to give a p. the lie; e-n e-s Verbrechens ⌣ to charge (or tax) a p. with a crime, to impute a crime to a p.
Zeiland ⟋ (⌣⌣) [mhd.: Zeidel-...] m ⒹD. laurel-herb (= Kellerhals b).
Zeile (⌣⌣) [ahd.: Ziel] f 48 1. geschriebene oder gedruckte ~ line, f. Paar III am Ende und schreiben 2 am Ende; zwischen den ~n lesen to read between the lines; zwischen zwei ~n geschrieben interlinear, typ. ~ halten to keep to the line. — 2. (Reihe): a) von Personen: lane; b) von Gegenständen: range; c) (Häuserreihe) row of houses, bisw. auch: street (= Straße); d) hort. in ~n pflanzen to plant in rows or straight lines.
Zeilen-breite (⌣⌣...) f 22 typ. measure; **=gieß-maschine** ⊙ f Schriftgießerei: line-casting machine; **=länge** ⊙ f length of a line, typ. justification; **=maß** n, typ. type-scale, -gauge; **⌣weise** adv.(a.) by the line, in (or by) lines, in rows.
...zeilig (...⌣́) a. 46: drei⌣ three-lined.
Zeisig (⌣⌣) [mhd.; *poln., tichech.] m 23 1. orn. siskin, aberdevine (Fringilla spinus). — 2. fig. ein lockerer ~ a loose (or fast) fellow; vgl. locker 2 am Ende.
zeisig-grün (⌣⌣⌣) a. 46 siskin-green.
Zeißing ⚓ = Seising.
Zeit¹ (⌣́) [ahd.: tide] f 46 1. time, ~(abschnitt) epoch, period, space of time; ~(alter) age, generation; der größte Dichter seiner ~ the greatest poet of his time or age; med. ihre ~ ist noch nicht da her time (of confinement) has not yet arrived; gram. von Zeitwörtern: (past, present, future) tense; ♪ pros. = Zeitmaß. — 2. mit a. f. allezeit; alte ~(en pl.) old (or ancient, past) times pl.; f. frei 4, geraum, gut 2 am Schluß; harte, schlechte, schwere ~(en) hard times pl.; f. hoch 2 am Ende; ist die höchste ~ it is the highest

---

Zeichen (f. S. XVII): F familiär; P Volkssprache; F Gaunersprache; ⟋ selten; † alt (auch gestorben); * neu (auch geboren); ⁓ unrichtig.

[zeit] — 1145 — [Zeitraum]

time, it is most urgent; s. jederzeit, kurz 2 gegen Ende, lang 3; du liebe (auch meine) ~! good gracious!, dear me!, F what, oh!; s. still 2 gegen Ende u. teuer 2. — 3. *adv.*: a) im *acc.* meist mit *adv.*: eine ~lang s. ~lang; einige ~ nachher (vorher) some time after (before); 2 seines Lebens (= zeitlebens) all his life-time; b) im *gen.*: du warst deinerzeit ein tüchtiger Ruderer you were, in your time, a splendid oarsman; ich werde dir das seinerzeit (zu geeigneter ~) (s. 3.) mitteilen I will tell you in due season or when the (proper) time arrives. — 4. mit *verbs*: eine ~ festsetzen to fix (or appoint) a time; die ~ s-r Ankunft ist auf 4 Uhr festgesetzt he is timed to arrive at four o'clock; mit der ~ gehen to go (or advance) with the times, to keep pace with the age; ~ gewinnen to gain (or save) time; einem ~ gönnen to give a p. time (to do a th.); ich werde mir ~ gönnen I shall take my time (to do it or to consider it); (keine) ~ haben to have (no) time; er hat viel (freie) ~ he has plenty of leisure or (spare) time; das hat ~, damit hat es gute ~ there is plenty of time (or no hurry) for that; es hat ~ bis nächste Woche it need not be (done) until next week; es hat ~ (wird lange währen), bis // it will be some time before //; man muß sich ~ lassen you must give yourself (sufficient) time, you must take your time; es ist oder wird ~ schlafen zu gehen oder zum Schlafengehen it is time to go to bed, s. 5 am Anfang; wie die ~en (jetzt) stehen as times go. — 5. mit *prp.*: es ist an der ~ (a. es wäre ~) zu handeln it is now the (proper) time to act; dies ist nicht mehr an der ~ the suitable (or favourable) time (or hour) has passed, it is out of season; wie viel (ob. wie hoch) ist es an der ~? what is the (right) time?, what time is it?; es ist früh an der ~ it is early (yet); auf einige ~ leihen to lend out for a certain time, ☿ auf ~ on credit, on account; außer der ~ at the wrong time, out of season, unseasonable, untimely; beizeiten (⌣‿⌢) in time; bei guter ~ in good time; bei diesen unseren ~en as times are or go, nowadays; für alle ~en for all times (to come), for ever; in der ~ oder den ~en des Krimkrieges at the time (or in the days) of the Crimean War; s. alt 3; in kurzer ~ within a short time, vgl. kurz 2 gegen Ende; s. letz 6; in (bei) ~en in (good) time; in ~ von drei Wochen in three weeks' time, within three weeks; mit der ~ in (the) course of time, as time goes on, in the long run; nach einiger ~ after some time, after a time; nach geraumer ~ after a considerable interval or period; seit der ~ since that time, ever since (then); es sind schon zwei Tage über die ~ it is now ... past the time or over time; um die ~ der Ernte about (or near) harvest-time; übers Jahr um dieselbe ~ about the same time next year; von ~ zu ~ from time to time; occasionally; vor kurzer ~ a short time (or a little while) ago or since, not long ago; vor der (gehörigen) ~ before the time (had arrived); prematurely; vorzeiten (⌣‿⌢), vor langer ~ once (upon a time), long ago, in olden times; während der ~ during that time or interval, in the meantime, all the while; während der ~, daß // whilst //, while /; zu allen ~en, jederzeit at all times; zur ~ Jesu in the days of Jesus, at the time of our Lord; noch zu gehöriger ~ in proper time; s. gelegen 2 am Schluß; zu gleicher ~ at the same time or hour; simultaneously; zu meiner ~ in my time; zur ~ vgl. zurzeit: zu rechter ~ at the right time or moment, in (the very nick of) time, opportunely; zu seiner ~ in his (or its) time; ein Wort zu seiner ~ a word in season; zu ungelegener ~ at an inconvenient (or awkward) time or moment; zuzeiten (bisweilen) sometimes, at times. — 6. Sprichw.: andere ~en, andere Sitten times change customs or manners; ~ ist Geld time is money; ~ gewonnen, alles gewonnen time (gained) is everything (gained); wer nicht kommt zur rechten ~, der muß essen, was übrig bleibt last come last served; jedes Ding währt seine ~ everything lasts (but) a certain time; alles zu seiner ~ everything in due season, there is a time for all things; *bibl.* ein jegliches hat seine ~ (Prediger 3,1) to everything there is a season; s. Rat 1 gegen Ende; spare in der ~, so hast du in der Not lay (or put) by for a rainy day.

zeit² (⌣) *adv.* s. Zeit 3.

Zeit¹-abschnitt (⌢‿⌢) *m* ⊗ (apportioned) space of time; period, epoch; =alter (brazen, golden, &c.), age, generation; in jenem ~ in those days, at that period; =angabe *f* date; ohne ~ without date, undated; =anwendung *f* employment (or use) of time; =aufwand *m* waste (or loss) of time; =ball ↓ *m* time-ball; =begebenheit *f* event of the day, contemporary event; =behelf *m* temporary expedient; =berechnung, =bestimmung *f* computation of the time or the date, chronology; =beschreibung *f*: ⚘ chronography; =biegung* *f*, *gram.* = Konjugation; =bogen *m*, *ast.* arc of time; =buch *n* chronicle (Jahrbücher) annals *pl.*; =dauer *f* duration (or space) of time, period; =differenz *f*, *ast.*, &c. difference of time (between two places); =droschke *f* cab taken (or engaged, hired) by the hour, selbstregistrierende: taxicab. [spout.

Zeite (⌣‿) *f* ⊗ (Schnauze eines Topfes 2c.)

Zeit-einheit (⌢‿⌢) *f* ⊗: a) im Drama: unity of time; b) *phys.*, &c. unit of time; =einteilung *f* division of time.

..zeiten (...⌢‿) *adv.*, zB. bei 2 betimes.

zeit¹-ersparend (⌢‿⌣) *a.* ⊗ time-saving; =ersparnis *f* ⊗ saving (or economy) of time; =folge *f*: a) chronological sequence or order; b) *gram.* =(en)folge (*consecu'tio te'mporum*) concord of tense(s); =form *f*, *gram.* tense; =forscher *m* chronologist; =forschung *f* chronology; =frage *f* question (or topic) of the day; =geist *m* spirit of the age; ⚶gemäß *a.* in conformity (or harmony) with the (spirit of the) age; seasonable, opportune, F up to date; =gemäßheit *f* seasonableness, opportuneness; =genosse *m*, =genossin *f* contemporary; =genossenschaft *f* s. Gleichzeitigkeit; ⚶genössisch *a.* contemporary; =geschäft ☿ *n* time-bargain, business by option; =geschichte *f* contemporary history, history of our time; =gewinn *m* economy (or saving) of time; =gleichung *f* s. Gleichung 2; =hafen ↓ *m* tidal harbour; ⚶her (⌢‿) *adv.*, ⚶herig (⌢‿⌢) *a.* = bisher(ig).

zeitig (⌢‿) [ahd.] *a.* ⊗ 1. = damalig. — 2. (der Zeit gemäß) opportune, coming in the nick of time, seasonable, well-timed. — 3. (früh) early, timely; 2 (*adv.*) kommen to come in good time. — 4. (reif) ripe(ned), mature, well-seasoned; 2 werden to ripen, to mature.

zeitigen (⌢‿⌢) I *v/a.* und *v/n.* (h.) ⊗ to ripen, to mature, *med.* to bring (*v/n.* to come) to a head; *a.* reifen¹. — II **Zeitigung** *f* ⊗ ripening; die ~ s-r Pläne the maturing of his plans.

Zeit-karte (⌢...) *f* ⊗ season-ticket; =kauf ☿ *m* time-bargain or purchase; =kunde *f* chronology; ⚶kundig *a.* ⊗ versed in chronology; ⚶kürzend *a.* whiling away the time; entertaining, amusing; =kürzung *f* = =vertreib; =lage *f* juncture; =lang *f*: eine ~ for some time, for a (long) while; =lauf *m*: a) lapse of time, course of events; b) =läuf(t)e *pl.* times *pl.*; ⚶lebens (⌢‿⌢) *adv.* all one's life(-time. for life; =lehen *n* temporary fief or fee.

zeitlich (⌢‿) [mhd.] *a.* ⊗: a) (*ant.* ewig) temporal, worldly, (irdisch) earthly, (vergänglich) fleeting; das ~e segnen to depart this life, (*sh.*) to shuffle off one's mortal coil, F to kick the bucket, to hop the twig, to peg out; b) (*ant.* geistlich) temporal, secular; 2e Güter *pl.* temporal possessions, temporalities.

Zeitlichkeit (⌢‿⌢) *f* ⊗ 1. earthly life, temporal concerns *pl.*; *rel.* aus dieser (irdischen) ~ abscheiden to pass away from our earthly home, to depart this life. — 2. ~en *pl.* temporalities (= Temporalien).

Zeit-lose ⚘ (⌢‿⌢) *f* ⊗ = Herbstzeitlose; =mangel *m* want of time; =maß *n* measure of time; ♪ und Tanzkunst: measure, time; *gram. pros.* ~ der Silben: quantity; =messer *m*, *ast.*, &c. chronometer; =meßkunst, =messung *f* measurement of time, ⚘ chronometry; *gram.* prosody; =ordnung *f* chronological order; =pacht *f* lease (held) for a certain number of years; =punkt *m* point of time, moment; geschichtlicher: epoch; den günstigen (oder richtigen) ~ verpassen to miss one's opportunity; ⚶raubend *a.* ⊗ taking up much time; wearisome; 2e Studien time-consuming studies *pl.*; =raum *m* space of time; interval; period;

♪ Musik; ⚘ Wissenschaft; ⚥ Pflanze; ⊕ Geographie; ⊗ Technik; ⚒ Bergbau; ⚔ Militär; ↓ Marine; ☿ Handel; ✉ Post; ⚏ Eisenbahn.

[Zeitrechner] — 1146 — [Zensur]

=rechner m chronologist; =rechnung f time-computation, chronology, christliche: Christian era; Fehler gegen die ~: ⚇ anachronism; =register n = =tafel; =rente f annuity (for a certain number of years); =schrift f periodical (publication); wöchentliche, monatliche ~ weekly, monthly (magazine or journal); =sinn m, phls. time-sense; =spanne f span of time: =tafel f chronological table; =umstände m/pl. circumstances pl. (of the time); (Zutreffen von Umständen) juncture; unter den heutigen =umständen in the present condition of affairs; as times go.

Zeitung (⸗⸗) [mhd. (ndd.): tiding] f 1. (news)paper, journal, public print, fast contp. (local) sheet, amtliche: gazette, tägliche: daily paper, pl. oft: dailies (sich dat.) eine ~ halten to take in a paper; was die ~en schreiben what's written in the papers; in die ~ setzen to insert in a paper; das steht in der ~ that's (written) in the paper(s), the newspaper says so; in einer ~ veröffentlichen to publish in a paper. — 2. † (Nachricht) tidings pl., news; eine (un)angenehme ~ bekommen to receive (un)pleasant news or good (ill) tidings. Zeitungs-abonnement (⸗⸗⸗...) n (=abonnent m) subscription (subscriber) to a paper; =amt n newspaper office; =annonce, =anzeige f advertisement (in a paper); =artikel m newspaper-article, article (appearing) in a paper, kurzer: paragraph, F item; =ausschnitt m newspaper cutting, clipping; =beilage f supplement of (or to) a newspaper; =blatt n: a) (single) copy of a (news)paper; b) = Zeitung 1; =druck ⊙ m, typ. news(paper) work; =druckerei f, typ. news-house; =ente f = Ente 2; =expedition f = =amt; =frau f woman carrying about newspapers; =händler(in f) m newsagent; =inserat n (newspaper-)advertisement; =junge m (news)paper-boy, boy selling papers; =kiosk m newspaper stall; =kopf m, typ. newspaper heading; =korrespondent m newspaper correspondent; =krieg m newspaper war; =lesehalle f newsroom; =leser m newspaper reader; =nachricht, =neuigkeit f news report; =notiz f notice (inserted in a paper); =redakteur m editor of a (news)paper; =rubrik f newspaper column; =satz m, typ. news(paper)-work; =schreiber m journalist, (Berichterstatter) reporter; =stempel m newspaper stamp; =träger m newspaper carrier or man or boy; =verkäufer(in f) m newspaper man, newsvender, (wo)man selling (daily) papers; =wesen n journalism, newspapers pl., the (daily) press; =winkelhaken ⊙ m, typ. news-stick.

Zeit-verderb ("...) m = waste of time, wasting (one's) time; =vergeudend a. ⊕ wasting (one's) time; =verhältnisse n/pl. = =umstände; =verlauf m = =lauf a; =verlust m loss of time; ohne ~ without losing time, without delay; =verschwender(in f) m one who wastes (his, f her) time; =verschwendung f

waste of time; =vertreib m pastime, amusement; zum ~ to pass away the time, as a pastime, for (an) amusement; ⚇vertreibend a. whiling away the time, entertaining, amusing; ⚇weilig a. temporary, lasting a (short) while; (einstweilig) provisional; ⚇ (adv.) for a time, ⚇ bewußtlos, irre temporarily unconscious, insane; ⚇weise adv. (F a. a.): a) for a time, temporarily; b) from time to time, occasionally; =wind m periodical wind; =wort n, gr. verb; =zünder ⊕ m, artill. time-fuse (= Brennzünder).

Zelebrant (⸗⸗⸗) [lt.] m ⊕ Cath. eccl. (Messe lesender Priester) officiating priest, = celebrant; zelebrieren (⸗⸗⸗⸗) v/a. ⊕ to celebrate (high) mass. [Berühmtheit.) Zelebrität (⸗⸗⸗⸗) [lt.] f ⊕ celebrity (=f Zölibat (-⸗) n = ⊕c. f. Zölibat. Zell-bruder (⸗⸗⸗) m ⊕ (Klausner) one living in a cell, recluse. Zellchen (⸗⸗) n (dim. v. Zelle) small (or minute) cell, ⚇ cellule. Zelle (⸗⸗) [mhd. = cell; *lt. cella] f ⊕ 1. a) enger Wohnraum. b) ⚇ und anat. Grundstoff des Gewebes: cell; f. Zellulartheorie. — 2. = Badezelle. — 3. ~ der Bienenwaben: cell, ⚇ alveolus. — 4. anat. (Behältnis für eine Zahnwurzel) socket (of a tooth), ⚇ alveolus.

zellen-artig (⸗⸗...) a. ⊕ cellular; =bildung f ⊕ cell-formation; =förmig a. cellular, celliform, ⚇ alveolar; =gang m, anat. &c.: ⚇ cellular duct; =gefängnis n prison on the solitary (or Pennsylvania) system, a. cell; =gewebe n f. Zellgewebe; =koralle f = Cellepore; =rad ⊙ n bucket-wheel; =sprossung f; ⚇ cell-proliferation; =system n in Gefängnissen: system of solitary confinement (in cells), auch Pennsylvania system.

Zell-gewebe (⸗⸗...) n ⊕ physiol. cellular tissue, ⚇ parenchyma; =gewebepflanze f ⊕ cellular plant; =gewebesystem n cellular system; =horn* n = Zelluloid. [...ous, a. = zellenförmig.) zellicht, mst zellig (⸗⸗) a. ⊕: ⚇ cellulose. Zell-knoten (⸗...) m ⊕ ⚇ cellulose; =stoff* m = Zellulose. a. protoplasm (a). Zellular-pathologie ⚇ (⸗⸗⸗...) f ⊕ (Lehre v. krankhaften Gewebezellen) cellular pathology; =theorie f (Lehre v. d. Zellen) cellular theory. [(Eisenbahn) celluloid.] Zellulo-id ⚇ (⸗⸗⸗⸗) [lt.] n ⊕c. (Kunststoffes) Zellulose ⚇ (⸗⸗⸗) [lt.] f ⊕ chm. (Pflanzenfaserstoff) cellulose (C₆H₁₀O₅). Zelot (⸗⸗) [grch. Eiferer] m ⊕ ~in f ⊕ zealot, fanatic; ~entum (-⸗⸗) n (2d.) zealotism, ...ry. fanaticism; Zisch (-⸗⸗) a. ⊕ fanatical, seltener: zealotical; ~ismus (-⸗⸗⸗) m ⊕ = ~entum. Zelt¹ (⸗) [ahd.: tilt; *lt. tentum] n ⊕b., (P a. ⚇b.) tent, glockenförmiges: bell-tent, größeres: pavilion, marquee; ↓ (Sonnenzelt) awning, fast nur bibl. (Hütte) tabernacle; f. Himmelszelt; ein ~ aufschlagen (abbrechen) to pitch (to strike) a tent; unter =en wohnen to live in tents, ⚇ in =en under canvas. Zelt² (⸗) [mhd. tilt; *span.] m ⊕b. (o. pl.) man. (Paßgang) amble, ambling-pace. Zelt³ obd. (⸗) [ahd.] m ⊕b. flat cake.

Zelt¹-baracken ⚇ (⸗...) f/pl. ⊕ tent-barracks pl.; =bett n canopy-bed; =bude f tent-booth. Zeltchen (⸗⸗) n (dim. v. Zelt³) (Zuckerplätzchen) sugar tablet. Zelt¹-dach (⸗...) n ⊕: a) roof of a tent; b) arch. pavilion-roof; =ecke f awning. Zelter (⸗⸗) [ahd. *Zelt²] ⊕ m man. (Paßgänger) ambler, ambling horse; ehm.: Reitpferd für Damen) palfrey; =gang, =schritt m = Zelt². Zelt¹-haus (⸗...) n ⊕ pavilion; =lager ⚇ n camp formed of tents; =leinwand f tent-cloth, canvas for tents; =pfahl m tent-pole; =pflock m tent-peg, picket; =stange f = =pfahl; =stuhl m camp-stool; =wagen m: a) luggage-van; b) van (or wagon) with an awning or a tilt; f. Planwagen. Zement ⊙ (⸗⸗) [lt. caementum n Bruchstein] m (⚇ n) ⊕c. cement. zement-artig ⊙ (⸗⸗...) a. ⊕ cement-like; =fabrik f ⊕ cement-works pl. zementieren ⊙ (⸗⸗⸗⸗) [lt.] I v/a. ⊕ 1. (mit Mörtel befestigen) to cement. — 2. (Zementstahl verfertigen, fällen) to cement, to convert into steel, to precipitate. — II ⚇ 3. f. Zementierung; auf =n bezüglich cementing, cementatory. Zementierer ⊙ (⸗⸗⸗⸗) m ⊕ cementer. Zementierung (⸗⸗⸗⸗) f ⊕ des Eisens: cementation, converting. Zementier(ungs)-ofen ⊙ (⸗⸗"⸗...) =prozeß m ⊕ cementing- (or converting-)furnace, process; =pulver n cementing-powder, a. cement. Zement-kupfer (⸗⸗...) metall. precipitated copper, metal: =ofen m = Zementier(ungs)ofen; =silber n precipitated silver; =stahl m steel of cementation, converted steel; ~ herstellen to convert steel; =stahlbereitung f cementation of steel; =stein m cement-stone; =tiegel m cement (or cementation)-crucible; =wasser n cement (or cementing)-water. Zend (⸗) [alt-pers. = Kommentar] n ⚇ (ohne pl.), auch ~sprache f ⊕ (Sprache der alten Perser) Zend (language). Zenit ⚇ (⸗⸗) [+ ar.] m (n) ⊕c. (o. pl.) ⊕ (Scheitelpunkt) zenith, fig. = Gipfelpunkt. Zenotaphium ⚇ (⸗⸗"⸗...) [lt., *grch.] n ⚇ (Ehrengrab) cenotaph (= Kenotaphion). zensieren (⸗⸗⸗⸗) [lt. cense're] v/a. ⊕ 1. allg.: to pass an opinion (on), (scharf beurteilen) to censure, to criticize (keenly or sharply), to cavil (or carp) at; (besprechen) to review (tadelnd oft: F to slate) a book, &c. — 2. (über die Zulässigkeit zum Drucke urteilen) to examine as censor; ein Buch ⚇ to license ... Zensor (⸗⸗) [lt.] m ⚇ röm. Alt.: (Sittenaufseher) und jetzt: (Aufsichtsbeamter für das Schrifttum) censor; in Engl. (Unterbeamter des Lord Chamberlain für die Beurteilung v. Bühnenstücken) examiner (or censor) of plays; ~amt n, ~würde f ⊕ (a. Zensora't n) censorship. [sorian.] zensorisch (⸗⸗⸗⸗) a. ⊕ censorial, cen-Zensur (⸗⸗) [lt.] f ⊕ 1. röm. Alt. u. jetzt: (amtliche Prüfung der Druckschriften) censorship; censorial office or officer (pl.). — 2. (Zeugnis) certificate; marks pl. (obtained in an examination); für

---

Signs (see page XVII): F familiar; P vulgar; F flash; ⚇ rare; † obsolete (died); * new word (born); ⁓ incorrect; ♪ music.

Schüler: (term's) report; gute, schlechte ~ (Note) good, bad mark.

Zensur=behörde (*v*ᴸ...) f © für das Schrifttum: censorship of the press; =(en)=buch n e-r Klasse: mark-(weitS. conduct-)book; =liste f list of marks; =schema n printed certificate-form; =(en)=verteilung f distribution of (term's) reports.

Zensus (ˢᴗ) [lt.] m, inv. (a. ⑯) 1. röm. Alt.: (Steuerquote) census, property qualification. — 2. jetzt: (Volkszählung) census; e-n ~ vornehmen to take a census.

Zent (ᵛ) [mlt. cent(e'n)a Hundertschaft] f ® ehm.: 1. (Gau) hundred. — 2. (peinliche Gerichtsbarkeit; Kriminalgericht) criminal (or penal) jurisdiction or court.

Zentaur (ᵛˈ) [grch.] m ⑫ (⑤d.) 1. myth. (fabelhaftes Wesen, halb Mensch u. halb Pferd) centaur; wie ein ~ (Zen=artig, ²haft, ²isch a. ⑯) centaurlike. ...ian; ~en=kampf m ⑫, ~en=schlacht f: ⚔ centauromachy. — 2. ast. (südliches Sternbild) Centaur(us).

Zent=ding (ˢ..) n ⑫ = Zentgericht.

zentenar (ˢᵛᴸ) [lt.] a. ⑯ (hundertjährig) centenary,...ian; ~=feier f® centenary.

zentesimal (ˢᵛ⁻ᴸ) [lt.] a. ⑯ (hundertteilig) centesimal; ~=(ein)teilung f (...) f centesimal division, für Thermometer ꝛc.: centigrade scale;~=thermometer n (m) centigrade thermometer; ~=wage f centesimal balance.

Zent=gericht (ˢ...) n ⑫ ehm. hundred-court; =graf m ehm. criminal judge.

Zentifoli=e (ˢᵛ⁻ᴸ(ᵛ)ᵛ) [lt. hundertblätterige] f ⑯ cabbage-rose (Rosa centifo'lia).

Zenti=gramm (ˢᵛ⁻ᴸ...") [lt.] n ⑳⑥ (0,01 Gramm; abbr. cg) centigram, vgl. Gramm; =liter n (m) (0,01 Liter; abbr. cl) centi-litre; =meter n (m) (0.01 Meter; abbr. cm) centimetre, vgl. Meter.

Zentner (ˢᵛ) [mhd.; *mlt. hunderter] m ⑫ (Maßgewicht = 50 kg) hundredweight (abbr. cwt); auch: (dtsch) centner.

Zentner=gewicht (ˢ...) n ⑫ hundred-weight; =last f heavy weight; fig. das nahm mir eine ~ vom Herzen that took a heavy burden off my mind or a heavy weight off my heart; ²schwer a. ⑯ weighing a hundredweight; fig. excessively (or very) heavy; fig. das lag ihm ² auf dem Herzen that weighed heavily on his mind, it greatly depressed him.

zentral (ᵛᴸ) [lt.] a. ⑯ (mittelständig) central.

Zentral=amerika ♀ (ᵛᴸ...), =asien n ⑫ Central America, Asia; =bahn f central railway; =behörde f central authority; =blatt n central journal or organ.

Zentrale (ᵛᴸ) f ⑱ 1. math. line joining two centres. — 2. ⊕ central station.

Zentral=kraft (ᵛᴸ...) f ⑫ central force or power; =heizung ⊕ f (Sammelheizung) central system of heating.

Zentralisation (ˢᵛ⁻⁻ᴸᴸ) [lt.] f ⑯ centralization; Anhänger(in) der ~ centralist; die ~ abschaffen, von der ~ befreien to decentralize.

zentralisieren (ˢᵛ⁻ᴸᴸ) [lt.] I v/a. ⑨³ (ziehen) to centralize. — II ~ n ㉓ u. **Zentralisierung** f ⑯ = Zentralisation.

Zentral=punkt (ᵛᴸ...) m ⑫ centre; =schwenkung ⚔ f centric evolution or movement; =stelle f central (or chief)

office or bureau, centre; =turn=anstalt f central gymnasium; =viehhof m in großen Städten: (town) abattoir, central slaughter-house; =zündung ⚔ f central (or centre-)fire.

Zent=richter (ˢ,ᵛ) m ⑫ = Zentgraf.

zentrieren ⊕ (ᵛᴸ) [lt.] v/a. ⑨³: e-e Linie, ein zu bohrendes Stück ⚔ to centre...

zentrifugal ⚛ (ˢᵛ⁻ᵛ⁻ᴸ) [lt.] a. ⑯ phys., &c. centrifugal (ant. zentripetal); ~=kraft f ⑫ phys. centrifugal (or tangential) force, ⚛ centrifug(i)ence; ~=maschine f centrifugal machine, centrifuge; ~=pendel m u. n centrifugal pendulum.

zentripetal ⚛ (ˢᵛ⁻ᵛ⁻ᴸ) [lt.] a. ⑯ phys., &c. centripetal (ant. zentrifugal); ~=kraft f ⑫ phys. centripetal force.

Zentri=winkel ⚔ (ˢᵛ⁻ᵛ) m ⑫ math. angle at the centre (of a circle).

Zentrum (ˢᵛ) [lt.] n ㉘ 1. (Mittelpunkt) centre; ins ~ treffen (schießen) to hit the bull's-eye, F to make a bull. — 2. parl. (Mittelpartei) centre, (bsd. die katholische Zentrumspartei) central party.

Zentrum=bohrer ⊕ (ˢᵛ...) m ⑫ carp. centre-bit; =(s=)fraktion, =(s=)partei f, parl. = Zentrum 2; =schuß m (hit in the) bull's-eye, F bull.

Zentumvir (ᵛ⁻ᵛ⁻ᵛ) [lt.] m ⑯ röm. Alt.: centumvir; ~at (ˢᵛ⁻ᵛᴸ) n ⑪c. (Richterkollegium) centumvirate.

Zenturiat=komiti=en (ˢ⁻⁻)⁻ᴸ⁻tˢ(ᵛ)ᴸ) [lt.] n/pl. röm.Alt.:(Gauversammlung)centuriate comitia, (lt.) comitia centuriata pl.

Zenturi=e (ᵛᴸᴸᵛ) [lt.] f ⑱ röm. Alt.: a) politischer Bezirk [nach Servius Tullius]; b) ⚔ (röm. Truppenabteilung, Kompagnie) centuria,...y. f (Hauptmann) centurion.

Zenturio (ᵛᴸ(ᵛ)⁻) [lt.] m ⑯⑳ röm. Alt. ⚔.:

Zeolith ⚛ (ˢᵛ⁻ᴸ) [grch.] m ⑪c.⑫ min. zeolite; ²isch a. ⑯ zeolitic.

Zephanja (ᵛf⁻) [hebr.] npr/m. ⑯④α. Zephaniah.

Zephir (ᴸf⁻) [grch.] ⑦d. I npr/m., a. ~us (ᴸfᵛᵛ) inv. myth. (Südwestwind als Gott) Zephyr(us). — II m (Südwestwind) south-westerly breeze; (lauer Wind) zephyr, soft wind or breeze.

Zephir=garn (ᴸf⁻...) n ② zephyr; **zephirhaft** (ᴸf⁻ᵛ), **zephirisch** (⁻fᴸᵛ) a. ⑯ zephyr-like; balmy (breeze).

Zephir=schal (ᴸf⁻...) m ⑫, =wolle f zephyr.

Zepter (ˢᵛ) [mhd.; *lt.] n (m) ⑫ sceptre, des engl. 'Sprechers', des Lordmayors ꝛc.: mace; das ~ führen to wield the sceptre; ~=träger m ⑫: a) sovereign; b) (Beamter) mace-bearer.

Zer (ᴸ) [Cerium] n ⑯ (o. pl.) chm. (seltenes Metall) cerium (Ce).

zer=..., **Zer=...** (ˢ) [ahd.: lt. dis] Vorsilbe in Zssgn mit verbs und daraus abgeleiteten nouns u. adjectives, immer untrennbar (*), bz. Auflösung, Trennung, Beschädigung, Vernichtung, im v/refl. Übermaß, gänzliche Erschöpfung, z.B.: zer=ätzen, zer=beizen to destroy with caustics; zer=lesen to spoil with (much) reading.

zer=arbeiten (ᵛᵛ⁻ᵛ⁻ᵛ) ⑨*ᴸ I v/a. to destroy with (or by) working; (zermalmen) to crush; F e-n (derb) ² = prügeln. — II v/refl. sich ² to wear o.s. out with hard work, to overwork o.s., F to fag o.s. out or to death.

zer=ätzen (ᵛᵛᵛ) v/a. ⑨* f. zer=...

zer=beißen (ᵛᴸ) v/a. ⑨a* to bite through or to pieces, to break with one's teeth; to crunch a bone, to crack a nut.

zer=beizen (ᵛᴸ) v/a. ⑨* f. zer=...

zer=bersten (ᵛᴸ) v/n. (sn) ⑨e⑥b* to burst (or split) asunder.

Zerberus (ˢᵛᵛ) [lt., *grch.] npr/m. ⑯ grch. myth. (Höllenhund) Cerberus.

zer=blasen (ᵛᴸ) v/a. ⑨a* to blow apart.

zer=blättern (ᵛᵛ) v/a. u. v/refl. ⑨a* to strip of leaves; sich ² to peel off, to exfoliate. [thrash) unmercifully.]

zer=bleuen (ᵛᴸ) v/n. ⑨* to beat (or)

zer=borsten (ᵛᴸ) p.p. v. zerbersten.

zer=brechbar (ᵛᵛ) ꝛc. = zerbrechlich ꝛc.

zer=brechen (ᵛᵛᵛ) ⑨a* I v/a. to break (to pieces), stärker: to shatter, to smash, in kleine Stücke: to shiver (to atoms), to smash (up), F to break to smithereens; (durchbrechen) to break through, to snap (off) wood, metal, &c., bsd. Knochen, Glieder: to fracture; fig. (dat.) das Kreuz ² to break (or fracture) one's back; fig. sich den Kopf ² to rack (or worry) one's brain about a th., to puzzle over a th.; zerbrochen broken, shattered; alles Zerbrochene all breakages pl. — II v/n. (sn) (f. I) to break (to pieces), to smash, to snap (in two); to go to pieces or to bits, to get broken or smashed.

Zer=brecher (ᵛᵛᵛ) m ⑫ one that breaks crockery, &c., a. breaker, F smasher.

zer=brechlich (ᵛᵛᵛ) a. ⑯ breakable, apt (or liable) to break; brittle (glass, &c.), fragile (ware, &c.), shaky (furniture, &c.), als Aufschrift: ²! with care!; schwach und ² frail and fragile, delicate; ~=keit f ⑯ brittleness, fragility.

zer=brochen (ᵛᵛᵛ) p.p. v. zerbrechen.

zer=bröckeln (ᵛᵛᵛ) ⑨a* I v/a. to crumble (to pieces), Brot a. to crumb. — II v/n. (sn) to crumble (away or to pieces).

zer=dreschen (ᵛᵛᵛ) v/a. ⑨e(⑥b)* to crush to pieces; F fig. = zerbleuen.

zer=drücken (ᵛᵛᵛ) v/a. ⑨* to crush; (breit drücken) to squeeze flat; (zerknittern) to crumple, to crease.

Zereali=en (⁻ᵛᴸ⁻ᵛ) [lt.] f/pl. ㉙ 1. Alt.: (Ceresfeste) cerealia pl. — 2. jetzt: (Getreidearten) cereals, ...ia; ⚘ bread-stuffs.

Zerebral=system ⚛ (ᵛᵛ⁻ᴸ⁻ᵛᴸ) [lt.] n anat. cerebral system.

zerebro=spinal ⚛ (ᵛᵛᵛᵛ⁻⁻ᴸ) [lt.] a. ⑯ (Gehirn u. Rückenmark betr.) cerebro-spinal.

Zeremonial (⁻ᵛ⁻(ᵛ)ᴸ) [lt.] n ⑪c. (Kirchenꝛc. gebrauch) ceremonial; ~=gesetz n der Juden the Jewish (or Mosaic) law.

Zeremonie (⁻ᵛ⁻ᴸ) [lt. caerěmō'nĭa] f ⑨ ceremony; zu e-r ~ gehörig ceremonial; in ~n bestehend ceremonious.

Zeremoniell (⁻ᵛ⁻(ᵛ)ᴸ) [lt.] I n ⑪d. = Zeremonial; zum ~ gehörig ceremonial. — II ² a. ⑯ ceremonious, formal; precise (vgl. auch zeremoniös).

Zeremoni=en=buch (⁻ᵛᴸ(ᵛ)...) n ⑫ book of ceremonies, rel. ceremonial; =kleid n = Galakleid; =meister m master of (the) ceremonies; in Engl.: Erster ~ bei Kapiteln des Hosenbandordens, bei parlamentarischen Feierlichkeiten ꝛc.: (Gentleman Usher of the) Black Rod.

zeremoniös (⁻ᵛ⁻(ᵛ)ᴸ) [lt.] a. ⑯ (D 10) (f. Zeremoniell II) ceremonious, formal;

⚛ scientific; ⚘ botanical; ♀ geography; ⊕ machinery; ⚒ mining; ⚔ military; ⚓ marine; ⊛ commercial; ⌬ postal; 🚂 railway.

(steif) stiff; (peinlich genau) punctilious, precise, F fussy.

Zerevis (⏑‑⏑‑)[lt. *cerevi'sia*; *flt.] *n, inv.* (auch ⓂA.) studentisch: **1.** = ~-kappe. — **2.** Beteuerung: auf ~!, etwa: upon (a student's) honour!; ~-kappe (“...) *f* ⓔ, ~-mütze *f* student's gala cap (with the colours of his club or association).

zer-fahren (⏑‑⏑) ⓈB* **I** *v/a.* **1.** to crush (or break, smash) by (or in) driving over a th., die Wege: to ruin (or spoil) with heavy carting or traffic. — **II** *v/n.* (fn) **2.** (aus-ea.-fahren) to burst (or go) asunder. — **III** *p.p. u. a.* ⓖ (D 9) **3.** Bed. des *inf.* — **4.** *fig.* (unzusammenhängend) disconnected, desultory, confused; v. Personen: (sehr zerstreut) absent-minded, very inattentive or thoughtless, (unachtsam) heedless; (unbesonnen) unsteady, (highty-)flighty. giddy; der Mensch harum-scarum.

Zer-fahrenheit (⏑‑⏑‑) *f* ⓰ desultoriness; von Personen: absent-mindedness, inattentiveness, thoughtlessness. heedlessness; unsteadiness.

Zer-fall (⏑‑) *m* Ⓓc. (o. *pl.*) crumbling away, dilapidated state, (utter) decay, ruin; vgl. zerfallen III.

zer-fallen (⏑‑⏑) ⓈA* **I** *v/n.* (fn) **1.** to fall (or go, come) to pieces, to tumble down; (aus den Fugen weichen) to come undone, to go asunder; (verwittern) to crumble away, to fall to dust, to decay; (einstürzen) to collapse; *p.p.* auch: in ruins, wrecked; ein Les Gebäude a dilapidated (or tumble-down) building; *fig.* (scheitern, mißglücken) to fail, to miscarry. — **2.** in mehrere Teile Ⓛ (sich teilen I.) to fall (or to be divided, to be divisible) into several parts. — **3.** mit e-m Ⓛ (sich entzweien) to fall out (or quarrel) with a p.; mit e-m Ⓛ sein to be at variance (or at loggerheads) with a p. — **II** *v/a.* **4.** *sich (dat.)* den Kopf Ⓛ to break (or injure) one's head by a fall. — **III** ~ *n* Ⓑ **5.** falling to pieces, &c. (f. I); decay, decomposition; dilapidation; *fig.* failure.

Zer-fallenheit (⏑‑⏑‑) [zerfallen *p.p.*] *f* ⓰ ruinous state. dilapidated (or tumble-down) condition, decay(ed state).

zer-fasern (⏑‑⏑) *v/a.* ⓈA* to reduce to fibres or threads, ein Gewebe: to unravel, Wollstoff ⓡc.: to fuzz, to fray out.

zer-feilen (⏑‑⏑) *v/a.* ⓈB* to file to pieces or to powder, (durchfeilen) to file through or asunder, to cut with the file.

zer-fetzen (⏑‑⏑) **I** *v/a.* ⓂA* to tear in (or to) rags (and tatters), to cut to pieces; (zerhauen) to hack to pieces; (zerschlitzen) to slit up; (verstümmeln) to mutilate, (an (ob. e-m das Gesicht) fechtend ⓡc.) Ⓛ to slash (or gash) a p.'s face; zersetzt aussehen to look tattered and torn; in zerfetzten Schuhen out at heels. — **II** ~ *n* u. **Zer-fetzung** *f* ⓰ tearing, &c. (f. I); mutilation.

zer-fleischen (⏑‑⏑) **I** *v/a.* ⓂA* to lacerate. weits. to tear (or pull) to pieces; to mangle; der Löwe zerfleischte ihn mit seinen Krallen ... tore (or mawled) him with his claws; stark zerfleischt fearfully lacerated or mangled, durch ein wildes Tier: badly mawled. — **II** ~ *n* Ⓑ, **Zer-fleischung** *f* ⓰ laceration.

zer-fliegen (⏑‑⏑) *v/n.* (fn) ⓌD* to fly asunder, to (fly away) and disperse.

zer-fließbar (⏑‑‑) *a.* ⓖ liquefiable, liable to melt away, *chm.*: ⇗ deliquescent; **Zer-fließbarkeit** (⏑‑⏑‑) *f* ⓰: ⇗ deliquescence.

zer-fließen (⏑‑⏑) **I** *v/n.* (fn) ⓌD* to melt (or flow) away, to liquefy, to dissolve, *chm.*: ⇗ to deliquesce; *fig.* in Tränen Ⓛ to melt into tears; wie Niobe in Tränen zerflossen like Niobe all tears (*SH.*); die Königin, zerflossen in Wehmut und in Lust (*v.*) the Queen with sadness and rapture o'ercome. — **II** ~ *n* Ⓑ u. **Zer-fließung** *f* ⓰ melting away of snow, &c., liquefaction, *chm.*: ⇗ deliquescence.

zer-flossen (⏑‑⏑) *p.p.* von zerfließen; ~heit *f* ⓰ melted (or liquefied) state, *chm.*: ⇗ deliquescence.

zer-fressen (⏑‑⏑) **I** *v/a.* ⓈB* to eat (or gnaw) away or through; (beizend zerstören) to corrode; vom Roste Ⓛ rust-eaten; von Würmern Ⓛ worm-eaten; *chm., med.* Ⓓb (ätzend) corrosive; (Fäulnis erregend) septic. — **II** ~ *n* Ⓑ u. **Zer-fressung** *f* ⓰ corrosion.

zer-geh(e)n (⏑‑⏑) **I** *v/n.* (fn) ⓌA* to melt, dissolve, liquefy, vom Nebel: to disperse, *chm.* v. Salzen: ⇗ to deliquesce; in Luft, in nichts Ⓛ to melt into thin air, to dwindle (away) to nothing, to vanish. — **II** ~ *n* Ⓑ liquefaction.

zergen *provc.* (⏑‑) *v/a.* ⓈB = necken.

Zer-gliederer (⏑‑⏑‑) *m* ⓑ *anat.* dissector, ⇗ anatomist; *fig.* analyst; critic.

zer-glieder|n (⏑‑⏑‑) **I** *v/a.* ⓂA* to dismember, *anat.* to dissect, ⇗ to anatomize; *gr., log., chm.* to analyse, to decompose. — **II** ~ *n* Ⓑ und **~ung** *f* ⓰ dismemberment, *anat.* dissection, ⇗ anatomy, lebender Tiere: vivisection; *gr., log., &c.* analysis, decomposition.

Zer-gliederungs-kunst (⏑‑⏑‑...) *f* Ⓔ: ⇗ anatomy; **=messer** *n* dissecting-knife, mit fester Klinge: ⇗ scalpel; **=saal** *m* dissecting-room, anatomical theatre.

zer-hacken (⏑‑⏑) *v/a.* ⓈB* to cut to pieces, to chop to mince-meat; to hack, to chop up (small), to mince; ⚔ zerhacktes Eisen oder Blei slug.

zer-hauen (⏑‑⏑) *v/a.* Ⓓc(Ⓢ)* to cut asunder or in two, to hew; vgl. zer-hacken; in Stücke Ⓛ to cut (or hack, chop) to pieces, Schlächterei: to cut up a sheep, &c.; im Gesichte Ⓛ (*p.p.*) cut about (or slashed) in the face; *fig.* den (gordischen) Knoten Ⓛ to cut the Gordian knot.

zer-kauen (⏑‑⏑) *v/a.* ⓈB* to chew (or masticate) well or thoroughly.

zer-kleine(r)n (⏑‑⏑) *v/a.* ⓈB (ⓂA)* to make small pieces of, to cut (or split) in(to) small bits, ⚔ Erz ⓡc.: to break up, to spall; (zu Staub m.) to grind (or reduce) to powder, to pulverize, ⇗ to triturate. — **II** ~ *n* Ⓑ und **Zer-kleinerung** *f* ⓰ cutting in(to) bits, breaking up; pulverization, ⇗ trituration.

zer-klopfen (⏑‑⏑) *v/a.* ⓈB* to knock (or pound) to pieces, to smash, break (up).

zer-klüftet (⏑‑⏑) *a.* ⓖ cleft, cloven; rifted, riven, fissured; **Zer-klüftung** *f* ⓰ cleft, cleavage; rift, fissure.

zer-knacken (⏑‑⏑) *v/a.* ⓈB* to crack (open) a nut, &c., to crunch a bone, &c., to break (or crush) with one's teeth.

zer-kn(a)utschen P (⏑‑⏑) *v/a.* ⓆI* to crumple, to crease; vgl. zerknittern.

zer-knirschen (⏑‑⏑) *v/a.* ⓆI* to crunch, to crush, bsd. *rel.* zerknirscht (reumütig) contrite, penitent; **Zer-knirscht-heit** (⏑‑⏑‑), **Zer-knirschung** (⏑‑⏑‑) *f* ⓰ contrition. penitence, remorse.

zer-knittern ⓌA*, **zer-knüllen** ⓈB* (⏑‑⏑) *v/a.* Kleider ⓡc.: to (c)rumple, ruffle, tumble, crush, crease.

zer-kochen (⏑‑⏑) *v/a. u. v/n.* (fn) ⓈB* to boil to rags or to pulp or F to death.

zer-kratzen (⏑‑⏑) *v/a.* ⓂA* to scratch, to mark (or spoil) with scratches.

zer-krümeln (⏑‑⏑) *v/a., v/n.* (fn) u. *sich* Ⓛ *v/refl.* ⓂA* = verkrümeln.

zer-lassen (⏑‑⏑) *v/a.* ⓈA* = auslassen 4, *a.* to liquefy (auflösen) to dissolve.

zer-laufen (⏑‑⏑) ⓌA* **I** *v/n.* (fn) **1.** = verlaufen 3. — **2.** = zerfließen. — **II** *v/a.* **3.** sich (*dat.*) die Stiefel Ⓛ to run (or wear) down one's boots.

zer-legbar (⏑‑‑) *a.* ⓖ that can be taken apart or asunder or to pieces; decomposable (a. *chm.*), divisible (a. *math.*), Ⓞ von Brücken ⓡc.: portable; **~keit** *f* ⓰ *chm.* decomposability.

zer-legen (⏑‑⏑) **I** *v/a.* ⓈB* to take apart or to pieces, to disjoin(t), to undo, Ⓞ to disintegrate, mit dem Messer: to cut up (a. Kocht. u. Schlächterei); *anat.* to dissect a body; in f-e Bestandteile Ⓛ to split up (or dissolve) into its component parts; in zwei Teile Ⓛ to divide into two parts, to cut in two; bei Tische: einen Braten Ⓛ (vorschneiden) to carve a joint; *chm.* e-n Stoff Ⓛ to analyse (or decompose) a substance; *math.* e-n Wert (in Faktoren) Ⓛ to split up ... into factors, to factorize ...; *mech.* Kräfte Ⓛ to resolve forces. — **II** ~ *n* Ⓑ u. **Zer-legung** *f* ⓰ Ⓞ disintegration, *anat.* dissection; *chm.* analysis, decomposition, *math.* factorizing; *mech.* resolution of forces.

zer-lesen (⏑‑⏑) *v/a.* ⓈA* f. zer=...; ein Les Buch a well-thumbed volume.

zer-löchern (⏑‑⏑) = durchlöchern.

zer-lumpt (⏑‑) *a.* ⓖ ragged, tattered (and torn), in rags (and tatters), auch: out at elbows, shabby; der Mensch ragamuffin, tatterdemalion; ~heit *f* ⓰ raggedness, ragged (or tattered) condition.

zer-mahlen (⏑‑⏑) *v/a.* ⓈB* to grind (up), zu Staub: to pulverize.

zer-malmen (⏑‑⏑) *v/a.* ⓈB* to crush, to crunch, to smash (up), F to scrunch (up); (zerstoßen) to bruise, pound, bray; (zermahlen) to grind (to powder), to pulverize; vgl. zerreiben.

zer-martern (⏑‑⏑) *v/a.* und *sich* Ⓛ *v/refl.* ⓂA* = martern I.

zer-nagen (⏑‑⏑) *v/a.* ⓈB* to gnaw through, beizend ⓡc.: to corrode.

zer-nähen (⏑‑⏑) *v/a.* ⓈB*: sich (*dat.*) die Finger Ⓛ to prick one's fingers in (or to spoil one's fingers with) sewing.

[zernieren] — 1149 — [zerstäuben]

zernieren bsd. ⚔ (‿‿‿) [lt.] **I** v/a. 🟢* (einschließen) to invest, besiege, beleaguer, blockade. — **II** ~ n ㉓, **Zernierung** f 🌐 investment, siege, blockade.

Zernierungs-armee ⚔ (‿‿‿‿‿) f ㉖ investing, &c. (s. zernieren) army, army of investment.

zer-pflücken (‿‿‿) v/a. ⑧* to pluck (or pick) to pieces; (rupfen) to pluck.

zer-platzen (‿‿‿) **I** v/n. (sn) ⑨⓪* to burst (asunder or apart), to shiver into atoms, mit e-m Knall: to explode, to burst with a loud report, to blow up, von Glas ⁊c. auch: to crack, to split, F to fly. — **II** ~ n ㉓ bursting (asunder), explosion.

zer-quetschen (‿‿‿) v/a. ①* to (s)quash, crush, bruise, jam, zu Brei: to turn to pulp, Kartoffeln ⁊c.: to mash.

zer-raufen (‿‿‿) v/a. ⑧* to pull to pieces, to pluck asunder; vgl. zerreißen; e-m das Haar ⚡ to tear a p.'s hair (out by handfuls).

Zerr-bild (⚹…) n ㊷ caricature; ⚡bildlich a. ⑥ like a caricature; ⚹bildner m caricaturist. [able, ⚡ triturable.]

zer-reibbar (‿‿‿) a. ⑥ friable, levig-⎤
zer-reiben (‿‿‿) **I** v/a. ⑨* to rub (or grind, reduce) to powder, to grind down, to levigate, ⚡ to triturate. — **II** ~ n ㉓ u. **Zer-reibung** f ㊻ grinding (down), levigation, ⚡ trituration.

zer-reißbar (‿‿‿) a. ⑥ that can be torn, auch: easily tearing or torn.

zer-reißen (‿‿‿) ⑨⓪a* **I** v/a. und sich ⚡ v/refl. to tear (up); to rend (asunder), fig. to sever; Fäden ⁊c.: to break, path. Muskelbänder ⁊c.: to rupture; (zerfleischen) to lacerate, to mangle; in Stücke ⚡ to tear to pieces; to dismember; seine Ketten ⚡ to break (or burst) one's chains (auch fig.); viel Stiefel, Kleider ⚡ to wear out many …; fig. v. Mißtönen: e-m das Ohr ⚡ to grate (or jar) upon a p.'s ear; er würde sich für sie ⚡ lassen, etwa: he would go through fire and water for them; er ließe sich lieber in Stücke ⚡ he would rather be torn to pieces or rather suffer a martyrdom; zerrissen torn, rent, ⚡: ⚡ laciniate; in zerrissenen Kleidern tattered and torn, out at elbows; in zerrissenen Schuhen out at heels. — **II** v/n. (sn) (f. I) to tear, to rend, to be rent, von Fäden ⁊c.: to snap, to break, von Kleidern: to wear out; zerrissener Faden broken thread. — **III** ~ n ㉓ und **Zer-reißung** f ㊻ (f. I) tear(ing), rending, fig. severance, disruption; laceration; dismemberment; path. rupture.

zerren (⚹‿) [ahd.: tear] v/a., v/n. (h.), v/recip. und (‿‿‿) ⚡ to pull, to tug (an et. at a th.); (schleppen) to drag, haul, lug; beim Rocke ⚡ to pull by the coat-tail; in den Kot ⚡ to drag into (or through) the mud (a. fig.); e-m die Kleider vom Leibe ⚡ to drag (or tear) the clothes off a p.('s body); sich (mit⚹ea.) ⚡ to pull each other about, to (have a) scuffle or romp.

Zer-renn=herd (‿⚹‿) m ㉘ (Treibherd) refining-hearth. [tesque) figure.⎤
Zerr=gestalt (⚹.‿⚹) f ㉖ comical (or gro-⎦

zer-rinnen (‿‿‿) v/n. (sn) ⓽b(a)* to melt away, to dissolve; fig. to vanish (away); in ein Nichts ⚡ to dwindle away, to go to nothing, to fade away; Sprichw. s. gewinnen 1 am Schluß; ⚡d melting away, fig. evanescent.

zer-rissen (‿‿‿) p.p. von zerreißen (s. ds I); **⚡heit** f torn (or tattered) condition; eines Landes ⁊c.: dismemberment; (Zerlumptheit) raggedness; fig. bisw. = Weltschmerz.

zer-rühren (‿‿‿) v/a. ⑧* to stir to a pulp, to mix in stirring round, Kartoffeln ⁊c.: to mash, Eier: to beat up.

zer-rupfen (‿‿‿) v/a. ⑧* = zerpflücken.

zer-rütten (‿‿‿) **I** v/a. ⑧* to unsettle, to throw into disorder or confusion; fig. to disorganize, to break up; den Geist: to unhinge, derange, upset, die Gesundheit: to ruin, shatter, destroy. — **II** zer-rüttet p.p. u. a. ⑥ in disorder, confused, geistig: (mentally) deranged, distracted; zerrüttete Gesundheit shattered (or broken) health; in zerrütteten Verhältnissen in decayed circumstances, (financially) ruined; zerrütteter Zustand disorganized state. — **III Zer-rüttet-heit**, **Zer-rüttung** f ㊻ disorder, confusion; fig. disorganization; des Geistes: derangement, distraction.

zer-sägen (‿‿‿) v/a. ⑧* to saw to pieces, to saw through or asunder.

zer-schaben (‿‿‿), **zer-scharren** (‿‿‿) v/a. ⑧* to spoil (or wear out) by scraping, to scrape to pieces.

zer-schellen (‿‿‿) [mhd.] **I** v/a. dash to pieces, to shatter, shiver, smash, crush. — **II** v/n. (sn) to be dashed (or break) to pieces, to shiver (to atoms), ⚓ von Schiffen: to be wrecked, to split (on a rock).

zer-schießen (‿‿‿) v/a. ⑩c(es)t* to break (or smash) with a shot, to riddle (or pierce, wreck, destroy) with bullets, ⚔ ⚓ to pound away at, to batter to pieces, to bombard, to shell.

zer-schlagen (‿‿‿) v/a. und v/refl. ⑧b* 1. to knock (or break, dash) to pieces or F to smithereens, to batter, to smash (up); vom Hagel ⚡ (p.p.) beaten down by hail(stones). — 2. von Personen: (ganz) ⚡ sein to be bruised (all over); ich bin an allen Gliedern ⚡, oder: alle Glieder sind mir (wie) ⚡ I feel thoroughly knocked (or done) up. — 3. fig. große Güter ⚡ (zerteilen) to parcel out (or split, divide) large estates. — 4. fig. sich ⚡: a) von einem Handel ⁊c.: to fall to the ground, to come to nothing or to nought; (wieder zurückgehen) to be broken off; b) von seiner Hoffnung ⁊c.: to be disappointed; c) ⚡ v. e-m Gang: to branch out or off.

zer-schlitzen (‿‿‿) v/a. ⑨⓪* to slit up, to rive, ein Kleid, auch: to rend.

zer-schmeißen F (‿‿‿) v/a. ⓾a* to knock (or dash) to pieces, to smash (up or F to atoms). [schmelzen ⁊c.=⎦
zer-schmelzen (‿‿‿) ⑨⓪b* v/a. =⎤
zer-schmettern (‿‿‿) ⑨a* **I** v/a. to smash (up), to shatter (to pieces), to break to bits; (zermalmen) to crush;

mit zerschmettertem Leibe with every bone (in his body) broken. — **II** v/n. (sn) to get smashed, to (break with a) crash, F to go to smithereens.

zer-schneiden (‿‿‿) v/a. ⑨c* to cut in pieces, to cut (or carve) up, in kleine Stücke ⚡ to cut in(to) shreds, to shred, Fleisch ⁊c.: to mince (up), to chop into bits; (durchschneiden) to cut through; fig. e-m das Herz ⚡ to grieve a p. to the core, to cut a p. to the quick, to wring a p.'s heart; ein zerschnittener Faden a cut (or broken) thread; ⚡ fiederförmig zerschnitten: ⚡ pinnatisect. [schnippeln.⎦

zer-schnipp(f)eln (‿‿‿) ⑧a* = ⎤
zer-schroten (‿‿‿) v/a. ⑧* to bruise, to rough-grind; vgl. schroten 1b u. c.

zer-setzbar (‿‿‿) a. ⑥ decomposable; **⚡keit** f ㊻ decomposability.

zer-setzen (‿‿‿) **I** v/a. u. v/refl. ⑨⓪* chm., &c. (sich) ⚡ to decompose, disintegrate; sich ⚡ (vermittern), auch: to decay; (sich auflösen) to dissolve. — **II** ~ n ㉓ und **Zer-setzung** f ㊻ (s. I) decomposition, disintegration, decay, dissolution.

Zer-setzungs-kunst (‿‿…) f ㉖: ⚡ analysis; ⚡prozeß, ⚡vorgang m process of decomposition or disintegration.

zer-spalten (‿‿‿) v/a. ⑧* = spalten.

zer-splittern (‿‿‿) ⓽a* **I** v/a.u.v/refl.: e-e Lanze ⁊c. ⚡ to splinter … (a. surg.), to break … in(to) splinters, to shiver … (to pieces); ⚔ seine Truppen ⚡ to disperse (or scatter) one's troops, to divide (or split up) one's forces; fig. seine Kräfte (a. sich) ⚡ to fritter away one's strength, to dabble in too many things; zersplittert splintered, surg. auch: ⚡ comminuted; parl. eine zersplitterte Partei a divided (or disunited) party. — **II** v/n. (sn) und sich ⚡ v/refl. to splinter (a. surg.); to split (up), to disperse, von Bomben ⁊c.: to burst; s. a. I fig. — **III** ~ n ㉓ und **Zer-splitterung** f ㊻ splintering, &c. (s. I und II), ⚔ dispersal of troops, fig. frittering away one's means, &c.

zer-sprengen (‿‿‿) v/a. ⑧* to burst (open), to blast with gunpowder, &c., to blow up, to explode, weitS. = zerschlagen 1; ⚡de Kraft explosive force. — 2. eine Menschenmenge ⚡ to disperse (or scatter) a crowd, ⚔ Truppen: to rout. — 3. Saiten ⁊c. ⚡ to burst (or snap) …

zer-springen (‿‿‿) **I** v/n. (sn) ⓽st* to burst (or fly) asunder, v. Saiten: to break, von Holz ⁊c.: to split, von Glas auch: to crack (s. zerplatzen); fig. der Kopf will mir ⚡ my head is ready to burst or is splitting. — **II** ~ n ㉓ bursting (asunder), mit lautem Knall: explosion, path. eines Blutgefäßes ⁊c.: breaking, rupture.

zer-stampfen (‿‿‿) v/a. ⑧* to crush by stamping or with stamps (a. ⚙ u. ⚒), im Mörser: to pound, to bray, zu Pulver: to pulverize; auch = zertreten.

zer-stäuben (‿‿‿) ⑧* **I** v/a. to reduce to (or to turn into) dust, bsd. Wasser: to convert into spray; fig. to disperse, dispel, dissipate. — **II** v/n. (sn) to fall to dust, to turn into dust

♪ Musik; ⚡ Wissenschaft; ⚹ Pflanze; 🌐 Geographie; ⚙ Technik; ⚒ Bergbau; ⚔ Militär; ⚓ Marine; 🌐 Handel; 🖃 Post; 🚂 Eisenbahn.

[Zerstäuber] — 1150 — [Zettelträgerin]

or spray; ⚭ vom Quecksilber: 2 (sich in kleine Kügelchen brechen) to flour.
Zer-stäuber (⌣⌣́) m ㉒, **Zer-stäubungs-apparat** (⌣⌣́⌣⌣́) m ⑪c. ☉ spray-diffuser or -instrument, sprayer (a. ☉), med. a. vaporizer, atomizer.
zer-stechen (⌣⌣́) v/a. ㉘a* to pierce (with pricks), to prick (or sting) all over; v. Flöhen zerstochen flea-bitten, covered with flea-bites.
zer-stieben (⌣⌣́) v/n. (fn) ㉘a☉* to fly away (like dust), to vanish. von Personen: to disperse; und wie vom Sturm zerstoben ist all der Hörer Schwarm (v.) his hearers all are scattered as if by a mighty storm.
zer-störbar (⌣⌣́) a. ⓖ destructible, perishable; ~keit f ㊻ destructibility.
zer-stören (⌣⌣́) I v/a. ㉘* to destroy, Gebäude ꝛc.: to demolish, to pull down; (niederwerfen) to overthrow, nur fig. to subvert; (in Trümmer legen) to wreck, (verwüsten) to lay waste, ravage, devastate; (zugrunde richten) to (bring to) ruin, (vernichten) to annihilate, overthrow, undo, Hoffnungen: to frustrate, dissipate, blight; ⚭ die Telegraphendrähte 2 to cut the wires; 2d destructive; (Umsturz bewirkend) subversive; zerstörte Gesundheit ruined (or broken, shattered) health. — II ~ n ㉓ f. Zerstörung.
Zer-störer (⌣⌣́) m ㉒, ~**in** f ㊻ destroyer, demolisher, wrecker, von Häusern auch: housebreaker, vandal, (Bilderstürmer) ⚛ iconoclast; fig. subverter.
Zer-störung (⌣⌣́) f ㊻ (f. zerstören I) destruction, demolition; overthrow, fig. subversion; ravaging, ravages pl. (of time, &c.); ruin, havoc wrought on; die ~ Karthagos the fall of Carthage.
Zer-störungs-geist (⌣⌣́...) m ㉒ spirit of destruction, destructive spirit; vgl. ⸗trieb; **⸗krieg** m war of destruction; **⸗sinn, ⸗trieb** m destructiveness, mit Bezug auf Kunstwerke: vandalism, eccl. hist.: ⚛ iconoclasm; **⸗werk** n work of destruction; (Verwüstung) devastation; **⸗wut** f = ⸗trieb.
zer-stoßen (⌣⌣́) ㉘a* I v/a. to knock to pieces, to bruise, in e-m Mörser: to pound, to bray; vgl. zerreiben. — II sich 2 v/refl. to hurt o.s., v. Sachen: to break (through rough wear), to get knocked off or battered about.
zer-streuen (⌣⌣́) I v/a. und v/refl. ㉘* 1. (ausstreuen) to disseminate, to scatter; (verschwinden m.) to dissipate; (vertreiben) to dispel, (aus-ea.-treiben) to disperse; j-s Gedanken 2 (abziehen) to divert (or turn off) a p.'s attention, auch: to take a p. off his guard. — 2. e-n 2 (belustigen) to divert (or amuse) a p.; sich 2 to seek diversion or recreation, to enjoy o.s. — II ~ n ㉓ 3. f. Zerstreuung.
zer-streut (⌣⌣́) a. ⓖ 1. scattered, dispersed; detached (house, &c.), straggling (village, &c.), loose (papers, &c.); 2e Bevölkerung sparse (or roving) population; 2e Gedanken wandering (or rambling) thoughts pl. — 2. (nhd. nach fr. distrait) (mit den Gedanken abwesend) absent-minded, thinking of

other things, F wool-gathering; stärker: distracted; 2 aussehen (sein), auch: to look (to be) absent-minded or inattentive; 2es Wesen = Zerstreutheit.
Zer-streut-heit (⌣⌣́) f ㊻ absent-mindedness, absence of mind, inattentiveness, lack of attention, F wool-gathering; stärker: distractedness.
Zer-streu-ung (⌣⌣́) f ㊻ (f. zerstreuen) 1. scattering (about), dissemination, dissipation; dispersal, phys. von Lichtstrahlen ꝛc.: divergence. — 2. (Erholung) diversion (of one's thoughts), distraction, recreation, amusement; sich ~ m. ob. verschaffen to amuse o.s., F to go out pleasuring; ~ suchen to seek diversion, F to go (out) pleasure-making.
Zer-streuungs-bild (⌣⌣́...) n ㉒ opt. virtual image; **⸗glas** n, **⸗linse** f, opt. diverging-glass, -lens; **⸗punkt** m, opt. point of divergence; **⸗sucht** f mania (or great love) for amusement(s); **2süchtig** a. ⓖ (madly) fond of amusement(s), pleasure-hunting; **⸗vermögen** n, phys. dispersive power.
zer-stücke(l)n (⌣⌣́) I v/a. ㉘(㉒a)* to cut into (little) pieces or bits or morsels, mit dem Hackmesser: to chop up, fein: to mince; to cut up (auch Schlächterei), e-n Leib: to dismember (a. fig.); (zerteilen) to divide, to parcel out, Gitter a.: to partition; zerstückelt, oft: piecemeal. — II ~ n ㉓ und **Zer-stück[e]lung** f ㊻ cutting, &c. (f. I); dismemberment; parcelling (out), einer Erbschaft ꝛc.: partition.
Zertamen (⌣⌣́⌣́) [lt.] n ㉓ Schule: competitive (class-)examination; theme for (class-)competition; vgl. zertieren.
zer-tanzen (⌣⌣́) v/a. ㊼* Kleider ꝛc.: to wear out (or ruin) in dancing.
zer-teilbar (⌣⌣́) a. ⓖ divisible, ~**keit** f ㊻ divisibleness, divisibility.
zer-teilen (⌣⌣́) I v/a. und v/refl. ㉘* 1. to divide; (zerspalten) to split up; (zerstückeln) to cut up, to dismember; sich 2 to be divided, to divide (o.s.), med. to disperse; die Wolken 2 sich the clouds are dispersing, it is clearing up; 2des Mittel resolvent. — 2. (teilend zerlegen) Begriffe ꝛc.: to analyse, mech., &c. Kräfte ꝛc.: to decompose, math. zj. ⸗gesetzte Größen: to resolve into factors, to factorize. — 3. (zergehen m.) to dissolve. — II ~ n ㉓ und **Zer-teilung** f ㊻ 4. (f. 1) division; dismemberment, med. dispersal; resolution of a tumour, &c.; (f. 2) analysis; mech., &c. decomposition of forces, &c.; math. resolution into factors; (f. 3) dissolution; **Zer-teilungs-mittel** n, med.: ⚛ resolvent, dispersive, discutient.
zertieren (⌣⌣́) [lt.] I v/n. (h.) ㊼ Schule: (wetteifern) to compete (for a place or prize). — II ~ n ㉓ = Zertamen.
Zertifikat (⌣⌣⌣́) [lt.] n ⑪c. (Zeugnis) certificate; ein ~ ausstellen ob. **zertifizieren** (⌣⌣⌣́) [lt.] v/a. to certify.
zer-trampeln (⌣⌣́) v/a. ㉒a* to trample down or under foot; f. zertreten.
zer-trennen (⌣⌣́) v/a. und sich 2 v/refl. ㉘* = trennen, ein Kleid 2 to rip up.
zer-treten (⌣⌣́) ㉘d* 1. to crush (or tread) under foot; f. zertrampeln.

— 2. fig. (mit Füßen treten) to crush under one's heel(s). [demolisher.]
Zer-trümmerer (⌣⌣́⌣) m ㉒ destroyer,]
zer-trümmern (⌣⌣́) ㉒a* I v/a. to lay in ruins, to wreck, to demolish, weitS. = zerschlagen 1 und zerstören I. — II v/n. (fn) to break (to pieces). — III ~ n ㉓ und **2/ung** f ㊻ wreckage, demolition; havoc wrought on; (Zerstörung) destruction.
Zervelat-wurst (⌣w⌣́...) [lt.⸗dtsch] f ㉒, etwa: (superior kind of) saveloy.
zer-waschen (⌣⌣́) ㉘b* to wash linen, &c. to rags, to spoil (or ruin) clothes, &c. by washing. [der.]
zer-wehen (⌣⌣́) v/a. ㉘* to blow asun-]
zer-wühlen (⌣⌣́) v/a. ㉘* to root (or grub) up; (durchstöbern) to rummage in a chest full of clothes, &c.; mit zerwühltem Haar with dishevelled hair.
Zer-würfnis (⌣⌣́) n ⑰ difference (of opinion), dissension, disagreement, discord; (Streit) strife, quarrel, dispute.
zer-zausen (⌣⌣́) v/a. ㉘* = zausen; (zerknittern) to crumple, to crease; fig. e-n tüchtig 2 to pull a p. about, to handle a p. roughly; von Kleidern: zerzaust creased, disarranged, (zerrissen) torn.
zer-zupfen (⌣⌣́) v/a. ㉘* to pick (or pull) to pieces or to rags or to threads.
Zession (⌣⌣́) [lt.] f ㊻ jur. assignment, transfer, cession; von Ansprüchen: abandonment of claims; vgl. zedieren.
Zessionar (⌣⌣⌣́⸗) [lt.] m ⑨d. jur. (Bevollmächtigter) assignee, transferee.
Zessions-akte (⌣⌣́⌣...), **⸗urkunde** f ㊻ jur. deed of assignment or transfer.
Zetaze-e (⸗⌣⸗tiʒ́⸗) [lt.] f ㊻ (Fischsäugetier) sg. cetacean, ~n pl. cetacea pl.
Zeter! (⌣́⌣) int. und **Zeter** (⌣́⌣) [(mhd.) nbd.] n ㉓ cry of distress, cry for help, 2 (und Mord) schreien to cry murder, to raise an outcry; 2 (a. ~) über e-n schreien: a) to raise a hue and cry after a p.; b) to cry shame upon a p.; **~geschrei** [mhd.], **~mordio** n ㉒ = Zeter, a. loud shouts pl. (for help), (loud) outcry; **2-mordio!** int. murder!, (stop) thief!
zetern (⌣́⌣) v/n. (h.) ㊼a. to raise an outcry after (or against) a p.; (schimpfen) to storm, to utter (forth) a volley of abuse.
Zettel¹ (⌣́⌣) [mhd.: schedule; *it. f] m ㉒ slip (or scrap) of paper, bedruckter: handbill, beschriebener: note, zum Anhängen: label (auch ✱), zum Ankleben: ticket (a. ✱), zum Anschlagen: placard, bill, poster, (Theater⸗)~ play-bill; (Wahl⸗)~ voting-paper; mit einem ~ versehen to label, to ticket (auch ✱); Anschlag: hier dürfen keine ~ angeklebt w.! stick no bills!; vgl. anschlagen.
Zettel² ☉ (⌣́⌣) [mhd.: ted] m ㉒ Weberei: (Kette) chain, warp.
Zettel¹⸗ankleber(in f) m (⌣́⌣...) ㉒, **⸗anschläger(in** f) m ⑪ bill-sticker or -poster; **⸗anschlagen** n bill-sticking; das ~ ist verboten! bill-stickers beware!, stick no bills (here)!; **⸗bank** f bank of issue; **⸗²baum** ☉ warpbeam; **⸗stößer** m warp-cop. [anzetteln.]
zetteln (⌣́⌣) [mhd.: ted] v/a. ☉ u. fig.=]
Zettel¹⸗träger(in f) m (⌣́⌣...) ㉒ distributer of bills, person carrying (or

[Zettelwahl]

distributing) bills, m bisw. bill-boy; =wahl f election by means of voting-papers, (election by) ballot, balloting. zeuch, fast † (¹) 2. Person des imper., zeuchse 2. u. zeucht 3. Person sg. pres. ind. von ziehen.

Zeug (¹) [ahd.: toy; *ziehen] n (m) ⓓc.
1. stuff, material; gewebtes: textile material, fabric, ⊕ textile goods pl.; (Tuch) cloth; f. Leinw. u. Weißzeug; gewürfelte ~e checked goods, checks pl.; seidene ~e silk goods, silks pl.; (Kleidungsstücke) clothes, garments, F togs pl. — 2. a) ⊕ utensils, implements pl., (Handwerkszeug) tools pl.; mach. gear; gehendes ~ machinery; metall. ore to be smelted; Bäckerei: α) Teig; β) (Backpulver) baking powder; (Aufsatzhefe) baker's yeast; Papierfabr.: (die zerstampften Lumpen) pulp; Schriftgießerei, typ.: (Schrift)~ m und n type-metal; b) ⚓, ⚔ tackle, tackling. — 3. (Geschirr für Reit- und Wagenpferde) harness(ing), trappings pl. — 4. hunt. = Jagdgerät. — 5. Haushaltung: (cooking-)utensils, pots and pans pl.; irdenes ~ (Geschirr) crockery(-ware). — 6. fig. ~ oder ~s inv. contp. (Kollektiv zu Ding) things, sundries, F concerns pl.; albernes ~ (foolish or silly) stuff, trash, stuff and nonsense; allerhand ~ all sorts of stuff or rubbish; s. dumm 2; iro. das ist schönes ~ that's a nice business; tolles ~ treiben to do silly things, to carry on mad pranks; wertloses ~ trash, rubbish. — 7. Redensarten: a) das ~ (die Anlagen) haben zu // to have the qualifications (or the ability) required for //; sie hat das ~ zu einer Schauspielerin she is cut out for an actress, F she has the making (or the stuff) of an actress in her; er hat nicht das ~ dazu he is not the man for it; b) F was das ~ hält oder halten will (soviel irgend angeht) with might and main, with a mighty pull, F with a vengeance; c) s. flicken² am Schluß; d) ins ~ (Geschirr) geh(e)n od. sich legen od. sich werfen (mit Eifer vorgehen) to put one's shoulder(s) to the wheel, to set to (work) with a will.

Zeug=amt ⚔ (¹¹...) n ⓑ² ordnance department; =baum ⊕ m Weberei: (weaver's) cloth-beam; =bütte f Papierfabr.: pulp-vat; =druck m cloth- (or calico-)printing, printing of textile goods; =drucker ⊕ m cloth- (or calico-)printer; =druckerei f print-works pl. Zeuge (¹) [mhd.: ziehen] m ⒠, Zeugin f ⒡ (male, f female) witness, (one who gives) evidence; falscher ~ false witness; vereidigter ~ sworn witness; vor zwei ~n in the presence of two witnesses; e-n zum ~n nehmen (od. anrufen) to take a p. to (or to call a p. as) witness; ~ sein von et. to be witness of a th., to witness a th.; to be present at a th.; s. stellen 6; et. als ~ unterschreiben to witness a th. zeugen¹ (¹) [mhd.: team; *Zeug] I v/a. 1. ⊕ to engender, Kinder: to beget, procreate; weitS. = erzeugen 2; ⒮ generative, procreative; die ~den the parents pl. — II ~ n ⓑ s. Zeugung.

zeugen² (¹⌣) [mhd.; *Zeuge] v/n. (h.) ⓑ to (appear as) witness, to give evidence for (or against) a p.; to testify (or bear witness) to a th., bsd. jur. to depose (to) a th. (in a court of law); fig. ⓑ von to show, to prove; die Verse ⓑ von dichterischer Gabe ... are evidence (or give proof) of ...

Zeugen=abhörung (¹¹...) f ⓑ² Gericht: =verhör; =aussage f evidence (or deposition, testimony) of a witness; =bestechung f suborning (or corruption) of witnesses; =beweis m proof by (sworn) evidence; =eid m oath of a witness; ⒠eidlich a. ⓑ Le Vernehmung examination of sworn witnesses; =gebühren f/pl. fees pl. paid to a witness. Zeug(en)schaft (¹(⌣)⌣) f ⓑ deposition (of witnesses), (sworn) evidence. Zeugen=stand (¹¹...) m ⓑ² Gerichtshof: witness-box; =verhör n, =vernehmung f vor Gericht ꝛc.: hearing (or examination) of witnesses, taking evidence.

Zeuger (¹¹) m ⒠, ~in f ⒡ = Erzeuger. Zeug=fabrik (¹¹...) f ⓑ² (=fabrikant m) manufactory (manufacturer) of textile fabrics; =handel ⊕ m textile trade; =haus ⚔ n arsenal, armoury; =hausverwalter ⚔, ehm. =herr m superintendent of the arsenal; =kammer f: a) tool-room; b) ⚔ armoury; =kapitän ⚓ m officer who directs the (ship's) ordnance; =karren ⊕ m Papierfabr.: paper-pulp cart; =kasten m: a) linen-chest; b) Papierfabr.: stuff-chest; c) typ. batter-box; =kiste f, typ. hell-box; vgl. =kasten c; =laus f = Kleiderlaus.

Zeugma ⚉ (¹⌣) [grch.] n ⓑ ⓑ gr. (Verbindung von zwei Subjekten mit einem Prädikat, das nur zu einem Subjekt paßt) zeugma.

Zeug=meister ⚔ (¹¹⌣) m ⓑ² master of (the) ordnance; vgl. Feldzeugmeister.

Zeugnis (¹⌣) [mhd.; *zeugen²] n ⓑ² 1. (bezeugende Aussage) witness, testimony, vor Gericht auch: evidence, deposition (s. ablegen 5); jur. zu(m) ~ dessen in witness whereof; bibl. du sollst kein falsch(es) ~ reden wider deinen Nächsten thou shalt not bear false witness against thy neighbour. — 2. (schriftliche Bescheinigung) certificate, attestation, über das Betragen, bsd. von Dienstboten: character, bsd. über gute Führung: testimonial, in Schulen auch: good conduct-marks pl.; (Schul=)~ school-certificate, vgl. Zensur 2; ~ der Reife = Maturitätszeugnis; e-m ein gutes ~ geben to give a p. a good reference or character.

Zeugnis=ablegung (¹¹...) f ⓑ² giving (legal) evidence, (making a) deposition; =brief m, etwa: letter of recommendation, testimonial; =verweigerung f jur. v. Zeitungen: refusal to give the name of a contributor as evidence; =zwang m der Redakteure ꝛc.: obligation to give evidence or to divulge the authorship of a newspaper article.

Zeug=offizier ⚓ (¹¹...) m ⓑ² = =kapitän; =presse ⊕ f clothes-press, calender; =pressen n calendering; mangling; =rolle f = Mange; =schmied ⊕ m tool-smith, edge-tool maker; =schmiede f tool-smithy; =schmiede=arbeit f tool-making or -smithery; =schuhe, =stiefel

[Ziegeldach]

m/pl. cloth shoes, boots pl.; =tapete f tapestry. Zeugung (¹⌣) [mhd.] f ⓑ physiol. (das Zeugen) generation, procreation. zeugungs=fähig (¹¹...) a. ⓑ capable of begetting; generative, procreative; (fruchtbar) prolific; =fähigkeit f ⓑ procreative faculty, procreativeness; =glied n, anat. genital member; =kraft f generative (or procreative) power; =organe, =teile n/pl. generative (or genital) organs, privy parts pl.; =trieb m procreative (or sexual) instinct; =unfähig a. impotent; =unfähigkeit f impotency; =vermögen n = =kraft. Zeug=wagen (¹¹...) m ⓑ hunt. cart for conveying requisites for hunting; =waren ⊕ f/pl. textile fabrics pl.; ehm. =wärter ⚔ m inspector of an arsenal, =weber, =wirker ⊕ m weaver (or manufacturer) of textile goods.

Zeus (¹) [grch.] npr/m. ⓑγ. myth. (Götterkönig) Zeus, mehr gbr.: Jupiter; beim ~! by Jove!, F by jingo! z. H. abbr. = zu Händen, zuhanden: (in) care of, to be delivered to.

Zibebe (¹⌣) [it.; *ar. Traube] f ⓑ (große Rosinenart) large raisin.

Zibet (⌣¹) [it., *ar.] m ⓓc. (moschusartige Absonderung der Zibetkatze) civet, zibetum; ~=katze, ~=tier ⓑ zo. civet-cat (Vive'rra cive'tta); ~=maus f, zo. = Bisamratte.

Zichori=e (⌣¹(⌣)⌣) [it., grch., *ägypt.] f ⓑ: a) ♀ chicory, succory (Cicho'rium i'ntybus); b) ⓑ (Kaffeesurrogat) chicory; ⒠n=artig (⌣¹¹(⌣)⌣) ♀ a. cichoraceous; ~n=kaffee ⊕ m ⓑ² roasted chicory.

Zicke P (¹⌣) [ahd.] f ⓑ = Ziege; in guter Rede gbr. als dim. Zickel (¹⌣) n ⓑ², Zickelchen (¹⌣⌣) n ⓑ (little) kid. zickeln (¹⌣) v/n. (h.) ⓑ a. v. Ziegen: to kid. Zicklein (¹⌣) [mhd.] n ⓑ f. Zicke.

zickzack (¹¹) [fr., *dtsch] I adv. (in) ⚐ zigzag. — II ~ m (n) ⓓc. ⚐ zigzag (line), crinkum-crankum; ⚓ im ~ segeln to tack about; ⚓ laufen, im ~ laufen to run zigzag, von Hasen: to double.

Zickzack=blitz (¹¹...) m ⓑ fork-lightning; ⒠förmig a. ⓑ zigzag-shaped; zickzackig (¹¹⌣⌣) a. ⓑ (shaped in) zigzag. Zickzack=lini=e (¹¹⌣(⌣)⌣) f ⓑ² zigzag line. Ziber f [fr.; *hebr. Rausch] m ⓑ (Apfelwein) cider; ~=essig m = cidervinegar; ~=fabrikant m cider-maker.

Zieche prov. (¹⌣) [ahd.: tick; lt. (*grch.) theca] f ⓑ = Bettüberzug.

Ziege (¹) [ahd.] f ⓑ zo. und Viehzucht: she-goat, F nanny-goat (Capra); junge ~ = Zicklein (f. Zicke).

Ziegel ⊕ (¹⌣) [ahd.: tile; lt. te'gula f] m ⓑ Bauwesen: 1. (Mauer=)~ brick; ~ brennen to make (or burn) bricks. — 2. (Dachziegel) tile; mit ~n decken to cover (or roof) with tiles, to tile. Ziegel=arbeit (¹¹...) f ⓑ: a) brickwork; b) (Pflastern mit Ziegeln) tiling; =arbeiter m = Ziegler; ⒠artig a. like a tile, ⚉ tegular; =bau m brick structure or building; =brennen n burning of bricks or tiles, brickmaking; =brenner m brick- (or tile-)maker; f. auch Brenner 2; =brennerei f: a) = =ofen; b) = Ziegelei a; =dach

⚉ scientific; ♀ botanical; ⚐ geography; ⊕ machinery; ⚔ mining; ⚔ military; ⚓ marine; ⊕ commercial; ⊕ postal; ⛭ railway.

[ziegeldachförmig] — 1152 — [ziehen]

n tiled roof; ̰dach=förmig ̰ a. ⊕ ⚭ imbricate(d); =decker m tiler.

Ziegelei (-́-́) f ⊕: a) brick- (or tile-) yard or field, tile-works pl.; b) = Ziegelofen; ~arbeiter m = Ziegler; ~besitzer m owner of a brick-yard, proprietor of tile-works.

Ziegel=erde ⊙ (́̆-...) f ⊕ brick-clay or -earth; =erz ⚹ n red copper-ore; =farben, =farbig a. ⊕ brick-coloured, med.: ⚬ latericeous; =form f brick- (or tile-)mould; =(form)maschine f =presse; =hütte f = =brennerei; =mauer f brick wall; =mauerung f brick-masonry; =maurerei f brick-laying; =mehl n brick-dust; =meister m = Ziegler; =ofen m brick- (or tile-)kiln; =presse f brick-machine; =rohbau m bricking, vgl. =werk; =rot a. brick-red; vgl. =farben; =stein m brick; =streichen n brick- (or tile-)moulding or making; =streicher m brick-, tile-moulder or -maker; =werk f brick-work.

ziegen=artig (́̆-...) a. ⊕ zo. goat-like, goatish, ⚬ caprid, caprine. capriform; =artigkeit f ⊕ goatishness; =auge n: a) goat's eye; b) path. (Geschwür im inneren Augenwinkel) ⚬ ægilops; =bart m: a) von Ziegen: beard of a goat; b) von Menschen: imperial, seltener: F co. goatee; =bock m: a) he-goat, F billy-goat; b) P fig. (Schneider) snip; =böckchen n young he-goat; =fell n goat's skin, goatskin; =fleisch n goat's flesh; =fuß m goat's foot; =füßig a. with goat's feet, ⚬ capriped; =hainer [Ziegenhain ♀. Dorf bei Jena] m stout knotty stick; =hären a. (made) of goat's hair; =hirt m goatherd, goat-keeper; =käse m cheese made from goat's milk, goatcheese; =lab n goat's rennet; =lamm n kid; =leder ♥ n goat's leather, kid (-leather); =melker m: a) person who milks goats; b) orn. europäischer ~ goatsucker, a. goat-milker or -owl (Caprimu'lgus Europae'us); =milch f goat's milk; =peter m, path. (Entzündung der Ohrspeicheldrüsen) mumps; =pferch m goat-fold; =stall m shed for goats, a. goat-fold; =stein m, pharm. bezoar; =weide ♀ f goat-willow (Salix ca'prea).

Zieger (́̆-) [Ziege] m ⊕ (festere Masse im Käsewasser) solid component of curdled milk; vgl. Schab2.

Ziegler ⊙ (́̆-) [Ziegel] m ⊕ (master) brick- (or tile-)maker.

zieh(́) ind.impf.v.ziehen; imper.v.ziehen.

Zieh=arm ⊙ (́̆...) m ⊕ crank; =band n: a) ribbon (or rope) by which to pull a th. along; b) ⊙ (eisernes Band) iron band or clamp, Stellmacherei: tire-clip; =bank f Büchsenmacherei: rifling-bench or -machine; Drahtzieherei: wire-drawing bench; Glaserei: glazier's bench; carp. draw-horse.

ziehbar (́-) a. ⊕ phys. u. ⊙ von Metallen: ductile; ~keit f ⊕ ductility.

Zieh=brücke (́̆...) f ⊕ = Zugbrücke; =brunnen m draw-well; =eisen ⊙ n Drahtzieherei: wire-drawing iron or plate.

ziehen (́̆-) [ahd.: tie, tow: lt. du´cer] ⊕ b. I v/a. 1. to draw, zu sich heran: to pull, (schleppen) to drag, meist F to lug, bjp. ↓

to haul, to tow a ship, &c.; (anziehen) to attract; heftig ⚬ to give a strong (or hearty) pull; abs. (verlockend sein) to be attractive or charming or fascinating. F to draw, vgl. 7 b thea.; pharm. das Pflaster zieht gut the plaster draws well. — 2. (Redewendungen) mit nouns: (tief) Atem ⚬ to draw (a deep) breath; hort. Bäume ⚬ to rear (or nurse) trees; ⊙ die Bilanz ⚬ to strike (or make up) the balance; med. Blasen ⚬, auch: abs. ⚬ (von einem Zugpflaster) to (bring up a) blister; Blumen ⚬ to grow (or cultivate) flowers; ↓ ein Boot ⚬ to tow (or pull, haul) a boat (along); ⊙ den Draht ⚬ to draw wire; ⊙ Federn ⚬ to dress feathers or quills; eine Fratze ⚬ to make grimaces; Geld aus einer Bank ⚬ to draw money (from a bank); ein schiefes Gesicht ⚬ to pull a long face, to make a grimace; agr. Furchen ⚬ to make furrows; ⊙ Waffenfabr.: ein Geschützrohr ⚬ (mit Zügen versehen) to rifle a gun; die Glocke ⚬ to pull (or ring) the bell; einen Graben ⚬ to make a ditch, to dig a trench; ein Kind ⚬ (groß ⚬, vgl. 3) to bring up a child; vgl. a. erziehen; s. kurz 3 am Schluß; s. Licht 5; eine Linie ⚬ to draw a line; s. Los 1; eine Mauer ⚬ to build (or construct) a wall; s. Nase 3 gegen Ende; Lotterie: eine Niete ⚬ to draw a blank; Fischerei: ein Schleppnetz ⚬ to drag a net; das Schwert ⚬ to draw the sword; s. Schluß 6 am Ende; geom. eine Senkrechte ⚬ to draw (or drop) a perpendicular (line); Brettspiel: einen Stein, eine Figur, auch abs. ⚬ to move a piece, im Schach auch: to move (one of the men); Telegraphendraht ⚬ to stretch telegraph wire; fig. einen Vergleich ⚬ zwischen zwei Dingen: to draw (or make) a comparison between ...; Vieh ⚬ to breed (or raise, rear) cattle; e-n Wagen ⚬ to draw (or pull) a carriage; Wasser ⚬ to draw water; der Schwamm zieht Wasser ... draws in (or sucks up) water; die Sonne zieht Wasser ... attracts (or absorbs, draws up) the water; die Stiefel ⚬ Wasser ... let in (the) water; ↓ das Schiff zieht Wasser ... leaks, ... has sprung a leak; ♥ einen Wechsel ⚬ to make out (or draw, issue) a bill (of exchange). — 3. mit adjectives u. adverbs: fest, stramm ⚬ to pull tight(ly), to tighten; groß ⚬ to rear (or train, bring up) a child; von Wagen: leicht zu ⚬ of easy draught. — 4. mit prp.: an et. ⚬ to pull (at) a th., to tug at a th.; e-n am Ärmel ⚬ to pull (or pluck) a p. by the sleeve; e-n an (od. bei) den Haaren ⚬ to pull a p. by the hair, to pull a p.'s hair; s. Strang 2 am Schluß; ↓ ans Land ⚬ to haul a boat, &c. ashore; hort. s. Spalier 1; an sich ⚬ to attract, to draw towards one or o.s., zum eigenen Vorteile: to monopolize, to usurp; auf sich ⚬ to draw upon o.s.; j-s Blicke auf sich ⚬ to attract a p.'s glances; ⚔ das Feuer des Feindes auf sich ⚬ to draw the enemy's fire;

auf e-n Faden ⚬ to (string on a) thread; s. Flasche 1; Saiten auf die Geige ⚬ to put (new) strings on (or to string) the violin; e-n auf die Seite (oder beiseite) ⚬ to draw a p. aside; einen auf seine Seite ⚬ to draw (or bring) a p. over to one's side; et. aus dem Wasser ⚬ to pull (or haul) a th. out of the water; den Kork oder Pfropfen aus einer Flasche ⚬ to take the cork out of (or to uncork) a bottle; viel Geld, Gewinn aus et. ⚬ to derive large profits from a th.. to make much money by a th.; s. Nutzen am Ende; er weiß aus allem Vorteil zu ⚬ he knows how to turn everything to account; ich werde mir eine Lehre daraus ⚬ it will be a lesson to me, I shall take it to heart; s. Schlinge 1 b fig. u. Nase 3 unter „aus"; et. aus=ea. ⚬: a) et. Elastisches: to pull a th.: b) et. Verbundenes: to pick (or pull) a th. apart or asunder; ein Band durch ein Schnürloch ⚬ to pass a lace through an eye(let); Flachs, fig. e-n durch die Hechel ⚬ = durchhecheln I; durch (oder in) den Kot (oder Schmutz) ⚬ to drag into (or through) the mud or mire; a. to blacken a p.'s character, &c.; in sich ⚬ (schlürfen) to absorb, Wasser &c.: to suck up, to imbibe; in Beratung ⚬ to deliberate upon; in Betracht ob. Erwägung ⚬ to take into consideration; s. Falte 1; e-n ins Geheimnis ⚬ to let a p. into the (or to confide a p. one's) secret; in die Höhe ⚬ to hoist (or pull) up; e-n in sein Interesse ⚬ to attach a p. to one's interest(s). to obtain a p.'s support; ins Lächerliche ⚬ (turn into) ridicule; s. Länge 2; e-n ins Unglück ⚬ to involve a p. in a misfortune, F to drag a p. in(to an unfortunate affair); e-n ins Vertrauen ⚬ to take a p. into (one's) confidence; in Zweifel ⚬ to be in doubt about, to doubt, to (call in) question; fig. nach sich ⚬ to bring on, to cause, entail, involve, to be attended with; ernste Folgen nach sich ⚬ to have serious consequences; ein Kleid über das andere ⚬ to put one dress over another; fig. s. Fell 2 am Schluß; den Hut über das Gesicht ⚬ to pull one's hat over one's eyes; einen Schleier über et. ⚬ to draw a veil over a th.; von: einem die Larve vom Gesicht ⚬ to tear the mask from a p.'s face. to unmask a p.; Vorteil von et. ⚬ to derive advantage from a th.. to benefit by a th.; e-n vor Gericht ⚬ to summon (F to haul) a p. before a court of law; s. Hut 1; e-n zu sich ⚬ to attract a p.; zu Boden ⚬ (or weigh) down; sich et. zu Herzen, zu Gemüte ⚬ to take a th. to heart; einen zu Rate ⚬ to consult a p.; e-n zur Strafe ⚬ to inflict a punishment (or a fine) upon a p.; e-n zur Tafel ⚬ to invite a p. to dinner or to one's table; zur Verantwortung ⚬ to call to account. — II sich ⚬ v/refl. 5. von Stoffen &c.: to stretch; ⊙ = werfen 6; sich ⚬ lassen to stretch, ⊙ to be ductile. — 6. das

Zeichen (f. S. XVII): F familiär; P Volkssprache; Г Gaunersprache; ⚹ selten; † alt (auch gestorben); * neu (auch geboren); ⚹ unrichtig;

[Zieher] — 1153 — [ziemlich]

Gebirge zieht (erstreckt) sich bis an den Fluß the mountains extend (or stretch) as far as the river; diese Vorstellungen 2 sich durch das ganze Buch ... continue (or run) through the whole book; sich in et. 2 (in et. eindringen) to penetrate into a th., von Flüssigkeiten: to soak into a th.; sich nach et. 2 (gestalten) to shape o.s. after a th.; Strümpfe 2 sich nach dem Fuße stockings take the shape of (or give to) the foot; sich wohin 2 (begeben) to move to a place; der Leim zieht sich (zu Fäden) the glue (all) goes to threads, auch: the glue is ropy. — **III** v n. (h., bei Ortsveränderung sn) 7. a) = 2 1 u. 2 abs.; b) mit zu ergänzendem Objekt: der Tee muß noch eine kleine Weile 2 the tea must draw a little while longer; den Tee 2 lassen to let the tea draw; der Kamin zieht (gut) the chimney draws well or has a good draught; der Schraubenzieher zieht schlecht the screw-driver does not bite well; thea. das Stück zieht gut the play draws (large audiences); fig. dieser Grund zieht bei mir nicht that reason does not weigh (or F go down) with me; die Sache zieht nicht .. has no effect, .. does not answer; s. unter 2 Blasen 2 und einen Stein 2. — **8.** mit prp. statt des Objekts, zB. an einem Karren 2 to drag (or pull) a cart (along); Schach: mit dem Könige 2 to move the king; ⚔ vom Leder 2 to draw one's sword. — **9.** impers. es zieht (herrscht Zugluft) hier there is a draught here, it is draughty here; es zieht durch diese Tür there is a draught at (or a draught comes through) that door; path. es zieht mir (ob. mich) in der Schulter I have twitches or (rheumatic) pains in the shoulder. — **10.** burschikos: (trinken) to take (a good) draught, to imbibe, to drink. — **11.** Spiel: 2 wer gibt to cut for the deal. — **12.** (sn) (stetig vorrücken, sich fortbewegen): a) to move (by degrees), to march along (slowly); gezogen kommen to come (marching) along (in einem Haufen in a body), von Volksstämmen, Vögeln ꝛc.: to migrate; (in) die Kreuz und Quer 2 to travel hither and thither, to rove (in all directions); laß(t) mich 2! let me depart (in peace)! s-r Wege 2 to go one's way, to pursue one's journey; b) mit prp.: auf die Messe 2 to go (or travel) to the fair; s. Wache 1 a; die Wolken 2 aus Süden ... are travelling (or coming) from the south; in das Feld, den Krieg 2 to take the field, to go to the war(s); in die Fremde 2 to go abroad; der Rauch zieht ins Zimmer ... is coming into the room; nach Hause 2 to return homeward, to make for home; die Vögel 2 nach Süden the birds are flying southward or are bound for the south; übers Meer 2 to cross (or to travel across) the sea; c) (sine Wohnung verändern) to (re)move (to new quarters), to change one's residence or apartments; auf ein anderes Zimmer 2 to take another room; aus einem Orte 2 to remove from (or leave, quit) a place; in ein Haus 2 to move (or go) into a house; in die Stadt 2 to go to live in the town; zu e-m 2 to go to live with a p.; d) von Dienstboten: aus einem Dienst 2 to leave a situation; in e-n Dienst 2 to go into (or to take) a situation or place. — **IV** ~ n 23 **13.** drawing, pull, haul, tug, &c. (s. I). von Karren ꝛc. auch: draught, bsd. 🜚 und mach. traction by steam, by electricity. &c.; ⚓ hauling, towage of boats; Pferd zum ~ draught-horse; ~ von Blumen ꝛc.: cultivation, von Kindern: rearing, training, education; in Brettspielen: move; (Anziehung) attraction, charm. — **14.** (s. II) draught of a chimney. &c.; thea. attractiveness (or run) of a play; path. ~ (Reißen) in den Gliedern twitches, (rheumatic) pains pl. — **15.** (s. III) (Wandern) migration, von Vögeln, auch: passage; (Reisen) travelling; (Umziehen) removal, change of residence or apartments. — **V** ge-zogen p.p. u. a 🜚 (D9) **16.** in den Bed. des inf., bsd. 2er Federkiel dressed quill; 2e Lichte dipped candles, dips pl.; ⚔ 2es Rohr [Zug 10d] rifled barrel.

Zieher (2ʰ) m 22 **1.** (auch ~in f 40): a) one who draws; ⚓ (s. der Boote zieht) tower; b) 🜚 drawer (= Trassant). — **2.** instrument for drawing or pulling (out); s. Kork-, Schrauben-, Stiefel-.

Zieh-fenster 🜚 (²ʰ…) n 🜚 sash-window; ‐garn n, hunt. draw-net; ‐gelder n/pl. für die Pflege von Kindern: fee for nursing (or bringing up) children; ‐harmonika 🎵 f accordion, concertina; ‐hund m (in England unbekannt) dog used for drawing (light carts); ‐klimmen n Turnerei: climbing a ladder with the aid of one's hands only; ‐klinge 🜚 f, join. scraper; ‐kloben 🜚 m pulley; ‐kraft f: a) traction-power; b) (Anziehungskraft) attractive force; ‐leine f einer Lauframme: draw-line; ‐maschine 🜚 f Drahtzieherei: drawing-machine; ‐mutter f foster-mother; ‐ochs m draught-ox; ‐pflaster n = Zugpflaster; ‐säge 🜚 f, carp. &c. jack-saw; ‐schacht ⚒ m = Förderschacht; ‐schleife f noose, slip-knot; ‐schraube 🜚 f Schiffbau: draw-screw; ‐seil n rope for hauling or pulling or dragging; ‐stange 🜚 f der Büchsenmacher: rifling-rod; ‐strang, ‐strick m trace; ‐tag m day of removal; ‐tochter f Pflegetochter.

Ziehung (2ʰ) f 🜚: ~ der Lose, der Lotterie: drawing of lots, in a lottery; ~s-liste f 🜚 list of prizes (drawn in a lottery), lottery-list; ~s-tag m day fixed for a lottery-drawing, drawing-day.

Zieh-vater (²ʰ…) m 🜚 foster-father; ‐weg ⚓ m (Leinpfad) towing-path; ‐werk 🜚 n engine for hauling or pulling or dragging; ‐werkstätte f wire-drawing shop or room; ‐zange f pliers, nippers pl.; ‐zeit f time of removal.

Ziel (¹) [ahd.] n 🜚 c. **1.** (Ende, Grenze) term, limit; (Schranke) boundary, bounds pl.; s. Maß 1; e-m, j-s Ehrgeize ein ~ machen oder setzen to set bounds to (or to put a check on) a p.'s ambition; am ~e seines Lebens sein to reach (or get to) the end of one's life or days; das ~ überschreiten to exceed the limits, to overstep the mark; ohne Maß und ~ without moderation, beyond all bounds; 🜚 auf drei Monate ~ at three months' date. — **2.** (zu erreichender Punkt) aim (auch des Schützen), ⚔ verdecktes freistehendes ~ covered, exposed target, s. Zielscheibe; e-r Reise: destination, einer Rennbahn: (winning-)post, des Strebens: goal, end (in view); am ~e seiner Wünsche angelangt sein to have attained one's end or the object of one's desire; ans ~ gelangen to reach one's goal, Sport: to get home; nicht zum ~e führen to miscarry, to fail; zum ~ gelangen to attain one's object, to carry one's point; s. erreichen 2, treffen 1. hinausschießen. — **3.** — Zweck.

ziel-bewußt (²ʰ‿ʰ) a. 🜚 consciously (or steadily) pursuing one's aim; clear-headed or -sighted.

zielen (²ʰ) [ahd.] v/n. (h.), bisw. v/a. 🜚 to aim at (auch fig.), ⚔ mit Geschossen auch: to take aim at, mit der Flinte auch: to sight, to level one's gun at, mit der Kanone: to train a cannon at; gut 2 to take (a) good aim; fig. auf et. 2 to aim at a th., to tend to (bring about) a th., to point to a th.; in der Rede: to refer (or allude, make allusion) to a th.; gr. *~des Zeitwort = Transitiv.

Zieler ⚔ (²ʰ) m 22 one who takes aim, person aiming at a th.; ⚔ artill. trainer of cannon, marksman.

ziel-los (²ʰ…) a. 🜚 aimless, without aim. a. = zwecklos; gram. * ~loses Zeitwort = Intransitiv; ‐punkt m 🜚 goal, in der Zielscheibe: bull's-eye, white; ‐scheibe f target (a. fig.), butt, mark; ~ des Witzes oder Spottes laughing-stock; er war die ~ ihrer Spötterein he served as a butt (or target) for their mockery.

ziemen (²ʰ) [ahd.;*zähmen] v/n.(h.) u. sich 2 v/refl. 🜚 to be seemly or meet (= ge2).

Ziemer (²ʰ) [mhd.; *fr. cimier?] m 🜚 **1.** a) (Rücken, bsd. des Hinterviertels v. Wildbret) haunch of venison; b) (Lendenstück v. Schlachttieren) loin, chine. — **2.** (männl. Glied größerer Tiere) yard; s. Ochsenziemer.

ziemlich (²ʰ) [mhd.] ursprünglich a. 🜚, aber jetzt mst als adv. gbr.; zB. 2 gut pretty good or well, tolerable, passable; 2 lang longish; 2 oft pretty often; 2 spät rather (or somewhat) late; es waren 2 viel Fremde da there were a good (or a great) many strangers, et. 2 Schweres a tidy weight; er ist so 2 von meinem Alter he is pretty much (or just about) the same age as I (am); so 2 dasselbe very nearly the same thing, much of a muchness, almost alike or identical; seltener als attrib. a. = bedeutend, zB. eine 2e (ziemlich große) Anzahl von Läden a fair number of (or a good many) shops; es ist eine 2e Strecke Wegs it's a good (F it's rather a) long way (from here); als s/n.: er hat ein ~es dabei verdient he made a fairly good profit over (F a pretty good thing of) it.

🎵 Musik; ⚛ Wissenschaft; 🌱 Pflanze; 🜚 Geographie; 🜚 Technik; ⚒ Bergbau; ⚔ Militär; ⚓ Marine; 🜚 Handel; ✉ Post; 🚂 Eisenbahn.

[ziepen] — 1154 — [Zimmermann]

ziepen prov. (´‿) [ndd.: zupfen] v/a. ⊛: e-n an den Haaren 2 (ziehen) to pull a p. by the hair.
Zier (´) [ahd.] f ⊛ = Zierde.
Zier-affe (ˮ...) m ⓺, **-äffchen** n person fond of fine attire, fop, dandy, F masher, fashion-plate, von Frauen: F dressy (or showy, affected) little body or thing, (mere) doll; vgl. puppe.
Zierat (´‿) [mhd.; *Zier] m ⒸC., obb. f ornament, adornment; (Ausschmückung) decoration, embellishment, sculp.: ⚘ agalma; (Schnörkel) flourish; (Schmucksachen) finery; (Tand) gewgaw, bauble; zum ~ ornamental, decorative; **-en-maler** m ⓺ decorative painter.
Zier-beet (ˮ...) n ⊛ hort. ornamental bed; **-bengel** F m (dressed up) fop, young spark, F swell, masher, puppy; f. a. Geck 2; **-blume** (‿) f pflanze; **-buchstabe** ⊛ m, typ. ornamental letter.
Zierde (´‿) [ahd.; *Zier] f ⊛ ornament; f. Zierat; er war eine ~ der Stadt he was an ornament (or a credit) to the town, he shed lustre on the town.
zieren (´‿) [ahd.] ⊛ I v/a. 1. (zur Zierde dienen) to be (or to serve as) an ornament to, to adorn, grace, set off; (verschönern) to embellish; (ausschmücken) to decorate, to ornament. — II **sich** 2 v/refl. 2. b. s. to be affected or formal, to give o.s. (or to put on) airs and graces, to stand on ceremony, von Frauen auch: to be prim or prudish or old-maidish or coy; (sich affettiert sträuben) to refuse (or resist) prudishly or from sheer affectation, ziere dich nicht so! don't be so prim or so finical or so fussy! — III ~ n ⓷ 3. adornment; ornamentation, auch = Ziererei. — IV **ge-ziert** p.p. u. a. ⊛ 4. geziert mit et. adorned with s.th. — 5. zu II: f. geziert, bsb. Artikel; geziert reden, oft: to mince one's words.
Ziererei (-‿´) f ⊛ affectation, formal (or prim, prudish) ways pl., coy manner, (putting on) airs and graces.
zierisch ↘ (´‿) a. ⊛ affected, prim.
Zier-garten (ˮ...) m ⓺ pleasure-garden or -grounds pl.; **-gärtner** m ⓺ ornamental or fancy-gardener; **-gärtnerei** f ornamental gardening; **-giebel** m, arch. gablet; **-leiste** ⊛ f, typ. flourish, vignette, ornamental head-piece.
zierlich (´‿) a. ⊛ graceful, elegant, (fein) fine; (Schmuck) buxom (girl); (hübsch) pretty, (neu) nice, neat; 2 gekleidet smartly (or neatly) dressed, spruce; **~keit** f ⊛ gracefulness, elegance, im Benehmen: graceful ways pl.; pretty shape or figure, nicety, neatness.
Zier-linie (ˮ...) f ⊛ typ. ornamented rule; **-pflanze** f, hort. ornamental plant; **-puppe** f F dressed-up doll, showily dressed girl; vgl. affe; **-rahmen** m f. Kartusche 2; **-redner** m flowery speaker; **-rippe** f, arch. surface-rib; **-schrift** ⊛ f, typ. ornamented type, fancy-letters pl.; **-stich** ⊛ m Näherei: festoon-stitch; **-stück(e** pl.) n, typ. fancy-type; **-werk** n fancy-work.
Ziesel (´‿) [mhd.; *lt. ci'simus; m (n) ⓶ **~-maus**, **~-bär** m 2 = Honigbär; **~-maus** f ground-squirrel.

Ziest ↘ (´) m ⒷB. hedge-nettle, woundwort (Stachys).
Ziffer (´‿) [mhd.: cipher; *ar.] f ⊛ 1. (Zahlzeichen) figure, numeral (character). arith. Zahl von drei ~n (Stellen) number (consisting) of three digits; arabische, römische ~n Arabic, Roman numerals or numbers pl. — 2. (Schriftzeichen) cipher; in ~n schreiben to write in cipher(s).
Ziffer-blatt (‿...) n ⊛ der Uhr: dial- (or hour-)plate, face (of a clock or watch); **-blatt-rahmen** ⊛ m dial-case; **-brief** m letter (written) in cipher; **-kasten** m, typ. figure-case.
ziffern (‿‿) v/n. (h.) und v/a. ⒽH. to cipher.
ziffer(n)-mäßig (‿‿‿) a. ⊛ numerical; adv. auch: by figures.
Ziffer-rechnung (‿...) f ⊛ ciphering; **-schlüssel** m cipher-key; **-schrift** f cipher (writing), tel. auch: code; **-telegramm** n cipher- (or code-)telegram.
...zig (...‿) [ahd.: ...ty: zehn] 1. Nachsilbe in Zssgn mit den Zahlen von 2–9, bz. die entsprechende Anzahl von Zehnern, z.B.: a) inv. achtzig, vierzig eighty, forty, b) flektiert, zur Bezeichnung des Jahrzehnts, worin f. steht, z.B. über die Zwanzig(e) hinaus sein, in den Zwanzigern sein to be between twenty and thirty (years of age). — Weitere Fortbildungen: 2. **...ziger**: a) als a. u. s/m. mit beigefügtem ob. zu ergänzendem Substantiv: im Anfang ihrer zwanziger Jahre when she was just over twenty; b) vom Jahrzehnt des Jahrhunderts: in den zwanziger Jahren in the twenties; c) (j. nach dem Jahrzehnt seines Lebensalters, auch mit f: ...zigerin), vgl. Vierziger 1; d) Mitglied e-s Rates oder Kollegs von 20, 30 2c. Personen) einer von den Vierzigern one of the Forty; e) ⚔ f. Vierziger 2; f) Gesamtheit von 20, 30 2c. Dingen, z.B. Zwanzigpfennig piece, &c. — 3. **...zigst** zur Bildung von ordinal numbers, z.B. vierzigst(e, er) fortieth. — 4. **...zigstel**, zur Bildung von Brüchen, z.B. Zwanzigstel n twentieth (part).
Zigarette (‿‿‿) [fr. dim. v. Zigarre] f ⊛ (Papierzigarre) cigarette, bisw. paper-cigar; eine ~ drehen to make a cigarette.
Zigaretten-arbeiter(in f) m (‿‿‿...) cigarette-maker; **-(füll-)maschine** ⊛ f cigarette-filler or -machine; **-hülse** f c.-holder; **-papier** n c.-paper; **-spitze** f c.-holder; **-tabak** m tobacco (suitable for cigarettes); **-tasche** f c.-case.
Zigarre (‿´‿) [mhd. 19. sae.; fr.; *span.] f ⊛, dim. Zigärrchen n ⊛ cigar, F cig, weed; leichte, schwere ~ light, heavy cigar; e-e ~ anzünden, rauchen to light, to smoke a cigar; immer(fort) eine ~ im Munde führen to have always a cigar in one's mouth, to be for ever puffing at a cigar; ~n wickeln to roll cigars; die ~ hat keine Luft the cigar does not draw; e-e Kiste (abgelagerter) ~n a box of (well-seasoned) cigars.
Zigarren-abfall ⊛ (‿‿...) m ⊛ cigar-waste or -ends pl. or -tips pl.; scraps pl. of cigars; **-abschneider** m cigar-cutter; **-deckblatt** n wrapper; **-einlage** f filling (of a cigar); **-etui** n c.-tasche; **-kistchen** n (small) cigar-box.

-kiste f cigar-box or -case; **-kistenholz** n cigar-box wood; **-laden** m c.-shop; **-raucher** m c.-smoker; **-spitze** f: a) (zum Halten der Zigarre) c.-holder or -tube: b) bsd. abgeschnittene ~ c.-tip; **-spitzen-abschneider** m cigar-cutter; **-spitzen-futteral** n case of a c.-holder; **-ständer** m c.-stand; **-stummel** m cigar-end; **-tasche** f cigar-case.
Zigeuner (‿´‿) [mhd. 15. sae.] m ⓶, **~in** f ⓸ gipsy, seltener: Bohemian, bsb. unter Zigeunern und im Schrifttum: Romany; ~in gipsy woman, female gipsy, weitS. fortune-teller; **~-bande** f ⊛ band of gipsies, gipsy band; **~-bursch** m gipsy lad, auch: Romany rye; 2haft, 2isch (-´‿) a. ⊛ gipsy-like, weitS. vagrant, nomadic; **~-leben** n gipsy (weitS. wandering, roving) life; **~-mädchen** n gipsy girl; 2n (´‿) v/n. (h.) ⒶA. to lead a gipsy life, weitS. to rove (or wander) about; **~-sprache** f gipsy language, Romany; **~-tanz** m gipsy dance; **~-tum** (-‿)n⊛c. gipsydom, gipsyism; **~-volk** n gipsies pl., gipsy tribe; **~-wagen** m gipsy van or caravan; **~-weib** n gipsy woman; **...zigst(el)** f. ...zig 3 u. 4.
Zikade (‿´‿) [lt.] f ⊛ ent. (Baumgrille) Zirpe) cicada. [ciliary gland.
Ziliar-drüse ⚘ (‿´‿‿) f ⊛ anat.⌐
Zilizi-en ♀ (‿´‿(‿)) npr/n. ⓶a. Alt.: (Teil von Kleinasien) Cilicia; **Zilizi-er(in** f ⊛) m ⓶, **zilizisch** (‿´‿) a. ⊛ Cilician.
Zille ↕ prov. (´‿) [mhd.] f ⊛ (Flußkahn) (small) boat, skiff; **~-fahrer** m bargeman.
Zimbel ♪ (´‿) [ahd. *lt.] f ⊛ cymbal.
Zimbern (´‿) m/pl. ⓶ germ. Volk: Cimbri pl.; **zimbrisch** a. ⊛ Cimbric.
Zimmer¹ (´‿) [ahd.: timber] n ⓶ 1. room, apartment, f. hinten u. vorn 2; (Kammer) chamber; Haus mit acht ~n eight-roomed house; möblierte ~ furnished rooms or apartments pl.; f. hüten 1 u. vermieten. — 2. ⚔ Pelzhandel: bale of forty skins. — 3. (Bauholz) timber.
Zimmer²-arbeit ⊛ (‿‿...) [zimmern] f ⊛ carpenter's work; **-axt** f, **-beil** n carpenter's (broad) axe, auch: adze; **-bekleidung** f wainscotting.
Zimmerchen (‿‿) n ⊛ (dim. v. Zimmer) small (or cosy little) room, boudoir, seltener: closet; arch.: ⚘ zeta.
Zimmer¹-decke (‿‿) f ⊛ ceiling.
Zimmerei (‿‿´) f ⊛ bisw. = Zimmerhandwerk.
Zimmerer (´‿‿) m ⓶ = Zimmermann.
Zimmer²-flöße (‿‿...) ⊛ f ⊛ floating of timber; **-flucht** f suite of apartments; **-gerät** n (Mobiliar) furniture; **-²gesell** m journeyman carpenter; **-¹gymnastik** f indoor gymnastics; **-²handwerk** n carpenter's trade, carpentry; **-¹herr** m gentleman lodger; **-²hof** m timber- (or building-)yard; **-holz** n; **-jungfer** f housemaid (= Stubenmädchen); **-kellner** m waiter in a hotel who attends on visitors in their rooms, room-waiter; **-²lehrling** m carpenter's apprentice; **-¹mädchen** n chambermaid; **-mann** m (pl. -leute) carpenter; fig. e-m zeigen, wo der Zimmermann das Loch gelassen (ob. gemacht) hat to

---

Signs (see page XVII): F familiar; P vulgar; F flash; ↘ rare; † obsolete (died); * new word (born); ⁓ incorrect; ♪ music;

[Zimmermeister] — 1155 — [zinsfrei]

how a p. the door; **meister** m master carpenter; **¹miete** f rent of a room.
zimmern ⊙ (⌣⌣) [ahd.] **I** v/a. u. v/n. (h.) ⓐa. das Holz ♃ to cut (or hew, frame, square) ... with an axe; ein Haus ♃ to timber ... — **II** ~ n ㉓ f. Zimmerung.
Zimmer²-nagel ⊙ (⌣⌣...) m ⓒ carpenter's nail; **¹orgel** ♪ f reed-organ; harmonium; **pflanzen** f/pl. plants pl. grown indoors, indoor plants pl.; **²platz** m = hof; **polier(er)** (uspr. **parlier**) m carpenter's foreman; **²¹reich** a. containing many rooms; spacious; **reihe** f = flucht; **sport** m parlour game(s pl.); **²stück** n: a) piece of carpentry; b) paint. indoor scene; **¹tapete** f wall-paper.
Zimmerung (⌣⌣⌣) f ⓐ carpentering; timbering, ⚒ timber-work, framework; in ~ setzen to tub.
Zimmer²-verband ⊙ (⌣⌣...) m ⓒ carp. timber-band; **¹vermieter(in** f) m one who lets (furnished) apartments, lodging-house keeper; **verzierer** m house-decorator; **²werk** = ²arbeit; **werkstatt** f carpenter's workshop.
Zim(me)t (⌣⌣) [ahd.; grch.; *malai.] m ⓒc. cinnamon (= Kanzel); eine Röhre (ob. Stange) ~ a stick of cinnamon.
Zim(me)t-alkohol (⌣⌣)...) m ⓒ chm.: ♋ cinnamic alcohol; **apfel** m custardapple (Ano'na squamo'sa); **baum** m = Kaneelbaum; **blüten** f/pl. (Gewürz) cinnamon-flowers, cassia-buds pl.; **²braun** a. ⓐ = ²farben.
zim(me)ten (⌣⌣⌣) a. ⓐ of cinnamon.
zim(me)t-farben (⌣⌣⌣⌣) a. ⓐ cinnamon-coloured, (as) brown as cinnamon; **nägelein** ♣ n/pl. ⓒ = blüten; **öl** ♃ n (essential) oil of cinnamon; **rinde** f cinnamon-bark; **röhrchen** n, **röhre** f = stange, **stange** f stick of cinnamon; **säure** f, chm.: ♋ cinnamic acid $(C_9H_8O_2)$; **säure-salz** n: ♋ cinnamate; **wasser** n, pharm. cinnamon-water.
zimperlich (⌣⌣⌣) [ndd. simper] a. ⓐ prim, demure, very proper, F finical; (übertrieben sittsam) prudish, coy, straight-laced; too modest or bashful, squeamish, a. geziert II; ♃ tun to put on a prim, &c. appearance or behaviour; **~keit** f ⓐ primness; prudishness, coyness; affectation, affectedness.
Zimper-liese F (⌣⌣⌣) f ⓑ prudish (or prim, bashful, simpering) girl, prude.
zimpern (⌣⌣) v/n. (h.) ⓐa. = zimperlich (f. bes tun; auch: to simper.
Zimt (⌣) 2c. f. Zimmet 2c.
Zindel (⌣⌣) ⓑ [mhd.; it.; *grch. „indischer"] m ⓑ, ~taf(fe)t m ⓒ light taffeta.
Zink (⌣) [nhd.; *pers.?] m u. n ⓑ. ⊙ metall., chm. zinc (Zn); rohes ~ spelter; schwefelsaures ~ = Zinkvitriol; mit ~ belegen to (coat with) zinc, to cover (or line) with zinc; mit ~ gedeckt, überzogen zinc-covered.
Zink-arbeiter ⊙ (⌣⌣...) m ⓒ zinc-worker; **²artig** a. ⓐ zinky; **asche** f dross of zinc; **ätzer** m zinco-etcher; **ätzung** f zincography; typ. zincograph-process (block); **bedachung** f zinc roofing; **blech** n zinc-plate, sheeted (or laminated, rolled) zinc; **blende** f, min. zinc-blende, native sulphide of

zinc; f. a. Blende 4; **blume, blüte** f (Zinkoxyd) flowers pl. (or bloom) of zinc; **butter**, **chlorid** n, chm. chloride of zinc $(ZnCl_2)$; **dach** n zinc roof.
Zinke¹ (⌣⌣) [ahd.] f ⓐ = Zacke 1; F co. (große Nase) proboscis, F u. P beak, conk.
Zinke² (⌣⌣) [spät-mhd.] f ⓐ: a) Art Blasinstrument) etwa: clarion, cornet; b) = Zinkenregister.
Zinken¹ (⌣⌣) (⌣⌣) m ㉓ = Zinke¹.
zinken² (⌣⌣) [Zint] a. ⓐ (D9) (of) zinc.
zinken³ (⌣⌣) (⌣⌣) v/a. ⓐ (mit Zinten versehen) to furnish with prongs or spikes; bsd. im p.p., z.B. dreigezinkte Gabel three-pronged fork.
zinken⁴ ♪ (⌣⌣) [Zinke²] v/n. ⓐ ehm. to play (on) the cornet.
Zinken⁵-bläser ♪ (⌣⌣.⌣) [Zinke²] m ehm. cornet-player, cornetist.
Zinkenist ♪ (⌣⌣.⌣) m ⓐ ehm. = Zinkenbläser; weitS. = Mufikant.
Zinken⁵-register (⌣⌣...) n ⓐ, **zug** m e-r Orgel: cornet-register.
Zink-erz ⚒ (⌣...) n ⓐ min. zinc-ore; **gelb** n, chm. (chromsaures Zint) chromate of zinc $(ZnCrO_4)$; **gießer** m zinc-founder; **glas-erz** n, min. zinc-glance or -glass, silicious oxide of zinc; **haltig** a. ⓐ zinkiferous; **hochätzung** f = ätzung; **hütte** ⚒ f zinc-works pl.; **hütten-rauch** m zinc-fume(s pl.).
zinkig a. [Zinke¹] ⓐ ⓐ pronged, spiked; bfd. in Zssgn zwei-, zweigliedrig two-pronged.
Zink-kalk (⌣.⌣) m ⓐ = Zinkasche.
Zinkographie (⌣⌣⌣f⌣) [dtsch-grch.] f ⓐ (Zinkhochätzung für Druckzwecke) zinco-graphy; **zinkographisch** (⌣⌣.⌣.⌣) a. ⓐ zincographic, zincographical.
Zink-oxyd (⌣..⌣) n ⓐ chm. zinc-oxide, oxide of zinc (ZnO); **platte** f zinc-plate, geätzt: zincograph, zincotype; **pol** m, elect. zincoid pole; **salbe** f, pharm. zinc-ointment; **salz** n, chm. zinc-salt; **schaum** m zinc-scum; **sender** m, tel. (selbsttätiger Umschalter für Kabelbetrieb) zinc-sender; **spat** m, min. zinc-spar, native carbonate of zinc; **staub** m zinc-powder or -dust; **stechkunst** ⊙ f zinco-graphy; **vitriol** m (n) min. white vitriol or copperas, chm. sulphate of zinc $(ZnSO_4)$; **waren** f/pl. zinc ware(s pl.) or goods; **weiß** ⊙ n (reines Zinkoxyd für weiße Ölfarbe 2c.) zinc-white.
Zinn (⌣) [ahd.: tin] n ⓒc. tin (Sn); englisches (mit Blei vermischtes) ~ pewter.
Zinn-ader ⚒ (⌣...) f tin-lode; **²ähnlich**, **²artig** a. ⓐ tin-like, ♋ stannous; **asche** f tin-ashes pl., (tin-)putty; **berg-werk** n tin-mine, stannary; **blättchen** n tin-foil, leaf-tin; **blech** n tin-plate; **block** m tin-block; **butter** f, chm. butter of tin, tin-butter; **chlorid** n stannic chloride $(SnCl_4)$; **chlorür** n stannous chloride $(SnCl_2)$.
Zinne (⌣⌣) [ahd.] f ⓐ arch. (Helmbach) pinnacle (of the temple, &c., a. bibl.); auch: ≈ frt. (Mauer-)~ battlement, crenel(l)ation; mit ~n versehen crenel(l)ated, embattled.
zinnen¹ (⌣⌣) [ahd.] a. ⓐ = zinnern.
zinnen² (⌣⌣) [Zinne] a. ⓐ arch. u. ⚔ frt. crenel(l)ated; **krönung** f ⓑ crenel(l)ation; **zahn** m merlon.
zinnern (⌣⌣) a. ⓐ (of) tin or pewter.

Zinn-erz ⚒ (⌣...) n ⓐ tin-ore, tinstone; **foli-e** ⊙ f/tin-foil; **gekrätz** n tin-ashes, refuse of tin; **gerät**, **geschirr** n, coll. tin (or pewter) vessels or pots or utensils pl.; **geschrei** n creaking (or crackling) of tin; **gießer** m tinman, tin-moulder, tinner, pewterer; **gießerei** f tin-foundry, pewterer's (work-)shop; **glasur** f Töpferei: tin-glaze; **grube** f tin-mine; **²haltig** a. ⓐ containing tin, stanniferous; **inseln** n pr/f pl. ♀ Alt. (Westen von England) Cassiterides pl.; **kalk** m calcinated tin; **kies** n, min. tin-pyrites, sulphuret of tin; **kräze** f = asche; **löffel** m tin (or pewter) spoon or ladle; **lot** n tin (or soft) solder.
Zinnober (⌣⌣⌣) [mhd., *grch.] m ⓐ min. (rotes Schwefelquecksilber), paint. cinnabar, native red sulphide of mercury (HgS); chm. künstlicher ~: ♋ vermilion.
Zinnober-erz ⚒ (⌣⌣...) n ⓐ (Quecksilbererz) ore of cinnabar; **grün** n chrome-green; **rot** n u. ♃ a. ⓐ vermilion.
Zinn-oxyd (⌣...) n ⓐ chm. stannic oxide (SnO_2); **oxydul** n stannous oxide (SnO); **platte** f plate of tin; **salz** n, chm. tin-(or stannic, stannous) salt; **sand** m grain-tin; **²sauer** a. ⓐ chm.: ♋ stannic; **²saures Salz** stannate; **säure** f stannic acid (H_2SnO_3); **schmelzer** ⊙ m blower; **schmelzhütte** f, metall. blowing-house; **soldat** m tin soldier; **stufe** ⚒ f lump of tin-ore; **sulfid** n, chm. stannic sulphide (SnS_2); **sulfür** n stannous sulphide (SnS); **teller** f tin (or pewter) plate; **ware** f tin (or pewter) ware or goods pl.; **wäsche** ⚒ f tin-buddle.
Zins (⌣) [*lt. cens-us Abschätzung] m ㉕ⓐ a. 1. bfd. bibl. tribute. — 2. (Abgabe an den Grundherrn) ground-rent. — 3. ⓐa. (Miete) (house-)rent. — 4. ⚒a. (ant. Kapital) interest; ~ auf (od. vom) ~ compound interest; f. ausliegen I; von f-n Zinsen leben to live on one's interest or income; 3 Prozent Zinsen tragen to bear three per cent. interest, to bear interest at the rate of 3 per cent.; fig. e-m et. mit Zinsen zurückzahlen to return a p. a th. with interest or usury; (heimzahlen) to give a p. as good as (s)he sent.
Zins-acker (⌣⌣...) m ⓐ field let out at a rent(al), rented field.
zinsbar (⌣⌣) a. ⓐ = zinspflichtig; **Zins-barkeit** f ⓐ = Zinspflicht.
Zins-bauer (⌣⌣...) m ⓐ chm. peasant paying tithe(s), copyholder; **brief** m copyhold- (or leasehold-)deed; **buch** n rent-roll, rental; **coupon** ♣ m = schein.
zinsen (⌣⌣) a. ⓐ *Zins] v/a. und v/n. (h.) ⓐ to pay in the shape of tribute or rent or interest; (Zins einbringen) to bring in (or yield) rent or interest, to bear interest.
Zinsen-berechnung (⌣⌣...⌣) f ⓐ arith. calculation (or computation) of interest, interest-account.
Zinses-zins (⌣⌣.⌣) m ⓐ arith. (Zins auf Zins) compound interest.
zins-fällig a. ⓐ = ²pflichtig; **frau** f ⓐ f. **mann**; **²frei** a.: a) exempt from (paying) rent; Les Gut, Land

---
⚛ scientific; ♦ botanical; ♀ geography; ⊙ machinery; ⚒ mining; ⚔ military; ⚓ marine; ⚘ commercial; ⚐ postal; 🚂 railway.

[Zinsfreiheit] — 1156 — [Zitierung]

freehold (estate, land), ehm. allodium; b) 2 wohnen to live rent-free; e-m ein Kapital 2 leihen to lend a p. ... free of (or without asking any) interest; =freiheit f exemption from paying rent, living rent-free; =fuß m rate of interest; zu e-m hohen (niedrigen) ~ at a high (low) rate of interest; =groschen m, bibl. tribute-money; =gut n copyhold, leasehold; vgl. =lehen; =hahn m nur gbr. in: rot wie ein ~ (as) red as a turkey-cock; =haus n: a) house let out at a rent, house to let, b) house subject to ground-rent; =herr m ground-landlord, lessor, lord of the manor; =korn n ehm. corn paid in lieu of rent, cense-corn; =lehen n Feudalwesen: fee-farm; vgl. =gut; =leiste ⚘ f =schein; =leute pl. f. =mann; 2los a. free of interest, rent-free; =mann m, =frau f: a) Feudalwesen: feoffee, copyholder; b) = Miet(s)-mann, =frau; =pflicht f obligation to pay rent; =pflichtig a. subject to rent, (tributpflichtig) tributary; =rechnung f, arith. interest-account or sum; =register n = =buch; =schein m coupon, für Aktien: dividend-warrant; =tabelle f table of interest, ready reckoner; =tag m rent-day, vierteljährlicher: quarter-day; 2tragend a. bearing interest; =vergütung f =zahlung; 2weife adv. by way of interest or rent; =zahl f: a) röm. Alt.: (Zeitrechnung) indiction, b) ~en pl. Buchführung: red numbers; =zahlung f payment of interest or rent.

Zion (ˊ‿) [hebr.] npr/m. ⓐ a. (höchster Hügel Jerusalems mit der Burg Davids), fig. n ⓑ (die rechtgläubige Kirche) Sion (Zion).

Zionismus (-‿‿) [Zion] m ㉗ (Bewegung unter den Juden, zur Gründung eines jüdischen Staates hinzielt) Zionism.

Zions-brüder (ˊ‿…) m/pl. ⓒ christl. Sekte: Sionites; =schwestern f pl. Nonnen: sisters of Zion; =wächter m guard(ian) of Zion, iro. fanatic divine or minister; (Eiferer) zealot, fanatic.

Zipfel (ˊ‿) [mhd. Zapf(en)] m ⓑ tip, point, e-s Taschentuches: corner, e-s Rockes: flap, lappet; F fig. et. beim rechten ~ anfassen to tackle a th. in the right fashion, to go the right way to work.

zipf(e)lig (ˊ(‿)‿) a. ⓒ having tips or points, ⚘: ↘ laciniolate(d), laciniform; bsd. in Zssgn. z.B. drei-2 with three tips or points.

Zipfel-mütze (ˊ‿…) f ⓑ night-cap; =perücke f pointed (or full-bottomed) wig, wig with lappets.

Zipolle ⚘ (-‿‿) [it.] f ㊽ onion (= Zwiebel). [= Singdrossel.]

Zipp-drossel (ˊ‿‿) f ⓑ, Zippe (ˊ‿) f ㊽ Zipperlein (ˊ‿‿) [mhd.] n ㉓ path. gout, bsd. = Fuß-, Handgicht.

Zipp-lerche (ˊ‿‿) f ⓑ = Wiesenlerche.

Zirbel ⚘ (ˊ‿) [vgl. ahd. zirben wirbeln] m ⓑ, a. f ⓑ = Zirbelkiefer.

Zirbel-drüse (ˊ‿…) f ⓑ anat. ↘ pineal body or gland; =fichte f = =kiefer; =holz ⚘ n cembra-wood (v. Pinus cembra); =kiefer ⚘ f cembra-pine (Pinus cembra); =nuß f cedar-nut.

zirka (ˊ‿) [it.] adv. (abbr. ca.) about, nearly (= ungefähr).

Zirkassi-en ⚘ (‿ˊ(‿)‿) npr/n. ㉓ α. (russ. Provinz am Kaukasus) Circassia.

Zirkassi-er (‿ˊ(‿)‿) m ㉒, ~in f ⓒ, zirkassisch (‿ˊ(‿)‿) a. ⓒ Circassian.

Zirkel (ˊ‿) [ahd: circle; *lt.] m ㉒ 1. circle (a. math.). — 2. fig. (gesellschaftliche Vereinigung) (social) circle, set of people), society; vgl. Kreis 3 gegen Ende und Lesezirkel. — 3. ⊙ (Werkzeug zum Ziehen von Kreislinien) (pair of) compasses; fig. alles mit dem ~ abmessen to do everything by rule and compass or with minute care or most precisely.

Zirkel-beweis (ˊ‿…) m ⓑ log. =schluß; =bogen m = Kreisbogen; =förmig a. ⓒ circular; =lini-e f circular line.

zirkeln (ˊ‿) v/a. ㉒a. = abzirkeln.

zirkel-rund (ˊ‿…) a. ⓒ circular; =säge ⊙ f ⓒ circular saw; =schenkel m shank of (a pair of) compasses; =schluß m, log. vicious circle; =spitze f point of the compasses; =weite f span of (a pair of) compasses; =zug ⊙ u. ↓ m circular flourish or trace.

Zirkon ⚘ (‿ˊ) [perſ.] m ⓑd. min. zircon; ~erde f ⓒ zirconia (ZrO₂).

Zirkonium ↘ (‿ˊ(‿)‿) n ㊿ (o. pl.) chm. (im Zirkon enthaltenes Metall) zirconium (Zr); ~oxyd n ⓒ = Zirkonerde.

Zirkular (‿‿ˊ) [lt.] n ⓑd. (Rundschreiben) circular (letter); ein ~ erlassen to send round (or out) a circular; ❀ ~e an die Kunden aussenden to send out circulars to (or to circularize) the customers; ~erlaß m ⓑ order issued in form of a circular; ~pumpe ⊙ f circulating-pump; =säge f = Kreissäge; =schreiben n = Zirkular.

Zirkulation (‿‿‿ˊ‿ᵗˢ(‿)ⁿ) [lt.] f ㊻ (Umlauf) circulation; in ~ sein = zirkulieren; in ~ setzen to put in circulation, to circulate; ~röhre f ⓒ circulating pipe or tube.

zirkulieren (‿‿ˊ‿‿) [lt.] I v/n. (h.) ⓓ (die Runde machen, umlaufen) to circulate; 2 lassen to put in circulation, to let go the round; von Gerüchten auch: to spread (about). — II ~ n ㉓ = Zirkulation.

Zirkulier-gefäße (‿‿ˊ‿…) n/pl. ⓒ chm. circulating vessels pl.; =ofen m ⓒ circulating oven or furnace.

Zirkulierung (‿‿ˊ‿‿) f ㊻ = Zirkulation.

Zirkumflex (ˊ‿‿) [lt.] m ⓑa. gr. (Dehnungszeichen) circumflex (ˆ, ˆ, ˜); mit einem ~ bezeichnen to mark with a circumflex.

Zirkus (ˊ‿) [lt. Kreis] m, inv. ob. ⓒ (Kunstreiterbude) circus; ~reiter(in f) m ⓑ circus-rider, a. equestrian (performer).

Zirp-apparat (ˊ‿‿‿ˊ) m ⓑ ent.: stridulating organ.

Zirpe (ˊ‿) f ㊽ ent. cicada (= Zikade).

zirpen (ˊ‿) [nhd. lautm.: chirp] I v/n. (h.) u. v/a. ⓑ von Vögeln u.: to chirp; von Insekten ꝛc. auch: to utter a sharp (or strident) note, ↘ to stridulate; von jungen Vögeln auch: to squeak; ent. 2o: ↘ stridulant, …atory. — II ~ n 23 chirping, ent.: stridulation.

Zirrus ↘ (ˊ‿) [lt. cirrus Locke] m, inv. (a. ~wolke f ㊽ (Federwolke) cirrus (cloud).

zirzensisch (‿ˊ‿‿) (‿ˊ‿) [lt. circus] a. ⓒ röm. Alt.: 2e Spiele (zur Unterhaltung des Volkes) circensian (or circus-) games pl.

zis-alpin(isch) ⚘ (ˊ‿‿(‿)) a. ⓒ cisalpine.

Zisch (ˊ) m ⓑa. hiss, whiz.

Zischelei (‿‿ˊ) f ⓒ = Gezischel.

zischeln (ˊ‿) [mhd. lautm.] I v/n. (h.) u. v/a. ⓑa. to whisper, to speak in an undertone. — II ~ n 23 = Gezischel.

zischen (ˊ‿) [nhd. (LU.) lautm.] I v/n. (h., bei Ortsveränderungen fn) ⓑ to hiss (auch als Ausdruck des Hohnes u. als v/a. = auszischen); sausend, sprühend 2 to fizz(le), seltener: to sizzle, to swish; schwirrend 2 to whiz, to whir, sprühend: to sputter; das Wasser kocht noch nicht, aber es (ob. der Kessel) fängt an zu 2 … it (or the kettle) is beginning to sing; 2d gr.: ↘ sibilant; 2d sprechen: ↘ to sibilate. — II ~ n 23 hissing, gr.: ↘ sibilance, sibilation, whir, sputter, der Kugeln: whizzing, ping.

Zischer (ˊ‿) m ㉒ hisser.

Zisch-laut (ˊ‿…), =ton m ⓑ hissing sound, ↘ sibilation, gr. hiss, ↘ sibilant.

Ziseleur (‿‿ˊ) (‿ˊ‿ɜːr) [fr.] m ⓑd. (㊿) (Glattmeißler) (en)chaser, carver.

Ziseleur-arbeit (‿‿ˊ‿…) f ⓑ chased (or chisel-) work.

ziselier-en (‿‿ˊ‿‿) [fr.] I v/a. ⓑ to (en)chase; to carve. — II ~ n 23 = 2ung.

Ziselier-hämmerchen (‿‿ˊ‿…) n ⓑ chasing hammer; =kunst f chaser's art; chasing; art of carving.

Ziselierung (‿‿ˊ‿‿) f ㊻ chasing, carving.

zis-leithanisch ⚘ (ˊ‿‿‿ˊ‿) a. ⓒ (diesseits der Leitha, in Deutsch-Österreich, gelegen) Cisleithan; 2padanisch a. (diesseits des Po, von Rom aus, gelegen) Cispadane.

Zisso-ide (‿‿ˊ‿‿) [grch. kisso's Efeu] f ⓑ math. cissoid; 2 an den ~ gehörig cissoidal.

Zisterne (‿ˊ‿) [lt.] f ㊽ cistern.

Zisterzi-enser (‿ˊ‿‿‿) [lt.] m ㉒, ~in f ㊼ Cistercian (monk m. nun f); ~kloster n ⓒ Cist. convent; ~mönch (~nonne f) m ⓑ Zisterzienser(in); ~orden m Cistercian order.

Zist-rose ⚘ (ˊ‿…) [lt., *grch.] f ㊽, =röschen n (sweet) cistus, rock-rose (Cistus heli-a'nthemum), =rosen-harz n la(b)danum.

Zitadelle ⚔ (‿‿ˊ‿) [it.] f ㊽ frt. citadel.

Zitat (‿ˊ) [lt.] n ⓑc. (angeführte Stelle) quotation, quoted passage, auch: citation; falsches ~ misquotation.

Zitation (‿‿ˊ‿ᵗˢ(‿)ⁿ) [lt.] f ㊻ jur. (Vorladung) summons, citation.

Zither ♪ (ˊ‿) [ahd.; grch.; *perſ. Drei-Saite; f. Gitarre] f ㊽ Saiten-instrument: a) der Alten: cithara, lute, lyre; Ari'on war der Tone Meister, die ~ lebt' in seiner Hand (SCHLEGEL) … the lute responded to his hand; b) jetzt (Schlag-)~ zither, seltener: cithern; vgl. Streichzither; die ~ schlagen, spielen to play the zither; ~ring m ⓑ ring for playing the zither; =schlagen, ~spiel(en) n playing the zither; =schläger(in f) m, ~spieler(in f) m ⓑ zither-player, seltener: zitherist, citharist.

zitieren (‿ˊ‿‿) [lt.] I v/a. ⓑ 1. einen Autor ꝛc. 2 to cite …; einen Schriftsteller ꝛc. 2 to quote …; falsch 2 to misquote. — 2. jur. (vorladen) to summon, bisw. to cite. — 3. Geister 2 (heraufbeschwören) to raise …, to call (or conjure) up … — II ~ n 23 und Zitierung f ㊻ 4. (f. 1) citation; quotation. — 5. (f. 2) summons. — 6. (f. 3) conjuration.

Zeichen (f. S. XVII): F familiär; P Volkssprache; ⚞ Gaunersprache; ↘ selten; † alt (auch gestorben); * neu (auch geboren); ⁺ unrichtig;

[zitissime] — 1157 — [Zollgesetz]

zitissime (⸺‿‿) **zito** (‵‿) [lt. schnell(stens)] adv. auf Briefen: Immediate!, Urgent!
Zitrin ⚗ (‿‵) [lt.] m ⓐd. min. citrine.
Zitronat ⚘ (⸺‵) [lt.] n ⓐ ⓒ. (verzuckerte Zitronenschale) preserved citron, candid lemon-peel, succade.
Zitrone (⸺‵‿) [fr., lt.; *medisch?] f ⓐ 1. Frucht: citron, lemon; mit ~ u. gewürzt flavoured with lemon. — 2. ⚘ = Zitronenbaum.
Zitronen-äther (⸺‵‿...) m ⓑ chm.: ⚗ citric ether; **-baum** ⚘ m lemon-tree, citron (Citrus me'dica a'cida); **-blüte** f lemon-blossom; **-falter** m, ent. brimstone butterfly (Gono'pteryx rhamni); **-farbe** f ~ gelb a; **-farbig** a. ⓑ ⚘ gelb ⓑ; **-gelb**: a) n citrine, lemon-colour or -yellow; b) ⚗ a. citrine, citrinous, lemon(-coloured); **-limonade** f lemon-squash, (home-made) lemonade; **-melisse** ⚘ f lemon-balm (Meli'ssa officina'lis); **-öl** ⚘ n oil of citron, lemon-oil; **-saft** m lemon-juice; **-sauer** a. chm.: ⚗ citric; **-saures Salz** ⚗ citrate; **-säure** f, chm. citric (or lemon-) acid; **-schale** f lemon-peel; **-scheibe** f slice of a lemon; **-vogel** m = -falter; **-wasser** n lemon-water.
Zitter-aal (‵‿...) m ⓑ ichth. electric eel, gymnotus (Gymno'tus ele'ctricus); **-affe** m, zo. = Kapuziner-affe; **-alge** ⚘ f star-jelly (Nostoc); **-anfall** m shivering fit, fit of trembling.
Zitterer (‵‿‿) m ⓑ trembler.
Zitter-fisch (‵‿...) m ⓑ = -aal, -roche(n), -wels; **-gold** n = Flittergold; **-gras** ⚘ n quaking-grass (Briza me'dia).
zitterhaft, zitterig (‵‿‿) a. ⓑ trembling, tremulous, shaking, shivering.
zittern (‵‿) [ahd.: titter] I v/n. (h.) ⓑ a. to tremble with cold, excitement. fear, &c., vor Kälte auch: to shiver, vor Furcht, Schwäche auch: to quake, to shake (in one's shoes), vor Unruhe: to flurry, to flutter; schwingend: to vibrate, to oscillate, zuckend: to quiver; 2 u. beben to shake and tremble; 2 und zagen f. zagen I; er zittert am ganzen Leibe he trembles all over (his body) or in every limb, F. u. P he's all of a tremble; f. Espenlaub; vor einem 2 to tremble before a p.; leise 2d tremulous; mit 2der Stimme with a faltering voice. — II ~ n ⓑ trembling, &c. (f. I); flutter(ing); vibration; med.: ⚕ tremor; aus Furcht: trepidation, der Stimme: faltering, tremulousness; ♪ f. beben 4; mit ~ und Zagen with fear and trepidation; vgl. zagen II.
Zitter-nadel (‵‿...) f ⓑ am Kopfputze, etwa trembling ornament on a lady's bonnet, &c., auch aigrette, egret(te); **-pappel** ⚘ f trembling-poplar, aspen (Po'pulus tre'mula); **-pilz** ⚘ m: ⚗ tremella; **-pilz-artig** a. ⓑ ⚗ tremelloid; **-roche(n)** m, ichth. cramp-(or numb-)fish, electric ray (Torpe'do); **-spiel** n (Geduldspiel) spillikins; **-stimme** f trembling (or tremulous) voice; **-tierchen** n, zo. thread-animalcule, vibrio(n); **-wels** m electric cat-fish, thunder-fish, ⚗ malapteruroid (Malapteru'rus ele'ctricus).
Zitwer ⚘ (‵‿) [ahd., lt., *ar.] (in pharm.) zedoary (Cu'rcuma zedoa'ria); **-wurzel** ⚘ (‵...) f zedoary(-root).

Zitz ⚘ (‵) [engl., *bengal.] m ⓐ a. chintz, printed calico.
Zitze (‵‿) [mhd.: tit (teat)] f ⓐ 1. (Brustwarze) nipple. — 2. zo. ~ am Euter der Kühe, Ziegen ꝛc.: teat, dug.
zitzen-förmig (‵‿...) a. ⓑ nipple-shaped, zo. mammiform; **-los** a. without nipples, udderless; **-tiere** n/pl. zo. mammals. | calico (or printed dress.)
Zitz-kattun ⚘ (‵...) m ⓑ chintz; **-kleid** n
zivil (‿‿‵) [lt.] I a. ⓑ 1. a) bürgerlich (ant. kriminal), b) höflich, gesittet: civil. — 2. (mäßig, billig) moderate, reasonable, um sehr den Preis at a very reasonable (or fair) price. — II ~ n ⓑ 3. (ant. Militär) civil population; in ~ in plain (or private) clothes, ⚔ auch: in mufti.
Zivil-amt (‿‿‵...) n ⓑ civil-service (or government) appointment; **-anwärter** m pensioner (or person) who has a claim (or is entitled) to a government appointment; **-anzug** m civilian's dress or garb, ⚔ a. mufti, vgl. -kleidung; **-ehe** f civil marriage, marriage before a registrar; **-gesetzbuch** n code of civil law; **-ingenieur** m civil engineer.
Zivilisation (‿‿‿‵) [lt.] f ⓐ (Bildung, Gesittung) civilization, culture; **~s-bestrebungen** (‵‿...) f/pl. ⓑ civilizing efforts pl.; striving after culture or refinement; **~s-fähig** a. ⓑ = zivilisierbar.
zivilisatorisch (‿‿‿‵) a. ⓑ (die Gesittung fördernd) civilizing, promoting (the cause of) civilization.
zivilisierbar (‿‿‵‿) a. ⓑ civilizable, amenable to civilization.
zivilisieren (‿‿‵‿) [lt.] v/a. ⓑ (bilden, verfeinern) to civilize, auch: to humanize; fig. to polish.
Zivilist (‿‿‵) [lt.] m ⓑ 1. civilian. — 2. jur. (ant. Kriminalist) civil jurist, one (deeply) versed in civil law.
ziviliter (‿‿‵‿) [lt.] adv. jur. by civil process, in the civil courts.
Zivil-kleidung (‿‿‵...) f ⓑ plain clothes pl., vgl. -anzug; **-liste** f eines Fürsten: civil list; **-person** f = Zivilist; **-rechtlich** a. ⓑ u. adv. jur. civil, according to civil law; e-n 2 verfolgen to bring a civil suit against a p.; **-stand** m: a) legal status of a p.; b) (the) middle class(es pl.) (= Bürgerstand); **-stands-amt** n registration-office, registrar's office; **-tracht** f = -anzug, -kleidung; **-versorgungs-berechtigt** a. entitled to a post in the civil-service or a government appointment; **-versorgungs-schein** m. etwa: certificate stating the claims of a government pensioner.
Zobel (‵‿) [mhd.; *russ.] m ⓐ 1. zo sable (Muste'la zibelli'na). — 2. ⚘ = -balg, -pelz.
Zobel-balg (‵‿...) m ⓑ, **-fell** n sable (-skin); **-fang** m sable - hunting; **-fänger** m sable-hunter; **-jagd** f = -fang; **-pelz** m sable-fur, als Gewand: sable-cloak or -cape; **-tier** n = Zobel; **-verbrämung** f sable-trimming.
Zober (‵‿) m ⓑ = Zuber.
zockeln provc. (‵‿) v/n. (sn) ⓑ a. (wackelnd gehen) to toddle (along), to waddle.
Zodiakal-licht (‿‿‿‵‿) [grch.] n ⓑ ast. (= Tierkreis...) zodiacal light.

Zodiakus ⚗ (‵‿‿‿) [grch.] m ⓑ ast. zodiac (= Tierkreis).
Zofe (‵‿) [nhd. zu mhd. zafen schmücken] f ⓐ (lady's) maid; vgl. Kammerfrau.
zog (‵) ind., **zöge** (‵‿) subj. impf. v. ziehen.
Zögerer (‵‿‿) m ⓑ = Zaud(e)rer.
zögern (‵‿) [nhd.; *(Ver)zug, ziehen] ⓑ a. I v n. (h.) 1. = säumen I. — 2. (zurückweichen) to draw back; (sich bei etwas aufhalten) to linger, to dawdle; 2d dilatory, tardy, slow, dawdling. — II ~ n ⓑ und **Zögerung** f ⓑ 3. = säumen³ II, auch: dilatoriness; ohne ~ without hesitation or delay.
Zögling (‵‿) [nhd.; *zog] m ⓐ d. pupil, (Schüler[in])scholar, (Kostschüler)boarder.
Zölestin ⚗ (‿‿‵) [lt.] m ⓐ d. min. celestite. celestine, cœlestine.
Zölibat (‿‿‵) [lt.] m u. n ⓑ c. celibacy; bachelordom; im ~ (als Junggeselle) leben to lead a bachelor's life, co. to live in single blessedness.
Zoll¹ (‵) [mhd.] m ⓑ c,6. 1. ($^{1}/_{12}$ oder $^{1}/_{10}$ Fuß), etwa 2½ cm) inch; drei Viertel ~ breit three-quarters of an inch wide; zwei ~ dickes Brett two-inch board, plank two inches thick; fig. auf ~ u. Linie (ganz genau) to the very inch. very accurate(ly); jeder ~ (an ihm) ein König every inch a king; a king. every inch of him. — 2. ast. (Zwölftel des Sonnen- oder Mond-durchmessers) digit.
Zoll² (‵) [ahd.: toll; *lt.] m ⓑ c. 1. (Wegegeld) toll; meist ⚘ (Abgabe, Steuer) duty. custom; f. Ausfuhr-. Eingangs-zoll. — 2 fig. (zu entrichtender Zins) tribute. — 3. = Zoll-haus.
Zoll-amt (‵...) n ⓑ board of customs: vgl. **-behörde, -haus**; **-amtlich** a. ⓑ relating to the custom-house; 2e Untersuchung examination by revenue-officers; **-angabe** f entry at the custom-house; **-ansatz. -anschlag** m tariff of rates or customs; **-anschluß** m accession to a customs-union; **-aufseher** m surveyor of customs.
zollbar (‵‿) a. ⓑ = zollpflichtig.
Zoll²-beamte(r) ⚘ (‵...) m ⓑ custom-house (or revenue-)officer; **-behörde** f c.-house authorities pl.; **-breit** a. ⓑ an inch wide; **-defraudant** m, defraudation f defrauder. defraudation of the customs or revenue; **-deklaration, -deklarierung** f c.-house clearance; **-einnehmer** m: a) receiver (or collector) of customs; b) toll-gatherer.
zollen (‵‿) v/n. (h.) u. v/a. ⓑ 1. to pay custom or duty. — 2. fig. to pay by way of homage; einem Achtung 2 to show (or express) one's esteem for a p., to pay a p one's respects, f. Beifall; am Schluß; e-m Dank 2 to express one's thanks (or gratitude) to a p.
Zoll²-ermäßigung ⚘ (‵...) f ⓑ reduction (or abatement) of duty; **-formalitäten** f/pl. custom-house formalities pl; **-frei** a. ⓑ exempt from duty, duty-free; Sprichw. Gedanken sind 2 thoughts are free, our thoughts are our own, you cannot stop people from thinking what they like; **-freiheit** f exemption from duty; **-gebiet** n customs-district; **-gebühr** ⚘ f duty; vgl. Zoll² 1; **-geleit-schein** m permit, pass; **-gesetz** n law

♪ Musik; ⚗ Wissenschaft; ⚘ Pflanze; ⚱ Geographie; ⚙ Technik; ⛏ Bergbau; ⚔ Militär; ⚓ Marine; ⚖ Handel; ✉ Post; 🚂 Eisenbahn.

[Zollgrenze] — 1158 — [zu]

relating to customs or to the collection of revenue; =grenze f customs-frontier; =haus n custom-house; ²hoch a. an inch high.

...zollig. ..zöllig (...²) a. ⓖ 1. (ein.²) of (or measuring) one inch. — 2. in Zssgn mit Zahlen, zB. drei² of (or measuring) three inches, three-inch.

Zoll²-inhalts-erklärung (²´⌣`) f ⓖ = -angabe. [of custom-houses.]
Zollini-e (²´(⌣`)) [Zoll²-linie] f ⓖ line
Zoll²-inspektor (²´...) m ⓖ = -aufseher; -krieg ⚔ u. pol. tariff war; -lini-e i. Zollinie; -maß n measure(ment) in inches; inch-measure.

Zöllner (²`) [ahd.: *Zoll²] m ²¹ 1. bibl. publican; vgl. Zollwächter. — 2. = Zolleinnehmer; poet. O ~, o ~. entfleuch geschwind! (B.) oh, tollman, tollman, speed away!

Zoll²-ordnung (²`...) f ⓖ custom-house regulations pl.; bid. ehm. =pächter m farmer of taxes; =papiere n pl. custom-house papers; =passier-schein m = -geleitschein; =pflichtig a. ⓖ subject to duty, dutiable; =pflichtigkeit f liability to pay duty; =pfund n pound of the Zollverein, one half kilogram; =plackereien f pl. bother (or trouble) at the custom-house; =politik f customs-policy; =quittung f = -schein; =revision f ⚓ u. 🚂 examination of passengers' luggage; =schein m clearance(-bill); vgl. -geleitschein; =schiff ⚓ n revenue-cutter; =schikanen f pl. c.-house chicanery, vgl. -plackereien; =schreiber m c.-house clerk; =speicher m c.-house store, Lo. bonded (or bonding-)warehouse; =spesen ⚖ f pl. c.-house charges pl.; =stab, =stock O m foot-rule, carpenter's rule; =stätte, =stelle, =system n custom-house (or tariff) system; =tafel f, =tarif m tariff; =umgehung f defraudation of the customs; =verband, =verein n customs-union; ehm. der Deutsche =verein the German Zollverein; =vergütung f drawback; =verschluß m customs-seal, leads pl.; Waren unter ~ goods in bond, bonded goods pl.; =vertrag m customs-treaty; =verwaltung f management (or administration) of customs; =wächter m = -beamte(r), in Seehäfen: tide-waiter; =wachtschiff ⚓ n revenue-cutter; =²weise adv. by inches; =²wesen n custom-house affairs pl., fiscal system; Stelle im ~ appointment (or situation) in the Customs.

Zone (²`) [grch.(Erd-)Gürtel] f ⓖ 1 ast.. ♀. math. ⚗ u. fig. zone; ♀ i. gemäßigt ², heiß ¹: kalte = frigid zone; in ~n einteilen ² to divide into zones, to zone. — 2. ♀ u. zo. (Fund-ort) ⚗ habitat.

Zonen-einteilung (²´...) f ⓖ division into zones; =tarif ⚒ m ⓖ (ermäßigtes Fahrgeld für lange Strecken) zone-tariff. [der Wesen) zoochemistry.]
Zo-o-chemie ⚗ (²´⌣´) f ⓖ (Chemie leben-
Zo-o-lith ⚗ (²´⌣) m ⓖc. ⓖ geol. (Tierversteinerung) zoolite.
Zo-o-log ⚗ (²´⌣) m ⓖ. ~e ⓖ (Tierkenner) zoologist; ~ie (²´⌣) f ⓖ (Tierkunde)

zoology; ²isch (⌣´⌣`) a. ⓖ zoological, i. Garten. [animal plant. zoophyte.]
Zo-ophyt (²´⌣) m. n ⓖ (Tierpflanze)
Zopf (²) [ahd.: top: Zipfel] m ⓖb. 1. Haartracht: a) ehm. von Männern, noch jetzt in China: pigtail; b) bei Frauen: geflochtener ~ (long) plait (or tress) of hair; das Haar in Zöpfe flechten to plait (or braid) one's hair; vgl. flechten I; c) fig. e-m einen ~ anstecken, drehen ob. machen (einen Schabernack spielen) to play a p. a trick, to hoax a p.; einem auf den ~ kommen ob. P spucken f. spucken; sich e-n ~ trinken to get tipsy; d) fig. (altsteife Sitte oder Beschränktheit) antiquated formalism, absurd pedantry, pettifoggery, der Beamten: red-tape or -tapism, ⚓ pipe-clay. — 2. for. ~(ende) eines Baumes: top of a tree.

Zopf-band (²´⌣) n ⓖ ribbon tied to tresses or to a pigtail.

zöpfen, † zöpfen (²`) v.a. ⓖ 1. die Haare ² to plait (or braid) the hair. — 2. O carp. einen Baum ² (ihm das Zopfende abschneiden) to top a tree.

Zopf-ende (²´...) n ⓖ i. Zopf 2; =holz n, for. top branches pl. of a tree.
zopfig (²`) a. ⓖ 1. pigtailed, wearing a pigtail, von Frauen: with (hair in) tresses, with plaited hair. — 2. fig. pedantic, antiquated, old-fashioned, fossil(ized), im Beamtentum: red-tape (regulations. &c.), ⚓ pipe-clay (system, &c.).
Zopf-lerche (²`...) f ⓖ = Haubenlerche; =mensch m pedant; (Beamter) red-tapist; =periode f = -zeit; =perücke f tie-wig, wig with a pigtail (attached to it); =stil m pedantic (or formal, superannuated) style.

Zopftum (²`..) n ⓖc. Kunst x.: pedantry, formalism; weitS. = Zopf 1 d.
Zopf-zeit (²`..) f ⓖ fig. age of pigtails, hist. Englands, etwa: Georgian era.

Zorillo (²´⌣`) [span.] m ⓖ zo. (Stinktier) maripurt (Mephi'tis zori'lla).

Zorn (²) [ahd.: zehren] m ⓖb. (pl. mst ~ausbrüche) wrath, anger, F u. P wax. poet. ire; (Leidenschaft) passion, temper, (Unwille) indignation; (Gereiztheit) irritation; (Galle) bile; e-n in ~ bringen, zum ~ reizen to rouse a p.'s anger, to put a p. into a passion or P a paddy, to exasperate a p ; f. ausgießen 1 und geraten ² unter in".

Zorn-anfall (²`..) m ⓖ, =ausbruch m fit (or burst) of anger or passion; =(es-)blick m angry look, furious glance; =entbrannt, =glühend a. ⓖ inflamed (or burning) with anger, boiling with rage, red-hot with passion.

zornig (²`) a. ⓖ 1. (f. Zorn) angry, geh. Spr.: wrathful, F u. P waxy, fast poet. irate; worked up (into a passion), F in a temper; (wütend) enraged, F wild. — 2. biSw. = zornmütig. — 3. (v. Zorn zeugend) passionate (words), hasty (remark), angry (look).

zorn-mütig (²`..) a. ⓖ irascible, choleric, hot-tempered; =(es-)röte f ⓖ flush of anger, glow of passion; =rute f, theol. rod of God's wrath; =wütig a. furious, enraged.
Zoroaster (²`⌣⌣) npr/m. ⓖα. (persischer Religionsstifter, um 600 v. Chr.) Zoroaster,

Zarathus(h)tra; Zoroastrianismus (⌣´⌣⌣`⌣`) m ⓖ (Religion der alten Perser) Zoroastrianism, Zarathus(h)trism; zoroastrisch a. ⓖ Zoroastrian, Zarathus(h)trian.

Zote (²´) [nhd.: *fr., it.] f ⓖ obscenity, obscene (or smutty, filthy, ribald, indecent) expression or word or joke, ribaldry, smut; ~n reißen (auch zoten v.n.(h.) ⓖ) to make obscene (or smutty, indecent) jokes or remarks, to use filthy language, F to talk smut.
zotenhaft (²´..) a. ⓖ = zotig.
Zoten-lied (²´..) n ⓖ obscene (or smutty) song; =reißen n, =reißerei f obscene (or smutty, filthy, indecent) talk or conversation or language, ribaldry, smut; =reißer(in f) m one who makes smutty (or filthy) jokes or remarks, smutty person.

zotig (²`) a. ⓖ obscene, smutty, filthy.

Zotte(1) (²`) [ahd.: tod] f ⓖ 1. tuft of hair; (verflochtenes Haar) matted (or shaggy, tangled) hair. — 2. ⚗ anat. villus.
Zottel-bär (²´..) m ⓖ zo. shaggy bear; =bart m tangled (or rough-looking) beard; =blume ⚘ f = Fieberklee.
Zottelei F (²´⌣`) f ⓖ toddling (along), dawdling. [ruffled, shaggy) hair.]
Zottel-haar (²´..) n ⓖ matted (or
zott(e)lig (²`(⌣)`) a. ⓖ shaggy.
Zottel-kopf (²´..) m ⓖ (person with a) shaggy head, auch: shock-head.
zotteln F (²`) v/n. (fn.) ²a. to toddle (along), to dawdle.
Zottel-wolle ⚘ (²´⌣`) f ⓖ shaggy wool.
zottig (²`) a. ⓖ bsd. von Haaren: (arranged) in tufts; (struppig) shaggy, rough, shagged, matted, ruffled, F tousled, ², ⚗ villous.
zottlig (⌣`) a. ⓖ f. zott(e)lig.
Bötus F (²`) [it.] m ⓖ (Abteilung e-r Schulklasse, Lehrstufe) section (or division) of a form or class, parallel form or class.

z. T. abbr. = zum Teil.
Ztr. abbr. = Zentner.

zu (²) [ahd.: to] I prp mit dat., verschmelzend mit dem Artikel: zum = zu dem, zur = zu der. 1. örtlich: meist to: (in j-s Wohnung) to a p.'s (house); (in j-s Nähe) near a p., by a p.('s side); (in der Richtung nach e-m, et. hin) towards a p., a th.; f. fahren 1 u. 4 gegen Ende und Fuß 7; zu Bett(e) gehen to go to bed, to retire to rest; er geht zu seinem Bruder he goes to (see) his brother, he is going to his brother's (house); er setzte sich zu s-m Freunde he went to sit near (or by the side of) his friend; f. Feld 2 gegen Ende und 3; zugrunde; der Weg zur Kirche the way to church; f. zutage, zuwege; zum (aus dem) Tore (Fenster) hinaus out of the gate (the window); von Haus zu Haus from house to house. — 2. hinzu-fügend, -tretend: with, in addition to; Brot zum Fleisch essen to eat bread with meat; Wasser zur (in die) Milch gießen to pour water into (or to add water to) the milk. — 3. ein Verweilen bz..: a) zu Hause at home; zur Linfen on the left hand (side); zur See at sea; zu Wasser und zu Lande by land and by water (vgl. zulande).

Signs (see page XVII): F familiar; P vulgar; P flash; ⌐ rare; † obsolete (died); * new word (born); ⫞ incorrect; ♪ music.

[Zu-...] — 1159 — [Zubiß]

b) vor Ortsnamen: a) at, z.B. zu Potsdam at Potsdam; b) vor den Namen von Großstädten meist: in, z.B. zu Berlin in Berlin. — 4. zeitlich, meist: at, z.B. zu Mittag, Mitternacht at noon, midnight; f. speisen 1; zur selben Stunde at the same hour; von Tag zu Tag from day to day; f. Unzeit. — 5. Art und Weise bz.: zu meinem Erstaunen to my astonishment; zu Fuß on foot; et. zur Genüge h. to have plenty (or enough) of s.th.; zum Glück für ihn luckily (or fortunately) for him; f. zuhauf; mir ist nicht zum Lachen I don't feel in a laughing humour or mood; f. Not 6 am Ende, Preis¹ 1 ✱; zum Teil (abbr. z. T.) partly, partially. — 6. als Ersatz für einen (objektiven) Genitiv: aus reiner Liebe zu euch from sheer affection for you; der Eingang zu e-m Hause the entrance to (or of) a house. — 7. bei Wünschen ꝛc. die Veranlassung bz.: e-m zu et. Glück wünschen, gratulieren to congratulate a p. upon a th.; f. Glück 1 gegen Ende. — 8. vor Zahlwörtern: a) vor *cardinal numbers*: zu (+ ad) 1; hinweisend: respecting 1, in reference to 1; zu zweien, zu zweit two and two, by twos, in couples; zu Hunderten by hundreds; sie kamen zu Hunderten und Tausenden they came in their hundreds and thousands; b) vor *ordinal numbers*: zu dritt (als dritter) we (you, &c.) three; in Auktionen: zum ersten, zum andern, zum dritten (und letzten) Male going, going, gone! — 9. vor *sup*.= auf³ (f. auf 7): zum besten (vgl. best 6) in the best way (possible), for the best; zum ersten for the first time; f. zu-(aller=)erst, =letzt, zumeist, zuvörderst; vgl. ober 2, unter 7 u. 8. — 10. *math*. zur Bezeichnung des Verhältnisses: drei verhält sich zu sechs wie fünf zu zehn three is (in the same proportion) to six as five to ten); f. Verhältnis 2 und umkehren. — 11. zur Anknüpfung prädikativer Bestimmungen: a) Zweck: das dient zum (mehr gbr. als) Beispiel, Exempel that serves as an example; aber: zum Beispiel, zum Exempel (abbr. z.B., z.E.) for example, for instance (abbr. e. g. = *exempli gratia*); es geschieht zu deinem Besten it is done for your best; Gott schuf den Menschen ihm zum Bilde God created man in his own image; er tut es Ihnen zu Gefallen he does it to please you; sie rüsten sich zum Kriege they are preparing for war; zunichte m. f. nicht II; zu Rate ziehen to consult; zu Recht besteh(e)n to be valid or legal; Tuch zu einem Rocke cloth for a coat; mir zum Schaden to my detriment; es ist zum Sterben it is enough to kill one; Wasser zum Trinken ... for drinking; er hat e-n Engel zum Weibe he has an angel of a wife; zum Zwecke f. Zweck 2; ✱ zur Disposition f. Disposition; zu Händen (od. zuhanden, f. ds) *(abbr. z. H.)* des Herrn N. in(to) the hands of Mr. N.; b) Grund: zu (über) et. lachen to laugh at a th.; c) Übergang, Umwandlung: e-n

sich zum Feinde m. to make an enemy of a p.; zum Narren w. to grow foolish, stärker: to go mad; f. zustande, zustatten; zu Staub w. to turn to dust; *ell*. (kommt) zur Sache! (come) to the point!; d) zu et. ernennen, erwählen, geboren werden, machen ꝛc.: e-n zum Fürsten erheben to raise a p. to the rank of a prince; der König ernannte ihn zum General ... appointed (or made) him a general; zum Führer erwählen to elect (or choose) as a leader; zum Erfinder geboren a born inventor. — 12. tonloses Bindewort zu als Anknüpfung e-s *inf*.: a) sie erinnert sich nicht, dort gewesen zu sein she does not remember having been there; ich erlaube dir zu kommen I allow you to come; ich habe zu arbeiten I have to work; es ist zu haben it is to be had, it can be had; ich komme Sie abzuholen I come to fetch you; es ist schwer zu unterscheiden it is difficult to distinguish; dagegen: es ist zu unterscheiden (es muß unterschieden werden) one must discriminate, a distinction must be made; Haus zu vermieten house to let; dagegen: das Haus ist zu verkaufen ... to be sold; b) nach *prp*.: **anstatt** hinzugehen instead of going there; **ohne** es zu wissen without knowing it; **um** mich zu täuschen in order to deceive me; c) dessen zu geschweigen f. geschweigen 1. — 13. mit *p.pr*., entsprechend dem von „sein" abhängigen *inf*.: das zu verkaufende Haus the house (which is) to be sold; ein wohl zu überlegender Schritt a step requiring careful consideration or which has to be well considered. — **II** *adv*. **14.** vor *a*. u. *adv*., ein Übermaß bz.: zu groß too big; zu klein too small; zu sehr, zuviel too much; f. zuviel; zu vorsichtig over-cautious; gar zu klein rather (or much) too small; f. gar 3; zuwe"nig u. zu wenig too little. — 15. (verschlossen, *ant*. offen) closed; die Tür ist zu ... is shut; mach' sie (die Tür) zu! shut it (to)!, close it! — 16. ab und zu, f. ab 5. — 17. Richtung bz.: nach (gegen ob. gen) Norden zu towards (the) north, to the north, north(ward); nach der Stadt zu in the direction of the town; bf. von e-r Bewegung nach e-m Ziele hin: auf et. zu gehen to walk towards a th.; oft: mit zu ergänzendem *imper*.: zu!, immer(=)zu!, nur zu! set to!, go (it)!, now then!, (fire) away! — 18. neben *verbs*, ununterbrochene Tätigkeit bz.: der Wind bläst immer(=)zu ... is for ever (or keeps on) blowing; er lief immer(=)zu he ran on and on, he kept on (or never stopped) running.

Zu-..., zu-... *(" ...)* Vorsilbe in Verbindung mit *verbs*, immer trennbar, bz. **1.** Verschließung, z.B. zu-klinken ⊕✱✱ to fasten with a latch, to latch (up). — **2.** Streben, Richtung, z.B. dem Gipfel zu-arbeiten ⊕✱✱ to toil (or struggle) towards the summit. — **3.** Hinzufügung, z.B. zu-arbeiten to add in working. — **4.** Fortfahren in einer Tätigkeit, Beschleunigung derselben, oft zj. mit

immer, z.B. zu-arbeiten ⊕✱✱ to pursue (or continue) one's work; zu-läuten ⊕✱✱ to go on ringing (the bells). — **5.** Erteilung, Zueignung, z.B. e-m eine Strafe zu-diktieren to impose a punishment (or penalty) on a p.

zu-ackern (‖‿) *v/a*. ⊕a✱✱ *agr*. to cover (or fill) up in ploughing.

zu-aller=erst, =letzt (-‿‿) *adv*. first of all, last of all.

Zuave ✕ (-‿‿, r-r f-‿‿) [⚥ fr. ar.✱] **zu-bauen** ⊙ (‖‿) *v/a*. ⊛✱✱ to build (or wall) up, to block up a view, &c. with buildings or with walls.

zu-behalten (‖‿‿) *v/a*. ⊛a✱/✱ to keep shut, den Rock: to keep buttoned up.

Zu-behör (‖‿✓) f ⊛, n ⊛c. (o. *pl*.) what belongs to a th.; appurtenances, accessories *pl*.; (Anhängsel) appendage to a th.; zu e-m Gute: (zugehörige Grundstücke) premises, buildings, outhouses, offices *pl*.; Wohnung von 6 Zimmern mit ~ six-roomed flat with all (the usual) conveniences or appointments; ⊕ (das nötige Gerät) appliances *pl*., gear, tools and machinery; bei Handwerkern: Arbeit und ~ work with (tools and) materials; Kocht.: ~ zu den Speisen: dressing, seasoning, relish; Tee mit ~ tea and turn-out, tea with something to eat.

zu-beißen (‖‿) ⊛a✱ **I** *v/n*. (h.): a) to snap at, to take (or have) a bite at a th., *fig*. to jump at (an offer), to accept (eagerly), to snatch at; b) F wacker 2 to eat away to one's heart's content, *co*. to play a good knife and fork, F to pack away one's food or grub. — **II** *v/a*. F Brot 2 to eat bread with one's meat, &c.

zu-bekommen (‖‿‿) *v/a*. ⊛✱/✱ **1.** to receive (or get) in addition or into the bargain. — **2.** to succeed in closing (up) or in fastening a door, a coat, &c.

zu-benam(s)en (‖‿‿) *v/a*. ⊛(⊛)✱/✱ to surname.

zu-benamt (‖‿✓), **zu-benannt** (‖‿✓) *a*.

Zuber (‿‿) [ahd. tub, (P) „zwie-bar", *ant*. Einer] *m* ⊛ (two-handled) tub; ein ~ voll Wasser a tubful of water.

zu-bereiten (‖‿‿‿) **I** *v/a*. ⊛✱/✱ to prepare, to get ready, ⊙ to dress, Speisen auch: to cook, to dish up; (fertig m.) to finish (a. ⊙); vgl. bereiten 2a. — **II** ~ n 🜙 f. Zubereitung.

Zu-bereiter (‖‿‿‿) *m*⊛ one who prepares, ⊙ dresser, finisher; **Zu-bereitung** (‖‿‿✓) *f* ⊛ preparation, ⊙ dressing, cooking of food; vgl. Bereitung.

Zu-bette-geh(e)n (‖‿‿‿) *n* 🜚 going to bed, F turning in; beim ~ auch: on retiring to rest, F on going to roost.

zu-billigen (‖‿‿) **I** *v/a*. ⊛✱✱: e-m et. 2 to grant (or concede, allow) a p. a th. — **II Zu-billigung** *f* ⊛ concession.

zu-binden (‖‿‿) *v/a*. ⊕✱✱ to tie up a sack, &c.; to bind up a wound, &c.; mit e-m Strick: to cord (up), to tie (or fasten) up with a rope; e-m die Augen 2 to bandage a p.'s eyes, to blindfold a p.

Zu-biß (‖‿) *m* ⊛a.: ein Glas Wein mit einem ~ a glass of wine with (a morsel of) s.th. to eat; vgl. Imbiß.

⚛ scientific; ⚘ botanical; ⚲ geography; ⊕ machinery; ⚒ mining; ⚔ military; ⚓ marine; ⚖ commercial; ✉ postal; 🚂 railway.

[zublasen] — 1160 — [Zuckermelone]

zu-blasen (ᵘᴸ∨) v/a. ⑱a** 1. vom Winde ꝛc.: to close (or shut) in (or by) blowing, a. to blow to. — 2. auf e-n ⸗ to blow towards a p. — 3. fig. e-m et. ⸗ = einblasen 2.

Zu-bläser (ᵘᴸ∨) m ㉒, ~in f ㊼ prompter.

zu-bleiben (ᵘᴸ∨) v/n. (ſu) ⑳** to remain closed or shut or locked.

zu-blinze(l)n (ᵘᴸ∨) v/n.(h.) ⑳ (㉒a)**: e-m ⸗ to wink at a p., to give a p. a wink.

zu-bringen (ᵘᴸ∨) v/a. ⑰** 1. e-m et. ⸗ to bring a p. a th.; Klatſch, Neuigkeiten ꝛc.: to carry, to report; jur.: die zugebrachten Kinder pl. the children by a former husband or wife; das zugebrachte Vermögen, das Zugebrachte the money brought into the marriage, the wife's dowry. — 2. die Zeit mit et. ⸗ to pass away one's time with a th., to spend (or employ) one's time in doing a th.; er brachte die Nacht unter freiem Himmel zu he spent the night in the open (air), he slept out in the fields. — 3. et. ⸗ to succeed in closing (up) or fastening a th.

zu-brocken (ᵘᴸ∨) v/a. ⑱** 1. = brocken³. — 2. F fig. etwas ⸗ to contribute s.th. (of one's own); et. zuzubrocken haben to have s.th. to live upon or to do with, to have an independent income or a competency.

Zu-brot (ᵘᴸ) n ⓝc. (ohne pl.) = Zufoſt.

Zu-buße (ᵘᴸ∨) [mhd.] f ㊸ 1. ⚔ (additional) contribution, share in a mine. — 2. auch von anderen Geſchäften und fig. new supply of funds; ~ geben to contribute (or pay) one's share towards a th.

zu-büßen ⚔ (ᵘᴸ∨) v/a. ⑨** to contribute funds towards the working of a mine, weitS. to sink money in a mine, &c.

Zucht (ᵉᶜʰᵗ) [ahd.; *ziehen] f ㊹ (pl. ⥀ i. 3) 1. a) rearing, breeding of cattle, &c., von Obſtbäumen ꝛc.: growing, cultivation; b) weitS. (Raſſe) breed, stock. — 2. ~ (Erziehung) von Perſonen: education, training, schooling; (Schul-, Manns-, ⚔ Kriegs-)~ discipline; der ~ entwachſen ſein to have outgrown the rod, to be beyond control; an ~ und Ordnung gewöhnen to (accustom to) discipline; in ~ und Ordnung halten to keep under discipline (auch ⚔), to keep a strict hand (or an iron rod) over, ſchwächer: to keep in order; ſich der ~ unterwerfen to submit (or yield) to discipline. — 3. (anſtändiges, geſittetes Benehmen) decency, propriety (of conduct), modesty; in aller ~, a. in allen Züchten u. Ehren with due decorum or propriety, most respectably. — 4. mit tadelndem Beiworte: das iſt ja eine wilde (oder tolle) ~ (Handlungsweiſe) that's a mad way of acting or proceeding, F that's Bedlam let loose.

Zucht-biene (ᵉᶜʰᵗ...) f ㊷ queen-bee; ⸗**buch** n Rennſport: stud-book; ⸗**bulle** m = ⸗ſtier.

züchten (ᵈ∨) [ahd.; *Zucht] I v/a. ⑱ Haustiere, Seidenwürmer ꝛc.: to breed, keep, rear, auch: to raise cattle; Zieroder Nutzpflanzen ꝛc.: to rear, grow, cultivate; Kinder ꝛc. 2 (in Zucht nehmen) to train ...; F to take ... in hand; vgl. ziehen 2. — II ~ n ㉓ i. Züchtung.

Züchter (ᵈ∨) m ㉒ breeder (of cattle, &c.), keeper (of bees, &c.); grower (of roses, potatoes, &c.), cultivator (of barley, &c.).

zucht-fähig (ᵉᶜʰᵗ...) a. ⑥ yielding to discipline, ſeltener: disciplinable; ⸗**geſetz** n ㉒ disciplinary law; ⸗**gewohnt** a. disciplined; ⸗**haus** n house of correction, penitentiary; im ⸗hauſe ſitzen to undergo (a sentence of) penal servitude, a. to serve (F to do) one's time, F to pick oakum; ⸗**haus-aufſeher** m inspector of a house of correction; ⸗**haus-gefangen(er)** s., ⸗**häusler(in** f) m, ⸗**häusling** m convict, person in (or undergoing) penal servitude, F jailbird; ⸗**haus-ſtrafe** f penal servitude; ⸗**hengſt** m stallion (for breeding).

züchtig (ᵈ∨) [ahd.; *Zucht] a. ⑥ modest, bashful, demure, maidenly; (ehrbar) decent, respectable; (keuſch) chaste.

züchtigen (ᵈ∨) [mhd.] I v/a. ⑱ to chastise, punish, correct, mit der Rute ꝛc.: to scourge, whip, lash, mit Worten: to reprove, reprimand, censure, scold; bibl. wen der Herr lieb hat, den züchtigt er (Hebr. 12, 6) whom the Lord loveth He chasteneth. — II ~ n ㉓ i. Züchtigung.

Züchtiger (ᵈ∨) m ㉒ chastiser.

Züchtigkeit (ᵈ∨) f ㊹ (f. züchtig) modesty, bashfulness, demureness; decency, propriety, chastity.

züchtiglich (ᵈ∨) a. ⑥ bsd. adv. = züchtig.

Züchtigung (ᵈ∨) f ㊺ chastisement, punishment, castigation, correction, mit Worten: reprimand(ing); körperliche ~ corporal punishment; (Selbſtkaſteiung) flagellation. [chastise (or punish.]

Züchtigungs-recht (ᵈ∨∨) n ㉒ right to⌐

Züchtling (ᵈ∨) m ⓓd. = Zuchthäusler; ~s-**anzug** m ㉒, ~s-**kleidung** f convict's (or prisoner's) garb or dress; ⸗s-**arbeit** f convict's work, picking oakum.

zucht-los (ᵉᶜʰᵗ...) a. ⑥ insubordinate, undisciplined (beide a. ⚔); (liederlich) dissolute, loose; ⸗**loſigkeit** f insubordination, want of discipline, dissoluteness, looseness; ⸗**meiſter** m task-master, F nigger-driver, terror; ⚔, Schule ꝛc.: ſtrenger ~ severe disciplinarian, bsd. ⚔: a martinet; ⸗**mittel** n means of correction, corrective; ⸗**pferd** n horse (kept) for breeding, stud-horse; ⸗**polizei** f correctional police; ⸗**polizei-gericht** n police-court; ⸗**rute** f rod of correction, rel., &c. a.: scourge; ſ. a. Fuchtel; ⸗**ſau** f broodsow; ⸗**ſchaf** n ewe (kept for breeding); ⸗**ſchule** f seminary; ⸗**ſtier** m bull (kept for breeding); ⸗**ſtute** f brood-mare; ⸗**tier(e** pl.) n, ⸗**vieh** n cattle (kept for breeding). [cultivation; training.]

Züchtung (ᵈ∨) f ㊺ breeding, growing,⌐

Zucht-wahl (ᵉᶜʰᵗ⸗ᴸ) f ㊸ Biologie: natürliche ~ (nach Darwin) natural selection.

Zuck (ᵈ) [mhd.; *ziehen] I m ⓝc. (sudden) jerk, twitch, start. — II zuck! int. etwa: bang!, there (goes)!

zuckeln F (ᵈ∨) v/n. (ſn) ⑳a. (ſchlotterig gehen) to toddle (or dawdle) along, to waddle.

zucken (ᵈ∨) [ahd.: tuck; *ziehen] ⑱ I v/n. (h.) to jerk, krampfhaft: to move convulsively, to twitch, zitternd: to quiver, to palpitate; der Blitz zuckte durch die Luft ... flashed through the air; das zuckt ihm durch alle Glieder it makes all his limbs twitch, ſchwächer: it sends a thrill through his whole body; im Herzen: ſtark ⸗ violently throbbing or palpitating, F bumping. — II v/a. und v/n. mit perſönlichem Subjekt: in die Höhe ⸗ to jerk up; er hat nicht gezuckt he did not wince or move (a muscle); die Achſeln (oder mit den Achſeln) ⸗ to shrug one's shoulders. — III ~ n ㉓ i. Zuckung. — IV ⸗d p.pr. und a. ⑥ jerking, krampfhaft ⸗d twitching, convulsive, spasmodic.

zücken (ᵈ∨) [mhd.: zucken] v/a. ⑱ bsd. den Degen ⸗ to draw the sword; den Dolch auf e-n ⸗ to point one's dagger at a p.

Zucker (ᵈ∨) [ahd.: sugar; it., ar., *ind.] m ㉒ sugar, chm.: 🜍 saccharum; 🜨 erſter ~ aus dem Zuckerrohre = Rohrzucker; ſ. Farin i. Hut¹ 3; in ~ verwandeln, zu ~ werden to turn to sugar, 🜍 to saccharify; ~ in et. tun to put sugar into (or to add sugar to) a th., to sugar (or to sweeten) a th.

Zucker-ahorn ♃ (ᵈ∨...) m ㉒ sugar-maple (Acer saccharinum) [auch Nationalemblem Kanadas]; ⸗**apfel** ♃ m custard-apple (Ano'na squamo'sa); ⸗**artig** a. ⑥ sugarlike, sugary, saccharine, ...oid; ⸗**bäcker** (⸗**in** f) m confectioner; ⸗**bäckerei** f confectioner's (or sweet-stuff) shop; ⸗**back-werk** n confectionery; (Kuchen) pastry; ⸗**bau** m cultivation of the sugar-cane; ⸗**bildung** f formation of sugar, 🜍 saccharification; ⸗**bohne** f (Konfekt) sugar-plum; ⸗**bonbon** m = Bonbon; ⸗**brot** n: a) (Konfekt) sweet cake, b) = ⸗hut; ⸗**büchſe** f sugar-box, canister for sugar; ⸗**doſe** f = ⸗büchſe; ⸗**erbſe** f: a) ♃ sweet-pea, b) (Konfekt) (su.-)drop; vgl. ⸗bohne; ⸗**fabrik** f su.-factory or ⸗works pl.; vgl. ⸗ſiederei; ⸗**fabrikant** m = ⸗ſieder; ⸗**faß** n su.-cask, größeres: hogshead; ⸗**form** ⚒ f sugar-mould; ⸗**freſſer** m. orn. sugar-eater (Ce'rthia flave'ola); ⸗**früchte** ♃ f/pl. candied fruit sg.; ⸗**gärung** f: 🜍 saccharine fermentation; ⸗**gaſt** m, ent. su.-mite (Lepi'sma saccha'rina); ⸗**gebäck(en)** n confectionery; ⸗**gehalt** 🜍 m proportion (or percentage) of (pure) sugar contained in a th.; ⸗**gehalt-meſſer** m, ⸗**gehalts-wage** f = ⸗meſſer a.; ⸗**geſchmack** m sugary taste; ⸗**guß** m Konditorei: sugar-icing or ⸗ice; ⸗**haltig** a. containing sugar. 🜍 sacchariferous, saccharine; ⸗**hammer** m hammer for breaking sugar; ⸗**handel** m sugar-trade; ⸗**harn-ruhr** f = ⸗krankheit; ⸗**honig** ♃ m = Steinhonig; ⸗**hut** m sugar-loaf.

zuck(e)rig (ᵈ∨∨) a. ⑥ 1. = zuckerhaltig. — 2. sugary, 🜍 saccharine.

Zucker-kalk (ᵈ∨...) m ㉒ chm. sugar-lime, 🜍 sucrate of lime; ⸗**kand(is)** 🜨 (ᵈ∨∨∨) [i. Kandis] m sugar-candy; ⸗**kind** n (Koſewort) sweet child, darling; ⸗**krankheit** f path. diabetes, 🜍 glucosuria; an ~ leidend diabetic(al); ⸗**kuchen** m sugared cake; ⸗**löffel** m sugar-spoon; ⸗**mandel** f (Konfekt) sugared almond, (gebrannte Mandel) burnt almond; ⸗**maul**, ⸗**mäulchen** F n person with a sweet tooth, co. sugar-baby; ⸗**mehl** n powdered sugar; ⸗**melone** f (sweet)

[Zuckermesser] — 1161 — [zufalten]

melon (Cu'cumis melo); =**messer**: a) *m*, *phys*. saccharometer, sugarmeter; b) *n* sugar-cleaver; =**messung** *f*: ⚗ saccharometry; =**milbe** *f*, *ent*. sugar-louse (*Glyciphagus sa'cchari*); =**muud** F *m* = maul.
zuckern (⌣⌣) I *v/a*. ❷a. to (sweeten with) sugar; ❷ zuckert sugared, auch = **zuckersüß** b. — II *a*. ❺ (of) sugar.
Zucker-palme ⚘ (⌣⌣...) *f* ❷ Ost-indien: arenga(*a*) (*Are'nga sacchari'fera*); =**papier** *n* paper for covering sugar-loaves, a.: su.-paper; =**pflanzer** *m* su.-grower; =**pflanzung** *f* su.-plantation; =**plätzchen** *n* (Konfekt) (sugar-)drop, lozenge; =**prämi-e** 💰 *f* bounty paid to exporters of sugar; =**probe** *f* sugar-test; =**puppe** *f*, =**püppchen** *n* = **=kind**; =**quetscher** ⚙ *m* su.-crusher; =**raffinerie** ⚙ *f* su.-refinery; =**raffinierer** *m* su.-refiner; =**rohr** ⚘ *n* su.-cane (*Sa'ccharum officina'rum*); afrikanisches ~ imphee (*Holcus sacchara'tus*); chinesisches ~ sorghum, sorgho (*Sorghum sacchara'tum*); =**rohr-mühle** ⚙ *f* cane-mill; =**rohr-rückstände** *m/pl*. cane-trash, bagasse; =**rohr-saft** *m* juice of the sugar-cane; =**rübe** ⚘ *f*: a) weiße ~ sweet turnip; b) rote ~ sugar-beet: =**ruhr** *f*, *path*. diabetes; =**sachen** *f/pl*. = =waren; =**satz** *m* = sirup; ⚬**sauer** *a*. *chm*.: ⚗ saccharic, ⚬saures Salz saccharate; =**säure** *f* saccharic acid ($C_6H_{10}O_8$); =**schale** *f* sugar-basin; =**schneidemaschine** *f* ⚙ sugar-cutting machine; =**schote** ⚘ *f* = =erbse a; =**sieden** ⊙ *n* su.-refining; =**sieder** *m* su.-refiner; =**siederei** *f* su.-boilery or -refinery, als Gebäude: su.-house; *vgl*. =fabrik; =**sirup** 🍯 *m* molasses *pl*., treacle; =**stange** *f* su.-stick; =**steuer** *f* duty on sugar; =**stoff** *m*, *chm*. saccharine matter; =**streu-büchse** *f* su.-caster or -sifter; =**streuer**, =**streu-löffel** *m* su.-dredger; ⚬**süß**: a) (as) sweet as sugar; b) sugary, sugared, *fig*. auch: honeyed, honied (words, &c.); =**verbindungen** *f/pl*. *chm*.: ⚗ sucrates, saccharates *pl*.; =**waren** *f/pl*.; =**werf**; =**wasser** *n* sugared water, sugar and water; =**werk** *n* confectionery, sweetmeats *pl*., F sweets, lollipops *pl*.; =**worte** *n/pl*. honeyed words; =**wurzel** ⚘ *f* skirret (*Sium Si'sarum*); =**zange** *f*: a) zum Zerkleinern: sugar-nippers *pl*.; b) zum Fassen: sugar-tongs *pl*.; =**zentrifuge** ⊙ *f* sugar-drainer; =**zwieback** 🍞 *m* sweet biscuit.
Zuck-krampf (⌣...) *m* ⚕ *path*.: ⚗ clonic spasm; =**mücke** *f*, *ent*. f. Mücke 1.
Zuckung (⌣⌣) *f* ⚕ jerking, convulsion, convulsive action or movement or fit; twitching, palpitation, thrill; ~en bekommen to be seized with (F to go into) convulsions or spasms.
zu-dämmen ⊙ (⌣⌣) *v/a*. ❽** 1. ein Loch im Pflaster. ❷ to stop up — 2. (mit e-m Deich verschließen) to dam up.
zu-decken (⌣⌣) *v/a*. ❽** to cover (up), mit einem Tuch: to cover over, to tuck up: mit einem Deckel ❷ to put a lid on a saucepan, &c.. to cover; *hort*. mit Dünger, Stroh ⚡. ❷ to dress with manure, straw, &c.; *fig*. mit dem Mantel der Liebe ❷ to palliate, to put a charitable construction on.

zu-dem (⌣') *adv*. besides, moreover, in addition to that; to which must be added; = außerdem und überdies.
zu-denken (⌣⌣⌣) *v/a*. ❽** 1. e-m ein Geschenk, eine Strafe ⚡. ❷ to purpose (or intend) making a p. a present, giving a p. a punishment, &c.; die mir zugedachte Ehre the honour intended (or in store) for me. — 2. = hinzudenken.
zu-diktieren (⌣⌣⌣) *v/a*. ❾** f. zu-... 5.
Zu-drang (⌣⌣) *m* ⓓc. (o. *pl*.) 1. rush to (or throng outside) a place, zu einer Bank, e-m Theater ⚡.: crowd besieging (the doors of) a bank, a theatre, &c.; der unerwartete ~ der Gäste the unexpected influx (or inrush) of visitors. — 2. *path*. ~ des Blutes zum Gehirn: ⚗ cerebral congestion.
zu-drängen (⌣⌣⌣) *v/refl*. ❽**: sich ❷ to rush (or crowd, throng) to a place, to besiege a place; *fig*. to intrude, to obtrude o.s., to press o.s. forward; sich überall ❷ to push (or force) one's way in everywhere.
zu-drehen (⌣⌣) *v/a*. ❽** 1. to close by turning, to shut off, e-n Hahn: to turn off. — 2. e-m den Rücken ❷ to turn one's back upon a p.; *vgl*. zufehren 1).
zu-dringlich (⌣⌣⌣) *a*. ❽ intruding, intrusive, obtrusive, im Benehmen: forward, officious, im Bitten: importunate; ~**keit** *f* ❷ obtrusiveness, forwardness, officiousness, importunity.
zu-drücken (⌣⌣) *v/a*. ❽** 1. to close by pressing or squeezing, to shut (to); *fig*. ein Auge bei et. ❷ to pretend not to see a th., to overlook a th., (es nicht genau damit nehmen) to wink (or connive) at a th. — 2. (immer) ❷ to go on pressing, *fig*. to push on.
zu-eignen (⌣⌣⌣) I *v/a*. ❷b**: e-m et. ❷ = zuerteilen, (zuschreiben) to attribute (or ascribe) a th. to a p.; e-m ein Buch ⚡. ❷ to dedicate ... to a p.; sich (*dat*.) et. ❷ to appropriate a th. (to o.s.), to help o.s. to a th., als sein Eigentum: to take possession of a th., widerrechtlich: to usurp a th., to arrogate a th. to o.s. — II ~ *n* ❷ f. Zueignung.
Zu-eigner (⌣⌣⌣) *m* ❷ appropriator, e-s Buches: dedicator.
Zu-eignung (⌣⌣⌣) *f* ❹ (f. zueignen I) allotment; dedication of a book; appropriation; (widerrechtliche Aneignung) usurpation; ~**s=schrift** (⌣⌣⌣,⌣) *f* ❷ dedicatory letter or preface, (letter of) dedication.
zu-eilen (⌣⌣⌣) *v/n*. (fn) ❽**: auf e-n, et. ❷ to hasten (or run, rush) towards a p., a th.; *fig*. f-m Verderben ❷ to rush (headlong) into destruction.
zu-ein-ander (--⌣⌣) *adv*. to(wards) each other, auch: one to another.
zu-erkennen (⌣⌣⌣) I *v/a*. ❾b*/* *jur*.: e-m et. ❷ to adjudge (or adjudicate) a th. to a p., weit⚬. = zuerteilen; e-m einen Preis ❷ to award a p. a prize; e-m eine Würde, Ehre ❷ to confer ... on a p. — II ~ *n* ❷ u. **Zu-erkennung** *f* ❹ adjudication; award; **Zu-erkennungs-urteil** *n* ❷ adjudicative sentence.
zu-erst (⌣', ⌣') [ahd.] *adv*. in the first place; (als der ob. die erste) first (of all), before everybody; (vor allem übrigen)

first and foremost, before everything; gleich ❷ (anfangs) from the (very) first, to begin with, at first; ❷ am Platz, ❷ zur Stelle first on the spot, first in the field; der ❷ Angekommene. Antommende the first comer or arrival; ❷ trank er ein Glas Bier he began by drinking a glass of beer; wer schoß ❷? who shot (or fired) first?, who was the first to shoot?, who started (or began the) shooting?
zu-erteilen (⌣⌣⌣) I *v/a*. ❽*.*: e-m et. ❷ to allow (or apportion, assign) a th. to a p., to bestow (or confer) a th. on a p. — II ~ *n* ❷ u. **Zu-erteilung** *f* ❹ allotment, apportionment, assignment.
zu-essen (⌣⌣⌣) *v/a*. u. *v/n*. (h.) ❽** 1. = zubeißen II. — 2. iß (nur) zu! go on eating!, eat away (as much as you like or can)!, F peg away (at it)!
zu-fächeln (⌣⌣⌣) *v/a*. ❷a**: e-m Kühlung ⚡. ❷ to waft coolness, &c. to(wards) a p.; sich Luft ❷ to fan o.s.
zu-fahren (⌣⌣⌣) *v/n*. (fn und h.) ❺b** 1. dem Dorfe ❷ to drive towards (or in the direction of) the village; ⚓ auf das Land ❷ to make for land, to sail (or steam) towards (the) land; *fig*. auf e-n ❷ (losspringen) to rush (or spring) upon a p., to fly at a p.; unbesonnen (drauf) ❷ to go headlong, to act hastily or rashly, f. blind ❷ am Schluß. — 2. gut ❷ to drive at a good (or brisk, rattling) pace.
Zu-fahrt (⌣') *f* ❹ zu e-m Hause: drive.
Zu-fall (⌣') [mhd.] *m* ⓓc. chance, hazard, casual event; (Möglichkeit) contingency; (Vorfall) incident. occurrence, (Unfall) accident, casualty: *path*. = Anfall 3; durch (bloßen) ~ by (a mere) accident, (quite) accidentally; glücklicher ~ lucky hit; widriger ~ ill luck, misfortune, mischance; es hängt ganz vom ~ ab, ob ⚡. it is quite a matter of chance whether ⚡.; et. dem ~ überlassen to leave a th. to chance; Launen des ~s freaks (or whims) of fortune.
zu-fallen (⌣⌣⌣) *v/n*. (fn) ❺a** 1. (ant. auffallen 3) to close in falling, von einer Tür auch, to shut (of) itself; von selbst ❷de Tür swinging door, swingdoor; die Augen fallen ihm zu his eyes (or eyelids) are closing or falling to. — 2. (zu et. hinfallen) to fall towards a th. — 3. e-m ❷ (zuteil w.) to fall to a p.'s share, to accrue to a p., von einer Erbschaft auch: to come to a p., von e-r Aufgabe: to devolve upon a p., *jur*. von einem zu liefernden Beweise: to rest (or lie) with a p.
zu-fällig (⌣⌣⌣) [Zufall] *a*. ❺ (nicht wesentlich) accidental, (gelegentlich) incidental, casual, haphazard, random, (möglich) contingent; (unerwartet) fortuitous, *adv*. ❷, ❷**er-weise** incidentally, by chance, by hazard, F by a fluke; (gelegentlich) casually, occasionally; wenn ich ihn ❷ treffe if (or whenever) I happen (or chance) to meet him; ~**keit** *f* ❹ accidentalness, contingency; *bsd*. im *pl*. = Zufall.
Zu-fall-spiel (⌣⌣⌣) *n* ❷ = Hasardspiel.
zu-falten (⌣⌣⌣) *v/a*. ❽**: e-n Brief ❷ to fold up .... die Hände ❷ to fold one's hands.

♪ Musik; ⚗ Wissenschaft; ⚘ Pflanze; ♀ Geographie; ⊙ Technik; ⚒ Bergbau; ⚔ Militär; ⚓ Marine; 💰 Handel; ✉ Post; 🚂 Eisenbahn.

[zufassen] — 1162 — [Zugang]

zu-fassen (⸗⸗) v. n. (h.) ⊕** to seize (hold of) a th., to catch on to a th., to clutch, F to grab (at) a th.

zu-fertigen (⸗⸗) I v/a. ⊕**: e-m et. ⸗ to dispatch a th. to a p.; e-m einen Auftrag ⸗ to send (or transmit) a p. an order. — II ~ n 23 und **Zu-fertigung** f ⊕ dispatch(ing), transmission.

zu-flechten (⸗⸗) v/a. ⊕b** to (en)close (or bar, fence, protect) with wickerwork, to plait (or twist) together.

zu-flicken (⸗⸗) v/a. ⊕** to mend, patch, repair, darn: Löcher in e-m Kleide ⸗ to patch up holes (or tears) in a dress.

zu-fliegen (⸗⸗) v n. (jn) ⊕** 1. einem Orte ⸗ to fly to(wards) a place. — 2. (immer) ⸗ to exert o.s. in (or to keep on) flying. — 3. die Tür flog zu ... (was) slammed, ... closed with a bang. ⸗ ... (was) banged to.

zu-fließen (⸗⸗) I v n. (jn) ⊕d** to flow in or to(wards). fig. to flow in upon: die Gedanken fließen ihm zu (the) ideas come readily to him; das Geld floß ihm von allen Seiten zu ... was showered upon him from all sides; e-m et. ⸗ (angedeihen) l. to bestow a th. upon a p.: die dem Meere ⸗den Ströme the rivers flowing (or emptying) into the sea. — II ~ n 23 f. **Zufluß** 1.

Zu-flucht (⸗⸗t) f ⊕ (o. pl.) refuge; (Obdach) (place of) shelter: seine ~ zu e-m nehmen to take refuge (or shelter) with a p. or under a p.'s roof; seine ~ zu et. nehmen to have recourse (F to fly) to a th.; fig. meine letzte ~ my last resource, my sheet-anchor.

Zu-fluchts-hafen (⸗⸗ts...) m = =ort; **=haus** n house of refuge, ehm.: (Heiligtum) sanctuary; **-ort, -platz** m, **-stätte** f place (or harbour) of refuge, (place of) shelter, retreat, für Alte, Kranke ⸗c.: home, asylum.

Zu-fluß (⸗⸗) m ⊕a. 1. (das Zufließen) flowing in, (in)flow, influx (of various, &c.); med.: des Blutes ⸗c. ⸗ afflux. — 2. (das Zufließende) die Zuflüsse des Rheins the affluents (or feeders, tributaries) pl. of the Rhine: ⊕ ~ von Waren supply of goods.

Zu-fluß-graben, -kanal (⸗⸗...) m ⊕ feeder of a lake, pond, &c.; **-röhre** ⊕ f. Wasser ⸗c.: feed(ing)-, service-, supply-pipe.

zu-flüstern (⸗⸗) v/a. ⊕a**: e-m et. ⸗ to whisper (or breathe) a th. to a p. or in(to) a p.'s ears. fig. to insinuate (or hint) a th. to a p.

Zu-flüsterung (⸗⸗) f ⊕ whisper, words whispered to a p., fig. insinuation.

zu-folge (-⸗⸗) prp. (mit dat., wenn fie nachfleht, mit gen., wenn fie vorangeht) = gemäß, auch owing to: (auf Grund von) by virtue (or on the strength) of: (infolge von) in consequence of; dem⸗ in consequence (or pursuance) of which.

zu-frieden (-⸗⸗) [adv.] a. ⊕ 1. adv. at peace: fich ⸗ geben to rest satisfied: fich mit et. ⸗ geben to acquiesce in a th., to bear up with a th.: laß ihn ⸗! let (or leave) him alone! — 2. content(ed), (zufriedengeftellt) satisfied, gratified, (glücklich) happy; mit e-m etwas ⸗ fein to be satisfied (or pleased) with a p., a th.; mit e-m et. nicht ⸗ fein to be dissatisfied (or displeased) with a th.; er ift mit allem ⸗ he puts up with anything; Sprichw. der ⸗e hat immer genug a contented mind is a continual feast. — 3. ich bin es ⸗ (damit einverftanden) I agree (or am agreeable) to it, I (give my) consent to it, F all right!, alright!

Zu-friedenheit (-⸗⸗⸗) f ⊕ content(ment), contentedness, contented (or satisfied) state; (Wohlfein) ease, comfort.

zu-frieden-ftellen (-⸗⸗⸗) v/a. ⊕**: e-m ⸗ to satisfy a p., to accede to a p.'s request, to gratify a p.'s wish(es); **⸗ftellend** (-⸗⸗⸗) a. ⊕ giving satisfaction, satisfactory, gratifying, pleasant; **-ftellung** f ⊕ satisfying a p., giving a p. satisfaction, gratification of a p.('s wishes).

zu-frieren (⸗⸗) v n. (jn) ⊕c** to freeze up, to get frozen up, von Seen ⸗c. auch: to be(come) covered with (a sheet of) ice; zugefroren frozen up or over.

zu-fügen (⸗⸗) v/a. ⊕** 1. (hinzufügen) to add. — 2. = antun 2.

Zu-fuhr (⸗⸗) f ⊕ 1. importation (or introduction, supply) of goods, &c. — 2. (das Zugeführte) supplies, imports, arrivals pl., stock; (Lebensmittel) provisions pl.; ⨯ dem Feinde die ~ abschneiden to cut off (or intercept) the enemy's supplies.

zu-führen (⸗⸗) I v a. ⊕** 1. to import (or supply) goods, &c., to introduce a friend, &c., to bring customers, &c.; ⨯ e-m Heere Lebensmittel ⸗ to provision an army; ⊕ mach. (der Maschine) Zugeführtes feed; e-m Hause Gas, Wasser ⸗ to lay on gas, water in a house, to connect a house with the (gas-, water-)main. — 2. ⚒ (erweitern) to enlarge a gallery, &c. — II ~ n 23 3. f. **Zuführung**. — III ⸗d p.pr. u. a. ⊕ 4. in den Bed. des inf. — 5. Luft ⸗d ventilating: ⸗, anat. ⸗de Gefäße, Kanäle ⸗ afferent vessels, ducts pl.

Zu-führer (⸗⸗) m ⊕. **~in** f ⊕ meift b.s. (Kuppler[in]) procurer, f procuress.

Zu-führung (..) f ⊕ (f. zuführen 1) supply, supplying, importation, introduction.

zu-füllen (⸗⸗) v/a. ⊕** Wasser ⸗c. to add, to pour in; einen Graben ⸗c. ⸗ (ausfüllen) to fill up ... with earth, &c.

Zug (⸗, ⨯ ⸗, pl. Züge: ⸗) [ahd.: tugziehen] m ⊕c. 1. (das Ziehen) drawing, pull(ing), tug(ging), von Zugtieren ⸗c.: draught. mech. traction; (Ruck) jerk; mit e-m gewaltigen ~ with a mighty pull or effort; e-n ~ an der Glocke tun to pull (or ring) the bell. — 2. ~ eines Heeres: march, expedition, progress; f. Kreuz-, Rück-zug; der Vögel ⸗c.: passage, migration; der Wolken ⸗c.: course; der Luft, des Windes: draught, current of air; zur Lüftung: ventilation; hier herricht ein arger (Luft-)~ there is a strong draught here; der Ofen hat feinen ~ the stove has no draught or does not draw (well). — 3. (Gesamtheit von Ziehenden): a) von Perfonen: file, ⨯ auch: squad, column, section; train of artillery; bjb. ecc. procession: vgl. Leichenzug; b) von Tieren: troop, flock, herd, von Vögeln: flight, von Fischen: shoal; ~ Ochsen, Pferde team of oxen, horses. — 4. (Gesamtheit von Fahrzeugen, Wagen) train (auch 🚂); ~ von Wagen file (or line) of carriages, ⨯ train of artillery; 🚂 den ~ (rechtzeitig) erreichen to catch the train; den ~ verfehlen to lose (or miss) one's train; abgehender ~ departing train, train while starting or leaving; ankommender ~ incoming train, train arriving at a place or steaming into the station. — 5. a) (Linie, Strich) stroke (or dash) of the pen, pencilled line; touch of the pencil; in kurzen Zügen in a few strokes, in brief outline; in kräftigen Zügen in bold outlines; b) die Züge eines Bildes, weitS. eines Gesichts: the features or lineaments pl. ...; c) fig. (Eigentümlichkeit) (characteristic) trait, (peculiar) feature, ein ~ der Zeit a sign of the times. — 6. (Bewegung von et. Gezogenem; fig. Neigung) ~ mit dem Netze draught of the net; Brettspiel: move; Sie find am ~e it is your move; Weiß ift am Zuge white to play; fig. ~ des Herzens inclination, bent; (Trieb) (natural) impulse; dem ~e des Herzens folgen to obey the inner voice; aus dem ~ kommen to get out of practice or touch; im besten (ob. fo recht im) ~e fein to be in full swing or motion or play or activity; in ~ bringen to set going or in motion; to bring into vogue or fashion; in (ob. mit) einem ~e (Male), auf einen ~ (ohne Unterbrechung) at one stretch or pull, without a break, F at one go, straight off; in einem ~e schlafen to sleep without (once) waking; ~ um ~ for (ready) cash; ~ um (ob. für) ~ handeln to have a ready-money business, to have a quick turnover. — 7. a) beim Trinken: draught; kleiner ~ sip; e-n ~ aus der Flasche tun to take a draught (or F pull) at the bottle; das Glas auf einen ~ austrinken to empty ... at one draught or F at one go; in langen Zügen trinken to take deep draughts; b) beim Rauchen: whiff; ein paar Züge tun to take a few whiffs at a pipe, cigar, &c. — 8. (Zucken im Todeskampfe) agony, jetzt nur gbr. in: in den letzten Zügen liegen to lie in the agonies of death or med. in extremis, mehr gbr.: to be dying or at the last gasp, to be breathing one's last. — 9. ♪ = **Pianozug**, **Orgelftimme**. — 10. ⊙ = a) = **Flaschenzug**; b) (Kolben an einer Pumpe) piston; ~ (Heizkanal) eines Ofens: flue; c) ~ an der Tür cord for opening a street-door from within; d) ⨯ ⊕ Züge pl. rifling, (spiral) grooves pl.; ohne Züge unrifled; e) ehm. ~ am Damenkleide: dressholder; f) Schuhm.: elastischer ~ am Stiefel: elastic side-spring.

Zu-gabe (⸗⸗) [zugeben] f ⊕ 1. s.th. given as an addition or extra, s.th. thrown in. Buchhandel: supplement, beim Messen: s.th. over (the full measure), beim Wiegen: make-weight, surplus: et. als ~ erhalten to get s.th. in(to) the bargain. — 2. = **Prämie**.

Zu-gang (⸗⸗) [ahd.] m ⊕e. 1. = zu e-m access (or admittance) to a p. — 2. (ßej.

Signs (see page XVII): F familiar; P vulgar; ⸗ flash; ⨯ rare; † obsolete (died); * new word (born); ** incorrect; ♪ music.

[Zugangel] — 1163 — [zugrunde]

der zu etwas führt) avenue, approach, road which leads (up) to a th.; gate, gateway; (Eingang) entrance to, entry, (Vorhalle) entrance-hall; die Zugänge versperren to stop (or block up) every approach or avenue. [ground-line.)
Zug-angel ☉ (⸗⸗) f ⊕ Fischerei:
zu-gängig a. ⊕ = zugänglich.
zu-gänglich (⸗⸗⸗) a. ⊕ accessible, approachable, von Personen auch: affable; F come-at-able; leicht (schwer) 2 of easy (difficult) access; fig. 2 für et. susceptible of a th., open to a th.; 2 m. to render accessible, to pave the way to, fig. a. to throw open to the public; wissenschaftliche Dinge: to popularize; ~keit f ⊕ accessibility, approachableness, von Personen auch: affability; ~machung f bsd. fig. opening up, won Ländern: popularization.
Zug-anker ☉ (⸗...) m carp. tension-rod, iron brace or tie; =**artikel** ⚭ m article which draws, very saleable (or popular) article, F draw; =**balken** ⊕ m tie-beam; =**band** n ribbon to pull s.th. by; =**bohrer** m der Böttcher: turrel; =**brücke** f draw-bridge; =**brunnen** m = Ziehbrunnen; =**dynamometer** n (m), mach. traction-dynamometer.
zu-geben (⸗⸗⸗) v/a. ⚭c*** 1. to add, bei einem Handel: to give into the bargain, ⚭ to throw in with. — 2. Kartenspiel: to follow suit. — 3. (einräumen) to accede to; to grant, allow, admit; (gestehen) to confess; sein Unrecht 2 to admit being in the wrong, to own one's mistake or error.
zu-gedacht (⸗⸗cht) p.p. von zudenken (s. ds. bsd. 1) u. a. ⊕ intended, meant for.
zu-gegen (-⸗⸗) a. nur prädikativ; 2 sein bei etwas to be present at (or to attend) a meeting, to assist at a ceremony.
zu-geh(e)n (⸗⸗(⸗)) v n. (jn) ⚭⚭** 1. (sich schließen) to close (a. von Wunden 2c.), to shut (auch von Türen 2c.); der Rock geht nicht zu ... won't button or F meet. — 2. auf n, et. 2 to walk towards a p., a th.; diese Arbeit geht dem Ende zu .. is coming to an end or drawing to a close. — 3. spitzig 2 (ausgehen) to end in (or run to) a point, to taper off. — 4. von Sachen: e-m 2 = zukommen 2; ⚭ die Waren sind uns soeben zugegangen the goods have just reached us. — 5. (geschehen) to happen; wie geht es zu, daß //? how is it that //?; wie ging es zu, daß // how came it (to pass) that //?; es geht sonderbar in dieser Welt zu strange things happen in this world (of ours), it is a queer world (to be in); es müßte mit dem Teufel 2, wenn // the devil 2 (F Old Nick) must be in it if //; im Kriege geht es nicht anders zu war (or such) is war; s. Ding 4 gegen Ende. — 6. gut 2 to walk a good pace, to trot along briskly; 2 geh(t) zu! move on (faster)!, get along!, walk faster!
Zu-gehör (⸗⸗⸗) n (m) ü c. = Zubehör.
zu-gehören (⸗⸗⸗⸗) v n. (h.) ⚭⚭** 1. e-m 2 to belong (or appertain) to a p. — 2. abs. nicht jedes Fleisch allein, es gehört Brot zu (dazu) .. bread should be eaten (or F go) with it.

zu-gehörig (⸗⸗⸗⸗) a. ⊕ = gehörig 1 u. 2, auch: proper, becoming; pertinent; das Haus mit dem 2en Mobiliar the house with the requisite (or appropriate) furniture; ~keit f ⊕ = Gehörigkeit 1; (Mitgliedschaft) membership of a club, &c.; [~ e-r Kettenbrücke: tie-rod.
Zug-eisen (⸗⸗⸗) n mach. tie-bar.
Zügel (⸗⸗) [abd.; *Zug] m ⊕ 1. man. Fahrkunst: bridle, bsd. des Reitpferdes: mst pl. ⸗ (driving-)reins, F ribbons pl.; dem Pferde die ~ anziehen to pull (or rein) in a horse; s. fallen 4 unter „in"; ein Pferd am ~ führen to lead ... by the bridle; mit verhängtem ~ reiten, dem Pferde die ~ schießen lassen to ride at full gallop or speed, to give the horse the reins or his head. — 2. fig. curb, check, restraint; e-m die ~ schießen l. to let a p. have his fling, to indulge in a p.; s. schießen 4; die ~ der Regierung in Händen haben (ergreifen) to hold (to seize) the reins of government.
Zügel-fabrikant ☉ (⸗⸗⸗...) m ⊕ bridle-maker; =**hand** f (des Reiters Linke) bridle-hand, left (or near) hand; =**los** a. ⊕ without a bridle, unbridled; fig. auch: unrestrained, licentious, unruly; =**losigkeit** f ⊕ unbridled (or unrestrained) state, fig. licentiousness.
zügeln (⸗⸗) v/a. ⊕ a. ein Pferd: to bridle, to pull (or rein) in ..., fig. e-n, j-s Leidenschaft: to curb (or check, restrain).
Zügel-pflock ☉ (⸗⸗⸗) m ⊕ bridle-jack; =**ring** m Sattlerei: bridle- (or bit-)ring; =**schieber** m bridle-slide. [(s. zügeln.)
Züg(e)lung (⸗⸗(⸗)) f ⊕ bridling, &c.
Zu-gemüse (⸗⸗⸗⸗) n ⊕ vegetables pl. eaten (or served up) with (the) meat; weit 2. garnishing of a dish.
zu-genannt (⸗⸗⸗⸗) a. ⊕ surnamed.
Zug-entgleisung ⛙ (⸗⸗⸗⸗) f ⊕ derailing (or derailment) of a train. [nete(r).
Zu-geordnete(r) (⸗⸗⸗⸗⸗) m f = Beigeord-
Zuger [Zug 2, schwz. Kanton und Stadt] m ⊕ **-in** f ⊕ inhabitant of Zug; ~ See m Lake of Zug.
zu-geritten (⸗⸗⸗⸗) p.p. v. zureiten (s. ds) u. a. ⊕(D9) broken in (for riding).
zu-gesellen (⸗⸗⸗⸗) v/a., v/refl. ⚭⚭*/*; (sich) e-m 2 to associate with a p., to join a p.
zu-gestanden (⸗⸗⸗⸗) p.p. v. zugestehen; ⸗er-maßen (⸗⸗⸗⸗⸗⸗) adv. admittedly.
Zu-geständnis (⸗⸗⸗⸗⸗) n ⊕ concession.
zu-gesteh(e)n (⸗⸗⸗(⸗)) v/a. ⚭⚭** 1. = gestehen. — 2. e-m et. 2 = einräumen 2.
zu-getan (⸗⸗⸗) [zutun] a. ⊕: e-m 2 attached (or devoted) to a p.; e-m sehr (od. von Herzen) 2 sein to be very fond of a p., to have a great (or strong) affection (or liking) for a p.
zu-gewandt (⸗⸗⸗⸗) a. ⊕ 1. p.p. von zuwenden (s. ds.). — 2. (als verbunden angehörig) hist. die Schweiz mit ihren 2en Orten Switzerland with her associates or her confederate districts.
Zug-exerzieren ⚔ (⸗⸗⸗) f ⊕ drilling in files or squads; =**feder** f draw-spring; ⛙ am Tender: drag-spring; =**festigkeit** f tensile strength; =**fisch** m (Hering 2c.) migratory fish; =**führer** m: a) ⛙ chief guard, guard in charge (Am. conductor) of a train; b) ⚔ file-

leader; =**garn** n = =netz; =**geschirr** n Sattlerei: harness, draw-gear; =**hafen** m Fuhrwesen: pole-hook, draw-hook, an der Gabeldeichsel: tug-iron or -hook; =**heuschrecke** f = Wanderheuschrecke.
zu-gießen (⸗⸗(⸗)) v/a. ⚭d** 1. to add by pouring in, to pour into. — 2. das Loch mit Blei 2 to fill (or stop) up ... with lead. — 3. (immer) 2 to go on pouring in.
zugig (⸗⸗) a. ⊕ draughty (room. &c.), exposed to the draught; bleak (hill).
zu-gittern (⸗⸗⸗) v/a. ⚭a** to fence (or rail) in, to enclose with a railing.
Zug-karre ☉ (⸗...) f ⊕ truck, hand-barrow; =**kessel** m (Dampfkessel mit innen liegenden Feuerzügen) flue-boiler; =**kette** f draught-chain; =**kraft** f: a) mech. power of traction, tractive force; typ. (Elastizität der Walze) suction; b) (Anziehungskraft) attractive force; =**kräftig** a. ⊕: a) tractive; b) attractive.
zu-gleich (-⸗) [nhd.] adv. at the same time (mit mir as I), simultaneously with a p.; (alle auf einmal) together, jointly; 2 mit // along with ...; 2 bestehen oder sein to co-exist; sie ist schön und 2 höchst gebildet she is both handsome and most accomplished; sie verließen alle 2 den Saal they all left the hall together or in a body.
Zug-leine ☉ (⸗...) f ⊕ drag- (⛢ tow-) line; =**lini-e** f: a) math. (Kurve) tra(je)ctory, tractrix; b) mech. line of traction; =**loch** n, metall. u. Bauwesen: vent- (or draught-)hole of a furnace; =**luft** f current of air, draught.
Züglung (⸗⸗) f. = Zügelung.
Zug-maschine (⸗...) f ⊕ traction-engine, locomotive; =**material** ⛙ n rolling-stock; =**mittel** n: a) means of attracting the multitude, attraction, F draw; b) pharm. blister, ⚭ vesicatory; =**netz** n drag- (or draught-, sweep-, raffle-)net; =**ochse** m, agr. draught-ox; =**ofen** m, metall. air-draught furnace, blast-furnace; =**personal** ⛙ n staff (or officials pl., (fr.) personnel) of a train; =**pferd** n draught-horse; =**pflaster** n, pharm. blister, ⚭ vesicatory.
zu-graben (⸗⸗⸗) v/a. ⚭b** 1. to dig in, to cover (up or over) with earth; 2. (drauf) 2 to go on digging.
zu-greifen (⸗⸗⸗) v/n. (h.) ⚭b** 1. to stretch out one's hand (to seize a th.), to snatch at a th.; to fall to, F to (make a) grab; bei Tisch: greifen Sie zu! help yourself or yourselves!, make yourself (or yourselves) at home!; fig. mit allen fünf (oder zehn) Fingern nach etwas 2 to accept a th. willingly or eagerly, F to jump (or rush) at a th. — 2. ⛢ der Anker greift zu ... bites, ... acts well.
Zug-riemen ☉ (⸗...) m ⊕ Sattlerei: draught-tug, trace; =**rohr** n, =**röhre** f air- (or vent-)pipe; =**rolle** f pulley.
zu-grunde (-⸗⸗...) adv. 2 geh(e)n; a) von Schiffen: to founder; to be lost; b) fig. (verderben) to run into destruction, to perish; to be ruined; 2 legen v/t. to put as a foundation, to take as basis or point of departure; e-r Sache (dat.) 2 liegen to be at the bottom (or root)

⚭ scientific; ⚘ botanical; ⚲ geography; ⊕ machinery; ⚒ mining; ⚔ military; ⛢ marine; ⚭ commercial; ⚮ postal; ⛙ railway.

[Zugrundegehen] — 1164 — [Zukunft]

of a th.; ⁂ richten to ruin, wreck, destroy; sich ⁂ richten to ruin (or undo) o.s.
Zu-grunde-geh(e)n (-⸚) n ㉓ perishing, ruin, ruination; =legung f ㊻ laying a foundation; mit ~ von ... taking as a basis to operate (or work) upon ...; =richten n ㉓ destruction, demolition, ruination.
Zug=rute ⊙ (⸚...) f ㉖ (Schwengel) e-r Zugbrücke: draw-beam; =scheibe ⚔ f movable target; =schnur f string pulling a curtain, &c.; =seil n towing-line, hawser; =stange f, mach. draw-rod (auch ⚒), an der Lokomotive: connecting-rod, bsd. ↯ drag-link; =stiefel m Schuhmacherei: boot with elastic sides; =strang m Sattlerei: harness-rope; =stück n, thea. piece that draws (full houses), popular play, F draw; =tier n draught-animal, beast of draught.
zu-gucken F (⸚⸗) v/n. (h.) ⑧** = zusehen.
zu-gunsten (-⸚) prp. mit gen. in favour of, for the benefit (or sake) of.
zu-gürten v/a. ⑨** to strap with a belt, to gird (round), to buckle to.
Zu-guß (⸚) m ⑧a. 1. pouring in, infusion. — 2. liquid (or fluid) added: addition(al fluid).
zu-gute (-⸚) adv.: e-m et. ⁂ halten (Rechnung tragen) to account to a p. for a th.; (verzeihen) to pardon (or condone) a p. a th.; e-m et. ⁂ kommen lassen to give a p. the benefit of a th.; e-m et. ⁂ schreiben = gutschreiben (s. gut 8); e-m etwas ⁂ tun (zum Ersatz geben) to compensate a p. for a th.; (zum besten geben) to treat a p. to a th.; sich (dat.) et. ⁂ tun to indulge in a th., to enjoy (or to feast upon) a th., sich (et.) auf et. ⁂ tun (auf et. stolz sein) to pride o.s. on a th., to glory in a th.
zu guter Letzt F (-⸚⸗) adv. in the end, last of all, at the eleventh hour.
Zug=verspätung ⚒ (⸚...) f ㉖ lateness of a train; =vieh n draught-cattle pl.; =vogel m; a) orn. bird of passage; b) fig. (Landstreicher) tramp, vagabond; =vorhang m drawing-curtain; =vorrichtung ♪ f der Posaune: slide-action; ⁂weise adv. (Γ u. i.) in flocks or troops, ⚔ in squads; =wind m sharp (or cold) wind, auch = =luft; =winde f pulley; =winkel m. mech. angle of traction.
zu-haben (⸚⸗) v/a. ⑨b** 1. to have (or keep) shut (vgl. zuhalten); er hatte den Rock zu he had his coat buttoned up. — 2. nur im inf. er will (beim Tausch) noch Geld ⁂ he wants money in(to) the bargain.
zu-häfeln ㉒a** **zu-haken** ⑧*** (⸚⸚) v a. to fasten (up) with a hook or clasp.
zu-halten (⸚⸚) ⑧a** I v a. 1. to keep closed or shut or locked up: die Hand ⁂ to clench one's fist. — II v n. (h.) 2. auf et. ⁂ (lossteuern) to make (straight) for a th., to bear down upon a th. — 3. mit e-m ⁂ (unerlaubten Umgang haben) to have illicit intercourse with a p. — III sich ⁂ v refl. 4. (eilen) to hurry forward, to bestir o.s. — IV ~ n ㉓ 5. keeping closed, &c. (!); ⁂ das ⁂ der Tür ist nötig it is necessary to keep the door shut; vgl. Zuhaltung.

Zu-halter, -hälter (⸚⸚) m ㉒ protector or bully of a loose woman or prostitute, ehm. a.: fancy-man.
Zu-haltung ⊙ (⸚⸚) f ㊻; ~ am Türschloß: tumbler; Schloß mit ~ tumbler-spring.
zu-hämmern (⸚⸚) v/a. ㉒a** to close by hammering, to fasten (or clinch) with the hammer, to hammer down.
zu-handen (-⸚) [mhd.] adv.: a) close at hand, ready, in readiness; b) in (or to) hand; ⁂ kommen to come to hand; s. zu Händen (Hand 4 gegen Schluß).
zu-hängen (⸚⸚) v/a. ⑧*** to hang (or cover) with curtains or drapery.
zu-hauen (⸚⸚) ⑨c** I v/n. (h.) 1. auf e-n ⁂ to deal (out) blows to a p., to belabour a p.; hau ihn zu! strike (hard)!, F give it them! — 2. abs. to go on striking. — II v/a. ⊙ (hauend zurichten) carp...&c. 3. to rough-hew, to shape, to frame; Schlächterei: ein Schwein ⁊. ⁂ to cut up; Steinhauerei: Steine ⁂ to carve ...
zu-hauf (-⸚) adv. in a body or a crowd, in dense masses, together.
zu-hefteln (⸚⸚) v/a. ㉒a** to clasp.
zu-heften (⸚⸚) v/a. ⑨*** to stitch (or sew) up, weit⁂ to patch up.
zu-heilen (⸚⸚) I v/n. (sn) ⑧*** von Wunden: to heal (or close) up; (vernarben) to form a scar, to cicatrize. — II ~ n ㉓ u. **Zu-heilung** f ㊻ healing up, healing process; cicatrization.
zu-herrschen (⸚⸚) v/a. ⑨¹** geh. Spr.: e-m et. ⁂ to say a th. to a p. in a domineering (or overbearing, bullying) manner or in a harsh tone.
Zu-hilfe-nahme (-⸚⸚⸚) f ㊻: mit (ohne) ~ von // by (without) having recourse to //, by (without) the aid of //.
zu-hinterst (-⸚) adv. quite at the end or in the rear, rearmost, last of all.
zu-horchen (⸚⸚) v/n. (h.) ⑧***; e-m ⁂ to listen (attentively) to a p.; heimlich ⁂ to stand listening or eavesdropping.
zu-hören (⸚⸚) v/n. (h.) ⑧**, j-s Erzählung ⁂ to listen (aufmerksam; to give an ear, to attend) to a p., a p.'s narrative, poet. to hearken; sie hörten mit gespannter Aufmerksamkeit zu they were all ears.
Zu-hörer (⸚⸚) m ㉒, ~in f ㊼ hearer, listener; der Professor hat viele ~ the professor has (a great) many hearers, the professor's lectures are well attended; ~raum m ㉖ space (or hall) for the audience, auch: auditory.
Zu-hörerschaft (⸚⸚) f ㊻ audience, aufmerksame u. a. attentive crowd of listeners, eagerly listening assembly.
Zuider-see ⚓ (ſen~⸚) [ndl. Süd(er)fee] npr f. od. m. inv. Zuyder Zee.
zu-innerst (-⸚) adv. innermost, in the very centre or core, quite inside, (tief im Herzen) (with)in one's deepmost (or innermost) heart.
zu-jagen (⸚⸚) ⑧*** I v/n. 1. (in) einem Orte ⁂ to gallop (or speed, rush) towards ..., mit dem Wagen, Automobil ⁊c. ⁂ to drive (or ride, race) furiously to (-wards) ..., auch: to scorch (along). — 2. (h.) jag' zu! ride at full speed!, speed on!, F go it! — II v/a. 3. e-m ein Wild ⁂ to drive game towards a p.

zu-jauchzen (⸚⸚) ⑨*, **zu-jubeln** (⸚⸚) ⑨a** I v/n. (h.) u. v/a.: e-m ⁂ to shout (in a jubilant tone) to cheer (or hail) a p.; e-m Beifall ⁂ to applaud (or welcome) a p. with loud acclamations. — II ~ n ㉓ cheers pl.; shouts pl. (of acclamation or of joy). [purchase) in addition.]
zu-kaufen (⸚⸚) v/a. ⑧*** to buy (or
zu-kehren (⸚⸚) v/a. und v/refl. ⑧** 1. (sich) ⁂ to turn to(wards); e-m das Gesicht ⁂ to face a p.; s. zudrehen 2; her. mit zugekehrtem Kopfe spectant. — 2. (zufegen): a) to sweep to(wards); b) eine Öffnung ⁂ to close or block up ... in (or by) sweeping.
zu-feilen v/a. ⑧** to close with wedges, to wedge (or plug) up
zu-ketteln (⸚⸚) v/a. ㉒a** to lock with a small chain, to chain up.
zu-kitten (⸚⸚) v/a. ⑧** to (stop up with) putty, to (close with) cement.
zu-klappen (⸚⸚) v n. (sn) und v/a. ⑨** von e-r Klappe, Tür ⁊c.: to close (or shut) with a bang, F to bang (or slam) to.
zu-klatschen (⸚⸚) v/n. (h.) u. v/a. ⑨¹**: e-m ⁂ to clap (one's hands to) a p.; e-m Beifall ⁂ to applaud a p. (by clapping).
zu-kleben (⸚⸚), **zu-kleistern** ㉒a** (⸚⸚) v/a. to paste (or glue) up, to stick fast (with size or glue).
zu-klemmen (⸚⸚) v/a. ⑧** to close by pinching, to squeeze together.
zu-klinken (⸚⸚) v/a. ⑧** s. zu... 1.
zu-knöpfen (⸚⸚) v/a. u. v/refl. ⑧**: (sich) ⁂ to button (up); der Rock läßt sich nicht ⁂ ... does not button (up); fig. er ist sehr zugeknöpft he is very reserved or close or haughty.
zu-knüpfen (⸚⸚) v/a. ⑧** to tie up (with a knot); enger ⁂ to tie faster.
zu-kommen (⸚⸚) v/n. (sn) ⑨** 1. auf e-n ⁂ to come (or go) up to a p., to approach a p. — 2. e-m ⁂ (zu ihm gelangen) to come to a p., to reach a p.('s hands); (zuteil werden) to fall to a p.'s share; e-m et. ⁂ lassen to let a p. have a th.; (hinlangen) to pass a th. on to a p.; (überlassen) to give a th. up to a p.; e-m Nachrichten ⁂ lassen to communicate (or correspond) with a p., to send (or forward) news to a p. — 3. e-m ⁂ = gebühren 1; das mir ~be what is due to me, my due, my share; Sprichw. jedem, was ihm zukommt! give every one his due!
zu-können (⸚⸚) v/n. (h.) ⑧**: zu et. ⁂ to be able to approach (or get near, get at, get to, reach) a th.
zu-korken (⸚⸚) v/a. ⑧**; Flaschen ⁂ to cork up ..., to stopper ...
Zu-kost (⸚⸚) f ㊻ s.th. eaten with bread or meat, vgl. Zugemüse, Kompott; fig. (Würze) seasoning, condiment.
zu-kratzen (⸚⸚) v/a. ⑨** to fill (or cover) up by scratching. [kommen.]
zu-kriegen F (⸚⸚) v/a. ⑩ s. zu-
Zu-kunft (⸚⸚) f ⑩ (o. pl.) future (a. gr.), future time, coming ages pl.; für die ~ for the future; (von jetzt ab) henceforth; in ~ in the future, in times to come, hereafter; Mann der ~ rising star, coming man; ihm sieht eine glänzende ~ bevor he has

Zeichen (s. S. XVII): F familiär; P Volkssprache; Ϝ Gaunersprache; ⸜ selten; † alt (auch gestorben); * neu (auch geboren); ‡ unrichtig.

[zukunftahnend] — 1165 — [Zündloch]

brilliant prospects (before him); weit in die ~ blickend far-seeing. [future.]
zu-kunft-ahnend (⏑⏑⌣⏑) a. divining the
zu-künftig (⏑⌣⏑) a. ⑯ = künftig.
zu-kunft-schauend (⏑⏑⌣⏑) a. ⑯ peering into the future, far-seeing, far-sighted.
Zu-kunfts-musik (⏑⌣...) f ⑫ music of the future, engs. Wagnerian music; fig. dreams pl. of the future. airy castles pl.; =pläne m/pl. plans (or schemes) pl. for the future.
zu-lächeln (⏑⌣⏑) v/n. (h.) und v/a. ②a**: e-m ⌣ to smile at a p.; e-m Beifall ⌣ to (express by a) smile one's approval to a p.
Zu-lage (⏑⌣) f ㊽ 1. increase of salary; (besondere Bezahlung) extra pay, bonus; e-m eine ~ geben to raise (or increase) a p.'s pay or salary. — 2. = Beilage 1.
zu-lande (⏑⌣⏑) adv.: bei uns ⌣ (daheim) in my (native) country; vgl. hier⌣.
zu-langen (⏑⌣⏑) ⑧** I v/n. (h.) 1. to stretch out one's hand (to seize a th.), beim Essen ꝛc.: to help o.s., gierig: to fall to. — 2. (genug sein) to be sufficient, to suffice; das wird nicht ⌣ that will not be enough, that won't do. — II v/a. 3. e-m et. ⌣ (hinreichen) to hand (or pass) a p. a th. (on) to a p.
zu-länglich (⏑⌣⏑) a. ⑯ (hinlänglich) sufficient, adequate; ~keit f ㊻ sufficiency, adequacy.
Zu-laß (⏑⌣) m ⑧a. = Zulassung.
zu-lassen (⏑⌣⏑) I v/a. ⑥a** 1. die Tür ꝛc. to leave ... shut or closed. — 2. (einlassen) to admit, welcome, receive; ⊙ to turn on gas, steam, &c. — 3. (geschehen lassen) to permit, allow, suffer, agree to; (gewähren) to grant; et. nicht ⌣ to object to (F to kick against) a th.; meine Mittel lassen es nicht zu my means do not (F won't) allow it, I cannot afford it. — II ~ n ㉔ 4. f. Zulassung.
zu-lässig (⏑⌣⏑) a. ⑯ admissible; f. a. statthaft; ~keit f ㊻ admissibility.
Zu-lassung (⏑⌣⏑) f ㊻ (zu zulassen 2:) admission, reception; (zu 3:) permission.
Zu-lassungs-gesuch (⏑⌣⏑...) n ⑫ application for admission; =prüfung f examination for admission (to a college, &c.) or entrance - examination; =schein m ticket of admission, pass.
Zu-lauf (⏑⌣) m ⑦c. (ohne pl.) rush or concourse, great pressure of people; großen ~ haben to be (greatly) in vogue, to be much run (or sought) after, von Predigern auch: to draw large congregations, von Ärzten: to have an extensive practice, von Theaterstücken: to have a great (or long) run, to draw full houses.
zu-laufen (⏑⌣⏑) I v/n. (fn) Sätn** 1. to run fast, to race (along); lauf zu! run on!, be quick!; zugelaufener (herrenloser) Hund, etwa: (stray) dog which has found a (new) home. — 2. auf e-n ⌣ to run up to a p. — 3. e-m ⌣ to flock to (hear or see) a p. — 4. spitz ⌣ to run to a point, to taper. — II ~ n ㉓ 5. = Zulauf; Ab- und ~ running to and fro.

Zu-lege-messer ⊙ (⏑⌣⏑⌣) n ⑫ claspknife.
zu-legen (⏑⌣⏑) ⑧** I v/a. 1. ein Loch ꝛc. mit Brettern ⌣ to cover up ... with planks, to board (or plank) up ...; ein Messer ⌣ to shut (or clasp) ... — 2. (hinzufügen; ant. abbrechen) to add to, to give in addition to; sie haben 200 Mark zu seinem Gehalte zugelegt they have added ten pounds to his pay or raised his salary (by) ten pounds. — 3. sich (dat.) ... (anschaffen) to provide o.s. with a th. ⌣, to secure a th., lang Erwünschtes: to treat o.s. to a th.; sich ein neues Kleid ⌣ to have ... made, F to get ... (made); sich ein Zweirad ⌣ to buy o.s. a bicycle. — II F v/n. (h.) 4. to grow stout, to put on flesh, to fill (or widen) out.
zu-leide (⏑⌣⏑) adv.: was habe ich ihm ⌣ getan? what (harm) have I done him?; er hat ihnen nichts ⌣ getan, oft: he has done nothing to hurt them.
zu-leimen (⏑⌣⏑) v/a. ⑧** to glue up.
zu-leiten (⏑⌣⏑) v/a. ⑧** to direct (or conduct, convey) to(wards), Wasser: to let in. [Zufluß-...]
Zu-leitungs-... (⏑⌣⏑...) in Zssgn =
zu-lernen (⏑⌣⏑) ⑧** to learn (or acquire) in addition to what one knows, to add to one's stock of knowledge; wir lernen immer zu we never cease learning, we live and learn.
zu-letzt (⏑⌣) [ahd.] adv. at last, finally, ultimately; (zum letzten Male) (for) the last time; ⌣ kommen to be the last (to come), to come (or arrive) last of all); ⌣ kam er doch noch in the end (or eventually) he did come, he came after all; Sprichw. f. lachen¹¹ gegen Ende.
zu-liebe (⏑⌣⏑) adv.: e-m et. ⌣ tun to do a th. to please a p. [flüstern.]
zu-lispeln (⏑⌣⏑) v/a. ②a** = zu=
zu-löten (⏑⌣⏑) v/a. ⑧** to solder up.
Zulu (⌣-, r-r f⌣) [afrik.] m ㊿ (pl. auch inv.), ~, ~frau f ㉒, ~weib n Zulu(-Kafir) [f auch: Zulu woman; ~kaffer m Zulu-Kafir or -Kaffir, Zulu; ~land n Zululand; ~sprache f Zulu language.
zum (⌣) = zu dem (f. zu I).
zu-machen (⏑⌣ch⏑) ⑧** I v/a. die Tür, die Augen, das Geschäft ꝛc.: to close, to shut, einen Brief auch: to seal (or fasten) up, eine Flasche: to cork up, den Rock: to button up; mach' die Tür zu! shut (or close) the door! — II v/n. (h.) mach' zu! make haste!, look sharp!, get on!, F P buck up!
zu-mal (⏑⌣) [ahd.] adv. 1. principally, chiefly, especially; ⌣ da all the more since, more particularly as. — 2. = zugleich.
zu-mauern (⏑⌣⏑) v/a. ⑧a** to wall (or build, brick) up, to block up with a wall or with brick-work.
zu-meist (⏑⌣) adv. in most cases, for the most part, vgl. meist III.
zu-messen (⏑⌣⏑) v/a. ⑧**: e-m et. ⌣ to measure (or mete) out a th. to a p., in kleinen Mengen: to dole out; e-m das Essen knapp ⌣ to stint a p. in the matter of food, bfd. ⌣ ↓ to keep a p. at short rations; der zugemessene Teil

the allotted (or apportioned) part or share; das ihm Zugemessene his (allotted) share or portion, Phis whack.
zu-mute (⏑⌣⏑) adv.: mir ist schlecht ⌣ f. Mut...
zu-muten (⏑⌣⏑) v/a. ⑧**: e-m et. ⌣ to expect a p. to do s.th. (difficult or unpleasant), to exact s.th. from a p.; e-m zu viel ⌣ to expect too much of (or from) a p., to be too hard on a p., to overwork (or overtask) a p.
Zu-mutung (⏑⌣⏑) f ㊻ exacting (or unreasonable) demand; e-m eine starke ~ stellen to ask a p. to do more than is fair or right; was für eine ~! what a thing to ask for!, the idea of expecting such a thing!
Zum-vorschein-kommen (⌣f-⌣⌣) n ㉓ coming to light, emerging, appearing on the scene, F popping up.
zu-nächst (⏑⌣) adv. 1. örtlich: nearest; ihm ⌣ next to him; auch als prp.: dem Tore, ⤡ des Tores close to the gate. — 2. reines adv.: (in erster Linie) first of all, above all; in the first instance or place; das ⌣=liegende that which lies nearest to hand.
zu-nageln (⏑⌣⏑) v/a. ⑧a** to nail up, e-n Kisten, Sarg-deckel ꝛc. to nail down.
zu-nähen (⏑⌣⏑) v/a. ⑧** to sew (up).
Zu-nahme (⏑⌣⏑) f ㊻ increase, augmentation, rise; (Wachstum) growth; (Fortschreiten) progress, improvement, advance. [(Beiname) surname.]
Zu-name(n) (⏑⌣⏑) m ⑧⑦(㉓) family name,
Zünd-apparat (⌣⌣⌣⌣) m ⑫ priming-apparatus. [f ㊻ inflammability.]
zünd-bar (⌣⌣⏑) a. ⑯ inflammable; ~keit
Zünd-draht ⊙ (⌣⌣⏑) m ⑫ primer, priming-iron or -wire.
zünden (⌣⏑) [ahd.: Zunder] ⑧ I v/a. to kindle, to set alight or ablaze; (in Brand setzen) to set on fire; vgl. anzünden; auch abs., bfd. fig. to cause a conflagration; ⌣d inflammatory, nur fig. fiery, inciting, stirring (speech, &c.). — II v/n. (h.) to catch fire, to kindle, to ignite. — III ~ n ㉓ f. Zündung.
Zunder (⌣⏑) [ahd.: tinder] m ㉒ (German) tinder, touchwood, spunk, fig. inflammable substance; es brennt wie ~ it burns like tinder or F like (old) blazes.
Zünder (⌣⏑) [ahd.] m ㉒ 1. one who kindles, &c. (f. zünden I). — 2. (et. zum Zünden Dienendes) bfd. ✕ fusee for a projectile, (slow) match, train of gunpowder; vgl. Zünd=papier, =schnur.
Zunder-büchse (⌣⌣st⏑) f ㊻ tinder-box.
Zünder-maschine ✕ (⌣⌣⌣⌣) f ⑫ fuse-engine. [paper.]
Zunder-papier ⊙ (⌣⌣⌣) n ⑫ touch-
zünd-fertig ⊙ (⌣...) a. ⑯ primed; =holz, =hölzchen ⊙ n ⑫ match, schwedisches: safety-match; =holz-büchse f match-box; =hütchen n (für Perkussionswaffen) (percussion-)cap; =kanal ⊙ m im Piston: nipple-bore; =kegel m eines Perkussionsgewehrs: nipple, cone; =kegel-zieher m nipple-wrench; =kraut n Feuerwerkerei: prime, auch == pulver; =kugel f explosive shell or bomb, ehm. a. =Brandkugel; =leine ↓ f slow-match, match-cord; ~ ↓ n, artill. port-fire; =loch ✕ n touch-hole, ✕ ~ einer Kanone: vent;

♪ Musik; ⚷ Wissenschaft; ⚘ Pflanze; ♀ Geographie; ⊙ Technik; ⚒ Bergbau; ✕ Militär; ↓ Marine; ⊕ Handel; ✉ Post; 🚂 Eisenbahn.

[Zündlochbohrer] — 1166 — [Zurateziehung]

=loch=bohrer *m* vent-bit; =loch=deckel *m* vent-cover; =loch=stollen *m* vent-punch; =loch=stempel *m* vent-piece; =masse *f* = =satz; =nadel *f* needle of a needle-gun; =nadel=gewehr ⚔ *n* needle-gun; =papier *n* = Fidibus; in Salpeter getränktes: touch-paper, (slow) match; ehm. =pfanne *f* am Steinschloßgewehr touch-pan; =pille ⊕ *f* primer; =pulver *n* priming-powder; ~ aufschütten to prime; =rakete ⚔ *f* rocket for firing mines; =röhrchen *n* quick-match tube; =satz *m* artill. u. Feuerwerkerei: priming-matter or -composition; =schnur(=haspel) *f* quick-match (reel); =schwamm *m* = Zunder; =stoff *m* inflammable (or combustible) matter, fuel, *fig. auch*: matters *pl.* which may easily cause a conflagration; seeds *pl.* of discontent; =strick *m* match-rope, = =schnur.

Zündung (⌣́‿) *f* ㊻ kindling, ignition, ⚔ Feuerwerkerei: priming.

Zünd=waren ⊕ (⌣́...) *f pl.* ㊷ combustibles, explosives, matches *pl.*; =waren=fabrik *f* match-factory.

zu=nehmen (⌣⌣́‿) ㋐a** I *v/n.* (h.) (*ant.* abnehmen) 1. to increase; (anwachsen) to grow (larger or bigger), von einem Übel: to grow (or get) worse; (Fortschritte m.) to advance, progress, improve; (steigen) to rise; (dicker w.) to swell out, von Personen: to grow stout(er), to put on flesh or weight, to fill out; (länger w.) to grow longer, to lengthen; (auch von den Tagen) an Kräften 2 to gather strength; im Werte 2 to advance, to improve (in value); 2b increasing, ⚔ (ac)crescent; 2de Geschwindigkeit increasing speed, *mech.* accelerated motion; der 2de Mond the waxing (⚔ crescent) moon; bei (oder mit) 2den Jahren with advancing years, as people grow older. — 2. b. Stricken: to increase the number of stitches. — II *v/a.* 3. noch et. (hin=)2 to take s.th. more or in addition. — III *~ n* ㉓ 4. = Zunahme; der Mond ist im ~ ... is increasing or waxing.

zu=neigen (⌣⌣́‿) *v/a.* u. *v/refl.* ㊸**: (sich) 2 to incline, to bend (forward).

Zu=neigung (⌣⌣́‿) *f* ㊻ affection, attachment; (Seelenverwandtschaft) sympathy, congeniality; ~ zu e-m fassen to take a liking (or to grow attached) to a p., to grow fond of a p.

Zunft(⁵) [ahd.: ziemen] *f* ㉑ 1. Handwerker=~ guild, corporation, in *Lo.* auch: city-company, livery; e-n in e-e ~ aufnehmen to make a p. free of a corporation or livery. — 2. weitS. profession, brotherhood, fraternity, craft, oft *b.s.* clique, set, tribe, gang, band.

Zunft=brief (⁵...) *m* ㊷ charter of a guild or city-company; =geist *m* corporative spirit, trade-unionism, (fr.) esprit de corps, *b.s.* cliquism, caste feeling; =gelehrte(r) *m* member of a learned profession; ²gemäß *a.* ㊺ according to the statutes of a guild; corporative, *b.s.* exclusive, F shoppy; =genosse *m* member of a guild or corporation, in *Lo.* a. liveryman; weitS. one of the same trade or craft; =haus *n* hall (or meeting-place) of a guild.

zünftig (⌣́‿) *a.* ㊺ 1. = zunftgemäß. — 2. belonging to a guild, corporate; 2 w. to be admitted into a guild, bisw. ~ to receive the freedom of a city-company.

Zünftigkeit (⌣́‿‿) *f* ㊻ corporateness.

Zünftler (⌣́‿) *m* ㊷ 1. = Zunftgenosse. — 2. adherent of (the system of) guilds.

Zunft=meister (⁵...) *m* ㊷ master (or warden) of a guild; =wesen *n* (everything relating to) guilds or corporations; weitS. trade-unionism; =zwang *m* obligation imposed upon artisans, tradesmen, &c. to join a guild.

Zunge (⌣́‿) [ahd.: tongue] *f* ㊸ 1. tongue, P clack, red rag; *anat.*: ⚔ glossa, i. anstoßen 5, beißen 1; belegte ~ furred tongue; f. lösen 1; e-e feine ~ h. to have a delicate taste or palate; die ~ klebt mir am Gaumen my tongue cleaves (or adheres) to the roof of my mouth; *fig.* eine böse (od. lose) ~ haben to have a wicked (or loose, F long) tongue; f. schweben 2; er trägt das Herz auf der ~ he is very outspoken, a.: he wears his heart on his sleeve. — 2. (Sprache) language; soweit die deutsche ~ klingt wherever German speech resounds; in fremden ~n reden to speak in foreign tongues; *bibl.* ... fingen an zu predigen mit andern ~n (Apostelgesch. 2, 4) ... began to speak with other tongues. — 3. meist ⊕: e-r Flagge, Flamme, Rohrpfeife, Wage ꝛc.: tongue, ~ e-r Schnalle, a. catch ⊕ (Weichen)~ switch-tongue; ♪ ~ an Blasinstrumenten reed, mouthpiece. — 4. *ichth.* = Scholle²; vgl. Seezunge.

Züngelchen (⌣́‿‿) *n* ㉓ (*dim. v.* Zunge) little tongue, *auch*: tonguelet, ⊕ e-r Wage: tongue, needle index.

züngeln (⌣́‿) *v/n.* (h.) ㊶a. to play with the tongue, von Flammen: to lick, to shoot (or leap) up, to play around, *v.* Schlangen: to hiss; 2de Flammen *poet.*, auch: lambent flames.

Zungen=ader (⁵...) *f* ㊷ *anat.*: ⚔ lingual (or ranular) vein; =band *n*, *anat.* ligament of the tongue; =bein *n*, *anat.* tongue-bone, ⚔ hyoid bone; =besichtigung *f*, *med.* examination of the tongue, ⚔ glossoscopy; =blüte ♀ *f*: ⚔ ligulate(d) flower; =blütig ♀ *a.* ⚔ ligulate, ligulated; =buchstabe *m*, *gr.* lingual letter; =drescher *m* babbler, word-spinner; =drescherei *f* babbling; (Zänker) wrangling, bisw. auch: tongue-lashing; =drüse *f*, *anat.*: ⚔ lingual gland; =entzündung *f*, *path.* inflammation of the tongue, ⚔ glossitis; =fehler *m*: a) defect in one's speech; b) (Verstoß beim Sprechen) slip of the tongue, (lt.) lapsus linguae; ²fertig *a.* voluble, fluent, loquacious; =fertigkeit *f* volubility, fluency of speech, glibness of tongue, F gift of the gab; =förmig *a.* tongue-shaped, ⚔ linguiform; =gebiß ⊕ *n* für hartmäulige Pferde: tongue-bit; =häutchen *n*, *anat.*: =held F *m* = Maulheld; =krebs *m*, *path.* cancer of (or on) the tongue; =lähmung *f*, *path.* paralysis of the tongue; =laut *m*, *gr.* lingual (sound); =löffel *m*, *surg.* tongue-depressor; =muschel *f*, *zo.* tongue-shell (*Li'ngula*); =muskel *m*, *anat.*: ⚔ lingual muscle; =pfeife ♪ ⊕ Orgelbau: reed-pipe; =register ⊕ *n* Orgelbau: flute-stop; =schaber *m* tongue-scraper; =schiene ♀ ⊕ tongue-rail; =schiff *n*, *typ.* slice-galley; =schlag *m*: F *fig.* e-n guten ~ h. to have a good long tongue; =schnitt *m*, *surg.*: ⚔ glossotomy; =spitze *f* tip of the tongue; =vorfall *m*, *path.*: ⚔ glossocele; =weiche ♀ ⊕ *f* siding with tongue-rails.

...zungig, ...züngig (...⌣́‿) *a.* ㊺ in Zssgn, z.B.: schmal-2 narrow-tongued, with narrow tongue(s); vgl. doppelzüngig.

Zünglein (⌣́‿) *n* ㉓ = Züngelchen.

zu=nicht(e) (⌣‿⌣́) [mhd.] *adv.* f. nicht II; 2 schlagen to beat to death.

zu=nicken (⌣́‿‿) ㊸** I *v/n.* (h.): e-m 2 to nod to a p. — II *v/a.* to express by nodding; e-m Beifall 2 to nod approbation to a p. (motte): ⚔ pyralid.

Zünsler (‿‿) [erst nhd.] *m* ㊷ *ent.* (Licht-)

zu oberst (‿⌣́‿) f. ober 2.

zu=ordnen (⌣́‿‿) I *v/a.* ㊶b** = beiordnen 1 u. 2; zugeordnet confederate, *math., &c.*: ⚔ co-ordinate. — II *n* ㉓ u. Zu=ordnung *f* ㊻ co-ordination.

zu=packen (⌣́‿‿) ㊸** I *v/n.* (h.) = zugreifen. — II *v/a.* to pack.

zu=paß (⌣‿⌣́), zupasse (⌣‿⌣́‿) *adv.* nur in: kommen to come at the right (or in the nick of) time.

zu=peitschen (⌣́‿‿) *v/n.* (h.) ㊸** 1. e-m 2 to whip (or lash) a p.; Kutscher, peitsch zu! use the whip, coachman! — 2. to go on smacking the whip.

zu=pfeifen (⌣́‿‿) *v/n.* (h.) ㊺b**: e-m 2 to whistle to a p.

zupfen (⌣́‿) [nhd.: Zopf] *v/a.* ㊸ 1. to tug, to pluck; e-n am Ärmel, an den Haaren, Ohren 2 to pull a p. by the sleeve, hair, ears; *fig.* zupf dich an deiner Nase! mind your own business! — 2. Leinwand ꝛc. 2 (ausfasern) to unravel ...; (Leinwand zu) Scharpie 2 to make (or prepare) lint; ⊕ Spinnerei: Wolle 2 to pick wool.

zu=pflastern (⌣́‿‿) *v/a.* ㊶a** 1. = zudämmen 1. — 2. *surg.* to plaster up or over, to bind up with plaster.

Zupf=leinwand (⁵...) *f* ㊺ = lint.

zu=pflöcken (⌣́‿‿) *v/a.* ㊸** to plug up.

zu=pflügen (⌣́‿‿) *v/a.* ㊸** to cover up in ploughing. [to put a stopper on.]

zu=pfropfen (⌣́‿‿) *v/a.* ㊸ to cork up.]

Zupf=seide ⊕ (⁵...) *f* ㊷ (un)ravelled (or loose threads) of silk; =wolle *f* picked wool, wool-pickings *pl.*

zu=pichen ⊕ (⌣́‿‿) *v/a.* ㊸** to fasten with pitch, bisw. to pitch up.

zu=pressen (⌣́‿‿) *v/a.* ㊻** to close by pressing or squeezing.

zur (⌣́, ‿) = zu der (f. zu I).

Zu=rate=halten (⌣⌣́‿‿) [f. Rat] *n* ㊷ =haltung *f* der Mittel ꝛc. husbanding (or sparing) one's resources, &c.

zu=raten (⌣́‿‿) I *v/a.* ㊶a**: e-m 2 to advise a p. to do a th.; ich kann dir weder zu= noch ab=raten I cannot advise you either for or against or either one way or the other. — II *n* ㉓ encouraging advice; auf sein ~ by (or on) his advice, at his suggestion.

Zu=rate=ziehung (⌣⌣́‿‿) *f* ㊻: ~ e-r Person consultation with a p.

Signs (see page XVII): F familiar; P vulgar; F flash; ⚲ rare; † obsolete (died); * new word (born); ‡ incorrect; ♪ music;

[zuraunen] — 1167 — [zurückbringen]

zu-raunen (⁻¹⌣) ⊛** ꝛc. = zuflüstern ꝛc. **Zürch** ♀ (⸜), ~er m ⚁ u. a. inv. **Zerisch** a. ⊛, ~er See f. Züricher ꝛc.
Zur=disposition=stellung (⸜⸍⸜⸍⸌⸃(⸜)⸍⸍) f ⊛ putting an officer, &c. on half-pay.
zu-rechn/en (⁻¹⌣) **I** v/a. ⊛²b** **1.** to add in reckoning, to reckon (or add) on to. — **2.** e-m et. ² (aufs Konto setzen) to put a th. to a p.'s account, (zuschreiben) to ascribe (or to attribute, et. Schlechtes: to impute) a th. to a p.; das ihm Zuzurechnende what's attributable to him. — **II ~** n ⚁ **3.** = ³/ung.
Zu-rechnung (⸜) f ⊛ **1.** addition; mit ~ aller Kosten including all charges. — **2.** imputation; **²s=fähig** a. ⊛ accountable (or responsible) for one's actions, of sound mind; rational; **~s=fähigkeit** f ⊛ accountability, mehr gbr.: soundness of mind, sound judgment.
zu-recht (⸍⸜) [ahd.] in good (or due) order, F in good form, trim, fit; well prepared; (wie es sich gehört) as it should be; (am rechten Orte) in the right place, (a)right; in Verbindung mit verbs, stets trennbar (**): **zurecht-bringen** (⸍⸜...) v/a. ⊛⁷* to set right, to put in order; to adjust, arrange, accommodate; **sich² finden** v/a. ⊛b** to find one's way (about), fig. a. to see one's way in a th.; e-m **helfen** v/a. ⊛b** to come to a p.'s aid, to set a p. right; **²kommen** v/n. (fn) ⊛²** to get on well, to succeed; ich kann mit ihm nicht ² I cannot get on with him; wie kommt er zurecht? how is he getting on?, how does he manage?; et. ²**legen** v/a. ⊛** to lay out a th. in order, to put (or arrange) a th., to get a th. ready; fig. et. schön ² to give a nice explanation of a th.; **²legung**/preparation; **²machen** v/a. ⊛** to arrange, prepare, organize; to get ready, to do up a parcel, &c., to trim (up) a dress, &c.; den Salat ² to mix the salad; sich ² to get (o.s.) ready; **~n** ⚁ arrangement; **²rücken** v/a. ⊛** to move (or push, put) in(to) the right place; fig. e-m den Kopf ² to give a p. a sharp talking-to; **²setzen** ⊛⁰**, **²stellen** ⊛** v/a. to put in(to) the right place, to set (a)right or to rights; fig. e-m den Kopf ² to bring a p. (back) to reason or to his senses; e-n **²weisen** v/a. ⊛¹** to show a p. the (right) way, fig. to guide (or advise, instruct) a p.; (aus dem Irrtum ziehen) to disabuse a p.('s mind); (streng tadeln) to reprimand (or chide, reprove) a p.; **²weisung** f ⊛ guidance, advice, instruction; ²**weis**) reprimand, reproof.
Zu-rede (⁻¹⌣) f ⊛ = zureden II.
zu-reden (⁻¹⌣) **I** v/n. (h.) ⊛**: e-m ² to advise (or urge) a p. to do a th., to try to persuade a p., tröstend: to speak words of comfort to a p., ermutigend: to encourage a p.; er läßt sich nicht ² he won't be talked over. — **II ~** n ⚁ advice, persuasion, comforting (or encouraging) speeches or words pl.; (Ermahnung) admonition; auf vieles ~ seiner Freunde tat er es he did it at the urgent request (or entreaty) of his friends; Sprichw. ~ hilft good counsel (or advice) prevails.

zu-reichen (⁻¹⌣) **I** v/n. (h.) ⊛** to suffice; **²d** sufficient; (genug) (just) enough. — **II** v/a. = reichen II.
zu-reiten (⁻¹⌣) ⊛b** **I** v/a. (fn) **1.** e-m Orte (auf e-n) ² to ride up to a place (to a p.). — **2.** tüchtig ² to ride at a brisk pace, to gallop (or race) along. — **II** v/a. **3.** ein Pferd: to break in (thoroughly), to train. — **III ~** n ⚁ **4.** breaking-in a horse. [trainer.]
Zu-reiter (⁻¹⌣) m ⚁ rough-rider,|
zu-rennen (⁻¹⌣) v/n. (fn) ⊛b** = laufen 1 bis 3.
Zür(i)cher (²⌣) [Zürich ♀ schwz. St.] **I** m ⚁, **~in** f ⊛ inhabitant of Zürich. — **II** a. inv. und **Zisch** a. ⊛, ~er See Lake of Zürich or Zurich.
Zu-richt(e)-bank ⊙ (⁻¹⌣(⸜)...) f ⊛ metall. dressing-bench; **=bogen** m. typ. register-sheet; **maschine** f finishing-machine; **messer** n dressing-knife, typ. overlay-knife, cutting-out knife.
zu-richten (⁻¹⌣) **I** v/a. ⊛** **1.** to turn (or direct) to(wards). — **2.** (zum Gebrauche fertig m.) to get ready, to prepare, to do up; Kochkunst: die Speisen ² to prepare the food, to serve up the dinner; eine Gans, einen Hasen ꝛc. zum Braten ² to truss ..., ⊙ to dress, to trim; Holz, Stein aus dem groben ² to hew ..., to square ...; Gerberei: das Leder ² to dress ..., to curry ...; Seidenfabr.: die Seide ² to shake ..., (zwirnen) to twist ...; Tuchmacherei, Weberei: ein Zeug ² to finish a cloth; Färberei: die Küpe ² to prepare the vat; typ. die Form ² to get the form ready, to make ready the form. — **3.** iro. e-n arg, schlimm, übel ² to ill-use (or maltreat) a p., to handle a p. roughly; schrecklich zugerichtet in a terrible state or condition, F in an awful mess; f-e Kleider übel ² to tear out (or mess up) one's clothes. — **II ~** n ⚁ f. Zurichtung.
Zu-richter (⁻¹⌣) m ⚁ one who prepares a meal, &c.; ⊙ dresser, finisher, mounter, des Leders: leather-dresser, currier. [finishing-room.|
Zu-richt(e)-zimmer ⊙ (⁻¹⌣(⸜)⸍⸜) n ⚁|
Zu-richtung (⁻¹⌣) f ⊛ preparation; dressing, trimming, finishing.
zu-riegeln (⁻¹⌣) v/a. ⊛a** to bolt up.
zürnen (²⌣) [ahd. Zorn] **I** v/n. (h.) ⊛ to be angry or wroth (über od. um et., wegen e-r Sache at a th., about a th.); e-m (auf e-n, mit e-m) ² to be angry (or cross) with a p., to have a grudge against a p. — **II ~** n ⚁ anger, wrath.
zu-rollen (⁻¹⌣) ⊛** **I** v/n. (fn) to roll towards. — **II** v/a. to roll up.
zu-rosten (⁻¹⌣) v/n. (fn) ⊛** to be (or become) covered (or closed, stopped up)|
zurren (²⌣) v/a. = zorren. [with rust.|
Zur-schau-stellung (⸜⸍⸍⸍, ⸜⸍⸜⸍) f (f. ausstellen 2) exhibition, (public) display, (setting out for) show, auch: parading.
zu-rück (⸜⸃), ⊛ **²e** (⸜⸍⸜) [ahd. zu Rücken] adv. **1.** back, backward(s); (hinten) behind(hand), in the rear; (im Rückstande) in arrears; ↓ hin und ² out and home. — **2.** ell. ², du rettest den Freund nicht mehr (SCH.) turn back, you cannot save your friend; er ist noch nicht ² (zurückgekehrt) he has not come (or is

not) back yet; ich bin wieder ² I am back again. — **3.** (wenig reif od. fortgeschritten) er (der Schüler) ist weit im Lateinischen ² he is very backward in (his) Latin; die Kirschen sind sehr ² the cherries are very backward or late.
zu-rück... (⸜⸃...), bisw. nachdrücklicher Rücksichten: **zu-rücke** (⸜⸍⸜...), Vorsilbe in Zssgn mit verbs, immer trennbar (**), mit verbal nouns u. adjectives, z.B.: **²arbeiten** v n. (h.) ⊛** von Maschinen: to work backward; **²beben** v/n. (fn) ⊛** to start back (with fright), to recoil, to shrink back; sich **²begeben** v/refl. ⊛c*/* to return, to go back (an einen Ort to a place); **²begehren** ⊛*/*: v/n. (h.) to (have a) wish to return, to wish o.s. back; v/a. to demand (or ask) back; **²begleiten** v/a. ⊛*/* to accompany (or conduc't, escort) back; e-n nach Hause ² to see a p. (safely) home; **=begleitung**/⊛(safe) co'nduct (or escort) on the way back; **²behalten** v/a. a*/* to keep back, to retain; e-n gegen seinen Willen ² to detain a p.; **=behaltung** f ⊛ retention, detention; **=behaltungs=recht** n ⊛ right to retain a th., right of retention; **²bekommen** v/a. ⊛*/* to receive (or get) back, to recover, to retrieve; ich habe das Buch ² I have got ... back, ... has been restored to me; **²berufen** v/a. ⊛b*/* to call back; (absetzen) to recall; **²berufung** f recall; **²beugen** v/a. ⊛** = ²biegen; **²bewegen** v/refl. ⊛*/* to move backward, to back; **²bezahlen** v/a. ⊛*/* to pay back or home, to repay, refund, reimburse; **=bezahlung** f repayment, reimbursement; sich **²beziehen** v/refl. ⊛b*/* to refer back to, gram. von Zeitwörtern: to be reflexive; **²bezüglich** a. ⊛ gram. reflective, reflexive; **²biegen** v/a. ⊛aft** und v/refl. (sich) ² to bend back(wards), to recurve; ⸜, zo., &c. **²gebogen**, auch: ⸜⸜ reflexed, recurvous; **=biegung** f backward bend(ing), recurvation; **²bleiben** v/n. (fn) ⊛** to remain (or to be left) behind, hinter den anderen: to lag behind, mit Bezug auf Fertigkeiten, Kenntnisse a. to be backward, not to be up to the mark, to be below (or to fall short of) the standard of a class, &c.; auf der Rennbahn ² to be outdistanced; von Obst ꝛc.: to be late; meine Uhr bleibt zurück gegen die Bahnhofsuhr ... is behind (or is slow compared with) the station-clock; hinter der Zeit ² to be behind the times; tel. ²gebliebene Drahtmeldung F belated wire; (dableiben) to stay behind, in der Schule: to be kept in or detained; (überleben) to survive; **~** n backward (or belated) state; **²blicken** v/n. (h.) ⊛** to look (or glance) back; in die Vergangenheit ² to review the past; **²d** retrospective; **²bringen** v/a. ⊛⁷**: a) to bring (or take) back a th.; fig. die Rebellen zum Gehorsam ² to reduce the rebels to obedience; einen ins Leben ² to recall a p. to life; b) fig. diese Verluste haben ihn sehr ² (in seinen Verhältnissen) ²gebracht these losses have greatly reduced him (in circumstances) or F

⚆ scientific; ♀ botanical; ♀ geography; ⊙ machinery; ⚒ mining; ⚔ military; ↓ marine; ⊛ commercial; ✉ postal; 🛤 railway.

[zurückbugsieren] — 1168 — [zurückmarschieren]

have pulled him down very much; ⸗**bugsieren** v./a. ⓖ** to tow back, weit⸗ to take back; ⸗**dampfen** v.n. (fn) ⓖ** to steam back; ⸗**datieren** v./a. ⓖ³** to antedate; ⸗**denken** v./n. (h.) ⓖ⁷** to think back on, to carry back one's memory to; an f-e Jugendtage ⸗ to recall (to mind) one's early days; vgl. (sich) ⸗erinnern; ⸗**drängen** v./a. ⓖ⁸** to push (or press) back, den Feind ⁊c.: to drive back, to repel; fig. eine Träne ⁊c. ⸗ (unterdrücken) to repress …, to restrain …; ⸗**drehen** v./a. ⓖ** to turn back, typ. e-e Maschine: to back up; ⸗**drücken** v./a. ⓖ⁸** to press back; ⸗**dürfen** v./n. (h.) ⓖ** ell. to be allowed to return; ⸗**eilen** v./n. (fn) ⓖ** to hasten (or hurry) back; ⸗**erbitten** v./a. ⓖ⁴*/* to solicit the return of, to ask for a th. back; ⸗**erhalten** v./a. ⓖ** = ⸗**bekommen**; ⸗**erinnern** v./a. u. v./refl. ⓖ²a*/*: e-n an et. ⸗ to remind a p. of a th.; sich an et. ⸗ to recollect a th.; soweit ich mich ⸗ kann as far as I can remember, as far as my memory carries me (back); vgl. ⸗**denken**; ⸗**erinnerung** f ⓖ reminder; recollection, reminiscence (of the past); ⸗**erlangen** v./a. ⓖ⁸*/* to recover; ⸗**erobern** v./a. ⓖ²a*/* to reconquer; ⸗**erstatten** v./a. ⓖ⁰** = wiedererstatten; ⸗**fahren** ⓢb** v./n. (fn): a) to drive (or sail, steam, row, cycle, motor, ride) back. 🚂 to return (or go back) by train; engS. to return the same way; b) (sich plötzlich rückwärts bewegen) to start back, to recoil, vom Pferde c. ⁊c. to jib; v./a. to convey (or drive, row) back, to take back in a carriage, boat, &c.; ~ n ㉓ return-drive; ~ einer Schußwaffe: recoil; ⸗**fahrt** f ⓖ return(ing) by carriage, boat, &c.; ⸗**fallen** v./n. (fn) ⓖa**: a) to fall back; fig. in denselben Fehler ⸗ to fall into the same mistake again, in ein Laster, eine Krankheit ⁊c.: to relapse; b) (zurückgestrahlt werden) to be reflected; fig. die Schande davon fällt auf uns zurück the disgrace of it falls upon us; c) jur. an einen ⸗ (von Gütern, Ländern ⁊c.) to revert to a p.; ⸗v reversionary; ~ n ㉓ falling back, fig. relapse; ⸗**finden** v./n. (h.) ⓣ** und sich ⸗ v./refl. to find one's way back (again); ⸗**fliegen** v./n. (fn) ⓖa** to fly back; ⸗**fliehen** v./n. (fn) ⓖb** to flee back, to retire hastily; ⸗**fließen** v./n. (fn) ⓣd** to flow (or run) back, von der See bei der Ebbe: to recede, to ebb, to go out; fig. eine Wohltat fließt zu dem Wohltäter zurück a good deed comes home to the benefactor; ⸗**fordern** v./a. ⓖa** to ask (or demand) back (again), als einem zukommend: to claim back, to reclaim; ⸗**forderung** f reclamation; ⸗**führbar** a. ⓖ reducible to; traceable to; ~**keit** f reducibility; ⸗**führen** v./a. ⓖ** to lead (or take) back, to reconduct, to reconvey; fig. auf et. ⸗ to reduce to a th.; als Ursprung, Ursache: to trace back to a th.; auf seinen wahren Wert ⸗ to reduce to its true value; auf andere Ursachen zurückzuführen attributable (or traceable) to other causes; ⸗**führung**

f leading back; log., &c. ~ auf das Unmögliche reduction to the impossible. (it.) reductio ad absurdum, geom. indirect proof; ⚔ ~ des Heeres auf den Friedensstand reduction of the army to its peace-footing; ⸗**gabe** f ⓖ giving back; vgl. Rückgabe, ⸗**geben** v./a. ⓢ²c** to give back, to return; (wieder herausgeben) to restore; ⸗**geh(e)n** v./n. (fn) ⓖ⁴**: a) to go back, to return, to retrace one's steps; ⚔ Waren ⸗ lassen to return …, to send back …; b) (rückwärts gehen) to go backwards, to retrograde, von den Preisen auch: to recede, to go down, to give way, to (have a) fall; (Rückschritte machen) to decline, to fall off, to deteriorate; von einem Geschäfte auch: to go down, seine Geschäfte gehen zurück, auch: his business is coming to grief or F going to the dogs; c) fig. auf den Grund von et. ⸗ to search for the (original) cause of a th.; bei et. auf die Quelle oder den Ursprung ⸗ to retrace (or follow up) a th. to its source or origin; in sich selbst ⸗ to commune with o.s., to search one's (own) heart; d) (nicht zustande kommen) not to succeed, to come to nothing, von einem Handel ⁊c. auch: to fall to the ground, F to be off, von einer Heirat, von Verhandlungen: to be broken off; ~ n ㉓ = Rückgang, ⸗**gekrümmt** ⸗ a.: ⚚ replicate; ⸗**geleiten** v./a. ⓖ⁹** to lead back, to reconduct; ⸗**gezogen** a. ⓖb**: a) p.p. von ⸗ziehen (f. bs); b) (in der Einsamkeit) secluded, leading a retired (or solitary) life; ~**heit** f ⓖ seclusion, retirement, retired (or solitary) life, privacy, obscurity; ⸗**greifen** v./n. (h.) ⓖb**: a) to turn round to seize a th.; b) fig. weiter ⸗ to begin (or go) farther back; ⸗**haben** v./a. ⓣb** to have back; er möchte sein Wort gern ⸗ he would like to be released from (or to cancel) his promise; ⸗**halten** v./a. u. v./refl. ⓖa** (sich) ⸗ to keep back or in the background, to hold back, einen ⸗, et. zu tun to keep (or restrain) a p. from doing a th.; f-n Atem ⸗ to hold one's breath; seine Gefühle ⸗ to repress (or check, verbergend: to hide) …; ein Kind, ein Bäumchen im Wachstum ⸗ to stunt … in its growth; sich ⸗ (in Schranken halten) to contain o.s., to keep within bounds; sein Urteil (oder v./n. mit seinem Urteil) ⸗ to reserve one's opinion; v./n. (h.) to keep aloof; mit et. ⸗ (nicht hervortreten) to conceal (or hide) a th.; mit seinem Ausspruche über et. ⸗ to suspend one's judgment; ⚔ die Käufer halten sehr zurück buyers are very cautious or shy or loath to buy; ~ n ㉓ f.⸗**haltung** ⓢd p.pr. u. a. ⓖ: a) sachlich: retentive; b) von Personen: im Benehmen ⁊c. ⸗ reserved, discreet, guarded, cautious, shy, von Mädchen auch: coy, demure; sich ⸗ (adv.) benehmen to show (great) reserve, to keep one's distance, to stand aloof; ⸗**haltung** f ⓖ: a) keeping back; retention (a. med.); der Gefühle: restraint (or check) put upon one's feelings; b) nur ~ keeping aloof, aloofness; reserve, discretion, shy-

ness, von Frauen: coyness, demureness; (Verschämtheit) bashfulness; ⸗**helfen** v./n. (h.) ⓣb**: e-m ⸗ to aid a p. in returning; ⸗**holen** v./a. ⓖ** to fetch (or bring) back; ⸗**jagen** v./a. ⓖ⁸** to drive back; v./n. (fn) to gallop (or rush, race) back; ⸗**kämmen** v./a. ⓖ** to comb back a p.'s hair; ⸗**kaufen** v./a. ⓖ** to buy back, to repurchase; ⸗**kehren** v./n. (fn) ⓖ** to return, zum Sprechenden hin: to come back; nach Hause ⸗ to return home; ein ins Vaterland ~der a person returning (or going back) to his native country; ~ n ㉓ = Rückkehr, ⸗**kommen** v./n. (fn) ⓖ⁴**: a) to come back; b) von seiner Meinung ⸗ to change (or alter) one's opinion; c) auf e-n Gegenstand ⸗ to revert (or return) to a subject; d) mst ⚔ to go down, to be doing badly, to fail in (one's) business; sehr ⸗ gekommen greatly reduced; ⸗**können** v./n. (h.) ⓖ⁸** ell. to be able to return; ⸗**kunft** f ⑩ = Rückkehr, ⸗**lassen** v./a. ⓖa**: a) to leave behind, not to take away, ⚔ auf dem Schlachtfelde: to leave (dead) on the battle-field; die Zurückgelassenen those (who are) left behind; b) hinter sich im Laufen, Lernen ⁊c. ⸗ to outstrip, to outdo; Bescheid ⸗ to leave word; c) ell. e-n zurück (⸗gehen, ⸗kehren) lassen to allow a p. to go back, to let a p. return; ⸗**lassung** f ⓖ: ⚔ sie flohen mit ~ von 10 Kanonen … leaving ten guns behind (them); ⸗**laufen** v./n. (fn) ⓢa** to run back, von Gewässern: to flow back, ast.: ⚚ to retrograde; ~ n = Rücklauf, ⸗**legen** v./a. ⓖ**: a) to lay (or put) back; a. v./refl. sich ⸗ to recline; (beiseite legen) to put aside, to lay by, jur. u. fig. to put on the shelf, to shelve; b) Geld ⸗ (sparen) to put (or lay) … by, to save (up) …; c) einen langen Weg ⸗ to go (or travel) a long distance or way, to get over a good deal of ground; eine kurze Strecke zu Fuß (auf dem Fahrrad, im Wagen, in der Droschke) ⸗ to walk (to cycle, drive, cab) a short distance; das dreißigste Jahr ⸗gelegt haben to have reached (or attained) the age of thirty; nach ⸗gelegtem neunzehntem Lebensjahre after completing one's nineteenth year; die Schule ⸗gelegt haben to have gone through a complete school-course; ~ n u. ⸗**legung** f putting aside, von Erspartem: laying by, economizing, saving; ⸗**lehnen** v./refl. ⓖ**: sich ⸗ to lean back; ⸗**leiten** v./a. ⓖ⁹** to lead back, to reconduct; fig. zu et. ⸗ to trace back to a th.; ⸗**lenken** v./a. ⓖ** to guide (on the way) back; ⸗**leuchten** v./n. (h.) ⓖ**: a) to be reflected, to shine forth; b) einem ⸗ to accompany a p. back with a light; ⸗**liefern** v./a. ⓖa** to send back, to return (by post, &c.), ⚔ auch: to redeliver; ⸗**liegen** v./n. (h.) ⓣ⁴** to lie back, zeitlich: to belong to the past; diese Dinge liegen nicht allzu lange zurück these things happened not so very long ago; ⸗**marsch** ⸗ m = Rückmarsch; ⸗**marschieren** v./n. (fn)

Zeichen (s. S. XVII): F familiär; P Volkssprache; Γ Gaunersprache; ⸗ selten; † alt (auch gestorben); * neu (auch geboren); ⁒ unrichtig;

[zurückmelden] — 1169 — [zurücktreten]

⑬** to march back. eng☉. ⚔ to fall back; ℨmelden v/refl. ⑧**: sich ℨ to report one's return; ⚔ sich von Urlaub ℨ to report o.s. after a furlough; ℨmögen v/n. (h.) ⑧** ell. to feel inclined (or disposed) to return, to wish o.s. (stärker: to long to get) back; ℨmüssen v/n. (h.) ⑧** ell.: a) von Personen: to be obliged to return; b) von Sachen: das Buch muß zurück ... has to be returned; der Tisch muß zurück ... must be moved (or pushed) back; =nahme f ㊽: a) taking (or receiving) back; b) fig. withdrawal of an insulting remark, &c., retract(at)ion of a promise, &c., (Widerruf) revocation of an edict, &c., recantation of a doctrine, &c.; ℨnehmen v/a. ㊾a**: a) to take back, to withdraw a remark, a statement, &c., to countermand (or cancel) an order, to rescind an injunction, a prohibition, &c.; sein Wort ℨ to retract one's promise, mehr gbr.: to go back from one's word; b) einen Schüler aus der Schule ℨ to take a boy away from school; ~ n ㉓ = =nahme; ℨnötigen v/a. ⑧** to force (or compel) to return or to retreat; ℨprallen v/n. (jn) ⑧** to rebound, to be thrown (or to fly) back, to recoil, phys. auch: to reverberate, vom Lichte: to be reflected; fig. vor Schreck ℨ to start back with fright; ~ n ㉓ rebound(ing), recoil, reverberation; ℨrechnen v/a. u. v/n. (jn) ⑧** to count back; ℨreichen v/n. (h.) ⑧** to reach back; mein Gedächtnis reicht weit bis in meine Kinderjahre zurück my memory carries me far back to the years of my childhood; =reise f ㊽ = Rückreise; ℨreisen v/n. (jn) ⑨** to journey back, to return by train, ship, &c.; ℨreißen v/a. ㊾a** to pull back; ℨreiten v/n. (jn) ⑨b** to ride back, to return on horseback; ℨrennen v/n. (jn) ⑯b** to run back; ℨrollen v/a. und v/n. (jn) ⑧** to roll back; ℨ gerollt: ⚛ revolute; ℨrücken v/a. ⑧** to move (or push) back; ℨrudern v/n. (jn) ㊾a**: a) to row back; b) (rückwärts rudern) to back-water; ℨrufen v/a. ⑯b** to call (or summon) back; fig. sich et. ins Gedächtnis ℨ to recall a th. to mind, to freshen up memories (or reminiscences) of the past; ins Leben ℨ to recall (or restore) to life, to revive; ~ n ㉓ =rufung f ㊽ recall; ℨsagen v/a. ⑧** to say in return, to reply; ein Kompliment ℨ to return ...; ich ließ ihm ℨ, daß // I sent him back word that //; ℨschaffen v/a. ⑧** to convey (or take, haul) back; ℨschallen v/n. (jn) ⑦a⑧** to resound, to re-echo, phys. to reverberate; ℨschaudern v/n. (jn) ㊾a** to recoil, to shrink back; ℨschauen v/n. (h.) ⑧** = ℨsehen; ℨscheuchen v/a. ⑧** to scare (or frighten) back or away; ℨschicken v/a. ⑧** to send back, to return by post, &c.; einen in sein Vaterland ℨ to repatriate a p.; ✠ Ware(n) ℨ to reconsign (zu Wasser: to reship) goods; ℨschieben v/a. ⑯c** to push (or shove) back; fig. e-n ℨ (in Bezug auf ein Amt) to pass over a p.; einem et. ℨ

(an ihn zurück verweisen) to refer a th. back to a p.; bid. jur. (jetzt gbr. für referieren): einen Beweisgrund (des Gegners) ℨ (gegen ihn selbst gebrauchen) to turn the tables upon one's opponent, to (make a) retort; ℨschiffen v/n. (jn) ⑧** to return in a boat, to sail (or steam) back or home; v/a. to take back (or home) by boat or by steamer; ℨschlagen v/a. ⑯b**: a) to strike (or beat, knock) back; b) eine Decke ℨ to throw off a covering or wrap; den Mantel ℨ to fling back one's cloak; ℨgeschlagener Wagen open carriage; den Ball ℨ to send back (or drive home) the ball; v/n. (jn): a) to fall back or backwards; b) ♣ von Preisen: to recede, fall, decline, go down; c) path. auf die Lunge ℨ to attack (or to settle on) the lungs, &c.; d) Biologie: to revert to the original species, ⚛ to retrograde; ~ n ㉓ (i. v/n. b) ♣ fall (or decline) of prices; (j. v/n. d) ⚛ retrogression, von Tieren und Menschen auch: atavism; ℨschleichen v/n. (jn) ㊾a** u. sich ℨ v/refl. to sneak (or slink) back; ℨschleppen v/a. ⑧** to drag back; ℨschleudern v/a. ⑧** to hurl (or fling) back; ℨschließen v/n. (h.) ⑦d** log. to draw a conclusion from the effect to the cause or from the known to the unknown, to reason (it.) a posterio'ri; ℨschnellen v/a. ⑧** to jerk back; v/n. (jn) to fly back, rebound, recoil; ℨschrecken v/a. ⑧** to frighten away, scare, deter; v/n. (jn) ㊾a**: vor e-r Sache ℨ to shrink back (or to recoil) from a th.; ℨschreiben v/a. ⑪** to write back or in reply; ⚔ to put on the list of reserves; ℨschreiten v/n. (jn) ⑯b**: a) to stride (or step) back; b) (rückwärts gehen) to walk backwards; ℨschwimmen v/n. (jn) ⑫a(b)** to swim back; ℨsegeln v/n. (jn) ⑫a** to sail back; ℨsehen v/n. (h.) ⑫a** to look back, auf die Vergangenheit ℨ to review the past; ℨsehnen v refl. ⑧**: sich nach der Heimat ℨ to have a longing (or to be sighing) for home; abs. er sehnt sich zurück he wishes himself back; ℨsein v/n. ⑫a** f. zurück; man ist hier noch sehr zurück people here are very backward or very much behind (the times) or very old-fashioned; ℨsenden v/a. ⑯a** u. =sendung f ㊽ = ℨschicken; ℨsetzen v/a. ⑨**: a) to set (or put) back, e-n Tisch: to push back; das Datum ℨ = ℨdatieren; b) an die vorige Stelle ℨ to put back in the old place; auch ~ v/refl. sich zehn Jahre ℨ to carry o.s. (in thoughts) back (bsd. ℨversetzen); c) et. für e-n ℨ to put a th. by for a p.; d) Waren (als Ausschuß) ℨ to cast off..., to put ... aside as waste or refuse; e) fig. e-n ℨ (geringschätzig behandeln) to treat a p. with neglect or disdain, to slight (or snub) a p.; v/n. (jn): über einen Graben ℨ to leap (or jump) back across a ditch; =setzung f ㊽ disregard shown (to) a p., disdainful treatment of a p., slight put upon a p., snub suffered by a p.; ℨsinken v/n. (jn)

①** to sink (or fall) back, fig. to relapse into vice, &c.; ℨsollen v/n. (h.) ⑧** ell. to be ordered back; er soll zurück he shall return, he is to come back; ℨspiegeln v/a. ⑫a** to reflect; ℨspießen v/a. ⑧**: e-n Ball ℨ to send back ...; ℨsprengen v/n. (jn) ⑧** to gallop back; ℨspringen v/n. (jn) ⑲f**: a) to spring (or leap) back; f nach Hause ℨ to run back home; b) phys. von Kugeln ꝛc.: to rebound, ⚛ to reverberate; ℨd rebounding, resilient; c) arch. to stand back, to recede; geom., ⚔ frt. ℨder Winkel re-entering angle; ℨstecken v/a. ⑧** to put back a peg, &c.; fig. e-n Pflock ℨ to come down a peg or two; ℨsteh(e)n v/n. (jn) ⑭**: a) to stand back, (ℨtreten) to step back; b) fig. hinter e-m (od. gegen e-n), et. ℨ to be below (or inferior to) a p., a th.; ℨstellen v/a. ⑧**: a) to put back (auch eine Uhr), to move (or push) back, to replace; b) (beiseite setzen) to set (or put) aside for a p.; ⚔ einen Militärpflichtigen ℨ to send back a candidate for military service for another year or until (fully) qualified; ⚔ =stellung f ㊽ replacement, e-s Militärpflichtigen: temporary rejection; ℨstoßen v/a. ㊾a**: a) to push (or thrust) back; b) (von sich stoßen) phys. &c., fig. to repel; ℨd (anwidernd) repulsive, revolting; ~ n ㉓ u. =stoßung f ㊽ pushing back, phys. repulsion, fig. repulse, rebuff; =stoßungs-kraft f ㊷ repulsive force; ℨstrahlen v/n. (jn) ⑧** phys. to be reflected; v/a. to reflect (back), to reverberate; =strahlung f ㊽ reflexion, reverberation; ℨstreichen v/a. ㊾a** to stroke (or smooth) back; v/n. (jn) von Zugvögeln: to fly back, to return; ℨstreifen v/a. ⑧** to turn (or tuck) up one's sleeves, &c.; ℨströmen v/n. (jn) ⑧** to flow (or stream) back; die ℨde Flut des Meeres the receding tide; ~ ↓ n ㉓ der Meeresflut turn(ing) of the tide; ℨstürzen v/n. (jn) ⑨**: a) to fall back(wards); fig. = ℨsinken; b) nach Hause ℨ to rush back home, &c.; ℨtaumeln v/n. (jn) ㊾a** to reel (or totter) back; ℨtelegraphieren v/a. u. v/n. (h.) ⑧** to telegraph (or wire) back; ℨtragen v/a. ⑧** to carry (or take) back; ℨtrassieren ✉ v/a. ⑧** to redraw; ℨträumen v refl. ⑧**: sich in et. ℨ to be carried back to a th. in a dream; ℨtreiben v/a. ⑧**: a) to drive back, to repel (beide auch ⚔); b) med. den Schweiß ꝛc. ℨ (ℨtreten I.) to drive (or send) ... inwards; ℨd: ⚛ repellent; =treibung f repulse; ℨtreten v/n. (jn) ㊾d**: a) to step back; fig. to withdraw from a society, &c.; in das Privatleben ℨ to retire (or withdraw) into private life; ⚔ in Reih' und Glied ℨ to fall back into the ranks; von seinem Amte ℨ to resign (or leave) one's post, von Ministern: to resign (one's) office; b) vom Wasser ꝛc.: to subside; der Fluß tritt in sein Bett zurück ... retires within its own banks; c) path. von Krankheiten ꝛc.: to strike inwards, to settle internally;

♪ Musik; ⚛ Wissenschaft; ♀ Pflanze; ♆ Geographie; ⊙ Technik; ⚒ Bergbau; ⚔ Militär; ↓ Marine; ✉ Handel; ✉ Post; 🚂 Eisenbahn.

[zurücktun] — 1170 — [zusammendrucken]

d) *paint.* to form (part of) the background, to recede: nicht genug ☉ to be too forward or too prominent; ☉ lassen to put in the background; e) ☉e Stirn receding forehead; ~ n = Rücktritt; ☉tun *v.a.* ⊕** to put back (in its place); einen Schritt ☉ to step back; ☉übersetzen *v.a.* ⊕** to retranslate; ☉verlangen *v.a.* ⊕*/* ☉fordern; *v/n.* (h.) = sich sehnen; ☉versetzen *v.a.* ⊕**/** to reinstate; in den früheren Zustand ☉ to put back in its former state, to restore to its previous condition. e-n Schüler : to send back to a lower form; *v refl.* sich in eine frühere Zeit ☉ to be carried back (in one's thoughts) to a former period; ~ *n* 23 u. **versetzung** *f* ⊕ putting (or setting) back, eines Beamten 2c.: reinstatement, e-s Schülers: return to a lower form; ☉wälzen *v/a.* ⊕**: a) to roll back; b) to push back; ☉wandern *v/n.* (ſn) ⊕a** to wander (or F tramp) back, to return (on foot); ☉weichen *v/n.* (ſn) ⊕ań** to recede (a. *arch.*); × to fall back, to retreat; (nachgeben) to give way, yield, give in, F to climb down; vor et. ☉ to shrink back from a th.; ~ *n* 23 receding. F climb-down; ↓ turn of the tide; (Rückzug) retreat; ☉weisen *v/n.* (h.) ⊕**: auf (ob. zu) et. ☉ to refer (back) to a th.; *v/a.* e-n an seine Stelle ☉ to make signs to a p. to return to his place; e-n auf eine Anmerkung ☉ to refer a p. (back) to a note; (abweisen) to reject, to repel, ein Geschenk: to decline; e-n (j-s Bitte) ☉ to refuse a p.('s petition or request); e-n in f-e Schranken ☉ to keep a p. within bounds or in his (proper) place; **weisung** *f* ⊕ (ſ. *v/a.*) rejection, repulse; refusal; ☉wenden *v/a.* u. *v/refl.* ⊕a**: (sich) ☉ to turn back; ☉werfen *v/a.* ⊕b**: a) to throw back(wards); den Kopf ☉ to toss up (stärker: to fling back) one's head; b) den Ball ☉ to throw (or send) back the ball; c) *phys.* Lichtstrahlen 2c. ☉ to reflect ..., ⊕ to reverberate ...; d) × den Feind ☉ to drive (or chase) back ..., to repulse ...; **werfen** *n* 23 und **werfung** *f* ⊕ throwing (or flinging, driving) back, *phys.* reflexion, ⊕ reverberation; ☉wirken *v/n.* (h.) ⊕**: auf et. ☉ to react upon a th.; v. Gesetzen: ☉d retrospective; ~ *n* 23 u. **wirkung** *f* ⊕ = Rückwirkung; ☉wollen *v/n.* (h.) ⊕* *ell.* to want to return; ☉wünschen *v/a.* ⊕**: et. (e-n) ☉ to wish s.th. (a p. to come) back; sich ☉ to wish o.s. back in a place; ☉zahlen *v/a.* ⊕** to pay back, to repay, to refund, to reimburse; ☉zählen *v/a.* ⊕** to count backwards; **zahlung** *f* ⊕ repayment, reimbursement; ☉ziehen *v/a.* und *v/refl.* ⊕b**: a) (sich) ☉ to draw back, to withdraw; sich auf (ob. in) sich selbst ☉ to become absorbed (or wrapt up) in o.s.; sich aus einer Sache ☉ to retire from (or to back out of) a th.; × e-n Posten ☉ to withdraw a post; sich ☉ to retreat (before the enemy); b) sich von der Bühne 2c. ☉ to quit (or leave,

give up) the stage, &c.; *v n.* (ſn): an einen Ort (in seine frühere Wohnung) ☉ to move back to a place (to one's old apartments); von Zugvögeln 2c.: to return; ~ *n* 23 u. **ziehung** *f* ⊕ (ſ. *v/a.*) withdrawal; (das Sich-) ~ retirement, 𝔐 retreat. (ſ. *v/a.*) return.

Zu-ruf (⁻⁻) *m* 2c. call, shout; (Gruß) acclamation, cheering; (loud) salutation.

zu-rufen (⁻⁻ᵛ) I *v/n.* (h.) u. *v.a.* ⊕b**: auf e-n ☉ to call (or shout) after a p.; e-m et. ☉ to call (out) a th. to a p.; e-m Beifall ☉ to acclaim a p.; beifällig ☉d acclamatory. — II ~ *n* 23 = Zuruf.

zu-rüsten (⁻⁻ᵛ) I *v a.* ⊕** to fit out, to equip, F to rig out; (bereit-m.) to prepare, to get ready. — II ~ *n* 23 und **Zu-rüstung** *f* ⊕ fitting out, equipment, F rig-out; preparation, getting ready. × für den Krieg: armament, mobilization.

zurzeit (⁻⁻) at the time, for the time being, (ſetzt) at the present time; ſ. Zeit 5.

Zu-sage (⁻⁻) *f* ⊕ (verbal) promise, pledged word; (Annahme) acceptance; (Einwilligung) consent.

zu-sagen (⁻⁻ᵛ) ⊕** I *v/a.* 1. e-m et. auf den Kopf ☉ to tell a p. a th. to his face, to say a th. to a p.'s face. — 2. e-m etwas ☉ (versprechend zusichern) to promise a p. a th. (by word of mouth), to pledge o.s. (one's word) to a p. to do a th.; die eingeladenen Herren haben alle zugesagt (zu kommen) the gentlemen invited have all accepted (the invitation). — II *v/n.* (h.) 3. = entsprechen 1. — 4. e-m ☉ (behagen) to be suitable or agreeable, congenial to a p., to suit a p.('s taste); (gefallen) to please a p.; das feuchte Wetter sagt mir nicht zu ... is not to my taste or liking, ... does not agree with (or suit) me. — III ~ *n* 23 u. **Zu-sagung** *f* ⊕ 5. = Zusage.

zu-sammen (-⁻) [ahd.] *adv.* (bei- und mit-ea., *vgl. beisammen,* welches bloß örtliche Nähe bz.) together, nur zeitlich: at the same time; alles ☉ all in all, F the whole lot or concern; mit e-m ☉ (gemeinschaftlich) (con)jointly (or in company) with a p.; wir (sie) bezahlen es ☉ we (they) pay it between us (them); alle gingen ☉ all went in a body; wir fünf kommen ☉ (zugleich) we five come at the same time or in a body; *vgl. zusammenkommen;* ☉ machen to make together; das macht 1000 Mark ☉ it makes altogether (or it totals up to, *einfacher:* it comes to) five pounds; *vgl. zusammenmachen;* wir tragen die Kosten ☉ we bear the costs together or in common; *vgl. zusammentragen.*

zu-sammen-..., **zusammen**-... (-⁻...) Vorsilbe in Zssgn mit *verbs,* immer trennbar (**), mit *verbal nouns* und *adjectives,* zB.: ☉**addieren** *v/a.* ⊕** to add together, to sum (or total, add) up; ☉**arbeiten** *v/n.* (h.) ⊕** und *v/a.* ⊕** to work together; gut ☉, auch: F to pull well together; b) *fig.* e-n ☉ (arg mitnehmen) to maltreat (or ill-use) a p.; *v/a.*: a) to earn (together); b) (zusammenkleben) to stick together; ~ *n* 23 co-operation; ☉**backen** *v/n.* (h. u. ſn)

⊕(⊕b)** to adhere (or stick together) when heated, to cake together; ☉**ballen** *v/a.* und *v/refl.* ⊕**: (sich) ☉ to conglomerate, agglomerate, stick together; ☉ ☉geballt: ⊕ conglobate(d); ~ *n* 23 u. **ballung** *f* ⊕ conglomeration; ☉**beißen** *v/a.* ⊕a** to chew; die Zähne ☉ to set one's teeth; ☉**bekommen** *v a.* ⊕*/* to succeed in joining; Geld genug ☉ to get (or scrape) enough money together; to collect enough money; ☉**berufen** *v/a.* ⊕b** to call together; das Parlament, e-e Versammlung: to convoke, convene, summon, assemble; **berufung** *f* ⊕ convocation, convening, summoning; ☉**bestehen** *v n.* (h.) ⊕** to exist together; to be consistent (or compatible) with; ☉**betteln** *v/a.* ⊕a** to beg together, to collect (or obtain) by begging; ☉**biegen** *v/a.* ⊕ań** to bend up; ☉**binden** *v/a.* ⊕** to bind (or string, tie, fasten) together, ↓ (ſorren) to seize, to lash; ſeine Wäsche ☉ to put one's washing together in a bundle; feſt ☉ to lace tightly; ☉**bitten** *v/a.* ⊕** to invite together; ☉**blasen** *v/a.* ⊕a**: a) to assemble (or summon) by sound of trumpets; b) ⊕ Glasmacherei 2c. to blow together, to join by blowing; c) ein Kartenhaus 2c. ☉ to blow down ...; ☉**bleiben** *v/n.* (ſn) ⊕** to remain (or keep) together; ☉**bolzen** ☉ *v/a.* ⊕** *carp.* to pin together; ☉**borgen** *v/a.* ⊕** to raise (or collect) by borrowing; ☉**brauen** *v/a.* ⊕** to brew, *b.s.* to concoct; *fig.* es braut sich etwas zuſ. there is s.th. in the wind, a storm is brewing; ☉**brechen** *v/n.* (ſn) ⊕a**: a) to break to pieces, F to go to smash; ſ-e Knie brechen unter ihm ☉ his knees give way under him; b) v. Perſonen, Unternehmungen 2c.: to break down, to collapse; ~ *n* 23 **brechung** *f* ⊕ (ſ. *v/n.*: b) break-down, collapse; ☉**bringen** *v/a.* ⊕?**: a) to bring (or get) together, to amass, (ſammeln) to gather, collect, assemble (auch ×), Geld: to raise; Perſonen: to bring into contact (with each other), to arrange an interview between; Verfeindete wieder ☉ to reconcile ...; bſd. *jur.*: das ☉gebrachte Vermögen the joint estate; ☉gebrachte Kinder children by two marriages, half-brothers and -sisters *pl.*; ~ *n* 23 collection, assemblage; ☉**drängen** *v/a.* u. *v/refl.* ⊕**: a) (sich) ☉ to crowd together, to press (or squeeze) close(ly) together; b) (enger begrenzen) to compress (into a narrow space), to condense, × Truppen: to mass (together); vom Stil: ☉gedrängt concentrated, concise, terse; ~ *n* 23 u. **drängung** *f* ⊕ (ſ. *v/a.*: a) crowding, (tight) squeeze; (ſ. *v/a.*: b) condensation, concentration; ☉**drehen** *v/a.* und *v/refl.* ⊕**: (sich) ☉ to twist (or twine, coil) together; ☉ ☉gedreht: ⊕ contorted; ☉**drückbar** *a.* ⊕ compressible; **~keit** *f* ⊕ compressibility; ☉**drücken** *v/a.* ⊕ *typ.* ⊕**: a) to print together or in one volume; b) in ein Werk ☉ to collect in one

Signs (see page XVII): F familiar; P vulgar; F flash; × rare; † obsolete (died); * new word (born); +* incorrect; ♪ music;

[zusammendrücken] — 1171 — [zusammenkommen]

work; ⇄drücken v/a. ⚌** to press together, to compress; ⚇ ⇄gedrückt compressed; ~ n ⚌ und =drückung f ⚌ compression; ⇄eilen v/n. (fn) ⚌** to gather (or assemble) quickly; ⇄fahren v/n. (fn) ⚇b**: a) to drive together (in a carriage). to cycle (or motor, sail) together or in company with a p., 🚂 to travel (or ride) together or in the same carriage; b) zwei Züge sind ⇄gefahren ... have collided, ... have come into collision; c) (aneinandergeraten) to have an encounter. fig. to fall foul of each other; d) vor Angst, Schreck ⇄ to start with fright, to suffer a shock; v/a. to convey in (one and) the same carriage or vehicle; =fall m⚆c.(down)fall, collapse, crash; ⇄fallen v/n. (fn) ⚇a**: a) to fall (or tumble) down. to collapse: (verfallen) to crumble away: v. Personen: to fall away, to lose in strength or flesh; v. et. Aufgeblähtem: to go down, to shrink; b) von mehreren Gegenständen: to fall together or at the same time; c) (auf demselben Raum fallen) to collect (in the same place); math. (sich decken) to coincide; d) der Zeit nach ⇄ to coincide, to concur, to happen at the same moment, phys. to synchronize (with); ⇄d coincident; e) (sich vereinigen) von Lichtstrahlen: to assemble in one ray or focus; ~ n ⚌ (f. ⇄ a) collapse, (f. ⇄ c) coincidence; ⇄falten v/a. ⚌** to fold up, Segel: to furl (up); ⇄fassen v/a. ⚇**: a) to grasp, to seize with the hand, to gather up; b) fig. das Ganze ⇄ to comprehend (or comprise, embrace) everything; als Ganzes ⇄ to treat as a whole, to take collectively; kurz ⇄ to compress, to condense, ein Werk, auch: to summarize, to epitomize, kurz ⇄gefaßt summary, (short and) comprehensive, concise; noch einmal ⇄ to sum up, to recapitulate; s-e Gedanken ⇄ to collect one's thoughts; ~ n ⚌ u. =fassung f ⚌ (f.v/a.: b) comprehension; condensation; ⇄fegen v/a. ⚌** to sweep together; ⇄finden sich ⇄ to meet (together); ⇄flechten v/a. ⚇b**: to braid (or plait, twine) together; ⇄flicken v/a. ⚌** to patch together or up; fig. Stellen aus fremden Büchern ⇄ to extract (from other books), to compile (from divers sources); b.s. to plagiarize; ⇄fliegen v/n. (fn) ⚇a**: a) to fly together; b) to meet in flying; ⇄fließen v/n. (fn) ⚇d** to flow together, to flow in(to) one channel, schmelzend: to fuse; ⇄d: ⚇ confluent; ~ n ⚌, =fluß m ⚇a.: a) confluence, junction, v. Farben ac.: fusion; b) fig. =fluß (=treffen) von Umständen juncture; =fluß von Menschen concourse, crowd, throng, assemblage of people; ⇄frieren v/n. (fn) ⚇c**: a) to freeze together, to congeal; b) to contract (or shrink) in freezing; ~ n ⚌ und =frierung f ⚌ congelation; ⇄fügen v/a. ⚌** to join, to unite (auch sich ⇄ v/refl.), to construct; ⇄schickt ⇄ to put (or fit) cleverly together, to match well; gr. to construe; durch Nähen: to sew (or piece, join) together; ⚆ Bretter ⇄ to assemble ..., (verzapfen) to mortize; ~ n u. =fügung f ⚌ joining, junction, juncture; anat. der Gelenke: articulation; gr. construction; ⇄führen v/a. ⚌** to bring together, to assemble; ⇄geben v/a. ⚆c** to join in wedlock, to marry; ⇄geh(e)n v/n. (fn) ⚇**: a) to go together, to go hand in hand; fig. to agree well, F to hit it off well, to jog on together; b) (sich ⇄ziehen) to shrink, schmelzend: to melt away; c) von Türen ac.: to shut, to close; ⇄gehören v/n. (h.) ⚌*/* to belong together, paarweise: to form a pair or couple; ⇄gehörig a. ⚆ belonging together, adapted for each other, (gleichartig) homogeneous; ~keit f ⚌ homogeneousness; ⇄gesellen v/a. ⚌*/* to associate, in Paaren: to couple; ⇄gesetzt p.p. u. a. ⚆ composite (auch ⚇), compound (auch gr., math., &c.); (verwickelt) complex, complicated; ⇄ sein aus ⫽ to be compounded from ⫽, to consist of ⫽, to be made up of ⫽; sie sind aus lauter Eitelkeit ⇄ they are crammed full (or brimful) of vanity or conceit; das ~e the compound, the composite; ~heit f ⚌ composite (or compound) nature or state, complexity; ⇄gießen v/a. ⚆d** to pour together or into one vessel; ⇄grenzen v/n. (h.) ⚇** to adjoin (or bound) each other, to be contiguous; ⇄grenzend adjacent; ⇄haben v/a. ⚇b** to have collected or (put) together; =halt m ⚆c. holding together, coherence, consistency, phys. der Teilchen: ⚇ cohesion; fig. agreement, unity, concord; ⇄halten ⚇a** v/a.: a) to hold (or keep) together, sein Geld ac.: to take (good) care of; b) vergleichend: to put side by side, to compare; c) to hold (or keep) jointly; wir halten uns einen Wagen (e-e Zeitung) zs. we keep a carriage (take in a paper) together; v/n. (h.) (an=ea.=haften) to hold together, cohere, stick; fig. von Menschen: to stick (or pull) together; ~ n ⚌ u. =haltung f ⚌ ⚇ = =halt; =hang m⚆c.: a) (Beziehung) relation(ship) (Verkettung) concatenation, association of ideas, &c.; (fortlaufender Faden) continuity; sequence; ich kann mir den ~ nicht erklären I cannot make out the connexion (or history) of it; aus dem ~e reißen to detach (from the context); keinen ~ haben mit ⫽ not to be connected (or associated) with ⫽; sind Sie im ~e? are you following (the thread)?; in (logischen, grammatischen) ~ setzen to associate ideas, to construe sentences; im ~ stehen mit ⫽ to be connected with ⫽, to relate to ⫽, to have reference to ⫽; ohne ~ incoherent; ohne ~ mit ⫽ unconnected with ⫽, independent of ⫽; b) phys.: ⚇ cohesion; ⇄hangen v/n. (h.) ⚇b**: a) to hang together, to be connected; b) alles, was damit ⇄hängt everything connected with (or involved in) it or relating to it; sagen Sie mir doch, wie das alles zusammenhing please tell me how it all came about; b) to be bound up together, phys.: ⚇ to cohere; ~ n ⚌ = =hang; ⇄hängen v/a. ⚌** v/a.: a) to hang side by side, b) = in =hang (f. bs a) setzen; v/n. (h.) = ⇄hangen; ⇄hangend od. ⇄hängend a. ⚆ connected, coherent, (fortlaufend) continuous; ⇄hangslos a. ⚆ incoherent, desultory (remark, &c.); loose, detached; =hangslosigkeit f ⚌ incoherency, ..., e; ⇄hauen v/a. ⚆c**: a) to cut (or hew) to pieces, to cut up; ⚔ ein Heer gänzlich ⇄ to inflict terrible losses on ..., F to cut ... into mince-meat; b) F einen ⇄ (durchprügeln) to thrash a p. soundly; ⇄häufen v/a. ⚌** to heap (or pile) up, to accumulate, Schätze ac.: to amass; phys., geol. oft: ⚇ to conglomerate; =häufung f ⚌ heap(ing) up, accumulation, aggregation, amassing of treasures, ⚇ conglomeration; ⇄heften v/a. ⚌** to stitch together or up; (verbinden) to join (together); ⇄heilen ⚌** v/n. (fn) von Wunden: to heal (or close) up; v/a. surg. to heal up, to cure; ~ n ⚌ und =heilung f ⚌ healing process; ⇄hetzen v/a. ⚇** to set (together) by the ears, to set against each other; ⇄holen v/a. ⚌** to bring together, to fetch from all sides; to collect; ⇄jagen v/a. ⚌** to drive together; ⇄jochen v/a. ⚌** to yoke together; ⇄kauern v/refl.: sich ⇄ to cower (down), to squat down (in a corner); ⇄kaufen v/a. ⚌** to buy up, to purchase wholesale, stärker: to monopolize; 🚂 alles Blei ac. ⇄ to form a corner (or a ring) in lead, &c., F to corner lead, &c.; vgl. aufkaufen; ~ n ⚌ wholesale (or extensive) purchase, F cornering; ⇄ketten v/a. ⚌** to chain (fig. to link) together; ~ n ⚌ u. =kettung f ⚌ chaining together, fig. enchainment, concatenation; ⇄kitten v/a. ⚌** to cement (together), chm. to lute; ⇄klammern ⚇ v/a. ⚌** to fasten (or join, bind) with clamp-irons; =klang m ⚆c. consonance, mehr gbr.: concord, accord, ♪ harmony; ⇄klappen v/a. ⚌** to fold up a fan, to shut a penknife, &c.; v/n. (fn): a) seine Zähne klappten zs. (aneinander) ... were chattering; b) F er ist recht ⇄geklappt (mager geworden) he looks very emaciated, he is quite a wreck; er ist vor Aufregung ac. ⇄geklappt (zs.=gesunken) he broke down (or F collapsed) with excitement, &c.; ⇄klauben v/a. ⚌***, etwa: to scrape together, eine Chronik ac. to compile; ⇄kleben ⚌** v/n.(h.) to stick together; v/a. to glue (or paste) together, ⚇ to agglutinate; ⇄d: ⚇ agglutinant; ~ n ⚌ u. =klebung f ⚌: ⚇ agglutination; ⇄kleistern v/a. ⚇a** to paste together; ⇄klingen v/n. (h.) ⚇i**: a) to harmonize, to chime in; ⇄ lassen to set chiming, to chime; b) mit den Gläsern ⇄ to touch (or chink) glasses together; ⇄kneten v/a. ⚌** to knead; ⇄knüpfen v/a. ⚌** to tie (or knot) together; ⇄kommen v/n. (fn) ⚌**: a) to come together; b) (sich versammeln) to meet, to assemble; mit e-m ⇄ to (go

[zusammenkönnen] — 1172 — [zusammenschließen]

to) meet a p.; c) scharf mit e-m 2 (aneaгeraten) to have a sharp encounter (or high words) with a p.; 2können v/n. (h.) ⓼⁂ ell. to be able to meet; 2koppeln v/a. ⓶a⁂ to couple together; 2krachen v/n. (fn) ⓼⁂ to crash; 2krampfen v/a. ⓼⁂: die Hände 2 to wring one's hands; 2kratzen v/a. ⓺⁂ to rake (or scrape) together; 2kriechen v/n. (fn) ⓻dfl⁂: a) to creep together; b) to crouch down; 2kugeln v/refl. ⓶a⁂: sich 2 to roll o.s. up (into a ball); =kunft f ⓾: a) vieler Personen: gathering, meeting, assembly, zur Beratung: conference, convention, der Gemeinde: congregation, von zwei Personen interview, verabredete: appointment, seltener: (fr.) rendezvous; b) ast. ~ zweier Planeten: ⚭ conjunction; =kunfts-ort m ⓼ place of meeting, Liebespaares, a.: trysting-place; 2lassen v/a. ⓼a⁂: a) to leave together; b) ell. (2kommen I.) to allow to come together or to meet; 2laufen v/n. (fn) ⓺aft⁂: a) to run to the same place, to flock (or crowd) together; (e-n Auflauf bilden) to raise a riot or tumult; (auf-ea.-stoßen) to jostle (each other); (zf.-treffen) to meet; b) von Flüssigkeiten: to flow in the same direction, to collect (in the same spot); c) von Farben: to run together or into each other, to get mixed; d) math. von Linien ꝛc.: to converge; e) sie liefen mit den Köpfen zs. they knocked their heads together; f) (gerinnen) to curdle; g) bei der Wäsche 2 (einlaufen) to shrink in the wash; ~ n ⓶⓷ concourse of people; running (or mixture) of colours; math. convergence of lines; 2läuten v/n. (h.) ⓽⁂: alle Glocken 2 lassen to let all the bells ring together, to set all the bells ringing; v/a. to assemble (or call) with pealing of bells; ~ n ⓶⓷: unter dem ~ der Glocken amid the pealing (or ringing) of bells; 2leben v/n. (h.) ⓼⁂ to live together, geschlechtlich: to cohabit; mit e-m 2 to live with a p.; ~ n ⓶⓷ living together, companionship, geschlechtliches: cohabitation. eheliches: married (or wedded) life; 2legbar a. ⓼ foldable; 2legen ⓼⁂ v/a.: a) to lay (or put) together, auf einen Haufen: to pile (or heap) up; b) Geld 2 to collect (a sum of) money; vgl. 2schießen; c) einen Brief, Wäsche ꝛc. 2 to fold up …; ein Taschenmesser 2 to shut up …; sich 2 v/refl. to lie together or in one bed; die Wolldecke läßt sich 2 the blanket can be folded; 2leihen v/a. ⓽⁂: sich eine Summe 2 to make up a sum of money by borrowing on all sides; 2leimen v/a. ⓼⁂ to glue together, ⚭ to agglutinate; 2lesen v/a. ⓶a⁂: a) Ähren, Früchte ꝛc. to glean, to gather; b) aus Büchern: to collect in reading; 2liegen v/n. (h.) ⓻⁂ to lie together, von Grundstücken: to adjoin (or to lie near) each other; ⚔ von Soldaten: to be quartered together, to share the same quarters; 2löten ⓾ v/a. ⓽⁂ to solder together, e-e offene Stelle: to solder up; 2machen v/a. ⓼⁂ to put together; vgl. zu-

sammen; 2münden v/n. (h.) ⓼⁂: a) die Flüsse münden zusammen the rivers join (each other) at their mouths; b) anat. von Gefäßen: ⚭ to inosculate; ~ n ⓶⓷: a) juncture, confluence; b) anat.: ⚭ anastomosis; 2nageln v/a. ⓶a⁂ to nail together; 2nähen v/a. ⓼⁂: a) to sew (or stitch) together, einen Riß: to sew up; b) die Kleidermacherin hat sich ein Vermögen 2genäht the dressmaker has made a fortune by sewing or with her needle; 2nehmen v/a. ⓶a⁂: a) ein Los mit e-m 2 to take a lottery-ticket (together) with a p.; b) = 2fassen; alles 2genommen taking everything into consideration, all in all, upon the whole; alle übrigen 2genommen all the rest taken together; die Kleider 2 (aufschürzen) to tuck (or gather, take) up one's clothes, Spiel: die Karten 2 to pick up the cards; c) fig. (all) seine Gedanken 2 to collect one's thoughts, F to keep one's wits together; ſ-e Kräfte 2 to use (or summon up, collect) all one's strength, to make a great (stärker: desperate, supreme) effort; sich 2 v/refl.: a) = 2 c; nimm dich zusammen!, auch: pluck up courage!, never say die!; b) (sich fassen) to collect o.s.; c) (auf der Hut sein) to be on one's guard, to pay attention; nimm dich zf.! be on your guard!, be careful!, take care!; 2ordnen v/a. ⓶b⁂ to arrange together, to classify; =ordnung f ⓾ classification; 2packen v/a. ⓼⁂ to pack up (together); alles in e-n Ballen 2 to put everything into one bale or packet; 2passen v/n. (h.) ⓾⁂ to be adapted for each other, to go well together, von Personen: to agree, to harmonize, to pull together, v. Handschuhen, Schuhen: to be pairs; gut (schlecht) 2d well (ill) assorted, well (ill) adapted for each other (auch von Eheleuten); v/a. (anpassen) to fit, to adapt; (geschickt verbinden) to adjust; Kleidungsstücke: to match, Handschuhe, Schuhe: to pair; 2pfarren v/a. ⓼⁂: Dörfer 2 to form … into one parish; 2pferchen v/a. ⓼⁂ Vieh: to pen up, to put into one fold. Menschen: to crowd together; 2pressen v/a., ~ n u. -pressung f = 2drücken; 2raffen v/a. ⓼⁂ to snatch up, to scrape (or rake, scramble) together or up; seine Kräfte 2 oder v/refl. sich 2 to summon up (all) one's strength; seinen Mut 2 to pluck up courage; die Kleider 2 to gather up one's clothes; 2rechnen v/a. ⓶b⁂: a) to reckon (or sum, add, cast, figure) up; alles 2gerechnet taking everything into account. including everything; b) wir wollen die Exempel 2 (ob. zusammen rechnen) we'll do the sums together; =rechnung f ⓾ addition (sum); 2reimen v/a., v/n. v/refl. ⓼⁂: to rhyme; fig. sich 2 to agree, to tally; können Sie (sich) das alles 2? can you see the drift (or purport) of all that?; 2reisen v/n. (fn) ⓾⁂ to travel together; ~ n ⓶⓷ travelling together, companionship in travelling;

2reißen v/a. ⓼a⁂ to pull down, to demolish; 2reiten v/n. (fn) ⓼b⁂: a) to ride (out) together on horseback; b) 2rennen v/n; v/a. ein Pferd 2 to overwork (or ruin) a horse in riding. seltener: to override a horse; 2rennen v/n. (fn) ⓼⁂: a) = 2laufen a und b; F fig. mit e-m 2 (have a) quarrel with a p.; 2ringeln ⓼a⁂, 2rollen ⓼⁂ v/a. u. v/refl. (sich) 2 to roll o.s. up, to coil o.s. up; das Insekt rollt sich zf. … rolls itself up into a ball; bsd. ent. sich 2d: ⚭ convolvent; 2 2gerollt: ⚭ convolute; 2rotten ⓼⁂ v/a. to collect (or assemble) a mob; v/refl. sich 2 to band together (as rioters or rebels), to cause a riot or to assemble; =rottung f ⓾ tumultuous assembly or gathering, riotous mob or crowd; 2rücken ⓼⁂ v/a. to push (or put) together or near each other; die Stühle 2 to put the chairs closer; v/n. (fn) to move close (or to draw near) each other, von Sitzenden: to sit closer together; ⚔ nach rechts 2 to file off to the right; =ruf m ⓼c. convocation; 2rufen v/a. ⓼b⁂ to call together, to convoke a meeting, parliament, &c.; =rufung f ⓾ =ruf; 2rühren v/a. to mix (up) in stirring, to mix together, Eier: to whip; 2rütteln v/a. ⓶a⁂ to jumble (or shake) up; 2scharren v. a. u. sich 2 v/refl. ⓼⁂ = 2scharren; 2scharren v/a. ⓼⁂ to scrape (or rake) together, Geld, auch: to amass, to pile (or hoard) up; 2schau(d)ern v/n. (fn) ⓶a⁂ to shudder, to shake in one's shoes; ~ n ⓶⓷ shudder; 2schaufeln v/a. ⓶a⁂ to shovel up or together; 2schichten v/a. ⓽⁂ to arrange in layers, weitS. (anhäufen) to heap (or pile) up; 2schieben v/a. ⓼⁂ to shove (or push) together; 2schießen ⓻d⁂ v/a.: a) to shoot (mit Kanonen: to batter) down, to knock over (with shot and shell); b) eine Summe 2 (durch Beisteuern zf.-bringen) to make up a sum by contributions, abs. 2 to club (money) together, um e-n zu ehren oder zu unterstützen: to get up a subscription (for a p.); bei Wetten: 2geschossenes Geld sweepstake; v/n. (h.) ⓼⁂ to shoot at the same time; 2schlagen: v/n. (fn) ⓼b⁂ to strike (or knock, dash) against each other, to clash (together); die Wellen schlugen über ihm zf. the waves closed over him or engulfed him; v/a.: a) to strike (or knock) together; die Hände 2 to clap one's hands; (vor Erstaunen) die Hände über dem Kopfe 2 to throw (or put) up one's hands in astonishment; b) eine Serviette 2 (falten) to fold (up) …; ⚭ rückwärts 2geschlagen: ⚭ reduplicate; c) to join (or fasten) by knocking; d) agr. den Lehm der Tenne 2 to batter down …; e) (schlagend vernichten) to smash (up), to knock (or batter) to pieces; f) ⚡ Geld aus et. 2 to make money out of a th.; mehrere Posten 2 to sum (or total, lump) up several items; 2schleppen v/a. ⓼⁂ to drag (or haul, lug) into one place; 2schließen ⓼⁂: a) v/a. to link together, Verbrecher ꝛc.:

Zeichen (s. S. XVII): F familiär; P Volkssprache; Γ Gaunersprache; ⚹ selten; † alt (auch gestorben); * neu (auch geboren); ⁺⁺ unrichtig;

[Zusammenschließung] — 1173 — [zusammenwirken]

to chain ... together; ⚭ die Reihen ⚭ to close the ranks; b) v.n. (h.) gut ⚭ to shut well, to fit tightly; c) sich ⚭ v/refl. to join, to unite, von Personen auch: to form a union or a bond or an alliance; ~ n ㉓ und =schließung f ㊻ (f. b) tight fit; (f. c) union, bond, alliance; ⚭schmeißen F v/a. ⑳a** =werfen; ⚭schmelzen v/n. (fn) ⑬b** to melt away, to dissolve, fig. to dwindle (away), to vanish; ⚭ n ㉓ u. =schmelzung f ㊻ fusion; ⚭schmieden ⊙ v/a. ㊾ to weld together; fig. ein Bühnenstück, ein Heldengedicht ⚭ to build up (or construct) a stage-play, an epic; ⚭schmiegen v/refl. ⑱**: sich ⚭ to snuggle (or cuddle) o.s. up; ⚭schmieren F v/a. ⑱** Bücher: to scribble (or compile) ...; ~ n ㉓ und =schmierung f ㊻ compilation; ⚭schnallen v/a. ⑱*** to buckle up, to strap together; ⚭schnüren v a. ⑱*** to lace (or tie) up, e-n Ballen: to cord up; fig. das schnürt mir den Hals od. die Kehle zs. that makes me choke; ⚭d constrictive; ⚭schrauben v/a. ⑰c ⑱** to screw together; ⚭schrecken v/a. (fn) ⑬a** to startle, to get alarmed; ⚭schreiben v/a. ⑱**: a) (zf.-stellen) to compile; b) (in einem Worte schreiben) to write in one word; c) was er alles ⚭schreibt! what a number of things he writes (about)!, F what a lot of scribbling he does!; d) der Romanschreiber hat sich einen Haufen Geld ⚭geschrieben the novelist has made a pile of money by his pen; ⚭schrumpfen ⑱**, P ⚭schrumpeln ⑫a** v/n. (fn) to shrink (or shrivel) up; (sich runzeln) to wrinkle; (sich zf.-ziehen) to contract; fig. (abnehmen) to diminish, to dwindle away, von Vorräten ꝛc.: to run short, to get low; ⚭schustern v/a. ⑫a** = ⚭flicken; ⚭schütteln v/a. ⑫a** to shake up well; ⚭schütten v/a. ㊾** to pour together, to mix up fluids (in one vessel); ⚭schweißen v/a. ㊾** Schmiede: to weld (together); fig. eine Oper ⚭ to compose an opera; =schweißer ⊙ m ㉒ welder; =sein n ㉓ being together, companionship; ⚭setzbar a. ㊻ compoundable; ⚭setzen ㊿** v/a.: a) Personen: to put together; sich ⚭ to sit together; ⚔ die Gewehre ⚭ to pile arms; b) (zu einem Ganzen vereinigen) to compose, chm. u. math. to combine, Arzneistoffe, Speisen ꝛc.: to compound, Maschinen: to construct, to mount; ⚭gesetzt sein aus //, sich ⚭ aus // to be composed of //, to consist of //, to be made up of //; fig. aus (lauter) Vorurteilen ⚭gesetzt sein to be (crammed) full of prejudice; f. a. ⚭gesetzt; ~ n = =setzung a; =setzer m ㉒ one who (makes up) compounds, compounder, von Maschinen: constructor, mounter, =setz-spiel n ㊷ Chinese puzzle; =setzung f ㊻: a) composing, compounding, chm., math. ꝛc. combination, ☌ synthesis, von Maschinen ꝛc.: construction; b) composition, mit Hinsicht auf die Bestandteile: compound, (Mischung) mixture, medley, (Bau) structure (a. gr.); ⚭singen v/n. (h.) und v/a. ⑪fi**: a) to sing (or chant) together, to sing in chorus; b) v/a. sich ein Vermögen ⚭ to make a fortune by singing; ⚭sinken v/n. (fn) ⑪fi** to sink (or break) down, to fall to the ground, von Bauten ꝛc.: to crumble into dust, to collapse; f. a. einfallen 7; =sinken n ㉓ von Personen: prostration (auch med.), von Bauten ꝛc.: collapse; ⚭sitzen v/n. (h.) ⑭** to sit together or near to each other, von Sachen oft: to be grouped (or classed) together; ⚭spannen v/a. ⑱** to yoke (or harness) together; ⚭sparen v/a. ⑱** to save up, to economize; ⚭sperren v.a. ⑱** to shut (or lock) up together; =spiel n ㉑d. thea. acting in unison, collective acting, seltener: (fr.) ensemble; Fußball: combination; ⚭stecken v/a. ⑱** to pin together; die Köpfe ⚭ to lay (or put) one's heads together; v/n. (h.): immer ⚭ to be always together; ⚭steh(e)n v/n. (h.) ⑭**: a) to stand together; b) fig. to stand by one another, to be on the same side or of the same party, F to stick together; c) gut ⚭ to be on good (or friendly) terms (with each other); ⚭stellbar a. ㊻ compoundable; ⚭stellen v a. ⑱** to put (or place) together, Getrenntes: to join, to assemble, Ideen, Wörter: to associate; nach Klassen ⚭ to classify, in Gruppen: to group, to assort, zur Vergleichung: to put side by side, to compare; (zf.-fassend vereinigen) to combine; das Wahlergebnis ⚭ to count the votes, to examine the voting-papers; ~ n ㉓ und =stellung f ㊻ putting together or side by side, juxtaposition; assemblage, association; classification, assortment, comparison, combination; ⚭steuern v/a. ⑫a** to collect in the way of contributions, abs. to club together; ⚭stimmen v/n. (h.) ⑱**: a) ♪ u. weitS. to harmonize, to be in accord; mit etwas ⚭ (übereinstimmen) to agree (or chime in) with a th., to be in keeping (or in harmony, in agreement) with a th., F to gee in with a th.; nicht ⚭ to be discordant, to disagree, to jar; b) to vote together; =stimmung f ㊻ harmony, concordance, agreement; ⚭stoppeln v/a. ⑫a** = =stoppeln; =stoppelung f ㊻ patch-work, compilation; vgl. ⚭stoppelwerk; =stoppelgedicht; =stoß m ㉑a. shock, clashing, concussion, ⚔ encounter; phys. collision (auch 🚂); fig. (Widerstreit) conflict, clashing of opinions; ⚭stoßen v/a. ⑭a**: a) to knock (or push) against each other; die Gläser (od. v/n. mit den Gläsern) ⚭ to touch (or chink) glasses; b) to join by pushing; ⊙ Schneiderei: to piece together; ⊙ Mörser ⚭ to pound, to crush; d) einstürzen machen) to knock over, to upset; v/n. (h. und fn): a) to knock (or dash, rush) against each other, to clash, 🚂 to run into each other, to collide, to come into collision; b) = ⚭grenzen; ⚭stoßend contiguous, adjacent, adjoining; von Truppen: (zu-e.-stoßen) to effect a junction, auch ⚭ to join forces or hands; ~ n: a) = =stoß; b) (Vereinigung) junction, union; ⚭streichen v/a. ㊾fi**: a) Geld ⚭ to amass (or make) ...; b) thea. to cut down a piece (by striking out certain parts or passages); ⚭strömen v/n. (fn) ⑱** to flow together or in one channel, von Menschen: to crowd (or flock) together; ~ n ㉓ flowing together, confluence, conflux; ⚭stücke(l)n v/a. ⑱ (⑫a)** to piece together, to patch up; ⚭sturz n ㉑a. downfall, crash, collapse; ⚭stürzen v/n. (fn) ⑳** to fall to the ground, to tumble down, to collapse, von Gebäuden ꝛc. auch: to crumble away; ~ n ㉓ = =sturz; ⚭suchen v/a. ⑱** to gather, pick up, collect; ⚭tragen v/a. ⑬b** to carry to the same place; to collect, aus Büchern: to compile; ~ n ㉓ collection, compilation; ⚭treffen v/n. (fn) ⑬a**: a) von Personen: mit ea. ⚭ to meet (by chance), to come across each other; hart ⚭ to have a violent encounter; b) (gleichzeitig geschehen) to coincide; (mitwirken) to concur, to combine (zu et. in doing a th.); das traf sehr unglücklich zusammen it all happened very unfortunately; c) (übereinstimmen) to correspond to a th., mit j-s Erwartungen: to come up to a p.'s expectations; ~ n: a) (f. ⚭ a) (chance) meeting, feindliches: (hostile) encounter, collision; b) (f. ⚭ b) coincidence, concurrence; (Gleichzeitigkeit) simultaneousness; ~ von Umständen juncture; ein glückliches ~ a happy coincidence; ⚭treiben v/a. ⑪** das Vieh ꝛc.: to drive together, hunt. das Wild: to beat up; ⚭treten v n. (fn) ⑭d**: a) to step up to each other; b) (sich vereinigen) to meet, to come together; c) (gemeinschaftliche Sache m.) to unite, to combine, to join (in defence of the same cause); v/a. to tread down; ~ n ㉓ = =tritt; =tritt m ㉑c. meeting (or opening) of parliament; ⚖ ~ der Gläubiger meeting (or gathering) of creditors; ⚭trommeln v/a. ⑫a** to call together with sound of drums; ⚔ Rekruten ⚭ to beat up recruits; weitS. (zf.-bringen) to bring together (by a great effort), to assemble; ⚭tun v/a. ㊾** to put together; sich ⚭ v/refl. to join, unite, associate, ✚ to join (or go into) partnership, to form a syndicate or ring; ⚭wachsen v/n. (fn) ⑬b** to grow together, bsd. fig. to coalesce, ☌ ⚭gewachsen grown together, anat.: anchylosed, ⚘: ☌ accrete, connate; Pflanzen mit ⚭gewachsenen Staubbeuteln: ☌ syngenesia; ~ n ㉓ coalescence, ☌ concrescence; ⚭wehen v/a. ⑱** to blow (or waft) together, ⚭gewehter Schnee drifted snow; ⚭werfen v/a. ⑬b** to throw together; in e-n Haufen: to lump, unordentlich: to jumble up; (vermengen) to mix up; (verwechseln) to confound, to mistake; (stürzen machen) to throw (or knock) down, to overthrow; ⚭wickeln v/a. ⑫a** to wrap (or roll) up; ⚭wirken v/n. (h.): ⑱** a) von Personen: to act (or work) together, to co-operate;

♪ Musik; ☌ Wissenschaft; ⚘ Pflanze; 🜨 Geographie; ⊙ Technik; ⚒ Bergbau; ⚔ Militär; ⚓ Marine; ✚ Handel; ✉ Post; 🚂 Eisenbahn.

[zusammenwohnen] — 1174 — [zuschrauben]

b) (zu etwas mithelfen) to contribute towards a th.; ⚭ co-operative, concurrent; ~ n acting together, concerted action, combined (or united) effort(s pl.), co-operation; ⚭wohnen v/n. (h.) ⚭** to live together; eng ⚭ to be huddled together; ⚭würfeln v/a. ⚭a** to pack (or mix) up in a haphazard fashion, to jumble up; eine bunt ⚭gewürfelte Gesellschaft a strange mixture (or medley) of people, a very mixed company, F a motley crew; ⚭zählen v/a. ⚭** to add (or sum, total) up; ⚭ziehbar a. ⚭ physiol., &c.: ⚭ contracti(b)le; ~keit f: ⚭ contracti(bi)lity; ⚭ziehen v/a. u. v/refl. ⚭b**: a) (sich) ⚭ to draw together, to assemble (beide auch ⚭), beim Nähen: to gather (up), es zieht sich ein Gewitter zusammen a storm is gathering or brewing; (ziehend verkürzen) (sich) ⚭ to contract; fest ⚭ (schnüren) to pull (or lace) tightly; die Lippen (oder den Mund) ⚭ to screw (or pucker) up one's lips or mouth; ⚭ Truppen ⚭ to concentrate (or assemble) ...; ⚭gezogen werden, oft: to contract; ⚭ phys. contractive, constringent, med.: ⚭ astringent; ~ n ⚭ u. ⚭ziehung f ⚭ (f. ⚭ b) contraction; ⚭ concentration of troops; med.: ⚭ astriction, des Herzens: ⚭ systole; krampfhafte ⚭ziehung convulsion; ⚭zwängen v/a. ⚭** to force together, to join by main force.

zu-samt ⚭ (-⚭) [nhd.] adv. (all) together, (con)jointly, in a body.

Zu-satz (⚭) m ⚭a. (das Zugesetzte ⚭) addition; (Beimischung) admixture, zu Metallen: alloy; (Anhang) addendum, appendix, als Bemerkung: appended note, (Ergänzung) supplement, math., &c. corollary; (Nachschrift) postscript to a letter, rider or additional clause to a bill, codicil to a will; Wasser mit e-m ~ von Kognak water with a dash (or a thimbleful, F a small drop) of brandy; ohne weiteren ~ without any further addition.

Zu-satz-artikel (⚭...) m ⚭ additional article, zu e-m Gesetze ⚭: extra (or additional) clause, rider; parl. ⚭budget supplementary estimates pl.

zu-schanden (-⚭) adv. (zunichte) ruined, marred, done for, lost; ⚭ geh(e)n od. werden to come to nought or to grief, F to go to the bad or to the dogs; (untergehen) to perish; ⚭ hauen, schlagen to knock (or smash) to pieces, F co. to beat into a pulp or a cocked hat; Pläne ⚭. ⚭ machen to foil, overthrow, confound, thwart, Hoffnungen: to destroy, blast, frustrate, defeat; ein Pferd ⚭ reiten to founder a horse.

zu-schanzen F (⚭) ⚭** = zuschieben 2 b.

zu-schärfen ⚭ (⚭) v/a. ⚭** to sharpen a tool, &c., to whet a blade; zugeschärfte Kante fine edge, auch: feather-edge, bevel.

zu-scharren (⚭) v/a. ⚭**: ein Loch ⚭ to fill up ... by scratching or scraping.

zu-schauen (⚭) v/n. (h.) ⚭**: e-r Sache (dat.) ⚭ to look on at a th.; e-m ⚭ to watch a p. doing a th.; vgl. zusehen 1.

Zu-schauer (⚭) m ⚭, ~in f ⚭ spectator (f bisw. auch: spectatress), looker-on; (Zeuge) witness; ~plätze m/pl. ⚭ places (or stands, seats) pl. for spectators; ~raum m, thea. space allotted to (or set apart for) the audience, türsis: house; ~schaft (⚭) f ⚭ (the) spectators pl., (the) audience (a. thea.).

zu-schaufeln (⚭) v/a. ⚭a**: einen Graben ⚭ to fill up ... by shovelling.

zu-schicken (⚭) v/a. ⚭**: e-m et. ⚭ to send (or forward) a p. a th., Geld: to remit money to a p.; ⚭ e-m Waren ⚭ to consign ... to a p. — II ~ n ⚭ sending, &c., ⚭ consignment of goods.

zu-schieben (⚭) v/a. ⚭c** 1. to push (or shove) to, to close by pushing; einen Riegel ⚭ to shoot a bolt; eine Schublade ⚭ to close (or shut) a drawer. — 2. e-m ⚭: a) to push a th. towards a p.; b) fig. (e-m et. in die Hände spielen) to pass (or shift) a th. on to a p., et. Lästiges: to shuffle a th. on to a p.; jur. e-m den Haupteid ⚭ to tender an oath to a p., to put a p. upon his oath; e-m die Schuld an et. ⚭ to lay (or put) the blame for a th. on a p., to blame a p. for a th.

zu-schießen (⚭) ⚭c(es)t ** I v/n. 1. (h.) to (give) fire; immer ⚭ to go on shooting, to fire away at the enemy, &c. — 2. (sn) — losschießen b. — II v/a. 3. dem Feinde Kugeln ⚭ to ply the enemy with bullets; fig. e-m Blicke ⚭ to dart glances at a p. — 4. Geld ⚭ (beisteuern) to contribute money; noch mehr Geld ⚭ to put in more money. — III ~ n ⚭ 5. Zuschuß.

zu-schiffen (⚭) v/n. (sn) ⚭**: auf einen Ort ⚭ to sail (or steam) to(wards) a place, to make for a place.

Zu-schlag (⚭, ⚭) m ⚭c. 1. auf Versteigerungen: knocking down a th. (to the last bidder), bsd. jur. (public) adjudication. — 2. (Vermehrung) increase; (Zusatz) addition; ⚭ ein Billett excess fare; ⚭ ein ~ von 3 Mark die Elle an extra (or additional) charge of three shillings a yard. — 3. ⚭ metall. (Flußmittel) flux.

Zu-schlag-billett ⚭ (⚭...) n ⚭ extra ticket; ~gebühr f extra (or additional) fee, ⚭ excess fare.

zu-schlagen (⚭) ⚭b** I v/n. 1. (h.) to strike (a blow), to hit (out), auf eine Person: to lay it on; schlag zu! hit hard!; die Augen ⚭ to close one's eyes; ein Buch ⚭ to shut up a book; ⚭ Schmiede: kurz ⚭ to strike (or hammer) briskly. — 2. (sn) von einer Tür, einem Falleisen ⚭: (sich schließen) to shut suddenly. — II v/a. 3. die Tür ⚭ to slam (or bang) ... (to). — 4. e-m et. ⚭: a) to strike (or knock) a th. towards a p.; e-m den Ball ⚭ to drive (or bat) the ball towards a p.; b) auf Versteigerungen: to knock a th. down (bsd. jur. to adjudicate a th.) to a p. — 5. ⚭ metall. to add as a flux. — 6. ⚭ = zuhauen II.

Zu-schläger ⚭ (⚭) m ⚭ des Schmieds: smith's assistant, hammerman.

Zu-schlag-kalkstein ⚭ (⚭...) m ⚭ metall. calcareous flux; ~karte f additional

ticket; ~porto n excess postage; ~prämie f extra premium; ~steuer f additional tax, extra impost or duty; ~taxe f extra tax.

zu-schleifen (⚭) [schleifen¹] v.a. ⚭b**: to sharpen, ⚭ (to grind to a) point, to polish; e-n Edelstein vieleckig ⚭ to cut ... into facets.

zu-schleppen (⚭) ⚭** : e-m et. ⚭ to drag (or haul) a th. to(wards) a p., b.s. to get (or procure) a th. for a p. (in an underhand or illegal way).

zu-schließen (⚭) v/a. ⚭d** to lock up with a key, mit einem Vorhängeschloß ⚭: to padlock, weitS. to shut up, to close.

zu-schmeißen F (⚭) v/a. ⚭a**: eine Tür ⚭.: to fling (or slam, bang) ... to.

zu-schmelzen (⚭) v/a. ⚭** to close up by (s)melting or fusion, luftdicht: to seal hermetically.

zu-schmieren (⚭) v/a. ⚭** to smear (or daub) over.

zu-schnallen (⚭) v/a. ⚭** to buckle (up), mit Riemen: to strap up; Gürtel (od. Riemen) enger ⚭ to draw in one's belt (strap) more tightly.

zu-schnappen (⚭) v/n. ⚭** 1. (sn) von Schlössern ⚭: to shut with a snap, to snap to, von Schnallen ⚭: to catch. — 2. (h.) nach et. ⚭ to snap at a th.

Zu-schneide-brett ⚭ (⚭...) n ⚭ der Sattler, Schuhmacher: cutting-out board; ~kunst f Schneiderei ⚭: art of cutting out; ~kursus m course of instruction in cutting out coats, dresses, &c.; ~messer ⚭ n cutting-out knife.

zu-schneiden (⚭) v/a. ⚭c** 1. to cut up, bsd. ⚭ Näherei, Schneiderei: to cut out a shirt, dress, coat, &c., carp. Bauholz: to cut up, to dress, to scantle. — 2. fig. et. sehr knapp ⚭ to cut a th. very fine; e-m et. spärlich ⚭ (or serve) a p. very slender portions of a th., to keep a p. short of a th.

Zu-schneider ⚭ (⚭) m ⚭, ~in f ⚭ cutter(-out) of dresses, coats, &c.

Zu-schneiderei ⚭ (⚭) f ⚭ 1. cutting-(out) room. — 2. Schneiderei ⚭: cutting-out, carp. scantling, squaring. — 3. b.s. slovenly (style of) cutting out, bad (or inferior) cut.

Zu-schneide-tisch ⚭ (⚭...) m ⚭ der Schneider ⚭: cutting-out table.

zu-schneien (⚭) v/n. (sn) ⚭** to get snowed up; ⚭ zugeschneit (von einer Bahnstrecke) blocked (up) with snow.

Zu-schnitt (⚭) [zuschneiden] m ⚭c. cut (or cutting out) of a garment; (Anordnung) arrangement; fig. (äußeres Wesen, Stil) (outside) appearance, look, style, fashion; in großartigem ~ in magnificent style or trim, on a grand (or elaborate) scale.

zu-schnüren (⚭) v/a. ⚭** to lace up a dress, &c.; einem die Kehle ⚭ to strangle (or throttle, garrotte) a p., fig. es schnürte mir das Herz zu it wrung my very heart; es schnürte mir die Kehle zu it made a lump rise in my throat; vgl. Kehle 1.

zu-schrauben (⚭) v/a. ⚭c ⚭** to screw up, einen Deckel ⚭: to screw down, (fest schrauben) to fasten (or tighten) with a screw.

Signs (see page XVII): F familiar; P vulgar; ⚭ flash; ⚭ rare; † obsolete (died); * new word (born); ⚭ incorrect; ♪ music;

zu-schreiben (⁀⁀᪽) v/a. ⓮** 1. einige Zeilen ᪽ to add a few lines. — 2. e-m et. ᪽ to assign a th. to a p. in writing; ⚇ e-m eine Summe ᪽ to put ... to a p.'s credit, to credit ... to a p. — 3. = beilegen 2; e-m eine Tat, Handlung ꝛc. ᪽ to ascribe ... to a p., to set (or put) ... down to a p., to father s.th. upon a p.; das muß er sich selbst ᪽ he has to blame (or thank) himself for it; das alles ist ihm zuzuschreiben it is all due to him, the blame rests entirely with him. — 4. (schriftlich versprechen, annehmen) to accept by letter, to promise in writing; ich habe ihnen zugeschrieben I have accepted their invitation, auch: I have written to them to say we were coming.

zu-schreien (⁀⁀᪽) v/a. u. v/n. (h.) ⓮**: e-m et. ᪽ to cry (or bawl. scream. shout) out a th. to a p.

zu-schreiten (⁀⁀᪽) v/n. (ſn) ⓮b**: 1. auf e-n ᪽ to step (or walk) up to a p. — 2. tüchtig (od. wacker) ᪽ to step out well, to walk (or stride along) briskly, F to put one's best leg (or step) forward.

Zu-schrift (⁀᪽) [zuschreiben] f ⓯ writing (addressed) to a p.; letter, epistle; amtliche ~ official communication. (Widmung) inscription, dedication.

zu-schriftlich (⁀⁀᪽) adv. by letter.

zu-schulden (⁀᪽⁀) adv.: sich (dat.) et. ᪽ kommen lassen to make o. s. guilty of a th., to do s. th. wrong.

Zu-schuß (⁀᪽) [zuschießen 4] m ⓮a. contribution, addition(al supply or payment); e-m Zuschüsse gewähren to make a p. extra allowances; typ. ~ von Papier overs pl.; ~bogen ⊕ m ⓰ typ. extra sheet: ~steuer f additional tax or duty.

zu-schütten (⁀⁀᪽) v/a. ⓮** 1. to pour on ꝛc. to add to. — 2. e-n Brunnen ꝛc. ᪽ to fill up ... with earth, rubbish, &c.

zu-schwären (⁀⁀᪽) v/n. (ſn) ⓮a ⓮a** to close by ulceration or suppuration.

zu-sehen (⁀⁀᪽) I v/n. (h.) ⓮a** 1. to look on, to be a spectator or an eyewitness: e-r Sache ᪽ to watch a th., als Zeuge: to witness a th.; sie sahen zu, wie er es machte they watched him doing it. — 2. = hinsehen, weiter = nachsehen a und b. — 3. (sorgen) to take care, to pay attention; (sich in acht nehmen) to be on one's guard; da muß er selbst ᪽ he must see (or look) to it himself. — 4. (zögern) to delay; eine kleine Weile ᪽ to wait a little while; da kann ich nicht länger ᪽ I cannot stand this any longer. — II ~ n ㉓ 5. looking on, &c. (ſ. I); er hat das (bloße) ~ he is a mere looker-on, he gets nothing for his pains.

zu-sehends (⁀⁀᪽) adv. visibly, obviously, evidently, manifestly, noticeably.

zu-sein (⁀⁀) v/n. (ſn) ⓮a** to be shut or closed or locked or fastened (up).

zu-senden (⁀⁀᪽) v/a. ⓮a** = zuschicken.

zu-setzen (⁀⁀᪽) ⓮** I v/a. 1. (hinzufügen) to add, to contribute; (beimengen) to mix up with, Metalle: to alloy with; es ist zuzusetzen, daß ɉɉ it must be added that ɉɉ, it must also be noticed that ɉɉ. — 2 (einbüßen) to lose; seine Gesundheit dabei ᪽ to sacrifice one's health over (or to) it. — 3. (versperren) to obstruct, block, bar; Dominospiel: to place a domino so as to end the game. — II v/n. (h.) 4. e-m hart (oder scharf) ᪽ to press a p. hard. to be hard upon a p.; e-m mit Bitten stark ᪽ to beg hard of a p., to importune (or besiege) a p. (with one's petitions); e-m mit Fragen ᪽ to ply a p. with questions; e-m mit eitelem Gerede, Geschwätz ᪽ to bother (or worry) a p. with empty talk or twaddle; e-m so ᪽, daß er nicht mehr aus noch ein weiß to drive (or push) a p. into a corner; es wurde ihm von seinen Gläubigern scharf zugesetzt he was cruelly dunned (or worried) by his creditors.

zu-sichern (⁀⁀᪽) I v/a. ⓰a**: e-m et. ᪽ to assure a p. of a th., to promise a p. a th. (faithfully). — II ~ n ㉓ u. Zusicherung f ⓯ assurance; ⚇ unter Zusicherung pünktlicher Bedienung promising you our strictest attention to your orders.

zu-siegeln (⁀⁀᪽) v/a. ⓰a** to seal up.

Zu-speise (⁀⁀᪽) f ⓯ = Zukost.

zu-sperren (⁀⁀᪽) v/a. ⓮** to bar up, to close, to shut (up), to fasten (up).

zu-spielen (⁀⁀᪽) v/a. ⓮**: e-m et. ᪽ to play a th. into a p.'s hands; Fußball: to pass; fig. e-m et. ᪽ to pass a th. on to a p. in a sly (or cunning) manner; vgl. zustecken 1.

zu-spitzen (⁀⁀᪽) v/a. u. v/refl. ⓰** 1. to (sharpen to a) point, to taper, (dünner schneiden) to thin (off); fig. to bring to a point; sich ᪽ to run to a point, to taper (off), fig. to come to a (critical) point; zugespitzt pointed, ¶: ⚇ acuminate(d). ⊕ coned; arch. bogenförmig to cope; kegelförmig zugespitzt conical, conic-acute; spitzartig zugespitzt spired. — fig. epigrammatisch ᪽ to put in the form of an epigram, to express epigrammatically.

Zu-sprache (⁀⁀᪽) f ⓯ = Zuspruch 1.

zu-sprechen (⁀⁀᪽) ⓰a** I v/a. 1. e-m Mut ᪽ to cheer a p. up, to raise a p.'s courage; e-m Trost ᪽ to speak (words of) comfort to a p., to comfort a p. — 2. jur. e-m etwas ᪽ to adjudge (or adjudicate) a th. to a p. — II v/n. (h.) 3. e-m (freundlich) ᪽ to speak (kindly or cheeringly) to a p. — 4. fig. der Flasche fleißig ᪽ to partake freely of the bottle, to drink copiously; einer Speise gehörig ᪽ to eat heartily of (or to do full justice to) a dish. — III ~ n ㉓ u. Zusprechung f ⓯ 5. (ſ. 1) (words of) comfort or cheer; (ſ. 2) jur. adjudication.

zu-springen (⁀⁀᪽) v/n. (ſn) ⓰f** 1. auf e-n ᪽ to spring (or leap) towards a p., to run up to a p. — 2. (immer) ᪽ to continue leaping. — 3. = zuschnappen 1.

Zu-spruch (⁀⁀ɗ) m ⓮c. 1. words addressed to a p.; (tröstendes Zusprechen) comforting (or cheering) words pl.; (Ermunterung) encouragement; (Ermahnung) exhortation. — 2. guten ~ (gute Kundschaft) h.: a) von Geschäften: to have a good circle of customers or a good connexion; b) v. Gasthäusern, Bädern ꝛc. to be much resorted to or frequented.

zu-spunden (⁀⁀᪽) v/a. ⓮** to bung up.

Zu-stand (⁀⁀) m ⓮c. state, condition; (Lage) situation. position; (Los) lot; in gutem ~e in good state or trim or order, von Gebäuden: in good repair.

zu-stande (⁀⁀᪽) adv.: et. ᪽ bringen to achieve (or bring about. accomplish) a th.; ᪽ kommen to come about; die Reise ꝛc. wird ᪽ kommen (stattfinden) ... will take place; parl. das Gesetz kommt ᪽ the bill will pass; nicht ᪽ kommen, oft: to fail, to come to grief or to nought, not to come off.

Zu-stande-bringen (⁀⁀᪽...) n ㉒ achievement. accomplishment; ~kommen n success, realization; das ~ des Kongresses ist gesichert it is settled that the congress will be held. a. the meeting of the congress is secured.

zu-ständig (⁀⁀᪽) a. ⓰ 1. e-m ᪽ (angehörig) belonging (or appertaining) to a p. — 2. jur. Der Richter (vor den die Sache gehört) competent judge: ~keit f ⓯ competence; ~keits-kreis m ⓰ department, eines Richters: venue. [active.

zu-ständlich (⁀⁀᪽) a. ⓰ neutral, not]

zu-statten (⁀᪽⁀) [ahd.] adv.: e-m ᪽ kommen to be (or prove) useful (or advantageous) to a p.

zu-stechen (⁀⁀᪽) v/n. (h.) ⓮a** I v/a. to stitch up. — II v/n. (h.): auf e-n ᪽ to (make a) thrust at a p., to stab at a p.

zu-stecken (⁀⁀᪽) v/a. ⓮** 1. e-m et. ᪽ slip a th. into a p.'s hands or pockets, to give (or hand) a p. a th. secretly or F on the sly; vgl. zuspielen fig. — 2. (mit einer Nadel schließen, festmachen) to pin up, to fasten with a pin.

zu-steh(e)n (⁀⁀᪽) v/n. ⓮a**: e-m ᪽ (zukommen) to appertain (or belong) to a p., weitS. = gebühren 1; es steht ihm nicht zu, hier zu befehlen he has no right (or it is not for him) to give orders here; es steht uns nicht zu, eine Entscheidung zu fällen it is no business of ours (or it is not incumbent on us) to give a decision.

zu-stellen (⁀⁀᪽) I v/a. ⓮** 1. to put in front of, to obstruct (or block up) with s.th. put before. — 2. e-m et. ᪽ (überhändigen) to hand a p. a th., to deliver (or present, convey) a th. to a p., jur. to serve a th. on a p., to notify a th. to a p. — II ~ n ㉓ u. Zu-stellung f ⓯ 3. (ſ.1,2) delivery. presentation, conveyance, gerichtliche: service, notification.

Zu-stellungs-beamte(r) (⁀⁀᪽...) m ⓰ Gericht: officer of the court serving writs; ~gebühr f fee for conveyance, carrier's charges pl., gerichtliche: fee for serving (or for the service of) writs; ~urkunde f jur. writ of summons.

zu-steuern (⁀⁀᪽) ⓮a** I v/a. u. v/n. (h.) (beisteuern) to contribute to a th. — II ↧ v/n. (ſn): a) der Küste ᪽ to steer towards (or to head for, make for) the coast: b) (immer) ᪽ (steadily) to pursue one's course.

zu-stimmen (⁀⁀᪽) I v/n. (h.) ⓮** to (give one's) consent to a th.; vgl. beistimmen I; nickend ᪽ to nod assent; ᪽d assenting, assentient, affirmative. — II ~ n ㉓ u. Zu-stimmung f ⓯ consent; vgl. Beistimmung.

⚇ scientific; ⚹ botanical; ⚇ geography; ⊕ machinery; ⚒ mining, ⚔ military; ↧ marine; ⚇ commercial; ⚇ postal; ⚇ railway.

[zustopfen] — 1176 — [zuverlässig]

zu-stopfen (᷼͝ ᷽) v/a. ⑧⁎⁎ 1. ein Loch ꝛc. ᷾ to stop (or stuff) up …; die Ohren ᷾, auch: to close one's ears. — 2. e-n Riß ꝛc. mit der Nadel ᷾ to darn (up) …, to mend …, to patch (up) …

zu-stöpseln (᷼͝ ᷽) v/a. ⓐ⁎⁎ to stopper, mit Kork: to cork (up) a bottle, &c.

zu-stoßen (᷼͝ ᷽) ⁎⁎ I v/a. 1. e-m et. ᷾ to push a th. towards a p.; to thrust a th. at a p. — 2. die Tür ᷾ to push …, to slam or bang … — II v/n. 3. (h.) kräftig ᷾ to give a hard push. — 4. (sn) v. et. Widrigem: to befall a p.; es ist ihm ein Unglück zugestoßen a misfortune has befallen (or overtaken) him, he has met with an accident; falls mir et. ᷾ sollte in case anything (unforeseen) should happen to me.

zu-streben (᷼͝ ᷽) v/n. (h.) ⑧⁎⁎: dem Ziele ᷾ to endeavour to attain one's object, to strive for (or after, towards) s.th. (in view), to make for the goal.

zu-streichen (᷼͝ ᷽) ⓐst⁎⁎ I v/n. (sn): auf ein Ziel ᷾, dem Ziele ᷾ = zustreben. — II v/a. Ritzen ꝛc. ᷾ to stop up with clay, putty, &c., to smear over … with tallow, grease, &c.

zu-stricken (᷼͝ ᷽) v/a. ⑧⁎⁎: e-n Strumpf ᷾ to finish (or close, complete) (the knitting of) a stocking.

zu-strömen (᷼͝ ᷽) ⑧⁎⁎ I v/n. (sn) to stream (or flow) towards, v. Personen: to pour (or flock, crowd) in. — II ~ n ㉓ v. Personen ꝛc.: influx, v. Ideen ꝛc.: inflowing, (rich) flow.

zu-stülpen (᷼͝ ᷽) v/a. ⑧⁎⁎ to (put a) cover over, to cover with a lid.

zu-stürmen (᷼͝ ᷽) v/n. (sn) ⑧⁎⁎: auf e-n ᷾ to (make a) rush at (or upon) a p., to dash at a p.

zu-stürzen (᷼͝ ᷽) v/n. (sn) ⑨⁰⁎⁎: auf e-n ᷾ to fall upon a p., to rush upon (or towards) a p., to hurry up to a p.

zu-stutzen (᷼͝ ᷽) v/a. ⑨⁰⁎⁎ to dress (or fit) up, to (put into) shape, to fashion; einen Hut: to trim, einen Baum: to lop; ein Stück für die Bühne ᷾ to adapt a piece for the stage; F e-n zu et. ᷾ to train a p. for a th.

zu-tage (᷻͝͝) adv.: ᷾ bringen, ᷾ fördern fig. to bring to light; ᷾ bringen to bring to the surface or F to grass, to extract (ore, &c.), fig. to unbury, uncover; ᷾ kommen = ᷾ treten; ᷾ liegen fig. to be evident or manifest, ⚔ to appear (or show) on the surface, ᷾ treten fig. to come to light; ⚔ to crop out.

Zu-tage-streichen ⚔ (-᷼͝ ᷽) n ㉓ cropping out of a lode or a seam.

zu-tappen (᷼͝ ᷽) v/n. (h.) ⑧⁎⁎ 1. to grope on or along, F to fumble (or poke) about (in the dark); fig. to blunder along. — 2. (plump zugreifen) to seize clumsily, fig. to use no (or to act without) discretion.

Zu-tat (᷻͝) f ㊻ 1. a) Schneiderei: (Futter, Knöpfe, Einfassung ꝛc. für ein Kleidungsstück) lining and trimming(s pl.); b) Kochkunst: ~en zu einer Speise ingredients pl. (als Verzierung: garnishing) of a dish. — 2. (Rohmaterial) raw material.

zu-teil (᷻͝) adv.: e-m ᷾ w. to fall to a p.'s share or lot; e-m et. ᷾ w. lassen to allot (or grant, apportion) a p. a th.

zu-teilen (᷻͝ ᷽) I v/a. ⑧⁎⁎: e-m et. ᷾ to apportion (or allot, assign) a th. to a p., in reichem Maße: to lavish a th. on a p., gerichtlich: to adjudge (or adjudicate) a th. to a p.; (austeilen) to distribute, divide, mete out; e-m e-n Titel, e-e Würde ᷾ to confer (or bestow) a title, a dignity on a p.; das mir zugeteilte Stück the piece which has fallen to my share. — II ~ n ㉓ u. **Zu-teilung** f ㊻ allotment, assignment, adjudication, distribution.

zu-traben (᷻͝ ᷽) v/n. (h.) ⑧⁎⁎ 1. auf e-n Ort ᷾ to trot towards a place. — 2. kräftig ᷾ to trot (or step) along at a brisk pace.

zu-tragen (᷻͝ ᷽) ⑧b⁎⁎ I v/a. 1. a) e-m et. ᷾ to carry a th. to a p.; b) Neuigkeiten und Klatsch ᷾ to report (or retell, repeat, bring, take) all the news; er trug es ihnen brühwarm zu he carried them the news in hot haste, he hurried to tell them what had happened. — II v/n. (h.) 2. von Bäumen, Äckern: (reichlich tragen) to bear (or produce) good fruit or crops. — 3. sich ᷾ v/refl. = sich ereignen.

Zu-träger (᷻͝ ᷽) m ⓶, ~in f ㊼: a) carrier; b) von Neuigkeiten: tell-tale, gossip, scandalmonger; f. a. Angeber 3.

Zu-trägerei (᷻͝-᷽) f ㊻ tale-bearing, gossip, circulating reports, F fetching and carrying (news); f. a. Angeberei.

zu-träglich (᷻͝ ᷽) [zutragen 2] a. ㊻ productive (of), conducive (to); weitS. (vorteilhaft) advantageous, profitable, beneficial, (nützlich) useful; (heilsam) salutary, der Gesundheit ᷾ conducive to health, wholesome (food, habit. &c.), salubrious (climate, &c.); schwere Speise ist ihm nicht ᷾ rich food is not good for him or does not agree with him.

Zu-träglichkeit (᷻͝ ᷽-) f ㊻ conduciveness; advantageousness; usefulness; wholesomeness, salubrity.

zu-trauen (᷻͝ ᷽) I v/a. ⑧⁎⁎: e-m et. ᷾ to believe a p. able to do a th., to put one's trust in (or to rely on a p.) for s.th.; das hätte Ihnen niemand zugetraut nobody would have thought you capable of that; ich traue ihm nicht viel Gutes zu I have no (or I don't put) great confidence in him. — II ~ n ㉓ trust, confidence; e-m unbedingtes ~ schenken to put implicit confidence (or faith) in a p.; kein ~ zu e-m h. to place no reliance on a p., not to trust a person, to mistrust a person.

zu-trauen-erweckend (᷻͝-᷽᷼) a. ㊻ inspiring confidence.

zu-trauens-voll (᷻͝-᷽fl) a. ㊻ full of confidence, confident; (vertraulich) confidential, friendly.

zu-traulich (᷻͝ ᷽) a. ㊻ = vertraulich 2; ~keit f ㊻ = Vertraulichkeit 2.

zu-treffen (᷻͝ ᷽) I v/n. (h.) ⓐa⁎⁎ v. Vorausgesagtem: to come true, to prove correct (= eintreffen 2), von Beweisen: to be conclusive or clinching; das trifft nicht in allen Fällen zu that does not hold good in all cases, that does not always follow. — II ~ n ㉓ coming true of a prediction, &c., conclusiveness of a proof, &c. — III ᷾d p.pr.

u. a. ㊻ = treffen III; Den-falls in the event of s.th. happening, eventually. should such a case occur.

zu-treiben (᷻͝ ᷽) ⓑ⁎⁎ I v/a. 1. to drive to(wards); Vieh der Weide ᷾ to drive (or lead) cattle to pasture; ⚹ Kunden ᷾ to attract custom(ers), to tout (for customers). — 2. die Pferde ᷾ (antreiben) to urge on …, mit der Peitsche: to whip up … — II v/n. 3. (sn) von einem Schiffe: von Klippen ᷾ to drift towards the cliffs, to be carried (or borne, driven) towards the rocks.

zu-treten (᷻͝ ᷽) ⓐd⁎⁎ I v/n. (sn) 1. to step up to, näher: to step (or come) nearer to. verstärkend, helfend: to intervene, to come to the rescue. — 2. (hinzutreten) to be added to. v. Krankheiten: to produce complications. — 3. (immer) ᷾ to go on treading; sobald er auf dem Zweirade saß, trat er aus allen Kräften zu as soon he had mounted his bicycle he pedalled away (or worked the pedals) with all his might. — II v/a. 4. ein Loch in der Erde ᷾ to stop (or fill) up … by treading or stamping. — III ~ n ㉓ 5. (f. 1) stepping up or nearer, approach, intervention.

zu-trinken (᷻͝ ᷽) v/n. (h.) ⓐst⁎⁎ 1. e-m ᷾ to drink to a p.'s health, seltener: to pledge a p. — 2. (immer) ᷾ to go (or keep) on drinking, to imbibe (freely).

Zu-tritt (᷻͝) [zutreten] m ⓒc. access, admittance. bei Hofe ꝛc.: admission to court, &c.; thea. freier ~ free admission, free pass; bei e-m freien ~ h. to have free access to (or F the free run of) a p.'s house. to be allowed to visit a p.('s house), F to go freely in and out of a p.'s house; ~ bei Hofe h. to be admitted at court; überall ~ h. to be welcome everywhere.

zu-tulich (᷻͝ ᷽) ꝛc. f. zutunlich ꝛc.

zu-tun (᷻͝) I v/a. u. v/refl. ⑨⁵⁎⁎ 1. = hinzufügen. — 2. die Augen ᷾ (schließen): a) to close (or shut) one's eyes; f. Auge 1 am Schluß; b) fig. = sterben. — 3. e-m ᷾ (anschmiegen) to make up to (or to curry favour with) a p. — II ~ n ㉓ 4. (Mitwirkung) co-operation, participation; ohne sein ~ without his aid or assistance or interference, had it not been for him. — III zugetan p.p. u. a. ㊻ 5. in den Bed. des inf. — 6. f. bsd. Artikel.

zu-tu(n)lich (᷻͝ ᷽) a. ㊻ (dienstbeflissen) officious, obliging, complaisant; (zutraulich) engaging; ~keit f ㊻ officiousness, complaisance; engaging (or insinuating) manners or ways pl.

Zu- und Ab-strömen (᷽᷻᷻͝͝) n ㉓ flowing to and fro, ⚓ (in)flux and reflux, ⚓ der Gezeiten: incoming and receding tide.

zu-ungunsten (-᷽᷼) adv. f. Ungunst.

zu unterst (-᷽) f. unterst.

zu-verlässig (᷻f᷽᷼) a. ㊻ von Personen u. Nachrichten: to be relied (or depended) upon, reliable, dependable, trustworthy; von Nachrichten auch: sure, certain, authentic (news), authoritative (statement); (ganzbestimmt) positive, (positively) true, (glaubwürdig) credible; von ᷾er Seite erfahren, daß // to

---

Zeichen (s. S. XVII): F familiär; P Volkssprache; ⸹ Gaunersprache; ~ selten; † alt (auch gestorben); * neu (auch geboren); ⁺⁺ unrichtig;

[Zuverlässigkeit] — 1177 — [zuziehen]

have it on good (or safe) authority that ||; ~feit f ⁴⁶ reliability, reliableness, trustworthiness; certainty, authenticity; credibility.

Zu-versicht (-ᵘˡ~) [mhd.: *versehen 8] f (full or entire) confidence, (positive) assurance; (feste Hoffnung) confident hope; (volle Überzeugung) firm conviction; (Vertrauen) trust (zu Gott in God); ich hege die volle ~, daß || I fully trust that ||; Sie dürfen mit ~ darauf rechnen you may confidently rely upon it; wir setzen unsere ganze ~ auf ihn we put our whole trust in him, we entirely rely on him.

zu-versichtlich (-ᵘˡ~) a. ⁶⁶ confident, assured; (hoffnungsvoll) hopeful; mit höchst ⁶er Miene with an air of great assurance; ⁶ (adv.) auf et. hoffend resting one's hope and trust on a th., trusting in a th.; ~feit f ⁴⁶ confidence, dünkelhafte: assurance, conceit. hoffnungsvolle: hopefulness, trust.

zu-viel (-f¹) I adv. (a. zu viel): ⁶(e) too much (many); i. a. all⁶: drei ⁶ three too many; mehr als ⁶ more than enough; viel ⁶ by far too much; das ist (des Guten) ⁶ that is too much (of a good thing); des Guten ⁶ tun, auch: to go too far; was ⁶ ist, ist ⁶ too much is too much; f. Kopf 7 am Schluß; beſſer ⁶ als zuwenig better too much than too little. — II ~ n, inv. excess, s.th. beyond (the right) measure; ein ~ iſt beſſer als ein Zuwenig too much (of a good thing) is better than too little.

zu-vor (-f¹) [mhd.] I adv. = vorher 1. — II ~ n. inv. das ~ und Hernach the (events) before and after.

zu-vor-.... Zu-vor-.... in Verbindung mit verbs, immer trennbar (**), u. in Zſgn mit verbal nouns u. adjectives. zB. ⁶bedenken (-ᵘ~) v/a. ⁷⁷** to consider (or think over) beforehand.

zu-vorderſt (-f¹~) adv. in the front rank.

zu-vörderſt (-f¹~) adv. first of all, in the first place; (vor allem andern) before everything else, first and foremost, to begin with.

zu-vor-einnehmen (-f¹...) v/a. ⁷ᵃ** = einnehmen 6; ⁶erwägen v a. ⁷ᵃ(⁸⁸)*/* = ⁶bedenken. auch: to weigh beforehand; ⁶kommen v n. (ſn) ⁸⁸**; a) e-m ⁶ to come before a p., to forestall or anticipate a p., to get the start of a p.; ich bin ihren Wünſchen ſtets zuvorgekommen I always anticipated her wishes; b) e-r Sache (vorbeugen) to prevent a th.; ⁶d p.pr. u. a. ⁶⁶: a) anticipatory; b) (gefällig) obliging, complaisant; (höflich) civil, courteous; aufs ⁶ſte most obligingly, in the most courteous way; ~heit f ⁴⁶ obligingness, complaisance; civility; ⁶tun v/a. ⁹⁵**: es e-m ⁶ (ihn übertreffen) to surpass (or excel, outdo, outshine) a p.; es e-m ⁶ zutun ſuchen to vie (or compete) with a p.

Zu-wachs (-ᵘſf¹) m ⁸a. (pl. ~) growth, ⁷⁷ accrescence, accretion; (Vermehrung) increase, augmentation, increment, addition(al number); (Vergrößerung) enlargement, extension; (Ausdehnung) expansion, extension; Kleider auf (den)

~ machen to make clothes so (long and wide) as to allow for growing.

zu-wachſen (-ᵘˡ~) v/n. (ſn) ⁸ᵇ** 1. to close (up) in growing, von Wunden: to heal up. — 2. e-m ⁶ (zuteil werden): a) eigentlich: dem Landmanne wachſen die Früchte ⁶ the growing crops are the husbandman's reward; es ſind ihm viele Lämmer zugewachſen he has many lambs growing up; b) weit⁶. to fall to a p.'s lot or share, to accrue to a p.

zu-wägen (-ᵘˡ~) v a. ⁷ᵃ⁸⁸** 1. et. ⁶ to weigh a th. out to a p.; fig. Lob und Tadel ⁶ to dispense ... — 2. (wägend zufügen) to add in weighing.

zu-wälzen (-ᵘˡ~) v/a. ⁹⁰** 1. to roll to or towards; der Strom wälzt ſeine Fluten dem Meere zu ... rolls (or carries) its waters towards the sea. — 2. den Eingang der Höhle mit Felſen ⁶ to bar (or block) up the entrance to a cave with rocks.

zu-wandern (-ᵘˡ~) v/n. (ſn) ⁹²ᵃ** to wander (or migrate) to(wards); zu"- gewandert kommen to immigrate; ein Zu"gewanderter ⁶⁷ an immigrant, a new settler, a fresh comer.

zu-wanken (-ᵘˡ~) v/n. (ſn) ⁶⁸**: auf et. ⁶ to totter (or reel, stagger) towards a th.

zu-warten (-ᵘˡ~) I v/n. (h.) ⁶⁹** to wait patiently (or quietly), ⁶d. auch: expectant. — II ~ n ²³ patient waiting; durch ~ zu gewinnen ſuchen to play a waiting game.

zu-wege (-ᵘˡ~) [ahd.] adv.: et. ⁶ bringen to bring about a th., to effect (or accomplish) a th., to set a th. on foot; gut ⁶ (ſein) (to be) quite well, (to be) in good health.

zu-wehen (-ᵘˡ~) v/a. ⁷⁹ᵇ** 1. to blow (or waft) to(wards); e-m (ſich) Luft ⁶ to fan a p. (o.s.). — 2. der Wind hat die Wege mit Schnee zugeweht ... has blocked up the roads with (drifted) snow.

zu-weilen (-ᵘˡ~) [nhd.] adv. sometimes, at times, now and then, now and again, occasionally, a.: between whiles.

zu-weiſen (-ᵘˡ~) I v/n. (h.): auf etwas ⁶ = hinweiſen. — II v a.: e-m et. ⁶ (zuerteilen) to assign (or apportion) a th. to a p.; e-m Kunden ⁶ to send (or introduce) customers to a p.; der ihm zugewieſene Teil, das ihm Zugewieſene his allotted portion.

Zu-weiſung (-ᵘˡ~) f ⁴⁶ (f. zuweiſen II) assignment, von Kunden: introduction.

zu-wenden (-ᵘˡ~) I v/a. u. ſich ⁶ v/refl. ⁹⁶ᵃ** 1. den Schritt (od. ſich) nach einem Orte ⁶ to turn one's steps or to wend one's way towards a place. — 2. e-m das Geſicht ⁶ to turn one's face towards a p., to face a p.; e-m den Rücken ⁶ to turn one's back upon a p.; e-m ſ-e Liebe ⁶ to bestow one's affection(s) upon a p.; ſeine Freundlichkeit wandte ihm alle Herzen zu his kind ways drew all hearts towards him or won every heart (for him). — 3. e-m et. ⁶ (zukommen l.) to obtain (or procure) a th. for a p., to put (or throw) s.th. in a p.'s way; einer Sache ſeine volle Aufmerkſamkeit ⁶ to bestow one's undivided attention upon a th., to pay (or give) the strictest (or greatest)

attention to a th. — II zu-gewandt p.p. 4. f. bib. Artikel.

zu-wenig (-ᵘˡ~) adv. too little.

zu-werfen (-ᵘˡ~) v/a. ⁷⁹ᵇ** 1. e-m Hunde ein Stück Brot ⁶ to throw a dog a piece of bread, to throw (or cast) a piece of bread to a dog; e-m (verſtohlene, heimliche) Blicke ⁶ to cast (sly, furtive) glances at a p.; e-m verliebte Blicke ⁶ to make sheep's eyes at a p.; vgl. Blick 1 am Ende. — 2. Kartenſpiel: to play. — 3. die Tür ⁶ to slam the door. — 4. e-n Graben ⁶ to fill up a ditch with earth, rubbish, &c.

zu-wider (-ᴵ~) [erſt nhd.] adv. und prp. mit dat. nachſtehend: contrary to (or in contravention of) the law.

zu-wider-handeln (-ᴵ~...) v n. (h.) ⁹ᵃ** to act contrary to or in contravention of: dem Geſetze ⁶, a. to offend against ...; ~ n ²³. Handlung f ⁴⁶ contravention of the law, &c.; ⁶laufen v/n. (ſn) ⁶ᵃſt** to run counter to (a. fig.); ⁶machen v a. ⁸⁸**: e-m et. ⁶ to set a p. against a th.; ⁶ſein v/n. (ſn) ⁶ᵃſt**: a) das Glück iſt uns zuwider fate is against us; Wünſche, die ſeiner Pflicht ⁶waren ... which clashed with his duty; b) e-m ⁶ (verhaßt ſein) to be repugnant (or distasteful, objectionable, ſtärker: loathsome) to a p.; er iſt mir in den Tod zuwider he is my aversion, I abominate (ſtärker: I loathe) him; ⁶tun v/a. ⁹⁵** to do in opposition to or in spite of.

zu-winken (-ᵘˡ~) v n. (h.) ⁶: einem ⁶ to nod (or beckon) to a p.

zu-wölben (-ᵘˡ~) v/a. ⁸⁸** arch. to vault (or arch) over or up.

Zu-wuchs (-ᵘˡ~) m ⁸a. = Zuwachs.

zu-zahlen (-ᵘˡ~) I v a. ⁹ᵃ** to pay extra or additionally. — II ~ n ²³ = Zuzahlung.

zu-zählen (-ᵘˡ~) v/a. ⁸⁸** 1. et. ⁶ to add s.th. in counting, to reckon (or F throw) s.th. in with. — 2. e-m et. ⁶ to count s.th. out to a p. [ditional) payment.|

Zu-zahlung (-ᵘˡ~) f ⁴⁶ extra (or ad-

zu-zeiten (-ᵘˡ~) adv. (bisweilen) at times.

zu-ziehen (-ᵘˡ~) ⁹ᵇ** I v/a. 1. einen Knoten ⁶ to tighten ...; die Tür ⁶ to pull the door to; die Vorhänge ⁶ to draw the curtains; ſ. aufziehen 3. — 2. e-n dem Abgrunde ⁶ to draw (or pull) a p. towards the gulf, to bring a p. to the brink of ruin. — 3. e-n (als Teilnehmer) zu et. ⁶ to call in a p.('s assistance), to invite a p. to participate in a th., zur Beratung: to consult a doctor, &c., to take the advice of a physician, &c.; bei Hofe: zur Tafel ⁶ to command to dinner. — 4. ſich (dat.) Äußerungen ⁶ to draw down remarks upon o.s., to expose o.s. to criticism; ſich j-s Feindſchaft ⁶ to incur a p.'s enmity; ſ. Handel; ſich einen Tadel ⁶ to incur censure or blame; ſich eine Krankheit ⁶ to contract (or catch) a disease. — II ſich ⁶ v/refl. 5. die Schleife zieht ſich zu the slip-knot tightens. — III v n. 6. (h.) kräftig ⁶ to pull with all one's might. — 7. (ſn) to move to or towards; v. Dienſtboten: to go into service, to (under)take a (new) situation; er iſt in dieſem Orte zugezogen he has come to settle down

[Zuziehung] — 1178 — [zwei]

at this place. — **IV** ~ n ⓩ 8. (f. 7) von Dienstboten: entering service; v. Einwandernden: settling down, immigration.

Zu-ziehung (ᴵᴸ˘) f ㊻ 1. (f. zuziehen 3) calling in a p., consultation of a doctor, &c.; (Hilfe) assistance, aid. — 2. ⚜ unter ⟨ Ihrer Spesen by adding (on) your charges. [pl., fresh breed or stock.

Zu-zucht (ᴵᴸ˘q1) f ㊉ agr. young animals)

Zu-zug (ᴵᴸ, ᴵᴸ˘) m ㊉c. 1. immigration (of fresh settlers), addition to the (adult) population. — 2. ⚔ reinforcements, auxiliary (or fresh) troops pl. — 3. = zuziehen IV.

Zu-zügler (ᴵᴸ˘) m ⓶ 1. bsd. ⚔ volunteer; ~ pl. = Zuzug 2. — 2. new comer or settler, immigrant, fresh arrival.

zu-zwängen (ᴵᴸ˘) v/a. ⑱** to close (or shut, bar, bolt) with a great effort, a. to force to.

zwacken (˘ᴗ) [mhd.: zwicken] v/a. ⑱ 1. to pinch, squeeze, twitch; fig. e-n zwicken und 2 to bother and torment a p., to vex and worry a p., to be for ever nagging at a p. — 2. F et. an sich 2 (reißen) to grab a th.

zwang¹ (˘) ind. impf. v. zwingen.

Zwang² (˘) [ahd.: *zwang¹] m ㊉b. (o. pl.) (ant. freier Wille) 1. compulsion, moralischer: constraint, restraint, check, gesetzlicher: coercion; (Gewalt) force, violence; (Verpflichtung) obligation; (Druck) pressure; (Unfreiheit) want of freedom; aus ⟨ under compulsion; e-m (sich) ~ antun, auferlegen to impose restrictions on a p. (o.s.), seinen Gefühlen: to check (or curb. restrain) o.s.; fig. dem Sinne einer Stelle ⟨ (Gewalt) antun to twist (or strain, distort) the meaning of a passage. — 2. path. (schmerzhafter Drang) painful pressure; bsd. in 3ssgn, f. zB. Stuhlzwang.

zwängen (˘ᴗ) [mhd.] v/a. ⑱ 1. to constrain. to press (hard); abs. enge Schuhe 2 tight boots pinch the feet. — 2. mit Angabe der Wirkung: den Kopf durch ein Loch 2 to force one's head through an opening.

zwang-los (˘⋅ᴵ) a. ㊻ unconstrained, unrestricted, von Pers., vom Umgange ꝛc.: free and easy, unceremonious; von Sitten ꝛc.: unconventional; ⬥ in losen Heften erscheinen to appear in occasional numbers or at indefinite periods; **=losigkeit** f ㊻ unconstraint, freedom. ease. auch: (fr.) laisser-aller.

Zwangs-anleihe (˘⋅…) f ㊷ pol. forced loan; **=arbeit** f forced (or compulsory) labour. im Zuchthause: hard labour, penal servitude; **=dienst** m compulsory service. ehm.: corvée; vgl. =arbeit; **=enteignung** f forcible (or compulsory) expropriation; **=erziehung** f ehm. jur. education in a reformatory; **=gesetz** n pol. coercive law; **=herrscher** m despot; 2häufig a. ㊻ = hufzwangig; **=jacke** f strait-jacket; **=kurs** m (von Papiergeld) forced currency; **=lage** f position of constraint, embarrassing situation; **=maßregel** f coercive measure; **=maßregeln anwenden** to adopt coercive measures, to use force; **=mittel** n means of coercion, auch = maßregel; **=paß** m passport prescribing

the route to be followed; **=pflicht** f corpulsory duty; **=recht** n jur. des Gutsherrn: banality; **=verfahren** n coercive measures pl.; **=versteigerung** f forced sale; **=vollstreckung** f jur. distress levied upon a p..; distraint. execution; 2weise adv. (F a. a.) compulsorily. forcibly, by (main) force.

zwanzig (˘ᴗ) [ahd.: twenty] numer. I card. numb. twenty; etwa 2 Leute (about) a score of people. — II (die Zahl) ~ f ㊻ (number) twenty; fie ist über die ~ hinaus … over (or turned) twenty, … out of her teens; zu ~en by scores; in den 2er Jahren (oder Zwanzigern) e-s Jahrhunderts in the twenties of a century.

Zwanzig-eck (˘ᴗ⋅˘) n ㊷ geom. icosagon.

Zwanziger (˘ᴗᴗ) m ⓶ 1. (~in f ㊼) person twenty (and more) years old. young (wo)man between twenty and thirty years of age. — 2. f. zwanzig II; in den ~n fein, steh(e)n to be between twenty and thirty (years old), to be out of one's teens. — 3. everything marked with 20. — 4. Münze: (20 Pfennig, abbr. 20 ₰) twenty-pfennig piece, two-pence half-penny (abbr. 2¹⁄₂ d.)

zwanziger-lei (˘ᴗᴗ⋅) a. inv. of twenty (different) kinds or sorts, twenty kinds of.

zwanzig=fach (˘ᴗ⋅…) a. ㊻, =fältig twenty-fold; **=flach** n ㊷, **=flächner** m, math. cryst.: ⚆ icosahedron; 2flächig a. icosahedral; **=jährig** a. of twenty years, twenty years old; 2mal adv. twenty times; 2männig ᛚ a. (mit 20 oder mehr Staubgefäßen): ⚆ icosandrous; **=mark-stück** n (Goldstück von 20 ℳ) twenty-mark piece. (German) sovereign; **=pfennig-stück** n: a) = Zwanziger 4; b) ehm.: two-groschen piece; **=pfünder** ⚔ m, artill. twenty-pounder.

zwanzigste (˘ᴗᴗ) ord. numb. twentieth; Datum: den (oder am) 2n März on the twentieth of March. March the twentieth (geschrieben 20th March, March 20th, in Briefen auch: 20. March); ~l (˘ᴗᴗ) n ㉒, 2l a. inv. twentieth (part); fieben ~l (⁷⁄₂₀) seven twentieths; nicht ein ~l des Ganzen not one-twentieth (or not the twentieth part) of it all; (or ⟨ 2ns (˘ᴗᴗ) adv. in the twentieth (20th) place.

zwar (⋅ᴵ) [ahd.; *zu ⫶ wahr in Wahrheit] adv. 1. und 2 (zur Bekräftigung des Vorangehenden, meist schwer, oft gar nicht zu übersetzen): er hat geschrieben, und 2 recht ausführlich he has written (and, what is more,) a very explicit letter or and very explicitly (too); fie haben nur ein Kind, und 2 einen Sohn … but one child, and that one (or and he is) a son. — 2. et. einräumend, doch zugleich beschränkend, meist mit folgendem „aber, doch, dennoch": er ist 2 gescheit, aber liederlich he is clever, it is true (or I admit, I grant, I must confess), but fast; er kam 2. doch war's zu spät indeed, he came, but …; he did come, in the end, but …; fie spielt 2. ist aber keine Künstlerin (al)though she plays, (still) she is …; so 2 (oder und 2 (so), daß man es versteht, aber // (and) though intelligible, yet //.

Zweck (⋅) [mhd.] m ⓶b. 1. = Pflock (Schützenziel) butt. — 2. fig. (Ziel e-s Strebens) goal; object, end in view, aim, (Absicht) design, intention; für einen bestimmten ~ for a set purpose, for a particular object; zum ~ der Bekanntmachung for the purpose of (or with a view to) advertisement; vgl. ~s; zu diesem ~e for this purpose; zu welchem ~e ? for what purpose? Sprichw. der ~ heiligt die Mittel the end justifies the means; das hat nur wenig ~ that's of little avail or use; F sonst hat es (weiter) keinen ~ and that's all it's intended (or meant) for; er macht alles seinen ~en dienstbar he makes everything subservient to his ends or serve his purpose.

zweck-dienlich (⋅…) a. ㊻ answering (or serving) its purpose, to the purpose, serviceable, useful; (wirksam) efficacious, efficient; vgl. 2mäßig; **=dienlichkeit** f ㊻ serviceableness; usefulness.

Zwecke ⊙ (⋅ᴗ) f ㊼ [= Zweck] (sharp) wooden peg. Schuhmach. ꝛc.: tack, brad, sparable; (grober Schuhnagel) hobnail.

zwecken¹ (˘ᴗ) v/a. ⑱ = zwacken, zwicken.

zwecken² ⊙ (˘ᴗ) [Zwecke] v/a. ⑱ to fasten with pegs or tacks, to tack.

zweck-entsprechend (⋅…) a. ㊻ = 2dienlich; **=essen** n ㊷ public dinner given for charitable or other purposes, public banquet; **=lehre** f, phls. doctrine of cosmic designs or ends, ⚆ teleology; 2los a. aimless, purposeless, without an object, (unnütz) useless; (nichtig) frivolous; ger. auch: to no purpose; **=losigkeit** f ㊻ aimlessness. uselessness; 2mäßig a. (ant. 2widrig) suitable, fitted for the purpose, to the purpose, appropriate; (zeitgemäß) opportune, expedient; vgl. 2dienlich; für 2 halten to deem expedient; **=mäßigkeit** f suitableness, fitness; expediency.

zwecks (⋅) prp. gen. for the purpose of (= zum Zweck, f. b. 2).

zweck-widrig (⋅…) a. ㊻ (ant. 2mäßig) unsuited to the end in view, unsuitable, inexpedient; **~keit** f ㊻ unsuitableness, inexpediency.

zween † (⋅) card. numb., mft inv. bisw. a. ㊻ (nur gbr. mit s/m.) = zwei.

Zwehle prov. (⋅ᴵ) f ㊻ = Quehle.

zwei (⋅) [ahd.: two: lt. duo: grch. dyo] numer. I card. numb. (ohne s. auch 2e) inv. (jedoch als gen. ohne art. 2er; als dat., wenn kein zugehöriges s. folgt, meift 2en, das in geh. Spr. auch als dat. des attributiven Zahlworts gebraucht wird) 1. two; alle 2 Monate every two months, every second month; von der Uhr: es ist halb 2 it is half past one; um drei Viertel auf 2 at a quarter to two; Sprichw. f. Seite 3; aus 2 bestehend, in 2 zerfallend; ⚆ binary. — 2. mit Beinen, Köpfen ꝛc. zweibeinig, zweiköpfig; mit 2en (zwei Pferden) fahren to drive a coach and pair; zu 2en by twos. two by two, two and two, in pairs; zu 2en hintereinander in double file; ⚆ 2 zu 2(en) standing double. in double rows; vgl. zweireihig; phys. in 2 Farben (spielend); ⚆ dichromic. —

Signs (see page XVII). F familiar; P vulgar; ℓ flash; ⟍ rare; † obsolete (died); * new word (born); ,+ incorrect; ♪ music;

[Zwei] — 1179 — [Zweimarkstück]

II (die Zahl) **Zwei** f ⑮ 3. (number) two, auf Karten und Würfeln: the deuce. — 4. = Zweiheit. — **III** ~ n, inv. 5. (Paar) pair, couple, brace (of partridges, &c.). **zwei-achselig** (ᴴ...) a. ⑯ fig. double-faced; ⁀**armig** a. two-armed; ⁀**ästig** a. bifurcate(d), biforked; ⁀**äugig** a. two-eyed; ⁀**bändig** a. two-volume, in two volumes; ⁀**basisch** a. chm.: dibasic; ⁀**beinig** a. two-legged, bi-crual; vgl. ⁀**füßig**; Les Tier biped (auch = Mensch); ⁀**blatt** ⚥ n ⑫: cibätteriges ~ twayblade (*Li'stera ova'ta*); ⁀**blätt(e)rig** a. two-leaved, bifoliate, diphyllous, von der Blüte: ⁂ bipetalous; ⁀**blumig**. ⁀**blütig** ♀ a. with two flowers, ⁂ biflorate, biflorous; =**brücken** [dat. pl.] npr/n. ♀ (Stadt in der bayrischen Pfalz) Zweibrücken, (fr.) Deux-Ponts; in ~ erschienene Ausgabe der Klassiker Bipontine edition; ⁀**brüd(e)rig**. ⁀**bündelig** ♀ a.: ⁀**diadelphian**; =**decker** ⬇ m (Schiff) two-decker; =**deutelei** f: (habit of) equivocation, (Doppelsinn) ambiguity; ⁀**deuteln** v/n. (h.) a*⃰⁎ to equivocate; to speak ambiguously; ⁀**deutig** a. ⑯ equivocal, (Doppelsinnig) ambiguous, ⁂ amphibological, amphibolous; (e⸗e doppelte Rolle spielend) double-dealing; Les Betragen, Wesen double-dealing, duplicity; ~**keit** f: a) equivocalness, equivocation; ambiguity; b) duplicity (of character); ⁀**doppelt** a.: a) F double; b) ♀ binate, =**drittel-majorität**. =**mehrheit** f majority by (or of) two-thirds of the votes; ⁀**eckig** ♀ a.: ⁂ digonous; ⁀**ehig** ♀ a.: ⁂ digamous. **Zweier** (¹⋎) m ㉒ 1. two-pfennig piece, (German) farthing. — 2. anything marked with two; soldier of the second regiment, &c. **zweier-lei** (¹⋎¹) a. inv. of two (different) kinds or sorts. two kinds of; auf ♀ Art in two different ways; das ist ♀ those are two different things; ♀ (Herren von) ♀ Tuch the military (profession); soldiers pl., in England auch: redcoats pl. **zwei-fach** (ᴴ...) a. ⑯ twofold, double; chm. ♀ Schwefeleisen = Doppeltschwefeleisen; ⁀**fächerig** a. two-celled, ⁂ bilocular; =**falter** ⸺ m ⑫ ent. = Schmetterling; ⁀**fältig** a. = ⁀**fach**; ⁀**farbig** a. two-coloured; F fig. Les Tuch uniform. **Zweifel** (¹⋎) m ㉒ 1. (ant. Glaube) doubt (-fulness), scepticism. — 2. (Ungewißheit) uncertainty, (Unschlüssigkeit) hesitation, wavering, (Bedenken) scruple; ohne ~: a) undoubtedly; b) (sicher, gewiß) certainly, surely; das unterliegt keinem ~ there is no doubt about it; ohne allen ~ without any doubt (whatever), undoubtedly, auch: most assuredly. **Zwei-felder-wirtschaft** (¹⋎¹⋎¹⋎) f ⑫ agr. farming with (a rotation of) two crops. **Zweifelei** (−⋎¹) f ㊻ (bad) habit of doubting (everything). scepticism. **zweifel-frei** (ᴴ...) a. ⑯ free from doubt; =**geist** m ⑫ sceptical spirit; vgl. =sucht. **zweifelhaft** (¹⋎⋎) a. ⑯ doubtful, dubious, (fraglich) questionable, problematic(al); (ungewiß) uncertain, (unsicher) precarious; (verdächtig) suspicious; et.

♀ lassen to leave a th. undecided or in suspense; etwas ♀ machen to cast doubts upon a th.; ♀ sein, ob man et. tun soll (ob. nicht) to be wavering (or in two minds) about (doing) a th. **Zweifelhaftigkeit** (¹⋎⋎⋎-) f ㊻ doubtfulness, dubiousness; uncertainty. **zweifel-los** (ᴴ...) a. ⑯ doubtless, certain, auch = zweifelsohne; =**losigkeit** f ♀ doubtlessness; =**mut** m indecision, irresolution, wavering. vacillation; ⁀**mütig** a. irresolute. **zweifeln** (¹⋎) [ahd.] **I** v/n. (h.) ⑫ a. to doubt (of) a th., to have one's doubts about a th.; wer kann daran ♀? who can doubt (or question) it?; ich zweifle nicht, daß er kommen wird I do not (or I have no) doubt but that (seltener but allein) he will come. F I don't doubt but what he'll come; ich zweifelte nicht, daß er kommen würde I had no doubt (but) that he would come; wir ♀, ob das wahr ist oder sei we doubt (or are doubtful) whether that be true, we have (our) doubts about (or as to) the truth of it; wir ♀, ob er es kann we doubt whether he can (or his ability to) do it; Le doubting, doubtful, sceptical. — **II** ~ n ㉓ doubt(ing), scruple; vgl. Zweifelei. **Zweifels-fall** (ᴴ...) m ⑫ case of doubt, doubtful case; =**grund** m reason for doubt; ⁀**ohne** (¹⋎⋎) adv. doubtless(ly), without doubt, auch F als prädikatives a. not to be doubted, indubitable. **Zweifel-sucht** (¹⋎⋎) f ⑫ scepticism; ⁀**süchtig** a. ⑯ inclined to doubt (everything), sceptical. **Zweifler** (¹⋎) m ㉓, ~**in** f ㊼ person who doubts, ⁀**doubter**; engl. sceptic. **zwei-flügelig** (ᴴ...) a. ⑯: a) two-winged, ♀ und ent.: ⁂ dipterous, ...al; b) Le Tür folding-door(s pl.); =**flügler** m ⑫ ent.: ⁂ dipterous insect, dipteran, pl. auch: diptera; ⁀**früchtig** ♀ a. with double fruit, ⁂ dicarpellary, =**fünftel-schein** m., astrol.: ⁂ biquintile (aspect); ⁀**füßig** a. two-footed ⁀**füß(l)er** m, zo. two-footed animal, biped. **Zweig** (¹) [ahd.: twig; *zwei] m ⑫ c. (Teil des Astes) twig. kleinerer: spray, sprig, branchlet; (Ast) branch, bough; grüne ~e green branches pl.; ~e treiben to ramify, to branch forth; fig. er wird nie auf einen grünen ~ kommen (nach Hiob 15,32) he will never prosper or thrive or meet with success or F make his way (in the world). **Zweig-abteilung** (ᴴ...) f ⑫ section; =**anstalt** f branch-establishment, -institution, branch; =**bahn** ⚞ f branch-line; =**bank** ⚙ f branch of a bank. **Zweigelchen** (¹⋎⋎) n ㉓ = Zweiglein. **zwei-g(e)leisig** (ᴴ...) a. ⑯ ⁀**spurig**. =**gesang** ♫ m ⑫ duet; ⁀**geschlechtig** a. of double sex, ⁂ hermaphrodite, ♀ bisexual, androgynous, =**gespann** n: a) two-horse team; b) (zweispänniger Wagen) carriage and pair; =**gespräch** n = Zwiegespräch; ⁀**gestaltig** a. in two shapes or forms, ⁂ dimorphous, ⁀**gestrichen** ♫ a. twice-marked or -accented; Le Note a. semiquaver; ⁀**geteilt** a. bipartite.

zweig-förmig (ᴴ...) a. ⑯ branched, branchy, ⁂ rameous; =**geschäft** ⚙ n ⑫ branch of a business, branch-office; =**gesellschaft** ⚙ f branch of a company. **Zweiglein** (¹⋎) n ㉓ (dim. von Zweig) branchlet. small bough, twig; (kleines Reis) sprig, spray. **zwei-gleisig** (ᴴ...) a. ⑯ ⁀**spurig**; ⁀**glied(e)rig** a. having two li nbs, zo.: ⁂ biarticulate. ⁎⁎ in two ranks, math. binomial; ⁀**griff(e)lig** ♀ a. = Zweibig. **Zweig-station** ⚞ (ᴴ...) f ⑫ (railway-) junction; =**stelle** ⚙ f (Postagentur) branch post-office; =**strecke** ⚞ f branch-gallery; ⁀**tragend** ♀ a. ⑯: ⁂ ramiferous, ramous, ramose; =**verein** m affiliated (or branch-)society, branch of an association; =**werk** n branches, boughs pl. **Zwei-händer** (ᴴ...) m ⑫ : a) two-handed sword; b) zo. bimanous animal. pl. auch: bimana; ⁀**händig** a. ⑯: a) two-handed, bimanous: b) Les Schwert two-handed sword; ♫ Les Stück piece for two hands; ⁀**häusig** ♀ a.: ⁂ diœcious. **Zweiheit** (¹⋎) f ㊻ phls., &c.: ⁂ duality; Lehre von der ~: ⁂ dualism. **zwei-henk(e)lig** (ᴴ...) a. ⑯ two-handled; =**herr** m ⑫ Alt.: duumvir; =**herrschaft** f duumvirate; ⁀**höck(e)rig** a. two-humped; f. Kamel; ⁀**hörnig** a. two-horned, ⁂ bicorn(u)ous, bicornute; =**hufer** m. zo. cloven-footed (⁂ bisulcate) animal; ⁀**hufig** a. cloven-footed, cloven-hoofed, ⁂ bisulcate; ⁀**hundert** numer., a. two hundred; ⁀**hundertjährig** a. lasting (or of) two hundred years; Ler Geburtstag von // bicentennial anniversary of the birth of //; ⁀**hundertste(r)** a. u. s. two-hundredth. ⁀**jährig** a.: a) two years old; ein Les Kind a two-year-old child, a child of two years; Sport: Rennen für Le Füllen two-year-old race or event; b) (zwei Jahre lang dauernd) lasting two years, v. Pflanzen: biennial; ⁀**jährlich** a. occurring every two years, biennial; =**kammer-system** n, parl. two-chamber system; =**kampf** m single combat, mit hergebrachten Formen: duel; =**kämpfer** m person engaged in single combat, duellist; ⁀**kaps(e)lig** ♀ a. two-capsuled, ⁂ bicapsular; ⁀**klappig** a. two-valved, ♀ bivalved, bivalvular; Le Frucht: ♀ bivalve; ⁀**knospig** ♀ a.: ⁂ bigeminal, bigeminate; ⁀**köpfig** a. two-headed; ⁀**kuppig** a. with two peaks; ⁀**lappig** ♀ a. two-lobed, ⁂ bilobate, von Fruchtknoten: ⁂ dicoccous; ⁀**lastig** a.: Les Schiff f. lastig; ⁀**lebig** ♀ a. amphibious; ⁀**lippig** ♀ a.: ⁂ bilabiate; ⁀**lötig** a. weighing (or of) one ounce; ⁀**mächtig** ♀ a.: ⁂ didynamic. ...ian; vgl. didynamisch; ⁀**mal** adv. twice; ♀ so viel(e) twice as much (as many); ♀ im Jahre (im Monate, in der Woche) erscheinend biannual (bimonthly, biweekly); Tennis: ♀ auf second bound (bounce); er wird sich das nicht ♀ sagen lassen he won't require telling (or being told) twice, F he will jump at it; ⁀**malig** a. done (or occurring) twice; (wiederholt) repeated, reiterated; ⁀**männ(e)rig** ♀ a.: ⁂ diandrian, ...ous; =**mark-stück** n two-mark piece, (German) florin;

⁂ scientific; ♀ botanical; ⚱ geography; ⚙ machinery; ⚒ mining; ⚔ military; ⚓ marine; ⚙ commercial; ✉ postal; ⚞ railway.

[Zweimaster] — 1180 — [Zwiebelmuschel]

=master ↓ m two-master, two-masted vessel; brig; ≈mastig ↓ a. two-masted; ≈monatig (2 Monate dauernd) of two months(' duration); ≈monatlich a. (alle 2 Monate) occurring once in two months; ≈paarig a. forming two pairs; ≈ ≈ gefiedert ⇒ bijugate, ...ous; ≈plattig a.: ⇒ bilamellar, ...ate(d); ≈polig a. phys. bipolar; =rad n bicycle, F bike, wheel, machine, für Wettfahrten: racer, für Touren: roadster; ≈räd(e)rig a. two-wheeled a. (or on) two wheels; ≈rädriger Wagen two-wheeled carriage, two-wheeler, als Droschke: hansom; =rad-fahren n bicycling; =rad-fahrer m bicyclist; vgl. Radfahrer; ≈reihig a. two-(or double-)rowed, ⇒ distichous; ≈rippig a. ≈ u. ent.: ⇒ bicarinate, binervate; =rud(e)rer ↓ m galley (or boat) with two rows of oars, Alt.: bireme; ≈rud(e)rig ↓ a. with two rows of oars; ≈samenlappig ≈ a.: ⇒ dicotyledonous; ≈schalig a. zo. bivalvous, ...ed, ...ular; ≈e Muschel bivalve; ≈schattig a. ≈: ⇒ amphiscian; ≈schläfig a.: ≈es Bett double bed, bed for two persons; =schlitz m, arch. diglyph; ≈schneidig a. two-edged, bisw.: ancipital, ...ous; ≈schürig a.: a) von Schafen: twice shorn, shorn twice a year; b) von Wolle: of the second shearing; ≈seitig a. two-sided, bilateral; ≈silbig a. gram. dissyllabic; ≈sitzig a. with two seats, double-seated; ≈spaltig a.: a) doubly cleft or split, ≈ bifid; b) ⊕ typ. in two columns; =spänner m = =g spann b; ≈spännig a. drawn by tw≈ horses; ≈ (adv.) fahren to drive (in) a carriage and pair; =spitz m (Hutform der Gesandten) two-cornered hat; ≈spitzig a. two-pointed, with two points or peaks, ≈ bicuspid; ≈sprachig a. in two languages, bilingual; ≈spurig a. double-tracked; ≈e Bahn, auch: double line; ≈stimmig ♪ a. for two voices; ≈er Gesang a) (zwei Personen allein) duet; b) singing in two (different) voices; ≈stündig a. (2 Stunden dauernd) of two hours(' duration), lasting two hours; ≈stündlich a. (alle 2 Stunden) occurring every two hours. zweit (¹) adv.: wir sind zu ≈ there are two (or F a pair) of us, we are two. zweit-ältest (⁻¹⁻) a. ≈ second (by age), von nur zweien: younger, junior. zwei-tausend (⁻¹⁻) a. ≈ two thousand. zweit-best (⁻¹⁻) a. ≈ second (or next) best. zweite (¹⁻) [erst nhd.] ord. numb. ≈ (the) second; ≈ Gesicht 2: Tennis: ≈r Aufsprung (=schlag) second bound (bounce); eine ≈ Niederlage another defeat; der ~ des Monats the second day of the month; ≈s Ich one's other self, (lt.) alter ego; sein ≈s Ich his double; Heinrich der ~ (gschr. II.) Henry the Second (gschr. II); zum ≈n-mal for the second time; ≈ aus ≈r Hand kaufen to buy second-hand; Möbel, Waren aus ≈r Hand second-hand furniture, goods. zwei-teilig (⁻¹⁻) a. ≈ in two parts, ≈ bipartite, zo. = ≈klappig; =teilung f ≈ bipartition, math. bisection, (Gabelung) bifurcation.

zweitens (⁻¹⁻) adv. secondly (2ˡʸ), in the second place. zweit-geboren (⁻¹⁻) a. ≈ second, younger; ≈höchst a. highest but one, second in height; ≈jüngst a. youngest but one; ≈letzt a. last but one, gram. penultimate; ≈nächst a. next but one; am 2en Tage (on) the second day after, weniger genau: two days later. zwei-und-dreißig (⁻¹⁻) numer. thirty-two, seltener: two-and-thirty; ~er, ~er(=format) ≈ ≈ typ. thirty-twomo (abbr. 32 mo, 32⁰); ~stel-note ♪ f demisemiquaver; ~stel-pause ♪ f demisemiquaver-rest. zwei-und-siebzig (⁻¹⁻) numer.: er ist ≈ (Jahre alt) ... seventy-two (years of age). Zwei-viertel-note (¹ ⁻) (⁻¹⁻) n ≈ minim; =viertel-pause ♪ f minim-rest. =viertel-takt ♪ m measure of two crotchets; =weiberei f bigamy; ≈weibig a. ≈ bigamous, ≈ digynian, ...ous; ≈wertig a. chm.: ⇒ divalent; ≈es Element dyad; ≈wüchsig a. path. rickety; =zack m two-pronged fork or instrument, ⊕ agr. bident; ≈zackig a. two-pronged, auch = ≈ästig; =zahl f: a) phls. duad, chm., &c. dyad; b) gram. dual (= Dualis); =zahn ≈ m, etwa: bur-marigold (Bidens); ≈zähnig a. with two teeth, ≈ bidental, ...ated; (mit zwei Spitzen) bicuspid; ≈zehig a. zo. two-toed, ⇒ didactyle; ≈zeilig a. of (or in) two lines, two-lined, ≈ distichous; ≈es Gedicht distich, couplet; ≈zeitig a.: a) ≈ dichronous; b) pros. ≈e Silbe (die lang oder kurz sein kann) doubtful syllable; ≈züngig ≈. doppelzüngig ≈. zwerch prov. (¹) [ahd.]: thwart: quer! a. ≈ u. adv. = quer; bsd. gbr. in ≈ssgn. Zwerchfell (⁻¹⁻) n ⓒc. anat.: ⇒ diaphragm, seltener: midriff; einem das ~ erschüttern (e-n lachen machen) to make a p.('s sides) split (or shake) with laughing; ~entzündung f ≈² path. inflammation of the diaphragm. ⇒ diaphragmatitis; ~erschütterung f fit (or outburst) of laughter. Zwerg (¹) [ahd.] m ⓐb., ~in f ≈ dwarf, diminutive person, (urspr. myth.) pygmy; F (mere) shrimp, (little) mite or dot, (am m) mannikin (s. Däumling 2). Zwerg-alpenrose ≈ (⁻¹⁻) f ≈² dwarf rose-bay (Rhodode'ndron chamaeci'stus); =apfel ≈ m dwarf-apple (Pirus paradisi'aca); =apfelsine ≈ f mandarin (Citrus no'bilis), aus Tanger: tangerine; ≈artig a. ≈ dwarfish, of diminutive size or stature, pygmy(-like), pygmean, puny, ⇒ nanoid; ≈es Weibchen, auch: F little dot of a woman; =baum ≈ m dwarf-tree, stunted tree; =bildung f dwarfishness, ⇒ nanism; =birke ≈ f dwarf-birch (Be'tula nana); =bisamhirsch m, zo. dwarf musk-deer; =fledermaus f ≈ pipistrel(le) (Vesperu'go pipistrel'lus); =gestalt f dwarfish shape or form. zwerghaft (⁻¹) a. ≈ = zwergartig. Zwerg-haftigkeit (⁻¹⁻), bisw. Zwerg-heit (¹-) f ≈² dwarfishness, diminutive size or stature, ⇒ nanism. [artig. zwergicht, mst zwergig (⁻¹⁻) a. ≈ = zwerg-. Zwerg-kastani-e (⁻¹⁻) f ≈² dwarf chestnut-tree (Casta'nea pu'mila); =kiefer

≈ f dwarf-pine (Pinus pumi'lio); =kirsche ≈ f ground-cherry (Prunus chamaece'rasus); =maki m, zo. dwarf-lemur (Microce'bus); =maus f, zo. harvest-mouse (Mus minu'tus); =mensch m, myth. pygmy; =obstbaum m dwarf fruit-tree; =palme ≈ f dwarf-palm (Chamae'rops hu'milis), palmetto (Chamae'rops palme'tto); =trappe f, orn. little (or lesser) bustard (Otistetrax); =volk n dwarf (or pygmy) tribe. Zwetsch(g)e ≈ (⁻¹⁻) [nhd.] f ≈² = Pflaume — ~n=kern m plum-stone; ~n=mus n plum-preserve. Zwick (¹) [mhd.] m ⓐb. 1. = Zwecke. — 2. (Kneifen) pinch(ing), twinge. — 3. a) = Schmitze; b) (Hieb damit) lash, lashing, smack, cut. [wimble. Zwick-bohrer (⁻¹⁻) m ≈ (⁻¹⁻) ≈ gimlet. Zwicke (⁻¹⁻) f ≈² = Zwickzange. Zwickel (⁻¹⁻) [mhd.] m ≈²: a) wedge; b) am Kleid ≈c.: gusset, am Segel ≈c.: gore; (Verzierung an der Seite eines Strumpfes) clock of a stocking. [Kinnbart]. Zwickel-bart (⁻¹⁻) m ≈² imperial (= ¹ zwickeln (⁻¹⁻) v/a. ≈a.: Strümpfe ≈ to clock stockings, Unterröcke ≈c. ≈ to gore skirts, &c. [stocking. Zwickel-strumpf (⁻¹⁻) m ≈² clocked ≈ zwicken (⁻¹⁻) [mhd.]: twitch: zwacken] v/a. ≈¹ 1. a) e-n ≈ to pinch (or twinge, tweak, twitch) a p., von der Kälte ≈c. to nip a p.; fig. e-n ≈ (quälen) to torment a p., (necken) to tease (or chaff) a p.; i. zwacken 1; b) v/impers. es zwickt mich im Leibe I have a (gnawing) pain in the stomach, F I have the gripes. — 2. den Bart ≈ (mit e-r Schere kürzen) to clip (or trim) one's whiskers or beard. Zwicker (⁻¹⁻) [zwicken] m ≈² 1. = Kneifer 1. — 2. (Augenglas) eye-glasses pl., (fr.) pince-nez. — 3. ⊕ = Zwickzange. Zwick-mühle (⁻¹⁻) f ≈² Mühlspiel: (wenn 5 Steine so stehen, daß man durch das Aufmachen der einen Mühle die andere jedesmal zumacht) double mill or row; Whistspiel: (zweiseitiges Trumpfen) seesaw; fig. (et. wobei man auf jeden Fall Gewinn macht) most profitable game, safe trick or dodge, Rennsport: hedging; =zange f pincers, pliers, kleinere: tweezers pl. Zwieback (⁻¹⁻) [nhd. 1600; * (Biskuit)] m ⓐⓒc. (ant. Einback) biscuit, rusk. Zwiebel (⁻¹⁻) [ahd. (P: Zwie=bolle) * lt. caepu'lla] f ≈² 1. a) ≈ u. hort.. a) Kocht.: echte ≈ onion (A'llium Cepa); b) (knollige Wurzel) bulb(ous root). — 2. F fig. (dicke Uhr) turnip, potato, clumsy (old) watch or ticker. Zwiebel-artig ≈ (⁻¹⁻) a. ≈ : a) like an onion, bisw. ≈ cepaceous; b) bulbous; =beet n ≈² bed of onions; =brühe f ≈ Kocht.: onion-sauce; =dach n. arch. imperial; =fische ≈ m/pl. typ. (in Unordnung geratener Satz) jumbled (or mixed) type, pie; zu ≈n ≈ fallen to go to pie; =fliege f, ent. onion-fly (Anthomy'ia cepa'rum); ≈förmig a.: ⇒ bulbiform; =gericht n Kocht.: dish flavoured with onions; =geruch m smell of onions; =geschmack m taste of onions; =gewächs ≈ n bulbous plant; =knollen ≈ m bisw. bulbotuber; =lauch ≈ m = Zwiebel 1 a; =marmor m, min.: ⇒ cipolin; =muschel f, zo. clink-shell (Ano'mia).

Zeichen (s. S. XVII): F familiär; Ⱶ Volkssprache; Ⱡ Gaunersprache; ` selten; † alt (auch gestorben); * neu (auch geboren); ++ unrichtig;

[zwiebeln] — 1181 — [Zwischenhändler]

zwiebeln (´‿) ⓥa. I v/n. (h.) 1. to smell of onions. — II v/a. 2. to rub (or flavour) with onions. — 3. F fig. e-n ⁓ (hart bedrängen) to plague (or torment, worry) a p., Arbeiter ꝛc.: to treat harshly, F to drive (like niggers), to grind, to sweat.

Zwiebel=same(n) (´‿...) m ⓶ hort. onion-seed; =sauce f = ⁓tunke; =schale f onion-skin, skin of an onion; =suppe f Kochk.: onion-soup; ⁓tragend ⸜ a. ⓺⓺ bulb-bearing, ⸙ bulbiferous: =tunke f onion-sauce; =wurzel f = Zwiebel 1 b.

Zwie=brache (´‿...) [= zwei-] f ⓺⓺ agr. (zweimaliges Pflügen) double ploughing, bisw.: twifallow(ing); ⓶ brachen v/a. ⓺⓺ agr. to plough a second time; ⓶fach [mhd.], ⓶fältig [mhd.] a. = zwei=f.; =gespräch n dialogue, colloquy, vertraulicher: (confidential) chat; vgl. =sprache; =licht n twilight; im ⁓ in the dusk, between the lights.

zwier † (´) [ahd.] adv. = zweimal.

Zwiesel (´‿) [ahd.] * zwei, Zweig] f ⓺⓺ (⸺ am Sattel; m ⓶) fork(ed branch), bifurcation; zwieselig (´‿...) a. ⓺⓺ forked, bifurcate; zwieseln v n. und sich ⁓ v refl. ⓺⓺a. to (branch out like a) fork, to bifurcate.

Zwie=spalt (´‿...) [= zwei-] m ⓺⓺ disunion, (Mißhelligkeit) dissension, disagreement, rel. schism; vgl. =tracht; in ⁓ geraten mit to fall out with; (⓶spaltig) ⓶spältig [mhd.] a. ⓺⓺ disunited, divided; =spältigkeit f disagreement; =sprache [nhd.] f dialogue, conversation; mit e-m ⁓ halten to converse with a p.; =tracht [mhd.] f discord; vgl. =spalt; ⁓ säen to sow the seeds of discord, Göttin der ⁓ goddess of discord, Eris; ⓶trächtig [mhd.] a. discordant, at variance; =tracht=stifter m breeder of discord, mischief-maker.

Zwil(lich) (´‿) [ahd., nach lt. bilix; vgl. Drillich] m ⓺c. ⓺ u. Weberei: (f. Betten ꝛc.) tick(ing), a. drill(s pl.); ⁓en (´‿) a. ⓺⓺ of ticking; =kittel, =rock m ⓶ blouse, frock made of coarse linen.

Zwilling (´‿) [ahd.] * zwei] m ⓶d. 1. ⁓(s=knabe) twin boy, ⁓(s=mädchen) twin girl; die siamesischen ⁓e the Siamese twins a.; ⁓e gebärend bearing twins, zo.: ⸙ biparous. — 2. ast. die ⁓e pl. (Sternbild des Tierkreises) Gemini, Twins pl., Castor and Pollux. — 3. ⓹ Büchsenmacher: double-barrelled gun.

Zwillings=achse ⸙ (´‿...) f ⓺⓺ cryst. twinning-axis; =bildung f, ⸙ congemination; ⓶bstätig ⓺⓺ a. ⓺⓺ geminiflorous; =bruder m twin brother; =dampf=maschine ⓺ =twin-cylinder engine; =geschwister pl. twins pl.; =gestirn n = Zwilling 2; =knabe m, =mädchen n f. Zwilling; =kristall m twin crystal; =muskeln m/pl. anat. twin muscles, ⸙ gemelli; =paar n pair of twins; =pflaume ⸓ f li(t)chi (Frucht von Nephe´lium litchi); =schraube ⓺ f twin-screw; =schwester f twin sister; =ventil ⓺ n twin valve.

Zwing=burg (⸗´‿) f ⓺⓺ (tyrant's) strong castle (or stronghold, citadel) overawing a country.

Zwinge ⓺ (´‿) [nhd.: zwingen] f ⓺⓺ 1. (schützender Beschlag aus Metall am unteren Ende von Stöcken, Schirmen ꝛc.) ferrule, auch: (iron) tip; mit e-r ⁓ versehen to (furnish with a) ferrule. — 2. (Vorrichtung, worin etwas fest zs.-gehalten wird) holdfast, holder, clamp, collar; (Schraubstock) vice; (Schraub-) ⁓ vice-pin.

zwingen (´‿) [ahd.] I v/a. u. v/refl. ⓵(⓶)ft 1. to constrain, mit Gewalt: to compel, to force, to do violence to; (überwältigen) to subdue, to conquer; (einschränken) to coerce, (nötigen) to oblige, to constrain (zu et. to do a th.); sie ⁓ ihn zu arbeiten they compel him to (or make him) work; sich zum Lachen, Lächeln ⁓ to affect a laugh, to put on a forced smile; sich zur Lustigkeit ⁓ to pretend being merry; ich muß mich ⁓, es zu tun I must force myself to do it, I must do it against my own inclination; das läßt sich nicht ⁓ it cannot be done by force; er läßt sich nicht ⁓ he won't be driven (into a th. or to do a th.); sich gezwungen sehen zu et. oder et. zu tun to see o.s. compelled (schwächer: obliged) to do a th. — 2. mit Angabe des Wohin oder der Wirkung: e-n in Fesseln ⁓ to cast a p. (forcibly) in(to) chains; × e-e Festung zur Übergabe ⁓ to reduce ..., durch Hunger: to starve ... into surrender. — II ⓶d p.pr. und a. ⓺⓺ 3. coercive or forcible (measures, ꝛc.), cogent (reason, &c.); ⓶de Kraft cogency, urgency; ⓶e Umstände urgent (or overpowering) circumstances pl. — III ge=zwungen pl. u. a. ⓺⓺(D9) 4. ⁓ gezwungen, bsd. Artikel II. 5. (adv.) lachen, oft: to laugh on the wrong side of the mouth.

Zwinger (´‿) [mhd.] m ⓺⓺ 1. (a. =in f ⓺⓺) one who compels (or forces, drives) people to do a th. — 2. (umschlossener Raum) enclosure, für Jagdhunde: kennel, für Bären: bear-pit, (Kampfplatz für wilde Tiere) arena (or ring) for wild beasts. — 3. ehm. (fester Turm) dungeon, donjon; (Schloßburg) keep, fortified castle.

Zwing=herr (´‿...) m ⓺⓺ tyrant, despot; =herrschaft f tyranny, despotism.

Zwinglianer (´‿...) [Ulrich Zwingli, schwz. Reformator, 1484—1531] m ⓺⓺, =in f ⓺⓺ Zwinglian, follower of Zwingli.

Zwing=schraube ⓺ (´‿...) f Tischlerei: ferrule-screw; am Wagen: coupling-screw; ⁓ m = Schraubstock; ehm. =Uri npr/n. ⓺ citadel of Uri.

zwinke(r)n (´‿) [mhd.: twinkle] v/n. (h.) ⓺⓺(⓺⓺a.) to wink (one's eyes), to cast side-glances at; (zappeln) to wriggle (about), F to fidget (about). [to twirl.]

zwirbeln (´‿) [mhd.] twirl] v/a. ⓺⓺a.]

Zwirl=bohrer ⓺ (⸗´‿) m ⓺⓺ centre-bit.

Zwirn (´) [mhd.; * zwier] m ⓶b. 1. ⓺ u. ⓺ twine, twisted (or two-cord) yarn, (Faden) thread; ⁓ aus Roh-seidenfaden: thrown singles pl.; F co. fig. Meister ⁓ (Schneider) Master Snip. — 2. F fig. (Gedanken, Verstand) ideas pl.; ⁓ im Kopfe haben to have (plenty of) good sense, to be a sensible (or shrewd) person, F to have s.th. (good) in one's head.

Zwirn=band ⓺ n. ⓺ (⸗´‿) n ⓺⓺ thread-tape. [of thread.]

zwirnen¹ (´‿) a. ⓺⓺ of yarn, (made)]

zwirnen² (´‿) I v/a. ⓺⓺ to twine thread, &c., to (double and) twist yarn, &c., to throw silk; gezwirnte Seide twisted (or thrown) silk. — II v/n. (h.) von Katzen: to purr = spinnen 3).

Zwirner ⓺ (´‿) m ⓺⓺, =in f ⓺⓺ twister, Seidenspinnerei: throw(st)er of silk.

Zwirn=fabrikation ⓺ (⸗´‿...) f ⓺⓺ manufacture of twine, thread-making; =(s=)faden m (linen) thread; =gardinen f/pl. thread-curtains; =glätt=maschine f thread-finisher; =handschuh m thread-glove; =kästchen n thread-box, mehr gbr.: (lady's) work-box; =knäuel n ball of thread; =maschine f twine-.achine, twist-frame or -machine, =mühle f Spinnerei: twisting-mill or -machine, thread-frame; a.: doubling machine, doubler; =seide f twisted (or thrown) silk; =spitze f thread-lace or -bobbin; =wickel m thread-paper; =winde f thread-reel, reel for (winding) thread.

zwischen (´‿)[ahd.; *zwei] I prp. (mit dat. auf die Frage: wo?, mit acc. auf die Frage: wohin?) between, bsd. in geh. Spr. auch betwixt, abbr. 'twixt; ⓶ 20 und (Tonnen &c.); f. Angel¹ 1; ⓶ heute und morgen between this (time) and tomorrow; ⓶ Himmel und Erde, oft: 'twixt heaven and earth; ⓶ Lipp' und Kelches Rand schwebt der finstern Mächte Hand (FR. KIND „Antäos") there's many a slip 'twixt the cup and the lip; anat. ⓶ zwei Rückenwirbeln liegend: ⸙ intervertebral; f. Unterschied, Zeile 1. — II adv. = dazwischen.

Zwischen=akt (´‿...) m ⓺⓺ thea. interval between two acts, (fr.) entr'acte; vgl. =spiel; =akts=vorhang m = =vorhang; =artikel m e-r Zeitung ꝛc.: padding; =balken m, arch. mid-beam; =band n. anat.: ⸙ intervertebral ligament; =begebenheit f episode; =bemerkung f incidental remark, unterbrechende: interruption, abschweifende: digression; =deck ⸘ n between deck(s), steerage; =decks=passagier m steerage-passenger; =ding n s.th. intermediate, s.th. between two things, (Bastard) cross (breed); ⓶durch (mst ⸗´‿) adv.: a) (right) across; b) zeitlich: between whiles, at intervals, occasionally, a. in between; =essen n = =gericht; =fall m incident, episode; plötzlicher ⁓ von entscheidender Wirkung sudden blow, F bolt from (or out of) the blue; =farbe f colour (or shade) between, paint. half-tint; =gang m, arch. corridor; =gebäude n, arch. intermediate wing; =gericht n, Kochk.: intermediate course, extra dish; (fr.) entremets; =gesang m song (coming) between, inserted song; =geschoß n, arch. intermediate story; =glied n intermediate (or connecting) link; =hafen ⸘ m, etwa: commercial (or international) port; =handel ⓺ m carrying trade, eng⸗: commission-business or -agency; =händler m intermediary, agent, ⓺ commission-agent or -merchant, middleman; vgl. Unter-

[Zwischenhandlung] — 1182 — [zyklisch]

händler; =handlung f episode; vgl. =fall; ⚥her (mst ̮ ͜ ͜) adv. in the meantime, meanwhile, during the interval; =herrschaft f s. Interregnum; ⚥hin adv. (in) between; ⚥inne (mst ̮ ͜ ͜) adv. between (or amid) the two; =kiefer(=bein n) m, anat.: ↻ intermaxillary (bone); =könig m ursvr. röm. Alt.: interrex: =königtum n interregnum; =lage f interposition; ⚥liegend a. ⑯ lying between, interposed, intermediate; intervening (space, &c.); =mahlzeit f intermediate meal, (light) collation; (Gabelfrühstück) lunch(eon); =mauer f Bauwesen: partition- (or party-)wall; =meister m Schneiderei ꝛc.: middleman between the wholesale dealer and the worker, b.s. sweater; =pause f interval; =pfeiler ⊙ m Bauwesen: intermediate pillar, pier; =pfosten ⊙ m Bauwesen: intermediate (or middle) post; =platz m place (or seat) between; ⚥ emporium; =raum m: a) räumlich: space between, intervening space; (Lücke) interstice, ↻ lacuna; (Entfernung) distance (between); ⊙ typ. space, blank (space); b) zeitlich: interval; in langen =räumen at long intervals; in =räumen stattfindend intermittent; =rede f: a) interruption: b) (Abschweifung) digression; =redner m interlocutor; =regierung f. =reich n interregnum; =reihe f row between, intermediate row; =rippen=muskel m, anat.: ↻ intercostal muscle; =ruf m loud interruption, exclamation; =satz m: a) in der Wäsche ꝛc.: insertion, piece let in; b) gr. inserted sentence or clause, parenthesis; =schlag m: a) = =mauer; b) ⊙ typ. = Durchschuß 2; =speise f = =gericht; =spiel n, thea., &c. interlude, fig. auch: intermezzo; =stab m, arch. (schmale Leiste) fillet; =stadt f intermediate town; =stand m intervening (or intermediate) position; =ständer ⊙ m = =pfosten; =station ⛃ f intermediate (or subordinate) station; =stellung f = =stand; =stock(=werk n) m arch. = =geschoß; =streit m jur. intervention; =stück n: a) intermediate piece; b) = =spiel; =stufe f intermediate stage or grade; =stunde f: a) intermediate hour, weitS. interval; b) (Pause zwischen den Lehrstunden) hour (or time) of recreation, playtime; =ton ♪ m intermediate tone or note; =träger(in f) m meist b.s. gobetween, tell-tale, scandalmonger; =trägerei = Zuträgerei; =umstand m incident(al circumstance); =verkehr m intercommunication; =vorfall m incident(al occurrence); =vorhang m, thea. drop-scene; =wall ⚔ m, frt. partition-wall, curtain; =wand ⊙ f = =mauer; =weite f distance between; =wort ↘ n, gr. interjection; =zaun m boundary-fence between fields, &c.; =zeile f intermediate line; ⚥zeilig a.: ₂e Übersetzung interlinear translation; =zeit f intervening time, interval; in der ~ (in the) meanwhile; =zustand m intermediate state.

Zwist (²) [(mhd.) ndd.: twist] m ①b. dissension, difference; (Zwietracht) discord; (Streit) quarrel, dispute, F tiff; mit c-m über et. in ~ geraten to begin to quarrel or F to spar (or to start a dispute) with a p. about a th.

zwistig (̮ ͜) a. ⑯: a) von Personen: at variance, F at loggerheads; (streitend) quarrelling, squabbling, F sparring; b) v. Sachen: = streitig 2.

Zwistigkeit (̮ ͜ ͜) f ㊻ = Zwist.

zwitschern (̮ ͜ ͜) [ahd. lautm.] I v/n. (h.) u. v/a. Wa. v. Vögeln: to twitter, to chirp, v. Lerchen ꝛc.: to warble, to carol; als v/a. ein Lied ₂ to chirp (or sing) a song; Sprichw. f. Alte 1. — II ~ n ㉓ twitter(ing), chirp(ing), warbling.

Zwitter (̮ ͜) [ahd. zwei] m ㉓ 1. allg.: being in which two opposite natures are blended or united; (Bastard) bastard, zo. cross (-breed), half-breed, mongrel, v. ⚥: ↻ hybrid. — 2. (Wesen mit männlichen u. weiblichen Geschlechtsteilen) physiol.: ↻ hermaphrodite, ⚥ auch: androgynous plant.

Zwitter=art (̮ ͜ ͜...) f ㊷ mongrel (or cross-) breed, ⚥ u. zo.: ↻ hybrid species; ⚥artig a. ⑯ = zwitterhaft; =bildung f: ↻ hermaphroditism, androgyny, weitS. hybridism, hybrid(iz)ation; =blume, =blüte ⚥ f: hermaphrodite (flower), androgynous flower; ⚥blütig a.: ↻ hermaphrodite, androgynous; =form f = =bildung; =cross breed; =geschlecht n mongrel (or mixed) race, ↻ hybrid stock; =geschöpf n. =gestalt f = Zwitter.

zwitterhaft (̮ ͜ ͜) a. ⑯: a) bastard, mongrel, ↻ hybrid; b) physiol.: hermaphrodite, hermaphroditic(al), ⚥: ↻ androgynous.

Zwitterhaftigkeit (̮ ͜ ͜ ͜-) f ㊻ a) mongrelism, ↻ hybridism; b) ↻ hermaphroditism, ⚥ a. androgyny.

zwitterig (̮ ͜ ͜) a. ⑯ = zwitterhaft.

Zwitter=pflanze ⚥ (̮ ͜.̮ ͜) f ㊷: ↻ hybrid(ous) plant.

Zwitterschaft (̮ ͜ ͜) f ㊻. Zwittertum (̮ ͜-) n ②c. = Zwitterhaftigkeit.

Zwitterwesen (̮ ͜ ͜...) n ㉒: a) ↻ hybrid nature or condition; b) = Zwitter; =wort n word of mixed (or hybrid) origin.

zwo † (²) = zwei (nur mit s/f. verbunden; vgl. zwen); ₂ Reihen two rows.

zwölf (²) [ahd.: twelve: zwei] numer. I card. numb. (ohne s. a. ₂c) twelve; etwa ₂ (about) a dozen; ₂ Flaschen a dozen bottles; um 12 Uhr at twelve o'clock, mittags, auch: at noon, nachts, auch: at midnight; um halb ₂ at half past eleven (o'clock); um ³/₄ auf ₂ at a quarter to twelve; wir sind unser ₂(e) we are twelve, there are a dozen of us. — II (die Zahl) ~ f ㊻ (number) twelve.

Zwölf=eck (²...) n ㊷ geom. dodecagon; ⚥eckig a. ⑯ geom. dodecagonal.

Zwölfer (²...) m ㉓ 1. anything marked with 12; soldier of the twelfth regiment. — 2. member of a council (or a body) of twelve. — 3. ⊙ ~ pl. Flachsspinnerei: (Art Flachsbecheln) twelves pl.

zwölfer=lei (²...) a. ⑯ inv. of twelve (different or distinct) kinds or sorts.

zwölf=fach (²...) a. ⑯ twelvefold; =fingerdarm m ⑥², anat.: ↻ duodenum; =fingerdarm=entzündung f, path.: ↻ duodenitis; =flach n.geom.,min.dodecahedron; ⚥flächig a. geom. dodecahedral; =flächner m = =flach; =fürst m Alt: dodecarch; ⚥griff(e)lig a.: ↻ dodecagynian, ...ous; ⚥jährig a. of twelve years, twelve years old; ein ₂er Knabe auch: a twelve-year-old boy; ⚥lötig a. of six ounces; ⚥malig a. taking place twelve times; ⚥männ(er)ig ⚥ a.: ↻ dodecandrian, ...ous; =pfünder ⚔ m, artill. twelve-pounder; ⚥seitig a. twelve-sided; ⚥stündig a. of (or lasting) twelve hours; ⚥stündlich a. occurring every twelve hours; =tafelgesetz n röm. (450 v.Chr.) TwelveTables pl.

zwölfte (̮ ͜) I ord. numb. ⑯ twelfth; Karl der ~ (gschr. XII.) Charles the Twelfth (gschr. XII); der ~ des Monats the twelfth (oder: 12th) of the month. — II die Zwölften pl. the twelve days (or nights) between Christmas and Twelfth-night.

zwölf=teilig (²...) a. ⑯ consisting of twelve parts, ⚥: ↻ dodecafid, dodecamerous, math. duodecimal; ~teit f ㊻ math. duodecimal system.

Zwölftel (̮ ͜) n ㉒, ₂ a. inv. twelfth (part); ~form ⊙ f ㊷ typ. twelves pl.; ~format n duodecimo (volume or book). [in the twelfth place,|

zwölftens (̮ ͜ ͜) adv. twelfthly (12ly).)

zwölf=weib(er)ig ⚥ (²...) a. ⑯: ↻ dodecagynian, ...ous; =zahl f ㊷ duodecimal.

Zyan ↻ (∪-²) [grch. blau] n ①d. chm. cyan, mehr gbr. cyanogen (Symbol als Radikal: Cy, sonst: CN); ~=äther m ㉓ cyanic ether.

Zyane ⚥ (∪-²) [grch.] f ㊸ (Kornblume) corn-flower, blue-bottle (Centaure'a cy'anus); Zyaneen ⚥ (∪-²-) f pl. inv. ↻ centaureae pl.

Zyan=eisen ↻ (∪-²...) n ㉒ cyanide of iron, iron cyanide; ⚥haltig a. ⑯ cyanous.

Zyanid ↻ (∪-²) [grch.] n ①c. chm. (Zyanverbindung) cyanide; ⚥zyanig ↻ (∪-²) a. ⑯ cyanous; ₂e Säure cyanous acid; zyanisieren ⊙ ⁺⁺ (∪-∪-²) v/a. ₂ Holz: to cyanize (= kyanifieren).

Zyan=kali=salz ⊙ (∪-²...) n ㉒ für galvanische Vergoldung ꝛc.: cyanide powder; =kali(um) n, chm. (starkes Gift) cyanide of potassium, potassium cyanide (KCN); =metall n metallic cyanide. [Zyan.)

Zyanogen ↻ (∪∪-²) [grch.] n ①c. chm. =)

Zyanometer ↻ (∪∪-∪-²) [grch.] n (m) ㉒ zum Messen der Himmelsbläue: cyanometer.

Zyanotyp ↻ (∪∪-²) [grch.] n ①c. phot.: (Schnellphotographie) cyanotype; ~papier n ㉒ cyanotype-paper.

zyan=sauer (∪-²...) a. ⑯ chm.: ↻ cyanic; ₂saures Salz cyanate; =säure f cyanic acid (CN. HO); =silber n cyanide of silver; =verbindung f cyanide; =wasserstoffsäure f (Blausäure, Gift) hydrocyanic (or prussic) acid (HCN).

Zychoma ⚥ (∪-²) [grch.] n ㉓ = Zochbein.

Zykladen ⚥ (∪-²) [grch. kyklos Kreis] npr/f pl. ㊸ (ant. Sporaden) (Inseln im Ägäischen Meere) Cyclades pl.

Zyklamen (∪-²) [grch.] n ㉓ (Alpenveilchen) cyclamen (Cycla'men Europae'um).

Zykliker ↻ (²...) [grch. Kreis] m ㉒ grch. Alt.: (Sagen,,kreis''=dichter) cyclic poet.

zyklisch ↻ (²...) [grch.] a. ⑯ cyclic.

Signs (see page XVII): F familiar; P vulgar; ℉ flash; ↘ rare; † obsolete (died); * new word (born); ⁺⁺ incorrect; ♪ music;

[Zyklode] — 1183 — [z. Z.]

Zyklode 🜚 (-⏑-⏑) [grch.] f ⊕ math. (nte Involute eines Kreises) cycloide.

Zyklo-ide 🜚 (-⏑-⏑) [grch.] f ⊕ geom. u. mach. (Radlinie) cycloid.

Zyklon (-⏑) [grch.] m ⊕ d.(N.), ~e (-⏑-⏑) f ⊕ (Wirbelwind) cyclone.

Zyklop (-⏑) [grch.] m ⊕ myth. (einäugiger Riese) Cyclops, pl. Cyclopes; ~en-bau m ⊕ Cyclopean architecture; Lenhaft (-⏑⏑-), Zisch (-⏑-) a. ⊕ Cyclopean.

Zyklus (⏑-) [grch.] m ⊕ 1. ast., Zeitrechnung: cycle; metonischer ~ (von 19 Jahren, in dem sich die Mondphasen wiederholen) Metonic (or lunar) cycle; Alt.: (epischer Sagenkreis) (epic) cycle. — 2. Reihe von Vorlesungen ꝛc.: series (or course) of lectures, &c.

Zylinder (tsi-⏑-⏑) [grch.] m ⊕ 1. math., mech. (Walze) cylinder. — 2. chm. (Probierglas)~ test-tube. — 3. ⊕ (Lampen-)~ cylinder (or glass, chimney) of a lamp; lamp-glass. — 4. F (hoher Hut) high (or silk) hat, F top-hat, topper; co. chimney-pot.

zylinder=ähnlich (-⏑-⏑...) a. ⊕ cylinder-like; =bohrmaschine ⊕ f ⊕ cylinder-boring machine; =dampfkessel m cylindrical boiler; =deckel m. mach. cylinder-cover; =drehbank f slide-lathe; =elektrisier=maschine f cylinder-electrical machine; =fläche f, geom. cylindrical surface; =förmig a. cylindriform, cylindrical; =gebläse n cylinder-blast engine, cyl.-blower; =hahn m eines Dampfzylinders: cylinder-cock; =hemmung f einer Uhr: cylinder-escapement; =hut m = Zylinder 4; =kratze ⊕ f Spinnerei: cylinder-card; =mange(l) f Tuchfabr.: calender; =mantel m Dampfm.: cylinder-jacket, steam-case or -casing; =maschine f Dampfm.: cylinder-engine.

zylindern ⊕ (-⏑-⏑) va. (p.p. zyli'ndert ohne ge-) (calandern) to calender.

Zylinder-presse ⊕ (-⏑-⏑...) f ⊕ = =mange; =rad n Uhren: cylinder-wheel; =scheibe f = Kolben; =schreibtisch m cylinder-desk; =stopfbüchse f Dampfm.: cylinder stuff-box; =uhr f watch with cylinder-(or horizontal) escapement; =zapfen ↧ m (Döbel) dowel.

zylindrieren (-⏑-⏑) va. ⊕ = zylindern.

zylindrisch (-⏑-⏑) a. ⊕ (walzenförmig) cylindrical. [(elliptische Walze) cylindroid.↧

Zylindro-id (-⏑⏑-) [grch.] n ⊕ c. math.

Zymologie 🜚 (-⏑⏑-⏑) f ⊕ chm. (Gärungslehre) zymology.

Zyniker (⏑-⏑⏑) [grch. ky'ōn Hund, Spottname des Dio'genes von Athen] m ⊕ phls. Cynic. fig. (schamloser Mensch) cynic(al p.).

zynisch (-⏑) a. ⊕ cynical, shameless fig. auch: indecent, offensive.

Zynismus (-⏑⏑) [grch.] m ⊕ phls. cynical (school of) philosophy; fig. cynicism. cynical view (of life), contemptuous disregard of the rules of decency, shamelessness.

Zyper=gras (⏑-...) n ⊕ cypress-grass. 🜚 cyperus; =gräser pl.: 🜚 cyperaceæ; =gras=artig ♃ a. ⊕: 🜚 cyperaceous.

Zypern ♀ (-⏑) npr/n. Ba. (türk. Insel unter engl. Schutzherrschaft) Cyprus.

Zyper=wein (⏑-...) m ⊕ Cyprus-wine; =wurz ♃ f (English) galanga (Cype'rus longus).

Zypresse ♃ (⏑-⏑) [grch.; *semit.] f ⊕ cypress (-tree) (Cupre'ssus); vgl. Lebensbaum.

zypressen=artig (-⏑-⏑...) a. ⊕: Le Zapfenträger m pl.: 🜚 cupressineæ pl.; =hain m ⊕ = =wald; =holz n cypress-wood; =nuß ♃ f cypress-cone; =wald m cypress-grove or -wood.

Zypri-er (-⏑⏑) [grch.] m ⊕, ~in f ⊕, **zyprisch** (-⏑) a. ⊕ Cypriote, Cyprian.

Zyste 🜚 (⏑-⏑) [grch.] f ⊕ path. (Eiterblase. Balggeschwulst) cyst; ~n=flüssigkeit f ⊕ cystic fluid. [Goldregen.

Zytisus 🜚 ♃ (⏑-⏑) [grch.] m, inv. = ↧

z. Z. abbr. = zurzeit.

∗ METHODE TOUSSAINT-LANGENSCHEIDT ∗

Nachtrag

zu

MURET-SANDERS

Enzyklopädisches englisch-deutsches
und deutsch-englisches Wörterbuch

Mit Angabe der Aussprache nach dem phonetischen System der
METHODE TOUSSAINT-LANGENSCHEIDT

Hand- und Schulausgabe

TEIL II: DEUTSCH-ENGLISCH

Zusammengestellt von
Professor E. Klatt

Published and Distributed in the
Public Interest by Authority of the
Alien Property Custodian under
License No. A-548, by

FREDERICK UNGAR PUBLISHING COMPANY
NEW YORK

Die mit einem Stern * versehenen Titelköpfe kommen schon im Texte des Wörterbuches vor; die Aussprache und die Merke sind daher nur bei neuen Wörtern gegeben.

Wird bei einem englischen Wort, das abgeteilt ist, der Trennungsstrich vor der auf die nächste Zeile kommenden Silbe wiederholt, so handelt es sich um ein Wort, das immer mit Bindestrich geschrieben wird, z. B. tee-shot beim Stichwort „Abschlag".

Neue, im Hauptteil noch nicht angewendete bildliche Zeichen:

✈ = Flugwesen aviation.   mot. = motoring Kraftfahrwesen.   mount. = mountaineering Bergsteigerei.

A

*ab zu II 8b: ab heute from to-day; ✈ ab Spesen less (or deducting) charges.

*Ab-bau 4. v. Maßnahmen, Gesetzen usw.: withdrawal; ~ der Zwangswirtschaft in Milch usw. decontrol of milk, &c.; der Preise, Löhne usw. reduction; v. Beamten: dismissal, F the axe; der Behörden, Verwaltung: retrenchment.

*ab-bauen zu III: 7. Maßnahmen, Gesetze usw.: to withdraw; die Zwangswirtschaft (in Milch usw.) ~ to decontrol (milk, &c.); Preise, Löhne, Steuern: to reduce; Beamte: to dismiss, F to axe; Behörde, Verwaltung: to retrench.

ab-blenden (⌣⌣) v/a. ⓕ ** helles Licht: to dim, to screen; phot. to stop down.

*Ab-bruch 5. mount. — Gletscherabbruch; e-s Berggrates usw.: drop, descent, precipice.

Ab-bruch-unternehmer (⌣⌣⌣ch...) m ⓑ [housebreaker.

*ab-büßen zu I: jur. Strafe: to serve.

*ab-decken 3. ⊙ (verdecken) to mask, to cover.

ab-drosseln (⌣⌣⌣) v/a. ⓟa. ** to choke; mot. to throttle down.

ab-ducken (⌣⌣⌣) v/a. ⓕ ** Boxen: to dodge, F to duck, F to side-step a blow.

*ab-fahren zu I: mount. to glissade.

*Ab-fahrt 4. mount. glissade.

Ab-fahrts-bahn-steig 🚂 (⌣⌣...) m ⓑ starting-platform.

ab-filmen (⌣⌣⌣) v/a. ⓕ ** to film.

*ab-finden zu II: sich 2 mit et. to put up with a th.

Ab-gas (⌣⌣) n ⓓa. waste gas, bsd. mach., mot. exhaust gas.

ab-geklärt (⌣⌣⌣) I s. abklären II. — II a. ⓕ fig. Alter, Charakter, Urteil: mellow.

ab-gelten (⌣⌣⌣) v/a. ⓔ ** to discharge.

Ab-geltung (⌣⌣⌣) f ⓕ discharge.

*Ab-geneigtheit: ~ et. zu tun unwillingness to do a th.

*ab-hauen II P [+ abbauen I] v/n. ⓕ ** (fn) (ausreißen) to cut off, to slope (off).

*ab-hören zu I: teleph. to listen in.

Abiturienten-zeugnis n ⓑ Higher Certificate. [Strickerei: to close off.)

ab-ketteln ⊙ (⌣⌣⌣) v/a. u. v/n. ⓟa. **

Ab-kettelung (⌣⌣(⌣)⌣) f ⓕ Strickerei: purl-edge.

*ab-klopfen 5. fig. F Gegend usw. to beat.

*ab-kochen II v/n. (h.) ⓕ ** to do one's cooking.

*ab-kommen zu I 1: Rennsport: gut 2 to get a good start. [zungszeichen.)

*Ab-kürzungs-zeichen Kurzschrift: s. Kür-

*ab-legen zu I: Briefe, Akten: to file.

*Ab-leitung 3. elect. leakage (conductance), leakance.

*Ab-messung 2. ~en pl. (Größe) dimensions pl. [knock down.)

*ab-montieren ⊙ to dismantle, to

*Ab-nahme zu 3: ~-r Ware: acceptance.

Ab-nahme-prüfung ⊙ (⌣⌣...) f ⓕ acceptance test. [removable.)

ab-nehmbar ⊙ (⌣⌣⌣) a. ⓕⓕ detachable,)

Ab-rechnungs-verkehr m clearing arrangement. [-down.)

*Ab-reibung: nasse ~ des Körpers sponge-)

*ab-riegeln Straße: to block.

*ab-rollen zu I: ✈ to forward.

*Ab-ruf: ✈ auf ~ at (or on) call.

*ab-rutschen zu I: ✈ to side-slip; in der Kurve: to skid.

Ab-satz-methode f method of marketing. [deport.)

Ab-schieben zu I: lästige Ausländer: to

Ab-schiebung (⌣⌣⌣) f ⓕ lästiger Ausländer: deportation. [certificate.)

Ab-schieds-zeugnis (⌣⌣⌣...) n ⓕ leaving)

*ab-schießen zu I 1: abgeschossene (verbrauchte) Patrone spent cartridge.

*Ab-schlag 9. Golf (Spieleröffnung) tee-shot.

*ab-schlagen zu I: Raum (durch e-e Scheidewand): to partition off.

*ab-schleppen zu I: ↓ u. mot. to (take in) tow. [to settle accounts with life.)

*ab-schließen zu II: mit dem Leben 2)

*ab-schmelzen zu I u. II: elect. Sicherung: to fuse, to blow.

Ab-schmelz-sicherung ⊙ (⌣⌣...) f ⓕ elect. (safety) fuse, safety cut-out.

*ab-schmieren zu I: ⊙ mach. to grease duly or sufficiently.

ab-schminken (⌣⌣⌣) v/a. ⓕ ** to remove the paint from a p's face.

ab-schmirgeln ⊙ (⌣⌣⌣) v/a. ⓟa. ** to sand-paper. [sector.)

*Ab-schnitt zu 3: ⚔ (Operationsbezirk))

ab-seilen ⊙ (⌣⌣⌣) ⓕ ** v/a. u. v/refl. (sich 2) mount. to rope down.

Ab-seil-schlinge (⌣⌣⌣) f ⓕ mount. safety-sling. [hausted.)

*ab-sein 2. F (ermattet sein) to be ex-)

*ab-seits zu I: Fußball: off-side.

*Ab-sprung 4. (-stelle) take-off.

*ab-stellen zu I 2: ✈ u. mot. den Motor: to shut off, to stall.

*ab-stimmen zu 1: Radio: to tune (in) (auf acc. to), to syntonize.

Ab-stimm-schärfe (⌣⌣⌣) f ⓕ Radio: sharpness of tuning or resonance; -spule f Radio: tuning coil.

*Ab-stimmung 2. Radio: (Vorgang) tuning (in), selection (auf acc. to), syntonization; (Vorhandensein der) ~ syntony. [Radio: tuner.)

Ab-stimm-vorrichtung (⌣⌣⌣) f ⓕ

*ab-stoßen zu I: F fig. = erübrigen.

*Ab-strich 3. med. (bei Diphtherie usw.): swab.

*Ab-sturz zu I: ✈ crash.

*ab-stürzen zu II 3: ✈ to crash.

*ab-töten zu I: Bakterien: to destroy.

*Ab-tötung v. Bakterien: destruction.

Ab-treibungs-mittel (⌣⌣...) n ⓕ med. 7 abortifacient. [to shift off.)

*ab-wälzen 2. Arbeit, Bürde von sich 2)

ab-wandern (⌣⌣⌣) v/n. (fn) ⓟa. ** to wander away.

Ab-wanderung (⌣⌣⌣) f ⓕ wandering away; ~ des Kapitals exodus of capital.

*ab-warten zu I 1: das bleibt abzuwarten that remains to be seen,

Ab-wehr-... (⌣⌣⌣) mst defensive.

*ab-wehren Dank, Lob usw.: to refuse (gently).

Ab-wick(e)lungs-behörde (⌣⌣(⌣)...) f ⓕ Liquidation Department.

Ab-zähl-reim (⌣⌣⌣) m ⓕ bei Kinderspielen: counting-out rhyme.

Ab-zahlungs-kauf (⌣⌣...) m ⓕ hire purchase; -system n hire-purchase system, instalment plan; -wesen n instalment buying.

*Ab-zieh-bild transfer (picture).

Ab-zugs-stange ⊙ (⌣⌣...) f ⓕ im Gewehr-schloß: sear.

Ab-zweig (⌣⌣⌣) m ⓓc. branch.

Ab-zweig-dose (⌣⌣⌣...) f ⓕ elect. junction (or connector) box; -klemme ⊙ f branch terminal.

Achs-kasten ⊙ (⌣tß...) m ⓑ ⓯ axle-box; -schenkel ⊙ m mot. steering knuckle spindle. [eights race.)

Achter-rennen (⌣⌣⌣...) m ⓕ Ruderport:)

adenoid ⁊ (⌣⌣⌣´) [grch.] a. ⓕⓕ path. ~-e Wucherungen f/pl. im hinteren Nasenraum adenoids pl.

Adrenalin ⁊ (⌣⌣⌣-⁗) [lt.] n ⓓd. med. (blutstillendes Mittel) adrenalin.

A.E.G. abbr. = Allgemeine Elektrizitäts-gesellschaft General Electric Company.

Aerophon ⁊ (⌣⌣⌣´⁗) [grch.] n ⓓe. Radio: acrophone.

Aeroplan ✈ (⌣⌣⌣´⁗) [grch.-lt.] m ⓓd. aeroplane, airplane.

Afa abbr. = Allgemeiner Freier Angestelltenbund Federation of Employees' Free Trade Unions.

*After-miete: in ~ wohnen bei j-m to be a p.'s sub-tenant. [interest.)

After-zins (⌣⌣⌣) m ⓕ ⓯ compound)

A.G. abbr. = Aktiengesellschaft (s. ds)

a.G. abbr. = auf Gegenseitigkeit Mutual vor dem Namen der Gesellschaft.

Agrariertum (⌣⌣´´(⌣)⌣´) n ⓓd. landed interest.

Akkord-lohn (⌣⌣⌣´) m ⓕ piece-wages pl.

1*

Akkumulatoren-batterie ⊙ (⌣⌣⌣‼⌣...) f ⓶ elect. storage battery.
Akquisiteur ❋ (⌣--tŏ'r) [fr.] m ⑪e. (Anzeigeneinholer) tout, canvasser.
Akrobatentum (⌣⌣⌣⌣) n ②d., **Akrobatik** (⌣⌣⌣⌣) [grch.] f ㊻ acrobatism.
*Akt 3. paint., sculp. (Darstellung des nackten Körpers) nude.
Akten-hefter (⌣⌣...) m ⓶ (Gerät) document file; **=klammer** f paper-clip; **=schwanz** m docket; **=zeichen** n reference (or file) number. ⟦lot⟧ of shares.⟧
Aktien-paket (⌣tḫ⌣⌣...) n ⓶ parcel (or)
Aktinium ⌒ (⌣′⌣⌣) [grch.] n ⓶ phys. (radioaktives Element) actinium.
Aktiv-posten (⌣‼⌣...) m ⓶ credit item, (a. fig.) asset; **=wert** ❋ m active value.
Akt-studie (⌣′...) f ⓶ paint., sculp. nude.
Akzelerator ⊙ (⌣⌣⌣‵⌣) [lt.] m ㉛ mot. accelerator.
*Alarm-bereitschaft: in ~ on the alert.
*Alimente: ~ für die geschiedene Frau separation allowance.
alkohol-frei (⌣⌣⌣...) a. ㊻ non-alcoholic; **=gehalt** m ⓶ chm. percentage of alcohol; **=schmuggel** m spirit-smuggling, F rum-running, Am. F bootlegging; **=schmuggler** m spirit-smuggler, F rum-runner, Am. F bootlegger; **=verbot** n Prohibition; **=vergiftung** f alcoholic poisoning.
Allein-vertreter ❋ (⌣‼...) m ⓶ sole agent or distributor.
Allgemein-unkosten ❋ (⌣⌣‼...) pl. ⓶ overhead cost(s pl.).
Allheil-mittel (⌣‼...) n ⓶ universal remedy, panacea.
*Almosen-pfleger hist. almoner.
*Alse: weiße ~ whitebait.
Alt-besitz (⌣′...) m ⓶ old holding; **=besitzer** m old holder; **=eisen** n scrap iron; **=papier** n (old) waste paper.
*ambulant med. ℒ behandelter Patient outpatient.
*amerikanisch ❋ ℒe Buchführung columnar (or tabular) book-keeping.
Ammeter ⊙ (⌣′⌣) [Ameremeter] n (m) ⓶ elect. ammeter.
Amöben-ruhr ⌒ (⌣‼⌣′) f ⓶ path. entamœbial dysentery.
Amplitüde ⌒ (⌣-′⌣) [fr., *lt.] f ㊸ phys. amplitude.
Ampulle ⌒ (⌣⌣) [lt.] f ㊸ med. (Glaskapsel mit Injektionsflüssigkeit) ampoule.
*an zu Ia): es ist an mir zu tun it is up to me to do. ⟦literacy.⟧
Analphabetentum (⌣⌣⌣′⌣⌣) n ②d. il-⟧
An-biet-arbeit ❋ (⌣′-...) f ⓶ advertising work, publicity work.
An-binden ⚔ (⌣⌣) n ㉓ (Strafe im Felde) crucifixion. ⟦cation.⟧
*An-bringung zu 1: (Einbau) appli-⟧
An-dreh-kurbel (⌣′-...) f mot. starting crank; **=klaue** f, mot. starting crank jaw. ⟦price.⟧
An-fangs-kurs (⌣⌣⌣) m ⓶ Börse: opening⟧
an-fräsen ⊙ (⌣′⌣) v/a. ㉙ to trepan.
*an-gehend zu III 10: Kunde: prospec-⟧
*angeln² zu II: Sport: angling. ⟦tive.⟧
an-geschlagen (⌣⌣⌣⌣) p.p. f. anschlagen; v. Porzellan, Steingut usw.: chipped.
*An-gesicht zu 1: ℤℬ (in Erwägung) e-r Sachlage usw. in view of.

an-gliedern (⌣′⌣⌣) v/a. ⓶a.** to annex, to affiliate, Person: to attach (dat. ob. an acc. to).
An-gliederung (⌣′⌣⌣) f ㊻ annexation, affiliation (an acc. to).
an-griffs-lustig (⌣⌣...) ㊻ a. aggressive.
*an-hängen zu I: Fernspr. to hang up, to restore the receiver; abs. to clear (out), to touch off.
*An-hänger 2. = Anhängewagen.
An-hänge-wagen (⌣⌣⌣...) m ⓶ supplementary car; der Straßenbahn: trailer.
*An-hieb 2. univ. sl. u. F auf ~ (sofort) at (the) first go-off. ⟦push rod.⟧
An-hub-stange ⊙ (⌣′⌣⌣) f ⓶ mach.⟧
*Anker (Verspannung) z.B. e-r Telegraphenstange stay, guy.
Anker-mast ⚓ (⌣′⌣) m mooring-mast.
*an-klingeln zu I: Fernspr. to call.
an-kurbeln ⊙ (⌣⌣⌣) v/a. ⓶a.** mot. to crank (up).
An-kurbelungs-kredit ❋ (⌣⌣⌣⌣′) m ⓶ reconstruction credit.
Ankylose ⌒ (⌣-′⌣) [grch.] f ㊸ path. (Gelenksteifheit) ankylosis.
*An-lage ⊙ (Gesamtheit e-s technischen Betriebes) plant; z.B. Fernsprechanlage telephone plant.
*An-lasser mach. starter.
An-laß-kurbel ⊙ (⌣⌣...) f ⓶ mot. starting handle; **=motor** m starting motor; **=schalter** m starting switch.
*an-legen zu I1: typ. to feed, to lay on.
An-leihe-ablösung (⌣′⌣⌣) f ㊸ loan-liquidation, loan-redemption.
*an-muten zu I: seltsam (ob. eigenartig) ℒ to seem somewhat curious (j-n to a p.).
An-näherungs-schlag (⌣′⌣⌣) m ⓶ Golf: approach-shot. ⟦cancellation.⟧
Annullierung (⌣⌣′⌣) f ㊻ annulment,⟧
Anoden-... ⌒ (⌣′⌣) elect. anode.
Anoden-batterie (⌣‼⌣...) f ⓶ Radio: anode battery, B battery.
an-prangern (⌣′⌣⌣) v/a. ⓶a.** to pillory.
An-probe (⌣′⌣) f ㊸ Schneiderei: try-on.
*an-pumpen F to bite a p.'s ear.
*An-regung (Vorschlag) suggestion.
*an-reihen zu II 3: sich anderen ℒ to join others. ⟦the season.⟧
*an-rudern II ~ n ㉓ opening row of⟧
*An-sager Radio: announcer.
An-schlag (Hemmung) stop, catch.
*an-schlagen zu I: angeschlagen sein Boxen: to be injured.
*an-schließen zu II4: sich e-r Meinung usw. ℒ to join, to follow, to adopt.
*An-schluß zu 5: Fernspr. communication, connexion. — 6. ⊙ (Wasser-, Gas- usw.ℒ) supply. — 7. (Umgang) ~ finden to find congenial company.
An-schluß-klemme ⊙ (⌣⌣...) f ⓶ elect. binding post; **=schnur** f, elect. flex.
An-schrift (⌣⌣) f ㊻ address.
*an-segeln II ~ n ㉓ opening sail of the season.
*an-seilen v/a. u. v/refl. (sich ℒ) mount. to rope; mehrere: to rope together; angeseilt a. on the rope.
*an-spielen zu I3: Sport: to lead off.
*an-sprechen zu I1: v. Bettlern und Prostituierten: to solicit.
*An-stand zu 3: keinen ~ nehmen zu tun to have no hesitation in doing.

An-stands-formen (⌣⌣...) f/pl. ⓶ die ~ the proprieties pl.
*an-stehen (e-e Reihe bilden) to stand in a queue or in queues, F to queue (nach Lebensmitteln usw. for).
*an-stellen zu II6: sich ℒ in e-r Reihe to take one's place in the queue, to queue (on or up) (nach Lebensmitteln usw. for).
*Antenne 3. Radio: aerial, a. antenna
Antennen-draht ⊙ (⌣⌣′⌣) m ⓶ Radio aerial wire.
Anti-körper ⌒ (⌣⌣⌣) m ⓶ physiol. (Schutzmittel im Blutkörperchen) antibody.
An-triebs-welle ⊙ (⌣′...) f ⓶ mach. clutch shaft.
An-zeigen-annahme (⌣′⌣⌣...) f ⓶ advertising office; **=büro** n advertising agency. ⟦(Strolch) apache.⟧
Apache (⌣⌣⌣⌣) [fr., *indianisch] m ⓸⟧
Apachentum (⌣⌣ch⌣⌣) n ②d. apachism.
aperiodisch ⌒ (⌣⌣(⌣)′⌣) [grch.] a. ㊻ elect. v. Stromkreis: aperiodic.
*Apparat Fernspr. am ~! (Antwort des Angerufenen) speaking!
April-scherz (⌣⌣′) m ⓶ April fish.
*Arbeit zu 1: ~(en pl.) (Tätigkeit bestimmter Art) operation(s pl.), z.B. building operations are going on. ⟦Bank.⟧
Arbeiter-bank ❋ (⌣′-⌣⌣) f ⓶ Labour⟧
Arbeiter- und Soldaten-rat (⌣′-⌣...) m ⓶ Workers' and Soldiers' Council.
Arbeits-abkommen (⌣′⌣...) n ⓶ Labour Convention; **=dienst-pflicht** f compulsory labour service; **=einkommen** n earned income; **=einteilung** f division of labour; **=freudigkeit** f pleasure in one's work; **=gebiet** n scope of labour; **=gemeinschaft** f working association or co-operation; **=gericht** n industrial court; **=kommando** ⚔ n fatigue-party; **=losen-fürsorge** f Welfare Work for the Unemployed; **=losen-unterstützung** f unemployment benefit, the dole; **=losen-versicherung** f unemployment insurance; **=minister** m Minister of Labour; **=programm** n programme; **=ruhe** f rest from work; *⁂scheu I a. ㊻ work-shy. — II ~e(r) m, f ⓶ work-shy; **=vermittlung** f provision of employment; **=verweigerung** f refusal to work; **=willige(r)** m would-be worker, non-striker; **=zeit-abkommen** n hours convention.
Armaturen-brett (⌣⌣‼⌣) n ⓶ mot. u. ⚓ instrument board.
Arm-band-uhr (⌣′...) f ⓶ wrist(let) watch; an e-m Schmuckarmband: bracelet watch; **=blatt** n im Kleid zum Schutz gegen Schweiß: dress preserver, dress shield.
Armierungs-soldat ⚔ (⌣‼...) m ⓶ private in a labour battalion, pioneer.
arrivieren Gallizismus (⌣-′⌣) [fr.] v/n. (fn) ⑨ (emporkommen) to arrive.
Art-genosse (⌣‼...) m ⓶ one of one's own kind; **⁀verschieden** a. ㊻ different in kind. ⟦-path.⟧
Aschen-bahn (⌣⌣′) f ⓶ Sport: cinder-⟧
Aspirin (⌣-′) [lt.] n ⓶c. pharm. aspirin.
Atem-filter ⊙ (⌣‼⌣) m ⓶ respirator; **=pause** f breathing-time, b.-pause; **=übungen** f/pl. deep-breathing.
Äther-wellen (⌣‼...) f/pl. ⓶ phys. ether-waves pl.

Audion (⏑–⏑⏑) [lt.=grch.] n ⓔⓦ Radio: (Hauptaufnahmeröhre) audion, valve detector, detecting tube or valve.

*****Auf-bau** zu 1: e-s Dramas usw.: construction. [construct.]

*****auf-bauen** zu 1: ein Drama usw.: to

Auf-bewahrungs-raum (verschließbarer) lock-up.

*****auf-fallen** zu IV: 2d (deutlich sichtbar) conspicuous, prominent, outstanding.

Auf-forstung (–⏑⏑) f ⓖ for. afforestation.

*****Auf-gabe** zu 1: Tennis: service.

Auf-gabe-spiel (–⏑–⏑) n ⓖ Tennis: service game.

*****auf-geben** zu 16: Sport: (nicht weiter spielen; a. abs.) to give up, to abandon.

*****Auf-gebot** zu 1: eccl. das ~ bestellen to ask the banns.

*****auf-hellen** zu I: (sich) 2 fig. Gesicht, Miene: to brighten, to clear up.

*****Auf-klärung** zu 2: sexuelle ~ sex instruction.

Auf-klärungs-film (–⏑–⏑...) m ⓖ sex-film; =**periode** f, =**zeit-alter** n, hist. enlightening age. [to mount.]

auf-klotzen (–⏑–⏑) v/a. ⓜ ** typ. Platten:

*****auf-knabbern**, *****auf-knacken** f sl. Geldschrank: to crack. [yield of a tax.]

*****auf-kommen** zu II: = aus e-r Steuer:

*****Auf-lage** zu 3: b) = Auflageziffer. — 4. ⓞ ~ v. Metall usw.: coating.

Auf-lage-matratze (–⏑–⏑...) f ⓖ overlay mattress; =**ziffer** f e-r Zeitung usw.: circulation, issue.

auf-liefern ⟳ (–⏑–⏑) v/a. ⓖ a. ** to post.

*****auf-machen** zu I: ⓞ Dampf 2 to get up (or raise) steam.

*****Auf-machung** 2. (Äußeres) make-up, get-up; contp. (Blendwerk) window-dressing.

Auf-näher (–⏑–⏑) m ⓖ im Kleid: tuck.

Auf-nahme-apparat (–⏑–⏑...) m ⓖ für Wiedergabe auf dem Grammophon: recording apparatus; *=**fähig** vom Geist: receptive; *=**fähigkeit** 2. ⓜ capacity for absorbing goods. — 3. (geistige ~) receptive; Schallplatte: to record.

*****auf-nehmen** zu 10: Film: to shoot.

Auf-rüstung ⚔ (–⏑–⏑) f ⓖ (ant. Abrüstung) armament. [vice(-ball).]

Auf-schlag-ball (–⏑–⏑) m ⓖ Tennis: ser-

*****auf-schlagen** zu II: Tennis: to serve.

Auf-schlag-linie (–⏑–⏑) f ⓖ Tennis: service-line; innere ~ service side-line; =**spiel** n Tennis: service. [label.]

Auf-schrift-zettel (–⏑–⏑) m ⓖ ticket,

Auf-sichts-beamte(r) (–⏑–⏑) m ⓖ, =**beamtin** f supervisor; =**dame** f, =**herr** m in Kaufhäusern shop-walker; *=**rat** b) (Person) director.

*****auf-stellen** zu 14: e-n Rekord: to set, to establish, to constitute.

*****auf-treten** zu 13: Bühnenanweisung: ... tritt auf, ... treten auf enter ...

Auf-wärts-haken (–⏑–⏑) m ⓖ Boxen: uppercut. [foot down.]

*****auf-trumpfen** zu 1: fig. to put one's

auf-werten (–⏑–⏑) v/a. ⓖ ** to revalorize, to revalue. [revaluation.]

Auf-wertung (–⏑–⏑) f ⓖ revalorization,

*****Auge** zu 5: F et. fürs ~ (Blendwerk) F eyewash, window-dressing; dem Tod ins ~ sehen to stare at death.

*****aus-bleichen** zu I: nicht 2d v. Farben: fadeless, unfading.

*****aus-drücken** zu I3: Zigarette im Aschbecher: to mushroom.

aus-dünnen (–⏑⏑) v/a. ⓖ ** Pflanzen od. Haare: to thin out.

*****Aus-fahrt** zu 2: ⚓ e-s Hafens: mouth.

Aus-fall-straße (–⏑–⏑...) f ⓖ (aus der Innenstadt zum Weichbild führende Hauptverkehrsstraße) arterial road. [=stelle.]

*****Aus-gabe-büro** n = Ausgabe=schalter,

*****aus-gehen** zu I6: gut (schlecht, unglücklich usw.) 2 to turn out well (ill, disastrously, &c).

*****aus-genommen** zu II: ... nicht 2 not excepting ...

aus-gestoßen (–⏑–⏑) I p.p. v. ausstoßen. — II a. ⓖ, **Aus-gestoßene(r)** ⓖ outcast.

*****Aus-gleich** Sport: (~ der Spiel= usw. stärke) handicap; Tennis: (Einstand) deuce.

*****aus-gleichen** zu I: Sport: die Spiel= usw. stärke: to handicap; ausgeglichen v. Charakter usw.: equable, level.

Aus-gleich-getriebe ⓞ (–⏑–⏑...) n ⓖ mot. differential (gear); =**hebel** ⓞ m ⓖ equalizer. [Office.]

Aus-gleichs-amt (–⏑–⏑) n ⓖ Clearing

Aus-gleichs-stern ⓞ (–⏑–⏑) m ⓖ mot. differential spider.

Aus-guß-eimer (–⏑–⏑) m ⓖ slop-pail.

Aus-hilfe-mädchen (–⏑–⏑...) n ⓖ between-maid. [gen) to scale (off).]

*****aus-klopfen** ⓞ Kessel: (v. Kesselstein reini-

aus-knobeln 2. = austüfteln.

*****aus-koppeln** Radio: to tune out.

Aus-kunfts-beamte(r) (–⏑–⏑...) m ⓖ, =**beamtin** f inquiry clerk. Fernspr. information operator; =**stelle** f inquiry office.

Aus-lands-deutsche(r) (–⏑–⏑) m, f ⓖ German (woman) living abroad; =**reise** f outward journey or voyage.

Aus-laß-ventil ⓞ (–⏑–⏑) n ⓖ exhaust valve. [run.]

*****Aus-lauf** zu 2: für Käfigtiere usw.: outlet,

Aus-lauf-platz (–⏑–⏑) m ⓖ = dem vorigen.

*****aus-laufen** zu I (sich verwischen) v. Farbe: to blot, to blur.

Aus-leihe-bibliothek (–⏑–⏑...) f ⓖ e-r großen öffentlichen Bücherei: lending library. [release, phot. a. trigger.]

Aus-löser ⓞ (–⏑–⏑) m ⓖ mach., phot.

Aus-lösungs-hebel ⓞ (–⏑–⏑...) m ⓖ = Auslöser.

Aus-maß (–⏑) n ⓖ a. measurement(s pl.), dimension(s pl.); fig. extent; in weitem ~ to a great extent.

aus-puffen ⓞ (–⏑–⏑) v/a. ⓖ ** mach. to exhaust.

Aus-puff-gas (–⏑–⏑) n ⓖ mot. exhaust gas, burnt gas; =**klappe** f, mot. (exhaust or muffler) cut-out; =**leitung** f, mot. exhaust manifold; =**rohr** n exhaust pipe; =**topf** m, mot. silencer, Am. muffler; =**ventil** n exhaust valve.

*****aus-räumen** zu II: fig. Schwierigkeiten usw.: to remove, to clear away.

*****aus-scheiden** zu III3: to drop out, to retire (beide a. im Sport).

Aus-scheidungs-kampf (–⏑–⏑) m ⓖ, =**spiel** n Sport: eliminating-bout.

*****aus-schlachten** 2. F fig. (ausnutzen) to exploit, to turn to account.

*****aus-schließen** zu II1: Sport: to disqualify; (zeitweilig 2) to suspend.

Aus-schließung, **Aus-schluß** zu 1: Sport: disqualification; (zeitweilige[r] ~) suspension.

*****aus-schwärmen** zu I1: ⚔ 2 lassen to extend; ausgeschwärmte Schützenlinie extended order.

*****aus-seilen** (–⏑–⏑) v/a. u. v/refl. (sich 2) ⓖ ** mount. to unrope.

Außen-aufnahme (–⏑–⏑) f ⓖ Film: auf ~ on location; =**bord-motor** ⚓ m outboard (or detachable) motor; =**politik** f foreign policy; =**politisch** a. ⓖ of (or pertaining to or referring to, adv. with regard to) foreign policy; =**seiter** m ⓖ Rennsport: outsider (a. fig.). [on the face of it.]

*****äußerlich** zu I1: schon rein 2 betrachtet

*****aus-setzen** zu I1: mot. to misfire.

Aus-setzer ⓞ (–⏑–⏑) m ⓖ mot. misfire.

*****aus-spannen** zu I2: F fig. e-m et. 2 (entwenden) to relieve a p. of a th.

Aus-sparung (–⏑–⏑) f ⓖ 1. leaving free or open. — 2. (Lücke) hollow.

*****aus-spucken** fig. Geld: (= zahlen müssen) to cough up. [fitment.]

*****Aus-stattungs-stück** 2. (Möbelstück usw.)

*****aus-stehen** zu I 2 b): noch 2 to be lacking or expected. [decided.]

*****Aus-trag** zu 2: zum ~ kommen to be

*****aus-tragen** zu I6: Sport: to decide.

*****aus-treten** zu I: pol., eccl. to secede (aus from). — zu I: (seine Notdurft verrichten) to relieve nature.

Aus-tritts-pupille (–⏑–⏑) f ⓖ opt. exit pupil.

*****Aus-übung** zu 1: e-s Berufes: practice.

*****aus-wählen** zu I: das Beste unter vielem: to select. [select team.]

Aus-wahl-mannschaft (–⏑–⏑...) f ⓖ Sport:

aus-wechselbar (–⏑–⏑) a. ⓖ interchangeable. [deport.]

*****aus-weisen** zu I: lästige Ausländer: to

*****Aus-weisung** zu 1: lästiger Ausländer: deportation.

aus-werten (–⏑–⏑) v/a. ⓖ ** 1. (dem Werte nach bestimmen) to evaluate. — 2. (ausnützen) to make full use of.

Aus-wertung (–⏑–⏑) f ⓖ (s. auswerten) 1. evaluation. — 2. using to the full.

*****aus-wirken** III v/refl. (sich 2) 5. Maßnahme usw.: to operate. [out.]

*****aus-zählen** 4. parl. u. Boxen: to count

*****Auto**²: sich im ~ mitnehmen l. to hitch-hike.

autogen ⟳ (–⏑–⏑) [grch.] a. ⓖ med. u. ⓞ autogenous.

Automaten-restaurant (–⏑–⏑...) n ⓖ self-service restaurant.

Auto(mobil)-falle (⏑⏑..., –⏑–⏑...) f ⓖ police-trap; =**garage** f motor-garage; =**sport** m motoring, automobilism; =**steuer** f motor car duty.

Autosuggestion ⟳ (–⏑⏑⏑(⏑)–⏑) [grch.=lat.] f ⓖ auto-suggestion.

*****Autotypie** half-tone (engraving). — 2. (Druckverfahren) autotypy, half-tone printing. [Ausgang) autocide.

Autounfall (⏑⏑...) m ⓖ c.: ~ mit tödlichem

Averbo ⟳ (–⏑⏑–) [lt.] n ⓖ gram. principal parts pl. of a verb.

Azetat-seide ⓞ (–⏑⏑–⏑...) f ⓖ acetate silk.

B

Baby-ausstattung (bēˮbĭ...) f ⊕ = Säuglingsausstattung.
Bade-kappe (ᴗ–...) f ⊕ bathing cap; **-laken** n bath-sheet; **-ofen** m bathing-stove; (Gas²) geyser; **-trikot** n bathing tricot.
***Bahn** zu 5: Rennsport: track.
Bahn-übergang ⚂ (ᴗ–...) m ⊕ railway-crossing.
Bakelit ⊙ (–ᴗ–) [Baekeland, Entdecker] n ⊕c. (dem Hartkautschuk ähnliches Kunstprodukt) bakelite.
Bakkarat (ᴗᴗᴗ) [fr.] n ⊕e. baccara(t).
Balgen² (–ᴗ) [Balg] m ㉓ phot. bellows.
***Ballen¹** 6. path. (entzündliche Schwellung am Fuß) bunion.
Ball-junge (–...) m ⊕ Tennis: ball-boy; **-mutter** f chaperon.
Ballonett (ᴗᴗ–) [fr.] n ⊕d. (Gaszelle e-s lenkbaren Luftschiffes) ballonet.
Ballon-stoff (ᴗᴗᴗ–) m ⊕ (gummierter Baumwollstoff) ballon-fabric.
Bananen-stecker (ᴗ–ᴗᴗ...) m ⊕ elect. spring (contact) plug.
***Band²** zu II 8: ⊙ laufendes ~ running belt, conveyor. — zu II: mount. (Felsleiste) ledge.
Banden-mitglied (–ᴗᴗ...) n ⊕ member of a gang (of criminals), Am. gangster.
Banderole (ᴗᴗ–ᴗ) [fr.] f ⊕ Steuerwesen: revenue stamp.
Bandonion ♪ (–ᴗ[ᴗ]ᴗ) [Band, Erfinder] n ㉘ u. ㊵ (Art Handharmonika) concertina.
Bange-macher (–ᴗᴗ...) m ⊕ alarmist, panic-monger.
***Bank²-ausweis** bank(ing) (or bank's) return; **-geheimnis** n ⊕ banker's discretion.
Bantam-gewicht ☨ (–ᴗᴗ...) [engl.] n ⊕ Boxen: bantam-weight.
Bar-geld (–...) n ⊕ cash, ready money; **²geld-los** ⊙ a. ⊕ cashless.
***barock** arch. baroque. — II n ㊿ (Kunststil des 17. Jahrhunderts) baroque.
Bar-scheck (–ᴗ) m ⊕ cash-cheque.
Barsoi (ᴗ–) [russ.] m ㊱ zo. (russ. Windhund) borzoi. [or dead) loss.⎦
Bar-verlust ☨ (ᴗ–...) m ⊕ clear (or net
***basteln** ⊙ v/a. (mit kleinen Mitteln zs.-bauen) to tinker (up), to rig up.
Bastler (–ᴗ) m ⊕ trifler; (der etwas mit kleinen Mitteln zs.-baut) one who rigs up an apparatus &c., amateur (constructor).
Batik (–ᴗ) [malaiisch] m ⊕ (indischer Baumwollstoff mit unregelmäßigem Farbdruckmuster; das Farbdruckmuster; das Verfahren) batik.
batiken v/a. ⊕ to batik.
Bau¹ zu 1: im ~ under construction.
***Bauch** zu 2: F j-m ein Loch in den ~ fragen to pump a p. dry.
bauch-reden (–ᴗ–) v/n. (h.) ⊕** to ventriloquize. [ant proprietor.⎦
Bauern-guts-besitzer (–ᴗᴗ–ᴗ...) m ⊕ peas-
Bau-gelände (–ᴗ–...) n ⊕ building land; **-gelder** n/pl. building funds pl.; **-genossenschaft** f (benefit) building society; **-ingenieur** m constructional engineer; **-land** n = **-gelände**.
Baum-grenze ♀ (–ᴗ...) f ⊕ timber-line.
Bau-polizei (–ᴗᴗ–) f ⊕ Board of Surveyors; **²reif** a. ⊕ developed; ² machen

to develop; noch nicht ² undeveloped; **-tätigkeit** f building activity; **-wächter** m watchman (of a new building).
Bazillen-träger ⚕ (ᴗ–ᴗ...) m ⊕ med. carrier.
be-achtlich (ᴗ–ᴗ) a. ⊕ = beachtenswert.
***Be-achtung** (Befolgung) observance.
Be-amten-wirtschafts-verein (ᴗ–ᴗ...) m ⊕ Civil Service Co-operative Stores pl.
***be-bildern** to illustrate.
Becken zu 1: c) e-s Klosetts: bowl, flushing-pan.
***Be-darf²** zu 1: ~ haben an (dat.) to require, to want, to need; nach ~ according to requirements, when needed.
Be-darfs-artikel (ᴗ–ᴗ...) m ⊕ article of consumption; pl. necessaries, necessities, requisites. [nience.⎦
***Be-dürfnis-anstalt** public conve-
***Be-fehl** zu 1a: ~ haben et. zu tun to have orders to do a th.
***be-frieden** 3. ein Land: to pacify.
Be-friedung (ᴗ–ᴗ) f ⊕ e-s Landes: pacification. [timed.⎦
be-fristet (ᴗ–ᴗ) a. ⊕ limited in time,
Be-gehrtheit (ᴗ–ᴗ) f ⊕ desiredness.
Be-gleit-adresse ⚓ (ᴗ–ᴗ...) f ⊕ way-bill.
be-griffs-stutzig (ᴗ–ᴗ...) a. ⊕ puzzle-headed. [(ᴗ–ᴗ...) emergency.⎦
be-helfs-mäßig (ᴗ–ᴗ) a. ⊕, **Be-helfs-**...
Bein-arbeit (–ᴗ...) f ⊕ Sport: foot-work.
***Bei-trag** zu 2: (Mitgliedsbeitrag) subscription.
***Bei-wagen** 2. des Motorrades: side-car.
***Beize** zu 2: Kocht. pickle.
Be-kenntnis-schule (ᴗ–ᴗ...) f ⊕ denominational school. [to bait.⎦
be-ködern (ᴗ–ᴗ) v/a. ⊕a. * Angel, Falle:
***Be-lang** 2. pl. ~e interests pl. [taint.⎦
***Be-lastung:** path. erbliche ~ hereditary
***Be-legschaft** 2. e-r Fabrik usw.: personnel, workers pl.
Be-leg-schein (ᴗ–⎯) m ⊕ voucher.
***Be-leuchtungs-körper** (Kronleuchter usw.) (light) fixture, pl. oft (light) fittings; **-kosten** pl. lighting charges pl.
Be-lichtungs-messer (ᴗ–ᴗ...) m ⊕ phot. exposure-meter.
be-liefern (ᴗ–ᴗ) v/a. ⊕a. * to supply, to provide, to furnish (mit with).
***be-messen** zu 1: zeitlich: to time.
be-mustern ⚓ (ᴗ–ᴗ) v/a. ⊕a. * Angebot, Waren: to sample; j-n: to send samples to. [line, (motor) spirit.⎦
***Benzin** mot. petrol, bsd. Am. gaso-
Benzin-motor ⊙ (ᴗ–...) m ⊕ mot. petrol-engine.
***be-ob-achten** zu I 1: polizeilich: to shadow.
Be-ob-achtungs-ballon ✈ (ᴗᴗ–ᴗ...) m ⊕ observation balloon; **-station** f im Krankenhaus: observation ward.
Be-ratungs-stelle (ᴗ–ᴗ...) f ⊕ Advisory Board. [Abteilung der Polizei) squad.⎦
***Be-reitschaft** 2. (mit pl.) (dienstgabende
***Berg** zu 2: fig. über den ~ kommen (die Schwierigkeiten überwinden) to turn the corner.
Berg-arbeiter-verband ⚒ (–ᴗ...) m ⊕ Miners' Federation; ²baulich a. ⊕ of (or pertaining to) mines, mining; **-krankheit** f path. mountain-sickness; **-rennen** n, mot. hill-climbing

contest; **-seil** n, mount. Alpine rope
***-steiger** c) mot. (Kraftwagentyp) hill -climber; ²**steigerisch** a. ⊕ mountaineering; **-stütze** ⊙ f ⊕ am Wagen: sprag; **-tour** f mount. climb.
***Be-rieselungs-anlage** zum Löschen von Bränden: sprinkler.
***Berta:** ⚔ dicke ~ (schwerer deutscher Mörser im Weltkriege 1914-1918) Big Bertha.
***Be-ruf** zu 1: von ~ by profession.
Be-rufs-beratung (ᴗ–ᴗ...) f ⊕ vocational guidance; **-fahrer** m Radfahrsport: professional (cyclist); mot. professional (driver); **-schule** f vocational (or occupational) school; **-spieler** m Sport: professional (ant. Amateur); ²**tätig** a. ⊕ employed in an occupation or calling. [(in dat. of).⎦
Be-schlagenheit (ᴗ–ᴗ–) f ⊕ experience
be-schriften (ᴗ–ᴗ) v/a. ⊕* to inscribe.
Be-schriftung (ᴗ–ᴗ) f ⊕ inscription, e-r Münze: legend; e-r Illustration: caption. [squiffy.⎦
be-schwipst F (ᴗ–) a. ⊕ fuddled, tipsy,
Be-segelung (ᴗ–ᴗᴗ) f ⊕ Segelsport: sail outfit.
***be-sorgen** zu I 2: Mittag(brot) ² to provide (for) dinner. — zu I: = beschaffen 1; ⚔ sl. sich et. ² (irgendwo wegnehmen) to scrounge.
***besser** zu 5: er ist doch et. ²es he is a superior man. [-taking.⎦
Be-stands-aufnahme (ᴗ–ᴗ...) f ⊕ stock-
***be-stäuben** zu 1: ♀ (befruchten) to pollinate.
***Be-stäubung** ♀ (Befruchtung) pollination.
Be-stell-gang (ᴗ–ᴗ...) m ⊕ delivery; **-schein** ⚓ m order-form. [rays.⎦
***be-strahlen** zu 1: med. to treat with
***Be-strahlung** med. ray treatment.
be-streifen (ᴗ–ᴗ) v/a. ⊕* to fight an undertaking with a strike, to strike.
***Be-streitung** zu 1: jur. allgemeine ~ (e-r Klageschrift) joinder of issue.
Beta-strahlen ☢ (–ᴗ...) [grch.] m/pl. ⊕ phys. beta-rays pl.
Be-tätigungs-hebel ⊙ (ᴗ–ᴗᴗ...) m ⊕ mach. control lever.
***be-teiligen** zu 1: beteiligt an (dat.) interested (or concerned) in.
***Beton:** armierter ~ reinforced concrete.
***Be-trieb¹** zu 2: den ~ schließen to close (or shut) down; den ~ wiederaufnehmen to reopen; in ~ at work, in operation, working, running; in ~ setzen to put ... in operation, to set ... working or going, to start. — 3. tontr. establishment, (industrial or agricultural) undertaking; (Gewerbe) trade, business; (Werkstatt) (work)shop; (Fabrik) factory, größer: works pl. (oft sg.); separate branch of a factory; lebenswichtiger ~ essential supply service; öffentlicher ~ public utility.
Be-triebs-einstellung (ᴗ–ᴗ...) f ⊕ e-r Fabrik usw.: shut-down; ²**fähig** a. ⊕, ²**fertig** a. ready for service, in working (or running) order; **-fähigkeit** f ⊕ working order; **-koeffizient** m operating ratio; **-leiter** m ma ager; ~rat m a) (Ausschuß) works council, shop committee; b) (Person) shop steward or deputy; ²**sicher** a. ⊕ reliable (in operation), foolproof; **-sicherheit** f ⊕

Betriebsstoff reliability (of operation); =stoff m mot. combustible (material); =wirtschaft f organized economy, industrial administration; =wirtschafts=lehre f doctrine (or science) of industrial administration.

Be-völkerungs-abnahme (⌣⌣⌣...) f ② decrease of population.

Be-währungs=frist (⌣⌣...) f jur. probation.

*be-zahlen zu I 1: gekaufte Ware: to pay for.

*be-ziehen zu I: Zeitung: to take in.

*Be-zug 3. ⊛ procuring or obtaining of goods, supply; e-r Zeitung: subscription (to); bei ~ von 100 Stück on orders for 100. [drayman.⟩

Bier=fahrer (⌣...) m ②, =kutscher m⟩

Bilanz verschleierung (⌣⌣...) f ② jur. cooking (or doctoring or faking) of balances.

Bild=brief(⌣...) m ② tel. = =telegramm; =brief=sender m, tel. = =telegraph; =karte f Kartenspiel: court-card; =(rund)funk m Radio: wireless picture transmission; =sendung f, tel. = übertragung; =telegramm n, tel. picture telegram, ↻ telautogram; =telegraph m, tel. picture telegraph, ↻ telautograph or phototelegraph or telescriptor; =telegraphie f, tel. picture telegraphy, ↻ telautography or phototelegraphy; =übertragung f, tel. picture transmission.

*binden zu V 10: man ist durch Kinder usw. sehr gebunden children &c. are a great tie.

Binde=strich=amerikaner (⌣⌣...) m ② hyphenated American (z.B. German--American).

*Bindung Stijsport: binding.

Bio-chemie ↻ (-⌣⌣-ˊ) [grch.] f ② (heilkundlich auf Lebensvorgänge angewendete Chemie) biochemistry. [chemist.⟩

Bio-chemiker ↻ (-⌣⌣⌣⌣) m ② bio-⟩

bio-chemisch ↻ (-⌣⌣⌣) a. ⑥ biochemical.

*Birne zu 3: elect. bulb.

*blank zu 1: ⚔ ℒe Waffe white arm.

blank=gescheuert (⌣...) a. ⑥, =getragen a. v. Anzug: glossy, shiny.

Blanko=vollmacht (⌣...) f ② jur. unlimited power.

Blau=beutel (⌣...) m ② (Beutel mit Waschblau) blue-bag; =stift m blue pencil.

*blechern v. Klang: tinny.

*bleiben zu I 4: Fernspr. in der Leitung ℒ to hold the line.

Blei=stift=hülse (⌣...) f ② pencil-point-protector.

Blend=anstrich ⚔ (⌣...) m ② camouflage; ↓ dazzle-paint(ing); mit ~ versehen to camouflage; ↓ to dazzle-paint.

Blick=fang (⌣ˊ) m ② eye-catcher.

Blinden=führer=hund (⌣⌣...) m ② blind man's dog; =schrift f lettering for the blind.

Blink=licht (⌣...) n ② flash light; =zeichen n flash signal; ~ geben to flash.

Blitz=pfeil ⊙ (⌣...) m ② elect. danger arrow; =schutz m, tel. lightning arrester.

*Block 6. parl. (Verbindung mehrerer Parteien zu einem bestimmten Zweck) bloc.

*blocken² ⚒ to block.

*blockieren zu I: ⚒ to block.

Block=kondensator ⊙ (⌣...) m ② elect. block(ing) (or stopping or fixed) condenser. [pressure.⟩

Plut=druck (⌣ˊ) m ② physiol. blood⟩

Bob(sleigh) ⊤ (ℒ(-) [engl.] m ⑩ Wintersport: (Mannschaftsrennschlitten mit Steuerung) bobsleigh. [pl. of the soil.⟩

Boden=schätze (⌣⌣...) m/pl. ② treasures⟩

bogen=bildend (⌣⌣...) a. ⑥ elect. arcing.

Bohn(er)=schrubber (⌣(⌣)...) m ② floor--polisher. [shevik.⟩

Bolschewik (⌣⌣) [russ.] m ② pol. Bol-⟩

bolschewisieren (⌣⌣-ˊ⌣) v/a ⑨ pol. to bolshevize. [Bolshevism.⟩

Bolschewismus (⌣⌣⌣⌣) [russ.] m ② pol.⟩

Bolschewist (⌣⌣ˊ) m ②, ~in (⌣⌣⌣) f ④⟩ pol. Bolshevist. [shevist(ic).⟩

bolschewistisch (⌣⌣⌣) a. ⑥ pol. Bol-⟩

Bomben=flugzeug ⚔ (⌣...) n ② bomber; =überfall ⚔ m bombing-raid; =werfer ⚔ m (Person u. Maschine) bomb-thrower.

Bord=funker ⚔ u. ⚓ (⌣...) m ② wireless officer; =funk=stelle ⚔ u. ⚓ f ship radio station; =monteur ⚔ m air-mechanic. [ointment.⟩

Bor=salbe (⌣...) f ② pharm. boric⟩

Bourgeoisie (būr-ğoa-fiˊ) [frz.] f ⑤ pol. bour-⟩

*Bourgeois pol. bourgeois. [geoisie.⟩

Box=handschuh (⌣...) m ② boxing glove.

Brause=limonade=würfel (⌣⌣...) m ② sparklet. [tail.⟩

Breit=schwanz ⚔ (⌣ˊ) m ② (Pelzart) broad-⟩

Brems=ausgleich ⊙ (⌣...) m ② mot. brake equalizer; =fuß=hebel ⊙ m, mot. brake pedal; =leistung f, mech. braking efficiency. [a pancake⟩

*Brett zu 9: flach wie ein ~ as flat as⟩

Brief=kasten (Zeitungsrubrik) Question and Answer Column; =kurs ⚹ m Börse: selling (or asked) rate; =locher m file-punch, perforator; =öffner m letter-opener; =ordner m letter-file; =tasche zu a): letter-case, wallet; =telegramm ⚹ n night telegraph letter, Am. lettergram; =trägerin f postwoman. [high explosive.⟩

Brisanz=pulver ⚔ (-⌣...) n ② artill.⟩

*Broschüre zu 1: brochure; ⚹ booklet.

*Bruch² zu 1: ⚒ ~ machen to crash.

Bruch=festigkeit (⌣...) f ② mech. ultimate (or bursting) stress, breaking load; =strich m, arith. fraction line, fraction stroke.

*Brücke 4. Zahnheilkunde: bridge(-work).

Brunft=schrei (⌣ˊ) m ② hunt. bell.

Brust=schwimmen (⌣...) n ② breast--stroke.

Buben=, Bubi=kopf (⌣⌣...) m ② (am Hinterkopf kurz) shingled hair; (Pagenkopf) bobbed hair; j-m e-n ~ schneiden to shingle (or bob) a p.'s hair.

Buch=drama (⌣...) n ② (das nicht bühnenfähig ist) closet-play; =eigner=zeichen n book-plate.

*Bücher=schrank: aus einzelnen Abteilungen zs.=setzbarer ~ sectional (or expanding) book-case; =stütze f book-end.

*Buch=halterei, =haltung 2. (Raum) Counting House, Accountancy Department; =haltungs=maschine ⚹ f book-keeping (or accounting) machine; =kunst f book(-printing) art; =messe f book(-trade) fair.

Bügel=falte(⌣...)f ② Schneiderei: crease.

*Bühne zu 1: zur ~ gehen (Schauspieler werden) to go on the stage.

Bühnen=größe (⌣...) f ② star of the stage; =inspizient m. thea. stage-manager; =licht n limelight; =stern m = =größe.

*bullern (Feuer im) Ofen: to roar.

bündeln² (⌣⌣) [Bündel] v/a. ⑨a. to bundle (up), a. to bunch (together).

*Bürger=kunde civics pl. u. sg.

Büro(bedarfs)artikel (bü-rōˊ...) m/pl. ② office appliances pl.; =klammer f paper-clip; =möbel n/pl. office furniture. [mit brassière.⟩

Büsten=halter (⌣...) m ② bust bodice,⟩

Butter=brot=papier (⌣...) n ② (fettdicht) grease-proof paper; =kugel f butter--pat; =sauce f Kocht. melted butter; =stecher m Scotch hand.

C

Chassis ⊙ (scha-si') [fr.] m ㉓ (Rahmen, Fahrgestell) chassis.

Chaussee=floh ⦃ (schō-sē'ˊ) m ② (daherrasender Motorfahrer usw.) road-hog.

Chef-arzt (schēˊf⌣) m ② Medical Superintendent. [=number.⟩

Chiffre=nummer (schiˊf=⌣⌣...) f ② box-⟩

*chinesisch zu 1: Ces Papier India paper.

Chiropraktik ↻ (ch-⌣⌣⌣) [grch.] f ⑨ med. (Heilung von Krankheiten durch Behandlung des Rückgrates mit besonderen Handgriffen) chiropractic; ~er (ch-⌣⌣⌣) m ② chiropractor.

chiropraktisch ↻ (ch-⌣⌣⌣) a. ⑥ chiropractic(ally adv.).

D

Dach-antenne (⌣...) f ② Radio: outdoor aerial; =garten m roof-garden; =gesellschaft ⚹ f holding company.

Daktylographie ↻ (⌣⌣⌣-fiˊ) [grch.] f ② (Studium der Fingerabdrücke) dactylography.

Daktyloskopie ↻ (⌣⌣⌣⌣-ˊ) [grch.] f ② (Fingerabdruckverfahren) dactyloscopy.

Damen=binde (⌣...) f ② sanitary towel; =doppel(=spiel) n Tennis: women's doubles pl.; =einzel(=spiel) n Tennis: women's singles pl.; =mannschaft f Sport: women's team.

*Damm zu 2: fig. auf dem ~ sein to be all right, to feel up to it.

*dämmern zu I 2: fig. es dämmert bei ihm it is beginning to dawn on him.

Dämmer=schlaf (⌣...) m ② med. um das Gebären schmerzlos zu machen: twilight sleep; =schoppen m sundowner.

*Dämpfung 3. ⚓ stabilization.

Dämpfungs=fläche ⚓ (⌣...) f ②, =flosse ⚓ f stabilizer.

*dänisch: ⚹ Ces Butter Kiel butter.

*dar-stellen zu 12 b): aus e-r Verbindung to liberate, to disengage. — zu 13: Filmwesen: bsd. die Hauptrolle ℒ to feature; graphisch ℒ (als Kurve usw.) to plot; schematisch ℒ to skeletonize.

*Dar-stellung zu 2: liberation, disengagement. — zu 3: graphische ~ (als Kurve usw.) plotting.

*darüber zu IV: fig. ℒ geht nichts! that is the limit!

dasein — 8 — Edelvaluta

*da-sein zu I: noch nie dagewesen unprecedented.
Dauer-ausstellung (ᵘ⸍…) f ② permanent exhibition; =betrieb m continuous running; =fahrer m Rennsport: stayer; =fahrt f Sport: endurance run, long-distance trial; =karte f season-ticket; =lauf m endurance run; =läufer(in f) m stayer; =rennen n Sport: =fahrt; =wellen f/pl. im Haar: permanent waves pl.; (Herstellung f von) ~ permanent waving; mit ~ permanent(ly) waved; sich ~ machen lassen, ~ tragen to have one's hair permanent(ly) waved.
Daumen-abdruck (ᵘ⸍…) m ② zu polizeilichen Erkennungszwecken: thumb-print; =lutscher m im Märchen: suck-a-thumb.
Dawes-gut-achten (dāˊf…) [Dawes, amerikan. Finanzmann] ② Dawes Report; =plan m (1924 aufgestellter Plan zur Zahlung der deutschen Weltkriegsentschädigungen) Dawes Plan.
Deck-adresse ⚓ (ᵘ⸍…) f ② cover (address).
*Decke zu 1: mot. e-s Luftreifens: cover, [shoe.]
Defaitismus, Defätismus (-fā̆ˊ) [fr.] m ㉗ (Flaumacherei) defeatism.
Defaitist, Defätist (-fā̆ˊ) [fr.] m ② (Flaumacher) defeatist.
Deflation (--tß(ᵛ)ˊ) [lt.] f ㊻ der Währung: deflation (ant. Inflation).
Deformation (-ᵛ-tß(ᵛ)ˊ) [lt.] f ㊻ (Verunstaltung) deformation.
deformieren (-ᵛ⸍ᴸᵛ) [lt.] v/a. ㊳ (verunstalten) to deform.
Deformierung (-ᵛ⸍ᴸᵛ) f ㊻ deformation.
deichseln P (⸍tɞˇ) [Deichsel²] v/a. ㊳a. (zustande bringen) to wangle.
Depeschen-büro (-ᵋ⸍…) n ② dispatch-agency.
Depolarisation ⚡ (-ᵛ-ᵛᵛtß(ᵛ)ˊ) [lt.] f ㊺ opt., elect. depolarization.
depolarisieren ⚡ (-ᵛ-ᵛᴸᵛ) v/a. ㊳ opt., elect. to depolarize.
*Depositen-kasse branch-office of a bank; =konto n deposit-account.
*Depot zu 1 a): Bankwesen: deposit.
Derby ⚡ (dŏˊrbi) [engl. St.] n ㊽㊾ (Pferderennen) derby; =sieger m ② derby-winner. [empfänger.]
Detektor (-ᵋ⸍) [lt.] m ② Radio: (Wellen=)
*deuteln II v/n. ㉒ an (dat.) = v/a.
*Deutschtum: Verein für das ~ im Auslande Society for Germans living abroad.
Devisen-bank ⚡ (-wᵘ⸍ᵋ) f ② bank allowed to conduct transactions in foreign exchange.
Diapositiv ⚡ (ᵛᵛ-ᴸ⸍f) [grch.-lt.] n ②d. phot. (positives Durchscheinbild) lantern slide.
Diathermie ⚡ (ᵛᵛᵛᴸ) [grch.] f ㊸ phys., med. (Wärmedurchdringung) diathermy.
*Dichtung¹ mach. packing; bsd. Rohrlegerei: gasket.
*dick zu 7: ⚓ sl. es ist ²e Luft there is a great wind up, there is a (vertical) breeze.
Dienst-gewehr ⚔ (ᵘ⸍) n ② service rifle; =herrin f mistress; =pistole ⚔ f service pistol.
Diesel-motor ⊕ (ᵘ⸍…) [Diesel, deutscher Erfinder] m ② mach. ⚡ Diesel engine.

*Differential: mot. = ⸗getriebe.
Diktier=maschine (ᵛᵘ…) f ② dictating machine. [dioxide.]
Dioxyd ⚡ (-ᵛˊ) [grch.] n ②d. chm.
*Direktive rule.
*Diskont Bankwesen: den ~ erhöhen, herabsetzen to raise, lower the bank-rate. [cus-throw(ing).]
Diskus=werfen (ᵋ⸍…) n ② Sport: dis-
*Disposition: ⚔ zur ~ stellen to place an officer on half-pay.
Dollen=boot ⚓ (ᵋᵋᴸ) n ② rowlock-boat (ant. Auslegerboot).
dopen ⚡ (ᴸᵛ) [engl.] v/a. ㊸ Sport: (durch Nervenmittel anreizen) to dope.
*Doppel 2. Tennis: = Doppel=spiel.
Doppel=decker ✈ (ᵋ⸍…) m ② biplane; =kapsel ⊕ f der Taschenuhr: hunting-case; =kapsel=uhr ⊕ f hunter; =kopf=hörer m Radio: (ein = a pair of) head-phones pl., head-set; ²motorig ✈ twin-engined; *²reihig Jackett: double-breasted; =ruder n Sport: paddle; ²seitig a. ㊺ double-sided; Gewebe, Teppich usw. reversible; med. ²e Lungenentzündung double pneumonia; =skuller ⚓ m ② Rudern: double scull; =spiel n Tennis: doubles pl.; =gemischtes ~ mixed doubles pl.; =stecker ⊕ m, elect. double plug, two-way plug adapter.
Dosen-öffner (ᵘ⸍…) m ② tin-opener.
Draht=funk (ᵘ⸍…) m Radio: wired wireless; =lehre ⊕ f wire gauge; =verhau ⚔ m = ⸗hindernis.
Dreh=blei=stift (ᵘ⸍…) m ② propelling pencil; =buch n Filmwesen: scenario, script; =bühne f, thea. rotatory (or revolving) stage.
*drehen zu I 4: e-n Film: to shoot.
Dreh=kondensator (ᵘ⸍…) m ⚡ elect. rotating plate condenser, variable condenser; =moment n, mech. torque; =schalter m elect. rotary switch; =zapfen ⊕ m trunnion.
*Drei=decker ⚓ triplane; ²eckig (ᵋ⸍…) ²es Verhältnis in e-r Ehe triangular situation; =gestirn n three companion stars pl.; ²jährig Rennsport: Rennen n für Dreijährige three-year-old race; =kampf m Leichtathletik: triathlon; =röhren-apparat m Radio: three-valve (wireless) set; =satz=kampf m Tennis: three-set match; ²stellig a. ㊺ of three places; ²e Zahl a. three-figure number.
dribbeln ⚡ (ᵋ⸍…) [engl.] v/n. ㉒a. Fußball: (den Ball vor sich hertreiben) to dribble.
*dringen zu I 3: auf Antwort ² to press for an answer; auf Maßnahmen usw. ² to urge measures, &c.
Droschken=auto (ᵋ⸍…) n ② taxi(-cab); =chauffeur m taxi-man.
*Drossel² ⊕ mach. = ⸗klappe; elect. = ⸗spule, a. choke.
Drossel=spule ⊕ (ᵋ⸍…) f ② elect. choking coil, inductance.
Drosselung ⊕ (ᵋᵛᵛ) f ㊻ = Drossel-klappe, ⸗spule.
*Druck¹ zu 4: Dampf unter ~ live steam.
*drücken zu I: Sport: e-n Rekord: to lower.
Druck=fehler=teufel (ᵋ⸍…) m ② printer's devil; *=knopf am Kleid: press button, press fastener, snap fastener; am

Handschuh: glove-dome; elect. push-button; =posten ⚔ sl. m funk-hole; =schmierung ⊕ f, mach. force-feed lubrication, pressure-feed l. [(unfit).]
d. u. ⚔ abbr. (= dauernd untauglich) C 3
Dublee (-ᴸˊ) [fr.] n ㊿ 1. ⊕ = ~=gold. — 2. Billard: double.
Dublee=gold ⊕ (-ᵘᴸ) n ② rolled gold.
*Dublette hunt. right-and-left (shot).
Dünge=salze (ᵋᵛ…) n/pl. ② agr. manure salts pl.
Dünn=druck=papier (ᵋ⸍…) n ② typ. thin printing paper; für Wertpapiere usw. bond-paper.
*Dunst zu 1: Wetterkunde: haze.
*dunsten, dünsten zu II: Eier: to poach.
Dünster (ᵋᵛ) m für Eier: poacher.
Duralumin(ium) ⊕ (ᵘ-ᴸ⸍[(ᵛ)⸍]) [lt.] n ⓑ o. pl. (dauerhaftes Aluminium, bsd. zum Bau v. Flugzeugen verwendet) duralumin(ium). [to blow, to fuse.]
*durch-brennen zu I: elect. Sicherung:
*Durch-bruch zu 1: bsd. ⚔ break-through.
Durch-bruch=hürde (ᵋᵛᶜʰ…) f ② Rennsport: bullfinch.
Durch-bruchs=schlacht ⚔ (ᵋᵛᶜʰ…) f ② break-through. [dringlich.]
durch-dringbar (ᵋᵛ-) a. ㊺ = durch-
*Durch-dringung: pol. friedliche ~ peaceful penetration.
*durch-fallen zu I 1: ² lassen to reject, thea. to damn.
Durch-führungs=bestimmungen (ᵍᴸᵛ…) f/pl. jur. ~ zu einem Gesetz provisions pl. in execution of a law.
*durch-gängig: ⚡ ²er Preis all-round price.
*durch-gehen zu I 4: ⊕ v. Motor: to race.
*durch-leuchten zu II: mit X-strahlen: to x-ray, to radio(graph).
Durch-leuchtung (ᵍᴸᵛ…) f ㊻ mit X-strahlen: ray examination.
Durch-lochung (ᵋᵛ…) f ㊻ mot., Radsport: des Luftreifens: puncture.
*Durch-querung: ~ des Kanals cross-Channel swim.
durch-rufen (ᵋᴸᵛ) v/n. (h.) ㊲b. ** Fernspr. to ring through.
durch-schalten (ᵋᴸᵛ) v/a. ㊴ ** elect., Fernspr. to connect (or put) through.
*Durch-schlag 4. v. Maschinenschrift: carbon copy; =papier n carbon paper.
durch-schmelzen (ᵍᴸᵛ) v/a. u. v/n. (ſn) ㊳b. ** to melt, to fuse.
*durch-schnittlich zu II: ² betragen to average; kosten, leisten to average.
Durch-schnitts=geschwindigkeit (ᵍᵍ…) f ② average speed.
Durch-schreibe-buch ⚡ (ᵍᴸᵛ…) n ② duplicate book; =buch-führung ⚡ f mechanical (system of) book-keeping.
*Düse allg. ⊕ nozzle; (zum Spritzen) jet.
Dutzend-ware (ᵋᵛ…) f ② article sold by the dozen.

E

Echo-lot (ᵋ…) n ② phys. zu Tiefseemessungen: echo-sounder; =lotung f echo-sounding.
*echt v. Farben: fast, fadeless, unfading.
Edel-obst (ᵘ⸍…) n ② hort. dessert fruit; =valuta ⚡ f high-value currency.

Effekten-abteilung (⌣́⌣̆...) f ② Securities Department of a bank.

ego-zentrisch ⚘ (⌣̆⌣̆́) [lt.] a. ⑥⓪ self-centred, ⚘ egocentric(ally adv.).

ehren-amtlich (⌣́⌣̆...) a. ⑥⓪ honorary; adv. as an honorary official; **bürger-urkunde** f ② city's scroll of honour; **-mal** n cenotaph; **-tafel** ⚔ f roll of honour.

***Ei²** zu 1: kocht. verlorene ⁓er pl. poached eggs pl.

Eier-hand-granate ⚔ (⌣́⌣̆...) f ② egg(-shaped hand-)grenade; britische ⁓ Mills bomb.

Eigen-bedarf (⌣́⌣̆...) m ② one's own needs or requirements pl.; ⁓gebacken a. ⑥⓪ home-made. [-test.]

Eignungs-prüfung (⌣́⌣̆...) f ② aptitude-

Ein¹-bahn-straße (⌣́⌣̆...) f ② (mit Wagenverkehr nur nach einer Richtung) one-way traffic road.

*****Ein²-bauen** zu II allg. to build in; Apparat, Motor usw.: a. to install, fit, fix.

*****Ein²-bruch** ⚘ Börse: setback.

*****Ein-bruch(s)-diebstahl**: Versicherung gegen ⁓ burglary insurance.

*****ein-decken** zu I: Börse: to repurchase, buy in. — v/refl. (sich 2) to lay in stocks.

Ein¹-decker ✈ (⌣́⌣̆...) m ② monoplane.

Ein¹-ehe (⌣́⌣̆...) f ② monogamy.

*****Einer** Rudersport: skiff.

*****Ein-fahrt** zu 2: ⚒ mouth of a shaft, a. collar.

*****Ein-fall** zu 5: glücklicher ⁓ brain-wave.

*****ein-frieren**: ⚘ eingefrorene Kredite m/pl. frozen credits pl.

Ein²-fühlung (⌣́⌣̆...) f ㊵, ⁓s-vermögen n ㊶ Psychologie: empathy.

Ein²-fuhr-schein ⚘ (⌣́⌣̆...) m ② free-import permit.

Ein²-füll-öffnung ⊙ (⌣́⌣̆...) f ② filling-hole; ⁓stutzen ⊙ m, mot. tank filler cap.

ein²-gabeln ⚔ (⌣́⌣̆...) v/a. ②a.** artill. (durch Abgeben eines zu weiten u. eines zu kurzen Schusses sich auf ein Ziel einschießen) to bracket, ⚓ to straddle.

Ein²-gemeindung ⚔ (⌣́⌣̆...) f ㊶ incorporation, communalization.

ein-gezogen 3. ⊙ mot. Der Rahmen inswept frame.

Ein²-glas (⌣́⌣̆...) n ② single eyeglass.

ein²-gliedern (⌣́⌣̆...) v/a. ②a.** to insert (in acc. in[to]), to make a member (of).

Ein¹-heits-preis ⚘ (⌣́⌣̆...) m ② flat (or uniform or standard) price; **-preis-geschäft** ⚘ n uniform price business; **-schule** f standard school; **-staat** m unitary state; **-tarif** m uniform (or standard) tariff.

Ein¹-jährigen-dienst ⚔ (⌣́⌣̆...) m ② ehm.: one year's military service.

Ein¹-jährige(r) F (⌣́⌣̆...) n ⑥⑦ = **Ein-jährig-Freiwilligen-prüfung** f ② examination to qualify for one year's military service.

Ein¹-jährig-Freiwilligen-zeugnis n ② qualification certificate for one year's military service.

Ein¹-kaufs-genossenschaft ⚘ (⌣́⌣̆...) f ② co-operative buying society.

Ein¹-kommen-steuer-erklärung (⌣́⌣̆...) f ② income-tax return; **-steuer-zuschlag** m supertax.

Ein¹-kreis-empfänger (⌣́⌣̆...) m ② Radio: single-circuit receiver, primary receiver. [-kitchen house.]

Ein¹-küchen-haus (⌣́⌣̆...) n ② one-

*****Ein-lage** 5. (gegen Senkfuß) arch-support, instep-raiser, foot-easer.

*****Ein-lauf** 2. med. enema.

Ein²-lauf-tour (⌣́⌣̆...) f ② training-tour, mount. training-climb.

*****ein-lochen** 3. Golf: (a. v/n. [h.]) to put. — II ⁓ n ② Golf: putting.

Ein¹-mast-jacht ⚓ (⌣́⌣̆...) f ② sloop.

ein²-nebeln ⚔ (⌣́⌣̆...) v/a. ②a.** to envelop in (or to cover by) a smoke-screen, to smoke, to screen.

ein¹-polig (⌣́⌣̆...) a. ⑥⓪ elect. single-polar, unipolar.

ein-puppen zu I: F v/a. u. v/refl. (fein anziehen) to doll up. [put in.]

*****ein-schalten** zu I: mot. e-n Gang: to

*****ein-schießen** zu II: sich 2 auf ein Ziel to find the range of.

*****Ein-schlag** Golf: put(t).

*****ein-schleifen² Stöpsel usw.: to lap.

*****ein-seitig: path. 2e Lungenentzündung single pneumonia.

*****ein-senden zu I: abs. Fußball: to score.

Ein¹-sitzer (⌣́⌣̆...) m ② (Wagen usw. mit einem Sitz) single-seater.

ein²-sparen (⌣́⌣̆...) v/a. ②** to save materials by careful methods; to make (or gain) money by economics.

*****ein-springen zu 5: als Ersatz für j-n 2 to act as a p.'s substitute.

Ein²-steck-lauf (⌣́⌣̆...) m ② für Gewehre größeren Kalibers: Morris (or morris) tube. [withdraw the suit]

*****ein-stellen zu I: jur. die Verfolgung 2 to

Ein²-stell-scheibe (⌣́⌣̆...) f ② phot. focussing screen.

*****ein-stürzen zu I: ⚒ Stollen: to cave in.

Ein¹-und-zwanzigstel (⌣́⌣̆...) n ②, 2 a. inv. one-and-twentieth (part).

*****ein-weihen zu I4: eingeweiht sn (um die Sache wissen) to be in the secret, F to be in the know.

*****ein-werfen zu I4: (j-s Rede unterbrechen) to throw in, to interject.

Ein²-wickel-papier (⌣́⌣̆...) n ② wrapping paper.

Ein²-wohner-wehr ⚔ (⌣́⌣̆...) f ② Civic Guard, Citizen Guards pl.

Einzel-firma ⚘ (⌣́⌣̆...) f ② single firm; **-handel** ⚘ m retail trade; **-händler** ⚘ m retailer; **-haus** n detached house; **-lader** m single-loader, single-shot gun or rifle (ant. Mehrlader); **-teile** ⊙ m/pl. components pl.; **-zelle** f im Gefängnis solitary cell. [-fall.]

*****Eis-bruch mount. e-s Gletschers: ice-

*****Eisen zu 1: zwei ⁓ im Feuer h. to have two strings to one's bow.

Eisenbahn-fähre ⚓ (⌣́⌣̆...) f ② train-ferry. [crete, reinforced concrete.]

Eisen-beton ⊙ (⌣́⌣̆...) m ② ferro-con-

*****eisern zu 2: ⚔ 2e Ration iron ration.

Eis-hockey ⚐ (⌣́⌣̆...) n ② Sport: ice-hockey; **-pickel** m, mount. ice-axe; **-schnellauf(en** n) m speed skating.

ekzem-artig ⚘ (⌣́⌣̆...) a. ⑥⓪ path. eczematous.

elektrisizieren ⊙ (-⌣́⌣̆-⌣́⌣̆) [grch.-lt.] v/a. ⑬ (für elektrischen Betrieb einrichten) to electrify.

Elektrisierung ⊙ (-⌣́⌣̆-⌣̆) f ⑯ electrification.

Elektrizitäts-gesellschaft (-⌣̆⌣̆-⌣́⌣̆...) f ② electricity supply company.

Elektro-lyt ⚘ (-⌣́⌣̆) m ② phys. (durch elektrischen Strom zersetzbarer Körper) electrolyte; **-lytisch** ⚘ a. ⑥⓪ electrolytic(ally adv.).

*****Element 4. elect. cell.

Eltern-(bei)rat (⌣́⌣̆...) m ② Parents' Council.

*****Emission phys. emission.

*****Empfang 3. Radio: reception; auf ⁓ stehen to stand by.

*****empfangen zu I: Radio: to receive.

Empfangs-gerät (⌣́⌣̆...) n ② receiving set. [gown.]

Empire-kleid (a-vīːrˈ) n ② empire

*****empor-ragen allg. to stand up, to rise; ⁓schrauben ⚙ (sich 2) v/refl. ②** to spiral up(wards).

End-kampf (⌣́⌣̆...) m ② finish; **-moräne** f geol. terminal moraine.

endothermisch ⚘ (⌣́⌣̆⌣̆) [grch.] a. ⑥⓪ phys. (Wärme bindend) endothermic.

End-spurt ⚐ (⌣́⌣̆...) m ② Sport: final spurt; **-summe** f (sum) total.

Engagement (a-ga-ʒ-mã:ˈ) [fr.] n ⑨ engagement; (Stellung) position, berth; ⚘ Börse: commitment.

Engländer 2. ⊙ (Schraubenschlüssel) monkey wrench.

eng-maschig (⌣́⌣̆...) a. ⑥⓪ close-meshed.

Ent-fernungs-messer (⌣̆⌣̆...) m ② range-finder. [decohere.]

ent-fritten (⌣̆⌣́⌣̆) v/a. ②* Radio: to

Ent-fritter (⌣̆⌣́⌣̆) m ② Radio: decoherer.

ent-gasen (⌣̆⌣́⌣̆) v/a. ②* to outgas.

*****Ent-gleisung: zur ⁓ bringen to derail.

ent-haften (⌣̆⌣́⌣̆) v/a. ②* to release from detention.

ent-jungfern (⌣̆⌣́⌣̆) v/a. ②a.* to deprive of virginity, to deflower.

Ent-jungferung (⌣̆⌣́⌣̆⌣̆) f ② defloration.

*****ent-koppeln 2. Radio: to tune out.

Ent-lastungs-straße (⌣̆⌣́⌣̆...) f ② zur Ablenkung übermäßigen Verkehrs: by-pass road.

ent-laus/en (⌣̆⌣́⌣̆) I v/a. ②* to delouse. — II ⁓ n ② u. ⁓ung f ㊶ delousing.

Ent-lausungs-anstalt (⌣̆⌣́⌣̆...) f ② delousing station.

Ent-leerungs-ventil ⊙ (⌣̆⌣́⌣̆...) n ②d relief valve.

ent-lüften (⌣̆⌣́⌣̆) v/a. ②* to ventilate.

Ent-lüftung (⌣̆⌣́⌣̆) f ㊶ ventilation.

ent-magnetisier/en (⌣̆⌣̆-⌣́⌣̆) I v/a. ②* to demagnetize. — II ⁓ n ② u. ⁓ung f ㊶ demagnetization.

*****ent-puppen: sich als Betrüger usw. 2 to prove (or to turn out) to have been an impostor, &c. [(f. verzücken).]

*****ent-rücken zu I: entrückt fig. = verzückt

*****ent-scheiden zu I: v/n. to decide (über acc. on).

Ent-scheidungs-spiel (⌣̆⌣́⌣̆⌣̆́) n ② Sport: deciding game, conqueror, tie.

*****ent-schuldigen: j-n 2 bei ... to make a p.'s excuses to ...

ent-spannen (⌣̆⌣́⌣̆) v/a. u. sich 2 v/refl. ②* to unbend, slacken, relax (a. fig.).

Ent-spannung (⌣̆⌣́⌣̆) f ㊶ unbending, slackening, relaxation (a. fig.): pol. détente.

Ent-wickler (⌣⌣⌣) m ㉒ phot. developer.
epidemisch ⚁ (⌣⌣⌣⌣) [grch.] a. ㊿ path. epidemic(ally adv.).
epigonenhaft ⚁ (⌣⌣⌣⌣⌣) a. ㊿ epigonous.
erden³ (⌣⌣) elect. I v/a. ㊾ to earth, ground. — II ~ n ㉓ u. E/ung f ㊿ earthing, grounding, earth- (or ground-) connexion.
Erd-kabel (⌣⌣...) n ㉒ tel. buried cable; =**leiter** m, elect. ground wire.
Er-drosselungs-steuer (⌣⌣⌣...) f ㉒ destructive (or prohibitive) tax.
Erdungs-schalter (⌣⌣⌣...) m ㉒ elect. earthing switch.
*****Er-füllung**: in ~ gehen = sich erfüllen (s. erfüllen II).
*****er-gänzen** zu I: ✱ Lager: to replenish.
er-gebnis-los (⌣⌣⌣...) a. ㊿ without result, fruitless; ⁰reich a. fruitful.
*****er-härten** zu I v/n. ㊾* to harden.
Er-holungs-fähigkeit (⌣⌣⌣...) f ㊿ elect. recuperability.
Er-nährungs-minister (⌣⌣⌣...) m ㉒ Minister of Food and Agriculture; in England: Food Controller.
Ernte-aussicht (⌣⌣...) f ㊿ harvest- (or crop-) prospect.
*****er-öffnen** zu II: jur. den Konkurs ⁰ to institute bankruptcy proceedings.
er-rechn/en I v/a. ㉒b.* to calculate, compute. — II ~ n ㉓ u. E/ung f ㊿ calculation, computation.
Er-reger-kreis (⌣⌣⌣⌣) m ㉒ Radio: exciting circuit.
*****Er-satz** (Ersatzmittel) substitute, surrogate; ~ leisten to make restitution (für of).
Er-satz-blei (⌣⌣...) n ㉒ für Füllbleistifte: spare lead, refill; =**reifen** m, mot. spare tyre, stepney; =**spieler** m Sport: emergency man; =**teil** m od. n spare (part).
*****er-scheinen** zu I 1: in Buchhändleranzeigen: erscheint demnächst to be published shortly.
*****Er-scheinung** zu 2: eine glänzende ~ in v. Mann: to cut a fine figure; v. b. Frau: to be of dazzling beauty.
*****er-schließen** 3. Baugelände: to develop.
*****erste** zu I 1: med. ⁰ Hilfe bei Unfällen first aid.
er-strebens-wert (⌣⌣⌣⌣) a. ㊿ desirable.
Er-trags-wert (⌣⌣⌣⌣) m ㉒ income (or capitalized) value.
er-tüchtig/en (⌣⌣⌣) I v/a. ㊾* to make efficient, to train. — II ~ n ㉓ u. E/ung f ㊿ making efficient, training; körperliche E/ung physical drill.
*****er-weitern** zu I 2: gr. erweiterter Satz compound sentence.
er-werbs-los (⌣⌣⌣) a. ㊿ usw. s. arbeitslos; ⁰tätig a. gainfully employed, employed in industry or trade.
Er-zeuger zu I: Volkswirtschaft: producer (ant. Verbraucher).
Esperantist (⌣⌣⌣) m ㉒, ~in f ㊿ (Anhänger[in] des Esperanto) Esperantist.
Esperanto (⌣⌣-) [it. spera're] n ㉓ o. pl. (künstliche Weltsprache) Esperanto.
*****Etappe** (militärischer Stützpunkt) base, basis; fig. (Teilstrecke e-r Reise usw.) stage.
*****etat-mäßig** 2. Beamter usw.: permanent.

Eugenik ⚁ (-⌣-) [grch.] f ㊺ (Lehre von der Rassenveredlung) eugenics.
E. V. abbr. = Eingetragener Verein Inc(or). (= Incorporated).
*****exemplarisch**: ²e Strafe signal punishment.
Existenz-mittel (⌣⌣⌣...) n/pl. ㉒ means of existence.
Explosions-motor ⚁ (⌣⌣⌣⌣⌣"...) m ㉒ mot. internal combustion engine.
Expressionismus (⌣⌣(⌣)⌣⌣⌣) [it.] m ㉗ Kunst: expressionism.
Expressionist (⌣⌣(⌣)⌣⌣) m ㉒ expressionist.
expressionistisch (⌣⌣(⌣)⌣⌣⌣) a. ㊿ expressionist.
Extensität (⌣⌣⌣") [it.] f ㊺ (Umfang) extensity.
extensiv (⌣⌣") a. ㊿ (der Ausdehnung nach) extensive; agr. ²e Wirtschaft extensive farming.
exterritorial (⌣⌣⌣⌣(⌣)") [it.] a. ㊿ (den Landesgesetzen nicht unterworfen) ex(tra)territorial.
Exterritorialität (⌣⌣⌣⌣(⌣)-⌣") f ㊺ ex(tra)territoriality.

F

Fabrik-marke (⌣"...) f ㉒ trade-mark.
*****facettieren** Spiegel usw.: to bevel.
Fach-arbeit (⌣ch...) f ㉒ expert (or skilled) work; =**arbeiter(in** f) m expert (or skilled) worker; =**arzt** m (medical) specialist; =**ausstellung** f trade exhibition; =**kenntnisse** f/pl. technical knowledge; ⁰**kundig** a. ㊿ competent, expert; =**literatur** f ㊺ technical (or trade) literature; =**minister** m Expert Minister.
*****fahren** zu I u. II: (im Kraftwagen ⁰) to motor. — zu II: aus der Haut ⁰ to jump out of one's skin.
Fahr-gestell ⓞ (⌣"...) n ㉒ under-carriage, mot. a. chassis; =**mantel** m driving coat; =**pelz** m driving furs pl.; =**preis-anzeiger** m fare-indicator; =**preis-zone** f fare-stage; =**schalter** m, mot. controller; =**stuhl-führer** m lift-attendant.
Fälligkeits-termin (⌣⌣-...) m ㉒ maturity, due date.
Fall-schirm-künstler(in f) m (⌣"...) =**schirm-springer(in** f) m parachutist; =**wind** m Wetterkunde: fall-wind.
Falsch-münzer-werkstatt (⌣"...) f ㉒ coiner's den.
Falt-schachtel (⌣"...) f ㉒ folding box.
Famili-en-unterstützung ⚔ (⌣"⌣⌣⌣...) f ㉒ für die Familie e-s im Felde stehenden Soldaten: separation allowance.
Fang-vorrichtung (⌣"...) f ㉒ am Straßenbahnwagen: tray.
Farb-band ⓞ (⌣"...) f ㉒ der Schreibmaschine: typewriter (a. typewriting) ribbon; ⁰**echt** a. ㊿ fast, fadeless.
Färbe-mittel n ㉒ dye(-stuff).
*****färben** zu I: Haar: to tint.
Farben-industrie (⌣"...) f ㊺ dyeing industry; =**kasten** m colour-box, box of paints; =**photographie** f direct colour photography.
Farb-stift (⌣"...) m ㉒ coloured pencil.
Faschismus (⌣"") [it.] m ㉗ pol. (italienischer Nationalismus) Fascism.
Faschist (⌣") [it.] m ㉒, ~in (⌣"⌣) f ㊺ pol. Fascist.

faschistisch (⌣"⌣) a. ㊿ pol. Fascist(ic).
Fascismus usw. s. Faschismus usw.
Fassaden-kletterer (⌣"...) m ㉒ cat burglar, pipe-climber.
faß-reif (⌣"...) a. ㊿ v. Wein usw.: vatted; ⁰**wein** m ㉒ wine in (or from) the wood.
Faszismus usw. s. Faschismus usw.
Faxe: ~n machen (to play the) fool, (to play the) buffoon, to tomfool; mach' keine ~n! stop your fooling!
Fecht-maske (⌣"...) f ㉒ fencing mask =**schurz** m plastron.
Feder-gabel (⌣"...) f ㉒ am Fahrrad: spring-fork; =**gewicht** n Boxen: feather-weight; =**klemme** ⓞ f clip.
Federung ⓞ (⌣⌣⌣) f ㊺ e-s Wagens: spring suspension.
Fehler-quelle (⌣"...) f ㉒ source of error.
*****Fehl-farbe** ✱ (⌣"...) f ㉒ off shade; =**spruch** m Fernspr. miscarriage of justice; =**urteil** n misjudg(e)ment; ⁰**zünden** v/n. (h.) ㊾*** mot. to miss fire, to misfire; =**zündung** f ㉒ mot. misfire.
Feier-schicht (⌣"⌣) f ㉒ ~en einlegen to drop shifts.
Fein-einstellung ⓞ (⌣"...) f ㉒ fine adjustment; =**(ein)stell-vorrichtung** ⓞ f vernier; =**gehalts-stempel** ⓞ m hall-mark.
*****Feist**: im ~ in (pride or prime of) grease.
Feld-bahn ⓞ (⌣"...) f ㉒ field-railway, portable railway; =**gericht** ⚔ n drum-head court-martial; ⁰**graue(r)** ⚔ m ㊾ field-gray ⚔ a. ㊿, =**kriegs-gericht** ⚔ n = =gericht.
*****Felge** zu 1: mot. geteilte ~ demountable rim. [rad: rim.]
Felgen-band ⓞ (⌣⌣⌣) n ㉒ am Wagen, =**Fels-kletterer** (⌣"...) m ㉒ mount. rock-climber, cragsman.
Fenster-dekorateur (⌣"...) m ⓐd window-dresser; =**leder** n chamois (leather), shammy.
Fern-amt (⌣"...) n ㉒ Fernspr. trunk-exchange, F Trunks (sg., o. art.); =**anruf** m Fernspr. trunk-call; =**drucker** m tel. teletyper; =**empfang** m Radio: long-distance reception.
*****ferner²** zu II: in Rennberichten: ⁰ liefen ... also ran.
Fern-flug ⚔ (⌣"...) m ㉒ long-distance flight; =**geschütz** ⚔ n long-range gun; =**gespräch** n Fernspr. trunk-call; =**heizung** f distant (or district) heating; =**leitung** f, elect., Fernspr. trunk-line; =**rohr-büchse** f ⚔ u. hunt. telescopic (or telescope sight) rifle; =**ruf** m = =anruf; =**sehen** n, tel. television; =**seher** m, tel. television apparatus, televisor.
Fernsprech-apparat (⌣⌣"...) m ㉒ telephone instrument; =**automat** m automatic telephone, coin collector telephone (station); =**zelle** f telephone box or cabin, call-box.
Fern-steuerung ⓞ (⌣"...) f ㉒ remote (or distant) control, ⚁ telautomatics (pl.). [goods.]
Fertig-waren ✱ (⌣⌣...) f/pl. ㉒ wrought
fest-besoldet (⌣"...) a. ㊿ in receipt of a fixed salary, salaried.

fest-halten zu 1: *paint., phot.* im Bilde ~ to register.
festigen 3. e-e Währung: to stabilize.
Festigung (⁻⁻) f ⓯ e-r Währung: stabilization. [capital.]
fest-liegen: ⚓ ⚓des Kapital fixed⟨
fest-stellen Persönlichkeit: to identify.
Fest-stellung der Persönlichkeit: identification.
Fett-büchse ⊙ (⁻⁻) f ⚙ *mach.* grease-box; **-druck** m, *typ.* bold print; **-geschwulst** f. *path.* fatty tumour; **-herz** n. *path.* fatty heart; **-kohle** ⚒ f bituminous coal; **-papier** n grease-proof paper.
Feuer-überfall ⚔ (⁻⁻) m ⚔ strafe.
Feuerungs-raum ⊙ (⁻⁽⁻⁾⁻) m ⚙ furnace (chamber); ↕ stoke-hole.
Feuer-vorhang ⚔ (⁻⁻) m ⚙ *thea.* fire-curtain; **-walze** ⚔ f creeping barrage; ***zeug** (mechanisches, bsd. für die Tasche) lighter.
Fieber-tabelle (⁻⁻) f ⚕ *med.* temperature-chart; **-thermometer** n, *med.* clinical thermometer.
***Film** (Filmbild[er]) mst moving picture, F movie; der ~ als Gattung the moving pictures *pl.*, F the movies *pl.*
Film-atelier (⁻⁻) n ⚙ moving-picture (or film) studio; **-aufnahme** f (Vorgang) shooting of a film; **-band** n reel; **-darstellung** f e-s wirklichen Ereignisses screen record; **-diva** f film star.
filmen (⁻⁻) v/a. ⚙ to film, to screen.
Film-industrie (⁻⁻) f ⚙ film (or moving-picture) industry; **-künstler(in** f) m moving-picture (or screen) artist; **-pack** n. *phot.* film pack; **-regisseur** m film producer; **-reklame** f screen advertising; **-rolle** f reel; **-schauspiel** n picture-play, photo-play; **-schauspieler(in** f) m moving-picture (or screen) actor m (actress f); **-theater** n picture-theatre; **-vorstellung** f moving-picture show; **-welt** f screendom.
filtrierbar (⁻⁻) a. ⚙ filtrable.
Fimmel² F (⁻⁻) m ⚙ (Schrulle) craze.
Finanz-amt (⁻⁻) n ⚙ revenue-board, revenue-office.
finanzieren (⁻⁻) v/a. ⚙ to finance.
Finanz-politik (⁻⁻) f ⚙ financial (or fiscal) policy; **-wirtschaft** f finance economy.
Firmen-inhaber ⚔ (⁻⁻) m ⚙ principal; **-schild** n sign(board), facia.
Firn² zu 1: *mount.* névé; **~feld** n ⚙ *mount.* névé field.
Fixier-bad (⁻⁻) n ⚙ *phot.* fixing solution, fixer.
Flach-ball (⁻⁻) m ⚙ Tennis: drive.
Flächen-blitz (⁻⁻) m ⚙ *phys.* sheet lightning.
Flach-kopf ⊙ (⁻⁻) m ⚙ (Musterklammer) flat-headed paper-fastener.
Flammen-werfer ⚔ (⁻⁻) m ⚙ (Kampfgerät) flame-projector.
Flamm-punkt (⁻⁻) m ⚙ *phys., chm.* flash-point.
***Flanke** 2. *mount.* e-s Berges: face.
Flaschen-kind (⁻⁻) n ⚙ bottle baby.
Flau-macher (⁻⁻) m ⚙ alarmist; Börse: bear. [(shot.)]
Fleck-schuß (⁻⁻) m ⚙ point-blank⟨

Fleisch-vergiftung (⁻⁻) f ⚙ *path.* ptomaine poisoning.
fliegen zu II: ✈ to fly, to aviate. — zu III6: ✈ flying, aviation.
Fliegen-gewicht (⁻⁻) n ⚙ Boxen: fly-weight.
***Flieger** 3. ✈ airman, aviator; (berufsmäßiger ~) pilot. — 4. Rennsport: sprinter.
Flieger-abwehr-... ✈ (⁻⁻) in Zssgn: anti-aircraft; **-aufnahme** f ⚙ aerial photo; **-geschütz** ⚔ n anti-aircraft gun, aerogun.
Fliegerei ✈ (⁻⁻) f ⚙ flying, aviation.
Flieger-hauptmann ✈ (⁻⁻) m ⚙ flight-lieutenant. [aviator.⟩
Fliegerin (⁻⁻) f ⚙ airwoman,⟨
Flieger-kamera ✈ (⁻⁻) f ⚙ zum Photographieren des überflogenen Gebiets: aero-camera; **-korps** ✈ n Flying Corps; im Britischen Reich: Royal Air Force; **-leutnant** ✈ m pilot officer; **-oberleutnant** ✈ m flying-officer; **-offizier** ✈ m Air Force officer; **-pfeil** ✈ m aircraft arrow, aerodart; **-schuppen** ✈ m hangar; **-station** ✈ f air-base; **-truppe** ✈ f = **-korps**; [duction.⟩
Fließ-arbeit ⊙ (⁻⁻) f ⚙ serial pro-⟨
***flimmern** zu 1: v. Film: to flicker. — II ~ zu 3: v. Film: flicker.
Flotten-station ⚓ (⁻⁻) f ⚙ naval station.
flottierend ⚔ (⁻⁻) a. ⚙ v. Staatsschulden: floating.
Flug-ball (⁻⁻) m ⚙ Tennis: volley; e-n Ball als ~ nehmen to volley; **-boot** ✈ n flying-boat.
Flügel-nagel (⁻⁻) m ⚙ *mount.* für den Sohlenrand des Bergschuhs: clinker.
Flug-gast ✈ (⁻⁻) m ⚙ air-passenger; **-hafen** ✈ m aerodrome, a. air-base; **-kapitän** ✈ m flight-commander; **-platz** ✈ m aerodrome, aviation field; **-post** f air-post, air-mail; **-(post-)linie** ✈ f air-way; **-schüler** ✈ m pilot pupil; **-station** ✈ f air-base; **-strecke** f covered distance; Golf: carry; **-wesen** ✈ n flying, aviation; ***zeit** ✈ f flying time; **-zeug** ✈ n aeroplane, Am. airplane; *pl. a.* aircraft; **-zeug-führer** ✈ m pilot; **-zeug-lande-insel** f langley; **-zeug-motor** ✈ m aero-motor; **-zeug-mutter-schiff** ⚓ n aircraft-carrier; **-zeug-schraube** ✈ f air-screw.
flüssig zu 1: v. Stil, Schrift: s. fließend 7. — zu 3: Kapital ~ machen to release capital.
Flüster-galerie (⁻⁻) f ⚙ whispering galery.
Föhn 2. ⊙ (Haartrockner) hair-dryer.
Fondant (fr. fȣdā') [fr.] m ⚙ e. (gefülltes Zuckerplätzchen) fondant.
Förder-kohle ⚒ (⁻⁻) f ⚙ pit-coal.
forkeln (⁻⁻) [:Forke] v/a. ⚙ *hunt.* (mit dem Geweih ob. Gehörn durchbohren) to gore.
***Form** 5. Sport: (guter Zustand) form, condition.
Formalin ⚗ (⁻⁻) n ⚙ c. *chm.* formalin.
Forscher-drang (⁻⁻) m ⚙ = Forschbegierde.
***Foyer** e-s Theaters usw. lounge.
Foxtrott ⊤ (⁻⁻) [engl.] m ⚙ d. (Tanz amerikanischen Ursprungs im Vierviertelbakt) foxtrot. [business.⟩
Frachterei (⁻⁻) f ⚙ shipping⟨

Fracht-kosten (⁻⁻) *pl.* ⚙ freight-charges *pl.* [suit.⟩
Frack-anzug (⁻⁻) m ⚙ evening-dress⟨
Franzosen-feind(in f) m (⁻⁻) Francophobe; **-freund(in** f) m Francophil.
Frauen-rechtlertum (⁻⁻) n ⚙ feminism; **-sport** m women's sports *pl.*; **-stimm-recht** n, **-wahl-recht** n women's suffrage.
***Fräulein**: Fernspr. das ~ vom Amt the operator.
***frech**: F ~ wie Oskar as cool as a cucumber.
***frei** zu 2: ~er Beruf liberal profession. — zu 4: bei Kinderspielen: ~! pax!, fay-nights!
Frei-ballon (⁻⁻) m ⚙ free balloon; **-bleibend** ✳ *a.* ⚙ v. Preis: subject to change without notice, subject to market fluctuations, without engagement; **-börse** ✳ f ⚙ kerb(-market); **-fläche** f Städtebau: open space; ***gabe**: c) des Handels usw.: decontrol; **-geben**: b) to restore property; c) to decontrol trade, &c.; ***händig**: ✳ ⚙er Verkauf sale in the open market; **-lauf-rad** n am Fahrrad: free wheel; **-stil** m Sport: free style, a. any style; **-stoß** m Fußball: free kick; **-tod** m voluntary death; **-verkehr** ✳ m Börse: kerb-market; weiteS.: open market, free trade; im ~ on the kerb; **-verkehrs-kurse** ✳ m/pl. Börse: kerb prices *pl.*; **-wild** n *hunt.* fair game (a. *fig.*); **-zeichen** ✳ n free trade-mark.
Fremden-industrie (⁻⁻) f ⚙ tourist industry; **-verkehr** m tourist traffic or travel(l)ing; den ~ heben to attract foreign visitors, to encourage tourist travel(l)ing).
Frequenz *phys.* frequency; density of traffic.
Freuden-haus (⁻⁻) n ⚙ disorderly house.
friderizianisch (⁻⁽⁻⁾⁻) *a.* ⚙ of (or pertaining to) Frederick the Great.
Friedens-konferenz (⁻⁻) f ⚙ peace conference; **-miete** f pre-war rent; **-preis** m pre-war price.
frisieren zu 1: F fig. e-n Bericht usw.: to cook, doctor, garble.
***Frisier-mantel** der Frauen: peignoir; **-tisch** m dressing-table.
Fritter (⁻⁻) m ⚙ Radio: coherer.
***früher** zu 2: ~ schrieb ich viel (ant. jetzt tue ich es nicht mehr) I used to write a great deal.
Früh-zündung (⁻⁻) f ⚙ *mot.* premature ignition, pre-ignition, early spark. [want.⟩
***fühlbar** zu b): ein ~er Mangel a felt⟨
***Führer** zu 1: *mot.* driver; ✈ pilot.
Führer-partie (⁻⁻) f ⚙ *mount.* guided party; **-schein** m, *mot.* u. ✈ driving licence; **-sitz** m, *mot.* u. ✈ driver's seat; ✈ oft cockpit.
Füll-blei-stift (⁻⁻) m ⚙ magazine pencil, eversharp.
Fünf-kampf (⁻⁻) m ⚙ Leichtathletik: pentathlon. [radio.⟩
Funk-... (⁻⁻) in Zssgn mst wireless,⟨
Funk-anlage (⁻⁻) f ⚙ wireless plant; **-bastler** m radio fan; **-beamte(r)** m

Funkeinrichtung wireless officer or operator; =**einrichtung** f wireless set or plant.
funken (‿‿) v/a. u. v/n. ⊕ Radio: to wireless.
*****Funken=strecke** elect. (spark-)gap; =**telegramm** n, tel. wireless (telegram), radio(tele)gram; ⚷**telegraphisch** a. ⊕ radiotelegraphic.
*****Funker** weitS. wireless operator.
Funk=kompaß (‿‿) m ⊕ wireless compass; =**offizier** m wireless officer; =**sprech=**... in Zssgn: radiophonic, radiophone; =**sprecher** m (Gerät) radiophone; =**technik** f radio art or engineering.
*****funktionieren** to function, operate.
Funk=turm (‿‿) m ⊕ tel. radio tower; =**verkehr** m radio service; =**wesen** n radio(telegraphy).
*****Für=sorge** 2. (soziale ~) social (or welfare) work; =**sorge=amt** n Welfare Centre; =**sorge=erziehung** f trustee education; =**sorger(in** f) m social (or welfare) worker; =**sorge=tätigkeit** f social (or welfare) work; =**sorge=wesen** n social administration.
fusionieren (-‿-‿) ⊕ v/a. u. v/refl. (sich 2) (verschmelzen) to amalgamate.
Fuß=gas=hebel ⊙ (″...) m ⊕ mot. foot throttle; =**hebel** ⊙ m pedal; =**stütze** f foot support; med. (gegen Senkfuß) arch-support, instep-raiser, foot-easer.
Futter=krippen=politiker (‿‿...) m pol. placeman; =**krippen=system** n, pol. spoils system; =**mittel** n, agr. feedstuff, feeding stuff. [futurism.]
Futurismus (-‿-‿) [lt.] m ⊕ paint.⎦
Futurist (-‿-‿) m ⊕ paint. futurist.
futuristisch (-‿-‿) a. ⊕ paint. futurist.

G

*****Gabel** zu 5: ↓ a. straddle; ~ bilden to bracket, ↓ a. to straddle. — 6. am Fahrrad: fork.
Galalith ⊙ (‿‿‿) [grch. = Milchstein] m ⊕c. galalith (Ersatz für Zelluloid).
*****Gang** zu 4: mot. (Geschwindigkeit) speed.
Gang=zahl (‿‿) f ⊕ mot. number of gears.
*****Gans** zu 1: junge ~ b) Kocht. green goose; Sprichw. wie die ~, wenn's wetterleuchtet like a duck in a thunderstorm.
Ganz=fabrikat ⊛ (‿‿) n ⊕ wholly manufactured article; =**stahl=**... ⊕ all-steel; =**wolle** ⊛ f all wool; ⚷**wollen** ⊛ a. ⊕ all-wool.
Garagen=besitzer (‿″‿‿) m ⊕ garage proprietor; =**wärter** m garageman.
Garderoben=marke (‿″‿‿...) f ⊕ check.
Garnison=prediger ⚔ (‿″‿) m ⊕ chaplain to the garrison.
Garten=stadt (‿‿) f ⊕ garden city.
*****Gas:** mot. ~ geben to open out the throttle, to step on the gas; mot. ~ wegnehmen to shut off gas.
Gas=angriff ⚔ (‿‿) m ⊕ gas-offensive; =**arbeiter** m gas-fitter; =**bereitschaft** ⚔ f gas alert; ⚷**dicht** a. ⊕ gas-tight; *****druckmesser** zur Messung des in Feuerwaffen beim Schuß entwickelten Gasdrucks: accelerometer; =**fuß=hebel** m, mot. accelerator; =**granate** ⚔ f gas-shell; =**hebel** m, mot. throttle (hand) lever; =**herd** m gas-range; ⚷**krank** a. ⊕ gassed; =**licht=papier** n ⊕ phot. gas-light paper; =**maske** ⚔ f gas-mask; mit Filterkasten: box-respirator; =**pedal** n, mot. accelerator.
Gassen=schank (‿‿) m ⊕ off-licence.
Gäste=buch (‿‿) n ⊕ visitors' book, guest book.
Gas=vergiftung (‿‿) f ⊕ gas poisoning; =**versorgung** f gas supply; =**zelle** f e-s lenkbaren Luftschiffes: gas-bag, ballonet. [plate.⎦
Gaumen=platte (″‿...) f Zahnheilkunde:⎦
geben zu 19: etwas (nichts) 2 auf (acc.) to make (no) account of; viel 2 auf (acc.) to make much of. — zu 1: tel. to transmit, send.
*****ge=brauchen** zu 1: er ist zu allem zu 2 he can turn his hand to anything.
Ge=brauchs=artikel (‿‿ch...) m ⊕, =**gegenstand** m commodity, requisite; ⚷**fertig** a. ⊕ ready for (or to) use; =**graphik** f ⊕ advertising art; =**muster=schutz** m jur. legal protection for registered designs.
*****ge=braucht** (für alt gekauft) v. Kleidern, Möbeln, Büchern usw.: second-hand.
Ge=bühren=ordnung (‿″‿...) f ⊕ tariff of fees or charges; ⚷**pflichtig** a. ⊕ subject (or liable) to a fee or duty.
Ge=burten=beschränkung (‿″‿...) f ⊕ birth-control; =**überschuß** m excess of births; =**ziffer** f birth-rate.
Ge=dächtnis=hilfe (‿″‿...) f ⊕ aid to memory; =**rennen** n Rennsport: memorial stakes pl.
Ge=fangenen=fürsorge (‿‿‿...) f ⊕ prison welfare-work.
Ge=fechts=einheit ⚔ (‿‿...) f ⊕ fight- [ing unit.⎦
Ge=frier=fleisch (‿″...) n ⊕ frozen meat; =**kammer** f freezer, refrigerator.
*****Gegen=seitigkeit:** Lebensversicherungsgesellschaft auf ~ Mutual Life Insurance Society.
*****gegen=über** zu 11: sich einer Aufgabe usw. 2 sehen to be up against a task. &c.
Ge=halts=empfänger (‿″...) m ⊕ salary-earner, salaried employee.
*****Gehäuse** zu 1: body.
Geh=bahn (″‿) f ⊕ = Bürgersteig.
Ge=heim=konto ⊛ (‿″...) n ⊕ private (or secret) account.
*****gehen** zu I 10: F mit e-m Mädchen 2 to walk out with; das Fenster geht nach Norden the window faces (or looks) north.
Geher (‿‿) m ⊕ Sport: walker.
*****ge=hoben:** Mensch m in ~er Stellung superior man.
*****ge=horchen** zu I: mach. to respond.
*****Geißler** II npr.: elect. ~sche Röhre vacuum tube.
Geistes=arbeiter (″‿...) m ⊕ brain-worker; =**blitz** m stroke of genius, brain-wave; =**verfassung** f state of mind.
*****geistig** zu 2: 2e Arbeit brain-work.
*****ge=laden** 2. (eingeladen) invited; Ausstellungs=Besichtigung durch (ob. für) 2e Gäste private view.
Ge=lände=lauf (‿‿...) m ⊕ Sport: cross-country run; =**ritt** m Rennsport: cross-country (or point-to-point) race.

Geld=einwurf (‿″...) m ⊕ coin slot; =**entwertung** f depreciation of money; *****geschäft:** ~e machen contp. to financier; =**knappheit** f shortness of money.
*****Ge=leise** zu 3: aus dem ~ off the rails.
Ge=leit=wort (‿″‿) n ⊕ preface, foreword. [normal value.⎦
*****ge=mein** zu I2: 2er Wert ordinary (or⎦
Ge=meinde=bestimmungs=recht (‿″‿‿‿) n ⊕ jur. local option; =**steuer** f rate; Am. local tax; =**verband** m, pol. association of communes.
*****ge=mein=nützig:** 2e Einrichtung, 2es Unternehmen public utility.
*****Gendarm** 2. mount. (Gratturm) gendarme. [strike.⎦
General=streik (‿‿‿) m ⊕ general⎦
Genetik ⚗ (‿‿) [grch.] f ⊕ (Entstehungslehre) genetics pl.
Geo=politik ⚗ (-‿‿‿) [grch.] f ⊕ (Lehre von der Bestimmung der Politik durch die geographischen Verhältnisse) geopolitics pl. u. sg.
Ge=päck=aufbewahrungs=stelle ⛬ (‿‿...) f ⊕ left-luggage office; =**halter** m am Wagen: (trunk) rack; am Fahrrad: carrier; =**netz** n luggage-rack; =**stück** n parcel.
*****ge=rade¹** zu II: 8. Rennsport: die (Schlußstrecke der Rennbahn) the straight.
Ge=rade=halter (‿″‿...) m ⊕ med. back-board.
*****Ge=rät¹** Fernspr., Radio: set.
Ge=röll=halde (‿‿‿) f ⊕ geol. débris (or scree) slope, scree(s pl.).
Ge=samt=preis ⊛ (‿‿...) m ⊕a lump sum price; =**versicherung** f all-in insurance.
Ge=schäfts=aufsicht ⊛ (‿‿...) f ⊕ jur. legal (or official) supervision (or control), temporary receivership; =**bereich** m sphere of action, scope; =**karte** ⊛ f business-card, trade-card; =**wagen** m delivery van. [game of skill.⎦
Ge=schicklichkeits=spiel (‿‿‿‿) n ⊕⎦
Ge=schwader=führer ↓ u. ⚔ (‿″‿...) m ⊕ squadron-leader.
Ge=sellen=stück (‿‿‿) n ⊕ journeyman's piece of work. [ception room.⎦
Ge=sellschafts=raum (‿‿‿...) m ⊕ re-⎦
*****Ge=setzes=kraft:** e-r Sache ~ geben to enact a th., e-r Sache ~ erlangen to pass a th. into law.
*****Ge=sicht** zu 2: F fig. j-m ins ~ springen vor Wut to fly out at a p.
*****Ge=spräch** 3. Fernspr. call.
*****Ge=stalt** zu 2: ~ annehmen (sich verwirklichen) to take shape; e-m Gedanken ~ geben to get an idea into shape.
Ge=stehungs=kosten ⊛ (‿″‿...) pl. ⊕ cost-price, prime cost.
*****Ge=sund=beter(in** f) m ⊕ ⊕ faith-curer; =**beterei** f faith-healing, faith-curing.
*****Ge=sundheit** zu 1: öffentliche ~ public hygiene. [-tax.⎦
Ge=tränke=steuer (‿″‿...) f ⊕ beverage-⎦
Ge=treide=produkte ⊛ (‿″‿...) n pl. ⊕ cereal products pl.
Ge=wehr=futteral (‿″‿...) n ⊕ hunt. gun-case; =**granate** ⚔ f rifle-grenade.
Ge=werbe=aufsicht (‿″‿...) f ⊕ trade (or industrial) inspection; =**inspektor** m trade (or factory) inspector; =**kunde**

f technology; =recht n trade (or industrial) law; =stand m class of tradespeople and handicraftsmen; =unterricht m technical education; =zählung f census of industry.
Ge-werkschafts-bund (⌣⌢⌣...) m ⓶ federation of trade(s)-unions; =wesen n trade-unionism.
*Ge-wicht: mech. totes ~ dead load.
Ge-winn|er (⌣⌢⌣) m ⓶ profiteer.
Ge-winn-realisierung (⌣⌢...) f ⓶, =sicherung f profit-taking; =steuer f profits tax.
Gift-gas ⚔ (⌢⌣...) n ⓶ poison-gas; =schein m, pharm. permit to purchase poison.
Giro-konto (g⁻...) n ⓶ current- (or clearance-)account; =zentrale ⓶ f clearing-house.
*Gitter zu 2: Radio: grid; ~-batterie f Radio: grid battery, C battery; ~-bett n für Kinder: cot; ~-spannung f Radio: grid tension or voltage; ~-widerstand m Radio: grid leak resistance.
Glanz-lichter (⌢⌣...) n/pl. ⓶ paint. high lights pl.   [-glass insurance.]
Glas-versicherung (⌢⌣...) f ⓶ plate-
glatt-stellen ⓶ (⌢⌣...) v/a. ⓷** to settle; Börse: to even up, to square obligations.
*glauben² zu II 4: ich glaube wohl (zögernde Zustimmung) I suppose so.
Gläubiger-schutz-verband (⌢⌣⌣⌣...) m ⓶ jur. creditors' defence association.
gleich-gültig: es ist mir ⌢ I don't care (for it); ⌢macherisch a. ⓶ egalitarian; ⌢richten ⓶ v/a. ⓷** elect. to rectify; ⌢ziehen v/n. (h.) Sb.** Sport: to draw level.
Gleit-boot (⌢⌣...) n ⓶ gliding boat, hydroplane; =flieger ⚔ m gliding machine, glider; =flug ⚔ m gliding flight, glide, volplane; e-n ~ machen, im ~ niedergehen to volplane; =laut m Sprachwissenschaft: glide; =schutz ⊙ m, mot., Radsport: non-skid; =schutz-reifen ⊙ m, mot., Radsport: non-skid tyre.
Gletscher-(ab)bruch (⌢⌣...) m ⓶ geol. icefall; =mühle f, geol. (Strudelloch) pot-hole; =seil n, mount. Alpine rope; =topf m, geol. = =mühle.
Glücks-beutel (⌢⌣...) m ⓶ lucky-bag; =bringer(in f) m mascot, =pfennig m lucky penny; =puppe f bsd. mot. mascot.
*Glück-wunsch zu Neujahr usw.: compliments pl. (of the season); =wunsch-karte f congratulatory card.
Glüh-birne ⊙ (⌢⌣...) f ⓶ elect. electric bulb; =faden m, elect. filament; kathoden-röhre f, elect., Radio: thermionic valve.
Glyzine ♀ (⌣⸺t⌣⌣) [grch.] f ⓷ wistaria
*gnädig zu 1: Gott sei ihm ⌢! God be merciful (un)to him!, the Lord have mercy upon him!
Gold-anleihe (⌢⌣...) f ⓶ gold loan; =bestand m gold reserve; =feder f gold nibo; =fisch-glas n fish-bowl; =prägung f gold stamping.
Golf² (⌢) [schott.] n (Art Ballspiel) golf.
Golf-ball (⌢...) m ⓶ golf-ball, sl. gutty; =platz m links pl.; =schläger m (Gerät) golf-club; =spiel n golf; =spieler(in f) m golfer.
Graben-bruch (⌢⌣...) m ⓶ geol. rift--valley (a. =bruch-tal n); =krieg ⚔ m

trench warfare; =mörser ⚔ m trench mortar; =stellung ⚔ f entrenchment.
Grabes-stimme (⌢⌣...) f ⓶ sepulchral voice.
Grammophon-nadel (⌢⌣f⌢...) f ⓶ gramophone needle; =stift m style.
Granat-trichter ⚔ (⌣⌢...) m ⓶ shell--crater.
*Grätsche = Grätschsprung.
Grat-schneide (⌢...) f ⓶ mount. crest of an arête.
Grätsch-sprung (⌢⌣) m ⓶ Turnerei: straddling vault.
Grat-turm (⌢⌣) m ⓶ mount. gendarme.
*greif-bar: ⓶ available, ready, on
*Greifer zu 2: mach. grip.   [hand.]
*Grenze: Volkswirtschaft: margin.
Grenz-krieg ⚔ (⌢⌣) m ⓶ border-war.
*Griff² 9. mount. hold.
griffig (⌢⌣) a. ⓶ typ. das Papier ist ⌢ the paper bulks well.
grob zu 11: ⌢ werden gegen j-n od. zu j-m to fly out at a p.
Grob-futter (⌢⌣...) n ⓶, =kost f roughage; =waren ⓶ f/pl. coarse goods pl.
Groß-aufnahme (⌢⌣...) f ⓶ phot., bsd. Filmwesen: close-up; =flug-zeug ⚔ n giant aeroplane; =folio ⓶ n (Papiergröße) large foolscap; =funk-stelle f Radio: long-distance (or high-power) radio (or wireless) station; =kampf-tag ⚔ m big battle; =kapital ⓶ n High Finance, big capital interests pl.; =schiffahrt ⚓ f large-scale shipping; =unternehmer m big industrialist or manufacturer; ⌢zügig v. Charakter: liberal; =zügigkeit f ⓶ liberality.
Gruben-holz ⚔ (⌢⌣⌣) n ⓶ pit-props pl.
*Grund-buch-amt land-registry.
Grund-moräne (⌢⌣...) f ⓶ geol. ground moraine; =platte ⊙ f base-plate; =stock m stock; =vermögens-steuer f landed--property tax.
Gschaftlhuber südd. (⌢⌣⌣) m ⓶ busy-body, F Nosy Parker.
Gummi-druck (⌢⌣...) m ⓶ typ. (rubber) offset (printing); =handschuh m rubber glove; =lösung ⊙ f rubber solution; =lutscher m für Säuglinge rubber teat; =mantel m mackintosh, waterproof; =schrubber m (Holzgerät mit Gummikante zum Straßenreinigen) squeegee; =sohle f rubber sole; =stempel m rubber stamp.
Gut-achter (⌢...) m ⓶ surveyor.
Güter-trennung (⌢⌣...) f ⓶ jur. separate (ownership of) property.
gut-gläubig (⌢...) a. ⓶ acting (or done) in good faith; =sager m jur. surety; =schein ⓶ m voucher; =schrift f Bankwesen: credit(ing).
Guts-hof (⌢⌣') m ⓶ farm-yard.
*gut-tun: das tut gut! that's a comfort!

H

Haar-ersatz (⌢...) m ⓶ transformation; *=färbe-mittel n bsd. Am. hair-colo(u)r; =nadel-kurve f Verkehrswesen: hair-pin bend; =trockner m (Gerät) hair-dryer; =wuchs-mittel n hair restorer.
Hack-bau (⌢⌣) m ⓶ agr. tillage by means of the hoe.
Hafen-anlagen ⚓ (⌢⌣...) f/pl. ⓶ docks pl.; =behörde f port-authority.

*haften zu 12: ⌢ für e-n Schaden to be liable (or answerable) for.
Haft-pflicht-versicherung (⌢⌣...) f ⓶ liability insurance.
*Haftung: = Haftpflicht.
Hahn-flinte (⌢...) f ⓶ ⊙ u. hunt. hammer--gun; ⌢los a. ⓶ ⊙ u. hunt. v. Gewehren: hammerless.
*Haken¹ 5. Boxen: hook.
Haken-kreuz (⌢⌣⌢) n ⓶ hooked cross, swastika, fylfot.
Halb-(fertig-)fabrikat ⓶ (⌢⌣...) n ⓶ semi--manufactured product; =geviert ⊙ n. typ. en quad; =schwer-gewicht n Boxen: light-heavy-weight; ⌢starr a. ⓶ v. Luftschiff: semi-rigid; =ton-ätzung f Chemigraphie: half-tone (engraving); =zeit f Sport: half-time.   [supply.]
Halden-vorrat ⚔ (⌢⌣...) m ⓶ pit-head
*Halle 5. Tennis: covered court.
*Hals 6. hunt. (Stimme des Hundes) tongue; ~ geben to give tongue.
Halte-riemen (⌢⌣...) m für die Stehenden im Omnibus usw.: (hanger-)strap.
Hammel-füße (⌢⌣...) m/pl. ⓶ Kocht. sheep's trotters pl.; =rücken m Kocht. saddle of mutton.
*hämmern zu II: v. Motor: to knock. — zu III: v. Motor: knocking.
Hammer-werfen (⌢⌣...) n ⓶ Sport: throwing the hammer.   [hoarder.]
Hamsterer (⌢⌣⌣) m ⓶ (vgl. hamstern)
hamstern (⌢⌣) v/a. u. v/n. (h.) ⓶ a. (große Vorräte bsd. v. Lebensmitteln anlegen) to hoard.
*Hand zu 1: die öffentliche ~ (business activity of) the State (or public) authority. — zu 4: aus erster (zweiter) ~ at first (second) hand.
*Hand-arbeit (ant. Maschinenarbeit) handwork; =ball m Sport: handball, net-ball; =bremse ⊙ f hand-brake.
Handels-bericht ⓶ (⌢⌣...) m ⓶ commercial report; =erlaubnis ⓶ f permission to trade; ⌢gerichtlich adv. ⌢ eingetragen officially registered; =hochschule f University of Commerce; =kolonie f trading colony; =krieg m trade-war; =marke f trade-mark; =nachrichten f/pl. commercial news pl.; als Zeitungsrubrik auch City news pl.; =politiker m one interested in commercial policy; ⌢rechtlich a. ⓶ of (or pertaining to) commercial law; adv. according to c. l.; =richter m jur. commercial judge; ⌢üblich a. ⓶ usual in (the) trade; =vertreter m mercantile agent; =wechsel ⓶ m commercial bill; =wert ⓶ m trade-value, commercial (or selling) v.; ⌢wissenschaftlich a. ⓶ of (or pertaining to) the science of commerce.
Hand-feger m ⓶ dusting brush; =gelenk-halter (⌢⌣...) m, =gelenk-schützer m Sport, bsd. Tennis: wristlet; ⌢geschöpft ⓶ a. ⓶ v. Papier: hand-made.
Händler-preis ⓶ (⌢⌣...) m ⓶ trade-price.
Handlungs-spesen ⓶ (⌢⌣...) f/pl., =un-kosten ⓶ pl. overhead charges.
Hand-täschchen (⌢⌣...) n ⓶ für Damen: pochette; mit Spiegel, Puderdose usw.: vanity-bag; =tasche f hand-bag; =taschen-räuber m bag-snatcher; *=tuch: Boxen: das ~ werfen (sich für be-

Hand- und Fußpflege — 14 — **Höhensonne**

fiegt erklären) to throw in the towel; **= und Fuß-pflege** f chiropody; **zettel** m hand-bill, leaflet.
Hänge-licht (⸗ᴗ) n ⑫ drop light.
Harsch-schnee (ᵍᴸ) m ⑫ mount. crusted snow.
*Härte 5. (Ungemach, Unbill) hardship.
Hart-geld (ˮ...) n ⑫ hard cash, coin, metallic currency; **=holz** ⊙ n hardwood; **löten** ⊙ v/a. ⑨** to braze; **=plätze** m/pl. ⑫ Tennis: hard courts pl.
hasen-rein (ˮᴸ) a. ⑥ hunt. v. Hund: steady from hare.
*Haube zu 4: des Motors am Kraftwagen: bonnet, motor-hood.
hauch-dünn (ᴸˢ) a. ⑥ filmy. [steps.
hauen zu II 3: mount. Stufen ♀ to cut ʃ
*Haupt zu 1: an ~ und Gliedern reformieren to reform root and branch.
Haupt-aktionär (ˮ...) m ⑫ chief (or principal) shareholder; **=amt** n Fernspr. usw.: head (or main) office; **=anschluß** m Fernspr.: main station; **=geschäft** ✱ n chief (or principal) business; (ant. Filiale) head office; **=geschäfts-stunden** f/pl. rush hours pl., busy period; **=rolle:** thea. in der ~ auftreten, die ~ spielen to star; Filmwesen: die ~ spielen in e-m Stück to feature; in der ~ N.N. featured by N.N., N.N. featured; **=schalter** m, elect. main switch; **=sicherheit** f jur. primary security; **=verkehr** m rush of traffic; **=verkehrs-stunden** f/pl., **=verkehrs-zeit** f crowded (or rush) hours pl., busy period; **=verwaltung** f central administration; **=welle** ⊙ f, mach. transmission shaft.
Haus-angestellte(r) f, m (ˮ...) ⑫ domestic servant; **=ball** m carpet dance; **=brand** m (Feuerung für den Privathaushalt) domestic fuel.
Häuser-makler ✱ (ˮᴗ...) m ⑫ = Hausmakler; **=schlächter** m (Aufkäufer v. alten Häusern zu Abbruchzwecken) house-knacker.
Haus-halts-ausschuß (ˮ...) m ⑫ parl. Committee of Way's and Means, C. of Supply; **=halt(s)-plan** m, parl. budget; **=halts-(vor)anschlag** m, parl. the Estimates pl.; **=haltungs-vorstand** m head of the household, householder; **=makler** ✱ m house-agent; **=pflege** f 1. med. home-nursing, h.-treatment. — 2. Armenpflege: outdoor relief; *segen: c) (Brett usw. mit Spruch) wall-text; **=trunk** m brewers' tax-free beer for their own domestic requirements; **wirtschaftlich** a. ⑥ domestic, household-...; **=zins-steuer** ⊙ f rents tax.
Haut-pflege (ˮ...) f ⑫ care of the skin; **=schere** f (eine ~ a pair of) cuticle scissors pl. [-list.
Hebe-liste (ˮ...) f ⑫ Steuerwesen: tax-ʃ
Hebel-schalter (ˮ...) m ⑫ elect. rocker switch. [office.ʃ
Hebe-stelle (ˮᴗ) f ㊽ (tax-)collectingʃ
Heeres-bedarf ⚔ (ˮᴗ...) m ⑫ army-requirements pl., a. -supplies pl.; **flüchtig** ⚔ I a. ⑥ ♀ sein to be a deserter; ♀ werden to desert. — II -e(r) m ⑰ deserter.
Heft-klammer (ˮ...) f ⑫ paper-fastener; **zwinge** f clip.
heilen zu II: Kindersprache: heile, heile, Kätzchen! diddums!

Heimat-hafen ⚓ (ˮᴗ...) m ⑫ home-port, port of registry; **=krieger** ⚔ m, iro. (Reklamierter, Drückeberger) stay-at-home warrior; **=schuß** ⚔ m, sl. Blighty (one or touch), cushy one; **=wehr** ⚔ f Österreich: Home Defence Force.
Heim-kehrer (ˮ...) m ⑫ repatriated soldier or emigrant; **=wehr** f = Heimatwehr.
Heirats-markt (ˮ⸗ᴗ) m ⑫ marriage-market.
*heißen¹ zu II 5: was soll es ♀, daß Sie hierher kommen? what do you mean by coming here?
heiß-laufen ⊙ (ˮ...) v/n. (ʃn) ⓒⓒ ** mach. to overheat o.s.
Heiz-batterie (ˮ...) f ⑫ Radio: heating (or A) battery; **=faden** m, elect. filament; **=kissen** n, elect. heating cushion or pad; **=körper** der Zentralheizung usw. radiator; **=öl** n, mach. oil-fuel; **=schlange** f radiator, heating coil; **=sonne** f, elect. heating bowl, bowl fire, pedestal heater; **=strom** m Radio: filament current; **=wert** m, phys. heat (or ⚭ thermal or calorific) value; **=widerstand** m, elect. filament resistance.
Helio-therapie ⚭ (ᴵᴗᴗᴗˮ) [grch.] f ⑭ med. (Sonnenlichtheilverfahren) heliotherapy.
Helium ⚭ (ᴵᴗᴗ) [lt.; *grch.] n ⑧ chm. (Gasart) helium.
*Hell-dunkel paint. clear-obscure, chiaroscuro.
Hemd-bluse (ᴮ...) f ⑫ shirt-blouse; **=brust** f shirt-front; **=hose** f (eine ~ a pair of) combinations, für Damen mst cami-knickers, cami-bockers pl.
*Hemmung zu 1: Psychologie: inhibition, restriction.
*her-an-kommen: v. Angreifer, Unwetter usw.: to come on. — (näher kommen) to approach (an j-n a p.); unmittelbar ~ an j-n to come up to a p. — (erreichen) ♀ an et. to get to (or at) a th. — fig. ♀ an e-e Zahl, Summe usw. to approach (to), to approximate (to); **nehmen** v/a. ⑧ㄒ.** Schule: to put a pupil on; *treten: fig. mit e-m Angebot usw. ♀ an j-n to approach a p.
her-aus-klingeln (ᴗ⸗...) v/a. ⑧ㄒ.** Arzt usw.: to ring up.
Her-ein-fall (Mißerfolg) failure, F frost; *fallen (Mißerfolg haben) to fail.
Herren-doppel(-spiel) (ˮ⸗ᴗ) n ⑫ Tennis: men's doubles pl.; **=einzel(-spiel)** n Tennis: men's singles pl.; **=fahrer** m Rennsport: gentleman (or amateur) driver; **=schnitt** m (Damenfrisur) Eton crop; **=socken** f/pl. ✱ half hose; **=zimmer** n e-r Wohnung: study; e-r großen Wohnung: smoking-room.
Hertz (♪) npr., id. (Heinrich ~, deutscher Physiker, 1857-1894); elect. ~sche Wellen Hertzian waves pl.
Her-vor-ruf (ᴗ⸗ᴸ) m ⑫ thea. recall.
hetzerisch (⸗ᴗ) a. ⑥ inflammatory.
Hetz-rede (⸗ᴗ) f ⑫ inflammatory speech; **=redner(in** f) m agitator; **=schrift** f inflammatory writing.
*heulen zu I: v. der Heulsirene usw.: to hoot.
*Heuler (Heulsirene) hooter.
*hiesig: ♀es Bier home-brewed beer.

Hilfs-kraft (♂...) f ⑫ subsidiary worker, assistant; **=kreuzer** ⚓ m boarding-ship, b.-steamer; **=motor** ⊙ m auxiliary motor; **=organ** n subsidiary; **=schule** f school for backward children.
*Himmel zu 1: fig. vom ~ (herab)fallen to come out of the blue.
*himmeln 3. hunt. (senkrecht in die Luft steigen) v. töblich getroffenem Federwild: to tower.
Himmels-schrift ⚙ (⸗ᴗ) f ⑫ (Art Reklame) sky-writing.
hin-auf-setzen (ᴗᴸˮᴗ) v/a. ⑨** Preise: to raise.
*Hindernis Rennsport: fence.
hin-hauen F (ˮ...) v/a. ⑧ㄒ. u. ⑧** (schmeißen) to bung, whang; *richten: durch Elektrizität ♀ to electrocute.
Hinter-asien ⚐ (ˮᴗ...) ⑬ α. Farther Asia, the Far East; **=grund** thea. (gemalte Dekoration) flat; **lastig** ⚙ a. ⑥ tail-heavy; **legen:** hinterlegte Gelder pl. cautionary deposits; **=pommern** ⚐ npr/n. ⑬ α. Farther Pomerania.
Hitze-welle (⸗ᴗ...) f ⑫ heat-wave.
*hoch zu I 6: ♪ ♀ zu ♀ singen to sing sharp. — zu V: 19. Wetterkunde: high.
Hoch-antenne ⊙ (⸗ᴗ...) f ⑫ Radio: high aerial; **=bau:** arch. overground building; **=bau-amt** n Building Surveyor's Office; **=betrieb** m im Geschäft usw.: intense activity, F hustle; ~ haben F to hustle; **=burg** f, fig. stronghold; **=druck** fig. mit ~ arbeiten F to hustle; **=druck-gebiet** n Wetterkunde: high-pressure area; **empfindlich** a. ⑥ phys. highly sensitive; **=finanz** ⊙ f High Finance; **=format** ⊙ n upright size; **frequent** a. ⑥ elect. high frequent; **=frequenz** f elect. high frequency; **=geschwindigkeit...** v. Patronen usw.: high-velocity; **=haus** n, arch. skyscraper; **=konjunktur** ✱ f business prosperity, boom, peak season; **machen** v/a. ⑧** hunt. (aufjagen) to put up; **pumpen** v/a. ⑧** to pump up; **=spannungs-pfeil** m ⑫ elect. danger arrow; **=stand** m high standing; fine condition; high rate of prices, &c.
Höchst-belastung ⊙ (ˮ...) f ⑫ mech. maximum load; **=form** f Sport: top form; *geschwindigkeit: mot. zulässige ~ speed-limit; **=leistung** e-r Fabrik: maximum output; Sport: record; **=lohn** m maximum wage (s pl.); **=preis** ✱ m maximum price; **=satz** m maximum rate.
Hoch-tour (ˮ...) f ⑫ mount. high-level climb; **verzinslich** a. ⑥ bearing high rates of interest; **=wasser-katastrophe** f ⑫ flood-disaster; **wertig** a. ⑥ of high value, valuable, high-class.
*Hocke zu 2: = Hocksprung.
Hocker-steuer (⸗ᴗ...) f ⑫ fine for staying in inns beyond the legal hour.
Hock-sprung (ᵍᴸ) m ⑫ Turnerei: squatting vault.
*Höhe zu 2: F das ist (doch wirklich) die ~! that's the (absolute) limit!
Höhen-rekord ⚙ (ˮᴗ...) m ⑫ altitude record; **=sonne** f (künstliche artificial

Alpine (or mountain) sun, med. ultra-violet rays pl.; **-steuer ⚥** n elevator, horizontal rudder.

Hohl-hering (⁻ᵘ...) m ⊕ (ant. Vollhering) spent herring. [at).

*****höhnisch**: ≈ lächeln to sneer (über acc.

Hol-schuld (ᴗ⁻) f ⊕ jur. debt payable in the domicile of the debtor (ant. Bringeschuld). [wood pulp.

Holz-masse ⊙ (⁻ᵘ...) f ⊕, **-schliff** ⊙ m

homosexuell ⌐ (ᴗᴗᴗ⁻) [grch.-lt.] a. ⊕ homosexual; ≈ Veranlagte(r) invert.

Homosexualität ⌐ (ᴗᴗᴗ-ᵘ) f ⊕ homosexuality.

*****Hops** zu II: F hops gehen to go West.

Horch-posten ⚔ (⁻ᵘ...) m ⊕ listening-post.

*****hören** zu I 3: Radio: to listen (in). — zu III 9: Radio: listening(-in).

*****Hörer** zu 1: Radio: listener(-in).

Hör(er)muschel (⁻ᵘ(ᴗ)...) f ⊕ Fernspr. ear-piece.

Hormon ⌐ (ᴗ⁻) [grch. = anspornend] n ⊕ d. physiol. (eine der inneren Körperaussonderungen, die die Organe anregen) hormone.

*****Hörnchen** (hornförmiges Gebäck) crescent.

Hosen-strecker (⁻ᵘ...) m ⊕ (Gerät) trouser-stretcher.

Hotel-gewerbe (-ᵘ...) n ⊕ hotel in- [dustry.

*****Huhn** zu 1: er ist ein blindes ~ he is as blind as a bat.

Hühner-nest (⁻ᵘᴗ) n ⊕ hen's nest; ~er ausnehmen to rob the hen-roosts.

*****Hülle** zu 1: e-s Ballons od. Luftschiffs: envelope. [pulse.

*****Hülsen-frucht**: Hülsenfrüchte pl. coll.

*****Hummel**¹ zu 2: F leichte ~ (leichtfertiges Mädchen) bird.

Humpel-rock (ᴗᴗ⁻) m ⊕ (um die Knöchel enger als oben) hobble-skirt.

Hunde-abteil ⊕ (⁻ᵘ...) n ⊕ dog-box; ≈elend F a. ⊕: sich ≈ fühlen (aussehen) to feel (look) like nothing on earth; **-rennen** n ⊕ greyhound race.

hundert-prozentig (ᴗᴗ⁻...) a. ⊕ ≈er Sprechfilm all-talking film; **-satz** ⚥ m ⊕ percentage.

Hunger-blockade (ᴗᴗ⁻...) f ⊕ starvation blockade; **-krieg** m war of starvation; **-streik** m (hartnäckige Verweigerung der Nahrungsaufnahme seitens e-s Gefangenen) hunger-strike. [to hoot.

hupen (⁻ᴗ) v/n. (h.) ⊕ mot. to honk, a.

Hurra-patriot(in f) m (ᴗ⁻..., ᴗ⁻...) patrioteer; **-patriotentum** n patrioteering.

Hut-stumpen ⊙ (⁻ᵘ...) m ⊕ hat stump]

*****Hütte** 4. mount. (Schutzhütte) refuge.

Hütten-industrie ⚒ (ᴗ⁻...) f ⊕ smelting- (or foundry-) business; **-wirt** m, mount. hut-keeper.

Hydrophon ⌐ (ᴗᴗ⁻) [grch.] n ⊕ d. wasserapparat zur Meldung sich nähernder Schiffe durch Auffangen der von ihnen ausgehenden Geräusche) hydrophone.

Hydroplan ⌐ (ᴗᴗ⁻) [grch.-lt.] m ⊕ c. [a] Gleitboot; b) Höhen- und Tiefensteuer des Unterseebootes] hydroplane.

*****Hypothek**: e-e ~ aufnehmen to raise (or effect) a mortgage.

Hypotheken-forderung (ᴗᴗ⁻...) f ⊕ jur. hypothecary claim.

hypothekieren (ᴗᴗ⁻ᴗ) v/a. ⊕ jur. to hypothecate, mortgage.

J

i. e. R. abbr. = im einstweiligen Ruhestand, en disponibilité. [(f. ds).

J. G. abbr. = Interessengemeinschaft

Ikonometer ⌐ (⁻ᴗᴗ⁻) [grch.] n ⊕ phot. (Rahmensucher) iconometer.

Immobilien-gesellschaft ⚒ (ᴗ⁻ᵘᴗ...) f ⊕ real estate company.

immobilisieren (ᴗᴗᴗ⁻ᴗ) v/a. ⊕ to immobilize.

*****Immunität** parl. e-s Abgeordneten: privilege of parliament. immunity from arrest.

*****imprägnieren** Webstoffe: (wasserdicht machen) to (water)proof.

Index-zahl (ᴗ⁻...) f ⊕, **-ziffer** f (amtlich errechnete Preislage) index number.

individualistisch (ᴗ-mᴗᴗᴗ⁻) a. ⊕ individualistic(ally adv.).

Induktanz ⌐ (ᴗᴗ⁻) f ⊕ elect. inductance.

industrialisieren (ᴗᴗᴗᴗ⁻ᴗ) I v/a. ⊕ to industrialize. — II ~ n ⊕ u. **Industrialisierung** f ⊕ industrialization.

Industrialismus (ᴗᴗᴗᴗ⁻...) m ⊕ (Vorherrschen des Gewerbfleißes) industrialism.

Industrie-arbeiter (ᴗᴗ⁻ᵘ...) m ⊕ industrial worker; **-baron** m = **-führer**; **-bezirk** m industrial (or manufacturing) district; **-führer** m captain of industry; **-könig** m = **-führer**; **-land** n, **-staat** m industrial (or manufacturing) country.

Inflation (ᴗ-tᶠ(ᴗ)⁻) [lt.] f ⊕ (Aufblähung der Zahlungsmittel) inflation, **~s-zeit** f ⊕ inflationary period.

Initiativ-antrag (ᴗᴗtᶠ(ᴗ)⁻ᵘ-i...) m ⊕ parl. private bill.

Inkasso-büro (ᴗ⁻ᵘ...) n ⊕ debt-collecting office; **-wechsel** m bill to be cashed.

In-kurs-setzung (ᴗ⁻ᵘ⁻ᴗ) f ⊕ (putting into) circulation.

Innen-lenkung ⊙ (⁻ᵘ...) f ⊕, **-steuerung** f, mot. inside control or drive.

Innungs-wesen (⁻ᵘ...) n ⊕ guild-system; **-zwang** m compulsion to form a guild.

Insekten-vertilgungs-mittel (ᴗᵘ⁻...) n ⊕ insecticide.

Inseraten-annahme (ᴗᴗ⁻ᵘ...) f ⊕ advertisement office; **-büro** n advertising agency; **-wesen** n advertising.

*****Inspizient** thea. stage manager.

Installateur ⊙ (ᴗᴗᴗtᵉ⁻ᵉr) m ⊕ d. plumber; für Gasanlagen: gas-fitter.

Installation ⊙ (ᴗᴗᴗtᶠ(ᴗ)⁻) f ⊕ installation.

Instrumenten-brett ⊙ (ᴗ-ᴗᴗ⁻) n ⊕ mot. u. ⚔ instrument-board, dashboard.

intensivieren ⌐ (ᴗᴗᴗ⁻ᴗ) I v/a. ⊕ (verstärken) to intensify. — II ~ n ⊕ u. **Intensivierung** f ⊕ intensification.

Interessen-gemeinschaft (ᴗᴗᴗ⁻...) f ⊕ 1. community of interests. — 2. ⚒ (Vereinbarung) pooling agreement. — 3. ⚒ (Kartell) pool, trust.

*****Interessent** ⚒ prospective customer.

Interferenz ⌐ (ᴗᴗᴗtᶠ⁻) [lt.] f ⊕ phys. (gegenseitige Beeinflussung s. treffender Wellen) interference.

---

interkonfessionell ⌐ (ᴗᴗᴗ(ᴗ)ᴗ⁻) a. ⊕ interdenominational.

*****Internationale** pol. die ~ (Trutzlied der Sozialisten) the internationale.

internationalisieren (ᴗᴗ-tᶠ(ᴗ)ᴗᴗ⁻ᴗ) I v/a. ⊕ to internationalize. — II ~ n ⊕ u. **Internationalisierung** f ⊕ internationalization.

Internationalismus (ᴗᴗ-tᶠ(ᴗ)ᴗᴗ⁻...) m ⊕ internationalism.

Internationalität (ᴗᴗ-tᶠ(ᴗ)ᴗᴗ-ᵘ) f ⊕ internationality.

*****internieren** zu I: to intern. — zu II: internee.

Internierung (ᴗᴗ⁻ᴗ) f ⊕ internment.

Internierungs-lager ⚔ (ᴗᴗ⁻ᵘ...) n ⊕ detention-camp.

Inventar zu 1: c) lebendes ~ live stock; totes ~ dead stock.

Inventur-ausverkauf ⚒ (ᴗᴗ⁻ᵘ...) m ⊕ stock-taking sale.

*****Investierung** 2. ⚒ v. Kapital: investment.

ionisieren ⌐ (ᴗ-ᴗ⁻ᴗ) elect. I v/a. ⊕ (elektrisch leitfähig machen) to ionize. — II ~ n ⊕ u. **Ionisierung** f ⊕ ionization.

Ionium ⌐ (⁻ᴗ(ᴗ)) [lt. *grch.] n ⊕ chm. ionium (radioaktives Element).

Irrigator ⌐ (ᴗᴗ⁻ᴗ) [lt.] m ⊕ surg. irrigator, douche.

Isolier-band (-ᴗ⁻...) n ⊕ elect. insulating tape; **-baracke** f, med. isolation hospital; **-flasche** f vacuum bottle or flask.

i. W. abbr. = in Worten in words.

J

*****ja** zu I 1: wenn ja if so (ant. wenn nein).

Jacken-kleid (ᴗ⁻...) n ⊕ suit.

Jagd-gewehr (⁻"...) n ⊕ shooting-gun.

Jahres-abonnement (⁻ᵘ...) n ⊕ annual subscription.

*****Jahr-gang** v. Wein: vintage; **-tausendfeier** f millenary.

Jammer-lappen F (⁻ᵘ...) m ⊕ contp. crock.

Japan-lack (⁻ᴗ⁻...) m ⊕ japan; mit ~ überzogen japanned; **-papier** n Japanese (or India) paper.

Jazz ♪ ♪ (⁻) [?] m ⊕ (neue Musik- u. Tanzart) jazz; ~ spielen od. tanzen to jazz.

jazzen ♪ ♪ (⁻ᴗ) v/n. (h.) ⊕ to jazz.

Jazz-kapelle ♪ (⁻ᵘ...) f ⊕ jazz-band.

Jiu-Jitsu (dschiu-dschit'tsu) [japanisch] n inv. o. pl. (japanische Kunst des Ringens u. der Selbstverteidigung ohne Waffen) ju-jitsu, jiu-jitsu.

Joghurt (⁻gurt) [türk.] n ⊕c. o. pl. (Art Sauermilch) yog(ho)urt.

Jugend-amt (⁻ᵘ...) n ⊕ Youth Commission, Juvenile Board; **-bewegung** f youth-movement; **-gericht** n jur. juvenile court, a. children's court; **-herberge** f youth-hostel.

*****jugendlich** zu a): der Verbrecher youthful offender; jur. Amtsstil: juvenile delinquent. — II ~e(r) m ⊕ juvenile.

Jugend-pflege (⁻ᵘ...) f ⊕ welfare work among the young; **-schutz** m protection of the young; **-werk** n e-s Dichters usw.: early work.

Jugo-slawe ♀ (-‿⸱‿) [serbisch = Süd-slawe] *m* ㊹, **-slawien** *f* ㊼ Yugo-Slav; **-slawien** npr/n. ㉓ α. Yugo-Slavia; **-slawisch** *a.* ㊿ Yugo-Slav(ic).

Jujitsu = Jiu-Jitsu.

Jumper ⊤ (bǧŏ″m″) [engl.] *m* ㉒ (Schlupfbluse) jumper.

jung zu 2: ⚤ ℒe Aktien *pl.* new shares.

Jungfern-rennen (‿⸱‿…) *n* ㉒ Rennsport: maiden race.

Jung-gesellin (‿⸱‿…) *f* ㉒ bachelor-girl; **-türken** *m/pl., pol. hist.* the Young Turks.

Junker 2. (adliger Grundbesitzer) squire; bsd. in Preußen: ⊤ *junker*.

*****juristisch**: *jur.* ℒe Person body corporate, (legal) corporation.

K

Kabel-depesche (‿″…) *f* ㉒ *tel.* cablegram.

Kabinetts-beschluß (‿‿ʊ…) *m* ㉒ *pol.* Cabinet decision.

*****Kabriolett** *mot.* cabriolet.

*****Kaffee** zu a): ∼ verkehrt milk with a dash.

Kahl-schlag (‿⸱) *m* ㉒ *for.* **1.** complete deforestation. — **2.** (Lichtung) clearing.

Kai-arbeiter ⚓ (″…) *m* ㉒ docker, longshoreman.

Kalender-block (‿ʊ‿…) *m* ㉒ date-block.

Kalk-stick-stoff (ʊ‿…) *m* ㉒ *chm.* calcium cyanamid(e).

Kälte-industrie (ʊ‿…) *f* ㉒ freezer- (or cold-storage) industry.

Kamera-mann (‿″ʊ‿ʊ) *m* ㉒ Filmwesen: cameraman.

Kamin zu 2: *mount.* chimney.

Kamm-garn-spinnerei 2. (Fabrik) worsted (spinning-)mill; **-garn-stoff** *m* worsted.

Kampf-bahn (ʊ″…) *f* ㉒ Sport: stadium; **-flug-zeug** ✈ *n* fighting plane; *-preis *m* Sport: fighting-prize.

Kanal-dampfer ⚓ (‿″…) *m* ㉒ zwischen England u. Frankreich: cross-Channel steamer; **-flieger** ✈ *m* cross-Channel pilot.

*****Kanalisation** 2. (Entwässerung) drainage; e-r Stadt: sewerage (auch = Kanalsystem).

Kanal-strahlen ⚡ (‿″…) *m/pl. phys.* canal rays *pl.*

Kannel-kohle ⊤ (ʊ‿…) [engl.] *f* ㉒ cannel-coal.

*****Kanone** 4. F (Hauptkerl) crack (hand).

*****Kapital** zu I 1: stehendes ∼ fixed capital.

Kapital-abwanderung (ʊʊ‿…) *f* ㉒ migration of capital to foreign countries; **-bildung** *f* formation of (new) capital; **-erhöhung** *f* increase of c.; **-ertrag** *m* c. yield; **-ertragssteuer** *f* tax on c. yield; **-flucht** *f* flight of capital (abroad); **-herabsetzung** *f* decrease of c.

kapitalistisch (ʊʊ‿ʊ) *a.* ㊿ capitalistic(ally *adv.*).

*****Kappe** zu 4: e-s Zahnes: crown; e-n Zahn mit e-r ∼ versehen to crown.

Karborund ⊙(‿ʊ‿) [lat. + indisch (Korund)] *n* ⓓd. (Poliermittel) carborundum.

Kardan-gelenk ⊙ (‿″…) *n* ㉒ cardan-joint.

*****Karosserie** (car-)body.

Kartei (‿⸱) *f* ㊻ card-index, c.-registry, filing-cabinet.

Kartoffel-bauch P (‿ʊ‿⸱) *m* ㉒ pot-belly.

Kartonagen-fabrik ⊙ ‿(‿″ʊ‿…) *f* ㉒ cardboard box factory.

Kartothek (‿‿⸱) *f* ㊻ = Kartei.

*****Kasse** zu 3: gegen ∼ verkaufen to sell for cash; per ∼ zahlen to pay per cash.

Kassen-arzt (‿ʊ⸱) *m* ㉒ panel doctor.

*****Kassette** 3. *phot.* plate-holder.

*****kassieren** zu 1: ⚔ = einkassieren.

Kataster-amt (‿ʊ‿⸱) *n* ㉒ land registry.

katastrophal (‿‿⸱f‿) *a.* ㊿ catastrophic(ally *adv.*).

Kathoden-strahlen ⚡ (‿″‿…) *m/pl. elect.* cathode rays *pl.*

*****Kauf-geld** 2.(Angeld) earnest(-money); *****-lustig** disposed or inclined to buy; **-zwang** *m* obligation to buy; fein ∼ free inspection invited. [stamp.]

Kautschuk-stempel (‿″‿…) *m* ㉒ rubber)

Kegel-rad ⊙ (″…) *n* ㉒ bevel wheel; **-rad-getriebe** ⊙ *n* bevel gear.

*****Kehre** zu 1: e-r Gebirgsstraße: bend, turn. — 3. Turnerei: rear-vault.

Keil-schnitt (″⸱) *m* ㉒ beim Zigarrenabschneiden: wedge-cut.

Keim-träger (″…) *m* ㉒ *med.* carrier.

Keks (-) *m*(*n*)/*pl.* biscuits *pl.*

Kerosin ⚡ (-‿⸱) [grch. *kērós* = Wachs] *n* ⓓd. (Art Leuchtöl) kerosene.

Kerzen-schirm (‿ʊ‿) *m* ㉒ candle-shade.

*****Kette** 6. (Reihe wartender Personen, Wagen usw.) queue; ∼ stehen to stand in (a) queue.

Ketten-geschäft ⊙ (‿ʊ‿…) *n* ㉒ multiple store, Am. chain-store; **-handel** ⚖ *m* chain-trade; **-laden** ∼ = -geschäft; **-rad** ⊙ *n* am Fahrrad usw.: sprocket-wheel; **-raucher** *m* chain-smoker.

Kilometer-zähler ⊙ (-‿″‿…) *m* ㉒ (h)odometer.

Kilowatt-stunde (-‿ʊ‿) *f* ㉒ *elect.* kilowatt hour, Board of Trade unit (*abbr.* B.T.U.).

Kinder-fürsorge (‿″…) *f* ㉒ child welfare; **-hort** *m* day-nursery; **-lähmung** *f, path.* infantile paralysis; **-reichtum** *m* abundance of children.

Kindes-entführer (‿″…) *m* ㉒, **-räuber** *m* baby-snatcher.

Kinn-haken (‿″…) *m* ㉒ Boxen: uppercut.

Kino² P (‿⸱) [Kinematograph] *n* ㊿ cinema, the pictures *pl.*; **-besucher(in** *f*) *m* ㉒ picture-goer; **-vorstellung** *f* cinema-show, the pictures *pl.*

Kipp-lauf-gewehr (‿ʊ‿…) *n* ㉒ break-joint gun.

Kirchen-steuer (‿ʊ‿…) *f* ㉒ church-rate.

*****Kiste** 2. *mot.* u. ⚔ *sl.* bus.

Kitsch (ʊ) *m* ⓐa. trumpery, trash.

kitschig (‿ʊ) *a.* ㊿ trumpery, trashy.

Kittel-kleid (‿⸱) *n* ㉒ Schneiderei: woman's or child's tunic.

*****Klage-schrift** statement of claim.

Klang-fülle ♪ (‿″…) *f* ㉒ sonority.

Klappen-kasten (‿ʊ‿…) *m* ㉒ e-r elektr. Klingelanlage: annunciator.

Klapper-decklein (‿ʊ‿) *n* ㉒ unter Teller usw. zu legen: doily, doyly.

Klapp-kamera (ʊ‿…) *f* ㉒ *phot.* folding camera; *-sitz *m* *thea. a.* tip-up seat.

*****Klasse** 2. ⚓ = Segelklasse.

klassen-bewußt (‿ʊ‿…) *a.* ㊿ class-conscious; **-bewußtsein** *n* ㉒ class-consciousness; **-justiz** *f* class-justice; **-kampf** *m* class-war(fare), c.-conflict, c.-struggle.

*****klatschen** zu I 2: mit den Flügeln ♀ to flap, clap. — zu II: mit der Fliegenklappe ♀ to flap.

Klavier-vortrag ♪ (‿″…) *f* ㉒ pianoforte-recital.

Klebe-mittel adhesive.

Kleider-bügel (″…) *m* ㉒ coat-hanger; **-puppe** *f* in Bekleidungsgeschäften: lay-figure.

*****klein** zu I 3: Kleine Anzeigen *f/pl.* (Zeitungsrubrik) Smalls *pl.*

Klein-auto (″…) *n* ㉒ *mot.* light (or small) car, runabout; **-bauern-siedlung** *f* home-croft; **-flug-zeug** ✈ *n* baby aeroplane; **-kaliber-büchse** *f* miniature rifle; **-kaliber-schießen** *n* miniature rifle shooting; **-luft-schiff** ✈ *n* baby airship; **-rentner** *m* small investor or capitalist; **-steller** *m* der Gaslampe: by-pass.

*****Klemme** zu 1: *elect.* clamp, binding post, connector.

Klemm-schraube ⊙ (‿″…) *f* ㉒ fixing (or clamping) screw. [rope.]

Kletter-seil (‿ʊ‿) *n* ㉒ *mount.* climbing)

*****Klinik** nursing home.

*****Klinke** *elect.* jack.

*****Klischee** block, cut, electro.

*****klopfen** zu I 1: es klopft there's a knock at the door.

*****Klopfer** zu 2: Radio: decoherer.

klopf-fest ⊙ (‿″…) *a.* ㊿, **-frei** *a., mot.* v. Kraftstoff: anti-knock.

Kloset-becken (‿⸱‿…) *n* ㉒ lavatory bowl, flushing-pan; **-bürste** *f* W.C. brush. [quenelle.]

*****Klößchen** Kocht. ∼ v. Fleisch od. Fisch)

*****Koch-geschirr** ⚔ mess-tin, canteen; *-kiste hay-box.

Ko-edukation ⚡ (-‿-‿(″)…) [it.] *f* ㉒ (gemeinschaftlicher Unterricht für Knaben u. Mädchen) co-education.

Koffer-grammophon ♪ (‿ʊ‿…) *n* ㉒ portable gramophone.

Kognak-bohne ⚘ (kŏ″n-jäk…) *f* ㉒ brandy-ball.

Kohle-hydrat ⚡ (″‿…) *n* ㉒ *chm.* carbohydrate.

Kohlen-anzünder ⚘ (‿″…) *m* ㉒ (Brennstoff) fire-lighter; **-bergbau** ⛏ *m* coal-mining; **-faden-lampe** *f, elect.* carbon filament lamp; **-not** *f* coal famine; **-revier** ⛏ *n* coal-district, c.-field; **-säure-schnee** *m, chm.* carbon dioxide snow; **-syndikat** ⚘ *n* coal-syndicate.

Kohle-papier (‿″…) *n* ㉒ carbon paper; **-zeichnung** *f* charcoal drawing.

Kokerei (-‿⸱) *f* ㊻ coking kiln.

Kolben-lager ⊙ (‿ʊ‿…) *n* ㉒ *mach.* piston-bearing.

Kolonial-wirtschaft (‿-‿″…) *f* ㉒ colonial trade or commerce.

Kolonisator (‿‿⸱‿) *m* ㉛ colonizer.

Komitadschi (‿‿‿⸱) [serb., *It.* co'mes = Gefährte] *m* ㉒ (Aufständischer auf dem Balkan) comitadji, komita(d)ji.

*****kommen** zu I 10: zu et. ℒ (in den Besitz e-r S. kommen) to come by a th.

kommerzialisieren (⌣⌣́(⌣)-⌣⌢́⌣) I v/a. ⑬ (in den Handel bringen) to commercialize. — II ~ n ㉓, **Kommerzialisierung** f ㊻ commercialization.
Kommunal-betrieb (⌣⌣⌢́⌣...) m ㉒ communal trading; konkret: c. (trade-) undertaking.
kommunalisieren (⌣⌣-⌣⌢́⌣) I v/a. ⑬ (e-r [Stadt=]Gemeinde unterstellen) to communalize. — II ~ n ㉓, **Kommunalisierung** f ㊻ communalization.
Kompagnie-offizier ⚔ (⌣pa-nī"...) m ㉒ company officer.
*Komplex zu I: Psychologie: complex.
*komplizieren: kompliziert surg. v. e-m Knochenbruch: compound.
Kompressions-hahn ⊙ (⌣⌣(⌣)⌢́⌣) m ㉒ compression-tap.
*Konjunktur: ⚕ sinkende ~ business recession; steigende ~ business revival.
Konjunktur-bericht ⚕ (⌣⌣⌢́⌣...) m ㉒ report on business-conditions; -bewegung f cyclical movement; -forschung f research into economic cycles; -gewinn m market profit; -lage f market condition, business; -schwankung f market vacillation; -verkauf m seasonal sale.
*konkret: Ɛe Frage actual question.
*Konkurrenz (Einzelnummer innerhalb e-r größeren sportlichen Veranstaltung) event; außer ~ not competing, hors concours.
Konkurrenz-kampf (⌣⌣⌢́⌣...) m ㉒ (struggle of) competition, trade rival; -preis m competitive price.
Konkurs-verwalter (⌣⌣⌢́⌣...) m ㉒ trustee (in bankruptcy), receiver.
Konserven-büchse (⌣⌣⌢́⌣...) f ㊻, -dose f tin, Am. can; -industrie f tinning industry, Am. canning (or packing) i.
*konstituieren: parl. das Haus konstituiert sich als ... the House resolves itself into ...
Kontakt-knopf ⊙ (⌣⌢́⌣) m ㉒ elect. push-button; -schalter m contact switch; -schnur f flex; -stecker, -stöpsel m contact plug.
kontern ⚔ (⌢́⌣) [engl.] v/n. ⓐ. Boxen: (e-n Schlag durch Gegenschlag parieren) to counter.
Konto-auszug ⚕ (⌢́-...) m ㉒ abstract of account.
Kontoristin ⚕ (⌣-⌢́⌣) f ㊼ female (or lady) clerk.
kontrakt-widrig (⌣⌢́⌣...) a. ㊺ contrary to the contract.
Kontroll-abschnitt (⌣⌢́⌣...) m ㉒, -blatt n counterfoil.
*kontrollieren (nachprüfen) to verify.
Kontroll-kasse (⌣⌢́⌣...) f ㊻ cash-register; -marke f in großen Betrieben: time-keeping check; -schein m counterfoil; -uhr f controlling (or tell-tale) clock.
Konzentrations-lager ⚔ (⌣⌣-⌣ts(⌣)⌢́⌣...) n ㉓ concentration camp.
Konzern ⚕ (⌣⌢́⌣) [engl., *It.*] m ⓐd. combine. [knob.↑
*Kopf zu 1: ⦾ Radio: ~ der Stalenscheibe
Kopf-arbeiter (⌣⌢́⌣...) m ㉒ brain-worker; -ball m Fußball: heading.
*köpfen zu 1: Fußball: to head.
Kopf-hörer ⊙ (⌣⌢́⌣...) m ㉒ Fernspr., Radio: head-receiver, headphone; -hörer

bügel m head-band; -reim m, pros. head-rhyme; -schützer m Balaclava helmet; -zeile f head-line.
*koppeln 5. tel., Radio: to couple.
Koppler (⌢́⌣) m ㉒ tel., Radio: coupler.
Korb-möbel (⌢́⌣...) n/pl. ㉒ wicker furniture; *-stuhl m wicker chair.
Körner-fritter (⌢́⌣...) m ㉒ drahtlose Telegraphie: granular coherer.
Körper-kultur (⌢́⌣...) f ㉒, -pflege f physical culture.
Körperschafts-steuer (⌢́⌣...) f ㉒ corporation profits tax.
Körper-treffer (⌢́⌣...) m/pl. Boxen: rechte und linke ~ rights and lefts to the body.
*Korrespondent 2. ⚕ in e-r Bank usw.: clerk in charge of the correspondence.
Korrespondenz-büro (⌣⌣-⌣⌢́⌣...) n ㉒ press-agency, news-agency.
Kosaken-stiefel ⚔ (⌣⌢́⌣...) m/pl. Russian boots pl.
Kosten-berechnung (⌢́⌣...) f ㊻ calculation of cost, costing; -frage f question of cost; ⁰pflichtig a. ㊻ with costs, bound (or liable) to pay costs.
*Kostüm 2. für ein Kostümfest: fancy dress. — 3. Schneiderei: (Jackettkleid) suit.
Kostüm-probe (⌣⌢́⌣...) f ㉒ thea. dress rehearsal.
Kot-flügel ⊙ (⌢́⌣...) m ㉒ am Wagen: mud-guard, mot. a. fender.
Krabbe zu 1: (Garnele) shrimp.
Kraft-anlage (⌢́⌣...) f ㉒ power-plant; -droschke f taxi(-cab); -fahrer(in f) m motorist, automobilist; -fahr-schule f school of motoring; -fahr-truppe(n pl.) ⚔ f mechanical transport service; -fahr-wesen n motoring, automobilism; ⚔ = -fahrtruppe; -fahr-zeug n motor vehicle; -futter n concentrated feed.
*kräftig zu 1: paint., phot. Ɛe Lichter n/pl. high lights pl.
Kraft-last-wagen (⌢́⌣...) m ㉒ motor lorry; -omnibus m motor (omni)bus; -rad n motor (bi)cycle; -stoff m, mot motor spirit, fuel; -stück n stunt.
Kranken-auto (⌣⌢́⌣...) n ㉒ motor ambulance; -geld n sick(ness) benefit; -kassenarzt m panel doctor; Liste f der Krankenkassenärzte panel; -schwester f hospital nurse; -unterstützung f = -geld; -versicherung f sick(ness) insurance.
Kräusel-stoff ⚕ (⌣⌢́⌣) m ripple-cloth.
*Krebs zu 1: fig. Ruderei: e-n ~ fangen to catch a crab.
Kredit-reise-brief (-⌣⌢́...) m ㉒ traveller's letter of credit; -wirtschaft f credit economy.
Kreide-papier (⌢́⌣...) n ㉒ coated (or art) paper.
*Kreis zu 3: in Parlamentskreisen in Parliamentary quarters.
Kreisel-kompaß (⌢́⌣...) m ㉒ phys. gyro-compass; -pumpe ⊙ f centrifugal pump.
Kreis-teil-maschine f circular dividing machine; -verkehr (⌢́⌣...) m ㉒ auf verkehrsreichen öffentlichen Plätzen: gyratory (or roundabout) system (of traffic).
Krepp-gummi ⊙ (⌣⌢́⌣...) n u. m ㉒ crêpe rubber; -papier n crêpe paper.

Kreuz-gelenk ⊙ (⌢́⌣...) n mech. universal joint; -wort-rätsel n (bei dem e-e Reihe bestimmter einander kreuzender Wörter gefunden werden muß) crossword puzzle. [-serviceman.↑
*Krieger: alter (ob. ehemaliger) ~ ex-/
Krieger-grab (⌣⌢́⌣′) n ㉒ war-grave.
Kriegs-anleihe (⌢́⌣...) f ㉒ war-loan; -beschädigte(r) m war-invalid, disabled ex-serviceman; -blinde(r) m blind(ed) ex-serviceman; -gebiet n war-zone; -gewinn m war-profit; -gewinnler m war-profiteer; -industrie f war-industry; -kind n war-baby; -lasten f/pl. burdens (or charges) of war; -schieber m war-profiteer; -schuld f 1. (Schuld aus e-r Kriegsanleihe) war-debt. — 2. (Schuld am Kriege) war-guilt; -schuldverschreibung f war-bond; -teilnehmer m combatant, ehemaliger ~ ex-serviceman; -trauung f war-wedding.
Kriminal-polizei (-⌣⌢́...) f ㉒ detective police; Lo. Criminal Investigation Department; -polizist m detective; -roman m detective novel.
*Krippe 2. (Säuglingsheim) crèche.
Krisen-fürsorge (⌢́⌣...) f ㉒ emergency unemployment relief.
Kristall-detektor (⌣⌢́⌣...) m ㉒ Radio: crystal detector.
*Kröpfung 3. ⊙ bend, shoulder.
krumig (⌢́⌣) a. ㊺ v. Brot: crumby.
Kruschen-salz (⌣⌢́⌣) n ㊻ chm. Kruschen salts pl.
Kubismus (⌣⌢́⌣) [lt.] m ㉗ paint. (moderne Richtung, bei der das Bild aus einer Vereinigung geometrischer Figuren besteht) cubism.
Kubist (⌣⌢́) m ㉒ paint. cubist.
kubistisch (⌣⌢́⌣) a. ㊺ paint. cubistic(ally adv.), cubist.
*Kufe² ✈ ~ e-s Landflugzeuges: skid.
*Kugel-gelenk ⊙ ball-joint; -lager ⊙ n, mach. ball-bearing; -spitz-feder f ball-pointed pen; -stange f Turnerei: bar-bell; ⁰stoßen Leichtathletik: I v/n. ⓐa.** to put the weight. — II ~ n ㉓ putting the weight.
Kühl-anlage ⊙ (⌢́⌣...) f ㉒ cold-storage plant.
*Kühler 3. mot. radiator.
Kühler-figur (⌢́⌣...) f ㉒ mot. radiator mascot; -verschraubung f, mot. radiator (filler) cap.
Kühl-haus (⌢́⌣...) n ㉒ cold-storage building; -mantel ⊙ m cooling jacket; -rippe ⊙ f, mot. gill, radiator fin.
Kultur-land (⌢́⌣...) n ㉒ agr. cultivated (or tilled or arable) land; -stufe f stage of civilization.
*kündbar c) v. Anleihen: redeemable; d) v. Rentenbriefen: terminable.
Kunden-dienst ⚕ (⌢́⌣...) m ㉒ custom-work; -fang m snaring of customers; -wechsel m customer's acceptance; -werbung f solicitation of customers.
*kündigen ⚕ Kapital: to recall.
*Kündigung call of securities; calling in of money lent; mit monatlicher ~ subject to a month's notice.
Kunst-anstalt (⌢́⌣...) f ㉒ art printing works or office; -blatt n art print,

Kunstdruckerei — 18 — **Lichtbildnerei**

=druckerei f = anſtalt; =eis n artificial ice; =fahrer(in f) m =radfahrer; =laufen n Eisſport: figure-skating; =leder n imitation leather, leatherette; =radfahrer(in f) m trick-cyclist; =ſeide f artificial silk, rayon; =ſpringen n Schwimmſport: diving; =ſtein m artificial stone; *=ſtück (Kraftſtück) stunt; =wart m Art Adviser.
Kupp(e)lungs-fuß-hebel ⊙ (ˈ(ˇ)ˇ...) m ⊕ mot. clutch lever or pedal; =ſtange f, mach. draw-bar.
*kurbeln II v/a. e-n Film: to crank off.
Kurbel-gehäuſe ⊙ (ˇˇ...) n ⊕, =kaſten m, mach. crank-case; =zapfen ⊙ m, mach. crank-pin.
Kurs-feſt-ſetzung ⊕ (ˇ...) f ⊕ Börſe: rate-fixing; =gewinn m profit by exchange; =makler m sworn (or inside) broker; =wert m market-value.
***Kurve** (Krümmung e-r Straße uſw.) bend, curve; ⚓ in die ~ gehen to bank.
Kurven-blatt (ˇˇ...) n ⊕, =darſtellung f, math., chm., phys. graph.
Kurz-arbeit (ˇˇ...) f ⊕ ⊕ short time; =arbeiter m worker on short time.
Kürzel (ˇˇ) [kurz] n ⊕ Kurzſchrift: grammalogue.
kurz-friſtig (ˇˇ...) a. ⊕ short-dated; ⚡ ſchließen v/a. ⊕ d. ** elect. to short-circuit; =ſtrecken-fahrer m, =ſtrecken-läufer m Sport: sprinter.
***Kürzung** 3. ~ der Ausgaben retrenchment of expenses; ~ des Lohnes reduction of (or cut in) wages. — 4. Kurzſchrift: = ~s-zeichen.
Kürzungs-zeichen (ˇˇ...) n ⊕ Kurzſchrift: grammalogue.
Kurz-wellen (ˇ...) f/pl. ⊕ elect. short waves pl.; =wellen-..., ⚡ wellig a. ⊕ elect. short-wave(d); =wort n ⊕ shortened word, abbreviation. [proof.]
kuß-feſt (ˇˇ) a. ⊕ v. Lippenſchminke: kiss-
Küſten-dampfer ⚓ (ˇˇ...) m ⊕ coasting-steamer; =dienſt m gegen Schmuggelei: preventure service.
k. v. ⚔ abbr. = Kriegsverwendungs-fähig A 1.

L

labil ⚛ (ˇˇ) [lt.] a. ⊕ bſd. mech. unstable.
***lächerlich** zu I 1: (unbedeutend) derisory.
Lade-fläche ⊙ (ˇˇ...) f ⊕ e-s Wagens: loading area; =hemmung f e-r Feuerwaffe: jam; ~ haben to jam; =linie ⚓ f load-line.
***laden²** zu I: elect. e-e Batterie: to charge.
Laden-gehilfin (ˇˇ...) f ⊕ shop-assistant, shop-girl; =ſchild n facia, sign.
***Lade-platz** c) ⚓ (Verſandhafen) port of shipment; =ſtation f, elect. battery-charging station.
Lage zu 1: j-n in die ~ (ver)ſetzen, et. zu tun to enable a p. to do a th.
***Lager** zu 2 b) e-s Haſen: form. — zu 6: ⚑ ab ~ ex warehouse.
Lager-bock ⊙ (ˇˇ...) m ⊕ bearing bracket or support or stand; =feuer n camp-fire; =genoſſenſchaft f Agricultural Co-operative Warehouse Society; =halter m distributor; =koſten pl. warehousing (expenses), storage;

=metall ⊙ n antifriction metal, bearing metal.
Laien-richter (ˇˇ...) m ⊕ jur. lay judge.
***Lamelle** elect. lamina (pl. laminæ), bar; ⚘ der Pilze: gill; ⊙ mot. ⌣ n pl. der Kupplung: clutch disks pl.
Lamellen-kupplung ⊙ (-ˇˇ...) f ⊕ mot. disk clutch.
Lampion (ˇ(ˇ)ŏ'ng) [fr.] m u. n 🏮 Japanese (or Chinese) lantern.
***lancieren** fig. to launch, float.
Landaulette (läng-do-lĕ't) [fr.- *dtſch. (Stadt Landau)] f ⊕ mot. (Kraftwagenform) landaulet.
Land-bank ⚑ (ˇ...) f ⊕ farmers' (or agricultural) bank; =bund m, pol. im Deutſchen Reich: Farmers' Union; =brücke f, geol. land-bridge; =hunger m a) greed for land; b) pol. greed for territory. [cultural loan-bank.]
Landſchafts-bank ⚑ (ˇˇ...) f ⊕ agri-
Land-ſtraßen-ſchreck F (ˇˇˇˇ) m (rückſichtsloſer Automobiliſt) road-hog.
Langette ⊙ (ˇˇˇ) [fr.] f 🪡 (Ausbogung) scallop.
***langettieren** to scallop.
lang-friſtig (ˇ...) a. ⊕ long-dated; =geſchoß n ⚔ u. hunt. (ant. Rundkugel) long shot.
langſam zu 1: ⚔ Der Schritt goose-step.
Lang-ſchäfter (ˇˇ...) m/pl. ⊕ high boots, Wellingtons pl. [side-member.]
Längs-träger ⊙ (ˇˇ...) m ⊕ mot. (frame)
Lang-ſtrecken-läufer ⊙ (ˇˇ...) m ⊕, =ſtreckler m Sport: stayer; =wellen-..., ⚡ wellig a. ⊕ elect. long-wave(d).
***läſtig**: pol. Der Ausländer undesirable alien.
Laſt-kraft-wagen ⊙ (ˇˇ...) m ⊕ motor lorry or truck; =ſchrift f Bankweſen: (act of) debiting; debit-item.
Latifundien-beſitz (-ˇˇ(ˇ)ˇ...) m ⊕ large landed property.
***Latrine** bſd. ⚔ latrine.
Laub-baum ⚘ (ˇˇ) m ⊕ deciduous (or broad-leaf or broad-leaved) tree, foliage-tree. [garden.]
Lauben-kolonie (ˇˇˇ...) f ⊕ allotment]
***Laub-holz** ⚘ = Laubbaum.
Lauf-decke (ˇˇ...) f ⊕ mot. tyre shoe, tyre cover.
***Läufer** zu 2: f) elect. an der Dynamo: rotor.
***Lauf-ſchritt** als Kommando: ~! at the double!
Laut-film (ˇˇ...) m ⊕ sound-film, phonofilm; im ~ darſtellen to phonofilm; ⚡ hals adv., hunt. (laut bellend) in full cry; =ſprecher m Radio: loud-speaker; =ſtärke f intensity (ob. bſd. Radio: volume) of sound; =ſtärke-regler m Radio: volume regulator or control.
Lazarett-ſchiff ⚓ (ˇˇˇ...) n ⊕ hospital-ship.
Lebens-gewicht ⚑ (ˇˇ...) n ⊕ live)
***Lebens-führung** b) mode (or way) of life or living; =gemeinſchaft f partnership for life; =mittel-karte f food-card, ration-book; =mittel-knappheit f food-shortage; =mittel-verſorgung f food-supply; =ſtellung b) (lebenslängliche Berufsſtellung) permanent position (or situation); ⚡ wichtig a. ⊕ essential to life, vital(ly important); vgl. Betrieb.

Leber-knödel (ˇˇ...) m ⊕ Kocht. faggot.
Leder-fett ⊙ (ˇˇ...) n ⊕ leather-fat, dubbin(g); =gamaſchen f/pl. leather gaiters; leggings; =öl n leather-oil.
Ledigen-ſteuer (ˇˇˇ...) f ⊕ tax on bachelorhood.
***leer** zu II 1: mach. ⚙ laufen to run free or idle.
***leeren** zu I: ⚘ Poſtkaſten: to clear.
Leer-gewicht ⚑ (ˇˇ...) n ⊕ weight empty, deadweight; =gut ⚑ n empties pl.; =lauf m, mach. light running, no-load work; ⚡ laufend ⊙ a. ⊕ a) mach. idle; b) ⚓ travelling in ballast; ⚡ pumpen v/a. ⊕ ** to pump dry; =verkauf ⚑ m ⊕ short sale.
Lehr-film (ˇˇ...) m ⊕ instructional film; =kurs m course of instruction.
***leicht** zu 3: ⚛ entzündlich highly inflammable.
Leicht-athletik (ˇˇˇ...) f ⊕ Sport: athletics sg. u. pl.; =gewicht n Boxen: light-weight; =metall ⊙ n light metal.
Leidens-weg (ˇˇˇ) m ⊕ eccl. way of the Cross.
***leider** oft: I am afraid, z.B. ⚙ muß ich gehen I am afraid I have to go.
Leinen-papier ⊙ (ˇˇ...) n ⊕ linen paper.
***Leinwand** im Filmtheater: screen; e. Bild auf die ~ werfen to screen.
Leinwand-ſchirm (ˇˇ...) m ⊕ im Filmtheater uſw.: screen.
***Leiſtung** zu 2: Sport: performance; mach., elect. power; e-r Fabrik uſw.: (Produktionsmenge) output.
Leiſtungs-wucher (ˇˇ...) m ⊕ jur. extortionate price demanded for services (to be) rendered.
***leiten** zu II 1: phys. to conduct; tel. Fernſpr. über e-e Linie ⚙ to route over a trunk.
***Leit-hund** 2. e-s Schlittengeſpanns: outrunner.
***Leitung** zu 2: elect. fontret: lead. — zu 3: b) = Waſſerleitung.
Leitungs-aufſeher (ˇˇ...) m ⊕ tel. Fernſpr. lineman; =netz n, elect. supply network, distribution system; =waſſer n company's (or tap) water.
Lenk-rad ⊙ (ˇˇ...) n ⊕ mot. steering wheel; =ſäule f, mot. steering column; =ſchnecke f, mot. steering worm; *=ſtange e-s Fahrrades: handle-bar.
***lernen** zu III gelernt 6: v. Arbeit(er): skilled.
***letzt** zu II 1: Die Nachrichten f/pl. e-r Zeitung: late (or stop-press) news pl.
Leucht-mittel (ˇˇ...) n ⊕ illuminant; =mittel-ſteuer f tax on illuminants; =piſtole ⚔ f Very pistol; =rakete ⚔ u. ⚓ f star-light; =uhr f luminous clock or watch; =ziffer-blatt n luminous dial; =ziffern f/pl. in Uhren: luminous figures pl.
Leukämie ⚛ (--ˇ) [grch. = Weißblütigkeit] f ⊕ path. leucocytæmia.
Leute-not (ˇˇ) f ⊕ scarcity of workpeople.
Levante-handel (ˇˇˇˇ...) m ⊕ trade with the Levant.
Licht-anlage (ˇˇ...) f ⊕ lighting plant or system; =bad n solar bath, insolation; =bild-kunſt f, =bildnerei

photography; =bogen m, elect. (offener, geschlossener) ~ (open, enclosed) arc; =bogen-bildung f, elect. arcing; ℒecht a. 🜨 fast to light, fadeless; ℒelektrisch a., phys. photo-electric(ally); *ℒempfindlich: ℒ machen chm. to sensitize; =empfindlichkeit f sensibility to light. *lichten¹ zu I: hort. junge Pflanzen: to thin out.
Licht-heil-kunde (ˉ...) f med. ⚚ phototherapeutics sg., a. pl.; =heil-verfahren n, med. light (or sunray) treatment, ⚚ phototherapy; ℒhof-frei a. 🜨 (D 1,7) phot. anti halo; =jahr n, ast. light-year; =leitung f, elect. lighting circuit; =maschine f, mot. generator; =paus-apparat m Kunstdruck: copying apparatus; =pause f Kunstdruck: photographic (or blue) print; =paus-lampe f copying lamp; =paus-verfahren n photographic printing; =reklame f illuminated advertising; =signal n luminous signal; =spiel-leinwand f Filmwesen: (film) screen; =spiel-theater n cinematograph theatre, picture-theatre, p.-house, p.-palace.
Liebes-knochen F (ˉ...) m 🜨 (Art Gebäck) Cupid's whisper.
Lieb-haber-wert (ˉ...) m 🜨 sentimental value.
Lieder-abend (ˉ...) m 🜨 ballad concert.
Lieferungs-werk (ˉ...) n 🜨 Buchhandel: serial.
Liefer-wagen ☗ (ˉ...) m 🜨 delivery van.
Liege-kur (ˉ...) f 🜨 med. rest-cure; =stuhl m deck-chair, long-chair; *=tage ⚓ lay-days pl.
Liga-spiel (ˉ¹) n 🜨 Sport: league-match.
Liliputaner (ˇˇˉ) m 🜨, ~in f 🜨, liliputanisch a. 🜨 Lilliputian.
Limousine ⊙ (ˇˉˇ) [fr.] f 🜨 mot. (Kraftwagenform) limousine; ~ mit Innenlenkung sedan.
*link zu II 4: parl. bsd. im Deutschen Reich: the Left. — III ~e(r) m 🜨 5. Boxen: left; gerader ~er straight left, jab.
Linkrusta ⊙ (ˇˇˇ) [it.] f 🜨 (künstliches Leder) lincrusta.
Links-außen(-stürmer) (ˉ...) m 🜨 Fußball: outside left; =drall ⊙ m left-handed lay or twist; =gewinde ⊙ n left-handed thread.
Linoleum-schnitt (ˉˇˇˇ) m 🜨 typ. Kunstgewerbe: linoleum engraving, lino cut.
Lippen-stift (ˉˇˇ) m 🜨 lip-stick.
*Liquidation (Honorarforderung) bsd. vom Arzt: charge.
*liquidieren zu I: b) (als Honorar verlangen) bsd. vom Arzt: to charge.
Listen-wahl (ˉˇˇ) f 🜨 parl. election by ticket.
*Litze 4. elect. strand(ed wire), flexible.
Lizenz-geber (ˇˇ...) m 🜨 licenser; =gebühren f/pl. royalties pl.; =nehmer m licensee.
Lobeli-e ⚘ (ˉˇˇˇ) [Prsn.] f 🜨 lobelia.
*Loch zu 1: im Luftreifen: puncture.
*Locher für abzulegende Briefe usw.: file-punch, perforator.
Loch-wett-spiel (ˉˇˇ) n 🜨 Golf: (ant. Zählwettspiel) match play.

Lohn-büro ☗ (ˉ...) n 🜨 wage-office, pay-office; =empfänger m wage-earner.
=löhnen v/n. to pay wages.
Lohn-erhöhung (ˉ...) f 🜨 raising of wages, rise in wages; =forderung f demand for (higher) wages; =herabsetzung f decrease of wages, fall in wages; =liste f list of wages, wage(s)-sheet; =steuer f tax on wages; =wesen n matters pl. relating to wages.
lombardieren ☗ (ˇˇˉˇ) v/a. 🜨 a) to advance money on securities; b) to deposit pledges as security for a loan.
*Lorgnette lorgnette.
Lösch-bombe (ˉ...) f 🜨 fire-grenade; =mittel n fire-extinguisher.
Lose-blatt-bücher ☗ (ˉˉˇ...) n/pl. loose-leaf books pl.
*los-kommen ⚡ ℒ vom Land od. Wasser to take off; ℒlöten ⊙ v/a. 🜨** to unsolder.
Löt-naht ⊙ (ˉ...) f 🜨, =stelle f soldered seam or joint.
Luft-amt ⚡ (ˉ...) n 🜨 Air Board; =angriff ⚡ m air raid; =bad n air-bath; =bombe ⚡ f aerobomb; =dienst ⚡ m air-service; =draht m Radio: aerial; ℒelektrisch a. 🜨 phys. ℒe Störungen f/pl. atmospherics pl.; =fahrt-ministerium n im Britischen Reich: Air Ministry; =fahr-zeuge n/pl. jeder Art: coll. aircraft; =fanatiker m fresh-air fiend; ℒgefühlt ⊙ a. air-cooled; =hafen ⚡ m air-port; ℒkrank a., path. air-sick; =krankheit f, path. air-sickness; =leiter ⊙ m, elect. aerial; =loch ⚡ n (Stelle dünner Luft) air-pocket; =macht f air-power; =post f air-mail; =reifen m, mot. (pneumatic) tyre; =reiniger m air-filter, air-cleaner; =reisende(r) 🜨 air-passenger; =reklame f sky-line advertising; =saug-ventil n air suction valve; =schiff-hafen m airship depot; =schiff-halle f airship shed; =schlauch m, mot. (inner) tube; =schlauch-beschädigung f mot., Radsport: puncture; =schlitz m, mot. in der Motorhaube: louver, louvre; =sog ⚡ m wake; =störungen f/pl., phys. atmospheric disturbances, atmospherics pl.; =streitmacht f air-force; =stoß m, phys. air-eddy; =stütz-punkt ⚡ m air-base; =torpedo ⚡ m aerial torpedo; =überfall ⚡ m air-raid; =verkehrs-linie f air-way; =zufuhr f air supply.
Lüge: ~n strafen to belie one's words, &c.
Lumineszenz ⚚ (ˉˇˇˇ) [it.] f 🜨 phys. (Lichterregung) luminescence.
*Lustbarkeit: (öffentliche) ~ (public) entertainment; ~s-steuer f 🜨 entertainment(s) tax.
*Lust-mord lustful murder.
Lute-in ⚚ (-ˇˉ) [it.] n 🜨c. (gelber Farbstoff) lutein.
Lutscher (ˉˇ) m 🜨, Lutsch-pfropfen (ˉ...) m 🜨 für Säuglinge: (rubber) teat.
Luxus-auto (ˉˇ...) n 🜨 saloon-car.
*Luzerne ✿ alfalfa.
Lysol (-ˉ) [grch.] n 🜨c. pharm. lysol.
*Lyze-um b) (höhere Mädchenschule) Girls' High School.

M

Macht-politik (ˉ...) f 🜨 policy of the strong hand.
*Magen F little Mary, co. tub, Kindersprache: tummy.
Magnet-feld (ˇˉ...) n 🜨 phys. magnetic field; =zünder ⊙ m, mot. magneto.
Mai-feier (ˉ...) f 🜨 celebration of May-day, May-day Demonstration.
*Majorat 2. (~sgut) entail(ed estate).
Mako ☗ (ˇ-) [Prsn.] f 🜨 (feine [ägyptische] Baumwolle) maco.
Mal¹-mann (ˉˉ) m 🜨 Sport: scratch (man).
Malthusianismus (ˇ-(ˇ)-ˇˇ) [Malthus, engl. Volkswirtschaftler, 1766-1834] m 🜨 (Lehre v. der Notwendigkeit, die Bevölkerungszahl einzuschränken) Malthusianism.
Malz-bonbon (ˉ...) m 🜨 cough-lozenge.
Mal²-zeichen (ˉ...) n 🜨 arith. sign of multiplication, m. mark.
Malz-kaffee (ˉ...) m 🜨 malt-coffee.
Manchester ⓉⒻ (mä'n-tschö̈̈') [engl. St.] m = Manchester.
maniküren (ˇˇˉˇ) v/a. 🜨 (Hände, bsd. Nägel pflegen) to manicure.
Maniküre-kasten (ˇˇˉˇ...) m 🜨 manicure-case.
Mannequin (ˇˇtä'ng) [fr., *flämisch (ndd. = Männchen)] m 🜨 (Vorführdame) mannequin, ...kin.
Mannschafts-rennen (ˉˇˉ...) n 🜨 Sport: team-race.
*Manns-leute bsd. in e-m Haushalt: mankind.
*Manschester [Manchester] m 🜨, a. ~samt m 🜨 velveteen; gerippter: corduroy.
Manchestertum (ˇˇˉ-) n 🜨d. o. pl.; pol. (Befürwortung des Freihandels u. der politischen u. persönlichen Ungebundenheit) Manchesterism.
*Manschette zu 2: ~n haben vor (dat.) to funk.
*Mantel zu 3: mot., Radsport: cover, shoe of a tyre. — 5. ☗ Börse: ~ e-s zinstragenden Papiers scrip (or share) without the coupon-sheet.
Mantel-geschoß (ˉˇ...) n 🜨 metal-cased (or m.-covered) bullet; =gesetz n, parl. skeleton law; =tarif m skeleton agreement.
*Mappe zum Ablegen von Briefen usw.: file.
Marathon-lauf (ˉˇˇˉ) [grch. St.] m 🜨 Sport: Marathon race.
*Mariechen: ~ saß auf einem Stein (Kinderspiel) Poor Mary sits a-weeping, Poor Jenny is a-weeping.
Marien-verehrung (ˇˉˉ...) f 🜨 eccl. Mariolatry.
Marine-flug-zeug ⚓ (ˇˉˇ...) n 🜨 sea-plane; =station f naval base.
*Marke zu 2: (Fabrikat) make.
Marken-artikel ☗ (ˉˇ...) m 🜨 proprietary (or patent or branded) article.
*Markt zu 3: an (ob. auf) den ~ kommen to come to market. — 8. (Absatzgebiet) market(-area).
Markt-aushelfer (ˉ...) m 🜨 vanboy; ℒfähig a. 🜨 marketable, sal(e)able;

Marktfähigkeit — **Morphologie**

=fähigkeit f ⓐ marketability, salability; =wert m market-value.
*Marsch=anzug: Nacherzerzieren n im ~ pack-drill.
Marxismus (‿‿) [Karl Marx, 1818–1883, deutscher Sozialist] m ㉗ Marxism, a. Marxianism.
Marxist (‿‿) m ㊷ Marxian, Marxite; ‿isch (‿‿) a. ⓰ Marxian.
maschen=fest ⊙ (‿‿) a. ⓰ v. Strümpfen usw.: ladderproof.
Maschinen=antrieb ⊙ (‿‿‿) m ⓐ machine drive; mit ~ machine driven; =bau m construction of machines, mechanical engineering; =bau=anstalt f machine - factory, engineering works; =bau=wesen n mechanical engineering; =defekt m == schaden; =gewehr ⚔ n machine-gun; =gewehr=nest ⚔ n m.-gun nest; =meister zu b) thea. stage-mechanician; =schaden m engine trouble; =schreiben n typewriting; =schrift f typewriter type.
Maß=abteilung (‿‿) f ⓐ e-s großen Kleidergeschäfts: bespoke department.
Massen=absatz ✴ (‿‿) m ⓐ wholesale (or bulk) selling; =artikel m article made in bulk, bulk article; =aus=sperrung f general lock-out; =erzeugung f, =fabrikation f mass production, production in bulk; =grab n common grave; =herstellung f, =produktion f == erzeugung; =streik m general strike; =suggestion f mass suggestion; =verbrauch m mass consumption, bulk consumption.
*Maß=nahme 2. = Maßregel; =schneider m bespoke tailor; =schneiderei f bespoke tailoring; =schuster m bespoke bootmaker.
Material=kosten (-‿‿) pl ⓐ cost(s pl.) of material; =prüfung f testing of materials; =prüfungs=amt n testing station.
*Matinee 2. (Morgenkleid) peignoir.
mattieren ⊙ (‿‿) [matt] v/a. ⓷ to mat.
Matt=scheibe (‿‿) f ⓐ phot. ground glass.
Mauer=haken (‿‿) m ⓐ mount. piton.
*mauern zu 2: to stone-wall.
Maurer=fräse P (‿‿) f ⓐ (Bartkranz unter dem rasierten Kinn) Newgate fringe.
M.d.L. abbr. = Mitglied des Landtags Member of the Diet.
*mechanisch: 2e Leiter fire escape; 2er (Arbeits=)Mensch robot; 2er Webstuhl power-loom.
mechanisieren ⊙ (‿‿‿) I v/a. ⓷ to mechanize. — II ~ n ㉓ u. **Mechanisierung** f ⓰ mechanization.
Megaphon (‿‿‿) [grch.] n ⓓd. (Schallverstärker) megaphone.
*mehr zu 12: ich habe niemand (od. nichts) 2 I have no one (or nothing) left.
Mehr=arbeit (‿‿) f ⓐ surplus labour; =bedarf m surplus (or excess) demand; =einkommen n excess of income; =erlös m over-proceeds; =ertrag m increment; =gewinn m increased profit; excess profit; =kosten pl. additional cost; =leistung f a) increased performance or production; b) Versicherungs=

wesen: extended benefit; =preis m surplus price.
*Meinung zu 1: der ~ sein, daß ... to be of opinion that ...
Meister(in f) m 5. Sport: champion.
Meister=prüfung (‿‿‿) f ⓐ examination for the title of master.
Melde=fahrer ⚔ (‿‿‿) m ⓐ == Meldereiter; =gänger ⚔ m dispatch-runner.
*melden zu 1: v/n. Sport: to enter (zu for).
Melder (‿‿) m ㊷ 1. ⊙ alarm, signal. — 2. ⚔ == Melde=fahrer, =gänger, =reiter.
Melde=reiter ⚔ (‿‿‿) m ⓐ dispatch-rider; =schluß m Sport: closing (date) for entries.
Melioration (‿(‿)‿-t‿(‿)‿) [lt.] f ㊻ (a)melioration, improvement; jur. betterment.
*melken zu II: 2de Kuh milch cow.
*Melone 2. F (runder, steifer Männerfilzhut) bowler.
Menschen=material (‿‿‿) n ⓐ bsd. ⚔ verfügbares ~ man-power; =schinder m oppressor.
Menü=karte (‿‿) f ⓐ menu-card.
Merkantil=lithograph (‿‿‿) m ⓐ commercial lithographer.
Merk=blatt (‿‿) n ⓐ leaflet.
*merzerisieren II ~ n ㉓ u. **Merzerisierung** f ⓰ mercerization.
*messen zu II: med. j-s Temperatur 2 to take a p.'s temperature.
Messer=stecherei (‿‿‿) f ⓐ knife-battle; =(schmiede=)waren f/pl. cutlery.
Meß=ziffer (‿‿) f ⓐ index-number.
Metall=bestand (‿‿‿) m ⓐ Währungswesen: bullion (or specie) in hand; =deckung f Währungswesen: metallic cover; =industrie f metallurgical industry; =säge f hack-saw; =vorrat m Währungswesen: stock of bullion or specie; =währung f metallic standard or currency.
*Meter=maß 2. konkret: metre measure; =tonne f metre-ton.
methodisieren (‿‿‿‿) v/a. ⓷ to method.
M. G. ⚔ abbr. = Maschinengewehr m.g.
Mies=macher F (‿‿) n ⓐ alarmist.
Miet=auto (‿‿) n ⓐ motor hackney vehicle; =einigungs=amt n Housing Conciliation Board.
*Mieter einzelner Zimmer: lodger.
Mieter=schutz (‿‿‿) m ⓐ tenants' protection.
Miet=ertrag (‿‿) m ⓐ yield from rent, rental; =recht n rent (or housing) law.
Miets=taler (‿‿) m ⓐ earnest(-money).
Miet=verlust (‿‿) m ⓐ loss of rent; *=vertrag 2. ⚓ charter-party; =vorschuß m advance on the rent; =wert m rental value.
Milch=geschäft (‿‿) n ⓐ dairy; =pan(t)scher m adulterator of milk; =schleuder(=maschine) ⊙ f (milk-)separator; =wagen m milk-float.
Militär=flug=zeug ⚔ (‿‿‿) n ⓐ military aeroplane, war-plane.
Mille bsd. ✴ (‿‿) [lt.] n inv. thousand.
Minder=ausgabe (‿‿‿) f ⓐ a) reduced expenditure; b) ✴ von Wertpapieren: reduced issue; =bedarf m reduced demand; 2bemittelt a. ⓰ of moderate means; =ertrag b) reduction (or

falling-off) in output or yield; =gebot n lower bid; =preis m reduced price.
Mindest=gebot (‿‿‿) n ⓐ lowest bid; =lohn m minimum wage; =preis m minimum price.
Minen=leger ⚓ (‿‿‿) m ⓐ mine-layer; =sucher ⚓ m mine-sweeper; =werfer ⚔ m mine-thrower, ⚙ minenwerfer, trench mortar.
Minier=arbeit ⚔ (‿‿‿) f ⓐ sap(ping) (a. fig.).
*Minister: ~ für die besetzten Gebiete im Deutschen Reich Minister for the Occupied Areas.
Ministerial=direktor (‿‿(‿)‿‿) m ⓐ Permanent Secretary in a ministry.
Miß=wirtschaft (‿‿) f ⓐ maladministration, mismanagement.
*Mit=arbeit collaboration.
*Mit=esser blackhead, ⚕ comedo.
Mit=glieds=beitrag (‿‿‿) m ⓐ membership subscription; =glieds=karte f membership card, (member's) ticket; 2hören v/n. (h.) ⓰** Fernspr. to listen in, tap; 2klingen v/n. (h.) ⓓ** to resonate.
Mittags=ausgabe (‿‿‿) f ⓐ einer Zeitung: noon edition.
*mittel¹ (durchschnittlich) average.
Mittel=asi=en (‿‿‿) ⚥ npr/n. ⓑ α. Central Asia; =gewicht n ⓓ Boxen: middle-weight; =land=kanal m Midland Canal; =läufer m Fußball: centre half; =mächte f/pl., pol. Central Powers pl.; =meer=gebiet ⚥ n Mediterranean territory; =moräne f geol. medial moraine; =stands=... middle-class; =wert m average (or mean) value.
Mit=verschulden (‿‿‿) n ⓐ jur. contributory negligence.
Möbel=stück (‿‿‿) n ⓐ piece of furniture, fitment. [securities.]
*mobil ✴ easily realizable capital or]
mobilisieren zu I: ✴ to realize land. — zu II: ✴ realization of land.
modal ⚕ (‿‿) [lt.] a. ⓰ modal.
Modell=tischler ⊙ (-‿‿) m ⓐ pattern-maker.
Moden=schau ✴ (‿‿‿) f ⓐ dress parade.
Modulation bsd. ♪ (‿‿-t‿(‿)‿) [lt.] f ⓐ modulation. [dication.)
Mohren=wäsche (‿‿‿) f ⓐ fig. vin-]
*Moment=aufnahme: e-e ~ machen (von j-m od. et.) to snapshot (a p. or a th.).
Monats=binde (‿‿‿) f ⓐ sanitary towel; =karte f monthly season-ticket, Am. commutation(-ticket); =lohn m monthly wages or pay.
*Montage (Zusammenbau) assembling, assemblage of parts.
*Monteur assembler; bsd. mot. u. ⚔ mechanic(ian).
*montieren zu 11: (zusammenbauen) to assemble parts.
Moor=kultur (‿‿) f ⓐ cultivation of moorland; =wirtschaf f moorland farming. [morainic.)
Moränen=... (‿‿‿) geol. morainal,]
Morgen=haube (‿‿‿) f ⓐ boudoir-cap.
Morphologe ⚕ (‿‿‿) [grch.] m ㊸ morphologist.
Morphologie ⚕ (‿‿‿‿) f ㊺ (Gestaltlehre) morphology.

morphologisch ⚡ (⸗⸗⸗) *a.* 🌐 morphological.

*****Motor-barkasse** ⚓ (⸗⸗⸗) *f* 🚗 motor launch; **=haube** ⚙ *f, mot.* bonnet, motor-hood.

motorisieren ⚙ (⸗⸗⸗⸗) **I** *v/a.* 🚗 (auf Kraftfahrbetrieb umstellen) to motorize. — **II** ~ *n* u. **Motorisierung** *f* 🚗 motorization.

Motor-pflug ⚙ (⸗⸗⸗) *m* 🚗 *agr.* motor (or tractor) plough; ***=rad** motor cycle; **=rad-fahrer** *m* motor cyclist; **=schiff** *n* motor ship; **=schlitten** *m* motor sled or sleigh; **=unterschutz** *m* pan, engine shield; **=zwei-rad** *n* motor bicycle or F bike.

Mühlen-fabrikat ✱ (⸗⸗⸗) *n* 🏭 milling product.

Müll-abfuhr (⸗⸗⸗) *f* 🏭 removal of refuse.

müllern (⸗⸗⸗) [Prsn.] *v/n.* (h.) 🏭 *a.* to do Muller exercises.

Müll-verbrennungs-ofen ⚙ (⸗⸗⸗⸗) *m* 🏭 destructor, incinerator.

*****mündel-sicher**: 2e Anlage trustee investment; 2es Papier trustee (or gilt--edged) security.

Mund-pflege (⸗⸗⸗) *f* 🏭 care of the mouth; *****=stück** e-r Zigarette: tip; mit Gold-2 gold-tipped.

Munitions-arbeiter ⚔ (⸗⸗tf(⸗)⸗⸗⸗) *m* 🏭, **=arbeiterin** *f* munition-worker, *m. a.* munitioneer, *f. a.* munitionette; **=fabrik** *f* munition-factory.

Münz-fern-sprecher (⸗⸗⸗) *m* 🏭 Fernspr. coin-box call station or office; **=um-lauf** *m* monetary circulation.

Muster-einband (⸗⸗⸗) *m* ⓘc dummy binding; **=gut** *n* *agr.* model farm; **=klammer** *f* paper-fastener; *****=lager** show-room(s *pl.*); **=schutz-gesetz** *n* (Copyright in) Designs Act; **=staat** *m* model State.

Musterungs-kommission ⚔ (⸗⸗⸗) *f* 🏭 tribunal.

Mutter-fürsorge (⸗⸗⸗) *f* 🏭 maternity care or welfare; **=gesellschaft** ✱ *f* parent company; **=haus** *n, fig.* (Stammhaus) parent house; **=schutz** *m* protection of motherhood.

N

Nach-*bestellung ✱ *sl.* repeat-order; **=börse** ✱ (⸗ch⸗) *f* 🏭 kerb-market; 2börslich *a.* 🌐 kerb-...; *****=gehen** e-m Vorfall usw.: to trace out; **=hut-gefecht** ⚔ *n* rear-guard action; **=kriegs-...** post-war; 2**lösen** *v/a.* 🚂** (e-e Fahrkarte) ~ to take a supplementary ticket.

Nachmittags-kleid (⸗ch⸗⸗⸗) *n* 🏭 tea-gown.

nach-prüfen (⸗ch⸗) *v/a.* 🚂** to re--examine, check (again), counter--control; die Richtigkeit e-r S.: to verify; **=prüfung** *f* 🏭 re-examination, counter--control; verification; **=richten-amt** *bsd.* ⚔ *n* Intelligence Department; **=richten-büro** *n* news (or press) agency; **=richten-technik** *f* communication art; **=richten-truppe** ⚔ *f* Signal Corps; **=richten-übermittlung** *f* transmission of intelligence;

=saison ✱ *f* after-season; **=schlage-bibliothek** *f* (ant. Ausleihebibliothek) reference library; *****2=sehen** **II** ~ *n* 🏭 Sport: dem Gegner das ~ geben to dismiss one's opponent (mit dem und dem Spielergebnis for); *****2=stellen** ⚙ Stell-schraube: to adjust; 2**stell-vorrichtung** *f* readjusting gear. [night-club.)

Nacht-(betriebs-)lokal (⸗ch⸗) *n* 🏭

Nach-versicherung (⸗ch⸗) *f* 🏭 additional insurance; *****2=ziehen** *zu v/a.* e-e Schraube: to screw up, tighten; die Augenbrauen: to pencil; **=zündung** ⚙ *f, mot.* retarded (or delayed or late) ignition.

Nagel-pflege (⸗⸗⸗) *f* 🏭 care of the nails, manicure; **=pflege-kasten** *m* manicure-case.

Nah-aufnahme (⸗⸗⸗) *f* 🏭 Filmwesen: e-s Gesichts: close-up; e-s Gegenstandes: bust.

*****näher¹**: 2e Bestimmungen *f/pl.* specific regulations.

Nähr-mittel (⸗⸗⸗) *n* 🏭 prepared food-stuff, patent food.

Nah-verkehr 🚂 (⸗⸗⸗) *m* 🏭 local traffic.

*****Name** *zu* 1: e-n ~*n* tragen to bear a name.

*****Nase** *zu* 1: (Geruchssinn) nose, bsd. vom Hund: scent. — *zu* 2: e-e lange ~ machen (verächtliche Gebärde) to cock a snook.

Nasen-länge (⸗⸗⸗) *f* 🏭 Rennsport: um e-e ~ by a short head; **=schleim** *m* nasal mucus.

National-sozialist (⸗⸗tf(⸗)⸗⸗⸗) *m* 🏭 *pol.* National Socialist. [kind.)

Natural-wert (⸗⸗⸗) *m* 🏭 value in)

Natur-schutz (⸗⸗⸗) *m* 🏭 preservation of natural beauty.

Nebel-bombe ⚔ (⸗⸗⸗) *f* 🏭 smoke--ball, s.-bomb; **=schleier, =vorhang** ⚔ *m* (künstlicher) smoke-screen.

Neben-anschluss (⸗⸗⸗) *m* 🏭 Fernspr. extension (station).

Neben-einander-schaltung ⚙ (⸗⸗⸗⸗) *f* 🏭 *elect.* parallel connexion.

Neben-gelass (⸗⸗⸗) *n* 🏭 e-r Wohnung offices *pl.*; **=geleise, =gleis** 🚂 *n* siding, *Am.* side-track, shunt; **=kläger(in** *f*) *m jur.* co-plaintiff; **=nieren-...** *anat.* ⚡ adrenal; **=nieren-extrakt** *m, med.* ⚡ adrenalin. [to the dregs.)

*****Neige** *zu* 4: bis zur ~ leeren to drain)

Renn-geld (⸗⸗⸗) *n* 🏭 Sport: entry-fee.

Nennungs-liste (⸗⸗⸗) *f* 🏭 Sport: list of competitors, entries *pl.*; **=schluss** *m* Sport: close of entries.

Neon ⚡ (⸗⸗) [grch.] *n* ⓓ. *o. pl., chm.* (Edelgas) neon.

Netz-anode (⸗⸗⸗) *f* 🏭 Radio: grid terminal; **=anschluss** *m elect.* public supply, commercial current supply; Radio: lighting-circuit supply; **=emp-fänger** *m* Radio: lighting-circuit receiving-set; **=hemd** *n* cellular shirt; **=stoff** *m* cellular cloth.

neu-artig (⸗⸗) *a.* 🌐 novel.

neun-mal-klug (⸗⸗) *a.* 🌐 *iro.* sapient.

Neu-regelung (⸗⸗⸗) *f* 🏭 re-arrangement; **=reiche** *m/pl.*: die ~*n* the new rich; **=wert** *m* value (when or as) new.

Nicht-einhaltung (⸗⸗⸗) *f* 🏭 non-compliance (*gen.* ob. von with); **=mitglied** *n* non-member.

nieder-frequent (⸗⸗...) *a.* 🌐 *elect.* low frequent; **=frequenz** *f, elect.* low frequency; *****2=gehen** ⚡ to alight; *****=schlag** d) Boxen: knock-out; j-n durch ~ besiegen to knock a p. out; *****2=schlagen** *zu* d): to cancel costs or a tax; *****=schla-gung** cancellation of costs or taxes; **=spannung** *f. elect.* low tension; **=wild** *n, hunt. coll.* small game.

Nippel ⚙ (⸗⸗) [ndd.] *m* 🏭 nipple.

Nist-platz (⸗⸗⸗) *m* 🏭, **=stätte** *f* breeding place.

Nocken-welle ⚙ (⸗⸗⸗) *f* 🏭 *mach.* camshaft.

*****nordisch**: die 2e Rasse the Nordic race.

normen ⚙ (⸗⸗) [Norm] **I** *v/a.* 🚂 to standardize. — **II** ~ *n* 🏭 u. **Nor-mung** *f* 🏭 standardization.

Not-bedarf (⸗⸗...) *m* 🏭 necessary requirements *pl.*, necessaries *pl.* of life; **=etat** *m, parl.* emergency budget; **=geld** *n* emergency money; **=gesetz** *n* emergency law; **=hilfe** *f*: Technische ~ Organization for the Maintenance of Supplies.

*****notieren** *zu* I: ✱ das Pfund notiert 145 Frank the pound is quoted at 145 francs.

Notiz-block (⸗⸗...) *m* 🏭 note block.

not-landen ⚡ (⸗⸗) *v/n.* (sn) 🚂*, *p.p.*** to be forced to land; **=landung** ⚡ *f* 🏭 forced landing; **=sitz** ⚙ *m* Wagenbau: emergency seat, dicky; **=stands-ar-beiten** *f/pl.* für Arbeitslose: relief works *pl.*; **=verordnung** *f, parl.* emergency decree.

Novellette (⸗w⸗⸗) [fr., *lt.] *f* 🏭 (kleine Novelle) novelette.

Novokain ⚡ (⸗w⸗⸗) [*lt. no'vus* neu + (Ko)kaïn] *n* ⓓ. *med.* (örtlich unempfindlich machendes Mittel) novocaine.

*****numerieren** *zu* 1: *thea.* numerierter Platz reserved seat.

Nummern-scheibe ⚙ (⸗⸗⸗) *f* 🏭 Fernspr. dial(-plate); **=schild** *n, mot.* number-plate.

Nuss-kohle ⚒ (⸗⸗⸗) *f* 🏭 screened coal, nuts *pl.*

nuten ⚙ (⸗⸗) *v/a.* 🚂 to groove.

Nutz-last (⸗⸗⸗) *f* 🏭 *mech.* useful load; **=leistung** *f* useful output; **=pflanze** ✻ *f* useful plant.

O

o-beinig F (⸗⸗⸗) *a.* 🌐 bandy-legged.

Ober-ingenieur (⸗⸗⸗) *m* 🏭 engineer--in-chief; **=klasse** *f* a) upper (or higher) class of society; b) better sort (or grade or quality) of goods; c) senior (or top) form in schools; **=reichs-anwalt** *m* Chief Director of Public Prosecutions; **=schwester** *f* e-s Krankenhauses: sister; **=verwaltungs-gericht** *n* Chief Administration Court.

objektivieren ⚡ (⸗⸗w⸗⸗) *v/a.* 🚂 to objectify, objectivize.

Objektivismus ⚡ (⸗⸗w⸗⸗) *m* 🏭 objectivism.

Objekt-träger (⸗⸗⸗) *m* 🏭 des Mikroskops:)

Obligations-gläubiger (⸗⸗⸗tf(⸗)⸗⸗) *m* 🏭 *jur.* obligee; **=schuld** *f jur.* bond(ed) debt; **=schuldner** *m jur.* obligor.

Obrigkeits-staat (⸚⸚⸌) m 🇬🇧 authoritarian state.
***Obstruktion** in Fabriken: ca'canny.
***öde**¹ F (langweilig) dull.
***Ödigkeit** F (Langweiligkeit) dulness.
***offen** zu 2: 2e Stadt unfortified town. — zu 3: 2e Handelsgesellschaft private firm or partnership.
***Öffentlichkeit**: sich in die ⁓ flüchten to rush into print; Flucht in die ⁓ rushing into print; vor die ⁓ bringen to bring before the public.
öffentlich-rechtlich (⸚⸚...) a. 🇬🇧 jur. of public law standing, quasi-public, semi-governmental.
***Offizier** zu 1: ⁓ mit Generalsrang general officer.
Offset-druck ⊤ ⊙ (⸌⸚...) [engl.] m 🇬🇧 typ. (Flach-, Gummi-druck) offset printing; **-presse** f offset machine.
Okkupation (⸚⸚-tß(⸍)⸌) [fr., *It.] f 🇬🇧 1. ⚔ occupation. — 2. jur. seizure; **⁓s-heer** ⚔ n 🇬🇧 army of occupation.
***Ökonom** (Wirtschafter e-s großen Unternehmens ob. Vereins) catering manager.
***ölen** zu I: F wie ein geölter Blitz like a greased lightning.
Öler ⊙ (⸌⸍) m 🔧 mach. oiler, lubricator; oil cup.
Öl-feuerungs-maschine ⊙ (⸌...) f mach. oil-engine; **-fund** m, geol. oil-find.
Oligozän ⏁ (⸚⸚⸚tß⸌) [grch.] geol. I n 🇬🇧 d. Oligocene. — II 2 a. 🇬🇧 oligocene.
Öl-quelle (⸌...) f 🇬🇧 oil-spring; **-schalter** ⊙ m, elect. oil-switch; **-schau-glas** n, mach. circulating indicator, tell-tale; **-stand-zeiger** ⊙ m, mach. oil (level) gauge.
ondulieren (⸚⸚⸌⸍) [fr., *It.] I v/a. 🇬🇧 Haar: to wave. — II ⁓ n 23 u. **Ondulierung** f 🇬🇧 waving.
Opfer-stätte (⸌...) f 🇬🇧 place of sacrifice; **-tag** m zugunsten e-r Spende flag-day.
Optant (⸚⸌) [It.] m 🇬🇧, **⁓in** (⸚⸚⸌) f 🇬🇧 pol. (seine Staatsangehörigkeit Wählende[r]) optant.
Option (⸚tß(⸍)⸌) [It.] f 🇬🇧 pol. u. 💼 option.
***Ordner** in der Schule: prefect, monitor; bei e-m Fest, e-r Versammlung usw. steward.
Ordnung zu 3: Straße erster (zweiter) ⁓ first-class (second-class) road.
Organisations-zwang (⸚⸚⸍-tß⸌⸚⸌) m 🇬🇧 compulsion to join (or form) organization.
***organisieren** zu I: organisiert(er Arbeiter) unionist; nicht organisiert(er Arbeiter) non-unionist.
Orgasmus ⏁ (⸚⸚⸌) [grch.] m ⚕ (äußerste Erregung) orgasm.
orts-ansässig (⸌...) a. 🇬🇧, **-ansässige(r)** 🇬🇧 resident; **⁓fremd** a. 2er Kaufmann merchant who is a stranger to the locality; **-gespräch** n 🇬🇧 Fernspr. local call, a. l. connexion; **-gruppe** f local group or branch; **-unterkunft** ⚔ f cantonment; **-verkehr** m 🚚 u. Fernspr. local traffic; **-zulage** f, **-zuschlag** m local bonus.
Ost-elbien ⊙ (⸌...) npr/n. 🌎α Prussia east of the river Elbe, East Elbia;

-elbi-er m 🇬🇧 Prussian from the east of the Elbe, East Elbian.
***Osten**¹ ♀ der Nahe ⁓ (Südost-Europa) the Near East; der Ferne ⁓ (Ostasien) the Far East.
Oxford-hosen (⸌⸚...) f/pl. 🇬🇧 (sehr weite Hosen) Oxford bags pl.
Ozean-flieger ✈ (⸌⸚⸚...) m 🇬🇧 trans-Ocean airman; **-flug** m trans-Ocean flight.
Ozeanographie ⏁ (⸚⸚⸚⸚f⸌) [grch.] f 🇬🇧 (Meerbeschreibung) oceanography.
ozeanographisch ⏁ (⸚⸚⸚⸌⸍⸚) a. 🇬🇧 oceanographic.

P

Paar-laufen (⸌...) n 🇬🇧 Eissport: couple-skating.
Pacht-ertrag (⸌⸚...) m 🇬🇧 rental; **-land** n leasehold land; **-wert** m rental value.
***Packerei** 2. = Packraum a).
***Paddel-boot** (⸌⸚⸌) n 🇬🇧 Rudersport: canoe.
***paddeln** Rudersport: to paddle, canoe.
Paddel-ruder (⸌⸚...) n 🇬🇧 (kurzes Doppelruder) paddle.
Pagen-kopf (⸌⸚⸚⸌) m 🇬🇧 (Haartracht) bobbed hair.
Paket-annahme (⸚⸌...) f 🇬🇧 parcels receiving office.
Paneuropa (⸚⸚⸌⸚) [grch.] npr/n. 🌎α. pol. Pan-Europe.
***Panne** break-down, mishap.
Panzer-gewölbe (⸌⸚...) n 🇬🇧 e-r Bank: strong-room, vault; **-wagen** ⚔ m armoured car.
***Papier-gewicht** (⸚⸌...) n 🇬🇧 Lager: paper-weight; **-laterne** f Chinese lantern; **-masse** ⊙ f pulp; **-schlange** f (Scherzartikel zum Werfen) paper streamer; **-waren** f/pl. stationery.
Paraphe 2. provisional signing of a treaty.
paraphieren (⸚⸚f⸌) v/a. 🇬🇧 to sign provisionally.
Paratyphus ⏁ (⸚⸚⸌⸚) [grch.] m inv., path. paratyphoid.
parken ⊤ (⸚⸌) [engl.] v/n. (h.) u. v/a. 🇬🇧 v. Straßenfuhrwerk: to park.
Parmäne ♀ (⸚⸌⸍) [alt-fr., *it. St. Pa'rnna?] f 🇬🇧 (Apfelart) pearmain.
Partei-buch (⸚⸌...) n 🇬🇧 pol. membership book; **-tag** m, pol. party-conference, caucus.
Partie-waren-geschäft 💼 (⸚⸌...) n 🇬🇧 a) job-goods trade; b) job-goods shop; **-waren-händler** m dealer in job-goods; **-waren-handlung** f = **-warengeschäft** b).
Passagier-flug-zeug ✈ (⸚⸚G⸌...) n 🇬🇧 air-liner.
***passen** zu IV: in Farbe usw. dazu 2d to match, z.B. note-paper and envelope to match.
passiv zu I: 2er Widerstand passive resistance, in Fabriken a. working to rule, ca'canny.
***Patent** zu I: ⚓ (Kapitäns2) master certificate or ticket; ⁓ für große Fahrt master certificate for foreign going ship. — zu I 3: ein ⁓ erteilen to grant a patent; **-antrag** m patent application.
patent-fähig (⸚⸌...) a. 🇬🇧 patentable.
***patentieren** zu I: (sich) et. 2 lassen to take out a patent for a th.

Patronen-auswerfer ⊙ (⸚⸌⸚...) m 🇬🇧 (Vorrichtung am Gewehr) ejector.
Patrouillen-lauf (⸚trü"l-j⸚⸌) m 🇬🇧 Sport: (militär) patrol race.
***paufen** 5. Schul-sl. to cram, grind.
***Pauker** 3. Schul-sl. (Lehrer) crammer, grinder.
***Paukerei** 2. Schul-sl. cramming, grinding.
***Pause**¹ (Unterbrechung der Arbeit) break, in der Schule a. playtime.
Pazifismus (⸚⸚⸌⸍) [fr., *It.] m ⚖ (Friedensschwärmerei) pacifism.
Pazifist (⸚⸚⸌) m 🇬🇧, **⁓in** f 🇬🇧 pacifist; 2isch a. 🇬🇧 pacifistic(ally adv.).
Peil-antenne (⸌...) f 🇬🇧 Radio: direction-finder aerial; **-funk...** Radio: direction-finding; **-funk-einrichtung** f direction-finder.
Pendel-verkehr 🚚 (⸌⸚...) m 🇬🇧 pendulum traffic, shuttle movement.
***Penne** 2. Schul-sl. = Pennal 2.
***pensionieren** zu I: sich 2 lassen to retire.
***per**: ⸱ 2 1. März per (or due on) 1 March.
***perfekt** zu I: Vertrag usw.: settled, concluded.
Periskop ⏁ (⸚⸚⸌) [grch. = Ringsumschauer] n ⚓, ⚔ u. ⚕ (Sehrohr) periscope.
***perlen** zu I: fig. vom Lachen: to ripple.
Personen-verwech(s)lung (⸚⸚⸌...) f 🇬🇧 mistaken identity; ***-wagen** m mot. passenger car, a. private car.
***Pfad-finder** (Mitglied der ⁓ genannten Jugendorganisation) boy scout.
***pfeifen** zu II 1: Radio: v. den Verstärkern: to sing, squeal, howl; seinem Hunde 2 to whistle one's dog.
Pfeil-rad-getriebe ⊙ (⸌⸚...) n 🇬🇧 mach. herringbone gear.
***Pferd** 4. Turnerei: vaulting-horse.
***Pferde-koppel** (⸌⸚...) f 🇬🇧 (Gehege) paddock.
***Pflanzen-butter** 💼 (⸌⸚...) f 🇬🇧 vegetable butter; **-fett** n v. fat; **-öl** n v. oil.
***Pflege-heim** (⸌⸚⸌) n 🇬🇧 charity; med. nursing home.
***Pflegschaft** (Vormundschaft) guardianship; (Vermögensverwaltung) trust.
***Photo-chemigraphie** ⏁ (⸌...) f 🇬🇧 photo-engraving; **-montage** f photo-mounting.
***physisch** jur. 2e Person natural person.
Pianola ♪ (⸚⸚⸌⸍) [it.] n 🎵 (selbsttätig spielendes Klavier) pianola.
***pikant** Kocht. 2es Vorgericht appetizer, hors d'œuvre; 2e Nachspeise savoury.
Pikanterie (⸚⸚⸚⸌) [fr.] f 🇬🇧 1. piquant (or spicy) story or remark. — 2. = Stichelei.
***Pikkolo** zu 1: (Kellnerlehrling) omnibus.
pinkeln F (⸚⸌) [pinf] v/n. (h.) 🇬🇧 a. to make water, F to piddle.
Pipette (⸚⸌⸍) [fr.] f 🇬🇧 (Stechheber) pipette.
Pipi F (-⸌) [lautm.] f inv. o. pl. Kindersp. urine; ⁓ machen to make water, F to piddle.
***placieren** 💼 to negotiate a bill; to realize securities. [-man-]
Plakat-träger (⸚⸌...) m 🇬🇧 sandwich]
Plakette (⸚⸌⸍) [fr.] f 🇬🇧 (Gedenktafel, Denkmünze) plaquette.

planmäßig — 23 — **Quarzlampe**

***plan-mäßig:** Der Angestellte regular member of the staff; **=wirtschaft** f ⑫ economy according to plan, systematized economy.
Plastilin ⊙ (˘-´) [grch.] n ⑬c., **~a** (˘-´-) f inv. o. pl. (Knetmasse) plasticine.
Platte zu 3: (Grammophon⊙) disk, record.
Platten-anker (ˊ˘...) m ⑫ gusset.
Platt-fuß-einlage (ˊ˘...) f ⑫ arch-support, instep-raiser, foot-easer.
*****platzen** zu II: *mot.*, Radsport: ~ des Luftreifens blow-out. 【man.】
Platz-wärter (ˊ˘...) m ⑫ Sport: ground(s)-/
plissieren ⊙ (˘-˘) v/a. ⑬ to pleat.
Plural-wahl-recht (-˘˘...) n ⑫ parl. plural vote.
Pogrom (-´) [russ.] m ⑬c. (Judenverfolgung) pogrom.
*****Pokal** als sportlicher Ehrenpreis: cup; **~spiel** n ⑫ Sport: cup-tie.
*****Pol**¹ elect. e-s Elements, e-r Leitung: a. terminal.
*****Polizei-aufsicht:** unter ~ under police supervision; v. e-m vor Ablauf seiner Strafzeit entlassenen Strafgefangenen: on ticket of leave; unter ~ Stehender ticket-of-leave man; **=büro** n police-station.
*****polizeilich:** unter Der Bewachung ob. Bedeckung, unter Dem Schutz in the care of policemen.
Polizei-präsidium (˘-˘ˊ...) n ⑫ Police Head-quarters pl., Police Office; **=schule** f police training-school; **=streife** f raid; **=widrigkeit** f offence against police regulations.
Polizistin (˘-ˊ˘) f ⑰ policewoman.
Pol-klemme (ˊ˘...) f ⑫ elect. pole terminal, terminal post.
Polonium ⚛ (-´˘(˘)) [lt. *Polo'nia* = Polen] n ⑬ (o. pl.) chm. (radioaktives Element) polonium.
Polter-geist zu b) Spiritismus: noisy ghost, ⸸ poltergeist.
Porto-auslagen (ˊ˘...) f/pl. ⑫ = **=kosten**; **=kasse** ✲ f petty cash; **=kosten** pl. postal expenses pl.
*****Position** in e-r Aufstellung, e-m Tarif usw. item.
Post-bestellung (ˊ˘...) f ⑫ delivery of post or mail; **=betrieb** m postal service; **=einlieferungs-schein** m post-office receipt.
Posten-dienst ⚔ (ˊ˘...) m ⑫ sentry duty; **=gang** m sentry-go.
Post-fach (ˊ˘...) n ⑫ post-office box (mit P. O. Box); **=flug-zeug** ✈ n mail (aero-)plane; **=hilfs-stelle** f branch post-office; *****karte** zu c) mit (Rück=)- Antwort reply postcard; **=kraft-wagen-verkehr** m service of post-office motor vans; **=scheck** m postal cheque; **=scheck-amt** n postal cheque office; **=scheck-konto** n postal cheque account, post-office transfer account; **=schließ-fach** n =fach; **=spar-schein** m savings certificate. 【potential.】
potentiell ⚛ (˘-˘(˘)ˊ) [fr., *lt.*] a. ⑯
p.p., p.pa., ppa. ✲ abbr. = per procura, englisch per pro.
Prädikats-nomen ⚛ (-˘˘...) n ⑫ gr. complement.
Praline (˘-´˘) [fr.] f ㊽ = Praliné.
*****Prämie** 3. Lotteriewesen: prize.

prämi-en-frei (ˊˊ(˘)˘-´) a. ㊅㊅ Versicherungswesen: free of premium.
Präsentant (-˘ˊ) [lt.] m ⑫ e-s Wechsels: bearer, holder.
Präsenz-geld (-ˊˊ) n ⑫ attendance-fee.
Preis-abbau (ˊˊ...) m ⑫ (gradual) reduction of prices; **=bewegung** f movement of prices; **=differenz** f = =unterschied; **=drücker** m close bargainer; price-cutter; **=drückerei** f close bargaining, forcing down the market; price-cutting; **=erhöhung** f advance (or rise or increase) in prices; **=gabe** f = =gebung; *****geben** (bloßlegen) to reveal; *****gebung** (Bloßlegung) revelation; **=gestaltung** f formation of prices; **=grenze** f (price-)limit; **=lage** f range of price; in dieser ~ at (or about) this price; **=nachlaß** m rebate, discount; **=notierung** f quotation; **=senkung** f lowering of prices, price-cut; **=steigerung** f = =erhöhung; **=träger** m prize-winner; **=treiber** m bull; **=treiberei** f forcing up the market or prices; **=unterbietung** f am Auslandsmarkt: dumping; **=unterschied** m difference in price; **=veränderung** f change in price; **~en** vorbehalten subject to alteration(s); **=wucher** m profiteering.
Presse-amt (ˊ˘...) n ⑫ Press Council, Press Board; **=tribüne** f press-gallery.
Preß-heu (ˊ˘...) n ⑫ pressed hay; **=stroh** n pressed straw.
Primitivität (-˘-˘˘ˊ)/f ㊻ primitiveness, primitivism.
Prinzeß-rock ✲ (-˘ˊˊ) m ⑫ (Art Unterrock) princess slip or petticoat.
Prismen-(fern-)glas (ˊ˘...) n ⑫ opt. prism(atic) binocular.
Privat-wirtschaft (˘-ˊ...) f ⑫ private enterprise; **⦾wirtschaftlich** a. ㊅㊅ Der Betrieb = =wirtschaft; **=wirtschafts-lehre** f doctrine (or science) of private enterprise. 【num.】
*****pro** zu I: soundso viel ⦾ Jahr per an-/
*****Probe** zu 1: auf ~ v. Warensendungen on approval.
Probe-bild (ˊ˘...) n ⑫ phot. proof; **=einband** m dummy binding; **=spiel** n Sport: trial.
Produkten-markt ✲ (˘-ˊ˘ˊ) m ⑫ produce market.
Produktions-ausfall (˘-˘ˊ(˘)ˊˊ...) m ⑫ falling off (or deficiency) in production; **=beschränkung** f, **=einschränkung** f restriction of output; **=kosten** pl. cost of production; **=land** n producing country; **=menge** f output; **=wirtschaft** f producing industry.
*****Prognose** des Wetters u. *fig.* forecast.
Prohibition (-˘-˘˘(˘)ˊ) [lt.] f ㊻ (Alkoholverbot in U. S.) prohibition.
Projektions-apparat (˘-˘ˊ(˘)ˊ...) m ⑫ opt. projection apparatus, projector; **=bild** n lantern slide; **=schirm** m screen.
Prolet (˘ˊ) [lt.] m ⑫ contp. = Proletarier; *fig.* (ungebildeter Mensch) cad.
proletarisieren (-˘-˘-´˘) v/a. ⑬ to proletarianize.
*****Prolongation:** in ~ geben to carry on, to give on stock, to hold over; in ~ nehmen to take in (stock), to carry over.

Promenaden-anzug (˘˘-´˘...) m ⑫ lounge-suit.
*****Propaganda:** ~ der Tat direct action.
Propeller ⸸ (˘-ˊ˘) [engl., *lt.*] m ⑫ ⚓ u. ✈ propeller; **=flügel** m blade.
Proportionalität ⚛ (-˘-˘(˘)˘-´) f ㊵ proportionality.
Proporz-wahl (˘-ˊˊ) f ⑫ parl. = Verhältniswahl.
Protest-gebühr (˘-ˊ...) f ⑫ Sport: protest fee; **=versammlung** f meeting of protest.
Prozent-gehalt (˘-ˊ...) m ⑫ percentage.
Prozeß-bevollmächtigte(r) (˘-ˊ...) m ⑫ jur. mandatary; **=vollmacht** f power of attorney. 【per pro.
pr.pa. ✲ abbr. = per procura, englisch
Prüf-stand ⊙ (-ˊˊ) m ⑫ testing stand or shop or block.
Prüfungs-apparat(e pl.) ⊙ (-´˘...) m ⑫ testing apparatus; **=stelle** f inspection office; **=termin** m a) public examination of bankrupt; b) time allowed to test goods bought. 【(or stately) hall.】
Prunk-saal (ˊ-) m ⑫ magnificent
Psycho-analyse ⚛ (-´˘˘-˘) [grch.] f ㊽ med. (Seelenerkundung) psycho-analysis; **~analytiker** (-´˘˘-´˘) m ⑫ psycho-analyst, ps.-analyst; **=analytisch** (-´˘˘-´) a. ㊅㊅ psycho-analytic(ally adv.) 【(Seelenstörung) psychosis.】
Psychose ⚛ (-´˘) [grch.] f ㊽ path.
Puddel-eisen ⊙ (ˊ˘...) n ⑫ puddled iron; **=werk** n puddle ironworks, forge.
pud(d)eln² (ˊ˘, ˊ˘) [ndd.] Schwimmsport: I v/n. (h.) ⑭a. Λo trudge. — II ~ n ㉓ trudge(n stroke).
Puder-dose (ˊ˘...) f ⑫ powder-box.
*****Puff** zu 15: (Sitzmöbel) pouffe.
Pullover ⸸ (˘-´˘) [engl.] m ⑫ (Schlupfbluse) pull-over.
*****Punkt** zu 1: Boxen: nach ~en siegen to win on points.
Punkt-roller (ˊ˘...) m ⑫ (Massagegerät) massage suction roller; **=sieg** m Boxen: winning on points; **=sieger** m Boxen: winner on points. 【tooling.】
Punz-arbeit (ˊ˘...) f ⑫ v. Lederarbeiten:
Pup P (´) [lautm.] m ⑬c. fart.
pupen P (´˘) v/n. (h.) ⑭ to fart.
Pupin-spule ⚛ (˘-ˊ...) [Prsn.] f ⑫ Fernspr. load(ing)-coil, Pupin coil.
Puppen-spielerei (ˊ˘...) f ⑫ puppetry; **=wagen** m doll's pram.
Putz-kasten (ˊ˘...) m ⑫ box for polishing material; **=leder** n chamois (leather), shammy; **=mittel** n polish(ing material).
Pyjama (-´˘) [persisch-hindostani] n, a. m ㊿ (Schlafanzug) pyjamas pl.; ein ~ a pyjama suit.

Q

Quadrat-rute (˘-ˊ...) f ⑫ (Grundstücksmaß) square rod or perch or pole.
Qualitäts-arbeit (-˘-ˊ...) f ⑫ work (-manship) of (high) quality; **=ware** ✲ f article of quality, superior (or high-class) article.
Quanten-theorie ⚛ (ˊ˘...) f ⑫ phys. quantum theory.
Quarz-lampe (ˊ˘...) f ⑫ elect., med. quartz lamp.

Quellen-angabe (ˇ˘...) f ② mention of one's sources or authorities; **-nach-weis** m indication of sources used.
queren (˘ˊ) [quer] v/a. u. v/n. (h.) ⑧ mount. to traverse. [run, &c.
*****quer-feld-ein** in Zssgn: cross-country;
Quer-gang (ˊˊ...) m ② traverse; **-holz** Kricket: bail; **-schlag** ✕ m cross-cut; **-träger** ⊙ m traverse; mot. transverse member, (frame) cross member; **-verbindung** f cross connexion.
quotieren ⓒ (-ˊ˘) v/a. ⑨ (den Preis angeben für et.) to quote.

R

*****Radau**: ~ machen to make a row, bsd. v. Kindern: to rag.
Rad-fahrer-(erfrischungs-)station (ˊ...) f ② cyclist's rest; **-fahrer-falle** f der Polizei: police-trap; **-fahr-künstler(in** f) m trick-cyclist. [calize.
radikalisieren (-˘-ˊ˘) v/a. ⑨ to radi-
Radio (ˊ(˘)-) [it.] n wireless, radio; **~anlage** (ˊˊ...) f ② wireless (or radio) plant; **~apparat** m wireless set; **~einrichtung** f wireless equipment.
Radiologe ⊘ (ˊ(˘)˘ˊˊ) [it.-grch.] m ㊹ phys. (Strahlenforscher) radiologist.
Radiologie ⊘ (ˊ(˘)˘˘ˊ) f ⑧ radiology.
radiologisch ⊘ (ˊ(˘)˘ˊ˘) a. ⑥⑥ radiological.
Radium-heil-verfahren (ˊ(˘)˘...) n ② med. radiotherapy, radiotherapeutics pl.
Rad-kappe ⊙ (ˊ...) f ② mot. hub-cap; **-renn-bahn** f cycling ground; **-stand** ⊙ m Wagenbau: wheel-base; **-stern** m Wagenbau: wheel-spider.
Rahmen-akkumulator ⊙ (ˊˊ...) m ㉛ frame accumulator; **-antenne** f Radio: frame aerial; **-gesetz** n, parl. skeleton law; **-sucher** m, phot. frame (view-) -finder; **-vertrag** m skeleton agreement.
Raiffeisen-genossenschaft (ˊˊ-˘...) [F. W. Raiffeisen, 1818—1888, Begründer] f ②, **-kasse** f, **-verein** m Agricultural Co-operative Credit Society.
Raketen-flug-zeug ✕ (ˊˊˊ...) n ② rocket plane; **-wagen** m, mot. rocket car.
*****Ramsch 2.** = Ramschverkauf.
Ramsch-verkauf ❀ (ˊ...) m ② (Verkauf aller möglicher billiger Waren) jumble-sale.
Rand-staat ⚥ (ˊˊ) m ② Border State.
Rang-liste Sport: ranking list.
Raps-öl (ˊˊ) n ② rape-oil.
rasant ⊙ (-ˊ) [fr.] a. ⑥⑥ (flach) v. d. Flugbahn e-s Geschosses: flat.
Rasanz ⊙ (-ˊ) f ㊻ (f. rasant) flatness.
Rasen-sprenger ⊙ (ˊˊ˘...) m ② hort. (Gerät) lawn-sprinkler.
Rasier-apparat (˘ˊˊ...) m ② safety-razor; **-spiegel** m shaving-mirror.
Rassen-haß (ˊˊ...) m ② race-hatred; **-hygiene** ⊘ f eugenics pl.; **-hygienisch** ⊘ a. ⑥⑥ eugenic(ally adv.); **-(ver-)mischung** f miscegenation.
*****rasten** v/n. Tennis: to have drawn a bye, to be a bye.
Raster ⊙ (ˊ˘) [it.] m ② Photochemigraphie: (fein liniierte Glasplatte) screen; **~(tief-) druck** (ˊˊ...) m ② screen process.

rastern ⊙ (ˊ˘) (h.) ㉒ v. I v/n. provc. = rasseln, rauschen. — II [Raster] v/a. to print by screen process.
*****Rate** (verhältnismäßiger Teil) rate.
*****raten** zu I 3: rate mal! give a guess!
Raten-kauf ❀ (ˊˊ...) m ② hire-purchase, purchase on the instalment system; **-system** n hire-purchase (or instalment) system; **-(zahlungs-)geschäft** n hire-purchase business.
Räte-regierung (ˊˊ˘...) f ② pol. in Rußland: Soviet government.
rationalisieren (˘ˊß(˘)˘˘ˊ˘) I v/a. ⑨ (Wirtschaft auf möglichste Einheitlichkeit einstellen) to rationalize. — II ~ n ㉓ u. **Rationalisierung** f ㊻ rationalization.
rationieren (˘ˊß(˘)˘ˊ˘) v/a. ⑨ (ein-, zuteilen) to ration.
*****Raub-bau**: ~ treiben agr. to exhaust the land; ✕ to rob a mine.
Rauch-bombe ✕ (ˊˊ...) f ② smoke-ball, smoke-bomb.
*****räuchern** zu I: ⊙ Eichenmöbel: to fume.
Rauch-helm (ˊˊ...) m ② der Feuerwehr: smoke-helmet; **-schrift** f als Flugzeugreklame: sky-writing; **-vorhang** ✕ u. ⚓ m beim Einnebeln: smoke-screen; **-verzehrer** ⊙ m (Gerät) smoke-consumer.
*****rauh** fig. die ⚥ Wirklichkeit the hard (or stubborn) facts pl.
Raum-kunst (ˊˊ...) f ② (art of) interior decoration; **-maß** n measure of capacity.
Räumungs-(aus)verkauf ❀ (ˊˊ˘...) m ② clearance sale.
*****Raupe** zu 1: F er hat ~n im Kopf he's got maggots in his head or brain, he's got bats in the belfry.
Raupen-rad (ˊˊ...) n ② caterpillar wheel; **-schlepper** ⊙ m caterpillar (or creeper type) tractor.
Rausch-gift (ˊˊ...) n ② med. narcotic (drug); **-gift-sucht** f addictedness (ob. addiction) to drug-taking; **-gift-süchtig** a. ⑥⑥ addicted to drug-taking; **-gift-süchtige(r)** drug addict.
Raus-schmeißer P (ˊˊ...) m ② zur Entfernung v. Störenfrieden in Lokalen: chucker-out.
realisierbar (˘ˊ-˘ˊ) a. ⑥⑥ realizable.
Realisierbarkeit (˘ˊ-˘ˊ--) f ㊻ realizability. [realty.
*****Realität**: jur.: ~en pl. real property,
Real-last (-ˊˊ...) f ② jur. recurrent charge on landed property; **-politik** f realistic policy, practical politics; **-steuern** f/pl. taxes on real estate and commercial transactions.
Rechen-schieber (ˊˊ˘...) m ② slide-rule; **-tabelle** f ready reckoner. [office.
Rechnungs-stelle (ˊˊ˘...) f ② accounting
*****recht¹** zu 1 b) die **~e** pol. im Deutschen Reich: the Right; d) s/m. **~e(r)** Boxen: right. [come into one's own.
*****Recht²** zu 1: zu seinem ~ kommen to
Rechts-auskunft (ˊˊ...) f ② legal information; **-außen(-stürmer)** m Fußball: outside right; **-belehrung** f der Geschworenen durch den Richter: summing up; **-drall** ⊙ m right-hand lay or twist; **-frage** im Prozeß: issue of (or in) law; **-gewinde** ⊙ n right-hand thread; **-handlung** f legal action; **-innen(-stürmer)** m Fußball:

inside right; **-irrtum** m mistake in law, error of judgment; **-läufig** ⊙ a. ⑥⑥ right-hand; **-nachfolge** f (right of) succession; **-person** f body corporate; **-ungültig** a. ⑥⑥ illegal, invalid; **-ungültigkeit** f ② (legal) invalidity, illegality; **-vertreter** m legal representative, proxy; **-widrigkeit** f illegality; **-wirkung** f legal effect; **-zustand** m state of law.
Reederei (ˊfirma) shipowner's firm.
Reflektant prospective customer.
Regie-betrieb (˘ˊgiˊˊ...) m ② State trading or manufacture or undertaking; **-kosten** ❀ pl. overhead expenses pl. [gister.
Registrier-kasse (˘˘ˊˊ...) f ② cash re-
*****regnen** v/a. fig. es regnete Einladungen usw. it rained invitations, &c. (auf acc. upon).
Regreß-anspruch (˘ˊˊ...) m ② = **-recht**; **-pflichtig** a. ⑥⑥ liable to remedy or recourse; j-n ⚥ machen to have recourse against a p.
Regulier-schraube ⊙ (-ˊˊ...) f ② adjusting screw.
*****Reh** Kocht. (-fleisch) venison.
Reh-rücken (ˊˊ...) m ② Kocht. saddle of venison. [oft T the Reich.
*****Reich²**: das Deutsche ~ nach dem Kriege
Reichs-... (ˊˊ...) vom Deutschen Reich nach dem Kriege: of the Reich, (German) National, a. Federal; vor dem Kriege: (German) Imperial.
Reichs-angehörige([r] m) (ˊˊ...) f ② subject (or citizen) of the Reich; **-anwalt** m Public Prosecutor in the Reichsgericht; **-archiv** n (German) National Archives pl.; in England: Public Record Office; **-bahn** ⌘ f: die deutsche ~ the Reich railway; **-bund** m National League; **-flagge** f National Flag; **-flucht-steuer** f emigration-tax; **-kassenschein** m currency note, treasury note; **-konferenz** f des Britischen Reichs: Imperial Conference; **-rat** m des Deutschen Reichs: T Reichsrat; **-verband** m National Federation; **-wehr** ✕ f T Reichswehr; **-wehr-minister** m Minister of National Defence.
Reich-weite (ˊˊ...) f ② reach, range, scope.
*****reif¹**: ⚥ sein für die Pensionierung to qualify for the pension.
Reifen-schaden (ˊˊ...) m ② mot., Radsport: tyre trouble, burst.
Reife-zeugnis (ˊˊ...) n ② certificate of maturity.
Reihen-fabrikation ⊙ (ˊˊ...) f ②, **-fertigung** f serial manufacture; **-häuser** n/pl. serial houses; **-schaltung** f, elect. series connexion.
Reiher-horst (ˊ˘ˊ) m ② heronry.
Rein²-fall (ˊˊ...), **-fallen** F = Hereinfall, hereinfallen.
*****Rein¹-kultur** pure culture (a. fig.) **-rassig** a. ⑥⑥ thoroughbred.
Reise-gepäck-versicherung (ˊˊ...) f traveller's luggage insurance; **-grammophon** n portable gramophone.
*****reisen** zu I: fig. ⚥ auf et. (acc.) (ausnutzen) to trade on a th.
Reise-scheck ❀ (ˊˊ...) m ② traveller's cheque; **-spesen** ❀ pl. travelling ex-

penses; =unfall-versicherung f traveller's accident insurance; =verkehr m tourist traffic; *=wagen mot. touring car; =zeit f travelling (or tourist) season.

Reiß-dreieck (″...) n ② geom. set-square; =verschluß m an Handtaschen usw.: zip fastener or fastening, lightning fastener; mit ~ (versehen) zip-fastened.

*Reiter¹ 5. ⊙ auf Karteikarten usw.: tab. reiterlich (″⌣⌣) a. ⑥ ≃e Fähigkeiten pl., ≃es Geschick horsemanship.

Reiz-gas (″...) n ② chm. ✕ irritant gas; =schwelle f, physiol. threshold of sensation.

*Reklame (Schaufenster₂) u. fig. window-dressing.

Reklame-... (⌣″⌣...) mst advertising.

Reklame-artikel (⌣″⌣...) m ② advertising article; =büro n a. office; =chef m a. manager; =druck-sache ✎ f a. printed matter; =fachmann m a. expert; =künstler m a. artist; *=macher (-in) fig. window-dresser; =schild n advertising sign; =zeichner m a. designer.

Reklamierte(r) ✕ (⌣″⌣⌣) m ⑥⑦ indispensable one, sl. Cuthbert.

*Rekord: e-n ~ aufstellen to set (or establish) a record; e-n ~ brechen to break (or cut) a r.; e-n ~ schlagen to beat a r.; e-n ~ verbessern to ameliorate a r.; ~lauf m ② record run; ~versuch m attempt to beat a record; ~zeit f record time.

Relief-schreiber ⊙ (⌣(⌣)″...) m ② embosser; =schrift f embossed writing.

Religions-gemeinschaft (⌣⌣(⌣)″...) f ② religious society.

Rembrandt-hut (″⌣¹) m ② (breitkrämpig) picture (or Gainsborough) hat.

rennen zu IV 5: (Einzel₂) heat; das ~ machen to make the running.

Renn-fahrer (″...) m ② racing cyclist or motorist; =mannschaft f Sport: race-crew; =saison f racing season; =straße f racing road; =strecke f distance to be run; =tag m racing day; =termin m racing fixture. [repair.]

Renovierung (⌣⌣″⌣) f ⑥ renovation.

Renten-empfänger(in f) m (″⌣...) ② annuitant; =mark f ᛏ rentenmark.

Reparation (⌣⌣⌣″tß(⌣)″...) [fr. *ft.] f ② (Wiedergutmachung) bsd. von Kriegsschäden: reparation; ~(en) leisten to make reparation.

Reparations-abkommen (⌣⌣tß(⌣)″...) n ② pol. Reparations Agreement; =ausschuß m, =kommission f Reparation(s) Committee; ⊙pflichtig a. ⑥ liable to make reparation; =zahlung f ② reparation-payment.

Reparatur-werkstatt (⌣⌣⌣″...) f ② repairing-(work)shop.

*Replik jur. reply.

*repräsentieren II v/n. to keep up appearances.

Reproduktions-kamera ⊙ (⌣⌣⌣″tß(⌣)″...) f ② camera for process-work.

Reserve-rad (⌣⌣″⌣⌣¹) n ② mot. spare wheel.

Respirator ⌣ (⌣⌣″⌣) [lt.] m ⑪ (Atemfilter) respirator, inhaler.

Rest-auflage ✱ (⌣″...) f ② Buchhandel: remainder; =gut n remainder of an estate; =kauf-geld n balance of purchase price; =lager ✱ n stock of remnants.

restlich (⌣⌣) a. ⑥⑥ remaining, left over.

Rest-summe (⌣″...) f ② balance; =zahlung f payment of balance.

*Resultat Sport: score.

Revanche-partie (⌣wa″-jch...) f ② return match.

revieren (⌣⌣″⌣) [Revier] v/n. (h.) ② hunt. v. Jagdhunden: (hin und her suchen) to [quarter.]

*Revue thea. revue (fr.).

Rhön-rad (″¹) n ② Sport: gyro-wheel.

richtig zu 1: der, die ~e (Zukünftige) Mr. (Miss) Right.

Richt-kanonier ✕ (″...) m ② artill. gun-layer; =linien f/pl. terms of reference; =preis ✱ m standard (or guiding) price; =zahl f coefficient.

*Riemen¹ mach. = Treibriemen.

Riesel-gut (″⌣¹) n ② agr. sewage-farm. [the prize-ring.]

*Ring¹ 5. der ᛏ Boxen: the ring, a.

ringen² zu II 3: nach Atem ≃ to gasp for breath.

Ritzel ⊙ (⌣⌣) m ② pinion.

Rodel (⌣″) f ④⑧ Wintersport: luge, toboggan; ~bahn (″¹) f ② luge-ing-track, tobogganing-track, t.-slide.

rodeln (⌣″) I v/n. (h.) ⑫a. to luge, to boggan. II ~ n ② luge-ing, tobogganing.

Rodel-schlitten (″⌣...) m ② = Rodel.

*roden zu I: to root up (or out) trees. ~ zu II: rooting up (or out) trees. (nur: Rodung) = Rodeland.

Roggen-bau (″⌣¹) m ② agr. rye-growing, cultivation of rye.

Rohling (⌣″) [roh] m ⑪d. brutal fellow, ruffian.

Roh-öl ⊙ (″¹) n ② crude oil.

*Röhre zu 1: Radio: valve, Am. tube.

Röhren-apparat (″...) m ② Radio: valve-set; =empfänger m Radio: valve-receiver.

Rohr-leitung ⊙ (″...) f ② pipe-line; =spanner ⊙ m ② box-spanner.

Rollen-lager ⊙ (″...) f ② mach. roller-bearing.

*Roller 3. (Kinderspielzeug) scooter. — 4. orn. (Kanarienvogel) roller.

Roll-film (″...) m ② phot. roll-film; =schuh-laufen n roller-skating; =sitz m im Ruderboot: sliding seat; =treppe f moving staircase, escalator.

*Romantik (romantisches Wesen) romanticism. [röntgenologist.]

Röntgenologe ⌣ (⌣⌣″...) m ⑪ phys.

Röntgen-photographie (⌣⌣″...) f ② (Verfahren) röntgenography.

röntgen (⌣″) v/a. ② (mit Röntgenstrahlen durchleuchten; bestrahlen) to röntgenize, radio.

rost-frei (⌣″...) a. ⑥⑥ rustless; ⊙ v. Stahl: stainless; =schutz m ② anti-rust.

*rot zu III 4 b): pol. red.

Rotations-druck (⌣⌣″tß(⌣)″¹) m ② typ. rotary press printing.

Rotogravüre ⊙ (⌣⌣⌣″⌣) (Art Photogravüre) rotogravure.

Rotor (⌣″) [neu-lt. = Dreher] m ⑪ [a] ⊙ mach., elect. sich drehender Maschinen-teil; ant. Stator; b) ↓ Flettnerscher Drehmast] rotor. [foreman.]

*Rotten-führer v. Arbeitern: ganger,

Rotz-lappen P (″...) m ② (Taschentuch) snot-rag.

*Rück-antwort: ✉ Postkarte f mit ~ reply postcard; Telegramm mit bezahlter ~ reply-paid.

Rück-bildung (″...) f ② retrograde change or development; ⊙datieren v/a. ② to postdate. [of mutton, &c.]

Rücken¹ zu 1: Kocht. (Rückenstück) saddle

Rücken-deckung (⌣⌣...) f ② cover; fig. (Unterstützung) backing, support; =schwimmen n back-stroke; =wind m following wind.

rück-erstatten (″...), Rück-erstattung wiedererstatten usw.; =fall-fieber n ② path. relapsing fever; =hand-schlag m Tennis: backhand stroke; =kaufs-wert m repurchase value, redemption v.; Versicherungswesen: =koppeln (″...) Radio: I v/a. u. v/n. (h.) ②a. ** to couple (or feed) back. — II ~ n ② u. Rück-kopp(e)lung f ⑥ reaction coupling, back-coupling, feed-back; =kopp(e)lungs-... Radio: regenerative; =kopp(e)lungs-verstärkung f regeneration; =läufer m Billard: drag.

*Ruck-sack ᛏ rucksack.

Rück-spiel (″...) n ② Sport: return match; =strömung f reflux; =tritt-bremse f Radsport: back-pedalling brake; =tritts-gesuch n resignation; ⊙übersetzen v/a. ②; =wanderer m immigrant returning home; =wärts=gang m, mach. reverse; ⊙wärts=treten v/n. (h.) ②d. ** Radsport: to back-pedal.

Rud(r)erin (⌣⌣) f ④⑦ (female) rower, oarswoman.

Ruder-stange (″⌣...) f oar; zum Staken: punt-pole; =verein m rowing-club.

Ruf-zeichen (″...) n ② Fernspr. call-sign(al).

*ruhig zu 1: ✱ vom Markt: quiet, dull.

Ruhr-einbruch (″...) m ② hist. invasion of the Ruhr (1923).

Rühr-seligkeit (″...) f ② sentimentality.

ruinös bsd. ✱ (⌣⌣″) [fr.] a. ⑥ (zugrunde richtend) ruinous.

Rummel-platz P (⌣⌣″) m ② place of amusement.

Rummy (⌣″) [fr.] n inv. (o. pl.) (Kartenspiel) rummy. [lage.]

*Rumpf ✗ e-s Flugzeugs: body, fuse-

*Runde zu 1: Rennsport u. ✗ lap. — zu 2: die ~ machen to make (or go) one's rounds.

Rund-frage (″...) f ② inquiry by means of a circular; ⊙ Radio: broadcast(ing); durch ~ verbreiten to broadcast; im ~ Vortragende pl. broadcasters; =funk-empfänger m ② broadcast receiver; ⊙funken v/a. u. v/n. (h.) ② **; ** to broadcast; =funk-hörer ⊙ m listener-in; =funk-programm n broadcast programme; =funk-sender m broadcast transmitter; =funk-station, =funk-stelle f broadcast(ing) station; =funk-teil-nehmer m listener-in; =kopf ⊙ m (Musterklammer) round-headed paper fastener; =kugel f (ant. Lang-

geschoß round shot; **Spitz-feder** f circular-pointed pen; **Spruch** m Radio: broadcasting.

Rüstungs-industrie (ˈ…) f armaments industry. [lehrten.)

Rüst-zeug fig. equipment (z.B. e-s Ge-

S

Saaten-stand (ˈ…) m agr. a) young (or green) crops pl.; b) condition of the crops; **-stand-bericht** m crop report.

Saat-gut (ˈ) n agr. seed(-corn).

Sabotage (ˈˑˑ) [fr.] f (absichtliches Verderben v. Betriebsmitteln) sabotage.

sabotieren (ˈˑˑˑ) v/a. to sabotage.

Sach-beschädigung (ˈ…) f jur. damage to property; **-katalog** m subject catalogue; **-leistung** f jur. performance (or payment or service) rendered in kind.

*sachlich (unparteiisch) unbiassed, impartial; bsd. arch. (zweckdienlich) practical.

*Sachlichkeit impartiality; bsd. arch. die neue ~ the new practicality.

Sach-lieferung (ˈ…) f delivery in kind; **-versicherung** f property-insurance; **-wucher** m jur. exorbitant charges for commodities.

Sadismus (ˈˑˑ) [Marquis de Sade, 1740—1814] m path. sadism.

Sadist (ˈˑˑ) m , **~in** f path. sadist; **sadisch** a. sadistic(ally adv.).

Saison-arbeit (sä-, kä-fg"…) f seasonal work; **-(aus)verkauf** m seasonal sale; **-geschäft** n seasonal business; **-gewerbe** n seasonal trade; **-mäßig** a. seasonal.

Sakko (ˈˑ) [it.] m Schneiderei: lounge jacket; **~anzug** (ˑˑ…) m lounge suit.

sakral (ˈˑ) [it.] a. (Heiligtümer betreffend) sacral.

Sakrileg (ˈˑˑ) [it.] n (Entweihung v. Heiligtümern) sacrilege.

säkular (ˈ-ˑˑ) [it.] a. (alle hundert Jahre wiederkehrend; eccl. weltlich) secular.

Saloniki (ˈˑˑˑ) npr/n. α. (grch. Hafenstadt) Salonika.

Sammel-güter (ˈ…) n/pl. miscellaneous goods pl.; **-schule** f pooled school.

Sammler-batterie (ˈ…) f elect. storage battery. [-blast.)

Sand-strahl-gebläse (ˈ…) n sand-)

*sanft: der Zwang non-violent coercion.

*sanieren zu I: to reorganize an undertaking. — zu II: reorganization.

*Sanktion pol. (Zwangsmaßnahme) sanction.

*satt: es ~ haben to be fed up with.

*Sattel zu 1: ♀ ~ im Gebirgsstamm saddle.

*Satz zu 8: gram. einfacher ~ simple sentence, erweiterter ~ compound s., zusammengesetzter ~ complex s.

Satz-aussage (ˈ…) f gram predicate; **-gefüge** 2. gram. (Hauptsatz mit Nebensatz usw.) complex sentence; **-spiegel** m, typ. page proof.

Sauer-stoff-apparat (ˈ…) m oxygen apparatus. [gas plant.)

Saug-gas-anlage (ˈ…) f suction)

Säuglings-ausstattung (ˈ…) f (Windeln, Wäsche usw.) layette; **-fürsorge** f

infant welfare work; **-fürsorge-anstalt** f. **-fürsorge-heim** n baby-nursery; **-sterblichkeit** f infant mortality. [(rubber) teat.)

Saug-pfropfen (ˈ…) m für Säuglinge:)

säure-fest (ˈˑˑ) a. acid-proof.

Saxophon (ˑˑˑ) [vgl. Saxhorn] n d. saxophone.

Schachtel-gesellschaft (ˈ…) f (Unterabteilung einer Dachgesellschaft) subsidiary company; **-wort** n, gram. (Verschmelzung zweier Einzelwörter) portmanteau word.

Schadens-fall (ˈˑˑ) m jur. case of damage.

*Schäfer-hund zo. deutscher ~ Alsatian.

*schaffen zu II 2: ich hab's geschafft (fertiggebracht) I did it. [die cast.)

Schalen-guß (ˈˑˑ) m metall.)

*Schall-dämpfer ⊙ silencer; ⁰dicht a. sound-proof, sound-tight; **-dose** f e-s Grammophons sound-box; **-platte** f record. [(shift) gears.)

*schalten zu I: mot. to change (or)

*Schalter zu 3: interrupter.

Schalter-dienst (ˈˑˑ) m counter-service.

Schalt-hebel ⊙ (ˈ…) m mach. gear shift(ing) lever; **-kasten** m, elect. switch-box; **-tafel** f, elect. switch-board; mot. u. instrument-board.

Schank-betrieb (ˈ…) m Schank-geschäft, -wirtschaft; **-gerechtigkeit** im eigenen Lokal: on-licence; für den Straßenschank: off-licence; **-gewerbe** n = Schankgeschäft a); **-konzession** f = Schankgerechtigkeit; **-stätte** f = Schankwirtschaft; **-verzehr-steuer** f restaurant tax. [play, F thriller.)

Schauer-drama (ˈˑˑ) n sensational)

Schau-fahne (ˈ…) f (Stückchen Stoff an e-m Stoffballen, um Farbe u. Musterung zu zeigen) tab; **-fechten** n Sport: assault at arms; **-fenster-dekorateur** m window-dresser, window display man; **-fenster-dekoration** f window-dressing, window display; **-fenster-reklame** f window display; **-fenster-wett-bewerb** m window display competition; **-kampf** m Sport: exhibition bout; **-öler** ⊙ m, mach. sight feed, circulation indicator; **-packung** f dummy; *-spieler fig. (Heuchler) play-actor. [in cheques.)

Scheck-verkehr (ˈ…) business)

Scheiben-gardinen (ˈ…) f/pl. casement-curtains pl.; **-wischer** m, mot. wind-screen wiper.

*scheinen zu I 2: es könnte ~ it should (or would) seem.

Schein-auktion (ˈ…) f mock auction; **-blüte** f sham boom (in trade), specious prosperity; **-gebot** n feigned (or sham) bid; **-verkauf** m fictitious (or sham) sale; *-werfer mot. a. headlight, headlamp; thea. spot-light (a. = werfer-licht n).

*scheitern zu I: to fall through.

Scheren-fern-rohr (ˈˑˑ…) n opt. periscope.

*Scherz-artikel (ˈ…) m trick.

*Scheuer-leiste über dem Fußboden: skirting-board.

Scheunen-viertel (ˈˑˑ) n e-r Stadt: slum(s pl.).

Schichten-kopf (ˈˑˑ) m geol. outcrop.

*schicken zu 12: ~ nach, ~ zu (holen lassen) to send for.

*schieben zu I: F (auf gerissene u. nicht ganz einwandfreie Weise erlangen) to put through by sharp practice, to manipulate, to wangle; (Wuchergeschäfte machen, bsd. mit Lebensmitteln) nur v/n.) to profiteer.

*Schieber 3. F (gerissen u. nicht ganz einwandfrei Vorgehender) wangler; (Wuchergewinne Erzielender) profiteer; **~geschäft** F n profiteering job; **~e** machen to profiteer.

Schiebe-wind (ˈˑˑ) m (v. hinten kommend) following wind.

*Schiebung F (s. schieben u. Schieber im Nachtrag) wangling; profiteering; eine ~ a put-up job.

*Schieds-gericht Sport: arbitration committee; **-richterlich** a. arbitral, arbitror's; adv. by arbitration; **-richtern** F v/n. (h.) ~ a. * Sport: to referee, umpire; **-verfahren** n arbitration; **-vertrag** m arbitration treaty.

*Schiene¹ zu 1: ~n pl. (um verkrümmte Beine gerade zu richten) irons pl.

Schieß-bude (ˈˑˑ) f auf Vergnügungsplätzen: shooting gallery, miniature rifle-range.

Schiffahrts-gesellschaft ⊥ (ˈ…) f shipping company; **-kanal** m ship-canal.

Schiffer-patent ⊥ (ˈ…) n ~ für große Fahrt master's certificate or patent; ~ für kleine Fahrt mate's certificate or patent.

Schiffs-klasse ⊥ (ˈ…) f (ship's) rating; **-körper** m (ship's) hull; **-schlächter** m (der alte Schiffe zum Abwracken aufkauft) ship-knacker; **-verkehr** m shipping traffic.

Schinken-brötchen (ˈˑˑ) n ham-roll.

*Schiß¹ (Angst) funk.

Schlacht-gewicht (ˈ…) n dead weight; **-kreuzer** ⊥ m battle-cruiser; **-reihe** × f line of battle.

Schlaf-anzug (ˈ…) m sleeping-suit; **-sack** m sleeping-bag; **-sofa** n chesterfield; **-wandler(in** f) m sleep-walker.

*Schlag-ball(-spiel n) m: deutscher ~ rounders pl. [recoil.)

*schlagen zu II 8: vom Gewehr: to kick.)

*Schläger zu 1: Golf: (Golfstock) putter.

Schlag-platz (ˑ…) m Golf: putting-green.

Schlager-melodie ♪ (ˈ…) f song-hit; **-preis** ♥ m, sl. rock-bottom price.

*Schlag-wort bsd. pol. u. ♥ slogan; **-zeile** f, typ. catch-line; **-zeug** ♪ n percussion instruments pl.

*Schlange 3. F fig. (Reihe hintereinander stehender Personen) queue; ~ bilden od. stehen to stand in queue, to queue (up).

Schlangen-mensch (ˈˑˑ) m im Zirkus contortionist.

*schlank zu 1: die ~e Linie in der Damenkleidung the slimming line, the waistline; ~ machen v. der Kleidung to slim, slenderize.

Schlankheits-bad (ˈ-ˑ) n med. slimming bath.

Schlapp-macher F (ˈ…) m slacker.

Schlauch-anschluß ⊙ (″...) m ⓢ hose union; =**ventil** ⊙ n. mot. u. Radsport: tyre valve. [⚙ loop.]
Schlaufe ⊙ (⌣⌣) [mhd.: vgl. Schleife] f⚙
Schleier-stoff ✱ (″⌣) m ⓢ veiling. (fr.) voile.
*Schleppe hunt. (künstliche Fährte) drag.
*schleppen zu III: ✱ (Kunden werben) to tout.
*Schlepper 3. ⊙ für Lastwagen: tractor.
Schlepp-jagd (⌣⌣′)f⓶hunt. drag(-hunt); *=**seil** 2. =s Freiballons: trail-rope.
Schleuder²=**artikel** ✱ (″⌣...) m ⓢ catch-penny article; =²**ausfuhr** f dumping; =¹**guß** m, metall. centrifugal cast; =¹**guß**... centrifugally cast; *=¹**maschine** zu a): Milchwirtschaft: separator, =¹**milch** f separated milk.
*schleudern¹ zu II: vom (Kraft=)Wagen: to skid, side-slip.
Schleuder¹=**pumpe** ⊙ (″⌣...) f ⓢ centrifugal pump; =²**ware** ✱ f catch-penny article(s pl.).
Schleusen-hafen ⚓ (″⌣...) m⓶wet dock.
*Schlichter zu 1: bei Lohnstreitigkeiten usw.: (official) arbitrator.
Schlichtungs-ausschuß (⌣⌣...) m ⓢ Arbitration (or Conciliation) Committee, Committee (or Board) of Arbitration; =**stelle** f Conciliation (or Arbitration) Authority or Court or Board.
*schließen zu II: e-n Betrieb, bsd. um Arbeiter auszusperren: to close down.
Schlitz-verschluß ⊙ (″...) m ⓢ phot. focal plane shutter.
Schlüpfer ⊙ m ⓢ 1. (bequemer Mantel) raglan (coat). — 2. (Damenunterkleid) (ein ~ a pair of) knickers pl.
*Schlüssel tel. (Chiffrier²) code; ✱ (Verteilungs²) ratio.
Schlüssel-industrie (⌣⌣...) f ⓢ (welche die Grundlage mehrerer anderer Industrien bildet) key-industry.
schlüsseln (⌣⌣) v/a. ⓶a. tel. (chiffrieren) to key, code, cipher.
Schluß-laterne (″...) f ⓢ 🚗 mot., &c. tail-light, tail-lamp; =**runde** f Sport: final; =**runden-spieler** m/pl., =**runden-teilnehmer** m/pl. Sport: finalists pl.
Schmarotzertum (⌣⌣-) n ⓶d. parasitism.
*schmeißen¹ F e-e S. ² to manage a th. successfully, F to pull off a th.
Schmelz-eisen ⊙ (″...) n ⓢ metall. cast (or pig) iron; =**koks** ✱ m foundry-coke; =**stahl** ⊙ m, metall. cast (or natural or rough) steel.
*schmerz-los: med. ² machend(es Mittel) ⊛ analgetic. [smash.]
Schmetter-ball (⌣⌣) m ⓢ Tennis:]
*schmieden zu 1: ⊙ geschmiedetes Eisen wrought iron, geschmiedeter Stahl wrought steel. [steel.]
Schmiede-stahl ⊙ (″⌣¹) m⓶wrought]
Schmieren-schauspieler (″...) m⓶ thea. strolling player, stroller.
Schmier-fett ⊙ (″...) n ⓢ grease; =**geld**(er pl.) n F palm-oil; *=**öl** ⊙ m ⓢ lubricating oil.
Schmierung ⊙ (⌣⌣) f ⓦ lubrication.
Schmirgel-leinwand ⊙ (⌣⌣...) f ⓢ emery-cloth. [F punch.]
*Schmiß 2. F (Lebendigkeit) go, verve,]

schmissig F (⌣⌣) a. ⓖⓖ (lebendig) smart, dashing, full of go or verve.
Schmuggel-ware (⌣⌣...) f ⓢ contraband, smuggled goods pl.
Schmutz-blech ⊙ (″...) n ⓢ über dem Wagenrad: mudguard; =**presse** f gutter press; =**schrift** f obscene publication.
Schnabel-tasse (″...) f ⓢ zur Kinder- u. Krankenpflege: feeding cup.
*Schnecke zu 2: c) ~n pl. (weibliche Haartracht) earphones pl.
Schnecken-antrieb ⊙ (″...) m ⓢ mach. worm drive; =**getriebe** ⊙ n, mach. worm gear.
Schnee-fahne (″...) f ⓢ mount. (loser Schnee, den der Wind vom Berggipfel in die Luft weht) snow-banner; =**schmelze** f snow-break; *=**schuh**: ~ laufen to ski; *=**schuh-läufer**(in) skier.
Schneide-backe ⊙ (″...) f ⓢ die.
*schneiden zu I3: Sport, bsd. Tennis: e-n Ball: to cut. [skating.]
*Schnellauf(en n) m Eissport: speed]
Schnell¹=**bahn** 🚇 (⌣¹) f ⓢ quick (railway) line. [speed record.]
Schnelligkeits-rekord(⌣⌣...)m⓶Sport:]
Schnell¹=**pause** ⊙ (⌣...) f ⓖ velograph; =**zeichner** m im Varieté: lightning artist.
Schnitt-ball (⌣⌣) m ⓢ Sport, bsd. Tennis: cut.
*schön zu I2: ²e Literatur polite literature. — zu I3: ² machen vom Hund: to beg.
Schönheits-pflege (″...) f ⓢ beauty culture; Salon für ~ beauty parlour.
Schranken-wärter 🚂 (⌣⌣...) m ⓢ gateman.
Schrank-fach (Bankschließfach) safe; =**koffer** m wardrobe-trunk.
Schrauben-flug-zeug ✈ (″...) n ⚙ screw-propelled flying-machine, 🚁 helicopter.
Schreber-garten(″...) [Daniel Schreber, 1808—1861] m ⓢ allotment(-garden).
Schreib-block (″...) m ⓢ writing block; =**maschinen-papier** n typewriting paper; ⁹**unkundig** ⓢ ignorant of writing; =**waren-händler** m ⓢ stationer.
*schreien zu II: hunt. vom Hirsch in der Brunft: to bell.
Schrift-bild (⌣...) n ⓢ typ. face; *=**satz** jur. written pleading or statement; =**verkehr** m correspondence.
Schritt¹ zu 2: diplomatischer ~ démarche; ²e unternehmen to take steps.
Schrot²=patrone (″...) f ⓢ hunt. shot-gun cartridge.
*Schub zu 6: batch a. fig. v. gleichzeitig eingehenden Briefen, gleichzeitig vorgenommenen Ernennungen usw.
Schuh-schrank (″...) m ⓢ boot-cabinet; =**zeug** n footgear, footwear.
Schul-aufsicht (″...) f ⓢ school-inspection; =**beispiel** n test-case.
*Schuld zu 3: mst guilt.
*Schuld-buch b) State or municipal Debt Register; =**buch-forderung** f inscribed stock holding. [the debts.]
Schulden-dienst (⌣⌣¹) m ⓢ service of]
*Schuld-verschreibung b) staatliche: debenture, bond.
Schul-speisung (″...) f ⓢ feeding of school-children;=**weg** m way to school.

Schund-roman (″...) m ⓢ shilling shocker, penny dreadful.
Schupo (⌣⌣) 1. f, inv. o. pl. Kurzwort für Schutzpolizei. — 2. m ⓢ (F = Schutz-polizist). a. ~**mann** (⌣″) m⓶etwa: Bobby.
Schnß-kreis (⌣¹) m ⓢ Hockeysport: striking circle.
Schüttel-reim (⌣⌣¹) m ⓢ spoonerism.
schütter obd. (⌣⌣) [: schütten¹] a. ⓖⓖ (lose dünnstehend) sparse.
Schutt-halde (⌣⌣) f ⓢ, =**hang** m, geol., mount. (slope of) scree(s pl.).
Schutz-anstrich (″...) m ⓢ 1. protective coat. — 2. ✕ u. ⚓ = Blendanstrich; =**ärmel** m oversleeve; =**belag** m, mot. des Laufbretts: step mat.
*Schütze zu 1: Ballsport: shooter.
Schützen-graben-fieber (⌣⌣...) n ⓢ path. trench fever; =**graben-krieg** ✕ m trench warfare; =**schleier** ✕ m screen of skirmishers.
Schutz-färbung (″...) f ⓢ zo., orn. protective colouring; =**frist** f jur. term of copyright; =**gitter** n barrier guard; Radio: screening grid or net; =**haft** f jur. preventive arrest; *=**hütte** mount. mst refuge; =**insel** f auf der Fahrbahn: safety island, refuge; =**maske** f protective mask; =**polizei** f constabulary; =**polizist** m policeman, constable; =**verband** m, =**vereinigung** f Defence Association, Protection Society; =**weg** m für Fußgänger auf der Fahrbahn: safety zone; =**zoll-politiker** m protectionist.
Schwanz-fläche ✈ (″...) f ⓢ tail-surface, tail-plane.
*Schwarm 2. F (Gegenstand besonderer Vorliebe) ideal, F craze.
*schwärmen zu 1: ✕ ² lassen to extend.
Schwarm-linie ✕ (″...) f ⓢ extended order.
Schwarz-arbeit (″...) f ⓢ illicit work; =**fahrer** m, bsd. mot. joy-rider; =**fahrt** f, bsd. mot. joy-ride; =**hemden** n/pl., pol. in Italien: Black Shirts pl.; =**hörer** m Radio: wireless pirate; =**kauf** m illicit sale; =**pulver** n, hunt. black powder; =**weiß-künstler** m, paint. black-and-white artist; =**weiß-zeichnung** f, paint. black-and-white drawing.
*Schwebung c) Radio: beat, surge; ~en bilden mit to beat with.
Schwebungs-empfang m (″...) ⓢ Radio: beat (or 🔄 heterodyne) reception.
Schweige-pflicht (″⌣) f ⓢ business (or professional) discretion.
Schweißung ⊙ (⌣⌣) f ⓦ metall. welding.
Schwel-gas-anlage f) n (″...) ⓢ chm. low-temperature carbonization (plant).
*Schwelle 3. Psychologie: threshold.
*schwer zu 2: ² von Begriff slow of perception, slow-witted.
*Schwer-gewicht 2. Boxen: heavy-weight; =**industrie** f heavy industry; =**kriegs-beschädigte(r)** m man badly injured in war; =**öl** n, chm. heavy oil. [bility.]
Schwert-adel (″...) m ⓢ military no-]
*Schwester (Kranken²) nurse.

Schwimmer-nadel ⊙ (⸗⌣...) f ⊕ mot. carburettor float valve or spindle.
Schwimm-weste ⚓ (⸗⌣...) f ⊕ life-jacket.
Schwing-achse ⊙ (⸗⌣...) f ⊕ mot. oscillating axle shafts pl.
Schwinger (⸗⌣) m ⊕ Boxen: swing.
*__Schwund__ Radio: fading.
*__Schwung__[1] zu 2: (Lebendigkeit) go, verve, F punch; ~ in die Sache bringen to put (a) jerk in(to) it.
*__Sechser__ 4. hunt. = Sechserbock.
Sechser-bock (⸗⌣⌣) m ⊕ hunt. (Bock mit sechs Gehörnprossen) buck of six points.
Sechs-tage-rennen (⸗"⌣...) n ⊕ Radsport: six-day (bicycle) race.
See-gefahr ⚓ ("...) f ⊕ sea-risk; Versicherung gegen ~ marine insurance; =**geltung** f, pol. naval prestige; =**hunds-fell** n sealskin; =**kriegs-recht** n law of naval warfare; =**manns-amt** ⚓ n Mercantile Marine Office; =**manns-ordnung** ⚓ f Ships' Crews' Ordinance; =**not** f distress at sea.
*__Segel-boot__ Sport: yacht; =**flieger** ⚓ m gliding machine, glider; =**flug** m als Sport: aerial sailing; einzelner: gliding flight, glide; =**klasse** ⚓ f rating. [II 4: Sport: yachting.]
*__segeln__ zu II: Sport: to yacht. — zu
Segel-sport ("⌣) m ⊕ yachting.
*__Segler__ Sport: yachtsman, ~in f ⊕ Sport: yachtswoman.
Segler-verein ("...) m ⊕ yacht-club.
*__Seh-rohr__ ⚓ des Unterseeboots: periscope.
*__Seiden-glanz__ v. Webwaren: mit ~ silk-finished.
*__Seil__ zu 1: mount. am ~ on the rope; ~ springen to skip.
*__Seil-bahn__ rope railway.
*__Seilerei__ 2. (Werkstatt) ropery.
Seil-ring ("...) m ⊕ mount. rope-ring; =**schlinge** f loop of rope.
Seiten-moräne ("...) f ⊕ geol. lateral moraine; =**schwimmen** n Sport: side-stroke; *=**sprung** fig. (Ausflucht) evasion; (leichtsinniger Streich) escapade; =**steuer** ✈ n vertical rudder; =**wagen** m des Motorrades: side-car.
Selbst-anlasser ⊙ (⸗"...) m ⊕ mach. self-starter, automatic starter; =**anschluß** m Fernspr. automatic telephone; =**anschluß-amt** n Fernspr. automatic (telephone) exchange; =**bedarf** m personal requirements pl.; =**bedienung** f serving oneself; =**binder** m self-tying knot; =**erhaltungs-trieb** m instinct of self-preservation; *=**fahrer** c) (Rollstuhl für Invalide) self-propelling chair, manumotor; d) (Person) owner-driver; =**füller** m self-filling pen; *⚬**gemacht** (im eignen Haus[halt] hergestellt) home-made; ⚬**gesponnen** a. ⊕ homespun; =**kosten** ★ pl. ⊕ first (or prime) cost; =**lade-gewehr** n ⊕ automatic gun; =**lade-pistole** ⊙ f automatic pistol; =**lade-vorrichtung** ⊙ f automatic loader; ⚬**spielend** a. ⊕: ♩ des Klavier player-piano, autopiano; =**verbrauch** m ⊕ private consumption; =**versorger** m self-supporter; =**versorgung** f self-supply; =**verständlichkeit** f 1. self-evidence. — 2. (etwas Selbstverständliches) foregone conclusion; =**wert** m proper value.

Selektivität ⚡ (-⌣-⌣⸗) [lt.] f ⊕ Radio: selectivity.
Sende-bühne (⸗⌣...) f Radio: transmitting stage.
*__senden__ zu I: tel., Radio: to transmit, send, Radio: a. to broadcast.
*__Sender__ zu 2: Radio: transmitter.
Sende-röhre (⸗⌣...) f ⊕ Radio: transmitter valve; =**spiel** n Radio: transmitted play; =**stelle** f, tel., Radio: transmitter (or transmitting) station.
*__Sendung__ zu 1: tel., Radio: transmission.
Senk-fuß ("...) m ⊕ path. flat foot; =**fuß-einlage** f arch support, instep-raiser.
Sensations-bedürfnis (⸗-tß(⌣)"...) n ⊕ sensationalism; =**stück** n, thea. sensational play, F thriller; =**sucht** f sensationalism.
Serien-arbeit ⊙ ("(⌣)...) f ⊕ serial work; =**fabrikation** f serial manufacture; ⚬**mäßig** a. ⊕ u. adv. in series; =**schaltung** f, elect. series (or tandem) connexion.
*__Serpentine__ (Schlangenlinie) serpentine line; (Straßenkehre) bend, turn.
*__Setz-ei__(er pl.) fried egg(s).
Seufzer-spalte F ("...) f ⊕ in Zeitungen: (Verlustanzeigen, Korrespondenz v. Liebespärchen usw.) agony column.
sexual (⌣⸗⌣) [lt.] a. ⊕ (geschlechtlich) sexual.
Sexual-drama (⌣⸗"...) n ⊕ sex-play; =**film** m sex-film; =**roman** m sex-novel.
*__sicher__ zu 2: ♣ ☷ Le Außenstände pl. good claims; ☷ Papier first-rate stock; ☷er ☷ Papier good (or fine) bill.
Sicherheits-klausel (⸗⌣...) f ⊕ jur. safeguard; =**schloß** n safety-lock.
*__sichern__ zu II 1: mount. to belay. [-out.]
*__Sicherung__ 3. elect. (safety) fuse, cut-
Sicht-geschäft ⊙ ("...) f ⊕ Börse: forward transaction; ~e pl. futures pl.
Sichtigkeit (⸗⌣...) f ⊕ Wetterkunde: visibility. [paß: visé, visa.]
Sicht-vermerk ("...) m ⊕ auf e-m Reise-
Siedler-stelle ("...) f ⊕ settler's holding. [-settlement society.]
Siedlungs-gesellschaft ("...) f ⊕ land-
*__siegen__ zu I: bes. Sport: to win.
*__Silber__ 2. = Silbergerät.
*__Sims__ ledge (Wandbrett) shelf, ⊙, arch. = Gesims.
*__simulieren__ 3. v/n. (Krankheit vortäuschen) to feign sickness; bes. ✕ to malinger.
*__Sinn__ zu 2: ohne ~ und Verstand without rhyme or reason.
Sinnes-art (⸗⌣⸗) f ⊕ habit of mind.
sinn-getreu ("...) a. ⊕ faithful.
...**sitzer** ("...) m in Zssgn ...-seater; z.B. Viersitzer four-seater.
Sitz-gelegenheit ("...) f ⊕ seating accommodation. [empfangsgerät: dial.]
Skalen-scheibe ⊙ ("...) f ⊕ z.B. am Funk-
Skandal-presse ("...) f ⊕ gutter press.
*__Ski__: ~ laufen to ski.
Ski-lang-lauf (sht "...", "...) m ⊕ Sport: ski (long-)distance race; =**läufer**(in f) m skier; =**sprung-lauf** m ski jumping (race). [paper, writing.]
*__Skriptur__ ⚡ (⌣⸗) [lt.] f ⊕ (Schriftstück)
Skull-boot ⚓ (⸗¹) n ⊕, **Skuller** ⚓ (⸗⌣) [engl.] m ⚓ Art Ruderboot: sculling-boat, scull.

Smoking ⊤ (⸗⌣) [engl.] m ⊕ (Gesellschaftsjackett) dress (or dinner) jacket; ~**anzug** ("...) m ⊕ dress jacket suit.
*__Socke__: ~n pl. ✱ half hose.
Socken-halter (⸗⌣...) m/pl. ⊕ suspenders pl. [cassar, tidy.]
Sofa-schoner (⸗"⸗...) m ⊕ antima-
*__so-fort__ ⚓ v. Zahlungen: down.
*__so-fortig__ ✱ Le Kasse ready cash, cash down.
*__solid__ zu 1: ♣ v. Preisen: reasonable.
Soll-ausgabe ("...) f ⊕ estimated expenditure; =**einnahme** f estimated receipts pl. or revenue; =**etat** m, parl. Estimates pl.
Sonder-angebot (⸗⌣...) n ⊕ special offer; =**beilage** f e-r Zeitung usw.: inset, supplement; =**belastung** f specific lien; =**bericht** m special report; =**bericht-erstatter** m special correspondent; =**druck** m reprint; =**einnahme** f specific revenue; =**gericht** n jur. special court; =**gesetz** n special law; =**klasse** f special class; =**sonderclass**; der ~ angehörig T sonder-; =**nummer** f e-r Zeitschrift: special edition; =**zulage** f special (or extraordinary) bonus.
*__sonntäglich__ zu 2: (angezogen od. still wie am Sonntag) Sundayfied.
Sonntags-anzug (⸗⌣...) m ⊕ Sunday dress, F S. best; =**ausflügler** m week-ender; =**fahr-karte** f week-end ticket.
Sore F (⸗⌣) [hebr.] f ⊕ (gestohlenes Gut) swag, haul.
Sowjet (⸗⌣, ⌣⸗) [russ. = Volks-]Rat] m ⊕ pol. Soviet.
Sozial-beamte(r) (⌣⸗(⌣)"...) m ⊕ social (or welfare) worker; =**beamtin** f woman (or lady) social (or welfare) worker.
sozialisieren (⌣⸗(⌣)⸗⌣⸗) I v/a. ⊕ to socialize. — II ~ n ⚭ u. **Sozialisierung** f ⊕ socialization.
Sozial-politik (⌣⸗(⌣)"...) f ⊕ social policy; =**politiker** m social thinker; ⚬**politisch** a. ⊕ socio-political; =**rentner** m ⊕ annuitant under a social insurance scheme; =**zulage** f family bonus.
soziologisch ⚡ (⌣⸗(⌣)⸗⌣⸗) a. ⊕ sociologic(al); adv. sociologically.
Sozius-fahrer(in f) m ("(⌣)...) ⊕ Motorradsport: pillion-rider; =**sitz** m Motorradsport: pillion; auf dem ~ mitfahren to ride pillion.
*__Spange__ ⊙ am Damenschuh: bar.
*__Spanne__ 3. fig. (Spielraum) margin between prices, &c.
*__Spannung__ zu 2: elect. tension, voltage. — 4. fig. (Spielraum) margin between numbers, prices, &c.
*__Spann-weite__ c) fig. range.
Spar-gut-haben ("...) n ⊕ balance at a savings bank; =**kocher** m high-economy cooking apparatus; =**kommissar** m (Government) Economy Commissioner; =**marke** f thrift-stamp.
*__sparsam__ v. e-m Verfahren usw.: economical. [nomicalness.]
*__Sparsamkeit__ v. e-m Verfahren usw.: eco-
Spar-sinn ("...) m ⊕ thrift; =**trieb** m saving (or thrifty) instinct; =**verein** m savings association.

Spartakist (⌣⌣⌣) [*Spa'rtacus*, Führer im römischen Sklavenaufstand] *m* ⑫ *pol.* (extremer Revolutionär), **spartakistisch** *a.* ⑥⑥ Spartacist.

Spät-zündung ⓪ (″...) *f* ⑫ *mot.* = Nachzündung (im Nachtrag).

*****Spediteur** (Möbel⚶) (furniture) remover.   [the javelin.]

Speer-werfen(″...)*n* ⑫ Sport: throwing.

Speicher-anlage ⓪ (″...) *f* ⑫ accumulating plant; **-geld** *n* storage.

Speise-eis (″⸋) *n* ⑫ ice-cream.

Spekulations-geschäft (⸌⸜-t⸜(⸝)″...) *n* ⑫ speculative operation or transaction; **-gewinn** *m* profit from speculation; **-papier** *n* Börse: speculative (or fancy) stock or security.

*****Spende** zu 2: (Beitrag) contribution.

*****spenden** zu I: (beitragen; a. *v/n.* [h.]) to contribute (zu, für to).

Spender(in) (Beitragender) contributor.

Sperre zu 1: ⚕ (Gesundheits⚶) quarantine. — zu 2: 🚆 (Kontrollschranke) barrier.

Sperr-feuer ⚔ (⸜...) *n* ⑫ barrage, curtain-fire; **-holz** *n* Tischlerei: plywood; **-kreis** *m* Radio: stopper (or rejector) circuit.

Spezial-geschäft (⸌⸝-″...) *n* ⑫ oneline (or special) shop.   [cialize in.]

*****Spezialist**: ~ sein in (*dat.*) to spe-

Spiegel 6. ⚔ am Kragen e-r Offiziersuniform: tab.

Spiegel-ei(er *pl.*) (″⸜...) *n* ⑫ Kochk.: fried egg(s); **-schrift** *f* ⑫ *typ.* reflected face.

*****Spiel** zu 1: beim ~ at play; Tennis: (Sieg *m*) ohne ~ walk-over.

Spiel-anzug (″...) *m* für Kinder: rompers, jumpers *pl.*

*****spielen** zu I1: *fig.* ⚶ᵈ erledigen easily.

Spiel-gewinn (″...) *m* ⑫ gambling profit; *****-raum** zu b): *mach.* clearance.

Spinn-düse ⓪ (⸜...) *f* ⑫ spinning nozzle, spinneret.

Spiritus-gehalt (″⸜...) *m* ⑫ *chm.* percentage of spirit; **-kocher** *m* spirit stove; kleiner u. einfacher: etna.

Spitz-bein (⸜⸜) *n* ⑫ Schlächterei:(Schweinsfuß) pettitoes *pl.*

Spitzen-belastung (⸜⸜...) *f* ⑫ *elect.*, 🚆 🌑 usw. peak load; **-leistung** *f* peak performance, record; *mach.*, ⚔ maximum amount of work; *elect.* peak power; **-lohn** *m* peak wage(s *pl.*); **-organisation** *f*, **-verband** *m* head (or central) organization.   [party.]

Splitter-partei (⸜⸜...)*f* ⑫ *parl.* splinter.

Sport-anlage (⸜⸜...) *f* ⑫ playing-ground, recreation ground; **-anzug** *m* sports suit; **-ausrüstung** *f* sports kit; **-(be)kleidung** *f* sports wear; **-dame** *f*, **-freundin** *f* = **-liebhaberin**; **-haube** ⓪ *f*, *mot.* der Karosserie: apron, cowl; **-jacke** *f* sports jacket; **-lehrer(in** *f*) *m* trainer.   [liebhaber(in).]

Sportler (⸜⸜) *m* ⑫, **~in** *f* ④⑦ = Sport-

*****sportlich** mst sporting; vom Benehmen usw.: sportsmanlike.

Sport-liebhaberin (⸜⸜...) *f* ⑫ sportswoman; **-mantel** *m* sports coat; ⚶**mäßig** *a.* ⑥⑥ = sportlich; ⚶ gute Gewinnaussicht sporting chance; **-mütze** *f* ⑫ sporting cap; **-nachrichten** *f/pl.* sporting news *pl.*; **-platz** *m* = **-an-**

-lage; **-waren-händler** *f* sports outfitter.   [talkie.]

Sprech-film (⸜⸜) *m* ⑫ talking film, F

Spreiz-fuß (″...) *m* ⑫ *path.* splayfoot; **-schritt** *m* Turnerei, *mount.* straddle.

*****springen** zu I1: in den Sattel ⚶ to get into the saddle; F *fig.* etwas ⚶ lassen (etwas zum besten geben) to stand treat.

*****sprechen** zu I1: Laßt Blumen ⚶! Say it with flowers! [hörn: tine, point.]

Sprosse¹ 3. *zo.*, *hunt.* am Geweih u. Ge-

*****Sprung** zu 1: ⚔ e-r vorgehenden Gruppe: dash; Turnerei: ~ mit Anlauf flying jump; ~ aus dem Stand standing jump.

Sprung-brett mst spring-board, a. jumping-board; *fig.* (Stufe zu Höherem) stepping-stone; **-lauf** *m* Skisport: ski jumping (race); **-pferd** *n* Turnerei: vaulting-horse; **-stab** *m* Sport: jumping-pole.   [flushing-pan.]

Spül-becken ⓪ (″...) *n* ⑫ des Klosetts:

Spur-halter (″...) *m* ⑫ *hunt.* vom Spürhund: tracker, trailer.

Staats-aufsicht (″...)*f* ⑫ State control; **-bank** *f* National Bank; **-druckerei** *f* State Printing Works; ⚶**eigen** *a.* ⑥⑥ belonging to the State; **-eigentum** *n* ⑫ State (or national) property; ⚶**feindlich** *a.* ⑥⑥ hostile (or inimical) to the State.

stabil(if)ieren (⸌⸜(⸝)⸌⸜) I *v/a.* ⑨③ (stetig machen) to stabilize. — II ~ ⓘ ② u. **Stabilisierung** *f* ④⑥ stabilization.

Stabilisierungs-fläche ⚔ (⸌⸜⸜″...) *f* ⑫ stabilizer.   [-officer.]

*****Stabs-offizier** e-s Regimentsstabes: field-

stab-springen (″...) *v/i.* (fn) Sport: I *v/n.* (fn) ⑪⚶ʰ to pole-jump. — II ~ ⓘ ② pole-jumping; **-sprung** *m* ⑫ pole-jump.

Stadion (¹(⸝)⸜) [grch.] *n* ②⑧ Sport: (Kampfspielbahn) Stadium.

Stadt-anleihe (⸜⸜) *f* ⑫ municipal loan; in England: corporation loan; **-bank** *f* Municipal Bank; **-bau-plan** *m* town-plan.

Städte-bau (⸜⸜...) *m* ⑫ *arch.* town-planning; **-bauer** *m* town-planner.

Stadt-koch (⸜⸜) *m* ⑫ (der Speisen für Privatfestlichkeiten zubereitet u. liefert) caterer; **-koffer** *m*, **-köfferchen** *n* attaché case, F tachy case; **-küche** *f* (f. **-koch**) catering establishment.

*****Stafette** Sport: relay; **~n-lauf** *m* ⑫ Sport: relay race.

*****Staffel** Sport: relay.

Staffel-auszug (⸜⸜...) *m* ⑫ Bankwesen: equated abstract of account; **-lauf** *m* Sport: relay race; **-methode** *f* Bankwesen: equated calculation of account.

*****staffeln** I ②. Steuern, Löhne, Zölle usw.: to graduate, differentiate; Bankwesen: to equate. — II ~ ⓘ ② u. **Staffelung** *f* ④⑥ 3. graduation, differentiation; equation.

Staffel-rechnung (⸜⸜...) *f* ⑫ Bankwesen: equated interest-account; **-schwimmen** *n* Sport: relay swimming; **-zinsen** *m/pl.* Bankwesen: compound interest.

Stahl-helm ⚔ (″...) *m* ⑫ steel helmet; der ~ (Verein deutscher Fronttrieger) the Steel Helmets *pl.*; **-helmer** *m* Steel Helmeter; **-kammer** *f* e-r Bank: strong-

-room, bsd. *Am.* vault; **-kassette** *f* strong-box.

Stamm-baum v. Pferden, Hunden usw.: pedigree; *****-form**: **~en** *pl.* eines Zeitworts principal parts.

*****Stand²** zu 2: (fester Halt für den Fuß) bsd. *mount.* footing. — zu 4: j-n in den ~ setzen et. zu tun to enable a p. to do a th.   [gauge glass.]

Stand-anzeiger ⓪ (⸜...) *m* ⑫ *mach.*

Stander ⚓ (⸜⸜) *m* ⑫ (Flaggzeichen) burgee.

Ständer *elect.* an der Dynamo: stator.

Ständer-lampe (⸜⸜...) *f* ⑫ (auf dem Fußboden stehende Lampe) floor-lamp.

Standes-dünkel (⸜⸜...) *m* ⑫ pride of place.

Stand-glas ⓪ (⸜...) *n* ⑫ *mach.* glass gauge; **-rohr** ⓪ *n* standing-pipe; *****-uhr** große, auf dem Fußboden stehende: grandfather's clock.

*****Stange** zu 2: F fertiggekauften Kleidern: (ein Anzug od. Kleid) von der ~ (a) reach-me-down.   [*thea.* star.]

Star³ ♀ (¹) [engl. = Stern] *m* ⑩ bsd.

Stark-strom-leitung ⓪ (⸜...) *f* ⑫ *elect.* power circuit.

*****starr** zu 2: ⚔ vom Luftschiff: rigid.

*****Start**: fliegender ~ (mit Anlauf) flying start; stehender ~ (ohne Anlauf) standing start.

Start-band (⸜...) *n* ⑫ Sport: starting band; **-ordnung** *f* order of starting.

*****Station** 4. (Abteilung im Krankenhaus)

*****Stativ** *phot.*, *surv.* tripod.   [ward.]

Stator ⓪ (¹) [lt. = Steher] *m* ⑪ *mach.*, bsd. *elect.* (feststehender Teil e-r Maschine; *ant.* Rotor) stator.   [statuesque.]

statu-enhaft (⸌⸜⸜) *a.* ⑥⑥ statue-like,

*****Statut**: 🌑 **~en** *pl.* e-r Gesellschaft articles *pl.* of association.

Stau-anlage ⓪ (⸜...) *f* barrage.

staub-dicht (″...) *a.* ⑥⑥ dust-proof; **-sauger** *m* ⑫ vacuum cleaner, suction cleaner or sweeper.

Stauffer-büchse ⓪ (″⸜...) [Prsn.] *f* ⑫ *mach.* grease-cup.

Staupe² *vet.* bsd. bei Hunden: distemper.

Stau-werk ⓪ (⸜⸜) *n* ⑫ barrage.

*****stechen** zu I: Sport, Kartenspiel: (bei gleicher Punktzahl nochmals spielen usw.) to play (or run, shoot, &c.) off the tie.

Stech-schritt ⚔ (⸜...) *m* ⑫ the goose-step.

Steck-dose ⓪ (⸜...) *f* ⑫ *elect.* wall-socket, plug-socket, plug-box.

Stecker (⸜⸜) *m* ⑫ *elect.* plug.

Steck(er)-kontakt (⸜(⸝)⸜...) *m* ⑫ *elect.* plug-contact, plug-point.

*****stehen** zu I9: ⚶ zu j-m to stand by a p.; ⚶ zu e-m Versprechen, e-r Behauptung usw. to stand to. — zu III 20: ⚶de Schuld consolidated debt; f. Kapital im Nachtrag.

*****steh(e)n-bleiben** *mot.* to stall, aus Benzinmangel: to starve.

Steh-lampe (″...) *f* ⑫ standard (lamp); **-umlege-kragen** *m* turn-down (collar).

Steig-leitung ⓪ (″...) *f* ⑫ *elect.* rising main.

Steil-feuer ⚔ (″...) *n* ⑫ *artill.* high-angled fire; **-hang** *m* steep slope, precipice; **-schlucht** *f*, *mount.* couloir.

Stein-mann (″...) *m* ⑫ *mount.* (Wegzeichen) cairn; **-schlag** *m*, *mount.* fall-

steinschlaggefährlich — **30** — **Tagelohn**

ing stones pl.; ²**Schlag-gefährlich** a. ⓖ mount. stone-swept. [lien loan.]
Stelle zu 1: Darlehen an erster ~ prior
****stellen**¹ zu 8c): artill. Zünder: to time.
Stellen-angebot (ᵍ⌣...) n ⓖ a) offer(ing) of a post; b) position offered; =**nach-weis** m = Arbeitsnachweis: =**suche** f looking for a post or sl. job; =**vermittler(in** f) m employment agent.
Stell-keil ⓖ (ᵍ...) m ⓖ c adjusting or tightening wedge.
Stellungs-krieg ᵘ (ᵍ...) m ⓖ stabilized warfare; =**manöver** ⚔ u. ⚓ n manœuvre for position; =**wechsel** ⚔ m evolution.
****stempeln** zu 1a): sl. ⌢ **gehen** (Arbeitslosenunterstützung beziehen) to go (or be) on the dole, to draw the dole.
Stereo(skop)-kamera(⌣⌣⌣..., ⌣⌣⌣...) f ⓖ phot. stereoscopic (or binocular) camera.
Steuer²-abzug (ᵘ...) m ⓖ deduction of (income-)tax (von from); =**anfall** m incidence of taxation; =**aufkommen** n yield of a tax; =**druck** m pressure of taxation; =¹**elektrode** f Radio: control electrode; =**erklärung** f (income-)tax return; ⌢**fähig** a. ⓖ dirigible; =¹**fläche** ⚔ f control surface; =**flosse** ⚔ f fin; =²**hinterziehung** f defraudation of the revenue; =¹**knüppel** ⚔ m control lever, joystick.
steuerlich (⌣⌣⌣) a. ⓖ of (or pertaining to) taxation, taxative, tax-...
²**Steuer**¹=**mann** Bootrennen: ohne ~ coxswainless; =²**marke** f revenue stamp.
****steuern**¹ zu 11: c) Radio: to control.
Steuer²-politik (ᵘ⌣...) f f fiscal policy; =**röhre** f Radio: control valve; =²**schuld** f tax(es pl.) due; =**senkung** f lowering of taxation; =¹**welle** ⚙ f, mach. camshaft.
****Steu(e)rung** zu 1: Radio: control.
Stich-tag (ᵍ⌣) m ⓖ fixed day, key-day, key-date.
Stil-gefühl (ᵘ...) n ⓖ stilistic sense.
****still** zu 2: ⌢e **Reserven** f/pl. secret reserves. [Betrieb: to shut down.]
stillegen (ᵍ⌣) [still-legen] v/a. ⓖ** e-n
Still-wein (ᵍ⌣) m ⓖ (ant. Schaumwein) still (or dead) wine. [position.]
Stil-übung (ᵘ...) f ⓖ exercise in com-
****Stimme** 4. (Preßeäußerung) comment.
Stimmungs-mensch (ᵍ⌣...) m ⓖ moody creature; =²**voll** impressive.
Stirn-rad-getriebe (ᵍ⌣...) n ⓖ mech. spur-gear; =**wunde** f, surg. frontal wound.
****stocken** zu 14: v. Zähnen: to decay, rot.
Stock-fleck: ⌢e pl. bsd. ⚘ mildew; ⌢**fleckig** a. ⓖ foxed, foxy, bsd. ⚘ mil-
****stockig²** v. Zähnen: decayed. [dewy.]
Stock-laterne (ᵍ...) f ⓖ cresset (light); =**träger** m Golf: caddie.
Stoff-handschuh (ᵍ...) m ⓖ fabric glove; =**veredlung** f improvement (or finishing) of materials.
stopp(e)lig (⌣⌣⌣) a. ⓖ stubbly.
Stopp-uhr (ᵍ⌣) f ⓖ Sport: stopwatch.
Stör-befreiung (ᵘ...) f ⓖ Radio: elimination of interference or jamming; v. Luftstörungen: X. stopping; =**befreiungs-drossel** f Radio: X. stopper.

****stören** zu I: Radio: durch fremde Sender: to jam, to interfere (with).
****Störung** zu 2: Radio: jamming, interference; vgl. a. Luftstörungen.
Störungs-sucher (ᵘ...) m ⓖ tel., Fernspr. faultsman, troubleman.
****Stoß** zu 1: mit der Faust: punch.
Stoß-borte (ᵘ...) f ⓖ Schneiderei: tail-braid; =**dämpfer** ⓖ m, mot. shock-absorber; ~ **mit Riemen** snubber.
****Stößel** mot. tappet, lifter.
Stoß-fänger (ᵘ...) m ⓖ mot. bumper (rod), buffer bar; =**trupp** ⚔ m shock-troops.
****Strafe**: jur. ~ **zahlen** to pay a fine.
****straff** 3. fig. vom Stil: concise.
Straf-mandat (ᵘ...) n ⓖ jur. summons; =**punkt** m Sport: bad point, penalty; =**register** n jur. penal register; =**zuschlag** m surcharge.
Strahlen-forscher (ᵘ...) m ⓖ phys. radiologist; =**forschung** f, phys. radiology. [=**rohr** ⓖ n jet (nozzle).]
Strahl-ofen ⓖ (ᵘ...) m ⓖ radiator;
****stramm** 2. Marsch, Ritt, Kletterei usw.: stiff.
Strand-nixe (ᵍ⌣) f ⓖ co. seaside girl; =**schuhe** m/pl. sand-shoes.
****strapazieren** v. Stoffen usw.: zum ~ **for hard wear.**
strapazier-fähig (⌣⌣ᵘ...) a. ⓖ Stoff usw.: (for) hard wear, nur attributiv hard-wearing.
Straßen-anzug (ᵘ⌣...) m ⓖ Schneiderei: lounge suit; =**bahn-halte-stelle** f tramway stop; =**bau-amt** n Road Board; =**händler** m street-trader, street-vendor; =**rennen** n Sport: road-race; =**schank(gerechtigkeit** f) m off-licence; =**schild** n street sign; =**schreck** F m (bei herrasender Motorfahrer usw.) road-hog; =**überführung** f overpass; =**unfall** m street accident; auf der Landstraße: road accident; =**zug** m road train.
Strecke zu 5: hunt. (Gesamtzahl des erlegten Wildes) bag. — 6. Sport: (Rennen) distance.
****strecken** zu 13: Mehl usw.: (durch Beimengung minderwertiger Stoffe den Vorrat vermehren) to lengthen. — zu I: hunt. (erlegen) to kill, shoot down, bag.
****Streckung** v. Mehl usw.: lengthening.
****streichen** zu 1: (nur h.) Sport: (seine Meldung zurückziehen) to scratch.
****Streife** v. d. Polizei: a) (Streifzug) raid, razzia; b) (Streifwache) patrol.
Streik: **sich im** ~ **befinden** to be on strike; **in den** ~ **treten** to go on strike.
Streik-arbeit (ᵘ...) f ⓖ blackleg-work, scab-work.
****streifen** II **Streifende(r)** m ⓖ striker.
Streik-lohn (ᵘ...) m ⓖ strike-pay; =**posten**: ~ **ausstellen vor e-r Fabrik** usw., mit ~ **besetzen** to picket; ~ **stehen** to picket.
Strich-ätzung (ᵍ...) f ⓖ Chemigraphie: line-plate; =**zeichnung** f Kunst: line-drawing.
Strick-waren ⚔ (ᵍ...) f/pl. knit(ted) goods pl., hosiery sg.
Strom-dichte (ᵍ...) f ⓖ elect. current density; =**linie** f phys. stream-line; =**linien-form** f, mot. u. ⚓ streamline form or shape; **Wagen mit Stromlinienform** stream-lined car;

=**schiene** ⓖ f, elect. electric current rail; =**verbrauch** m, elect. current consumption.
****Strumpf**: **Strümpfe** pl. ⚘ hose. [pl.]
Strumpf-halter (ᵍ...) m ⓖ suspenders
Struw(w)el-bart F (ᵍ⌣, ᵘ⌣) m ⓖ scrubby beard, F bootbrush.
Stück-lohn (ᵍ⌣) m ⓖ piece-wage (s pl.)
Studi-en-anstalt (ᵘ(⌣)⌣...) f ⓖ girls' secondary school; *=**direktor** headmaster of a secondary school; *=**rat** zu b): assistant master of a secondary school; =**reise** f educational journey or trip. [development.]
Stufen-gang (ᵘ⌣⌣) m ⓖ fig. gradual.
Stumpen ⓖ (ᵍ) m ⓖ Hutmacherei: body.
Stunden-durchschnitts-geschwindigkeit (ᵍ⌣...) f ⓖ Sport: average hourly speed.
****Sturm-riemen** ⚔ chin-strap; =**truppen** ⚔ f/pl. storm-troops; =**wagen** ⚔ m tank.
Sturz-flug ⚓ (ᵍ⌣...) m ⓖ (nose-)dive; **einen** ~ **machen** to (nose-)dive; =**helm** m, mot. u. ⚓ crash helmet.
****Stutzen²** 2. ⓖ (Ansatzrohrstück) nozzle.
****stützen** zu II: Börse: e-e **Valuta**: to peg, pin.
****Stütz-punkt** ⚔ u. ⚓ basis, base.
Stützung (ᵍ⌣) f ⓖ = stützen II; Börse: pegging, pinning; =**s-aktion** (⚘ "...) f ⓖ pegging the market.
****Substanz** 2. ⚘ real (or actual) capital.
****Sucher** 3. opt. am Fernrohr: finder; phot. an der Kamera: view-finder; =**lampe** ⓖ (⌣...) f ⓖ spot-light.
Such-schein-werfer ⓖ (ᵘ...) m ⓖ spot-light.
****süchtig** zu 2: b) (e-m **Rauschgift** usw. verfallen) addicted to, mit in Zssgn. z. B. **Kokain-**⌢ addicted to cocaine. II ⌢**e(r)** m, ⌢**e** f ⓖ 3. wie 2 b), z. B. **Kokain-**⌢ cocaine addict.
Süd-frucht-handlung ⚘ (ᵘ...) f ⓖ Italian warehouse.
Suhle (ᴸ⌣) f ⓖ hunt. (Lache) wallow.
Summer ⓖ (ᵍ⌣) [summen¹] m ⓖ Fernspr.
****Sumpf** ⚔ u. mot. sump. [bauer.]
Süß-stoff (ᵘ...) m ⓖ chm sweetening substance; =**waren** ⚘ f/pl. sweets pl., confectionery. [pathetic strike.]
Sympathie-streik (ᵍ⌣ᵘ...) m ⓖ sym-
****sympathisch**: **er ist mir** ⌢ I like him.
synchronisieren ⚙ (⌣⌣⌣ᵘ⌣) [grch.] I v/a. ⓖ to synchronize. — II ⌢ n ⓖ n.
Synchronisierung f ⓖ synchronization.
Syndikalismus (⌣⌣⌣ᵘ⌣) [lt., *grch.] m ⓖ pol. (linksradikale Richtung) syndicalism. [syndicalist.]
Syndikalist (⌣⌣⌣ᵘ) m ⓖ pol. Lisch a. ⓖ
****Szene**: fig. **sich in** ~ **setzen** to show off.

T

Tabak-handel (⌣ᵘ⌣...) m ⓖ tobacco trade; =**regie** f =**verwaltung**; =**waren** f/pl. smokes pl. [late.]
tabellarisieren (⌣⌣⌣⌣ᴸ⌣) v/a. ⓖ to tabu-
Tabellen-form (⌣ᵘ⌣...) f ⓖ tabular form; =**werk** n tabular compilation.
Tachometer ⓖ u. ⚙ (ᵍ⌣ᵘ...) [grch.] n ⓖ bsd. mot. (Schnelligkeitsmesser) tachometer, speedometer. [work by the day.]
****Tage-lohn**: **auf** (od. **in**) ~ **arbeiten** to

*Tages-ordnung: parl. die ~ beantragen to move the previous question; e-r Versammlung usw. agenda; -preis m to-day's (or current or actual or latest) price; -wert m to-day's (or present or current or actual) value.
*täglich zu 1: ❷ Des Geld call-money; auf De Kündigung at call.
*Tal zu 1: b) phys. (Wellen2) trough.
*Talisman mascot.
*Tal-sperre barrage.
Tank ⊤ (ᵛ) [engl.] m ⑪ c. ❸ c. [a] ⊕ Behälter für Flüssigkeiten; b) ⚔ gleitendes Panzerauto] tank.
Tank-dampfer ⚓ (ᵛ...) m ❷ tanker.
tanken ⊕ (ᵛᵛ) v/n. (h.) ❽ mot. (Kraftstoff einnehmen) to take in petrol.
Tank-schiff ⚓ (ᵛ...) n ❷ tank-ship, tanker; -stelle f, mot. (petrol) filling station; -wagen 🚂 m cistern (or tank) wagon. [danseuse.)
*Tänzer(in) thea. m danseur, f)
Tapisserie-waren ❀ (ᵛᵛᵘ...) f/pl. ❷ tapestry goods, tapestries pl.
Tarif-bruch (ᵛᵘᵘ) m ❷ breach of the tariff.
tariflich (ᵛᵛ) a. ❻❻ of (or pertaining to) the tariff; conforming to the tariff; adv. according to the tariff; in (or by) the tariff; ₂ erfassen to include in the tariff.
Tarif-lohn (ᵛᵘ...) m ❷ wage(s pl.) conforming to the tariff, standard wage(s pl.); -vertrag m tariff-treaty.
tarnen ⚔ u. ⚓ (ᵛᵛ) [mhd.] I v/a. ❸ (für den Feind unsichtbar ob. unkenntlich machen) to camouflage. — II ~ n ㉓, Tarnung f ㊻ camouflage. [turnover.)
*Tasche 3. Bäckerei: (z.B. Apfel₂ apple-)
Taschen-apotheke (ᵛᵛᵛ...) f ❷ pocket medicine case; -feuerzeug n pocket lighter; -lampe f pocket lamp.
tätigen ⊕ (ᵛᵛᵛ) v/a. ❽ to carry out, to effect a sale; to conclude a transaction.
Tat-sachen-frage (ᵘ...) f ❷ jur. issue in fact. [(boat.))
Tauch-boot ⚓ (ᵘᵘ) n ❷ submersible)
*tauchen zu II 2: ⚓ vom Unterseeboot: to submerge.
tauch-fähig ⚓ (ᵘ...) a. ❻❻ vom Unterseeboot: submersible; -fähigkeit ⚓ f ❷ submersibility; -sieder ⊕ m immersion heater. [(part) exchange.)
*Tausch: ❀ in ~ nehmen to take in)
Tausch-mittel (ᵘ...) n ❷ medium of exchange; -objekt n object of value in exchange; -wert m exchangeable value.
Tau-tropfen-form ⊕ (ᵘ...) f ❷ mot. u. ⚡ stream-line form or shape.
Taxe² (ᵛᵛ) [abbr. Taxameter(droschke)] f ❷ taxi.
taxierbar (ᵛᵛ) a. ❻❻ appreciable; amtlich: assessable. [logical.)
technologisch ⚗ (ᵛᵛᵛ) a. ❻❻ techno-)
Teddy-bär ⊤ (ᵛᵛᵛ) [engl.] m ❷ (Kinderspielzeug aus Stoff) Teddy bear.
Tee-wagen (ᵘ...) m ❷ (Teetisch auf Rädern) tea wagon.
Teil-betrag (ᵛᵛ...) m ❷ partial (or fractional) amount, instalment; *-nehmer Fernspr. subscriber; ~ antwortet nicht there's no reply; -wert m partial (or fractional) value.

Telegramm-adresse ❀ (-ᵛᵛ...) f ❷ telegraphic address.
Telegraphen-arbeiter (-ᵛᵘᵛ...) m ❷ line(s)man; -truppe ⚔ f Signal Corps.
Telepathie ⚗ (-ᵛᵛ) [grch.] f ㊻ (passive Fernbeeinflussung) telepathy.
telepathisch ⚗ (-ᵛᵛ) a. ❻❻ telepathic (-ally adv.). [box.)
Telephon-zelle (-ᵛᵘ...) f ❷ telephone)
Telergie ⚗ (-ᵛᵛ) [grch.] f ㊻ (aktive Fernbeeinflussung) telergy.
tempel-schänderisch (ᵛᵛ...) a. ❻❻ sacrilegious; -schändung f ❷ sacrilege.
*Temperament (Lebhaftigkeit) spirits pl., mettle; ₂-los (ᵛᵛᵛᵛ) a. ❻❻ spiritless.
Temperatur-schwankungen (ᵛᵛᵛᵛ...) f/pl. ❷ swinging temperature(s pl.).
Temper-guß ⊕ (ᵛᵛᵛ) m ❷ metall. malleable cast iron.
Teppich-kehr-maschine ⊕ (ᵛᵛᵛ...) f ❷ carpet-sweeper.
*Termin zu 1 a): Sport: fixture.
*Termin-geschäft (Lieferungsgeschäft) forward transaction, pl. a. futures.
*Terrain (Grundstück) plot of land, building site.
Terrain-gesellschaft ❀ (vä"nᵛ...) f ❷ real estate (or proprietary) company; -spekulation ❀ f speculation in real estate, land speculation; -unternehmen ❀ n real estate firm or business.
Terror (ᵛᵛ) [lt.] m ❷ o. pl. (Schrecken[sherrschaft]) terror.
*teuer zu 1: De Preise pl. high prices.
Teurungs-welle (ᵘ...) f ❷ wave of high prices; *-zulage (cost of living) bonus; -zuschlag ❀ m advance in price due to increased cost.
Textili-en ⊕ (ᵛᵛᵛ) n [lt.] pl. inv. (Webwaren) textiles pl.
Theater-fieber (ᵛᵛᵛ...) n ❷ stage-fever.
Thermion (ᵛᵛᵛ) [grch.] n ㉛ elect. (v. e-r glühenden Substanz ausgehendes elektrisch geladenes Teilchen) thermion.
thermionisch ⚗ (ᵛᵛᵛ) a. ❻❻ elect. thermionic.
thermisch ⚗ (ᵛᵛ) [grch.] a. ❻❻ phys. (die Wärme betreffend) thermic, thermal.
Thermos-flasche ⊕ (ᵛᵛ...) f ❷ thermos flask or bottle, vacuum flask.
Thermostat ⚗ (ᵛᵛᵛ) [grch.] m ⑪ c. phys. (selbsttätiger Wärmeregler) thermostat.
thesaurieren (---ᵛᵛ) [grch.] v/a. ❽ (aufspeichern) to lay up, to store (up).
Thomas-eisen ⊕ (ᵛ...) n ❷ metall. basic iron; -schlacke f basic slag; -stahl m basic steel.
Thrombose ⚗ (ᵛᵛᵛ) [grch.] f ㊻ path. (Verstopfung der Gefäße durch e-n Blutpfropfen) thrombosis.
Ticker ⊤ (ᵛᵛ) [engl.] m ❷ Radio: (Schnellunterbrecher) ticker.
*tief zu 13: zu ₂ singen to sing flat. — zu II 6: Wetterkunde: low, depression.
*Tief-blick (Blick in die Tiefe) bird's eye view (auf acc. of); *-druck 2. Wetterkunde: low pressure, depression; -druck-gebiet n Wetterkunde: low-pressure area; ₂gebeugt ❀ fig. deeply afflicted; ₂gefühlt a. heartfelt; -konjunktur ❀ f trade depression; -schlag m Boxen: deep hit; -stand m low state or level.

Tier-zucht (ᵘᵛ) f ❷ animal husbandry.
Tikker ⊤ (ᵛᵛ) m ❷ = Ticker.
Tilgungs-plan (ᵛᵛᵛ) m ❷ plan (or scheme) of redemption.
*tippen 2. sl. (auf der Schreibmaschine schreiben) to type.
*Tisch zu 1: Konferenz am grünen ~ round-table conference.
Tisch-apparat (ᵛ...) m ❷ Fernspr. desk-telephone; -butter f = Tafelbutter; *-karte (die dem einzelnen Gast seinen Platz anweist) dinner guest card; -lampe f table lamp; -tennis n Sport: table-tennis, ping-pong.
Titel-halter (ᵘ...) m ❷, -verteidiger m Sport: title-holder.
Tizian (ᵛᵛ) npr/m. ❺α. (it. Maler 1477-1576) Titian.
Tochter-gesellschaft ❀ (ᵛᵛᵛ...) f ❷ daughter (or subsidiary) company.
*Toleranz erlaubte Spanne: allowance, deviation.
*Tolpatsch F butter-fingers.
Tombola (ᵛᵛᵛ) [it.] f ㊾ (Lospiel) tombola. [toning-solution.)
Ton-bad (ᵘᵛ) n ❷ phot. toning-bath.)
tonen² (ᵛᵛ) [Ton² 5.] v/a. ❽ phot. to tone.
*Ton¹-erde: essigsaure ~ alumina acetate; *-fall beim Sprechen: intonation, accent; -film m sound-film, phono-film; im ~ darstellen to phonofilm; -fixier-bad n, phot. = -bad; -fülle ♪ f sonority. [halt; Tonnengeld) tonnage.)
Tonnage ⚓ (ᵛᵛᵛ) [fr.] f ❷ (Tonnenge-)
Ton¹-taube (ᵘ...) f ❷ Schießsport: clay pigeon or bird; -tauben-schießen n clay pigeon shooting.
Torf-streu (ᵛᵛ) f ❷ peat-litter.
Tor-latte (ᵘ...) f ❷ Fußball: cross-bar; -linie f Fußball: goal-line; -schütze m Fußball usw.: scorer.
Torsions-festigkeit (ᵛ(ᵛ)ᵘ...) f ❷ mech. torsional strength.
Tot-punkt (ᵘ...) m ❷ mech. dead centre; ₂sicher F a. ❻❻ cocksure; ₂stechen v/a. ❸ a.** to stab to death.
*Tour zu 1: auf (der) ~ on the road; mot. auf ~en kommen to pick up.
Touren-fahrt (tü"ᵛ...) f ❷ Sport: touring competition; -wagen m, mot. touring car. [Herr.)
*Tourist mount. im Verhältnis zu f-m Führer:)
Touristen-verkehr (tuᵛᵛ...) m ❷ tourist traffic or travelling.
Toxin ⚗ (-ᵛᵛ) [grch.] n ⑪ c. (Giftstoff) toxin. [toxic(ally adv.))
toxisch ⚗ (ᵛᵛ) [grch.] a. ❻❻ (giftig))
*Trab u b): F im ~ (auf den Beinen) on the run. [sulky.)
Traber-wagen (ᵘ...) m ❷ Rennsport:)
*tragbar 3. = erträglich 1.
*tragen zu I 3: den Verlust ₂ to bear (or stand) the loss.
Trag-fläche ⚔ (ᵘ...) f ❷ supporting surface, plane, a. aerofoil.
Trainer ⊤ (trä"ᵛ) [engl.] m ❷ Sport: trainer. [training, coaching.)
Training ⊤ (trä"ᵛᵛ) [engl.] n ❸ e. o. pl.)
Traktor ⊕ (ᵛᵛ) [it.] m ❷ c. (Motorzugmaschine) tractor.
Tranchier-besteck (trän"sch"...) n ❷ (Messer und Gabel zum Vorschneiden) (ein ~ a pair of) carvers pl.

Tränen=gas (⏑⏑...) n ⓶ chm. tear-gas, lachrymatory gas; **=gas=granate** ⚔ f tear-shell, lachrymatory shell.
Transaktion ❀ (⏑⏑tz(⏑)¹) [lt.] f ㊻ (Tätigung e-s Geschäfts) transaction.
Transfer ❀ (⏑⏑) [lt.] m, inv. ob. ⓔ e. o. pl. (Verrechnung v. Geldsummen) transfer.
transferieren (⏑⏑⏑⏑) [lt.] v/a. ㊓ (übertragen) to transfer.
Transmissions=welle ❀ (⏑⏑(⏑)¹...) f ⓶ mach. connecting shaft. [oceanic.]
trans=ozeanisch ♀ (⏑⏓⏑⏑) a. ㊻ trans-
Transplantation ⚢ (⏑⏑⏑tz(⏑)¹) [lt.] f ㊻ (Überpflanzung [bes. surg. v. Hautteilen]) transplantation.
Transport=arbeiter (⏑⏓...) m ⓶ transport-worker; **=arbeiter=verband** m Transport Workers' Federation; **=versicherung** f insurance against risk of transport. [trapezing.]
Trapez=akt (⏑⏑⏑) m ⓶, **~e** m/pl. Zirkus:
Traverse (⏑w⏑⏑) [fr., *lt.] f ㊻ 1. ⓔ (Querträger) arch. traverse; mot. cross-member. — 2. mount. (Quergang) traverse.
traversieren (⏑w⏑⏑¹) [fr.] v/a. u. v/n. (h. u. sn) ㊓ (queren) to traverse.
Trecker ❀ (⏑⏑) m ⓶ = Traktor.
Treff=punkt (⏑⏑) [m] ㊻ meeting-place, rendezvous.
***treiben** zu I7: Sport ♀ to engage in sports; Sprachen ♀ to study languages.
Trembleur (trɑ̃blœ̈'r) [fr.] m ㊵ e. elect. trembler, vibrator.
***trennen** zu I1: Fernspr. to cut off.
***Tresor** (Stahlkammer e-r Bank) strong-room, Am. vault; **~fach** n safe.
Tret=zweirad (⏑...) n ⓶ (ant. Motorrad) push-bicycle, F push-bike.
Treu=gut (⏓...) n ⓶ jur. trust-property; **=hand** f jur. (legal) trust; **=hand=gesellschaft** f trust-company; **=hand=vermögen** n = gut.
***Trichter** des Grammophons, Lautsprechers usw.: horn; ⚔ (Granatloch usw.) crater.
Trick=film (⏑⏑) [engl.] m ⓶ trick film, a. stunt film.
Trieb=wagen 🚋 (⏓...) m ⓶ rail-car, railway motor car; **=wagen=zug** m motor train.
Trikoline ❀ (⏑⏑⏓⏑) [fr.: Trikot] f ⓶ (Art Baumwollstoff) tricoline.
Trikotagen ❀ (⏑⏑⏑ɑ̃) [fr.] f/pl. ㊸ = Trikotwaren. [knitted goods pl.]
Trikot=waren (⏓ or -to̅...) f/pl. ⓶ hosiery.]
Trink=branntwein (⏓...) m ㊻ potable spirit(s pl.); **=fest** a. ㊻ able to stand alcohol; ***=halle** c) offene **~** auf der Straße: coffee-stall; **=kur** f, med. e-e **~** machen to drink the waters; **=reif** a. ㊻ ready (or fit) for drinking.
***Tritt²** zu 1: im **~** in step; aus dem **~** in falschem **~** out of step; **~** fassen, **~** halten, im **~** sein ob. marschieren to keep step; aus dem **~** kommen, ohne **~** marschieren to break step. — 4. mount. (Halt für den Fuß) foothold.
***Tritt=brett** mot. u. 🚋 running-board.
Trocken=bagger ⓔ (⏑⏑) m ⓶ (steam) navvy; **=batterie** ❀ f, elect. dry (cell) battery, dry pile; **=element** ❀ n, elect. dry cell; ***=legen** 2. e-n Säugling: to change. — 3. fig. durch Alkoholverbot:

to make a country dry (by prohibition);
***=legung** making a country dry (by prohibition); **=maß** n dry measure.
Trommel=feuer ⚔ (⏓⏑...) f ⓶ artill. drumfire.
Trost=preis (⏓...) m ⓶ Sport: consolation prize, F booby-prize; **=rennen** n Sport: consolation race.
trügerisch v. Wetter, Eis, Gedächtnis usw.: treacherous.
Truppen=reserve ⚔ (⏑⏓⏑) f ⓶ mass of manœuvre; **=verband** ⚔ m unit.
Trust ⓣ ❀ (trɒ̈st) [engl.] m ⑪ a. (Verband, Ring) trust, corner.
Tschechoslowak|e ♀ (⏑⏑⏑⏓⏓) m ㊹, **~in** f ㊻ Czecho-Slovak; **Zisch** a. ㊻ Czecho-Slovak(ian); **~ei** (⏑⏑⏑⏓⏓¹) npr/f. ㊻ die **~** Czecho-Slovakia.
Tupfer (⏓⏑) m ⓶ surg. tampon.
***Tür** zu 1: in (ob. unter) der **~** in the doorway.
***Türke**: F fluchen wie ein **~** to swear like a trooper.
***türkisch**: ❀ Der Honig Turkish delight.
türmen² F (⏓⏑) [?] v/n. ㊓ (sich heimlich davonmachen) to abscond, sl. to hook it.
Turm=springen (⏓...) n ⓶ Schwimmsport: high diving; **=wagen** m, elect. tower-wag(g)on.
Turn=hose (⏓...) f ⓶ (eine **~** a pair of) shorts pl.; **=schuh** m pump for gymnastics, gym(nasium)-shoe.
***typisch**: das **~e** the typical character.
typisieren (-⏑⏓⏑) I v/a. ㊓ (vereinheitlichen) to standardize. — II **~** n ㉓, **Typisierung** f ㊻ standardization.
Tyrannen=mörder(in f) m (-⏓⏑...) ⓶ tyrannicide.

U

über=angebot ❀ (⏓⏑⏓-) n ⑪ d. excessive supply; **=arbeitung** (⏓⏑⏓⏑) f ㊻ (zuviel Arbeit) overwork, over-exertion; ♀**belichten** (⏓⏑⏑⏑) v/a. ㊹*/* phot. to over-expose; **=belichtung** (⏓⏑⏑⏑) f ㊻ phot. over-exposure; ♀**be-werten** (⏓⏑⏑⏑) v/a. ㊹*/* to overvalue; **=bewertung** (⏓⏑⏑⏑) f ㊻ overvaluation;
***♀drehen** to strip the thread of a screw;
♀**drucken** (⏓⏑⏓⏑) v/a. ㊹ b.* jur. to make over, to assign, convey, transfer; **=eignung** (⏓⏑⏑⏑) f ㊻ jur. assignment, conveyance; **=erzeugung** (⏓⏑⏓⏑) f ㊻ over-production; **=exponieren** (⏓⏑⏑⏓⏑) v/a. ㊹*/* phot. = belichten; **=exposition** (⏓⏑⏑⏑⏑tz(⏑)¹) f ㊻ phot. = belichtung; **=fall=kommando** (⏓⏑⏓...) n ⓶ der Polizei: flying squad; ♀**feinern** (⏓⏑⏑⏑) v/a. ㊹.* to over-refine; **=feinerung** (⏓⏑⏑⏑⏑) f ㊻ over-refinement; ♀**fremden** (⏓⏑⏓⏑) v/a. ㊹* to bring into foreign control, to control by foreign capital; **=fremdung** (⏓⏑⏓⏑) f ㊻ foreign control; **=führung** 2. 🚋 usw.: viaduct, overpass.
übergangs=stadium (⏓⏑⏓...) n ⓶ transitional stage.
über=gewinn (⏓⏑⏓⏑) m ⑪ b. surplus profit; ***=hang** bes. mount. (überhängendes Felsstück) overhang; ***♀haupt**: **~** kein ... no ... whatever; gibt es ♀ eine Möglichkeit? is there any chance

whatever?; ♀**heblich** (⏓⏑⏑⏑) a. ㊻ presumptuous, arrogant; **=heblichkeit** (⏓⏑⏑⏑) f ㊻ presumption, assumption, arrogance; *♀**hitzen** bes. ⓔ Dampf usw.: to superheat; **=hitzer** ⓔ (⏓⏑⏑⏑) m ⓶ superheater; *♀**holen** (⏓⏑⏑⏑) ⓔ (nachsehen u. ausbessern) to overhaul; ⚓/n. (h.) ⚓ vom Schiff: to heel; ♀**kapi-talisieren** (⏓⏑⏑⏑-⏑⏑) v/a. ㊹*/* to overcapitalize; **=kapitalisierung** ❀ (⏓⏑⏑⏑⏑⏑⏑) f ㊻ overcapitalization; **=kleidung** (⏓⏑⏑⏑) f ㊻ (ant. Unterkleidung) outerwear; **=kultur** f ㊻ over-refinement; ♀**lagern** (⏓⏑⏑⏑) I v/a. ㊓ a.* to super(im)pose; Radio e-e abweichende Schwingung: to heterodyne. — II **~** n ㉓ u. **Überlagerung** f ㊻ super(im)position; Radio: heterodyne; **=lagerungs=empfang** (⏓⏑⏑⏑⏑⏑...) m ⓶ Radio: heterodyne reception; **=lag=flug** ⚓ (⏓⏑⏑⏑) n ⓶ cross-country flight; **=land=zentrale** f, elect. super-power station; ♀**modern** (⏓⏑⏑⏓) a. ㊻ ultra-fashionable; *♀**nehmen** ❀ ❀ to contract for a loan, new issue, &c.; Bürgschaft ♀ to become (or stand) surety; ***=nehmer** ❀ receiver, assignee of goods, drawee of a bill, contractor for a loan; **=preis** (⏓⏑⏑) m ⑪ a. excessive (or exorbitant) price; ♀**prüfen** (⏓⏑⏑⏑) v/a. ㊹* to examine, scrutinize; **=prüfung** (⏓⏑⏑⏑) f ㊻ examination, scrutiny; *♀**schicht**: **~en** machen to work overtime; *♀**schlag** (⏓⏑⏑⏑) looping (the loop); *♀**schlagen** (⏓⏑⏑⏑) sich ♀ ⚓ to loop the loop; ♀**schneiden** (⏓⏑⏑⏑) I v/a. u. v/refl. ㊹ c.* to intersect, overlap. — II **~** n ㉓ u. **Überschneidung** f ㊻ intersection, overlapping; *♀**schreiben** (⏓⏑⏑⏑) ❀ to transmit, send, mail, post an order; **=see=handel** ❀ (⏓⏑⏓⏑) m ⓶ oversea trade; **=see=verkehr** ⚓ m oversea (or transoceanic) traffic; *♀**sehen** (⏓⏑⏑⏑) (erkennen) die Gefahr, Lage usw.: to realize, perceive; *♀**setzen** (⏓⏑⏓⏑) v/a. j-n über e. Wasser ♀ to carry a p. over; *♀**setzung** am Fahrrad usw.: gear ratio; **=setzungs=büro** (⏓⏑⏓⏑) n ⓶ translation bureau; **=sichts=tabelle** (⏓⏑⏑⏑...) f ⓶ tabular summary; **=spannung** (⏓⏑⏑⏑) f ㊻ elect. excess voltage; ♀**spielen** (⏓⏑⏑⏑) v/a. ㊹ * Sport: dem Gegner: to pass; *♀**stürzen**: sich ♀ v. Ereignissen usw.: to press one another; **=tag=arbeiter** ⚒ (⏓⏑⏑"...) m ⓶ surface-worker; *♀**tragen** (⏓⏑⏑⏑) zu d): Kurzschrift usw. in gewöhnliche Schrift: to transmit, relay; zu d): Kurzschrift usw. in gewöhnliche Schrift: to transcribe; *♀**tragung** zu a) Radio: transmission; v. Kurzschrift usw. in gewöhnliche Schrift: transcription; ♀**trainieren** (⏓⏑⏑⏑⏑) ㊓*/* Sport: to overtrain; *♀**tritt** am Zaun an Stelle e-r Tür: stile; *♀**wachen**: j-n polizeilich ♀ to shadow a p.; *♀**wachtet** (⏓⏑⏑⏑) a. ㊻ mount. corniced; **=wachungs=ausschuß** (⏓⏑⏑⏑) m ⓶ commission of control; *♀**weisen** zur Entscheidung: to refer, remit (dat. ob. an e-n Ausschuß usw. to), parl. a. to devolve (upon a committee); Geld: to transfer, remit; **=weisung** zur Entscheidung: reference, remitting (an acc. to), parl. a. devolution (upon);

Überweisungsscheck v. Geld: transfer(ring), remitting, remittance; **weisungs-scheck** (⁻ᵘ‿⁻) m ⓶ transfer-cheque; **wert** (ᵘ‿¹) n ⑪b. surplus (or excess) value; **wertig** (ᵘ‿¹‿) a. ⓺ (standing or quoted) above (the) value, superior; **wurf-mutter** (¹‿...) f ㉑ cap screw or nut; *zieh**en** (¹‿‿) e. Guthaben usw.: to overdraw; **zieh-socken** (ᵘ‿¹...) f/pl. ⓺ in Halbschuhen zu tragen: golf sock s pl.; **ziehung** (¹‿ᵘ‿) f ㊻ e-s Guthabens usw.: overdrawing, overdraft.

U-Boot ⚓ (ᵘ¹) n ⑪c. (Unterseeboot) U-boat.
*übrigens (beiläufig) by the by.
Übungs-marsch ⚔ (‿ᵘ‿) m ⓶ route-march.
Ufer-recht (ᵘ‿...) n ㉒ jur. riparian right; =**staat** ♀ m riparian state.
Uhr-arm-band (ᵘ‿...) n ⓶ watch bracelet. **Uhren-industrie** (‿‿‿) f ⓶ watch-making industry.
*Ulk: ~ treiben mit to make fun of.
Ulk-bild (ᵘᵘ) n ⓶ caricature.
*Ultimo: per ~ for the monthly settlement.
Ultimo-geld ♣ (ᵘ‿‿‿) n ⓶ monthly loan.
um-buchen ♣ (ᵘ‿‿) v/a. ⓾** to transfer (to another account).
*um-gehen zu I 3: ~d (sofort[ig]) immediate(ly adv.); ♣ höflich: at your earliest convenience. — zu II 3: das Gesetz ⚖ to evade the law.
um-gruppieren (ᵘ‿‿‿) I v/a. ⓽*/* to regroup. — II ~ n ㉓ u. **Umgruppierung** f ㊻ regrouping; =**hänge-tasche** (ᵘ‿‿) f ㊽ shoulder-bag.
um-her-fuchteln (ᵘ¹‿...) v/n. (h.) ⓽² a.** to saw the air; *ziehen: **Handel** im ~ = Hausierhandel.
*um-klammern v/refl. (sich ♀) Boxen: to clinch; =**klammerung** f ㊻ Boxen: clinch; =**kleide-raum** (ᵘ‿¹‿) m ⓶ dressing-room; *=**lage** (Verteilung v. Unkosten) apportionment, levy of costs; (Sonderbeitrag) extra payment, contribution; *=**lagern** (ᵘ‿¹) Vorräte: to re-store; *=**lauf** zu b): außer ~ setzen to withdraw from circulation, to call in; *=**legung** apportionment of costs (auf acc. among); ⓺**randet** (ᵘ‿‿) a. ⓺ bordered, rimmed; =**rechnungs-kurs** (ᵘᵘ‿) m ⓶ Börse: rate of exchange; *=**satz** ♣ schneller ~, kleiner Nutzen quick returns, small profits; ♣ **Umsätze** pl. transactions, sales pl., business; bei guten Umsätzen business being fair, with a brisk market; =**satz-steuer** (ᵘ‿...) f ⓶ turnover (or sales) tax; *=**schichten** fig. Bevölkerung, Kapital: to shift, regroup; =**schiffen** B (ᵘᵘ‿) v/a. ⓾** to tran(s)ship; *=**schlag** zu b): Schneiderei: ~ an der Hose cuff; (eine) Hose mit ~ (a pair of) cuff-trousers pl.; (eine) Hose ohne ~ (a pair of) straight trousers pl.; Buchhandel: jacket of a book.
*um-schlagen zu B: 11. hunt. (herumgehen um) to walk round; (umgehen) to avoid, shun.
Umschlag-hafen ⚓ (ᵘ‿¹...) m ⓶ port (or harbour) of tran(s)shipment; =**platz** m place of tran(s)shipment.

um-schulden (ᵘ‿‿) I v/n. (h.) ⓽** to convert a debt. — II ~ n ㉓ u. **Umschuldung** f ㊻ conversion of a debt; *=**setzen** zu A d): £ 1000 wöchentlich ♀ to turn over £ 1000 a week. — zu A: e) in die Tat, Musik usw. ♀ to translate into; =**sied(e)lung** (ᵘ‿¹‿(‿)‿) f ㊻ removal; *=**spannen** elect. Strom: to transform; =**spanner** (ᵘ‿‿) m ⓶ elect. transformer.
*Um-stand zu 1: unter Umständen circumstances permitting.
Um-stands-korsett (ᵘ‿...) n ⓶ maternity corset.
*um-stellen zu A: Fabrikbetrieb, Valuta: to convert (auf acc. to); auf Kraft(fahr)betrieb ♀ to motorize; auf Maschinenbetrieb ♀ to mechanize; v/refl. (sich ♀) to adapt o. s. (auf acc. to); *=**stellung** conversion, adaptation (auf acc. to); ⓺**wandelbar** (ᵘ‿‿) a. ⓺ v. Wertpapieren: convertible; =**welt** f ㊻ environment; *=**zug**: Wohnungs-Umzüge unternehmen od. besorgen to remove furniture.
Un-abkömmliche(r) ⚔ (ᵘ‿ᵘ‿) m ⓺⑦ im Weltkrieg: indispensable, sl. Cuthbert; ⓺**ausgeglichen** (ᵘ¹‿‿) a. ⓺ unbalanced; *=**befugt**: Unbefugten ist der Eintritt untersagt no admittance except on business; *=**bequem** (unhandlich) unmanageable, unwieldy; *=**besiegt** (frei v. Sport: undefeated; *=**besorgt** (frei v. Sorge) care-free; ⓺**einlösbar** (ᵘ‿¹‿) a. ⓺ v. Wertpapieren: irredeemable; =**entölt** (ᵘ‿¹) a. ⓺ v. Wolle: wool in the grease; *=**entwegt**, =**entwegte(r)** m ⓺⑦ pol. die-hard; ⓺**erschlossen** (ᵘ‿‿) a. ⓺ (noch nicht baureif) undeveloped; *=**erschütterlich** (nicht leicht erregbar) stolid (a. vom Widerstand); *=**fall**: Tod m durch ~ accidental death; =**fall-station** (ᵘᵘ...) f ⓶ ambulance station; *⓺**gar¹** Gerberei: un(der)tanned; ⓺**gedämpft** (ᵘ‿‿) a. ⓺ elect. undamped; =**ge-erdet** (ᵘ‿¹‿) a. ⓺ elect. ungrounded; =**ge-federt** ⊙ (ᵘ‿¹‿) a. ⓺ Wagenbau: unsprung; =**gelernt** (ᵘ‿‿) a. ⓺ v. Arbeit(ern): unskilled; ⓺**geschlagen** (ᵘ‿‿) a. ⓺ unbeaten; ⓺**geschlechtlich** (ᵘ‿‿) a. ⓺ asexual; (♀ veranlagt) a. unsexed; *⓺**glücklich**: ♀e Liebe disappointment in love; ⓺**handlich** (ᵘ‿‿) a. ⓺ unmanageable, unwieldy.
unipolar ⚡ (‿ᵘ¹) [lt.] a. ⓺ elect. (einpolig) unipolar.
Universal-gelenk ⊙ (‿ᵛᵘ...) n ⓶ mech. universal joint.
unken (ᵘ‿) v/n. (h.) ⓽⑧ (Unglück prophezeien) to croak.
*un-kündbar v. Anleihen: irredeemable; v. Kapital: not to be called in or recalled; v. Stellungen: permanent; *=**kündbarkeit** e-r Stellung: permanency; *=**lust** v. Börse, Markt: dullness, slackness; *⓺**lustig** v. Börse, Markt: dull, slack, listless; ⓺**magnetisch** (ᵘ‿‿) a. ⓺ elect. non-magnetic; ⓺**notiert** (‿‿¹) a. ⓺ Börse: unquoted, unlisted; ⓺**pfändbar** (ᵛ‿‿) a. ⓺ jur. unseizable, not attachable; =**pfändbarkeit** f ㊻ unseizableness, freedom from distraint; ⓺**sportlich** (ᵘᵘ‿) a. ⓺ unsportsmanlike; ⓺**ständig** (ᵘᵘ‿) a. ⓺ impermanent; ♀ Beschäftigter casual worker; ⓺**starr** (ᵘᵘ) a. ⓺ vom Luftschiff: non-rigid; ♀

stimmig (ᵘᵘ‿) a. ⓺ inconsistent; =**stimmigkeit** f ㊻ inconsistency; ⓺**sympathisch** (ᵘ‿‿) a. ⓺ unpleasant; er ist mir ♀ I don't like him, he's not my sort.
unter-baut ⊙ (ᵘ‿¹) a. ⓺ Wagenbau: v. Rahmen, Feder: underslung; ⓺**belichten** (ᵘ‿‿) phot. I v/a. ⓽*/* to under-expose. — II ~ n ㉓ u. **Unterbelichtung** f ㊻ under-exposure; ⓺**bewerten** (ᵘ‿‿) v/a. ⓽*/* to undervalue; =**bewertung** (ᵘ‿‿) f ㊻ undervaluation; ⓺**bewußt** (ᵘ‿‿) a. ⓺ subconscious; =**bewußtsein** n ㉓ subconsciousness; ⓺**bieten** (ᵘ‿‿) v/a. ⑲ a.* bei Auktionen: to underbid; ♣ Preise: to undercut; ♣ Konkurrenz: to undersell; Sport: im Rekord: to lower; *=**bilanz**: mit ~ arbeiten to work at a loss; *⓺**binden** (ᵘ‿‿) fig. (verhindern) to prevent, paralyse; ⓺**ernährt** (ᵘ‿¹) a. ⓺ underfed, undernourished; =**ernährung** (ᵘ‿‿) f ㊻ underfeeding, malnutrition; =**gebot** ♣ jur. (ᵘ‿¹) n ⑪c. (ant. Übergebot) lower bid, counter-offer; *=**gestell** zu a) ♣ im Straßenbahn: drehbares ~ truck; =**halts-mittel** (ᵘ‿¹...) n ⓶ means of subsistence; *=**haltungs-kosten** bsd. für Gebäude u. Grundstücke upkeep; *=**hose(n)** (bis zum Knie reichend) trunk drawers pl.; ⓺**kühlen** (ᵘ‿‿) v/a. ⓽** to super-cool; *=**lage** (Beweis) evidence; (Beleg) voucher; =**lag-scheibe** ⊙ (ᵘ‿¹...) f ⓶ washer; **lassungs-klage** (ᵘ‿‿‿) f ⓶ jur. action to gain an injunction; ⓺**lastig** ⚓ (ᵘ‿‿) a. ⓺ insufficiently ballasted; ⓺**produktion** (ᵘ‿‿‿(‿)¹) f ㊻ under-production; =**schreiten** (ᵘ‿‿) v/a. ⑳b.* to undercut prices; =**see-boot-falle** ⚓ (ᵘᵘ¹...) f ⓶ (als Handelsschiff u. dgl. verkleidetes Kriegsschiff) mystery-ship, Q-boat; *=**stand** ⚔ dug-out; ⓺**steh(e)n** (ᵘ‿‿) j-m ♀ to be under a p.'s control or command; ⓺**stellen** (ᵘ‿‿) j-m zur Beaufsichtigung ♀ to put under a p.'s control or command; *=**stützung** aus e-r Kranken- od. Arbeitslosenversicherung benefit.
*Unter-suchungs-haft: in ~ nehmen to commit for trial (wegen on a charge of).
Unter-titel (ᵘ‿‿) m ㉒ typ. subtitle; ⓺**vermieten** (ᵘ‿‿) v/a. ⓽*/* to sublet; ⓺**versichern** (ᵘ‿‿) v/a. ⓽*/* to under-insure; =**versicherung** (ᵘ‿‿‿) f ㊻ under-insurance; =**wasser-bombe** ⚓ u. ⚓ (ᵘ‿‿‿) f ㊻ gegen Unterseeboote verwendet: depth-charge; =**wasser-mikrophon** ⚓ n hydrophone; *⓺**ziehen** (ᵘ‿‿) e-r Prüfung usw.: to subject to an examination, &c.
un-tragbar (ᵘᵘ‿) a. ⓺ = unerträglich; ⓺**übersichtlich** (ᵘ‿‿‿) a. ⓺ badly arranged; ⓺**umstritten** (ᵘ‿‿) a. ⓺ = unbestritten; *⓺**verkäuflich** (nicht zum Verkauf bestimmt) not for sale; ⓺**weidmännisch** (ᵘ‿‿) a. ⓺ hunt. unsportsmanlike.
*Ur-aufführung e-s Films: release.
urbanisieren (‿‿ᵘ¹) [lt.] v/a. ⓽ (mit städtischem Wesen erfüllen) to urbanize.
Urbanisierung (‿‿ᵘ‿‿) f ㊻ urbanization.
Ur-erzeuger (ᵘ‿‿) m ㉒ primary producer; =**produkt** (ᵘ‿¹) n ⑪c. primary product.

***Ur-teil** zu 2: sich ein ~ bilden über (*acc.*) to form (a) judgment of or on.
Ur-teils-sammlung (¨´…) *f* [62] jur. Law Reports *pl.*
u. U. *abbr.* = unter Umständen circumstances permitting.
u. ü. V. *abbr.* = unter üblichem Vorbehalt with the usual preserves or proviso.

V

Vakuum-röhre (¯″◡¨…) *f* [62] *elect.* vacuum tube.
valorisieren ✻ (w¯¯◡´◡) [lt.] **I** *v/a.* [93] (werten) to valorize. — **II** ~ *n* [23] u. **Valorisierung** *f* [46] valorization.
***variabel: II Variable** ⚗ *f* [67] bsd. *math.* (veränderliche Größe) variable.
Varieté-theater (w¯(◡)◡´…) [fr.] *n* [62] variety theatre; **-vorstellung** *f* variety entertainment, variety show.
Variokoppler ⊙ (w¯″(◡)¯¨◡) [lt. + koppeln] *m* [22] Radio: variocoupler.
Variometer ⚗ (w¯(◡)¯´◡) [lt.] *n* [22] *elect.* variometer.
***Ventilator** bsd. *mot.* fan.
***ver-ankern** zu 1: eine Stange usw.: to stay. — **II** ~ *n* u. **Verankerung** *f* [46] staying; nur Verankerung konkret: stay.
ver-antwortungs-freudig (f◡¨◡◡…) *a.* [66] ready to take responsibility.
***ver-arbeiten** zu 12: ~de Industrie finishing (or transforming) industry.
ver-auslagen (f◡´-◡) *v/a.* [88]* to lay out; (vorschießen) to advance.
Ver-bands-preis ✻ (f◡¨´) *m* [62] combine-price.
Ver-band-stoff(e *pl.*) (f◡¨…) *m* [62] *surg.* bandaging material.
***ver-bessern** zu 11: Sport: e-n Rekord: to improve.
***Ver-bindung** zu 4: Fernspr. connexion; eine ~ herstellen to set up a connexion, to complete a call; ~ bekommen to get through.
Ver-bindungs-graben ⚔ (f◡¨◡…) *m* [62] communication-trench; **-offizier** ⚔ *m* liaison officer.
***ver-blenden** zu 12: mit Zweigen usw.: to mask, screen, bsd. ⚔ to camouflage.
***Ver-blendung** zu 2: masking, screening, bsd. ⚔ camouflage.
***ver-bodm/en** 2. ⚓ (verpfänden) to bottomry; **V/ung** 2. ⚓ bottomry(-loan).
ver-bolzen ⊙ (f◡¨◡) *v/a.* [90]* to bolt.
Ver-braucher (f◡´◡) *m* [22], **~in** *f* [47] (*ant.* Erzeuger) consumer.
***Ver-brecher** Rennsport: rogue.
***ver-brennen** zu II: Leichen: to cremate.
Ver-brennungs-maschine ⊙ (f◡¨◡…) *f* [62], **-motor** ⊙ *m* internal combustion engine.
***ver-büßen:** seine Strafe ~ to complete one's sentence, to serve one's time.
Ver-dampfer ⊙ (f◡¨◡) *m* [22] evaporator, vaporizer.
Ver-dienst-ausfall (f◡″…) *m* [62] broken time; **-spanne** ✻ *f* margin.
***ver-donnern** zu 2: *univ.sl.* to sconce.
ver-drahten ⊙ (f◡´◡) *v/a.* [89]* to wire.
***Ver-drängung:** Psychologie: repression.
***ver-edeln** zu 12: to finish goods. — zu 113: finishing of goods.
Ver-ed(e)lungs-industrie (f◡″(◡)◡…) *f* [62] finishing industry.
ver-einheitlich/en (f◡´-◡◡) *v/a.* [88]* to unify, standardize; **V/ung** *f* [46] unification, standardization.
Ver-eins-bruder (f◡″…) *m* [62] clubmate.
Ver-elendung (f◡´◡◡) *f* [46] increasing misery, pauperization.
***Ver-fahren** zu IV 7: jur. das ~ einleiten gegen to take (or institute) proceedings against.
***ver-fallen** zu 11: ~e Gesichtszüge *m/pl.* worn (or faded) features. — zu 2: ~n *a.* [66] e-m Laster usw.: addicted to; dem Rauschgift usw. ~er drug addict.
Ver-fassungs-recht (f◡¨◡…) *n* [62] constitutional law; **-staat** *m* constitutional State; **-tag** *m* Constitution Day.
Ver-femung (f◡´◡) *f* [46] outlawry.
ver-filmen (f◡¨◡) *v/a.* [88]* to film, picturize.
Ver-fügungs-recht (f◡″◡¨) *n* [62] right of disposal.
***ver-fumfei-en** (verpfuschen) to bungle.
ver-gällen (f◡¨◡) *v/a.* [88]* *chm.* Alkohol: to methylate, denature.
***ver-gasen** ⊙ *mot.* to carburet; ⚔ to gas.
Ver-gaser ⊙ (f◡´◡) *m* [22] *mot.* carburett*or*, -er.
***ver-geben** zu 11: ✻ e-n Auftrag ~ to give (or place) an order.
***Ver-gebung** ✻ giving, placing of an order.
Ver-geltungs-maßregel (f◡¨◡…) *f* [62] reprisal.
ver-gemeinschaft/en (f◡◡´◡◡) *v/a.* [89]* to communize; **V/ung** *f* [46] communization.
***ver-gesellschaften** zu I: = sozialisieren. — zu II: = Sozialisierung.
***ver-gessen** zu I: nicht zu ~ … not forgetting …
ver-gipsen ⊙ (f◡¨◡) *v/a.* [90]* to plaster.
Ver-gnügungs-steuer (f◡″◡…) *f* [62] amusement(s) tax, entertainment(s) tax.
Ver-größerungs-apparat (f◡″◡◡…) *m* [62] *phot.* enlarging apparatus.
Ver-günstigungs-tag (f◡¨◡◡…) *m* [62] day of respite or grace; **-zoll** *m* preferential duty.
***ver-halten** zu 11: Rennsport: sein Pferd ~ (a. *abs.*) (zurückhalten, um das Rennen absichtlich zu verlieren) to rope one's horse.
Ver-hältnis-wahl (f◡¨◡´) *f* [62] *parl.* proportional representation.
***ver-handeln** zu 11: gerichtlich ~ über e-e Sache, gegen j-n to try a case, a p.
***ver-harschen** zu I: v. Schnee: to crust.
Ver-jüngungs-kur (f◡¨◡´) *f* [62] *physiol.* rejuvenating cure, (monkey-)gland cure.
Ver-kaufs-abteilung ✻ (f◡″…) *f* [62] sales department; **-rennen** *n* Rennsport: claiming stakes *pl.*; **-wert** ✻ *m* sale (or selling) value.
***Ver-kehr** zu 2: aus dem ~ ziehen v. Wagen: to withdraw from service; v. Geld: to withdraw from circulation.
***ver-kehren** zu I: **3.** 🚂, ⚓, ⛴ (regelmäßig ~) to run, ply. — **4.** ✻ v. Börsenpapieren: to be sold (zu at).
Ver-kehrs-ampel (f◡″…) *f* [62] traffic light; **-amt** *n* a) Traffic Bureau; b) Tourist Bureau; **-andrang** *m* rush of traffic; **-anstalt** *f* traffic institution; **-dienst** *m* der Polizei: point-duty; ~**fähig** ✻ *a.* [66] marketable, current; **-flugzeug** ✈ *n* [62] air-liner; **-inspektor** 🚂 *m* traffic inspector; **-karte** *f* road-map; **-minister** *m*, **-ministerium** *n* Minister, Ministry of Communications, in England: M. of Transport; **-netz** *n* network of communication; **-posten** *m* der Polizei = -schutzmann; **-posten-dienst** *m* der Polizei: point-duty; ~**reich** *a.* [66] v. Straßen: congested; v. Zeiten: = ~stark; **-schutzmann** *m* [62] policeman on point-duty, point-policeman; ~**schwach** *a.* [66] ~e Zeit slack period; ~**stark** *a.* ~e Zeit busy period, rush hours *pl.*; **-stauung** *f* congestion of traffic; ***-stockung** stoppage of traffic, traffic-jam; ***-straße** in der Stadt: thoroughfare; **-tafel** *f* [62] = -zeichen; **-truppen** ⚔ *f/pl.* traffic troops *pl.*; **-unternehmen** *n* transport(ation) undertaking or firm; **-zählung** *f* traffic census; **-zeichen** *n* zur Regelung des Straßenverkehrs: traffic-sign.
ver-klemmen (f◡´◡) *v/a.* u. *v/refl.* [88]* v. Tauen usw.: to jam.
Ver-knappung ✻ (f◡¨◡) *f* [46] shortcoming, scarcity.
***ver-krachen** *v/refl.* (sich veruneinigen) to fall out (mit with).
***ver-krümeln** *v/refl.* (sich davonmachen) to make off, F to skedaddle.
***ver-kürzen** zu 11: verkürzte Arbeitszeit short time.
ver-lagern (f◡´◡) *v/a.* u. *v/refl.* [92]a.* to shift.
Ver-lags-anstalt (f◡″…) *f* [62] publishing firm or house.
Ver-längerungs-spule ⊙ (f◡¨◡◡…) *f* [62] Radio: load(ing)-coil.
***ver-legen**[1] zu 11 a): ⊙ (legen) Kabel, Rohre usw.: to lay.
Ver-leih (f◡´) *m* [11]c. = Verleihung.
***ver-lustig:** j-n e-r S. für ~ erklären to declare a p. to have forfeited a th.
Ver-messungs-amt (f◡¨◡¨) *n* [62] *surv.* Surveyor's Office; **-wesen** *n* surveying.
Ver-mittlungs-amt (f◡¨◡¨) *n* [62] Fernspr. exchange.
Ver-mögens-abgabe (f◡″◡…) *f* [62] capital levy; **-anfall** *m* jur. accession of property.
***ver-mutlich** *adv.* I suppose.
ver-nebeln ⚔ (f◡´◡) *v/a.* [92]a.* = einnebeln.
***ver-nichten** zu III: ~d Kritik, Blick: scathing.
Veronal ⚗ (w-◡´) [?] *n* [11]c. *pharm.* (Schlafmittel) veronal.
ver-petzen F (f◡¨◡) *v/a.* [90]* to peach (up)on a p., bsd. Schule: to sneak against a p.
***Ver-pflegung** bsd. ⚔ = Proviant.
ver-qualmt (f◡¨) *a.* [66] filled with smoke.
***ver-räuchern II** verräuchert *p.p.* u. *a.* [66] (v. Rauch dunkel gebeizt) smoky.
Ver-rechnungs-scheck ✻ (f◡¨◡…) *m* [62] not negotiable cheque; **-stelle** *f* clearing-house.
Ver-rufs-erklärung (f◡″…) *f* [62] boycott.
Ver-sager (f◡´◡) *m* [22] (nicht losgehender Schuß) misfire.
***ver-schicken** zu I: e-n Sträfling: to deport. — zu II: e-s Sträflings: deportation.
Ver-schiebe-bahnhof 🚂 (f◡″◡…) *m* [62] shunting-station.

ver-schieben zu I: ❋ b.s. to sell goods illicitly or underhand. — zu II: ❋ b.s. illicit (or underhand) sale.
ver-schießen zu III 7: nicht 2d fadeless, unfading.
*ver-schleiern ≈ to screen an evolution, attack; ❋ b. s. to cook, doctor an account, &c. [wear and tear.)
*Ver-schleiß¹ (v⁻¹) m u. a. (Abnutzung)/
*verschleudern Waren aus Ausland: to damp.
*Ver-schluß zu 2: (Mittel) fastener; (Zollplombe) seal: Ware in Zoll-2 legen to bond.
*ver-schmutzen v n. (in) to get soiled or dirty, to soil.
*ver-schneiden zu I 5: (mischen) Wein, Spirituosen usw.: to blend.
*Ver-schnitt¹ (Mischung) v. Wein, Spirituosen usw.: blend.
Ver-schwendungs-sucht (v⁻⁻⁻) f ⑯ prodigality, squandermania.
*ver-senken zu II: ⊙ Schrauben: to countersink.
ver-sicherungs-fähig (v⁻⁻⁻) a. ⓖ insurable; **-fonds** m ⑫ benevolent (or benefit) fund; **-nehmer** m insurant, the insured: bei der Lebensversicherung: the assured; **-recht** n jur. law of insurance; **-statistiker** m actuary; **-wert** m insurance (or insured) value.
versiert ⟨⟩ (w⁻¹) [lt.] a. ⓖ (bewandert) versed (in dat. in).
Ver-sorgungs-betrieb (v⁻⁻⁻) m ⑫ public supply undertaking.
ver-spannen ⊙ (v⁻⁻) I v/a. ⓖ* to guy, stay; a. = verstreben. — II ~ n ㉓ u. **Verspannung** f ⑯ guying, staying; nur **Verspannung** konkret: guy, stay.
ver-städtern (v⁻⁻) I v/a. ⓖ a.* (mit städtischem Wesen erfüllen) to urbanize. — II ~ n ㉓ u. **Verstädterung** f ⑯ urbanization.
ver-stadtlichen (v⁻⁻⁻) I v/a. ⓖ* (in städtische Verwaltung übernehmen) to municipalize. — II ~ n ㉓ u. **Verstadtlichung** f ⑯ municipalization.
ver-stärken zu I: elect., Radio: to amplify. — zu II: amplification.
Ver-stärker (v⁻⁻) m ⑫ elect., Radio: amplifier; **-röhre** (⁻⁻) f ⑫ Radio: amplifier (or amplifying) valve.
ver-stauen (v⁻⁻) v/a. ⓖ* to stow away.
*ver-steckt zu 1: (absichtlich nicht geäußert) v. Gedanken, Absichten usw.: ulterior.
ver-steifen zu I: v a. ⓖ to strut, prop; v/refl. sich 2 auf (acc.) to make a point of. — zu II: ⊙ strutting, propping; konkret: strut, prop.
*Ver-stimmung zu 2: zwischen zweien: ill-feeling.
ver-streben ⊙ (v⁻⁻) I v.a. ⓖ* to strut. — II ~ n ㉓ u. **Verstrebung** f ⑯ strutting; nur **Verstrebung** konkret: strut.
Ver-suchs-anstalt ⊙ (v⁻⁻⁻) f ⑫ experimental station; **-ballon** m, fig. kite, (fr.) ballon d'essai; **-gut** n, agr. experimental farm; **-rennen** n Rennsport: trial; **-stück** ⊙ n test piece.
Ver-teilungs-plan (v⁻⁻⁻) m ⑫ plan of distribution; **-schlüssel** m ratio of distribution.
ver-tobacken P (berlinisch) (v⁻⁻⁻) v.a. ⓖ* (verprügeln) to whop.

Ver-trags-erbe (v⁻"...) m ⑫ jur. heir under settlement; **-hafen** ⊥ m treaty port. [spiring trust.)
ver-trauen-erweckend (v⁻⁻⁻...) a. ⓖ in-)
Ver-trauens-bruch (v⁻⁻⁻) m ⑫ breach of confidence.
*ver-treiben zu 3: mit to distribute.
Ver-trieb mit distribution.
ver-trusten ⊤ ❋ (v⁻tr̆ŏ"sts) [engl.] v.a. ⓖ* to corner, pool, trustify.
ver-ulken (v⁻⁻⁻) v/a. ⓖ* to make fun of.
Ver-vielfältigungs-apparat (v⁻⁻⁻⁻⁻⁻) m ⑫ manifold writer.
Ver-waltungs-bericht (v⁻⁻⁻) m ⑫ statement of administration; **-gericht** n Administrative Court; **-recht** n jur. administrative law.
Ver-wandlungs-dekoration (v⁻⁻⁻) f ⑫ thea. shift-scene; **-szene** f. thea. transformation scene.
ver-wanzt (v⁻⁻) a. ⓖ buggy.
*ver-weisen² zu I 2: Sport: j-n von e-r Bahn 2 to warn a p. off a track.
Ver-weisungs-zeichen (v⁻⁻⁻...) n ⑫ typ. (mark of) reference.
*Ver-werfung geol. dislocation; **~s-linie**, **~s-spalte** (⁻...) f ⑫ geol. fault.
*ver-winden 2. ⊙ to distort; ≈ Tragfläche: to warp. — II ~ n ㉓ u. **Verwindung** f ⑯ ⊙ distortion; ≈ warping. [⑫ casualty clearing-station.)
Ver-wundeten-sammelstelle ≈ (v⁻⁻⁻...)/
*ver-zahnen zu I: fig. v. Besoldungsgruppen usw.: to link together.
*Ver-zahnung 3. fig. linking together.
Ver-zehr (v⁻¹) m ⓒ c. consumption of food.
Ver-zugs-aktien ❋ (v⁻⁻"...) f/pl. deferred shares; **-tage** ❋ m/pl. days of grace. [puzzle, picture-puzzle.)
Vexier-bild (w⁻⁻⁻) n ⑫ pictorial)
v.H. abbr. = vom Hundert per cent.
Vibrations-massage ⟨⟩ (w⁻⁻iʒ(v)⁻"...) f ⑫ med. vibro-massage.
Vieh-haltung (i⁻"...) f ⑫ cattle-farming, stock-raising; **-versicherung** f cattle (or live stock) insurance; **-zählung** f cattle census.
Viel-staaterei (i⁻"...) f ⑫ pol. tendency to split up into many states.
*Vierer 4. Sport: (Spiel zu vieren) foursome. — 5. Ruderssport: four.
Vierer-rennen (i⁻"...) n ⑫ Ruderssport: fours-race; **-spiel** n foursome; **-zug** m (Viergespann) four-in-hand.
Vier-rad-bremse ⊙ (i⁻"...) f ⑫ mot. four-wheel brake; **-sitzer** m, bsd. mot. four-seater; **-takt-motor** ⊙ m, mot. four cycle (or stroke) engine; **-takt-prozeß** ⊙ m, mot. four (stroke) cycle.
vignettieren (win-jĕ-tī'-rĕn) [fr.] v/a. ⑫ typ., phot. to vignette.
Villen-kolonie (w⁻⁻⁻...) f ⑫ garden-suburb.
*Visier-linie sighting-line. [a visit.)
*Visite: (bei) j-m ~ machen to pay a p./
viskos ⟨⟩ (w⁻¹) [lt.] a. ⓖ (zähflüssig) viscous. [Kunstseide) viscose silk.)
Biskose-seide ⊙ (w⁻⁻⁻...) f ⑫ (Art)
Biskosität (w⁻⁻¹) f ⑯ [lt.] (Zähflüssigkeit) viscosity.
Vitamin ⟨⟩ (w⁻⁻¹) n ⑫ c. physiol., chm. (lebensnotwendiger Ergänzungsstoff) vitamin(e).

Voile ⊙ (wȧ't) [fr.,*lt.] m ⑫ (Schleierstoff) (fr.) voile.
Volapük (w⁻⁻¹) [künstliches Wort = Weltsprache] n ⑫ e. o. pl. (ersonnene Sprache) Volapük.
Völker-bund (i⁻⁻...) m ⑫ pol. (1919 geschlossen) League of Nations; **~s-rat** m Council of the League of Nations.
Volks-beauftragte(r) (i⁻"...) m ⑫ pol. People's Delegate or Commissar; **-begehren** n, parl. initiative; **-beglücker** m, iro. public benefactor; **-bildungs-kursus** m direct contact class; **-eigentum** n national property; **-entscheid** m, parl. referendum, plebiscite; **-erhebung** f a) rising of the (common) people, popular rising; b) national rising; **-gemeinschaft** f community of the people; **-hochschule** f People's University, University Extension; **-hochschul-kurse** m/pl. University Extension Lectures, Extramural Lectures; **-hymne** f national anthem; *-redner b. s. (Wahlagitator) mob-orator, tub-orator, tub-thumper; **-wirtschaftler** m = wirt; **-wohl** n national welfare; **-wohlfahrt** f national welfare work, national social service.
voll-beschäftigt (i⁻"...) a. ⓖ fully (or completely) employed; **-bier** n ⑫ entire (beer); **-brot** n whole-meal bread; **-erbe** m jur. sole heir; **-gummi** n solid rubber; **-gummi-reifen** m Radsport, mot. solid(-rubber) tyre; mit ~ solid(-rubber) tyred; **~ mit Luft-kammern** cushion tyre; **-mehl** n whole meal; **-sitzung** f, parl. plenary session; ○**spurig** a. ⓖ, **-spur-** ... ⚑ broad-gauge; **-streckungs-beamte(r)** m ⑫ jur. executory officer.
Vor-anmeldung (i⁻"...) f ⑯ preliminary announcement.
Vor-aus-klage (i⁻"...) f ⑫ jur. previous action or suit; unter Verzicht auf die ~ waiving preliminary proceedings against the debtor; **-leistung** f advance payment of a tax; *-sage bei: Pferderennen; über Marktpreise: tip; vom Wetter u. fig. forecast; **~n** pl. als sportliche Zeitungsrubrik: Selections.
Vor-behalts-klausel (i⁻"...) f ⑫ jur. proviso clause.
vor-bei-reden (i⁻"...) v/n. (h.) ⓖ** an ca. 2 to be at cross purposes.
vor-börslich ❋ (i⁻"...) a. ⓖ u. adv. (noted) before the official hours; **-bühne** f ⑫ thea. (Bühnenteil vor dem Vorhang) apron. [-heavy.)
vorder-lastig ≈ (i⁻"...) a. ⓖ nose-)
*Vor-druck² 2. (Formular) (printed) form; **○ehelich** a. ⓖ prenuptial; **-führ-dame** ⓖ mannequin; **-führer** m Filmwesen: (cinema) operator; *○gehen zu c): gerichtlich 2 gegen to proceed against; **-gelege-rad** ⊙ n, mach. clutch gear; **-gelege-welle** ⊙ f, mach. counter-shaft; **-halle** e-s Hotels, Theaters usw. lounge; *-kämpfer protagonist; **-kriegs-**... pre-war; ○**kühlen** ⊙ v/a. ⓖ* to precool; *-lage (Muster) model, pattern; ○**legen** zu I: to produce documents; *-legung production of documents; *○merken to book a seat.

Vormerkung &c.; ↓ seine Fahrkarte 2 lassen to book one's passage; *=**merkung** booking of a seat, &c.; *=**prüfung** Sport: trial; =**runde** f Tennis: preliminary round; =**saison** f pre-season; =**schlußrunde** f Tennis: semifinal; Teilnehmer(=in) an der ~ semifinalist; *=**spieg(e)lung** jur. ~ falscher Tatsachen misrepresentation of facts; unter ~ f. T. under false pretences; =**strafe** f jur. previous conviction.

Vortizismus ⚤ (w⁓⌣⌣) [It.] m 🎨 paint. (moderne Richtung, die spiralige Farbwirbel zur Darstellung verwendet) vorticism.

vor=täuschen (f⁓...) v/a. ⑨¹** to feign, counterfeit; =**trags=künstler**(in f) m ⑫ rhet. elocutionist; ♂ executant, performer; =**verkauf** m, thea. booking; im ~ zu haben bookable; ⁰**wärmen** v/a. ⑧⁸** to preheat; =**wärmer** m ⑫ preheater.

Vor=zugs=bedingung ⚤ (í⁻⁻'...) f ⑫ preferential term; =**gläubiger** m jur. preferential creditor; =**zoll** m preferential duty.

Vor=zündung ⓞ (í...) f ⑫ mot. pre-ignition, premature ignition, early spark.   [fibre.⌐

Vulkan=fiber ⓞ (w⁓⌣...) f ⑫ vulcanized⌐

W

Wächte (ᴖ⌣) f ⛰ mount. (überhangender Schneegrat) cornice.   [-running.⌐

Waffen=schmuggel (ᴖ⌣...) m ⑫ gun-⌐

***wagen**¹ zu 1: Sprichw. wer nicht wagt, der nicht gewinnt nothing venture nothing have.

Wagen==**heber** ⓞ (ᴗ⌣...) m ⑫ (lifting-) jack; =**mangel** ⚔ m shortage of rolling-stock; =**material** ⚔ n rolling-stock.

Wähler=scheibe ⓞ (ᴗ⌣...) f ⑫ Fernspr. (Nummernscheibe am Selbstanschlußapparat) dial switch.

Wahl=geschäft (ᴗ...) n ⑫ management of an election; =**konsul** m honorary consul; =**leiter** m = **kommissar**; =**vorsteher** m = **kommissar**.

***wahren** Interessen: to protect.

Wahrung (ᴗ⌣) f ⑫ s. wahren; v. Interessen: protection.

Waisen=pflege (ᴖ⌣...) f ⑫ care of orphans; =**rat** m Orphans' Welfare Board.

Wald=grenze ♀ (ᴗ...) f ⑫ = Baumgrenze; =**reichtum** m abundance of forests.   [Hotels usw. lounge.⌐

***Wandel=gang, =halle** e-s Theaters,⌐

Wander=ausstellung (ᴖ⌣...) f ⑫ itinerant (or flying) exhibition; =**gewerbe** n itinerant trade; =**gewerbeschein** m pedlar's licence; =**handel** m = Hausierhandel; *=**vögel** fig. Name v. Wandervereinen: Ramblers pl.

Waren=wechsel (ᴖ⌣...) n ⑫ bill on goods; =**zeichen** n mark brand; (Schutzmarke) trade-mark.

Warm=wasser=bereiter ⓞ (ᴗ...) m ⑫ geyser; =**wasser=versorgung** f hot water supply.

***warnen** zu 1: j-n 2 et. zu tun to warn a p. not to do a th.

***warten** zu II 1: j-s 2 v. Bevorstehendem: to be in store for a p.

***Warte=zeit** allg. waiting period; Versicherungswesen: gap.

Wasch=samt (ᴖ...) m ⑫ washing velvet; =**seide** f washing silk; *=**zettel** Buchhändler=sl. dope.

Wasser=ball(=**spiel**) m (ᴗ⌣...) ⑫ Schwimmsport: water polo; =**erhitzer** m geyser; =**flug=zeug** ⚙ n water-plane, sea-plane, hydro-aeroplane; ⁰**gefühlt** ⓞ a. ⑥⑥ water-cooled; =**kühlung** ⓞ f ⑫ water-cooling; mit ~ water-cooled; *=**leitung** zu a): im Hause (tap and) sink; =**leitungs=hahn** m water tap; =**mantel** ⓞ m water-jacket; *=**recht** (Recht, Wasser zu entnehmen od. zu benutzen) water-right; =**versorgung** f water supply.

***Webe=art** e-s Stoffes: weave; =**stoff** m woven material, pl. textiles.

***Wechsel** zu 5: runway.

Wechsel=getriebe ⓞ (ᴗ⌣...) n ⑫ mach. change-gear, variable gear; =**jahre** n/pl., physiol. climacteric period; =**schaltung** ⓞ f, elect. two-point control switch arrangement; =**stube** ⚔ f exchange-office.

***Weg**¹ zu 4: auf dem besten ~e sein fig. to be getting on.   [from a p.⌐

***weg**²=**nehmen**: j-m et. 2 to take a th.⌐

weh=leidig (ᴗ...) a. ⑥⑥ lackadaisical.

wehr=fähig (ᴗ...) a. ⑥⑥ capable of bearing arms, able-bodied.

***weiblich** zu 1: das ewig Weibliche the Eternal Woman.

***Weiblichkeit**: die holde ~ the fair sex.

***weichlich** v. Nahrung, Gefühlen: sloppy.

Weidmanns=heil (ᴗᴗ⌣) n ⑫ hunt. good sport.   [Festgruß: Christmas card.⌐

Weih=nachts=karte (ᴗ⌣chts...) f ⑫ als⌐

Weiß=metall ⓞ (ᴗ...) n ⑫ white metal or bronze; =**wurst** f white pudding.

Weit=flug ⚙ (ᴗ...) m ⑫ long-distance flight; ⁰**herzig** a. ⑥⑥ large-hearted, large-minded.

***wellen** Haar: to wave.

Wellen=anzeiger (ᴗ⌣...) m ⑫ Radio: detector, ⚙ cymoscope; =**bereich** m Radio: wave-range; =**erreger**, =**erzeuger** m Radio: wave generator, oscillator; =**länge** f wave-length; =**messer** m Radio: wavemeter, ⚙ cymometer; =**reiten** n Sport: surf-riding.

Well=pappe ⓞ (ᴗ...) f ⑫ corrugated (or grooved) cardboard or paste board.

Welt=***anschauung** philosophy of life; =**bund** m international union; =**krieg** ⚔ m world-war; der ~ (1914-1918) mst the Great War.

***weltlich** 2e Schule secular school.

Welt=politik (ᴗ...) f ⑫ international (or world) policy; =**meister**(in f) m Sport: champion of the world; =**meisterschaft** f Sport: the world's championship; =**reise** f journey round the world; =**rekord** m Sport: world('s) record; =**ruf** m world-wide renown, international reputation; =**wirtschaft** f world (or international) economy; ⁰**wirtschaftlich** a. ⑥⑥ of (or pertaining to, adv. with respect to) world economy.   [turning buoy.⌐

Wende=boje ↓ (ᴗ⌣...) f ⑫ Segelsport:⌐

wendig (ᴗ⌣) a. ⑥⑥ (behend) nimble, lithe; vom Boot, Auto: easily steered.

Werbe=abteilung ⚔ (ᴗ⌣...) f ⑫ advertising (or publicity) department; =**film** m advertising film; =**kosten** pl. a) advertising expenses; b) = Werbungskosten a); =**mittel** n means of advertisement or publicity.

***werben** zu 13: 2d ⚔ v. Ausgaben, Kapital usw.: earning, productive.

Werbe=wesen ⚔ (ᴗ⌣...) n ⑫ publicity.

Werbungs=kosten (ᴗ⌣...) pl. ⑫ a) professional outlay; b) = Werbekosten a).

*=**Werbe=gang** development, career.

***werden** zu 15 a): was will er 2? what is he going to be?

Werft=arbeiter ↓ (ᴗ...) m ⑫ a) docker, longshoreman; b) ship-wright.

Werk=bund (ᴗ...) m ⑫ Arts and Craft Society; =**lohn** m wages pl.; =**stück** n piece of material to be worked up; =**student** m, univ. working student; =⁰**tätig** (arbeitend) working, labouring, (ant. theoretisch) practical.

Werkzeug=ausrüstung ⓞ (ᴗ⌣...) f ⑫ bsd. mot. tool-kit; =**stahl** ⓞ m tool steel.

wert=beständig ⚔ (ᴗ...) a. ⑥⑥ of fixed value, fixed in value; 2e Anleihe fixed-value loan; =**beständigkeit** f ⑫ fixed value, stability of value; =**gegenstand** m object (or article) of value; =**minderung** f decrease in value, depreciation; =**nehmer** ⚔ drawer of a bill; ⁰**schaffend** a. ⑥⑥ productive; =**steigerung** f ⑫ increase in value, appreciation; =**stück** n = =gegenstand; =**urteil** n judgment as to value; =**zuwachs** m unearned increment, increment-value; =**zuwachs=steuer** f increment-value duty or tax.   [mation.⌐

Wertung (ᴗ⌣) f ⑫ valuation, esti-⌐

wett=bewerbs=mäßig (ᴗ⌣...) a. ⑥⑥ competitive.

***wetten** zu 1: ich wette mit Ihnen um einen Schilling I bet you a shilling.

Wetter=schutz (ᴗ⌣) m ⑫ weather protection.

Wett=kurs (ᴗ...) m ⑫ Rennsport: odds pl., oft sg.; =**markt** m betting market; =**steuer** f betting tax; =**zettel** m betting slip.

Wickel=gamasche (ᴗ⌣...) f ⑫ puttee.

***Wider=ruf**: gültig usw. bis auf ~ until recalled or counter-manded.

***wie** zu 14 a): Sprichw. 2 du mir, so ich dir tit for tat.

Wieder=au***fnahme=verfahren** (ᴗ⌣...) n ⑫ jur. retrial; das ~ einleiten in e-m Prozeß od. gegen e-e Person to retry; ⁰**ergrei*****fen** I v/a. ⑧ b.*/* Flüchtling: to reseize. — II ~ n ⚔ u. **Wieder=ergreifung** f ⚔ reseizure; =**"bescha******ffungskosten** ⚔, pl. ⑫ a) = "bescha**ffungs=preis m cost (or price) of replacement; *⁰**geben** zu b): (bildlich od. lautlich nachbilden) to reproduce; =**gu*****tmachung** f ⑫ a) restoration; b) pol. reparation; ⁰**er=kau*****fen** v/a. ⑧*/* to resell, in kleinen: to retail; *=**verkäufer**: Preis für ~ trade-price.   [-strike.⌐

***wild** zu 12: 2er Streit lightning-⌐

Willens=schwäche (ᴗ⌣...) f ⑫ weak will.

Wind=flügel ⓞ (ᴗ...) m ⑫ mot. fan; =**jacke** f wind-jacket, trench-jacket; =**mühlen=flugzeug** ⚙ n windmill

Windrichtung — **zufassen**

(aero)plane; =richtung f direction of the wind; =schutz=scheibe ⊙ f, mot. wind-screen, bsd. Am. wind-shield.
*Winkel 4. ⚔ (Abzeichen am Ärmel) chevron.
Winkel=lineal (ˊ˘...) n ⑫ geom. set--square. [phore.\
*winken 4. ⚔ bsd. mit Flaggen: to sema-⌉
Wink=zeichen ⚔ (ˊ˘...) n/pl. ⑫ semaphore; ~ geben, durch ~ mitteilen to semaphore.
Winter=sport (ˊ˘˘) m ⑫ winter sports pl.
Wirtschafts=geographie ⚥ (ˊ˘...) f ⑫ economic geography; =jahr n financial year; =krieg m economic war; =lage f economic situation; =leben n economic life; =lehre f economics pl.; =politisch a. ⑥⑥ of (or pertaining to, adv. with respect to) economic policy; =rat m ⑫ Advisory Economic Council; =schürze f overall.
Wisch=strick ⚔ (ˊ˘) m ⑫ zum Reinigen des Gewehrlaufs: pull-through.
Witwen=schneppe (ˊ˘...) f ⑫ (Kopfbekleidung aus Trauerkrepp) widow's peak; =trauer f (Kleidung) widow's weeds pl.
*Woche zu 1: ❋ weiße ~ white sale.
Wochen=(bei)hilfe (ˊ˘...) f ⑫ maternity relief; =end=..., =ende n week-end; =endler m week-ender; =markt m weekly market; =pflegerin f monthly nurse.
wohl=beraten (ˊ˘...) a. ⑥⑥ well-advised; ºerworben a. duly acquired, legally obtained; Se Rechte pl. vested (or well established) rights.
Wohlfahrts=einrichtung (ˊ˘˘...) f ⑫ establishment for welfare work; =marke f charity (postage-)stamp; =minister m Minister of Social Welfare; =pflege f welfare work.
Wohlstands=index (ˊˊ˘...) m ⑫ prosperity index.
Wohn=raum (ˊˊ) m ⑫ living room.
Wohnungs=amt (ˊ˘...) n ⑫ Housing Board; =nachweis m Housing Registry or Office; =tausch m exchange of dwellings; =zuschuß m bonus for rent; =zwangs=wirtschaft f housing control.
Wohn=viertel (ˊ˘...) n ⑫ residential quarter of a town; =wagen m caravan.
*Wort zu 2 c): auf ein ~! a word with you! (of words); b. s. verbosity.
Wort=reichtum (ˊ˘...) m ⑫ abundance⌉
*Wucher zu 1: mit Waren, Eintrittskarten usw.: profiteering. [profiteer.\
*Wucherer mit Waren, bsd. im Weltkrieg.⌉
Wucher=gewinn (ˊ˘...) m ⑫ excess profit; =gewinn=steuer f excess profits duty; =kredit m usurious credit; =miete f rack-rent; =preis m usurious price, exorbitant charge.
Wucherung (˘ˊ˘) f ⑯ ⚕ u. med. (Auswuchs) exuberance.
Wühl=arbeit (ˊ˘...) f ⑫ fig. insidious agitation.
*wulstig v. Lippen: protruding, pouting.
wunsch=gemäß (ˊ˘...) adv. conformably to a p.'s wishes; (auf Verlangen) by request.
*Wurf=maschine c) zum Tontaubenschießen: trap; =taube f Sport: clay pigeon.
Würge=bohrung ⊙ (ˊ˘...) f e-s Flintenlaufes: choke-bore (a. Flinte f mit ...).

*würgen zu II: ⊙ e-n Flintenlauf: (nach der Mündung hin verengern) to choke.
*Würgung 3. ⊙ e-s Flintenlaufs: choke.
Wurm=fortsatz (ˊ˘...) m ⑫ anat. appendix.
Wurst=blatt (ˊ˘...) n ⑫ iro. v. e-r Zeitung: rag; =vergiftung f, path. sausage--poisoning, ⚕ botulism.
Wurzel=behandlung (ˊ˘...) f ⑫ med. root-treatment.

3

zäh=flüssig (ˊˊ˘) a. ⑥⑥ viscous, sticky; ºflüssigkeit f ⑫ viscosity, stickiness.
zahlen=mäßig (ˊˊ˘...) a. ⑥⑥ numerical.
Zahl²=karte ✍ (ˊˊ...) f ⑫ paying-in form or slip.
*Zähl=karte Sport: scoring card.
Zahl²=schein (ˊˊ) m ⑫ a) ✍ = =karte; b) ❋ cheque. [part payment.\
*Zahlung zu 1: in ~ nehmen to take in⌉
Zahlungs=aufforderung (ˊˊ˘...) f ⑫ application (or demand) for payment; =bedingungen f/pl. terms (or conditions) of payment; =bestätigung f acknowledgment of receipt of payment; =ort m place of payment; v. Wechseln: domicile; =schwierigkeiten f/pl. pecuniary difficulties or embarrassment. [play.\
Zähl=wett=spiel (ˊˊ...) n ⑫ Golf: medal-⌉
Zahn=pflege (ˊˊ...) f ⑫ care of the teeth; =pflege=mittel n, =reinigungs=mittel n dentifrice; =rad=fräs=maschine f gear cutting machine, gear hobbing machine.
Zapf=säule ⊙ (ˊˊ...) f mot. ~ für Benzin (roadside) petrol pump.
Zarentum (ˊˊ˘) n ⑨d. Tsarism, Czarism.
*Zarge Böttcherei: chime.
Zechen=gemeinschaft ⚒ (ˊˊ...) f ⑫ Mining (or Miners') Co-operative Association; =koks m foundry-coke; =preis m pithead price.
Zehn=kampf (ˊˊ...) m ⑫ Sport: decathlon; =stunden=tag m ten-hour day; *Tausend b) ~e pl. von Exemplaren tens of thousands of copies.
*zehnten 3. (den zehnten Mann hinrichten) to decimate (a. fig.).
*zeigen zu 13: ⚕ auf ... (acc.) to point at.
Zeige=stock (ˊˊ˘) m ⑫ pointer.
Zeit=abstand (ˊˊ...) m ⑫ interval; =aufnahme f, phot. time exposure; =freiwillige(r) ⚔ m temporary volunteer; =lupe f Filmwesen: slow-motion apparatus; =lupen=aufnahme f slow-motion picture; =nehmer m Sport: timekeeper, timer; =raffer m Filmwesen: quick-motion apparatus.
Zeitungs=halter (ˊˊ...) m ⑫ newspaper-holder; =kunde f science of journalism; =papier n news-print; =verleger m newspaper publisher.
Zeit=zeichen (ˊˊ...) n ⑫ bsd. Radio: time--signal.
*zensieren zu 1: Schule: to give (or award) marks for school work.
*Zentrale 3. main (or head) office, m head-quarters pl.
Zentral=schmierung ⊙ (˘ˊˊ...) f ⑫ mach. centralized (or one-shot) lubrication.

Zentrierung ⊙ (˘ˊ˘) f ⑯ Am. cent(e)ring.
Zentrifugal=pumpe ⊙ (˘˘˘ˊˊ...) f ⑫ centrifugal pump.
Zentrifuge (˘˘ˊ˘) f ⑫ ([lt.] ⑬ ([Milch-]Schleudermaschine) centrifuge.
zentrisch ⚘ (ˊ˘) a. ⑥⑥ (im Mittelpunkt befindlich) centric(al[ly adv.]).
Zeppelin (ˊ˘˘) n ⑫ [Graf Zeppelin, 1838-1917, deutscher Erfinder] m ⑪ e. (Luftschiff) Zeppelin, F Zepp; ~=luftschiff n ⑫ Zeppelin airship.
zer=knicken (˘ˊ˘) v/a. ⑥⑧* to break.
zer=mürben (˘ˊ˘) v/a. ⑥⑧* to wear (down).
Zer=mürbung (˘ˊ˘) f ⑯ wearing (down), attrition; ~s=krieg (ˊˊ...) m ⑫ war of attrition.
*zer=stören zu I: im Weltkrieg 1914-1918 zerstörte Gebiete pl. devastated districts.
*Zer=störer ⚓ (Kriegsschiff zur Vernichtung v. Torpedo- u. Unterseebooten) destroyer.
Zettel=kasten (ˊ˘...) m ⑫ filing-cabinet.
Zibbe P (ˊ˘) [nordd.] f ⑬ Weibchen des Hasen od. Kaninchens) doe.
Zieh=kind (ˊˊ) n ⑫ = Pflegekind.
Ziel=fern=rohr (ˊˊ...) n ⑫ opt. telescope sight; =richter m Sport: judge; =setzung f (setting up a particular) object in view.
*...zig zu 1: c) F (sehr viele) umpteen. — zu 3 ...zigst: b) F ...zigst(e, er) umpteenth. [whiff, a. cigarillo.\
Zigarillo ❋ (-˘ˊ-, -˘ˊˊtso) [span.] m ⑫⌉
Zimmer¹=antenne (ˊ˘˘...) f ⑫ Radio: indoor aerial; =büchse f saloon rifle; =pistole f saloon pistol.
Zins=abschnitt (ˊˊ...) m ⑫ (interest-)coupon; für Aktien: dividend-warrant; =bogen m coupon-sheet. [Zionist.\
Zionist (˘˘ˊ) m ⑫, ~in f ⑭, Zisch a. ⑥⑥⌉
Zisch=hahn ⊙ (ˊˊ) m ⑫ mot. compression cock or tap, priming cock; Benzin in die Zischhähne gießen to prime.
Zitronen=presse (˘ˊˊ˘...) f ⑫ lemon--squeezer.
Zivil=prozeß (˘˘ˊ...) m ⑫ jur. civil action or suit; =prozeß=ordnung f Civil Procedure Code.
Zoll=abfertigung (ˊˊ...) f ⑫ customs clearance or clearing; =begleit=schein m bond-note; =einfuhr=schein m bill of entry; =erhöhung f increase of customs or duty; =gewicht n customs--union weight; =hinterzieher m = =defraudant; =hinterziehung f = =defraudation; =niederlage f bonded warehouse; =rückgabe=schein m customs debenture; =satz m tariff-rate, rate of duty; =schranke f customs--barrier; =schutz m (tariff) protection.
*zu 1: zur Tür hinausgehen to go out by the door.
Zu=behör=teile (ˊ˘ˊˊ˘) m/pl. ⑫ accessories. [feeder-line.\
Zu=bringer=linie 🚆 (ˊ˘˘ˊ˘) f ⑫⌉
*Zucht zu 1: c) (künstlich gezüchtete Bakterien) culture.
*Zucht=haus b) — =hausstrafe; =henne (ˊ˘...) f ⑫ brood-hen.
*zucken zu II: ohne mit der Wimper zu ~ without turning a hair. [-vote.\
Zu=falls=stimme (ˊˊ˘...) f ⑫ parl. snap-⌉
*zu=fassen helfend: to lend a hand.

*zu-führen zu I1: ⊙ mach. to feed material, &c. to a machine.
*Zu-führung elect. (Drahtleitung) lead; ~s-draht m ⓶ feed wire, feeder.
*Zug zu 3 a): ⚔ (Unterabteilung e-r Kompagnie) platoon. — zu 10: g) (englische) Züge pl. im Schreibtisch usw. sliding shelves.
*Zu-gang 3. (Vermehrung) increase.
*zu-greifen zu 1: helfend: to lend a hand.
*zu-gute: j-m ⚰ kommen to be for the benefit of a p.
*zu guter Letzt ultimately.
Zu-kunfts-staat (ᴴᴶᴸ) m ⓶ State of the future. 〚admit of.〛
*zu-lassen zu I3: Deutung, Zweifel: to
Zu-leitung (ᴴᴸᵛ) f ⓺ elect. (Drahtleitung) lead; ~s-draht m ⓶ lead(ing)-in wire.
Zünd-holz-steuer (ᵟ...) f ⓶ tax on matches; -kerze ⊙ f, mot. sparking plug, bsd. Am. spark plug; -ladung ⚔ f firing-charge; -schalter ⊙ m, mot. ignition switch. 〚to a close.〛
*zu-neigen: sich dem Ende ⚰ to draw
*zu-recht-machen: sich ⚰ v. Frauen (sich pudern usw.) to make up.
zu-rück-verweisen (-ᵟ...) v/a. ⊕*/* parl. to refer back (an e-n Ausschuß usw. to).
Zu-sammen-arbeit (-ᵟᵛ...) f ⓶ co-operation, team-work; -bruch m break-down, collapse, downfall, failure; -gehörigkeits-gefühl n (Korpsgeist) team-spirit; *⚰legen d) ⓸ Aktien: to consolidate; Firmen: to unite, merge; -legung f v. Aktien: consolidation; v. Firmen: union, merger; *⚰reißen: sich ⚰ F fig. to pull o. s. together; *-schluß m = -schließung; ⓸ v. Firmen: union, merger; *⚰setzen zu b) gr. zusammengesetzter Satz complex sentence; *⚰stellen aus Einzelteilen, z. B. Arznei, Eisenbahnzug, Liste: to make up; *-stoß zwischen ea. entgegenkommenden Straßenfuhrwerken: end-on (or head-on) collision.
Zu-satz-antrag (ᴴᴶ...) m ⓶ parl. amendment; -batterie f, elect. booster battery; -patent n additional patent; -versicherung f supplementary (or additional) insurance.
zu-sätzlich (ᴴᴸᵛ) a. ⓺ additional.
*Zu-schlag 4. (Steuer⚰) additional tax, supertax, surtax. 〚duty.〛
Zu-schlag-zoll (ᴴᵛᴶ) m ⓶ additional
Zu-schuß-betrieb (ᴴᴶ...) m ⓶ undertaking that requires a subsidy; -kasse f benefit-fund. 〚delivery.〛
*Zu-stellungs-urkunde ⚰ notice of
*zu-teilen zu I: Aktien, Anleihestücke: to allot; ⚔ u. pol. to attach. — zu II: v. Aktien usw.: allotment; ⚔ u. pol. attachment. 〚allotment.〛
Zu-teilungs-schein (ᴴᴸᵛᴸ) m letter of
Zu-verlässigkeits-fahrt (ᴴᵢᵛᴸᵛᴸ) f ⓶ u. Sport: realibility run. 〚tax.〛
Zu-wachs-steuer (ᴴᵟᵟ...) f ⓶ increment
Zu-wanderung (ᴴᴸᵛᵛ) f ⓺ immigration.
Zu-wider-handelnde(r) (-ᴴᵛ...) m ⓻ trespasser.
Zwangs-aushebung ⚔ (ᵟ...) f ⓶ compulsory levy; -ausverkauf m forced (or compulsory) sale; -bewirtschaftung = -wirtschaft; -ernährung f forcible feeding; -erziehungs-anstalt f reformatory; -gestellung f durch die Polizei: arrest; -innung f obligatory guild; -kauf m forced (or compulsory) purchase; ⚰läufig a. ⓺ mach. constrained; -pensionierung f compulsory retirement on a pension; -regulierung f, -vergleich m compulsory arrangement or settlement; -verkauf m forced (or compulsory) sale; -verwalter m jur. sequestrator; -verwaltung f jur. forced administration, sequestration; -versicherung f compulsory insurance; -vorstellung f, path. hallucination; -wirtschaft f Government control; die ~ für e. Gewerbe usw. aufheben od. abbauen to decontrol a trade, &c.; Aufhebung (od. Abbau) der ~ decontrol.
zweck*-dienlich effective; -verband m local administrative union.
Zwei-bund (ᴴ...) m ⓶ pol. Dual Alliance; -decker ⚔ m biplane.

Zweig-niederlassung ⓸ (ᴴ...) f ⓶ branch(-office); -stelle ⚰ f sub-post-office.
Zwei-kinder-system (ᴴ...) n ⓶ two-child system; -kreis-empfänger m Radio: double-circuit receiver; ⚰motorig ⚔ a. ⓺ bi-motored; ⚰phasig a., elect. two-phase; *⚰reihig v. e-m Jackett usw.: double-breasted; -röhren-empfänger m ⓶ Radio: two-valve receiver; -sitzer m (zweisitziger Wagen) bsd. mot. two-seater; mot. offener ~ runabout, roadster, geschlossener ~ coupé. 〚twos.〛
*zweit: zu ⚰ (paarweise) gehen usw. by
Zwei-takt-motor ⊙ (ᴴ...) m ⓶ mot. two-cycle (or two-stroke) engine.
*zweite Sport: Zweite(r) m, f runner-up.
*zwei-teilig Kleid, Anzug: two-piece (nur attr.).
Zwei-weg(e)-hahn ⊙ (ᴴ...) m ⓶ two-way tap.
Zwirn-garn ⓸ u. ⊙ (ᵟᴶ) n ⓶ yarn, twist.
Zwischen-abschluß ⓸ (ᵟᵛ...) m ⓶ interim balance; -akt-zigarre ⓸ f tweeny; -bescheid m jur. interlocutory decree; -bilanz ⓸ f = -abschluß; -ergebnis n bsd. Sport: provisional result; -futter ⊙ n Schneiderei: interlining; -gewinn m middleman's profit; -klage f jur. interpleader; -kosten ⓸ pl. intermediate cost(s pl.); -landung ⚔ f intermediate landing; Flug m ohne ~ non-stop flight; -schein m für Staatspapiere usw.: scrip; -staat m, pol. buffer-state; ⚰staatlich a. ⓺ international, inter-state; -stecker ⊙ m ⓶ elect. intermediate plug, adapter; *-stück zu a): ⊙ inset; -urteil n jur. interlocutory judgment; -verkauf m sale in the meantime; ~ vorbehalten subject to being unsold.
Zyklonette ⊙ (ᴸᵛᵟ) [fr., *grch.] f ⓸ mot. (leichter Kraftwagen) cycle-car.
Zylinder-block ⊙ (tṡiᵟᵛ...) m ⓶ mach. cylinders pl. cast in block; -büro n (durch Rolljalousie verschließbarer Schreibtisch) roll-top desk.